CW01368014

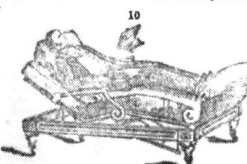

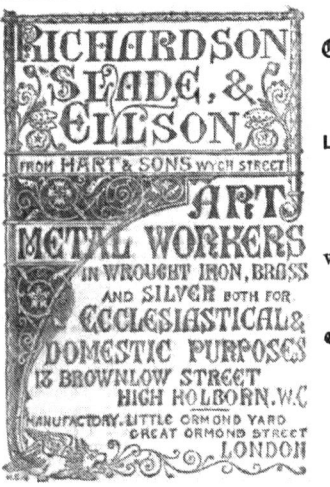

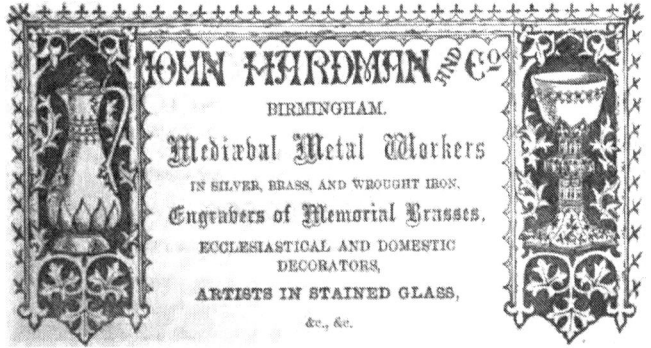

CROCKFORD'S

Clerical Directory

FOR

1868:

BEING A

BIOGRAPHICAL AND STATISTICAL BOOK OF REFERENCE FOR FACTS RELATING TO THE CLERGY AND THE CHURCH.

FOURTH ISSUE.

London:
HORACE COX, 10, WELLINGTON-STREET, STRAND, W.C.
1868.

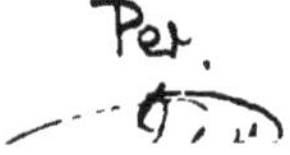

LONDON:
PRINTED BY HORACE COX, WELLINGTON-STREET, STRAND, W.C.

PREFACE.

ANOTHER Edition of "CROCKFORD'S CLERICAL DIRECTORY," after an interval of three years, is here produced. The favour with which former editions have been received has induced the Proprietor to spare neither pains nor expense in the preparation of the present Edition. A circular was posted to every clergyman in England and Wales soliciting the revision of the particulars under his own name. The replies to these circulars were eminently satisfactory, as improvements on every page of the present volume will testify. In the majority of cases the account of each benefice has been supplied by its incumbent. There has occasionally been some difficulty about the statement of income, whether gross or nett. As far as possible, the gross income has been given. The deductions requisite to ascertain nett income are so variously estimated as to render any approach to uniformity unattainable.

In a work of such extent and complexity mistakes are inevitable. We believe there are few which care could have prevented. Particulars are sometimes omitted, because they could not be furnished with any assurance of accuracy. For whatever mistakes and omissions may be found, the Editor must plead the difficulty, magnitude, and novelty of his undertaking. Corrections and additions will be thankfully received and registered for future use.

To Alexander Thom, Esq., of Dublin, we have once more to render thanks for permission to extract the List of the Irish Clergy from his admirable "Irish Almanac and Official Directory."

February, 1868.

Table of Contents.

Chapel Royal, St. James'.

Dean of the Chapel—Rt. Hon. and Rt. Rev. Archibald Campbell Tait, D.C.L., Lord Bishop of London.
Sub-Dean—Francis Garden, M.A.
Clerk of the Queen's Closet—Rt. Rev. Henry Philpott, D.D., Lord Bishop of Worcester.
Deputy-Clerks—Hon. E. S. Keppel, M.A.; Lord Wriothesley Russell, M.A.; Dean of Westminster, D.D.
Domestic Chaplain to Her Majesty—Hon. G. Wellesley, M.A., Dean of Windsor.
Chaplain of Her Majesty's Household, St. James'—Francis Garden, M.A.

CHAPLAINS IN ORDINARY TO HER MAJESTY.

January.		*June.*		*November.*	
Sir J. H. Seymour, M.A.* ...	1827	*Dean of Chichester, D.D. ...	1827	Archdeacon Tattam, D.D. ...	1853
Wm. Rogers, M.A....	1857	Henry M. Birch, M.A.	1852	Henry Howarth, B.D.	1855
George Mathias, M.A.	1858	Hon. A. F. Phipps, M.A. ...	1847	Thomas Protheroe, M.A. ...	1853
February.		*July.*		*December.*	
Chas. J. Vaughan, D.D.... ...	1851	Richard Harvey, M.A.	1847	Charles Kingsley, M.A.	1859
W. H. Brookfield, M.A.... ...	1862	Henry Melville, B.D.	1853	Calvert Moore, M.A.	1825
Frederick Temple, D.D.... ...	1856	Hon. C. L. Courtenay, M.A....	1851	Edward Bouverie, M.A.... ...	1819
March.		*August.*		*Hon. Chaplains.*	
C. V. H. Sumner, M.A.... ...	1830	Chas. A. S. Morgan, M.A. ...	1829	Lord W. Russell, M.A.	1862
John Ryle Wood, M.A.	1837	C. F. Tarver, M.A....	1858	Dean of Christ Church, D.D....	1862
John Vane, B.D.	1831	Hon. D. Hamilton Gordon, M.A.	1857	Dean of Westminster, D.D. ...	1862
April.		*September.*		J. B. Lightfoot, D.D.	1862
F. B. Zincke, M.A.	1858	Henry Moseley, M.A.	1855	J. St. John Blunt, M.A.... ...	1863
Evan Nepean, M.A.	1847	William Selwyn, D.D.	1859	J. E. Kempe, M.A.	1864
G. A. F. Hart, M.A.	1848	Fred. C. Cook, M.A.	1857	Geo. Protheroe, M.A.	1865
May.		*October.*		T. J. Rowsell, M.A.	1866
Thomas Mills, M.A.	1816	Alan G. Cornwall, M.A.... ...	1848	B. Morgan Cowie, B.D.	1866
Thomas Randolph, M.A. ...	1825	W. Drake, M.A.	1862	Daniel Moore, M.A.	1866
Hon. R. C. T. Boyle, M.A. ...	1847	James Cartmell, D.D.	1851	Jas. Russell Woodford, M.A....	1866
				Stopford A. Brooke, M.A. ...	1867
				Hon. F. E. C. Byng, M.A. ...	1867

PRIESTS IN ORDINARY.

J. W. Vivian, D.D....	1815	John V. Povah, M.A.	1833	John Antrobus, M.A.	1855
Christopher Packe, M.A. ...	1821	John Clarke Haden, M.A. ...	1834	Alfred H. Sitwell, M.A.... ...	1864
R. C. Packman, B.A.	1825	Thomas Helmore, M.A.	1847		

Organist—Mr. G. Cooper. | *Composer*—Mr. John Goss.

Chapel Royal, Whitehall.

Dean of the Chapel—Rt. Hon. and Rt. Rev. Archibald Campbell Tait, D.C.L., Lord Bishop of London. (1857.)
Sub-Dean—Francis Garden, M.A. (1859.)

Preachers.
George W. Kitchin, M.A. Christ Ch. Ox.
Joseph B. Lightfoot, D.D., Trin. Coll. Cam.

Permanent Preachers and Readers.
W. C. Lake, M.A., Ball. Coll. Ox.
W. F. Erskine Knollys, M.A., Merton Coll. Ox.

Organist—Mr. Richard Massey. (1863.)

Chapel Royal, Savoy.

Chaplain—Henry White, M.A. (1860.)
Assistant Chaplains— Thomas Wodehouse, B.A. (1862.) Henry A. Giraud, M.A. (1867.)

Preachers, &c., at Inns of Court.

TEMPLE, founded 1185.
Master—Thomas Robinson, D.D. (1845.)
Reader—A. Ainger, M.A. (1866.)
Assistant Preacher—G. F. Maclear, B.D. (1865.)

GRAY'S INN, founded 1357.
Preacher—James A. Hessey, D.C.L. (1850.)
Reader—A. Taylor, M.A. (1861.)

LINCOLN'S INN, founded 1310.
Preacher—F. C. Cook, M.A. (1862.)
Assistant Preacher—James G. Lonsdale, M.A. (1862.)
Chaplain—Charles J. D'Oyly, M.A. (1860.)

ROLLS CHAPEL.
Preacher—J. S. Brewer, M.A.
Chaplain—W. H. Brookfield, M.A.

Deans of Peculiars.

Battle	Very Rev. E. Neville Crake, M.A.
Bocking	„ Henry Carrington, M.A.
	„ Henry Barry Knox, M.A.
Guernsey.........	Very Rev. William Guille, M.A.
Jersey............	„ Wm. Corbet Le Breton, M.A.
Stamford.........	„ Ed. Reginald Mantell, M.A.

List of Bishops,

FROM THE YEAR 1774 TO 1868, INCLUSIVE.

See	Bishop	From	To
Canterbury	John Moore	1783	1805
	Charles Manners Sutton	1805	1828
	William Howley	1828	1848
	John Bird Sumner	1848	1862
	Charles Thomas Longley	1862	
York	William Markham	1776	1807
	Hon. Edward V. Harcourt	1807	1847
	Thomas Musgrave	1847	1860
	Charles Thomas Longley	1860	1862
	William Thomson	1862	
Bangor	William Cleaver	1800	1807
	John Randolph	1807	1809
	Henry William Majendie	1809	1830
	Christopher Bethell	1830	1859
	James Colquhoun Campbell	1859	
Bath and Wells	Charles Moss	1774	1802
	Richard Beaden	1802	1824
	George Henry Law	1824	1845
	Richard Bagot	1845	1854
	Hon. Robert John Eden	1854	
Bristol	F. H. W. Cornewall	1797	1802
	George Pelham	1802	1807
	John Luxmore	1807	1808
	William Lort Mansel	1808	1820
	John Kaye	1820	1827
	Robert Gray	1827	1834
	Joseph Allen	1834	1836
Carlisle	Samuel Goodenough	1808	1827
	Hon. Hugh Percy	1827	1856
	Hon. Henry Montagu Villiers	1856	1860
	Hon. Samuel Waldegrave	1860	
Chester	Henry William Majendie	1800	1809
	Bowyer Edward Sparke	1809	1812
	George Henry Law	1812	1824
	Charles James Blomfield	1824	1828
	John Bird Sumner	1828	1848
	John Graham	1848	1865
	William Jacobson	1865	
Chichester	John Buckner	1797	1824
	Robert James Carr	1824	1831
	Edward Maltby	1831	1836
	William Otter	1836	1840
	Philip Nicholas Shuttleworth	1840	1841
	Ashhurst Turner Gilbert	1841	
Durham	Hon. Shute Barrington	1791	1826
	William Van Mildert	1826	1836
	Edward Maltby	1836	1856
	Thomas Charles Longley	1856	1860
	Hon. Henry Montagu Villiers	1860	1861
	Charles Baring	1861	
Ely	James Yorke	1781	1808
	Thomas Dampier	1808	1812
	Bowyer Edward Sparke	1812	1836
	Joseph Allen	1836	1845
	Thomas Turton	1845	1864
	Edward Harold Browne	1864	
Exeter	Henry Reginald Courtenay	1797	1803
	John Fisher	1803	1807
	Hon. George Pelham	1807	1820
	William Carey	1820	1830
	Christopher Bethell … April 7	1830	
	Henry Phillpotts … Nov. 11	1830	
Gloucester and Bristol	George Isaac Huntingford	1802	1815
	Hon. Henry Ryder	1815	1824
	Christopher Bethell	1824	1830
	James Henry Monk	1830	1856
	Charles Baring	1856	1861
	William Thomson	1861	1862
	Charles John Ellicott	1863	
Hereford	John Butler	1788	1802
	F. H. W. Cornewall	1802	1808
	John Luxmore	1808	1815
	George Isaac Huntingford	1815	1832
	Hon. Edward Grey	1832	1837
	Thomas Musgrave	1837	1847
	Renn Dickson Hampden	1847	

LIST OF BISHOPS.

		FROM	TO
Lichfield and Coventry	Hon. James Cornwallis	1781	1824
	Hon. Henry Ryder	1824	1836
	Samuel Butler	1836	1839
	James Bowstead	1839	1843
	John Lonsdale	1843	1867
	Charles Augustus Selwyn	1867	
Lincoln	George Pretyman Tomline	1787	1820
	Hon. George Pelham	1820	1827
	John Kaye	1827	1853
	John Jackson	1853	
Llandaff	Richard Watson	1782	1816
	Herbert Marsh	1816	1819
	William Van Mildert	1819	1826
	Charles Richard Sumner	1826	1827
	Edward Copleston	1827	1849
	Alfred Ollivant	1849	
London	Beilby Porteus	1787	1809
	John Randolph	1809	1813
	William Howley	1813	1828
	Charles James Blomfield	1828	1856
	Archibald Campbell Tait	1856	
Manchester	James Prince Lee	1847	
Norwich	Charles Manners Sutton	1792	1805
	Henry Bathurst	1805	1837
	Edward Stanley	1837	1849
	Samuel Hinds	1849	1857
	Hon. John Thomas Pelham	1857	
Oxford	John Randolph	1799	1807
	Charles Moss	1807	1811
	William Jackson	1812	1815
	Hon. Edward Legge	1815	1827
	Charles Lloyd	1827	1829
	Richard Bagot	1829	1845
	Samuel Wilberforce	1845	
Peterborough	Spencer Madan	1794	1813
	John Parsons	1813	1819
	Herbert Marsh	1819	1839
	George Davys	1839	1864
	Francis Jeune	1864	
Ripon	Thomas Charles Longley	1836	1856
	Robert Bickersteth	1856	
Rochester	Samuel Horseley	1793	1802
	Thomas Dampier	1802	1808
	Walter King	1808	1827
	Hon. Hugh Percy ... June 28	1827	
	George Murray ... Nov. 14	1827	1860
	Joseph Cotton Wigram	1860	1867
	Thomas Legh Claughton	1867	
St. Asaph	Lewis Bagot	1790	1802
	Samuel Horseley	1802	1806
	William Cleaver	1806	1815
	John Luxmore	1815	1830
	William Carey	1830	1846
	Thomas Vowler Short	1846	
St. David's	William Stuart	1793	1800
	Lord George Murray	1800	1803
	Thomas Burgess	1803	1825
	John Banks Jenkinson	1825	1840
	Connop Thirlwall	1840	
Salisbury	John Douglas	1791	1807
	John Fisher	1807	1825
	Thomas Burgess	1825	1837
	Edward Denison	1837	1854
	Walter Kerr Hamilton	1854	
Winchester	Hon. Brownlow North	1781	1820
	George Pretyman Tomline	1820	1827
	Charles Richard Sumner	1827	
Worcester	Richard Hurd	1781	1808
	F. H. W. Cornewall	1808	1831
	Robert James Carr	1831	1841
	Henry Pepys	1841	1861
	Henry Philpott	1861	

Crockford's Clerical Directory

FOR THE YEAR 1868.

It is requested that this Work be cited as "CROCKFORD'S CLERICAL DIRECTORY."

ABBES, George Cooper, *Cleadon Hall, Sunderland.*—St. John's Coll. Cam. B.A. 1821; Deac. 1823 and Pr. 1824 by Bp of Dur. Patron and Lay Impro. of Ingleby Arnecliffe, Yorks. Formerly C. of Dalton-le-Dale 1823, Gateshead 1825, Whitburn 1836, Chap. to the late Earl of Beverley 1826. [1]

ABBEY, Charles John, *Checkendon, Henley-on-Thames.*—Univ. Coll. Ox. 2nd cl. Lit. Hum. Ellerton Theo. Ess. 1857, Denyer Theol. Ess. 1861 and 1862, B.A. 1856, M.A. 1859; Deac. 1858 and Pr. 1859 by Bp of Roch. R. of Checkendon, Dio. Ox. 1865. (Patron, Univ. Coll. Ox.; R.'s Inc. 600*l* and Ho.; Pop. 357.) Formerly Tut. and Theol. Lect. Trin. Coll. Glenalmond, 1859; Fell. of Univ. Coll. Ox. 1862; 2nd Mast. of Dedham Gr. Sch. 1857–59. [2]

ABBEY, William, *Salton, Oswaldkirk, York.*—Deac. 1845 and Pr. 1846 by Bp of Nor. V. of Salton, Dio. York, 1847. (Patron, John Woodall, Esq; Tithe—Imp. 257*l* 10*s*, V. 13*l*; Glebe, 58 acres; V.'s Inc. 140*l*; Pop. 384.) [3]

ABBISS, John, 41, *Myddelton-square, Clerkenwell, London, E.C.*—Trin. Coll. Ox. B.A. 1814, M.A. 1817; Deac. 1818, Pr. 1819. R. of St. Bartholomew the Great, City and Dio. of Lon. 1819. (Patrons, Trustees of the late W. Phillips, Esq; R.'s Inc. 700*l*; Pop. 3426.) [4]

ABBOT, Bradley, *Parsonage, Christ Church, Clapham, London, S.W.*—Dub. A.B. 1852, A.M. 1864; Deac. 1852, Pr. 1853. P. C. of Ch. Ch. Clapham, Dio. Win. 1856. (Patron, R. of Clapham; P. C.'s Inc. 500*l*; Pop. 4600.) Formerly C. of Holy Trinity, Brompton, 1852–53, St Mark's, Whitechapel, 1854–55. [5]

ABBOT, Charles H. P., *Weston-super-Mare.*—Ch. Ch. Ox. M.A., Stud. of Ch. Ch. Ox. C. of Emmanuel's, Weston-super-Mare. [6]

ABBOT, Frederick James, *North Camp, Aldershot.*—Corpus Coll. Cam. B.A. 1846; Deac. 1846 and Pr. 1847 by Bp of G. and B. Chap. to the Forces, Aldershot. Formerly C. of St. Luke, Berwick-street, Lond. and of Torquay; Precentor of the High Ch. Hull. [7]

ABBOTT, Charles, *Corney, Ravenglass, Cumberland.*—R. of Corney, Dio. Carl. 1848. (Patron, Earl of Lonsdale; R.'s Inc. 150*l*; Pop. 256.) [8]

ABBOTT, Charles, *Tunstall, Burstwick, Hull.*—St. Bees; Deac. 1851, Pr. 1852. R. of Tunstall, Dio. York, 1858. (Patron, Succentor of York; Glebe, 22 acres; Tithe, 34*l*; R.'s Inc. 100*l* and Ho.; Pop. 166.) R. of Hilston, Dio. York, 1866. (Patron, Sir Tatton Sykes; Glebe, 46 acres; Tithe, 12*l*; R.'s Inc. 80*l*; Pop. 30.) Formerly C. of St. Paul's, Staley, Mottram-in-Longendale. [9]

ABBOTT, E. A., *City of London School.*—St. John's Coll. Cam. Fell. of; Head Mast. of City of London Sch. Formerly Asst. Mast. King Edward's Sch. Birmingham. [10]

ABBOTT, George, *Stokewake, Blandford.*—Magd. Hall, Ox. B.A. 1831; Deac. 1833 by Bp of B. and W. Pr. 1836 by Bp of Salis. C. of Stokewake, 1845. Formerly C. of Lytchet Minster; Chap. to Earl of Castlestuart. [11]

ABBOTT, James Swift, *Woodhouse, Leeds.*—Queen's Coll. Birmingham; Deac. 1859 and Pr. 1861 by Bp of Rip. C. of St. Mark's, Woodhouse, 1861. Formerly C. of St. John's, Holbeck, Leeds, 1859. [12]

ABBOTT, John, *Meavy, Tavistock.*—Pemb. Coll. Ox. 3rd cl. Lit. Hum. B.A. 1821, M.A. 1823; Deac. 1822 and Pr. 1823 by Bp of Ex. R. of Meavy, Dio. Ex. 1831. (Patron, Ld Chan; Tithe comm. at 224*l* 10*s*; Glebe, 23 acres, let for 35*l*; R.'s Inc. 255*l*; Pop. 269.) Formerly C. of Heavitree 1822, St. David's, Exeter, 1823–31. [13]

ABBOTT, John Holmes, *Abbey, Middleton, Kirkby-Lonsdale.*—St. Bees; Deac. 1839 and Pr. 1840 by Bp of Rip. P. C. of Middleton, Dio. Carl. 1840. (Patron, V. of Kirkby-Lonsdale; Tithe—App. 1*l* 19*s*, Imp. 300*l*; Glebe, 92 acres; P. C.'s Inc. 130*l* and Ho; Pop. 366.) Formerly C. of Slaidburn, Clitheroe, 1839. [14]

ABBOTT, Richard H., *West Town, Dewsbury.*—P. C. of St. Matthew's, West Town, Dio. Rip. 1850. (Patron, V. of Dewsbury; P. C.'s Inc. 70*l* and Ho; Pop. 3431.) [15]

ABBOTT, Walter, *Saxon-street, Lincoln.*—Ch. Coll. Cam. B.A. 1859; Deac. 1861 by Bp. of Cant. Pr. 1862 by Bp of Lich. V. of St. Martin's, Lincoln, Dio. Lin. 1865. (Patron, Bp of Lin; V.'s Inc. 130*l*; Pop. 3232.) Surrogate. Formerly C. of Wickham, Kent, 1861; Swanwick, Derbyshire, 1862, St. John's, Ladywood, Birmingham, 1864. [16]

ABBOTT, Walter Guppy, *College Green, Gloucester.*—Queens' Coll. Cam. B.A. 1856; Deac. 1857 by Bp of Ex, Pr. 1857 by Bp of Lon. Organizing Sec. for the Western Dioceses, of Additional Curates' Society, 1866. Formerly C. of St. Peter's, Plymouth, 1857, St. Thomas's, Bethnal Green, 1859, St. Paul's, Walworth, 1862. Author, *Baptismal Regeneration*, being reply to Rev. C. H. Spurgeon, 1*d*; *Mr. C. H. Spurgeon on Infant Baptism and the Greek Testament*, 1d. [17]

ABDY, Albert Channing, *Streatham Surrey.*—Wor. Coll. Ox. B.A. 1852, M.A. 1854; Deac. 1854 and Pr. 1855 by Bp of Win. C. of Streatham, 1866. Formerly C. of Broughton, Hants, 1854, St. Martin's, Worcester, 1856, Chipping Norton 1859, Holy Trinity, Tottenham, 1862. [18]

ABELL, John, *East Ferring, Kirton-in-Lindsey, Lincolnshire.*—C. of East Ferring. [19]

ABERGAVENNY, The Right Hon. William Neville, 4th Earl of, 38, *Portland-place, London, W; Eridge Castle, Tonbridge Wells.*—

Magd. Coll. Cam. M.A. 1816; Deac. 1817, Pr. 1818. Formerly R. of Birling, Kent, and V. of Frant, Sussex. [1]

ABNEY, Edward Henry, *St. Alkmund's Vicarage, Derby.*—Ex. Coll. Ox. B.A. 1833. V. of St. Alkmund's, Derby, Dio. Lich. 1841. (Patron, the present V; V.'s Inc. 246*l* and Ho; Pop. 7990.) Rural Dean; Dom. Chap. to Lord Belper. [2]

ABRAHALL, John Charles James, Hoskyns, *Butterleigh, Collumpton, Devon.*—Wad. Coll. Ox. Scho. 2nd cl. Lit. Hum. B.A. 1823, M.A. 1826; Deac. 1824, Pr. 1825. R. of Butterleigh, Dio. Ex. 1864. (Patron, Ld Chan; Tithe, 84*l* 11*s*; Glebe let for 88*l* 9*s*; R.'s Inc. 173*l* and Ho; Pop. 100.) Formerly Mast. of Bruton Gr. Sch. Somerset. [3]

ABRAHALL, John Hoskyns, *Combe Longa, Woodstock, Oxon.*—Ball. Coll. Ox. Chan. Prize for Latin Poem 1850, 2nd cl. Lit. Hum. 1852, B.A. 1852, Fell. of Lin. Coll. 1853, M.A. 1854; Deac. 1854 and Pr. 1855 by Bp of Ox. P. C. of Combe Longa, Dio. Ox. 1861. (Patron, Lin. Coll. Ox; P. C.'s Inc. 150*l* and Ho; Pop. 627.) Formerly Prin. of Trin. Coll. Sch. Toronto; late Fell. of Lin. Coll. Ox. Author, *The Body of Christ, or Human Society and Christianity*, 1861, 1*s*; *Versiculi, or Verselets, Latin and English*, 4*s* 6*d*; *Western Woods and Waters, Poems and illustrative Notes*, 1864, 8*s*. 6*d*., Contributor to *Lyra Mystica*; *Pictures of Society, Grave and Gay*; *Cassell's Illustrated Book of Sacred Poems*; and sundry periodicals. [4]

ABRAHAM, Thomas Edward, *Risby, Bury St. Edmunds.*—Ball. Coll. Ox. 1st cl. Math. 2nd cl. Lit. Hum. B.A. 1833, M.A. 1836; Deac. 1835 and Pr. 1836 by Bp of Lon. R. of Risby with Fornham R. Dio. Ely, 1863. (Patron, Ld Chan; Tithe, 755*l*; Glebe, 21 acres; R.'s Inc. 800*l* and Ho; Pop. Risby 427, Fornham 64.) [5]

ABSOLOM, Charles Severn, *Manningtree, Essex.*—Trin. Coll. Cam. M.A. 1832; Deac. 1832 and Pr. 1833 by Bp of Ches. P. C. of Manningtree, Dio. Roch. (Patron, R. of Mistley; P. C.'s Inc. 220*l* and Ho; Pop. 880.) [6]

ABUD, Henry, *Uttoxeter, Staffs.*—Wad. Coll. Ox. B.A. 1843, M.A. 1850; Deac. 1845, Pr. 1846. V. of Uttoxeter, Dio. Lich. 1854. (Patrons, D. and C. of Windsor; Tithe—Apps. 725*l* 5*s* and 55½ acres of glebe, Imp. 3*l* 2*s*, V. 199*l* 15*s*; V.'s Inc. 280*l* and Ho; Pop. 4515.) Surrogate. Patron of P. C. of Stramshall, Staffs. Author, *A Church Hymn-book for every Sunday and Holy Day throughout the year, arranged according to the order of the Book of Common Prayer*, Masters. [7]

ACE, Daniel, *Dacre, near Penrith.*—St. John's Coll. Cam. B.D. 1861, D.D. 1862, D.D. of Ox. *comitatis causa*, 1866; Deac. 1849 and Pr. 1850 by Bp of Rip. V. of Dacre, Dio. Carl. 1864. (Patron, Ld Chan; Glebe, 4½ acres; V.'s Inc. 170*l* and Ho; Pop. 967.) Formerly C. of St. Leonard's, Malton, Mariner's Ch. Lond. St. James's, Clerkenwell, Ordnance Chap. Plumstead, Edmonton, and St. Andrew's, Plymouth. Author, Sermons in *Pulpit* and *Church of England Magazine*; *Lectures on Education*; *The Age we Live in*; *Chemistry of the Seasons*; *Auricular Confession*, Westerton, 5*s*. [8]

ACHESON, Johnston Hamilton, *The Parsonage, Upton, Birkenhead.*—Dub. A.B. 1860; Deac. 1860 by Bp of Meath, Pr. 1862 by Bp of Ches. P. C. of Upton or Overchurch, Dio. Ches. 1862. (Patron, W. Inman, Esq; P. C.'s Inc. 64*l* and Ho; Pop. 293.) Formerly C. of Newton, Kells, Co. Meath, 1860, C. of Liverpool and Chap. to the Reformatory Ship "Akbar" 1860–62. [9]

ACKERLEY, George Biglands, *Whalley, Lancashire.*—St. Mary Hall, Ox. B.A. 1861; Deac. 1861 and Pr. 1862 by Bp. of Man. C. of Whalley 1861. [10]

ACKLAND, Charles Tabor, 25, *Kensington-square, London, W.*—Dub. A.M. 1862; Deac. 1861 and Pr. 1862 by Bp of Lon. Asst. Min. of Curzon Chapel 1865; Asst. Mast. of Kensington Sch. 1857. Formerly C. of St. Barnabas', Kensington, 1861–67. [11]

ACKLAND, Thomas Suter, *Pollington, Selby.*—St. John's Coll. Cam. 21st Wrang. 1838, Scho. of St. John's 1838, B.A. 1839, Fell. of Clare Hall 1842, M.A. 1843; Deac. 1841 and Pr. 1842 by Bp. of Ches. P. C. of Pollington-cum-Balne, Dio. York, 1864. (Patron, Viscount Downe; P. C.'s Inc. 150*l* and Ho; Pop. 863.) Formerly Math Mast. in Royal Institution Sch. Liverpool, 1840–47; P. C. of St. Stephen's, Liverpool, 1843–53; 2nd Mast. of St. Peter's Coll. Sch. Eaton-square, London, 1854–64. Author, *The Apostolic Commission* (a Sermon), 1862; *Summary of the Evidence for the Bible*, 3*s*, 1866. [12]

ACLAND, Charles Lawford, *Radley, Abingdon, Berks.*—Jesus Coll. Cam. B.A. 1856, M.A. 1859; Deac. 1859 and Pr. 1860 by Bp of Lon. Fell. 1864 and Sen. Math. Tut. 1866 of St. Peter's Coll. Radley. Formerly C. of Trin. Ch. Gray's-inn-road, 1859, and St. Olave's, Hart-street, Mark-lane, Lond. 1863. [13]

ACLAND, Peter Leopold Dyke, *Broad Clyst, Exeter.*—Ch. Ch. Ox. B.A. 1841, M.A. 1844, *ad eund.* Dur; Deac. 1843, Pr. 1844. V. of Broad Clyst, Dio. Ex. 1845. (Patron, Sir Thomas Dyke Acland, Bart; Tithe—Imp. 990*l*; V. 495*l*; Glebe, 73 acres; Corn rent-charge out of Cutton Estate 322*l*; V.'s Inc. 975*l* and Ho; Pop. 2318.) Preb. of the Cathl of Exeter, 1866. [14]

ACOCK, Edgar Morton, *Christ Church. Oxford.*—Madg. Coll. Ox. 3rd cl. Lit. Hum. B.A. 1859, M.A. 1862; Deac. 1860 by Bp of Salis. Pr. 1862 by Bp of St. D. Chap. of Ch. Ch. Ox. Formerly, Asst. Mast. in King's Sch. Sherborne, Dorset, 1859–60; Vice-Prin. of Training Coll. Caermarthen, 1861–63; Asst. Mast. in Magd. Coll. Sch. Oxford, 1864. [15]

ACRAMAN, William, *Oakham, Rutland.*—St. Aidan's; Deac. 1865 by Bp of Herf, Pr. 1866 by Bp of Pet. C. of Oakham 1866. Formerly C. of St. Peter's, Hereford, 1865. [16]

ACRES, John, *Clevedon, Bristol.*—Lin. Coll. Ox. B.A. 1840, M.A. 1846; Deac. 1841 by Bp of B. and W. Pr. 1843 by Bp of G. and B. P. C. of Kenn, Dio. B. and W. 1847. (Patron, V. of Yatton; Tithe, 90*l*; Glebe, 7 acres; P. C.'s Inc. 105*l*; Pop. 282.) [17]

ACTON, John, *Iwerne Minster, Shaftesbury.*—Ex. Coll. Ox B.A. 1844, M.A. 1846; Deac. 1848 and Pr. 1849 by Bp of Salis. V. of Iwerne Minster, Dio. Salis. 1860. (Patrons, D. and C. of Windsor; Tithe, 180*l*; Glebe let for 60*l*; V.'s Inc. 240*l*; Pop. 712.) Formerly C. of East Orchard and St. Margaret's Marsh 1848–60, of which livings with Hinton he is Patron. [18]

ACTON, William, *Wicklewood, Wymondham, Norfolk.*—Ball. Coll. Ox. B.A. 1846; Deac. 1847, Pr. 1848. V. of Wicklewood, Dio. Nor. 1854. (Patrons, A. C. Heber Percy, Esq. and Rev. M. B. Darby; Tithe—Imp. 340*l*, V. 130*l*; Glebe, 30 acres; V.'s Inc. 174*l*; Pop. 806.) [19]

ACWORTH, William, *Farrs, near Wimborne, Dorset.*—Queens' Coll. Cam. B.A. 1829, M.A. 1832; Deac. 1832 and Pr. 1833 by Bp of Lin. Formerly C. and afterwards V. of Rothley, Leic; V. of Plumstead, Kent, 1856–64. Author, *Sermon on the death of Thomas Babington, Esq. of Rothley Temple*, 1837; many Letters to *The Times* on the undrained state of the Marsh Lands on the south side of the Thames; and of a Letter to Abp of Cant. on Ritualistic Practices in the Dio. of Oxford. [20]

ACWORTH, William Pelham, *Thorpe, Norwich.*—C. of Thorpe. [21]

ADAIR, Hugh Jenison, *Bradford, Taunton.*—Ch. Ch. Ox. B.A. 1859, M.A. 1865; Deac. 1859 and Pr. 1860 by Bp of B. and W. V. of Bradford, Dio. B. and W. 1861. (Patron, the present V; Tithe, 150*l*; Glebe, 27 acres; V.'s Inc. 150*l* and Ho; Pop. 552.) Formerly C. of Westbury-cum-Priddy, 1859–61. [22]

ADAM, George Robert, *Isle of Cumbrae, Scotland.*—St. Edm. Hall, Ox. B.A. 1860, M.A. 1863; Deac. 1861 and Pr. 1862 by Bp of Wor. Formerly C. of Newland, Great Malvern, 1861–66, Dorking 1866; Dom. Chap. to Earl of Strathmore 1866–67. [23]

ADAM, Stephen Condon, 11, *Buckingham-street, Adelphi, London, W.C.*—St. John's Coll. Cam. 31st Wrang. Foundation Scho. of St. John's, B.A. 1858, M.A. 1861; Deac. 1858 and Pr. 1859 by Abp of York.

Assoc. Sec. of the Society for Irish Church Missions to the Roman Catholics. Formerly C. of Holy Trin. Wicker, Sheffield, 1858–59. [1]

ADAMS, Augustus Crichton, *Toft, Knutsford, Cheshire.*—St. Bees; Deac. 1856 and Pr. 1857 by Bp of Lich. P. C. of Toft, Dio. Ches. 1865 (Patrons, Leycester Family; P. C.'s Inc. 43*l*. and Ho; Pop. 240.) Formerly C. of Winster, Derbyshire, 1856–58, St. Nicholas' Rochester, 1859–64, Watton, Herts, 1864–65. [2]

ADAMS, Benjamin, *Belton, near Great Yarmouth.*—St. John's Coll. Cam. B.A. 1848; Deac. 1852 and Pr. 1853 by Bp of Lich. C. of Belton 1866. Formerly C. of Shottisham, Bradwell, Hales, Riddings, and Ch. Ch. Burton-on-Trent. [3]

ADAMS, Cadwallader Coker, *Ansty, Coventry.*—Mert. Coll. Ox. B.A. 1843, M.A. 1846. V. of Ansty, Dio. Wor. 1852. (Patron, Ld Chan; Tithe—Imp. 12*l* 12*s*, V. 40*l*; V.'s Inc. 165*l*; Pop. 171.) P. C. of Shilton, Warw. Dio. Wor. 1852. (Patron, Ld Chan; Tithe—Imp. 37*l*, P. C. 4*l* 1*s* 4½*d*; P. C.'s Inc. 90*l*; Pop. 487.) [4]

ADAMS, Charles, *Caynham, Ludlow, Salop.*—St. Bees; Deac. 1833 and Pr. 1835 by Bp of Ches. V. of Caynham, Dio. Herf 1850. (Patron, C. K. Mainwaring, Esq; Tithe, 90*l* 5*s*; Glebe, 146 acres; V.'s Inc. 450*l* and Ho; Pop. 368.) Formerly C. of Eartham 1833–36, Caynham 1836-50. [5]

ADAMS, Coker, *New College, Oxford.*—New Coll. Ox. B.A. 1851, M.A. 1854; Deac. 1853 and Pr. 1855 by Bp of Ox. [6]

ADAMS, Dacres, *Bampton, Witney, Oxon.*—Ch. Ch. Ox. B.A. 1827, M.A. 1838; Deac. 1829, Pr. 1830. V. of Bampton, 2nd Portion, Dio. Ox. 1837. (Patrons, D. and C. of Ex; Tithe—Apps. 143*l*. 8*s*; to the three V.'s 919*l*; V.'s Inc. 450*l* and Ho; Pop. 1713.) Rural Dean of Witney. [7]

ADAMS, Daniel Charles Octavius.—St. John's Coll. Ox. B.A. 1845, M.A. 1852; Deac. 1846, Pr. 1847. Formerly C. of Ch. Ch. St. Pancras, Lond. [8]

ADAMS, Edward Aurelius, 64, *Wimpole-street, London, W.*—Caius Coll. Cam. 19th Sen. Opt. B.A. 1860; Deac. 1860 and Pr. 1861 by Bp of Ely. Formerly C. of St. Mary's, Bury St. Edmund's, 1860, and Trin. Ch. Marylebone, Lond. 1863. [9]

ADAMS, Edward Charles, *Worcester College, Oxford.*—Wor. Coll. Ox. 2nd cl. Lit. Hum. and B.A. 1851; Deac. 1852. Fell. and Div. Lect. of Wor. Coll. Ox. [10]

ADAMS, Edward Cray, *Hawkchurch, near Axminster.*—Magd. Hall, Ox. B.A. 1842. R. of Hawkchurch, Dio. Salis. 1852. (Patron, the present R; Tithe, 536*l*; R.'s Inc. 640*l* and Ho; Pop. 706.) [11]

ADAMS, Edward Richard, *Luton.*—Caius Coll. Cam. B.A. 1864; Deac. 1864 and Pr. 1865 by Bp of Ox. P. C. of Limbury with Biscot, Dio. Ely, 1866. (Patron, J. S. Cranley, Esq; Tithe, 148*l*; P. C.'s Inc. 198*l*; Pop. 800.) Formerly C. of Linslade, Bucks, 1864–65. [12]

ADAMS, Frederick Morice, *Teffont Ewyas, near Salisbury.*—Ex. Coll. Ox; Deac. 1849 and Pr. 1850 by Bp of Ex. R. of Teffont Ewyas, Dio. Salis. 1866. (Patron, W. Fane De Salis, Esq; Tithe, 190*l*; Glebe, 33 acres; R.'s Inc. 241*l* and Ho; Pop. 163.) Formerly C. of Stoke Canon 1849-51, Uffculme 1851-66. [13]

ADAMS, George Dacres, *East Budleigh Salterton, Devon.*—Deac. 1848 and Pr. 1849 by Bp of Ex. V. of East Budleigh with Budleigh Salterton C. Dio. Ex. 1852. (Patrons, Lord Clinton, Lord Churston, and Lieut.-Col. Sir G. Stucley, Bart, Trustees under the will of the late Lord Rolle; Tithe, Imp. 320*l*; V. 223*l*; Glebe, 9 acres; V.'s Inc. 325*l* and Ho; Pop. 2496.) Dom. Chap. to the Earl of Kintore 1849. [14]

ADAMS, Henry Cadwallader, *Bromley College, Kent.*—Magd. Coll. Ox. 2nd cl. Lit. Hum. and B.A. 1840, M.A. 1842; Deac. 1846 and Pr. 1852 by Bp of Ox. Chap. of Bromley Coll. 1855 (Value 170*l* and Res.) Formerly Fell. Magd. Coll. Ox. Author, *The Cherrystones*, 1851, 2*s*; *The First of June*, 1856, 2*s*; *Sivan the Sleeper*, 1856, 5*s*; *Schoolboy Honour*, 1861, 3*s* 6*d*; *White Brunswickers*, 1864; *Balderscourt or Holiday Tales*, 1865; *Barford Bridge*, 1867; *Twelve Foundations and other Poems*, 1858; *Sundays at Encombe*, 1866; *Judges of Israel*, 1867; *Adams's Greek Delectus*, 1851, 3*s* 6*d*; *Greek Exercises*, 1836, 3*s* 6*d*; *Latin Delectus*, 1852; *Latin Exercises*, 1858; *Greek Text of the Gospels, with Notes and References—St. Matthew*, 2*s* 6*d*, *St. Mark*, 1*s* 6*d*, *St. Luke*, 2*s*, *St. John*, 2*s*, 1855. [15]

ADAMS, Henry Willoughby, *Great Parndon Rectory, near Harlow.*—Ex. Coll. Ox. B.A. 1843, M.A. 1847. R. of Great Parndon, Dio. Roch. 1863. (Patrons, Govs. of St. Thomas's Hospital, Reps. of the late Earl of Mornington, and Rev. W. C. Adams; Tithe, 599*l*; Glebe, 28 acres; R.'s Inc. 649*l* and Ho; Pop. 491.) [16]

ADAMS, James Williams, *Shottesbrook, Maidenhead.*—Dub. A.B. 1861; Deac. 1863 and Pr. 1864 by Bp of Win. C. of Shottesbrook. Formerly C. of Hyde, Hants. [17]

ADAMS, John, *Stockcross, Newbury, Berks.*—Magd. Hall, Ox. Newdigate Prize for English Poetry, M.A. 1852; Deac. 1848 and Pr. 1850 by Bp of Ex. P. C. of Stockcross, Dio. Ox. 1858. (Patron, V. of Speen, Berks; Glebe, 38 acres; P. C.'s Inc. 138*l* and Ho; Pop. 815.) [18]

ADAMS, John Exley, *Ashmore (Dorset), near Salisbury.*—Emman. Coll. Cam. LL.B. 1816. R. of Ashmore, Dio. Salis. 1854. (Patron, Rev. C. Chisholm; Tithe, 351*l*; R.'s Inc. 360*l* and Ho; Pop. 254.) [19]

ADAMS, Philip B., *The Rectory, Hopesay, near Bishop's Castle, Salop.*—R. of Hopesay, Dio. Herf. (Patroness, Mrs. Adams; Tithe, 511*l*; Glebe, 62 acres; R.'s Inc. 604*l* and Ho; Pop. 676.) [20]

ADAMS, Reginald Samuel, *Sebergham, Carlisle.*—Caius Coll. Cam. 6th Sen. Opt. B.A. 1862, M.A. 1865; Deac. 1862 and Pr. 1863 by Bp of Carl. R. of Sebergham, Dio. Carl. 1865. (Patrons, D. and C. of Carl; Tithe, from 80*l* to 110*l*; Glebe, 82 acres; R.'s Inc. 160*l* and Ho; Pop. 745.) Formerly C. of Ch. Ch. Carlisle, 1862-65. [21]

ADAMS, Richard, 234, *City-road, Manchester.*—Magd. Coll. Cam. B.A. 1854, M.A. 1861; Deac. 1857 by Bp of Man. for Bp of Rip. Pr. 1858 by Bp of Rip. C. in sole charge of Dist. of St. Stephen, Hulme, 1865. Formerly C. of St. John's, Huddersfield, of Norton, Durham, and Gorton, Manchester. [22]

ADAMS, Richard Leonard, *Shere, near Guildford.*—Ch. Ch. Ox. Stud. of, B.A. 1824, M.A. 1826; Deac. 1826 and Pr. 1827 by Bp of Ox. R. of Shere, Dio. Win. 1859. (Patron, the present R; R.'s Inc. 800*l* and Ho; Pop. 1503.) Formerly P. C. of Wimbledon 1846-49. [23]

ADAMS, Richard Leonard, *Framfield Vicarage, Hurst Green, Sussex.*—V. of Framfield, Dio. Chich. 1866. (Patron, Rev. R. L. Adams, Sen; V.'s Inc. 540*l* and Ho; Pop. 1355.) [24]

ADAMS, Richard Newton, *Rempstone, Loughborough.*—Sid. Coll. Cam. 7th Wrang. B.A. 1814, M.A. 1817, B.D. 1824, D.D. 1830; Deac. 1815 and Pr. 1816 by Bp of Nor. R. of Rempstone, Dio. Lin. 1839. (Patron, Mast. of Sid. Coll. Cam; R.'s Inc. 478*l* and Ho; Pop. 377.) Author, *Commencement Sermon*, at Cambridge, 1830; *The Opening of the Sealed Book in the Apocalypse shown to be a Symbol of a future Republication of the Old Testament*, 1838, 8*s* 6*d*; "*Reading-in*" *Sermon*, at Rempstone, 1840; *Visitation Sermon*, at Nottingham, 1840; *The Jewish Missionary*, 1849; *Letter to the Archbishop of Canterbury*, 1850. [25]

ADAMS, Samuel, *Thornton, Market-Bosworth, Leicestershire.*—Sid. Coll. Cam. B.A. 1824, M.A. 1837; Deac. and Pr. 1826. V. of Thornton with Bagworth C. and Stanton C. Dio. Pet. 1857. (Patrons, Trustees of late Viscount Maynard; V.'s Inc. 220*l*; Pop. Thornton 446, Bagworth 534, Stanton 312.) Formerly C. of Thornton and Bagworth 1838–57. [26]

ADAMS, Samuel, *Monte Video.*—St. John's Coll. Cam. B.A. 1853; Deac. 1853 and Pr. 1854 by Bp of Ches. British Chap. at Monte Video. Formerly P. C. of Holy Trin. Runcorn, Cheshire, 1854–58. [27]

ADAMS, Simon Thomas, *The Rectory, Horwood, Winslow, Bucks.*—New Coll. Ox. B.A. 1831, M.A. 1835; Deac. 1832 and Pr. 1833 by Bp of Ox. R. of Great Horwood, Dio. Ox. 1839. (Patron, New Coll. Ox.; Tithe, 445*l* 2*s*; R.'s Inc. 452*l* and Ho; Pop. 845.) Rural Dean of Mursley 1851. [1]

ADAMS, William, *The Rectory, Throcking, Buntingford, Herts.*—Queens' Coll. Cam. B.A. 1829, M.A. 1832; Deac. 1829, Pr. 1831. R. of Throcking, Dio. Roch. 1841. (Patron, the present R; Tithe, 290*l* 4*s* 6*d*; R.'s Inc. 320*l* and Ho; Pop. 97.) Author, (Pamphlets), *The Poor Law*; *Management of the Poor in Agricultural Districts*; *Remarks on Grand Juries.* [2]

ADAMS, William Cockayne, *Dummer, Rectory, near Basingstoke.*—Ball. Coll. Ox. B.A. 1835, M.A. 1839. R. of Dummer, Dio. Win. 1848. (Patron W. Adams, Esq; Tithe, 472*l*; Glebe, 83 acres; R.'s Inc. 578*l* and Ho; Pop. 400.) [3]

ADAMS, William Joshua, *Dolphinholme, near Lancaster.*—Caius Coll. Cam. B.A. 1859; Deac. 1859 and Pr. 1860 by Bp of Man. P. C. of Dolphinholme, Dio. Man. 1859. (Patron, H. Garnett, Esq; P. C.'s Inc. 76*l*; Pop. 800.) [4]

ADAMSON, Edward Hussey, *St. Alban's, near Gateshead.*—Lin. Coll. Ox. B.A. 1839, M.A. 1841; Deac. 1840 and Pr. 1841 by Bp of Dur. P. C. of St. Alban's, Heworth, Dio. Dur. 1843. (Patron, P. C. of Heworth; P. C.'s Inc. 300*l* and Ho; Pop. 2635.) Surrogate 1858. Formerly C. of Wallsend. Author, *Catechetical Exercises on the Saints' Days*; *The Parochial System* and *The Parish Church* (Sermons). [5]

ADAMSON, Henry Thomas, 14, *Portland-place, Lower Clapton, London, N.E.*—St. John's Coll. Cam. B.D. 1864; Deac. 1854 and Pr. 1855 by Bp of S. and M. C. of Hackney 1866. Formerly C. of St. Barnabas', Douglas; Sen. C. of Great Malvern, 1856–58 and St. Andrew's, Holborn, Lond. 1858–62. Author, *The Seventh Day, an Argument for the Observance of the Sabbath hitherto untouched*, 8*d.* [6]

ADAMSON, Sanford John Cyril, *Moorside, Altham, near Accrington.*—Deac. 1821, Pr. 1822. Formerly P. C. of Padiham, Lancashire, 1823–65. [7]

ADAMSON, William, *The Parsonage, Winster, Kendal.*—Dub. A.B. 1833; Deac. 1833 and Pr. 1834 by Bp of Killaloe. P. C. of Winster, Dio. Carl. 1856. (Patron, V. of Kendal; P. C.'s Inc. 90*l* and Ho; Pop. 110.) Formerly P. C. of St. Augustine's, Ticehurst, Sussex, 1844–56. [8]

ADAMSON, William, 7, *Torrington-place, Plymouth*—L. C. S. Edin. and Lond. Deac. 1866. C. of Charles the Martyr's, Plymouth. [9]

ADAMSON, William Collinson, *Ulrome, Hull.*—St. Bees; Deac. and Pr. 1835. P. C. of Cumberworth, Dio. Rip. 1855. (Patron, W. B. Beaumont, Esq; Glebe, 120 acres; P. C.'s Inc. 147*l* and Ho; Pop. 813.) C. of Ulrome 1866. Formerly C. of Newchurch, near Burnley, of Burscough, near Ormskirk, and West Witton, near Bedale. [10]

ADCOCK, Halford H., 29, *Upper Brunswick-place, Brighton.*—Trin. Coll. Cam. B.A. 1839, M.A. 1842; Deac. 1839 by Bp of Lin. Pr. 1840 by Bp of Pet. Formerly C. of Scraptoft, Lincolnshire; V. of Humberston, Leicestershire, 1856–61. Editor, *Churchman's Manual of Private Devotion*, 3rd ed. 3*s.* 6*d.* [11]

ADDENBROOKE, Edward, *Smethwick, Birmingham.*—P. C. of Smethwick, Staffs, Dio. Lich. 1850. (Patrons, Trustees; P. C.'s Inc. 300*l.* and Ho; Pop. 1058.) [12]

ADDERLEY, B., *Fillongley Hall, Coventry.*— [13]

ADDINGTON, Henry, *Langford, Biggleswade, Beds.*—Lin. Coll. Ox. B.A. 1843, M.A. 1860; Deac. 1844 and Pr. 1845 by Bp of Pet. V. of Langford, Dio. Ely, 1850. (Patron, Ld Chan; Glebe, 103 acres; V.'s Inc. 300*l*; Pop. 1086.) [14]

ADDISON, Berkeley, *Jesmond, Newcastle-on-Tyne.*—St. Peter's Coll. Cam. Classical Prizeman 1836, B.A. 1839, M.A. 1842; Deac. 1839 and Pr. 1840 by Bp of Chich. P. C. of Jesmond, Newcastle, Dio. Dur. 1861. (Patrons, Five Trustees; P. C.'s Inc. 630*l* and Ho; Pop. 3442.) Surrogate; Dom. Chap. to Earl of Caithness. Formerly R. of Collyhurst, Manchester, 1855–61. Author, *The Ark of Israel*, 5*s*; *Rod of Moses* (Sermons), 5*s*; *Manchester Lectures*; and various pamphlets on Romanism. [15]

ADDISON, Frederic, *Cleator, Cumberland.*—Univ. Coll. Dur. B.A. 1852; Deac. 1852 and Pr. 1853 by Bp of Ches. P. C. of Cleator, Dio. Carl. 1855. (Patron, Earl of Lonsdale; Glebe, 32 acres; P. C.'s Inc. 100*l*; Pop. 6500.) Formerly C. of Trin. Ch. Whitehaven, 1852, and Ossett, Yorkshire, 1854. [16]

ADDISON, John Aspinall, *Hound, Southampton.*—St. John's Coll. Cam. B.A. 1838, M.A. 1842; Deac. and Pr. 1839. V. of Hound, Dio. Win. 1862. (Patron, Win. Coll; Tithe, 154*l*; Glebe, 18 acres; V.'s Inc. 190*l* and Ho; Pop. 500.) Formerly C. of Wallasea, Cheshire, 1839–40; P. C. of Middleton and Barbon, Westmorland, 1840–41; V. of Mitton, Yorkshire, 1841–49; Min. of St. Mary's, Windermere, 1849–55; C. of Plympton and Brixton, Devon, 1856–59; C. of Hound, 1860–62. [17]

ADDISON, John Cramer, *Wootton-under-Wood, Aylesbury, Bucks.*—St. John's Coll. Cam. B.A. 1854; Deac. 1854 and Pr. 1855 by Bp of Lich. P. C. of Wootton-under-Wood, Dio. Ox. 1856. (Patron, Duke of Buckingham; P. C.'s Inc. 80*l.* and Ho; Pop. 266.) Dom. Chap. to the Duke of Buckingham. [18]

ADDISON, John Dupre, *Rodwell House, Weymouth.*—Ex. Coll. Ox. B.A. 1835, M.A. 1838; Deac. 1837, Pr. 1839. P. C. of Holy Trinity, Weymouth, Dio. Salis. 1863. (Patron, Rev. W. G. S. Addison; Pop. 4438.) Chap. of the Weymouth Union. Formerly V. of Fleet, near Weymouth, 1857–63. [19]

ADDISON, Leonard, *The Marble House, Warwick.*—Corpus Coll. Cam. B.A. 1861; Deac. 1863 and Pr. 1864 by Bp of Wor. Lect. at New Milverton, Leamington, 1865. Formerly C. of St. Paul's, Warwick, 1863. [20]

ADDISON, Richard, *Pernambuco.*—Literate; Deac. 1856 by Bp of Capetown, Pr. 1858 by Bp of Lich. British Chap. at Pernambuco. Formerly C. of King William's Town, S. Africa, 1856, Wolverhampton 1858, St. Mary Magdalen's, Taunton, 1861. [21]

ADDISON, William Fountaine, *Reading.*—Wad. Coll. Ox. B.A. 1840. P. C. of Ch. Ch. Reading, Dio. Ox. 1863. (Patron, Bp of Ox; P. C.'s Inc. 120*l.*) [22]

ADDISON, William George Sinclair, *Hartpury, Gloucester.*—Magd. Hall, Ox. B.A. 1839, Kennicott Hebrew Scho. 1840, Pusey and Ellerton Scho. 1840, M.A. 1841; Deac. 1841 and Pr. 1842 by Bp of G. and B. V. of Hartpury, Dio. G. and B. 1856. (Patron, Bp of G. and B; V.'s Inc. 200*l* and Ho; Pop. 843.) Formerly P. C. of Dearhurst 1846–56. [23]

ADENEY, John, *Flowton Rectory, near Ipswich.*—Queens' Coll. Cam. B.A. 1825, M.A. 1843; Deac. 1825 and Pr. 1826 by Bp of Lon. R. of Flowton, Dio. Nor. 1844. (Patron, H. S. Thornton, Esq; Tithe, 135*l*; Glebe, 16 acres; R.'s Inc. 107*l* and Ho; Pop. 151.) Author, *Christian Recreations.* [24]

ADEY, Francis William, *Markyate Cell, near Dunstable.*—Trin. Hall, Cam. Min. of St. John's, Caddington, a private donative chapel, Dio Roch. 1847. (Patron, D. G. Adey, Esq; Min.'s Inc. 150*l.*) [25]

ADLEY, George Frederick, *St. Helens, Lancashire.*—Caius Coll. Cam. B.A. 1855; Deac. and Pr. 1858 by Abp of York. C. of Gerard's Bridge Dist, St. Helens, 1865. Formerly C. of St. Mark's, Hull, 1858–59; and Beverley Minster 1859–65. [26]

ADLEY, William, *Rudbaxton, Haverfordwest.*—Deac. 1823 by Bp of Lon. Pr. 1824 by Bp of St. D. R. of Rudbaxton, Dio. St. D. 1857. (Patron, Ld Chan; R.'s Inc. 200*l*; Pop. 586.) Formerly C. of Privett, and Ch. Miss. in Ceylon. Author, *A Missionary Sermon*; *Samuel the Malabar* (a Tract); Compiler of *A Selection of Psalms and Hymns.* [27]

ADLINGTON, John, *Worcester.*—Chap. of the County Gaol and Union, Worcester. [28]

ADNUTT, R. T., *Cadeby Rectory, Hinckley, Leicestershire.*—R. of Cadeby, Dio. Pet. 1836. (Patron,

Sir Alexander Dixie, Bart; R.'s Inc. 260*l* and Ho; Pop. 422.) R. of Croft, Dio. Pet. 1826. (Patron, the present R; R.'s Inc. 620*l*; Pop. 319.) [1]

ADOLPHUS, Otto, *Hope House, Cintra Park, Upper Norwood, London, S.*—Corpus Coll. Cam. B.A. 1851, M.A. 1854; Deac. 1851 and Pr. 1852 by Bp of Win. Cl. Mast. in King's Coll. Sch. Lond. Formerly Vice-Prin. of North Lond. Collegiate Sch; C. of St. Matthias', Bethnal-green, Lond. Great Bookham, Surrey, and St. Barnabas', King-square, Goswell-street, Lond. Author, *Compendium Theologicum*, 3rd ed. 1866, 6*s*. 6*d*. [2]

ADY, the Ven. William Brice, *Little Baddow Rectory, Chelmsford.*—Ex. Coll. Ox. 2nd cl. Lit. Hum. 1838, B.A. 1838, M.A. 1841; Deac. 1839 and Pr. 1840 by Bp of Lon. R. of Little Baddow, Dio. Roch. 1857. (Patron, Lord Rayleigh; Tithe, comm. at 623*l*; Glebe, 13 acres; R.'s Ice. 640*l*. and Ho; Pop. 605.) Archdeacon of Colchester 1867; (Sal. 600*l*;) Chap. to Bp of Roch. Formerly C. of Little Baddow 1839–42, and V. of same 1842–57. [3]

AGASSIZ, Rodolph, *Great Clacton, Colchester.*—St. John's Coll. Cam. B. A. 1861, M. A. 1866; Deac. 1862 and Pr. 1863 by Bp of Roch. V. of Great Clacton, with Little Holland, Dio. Roch. 1864. (Patron, L. Agassiz, Esq. Stour Lodge, Essex; Tithe, 308*l*; Glebe, 3½ acres; V.'s Inc. 315*l* and Ho; Pop. 1400.) Formerly C. of Radwell, Herts, 1862–63. [4]

AGER, William, *Grammar School, Kimbolton.*—St. John's Coll. Cam. B.A. 1845, M.A. 1848; Deac. 1846 and Pr. 1847 by Bp of Pet. Head. Mast. of Kimbolton Gr. Sch. 1865. (Stipend, 125*l*, Ho. and capitation fees.) Formerly C. of Barningham, Suffolk, 1858–62, and Irthlingborough, Northants, 1863–65. [5]

AGLEN, Anthony Stacker, *Scarborough.*—Univ. Coll. Ox. Newdigate prize, 1859, 2nd cl. Maths. 1860, B.A. 1860, M.A. 1863; Deac. 1862 and Pr. 1863 by Bp of Salis. C. of Scarborough 1865. Formerly Asst. Mast. of Marlborough Coll. 1860–65. [6]

AINGER, Alfred, 18, *Westbourne-square, London, W.*—Trin. Coll. Cam. B.A. 1860, M.A. 1865; Deac. 1860 and Pr. 1863 by Bp of Lich. Reader at the Temple Ch. Lond. Formerly C. of Alrewas, Staffs. [7]

AINGER, Edward Barnard, *Ascot Heath, Staines.*—Pemb. Coll. Ox. B.A. 1857, M.A. 1859; Deac. 1858 by Bp of Lon. Pr. 1859 by Bp of Wor. Fell. of Pemb. Coll. Ox; C. of All Saints', Ascot, 1867. Formerly C. of St. John's, Worcester. [8]

AINGER, George Henry, *St. Bees College, Whitehaven, Cumberland.*—St. John's Coll. Camb. Bell's Univ. Scho. 19th Wrang. 2nd cl. Cl. Trip. B.A. 1842, M.A. 1845, D.D. 1859; Deac. 1845 and Pr. 1846 by Bp of Ely. Principal of St. Bees Coll.; P. C. of St. Bees, Dio. Carl. 1858. (Patron, Earl of Lonsdale; P.C.'s Inc. 103*l* and Ho; Pop. 2327.) Late Fell. of St. John's Coll. Cam; C. of Alford, Somerset, 1846–47; Tut. of St. Bees Coll. 1849–57. [9]

AINSLIE, Alexander Colvin, *Corfe, near Taunton.*—Univ. Coll. Ox. B.A. 1852, M.A. 1855; Deac. 1853 by Bp. of G. and B. Pr. 1854 by Bp of B. and W. P. C. of Corfe, Dio. B. and W. 1854. (Patron, F. W. Newton, Esq; Tithe—Imp. 87*l* 11*s*; Glebe, 2¼ acres; P. C.'s Inc. 152*l*. and Ho; Pop. 381.) Formerly C. of Sopworth, Wilts, 1853. [10]

AINSLIE, George, *Church Building Society*, 7, *Whitehall, London, S.W.*—Eman. Coll. Cam. B.A. 1825, M.A. 1829. Secretary to the Church Building Society. [11]

AINSLIE, Gilbert, *Pembroke College, Cambridge.*—Pemb. Coll. Cam. B.A. 1815, M.A. 1818, D.D. 1828; Deac. 1816, Pr. 1818. Mast. of Pemb. Coll. Cambridge, 1828. [12]

AINSLIE, Henry, *Easingwold, Yorks.*—Trin. Coll. Cam. B.A. 1846, M.A. 1849; Deac. 1847, Pr. 1848. V. of Easingwold, Dio. York, 1856. (Patron, Bp of Ches.; Tithe, 205*l*; Glebe, 10 acres; V.'s Inc. 260*l* and Ho; Pop. 2147.) Formerly C. of Bury. Author, *Preparations for Holy Communion*, 1848, 1*d*; *Weapons of God's Warfare*, 1851, 6*d*; *Pattern of Church Ordinances*, 1853, 6*d*; *Godliness, not Gain, the Business of Life*, 1855, 1*d*. [13]

AINSLIE, Robert, *Great Grimsby, Lincolnshire.*—Emman. Coll. Cam. B.A. 1840, M.A. 1843. V. of Great Grimsby, Dio. Lin. 1856. (Patron, G. F. Heneage, Esq.; Tithe 57*l* 2*s*; V.'s Inc. 544*l*; Pop. 11,067.) Rural Dean; Preb. of Lincoln 1864. Formerly Warden of the House of Charity, Soho, London. [14]

AINSWORTH, Thomas, *Kimbolton, Hunts.*—St. Cath. Coll. Cam. 24th Wrang. and Prizeman, B.A. 1839, M.A. 1843; Deac. 1839 and Pr. 1840 by Bp of Lon. V. of Kimbolton, Dio. Ely, 1845. (Patron, Duke of Manchester; Tithe, 48*l* 15*s*; Glebe 112 acres; V.'s Inc. 240*l* and Ho; Pop. 1661.) Dom. Chap, to Duke of Manchester. Formerly V. of Carbrook, Norfolk; C. of Trin. Ch. Chelsea. Author, *Pastoral Duties* (a Visitation Sermon), 1*s*; *True Riches* (a Sermon); *Pure and Undefiled Religion* (a Sermon.) [15]

AIREY, George, *Peel, Bolton-le-Moors.*—St. Bees; Deac. 1859, Pr. 1861; P. C. of Peel, Dio. Man. 1862. (Patron, Lord Kenyon; Glebe 10 acres; P. C.'s Inc. 178*l* and Ho; Pop. 3390.) Formerly C. of St. Matthew's, Manchester, 1859–62. [16]

AIREY, Henry Holme, *Selside, Kendal.*—Literate; Deac. and Pr. 1821 by Bp of Ches. P. C. of Selside, Dio. Carl. 1831. (Patrons, the Landowners; Glebe, 168 acres; P.C.'s Inc. 115*l* and Ho; Pop. 308.) Formerly 2nd Mast. of Sedberg Gr. Sch. 1823–30. [17]

AIREY, John Alfred Lumb, *Merchant Taylors' School*, 6, *Suffolk-lane, Cannon-street, London, E.C.*—Pemb. Coll. Cam. B.A. 1846, M.A. 1843; Deac. 1846 and Pr. 1847 by Bp of Dur. Townshend Lect. at St. Magnus the Martyr, Lond. Bridge, 1853 (Value, 75*l*); Head Math. Mast. and First Mast. Under Cl. in Merchant Taylors' Sch. [18]

AIREY, John Postlethwaite, *Clerk's Hill, Prestwich.*—Queen's Coll. Ox. 3rd cl. Lit. Hum. Hon. 4th in Maths. B.A. 1858, M A. 1861; Deac. 1859 and Pr. 1860 by Bp of Man. C. of Prestwich 1866. Formerly C. of Stretford 1859–66. [19]

AIREY, Robert, *St. Mark's, Douglas, Isle of Man.*—Deac. 1850 and Pr. 1852 by Bp of S. and M. P. C. of St. Mark's, Dio. S. and M. 1865. (Patron, V. of Malew; Glebe, 60 acres; P. C.'s Inc. 98*l* and Ho; Pop. 600.) Formerly C. of Lezayre, 1850–58, Jurby 1858; Chap. of Baldwin 1859–62; C. of St. George's, Douglas, 1862–65. [20]

AIREY, Thomas, *Holme Park, Lambrigg, Kendal.*—Mert. Coll. Ox. *ad eund.* Trin. Coll. Cam. B.A. 1814, M.A. 1817; Deac. 1814 by Bp of G. and B, Pr. 1815 by Bp of Pet. Late 2nd Mast. of the Lewes Gr. Sch; formerly C. of St. George's, Kendal, 1827–29; P. C. of Gray-Rigg, Westmorland, 1829–34. [21]

AIREY, Thomas Charles, 30, *Cousin-street, Sunderland.*—Late Chap. of the Union, Wigan. [22]

AIREY, William, *Bramley, Basingstoke, Hants.*—Queen's Coll. Ox. 3rd cl. Lit. Hum. and B.A. 1822, M.A. 1826; Deac. 1824 and Pr. 1826 by Abp of York. V. of Bramley, Dio. Win. 1845. (Patron, Queen's Coll. Ox; Tithe—Imp. 510*l*, V. 150*l*; Glebe, 4½ acres; V.'s Inc. 441*l* and Ho; Pop. 467.) Formerly C. and P. C. of Hexham 1824–45. [23]

AIRY, William, *Keysoe, near Kimbolton, Beds.*—Trin. Coll. Cam. B.A. 1829, M.A. 1832; Deac. 1830 and Pr. 1831 by Bp of Nor. V. of Keysoe, Dio. Ely, 1836. (Patron, Trin. Coll. Cam; Tithe—Imp. 54*l* 14*s*, V. 1*l* 15*s* 4*d*; Glebe, 176 acres; V.'s Inc. 205*l* and Ho; Pop. 867.) R. of Swynshed, Hunts, Dio. Ely, 1845. (Patron, Duke of Manchester; Glebe, 250 acres; R.'s Inc. 275*l*; Pop. 275.) Rural Dean of Eaton 1839; Dom. Chap. to Duke of Manchester. Formerly C. of Rushbrooke 1830–34; R. of Bradfield St. Clare 1832–36. Author various Archæological Essays. [24]

AISLABIE, William John, *Alpheton Rectory, Sudbury, Suffolk.*—Trin. Coll. Cam. B.A. 1829; Deac. 1829 and Pr. 1833 by Bp of Nor. R. of Alpheton, Dio. Ely, 1848. (Patron, John Hodgson, Esq; Tithe, 286*l*; Glebe, 40 acres; R.'s Inc. 326*l* and Ho.; Pop. 298.) [25]

AITKEN, James, *Womersley, Pontefract.*—Ex. Coll. Ox. B.A. 1851, M.A. 1854; Deac. 1852 and Pr.

1853 by Bp of Win. V. of Womersley, Dio. York, 1865. (Patron, Lord Hawke; V.'s Inc. 300*l* and Ho; Pop 998.) Formerly C. of Woodmansterne 1852–54 and 1859–65, Beddington 1854–59. [1]

AITKEN, Robert, *Pendeen Parsonage, Penzance, Cornwall.*—Univ. of Edinburgh; Deac. 1823 and Pr. 1824 by Bp of Ox. P. C. of Pendeen, Dio. Ex. 1849. (Patron, the present P. C.; P. C.'s Inc. 180*l* and Ho; Pop. 3516.) Dom. Chap. to the Earl of Seafield. Author, *Truth against Truth, or the Battle of the Covenants,* 1851, 1*s* 6*d*; *Spiritual Vitality,* 1852; *A Letter to one of the Leeds Clergy on the Difference between Salvation and Regeneration,* 1852; *The Conversion and Holy Life of St. Augustine,* 1853; *The Teaching of the Types,* 1854, 10*s* 6*d*; *The Power of Christ's Name, or Church and Dissent,* 1856, 1*s* 6*d*; *A Word for the Truth, for the Church, and for God—on the Denison Controversy,* 1857, 2*s*; *Hints, Suggestions, and Reasons for the Provisional Adjustment of the Church Rate,* 1859, 2*s* 6*d*; *The Prayer-Book Unveiled in the Light of Christ,* 1863, 2nd ed. 1867, 5*s* 6*d*; *High Truth, the Christian's Vocation, Progress, Perfection, and State in Glory,* 1866, 2*s* 6*d*; Tracts and various Sermons. [2]

AITKEN, Robert Wesley, *Kirk Marown, Isle of Man.*—St. Bees; Deac. 1858 by Abp of York. V. of Kirk Marown, Dio. S. and M. 1862. (Patron, The Crown; V.'s Inc. 150*l*; Pop. 1161.) Formerly C. of Grosmont, York. [3]

AITKEN, William Hay Macdowall Hunter, 1, *Mildmay-road, London, N.*—Wad. Coll. Ox. 2nd cl. Lit. Hum. B.A. 1865, M.A. 1867; Deac. 1865 by Bp of Lon. Pr. 1866 by Bp Anderson. C. of St. Jude's, Islington, 1865. [4]

AITKENS, Charles Haughton, *The Rectory, Mavesyn Ridware, near Rugeley, Staffs.*—New Inn Hall Ox. B.A. 1839, M.A. 1842; Deac. and Pr. 1840. R. of Mavesyn Ridware, Staffs, Dio. Lich. 1852. (Patrons, H. M. Chadwick and J. N. Lane, Esqrs; Tithe, 472*l* 15*s*; Glebe, 14 acres; R.'s Inc. 456*l* and Ho; Pop. 462.) [5]

AITKINS, Albert, *Highcliffe, Christchurch, Hants.*—St. John's Coll. Cam. B.A. 1850; Deac. 1851 and Pr. 1852 by Abp of Cant. P. C. of Highcliffe, Dio. Win. (Patroness, Lady Stuart de Rothesay; P. C.'s Inc. 40*l*.) [6]

AKEHURST, George, 38, *Carlton-hill East, London, N.W.*—Trin. Coll. Dub. and King's Coll. Lon. A. K. C; Deac. 1857 and Pr. 1858 by Bp of Lon. Chap. of the Strand Union; C. of St. Mark's, Regent's Park; Chap. to the Home, Great Ormond-street. Formerly C. of Regent-square Ch. of St. Saviour's, Paddington, and St. Thomas's, Chancery-lane. Author, *Imposture instanced in the Life of Mahomet*; *The Prayer-Book and its History.* [7]

AKENHEAD, David, *Sandhutton, York.*—Univ. Coll. Ox. B A. 1842, M.A. 1844; Deac. 1843 by Bp of Ely, Pr. 1844 by Bp of Dur. P. C. of Sandhutton, Dio. York, 1861. (Patrons, D. and C. of York; P. C.'s Inc. 200*l*; Pop. 400.) Formerly C. of Bishop Wearmouth 1843–48, and Ryton 1848–61. [8]

AKERS, George, *Mission House, Wellclose-square, London, E.*—Oriel Coll. Ox. B.A. 1859; Deac. 1860 and Pr. 1861 by Bp of Roch. Missionary C. of St. Saviour's, Wellclose-square, 1864. Formerly C. of Northfleet, Kent, and St. Mary's, Aberdeen. Author, sundry Tracts and Pamphlets. [9]

AKROYD, Jonathan, *Elmton, Chesterfield.*—Dub. and St. Bees; Deac. 1863 by Bp of Lich. C. of Elmton. Formerly C. of Gayton and Stowe, Staffs. [10]

ALCOCK, Henry Jones, *Eccleston, Lancashire.*—C. of St. Thomas's, Eccleston. [11]

ALCOCK, John Price, *The College, Ashford, Kent.*—St. John's Coll. Cam. B.A. 1831, M.A. 1834; Deac. 1831 by Bp of Lich. Pr. 1834 by Abp of Cant. V. of Ashford, Dio. Cant. 1847. (Patrons, D. and C. of Roch; Tithe—Imp. 210*l*, V. 456*l* 7*s*; Glebe, 10 acres; V.'s Inc. 532*l* and Ho; Pop. 6950.) Rural Dean of East Charing 1848; Surrogate 1848; one of the Six Preachers in Canterbury Cathedral 1858; Hon. Can. of Cant. 1866. [12]

ALCOCK, John Price, *Bickley, Bromley, Kent*—P. C. of Bickley, Dio. Cant. 1864. [13]

ALCOCK, J. E., *Hawling Rectory, Cheltenham.*—R. of Hawling, Dio. G. and B. 1859. (Patron, H. T. Hope, Esq; R.'s Inc. 130*l* and Ho; Pop. 171.) [14]

ALDER, Edward, *Swaffham Prior, Cambridge.*—C. of Swaffham Prior. [15]

ALDER, Gilbert, *Hurstbourne-Tarrant, Andover, Hants.*—Trin. Hall Cam. B.C.L. 1823; Deac. 1823, Pr. 1824. V. of Hurstbourne-Tarrant with Vernhams-Dean C. Dio. Win. 1846. (Patron, Bp of Win; Tithe—App. 1340*l* and 100 acres of Glebe, V. 402*l* 11*s* 6*d*; Glebe, 50 acres; V.'s Inc. 490*l* and Ho; Pop. Hurstbourne-Tarrant 839, Vernhams-Dean 727.) Rural Dean; Surrogate. [16]

ALDER, Henry Robert.—Trin. Coll. Cam. B A. 1849, M.A. 1850; Deac. 1847, Pr. 1850. Formerly P. C. of St. Mary's, Barnsley, 1852–63. [17]

ALDER, Richard, *Gibraltar.*—Canon of Gibraltar 1855; Chap. to the Convict Establishment, Gibraltar; Dom. Chap. to Dowager Baroness Truro. [18]

ALDERMAN, Francis Charles, *Kintbury, Hungerford, Berks.*—Ex. Coll. Ox. B.A. 1826, M.A. 1828. P. C. of the District Chapel of Denford, Kintbury, Dio. Ox. 1839. (Patron, G. C. Cherry, Esq; P. C.'s Inc. 48*l*; Pop. 77.) [19]

ALDERSEY, John, *Kirkland, Penrith.*—Queen's Coll. Ox. B.A. 1835, M.A. 1838; Deac. 1836, Pr. 1837. C. of Kirkland. [20]

ALDERSON, Christopher, *Kirkheaton Rectory, Huddersfield.*—Magd. Hall Ox. B.A. 1829, M.A. 1836; Deac. 1829 and Pr. 1830 by Abp of York. R. of Kirkheaton, Dio. Rip. 1836. (Patrons, Trustees; R.'s Inc. 620*l* and Ho; Pop. 7201.) [21]

ALDERSON, Edmund, *Aslackby, Folkingham, Lincolnshire.*—St. John's Coll. Cam. B.A. 1831; Deac. 1832, Pr. 1833. V. of Aslackby, Dio. Lin. 1851. (Patron, R. F. Barstow, Esq; Tithe—Imp. 429*l* 15*s* 6*d*, V. 352*l*; Glebe, 38 acres; V.'s Inc. 410*l* and Ho.; Pop. 534.) [22]

ALDERSON, Edmund Albert, *Colchester.*—St. John's Col. Cam. B.A. 1862; Deac. 1864 and Pr. 1865 by Bp of Roch. C. of St. Peter's, Colchester. [23]

ALDERSON, Frederick Cecil, *Holdenby Rectory, Northampton.*—Trin. Coll. Cam. B.A. 1857, M.A. 1861; Deac. 1861 by Abp of York, Pr. 1862 by Bp of Ely. R. of Holdenby, Dio. Pet. 1865. (Patron, the Crown; Glebe, 5 acres; R.'s Inc. 580*l* and Ho; Pop. 180.) Formerly C. of Ampthill, Beds, 1861–63, Hursley, Hants, 1863–65. [24]

ALDERSON, George, *Hornby Vicarage, Catterick, Yorks.*—Pemb. Coll. Cam. B.A. 1822, M.A. 1836; Deac. 1822 and Pr. 1823 by Abp of York. V. of Hornby, Dio. Rip. 1829. (Patrons, D. and C. of York; Tithe—93*l* 8*s* 8*d* to the V, 640*l* to the Duke of Leeds; Glebe, 66 acres to Duke of Leeds; V.'s Inc. 280*l*; Pop. 615.) Dom. Chap. to Duke of Leeds. Formerly C. of Hart-hill, Yorks, 1822–24, Sutton and Wingerworth 1824–26, Hornby 1826–29. [25]

ALDERSON, James Thomas, *Ravenstone Rectory, near Ashby de-la-Zouch.*—R. of Ravenstone, Dio. Lich. 1855. (Patron, Ld Chan; R.'s Inc. 305*l* and Ho; Pop. 392.) Late C. of Denham, Suffolk. [26]

ALDERSON, Richard W. S. A., *Swan River, West Australia.*—Chap. to the Convict Establishment, Swan River. [27]

ALDERSON, Robert Jervis Coke, *Wetherden, Stow Market, Suffolk.*—Ex. Coll. Ox. B.A. 1825, M.A. 1827. R. of Wetherden, Dio. Nor. 1844. (Patron, Ld Chan; Tithe, 490*l* 11*s* 9*d*; R.'s Inc. 500*l* and Ho; Pop. 479.) [28]

ALDERSON, William Thompson, *Wakefield.*—St. Cath. Coll. Cam. B.A. 1829; Deac. 1829 and Pr. 1830 by Abp of York. Chap. to the West Riding House of Correction, Wakefield. [29]

ALDHAM, Harcourt, *Stoke Prior Vicarage, Bromsgrove.*—Wor. Coll. Ox. B.A. 1831; Deac. and Pr. 1832 by Bp of Wor. V. of Stoke Prior with C. of St. Godwald's, Dio. Wor. 1842. (Patrons, D. and C. of Wor;

Tithe—Imp. 430*l*; Glebe, 154 acres; V.'s Inc. 350*l* and Ho; Pop. 1579.) Formerly C. of St. Helen's and St. Alban's 1832-33, Wichenford 1833-4, Hartlebury 1834-35, Stoke Prior 1836-42, all in Worcestershire. Late Chap. to the Bromsgrove Union. [1]

ALDINGTON, G.—C. of St. George the Martyr's, Southwark. [2]

ALDIS, C. M., *Wrenbury, Nantwich, Cheshire.*—P. C. of Wrenbury, Dio. Ches. 1848. (Patron, V. of Acton; P. C.'s Inc. 150*l* and Ho; Pop. 2505.) [3]

ALDOM, John Wesley, *Penistone, Yorks.*—Mast. of the Penistone Gr. Sch. [4]

ALDOUS, John, *Trinity Parsonage, Sheffield.*—St. Cath. Hall, Cam; Deac. 1848, Pr. 1849. P. C. of Holy Trin. Wicker, Sheffield, Dio. York, 1853. (Patroness, Miss Harrison; P. C.'s Inc. 280*l* and Ho; Pop. 10,796.) Surrogate. [5]

ALDRED, John Thomas Foster, *Dore Parsonage, Sheffield.*—Lin. Coll. Ox. B.A. 1842, M.A. 1844; Deac. 1843 by Bp of Lin, Pr. 1844 by Abp of York. P. C. of Dore, Dio. Lich. 1849. (Patron, Earl Fitzwilliam; Glebe, 48 acres; P. C.'s Inc. 110*l* and Ho; Pop. 1006.) Author, A *Lecture on the Advantages and Uses of General Knowledge*, 1851. [6]

ALDRICH, John Cobbold, *Ipswich*—Lin. Coll. Ox. B.A. 1829, M.A. 1832; Deac. 1830 and Pr. 1831 by Bp of Nor. P. C. of St. Lawrence's, Ipswich, Dio. Nor. 1830. (Patrons, the Parishioners; P. C.'s Inc. 180*l*; Pop. 502.) [7]

ALDRICH-BLAKE, Frederic James, *The Old Hill Court, Ross, Herefordshire.*—Pemb. Coll. Cam. B.A. 1852, M.A. 1856; Deac. 1853 and Pr. 1854 by Bp of Ely. Formerly C. of Stanningfield, Suffolk, 1853-55, St. Martin's-in-the-Fields, Lond. 1859-62, and Chingford, Essex, 1862-66. [8]

ALDRIDGE, Augustus Edward, *Worton, Devizes, Wilts.*—St. John's Coll. Cam; Deac. 1846, Pr. 1848. P. C. of Worton with Marston, Dio. Salis. 1853. (Patron, V. of Potterne; Tithe, 125*l*; P. C.'s Inc. 180*l*; Pop. 591.) [9]

ALDRIDGE, Edward H., *Park-road, Chorley, Lancashire.*—C. of Chorley. [10]

ALDRIT, William, *Hutton, near Weston-super-Mare.*—Magd. Coll. Cam. B.D. 1844; Deac. 1836, Pr. 1837. C. of Hutton. Formerly Mast. of Wells Cathl. Gr. Sch. [11]

ALDWELL, Basil Duckett, *Southsea, Hants.*—Dub. A.M; Deac. 1842 by Bp of Ossory and Ferns, Pr. 1843 by Bp of Cashel and Waterford. P. C. of St. Luke's, Southsea, Dio. Win. 1864. (Patron, Bp of Win; P. C.'s Inc. 330*l* and Ho; Pop. 11,000.) Formerly C. of St. Luke's, Southsea. [12]

ALDWORTH, John, *Little Walsingham, Norfolk.*—Dub. A.B. 1855; Deac. 1856 by Abp of Dub., Pr. 1856 by Bp of Cork. V. of West Barsham, Dio. Nor. 1857. (Patron, Major-Gen. Balders, C.B; Tithe, 168*l*; Bounty Land, 7½ acres; V.'s Inc. 188*l* 19*s* 4*d*; Pop. 92.) [13]

ALDWORTH, John, *Haigh, near Wigan.*—Wor. Coll. Ox. M.A; Deac. 1857 and Pr. 1858 by Bp of Ox. P. C. of Haigh, Dio. Ches. 1868. (Patron, R. of Wigan; P. C.'s Inc. 300*l*; Pop. 5461.) Formerly C. of Somerton, Oxon. [14]

ALEXANDER, Alexander Benjamin, *The Cottage, Earlswood Common, Red Hill.*—Ch. Coll. Cam. Sen. Opt. and B.A. 1863; Deac. 1863, Pr. 1864. C. of St. John's, Red Hill, 1863. [15]

ALEXANDER, C.—Dom. Chap. to the Earl of Caledon. [16]

ALEXANDER, Charles Leslie.—Deac. 1852, Pr. 1853. Formerly C. of St. Mary's, Lambeth. [17]

ALEXANDER, David M.—P. C. of Hanover Chapel, Regent-street, Dio. Lon. 1864. (Patron, R. of St. George's, Hanover-square; P. C.'s Inc. 700*l*; Pop. 2923.) Formerly P. C. of Oldham 1861-64. [18]

ALEXANDER, Disney Legard, *Ganton Vicarage, Yorks.*—St. Mary Hall, Ox. B.A. 1847; Deac. 1847 and Pr. 1848 by Bp of Dur. V. of Ganton; Dio. York, 1852. (Patron, Sir T. D. Legard, Bart; V.'s Inc. 186*l* and Ho; Pop. 352.) Formerly C. of Willerby, Yorks. [19]

ALEXANDER, Godfrey Edward, *Stoke Bliss, Tenbury.*—Trin. Coll. Ox. B.A. 1840, M.A. 1843; Deac. and Pr. 1842 by Abp of Armagh. V. of Stoke Bliss, Dio. Herf. 1865. (Patron, Ld Chan; Tithe, 350*l*; Glebe, 74 acres; V.'s Inc. 430*l* and Ho; Pop. 298.) Dom. Chap. to the Earl and Dowager Countess of Caledon. Formerly V. of Woodford, Northants, 1855-65. [20]

ALEXANDER, Harvey, *Stoke Rivers Rectory, Barnstaple.*—Wor. Coll. Ox. B.A. 1844; Deac. 1845 and Pr. 1846 by Bp of Ex. R. of Stoke Rivers, Dio. Ex. 1854. (Patroness, Mrs. Hutton; Tithe—Imp. 245*l*; Glebe, 60 acres; R.'s Inc. 316*l* and Ho; Pop. 242.) [21]

ALEXANDER, Henry.—Chaplain Royal Navy. [22]

ALEXANDER, H., *Shelford, Nottingham.*—P. C. of Shelford, Dio. Lin. 1857. (Patron, Earl of Chesterfield; P. C.'s Inc. 60*l*; Pop. 692.) [23]

ALEXANDER, Richard Dobson, *South Pool, Kingsbridge, Devon.*—Ex. Coll. Ox. B.A. 1854; Deac. 1855 by Bp of Ex. Pr. 1858 by Bp of Win. R. of South Pool, Dio. Ex. 1861. (Patrons, A. Kelly, Esq. two turns, Mrs. A. F. Praed, one turn; Tithe, comm. at 387*l*; Glebe, 50 acres; R.'s Inc. 470*l* and Ho; Pop. 418.) Formerly C. of Tavistock and Brentor 1855-57; P. C. of St. Matthew's, Hatchford, Surrey; and Dom. Chap. to the late Dow. Countess of Ellesmere 1857-61. [24]

ALFORD, Bradley Hurt, *Leavenheath Colchester.*—Trin. Coll. Cam. 2nd cl. Cl. Trip. B.A. 1859, M.A. 1862; Deac. 1862, and Pr. 1863 by Bp of Lon. P. C. of Leavenheath, Dio. Ely, 1865. (Patron, V. of Stoke; P. C.'s Inc. 100*l* and Ho; Pop. 520.) Formerly C. of St. Michael's, Chester-square, Pimlico, 1862-65. [25]

ALFORD, Charles, *West Quantoxhead, Bridgwater, Somerset.*—Ball. Coll. Ox. B.A. 1809; Deac. 1810, Pr. 1811. R. of West Quantoxhead, Dio. B. and W. 1814. (Patron, H. Harvey, Esq.; Tithe, 220*l*; Glebe, 38 acres; R.'s Inc. 330*l* and Ho; Pop. 223.) Surrogate 1820. [26]

ALFORD, Clement, *Willesden, Middlesex.*—Corpus Christi Coll. Ox. B.A. 1863, M.A. 1866; Deac. 1864, and Pr. 1865 by Bp of Ex. C. of Willesden 1866. Formerly of Ch. Ch. Plymouth, 1864. [27]

ALFORD, George, *Downend, near Bristol.*—Queen's Coll. Ox. B.A. 1846, M.A. 1849; Deac. 1846 and Pr. 1847 by Bp of Ox. C. of Mangot's-field with Downend 1866. Formerly C. of Aston Sandford 1846; Holy Trinity, Tewkesbury, 1849, Holy Trinity, St. Pancras, Lond. 1852; P. C. of Arkley, Barnet, 1856; R. of Aston Sandford 1858; P. C. of Cookley, Worcestershire, 1862-66. [28]

ALFORD, The Very Rev. Henry, *The Deanery, Canterbury.*—Trin. Coll. Cam. Bell's Univ. Scho. Latin Members' Prizeman 1831, 37th Wrang. 1st cl. Cl. Trip. and B.A. 1832, M.A. 1835, B.D. 1849, D.D. 1859; Deac. 1833 by Bp of Ex. Pr. 1834 by Bp of Roch. Dean of Canterbury 1857 (Value 2000*l* and Res). Fell. of Trin. Coll. Cam. 1834, Hulsean Lecturer 1841 and 1842. Formerly C. of Ampton, Suffolk, 1833-35; V. of Wymeswold, Leicestershire, 1835-53; Min. of Quebec Chapel, Lond. 1853-57; Examiner in Logic in the Univ. of Lond. 1842. Author, *Poems*, 2 vols. Cambridge Univ. Press, 1835, and various later editions in England and America; *Hulsean Lectures*, 2 vols.; *Chapters on the Poets of Ancient Greece*, 1842; *Sermons*, 1848; *Greek Testament, with a critically revised Text, Prolegomena and English Notes*, 4 vols. 1849-62; *Quebec Chapel Sermons*, 7 vols. 1854-57; *Homilies on the First Ten Chapters of the Acts of the Apostles*, 1858; *Memoir of the late Rev. H. Alford* (Father of the Author); *The Odyssey of Homer in English Verse*, 1861; *The New Testament for English Readers*, 2 vols. 1863-65; *The Queen's English*, 1863; *The Year of Prayer, or Family Prayers adapted to the Seasons of the Church*, 1866; *Letters from Abroad*, 1864; *How to Use the New Testament*, 1866; *Sermons on Christian Doctrine, preached in Canterbury Cathedral*, 1863; Contributions to Magazines; etc. [29]

ALFORD, Samuel, *Glasbury, near Hay, South Wales.*—Queens' Coll. Cam. B.A. 1841, M.A. 1845; Deac. 1841, Pr. 1842. C. of Glasbury. [1]

ALFORD Walter, *Drayton Parsonage, Taunton.*—St. Edm. Hall, Ox. B.A. 1830, M.A. 1834; Deac. 1831 and Pr. 1832 by Bp of B. and W. P. C. of Muchelney, Somerset, Dio. B. and W. 1843. (Patron, W. Long, Esq; Tithe—Imp, 336*l* 11*s* and 11½ acres of Glebe; P. C. 10*l*; Glebe, ¾ acres; P. C.'s Inc. 94*l*; Pop. 309.) P. C. of Drayton, Somerset, Dio. B. and W. 1848. (Patrons, D. and C. of Bristol; Tithe—Apps. 330*l* and 34 acres of Glebe; P. C.'s Inc. 101*l* and Ho; Pop. 559.) Author, *The Old and New Testament Dispensations Compared*, 1858, 12*s*, 2nd ed. 1862, 7*s* 6*d*. [2]

ALINGTON, Alan Marmaduke, *Benniworth Rectory, Wragby, Lincolnshire.*—Wor. Coll. Ox. B.A. 1857, M.A. 1860; Deac. 1860 by Bp of Ox. Pr. 1861 by Bp of Lin. R. of Benniworth, Dio. Lin. 1864. (Patron, G. F. Heneage, Esq; R.'s Inc. 600*l* and Ho; Pop. 431.) Formerly C. of Croxby and Beelsby 1861–64. [3]

ALINGTON, Charles Argentine.—Mert. Coll. Ox. B.A. 1851; Deac. 1851, Pr. 1852. Missionary Chap. to the Right Rev. Bp Tozer, Central Africa. Formerly R. of Muckton and V. of Burwell, Dio. Lin. [4]

ALINGTON, Henry Giles, *Education Department, Privy Council Office, London, S.W.*—Magd. Coll. Ox. B.A. 1859, M.A. 1865; Deac. 1866 by Bp of Salis. [5]

ALINGTON, John, *Candlesby Rectory, Spilsby, Lincolnshire.*—Magd. Coll. Ox. B.A. 1822, M.A. 1825. R. of Croxby, Lincolnshire, Dio. Lin. 1832. (Patron, Ld Chan; Tithe, 313*l*; Glebe, 12 acres; R.'s Inc. 329*l*; Pop. 147.) R. of Candlesby, Dio. Lin. 1834. (Patron, Magd. Coll. Ox; R.'s Inc. 206*l* and Ho; Pop. 240.) [6]

ALINGTON, John Wynford, 2, *Foley-place, Gloucester.*—Magd. Coll. Ox. Deac. 1863, Pr. 1864. C. of St. James's, Gloucester. [7]

ALINGTON-PYE, Richard, *Swinhope, Binbrook, Great Grimsby.*—St. John's Coll. Cam. B.A. 1835; Deac. 1835, Pr. 1836. R. of Swinhope, Dio. Lin. 1837. (Patron, George Marmaduke Alington, Esq; Tithe, 230*l* 16*s* 10*d*; Glebe, 14 acres; R.'s Inc. 234*l*; Pop. 105.) R. of Stenigot Horncastle, Dio. Lin. 1837. (Patron, George Marmaduke Alington, Esq.; Tithe, 282*l* 9*s* 2*d*; Glebe, 38 acres; R.'s Inc. 332*l*; Pop. 96.) [8]

ALKER, George, *Maudland Bank, Preston.*—Dub. A.B. 1850; Deac. 1851 by Bp of Man. Pr. 1852 by Bp of Ches. P. C. of St. Mary's, Preston, Dio. Man. 1857. (Patron V. of Preston; P. C.'s Inc. 170*l*; Pop. 9025.) Formerly C. of St. Mary's, Preston. Author, *Tracts on Purgatory and Transubstantiation.* [9]

ALLAN, George, *Hazlemere, High Wycombe, Bucks.*—Deac. 1828, Pr. 1829. P. C. of Hazlemere, Dio. Ox. 1851. (Patroness Miss H. Carter; Glebe, 3 acres; P. C.'s Inc. 47*l* and Ho; Pop. 966.) [10]

ALLAN, Hugh, *Cricklade, Wilts.*—Dub. A.B. 1827, A.M. 1830; Deac. 1828 and Pr. 1829 by Bp of Carl. R. of St. Mary's, Cricklade, Dio. G. and B. 1834. (Patron Bp of G. and B; Tithe—Imp. 19*l*, R. 15*l*; Glebe, 50 acres; R.'s Inc. 95*l* and Ho; Pop. 367.) Surrogate for Consistory Courts of Salisbury and Bristol. [11]

ALLAN, Hugh, *Sherborne, Dorset.*—Wad. Coll. Ox. B.A. 1856, M.A. 1859; Deac. 1859, Pr. 1860. C. of Haydon, Dorset, 1865. Formerly C. of St. Paul's, Bristol, 1859, St. Jude's, Southwark, 1861, Hazlemere, Bucks, 1861, Woodlands, Dorset, 1862, and Hazlemere 1865. [12]

ALLAN, William, 75, *Elgin-crescent, Notting-hill, London, W.*—Wor. Coll. Ox. B.A. 1859, M.A. 1862; Deac. 1860 and Pr. 1861 by Bp of Win. Assoc. Sec. of Lord's Day Observance Soc. 1862. Formerly C. of St. Andrew's, Lambeth, 1860–62. [13]

ALLCROFT, Walter, *Gunness, Brigg, Lincolnshire.*—Dub. A.B. 1853; Deac. 1853 and Pr. 1854 by Bp of Lin. R. of Gunness with Burringham C. Dio. Lin. 1861. (Patron, Bp of Nor; Tithe, 200*l*; Glebe, 1 acre; R.'s Inc. 220*l* and Ho; Pop. 791.) Formerly C. of Messingham. [14]

ALLCROFT, William Rowley, *Belton, Bawtry, Lincolnshire.*—Literate; Deac 1831 and Pr. 1832 by Abp of York. P. C. of West Butterwick, Lincolnshire, Dio. Lin. 1852. (Patron, V. of Owston; P. C.'s Inc. 95*l*; Pop. 907.) Editor of *Read's History of the Isle of Axholme*, Gainsborough, 1860, 16*s*. [15]

ALLEN, Alfred, *Barcombe, Lewes, Sussex.*—Pemb. Coll. Cam. B.A. 1845, M.A. 1849; Deac. 1845, Pr. 1846. C. of Barcombe. Formerly C. of Burton-Coggles. Author, *Supremacy of the Scriptures as the Rule of Faith*, 1851, 1*s*; *A Tract for Navvies*, 1851. [16]

ALLEN, Charles, *Bushley (Worcestershire), near Tewkesbury.*—Brasen. Coll. Ox. B.A. 1843, M.A. 1846; Deac. 1844 and Pr. 1855 by Bp of Wor. P. C. of Bushley, Dio. Wor. 1846. (Patron, W. Dowdeswell, Esq; P. C.'s Inc. 356*l*; Pop. 282.) [17]

ALLEN, Charles Jefferies, *Stocklinch-Ottersay, Ilminster, Somerset.*—R. of Stocklinch Ottersay, Dio. B. and W. 1823. (Patron, J. Allen, Esq; Tithe, 108*l* 15*s*; Glebe, 21¾ acres; R.'s Inc. 153*l*; Pop. 69.) [18]

ALLEN, Ebenezer Brown, 14, *Foulis-terrace, Brompton, London, S.W.*—Queens' Coll. Cam. B.A. 1834; Deac. 1834, Pr. 1835. Chap. to Brompton Hospital for Consumption 1849. [19]

ALLEN, Edmund Edward, *Porth Kerry, Cowbridge.*—Trin. Coll. Cam. B.A. 1846, M.A. 1860; Deac. 1847, Pr. 1848. R. of Porth Kerry with Barry R. Dio. Llan. 1865. (Patrons, Sons of late Sir S. Romilly; Tithe, 183*l*; Glebe, 100*l*; R.'s Inc. 292*l* and Ho; Pop. Porth Kerry, 168, Barry, 87.) Formerly C. of St. Mary's, Shrewsbury, 1847, Yerbeston 1850; V. of Millom 1854; Rural Dean of Gosforth, 1859. [20]

ALLEN, Edward, *Dartford, Kent.*—Brasen. Coll. Ox. B.A. 1808, M.A. 1810. R. of Hartley, Kent, Dio. Roch. 1827. (Patron, the present R; Tithe, 362*l*; Glebe, 13 acres; R.'s Inc. 375*l*; Pop. 244.) [21]

ALLEN, Edward, *Castle Church, near Stafford.*—St. John's Coll. Cam. B.A. 1845, M.A. 1849; Deac. 1845, Pr. 1846. P. C. of Castle Church, Dio. Lich. 1853. (Patron, Ld Chan; Tithe—Imp. 91*l* 16*s* 8*d*; Glebe, 29 acres; P. C.'s Inc. 143*l* and Ho; Pop. 831.) Formerly P. C. of St. Paul's, Forebridge, Staffs, 1847. [22]

ALLEN, Edward, *Trinity Rectory, Salford, Manchester.*—R. of Trinity, Salford, Dio. Man. 1860. (Patron, Sir R. G. Booth; R.'s. Inc. 550*l*; Pop. 12,192.) [23]

ALLEN, Edward Henry, *Hampton Bishop, Hereford.*—Trin. Coll. Cam. B.A. 1861, M.A. 1865; Deac. 1861 and Pr. 1862 by Bp of Herf. C. of Hampton Bishop 1861. [24]

ALLEN, Fletcher, *Frier Field, Derby.*—Ch. Coll. Cam. B.A. 1858; Deac. 1858 and Pr. 1860 by Bp of G. and B. C. of Radborne, near Derby, 1863, and Head Mast. of St. Clement's Sch. Derby. Formerly C. of Awre, near Newnham, 1858. [25]

ALLEN, George.—P. C. of St. Thomas's Islington, Dio. Lon. 1860. (Patrons, Trustees; P. C.'s Inc. 300*l*; Pop. 5598.) [26]

ALLEN, George, *Little Driffield, Yorks.*—Deac. 1816 and Pr. 1817 by Abp of York. P. C. of Driffields-Ambo, Dio. York 1833. (Patron, Abp. of York; Tithe, 127*l* 15*s*; Glebe, 46 acres; P. C.'s Inc. 300*l* with 35*l* for Ho.) Formerly V. of Kirkburn, 1826–65; Surrogate, 1833. [27]

ALLEN, George Samuel, *Manchester.*—Dur. B.A. 1853, M.A. 1854; Deac. 1856 and Pr. 1857 by Bp of Man. Min. of temporary Ch. Lower Broughton, 1864. Formerly C. of St. Andrew's, Manchester, 1856; Dep. Asst. Min. Can. of Man. Cathl. 1860. [28]

ALLEN, Hugh, 231, *New Kent-road, London, S.E.*—Dub. A.B. and A.M. 1835, B.D. and D.D. 1861, *ad eund.* Cam. 1861; Deac. 1835 and Pr. 1836 by Bp of S. and M. R. of St. George the Martyr's, Dio. Win. 1859. (Patron, Ld Chan; R.'s Inc. 750*l* and Ho; Pop. 26,300.) Surrogate. [29]

ALLEN, Humphrey, *Clifton.*—Wor. Coll. Ox. B.A. 1821, M.A. 1825; Deac. 1824 and Pr. 1825 by Bp of St. D. P. C. of Trinity, Clifton, Dio. G. and B. 1845. (Patrons, Simeon's Trustees; P. C.'s Inc. 300*l*; Pop. 3400.) Hon. Can. of Bristol Cathl. 1862. Formerly C. of Hay, Brecon 1824–44. [30]

ALLEN, H. B., *Stanton Prior, Bristol.*—C. of Stanton Prior. [1]

ALLEN, James, *Castle-Martin, Pembrokeshire.*—Trin. Coll. Cam. B.A. 1825, M.A. 1829; Deac. 1834 and Pr. 1835 by Bp of G. and B. V. of Castle-Martin, Dio. St. D. 1839. (Patron, Earl of Cawdor; Tithe—Imp. 190*l*, V. 193*l*; Glebe, 63 acres; V.'s Inc. 300*l* and Ho; Pop. 404.) Preb. of St. David's; Rural Dean of Castle-Martin 1840. [2]

ALLEN, The Venerable John, *Prees Vicarage, Shrewsbury.*—Trin. Coll. Cam. 18th Sen. Opt. B.A. 1832, M.A. 1835; Deac. 1833 and Pr. 1834 by Bp of Lon. V. of Prees, Dio. Lich. 1846. (Patron, Bp of Lich; Tithe—App. 1041*l* 1*s*, V. 636*l*; Glebe, 62 acres; V.'s Inc. 720*l* and Ho; Pop. 2259.) Chap. of King's Coll. Lond. 1833; Exam. Chap. to Bp of Chich. 1836; Her Majesty's Inspector of Schools 1839; Exam. Chap. to the Bp of Lich. 1843; Archd. of Salop 1847; Preb. of Ufton Cantoris in Lich. Cathl. 1848. Editor of *Cudworth on Free Will*, 1835; Author, *History of St. Christopher* (an Allegory), 1843; occasional Sermons; Reports in the Minutes of the Committee of Council on Education. [3]

ALLEN, John, *Brighton.*—Dub. A.B. 1835; Deac. 1837 by Bp of Derry, Pr. 1839 by Bp of Chich. V. of Patcham, Dio. Chich. 1865. (Patron, Ld Chan; Tithe, 138*l*; Glebe, 2½ acres; V.'s Inc. 160*l* and Ho; Pop. 638.) Formerly C. of Kilcar and Dunfanaghy, Donegal, and of Steyning, Sussex; Chap. to Workhouse and Industrial Schools, Brighton. [4]

ALLEN, John, *Coggeshall, Essex.*—Brasen. Coll. Ox. B.A. 1863; Deac. 1864 and Pr. 1866 by Bp of Roch. C. of St. Peter's, Coggeshall, 1864. [5]

ALLEN, John, 28, *Storey-square, Barrow-in-Furness.*—Lond. Univ. B.A. 1859; Deac. 1862 and Pr. 1863 by Bp of Dur. C. of St. George's, Barrow-in-Furness, 1866. Formerly C. of St. Paul's, Ryhope, 1862, and St. Cuthbert's, Durham. [6]

ALLEN, John. — Min. of Peckham Chapel, Surrey. [7]

ALLEN, John Henry, *Mappowder, Blandford, Dorset.*—Brasen. Coll. Ox. B.A. 1831, M.A. 1834; Deac. 1833, Pr. 1834. R. of Mappowder, Dio. Salis. 1835. (Patron, Earl of Beauchamp; Tithe, 330*l*; Glebe, 89 acres; R.'s Inc. 464*l*; Pop. 238.) [8]

ALLEN, Mundeford, *Melbourne, near Royston, Cambs.*—King's Coll. Lond. 1st cl. Assoc. 1862; Deac. 1862 and Pr. 1863 by Bp of Herf. C. of Melbourne 1864. Formerly C. of Iron Bridge 1862–64. [9]

ALLEN, Peregrine S., *Mainstone, Bishop's Castle, Salop.*—R. of Mainstone, Dio. Herf. 1866. (Patron, Ld Chan; R.'s Inc. 300*l*; Pop. 365.) [10]

ALLEN, Richard, *Gipsey Hill, Norwood, Surrey.*—P. C. of Ch. Ch. Gipsey Hill, Dio. Win. 1862. (Patron, P. C. of St. Luke's, Lower Norwood; P. C.'s Inc. 300*l*.) [11]

ALLEN, Richard John, *Swilland Vicarage, Ipswich.*—Queens' Coll. Cam. B.A. 1836; Deac. 1837 and Pr. 1838 by Bp of Rip. V. of Swilland, Dio. Nor. 1847. (Patron, Ld Chan; Tithe, 252*l*; Glebe, 42 acres; V.'s Inc. 294*l* and Ho; Pop. 243.) [12]

ALLEN, Robert, *Battersea Rise, Wandsworth, London, S.W.*—New Coll. Ox. LL.B. 1819; Deac. 1816; Pr. 1817 by Bp of Herf. R. of Barcombe, Sussex, Dio. Chich. 1826. (Patron, Ld Chan; Tithe—Imp. 3*l* 12*s*, R. 960*l* 4*s* 3*d*, Glebe, 49 acres; R.'s Inc. 960*l* and Ho; Pop. 1090.) Preb. in Chich. Cathl. 1841 (Value 5*l* 3*s* 8*d*); Rural Dean. [13]

ALLEN, Robert James, 2, *Courtland-terrace, The Mall, Kensington, W.*—Ball. Coll. Ox. B.A. 1854, M.A. 1857; Deac. 1857 and Pr. 1858 by Bp of Salis. C. of St. George's, Campden Hill, 1866. Formerly Cl. Mast. at the Priory, Croydon, 1854–56; C. of Westbury, Wilts, 1857–59; Vice Prin. of the Wor. Dio. Training Coll. Saltley, 1859–60; C. of St. Martin's, Leicester, 1861; Dio. Org. Sec. for Nat. Soc. 1861–65; Asst. Mast. of Leicester Coll. Sch. 1862–66. [14]

ALLEN, Robert Pinhorn, *Westbourne (Sussex), near Emsworth, Hants.*—Magd. Hall, Ox. B.A. 1835, M.A. 1837; Deac. 1835, Pr. 1836 by Bp of Lin. [15]

ALLEN, Samuel, 2, *Cambridge-terrace, Hastings.*—Trin. Coll. Cam. B.A. 1852; Deac. 1854 and Pr. 1855 by Bp of Pet. Chap. to the Hastings Borough Cemetery, and Chap. to Lord Muncaster. Formerly C. of Higham Ferrers, Northants. [16]

ALLEN, Stephen.—Trin. Coll. Cam. B.A. 1835, M.A. 1839, D.D. 1851; Deac. 1836, Pr. 1837. Late C. of St. Cuthbert's, Wells, Somerset. [17]

ALLEN, Thomas Dawson, *North Cerney Rectory, Glouc.*—Univ. Coll. Ox. B.A. 1808, M.A. 1811; Deac. 1811, Pr. 1812. R. of North Cerney, Dio. G. and B. 1827. (Patron, Univ. Coll. Ox; Tithe, 730*l*; Glebe, 104½ acres; R.'s Inc. 830*l* and Ho; Pop. 692.) [18]

ALLEN, Thomas Kingdon, *Girlington, Bradford, Yorks.*—Literate; Deac. 1857 and Pr. 1858 by Bp of Rip. P. C. of St. Philip's, Girlington, Bradford, Dio. Rip. 1860. (Patrons, Trustees of the Rev. Chas. Simeon; P. C.'s Inc. 135*l*; Pop. 2227.) Formerly C. of St. Andrew's, Bradford, 1857–60. [19]

ALLEN, Udney John Thomas, *The Vicarage, Throwley, near Faversham.*—Magd. Hall, Ox. B.A. 1846, M.A. 1863; Deac. 1846 and Pr. 1847 by Abp of York. V. of Throwley, Dio. Cant. 1862. (Patron, Abp of Cant; Tithe—Imp. 610*l*. and Glebe 73 acres; V. 257 and Glebe, 25 acres; V.'s Inc. 330*l* and Ho; Pop. 635.) Formerly C. of Warmfield, Yorks. 1847; Min. of St. John's, Bradford, 1848; C. of Frating 1849; Sen. C. of Chiddingstone, Kent, 1851; V. of Leysdown with Harty, Kent, 1852–62, and at same time C. of Goudhurst, Kent, 1857–60. Author, *The Work of the Ministry* (a Visitation Sermon), 1854. [20]

ALLEN, William, *Bosherston, Pembroke.*—Ox. B.A. 1820, M.A. 1823; Deac. 1823 by Bp of Ox. Pr. 1824 by Bp of St. D. R. of St. Brides, Dio. St. D. 1825. (Patrons, S. Philipps and J. J. Allen, Esqrs; Tithe, 195*l* 5*s*; Glebe, 1 acre; R.'s Inc. 197*l* and Ho; Pop. 151.) R. of Stackpole Bosher, Dio. St. D. 1831. (Patron, Earl of Cawdor; Tithe, 110*l* 10*s*; Glebe, 65 acres; R.'s Inc. 175*l* and Ho; Pop. 200.) [21]

ALLEN, William, *St. George's Parsonage, near Wellington, Shropshire.*—St. John's Coll. Cam. Scho. and Prizeman of B.A. 1853, M.A. 1856; Deac. 1853 and Pr. 1854 by Bp of Lich. P. C. of St. George's, Pain's-lane, Dio. Lich. 1857. (Patron, Duke of Sutherland; Glebe, 3 acres; P. C.'s Inc. 205*l* and Ho; Pop. 2180.) Formerly C. of Mucklestone, Shropshire, 1853–57. [22]

ALLEN, William, *Newtown, Bishops Waltham, Hants.*—Magd. Hall, Ox. P. C. of Newtown, Dio. Win. 1851. (Patrons, Trustees; Glebe, 10 acres; P. C.'s Inc. 168*l* and Ho; Pop. 635.) [23]

ALLEN, William Arthur, *Nether Stowey, Bridgwater.*—Deac. 1861 and Pr. 1862 by Bp of B. and W. C. of Nether Stowey 1864. Formerly C. of Drayton Muchelney 1861–64. [24]

ALLEN, William Maxey, *Shouldham, Downham-Market, Norfolk.*—Ch. Coll. Cam. B.A. 1848, M.A. 1852; Deac. 1849, Pr. 1850. P. C. of Shouldham with Shouldham Thorpe, Dio. Nor. 1850. (Patron, Sir Thomas Hare, Bart. Stow Hall, Downham-Market; Shouldham, Tithe—Imp. 245*l*; Shouldham Thorpe, Tithe—App. 115*l* 13*s*, Imp. 171*l* 18*s*; P. C.'s Inc. 120*l*; Pop. Shouldham 727. Shouldham Thorpe 298.) [25]

ALLEN, William Taprell, *St. Briavels Vicarage, Coleford.*—St. Mary Hall, Ox. B.A. 1849, M.A. 1867; Deac. and Pr. 1849 by Bp of Salis. V. of St. Briavels, Dio. G. and B. 1866. (Patrons, D. and C. of Herf; Tithe, comm. at 229*l*; Glebe, ¼ acre; V.'s Inc. 223*l* and Ho; Pop. 1261.) Formerly C. of Beaminster, Dorset, 1849; Bower Chalke, Wilts, 1849, Fifield Bavant, Wilts, 1850, and Brinsop, Hereford, 1855. [26]

ALLEY, Frederick Augustus, *Upton Scudamore, Warminster, Wilts.*—C. of Upton Scudamore. [27]

ALLEY, John Peter, M.A.—British Chap. at Ghent. [28]

ALLEY, J. P. D., *Corpus Christi Buildings, Cambridge.* [29]

ALLEYNE, A. O. G., *Exeter.*—R. of St. Edmund's, City and Dio. Ex. 1863. (Patron, G. Hyde, Esq; R.'s Inc. 200*l*; Pop. 1525.) [30]

ALLEYNE, John Forster, *Kentisbere, Collumpton, Devon.*—Ball. Coll. Ox. B.A. 1826, M.A. 1829; Deac. 1829 and Pr. 1830 by Bp of Lin. R. of Kentisbere, Dio. Ex. 1854. (Patrons, Trustees of late Earl of Egremont; Tithe, 400*l*; Glebe, 60 acres; R.'s Inc. 470*l* and Ho; Pop. 1068.) [1]

ALLFREE, Edward, 62, *Myddelton-square, London, E.C.*—St. John's Coll. Cam. B.A. 1829, M.A. 1850; Deac. 1830 and Pr. 1831 by Bp of Lon. R. of St. Swithin with St. Mary Bothaw, City and Dio. of Lon. 1850. (Patrons, D. and C. of Cant. and Rev. H. G. Watkins, alt; R.'s Inc. 450*l*; Pop. St. Swithin 297, St. Mary Bothaw 161.) [2]

ALLFREE, Frederick Charles, *Rose Hill, Tonbridge Wells.*—St. John's Coll. Cam. B.A. 1835, M.A. 1838; Deac. 1836, Pr. 1837. [3]

ALLFREE, George Frederic, *Holland-road, Brighton.*—St. John's Coll. Cam. B.A. 1851, M.A. 1854; Deac. 1851, Pr. 1852. [4]

ALLFREE, William Edward, *Narburgh Rectory, Swaffham, Norfolk.*—Wad. Coll. Ox. B.A. 1839, M.A. 1843; Deac. and Pr. 1840 by Bp of Chich. R. of Narburgh with Narford V. Dio. Nor. 1864. (Patron, the present R; Narburgh, Tithe—R. 373*l*; Narford, Tithe—App. 185*l*, V. 145*l*; Glebe, 118 acres, R. and V.'s Inc. 540*l* and Ho; Pop. Narburgh 387, Narford 123.) Formerly R. of Southease, Sussex, 1843–64. [5]

ALLGOOD, James, *Ingram Rectory, Alnwick, Northumberland.*—Brasen. Coll. Ox. B.A. 1849, M.A. 1851; Deac. 1851 and Pr. 1852 by Bp of Dur. R. of Ingram, Dio. Dur. 1852. (Patron, Hunter Allgood, Esq; Tithe—Imp. 76*l* 13*s*, R. 299*l* 8*s* 1*d*; Glebe, 41½ acres, with water cornmill; R.'s Inc. 480*l* and Ho; Pop. 200.) [6]

ALLIN, Thomas May, *East Brendon, Sutcombe, Holsworthy, Devon.*—Queens' Coll. Cam. B.A. 1836; Deac. 1839 by Bp of Roch. Pr. 1846 by Bp of Ex. C. of Tawstock 1865. Formerly C. of Hatherleigh and Honeychurch 1839, Nether Ham 1842, Phillack and Gwithian 1846, St. Paul's, Truro, 1848, St. Mary's, Ware, 1851, Shute 1853. [7]

ALLIN, William Henry, *Stonehouse, Plymouth.*—St. Bees; Deac. 1861 and Pr. 1862 by Bp of Ches. C. of East Stonehouse 1866. Formerly C. of St. John's, Dukinfield, 1861–63, and St. Mary's, Kirkdale, 1863–66. [8]

ALLMATT, Francis John, *Abbey Street, Carlisle.* [9]

ALLNUTT, Richard Lee, *Tonbridge, Kent.*—St. Peter's Coll. Cam. B.A. 1841, M.A. 1845; Deac. 1841 and Pr. 1842. P. C. of St. Stephen's, Tonbridge, Dio. Cant. 1862. (Patron, V. of Tonbridge; Pop. 3400.) [10]

ALLNUTT, Thomas, *Gorleston, Great Yarmouth.*—St. Cath. Coll. Cam. B.D. 1856; Deac. 1844 and Pr. 1845 by Bp of Pet. C. of Gorleston with Southtown 1865. Formerly C. of Burton Latimer 1844, Tankersley 1846, Malton 1848, Eyam 1850, and Thriplow 1855. [11]

ALLNUTT, Walter, *Glastonbury.*—St. Cath. Hall, Cam; Deac. and Pr. 1841 by Bp of B. and W. P. C. of St. Benedict's, Glastonbury, Dio. B. and W. 1845. (Patron, Bp of B. and W; P. C.'s Inc. 112*l*; Pop. 1798.) Formerly C. of East Brent, East Pennard, and West Bradley. [12]

ALLOTT, George, *South Kirby, Pontefract, Yorks.*—Jesus Coll. Cam. B.A. 1841; Deac. 1842 and Pr. 1843 by Bp of Lin. V. of South Kirby, Dio. York 1848. (Patron, the present V; Tithe—App. 25*l*, Imp. 315*l*, V. 4*l*; Glebe, 90 acres; V.'s Inc. 290*l* and Ho; Pop. 1200.) [13]

ALLOTT, John, *Maltby-le-Marsh, Alford, Lincolnshire.*—St. John's Coll. Cam. B.A. 1836; Deac. 1835, Pr. 1836. R. of Maltby-le-Marsh, Dio. Lin. 1836. (Patron, the present R; Tithe, 300*l*; Glebe, 28 acres; R.'s Inc. 345*l* and Ho; Pop. 332.) [14]

ALLOTT, Joseph, *Thornhill, Dewsbury.*—St. Bees; Deac. 1863 and Pr. 1864. C. of Thornhill 1865. Formerly C. of Bishop Mankton 1863–65. [15]

ALLOWAY, Josiah William, *Newport, Salop.*—St. John's Coll. Cam. B.A. 1858; Deac. 1858 by Bp of Win. 2nd Mast. of Gr. Sch. Newport, and C. of Woodcote, Salop. Formerly C. of St. Thomas's, Lambeth. [16]

ALLPORT, Josiah, *Sutton-on-Trent, Newark, Notts.*—Deac. 1811 and Pr. 1812 by Bp of Llan. V. of Sutton-on-Trent, Dio. Lin. 1859. (Patron, Daniel Douglas, Esq; Tithe, 77*l* 5*s* 8*d*; V.'s Inc. 280*l*; Pop. 1147.) Late P. C. of St. James, Ashted, near Birmingham, 1829–59. Author, *Translation of Bp Davenant's Expositio Epistolæ Pauli ad Colossenses*, 1831, 2 vols; *The Protestant Journal*, monthly, 1831–34; *Baxter's Key for Catholics*, 1839; *Dr. Ball's Catholic Religion Maintained in the Church of England*, 1840; *Translation of Bp Davenant's Disputatio de Justitia*, 2 vols. 1846, 24*s*; various Tracts and Sermons. [17]

ALLSOPP, George Lewis, *Ilketshall, Bungay, Suffolk.*—Emman. Coll. Cam. B.A. 1842, M.A. 1846; Deac. 1843 and Pr. 1844 by Bp of Nor. V. of St. Margaret's, Ilketshall, Dio. Nor. 1847. (Patron, Duke of Norfolk; Tithe—Imp. 536*l* 8*s*, V. 121*l*; Glebe, 40 acres; V.'s Inc. 175*l* and Ho; Pop. 326.) Formerly C. of Tressingfield 1843–46. [18]

ALLSOPP, Richard Winstanley, *Coleshill, Berks.*—Emman. Coll. Cam. S.C.L. 1855, L.L.B. 1864; Deac. 1856 and Pr. 1857 by Bp of Ox. C. of Coleshill 1857. Formerly C. of Shrivenham 1856–57. [19]

ALMACK, Henry, *Fawley, near Henley-on-Thames.*—St. John's Coll. Cam. B.A. 1828, M.A. 1831, B.D. 1835, D.D. 1844; Deac. 1830, Pr. 1831. R. of the Sinecure R. of Aberdaron, Dio. Ban. 1843. (Patron, St. John's Coll. Cam; R.'s Inc. 241*l*.) R. of Fawley, Dio. Ox. 1846. (Patron, W. P. W. Freeman, Esq; Tithe, 742*l* 10*s*; Glebe, 24 acres; R.'s Inc. 330*l* and Ho; Pop. 272.) [20]

ALMOND, William Russell, *Stapleford, near Nottingham.*—St. Peter's Coll. Cam. B.A. 1838; Deac. 1838, Pr. 1839. P. C. of Stapleford, Dio. Lin. 1848. (Patron, J. Jackson, Esq; P. C.'s Inc. 120*l*; Pop. 1730.) [21]

ALSOP, James Richard, *West Houghton, Bolton-le-Moors.*—Brasen. Coll. Ox. B.A. 1839; Deac. 1840 and Pr. 1841 by Bp of Ches. P. C. of West Houghton, Dio. Man. 1842. (Patron, V. of Deane; Tithe, 65*l* 13*s* 7*d*; Glebe, 14 acres; P. C.'s Inc. 164*l* and Ho; Pop. 3679.) Author, *Faith and Practice*, 1858, 10*s* 6*d*; various Tracts. [22]

ALSTON, Albert, *St. John's College, Finchley-road, London, N.W.*—St. John's Coll. Cam. Scho. of, Sen. Opt. B.A. 1843, M.A. 1846, B.D. 1864; Deac. 1844 and Pr. 1845 by Bp of Lon. Lumley Lect. St. Helen's, Bishopsgate, 1847 (sal. 20*l*); C. of All Saints, St. John's Wood, 1858. Formerly C. of Trinity, Marylebone, 1845, St. George's, Hanover-square, 1848–57, and St. Botolph's, Aldgate; Chap. to Lord Mayor of Lond. Author, *How can I get into an hospital?* Sermons, *Purgatory*, *Election of Lord Mayor*, etc. [23]

ALSTON, Charles William Horace, *Wembdon, Bridgwater, Somerset.*—St. Mary Hall, Ox. B.A. 1831, M.A. 1832; Deac. 1830, Pr 1831. V. of Wembdon, Dio. B. and W. 1845. (Patron, the present V; Tithe—App. 22*l*, Imp. 200*l*, V. 575*l*; Glebe, 7 acres; V.'s Inc. 578*l* and Ho; Pop. 934.) Chap. to the Earl of Bessborough 1853. [24]

ALSTON, Edward.—Fell. of St. John's Coll. Ox. [25]

ALSTON, Edward Constable, *Dennington, Framlingham, Suffolk.*—Caius Coll. Cam. B.A. 1839, M.A. 1842; Deac. 1839 and Pr. 1840 by Bp of Nor. R. of Dennington, Dio. Nor. 1855. (Patron, the present R; Tithe, 1050*l*; Glebe, 152 acres; R.'s Inc. 1100*l* and Ho; Pop. 895.) [26]

ALSTON, George, *Studland, Wareham.*—Dub. A.B. 1835; Deac. 1836 by Abp of Dub. Pr. 1838 by Bp of Rip. R. of Studland, Dio. Salis. 1853. (Patroness, Mrs. Michel; Tithe, 138*l* 10*s*; Glebe, 62 acres; R.'s Inc. 180*l* and Ho; Pop. 472.) [27]

ALT, Just Henry, *Enford Vicarage, Marlborough, Wilts.*—Pemb. Coll. Cam. B.A. 1819, M.A. 1824; Deac. 1827 and Pr. 1828 by Bp of Lon. V. of Enford, Dio. Salis. 1833. (Patrons, Govs. of Christ's Hospital; Glebe, 350 acres; V.'s Inc. 450*l* and Ho; Pop. 950.) Formerly Prof. of Languages, Bishop's College, Calcutta; C. of St. Giles', Cripplegate, Lond. [1]

ALTHAM, I., *Holmpton, Withernsea.*—York Dioc. Coll. 1827; Deac. 1830 by Bp. of Roch., Pr. 1831 by Abp of York. C. of Holmpton and Welwick 1865. Formerly C. of Dalton 1830, Attenborough 1841, Hawton 1846, Anderby 1848, Bicker 1851, Lanebam 1856. Author, *The Force of Example, The Power of Conscience,* Sermons, &c. [2]

ALTMAN, J. S.—P. C. of St. Andrew's, Thornhill-square, Islington, Dio. Lon. 1853. (Patron, P. C. of Trinity, Islington; P. C.'s Inc. 300*l*; Pop. 6193.) [3]

ALVIS, Edward John, *The Mount, Chilton, Sudbury.*—Christ's Coll. Cam. B.A. 1862, M.A. 1866; Deac. 1866 by Bp of Ely. C. of Newton, by Sudbury, 1866. [4]

AMBROSE, John, B.A., *Copford Lodge, Colchester.* [5]

AMBROSE, John Cole, *North Lopham, Thetford.*—Corpus Christi Coll. Cam. B.A. 1860, M.A. 1864; Deac. 1861 and Pr. 1862 by Bp of Ely. C. of North and South Lopham 1863. Formerly C. of Nayland, Suffolk, 1861. [6]

AMERY, Edmund Verdon, *Munsley, near Ledbury.*—Brasen. Coll. Ox. B.A. 1851, M.A. 1852; Deac. 1852 and Pr. 1853 by Bp of Wor. Munsley Stipendiary Curacy, Dio. Herf. 1864. (Patron, Rev. John Hopton; value, 227*l*; Pop. 160.) Formerly C. of Eyam; P.C. of Bamford, Derbyshire. [7]

AMES, Francis William.—C. of St. Jude's, Bethnal-green. [8]

AMORY, Thomas, *St. Teath, Camelford.*—V. of St. Teath, Dio. Ex. 1838. (Patron, Bp of Ex.; V.'s Inc. 250*l* and Ho; Pop. 1980.) [9]

AMOS, James, 8, *Paragon, New Kent-road, Southwark, London, S.E.*—Clare Coll. Cam. Scho. of, 14th Sen. Opt. B.A. 1851, M.A. 1854; Deac. 1852 and Pr. 1853 by Bp of Ely. P. C. of St. Stephen's, Southwark, 1861. (Patrons, Trustees; P. C.'s Inc. 300*l*; Pop. 5260.) Hon. Clerical Examiner to the Scripture Readers' Association. Formerly C. of Brent Eleigh, Suffolk, 1852–54, Trinity, Marylebone, 1854–61. Author, *Seven Chapters on Confirmation,* 1858; *Five Years in Kent-street,* 1866; etc. [10]

AMOS, William, *Braceborough, Stamford, Lincolnshire.*—R. of Braceborough, Dio. Lin. 1860. (Patron, Ld Chan; R.'s Inc. 160*l* and Ho; Pop. 220.) [11]

AMPHLETT, Charles, *Four Ashes Hall, Bridgnorth.*—Wor. Coll. Ox. [12]

AMPHLETT, Joseph, *Hampton-Lovett, near Droitwitch, Worcestershire.*—Trin. Coll. Ox. B.A. 1823, M.A., 1826; Deac. 1823 and Pr. 1825 by Bp of Wor. R. of Hampton-Lovett, Dio. Wor. 1834. (Patron, Right Hon. Sir J. S. Pakington, Bart; Tithe, 318*l*; Glebe, 33 acres; R.'s Inc. 368*l* nett and Ho; Pop. 185.) Chap. to Bp of Man. [13]

AMPHLETT, Martin, *Church-lench, near Evesham, Worcestershire.*—St. Peter's Coll. Cam. Sen. Opt. B.A. 1836, M.A. 1839; Deac. 1837, Pr. 1838. R. of Church-lench, Dio. Wor. 1844. (Patron, Bp of Wor; Tithe—App. 242*l*, R. 280*l*; Glebe, 80 acres; R.'s Inc. 400*l* and Ho; Pop. 488.) [14]

AMPS, James Henry, *Calstock, Cornwall.*—Lond. Univ. B.A. 1864; Deac. 1865 and Pr. 1866 by Bp of Ches. C. of Calstock 1867. Formerly C. of St. Thomas's, Wigan, 1865–67. [15]

ANDERS, Henry, *Kirkby-la-Thorpe Rectory, Sleaford.*—Caius Coll. Cam. B.A. 1839; Deac. 1842, Pr. 1843. R. of St. Denis with St. Peter's V. Kirkby-la-Thorpe and Asgarby R. Dio. Lin. 1854. (Patron, Marquis of Bristol; Kirkby-la-Thorpe, Tithe—Apps. 130*l*, R. 300*l*; Glebe, 47 acres; Asgarby, Tithe—R. 200*l*; Glebe, 19 acres; R.'s Inc. 600*l* and Ho; Pop. Kirkby-la-Thorpe 208, Asgarby 83.) [16]

ANDERSON, Andrew, *Porlock, Somerset.*—Trin. Coll. Cam. B.A. 1826; Deac. 1826 and Pr. 1827 by Bp of Lon. R. of Culbone *alias* Kitner, Somerset, Dio. B. and W. 1848. (Patron, Earl of Lovelace; Tithe, 37*l* 5*s*; Glebe, 32 acres; R.'s Inc. 62*l*; Pop. 41.) R. of Oare, Somerset, Dio. B. and W. 1855. (Patron, Rev. W. S. Halliday; Tithe, 81*l* 10*s*; Glebe, 11 acres; R.'s Inc. 152*l* and Ho; Pop. 60.) [17]

ANDERSON, Charles.—C. of St. Paul's, Brighton. [18]

ANDERSON, Charles George, *Countesthorpe, near Leicester.*—St. Bees, 1860–62; Deac. 1862 and Pr. 1863 by Bp of Pet. C. of Blaby with Countesthorpe, 1866. Formerly C. of Walton-le-Wolds 1862–66. [19]

ANDERSON, The Right Reverend David, *Clifton, Bristol.*—Ex. Coll. Ox. 3rd cl. Math. et Phy. 4th cl. Lit. Hum. and B.A. 1836, M.A. 1839, B.D. and D.D. 1849; Deac. and Pr. 1837. P. C. of Ch. Ch. Clifton, Dio. G. and B. 1864. (Patrons, Simeon's Trustees; P. C.'s Inc. 800*l*; Pop. 10,413.) Formerly P. C. of All Saints, Derby; Vice-Prin. of St. Bees Coll.; Bp of Rupert's Land 1849–64. [20]

ANDERSON, Drummond, *Liverpool.*—P. C. of St. Mark's, Liverpool, Dio. Ches. 1857. (Patrons, Trustees; P. C.'s Inc. 380*l*; Pop. 10,066.) Formerly P. C. of St. Stephen-the-Martyr, West Derby, 1850–57. [21]

ANDERSON, Ebenezer, *Lilley Rectory, Luton, Beds.*—Wor. Coll. Ox. B.A. 1855; Deac. 1857 and Pr. 1858 by Bp of Wor. C. in sole charge of Lilley 1867. Formerly C. of St. Andrew's, Worcester, 1857–58, Frankley, Worcestershire, 1859; R. of Frankley 1861–66; C. of Stapleford Abbotts, Essex, 1865–67. [22]

ANDERSON, Frederick, *Balby, Doncaster.*—Lon. Coll. of Divinity; Deac. 1866 by Abp of York. C. of Balby with Hexthorpe 1866. [23]

ANDERSON, F. L., *Harworth, Bawtry, Notts.*—C. of Harworth. [24]

ANDERSON, Frederick West, *Rochdale.*—St. Peter's Coll. Cam; B.A. 1864; Deac. 1865 by Bp of Man. C. of St. Alban's, Rochdale. [25]

ANDERSON, Henry Robert, *Sneinton, Nottingham.*—Magd. Coll. Ox; Deac. 1865 and Pr. 1866 by Bp of Lin. C. of Sneinton 1865. [26]

ANDERSON, James Richard, *Metton Rectory, Cromer.*—Trin. Coll. Cam. B.A. 1846; Deac. 1846 by Bp of Ely, Pr. 1847 by Bp of Wor. R. of Felbrigge with Metton R. Dio. Nor. 1866. (Patron, John Ketton Esq; R.'s Inc. 390*l* and Ho; Pop. Felbrigge 136, Metton, 78.) Formerly R. of Barningham Town, Norfolk, 1851–66. [27]

ANDERSON, James Stuart Murray, *Chippenham.*—Ball. Coll. Ox. B.A. 1820, M.A. 1823; Deac. 1823 and Pr. 1824 by Bp of Bristol. R. of Tormarton with Acton Turville V. and West Littleton C. Dio. G. and B. 2851. (Patron, Duke of Beaufort; Tormarton, Tithe—R. 731*l* 12*s*; Glebe, 96 acres; Acton Turville, Tithe—V. 52*l* 14*s* 5½*d*; Glebe, 19 acres; West Littleton, Tithe—R. 220*l*; R.'s Inc. 1020*l* and Ho; Pop. Tormarton, 454, Acton Turville 310, West Littleton 120.) Chap. in Ordinary to the Queen 1836; Preacher of Lincoln's Inn 1844–58; Hon. Can. of Bristol Cath. 1856; British Chap. at Bonn. Author, *Sermons on Various Subjects,* 8*s* 6*d*; *Christian Philanthropy* (a Spital Sermon), 1*s* 6*d*; *The Christian Watching against the Suddenness of Death* (a Sermon for the Humane Society), 1*s*; *The Importance of an Established Ministry* (a Consecration Sermon), 1*s*; *Redemption in Christ the True Jubilee* (a Sermon for the Deaf and Dumb), 1*s*; *Giving no Offence in Anything, that the Ministry be not blamed* (a Visitation Sermon), 1*s* 6*d*; *The Trials of the Church a Quickening of her Zeal and Love* (Two Sermons on the Gorham Case), 1*s* 6*d*; *A Minister's Farewell to his People* (Two Sermons preached at St. George's, Brighton), 1851, 1*s* 6*d*; Editor, with *Notes and Preface,* of a hitherto unpublished "Letter" of Bishop Berkeley, "On the Roman Catholic Controversy," 6*d*; *The History of the Church of England in the Colonies and Foreign Dependencies of the British Empire,* 3 vols. 24*s*; *Addresses, chiefly to Young Men, on Miscellaneous Subjects,* 5*s*; *Memoir of the Chisholm,* 4*s* 6*d*; *The Present Crisis* (Four Sermons preached before the Hon. Soc. of

Lincoln's Inn, with Notes and Appendix), 4s 6d; *The Cloud of Witnesses*, 2 vols. 18s; *Discourses on Elijah and St. John the Baptist*, 9s; Funeral Sermons—*On Queen Adelaide* (preached at St. George's, Brighton), 1s; *On Sir Robert Peel* (preached at St. George's, Brighton), 1s; *On the Duke of Wellington* (preached at Lincoln's Inn), 6d; *On the Rev. Robert Anderson* (with Appendix, preached at Trinity Chapel, Brighton), 2s; *On the Rev. Frederick W. Robertson* (preached at Trinity Chapel, Brighton), 1s. [1]

ANDERSON, John, *Norton-on-the-Moors, Newcastle-under-Lyne.*—Mert. Coll. Ox. B.A. 1838, M.A. 1841; Deac. 1839 and Pr. 1840 by Bp of G. and B. R. of Norton-on-the-Moors, Dio. Lich. 1854. (Patron, Rt Hon C. B. Adderley, M.P; Tithe comm. 550*l*; R.'s Inc. 550*l* and Ho; Pop. 1991. Formerly P. C. of Lee, Bucks. [2]

ANDERSON, John Dauncey, *Thornton Watlass, Bedale, Yorks.*—Dur. B.A. 1846, M.A. 1849; Deac. 1848 and Pr. 1849 by Bp. of Rip. P. C. of Leeming, Dio. Rip. 1849. (Patron, V. of Burneston; Glebe, 33 acres; P. C.'s Inc. 120*l*; Pop. 780.) C. of Thornton Watlass 1866. Formerly C. of West Wilton. [3]

ANDERSON, Mason, *Sherrington, Heytesbury, Wilts.*—Literate; Deac. 1828 and Pr. 1829 by Bp of Salis. R. of Sherrington, Dio. Salis. 1831. (Patron, Rev. A. Fane; Tithe, 252*l* 3*s*; Glebe, 21 acres; R.'s Inc. 310*l* and Ho; Pop. 187.) [4]

ANDERSON, Matthew, *Buckland Vicarage, Dover.*—V. of Buckland, Dio. Cant. 1866. (Patron, Bp of Cant; V.'s Inc. 160*l* and Ho; Pop. 2162.) [5]

ANDERSON, Matthew, *Herne-hill, Dulwich, Surrey.*—St. John's Coll. Cam. B.A. 1823, M.A. 1827; Deac. 1824, Pr. 1825. V. of St. Paul's, Herne-hill, Dio. Win. 1844 (Patron, W. H. Stone, Esq. M.P; P.C.'s Inc. 500*l*; Pop. 911.) Author, *Discourses on the Principal Events in the Life of Moses*, 1834, 6*s*; Various Sermons. [6]

ANDERSON Michael James, *Hockering, East Dereham, Norfolk.*—Dub. A.B. 1847, A.M. 1854; Deac. 1847 and Pr. 1848 by Bp of Ches. R. of Hockering with Burgh Mattishall R. Dio. Nor. 1856. (Patron, T. T. Berney, Esq; Hockering, Tithe, 539*l* 10*s*; Glebe, 50 acres; Burgh-Mattishall, Tithe 200*l*; Glebe, 20 acres; R.'s Inc. 859*l* and Ho; Pop. Hockering 387, Burgh Mattishall 191.) Formerly C. of Pendleton, Manchester. [7]

ANDERSON, Richard, *Leeming, Bedale, Yorks.*—C. of Leeming. [8]

ANDERSON, Robert Gerard, *Falkingham, Lincolnshire.*—Trin. Coll. Cam. B.A. 1858; Deac. 1858 and Pr. 1859 by Abp of York. P. C. of Walcot, Dio. Lin. 1866. (Patron, Lord Auckland; P. C.'s Inc. 215*l* and Ho; Pop. 200.) Formerly C. of Lythe-cum-Ugthorpe, Yorks, 1858–59; V. of Manton, Rutland, 1859–66. [9]

ANDERSON, Samuel Ruthven, *Otley.*—Trin. Coll. Cam. B.A. 1852; Deac. 1852 and Pr. 1853 by Bp of Lon. V. of Otley, Dio. Rip. 1865. (Patron, Ld Chan; Tithe, 28*l*; Glebe, 85*l*; V.'s Inc. 306*l* and Ho; Pop. 5080.) Formerly C. of Trinity, Hounslow, and Chap. to Middlesex Volunteers. [10]

ANDERSON, Thomas, *Felsham, near Woolpit, Suffolk.*—R. of Felsham, Dio. Ely, 1822. (Patron, the present R; Pop. 394.) [11]

ANDERSON, Thomas Wilson, *Weedon, Northants.*—Jesus Coll. Cam. B.A. 1852; Deac. 1854 and Pr. 1855 by Bp of Pet. C. of Brockhall, Northants, 1854. Formerly C. of Watford 1854. [12]

ANDERSON, William, *Ashford, Kent.*—Trin. Coll. Cam. B.A. 1849, M.A. 1854. C. of Ashford. Formerly C. of Heckington 1860. [13]

ANDERSON, William Dyer, *Milton Damerell, Brandis-Corner, Devon.*—Deac. 1846 and Pr. 1847 by Bp of Ex. R. of Milton Damerell with Cookbury C. Dio. Ex. 1852. (Patron, the present R; Milton Damerell, Tithe, 325*l*; Glebe, 86 acres; Cookbury, Tithe, 118*l* 2*s* 6*d*; Glebe, 50 acres; R.'s Inc. 500*l* and Ho; Pop. Milton Damerell 684, Cookbury 249.) [14]

ANDERSON, William Paley, *Winsford, Dulverton, Somerset.*—St. John's Coll. Cam. Jun. Opt. 1st cl. Cl. Trip. and B.A. 1847, M.A. 1850; Deac. 1853 and Pr. 1854 by Bp of Ely. V. of Winsford, Dio. B. and W. 1857. (Patron, Emman. Coll. Cam; V.'s Inc. 362*l*; Pop. 574.) Fell. and Tut. of Emman. Coll. Cam. 1850. [15]

ANDERTON, Joseph Heywood, *Clitheroe, Lancashire.*—St. John's Coll. Cam. B.A. 1828, M.A. 1831; Deac. 1829 and Pr. 1830 by Bp of Ches. V. of Clitheroe, Dio. Man. 1835 (Patron, the present V; Glebe, 50 acres; V.'s Inc. 200*l* and Ho; Pop. 2500.) [16]

ANDRAS, Charles Henry, *Blackheath College, Kent, S.E.*—St. John's Coll. Cam. Sen. Opt. B.A. 1860. M.A. 1863; Deac. 1861 and Pr. 1862 by Bp of Lon. Formerly C. of Greenwich and Vice-Prin. of Blackheath Coll. 1861–63. [17]

ANDRAS, John Abraham, *Blackheath College, Kent, S.E.*—St. John's Coll. Cam. 11th Sen. Opt. Scho. of St. John's, B.A. 1833, M.A. 1851; Deac. 1833 by Bp. of Ches, Pr. 1835 by Bp. of Ex. Prin. of Blackheath Coll. and Chap. of Lewisham Union. Formerly C. of South Shields 1833, East Allington, Devon, 1835. [18]

ANDREW, Charles, *Hemsworth, Pontefract, Yorks.*—Head Mast. of Hemsworth Free Gr. Sch. [19]

ANDREW, James Hardy, *Tideswell, Derbyshire.*—Christ's Coll. Cam. B.A. 1865; Deac. 1865 and Pr. 1866 by Bp of Lich. C. of Tideswell. [20]

ANDREW, Jean Baptiste, *King's Hill, Wednesbury.*—C. of King's Hill. [21]

ANDREW, John.—St. John's Coll. Ox. B.A. 1836; Deac. 1836, Pr. 1837. Formerly P. C. of Worsboro, Barnsley, 1837–62. [22]

ANDREW, John Chapman, *Canterbury, New Zealand.*—Univ. Coll. Ox. B.A. 1844, M.A. 1847; Deac. 1847, Pr. 1848. Formerly Fell. and Tut. of Lin. Coll Ox. 1846–60. [23]

ANDREW, Samuel, *Halwell Rectory, Launceston.*—Lin. Coll. Ox. 2nd cl. Lit Hum. B.A. 1840, M.A. 1841; Deac. 1840 and Pr. 1841 by Bp of Pet. R. of Halwell, Dio. Ex. 1852. (Patron, Ld Chan; Tithe, 176*l*; Glebe, 125 acres; R.'s Inc. 240*l* and Ho; Pop. 257.) Formerly Head Mast. of the Truro Gr. Sch. 1852–54. [24]

ANDREW, Samuel, *Tideswell Vicarage, Derbyshire.*—St. Bees. and St. John's Coll. Cam; Deac. 1853 and Pr. 1854 by Bp of Lich. V. of Tideswell, Dio. Lich. 1864. (Patrons, D. and C. of Lich; V.'s Inc. 270*l* and Ho; Pop. 3094.) Rural Dean and Surrogate. Formerly C. of St. Michael's, Lichfield, and P. C. of Wall, near Lichfield. [25]

ANDREW, Thomas, *Thriplow, Royston, Cambs.*—Pem. Coll. Cam. B.A. 1840, M.A. 1844; Deac. 1841, Pr. 1842. V. of Thriplow, Dio. Ely, 1849. (Patron, Bp of Ely; Tithe—Imp. 634*l* 14*s*; Glebe, 55 acres; App. 2*l* 8*s*; V. 134*l* 10*s*; Glebe, 3 acres; V.'s Inc. 199*l* 10*s* and Ho; Pop. 502.) [26]

ANDREW, Thomas Prynn, *Illogan, Redruth, Cornwall.*—Lin. Coll. Ox. B.A. 1853; Deac. 1853, Pr. 1854. C. of Illogan. [27]

ANDREW, William, *Whitfield, Brackley, Northants.*—Wor. Coll. Ox. 1st cl. Lit. Hum. B.A. 1842, M.A. 1860; Deac. 1843, Pr. 1845. R. of Whitfield, Dio. Pet. 1862. (Patron. Wor. Coll. Ox; R.'s Inc. 258*l*; Pop. 265.) Dioc. Inspector of Schs. Late Fell. and Tut. of Wor. Coll, Public Examiner 1853, Select Preacher 1855–56; formerly P. C. of Kirkdale, Yorks. [28]

ANDREW, William Wayte, *Wood Hall, Hethersett, Wymondham, Norfolk.*—St. Mary Hall, Ox. B.A. 1830, M.A. 1834; Deac. 1831 and Pr. 1832 by Bp of Nor. V. of Ketteringham, Dio. Nor. 1835. (Patron, Sir T. P. Boileau, Bart; Tithe, 170*l*; Glebe, 38 acres; V.'s Inc. 194*l*; Pop. 198.) Rural Dean of Humbleyard 1843. Author, *Sermon on Rush, the Murderer*; *The Legacy*, 1856; *The Cottager's Guide.* [29]

ANDREWES, Charles Gerrard, *Wouldham Rectory, Rochester.*—R. of Wouldham, Dio. Roch. 1866. (Patron, Bp of Roch; R.'s Inc. 340*l* and Ho; Pop. 433.) [30]

ANDREWES, William Gerrard, *Morden, Mitcham, Surrey.*—Magd. Hall, Ox. B.A. 1846, M.A.

1848; Deac. 1847 and Pr. 1848 by Bp of Lon. C. of Morden 1850. [1]

ANDREWS, Charles Henry, 25, *Hunter-street, Brunswick-square, London, W.C.*—King's Coll. Lond; Deac. 1852 and Pr. 1853 by Bp of Lon. P. C. of St. Luke's, King's-cross, St. Pancras, Dio. Lon. 1816. (Patrons, Crown and Bp of Lon. alt; P. C.'s Inc. 220*l*; Pop. 8020.) Formerly C. of St. Pancras and Even. Lect. at St. Matthew's, Oakley-square. St. Pancras, Lond. [2]

ANDREWS, Christopher Robert, *Hough-on-the-Hill, Grantham, Lincolnshire.*—Emman. Coll. Cam. B.A. 1844; Deac. 1844 and Pr. 1845 by Bp of Lin. V. of Hough-on-the-Hill with Brandon C. Dio. Lin. 1855. (Patron, Ld Chan; Tithe—Imp. 3*l* 14*s*, V. 88*l*; Glebe, 5 acres; V.'s Inc. 105*l* and Ho; Pop. 655.) Formerly C. of Manea 1845-55. [3]

ANDREWS, Evan, *Glanmorlais, Llandefeilog, Kidwelly.*—Trin. Coll. Cam. B.A. 1833; Deac. 1840 and Pr. 1841 by Bp of St. D. V. of Llandefeilog, Dio. St. D. 1865. (Patrons, Trustees; Tithe—Imp. 742*l*, V. 11*l* 13*s* 4*d*; Glebe, 35 acres; V.'s Inc. 71*l* 9*s*; Pop. 1247.) C. of Llangendeirne 1865. Formerly C. of Ishmael's, Kidwelly, 1840–44; Head Mast. of Gr. Sch. and C. of Dolgellan 1844–49; R. of Llanfrothen 1849-65. Author, *Sermons*, 1844, 2*s* 6*d*; *Discussion of Church and State Question*, 1846, 6*d*; *Pregethau, or Welsh Sermons*, 1847, 3*s* 6*d*; *Ymddyddanion ar Fedydd, or a Dialogue on Infant Baptism*, 1855, 3*d*; *A Translation of, with a Commentary on, the Septuagint, in Welsh*, 3 vols. 1867; etc. [4]

ANDREWS, Frederick Gould, *Eccleston, St. Helens.*—C. of St. Thomas's, Eccleston. [5]

ANDREWS, John Marshall, 38, *Argyle-square, Euston-road, London, W.C.*—King's Coll. Lond; Deac. 1853 and Pr. 1854 by Bp of Lon. P. C. of St. Jude's, Gray's-inn-road, Dio. Lon. 1858. (Patrons, Crown and Bp of Lon; Pop. 8427.) Chap. to Lord Rolle. Formerly C. of St Jude's. [6]

ANDREWS, Percy, *Lilleshall, Newport, Salop.*—Ball. Coll. Ox. B.A. 1861, M.A. 1864; Deac. 1862 and Pr. 1863 by Bp of Lich. C. of Lilleshall 1862. [7]

ANDREWS, Robert, *Middleton (Essex), near Sudbury.*—Emman. Coll. Cam. B.A. 1821, M.A. 1824, B.D. 1831; Deac. 1822, Pr. 1823. Fell. of Emman. Coll. Cam. 1827. [8]

ANDREWS, Samuel Wright, *Claxby, Market Rasen, Lincolnshire.*—Caius Coll. Cam. B.A. 1847, M.A. 1850; Deac. 1847, Pr. 1848. C. of Claxby with Normanby-on-the-Wolds, Lincolnshire. [9]

ANDREWS, Septimus, *The Parsonage, Market Harborough.*—Ch. Ch. Ox. Stud. of, 1851, B.A. 1855, M.A. 1858; Deac. 1857 and Pr. 1862 by Bp of Ox. P.C. of Market Harborough, Dio. Pet. 1865. (Patron, Ch. Ch. Ox; P. C.'s Inc. 290*l* and Ho; Pop. 2302.) Formerly Fell. of St. Peter's Coll. Radley, 1857–60; Asst. Mast. of Westminster Sch. 1860–65. [10]

ANDREWS, Thomas Desborough.—Corpus Coll. Ox. B.A. 1838, M.A. 1841, B.D. 1845; Deac. 1841 and Pr. 1842 by Bp of Ox. Fell. of Corpus Coll. Ox. Formerly C. of Bredhurst, Kent. [11]

ANDREWS, William, *Stowe, near Buckingham.*—V. of Stowe, Dio. Ox. 1833. (Patron, Duke of Buckingham; Tithe—Imp. 200*l*, V. 160*l*; Glebe, 4 acres; V.'s Inc. 167*l*; Pop. 352.) [12]

ANDREWS, William, *Broad-Somerford, Chippenham.*—Queen's Coll. Ox. B.A. 1835; Deac. 1835 and Pr. 1845 by Bp of Ox. R. of Broad-Somerford, Dio. G. and B. 1854. (Patron, Ex. Coll. Ox; R.'s Inc. 350*l* and Ho; Pop. 522.) Late Fell. of Ex. Coll. Ox. [13]

ANDREWS, W., *Westborough, Grantham.*—C. of Westborough with Dry Doddington. [14]

ANDREWS, William Hale, *Carlton-Colville, Lowestoft.*—St. John's Coll. Cam. B.A. 1844, M.A. 1847; Deac. 1844 and Pr. 1845 by Bp of Ex. R. of Carlton-Colville, Dio. Nor. 1848. (Patron Wm. Andrews, Esq; Tithe—Imp. 342*l* 15*s* 6*d*, R. 397*l*; Glebe, 18 acres; R.'s Inc. 410*l* and Ho; Pop. 946.) R. of Ermington, Sinecure, Dio. Ex. 1866. (Patron, Wm. Andrews, Esq; Val. of Tithe and 85 acres of Glebe, 588*l*.) [15]

ANDREWS, William Nesfield, *Chilton, Sudbury, Suffolk.*—Jesus Coll. Cam. B.A. 1828, M.A. 1832 Deac. 1829, Pr. 1830. R. of Chilton, Dio. Ely, 1853. (Patron, W. Parmenter, Esq.; Tithe—App. 90*l*, R. 200*l*; Glebe, 25¾ acres; R.'s Inc. 240*l*; Pop. 149.) Formerly Under Mast. of Durham Coll. Sch. 1828; C. of Pittington, Durham, 1829, Bulmer, Essex, 1836–53. [16]

ANDREWS, William Ryton, *East Hill-place, Hastings.*—Wad. Coll. Ox. 2nd cl. in Sci. and B.A. 1857, M.A. 1859; Deac. 1859, and Pr. 1860 by Bp of Ox. C. of All Saints', Hastings. Formerly C. of Culham, Oxon, 1859–60, Maldon with Chessington, Surrey, 1860–63, and Long Ditton, Surrey, 1863–66. [17]

ANGELL, Charles Henry, *Hostingley House, Horbury-bridge, near Wakefield.*—Queen's Coll. Ox. B.A. Formerly C. of Earls-Heaton, Yorks. [18]

ANGELL, William, *Prior's-Lee, Shiffnal, Shropshire.*—Dub. A.B.; Deac. 1847 and Pr. 1848 by Bp of Ches. P. C. of Prior's-Lee, Dio. Lich. 1857. (Patron, V. of Shiffnal; P. C.'s Inc. 160*l*; Pop. 1721.) [19]

ANGELL, William John Brown, *Overton, Marlborough.*—Queen's Coll. Ox. B.A. 1826, M.A. 1830; Deac. 1828 and Pr. 1829 by Bp of Herf. V. of Overton with Fyfield V. and Alton Priors V. Dio. Salis. 1848. (Patron, Duke of Marlborough; Tithe, 236*l*; Glebe, 39 acres; V.'s Inc. 300*l* and Ho.; Pop. Overton 703, Fyfield 200, Alton Priors 207.) [20]

ANGLEY, John Godfrey, *East Meon, Petersfield, Hants.*—Dub. A.B. 1841, A.M. 1846, *ad eund.* Cam. 1846 and Ox. 1861; Deac. 1841 by Abp of Dub. Pr. 1843 by Bp of Rip. C. of East Meon. Formerly C. of Great Munden, Herts; Head Mast. and Div. Lect. of the Class. and Theol. Coll. Southampton-place, Euston-square. Author, *Alaric De Lisle*, 1842, 2*s* 6*d*; *Faith, Hope, and Charity*, 1845, 2*s* 6*d* *De Clifford, the Philosopher*, 1847, 10*s* 6*d*; *The Sceptre, the Sword, and the Lyre; with War Collects* (an original Greek allegory), 3 vols. 1854; *The Bible, the Mother of all Books*, 1856; *Hezekiah and Sennacherib, with contemporaneous Jewish and Assyrian History*, 1857; *The Angel of the Lord and the Millennium*, 1858; *Wellington, an Historical Poem, with an Analysis of the Duke's Life and Character*, 1859, 2*s* 6*d*; *Golden Thoughts*; several Sermons in *The Pulpit*, &c. [21]

ANGUS, George, *Prestbury, near Cheltenham.*—St. Edm. Hall. Ox. B.A. S.C.L. 1866; Deac. 1866 by Bp of G. and B. C. of Prestbury 1866. [22]

ANNESLEY, Charles Henry, *Kingsdown, Bristol.*—Wad. Coll. Ox. B.A. 1863, M.A. 1866; Deac. 1864 and Pr. 1865 by Bp of Win. C. of St. Matthew's, Kingsdown 1866. Formerly C. of Wonston 1864, and Micheldever, Hants, 1865. [23]

ANNESLEY, Francis, *Clifford Chambers, near Stratford-on-Avon.*—St. John's Coll. Ox. B.A. 1824, M.A. 1826; Deac. 1824 and Pr. 1825 by Bp of G. and B. R. of Clifford Chambers, Dio. G. and B. 1845. (Patron, the present R; Tithe 44*l* 17*s*; Glebe, 66 acres; R.'s Inc. 190*l*; Pop. 344.) [24]

ANNESLEY, Francis Hanbury, *Horseheath, near Cambridge.*—Trin. Coll. Ox. B.A. 1861, M.A. 1863; Deac. 1861 and Pr. 1862 by Bp of Win. C. in sole charge of Horseheath 1864. Formerly C. of Titsey, Surrey, 1861. [25]

ANNESLEY, William, *The Vicarage, Abbot's Leigh, near Bristol.*—Univ. Coll. Ox. B.A. 1827, M.A. 1830; Deac. 1829, and Pr. 1830 by Bp of Wor. V. of Abbot's Leigh, Dio. G. and B. 1861. (Patron, Bp of G. and B; V.'s Inc. 85*l* and Ho; Pop. 366.) Formerly P. C. of Flax-Bourton 1860. [26]

ANSON, The Hon. Adelbert, J. R., *St. Leonard's Parsonage, Bilston.*—Ch. Ch. Ox. B.A. 1862, M.A. 1867; Deac. 1864 and Pr. 1865 by Bp of Lich. C. in sole charge of St. Leonard's, Bilston, 1866. Formerly C. of St. John's, Wolverhampton, 1864–66. [27]

ANSON, Frederick, *Sudbury, Derby.*—Ch. Ch. Ox; All Souls Coll. Ox. B.A. 1833, M.A. 1839; Deac. and Pr. 1834 by Bp of Ox. R. of Sudbury, Dio. Lich. 1836. (Patron, Lord Vernon; Tithe, 618*l*; Glebe, 134 acres; R.'s Inc. 800*l* and Ho; Pop. 587.) Can. Res. of

St. George's Free Chapel, Windsor, 1845. (Value, 900*l* and Res.) Late Fell. of All Souls Coll. Ox. [1]

ANSON, George Henry Greville, *Birch-in-Rusholme, Manchester.*—Ex. Coll. Ox. B.A. 1843, M.A. 1846; Deac. 1843, Pr. 1846. R. of Birch-in-Rusholme, Dio. Man. 1846. (Patron, Sir J. W. H. Anson, Bart; R.'s Inc. 520*l* and Ho; Pop. 2043.) [2]

ANSON, Thomas Architel, *Longford Rectory, Derbyshire.*—Jesus Coll. Cam. 1843, M.A. 1847; Deac. 1842, Pr. 1843. R. of Longford, Dio. Lich. 1850. (Patron, Hon. E. W. R. Coke; Rent Charge in lieu of Tithe, 410*l* 6*s* 3½*d*; Glebe, 193 acres; R.'s Inc. 683*l* and Ho; Pop. 993.) [3]

ANSTED, Joseph Boord, *Stilton, Hants.*—Ch. Coll. Cam. 18th Wrang. B.A. 1843, M.A. 1846; Deac. 1843 and Pr. 1844 by Bp of Lon. R. of Morborne, Dio. Ely, 1861. (Patron, Rev. Dr. Vincent; Tithe, 164*l*; Glebe, 81 acres let for 105*l*; R.'s Inc. 269*l*; Pop. 133.) Formerly C. of Whitechapel 1843; P. C. of St. Simon Zelotes, Bethnal-green, 1847–57; P. C. of Stoney Stratford 1857; V. of Longdon, Staffs. 1859–61 [4]

ANSTEY, Charles Christopher, *Tilehurst, near Reading.*—Caius Coll. Cam. B.A. 1849, M.A. 1852; Deac. 1850 and Pr. 1851 by Bp of Wor. Surrogate. Formerly C. of Hillmorton, near Rugby, 1854–59, Calthorpe, Leic. 1853–54, Evesham, Wor. 1850–53; Chap. at Fyzabad, Oude, 1860. [5]

ANSTEY, Henry, *St. Mary Hall, Oxford.*—Univ. Coll. Ox. B.A. 1850, M.A. 1854; Deac. 1852 and Pr. 1856 by Bp of Wor. Vice Prin. of St. Mary Hall 1858; Chap. of Queen's Coll. 1849. Late Asst. Mast. of King Edward's Sch. Birmingham, 1852–56; formerly Asst. Mast. of Rossall Sch. 1850–52. [6]

ANSTEY, John Filmer, *Cirencester.*—Oriel Coll. Ox. B.A. 1848, M.A. 1850; Deac. 1849 and Pr. 1850 by Bp of G. and B. Formerly C. of Ampney-Crucis, Cirencester. [7]

ANSTICE, Joseph Ball, *Hungerford.*—St. John's Coll. Cam. Scho. of, B.A. 1850 M.A. 1853; Deac. 1851 and Pr. 1852 by Bp of Ex. V. of Hungerford, Dio. Ox. 1866. (Patrons, D. and C. of Windsor; Tithe, 525*l*; V.'s Inc. 550*l* and Ho; Pop. 3001.) Chap. to Hungerford Union Workhouse 1866. Formerly C. of Kilton 1850–56, and Bovey Tracey 1856–66. [8]

ANSTISS, George William, *Tynemouth.*—Lon. B.A. 1863; Deac. 1864 and Pr. 1866 by Bp of Dur. C. of St. Peter's, Tynemouth, 1864. [9]

ANTRIM, Richard, *Slapton, Dartmouth, Devon.*—Queen's Coll. Ox. B.A. 1825, M.A. 1827; Deac. and Pr. 1826 by Bp of Ely. P. C. of Slapton, Dio. Ex. 1850. (Patron, William Paige, Esq; Tithe—Imp. 60*l* 3*s*; P. C.'s Inc. 96*l*; Pop. 681.) Formerly R. of Lydlinch, Dorset, 1833–48; V. of Tollesbury, Essex, 1848–50. [10]

ANTROBUS, George, *Beighton Vicarage, near Sheffield.*—Brasen. Coll. Ox. B.A. 1840, M.A. 1844; Deac. 1842 by Bp of Rip. Pr. 1842 by Abp of York. V. of Beighton, Dio. Lich. 1865. (Patron, Earl Manvers; Tithe, 180*l*; Glebe, 1 acre; V.'s Inc. 247*l* and Ho; Pop. 1300.) Formerly C. of Shelton, Yorks, 1842–43, Farnham Royal, Bucks, 1843–47, St. John's, Withyham, Sussex, 1847–62; St. Gabriel's, Warwick-square, Lond. 1862–65. [11]

ANTROBUS, John, *Little Cloisters, Westminster, S.W.*—Min. Can. of Westminster. [12]

APPLEBY, Philemon.—Min. Can. of St. David's Cathl. [13]

APPLEBY, Thomas, *Haverstock-hill, London, N.W.*—Chap. of the Tailors' Almshouses, Haverstock-hill. [14]

APPLEFORD, William, 19, *Penn-road Villas, Holloway, London, N.*—Caius Coll. Cam. B.A. 1858; Deac. 1858, Pr. 1859. 2nd Chap. Convict Prison, Pentonville, 1867. Formerly C. of Trinity, St. Giles-in-the-Fields, Lond. 1858–60; Chap. of Convict Department, House of Correction, Wakefield, 1865–67. [15]

APPLETON, James, *Worksop, Notts.*—St. John's Coll. Cam. B.A. 1828, M.A. 1833; Deac. 1828, Pr. 1829. V. of Worksop, Dio. Lin. 1847. (Patron, Duke of Newcastle; Glebe, 8 acres; V.'s Inc. 388*l* and Ho; Pop. 8361.) [16]

APPLETON, J. A., *Limber Magna, Ulceby, Lincolnshire.*—C. of Limber Magna. [17]

APPLETON, John H., *Staplefield, Crawley, Sussex.*—Pemb. Coll. Ox; Deac. 1858 and Pr. 1859 by Bp of Ox. P. C. of St. Mark's, Staplefield, Dio. Chich. 1866. (Patron, V. of Cuckfield; P. C.'s Inc. 60*l* and Ho; Pop. 798.) [18]

APPLETON, Richard, *Chaplain's-house, Kirkdale, Liverpool.*—Trin. Coll. Cam. Sen. Opt. and 2nd cl. Cl. Trip. B.A. 1827, M.A. 1830; Deac. and Pr. 1830 by Bp of Ches. Chap. to Kirkdale County Gaol 1839. [19]

APPLETON, Robert T., *Staplefield, Crawley, Sussex.*—Pem. Coll. Ox. B.A. 1826, M.A. 1828; Deac. 1826 by Bp of Ox. Pr. 1826 by Bp of Cashel. Formerly Head Mast. of Reading Gr. Sch. [20]

APPLETON, W., *Gleadless, Sheffield.*—C. of Gleadless. [21]

APPLEYARD, E. S., *Crawley, Essex.* [22]

APPLEYARD, Edwin William, *Prestolee Parsonage, near Manchester.*—Magd. Hall, Ox. B.A. 1844; Deac. 1844 and Pr. 1845 by Bp of Ches. P. C. of Holy Trinity, Prestolee, Dio. Man. 1863. (Patron, W. J. Rideout, Esq; P. C.'s Inc. 300*l* from chief rents; Pop. 1500.) Formerly C. of St. Saviour's, Ringley, 1852–62. [23]

APPLEYARD, William, *Batley Carr, Dewsbury, Yorks.*—St. Bees; Deac. 1848, Pr. 1849. P. C. of Batley Carr, Dio. Rip. 1841. (Patron, V. of Dewsbury; P. C.'s Inc. 170*l* and Ho; Pop. 3859.) [24]

APTHORP, Charles Pretyman, *Stamford.*—Emman. Coll. Cam. 3rd cl. Cl. Trip. B.A. 1865; Deac. 1866 by Bp of Lin. C. of St. Michael's, Stamford, 1866. [25]

APTHORP, George Frederick, *Vicars'-court, Lincoln.*—Emman. Coll. Cam. 7th Jun. Opt. B.A. 1826; Deac. 1827 and Pr. 1828 by Bp of Lin. R. of Thorpe-on-the-hill, Dio. Lin. 1834. (Patrons, D. and C. of Lin; Tithe—Comm. 267*l*; Glebe, 266 acres; R.'s Inc. 330*l*; Pop. 427.) Succentor, Lib. and Preb. of Lin. Cathl. Formerly Sen. V. of Lin. Cathl. Author, *A Catalogue of the Books and Manuscripts in the Library of Lincoln Cathedral, with an Index of the Names of the Authors*, Lincoln, 1859. [26]

APTHORP, George Francis, *Birdsall, York.*—Emman. Coll. Cam. B.A. 1861, M.A. 1865; Deac. 1863 and Pr. 1864 by Bp of Lin. C. of Birdsall, and Chap. to Lord Middleton, 1867. Formerly C. of Barrow-on-Humber 1863, St. Swithin's, Lincoln, 1865. [27]

APTHORP, William Hutchinson, 5, *Southgate-place, Bath.*—Ch. Coll. Cam. B.A. 1830; Deac. 1832 by Abp of York, Pr. 1834 by Bp of Lin. Formerly P. C. of Blackford, Somerset, 1851–58. [28]

ARBUTHNOT, Robert Keith, *Kimpton, Welwyn, Herts.*—Dub. A.B. 1861, A.M. 1864; Deac. 1861 and Pr. 1862 by Bp of Lon. C. of Kimpton, Welwyn 1864. Formerly C. of St. Martin's-in-the-Fields, Lond. 1861–63. [29]

ARCHBOLD, Thomas.—Scho. of St. John's Coll. Cam. [30]

ARCHDALL - GRATWICKE, George, *Emmanuel College, Cambridge.*—Emman. Coll. Cam. B.A. 1815, M.A. 1818, B.D. 1825, D.D. 1835; Deac. 1819 by Bp of Ely, Pr. 1819 by Bp of Lon. Mast. of Emman. Coll. Cam. 1835; Can. of Nor. Cathl. 1842. [31]

ARCHER, Arthur William, 4, *Albert-terrace, Whalley Range, Manchester.*—Dub. A.M. 1840; Deac. 1841 and Pr. 1842 by Bp of Ches. P. C. of St. Mark's, Hulme, City and Dio. of Man. 1846, R. 1852. (Patrons, the Crown and Bp of Man. alt; R.'s Inc. 293*l*; Pop. 5687.) [32]

ARCHER, Charles Goodwyn, *Alderton, Woodbridge, Suffolk.*—Jesus Coll. Cam. B.A. 1846, M.A. 1849; Deac. 1847, Pr. 1848. R. of Alderton, Dio. Nor. 1856. (Patrons, T. Archer, Esq. and Bp. of Nor. every fourth turn; R.'s Inc. 720*l* and Ho; Pop. 634.) Formerly C. of Narburgh and Narford, Norfolk. [33]

ARCHER, Charles Harward, *Lewannick Vicarage, Launceston.*—V. of Lewannick, Dio. Ex. 1844. (Patron, Ld Chan; V.'s Inc. 260*l* and Ho; Pop. 685.) [1]

ARCHER, Edward, *West Barkwith Rectory, Wragby, Lincolnshire.*—R. of West Barkwith, Dio. Lin. 1860. (Patron, the present R; Tithe, 86*l*; Glebe, 113½ acres; R.'s Inc. 300*l* and Ho; Pop. 150.) Late Chap. to the Wandsworth and Clapham Union, Surrey; formerly C of Rochford, Essex. [2]

ARCHER, Samuel Haward, *Throwley, Okehampton, Devon.*—Ex. Coll. Ox. B.A. 1843, M.A. 1848; Deac. 1844, Pr. 1845. R. of Throwley, Dio. Ex. 1852. (Patron, Ld Chan; Tithe, 172*l*; R.'s Inc. 210*l*, and Ho; Pop. 327.) [3]

ARCHER, William John Bellew, *Churchill, near Bristol.*—P. C. of Churchill, Dio. B. and W. 1840. (Patrons, D. and C. of Bristol; Tithe—App. 585*l* 8*s*; P. C.'s Inc. 100*l*; Pop. 810.) [4]

ARCHIBALD, James, *Downton Vicarage, Herefordshire.*—V. of Downton, Dio. Herf. 1856. (Patron, Ld Chan; V.'s Inc. 160*l* and Ho; Pop. 184.) [5]

ARDEN, George, *Dunsford, Exeter.*—Wad. Coll. Ox. 3rd cl. Lit. Hum. B.A. 1840, M.A. 1842; Deac. 1842 and Pr. 1843 by Bp of Ex. V. of Dunsford, Dio. Ex. 1866. (Patron, Baldwin Fulford, Esq; Tithe, 365*l*; Glebe, 9½ acres; V.'s Inc. 400*l* and Ho; Pop. 921.) Formerly Chap. to the Earl of Devon; R. of Winterbourne-Came, Dorset, 1847–58; R. of North Bovey, Devon, 1859–66. Author, *A Manual of Catechetical Instruction*, 1851, 4th ed. 1867, 2*s*; *Breviates from Holy Scripture*, 1856, 2nd ed. 1860, 2*s*; *Lectures in Outline on Confirmation and Holy Communion*, 1857, 1*s*; *The Cure of Souls*, 1858, 2*s* 6*d*. [6]

ARDEN, Edward Thomas, *The Close, Lichfield.*—Ch. Coll. Cam. B.A. 1861; Deac. 1861 and Pr. 1863 by Bp of Lich. Asst. Pr. Vicar in Lich. Cathl. 1863; Sen. C. of St. Michael's, Lichfield, 1861. Formerly Asst. Chap. Lichfield Union 1865–66. [7]

ARGLES, George Marsham, *Doncaster.*—Ball. Coll. Ox. 2nd cl. Lit. Hum. B A. 1864, M.A. 1867; Deac. 1865 and Pr. 1866 by Abp of York. C. of Ch. Ch. Doncaster, 1865. [8]

ARGLES, Marsham, *Barnack Rectory, Stamford, Northants, and Prebendal House, Peterborough.*—Mert. Coll. Ox. 2nd cl. Lit. Hum B.A. 1835, M.A. 1838; Deac. 1837, Pr. 1838. R. of Burnack, Dio. Pet. 1851. (Patron, Bp of Pet; Tithe, 884*l* 10*s*; Glebe, 85 acres; R.'s Inc. 1036*l* and Ho; Pop. 948.) Exam. Chap. to the Bp of Pet. 1839; Can. of Pet. 1849; Chancellor of the Dio. of Pet. 1842–49. [9]

ARKELL, J., *Boxted, Colchester.*—C. of Boxted. [10]

ARKWRIGHT, Edwyn.—C. of Trinity, Twickenham. [11]

ARKWRIGHT, George, *Pencombe Rectory, Bromyard, Herf.*—R. of Pencombe, Dio. Herf. 1861. (Patron, J. H. Arkwright, Esq; R.'s Inc. 600*l* and Ho; Pop. 415.) [12]

ARKWRIGHT, Henry, *Bodenham, Leominster.*—Trin. Coll. Cam. B.A. 1835, M.A. 1838; Deac. 1836 by Bp of Lich, Pr. 1837 by Bp of Ches. V. of Bodenham, Dio. Herf. 1842. (Patron, Richard Arkwright, Esq; V.'s Inc. 660*l* and Ho; Pop. 1096.) Chap. to the Coningsby Hospital, Hereford. [13]

ARLETT, Henry, *Pembroke College, Cambridge.*—Pemb. Coll. Cam. B.A. 1824, M.A. 1827; Fell. of Pemb. Coll. Cam. Late Tut. of Pemb. Coll. [14]

ARMAND, A. W., *Roade, near Northampton.*—V. of Roade, Dio. Pet. 1866. (Patrons, Duke of Grafton and R. of Ashton; V.'s Inc. 100*l* and Ho; Pop. 644.) [15]

ARMGRISTER, W. A., *New Seaham, Durham.*—C. of New Seaham. [16]

ARMFIELD, Henry Thomas, *The Close, Salisbury.*—Pemb. Coll. Cam. Wrang. 1858, M.A; Deac. 1859 and Pr. 1860 by Bp of Wor. Min. Can. of Salis. 1863. Formerly 2nd Mast. of Gr. Sch. Atherstone; C. of Armley, Leeds. Editor, *Murray's Handbook for Belgium*. [17]

ARMISTEAD, Charles John, *Withcall Rectory, Louth.*—Magd. Hall, Ox. M.A. 1859; Deac. 1854 and Pr. 1855 by Abp of Cant. C. in sole charge of Withcall 1867; has pension of 136*l* a-year as retired Naval Chap. Formerly C. of Westwell, Kent, 1854–56; Chap. of Royal Naval Hospital, Hong Kong, China, 1856–61; Chap. of H.M.S. "Pembroke," at Harwich, 1862–67. Is a Fell. of the Soc. of Antiquaries and Royal Geographical Soc. [18]

ARMITAGE, Arthur, *Cheltenham.*—P. C. of St. John's, Cheltenham, Dio. G. and B. 1864. (Patrons, Simeon's Trustees; P. C.'s Inc. 250*l*; Pop. 2900.) Formerly C. of Cheltenham, and Chap. to the General Hospital and Female Refuge, Cheltenham. [19]

ARMITAGE, Braithwaite, *Peterchurch, Herefordshire.*—Trin. Coll. Cam. B.A. 1826; Deac. 1828 and Pr. 1829 by Bp of Herf. V. of Peterchurch, Dio. Herf. 1832. (Patrons, Rev. E. Williams and W. Farratt, Esq; Tithe—Imp. 307*l* 10*s* 1*d*, V. 374*l* 1*s* 2*d*; V.'s Inc. 390*l*; Pop. 710.) [20]

ARMITAGE, Edward, *Corscombe, near Dorchester.*—R. of Corscombe, Dio. Salis. 1858. (Patron, Rev. E. Armitage; R.'s Inc. 530*l* and Ho; Pop. 753.) [21]

ARMITAGE, Francis James, *Casterton, Kirkby Lonsdale.*—Ch. Coll. Cam. B.A. 1849, M.A. 1866; Deac. 1853 and Pr. 1854 by Bp of Lich. P. C. of Casterton, Dio. Carl. 1866. (Patrons, Trustees; P. C.'s Inc. 210*l* and Ho; Pop. 586. [22]

ARMITAGE, Frederick, M. A., *Paramatta, Sydney, New South Wales.*—Head Mast. of King's Sch. Paramatta. [23]

ARMITAGE, George, *Gloucester.*—C. of St. Luke's, Gloucester, 1866. [24]

ARMITAGE, George, *Silverdale, near Newcastle, Staffs.*—St. John's Coll. Cam. B.A. 1851; Deac 1851 and Pr. 1852 by Bp of Lich. P. C. of Silverdale, Dio. Lich. 1853. (Patron, R. Sneyd, Esq; P. C.'s Inc. 300*l*; Pop. 4673.) [25]

ARMITAGE, Joseph Akroyd, *Methley, near Leeds.*—Dub. A.B. 1852, A.M. 1859; Deac. 1852 and Pr. 1853 by Bp. of Rip. P. C. of Whitwood, Dio. York, 1862. (Patrons, D. and C. of Ch. Ch. Ox; Tithe, 120*l*; Glebe, 1 acre; Pop. 930.) Formerly C. of Farnley, Leeds, 1852–57, and Thornley and Tow-Law, Durham, 1857–61. [26]

ARMITAGE, W.—Chap. of Industrial Ragged Sch. and C. of St. Bride's Liverpool. [27]

ARMITSTEAD, H. S, *Sandbach Heath, Cheshire.*—P. C. of St. John's, Sandbach Heath, Dio. Ches. 1862. (Patron, V. of Sandbach; P. C.'s Inc. 150*l*; Pop. 1500.) [28]

ARMITSTEAD, John, *Sandbach, Cheshire.*—Trin. Coll. Ox. B.A. 1823, M.A. 1827; Deac. 1824, Pr. 1825. V. of Sandbach, Dio. Ches. 1828. (Patron, the present V; Tithe—App. 14*l* 8*s* 9*d*, Imp.—1024*l* 0*s* 9½*d*. V. 1165*l* 15*s* 11*d*; Glebe, 4 acres; V.'s Inc. 1307*l* and Ho; Pop. 4301.) [29]

ARMITSTEAD, Thomas Bell.—Brasen. Coll. Ox. Scho. of, B.A. 1863; Deac. 1864 by Bp of Lich. Pr. 1866 by Bp of Ches. Formerly C. of Silverdale, Staffs, 1864–66, Wolstanton, Staffs. 1866–67. [30]

ARMITSTEAD, William, *Garstang, Lancashire.*—Deac. 1829 and Pr. 1830 by Bp. of Carl. P. C. of St. Thomas's, Garstang, Dio. Man. 1835. (Patron, V. of Churchtown; P. C.'s Inc. 150*l* and Ho; Pop. 2300.) [31]

ARMSTRONG, Alfred Thomas, *Ashton, Preston.*—Dub. A B. 1830, A.M. 1833; Deac. and Pr. 1832. P. C. of Ashton-on-Ribble, Dio. Man. 1854. (Patron, V. of Preston; P. C.'s Inc 108*l* and Ho; Pop. 911.) [32]

ARMSTRONG, Benjamin John, *East Dereham, Norfolk.*—V. of East Dereham with Hoo C. Dio. Nor. 1850. (V.'s Inc. 560*l*; Pop. East Dereham 4368, Hoo 169.) Surrogate. [33]

ARMSTRONG, Charles, *Nottingham.*—P. C. of St. Paul's, Nottingham, Dio. Lin. 1838. (Patron, Bp of Lin; P. C.'s Inc. 300*l*; Pop. 6817.) [34]

ARMSTRONG, Charles Edward, *Holgate Lodge, Hemsworth, Pontefract.*—Wor. Coll. Ox. B.A. 1831, M.A. 1833; Deac. 1831, Pr. 1832. Mast. of Hemsworth Hospital 1832 (Value, 555*l*). Author, *England under the Popish Yoke, from A.D. 600 to 1534*, 1*s* 6*d*; *A Tar of the Last War, being the Naval Services and Anecdotes of Vice-Admiral Sir Charles Richardson, K.C.B.* 5*s* 6*d*. [1]

ARMSTRONG, Edward Pakenham, *Skellingthorpe, near Lincoln.*—V. of Skellingthorpe, Dio. Lin. 1838. (Patron, Master of Spital Hospital; V.'s Inc. 35*l*; Pop. 662.) [2]

ARMSTRONG Henry William Gleed, *Bierton Vicarage, Aylesbury.*—St. John's Coll. Ox. B.A. 1828, M.A. 1829. V. of Bierton with Quarrendon V. Dio. Ox. 1863. (Patrons, D. and C. of Lin; V.'s Inc. 348*l* and Ho; Pop. Bierton 691, Quarrendon 58.) Formerly V. of Willesden 1854–63. [3]

ARMSTRONG, James, B.A.—British Chaplain at Morro Velho. [4]

ARMSTRONG, John, *Wallsend, Newcastle-on-Tyne.*—P. C. of Wallsend, Dio. Dur. 1830. (Patrons, D and C. of Durham; Tithe—App. 459*l* 13*s* 4*d*; P. C. 167*l*; Glebe, 41½ acres; P. C.'s Inc. 290*l*; Pop. 2477.) [5]

ARMSTRONG, John Echlin, *Burslem, Staffs.*—Dub. A.B. 1831, A.M. 1842, LL.D. 1849, D D. 1853; Deac. 1840 and Pr. 1841 by Bp. of Ches. R. of Burslem, Dio. Lich. 1850. (Patron the present R; Tithe, 400*l*; Glebe, 82 acres; R.'s Inc. 660*l* and Ho; Pop. 8077.) Surrogate; Chap. to Lord Gray of Gray, and to the Earl of Shrewsbury and Talbot. [6]

ARMSTRONG, John Hopkins, *Reading.*—Dub. 1st cl. Div. A.M. 1854; Deac. 1843 and Pr. 1844 by Abp of Dub. Chap. of Alnut's Hospital, Goring Heath, 1864 (Stipend 109*l*.) Formerly C. of St. Stephen's, Dublin; V. of Bicknoller, Somerset; C. of St. Giles's, Reading. [7]

ARMSTRONG, Robert Lovett, 113, *Cross Lands, Salford, Manchester.*—B.A. 1853, M.A. 1866; Deac. 1855 and Pr. 1856 by Bp of Lich. Assoc. Sec. to the Soc. of Irish Ch. Missions. Formerly P. C. of Heywood, Wilts, 1862. [8]

ARMSTRONG, Rowley, *Ripley, Yorks.*—St. Bees 1854–55; Deac. 1856 and Pr. 1857 by Bp of Ches. C. of Ripley 1857. Formerly C. of Bollington, Cheshire, 1856–57. Author, *Sermon on the Mount*, in verse, 1856, 6*d*. [9]

ARMYTAGE, Joseph North Green, *Clifton.*—St. John's Coll. Cam. B.A. 1830, M.A. 1834; Deac. 1831, Pr. 1832. R. of Flax Bourton, Dio. B. and W. 1866. (Patron, R. of Nailsea; R.'s Inc. 90*l*; Pop. 215.) [10]

ARNEY, Edward Francis, *The Vicarage, Monmouth.*—Brasen. Coll. Ox. B.A. 1821, M.A. 1824. V. of Monmouth, Dio. Llan. 1849. (Patron, Duke of Beaufort; Tithe—Imp. 592*l* 13*s* 5*d*; V.'s Inc. 200*l* and Ho; Pop. 4131.) Surrogate. [11]

ARNOLD, B. North, *Caverswall, near Cheadle, Staffs.*—Edin. 1836, Fell. of the Royal Coll. of Physicians Edin. and of the Royal Coll. of Surgeons, Lond; Deac. 1862, Pr. 1863. V. of Caverswall, Dio. Lich. 1865. (Patron, Hon. E. S. Jervis; Tithe—App. 2*l*, Imp. 200*l* 1*s* and Ho; Pop. 3046.) [12]

ARNOLD, Charles, *Tinwell Rectory (Rutland), near Stamford.*—Caius Coll. Cam. B.A. 1824, M.A. 1827; Deac. 1825 by Bp of Pet. Pr. 1826 by Bp of Nor. R. of Tinwell, Dio. Pet. 1827. (Patron, Marquis of Exeter; Tithe—Imp. 110*l*, R. 6*s*; Glebe, 148 acres; R.'s Inc. 305*l* and Ho; Pop. 235.) Hon. Can. of Pet. Cathl. 1854; Rural Dean. Formerly Fell. of Caius Coll. Cam. Author, *The Boys' Arithmetic*, 2 parts, 1844, 3*s*. 6*d*. [13]

ARNOLD, Charles Maddock, *South Norwood, Surrey.*—St. John's Coll. Cam. B A. 1839, M.A. 1842; Deac. 1839 and Pr. 1840 by Bp of Ches. Min. Can. of Westminster Abbey; P. C. of St. Mark's, South Norwood, Dio. Cant. 1859. (Patron, P. C. of All Saints, Norwood; P. C.'s Inc. about 160*l*; Pop. 1489.) Dom. Chap. to the Dowager Marchioness of Bath. [14]

ARNOLD, Charles Thomas, *Rugby.*—Magd. Hall and Ball. Coll. Ox. B.A. 1840, M.A. 1843; Deac. 1841 and Pr. 1842 by Bp of Wor. Asst. Mast. in Rugby Sch. 1841. [15]

ARNOLD, Charles William, *Royal Naval School, Newcross, Kent, S.E.*—Trin. Coll. Cam. Wrangler and Prizeman, B.A. 1854, M.A. 1858; Deac. 1854 by Bp of Pet. Pr. 1859 by Bp of Wor. Head Mast. and Chap. of the Royal Naval Sch. Newcross, 1867; Head Mast. of Chelmsford Gr. Sch. 1855; C. of Chignal-Smealy, near Chelmsford, 1859, and of Downham, near Chelmsford, 1864. Formerly C. of Eaton Astbury, Cheshire, and Head Mast. of Congleton Gr. Sch. 1854. [16]

ARNOLD, Edward Gladwin, *Barrow Rectory, Chester.*—Ex. Coll. Ox. B.A. 1847; Deac. 1847, Pr. 1848. R. of Barrow, Dio. Ches. 1862. (Patron, Lord H. Cholmondeley; Tithe, 460*l*; Glebe, 2½ acres; R.'s Inc. 460*l* and Ho; Pop. 615.) Formerly R. of Stapleford, near Hertford, 1852–62. [17]

ARNOLD, Edward Penrose, *Privy Council Office, Whitehall, London, S.W.*—Ball. Coll. Ox. B.A. 1848, M.A. 1851; Deac. 1852 and Pr. 1855 by Bp of Ox. Late Fell. of All Souls' Coll. Ox. One of Her Majesty's Assistant Inspectors of Schools. [18]

ARNOLD, Frederick, *Brimington, Chesterfield.*—Queens' Coll. Cam. B.A. 1830; Deac. 1830 and Pr. 1831 by Bp of Lin. P. C. of Brimington, Dio. Lich. 1852. (Patron, V. of Chesterfield; Glebe, 4 acres; P. C.'s Inc. 300*l* and Ho; Pop. 1806.) Surrogate 1852. Author, *Sermons*, 1840; *Practical Lectures on the Fulfilled Prophecies*, 1850. [19]

ARNOLD, Frederick Henry, *Ashling, Chichester.*—Dub. A.B. 1859, A.M. 1862, LL.B. 1864; Deac. 1859 and Pr. 1860 by Bp of Chich. R. of Racton with Lordington C. Dio. Chich. 1865. (Patrons, D. and C. of Chich; Tithe, 183*l*; R.'s Inc. 183*l*; Pop. 95.) Formerly C. of Barlavington 1859; P. C. of Appledram 1861; Sequestrator of St. Martin's, and Mast. of Cath. Sch. Chichester, 1865. Author, *Petworth, its History and Antiquities*, 1864; *The Libretto of Dr. Arnold's Oratorio Ahab*, 1864; *Parochial History of Appledram*, 1866; etc. [20]

ARNOLD, Frederick Montagu, *Kingston-on-Thames.*—Late Scho. of Caius Coll. Cam. Wrang. and B.A. 1848, M.A. 1851; Deac. 1848 and Pr. 1849 by Bp of Chich. Late Sen. Fell. of St. Nicholas' Coll. Shoreham, Sussex. [21]

ARNOLD, John Muehleisen, *Batavia.*—Tübingen, M.A. and Ph. D; Basle B.D; Theol. Licen; Deac. and Pr. by Bp of Jerusalem, 1842. Consular Chap. at Batavia 1865. Late Missionary of C. M. S. in Abyssinia and India; Chap. to Bp of Gibraltar; Chap. to St. Mary's Hospital, Paddington; C. of East Ham, London; and Hon. Sec. to the Moslem Mission Society. Author, *Anti-Papal Aggression*, Seeleys, 1851; *True and False Religion*, Seeleys, 1852; *Scripture Answers to Questions on the Church Catechism*, 1*s* 6*d*, Rivingtons, 1859; *Ishmael, or a Natural History of Islamism and its Relation to Christianity*, 10*s* 6*d*, Rivingtons, 1859; *The Moslem Mission Field*, 1*d*, Rivingtons, 1860; *English Biblical Criticism and the Authorship of the Pentateuch from a German point of view*, 1864. [22]

ARNOLD, Kerchever William.—Ball. Coll. Ox. B.A. 1855; Deac. 1855 by Abp of York. Formerly C. of Topcliffe, Yorks. [23]

ARNOLD, Richard Aldous, *Ellough, Beccles, Suffolk.*—Trin. Coll. Ox. B.A. 1815; Deac. 1817, Pr. 1819. R. of Ellough, Dio. Nor. 1830. (Patron, Rev. H. Golding; Tithe, 305*l* 3*s* 10*d*; Glebe, 35 acres; R.'s Inc. 300*l* and Ho; Pop. 126.) [24]

ARNOLD, R. Stedman, *Gateshead.*—C. of St. Mary's, Gateshead. Formerly C. of Ferry Fryston Yorks. [25]

ARNOLD, William, *Evercreech, Somerset.*—Pemb. Coll. Ox. B.A. 1856, M.A. 1859; Deac. 1857 and Pr. 1858 by Bp of B. and W. C. of Evercreech with Chesterblade 1859. Formerly C. of Midsomer Norton, Somerset, 1857. [26]

ARNOTT, Samuel, *Rectory, Ilketshall, Bungay, Suffolk.*—Emman. Coll. Cam. Jun. Opt. and 3rd cl. Cl. Trip. B.A. 1843, M.A. 1846; Deac. 1845 and Pr. 1846 by Bp of Lon. R. of Ilketshall St. John's, Dio. Nor. 1866. (Patron, Ld Chan; R.'s Inc. 361*l* and Ho; Pop. 75.) Formerly P. C. of St. Luke's, Berwick-street, Lond. 1854–58; V. of Chatham 1858–66. Author, various single Sermons, etc. [1]

ARNOTT, Samuel Brazier, *Englefield-green, Egham, Surrey.*—St. John's Coll. Ox. B.A. 1836, M.A. 1841; Deac. 1841, Pr. 1842. [2]

ARROWSMITH, James, *Stoke Row, Henley-on-Thames.*—St. Edm. Hall, Ox. B.A. 1845, M.A. 1848; Deac. 1845 by Bp of Lich. Pr. 1846 by Bp of Rip. P. C. of Stoke Row, Dio. Ox. 1850. (Patron, St. John's Coll. Cam; P. C.'s Inc. 100*l* and Ho; Pop. 386.) [3]

ARROWSMITH, Robert, *Ludlow, Shropshire.*—Oriel Coll. Ox. B.A. 1846, M.A. 1849; Deac. 1847 by Bp of Ox. Pr. 1850 by Bp of Wor. R. of Ludlow, Dio. Herf. 1866. (Patron, Ld Chan; R.'s Inc. 200*l* and Ho; Pop. 5171.) Formerly V. of Stoke with Walsgrave, Coventry, 1856–66. [4]

ARROWSMITH, William Robson, 82, *Charrington-street, Oakley-square, London, N.W.*—P. C. of Old Church, St. Pancras, Lond. Dio. Lon. 1859. (Patron V. of St. Pancras; P.C.'s Inc. 220*l*; Pop. 11,161.) Formerly R. of Byton, Herefordshire, and Head Mast. of the Leominster Gr. Sch. 1853–59. [5]

ARTHUR, David, *Fort St. George, Inverness.*—Chap. to the Garrison, Fort St. George. [6]

ARTHUR, George Frederick, *Tamerton-Foliott, Plymouth.*—Trin. Coll. Ox. B.A. 1827, M.A. 1832; Deac. 1829 by Bp of Ex. Pr. 1830 by Bp of B. and W. V. of Tamerton-Foliott, Dio. Ex. 1830. (Patron, Ld Chan; V.'s Inc. 315*l* and Ho; Pop. 1170.) [7]

ARTHUR, James, *Atherington, Barnstaple, Devon.*—Pemb. Coll. Cam. B.A. 1823; Deac. 1824, Pr. 1825. R. of Atherington, Dio. Ex. 1829. (Patron, the present R.; Tithe, 400*l*; Glebe, 200 acres; R.'s Inc. 600*l* and Ho; Pop. 598.) [8]

ARTHUR, Lucius, *Cromford-bridge House, Matlock.* [9]

ARTHUR, Pellew, *Guildford Surrey.*—Trin. Coll. Cam. B.A. 1859; Deac. 1860 by Bp of Win. Asst. Mast. at the Gr. Sch. Guildford, 1860. [10]

ARTHUR, Thomas Freke, *Eastdowne Rectory, Barnstaple.*—Caius Coll. Cam. B.A. 1851; Deac. 1851 and Pr. 1852 by Bp of Ex. R. of Eastdowne, Dio. Ex. 1856. (Patron, John Wills, Esq; Tithe, 385*l*; Glebe 100 acres; R.'s Inc. 485*l* and Ho; Pop. 350.) Rural Dean. Formerly C. of Atherington. [11]

ARTHURE, Benedict, *All Saints' Rectory, Worcester.*—Deac. 1842 and Pr. 1843 by Bp of Ches. R. of All Saints', City and Dio. Wor. 1860. (Patron, Ld Chan; R.'s Inc. 200*l* and Ho; Pop. 2421.) Formerly P. C. of St. Catherine's, Tranmere, Cheshire, 1846–60; previously R. of St. Lawrence, Isle of Wight. [12]

ARTHY, John, *Caistor, near Norwich.*—Jesus Coll. Cam. B.A. 1824, M.A. 1828; Deac. 1825, Pr. 1826. R. of Caistor with Markshall, Dio. Nor. 1842. (Patroness, Mrs. H. Dashwood; Tithe, 445*l*; Glebe, 58¾ acres; R.'s Inc. 512*l* and Ho; Pop. Caistor 162, Markshall 34.) [13]

ARTHY, N. Hopper, *Whitby.* [14]

ARTHY, Walter Bridge.—Chap. of H.M.S. "Defence." Formerly Chap. and Naval Instructor H.M.S. "Calypso," and of H.M.S. "Horatio." [15]

ARTHY, William Robert Bridge, *Sutton, Macclesfield.*—St. Bees and St. John's Coll. Cam; Deac. 1846 and Pr. 1847 by Bp of Ches. P. C. of St. George's, Sutton, Prestbury, Dio. Ches. 1848. (Patrons, Trustees; P. C.'s Inc. 270*l* and Ho; Pop. 5308.) Author, Sermons, *Tercentenary of the Prayer-book*, 1849; *Cholera, the Voice of God*, 1849; *Death of the Righteous*, 1850; *Our National Advantages and Duties*, 1853; *Sabbath Observances*, 1855; *Lectures on the Theology of Dr. Newman*, 1851; *The Blessings of the Reformation*, 1858. [16]

ARUNDEL, William Harris, *Cheriton-Fitzpaine, Crediton, Devon.*—Caius Coll. Cam. B.A. 1820, M.A. 1823; Deac. 1822 and Pr. 1823 by Bp of Ex. R. of Cheriton-Fitzpaine, Dio. Ex. 1824. (Patron, the present R; Tithe, 992*l*; Glebe 37 acres; R.'s Inc. 992*l* and Ho; Pop. 1111.) Formerly C. of Cheriton-Fitzpaine 1822 [17]

ARUNDELL, Thomas, *Hayton Vicarage, York.*—St. John's Coll. Cam. B.A. 1851; Deac. 1852 and Pr. 1853 by Bp of Win. V. of Hayton with Bealby, Dio. York, 1860. (Patron, Abp of York; V.'s Inc. 388*l* and Ho; Pop. Hayton 210, Bealby 268.) Formerly C. of Ch. Ch. Blackfriars, Lond. 1853–54; All Saints', Gordon-square, and Reader of Ch. Ch. Newgate-street, Lond. 1854–56; P. C. of St. Peter's, Hammersmith, Middlesex, 1856–60. Author, *Address to Parishioners of Hammersmith*, 1860; various Sermons. [19]

ARUNDELL, William Henry, *Huntspill, Bridgwater.*—Ex. Coll. Ox. B.A. 1864; Deac. 1865, Pr. 1866. C. of Huntspill 1865. [18]

ASH, Charles, *Holbeach, Lincolnshire.*—Deac. 1820 and Pr. 1821 by Bp of Lin. [20]

ASH, Drummond, *Cocking Vicarage, Midhurst, Sussex.*—B.A. 1851, M.A. 1852; Deac. 1852, Pr. 1853. V. of Cocking, Dio. Chich. 1860. (Patron, Bp. of Ox; Tithe, 340*l*; Glebe, 35 acres; V.'s Inc. 430*l*; Pop. 430.) [21]

ASH, Robert Halcott, *Sunningdale, Berks.*—Deac. 1864 and Pr. 1865 by Bp of Ox. C. of Sunningdale 1866. Formerly C. of Bracknell 1864, and Folkestone 1865. [22]

ASH, T. E.—C. of St. Michael's, Liverpool. [23]

ASHBY, Edward Queenby, *Dunton, Aylesbury, Bucks.*—Ch. Ch. Ox. B.A. 1826, M.A. 1833. R. of Dunton, Dio. Ox. 1842. (Patron, Abel Smith, Esq; R.'s Inc. 210*l* and Ho; Pop. 106.) [24]

ASHBY, Samuel, *Saxthorpe, Reepham, Norfolk.*—Pemb. Coll. Cam. B.A. 1835, M.A. 1838; Deac. 1838 and Pr. 1839 by Bp of Ely. V. of Saxthorpe, Dio. Nor. 1840. (Patron, Pemb. Coll. Cam; Tithe—Imp. 302*l* 10*s*, V. 91*l*; Glebe, 45 acres; V.'s Inc. 136*l* and Ho; Pop. 328.) V. of Corpusty, Norfolk, Dio. Nor. 1844. (Patron, J. R. Ives, Esq; Tithe—Imp. 256*l*; V.'s Inc. 62*l*; Pop. 425.) Fell. of Pemb. Coll. Cam. [25]

ASHE, George A. Hamilton, *Witton, Blackburn.*—Dub. A.B. 1835; Deac. 1838 and Pr. 1839 by Abp of Cant. P. C. of Witton, Dio. Man. 1839. (Patron, V. of Blackburn; Tithe, comm. 244*l*; P. C.'s Inc. 300*l*; Pop. 5297.) [26]

ASHE, James William, *Garton-in-Holderness, Yorks.*—St. Bees; Deac. 1855 and Pr. 1856 by Abp of York. V. of Garton-in-Holderness, Dio. York, 1858. (Patron, Ld Chan; V.'s Inc. 105*l*; Pop. 195.) Late C. of Witherwick, Yorks. [27]

ASHE, Thomas.—Chaplain of H.M.S. "Racoon." [28]

ASHE, William, *Dalwood, Honiton.*—Dub. A.B; Deac. 1824, Pr. 1825. C. of Dalwood 1866. Formerly C. of Treneglos and Warbstow, Cornwall, 1826, Milton Abbott 1846, Shute 1848, Trusham 1862, and Chivelstone, Devon, 1864. [29]

ASHFIELD, Charles Robert, *Burgate, (Suffolk), near Scole, Norfolk.*—Brasen. Coll. Ox. B.A. 1812; Deac. 1813 and Pr. 1814 by Bp of Lin. R. of Great Blakenham, Suffolk, Dio. Nor. 1827. (Patron, Eton Coll; Tithe, 195*l*; Glebe, 8½ acres; R.'s Inc. 203*l*; Pop. 291.) R. of Burgate, Dio. Nor. 1834. (Patron, Bp of Nor; Tithe, 550*l*; Glebe, 74 acres; R.'s Inc. 639*l* and Ho; Pop. 359.) [30]

ASHFIELD, Edmund Wodley, *Berrow, near Ledbury.*—Trin. Coll. Cam. 1st cl. Cl. Trip. B.A. 1859, M.A, 1862; Deac. 1861 and Pr. 1862 by Bp of B. and W. C. of Berrow 1866. Formerly C. of Ch. Ch. Frome, 1861, and North and South Stoke, near Grantham, 1864. [31]

ASHHURST, James Henry, *Waterstock Rectory, Wheatley, Oxon.*—Ex. Coll. Ox. B.A. 1841, M.A. 1844; Deac. 1842 and Pr. 1843 by Bp of Ox. R. of Waterstock, Dio. Ox. 1856. (Patron, John Henry Ashhurst, Esq; Tithe, 250*l*; Glebe, 13 acres; R.'s Inc. 275*l* and Ho; Pop. 147.) Surrogate 1849; Rural Dean;

Treas. of Dioc. Ch. Build. Soc. Formerly C. of Aston, Oxon, 1842–44; P. C. of Little Milton, Oxon, 1844–48; V. of Great Milton 1848–56. [1]

ASHINGTON, Henry, *Anwick, Sleaford, Lincolnshire.*—Trin. Coll. Cam. Sen. Opt. 1st cl. Cl. Trip. B.A. 1826, M.A. 1828; Deac. 1832, Pr. 1833. R. of Brauncewell with Anwick V. Dio. Lin. 1854. (Patrons, Marquis of Bristol and Mrs. Robinson alt; Brauncewell, Tithe, 640*l*; Glebe, 9 acres; Anwick, Tithe, 93*l*; Glebe, 81 acres; R.'s Inc. 850*l* and Ho; Pop. Brauncewell 112, Anwick 277.) Author, *A Visitation Sermon*, 1847; *A Funeral Sermon*, 1848. [2]

ASHLEY, Francis Busteed, *Wooburn, Beaconsfield, Bucks.*—Deac. 1844 and Pr. 1845 by Bp of Ches. V. of Wooburn, Dio. Ox. 1847. (Patron, James Dupré, Esq; Tithe—Imp. 18*l*, V. 9*l*; Glebe, 90 acres; V.'s Inc. 150*l* and Ho; Pop. 2450.) Author, *The Domestic Circle*, 3*s* 6*d*; *Health*, S. P. C. K; *Mormonism*, Hatchards; *Romanism*; *The Bible Chart*; *Confirmation*; *The Christian Ministry*; *Confession*; *Roman Catholicism Modern and Protestant Catholicism Ancient*; *Wooburn Handbills* Nos. 1–33; &c. [3]

ASHLEY, George Edward, *The Close, Lichfield.*—Oriel Coll. Ox. B.A. 1854, M.A. 1865; Deac. and Pr. 1856 by Bp of Lich. Formerly C. of St. Mary's, Lichfield, 1856–60, and Weeford with Hints 1861–66. [4]

ASHLEY, John, *Milford Cottage, Greville-road, Kilburn, London, N.W.*—Trin. Coll. Cam. LL.D. 1821; Deac. 1824, Pr. 1828. [5]

ASHLEY, John Marks, *Swanscombe, Dartford.*—Caius Coll. Cam. S.C.L. 1856, B.C.L. 1859; Deac. 1857 and Pr. 1858 by Bp of Lon. C. of Swanscombe, Kent, 1858; Sunday Even. Lect. at St. Mary's, Greenhithe, 1860. Formerly C. of St. Ethelburga's, Lond. 1857. Author, *The Relations of Science*, 1855, 6*s*; *Victory of the Spirit*, Masters, 1865, 2*s*; *Homilies of St. Thomas Aquinas*, Church Press Co. 1866–67; etc. [6]

ASHMORE, Paul, 14, *Queen's-gardens, Hyde Park, London, W.*—Ch. Coll. Cam. LL.B. 1826; Deac. 1827, Pr. 1828. Formerly R. of Porthkerry, Glamorgan, 1838–65. [7]

ASHPITEL, Francis, *Hampden Rectory, Great Missenden, Bucks.*—R. of Great Hampden, Dio. Ox. 1859. (Patron, D. Cameron, Esq; R.'s Inc. 400*l* and Ho; Pop. 266.) [8]

ASHTON, Ellis, *Huyton, Prescot, Lancashire.*—Brasen. Coll. Ox. B.A. 1811, M.A. 1813, B.D. 1821; Deac. 1813 by Bp of Ox. Pr. 1818 by Abp of York. V. of Huyton, Dio. Ches. 1818. (Patron, Earl of Derby; Tithe—Imp. 600*l*, V. 690*l*; Glebe, 1 acre; V.'s Inc. 690*l* and Ho; Pop. 1641.) R. of Begbroke, Dio. Ox. 1821. (Patrons, Brasen. Coll. Ox; Tithe, 155*l*; Glebe, 37 acres; R.'s Inc. 180*l* and Ho; Pop. 87.) Rural Dean of Prescot 1845. Late Fell of Brasen. Coll. Ox. Formerly Chap. to Abp of Cant. [9]

ASHWELL, Arthur Rawson, *Training College, Durham.*—Trin. Coll. Cam. 1843, Foundation Scho. Caius Coll. 1846, 15th Wrang. B.A. 1847, M.A. 1850; Deac. 1848 and Pr. 1849 by Abp of Cant. Prin. of Dioc. Training Coll. Durham, 1865. Formerly C. of Speldhurst, Kent, 1848–49, and St. Mary's the Less, Cam. 1849–50; Vice-Prin. of St. Mark's Coll. Chelsea, 1851–52; Prin. of Ox. Dio. Training Coll. at Culham 1853–62; Min. of Trin. Ch. Conduit-Street, Lond. 1862–64. Author, *The Schoolmaster's Studies*, 1860, 1*s* 6*d*; *God in His Work and in His Nature*, 1863, 3*s*; Contributor to Series III. of *Tracts for Christian Seasons*, and various periodicals. [10]

ASHWELL, Seymour, *Finmere, Bicester.*—R. of Finmere, Dio. Ox. 1866. (Patron, W. Ashwell, Esq; R.'s Inc. 370*l* and Ho; Pop. 338.) [11]

ASHWIN, Charles Godfrey, 1, *Cambridge Terrace, Whalley Range, Manchester.*—Caius Coll. Cam. B.A. 1858; Deac. 1858 and Pr. 1859 by Bp of G. and B. Assoc. Sec. to Lond. Soc. for Promoting Christianity amongst the Jews. Formerly C. of St. Philip's, Bristol. [12]

ASHWIN, Forster, *Wigtoft, Spalding, Yorks.*—Dub. A.B. 1852; Deac. 1852 by Bp of St. D. Pr. 1853 by Bp of Llan. C. of Wigtoft with Quadring 1862. Formerly C. of St. Paul's, Newport, Monmouthshire, 1852; Incumb. of Holy Trin. Sydney, 1855; Incumb. of Ch. Ch. Kiama, New South Wales, 1858. [13]

ASHWIN, Hamilton, 5, *Holly-terrace, Stoneycroft, Liverpool.*—Dub. A.B. 1858; Deac. 1858 and Pr. 1859 by Bp of Rip. Assoc. Sec. of Colonial and Continental Ch. Soc. 1864. Formerly C. of Ossett, Yorks, 1858, Tamworth 1860, and St. Mary's, Southampton, 1862. [14]

ASHWORTH, Arthur, *Holm Cultram Vicarage, Abbey Town, Carlisle.*—Magd. Hall, Ox. B.A. 1855, M.A. 1863; Deac. 1857 and Pr. 1858 by Bp of Man. V. of Holm Cultram, Dio. Carl. 1865. (Patron, Univ. of Ox; V.'s Inc. 170*l* and Ho; Pop. 980.) Formerly C. of Belmont 1857–59, Wigton 1859–62, and Holm Cultram 1862–65. Author, *Addresses to Sunday School Teachers and Scholars.* [15]

ASHWORTH, Arthur Howard, *Nether-Wallop, Stockbridge, Hants.*—Oriel Coll. Ox. B.A. 1842, M.A. 1845. V. of Nether-Wallop, Dio. Win. 1857. (Patrons, Vicars Choral in York Cathl; V.'s Inc. 294*l*; Pop. 946.) Min. Can. of York Cathl. 1853 (value 150*l*). Formerly V. of St. Mary Bishopshill Junior, York. [16]

ASHWORTH, John Ashworth, *Didcot, Abingdon, Berks.*—Ch. Ch. Ox. B.A. 1836, Brasen. Coll. Ox. M.A. 1839. R. of Didcot, Dio. Ox. 1851. (Patron, Brasen. Coll. Ox; R.'s Inc. 399*l*; Pop. 349.) Late Fell. of Brasen. Coll. Ox. [17]

ASHWORTH, John Hervey, *East Woodhay, Hants.*—Univ. Coll. Ox. B.A. 1819, M.A. 1825; Deac. 1821, Pr. 1822. Author, *The Saxon in Ireland*, Murray, 5*s*. [18]

ASKER, Henry.—Corpus Coll. Cam. B.A. 1835; Deac. 1836 by Bp of Lin. Pr. 1836 by Bp of Nor. Late C. of Denver 1850; Chap. to Downham Market Union 1851. [19]

ASKEW, John, 4, *Holland-place, Notting-hill, London, W.*—Emman. Coll. Cam. B.A. 1828, M.A. 1831; Deac. 1830, Pr. 1833. [20]

ASKEW, Richard, *Stonham-Parva, Suffolk.*—Dur. M.A. R. of Stonham-Parva, Dio. Nor. 1856. (Patron, the present R; Tithe, 336*l*; Glebe, 30 acres; R.'s Inc. 420*l* and Ho; Pop. 391.) [21]

ASPIÑALL, George, *Mayfield Cottage, Sevenoaks, Kent.*—Heidelberg, Ph. D. 1840; Deac. 1846 by Bp of Ches. Pr. 1848 by Bp of Man. Chap. of the Iron Ch. and C. of Sevenoaks. Formerly C. of Almondbury, Yorks. [22]

ASPLEN, George William, *Wadmore House, Panton-street, Cambridge.*—Corpus Coll. Cam. B.A. 1849, M.A. 1852; Deac. 1859 and Pr. 1860 by Bp of Ely. Chap. of Corpus Christi Coll. Cam. 1864; English Mast. of Perse Gram. Sch. Cambs. 1855. Formerly C. of Stapleford, Cambs. 1859–60, St. Andrew's the Great, Cam. 1861. Author, *A Lively Sketch of a Trip to Killarney and the South of Ireland*, 1858, 1*s*; *The Seven Churches of Asia, a Poem.* [23]

ASSHETON, R. O., *Bilton Rectory, Rugby.*—R. of Bilton, Dio. Wor. 1862. (Patron, the present R; R.'s Inc. 700*l* and Ho; Pop. 1100.) [24]

ASTBURY, Charles John, 66, *Fishergate, Preston.*—Brasen. Coll. Ox. B.A. 1859, M.A. 1862; Deac. 1861 and Pr. 1862 by Abp of Cant. C. of Preston, 1866. Formerly C of Seal, Kent, 1861, and Walton-le-Dale, Lancashire, 1863. Author, *A Continental Tour*, 1861, and *Political Reform, a Plea for Conservatism*, 1860. [25]

ASTLEY, Benjamin Buckler Gifford, *Merevale, Atherstone, Leicestershire.*—St. Alban's Hall, Ox. B.A. 1840, M.A. 1849; Deac. 1842, Pr. 1843. R. of Pitney-Yeovil, Somerset, Dio. B. and W. 1857. (Patrons, Mrs. H. Mitchell and W. Uttermere, Esq; R.'s Inc. 170*l*; Pop. 390.) P. C. of Merevale, Dio. Wor. 1855. (Patron, W. S. Dugdale, Esq; P C.'s Inc. 75*l*; Pop. 212.) Formerly R. of Draycot-Foliatt, Wilts; previously C. of Everley, Wilts. [26]

ASTLEY, Charles Tamberlane, *Brasted Rectory, Sevenoaks, Kent.*—Jesus Coll. Ox. B.A. 1847, M.A. 1849; Deac. and Pr. 1849. R. of Brasted, Dio. Cant. 1864. (Patron, Abp of Cant; Tithe, 854*l* 19*s* 6*d*;

R.'s Inc. 880*l* and Ho; Pop. 1182.) Formerly V. of Margate, 1854–64. [1]

ASTLEY, Hon. Delaval Loftus, *East Barsham, Fakenham, Norfolk.*—Trin. Coll. Cam. M.A. 1846; Deac. 1851, Pr. 1852. V. of East Barsham with Little Snoring R. Dio. Nor. 1855. (Patron, Ld Hastings; East Barsham, Tithe—V. 314*l*; Little Snoring, Tithe—R. 363*l*; V.'s Inc. 680*l* and Ho; Pop. East Barsham 221, Little Snoring 311.) [2]

ASTLEY, John Wolvey, *Chalton, Horndean, Hants.*—King's Coll. Cam. B.A. 1829, M.A. 1834; Deac. 1830 and Pr. 1834 by Bp of Lin. R. of Chalton with Clanfield R. and Idsworth C. Dio. Win. 1848. (Patron, King's Coll. Cam; Chalton, Tithe, comm. 218*l*; Glebe, 77 acres; Clanfield, Tithe, 130*l*; Glebe, 62½ acres; Idsworth, Tithe, 257*l*; R.'s Inc. 605*l* and Ho; Pop. Chalton 286, Clanfield 265, Idsworth 333.) [3]

ASTLEY, Richard, *Perran-Uthnoe, Marazion, Cornwall.*—Pemb. Coll. Ox. B.A. 1842. R. of Perran-Uthnoe, Dio. Ex. 1850. (Patroness, Lady Carrington; Tithe, 295*l*; Glebe, 16 acres; R.'s Inc. 700*l* and Ho; Pop. 1507.) [4]

ASTLEY, William Dugdale, *East Langdon, near Dover.*—Pemb. Coll. Ox. B.A. 1838, M.A. 1847; Deac. 1840 and Pr. 1841 by Abp of Cant. R. of East Langdon, Dio. Cant. 1852. (Patron, Earl of Guilford; Tithe—Imp. 65*l*, R. 175*l* 2*s*; Glebe, 2 acres; R.'s Inc 240*l* and Ho; Pop. 362.) [5]

ASTON, Frederick, *Todenham, Moreton-in-the-Marsh, Glouc.*—Univ. Coll. Ox. B.A. 1820, M.A. 1824; Deac. 1821 and Pr. 1822 by Bp of Glouc. R. of Todenham, Dio. G. and B. 1855. (Patron, Bp of G. and B.; Tithe, 181*l* 4*s*; Glebe, 188 acres; R.'s Inc. 500*l* and Ho; Pop. 408.) Hon. Can. of Glouc. Cathl. 1855; Surrogate. Formerly C. of Stanway, Glouc. 1821–38; V. of Northleach, Glouc. 1838–55; Rural Dean of Cirencester 1849–55. Hon. Can. of Bristol Cathl. 1850–55. [6]

ASTON, John Astbury, 2, *Elvaston-place, South Kensington, W.*—Dub. and Ox. B.A. 1848, M.A. 1851; Deac. 1850 and Pr. 1851 by Bp of Lich. P. C. of St. Stephen's, South Kensington, Dio. Lon. 1867. (Patron, present P. C.) Formerly C. of Norton, Derbyshire, 1851–52; P. C. of Bollington, Cheshire, 1853–56; R. of Kimberton, Shropshire, 1856–60; P. C. of Tulse-hill, Surrey, 1860–66. [7]

ASTON, John Meredith L., *King's Norton, near Birmingham.*—Ex. Coll. Ox. B.A. 1848, M.A. 1851; Deac. 1850 and Pr. 1851 by Bp of Wor. V. of King's Norton, Dio. Wor. 1859. (Patrons, D. and C. of Wor; V.'s Inc. 290*l* and Ho; Pop. 2005.) Surrogate. Formerly C. of St. Philip's, Birmingham, 1850–59, and Edgbaston 1859. Author, *Antiquities of King's Norton*, 1866, 1*s*, with photographs, 3*s*. [8]

ASTON, T. B., *Chilwell, Notts.* [9]

ATCHESON, Alfred S., *Teigh, Oakham, Rutland.*—R. of Teigh, Dio. Pet. 1836. (Patron, Earl of Harborough; Tithe, 305*l*; R.'s Inc. 405*l* and Ho; Pop. 128.) [10]

ATCHESON, Henry, *Kingsbury, Middlesex.*—Jesus Coll. Cam. M.A. 1823; Deac, 1828, Pr. 1830. V. of Kingsbury, Dio. Lon. 1833. (Patrons, D. and C. of St. Paul's, Lon; Tithe—App. 500*l* and 2½ acres of Glebe; V.'s Inc. 92*l*; Pop. 536.) [11]

ATCHESON, Robert Steven Eden.—Trin. Coll. Cam. B.A. 1853, M.A. 1857; Deac. 1858 and Pr. 1859 by Bp of Carl. Formerly C. of Dalston, Cumberland, 1858–60, and Houghton-le-Spring, Durham, 1860. [12]

ATHAWES, John Thomas, *Loughton, Bucks.*—Clare Coll. Cam. B.A. 1861, M.A. 1864; Deac. 1862 and Pr. 1864 by Bp of Ox. Formerly C. of Loughton. [13]

ATHERLEY, Arthur Gauntlett, *Hartham, Chippenham.*—Ch. Ch. Ox. B.A. 1845; Deac. 1847 and Pr. 1848 by Bp of B. and W. Min. of Hartham Chapel, Dio. G. and B. 1864. (Patron, T. H. A. Poynder, Esq; Min.'s Inc. 100*l*.) Formerly C. of Biddestone, Wilts; P. C. of Alderton, Wilts, 1859–64. [14]

ATHERLEY, Henry Fox, *Staverton, Totnes, Devon.*—Trin. Coll. Cam. B.A. 1828, M.A. 1831; Deac. 1829 and Pr. 1830 by Bp of Chich. V. of Staverton, Dio. Ex. 1850. (Patrons, D. and C. of Ex; V.'s Inc. 300*l* and Ho; Pop. 550.) [15]

ATHERTON, Charles Isaac, *Pensnett Parsonage, near Dudley.*—St. John's Coll. Cam. B.A. 1863, M.A. 1866; Deac. 1863 by Bp of Ely, Pr. 1864 by Bp of Lich. P. C. of Pensnett, Dio. Lich. 1867. (Patron, Earl of Dudley; Glebe, 3 acres; P. C.'s Inc. 260*l* and Ho; Pop. 5600.) Formerly C. of Pensnett. Author, *Nature's Parables*, Longmans, 1866, 2*s* 6*d*. [16]

ATHERTON, Robert Heys, *Ratcliffe Parsonage, Butcher-row, London, E.*—St. John's Coll. Cam. P. C. of Ratcliff, Dio. Lon. 1855. (Patron, Bp of Lon; P. C.'s Inc. 300*l* and Ho; Pop. 8445.) [17]

ATHERTON, Thomas, *Highfield Terrace, Bury, Lancashire.*—St. John's Coll. Cam. B.A. 1861, M.A. 1865 Deac. 1861 and Pr. 1862 by Bp of Man. P. C. of St. Thomas's, Bury, Dio. Man. 1866. (Patron, R. of Bury; P. C.'s Inc. 150*l*; Pop. 2600.) Formerly C. of St. John's, Bury, 1861. [18]

ATHORPE, George, *Langton-en-le-Morthen, Rotherham.*—C. of Langton-en-le Merthen. [19]

ATKINS, Stephen Hastings.—Dub. A.B. 1836, A.M. 1842; Deac. 1840 by Bp of Lin. Pr. 1841 by Bp of Rip. [20]

ATKINSON, Arthur, *Audlem Vicarage, Nantwich, Cheshire.*—Emman. Coll. Cam. B.A. 1856, M.A. 1859; Deac. 1857 and Pr. 1858 by Abp of York. V. of Audlem, Dio. Ches. 1865. (Patron, Viscount Combermere; Tithe, comm. 700*l*; Glebe, 2 acres; V.'s Inc. 700*l* and Ho; Pop. 2287.) Formerly C. of Scalby, Yorks, St. Jude's, Bradford, Settrington, Yorks, Sidmouth, Devon, and Petworth, Sussex; Chap. to Lord de Tabley. [21]

ATKINSON, Charles Slingsby, *Harswell, Yorks.*—St. Edm. Hall Ox. B.A. 1864; Deac. 1865 and Pr. 1866 by Abp of York. R. of Harswell, Dio. York, 1867. (Patron, Sir Charles Slingsby, Bart; R.'s Inc. 200*l* with Ho; Pop. 70.) Formerly C. of Helmsley, York, 1865. [22]

ATKINSON, Edward, *Clare College, Cambridge.*—Clare Coll. Cam. B.A. 1842, M.A. 1845, B.D. 1853, D.D. 1859; Deac. 1844 and Pr. 1846 by Bp of Ely. Mast. of Clare Coll. Cam. 1856. Formerly Senior Fell. and Tut. of Clare Coll. Cam. [23]

ATKINSON, Francis Home, *Freshwater, Isle of Wight.*—Caius Coll. Cam. B.A. 1861, M.A. 1865; Deac. 1864 and Pr. 1865 by Bp of Nor. C. of Freshwater 1866. Formerly C. of East Dereham, Norfolk, 1864–65. [24]

ATKINSON, Frederic, *Long Eaton, Nottingham.*—Trin Coll. Cam. B.A. 1853, M.A. 1856; Deac. 1854 and Pr. 1855 by Bp of Pet. P. C. of Long Eaton, Dio. Lich. 1864. (Patron, Bp of Lich; P. C.'s Inc. 300*l* and Ho; Pop. 2000.) Formerly C. of Sapcote, Leicestershire, 1854–55, Sheffield 1856–60, and Long Eaton 1860–64. [25]

ATKINSON, George, *Arnold, Nottingham.*—C. of Arnold. [26]

ATKINSON, George Barnes, *Sheffield.*—Trin. Hall. Cam. B.A. 1856, M.A. 1859; Deac. 1857 and Pr. 1858 by Bp of Ely. Head Mast. of the Coll. Proprietary Sch. Sheffield. Formerly Fell. and Asst. Tut. of Trin. Hall Cam. [27]

ATKINSON, George James, *Kettlethorpe (Lincolnshire), near Newark.*—R. of Kettlethorpe, Dio. Lin. 1836. (Patron, Weston Cracroft Amcotes, Esq; Tithe—Imp. 20*l*; R.'s Inc. 560*l* and Ho; Pop. 486.) [28]

ATKINSON, George Wilkinson, *Culgaith, Penrith.*—Queen's Coll. Ox. B.A. 1848, M.A. 1851; Deac. 1849 and Pr. 1850 by Bp of Dur. P. C. of Culgaith, Dio. Carl. 1852. (Patron, V. of Kirkland; P.C.'s Inc. 80*l*; Pop. 323.) [29]

ATKINSON, Henry Alford, *Barton, Yorks.*—Jesus Coll. Cam. B.A. 1852; Deac. 1853, Pr. 1854. Formerly C. of Rugeley, Staffs. [30]

ATKINSON, Henry Arthur, *Escomb, Bishop-Auckland, Durham.*—Queen's Coll. Ox. M.A. 1811; Deac. 1811, Pr. 1812. P. C. of Escomb, Dio. Dur. 1848. (Patron, Bp of Dur; Tithe—Imp. 42*l* 5*s*; Glebe, 30 acres; P. C.'s Inc. 220*l*; Pop. 12,234.) Formerly Michel Fell. of Queen's Coll. Ox. 1811–22. Author, *Sermons*, 2 vols. [1]

ATKINSON, Henry Dresser, *Pembroke Villa, London-road, Worcester.*—Magd. Coll. Cam. 1860–62, *ad eund* Dub. A.B. 1864; Deac. 1865 and Pr. 1866 by Bp of Wor. C. of Trinity, Shrub Hill, Worcester, 1865. Formerly Asst. Mast. in Leamington Coll. [2]

ATKINSON, James Augustus, *Longsight, Manchester.*—Ex. Coll. Ox. B.A. 1853, M A. 1856; Deac. 1854 and Pr. 1855 by Abp of Cant. R. of Longsight, Dio. Man. 1861. Patrons, Trustees; Pop. 3000.) [3]

ATKINSON, John, *Fishtoft, Boston.*—Jesus Coll. Cam. B.A. 1809; Deac. 1809 and Pr. 1810 by Bp of Lon. R. of Fishtoft, Dio. Lin. 1860. (Patron, Wm. Hopkinson, Esq; R.'s Inc. 700*l* and Ho; Pop. 600.) [4]

ATKINSON, John, *Kirkham, Lancashire.*—St. Bees; Deac. 1849 and Pr. 1850 by Bp of Man. C. of Kirkham 1863. [5]

ATKINSON, J. B., *Aycliffe, Durham.*—C. of Aycliffe. [6]

ATKINSON, John Breeks, *The Parsonage, West Cowes, Isle of Wight.*—P. C. of West Cowes, Dio. Win. 1827. (Patron, V. of Carisbrooke; P. C.'s Inc. 159*l* 12*s* 10*d* and Ho; Pop. 4591.) R. of Kingston, Isle of Wight, Dio. Win. 1831. (Patron, G. H. Ward, Esq; Tithe, Rent Charge, 220*l*; Glebe, 20*l*; R.'s Inc. 240*l*; Pop. 68.) Surrogate. [7]

ATKINSON, John Christopher, *Danby, Yarm, Yorks.*—P. C. of Danby, Dio. York, 1847. (Patron, Viscount Downe; P. C.'s Inc. about 100*l*; Pop. 1637.) [8]

ATKINSON, Joseph W., *Brodsworth, Doncaster.*—V. of Brodsworth, Dio. York, 1860. (Patron, Abp of York; V.'s Inc. 367*l* and Ho; Pop. 412.) [9]

ATKINSON, Matthew, *Chesterfield.*—St. Bees; Deac. 1849 and Pr. 1849 by Bp of Man. C. of Chesterfield 1859. Formerly C. of St. Thomas's, Preston, 1848, Jarrow 1849, Tynemouth 1851, Walsingham 1856, and St. John's, Newcastle, 1858. [10]

ATKINSON, Michael Angelo, *Fakenham, Norfolk.*—Trin. Coll. Cam. 16th Wrang. 12th in 1st cl. Cl. Trip. B.A. 1836, M.A. 1839; Deac. 1842 and Pr. 1843 by Bp of Ely. R. of Fakenham with Alethorpe, Dio. Nor. 1855. (Patron, Trin. Coll. Cam; Fakenham, Tithe, 762*l* 5*s* 6*d*; Alethorpe, Tithe, 60*l* 13*s* 9*d*; Glebe, 81 acres; R.'s Inc. 984*l* and Ho; Pop. 2456.) Formerly Sen. Fell. and Tut. of Trin. Coll. Cam. [11]

ATKINSON, Miles, *Harewood, near Leeds.*—Queen's Coll. Ox. B.A. 1833, M.A. 1836. V. of Harewood, Dio. Rip. 1854. (Patrons, Earl of Harewood and Rev. C. Wheeler, alt; V.'s Inc. 450*l* and Ho; Pop. 1737.) [12]

ATKINSON, Nathaniel, *Great Hampton, Worcestershire.*—Dur. M.A. 1846; Deac. 1845, Pr. 1846. C. of Great and Little Hampton. Formerly P. C of Horton, Northumberland, 1847–55. [13]

ATKINSON, P. R., *Pusey, Farringdon.*—R. of Pusey, Dio. Ox. 1860. Patron, Bp. of Ox; R.'s Inc. 163*l* and Ho; Pop. 134.) [14]

ATKINSON, Richard, *The Lodge, Wyton, Hull.*—St. Cath. Hall, Cam. B.A. 1818, M.A. 1822; Deac. 1818, Pr. 1819. R. of Claxby with Normanby-on-the-Wolds, Lincolnshire, Dio. Lin. 1820. (Patron, Rev. S. Wright Andrews; Claxby, Tithe, 303*l* 11*s*; Glebe, 88 acres; Normanby-on-the-Wold, Tithe, 511*l* 9*s*; Glebe, 47 acres; R.'s Inc. 930*l* and Ho; Pop. Claxby 237, Normanby-on-the-Wolds 138.) P. C. of Usselby, Lincolnshire, Dio. Lin. 1820. (Patron, Hon. G. T. D'Eyncourt; Glebe, 36 acres; P. C.'s Inc. 78*l*; Pop. 76.) [15]

ATKINSON, Richard, *Cockerham Vicarage, Torquay.*—St. John's Coll. Ox. B.A. 1843, M.A. 1845; Deac. 1850 and Pr. 1851 by Bp of Ex. V. of Cockerham, Dio. Man. 1858. (Patrons, V. and others as Lords of the Manor; Tithe—Imp. 236*l* 5*s*, V. 600*l*; Glebe, 10 acres; V.'s Inc. 640*l* and Ho; Pop. 778.) [16]

ATKINSON, Robert Moulton, *Bath.*—St. John's Coll. Cam. B.A. 1830, M.A. 1834; Deac. 1830 and Pr. 1831 by Bp of Pet. Formerly C. of Wardley with Belton, Rutland, 1830–34; R. of Cheverel Magna, Wilts, 1841–65. [17]

ATKINSON, Samuel, *Eighton Banks, Chester-le-Street, Durham.*—St. Aidan's; Deac. 1858 and Pr. 1859 by Bp of Dur. P. C. of Eighton Banks, Dio. Dur. 1865. (Patron, Bp of Dur; P. C.'s Inc. 150*l*; Pop. 2286.) Formerly C. of Gateshead, and Chap. of the Union, Newcastle, 1860–65. [18]

ATKINSON, Thomas, *Colesbourne, Cheltenham.*—Lin. Coll. Ox. B.A. 1839; Deac. 1840, Pr. 1841. C. of Colesbourne 1864. Formerly C. and P. C. of Ch. Ch. Liversedge, Yorks, 1840–64. [19]

ATKINSON, Thomas, *Great Ouseburn, Yorks.*—Deac. 1835, Pr. 1836. V. of Great Ouseburn, Dio. Rip. 1846. (Patron, Ld Chan; Glebe, 124 acres; V.'s Inc. 220*l* and Ho; Pop. 599.) [20]

ATKINSON, Thomas, *Hillingdon, Middlesex.*—Univ. Coll. Ox. B.A. 1863, M.A. 1865; Deac. 1864 and Pr. 1865 by Bp of Lon. C. of Hillingdon 1864. [21]

ATKINSON, Thomas Goodall.—Queen's Coll. Ox. B.A. 1852, M.A. 1855; Deac. 1856 by Bp of Man. Formerly C. of Upton-Scudamore, Wilts. [22]

ATKINSON, William, *Gateshead Fell, Gateshead*—Univ. Coll. Ox. B.A. 1831; Deac. 1834, Pr. 1835. R. of Gateshead Fell, Dio. Dur. 1838. (Patron, Bp of Dur; Tithe, 96*l*; Glebe, 2 acres; R.'s Inc. 300*l* and Ho; Pop. 3327.) Hon. Can. of Dur. Cathl. 1854. [23]

ATKINSON, William Raine, *Barton St. Cuthbert, Darlington.*—P. C. of Barton St. Cuthbert with St. Mary P. C. Dio. Rip. 1835. (Patrons, V. of Stanwick and V. of Gilling; P. C.'s Inc. 110*l* and Ho; Pop. 584.) [24]

ATKYNS, John, *Ombersley, Droitwich, Worcestershire.*—Wor. Coll. Ox. B.A. 1826, M.A. 1829; Deac. 1826 and Pr. 1827 by Bp of Ex. V. of Ombersley, Dio. Wor. 1855. (Patron, Ld Sandys; V.'s Inc. 390*l* and Ho; Pop. 2463.) Chap. to Ld Sandys 1839. Formerly V. of Littlehampton and R. of Ford, Sussex. [25]

ATLAY, Brownlow Thomas.—St. John's Coll. Cam. B.A. 1854, M.A. 1857; Deac. 1856 and Pr. 1857 by Bp of Ely. C. of St. Peter's, Vauxhall, Lambeth. [26]

ATLAY, Charles, *Barrowden, Stamford.*—St. John's Coll. Cam. B.A. 1816, M.A. 1819; Deac. 1817 and Pr. 1819 by Bp of Lin. R. of Barrowden, Dio. Pet. 1840. (Patron, Marquis of Exeter, Burghley House, near Stamford; Tithe, 565*l* 13*s*, Glebe, 25½ acres; R.'s Inc. 593*l* and Ho; Pop. 653.) Formerly C. of All Saints', Stamford, 1819–23; R. of St. George's, Stamford, 1823–40. [27]

ATLAY, James, *Vicarage, Leeds.*—St. John's Coll. Cam. Bell's Univ. Scho. Sen. Opt. 1st cl. Cl. Trip. B.A. 1840, M.A. 1843, S. T. B. 1850, S. T. P. 1859; Deac. 1842 by Bp of Ely, Pr 1843 by Bp of Lin. V. of Leeds, Dio. Rip. 1859. (Patrons, 25 Trustees; V.'s Inc. 1150*l* and Ho; Pop. 20,000.) Can. of Rip. 1861; Rural Dean. Formerly Fell. and Coll. Tut. of St. John's Coll. Cam; C. of Warsop, Notts, 1842; V. of Madingley, Cambs. 1847–52. [28]

ATTENBOROUGH, William Frederick, *Fletching Vicarage, Sussex.*—St. John's Coll. Cam. Jun. Opt. 3rd cl. Cl. Trip. B.A. 1849, M.A. 1852; Deac. 1854 and Pr. 1855 by Bp of Ches. V. of Fletching, Dio. Chich. 1863. (Patron, Earl of Sheffield; Tithe, 340*l*; Glebe, 13 acres; V.'s Inc. 360*l* and Ho; Pop. 1210.) Dom. Chap. to Earl of Sheffield. Formerly C. of Runcorn, Cheshire, 1854–63. [29]

ATTHILL, Richard, *Somerton, Somerset.*—V. of Somerset, Dio. B. and W. 1857. (Patron, Earl of Ilchester; Tithe—App. 686*l* 15*s* and 197 acres of Glebe; V. 252*l*; Glebe, 40 acres; V.'s Inc. 326*l* and Ho; Pop. 2206.) Chap. to the Earl of Bantry; Surrogate, Lect. of Langport. [30]

ATTHILL, William.—Caius Coll. Cam. B.A. 1830, M.A. 1851; Deac. 1830 by Bp of Killaloe, Pr. 1832 by Bp of Kilmore. Formerly Sub-Dean, Canon and Commissary of the Collegiate Church of Middleham, Yorkshire. Author, *History and Antiquities of the Collegiate Church of Middleham*, 1847; Articles in Burke's *Historic Lands of England*, 1849. [1]

ATTLEE, Simmonds, *Newland Parsonage, near Hull.*—Trin. Coll. Cam. B.A. 1859, M.A. 1862; Deac. 1859 by Bp of Carl. Pr. 1862 by Bp of Ches. P. C. of Newland, Dio. York, 1863. (Patron, V. of Cottingham; Glebe, 12 acres; P. C.'s Inc. 105*l* and Ho; Pop. 675.) Formerly C. of Alderley Edge, Cheshire, 1861–63; previously Miss. of Ch. Miss. Soc. at Lucknow, North India, 1859–61. [2]

ATTWOOD, George, *Framlingham, Woodbridge, Suffolk.*—Pemb. Coll. Cam. B.A. 1818, M.A. 1821. R. of Framlingham with Saxted C. Dio. Nor. (Patron, Pemb. Coll. Cam; Framlingham, Tithe, 1272*l*; Glebe, 70 acres; Saxted, Tithe, 340*l* 2*s*; Glebe, 2 acres; R.'s Inc. 1701*l* and Ho; Pop. Framlingham 2252, Saxted 448.) Rural Dean of Framlingham; Surrogate. [3]

ATTWOOD, William Denton.—Emman. Coll. Cam. Dixie Fell. of, B.A. 1860, M.A. 1863; Deac. 1862 by Bp of Ely, Pr. 1863 by Bp of Wor. Formerly C. of Hanbury 1862–64; Chap. of the Orsett Union, C. of Orsett, 1864–66. [4]

ATTWOOD, William Hamilton, *Gosbeck, Ipswich.*—Pemb. Coll. Cam. B.A. 1829; Deac. 1830 by Bp of Roch. Pr. 1831 by Bp of Chich. R. of Gosbeck, Dio. Nor. 1847. (Patron, Pemb. Coll. Cam; Tithe, 398*l* 13*s* 5*d*; Glebe, 13 acres; R.'s Inc. 406*l* and Ho; Pop. 301.) [5]

ATWOOD, Alban Thomas, *Kneyton in Leake, near Thirsk, Yorks.*—Wor. Coll. Ox. B.A. 1836, M.A. 1843; Deac. 1837 and Pr. 1838 by Bp of Rip. V. of Leake with Nether-Stilton, Dio. York. 1852. (Patron, Bp of Rip; Tithe, 282*l* 18*s* 9*d*; Glebe, 30 acres; V.'s Inc. 306*l*; Pop. 1092.) Formerly C. of Almondbury 1837, Goldsborough 1838. [6]

ATWOOD, Arthur Thomas, *Burgate, Suffolk.*—Brasen. Coll. Ox. B.A. 1855; Deac. 1856 and Pr. 1857 by Bp of Ches. C. of Burgate 1859. Formerly C. of Halsall, Lancashire. [7]

ATWOOD, Francis John, *Cowes, Isle of Wight.*—C. of Trinity, Cowes. [8]

ATWOOD, George Dewhurst, *Hinton-in-the-Hedges, Brackley, Northants.*—R. of Hinton-in-the-Hedges with Stean R. Dio. Pet. 1864. (Patron, Earl Spencer; R.'s Inc. 400*l* and Ho; Pop. Hinton 178, Stean 25.) Formerly C. of Ashelworth, Glouc. and Thelveton, Norfolk. [9]

ATWOOD, Henry Adams Sergison, *Ashelworth, Glouc.*—Queen's Coll. Ox. M.A. 1824; Deac. 1823, Pr. 1824. V. of Ashelworth, Dio. G. and B. 1839. (Patron, Bp of G. and B; V.'s Inc. 280*l*; Pop. 547.) Fell. of the Royal Astronomical Society. Formerly Chap to Bp of Lichfield. [10]

ATWOOD, Thomas George Patrick, *Froxfield, Hungerford, Wilts.*—Pemb. Coll. Ox. B.A. 1825; Deac. 1828, and Pr. 1829 by Bp of Salis. V. of Froxfield, Dio. Salis. 1828. (Patrons, D. and C. of Windsor; Tithe—App. 720*l*, Imp. 10*l*; V.'s Inc. 128*l* and Ho; Pop. 530.) [11]

AUBER, Charles Bransby, *Clannaborough, Crediton, Devon.*—Trin. Coll. Cam. B.A. 1844; Deac. 1845, Pr. 1846. R. of Clannaborough, Dio. Ex. 1853. (Patron, Ld Chan; Tithe, 95*l*; Glebe, 42 acres; R.'s Inc. 145*l* and Ho; Pop. 61.) [12]

AUBERTIN, Peter, *Chipstead, Red Hill.*—Wad. Coll. Ox. B.A. 1834, M.A. 1839; Deac. 1837, Pr. 1838. R. of Chipstead, Dio. Win. 1861. (Patron, Lord Hylton; R.'s Inc. 450*l* and Ho; Pop. 540.) [13]

AUBERTIN, Thomas, *Melton-Ross, Ulceby, Lincolnshire.*—St. John's Coll. Cam; P. C. of Melton-Ross, Dio. Lin. 1858. (Patron, Earl Manvers; Tithe—App. 566*l* 10*s*; Glebe, 11 acres; P. C.'s Inc. 220*l* and Ho; Pop. 166.) Formerly C. of Great Bradley and South Ormsby. [14]

AUBREY, Henry George Windsor, *Hale, Salisbury.*—Ex. Coll. Ox. 3rd cl. Lit. Hum. B.A. 1849; Deac. 1850 and Pr. 1851 by Bp of Wor. R. of Hale with South Charford (Don. R.), Dio. Win. 1865. (Patron, Joseph Goff, Esq; Tithe, 250*l*; Glebe, 4 acres; R.'s Inc. 262*l*; Pop. 213.) Formerly C. of St. George's, Kidderminster, 1850; Incum. of St. Mary's, Dalmahoy, Scotland, 1851–59, and St. Peter's, Galashiels, 1859–65. [15]

AUCHINLECH, Armar, *Shirley, Southampton.* [16]

AUCHINLECK, Alexander E., *Dronfield, Derbyshire.*—C. of Dronfield. [17]

AUCHMUTY, Samuel Forbes, *Broad Blunsdon, Highworth, Wilts.*—Brasen. Coll. Ox. B.A. 1834, M.A. 1836. P. C. of Broad Blunsden, Dio. G. and B. 1864. (Patron, Bp of G. and B; P. C.'s Inc. 300*l*; Pop. 806.) C. of Blunsden St. Andrew. [18]

AUDEN, John, *Horninglow, Burton-on-Trent.*—St. John's Coll. Cam. B.A. 1853, M.A. 1856; Deac. 1854 and Pr. 1855 by Bp of Wor. P. C. of Horninglow, Dio. Lich. 1866. (Patron, W. Hopkins, Esq; P. C.'s Inc. 200*l*; Pop. 2500.) Formerly C. of Hill, Sutton Coldfield, 1854, Silverdale 1857, Carisbrooke 1864. [19]

AUDEN, Thomas, *Wellingborough.*—St. John's Coll. Cam. B.A. 1858, M.A. 1861; Deac. 1859 and Pr. 1860 by Bp. of Roch. Head Mast. of the Gr. Sch. Wellingborough, 1863. Formerly 2nd Mast. of Dedham Gr. Sch. Essex. [20]

AUDEN, William, *Church Broughton, Derby.*—St. John's Coll. Cam. B.A. 1856, M.A. 1859; Deac. 1860 and Pr. 1861 by Bp of Wor. V. of Church Broughton, Dio. Lich. 1864. (Patron, Wm. Hopkins, Esq; Glebe, 80 acres; V.'s Inc. 220*l*. and Ho; Pop. 651.) [21]

AUDUS, George, *Kirkby-in-Malham-Dale, Leeds.*—V. of Kirkby-in-Malham-Dale, Dio. Rip. 1862. (Patron, W. Morrison, Esq; V.'s Inc. 150*l*; Pop. 850.) [22]

AURIOL, Edward, 35, *Mecklenburgh-square, London, W.C.*—Ch. Ch. Ox. B.A. 1828, M.A. 1832. R. of St. Dunstan's-in-the-West, Fleet-street City, and Dio. Lond. 1841. (Patrons, Simeon's Trustees; R.'s Inc. 500*l*; Pop. 2511.) [23]

AUSTEN, Benjamin, *The Grove, Upper Deal.*—C. of Mongeham with Sutton-by-Dover 1867. Formerly C. of St. George's, Canterbury, 1864, Dudley 1863, Tong, Salop, 1861–62. [24]

AUSTEN, Edward Thomas, *Barfreystone, Wingham, Kent.*—St. John's Coll. Ox. B.A. 1846. R. of Barfreystone, Dio. Cant. 1854. (Patron, St. John's Coll. Ox; Tithe, 139*l* 6*s* 1*d*; R.'s Inc. 200*l* and Ho; Pop. 144.) [25]

AUSTEN, George, *Hill-terrace, Middlesborough.*—St. John's Coll. Cam. Carus Prizeman, 1861, 1st in 1st cl. Moral Sci. Trip. 1862, B.A. 1863, M.A. 1866; Deac. 1864 and Pr. 1865 by Bp of Lin. C. to organize new dist. of St. Paul's, Middlesborough, 1867. Formerly C. of St. Mary's, Nottingham, 1865–66. [26]

AUSTEN, George, *St. John's Rectory, Havant, Hants.*—St. John's Coll. Ox. B.A. 1834, M.A. 1837; Deac. 1835 and Pr. 1836 by Bp of Win. R. of Red Hill, Dio. Win. 1856. (Patrons, Rs. of Havant and Warblington, alt; Tithe, 83*l*; Glebe, 4 acres; R.'s Inc. 131*l* and Ho; Pop. 343.) Formerly P. C. of St. Thomas', Elson, Hants, 1855–57. [27]

AUSTEN, Henry Morland, *Crayford, Kent.*—Ch. Ch. Ox. B.A. 1845, M.A. 1849; Deac. 1846, Pr. 1847. R. of Crayford, Dio. Cant. 1851. (Patron, J. Francis Austen, Esq; Tithe, 595*l*; Glebe, 56½ acres; R.'s Inc. 850*l* and Ho; Pop. 3103.) [28]

AUSTEN, John Hiley, *Tarrant Keyneston, Blandford.*—Jesus Coll. Cam. B.A. 1839, M.A. 1843; Deac. 1847 and Pr. 1848 by Bp of Salis. R. of Tarrant Keyneston, Dio. Salis. 1865. (Patrons, Trustees of G. H. H. Austen; Tithe, 395*l*; Glebe, 56 acres; R.'s Inc. 365*l* and Ho; Pop. 309.) Formerly C. of Verwood, Dorset, 1847–49, and Langton Maltravers 1849–52; R. of Tollard Royal, Wilts, 1860–65. Author, *Guide to the Geology of the Isle of Purbeck*, 1852. [29]

AUSTEN, John Thomas, *West Wickham, Bromley, Kent.*—St. John's Coll. Cam. B.A. 1817, M.A.

1820, B.D. 1827; Deac. 1819, Pr. 1820. R. of West Wickham, Dio. Cant. 1848. (Patron, Col. Lennard; Tithe, 495*l*; Glebe, 35 acres; R.'s Inc. 480*l* and Ho; Pop. 787.) Formerly Fell. of St. John's Coll. Cam. 1817; V. of Aldworth, Berks. [1]

AUSTEN, Joseph Mason, *Salisbury.*—Brasen. Coll. Ox. Scho. and Hulme Exhib. 2nd cl. Lit. Hum. 2nd cl. Law and Modern Hist. Johnson Theol. Scho. (Univ.) 1859, B.A. 1858, M.A. 1861; Deac. 1860 and Pr. 1861 by Bp of Ox. C. of St. Edmund's, Salisbury, 1863. Formerly C. of Sonning, Berks, 1861. [2]

AUSTIN, C. E. Lefroy, *West Littleton, Chippenham.*—C. of West Littleton. [3]

AUSTIN, Edward, *St. Mary's Parsonage, Broughton, Chester.*—Queen's Coll. Ox. B.A. 1847, M.A. 1849; Deac. 1846, and Pr. 1848 by Bp of Wor. C. of Broughton in Hawarden 1853. Formerly C. of St. Lawrence's, Evesham, 1846, and Marshwood-in-Whitchurch Canonicorum, Dorset, 1849. [4]

AUSTIN, John Southgate, *Leigh, Cheltenham.*—Trin. Coll. Ox. B.A. 1834, M.A. 1838; Deac. 1838 by Bp of B. and W. Pr. 1840 by Bp of G. and B. V. of Leigh, Dio. G. and B. 1851. (Patron, Ld Chan; Glebe, 125 acres; V.'s Inc. 266*l* and Ho; Pop. 428.) [5]

AUSTIN, W. G. G., *Radley, near Abingdon.*—Fell. of St. Peter's Coll. Radley. [6]

AUSTIN-GOURLAY, William Edmund Craufurd, *Stoke Abbas, near Beaminster, Dorset.*—New Coll. Ox. B.A. 1843, M.A. 1847; Deac. 1844 and Pr. 1845 by Bp of Ox. R. of Stoke Abbas, Dio. Salis. 1862. (Patron, New Coll. Ox.; Tithe, 420*l*; Glebe, 60 acres; R.'s Inc. 520*l* and Ho; Pop. 703.) Fell. of New Coll. Ox. 1842–63; Tut. of New Coll. 1848–61. [7]

AUTRIDGE, Francis Charles.—St. John's Coll. Cam. B.A. 1853; Deac. 1854 and Pr. 1855 by Bp of Ox. Chap. of H.M.S. "Cossack." Formerly Math. Mast. of All Saints' Gr. Sch. Bloxham, Ox. 1854–58; C. of Sneaton, Notts. [8]

AVARD, Theodore John, *The Parsonage, Warton, Kirkham, Lancashire.*—Dub. A.B. 1840; Deac 1843 by Bp of Herf. Pr. 1844 by Bp of Lich. C. in sole charge of Warton 1861. Formerly P. C. of Trinity, Hinckley, Leic. 1850–62. [9]

AVENT, John, *Broughton, Lechlade, Glouc.*—Caius Coll. Cam. B.A. 1859, M.A. 1863; Deac. 1860 and Pr. 1861 by Bp of Ches. R. of Broughton, Dio. Ox. 1867. (Patron, the present R.; Tithe, 268*l*; Glebe, 39 acres; R.'s Inc. 400*l* and Ho; Pop. 135.) Formerly C. of Capenhurst, Chester, 1860–62; St. Thomas's, Islington, Lond. 1862–63, and Marlborough, Devon, 1863–67. [10]

AVERELL, Thomas, *Tynemouth, North Shields.* St. Aidan's, 1863; Deac. 1863 and Pr. 1864 by Bp of Rip. C. of Holy Saviour's, Tynemouth, 1866. Formerly C. of St. John's, Golcar, Huddersfield, 1863. [11]

AVERILL, George, 2, *Prior-park Buildings, Widcombe, Bath.*—Wad. Coll. Ox. B.A. 1864; Deac. 1864 and Pr. 1865 by Bp of B. and W. C. of Widcombe 1864. [12]

AVERY, John Symons, *Budehaven, Stratton, Cornwall.*—Magd. Hall, Ox. B.A. 1827. P. C. of St. Michael's, Budehaven, Dio. Ex. 1843. (Patron, Sir Thomas Dyke Acland, Bart.; P. C.'s Inc. 150*l*; Pop. 766.) [13]

AVERY, William, *St. Ewe's Rectory, St. Austell, Cornwall.*—St. Bees; Deac. 1846 and Pr. 1847 by Bp of Ches. R. of St. Ewe. Dio. Ex. 1864. (Patrons, Sir Jos. Sawle, Bart. and E. Carlyon, Esq; R.'s Inc. 450*l* and Ho; Pop. 1450.) Formerly P. C. of Belventor, Launceston, 1850–64. [14]

AWDRY, Charles, *Worthen, Shrewsbury.*—New Coll. Ox. B.C.L. 1828, M.A. 1856; Deac. 1828 and Pr. 1829 by Bp. of Herf. R. of Worthen, Dio. Herf. 1840. (Patron, New Coll. Ox; Tithe, 1204*l* 17*s*; Glebe, 106 acres; R.'s Inc. 1345*l* and Ho; Pop. 1321.) Preb. of Herf. Cathl. 1855; Rural Dean of Pontesbury. Formerly Fell. of New Coll. Ox; C. of Wood-Eaton, Oxon. 1832–38; R. of Little Sampford, Essex, 1838–40. [15]

AWDRY, Charles Hill, *Seagry, near Chippenham.*—Queen's Coll. Ox. B.A. 1846, M.A. 1849; Deac. 1848, Pr. 1849. V. of Seagry, Dio. G. and B. 1854. (Patron, Earl of Carnarven; Tithe—Imp. 163*l*; V. 159*l*; Glebe, ½ acre; V.'s Inc. 166*l* and Ho; Pop. 263) Surrogate. [16]

AWDRY, Charles Roston Edridge, *Draycot Cerne, near Chippenham.*—St. John's Coll. Cam. B.A. 1834; Deac. 1835, Pr. 1836. R. of Draycot Cerne, Dio. G. and B. 1850. (Patron, Earl Cowley; Tithe, 265*l*; Glebe, 50 acres; R.'s Inc. 345*l* and Ho; Pop. 158.) [17]

AWDRY, Edward Charles, *Kington St. Michael, near Chippenham.*—St. Cath. Coll. Cam. B.A. 1836; Deac. 1836, Pr. 1837. V. of Kington St. Michael, Dio. G. and B. 1856. (Patron, Earl Cowley; Glebe, 20 acres; V.'s Inc. 350*l* and Ho; Pop. 1089.) Formerly C. of Grittleton, Wilts. [18]

AWDRY, William, *Queen's College, Oxford.*—Ball. Coll. Ox. B.A. 1865; Deac. 1866 by Bp of Ox. C. of St. Peter's-in the-East, Oxford. 1866. [19]

AWDRY, William Henry, *Ludgershall, Andover, Hants.*—Ex. Coll. Ox. B.A. 1857, M.A. 1860; Deac. 1858 and Pr. 1859 by Bp of Lich. C. in sole charge of Ludgershall 1862. Formerly C. of West Felton, Salop, 1858–60, Quedgeley, Glouc. 1860, Compton Bassett, Wilts, 1860–62. [20]

AYERST, William, *Egerton, Ashford, Kent.*—St. John's Coll. Cam. B.A. 1825, M.A. 1837; Deac. and Pr. 1826 by Bp of Nor. P. C. of Egerton, Dio. Cant. 1853. (Patrons, D. and C. of St. Paul's; Tithe—App. 603*l* 18*s* 4*d*; Glebe, 11 acres; P. C.'s Inc. 125*l*; Pop. 816.) [21]

AYERST, William, *Fyzabad, Bengal.*—Caius Coll. Cam. B.A. 1853; Deac. 1853, Pr. 1854. Chap. Fyzabad. Formerly Head Mast. St. Paul's Sch. Calcutta, 1860; previously C. of St. Giles-in-the-Fields, and of St. Paul's, Lisson-grove, Lond. [22]

AYLING, Henry, *Frampton-Cotterell, near Bristol.*—Magd. Hall, Ox. B.A. 1820, M.A. 1820; Deac. and Pr. 1820 by Bp of Glouc. R. of Frampton-Cotterell, Dio. G. and B. 1851. (Patron, Rev. W. C. Fox; Tithe, 560*l* 12*s*; Glebe, 62 acres; R.'s Inc. 650*l* and Ho; Pop. 1011.) Dom. Chap. to the Duke of Beaufort 1853. Formerly R. of St. Mary's with Holy Trinity, Guildford, 1836–51; Head Mast. of the Royal Gr. Sch. Guildford, 1838–51. [23]

AYLWARD, Adolphus Frederick, *Chesham, Bucks.*—St. Edmund Hall, Ox. B.A. 1844, M.A. 1850; Deac. 1844, Pr. 1845. V. of Chesham, Dio. Ox. 1847. (Patron, Duke of Bedford; Tithe—Imp. 2366*l* 9*s*, V. 550*l*; V.'s Inc. 520*l* and Ho; Pop. 5985.) [24]

AYLWARD, Augustus Anthony, *Brede, Northiam, Sussex.*—Wor. Coll. Ox. B.A. 1841, M.A. 1848; Deac. 1847 and Pr. 1848 by Bp of Pet. R. of Brede, Dio. Chich. 1851. (Patron, T. Frewen, Esq; Tithe, 1055*l* 6*s* 6*d*; Glebe, 1 acre; R.'s Inc. 1012*l* and Ho; Pop. 1088.) [25]

AYRE, John, *Hyde Hall, Herts.*—Caius Coll. Cam. B A. 1823, M.A. 1827. Dom. Chap. to Earl of Roden. [26]

AYRE, Joseph Watson, 80, *Green-street, Grosvenor-square, London, W.*—St. Peter's Coll. Cam. B.A. 1841, M.A. 1844; Deac. 1842 and Pr. 1843 by Bp of Pet. P. C. of St. Mark's, North Audley-street, Dio. Lon. 1851. (Patron, R. of St. George's, Hanover-square; P. C.'s Inc. 700*l*; Pop. 4972.) Author, *Diary of Eastern Travel*, Seeleys, 1844. [27]

AYRE, Legh Richmond, *Rusland, Newton-in-Cartmel, Lancashire.*—Emman. Coll. Cam. B.A. 1850, M.A. 1853; Deac. 1850 by Bp of Wor. Pr. 1851 by Bp of Herf. P. C. of Rusland, Dio. Carl. 1860. (Patron, P. C. of Colton, Lancashire; P. C.'s Inc. 67*l* and Ho; Pop. 178.) Formerly C. of the Temporary Ch. of St. Michael's, Islington, Lond. 1853–60. [28]

AYRES, Benjamin, *Trent, Sherborne, Dorset.*—Queens' Coll. Cam. B.A. 1836; Deac. 1838 by Bp of Ex. Pr. 1841 by Bp of B. and W. R. of Stockwood, Dorset, Dio. Salis. 1856. (Patroness, Mrs. Eliza Matthews; Tithe, 125*l*; Glebe let for 55*l*; R.'s Inc. 180*l*; Pop. 60.) C. of Trent, Somerset, 1841. Formerly C. of Chilton-Canteloe 1838. [29]

AYRES, George, *Talbotstown House, Brittas, Co. Dublin.*—St. John's Coll. Cam. B.A. 1849, M.A. 1852; Deac. 1851 and Pr. 1852 by Bp. of Ely. V. of Kilbride, Dio. Dub. 1857. Formerly C. of Layham, Hadleigh, Suffolk, 1851–56. [1]

AYTOUN, William Alexander, *Parsonage, Oakengates, Wellington, Shropshire.*—Trin. Hall, Cam. B.A. 1841; Deac. 1842 by Abp of Cant. Pr. 1843 by Abp of York. P. C. of Trinity, Oakengates, Dio. Lich. 1863. (Patron, Bp of Lich; Glebe, 1 acre; P. C.'s Inc. 125*l* and Ho; Pop. 1821.) Formerly R. of Scampton, near Lincoln, 1850–63. [2]

BABB, George, *Asterby, Horncastle, Lincolnshire.*—St. John's Coll. Cam. B.A. 1843, M.A. 1847; Deac. 1844, Pr. 1845. R. of Asterby, Dio. Lin. 1860. (Patron, W. H. Trafford, Esq; R.'s Inc. 250*l* and Ho; Pop. 304.) V. of Cawkwell, near Horncastle, Dio. Lin. 1860. (Patron, Lord Yarborough; V.'s Inc. 65*l*; Pop. 36.) Formerly V. of East Halton, Lincolnshire, 1855–60. [3]

BABER, Charles, *Moor Cottage, Maidenhead, Berks.*—St. Bees; Deac. 1856 and Pr. 1857 by Bp of Herf. C. of St. Mary's, Maidenhead, 1865. Formerly C. of Glazely, Shropshire, 1856, and of Cookham, Berks, 1859. [4]

BABER, Harry, *Whitelands Training School, Chelsea, London, S.W.*—Trin. Coll. Cam. B.A. 1839, M.A. 1842; Deac. 1840, Pr. 1841. Chap. of the National Society's Female Training Institution, Whitelands, Chelsea, 1847. Formerly Asst. Min. of St. Mary's, Park-street, Lond. [5]

BABER, Henry Hervey, *Stretham, near Ely.*—All Souls Coll. Ox. B.A. 1799, M.A. 1805; Deac. 1800, Pr. 1801. R. of Stretham, Dio. Ely, 1827. (Patron, Bp of Ely; Tithe, 620*l*; R.'s Inc. 780*l* and Ho; Pop. 1462.) Editor, *Wickliffe's Trans. of the New Testament*, Lond. 1811; *Psalterium Græcum ex Cod. MS. Alexandrino*, Lond. 1812; *Vetus Testamentum Græcum ex Cod. MS. Alexandrino*, 4 vols. fol. Lond. 1816–28, 36*l* 15*s*. [6]

BABER, John George.—Caius Coll. Cam. B.A. 1850, M.A. 1855; Deac. 1851, Pr. 1852. Formerly C. of Uttoxeter. [7]

BABINGTON, Arthur, *Wanlip, near Leicester.*—R. of Wanlip, Dio. Pet. 1860. (Patron, Sir G. J. Palmer, Wanlip Hall, Leicester; R.'s Inc. 375*l* and Ho; Pop. 117.) [8]

BABINGTON, Churchill, *Cockfield Rectory, Sudbury, Suffolk.*—St. John's Coll. Cam. Sen. Opt. 1st cl. Cl. Trip. B.A. 1843, M.A. 1846, B.D. 1853; Fell. of St. John's Coll. Cam. 1846; Deac. 1846 and Pr. 1848 by Bp of Ely. Disney Prof. of Archæology in Univ. of Cam. 1865; R. of Cockfield, Dio. Ely, 1866. (Patrons, St. John's Coll. Cam; R.'s Inc. 1100*l* and Ho; Pop. 988.) Formerly P. C. of Chapelry of Horningsea, Cambs, 1848–66. Author, *The Influence of Christianity in promoting the Abolition of Slavery in Europe* (Hulsean Prize Essay), Cam. 1846, 5*s*; *Macaulay's Character of the Clergy in the Seventeenth Century, considered*, Cam. 1848, 4*s* 6*d*; *An Introductory Lecture on Archæology, delivered before the University of Cambridge*, Cam. 1865; *The Oration of Hyperides against Demosthenes respecting the Treasure of Harpalus*, edited from the fac-simile of the MS. discovered at Thebes in 1847, 4to plates, Cam. 1850, 6*s* 6*d*; *The Orations of Hyperides for Lycophron and Euxenippus*, in fac-simile, with notes, &c. 4to. 16 tinted plates, Cam. 1853, 21*s*; *The Funeral Oration of Hyperides* (edited from the Papyrus in the British Museum), 4to. tinted plates, Cam. 1858, 15*s*; *Hyperidis quæ supersunt*, with Notes, Memoir, &c. 8vo. Cam. 1859; *The Benefit of Christ's Death, probably written by Aonio Paleario*, facsimile reprint of the Italian edition of 1543, with the English version of 1548, and the French version of 1552, with an *Introduction and Notes*, 8vo. Cam. 1855, 7*s* 6*d*; *The Repressor of over-much Blaming of the Clergy*, by Bishop Reginald Pecock, 2 vols. 8vo, Lond. 1859, and *Polychronicon Ranulphi Higden*, with two ancient English versions, Vol. I. 1865, Vol. II. in the press, edited in the series of English Historical Works published by the authority of Her Majesty's Treasury; *Catalogue of MSS. in the Cambridge University Library* (the Classical Portion), Vol. I. Cam. 1856, Vol. II. ib. 1857, Vol. III. 1858, Vol. IV. 1859; *Catalogue of Adversaria* in same Library, 1864; Contributor to Sir W. J. Hooker's *Journal of Botany and Kew Miscellany*; *Cambridge Journal of Classical and Sacred Philology*; to Transactions of the Royal Society of Literature, and the Cambridge Antiquarian Society; to the *Numismatic Chronicle* and Watson's *Botanist's Guide to England and Wales*; the Ornithology and Botany in Potter's *History of Charnwood Forest*, the Lichens in Seeman's *Botany of the "Herald,"* and in Hooker's *Flora of New Zealand*. [9]

BABINGTON, John, *Peterborough.*—Magd. Coll. Cam. B.A. 1814, M.A. 1817; Deac. 1814, Pr. 1815. Hon. Can. of Pet. Cathl. 1849. Formerly R. of Cossington, Leicestershire, 1820–59. [10]

BABINGTON, William Marshall Sargent, *Madras.*—Clare Coll. Cam. B.A. 1862; Deac 1863 by Bp of Pet. Formerly C. of St. Mary's, Peterborough, 1863. [11]

BABINGTON, William Peile, *Staunton-on-Arrow, Herefordshire.*—Pemb. Coll. Cam. B A. 1843, M.A. 1846; Deac. 1844, Pr. 1846. V. of Staunton-on-Arrow, Dio. Herf. 1865. (Patron, Ld Chan; Tithe, 230*l* 11*s*; Glebe, 36 acres; V.'s Inc. 302*l* and Ho; Pop. 376.) Formerly C. of Great Yarmouth, Norfolk, 1844–48, St. Martin-in-the-Fields, Westminster, 1848–54; P. C. of Manningtree, Essex, 1854–65. [12]

BACHE, William Charles, *Longridge, near Preston.*—Brasen. Coll. Ox. B.A. 1843, M.A. 1846; Deac. 1846, Pr. 1847. P. C. of Longridge, Dio. Man. 1847. (Patrons, Hulme's Trustees; Glebe, 45 acres; P. C.'s Inc. 170*l* and Ho; Pop. 2057.) [13]

BACHELOR, C., *Coseley, Bilston, Staffs.*—C. of Coseley. [14]

BACK, Henry, *The Vicarage, Banbury.*—Trin. Coll. Cam. Scho. of, 1st cl. Cl. Trip. Jun. Opt. Math. Trip. B.A. 1847, M.A. 1850; Deac. 1850 and Pr. 1851 by Bp. of Lon. V. of Banbury with St. Paul Neithrop C. Dio. Ox. 1860. (Patron, Bp of Ox; Tithe, 56*l*; V.'s Inc. 300*l* and Ho; Pop. 6173.) Surrogate. Formerly C. of St. George's, Hanover-square, and Grosvenor Chapel, South Audley-street, London. [15]

BACK, James.—Chap. of St. George's Hanover-square Cemetery, Lond. [16]

BACK, John, *The Rectory, Great Ormond-street, London, W.C.*—Trin. Coll. Ox. 2nd cl. Lit. Hum. B.A. 1849, M.A. 1852; Deac. 1849 and Pr. 1850 by Bp. of Lon. R. of St. George-the-Martyr, Holborn, Dio. Lon. 1858. (Patron, Duke of Buccleuch; R.'s Inc. 300*l*; Pop. 9867.) Formerly C. of St. John's, Westminster, 1849–58. [17]

BACK, Samuel, *Powick, Worcester.*—Ch. Coll. Cam. B.A. 1847, M.A. 1850; Deac. 1848, Pr. 1850. V. of Powick with Cleveland C. Dio. Wor. 1866. (Patron, Earl of Coventry; Tithe, 330*l*; V.'s Inc. 344*l* and Ho; Pop. 2222.) Formerly C. of Berkeswell, near Coventry. [18]

BACKHOUSE, John Harris, *Felstead, Chelmsford.*—Brasen. Coll. Ox. 2nd cl. Lit. Hum. 1st cl. Maths. B A. 1848, M.A. 1851; Deac. 1850 and Pr. 1851 by Bp of Win. 2nd Mast. of Felstead Gr. Sch. 1852. [19]

BACKLER, Sotherton, *Blatherwycke, near Wansford, Northants.*—St. John's Coll. Cam. B.A. 1822, M.A. 1843; Deac. 1823, Pr. 1824. R. of Blatherwycke, Dio. Pet. 1838. (Patron, Stafford O'Brien, Esq; Tithe, 295*l* 3*s*; Glebe, 105 acres; R.'s Inc. 453*l* and Ho; Pop. 189.) Rural Dean of Weldon 1848. [20]

BACON, Francis, *Much Hadham, Ware, Herts.*—St. John's Coll. Cam. B.A. 1846, M.A. 1849; Deac. 1850, Pr. 1851. Formerly V. of Hundleby, Lincolnshire, 1860–63. [21]

BACON, Hugh, *Baxterley, near Atherstone.*—Trin. Coll. Ox. B.A. 1830, M.A. 1851; Deac. 1831 and Pr. 1852 by Bp of Lon. R. of Baxterley, Warwickshire

Dio. Wor. 1854. (Patron, Ld Chan. and W. S. Dugdale, Esq. alt; Tithe, 182*l*; Glebe, 45 acres; R.'s Inc. 260*l* and Ho; Pop. 273.) [1]

BACON, Hugh Ford, *Castleton, Derbyshire.*—Ch. Coll. Cam. B.A. 1836, M.A. 1839; Deac. 1838 and Pr. 1838 by Bp. of Ely. V. of Castleton, Dio. Lich. 1853. (Patron, Bp of Ches; Tithe—App. 150*l* and 87 acres of Glebe, V. 15*l*; Glebe, 21½ acres; V.'s Inc. 175*l*; Pop. 771.) [2]

BACON, John, *Wymondham, near Oakham.*—R. of Wymondham, Dio. Pet. 1863. (Patron, Ld Chan; R.'s Inc. 400*l* and Ho; Pop. 850.) Formerly P. C. of Lambourne Woodlands, Berks, 1837–63. [3]

BACON, J. H., *Great Grimsby.*—St. Bees; Deac. 1863 and Pr. 1864 by Bp of Lich. C. of Great Grimsby 1865. Formerly C. of Hope, Derbyshire, 1863. [4]

BACON, Samuel, *Chatham, New Brunswick.* [5]

BACON, Thomas, *Kingsworthy, near Winchester.*—Deac. 1846 and Pr. 1847 by Bp of Gibraltar. R. of Kingsworthy, Dio. Win. 1852. (Patron, Ld Northbrook; Tithe, 452*l* 10*s*; Glebe, 9 acres; R.'s Inc. 461*l* and Ho; Pop. 394.) Hon. Sec. of Winchester Dioc. Training Coll. Formerly a Lieutenant in the Bengal Horse Artillery; called to the Bar, Middle Temple, 1841; Chaplain of the Collegiate Church at Malta, 1846–48; Canon of Gibraltar, 1847–48; C. of Bedford Chapel, Exeter, 1848–49; Sen. C. of All Souls, St. Marylebone, Lond. 1849–52. Author, *First Impressions and Studies from Nature in Hindostan*, 2 vols. 1837; *The Oriental Annual*, 1839–40; *The Oriental Portfolio*, 1841, etc. [6]

BACON, Thomas, *Wiggenholt Rectory, Storrington, Sussex.*—R. of Wiggenholt with Greatham R. Dio. Chich. (Patron, Hon. R. Curzon; R.'s Inc. 250*l* and Ho; Pop. Wiggenholt 34, Greatham 51.) [7]

BADCOCK, Edward Baynes, *Training College, Ripon.*—St. John's Coll. Cam. B.A. 1852; Deac. 1852 and Pr. 1853 by Bp. of Man. Prin. and Chap. of the York and Ripon Female Training Sch. Rip. 1863. Formerly C. of Harpurhey, Manchester, 1852-54, and Sen. C. of St. Mary's, Battersea, 1854–63. [8]

BADCOCK, John, *Stroud.*—P. C. of Stroud with Trinity C. Dio. G. and B. 1865. (Patron, Bp of G. and B; P. C.'s Inc. 400*l* and Ho; Pop. 7171.) Surrogate. [9]

BADCOCK, Thomas, *Fleckney, Market-Harborough, Leicestershire.*—St. John's Coll. Cam. B.A. 1851; Deac. 1851 and Pr. 1852 by Bp of Man. V. of Fleckney, Dio. Pet. 1854. (Patron, Earl Lovelace; V.'s Inc. 148*l*; Pop. 581.) [10]

BADELEY, Edward, *Aldeby, Beccles, Suffolk.*—Deac. 1864 and Pr. 1865 by Bp of Pet. P. C. of Aldeby, Dio. Nor. 1865. (Patron, D. and C. of Nor; Glebe, 14 acres; P. C.'s Inc. 120*l* and Ho; Pop. 557.) Formerly C. of St. Margaret's, Leicester, 1864–65. [11]

BADELEY, John Joseph, *Mautby, near Yarmouth.*—Corpus Coll. Cam. B.A. 1856; Deac. 1857 and Pr. 1858 by Bp of B. and W. C. of Mautby 1859. Formerly C. of Chiselborough with West Chinnock, Somerset, 1857–59. [12]

BADGER, Albert.—Chap. of Brompton Cemetery, Lond. [13]

BADGER, Edwin, *Kingsdown, Dover.*—Queens' Coll. Cam. B.A. 1850; Deac. 1851, Pr. 1852. P. C. of Kingsdown, Dio. Cant. 1862. (Patrons, Trustees; P. C.'s Inc. 150*l*; Pop. 508.) [14]

BADGER, James, *Mayland, Maldon, Essex.*—V. of Mayland, Dio. Roch. 1859. (Patrons, Govs. of St. Bartholomew's Hospital, Lond; V.'s Inc. 150*l*; Pop. 225. [15]

BADGER, William Collins, *East Kennett, Marlborough, Wilts.*—Queens' Coll. Cam. B.A. 1844, M.A. 1851; Deac. 1844 and Pr. 1845 by Bp of G. and B. P. C. of East Kennett, Dio. Salis. 1863. (Patron, John Matthews, Esq; P.C.'s Inc. 113*l* and Ho; Pop. 80.) Chap. of the Union, Marlborough. Formerly C. of Calne, Wilts, Sherborne, Dorset, and Seend, Wilts. [16]

BADGLEY, C. H., *Hurstpierpoint, Sussex.*—Asst. Mast. in St. John's Sch. Hurstpierpoint. [17]

BADHAM, Charles, *All Saints, Sudbury, Suffolk.*—Emman. Coll. Cam. B.A. 1839, M.A. 1846; Deac. 1839, Pr. 1841. V. of All Saints, Sudbury, with Ballingdon V. and Brudon (Essex), Dio. Ely, 1847. (Patron, for this turn, D. Badham, Esq; Tithe—Imp. 156*l* 9*s* 3*d*, V. 35*l* 4*s* 3*d*; Endow. 84*l* 15*s* 2*d*; Glebe, 4 acres; V.'s Inc. 120*l* and Ho; Pop. All Saints 1850, Ballingdon and Brundon 861.) Surrogate for Dioc. of Nor. and Ely. Author, *Selections from Robert Hall*, 1840; *Aids to Devotion*, 1843; *History of All Saints, Church and Parish*, 1852; *Life and Writings of Archdeacon Wrangham*, etc. [18]

BADHAM, Charles, *Sydney, New South Wales.*—St. Peter's Coll. Cam. D.D. 1852; Deac. 1846, Pr. 1848. Professor of Classics, Sydney University. Formerly Head Mast. of the Edgbaston Sch. Author, *Euripides, Iphigenia and Helena*, 1851; *Platonis Phaedrus*, 1851; *Ion*, 1852; *Philebus*, 1855. [19]

BADNALL, The Ven. Hopkins, *George-town, Cape of Good Hope.*—Dur. B.A. 1844, M.A. 1851; Deac. 1845 and Pr. 1846 by Bp of Dur. Archd. of George-town. Formerly R. of Goldsborough, Yorks, 1855–58; C. of Canthorne; Dom. and Exam. Chap. to the Bp of Capetown 1847–51, and Fell. of the Univ. of Dur. 1845–7. [20]

BADNALL, James, *Endon, Leek, Staffs.*—P. C. of Endon, Dio. Lich. 1865. (Patron, Earl of Macclesfield; P. C.'s Inc. 110*l*; Pop. 1241.) [21]

BADNALL, William.—Brasen. Coll. Ox. B.A. 1825, M.A. 1828; Deac. 1826 by Bp of Lin. and Pr. 1827 by Bp. of Ches. Formerly P. C. of Trinity, Wavertree, near Liverpool, 1827–59; previously Queen's Lancashire Preacher, and Chap. to H.R.H. the late Duke of Cambridge. Author, *Sermon on the Cause and Effect of Sin, in reference to the Alarming Aspect of the Times*, 1831, 1*s*. [22]

BAGDON, J. C.—Formerly C. of Ch. Ch. Milton-next-Gravesend. [23]

BAGE, John Samuel, *Wharton, Winsford, Cheshire.*—St. John's Coll. Cam. B.A. 1843, M.A. 1846, Deac. 1843, Pr. 1844. P. C. of Wharton, Dio. Ches. 1859. (Patron, R. of Davenham; Tithe—App. 75*l* 1*s*, P. C.'s Inc. 150*l* and Ho; Pop. 2395.) Formerly C. of Davenham, Cheshire. [24]

BAGGE, James, *Crux-Easton (Hants), near Newbury, Berks.*—St. John's Coll. Cam. B.A. 1814, M.A. 1818; Deac. 1814 and Pr. 1815 by Abp of York. R. of Crux-Easton, Dio. Win. 1843. (Patron, the present R; Tithe, 200*l*; Glebe, 26 acres; R.'s Inc. about 206*l* and Ho; Pop. 76.) Author, *Remarks upon the Controversy between the Rev. Geo. Wilkins, Vicar of St. Mary's Nottingham, and the Rev. J. B. Stuart*, 1823; *Sufficiency of the Scriptures, and Salvation by Grace* (An Answer to the Rev. Mr. Barter's *Few Words to Lord Shaftesbury*); *Twelve Sermons* (preached at Melton Mowbray), 1835; *Church-rates binding on Dissenters as well as Churchmen* (A Sermon), 1837; *Popery in Alliance with Treason* (A Sermon), 1838; *The Gawthorne Correspondence and the Rev. W. B. Barter*, 1852. [25]

BAGGE, Philip Salisbury, *St. Peter's Lynn, Norfolk.*—Trin. Coll. Cam. B.A. 1840, M.A. 1843; Deac. 1843, Pr. 1844. R. of Walpole St. Peter with St. Edmund's C. Dio. Nor. 1853. (Patron, the Crown; Tithe—App. 1303*l* 16*s* 10*d*, R. 788*l* 3*s* 2*d*; Glebe, 14 acres; R.'s Inc. 800*l* and Ho; Pop. 1252.) [26]

BAGNALL, Henry, *Great Barr, Birmingham.*—Queens' Coll. Cam. M.A. 1824; Deac. 1824 and Pr. 1825 by Bp of Lich. P. C. of Great Barr, Dio. Lich. 1853. (Patrons, Trustees of late Sir F. E. Scott, Bart; Tithe, 568*l*; Glebe, 8 acres; P. C.'s Inc. 576*l* and Ho; Pop. 1075.) [27]

BAGNALL, Samuel, *Weston Point, Runcorn, Cheshire.*—Downing Coll. Cam. B.A. 1824, M.A. 1828; Deac. 1824 and Pr. 1825 by Bp of Ches. P. C. of Ch. Ch. Weston Point, Dio. Ches. 1844. (Patron, Bp of Ches; P. C.'s Inc. 150*l* and Ho; Pop. 1200.) Formerly P. C. of Aston, Cheshire, 1826–44. [28]

BAGNELL, Henry W., B.A.—Chap. Bombay. [29]

BAGNELL, William Webber, *Honiton Clyst, near Exeter.*—Trin. Coll. Cam. B.A. 1812; Deac. 1815, Pr. 1816. V. of Honiton Clyst, Dio. Ex. 1822. (Patrons, D. and C. of Ex; Tithe—App. 165l, V. 165l; Glebe, 2 acres; V.'s Inc. 150l; Pop. 416.) Author, *A Sermon* (Preached at the Peculiar Visitation of the Dean and Chapter of the Cathedral Church of Exeter), 1817; *A Sermon on the Death of the Princess Charlotte,* 1817; Two Pamphlets, 1s; various Tracts, 1d each; Contributor to *Oastler's Home.* [1]

BAGOT, Charles Walter, *Castle-Rising, Lynn, Norfolk.*—Ch. Ch. and All Souls Coll. Ox. M.A. 1833; Deac. 1835 and Pr. 1836 by Bp of Ox. R. of Castle-Rising with Roydon, Dio. Nor. 1846. (Patron, Hon. F. G. Howard; Tithe, 320l; Glebe, 17 acres; R.'s Inc. 520l and Ho; Pop. Castle-Rising 377, Roydon 196.) Chancellor of the Dio. of B. and W. Formerly Fell. of All Souls Coll. Ox. [2]

BAGOT, Frederic, *Harpsden, near Henley-on-Thames.*—Ch. Ch. Ox. B.A. 1844, All Souls Coll. B.C.L. and D.C.L. R. of Harpsden, Dio. Ox. 1859. (Patron, All Souls Coll. Ox; R.'s Inc. 700l and Ho; Pop. 261.) Preb. of Holcombe in Wells Cathl. 1851. Formerly R. of Rodney-Stoke, Somerset, 1846–59; previously Fell. of All Souls Coll. Ox. [3]

BAGOT, George, *Halifax.*—Dub. Queen's Scho. A.B. 1845, A.M. 1848; Deac. 1846 by Bp of Killaloe, Pr. 1847 by Bp of Ches. C. of Halifax. Formerly C. of Richmond 1859, previously C. of Bonsall, Derbyshire. [4]

BAGOT, The Hon. Hervey Charles, *Blithfield, Rugeley, Staffs.*—Ch. Ch. Ox. B.A. 1834, M.A. 1837; Deac. 1836, Pr. 1837. R. of Blithfield, Dio. Lich. 1846. (Patron, Lord Bagot; Glebe, 60 acres; R.'s Inc. 430l and Ho; Pop. 338.) Fell. of All Souls Coll. Ox. [5]

BAGOT, Lewis Francis, *Leigh, Cheadle, Staffs.*—Ch. Ch. Ox. B.A. 1834, All Souls Coll. M.A. 1836; Deac. 1836 and Pr. 1837 by Bp of Ox. R. of Leigh, Dio. Lich. 1846. (Patron, Lord Bagot; Tithe, 620l; Glebe, 70 acres; R.'s Inc. 730l and Ho; Pop. 1070.) Rural Dean of Uttoxeter 1846. [6]

BAGOTT, Elijah, *Charlestown, Halifax.*—St. Bees; Deac. 1855 and Pr. 1857 by Bp of Rip. P. C. of St. Thomas's, Charlestown, Dio. Rip. 1858. (Patron, V. of Halifax; V.'s Inc. 300l and Ho; Pop. 8000.) Formerly C. of Trinity, Holmfirth, 1855, and Huddersfield 1857. [7]

BAGSHAW, Charles Edward, *Ambrosden, Bicester.*—St. Aidan's; Deac. 1861 and Pr. 1862 by Bp of Rip. V. of Ambrosden, Dio. Ox. 1866. (Patron, Sir Edward Turner, Bart; V.'s Inc. 300l and Ho; Pop. 871.) [8]

BAGSHAW, Henry Salmon, *Enderby, Leicester.*—C. of Enderby. [9]

BAGSHAW, William Salmon, *Thrapston, Northants.*—Wor. Coll. Ox. B.A. 1817, M.A. 1821; Deac. 1818 by Bp of Glouc. Pr. 1820 by Bp of Pet. R. of Thrapston, Dio. Pet. 1837. (Patron, Ld Chan; Glebe, 218 acres; R.'s Inc. 400l and Ho; Pop. 1257.) [10]

BAGSHAW, William Salmon, jun., *Braunstone, Leicester.*—St. John's Coll. Cam. B.A. 1860, M.A. 1864; Deac. 1860 and Pr. 1861 by Bp of Pet. C. of Braunstone 1866. Formerly C. of Thrapstone 1860, Hale, Surrey, 1862, and Trinity, Bath, 1864. [11]

BAGSHAWE, Alfred Drake, *Shirland, Alfreton, Derby.*—C. of Shirland. [12]

BAGSHAWE, Augustus Adam, *Wormhill Parsonage, Miller's Dale, Bakewell.*—Corpus Coll. Cam. B.A. 1841, M.A. 1867; Deac. 1840 by Bp. of B. and W. Pr. 1841 by Bp of Lich. P. C. of Wormhill, Dio. Lich. 1843. (Patrons, Seven Trustees; P. C.'s Inc. 275l and Ho; Pop. 418.) [13]

BAGSHAWE, Charles Frederick, *New Bailey, Salford, Manchester.*—Chap. of the New Bailey, Salford. [14]

BAGSHAWE, Edward Benjamin, *Bath.*—Magd. Coll. Cam. B.A. 1823, M.A. 1827; Deac. 1823 and Pr. 1824 by Bp of B. and W. [15]

BAGSHAWE, Edward Salman, *Holm Cultram, Carlisle.*—C. of St. Cuthbert's, Holm Cultram. [16]

BAGSHAWE, Francis Lloyd, 15, *Coburg-place, Upper Kennington-lane, London, S.*—Trin. Coll. Cam. Scho. of, 19th Wrang. B.A. 1862, M.A. 1865; Deac. 1864 and Pr. 1865 by Bp of Win. C. of St. Mary's the Less, Princes-road, Lambeth, 1864. [17]

BAILEY, Anthony Winter, *Panton Rectory, Wragby, Lincolnshire.*—St. Cath. Coll. Cam. B.A. 1852, M.A. 1855; Deac. 1852 and Pr. 1853 by Bp of Pet. R. of Hatton, Dio. Lin. 1866. (Patron, C. C. W. Sibthorp, Esq; Glebe, 23 acres; R.'s Inc. 240l; Pop. 199.) Formerly C. of Nailstone 1852–54, and Cadeby, Leicestershire, 1854–56, St. George's, Everton, Lancashire, 1856–60, and Hainton, Lincolnshire, 1863–65. [18]

BAILEY, B., *Sheinton, Much Wenlock, Salop.*—R. of Sheinton, Dio. Lich. 1856. (Patron, John Anstice, Esq; R.'s Inc. 280l and Ho; Pop. 175.) [19]

BAILEY, Charles, *Vicarage, Marton-in-Cleveland, near Middlesborough.*—St. Cath. Coll. Cam. Scho. and Prizeman of, B.A. 1847, M.A. 1854; Deac. 1848 and Pr. 1849 by Abp of York. V. of Marton-in-Cleveland, Dio. York, 1860. (Patron, Abp of York; V.'s Inc. 300l and Ho; Pop. 587.) Formerly C. of Stainton 1849; V. of Marsk, Yorks, 1850–60. [20]

BAILEY, Ebenezer, *Ardwick, Manchester.*—Ch. Coll. Cam. B.A. 1866; Deac. 1866 by Bp of Man. C. of St. Jude's, Manchester, 1866. Author, *Conformity to the Church of England,* 1s. [21]

BAILEY, George, *Parson's Mead, Croydon.*—Dub. A.B. 1851, A.M. 1859; Deac. 1851 and Pr. 1852 by Bp of Roch. Chap. of Croydon Union 1866. Formerly C. of Dagenham, Essex, 1851–58; Chap. of Romford Union 1858–66. [22]

BAILEY, George Curling, *Shipdham Rectory, Norfolk.*—R. of Shipdham, Dio. Nor. 1850. (Patron, the present R; Tithe, 1240l; R.'s Inc. 1300l and Ho; Pop. 1644.) [23]

BAILEY, Hammond Roberson, *Great Warley, Brentwood, Essex.*—St. John's Coll. Cam. 1st Bell's Univ. Scho. 1851, 3rd in 1st Cl. Trip. and B.A. 1854, M.A. 1857; Deac. 1856 and Pr. 1857 by Bp of Ely. Cl. Lect. St. John's Coll. Cam; R. of Great Warley, Dio. Roch. 1866. (Patron, St. John's Coll. Cam; Tithe—Imp. 90l, R. 520l; Glebe, 12 acres; R.'s Inc. 530l and Ho; Pop. 422.) Formerly C. of Shipston-on-Stour 1856, Silsoe, near Ampthill, 1857. [24]

BAILEY, Henry, *St. Augustine's College, Canterbury.*—St. John's Coll. Cam, B.A. 1839; Tyrwhitt's Hebrew Scho. 1841. Warden of St. Augustine's Coll. 1850; Hon. Can. of Cant; Hon. Sec. of Soc. for Advancing the Christian Faith 1851. Formerly Fell. of St. John's Coll. Cam. Author, *Rituale Anglo-Catholicum,* 1847, 12s; *Ramsden Sermon* (at St. Mary's Cambridge), 1851; *Missionary's Daily Text Book,* 5s, etc. [25]

BAILEY, Henry Ives, *North Leverton, Retford, Notts.*—Deac. 1814 and Pr. 1815 by Abp of York. V. of North Leverton, Dio. Lin. 1844, with Habblesthorpe annexed, 1866. (Patron, Bp of Man; North Leverton—Glebe, 79½ acres; Pop. 329. Habblesthorpe—Glebe, 39¾ acres; Pop. 142; V.'s Inc. 300l.) Formerly Head Mast. of Abp Margetson's Gr. Sch. Drighlington 1814; P. C. of Drighlington 1815. Author, *The Liturgy compared with the Bible,* S. P. C. K. 1833, 6s. [26]

BAILEY, James Sandford, 6, *Clifton-terrace, Brighton.*—Jesus Coll. Cam. B.A. 1845, M.A. 1848; Deac. 1847 by Bp of Ox, Pr. 1848 by Bp of Win. Formerly V. of St. Clement's, Cambridge, 1849; Asst. C. of St. Paul's, Brighton, 1852–66. [27]

BAILEY, John, *Stoke Holy Cross, Norwich.*—St. Cath. Hall, Cam. B.A. 1834, M.A. 1837; Deac. 1834, Pr. 1835. V. of Stoke Holy Cross, Dio. Nor. 1838. (Patrons, D. and C. of Nor; Tithe—App. 360l, V. 210l; Glebe, 2 acres; V.'s Inc. 230l and Ho; Pop. 451.) Surrogate. Formerly Member of the Norwich Diocesan Training Institution Board; Hon. Sec. to the Norfolk and Norwich Diocesan Model Infant School; C. of St. Stephen's, Norwich, 1834–42; Chap. to the Henstead Union 1846–67. [28]

BAILEY, John, *Grosmont Parsonage, by York.*—St. John's Coll. Cam. B.A. 1854, M.A. 1857; Deac. 1854 and Pr. 1855 by Bp of Lich. Incumb. of Grosmont, Dio. York, 1863. (Patron, Abp of York; Glebe, 20 acres; Incumb.'s Inc. 300*l* and Ho; Pop. 1700.) Formerly P.C. of St. John's, The Pleck, Walsall. [1]

BAILEY, John Allanson, 5, *Mitre-court, Fleet-street, London, E.C.*—Caius Coll. Cam. B.A. 1857; Deac. 1857 by Bp of Ely, Pr. 1858 by Abp of Cant. Sec. of the Colonial and Continental Ch. Soc. Formerly C. of St. Stephen's, Tonbridge, Kent, 1857–60, St. Bride's, Liverpool, 1860–62, St. Dunstan's-in-the-West, Lond. 1862. [2]

BAILEY, John Hopkins, *White Notley, Witham, Essex.*—Trin. Coll. Cam. B.A. 1829, Tyrwhitt's Hebrew Scho. 1830; Deac. 1835, Pr. 1836. V. of White Notley, Dio. Roch. 1859. (Patron, Bp of Roch; Tithe—Imp. 254*l*, V. 249*l* 13*s* 6*d*; Glebe, 7 acres; V.'s Inc. 270*l* and Ho; Pop. 508.) Formerly P. C. of Billericay, Essex, 1845–59. [3]

BAILEY, Joseph Greenoak, *Rochester.*—Lin. Coll. Ox. 1st Cl. in Public Exam. B.A. 1862, M.A. 1864; Deac. 1862 and Pr. 1863 by Bp of Roch. Chap of the Chapel and Hospital of St. Bartholomew, Rochester, 1867. Formerly C. of Strood next Rochester 1862; Chap. of North Aylesford Union 1865. [4]

BAILEY, Richard Kemp, *Preston Rectory, Holderness, Yorks.*—Ox. B.A 1840, M.A. 1847; Deac. 1840 by Abp of Cant. Pr. 1841 by Bp of Lin. R. of Preston-in-Holderness, Dio. York, 1866. (Patron, Abp of York; R.'s Inc. 310*l* and Ho; Pop. 1061.) V. of Hedon, Dio. York, 1867. (Patron, Abp of York; V.'s Inc. 70*l* and Ho; Pop. 975.) Surrogate. Formerly P. C. of St. Paul's, Hull, 1844-66. Author, *Evils of Gaming, Death of the Duke of Wellington,* and *Sigglesthorne Harvest Home,* Sermons. [5]

BAILEY, Thomas John, *Lewes, Sussex.*—Corpus Coll. Cam. B.A. 1860; Deac. 1860 by Bp of Chich. C. of St. Michael's, Lewes. [6]

BAILEY, W. B., *Worcester.*—C. of St. Andrew's, Worcester. [7]

BAILLIE, The Hon. John, *Elsdon, Newcastle-on-Tyne.*—Trin. Coll. Cam. B.A. 1833, M.A. 1853; Deac. 1833 by Abp of York, Pr. 1834 by Bp of Lin. R. of Elsdon with Horsley C. and Otterburn C. Dio. Dur. 1854. (Patron, Duke of Northumberland; Tithe, 803*l*; Glebe, 40 acres; R.'s Inc. 860*l* and Ho; Pop. 1521.) Can. Res. of Wistow in York Cathl. 1854 (Value 600*l* and Res); Rural Dean of Rothbury. [8]

BAILLIE, John, *Wivenhoe Rectory, Colchester.*—Univ. Edinb. and Caius Coll. Camb. B.D; Deac. 1857 and Pr. 1858 by Bp of Lon. R. of Wivenhoe, Dio. Roch. 1866. (Patron, N. C. Corsellis, Esq; Tithe, 440*l*; Glebe, 60 acres; R.'s Inc. 510*l* and Ho; Pop. 1843.) Formerly Min. of Established and of Free Church of Scotland; also of Percy Episcopal Chapel, Lond. Author, *Memoir of Hewitson; Missionary of Kilmurray; Adelaide L. Newton; The Revival; Life of Capt. W. Thornton Bates, R.N; Life-Studies; Rivers in the Desert, a Narrative of the Awakening in Burmah; Scenes of Life, Historical and Biographical, chiefly from Old Testament times; Christ and Life;* and other works. [9]

BAILLIE, Robert, *Sywell Rectory, Northampton.*—Dub. A.B; Deac. 1847 by Bp of Tuam, Pr. 1848 by Bp of Derry. R. of Sywell, Dio. Pet. 1861; (Patron, Earl Brownlow; Tithe, 460*l*; Glebe, 70 acres. R.'s Inc. 630*l* and Ho; Pop. 241.) Formerly C. of Raphoe, Ireland, Lynn, Norfolk, St. John's, Derby. [10]

BALLIE-HAMILTON, The Hon. Arthur Charles, *Ridgmont, Woburn, Beds.*—Univ. Coll. Dur. B.A. 1859, M A. 1862; Deac. 1861 and Pr. 1863 by Bp of Lich. V. of Ridgmont, Dio. Ely, 1865. (Patron, Duke of Bedford; V.'s Inc. 138*l* and Ho; Pop. 1070.) Formerly C. of Pensnett, near Dudley, 1861–63; Sen. C. of Great Marlow 1864–65. [11]

BAILY, Henry George, *Swindon, Wilts.*—Ch. Coll. Cam. Scho. of, Wrang. B.A. 1842, M.A. 1845; Deac. and Pr. 1842 by Bp of Ches. V. of Swindon, Dio. G. and B. 1847. (Patron, Ld Chan; Tithe—Imp. 22*l* 3*s*, V. 269*l*; Glebe, 20 acres; V.'s Inc. 362*l* and Ho; Pop. 2689.) Surrogate. Author, *Litanies for Sunday Schools,* 2*d*; *Ten Reasons why I love my Church, and Ten Reasons why I love my Prayer-book,* 2*d*; *Contention for the Faith* (Sermon on the Popish Aggression.) [12]

BAILY, Johnson, *Bishop Middleham, near Ferry Hill Station, Durham.*—Trin. Coll. Cam. B.A. 1857, M.A. 1860, Sen. Opt; Deac. 1859 and Pr. 1860 by Bp. of Man. C. of Bishop Middleham 1863. Formerly C. of Christ Church, Salford, 1859–63. [13]

BAILY, Kitelee Chandos.—Univ. Coll. Dur. B.A. 1849; Deac. 1849 and Pr. 1850 by Bp of Lich. Formerly C. of Gnosall, Staffs, 1850–52; V. of Harwell, Abingdon, 1852–56; in 1856 went to India as Military Chap. in the E.I.Co.'s service, Madras Presidency; in 1862 returned to England on "sick leave," and still in the service; C. of Hinton-in-the-Hedges, Northants, 1863–64. [14]

BAILY, William Percival, *Great Waldingfield, Sudbury, Suffolk.*—Clare Coll. Cam. B.A. 1830, M A. 1833, B.D. 1854; Deac. 1832 by Bp of Roch. Pr. 1833 by Bp of Carl. R. of Great Waldingfield, Dio. Ely, 1858. (Patron, Clare Coll. Cam; R.'s Inc. 850*l* and Ho; Pop 622.) Formerly Fell. of Clare Coll. Cam. 1830–49; Chap. to her Majesty at Hampton Court Palace, 1849–58. [15]

BAIN, William Richard, *Flempton, Bury St. Edmunds, Suffolk.*—Ch. Coll. Cam. B.A. 1845, M A. 1848; Deac. 1845 and Pr. 1846 by Bp of Ely. R. of Flempton with Hengrave, Dio. Ely, 1851. (Patron, the present R.; Flempton—Tithe, 205*l* 18*s* 2*d*; Glebe, 40 acres; Hengrave—Tithe, 241*l* 0*s* 8*d*; R.'s Inc 520*l* and Ho; Pop. Flempton 190, Hengrave 219.) [16]

BAINBRIDGE, Francis, *Rothbury, Northumberland.*—St. Cath. Coll. Cam. B.A. 1831; Deac. 1831, Pr. 1832. C. of the Parochial Chapelry of Framlington, Northumberland; Head Mast. of Rothbury Gr. Sch. 1831. [17]

BAINBRIGGE, Joseph Henry, *Upton Warren, near Bromsgrove.*—Wad. Coll. Ox. B.A. 1845; Deac. 1851 by Bp of Wor. Pr. 1852 by Bp of Lich. C. in sole charge of Upton Warren 1866. Formerly C. of Ellaston 1851, and Yoxall 1854, Dio. Lich. [18]

BAINES, Charles Thomas Johnson, *Whissendine, Oakham.*—Ch. Coll. Cam. B.A. 1835, M A. 1836; Deac. 1836 by Bp of Nor. Pr. 1837 by Bp of Lin. [19]

BAINES, Edward, *Yalding, Staplehurst, Kent.*—Ch. Coll. Cam. Bell's Univ. Scho. Browne's Medallist, and B.A. 1824, M.A. 1827; Deac. 1825 by Bp of Herf. Pr. 1826 by Bp of G. and B. V. of Yalding, Dio. Cant. 1859. (Patron, James Warde, Esq; V.'s Inc. 1200*l* and Ho; Pop. 1762.) Author, *Notes on Æschylus*; *Art of Latin Poetry*; *First Form Latin Grammar on Analytical Principles,* 1855. [20]

BAINES, Francis A.—Formerly P. C. of Ch. Ch. Ware, Herts, 1858. [21]

BAINES, Haygarth, *Satterthwaite (Lancashire), near Milnthorpe, Westmoreland.*—Queens' Coll. Cam. B.A. 1827, M.A. 1830; Deac. 1828, Pr. 1829. P. C. of Satterthwaite, Dio. Ches. 1833. (Patron, P. C. of Hawkshead; Glebe, 180 acres; P. C.'s Inc. 120*l*; Pop. 397.) [22]

BAINES, Haygarth Taylor, *Hawkshead, Lancashire.*—Ch. Coll. Cam. B.A. 1847, M.A. 1850; Deac. 1847 and Pr. 1848 by Bp of Ches. Head Mast. of Hawkshead Gr. Sch. 1862. Formerly Mast. of Prescot Gr. Sch. 1851; Chap. of the Prescot Union 1857. [23]

BAINES, John, *Little Marlow, Marlow, Bucks.*—St. John's Coll. Ox. B.A. 1843, M.A. 1845; Deac. 1844 and Pr. 1845 by Bp of Lon. V. of Little Marlow, Dio. Ox. 1859. (Patron, S. Birch, Esq; V.'s Inc. 175*l* and Ho; Pop. 790.) Late Chap. of St. John the Evangelist's Asylum for Aged and Infirm Journeymen Tailors, Lond. 1848–59. Author, *Danger to the Faith,* 1850, 6*d*; *Papal Aggression,* 1850; *The Sword of the Lord,* 1851; *Tales of the Empire,* 1851, 1*s* 6*d*; *Honouring the Dead a Christian Duty* (Duke of Wellington's Funeral), 6*d*; *The*

Wisdom of Bezaleel, 1854, 6*d*; *Life of Archbishop Laud*, 1855, 3*s* 6*d*; *Twenty Sermons*, (Masters), 1857, 7*s*; *Hints for Harvest Services*, 1866, 1*s*. [1]

BAINES, Joseph, *St. John's Parsonage, Hawarden, Flints*.—Dub. A.B. 1858, Deac. 1860, and Pr. 1861 by Bp of Wor. C. of St. John's, Hawarden, 1865. Formerly C. of St. Andrew's, Birmingham, 1860–64, Hadleigh, Essex, 1864–65. [2]

BAIRD, James, *Southgate, Edmonton, Middlesex*.—Queens' Coll. Cam. B.A. 1845, M.A. 1848; Deac. 1845 and Pr. 1846 by Bp of Lon. P. C. of Southgate, Dio. Lon. 1858. (Patron, V. of Edmonton; P. C.'s Inc. 220*l*; Pop. 2226.) Formerly C. of Hornsey. [3]

BAIRD, Samuel Bawtree.—Emman. Col. Cam. B.A. 1854, M.A. 1857; Deac. 1854 and Pr. 1855 by Bp of Ches. Formerly C. of Marple, Cheshire, and Newton-in-Makerfield, Lancashire. [4]

BAIRD, William.—Lin. Coll. Ox. Scho. 1856, B.A. 1859; Deac. 1859 and Pr. 1860 by Bp of Lon. Chap. to Earl Beauchamp. Formerly C. of St. Bartholomew's, Moor-lane, Lond. [5]

BAKER, Arthur, *Broughton, Manchester*.—C. of Broughton. [6]

BAKER, Arthur, *Addington, Winslow, Bucks*.—Wad. Coll. Ox. B.A. 1840, M.A. 1850, Tunbridge Exhib. of 100*l* per ann; Deac. 1841 and Pr. 1842 by Bp of Lon. C. of Addington 1865. Formerly C. of Trinity, Marylebone, 1841–43; C. and Chap. of Aylesbury Union Workhouse and of Bucks County Infirmary 1843–49; C. of Newtown, Hants, and Chap. of Newbury Workhouse, 1849–51; C. of All Saints', Marylebone, 1851–53; Incumb. of St. Paul's, Wellington, New Zealand, 1854–59; C. of Kemerton, Glouc. 1860–65. Author, *Lectures on the Saints' Days*, 1846; *Sermons on Holy Joy, &c.*, 1847; *A Plea for Romanizers (so called) in the Anglican Communion*, Masters, 1850; *Joy in the Everlasting Benediction of the Heavenly Washing, a Sermon with Appendix on Canon XXIX*, 1861; *Temptation, its value, &c.* 1864; *The Christian Doctrine of Everlasting Punishment*, Mozley, 1864; and various Sermons and Pamphlets. [7]

BAKER, Charles, *Appleshaw Vicarage, Andover*.—Ex. Coll. Ox. M.A; Deac. 1856 by Bp of Win. Pr. 1857 by Bp of Salis. V. of Appleshaw, Dio. Win. 1864. (Patron, D. and C. of Chich; Tithe, 270*l* 11*s* 2*d*; V.'s Inc. 272*l* and Ho; Pop. 284.) Formerly R. of St. Martin's, Chichester, 1862–64. [8]

BAKER, Charles Francis, *Tellisford Rectory, Bath*.—Ex. Coll. Ox. B.A. 1840, M.A. 1861; Deac. 1841 and Pr. 1842 by Bp of Salis. R. of Tellisford, Dio. B. and W. 1861. (Patron, the present R; Tithe, 150*l*; Glebe, 60 acres; R.'s Inc. 220*l* and Ho; Pop. 112.) Formerly C. of Atworth, Wilts, and Road, Somerset. [9]

BAKER, E.—C. of Clare Portion, Tiverton. [10]

BAKER, Edward Turner, *Merstham, Surrey*.—C. of Merstham. [11]

BAKER, Frederick Augustus, *Godmanstone Rectory, near Dorchester*.—Wad. Coll. Ox. B.A. 1849, M.A. 1851; Deac. 1850, Pr. 1851. R. of Godmanstone, Dio. Salis. (Patron, the present R; Tithe, 240*l*; Glebe, 40 acres; R.'s Inc. 280*l* and Ho; Pop. 175.) Formerly C. of Corsham, near Bath, 1850, Stanley St. Leonard's, Glouc. 1853. [12]

BAKER, Frederick Walter, *Beaulieu, Southampton*.—Caius Coll. Cam. B.A. 1836, M.A. 1839; Deac. 1837 and Pr. 1838 by Bp of B. and W. P. C. of Beaulieu, Dio. Win. 1847. (Patron, Duke of Buccleuch; P. C.'s Inc. 340*l* and Ho; Pop. 1176.) Surrogate. Formerly C. of Bathwick 1838, and Rodney Stoke, Somerset, 1846. [13]

BAKER, George, *Freshford, Bath*.—Wad. Coll. Ox. B.A. 1825, M.A. 1833; Deac. 1826, Pr. 1827. Formerly C. of Fovant. [14]

BAKER, George Bayldon, *Glaseley Rectory, Bridgnorth, Salop*.—St. Cath. Coll. Cam. M.A; Deac. and Pr. by Bp of Ely. C. of Glaseley and Deuxhill 1861. Formerly C. of St. Andrew-the-Less, Cambridge. [15]

BAKER, George Rodney T., *Eton College*.—Ex. Coll. Ox. B.A. 1860; Deac. 1861 and Pr. 1862 by Bp of Ox. Conduct of Eton College and C. of Eton 1862. Formerly Asst. C. of Holy Trinity, Windsor, 1861–62. [16]

BAKER, Henry.—Church Miss. Coll. Islington; Deac. 1842 and Pr. 1843 by Bp of Ches. [17]

BAKER, Henry De Foe, *Thruxton, Andover Hants*.—Jesus Coll. Cam. B.A. 1855; Deac. 1855 by Bp of Pet. C. of Thruxton. [18]

BAKER, Henry Fowler, *Yarnscombe, Barnstaple, N. Devon*.—Emman. Coll. Cam. B.A. 1854; Deac. 1856 and Pr. 1857 by Bp of Herf. V. of Yarnscombe, Dio. Ex. 1861. (Patron, Ld Chan; Tithe, 136*l* 10*s*; Glebe, 30 acres; V.'s Inc. 172*l* 10*s*; Pop. 423.) Formerly C. of Presteign, Radnor, 1856–59, Bishop's-Tawton, Barnstaple, 1859–61. [19]

BAKER, Henry Martyn, *Almshouses, Kingsland-road, London, N.E.*—King's Coll. Lond. Theol. Assoc. 1853; Deac. 1854 and Pr. 1856 by Abp of Cant. Chap. to the Ironmongers' Co. Lond. 1864. Formerly C. of Bottesford 1862, previously C. of Tonbridge, Kent, 1854, Newport, Mon. 1856; Chap. of Silvertown, Essex, 1860. Author, *The Brother's Prayer*, 1848; *The Converted Bell-ringer*, 1852; *The New Comers*, 1855; *Secession*, 1856; *Nature and Grace*, 1857; *Daily Meditations on the Psalms of David*, 1855; *Mary Howell's Bible Difficulties*, etc. [20]

BAKER, Sir Henry Williams, Bart., *Monkland, Leominster*.—Trin. Coll. Cam. B.A. 1844, M.A. 1847; Deac. 1844, Pr. 1846. V. of Monkland, Dio. Herf. 1851. (Patrons, D. and C. of Windsor; Tithe, 250*l* 15*s*; Glebe, 3 acres; V.'s Inc. 253*l*; Pop. 211.) Author, *Daily Prayers for the use of those who have to work hard*; *Daily Text Book for the use of those who have to work hard*; other Small Tracts. [21]

BAKER, Hugh Ryves, 30, *Wood-street, Woolwich, S.E.*—Dub. A.B. 1854, A.M. 1858; Deac. 1856 and Pr. 1857 by Bp. of Ex. C. of Western Mission, Woolwich, 1865. Formerly C. of Ottery St. Mary, Devon. [22]

BAKER, James, *North Hill House, Winchester*.—Univ. Coll. Ox. B.A. 1847, M.A. 1851; Deac. 1851 and Pr. 1853 by Bp. of Ox. Chap. of Winchester Coll. [23]

BAKER, John, *St. John's Parsonage, Blackburn*. St. Bees; Deac. 1859, Pr. 1860. P. C. of St. John's Blackburn, Dio. Man. 1867. (Patron, V. of Blackburn; P. C.'s Inc. 300*l* and Ho; Pop. 8261.) Formerly C. of Trinity, Over Darwen, 1859–60, and St. Andrew's, Blackburn, 1861–66. [24]

BAKER, John Gerrard Andrews, *Old Warden, Biggleswade, Beds*.—Trin. Coll. Cam. B.A. 1838, M.A. 1841; Deac. 1839 and Pr. 1840 by Abp of Cant. V. of Old Warden, Dio. Ely, 1843. (Patron, W. H. Whitbread, Esq; Tithe, 6*l*; Glebe, 283 acres; V.'s Inc. 400*l* and Ho; Pop. 597.) Formerly C. of All Hallows, Bread-street, Lond. 1839–43. [25]

BAKER, John Julius, *Enfield, Middlesex*.—Ex. Coll. Ox. B.A. 1860, M.A. 1865; Deac. 1861 and Pr. 1862 by Bp of Ox. C. of St. Andrew's, Enfield, 1865. Formerly C. of Finstock, Oxon, 1861–63, and Welwyn, Herts, 1864–65. [26]

BAKER, John Norgrave, *How-Caple, Ross, Herefordshire*.—St. John's Coll. Cam. B.A. 1829; Deac. 1829 and Pr. 1830 by Bp of Herf. R. of How-Caple with Sollers Hope, Dio. Herf. 1851. (Patron, E. W. Pendarves, Esq; How-Caple, Tithe, 188*l*; Glebe, 44 acres; Sollers Hope, Tithe, 146*l*; Glebe, 63 acres; R.'s Inc. 390*l* and Ho; Pop. How-Caple 161, Sollers Hope 166.) [27]

BAKER, John Thomas Wright, *Fir-grove, West End, Southampton*.—Clare Hall, Cam. B.A. 1834, M.A. 1845; Deac. 1844 and Pr. 1845 by Bp of Win. Chap. to the South Stoneham Union 1847. Formerly C. of Botley 1844–55, Sholing 1855–59. [28]

BAKER, Joseph, *Neen Sollars, Cleobury-Mortimer, Shropshire*.—Wor. Coll. Ox. 2nd cl. Lit. Hum. B.A. 1840, M.A. 1843; Deac. 1841 and Pr. 1843 by Bp of Ox. R. of Neen Sollars with Milson C. Dio. Herf. 1855. (Patron, Wor. Coll. Ox; R.'s Inc. 420*l* and Ho; Pop. 346.) Formerly R. of Littleton-on-Severn, near Bristol, 1849–55; Fell. of Wor. Coll. Ox. [29]

BAKER, J. G., *Thorverton, Collumpton, Devon.*—C. of Thorverton. [1]

BAKER, Lawrence Palk, *Medbourne, Market-Harborough, Leicestershire.*—St. John's Coll. Cam. B.A. 1807, M.A. 1810; Deac. 1810 by Bp of Ely, Pr. 1817 by Bp of Bristol. R. of Medbourne with Holt C. Dio. Pet. 1825. (Patron, St. John's Coll. Cam; Medbourne, Tithe—Imp. 6*l* 6*s*; R. 570*l*; Glebe, 41 acres; Holt, Tithe—R. 166*l* 10*s* 6*d*; R.'s Inc. 780*l* and Ho; Pop. Medbourne 580, Holt 33.) [2]

BAKER, Ralph Bourne, *Hasfield Court, Gloucestershire,* and 6, *Royal York-crescent, Clifton.*—Trin. Coll. Cam. B.A. 1826, M.A. 1830; Deac. 1827 and Pr. 1828 by Bp of Lich. Formerly Rural Dean of Stone, Staffs, and P. C. of Hilderstone. Editor of *Psalms and Hymns*, 3rd ed. 1859, 2*s*; and Author of several parochial addresses. [3]

BAKER, Robert, *Nonington, Wingham.*—Corpus Coll. Cam. B.A. 1862; Deac. 1863 and Pr. 1864 by Abp of Cant. C. of Nonington 1864. Formerly C. of Brasted 1863. [4]

BAKER, R., *Aldringham, Aldeburgh, Suffolk.*—P.C. of Aldringham, Dio. Nor. 1858. (Patron, Rev. E. Hollond; P. C.'s Inc. 60*l*; Pop. 470.) [5]

BAKER, Robert, *King's-Walden, Welwyn, Herts.*—Magd. Hall, Ox. B.A. 1846, M.A. 1849; Deac. 1847 and Pr. 1848 by Bp of Ex. P. C. of King's-Walden, Dio. Roch, 1857. (Patron, C. C. Hale, Esq; P. C.'s Inc. 82*l*; Pop. 1183.) Formerly R. of Compton Martin with Nempnett C. Somerset. [6]

BAKER, Robert, *Friston, Saxmundham, Suffolk.*—V. of Friston with Snape V. Dio. Nor. 1841. (Patron, R. H. W. Vyse, Esq; Friston, Tithe—Imp. 256*l* 2*s* 3*d*, V. 129*l* 4*s* 10*d*; Snape, Tithe—Imp. 258*l* 19*s* 9*d*, V. 124*l* 9*s* 9*d*; V.'s Inc. 286*l*; Pop. Friston 432, Snape 554.) [7]

BAKER, Robert George, *Fulham, London, S.W.*—Trin. Coll. Cam. B.A. 1810, M.A. 1813; Deac. 1812 and Pr. 1813 by Bp of Lin. V. of All Saints, Fulham, Dio. Lon. 1834. (Patron, Bp of Lon; Tithe—Lessees of the Rectory, 90*l*, V. 800*l*; Glebe, 1 acre; V.'s Inc. 870*l* and Ho; Pop. 4906.) Preb. of St. Paul's Cathl. 1846 (Value, 2*l*.) Author, *The Olden Characters of Fulham*, 1847; *On Helping the Poor to Help themselves* (a Lecture); *Ten Sermons*; separate sermons. [8]

BAKER, Robert Lowbridge, *Ramsden, near Charlbury, Oxon.*—St. Peter's Coll. Cam. B.A. 1854, M.A. 1857; Deac. 1856 and Pr. 1857 by Bp of Lich. R. of Wilcote, Dio. Ox. 1860. (Patroness, Mrs. Pickering; R.'s Inc. 75*l*; Pop. 7.) P. C. of Ramsden, Dio. Ox. 1864. (Patron, Bp of Ox; Pop. 470.) [9]

BAKER, Robert Sibley, *Hargrave, Kimbolton.*—Magd. Coll. Cam. B.A. 1846; Deac. 1847 and Pr. 1850 by Bp of Pet. R. of Hargrave, Dio. Pet. 1865. (Patrons, Exors. of Rev. W. Lake Baker; Glebe, 312 acres; R.'s Inc. 320*l* and Ho; Pop. 310.) Formerly C. of Shilton, Beds, 1847–66. [10]

BAKER, Samuel Ogilvy, *North Cheriton Rectory, Wincanton, Somerset.*—St. John's Coll. Cam. B.A. 1858; Deac. 1859 and Pr. 1860 by Bp of B. and W. R. *pro tem.* of North Cheriton, Dio. B. and W. 1863. (Patrons, Trustees of late R. the Rev. T. Gatehouse; Tithe, 202*l* 17*s*; Glebe, 29 acres, let for 63*l* 17*s* 6*d*; R.'s Inc. 266*l* and Ho; Pop. 302.) Formerly C. of Muchelney and Drayton, near Langport, 1859–61, North Cheriton 1861–63. [11]

BAKER, Slade, *Clifton-on-Teme, Worcestershire.*—Univ. Coll. Ox. B.A. 1848, M.A. 1850; Deac. 1849 by Bp of G. and B. Pr. 1850 by Bp of Wor. V. of Clifton-on-Teme, Dio. Herf. 1853. (Patron, Sir T. E. Winnington, Bart; Tithe—Imp. 27*l* 10*s*, V. 207*l* 10*s*; Glebe, 2 acres; V.'s Inc. 215*l* and Ho; Pop. 542.) [12]

BAKER, Stephen Cattley, *Usk, Monmouthshire.*—St. John's Coll. Cam. Jun. Opt. and B.A. 1837; Deac. 1837 and Pr. 1838 by Abp of York. V. of Usk, Dio. Llan. 1860. (Patron, W. A. Williams, Esq; Tithe—Imp. 252*l* 10*s*, V. 285*l*; Glebe, 1 acre; V.'s Inc. 310*l*; Pop. 2112.) P. C. of Monkswood, Dio. Llan. 1857. (Patron, Duke of Beaufort; P. C.'s Inc. 90*l*; Pop. 179.) Hon. Chap. and Sec. of Monmouthshire Reformatory. Formerly C. of Birkin, Yorks, 1857, Ch. Ch. Leeds, 1839, St. Saviour's, York, 1841, St. Peter's, Colchester, 1845; Asst. Min. of St. Thomas's Episcopal Chap. Edinburgh, 1844; V. of Skenfrith, Mon. 1846; Chap. House of Correction, Usk, 1852. Author, *Cambridge Crepuscular Conversations*, 1837; *The Soul's Foundation*, 1846; *The Building of God*, 1846; *Early Grace* (a Memoir), 1846, 1*s* 6*d*; *A few Words from the late Curate* (a Tract), 1846; *The Blessed, or the First Psalm practically considered in Six Meditations*, 1855, 6*d*; *Reasons for a Reformatory for Monmouthshire*, 1856; *Hope founded on the Word*, 1861, etc. [13]

BAKER, Talbot Hastings Bendall, *Preston Vicarage, Weymouth, Dorset.*—Ch. Ch. Ox. B.A. 1843, M.A. 1847; Deac. 1844 and Pr. 1845 by Bp of Lich. V. of Preston with Sutton-Poyntz, Dio. Salis. 1848. (Patron, Preb. of Preston in Salis. Cathl; Tithe—App. 281*l*, V. 257*l*; Glebe, 3 acres; V.'s Inc. 271*l* and Ho; Pop. 723.) Chap. to Bp of Salisbury. [14]

BAKER, Thomas, *Hartlebury, Stourport, Worcestershire.*—Ch. Coll. Cam. B.A. 1822, M.A. 1825; Deac. 1822 by Bp. of G. and B. Pr. 1823 by Bp of Ches. R. of Hartlebury, Dio. Wor. 1835. (Patron, Bp of Wor; Tithe, 1778*l*; Glebe, 260 acres; R.'s Inc. 2188*l* and Ho; Pop. 2115.) Sen. Hon. Can. of Wor. Cathl. 1845; Rural Dean of Kidderminster. [15]

BAKER, William.—Fell. of St. John's Coll. Ox. [16]

BAKER, William, *Crambe Vicarage, York.*—Ch. Coll. Cam. Sen. Opt. M.A. 1849; Deac. 1846 and Pr. 1847. V. of Crambe, Dio. York, 1861. (Patron, Abp of York; V.'s Inc. 235*l* and Ho; Pop. 600.) Author, *Harmonic Maxims of Science and Religion*, Longmans, 1864, 3*s* 6*d*. [17]

BAKER, William De Foe.—Emman. Coll. Cam. Sen. Opt. B.A. 1854, M.A. 1859; Deac. 1856 and Pr. 1857 by Bp of Roch. Formerly C. of Orsett, Essex, 1856–63, and Chap. of the Orsett Union 1859–63, C. of St. Jude's, Southsea, 1863. [18]

BAKER, William John.—St. John's Coll. Cam. B.A. 1853, M.A. 1856; Deac. 1856 and Pr. 1857 by Bp of Lich. Formerly C. of Whaddon, Bucks. [19]

BAKER, William S., *Eversholt Rectory, Woburn, Beds.*—Clare Coll. Cam. B.A. 1854, M.A. 1857; Deac. 1854 and Pr. 1855 by Bp of B. and W. R. of Eversholt, Dio. Ely, 1861. (Patron, Duke of Bedford; Tithe, 480*l*; Glebe, 65 acres; R.'s Inc. 600*l* and Ho; Pop. 885. Formerly C. of Crewkerne, Somerset, 1854, Long Melford, Suffolk, 1858. [20]

BALCHIN, Henry James.—C. of St. Paul's, Charlton, Kent. [21]

BALDERSTON, William, *Bainbridge, Bedale, Yorks.*—St. John's Coll. Cam. Scho. of, Sen. Opt. B.A. 1842, M.A. 1846; Deac. 1842 and Pr. 1843 by Bp of Rip. P. C. of Stalling Busk, Yorks, Dio. Rip. 1856. (Patron, V. of Aysgarth; P. C.'s Inc. 95*l*; Pop. 332.) Mast. of the Yoresbridge Gr. Sch. Yorks. Formerly P. C. of Lunds, Yorks, 1843–58. [22]

BALDEY, Frederick, *St. Simon's, Southsea.*—Deac. 1853 and Pr. 1854 by Bp of Chich. Min. of St. Simon's, Southsea. Formerly C. of Binsted and Shindon, Sussex, 1853, Fareham, Hants, 1856, and St. Jude's, Southsea, 1858. [23]

BALDOCK, Charles, *The Sandbank, Southill, near Biggleswade, Beds.*—St. John's Coll. Cam. B.A. 1838; Deac. 1840 and Pr. 1841 by Abp of Cant. C. of Southill and Old Warden, Beds. Formerly C. of Snargate, Kent, 1840–42, Heslerton, Yorks, 1842–48. [24]

BALDOCK, Richard, *Kingsnorth, near Ashford, Kent.*—St. John's Coll. Cam. B.A. 1829, M.A. 1832; Deac. 1830 by Bp of Lon, Pr. 1832 by Abp of Cant. R. of Kingsnorth, Dio. Cant. 1832. (Patron, Denne Denne, Esq; Tithe, 635*l*; Glebe, 21 acres; R.'s Inc. 655*l* and Ho; Pop. 416.) Rural Dean. [25]

BALDOCK, Richard, *Carlton-le-Moorlands, Newark, Lincolnshire.*—St. John's Coll. Cam. B.A. 1840; Deac. 1842 by Bp of Lin. Pr. 1843 by Abp of York. V. of Carlton-le-Moorlands, with Stapleford, Dio. Lin.

1858. (Patron, Lord Middleton; V.'s Inc. 170*l*; Pop. 588.) Formerly C. of Langtoft, Cottam and Cowlam, Yorks. [1]

BALDOCK, W., *Appledore, Staplehurst, Kent.*—C. of Appledore. [2]

BALDWIN, Alfred, *Tonge, Sittingbourne, Kent.*—Jesus Coll. Cam. B.A. 1831, M.A. 1835; Deac. and Pr. 1837. V. of Tonge, Dio. Cant. 1837. (Patron, Rev. A. Baldwin; Tithe—App. 552*l* 10*s*; Glebe, 7 acres; V. 205*l*; Glebe, 3 acres; V.'s Inc. 205*l*; Pop. 277.) [3]

BALDWIN, Charles, *St. Stephen's Vicarage, Norwich.*—King's Coll. Lond. 1st in 1st cl. Assoc. 1853; Deac. 1853 and Pr. 1854 by Bp of Win. V. of St. Stephen's, City and Dio. Nor. 1863. (Patrons, D. and C. of Nor; Glebe, 28 acres; V.'s Inc. 265*l* and Ho; Pop. 4128.) [4]

BALDWIN, Frederick St. Leger, *Bearstead, Maidstone, Kent.*—Queen's Coll. Ox. B.A. 1825. V. of Bearstead, Dio. Cant. 1849. (Patrons, D. and C. of Roch; Tithe—Apps. 120*l*, V. 182*l* 9*s* 6*d*; V.'s Inc. 204*l*; Pop. 638.) [5]

BALDWIN, Nathaniel Evanson.—Dub A.B; Deac. 1849 by Bp of Lich. Pr. 1850 by Bp of Herf. Formerly C. of Eardisland, Herefordshire. [6]

BALDWIN, Octavius de Leyland.—Brasen. Coll. Ox. B.A. 1860; Deac. 1860 and Pr. 1861 by Abp of York. Formerly C. of Flamborough, Yorks, 1860–62. [7]

BALDWIN, Thomas Rigbye, *Leyland, Preston.*—Sid. Coll. Cam. B.A. 1845; Deac. 1846, Pr. 1847. V. of Leyland, Dio. Man. 1852. (Patron, the present V; Tithe—App. 247*l*, Imp. 771*l* 18*s*; V. 972*l* 6*s*; Glebe, 44 acres; V.'s Inc. 1310*l* and Ho; Pop. 4534.) Surrogate. [8]

BALDWIN, William, *Mytholmroyd, near Halifax.*—St. Edm. Hall, Ox. M.A. 1847; Deac. 1842 and Pr. 1843 by Bp of Rip. P. C. of Mytholmroyd, Dio. Rip. 1846. (Patrons, the Crown and Bp alt; P. C.'s Inc. 164*l*; Pop. 3063.) [9]

BALDWIN, William Henry, *Northleach, Gloucester.*—Dub. A.B. 1861, A.M. 1864; Deac. 1866. C. of Northleach 1866. [10]

BALE, George, *Odcombe, near South Petherton, Somerset.*—Ch. Ch. Ox. B.A. 1814, M.A. 1816; Deac. 1815 and Pr. 1816 by Bp of Ox. R. of Odcombe, Dio. B. and W. 1836. (Patron, Ch. Ch. Ox; Tithe, 387*l*; Glebe, 50 acres; R.'s Inc. 487*l* and Ho; Pop. 652.) [11]

BALFOUR, William, *Spa, Gloucester.*—Magd. Coll. Ox. B.A. 1844, M.A. 1846; Deac. 1844, Pr. 1845. P. C. of St. Bartholemew's with St. Nicholas', Gloucester, Dio. G. and B. 1852. (Patrons, Trustees of Charities; Glebe, 40 acres; P. C.'s Inc. 200*l*; Pop. 2348.) Formerly Fell. of Magd. Coll. Ox. 1844–48. [12]

BALFOUR, Willoughby William Townley, *Burbage, Hinckley, Leicestershire.*—Dub. A.B; Deac. 1829 by Bp of Waterford, Pr. 1832 by Bp of Killaloe. R. of Aston-Flamville with Burbage, Dio. Pet. 1837. (Patroness, Countess Cowper; Tithe, 707*l*; Glebe, 107 acres; R.'s Inc. 908*l* and Ho; Pop. 1946.) [13]

BALL, Charles Richard, *Lincoln-street, Leicester.*—Ch. Coll. Cam. B.A. 1858, M.A. 1863; Deac. 1858 and Pr. 1859 by Bp of Lich. C. of St. John's, Leicester, 1864. Formerly C. of Trentham, Staffs, 1858, and Belgrave, Leic. 1861. [14]

BALL, Frederick, *St. Mary's, Hoxton, London N.*—Caius Coll. Cam. B.A. 1860, M.A. 1864; Deac. 1861 and Pr. 1862 by Bp of Rip. P. C. of St. Mary's Hoxton, Dio. Lon. 1865. (Patron, The Crown; P.C.'s Inc. 200*l*; Pop. 6300.) Formerly C. of Trinity, Huddersfield, 1861–65. [15]

BALL, Thomas Preston, *Egremont, Birkenhead.*—Dub. A.B. 1850, A.M. 1857; Deac. 1850 by Bp of Kilmore, Pr. 1852 by Bp of Tuam. P. C. of St. John's, Liscard, Dio. Ches. 1862. (Patrons, Trustees; Pop. 3221.) Formerly Asst. Chap. to the Troops, Athlone, 1851; C. of Clifton 1852; Miss. to Roman Catholics, Kinvarra, 1853; C. of St. Jude's, Liverpool, 1854, Sefton 1855. [16]

BALL, Thomas Hanly.—Dub. A.B. 1843, K.D.C. of Aberdeen; Deac. 1843, Pr. 1844. C. of Wimbledon; Dom. Chap. to the Earl of Crawford and Balcarres. Author, *Sermons*, 1847, 5*s*; *Loyalty and Industry*, 6*d*; *Pros and Cons, being a Digest and Impartial Analysis of all the principal Reasons that have been given, and Arguments used for and against National Education, with brief Remarks*, 1850, 4*s* 6*d*; *The Third Person of the Trinity* (a Sermon), 1853, 1*s*; *An Address on Sabbath Desecration*, 1854, 6*d*. [17]

BALL, Thomas Otto Derville.—Univ. Coll. Dur. B.A. 1851; Deac. 1851, Pr. 1852. Formerly C. of Lower Guiting and Wyck Risington. [18]

BALLANCE, Josiah Descarrieres, *Horsford Vicarage, Norwich.*—Trin. Coll. Cam. B.A. 1852; Deac. 1852, Pr. 1853. V. of Horsford, Dio. Nor. 1863. (Patron, Ld Ranelagh; Tithe, 101*l* 4*s*; Glebe, 145 acres; V.'s Inc. 250*l* and Ho; Pop. 665.) P. C. of Horsham, Dio. Nor. 1863. (Patron, Ld Ranelagh; P. C.'s Inc. 90*l* and Ho; Pop. 967.) Chap. to the Union of St. Faith's (salary 50*l*.) Formerly C. of St. John's, Peterborough, St. Mary's Great Warley, Essex. [19]

BALLARD, John, *Rock House, Washington, Hurstpierpoint, Sussex.*—Trin. Coll. Ox. B.A. 1836, M.A 1839; Deac, 1837, Pr. 1838. [20]

BALLARD J. H.—C. of St. Mary's Newington, Surrey. [21]

BALLEINE, John James, *St Heliers, Jersey.*—Pemb. Coll. Cam. Jun. Opt. B.A. 1846, M.A. 1851, B.D; Deac. 1846 and Pr. 1847 by Bp of Win. C. of St. Simon's, St. Heliers. Formerly C. of St. Helier's 1846–48; Chap in R.N. 1849–66. [22]

BALLEINE, Le Couteur, *St Mary's Rectory, St. Helier's, Jersey.*—Trin. Coll. Cam. B.A. 1850, M.A. 1853; Deac. 1851 by Bp of Ox. Pr. 1852 by Bp of Win. R. of St. Mary's, Jersey, Dio. Win. 1856. (Patron, the Governor; R.'s Inc. 120*l* and Ho; Pop. 1040.) Formerly C. of St. Martin's, Jersey. [23]

BALSHAW, Edward, *Norton, Stockton-on-Tees.*—St. John's Coll. Cam. B.A. 1858; Deac. 1858 by Bp of Dur. Mast. of the Gr. Sch. Norton, 1859. Formerly Asst. C. of St. Thomas's, Stockton-on-Tees, 1858–59. [24]

BALSTON, Charles, *Stoke Charity, Andover Road, Hants.*—Corpus Coll. Ox. B.A. 1831, M.A. 1834, B.D. 1841; Deac. 1834 by Bp. of Ox. and Pr. 1835 by Bp. of Roch. R. of Stoke Charity, Dio. Win. 1846. (Patron, Corpus Coll. Ox.; Tithe, 377*l* 2*s*.; Glebe, 18 acres; R.'s Inc. 387*l* and Ho; Pop. 130.) [25]

BALSTON, Edward, *Eton.*—King's Coll. Cam. Fell. of, D.D. Head Mast. of Eton Coll. [26]

BAMFORD, Robert, *Little Dewchurch, Ross.*—Trin. Coll. Cam. B.A. 1847, M.A. 1850; Deac. 1848, Pr. 1849. P. C. of Little Dewchurch, Dio. Herf. 1865. (Patrons, D. and C. of Herf; Tithe, 90*l*; Glebe, ½ acre; P. C.'s Inc. 90*l* and Ho; Pop. 322.) Formerly C. of Uttoxeter 1848–49, Norbury with Snelston 1849–50, Highworth 1850–54, Abbott's-Ann 1855–57, Mickleton 1857–65. [27]

BAMPFIELD, J. R. McW.—Chap. of H.M.S. "Lord Clyde." [28]

BAMPFIELD, John William Lewis.—Chap. of H.M.S. "Prince Consort," Malta, 1866. [29]

BAMPFIELD, Robert Lewis, *Thorverton, near Cullompton, Devon.*—Trin. Coll. Ox. B.A. 1842, M.A. 1844; Deac. 1842 and Pr. 1843 by Bp of Ex. C. of Thorverton 1864. Formerly C. of Fowey, 1847–55, Mevagissey, Cornwall, 1858–62, St. Ewe 1863. [30]

BAMPTON, John B.—Ch. Coll. Cam. B.A. 1839; Deac. 1841 and Pr. 1842 by Bp of Nor. Dom. Chap. to Ld Wynford. [31]

BANCKS, Gerard, *Woolborough, Newton Abbott, Devon.*—St. Peter's Coll. Cam. B.A. 1854; Deac. 1855 and Pr. 1856 by Bp of Ches. C. of Woolborough. [32]

BAND, Charles Edward, *Combe-Rawleigh, Honiton, Devon.*—St. John's Coll. Cam. B.A. 1823, M.A. 1828; Deac. and Pr. 1825 by Bp of Ex. R. of Combe-Rawleigh, Dio. Ex. 1826. (Patron, E. S. Drewe, Esq; Tithe, 305*l*; Glebe, 40 acres; R.'s Inc. 350*l* and Ho; Pop. 299.) Formerly P. C. of Sheldon, Devon, 1826–66. [33]

BAND, Charles Edward, *Langton-on-Swale, Northallerton, Yorks.*—Ex. Coll. Ox. B.A. 1851; Deac. 1851 and Pr. 1852 by Bp of Ex. R. of Langton-on-Swale, Dio. Rip. 1856. (Patron, Hon. Capt. Duncombe; R.'s Inc. 324*l* and Ho; Pop. 239.) [1]

BANDINEL, James, *Emley, Huddersfield.*—Wad. Coll. Ox. B.A. 1836, M.A. 1844. R. of Emley, Dio. Rip. 1862. (Patron, Earl of Scarborough; R.'s Inc. 450*l*; Pop. 1450.) [2]

BANFATHER, Henry, *Sprowston, near Norwich.*—Jesus Coll. Cam. B.D. 1828; Deac. 1817, Pr. 1818. P. C. of Sprowston, Dio. Nor. 1818. (Patron, D. and C. of Nor; Tithe—App. 730*l*; P. C.'s Inc. 153*l*; Pop. 1407.) R. of Beeston St Andrew (no Ch.) Norfolk, Dio. Nor. 1849. (Patron, the present R; Tithe—App. 1*l* 10*s*; R. 190*l*; Glebe, 1 acre; R.'s Inc. 200*l*; Pop. 37.) [3]

BANGHAM, Thomas Alfred, *Christ Church Parsonage, Lichfield.*—Ch. Coll. Cam. B.A. 1846, M.A. 1849; Deac. 1846, Pr. 1847. P. C. of Ch. Ch. Lich. Dio. Lich. 1847. (Patron, Bp of Lich; P. C.'s Inc. 250*l* and Ho; Pop. 726.) Rural Dean. Formerly C. and P. C. of Great Wyrley 1847. Author, *Confirmation Questions on the Catechism*—to be answered on paper at home. [4]

BANGOR, The Right Rev. James Colquhoun CAMPBELL, Ld Bp of Bangor, *The Palace, Bangor, Carnarvonshire.*—Trin. Coll. Cam. Sen. Opt. and 2nd cl. Cl. Trip. and B.A. 1836, M.A. 1839; Deac. 1837 and Pr. 1838 by Bp of Llan. Consecrated Bp of Bangor 1859. (Episcopal jurisdiction, the Isle of Anglesey, and portions of the counties of Carnarvon, Montgomery and Merioneth; Gross Inc. of See, 4200*l*; Pop. 195,390; Acres, 985,946; Deaneries, 13; Benefices, 132; Curates, 60; Church sittings, 55,417.) His Lordship was formerly R. of Merthyr-Tydfil, Glamorganshire, 1844–59: Rural Dean of the Upper Deanery of Llandaff, Northern Division, 1844–57; Hon. Can. of Llandaff Cathl. 1852–57; Archd. of Llandaff 1857–59. Author, Charges and occasional Sermons. [5]

BANHAM, Daniel Beales Redfarn, 60, *Regent-street, Cambridge.*—Caius Coll. Cam. Fell. of, 6th Wrang, B.A. 1862, M.A. 1865; Deac. 1863, Pr. 1864. C. of St. Andrew's the Great, Cambridge, 1866. Formerly Math. Mast. in Bishop Stortford Gr. Sch. [6]

BANHAM, William, *Worsborough Dale, near Barnsley.*—Sid. Coll. Cam. Scho. of, B.A. 1855; Deac. 1855 by Abp of York, Pr. 1856 by Bp of Carl. P. C. of St. Thomas's, Worsborough Dale, Dio. York, 1860. (Patrons, Crown and Abp of York alt; P. C's Inc. 100*l* and Ho; Pop. 3500.) Formerly C. of St. Paul's, Sheffield, 1855–58. [7]

BANISTER, Edward, *Besthorpe, Attleborough, Norfolk.*—Deac. 1847 and Pr. 1848 by Bp of Roch. V. of Besthorpe, Dio. Nor. 1857. (Patron, Earl of Winterton; V.'s Inc. 250*l*; Pop. 554.) Formerly C. of Chiddingfold, Surrey. [8]

BANISTER, E. D., *Brighouse, Yorks*—C. of Brighouse. [9]

BANISTER, James Dawson, *Pilling, Fleetwood, Lancashire*—St. Bees; Deac. 1821, Pr. 1822. P. C. of Pilling, Dio. Man. 1825. (Patrons, E. Hornby, Esq. Rev. Dr. Gardner and H. Gardner, Esq; Tithe—Imp. 676*l*; Glebe, 33 acres: P. C.'s Inc. 105*l* and Ho; Pop. 1388.) Author, several Papers in *The Zoologist* and other Periodicals. [10]

BANISTER, John R., *Alton, Hants.*—Wor. Coll. Ox. B.A. 1810, M.A. 1814; Deac. 1810, Pr. 1811. P. C. of West Worldham, Hants, Dio. Win. 1828. (Patron, Win. Coll; Tithe—Imp. 140*l* 10*s*; P. C.'s Inc. 46*l*; Pop. 89.) R. of Kelvedon-Hatch, Dio. Roch. 1832. (Patron, E. Slocock, Esq; Tithe, 430*l*; Glebe, 28 acres; R.'s Inc. 467*l* and Ho; Pop. 454.) [11]

BANISTER, William, *St James's Mount, Liverpool*—Wad. Coll. Ox. B.A. 1838; Deac. 1839, Pr. 1840. Chap. of St. James's Cemetery, Liverpool, 1851. [12]

BANKES, Eldon Surtees, *Corfe Castle, Dorset.*—Univ. Coll. Ox. 3rd cl. Lit. Hum. B.A. 1852, M.A. 1864: Deac. 1853, Pr. 1854. R. of Corfe Castle, Dio. Salis. 1854. (Patrons, Trustees of H. J. P. Bankes, Esq; Glebe, 70 acres; R.'s Inc. 680*l* and Ho; Pop. 1966.) Formerly C. of Stapleton, near Bristol. [13]

BANKES, Frederick, *St Helen's College, Southsea.*—Magd. Hall. Ox. B.A. 1847, M.A. 1852 B.D. 1860; Deac. 1849 and Pr. 1851 by Bp of Wor. Principal of St. Helen's College. Formerly Lusby Scho. Magd. Hall, Ox. 1843; Head Mast. of the Dioc. Gr. Sch. Grahamstown, Cape of Good Hope, 1853–55; Principal of St. Andrew's Coll. Grahamstown, 1855–60; Head. Mast. of Mountswood Sch. Taunton, 1860-66. Author, *The Worship of the Body; being a few plain words about a plain duty; Cultus Animæ, or an Arraying of the Soul, being Prayers and Meditations which may be used in Church before and after Service, adapted to the days of the week; The Work of the Ministry* (an Ordination Sermon at St. George's Cathedral, Grahamstown), 1855; *Our Warning and our Work* (two sermons preached in St. George's Cathedral, Grahamstown, on occasion of the decease of Bp Armstrong), 1856; *The Observance of Holy Days, a duty in the English Church* (a sermon preached in St. Andrew's College Chapel, Grahamstown). [14]

BANKS, Edward, *Ibsley Rectory, Ringwood, Hants.*—New Inn Hall, Ox. 2nd cl. Maths. B.A. 1852; Deac. 1854 by Abp of Cant, Pr. 1855 by Bp of Win. R. of Ergham, Dio. York, 1860. (Patrons, Exors. of the late Col. Grimston; R.'s Inc. 22*l*; Pop. 27.) C. of Fordingbridge with Ibsley, Hants, 1860; Dom. Chap. to the Earl of Normanton. Formerly C. of Hyde District 1854–56. Fordingbridge 1856-60. [15]

BANKS, George Wilson, *Worth, Crawley, Sussex.*—Corpus Coll. Cam. B.A. 1852, M.A. 1855; Deac, 1853 and Pr. 1854 by Bp of Herf. R. of Worth, Dio. Chich. 1858. (Patron, present R; R.'s Inc. 610*l* and Ho; Pop. 1600.) [16]

BANKS, John Waters, *Portsmouth.*—St. Bees; Deac. 1849 and Pr. 1850 by Bp of Rip. Chap. to Convict Prison, Portsmouth, 1863. Formerly C. of St. Mary's, Barnsley, 1849, St. Thomas's, Brampton, Derbyshire, 1852, St. George the Martyr's, Southwark, 1855; Asst. Chap. Convict Prison, Portsmouth, 1856-63. Author, Tracts—*The Shunamite, Cane Polisher*, etc. [17]

BANKS, Robert John, *St. Catherine's, near Doncaster.*—St. Cath. Coll. Cam. B.A. 1845, M A. 1853; Deac. 1845 and Pr. 1846 by Abp of York. P. C of Loversall, Dio. York, 1847. (Patron, V. of Doncaster; Tithe, 10*l*; Glebe, 27 acres; P. C.'s Inc. 103*l*; Pop. 175.) Formerly C. of Brodsworth, Yorks. 1845–53. [18]

BANKS, Samuel, *Cottenham, near Cambridge.*—St. John's Coll. Cam. B.A. 1830, M.A. 1837; Deac. 1832 and Pr. 1833 by Abp of York. R. of Cottenham, Dio. Ely, 1851. (Patron, Bp of Ely; Tithe, 770*l*; Glebe, 133 acres; R.'s Inc. 980*l* and Ho; Pop. 2415.) Official of the Archd. of Ely; Rural Dean; Surrogate. Formerly Chap. to the British Merchants at Canton. [19]

BANKS, Samuel Horatio, *Dullingham, Newmarket, Cambs.*—Trin. Hall, Cam. LL.B. 1821, LL D. 1842; Deac. 1823, Pr. 1828. V. of Dullingham, Dio. Ely, 1828. (Patroness, Mrs. Pigott; Glebe, 87 acres; V.'s Inc. 148*l* and Ho; Pop. 800.) P. C. of Cowling, Suffolk, Dio. Nor. 1829. (Patron, Trin. Hall, Cam: Tithe—Imp. 924*l*; Glebe, 30 acres; P. C.'s Inc. 100*l*; Pop. 842.) [20]

BANKS, William, *Coleshill, Warwickshire.*—St. Cath. Coll. Cam. B.A, 1844, M.A. 1848; Deac. 1844 and Pr. 1846 by Bp of Rip. Head. Mast. of the Gr. Sch. Coleshill; P. C. of Water Orton, Aston, Dio. Wor. (Patrons, Trustees; P. C.'s Inc. 115*l*.) [21]

BANKS, William Thomas, *Mauritius.*—Dub. A.B. 1860; Deac. 1860 by Bp of Lich. [22]

BANNATYNE, Charles, *Aldham, Halstead, Essex.*—Ball. Coll. Ox. B.A. 1827, M.A. 1830. R of Aldham, Dio. Roch. 1840. (Patron, Bp of Roch; Tithe—Imp. 19*l* 11*s* 6*d*, R. 412*l* 6*s* 5*d*; R.'s Inc. 435*l* and Ho; Pop. 406.) [23]

BANNER, George John, *Roby Parsonage, near Liverpool.*—Brasen. Coll. Ox. B.A. 1845, M.A. 1847; Deac. 1847 and Pr. 1848 by Bp of Ches; P. C. of St. Bartholomew's, Roby, Dio. Ches. 1853. (Patron, the Earl of Derby; P. C.'s Inc. 200*l* and Ho; Pop. 715.) [1]

BANNER, Thomas, *Holy Innocents' Parsonage, Liverpool.*—P. C. of Holy Innocents', Liverpool, Dio. Ches. 1854. (Patrons, Trustees; P.C.'s Inc. 300*l* and Ho.) [2]

· **BANNERMAN, Edward,** *Natland Parsonage, near Kendal.*—Dub. A.B. 1852, A.M. 1865; Deac. 1855 by Bp of Derry, Pr. 1856 by Bp of Limerick. P. C. of Natland, Dio. Carl. 1866. (Patron, V. of Kendal; Glebe, 78 acres; P. C.'s Inc. 121*l* and Ho; Pop. 276.) Formerly C. of Listowel 1855, All Saints', Southampton, 1858, Alvanley, Cheshire, 1858, Heversham, Westmoreland, 1859-66. [3]

BANNERMAN, James Macleod.—Dub. A.B. 1854; Deac. 1856 and Pr. 1857 by Bp of Ches. Formerly C. of St. Andrew's and St. Barnabas', Liverpool. [4]

BANNING, Benjamin, *Wellington Vicarage, Shropshire.*—Trin. Coll. Ox. B.A. 1829, M.A. 1833; Deac. 1831 and Pr. 1832 by Bp of Ches. V. of Wellington with Eyton R. Dio. Lich. 1841. (Patron, T. C. Eyton, Esq; Wellington, Tithe—App. 560*l* 5*s* 9*d*, Imp. 1484*l*, V. 647 5*s* 9*d*; Glebe, 40 acres; Eyton, Tithe—App. 24*l* 19*s* 9*d*, Imp. 24*l* 19*s* 9*d*, R. 148*l* 6*s* 6*d*; V.'s Inc. 900*l* and Ho; Pop. Wellington 7690, Eyton 131.) Surrogate. Author, *Loyalty and Religion the Safeguard of the Nation* (a Sermon, 1848); *The Groundless Claims of the Papacy* (a Sermon, 1851); *The Groundless Claims of the Papacy re-asserted* (a Sermon), 1851. [5]

BANNING, Charles Henry, 16, *Lincoln's-inn-Fields, London, W.C.*—Dub. A.B. 1858, A.M. 1861; Deac. 1857 and Pr. 1858 by Bp of Dur. Association Secretary of the London Society for Promoting Christianity among the Jews, 1862. Formerly C. of Gateshead 1857–59; Asst. Chap. of St. Thomas's Church, Newcastle-on-Tyne, 1859–62. [6]

BANNISTER, Frederick, *Stanstead Vicarage, Ware, Herts.*—Sid. Coll. Cam. B.A. 1860; Deac. 1860 and Pr. 1861 by Bp of Ely. C. in sole charge of Stanstead Abbotts 1866. Formerly C. of Trinity, Bedford, 1860. [7]

BANNISTER, John, *St. Day, Truro, Cornwall.*—Dub. A.B. 1844, A.M. 1858; Deac. 1844 and Pr. 1845 by Bp of Lich. P. C. of Holy Trinity, St. Day, Dio. Ex. 1857. (Patron, V. of Gwennap; P. C.'s Inc. 200*l* and Ho; Pop. 3800.) Formerly P. C. of Christ Church, Belper, 1844–57. Author, *Benefits* (a Sermon), 1850. [8]

BANTON, Peake, *Duston, Northampton.*—V. of Duston, Dio. Pet. 1863. (Patroness, Viscountess Palmerston; V.'s Inc. 400*l* and Ho; Pop. 1162.) Author, *Sevenfold Mystery—Sermons on* 1 *Tim.* 1856; *Shellbound, a Tale of Macclesfield Forest in Verse,* 1859; and various Tracts. [9]

BARBER, Edward, *Rotherham.*—St. Bees; Deac. 1866 by Bp of Lin. Pr. 1867 by Abp of York. C. of Rotherham 1866. [10]

BARBER, Henry William, *Redland, Bristol.*—Queen's Coll. Ox. B.A. 1864; Deac. 1865 and Pr. 1866 by Bp of G. and B. C. of Trinity, St. Philip and St. Jacob's, Bristol, 1865. [11]

BARBER, John, *Bierley, near Bradford, Yorks.*—St. John's Coll. Cam. B.A. 1823, M.A. 1826. V. of Bierley, Dio. Rip. 1839. (Patron, W. Wilson, Esq; V.'s Inc. 176*l* and Ho; Pop. 3822.) Formerly Chap. to Bp of Gibraltar 1842. Author, *A Lecture on the Importance of the Occasional Offices of the Church of England,* 1845. [12]

BARBER, Richard, *Shalford, near Guildford.*—St. John's Coll. Cam. B.A. 1835, M.A. 1836; Deac. 1835 and Pr. 1836 by Bp of Lich. Formerly P. C. of Heage, Derbyshire, 1842–55; R. of Dorsington, Glouc. 1855–66. [13]

BARBER, Thomas, *Elmsett Rectory, Suffolk.*—Clare Coll. Cam. Fell. of, 1st cl. Cl. Trip. B.A. 1852, M.A. 1855; Deac. 1855 and Pr. 1857 by Bp of Ely. R. of Elmsett, Dio. Ely, 1864. (Patron, Clare Coll. Cam; Tithe, comm. 630*l*; Glebe, 50 acres; R.'s Inc. 700*l* and Ho; Pop. 459.) Formerly Head Mast. of Grassendale Park Sch. [14]

BARBER, William, *St. John's Parsonage, Leicester.*—Corpus Coll. Cam. B.A. 1834, M.A. 1837; Deac. 1835 and Pr. 1836 by Bp of Lin. P. C. of St. John's, Leicester, Dio. Pet. 1854. (Patron, Bp. of Pet; Pop. 4700.) [15]

BARBUT, Stephen, *Chichester.*—Mert. Coll. Ox. B.A. 1806, M.A. 1814; Deac. and Pr. 1806. Preb. of Ferring in Chich Cathl. 1841. Formerly P. C. of St. John's, Chichester, 1813–59. [16]

BARCLAY, Henry Alexander, *Ipswich.*—Ch. Ch Ox. B.A. 1854, M.A. 1857; Deac. 1857 and Pr. 1858 by Bp of Ox. Sub-Mast. of Queen Eliz. Gr. Sch. Ipswich. Formerly Asst. Mast. in Trin. Coll. Glenalmond. [17]

BARCLAY, John, *Runcorn, Cheshire.*—Ch. Ch. Ox. 1st cl. Lit. Hum. B.A. 1838, M.A. 1841; Deac. 1840, Pr. 1841. V. of Runcorn, Dio. Ches. 1845. (Patrons, D. and C. of Ch. Ch. Ox; Tithe—Apps. 1702*l* 9*s* 3*d*, Imp. 46*l* 1*s* 3*d*, V. 195*l* 7*s* 6*d*; Glebe, 30 acres; V.'s Inc. 400*l* and Ho; Pop. 9200.) [18]

BARCLAY, Robert Charles Colquhoun, *Bleasdale, Lancaster.*—Dub. A.B. 1845, A.M. 1850; Deac. 1846 and Pr. 1847 by Bp of Lich. P. C. of Bleasdale, Dio. Man. 1864. (Patron, V. of Lancaster; P. C.'s Inc. 80*l* and Ho; Pop. 272.) Formerly C. of Stalmine, Lancashire. [19]

BARCLAY, William, *Bishop-street, Portland-square, Bristol.*—Madg. Hall, Ox. B.A. 1849, M.A. 1857; Deac. 1850 and Pr. 1851 by Bp of Lin. C. of St. Barnabas', Bristol, 1862. Formerly C. of Evedon and Ewerby, Lincolnshire, 1851–52, Westbury, Wilts, 1852–60, Horfield, Bristol, 1860–62. [20]

BARDSLEY, George Waring, *St. Ann's, Manchester.*—Wor. Coll. Ox. B.A. 1864; Deac. 1864 and Pr. 1865 by Bp of Man. C. of St. Ann's, Manchester. [21]

BARDSLEY, James, *Manchester.*—Deac. 1833 and Pr. 1834 by Abp of York. R. of St. Ann's, Manchester, Dio. Man. 1857. (Patron, Bp of Man; R.'s Inc. 550*l*; Pop. 1416.) Author, *Introduction of Christianity into Britain, with a Sketch of the Early English Church,* Longmans; *Popery a Novelty; Rome the Mystic Babylon of the Apocalypse* (Tracts); *Mind your Rubrics,* 1*s* 6*d*. [22]

BARDSLEY, James Waring, *Greenwich, S.E.*—P. C. of St. Peter's, Greenwich, Dio. Lon. 1866. (Patrons, Trustees.) [23]

BARDSLEY, John Waring, *St. John's Parsonage, Bootle, Liverpool.*—Dub. A.B. 1858; Deac. 1858 and Pr. 1859 by Bp of Ches. P. C. of St. John's, Bootle. Formerly C. of Sale 1858, St. Luke's, Liverpool, 1859; Cler. Sec. Islington Protestant Institute 1861; Min. of St. Paul's Hulme, Manchester, 1863. [24]

BARDSLEY, Joseph, 79, *Pall Mall, London, S.W.*—Queens' Coll. Cam. B.A. 1849, M.A. 1858; Deac. 1849 and Pr. 1850 by Bp of Man. Sec. to the London Dioc. Home Mission; Lect. at St. Marylebone's. Formerly P. C. of St. Silas', Liverpool, 1857. [25]

BARDSLEY, Richard Waring, *Bootle, near Liverpool.*—C. of St. John's, Bootle. [26]

BARDSLEY, Samuel, *Battersea, London, S.W.*—Dub. A.B. 1853; Deac. 1851 and Pr. 1853 by Bp of Rip. P. C. of Ch. Ch. Battersea, Dio. Win. 1860. (Patron, V. of Battersea; Pop. 3500.) Formerly Sec. of Soc. of Irish Ch. Missions 1855. [27]

BARFF, Albert, *North Moreton, Wallingford, Berks.*—Pemb. Coll. Ox. B.A. 1852, M.A. 1855; Deac. 1852 and Pr. 1853 by Bp of Ex. V. of North Moreton, Dio. Ox. 1868. (Patron, Archd. of Berks; Tithe—App. 240*l*, Glebe, 23 acres; V. 105*l*, Glebe, 13 acres; V.'s Inc. 134*l* and Ho; Pop. 352. Formerly Chap. to Cuddesdon Theol. Coll. [28]

BARHAM, Richard Harris Dalton, *Lolworth, St. Ives, Hunts.*—Oriel Coll. Ox. B.A. 1837; Deac. 1839 by Bp of Llan, Pr. 1839 by Bp of Ely. R. of

Lolworth, Dio. Ely, 1840. (Patron, Richard Daintree, Esq; Tithe, 205*l*; Glebe, 22 acres; R.'s Inc. 225*l*; Pop. 133.) Author, *The Life and Works of Theodore Hook*, 1840. [1]

BARHAM, William, 3, *Alma Terrace, Parker's Piece Cambridge.*—Pemb. Coll. Cam. B.A. 1849, M.A. 1852; Deac. 1851 and Pr. 1852 by Bp of Ely. Chap. to Cambridge Borough Prison 1852; C. of St. Matthew's, Cambridge, 1865. Formerly C. of Chesterton, Cambs. 1851–53. Author, *A Parting Admonition to a Prisoner on Leaving Gaol*, 1854, 2*d*. [2]

BARING-GOULD, Baring, *Francis-road, Birmingham.*—Corpus Coll. Cam. B.A. 1865; Deac. 1866 and Pr. 1867 by Bp. of Wor. C. of St. George's, Edgbaston. [3]

BARING-GOULD, Sabine, *Horbury, Wakefield.*—C. of Horbury. [4]

BARKER, Alfred Greeley, *Sherfield Rectory, Basingstoke, Hants.*—Trin. Coll. Ox. B.A. 1857, M.A. 1860; Deac. 1860, Pr. 1861. R. of Sherfield-on-Lodon, Dio. Win. 1863. (Patron, George Barker, Esq; Tithe, 684*l*; Glebe, 35 acres; R.'s Inc. 744*l*; Pop. 693.) Formerly C. of St. Mary's, Warwick, and Easthampstead, Berks. [5]

BARKER, Alleyne Higgs, *Rickmansworth, Herts.*—Ch. Coll. Cam. B.A. 1829, M.A. 1832; Deac. 1829, Pr. 1830. V. of Rickmansworth, Dio. Roch. 1853. (Patron, Bp of Roch; Tithe—Apps. 1406*l* 18*s*, V. 608*l* 2*s*; Glebe, 108 acres; V.'s Inc. 570*l* and Ho; Pop. 3327.) Formerly R. of Wouldham, Kent, 1831-53. [6]

BARKER, Arthur Alcock, *East Bridgeford, Notts.*—Magd. Coll. Ox. B.D. 1853; Deac. 1843 by Bp of Ox. Pr. 1844 by Bp of Wor. R. of East Bridgeford, Dio. Lin. 1860. (Patron, Magd. Coll. Ox; R.'s Inc. 752*l* and Ho; Pop. 1080.) Formerly P. C. of St. Michael's-at-Thorn, Norwich, 1849–53. [7]

BARKER, C. A., *Chesterton, Newcastle-under-Lyne.*—C. of Chesterton; Dom. Chap. to Marquis of Queensbury. [8]

BARKER, Edward Algernon, *Ludlow.*—Trin. Coll. Cam. M.A; Deac. 1838 and Pr. 1839 by Bp of Herf. [9]

BARKER, E. S., *Heston, Hounslow, W.*—C. of Heston. [10]

BARKER, Frederick, *Nicholas-street, Chester.*—C. of Trinity, Chester; Min. Can. in Ches. Cathl. [11]

BARKER, Frederick Mills Raymond, *Bisley, near Stroud.*—Oriel. Coll. Ox. B.A. 1837, M.A. 1840; Deac. 1839, Pr. 1841. Fell. of Oriel Coll. Ox. [12]

BARKER, George Beevor, *Hurstmonceux, Hurst Green, Sussex.*—Wor. Coll. Ox. B.A. 1850; Deac. 1851 and Pr. 1852 by Bp of Lich. C. of Hurstmonceux. [13]

BARKER, George Llewellyn, *Watlington, Downham Market.*—Ch. Coll. Cam. B.A. 1839, M.A. 1843; Deac. 1841, Pr. 1842. R. of Watlington, Dio. Nor. 1860. (Patron, Gilbert Barker, Esq; Pop. 588.) [14]

BARKER, Henry, *Weare, Somerset.*—Trin. Coll. Cam. B.A. 1828, M.A. 1829; Deac. 1828 and Pr. 1829 by Abp of Cant. V. of Weare, Dio. B. and W. 1837. (Patrons, D. and C. of Bristol; Tithe—App. 40*l*, Imp. 75*l*, V. 386*l* 11*s*; Glebe, 37 acres; V.'s Inc. 420*l* and Ho; Pop. 680.) [15]

BARKER, Henry Charles Raymond, *Daglingworth, Cirencester.*—Mert. Coll. Ox. B.A. 1827, M.A. 1832; Deac. 1829, Pr. 1830. R. of Daglingworth, Dio. G. and B. 1841. (Patron, Ld Chan; Tithe, 261*l* 3*s* 6*d*; Glebe, 64 acres; R.'s Inc. 322*l* and Ho; Pop. 355.) [16]

BARKER, Henry Christopher, *Hexham, Northumberland.*—Caius Coll. Cam. Jun. Opt. 1840, B.A. 1840, M.A. 1845; Deac. 1845 and Pr. 1846 by Bp of Lin. R. of Hexham, Dio. Dur. 1866. (Patron, W. B. Beaumont, Esq; R.'s Inc. 139*l*; Pop. 6479.) Formerly C. of Gainsborough 1843–46; P. C. of Morton with East Stockwith 1846–62; Chap. of Huntingdon Episcopal Chapel, West Stockwith, 1849. Author, *A Visitation Sermon*, 1854. [17]

BARKER, John Collier, *Granville Lodge, Hinckley, Leicester.*—Jesus Coll. Ox. B.A. 1856, M.A. 1859; Deac. 1857 by Bp of Pet. Pr. 1858 by Bp of Man. P. C. of Trinity, Hinckley, Dio. Pet. 1865. (Patron, Thomas Frewen, Esq; P. C.'s Inc. 100*l*; Pop. 1862.) Formerly C. of Hoby with Rotherby 1862, Coventry 1860–62, Hinckley 1857–59. [18]

BARKER, John Ross, *Green-street, Enfield Highway, Middlesex, N.*—Dub. A.B. 1864; Deac. 1866 by Bp of Lon. C. of St. James's, Ponder's End, Enfield. [19]

BARKER, John T., *High Cross Parsonage, Ware, Herts.*—Trin. Coll. Cam. B.A. 1848, M.A. 1851; Deac. 1849 and Pr. 1850 by Bp of Win. P. C. of High Cross, Dio. Roch. 1864. (Patron, Rev. C. Puller; P. C.'s Inc. 150*l* and Ho; Pop. 819.) Formerly C. of Egham, Surrey, 1850–52, and St. Peter's, Pimlico, 1853–60; British Chap. at Dresden 1861–62. Author, occasional sermons. [20]

BARKER, Joseph, *Eardisland, Pembridge, Herefordshire.*—Ch. Coll. Cam. B.A. 1844, M.A. 1847; Deac. 1844 by Bp of Dur, Pr. 1845 by Bp of Wor. V. of Eardisland, Dio. Herf. 1867. (Patron, Bp of Wor; Tithe, 339*l* 11*s*; Glebe, 2½ acres; V.'s Inc. 350*l* and Ho; Pop. 894.) Formerly C. of Berkeswell, Warwickshire. [21]

BARKER, Joseph Henry, *Hereford.*—St. John's Coll. Cam. B.A. 1833, M.A. 1836; Deac. 1834 and Pr. 1835 by Bp of Herf. Chap. to the Hereford Infirmary 1843; Chap. to the Hereford County Gaol 1849. Author, *Puseyism according to the best Authorities*, 1837, 4*d*; *The Ages to Come, or the Future Destiny of our Globe*, 1853, 6*d*; *Apostolic Missions*, 1858, 4*s* 6*d*. [22]

BARKER, Matthias, *Warden Lodge, Cheshunt, Herts.*—Clare Hall Cam. B.A. 1844, M.A. 1847; Deac. 1846, Pr. 1847. P. C. of Trinity, Waltham Cross, Dio. Roch. 1866. (Patron, V. of Cheshunt; P. C.'s Inc. 140*l*; Pop. 2029.) Formerly C. of Kenilworth 1846, Barton-Latimer 1851, Bishop's Hatfield 1852, Holy Trinity, Tonbridge Wells, 1854; and Asst. Chap. Hon. E. I. Co.'s service, Peshawur, Punjab, 1855. [23]

BARKER, Ralph, *Pagham, near Chichester.*—St. Peter's Coll. Cam. B.A. 1821; Deac. 1821 and Pr. 1822 by Bp of Nor. V. of Pagham, Dio. Chich. 1850. (Patron, Abp of Cant; Tithe,—Imp. 1311*l* 12*s* 1*d*, V. 300*l*; V.'s Inc. 305*l* and Ho; Pop. 988.) Rural Dean of Chichester 1858. Author, *The Church's Safety in the Hour of Temptation* (a Sermon); *The Spiritual Life* (a Sermon); Occasional Sermons, Pamphlets, and Reviews; Co-Editor of *The Protestant Guardian*, 1827–29; Co-Editor of *The Quarterly Educational Magazine*, 2 vols. Home and Colonial School Society, Gray's-inn-road, 1847–49. [24]

BARKER, Richard Watts, *Norwich.*—St. Bees; Deac. 1848 and Pr. 1849 by Bp of Nor. C. of St. Martin's-at-Palace, Norwich. Formerly C. of Walpole St. Andrew, Norfolk. [25]

BARKER, Thomas, *Thirkleby, Thirsk, Yorks.*—V. of Thirkleby, Dio. York, 1804. (Patron, Abp of York; Tithe—App. 286*l* 2*s*, V. 207*l* 10*s* 3*d*; V.'s Inc. 225*l* and Ho; Pop. 300.) P. C. of Kilburn, near Easingwold, Dio. York, 1804. (Patron, Abp of York; Tithe—App. 670*l* 17*s*; P. C.'s Inc. 100*l*; Pop. 700.) [26]

BARKER, Thomas, *Revesby Parsonage, Boston, Lincolnshire.*—Queen's Coll. Ox. B.A. 1848, M.A. 1852; Deac. 1851 by Bp of Lon. Pr. 1856 by Bp of Roch. P. C. of Revesby, Dio. Lin. 1867. (Patron, J. B. Stanhope, Esq., M.P; P. C.'s Inc. 200*l* and Ho; Pop. 579.) Formerly C. of Broomfield 1857; Tut. of Codrington Coll. Barbados, 1852–4; C. of Wallasea, near Liverpool, 1854 56, Ware, Herts, 1856–57, Roding Aythorpe 1861, Aston, Rotherham, 1863, Gleadless, Sheffield, 1866. Author, *Plain Sermons preached in Parish Churches*, 1858, 6*s* 6*d*; *Strictures on Maurice's Doctrine of Sacrifice, deduced from the Scriptures*, 1858, 2*s* 6*d*; *The Canticles pointed for Anglican Chants*, 1863; *Letter to Archbishop of York on the* *fundamental principle of Anglican Chanting*, 1864; *Lecture on Penny Readings*, 1866; *Musical Fragments*, Novello, 1865. [1]

BARKER, Thomas Childe, *Spelsbury, Enstone, Oxon.*—Ch. Ch. Ox. B.A. 1850, M.A. 1853; Deac. 1851 by Bp of Ox. Pr. 1852 by Bp of Lich. V. of Spelsbury, Dio. Ox. 1856. (Patron, Ch. Ch. Ox; Glebe, 128 acres; V.'s Inc. 250*l* and Ho; Pop. 516.) Formerly Student of Ch. Ch. Ox. [2]

BARKER, Thomas Francis, *Thornton Rectory, Chester.*—Brasen. Coll. Ox. B.A. 1832, M.A. 1835; Deac. 1833 and Pr. 1834 by Bp of Ches. R. of Thornton-in-the-Moors, Dio. Ches. 1849. (Patrons, Hulme's Trustees; Tithe, 480*l*; Glebe, 120*l*; R.'s Inc. 600*l*; Pop. 943.) Formerly C. of Farndon 1833, St. George's, Everton, Liverpool, 1836–38; P. C. of Farndon 1838–44; Lect. of Wrexham 1839–42; C. of Whitchurch, Salop, 1844, Marbury 1848. [3]

BARKER, William, *Mitcheldean, Gloucestershire.*—P. C. of Trinity, Forest of Dean, Dio. G. and B. 1866. (Patron, the Crown; P. C.'s Inc. 150*l* and Ho; Pop. 3218.) [4]

BARKER, William, *Golcar, Huddersfield.*—St. Bees; Deac. 1855 and Pr. 1856 by Bp of Ches. P. C. of St. John's, Golcar, Dio. Rip. 1863. (Patron, V. of Huddersfield; P. C.'s Inc. 300*l* and Ho; Pop. 5110.) Formerly C. of Hindley 1856, Ch. Ch. Bradford, 1857, and Huddersfield 1858–63. [5]

BARKER, William, 99, *New Bond-street, London, W.*—Wor. Coll. Ox. B.A. 1861, M.A. 1863; Deac. 1862 and Pr. 1863 by Bp. of Lon. C. of Hanover Ch. Regent-street, 1862; Chap. to Royal London Ophthalmic Hospital, Moorfields, 1866. [6]

BARKER, William Chichester, 36, *Cecil-street, Carlisle.*—St. John's Coll. Cam. Sen. Opt. B.A. 1866; Deac. 1866 by Bp of Carl. C. of Ch. Ch. Carlisle, 1866. [7]

BARKER, William Gibbs, *The Green, Southgate, London, N.*—St. John's Coll. Cam. Sen. Opt. in Math. Trip B.A. 1833, M.A. 1836; Deac. 1835, Pr. 1837. Formerly C. of Combe St. Nicholas, near Chard, 1835–37, Abbey Ch. Shrewsbury, 1837–38, St. Mary's, Shrewsbury, 1838–39; Head Mast. of Walsall Gr. Sch. 1839–44; P. C. of Trinity, Matlock, 1844–53; Prin. of Ch. Miss. Children's Home 1853–63; P. C. of Trinity, New Barnet, 1864–66. Author, *Friendly Strictures on the Horæ Apocalypticæ*, 1847. [8]

BARKLEY, John Charles, *Little Melton, near Norwich.*—Emman. Coll. Cam. B.A. 1835, M.A. 1838; Deac. 1835 and Pr. 1836 by Bp of Roch. V. of Little Melton, Dio. Nor. 1839. (Patron, Emman. Coll. Cam; Tithe—Imp. 172*l* 6*s*, V. 95*l*; Glebe, 31 acres; V.'s Inc. 116*l*; Pop. 370.) [9]

BARKWAY, Frederick, *Bungay, Suffolk.*—Deac. 1824, Pr. 1825. C. of Trinity, Bungay. [10]

BARKWORTH, Shadwell Morley, *Reading.* Wor. Coll. Ox. B.A. 1842, M.A. 1845; Deac. 1843, Pr. 1844. P. C. of Grey Friars, Reading, Dio. Ox. 1864. (Patrons, Trustees; Pop. 2210.) Formerly P. C. of Southwold, Suffolk, 1860–64. [11]

BARLEE, W., *Caldecote, Baldock, Herts.*—C. of Caldecote. [12]

BARLEE, W. H., *Farmborough, near Bath.*—C. of Farmborough. [13]

BARLOW, Charles G. T., *Stanmer, Lewes.*—R. of Stanmer with Falmer, Dio. Chich. 1859. (Patrons, Abp of Cant. and Earl of Chich. alt; R.'s Inc. 150*l* and Ho; Pop. 660.) [14]

BARLOW, Charles Henry, *Willaston, near Chester.*—Dub. A.B. 1858, A.M. 1862; Deac. 1861 and Pr. 1862 by Bp of Ches. P. C. of Willaston, Dio. Ches. 1866. (Patron, D. Graham, Esq; P. C.'s Inc. 100*l*; Pop. 937.) Formerly C. (sole charge) of Willaston, Raby, and Thornton-Hough, all three villages in the parish of Neston. [15]

BARLOW, Edward William, *Cleveland Villa, Bathwick, Bath.*—Ex. Coll. Ox. B.A. 1834, M.A. 1836, D.D. 1865; Deac. 1837 and Pr. 1838 by Bp of Lon. Formerly C. of Rochford, Essex. Author, *A Brief Manual on Writing Latin*, 1834; *A Pamphlet on Church Music*, 1839; *A Treatise on the State of the Soul, with Reference to the Dead to this Mortal Life*, 1843; *Notes relative to the Church of England, Romanism, &c.* 1846; *Short Portions relative to Servants*, 1846; *Brief Considerations for the House of Mourning*, 1846; *The Apocrypha, its Use and Abuse*, 1850; *Twenty-five Useful Remarks for the Benefit of Young Clergymen*; *Index to the Rubric*, 1850; *A Few Testimonies relative to Lay Baptism*, 1850; *Sermons on Useful Subjects*; *Church Antiquity*; *St. Augustin's Reception-Testimony*, 1851; *Clerical Manual (2 Parts)* 1852; *The Mourner Met*, 1852; *Debt a Consideration for Young and Old*; *On the Registry of the Church of England*; *A Compilation on Dilapidations*, 1853; *Sermon on the Earthquake*, 1853; *Hymns in Use from the Book of Common Prayer*; *An Abridgment of a Proposed Index of Authorities*; Articles in *The Church Magazine*, *The Churchman*, *The Churchman's Sunday Companion*, *The British Magazine*, *Notes and Queries*, etc. [16]

BARLOW, George Hilaro Philip, *Sydenham, S.E.*—Brasen. Coll. Ox. Hulme Exhib. 3rd cl. Lit. Hum. B.A. 1862, M.A. 1865; Deac. 1863 and Pr. 1864 by Bp of Lon. C. of St. Bartholomew's, Sydenham. [17]

BARLOW, Henry, *Pitsmoor, Attercliffe, Sheffield.*—St. John's Coll. Cam. B.A. 1832, M.A. 1836; Deac. 1832 and Pr. 1833 by Bp of Lich. P. C. of Pitsmoor, Dio. York, 1845. (Patrons, the Crown and Abp of York, alt; P. C.'s Inc. 300*l*; Pop. 8921.) [18]

BARLOW, Henry Masterman, *Burgh, Woodbridge, Suffolk.*—Wad. Coll. Ox. B.A. 1834; Deac. 1834, Pr. 1835. R. of Burgh, Dio. Nor. 1850. (Patron, Frederick Barne, Esq; Dunwich, Suffolk; Tithe—Imp. 5*l* 4*s* 6*d*, R. 384*l* 15*s* 6*d*; Glebe, 11 acres; R.'s Inc. 368*l* and Ho; Pop. 299.) [19]

BARLOW, John, *Kensington Palace, London, W.*—M.A. F.R.S. Chap. to the Household at Kensington Palace. [20]

BARLOW, John James, *St. Mark's Parsonage, Gloucester.*—St. John's Coll. Cam. B.A. 1838, M.A. 1850; Deac. 1840 and Pr. 1841 by Bp of Lich. P. C. of St. Mark's, City and Dio. of Glouc. 1846. (Patron, Bp of G. and B; P. C.'s Inc. 175*l* and Ho; Pop. 2555.) Chap. of St. Margaret's with St. Mary Magdalen's, City and Dio. of Glouc. 1849. (Patrons, Charity Trustees; stipend, 70*l*.) [21]

BARLOW, John Mount, *Ewhurst Rectory, near Guildford, Surrey.*—Wor. Coll. Ox. B.A. 1836, M.A. 1840; Deac. 1838 and Pr. 1839 by Bp of Nor. R. of Ewhurst, Dio. Win. 1845. (Patron, Ld Chan; Tithe, 739*l*; Glebe, 60 acres; R.'s Inc. gross 772*l*, nett 462*l* and Ho; Pop. 881.) [22]

BARLOW, Peter.—Queen's Coll. Ox. B.A. 1830; Deac. 1831, Pr. 1832. [23]

BARLOW, Robert J., *Rudby-in-Cleveland, Stokesley, Yorks.*—V. of Rudby-in-Cleveland with Middleton P. C. and East Rounton P. C. Dio. York, 1831. (Patron, Lord Falkland; Rudby, Tithe—Imp. 246*l* 19*s*; Middleton, Tithe—Imp. 321*l* 6*s*, P. C. 5*l*; East Rounton, Tithe—Imp. 104*l* 17*s* 10*d*, P. C. 6*l* 4*s*; V.'s Inc. 190*l* and Ho; Pop. Rudby 925, Middleton 108, East Rounton 114.) [24]

BARLOW, Thomas Wotton, *Little Bowden (Northants), near Market Harborough.*—Wad. Coll. Ox. 3rd cl. Lit. Hum. and B.A. 1822, M.A. 1829; Deac. 1824 and Pr. 1825 by Bp of Ex. R. of Little Bowden, Dio. Pet. 1843. (Patron, the present R; Tithe, 4*l*; Glebe, 150 acres; R.'s Inc. 425*l* and Ho; Pop. 220.) [25]

BARLOW, William, *Toft Trees, Fakenham, Norfolk.*—Jesus Coll. Cam. B.A. 1833, M.A. 1836; Deac. 1835 and Pr. 1836 by Bp of Nor. V. of Toft-Trees, Dio. Nor. 1861. (Patron, Marquis of Townshend; V.'s Inc. 200*l*; Pop. 64.) [26]

BARLOW, William Hagger, 3, *Melcombe Villas, Sydenham-road, Bristol.*—St. John's Coll Cam. Scho. Prizeman and Exhib. of, 3rd in 2nd cl. Cl. Trip. Jun. Opt. 2nd cl. Theol. Trip. 2nd in 1st cl. Moral Sci. Trip. Carus Univ. Prize and B.A. 1857; Deac. 1858 and Pr. 1859 by Bp of G. and B. P. C. of St. Bartholomew's,

Bristol, Dio. G. and B. 1861. (Patrons, Trustees; P. C.'s Inc. 230*l* and Ho; Pop. 2500.) Formerly C. of St. James's, Bristol, 1858–61. [1]

BARMBY, James, *Durham.*—Univ. Coll. Ox. B.A. 1845, M.A. 1848, B.D. 1855; Deac. 1846 and Pr. 1847 by Bp of Rip. Prin. of Bp Hatfield's Hall, Durham. [2]

BARNACLE, Henry, *Knutsford, Cheshire.*—St. John's Coll. Cam. B.A. 1858; Deac. 1858 and Pr. 1860 by Bp of Man. V. of Knutsford, Dio. Ches. 1864. (Patrons, Lds of certain Manors, alt; V.'s Inc. 300*l*; Pop. 2898.) Formerly P. C. of Ringway, Cheshire, 1862–64. [3]

BARNARD, Charles Cary, *Brocklesby Rectory, Ulceby, Lincolnshire.*—Ex. Coll. Ox. B.A. 1850, M.A. 1852; Deac. 1851 and Pr. 1852 by Bp of Pet. R. of Brocklesby with Kirmington V. Dio. Lin. 1863. (Patron, Earl of Yarborough; Glebe, 104 acres; R.'s Inc. 450*l* and Ho; Pop. 640.) Formerly C. of Ashby-de-la-Zouch, 1851–53; R. of Ruckland and Maidenwell V. Lincolnshire, 1853–55. [4]

BARNARD, Charles James, *Bigby, Brigg, Lincolnshire.*—Emman. Coll. Cam. B.A. 1830, M.A. 1833. R. of Bigby, Dio. Lin. 1833. (Patron, R. C. Elwes, Esq; Tithe, 739*l* 1*s* 3*d*; Glebe, 28 acres; R.'s Inc. 771*l* and Ho; Pop. 250.) V. of Roxby with Risby V. Barton-on-Humber, Dio. Lin. 1833. (Patron, R. C. Elwes, Esq; Tithe—Imp. 5*l* 6*s* 4*d*, V. 436*l* 0*s* 10*d*; Glebe, 122 acres; V.'s Inc. 626*l*; Pop. 348.) [5]

BARNARD, Henry John, *Yatton (Somerset), near Bristol.*—St. John's Coll. Cam. B.A. 1845, M.A. 1856; Deac. 1845 and Pr. 1846 by Bp of B. and W. V. of Yatton, Dio. B. and W. 1846. (Patron, Bp of B. and W; Tithe—Comm. 399*l* 10*s*, 11 acres of Glebe, besides Ho and Garden; V.'s Inc. 426*l*; Pop. 1450.) Patron of the P. C. of Cleeve and Ken; Preb. of Wells; Rural Dean. Formerly C. of Compton Martin, Somerset, 1846. [6]

BARNARD, Markland, *Colney, near St. Albans, Herts.*—Trin. Coll. Cam. B.A. 1826, M.A. 1829; Deac. 1826 by Bp of Lin. Pr. 1826 by Bp of Lon. P. C. of Colney St. Peter, Dio. Roch. 1826. (Patroness, Countess of Caledon; Glebe, 9½ acres; P. C.'s Inc. 120*l* and Ho; Pop. 792.) V. of Ridge, Herts, near Barnet, Dio. Roch. 1832. (Patroness, Countess of Caledon; Tithe—Imp. 323*l* 12*s*, V. 242*l* 5*s*; Glebe, ½ acre; V.'s Inc. 242*l*; Pop. 300.) Dom. Chap. to the Countess of Caledon; Rural Dean of Barnet 1867. [7]

BARNARD, Mordaunt, 11, *Brunswick-square, Brighton.*—Ch. Coll. Cam. B.A. 1817, M.A. 1833; Deac. 1819, Pr. 1820. Surrogate. Formerly V. of Great Amwell, Herts, 1826–64, and R. of Little Bardfield, Essex, 1845–64. [8]

BARNARD, Mordaunt Roger, *Margaretting, Ingatestone, Essex.*—Ch. Coll. Cam. Jun. Opt. B.A. 1851; Deac. 1852 and Pr. 1853 by Bp of Roch. V. of Margaretting, Dio. Roch. 1863. (Patron, Rev. Mordaunt Barnard; Tithe, 191*l* 5*s*; Glebe, 6 acres; V.'s Inc. 191*l* 5*s* and Ho; Pop. 483.) Formerly British Chap. at Christiania; P. C of Oakengates, Shropshire. Author, *Sketches of Eminent English Authors*, Christiania, 1862; *Sport in Norway, and where to find it*; *Life of Thorwaldsen*; *Signe's History*; and *Gathered Flowers*. [9]

BARNARD, Thomas M. K., *Holdenhurst, near Christchurch.*—Ex. Coll. Ox. B.A. 1852, M.A. 1861; Deac. 1854 and Pr. 1855 by Bp of G. and B. C. of Holdenhurst 1856. [10]

BARNARD, William, *Alveston, Stratford-on-Avon.*—V. of Alveston, Dio. Wor. 1856. (Patron, R Hampton-Lucy, Esq; V.'s Inc. 220*l*; Pop. 850.) [11]

BARNARD, William Henry.—Ex. Coll. Ox. B.A. 1857; Deac. 1857 and Pr. 1858 by Bp of Lich. Late C. of Handsworth, Birmingham. [12]

BARNARDISTON, Arthur, *Metheringham, Sleaford.*—V. of Metheringham, Dio. Lin. 1863. (Patron, Marquis of Bristol; Tithe, 10*s*; Glebe, 262 acres; V.'s Inc. 470*l* and Ho; Pop. 1532.) [13]

BARNE, Charles Mark, *Tiverton, Devonshire.*—Sid. Coll. Cam. Blundell's Fell. for 10 years, B.A. 1825, M.A. 1828, S.T.B. 1835; Deac. 1826 by Bp of Roch, Pr. 1827 by Bp of B. and W. [14]

BARNE, Henry, *Faringdon, Berks.*—Ex. Coll. Ox. B.A. 1835, M.A. 1837; Deac. 1836, Pr. 1837. V. of Faringdon, Dio. Ox. 1851. (Patrons, Simeon's Trustees; Tithe—Imp. 546*l*, V. 74*l* 16*s* 9*d*; Glebe, 85 acres; V.'s Inc. 260*l* and Ho; Pop. 3365.) Surrogate; Dom. Chap. to the Earl of Radnor. [15]

BARNES, Barrington Syer, *Rectory, Chignal St. James, Chelmsford.*—St. John's Coll. Cam. B.A. 1857; Deac. 1857 by Abp of York, Pr. 1859 by Bp of Pet. R. of Chignal St. James and St. Mary with Mashbury R, Dio. Roch. 1863. (Patron, T. Barnes, Esq; Tithe, comm. 486*l*; Glebe, 54 acres; R.'s Inc. 530*l*; Pop. 378.) Formerly C. of Lythe, Yorks, 1857, Medbourne with Holt, Leic. 1858, Hundon, Suffolk, 1860. [16]

BARNES, Brooke Cremer, *Hawkhurst, Staplehurst, Kent.*—Jesus Coll. Cam. B.A. 1853, M.A. 1858; Deac. 1856 and Pr. 1858 by Bp of Nor. C. of Hawkhurst 1865. Formerly C. of Rotherfield, Sussex. [17]

BARNES, Charles, *Digby, Sleaford, Lincolnshire.*—Corpus Coll. Ox. B.A. 1863, M.A. 1866; Deac. 1863 and Pr. 1864 by Bp of Pet. C. of Digby 1866. Formerly C. of Harrowden 1863, and Cottingham, Northants, 1865. [18]

BARNES, E. J., *Lowestoft.*—P. C. of Ch. Ch. Lowestoft, 1867. (Patrons, Trustees; P. C.'s Inc. 150*l*.) [19]

BARNES, Francis, *Trinity Parsonage, Boo-street, Plymouth.*—Jesus Coll. Cam. B.A. 1847, M.A. 1851; Deac. 1848 and Pr. 1849 by Bp of Rip. P. C. of Trinity, Plymouth, Dio. Ex. 1851. (Patron, V. of St. Andrew's, Plymouth; P. C.'s Inc. 160*l* and Ho; Pop. 3809.) Formerly C. of Ch. Ch. Bradford, Yorks, 1848–49, and St. James's, Taunton, 1849–51. Author, *Twelve Sermons*, Longmans, 1860, 2*s* 6*d*. [20]

BARNES, Frederick, *Tideford, St. Germans, Cornwall.*—P. C. of Tideford, Dio. Ex. 1864. (Patron, P. C. of St. Germans; P. C.'s Inc. 102*l* and Ho; Pop. 913.) [21]

BARNES, George, 9, *Park-place, Grove-road, Mile-end, London, N.*—Univ. Coll. Dur. Found. Scho. B.A. 1852, M.A. 1861; Deac. 1852 and Pr. 1853 by Bp of Rip. C. of St. Luke's Mission (St. Simon Zelotes', Bethnal Green) 1865. Formerly C. of St. John the Baptist's, Hoxton. [22]

BARNES, Henry Frederick, *Bridlington, Yorks.*—Clare Hall, Cam. B.A. 1841, M.A. 1844; Deac. 1841 by Bp of B. and W. Pr. 1842 by Bp of Ely. P. C. of Bridlington, Dio. York, 1849. (Patrons, Simeon's Trustees; Tithe—Imp. 368*l* 2*s*; P. C.'s Inc. 250*l* and Ho; Pop. 3560.) Surrogate. Formerly C. of Doulting 1841–43, St. Luke's, Chelsea, 1843–44, St. James's, Ryde, Isle of Wight, 1844–49. Author, Two Visitation Sermons, 1852–53, 1*s*. each. [23]

BARNES, Herbert, *Alwington Rectory, Bideford.*—Ch. Ch. Ox. Stud. of, M.A. 1854; Deac. 1855, Pr. 1856. R. of Alwington, Dio. Ex. 1861. (Patron, Rev. J. R. Pine-Coffin; Tithe, 243*l*; Glebe, 70 acres; R.'s Inc. 310*l* and Ho; Pop. 320.) Formerly C. of Paignton 1855–57; Dom. Chap. to Bp of Madras and Chap. H. M.'s E. I. Service 1857–61. [24]

BARNES, Ismay.—Magd. Coll. Cam. Sen. Opt. B.A. 1857, M.A. 1860; Deac. 1858 and Pr. 1859 by Bp of Roch. Formerly C. of Great Berkhampstead, Herts, 1858–60. [25]

BARNES, James Alexander, *Gilling, near York.*—Trin. Coll. Cam. B.A. 1821, M.A. 1824; Deac. 1822, Pr. 1823. R. of Gilling, Dio. York. (Patron, Trin. Coll. Cam; R.'s Inc. 630*l* and Ho; Pop. 401.) Preb. of Barnby, York Cathl. 1857. Formerly Fell. of Trin. Coll. Cam. [26]

BARNES, Jeremiah, *Tissington, Ashbourn, Derbyshire.*—P. C. of Tissington, Dio. Lich. 1864. (Patron, Sir W. Fitz-Herbert, Bart; P. C.'s Inc. 100*l*; Pop. 406.) [27]

BARNES, Jocelyn, *Geddington, near Kettering, Northants.*—Wor. Coll. Ox. B.A. 1866; Deac. 1866 by Bp of Pet. C. of Geddington with Newton 1866. [28]

BARNES, Joseph, 2, *Darlington-street, Cheetham-hill, Manchester.*—St. Bees; Deac. 1862 and Pr. 1863 by Bp of Man. C. of St. Mark's, Cheetham-hill. Formerly C. of St. Michael's, Blackburn, 1862–64. [1]

BARNES, K. H., *Cattistock, Dorchester.*—R. of Cattistock, Dio. Salis. 1860. (R.'s Inc. 500*l* and Ho; Pop. 510.) [2]

BARNES, Ralph, *Christ Church, Oxford.*—Ch. Ch. Ox. B.A. 1833, M.A. 1835. V. of Ardington, near Wantage, Dio. Ox. 1839. (Patron, Ch. Ch. Ox; Tithe—Apps. 558*l* 7*s* 2*d*, Imp. 2*l* 12*s*, V. 139*l* 7*s* 11*d*; V.'s Inc. 165*l*; Pop. 854.) V. of Bampton, 3rd Portion, Dio. Ox. 1844. (Patrons, D. and C. of Ex; Tithe—Apps. 142*l* 16*s*; the Three V.'s of Bampton, 919*l* 10*s*; 3rd V.'s Inc. 610*l*; Pop. 968.) [3]

BARNES, Reginald Henry, *St. Mary Church, Torquay.*—Ch. Ch. Ox. Stud. of, M.A; Deac. 1854 and Pr. 1855 by Bp of Ex. V. of St. Mary Ch. Torquay with Coffinswell, Dio. Ex. 1860. (Patrons, D. and C. of Ex; Tithe, 310*l*; Glebe, 2 acres; V.'s Inc. 360*l* and Ho; Pop. 3425.) Dom. Chap. to Bp. of Ex. Preb. of Ex. 1865. Formerly C. of Kenwyn, Heavitree, Topsham, Torwood. Editor of the *Exeter Diocesan Calendar.* [4]

BARNES, Richard Nelson, *Kingsclere (Hants). near Newbury.*—Pemb. Coll. Cam. B.A. 1830, M.A. 1833; Deac. 1835 and Pr. 1836 by Bp of Ex. V. of Kingsclere. Dio. Win. 1849. (Patron, Lord Bolton; Tithe—Imp. 1850*l* and 78½ acres of Glebe, V. 444*l*; Glebe, 4 acres; V.'s Inc. 448*l* and Ho; Pop. 1600.) Surrogate. [5]

BARNES, Richard William, *Probus Sanctuary, Grampound, Cornwall.*—Queen's Coll. Ox. B.A. 1834, M.A. 1841; Deac. 1836, Pr. 1837. V. of Probus, Dio. Ex. 1849. (Patron, Bp of Ex; Tithe—App. 544*l* 5*s*, Imp. 328*l* 10*s*, V. 548*l* 18*s*; Glebe, 33 acres; V.'s Inc. 600*l* and Ho; Pop. 1450.) Preb. of Ex. 1853. [6]

BARNES, T., *Loxton Rectory, Axbridge, Somerset.*—R. of Loxton, Dio. B. and W. 1865. (Patron, the present R; R.'s Inc. 380*l* and Ho; Pop. 154.) [7]

BARNES, William, *Winterbourne Came, Dorset.*—St. John's Coll. Cam. B.D; Deac. 1847. Pr. 1848. R. of Winterbourne-Came with Winterbourne-Farringdon, Dio. Salis 1862. (Patron, Capt. S. W. Dawson Damer, M.P; Tithe, 270*l*; R.'s Inc. 270*l*; Pop. 248) Formerly C. of Whitcombe 1847. Author, *Poems*, last ed. 3 vols. 14*s* 6*d*; *Philological Grammar*, 9*s*; *T I W, or Roots and Stems of the English Language*, 5*s*; *Anglo-Saxon Delectus*, 2*s* 6*d*; *Notes on Ancient Britain*, 3*s*; *Views of Labour and Gold*, 3*s*; *Grammar and Glossary of Dorset Speech*; *Elements of Perspective*; *School Geography*; etc. [8]

BARNES, William, *Worthington, Ashby-de-la-Zouch.*—Literate; Deac. 1860 and Pr. 1861 by Bp of Lich. P. C. of Worthington, Dio. Pet. 1868. (Patron, present P. C; P. C.'s Inc. 105*l*; Pop. 1172.) Formerly C. of Elvastone, Derbyshire, 1860–62. [9]

BARNES, William, *Hasland Parsonage, Chesterfield.*—St. Bees; Deac. 1858 and Pr. 1859 by Abp of York. C. of Hasland 1862. Formerly C. of Rotherham 1858–62. [10]

BARNES, William Lawson, *Knapton, North Walsham, Norfolk.*—R of Knapton, Dio. Nor. 1837. (Patrons, Lord Suffield and the Master of Peter Ho. Cam. alt; Tithe—App. 6*l*, R. 475*l*; R.'s Inc. 500*l*; Pop. 310.) [11]

BARNES, William Miles, *Monkton Rectory, near Dorchester.*—St. John's Coll. Cam. B A. 1863; Deac. 1865 and Pr. 1866 by Bp of Salis. R. of Winterbourne Monkton, Dio. Salis. 1866. (Patron, Earl of Ilchester; Tithe, 125*l*; Glebe, part let for 65*l*; R.'s Inc. 200*l* and Ho; Pop. 85.) Formerly C. of Tincleton, Dorchester, 1865. [12]

BARNETT, Henry Martyn, *The Hearne, Charlton Kings, Cheltenham.*—Caius Coll. Cam. 2nd cl. Moral Sci. Trip. B.A. 1866; Deac. 1866 by Bp of G. and B. C. of Charlton Kings 1866. [13]

BARNETT, James Lewis, *Hessle, near Hull.*—Magd. Hall, Ox. B.A. 1859, M.A. 1865; Deac. 1859 by Bp of Rip. Pr. 1860 by Abp of York. C. of Hessle 1864. Formerly C. of Christ Ch. Hull 1859–61, Hanwell 1862–64. [14]

BARNETT, Robert Leighton, 72, *Ryland-road, Edgbaston, Birmingham.*—St. Peter's Coll. Cam. B.A; Deac. 1859 and Pr. 1860 by Bp of Ox. Sen. C. of St. Martin's, Birmingham, 1866. [15]

BARNETT, Samuel Whitehorne, *Towersey, (Bucks), near Thame, Oxon.*—Dub. A.B. 1820; Deac. 1822 and Pr. 1823 by Bp of Glouc. V. of Towersey, Dio. Ox. 1847. (Patrons, Trustees of the late Richard Barry Slater, M.D; Glebe, 60 acres; V.'s Inc. 110*l* and Ho; Pop. 450.) [16]

BARNEY, John, *Rattlesden, Bury St. Edmunds.*—R. of Rattlesden, Dio. Ely, 1861. (Patrons, Trustees; R.'s Inc. 930*l* and Ho; Pop. 1120.) [17]

BARNICOAT, Humphry Lowry, *Landrake Vicarage, St. Germans, Cornwall.*—St. John's Coll. Cam. 4th Sen. Opt. thrice 1st cl. Prizeman, B.A. 1843, M.A. 1846; Deac. 1846 and Pr. 1847 by Bp of Ex. V. of Landrake with St. Erney, Dio. Ex. 1866. (Patron, Earl of Mount Edgcumbe; Tithe, comm. 230*l*; Glebe, 50 acres; V.'s Inc. 305*l* and Ho; Pop. Landrake 714, St. Erney 79.) Formerly C. of Ladock 1846, and Penryn and St. Gluvias, Cornwall, 1847–48; C. of Beeralston and Beer Ferris, Devon, 1849–66. [18]

BARNSDALE, John Gorton, *Farnworth, Warrington.*—Dub. A.B. 1847, A.M. 1852; Deac. 1848, Pr. 1849. C. of Farnworth. [19]

BARNWELL, Charles Barnwell, *Mileham (Norfolk), near Swaffham.*—Caius Coll. Cam B.A. 1823; Deac. 1824 and Pr. 1825 by Bp of Nor. R. of Mileham, Dio. Nor. 1825. (Patron, the present R; Tithe, 650*l*; Glebe, 18 acres; R.'s Inc. 677*l* and Ho; Pop. 550.) [20]

BARNWELL, Edward Lowry, *Melksham House, Melksham, Wilts.*—Ball. Coll. Ox. 1st cl. Maths. Hon. 4th cl. Lit. Hum. B A. 1834, M.A. 1836; Deac. 1836, Pr. 1837. Formerly Head. Mast. of Ruthin Sch. 1830; C. of Malvern Wells 1836–39. Author, *An Account of the Perrot Families*, J. Russell Smith, Lond. 1867, 12*s* [21]

BARNWELL, John Clement, *Holford Rectory, Bridgwater.*—Wor. Coll. Ox. B.A. 1858, M.A. 1860; Deac. 1859 and Pr. 1861 by Bp. of Rip. C. of Holford. Formerly C. of St. Mary's, Leeds. [22]

BARNWELL, Lowry, *Deeping Fen, Spalding, Lincolnshire.*—Incumb. of the Don. of St. Nicholas, Deeping Fen, Dio. Lin. 1855. (Patrons, Exors. of the late W. Stevenson, Esq; Incumb's Inc. 210*l*; Pop. 1180.) [23]

BARON, John, *Upton Scudamore, Warminster, Wilts.*—Queen's Coll. Ox. B.A. 1838, M.A. 1841. R. of Upton Scudamore, Dio. Salis. 1850. (Patron, Queen's Coll. Ox; Tithe—App. 55*l*, Imp. 58*l* and 23½ acres of Glebe, R. 490*l*; Glebe, 22½ acres; R.'s Inc. 511*l* and Ho; Pop. 381.) [24]

BARON, William Joseph, *Hungerford, Berks.*—Queen's Coll. Ox. Hon. 4th cl. Math. et Phys. and B.A. 1850, M.A. 1857; Deac. 1851 and Pr. 1852 by Bp of Ox. C. of Hungerford 1854, and Chap. of Hungerford Union 1856. [25]

BARR, Ninian Hosier, *The Abbey, Romsey.*—St. Cath. Coll. Cam. B.A. 1863; Deac. 1863 and Pr. 1864 by Bp of Win. C. of Abbey Ch. of Romsey. [26]

BARR, John, *Wenden-Lofts, Saffron Walden.*—R. of Wenden-Lofts with Elmdon V. Dio. Roch. 1862. (Patron, Rev. R. Wilkes; R.'s Inc. 350*l* and Ho; Pop. 792.) [27]

BARRETT, Alfred, *Carshalton House, Surrey.*—Wor. Coll. Ox. B.A. 1842, M.A. 1845, D.D. 1865; Deac. 1842 and Pr. 1843 by Bp of Salis. Private Chap. Carshalton House grounds. Author, *Little Arthur's Latin Primer*, 1*s*; *Latin Exercises*, 3*s*. 6*d*; *Essays on Ancient Art Education*; *On the Advantages of a Decimal System* (read at the Social Science Congress, Liverpool), 1858. [28]

BARRETT, Benjamin, *Simonburn, Hexham.*—Bp Hatfield's Hall, Dur. Licen. in Theol; Deac. 1864 and Pr. 1866 by Bp of Dur. C. in sole charge of Simonburn 1866. Formerly C. of Southwick 1864–66. [29]

BARRETT, Henry, *Pelton, Fence Houses, Durham.*—Pemb. Coll. Cam. B.A. 1828, M.A. 1836; Deac.

1840 and Pr. 1840 by Bp of Dur. P. C. of Pelton, Dio. Dur. 1842. (Patron, P. C. of Chester-le-Street; P. C.'s Inc. 300*l* and Ho; Pop. 4344.) Surrogate, 1842; J. P. for co. Durham. Formerly of the Inner Temple 1836-40; C. of Gateshead 1840. [1]

BARRETT, Henry Alfred, *Chedgrave, Loddon, Norfolk.*—R. of Chedgrave, Dio. Nor. 1853. (Patron, Sir William B. Proctor, Bart. Langley Park, Norfolk; Tithe 221*l* 10*s*; Glebe 6 acres; R.'s Inc. 231*l*; Pop. 357.) P. C. of Langley, near Loddon, Dio. Nor. 1853. (Patron, Sir T. B. Proctor Beauchamp, Bart; Tithe—Imp. 400*l*; P. C.'s Inc. 68*l*; Pop. 316.) Dom. Chap. to Earl Waldegrave. [2]

BARRETT, James Michaelmas, *Dunholme, near Lincoln.*—Pemb. Coll. Ox. B.A. 1851; Deac. and Pr. 1853 by Bp. of Roch. V. of Dunholme, Dio. Lin. 1858. (Patron, Bp of Lin; V.'s Inc. 98*l*; Pop. 453.) Formerly C. of Willingdale-doe and Shellow-Bowells, Essex. [3]

BARRETT, John Casebow, *St. Mary's Parsonage, Birmingham.*—Ch. Ch. Ox. B.A. 1833, M.A. 1837; Deac. 1834 by Bp of B. and W. Pr. 1835 by Abp of York. P. C. of St. Mary's District Parish, Birmingham, Dio. Wor. 1837. (Patrons, Trustees; P. C.'s Inc. 400*l* and Ho; Pop. 7023.) Author, *God's Claims upon Youth's Obedience*, 1838; *National Education*, 1838; *The Christian Patriot's Duty* (a Sermon), 1839; *Minister's Trials*, 1846; *Death and the Resurrection* (Funeral Sermons), 1847; *Ministerial Caution* (Anniversary Sermon), 1848; *The Bible Burnt* (a Sermon), 1848; *Sermon on the death of Queen Adelaide*, 1849; *Papal Aggression*, 1850; *Romanism Hostile to Intellectual Advancement* (a Lecture), 1850; Sermons and Lectures, Controversial, Charitable, etc. contributed to various publications; *Church Hymns*, 1855. [4]

BARRETT, Richard Arthur Francis, *Stour-Provost, Blandford, Dorset.*—King's Coll. Cam. B.A. 1835, M.A. 1838, B.D. 1850; Deac. 1842 and Pr. 1848 by Bp of Lin. R. of Stour-Provost, with Todber, Dio. Salis. 1858. (Patron, King's Coll. Cam; Stour-Provost, Tithe, 100*l*; Glebe, 23 acres; R.'s Inc. 780*l* and Ho; Pop. Stour-Provost 889, Todber 122.) Sen. Fell. of King's Coll. Cam. Author, *Synopsis of Biblical Criticisms*, 20*s*. [5]

BARRETT, Thomas, *Stone, Staffs.*—St. John's Coll. Cam. B.A. 1854; Deac. 1854 and Pr. 1855 by Bp of Lich. Chap. of the Union, and C. of Ch. Ch. Stone. [6]

BARRETT, Tufnell Samuel, *St. George's Parsonage, Barrow-in-Furness, Lancashire.*—Ch. Ch. Ox. B.A. 1856, M.A. 1859; Deac. 1857, Pr. 1858. P. C. of St. George's, Barrow-in-Furness, Dio. Carl. 1861. (Patron, Duke of Devonshire; P. C.'s Inc. 189*l* and Ho; Pop. 16,000.) Formerly Asst. C. of St. John's and St. Nicholas', Hereford, 1857-58; P. C. of Rusland, Lancashire, 1858-60. [7]

BARRETT, William, *Saintbury, near Broadway, Glouc.*—Magd. Coll. Ox. B.A. 1823, M.A. 1826; Deac. 1826 and Pr. 1827 by Bp of Salis. R. of Saintbury, Dio. G. and B. 1851. (Patron, James Roberts West, Esq. Alscot, near Stratford-upon-Avon; Tithe, 196*l* 4*s*; Glebe, 115 acres; R.'s Inc. 415*l* and Ho; Pop. 121.) [8]

BARRINGTON, Hon. Lowther John, *Watton-at-Stone, Hertford.*—Oriel Coll. Ox. B.A. 1825, M.A. 1829; Deac. and Pr. 1830 by Bp of Lin. R. of Watton-at-Stone, Dio. Roch. 1850. (Patron, Abel Smith, Esq; Tithe, 676*l*; Glebe, 70 acres; R.'s Inc. 744*l* and Ho; Pop. 864.) Chap. to Bp of Roch; Rural Dean. Author, *Lectures*; *Child's Preacher*. [9]

BARROW, Christopher Brome, 15, *Marlborough Buildings, Bath.*—Caius Coll. Cam. Jun. Opt. 2nd cl. Cl. Trip. B.A. 1834, M.A. 1837; Deac. 1837 by Bp of Lin. Pr. 1838 by Bp of Nor. Formerly R. of Barwell, Leic. 1853-65. [10]

BARROW, George Martin, *Mistley, Manningtree, Essex.*—Trin. Coll. Cam. B.A. 1838; Deac. 1839 and Pr. 1840 by Bp of Roch. C. of Mistley 1865. Formerly C. of Ulcombe, Kent. [11]

BARROW, George Neale, *West-Kington, Chippenham.*—Univ. Coll. Ox. B.A. 1830, M.A. 1833; Deac. 1831 by Bp of Chich. Pr. 1832 by Bp of Llan. R. of West-Kington, Dio. G. and B. 1855. (Patron, Bp of G. and B; Tithe, 553*l* 14*s*; Glebe, 65 acres; R.'s Inc. 620*l* and Ho; Pop. 395.) Hon. Can. of Bristol 1844. Formerly C. of St. John the Baptist's, Bristol, 1831, and R. of same, 1834; V. of St. Nicholas', Bristol, 1840; Rural Dean of Bristol 1841; Ex. Chap. to Monk, Bp of G. and B. 1840. [12]

BARROW, George Stammers, *Thorpe-next-Haddiscoe, Loddon, Norfolk.*—St. John's Coll. Cam. B.A. 1826, M.A. 1833; Deac. 1833 and Pr. 1834 by Bp of Nor. R. of Thorpe-next-Haddiscoe, Dio. Nor. 1844. (Patrons, Ld Chan. and Ld Calthorpe alt; Tithe, 164*l* 16*s* 8*d*; Glebe, 15 acres; R.'s Inc. 195*l*; Pop. 84.) [13]

BARROW, George Staunton, *Northam, Southampton.*—Pemb. Coll. Ox. B.A. 1857, M.A. 1859; Deac. 1857 and Pr. 1858 by Bp of Lon. P. C. of Ch. Ch. Northam, Dio. Win. 1863. (Patron, Bp of Win; P. C.'s Inc. 240*l* and Ho; Pop. 3250*l*.) Surrogate. Formerly C. of Kensington 1857-58; P. C. of West Molesey, Surrey, 1859-62. [14]

BARROW, James, *North Wingfield, Chesterfield.*—St. John's Coll. Cam. Fell. of, 21st Wrang. B.A. 1815, M.A. 1818; Deac. and Pr. 1817 by Bp of Salis. R. of North Wingfield, Dio. Lich. 1861. (Patron, the present R; Tithe, 1200*l*; Glebe, 86 acres; R.'s Inc. 1300*l* and Ho; Pop. 2417.) Formerly R. of North with South Lopham, Norfolk, 1823-61. [15]

BARROW, John, *Bloxwich Parsonage, Walsall, Staffs.*—Univ. Coll. Dur. Barry Scho. 1858, Prizeman 1857, B.A. 1860, M.A. 1863; Deac. 1859 and Pr. 1860 by Bp of Ches. P. C. of Bloxwich, Dio. Lich. 1865. (Patrons, The Inhabitants; P. C.'s Inc. 300*l* and Ho; Pop. 7320.) Formerly C. of Hindley 1861, and Bloxwich 1861-65. [16]

BARROW, John Simeon, *Rogate, near Petersfield.*—Wad. Coll. Ox. 4th cl. Lit. Hum. B.A. 1848, M.A. 1857; Deac. 1849 and Pr. 1850 by Bp of Salis. V. of Rogate, Dio. Chich. 1867. (Patron, Ld Chan; Tithe, 290*l*; Glebe, 30*l*; V.'s Inc. 320*l*; Pop. 990.) Formerly C. of East and West Stower, Dorset, and Trinity, Ryde. [17]

BARROW, Thomas Forster, 14, *Clarendon-gardens, Maida-hill, London, W.*—St. Alban's Hall, Ox. 4th cl. Lit. Hum. B.A. 1833, M.A. 1850; Deac. 1834, Pr. 1835. Formerly P. C. of Barrow-Gurney, near Bristol, 1855-61. [18]

BARRY, Alfred, *The College, Cheltenham.*—Trin. Coll. Cam. Fell. of, 4th Wrang. 7th in 1st cl. Cl. Trip. Smith's Prizeman, and B.A. 1848, M.A. 1851, B.D. 1858, D.D. 1865; Deac. 1850 by Bp of Ely, Pr. 1853 by Bp of Ox. Prin. of Cheltenham Coll. 1862. Author, *Introduction to Old Testament*, J. W. Parker; *Notes on the Gospels*, Rivingtons; *Cheltenham College Sermons*, Bell and Daldy, 1865; *Notes on the Catechism*, 1867; *On Present Need of the Church*, Macmillan, 1867; *Life of Sir C. Barry, R.A.* Murray, 1867; *University Sermons*, Bell and Daldy, 1867. [19]

BARRY, Charles Upham, *Ryde, Isle of Wight.*—Trin. Hall, Cam. B.A. 1840, M.A. 1843; Deac. 1840 and Pr. 1841 by Abp of Cant. [20]

BARRY, David Thomas, *Birkenhead, Cheshire.*—Dub. A.B. 1844; Deac. 1845, Pr. 1846. P. C. of St. Anne's, Birkenhead, Dio. Ches. 1860. (Patron, Rev. A. Knox; P. C.'s Inc. 400*l* and Ho; Pop. 4200.) Formerly Secretary to the Church Missionary Society, for the North-Western District, 1857-60; P. C. of St. Barnabas', Liverpool, 1853-57. Author, *Psalms and Hymns for the Church, School, and Home.* [21]

BARRY, Edward Milner, *Scothorne, near Lincoln.*—Dub. A.B. 1848; Deac. 1849 and Pr. 1850 by Bp of Ely. V. of Scothorne, Dio. Lin. 1852. (Patron, Earl of Scarborough; Tithe—Imp. 1*s*, V. 12*l*; Glebe, 71 acres; V.'s Inc. 150*l* and Ho; Pop. 579.) Formerly C. of Eversholt, Beds, 1849, and Ifield, Kent, 1852. [22]

BARRY, Foster Stable, *Mercers' School, College Hill, London, E.C.*—Pemb. Coll. Cam. Scho. of, 1849, 30th Wrang. B.A. 1852, M.A. 1855; Deac. 1852 and Pr. 1853 by Bp of Lon. Head Mast. of Mercers' Sch. Lond. 1861; C. of St. Margaret's, Lothbury, 1866; Chap. of Skinners' Alms House, Mile End, 1861. Formerly C. of St. Peter's, Stepney, 1852–62; Chap. of Ophthalmic Hospital, Finsbury, 1862–64; Lect. of St. Andrew's, Holborn, 1864–66. [1]

BARRY, Henry, *Brockley, near Bristol.*—Trin. Hall, Cam. B.C.L. 1834, Coll. Prizeman, 1829 and 1830; Deac. 1831 and Pr. 1832 by Bp of B. and W. R. of Brockley, Dio. B. and W. 1834. (Patron, J. H. S. Pigott Esq; Tithe, 123*l*; Glebe, 14 acres; R.'s Inc. 140*l* and Ho; Pop. 93.) Surrogate 1847. Formerly C. of Compton Martin, Somerset. [2]

BARRY, Henry Boothby.—Queen's Coll. Ox. B.A. 1842, M.A. 1845; Deac. 1846, Pr. 1848. Michel Fell. of Queen's Coll, Ox; One of H. M.'s Inspectors of Schools; Dom. Chap. to the Earl of Yarborough. Author, *Thoughts on the Renovation of Cathedral Institutions,* 1852; *Remarks on the Three Proposals for Reforming the Constitution of the University of Oxford,* 1854; *A Few Words on the Constitution to be submitted to the Convocation of the University of Oxford by the Hebdomadal Board,* 1854. [3]

BARRY, Robert, *North Tuddenham, East Dereham, Norfolk.*—St. John's Coll. Cam. B.A. 1847, M.A. 1851; Deac. 1847 and Pr. 1848 by Bp of Lon. R. of North Tuddenham, Dio. Nor. 1851. (Patron, Robert Barry, Esq. Park-hill, Fylingdales, Whitby; Tithe, 700*l*; Glebe, 67 acres; R.'s Inc. 790*l* and Ho; Pop. 437.) Formerly C. of St. Pancras, Middlesex, 1847; R. of Hinderwell, Yorks, 1850. [4]

BARRY, William, *Blisworth, near Northampton.*—Trin. Coll. Cam. Sen. Opt. B.A. 1825, M.A. 1828; Deac. 1827 and Pr. 1828 by Abp of York. R. of Blisworth, Dio. Pet. 1839. (Patron, the present R; Tithe, 3*l* 8*s*; Glebe, 303 acres; R.'s Inc. 554*l* and Ho; Pop. 1020.) Rural Dean 1853. [5]

BARRY, William Thomas, *Upholland, Wigan.*—Trin. Coll. Cam. B.A. 1850; Deac. 1851 and Pr. 1852 by Bp of Rip. C. of Upholland. [6]

BARTER, Charles, *Sarsden, Chipping-Norton, Oxon.*—Ball. Coll. Ox. Fell. of, B.A. 1807, M.A. 1810; Deac. 1812 and Pr. 1813 by Bp of Ox. R. of Sarsden with Churchill V. Dio. Ox. 1817. (Patron, J. H. Langston, Esq; Sarsden, Glebe, 184 acres; Churchill, Glebe, 104 acres; R.'s Inc. 510*l* and Ho; Pop. Sarsden 166, Churchill 642.) R. of Cornwell, Ox. Dio. Ox. 1829. (Patron, Ld Chan; Glebe, 100 acres; R.'s Inc. 150*l*; Pop. 97.) Rural Dean. [7]

BARTER, Henry, *Lamborne, near Hungerford.*—Mert. Coll. Ox. 3rd cl. Lit. Hum. 2nd cl. Maths. B.A. 1858, M.A. 1860; Deac. 1859 and Pr. 1860 by Bp of Salis. V. of Lamborne, Dio. Ox. 1862. (Patron, Bp of Ox; Tithe, 8*l*; Glebe, 40 acres; V.'s Inc. 250*l* and Ho; Pop. 1900.) Formerly C. of Bradford-on-Avon 1859–61, Old Windsor 1861–62. [8]

BARTER, J. B., *Stevenage, Herts.*—C. of Stevenage. [9]

BARTER, J. C., *Hoby, near Leicester.*—C. of Hoby. [10]

BARTER, Robert Bruce, *Greinton Rectory, viâ Bath.*—Oriel Coll. Ox. B.A. 1858, M.A. 1861; Deac. 1859 and Pr. 1860 by Bp of Ex. R. of Greinton, Dio. B. and W. 1861. (Patron, S. T. Kekewich, Esq. M.P; R.'s Inc. 175*l* and Ho; Pop. 161.) Formerly C. of Broad Clyst, Exeter, 1859–60. [11]

BARTHOLOMEW, Charles Willyams Marsh, *Glympton, Woodstock, Oxon.*—Ex. Coll. Ox. B.A. 1848. R. of Glympton, Dio. Ox. 1856. (Patron, E. Way, Esq; Tithe, 255*l* 17*s* 6*d*; Glebe, 51 acres; R.'s Inc. 310*l* and Ho; Pop. 153.) Formerly C. of St. Mark's, North Audley-street, London. [12]

BARTHOLOMEW, Christopher Chadwick, *Cornwood Vicarage, Ivybridge.*—Jesus Coll. Cam. B.A. 1824, M.A. 1825; Deac. 1825, Pr. 1826. V. of Cornwood, Dio. Ex. 1862. (Patron, Bp of Ex; Tithe, 351*l*; Glebe, 95 acres; V.'s Inc. 500*l* and Ho; Pop. 1016.) [13]

BARTHOLOMEW, J., *Forest-hill, Kent, S.E.*—Chap. of the Cemetery, Forest Hill; C. of Camberwell. [14]

BARTHOLOMEW, Robert, *Harberton, Totnes, Devon.*—Ex. Coll. Ox. B.A. 1845; Deac. 1846 by Bp of B. and W. Pr. 1848 by Bp of Ex. V. of Harberton, Dio. Ex. 1860. (Patrons, D. and C. of Ex; V.'s Inc. 600*l* and Ho; Pop. 688.) [15]

BARTLE, George, *Walton-on-the-Hill, Lancashire.*—Dub. Giessen and Jena, A.M. Ph. D. and D. D; Deac. 1858 and Pr. 1859 by Bp of Ches. Prin. of Walton College. Formerly C. of St. Mary's, Kirkdale, 1858–60. Author, *Vulgar Fractions made Easy*; *An Epitome of English Grammar*; *Dissertation on the Sacrifice of Christ*; *Philosophical Discourse showing from the Hebrew that Moses taught the true system of Astronomy, and that Joshua did not command the Sun to stand still*; *Six Sermons on the Intermediate State*; *Synopsis of English History*; *The Reviewer of Dr. Bartle's Synopsis reviewed*; *Exposition of Church Catechism*; etc. [16]

BARTLEET, Samuel Edwin, *Shaw Parsonage, Oldham.*—Trin. Coll. Cam. B.A. 1857, M.A. 1860; Deac. 1858 and Pr. 1859 by Bp of Wor. P. C. of Shaw, Dio. Man. 1866. (Patron, R. of Prestwich; Glebe, 50 acres; P. C.'s Inc. 175*l* and Ho; Pop. 3618.) Formerly C. of Hallow, Worcester, 1858–60, and Prestwich 1861–66. [17]

BARTLET, James Tufton, *St. John's Parsonage, Mansfield.*—Corpus Coll. Cam. B.A. 1856, M.A. 1859, Member's Prize 1855; Deac. 1858 and Pr. 1859 by Bp of Lin. C. in sole charge of St. John's, Mansfield, 1867. Formerly C. of Caistor 1858–60, All Saints' 1860–66 and Trinity, Gainsborough, 1866–67. [18]

BARTLETT, Alfred Toms.—King's Coll. Lond. Theol. Assoc; Deac. 1860 and Pr. 1861 by Bp of Lon. Chap. Madras 1866. Formerly C. of St. Stephen's, Hammersmith 1860–66. [19]

BARTLETT, Frederick Augustus, *St. Olave's Parsonage, York.*—St. Bees; Deac. 1841 and Pr. 1842 by Bp of Ches. P. C. of St. Olave's with St. Giles's, City and Dio. of York, 1855. (Patroness, Countess Cowper; P. C.'s Inc. 220*l* and Ho; Pop. 2500.) Formerly R. of Newchurch, Lancashire. [20]

BARTLETT, Henry Charles, *Westerham, Edenbridge, Kent.*—Emman. Coll. Cam. B.A. 1849, M.A. 1852; Deac. 1849 and Pr. 1850 by Bp. of Roch. V. of Westerham, Dio. Cant. 1860. (Patron, John Board, Esq; Tithe, 420*l*; V.'s Inc. 500*l* and Ho; Pop. 1654.) Formerly C. of Tring 1849–51, Staines 1851–52, Spettesbury 1852–55, and Westerham 1856–60. [21]

BARTLETT, John, *Millbrook Parsonage, Devonport.*—Corpus Coll. Cam. Scho. and Prizeman, B.A. 1852; Deac. 1852 and Pr. 1853 by Bp. of Ex. P. C. of Millbrook, Dio. Ex. 1863. (Patron, Earl of Mount Edgcumbe; Glebe, 1 acre; P. C.'s Inc. 160*l* and Ho; Pop. 2986.) Surrogate. Formerly C. of Tywardreath 1852–53; V. of St. Blazey, Cornwall, 1853–63. Author, *Occasional Sermons*; and *The History of St. Blazey.* [22]

BARTLETT, John Moysey, *St. Michael's Mount, Cornwall.*—Wor. Coll. Ox. B.A. 1844; Deac. 1844 by Bp of G. and B. Pr. 1846 by Bp of Ex. Chap. of St. Michael's Mount 1849. Formerly P. C. of Marazion, Cornwall, 1847–57. [23]

BARTLETT, John Pemberton, *Exbury Parsonage, near Southampton.*—Deac. 1847, Pr. 1848. P. C. of Exbury, Dio. Win. 1863. (Patron, Bp of Win; P. C.'s Inc. 350*l* and Ho; Pop. 375.) Formerly C. of Exbury. [24]

BARTLETT, John Spencer, *Christ Church, St. Leonard's-on-the-Sea.*—Bishop Cosin's Hall, Dur. Barry Scho. and Theol. Prizeman 1857, B.A. 1858, Fellows' Prizeman 1859; Deac. 1858 and Pr. 1859 by Bp of Dur. C. of Ch. Ch. St. Leonard's 1863. Formerly C. of Morpeth 1858, Bothal 1861. Author, *Brief History of the Christian Church,* J. H. and J. Parker, Oxford, 1855. [25]

BARTLETT, Philip, *Weybridge, Surrey.*—Trin. Coll. Cam. B.A. 1856, M.A. 1859; Deac. 1857 and Pr. 1858 by Bp of Chich. C. of Weybridge 1867. Formerly C. of Rye Harbour, Icklesham, 1857. [26]

BARTLETT, Philip George, *Kirton, Woodbridge, Suffolk.*—R. of Kirton, Dio. Nor. 1861. (Patron, Ld Chan; R.'s Inc. 400*l* and Ho; Pop. 540.) [27]

BARTLETT, Robert Edward, *Pershore, Worcestershire.*—Trin. Coll. Ox. Fell. of, 1854-60, B.A. 1853, M.A. 1855, Denyer Theol. Prize 1856; Deac. 1856, Pr. 1859. V. of Pershore St. Andrew with Piovin C. Holy Cross C. Broughton C. and Bricklehampton C. Dio. Wor. 1865. (Patrons, D. and C. of Westminster; V.'s Inc. 500*l* and Ho; Pop. 4000.) Formerly P. C. of St. Mark's, Whitechapel, Lond. 1860-65. [1]

BARTLETT, Robert Leach, *Thurloxton, Taunton.*—Wad. Coll. Ox. B.A. 1848; Deac. 1849 and Pr. 1850 by Bp of Salis. R. of Thurloxton, Dio. B. and W. 1859. (Patron, Lord Portman; Tithe, 93*l* 14*s* 2½*d*; Glebe, 80 acres; R.'s Inc. 222*l* and Ho; Pop. 207.) Formerly C. of Yetminster 1850-51, Corton-Denham 1851-52, and Asst. C. of Durweston, 1852-58. [2]

BARTLETT, Symeon Taylor, *Everley, Marlborough, Wilts.*—Clare Coll. Cam. LL.B. 1840, LL.D. 1846; Deac. 1852 by Bp of Herf, Pr. 1854 by Bp of Wor. R. of Everley, Dio, Salis. 1857. (Patron, Sir F. Astley, Bart; Tithe, 708*l*; Glebe, 22 acres; R.'s Inc. 741*l* and Ho; Pop. 294.) Dom. Chap. to Lord Downe. Formerly C. of All Saints', Worcester, and Warndon, Worcester. Editor, *Cicero's Letters to his Friends*; *Xenophon's Anabasis*; *Satires of Horace*; *Cicero, De Oratore*; *Cicero, De Senectute*; etc. Author, *Personal Piety, the Nation's Safeguard* (a Sermon); *Journey of the Israelites from Marah to Sinai* (a Sermon); *The Law given from Mount Sinai* (a Sermon.) [3]

BARTLETT, Thomas, *Burton-Latimer Rectory, Kettering, Northants.*—St. Edmund Hall, Ox. B.A. 1813, M.A. 1817; Deac. 1812 by Bp. of Salis, Pr. 1814 by Bp of G. and B. R. of Burton-Latimer, Dio. Pet. 1857. (Patron, Rev. D. Barclay Bevan; Tithe—Glebe, 750 acres; R.'s Inc. 1000*l* and Ho; Pop. 1150.) Preacher of Cant. Cathl. 1832; Dom. Chap. to Marquis of Cholmondeley 1828-50. Formerly Asst. Min. of St. John's, Bedford-row, Lond. 1814; C. of Beckenham, Kent, 1815; V. of Luton, Beds, 1854-57. Author, *Memoirs of the Life and Writings of Bishop Butler*, 12*s*; *Confession of the Church of England, practically elucidated in Seven Discourses*, 3*s* 6*d*; *The Duty of Propagating Christianity among the Heathens* (a Sermon on behalf of the S.P.G.), 2*s*; *The Connection between Faith and Works* (a Sermon preached on the day of the Interment of the Princess Charlotte of Wales), 1*s* 6*d*; *Two Sermons*, preached on the opening of All Saints, Canterbury; *Sermon at the primary Visitation of the Archbishop of Canterbury*, 1832; *Two Sermons on Protestantism and Popery*; *A Sermon on the Fast Day*, 1832; *Defence of the Church Missionary Society, in a Letter to Sir Edward Knatchbull, Bart. M.P*; *The Protestant Rule of Faith Vindicated, with a Glance at Popery*, etc. [4]

BARTLETT, Thomas Bradford, *Roosdown, Axminster, Devon.*—Pemb. Coll. Ox. B.A. 1850; Deac. 1851 and Pr. 1853 by Bp of Salis. R. of Roosdown, Dio. Ex. 1858. (Patron, the present R; R.'s Inc. 35*l*; Pop. 13.) C. of Stocklinch Ottersay and Stocklinch Magdalen, Ilminster. Formerly C. of Clayhidon, Devon. [5]

BARTLETT, T. H. M., *Montreal.*—Chaplain to the Forces. [6]

BARTLETT, William Abraham, 1, *Waterloo-villas, New Wimbledon, Merton, S.*—Wad. Coll. Ox. B.A. 1853, M.A. 1857; Deac. 1855 and Pr. 1856 by Bp of Win. Sen. C. of Wimbledon 1860. Formerly C. of Wyke, near Winchester, 1855. Author, *The History and Antiquities of Wimbledon*, 1865, 6*s* 6*d*; *The Doubter Cured*, a Sermon, 1866. [7]

BARTON, Charles, *Flixton Rectory, Manchester*—Dub. A.B. 1846; Deac. 1847, Pr. 1848. R. of Flixton, Dio. Man. 1863. (Patron, Bp of Man; R.'s Inc. 300*l* and Ho; Pop. 2050.) Formerly P. C. of Bromborough, Cheshire, 1850-60; R. of Trusham, Devon, 1860-63. [8]

BARTON, Edwin, *Ross, Herefordshire.*—Ch. Coll. Cam. B.A. 1852; Deac. 1853 and Pr. 1854 by Bp of Wor. C. of Ross. Formerly C. of Ledbury 1854. [9]

BARTON, Henry Jonas, *Wicken Rectory, near Stoney Stratford.*—Brasen. Coll. Ox. B.A. 1818, M.A. 1820; Deac. 1822 and Pr. 1823 by Bp of Wor. R. of Wicken, Dio. Pet. 1838. (Patron, Sir C. Mordaunt, Bart; Tithe, 495*l*; Glebe, 127 acres; R.'s Inc. 650*l* and Ho; Pop. 530.) Hon. Can. of Pet. Cathl. 1854; Rural Dean. [10]

BARTON, Henry James, *St. Philip's Parsonage, Sheffield.*—St. Aidan's; Deac. 1865, Pr. 1866. C. of St. Philip's, Sheffield, 1867. Formerly C. of St. Matthew's, Sheffield, 1865. [11]

BARTON Henry Nowell, *St. Ervan Rectory, Padstow, Cornwall.*—Pemb. Coll. Ox. B.A. 1844, M.A. 1847. R. of St. Ervan, Dio. Ex. 1853. (Patron, the present R; Tithe, 380*l*; R.'s Inc. 418*l* and Ho; Pop. 437.) [12]

BARTON, James, *Hadley Parsonage, Wellington, Salop.*—St. John's Coll. Cam. B.A. 1849, M.A. 1852; Deac. 1850 and Pr. 1851 by Bp of Lich. P. C. of Hadley, Dio. Lich. 1856. (Patrons, Bp of Lich. and others; Glebe, ½ an acre; P. C.'s Inc. 110*l* and Ho; Pop. 1654) Formerly C. of Burton-on-Trent 1850-52, Emmanuel's, Bolton-le-Moors, 1852-53, Bolton 1853-54, Crumpsall, Cheetham Hill, Manchester, 1854-56. [13]

BARTON, James Warner, *Stramshall Parsonage, Uttoxeter.*—Ex. Coll. Ox. B.A. 1853; Deac. 1854 by Bp of Ex. Pr. 1855 by Bp of Pet. P. C. of Stramshall, Dio. Lich. 1859. (Patron, V. of Uttoxeter; P. C.'s Inc. 127*l* and Ho; Pop. 365.) Formerly C. of Cranley, Surrey. [14]

BARTON, John, *Rivenhall, Witham, Essex.*—Corpus Coll. Cam. B.A. 1853, M.A. 1856; Deac. 1853 and Pr. 1854 by Bp. of Salis. C. of Rivenhall. Formerly C. of Ramsbury, Wilts. Author, *The Reality, but not the Duration of Future Punishment is revealed*, Trübner, 1866, 1*s* 6*d*. [15]

BARTON, John, *Plaitford, Romsey, Hants.*—Wad. Coll. Ox. B.A. 1853; Deac. 1854 and Pr. 1855 by Bp of Win. R. of Plaitford, Dio. Salis. 1865. (Patron, Earl of Ilchester; R.'s Inc. 370*l*; Pop. 248.) Formerly C. of Sherfield, Hants. [16]

BARTON, John Lake, *Hinton House, Horndean, Hants.*—St. John's Coll. Cam. B.A. 1830; Deac. 1834, Pr. 1835. Head Mast. of St. Paul's Sch. Southsea. Formerly C. of Clanfield, Hants. [17]

BARTON, John Yarker, *Dover.*—Brasen. Coll. Ox. B.A. 1852; Deac. 1853, Pr. 1854. Chap. to the Forces, Dover. [18]

BARTON, Mathew Williams, *Thwing, near Bridlington.*—St. John's Coll. Cam. B.A. 1833, M.A. 1847; Deac. 1834, Pr. 1835. C. of Thwing. Formerly Head Mast. of the Chipping-Campden Gr. Sch. Gloucestershire, and afterwards of Queen Elizabeth's Hospital, Bristol. [19]

BARTON, Mordaunt, *Wicken Rectory, Stoney-Stratford.*—Ex. Coll. Ox. B.A. 1859; Deac. 1861 and Pr. 1862 by Bp. of Roch. C. of Hockerill, Herts, 1861. [20]

BARTON, Robert Gillbe, *Etchingham, Hurst Green, Sussex.*—Corpus Coll. Cam. B.A. 1845. R. of Etchingham, Dio. Chich. 1858. (Patron, the present R; Tithe, 613*l*; Glebe, 14 acres; R.'s Inc. 618*l*; Pop. 787.) Formerly C. of Oare, Sussex. [21]

BARTON, Thomas, *Donnington Square, Newbury, Berks.*—Queens' Coll. Cam. B.A. 1836, B.M. 1839; Deac. 1839 and Pr. 1840 by Bp of Pet. Formerly C. of Kettering 1839; P. C. of Midgham, Berks, 1858-66. [22]

BARTON, Thomas Haycraft, *Fridaythorpe, Pocklington, Yorks.*—St. Bees; Deac. 1848, Pr. 1849. V. of Fridaythorpe, Dio. York, 1862. (Patron, Abp of York; V.'s Inc. 200*l* and Ho; Pop. 332.) [23]

BARTRAM, William, *Sharncote, Cricklade, Wilts.*—Magd Hall, Ox. B.A. 1852, M.A. 1855; Deac. 1851 by Bp of Llan. Pr. 1852 by Bp of G. and B. Mast. of the Cirencester Gr. Sch; R. of Sharncote, Dio. G. and B. 1863. (Patron, Ld Chan; R.'s Inc. 130*l* and Ho; Pop. 19.) [24]

BARTRAM, W., *Leigh, Cricklade, Wilts.*—C. of Leigh. [25]

BARTRUM, Edward, *Great Berkhampstead, Herts.*—Pemb. Coll. Ox. B.A. 1856, M.A. 1858; Deac. 1857 and Pr. 1858 by Bp of B. and W. Head Mast. of King Edw. the Sixth's Gr. Sch. Berkhampstead. (Patron, the Crown.) Formerly the 2nd Mast. of King Edward's Sch. Bath, 1856–61; C. of Octagon Chapel, Bath, 1859, Widcombe, Somerset, 1857–59; Head Mast. of Hertford Gr. Sch. 1861-63. Author, *Promotion by Merit Essential to the Progress of the Church,* 1866, 1*s*. [1]

BARWELL, Arthur Henry Sanxay, *Southwater Parsonage, Horsham.*—Trin. Coll. Cam. B.A. 1860, M.A. 1863; Deac. 1860, Pr. 1861. P. C. of Southwater, Dio. Chich. 1864. (Patron, V. of Horsham; P. C.'s Inc. 85*l* and Ho; Pop. 600.) Formerly C. of Silsoe, Beds, 1860–64, and Wittersham, Kent, 1864. [2]

BARWIS, William Cuthbert, *Hoyland, Barnsley.*—Pemb. Coll. Cam. B.A. 1847, M.A. 1850, Licent. of Theol. Dur. 1848; Deac. 1848 and Pr. 1849 by Bp of Rip. C. of Hoyland 1866. Formerly C. of St. James's, Leeds, 1848–51; P. C. of Ch. Ch. Leeds, 1851–55; C. of Chipping Norton, Oxon, 1858-66. [3]

BASHALL, William, 3, *Cambridge-villas, Richmond, Surrey.*—St. John's Coll. Ox. B.A. 1852, M.A. 1855; Deac. 1853 and Pr. 1854 by Bp of Lon. C. of St. Mary's, Richmond, 1855. Formerly C. of Uxbridge, Middlesex, 1853-55. [4]

BASHFORTH, Francis, *The Royal Artillery Institution, Woolwich.*—St. John's Coll. Cam. 2nd Wrang. B.A. 1843, M.A. 1846, B.D. 1854; Deac. 1850 and Pr. 1851 by Bp of Ely. R. and V. of Minting, Dio. Lin. 1857. (Patron, St. John's Coll. Cam; Tithe, 451*l*; Glebe, 17 acres; R. and V.'s Inc. 490*l* and Ho; Pop. 422.) Prof. of Applied Mathematics to the Advanced Class, Woolwich. Late Fell. of St. John's Coll. Cam. Author, *Observations on some recent University Buildings, together with Remarks on the Management of the Public Library,* 1853; *Description of Chronograph,* Bell and Daldy, 1866, 2*s* 6*d*. [5]

BASKERVILLE, Charles Gardiner, *Wells, Somerset.*—Caius Coll. Cam. B.A. 1856; Deac. 1856 and Pr. 1857 by Bp of B. and W. C. of St. Thomas's, East Wells, 1865. Formerly Chap. of Bath Penitentiary 1858–64; P. C. of Stockingford, Nuneaton, 1864. Author, *Within the Veil, or Suggestions for Daily Prayer; What meaneth this Pestilence? Is your Money Safe?* Published by Hunt and Co. [6]

BASSET, Charles, 9, *Rock terrace, Talfourd-road, Camberwell, London, S.*—Trin. Coll. Cam. 3rd cl. Cl. Trip B.A. 1860, M.A. 1863; Deac. 1861 and Pr. 1862 by Bp of Lon. C. of Camberwell 1865. Formerly C. of St. Mary's, Fulham, 1861. [7]

BASSET, Walter St. Aubyn, *Ledsham, Milford Junction, Yorks.*—Ch. Ch. Ox. C. of Ledsham. [8]

BASSETT, Francis, *Heanton Punchardon, Devon.*—Trin. Coll. Ox. B.A. 1825; Deac. 1825 and Pr. 1827 by Bp of Ex. R. of Heanton Punchardon, Dio. Ex. 1836. (Patron, A. D. Bassett, Esq; Tithe, 406*l*; Glebe, 38 acres; R.'s Inc. 472*l* and Ho; Pop. 540.) [9]

BASSETT, Francis Tilney, *Healade House, Bath.*—Caius Coll. Cam. Scho. Prizeman and Exhib. B.A. 1852, M.A. 1857, *ad eund.* Ox. 1857; Deac. 1852 and Pr. 1853 by Bp of Ox. Sunday morn. Lect. at Widcombe, Bath, 1866. Formerly C. of Bucklebury Church and Marlston Chapel, Berks, 1852-57; Dist. Sec. of Lond. Soc. for Promoting Christianity among the Jews 1857–66. Author, *Elohism and Jehovism,* Bath, 1864, 1*s*; *The Prophets—What were they? A brief inquiry into the Titles of Prophet and Seer,* 1865; *Criticism and Interpretation of Psalm ii, 12,* 1866; *The Mission of Prophecy, and the Mission of Fulfilment,* 1866, etc. [10]

BASSETT, John Fardell, *Glentham Vicarage, Market Rasen, Lincolnshire.*—Caius Coll. Cam. B.A. 1830; Deac. 1850 and Pr. 1851 by Bp of Lin. V. of Normanby and Glentham, Dio. Lin. 1858. (Patrons, D. and C. of Lin; Glebe, 100 acres; V.'s Inc. 150*l* and Ho; Pop. 478.) Formerly C. of Willoughton, Linc. 1850–58. [11]

BASSETT, Mortimer W., *Alfreton, Derbyshire.*—C. of Alfreton. [12]

BASSETT, Richard Edward, *North Thoresby, Louth, Lincolnshire.*—Lin. Coll. Ox. B.A. 1837. R. of North Thoresby, Dio. Lin. 1852. (Patron, the present R; Tithe, 441*l* 12*s* 11*d*; R.'s Inc. 580*l* and Ho; Pop. 824.) [13]

BASTARD, Henry Horlock, *Haine's Hill, Taunton, Somerset.*—Wad. Coll. Ox. B.A. 1834, M.A. 1839; Deac. 1836 and Pr. 1837 by Bp of B. and W. Formerly C. of Dowlish-Wake, Somerset. [14]

BASTARD, William Pollexfen, *Lezant Rectory, Launceston.*—Ball. Coll. Ox. B.A. 1853, M.A. 1857; Deac. 1856 and Pr. 1857 by Bp. of Ex. R. of Lezant, Dio. Ex. 1866. (Patron, Bp of Ex; Tithe, 481*l*; Glebe, 158 acres; R.'s Inc. 663*l* and Ho; Pop. 815.) Formerly C. of Buckland-in-the-Moor 1856, and Cornworthy 1860; P. C. of Brixton 1862, all in Devon. [15]

BATCHELLOR, Edward William, *Trotton, Midhurst, Sussex.*—Ch. Ch. Ox. B.A. 1837. R. of Trotton, Dio. Chich. 1851. (Patroness, Mrs. Batchellor; Tithe, 424*l* 5*s*; Glebe, 39 acres; R.'s Inc. 454*l* and Ho; Pop. 452.) [16]

BATCHELOR, Frederick Shum, *Brixton, Surrey, S.*—King's Coll. Lond. and Pemb. Coll. Cam; Deac. and Pr. 1843. Chap. at the Female Convict Prison, Brixton. Formerly Asst. Chap. to the Dartmoor Prisons, and at Millbank Penitentiary. Author, *Address to Soldiers; Address to Prisoners.* [17]

BATCHELOR, Frederick Thomas, *Jacobstow Rectory, Stratton, Cornwall.*—Wad. Coll. Ox. B.A. 1848, M.A. 1852; Deac. and Pr. 1851 by Bp of St. D. R. of Jacobstow, Dio. Ex. 1865. (Patron, Earl of St. Germains; Tithe, 160*l*; Glebe, 90 acres; R.'s Inc. 280*l* and Ho; Pop. 462.) Formerly R. of Calstock, Cornwall, 1854–65. [18]

BATCHELOR, Thomas, *Sutton-on-Trent, Newark.*—Magd. Hall, Ox. 3rd cl. Lit. Hum. B.A. 1832; Deac. 1838 and Pr. 1839 by Bp of Nor. C. of Sutton-on-Trent 1864. Formerly C. of Woodbridge 1854–56, St. Matthew's, Gosport, 1857-59, Wilsden 1861–63. [19]

BATEMAN, Gregory, *Mowsley, near Rugby.*—Trin. Coll. Cam. B.A. 1833, M.A. 1837; Deac. 1836 and Pr. 1837 by Bp of Lich. V. of Ulrome, Dio. York, 1863. (Patron, the present V; Tithe, 18*l*; Glebe, 30 acres; V.'s Inc. 100*l* and Ho; Pop. 221.) Formerly Crown Chap. in Van Diemen's Land 1839–47. Author of various Sacred Poems and many Sermons. [20]

BATEMAN, Hugh Wilson, *Benenden, Staplehurst, Kent.*—Trin. Coll. Cam. B.A. 1864; Deac. 1865 and Pr. 1866 by Abp of Cant. C. of Benenden 1865. [21]

BATEMAN, John, *West Leake, near Loughborough.*—St. John's Coll Cam. B.A. 1822, M.A. 1826; Deac. 1826 and Pr. 1827 by Bp of Lich. R. of East Leake with West Leake, Dio. Lin. 1836. (Patron, the present R; Glebe, 470 acres; R.'s Inc. 715*l* and Ho; Pop. East Leake 1059, West Leake 171.) [22]

BATEMAN, J. Burleton Jones, *Sheldon, Birmingham.*—R. of Sheldon, Dio. Wor. 1849. (Patron, G. D. W. Digby, Esq; R.'s Inc. 490*l* and Ho; Pop. 434.) Rural Dean; Surrogate. [23]

BATEMAN, John Fitzherbert, *South Lopham Rectory, Harling, Norfolk.*—St. John's Coll. Cam. 2nd cl. Cl. Trip. and Jun. Opt. B.A. 1851, M.A. 1854, Fell. of St. John's Coll. 1851; Deac. 1853 and Pr. 1854 by Bp of Ely. R. of North with South Lopham, Dio. Nor. 1861. (Patron, Rev. J. Bateman, West Leake, Loughborough, who must present a Fell. of St. John's, Cam; North Lopham—Tithe, 303*l*; Glebe, 5½ acres; South Lopham—Tithe, 308*l*; Glebe, 45 acres; R.'s Inc. 865*l* and Ho; Pop. North Lopham 771, South Lopham 639.) Formerly C. of Lelcham 1855, Wymeswold 1856, Sutton St. Anne's, with Kingston-on-Soar, 1856–61. Author, *A Village Sermon in Aid of the Memorial Church at Constantinople,* 1856. [24]

BATEMAN, Josiah, *Vicarage, Margate.*—Queens' Coll. Cam. Scho. of, Sen. Opt. B.A. 1828, M.A.

1831; Deac. 1828 and Pr. 1829 by Bp. of Lich. V. of Margate, Dio. Cant. 1864. (Patron, Abp. of Cant; Tithe, 403*l*; Glebe, 12 acres; V.'s Inc. 540*l* and Ho; Pop. 5201.) Hon. Can. of Cant. 1863; Rural Dean. Formerly C. of Burslem 1828–30, St. Sepulchre, Lond. 1830–32; Chap. to the Hon. E.I.C. and Bp of Calcutta, 1830–38; V. of Marlborough 1838–40; V. of Huddersfield 1840–55, and Rural Dean; R. of North Cray, Kent, 1855–64. Author, *La Martiniere*, 1839, 1*s*; *Sermons Preached in India*, 1839, 4*s*; *Why do you believe the Bible to be the Word of God?* S.P.C.K. 1*s*; *Sermons preached in Guernsey*, 1842, 4*s*; *Sermons to Young Men, Parents, &c.* 1848, 1*s* 6*d*; *The Holmfirth Flood*, 1*s*; *The Life of Daniel Wilson, Bp of Calcutta and Metropolitan in India*, 2 vols. 1860, 28*s*; Single Sermons and Pamphlets. [1]

BATEMAN, Rowland, *St. John's Keswick.*—Magd. Coll. Ox. B.A. 1864, M.A. 1867; Deac. 1865 and Pr. 1866 by Bp of Carl. C. of St. John's, Keswick, 1865. [2]

BATEMAN, Stafford, *South Scarle, Newark, Notts.*—St. John's Coll. Cam. B.A. 1850; Deac. 1851, Pr. 1852. V. of South Scarle with Girton P.C. and Besthorpe C. Dio. Lin. 1857. (Patron, the Preb. of South Scarle in Lin. Cathl; South Scarle, Tithe, 60*l* 2*s* 6*d*; Glebe, 1½ acres; Girton, Tithe, 60*l* 2*s* 6*d*; Glebe, 50 acres; Besthorpe, Tithe, 44*l*; V.'s Inc. 249*l* 15*s* and Ho; Pop. South Scarle 175. Girton 188, Besthorpe 338.) [3]

BATES, Alfred Naunton, *Blaxhall Rectory, Wickham Market, Suffolk.*—Trin. Coll. Cam. Jun. Opt. B.A. 1854, M.A 1856; Deac. 1852 and Pr. 1853 by Bp of Ox. R. of Blaxhall, Dio. Nor. 1867. (Patron, the present R; R.'s Inc. 500*l* and Ho; Pop. 589.) P. C. of Wantisden, Dio. Nor. 1865. (Patron, N. Barnardiston, Esq; P. C.'s Inc. 64*l*; Pop. 106.) Formerly C. of Prestwood, Bucks, Melton, Suffolk, and St. Matthew's, Ipswich. [4]

BATES, Emery, *Middleton, near Manchester.*—Brasen. Coll. Ox. B.A. 1855, M.A. 1857; Deac. 1857 by Bp of Man. P. C. of Trinity, Middleton, Dio. Man. 1862. [5]

BATES, John, *Croyland, near Peterborough.*—Corpus Coll. Cam. Wrang. B.A. 1831, M.A. 1834; Deac. 1832 and Pr. 1833 by Bp of Pet. R. of Croyland, Dio. Lin. 1834. (Patrons, Marquis of Exeter and J. Whitsed, Esq. alt; Glebe, 35 acres; R.'s Inc. 174*l*; Pop. 3148.) Surrogate. [6]

BATES, J. C., *Castleton Moor, Rochdale.*—P. C. of St. Martin's, Castleton Moor, Dio. Man. 1862. (Patron, V. of Rochdale; P. C.'s Inc. 120*l*; Pop. 3000.) [7]

BATES, John Lockington, *Iden Rectory, Rye, Sussex.*—Trin. Coll. Ox. B.A. 1861, M.A. 1864; Deac. 1862 by Abp of Cant. Pr. 1864 by Bp of Chich. R. of Iden, Dio. Chich. 1864. (Patron, the present R; Glebe, 23 acres; R.'s Inc. 851*l* and Ho; Pop. 600.) Formerly C. of Wittersham, Kent, 1862, and Carisbrooke, Isle of Wight, 1864. [8]

BATES, Jonathan, *Kirkstead, Norwich.*—St. John's Coll. Cam. 11th Wrang. B.A. 1854, M.A. 1857; Deac. 1854 and Pr. 1856 by Bp of Roch. R. of Kirkstead with Langhale R. Dio. Nor. 1862. (Patron, Caius Coll. Cam; Tithe, 300*l*; Glebe, 38 acres; R.'s Inc. 327*l* and Ho; Pop. 241.) Late Fell. of Caius Coll. Cam. Formerly 2nd Mast. of Colchester Gr. Sch. 1854–57; Sen. Tut. and Chap. Queen's Coll. Birmingham 1857–58, C. of East Donyland, Essex, 1858–60; Vice-Prin. of Dioc. Coll. Chester, 1860–62. [9]

BATES, William, *Burnham-Westgate, Lynn, Norfolk.*—Ch. Coll. Cam. B.A. 1836, M.A. 1839, B.D. 1847, D.D. 1858, 20th Wrang; Deac. 1838 and Pr. 1839 by Bp of Rip. R. of Burnham-Westgate with Medieties of the Rectories of Burnham-Ulph and Burnham-Norton, Dio. Nor. 1849. (Patron, Ch. Coll. Cam; Glebe 130 acres; R.'s Inc. 1051*l* and Ho; Pop. Burnham-Westgate 721, Burnham-Ulph 338, Burnham-Norton 172.) Late Fell. Dean, Lect. and Tut. of Ch. Coll. Cam. Author, *College Lectures on Ecclesiastical History*, 6*s*, 3 editions; and *College Lectures on Ecclesiastical Antiquities*, 9*s*, Longmans. [10]

BATESON, John, *Taddington Parsonage, Bakewell, Derby.*—Dub. A.B. 1842; Deac. 1844, Pr. 1845. P. C. of Taddington, Dio. Lich. 1865. (Patron, V. of Bakewell; P. C.'s Inc. 90*l* and Ho; Pop. 500.) [11]

BATESON, Richard Kenyon, *Godley-cum-Newton Green, Hyde, Cheshire.*—St. Bees and Queens' Coll. Cam; Deac. 1844 and Pr. 1845 by Bp of Ches. P. C. of St. John's, Godley-cum-Newton Green, Dio. Ches. 1847. (Patrons, The Crown and Bp of Ches. alt; P. C.'s Inc. 150*l*; Pop. 2209.) [12]

BATESON, William, *Woodhead, Hadfield, Manchester.*—Queens' Coll. Cam. B.A. 1840; Deac. 1840, Pr. 1852. P. C. of St. James's, Woodhead, Dio. Ches. 1852. (Patron, J. Tollemache, Esq, M.P; Tithe, 47*l*; Glebe, 18 acres; P. C.'s Inc. 100*l* and Ho; Pop. 254.) [13]

BATESON, William Henry, *St. John's College, Cambridge.*—St. John's Coll. Cam. B.A. 1836, M.A. 1839, B.D. 1846, D.D. 1856. Mast. of St. John's Coll. Cam. 1857. Formerly Fell. of St. John's Coll. and Public Orator in the Univ. of Cam. 1848. [14]

BATH AND WELLS, The Right Rev. Robert John EDEN, Baron Auckland, Lord Bishop of Bath and Wells, 13, *Queen-square, Westminster, S.W.*, and *The Palace, Wells, Somerset.*—Eton Coll. and Magd. Coll. Cam. M.A. 1819, B.D. and D.D. per Literas Regias, 1847; Deac. 1823 by Bp of Nor. Pr. 1824 by Bp of Wor. Consecrated Bishop of Sodor and Man 1847; Translated to Bath and Wells 1854. (Episcopal Jurisdiction, the County of Somerset, with the exception of the parish of Bedminster; Inc. of See, 5000*l*; Pop. 422,527; Acres, 1,043,059; Deaneries, 13; Benefices, 473; Curates, 213; Church Sittings, 179,132.) His Lordship is Visitor of Wadham College, Oxford; was formerly R. of Eyam, Derbyshire, 1823–25; R. of Hertingfordbury, Herts, 1825–35; V. of Battersea, Surrey, 1835–47. Author, *The Churchman's Theological Dictionary*, 1845; Two *Charges* (at Visitation). [15]

BATHE, Stephen Brown, *Eastnor, Ledbury.*—Ball. Coll. Ox. B.A. 1865; Deac. 1865 by Bp of Herf. Pr. 1866 by Bp of Wor. C. of Eastnor with Pixley 1865. [16]

BATHER, Henry Francis, *Brace Meole, near Shrewsbury.*—St. John's Coll Cam B.A. 1856, M.A. 1858. V. of Brace Meole, Dio. Herf. 1858. (Patron, J. Bather, Esq; Tithe—Imp. 119*l*; V. 390*l*; Glebe, 12 acres; V.'s Inc. 428*l* and Ho; Pop. 1215.) [17]

BATHO, Frederick Goudge, *Cheshunt, Waltham Cross, Herts.*—Magd. Hall. Ox. B.A. 1848, M.A. 1851; Deac. 1848 by Bp of Chich. Pr. 1859 by Bp of Roch. C. of Waltham Holy Cross, Essex, 1859. Formerly C. of Ticehurst, Sussex, 1848. [18]

BATHO, George Best.—St. Bees; Deac. 1850 and Pr. 1851 by Abp of York. C. of Norton St. Philip, Bath. [19]

BATHURST, Frederick, *Diddington, near Huntingdon.*—Mert. Coll. Ox. B.A. 1849, M.A. 1852; Deac. 1852 by Bp of Ox. Pr. 1854 by Bp of Chich. V. of Diddington, Dio. Ely, 1857. (Patron, Mert. Coll. Ox; V.'s Inc. 150*l* and Ho; Pop. 204.) Rural Dean of St. Neots. Formerly C. of Maids-Morton, Bucks. [20]

BATHURST, Lancelot Capel, *Bramley, Guildford.*—Trin. Coll. Ox. B.A. 1842, M.A. 1845; Deac. 1843 by Bp of G. and B. Pr. 1844 by Bp of Salis. Formerly P. C. of Wythall, near Birmingham, 1854–58. [21]

BATHURST, Robert Andrew, *Brockworth, Gloucester.*—New Coll. Ox. B.A. 1839, M.A. 1843; Deac. 1840, Pr. 1841. V. of Brockworth, Dio. G. and B. 1864. (Patron, E. G. Davis, Esq; V.'s Inc. 150*l* and Ho; Pop. 475.) Formerly R. of Birchanger, Essex, 1851–64. [22]

BATHURST, Walter Apsley.—Wad. Coll. Ox. B.A. 1831, M.A. 1834. Asst. at All Saints', Kensington Park, Lond. Formerly Chap. of Wad. Coll. Ox. [23]

BATHURST, William Duncan Mackenzie, *Heckfield, Winchfield, Hants.*—New Coll. Ox. B.A. 1841, M.A. 1846; Deac. 1843, Pr. 1846; Fell. of New Coll. Ox; V. of Heckfield, Dio. Win. 1862. (Patron, New Coll.

Ox; Tithe, 396*l*; Glebe, 8 acres; V.'s Inc. 401*l* and Ho; Pop. 570.) Formerly C. of Hollesley, Suffolk, 1843; V. of Stradsett, Norfolk, 1846-47; C. of Marcham, Berks, 1849; R. of Stoke Abbott, Dorset, 1861-62. [1]

BATLEY, Beynon, *The Lodge, Braunton, North Devon.*—Wor. Coll. Ox. B.A. 1850, M.A. 1853; Deac. 1851 and Pr. 1852 by Bp of Ely. [2]

BATLEY, William, *Bedford Lodge, Tonbridge.*—Trin. Coll. Cam. M.A; Deac. 1862 and Pr. 1863 by Abp of Cant. C. of St. Stephen's, Tonbridge, 1864. Formerly C. of Folkestone 1862–64. [3]

BATT, Narcissus George, *Norton, Evesham.*—Dub. A.B. 1845, A.M. 1848; Deac. and Pr. 1848 by Bp of Down and Connor. V. of Norton with Lenchwick V. Dio. Wor. 1854. (Patrons, D. and C. of Wor; Tithe—App. 192*l* 6*s*, V. 39*l* 5*s*; Glebe 45 acres; V.'s Inc. 185*l* and Ho; Pop. 396.) [4]

BATTERSBY, James, 125, *Highfield-terrace, Sheffield.*—St. Aidan's; Deac. 1850 and Pr. 1851 by Bp of Ches. Min. of St. Simon's, Sheffield, 1856. (Patrons, Abp of York and others; Min.'s Inc. 200*l*.) [5]

BATTERSBY, John Casson, *Tollesbury, Kelvedon, Essex.*—St. John's Coll. Cam. B.A. 1843, M.A. 1846; Deac. 1844 and Pr. 1845 by Bp of Herf. V. of Tollesbury, Dio. Roch. 1857. (Patrons, Trustees; Glebe, 12 acres; V.'s Inc. 539*l* and Ho: Pop. 1393.) [6]

BATTERSBY, Thomas Dundas Harford, *St. John's Parsonage, Keswick.*—Ball. Coll. Ox. B.A. 1845, M.A. 1848; Deac. 1847 by Bp of Ox. Pr. 1849 by Bp of Win. P. C. of St. John's, Keswick, Dio. Carl. 1851. (Patron, R. D. Marshall, Esq; P. C.'s Inc. 270*l* and Ho; Pop. 1589.) Rural Dean, 1858; Surrogate; Hon. Can. of Carl. 1866. Formerly C. of Trinity, Gosport, 1847–49. Author, *What may the Church in general do to make the Rite of Confirmation more effectual?* 1857; *Christ in the Heart*, 1860; etc. [7]

BATTERSBY, William, *Pokesdown, Christchurch, Hants.*—P. C. of Pokesdown, Dio. Win. 1859. (Patron, V. of Christchurch; V.'s Inc. 80*l* and Ho; Pop. 457.) [8]

BATTISCOMBE, Henry, *Lee Park, Blackheath, Kent.*—Min. of St. German's Chapel, Charlton, near Blackheath. [9]

BATTISCOMBE, Richard, *Southmere, near Norwich.*—Mert. Coll. Ox. B.A. 1819, M.A. 1823. R. of Southmere, Dio. Nor. 1833. (Patron, Eton Coll; R.'s Inc. 300*l*; no church in the parish.) [10]

BATTISCOMBE, Robert Samuel, *Barkway, near Hertford.*—King's Coll. Cam. B.A. 1821, M.A. 1824; Deac. 1830 and Pr. 1831 by Bp of Pet. V. of Barkway with Reed R. Dio. Roch. 1840. (Patroness, the Hon. Mrs. Vernon Harcourt; V.'s Inc. 520*l* and Ho; Pop. Barkway 1221, Reed 224.) [11]

BATTISCOMBE, William, *Horseheath, Linton, Cambs.*—Pemb. Coll. Ox. B.A. 1822, M.A. 1826; Deac. 1827 and Pr. 1828 by Bp of Lon. R. of Horseheath, Dio. Ely, 1848. (Patron, Charter House, Lond; Tithe—App. 5*l* 2*s* and ½ acre of Glebe; Imp. 12*l* 10*s*, R. 450*l*; Glebe, 11 acres; R.'s Inc. 474*l* and Ho; Pop. 497.) [12]

BATTY, Benjamin N. R., *Mirfield, Dewsbury, Yorks.*—C. of Christchurch, Battyeford, near Mirfield. [13]

BATTY, George Staunton, *Holcroft Lodge, Fulham, S.W.*—Deac. 1861 and Pr. 1863 by Bp of Carl. C. of St. John's, Fulham, 1862. Formerly C. of Grange, Keswick. [14]

BATTY, Robert Eaton, *Birkenhead.*—Brasen. Coll. Ox. B.A. 1846, M.A. 1848; Deac. 1846 and Pr. 1847 by Bp of Ox. Formerly Incumb. of the Donative of Wragby, Yorks, 1851–59. Author, *History of Baptismal Fonts, with Four Lithographs of Norman Fonts in Bucks*, 1842, 2*s*; *Sermon on Fasting*, 1849; *Historic Sketch of Pontefract Castle*, 1852; *Sermon on the Life and Character of Wellington*, 1852. [15]

BATTY, William Edmund, *St. John's Parsonage, Fulham, S.W.*—Queen's Coll. Ox. B.A. 1845, M.A. 1848; Deac. 1846 and Pr. 1847 by Bp of Ox. P. C. of St. John's, Walham Green, Fulham. (Patron, V. of Fulham; P. C.'s Inc. 300*l*; Pop. 6931.) [16]

BATTYE, William Wilberforce, *Hever, Edenbridge, Kent.*—King's Coll. Lond. Theol. Assoc. 1849; Deac. 1849 by Bp of Chich. Pr. 1850 by Abp of Cant. R. of Hever, Dio. Cant. 1851. (Patron, E. W. Meade Waldo, Esq; Tithe, 602*l* 10*s*; Glebe, 16 acres; R.'s Inc. 622*l*, or nett 400*l*, and Ho; Pop. 544.) Formerly C. of Brighton 1849–50. [17]

BATY, Richard, *Worlabye, Brigg, Lincolnshire.*—St. Bees 1821; Deac. 1822 and Pr. 1823 by Bp. of Ches. V. of Worlabye, Dio. Lin. 1836. (Patron, J. Webb, Esq; Tithe, 342*l* 10*s*; Glebe, 12 acres; V.'s Inc. 364*l* and Ho; Pop. 526.) [18]

BATY, Thomas Jack, *Worlabye House, Roehampton, Surrey.*—Sid. Coll. Cam. B.A. 1855, M.A. 1858; Scho. Exhib. Prizeman, and late Fell. of his Coll. Formerly C. of Saunderton, Bucks, 1855–58; Asst. C. of Putney, Surrey, 1858–60. [19]

BAUGH Folliott, *Chelsfield, Bromley, Kent.*—Ex. Coll. Ox. B.A. 1831, All Souls Coll. Ox. M.A. 1836. R. of Chelsfield with Farnborough C. Dio. Cant. 1849. (Patron, All Souls Coll. Ox; Chelsfield, Tithe, 834*l*; Glebe, 53 acres; Farnborough, Tithe, 330*l* 1*s*; Glebe, 12 perches; R.'s Inc. 1212*l* and Ho; Pop. Chelsfield 784, Farnborough 955.) [20]

BAUGH, Henry, *St Mary Magdalen Parsonage, Low-hill, Liverpool.*—Queens' Coll. Cam. B.A. 1855, M.A. 1859; Deac. 1855 and Pr. 1856 by Bp of Ches. P. C. of St. Mary Magdalen's, Liverpool, Dio. Ches. 1859. (Patrons, Bp. of Ches. Archd. and R. of Liverpool; Min.'s Inc. 300*l* and Ho; Pop. 11,000.) Surrogate. Formerly C. of St. Peter's, Liverpool, 1855–59. [21]

BAUGH, Thomas, *Catherington, Horndean, Hants.*—Ch. Ch. Ox. B.A. 1851, M.A. 1855; Deac. 1852 by Bp of Madras, Pr. 1854 by Bp of Guiana. V. of Catherington, Dio. Win. 1860. (Patron, John Pritchard, Esq. M.P; V.'s Inc. 280*l* and Ho; Pop. 1160.) [22]

BAUGH, William Joseph, *Stawell, Bridgwater, Somerset.*—Magd. Hall, Ox. B.A. 1855; Deac. 1856 by Bp of B. and W. Pr. 1857 by Bp of G. and B. C. in sole charge of the Chapelries of Stawell and Sutton Mallett, Moorlinch, 1864. Formerly C. of St. Peter's, Cheltenham, Fareham, and St. James's, Halifax. [23]

BAUMGARTNER, Henry Algernon, *Mevagissey Vicarage, St. Austell.*—Caius Coll. Cam. B.A. 1844, M.A. 1847; Deac. 1845 by Bp of Salis. Pr. 1846 by Bp of B. and W. V. of Mevagissey, Dio. Ex. 1867. (Patron, J. Benbow, Esq; Tithe, 161*l*; Glebe, 23 acres; V.'s Inc. 220*l* and Ho; Pop. 1914.) Formerly P. C. of St. Paul's, Worcester, 1863–67. [24]

BAWDEN, Joshua, *South Molton, Devon.*—Ex. Coll. Ox. B.A. 1837; Deac. 1838 by Bp of G. and B. Pr. 1839 by Bp of Ex. Lect. of Molland Bothreaux (Stipend, 99*l* 16*s*.) Formerly C. of Knowstone. [25]

BAWDWEN, Walter, *Pleasington, near Blackburn.*—Trin. Coll. Cam. B.A. 1831; Deac. 1830 and Pr. 1831 by Bp of Ches. Formerly C. of Kirkham 1830–34, St. Helen's, Lancashire, 1834–38, Oswestry 1838–39; Chap. to Manchester Royal Infirmary 1839–64. [26]

BAXENDALE, Richard, *St. John's, Maidstone.*—Ch. Coll. Cam. LL.B. 1856; Deac. 1856 and Pr. 1857 by Bp of Wor. Dom. Chap. to the Earl of Romney 1858; P. C. of St. John's the Evangelist, Dio. Cant. 1860. (Patron, Earl of Romney; P. C.'s Inc. 107*l*; Pop. 330.) Formerly Asst. C. of St. Mary's, Warwick, 1856–58. [27]

BAXTER, Arthur George.—Wor. Coll. Ox. S.C.L. and B.A. 1840, M.A. 1844; Deac. 1841 and Pr. 1842 by Abp of Cant. Formerly R. of Hampreston, Dorset, 1845–57. Author, *Village Sermons*, 1848, 2nd vol. 1852. [28]

BAXTER, Henry Fleming, *Bushbury, Wolverhampton.*—Brasen. Coll. Ox. M.A. 1864; Deac. 1861 and Pr. 1862 by Abp of York. C. of Bushbury. Formerly C. of St. Thomas's, Scarborough, 1861–63. [29]

BAXTER, Thomas Preston Nowell, *Ravendale, near Grimsby, Lincolnshire.*—St. Cath. Coll. Cam. B.A. 1849, M.A. 1853; Deac. 1849 and Pr. 1850 by Bp of Ely. C. of Ravendale and Hatcliffe 1864. Formerly

Skirne Fell. of St. Cath. Coll. Cam; C. of Barton-on-Humber, and Great Coates, Lincolnshire. [1]

BAXTER, William George, *Haverhill, Suffolk.*—Dub. A.B. 1848; Deac. 1850 and Pr. 1851 by Bp of Llan. C. of Haverhill 1865. Formerly C. of Newport, Monmouthshire, 1850, Newington-Bagpath, Glouc. 1852, Basildon, Berks, 1858, Ovington, Norfolk, 1859. [2]

BAYLAY, Atwell Mervyn Yates, 44, *Jesus-lane, Cambridge.*—Trin. Coll. Cam. 26th Wrang. and B.A. 1866; Deac. 1866 by Bp of Ely. C. of St. Andrew's-the-Less, Cambridge, 1866. [3]

BAYLAY, Charles Frederick Rogers, *Kirkby-on-Bain, Horncastle, Lincolnshire.*—Trin. Coll. Cam. B.A. 1828, M.A. 1831; Deac. 1829, Pr. 1830. R. of Kirkby-on-Bain, Dio. Lin. 1846. (Patron, Ld Chan; Corn Rent, 209*l*; Glebe, 235 acres; R.'s Inc. 550*l* and Ho; Pop. 683.) Rural Dean. Author, *A Christian's Solicitude for the Ark of his Faith* (a Visitation Sermon), 1847; *On the "Essays and Reviews,"* Hatchard, 1*s* 6*d*. [4]

BAYLDON, George, *Cowling, near Cross-Hills, Yorks.*—St. Bees, 1844; Deac. 1846 and Pr. 1847 by Bp of Rip. P. C. of Cowling, Dio. Rip. 1850. (Patrons, The Crown and Bp of Rip. alt; Tithe—App. 77*l* 6*s*; P. C.'s Inc. 150*l*; Pop. 1870.) Formerly C. of Ossett, and afterwards P. C. of South Ossett, near Wakefield. Author, *Annals of the Christian Church*, 1852, 3*s*. [5]

BAYLDON, Joe Wood, *Brinkworth, near Chippenham.*—Sid. Coll. Cam. M.A. 1864; Deac. 1865 and Pr. 1866 by Bp of G. and B. C. of Brinkworth 1865. [6]

BAYLEE, Joseph, *St. Aidan's College, Birkenhead, Cheshire.*—Principal of St. Aidan's Coll. Birkenhead. [7]

BAYLEE, Joseph Tyrrell, 52, *Price-street, Birkenhead.*—Dub. A.B. 1856, A.M. 1859; Deac. 1856 and Pr. 1857 by Bp of Chich. P. C. of Trinity, Birkenhead, Dio. Ches. 1864. (Patrons, Trustees; P. C.'s Inc. 115*l* from endowment; Pop. 15,319.) Sen. Tut. of St. Aidan's Coll. Formerly C. of East Grinstead, Sussex, 1856–57, and Trinity, Birkenhead, 1857–64. Author, *Antiquity of the Church of England and Recent Origin of the Romish Sect in this Country*; *Sermon on the Man of Sin, compiled from the Notes of Wordsworth's Greek Testament*; *Questions on Books in the Course of St. Aidan's College, for use of the Students.* [8]

BAYLEE, William Cecil Percy, *Alston Vicarage, Carlisle.*—Dub. A.B. 1843, A.M. 1859; Deac. 1843 and Pr. 1845 by Bp of Lin. V. of Alston Moor with Garrigill C. Dio. Dur. 1862. (Patrons, Lords of Admiralty; Glebe, 9 acres; V.'s Inc. 175*l* and Ho; Pop. Alston 2918, Garrigill 1487, Nent Head 2039.) Formerly Chap. R. N. [9]

BAYLES, William, *Foston-on-the-Wolds, Lowthorpe, Hull.*—St. Bees; Deac. 1854 and Pr. 1855 by Bp of Lich. V. of Foston-on-the-Wolds, Dio. York, 1863. (Patroness, Miss Bayles; V.'s Inc. 102*l*; Pop. 759.) Formerly C. of Clay Cross 1854, Turton 1857. [10]

BAYLEY, Arden, *Edgcott Rectory, Banbury.*—Ex. Coll. Ox; Deac. 1819, Pr. 1821. R. of Edgcott, Dio. Pet. 1827. (Patron, Aubrey Cartwright, Esq; Tithe, 300*l*; R.'s Inc. 300*l* and Ho; Pop. 103.) Rural Dean. [11]

BAYLEY, Emilius, 1, *Montague-place, Bloomsbury, London, W.C.*—Trin. Coll. Cam; Deac. 1846 and Pr. 1847 by Bp of Ox. R. of St. George's, Bloomsbury, Dio. Lon. 1857. (Patron, Ld Chan; R.'s Inc. 800*l*; Pop. 17,392.) Rural Dean. Formerly P. C. of Woburn, Beds, 1853–56. Author, *The Choice—Lectures on Confirmation*, 2nd ed; *The Story of Nineveh*, a Lecture; *An Evangelic Ministry*; *Battles of the Bible*; Sermons, Lectures, etc. [12]

BAYLEY, Henry Marmaduke,—Trin. Coll. Cam. B.A. 1855; Deac. 1856 by Bp of Ex. Formerly Asst. C. of Appledore, Devon; and 2nd Mast. of the Bideford Gr. Sch. [13]

BAYLEY, H. E., *Cheltenham.*—Asst. Mast. in Cheltenham Coll. [14]

BAYLEY, John Arden, *Underdown House, near Pembroke.*—Oriel Coll. Ox. B.A. 1850; Deac. 1850 and Pr. 1851 by Bp of Pet. Chap. to the Forces at Pembroke. Formerly C. of Everdon, Daventry; previously C. of Staverton, Northants; Sen Chap. to the Forces in New Zealand. [15]

BAYLEY, Thomas, *Penn Street, near Amersham, Bucks.*—St. Edm. Hall, Ox. B.A. 1845, M.A. 1848; Deac. 1845, Pr. 1846. P. C. of Penn Street, Dio. Ox. 1860. (Patron, Earl Howe; P. C.'s Inc. 143*l* and Ho; Pop. 700.) [16]

BAYLEY, William Henry Ricketts, *Nailsea, Bristol.*—St. John's Coll. Cam. B.A. 1825, M.A. 1829; Deac. 1829 by Bp of Glouc. Pr. 1831 by Bp of Bristol. P. C. of Christ Ch. Nailsea, Dio. B. and W. 1860. (Patron, R. of Nailsea; P. C.'s Inc. 120*l* and Ho; Pop. 955.) Formerly P. C. of Stapleton, Glouc. 1842–47. [17]

BAYLEY, William Rutter, *Chadwell, Grays, Essex.*—Oriel Coll. Ox. B.A. 1858, M.A. 1860; Deac. 1859, Pr. 1860. R. of Chadwell St. Mary, Dio. Roch. 1864. (Patron, C. Harvey, Esq; Tithe, 480*l*; Glebe, 41½ acres; R.'s Inc. 520*l* and Ho; Pop. 457.) Formerly C. of Summertown, Oxford. [18]

BAYLIFF, Thomas Timothy Lane, *Albury, Ware, Herts.*—St. John's Coll. Ox. B.A. 1830, M.A. 1833; Deac. 1831 by Bp of Lich. Pr. 1833 by Bp of Lon. V. of Albury, Dio. Roch. 1846. (Patron, Treas. of St Paul's Cathl; Tithe—Apps. 750*l*, V. 250*l*; Glebe, 8 acres; V.'s Inc. 302*l* and Ho; Pop. 700.) [19]

BAYLIS, Edward, *Hedgerley, Gerrard's Cross, Bucks.*—St. John's Coll. Cam. B.A. 1839, M.A. 1842. R. of Hedgerley, Dio. Ox. 1845. (Patron, Edward Baylis, Esq; Tithe, 200*l* 10*s*; Glebe, 8 acres; R.'s Inc. 220*l* and Ho; Pop. 153.) [20]

BAYLISS, William Wyke, *Milton Parsonage, Portsea.*—St. John's Coll. Cam. Scho. of, B.A. 1858, M.A. 1862; Deac. 1858 by Bp of Nor. Pr. 1860 by Bp of St. D. P. C. of Milton, Dio. Win. 1865. (Patron, V. of Portsea; P. C.'s Inc. 100*l* and Ho; Pop. 2996.) Formerly C. of St. Mary's, Brecon, 1860, St. Mark's, Lakenham, Norwich, 1858–59, Ashwellthorpe, Norfolk, 1859–60, St. Mary's, Portsea, 1863–65. [21]

BAYLY, Charles Henville, *Stratton St. Peter, Long Stratton, Norfolk.*—New Coll. Ox. B.A. 1830, M.A. 1838. R. of Stratton St. Michael with Stratton St. Peter R. Dio. Nor. 1839. (Patron, New Coll. Ox; Tithe—App. 9*l* 11*s*, R. 390*l* 12*s*; Glebe, 22 acres; R.'s Inc. 430*l* and Ho; Pop. 231.) [22]

BAYLY, Edmund Goodenough, *Bedford.*—Pemb. Coll. Ox. B.A. 1825, M.A. 1827; Deac. 1827 and Pr. 1828 by Bp of Ox. C. of St. Mary's, Bedford. Formerly Fell. of Pemb. Coll. Ox; Sen. Proctor of the Univ. of Ox. 1836. [23]

BAYLY, Francis Turnour James, *Brookthorpe, near Gloucester.*—Pemb. Coll. Ox. B.A. 1831; Deac. 1831 and Pr. 1832 by Bp of Salis. V. of Brookthorpe 1839 with Whaddon P. C. 1841, Dio. G. and B. (Patrons, D. and C. of Glouc. 3 turns, and Sir John Neeld, Bart. 1 turn; Brookthorpe, Tithe—App. 155*l*, Imp. 4*l* 7*s*, V. 92*l*; Glebe, 24 acres; Whaddon, Tithe—Imp. 180*l*; Glebe, 12 acres; V.'s Inc. 222*l* and Ho; Pop. Brookthorpe 180, Whaddon 125.) Chap. to Earl of Dunraven. [24]

BAYLY, Henry Eastfield, *Leconfield, Cheltenham.*—Corpus Coll. Ox. B.A. 1840, M.A. 1851; Deac. 1853 and Pr. 1855 by Bp of G. and B. Vice Mast. in the Civil and Military Department, Cheltenham Coll. [25]

BAYLY, Thomas, 2, *Clifton, York.*—Magd. Hall, Ox. B.A. 1842; Deac. 1842 by Bp of Salis. Pr. 1846 by Bp of Chich. Min. Can. of York Cathl. 1851, Sub-chanter 1858; P. C. of St. Sampson's, City and Dio. of York, 1852. (Patrons, the Sub-chanter and Vicars-Choral of York Cathl; Glebe, 18 acres; P. C.'s Inc. 150*l*; Pop. 702.) [26]

BAYNE, George Smith, *South-Weald, Essex.*—Magd. Coll. Cam. B.A. 1851, M.A. 1854; Deac. 1851 and Pr. 1852 by Bp of Rip. C. of South-Weald 1856. Formerly C. of St. Andrew's, Wakefield, 1851, of St. John-Lee, Hexham, 1853. [27]

BAYNE, Robert Bicknell, *Cheshunt, Herts.*—Deac. 1865 and Pr. 1866 by Bp of Roch. C. of Cheshunt 1865 [28]

BAYNE, Thomas Vere, *Christ Church, Oxford.*—Ch. Ch. Ox. 2nd cl. Lit. Hum 1852, B.A. 1852, M.A. 1855; Deac. 1855 and Pr. 1856 by Bp of Ox. Student and Censor of Ch. Ch; Sen. Proctor 1867. [1]

BAYNES, Charles Alexander, *Lyndhurst, Hants.*—Trin. Coll. Cam. B.A. 1855; Deac. 1858, Pr. 1859. C. of Lyndhurst 1866. Formerly C. of Copford, Essex, 1859. [2]

BAYNES, Robert Hall, *Coventry.*—St. Edm. Hall, Ox. B.A. 1856, M.A. 1859; Deac. 1855 and Pr. 1856 by Bp of Win. V. of St. Michael's, Coventry, Dio. Wor. 1866. (Patron, the Crown; V.'s Inc. 350*l*; Pop. 15,000.) Surrogate. Formerly P. C. of St. Paul's, Whitechapel, Lond; P. C. of Trinity, Maidstone, 1862–66. Author, *Lyra Anglicana,* 36th thousand; *English Lyrics,* 5th thousand; *Canterbury Hymnal*; *Companion to the Communion Service,* with Preface by Villiers, Bp of Durham; Sermons, etc. [3]

BAYNHAM, Arthur, *Charlton, Marlborough, Wilts.*—Pemb. Coll. Ox. B.A. 1840, M.A. 1843; Deac. 1842 by Bp of Herf. Pr. 1843 by Bp of Wor. V. of Charlton, Dio. Salis. 1852. (Patron, Ch. Ch. Ox; V.'s Inc. 142*l*; Pop. 222.) Formerly Asst. C. of St. Bartholomew's, Birmingham, 1842–43; Sen. Asst. C. of Daventry 1843–53. [4]

BAYNHAM, John Francis, *Charlton-in-Dover, Kent.*—Ch. Coll. Cam. B.A. 1846, M.A. 1848; Deac. 1847 by Bp of Lon. Pr. 1848 by Abp of Cant. R. of Charlton, Dio. Cant. 1852. (Patrons, Exors. of Rev. John Monins; Tithe, 92*l*; R.'s Inc. 130*l* and Ho; Pop. 4093.) Chap. of the Dover Borough Gaol 1857 (Value 40*l*.) Formerly C. of Eastling, Kent, 1847–49, and St. John the Baptist's, Margate, 1849–52. Author, *The Voice of the Dead,* a Sermon, Dover, 1867. [5]

BAZELEY, Francis Ley, *Bideford, Devon.*—Queens' Coll. Cam. B.A. 1834, M.A. 1837; Deac. 1834 by Bp of Carl. Pr. 1836 by Bp of Roch. R. of Bideford, Dio. Ex. 1853. (Patron, Sir G. S. Stucley, Bart; Tithe, 618*l*; Glebe, 50 acres; R.'s Inc. 790*l* and Ho; Pop. 5742.) Surrogate. Formerly Rural Dean of East Cornwall 1842–45; R. of St. Dominick, Cornwall, 1835–53. [6]

BAZELEY, Francis Ley, Jun., 5, *Holyrood-place, Plymouth.*—Ch. Coll. Cam. B.A. 1863; Deac. 1863 and Pr. 1864 by Bp of Chich. Asst. C. of St. Andrew's, Plymouth, 1867. Formerly C. of Ferring-Kingston and East Preston, Sussex, 1863–67. [7]

BAZELY, John, *Cold Waltham, Petworth, Sussex.*—Brasen. Coll. Ox. B.A. 1857, M.A. 1860; Deac. 1858 and Pr. 1859 by Bp of Chich. C. of Cold Waltham and Hardham 1858. [8]

BAZETT, Alfred Young, *Quedgeley Rectory, Gloucester.*—Trin. Coll. Cam. B.A. 1837, M.A. 1840; Deac. 1838, Pr. 1839. R. of Quedgeley, Dio. G. and B. 1861. (Patron, J. C. Hayward, Esq; R.'s Inc. 161*l* and Ho; Pop. 408.) [9]

BEACH, W. R., 1, *Percy-terrace, Gloster-grove West, Kensington, S.W.*—Chap. to the Forces, Lond. [10]

BEADEL, Frank, *Dodworth, near Barnsley.*—Trin. Coll. Cam. B.A. 1864; Deac. 1865 by Bp of Rip. C. of Dodworth 1865. [11]

BEADON, Frederick, *North Stoneham, Southampton.*—Trin. Coll. Ox. B.A. 1800, M.A. 1804; Deac. 1801, Pr. 1802. Preb. of Compton Bishop in Wells Cathl. 1806; Can. Res. of Wells Cathl. 1811; Chan. of the Church of St. Andrew or Wells Cathl. 1823 (Value, 12*l*); R. of North Stoneham, Hants, Dio. Win. 1811. (Patron, J. Fleming, Esq; Tithe, 750*l*; Glebe, 50 acres; R.'s Inc. 750*l* and Ho; Pop. 968.) P. C. of Titley, Dio. Herf. 1811. (Patron, C. W. Greenly, Esq; P. C.'s Inc. 250*l*; Pop. 380.) [12]

BEADON, George Griffith, *Axbridge, Somerset.*—Deac. 1821, Pr. 1822. R. of Axbridge, Dio. B. and W. 1823. (Patron, Bp of B. and W; Tithe, 62*l* 2*s* 4*d*; Glebe, 30 acres; R.'s Inc. 155*l* and Ho; Pop. 799.) Author, *Sermons* (preached in Axbridge Church), 1840; *Ezekiel's Dry Bones* (Sermon), 1849; *Sermon on the Fast Day,* 1849; No. 2 of *The Wickliffe Club Papers,* 1849; *Remarks on a Work entitled "A Catechism of Baptism;" Letter to the Bishop of Bath and Wells,* 1850. [13]

BEADON, Hyde Wyndham, *Latton, Cricklade, Wilts.*—St. John's Coll. Cam. B.A. 1835, M.A. 1839; Deac. 1836, Pr. 1837. V. of Haslebury-Plucknett, near Crewkerne, Dio. B. and W. 1837. (Patron, Bp of B. and W; Tithe—App. 221*l* 17*s* 3*d*, and 55 acres of Glebe, V. 126*l* 6*s* 6*d*; Glebe, 7 acres; V.'s Inc. 190*l* and Ho; Pop. 834.) V. of Latton with Eisey V. Dio. G. and B. (Patron, Earl St. Germans; Eisey, Tithe, 153*l*; V.'s Inc. 300*l* and Ho; Pop. Latton 308, Eisey, 198.) Rural Dean. [14]

BEADON, Richard a'Court, *Cheddar, Weston-super-Mare.*—St. John's Coll. Cam. B.A. 1832, M.A. 1835; Deac. 1832, Pr. 1833. V. of Cheddar, Dio. B. and W. 1836. (Patrons, D. and C. of Wells; Tithe, 300*l*; Glebe, 40 acres; V.'s Inc. 423*l* and Ho; Pop. 1580.) V. of Wiveliscombe, Somerset, Dio. B. and W. 1837. (Patron, Preb. of Wiveliscombe in Wells Cathl; Tithe—V. 610*l*; V.'s Inc. 610*l* and Ho; Pop. 2735.) Preb. of Wiveliscombe 1827. [15]

BEADON, Richard John, *Sherwell, Barnstaple, Devon.*—Queen's Coll. Ox. B.A. 1826, M.A. 1829; Deac. 1827 and Pr. 1828 by Bp of B. and W. R. of Sherwell, Dio. Ex. 1834. (Patron, Sir A. Chichester, Bart; Tithe, 561*l*; Glebe, 91 acres; R.'s Inc. 651*l* and Ho; Pop. 609.) [16]

BEAL, Samuel.—Chap. of H.M.S. "Victory." [17]

BEAL, Samuel Gilbert, 29, *Delamere-terrace, London, W.*—Ex. Coll. Ox. Exhib. of, 1862, B.A. 1866; Deac. 1866 by Bp of Rupert's Land for Bp of Lon. Asst. C. of St. Mary Magdalene's, Paddington, 1866. [18]

BEAL, William, *Brooke Vicarage, Norwich.*—King's Coll. Lond. 1834, Trin. Coll. Cam. 1835–42; Univ. Aberdeen, M.A. and LL.D. 1845; Deac. 1841 by Bp of Ex. Pr. 1846 by Bp of Nor. V. of Brooke, Dio. Nor. 1847. (Patron, Ld Chan; Tithe, 325*l*, V. 240*l*; Glebe, 5 acres; V.'s Inc. 316*l* and Ho; Pop. 746); Dioc. Inspector of Schools; Surrogate; Fell. of the Society of Antiquaries; Vice-President of the Young Men's Christian Association; Corresponding Member of the Working Men's Educational Union; Corresponding Associate of the Genealogical and Historical Society of Great Britain. Formerly Head Mast. of Tavistock Gr. Sch. 1837–47; C. of Sampford Spiney, Devon, 1841–42; C. of Bray, near Dublin, 1843–47. Author, *First Book in Chronology,* 1840; *Christian Brotherhood,* 1841; *Young English Churchman's Commonplace Book,* 1845; *Certain Godlie Praiers,* &c. 1846; *Analysis of Origines Liturgicæ,* 1847; *Church Unions,* 1848; *People's Colleges,* 1851; *The Nineveh Monuments and Old Testament History,* 1853; *Practical Suggestions for the Celebration of Parochial Harvest Homes, &c.* 1855; *Letter to the Earl of Albemarle on the Origin, Progress and Management of Parochial Harvest Homes,* 1858; *The Triple Plea: Body, Soul and Spirit* (a Lecture delivered at Exeter Hall), 1858. Formerly Editor of the *West of England Magazine.* [19]

BEALE, S. C. Tress, *Eastgate, Tenterden, Kent.*—Wad. Coll. Ox. B.A. 1854, M.A. 1857; Deac. 1857 and Pr. 1858 by Abp of Cant. P. C. of St. Michael's, Tenterden, Dio. Cant. 1864. (Patron, Seaman Beale, Esq; P. C.'s Inc. 31*l* 13*s* 6*d*, int. of 1000*l* in Queen Anne's Bounty; Pop. 810.) Formerly C. of Capel-le-Ferne, Dover, 1857. [20]

BEALE, Th., *Hopton-castle, Aston-on-Clun.*—Brasen. Coll. Ox. R. of Hopton-castle, Dio. Herf. 1836. (Patron, T. Salwey Beale, Esq; Tithe, 294*l*; Glebe, 61 acres; R.'s Inc. 357*l* and Ho; Pop. 158.) [21]

BEALES, John Day.—St. John's Coll. Cam. B.A. 1861; Deac. 1862 and Pr. 1863 by Bp of Ely. Formerly C. of Newton, Suffolk, 1862. [22]

BEALEY, John Kay, *St. Hilda's, Middlesborough-on-Tees.*—Sid. Coll. Cam. B.A. 1855; Deac. 1855 by Abp of York, Pr. 1856 by Bp of Carl. P. C. of St. Hilda's, Middlesborough, Dio. York, 1865. (Patron, Abp of York, P. C.'s Inc. 300*l* and Ho; Pop. 11,000.) Surrogate. Formerly C. of Ch. Ch. Doncaster. [23]

BEAMISH, Henry Hamilton, *Wimbish, Saffron Walden.*—Dub. V. of Wimbish with Thunderley

V. Dio. Roch. 1865. (Patron, the present R; Tithe—Sinecure R. 564*l* 4*s* and 162 acres of Glebe, Imp. 204*l*. V. 283*l* 2*s* 10*d*; Glebe, 11 acres and 2 cottages; V.'s Inc. 303*l* and Ho; Pop. 1470.) Chap. to Earl of Bandon. Formerly Min. of Trin. Chapel, Conduit-street, Lond. 1832–62; V. of Old Cleeve, Somerset, 1862–65. Author, *Lectures on the Human Nature of Jesus Christ*; *Two Letters to Dr. Pusey*; *Treatise on Auricular Confession*; *Letters on Church Authority, Transubstantiation, &c*; *Truth spoken in Love*; *What, Where, and Who is Antichrist?* etc. [1]

BEAMISH, Thomas, *Harome Parsonage, Nawton, York.*—St. Aidan's; Deac. and Pr. by Abp of Cant. P. C. of Harome, Dio. York, 1863. (Patron, Ld Feversham; P. C.'s Inc. 143*l* and Ho; Pop. 447.) [2]

BEAMONT, William John, *Trinity College, Cambridge.*—Trin. Coll. Cam. B.A. 1850, M.A. 1853; Deac. 1853 by Bp of Ely, Pr. 1855 by Bp of Lon. P. C. of St. Michael's, Cambridge, Dio. Ely, 1857. (Patron, Trin. Coll. Cam; P. C.'s Inc. 150*l*; Pop. 376.) Formerly C. of St. John the Evangelist, Drury-lane, Lond; Fell. of Trin. Coll. Cam. Author, *Catherine*; *Cairo to Sinai and Sinai to Cairo*; *A Concise Grammar of the Arabic Language*; *Catechumen's Manual*; *Fine Art as a Branch of Academic Study*; *The Prayer Book interleaved*; etc. [3]

BEAN, Alexander Louis Wellington, *Sowerby, Halifax.*—Pemb. Coll. Ox. B.A. 1839, M.A. 1844; Deac. 1840 and Pr. 1841 by Bp of Rip. P. C. of Sowerby, Dio. Rip. 1852. (Patron, V. of Halifax; P. C.'s Inc. 198*l* and Ho; Pop. 4521.) [4]

BEANLANDS, Charles, 5, *Western Cottages, Brighton.*—Clare Hall, Cam. late Scho. of St. Cath. Hall, B.A. 1847, M.A. 1851; Deac. 1847 and Pr. 1849 by Bp of Rip. P. C. of St. Michael's, Brighton, Dio. Chich. 1860. (Patrons, Trustees; P. C.'s Inc. 150*l*.) Dom. Chap. to Earl of Crawford and Balcarres. Formerly C. of St. Paul's, Brighton. [5]

BEARCROFT, Edward Charles King, *Downham Market, Norfolk.*—Queens' Coll. Cam. LL.B. 1856; Deac. 1850 and Pr. 1856 by Bp of B. and W. C. of Downham Market 1859; Chap. to the Downham Union 1863; and Hon. Chap. to the 23rd Norfolk Volunteer Rifle Corps. Formerly C. of Bridgwater and Chilton, Somerset, and Whitchurch Canonicorum with Stanton St. Gabriel, Dorset. [6]

BEARCROFT, James, *Hadsor, Droitwich, Worcestershire.*—Oriel Coll. Ox. B.A. 1840; Deac. 1841, Pr. 1842. R. of Hadsor, Dio. Wor. 1842. (Patron, J. H. Galton, Esq; R.'s Inc. 210*l*; Pop. 158.) [7]

BEARCROFT, Thomas, *Ascot, near Shrewsbury.*—Queen's Coll. Ox. B.A. 1842, M.A. 1846; Deac. 1844 and Pr. 1845 by Bp of Wor. C. of Cruckton District in the second portion of Pontesbury Parish, Minsterley, Shropshire. [8]

BEARD, Arthur, *King's College, Cambridge.*—St. John's Coll. Cam. Scho. of, 29th Wrang. Goldsmith's Exhib. B.A. 1855, M.A. 1858; Deac. 1855 and Pr. 1856 by Bp of Lich. Chap. of King's Coll. Cam. 1858. Formerly C. of Weeford and Hints, Staffs. 1855–57. Joint Editor, with the Rev. F. H. Gray, of the *Oxford and Cambridge Psalter*, 1863, 3*s* 6*d*. [9]

BEARD, Thomas, *Stokesby Rectory, Norwich.*—Jesus Coll. Cam. B.A. 1864; Deac. 1865 and Pr. 1866 by Bp of Ely. R. of Stokesby with Herringby, Dio. Nor. 1866. (Patron, Charles Beard, Esq; Tithe, 526*l*; Glebe, 46 acres; R.'s Inc. 592*l* and Ho; Pop. 418.) Formerly C. of Godmanchester, Hunts, 1865-66. [10]

BEARD, William Day, *Norwich.*—Trin. Coll. Cam. B.A. 1846; Deac. 1847 and Pr. 1848 by Bp of Lich. [11]

BEARDSELL, George, 40, *Frenchwood-street, Preston.*—St. Bees; Deac. 1857 and Pr. 1858 by Abp of York. P. C. of All Saints, Preston, Dio. Man. 1863. (Patrons, Trustees; P. C.'s Inc. 230*l*; Pop. 4480.) Formerly C. of Seaton-Ross 1857–59, St. Matthias, Salford, 1859–61, Holy Trinity, Preston, 1861–63; Min. of St. Saviour's District, Preston, 1863. Author, Articles in various Magazines. [12]

BEARDSWORTH, George, *Selling, Feversham, Kent.*—St. John's Coll. Cam. Jun. Opt. B.A. 1837, M.A. 1843; Deac. by Abp of Cant. Pr. by Bp. of Lon; V. of Selling, Dio. Cant. 1851. (Patron, Ld Sondes; Tithe—Imp. 810*l*, V. 357*l*; Glebe, 6 acres; V.'s Inc. 363*l* and Ho; Pop. 575.) [13]

BEASLEY, Henry Frank, *Bishopston, near Shrivenham, Berks.*—Dub. A.B. 1829, A.M. 1833, *ad eund.* Ox. 1851; Deac. 1840 and Pr. 1842 by Bp of Ches. C. of Bishopston 1848. Formerly C. of Great Budworth 1840, and Wilmslow, Cheshire, 1843; Worsley, Lancashire, 1847. [14]

BEASLEY, Richard Dunkley, *Grammar School, Grantham.*—St. John's Coll. Cam. Fell. of, 6th Wrang. B.A. 1853, M.A. 1856. Head Mast. of Gr. Sch. Grantham, 1858. Author, *Elements of Plane Trigonometry*, 1858, 2nd ed. 1865, 3*s* 6*d*; *Arithmetic for Schools*, 1867, 3*s*. [15]

BEASLEY, Thomas Calvert, *Saffron-Walden, Essex.*—Trin. Coll. Cam. B A. 1859, M.A. 1862, Jun. Opt; Deac. 1859 and Pr. 1860 by Bp of Pet. C. of Saffron-Walden 1863. Formerly C. of Wellingborough 1859–63. [16]

BEATH, Henry.—St. John's Coll. Cam. B.A. 1837; Deac. 1837, Pr. 1838. Formerly V. of Billingshurst, Sussex, 1832–60. [17]

BEATSON, Benjamin Wrigglesworth, *Pembroke College, Cambridge.*—Pemb. Coll. Cam. B.A. 1825, M.A. 1828; Deac. 1828 by Bp of Lin. Pr. 1835 by Bp of Carl. Fell. of Pemb. Coll. Cam. 1827. [18]

BEATSON, Leonard Browne, *Twyford, Berks.*—Corpus Coll. Cam. B.A. 1859, M.A. 1862; Deac. 1860 and Pr. 1861 by Abp of Cant. C. in sole charge of Twyford 1865. Formerly C. of St. Clement and St. Mary's, Sandwich, 1860. [19]

BEATTIE, Henry, *London Orphan Asylum, Clapton, London, N.E.*—Dub. A.B. 1847, A.M. 1851, *ad eund.* Cam. 1852; Deac. 1847 and Pr. 1848 by Bp of Lon. Chap. and Head Mast. of the London Orphan Asylum. Formerly Vice-Prin. of the National Society's Training Institution, Westminster, 1843–52. [20]

BEATTIE, John, *Chapel House, Egham, Surrey.*—Dub. A.B; Deac. and Pr. by Bp of Salis. Chap. and Mast. of Cooper's Almshouses and Schools, Egham. Formerly C. of Bridport. [21]

BEAUCHAMP, G. C. P.—C. of St. Stephen's, Lewisham, Kent. Formerly C. of Haselbury Bryan, Dorset. [22]

BEAUCHAMP, James, *Crowell, Tetswell, Oxon.*—Clare Coll. Cam. B.A. 1828; Deac. 1829 and Pr. 1830 by Bp. of Ox. R. of Crowell, Dio. Ox. 1830. (Patroness, Miss Wykeham; Tithe, 243*l* 10*s*; Glebe, 9 acres; R.'s Inc. 249*l* and Ho; Pop. 162.) V. of Shirburn, Dio. Ox. 1832. (Patron, Earl of Macclesfield; Tithe, 80*l*, Corn Rent 14*l* 4*s*; V.'s Inc. 94*l*; Pop. 292.) [23]

BEAUCHAMP, Robert William, *Wickmere Rectory, Hanworth, Norwich.*—Ch. Coll. Cam. B.A. 1836, M.A. 1839; Deac. 1836 by Bp of Dur. Pr. 1838 by Bp of Nor. R. of Wolterton with Wickmere R. Dio. Nor. 1855. (Patron, Earl of Orford; Tithe, 550*l*; Glebe, 35 acres; R.'s Inc. 620*l*; Pop. Wolterton 48, Wickmere 268.) [24]

BEAUFORT, Daniel Augustus, *Warburton Rectory, near Warrington.*—Jesus Coll. Cam. B.A. 1837, M.A. 1840; Deac. 1838, Pr. 1839. R. of Lymm with Warburton, Dio. Ches. 1849. (Patron, R. E. Egerton Warburton, Esq; R.'s Inc. 400*l* and Ho; Pop. 484.) Author, *Scripture sufficient without Popish Tradition* (Norrisian Prize Essay), 1840; *The Customs of the Church* (a Sermon), 1843, 4*d*; *How shall I understand the Bible? or the True Nature of the Christian Church, the Real value of Tradition, and the Proper Use of Private Judgment familiarly explained*, 1844, 4*d*; *The House of Prayer for all People* (a Sermon), 1852. [25]

BEAUMONT, Francis Morton, 21, *Herbert-street, Hoxton, London, N.*—St. John's Coll. Ox. Fell. of, 3rd cl. Lit. Hum. B.A. 1861, M.A. 1864; Deac. 1864 and Pr. 1865 by Bp of Ox. Asst. C. of Trinity, Hoxton,

1865. Formerly Asst. Mast. in Rossall Sch. 1862-65. [1]

BEAUMONT, George Price, *Hokitika, New Zealand.*—Dub. A.M; Deac. 1858 and Pr. 1859 by Bp of B. and W. Miss. to Hokitika Gold Diggings 1866. Formerly C. of Monksilver, Taunton. [2]

BEAUMONT, George Richardson, *Clitheroe, Lancashire.*—Deac. 1856 by Abp of Cant, Pr. 1858 by Bp of Rip. Asst. Mast. of Clitheroe Gr. Sch. 1850. Formerly C. of Hurst-green, Whalley, 1856-59. [3]

BEAUMONT, Henry, 19. *Brunswick-square, Brighton.*—Dub. A.B. 1851, A M. 1854, B.D. and D.D. 1866, *ad. eund.* Ox. 1866; Deac. 1851 and Pr. 1852 by Bp of Ches. P. C. of St. Andrew's, Hove, Dio. Chich. 1866. (P. C.'s Inc. 150*l*.) Formerly R. of Freshford, Bath, 1854-56. Author, *Auricular Confession not the Doctrine of the Scriptures, nor of the Church of England,* Skeffington, 1857. [4]

BEAUMONT, James Akroyd.—Trin. Coll. Camb. B.A. 1841, M.A. 1844; Deac. 1842 by Bp of Herf. Pr. 1843 by Bp of Rip. Dom. Chap. to Earl Fitzwilliam 1842. Late R. of Poughill, Devon, 1850-61. [5]

BEAUMONT, John, *Askern, Doncaster.*—Trin. Coll. Cam. B.A. 1845, M.A. 1848; Deac. 1845, Pr. 1846. P. C. of Askern, Dio. York, 1857. (Patron, Abp of York; P. C.'s Inc. 93*l*; Pop. 863.) Formerly P. C. of Sneyd, Staffs, 1851-56. [6]

BEAUMONT, Matthias Henry, *Lowestoft, Suffolk.*—St. Cath. Coll. Cam. Scho. of, 14th Sen. Opt. B.A. 1847, M.A. 1851; Deac. 1847 by Bp of Ches. Pr. 1848 by Bp of Man. P. C. of St. John's, Lowestoft, Dio. Nor. 1854. (Patrons, Trustees; P. C.'s Inc. 320*l* and Ho; Pop. 2830.) [7]

BEAUMONT, Thomas George, *Chelmondiston, Ipswich.*—R. of Chelmondiston, Dio. Nor. 1863. (Patron, Ld Chan; R.'s Inc. 360*l* and Ho; Pop. 950.) [8]

BEAUMONT, William Beresford, *Cole-Orton Rectory, Ashby-de-la-Zouch.*—Ch. Ch. Ox. B.A. 1853, M.A. 1855; Deac. 1858 and Pr. 1859 by Bp of Herf. R. of Cole-Orton, Dio. Pet. 1864. (Patron, Sir G. Beaumont, Bart; Tithe, 292*l*; Glebe, 7½ acres; R.'s Inc. 292*l* and Ho; Pop. 550.) Formerly Stud. of Ch. Ch. Ox. 1852-60; C. of Church Stretton, Salop, 1858-60, and Seavington St. Mary, Somerset, 1862-63. [9]

BEAVAN, Thomas, *Much Birch, near Hereford.*—P. C. of Much Birch, Dio. Herf. 1850. (Patron, T. G. Symons, Esq; Tithe—App. 2*l* 4*s*, Imp. 192*l* 6*s*, P. C. 89*l* 1*s*; P. C.'s Inc. 104*l*; Pop. 496.) R. of Llandinabo, near Ross, Dio. Herf. 1850. (Patron, Kedgwin Hoskins, Esq; Tithe, 130*l*; R.'s Inc. 142*l*; Pop. 63.) [10]

BEAVAN, T. H.—C. of St. David's, Merthyr Tydvil. [11]

BEAVAN, Thomas Meredith, *Much Birch, near Ross, Herefordshire.*—St. John's Coll. Cam. B.A. 1861, M.A. 1865; Deac. 1862 and Pr. 1863 by Bp of Herf. C. of Llandinabo 1862. [12]

BEAZOR, John A., *Adderbury, Deddington, Oxon.*—C. of Adderbury. [13]

BEBB, William, *Simon's Town, Cape of Good Hope.*—St. John's Coll. Cam. B.A. 1853; Deac. 1853, Pr. 1854. Mast. of the Gr. Sch. Simon's Town. Formerly C. of Stanton-upon-Arrow, Herefordshire. [14]

BECHER, James Young, 20, *Norland-square, Notting-hill, London, W.*—Wor. Coll. Ox. B.A. 1837; Deac. 1838, Pr. 1839. Formerly Chap. Bengal Ecclesiastical Establishment and Acting Garrison Chap. St. Heliers, Jersey, 1862-65. [15]

BECHER, Michael Henry.—Jesus Coll. Cam. B.A. 1843; Deac. 1844 by Bp of Cork, Pr. 1844 by Bp of Killaloe. Formerly R. of Barnold-le-Beck, Lincolnshire, 1846-61. [16]

BECK, Andrew, *Lavenham, Suffolk.*—Caius Coll. Cam. B.A. 1855, M.A. 1858; Deac. 1855 by Abp of York, Pr. 1857 by Bp of Ely. C. of Lavenham 1856. Formerly C. of Kirk Fenton, Yorks, 1855-56. [17]

BECK, Cadwallader Coker, *Foleshill, Coventry.*—Ball. Coll Ox. B.A. 1841; Deac. 1842 and Pr. 1843 by Bp of Wor. P. C. of St. Paul's District, Foleshill, Dio. Wor. 1843. (Patron, V. of Foleshill; P. C.'s Inc. 148*l*; Pop. 3231.) [18]

BECK, Edward Josselyn, *Litlington Vicarage, Royston, Cambs.*—Clare Coll. Cam. B.A. 1855, M.A. 1858; Deac. 1856 by Bp of Ely, Pr. 1857 by Bp of Lon. Fell. of Clare Coll. Cam. V. of Litlington, Dio. Ely, 1867. (Patron, Clare Coll. Cam; Tithe, 230*l*; V.'s Inc. 230*l* and Ho; Pop. 697.) Formerly C. of Ch. Ch, St. Pancras, Lond. [19]

BECK, James, *The Cottage, Storrington, Sussex.*—Corpus Coll. Cam. B.A. 1839, M.A. 1842; Deac. 1842 and Pr. 1843 by Bp of Salis. R. of Parham, Sussex, Dio. Chich. 1859. (Patroness, Baroness De la Zouche; Tithe, 133*l*; Glebe, 15 acres; R.'s Inc. 150*l*; Pop. 71.) Formerly C. of Pulborough, Sussex, 1852-57. [20]

BECK, William, *Clannaborough Rectory, Bow, N. Devon.*—Pemb. Coll. Ox. 3rd cl Lit. Hum. B.A. 1850, M.A. 1853; Deac. 1851 and Pr. 1852 by Bp of Lon. R. of Clannaborough, Dio. Ex. 1867. (Patron, Ld Chan; Tithe, 95*l*; Glebe, 45 acres; R.'s Inc. 200*l* and Ho; Pop. 61.) Formerly C. of St. Mary's, Tothill-fields, Westminster, 1851-57, St. Philip's, Dalston, 1857-60, and St. Barnabas', Homerton, 1861-67. Author, *Bishop Latimer,* a Lecture, 1861; and *Sir Thomas More,* a Lecture, 1862, both published by S P.C.K. [21]

BECKER, Ferdinand William, 1, *St. George's-terrace, Regent's-park-road, London, N.W.*—Ex. Coll. Ox. B.A. 1830, M A. 1853; Deac. 1850 by Bp of Wor. Pr. 1831 by Bp of Ex. Formerly C. of Overbury, Worcestershire. [22]

BECKETT, Henry Frederick, *Orange Free State, S. Africa.*—St. Cath. Hall, Cam. B.A. 1840, M.A. 1844; Deac. 1840, Pr. 1841. [23]

BECKETT, Joseph Adkins, *Forest Row, East Grinstead, Sussex.*—Mert. Coll. Ox. B.A. 1836. P. C. of Forest Row, Dio. Chich. 1849. (Patron, V. of East Grinstead; P. C.'s Inc. 160*l*; Pop. 1411.) [24]

BECKETT, William Thomas, *Ingoldsthorpe, Lynn, Norfolk.*—Trin. Coll. Ox. B.A. 1840, M A. 1842; Deac. 1841 and Pr. 1842 by Bp of G. and B. R. of Ingoldsthorpe, Dio. Nor. 1855. (Patron, the present R; Tithe, 312*l*; Glebe, 47 acres; R.'s Inc. 380*l* and Ho; Pop. 372. Formerly C. of Abbenhall, Glouc. and Lacock, Wilts; P. C. of St. Mary Magdalen's, Harlow Bush, Essex. [25]

BECKETT, Wilson, *Heighington, Darlington.*—Trin. Coll. Cam. B.A. 1816; Deac. 1818, Pr. 1820. V. of Heighington, Dio. Dur. 1836. (Patrons, D. and C. of Dur; Tithe—App. 168*l* 12*s* 2*d*, V. 322*l*; V.'s Inc. 336*l* and Ho; Pop. 1214.) [26]

BECKFORD, Charles Douglas, 3, *Cumberland-place, Southampton.*—Brasen. Coll. Ox. B.A. 1819 and All Souls Coll. Ox. M.A. 1823; Deac. 1820, Pr. 1821. [27]

BECKWITH, George, *Winchester.*—New Coll. Ox. B.A. 1858, M.A. 1861; Deac. 1858 and Pr. 1859 by Bp of Carl. Min. Can. of Win. Cathl. 1860 and Chap. of St. Mary's Coll. Win. 1863. Formerly C. of Drigg, Cumberland, 1858-60, St. John's, Winchester, 1860-63. [28]

BECKWITH, George Langton, *Blymhill, Shiffnal, Salop.*—All Souls Coll. Ox. B.A. 1848, M.A. 1851; Deac. 1849, Pr. 1850. C. of Blymhill 1850. [29]

BECKWITH, Henry, *Eaton-Constantine, near Wellington, Shropshire.*—Jesus Coll. Cam. B.A. 1830; Deac. 1830, Pr. 1831. R. of Eaton-Constantine, Dio. Lich. 1832. (Patron, Duke of Cleveland; Tithe—App. 48*l* 6*s*, R. 130*l*; Glebe, 26 acres; R.'s Inc. 190*l*; Pop. 242.) [30]

BECKWITH, Henry William, *The Mount, York.*—Univ. Coll. Ox. B.A. 1843, M.A. 1853; Deac. and Pr. 1844 by Bp of Dur. R. of St. Mary Bishop-hill-the-Elder, City and Dio. York, 1854. (Patron, Ld Chan; Tithe, 151*l* 5*s*; Glebe, 47 acres; R.'s Inc. 330*l*; Pop 2340.) [31]

BEDDOES, Thomas Lewis, *Barton Grange, Irlam, Patricroft, Manchester.*—Deac. 1862 and Pr. 1863 by Bp of Ches. P. C. of Irlam, Dio. Man. 1866. (Patrons, Five Trustees; Pop. 4000.) Formerly C. of Hollinfare 1862–63, and Irlam 1864–65. [1]

BEDDOME, Arthur, *Clapham Common, London, S.*—Pemb. Coll. Ox. B.A. 1861, M.A. 1864; Deac. 1863 by Bp of Ely. Formerly C. of Shillington, Beds. [2]

BEDDY, Joseph Fawcett, *Monmouth.*—Dub. A.B. 1826, A.M. 1829, *ad eund.* Ox; Deac. 1823 by Bp of Lon. Pr. 1824 by Bp of Salis. P. C. of St. Thomas's, Monmouth, Dio. Llan. 1832. (Patron, Duke of Beaufort; P. C.'s Inc. 80*l*; Pop. 1140) Surrogate. [3]

BEDFORD, Charles, *Denton, Newhaven, Sussex.*—St. Peter's Coll. Cam. Scho. of, and 12th Sen. Opt. B.A. 1834; Deac. 1837 by Bp of Chich. Pr. 1838 by Bp of Lin. R. of Denton, Dio. Chich. 1838. (Patroness, Miss Catt; Tithe, 245*l*; Glebe, 65 poles; R.'s Inc. 264*l* 2*s* 6*d* and Ho; Pop. 250.) [4]

BEDFORD, Charles, *Allesley, Coventry.*—New Coll. Ox. B.A. 1839; Deac. 1841, Pr. 1842. [5]

BEDFORD, Henry, *Swanmore, Ryde, Isle of Wight.*—Emman. Coll. Cam. S.C.L. 1854, LL.B. 1857, B.C.L. *ad eund.* Ox. 1857, LL.D. 1865; Deac. 1854 and Pr. 1855 by Bp of Ex. C. of St. Michael's, Swanmore, 1867. Formerly C. of St. James's, Exeter, 1854–56, Frome Selwood, 1856–58, and 1860–62, Wilmslow 1858–59, Boyne Hill 1859–60, St. Thomas's, Oxford, 1863, Foxearth 1865–66, St. Paul's, Brighton, 1866. Author, *Despising the Poor*, a Sermon, Manchester, 1859. [6]

BEDFORD, James Gower, *Twyford, Winchester.*—New Coll. Ox. B.A. 1808, M.A. 1811; Deac. 1809, Pr. 1810. [7]

BEDFORD, John, *Scarborough.*—Lin. Coll. Ox. Scho. of, Goldsmith's Exhib. B.A. 1860, M.A. 1861; Deac. 1865 and Pr. 1866 by Abp of York. C. of St. Mary's, Scarborough. Formerly Head Cl. Asst. Mast. at Cheltenham Sch. 1860–65. [8]

BEDFORD, Thomas, *Iford, near Lewes.*—Emman. Coll. Cam. M.A; Deac. 1833, Pr. 1834. V. of Iford with Kingston V. Dio. Chich. 1864. (Patron, present V; Tithe, 394*l* 19*s*; Glebe, 4½ acres; V.'s Inc. 407*l* and Ho; Pop. Iford 167, Kingston 137.) Formerly R. of Old Cleeve, Somerset. [9]

BEDFORD, William, *Marshfield Vicarage, Chippenham.*—New Coll. Ox. B.A. 1838, M.A. 1842; Deac. 1838, Pr. 1840. V. of Marshfield, Dio. G. and B. 1858. (Patron, New Coll. Ox; Tithe—Imp. 680*l*, V. 321*l* 14*s*; Glebe, 10 acres; V.'s Inc. 342*l* and Ho; Pop. 1742.) [10]

BEDFORD, W. J. P., *Bramford, Ipswich.*—St. John's Coll. Cam. B.A. 1831; Deac. 1831 and Pr. 1832 by Bp of Lin. V. of Bramford with Burstall C. Dio. Nor. 1859. (Patrons, D. and C. of Cant; V.'s Inc. 80*l* and Ho; Pop. 1241.) [11]

BEDFORD, William Kirkpatrick Riland, *Sutton Coldfield, near Birmingham.*—Brasen. Coll. Ox. B.A. 1848, M.A. 1852; Deac. 1849 and Pr. 1850 by Bp of Wor. R. of Sutton Coldfield, Dio. Wor 1850. (Patron, the present R; R.'s Inc. 247*l* and Ho; Pop. 1947.) Rural Dean. Author, *The Blazon of Episcopacy*, 1858. [12]

BEDINGFELD, James, *Bedingfeld, Eye, Suffolk.*—Trin. Coll. Cam. B.A. 1831; Deac. and Pr. 1833. R. of Bedingfeld, Dio. Nor. 1833. (Patron, J. L. Bedingfeld, Esq; Tithe, 400*l* 10*s*; Glebe, 4 acres; R.'s Inc. 408*l* and Ho; Pop. 321.) Rural Dean of Hoxne; Dom. Chap. to Lord Henniker. Formerly V. of Debenham, Suffolk, 1840–59. [13]

BEDINGFIELD, Richard King, *Trowbridge, Wilts.*—Queens' Coll. Cam. B.A. 1833; Deac. 1833 and Pr. 1834 by Bp of Salis. C. of Trowbridge. [14]

BEDWELL, Francis, *Newport, Monmouth.*—Corpus Coll. Ox. B.A. 1860, M.A. 1865; Deac. 1861 and Pr. 1862 by Bp of Llan. C. of St. Woolos, Newport. [15]

BEE, John, *Jarrow Grange, Gateshead.*—Deac. 1863 by Bp of Dur. C. of Jarrow 1863. [16]

BEEBEE, Meyrick, *Simonburn, Hexham, Northumberland.*—St. John's Coll. Cam. B.A. 1828, M.A. 1847; Deac. 1829, Pr. 1830. R. of Simonburn, Dio. Dur. 1841. (Patrons, Governors of Greenwich Hospital; Tithe, 542*l* 10*s*; Glebe, 78 acres; R.'s Inc. 542*l* and Ho; Pop. 600.) Dom. Chap. to the Duke of Somerset 1831. Formerly Chap. R. N. [17]

BEEBY, William, *Birkby, Maryport, Cumberland.*—St. John's Coll. Cam. B.A. 1856; Deac. 1856 and Pr. 1857 by Bp of Carl. [18]

BEECHENO, James, *Walton, Peterborough.*—Queens' Coll. Cam. B.A. 1850, M.A. 1853; Deac. 1850 and Pr. 1851 by Bp of Pet. C. of Paston, near Peterborough. [19]

BEECHEY, Prince William Thomas.—Dub. A.B. 1862; Deac. 1863 and Pr. 1864 by Bp of Ox. [20]

BEECHEY, St. Vincent, *Worsley, Eccles, Manchester.*—Caius. Coll. Cam. B.A. 1826, M.A. 1829; Deac. 1829 and Pr. 1830 by Bp of Roch. P. C. of Worsley Dio. Man. 1850. (Patron, Earl of Ellesmere; P. C.'s Inc. 200*l* and Ho; Pop. 2000.) Incumb. of Ellenbrook Donative Chapel, Eccles, Dio. Man. 1854. (Patron, Earl of Ellesmere; Incumb.'s Inc. 175*l*.) Dom. Chap. to the Earl of Ellesmere and to Lord Grantley. [21]

BEEDHAM, Henry B., *Ellerburne, Pickering, Yorks.* [22]

BEEDHAM, Maurice John, *Spring Hill, Whitby.*—Caius. Coll. Cam. B.A. 1857; Deac. 1858 and Pr. 1859 by Bp of Herf. Formerly C. of Claverley, 1858–62, Kirby Moorside 1862–64, Westbury 1864. [23]

BEERS, John Banks, *Carlisle.*—C. of St. Mary's, Carlisle. [24]

BEEVER, William Holt, *St. Hilary, Glamorgan.*—V. of St. Hilary, Dio. Llan. 1854. (Patrons, D. and C. of Llan; V.'s Inc. 56*l*; Pop. 139.) Exam. Chap. to Bp of Llan. 1859; Hon. Can. of Llan. Formerly Fell of Jesus Coll. Ox. [25]

BEEVOR, Edward Rigby, *Hevingham, near Norwich.*—Corpus Coll. Cam. B.A. 1823; Deac. 1823 and Pr. 1824 by Bp of Nor. R. of Hevingham, Dio. Nor. 1837. (Patron, the present R; Tithe—App. 2*l* 16*s*; R. 547*l* 4*s*; R.'s Inc. 587*l* and Ho; Pop. 838.) [26]

BEEVOR, William Smythies, *Bury St. Edmunds.*—Jesus Coll. Cam. B.A. 1823, M.A. 1835; Deac. 1823 and Pr. 1824 by Bp of Lon. Formerly C. of Rampton, Cambs, and Cavendish, Suffolk. Author, *A Sermon on the Holy Sacrament*, 1843, 6*d*. [27]

BEGBIE, Alexander George, *Eton, Bucks.*—C. of Upton with Chalvey, Slough; Chap. of Eton Union. [28]

BEGBIE, Mars Hamilton, *Aldborough, Saxmundham, Suffolk.*—St. Peter's Coll. Cam. Gisborne Scho. 1854, 2nd cl. Cl. Trip. 1857, B.A. 1857; Deac. 1857 by Bp of Win. Pr. 1858 by Abp of Cant. Head Mast. of Aldborough Sch. Formerly Asst. Mast. of Clifton Coll. Bristol. [29]

BEHR, B. M.—C. of St. Stephen's, Old Ford, Middlesex, Bow. [30]

BEILBY, David, *Forsbrook Parsonage, near Stone, Staffs.*—Deac. 1852 and Pr. 1853 by Bp of Lich. P. C. of Forsbrook, Dio. Lich. 1859. (Patron, Bp of Lich; P. C.'s Inc. 158*l* and Ho; Pop. 765.) Formerly C. of Hilderstone, Staffs, 1852–59. [31]

BEILBY, G.—C. of Trinity, Bordesley, Birmingham. [32]

BEILBY, Jonathan, *Feniscowles, Blackburn, Lancashire.*—P. C. of Feniscowles, Dio. Man. 1845. (Patron, V. of Blackburn; P. C.'s Inc. 210*l* and Ho; Pop. 3500.) [33]

BELCHER, Andrew Holmes.—Emman. Coll. Cam. B.A. 1852; Deac. 1853, Pr. 1855. Formerly C. of Huntspill, Somerset. [34]

BELCHER, Brymer, 32, *Warwick-square, Pimlico, London, S.W.*—Wad. Coll. Ox. B.A. 1841, M.A. 1846; Deac. 1843 and Pr. 1844 by Bp of Win. P. C. of St. Gabriel's, Pimlico, Dio. Lon. 1853. (Patron, Marquis of Westminster; P. C.s Inc. uncertain; Pop. 12,000.) [35]

BELCHER, Evans, *Collingwood-terrace, Gateshead.*—Deac. 1866, Pr. 1867. C. of St. James's, Gateshead, 1866. [36]

BELCHER, George, *Heather, Market-Bosworth, Leicestershire.*—R. of Heather, Dio. Pet. 1836. (Patron, the present R; Tithe, 320*l*; R.'s Inc. 336*l*; Pop. 371.) [1]

BELCHER, George Paul, *Butterton, Leek, Staffs.*—Wor. Coll. Ox. B.A. 1822, M.A. 1826, B.D. 1837; Deac. 1823 and Pr. 1824 by Bp of Lich. P.C. of Butterton, Dio. Lich. 1834. (Patron, V. of Mayfield; P. C.'s Inc. 90*l*; Pop. 325.) [2]

BELCHER, William, *Walberswick, Southwold, Suffolk.*—P. C of Walberswick, Dio. Nor. 1866. (Patron, Sir J. R. Blois, Bart; P. C.'s Inc. 49*l* and Ho; Pop. 315.) P. C. of Blythburgh, Dio. Nor. 1866. (Patron, Sir J. R. Blois, Bart; P. C.'s Inc. 81*l*; Pop. 832.) [3]

BELCHER, William de Pipe, *Thurlby Rectory, Newark.*—Magd. Hall Ox. B.A. 1831; Deac. 1832 by Bp of Lich. Pr. 1834 by Bp of Lin. R. of Thurlby, Dio. Lin. 1864. (Patron, Bp of Lin; Tithe, 80*l*; Glebe, 30*l*; R.'s Inc. 110*l* and Ho; Pop. 150. [4]

BELCOMBE, Francis Edward, *Whitley Parsonage, Northwich, Cheshire.*—Edin. B.M. Deac. 1853 and Pr. 1854 by Abp of York. P. C. of Lower Whitley, Dio. Ches. 1856. Patron, Sir John N. L. Chetwode, Bart; P. C.'s Inc. 130*l* and Ho; Pop. 578.) Formerly C. of Church-Fenton, Tadcaster. [5]

BELEY, C. A. E.—C. of Cheddar, Weston-super-Mare. [6]

BELGRAVE, Charles William, *North Kilworth, Rugby.*—Lin. Coll. Ox. B.A. 1841, M.A. 1844; Deac. 1841, Pr. 1842. R. of North Kilworth, Dio. Pet. 1854. (Patrons, Exors. of Capt. Belgrave, R.N; Glebe, 411 acres; R.'s Inc. 567*l* and Ho; Pop. 409.) Formerly C. of South Kilworth 1841–45. [7]

BELGRAVE, William, *Preston Hall, Uppingham, Rutlandshire.*—St. John's Coll. Cam. B.A. 1813, M.A. 1817; Deac. 1814, Pr. 1815. R. of Preston, Dio. Pet. 1840. (Patron, present R; R.'s Inc. 340*l* and Ho; Pop. 350.) [8]

BELL, Arthur L'Argent, *Halliwell, Bolton le-Moors.*—Caius Coll. Cam. B.A. 1863; Deac. 1865. C. of St. Peter's, Halliwell, 1865. [9]

BELL, Charles Dent, *Ambleside, Westmoreland.*—Dub. A.B. 1842, A.M. 1852; Deac. 1843, Pr. 1844. P. C. of Ambleside, Dio. Carl. 1861. (Patron, Gen. Le Fleming; P. C.'s Inc. 80*l*; Pop. 1603.) [10]

BELL, Charles Lucas, *Willoughby Lodge, Enniskillen, Ireland.*—Dub. A.B. 1843; Deac. 1845 by Bp of Tuam, Pr. 1846 by Bp of Killaloe. Chap. R.N. 1846–56. [11]

BELL, David, *Goole, Snaith, Yorks.*—Glasgow, M.D. 1832, St. Bees 1850; Deac. 1850 and Pr. 1851 by Bp of Ches. P. C. of Goole, Dio. York. 1855. (Patron, Abp of York; P. C.'s Inc. 140*l*; Pop. 5613.) Surrogate. Formerly P. C. of Bleasdale, Lancashire, 1851–55; previously Physician to the Ludlow Dispensary. Author, *Address to Sunday-School Teachers*, 1844, 1*s*. [12]

BELL, Edward, *Gainford, Darlington.*—Trin. Coll. Cam Caius Univ. Prizeman, 1857, B.A. 1858, M.A. 1866; Deac. 1858 by Bp. of Chich; Pr. 1862 by Bp of Pet. C. of Gainford 1863. Formerly C. of Ore, Hastings, 1858, St. Michael-le-Belfrey, York, and Morcott, Rutland, 1862. [13]

BELL, Edward John, *Dalham Rectory, Newmarket.*—St. Cath. Coll. Cam. B.A. 1847, M.A. 1854; Deac. 1847 and Pr. 1848 by Bp of Nor. R. of Dalham, Dio. Ely, 1863. (Patron, Sir R. Affleck, Bart; Tithe, 378*l*; Glebe, 40 acres; R.'s Inc. 418*l* and Ho; Pop. 450.) Formerly R. of Crostwick, Norwich, 1848; Organizing Sec. to S.P.G. 1854. Author, *Mormonism*, a tract. [14]

BELL, Frederick, 4, *Medway-terrace, Exeter.*—Dub. A.B. 1839; Deac. 1840 by Bp of Ches. Pr. 1840 by Bp of Herf. Chap. to the City Workhouse, Exeter (Salary, 100*l*); Preb. of Endellion. [15]

BELL, George, *Kirklinton, Carlisle.*—Deac. 1826 by Bp of Ches. Pr. 1827 by Abp of York. R. of Kirklinton, Dio. Carl. 1836. (Patron, Joseph Dacre, Esq; Tithe, 68*l*; Glebe. 16 acres; R.'s Inc. 94*l* and Ho; Pop. 1749.) Surrogate. Formerly C. of Aspatria and Castle Sowerby, Cumberland. [16]

BELL, George Charles, *Dulwich College, S.*—Wor. Coll. Ox. B.A. 1855, M.A. 1857; Deac. 1857 by Bp of Ox. Math. Lect. and Fell. of Wor. Coll. Ox. 1857; 2nd Mast. of Dulwich Coll. 1865. [17]

BELL, George Robley.—St. John's Coll. Cam. B.A. 1842; Deac. 1843 and Pr. 1844 by Bp of Nor. Formerly V. of Field Dalling, Norfolk, 1856–59, previously V. of Llantrissant, Monmouthshire, 1851–56. [18]

BELL, Henry, *Nottingham.*—V. of Ruddington, near Nottingham, Dio. Lin. 1838. (Patrons, Simeon's Trustees; V.'s Inc. 135*l*; Pop. 2283.) P. C. of St. James's, Nottingham, Dio. Lin. 1849. (Patron, Ld. Chan; P. C.'s Inc. 200*l*.) [19]

BELL, Henry, *The College, Marlborough.*—Univ. Coll. Dur; Deac. 1860 by Bp. of Rip. Pr. 1864 by Bp of Salis. Asst. Mast. in Marlborough Coll. [20]

BELL, Henry Edward, *Long Houghton, Alnwick, Northumberland.*—Univ. Coll. Ox. B.A. 1834; Deac. 1836, Pr. 1837. V. of Long Houghton, Dio. Dur. 1842. (Patron, Duke of Northumberland; Tithe—App. 4*l*, Imp. 593*l* 12*s* 11*d*, V. 251*l* 19*s*; Glebe, 1 acre; V.'s Inc. 250*l* and Ho; Pop. 777.) [21]

BELL, James, *St. Botolph's, Bishopsgate, London, E.C.*—C. of St. Botolph's, Bishopsgate, Lond. [22]

BELL, John, *Oulton-green, near Wakefield.*—Univ. Coll. Ox. B.A. 1828, M.A. 1833; Deac. 1829, Pr. 1830. V. of Rothwell, Yorks, Dio. Rip. 1829. (Patron, C. J. Brandling, Esq; Tithe—Imp. 901*l* 2*s* 2*d*, the Public School at Rothwell, 4¾*d*, V. 900*l* 13*s* 9*d*; Glebe, 3 acres; V.'s Inc. 990*l*; Pop. 2762.) Rural Dean of Wakefield; Chap. to the Earl of Mexborough. [23]

BELL, John, *Fordham, Soham, Cambs.*—Jesus Coll. Cam. Fell. of, 1848–63, 21st Wrang. B.A. 1844, M.A. 1847; Deac. and Pr. 1848 by Abp of York. V. of Fordham, Dio. Ely, 1861. (Patron, Jesus Coll. Cam; Glebe, 270 acres; V.'s Inc. 430*l*; Pop. 1406.) Formerly C. and P. C. of Belsterstone, 1848–62. [24]

BELL, John, *Brington Rectory. Kimbolton.*—Clare Coll. Cam. Fell. 7th in 1st cl. Cl. Trip. Jun. Opt. and B.A. 1850, M.A. 1853; Deac. 1852 and Pr. 1854 by Bp of Ely. R. of Brington with Bythorn and Old Weston, Dio. Ely, 1857. (Patron, Clare Coll; Tithe, 460*l*; Rent from Glebe, 420*l*; R.'s Inc. 880*l*; Pop. Brington 191, Bythorn 292, Old Weston 426.) Formerly Head. Master's Asst. in King Edward's Sch. Birmingham. [25]

BELL, John, *Matterdale Parsonage, Penrith, Cumberland.*—St. Bees 1848; Deac. 1848 and Pr. 1849 by Bp of Lich. P. C. of Matterdale, Dio. Carl. 1851. (Patron, R. of Greystoke; Glebe, 3½ acres; P. C.'s Inc. 127*l* and Ho; Pop. 357.) [26]

BELL, John Dickinson, *Barnet, Middlesex, N.*—St. Bees; Deac. 1852, Pr. 1853. Formerly C. of Mansfield, Notts. [27]

BELL, Robert, *Newbottle Vicarage, Brackley.*—Dub. A.B. 1817, Edin. M.D. 1819, Wor. Coll. Ox. M.A. 1841; Deac. 1841 and Pr. 1842 by Bp of Pet. V. of Newbottle with Charlton, Dio. Pet. 1862. (Patron, W. C. Cartwright, Esq; Tithe, 159*l* 18*s* 6*d*; Glebe, 53 acres; V.'s Inc. 293*l* and Ho; Pop. 420.) Formerly C. of All Saints, Northampton, 1841–42; P. C. of Eye, Northants, 1848–62. [28]

BELL, Thomas, *Vale Rectory, Guernsey.*—Ex. Coll. Ox. B.A. 1843, M.A. 1846; Deac. 1845 and Pr 1846 by Bp of Ox. R. of the Vale, Guernsey, Dio. Win. 1859. (Patron, the Governor of Guernsey; Glebe, 10 acres; R.'s Inc. 150*l* and Ho; Pop. 2460.) Formerly C. of the Vale. [29]

BELL, Thomas, *Clun, Shrewsbury.*—Warden of Trinity Hospital and C. of Clun. [30]

BELL, Walter, *West Linton, Peebleshire.*—St Bees, 1847; Deac, 1847 and Pr. 1848 by Bp of Rip. Min. of St. Mungo's Episcopal Chapel, Linton, 1858. Formerly C. of Rowley 1856, and Cross-Stone, Yorks, 1847. [31]

BELL, William, *Wimbledon, Surrey.*—Brasen. Coll. Ox. 2nd cl. Lit. Hum. B.A. 1850, M.A. 1854; Deac. 1851 and Pr. 1853 by Abp of York. C. of Wimbledon 1865. Formerly C. of Ravenfield, Yorks, 1851; 3rd cl.

Mast. of Rossall Sch. 1852–54; Head Mast. of Wye Coll. Kent, 1854; Head Mast. of Carlisle High Sch. 1855; C. of Stepney 1861. [1]

BELL, William, *Lillingstone-Dayrell, near Buckingham.*—Corpus Coll. Cam. B.A. 1840; Deac. 1841. R. of Lillingstone-Dayrell, Dio. Ox. 1854. (Patron, R. Dayrell, Esq; Tithe, 278*l*; Glebe, 1 acre; R.'s Inc. 280*l* and Ho; Pop. 198.) [2]

BELL, William, *North Grove House, Southsea, Hants.*—Trin. Coll. Ox. B.A. 1844; Deac. and Pr. 1846 by Bp of Ely. Prin. of the Naval College of North Grove House. Formerly Chap. and Naval Instructor of H.M.S. "Royal William," and H M.S. "Superb;" previously Chap. of the Isle of Ascension. [3]

BELL, William, *St. John's Parsonage, Dukinfield, Manchester.*—St. Bees, 1st cl. Librarian and Rupert's Land Greek Prizeman; Deac. 1858 and Pr. 1859 by Bp of Ches. P. C. of Dukinfield, Dio. Ches. 1860. (Patron, R. of Stockport; P. C.'s Inc. 300*l* and Ho; Pop. 14,214.) Formerly C. of Dukinfield. Author, *Synopsis of Pearson on the Creed,* 2*s* 6*d*; *Synopsis of Paley's Evidences,* 1*s*; *Exposition of the Confirmation Service,* 3*d*; *The Witnessing Spirit,* 3*d*; and *The Blasphemy against the Holy Ghost,* 3*d*. [4]

BELL, William Lees, *Streatham, Surrey, S.*—C. of Ch. Ch. Streatham. [5]

BELL, William Robinson, *Laithkirk Parsonage, Mickleton, Barnard Castle.*—Univ. Coll. Dur. Sen. Hebrew Prizeman 1857, Divinity Prizeman 1858, Licen. in Theol. 1858; Deac. 1858 by Bp of Win. Pr. 1859 by Bp of Lich. P. C. of Laithkirk, Dio. Rip. 1864. (Patron, R. of Romaldkirk; P.C.'s Inc. as yet uncertain; Pop. 1311.) Formerly C. of Morton, Derbyshire, 1858, Kirkham, Lancashire, 1860, and Bakewell, Derbyshire, 1862. [6]

BELLAIRS, Charles, *Sutton Parsonage, near Mansfield.*—Wor. Coll. Ox. B.A. 1851; Deac. 1841 and Pr. 1842 by Bp of Wor. P. C. of Sutton-in-Ashfield, Dio. Lin. 1867. (Patron, Duke of Devonshire; Glebe, 22 acres; P. C.'s Inc. 350*l* and Ho; Pop. 7643.) Formerly P. C. of Ch. Ch. Coventry, 1845–46; P. C. of Deeping St. Nicholas, Linc. 1846–51; Chap. of Bedworth Hospital 1851–61; Min. of Buckley Mountain Chapelry, Flintshire, 1861–67. [7]

BELLAIRS, Frederic John Walford, *Sutton Parsonage, near Mansfield.*—Magd. Coll. Ox. B.A. 1865; Deac. 1866 and Pr. 1867 by Bp of St. A. C. of Sutton-in-Ashfield 1867. Formerly Asst. C. of Buckley Mountain 1866–67. [8]

BELLAIRS, Henry, *Cliffden, Teignmouth, Devon.*—Hon. Can. of Wor. 1853; V. of Hunsingore, Dio. Rip. 1832. (Patron, J. Dent, Esq; V.'s Inc. 400*l*; Pop. 561.) [9]

BELLAIRS, Henry Walford, *Privy Council Office, Whitehall, London, S.W.*—Corpus Coll. Ox. B.A. 1834, M.A. 1835; Deac. 1835, Pr. 1836. One of Her Majesty's Inspectors of Schools 1844. [10]

BELLAIRS, Stevenson Gilbert, *Goadby-Marwood, Melton Mowbray, Leicestershire.*—Magd. Hall, Ox. B.A. 1848, M.A. 1854; Deac. 1849 and Pr. 1850 by Bp of Pet. R. of Goadby-Marwood, Dio. Pet. 1856. (Patron, George Bellairs, Esq; R.'s Inc. 500*l* and Ho; Pop. 195.) C. of Caldwell with Wykeham 1866. Formerly C. of Deeping St. Nicholas, Linc. and Braunston and Waltham-le-Wolds, Leic. [11]

BELLAMY, Arthur, *Chichester.*—Educated at three Universities, Edin. Lond. and Oxford; studied Medicine at Edinburgh, Laws and Legislation at London, and Classics and Mathematics at Oxford; B.A. King's Coll. Lond. 1861; Deac. 1862 by Abp of Cant. Pr. 1863 by Abp of York. C. of the Subdeanery, Chichester. [12]

BELLAMY, David, *Gwalior, India.* [13]

BELLAMY, Edward, *Downham, Norfolk.*—St. John's Coll. Ox. B.A. 1813, M.A. 1816, B.D. 1822. V. of Dersingham, Castle Rising, Norfolk, Dio. Nor. 1840. (Patron, Marquis of Cholmondeley; Tithe—App. 350*l*; and 160 acres of Glebe, value 70*l*; V.'s Inc. 144*l*; Pop. 822.) [14]

BELLAMY, Franklin, A. S., *St. Mary's Parsonage, Devonport.*—St. Aidan's; Deac. 1854 and Pr. 1855 by Bp of Lin. P. C. of St. Mary's, Devonport, Dio. Ex. 1864. (Patrons, Crown and Bp alt; P. C.'s Inc. 300*l* and Ho; Pop. 6000.) Formerly C. of Trinity, Nottingham, 1854–55, Baumber with Sturton, Lincolnshire, 1855–57; Missions to Seamen, Liverpool; C. of St. Paul's, Devonport, 1859, Ch. Ch. Plymouth, and Royal Laboratory and Barracks, Devonport. [15]

BELLAMY, George, *Wark, Hexham, Northumberland.*—Lin. Coll. Ox. B.A. 1829, M.A. 1831; Deac. 1830, Pr. 1831. R. of Wark, Dio. Dur. 1858. (Patron, Greenwich Hospital; R.'s Inc. 275*l* and Ho; Pop. 900.) Formerly R. of Bellingham. [16]

BELLAMY, James, *St. John's College, Oxford.*—St. John's Coll. Ox. B.A. 1841, M.A. 1845, B.D. 1853. Fell. of St. John's Coll. Ox. [17]

BELLAMY, James William, *Sellindge, Ashford, Kent.*—St. John's Coll. Ox. B.A. 1816, Magd. Coll. Cam. M.A. 1820, B.D. 1822; Deac. 1813 and Pr. 1814 by Bp of Lon. V. of Sellindge, Dio. Cant. 1822. (Patron, Ld Chan; Tithe—App. 402*l* 2*s* and 5 acres of Glebe, V. 193*l* 18*s*; Glebe, 19 acres; V.'s Inc. 220*l* and Ho; Pop. 580.) Preb. of Harleston in St. Paul's Cathl. 1843; Rural Dean. [18]

BELLAMY, Joseph, *Laxey, Douglas, Isle of Man.*—Literate; Deac. 1860 by Bp of S. and M. P. C. of Laxey, Dio. S. and M. 1861. (Patron, Bp of S. and M; P. C.'s Inc. 100*l* and Ho.) [19]

BELLAMY, Richard, *Balham-hill, Streatham, Surrey, S.*—Pemb. Coll. Ox. B.A. 1829, M.A. 1832; Deac. and Pr. 1830. P. C. of St. Mary's, Streatham, Dio. Win. 1855. (Patron, R. of Streatham; P. C.'s Inc. uncertain.) [20]

BELLAS, Lancelot, *Bramshott, Liphook, Hants.*—Queen's Coll. Ox. B.A. 1825, M.A. 1828; Deac. and Pr. 1829. R. of Bramshott, Dio. Win. 1832. (Patron, Queen's Coll. Ox; Tithe, 785*l*; Glebe, 40 acres; R.'s Inc. 820*l* and Ho; Pop. 1367.) Formerly Fell. of Queen's Coll. Ox. [21]

BELLAS, Septimus, *Monk's-Sherborne, Basingstoke, Hants.*—Queen's Coll. Ox. B.A. 1826, M.A. 1829; Deac. 1827 and Pr. 1828 by Bp of Salis. V. of Monk's-Sherborne, Dio. Win. 1848. (Patron, Queen's Coll. Ox Tithe—Imp. 647*l* 3*s* 4*d*, V. 74*l* 2*s* 8*d*; Glebe, 65 acres; V.'s Inc. 90*l*; Pop. 649.) P. C. of Pamber, Dio. Win. 1848. (Patron, Queen's Coll. Ox; Tithe—Imp. 270*l*; Pop. 677; no Church.) Late Fell. of Queen's Coll. Ox. [22]

BELLAS, Thomas, *Bongate, Appleby, Westmoreland.*—Queen's Coll. Ox. B.A. 1813, M.A. 1816; Deac. 1815, Pr. 1816. V. of St. Michael's, Appleby, Dio. Carl. 1823. (Patron, Bp of Carl; Tithe, 104*l* 14*s* 6*d*; Glebe, 40 acres; R.'s Inc. 175*l* and Ho; Pop. 1255.) Surrogate. [23]

BELLETT, George, *St. Leonard's, Bridgnorth, Shropshire.*—Dub. A.B. 1820, A.M. 1828; Deac. 1821; and Pr. 1822 by Bp of Dromore. P. C. of St. Leonard's, Bridgnorth, Dio. Herf. 1835. (Patron, T. Whitmore, Esq; Tithe—Imp. 100*l*; P. C.'s Inc. 320*l* and Ho; Pop. 3080.) Rural Dean of Bridgnorth. Author, *The City of Rome* (a Lecture), 1854; *Antiquities of Bridgnorth,* 1856. [24]

BELLETT, John Crosthwaite, 7, *Albany-street, Regent's-park, London, N.W.*—Pemb. Coll. Ox. 1849, B.A. 1854, M.A. 1856; Deac. 1855 by Bp of Lon. Pr. 1856 by Bp of Win. C. of Trinity, St. Marylebone, 1855. Author, *Sermon on the Cattle Plague*; *Pictorial Handbills, explanatory of Pilgrim's Progress,* Religious Tract Society, etc. [25]

BELLEW, John Chippendall Montesquieu, 162, *Holland-road, Kensington, W.*—St. Mary Hall, Ox; Deac. 1849 and Pr. 1850 by Bp of Wor. Min. of Bedford Chapel, Bloomsbury, Lond. 1863. Formerly C. of St. Andrew's, Worcester, 1849; Prescot, Lancashire, 1850; Chap. St. John's Cathl. Calcutta, 1851–55; Assist. Min. St. Philip's, Regent-street, Lond. 1855–57; C. in sole charge of St. Mark's, Marylebone, 1857–62. Author, *Christ the Revealer of the Thoughts of many Hearts* (Sermon), 1856; *Sermons together with two Discourses delivered on the Days of National Thanksgiving,* 1855–56, 1856; *Five Occasional Sermons with a*

Discourses delivered on the Day of National Humiliation, Oct. 7, 1857, 1857; *What is the Chaff to the Wheat?* (a primary Sermon), 1857; *Sunday Trading in the Metropolis* (a Sermon), 1858; *The Lord's Prayer explained to Children*, 1860; *Christ in Life, Life in Christ* (Sermons), 1860; *Shakespere's Home at New Place, Stratford-upon-Avon, being a History of "the Great House" built by Sir H. Clopton and subsequently the property of W. Shakespere wherein he lived and died*, 1863; *History of the Seven Churches of Asia Minor*; *Blount Tempest*, 3 vols; *Baalbec*, etc. [1]

BELLEWES, George Clench, 7, *Taunton-place, Regent's-park, London, N.W.*—Lond. Univ; Deac. 1866 by Bp of Lon. C. of St. Mary's, Bryanston-square, 1866. [2]

BELLHOUSE, Albert Turner, *Shrewsbury.*—Oriel Coll. Ox. B.A. 1864; Deac. 1864 and Pr. 1865 by Bp of Lich. C. of St. Mary's, Shrewsbury, 1864. [3]

BELLHOUSE, William Cocker, *Tadcaster, Yorks.*—Magd. Coll. Cam. B.A. 1829; Deac. 1830 and Pr. 1831 by Abp of York. Mast. of the Tadcaster Gr. Sch. 1830. (Trustees, the Abp and Dean of York. [4]

BELLI, Charles Almeric, *South-Weald Vicarage, Brentwood, Essex.*—Ch. Ch. Ox. B.A. 1814, M.A. 1816; Deac. 1816 by Bp of Salis. Pr. 1817 by Bp of Lon. Precentor of St. Paul's Cathl. 1819. (Value, 47*l* 9*s*.) V. of South-Weald, Dio. Roch. 1823. (Patron, Bp of Roch; Tithe, 664*l*; Glebe, 17 acres, rented at 36*l*; V.'s Inc. 700*l* and Ho; Pop. 1359.) Formerly R. of Paglesham, Rochford, Essex, 1822–60. [5]

BELLINGHAM, John George, 4, *Holles-place, Brompton, London, S.W.*—Trin. Coll. Cam. B.A. 1832, M.A. 1837; Deac. 1833, Pr. 1834. Formerly P. C. of Aldsworth, Glouc. 1839–65. [6]

BELLIS, Richard, *St. Heliers, Jersey.*—King's Coll. Lond. Theol. Assoc; Deac. 1848 and Pr. 1849 by Bp of Lon. Min. of St. James's Chapel, St. Heliers Dio. Win. 1853. (Patrons, Proprietors; Min's Inc. 200*l*.) Formerly C. of St. Paul's, Lisson Grove, Lond. 1848–49, High Wycombe, Bucks, 1849–53. Author, *The Ark and other Sermons*, 1852. [7]

BELLMAN, Arthur Horatio, *Henham Vicarage, Bishop Stortford.*—Caius Coll. Cam. B.A. 1838; Deac. 1839 and Pr. 1840 by Bp of Nor. V. of Henham, Dio. Roch. 1853. (Patron, the present V; Tithe, 330*l*; Glebe, 70 acres; V.'s Inc. 485*l*; Pop. 875.) Formerly C. of Helmingham 1839, Great Snoring 1840, Potter Heigham 1842; P. C. of Aldeby 1843; C. of Great Linford, Bucks, 1852, Author, *Confirmation*, 1840, and *The Lord's Supper*, 1852, both tracts. [8]

BELLMAN, Augustus Frederic, *Moulton, near Acle, Norfolk.*—St. Peter's Coll. Cam. B.A. 1842; Deac. 1843, Pr. 1844. V. of Moulton St. Mary, Dio. Nor. 1853. (Patroness, Lady Catherine Melville; Tithe—Imp. 213*l* 2*s* 6*d*, V. 153*l* 2*s* 6*d*; Glebe, 33 acres; V.'s Inc. 200*l* and Ho; Pop. 260.) Chap. to Blofield Union. Formerly C. of Hemsby, Norfolk, 1843–53. Author, *A Word in Season* (a Sermon), 1858. [9]

BELLMAN, Edmund, 28, *Albion-square, Dalston, N.E.*—Queens' Coll. Cam. B.A. 1837; Deac. 1838 and Pr. 1843 by Bp of Nor. C. of St. Mary's, Haggerston, Lond. 1864. Formerly C. of Kirstead, Norfolk, 1843, and St. James's, Norwich, 1859. [10]

BELLSON, Robert, *Berlin.*—Chap. to the British residents, Berlin, 1847. [11]

BELOE, Robert Seppings, *Holton, Halesworth, Suffolk.*—Corpus Coll. Cam. B.A. 1846; Deac. 1846, Pr. 1848. R. of Holton St. Peter, Suffolk, Dio. Nor. 1855. (Patron, Ld Chan; Tithe, 310*l*; R.'s Inc. 320*l* and Ho; Pop. 470.) Formerly V. of All Saints', King's Lynn, 1850–55. [12]

BELT, Robert Wallis, *Emmanuel College, Cambridge.*—Emman. Coll. Cam. B.A. 1860. [13]

BELWARD, Henry Belward Moyse, *Wray-park, Reigate.*—Queen's Coll. Ox. B.A. 1817; Deac. and Pr. 1818. [14]

BENCE, George Wright, *Bishopston, Bristol.*—Emman. Coll. Cam. B.A. 1850, M.A. 1855; Deac. 1850, Pr. 1851. P. C. of Bishopston, Dio. G. and B. 1862. (Patron, Bp of G. and B; P. C.'s Inc. 120*l*; Pop. 2100.) Formerly C. of Lyddington, near Swindon. [15]

BENCE, John Britten, *Hayle, Cornwall.*—St. Mary Hall, Ox. S.C.L. 1854; Deac. 1858 and Pr. 1862 by Bp of Ex. C. of Phillack 1863. Formerly C. of East Budleigh, Devon, 1858–63; Dioc. Inspector of Schools 1864–67. [16]

BENDYSHE, Richard, *Harbridge, Ringwood, Hants.*—Trin. Coll. Cam. B.A. 1846, M.A. 1850; Deac. 1848, Pr. 1849. C. of Harbridge. [17]

BENEST, John William, *Southboro', Tonbridge Wells.*—Dub. A.B. 1848; Deac. 1849 and Pr. 1850 by Bp of Win. C. of Bidborough 1866. Formerly C. of St. Anne's, Alderney, 1849, Huddersfield 1854, Burnham Deepdale 1857, All Saints', Belvedere, 1865. [18]

BENGOUGH, Edward Stewart, *Weston in Gordano, near Clevedon.*—Oriel Coll. Ox. B.A. 1861, M.A. 1865; Deac. 1863, Pr. 1864. C. of Weston in Gordano 1866. Formerly C. of St. Mary's, Kidderminster. [19]

BENGOUGH, Samuel Edmund, *Victoria-road, Gipsy-hill, Norwood, S.*—Ch. Coll. Cam. B.A. 1855, M.A. 1860; Deac. 1856 by Bp of B. and W. Pr. 1857 by Bp of G. and B. Formerly C. of St. John's, Redland, Bristol, 1857, and Hadleigh, Essex, 1858. [20]

BENHAM, William, 322, *Fulham-road, London, S.W.*—King's Coll. Lond. The l. Assoc. 1857; Deac. 1857 and Pr. 1858 by Bp of Lon. Editorial Sec. S. P. C. K; Prof. of Modern History, Queen's Coll. Lond; C. of St. Lawrence's, Jewry, 1866. Formerly Tut. in St. Mark's Coll. and Lect. on English Literature, 1857–65. Author, *Sermon on the 21st Birthday of the Prince of Wales*, 1862, 4*d*; *Gospel of St. Matthew, with Notes and a Commentary*, National Society, 1862, 3*s*; *English Ballads, with Introduction and Notes*, National Society, 1863, 2*s* 6*d*; *The Epistles for the Christian Year, with Notes and Commentary*, National Society, 1864, various Tracts. [21]

BENISON, William, *Balsall Heath, Birmingham.*—Dub. A.B. 1847, A.M. 1852; Deac. 1847, Pr. 1848. P. C. of Balsall Heath, Dio. Wor. 1853. (Patron, the P. C. of King's Norton; P. C.'s Inc. 350*l* and Ho; Pop. 7651.) [22]

BENN, Anthony, *Woolfardisworthy, Crediton.*—Emman. Coll. Cam. B.A. 1859, M.A. 1865; Deac. 1860 and Pr. 1861 by Bp of Lich. R. of Woolfardisworthy, Dio. Ex. 1866. (Patron, present R; Tithe, 200*l*; Glebe, 99 acres; R.'s Inc. 350*l* and Ho; Pop. 180.) Formerly C. of Atcham, Salop, 1860–63. [23]

BENN, Thomas, *Brock Cottage, Goosnargh, Preston.*—St. Bees; Deac. 1822 and Pr. 1823 by Bp of Ches. P. C. of Whitechapel, Lancashire, Dio. Man. 1836. (Patrons, D. and C. of Ch. Ch. Ox; Tithe—App. 595*l*, P. C. from App. 80*l*; Glebe, 95 acres; P. C.'s Inc. 160*l*; Pop. 646.) [24]

BENN, William Heygate, *Churchover, near Rugby.*—Mert. Coll. Ox. B.A. 1838, M.A. 1841. R. of Churchover, Dio. Wor. 1853. (Patrons, Trustees of late Rev. Godfrey Arkwright; R.'s Inc. 290*l*; Pop. 357.) [25]

BENNET, Edward Kedington, *Cheveley, near Newmarket.*—Univ. Coll. Ox. B.A. 1858; Deac. 1858 and Pr. 1859 by Bp of Ely. C. of Cheveley 1859. Formerly C. of Swynshead, Hunts, 1858–59. [26]

BENNET, James Thomas, *Cheveley, near Newmarket.*—Ball. Coll. Ox. B.A. 1829, M.A. 1831; Deac. 1829 and Pr. 1831 by Bp of Nor. R. of Cheveley, Dio. Ely, 1832. (Patron, the present R; Tithe, 704*l*; Glebe, 38 acres; R.'s Inc. 750*l* and Ho; Pop. 607.) [27]

BENNET, William Poole, *Bothenhampton, Bridport.*—St. Bees; Deac. 1848 and Pr. 1850 by Bp of Rip. P. C. of Bothenhampton, Dio. Salis. 1860. (Patron, Sir H. M. Nepean; Tithe—Imp. 80*l*; Glebe, 8 acres; P. C.'s Inc. 95*l* and Ho; Pop. 546.) Formerly C. of Great Horton, Bradford, Yorks, Colnbrook, Bucks, Ilminster, Somerset, and Allington, Dorset. Previously practising as Surgeon in Cornwall 1835–45. [28]

BENNETT, Alexander, *Kepier Grammar School, Houghton-le-Spring.*—Lon. B.A. 1862, Dur. Licen. in

Theol; Deac. 1865 and Pr. 1866 by Bp of Dur. Mast. of Kepier Gr. Sch. 1866; C. of Seaham Harbour, Durham. [1]

BENNETT, Alexander Morden, *Bournemouth, Ringwood, Hants.*—Wor. Coll. Ox. B.A. 1830, M.A. 1832; Deac. 1831, Pr. 1832. P. C. of Bournemouth, Dio. Win. 1845. (Patron, Sir G. Gervis, Bart; Glebe, 2 acres; P. C.'s Inc. 50*l* and Ho; Pop. 3500. [2]

BENNETT, A. S., *Bournemouth, Ringwood, Hants.*—Asst. C. of Bournemouth. [3]

BENNETT, Alfred Robert, *Aylburton, Lydney, Glouc.*—St. Cath. Coll. Cam. B.A. 1864; Deac. 1866 and Pr. 1867 by Bp of G. and B. C. of Aylburton 1866. [4]

BENNETT, Barwell Ewins Worthington, *Jury-street, Warwick.*—Oriel Coll. Ox. B.A. 1853, M.A. 1859; Deac. 1856 and Pr. 1857 by Bp of Wor. C. of St. Nicholas', Warwick, 1861. Formerly C. of Whitnash, near Leamington, 1856–61. [5]

BENNETT, Edmund, *Ringmore, Teignmouth, Devon.*—P. C. of St. John's, Chittlehampton, Devon, Dio. Ex. 1839. (Patrons, Exors. of Lord Rolle; P. C.'s Inc. 150*l*.) [6]

BENNETT, Edward, *Pickering, Yorks.*—Dub. A.B. 1852; Deac. 1854 and Pr. 1855 by Bp. of Ches. C. in sole charge of Pickering 1863. Formerly C. of Rusland 1854–56; S.P.G. Missionary at St. Helena 1856–61, and V. of the Cathl. St. Helena 1860–62; C. of Hutton Bushell, Yorks, 1862–63. [7]

BENNETT, Edward Leigh, *Long Sutton, Lincolnshire.*—Mert. Coll. Ox. B.A. 1821; Deac. 1823, Pr. 1824. V. of Long Sutton, Dio. Lin. 1843. (Patrons, Exors. of the Rev. T. L. Bennett; Tithe—Imp. 3453*l* 2*s* 8*d*, V. 1108*l* 9*s* 4*d*; V.'s Inc. 1135*l* and Ho; Pop. 2490.) Rural Dean. [8]

BENNETT, Frederick, *Maddington, Devizes, Wilts.*—Wad. Coll. Ox. B.A. 1843, M.A. 1846; Deac. 1845, Pr. 1846. P. C. of Maddington, Dio. Salis. 1851. (Patron, L. P. Maton, Esq; Tithe—App. 128*l* 5*s*, Imp. 908*l*; P. C.'s Inc. 65*l* and Ho; Pop. 396.) V. of Shrewton, Wilts, Dio. Salis. 1853. (Patron, Bp of Salis; Tithe, 219*l*; Glebe, 40 acres; V.'s Inc. 257*l* and Ho; Pop. 710.) Archdiaconal Sec. to the S.P.G. [9]

BENNETT, George, *Gloster Villa, Sudbury, Middlesex, N.W.*—St. John's Coll. Cam. B.A. 1858, M.A. 1864; Deac. 1858 and Pr. 1860 by Bp of Lon. P. C. of St. George's, Campden Hill, Dio. Lon. 1864. (Patron, John Bennett, Esq; Pop. 6500.) Formerly C. of Willesden 1859–61, and Harrow-on-the-Hill 1861–64. [10]

BENNETT, George, *James Town, St. Helena.* [11]

BENNETT, George, *Chelmsford.*—2nd Mast. of Chelmsford Gr. Sch. [12]

BENNETT, George Bright, *Trinity Parsonage, Runcorn, Cheshire.*—St. John's Coll. Cam. B.A. 1853, M.A. 1864; Deac. 1853 and Pr. 1854 by Bp of Wor. P. C. of Trinity, Runcorn, Dio. Ches. 1864. (Patrons, John and Thomas Johnson, Esqs; P. C.'s Inc. 210*l* and Ho; Pop. 4500.) Formerly C. of St. Peter's, Coventry, 1853–55, Marsh Gibbon, Bucks, 1855–56, Fleet, Lincolnshire, 1856–64. Author, *The Last Harvest*, 2*d*; and *The Christian Governess*, 1863, 5*s*. [13]

BENNETT, George Peter, *Kelvedon, Essex.*—St. Cath. Hall, Cam. B.A. 1833; Deac. 1834 and Pr. 1835 by Bp of Lon. V. of Kelvedon, Dio. Roch. 1859. (Patron, Bp of Roch; Glebe, 57 acres; V.'s Inc. 600*l* and Ho; Pop. 1740.) Surrogate. Formerly V. of White Notley, Essex, 1850–59; previously Military Chap. at Weedon 1846–50. Author, *Addresses to Soldiers.* [14]

BENNETT, George T. Cull, *Elswick Dene, Newcastle-on-Tyne.*—St. Bees; Deac. 1863 and Pr. 1864 by Bp of Dur. C. of St. James's, Benwell, Newcastle. [15]

BENNETT, Henry, *St. Nicholas-at-Wade, Margate.*—St. Cath. Hall, Cam. B.A. 1850; Deac. 1850 and Pr. 1851 by Bp of Lich. V. of St. Nicholas-at-Wade, Dio. Cant. 1857. (Patron, Abp of Cant; V.'s Inc. 175*l*; Pop. 390.) Formerly C. of St. Dunstan's, Cranbrook, and Chap. to the Cranbrook Union, Kent, 1852–57. [16]

BENNETT, Henry, *Sparkford, Castle Cary, Somerset.*—Trin. Coll. Cam. B.C.L. 1822; Deac. 1822 by Bp of Glouc. Pr. 1823 by Bp of Ches. R. of Sparkford, Dio. B. and W. 1836. (Patron, the present R; Tithe, 256*l* 11*s* 6*d*; Glebe, 40 acres; R.'s Inc 332*l*; Pop. 305.) Formerly R. of South Cadbury, Somerset, 1836–66. [17]

BENNETT, Henry Leigh, *Thorpe Place, Chertsey, Surrey.*—Ch. Ch. Ox. B.A. 1817, M.A. 1819; Deac. 1818 and Pr. 1819 by Bp of Pet. V. of Thorpe, Dio. Win. 1849. (Patroness, Miss Ferguson; Tithe—Imp. 115*l*, V. 71*l* 5*s*; Glebe, 10 acres; V.'s Inc. 190*l* and Ho; Pop. 552.) [18]

BENNETT, Henry Leigh, *Sutton St. Mary, Long Sutton, Lincolnshire.*—Corpus Coll. Ox. B.A. 1858; Deac. 1856, Pr. 1858. C. of Sutton St. Mary. [19]

BENNETT, Hugh, *Elmley Castle, near Pershore.*—Wor. Coll. Ox. B.A. 1840, M.A. 1843; Deac. 1840 and Pr. 1841 by Bp of Ox. V. of Elmley Castle, Dio. Wor. 1860. (Patron, Bp of Wor; Tithe—App. 412*l*, V. 130*l*; Glebe, 30 acres; V.'s Inc. 225*l* and Ho; Pop. 470.) Organizing Sec. of Additional Curates' Soc. in Dio. Wor. Formerly C. of Lyme Regis, Dorset, 1841–51, Whitwick, Leicestershire, 1852–56; Fell. of Wor. Coll. Ox. 1840–59; Travelling Secretary for Additional Curates' Society 1856–60. Author, *Plain Statement of the Grounds on which it is contended that Marriage within the prohibited Degrees is forbidden in Scripture*, 1849, 1*s* 6*d*. [20]

BENNETT, James Arthur, *South Cadbury, Castle Cary.*—Univ. Coll. Dur. B.A. 1856; Deac. 1856 and Pr. 1858 by Bp of Dur. R. of South Cadbury, Dio. B. and W. 1866. (Patron, James Bennett, Esq; Tithe, comm. 260*l* 10*s*; Glebe, 32 acres; R.'s Inc. 300*l* and Ho; Pop. 287.) Formerly C. of Alvechurch 1860, and Ellingham, Northumberland. [21]

BENNETT, James Hatchard, *Solihull, near Birmingham.*—Ex. Coll. Ox. 2nd cl. Lit. Hum. and B.A. 1850, M.A. 1857; Deac. 1856 and Pr. 1857 by Bp of Roch. Head Mast. of Solihull Gr. Sch, and Chap. of Solihull Union 1864. Formerly 2nd Mast. of St. Albans Gr. Sch. 1855–60. [22]

BENNETT J.—C. of Kingswinford, Stourbridge. [23]

BENNETT, John, *Ibstock Rectory, Ashby-de-la-Zouch.*—R. of Ibstock with Hugglescote C. and Donington C. Dio. Pet. 1849. (Patron, Bp of Pet; R.'s Inc. 1000*l* and Ho; Pop. 2239.) Surrogate. [24]

BENNETT, John Bidgood, 90, *Waterloo-road, Manchester.*—Magd. Hall. Ox. B.A. 1828, M.A 1836; Deac. 1835 and Pr. 1836 by Bp of Ches. Formerly 2nd Mast. of Macclesfield Gr. Sch. [25]

BENNETT, Jonathan Henry Palmer, 2, *Kimberley-place, Falmouth.*—Corpus Coll. Cam. B.A. 1855; Deac. 1857 and Pr. 1859 by Bp of Ex. Head Mast. of the Gr. Sch. Falmouth 1856. Formerly C. of Gluvias with Budock, Penryn, 1857–58, Mabe, near Falmouth, 1858–66. [26]

BENNETT, J. W.—C. of Upminster, Romford. [27]

BENNETT, Joshua, *Caversham, near Reading, Berks.*—Ch. Ch. Ox. B.A. 1833, M.A. 1836; Deac. 1835 and Pr. 1836 by Bp of Herf. P. C. of Caversham, Dio. Ox. 1843. (Patrons, Ch. Ch. Ox; Tithe—Imp. 1067*l* 6*s* 1*d*; P. C.'s Inc. 160*l* and Ho; Pop. 1365.) [28]

BENNETT, Matthias John Bosse, *St. John's-terrace, Belle-vue-road, Leeds.*—Corpus Coll. Cam. B.A. 1865; Deac. 1866 by Bp of Rip. C. of St. Andrew's, Leeds, 1866. [29]

BENNETT, N., *Brixton, Surrey, S.* [30]

BENNETT, Newton C.—C. of Almondsbury, Bristol. [31]

BENNETT, Peter, *Warden, near Hexham.*—B.A; Deac. 1847 by Bp of Ches. Pr. 1848 by Bp of Man. C. of Warden with Newbrough 1865. Formerly C. of Saddleworth 1847–52, Brampton 1852–65. [32]

BENNETT, Simeon Hardy, *Roos, Hull.*—St. Aidan's; Deac. 1861 and Pr. 1863 by Abp of York. C. of Roos. [33]

BENNETT, Stephen, *Uphill, Axbridge, Somerset.*—Oriel Coll. Ox. B.A. 1845, M.A. 1848; Deac. 1850 and Pr. 1851 by Bp of Herf. R. of Uphill, Dio. B. and W. 1862. (Patron, T. Bennett, Esq; R.'s Inc. 300*l* and Ho; Pop. 450.) Formerly C. of Wyre-Piddle and Throckmerton, Worcestershire. [1]

BENNETT, Theophilus, 12, *Boon-place, Plymouth.*—Dub. A.B. 1844, A.M. 1849; Deac. 1847 by Bp of Ches. Pr. 1849 by Bp of Man. P. C. of Ch. Ch. Plymouth, Dio. Ex. 1865. (Patron, V. of St. Andrew's, Plymouth; P. C.'s Inc. 320*l*; Pop. 3984.) [2]

BENNETT, Thomas William.—Corpus Coll. Cam. B.A. 1833; Deac. 1834, Pr. 1835. Chap. R.N. 1841. [3]

BENNETT, William, *Exmouth Cottage, Hastings.* Dub. A.B. 1846, A.M. 1849; Deac. 1846 and Pr. 1847 by Bp of Ches. C. of St. Clement's, Hastings, 1861. Formerly C. of Witton, Cheshire, 1846, Chipping Norton 1848, St. Mary's, Walthamstow, 1850, Trinity and St. Mary's, Guildford, 1852, Stoke, next Guildford, 1856. Author, *Regeneration, its Type and Test,* 1849, 6*d*; *Popery as set forth in Scripture, its Guilt and Doom,* 1850, 6*d*; *What think ye of Christ?* 1853, 6*d*; *The Christian Sabbath, its Law and its Lord,* 1852, 6*d*; *The Signs of the Times,* 1853, 6*d*. [4]

BENNETT, William, *Gateshead.*—Dur. Licen. in Theol. 1839; Deac. 1839 and Pr. 1840 by Bp of Dur. P. C. of Trinity, Gateshead, Dio. Dur. 1864. (Patron, Bp of Dur; P. C.'s Inc. 450*l* and Ho; Pop. 5700) Formerly C. of Gateshead. [5]

BENNETT, William, *Plymouth.*—Head Mast. of the New Gr. Sch. Plymouth. [6]

BENNETT, William James Early, *Frome Selwood Vicarage, Frome, Somerset.*—Ch. Ch. Ox. B.A. 1827, M.A. 1829. V. of Frome Selwood with Woodlands and St. Mary's the Virgin (Chapels of Ease), Dio. B. and W. 1852. (Patron, Marquis of Bath; Tithe—Imp. 538*l* 13*s* 6*d*, V. 629*l* 15*s*; Glebe, 64½ acres; V.'s Inc. 762*l* and Ho; Pop. 4506.) Formerly P. C. of St. Paul's, Knightsbridge, with St. Barnabas', Pimlico, Lond. Author, *The Necessity of Prayer, particularly at the present Period of God's Visitation* (a Sermon), Lond. 1832; *Sermons on Marriage,* 1837; *Sermons on Miscellaneous Subjects,* with *Notes* and *Appendix,* 2 vols. 1838; *Neglect of the People in Psalmody and Responses,* 3 eds. 1841; *A Guide to the Holy Eucharist,* 2 vols. 1842; *Lecture-Sermons on the Distinctive Errors of Romanism,* 1842; *Letters to my Children on Church Subjects,* 2 vols. 1843; *The Principles of the Book of Common Prayer considered* (a course of Lecture-Sermons), 1845; *The Schism of Certain Priests and others lately in Communion with the Church of England,* 1845; *The Eucharist, its History, Doctrine and Practice, with Meditations and Prayers,* 1837; *Crime and Education* (a Pamphlet), 1846; *A Pastoral Letter to his Parishioners,* 1846; *Sins of the Church and People* (a Sermon on the National Fast-day), with an *Appendix concerning the Holy Communion on Days of Fasting,* 1847; *Apostacy* (a Sermon with a *Postscript*), 1847; *A Reply to* "A Statement of Facts," *made by A. Chirol, in Reference to a Late Event at St. Paul's, Knightsbridge,* 1847; *Lives of Certain Fathers of the Church in the Second, Third, and Fourth Centuries,* 3 vols; *Tales of Kirkbeck,* Two Series, 1849–50; *God's Judgment in the Pestilence* (a Sermon in two parts), 1849; *Calling upon God* (a Sermon on the Day of Consecration of the Church of St. Andrew's, Wells street), 1849; *A First Letter to Lord John Russell on the Persecution of a Certain Portion of the English Church,* with a *Sermon on Luke* xxi 17–19, 1850; *Three Farewell Sermons* (preached at St. Barnabas, Pimlico), 1851; *The Church, the Crown and the State, their Junction or their Separation* (two Sermons having reference to the Judicial Committee of the Privy Council), 1850; *Tales of a London Parish,* 1851; *Cousin Eustace, or Conversations on the Prayer-book,* 1851; *Farewell Letter to the Parishioners of St. Paul's, Knightsbridge, with Correspondence of the Bp of London on the Resignation of St. Paul's,* 2 eds. 1851; *Our Doctor, and other Tales of Kirkbeck,* 1852; *Mr. Horsman's Recent Motion in the House of Commons tested by Extracts from* "*Letters to my Children,*" 1852; *A Second Letter to Lord John Russell on the Present Persecution of a Certain Portion of the English Church,* 1852; *A Pastoral Letter to the Parishioners of Frome,* 1852; *St. John the Baptist's-day Sermons* (Preached at the Dedication of the Parish Church of Frome-Selwood), 1854; *Christian Zeal in Holy Places* (two Sermons on the re-opening of the Church at Bordesley, Birmingham); *An Examination of Archdeacon Denison's Propositions of Faith on the Holy Eucharist*; *Why Church Rates should be abolished* (a Pamphlet), 2 eds. 1861; *Lent Readings from the Fathers,* 1852; *Advent Readings from the Fathers,* 1853. Editor of *Sermons Preached at the Church of St. Barnabas during the Octave of its consecration,* with a *Preface,* 1850; Wagner's *Course of Sermons,* 1849; Fénélon's *Letter on Frequent Communion,* 1850; *The Theologian*; *The Old Church Porch,* 4 vols. from 1855 to 1860; etc. [7]

BENNETT, William John, D.D., *Dursley, Gloucestershire.* [8]

BENNETT, William Robert Lyon, *Northbourne Vicarage, Deal.*—St. Aidan's; Deac. 1851 and Pr. 1853 by Abp of Cant. V. of Northbourne, Dio. Cant. 1866. (Patron, Abp of Cant; Tithe, 180*l*; Glebe, 10 acres; V.'s Inc. 200*l* and Ho; Pop. 890.) Formerly C. of Bethersden 1851–54; P. C. of Trinity, Dover, 1854–56; Incumb. of Beechworth, Melbourne, Australia, 1856–60; C. in sole charge of Minster in Sheppey 1860–66; Chap. of Sheppey Union 1860–66. Previously an Officer in the Army. [9]

BENNETTS, John James, *West Coker, Yeovil.*—C. of West Coker. Formerly C. of Queen Camel, Somerset. [10]

BENNETTS, Thomas James, *Treverbyn, St. Austell, Cornwall.*—St. John's Coll. Cam. B.A. 1846; Deac. 1846 and Pr. 1847 by Bp of Ex. P. C. of Treverbyn, Dio. Ex. 1847. (Patrons, the Crown and Bp of Ex. alt; P. C.'s Inc. 157*l*; Pop. 2109.) [11]

BENNIE, James Noble, *Leicester.*—Glasgow, LL.B. 1854; Deac. 1854, Pr. 1855. V. of St. Mary's, Leicester, Dio. Pet. 1861. (Patron, Ld Chan; V.'s Inc. 250*l* and Ho; Pop. 8000.) [12]

BENNITT, William, *Bletchley, Fenny Stratford, Bucks.*—Trin. Coll. Ox. B.A. 1858, M.A. 1861; Deac. 1860 and Pr. 1861 by Bp of Ox. R. of Bletchley, Dio. Ox. 1861. (Patron, Jos. Bennitt, Esq; R.'s Inc. 630*l* and Ho; Pop. 670.) Formerly C. of Aylesbury 1859–61. [13]

BENNOCH, Archibald James, 128, *Camberwell-grove, London, S.*—Magd. Hall, Ox. B.A. 1860, M.A. 1864; Deac. 1861 and Pr. 1862 by Bp of Wor. Formerly Sen. C. of St. Matthew's, Duddeston, Birmingham, 1861–64; C. of St. Giles's, Camberwell, 1864–67. [14]

BEN-OLIEL, Maxwell Machluff, *St. Paul's Parsonage, Addiscombe, Croydon, S.*—St. Aidan's; Deac. 1860 by Bp of Carl. Pr. 1862 by Bp of Wor. Min. of St. Paul's Chapel, Addiscombe, Dio. Cant. 1867. (Patrons, Trustees; Min.'s Inc. 500*l*.) Formerly C. of Barbon, Westmoreland, 1860, St. Mary's, Edge Hill, 1862, St. Mary's, Leamington, 1862, Ch. Ch. Pentonville, Lond. 1863; Morn. Preacher Brompton Chapel 1864; Dom. Chap. to Dow. Duchess of Northumberland 1864. Author, *Sermon on the Death of the Duke of Northumberland,* 1*s*. [15]

BENSON, Alexander, *St. Thomas's, Birmingham.*—Dub; Deac. 1858 and Pr. 1859 by Bp of Rip. C. of St. Thomas's, Birmingham, 1864. [16]

BENSON, Christopher, *Woodfield, Ross, Herefordshire.*—Trin. Coll. Cam. B.A. 1802, M.A. 1815. Can. of Wor. Cathl. 1825. (Value, 700*l* and Res.) [17]

BENSON, Christopher, *Brampton, Cumberland.*—Queen's Coll. Ox. B.A. 1830, M.A. 1842. V. of Brampton, Dio. Carl. 1841. (Patron, Earl of Carlisle; Tithe, 21*l*; V.'s Inc. 300*l* and Ho; Pop. 3585.) Rural Dean; Surrogate. [18]

BENSON, Edward White, *Wellington College, near Wokingham.*—Trin. Coll. Cam. Sen. Chan. Medallist, 1st cl. Cl. Trip. Sen. Opt. 1852, Members' Prizeman, 1852, B.D. 1862; Deac. 1853 by Bp of Man. Pr. 1857 by Bp of Ely. Master of Wellington Coll. Late Fell. of Trin. Coll. Cam. [19]

BENSON, Henry, *Weald, Sevenoaks, Kent.*—P. C. of Weald, Dio. Cant. 1863. (Patron, V. of Sevenoaks; P. C.'s Inc. 90*l* and Ho; Pop. 824.) [1]

BENSON, Martin, *Ringwould Rectory, Dover.*—R. of Ringwould, Dio. Cant. 1866. (Patrons, Exors. of late Rev. J. Monins; R.'s Inc. 370*l* and Ho; Pop. 338.) [2]

BENSON, Percy George, *Mansfield Woodhouse, Mansfield, Notts.*—Magd. Coll. Cam. Scho. of, B.A. 1860; Deac. 1860 by Bp of Meath, Pr. 1861 by Bp of Kilmore. C. of Mansfield Woodhouse 1864. Formerly C. of Carnteel, Dio. Armagh, 1860, Bentham, Yorks, 1863. [3]

BENSON, Richard Meux, *Cowley, Oxon.*—Ch. Ch. Ox. Kennicott Hebrew Scho. B.A. 1847, M.A. 1849; Deac. 1848 and Pr. 1849 by Bp of Ox. P. C. of Cowley, Dio. Ox. 1850. (Patron, Ch. Ch. Ox; P. C.'s Inc. 90*l*; Pop. 1404.) Author, *Laying on of Hands, a Manual for Confirmation*, 4*d*; *Wisdom of the Son of David*, 5*s*; *Redemption* (a course of Sermons), 5*s*; *The Name of Jesus*, Sermon preached to Univ. of Ox. 1*s*; *The Free Action of God's Love amidst the Fixed Operations of His Power* (a Sermon), 1*s*; *The Divine Rule of Prayer*, 2*s* 6*d*; *Manual of Intercessory Prayer*, 1*s*. [4]

BENSON, R. G., *Hope-Bowdler, Church Stretton, Salop.*—R. of Hope-Bowdler, Dio. Herf. 1860. (Patrons, Trustees; R.'s Inc. 240*l* and Ho; Pop. 178.) [5]

BENSON, Samuel, 29, *King-street, Borough, Southwark, London, S.E.*—St. John's Coll. Cam. B.A. 1823, M.A. 1826; Deac. 1823 by Bp of Lin. Pr. 1824 by Bp of Win. Chap. of St. Saviour's, Southwark, Dio. Win. 1843. (Patrons, Parishioners; Chap.'s Inc. 360*l*; Pop. 14,057.) Formerly Chap. to the County Gaol, Surrey. [6]

BENSON, Thomas, *North Fambridge, Maldon, Essex.*—St. John's Coll. Cam. B.A. 1824; Deac. 1830, Pr. 1831. R. of North Fambridge, Dio. Roch. 1832. (Patron, Ld Chan; Tithe, 340*l*; Glebe, 22 acres; R.'s Inc. 380*l* and Ho; Pop. 191.) [7]

BENSON, William Peter, *Witheredge, N. Devon.*—Ex. Coll. Ox. B.A. 1825; Deac. 1826, Pr. 1827; V. of Witheredge, Dio. Ex. 1843. (Patron, the present V; Tithe, 350*l*; Glebe, 45 acres; V.'s Inc. 455*l* and Ho; Pop. 1237.) Formerly C. of South Molton 1826–32, Witheredge 1832–43. [8]

BENSTED, Thomas Barton, *Lockwood, Huddersfield.*—St. John's Coll. Cam. B.A. 1835, M.A. 1850; Deac. 1840, Pr. 1841. P. C. of Lockwood, Dio. Rip. 1848. (Patron, V. of Almondbury; Tithe—App. 36*l*, Imp. 9*s* 5*d*; P. C.'s Inc. 160*l* and Ho; Pop. 8783.) [9]

BENSTED, Thomas James, *Campden, Glouc.*—Sid. Coll. Cam. 15th Sen. Opt. B.A. 1862; Deac. 1866 by Bp of G. and B. C. of Weston-sub-Edge 1866. [10]

BENT, Frederick Charles Howard.—Univ. Coll. Dur. Licen. Theol. 1855; Deac. 1855 and Pr. 1856 by Bp of Rip. Formerly C. of Thornes, Wakefield, 1855, Lockwood, Huddersfield, 1856, Houghton Regis, Dunstable, 1858, Bulphan, Romford, 1860, Moulsham, Chelmsford, 1862. [11]

BENT, John Oxenham, *St. Mark's, North Audley-street, London, W.*—Pemb. Coll. Ox. B.A. 1855; Deac. 1856 and Pr. 1857 by Bp of Lin. C. of St. Mark's, North Audley-street. [12]

BENT, Robert Paul, *Melchbourne Vicarage, near Higham Ferrers.*—Pemb. Coll. Ox. B.A. 1850, M.A. 1856; Deac. 1850 by Bp of Wor. Pr. 1851 by Bp of Lich. V. of Melchbourne, Beds, Dio. Ely, 1864. (Patron, Lord St. John; V.'s Inc. 150*l* and Ho; Pop. 251.) Formerly C. of St. Matthew's, Wolverhampton, 1850–51, St. Nicholas', Great Yarmouth, 1852–53, Burnham, Bucks, 1853–60, Skeyton, Norfolk (sole charge), 860–64. [13]

BENTHALL, John, *Willen, Newport-Pagnell, Bucks.*—Trin. Coll. Cam. B.A. 1828, M.A. 1831; Deac. 1829, Pr. 1830. V. of Willen, Dio. Ox. 1852. (Patrons, Trustees; Tithe, 76*l*; Glebe, 20 acres; V.'s Inc. 132*l* and Ho; Pop. 80.) Chap. to the Marquis of Ailsa 1846. Formerly Asst. Mast. of Westminster Sch. 1828–46. Author, *Lectures on the Liturgy.* [14]

BENTINCK, The Ven. William Harry Edward, *Sigglesthorne Rectory, Hull.*—Ch. Ch. Ox. B.A. 1805, M.A. 1808. R. of Sigglesthorne, Dio. York, 1808. (Patron, the Crown; Tithe, 711*l* 15*s* 6*d*; R.'s Inc. 750*l* and Ho; Pop. 818.) Archd. and Rural Dean. Formerly Can. of Westminster 1809–64. [15]

BENTLEY, P. G., *Felton Grange, near Shrewsbury.* [16]

BENTLEY, Robert, *Kempsey, near Worcester.*—Bp Hat. Hall, Dur. Licent. in Theol. 1863, B.A. 1866; Deac. 1863 and Pr. 1864 by Bp of Dur. C. of Kempsey 1866. Formerly C. of St. Cuthbert's, Darlington, 1863. [17]

BENTLEY, Samuel, *Bridgnorth, Salop.*—St. Cath. Coll. Cam. B.A. 1849, M.A. 1852; Deac. 1849 and Pr. 1850 by Bp of G. and B. R. of St. Mary's, Bridgnorth, Dio. Herf. 1860. (Patron, T. Whitmore, Esq; R.'s Inc. 250*l* and Ho; Pop. 2683.) [18]

BENTLEY, William, *Oxted, near Godstone, Surrey.*—C. of Oxted. [19]

BENTLY, Thomas Rothwell, *St. Matthew's Rectory, Manchester.*—Emman. Coll. Cam. M.A; Deac. 1835, Pr. 1836. R. of St. Matthew's, City and Dio. of Man. 1840. (Patrons, D. and C. of Man; R.'s Inc. 300*l* and Ho; Pop. 11,257.) [20]

BENWELL, Augustus Frederick, 7, *Shornden Villas, Hastings.*—Deac. 1852 and Pr. 1855 by Bp of Chich. C. of St. Matthew's, Silver-hill, Hastings, 1866. Formerly C. of Laughton, Sussex, 1852, Soberton, Hants, 1856, Moor Critchell, Dorset, 1858, Laughton 1864; Chap. to Droxford Union 1858. [21]

BENWELL, Henry, *Aberystwith.*—Ex. Coll. Ox. 3rd cl. Lit. Hum. and B.A. 1858; Deac. 1862 and Pr. 1863 by Bp of St. D. Asst. C. of St. Michael's, Aberystwith, 1862. Formerly 2nd Mast. of Ystrad Mewrig Gr. Sch. 1859–1861. [22]

BENWELL, Henry.—— C. of Merton, Surrey. [23]

BENWELL, Henry Frederick, *Bassingham, Newark.*—Pemb. Coll. Ox. B.A. 1849; Deac. 1849 and Pr. 1850 by Bp. of Lin. C. of Bassingham 1856. Formerly C. of Fenton with Stragglesthorpe 1849. [24]

BENYON, Edward Richard, *Culford Hall, Bury St. Edmunds.*—St. John's Coll. Cam. B.A. 1825; Deac. 1826 by Bp of Bristol, Pr. 1827 by Bp of Nor. R. of the United R.'s of Culford, Ingham, and Timworth, Dio. Ely, 1839. (Patron, R. B. De Beauvoir, Esq; Culford, Tithe, 223*l* 6*s*; Ingham, Tithe, 340*l* 16*s* 6*d*; Glebe, 39*l* 2*s* 11*d*; Timworth, Tithe, 313*l* 2*s*; Glebe, 52*l* 1*s* 4*d*; R.'s Inc. 960*l* and 2 Hos; Pop. Culford 346, Ingham 236, Timworth 222.) [25]

BERE, Charles Sandford, *Uplowman, Tiverton, Devon.*—Ch. Ch. Ox. B.A. 1852; Deac. 1856, Pr. 1857. R. of Uplowman, Dio. Ex. 1858. (Patron, Rev. S. Pidsley; R.'s Inc. 625*l* and Ho; Pop. 444.) [26]

BERE, John, *Skilgate, near Wiveliscombe, Somerset.*—Emman. Coll. Cam. B.A. 1844; Deac. 1845 and Pr. 1846 by Bp of Ex. R. of Skilgate, Dio. B. and W. 1865. (Patrons, Exors. of Rev. R. Bere; Tithe, 205*l*; Glebe, 70 acres; R.'s Inc. 290*l* and Ho; Pop. 214.) P. C. of Upton, Dio. B. and W. 1865. (Patron, present P. C; P. C.'s Inc. 70*l*; Pop. 314.) Formerly P. C. of Upton 1846–58; C. of Withiell-Florey, Somerset, 1847–58, Selworthy, Somerset, 1858–64. [27]

BERE, J. L., *Weston Favell, Northampton.*—C. of Weston Favell. [28]

BERE, John, *Selworthy, Minehead, Somerset.*—C. of Selworthy. [29]

BERESFORD, Gilbert, *Hoby Rectory, Leicester.*—St. John's Coll. Cam. B.A. 1836, M.A. and B.D. R. of Hoby with Rotherby, consolidated living, Dio. Pet. 1843. (Patron, the present R; R.'s Inc. 800*l* and Ho; Pop. 503.) Hon. Can. of Pet. Cathl. 1854, and Rural Dean. Late Fell. of St. John's Coll. Cam. Author, *Sorrow, a Poem*, 1862. [30]

BERESFORD, John, *Walcot, Bath.*—Emman. Coll. Cam. B A. 1861, M.A. 1865; Deac. 1862 and Pr. 1863 by Bp of Nor. C. of Walcot, Bath, 1864. Formerly C. of St. Margaret's, Ipswich, 1862. Author, *The Priest-*

hood, the Covenant, and the Sacrifice of Christ, Three Sermons, 1864, 1s. [1]

BERESFORD, John George, *Bedale, Yorks.*—R. of Bedale with Burrill C. Dio. Rip. 1861. (Patrons, H. Beresford, Esq. and Lord Beaumont; R.'s Inc. 2000*l* and Ho; Pop. 2130.) [2]

BERESFORD, John James, *Peterborough.*—St. John's Coll. Cam. B.A. 1844, M.A. 1849, B.D. 1856; Deac. 1845 and Pr. 1846 by Bp of Lich. R. of Castor, Dio. Pet. 1864. (Patron, Bp of Pet; Tithe, 610*l*; R.'s Inc. 650*l* and Ho; Pop. 1111.) Formerly Fell. of St. John's Coll. Cam; C. of Tickenhall, Derbyshire, 1845; Chap. of Gaol, Northampton, 1849; Precentor of Pet. Cathl. 1850–64. [3]

BERGER, Theodore Thomas, *Bolton-le-Moors.*—King's Coll. Lond. B.A. 1854; Deac. 1856 and Pr. 1857 by Bp of Man. Sen. C. of St. George's, and C. in charge of St. James's, Bolton. Formerly C. of Padiham 1856, St. Bartholomew's, Salford, 1858. Author, *The Winding up of Earth's Story*, *God's Controversy*, and other Sermons [4]

BERGUER, Henry John, *Myddelton-square, London, N.*—King's Coll. Lond. Theol. Assoc. 1857; Deac. 1857 and Pr. 1858 by Bp of Lon. Min. of St. Peter's Mission Chapel, Limehouse. Formerly C. of St. James's, Pentonville. [5]

BERIDGE, Basil, *Algarkirk, Spalding, Lincolnshire.*—Deac. 1822, Pr. 1823. R. of Algarkirk with Fosdyke C. Dio. Lin. 1823. (Patron, the present R; Tithe, 1235*l*; Glebe, 503 acres; R.'s Inc. 2000*l* and Ho; Pop. Algarkirk 772, Fosdyke 549.) Rural Dean. [6]

BERKELEY, George Campion, *Southminster, Maldon, Essex.*—Pemb. Coll. Ox. B.A. 1835, M.A. 1838; Deac. 1836, Pr. 1837. V. of Southminster, Dio. Roch. 1839. (Patron, the Charter House; Tithe—Imp. 1414*l*, V. 422*l*; Glebe, 10 acres; V.'s Inc. 432*l* and Ho; Pop. 1424.) Rural Dean. [7]

BERKELEY, John Richard Pretyman, *St. Cleer, Liskeard.*—Dub. A.B. 1839; Deac. 1839 and Pr. 1840 by Bp of Kildare. V. of St. Cleer, Dio. Ex. 1844. (Patron, Ld Chan; Tithe—Imp. 330*l*, V. 300*l*; Glebe, 5 acres; V.'s Inc. 340*l* and Ho; Pop. 3930.) Formerly C. of Rosenallis 1839-41, St. Stephen's, Congleton, 1842, Gretton, Northants, 1843–44. [8]

BERKELEY, Miles Joseph, *King's Cliffe, Wansford, Northants.*—Ch. Coll. Cam. B.A. 1825, M.A. 1828; Deac. 1826 and Pr. 1827 by Bp of Pet. P. C. of Apethorpe, Northants, Dio. Pet. 1833. (Patron, Bp of Pet; P. C.'s Inc. 85*l*; Pop. 248.) P. C. of Wood Newton, Northants, Dio. Pet. 1833. (Patron, Bp of Pet; P. C.'s Inc. 135*l*; Pop. 529.) Rural Dean. Fell. of the Linnæan Society; Hon. Fell. of Royal Horticultural Society of Lond; Member of the Academy of Sciences of Sweden; Corresponding Member of the Society Naturæ Curiosum, the Societies of Agriculture of Paris and Lille, and of the Société de Biologie of Paris, etc. Author, *Gleanings of British Algæ*, 1833; The concluding Volume of *English Flora*, 1836; *Introduction to Cryptogamic Flora*, 1857; *Outlines of British Fungology*, 1860; *Handbook of British Mosses*, 1863; Articles on *The Diseases of Plants*, in *Encyclopædia of Agriculture*; A Series of Papers on *Vegetable Pathology* in *Gardener's Chronicle*; numerous Papers in *Linnæan Transactions*, *Zoological Journal*, *Annals of Natural History*, *Annales des Sciences Naturelles*, *Hooker's Journals of Botany*, *Journal of the Academy of Sciences of Philadelphia*, *Silliman's Journal*, *Hooker's Himalayan Journals*, *Antarctic and New Zealand Flora*, and *Sutherland's Journal*. [9]

BERKELEY, Sackville Hamilton, *Morebath, Tiverton.*—Oriel Coll. Ox. B.A. 1856, M.A. 1857; Deac. 1856 and Pr. 1857 by Bp of Ex. V. of Morebath, Dio. Ex. 1864. (Patron, Montague Bere, Esq; Tithe, 234*l*; Glebe, 4 acres; V.'s Inc. 240*l* and Ho; Pop. 430.) Formerly C. of Halberton, Tiverton, 1856–64. [10]

BERKELEY, W.—Trin. Coll. Ox. Fell. of. C. of St. Botolph's, Bishopsgate, Lond. [11]

BERKELEY, William Comyns, *Cotheridge Court, near Worcester.*—Jesus Coll. Cam. B.A. 1834; Deac. 1837, Pr 1839 P. C. of Cotheridge, Dio. Wor. 1850. (Patron, W. Berkeley, Esq; Tithe—App. 1*l* 15*s*, Imp. 1*l*; P. C.'s Inc. 100*l*; Pop. 233.) [12]

BERNAL, Charles.—Clare Coll. Cam. B.A. 1836; Deac. 1840 and Pr. 1841 by Bp of Lin. [13]

BERNARD, Henry Norris, *Twickenham Common, Surrey, S.W.*—Caius Coll. Cam. Moral Sci. Prize, M.A. LL.B. 1859; Deac. 1859 and Pr. 1860 by Bp of Win. C. of Trinity, Twickenham, 1864. Formerly C. of St. Anne's, Wandsworth, St. Giles's, Camberwell, St. Mary's, Balham Hill. [14]

BERNARD, John, *Woolton, Liverpool.*—Magd. Hall, Ox. M.A; Deac. 1845 and Pr. 1846 by Bp of Ches. Formerly C. of Toxteth Park, Liverpool, 1845–48. [15]

BERNARD, Samuel Edward, *Bath.*—Magd. Coll. Cam. B.A. 1829, M.A. 1832; Deac. and Pr. 1829 by Bp of Lich. Chap. to the Bath Penitentiary. Formerly C. of Cheltenham. [16]

BERNARD, Thomas Dehany, *Northfield House, Bath.*—Ex. Coll. Ox. 2nd cl. Lit. Hum. 1837, Ellerton Theol. Essay 1838, Chan's English Essay 1839, B.A. 1838, M.A. 1840; Deac. 1840 and Pr. 1841 by Bp of Lon. Select Preacher 1855 and 1862, and Bampton Lect. 1864. R. of Walcot, Dio. B. and W. 1863. (Patrons, Simeon's Trustees; Tithe, 130*l*; Glebe, 2 acres; R.'s Inc. 780*l*; Pop. 14,679.) Formerly C. of Gt. Baddow, Essex, 1840; V. of Gt. Baddow 1841; V. of Terling, Essex, 1848. Author, *The Witness of God* (University Sermons), Parker; *The Progress of Doctrine in the New Testament* (Bampton Lectures), Macmillan. [17]

BERNAU, John Henry, *Belvedere, Kent.*—Basle Miss. Coll. Deac. 1833 and Pr. 1834 by Bp of Lon. Min. of All Saints', Belvedere, Dio. Cant. 1856. (Patrons, Trustees; Min's Inc. 250*l* and Ho; Pop. 3000.) Formerly Miss. of Ch. Miss. Soc. 1834–53. Author, *Missionary Labours in British Guiana*. [18]

BERNAYS, Leopold John, *The Rectory, Great Stanmore, Middlesex.*—St. John's Coll. Ox. Fell. of, 2nd cl. Lit. Hum. B.A. 1843, M.A. 1846; Deac. 1844 and Pr. 1845 by Bp of Lon. R. of Great Stanmore, Dio. Lon. 1860. (Patron, the present R; Glebe, 25 acres; R.'s Inc. 500*l* and Ho; Pop. 1320.) Formerly C. of St. George-the-Martyr, Lond. 1844–45; Head Mast. of Church of England Gr. Sch. Hackney 1845. Author, *Translation of Goethe's Faust, 2nd part, &c. and other Poems*, 1839; *Translation of Couard's Sermons on Life of Early Christians*; *Manual of Family Prayers and Meditations*, 1845; *The Church in the Schoolroom* (Discourses to Schoolboys), 1851; *A Plea for Peace* (a Sermon preached before the University of Oxford), 1851; *God's Dwelling in his House* (a Sermon), 1853. [19]

BERNERS, H. A., *Harkstead, Ipswich.*—R. of Harkstead, Dio. Nor. 1865. (Patron, present R; R.'s Inc. 580*l* and Ho; Pop. 380.) [20]

BERNEY, Thomas, *Bracon Hall, Norwich.*—St. John's Coll. Cam. B.A. 1839, M.A. 1845; Deac. and Pr. 1839 by Bp of Nor. R. of Bracon Ash, Dio. Nor. 1855. (Patroness, Mrs. E. Berney; Tithe—App. 9*s* 2*d*; R. 248*l* 6*s* 2*d*; R.'s Inc. 263*l*; Pop. 270.) Formerly R. of Hockering, Norfolk, 1839–56. [21]

BERRIMAN, Richard, *Llanelly, Brecon.*—C. of Llanelly. [22]

BERRINGTON, William Morgan Davies, *Nolton, Haverfordwest, Pembrokeshire.*—Deac. 1837, Pr. 1838 by Bp of St. D. R. of Nolton, Dio. St. D. 1855. (Patron, Ld Chan; Tithe, 123*l*; Glebe, 29 acres; R.'s Inc. 154*l* and Ho; Pop. 205.) [23]

BERRY, Aubrey Brisbane, *Yoxall, near Burton-on-Trent.*—Ex. Coll. Ox. B.A. 1863, M.A. 1866; Deac. 1864 by Bp of Win. Pr. 1865 by Bp of Lich. C. of Yoxall 1864. [24]

BERRY, Charles, *Osborne-place, Soho-hill, Birmingham.*—St. Aidan's; Deac. 1865 and Pr. 1866 by Bp of Wor. C. of St. Stephen's, Birmingham, 1865. [25]

BERRY, E. F.—Chap. to Earl of Charleville. [26]

BERRY, Edward Sterling, *Helpringham, near Sleaford.*—Dub. A.B. 1838, A.M. 1844; Deac. 1238 by Bp of Lin. Pr. 1839 by Abp of Cant. V. of Scredington, Dio. Lin. 1861. (Patrons, D. and C. of Lin; Glebe, 154 acres; V.'s Inc. 200*l*; Pop. 397.) Formerly Incumb. of

St James's Episcopal Chapel, Edinburgh, 1856–61; previously Deputy Chap. of the Parish Ch. Sheffield, 1844–49; Chap. to the Cutlers' Company, Sheffield, 1849–56. Author, Sermons, *The Distress existing in Ireland and Scotland*, 1847; *Preaching Christ, its Manner and its End*, 1847; *The Ark of God in Danger*, Sheffield, 1850; *The Way of Duty the Way of Honour*; *on the Funeral of the Duke of Wellington*; *Sermons*, 1 vol. etc. [1]

BERRY, Joseph Walter, *Foxton (Cambs), near Royston.*—St. Peter's Coll. Cam. B.A. 1824, M.A. 1827; Deac. 1825 and Pr. 1826 by Bp of Lon. V. of Foxton, Dio. Ely, 1832. (Patron, Bp of Pet; Tithe—App. 538*l* 10*s* and 21 acres of Glebe, V. 122*l*; Glebe, 1¾ acres; V.'s Inc. 104*l* and Ho; Pop. 405.) [2]

BERRY, Marlborough Sterling, *West Ashton, Trowbridge, Wilts.*—Dub. A.B. 1837; Deac. 1840 and Pr. 1841 by Abp of Dub. P. C. of West Ashton, Dio. Salis. 1861. (Patron, W. Long, Esq; P. C.'s Inc. 220*l* and Ho; Pop. 314.) Formerly P. C. of Staverton, Wilts; previously C. of Trowbridge. [3]

BERRY, Thomas, *Bolton-le-Moors.*—Deac. 1841 by Bp of Rip. Pr. 1842 by Bp of Ches. P. C. of Ch. Ch. Bolton-le-Moors, Dio. Man. 1841. (Patrons, the Crown and Bp of Man. alt; P. C.'s Inc. 300*l* and Ho; Pop. 5635.) [4]

BERRY, T.—Asst. Cl. Mast. Atherstone Gr. Sch. [5]

BERRY, Thomas Brodbelt, *Ardeley Vicarage, Buntingford.*—Pemb. Coll. Cam. 1st in 2nd cl. Cl. Trip. 1860, B.A. 1860, M.A. 1864; Deac. 1862 and Pr. 1863 by Bp of Ches. C. in sole charge of Ardeley, Herts, 1865. Formerly C. of Neston, Cheshire, 1862–64. [6]

BERRY, Thomas Marlborough, *Burbage, Hinckley, Leicestershire.*—Dub. A.B. 1851; Deac. 1853, Pr. 1855. C. of Aston-Flamville and Burbage. [7]

BERRY, William, *Bircham-Newton, Rougham, Norfolk.*—R. of Bircham-Newton with Bircham-Tofts, Dio. Nor. 1835. (Patron, Marquis of Cholmondeley; Bircham-Newton, Tithe, 227*l* 12*s*; Glebe, 50 acres; Bircham-Tofts, Tithe, 221*l* 16*s*; Glebe, 32 acres; R.'s Inc. 505*l* 2*s* and Ho; Pop. Bircham-Newton 118, Bircham-Tofts 169.) [8]

BERRY, William, *Ullesthorpe House, Lutterworth.*—Dub. A.B. 1858; Deac. 1858 and Pr. 1859 by Bp of Pet. R. of Peatling Parva, Dio. Pet. 1866. (Patron, the present R; Tithe, 30*l*; Glebe, 104½ acres; Pop. 168.) Formerly C. of Ashby Parva 1858–59 and 1862–63, Peatling Parva 1863–66. [9]

BERRY, William Brodbelt, *Abbots Langley, Herts.*—Pemb. Coll. Cam. B.A. 1859; Deac. 1862, Pr. 1863. C. of Abbots Langley. Formerly C. of Capenhurst, Cheshire, 1862–63. [10]

BERRY, William Windsor, *Wadingham, Kirton-in-Lindsey, Lincolnshire.*—Ex. Coll. Ox. 2nd cl. Lit. Hum. 1822, B.A. 1823, M.A. 1826; Deac. 1832 and Pr. 1833 by Abp of Cant. R. of Wadingham, Dio. Lin. 1853. (Patron, the Crown; Tithe, 760*l*; Glebe, 130 acres; R.'s Inc. 930*l* and Ho; Pop. 812.) Preb. of St. Paul's Cathl. 1853. Formerly Asst. C. of Putney 1832–34; Chap. at Leghorn 1834–39; V. of Stanwell 1839–58; Rural Dean of Staines 1841–58. [11]

BERRYMAN, James Wise, *Emneth Vicarage, near Wisbech.*—St. Cath. Hall, Cam. B.A. 1845; Deac. 1845 by Bp of Rip. Pr. 1846 by Bp of Lin. V. of Emneth, Dio. Ely, 1858. (Patron, Bp of Ely; Tithe, 404*l*; Glebe, 2 acres; V.'s Inc. 420*l* and Ho; Pop. 1025.) Formerly C. of Carlton-in-Lindric, Notts, 1845–49, St. Mary's, Bury St. Edmunds, 1849–51, Newton, in Isle of Ely, 1851–59. Author, *The Vow Performed* (a Short and Plain Address to Young Persons after Confirmation), 1852, 1*d*; *The Vow Confirmed*, 1855, 2*d*; Tract, No. 1432 of S. P. C. K. List. [12]

BERTHON, Edward Lyon, *Romsey, Hants.*—Magd. Coll. Cam. B.A. 1845, M.A. 1848; Deac. 1845 and Pr. 1846 by Bp of Win. V. of Romsey, Dio. Win. 1860. (Patrons, D. and C. of Win; Tithe, 280*l*; Glebe, 50*l*; V.'s Inc. 430*l* and Ho; Pop. 5740.) Surrogate; Rural Dean. Formerly P. C. of Trinity, Fareham, 1847–57. [13]

BERTIE, Hon. Frederick, *Wytham (Berks), near Oxford.*—R. of Wytham, Dio. Ox. 1818. (Patron, Earl of Abingdon; R.'s Inc. 310*l* and Ho; Pop. 176.) R. of Albury, Wheatley, Oxon, Dio. Ox. 1820. (Patron, Earl of Abingdon; Tithe, 297*l* 2*s* 11*d*; R.'s Inc. 310*l* and Ho; Pop. 183.) P. C. of South Hincksey with Wootton P. C. Berks, Dio. Ox. 1820. (Patron, Earl of Abingdon; Wootton, Tithe, 250*l* 10*s* 6*d*; P. C.'s Inc. 300*l*; Pop. South Hincksey 636, Wootton, 384.) [14]

BERTIE, Hon. Henry William, *Great Ilford, Essex.*—Ch. Ch. Ox. 1833, All Souls Coll. S.C.L. 1836, B.C.L. 1840, D.C.L. 1847; Deac. 1836 and Pr. 1837 by Bp of Ox. V. of Great Ilford, Dio. Lon. 1844. (Patron, All Souls Coll. Ox; Glebe, 7 acres; V.'s Inc. 500*l*; Pop. 3353.) Fell. of All Souls Coll. Ox. [15]

BERTLES, William Dodsworth Bates, *Sevington, Ashford, Kent.*—Pemb. Coll. Cam. B.A. 1835, M.A. 1839; Deac. 1836, Pr. 1837. R. of Sevington, Dio. Cant. 1862. (Patron, Rev. W. H. Smith; R.'s Inc. 250*l*; Pop. 113.) Dom. Chap. to the Earl of Mountcashel. [16]

BERWICK, T. J.—C. of St. Thomas's, Charterhouse, Lond. [17]

BESANT, Frank, *Stockwell, Surrey, S.*—Emman. Coll. Cam. 28th Wrang. B.A. 1863, M.A. 1866; Deac. 1865 and Pr. 1866 by Bp of Win. 2nd Mast. of Stockwell Gr. Sch. [18]

BESANT, William, *Hulme Walfield, Congleton, Cheshire.*—Magd. Hall, Ox. B.A. 1837; Deac. 1857 and Pr. 1858 by Bp of Ches. Min. of Hulme Walfield. Formerly C. of Prestbury 1857–58. [19]

BESLEY, Charles John, *Burnley.*—St. Edm. Hall Ox. B.A. 1858, M.A. 1866; Deac. 1859 by Bp of Ex. Pr. 1860 by Bp of B. and W. C. of Burnley 1864. Formerly C. of Cheriton-Fitzpaine, Devon, 1859–64. [20]

BESLY, John, *Long Benton Vicarage, Newcastle-on-Tyne.*—Ball. Coll. Ox. B.A. 1821, Fell. of Ball. 1823, M.A. 1826, D.C.L. 1835; Deac. 1823 and Pr. 1824 by Bp of Ox. V. of Long Benton, Dio. Dur. 1830. (Patron, Ball. Coll. Ox; Tithe, 82*l*; Glebe, 80 acres; V.'s Inc. 887*l*; Pop. 2632.) R. of Aston Subedge, Glouc. Dio. G. and B. 1831. (Patron, Earl of Harrowby; Glebe, 104 acres; R.'s Inc. 280*l* and Ho; Pop. 121.) Formerly Tut. in Rugby School, 1823–28; Sub. Lib. in Bodleian Lib. 1828–31; Proctor in the Conv. of York, 1836–45, and again 1855–64. Author, *A Translation of Aristotle's Rhetoric, with Analysis by Hobbes*, 1833; The same, reprinted by Bohn; *The Principles of Christian Allegiance* (Sermon on the Birth of H.R.H. the Prince of Wales), 1841; *Desultory Notices of the Church and Vicarage of Long Benton*, 4to. Newcastle-on-Tyne, 1843; *The Duties of Masters and Servants* (a Sermon during the Strike of the Pitmen), 1844; *Visitation Sermons in* 1836 *and* 1843 *at Newcastle-on-Tyne*; *One Lord, One Faith* (Series of Discourses), 1850. [21]

BEST, James Kershaw, *Lane End Parsonage, High Wycombe.*—Deac. 1842 and Pr. 1845 by Bp of Madras. P. C. of Lane End, Dio. Ox. 1865. (Patron, R. of Hambleden; P. C.'s Inc. 110*l* and Ho; Pop. 1162.) Formerly Mis. S.P.G. Madras; C. of Chalfont St. Giles, Bucks. [22]

BEST, John, *Kirkoswald, Penrith.*—St. Bees; Deac. 1849 and Pr. 1850 by Bp of Man. V. of Kirkoswald, Dio. Carl. 1855. (Patron, Ld Chan; Tithe—Imp. 266*l* 19*s* 1*d*, V. 24*l*; Glebe, 74 acres; V.'s Inc. 168*l*; Pop. 944.) Formerly C. of Padiham, Whalley, Lancashire. [23]

BEST, J. H.—Min. at Fort Island, Essequibo. [24]

BEST, The Hon. Samuel, *Abbots-Ann, Andover, Hants.*—King's Coll. Cam. B.A. 1825; Deac. 1825, Pr. 1826. R. of Abbots-Ann, Dio. Win. 1831. (Patrons, Heirs of Sir J. Burrough, Knt; Tithe, 770*l* 6*s*; Glebe, 40 acres; R.'s Inc. 830*l* and Ho; Pop. 640.) Rural Dean of Andover. Late Fell. of King's Coll. Cam. Author, *Parochial Sermons*, 1836; *Afterthoughts on Dr. Buckland's Bridgwater Treatise*, 1837; *Discourses on*

Collects, Epistles and Gospels, 1853; *Manual of Parochial Institutions*, 1849; *Catechism on Collects, &c.* 1850; *On Catechising*, 1850; *Thoughts on Prudence, Savings Banks, &c.* 1850; *Education* (a Visitation Sermon), 1850; *Village Grammar*, 1852; *Village Reading Rooms and Libraries* 1854. [1]

BEST, William, *Campton Rectory, Biggleswade.*—Trin. Coll. Cam. B.A. 1849; Deac. 1849 and Pr. 1850 by Bp of Ox. R. of Campton with Shefford C. Dio. Ely. (Patron, Sir G. R. Osborn, Bart; R.'s Inc. 400*l* and Ho; Pop. Campton 529, Shefford 1015.) Formerly C. of Dinton, Bucks, 1849–55, Over Worton, Oxon, 1855–57, St. Paul's, Banbury, 1857–60, and Astley-Bridge, Lancashire, 1860–61, Campton with Shefford 1861–64. Editor of *The Church of Israel—A Study in Prophecy*, by the Rev. William Wilson. [2]

BEST, William Edward.—Corpus Coll. Cam. B.A. 1859; Deac. 1859 by Bp of Ox. Pr. 1860 by Bp of Lich. Formerly C. of Aylesbury 1859–60. [3]

BETHAM, Charles Jepson, *Brettenham, Bildeston, Suffolk.*—Emman. Coll. Cam. Exhib. Prizeman and B.A. 1845, M.A. 1848; Deac. 1846 by Bp of Pet. Pr. 1848 by Bp of Lin. R. of Brettenham, Dio. Ely, 1859. (Patron, Ld Chan; Tithe, 491*l* 2*s* 4*d*; Glebe, 24 acres; R.'s Inc. 506*l* and Ho; Pop. 426.) Formerly C. of Stanground with Farcet, Hunts, and Ibstock with Heekscote, Leic. Author, *The Lord my Banner* (a Sermon), 1857; *A Farewell Sermon*, 1859; *Arise and Build* (a Sermon), 1866. [4]

BETHELL, W., *Skipton, Yorks.*—C. of Skipton. [5]

BETHUNE, Angus, *Seaham, near Sunderland.*—King's Coll. Aberdeen, M.A. 1833; Deac. 1841 and Pr. 1842 by Bp of Dur. V. of Seaham, Dio. Dur. 1859. (Patron, Earl Vane; Tithe, 428*l*; Glebe, 232 acres; V.'s net Inc. 300*l* and Ho; Pop. 848.) Formerly C. of South Shields 1841, and P. C. of Seaham Harbour 1845. [6]

BETHUNE, George Cuddington, *Chumleigh, Devon.*—Trin. Coll. Ox. B.A. 1829, M.A. 1832, B.D. 1841; Deac. and Pr. 1830. R. of Chumleigh, Dio. Ex. 1859. (Patron, Rev. Robt. Hole; R.'s Inc. 740*l*; Pop. 1705.) Rural Dean. Dom. Chap. to Earl of Abergavenny. [7]

BETTISON, William James, *Plaistow, Essex.*—Corpus Coll. Cam. B.A. 1862; Deac. 1864 and Pr. 1865 by Bp of Roch. C. of St. Mary's, Plaistow, 1867. Formerly C. of Halstead, Essex. [8]

BETTON, Joseph.—Ch. Coll. Cam. B.A. 1833; Deac. 1833 and Pr. 1834 by Bp of Lin. Formerly R. of St. Michael's, Stamford, 1845–57. [9]

BETTS, Henry James, 26, *Price-street, Birkenhead.*—Dub. A.B. 1861; Deac. 1862 and Pr. 1863 by Bp of Ches. C. of St. Mary's, Birkenhead, 1862. [10]

BETTS, John, *Upton St. Leonard's, near Gloucester.*—Queens' Coll. Cam. B.A. 1829; Deac. 1829 and Pr. 1831 by Bp of B. and W. P. C. of Upton St. Leonard's, Dio. G. and B. 1860. (Patron, Bp of G. and B; Tithe—App. 678*l* 8*s*, Imp. 7*l*; Glebe, 29 acres; P. C.'s Inc. 110*l* and Ho; Pop. 1011.) Formerly Asst. C. of Avening, and C. of Wollaston, Glouc. [11]

BEVAN, Charles Hay, 6, *Theresa-terrace, Gloucester.*—St. Aidan's; Deac. 1856 and Pr. 1857 by Bp of Ches. Chap. of Mariner's Ch. Gloucester, 1863 (Stipend, 150*l*). Formerly C. in sole charge of Gee Cross, 1856, and Chadkirk, Cheshire, 1859; C. of Ch. Ch. Gloucester, 1861. Author, *Scriptural Lessons*, 1*s* 6*d*; *Is Baptism Regeneration?* 6*d*; *Address to the Confirmed*; *Church Rates no real Grievance to Dissenters*; etc. [12]

BEVAN, David Barclay, *Amwell Bury, Ware.*—Univ. Coll. Ox. B.A. 1836, M.A. 1838; Deac. 1837 and Pr. 1838 by Bp of Ches. Chap. of Little Amwell, Dio. Roch. 1864. (Patrons, Trustees; Chap.'s Inc. 70*l* and Ho; Pop. 600.) Formerly R. of Burton Latimer, Northants, 1848–57. Author, *Food for Babes*, 3*s*; *Minister's Letters*, 1 to 12, 1*d* each; *Heart's Looking-Glass*, 4*d*; etc. [13]

BEVAN, Ernest Charles, 4, *Denmark-terrace, Denmark-hill, S.*—Ex. Coll. Ox. B.A. 1861, M.A. 1864; Deac. 1865 and Pr. 1866 by Bp of Win. C. of St. Matthew's, Denmark-hill, 1865. [14]

BEVAN, Evan, *Nefyn, near Pwllheli, Carnarvon.* Deac. 1860 and Pr. 1861 by Bp of Llan. P. C. of Nefyn, Dio. Ban. 1862. (Patron, C. W. Finch, Esq; P. C.'s Inc. 125*l* and Ho; Pop. 1818.) Formerly C. of Cardiff 1860–62. [15]

BEVAN, Henry Bailey, *Malvern.*—Mert. Coll. Ox; Deac. 1851 by Bp of St. D. Pr. 1853 by Bp of Llan. Min. Can. of Llan. Cathl. [16]

BEVAN, William Henry Rawlinson, *Plumpton, Bury St. Edmunds.*—Trin. Coll. Cam. B.A. 1864; Deac. 1864 and Pr. 1865 by Bp of Lin. Formerly C. of East Retford 1864–65. [17]

BEVAN, William Latham, *Hay, South Wales.*—Magd. Hall, Ox. B.A. 1842, M.A. 1845; Deac. 1844, Pr. 1845. V. of Hay, Dio. St. D. 1845. (Patron, Sir J. Bailey, Bart; Tithe—Imp. 245*l* 18*s* 8*d*, V. 124*l* 12*s* 4*d*; Glebe, 50 acres; V.'s Inc. 200*l*; Pop. 1998.) Chap. of the Hay Union, Brecon. [18]

BEVERLEY, Henry Webber, *Worthing, Sussex.*—Caius Coll. Cam. B.A. 1862, M.A. 1866; Deac. 1862 and Pr. 1864 by Abp of Cant. C. of Chapel of Ease, Worthing, 1865. Formerly C. of Sturry, Kent, 1862–65. [19]

BEWSHER, Charles William, *Milton, near Canterbury.*—St. Peter's Coll. Cam. B.A. 1836; Deac. 1839, Pr. 1840. R. of Milton, Dio Cant. 1847. (Patron, M. Bell, Esq; Tithe, 65*l*; R.'s Inc. 76*l*; Pop. 11.) [20]

BEWSHER, Francis William, *Birtley Parsonage, Fence Houses, Durham.*—Dub. A.B. 1832, A.M. 1835, *ad eund.* Univ. Coll. Dur. 1840; Deac. 1833, Pr. 1834. P. C. of the Chapelry of St. John the Evangelist, Birtley, Dio. Dur. 1850. (Patron, P. C. of Chester-le-Street; P. C.'s Inc. 300*l* and Ho; Pop. 3888.) Formerly C. of Kirkhaugh 1833–34; 2nd Mast. High Sch. Carlisle, 1834–36; C. of Gateshead 1837–38, Gateshead Fell 1839–43, Long Benton 1843–45, South Hetton 1845–47, Birtley 1847–50. [21]

BEWSHER, George, *Lostock, Knutsford, Cheshire.*—St. Edm. Hall, Ox. B.A. 1824, M.A. 1837; Deac. 1829 and Pr. 1830 by Bp of Nor. P. C. of Lostock, Dio. Ches. 1846. (Patron, P. C. of Witton; P. C.'s Inc. 82*l*; Pop. 1294.) [22]

BEWSHER, Thomas.—St. Cath. Coll. Cam. LL.B. 1856; Deac. 1856 and Pr. 1857 by Bp of Carl. [23]

BEWSHER, Thomas James, *Cley-next-the-Sea, Holt, Norfolk.*—Univ. Coll. Dur. Licen. Theol. 1843; Deac. 1843 and Pr. 1844 by Bp of Dur. R. of Cley-next-the-Sea, Dio. Nor. 1859. (Patron, W. Bishop, Esq; R.'s Inc. 400*l*; Pop. 791.) [24]

BEWSHER, William, *Maryport, Cumberland.*—Dub. A.B. 1821; Deac. and Pr. 1823. P. C. of St. Mary's, Maryport, in the Parish of Cross Canonby, Dio. Carl. 1850. (Patroness, Mrs. Pocklington Senhouse; P. C.'s Inc. 170*l* and Ho; Pop. 6150.) Surrogate; Dom. Chap. to the Earl of Rosse. Formerly C. of Astbury, Cheshire, 1833. [25]

BEYNON, Edward Francis, *Stines Oaks, Chelsham, Croydon, Surrey.*—Trin. Coll. Cam. B.A. 1829, M.A. 1832; Deac. 1832 and Pr. 1833 by Bp of Pet. Formerly R. of Creaton, near Northampton, 1833–43. Author, *Words to Labourers*, 1858; *Progress, the Farmer's Watchword*, 1859. [26]

BEYNON, Frederick, *Bickenhill, near Birmingham.*—C. of Bickenhill. [27]

BEYNON, John, *Witston, Newport, Monmouthshire.*—Literate; Deac. 1826 and Pr. 1827 by Bp of Llan. V. of Witston, Dio. Llan. 1832. (Patrons, Chap. of Llan and Eton Coll. alt; Tithe—Imp. 1*l* 7*s*, V. 134*l*; Glebe, 45 acres; V.'s Inc. 220*l* and Ho; Pop. 25.) [28]

BEYNON, John Middleton, 30, *Delamere-terrace, Paddington, London, W.*—Jesus Coll. Ox. Scho. of, B.A. 1858, M.A. 1860; Deac. 1858 and Pr. 1859 by Bp of Llan. C. of St. Mary Magdalene's, Paddington, 1866. Formerly C. of Nash 1858, Penrith 1860, Ilford 1863. [29]

BEYNON, William Llewellyn, *Seale, near Farnham, Surrey.*—Magd. Hall, Ox. B.A. 1845, M.A

1846; Deac. 1845 by Bp of Wor. Pr. 1846 by Bp of Win. P. C. of Seale, Dio. Win. 1856. (Patron, Archd. of Surrey; P. C.'s Inc. 50*l* and Ho; Pop. 670.) Formerly C. of Fenny Compton, Warwickshire, 1853–56. [1]

BIBBY, Albert, *Gorey, Jersey.*—King's Coll. Lond. Deac. 1849 by Bp of Win. Pr. 1850 by Bp of Wor. P. C. of Gorey, Jersey, Dio. Win. 1857. (Patron, R. of St. Martin's, Jersey; P. C.'s Inc. 50*l*; Pop. 3558.) Formerly P. C. of Ch. Ch. Rotherhithe, Lond. 1854–57. [2]

BIBER, George Edward, *Roehampton, Surrey.*—Tübingen, Ph.D. Göttingen, LL.D; Deac. 1839, Pr. 1840. P. C. of Holy Trinity, Roehampton, Dio. Lon. 1842. (Patron, Bp of Lon; P. C.'s Inc. 250*l*; Pop. 974.) Formerly C. of St. John's, Putney Vale, 1839–46, St. Paul's, Hook, 1841–42. Author, Before Ordination:—*Lectures on Education*, delivered in 1828 and 1829; *Henry Pestalozzi and his Plan of Education, being an Account of his Life and Writings*, 1830; *Twenty-four Tales of the English Church*, 1832.—Since Ordination:—*The Standard of Catholicity, or an attempt to point out in a plain manner certain safe and leading Principles amidst the conflicting opinions by which the Church is at present agitated*, 1st edit. 1840, 2nd edit. 1844; *The Study of Holy Scripture recommended to the Young*; *God's Holy Presence*; *The Seal of the Covenant, or the Apostolic Ordinance of Confirmation, three Letters addressed to his Pupils*, 1841–42; *The Catholicity of the Anglican Church Vindicated, and the Alleged Catholicity of the Roman Church disproved*, 1842, 2nd edit. 1844; *Occasional Sermons on the more important Topics of the Present Day*, 1844; *Pictorial History of the Old Testament for the Use of the Young*, 1844; *The Ordinance of Confirmation considered as the Ordinance of the Holy Ghost*, 1844; *The English Church on the Continent*, 1845–47; *Sermons for Saints' Days*, 1846; *The Supremacy Question, or Justice to the Church of England*, 1847; *Church Emancipation and Church Reform*, 1847; *The Papal Bull* "In Cœna Domini," *translated, with a critical Introduction, and evidence of its present validity and recognition by the Romish Hierarchy in Ireland*, 1848; *A Letter to the Earl of Arundel and Surrey, on the Bull* "In Cœna Domini," 1848; *Papal Diplomacy and the Bull* "In Cœna Domini," 1848; *The Royal Supremacy over the Church, considered as to its Constitutional Limits in reference to Episcopal Promotions*, 1848; *The Life of St. Paul, for the Use of Young Persons*, 1849; *History and Present State of the Education Question*, 1850; *Fiat Justitia, a Letter addressed to the Rev. E. B. Pusey, D.D. in Reply to his Speech at the Meeting of the London Union on Church Matters*, 1850; *What English Churchmen should do*, 1851; *Opinions of Sir Frederic Thesiger, Sir W. Page Wood, and Dr. Robert Phillimore, upon a case submitted by the Society for the Revival of Convocation respecting the Constitutional Powers of Convocation, and the Right of the Suffragan Bishops to a Voice in the Question of Prorogation*, 1853; *Literature, Art, and Science considered as a Means of Elevating the Popular Mind*, 1854; *Sermons for the Times*, viz:—I. *The Church in her Day of Trial* (on the Gorham case), 1850; II.–IV. *The Exclusive Validity of Episcopal Ordinations*, 1851; V. *The Evidence of Popish Miracles not to be heard*, 1851; VI. *The Office of the Church as the Teacher of the Nation*, 1853; VII. *The Wrath of the Lamb, or the Doctrine of Everlasting Punishment set forth in the Gospel*, 1853; VIII. *Our National Sins and their Consequences*, 1855; *Church Biography for the Million—The Apostolic Age*, 1855; *A Plea for a new Edition of the Authorized Version of Holy Scripture*, 1857; *The Seven Voices of the Spirit, Sermons on the Promises to the Church Universal in the Apocalyptic Epistles*, 1857; *Bishop Blomfield and his Times*, 1857; *The Royalty of Christ and the Church and Kingdom of England* (sermons in reference to the Indian Revolt), 1857; *The Veracity and Divine Authority of the Pentateuch Vindicated, in a critical examination of Dr. Colenso's Book*, 1863; *The Integrity of the Holy Scriptures* (a sermon), 1863; *The Communion of the Faithful essential to the Celebration of the Holy Eucharist*, 1863; *Christian Worship: its nature, its pattern and primitive character*, 1864; *The Kingdom and Church of Hawaii*, 1865; *The Act of Suicide as distinct from the Crime of Self-Murder*, 1865; *The Supremacy Question considered in its successive Phases* (an Essay called forth by the judgment in the case of the South African Church), 1866; *The Upright Judge* (a Sermon on the death of Sir J. L. Knight Bruce), 1866. Besides the above, Dr. Biber has contributed largely to the current periodical literature, principally in the *English Review*, to which he contributed Essays on *The Scottish Episcopal Church*; *The English Church on the Continent*; *The Order of Jesuits*; *The Papacy and the Revolution*; *Church and State in France*; *Romanism and Protestantism in Germany*; *The Education Question*; *Irvingism*; *The Mormonites*; *Wesleyan Methodism*; *The British Anti-State Church Association*; *The Liturgical Question in Germany*; and a variety of other subjects 1844–51; in the *John Bull*, which he edited from 1848 to 1856; in the *Churchman's Magazine*, 1856–57; in the *Literary Churchman*, 1859–62; in the *Church Review*, January, 1862–June, 1864; and in the *Colonial Church Chronicle*. [Dr. Biber has been engaged in most of the Church movements of the last twenty years. He acted on the Committee of the "National Club" from its foundation in 1845 to 1850, when he withdrew on the issue of a circular to churchwardens inviting complaints against the clergy. He was concerned in the establishment, in 1849, of the "Metropolitan Church Union," and, in 1850, of the "Society for the Revival of Convocation," from which he withdrew, in 1855, on the question of lay representation. He was a member of the "Committee of June the Seventh," formed in 1849, whose operations, including the "Great Education Meeting" at Willis's Rooms in 1850, led to the settlement of the education question in 1852. Lastly, having joined the "English Church Union," he was elected a member of the Council in 1863, when he took a leading part in the action of the Union in the Colenso case, but resigned his seat in June 1864, on the ground of mediævalist tendencies and rationalistic sympathies in the Council.—*Communicated*.] [3]

BICKERDIKE, John, *St. Mary's Parsonage, Leeds.*—Trin. Coll. Cam. B.A. 1841; M.A. 1844; Deac. 1842, Pr. 1843. P. C. of St. Mary's, Leeds, Dio. Rip. 1848. (Patron, V. of Leeds; Glebe, 1 acre; P. C.'s Inc. 300*l* and Ho; Pop. 12,048.) Formerly C. of Bradford, Yorks, 1842–48. [4]

BICKERDIKE, Joseph Fletcher, *Girley, co Meath.* [5]

BICKERDIKE, Robert, 56, *Bridge-street, Southwark, London, S.E.*—Dub. A.B. 1847, A.M. 1850; Deac. 1847, Pr. 1848. C. of St. Saviour's, Southwark, 1852. Formerly C. of Stanley, Wakefield, 1847–52. [6]

BICKERSTAFF, Isaac, *Bonsall Rectory, Matlock.*—Lampeter, B.D. 1852; Deac. 1838 and Pr. 1839 by Bp. of St. D. R. of Bonsall, Dio. Lich. 1863. (Patron, Bp of Lich; Tithe, 128*l* 10*s*; Glebe, 108*l*; R.'s Inc. 240*l* and Ho; Pop. 1290.) Formerly C. of All Saints', West Bromwich, 1845–63. [7]

BICKERSTAFFE, Harry Lloyd.—St. Bees, 1849–42; Deac. 1851 by Bp of Wor. Pr. 1852 by Bp of Rip. Formerly C. of Thursley, Surrey, and Chorlton and Hardy, near Manchester. [8]

BICKERSTETH, The Venerable Edward, *Prebendal House, Aylesbury, Bucks.*—Sid. Coll. Cam. Sen. Opt. B.A. 1836, M.A. 1839, D.D. by Univ. of Cam. 1864; Licen. in Theol. of the Univ. of Dur. 1837; Deac. 1837 and Pr. 1839 by Bp of Herf. V. of Aylesbury, Dio. Ox. 1853. (Patron, Bp of Ox; Glebe, 90 acres; V.'s Inc. 400*l* and Ho; Pop. 5018.) Archd. of Buckingham, 1853 (value 300*l*); Prolocutor of Convocation of Cant. 1864, and again in 1866; Hon. Can. of Ch. Ch. Ox. 1866. Formerly C. of Chetton 1838, the Abbey, Shrewsbury, 1839; P. C. of Penn Street, Bucks, 1849; Rural Dean of Amersham 1849. Author, *Questions illustrating the XXXIX. Articles of the Church of England*, 4th edit. 1855, 3*s* 6*d*; *Catechetical Exercises on the Apostles' Creed*, 1846, 3*s*; *Prayers for the Use of the Clergy in the Present Times*, 1851, 1*s*; *Charges to the Clergy of the Archdeaconry of Buckingham*, 1855, '56, '58, '59, '61, '62, '64, and '65; *God's Judgments in India, a Warning to England* (a sermon), 1857; *Church Music*, 1857; *The*

Convictions of Balaam, 1858; *Joshua before Gibeon* (a sermon before the Rifle Volunteers), 1859; *The Conflict with the Spirit of Expediency* (an Oxford Lenten sermon), 1865; *The Name Jehovah*, and other tracts in the 3rd series of *Tracts for Christian Seasons*; *Diocesan Synods* (a Paper read at York Church Congress), 1866; *The Authority and Responsibilities of the Christian Ministry* (sermon preached at Ripon), 1866; etc. [1]

BICKERSTETH, Edward Henry, *Christ Church Parsonage, Hampstead, Middlesex, N.W.*—Trin. Coll. Cam. Sen. Opt. and B.A. 1847, M.A. 1850; Deac. 1848, Pr. 1849. P. C. of Christ Church, Hampstead, Dio. Lon. 1855. (Patrons, Trustees; P. C.'s Inc. 600*l*; Pop. 3000.) Chap. to Bp of Rip. Author, *Poems*, 5*s*; *Water from the Wellspring*, 2*s*; *Psalmody*; *The Rock of Ages, or Scripture Testimony to the Trinity in Unity*, 4*s*; *Commentary on the New Testament*, 32*s*; *Yesterday, To-Day, and For Ever, a Poem in 12 Books*, 10*s* 6*d*; *Hades and Heaven*, 2*s*. [2]

BICKFORD, Thomas Sydney, *Richmond, Yorks.*—2nd Mast. of Richmond Gr. Sch. [3]

BICKMORE, Charles, *Highlands, Leamington.*—Dub. A.B. 1840, A.M. 1843, *ad eund.* Ox. 1853, D.D. 1857; Deac. 1840, Pr. 1841. Min. of Christ Church Proprietary Chapel, Leamington. Formerly Asst. Min. of Temple Chapel, Balsall. Author, *A Humiliation Sermon*, 1854 (for the Benefit of Soldiers' Wives and Families), 1*s*; *A Course of Historical and Chronological Instruction, with Tables*; *A Series of Questions and Answers on Dr. Smith's History of Greece*; *Loyalty, Thankfulness and Godly Fear* (a Sermon on the Queen's Visit), Leamington, 1858. [4]

BICKMORE, Frederick Askew, *Cranwich, Brandon, Norfolk.*—Dub. A.B. 1843; Deac. 1843 and Pr. 1844 by Bp of Nor. R. of Cranwich with Didlington V. and Colveston R. Dio. Nor. 1855. (Patron, W. A. Tyssen Amhurst, Esq. Didlington Park; Tithe, 189*l*; Glebe, 19½ acres; Didlington, Tithe, 100*l*; Glebe, 100 acres; Colveston, Tithe, 100*l*; R.'s Inc. 600*l* and Ho; Pop. Cranwich 88, Didlington 80, Colveston 59.) [5]

BICKMORE, William Frederic, *Kenilworth, Warwickshire.*—Theol. Assoc. King's Coll. Lond. 1st cl. 1851; Deac. 1851 and Pr. 1852 by Bp of Lon. V. of Kenilworth, Dio. Wor. 1855. (Patron, Ld Chan; Tithe—Imp. 2*l* 2*s* 6*d*, V. 17*l* 10*s*; V.'s Inc. 288*l* and Ho; Pop. 2653.) Formerly Professor of History and Geography at the Ladies' College, Brompton, and C. of Chelsea. [6]

BICKNELL, Charles Brooke, *Stourton Rectory, Mere, Wilts vià Bath.*—Ex. Coll. Ox. B.A. 1848, M.A. 1851; Deac. 1850 and Pr. 1851 by Abp of Cant. R. of Stourton, Dio. Salis. 1858. (Patron, Sir H. A. Hoare, Bart; Tithe, 520*l*; R.'s Inc. 520*l* and Ho; Pop. 660.) [7]

BICKNELL, Clarence, 6, *Lorrimore-square, Walworth, S.*—Trin. Coll. Cam. B.A. 1865; Deac. 1866 by Bp Anderson for Bp of Lond. Asst. C. of St. Paul's, Lorrimore-square. [8]

BICKNELL, John, 41, *Highbury-hill, Islington, N.*—Trin. Coll. Cam. 2nd cl. in Cl. Trip. and Jun. Opt. B.A. 1843, M.A. 1846; Deac. 1844 and Pr. 1845 by Bp of Pet. P. C. of St. Saviour's, Aberdeen Park, Highbury, Dio. Lon. 1866. (Patron, Rev. W. D. Morrice; P. C.'s Inc. as yet *uncertain*; Pop. 400.) [9]

BICKNELL, Richard Henry.—Magd. Coll. Cam. B.A. 1847, M.A. 1850; Deac. 1848 and Pr. 1851 by Bp of Nor. Formerly C. of Southwold and Groton, Suffolk. [10]

BIDDICK, E. B. *Warton, Atherstone.*—P. C. of Warton, Dio. Wor. 1865. (Patron, V. of Polesworth; P. C.'s Inc. 122*l*; Pop. 582.) [11]

BIDDLE, Arthur John, *Painswick, Glouc.*—St. Mary Hall, Ox. B.A. 1848. V. of Painswick, Dio. G. and B. 1856. (Patron, J. Biddle, Esq; Tithe—Imp. 534*l* 0*s* 4*d*, V. 326*l*; V.'s Inc. 365*l* and Ho; Pop. 1845.) [12]

BIDDULPH, Henry, *Birbury, Rugby.*—Magd. Coll. Ox. B.A. 1817, M.A. 1820, B.D. 1830; Deac. 1819 and Pr. 1820 by Bp of Ox. R. of Birbury, Dio. Wor. 1826. (Patron, Sir T. Biddulph, Bart; Glebe, 167 acres; R.'s Inc. 150*l* and Ho; Pop. 184.) R. of Standlake, Oxon. Dio. Ox. 1832. (Patron, Magd. Coll. Ox; Tithe—App. 8*l* 2*s* 6*d*, R. 459*l* 15*s* 10*d*; R.'s Inc. 464*l* and Ho; Pop. 822.) Rural Dean. [13]

BIDDULPH, T. S.—Preb. of Brecon. [14]

BIDEWELL, George John, *Bodham Holt, Norfolk.*—St. Bees; Deac. and Pr. 1854 by Bp of Pet. R. of Bodham, Dio. Nor. 1861. (Patron, T. J. Mott, Esq; Pop. 316.) [15]

BIDWELL, George Henry Clarke, *Bressingham, Diss, Norfolk.*—Clare Hall, Cam. B.A. 1839, M.A. 1844; Deac. 1840, Pr. 1841. R. of Bressingham, Dio. Nor. 1841. (Patron, C. Bidwell, Esq; Tithe—App. 1*l* 10*s*, R. 613*l* 6*s*; R.'s. Inc. 690*l* and Ho; Pop. 596. [16]

BIDWELL, George Shelford, *Stanton Lodge, near Ixworth, Suffolk.*—St. John's Coll. Cam. B.A. 1852; Deac. 1855 and Pr. 1856 by Bp of Roch. C. of Stanton All Saints with St. John 1864. Formerly C. of Margaretting 1855–57, Yetminster 1858–60, St. Mary's, Chatham, 1862–64. [17]

BIDWELL, Woodward Clarke, *Potton, Beds.*—Clare Hall, Cam. B.A. 1843, M.A. 1846; Deac. 1843, Pr. 1844. V. of Potton, Dio. Ely, 1845. (Patron, Ld Chan; Land in lieu of Tithe, 280 acres; V.'s Inc. 450*l*; and Ho; Pop. 1944.) Rural Dean; Dom. Chap. to Lord Ashburton. [18]

BIGG, Charles, *Cheltenham College, Cheltenham.*—2nd Mast. of Cl. Department, Cheltenham Coll. Sen. Stud. of Ch. Ch. Ox. [19]

BIGG, Lionel Oliver, *Albury, Guildford.*—Univ. Coll. Ox. B.A. 1863; Deac. 1864 and Pr. 1865 by Bp of Win. C. of Albury 1864. [20]

BIGG, Thomas Frederick, *Cawnpore, Bengal.* [21]

BIGGE, George Richard, *Ovingham, Prudhoe Station, Northumberland.*—Univ. Coll. Dur. B.A. 1847, M.A. 1850; Deac. 1848 and Pr. 1850 by Bp of B. and W. P. C. of Ovingham, Dio. Dur. 1850. (Patron, Lieut.-Col. Bigge; Tithe—Imp. 1029*l*; Glebe, 38 acres; P. C.'s Inc. 147*l*; Pop. 2362.) [22]

BIGGE, Henry John, *Rockingham, Northants.*—Univ. Coll. Ox. B.A. 1838, M.A. 1841; Deac. 1841 by Bp of Dur. Pr. 1842 by Bp of Pet. R. of Rockingham, Dio. Pet. 1847. (Patron, G. L. Watson, Esq; Tithe, 150*l*; Glebe, 30 acres; R.'s Inc. 216*l*; Pop. 211.) [23]

BIGGE, John Frederic, *Stamfordham, Newcastle-on-Tyne.*—Univ. Coll. Dur. B.A. 1840, M.A. 1843; Deac. and Pr. 1840 by Bp of Dur. V. of Stamfordham, Dio. Dur. 1847. (Patron, Ld Chan; Tithe—App. 1083*l* 11*s* 9½*d*, V. 311*l* 10*s* 2*d*; Glebe, 315 acres; V.'s Inc. 549*l* and Ho; Pop. 1049.) Rural Dean. [24]

BIGGINS, Matthew Bennett, *Bucknall Rectory, Stoke-on-Trent.*—St. Bees; Deac. 1860 and Pr. 1861 by Bp of Lich. C. of Bucknall with Bagnall 1860, sole charge since 1862. [25]

BIGGS, George Hesketh, *Eatington Vicarage, Stratford-on-Avon.*—Wor. Coll. Ox. B.A. 1846, M.A. 1864; Deac. 1852 and Pr. 1853 by Bp of Wor. V. of Eatington, Dio. Wor. 1866. (Patron, E. P. Shirley, Esq; Tithe, comm. 13*l*; Glebe, 100 acres; V.'s Inc. 240*l* and Ho; Pop. 713.) Formerly C. of Shrawley, Worc. 1852; Chap. at Berne 1859–61; C. of Upton Warren, 1862. [26]

BIGGS, Louis Coutier, *Ipswich.*—St. Edm. Hall, Ox. B.A. 1863, M.A. 1866; Deac. 1864, Pr. 1865. Asst. Mast. in Ipswich Gr. Sch. 1867. Formerly C. of Grendon, Northants. Author, *Alphabetical Index of Texts to Hymns Ancient and Modern*, 1865, 1½*d*; *Hymns Ancient and Modern with Annotations, Translations, &c.* Novello, 1867, 6*d*. [27]

BIGGS, Michael, *Peckham, Surrey, S.E.*—Pemb. Coll. Cam. B.A. 1837, M.A. 1840; Deac. 1840 and Pr. 1841 by Bp of Lon. P. C. of St. Mary Magdalene's, Peckham, Dio. Win. 1859. (P. C.'s Inc. 330*l*; Pop. 8154.) [28]

BIGGS, William, *Tharston Vicarage, Long Stratton, Norfolk.*—St. Edm. Hall, Ox; Deac. and Pr. by Abp of York. V. of Tharston, Dio. Nor. 1844. (Patron, Bp of Nor; Tithe, 123*l* 6*s* 8*d*; Glebe, 52 acres; V.'s

Inc. 160*l* and Ho; Pop. 351.) Author, *Memoir of a Departed Friend*; *Sermons at Thaxted, Essex.* [1]

BIGLAND, John, *Finsthwaite, Newton-in-Cartmel, Lancashire.*—St. Bees; Deac. 1821 and Pr. 1822 by Bp of Ches. P. C. of Finsthwaite, Dio. Carl. 1822. (Patron, P. C. of Colton; P. C.'s Inc. 93*l*; Pop. 288.) [2]

BIGLAND, J. E., *Thorney, Newark.*—V. of Thorney, Dio. Lin. 1864. (Patron, C. Nevile, Esq; V.'s Inc. 180*l*; Pop. 93.) [3]

BIGNOLD, Samuel Frederic, *Tivetshall, Scole, Norfolk.*—Ball. Coll. Ox. B.A. 1842, M.A. 1849; Deac. 1842, Pr. 1843. R. of Tivetshall St. Mary with Tivetshall St. Margaret, Dio. Nor. 1845. (Patron, Earl of Orford; Tithe, 970*l*; Glebe, 28 acres; R.'s Inc. 1026*l* and Ho; Pop.—Tivetshall St. Mary 362, Tivetshall St. Margaret 375.) [4]

BIGSBY, Charles, *Bidborough Rectory, Tonbridge Wells.*—Trin. Coll. Cam. B.A. 1829, M.A. 1834, *ad eund.* Ox; Deac. 1830 and Pr. 1831 by Bp of Lin. R. of Bidborough, Dio. Cant. 1846. (Patroness, Mrs. Deacon; Tithe, 165*l*; Glebe, 118 acres; R.'s Inc. 270*l* and Ho; Pop. 208.) [5]

BIGSBY, Henry Julian, *Southborough, Tonbridge Wells.*—Wad. Coll. Ox. B.A. 1855, M.A. 1858; Deac. 1856 and Pr. 1857 by Abp of Cant. P. C. of St. Thomas's, Southborough, Dio. Cant. 1860. (Patroness, Mrs. Pugh.) Formerly C. of Hollingbourne 1856–58 and Nonington, Kent, 1858–60. [6]

BIGSBY, Robert Henry, *Leebrockhurst, Wem, Salop.*—C. of Leebrockhurst. [7]

BILLING, Joseph Phelps, *Seavington Rectory, Ilminster, Somerset.*—Sid. Coll. Cam. 1853; Deac. 1854 by Bp of Pet. Pr. 1856 by Bp of Salis. R. of Seavington St. Michael with Dinnington C. Dio. B. and W. 1861. (Patron, Earl Powlett; R.'s Inc. 300*l* and Ho; Pop. 390.) Dom. Chap. to Countess Powlett. [8]

BILLING, Robert Claudius, *Holy Trinity Parsonage, Louth, Lincolnshire.*—Wor. Coll. Ox. B.A. 1857; Deac. 1857 and Pr. 1858 by Bp of Roch. P. C. of Trinity, Louth, Dio. Lin. 1863. (Patron, Bp of Lin; P. C.'s Inc. 200*l* and Ho; Pop. 2500.) Formerly C. of St. Peter's, Colchester, 1857–60, Compton Bishop, Somerset, 1860; and Assoc. Sec. of the Church Miss. Soc. York, 1861–63. Editor of *The Church Missionary Juvenile Instructor.* [9]

BILLING, Robert Phelps, *South Petherton, Somerset.*—Giessen, M.A. and Ph. D. 1858; Deac. 1862 by Bp of Ex. Pr. 1865 by Bp of B. and W. Head Mast. of Gr. Sch. South Petherton; C. of Kingsbury Episcopi 1864. Formerly C. of Bickleigh, Devon, 1862. [10]

BILLINGS, Edward Thomas, *Prestwich, Manchester.*—Emman. Coll. Cam. B.A. 1853, M.A. 1861; Deac. 1854 and Pr. 1855 by Bp of Llan. C. of Prestwich 1857. Formerly C. of Monmouth 1854–56. [11]

BILLINGSLEY, John Richard Frederick, *Wormington Rectory (Gloucestershire), near Evesham, Worcestershire.*—Lin. Coll. Ox. B.A. 1828, M.A. 1830; Deac. 1831 and Pr. 1832 by Bp of Glouc. R. of Wormington, Dio. G. and B. 1838. (Patron, Samuel Gist, Esq; Glebe, 115 acres; R.'s Inc. 125*l* and Ho; Pop. 79.) [12]

BILLINGTON, George Henry, *Chalbury, Wimborne.*—Emman. Coll. Cam. 7th Sen. Opt. B.A. 1849, M.A. 1852; Deac. 1850 and Pr. 1851 by Bp of Herf. R. of Chalbury, Dio. Salis, 1861. (Patron, Earl of Pembroke; Tithe, 187*l*; Glebe, 30 acres; R.'s Inc. 197*l* and Ho; Pop. 194.) Formerly C. of St. Giles's, Dorset, 1859–61. [13]

BILLINGTON, John, *Kenardington, Ashford, Kent.*—Univ. Coll. Ox. Deac. 1821 and Pr. 1822 by Abp of Cant. R. of Kenardington, Dio. Cant. 1821. (Patroness, Mrs. Breton; Tithe, 200*l*; Glebe, 10 acres; R.'s Inc. 240*l*; Pop. 221.) V. of Boughton Aluph, Kent, Dio. Cant. 1822. (Patrons, Trustees of Dr. Breton; Tithe—Imp. 607*l*, V. 200*l*; V.'s Inc. 400*l*; Pop. 475.) [14]

BILLOPP, William T. N., *Halstead, Essex.*—P. C. of St. James's, Halstead, Dio. Roch. 1850. (Patron, Bp of Roch; P. C.'s Inc. 200*l* and Ho; Pop. 660) [15]

BINDER, William John, *Barnsley, Yorks.*—P. C. of St. John's, Barnsley, Dio. Rip. 1852. (Patrons, the Crown and Bp of Rip. alt; P. C.'s Inc. 150*l*; Pop. 4235.) [16]

BINDLEY, Frederick W., *St. Jude's, Moorfields, Sheffield.*—Sid. Coll. Cam. B.A. 1863; Deac. 1865 and Pr. 1866 by Abp of York. C. of St. Jude's, Moorfields, 1865. [17]

BINDLOSS, E., *Archangel, Russia.*—British Chaplain at Archangel. [18]

BINGHAM, Charles Hippuff, *Ramsey, near Huntingdon.*—Caius Coll. Cam. B.A. 1834, M.A. 1843; Deac. 1832 and Pr. 1834 by Bp of Lin. P. C. of Ramsey, Dio. Ely, 1847. (Patron, Edward Fellowes, Esq; Tithe—Imp. 648*l* 2*s* 10*d*; P. C.'s Inc. 200*l* and Ho; Pop. 3412.) Author, *Lectures on Psalm XXXII.* 1836, 5*s*; *Confirmation—Scriptural, Apostolical, Primitive* (a Sermon); *A Funeral Sermon on the Rev. H. Corrie, M.D. late R. of Kettering,* 1846; *The Story of Naaman the Syrian,* 1866, 2*s*; *The Christian Race* (a Sermon). [19]

BINGHAM, Charles William, *Bingham's Melcombe, Dorchester.*—New Coll. Ox. B.A. 1833, M.A. 1836; Deac. 1835 and Pr. 1836 by Bp of Ox. R. of Melcombe Horsey, Dio. Salis. 1842. (Patron, Lord Rivers; Tithe, 278*l* 6*s*; Glebe, 20 acres; R.'s Inc. 300*l* and Ho; Pop. 208.) Rural Dean 1863; Surrogate. Late Fell. of New Coll. Ox. Formerly V. of Sydling St. Nicholas, Dorset, 1838–46. Author, *Private Memoirs of John Potenger, Esq.* 1841, 2*s* 6*d*; *A Sermon* (for the Charitable Fund of the Dorset Lunatic Asylum), 1843; *Everlasting Consolation* (Farewell Sermon), 1846; *Poverty and Riches* (Sermon in aid of the Dorset County Hospital), 1847; *The Voice of the Bible Hawker* (Translated from the French of Felice), 1847, 2*s* 6*d*; *Commentaries on the Four Last Books of the Pentateuch* (Translated from the Latin of John Calvin), Calvin. Soc. 4 vols. 1852–55; *Confession and Absolution* (a Letter to the Bp of Salisbury), 1867. [20]

BINGHAM, Fanshawe, *West Cowes.*—Trin. Coll. Cam. B.A. 1865; Deac. 1866 by Bp of Win. C. of Kingston with West Cowes 1867. [21]

BINGHAM, John Batt, *Great Gaddesden (Herts), near Hemel Hempstead.*—Brasen. Coll. Ox. B.A. 1809, M.A. 1819. R. of St. Martin's, Ludgate, City and Dio. of Lon. 1819. (Patron, Bp of Lon; R.'s Inc. 279*l*; Pop. 1080.) V. of Great Gaddesden, Dio. Roch. 1820. (Patroness, Mrs. Halsley; Tithe—Imp. 750*l*, V. 260*l*; V.'s Inc. 275*l*; Pop. 1147.) [22]

BINGHAM, Richard, *Queenborough, Isle of Sheppey,* and 17, *Buckingham-street, Adelphi, London, W.C.*—Magd. Hall, Ox. B.A. 1821, M.A. 1827; Deac. 1821 and Pr. 1822 by Bp of Win. P. C. of Queenborough, Dio. Cant. 1856. (Patrons, Mayor and Corporation; P. C.'s Inc. 100*l*; Pop. 975.) Sec. to the Association for Promoting a Revision of the Prayer-Book. Formerly C. of Trinity, Gosport, for 20 years; P. C. of Harwood, Lancashire; C. of St. Mary's, Bryanston-square, Lond. 1854–56. Author, *Three Discourses on the Restoration and Conversion of the Jews,* 1826; *Practical Discourses,* 1827; *The Warning Voice,* 1829; *Sermons—Doctrinal, Practical and Experimental,* 1835; *Immanuel, or God with us* (a Series of Lectures on the Divinity and Humanity of our Lord), 1848; *Sermons at St. Mary's, Bryanston-square,* 1858; *Liturgia Recusa, or Suggestions for Revising and Reconstructing the Daily and Occasional Services of the Church,* 1860; *Liturgiæ Recusæ Exemplar, the Prayer-Book as it might be, or Formularies Old, Revised and New,* 1863. Editor of the last edition of the *Works of the Learned Joseph Bingham* (issued by the Oxford University Press). [23]

BINGHAM, Samuel Henry, *Sutton-le-Marsh, Alford, Lincolnshire.*—Wor. Coll. Ox. 3rd cl. Lit. Hum. B.A. 1863; Deac. 1865 and Pr. 1866 by Bp of Lin. C. of Sutton-le-Marsh 1865. [24]

BINGHAM, William Philip Strong, *Compton Valence, Dorchester.*—Ch. Ch. Ox. B.A. 1850, M.A. 1853; Deac. 1851 by Bp of Ex. Pr. 1852 by Bp of G. and B. C. of Compton Valence. Formerly P. C. of West Pinchbeck, Lincolnshire, 1859–63; C. of Thorverton

1858-59, St. Mary Redcliffe, Bristol, 1853–58, Dursley 1851–53, Edmonton 1863. Author, *Ecclesiastical Sculpture* (a Lecture), 1855, 1*s*; *A Few Words on the Divorce Bill*, 1857, 1*s*; *Divisions in the Church* (a Sermon), 1858, 3*d*; *Sermons on Eastern Subjects*, 1860, 4*s* 6*d*; *Why Parents may not be Sponsors*, 1861, 6*d*; *The Extension of the Diaconate*, 1862, 6*d*; *The Offertory* (a Prize Essay), 1865, 6*d*; *The Irish Church*, 1866, 4*d*. [1]

BINGLEY, John George, *St. Leonard's Rectory, Colchester.*—Brasen. Coll. Ox. M.A. 1857; Deac. 1858 and Pr. 1859 by Bp of Roch. R. of St. Leonard's, Colchester, Dio. Roch. 1864. (Patron, Ball. Coll. Ox; R.'s Inc. 104*l* and Ho; Pop. 1650.) Formerly C. of Margaretting 1858, and Springfield, Essex, 1858–64. [2]

BINGLEY, Robert Mildred, *Thornham, Eye, Suffolk.*—Trin. Coll. Cam. B.A. 1852; Deac. and Pr. 1853. R. of Braiseworth, Suffolk, Dio. Nor. 1853. (Patron, Sir E. Kerrison, Bart; Tithe, 200*l*; Glebe, 20 acres; R.'s Inc. 230*l*; Pop. 164.) [3]

BINNEY, D. B., *The Elms, Shirley, Southampton.* [4]

BINNS, Benjamin James, *Privy Council Office, London, S.W.* and *Swansea.*—Dub. A.B. 1842, A.M. 1858, *ad eund.* Ox. 1861; Deac. 1844 and Pr. 1845 by Bp. of Ban. One of H.M. Inspectors of Schs. Formerly P. C. of St. Ann's, Llandegai, Bangor, 1855–57, and Prin. of the Carnarvon Training Institution 1849–55. [5]

BINNS, Cornelius John, *Oswestry.*—St. Cath. Hall, Cam. B.A. 1855, M.A. 1858; Deac. 1855 and Pr. 1856 by Bp of Pet. C. of St. Mary's, Oswestry, 1865. Formerly C. of Isham, Northants, 1855–57, Chesham, Bucks, 1858–62, Ch. Ch. Plymouth, 1862–63, Irthlingboro', Northants, 1863–64, Feckenham, Worcester, 1864–65. [6]

BINYON, Frederick, *Burton-in-Lonsdale, near Lancaster.*—Trin. Coll. Cam. Jun. Opt. and B.A. 1860, M.A. 1863; Deac. 1861 and Pr. 1865 by Bp of Man. P. C. of Burton-in-Lonsdale, Dio. Rip. 1866. (Patron, V. of Thornton-in-Lonsdale; P. C.'s Inc. 94*l*; Pop. 597.) Formerly Asst. C. of St. Peter's, Blackburn, 1861–63; C. of Halton, near Lancaster, 1864–66. [7]

BIRCH, Augustus Frederic, *Eddlesborough Vicarage, Dunstable.*—King's Coll. Cam. Camden Gold Medallist 1848, M.A. 1852; Deac. 1859 and Pr. 1860 by Bp of Ox. V. of Eddlesborough, Dio. Ox. 1863. (Patron, Earl Brownlow; V.'s Inc. 700*l* and Ho; Pop. 1671.) Late Fell. of King's Coll. Cam. [8]

BIRCH, Charles, *Foot's Cray, Kent, S.E.*—St. John's Coll. Cam. late Scho. of, B.A. 1855, M.A. 1858 *ad eund.* Ox; Deac. 1856 and Pr. 1857 by Bp of G. and B. R. of Foot's Cray, Dio. Cant. 1861. (Patron, Ld Chan; Tithe, 265*l*; Glebe, 21 acres; R.'s Inc. 290*l* and Ho; Pop. 680.) Formerly C. of Upton St. Leonard's, afterwards of Bibury, Glouc. [9]

BIRCH, Charles, *Sawtrey All Saints, Stilton, Hunts.*—Trin. Hall. Cam. LL.B. 1827; Deac. 1828 and Pr. 1829 by Bp of Lich. R. of Sawtrey All Saints, Dio. Ely, 1835. (Patrons, Duke of Devonshire and J. C. Atherpe, Esq; Tithe, 250*l*; Glebe, 250 acres; R.'s Inc. 257*l* and Ho; Pop. 650.) P. C. of Kniveton, Derbyshire, Dio. Lich. 1833. (Patron, J. Harrison, Esq; Tithe—Imp. 108*l* 0*s* 3*d*, P. C. 25*l*; Glebe, 14 acres; P. C.'s Inc. 96*l*; Pop. 315.) C. of Sawtrey St. Andrew 1835. Formerly C. of Norbury, with Snelston, Derbyshire, 1828–35. [10]

BIRCH, Charles Edward, *Wiston, Colchester.*—St. John's Coll. Ox. B.A. 1829, M.A. 1835; Deac. 1830 and Pr. 1831 by Bp of Chich. R. of Wiston, *alias* Wissington, Dio. Ely, 1832. (Patron, Ld Chan; Tithe, 442*l* 5*s*; Glebe, 1½ acres; R.'s Inc. 443*l* and Ho; Pop. 254.) [11]

BIRCH, Charles George Robert, *Harlaxton, near Grantham.*—Trin. Hall, Cam. LL.B. 1861, LL.M. 1867; Deac. 1863 and Pr. 1864 by Bp of Ely. C. of Stretton 1865. Formerly C. of Sawtrey All Saints 1863–65. [12]

BIRCH, Edward, *St. Saviour's Rectory, Chorlton-on-Medlock, Manchester.*—St. John's Coll. Cam. B.A. 1831, M.A; Deac. 1832 and Pr. 1833 by Bp of Ches. R. of St. Saviour's, Manchester, Dio. Man. 1836. (Patron, the present R; R.'s Inc. 500*l* and Ho; Pop. 3409.) Hon. Can. of Man; Rural Dean. Formerly C. of All Saints', Manchester, 1832–36. [13]

BIRCH, Edward Jonathan, *Overstone Rectory, Northampton.*—Wad. Coll. Ox. B.A. 1849; Deac. 1850 and Pr. 1851 by Abp of Cant. R. of Overstone, Dio. Pet. 1857. (Patron, Lord Overstone; R.'s Inc. 320*l* and Ho; Pop. 206.) Formerly C. at Shirley and Addington, Surrey. [14]

BIRCH, Edwin Robert, *Idlicote, Shipston-on-Stour.*—St. John's Coll. Cam. B.A. 1850; Deac. 1850 and Pr. 1851 by Bp of Wor. R. of Idlicote, Dio. Wor. 1857. (Patron, H. P. K. Peach, Esq; Glebe, 2 acres; R.'s Inc. 300*l* and Ho; Pop. 115.) [15]

BIRCH, E. Mount, *Eastwood, Rochford, Essex.*—V. of Eastwood, Dio. Roch. 1866. (Patron, Ld Chan; V.'s Inc. 250*l*; Pop. 573.) [16]

BIRCH, Frederick, *Taxall, Stockport.*—New Inn Hall, Ox. B.A. 1849; Deac. 1851 and Pr. 1852 by Bp of Wor. C. of Taxall 1866. [17]

BIRCH, George Turner, 96, *Myrtle-street, Liverpool.*—Dur. Univ. Licen. in Theol. 1863; Deac. 1863 and Pr. 1864 by Bp. of Ches. Miss. C. of St. Clement's, Windsor, Liverpool, 1865. Formerly C. of St. Luke's, Liverpool, 1863. [18]

BIRCH, Henry Mildred, *Prestwich, Manchester.*—King's Coll. Cam. B.A. 1843, M.A. 1847. Hon. Can. of Man; Surrogate; Rural Dean; R. of Prestwich, Dio. Man. 1852. (Patron, Earl of Wilton; Tithe, 1184*l* 10*s*; Glebe, 116¾ acres; R.'s Inc. 1534*l* and Ho; Pop. 9830.) Chap. in Ordinary to the Queen 1852; Chap. to the Prince of Wales; one of the Nominators to the Hulme Exhibitions at Brasen. Coll. Ox. Late Fell. of King's Coll. Cam; and Tut. to the Prince of Wales. [19]

BIRCH, James Alexander, *Middleham, Yorks.*—New Inn Hall, Ox. B.A. 1841. R. of Middleham, Dio. Rip. 1856. (Patron, The Crown; Tithe, 232*l*; Glebe, 65½ acres; R.'s Inc. 298*l*; Pop. 922.) Formerly C. of Maidenhead; Chap. to the Cookham Union. [20]

BIRCH, James Wheeler, *All Saints Vicarage, Hertford.*—Magd. Hall, Ox. B.A. 1826, M.A. 1828; Deac. 1826, Pr. 1827. V. of All Saints' with St. John's R. Hertford, Dio. Roch. 1844. (Patron, Marquis of Townshend; Tithe—Imp. 70*l*, V. 480*l*; Glebe, 16 acres; V.'s Inc. 540*l* and Ho; Pop. All Saints 2516, St. John 2388.) Surrogate. Formerly Chap. at the River Plate. [21]

BIRCH, John, *Lower Gornal, Sedgeley, Staffs.*—C. of Lower Gornal. [22]

BIRCH, Joseph, *West Teignmouth, Devon.*—Pemb. Coll. Ox. B.A. 1831, M.A. 1837; Deac. 1831 and Pr. 1832 by Bp of Ches. V. of West Teignmouth, Dio. Ex. 1862. (Patrons, Trustees; Tithe, 157*l*; V.'s Inc. 200*l*; Pop. 3963.) Formerly C. of High Harrogate 1831, High Hoyland 1833, Bridlington 1840; V. of Bywell St. Andrew 1841; P. C. of Brighouse 1843; and Chap. to the Mayor of Bristol 1860–61. Author, *The Rev. C. Dodgson's New Tests of Orthodoxy* (a Letter addressed to the Earl of Shaftesbury, in consequence of the refusal of the Bishop of Ripon to confer Priest's Orders upon the Rev. George A. Hayward, nominated to the Curacy of Brighouse), 1853, 1*s*. [23]

BIRCH, Thomas Wickham, *Cheselborne, near Dorchester.*—Ch. Ch. Ox. B.A. 1813, M.A. 1814; Deac. 1815 and Pr. 1816 by Bp of B. and W. R. of Stokewake, Dorset, Dio. Salis. 1817. (Patron, H. K. Seymer, Esq; Tithe, 170*l*; Glebe, 13 acres; R.'s Inc. 193*l* and Ho; Pop. 112.) R. of Cheselborne, Dio. Salis. 1820. (Patron, Lord Rivers; Tithe, 315*l*; R.'s Inc. 360*l* and Ho; Pop. 432.) [24]

BIRCH, Wickham Montgomery, *Launceston.*—Trin. Coll. Ox. B.A. 1854, M.A. 1857; Deac. 1854 by Bp of G. and B. Pr. 1856 by Bp of B. and W. P. C. of Launceston, Dio. Ex. 1866. (Patron, A. H. Campbell, Esq, M.P; P. C.'s Inc. 175*l*; Pop. 2069.) Formerly C. of Abbenhall 1854, Long Ashton 1857; V. of Borton 1862–66. [25]

BIRCH, William Frederick, *St. Saviour's, Manchester.*—Caius Coll. Cam. 2nd cl. Cl. Trip. B.A.

1863, M.A. 1866; Deac. 1863 and Pr. 1864 by Bp of Wor. C. of St. Saviour's, Manchester. [1]

BIRCH, William Samuel, *Easton Grey, Malmesbury, Wilts.*—Oriel Coll. Ox. B.A. 1816, M.A. 1819; Deac. 1819 and Pr. 1822 by Bp of Glouc. R. of Easton Grey, Dio. G. and B. 1834. (Patron, the present R; Tithe, 260*l*; Glebe, 25 acres; R.'s Inc. 300*l* and Ho; Pop. 177.) [2]

BIRCHALL, Joseph, *Church Kirk House, near Accrington.*—Brasen. Coll. Ox. B.A. 1828, M.A. 1830; Deac. 1830 and Pr. 1831 by Bp of Ox. P. C. of Church Kirk, Dio. Man. 1840. (Patrons, Hulme's Trustees; Tithe, 24*l*; Glebe, 90 acres; P. C.'s Inc. 466*l* and Ho; Pop. 4753.) Surrogate; Rural Dean. Author, *Confirmation and other Sermons*, 1832–37; *Occasional Sermons*, 1840; *Visitation Sermon*, at Blackburn, 1841. [3]

BIRD, Charles James, *West Fordington, Dorchester.*—Trin. Coll. Cam. B.A. 1853, M.A. 1857; Deac. 1854 and Pr. 1855 by Bp of Chich. P. C. of West Fordington, Dio. Salis. 1861. (Patron, V. of Fordington; P. C.'s Inc. 60*l*; Pop. 1059.) Formerly C. of Ch. Ch. Ramsgate, St John's, Margate, St. Mary's, Brighton. [4]

BIRD, Charles Robinson, *Castle Eden, Durham.* R. of Castle Eden, Dio. Dur. 1860. (Patron, R. Burdon, Esq; R.'s Inc. 250*l* and Ho; Pop. 535.) [5]

BIRD, Christopher, *Chollerton, Hexham.*—St. Alb. Hall, Ox. B.A. 1806. V. of Chollerton, Hexham, Northumberland, Dio. Dur. 1826. (Patron, the present V; Tithe—Imp. 718*l* 19*s* 11*d*, V. 402*l* 0*s* 3*d*; V.'s Inc. 406*l* and Ho; Pop. 1156.) V. of Warden with Newborough C. and Haydon-Bridge C. near Hexham, Dio. Dur. 1827. (Patron, W. B. Beaumont, Esq; Warden, Tithe—Imp. 213*l* 6*s* 2*d*, V. 231*l* 12*s* 7*d*; Haydon-Bridge, Tithe—Imp. 700*l*, V. 354*l* 16*s* 6*d*; V.'s Inc. 590*l* and Ho; Pop. Warden 716, Newborough 703, Haydon-Bridge, 2221.) Rural Dean. [6]

BIRD, Christopher, jun., *High Hoyland, Barnsley, Yorks.*—Trin. Coll. Cam. B.A. 1838; Deac. 1839 and Pr. 1840 by Bp of Dur. R. of High Hoyland, Dio. Rip. 1855. (Patron, W. B. Beaumont, Esq; R.'s Inc 500*l* and Ho; Pop. 1536.) [7]

BIRD, Claude Smith, *Sandy, Beds.*—Trin. Coll. Cam. B.A. 1859, M.A. 1864; Deac. 1861 and Pr. 1862 by Bp of Lin. C. of Sandy 1866. Formerly C. of St. Michael's, Lincoln, 1861, Clareborough 1864. Author, *Sketches from the Life of the Rev. Charles S. Bird*, 7*s* 6*d*; *Memoir of G. Tyrrell*, 1861, 2*s* 6*d*, both pub. by Nisbet and Co. [8]

BIRD, George, *Blindley Heath (Surrey), near East Grinstead, Sussex.*—St. Edm. Hall, Ox. B.A. 1830, M.A. 1833; Deac. 1831, Pr. 1832. P. C. of Blindley Heath, Dio. Win. 1842. (Patron, R. of Godstone; Tithe, 25*l*; Glebe, 4½ acres; P. C.'s Inc. 120*l* and Ho; Pop 750.) [9]

BIRD, G. G., *Great Chart, Ashford, Kent.*—C. of Great Chart. [10]

BIRD, Godfrey, *Great Wigborough, Colchester.*—Univ. Coll. Ox. B.A. 1818, M.A. 1821; Deac. 1819, Pr. 1820. R. of Great Wigborough, Dio. Roch. 1832. (Patrons, Messrs. Bewes and Fookes; Tithe, 624*l* 2*s* 9*d*; Glebe, 96 acres; R.'s Inc. 710*l* and Ho; Pop. 329.) Rural Dean of Mersea. [11]

BIRD, Godfrey John, *Illington, Larlingford, Norfolk.*—St. Bees; Deac. 1852 and Pr. 1853 by Bp of Nor. R. of Illington, Dio. Nor. 1861. (Patron, R. K. Long, Esq; R.'s Inc. 150*l*; Pop. 88.) [12]

BIRD, Henry, *Rockland St. Peter, Attleborough, Norfolk.*—Corpus Coll. Cam. B.A. 1831; Deac. 1831 and Pr. 1832 by Bp of Nor. R. of Rockland St. Peter, Dio. Nor. 1838. (Patron, the present R; Tithe, 216*l*, App. 6*l* 15*s*; Glebe, 20¾ acres; R.'s Inc. 264*l*; Pop. 386.) [13]

BIRD, James, *Hull.*—Literate; Deac. 1849 and Pr. 1850 by Abp of York. [14]

BIRD, James Waller, *Foulsham, Thetford, Norfolk.*—Wad. Coll. Ox. B.A. 1832; Deac. 1833, Pr. 1834. R. of Foulsham, Dio. Nor. 1855. (Patron, Lord Hastings; Tithe, 780*l*; Glebe, 22¾ acres; R.'s Inc. 814*l* and Ho; Pop. 1022.) [15]

BIRD, Robert James, *St. Bartholomew's, Gray's Inn-road, London, W.C.*—St. Aidan's; Deac. 1859 and Pr. 1860 by Abp of Cant. P. C. of St. Bartholomews', Gray's Inn-road, Lond. Dio. Lon. 1863. (Patrons, Trustees; Pop. 5318.) [16]

BIRD, Samuel William Elderfield, 6, *Windsor-place, Plymouth.*—St. Mary Hall, Ox. B.A. 1860, M.A. 1863; Deac. 1862 and Pr. 1863 by Bp of Roch. Asst. C. of St. James's, Plymouth, 1864. Formerly Asst. Mast. in Felstead Gr. Sch. Essex, 1861–64; Chap. of Black Chapel, Great Waltham, 1862–64. [17]

BIRD, Thomas Hugh, *Yarkhill, near Ledbury, Herefordshire.*—Magd. Coll. Cam. B.A. 1828, M.A. 1831; Deac. 1831, Pr. 1837. P. C. of Morton-Jeffries, near Bromyard, Dio. Herf. 1844. (Patrons, D. and C. of Herf; Tithe—App. 95*l* 15*s*; P. C.'s Inc. 45*l*; Pop. 51.) V. of Yarkhill, Dio. Herf. 1849. (Patrons, D. and C. of Herf; Tithe—Imp. 138*l*, V. 220*l*; Glebe, 10½ acres; V.'s Inc. 230*l* and Ho; Pop. 568.) Surrogate. [18]

BIRD, William, *New Zealand.*—Trin. Coll. Cam. B.A. 1848, M.A. 1852; Deac. 1849, Pr. 1852. Formerly C. of Morton and East Stockwith, Lincolnshire. [19]

BIRDS, David, *Dudleston, Ellesmere, Shropshire.*—Queens' Coll. Cam. B.A. 1823; Deac. 1823 by Bp of Ches. Pr. 1834 by Bp of Lich. P. C. of Dudleston, Dio. Lich. 1838. (Patron, V. of Ellesmere; P. C.'s Inc. 238*l*; Pop. 1550.) Chap. to the Ellesmere Union 1855 (Value 50*l*.) [20]

BIRKBECK, John, *Denton, Darlington, Durham.*—Deac. 1824 and Pr. 1825 by Bp of Ox. P. C. of Denton, Dio. Dur. 1836. (Patron, V. of Gainford; Glebe, 38 acres; P. C.'s Inc. 100*l* and Ho; Pop. 244.) [21]

BIRKETT, George William, *St. Florence, near Tenby, Pembrokeshire.*—St. John's Coll. Cam. B.A. 1823, M.A. 1827; Deac. 1825, Pr. 1826. V. of St. Florence, Dio. St. D. 1829. (Patron, the Sinecure R; Tithe—R. 162*l* and 29 acres of Glebe; V. 81*l*; Glebe, 10 acres; V.'s Inc. 125*l*; Pop. 450.) Author, *The Trial of Creation and other Poems*, 1848, 3*s* 6*d*. [22]

BIRKETT, John, *Winsford, Cheshire.*—St. Bees; Deac. 1836 and Pr. 1837 by Bp of Ches. P. C. of Waterman's Church, Winsford, Dio. Ches. 1844. (Patron, Bp of Ches; P. C.'s Inc. 150*l* and Ho.) [23]

BIRKETT, John, *Cheltenham.*—Math. Mast. in Cheltenham Coll. [24]

BIRKETT, John Parker, *Graveley (Cambs), near Huntingdon.*—Jesus Coll. Cam. B.A. 1840, M.A. 1843; Deac. 1842 and Pr. 1843 by Abp of Cant. R. of Graveley, Dio. Ely, 1852. (Patron, Jesus Coll. Cam; R.'s Inc. 344*l* and Ho; Pop. 301.) Rural Dean of Bourn 1864. Late Fell. and Tut. of Jesus Coll. Cam. [25]

BIRKETT, Stephen, *Langdale, Ambleside, Westmoreland.*—Deac. 1822 and Pr. 1823 by Bp of Ches. Formerly P. C. of Langdale 1842–60. [26]

BIRKETT, Thomas, *Yealand Conyers, Lancaster.* [27]

BIRKETT, William, *Haseley, Tetworth, Oxon.*—Brasen. Coll. Ox. B.A. 1814, M.A. 1818; Deac. 1817 and Pr. 1818 by Bp of Ches. R. of Haseley, *alias* Great Haseley, Dio. Ox. 1846. (Patrons, D. and C. of Windsor; Tithe, 800*l*; Glebe, 97 acres; R.'s Inc. 950*l* and Ho; Pop. 714.) Dom. Chap. to the Earl of Buckinghamshire. Formerly Preb. and V. of Wolverhampton. [28]

BIRKS, Thomas Rawson, *Manor House, Cambridge.*—Trin. Coll. Cam. 2nd Wrang. Smith's Prizeman and B.A. 1834, M.A. 1837, Seatonian Prizeman 1843 and 1844; Deac. 1837, Pr. 1841. P. C. of Holy Trinity, Cambridge, Dio. Ely, 1866. (Patron, Rev. A. Peache; P. C.'s Inc. 210*l* and Lectureship 70*l*; Pop. 1949.) Formerly Fell. of Trin. Coll. Cam; R. of Kelshall, Herts, 1844–66. Author, *First Elements of Prophecy, and Examination of the Year-Day Theory*, 1843; *The Four Empires*, 1844; *Village Sermons*, 1845; *Mede's Apostacy, Introduction and Supplement*, 1845; *The Two Later Visions of Daniel*, 1846; *The Christian State*, 1847; *The Mystery of Providence*, 1848; *Paley's Evidences, Notes and Appendix*, 1849; *Modern Astronomy*, 1849; *Horæ Paulinæ et Apostolicæ*, 1850; *Memoirs of the Rev. E. Bickersteth*, 2 vols. 1851; *Horæ Evangelicæ*,

1852; *Modern Rationalism*, 1854; *Outlines of Unfulfilled Prophecy*, 1854; *The Treasures of Wisdom*, 1855; *Difficulties of Belief*, 1855; Lectures and Pamphlets, *On the Principles of Prophetic Interpretation*; *Letters on Maynooth*; *Protestantism the Basis of National Prosperity*; *National Responsibility*; *Popery in the Bud and the Flower*; *The Strength and Weakness of Popery as an Aggressive Power*; *Letter on the Evangelical Alliance*, 1846; *Letter to Lord John Russell on Jewish Emancipation*, 1848; *The Present Crisis, or the Need of Christian Union*, 1854; *The Bible and Modern Thought*, 1861; *Matter and Ether, or Secret Laws of Physical Change*, 1862; *The Exodus of Israel*, 1863; *The Ways of God*, 1864; *The Victory of Divine Goodness*, 1867. [1]

BIRLEY, Alfred, *Astley Bridge, Bolton-le-Moors.*—Ball. Coll. Ox. B.A. 1853, M.A. 1857; Deac. 1856 and Pr. 1857 by Bp of Man. P. C. of Astley Bridge, Dio. Man. 1859. (Patrons, Crown and Bp of Man. alt; P. C.'s Inc. 200*l* and Ho; Pop. 3210.) Formerly C. of Chorley, Lancashire, 1856–59. [2]

BIRLEY, Edward Hornby.—Asst. Min. of Quebec Chapel, Marylebone, Lond. [3]

BIRLEY, Hugh Hornby, *Cranfield Rectory, Newport Pagnell.*—Ball. Coll. Ox. B.A. 1848, M.A. 1852; Deac. 1849 and Pr. 1852 by Bp of Ex. R. of Cranfield, Dio. Ely, 1866. (Patron, Rev. G. G. Harter; R.'s Inc. 400*l* and Ho; Pop. 1591.) Formerly C. of Plymstock 1849; P. C. of Hooe, Devon, 1855; C. of Buckingham 1861, Trinity, Stepney, 1864; V. of Newport Pagnell 1865. [4]

BIRLEY, James Webber, *Caton, Lancashire.*—St. John's Coll. Cam. B.A. 1837, M.A. 1843; Deac. 1837 and Pr. 1838. P. C. of Littledale, Lancaster, Dio. Man. 1848. (Patron, V. of Lancaster; P. C.'s Inc. 50*l*; Pop. 93.) [5]

BIRLEY, John Shepherd, *Moss Lee, near Bolton-le-Moors.*—Brasen. Coll. Ox. B.A. 1827, M.A. 1830; Deac. 1830 and Pr. 1831 by Bp of Ches. Formerly C. of Brindle; R. of All Saints', Bolton, 1832–43; P. C. of Hoghton 1846–50. [6]

BIRLEY, Robert, *St. Philip's Rectory, Hulme, Manchester.*—Ball. Coll. Ox. 3rd cl. Lit. Hum. B.A. 1847, M.A. 1852; Deac. 1850 and Pr. 1852 by Bp of Lin. R. of St. Phillip's, Hulme, Dio. Man. 1860. (Patrons, Trustees; R.'s Inc. 300*l* and Ho; Pop. 8711.) Formerly C. of Lea, Lincolnshire, 1850–58, Holy Trinity, Hulme, 1858–60. [7]

BIRON, Edwin, *Lympne Vicarage, Hythe, Kent.*—Dub. A.B. 1826, A.M. 1830; Deac. and Pr. 1827 by Bp of Kildare. V. of Lympne, Dio. Cant. 1840 (Patron, Archd. of Cant; Tithe—App. 503*l* and 150 acres of Glebe, V. 239*l*; Rent from Glebe, 15*l*; V.'s Inc. 257*l* and Ho; Pop. 540.) V. of West Hythe, Kent, Dio. Cant. 1840. (Patron, Archd. of Cant; Tithe—App. 12*l*, V. 34*l*; Glebe, ½ acre; V.'s Inc. 35*l*; Pop. 130.) R. of Eastbridge, Kent, Dio. Cant. 1854. (Patron, Abp of Cant; Tithe, 83*l*; Rent from Glebe, 9*l*; R.'s Inc. 89*l*; Pop. 45.) Surrogate. [8]

BIRON, Henry Brydges, *Mersham, Kent.*—Trin. Hall, Cam. B.A. 1858; Deac. 1859, Pr. 1860 by Abp of Cant. C. of Mersham 1859. [9]

BIRRELL, Alexander Peters, *Oving, Chichester.*—Sid. Coll. Cam. B.A. 1832, M.A. 1836; Deac. 1826 and Pr. 1827 by Bp of Lon. V. of Oving, Dio. Chich. 1851. (Patron, Bp of Chich; Tithe, 270*l*; Glebe, 4 acres; V.'s Inc. 352*l* and Ho; Pop. 949.) Formerly Bishop's College, Calcutta, 1827–28; C. of Upwell with Welney 1832–39, Carlton Colville 1839–41; Prin. of Chich. Dioc. Training Coll. 1842–47; C. of Laindon with Basildon 1847–52. [10]

BIRTWELL, Geoffry, *Ashley, Bowdon, Cheshire.*—Queens' Coll. Cam. B.A. 1862; Deac. 1862 and Pr. 1863 by Bp of Win. C. of Ashley. Formerly C. of Hurstbourne-Tarrant with Vernham's Dean, Berks. [11]

BIRTWHISTLE, John Burton, *Minster Parsonage, Beverley, Yorks.*—Lin Coll. Ox. B.A. 1825, M.A. 1826; Deac. 1826 and Pr. 1827 by Abp of York. P. C. of Beverley-Minster St. John and St. Martin, Dio. York, 1844. (Patrons, Simeon's Trustees; St. John's Tithe—Imp. 143*l* 19*s*; Glebe, 23 acres; P. C.'s Inc. 182*l* and Ho; Pop. 5728.) P. C. of St. John's Chapel, Beverley, Dio. York, 1853. (Patrons, Trustees; Endow. 3*l*; P. C.'s Inc. 140*l*.) Formerly C. of Rylstone 1826 and Richmond, Yorks, 1832; P. C. of Trinity, Richmond, 1836. [12]

BIRTWHISTLE, Robert, *Minster Parsonage, Beverley.*—Lin. Coll. Ox. B.A. 1856, M.A. 1859; Deac. 1857 by Bp of Pet. Pr. 1858 by Bp of Man. C. of Beverley-Minster 1860. Formerly C. of Belton, Leic. 1857–59. [13]

BISCOE, Frederick, *Turkdean, Northleach, Glouc.*—Ch. Ch. Ox. 2nd cl. Lit. Hum. and 2nd cl. Math. et Phy. 1829, B.A. 1830, M.A. 1832; Deac. 1835, Pr. 1836. V. of Turkdean, Dio. G. and B. 1837. (Patron, Ch. Ch. Ox; Glebe, 200 acres; V.'s Inc. 210*l* and Ho; Pop. 276.) [14]

BISCOE, Robert, *Whitbourne Rectory (Herefordshire), near Worcester.*—Ch. Ch. Ox. B.A. 1823, M.A. 1825; Deac. 1827 and Pr. 1828 by Bp of Ox. R. of Whitbourne, Dio. Herf. 1833. (Patron, Bp of Herf; Tithe, 535*l*; Glebe, 34¾ acres; R.'s Inc. 600*l* and Ho; Pop. 891.) Preb. of Pratum Minus in Herf. Cathl. 1834 (Value 27*l*). [15]

BISCOE, William, *Edlington, Horncastle, Lincolnshire.*—Queens' Coll. Cam. B.A. 1830, M.A. 1833; Deac. and Pr. 1830 by Bp of Herf. V. of Edlington, Dio. Lin. 1857. (Patron, Ld Chan; Tithe, 217*l*; Glebe, 90 acres; V.'s Inc. 373*l* 12*s*; Pop. 212.) Formerly V. of Coombe-Bissett, near Salisbury, 1843–57. [16]

BISHOP, Alfred Cæsar, *Bramdean Rectory, New Alresford, Hants.*—Queen's Coll. Ox. B A. 1834, M.A. 1838. R. of Bramdean, Dio. Win. 1856. (Patron, Ld Chan; Tithe, 226*l*; Glebe, 11 acres R.'s Inc. 237*l* and Ho; Pop. 282.) Formerly R. of Worthy Martyr, Hants, 1851–66. [17]

BISHOP, Daniel Godfrey, *Buntingford, Herts.*—Deac. 1841, Pr. 1842. Mast. of the Buntingford Gr. Sch. 1841. Author, numerous Articles in *Penny Cyclopedia*, upon Biblical Criticism, Classical Literature, and General Biography. [18]

BISHOP, Everett, *Wiveton, Thetford.*—Ch. Coll. Cam. B.A. 1858; Deac. 1859 and Pr. 1860 by Bp of Nor. C. of Wiveton 1863. Formerly C. of Blakeney, Norfolk, 1859. [19]

BISHOP, Francis, *Sturminster Marshall, Wimborne, Dorset.*—Ch. Coll. Cam. B.A. 1861, M.A. 1865; Deac. 1865 and Pr. 1866 by Bp of Salis. C. of Sturminster Marshall 1865. [20]

BISHOP, Freeman Heathcote, *Bassingbourn, Royston, Cambs.*—Trin. Coll. Ox. B.A. 1835, M.A. 1847; Deac. 1836, Pr. 1837. V. of Bassingbourn, Dio. Ely, 1861. (Patrons, D. and C. of West; V.'s Inc. 250*l* and Ho; Pop. 2213.) Dom. Chap. to the Earl of Lanesborough. [21]

BISHOP, George, *Royal Berks Hospital, Reading.*—Magd. Hall, Ox. B.A. 1848; Deac. 1848 by Bp of Pet. Pr. 1852 by Bp of Herf. Chap. to Royal Berks Hospital 1866. Formerly Asst. Chap. Leicester County Gaol 1848; C. of Dynedor, Hereford, 1851, Wolvey, Warwickshire, 1853, Bottesford, Leic. 1857, Barnack, near Stamford, 1858, Sandy, Beds, 1859; P. C. of St. Jude's, Andreas, Isle of Man, 1859. [22]

BISHOP, John Rees, *Oake Rectory, Taunton.*—Jesus Coll. Ox. B.A. 1833, M.A. 1839; Deac. 1834 and Pr. 1835 by Bp of St. D. R. of Oake, Dio. B. and W. 1861. (Patrons, Trustees; Tithe, 200*l*; Glebe, 42 acres; R.'s Inc. 320*l* and Ho; Pop. 155.) [23]

BISHOP, William, *St. Andrew's Hill, Norwich.*—Deac. 1850 and Pr. 1851 by Bp of Nor. R. of St. Peter's, Southgate, City and Dio Nor. 1865. (Patron, Bp of Nor; Tithe, 4*l*; R.'s Inc. 78*l*; Pop. 457.) P.C. of St. Ethelred's, City and Dio. Nor. 1865. (Patrons, Trustees of Great Hospital, Norwich; Tithe—Imp. 3*l* 2*s*; P. C.'s Inc. 90*l*; Pop. 614.) Formerly C. of Heigham, Norwich, 1850–65; Chap. to the Norfolk and Norwich Magdalen. [24]

BISHOP, William Chatterley, *Cransley, near Wellingborough.*—St. John's Coll. Cam. 31st Sen. Opt. 2nd cl. Cl. Trip. and B.A. 1835, M.A. 1838; Deac. 1837 by Bp of Lon. Pr 1838 by Bp of B. and W. P. C. of Upton, near Peterborough, Dio. Pet. 1851. (Patron, Bp of Pet; Tithe—Imp. 224*l* 6*s*; P. C.'s Inc. 224*l*; Pop. 100.) C. of Cransley. Late Fell. of St. John's Coll. Cam. Author, *A Sermon on the Staffordshire Riots*, 1842; *Sermons*, 1846, 7*s*. [1]

BISSET, Charles, *Holland House, Wigan.*—P. C. of Upholland, Dio. Ches. 1844. (Patron, R. of Wigan; P. C.'s Inc. 300*l* and Ho; Pop. 6982.) Surrogate. [2]

BISSET, Thomas, *Pontefract.*—V. of Pontefract, Dio. York, 1865. (Patron, Ld Chan; V.'s Inc. 390*l* and Ho; Pop. 4987.) Formerly P. C. of Knottingley, Pontefract, 1861–65. [3]

BITTLESTON, Edwin, *Arncliffe, Skipton, Yorks.*—St. Edm. Hall, Ox. B.A. 1845, M.A. 1848; Deac. 1846, Pr. 1847. P. C. of Halton-Gill, near Skipton, Dio. Rip. 1847. (Patron, V. of Arncliffe; Tithe—Imp. 109*l* 18*s* 8*d*; Glebe, 200 acres; P. C.'s Inc. 100*l*; Pop. 83.) C. of Arncliffe. [4]

BLACK, Charles Ingham, *Burley, Wharfedale, Yorks.*—Dub. Queen's Scho. Univ. Scho. Vice-Chan. and Univ. Prizes, A.B. 1845; Deac. 1845 by Bp of Tuam, Pr. 1845 by Bp of Kilmore. P. C. of St. Mary the Virgin's, Wharfedale, Dio. Rip. 1855. (Patron, H. B. Crofton, Esq; Tithe—Head-rents, 16*l* 13*s*; Glebe, 17 acres, at rent, 40*l*; Queen Anne's Bounty, 40*l* 14*s* 8*d*; Eccl. Comm. 39*l*; Fees, 10*l*; P. C.'s Inc. 143*l* 5*s* 10*d* and Ho; Pop. 2454.) Formerly C. of St. Anne's, Soho, Lond. 1849, Homerton 1849, Poplar 1851. Author, *Messias and Anti-Messias*, 1853, 5*s*; *The Prayer of the New Covenant*, 1857, 2*s* 6*d*; *Spiritual Wedlock*, 2nd ed. 1859, 3*d*; *Memorialia Cordis, Sonnets, &c.* 1856, 2*s* 6*d*; *Little Primer of Christian Worship and Doctrine*, 1863, 8*d*. [5]

BLACK, James Frederick, *Kendal.*—Dub. A.B. 1839; Deac. 1842. Mast. of the Kendal Gr. Sch. 1845; Chap. of the Kendal Ho. of Correction, 1848. [6]

BLACK, John Whitmore, *Uxbridge, Middlesex.* Brasen. Coll. Ox. Scho. and Hulme's Exhib. of, 1st cl. in Lit. Gr. et Lat. 2nd cl. Lit. Hum. B.A. 1863, M.A. 1865; Deac. 1865 and Pr. 1866 by Bp of Lon. C. of Uxbridge 1865. [7]

BLACK, William Faussett, *Newchurch Rectory, Warrington.*—Dub. A.B. 1839, A.M. 1849, D.D. 1866; Deac. 1846 and Pr. 1847 by Bp of Rip. R. of Newchurch, Dio. Ches. 1864. (Patron, Earl of Derby; Tithe, 230*l*; Glebe, 70*l*; R.'s Inc. 300*l* and Ho; Pop. 2500.) Formerly C. of Bradford 1846–53; R. of Raheny, Ireland, 1853–64. [8]

BLACKALL, Samuel, *Earl's Colne, Halstead, Essex.*—St. John's Coll. Cam. Fell. of, 4th Wrang. B.A. 1838, M.A. 1841; Deac. 1841, Pr. 1842. V. of Earl's Colne, Dio. Roch. 1867. (Patron, H. Holgate Carwardine, Esq; Tithe, comm. 616*l*; Glebe, 4 acres; V.'s Inc. 630*l* and Ho; Pop. 1540.) Hon. Can. of Ely. Formerly P. C. of Ixworth, Suffolk, 1847–67. [9]

BLACKALL, Thomas Offspring, *Kemsing, Sevenoaks, Kent.*—Ch. Ch. Ox. Stud. of, B.A. 1844, M.A. 1848. V. of Kemsing with Seal C. Dio. Cant. 1846. (Patron, Earl Amherst; Kemsing, Tithe—Imp. 179*l* 19*s*, V. 133*l* 17*s* 6½*d*; Seal, Tithe—Imp. 152*l* 8*s*, V. 556*l*; V.'s Inc. 687*l*; Pop. Kemsing 366. Seal 1505.) [10]

BLACKBURN, Christopher, *Presteigne, Radnorshire.*—Corpus Coll. Cam. B.A. 1852; Deac. 1852, Pr. 1853. Chap. to the Radnorshire County Gaol 1853; Head Mast. of the Presteigne Gr. Sch. 1854. [11]

BLACKBURN, John, *Yarmouth, Isle of Wight.*—Late Scho. of St. John's Coll. Cam. B.A. 1815, M.A. 1818; Deac. 1815 by Bp of Ely, Pr. 1816 by Bp of Nor. R. of Yarmouth, Dio. Win. 1853. (Patron, Ld Chan. Tithe, 11*l* 0*s* 6*d*; Glebe, 32 acres; R.'s Inc. 100*l*; Pop. 726.) Preb. of Riccall in York Cathl. 1851; Surrogate for the Isle of Wight and County of Hants 1853. Formerly P. C. of Attercliffe, Yorks, 1817–52. Author, *Handbook round Jerusalem*, 1846; *Sermon* (on the Death of the Rev. Thomas Cotterill), 1824; *Sermon* (on the Consecration of Brightside Church, Yorks), 1854; *A Model of the Holy City*, executed by Smith of Sheffield. Inventor of Parabolic Sounding Board—Paper in *Transactions of Royal Society*, 1828, and Pamphlet on its Construction and Advantages, 1829. [12]

BLACKBURN, John, *Horton, Chipping Sodbury, Glouc.*—Pemb. Coll. Cam. M.A. R. of Horton, Dio. G. and B. 1848. (Patron, Rev. R. Brook; Tithe, 610*l*; Glebe, 39 acres; R.'s Inc. 660*l* and Ho; Pop. 454.) [13]

BLACKBURN, Robert, *Selham, Petworth, Sussex.*—Scho. of Ball. Coll. Ox. 1830, 1st cl. Lit. Hum. and B.A. 1834, M.A. 1837; Deac. 1838 and Pr. 1839 by Bp of Ox. R. of Selham, Dio. Chich. 1842. (Patron, Brasen. Coll. Ox; Tithe, 155*l*; Glebe, 27 acres; R.'s Inc. 180*l* and Ho; Pop. 123.) Late Fell. of Brasen. Coll. Ox. 1834. Author, *A Sermon in Aid of the Patriotic Fund*, 1854, 6*d*. [14]

BLACKBURN, Samuel, *St. John's College, Auckland, New Zealand.*—Ch. Coll. Cam. B.A. 1845, M.A. 1848; Deac. 1847 and Pr. 1848 by Abp of York. Principal of St. John's Coll. Auckland. Formerly Chap. R.N. and Dom. Chap. to Earl Ferrers. [15]

BLACKBURNE, Foster Grey, *Chester.*—Brasen. Coll. Ox. M.A. 1864; Deac. 1863 and Pr. 1864 by Bp of Ches. C. of St. Oswald's, Chester, 1867. Formerly C. of Bebington, Cheshire, 1863. [16]

BLACKBURNE, Francis Theophilus, *Abbotsford Cottage, Stockton, Tenbury.*—Jesus Coll. Cam. 1827, B.A. 1830; Deac. 1831, Pr. 1832. [17]

BLACKBURNE, Gilbert Rodbard, *Long Ashton, Bristol.*—Magd. Coll. Cam. B.A. 1824, M.A. 1830; Deac. 1826 by Bp of Lon. Pr. 1827 by Abp of York. V. of Long Ashton, Dio. B. and W. 1841. (Patrons, Sir J. Smyth, Bart. and W. Langton, Esq; Tithe—Imp. 59*l* 9*s* 10*d*, V. 450*l*; Glebe, 4 acres; V.'s Inc. 453*l* and Ho; Pop. 2000.) P. C. of Whitchurch, *alias* Filton, Somersetshire, Dio. B. and W. 1844. (Patrons, Sir J. Smyth, Bart. and W. Langton, Esq; Tithe—Imp. 21*l* 11*s* 6*d*, P. C. 150*l*; P. C.'s Inc. 163*l*; Pop. 394.) Formerly C. of Crofton, Yorks, 1826–37; V. of Church Minshull, Cheshire, 1837–42. [18]

BLACKBURNE, Henry Ireland, *Warmingham, Sandbach, Cheshire.*—Brasen. Coll. Ox. B.A. 1849, M.A. 1852; Deac. 1851 and Pr. 1852 by Bp of Ches. R. of Warmingham, Dio. Ches. 1858. (Patron, Lord Crewe; Tithe, 586*l*; Glebe, 130 acres; R.'s Inc. 666*l* and Ho; Pop. 786.) Formerly V. of Rostherne, Cheshire, 1855–58. [19]

BLACKBURNE, Thomas, *Clothall Rectory, Baldock, Herts.*—Brasen. Coll. Ox. B A. 1830, M.A. 1833. R. of Clothall, Dio. Roch. 1858. (Patron, Marquis of Salisbury; R.'s Inc. 700*l* and Ho; Pop. 492.) Surrogate; Rural Dean. [20]

BLACKDEN, Charles, *Melcombe-Regis, Dorset.*—Queens' Coll. Cam. B.A. 1841, M.A. 1844. C. of Melcombe-Regis with Radipole. [21]

BLACKER, Maxwell Julius, 121, *St. George's-road, Pimlico, London, S.W.*—Mert. Coll. Ox. M.A 1857; Deac. 1848 and Pr. 1849 by Bp of Nor. C. of St. Mary-the-Less, Princes-road, Lambeth, Lond. 1858. Formerly C. of North Cove, Suffolk, 1848–49; Chap. at Brussels 1850–56. [22]

BLACKER, Robert Shapland Carew, *Marholm Rectory, Peterborough.*—Dub. A.B. 1848, Silver Medallist in Ethics and Logic; Deac. 1850 and Pr. 1851 by Abp of York. R. of Marholm, Dio. Pet. 1860. (Patron, Hon. G. W. Fitzwilliam; Tithe, 311*l*; Glebe, 4 acres; R.'s Inc. 315*l* and Ho; Pop 141.) Dom. Chap. to Earl of Huntingdon. [23]

BLACKETT, Henry Ralph, 32, *Palace Gardens Villas, Kensington, W.*—St. John's Coll. Cam. B.A. 1846, M.A. 1849; Deac. 1846 by Bp of Win. Pr. 1847 by Bp of Ox. Formerly C. of Camden Ch. Camberwell, 1846, St. George's, Hanover-square, 1848, Kettering 1851; Chap. to St. George's Workhouse, Hanover-square, Lond. 1857–66. [24]

BLACKETT, William Russell.—Dub. A.B. 1858, A.M. 1862; Deac. 1860 and Pr. 1861 by Bp of Ches. Formerly C. of St. Simon's, Liverpool, and Trinity, Coventry. [25]

BLACKLEY, William, *Stanton-upon-Hine Heath, Shrewsbury.*—St. John's Coll. Cam. B.A. 1835,

M.A. 1852; Deac. and Pr. 1835. V. of Stanton-upon-Hine Heath, Dio. Lich. 1855. (Patron, Viscount Hill; V.'s Inc. 340*l*; Pop. 648.) Chap. to Viscount Hill 1837. Author, *Expository Lectures on the First Four Chapters of St. Matthew's Gospel, with one on Chap.* v. 21, 26, 1842, 5*s* 6*d*; *Diplomatic Correspondence of the Right Hon. Richard Hill*, 2 vols. 1845, 26*s*; *Scriptural Teaching* (Sermons) 1847, 5*s*; *The Seventy Weeks of the Prophet Daniel Explained, &c.* 1850, 1*s*; *Pastoral Letter to a Rural Congregation*, 1850, 6*d*; *The Gospel History between the Death of Christ and the Day of Pentecost, &c. set forth in a Harmony and Condensation of the Statements of the Four Evangelists, &c. in respect to that Period, with a few brief Notes*, 4to. 1855. [1]

BLACKLEY, William Lewery, *Frensham Parsonage, Farnham, Surrey.*—Dub. A.B. 1851, A.M. 1854; Deac. 1854 and Pr. 1855 by Bp of Win. C. in sole charge of Frensham 1855. Formerly C. of St. Peter's, Southwark. Author, *The Frithiof Saga, or Lay of Frithiof, Translated in the Original Metre from the Swedish of Esaias Tegner*, 1857; *The Practical German Dictionary*, Longmans, 1866, 14*s*.; *Abridgement of* Ditto. 1868, 6*s*; *The Critical English (New) Testament*, 3 vols. Strahan, 1866–67; Articles in *Quarterly Review, Fraser's Magazine, Good Words, Sunday Magazine, Churchman's Shilling Magazine*,, and other periodicals. [2]

BLACKMAN, Charles, *Chesham Bois, Amersham, Bucks.*—Deac. 1829, Pr. 1830. R. of Chesham Bois, Dio. Ox. (Patron, Duke of Bedford; Tithe, 160*l* 15*s*; Glebe, 2½ acres; R.'s Inc. 163*l* and Ho; Pop. 218.) [3]

BLACKMAN, Edward Lewis, *Newnham, Herts.*—Trin. Coll. Cam. B.A. 1856; Deac. 1856 and Pr. 1857 by Bp of Ex. Formerly C. of Ch. Ch. Plymouth 1856–58; P. C. of Walberswick and Blythburgh, Suffolk, 1858–66. Author, *Shall we Recognize the Confederate States?* 1862; *Our Relations with America, a reply to Mr. Cobden and Historicus*, 1863. [4]

BLACKMORE, Edmund, *Lancing College, New Shoreham, Sussex.*—Deac. 1861 and Pr. 1862 by Bp of Chich. Asst. Mast. Lancing Coll. [5]

BLACKMORE, Richard, *Charles Rectory, near Southmolton, North Devon.*—Ex. Coll. Ox. B.A. 1821, M.A. 1833; Deac. 1821 by Bp of B. and W. Pr. 1825 by Bp of Ex. R. of Charles, Dio. Ex. 1840. (Patron, the present R; Tithe, 240*l*; Glebe, 130 acres; R.'s Inc. 390*l* and Ho; Pop. 356.) P. C. of Cornelly, Cornwall, Dio. Ex. 1863. (Patron, V. of Probus; P. C.'s Inc. 47*l*; Pop. 99.) [6]

BLACKMORE, Richard White, *Donhead St. Mary, near Salisbury.*—Mert. Coll. Ox. B.A. 1813; Deac. 1814, Pr. 1815. R. of Donhead St. Mary, Dio. Salis. 1847. (Patron, New Coll. Ox; Tithe, 1099*l*; Glebe, 60 acres; R.'s Inc. 1200*l* and Ho; Pop. 1482.) Surrogate. Formerly Chap. to the Russia Company 1819–47. Author, *History of the Church of Russia*, Oxford, 1842; *The Doctrine of the Russian Church*, 1845. [7]

BLACKWELL, Christopher, *Lord-street, Cheetham, Manchester.*—Literate; Deac. 1830, Pr. 1835. Chap. to the Manchester Union Workhouse. Author, *A Sermon* (on the Death of a Friend), 1843; *Letter to Sir Robert Peel.* [8]

BLACKWELL, John William, *Mattingley, Winchfield, Hants.*—Emman. Coll. Cam. M.A. 1860; Deac. 1857 and Pr. 1858 by Bp of Ely. P. C. of Mattingley, Dio. Win. 1863. (Patron, New Coll. Ox; Tithe, 225*l* 10*s* 5*d*; P. C.'s Inc. 230*l* and Ho; Pop. 630.) [9]

BLACKWELL, Robert Edward, *Amberley, Stroud.*—St. Cath. Hall, Cam. B.A. 1828; Deac. 1829 and Pr. 1830 by Bp of Lin. R. of Amberley, Dio. G and B. 1836. (Patron, J. G. Frith, Esq; Tithe, 285*l*; Glebe, 21 acres; R.'s Inc. 353*l* and Ho; Pop. 1438.) [10]

BLACKWOOD, James Stevenson, *Middleton-Tyas, Richmond, Yorks.*—Dub. Barrister-at-Law, 1835, LL D 1845, D.D. 1857; Deac. 1847 and Pr 1848 by Bp of Win. V. of Middleton-Tyas, Dio. Rip. 1856. (Patron, Ld Chan; V.'s Inc. 750*l* and Ho; Pop. 775) [11]

BLAGDEN, Alfred John, *Newbottle, Fence-Houses, Durham.*—Pemb. Coll. Cam. B.A. 1853, M.A. 1856; Theol. Coll. Wells; Deac. 1854, Pr. 1855. P. C. of Newbottle with Herrington, Dio. Dur. 1865. (Patron, Bp. of Dur; P. C.'s Inc. 420*l* and Ho; Pop. 4000.) Formerly C of Houghton-le-Spring. [12]

BLAGDEN, Henry, *Newbury, Berks.*—Trin. Coll. Cam. B.A. 1855, M.A. 1858; Deac. 1855 and Pr. 1856 by Bp of Ely. C. of Newbury 1865. Formerly C. of St. Neots, Hunts, 1855–57 and 1859–62, Ch. Ch. St. Leonards, 1862–65. [13]

BLAGDEN, Henry Charles, *Milcombe Parsonage, Banbury.*—Queen's Coll. Ox. B.A. 1853, M.A. 1855; Stud. of Wells Theol. Coll. 1853–54; Deac. 1854 by Bp of Nor. Pr. 1855 by Bp of Wor. P. C. of Milcombe, Dio. Ox. 1860. (Patrons, Eton Coll. three turns out of every four, Jesus Coll. Ox. the fourth; P. C.'s Inc. 136*l* and Ho; Pop. 241.) Formerly C. of Shipmeadow 1854, Frankley 1855–57, Trysall 1858–59, Aldridge 1859–60. Author, *Simple Allegories*, 1860, and Contributions to *The Penny Post.* [14]

BLAGDEN, Richard Thomas, *Horfield Barracks, near Bristol.*—St. John's Coll. Cam. B.A. 1848, M.A. 1852; Deac. 1848 and Pr. 1849 by Bp of Win. Asst. Chap. at Horfield Barracks. Formerly P. C. of Claydon, Oxon, 1861–63, and King's Sterndale, Derby, 1863–65. [15]

BLAGG, Michael Ward, *Codrington College, Barbados.*—King's Coll. Lond. 1st cl. Theol. Certif. 1856; Deac. 1856 and Pr. 1857 by Bp of Salis. Chap. of the Trust Estates of the S.P.G. Barbados 1860. Formerly C. of Powerstock, Dorset, 1856–60. Author, *Christ the Second Adam* (Three Sermons), 1858–59. [16]

BLAIR, James Samuel, *Killingworth, Newcastle-on-Tyne.*—St. Bees and Dub; Deac. 1855 and Pr. 1856 by Bp of Man. for Bp of Dur. P. C. of Killingworth, Dio. Dur. 1865. (Patron, V. of Long Benton; P. C.'s Inc. 153*l*; Pop. 3364. Formerly C. of Heathery-Cleugh, Durham, 1855–58, and Long Benton 1858. [17]

BLAIR, R. H., *Worcester.*—R. of St. Michael's, Bedwardine, City and Dio. Wor. 1866. (Patrons, D. and C. of Wor; R.'s Inc. 90*l*; Pop. 570.) [18]

BLAIR, Thomas Richard Arthur, *Milborne St. Andrew, Blandford, Dorset.*—Pemb. Coll. Cam; Deac. 1839 by Bp of Calcutta, Pr. 1843 by Bp of Tasmania. V. of Milborne St. Andrew with Dewlish, Dio. Salis. 1854. (Patron, Gen. J. Michel; Milborne St. Andrew, Tithe—Imp. 150*l*, V. 209*l*; Glebe, ¼ acre; Dewlish, Tithe—Imp. 3*l*, V. 100*l*; V.'s Inc. 309*l* and Ho; Pop. Milborne St. Andrew 327, Dewlish 458. [19]

BLAKE, Edmund, *Bramerton, Norwich.*—Caius Coll. Cam. B.A. 1835, M.A. 1838; Deac. 1835 and Pr. 1836 by Bp of Win. R. of Bramerton, Dio. Nor. 1838. (Patron, R. Fellowes, Esq; Tithe, 250*l*; Glebe, 21 acres; R.'s Inc. 292*l* and Ho; Pop. 300.) R. of Oxwick, Norfolk, Dio. Nor. 1838. (Patron, J. Blake, Esq: Tithe, 224*l*; Glebe, 34¾ acres; R.'s Inc. 293*l*; Pop. 76.) [20]

BLAKE, Henry Bunbury, *Hessett, Bury St. Edmunds.*—Trin. Coll. Cam. B.A. 1842, Deac. and Pr. 1844 by Bp of Ely. R. of Hessett, Dio. Ely, 1844. (Patrons, M. E. Rogers and C. Tinling, Esqrs; Tithe, 350*l*; Glebe, 18 acres; R.'s Inc. 370*l* and Ho; Pop. 454.) [21]

BLAKE, Joseph Sewell, *Southsea.*—Corpus Coll. Cam. B.A. 1861; Deac. 1862 and Pr. 1863 by Bp of Nor. C. of St. Jude's, Portsea, 1866. Formerly C. of Felixstowe, Suffolk, 1862–64, Heigham, Norfolk, 1865–66. [22]

BLAKE, Vernon, *Stoke Poges Vicarage, Slough.*—Wad. Coll. Ox. B.A. 1850, M.A. 1857; Deac. 1851 and Pr. 1852 by Bp of Ox. V. of Stoke Poges, Dio. Ox. 1866. (Patron, Duke of Leeds; V.'s Inc. 500*l* and Ho; Pop. 1800.) Surrogate; Dom. Chap. to Duke of Leeds. Formerly C. of Banbury 1851–54, Bampton 1854–57, Stonehouse, Glouc. (sole charge), 1858–62; V. of Shiplake, Oxon, 1862–66. [23]

BLAKE, William, *Wetheral Parsonage, Carlisle.*—Trin. Coll. Cam. B.A. 1845; M.A, 1848; Deac. 1846 by Bp of Win. Pr. 1847 by Bp of Ex. P. C. of Wetheral and Warwick, Dio. Carl. 1861. (Patrons, D. and C. of Carl; Tithe, Eccl. Com. 1200*l*; Glebe, 47 acres; P. C.'s Inc. 182*l* 10*s* and Ho; Pop. 2515.) Formerly C. of Cam, Glouc. 1846-48; P. C. of High Legh 1849-53; C. of St. George's, Liverpool, 1854-56; Head Mast. of Penrith Sch. 1857-59; C. of Dalston, Carlisle, 1859-61. [1]

BLAKE, William Robert, *Great Barton, Bury St. Edmunds.*—Mert. Coll. Ox. B.A. 1822. V. of Great Barton, Dio. Ely, 1826. (Patron, Sir H. E. Bunbury, Bart; V.'s Inc. 398*l*; Pop. 848.) [2]

BLAKELOCK, Ralph, *Gimingham, North Walsham, Norfolk.*—St. Cath. Hall. Cam. 13th Wrang. 8th in 2nd cl. Cl. Trip. and B.A. 1825, Deac. 1831 and Pr. 1832 by Bp of Lin. R. of Gimingham, Dio. Nor. 1833. (Patron, St. Cath. Hall, Cam; Tithe, 404*l*; Glebe, 32 acres; R.'s Inc. 460*l* and Ho; Pop. 270.) Hon. Can. of Nor. 1864. Author, *Symbolical Edition of Euclid*; *Translation of Boucharlat's Differential Calculus, and Francœur's Pure Mathematics*; *Visitation Sermon* at North Walsham 1839; *Sermons* before the University of Cambridge, 1845. [3]

BLAKELY, George Armstrong, *Whitehall, Kinnerton, Old Radnor.*—Wor. Coll. Ox. B.A. 1838, M.A. 1842; Deac. 1839, Pr. 1840. C. of Kinnerton Chapel. [4]

BLAKENEY, John Edward, *Sheffield.*—Dub. A.B. 1848, A.M. 1855; Deac. 1849, Pr. 1850. P. C. of St. Paul's, Sheffield, Dio. York, 1860. (Patron, V of Sheffield; P. C.'s Inc. 170*l*; Pop. 6965.) [5]

BLAKENEY, Richard Paul, *Oxton, Birkenhead.*—Dub. A.B. 1842, 1st cl. Theol. 1843, LL D. 1852; Deac. 1843, Pr. 1844. P. C. of Ch. Ch. Claughton, Birkenhead, Dio. Ches. 1854. (Patrons, Trustees; P. C.'s Inc. from pew rents, 550*l*; Pop. 2154.) Surrogate 1866. Author, *Moral Theology of Alphonsus Liguori*, 2nd ed; *Manual of Romish Controversy*, 10th thousand; *Protestant Catechism*, 50th thousand; *Romanism in its Social Aspect*; *The Book of Common Prayer in its History and Interpretation with Special Reference to Existing Controversies*; and Sermons and Tracts. [6]

BLAKER, Richard Nathaniel, *Ifield, Crawley, Sussex.*—St. John's Coll. Cam. B.A. 1844, M.A. 1847; Deac. 1844, Pr. 1845. V. of Ifield, Dio. Chich. 1850. (Patroness, Mrs. Blaker; Tithe—Imp. 455*l* 17*s* 6*d*, V. 218*l*; Glebe, 3 acres; V.'s Inc. 220*l* and Ho; Pop. 1307.) [7]

BLAKESLEY, Joseph Williams, *Ware, Vicarage, Herts.*—Trin. Coll. Cam. Sen. Chan. Medallist, 21st Wrang. and B.A. 1831, M.A. 1834, B.D. 1850; Deac. 1833, Pr. 1835. V. of Ware, Dio. Roch. 1845. (Patron, Trin. Coll. Cam; Tithe—Imp. 1148*l* 15*s* and 171¾ acres of Glebe, V. 291*l*; Glebe, 5 acres; V.'s Inc. 431*l* and Ho; Pop. 3594.) Can. of Cant. Cathl. by the Crown 1863; elected Proctor in Conv. for the Chap. in 1864. Late Chap. of Ware Union 1845; Fell of Trin. Coll. Cam. 1831; Asst. Tut. 1834, Tut. 1839 to 1845, Select Preacher 1840 and 1843; Cl. Examiner to the Univ. of Lond. 1860-63. Author, *The Recommendations of the Ecclesiastical Commission considered* (a Pamphlet), 1837; *A Life of Aristotle, with a Critical Examination of some Questions of Literary History*, 1839; *The Majesty of the Law*; *The Dispensation of Paganism*; *Christian Evidences* (Ten Sermons preached before the University, and collected under the title of *Conciones Academicæ*), 1843; *Three Commemoration Sermons* (Preached in Trinity College Chapel, Cambridge, in 1836, 1839, and 1842); *The Effects of Private Tuition in the University of Cambridge* (a Pamphlet), 1844; *Latin Prælection* (delivered as Candidate for the Regius Professorship of Divinity in the University of Cambridge), 1850; *Address in the Town Hall, Ware, on the Opening of the Institute*, 1850; *The Way of Peace, with an Appendix containing a Critical Examination of the Original Text*, 1 Cor. i. 12, 1852; *An Edition of Herodotus, in the* "Bibliotheca Classica," 1854; *Four Months in Algeria, with a Visit to Carthage*, 1859. [8]

BLAKEWAY, Bennett, *Portwood, Stockport.*—St. Bees; Deac. 1865 by Bp of St. A. Pr. 1866 by Bp of Ches. C. of Portwood 1865. [9]

BLAKEY, Robert Healey, *Stockholm.*—Univ. Coll. Dur. B.A. and Licen. Theol. 1850, M.A. 1853; Deac. 1851, Pr. 1852. Fell. of Dur. Univ; British Chap. at Stockholm. Formerly Bursar and Chap. of Univ. Coll. Dur; Sub-Librarian of the Univ. of Dur. [10]

BLAKISTON, Horace Mann, *Benhall Vicarage, Saxmundham, Suffolk.*—Emman. Coll. Cam. B.A. 1842, M.A. 1845, B.D. 1855; Deac. 1843 and Pr. 1844 by Bp of Lin. V. of Benhall, Dio. Nor. 1860. (Patron, Rev. Edmund Hollond; Glebe, 6 acres; V.'s Inc. 216*l* and Ho; Pop. 678.) Formerly C. of Stainby, Lincolnshire, 1843-46, Romsey, Hants, 1846-47, Melksham, Wilts, 1847-50; Chap. to the British Embassy, Constantinople, 1851-58. [11]

BLAKISTON, John Richard, *Privy Council Office, London, S.W.*—Scho. of Trin. Coll. Cam. 1851-54, 2nd in 1st cl. Cl. Trip. and 5th Jun. Opt. B.A. 1855, M.A. 1856; Deac. 1855 and Pr 1856 by Bp of Pet. One of H.M.'s Inspectors of Schools. Formerly Sen. Cl. Mast. of Uppingham Sch. 1854-57; Head. Mast. of Preston Gr. Sch. 1858, of Giggleswick Sch. Yorks, 1859-65. [12]

BLAKISTON, Robert, *Ashington, Hurtspierpoint, Sussex.*—Queen's Coll. Ox. B.A. 1836, M.A. 1840; Deac. 1838 by Bp of Roch. Pr. 1840 by Bp of Chich. R. of Ashington with Buncton C. Dio. Chich. 1845. (Patron, Duke of Norfolk; Tithe, 288*l*; Glebe, 40 acres; R.'s Inc. 335*l* and Ho; Pop. 234.) Rural Dean 1852. Formerly C. of St. Paul's, Chichester, 1838; Sequestrator of Cold Waltham 1840. Author, *A Visitation Sermon* 1847, 1*s*. [13]

BLAMIRE, William Hodgson, *Over Darwen, Blackburn.*—St. Bees; Deac. and Pr. 1853 by Bp of Man. C. of St. James's, Over Darwen. Formerly C. of Much Marcle with Yatton 1857-60. [14]

BLANCHARD, Henry Dacre, *Middleton, Beverley.*—Trin. Coll. Cam. B.A. 1847, M.A. 1851; Deac. 1849 and Pr. 1850 by Bp of Nor. R. of Middleton-on-the-Wolds, Dio. York, 1863. (Patron, the present R; Glebe, 850 acres; R.'s Inc. 1100*l* and Ho; Pop. 701.) Formerly C. of Great Yarmouth 1849, St. John's, Worcester, 1851; P. C. of Kilnwick-by-Watton 1853-58. [15]

BLANCHARD, John, *Bridlington Quay.*—Trin. Coll. Cam. B.A. 1850, M.A. 1853; Deac. 1851 and Pr. 1852 by Bp of Lich. C. of Carnaby and Fraisthorpe, Yorks. [16]

BLAND, Albert Cockshott, *Skipton, Craven, Yorks.*—St. John's Coll. Cam. B.A. 1845, M.A. 1850; Deac. 1845 and Pr. 1846 by Bp of Rip. Formerly C. of Keighley 1845-47, Linton in Craven 1847-49, Burnsall 1849-60; and again 1862-63. [17]

BLAND, Edward Davison, *Kippax, Woodlesford, Yorks.*—Caius Coll. Cam. B.A. 1837, M.A. 1841; Deac. 1837 and Pr. 1838 by Abp of York. V. of Kippax, Dio. Rip. 1841. (Patron, Ld Chan; Tithe—Imp. 152*l* 8*s*, V. 20*l*; V.'s Inc. 329*l* and Ho; Pop. 2901.) [18]

BLAND, The Ven. George, *The College, Durham.*—Caius Coll. B.A. 1828, M.A. 1831; Deac. 1829, Pr. 1830. Archd. of Northumberland with Can. of Durham annexed, 1853 (Value of Archd. 213*l*, Value of Can. 1000*l* and Res.) Chap. to Abp. of Cant. Formerly R. of St. Mary-le-Bow, Durham, 1856-59. [19]

BLAND, Joseph, *Askham, Penrith.*—Dub. A.B. 1842; Deac. 1843 and Pr. 1844 by Bp of Carl. V. of Askham, Dio. Carl. 1863. (Patron, Earl of Lonsdale; Tithe, 130*l*; Glebe, 70*l*; V.'s Inc. 200*l* and Ho; Pop. 503.) Formerly C. of Warcop 1843-51, Kirkby Thore 1851-53, Patterdale 1853-58, Lowther 1858-63. [20]

BLAND, Miles, 5, *Royal-crescent, Ramsgate.*—St. John's Coll. Cam. 2nd Wrang. Smith's Math. Prizeman and B.A. 1808, M.A. 1811, B.D. 1818, D.D. 1826, Moderator 1814-15-16, Public Examiner 1817-18; Deac. 1809, Pr. 1810. R. of Lilley, Herts, Dio. Roch. 1823. (Patron, St. John's Coll. Cam; Tithe—Imp. 27*l* 19*s* 6*d*, R. 487*l* 6*s* 6*d*; Glebe, 33 acres; R.'s Inc. 500*l* and Ho; Pop. 480.) Preb. of Wells 1826. Late Fell. of St. John's Coll. Cam; Asst. Tut. 1809, Tut. resigned 1820. Fell. of the Royal Society, the Society of Antiquaries, and the Royal Astronomical Society. Author, *Algebraical*

Problems 1812, 10s 6d; *Geometrical Problems*, 1819, 10s 6d; *Elements of Hydrostatics*, 1824, 12s; *Mechanical and Philosophical Problems*, 1830; *Confession* (a Sermon). Whittaker, 1858. [1]

BLAND, Miles, jun., *Melbourne, Australia.*—St. John's Coll. Cam. B.A. 1851, M.A. 1854; Deac. 1852 by Bp of Ex. Pr. 1853 by Bp of B. and W. Formerly C. of Crewkerne 1857, Saltwood, near Hythe, 1858. [2]

BLAND, Philip Davison, *Warsop Rectory, Mansfield, Notts.*—Univ. Coll. Ox. B.A. 1847, M.A. 1850. R. of Warsop, Dio. Lin. 1860. (Patron, Sir W. Fitzherbert, Bart; R.'s Inc. 1020*l* and Ho; Pop. 1426.) [3]

BLAND, William Handley, *Braceby, Folkingham, Lincolnshire.*—Caius Coll. Cam. B A. 1830, M.A. 1833; Deac. 1830 and Pr. 1831 by Bp of Lin. V. of Braceby with Sapperton, Dio. Lin. 1832. (Joint Patrons, Sir G. E. Welby Gregory and V. of Grantham; V.'s Inc. 300*l*; Pop. 219.) V. of Middleton-Raisen, Dio. Lin. 1832. (Joint Patrons, Bp of Lin, and Hon. Charles Cust; V.'s Inc. 313*l*; Pop. 1144.) Formerly C. of Barrowby by Grantham. Pickworth, near Folkingham. [4]

BLANDFORD, Henry Weare, *Fryerning, Ingatestone, Essex.*—Wad. Coll. Ox. B.A; Deac. 1849. Pr. 1850. R. of Fryerning, Dio. Roch. 1861. (Patron, Wad. Coll. Ox; R.'s Inc. 300*l* and Ho; Pop. 707.) [5]

BLANDFORD, H. W., *Mappowder, Blandford, Dorset.*—C. of Mappowder. [6]

BLANDFORD, Josiah Jessop, *Spondon, Derby.*—Ch. Coll Cam. B.A. 1839; Deac. 1840, Pr. 1841. One of H.M.'s Inspectors of Schools. [7]

BLANDY, Francis Jackson, *Netheravon, Amesbury, Wilts.*—St. John's Coll. Ox. B.A. 1822, M.A. 1825; Deac. 1825 and Pr. 1826 by Bp of Ox. V. of Netheravon, Dio. Salis. 1838. (Patron, Bp of Salis; Tithe, 126*l*; Glebe, 5 acres; V.'s Inc. 332*l* 7*s* and Ho; Pop. 546.) [8]

BLANDY, William.—Deac. 1853 and Pr. 1854 by Bp of Lich. Formerly C. of Pickworth, Lincolnshire. [9]

BLANE, Henry, *Folkton, Scarborough.*—Brasen. Coll. Ox. B.A. 1833, M.A. 1836; Deac. 1836, Pr. 1837. Sinecure R. and V. of Folkton, Dio. York, 1856. (Patron, of the Sinecure R. Admiral Mitford; of the V. the present V; R. and V.'s Glebe, 1741 acres; R.'s Inc. 900*l*; V.'s Inc. 400*l* and Ho; Pop. 559.) Formerly R. of Warmley, Herts, 1853–56. [10]

BLANFORD, William West, *Oby Rectory, near Norwich.*—C. of Ashby Oby and Thirne, near Norwich. [11]

BLATCH, Frederick Roberts, *Little London, Leeds.*—Oriel Coll. Ox. B.A. 1862; Deac. 1866 by Bp of Rip. C. of St. Matthew's, Little London, 1866. [12]

BLATCH, William, *St. John's Parsonage, Perth, Scotland.*—Univ. of Edinburgh, Pantonian Theol. Stud; Deac. 1849 and Pr. 1850 by Bp of Edinburgh. Incumb. of St. John's, Perth, 1855; Synod Clerk of the United Dioceses of St. Andrew's, etc. Author, *Two Lectures on Historical Confirmation of the Scriptures.* 1843, 1*s*; *Lessons for the Living from the Experience of the Dying,* Edinburgh, 1850, 1*s*; *Memoir of Bishop Low, with Sketches of recent Scottish Ecclesiastical History,* Rivingtons, 1856, 7*s*; *Holding the Truth in Love, a Sermon on the Eucharistical Controversy,* Edinburgh, 1858; *The Bondage of Popery, a Sermon on the Tercentenary of the Reformation,* Edinburgh, 1859. [13]

BLATHWAYT, Charles, *Redlynch, Salisbury.*—Queens' Coll. Cam. B.A. 1823, M.A. 1828; Deac. 1824 and Pr. 1825 by Bp of B. and W. P. C. of Redlynch, Dio. Salis. 1865. (Patron, V. of Downton; Pop. 1170.) [14]

BLATHWAYT, Charles Welfitt, *Chelmarsh, Bridgnorth, Salop.*—Corpus Coll. Cam. B.A. 1844, M.A. 1867; Deac. 1844 and Pr. 1845 by Bp of Wor. V. of Chelmarsh, Dio. Herf. 1847. (Patron, Sir J. Sebright, Bart; Tithe—Imp. 369*l* 8*s*; V. 235*l*; Glebe, 24 acres; V.'s Inc. 294*l* and Ho; Pop. 514.) [15]

BLATHWAYT, John Calvert, *Leiston, Saxmundham, Suffolk.*—Corpus Coll. Cam. B.A. 1830, M.A. 1833; Deac. 1830 and Pr. 1832 by Bp of Lin. P. C. of Leiston with Sizewell, Dio. Nor. 1836. (Patrons, Christ's Hospital and the Haberdashers' Company alt; Leiston Tithe—Imp. 435*l* and 30 acres of Glebe Land in lieu of Tithe; P. C.'s Inc. gross, 440*l*; Pop. 2227.) [16]

BLATHWAYT, Raymond, *Woking, Surrey.*—Corpus Coll. Cam. B.A. 1844; Deac. 1844 and Pr. 1845 by Bp of Nor. Chap. to the Invalid Convict Establishment, Woking. Formerly C. of Iken and Theberton, Suffolk, Adlingfleet, Yorks, Mablethorpe, Linc; Asst. Preacher, St. Paul's, Covent garden, Lond; Asst. Chap. Portland Prison; Asst. Chap. Milbank Prison. [17]

BLATHWAYT, Richard Vesey, *Lillington, Sherborne, Dorset.*—Trin. Coll. Cam. B.A. 1849, M.A. 1853; Deac. 1850 by Bp of B. and W. Pr. 1851 by Bp of Pet. R. of Lillington, Dio. Salis. 1866. (Patron, G. D. W. Digby, Esq; Tithe, 186*l* 5*s* 6*d*; Glebe, 37 acres; R.'s Inc. 226*l* 5*s* 6*d*; Pop. 160.) Formerly C. of Stockland, Somerset, 1851, Catthorpe, Leicester, 1852–53, Langridge, Somerset, 1854; R. of Thornford, Dorset, 1856–63; P. C. of Redlynch, Wilts, 1864–66. [18]

BLATHWAYT, Wynter Thomas, *Langridge, Bath.*—Trin. Coll. Cam. B.A. 1847, M.A. 1851; Deac. 1848 and Pr. 1849 by Bp of Lich. R. of Langridge, Dio. B. and W. 1861. (Patron, present R; R.'s Inc. 111*l* and Ho; Pop. 101.) Formerly C. of Tean and Croxden, Staffs, 1848, Fisherton Delamere, Wilts, 1850, Langridge, Somerset, 1854. [19]

BLAYDES, Frederick Henry Marvell, *Harringworth, Uppingham.*—Ch. Ch. Ox. 2nd cl. Lit. Hum. and B.A. 1840, M.A. 1847; Deac. 1842, Pr. 1843. V. of Harringworth, Dio. Pet. 1843. (Patron, Ch. Ch. Ox; Glebe, 90 acres; V.'s Inc. 174*l* and Ho; Pop. 360.) Editor, *Aristophanis Aves,* 1843; *Aristophanis Acharnenses,* 1845. [20]

BLEASDALE, Anthony Cradwell, *Illingworth, Halifax.*—St. Bees; Deac. 1863 by Bp of Carl. Pr. 1864 by Bp of Dur. C. of Illingworth 1865. Formerly C. of West Hartlepool 1863–65. [21]

BLEAZBY, William, 10, *Church-road, St. Leonard's-on-Sea.*—Min. of Coghurst Chapel. Formerly C. of St. Mary Magdalene's, Taunton. [22]

BLEECK, Alfred George, *Preshute, Marlborough, Wilts.*—Trin. Coll. Ox. B.A. 1848, M.A. 1851; Deac. 1849 by Bp of G. and B. Pr. 1851 by Bp of Salis. V. of Preshute, Dio. Salis. 1859. (Patron, Bp of Salis; Tithe, 179*l*; Glebe, 1¼ acres; V.'s Inc. 212*l*; Pop. 1209.) Formerly C. of St. Jude's Bristol, 1849–50, Sutton Veney 1851–54, Stourton 1854–58, Boyton 1858–60, all in Wilts. [23]

BLEECK, William, *Huish, near Marlborough, Wilts.*—Magd. Hall, Ox. B.A. 1825; Deac. 1824, Pr. 1825. R. of Huish, or Hewish, Dio. Salis. 1830. (Patrons, Twelve Trustees; Tithe—Imp. 1*l* 15*s*, R. 185*l*; Glebe, 24 acres; R.'s Inc. 225*l* and Ho; Pop. 133.) [24]

BLENCOWE, Edward Everard, *West Walton Eliensis, Wisbeach, Norfolk.*—St. Alban's Hall, Ox. B.A. 1829; Deac. 1829, Pr. 1830. Mediety of the R. of West Walton, called Walton Eliensis, Dio. Nor. 1831. (Patron, Ld Chan; Tithe, 575*l*; Glebe, 2 acres; R.'s Inc. 579*l*; Pop. 950.) Late Rural Dean. [25]

BLENCOWE, Thomas, *Marston St. Lawrence (Northants), near Banbury.*—Wad. Coll. Ox. B.A. 1834, M.A. 1836; Deac. 1837 and Pr. 1838 by Bp of Ely. V. of Marston with Warkworth C. Dio. Pet. 1850. (Patron, J. J. Blencowe, Esq; V.'s Inc. 320*l* and Ho; Pop. Marston 535, Warkworth 85). [26]

BLENKARNE, J. C., *Great Easton, Great Dunmow, Essex.*—C. of Great Easton. [27]

BLENKIN, Frederick Beatson, *Minster Yard, Lincoln.*—Caius Coll. Cam. Sen. Opt. B.A. 1848, M.A. 1851; Deac. 1849 by Bp of Lin. Pr. 1850 by Bp of Pet. V. of St. Nicholas with St. John, Lincoln, Dio. Lin. 1862. (Patrons, D. and C. of Lin. and Rev. F. Swan; V.'s Inc. 270*l*; Pop. 1800.) Formerly C. of St. Martin's, Leicester, St. John's, Reading. [28]

BLENKIN, George Beatson, *The Vicarage, Boston, Lincolnshire.*—Corpus Coll. Cam; B.A. 1845, M.A. 1848; Sen. Opt. and 2nd cl. Cl. Trip. Deac. 1845 and

Pr. 1846 by Bp of Lin. V. of Boston, Dio. Lin. 1850. (Patroness, Mrs. Ingram; V's Inc. 885*l* and Ho; Pop. 18,948.) Surrogate 1851; Preb. of Lin. Cathl. 1858; Rural Dean of North Holland, 1860. Formerly C. of Navenby, Linc. 1845–50. [1]

BLENKINSOPP, Edwin Clennell Leaton, *Springthorpe Rectory, Gainsborough.*—Univ. Coll. Dur. B.A. 1839, M.A. 1842; Deac. 1842 and Pr. 1843 by Bp of Ches. R. of Springthorpe, Dio. Lin. 1863. (Patron, Ld Chan; Tithe, 180*l*; Glebe, 18 acres; R.'s Inc. 206*l* and Ho; Pop. 300.) Formerly P. C. of St. James's, Lathom, Lancashire, 1851–55; Chap. to the Army in Turkey 1855–56; Chap. to Bp of Argyll 1857; Chap. at Algiers 1859; and Chap. to Fortifications at Portsmouth 1862. Author, *Reunion of the Church*, an Essay in *The Church and the World*, 1865. [2]

BLENKINSOPP, Richard George Leaton, *Shadforth Parsonage, Durham.*—Trin. Coll. Cam. B.A. 1832, M.A. 1837, B.D. 1859; Deac. 1832, Pr. 1834. P. C of Shadforth, Dio. Dur. 1839. (Patrons, D. and C. of Dur; Glebe, 12½ acres; P. C.'s Inc. 300*l* and Ho; Pop. 2500.) Formerly C. of Ryton 1832-39. Author, *Earth's Coming Glory*, 6*d*; *Miner's Cry*, 4*d*; *Britain's Law and Britain's Duty*, 2*d*, etc. [3]

BLENKIRON, Bartholomew, *Portishead (Somerset), near Bristol.*—Late Scho. of Trin. Coll. Cam. 2nd Sen. Opt. 3rd cl. Cl. Trip. and B.A. 1840, M.A. 1843; Deac. 1842, Pr. 1843. V. of Coates Parva, Lincolnshire, Dio. Lin. 1843. (Patron, Trin. Coll. Cam; Tithe—Imp. 140*l*, V. 112*l* 5*s* 5*d*; V.'s Inc. 124*l*; Pop. 59.) C. of Portishead. [4]

BLENNERHASSETT, John, *Ryme Intrinseca, Sherborne, Dorset.*—Dub. A.B. 1824; Deac. 1826 by Bp of B. and W. Pr. 1827 by Bp of Bristol. R. of Ryme Intrinseca, Dio. Salis. 1830. (Patron, Prince of Wales; Tithe, 174*l*; Glebe, 20 acres; R.'s Inc. 200*l* and Ho; Pop. 217.) V. of Hermitage, Dorset, Dio. Salis. 1834. (Patron, Ld Chan; Tithe, 85*l*; V.'s Inc. 105*l* and Ho; Pop. 131.) [5]

BLEW, William John, *St. John's-next-Gravesend, Kent.*—Wad. Coll. Ox. B.A. 1830, M.A. 1832. Author (in conjunction with H. J. Gauntlett, Mus. Doc.), *The Church Hymn and Tune Book*; *Agamemnon the King* (from the Greek of Æschylus), *in English Verse, with a Preface, Notes and Illustrations*, 7*s* 6*d*. [6]

BLICK, Joseph Johnson, *Buxton, Norwich.*—St. John's Coll. Cam. B.A. 1857; Deac. 1857 and Pr. 1858 by Bp of B. and W. C. of Buxton 1861. Formerly C. of Batheaston, Bath, 1857–61. [7]

BLIGH, Hon. Edward Vesey, *Birling Vicarage, Maidstone.*—Downing Coll. Cam. M.A. 1854; Deac. 1855 and Pr. 1856 by Bp of Roch. V. of Birling, Dio. Cant. 1865. (Patron, Earl of Abergavenny; Tithe, 164*l*; Glebe, 16 acres; V.'s Inc. 400*l* and Ho; Pop. 650.) Chap. of the Queen's Own West Kent Yeomanry Cavalry. Formerly Attaché to the British Embassies at Hanover, Florence, and Berlin; C. of Snodland, Kent, 1855–56; R. of Rotherfield, Sussex, 1856–65. Author, *Church Rates—Concession advocated*, 1861, 3*d*; *A Catechism for the Use of Schools*, 1862, 1*d*; *Clerical Inconsistency*, 1863, 3*d*; *The Roots of Ritual and the Remedy*, 1867, 1*d*. [8]

BLIGH, The Hon. Henry, *Nettlebed, Henley-on-Thames.*—Oxford, and Salisbury Theol. Coll; Deac. 1863 and Pr. 1865 by Bp of Salis. Incumb. of Don. of Nettlebed, Dio. Ox. 1866. (Patroness, Dow. Lady Farquhar; Incumb.'s Inc. 112*l* and Ho; Pop. 737.) [9]

BLIGH, John, *Kimbolton, Hunts.*—V. of Easton near Kimbolton, Dio. Ely, 1826. (Patron, Bp of Ely; Tithe—Eccles. Commis. 16*l* 16*s*, App. 20*l*, V. 10*l* 15*s* 4*d*; V.'s Inc. 65*l*; Pop. 155.) P. C. of Barnham, near Kimbolton, Dio. Ely, 1826. (Patron, Bp of Ely; P. C.'s Inc. 65*l*; Pop. 115.) P. C. of Long-tow, near Kimbolton, Dio. Ely, 1826. (Patron, Bp of Ely; P. C.'s Inc. 53*l*; Pop. 208.) [10]

BLINCOE, Robert, 78, *Bunhill-row, London, E.C.*—Queens' Coll. Cam. B.A. 1848, M.A. 1857, *ad eund.* Ox; Deac. 1849 by Bp of Lich. Pr. 1850 by Bp of Roch. C. and Sunday Even. Lect. at St. Luke's, Old-street, Lond. 1852. Patron of R. of Swettenham, Cheshire. Formerly C. of St. George's, Wolverhampton, 1849–52. Author, various Sermons and Pamphlets. [11]

BLINK, Henry Simpson, *Watlington, Oxon.*—King's Coll. Lond. Theol. Assoc. 1855; Deac. 1856 and Pr. 1857 by Bp of Lich. C. of Watlington 1866. Formerly C. of Audley, Staffs, 1856, Reigate, Surrey, 1858, Battle 1861, Sittingbourne 1862, Little Munden, Herts, 1864. [12]

BLISS, James, 3, *Lansdowne-place, Plymouth.*—Oriel Coll. Ox. 1st cl. Lit. Hum. B.A. 1830, M.A. 1833, Deac. 1833 and Pr. 1834 by Bp of Glouc. P. C. of St. James's, Plymouth, Dio. Ex. 1858. (Patrons, Crown and Bp of Ex. alt; P. C.'s Inc. 160*l* and Ho; Pop. 3163.) Formerly V. of Ogbourne St. Andrew, Wilts. Editor, Bishop Andrews' Latin Works; Archbishop Laud's Works (except Vols. 1 and 2.) Translator of Vol. 3. St. Gregory on Job in *Library of the Fathers.* [13]

BLISS, John Worthington, *Betshanger Rectory, Sandwich, Kent.*—R. of Betshanger, Dio. Cant. 1866. (Patron, Sir Walter C. James, Bart; R.'s Inc. 180*l* and Ho; Pop. 43.) [14]

BLISS, Thomas, *Madras, India.*—Dub. A.B. 1839; Deac. 1840 and Pr. 1841 by Bp of B. and W. Head Mast. of Bp Corrie's School, Madras. Formerly C. of Ch. Ch. Clevedon, 1859. [15]

BLISS, William Blowers, *Wicken Bonant, Bishops Stortford.*—Trin. Coll. Cam. B.A. 1851, M.A. 1853; Deac. 1851 and Pr. 1852 by Bp of Rip. R. of Wicken Bonant, Dio. Roch. 1862. (Patron, H. Bliss, Esq; R.'s Inc. 350*l* and Ho; Pop. 173.) [16]

BLISS, William Henry, *King's School, Sherborne, Dorset.*—Ex. Coll. Ox. B.A. 1862, Mus. Bac. 1863; Deac. 1862 and Pr. 1863 by Bp of Ox. Asst. Mast. in the King's Sch. and Precentor of the Sch. Chapel. Formerly Precentor of Ex. Coll. Chapel. Author, Anthems, Hymns, etc. published by Novello. Editor, *Llandaff Church Music Associations' Festival Books*, 1863 and 1866. [17]

BLISSARD, John, *Hampsted Norreys, Newbury, Berks.*—St. John's Coll. Cam. B.A. 1826; Deac. 1827 and Pr. 1828 by Bp of Lin. V. of Hampsted-Norreys, Dio. Ox. 1843. (Patron, Marquis of Downshire; Tithe—Imp. 916*l* 13*s* 6*d* and 152½ acres of Glebe, V. 313*l* 14*s* 3*d*; Glebe, 135 acres; V.'s Inc. 430*l* and Ho; Pop. 924.) [18]

BLISSARD, John Charles, *Edgbaston, Birmingham.*—St. John's Coll. Cam. 34th Wrang. B.A. 1858, M.A. 1861; Deac. 1860 by Abp of Cant. Pr. 1863 by Bp of Wor. C. of Edgbaston 1862. [19]

BLISSARD, William, *Precincts, Canterbury.*—Emman. Coll. Cam. Burnley Moral Phil. Prize, B.A. 1860, M.A, 1863; Deac. 1860, Pr. 1862. First Math. Mast. in King's Sch. Cant; C. of Harbledown 1862. Formerly C. of Cantley 1860. Author, *The Moral Influences of Religious Worship*, Macmillan and Co. 1862. [20]

BLISSET, George, *Wells, Somerset.*—Ball. Coll. Ox. B.A. 1838, M.A. 1841; Deac. 1844 and Pr. 1846 by Bp of Lich. P. C. of St. Thomas the Apostle, East Wells, Dio. B. and W. 1857. (Patrons, D. and C. of Wells; P. C.'s Inc. 300*l* and Ho; Pop. 973). Chap. of the Wells Union. Formerly C. of Ch. Ch. Clifton, Bristol. [21]

BLISSET, Henry, *Letton, Weobly, Herefordshire.*—Ball. Coll. Ox. B A. 1831, M.A. 1837; Deac. 1835 by Bp of Pet. Pr. 1836 by Bp of Ely. R. of Letton, Dio. Herf. 1837. (Patron, the present R; Tithe, 235*l*; Glebe, 20 acres; R.'s Inc. 270*l* and Ho; Pop. 238.) R. of Willersley, Dio. Herf. 1837. (Patroness, Mrs. E. Blisset; Tithe, 60*l*; R.'s Inc. 78*l*; Pop. 13.) [22]

BLOFELD, Robert Singleton, *Great Yarmouth.*—Trin. Coll. Cam. B.A. 1860, M.A. 1864; Deac. 1862 and Pr. 1863 by Bp of Ely. V. of Ormesby St. Margaret with Scratby V. and Ormesby St. Michael V. Dio. Nor. 1866. (Patrons, D. and C. of Nor; Tithe, 304*l*; Glebe, 65 acres; V.'s Inc. 450*l*; Pop. Ormesby St. Margaret 777, Scratby 309, Ormesby St. Michael 311.) Formerly C. of Risby 1862–63, Woolpit, Suffolk, 1863–64, Ormesby 1864–66. [23]

BLOFELD, Thomas John, *Hoveton Hall, near Norwich.*—Trin. Coll. Cam. B.A. 1829, M.A. 1832; Deac. 1830, Pr. 1831. V. of Hoveton St. Peter with Hoveton St. John P. C. Dio. Nor. 1851. (Patron, Bp of Nor; Hoveton St. Peter, Tithe—App. 220l, V. 120l; Hoveton St. John, Tithe—App. 340l; P. C.'s Inc. 27l; V.'s Inc. 187l; Pop. Hoveton St. Peter 131, Hoveton St. John 285.) [1]

BLOMEFIELD, Charles D., *Calne, Wilts.*—C. of Calne. [2]

BLOMEFIELD, John, *St. George's Parsonage, Leeds.*—Trin. Coll. Cam. B.A. 1847, M.A. 1850; Deac. and Pr. 1848 by Abp of York. P. C. of St. George's, Leeds, Dio. Rip. 1857. (Patrons, Trustees; P. C.'s Inc. 580l and Ho; Pop. 8421.) Formerly Asst. Chap. of the Hon. E. I. Co's Establishment, and Dom. and Exam. Chap. to the Bp of Calcutta, 1850–56, P. C. of Drypool, Hull, 1856–57. [3]

BLOMEFIELD, R. A., *Spring Grove, near Hounslow, W.*—C. of Spring Grove. [4]

BLOMEFIELD, Samuel Edward, *Knottingley, Yorks.*—Ch. Coll. Cam. B.A. 1846; Deac. 1849 and Pr. 1850 by Bp of Melbourne. P. C. of Knottingley, Dio. York, 1866. (Patron, V. of Pontefract; P. C.'s Inc. 133l and Ho; Pop. 2198.) Formerly Asst. Min. of St. Peter's, Melbourne, 1849–52; C of Basildon, Berks, 1852–53; British Chap. at Vevey, Switzerland, 1853–60; C. of Kingswinford, Staffs, 1860–62; C. of St. Clement Danes, Strand, Lond. 1865. [5]

BLOMEFIELD, Sir Thomas Eardley Wilmot, Bart., *Pontefract.*—Trin. Coll. Cam. B A. 1843, M.A. 1846; Deac. 1844 and Pr. 1847 by Bp of Win. P. C. of All Saints', Pontefract, 1859. (Patron, Abp of York; P. C.'s Inc. 150l and Ho; Pop. 1392.) [6]

BLOMFIELD, Alfred, *St. Matthew's Parsonage, City-road, London, E.C.*—Ball. Coll. Ox. 1st cl. Lit. Hum; B.A. 1855, M.A. 1857; Deac. 1857 and Pr. 1858 by Bp of Ox. P C. of St. Matthew's, City-road, Dio. Lon. 1865 (Patron, Bp of Lon; P. C.'s Inc. 300l and Ho; Pop. 3700) Fell. of All Souls', Ox. Formerly P. C. of St. Philip's, Stepney, 1862 65. Author, *Memoirs of Bishop Blomfield*, 2 vols. Murray, 1863. [7]

BLOMFIELD, Arthur, *Barton le Cley, Ampthill, Beds.*—Ex. Coll. Ox. B.A. 1850, M.A. 1864; Deac. 1850 and Pr. 1851 by Bp of G. and B. R. of Barton, Dio. Ely, 1865. (Patron, the Crown; Glebe, 418 acres; R.'s Inc. 440l and Ho; Pop. 969.) Formerly C. of Tidenham, Glouc. 1851–54, Laycock, Wilts, 1854–64; Tetbury, Glouc. 1864–65. Author, *The Almost Christian*, 1861; *Abide in Him*, 1863; *Parting Words*, 1864; three Sermons. [8]

BLOMFIELD, Charles, *Churchstoke, Montgomeryshire.*—Jesus Coll. Cam. B.A. 1862, M.A. 1867; Deac. 1863 and Pr. 1864 by Bp. of Herf. C. of Churchstoke 1863. [9]

BLOMFIELD, Frederick George, *3 Finsbury Circus, London, E.C.*—Ball. Coll. Ox. 2nd cl. Lit Hum. and B.A. 1844, M A. 1846; Deac. 1846 and Pr. 1847 by Bp of Lon. R. of St. Andrew Undershaft, Leadenhall-street, with St. Mary-at Axe R. Dio. Lon. 1853. (Patron, Bp. of Lon; R.'s Inc. 1025l; Pop. 1071.) Preb. of St. Paul's; Chap. to Bp. of Lon; Rural Dean. [10]

BLOMFIELD, George Becher, *Stevenage, Herts.*—Ch. Coll. Cam. B.A. 1824, M.A. 1827; Deac. 1824 by Bp of Ches. Pr. 1825 by Bp of Ban. Can. Res. of Chester Cathl. 1827 (Value 500l and Res); R. of Stevenage, Dio. Roch. 1834. (Patron, W. R. Baker, Esq, Bayfordbury, Herts; Tithe, 1007l; Glebe, 27 acres; R.'s Inc. 1073l and Ho; Pop. 2352.) Rural Dean. Formerly C. of Hawarden, Flints, 1824; R. of Tattenhall and Coddington, Cheshire, 1827. Author, *Sermons adapted to Country Congregations*, 3 vols. 5s each. [11]

BLOMFIELD, George James, *Norton Rectory, Ilminster.*—Ch. Coll. Cam. B.A. 1853, M.A. 1858, and Theol. Coll. Wells; Deac. 1855 and Pr. 1856 by Bp of B. and W. R. of Norton-under-Hambdon, Dio. B. and W. 1861. (Patron, Rev. George Lock; Tithe, 240l; Glebe, 20 acres; R.'s Inc. 280l and Ho; Pop. 467.) Formerly C. of Bishops Lydiard 1854, Chilton-Canteloe 1855–61. [12]

BLOMFIELD, George John, *Dartford, Kent.*—Ex. Coll. Ox. B.A. 1845, M.A. 1847; Deac. 1846 and Pr. 1847 by Bp of Lon. V. of Dartford, Dio. Cant. 1857. (Patron, Bp of Wor; Tithe, 560l; Glebe, 17 acres; V.'s Inc. 650l and Ho; Pop. 6597.) Formerly R. of Bow with Broad Nymet, Devon, 1853–56. [13]

BLOMFIELD, James, *Orsett, Romford, Essex.*—Emman. Coll. Cam. B.D. 1829; Deac. 1820 and Pr. 1821 by Bp of Nor. R. of Orsett, Dio. Roch. 1842. (Patron, Bp of Roch; Tithe, 1227l; Glebe, 10 acres; R.'s Inc. 1237l and Ho; Pop. 1531.) Rural Dean. [14]

BLOMFIELD, James Charles, *Launton, Bicester, Oxon.*—Ex. Coll. Ox. B.A. 1843, M.A. 1844; Deac. 1845 and Pr. 1846 by Bp of Lon. R. of Launton, Dio. Ox. 1850. (Patron, Bp of Ox; Tithe, 52l; Glebe, 458 acres; R.'s Inc. 650l and Ho; Pop. 711.) Rural Dean of Bicester 1853; Hon. Organizing Sec. for the S P.G. in the Archd. of Ox. 1855. Formerly C. of Romford, Essex, 1845–50; R. of Offord Cluny, Hunts, 1850. [15]

BLOOD, William, *Temple Grafton, Alcester.*—Deac. 1843, Pr. 1844. P. C. of Temple Grafton, Warwickshire, Dio. Wor. 1851. (Patron, F. F. Bullock, Esq; P. C.'s Inc. 146l; Pop. 403.) Chap. to the Marquis of Hertford. Author, *Mercy to the Chief of Sinners* (a Narrative in French and English, interleaved), 14th edit; *The Amazon*, and *The Loss of the Amazon* (Four Sermons on the "Amazon"); *The Soul, its Nature and Destiny*; *The Blessedness of the Righteous*; *Salvation*; *Salvation by Faith*; *The Work of the Holy Spirit*; *The Love of God in Christ*; *Review of the Charge of the Bishop of Ossory*; *National Education*; *The Gospel, the Power of God to Salvation*; *The Divine Influence of the Holy Scriptures*; *A Missionary Visit to the Indians of Orialla.* [16]

BLOOM, John Hague, *Castle Acre, Swaffham, Norfolk.*—Caius Coll. Cam B.A. 1827; Deac. 1828, Pr. 1829. V. of Castle-Acre, Dio. Nor. 1835. (Patron, Earl of Leicester; Tithe—Imp. 610l 4s, V. 168l 7s; Glebe, 3½ acres; V.'s Inc. 174l; Pop. 1405.) V. of Newton-by-Castle-Acre, Dio. Nor. 1841. (Patron, Bp of Nor; Tithe—App. 210l 5s 8d, V. 97l 5s 8d; V.'s Inc. 100l; Pop. 84.) Surrogate. [17]

BLOOMFIELD, Edwin Newson, *Clare College, Cambridge.*—Clare Coll. Cam. B A. 1850, M.A. 1853; Deac. 1853 and Pr. 1854 by Bp of Ely; late Sen. Fell. of Clare Coll. Cam. R. of Guestling, Dio. Chich. 1863. (Patron, Clare Coll. Cam; R.'s Inc. 450l and Ho; Pop. 731.) [18]

BLOOMFIELD, Samuel Thomas, *Bisbrooke, Uppingham, Rutland.*—Sid. Coll. Cam. B.A. 1808, M.A. 1811, D.D. 1829; Deac. 1809, Pr. 1810. V. of Bisbrooke, Dio. Pet. 1814. (Patron, Duke of Rutland; Tithe—App. 4s 6d; V.'s Inc. 290l; Pop. 266.) Hon. Can. of Pet. Cathl. 1854. [19]

BLORE, Edward W., *Trinity College, Cambridge.*—Fell. of Trin. Coll [20]

BLORE, G. J., *Christ Church, Oxford.*—Ch. Ch. Ox. 1st cl. Lit. Hum. 2nd cl. Law and Mod. History, B.A. 1858, M.A. 1861; Deac. 1863 by Bp of Salis. Pr. 1864 by Bp of Ox. Sen. Stud. and Tut. of Ch. Ch. [21]

BLOSSE, The Ven. Henry Lynch, *New Castle, Bridgend, Glamorgan.*—Dub. Coll. Prizes and Certificates, A.B. 1835; Deac. 1836, Pr. 1837. Archd. of Llandaff 1859 (Val. 350l). Preb. of Caeran in Llan. Cathl, 1859; V. of New Castle, Dio. Llan. 1839. (Patron, Bp of Llan; Tithe—Imp. 164l 3s, V. 439l 1s 1d; V.'s Inc. 438l and Ho; Pop. 4828.) Surrogate. [22]

BLOW, John, *Goodmanham, Market Weighton, Yorks.*—St. John's Coll. Cam. 3rd Sen. Opt. B.A. 1839, M.A. 1843; Deac. 1839 and Pr. 1840 by Abp of York. C. of Goodmanham 1866. Formerly C. of Londesborough 1840–66. [23]

BLOW, William, *Goodmanham, Market Weighton, Yorks.*—Sid. Coll. Cam. B.A 1817; Deac. 1818 and Pr. 1819 by Abp of York. R. of Goodmanham, Dio. York, 1819. (Patron, the present R; Glebe, 732 acres; R.'s Inc. 1000l and Ho; Pop. 294.) [24]

BLOW, William, jun., *Layer-Breton, Kelvedon, Essex.*—St. Peter's Coll. Cam. B.A. 1846, M.A. 1849, Deac. 1847 and Pr. 1848 by Abp of York. R. of Layer-Breton, Dio. Roch. 1855. (Patron, the present R; Tithe, 302*l* 16*s* 5*d*; R.'s Inc. 360*l* and Ho; Pop. 298.) [1]

BLOWER, James, *Gwernesney Rectory, Usk, Monmouthshire.*—Jesus Coll. Ox. B.A. 1863; Deac. 1864 and Pr. 1865 by Bp of Llan. P. C. of Llangeview, Dio. Llan. 1866. (Patron, present P. C; P. C.'s Inc. 90*l*; Pop. 159.) C. of Gwernesney 1865. Formerly C. of Llansoy 1864. [2]

BLOXAM, Andrew, *Twycross near Atherstone.*—Wor. Coll. Ox. B.A. 1824, M.A. 1827; Deac. 1826 and Pr. 1827 by Bp of Ox. P. C. of Twycross, Dio. Pet. 1839. (Patron, Earl Howe; Tithe—App. 269*l* 6*s* 9*d*; Glebe, 3½ acres; P. C.'s Inc. 130*l* and Ho; Pop. 336.) Late Fell. of Wor. Coll. Ox. [3]

BLOXAM, John Rouse, *Beeding Priory, Hurstpierpoint, Sussex.*—Magd. Coll. Ox. 4th cl. Lit. Hum. B.A. 1832, M.A. 1835, B.D. 1843, D.D. 1847; Deac. 1832 and Pr. 1833 by Bp of Ox. V. of Upper Beeding, Dio. Chich. 1862. (Patron, Magd. Coll. Ox; V.'s Inc. 110*l*; Pop. 765.) Formerly Fell. of Magd. Coll. 1835–63; C. of Littlemore, near Oxford, 1836–40. Author, *Heylin's Memorial of Bishop Waynflete*, edited for the Caxton Society, 1851, 5*s* 6*d*; *A Register of S. M. Magdalen College, Oxford*, 3 vols. 1st vol. 10*s*, 2nd vol 15*s*, 3rd vol. 10*s*, 1864. [4]

BLOXAM, Richard Rowland, *Harlaston, Tamworth, Staffs.*—Wor. Coll. Ox. B.A. 1819; Deac. 1819 and Pr. 1820 by Bp of Pet. R. of Harlaston, Dio. Lich. 1850. (Patron, J. H. Pye, Esq. Clifton Hall; Tithe, 370*l*; Glebe, 43 acres; R.'s Inc. 424*l* and Ho; Pop. 239.) Dom. Chap. to Earl Ferrers 1848. Retired Naval Chap. with Pension (135*l* per ann.) 1845. [5]

BLOXAM, Thomas Lawrence, *Leamington.*—Lin. Coll. Ox. Scho. of, B.A. 1821; Deac. 1822 by Bp of Pet. Pr. 1824 by Bp of Lich. Formerly C. of Brinklow 1823–49. [6]

BLOXSOME, William Henry, *Stanton Rectory, Winchcomb, Glouc.*—Wad. Coll. Ox. B.A. 1832, M.A 1834; Deac. 1832, Pr. 1833. R. of Stanton with Snowshill C. Dio. G. and B. 1838. (Patron, the present R; Snowshill, Tithe, 76*l*; R.'s Inc. 423*l* and Ho; Pop. Stanton 260, Snowshill 235.) R. of Evesbach, near Bromyard, Herefordshire, Dio. Herf. 1838. (Patrons, Exors. of Dowager Countess of Berkeley; Tithe, 172*l* 3*s* 9¾*d*; R.'s Inc. 180*l*; Pop. 87.) [7]

BLOXSOME, William Henry, jun., *Stanton Rectory, Winchcomb, Glouc.*—Wad. Coll. Ox. B.A. 1859, M.A. 1862; Deac. 1860 and Pr. 1861 by Bp of Wor. C. of Stanton with Snowshill 1861. Formerly C. of Rowington, Warwick, 1860. [8]

BLUCK, John Hinton, *Eardisland, near Pembridge, Herefordshire.*—St. John's Coll. Cam. B.A. 1846; Deac. 1847, Pr. 1848. C. of Eardisland 1861. Formerly C. of Shrawardine and of More with Shelve, Shropshire. [9]

BLUCKE, William Strong, *Willoughby Waterless, Lutterworth.*—Magd. Hall, Ox. B.A. 1847, M.A. 1848; Deac. 1848 and Pr. 1849 by Bp of Pet. R. of Willoughby-Waterless with Peatling-Magna, Dio. Pet. 1858. (Patroness, Mrs. Blucke; R.'s Inc. 350*l* and Ho; Pop. 644.) [10]

BLUETT, Charles Courtney, *The Rectory, Barlow Moor, Manchester.*—Emman. Coll. Cam. B.A. 1851, M.A. 1854; Deac. 1852 and Pr. 1853 by Bp of Man. R. of Barlow Moor, Dio. Man. 1858. (Patron, Bp of Man; R.'s Inc. 240*l* and Ho; Pop. 1013.) Formerly C. of Didsbury 1852–58. [11]

BLUETT, Francis Robert Peter Clarke, *Abersychan, near Pontypool, Monmouthshire.*—Magd. Hall, Ox. B.A. 1833; Deac. 1834, Pr. 1835. P. C. of Abersychan, Dio. Llan. 1844. (Patron, V. of Trevethin; P. C.'s Inc. 300*l* and Ho; Pop. 7979.) [12]

BLUETT, John, *Lydford, Bridestow, Devon.*—Queens' Coll. Cam. B.A. 1835; Deac. 1839, Pr. 1841. C. of Lydford. [13]

BLUNDELL, Augustus Rickards, *Odessa.*—Queen's Coll. Ox. B.A 1862; Deac. 1863 by Bp of B. and W. British Chap. at Odessa. Formerly C. of Stoke Courcy 1863. [14]

BLUNDELL, Thomas B. H., *Halsall Rectory, Ormskirk.*—R. of Halsall, Dio. Ches. 1863 (Patron, H. H. Blundell, Esq; R.'s Inc. 3500*l* and Ho; Pop. 195.) [15]

BLUNT, Abel Gerald Wilson, *Rectory-house, Church-street, Chelsea, S.W.*—Pemb. Coll. Cam. B.A. 1850, M.A. 1860, Travelling Fell. of Univ; Deac. 1851, Pr. 1852. R. of St. Luke's, Chelsea, Dio. Lon. 1860, (Patron, Earl Cadogan; Tithe, 218*l*; R.'s Inc. 1400*l* and Ho; Pop. 20,000.) Dom. Chap. to Lord Crewe. Formerly P. C. of Crewe Green, Cheshire, 1856–60. [16]

BLUNT, Alexander Colvin, *Millbrook Rectory, Southampton.*—Ch. Ch. Ox. B.A. 1855; Deac. 1855 and Pr. 1856 by Bp of Win. R. of Millbrook, Dio. Win. 1866. (Patron, Bp of Win; Tithe, 502*l*; R.'s Inc. 542*l* and Ho; Pop. 5166.) Formerly C. of Alverstoke. [17]

BLUNT, Arthur Henry, *Bishops Stortford, Herts.*—Pemb. Coll. Cam. B.A. 1858; Deac. 1859 and Pr. 1860 by Bp of G. and B. Chap. and Sec. of Hockerill Training College, Bishops Stortford. Formerly C. of St. Philip's, Leckhampton, 1859. [18]

BLUNT, Edward Powlett, *Lytchett-Minster, Poole, Dorset.*—Corpus Coll. Ox. 2nd cl. Lit. Hum. Latin Verse 1825, B.A. 1826, M.A. 1827; Deac. 1829 and Pr. 1830 by Bp of Ox. V. of Lytchett-Minster, Dio. Salis. 1858. (Patron, Eton Coll; V.'s Inc. 300*l* and Ho; Pop. 802.) [19]

BLUNT, Henry George Scawen, *St. Andrew's Rectory, Holborn, London, E.C.*—R. of St. Andrew's, Holborn, Dio. Lon. 1858. (Patron, Duke of Buccleuch; R.'s Inc. 950*l* and Ho; Pop. 15,059.) [20]

BLUNT, James Henry Tomlinson, *Bombay.*—Ex. Coll. Ox. B.A. 1854, M.A. 1857; Deac. 1855 and Pr. 1856 by Bp of Man. Chap. Bombay. Formerly C. of Emman. Ch. Bolton, 1855–56, Davington, Kent, 1856–60, Chorley 1860. [21]

BLUNT, James St. John, *The Vicarage, Old Windsor.*—Ball. Coll. Ox. B.A. 1850, M.A. 1851; Deac. 1851 and Pr. 1852. V. of Old Windsor, Dio. Ox. 1860. (Patron, Ld Chan; Tithe, 200*l*; V.'s Inc. 270*l* and Ho; Pop. 1367.) Chap. to the Queen. [22]

BLUNT, Richard Frederick Lefevre, *The Vicarage, Scarborough.*—King's Coll. Lond. Theol. Assoc. 1857, M.A. by Abp of Cant. 1864; Deac. 1857 and Pr. 1858 by Bp of G. and B. V. of Scarborough, Dio. York, 1864. (Patron, Lord Hotham; V.'s Inc. 400*l* and Ho; Pop. 18,000.) Chap. of Scarborough Borough Gaol 1864; Hon. Chap. to Royal Northern Sea Bathing Infirmary; Surrogate. Formerly C. of St. Paul's, Cheltenham, 1857–60, St. Luke's, Chelsea, 1860–64. [23]

BLUNT, Walter, *Bicknor, Maidstone.*—Caius Coll. Cam. B.A. 1835, M.A. 1838; Deac. 1838 by Bp of Nor. Pr. 1841 by Bp of G. and B. R. of Bicknor, Dio. Cant. 1858. (Patron, Ld Chan; R.'s Inc. 115*l*; Pop. 53.) Formerly C. of St. Botolph-without, Aldgate. Author, *Hints for an Improved Course of Study in the University of Cambridge*; *Letters to the English Public on the Condition of the National Universities*; *Dissenting Baptisms and Church Burials*; *The English Church and the Roman Heresy*; *The Use and Abuse of Church Bells*; *Confirmation, or the Laying-on of Hands catechetically explained*; *Ecclesiastical Reformation and Reform*; *Church Rates*; *Education Question*; Hymns, *The Nativity*; *The Crucifixion*, etc. [24]

BLUNT, Walter, *Wallop House, Stockbridge, Hants.*—King's Coll. Cam. B.A. 1826, M.A. 1835; Deac. 1825 and Pr. 1826. Late Fell. of King's Coll. Cam. [25]

BLYTH, Charles Dethick, *Sutton, Biggleswade, Beds.*—St. John's Coll. Ox. B.A. 1819, M.A. 1824, B.D. 1829. R. of Sutton, Dio. Ely, 1830. (Patron, St. John's Coll. Ox; Tithe, 349*l*; Glebe, 32 acres; R.'s Inc. 370*l* and Ho; Pop. 438.) [26]

BLYTH, Edward Hamilton.—Univ. Coll. Ox. B.A. 1857; Deac. 1858 and Pr. 1859 by Bp of Ches.

Chap. Bengal. Formerly C. of Dunham Massey, Cheshire, 1858-59. [1]

BLYTH, Edward Keralake, *Burnham-Deepdale, Lynn, Norfolk.*—St. John's Coll. Cam. Sen. Opt. B.A. 1860; Deac. 1860 and Pr. 1861 by Bp of Nor. R. of Burnham-Deepdale, Dio. Nor. 1862. (Patrons, Trustees of the late H. Blyth, Esq; Tithe, 257*l*; Glebe, 26 acres; R.'s Inc. 290*l* and Ho; Pop. 81.) Formerly C. of Trowse with Lakenham 1860–62. [2]

BLYTH, Frederick Cavan, *Frittenden, Staplehurst, Kent.*—Oriel Coll. Ox. B.A. 1859; Deac. 1859 and Pr. 1860 by Bp of Lin. C. of Frittenden. Formerly C. of Kirkby, Lincolnshire. [3]

BLYTH, George Francis Popham, *Calcutta.*—Lin. Coll. Ox. B.A. 1854, M.A. 1858; Deac. 1855 by Bp of G. and B. Pr. 1856 by Bp of B. and W. Chap. Calcutta. Formerly C. of Westport St. Mary, Wilts. [4]

BLYTH, William, *Fincham, Downham, Norfolk.*—V. of Fincham St. Martin with St. Mitchael R. Dio. Nor. 1846. (Patrons, Ld Chan. and the present V. alt; Tithe,—Imp. 325*l*, V. 690*l*; V.'s Inc. 700*l* and Ho; Pop. 886.) Rural Dean. [5]

BLYTHE, Alfred T., *Staveley, Chesterfield.*—C. of Staveley. [6]

BLYTHE, Augustine, *High Harrogate, Yorks.*—Ch. Coll. Cam. Sen. Opt. B A. 1858; Deac. 1858 by Bp of Carl. C. of High Harrogate. [7]

BOARDMAN, Edward Hubbard, *Grazeley, Reading.*—King's Coll. Lon. Theol. Assoc; Deac. 1849, Pr. 1850. P. C. of Grazeley, Dio. Ox. 1863. (Patron, Bp of Ox; P. C.'s Inc. 35*l* and Ho; Pop. 648.) [8]

BOASE, Charles W., *Exeter College, Oxford.*—Fell. of Ex. Coll. Ox. [9]

BOCKETT, Benjamin Bradney, *Epsom, Surrey.*—Madg. Hall, Ox. B.A. 1833, M.A. 1836; Deac. 1832, Pr. 1834. V. of Epsom, Dio. Win. 1839. (Patron, Rev. W. Speer; Tithe—Imp. 225*l*, V. 350*l* 10*s* 10*d*; Glebe, 14 acres; V.'s Inc. 360*l* and Ho; Pop. 4890.) Author, *The Clergyman's Private Register*, 1838; *Right Baptism* (a Tract), 1850; *The Good Fight of Faith* (a Sermon), 1855. [10]

BOCKETT, Joseph, *Stoodleigh, Tiverton, Devon.*—Trin. Coll. Ox. B.A. 1815, M.A. 1818. R. of Stoodleigh, Dio. Ex. 1816. (Patron, T. Daniell, Esq; Tithe, 407*l*; Glebe, 30 acres; R.'s Inc. 462*l* and Ho; Pop. 499). Formerly Chap. to the Bp of Roch. [11]

BODDINGTON, Thomas Francis, *South Moreton, Wallingford.*—St. Peter's Coll. Cam. B.A. 1861, M.A. 1865; Deac. 1862, Pr. 1863. C. of South Moreton 1866. Formerly C. of Stapleton 1862, and Tetbury, Glouc. 1865. [12]

BODDINGTON, Thomas Fremeaux, *Badger Rectory, Shiffnal, Salop.*—Ball. Coll. Ox. B.A. 1826, M.A. 1827; Deac. 1828, Pr. 1829. R. of Badger, Dio. Herf. 1838. (Patron, R. H. Cheney, Esq; Tithe, 254*l* 10*s* 6*d*; Glebe, 25 acres; R.'s Inc. 324*l* and Ho; Pop. 137.) Formerly C. of Dinder, near Wells, 1831, Dynedor, Herefordshire, 1837. [13]

BODDY, George Yatman, 26, *Woolwich Common.*—St. John's Coll. Cam. B.A. 1843, M.A. 1847; Deac. 1844 and Pr. 1845 by Bp of Roch. 2nd Math. Mast. at the Royal Military Academy, Woolwich; Even. Lect. of Eltham, Kent. [14]

BODDY, James Alfred, *Red Bank, Manchester.*—St. John's Coll. Cam. B.A. 1838, M.A. 1842; Deac. 1838, Pr. 1839. R. of St. Thomas's, Red Bank, Dio. Man. 1844. (Patron, Bp of Man; R.'s Inc. 300*l* and Ho; Pop. 8167.) Author, *Euston Hall*, 1834, 5*s*; *The Christian Mission*, 1845, 2*s* 6*d*. [15]

BODE, George Cowling, *Great Barrington, Burford, Oxon.*—Madg. Hall, Ox. B.A. 1854, M.A. 1856; Deac. 1854 and Pr. 1856 by Bp of Ox. C. of Great Barrington 1857. Formerly C. of Westwell 1854, Kencot 1855, and Burford 1856. [16]

BODE, John Ernest, *Castle-Camps, Cambridge.*—Ch. Ch. Ox. 1st. cl. Lit. Hum. and B.A. 1837, M.A. 1840; Deac. 1841 and Pr. 1843 by Bp of Ox. R. of Castle-Camps, Dio. Ely, 1860. (Patron, Charter House, Lond; R.'s Inc. 580*l* and Ho; Pop. 901.) Formerly Tut. of Ch. Ch. 1841-47. Examiner in Lit. Hum. 1846, Select Preacher 1849, Bampton Lecturer 1855. Author, *Our Schoolboy Days viewed through the Glass of Religion* (a Sermon preached at the Charter House on Founder's Day), 1850; *Ballads from Herodotus*, 1853; *The Absence of Precision in the Formularies of the Church of England, Scriptural and Suitable to a State of Probation* (Bampton Lectures for 1855), 1855, 8*s*; *Short Occasional Poems*, 1858, 3*s*; *Hymns from Gospels*, 1860. [17]

BODEN, Edward, *The Hall, Clitheroe, Lancashire.*—St John's Coll. Cam. B.A. 1850, M.A. 1853; Deac. and Pr. 1851 by Bp of Rip. Head Mast. of the Gr. Sch. of Queen Mary and King Philip, Clitheroe, 1853. Formerly Scho. of St. John's Coll. Cam; and Vice-Prin. of Huddersfield Collegiate Sch. 1850–53. [18]

BODILY, Henry James, *St. Helena.*—St. Bees; Deac. 1853 and Pr. 1854 by Bp of Lich. R. of Longwood, St. Helena. Formerly C. of Pensnett 1859, Kingsthorpe, Northants, 1856–59, Pensnett 1853-56. [19]

BODINGTON, Alfred, *Markby, near Alford, Lincolnshire.*—St. Aidan's and Dub. A.B. 1854; Deac 1856 and Pr. 1857 by Bp of Herf. P. C. of Hannay, Dio Lin. 1864. (Patron, Rev. J. Allott; Glebe, 60 acres; P. C.'s Inc. 120*l*; Pop. 140.) Formerly C. of Little Hereford, 1856–58, Marston St. Lawrence 1858–59, Barton 1860 61, Mablethorpe 1861–63. [20]

BODY, Barnard Richard, *Trowbridge, Wilts.*—Magd. Hall Ox. M.A. 1862; Deac. 1865 by Bp of Salis. C. of Westwood, Wilts, 1867. Formerly C. of Trinity, Trowbridge, 1865–66. [21]

BODY, Elihu Edmund, *Wonersh, Guildford, Surrey.*—St. John's Coll. Cam. B.A. 1845, M.A. 1848; Deac. 1845 and Pr. 1846 by Bp of Win. V. of Wonersh, Dio. Win. 1852. (Patron, Ld Grantley; Tithe—Imp. 700*l*, V. 165*l* 13*s* 8*d*; Eccles. Commis. 26*l* 13*s* 4*d*; V.'s Inc. 210*l* and Ho; Pop. 1438.) Late 2nd Mast. and Chap. to the Clapham Gr. Sch. 1845–52. [22]

BODY, G.—C. of St. Peter's, Wolverhampton. [23]

BOGER, Edmund, *St. Saviour's Grammar School, Sumner-street, Southwark, London, S.E.*—Ex. Coll. Ox. 3rd cl. Lit. Hum. 1845, B.A. 1846, M.A. 1858; Deac. 1848 by Bp of Ox. Pr. 1855 by Bp of B. and W. Head Mast. of Queen Elizabeth's Gr. Sch. St. Saviour's, Southwark, 1859. Late P. C. of Knowle St. Giles, Somerset, 1855–59. Formerly Head Mast of the Helston Gr. Sch. 1850–55; Fell. of Ex. Coll. Ox. 1843-50. Author, *Outlines of Roman History*, 1864, 1*s* 6*d*. [24]

BOGGIS, Thomas, *Tavistock.*—Emman. Coll. Cam. B.A. 1841, M.A. 1860; Deac. 1841 and Pr. 1842 by Bp of Lon. P.C. of Sampford Spiney, Dio. Ex. 1866 (Patrons, D. and C. of Windsor; Tithe, 172*l*; Glebe, 9 acres; P. C.'s Inc. 210*l*; Pop. 150.) Formerly C. of White Colne, Sussex, 1841–47, Bourton-on-the-Water, Glouc. 1847–55, Chipping Camden 1855–57, Dursley 1857–60, Aldborough 1860–63, Landulph 1863–66. [25]

BOGIE, Brackenbury Dickson, *Bolingbroke, Spilsby, Lincolnshire.*—Dub. A.B. 1828; Deac. and Pr. 1828 by Bp of Lin. R. of Lusby, Lincolnshire, Dio. Lin. 1828. (Patron, Bp of Lin; Land in lieu of Tithe, 94 acres; R.'s Inc. 175*l*; Pop. 132.) P. C. of Asgarby, Dio. Lin. 1864. (Patron, Bp of Lin; P. C.'s Inc. 50*l* and Ho; Pop. 62.) [26]

BOGLE, Michael James.—Clare Coll. Cam. B.A. 1859; Deac. 1859 and Pr. 1860 by Abp of York. Formerly C. of St. Thomas's, Scarborough, 1859. [27]

BOISSIER, Peter Henry, *Barcheston Rectory, Shipston-on-Stour.*—Ex. Coll. Ox; Deac. 1847 and Pr. 1848 by Bp of Wor. C. (sole charge) of Barcheston 1862. Formerly C. of Leigh, Worcestershire, 1847, Turville, Bucks, 1850, Great Marlow, Bucks, 1857. [28]

BOLD, Hugh, *Llanfihangel-Tal-y-Llyn, Brecon.* Ch. Ch. Ox. B.A. 1820, M.A. 1825. R. of Llanfihangel-Tal-y-Llyn, Dio. St. D. 1822. (Patron, the present R; Tithe, 170*l*; Glebe, 18 acres; R.'s Inc. 188*l*; Pop. 149.) [29]

BOLDEN, C., *Worthenbury, Wrexham.*—C. of Worthenbury. [30]

BOLDEN, John Satterthwaite, *Rectory, Preston Bissett, near Buckingham.*—Trin. Coll. Cam. B.A. 1828, M.A. 1832; Deac. 1831 and Pr. 1832 by Bp of Ches. R. of Preston-Bissett, Dio. Ox. 1863. (Patron, the present R; Tithe, 200*l*; Glebe, 240 acres; R.'s Inc. 470*l* and Ho; Pop. 470.) Formerly C. of Dean, Lancashire, 1831; P. C. of Shireshead 1832. [1]

BOLDERO, Henry Kearney, *Grittleton, Chippenham.*—Trin. Coll. Cam. B.A. 1854. R. of Grittleton, Dio. G. and B. 1860. (Patron, Sir J. Neeld, Bart; Tithe, 400*l*; R.'s Inc. 430*l* and Ho; Pop. 361.) Formerly C. of Cirencester; R. of Yatton Keynal 1856–64. [2]

BOLDERO, John Simon, *Amblecote Parsonage, Stourbridge.*—Corpus Coll. Cam. B.A. 1856, M.A. 1859; Deac. 1855 and Pr. 1856 by Bp of Wor. P. C. of Amblecote, Dio. Wor. 1866. (Patron, Earl of Stamford; P. C.'s Inc. 100*l* and Ho; Pop. 2613.) Formerly C. of Martley, Worcestershire, 1855-57, Euville, Stourbridge, 1857–66. [3]

BOLES, James Thomas, *Ryll Court, near Exmouth, Devon.*—Ex. Coll. Ox. B.A. 1844, M.A. 1846; Deac. 1845 by Bp of G. and B. Pr. 1846 by Bp of Roch. R. of Elden, Hants, Dio. G. and B. 1864. (Patron, J. Hussey, Esq; Pop. 13.) C. of Littleham and Lect. at Exmouth. Formerly P. C. of St. Michael's, Ottery St. Mary 1846, and Chap. of Collegiate Ch. of Ottery St. Mary 1848. [4]

BOLLAND, Arthur, 4, *Frances-street, Leeds.*—Magd. Coll. Cam. B.A. 1853, M.A. 1856; Deac. 1853 and Pr. 1854 by Bp of Wor. P. C. of St. Thomas's, Leeds, Dio. Rip. 1859. (Patron, V. of Leeds; P. C.'s Inc. 230*l*; Pop. 5850.) Formerly Scho. of Magd. Coll. Cam; C. of St. Bartholomew's, Birmingham, 1853, St. Peter's, Leeds, 1855, St. Philip's, Leeds, 1856, St. Mark's, Woodhouse, 1857. Author, *The Sabbath from God*, 1856; and *The Lord is King* (a Thanksgiving Sermon for Harvest), 1861. [5]

BOLLAND, Henry, *St. James's Vicarage, Wolverhampton.*—Trin. Coll. Cam. B.A. 1853, M.A. 1856; Deac. 1853 and Pr. 1854 by Bp of Herf. V. of St. James's, Wolverhampton, Dio. Lich. 1863. (Patrons, Trustees; V.'s Inc. 300*l* and Ho; Pop. 4700.) Formerly C. of St. Mary Magdalen, Bridgnorth, 1853; Dom. Chap. to Viscount Hill 1856; C. of Trinity, Marylebone, Lond. 1861. [6]

BOLLING, Edward James, *Little Cressingham, Watton, Norfolk.*—Univ. Coll. Ox. B.A. 1850, M.A. 1853; Deac. 1853 by Bp of Man. R. of Little Cressingham, Dio. Nor. 1859. (Patroness, Mrs. Ann Baker; Tithe—App. 5*l* 14*s*, R. 365*l* 9*s* 4*d*; R.'s Inc. 400*l*; Pop. 243.) Formerly C. of Little Lever, Bolton-le-Moors. [7]

BOLTON, Augustus Charles Hope, *Shimpling Thorne, Bury St. Edmunds.*—Ch. Coll. Cam. B.A. 1847, M.A. 1851; Deac. 1848 by Bp of Nor. Pr. 1850 by Bp of Rip. R. of Shimpling Thorne, Dio. Ely, 1865. (Patron, the present R; Tithe, 620*l*; Glebe, 84 acres; R.'s Inc. 720*l* and Ho; Pop. 500.) Formerly C. of Kirkby Overblow 1849–55; P. C. of Stainburn, Yorks, 1852–55; Sen. C. of St. John's Notting Hill, Lond. 1855–64. [8]

BOLTON, Frederick Samuel, *Salt, near Stone, Staffs.*—St. John's Coll. Cam. Sen. Opt. B.A. 1839, M.A. 1842, B.D. 1849; Deac. 1841 and Pr. 1842 by Bp of Lich. P. C. of Salt, Dio. Lich. 1851. (Patron, Earl of Shrewsbury and Talbot; P. C.'s Inc. 100*l* and Ho; Pop. 808.) Late Fell. of St. John's Coll. Cam. 1840–51; Asst. Mast. of Bridgnorth Gr. Sch. 1839–50. [9]

BOLTON, Henry, *The Park, Nottingham.*—Ex. Coll. Ox. B.A. 1816, M.A. 1819; Deac. 1818, Pr. 1819. Author, *The Good of Evil, with Voice to Protestants, and suitable Prayers*, 1851, 1*s*; *Spiritual Impressions, with Job epitomised in verse*, 1*s*; *Tears Royal with Happiness, and Laylets*, 1*s*; *Grief's Relief for Mourning Christians*, 3*s*; etc. [10]

BOLTON, Horatio, *Oby Rectory, Flegg Burgh, Norfolk.*—Caius Coll. Cam. B.A. 1818, M.A. 1827; Deac. 1819 and Pr. 1821 by Bp of Nor. R. of Oby with Ashby R. and Thirne R. Dio. Nor. 1829. (Patron, Bp of Nor; Glebe, 26 acres; R.'s Inc. 690*l* and Ho; Pop. Ashby 16, Oby 80, Thirne 210.) V. of Docking, Norfolk, Dio. Nor. 1829. (Patrons, Eton Coll. and Bp of Nor; Tithe—Imp. 1114*l* 15*s*, V. 570*l*; Glebe, 58 acres; V.'s Inc. 628*l* and Ho; Pop. 1625.) [11]

BOLTON, James Beaumont, *Knowsley, Prescot.*—C. of Knowsley. [12]

BOLTON, John, *Swyre, Bridport, Dorset.*—Pemb. Coll. Cam. B.A. 1855; Deac. 1856 by Bp of Rip. Pr. 1857 by Bp of Dur. R. of Swyre, Dio. Salis. 1861. (Patron, Duke of Bedford; R.'s Inc. 150*l*; Pop. 277.) [13]

BOLTON, Richard Knott, *Newbold Parsonage, Chesterfield.*—Dub. 1st Math. and 2nd Cl. Hons. Vice-Chan. and Hebrew Prizeman, A.B. 1853, A.M. 1860; Deac. 1854 and Pr. 1855 by Bp of Lich. P. C. of Newbold with Dunstan, Dio. Lich. 1858. (Patron, V. of Chesterfield; Tithe, comm. 295*l*; P. C.'s Inc. 350*l* and Ho; Pop. 2320.) Formerly C. of Brierley Hill 1854–56, Ridgeway 1856–57, both in Dio. of Lich. [14]

BOLTON, Robert T., *Padbury, Buckingham.*—C. of Padbury and Hillesden. [15]

BOLTON, Thomas Ambler, *Stockhill House, Old Basford, Nottingham.*—Deac. 1841 by Bp of Rip. Pr. 1843 by Bp of Lin. P. C. of New Basford, Dio. Lin. 1848. (Patrons, the Crown and Bp of Lin. alt; P. C.'s Inc. 130*l*; Pop. 3241.) Formerly C. of Alverthorpe, Wakefield, 1841–42, Bawtry with Austerfield 1843–46. Author, numerous Letters (in newspapers) in defence of Church Principles; also Antiquarian Articles. [16]

BOLTON, T. De R., *Southampton.*—Min. of Zion Chapel, Southampton, 1864. Formerly C of Lunanaghan, Meath, 1857–64, Bisley, Surrey, 1864. [17]

BOLTON, William Jay, *The Grove, Stratford, Essex, E.*—Caius Coll. Cam. Hulsean Prizeman 1852, B.A. 1853, M.A. 1857; Deac. 1853 and Pr. 1854 by Bp of Ely. P. C. of St. John's, Stratford, Dio. Lon. 1866. (Patron, V. of West Ham; P. C.'s Inc. 310*l*; Pop. 6564.) Formerly C. of Ch. Ch. Cambridge, Trinity, Cheltenham, St. James's, Brighton, Chapel of Ease, Islington. Author, *Evidences of Christianity from the Early Fathers* (Hulsean Prize), 1853, 6*s*; *Fireside Preaching, Facts and Hints for Visitors of the Poor*, 1856, 2*s* 6*d*; *Footsteps of the Flock*, 1860, 3*s*; and Editor of *Selected Sermons by the late Rev. James Bolton*, 1st series, 1863, 5*s*., 2nd series, 1866, 5*s*. [18]

BOLTON, William Walter, *Frankfort-on-the-Maine.*—Chap. to the English residents at Frankfort-on-the-Maine; Dom. Chap. to Earl Cowley. [19]

BOMPAS, William Carpenter, *Fort Youcon, Canada.*—Literate; Deac. 1859 and Pr. 1861 by Bp of Lin. Formerly C. of Sutton-le-Marsh, Lincolnshire, 1859, New Radford, Nottingham, 1862, Trinity, Louth, Lincolnshire, 1863. [20]

BONAKER, William Baldwin, *Green Hill, Evesham.*—Wad. Coll. Ox. 1st cl. Lit. Hum. 2nd cl. Math et Phy. and B.A. 1807, M.A. 1810; Deac. 1809, Pr. 1810. V. of Church Honeybourne with Cow Honeybourne, Dio. Wor. 1817. (Patron, Rev. R. Poole; Church Honeybourne, Tithe—Imp. 156*l* 8*s* 2*d*, V. 91*l* 6*s* 8*d*; Glebe, 16 acres; Cow Honeybourne, Glebe, 7 acres; V.'s Inc. 258*l* and Ho; Pop. Church Honeybourne 144, Cow Honeybourne 360.) [21]

BOND, Alfred, *Freston, Ipswich.*—Trin. Coll. Cam. B A. 1849; Deac. 1851 and Pr. 1853 by Bp of Roch. R. of Freston, Dio. Nor. 1853. (Patron, the present R; Tithe, 376*l*; Glebe, 23 acres; R.'s Inc. 420*l* and Ho; Pop. 256.) [22]

BOND, Charles Watson, *Birkenhead.*—Ch. Coll. Cam. Scho. and Porteous Medallist, 16th Sen. Opt. B.A. 1862, M.A. 1866; Deac. 1862 and Pr. 1863 by Bp of Roch. C. of St. John's, Birkenhead, 1865. Formerly C. of Waltham Abbey, Essex, 1862–65. [23]

BOND, Edward Copleston, *Starcross, Exmouth.*—Ex. Coll. Ox. 2nd cl. Lit Hum. and B.A. 1846, M.A. 1851; Deac. 1849, Pr. 1850. P. C. of Starcross, Dio. Ex. 1865. (Patrons, D. and C. of Ex; Glebe, 6 acres; P. C.'s Inc. 200*l* and Ho; Pop. 800.) Formerly C. of St. Margaret's, Rochester. [24]

BOND, Frederick Hookey, *Grammar School House, Marlborough, Wilts.*—Ex. Coll. Ox. 2nd cl. Lit. Hum. and B.A. 1843, M.A. 1846; Deac. 1854 by Bp of Salis. Head Mast. of Royal Free Gr. Sch. Marlborough. Late Fell. of Ex. Coll. Ox. [1]

BOND, George, *Sutton Rectory, Coltishall, Norfolk.*—Lin. Coll. Ox. B.A. 1852, M.A. 1857; Deac. 1853 and Pr. 1854 by Bp of Rip. R. of Sutton, Dio. Nor. 1862. (Patron, Earl of Abergavenny; R.'s Inc. 300*l* and Ho; Pop. 338.) [2]

BOND, Henry, *South Petherton, Somerset.*—Ch. Coll. Cam. B.C.L. 1829; Deac. 1829, Pr. 1830. V. of South Petherton, Dio. B. and W. 1829. (Patrons, D. and C. of Bristol; Tithe—App. 155*l*, Imp. 623*l* 2*s*, V. 530*l* 2*s*; Glebe, 2¼ acres; V.'s Inc. 552*l* and Ho; Pop. 2423.) Preb. of Wells 1864; Rural Dean. [3]

BOND, John, *Anderby Rectory, Alford, Lincolnshire.*—R. of Anderby with Cumberworth R. Dio. Lin. 1865. (Patron, Magd. Coll. Cam; R.'s Inc. 620*l* and Ho; Pop. 542.) [4]

BOND, John, *Weston Vicarage, Bath.*—Wad. Coll. Ox. B.A. 1824, M.A. 1828; Deac. 1824 and Pr. 1825 by Bp of Bristol. V. of Weston with St. John's C. Dio. B. and W. 1826. (Patron, Ld Chan; Tithe—Imp. 21*l*, V. 396*l* 7*s*; Glebe, 15 acres; V.'s Inc. 500*l* and Ho; Pop. 3127.) Preb. of Cudworth in Wells Cathl. 1844; Rural Dean 1852. [5]

BOND, John.—C. of St. Mary's, St. George's-in-the-East, Lond. [6]

BOND, Nathaniel, *Creech Grange, Wareham, Dorset.*—Oriel Coll. Ox. B.A. 1829; Deac. 1831 and Pr. 1832 by Bp of Bristol. R. of Steeple with Tyneham, Dorset, Dio. Salis. 1852. (Patron, the present R; Tithe, 448*l*; Glebe, 28*l*; R.'s Inc. 565*l*; Pop. Steeple 262, Tyneham 272.) Preb. of Hurstbourne and Burbage, Salis. Cathl. 1859; Rural Dean. [7]

BOND, Richard, *Pulham, Harleston. Norfolk.*—Corpus Coll. Cam. B.A. 1829, M.A. 1832; Deac. 1831, and Pr. 1832 by Bp of Nor. R. of Pulham St. Mary-the-Virgin, Dio. Nor. 1858. (Patron, the Crown; Glebe, 30 acres; R.'s Inc. 662*l* and Ho; Pop. 863.) Formerly P. C. of Aldringham, Suffolk, 1838–57. [8]

BOND, William, *Ross, Herefordshire.*—Caius Coll. Cam. B.A. 1837, M.A. 1842; Deac. 1839 and Pr. 1840 by Bp of Pet. C. of St. Weonard's, Ross. [9]

BOND, William, *Beauchamp-Roding, near Ongar, Essex.*—Corpus Coll. Cam. B.A. 1817, M.A. 1821; Deac. 1818, Pr. 1819. R. of Beauchamp-Roding, Dio. Roch. 1839. (Patron, the present R.; Tithe—Imp. 1*l* 4*s*, R. 284*l*; Glebe, 38 acres; R.'s Inc. 300*l* and Ho; Pop. 226) [10]

BOND, William Henry, *Goldington Vicarage, Bedford.*—Queens' Coll. Cam. B.A. 1831; Deac. 1832 and Pr. 1833 by Bp of Lin. V. of Goldington, Dio. Ely, 1862. (Patron, Duke of Bedford; Tithe, 233*l* 8*s*; Glebe, 5 acres; V.'s Inc. 273*l* and Ho; Pop. 609.) Formerly C. of Great Woolstone, Bucks, 1832–41; R. of Wymington, Beds, 1834–39; P. C. of Stony Stratford, Bucks, 1841–49; V. of Stevington, Beds, 1849–62. Author, *A Concise View of Ancient Geography*, 4th ed. 1852, 4*s* 6*d*. [11]

BONE, John, *West Newton, Aspatria, Cumb.*—St. Bees; Deac. 1859 and Pr. 1856 by Bp of Win. P. C. of St. Matthew's, West Newton, Dio. Carl. 1857. (Patron, Bp of Carl; P. C.'s Inc. 100*l* and Ho; Pop. 422.) [12]

BONE, John, 4, *Hesketh-street, Southport, North Meols, Lancashire.*—King's Coll. Lond. 1st cl. in Theol. Theol. Assoc. 1861; Deac. 1861 and Pr. 1862 by Bp of Roch. C. of North Meols 1865. Formerly C. of Radwell, Herts, 1861; C. in sole charge of Poulton-le-Fylde, Lancaster, 1863. [13]

BONES, Henry Christopher, *Binsted, Arundel.*—Jesus Coll. Cam. B.A. 1854; Deac. 1856 by Bp of Nor. Pr. 1858 by Bp of Chich. R. of Binstead, Dio. Chich. 1863. (Patron, John Bones, Esq; Tithe, 187*l*; Glebe, 18 acres; R.'s Inc. 200*l* and Ho; Pop. 110.) Formerly C. of South Walsham, St. Lawrence, Norfolk, 1856; Walberton and Yapton, Sussex, 1858. [14]

BONNER, Arthur Thompson.—Lin. Coll. Ox. 1848, B.A. 1851, M.A. 1853; Deac. 1853, Pr. 1854. One of H.M.'s Inspectors of Schools. [15]

BONNER, James Tillard, *Dembleby Rectory, Folkingham, Lincolnshire.*—Lin. and New Colls. Ox. S.C.L. 1854, B.A. 1857; Deac. 1854 and Pr. 1855 by Bp of Ely. R. of Dembleby, Dio. Lin. 1856. (Patron, T. R. Buckworth, Esq; Tithe, 234*l*; Glebe, 16½ acres; R.'s Inc. 250*l* and Ho; Pop. 70) Formerly C. of Hadleigh, Suffolk, 1854–55, Sapiston, Suffolk, 1855–56. [16]

BONNETT, Stephen, *Northington, Alresford, Hants.*—Caius Coll. Cam. B.A. 1849; Deac. 1851 by Bp of Nor. Pr. 1854 by Bp of Down and Connor. C. of Northington and Swarraton. [17]

BONNEY, Thomas George, *St. John's College, Cambridge.*—St. John's Coll. Cam. 12th Wrang. 16th in 2nd cl. Cl. Trip. and B A. 1856, M.A. 1859, B.D. 1866; Deac. 1857 and Pr. 1858 by Bp of Lon. Fell. and Dean of St. John's Coll. Cam; Fell. of Geological Soc; Sec. to Philosophical and Antiquarian Socs. Formerly Math. Mast. of St. Peter's Coll. Westminster, 1856–61; C. of St. John's, Westminster, 1857–59. Translator, Pierotti's *Jerusalem Explored*, 2 vols. 1864; Pierotti's *Customs and Traditions of Palestine*, 1864. Author, *The Holy Places of Jerusalem*, 1864; *Outline Sketches in the High Alps of Dauphiné*, 4to. 1865; *Two Sermons preached in St. John's College Chapel*, 1866, The Text in *Walton's Peaks and Valleys of the Alps*, folio, 1867. [18]

BONNOR, The Very Reverend Richard Bonnor Maurice, *The Deanery, St. Asaph.*—Ch. Ch. Ox. 2nd cl. Math. et Phys. 3rd cl. Lit. Hum. B.A. 1826, M.A. 1852; Deac. 1827 and Pr. 1828 by Bp of St. A. Dean of the Dio. of St. A. 1859 (Value 700*l* and Res.) Chan. of the Dio. 1860 (Patron, Bp of St. A.); Treas. of the Dioc. Ch. Building Soc. Formerly V. of Ruabon, Denbighshire, 1842–59; Rural Dean of Wrexham 1848–59; Cursal Canon in St. Asaph Cathl. 1850–59. [19]

BONNOR, Robert Dempster, *Castle Caereinion, Welshpool.*—Trin. Coll. Cam. B.A. 1864; Deac. 1865 and Pr. 1866 by Bp of St. A. C. of Castle Caereinion 1866. Formerly C. of Holywell 1865. [20]

BONUS, Edward, *Hulcoth Rectory, Aylesbury.*—Corpus Coll. Cam. and Ox. LL.B. 1857, B.A. 1858, LL.M. 1860, M.A. 1861, Stud. at Cuddesdon; Deac. 1859 and Pr. 1860 by Bp of Ox. R. of Hulcott, Dio. Ox. 1864. (Patron, Baron de Rothschild; Glebe, 200 acres; R.'s Inc. 330*l* and Ho; Pop. 130.) C. of Buckland, Bucks (sole charge), 1859. Formerly C. of Aston Clinton, Bucks, 1862. [21]

BONWELL, James.—Deac. 1841 and Pr. 1842 by Bp of Ches. Formerly P. C. of St. Philip's, Stepney, Lon. 1845–61. Author, *Looking unto Jesus* (a Sermon to Candidates for Confirmation), Preston, 1*s*; *Perishing in the Gainsaying of Core* (a Lecture on the Swedenborgian Heresy), 1*s*; *Ministerial Engagements and Duties* (Farewell Sermon at Preston), 6*d*; *The Church, The Kingdom of God upon Earth* (Sermon for the S.P.G), 1842, 1*s*; *Sermons on the Holy Catholic Church and its Privileges*, 1844, 5*s*; *The Corruptions and Idolatry of the Church of Rome contrasted with the Pure Faith of the Church of England, with special reference to the late Schisms*, 1846, 2*s* 6*d*; *Two Pastoral Letters to his Congregation and Parishioners*, 6*d*. [22]

BOODLE, Adolphus, *Little Addington, Thrapstone, Northants.*—Caius Coll. Cam. B.A. 1840, M A. 1844; Deac. 1841 and Pr. 1842. V. of Little Addington, Dio. Pet. 1855. (Patron, the present V; V.'s Inc. 309*l* and Ho; Pop. 337.) [23]

BOODLE, John Adolphus, *West Malling, Maidstone.*—St. John's Coll. Cam. 2nd cl. Cl. Trip. and Jun. Opt. 1859, 1st cl. Theol. Trip. 1860, B.A. 1859, M.A. 1862; Deac. 1859 and Pr. 1861 by Bp of Ox. C. of West Malling 1867. Formerly C. of Buckingham, 1859–61; Tut. in St. Columba's Coll. Dublin, 1861–66. [24]

BOODLE, Richard George, *Mells, near Frome.*—Oriel Coll. Ox. 3rd cl. Lit. Hum. B.A. 1838, M.A. 1842; Deac. 1839 and Pr. 1840 by Bp of B. and W. C. of Mells 1861; English Commissary to Bp of Newcastle

1861; Dom. Chap. to Earl of Limerick 1866. Formerly C. of Compton Dando, Somerset, 1839; V. of same 1841; Incumb. of Muswell-brook, New South Wales, 1848, Morpeth, New South Wales, 1857-61; Exam. Chap. to Bp of Newcastle 1848-61; Canon of Newcastle 1856. Author, *Ways of Overcoming Temptation*, 1845, 4*d*; *The Misery of Sin*, *The Danger of Sin*, and *The Object of this Life*, three Tracts, published by Masters, London. [1]

BOODLE, Thomas, *Virginia Water, Chertsey, Surrey.*—Trin. Coll. Cam. B.A. 1830, M.A. 1834; Deac. 1831, Pr. 1832. P. C. of Ch. Ch. Virginia Water, Dio. Win. 1847. (Patrons, Trustees; P. C.'s Inc. 259*l*; Pop. 920.) [2]

BOOKER, Charles Francis, *Stanningley, Leeds.*—P. C. of Stanningley, Dio. Rip. 1864. (Patron, V. of Leeds; P. C.'s Inc. 200*l* and Ho; Pop. 2600.) [3]

BOOKER, George, 8, *Napier-road, Addison-road, Kensington, W.*—Trin. Coll. Cam. B.A. 1863; Deac. 1863 and Pr. 1864 by Bp of Lon. C. of St. Barnabas', Kensington, 1865. Formerly C. of St. Philip's, Kensington, 1863, St. Stephen's, Shepherd's Bush, 1864. [4]

BOOKER, John, *Benhilton Parsonage, Sutton, Surrey.*—Magd. Coll. Cam. B.A. 1844, M.A. 1855; Deac. 1844 and Pr. 1846 by Bp of Ches. P. C. of Benhilton, Dio. Win. 1863. (Patron, Thomas Alcock, Esq. M.P; Glebe, 1 acre; P. C.'s Inc. 200*l*; Pop. 950.) Formerly C. of Harpurhey 1844, and of Prestwich 1848, both in Lancashire, Ashurst, Kent, 1858, Litcham, Norfolk, 1859, Sevenoaks, Kent, 1862. Author, *Memorials of the Church in Prestwich*, 4to, Manchester, 1852; *A History of the Ancient Chapel of Blackley, in Manchester Parish*, 4to, ib. 1854; *Histories of the Chapels of Denton, Didsbury, Chorlton and Birch, in Manchester Parish*, 3 vols. 4to, 1855-58, privately printed in Cheetham Society's publications. [5]

BOOKER, John Kay, *South Broom, Devizes, Wilts.*—Queen's Coll. Ox. B.A. 1854, M.A. 1865; Deac. 1855 and Pr. 1856 by Bp of Ex. C. of South Broom 1863. Formerly C. of St. Mary Church, Devon, 1855-57, Dinton with Teffont, Wilts, 1857-58, Stroud 1858-59, Predon, Wor. 1859-63. [6]

BOOKER, Samuel Briddon, *Warwick.*—Jesus Coll. Cam. B.A. 1856, M.A. 1861; Deac. 1857 and Pr. 1858 by Bp of Lich. Pr. Chap. at St. Mary's, Warwick. Formerly C. of Hope, Derbyshire, 1857, Stockton Heath, Cheshire, 1859-64. [7]

BOOKER, William, *Brighouse, Normanton.*—St. Peter's Coll. Cam. B.A. 1850, M.A. 1858; Deac. 1851 and Pr. 1852 by Bp of Man. P. C. of Brighouse, Dio. Rip. 1862. (Patron, V. of Halifax; P. C.'s Inc. 230*l* and Ho; Pop. 4562.) Surrogate. [8]

BOOT, Richard Webster, *Pensnett, near Dudley.*—St. Bees; Deac. 1854 and Pr. 1855 by Bp. of Lich. P. C. of Pensnett, Dio. Lich. 1858. (Patron, Earl of Dudley; P. C.'s Inc. 150*l*; Pop. 5639.) Formerly C. of St. James's, Wednesbury. [9]

BOOTH, George Ayscough, *Clandown Parsonage, Bath.*—Ex. Coll. Ox. B.A. 1838, M.A. 1841; Deac. 1841 by Bp of Pet. Pr. 1844 by Bp of Nor. P. C. of Clandown, Dio. B. and W. 1861. (Patron, V. of Midsomer Norton; P. C.'s Inc. 22*l* and Ho; Pop. 1075.) Formerly C. of Barnack, Northants. [10]

BOOTH, H. E., *Marlborough.*—Asst. Mast. in Marlborough College. [11]

BOOTH, James, *Stone, Aylesbury, Bucks.*—Trin. Coll. Cam. B.A. 1835, M.A. 1842, LL.D. 1842; Deac. 1842 by Bp of Ex. Pr. 1842 by Abp of Cant. V. of Stone, Dio. Ox. 1859. (Patron, Royal Astronomical Soc; Tithe—Imp. 3*l*, V. 19*l*; Glebe, 100 acres; V.'s Inc. 300*l* and Ho; Pop. 1094.) Fell. of the Royal Society. Formerly Min. of St. Anne's, Wandsworth, Surrey. [12]

BOOTH, John, *Bromyard, near Worcester.*—Queens' Coll. Cam. B.A. 1827; Deac. and Pr. 1827 by Bp of Wor. P. C. of Wacton, near Bromyard, Dio. Herf. 1837. (Patron, Bp of Herf; P. C.'s Inc. 75*l*; Pop. 120.) P. C. of Stanford-Bishop, near Bromyard, Dio. Herf. 1837. (Patron, Bp of Herf; P. C.'s Inc. 75*l*; Pop. 234.) Div. Lect. of Bromyard 1838. Formerly C. of St. Edmund's, Dudley, 1827-35. Author, *A Sermon commemorative of the Third Centenary of the Reformation*, 1835. Editor, *Epigrams, Ancient and Modern*, 1863, 6*s*., 2nd ed. 1865, 7*s*. 6*d*. [13]

BOOTH, John Edmund, *Chorlton-cum-Hardy, Manchester.*—Brasen. Coll. Ox. B.A. 1843, M.A. 1851; Deac. 1843, Pr. 1844. R. of Chorlton with Hardy, Dio. Man. 1859. (Patrons, D. and C. of Man; R.'s Inc. 120*l*; Pop. 739.) Surrogate. [14]

BOOTH, Philip, *Little Wilbraham, Cambridge.*—Corpus Coll. Cam. B.A. 1826, M.A. 1829, B.D. 1836. R. of Little Wilbraham, Dio. Ely, 1848. (Patron, Corpus Coll. Cam; R.'s Inc. 350*l* and Ho; Pop. 353.) [15]

BOOTH, Thomas Willingham, *Friskney, Boston.*—Brasen. Coll. Ox. B.A. 1828; Deac. 1829, Pr. 1830. V. of Friskney, Dio. Lin. 1830. (Patron, John Booth, Esq; Tithe—Imp. 950*l*, V. 750*l*; Glebe, 9½ acres; V.'s Inc. 760*l* and Ho; Pop. 1604.) Rural Dean. [16]

BOOTHBY, Evelyn, *Whitwell, near Chesterfield.*—Univ. Coll. Ox. B.A. 1847; Deac. 1848, Pr. 1849. R. of Whitwell, Dio. Lich. 1851. (Patron, Duke of Portland; Tithe, 642*l*; Glebe, 143½ acres; R.'s Inc. 740*l* and Ho; Pop. 1487.) Formerly C. of Gosforth, Newcastle-on-Tyne, 1848-51. [17]

BOOTHBY, Henry Brooke, *Lissington Vicarage, Wragby, Lincolnshire.*—Dur. B.A. 1840; Deac. 1841 and Pr. 1842 by Abp of York. V. of Lissington, Dio. Lin. 1852. (Patrons, D. and C. of York; Tithe, 349*l*; Glebe, 56 acres; V.'s Inc. 444*l* and Ho; Pop. 240.) Formerly C. of Bishopthorpe, York; R. of Nunburnholme 1846-52. [18]

BOOTHBY, William Henry, *Hawkesbury, Chippenham.*—Corpus Coll. Cam. B.A. 1846; Deac. 1848, Pr. 1849. V. of Hawkesbury, Dio. G. and B. 1849, (Patron, Sir George Jenkinson, Bart; Tithe—Imp. 123*l* 17*s*, V. 350*l* 4*s*; Glebe, 3 acres; V.'s Inc. 350*l*, and Ho; Pop. 1599.) [19]

BOOTY, Charles S., *Hackness, near Scarborough.*—C. of Hackness. [20]

BOOTY, Miles Galloway, *Middleham Rectory, Bedale, Yorks.*—Trin. Coll. Cam. B.A. 1833, M.A. 1837; Deac. 1831 and Pr. 1832 by Bp of Ches. R. of Middleham, Dio. Rip. 1867. (Patron, the Crown; Tithe, 232*l*; Glebe, 63 acres; R.'s Inc. 460*l* and Ho; Pop. 912.) Formerly C. of Bedlington 1832, Warkworth 1835, Wensley 1839; P. C. of Coversham 1855-67. [21]

BORASTON, Gregory Birch, *Wendron, near Helston, Cornwall.*—Queen's Coll. Ox. 2nd cl. Lit. Hum. and B.A. 1824, M.A. 1828; Deac. 1826, Pr. 1827. V. of St. Wendron with Chapelry of Helston, Dio. Ex. 1837. (Patrons, Michel Visitors of Queen's Coll. Ox; Tithe—Imp. 584*l* 6*s* 6*d*, V. 877*l*; Glebe, 30 acres; V.'s Inc. 947*l* and Ho; Pop. 2914.) Late Michel Fell. of Queen's Coll. Ox. [22]

BORCKHARDT, Henry Jennings, *Burmarsh, Hythe, Kent.*—St. Peter's Coll. Cam. B.A. 1849; Deac. 1850, Pr. 1851. C. of Burmarsh. [23]

BORRISON, Louis, *Wheathampstead, St. Albans.*—St. Cath. Coll. Cam. B.A. 1865; Deac. 1866 by Bp of Roch. C. of Wheathampstead 1866. [24]

BORLAND, Robert Spencer, *Rownhams, Southampton.*—Trin. Coll. Cam. B.A. 1850, M.A. 1854; Deac. 1865 and Pr. 1866 by Bp of Win. C. of Rownhams 1865. [25]

BORLASE, William, *Zennor, St. Ives, Cornwall.*—St. Peter's Coll. Cam. B.A. 1832, M.A. 1837; Deac. 1833, Pr. 1834. V. of Zennor, Dio. Ex. 1851. (Patron, Bp of Ex; Tithe—Imp. 166*l* 18*s* 2*d*, V. 201*l* 13*s* 9*d*; Glebe, 5 acres; V.'s Inc. 220*l*; Pop. 933.) [26]

BORRADAILE, Abraham, *St. Mary's Parsonage, Vincent-square, London, S.W.*—Ch. Ch. Ox. B.A. 1836, M.A. 1839; Deac. 1838 and Pr. 1839 by Bp of Lon. P. C. of St. Mary's, Tothill-fields, Dio. Lon. 1841. (Patron, R. of St. John the Evangelist, Westminster; P. C.'s Inc. 500*l* and Ho; Pop. 6034.) [27]

BORRADAILE, Frederick, *East Hothley, Hurst Green.*—Brasen. Coll. Ox. B.A. 1820, M.A. 1824;

Deac. 1821 and Pr. 1822 by Bp of Lin. Preb. of Norton Episcopi in Lin. Cathl. 1826. (Patron, Bp of Lin.) [1]

BORRADAILE, Frederick, jun., *Bishop's Norton, Kirton-in-Lindsey, Lincolnshire.*—Trin. Coll. Cam. B.A. 1850, M.A. 1853; Deac. 1851, Pr. 1852. V. of Bishop's Norton with Atterby, Dio. Lin. 1853. (Patron, Preb. of Norton-Episcopi in Lin. Cathl; V.'s Inc. 270*l* and Ho; Pop. 459.) [2]

BORRADAILE, Robert Hudson, *Godstone Vicarage, Redhill.*—St. John's Coll. Cam. B.A. 1858; Deac. 1860 and Pr. 1861 by Bp of Win. V. of Godstone, Dio. Win. 1866. (Patron, the present V; Glebe, 8 acres; V.'s Inc. 545*l* and Ho; Pop. 1053.) Rural Dean. Formerly C. of Selworthy, Somerset, 1841–50, Lyndhurst, Hants, 1850–53; P. C. of Tandridge, Surrey, 1853–66. Author, *Village Museums*, 6*d*; *Letter Writer for the People*, 4*d*; *Notes on North Italy*, 6*d*; *Dare and Endure*, 6*d*. [3]

BORRER, Carey Hampton, *Hurstpierpoint Rectory, Sussex.*—Oriel Coll. Ox. Double Hon. 4th cl. B.A. 1836, M.A. 1840; Deac. 1838 and Pr. 1839 by Bp of Chich. R. of Hurstpierpoint, Dio. Chich. 1841. (Patron, the present R; Tithe, 1000*l*; R.'s Inc. 1000*l* and Ho; Pop. 2558.) Rural Dean; Surrogate; Chap. to Earl Manvers. Formerly C. of Cowfold, and C. of St. John's, Lewes. Author, *The Watchman of the Church* (a Visitation Sermon), 1845. [4]

BORROW, Henry John, *Lanivet, Bodmin.*—St. John's Coll. Cam. B.A. 1851; Deac. 1852, Pr. 1853. R. of Lanivet, Dio. Ex. 1862. (Patron, Rev. W. P. Flamank; R.'s Inc. 700*l* and Ho; Pop. 1151.) [5]

BORROW, William, *Higham Green, Bury St. Edmunds.*—Ex. Coll. Ox. B.A. 1854; Deac. 1854 and Pr. 1855 by Bp of Ox. V. of Higham Green, Dio. Ely, 1861. (Patron, Trin. Coll. Cam; V.'s Inc. 170*l* and Ho; Pop. 407.) [6]

BORTON, Charles, *Hartest, Bury St. Edmunds.*—R. of Hartest with Boxted R. Dio. Ely, 1853. (Patron, the Crown; R.'s Inc. 670*l* and Ho; Pop. Hartest 744, Boxted 192.) [7]

BORTON, William, *Thornton-le-Moor, Caistor, Lincolnshire.*—Caius Coll. Cam. B.A. 1832, M.A. 1835; Deac. and Pr. 1835. R. of Thornton-le-Moor, Dio. Lin. 1843. (Patron, Bp of Lin; Tithe, 315*l*; Glebe, 14 acres; R.'s Inc. 294*l*; Pop. 127.) [8]

BORTON, William Key, *Wickham St. Paul's, Halsted, Essex.*—St. Cath. Coll. Cam. B.A. 1828, M.A. 1831; Deac. 1829 and Pr. 1830 by Abp of York. R. of Wickham St. Paul's, Dio. Roch. 1835. (Patrons, D. and C. of St. Paul's; Tithe, 407*l*; Glebe, 20 acres; R.'s Inc. 437*l* and Ho; Pop. 409.) Rural Dean. Formerly C. of Kirby Misperton, Yorks, 1831–32, and Scarborough 1832–35. [9]

BORWELL, John Henry Coates, *Tregony, Cornwall.*—Queen's Coll. Ox. B.A. 1817, M.A. 1820; Deac. and Pr. 1818. V. of Tregony with Cuby, Dio. Ex. 1858. (Patron, Bp of Ex; V.'s Inc. 311*l*; Pop. 838.) Late Stip. C. of Chittlehamholt, Devonshire. [10]

BOSANQUET, Cecil, *Kirstead Rectory, Brooke, Norwich.*—Ex. Coll. Ox. B.A. 1863, M.A. 1865; Deac. 1864 and Pr. 1865 by Bp of Win. C. in sole charge of Kirstead 1867. Formerly C. of Crawley, Hants, 1864–67. [11]

BOSANQUET, Claude, *Rochester.*—V. of St. Nicholas' with St. Clement's, City and Dio. Roch. 1864. (Patron, Bp of Roch; V.'s Inc. 250*l* and Ho; Pop. 3442.) Formerly P. C. of St. Osyth, Colchester, 1861–64. [12]

BOSANQUET, Edward Stanley, *Old Bolingbroke, Spilsby, Lincolnshire.*—Trin. Coll. Cam. B.A. 1829; Deac. 1831 and Pr. 1832 by Bp of Llan. R. of Bolingbroke with Hareby R. Dio. Lin. 1841. (Patron, Sir William Smith Marriott, Bart; R.'s Inc. 600*l*; Pop. Bolingbroke 672, Hareby 93.) [13]

BOSANQUET, Edwin, *Forscote Rectory, Bath.*—Ch. Ch. Coll. Ox. B.A. 1823, M.A. 1826, *ad eund.* Cam; Deac. 1824, Pr. 1825. R. of Forscote, Dio. B. and W. 1846. (Patron, Sir Greville S. Smyth, Bart; Tithe, 106*l*; Glebe, 40 acres; R.'s Inc. 150*l* and Ho; Pop. 46.) Author, *Paraphrase on St. Paul's Epistle to the Romans*, 1840. [14]

BOSANQUET, Robert William, *Rock, near Alnwick, Northumberland.*—Ball. Coll. Ox. 2nd cl. Lit. Hum. and B.A. 1821, M.A. 1829; Deac. 1823 and Pr. 1824 by Bp of Lon. Formerly R. of Bolingbroke, Lincolnshire. [15]

BOSCAWEN, The Hon. John Townshend, *Lamorran, Truro.*—Magd. Coll. Cam. B.A. 1845, M.A. 1852; Deac. 1847, Pr. 1849. R. of Lamorran, Dio. Ex. 1849. (Patron, Viscount Falmouth; Tithe, 153*l*; Glebe, 42½ acres; R.'s Inc. 198*l* and Ho; Pop. 92.) Chap. to Earl of Falmouth. [16]

BOSCAWEN, William Henry, *Marchwiel Rectory, Wrexham.*—Magd. Hall Ox. B.A. 1845; Deac. 1846 and Pr. 1848 by Bp of Herf. R. of Marchwiel, Dio. St. A. 1867. (Patron, Bp of St. A; R.'s Inc. 760*l* and Ho; Pop. 536.) Surrogate; Rural Dean of Wrexham, and Dioc. Inspector of Schools. Formerly C. of Brampton Brian, Herefordshire, 1846, Hanmer, Flintshire, 1848. V. of same 1850–67. Author, *The Church's Work in extensive Parishes, Illustrated by Plans, etc. of Mission Houses*, 1*s*. [17]

BOSTOCK, James, *Barnslee, near Leek.*—St. John's Coll. Cam. B.A. 1829, M.A. 1832; Deac. 1829 by Bp of Lich. Pr. 1831 by Bp of Ches. P. C. of Wincle, Dio. Ches. 1832. (Patron, V. of Prestbury; P. C.'s Inc. 130*l*; Pop. 375.) Formerly C. of Horton, near Leek, 1830–31, Findon, Sussex, 1834–35. [18]

BOSWELL, James Philip, 445, *Mile End-road, London, E.*—Caius Coll. Cam. B.A. 1865; Deac. 1865 and Pr. 1866 by Bp of Lon. C. of Trinity, Stepney, 1865. [19]

BOSWORTH, Joseph, *Islip House, near Oxford.*—Univ. of Aberdeen M.A. and LL.D; Leyden M.A. and Ph. D; Trin. Coll. Cam. B.D. 1834, D.D. 1839; Deac. 1814, Pr. 1815. R. of Water Stratford, near Buckingham, Dio. Ox. 1858. (Patron, Bp of Ox; R.'s Inc. 400*l* and Ho; Pop. 179.) Prof. of Anglo-Saxon at the Univ. of Ox. 1858. Late V. of Waithe, Lincolnshire, 1840–58; formerly V. of Horwood Parva, Bucks, 1817–29; British Chap. at Amsterdam 1829–32, at Rotterdam 1832–40. Fell. of the Royal Society and of the Society of Antiquaries; Member of the Royal Institute of the Netherlands; Hon. F.R.S. of Sciences, Norway; F.S.A. of Copenhagen; Fell. of Lit. Socs. of Leyden, Utrecht, Rotterdam, Bristol, and Newcastle-on-Tyne. Author, *The Elements of Anglo-Saxon Grammar, with Notes*, London, 1823, 20*s*; *The Practical Means of Reducing the Poor's Rate*, 1824, 1*s* 6*d*; *A Compendious Grammar of the Primitive English, or Anglo-Saxon, Language*, 1826, 6*s*; *The Necessity of the Anti-Pauper System*, 1829, 2*s*; *Misery in the Midst of Plenty, or the Perversion of the Poor Laws*, 1833, 1*s*; *An Introduction to Latin Construing*, 6 eds. 1846, 2*s* 6*d*; *Latin Construing, with Rules for Translating Latin into English*, 5 eds. 1850, 2*s* 6*d*; *Dictionary of the Anglo-Saxon Language*, 1838, 42*s*; *The Contrast, or the Operation of the Old Poor Laws contrasted with the recent Poor Law Amendment Act*, 1838, 2*s*; *The Book of Common Prayer, English and Dutch*, Amsterdam, 1838, and S.P.C.K; *A Sermon on the Necessity of Humility*, preached at Rotterdam, 1838, 1*s*; *The Origin of the Danish and an Abstract of Scandinavian Literature*, London, 1838, 5*s*; *The Origin of the Dutch, with a Sketch of their Language and Literature*, 2 edits. 1838 and 1846, 5*s*; *The Origin of the English, Germanic and Scandinavian Languages and Nations, with a Sketch of their Language*, 1838 and 1848, 20*s*; *The Book of Common Prayer, arranged in the Direct Order in which the Prayers are used in the Morning and Evening Services*, 1839; *The Essentials of Anglo-Saxon Grammar*, 1841, 4*s*; *The Rudiments of Greek Grammar as used in the College of Eton*, 5 edits. 1842, 4*s*; *A Compendious Anglo-Saxon Dictionary*, 1848, 12*s*; *King Alfred's Anglo-Saxon Version of the Historian Orosius*, 1855, 16*s*; *The same, in Anglo-Saxon only*, 8*s*; *The same, in English only*, 8*s*; *A Description of Europe, and the Voyages of Othere and Wulfstan, written by King Alfred in Anglo-Saxon, with an English Translation, Notes and Map*, 1855, 5*s*; Two other editions of the last-mentioned; *A Description of Europe, Asia, Africa, and the Voyages of Others and Wulfstan, in fac-simile*, 4to. 52s 6d; *The History of the Lauderdale Manuscript of Orosius*, 1858. [1]

BOUCHER, Alfred Francis, *The Heath House, Cheddleton, Leek, Staffs.*—St. Peter's Coll. Cam. B.A. 1842, M.A. 1845; Deac. 1843, Pr. 1844. P. C. of Cheddleton, Dio. Lich. 1852. (Patrons, Mrs. Greenwood and others; Tithe, 14*l*; Glebe, 102 acres; P. C.'s Inc. 200*l*; Pop. 2050.) [2]

BOUCHER, Henry, *Thornhill House, Sturminster, Blandford, Dorset.*—Wad. Coll. Ox. B.A. 1819, M.A. 1821; Deac. 1820, Pr. 1821. Formerly V. of Hilton, Dorset, 1821–38. [3]

BOUCHER, James, *Exmouth.*—Wor. Coll. Ox. B.A. 1834, M.A. 1837; Deac. 1835, Pr. 1836. C. of Littleham and Exmouth. Formerly C. of Colyton Rawleigh. [4]

BOUCHER, John Sidney, *N.W. Training College, Carnarvon.*—St. John's Coll. Cam. Scho. Exhib. and Prizeman of, B.A. 1843, M.A. 1851; Deac. 1845 and Pr. 1846 by Bp of Lich. Prin. of N.W. Training Coll. Carnarvon, 1865. Formerly C. of Condover, Salop, 1845; Fell. and Tut. of St. Peter's Coll. Radley, 1849; Head Mast. of St. Paul's Gr. Sch. Knightsbridge, 1852, and of Hamilton-square Sch. Birkenhead, 1857; late 2nd Mast. of the King's Sch. Warwick, 1855. Author, *Mensuration, Plain and Solid*; *Analysis of Grecian, Roman, English, European, and Bible History*; *Ancient Greek and Latin Myths*; *Junior Greek and Latin Grammars*; *Practical Geometry*; *Trigonometry made Easy*; *Jesuitism in the Church*, sub vasto Genevæ; *The Who, When, and Where of Anti-Christ*; *Rationale upon Secession to Rome, Dissent, and Atheism*; *The Deficient Supply of well-qualified Clergy at the present time fully accounted for*; *Episcopal Ordination, or Miracles the Ministerial Warrant*; *Graphiology*; *The Best Means of Counteracting Dissent*; *St. Paul's Thorn in the Flesh*; *Choral Service, the Law of the Church of England*; etc. [5]

BOUDIER, Albert, *St. Mary's Vicarage, Warwick.*—Emman. Coll. Cam. Chap to Warwick Union; Dom. Chap. to Earl of Warwick. [6]

BOUDIER, George John, *Ewhurst Rectory, Hurst Green.*—King's Coll. Cam. B.A. 1844, M.A. 1848; Deac. 1844 and Pr. 1845 by Bp of Lin. R. of Ewhurst, Dio. Chich. 1863. (Patron, King's Coll. Cam; Tithe, 850*l*; Glebe, 30 acres; R.'s Inc. 900*l* and Ho; Pop. 1043.) Fell. of King's Coll. Cam. Formerly C. of St. Mary's, Warwick, 1844–46, Houghton-le Spring, 1848–50; Chap to the Army at Scutari and before Sebastopol and Kertch, Dec. 1854 to July, 1856; and Chap. to the Forces 1856–58. [7]

BOUDIER, John, *Vicarage, Warwick.*—Sid. Coll. Cam. B.A. 1809, M.A. 1813; Deac. 1809, Pr. 1810. V. of St. Mary's, Warwick, Dio. Wor. 1815. (Patron, Ld Chan; Tithe—Imp. 305*l*; V.'s Inc. 300*l* and Ho; Pop. 3526.) Hon. Can. Wor. Cathl; Rural Dean; Surrogate. Author, *Plain and Practical Sermons*, 1818, 9s; *Attendance on Daily Public Worship the Christian's Duty*, 1854, 6d; *Congregational Psalmody and Church Choirs*, 1857, 6d; *The Two Holy Sacraments of the Christian Church necessary to Salvation*, 1859, 1s. [8]

BOUGHEY, R., *Stoke-upon-Trent.*—C. of Stoke. [9]

BOUGHTON-LEIGH, Egerton Leigh Boughton Ward, *Harborough-Magna, Rugby.*—Trin. Coll. Cam. B.A. 1849, M.A. 1852; Deac. 1850 and Pr. 1851 by Bp of Wor. C. of Harborough-Magna. [10]

BOUGHTON-LEIGH, Theodosius Ward, *The Vicarage, Newbold-on-Avon.*—Trin. Coll. Cam. B.A. 1846, M.A. 1849; Deac. 1847 and Pr. 1848 by Bp of Nor. V. of Newbold-on-Avon with Long Lawford C. Dio. Wor. 1852. (Patron, John Ward Boughton-Leigh, Esq; Tithe—Imp. 303*l* 16s 10½d, V. 96*l* 6s 7¾d; Glebe, 185 acres; V.'s Inc. 690*l* and Ho; Pop. 1169.) [11]

BOULBY, Adam, *Aislaby, Whitby.*—C. of Aislaby. [12]

BOULGER, John, *Pennant Eglwysfach, near Llanrwst, Denbighshire.*—Ch. Ch. Ox. 3rd cl. Lit. Hum. 1811, B.A. 1813, M.A. 1816; Deac. 1813, Pr. 1814. [13]

BOULTBEE, James, *Wrangthorn, Leeds.*—King's Coll. Lon. Theol. Assoc; Deac. 1852, Pr. 1853. P. C. of Wrangthorn. [14]

BOULTBEE, R. Moore, B.D., *Iver Lodge, Uxbridge.* [15]

BOULTBEE, Thomas, *Salford, near Evesham.*—Deac. 1824, Pr. 1825. V. of Bidford, Warwickshire, Dio. Wor. 1830. (Patron, the present V; Tithe, 3*l* 4s; Glebe, 60 acres; V.'s Inc. 240*l*; Pop. 1565.) [16]

BOULTBEE, Thomas Pownall, *St. John's Hall, Highbury Park, London, N.*—St. John's Coll. Cam. 5th Wrang. Fell. of St. John's, B.A. 1841, M.A. 1844; Deac. 1844 and Pr. 1845 by Bp of Ely. Prin. of the London College of Divinity. Formerly Theol. Tut. and Chap. Cheltenham Coll. 1852–63. Author, *The Young Traveller to an Eternal Home*; *Chronicles of Ancient Faith*; *Rubrical and Canonical Reform*; and sundry Sermons. [17]

BOULTON, William, *Grammar School House, Wem, Salop.*—Ch. Ch. Ox. B.A. 1828, M.A. 1830; Deac. 1831 and Pr. 1833 by Bp of Herf. C. of Wem; Head Mast. of Wem Gr. Sch. 1839; P. C. of Lee Brockhurst, Dio. Lich. 1855. (Patron, J. Walford, Esq; Tithe—Imp. 68*l*; P. C.'s Inc. 66*l*; Pop. 133.) [18]

BOULTON, William Henry, *Aughton Rectory, near Ormskirk.*—Trin. Coll. Ox. B.A. 1831, M.A. 1834; Deac. 1831, Pr. 1832. R. of Aughton, Dio. Ches. 1834. (Patron, Col. Tempest; Tithe, comm. 800*l*; Rent from Glebe, 106*l*; R.'s Inc. 906*l* and Ho; Pop. 1869.) Formerly C. of Tarporley, Cheshire, 1831-34. [19]

BOURCHIER, Charles Spencer, *Great Hallingbury, Bishops Stortford.*—St. John's Coll Cam. B.A. 1812, M.A. 1838; Deac. 1814, Pr. 1815. V. of Sandridge, Herts, Dio. Roch, 1823. (Patron, Earl Spencer; Tithe—Imp. 753*l* 3s, V. 300*l*; V.'s Inc. 300*l* and Ho; Pop. 833.) R. of Great Hallingbury, Dio. Roch. 1838. (Patron, J. A. Houblon, Esq; Tithe, 720*l*; Glebe, 58 acres; R.'s Inc. 781*l* and Ho; Pop. 675.) Chap. to the Earl of Plymouth. [20]

BOURCHIER, Walter, *Sibford, Banbury.*—New Coll. Ox. B.A. 1860, M.A. 1863; Deac. 1863 by Bp of Win. Pr. 1864 by Bp of Ox. P. C. of Sibford, Dio. Ox. 1864. (Patron, New Coll. Ox; P. C.'s Inc. 250*l*; Pop. 800.) Formerly C. of Beaulieu, Hants, 1863–64. [21]

BOURDILLON, Francis, *Woolbeding Rectory, Midhurst, Sussex.*—Emman. Coll. Cam. Scho. and Prizeman, B.A. 1845, M.A. 1849; Deac. 1845 and Pr. 1846 by Bp of Ely. R. of Woolbeding, Dio. Chich. 1855. (Patroness, Hon. Mrs. Ponsonby; Tithe, 286*l*; Glebe, 26½ acres; R.'s Inc. 300*l* and Ho; Pop. 338.) Formerly V. of St. Mary's, Huntingdon, 1846–49; P. C. of Shipley, Sussex, 1849–51; P. C. of Trinity, Runcorn, Cheshire, 1851–54. Author, *Short Sermons for Family Reading*, 1860, 3s 6d, 2nd series, 1866, 3s 6d; *Bedside Readings*, 1864, 2s; 2nd series, 1866, 2s; and various Tracts. [22]

BOURKE, Cecil F. J., *Newbury, Berks.*—Corpus Coll. Ox. B.A. 1864, M.A 1867; Deac. 1865 and Pr. 1866 by Bp of Ox. C. of Newbury 1865. [23]

BOURKE, Hon. George Wingfield, *Coulsdon Rectory, Croydon.*—Univ. Coll. Dur. B.A. 1855, M.A. 1856; Deac. 1856 by Bp of Man. Pr. 1857 by Bp of Dur. R. of Coulsdon, Dio. Win. 1866. (Patron, Abp of Cant; Tithe, 858*l*; Glebe, 84 acres; R.'s Inc. 930*l* and Ho; Pop. 993.) Chap. to Abp of Cant. Formerly C. of Alnwick; R. of Wold Newton, Lincolnshire, 1858–66. [24]

BOURKE, Thomas, *Hyde, near Manchester.*—Dub. A.B. 1854; Deac. 1858 and Pr. 1859 by Bp of Ex. C. of St. Paul's, Gee Cross, Werneth, near Manchester, 1860. Formerly C. of Sampford Courtenay, Devon, 1858–60. [25]

BOURKE, Thomas Negus, *Appledore Vicarage, Staplehurst, Kent.*—St. Cath. Coll. Cam. Scho. and Cl. and Math. Prizeman, B.A. 1848; Deac. 1848 and Pr. 1849 by Abp of Cant. V. of Appledore with Ebony C. Dio. Cant. 1862. (Patron, Abp of Cant; Tithe, 184*l* 15s 2d;

Glebe, 14 acres; V.'s Inc. 270*l* and Ho; Pop. 824.) Formerly C. of Wye, Hythe, Trinity, Dover, St. Stephen's, Tonbridge, and Paddlesworth, all in Dio. of Cant. [1]

BOURLAY, Joseph Henry, *Frankley Rectory, Birmingham.*—Magd. Hall, Ox. B.A. 1856, M.A. 1858; Deac. 1857 and Pr. 1858 by Bp of Wor. R. of Frankley, Dio. Wor. 1866. (Patron, Lord Lyttelton; Pop. 132.) C. of Bartley Green. Formerly C. of All Saints', Evesham, 1857, Culford, Suffolk, 1863, Bartley Green 1865. [2]

BOURNE, Cornelius Alexander, *Fulstow, Louth, Lincolnshire.*—Deac. 1851 and Pr. 1852 by Bp of Nor. V. of Fulstow, Dio. Lin. 1860. (Patron, H. Allenby, Esq; V.'s Inc. 216*l* and Ho; Pop. 577.) Formerly C. of Lowestoft 1851, Mablethorpe 1854, Lutterworth 1860. [3]

BOURNE, George Drinkwater, *Weston-sub-Edge, Broadway, Chipping Campden, Glous.*—Oriel Coll. Ox. B.A. 1842, M.A. 1846; Deac. 1845 and Pr. 1846 by Bp of Ches. R. of Weston-sub-Edge, Dio. G. and B. 1846. (Patroness, Mrs. Peter Bourne; Tithe, 775*l*; Glebe, 70 acres; R.'s Inc. 900*l* and Ho; Pop. 369.) [4]

BOURNE, G. H., *Sandford, Oxford.*—C. of Sandford. [5]

BOURNE, John George, *Castle-Donington (Leicestershire), near Derby.*—Corpus Coll. Cam. B.A. 1846, M.A. 1849; Deac. 1846, Pr. 1847. V. of Castle-Donington, Dio. Pet. 1852. (Patron, Marquis of Hastings; Tithe, 1*l* 6*s* 5*d*; V.'s Inc. 246*l* and Ho; Pop. 2445.) Chap. to the Shardlow Union, Derbyshire. [6]

BOURNE, Joseph, *Broom, Kidderminster.*—R. of Broom, Dio. Wor. 1858. (Patron, Joseph Green Bourne, Esq; Tithe, 224*l* 1*s* 6*d*; Glebe, 53 acres; R.'s Inc. 337*l*; Pop. 118.) Formerly C. of Eatham, Cheshire. [7]

BOURNE, Robert Burr, *Donhead St. Andrew, near Salisbury.*—Ch. Ch. Ox. 2nd cl. Lit. Hum. 1820, B.A. 1821, M.A. 1823; Deac. 1826, Pr. 1827. R. and V. of Donhead St. Andrew, Dio. Salis. 1856. (Patron, the present R; Tithe, 691*l*; Glebe, 184 acres; R.'s Inc. 900*l* and Ho; Pop. 830.) Formerly C. of Grimley, Worcestershire, 1849–56. Author, *The Dangers of the Excuses commonly made for not Attending the Sacrament of the Lord's Supper* (Two Sermons). [8]

BOURNE, Samuel Whitbread, *Winfarthing, near Diss, Norfolk.*—Queens' Coll. Cam. B.A. 1850; Deac. 1850 and Pr. 1851 by Bp of Nor. C. (sole charge) of Winfarthing. Author, *Parochial Tracts on the New Year*, 1856. [9]

BOURNE, Thomas, *Stoke-Golding, Hinckley, Leicestershire.*—St. Edm. Hall, Ox. B.A. 1841, M.A. 1865; Deac. 1841, Pr. 1842. P. C. of Stoke-Golding with Dadlington, Dio. Pet. 1865. (Patrons, D. and C. of Westminster; P. C.'s Inc. 360*l*; Pop. 661.) Formerly C. of Stoke Golding and Mast. of Stoke-Golding Gr. Sch. [10]

BOUSFIELD, Alfred, *Ratley, Banbury.*—Queens' Coll. Cam. 1st Jun. Opt. and B.A. 1852, 1st in Nat. Sci. Trip. 1853, M.A. 1867; Deac. and Pr. 1854 by Bp of Wor. V. of Ratley, Dio. Wor. 1862. (Patron, Ld Chan; V.'s Inc. 150*l* and Ho; Pop. 476.) [11]

BOUSFIELD, George Benjamin Richings, 20, *Vineyards, Bath.*—St. Edm. Hall, Ox. B.A. 1847; Deac. 1847; and Pr. 1848 by Bp of Nor. Formerly C. of Carleton Rode, Norfolk, 1847–52, Swaffham 1852–53. [12]

BOUSFIELD, Henry Brougham, *Winchester.*—Caius Coll. Cam. Jun. Opt. B.A. 1855; M.A. 1858; Deac. 1855 and Pr. 1856 by Bp of Win. R. of Maurice, with St. Mary Kalendar (no ch.), Winchester, Dio. Win. 1864. (Patron, Bp of Win; R.'s Inc. 180*l*; Pop. 1982) Formerly C. of All Saints', Braishfield, Hants, 1855; P. C. of same 1856–61. [13]

BOUSFIELD, Henry Newham.—Queens' Coll. Cam. B.A. 1832; Deac. 1832, Pr. 1833. C. of St. Barnabas', Harvest-road, Islington. Formerly C. of St. Michael's, Stockwell. Author, *Sermon of one Syllable*, 12mo. [14]

BOUSFIELD, William, *Cublington, near Leighton Buzzard.*—Lin. Coll. Ox. 4th cl. Lit. Hum. and B.A. 1842, M.A. 1845; Deac. 1842 and Pr. 1843 by Bp of Ox. R. of Cublington, Dio. Ox. 1853. (Patron, Lin. Coll. Ox; Glebe, 200 acres; R.'s Inc. 347*l* and Ho; Pop. 288.) Formerly Fell. of Lin. Coll. Ox. [15]

BOUSTEAD, Thomas, *Kirby-Grindalyth, Malton, Yorks.*—St. John's Coll. Cam. Sen. Opt. and B.A. 1827, M.A. 1833; Deac. 1827, Pr. 1828. V. of Kirby-Grindalyth with Sledmere P. C. 1833. (Patron, Sir Tatton Sykes, Bart, Sledmere; Kirby-Grindalyth, Tithe—App. 40*l*, Imp. 253*l* 19*s* 11*d*, V. 84*l* 9*s* 2*d*; Glebe, 66 acres; V.'s Inc. 245*l*; Pop. Kirby-Grindalyth 570, Sledmere 486.) [16]

BOUTELL, Charles, *Penge, Surrey, S.E.*—Trin. Coll. Ox. M.A. 1836; Deac. 1837 by Bp of Ely, Pr. 1839 by Bp of Lon. Formerly C. of Hemsby, Norfolk, and Sandridge, Herts. Author, *Monumental Brasses and Slabs*, 1847, 25*s*; *Monumental Brasses of England and Wales*, 1849, 28*s*; *Christian Monuments in England and Wales*, 1854, 12*s* 6*d*; *Manual of British Archæologia*, 1854, 10*s* 6*d*; *Heraldry Historical and Popular*, 3rd edit. 1865, 21*s*; *Elementary English Heraldry*, 1867; *The First Church*, 1867, 1*s*. [17]

BOUTFLOWER, Charles William Marsh, *Dundry, Bristol.*—St. John's Coll. Cam. B.A. 1841, M.A. 1844; Deac. 1842 and Pr. 1843 by Bp of Win. P. C. of Dundry, Dio. B. and W. 1855. (Patron, V. of Clun Magna; Tithe—App. 200*l*, Imp. 15*l*; Glebe, 50 acres; P. C.'s Inc. 100*l* and Ho; Pop. 556.) [18]

BOUTFLOWER, Douglas John, *H.M.S. "Wolverine."*—Ch. Coll. Cam. Sen. Opt 2nd cl. Cl Trip. and B.A. 1849, M A. 1852, *ad eund.* Ox. 1853; Deac. 1852 and Pr. 1853 by Bp of Ex. Chap. of H.M.S. "Wolverine." [19]

BOUTFLOWER, Samuel Peach, *Old Brathay, Ambleside, Westmoreland.*—St. John's Coll. Cam. 22nd Wrang. B.A. 1838, M.A. 1841; Deac. 1838 and Pr. 1839 by Bp of Ches. P. C. of Brathay, Dio. Carl. 1856. (Patrons, Rev. J. Marriner, Clapham, Yorks, and two others; P. C.'s Inc. 140*l*; Pop. 422.) Hon. Can. of Carl. 1865; Rural Dean and Surrogate. Formerly C. of Coniston 1838, Seaforth 1842. [20]

BOUVERIE, Edward, *Coleshill, Faringdon, Berks.*—Ch. Ch. Ox. B.A. 1804, M.A. 1807; Deac. 1806 by Bp of Salis. Pr. 1807 by Bp of Win. V. of Coleshill, Dio. Ox. 1808. (Patron, Earl of Radnor; Tithe—Imp. 400*l*, V. 350*l* 10*s*; Glebe, 17 acres; V.'s Inc. 375*l* and Ho; Pop. 464.) Chap. in Ordinary to the Queen 1819; Preb. of Preston in Salis. Cathl. 1826. (Value, 23*l*.) [21]

BOUVERIE, Frederick William Bryon, *St Paul's, Aberdeen.*—College Bourbon, Paris, B. ès L. 1846; Deac. 1850 and Pr. 1851 by Bp of Win. Incumb. of St. Paul's, Aberdeen, 1858 (Stipend, 300*l*.) Formerly C. of St. Peter Fort and Chap. to Gaol, Guernsey. 1850–58. Author, *Life and its Lessons*, Seeleys; *Force et Faiblesse*, and other works in French, Guernsey; *Herbert Lovell*, and Short Stories, Hogg and Sons; *What is Truth?* Grant, Edinburgh. [22]

BOUVERIE, The Ven. William Arundell, *Denton Rectory, Harleston, Norfolk.*—Ch. Ch. Ox. B.A. 1817, Mert. Coll. Ox. M.A. 1820, B.D. 1829; Deac. 1821 and Pr. 1822 by Bp of Ox. R. of Denton, Dio. Nor. 1839. (Patron, Abp of Cant; Tithe, 761*l*; Glebe, 92 acres; R.'s Inc. 813*l* and Ho; Pop. 518.) Hon. Can. of Nor. Cathl. 1847; Archd. of Norfolk, 1850 (Value, 200*l*.) Late Fell. of Mert. Coll. Ox; and R. of West Tytherly, Hants, 1829–39. Author, *Charges to the Clergy and Churchwardens of the Archdeaconry of Norfolk.* [23]

BOUWENS, Theodore, *Stoke Hammond, Fenny-Stratford, Bucks.*—Mert. Coll. Ox. B.A. 1820, M.A. 1823. R. of Stoke-Hammond, Bucks, Dio. Ox. 1823. (Patron, Bp of Ox; R.'s Inc. 313*l* and Ho; Pop. 401.) R. of St. Mary's, Bedford, Dio. Ely, 1826. (Patrons, Bp of Lin. 2 turns, Ball. Coll. Ox. 1 turn; R.'s Inc. 300*l* and Ho; Pop. 1869.) Preb. of Brampton in Lin. Cathl. 1823 (Value, 40*l*). [24]

BOWCOTT, Richard, *Llanllwni, New Inn, Carmarthenshire.*—Deac. 1848, Pr. 1849. V. of Llanllwni with Llanfihangel Rhosycorn C. Dio. St. D. 1853. (Patron, Bp of St. D; Llanllwni, Tithe—App. 237*l* and 86 acres of Glebe; Llanfihangel Rhosyoorn, Tithe—App. 163*l* 9*s*; V.'s Inc. 158*l* and Ho; Pop. Llanllwni 776, Llanfihangel Rhosyoorn 634.) [1]

BOWDEN, Charles Edward, *Malvern Link.*—King's Coll. Lon. and St. John's Coll. Cam. B.A. 1855, M.A. 1860; Deac. 1855 and Pr. 1856 by Bp. of Ex. Formerly C. of St. Peter's, Vauxhall, 1864–65. [2]

BOWDEN, Ellis Treacher, *Rochford (Herefordshire), near Tenbury, Worcestershire.*—Late Scho. of St. Cath. Coll. Cam. B.A. 1853; Deac. 1853 and Pr. 1854 by Abp of Cant. R. of Rochford, Dio. Herf. 1857. (Patron, James P. Jones, Esq; R.'s Inc. 400*l*; Pop. 315.) Formerly C. of St. Mary's, Barnard's Green, Worcester. [3]

BOWDEN, James, *Staunton Rectory, near Gloucester.*—Univ. Coll. Ox. 2nd cl. Math. and B.A. 1856, M.A. 1858; Deac. 1858 and Pr. 1859 by Bp of Win. R. of Staunton, Dio. Wor. 1861. (Patron, J. Ford Sevier, Esq; Tithe, 385*l*; Rent from Glebe, 125*l*; R.'s Inc. 510*l* and Ho; Pop. 508.) Formerly C. of Crawley, near Winchester, 1858–61. [4]

BOWDEN, John, *Oakengates, Wellington, Shropshire.*—P. C. of Oakengates, Dio. Lich. 1861. (Patron, Bp of Lich; P. C.'s Inc. 89*l*; Pop. 1821.) [5]

BOWDEN, J., *Rokeby, Barnard Castle, Durham.*—R. of Rokeby, Dio. Rip. 1866. (Patron, Ld Chan; Tithe, 152*l*; Glebe, 5 acres; R.'s Inc. 162*l* and Ho; Pop. 180.) [6]

BOWDEN, Robert, *Stoke-Gabriel, Totnes, Devon.*—Wad. Coll. Ox. B.A. 1841; Deac. 1842, Pr. 1843. V. of Stoke-Gabriel, Dio. Ex. 1845. (Patrons, Sir S. H. Northcote, Bart. Exors. of the late Rev. J. Templar and John Belfield, Esq. alt; Tithe, 297*l* and 46 acres of Glebe, V. 128*l*; V.'s Inc. 198*l*; Pop. 622.) [7]

BOWDEN-SMITH, Frederick Hermann, *Fawley, Southampton.*—Trin. Coll. Ox. B.A. 1863, M.A. 1867; Deac. 1864 and Pr. 1866 by Abp of Cant. C. of Fawley 1867. Formerly C. of Marden, Kent, 1864–67. [8]

BOWDITCH, William Renwick, *Wakefield.*—St. Peter's Coll. Cam. B.A. 1843; Deac. 1843, Pr. 1844. P. C. of St. Andrew's, Wakefield, Dio. Rip. 1845. (Patrons, the Crown and Bp of Rip. alt; P. C.'s Inc. 152*l*; Pop. 2118.) Author, *Answer to Dr. Pusey's Sermon on the Eucharist*, 1*s*; *Church-rates, and what is given in return for them*, 4*d*; *Prize Essay on the Chemical Changes in the Fermentation of Manure*, Royal Agricultural Soc. 1855. [9]

BOWEN, Arthur J., *Winchester.*—C. of St. Thomas's, Winchester. Formerly C. of St. Mark's, Peterborough. [10]

BOWEN, Charles, *St. Mary's Rectory, Chester.*—St. Peter's Coll. Cam. B.A. 1833; Deac. 1835, Pr. 1836. R. of St. Mary-on-the-Hill, with Upton C. City and Dio. of Ches. 1856. (Patron, Marquis of Westminster; Tithe, 399*l* 15*s*; R.'s Inc. 490*l* and Ho; Pop. 4583.) Surrogate. Formerly P. C. of Revesby, Lincolnshire, 1851–56. Author, various Sermons. [11]

BOWEN, Charles James, *Thurgoland, Sheffield.*—P. C. of Thurgoland, Dio. Rip. 1865. (Patron, V. of Silkstone; P. C.'s Inc. 200*l* and Ho; Pop. 1783.) Formerly P. C. of St. Mary's, Bungay, 1861–65. Author, *Essays for the Times*, Longmans. [12]

BOWEN, Christopher, *St. Thomas's Rectory, Winchester.*—Dub. A.B. 1824, A.M. 1831; Deac. and Pr. 1825 by Bp of Killaloe. R. of St. Thomas's with St. Clement's, City and Dio. Win. 1855. (Patron, Bp of Win; Tithe, 60*l*; R.'s Inc. 198*l* and Ho; Pop. 4738.) Formerly C. of Bath Abbey 1838–43; P. C. of St. Mary Magdalen's, Southwark, 1843–55. Author, *Things to Come Practically Inquired into*, 1849; *Apostolic Resolve in Ministerial Difficulty*, 1853; *Suggestions respecting Church-rates*, 1855; *Esther, Sermon on the Marriage of the Prince of Wales*, 1863; *Heart-work essential to Personal Religion*, 1865. [13]

BOWEN, Craufurd Townshend, *Guisborough, Yorks.*—St. Bees; Deac. 1859 and Pr. 1860 by Abp of York. C. of Guisborough. [14]

BOWEN, Edward Charles Jackson, *Wickham Skeith, Stonham, Suffolk.*—Trin. Coll. Cam; Deac. 1861, Pr. 1862. C. of Wickham Skeith 1864. Formerly C. of Sparsholt, Berks, 1862–64. [15]

BOWEN, Jeremiah, *Walton Lewes, Wisbeach.*—All Souls Coll. Ox. B.A. 1825; Deac. 1825 by Bp of Ox. Pr. 1827 by Bp of Lich. R. of Walton Lewes, Dio. Nor. 1863. (Patron, Rev. C. Hare Townshend; R.'s Inc. 802*l*; Pop. 950.) Formerly C. of Mucklestone with Woore, Staffs, 1825, Hanford, Staffs, 1828; R. of West Lynn 1830. Author, *The Translation and Circulation of the Holy Scriptures, the True Cause of the Reformation in England*, 1836; *The Resurrection Defended against the Objections of the Mental Improvement Society*, 1838; *The Ministerial Gift conveyed by Ministerial Succession*, 1840; *Familiar Conversations on Infant Baptism; Circumcision and Baptism, the Signs and Seals of one and the same Covenant*; *The Call of Abraham*, 1847; *The Peace Society and the Militia Act*, 1852; *The War Abroad and the Church at Home*, 1854; *Revivalism*, 1859; *The Power of the Keys*; and *The Athanasian Creed*, 1860; Reviews, etc. [16]

BOWEN, John, *Newport, Monmouthshire.*—C. of Gelligaer Charity Schools Chapel, Newport. [17]

BOWEN, Percival, *Claughton Rectory, Lancaster.*—All Souls Coll. Ox. B.A. 1826, M.A. 1829; Deac. 1826 and Pr. 1827 by Bp of Lin. R. of Claughton in Lonsdale, Dio. Man. 1863. (Patrons, Trustees of late Thomas Fenwick, Esq; Tithe, comm. 150*l*; Glebe, 14 acres; R.'s Inc. 200*l* and Ho; Pop. 85.) Formerly Head Mast. of Sheffield Gr. Sch. 1831–63. [18]

BOWEN, William Clement, *Llanstinan Rectory, Haverfordwest.*—Late Scho. of Lampeter; Deac. 1840 by Bp of St. D. Pr. 1842 by Bp of Llan. R. of Llanstinan, Dio. St. D. 1847. (Patron, Bp of St. D; Tithe, 163*l*; R.'s Inc. 168*l* and Ho; Pop. 172.) C. of Hayscastle 1862. Formerly C. of Jordanston. [19]

BOWEN, W., Chaplain Royal Navy. [20]

BOWEN, William W. Webb, *Camrhôs, Haverfordwest.*—V. of Camrhôs, Dio. St. D. 1833. (Patron, H. W. Bowen, Esq; V.'s Inc. 100*l* and Ho; Pop. 1126.) [21]

BOWER, Anthony, *Grammar School House, Caistor, Lincolnshire.*—St. John's Coll. Cam. 10th Wrang. and B.A. 1846, M.A. 1849; Deac. 1851 and Pr. 1852 by Bp of Ely. Head Mast. of Caistor Gr. Sch. 1853. Late Fell. of St. John's Coll. Cam. [22]

BOWER, Charles Uppleby, *Grammar School, Walsall.*—St. John's Coll. Cam. Jun. Opt. B.A. 1860, M.A. 1865; Deac. and Pr. 1864 by Bp of Lich. 2nd Mast. of Gr. Sch. and C. of St. Paul's, Walsall, 1864. Formerly Asst. Mast. in Durham and Manchester Gr. Schs. [23]

BOWER, Edward, *Closworth, Sherborne, Somerset.*—Jesus Coll. Cam. B.A. 1824, M.A. 1828; Deac. 1825, Pr. 1826. R. of Closworth, Dio. B. and W. 1828. (Patron, Lord Portman; Tithe, 205*l*; Glebe, 11¾ acres. R.'s Inc. 206*l* and Ho; Pop. 184.) [24]

BOWER, Everard Hollier Spring, *Potterne, Devizes.*—Clare Coll. Cam. B.A. 1853; Deac. 1854, Pr. 1855. C. of Potterne. Formerly C. of Cucklington, Somerset. [25]

BOWER, George Henry, *Rossington, Doncaster.*—Trin. Coll. Cam. B.A. 1823, M.A. 1828; Deac. 1826 and Pr. 1827 by Abp of York. R. of Rossington, Dio. York, 1833. (Patron, James Brown, Esq; Tithe, 600*l*; Glebe, 65 acres; R.'s Inc. 665*l* and Ho; Pop. 400.) Formerly C. of Ganton, Yorks, 1828–30, Burythorpe 1830–34. [26]

BOWER, George Whitehead, *Newton Moor, near Manchester.*—Deac. 1822, Pr. 1823. P. C. of St. Mary's, Newton-Moor, Dio. Ches. 1839. (Patron, V. of Mottram; P. C.'s Inc. 150*l* and Ho; Pop. 5416.) Author, *Sermons*, 1836, 10*s*; *An Address to Adult Persons desirous of being Baptised*, 6*d*; *A Tract on Confirmation*, 2*d*; *Rules and Order of Instruction for a National Sunday School*, 2*d*; *An Address, chiefly directed to those who occupy Influential Stations in Life*, 6*d*. [27]

BOWER, Henry Tregonwell, *Fontmell Parva, Blandford, Dorset.*—St. Peter's Coll. Cam. B.A. 1831, M.A. 1834; Deac. 1832, Pr. 1833. C. of West Orchard, Dorset. [1]

BOWER, James, *Atherton, Manchester.*—C. of Atherton. Formerly C. of Newton-in-Makerfield. [2]

BOWER, James Henry, *Newnham, Sittingbourne, Kent.*—Ex. Coll. Ox. B.A. 1836, M.A. 1864; Deac. 1837 and Pr. 1839 by Bp of Salis. V. of Newnham, Dio. Cant. 1841. (Patron, the present V; Tithe, 115l; V.'s Inc. 145l and Ho; Pop. 409.) [3]

BOWER, John, *Lostwithiel, Cornwall.*—Ex. Coll. Ox. B.A. 1808, M.A. 1815; Deac. 1809 and Pr. 1812 by Bp of Ex. V. of Lostwithiel, Dio. Ex. 1816. (Patron, the present V; Tithe, 40l 5s 6d; Glebe, ½ acre; V.'s Inc. 100l; Pop. 1017.) [4]

BOWER, Robert Smith, 4, *Furnival's-inn, Holborn, London, W.C.*—Jesus Coll. Cam. B.A. 1828; Deac. 1828 and Pr. 1829 by Bp of B. and W. R. of St. Mary Magdalen's with St. Gregory's-by-St. Paul R. City and Dio. of Lon. 1845. (Patrons, D. and C. of St. Paul's; Fire Act Commutation, R. 200l; R.'s Inc. 240l; Pop. St. Mary Magdalen 732, St. Gregory 1154.) [5]

BOWERS, George Henry, *Boxley, Maidstone.*—Emman. Coll. Cam. B.A. 1860, M.A. 1864; Deac. 1861 and Pr. 1862 by Bp of B. and W. C. of Boxley 1863. Formerly C. of Westbury, near Wells, 1861–63. [6]

BOWERS, The Very Rev. George Hull, *Deanery, Manchester.*—Clare Coll. Cam. B.D. 1829, D.D. 1849; Deac. and Pr. 1819. Dean of Manchester 1847 (Value 2000l and Ho.) Select Preacher before the Univ. of Cam. 1830. Formerly R. of St. Paul's, Covent-garden, Lond. 1831–48. Author, *Sermons* (preached in Covent-garden Church), 1849; *Scheme for the Foundation of Schools for the Sons of Clergymen and others,* 1842. Founder, conjointly with the late Rev. E. Plater, of Marlborough Coll. Wilts. [7]

BOWERS, Thomas Smallwood, *Kirkstall Parsonage, near Leeds.*—Dub A.B. 1847, A.M. 1854; Deac. 1854 and Pr. 1855 by Bp of Rip. P. C. of Kirkstall, Dio. Rip. 1858. (Patrons, Trustees of Leeds Parish Ch; P. C.'s Inc. 320l and Ho; Pop. 8345.) Formerly Aft. Lect. of Leeds Parish Ch. 1854–56; and Clerk in Orders of same 1856–58. [8]

BOWES, George Seaton, *Tonbridge Wells.*—Corpus Coll. Cam. B.A. 1848; Deac. 1848 and Pr. 1849 by Bp of Win. Formerly R. of Chillenden, Kent, 1858–67. Author, *Illustrative Gatherings,* 1st and 2nd Series, 5s each. [9]

BOWKER, Henry Charles, *Christ's Hospital, London, E.C.*—Emman. Coll. Cam, 25th Wrang. and B.A 1862; Deac. 1864 and Pr. 1865 by Bp of Lon. Asst. Mast. in Christ's Hospital. Formerly Asst. C. of St. Mary's, Whitechapel, 1864–66. [10]

BOWLAN, William, 7, *Bentinck Crescent, Newcastle-on-Tyne.*—Dub. A.B. 1854, A.M. 1857; Deac. 1854 and Pr. 1855 by Bp of Ches. Chap. to the Newcastle Union 1863. [11]

BOULBY, Charles Edward, *Castle-Eaton Rectory, Fairford, Wilts.*—St. John's Coll. Cam. B.A. 1853, M.A. 1858; Deac. 1856 and Pr. 1857 by Bp of Roch. R. of Castle-Eaton, Dio. G. and B. 1863. (Patron, the present R; Tithe, 585l 10s; Glebe, 89 acres; R.'s Inc. 835l 10s and Ho; Pop. 286.) Late Scho. of St. John's Coll. Cam; R. of Stanwick, Northants, [illegible]–63. [12]

BOWLBY, Henry Bond, *Oldbury, near Birmingham.*—Wad. Coll. Ox. late Fell. of, B.A. 1844, M.A. 1849; Deac. 1846 by Bp of Ox. Pr. 1847 by Bp. of Dur. P. C. of Oldbury, Dio. Wor. 1850. (Patron, V. of Hales Owen; Glebe, 3 acres; P. C.'s Inc. 300l; Pop. 9780.) Author, *Lectures on the Resurrection of the Flesh,* [illegible], 4s 6d. [13]

BOWLES, Charles Bradshaw, *Woking, Surrey.*—[illegible] Coll. Ox. B.A. 1828, M.A. 1831; Deac. 1830, Pr. [illegible]. R. of Wisley with Pyrford, Dio. Win. 1866. (Patrons, Earl Onslow; Wisley, Tithe, 120l 10s; Glebe, 57 acres; Pyrford, Tithe, 78l 16s 10d; Glebe, 12 acres; R.'s Inc. [illegible] and Ho; Pop. Wisley 166, Pyrford 381.) Rural Dean 1850; Chap. to Earl Onslow 1831. Formerly V. of Woking 1837–66. [14]

BOWLES, Charles James Stillingfleet, *The Shrubbery, Great Malvern.*—Wad. Coll. Ox. B.A. 1842; Deac. 1843 and Pr. 1844 by Bp of Pet. C. of Malvern Link. Formerly C. of Towcester and of Budbrooke; P. C. of St. Barnabas', Warmley, Bristol, 1851; British Chap. at Malaga, Spain, 1863–64. [15]

BOWLES, Francis Alfred, *Singleton, near Chichester.*—Magd. Hall, Ox. B.A. 1837, M.A. 1840; Deac. 1837, Pr. 1838. R. of Singleton, Dio. Chich. 1849. (Patron, Duke of Richmond; Tithe—App. 501l, R. 115l; Glebe, 36 acres; R.'s Inc. 145l; Pop. 556.) [16]

BOWLES, George Cranley, *East Thorpe, Kelvedon, Essex.*—St. John's Coll. Cam. M.A. 1862 by Abp of Cant; Deac. and Pr. 1841 by Bp of Ches. R. of East Thorpe, Dio. Roch. 1844. (Patrons, Col. Onslow's Trustees; Tithe, 274l 9s; Glebe, 27 acres; R.'s Inc. 314l and Ho; Pop. 144.) Author, *An Address to the Soldiers of the 7th Fusileers.* [17]

BOWLES, George Downing, *Wendlebury Rectory, Bicester.*—Ch. Ch. Ox. Stud. of, B.A. 1849, M.A. 1852; Deac. 1850 by Bp of Ox. Pr. 1851 by Bp of Pet. R. of Wendlebury, Dio. Ox. 1866. (Patron, Ch. Ch. Ox; R.'s Inc. 270l and Ho; Pop. 237.) Formerly C. of Ravensthorpe 1850, Farthinghoe 1851 and 1863, Thenford 1854. [18]

BOWLES, Henry Albany, *Merrow, Guildford.*—St. John's Coll. Ox. B.A. 1841, M.A. 1844; Deac. 1842 and Pr. 1843 by Bp of Lon. R. of Merrow, Dio. Win. 1851. (Patron, Earl Onslow; Tithe, 250l; R.'s Inc. 250l; Pop. 370.) [19]

BOWLES, Henry Matthew John, *Gloucester.*—Dub. A.B. 1846, A.M. 1851, M.A. Ox. *ad eund.* 1856; Deac. 1851 by Bp of Llan. Pr. 1852 by Bp of G. and B. R. of St. Aldate's, City and Dio. Gloucester, 1867. (Patron, Bp of G. and B; Q. Anne's Bounty 47l 8s 2d; Glebe, 170l; R.'s Inc. 217l 8s 2d; Pop. 710.) Formerly C. of St. John's, Cheltenham, 1851–54; R. of Framilode, Glouc. 1854–67. [20]

BOWLES, Joseph, *Stanton-Lacey, Ludlow, Salop.*—Magd. Hall. Ox. 2nd cl. Lit. Hum. B.A. 1835, M.A. 1836, LL.D. 1837, D.D. 1841; Deac. 1836 and Pr. 1837 by Bp. of Lin. V. of Stanton-Lacey, Dio. Herf. 1847. (Patron, Earl of Craven; Tithe—Imp. 375l 9s 2d, V. 484l 12s; V.'s Inc. 564l and Ho; Pop. 1598.) Chap. of the D. of Sandford, Ox. 1838; Dom. Chap. to the Duchess of Inverness; Provincial Grand Master of the Freemasons of Herefordshire. Formerly R. of Stoke, Ox. 1837–38; R. of Woodstock, Ox. 1841–47; Chap. to H.R.H. the late Duke of Sussex 1838. Author, *Elegy on the Death of the Princess Charlotte; Monody on the Death of Sir John Throckmorton; Letters in Vindication of the Appointment of the Bishop of Hereford,* etc. [21]

BOWLES, Samuel James, *Beaconsfield, Bucks.*—Magd. Coll. Ox. B.A. 1848, M.A. 1851; Deac. 1852 and Pr. 1855 by Bp of Ox. Fell. of Magd. Coll. Ox. 1855. R. of Beaconsfield, Dio. Ox. 1867. (Patron, Magd. Coll. Ox; Tithe, 867l; Glebe, 8½ acres; R.'s Inc. 880l and Ho; Pop. 1662.) Formerly C. of Baltonsborough 1859–67. [22]

BOWLES, Thomas, *Milton Hall, Abingdon.*—Queen's Coll. Ox. B.A. 1846, M.A. 1850; Deac. 1848 by Bp of G. and B. Pr. 1849 by Bp of Salis. C. of Garsington. Formerly Incumb. of the Temporary Ch. Grafham, Surrey, 1854–59. [23]

BOWLES, William, *Erpingham Rectory, Norwich.*—Corpus Coll. Cam. B.A. 1849; Deac. 1849 and Pr. 1850 by Bp of Nor. C. of Erpingham 1859. Formerly C. of Tunstead 1849–58. [24]

BOWLEY, James William Lyon, *Bristol.*—Bp Hatfield's Hall, Dur. Barry Scho. and Licen. Theol. 1854; Deac. 1854 and Pr. 1855 by Bp of Win. V. of St. Philip and St. Jacob's, Bristol, Dio. G. and B. 1864. (Patrons, Trustees; V.'s Inc. 350l and Ho; Pop. 6500.) Formerly Chap. of Royal Naval Female School, Isleworth, Middlesex; C. of St. Barnabas', South Kennington, Lond. 1854–58. Author, *England's Mercies, England's Warning* (a Sermon), 1856. [25]

BOWLING, William, *Cosheston, Pembroke.*—Jesus Coll. Ox. B.A. 1829, M.A. 1831; Deac. 1829 and Pr. 1830 by Bp of Salis. R. of Loveston, Dio. St. D. 1830. (Patron, Baron de Rutzen; Tithe, 90*l* 10*s*; Glebe, 2 acres; R.'s Inc. 95*l*; Pop. 122.) R. of Cosheston, Dio. St. D. 1842. (Patron, G. Bowling, Esq; Tithe, 252*l*; R.'s Inc. 255*l*; Pop. 602.) R. of Yerbeston, Dio. St. D. (Patron, Baron de Rutzen; R.'s Inc. 138*l*; Pop. 118.) [1]

BOWMAN, Charles Henry. *Welshpool.*—Ch. Ch. Ox. B.A. 1858; Deac. 1865 and Pr. 1866 by Bp of St. A. C. of Welshpool 1865. [2]

BOWMAN, Edmund Burkitt, *Tidcombe Parsonage, near Marlborough, Wilts.*—Queens' Coll. Cam. B.A. 1851; Deac. 1851 and Pr. 1853 by Bp of Win. P. C. of Tidcombe, Dio. Salis. 1862. (Patrons, D. and C. of Windsor; Tithe—App. 480*l* 12*s* 6*d*; Glebe, 47 acres; P. C.'s Inc. 71*l* 10*s* and Ho; Pop. 90.) Formerly C. of Verulam Chapel, Kennington, 1851–54, St. John's, Horselydown, 1855–56; *pro. tem.* Chap. of St. Mary's Hospital, Paddington, 1857; C. of Chelmondeston, Suffolk (sole charge), 1857–58, St. James's, Oldham, 1858–59, Broad Chalke, Wilts (sole charge), 1859–61, Bulford, Amesbury, Wilts (sole charge), 1862–63. [3]

BOWMAN, Edward, *Croglin Rectory, Penrith, Cumberland.*—St. Bees; Deac. 1817 and Pr. 1818 by Bp of Ches. R. of Croglin, Dio. Carl. 1848. (Patron, Rev. J. H. Green; R.'s Inc. 320*l* and Ho; Pop. 54.) [4]

BOWMAN, Edward Lawson, *H.M.S. "Trafalgar."*—St. Peter's Coll. Cam. B.A. 1847; Deac. 1848, Pr. 1849. Chap. of H.M.S. "Trafalgar." [5]

BOWMAN, Isaac, *Burneside Parsonage, Kendal.*—Trin. Coll. Cam. B.A. 1854; Deac. 1854 and Pr. 1855 by Bp of Pet. C. of Burneside 1865. [6]

BOWMAN, Isaac, *Walton, near Carlisle.*—Literate; Deac. 1822 and Pr. 1823 by Bp of Ches. P. C. of Walton, Carlisle, Dio. Carl. 1854. (Patron, Joseph Dacre, Esq; Tithe—Imp. 197*l*, P. C. 27*l* 16*s*; Glebe, 94 acres; P. C.'s Inc. 125*l* and Ho; Pop. 407.) Rural Dean. [7]

BOWMAN, Thomas, *Clifton, Bristol.*—Dub. A.B. 1848, A.M. 1861; Deac. 1851 and Pr. 1852 by Bp of Ches. C. of St. Stephen's, Bristol, 1867. Formerly C. of St. Saviour's, Liverpool, 1851–56; Chap. to the Mayor of Bristol 1861–62. Author, *Catechism of Biblical Antiquities*, 1848, 2*s*; *Questions Adapted to Hall's Elementary Atlas*, 1850, 2*s*; *Questions on McLeod's Class Atlas of Physical Geography*, 1857, 1*s*. [8]

BOWNESS, George, *Orton, Westmoreland.* [9]

BOWNESS, John, *Northallerton, Yorks.*—Deac. 1821, Pr. 1822. Head Mast. of Northallerton Gr. Sch. Formerly Chap. to the North Riding Gaol, Yorks, 1824–56. [10]

BOWSTEAD, John, *St. Olave's Rectory, Southwark, London, S.E.*—St. John's Coll. Cam. Sen. Opt. 3rd cl. in Cl. Trip. B.A. 1832, M.A. 1835; Deac. 1834 and Pr. 1835 by Bp of Lin. R. of St. Olave's, Southwark, Dio. Win. 1862. (Patron, the Crown; R.'s Inc. 600*l*; Pop. 6197.) Preb. of Lincoln. Formerly V. of Messingham, Lincolnshire. Author, *Practical Sermons*, 2 vols. 1836; *The Village Wake*, 1846; *Regeneration not Salvation*, a letter to Mr. Spurgeon, 1864; and various single Sermons. [11]

BOWSTEAD, Joseph, *Etherley, Bishop Auckland, Durham.*—Queen's Coll. Ox. B.A. 1853, M.A. 1856; Deac. 1854 by Bp of Dur. Pr. 1855 by Bp of Man. C. of Etherley 1861. Formerly C. of Alston, Cumberland, 1854–57, Whickham, Gateshead, 1857–60. [12]

BOWSTEAD, Thomas, *Poulton Manor House, Cricklade, Wilts.*—Literate; Deac. 1817 and Pr. 1818 by Bp of Lin. Formerly P. C. of Poulton 1849. [13]

BOWYEAR, Thomas Kyrwood, *Harbledown, Canterbury.*—Caius Coll. Cam. Scho. of, B.A. 1833, M.A. 1837; Deac. 1834 and Pr. 1835 by Abp of Cant. R. of Harbledown, Dio. Cant. 1865. (Patron, Abp of Cant; Tithe, 385*l*; Glebe, 10 acres; R.'s Inc. 410*l* and Ho; Pop. 680.) Formerly C. of Hartlip; R. of Halstead, Kent, 1847–65. [14]

BOWYER, James, *Romford, Essex.*—Bishop's Coll. Calcutta, 1825–29; Deac. 1833 and Pr. 1835 by Bp of Calcutta. C. of Fobbing. Formerly Catechist in S. P. G. Missions, near Calcutta, 1829–33; in charge of Barripore and Howrah Missions, near Calcutta, 1833–43. [15]

BOWYER, John, *Spital, near Chesterfield.* [16]

BOWYER, William Henry Wentworth Atkins, *Clapham, Surrey, S.W.*—Brasen. Coll. Ox. S.C.L. 1831; Deac. 1832 by Bp of Lon. Pr. 1833 by Bp of Lich. R. of Clapham, Dio. Win. 1847. (Patron, H. A. Bowyer, Esq; Tithe, 500*l*; Glebe, 11 acres; R.'s Inc. 270*l* and Ho; Pop. 5650.) [17]

BOX, William George, *Metheringham, Sleaford, Lincolnshire.*—St. Bees, 1855; Deac. 1858 and Pr. 1859 by Bp of Win. C. of Metheringham. Formerly C. of St. Andrew's, Lambeth, 1858, St. Luke's, Lower Norwood, 1858; Hon. Chap. of Foreigners' Almshouses, Norwood, 1859; C. of Long Melford, Suffolk, 1859, Wixoe, Suffolk (sole charge), 1861, Hendon, Middlesex, 1862, St. Mary's-the-Less, Lambeth, 1864. [18]

BOYCE, Edward Jacob, *Houghton Rectory, Stockbridge, Hants.*—Trin. Coll. Cam. Sen. Opt. and B.A. 1840, M.A. 1843; Deac. 1840, Pr. 1841. R. of Houghton, Dio. Win. 1865. (Patron, Bp of Win; Glebe, 50 acres; R.'s Inc. 615*l* and Ho; Pop. 420.) Formerly C. of Holyrood, Southampton, 1840–41, Godalming, Surrey, 1841–47; V. of Godalming 1847–65. Author, *Parochial Sermons*, 2nd edit. 6*s*. [19]

BOYCE, Henry Le Grand.—Wor. Coll. Ox. B.A. 1834, M.A. 1840; Deac. 1838, Pr. 1839. Formerly C. of Oving, Aylesbury. [20]

BOYCE, John Cox.—Magd. Hall, Ox. B.A. 1854, M.A. 1859; Deac. 1853 by Bp of Lon. Pr. 1855 by Bp of Wor. Formerly C. of St. Mathias', Bethnal Green, 1853, Aston 1854, Walton-le-dale 1856, Topcliffe 1856–64; P. C. of Marton-le-Moor 1859–64. Author, *The Ground of Hope*, 1859, 2*s* 6*d*; *Pastoral Counsels*, 5*s*. [21]

BOYCE, Thomas White, *Clifton.*—Sid. Coll. Cam. Sen. Opt. and B.A. 1842; Deac. 1842, Pr. 1843. C. of St. Werburgh's, Bristol, 1856. Formerly P. C. of Danehill, Sussex, 1852–56. [22]

BOYCE, William, *Sandford-road, Cheltenham.*—Trin. Coll. Cam. B.A. 1845, M.A. 1848; Deac. 1846 and Pr. 1847 by Bp of G. and B. Mast. in Cheltenham Coll. [23]

BOYCOTT, William, *Wheatacre-Burgh (Norfolk), near Beccles, Suffolk.*—Magd. Coll. Ox. B.A. 1820, M.A. 1820; Deac. 1821, Pr. 1822. R. of Wheatacre-Burgh, Dio. Nor. 1829. (Patron, the present R; Tithe, 374*l*; Glebe, 16 acres; R.'s Inc. 400*l* and Ho; Pop. 298.) [24]

BOYD, Archibald, 13, *Sussex-gardens, Paddington, London, W.*—Trin. Coll. Cam. B.A. 1823, M.A. 1834. P. C. of Paddington, Dio. Lon. 1859. (Patron, Bp of Lon; P. C.'s Inc. 1200*l*; Pop. 5817.) Hon. Can. of Gloucester Cathl. 1857; Rural Dean. Formerly P. C. of Ch. Ch. Cheltenham, 1842–59. [25]

BOYD, Charles Twining, *Newport Pagnell, Bucks.*—Univ. Coll. Ox. B.A. 1865; Deac. 1866 by Bp of Lich. C. of Newport Pagnell, 1867. Formerly C. of All Saints', West Bromwich, 1866. [26]

BOYD, Francis Bacon, *Burghfield Rectory, Reading.*—Ch. Ch. Ox. B.A. 1858, M.A. 1862; Deac. 1861, Pr. 1862. R. of Burghfield, Dio. Ox. 1865. (Patron, Earl of Shrewsbury; Glebe, 13 acres; R.'s Inc. 1017*l* and Ho; Pop. 1139.) [27]

BOYD, Frederick, *Holwell Rectory, Hitchin.*—R. of Holwell, Beds, Dio. Ely, 1865. (Patron, F. D. Radcliff, Esq; R.'s Inc. 120*l* and Ho; Pop. 191.) [28]

BOYD, Henry, *Victoria Dock, Plaistow, Essex, E.*—Ex. Coll. Ox. B.A. 1853, M.A. 1856; Deac. 1854, Pr. 1856. P. C. of St. Mark's, Victoria Dock, Dio. Lon. 1863. [29]

BOYD, John William.—C. of St. Barnabas', West Kensington. [30]

BOYD, William, *Arncliffe, Skipton, Yorks.*—Univ. Coll. Ox. B.A. 1831, M.A. 1833; Deac. 1834, Pr. 1835. V. of Arncliffe, Dio. Rip. 1835. (Patron, Univ.

Coll. Ox. Tithe—Imp. 494*l* 0*s* 6*d*; Glebe, 28 acres; V.'s Inc. 74*l* and Ho; Pop. 320.) Rural Dean of North Craven; Hon. Can. of Rip. [1]

BOYD, William Frederick, *Clipstone Hospital, near Northampton.*—Trin. Coll. Ox. B.A. 1844, M.A. 1846; Deac. 1844 and Pr. 1845 by Bp of Ex. Head Mast. and Chap. of Clipstone Sch. and Hospital 1864. (Stipend, 100*l* and Ho.) Formerly C. of St. Paul's, Malmesbury, 1854–64. [2]

BOYDELL, Edward Neville Valentine, *Wingate Vicarage, Ferry Hill, Durham.*—Univ. Coll. Dur. Licen. Theol. 1840; Deac. 1840 and Pr. 1841 by Bp of Rip. V. of Wingate, Dio. Dur. 1843. (Patron, Bp of Dur; V.'s Inc. 210*l* and Ho; Pop. 1995.) Formerly C. of Bellerby, Yorks, 1840–42. Author, *Teetotalism and Temperance*; *The Patriotic Fund*; *Wrecks on the Eastern Coast*; *The Great Fire*, 1861; *A Few Observations, Illustrations, and Anecdotes Respecting Pitmen in a Northern Colliery Village*, 1862; *The Rock Forsaken*, 1863; and *Jesus at the Grave of Lazarus*, 2nd ed. 1867. [3]

BOYDEN, Henry, *Gosford-place, Highgate, Birmingham.*—Dub. A.B. 1867; Deac. 1856 and Pr. 1857 by Bp of Rip. P. C. of St. David's, Birmingham, Dio. Wor. 1866. (Patrons, Trustees; P. C.'s Inc. 300*l*; Pop. 9000.) Formerly, C. of St. Mary's, Honley, 1856–58; C. of St. Mary's 1858–64, St. George's 1865, and St. Luke's, Birmingham, 1865. Author, *Ministers of Health*, 2*s*; *Energy, a Lecture to Working Men*, 3*d*; *Counsel and Caution*, 3*d*; *Submission*, a Funeral Sermon; *Songs for the Household, Sacred and Secular*, 3*d*. [4]

BOYER, Richard, *Sywell House, Northampton.*—Trin. Coll. Cam. B.A. 1847, M.A. 1850; Deac. 1848 and Pr. 1849 by Bp of Pet. Formerly C. of Potterspury, Northants, 1848–51; R. of Northleigh, Honiton, Devon, 1861–64. [5]

BOYER, R. B., *Penarth, Cardiff.*—Chap. of Missions to Seamen, Penarth. [6]

BOYLE, George David, *Kidderminster.*—Ex. Coll. Ox. B.A. 1851, M.A. 1853; Deac. 1853, Pr. 1854. V. of Kidderminster, Dio. Wor. 1867. (Patron, Earl of Dudley; Tithe, 800*l*; Glebe, 150 acres; V.'s Inc. 1000*l* and Ho; Pop. 16 855.) Formerly C. of Kidderminster 1853–57, Hagley 1857-60; P. C. of St. Michael's, Handsworth, 1861–67. [7]

BOYLE, R. A. *Long Sutton, Wisbeach.*—C. of Long Sutton. [8]

BOYLE, Hon. Richard Cavendish, *Marston Rectory, Frome, Somerset.*—Ch. Ch. Ox. B.A. 1833, M.A. 1834; Deac. 1835, Pr. 1836. R. of Marston Bigot, Dio. B. and W. 1836. (Patron, Earl of Cork and Orrery; Tithe, 254*l*; Glebe, 46¾ acres; R.'s Inc. 323*l* and Ho; Pop. 369.) Chap. in Ordinary to the Queen 1847; Rural Dean. [9]

BOYNTON, Griffith, *Barmston Rectory, Hull.*—R. of Barmston, Dio. York, 1860 (Patron, Sir H. Boynton, Bart; R.'s Inc. 1160*l* and Ho; Pop. 206.) [10]

BOYS, Charles, *Wing, Uppingham, Rutland.*—Mert. Coll. Ox. B.A. 1833, M.A. 1836; Deac. and Pr. 1835. R. of Wing, Dio. Pet. 1839. (Patron, Ld Chan; Glebe. 140 acres; R.'s Inc 330*l* and Ho; Pop. 342.) Formerly V. of Shalford, Essex, 1835–39. [11]

BOYS, Edward, *Oakley, Thame, Bucks.*—V. of Oakley, Dio. Ox. 1864. (Patrons, Reps. of late Sir T. W. Aubrey; V.'s Inc. 270*l*; Pop. 420.) [12]

BOYS, James, *Biddenden, Staplehurst, Kent.*—Wad. Coll. Ox. B.A. 1815, M.A. 1818; Deac. 1816, Pr. 1817. R. of Biddenden, Dio. Cant. 1841. (Patron, Abp of Cant; Tithe, 572*l* 14*s* 6*d*; Glebe, 19¾ acres; R.'s Inc. 580*l* and Ho; Pop. 1412.) [13]

BOYS, The Ven Markby J. T.—P.C. of All Saints', Clapham-park, Dio. Win. 1865. (Patrons, Trustees; P. C.'s Inc. 550*l* and Ho; Pop. 3474.) Formerly Archd. of Bombay. [14]

BOYS, Thomas, 4, *Ashley-crescent, City road, London, N.*—P. C. of Trinity, Hoxton, Dio. Lon. 1848. (Patron, Bp of Lon; P. C.'s Inc. 290*l*; Pop. 18,911.) [15]

BOYS, Thomas James, *Ivychurch, Romney, Kent.*—C. of Ivychurch. [16]

BOYS, William James, *Egremont House, Delamere-terrace, London, W.*—King's Coll. Cam. Fell. of, B.A. 1861, M.A. 1864; Deac. 1861 and Pr. 1862 by Bp of Lin. C. of Trinity, Paddington, 1866. Formerly C. of St. John's, Leeds, 1861–64, Bakewell, Derbyshire, 1864–66. [17]

BRACE, Edmund C., *All Saints', Knightsbridge, London, W.*—C. of All Saints', Knightsbridge. [18]

BRACKENBURY, Algernon Charles, *Upton, Gainsborough.*—V. of Upton, Dio. Lin. 1858. (Patron, W. Cracroft-Amcotts, Esq; Glebe, 121 acres; V.'s Inc. 131*l* and Ho; Pop. 527.) Formerly C. of Great Coates, near Grimsby, Lincolnshire. [19]

BRACKENBURY, John Matthew, *Wimbledon, Surrey, S. W.*—St. John's Coll. Cam. B.A. 1838, M.A. 1841; Deac. 1841 and Pr. 1842 by Bp of Nor. Head Mast. of Wimbledon Sch. Formerly C. of St. Mary Magdalen, near Downham, Norfolk, 1841–43; Asst. Mast. of Marlborough Coll. 1843–49. [20]

BRADBURNE, Charles R., *Sheriff Hales, Newport, Shropshire.*—C. of Sheriff Hales. Formerly C. of Burton-on-Trent. [21]

BRADBURY, Walter.—Queens' Coll. Cam. B.A. 1851; Deac. 1852 and Pr. 1853. Formerly C. of St. George's, Brandon Hill, Bristol. [22]

BRADBY, Edward Henry, *Harrow, Middlesex.*—Ball. Coll. Ox. 1st cl. Lit. Hum. B.A. 1848, M.A. 1852; Deac. 1852 by Bp of Lich. Pr. 1857 by Bp of Lon. Asst. Mast. of Harrow Sch. 1853. Late Fell. and Tut. of Dur. Univ. and Prin. of Bp Hat. Hall, Dur. [23]

BRADDELL, Alexander, 3, *Sidney-terrace, Upper Leeson-street, Dublin.*—Dub. A.B. Formerly P. C. of St. Martin's-at-Palace, Norwich, 1853–60. [24]

BRADDON, Edward Nicholas, *St. Mary's Vicarage, Sandwich, Kent.*—Cam. B.A. 1825, M.A. 1828; Deac. 1827 and Pr. 1828 by Bp of B. and W. V. of St. Mary's, Sandwich, Dio. Cant. 1846. (Patron, Archd. of Cant; Tithe, 107*l* 6*s* 9*d*; Glebe. 8 acres; V.'s Inc. 124*l* and Ho; Pop. 919.) V. of St. Clement's, Sandwich, Dio. Cant. 1846. (Patron, Archd. of Cant; Tithe, 301*l* 13*s* 4*d*; V.'s Inc. 314*l*; Pop. 889.) Surrogate. [25]

BRADDY, Charles, 2, *Brunswick-terrace, Camberwell, London, S.*—St. John's Coll. Cam. B.A. 1841, M.A. 1845; Deac. 1844 by Abp of York, Pr. 1845 by Bp of Lon. Lect. at St. Magnus-the-Martyr, City of London, 1847; Asst. Mast. of the City of London Sch. Cheapside, 1847; Chap. of St. Margaret's and St. John's Union, Westminster, 1853. [26]

BRADFORD, Charles, *Oxford House, Parade, Southsea.*—R. of Greatham, Dio. Win. 1846. (Patron, Rev. T. A. Holland; Tithe, 247*l* 6*s* 8*d*; Glebe, 53½ acres; R.'s Inc. 275*l* and Ho; Pop 238.) [27]

BRADFORD, Charles William, *Clyffe-Pypard, Wootton Bassett, Wilts.*—Brasen. Coll. Ox. B.A. 1852, M.A. 1857; Deac. 1855 and Pr. 1856 by Bp of Salis. V. of Clyffe Pypard, Dio. Salis. 1863. (Patron, H. N. Goddard, Esq; V.'s Inc. 500*l* and Ho; Pop. 541.) Formerly C. of Beechingstoke, Wilts, 1855–57, Broughton, Oxon, 1857–63. [28]

BRADFORD, Frederick Fowler, *Market Bosworth, Hinckley, Leicestershire.*—C. of Market Bosworth and Carlton. [29]

BRADFORD, William Mussage Kirkwall, *West Meon, Petersfield, Hants.*—Magd. Hall, Ox. B.A. 1829, M.A. 1830; Deac. 1831 and Pr. 1832. R. of West Meon with Privett C. Dio. Win. 1844. (Patron, Bp of Win; West Meon, Tithe, 636*l*, Glebe, 32½ acres; Privett, Tithe, 213*l* 8*s*; R.'s Inc. 842*l* and Ho; Pop. West Meon 842, Privett 258.) Chap. to Lord Cranworth; Rural Dean. [30]

BRADLEY, Arthur, *Southampton.*—Queen's Coll. Ox. B.A. 1847, M.A. 1850; Deac. 1848 and Pr. 1849 by Bp of Win. R. of All Saints', Southampton, Dio. Win. 1863. (Patron, Bp of Win; R.'s Inc. 330*l* and Ho; Pop. 8695.) Surrogate. [31]

BRADLEY, Charles, 19, *Royal Parade, Cheltenham.*—St. Edmund Hall, Ox; Deac. 1812 by Bp of

Lon. Pr. 1814 by Bp of Lin. V. of Glasbury, Brecknock, Dio. St. D. 1823. (Patron, Bp of St. D; Tithe, 470*l*; V.'s Inc. 480*l* and Ho; Pop. 1396.) Formerly C. of High Wycombe, Bucks, 1813; Incumb. of St. James's Chapel, Clapham, 1828–55. Author, several volumes of Sermons and Classical School Books. [1]

BRADLEY, Charles, jun., *Southgate, Middlesex.* [2]

BRADLEY, Edward, *Denton Rectory, Peterborough.*—Univ. Coll. Dur. Thorpe Scho. Found. Scho. B.A. 1848, Licen. in Theol. 1849; Deac. 1850 and Pr. 1851 by Bp of Ely. R. of Denton with Caldecote, Hunts, Dio. Ely, 1859. (Patron, William Wells, Esq; Tithe, 127*l* 13*s* 11*d*; Glebe, 198 acres; R.'s Inc. 300*l* and Ho; Pop. 153.) Formerly C. of Glatton with Holme, Hunts, 1850–54, Leigh with Bransford, Worc. 1854–57; P. C. of Bobbington, Staffs, 1857–59. Author, various publications under the *nom-de-guerre* of "Cuthbert Bede;" *Verdant Green*, J. Blackwood, 1854–56, 3*s*; *Photographic Pleasures*, Maclean, 1855, 7*s* 6*d*, cheap ed. Day and Co, 1864, 1*s*; *Motley*, 1855, 1*s*; *Love's Provocations*, Ward and Lock, 1855, 1*s*; *Medley*, 1855, 1*s*; *Shilling Book of Beauty*, 1856, 1*s*; *Tales of College Life*, 1856, 1*s*; *Nearer and Dearer*, Bentley, 1857, 2*s*; *Fairy Fables*, Bentley, 1858, 5*s*; *Happy Hours*, 1858, 3*s* 6*d*; *Funny Figures*, 1858, 2*s*; *Glencreggan*, 2 vols. Longman, 1860, 25*s*; *Curate of Cranston*, Saunders, Otley and Co. 1862, 10*s* 6*d*; *Tour in Tartan-land*, Bentley, 1863, 10*s* 6*d*; *Guide to Rosslyn and Hawthornden*, 1864, 1*s*; *The White Wife*, S. Low and Co. 1864, 6*s*; *The Rook's Garden*, Ib. 1865, 8*s*; *Matins and Muttons*, Ib. 1866, 2 vols. 16*s*; contributions to *Bentley's Miscellany*, *Gentleman's Magazine*, *Sharpe's Magazine*, *Hogg's Instructor*, *Titan*, *The Month*, *George Cruikshank's Magazine*, *Illustrated News*, *Illustrated London Magazine*, *Leisure Hour*, *Sunday at Home*, *The Cottager*, *Church and State Review*, *Literary Budget*, *Field*, *Queen*, *Punch*, *London Society*, *Churchman's Family Magazine*, *Town and Country Magazine*, *Odd Fellows' Quarterly*, *Once a Week*, *Parish Magazine*, *Notes and Queries*, *St. James's Magazine*, *Cassell's Family Paper*, *The Quiver*, *The London Review*, etc. [3]

BRADLEY, George Granville, *The College, Marlborough, Wilts.*—Univ. Coll. Ox. Fell. of, 1st cl. Lit. Hum. and B.A. 1844, M.A. 1847; Deac. 1858 by Bp of Lon. Pr. 1858 by Bp of Salis. Mast. of Marlborough Coll. 1858. Formerly Asst. Mast. in Rugby Sch. 1846–58. [4]

BRADLEY, Gilbert, *Dunstall Parsonage, Burton-on-Trent.*—Univ. Coll. Ox. Math. Exhib. 2nd cl. Math. et Phy. and B.A. 1851, M.A. 1854; Deac. 1852 and Pr. 1853 by Bp. of Ely. P. C. of Dunstall, Dio. Lich. 1862. (Patron, John Hardy, Esq. M.P; P. C.'s Inc. 150*l* and Ho; Pop. 240.) [5]

BRADLEY, G., *Werneth, Stockport.*—C. of St. Paul's, Werneth. [6]

BRADLEY, James, *St. Peter's Parsonage, Walsall.*—Caius Coll. Cam. 27th Wrang. B.A. 1861, M.A. 1864; Deac. 1861 and Pr. 1862 by Bp of Rip. P.C. of St. Peter's, Walsall, Dio. Lich. 1863. (Patron, V. of Walsall; P. C.'s Inc. 300*l*; Pop. 10,418.) Formerly C. of St. Andrew's, Leeds. [7]

BRADLEY, James Chesterton, *Sutton-under-Brails, Shipston-on-Stour.*—Queen's Coll. Ox. B.A. 1841; Deac. 1842, Pr. 1843. R. of Sutton-under-Brails, Dio. G. and B. 1862. (Patron, Bp of G. and B; R.'s Inc. 350*l* and Ho; Pop. 227.) [8]

BRADLEY, James F., *Rudston, Bridlington, Yorks.*—C. of Rudston. [9]

BRADLEY, Reginald Robert, *Charteris Bay, Canterbury, New Zealand.*—Univ. Coll. Dur. B.A. 1844, M.A. 1851; Deac. 1849, Pr. 1850. Occasional Duty at Christchurch, N.Z. Formerly Chap. at Cape Coast Castle, Gold Coast, Africa; and C. of Crosby-Garrett, Westmoreland. [10]

BRADLEY, Richard, *Haxby, York.*—Bp Hat. Hall, Dur. Licen. Theol. 1848; Deac. 1848, Pr. 1849. P. C. of Haxby, Dio. York, 1865. (Patron, Abp of York; P. C.'s Inc. 300*l*; Pop. 597.) Formerly C. of St. Hilda's, Middlesborough. [11]

BRADLEY, Robert Augustus, 23, *Gloucester-terrace, Hyde-park, London, W.*—Mert. Coll. Ox. B.A. 1857; Deac. 1857 and Pr. 1858 by Bp of Lon. C. of St Augustin and St. Faith, City of London. [12]

BRADLEY, William, *Baddesley-Ensor, Atherstone, Warwickshire.*—Brasen. Coll. Ox. B.A. 1814, M.A. 1817. P. C. of Baddesley-Ensor, Dio. Wor. 1819. (Patrons, the Inhabitants; Tithe—Imp. 61*l* 15*s* 9*d*, P. C. 9*l* 14*s* 1*d*; P. C.'s Inc. 120*l*; Pop. 872.) P. C. of Nether Whitacre, Dio. Wor. 1826. (Patron, Earl Howe; P. C.'s Inc. 350*l* and Ho; Pop. 479.) [13]

BRADLEY, W. Windham, 101, *Marina, St. Leonards-on-Sea.*—Magd. Coll. Ox. late Demy of, B.A. 1845, M.A. 1847; Deac. 1855 by Bp of Win. Author, *Latin Prose Exercises*; *Lessons in Latin Prose*; and *Troy Taken*, Longmans. [14]

BRADNEY, Joseph, *Greet (Salop), near Tenbury.*—Late Scho. of Trin. Coll. Cam. 2nd Sen. Opt. and B.A. 1817, M.A. 1822; Deac. 1821, Pr. 1822. R. of Greet, Dio. Herf. 1844. (Patron, T. H. Hope Edwards, Esq; Tithe, 161*l* 5*s* 8*d*; Glebe, 40 acres; R.'s Inc. 191*l*; Pop. 129.) [15]

BRADSHAW, Edward, *Billington Rectory, Leighton Buzzard, Beds.*—St. John's Coll. Cam; Deac. 1849 and Pr. 1851 by Bp of Carl. R. of Billington, Dio. Ely, 1858. (Patrons, the Inhabitants; Tithe, 288*l* 13*s* 4*d*; Glebe, 3 acres; R.'s Inc. 290*l* and Ho; Pop. 484.) [16]

BRADSHAW, Francis Sands, LL.D., *Jamaica.* [17]

BRADSHAW, Henry Holden, *Lockington Vicarage, near Derby.*—Brasen. Coll. Ox. B.A. 1851; Deac. 1852 and Pr. 1853 by Bp of Ex. V. of Lockington, Dio. Pet. 1864. (Patron, J. B. Story, Esq; V.'s Inc. 238*l* and Ho; Pop. 571.) Formerly C. of Okehampton, Devon, 1852, Sudbury, Derby, 1853–64. [18]

BRADSHAW, James, *Christ Church, West Bromwich.*—St. Cath. Coll. Cam. B.A. 1843, M.A. 1846; Deac. 1843 by Bp of Herf. Pr. 1844 by Bp. of Lich. P. C. of Ch. Ch. West Bromwich, Dio. Lich. 1849. (Patrons, Earl of Dartmouth and Trustees; P. C.'s Inc. 350*l*; Pop. 16,246.) Surrogate 1849. Formerly C. of Darlaston 1843; P. C. of St. George's, Darlaston, 1844; P. C. of Coseley 1849. [19]

BRADSHAW, John, *Granby, Bottesford, Notts.*—St. John's Coll. Cam; Deac. 1836, Pr. 1837. V. of Granby, Dio. Lin. 1845. (Patron, Duke of Rutland; V.'s Inc. 123*l* and Ho; Pop. 479.) V. of Hose, Leicestershire, Dio. Pet. 1845. (Patron, Duke of Rutland; V.'s Inc. 105*l*; Pop. 477.) [20]

BRADSHAW, Samuel, *Basford Hall, Leek.*—Brasen. Coll. Ox. B.A. 1833, M.A. 1836; Deac. 1835 and Pr. 1836 by Bp of Lich. Rural Dean. [21]

BRADSHAW, Sandys Ynyr Burges, *Frederick-terrace, Didsbury, Manchester.*—Deac. 1859 and Pr. 1860 by Bp of Dur. C. of Didsbury 1867. Formerly C. of Alston Moor 1859–60, St. Hilda's, South Shields, 1860, Bucklebury, near Reading, 1860–67. [22]

BRADSHAWE, George, *Southampton.*—Chap. of the Gaol, and of the Union, Southampton. [23]

BRADSTOCK, W. E., *Farncombe, Godalming, Surrey.*—Brasen. Coll. Ox. M.A. C. of Farncombe. [24]

BRADSTREET, William, *Theberton Rectory, Saxmundham.*—Emman. Coll. Cam. B.A. 1837; Deac. 1838, Pr. 1839. R. of Theberton, Dio. Nor. 1865. (Patron, the Crown; Tithe, 420*l*; Glebe, 12 acres; R.'s Inc. 450*l* and Ho; Pop. 541.) Formerly C. of Lower Hardres, Kent. [25]

BRADY, Nicholas, *Ainsworth-street, Ulverston.*—Trin. Coll. Cam. 3rd cl. Nat. Sci. Trip. B.A. 1863, M.A. 1866; Deac. 1863 and Pr. 1865 by Bp of Carl. C. of Ulverston 1863. [26]

BRAGGE, Charles Albert, *Burstock, Beaminster.*—Trin. Coll. Cam, B.A. 1861, M.A. 1864; Deac. 1863 and Pr. 1864 by Bp of B. and W. C. of Burstock 1865. Formerly C. of Huntspill, Somerset, 1863. [27]

BRAGGE, John, *Thorncombe, near Beaminster.*—V. of Burstock, near Beaminster, Dorset, Dio. Salis. 1822. (Patron, John Bragge, Esq; Tithe—V. 177*l* 10*s*; Glebe, 1 acre; V.'s Inc. 180*l*; Pop. 220.) V. of Thorncombe,

Dio. Salis. 1838. (Patron, John Bragge, Esq; Tithe - Imp. 2l 6s, V. 500l; Glebe, 47 acres; V.'s Inc. 570l and and Ho; Pop. 1277.) [1]

BRAIKENRIDGE, George Weare, *Clevedon, Somerset.*—Univ. Coll. Ox. B.A. 1836, M.A. 1839; Deac. 1838 and Pr. 1839 by Bp of G. and B. Min. of Ch. Ch. Clevedon, Dio. B. and W. 1839. (Patrons, Trustees; Min.'s Inc. 200l.) [2]

BRAILSFORD, Edward, *Herne Bay.*—Trinity Hall, Cam. B.A. 1861. R. of Fordwich, Dio. Cant. 1852. (Patron, Earl Cowper; Tithe, 192l 19s 5d; R.'s Inc. 210l; Pop. 202.) Formerly C. of Radwell, Herts, 1860–61; P. C. of St. Stephen's, Selby, Isle of Man, 1846–49; C. of Charlton, near Dover, 1851. [3]

BRAILSFORD, Hodgson, *Exbourne, North Tawton, Devon.*—Dub. A.B. 1836, D.D. 1854; Deac. 1836, Pr. 1837. R. of Exbourne, Dio. Ex. 1845. (Patrons, the family of the present R; Tithe, 273l 1s 4d; Glebe, 63 acres; R.'s Inc. 400l and Ho; Pop. 459.) R. of Honeychurch, Devon, Dio. Ex. 1848. (Patron, the present R; Tithe, 45l; Glebe, 60 acres; R.'s Inc. 90l; Pop. 44.) Surrogate. Author, *Analysis of the Literature of Ancient Greece*, 1831, 5s; *Altar Denunciations*, 1848, 1s 6d. [4]

BRAIM, The Ven. Thomas Henry, *All Saints' Rectory, Dorchester.*—St. John's Coll. Cam. D.D. 1857; Deac. and Pr. 1848. R. of All Saints' Dorchester, Dio. Salis. 1866. (Patrons, Simeon's Trustees; R.'s Inc. 135l and Ho; Pop. 946.) Formerly Head Mast. of Bishop's Gr. Sch. Hobart Town, Tasmania, 1835; Prin. of Sydney Coll. 1841; Incumb. of St. John's, Belfast, 1848–66; Archd. of Portland, Dio. Melbourne, 1854. Author, *History of New South Wales*, 2 vols, Bentley; Australian Classical Text Books, and various Pamphlets. [5]

BRAITHWAITE, Francis Joseph, *Clare College, Cambridge.*—Clare Coll. Cam. B.A. 1860, M.A. 1863, 21st Wrang. 1860, Fell. of Clare Coll. 1861; Deac. 1861 and Pr. 1862 by Bp of Ely. Dean and Precantor of Clare Coll. 1865. Formerly C. of St. Peter's, Wisbeach, 1861. [6]

BRAITHWAITE, Frederick, 57, *York-terrace, Regent's-park, London, N.W.*—Clare Coll. Cam. B.A. 1835, M.A. 1839. Sexton and Clerk in Orders of St. Marylebone 1842. [7]

BRAITHWAITE, George, *Sub-Deanery, Chichester.*—Queen's Coll. Ox. B.A. 1840, M.A. 1843; Deac. 1841, Pr. 1842. V. of Sub-Deanery, and Sub-Dean of Chich. 1851. (Patrons, D. and C. of Chich; Tithe—App. 416l 5s 6d; V.'s Inc. 286l and Ho; Pop. 2098.) Author, *Sonnets and other Poems*, 2s 6d; *The Gospel Scheme of Man's Salvation*, 6d; *The Voice of the Lord—This is the will of God, even your Sanctification, that ye should abstain from Fornication*, 6d; *Sermon on Death of Prince Consort*, 6d; *Faith, Nominal and Real* (a Sermon), 1866, 6d [8]

BRAITHWAITE, Robert, *Clifton, Bristol.*—Literate; Deac. 1859 and Pr. 1860 by Bp of G. and B. C. of Clifton. Formerly C. of St. Mary's, Cheltenham, 1860. [9]

BRAITHWAITE, William, *Alne, Easingwold, Yorks.*—Jesus Coll. Cam. B.A. 1841, M.A. 1844; Deac. 1842, Pr. 1843. V. of Alne, Dio. York, 1850. (Patron, A. Braithwaite Esq; Tithe—Imp. 340l 4s 7d, V. 216l 4s; Glebe, 174 acres; V.'s Inc. 497l and Ho; Pop. 1592.) [10]

BRAMAH, Henry Salkeld.—King's Coll. Lond. Theol. Assoc. 1858; Deac. 1858 and Pr. 1859 by Bp of Lon. Asst. C. of Mission Ch. of St. James's-the-Less, Liverpool, 1863. Formerly C. of St. Mary's-the-Less, Lambeth. [11]

BRAMAH, Joseph West, *Davington Priory, Faversham, Kent.*—Min. of Davington; Chap. of the Faversham Union. [12]

BRAME, John, *Warrington.*—St. John's Coll. Cam. B.A. 1846; Deac. 1847, Pr. 1848. Travelling Sec. of the Additional Curates' Society. [13]

BRAMELD, George William, *East Markham, Tuxford, Notts.*—Lin. Coll. Ox. Hon. 4th cl. Lit. Hum. and B.A. 1839, M.A. 1841; Deac. 1840 and Pr. 1841 by Bp of Rip. V. of East Markham with West Drayton R. annexed, Dio. Lin. 1852. (Patron, the Duke of Newcastle; West Drayton, Tithe, 90l; V.'s Inc. 335l and Ho; Pop. East Markham 807, West Drayton 96.) Author, *Lecture on Liturgy of the Church of England*, 1843; *Dangers and Duties of the Times* (a Sermon preached before the Notts Yeomanry, at Mansfield), 1848; *Poems for Children*, 1849; *Practical Sermons*, 1st Series, 1852, 2nd ed. 1853, 2nd Series, 1855, 6s 6d, 2nd ed. 1858; *New Translation of the Gospels*, Longmans, 1863; Sundry Sermons and Pamphlets, 1849–63. [14]

BRAMELD, John Thomas, *St. John's Vicarage, Mansfield, Notts.*—St. Bees; Deac. 1854 and Pr. 1855 by Bp of Lin. P. C. of St. John's, Mansfield, Dio. Lin. 1856. (Patron, Bp of Lin; P. C.'s Inc. 300l and Ho; Pop. 4192.) C. of Folkingham, Lincolnshire. [15]

BRAMELL, John, *Hanley, Staffs.*—St. Bees; Deac. 1862 and Pr. 1863 by Bp of Lich. C. of Hanley 1867. Formerly C. of Fenton 1862–64, Lane End 1864–67. [16]

BRAMHALL, John, *Terrington St. John, King's Lynn, Norfolk.*—Ex. Coll. Ox. 4th cl. Lit. Hum. and B.A. 1832; Deac. 1837 and Pr. 1838 by Bp of G. and B. V. of Terrington St. John, Dio. Nor. 1843. (Patron, the Crown; Tithe, 206l 4s 11d; Glebe, 5 acres; V.'s Inc. 220l; Pop. 793.) Rural Dean 1865. [17]

BRAMLEY, Henry, *Exeter.*—Trin. Coll. Cam. B.A. 1852, M.A. 1855; Deac. 1853 and Pr. 1855 by Bp of Rip. C. of St. Sidwell's, Exeter. [18]

BRAMLEY, Henry Ramsden, *Magdalen College, Oxford.*—Magd. Coll. Ox. 1852, Scho. of Univ. Coll. Ox. 1853, 1st cl. Lit. Hum. and B.A. 1856, Fell. of Magd. Coll. Ox. 1857, M.A. 1858; Deac. 1856 and Pr. 1858 by Bp of Ox. P. C. of Horsepath, Dio. Ox. 1861. (Patron, Magd. Coll. Ox; P. C.'s Inc. 112l and Ho; Pop. 334.) Fell. and Tut. of Magd. Coll. Ox. 1857. Author, *An Answer to Professor Goldwin Smith's Plea for the Abolition of Tests in the University of Oxford*, Rivingtons, 1864, 1s 6d. [19]

BRAMLEY, Thomas, *Giggleswick, Settle.*—Queen's Coll. Ox. B.A. 1858, M.A. 1861; Deac. 1862 and Pr. 1863 by Bp of Rip. 2nd Mast. of Giggleswick Gr. Sch. 1865. Formerly C. of St. Mary's, Leeds, 1862, and Asst. Mast. in Leeds Gr. Sch. 1861. [20]

BRAMLEY-MOORE, William Joseph, *Gerrard's Cross, Bucks.*—Trin. Coll. Cam. B.A. 1853, M.A. 1856; Deac. 1855 and Pr. 1856 by Abp of Cant. P. C. of St. James's, Gerrard's Cross, Dio. Ox. 1861. (Patronesses, the Misses Reid; P. C.'s Inc. 160l; Pop. 550.) Formerly C. of Brenchley, Kent, 1855–56. Author, *The First Sabbath at Gerrard's Cross*, 1859; *The Six Sisters of the Valleys*, 3 vols. 1864, 4th ed. 1866; *The Great Oblation*, 1864; *The Seven Cries from Calvary*, 1867; *Scripture Training Lessons*, 1865. Editor, Foxe's *Book of Martyrs*, Cassell, 1867. [21]

BRAMSTON, Francis Thomas, *Layham, Suffolk.*—Trin. Coll. Cam. B.A. 1864; Deac. 1865 and Pr. 1866. C. of Layham 1865. [22]

BRAMSTON, John, *Witham, Essex.*—Oriel Coll. Ox. 2nd cl. Lit. Hum. and B.A. 1824, M.A. 1826; Deac. 1827 and Pr. 1828 by Bp of Lon. V. of Witham, Dio. Roch. 1840. (Patron, Bp of Roch; Tithe—App. 826l, Imp. 75l, V. 294l 9s; Glebe, 102 acres; V.'s Inc. 498l and Ho; Pop. 3455.) Fell. of Ex. Coll. Ox. 1825; Hon. Can. of Roch; Rural Dean; Proctor for Clergy Dio. Roch. 1861. [23]

BRAMSTON, John Trant, *Wellington College, Wokingham.*—New Coll. Ox; B.A. 1865; Deac. 1860 by Bp of Ox. Asst. Mast. in Wellington Coll. [24]

BRAMSTON, William, *Titsey, near Godstone.*—St. Peter's Coll. Cam. B.A. 1864; Deac. 1864 and Pr. 1865 by Bp of Win. C. of Titsey 1864. [25]

BRAMSTON, William Mondeford, *Willingale-Doe, Chipping-Ongar, Essex.*—Ball. Coll. Ox. B.A. 1856, M.A. 1859; Deac. 1859 and Pr. 1860 by Bp of Ox. R. of Willingale-Doe with Shellow-Bowels R. Dio. Roch. 1861. (Patron, T. W. Bramston, Esq; R.'s Inc. 560l;

Pop. 458.) P. C. of Berners Roding, Dio. Roch. 1861. (Patron, T. W. Bramston, Esq; P. C.'s Inc. 56*l*; Pop. 94.) [1]

BRAMWELL, Addison, *Thorington, Saxmundham, Suffolk.*—Trin. Coll. Cam. B.A. 1854, M.A. 1857; Deac. 1854 and Pr. 1855 by Bp of Nor. R. of Thorington, Dio. Nor. 1858. (Patron, H. A. S. Bence, Esq; Tithe, 283*l* 17*s*; Glebe, 11 acres; R.'s Inc. 290*l* and Ho; Pop. 121.) Late C. of Wrentham, Suffolk. [2]

BRAMWELL, Henry Rowland, *Buglawton, Congleton, Cheshire.*—P. C. of Buglawton, Dio. Ches. 1858. (Patron, R. of Astbury; P. C.'s Inc. 180*l* and Ho; Pop. 2014.) [3]

BRANCKER, Henry, *Thursley, near Godalming, Surrey.*—Wad. Coll. Ox. 2nd cl. Math. et Phy. 1839, B.A. 1840, M.A. 1841; Deac. 1840 and Pr. 1841 by Bp of Ches. P. C. of Thursley, Dio. Win. 1857. (Patron, V. of Whitley; Tithe, 95*l*; Glebe, 5 acres; P. C.'s Inc. 100*l*; Pop. 805.) Formerly C. of Warrington 1840; P. C. of Padgate 1841, P. C. of Bishopsworth 1847; C. of Mortlake 1854. [4]

BRANCKER, Peter Whitfield, *Scruton Rectory, Bedale, Yorks.*—Jesus Coll. Ox. B.A. 1836, M.A. 1839; Deac. 1838 and Pr. 1839 by Bp of Ches. R. of Scruton, Dio. Rip. 1857. (Patron, H. Coore, Esq; Tithe, 440*l*; Glebe, 80 acres; R.'s Inc. 550*l*; Pop. 408.) Late V. of Hatfield-Peverel, Dio. Roch. 1852–57. [5]

BRANCKER, Thomas, *Limington Rectory, Ilchester.*—Wad. Coll. Ox. Ireland Scho. 1831, B.A. 1834, M.A. 1837; Deac. 1836 and Pr. 1837 by Bp of Ox. R. of Limington, Dio. B. and W. 1849. (Patron, Wad. Coll. Ox; Tithe, 410*l*; Glebe, 8 acres; R.'s Inc. 424*l*; Pop. 348.) Preb. of Wells, and Inspector of Schools for the Deanery of Ilchester. Late Fell. of Wad. Coll. 1835–50, and Div. Lect. and Tut. of the same Coll. Editor of *Hammond on the Psalms*, 2 vols. Oxford Univ. Press, 1850. [6]

BRANDE, William Thomas Charles, *Pulborough, Sussex.*—New Inn Hall, Ox. B A. 1846, M.A. 1849; Deac. 1849 and Pr. 1850 by Bp of B. and W. R. of Egdean, Dio. Chich. 1860. (Patron, Hon. R. Curzon; Tithe, comm. 110*l*; R.'s Inc. 115*l*; Pop. 70.) C. of Coates 1861. Formerly C. of North Moor Green 1849, Bridgwater 1852, and St. Peter's, Pimlico, Lond. 1854. [7]

BRANDER, Boulton, *Beverley, Yorks.*—Queens' Coll. Cam. B.A. 1828, M.A. 1849; Deac. 1828, Pr. 1829. V. of St. Mary's with St. Nicholas R. Beverley, Dio. York, 1856. (Patron, Ld Chan; V. and R.'s Inc. 310*l* and Ho; Pop. 5241.) Dom. Chap. to Lord Dunboyne. Formerly P. C. of Christ Ch. Derry Hill, Wilts, 1848–56; Chap. of Calne Union 1854–56. Author, *A Sermon on the Death of the Marchioness of Lansdowne*, 1851; *Seven Sermons on different Subjects*, 1856. [8]

BRANDER, Gustavus, *Kingston, Modbury, Devon.*—Ball. Coll. Ox. B.A. 1861; Deac. 1865 by Bp of Ex. C. of Kingston 1865. [9]

BRANDON, Korah Nichols, *Walton Parsonage, Carlisle.*—King's Coll. Lon. Theol. Assoc. 1856; Deac. 1856 and Pr. 1857 by Bp of Lon. C. in sole charge of Walton 1866. Formerly C. of St. Peter's, Islington, 1856–60, St. Mary's, Balham, 1861; P. C. of Waltham Cross, Herts, 1862–66. [10]

BRANDRAM, Thomas P., *The Terrace, Wokingham.*—Oriel Coll. Ox. B.A. 1862, M.A. 1866; Deac. 1865 and Pr. 1866 by Bp. of Ox. C. of St. Paul's, Wokingham, 1865. [11]

BRANDRETH, William Harper, *Standish, Wigan.*—Ch. Ch. Ox. B.A. 1833, M.A. 1839; Deac. 1836, Pr. 1837. R. of Standish, Dio. Man. 1841. (Patron, the present R; Tithe, 1838*l* 3*s* 7*d*; Glebe, 271¼ acres; R.'s Inc. 2481*l* and Ho; Pop. 4902.) Hon. Can. of Man; Surrogate. [12]

BRANDT, F.—Dom. Chap. to the Marquis of Westminster. [13]

BRANDT, Henry, *Burrow-on-the-Hill, Melton Mowbray, Leicestershire.*—Trin. Coll. Cam. B.A. 1852; Deac. 1852 and Pr. 1854 by Bp of Ely. R. of Burrow, Dio. Pet. 1855. (Patron, Rev. G. Burnaby; Tithe, 248*l* 12*s*; Glebe, 74 acres; R.'s Inc. 410*l* and Ho; Pop. 138.) [14]

BRANFOOT, Thomas Redhead, *Lymm Rectory, Warrington.*—Trin. Coll. Ox. B.A. 1834, M.A. 1842; Deac. 1836 and Pr. 1837 by Bp of Jamaica. R. of 1st mediety of Lymm, Cheshire, Dio. Ches. 1863. (Patron, Egerton Leigh, Esq; Tithe—Rent-Charge, 254*l* 10*s*; Rent of Glebe 84*l*; R.'s Inc. about 400*l* and Ho. and Glebe attached; Pop. of the two medieties 3767.) Formerly Chap. and Sec. of the Bp of Jamaica, Registrar of the Dio. and Eccles. Commissary for Port Royal 1837; C. of Harrietsham, Kent, 1842, Kensington 1844, Cripplegate 1849. Ilford 1854, and Kensington 1862. Author, a Sermon, *Colonial Bishops' Fund*, 1842. [15]

BRANSCOMBE, George Henry Dacie, *Okehampton, Devon.*—Trin. Coll. Cam. B.A. 1853; Deac. 1854 and Pr. 1855 by Bp of Ex. C. of Okehampton 1859. Formerly C. of Exbourne and Honey Church, Devon, 1854–55, Par, Cornwall, 1856–58. [16]

BRANSON, George, *West Tisted, Alresford, Hants.*—P. C. of West Tisted, Dio. Win. 1863. (Patron, Magd. Coll. Ox; P. C.'s Inc. 58*l* and Ho; Pop. 282.) [17]

BRANSON, Henry John, *Armthorpe, Doncaster.*—Caius Coll. Cam. B.A. 1827, M.A. 1830; Deac. 1828, Pr. 1829. R. of Armthorpe, Dio. York, 1834. (Patron, Ld Chan; R.'s Inc. 300*l* and Ho; Pop. 424.) [18]

BRANT, William Crawley, *Albany Villas, Hove, Sussex.*—Oriel Coll. Ox. B.A. 1812, M.A. 1815; Deac. 1813, Pr. 1814. [19]

BRASHER, Samuel Benton, *St. Stephen's Parsonage, South Shields.*—Dub. A.B. 1840; Deac. 1840 by Bp of Nor. Pr. 1841 by Abp of York. P. C. of St. Stephen's, South Shields, Dio. Dur. 1847. (Patrons, D. and C. of Dur; Tithe, 236*l* 2*s*; Glebe, 1 acre; P. C.'s Inc. 280*l* and Ho; Pop. 6252.) Surrogate. [20]

BRASS, Henry, *Redhill, Surrey.*—Corpus Coll. Cam. Sen. Opt. in Math. and 2nd cl. Nat. Sci. Trip. 1854, B.A. 1854, M A. 1861; Deac. 1855 and Pr. 1856 by Bp of Roch. P. C. of St Matthew's Redhill, Reigate, Dio. Win. 1866. (Patron, Bp of Win; P. C.'s Inc. 350*l* and Ho; Pop. 4000.) Formerly C. of Brompton, Chatham, 1855–57, Tooting, Surrey, 1857–59, St. Stephen's, 1859–61, and St Mark's, Brighton, 1862, St. Matthew's, Redhill, 1862–66. Author, various sermons in *The Brighton Pulpit*. Fell. of the Geol. Soc. of Lond. 1857. [21]

BRASS, John.—Pemb. Coll. Ox. B.A. 1860; Deac. 1862 and Pr. 1863 by Bp of Chich. Formerly C. of Uckfield 1863. [22]

BRASSINGTON, William Henry, *Hoby, Leicester.*—Dub. A.B. 1849; Deac. 1851 and Pr. 1852 by Bp of Pet. P. C. of Ragdale, Dio. Pet. 1863. (Patrons, Trustees of Ragdale Estate; P. C.'s Inc. 40*l*; Pop. 120.) Formerly C. of Hoby and Rotherby 1851, Douglas, Cork, 1854, Castlemacadam, Wicklow, 1858. [23]

BRATHWAITE, Francis Gretton Coleridge.—Ball. Coll. Ox. B.A. 1858; Deac. 1859 and Pr. 1860 by Bp of Ox. Late C. of Banbury 1859. [24]

BRAUND, Ebenezer, 4, *Augusta-place, Bath.*—Dub; Deac. 1862 by Bp of Carl. C. of St. James's and Corn-street, Chapel, Bath, 1866. Formerly C. of Dean 1863 and Dean and Mosser, Cumberland, 1864. [25]

BRAUND, William Hockin, *Bath.*—Magd. Hall, Ox. B.A. 1828, M.A. 1839; Deac. 1830, Pr. 1831. C. of Trinity, Bath. Formerly P. C. of Ash, Somerset, 1845–65. Author, *Husbandman's Spiritual Monitor*, 1835, 3*s*; *Saint's Acrostic*, 1842, 1*s*. [26]

BRAUNE, George Martin, *Wistow, Selby, Yorks.*—Sid. Coll. Cam. B.A. 1833; Deac. 1834, Pr. 1835. V. of Wistow, Dio. York, 1839. (Patron, Abp of York; V.'s Inc. 360*l*; Pop. 849.) [27]

BRAY, E., *Poplar, London, E.*—C. of Poplar. [28]

BRAY, William, *Shidfield, Fareham, Hants.*—Ex. Coll. Ox. B.A. 1831, M.A. 1834; Deac. 1832 and Pr. 1833 by Bp of Win. P. C. of St. John's, Shidfield, Dio. Win. 1859. (Patron, R. of Droxford; P. C.'s Inc. 120*l* and Ho; Pop. 937.) [29]

BRAY, William Henry, *Etherley, Durham.*—St. John's Coll. Cam. B.A. 1865; Deac. 1866 by Bp of Dur. C. of Etherley 1866. [1]

BREALEY, Frederick, 38, *Rodney-street, Liverpool.*—Queens' Coll. Cam. B.A. 1846, M.A. 1853; Deac. 1846 and Pr. 1847 by Bp of Ches. P. C. of St. Michael's, Liverpool, Dio. Ches. 1865. (Patron, Rev. J. Lawrence; P. C.'s Inc. 400*l*; Pop. 8865.) Formerly C. of St. George's, Chorley, 1846, St. Saviour's, Southwark, 1848, Highgate 1852; Chap. of East London Union 1858; C. of St. Botolph's, Bishopsgate, 1861. [2]

BREAY, Henry Thomas, *Birmingham.*—Trin. Coll. Cam. B.A. 1852; Deac. 1853 by Bp of Wor. Pr. 1853 by Bp of Lich. P. C. of St. Mathias', Birmingham, Dio. Wor. 1859. (Patrons, Trustees; P. C.'s Inc. 300*l*; Pop. 10,934.) [3]

BREE, William, *Allesley Rectory, Coventry.*—Mert. Coll. Ox. B.A. 1845, M.A. 1847; Deac. 1847 and Pr. 1848 by Bp of Pet. R. of Allesley, Dio. Wor. 1863. (Patron, the present R; Tithe, 786*l*; Glebe, 39 acres; R.'s Inc. 860*l* and Ho; Pop. 974.) Formerly C. of Polebrook, Northants, 1847–62; R. of same 1862–63. [4]

BREESE, John, *Callcott-house, Bicton-heath, Shrewsbury.*—Queens' Coll. Cam. B.A. 1832; Deac. 1832, Pr. 1833. R. of Hanwood, Dio. Herf. 1852. (Patron, Rev. E. Warter; Tithe, 108*l*; Glebe, 48 acres; R.'s Inc. 200*l* and Ho; Pop. 288.) Chap. of the D. of Longdon, Salop, Dio. Herf. 1857. (Patron, D. Warter, Esq; Tithe—App. 330*l*; Chap.'s Inc. 75*l*; Pop. 88.) Formerly C. of Withington 1832, Burlastone 1837, Belper 1839, Mansfield 1840, Ipswich 1842, Forden 1844, Middleton 1845, Westbury 1846; P. C. of Bayston-hill 1847–52. [5]

BREHAUT, Thomas Collings, *Richmond, Guernsey.*—Pemb. Coll. Ox. B.A. 1853; Deac. 1849 and Pr. 1850 by Bp of Win. Chap. of the Gaol, Guernsey, 1858. Formerly C. of St. Martin's 1849–50 and Grouville, Jersey, 1850–58. [6]

BREMRIDGE, James Philip, *Chudleigh, Devon.*—Ex. Coll. Ox. B.A. 1841, M.A. 1844; Deac. 1844 and Pr. 1845 by Bp of Ex. C. of Chudleigh 1867. Formerly C. of Morchard-Bishop 1846. [7]

BREN, Robert, *Caister, near Yarmouth, Norfolk.*—Ch. Miss. Coll. Islington; Deac. 1848 by Bp. of Lon. Pr. 1850 by Bp of Colombo. C. of Caister. Late C. of Papworth St. Agnes 1859; formerly Missionary in Ceylon, 1849–59. Author, *Hinduism and Christianity Contrasted* (in Tamul), Ceylon; *The True Union.* [8]

BRENAN, Robert Hardy, 16, *Grafton-street, Brighton.*—Dub. A.B. 1859, A.M. 1864, *ad eund.* Ox. 1864; Deac. 1860 by Bp of Cork, Pr. 1861 by Bp of Down. C. of St. Mary's, Brighton, 1865. Formerly C. of Kenk Breda, Down, 1860, Trinity, Belfast, 1861, Stonehouse, Glouc. 1863. [9]

BRENT, Daniel, *Grendon Vicarage, Northampton.*—Univ. Coll. Ox. B.A. 1831, M.A. 1835, B.D. and D.D. 1850; Deac. 1832 and Pr. 1833 by Bp of Pet. V. of Grendon, Dio. Pet. 1835. (Patron, Trin. Coll. Cam; Tithe—Imp. 440*l*, V. 44*l*; Glebe, 28 acres; V.'s Inc. 140*l* and Ho; Pop. 610.) C. of Whiston. Formerly C. of Denton 1832, Whiston and Grendon 1835. Author, *Proposed Permissive Variations in the Use of the Church Service, Keeping the Prayer-Book intact,* 1863, 3*s* 6*d.* [10]

BRENT, Richard, *Grendon Vicarage, Northampton.*—Queens' Coll. Cam. Scho. of, B.A. 1861, M.A. 1865; Deac. 1863 and Pr. 1864 by Bp of Lin. Formerly C. of St. Peter's, Nottingham, 1863, St. Mary's, Abergavenny, 1865, Alresford, Colchester, 1866. [11]

BRERETON, Arthur Henry, *Mendham, Harleston, Norfolk.*—Queens' Coll. Cam. B.A. 1845; Deac. 1845 and Pr. 1846 by Bp of Nor. V. of Mendham, Dio. Nor. 1856. (Patroness, Mrs. Whitaker; Tithe—Imp. 486*l* 3*s* 6*d*, V. 84*l*; Glebe, 25 acres; V.'s Inc. 125*l* and Ho; Pop. 779.) [12]

BRERETON, Charles, *St. Mary's Rectory, Bedford.*—New Coll. Ox. B.C.L. 1840; Deac. 1838 and Pr. 1839 by Bp of Ox. C. of St. Mary's, Bedford (sole charge), 1860; Surrogate for the Archd. of Bedford; Sec. Asst. Cl. Mast. of Bedford Gr. Sch. Formerly Fell. of New Coll. Ox. [13]

BRERETON, Charles David, *Little Massingham, Swaffham, Norfolk.*—Queens' Coll. Cam. B.A. 1813, M.A. 1816; Deac. 1814, Pr. 1815. R. of Little Massingham, Dio. Nor. 1820. (Patron, H. Wilson, Esq; Tithe, 577*l*; R.'s Inc. 580*l* and Ho; Pop. 132.) Rural Dean. [14]

BRERETON, Charles David, Jun., *Rectory, Framingham Earl, Norwich.*—Trin. Coll. Cam. B.A. 1843, M.A. 1845; Deac. 1845 and Pr. 1846 by Bp of Nor. R. of Bixley with Framingham Earl, Dio. Nor. 1848. (Patron, Rev. C. D. Brereton; R.'s Inc. 606*l*; Pop. 297.) Rural Dean. [15]

BRERETON, C. J., *Thornage Rectory, Thetford, Norfolk.*—St. John's Coll. Cam. B.A. 1860; Deac. 1862 by Bp of Ely, Pr. 1862 by Bp of Lich. R. of Thornage with Brinton R. Dio. Nor. 1863. (Patron, Lord Hastings; Thornage, Tithe, comm. 331*l*; Glebe, 36 acres; Brinton, Tithe, comm. 177*l*; Glebe, 20 acres; R.'s Inc. 580*l* and Ho; Pop. Thornage 350, Brinton 150.) Formerly C. of Eccleshall, Staffs, 1862–63. [16]

BRERETON, Joseph Lloyd, *West Buckland, South Molton, Devon.*—Univ. Coll. Ox. Newdigate Prizeman 1844, B.A. 1846; Deac. 1847, Pr. 1848. R. of West Buckland, Dio. Ex. 1852. (Patron, J. F. Basset, Esq; Tithe, 190*l*; Glebe, 32 acres; R.'s Inc. 280*l* and Ho; Pop. 321.) Preb. of Ex. 1858. [17]

BRERETON, Randle Warwick, *Stiffkey, Wells, Norfolk.*—St. John's Coll. Cam. B.A. 1846; Deac. 1843, Pr. 1844. R. of Stiffkey (St. John with St. Mary) and Morston (All Saints), one Benefice with two Churches, Dio. Nor. 1845. (Patron, Capt. Townshend, R.N; Stiffkey, Tithe, 406*l* 19*s* 7*d*; Morston, Tithe, 280*l* 8*s*; R.'s Inc. 667*l* and Ho; Pop. Stiffkey 513, Morston 153.) [18]

BRERETON, Shovell, *Briningham, near Dereham, Norfolk.*—Queens' Coll. Cam. B.A. 1817, M.A. 1820; Deac. 1818 by Bp of Glouc. Pr. 1819 by Bp of Nor. P. C. of Briningham, Dio. Nor. 1861. (Patron, the present P. C; Tithe, comm. 353*l*; P. C.'s Inc. 353*l*; Pop. 200.) [19]

BRERETON, Thomas Joseph, *Metfield, Harleston, Suffolk.*—Ch. Ch. Ox. B.A. 1844; Deac. 1844 and Pr. 1845 by Bp of Nor. Chap. of D. of Metfield, Dio. Nor. 1859. (Patrons, Parishioners; Chap.'s Inc. 80*l* and Ho; Pop. 663.) Mast. of the Free Sch; and Morning Reader at Framlingham, Suffolk. [20]

BRESHER, Major Rider, *Coney-street, York.*—St. John's Coll. Cam. 10th Sen. Opt. B.A. 1850, M.A. 1854; Deac. 1850 and Pr. 1851 by Bp of Lich. V. of St. Martin's, Coney-street, City and Dio. York, 1858. (Patrons, D. and C. of York; Glebe, 36½ acres; V.'s Inc. 120*l*; Pop. 460.) Formerly C. of Weston, Yorks. [21]

BRETON, Edward Rose, *Charmouth, Dorset.*—Queen's Coll. Ox. B.A. 1825, M.A. 1828; Deac. 1826 and Pr. 1827 by Bp of Win. R. of Charmouth, Dio. Salis. 1843. (Patrons, Trustees; Tithe, 121*l* 4*s*; Glebe, 4 acres; R.'s Inc. 125*l* and Ho; Pop. 678.) [22]

BRETT, Edmund Percy, *Sandhurst, near Gloucester.*—St. John's Coll. Cam. 7th Jun. Opt. and B.A. 1847; Deac. 1847 and Pr. 1848 by Bp. of Pet. V. of Sandhurst, Dio. G. and B. 1854. (Patron, Bp of G. and B; Tithe—App. 480*l*; V. 205*l*; Glebe, 41 acres; V.'s Inc. 300*l* and Ho; Pop. 549.) [23]

BRETT, Francis Henry, *Carsington, Wirksworth, Derbyshire.*—St. John's Coll. Cam. 19th Wrang. and B.A. 1845, M.A. 1848; Deac. 1845 and Pr. 1847 by Bp. of Pet. R. of Carsington, Dio. Lich. 1859. (Patron, Bp of Lich; Tithe, 115*l*; Glebe, 46 acres; R.'s Inc. 190*l*; Pop. 269.) Formerly C. of Carsington, and Head Mast. of Wirksworth Gr. Sch. [24]

BRETT, George Russell, *Thwaite St. Mary Rectory, near Bungay.*—St. John's Coll. Cam. Jun. Opt. and Theol. Trip. B.A. 1858; Deac. 1858 and Pr. 1859 by Bp of Roch. R. of Thwaite St. Mary, Dio. Nor. 1866. (Patron, Edward Brett, Esq; Tithe, 179*l*; Glebe, 30 acres; R.'s Inc. 224*l* and Ho; Pop. 187.) Formerly C. of Metheringham 1863–64. [25]

BRETT, Philip, *Mount-Bures, Colchester.*—Emman. Coll. Cam. Sen. Opt. B.A 1840, M.A. 1844; Deac. 1841 and Pr. 1842 by Bp of Pet. R. of Mount-Bures, Dio. Roch. 1854. (Patron, the present R; Tithe, 455*l*; Glebe, 25 acres; R.'s Inc. 525*l* and Ho; Pop. 301.) Formerly C. of Passenham, Northants, and St. James's, Westminster. [1]

BRETTINGHAM, Thomas Clarke, *Fingringhoe Lodge, Colchester.*—Emman. Coll. Cam. B.A. 1848; Deac. 1850 and Pr. 1852 by Bp of Roch. V. of Fingringhoe, Dio. Roch. 1852. (Patrons, Trustees of late T. C. Brettingham, Esq; Tithe—Imp. 397*l*, V. 172*l* 2*s*; Glebe, 7 acres; V.'s Inc. 175*l*; Pop. 670.) Formerly C. of Fingringhoe 1850–52. [2]

BREWER, E. C., LL.D., 31, *St Luke's-road, Westbourne Park, London, W.* [3]

BREWER, James Sherrin, *King's College, Strand, London, W.C.*—Queen's Coll. Ox. B.A. 1833, M.A. 1835. Prof. of English Literature in King's Coll. Lond; Preacher at the Rolls Chap. Chancery-lane. Editor of *Field on the Church.* [4]

BREWER, William John, *Farningham, Kent.*—Queens' Coll. Cam. B.A. 1846, M.A. 1849; Deac. 1846 and Pr. 1847 by Abp of Cant. V. of Farningham, Dio. Cant. 1866. (Patron, Abp of Cant; Tithe, 255*l* 10*s*; Glebe, 10 acres; V.'s Inc. 283*l* and Ho; Pop. 900.) Formerly C. of Murston and Elmley, Kent, 1848–66; Chap. to Milton Union, and Inspector of Schools for Deanery of Sittingbourne 1854. [5]

BREWIN, George, *Wortley, near Sheffield.*—Scho. of Ch. Coll. Cam. 1837, B.A. 1839; Deac. 1839 by Bp of Roch. Pr. 1840 by Bp of Wor. P. C. of Wortley, Dio. York, 1845. (Patron, Lord Wharncliffe; Glebe, 19 acres; P. C.'s Inc. 120*l*; Pop. 1121.) [6]

BREWITT, Bellamy, *Westbury, near Wells, Somerset.*—St. Peter's Coll. Cam. Sen. Opt. and B.A. 1833; Deac. 1834, Pr. 1835. V. of Westbury, Dio. B. and W. 1857. (Patron, Bp of B. and W; Tithe, 183*l*; Glebe, 16 acres; V.'s Inc. 230*l* and Ho; Pop. 666.) Formerly C. of St. Cuthbert's, Wells. [7]

BREWSTER, Edward Jones, *Ampney, Cirencester.*—St. Mary Hall, Ox. B.A. 1849, M.A. 1852; Deac. 1853 and Pr. 1854 by Bp of Win. V. of Ampney Crucis, Dio. G. and B. 1864. (Patron the present V. (bought from the Ld Chan); Glebe, 20 acres; V.'s Inc. 320*l* and Ho; Pop. 648.) Formerly C. of St. Helen's, Isle of Wight; and Swindon, near Cheltenham. [8]

BREWSTER, Herbert Charles, *South Kelsey Rectory, Caistor, Lincolnshire.*—Queen's Coll. Ox. B.A. 1853; Deac 1855 and Pr. 1856 by Bp of Herf. R. of South Kelsey, Dio. Lin. 1865. (Patrons, Crown and J. Skipwith, Esq. alt; R.'s Inc. 750*l* and Ho; Pop. 633.) Formerly C. of Lucton, Herefordshire, 1855–56, Moore, Salop, 1856–57, Bulwell 1857–65. [9]

BREWSTER, James George, *Tottenham, London, N.*—Pemb. Coll. Ox. B.A. 1864; Deac. 1865 and Pr. 1866 by Abp of Cant. C. of Tottenham 1867. Formerly C. of Cranbrook, Kent, 1865–67. [10]

BREWSTER, Waldegrave, *Llandysilio Rectory, near Oswestry.*—Trin. Coll. Ox. 4th cl. Math. et Phy. 1838, B.A. 1839, M.A. 1842; Deac. 1839 and Pr. 1841 by Bp of Salis. R. of Llandysilio, Dio. St. A. (Patron, Bp of St. D; Tithe, 430*l*; Glebe, 20 acres; R.'s Inc. 465*l*; Pop. 689.) [11]

BRIANT, Henry, 2, *Clegg-street, Macclesfield.*—Queens' Coll. Cam B.A. 1842, M.A. 1848; Deac. 1842 and Pr. 1843 by Bp of Ches. P. C. of St. Paul's Macclesfield, Dio. Ches. 1844. (Patron, Bp of Ches; P. C.'s Inc. 300*l*; Pop. 5451.) Formerly C. of Cheadle 1842 and Wrenbury 1843, both in Cheshire. [12]

BRICE, Edward, *Humshaugh near Hexham.*—Wad. Coll. Ox. B.A. 1807; Deac. 1807 by Bp of Win. Pr. 1809 by Bp of Salis. P. C. of Humshaugh, Dio. Dur. 1832. (Patrons, Governors of Greenwich Hosp; Glebe, 3 acres; P. C.'s Inc. 120*l* and Ho; Pop. 558.) Formerly Chap. Royal Navy and R. of Thorneyburn, Northumberland, 1829–32. [13]

BRICE, Edward Cowell, *Newnham, Glouc.*—St. John's Coll. Cam. B.A. 1821; Deac. and Pr. 1821 by Bp of Bristol. P. C. of Newnham, Dio. G. and B. 1847. (Patrons, Mayor and Corporation of Gloucester; Tithe—App. 201*l* 5*s*; P. C.'s Inc. 150*l*; Pop. 1325.) [14]

BRICE, George Edward, *Humshaugh, Hexham.*—Univ. Coll. Dur. B.A. 1854, Licen. Theol. 1855, M.A. 1857, Barrington Scho. and Crewe Exhib; Deac. 1855 and Pr. 1856 by Bp of Man. C. of Humshaugh 1855. [15]

BRICE, Henry Crane, 5, *Richmond-hill, Clifton, Bristol.*—Ch. Coll. Cam. B.A. 1825, M.A. 1830; Deac. 1825, Pr. 1827. R. of St. Peter's, Bristol, Dio. G. and B. 1829. (Patrons, J. S. Harford, Esq. and Trustees; Glebe, 13 acres; R.'s Inc. 213*l*; Pop. 836.) [16]

BRICKDALE, Richard, *Felthorpe, Norwich.*—Ch. Ch. Ox. B.A. 1823, M.A. 1829; Deac. 1823 by Bp of Ex. Pr. 1824 by Bp of Glouc. R. of Felthorpe, Dio. Nor. 1833. (Patron, Bp of Nor; Tithe, 270*l*; Glebe, 24 acres; R.'s Inc. 300*l* and Ho; Pop. 514.) V. of Ringland, Dio. Nor. 1833. (Patron, Bp of Nor; Tithe—App. 162*l* 15*s*, V. 105*l*; V.'s Inc. 110*l*; Pop. 360.) [17]

BRICKEL, Robert, *The Manor House, Hoole, Preston.*—Dub. A.B. 1835; Deac. 1836, Pr. 1838. R. of Hoole, Dio. Man. 1848. (Patron, R. H. Barton, Esq; Tithe, 280*l*; R.'s Inc. 280*l*; Pop. 1132.) [18]

BRICKMANN, W. H. R., *The Elms, Wymondham, Norfolk.*—Chap. of the County Prison, Wymondham. [19]

BRICKNELL, Richard Nash, *Grove Parsonage, Wantage, Berks.*—St. Aidan's; Deac. 1862 and Pr. 1864 by Bp of Carl. C. in sole charge of Grove 1864. Formerly C. of Old Hutton, Westmoreland, 1862. [20]

BRICKNELL, William Simcox, *Eynsham, near Oxford.*—Wor. Coll. Ox. B.A. 1827, M.A. 1829. P. C. of Grove, Dio. Ox. 1836. (Patron, V. of Wantage; Glebe, 7 acres; P. C.'s Inc. 90*l* and Ho; Pop. 540.) V. of Eynsham, near Oxford, 1845. (Patroness, Mrs. W. S. Bricknell; V.'s Inc. 200*l* and Ho; Pop. 2096.) One of the Lecturers for the City of Oxford, at Carfax. [21]

BRICKWELL, Edward, *Hatley Cockayne, Potton, near St. Neots.*—Theol. Assoc. of King's Coll. Lond; Deac. 1851 and Pr. 1852 by Bp of Ox. R. of Hatley Cockayne, Dio. Ely, 1861. (Patron, Capt. H. F. Cockayne-Cust; Tithe, 194*l* 3*s* 4*d*; Glebe, 53 acres; R.'s Inc. 250*l* and Ho; Pop. 126.) Formerly C. of Cockayne-Hatley. [22]

BRICKWOOD, William, *Totternhoe Vicarage, Dunstable.*—V. of Totternhoe, Dio. Ely, 1866. (Patron, Earl Brownlow; V.'s Inc. 200*l* and Ho; Pop. 652.) [23]

BRIDGE, James Henry, *Barnes Green, Surrey, S.W.*—Sid Coll. Cam. Scho. of, Math. Exhib. 22nd Wrang. B.A. 1857, M.A. 1860; Deac. 1858, and Pr. 1859 by Bp of Lon. C. of Barnes 1864. Formerly C. of St. Mary-at-Hill and St. Andrew Hubbard, Lond. 1858–64. [24]

BRIDGE, Robert Lee, *Maldon, Essex.*—Queens' Coll. Cam. B.A 1828; Deac. 1828 and Pr. 1829 by Bp of Lon. R. of St. Mary's, Maldon, Dio. Roch. 1832. (Patrons, D. and C. of Westminster; R.'s Inc. 230*l*; Pop. 1278.) Formerly C. of Alphamstone, Essex, 1828. [25]

BRIDGE, Stephen, *Grove-place, Grove lane, Camberwell, London, S.*—Queens' Coll. Cam. B.A. 1834, M.A. 1839; Deac. 1836, Pr. 1837. P. C. of St. Matthew's, Denmark-hill, Surrey, Dio. Win. 1848. (Patrons, Trustees; P. C.'s Inc. 740*l*; Pop. 5240.) Formerly C. of St. John's, Hull, 1836; Sen. C. and Even. Lect. of St. Mary's, Islington. [26]

BRIDGE, Stephen Frederick, *Bedford.*—Trin. Coll. Cam. B.A. 1866; Deac. 1865 and Pr. 1866 by Bp of Ely. C. of St. Paul's, Bedford, 1865. [27]

BRIDGEMAN, Edmund Wolryche Orlando, *Kinnerley, Oswestry, Salop.*—Trin. Coll. Cam. B.A. 1847; Deac. 1848 and Pr. 1849 by Bp of Ches. V. of Kinnerley, Dio. Lich. 1849. (Patron, Ld Chan; Tithe—App. 1*l* 9*s*; Imp. 770*l* 19*s*, V. 160*l*; Glebe, 30 acres; V.'s Inc. 200*l* and Ho; Pop. 1310.) [28]

BRIDGEMAN, Hon. George Thomas Orlando, *The Hall, Wigan.*—Trin. Coll. Cam. M.A. 1845; Deac. 1849 by Bp of Roch. Pr. 1850 by Bp. of Herf. R. of Wigan, Dio. Ches. 1864. (Patron, Earl of Bradford;

R.'s Inc. 1600*l* and Ho; Pop. 11,000.) Formerly R. of St. Mary's, Blymhill, Salop, 1854–64. [1]

BRIDGEMAN. Hon. John Robert Orlando, *Weston-under-Lyziard (Staffs), near Shiffnal, Salop.*—Trin. Coll. Cam. M.A. 1853; Deac. 1857 and Pr. 1858 by Bp of Man. R. of Weston-under Lyziard, Dio. Lich. 1859. (Patron, Earl of Bradford; Tithe, 335*l* 4*s* 2*d*; Glebe, 93 acres; R.'s Inc. 460*l* and Ho; Pop. 335.) Formerly C. of Prestwich, Lancashire, 1857–59; Chap. to the Prestwich Union, 1858–59. [2]

BRIDGES, Alexander Henry, *Beddington House, near Croydon, S.*—Oriel Coll. Ox. 4th cl. Lit. Hum. B.A. 1835, M.A. 1838; Deac. 1836 and Pr. 1837 by Bp of Lon. R. of Beddington, Dio. Win. 1864. (R.'s Inc. 1380*l* and Ho; Pop. 1556.) Formerly C. of St. Mark's, Horsham, 1841–58; P. C. of Southwater, Sussex, 1858–64. [3]

BRIDGES, Brook Edward, *Haynes, near Bedford.*—Oriel Coll. Ox. 2nd cl. Lit. Hum. and B.A. 1835, M.A. 1839; Deac. and Pr. 1839 by Bp of Ox. V. of Haynes, Dio. Ely, 1843. (Patron, Sir G. Osborn, Bart; Tithe, 524*l* 18*s*; V.'s Inc. 525*l* and Ho; Pop. 932.) Formerly Fell. of Mert. Coll. Ox; P. C. of Holywell, Oxford, 1839–43. [4]

BRIDGES, Brook George, *Blankney, Sleaford, Lincolnshire.*—Oriel Coll. Ox. B.A. 1825; Deac. 1826 and Pr. 1827 by Bp of Pet. R. of Blankney, Dio. Lin. 1854. (Patron, H. Chaplin, Esq; Corn Rent, 428*l*; Glebe, 363 acres; R.'s Inc. 890*l* and Ho; Pop. 560.) [5]

BRIDGES, Charles, 5, *Great Ormond-street, Queen-square, Bloomsbury, London, W.C.*—Ch. Ch. Ox. B.A. 1852, M.A. 1855; Deac. and Pr. 1853. C. of St. George the Martyr's, Bloomsbury, 1860. Formerly C. of St. Mary's, Shrewsbury, 1853–56. [6]

BRIDGES, Charles, *Hinton Martell, Wimborne, Dorset.*—Deac. 1817, Pr. 1818. R. of Hinton Martell, Dio. Salis. 1855. (Patron, Earl of Shaftesbury; Tithe, 365*l*; Glebe, 22 acres; R.'s Inc. 387*l* and Ho; Pop. 357.) Surrogate. Author, *Sacramental Instruction*, 1844, 2*s* 6*d*; *Memoir and Correspondence of the Rev. J. T. Nottidge*, 1848, 8*s* 6*d*; *Manual for the Young, being an Exposition of Proverbs* i. 9, 2*s* 6*d*; *Exposition of Psalm* cxix. 7*s*; *The Christian Ministry*, 10*s* 6*d*; *Exposition of the Book of Proverbs*, 2 vols. 12*s*; *Memoir of Miss M. J. Graham*, 6*s*; *Address before and after Confirmation*, 3*d*; *Scriptural Studies*, 2 vols, 3*s*. [7]

BRIDGES, Frederick Hanson, *Dunkerton, Somerset.*—Trin. Coll. Cam. B.A. 1860, M.A. 1863; Deac. 1861 and Pr. 1862 by Bp of Lich. C. of Dunkerton 1865. Formerly C. of Earl Sterndale-with-Burbage, near Buxton, Derbyshire. [8]

BRIDGES, Nathaniel, *Henstridge (Somerset), near Blandford.*—Queens' Coll. Cam; Deac. 1812 and Pr. 1813 by Bp of Nor. V. of Henstridge, Dio. B. and W. 1813. (Patron, Bp of B. and W; Tithe—Eccles. Commis. 358*l* 2*s*, and 70 acres of Glebe; V. 557*l* 17*s*; V.'s Inc. 556*l* and Ho; Pop. 1173.) [9]

BRIDGES, Thomas Pym, *Danbury, Chelmsford.*—Ch. Ch. Ox. B.A. 1828; Deac. 1828 and Pr. 1830 by Bp of Lon. R. of Danbury, Dio. Roch. 1855. (Patron, Sir B. W. Bridges, Bart; Glebe, 22 acres; R.'s Inc. 450*l* and Ho; Pop. 1113.) Formerly C. of Danbury 1828–55. [10]

BRIDGES, William, *The Union, Bridge-street, Manchester.*—Deac. 1845, Pr. 1846. Chap. of the Manchester Workhouse 1860. Formerly P. C. of Lysse, Hants, 1847–58; C. of St. Peter's, Preston, 1858–60. [11]

BRIDGMAN, Arthur Alexander, *Padgate Parsonage, Warrington.*—Caius Coll. Cam. B.A. 1836; Deac. 1844, Pr. 1845. P. C. of Padgate, Dio. Ches. 1852. (Patron, R. of Warrington; P. C.'s Inc. 120*l*; Pop. 1510.) [12]

BRIDGWATER, Henry Hugh, *Snettisham, Lynn, Norfolk.* [13]

BRIERLEY, Edwin, *Great Broughton, Carlisle.*—St. Bees; Deac. 1858 and Pr. 1860 by Bp of Carl. P. C. of Great Broughton, Dio. Carl. 1863. (Patron, V. of Bridekirk; P. C.'s Inc. 100*l*; Pop. 1520.) Formerly C. of Bridekirk 1858–63. [14]

BRIERLEY, George Henry, *Pensnett, Dudley.*—St. Bees; Deac. 1867 by Bp of Lich. C. of St. Mark's, Pensnett, 1867. [15]

BRIERLEY, James, *Mossley Hall, Congleton, Cheshire.*—St. John's Coll. Cam. B.A. 1838, M.A. 1841; Deac. 1838 and Pr. 1839 by Bp of Ches. P. C. of Trinity, Mossley, Dio. Ches. 1846. (Patron, R. of Astbury; Tithe, 69*l*; P. C.'s Inc. 170*l*; Pop. 949.) Formerly C. of Rainhill, near Prescot. [16]

BRIERLEY, Joseph Henry, *The Priory, Leeds.*—Wad. Coll. Ox. B.A. 1863, M.A. 1865; Deac. 1866 and Pr. 1867 by Bp of Rip. C. of Leeds 1866. [17]

BRIERLEY, Thomas, *Ashton Wood Houses, Ashton-on-Mersey.*—Dub. A.B. 1855; Deac. 1855 by Bp of Ches. C. of Ashton-on-Mersey. Formerly C. of St. George's, Altrincham, and St. James's, Latchford, Lancashire. [18]

BRIGGS, Francis Brooking, *New Brentford, Middlesex.*—Trin. Coll. Cam. B.A. 1830, M.A. 1837; Deac. 1830, Pr. 1831. V. of New Brentford, Dio. Lon. 1853. (Patron, R. of Hanwell; Tithe, 85*l*; V.'s Inc. 350*l* and Ho; Pop. 1995.) [19]

BRIGGS, John, *Wollaston, near Wellingboro', Northants.*—C. of Wollaston. [20]

BRIGHT, James Franck, *Marlborough, Wilts.*—Univ. Coll. Ox. 1st cl. in History, M.A. 1854. Asst. Mast. in Marlborough Coll. [21]

BRIGHT, John Henry, *Adbaston, Newport, Shropshire.*—Scho. of St. John's Coll. Cam. B.A. 1823, M.A. 1828; Deac. 1825, Pr. 1826. P. C. of Adbaston, Dio. Lich. 1840. (Patron, Dean of Lich; Glebe, 3 acres; P. C.'s Inc. 100*l* and Ho; Pop. 610.) Formerly Travelling Fell. of St. John's Coll. Cam. Author, *A Visitation Sermon*; *Sermons on Family Worship*. [22]

BRIGHT, John Henry, *Westbury-upon-Trym, Bristol.*—St. Bees; Deac. and Pr. 1864 by Bp of Lich. C. of Westbury 1866. Formerly C. of St. Matthew's, Walsall, and St. Nicholas', Hereford. [23]

BRIGHT, Mynors, *Magdalen College, Cambridge.*—Magd. Coll. Cam. B.A. 1840, Tyrwhitt's Hebrew Scho. and M.A. 1843; Deac. 1842, Pr. 1844. President, Foundation Fell. and Tut. of Magd. Coll. Cam. [24]

BRIGHT, William, *University College, Oxford.*—Univ. Coll. Ox. 1st cl. Lit. Hum. 1846, B.A. 1846, Johnson's Theol. Scho. 1847, Ellerton Theol. Essay 1848, M.A. 1849; Deac. 1848 and Pr. 1850 by Bp of Ox. Fell. of Univ. Coll. Formerly Tut. Trinity Coll. Glenalmond, Perthshire. Author, *Ancient Collects selected from various Rituals*, 1857, 2nd ed. 1861, 5*s*; *History of the Church from Edict of Milan to Council of Chalcedon*, 1860, 10*s* 6*d*; and *Eighteen Sermons of St. Leo the Great on the Incarnation*, translated, with *Notes*, 1862, 5*s*. [25]

BRIGSTOCKE, Claudius Buchanan, *Turin.*—St. Edm. Hall, Ox. B.A. 1852; Deac. 1855 by Bp of Lon. Pr. 1856 by Bp of Carl. British Chap. at Turin. Formerly C. of St. George's, Bloomsbury, 1855, St. James's, Heywood, Manchester, 1856–58, Christ's Chapel, Maida-hill, Lond. 1858–62, Ockley, Dorking, 1863. [26]

BRIGSTOCKE, Decimus, 1, *St. Colme-street, Edinburgh.*—Jesus Coll. Ox. Exhib. B.A. 1862; Deac. 1862 and Pr. 1863 by Bp of G. and B. Asst. Min. of St. Paul's Episcopal Chapel, Edinburgh. Formerly C. of St. James's Chapel, Cheltenham. [27]

BRIGSTOCKE, Martin Whish, *Hope-Mansell Rectory, Mitcheldean, Herefordshire.*—Dub. A.B. 1849, A.M. 1852; Deac. 1851 by Bp of Lich. Pr. 1855 by Bp of Herf. C. of Hope-Mansell (sole charge) 1863. Formerly C. of Huntingdon 1854, Tretire 1860. [28]

BRIGSTOCKE, Silvanus, *Rhosmarket, Milford, Pembrokeshire.*—Deac. 1822, Pr. 1833. V. of Rhosmarket, Dio. St. D. 1856. (Patron, Ld Chan; V.'s Inc. 98*l*; Pop. 451.) Formerly C. of Holme Lacey, near Hereford. [29]

BRIGSTOCKE, Thomas, *Milford-Haven, Pembrokeshire.*—Trin. Coll. Cam. B.D 1830; Deac. 1817, Pr. 1818. R. of Whitton, Radnorshire, Dio. St. D. 1825. (Patron, Bp of St. D; Tithe, 141*l*; Glebe, 7 acres; R.'s Inc.

155*l* and Ho; Pop. 115.) P. C. of Milford-Haven, Dio. St. D. 1825. (Patron, Hon. F. R. Greville; P. C.'s Inc. *uncertain*.) Surrogate 1838; Rural Dean of Roose, Pembrokeshire, 1837. [1]

BRINDLE, Joseph, *Warrington.*—P. C. of Thelwall, near Runcorn, Dio. Ches. 1829. (Patron, James Nicholson, Esq; P. C.'s Inc. 150*l*; Pop. 468.) [2]

BRINDLE, Joseph Furnival, *Bacup, Whalley, near Manchester.*—Brasen. Coll. Ox. B.A. 1850, M.A. 1853; Deac. 1851 by Bp of Salis. Pr. 1852 by Bp of Chich. P. C. of St. John's, Bacup, Dio. Man. 1858. (Patrons, Hulme's Trustees; Glebe, 55 acres; P. C.'s Inc. 200*l* and Ho; Pop. 8981.) Formerly C. of Leckhampstead and Winterbourne, Berks. Editor, *Chants for our Choir*, 1864, 2*s*. [3]

BRINDLEY, Frederick, *Oakfield House, Collegiate Institution, Birkenhead.*—Dub. A.B. 1863, A.M. 1866; Deac. 1863 and Pr. 1864 by Bp of Ches. C. of Trinity, Liverpool. Formerly C. of St. Paul's, Tranmere, and All Saints', Nottingham. [4]

BRINE, Edward, *The Hague, Holland.*—Queens' Coll. Cam. B.A. 1842; Deac. 1843, Pr. 1844. Chap. to the British Embassy at the Hague. [5]

BRINE, George Augustus, *Croxton, Eccleshall, Staffs.*—Ex. Coll. Ox. B.A. 1863, M.A. 1866; Deac. 1865 and Pr. 1866 by Bp of Lich. C. of Croxton 1865. [6]

BRINE, James Gram, *Wiesbaden.*—St. John's Coll. Ox. 2nd cl. Lit. Hum. 3rd cl. Math. et Phy. and B.A. 1841, M.A. 1845. P. C. of All Saints', Chardstock, Dio. Salis. 1846. (Patron, Bp of Salis; P. C.'s Inc. 150*l* and Ho; Pop. 453.) Chap. at Wiesbaden. Late Fell. of St. John's Coll. Ox. [7]

BRINE, Percival John, *King's College Cambridge.*—King's Coll. Cam. B.A. 1845, M.A. 1848; Deac. 1846, Pr. 1847. Fell. of King's Coll. Cam. [8]

BRISCOE, John George, *Topcroft, near Bungay, Suffolk.*—St. Aidan's; Deac. 1851, Pr. 1852. C. of Topcroft 1858. Formerly C. of Ch. Ch. Chester, and St. Marylebone, Lond. 1855–58. [9]

BRISCOE, Richard, *Nutfield Rectory, near Redhill, Surrey.*—Jesus Coll. Ox. 3rd cl. Lit. Hum, 1829, B.A. 1830, M.A. 1833, B.D. 1841, D.D. 1845; Deac. 1831 and Pr. 1832 by Bp of Bristol. R. of Nutfield, Dio. Win. 1865. (Patron, Jesus Coll. Ox; Tithe, 725*l*; Glebe, 105 acres; R.'s Inc. 880*l* and Ho; Pop. 997.) Formerly C. of Llangollen 1831–33, Henllan, Denbigh, 1833–39; V. of Whitford, Dio. St. A. 1839–65; Fell. of Jesus Coll. Ox. 1831, and Sen. Fell. 1849–66. Author, *The Common Work of all the Members of the Church of Christ*, 1858. [10]

BRISCOE, Thomas, *Holyhead, Anglesey.*—Jesus Coll. Ox. 1st cl. Lit. Hum. B.A. 1833, M.A. 1836, B.D. 1843; Fell. of Jesus Coll. 1834 to 1859, and Tut. 1835 to 1839, and again from 1843 to 1857; Deac. 1836 and Pr. 1837 by Bp of Ox. P. C. of Holyhead, Dio. Ban, 1858. (Patron, Jesus Coll. Ox; Tithe—App. 613*l*; Glebe, 6 acres; P. C.'s Inc. 287*l*, fees about 50*l* and Ho; Pop. 8451.) Formerly P. C. of Henllan, Denbigh, 1839–40. Translator of Ellendorf's *Ist Petrus in Rom und Bischof der Romischen Kirche gewesen*, 1851, 2*s*; and from the Hebrew into Welsh of *The Prophet Isaiah*, 1853, 3*s* 6*d*; of *The Book of Job*, 1854, 2*s*; and of *The Books of Psalms and Proverbs*, 1855, 5*s* 6*d*. [11]

BRISCOE, William, *Jesus College, Oxford.*—Jesus Coll. Ox. 1846, 2nd cl. Lit. Hum. and B.A. 1850, M.A. 1852; Deac. 1851 and Pr. 1853 by Bp of Ox. Fell. and Tut. of Jesus Coll. Ox. Formerly C. of Mold, 1855–60. [12]

BRISTOW, E., *Cannington Vicarage, Bridgwater.*—V. of Cannington, Dio. B. and W. 1865. (Patron, Lord Clifford, or his Lessee; Pop. 1419.) [13]

BRISTOW, Richard Rhodes, 10, *Percy-circus, Pentonville, London, W.C.*—St. Mary Hall, Ox. B.A. 1866; Deac. 1866 by Bp Anderson for Bp of Lon. C. of St. Philip's, Clerkenwell, 1866. [14]

BRISTOW, Theodore, *Brattleby Rectory, near Lincoln.*—Trin. Hall, Cam. and Cuddesdon Theol. Coll. B.A. 1859; Deac. 1861 and Pr. 1863 by Bp of Ox. C. of Brattleby 1868. Formerly C. of Bierton, Bucks, 1861–63. [15]

BRISTOW, Whiston Timothy, *The Vicarage, Isle of Graine, Rochester.*—Sid. Coll. Cam. B.A. 1849; Deac. 1849 and Pr. 1851 by Bp of B. and W. V. of St. James's, Isle of Graine, Dio. Roch. 1862. (Patron, G. Henderson, Esq; Tithe, 358*l*; Glebe, 2 acres; V.'s Inc. 362*l* and Ho; Pop. 255.) Formerly C. of Luxborough, Somerset, 1849, Liverpool 1856, Ashton-in-Makerfield 1858, Great Tey, Essex, 1860. [16]

BRISTOW, William James, *Offenham Parsonage, Evesham.*—Ball. Coll. Ox. B.A. 1857, M.A. 1860; Deac. 1859 and Pr. 1860 by Bp of Ox. P. C. of Offenham, Dio. Wor. 1865. (Patrons, D. and C. of Ch. Ch. Ox; Glebe, 5 acres; P. C.'s Inc. 120*l* and Ho; Pop. 470.) Formerly Chap. of Ch. Ch. Ox. 1859; C. of Cassington, Oxon, 1860–64. [17]

BRITTAIN, Charles, 119, *Lodge-road, Winson-green, Birmingham.*—St. Bees 1852–53; Deac. 1854 and Pr. 1855 by Bp of Lich. Chap of the Workhouse, and of the Borough Lunatic Asylum, Birmingham, 1858 (Inc. 325*l*.) Formerly C. of Kingswinford, Wordsley, Staffs, 1854–57, Market Drayton, Salop, 1857–58. [18]

BRITTAIN, Isaac, *Wressel, Howden, Yorks.*—V. of Wressel, Dio. York, 1856. (Patron, Lord Leconfield; Tithe—Imp. 550*l*; V. 144*l* 10*s*; V.'s Inc. 160*l*; Pop. 423.) [19]

BRITTAN, Charles, *Wetherell-place, Clifton.*—St. John's Coll. Cam. Wrang. 1st cl. Nat. Sci. Trip. Scho. of St. John's, B.A. 1853, M.A. 1856; Deac. 1855 and Pr. 1856 by Bp of Ches. Chap. of the Bristol Gaol 1859. Formerly C. of St. Mark's, Liverpool, 1855, Bowdon, Cheshire, 1857, The Temple, Bristol, 1858. [20]

BRITTER, Thomas Candy, *Silverstone, Towcester, Northants.*—King's Coll. Lon. Assoc; Deac. 1866 and Pr. 1867 by Bp of Pet. C. of Whittlebury and Silverstone. [21]

BRITTON, J. P., *Brightlingsea, Essex.*—C. of Brightlingsea. [22]

BRITTON, Paul Ford, *Cadeleigh, near Tiverton, Devon.*—Ex. Coll. Ox. B.A. 1840, M.A. 1843; Deac. 1842 by Bp of Salis. Pr. 1843 by Bp of Ex. R. of Cadeleigh, Dio. Ex. 1845. (Patroness, Mrs. Moore; Tithe, 193*l*; Glebe, 55 acres; R.'s Inc. 270*l* and Ho; Pop. 358.) Rural Dean of Cadbury 1856. Formerly C. of Tawstock, Devon, 1842–45. [23]

BRITTON, Thomas Hopkins, *Cadeleigh, near Tiverton, Devon.*—Ex. Coll. Ox. Pusey and Ellerton Hebrew Scho. 1839, B.A. 1840, M.A. 1842; Deac. 1840 by Bp of Win. Pr. 1841 by Bp of Ex. V. of Newlyn, Dio. Ex. 1856. (Patron, Bp of Ex; Tithe—Imp. 700*l*, V. 470*l*; Glebe, 9 acres; V.'s Inc. 490*l* and Ho; Pop. 1641.) Late V. of Manaccan, Cornwall, 1854–56; Rural Dean of Pydar, Cornwall, 1856. Author, *Horæ Sacramentales* (*a Vindication of the Sacramental Articles, illustrating their meaning from the Writings of their Compilers and last Editor, and by other Documents published under the sanction of the Church between the years 1536 and 1571*), 1851, 6*s*; *An Examination of the Facts and Arguments addressed by Dr. Bayford to Dr. Lushington against the United Opinion of Historians that the 13th Eliz. cap. 12, referred to the Articles of 1562*, 1857, 4*s*. [24]

BROAD, John Samuel, *Newcastle-under-Lyme, Staffs.*—St. Edm. Hall, Ox. B.A. 1832, M.A. 1834; Deac. 1832, Pr. 1833. P. C. of St. George's, Newcastle-under-Lyne, Dio. Lich. 1840. (Patrons, Simeon's Trustees; P. C.'s Inc. 250*l*; Pop. 6807.) Head Mast. of the Newcastle-under-Lyne Gr. Sch. 1840. Author, *Ministers of Christ in their relation to Him and to one another* (a Visitation Sermon), 1846; *The True Ground of National and Individual Glory* (a Sermon on the Funeral of the Duke of Wellington), 1852; *The Divine Presence entreated for the Efficiency of the Ministry, and the Prosperity of the People of God* (a Visitation Sermon), 1854, etc. [25]

BROADBENT, Cornelius Farnworth, *Worfield, Bridgnorth, Salop.*—St. Mary Hall, Ox. B.A. 1832, M.A. 1836; Deac. 1832 and Pr. 1833 by Bp of

Lich. V. of Worfield, Dio. Lich. 1842. (Patron, W. Y. Davenport, Esq; Tithe—Imp. 1745*l*, V. 220*l*; Glebe, 17 acres; V.'s Inc. 260*l*; Pop. 1785.) Rural Dean of Trysull, Staffs, 1849. [1]

BROADBENT, Francis B., *Waterhead, Oldham.*—P. C. of Waterhead, Dio. Man. 1854. (Patrons, the Crown and Bp of Man. alt; P. C.'s Inc. 150*l*; Pop. 3941.) [2]

BROADE, George Edgar, *Torquay.*—Caius Coll. Cam. B.A. 1862, M.A. 1866; Deac. 1862 and Pr. 1863 by Bp of Win. Formerly Sen. C. of Romsey 1862–65, and C. of Wonston, Hants, 1865–66. [3]

BROADHEAD, George, *West Wycombe, Bucks.* —Trin. Coll. Cam. B.A. 1830, M.A. 1833; Deac. 1831 by Bp of Lin. Pr. 1833 by Bp of Nor. V. of West Wycombe, Dio. Ox. 1845. (Patron, Sir J. D. King, Bart; Tithe—Imp. 1248*l* 11*s* 7*d*, V. 294*l* 18*s*; V.'s Inc. 300*l*; Pop. 1786.) [4]

BROADLEY, Alexander, *Bradpole Vicarage, near Bridport, Dorset.*—Wad. Coll. Ox. B.A. 1836, M.A. 1839; Deac. 1838 and Pr. 1839 by Bp of Salis. V. of Bradpole, Dio. Salis. 1844. (Patron, Ld Chan; Tithe, 265*l*; Rent from Glebe, 55*l*; V.'s Inc. 320*l* and Ho; Pop. 1449.) Surrogate; Preb. of Winterborne Earls in Salis. Formerly C. of Bridport 1838; P. C. of Walditch. [5]

BROCK, Carey, *St. Peter-du-Bois Rectory, Guernsey.*—Trin. Coll. Cam. B.A. 1848; Deac. 1848 and Pr. 1849 by Bp of Win. R. of St. Peter-du-Bois, Dio. Win. 1850. (Patron, the Crown; Tithe, 80*l*; Glebe, 5 acres; R.'s Inc. 200*l* and Ho; Pop. 1141.) [6]

BROCK, Henry Frederick, *Doncaster.*—Trin. Coll. Cam. B.A. 1847, M.A. 1854; Deac. 1847 and Pr. 1848 by Bp. of Win. P. C. of Ch. Ch. Doncaster, Dio. York, 1854. (Patron, G. J. Jarratt, Esq; P. C.'s Inc. 400*l* and Ho; Pop. 9106.) [7]

BROCK, Isaac, *Park Cottage, Thornhill-road, Barnsbury Park, London, N.*—Queen's Coll. Ox. 1st cl Math. et Phy. B.A. 1851, M.A. 1865; Deac. 1852 and Pr. 1853 by Bp of Tuam. Min. of Chapel of Ease to St. Mary's, Islington, 1865. (Patron, V. of Islington; Min.'s Inc. about 500*l* from pew rents.) Formerly Miss. of Irish Ch. Missions in Connemara; Clerical Sec. of Islington Protestant Institute; Min. of Jews' Episcopal Chap. Bethnal Green. [8]

BROCK, Mourant, *Clifton, Bristol.*—St. Mary Hall, Ox. B.A. 1825, M.A. 1828; Deac. 1826, Pr. 1827. P. C. of Ch. Ch. Clifton, Dio. G. and B. 1856. (Patrons, Simeon's Trustees; P. C.'s Inc. 500*l*; Pop. 4176.) Formerly Chap. to Bath Penitentiary 1836. [9]

BROCK, Thomas, *Guernsey.*—Oriel Coll. Ox. B.A. 1838, M.A. 1848; Deac. 1839, Pr. 1840. P. C. of St. John's, Guernsey, Dio. Win. 1858. (Patrons, Trustees; P. C.'s Inc. 250*l* and Ho.) [10]

BROCK, William, *Bishop's Waltham, Hants.*—Queen's Coll. Ox. 2nd. cl. Lit. Hum. and B.A. 1827, M.A. 1834; Deac. 1828, Pr. 1829. R. of Bishop's Waltham, Dio. Win. 1833. (Patron, Bp of Win; Tithe, 1250*l*; Glebe, 98 acres; R.'s Inc. 1300*l* and Ho; Pop. 1628.) Author, *Tractarianism Schismatical and Dishonest*, 1850, 6*s*; *Popery in the Church of England* (a Letter to the Abp of York on Archd. Wilberforce's Doctrine of the Eucharist), 1854, 2*d*; *Lecture on Anglican Popery* 1855, 8*d*. [11]

BROCKBANK, John, *Ulverston.*—Dub. A.B. 1863, A.M. 1866; Deac. 1861 and Pr. 1864 by Bp of Carl. Mast. of Proprietary Sch. Ulverston, 1861; and C. of Kirkby Irleth, Lancashire, 1861. Formerly Mast. of Clergy Jubilee Sch. Newcastle-on-Tyne, 1853–55; Sec. at the Protestant Coll. Malta, 1855–58. [12]

BROCKLEBANK, Thomas, *King's College, Cambridge.*—King's Coll. Cam. B.A. 1849, M.A. 1852; Deac. 1850, Pr. 1851. Sen. Fell. of King's Coll. Cam. [13]

BROCKLEBANK, William, *Winchelsea, Rye, Sussex.*—Queens' Coll. Cam. B.A. 1831; Deac. and Pr. 1831. V. of Udimore, Dio. Chich. 1841. (Patrons, Trustees of late J. Langford, Esq; Tithe—Imp. 400*l* and 5 acres of Glebe; V.'s Inc. 106*l*; Pop. 444.) [14]

BROCKMAN, Ralph St. Leger, *Ipswich.*—Bp Hat. Hall, Dur. B.A. 1852, Licen. Theol. 1854; Deac. 1855 by Bp of Colombo, Pr. 1856 by Bp of Lon. C. of St. Matthew's Ipswich, 1866. [15]

BROCKMAN, Tatton, *Otham, Maidstone.*—Oriel Coll. Ox. B.A. 1815, M.A. 1818. R. of Otham, Dio. Cant. 1849. (Patron, the present R; Tithe, 415*l*; Glebe, 38 acres; R.'s Inc. 520*l* and Ho; Pop. 294.) [16]

BROCKWELL, John Cornthwaite, 9, *Harewood-street, Harewood-square, London, N.W.*—Ch. Ch. Ox. B.A. 1864; Deac. 1866 by Bp of Lon. C. of Ch. Ch. Marylebone, 1866. [17]

BRODHURST, Frederick, *Gawber, Barnsley, Yorks.*—Ch. Coll. Cam. B.A. 1854, M.A. 1857; Deac. 1855 and Pr. 1856 by Bp of Roch. P. C. of Gawber, Dio. Rip. 1858. (Patron, V. of Darton; P. C.'s Inc. 112*l* and Ho; Pop. 1421.) Formerly C. of Chelmsford. [18]

BRODIE, A., *Granborough, Rugby.*—V. of Granborough, Dio. Wor. 1866. (Patroness, Mrs. Halse; V.'s Inc. 200*l* and Ho; Pop. 462.) [19]

BRODIE, Caithness, 52, *Onslow-square, London, S.W.*—Trin. Coll. Cam. B.A. 1864; Deac. 1866 and Pr. 1867 by Bp of Lon. C. of St. Stephen's, Kensington, 1866. [20]

BRODIE, Peter Bellinger, *Rowington, near Warwick.*—Emman. Coll. Cam. B.A. 1838, M.A. 1842; Deac. 1838 and Pr. 1839 by Bp of Salis. V. of Rowington, Dio. Wor. 1853. (Patron, Bp. of Wor; Tithe—Imp. 603*l* 17*s* 3*d*, V. 231*l* 10*s*; Glebe, 40 acres; V.'s Inc. 313*l* and Ho; Pop. 995.) Surrogate. Formerly C. of Wylye, Wilts, 1838, Steeple Claydon, Bucks, 1840, Down Hatherley, Glouc. 1840. Author, *Fossil Insects in the Secondary Rocks*, Van Voorst, 1845; Papers on Geology in Transactions of Geological Society and British Association. [21]

BRODIE, William, *Alresford, Hants.*—Trin. Coll. Cam. 7th Sen. Opt. and B.A. 1843, M.A. 1846; Deac. 1844 and Pr. 1845 by Bp of Win. P. C. of New Alresford, Dio. Win. 1851. (Patron, Bp. of Win; Tithe, 240*l*; Glebe, 18 acres; P. C.'s Inc. 330*l* and Ho; Pop. 1541.) Formerly C. of Ewell 1844–47, Cheshunt 1847–51. [22]

BRODRIBB, William Jackson, *Wootton-Rivers, Pewsey, Wilts.*—St. John's Coll. Cam. R. of Wootton-Rivers, Dio. Salis. 1860. (Patrons, St. John's Coll. Cam. and Brasen. Coll. Ox. alt; Tithe, 405*l*; Glebe, 50 acres; R.'s Inc. 480*l* and Ho; Pop. 444.) Late Fell. of St. John's Coll. Cam. [23]

BRODRICK, Alan, *Bramshaw, near Lyndhurst.* —Ex. Coll. Ox. 3rd cl. Lit. Hum. B.A. 1849; Deac. 1850 and Pr. 1851 by Bp of Salis. V. of Bramshaw, Dio. Salis. 1860. (Patrons, D. and C. of Salis; Glebe, 8 acres; V.'s Inc. 153*l*; Pop. 750.) Formerly C. of Bishop's Lavington 1860–51, Chidcock, Dorset, 1852–53; P. C. of Baydon, Wilts, 1853–60. Author, *Songs of the People* with Preface by Bishop of Oxford, 1866; *Funeral Sermon* at Wyke Regis, 1866. [24]

BRODRICK, The Hon. Alan, *Stagsden Vicarage, Bedford.*—Ball. Coll. Ox. B.A. 1862, M.A. 1866; Deac. 1864, Pr. 1865. V. of Stagsden, Dio. Ely, 1867. (Patron, Lord Dynevor; Glebe, 7 acres; V.'s Inc. 300*l* and Ho; Pop. 708.) Formerly C. of Wrecklesham, Surrey, 1864–66, St. Matthew's, Denmark-hill, 1866–67. [25]

BRODRICK, Francis Edward, *Penwortham, near Preston.*—Wor. Coll. Ox. B.A. 1863, M.A. 1865; Deac. 1864 by Bp of Ches. Pr. 1866 by Bp of Man. C. of Penwortham 1865. Formerly Asst. C. of Stoke-upon-Trent. [26]

BRODRICK, John Barry, *Sneaton Rectory, Whitby.*—Queens' Coll. Cam. Scho. B.A. 1838, M.A. 1841; Deac. 1838 and Pr. 1840 by Bp of Ches. R. of Sneaton, Dio. York, 1848. (Patron, Ld Chan; Tithe, 269*l* 5*s* 4*d*; Glebe, 28 acres, let for 21*l* 5*s*; R.'s Inc. 290*l* and Ho; Pop. 268.) Formerly C. of Walmersley, St. Paul's, Warrington and Thorrington; Res. Chap. to the late Duchess of Gordon. Author, *Lays of the Sabbath*, 1859, 2*s* 6*d*; *Three Sermons on the Trinity*, 1846, 1*s*;

Lecture on Home Duties, 1857; *Lecture on Books, their Readers and Writers*, 1867. [1]

BRODRICK, The Very Rev. and Right Hon. William John (Viscount Middleton), *The Deanery, Exeter.*—Ball. Coll. Ox. 1st cl. Lit. Hum. and B.A. 1820, M.A. 1823; Deac. 1822 by Bp of Ban. Pr. 1822 by Bp of Win. Dean of Exeter 1863. Formerly C. of Ashstead, Surrey, 1822–25; R. of Castle Rising, Norfolk, 1825–39; R. of Bath 1839–54; Can. of Wells 1855–63; Chap. in Ordinary to the Queen. [2]

BROMAGE, James Gosling, *Bush Farm, Llansoy, near Usk.*—St. Edm. Hall, Ox. B.A. 1865; Deac. 1866 and Pr. 1867 by Bp of Llan. C. of Llansoy 1866. [3]

BROMBY, John Edward, *Melbourne, Victoria.*—St. John's Coll. Cam. Bell's Univ. Scho. 1829, 9th Wrang. 2nd cl. Cl. Trip. and B.A. 1832, M.A. 1835, B.D. and D.D. 1850; Deac. 1834, Pr. 1835. Head Mast. of the Gr. Sch. Melbourne, Australia. Formerly Prin. of Qu. Eliz. Coll. Guernsey. Author, *The Irregular Element in the Church* (Commencement Sermon at Cambridge), 1850. [4]

BROMBY, John Healey, *The Charter-house, Hull.*—Sid. Coll. Cam. 17th Wrang. and B.A. 1792, M.A. 1795; Deac. 1793 by Abp of York, Pr. 1797 by Bp of Lon. V. of Cheswardine, Market-Drayton, Salop, Dio. Lich. 1821. (Patron, Egerton W. Harding, Esq; Tithe, App. 605*l*, Imp. 213*l*, V. 197*l* 10*s*; Glebe, 30 acres; V.'s Inc. 295*l* and Ho; Pop. 993.) Master of the Charter-house, Hull, 1849; Surrogate 1799. Formerly Fell. of Sid. Coll. Cam; C. of Airmyn, East Yorks, 1793, Walkington 1795; V. of Trinity, Hull, 1797–66. Author, various Sermons, Essays and Lectures published in Hull. [5]

BROMEHEAD, A. C., *Newbold, near Chesterfield.* [6]

BROMEHEAD, Alexander Crawford, Jun., *Ridgeway, Chesterfield.*—Caius Coll. Cam. B.A. 1838; Deac. 1839, Pr. 1840. P. C. of Ridgeway, Dio. Lich. 1845. (Patron, R. of Eckington; P. C.'s Inc. 300*l*; Pop. 1745.) [7]

BROMEHEAD, William, 2, *Carholme-terrace, Lincoln.*—Lin. Coll. Ox. B.A. 1831; Deac. 1831 and Pr. 1832 by Bp of Lin. C. of St. Peter's-at-Gowts and St. Botolph's, Lincoln, 1831–37, North Hykeham 1837–55, South Hykeham 1837–67. [8]

BROMEHEAD, William Crawford, *Calcutta.*—Late Scho. of Trin. Coll. Cam. Jun. Opt. B.A. 1849, M.A. 1853; Deac. 1852, Pr. 1853. Chap. at Calcutta. Formerly P. C. of Rowsley, and C. of Bakewell, Derbyshire. [9]

BROMFIELD, Henry, *Blockley, Moreton-in-Marsh, Worcestershire.*—Wad. Coll. Ox. B.A. 1823; Deac. 1824 and Pr. 1825 by Bp of Lich. V. of Blockley, Dio. Wor. 1855. (Patron, Bp of Wor; Tithe, 520*l*; Glebe, 90 acres; V.'s Inc. 700*l* and Ho; Pop. 2337.) Formerly Sen. C. of Monks Kirby, Warwickshire. [10]

BROMHEAD, Alexander Leslie, *Winwick, Rugby.*—Caius Coll. Cam. B.A. 1844, M.A. 1848; Deac. 1846, Pr. 1847. R. of Winwick, Dio. Pet. 1848. (Patron, Bp of Pet; Tithe, 475*l*; Glebe, 100 acres; R.'s Inc. 596*l* and Ho; Pop. 122.) Rural Dean 1861; Hon. Can. of Pet. 1863. [11]

BROMLEY, Thomas, *Leamington.*—St. Cath. Hall, Cam. B.A. 1838, M.A. 1841; Deac. 1838 and Pr. 1839 by Bp of Chich. P. C. of St. Mary's, Leamington, Dio. Wor. 1856. (Patrons, Trustees; P.C.'s Inc. 350*l*; Pop. 3981.) Surrogate. Formerly V. of St. James's, Wolverhampton, 1843–56. [12]

BROOK, Alfred, *Mansfield-Woodhouse, Mansfield, Notts.*—Ex. Coll. Ox. 3rd cl. Lit. Hum. 1st cl. Math. B.A. 1850, M.A. 1852; Deac. 1851 by Bp of Llan. Pr. 1852 by Bp of G. and B. P. C. of Mansfield-Woodhouse, Dio. Lin. 1860. (Patron, Bp of Lin; V.'s Inc. 300*l*; Pop. 2266.) Rural Dean. Formerly C. of Tiddenham, Glouc. 1851–54; V. of East Retford, Notts, 1854–57; C. of Bournemouth, Hants, 1857–60. [13]

BROOK, Arthur, *Holbeach Vicarage, Lincolnshire.*—Univ. Coll. Ox. Scho. of, 3rd cl. Lit. Hum. 1st cl. Math. et Phy. and B.A. 1853, M.A. 1855; Deac. 1854 and Pr. 1855 by Bp of Lin. V. of Holbeach, Dio. Lin. 1865. (Patron, Bp of Lin; Tithe, 900*l*; Glebe, 16 acres; V.'s Inc. 1050*l* and Ho; Pop. 4960.) Chap. to Bp of Lin. Formerly V. of East Retford, Notts, 1857–65. [14]

BROOK, Charles A., *Hasketon, Woodbridge, Suffolk.* [15]

BROOK, James, *Helme, Huddersfield.*—Wor. Coll. Ox. B.A. 1854, M.A. 1862; Deac. 1854 by Abp of York. Pr. 1857 by Bp of Rip. P. C. of Helme, Dio. Rip. 1858. (Patrons, Wm. Brook, Esq. and V. of Almondbury; P. C.'s Inc. 150*l* and Ho; Pop. 787.) Formerly C. of Cottingham, Yorks, 1854–56, Meltham-Mills, Yorks, 1857–58. [16]

BROOK, John Oatway, *Hugglescote, Ashby-de-la-Zouch.*—St. Aidan's; Deac. 1855 and Pr. 1856 by Bp of Win. C. in sole charge of Hugglescote 1864. Formerly C. of Trinity, Southampton, 1855, Calne 1858; Chap. to the Calne Union 1858; C. of St. Jude's, Manchester, 1860, St. Michael's, Sutton Bonnington, 1862. [17]

BROOKE, Arthur George, *Ruyton-XI-Towns, Salop.*—St Bees; Deac. 1862 and Pr. 1863 by Bp of Lich. C. of Montford, Salop, 1864. Formerly C. of Ruyton-XI-Towns, 1862–64. Author, *The Dying Policeman.* [18]

BROOKE, John, *Haughton Hall, Shiffnal, Salop.*—Brasen. Coll. Ox. B.A. 1824, M.A. 1825; Deac. 1826 and Pr. 1827. Formerly V. of Shiffnal 1831–47. [19]

BROOKE, Joshua, *Colston Bassett, Bingham, Notts.*—Ex. Coll. Ox. B.A. 1832; Deac. 1833 and Pr. 1834 by Bp of Roch. V. of Colston-Bassett, Dio. Lin. 1834. (Patron, Ld Chan; Tithe, 202*l*; Glebe, 42 acres; V.'s Inc. 312*l* and Ho; Pop. 297.) P. C. of Tythby, Dio. Lin. 1843. (Patron, J. Chaworth, Esq; Glebe, 35 acres; P. C.'s Inc. 94*l*; Pop. 718.) [20]

BROOKE, Joshua Ingham, *Thornhill Rectory, Dewsbury.*—Univ. Coll. Ox. 2nd. cl. Lit. Hum. B.A. 1859, M.A. 1862; Deac. 1860 and Pr. 1862 by Bp of Lin. R. of Thornhill, Dio. Rip. 1867. (Patron, B. Ingham, Esq; Tithe, 988*l*; Glebe, 169 acres; R.'s Inc. 1200*l* and Ho; Pop. 3725.) Formerly C. of East Retford 1860–63, Bath-Easton 1863–66, Easthope, 1866–67. [21]

BROOKE, Richard England, *St. Mary's Parsonage, Spring Grove, Middlesex. W.*—Caius. Coll. Cam. 3rd Sen. Opt. B.A. 1844, M.A. 1847; Deac. 1844 and Pr. 1845 by Bp of Rip. P.C. of St. Mary's, Spring Grove, Dio. Lon. 1863. (Patron, H. D. Davies, Esq; P.C.'s Inc. 440*l* and Ho; Pop. 1495.) Hon. Can. of Man. 1862 and Exam. Chap. to Bp of Man. 1861. Formerly C. of Kirklinton 1844–46, Great Coates, 1846–49; P.C. of Sowerby, Halifax, 1849–52; R. of St. Luke's, Cheetham Hill, 1852–63; Rural Dean of Manchester 1860–63. Author, several single Sermons. [22]

BROOKE, Richard Sinclair, *The Rectory, Wyton, Huntingdon.*—Dub. A.B. 1828, A.M. 1857, B.D. and D.D. 1860, *ad eund.* Cam. 1863; Deac. 1828 by Bp of Kildare, Pr. 1829 by Bp of Killaloe. R. of Wyton, Dio. Ely, 1862. (Patron, Duke of Manchester; R.'s estate, 436 acres; R.'s Inc. 600*l* and Ho; Pop. 311.) Formerly C. of Kennity, King's Co. 1820, Letterkenny, Donegal, 1832, Abbeyleix, Queen's Co. 1835, and Min. of Mariners, Ch. Kingstown, Dublin, for 27 years. Author, *The Sheaf of Corn*, 1850; *The Three Voices*, 1851; *Poems*, 1852; *Christ in Shadow, being* 12 *Lectures on Isaiah L.*, 1858; *Biographical Sketches*, published separately in *Dublin University Magazine*; *Life and Times of Dr. John Owen, of Geoffry Chaucer, of Dr. Delany, of Henry Brooke, of Richard Savage*; *A Visit to Quilca, Rambles in Donegal*; *A Pilgrimage to Leix and Ossory*; *The Darragh*, etc. [23]

BROOKE, Stopford Augustus, 1, *Manchester-square, London, W.*—Dub. Downe's Prizeman, Vice-Chan.'s prizes for English verses, A.B. 1856, A M. 1858; Deac. 1857 and Pr. 1858 by Bp of Lon. Min. of St. James's Chapel, York-street, St. James's-square, 1866; Hon. Chap. in Ordinary to the Queen. Formerly C. of St. Matthew's, Marylebone, 1857–59, Kensington, 1860–63; Chap. to British Embassy, Berlin, 1863–65. Author, *Life and Letters of the late Frederick W. Robertson*, Smith, Elder, and Co. 1865, 25*s*. [24]

BROOKE, Thomas, *Wistaston, near Nantwich, Cheshire.*—Ch. Coll. Cam. B.A. 1815; Deac. 1814 by Bp of Lin. Pr. 1815 by Bp of Ban. R. of Wistaston, Dio. Ches. 1825. (Patron, E. Delves Broughton, Esq; Tithe, 200*l*; Glebe, 4½ acres; R.'s Inc. 210 and Ho; Pop. 331.) Author, *Baptismal Regeneration is not the Doctrine of Holy Scripture nor of the Church of England*, 1848, 3*s* 6*d*; *The Lord's Day, its Divine and Moral Obligation*, 1851, 5*s*. [1]

BROOKE, Thomas, 12, *St. Marie's-place, Bury, Lancashire.*—Dub. A.B. 1846, A.M. 1849; Deac. 1850 by Bp of Down, Pr. 1851 by Bp of Killaloe. Sen. C. of Bury 1859. Formerly C. of St. John's, Broughton, Manchester, 1855. [2]

BROOKE, William, *Ropsley Rectory, Grantham.*—King's Coll. Cam. Scho. 1828, Fell. 1831, B.A. 1833, M.A. 1836; Deac. 1833 and Pr. 1834 by Bp of Carl. C. in sole charge of Ropsley 1866. Formerly C. of Boxford 1833–37, Wetheringsett 1837–39, Bentley, Suffolk, 1839–41, and V. of same 1841–52; C. in sole charge of Moulton, Linc. 1852–66. [3]

BROOKES, Charles, *Congham, King's Lynn, Norfolk.*—Queen's Coll. Birmingham; Deac. 1863 and Pr. 1864 by Bp of Lich. C. in sole charge of Congham 1865. Formerly C. of Trinity, West Bromwich, 1863–65. [4]

BROOKES, James Bourne, *Gazeley, Suffolk.*—Ch. Coll. Cam. B.A. 1866; Deac. 1866 by Bp of Ely. C. of Gazeley 1866. [5]

BROOKES, John Henry, *Steeple Aston Rectory, Oxford.*—Brasen. Coll. Ox. Fell. of, B.A. 1845, M.A. 1848; Deac. 1846 and Pr. 1847. R. of Steeple Aston, Dio. Ox. 1863. (Patron, Brasen. Coll. Ox; R.'s Inc. 580*l* and Ho; Pop. 736.) Rural Dean. [6]

BROOKFIELD, William Henry, *Privy Council Office, Downing-street, London, S.W.*—Trin. Coll. Cam. B.A. 1833, M.A. 1836; Deac. 1834 and Pr. 1836 by Abp of York. One of H.M. Inspectors of Schools; R. of Somerby with Humby C. Dio. Lin. 1861. (Patron, Lord Willoughby d'Eresby; R.'s Inc. 700*l* and Ho; Pop. 234.) Chap. in Ordinary to the Queen; Chap. of Rolls Chapel, Lond. [7]

BROOKING, Arthur, *Bovingdon, Hemel-Hempstead, Herts.*—Trin. Coll. Cam. B.A. 1834, M.A. 1838; Deac. 1834 and Pr. 1835 by Bp of Ex. P. C. of Bovingdon, Dio. Roch. 1842. (Patron, Hon. G. D. Ryder; Tithe—App. 710*l*, P. C. 190*l*; Glebe, 11½ acres; P. C.'s Inc. 290*l*; Pop. 1155.) Chap. to Earl Spencer. [8]

BROOKMAN, H. J. T., *Madley, Hereford.*—C. of Madley. [9]

BROOKS, Edward Augustus, *Ibstock Rectory, Ashby-de-la-Zouch.*—Clare Coll. Cam. M.A. 1844; Deac. 1845 and Pr. 1846 by Bp of G. and B. C. of Ibstock 1855. Formerly C. of Christian-Malford, Avebury, and Seend, all in Wilts. [10]

BROOKS, Edward Brewer, *New England Parsonage, Peterborough.*—Wor. Coll. Ox. B.A. 1861, M.A. 1864; Deac. 1861 and Pr. 1862 by Bp of Ches. C. of St. Mark's, Peterborough, 1863. Formerly C. of Holy Trinity, Toxteth Park, Liverpool, 1861–63. [11]

BROOKS, Harvey William, 1, *Chepstow-villas-west, Westbourne-grove, London, W.*—Magd. Hall, Ox. B.A. 1851, M.A. 1854; Deac. 1851 and Pr. 1852 by Bp of Salis. P. C. of St. Stephen's, Westbourne-park, Dio. Lon. 1856. (Patrons, Trustees; P. C.'s Inc. 250*l*.) Formerly C. of Lyme-Regis, Dorset. Author, *The Christian Law of Mutual Burden-bearing*, 1853; *God is Love* (a Sermon). [12]

BROOKS, Jonah, *Barcelona.*—British Chap. at Barcelona. [13]

BROOKS, Joshua William, *Great Ponton, Colsterworth, Lincolnshire.*—M.A. by Abp of Cant; Deac. 1819 and Pr. 1820 by Abp of York. R. of Great Ponton, Dio. Lin. 1864. (Patron, Bp of Lin; R.'s Inc. 570*l* and Ho; Pop. 561.) Preb. of Lin. 1858. Formerly C. of East Retford and Dom. Chap. to Viscount Galway, 1821; V. of Clarsborough 1827; R. of Grove 1837; V. of Nottingham 1843–64, all Dio. Lin. [14]

BROOKS, Thomas William Dell, *Flitwick, Ampthill, Beds.*—Ch. Ch. Ox. B.A. 1851, M.A. 1854, Stud. of Wells Theol. Coll. 1851; Deac. 1852 and Pr. 1853 by Bp of Ox. V. of Flitwick, Dio. Ely, 1855. (Patroness, Mrs. Brooks; Glebe, 48 acres; V.'s Inc. 250*l* and Ho; Pop. 773.) Formerly C. of Cropredy, Ox. and Marston St. Lawrence, Northants. [15]

BROOKS, William, 9, *Jarratt-street, Hull.*—Sid. Coll. Cam. Scho. and Math. Prizeman of, B.A. 1857, M.A. 1861; Deac. 1866 by Abp of York. C. of St. Mary's, Hull, 1866. [16]

BROOKSBANK, Charles, *Blakeney, Glouc.*—Ch. Ch. Ox. B.A. 1853, M.A. 1838. P. C. of Blakeney, Dio. G. and B. 1843. (Patron, the Haberdashers' Company; P. C.'s Inc. 150*l*; Pop. 1079.) [17]

BROOKSBANK, Walter, *Lamplugh Rectory, Cockermouth.*—Univ. Coll. Dur. B.A. 1852, Licen. Theol. and M.A. 1855; Deac. 1853 and Pr. 1854 by Bp of Wor. R. of Lamplugh, Dio. Carl. 1854. (Patron, J. L. Lamplugh-Raper, Esq; Tithe, 300*l*; Glebe, 2 acres; R.'s Inc. 300*l* and Ho; Pop. 808.) Formerly C. of Fillongley, near Coventry, 1853–54. [18]

BROOME, John Henry, *Houghton Hall, Rougham, Norfolk.*—Queens' Coll. Cam. Literate, 1839; Deac. 1839, Pr. 1840. V. of Houghton *juxta* Harpley, Dio. Nor. 1845. (Patron, Marquis of Cholmondeley; Tithe, 108*l*; Glebe, 5½ acres; V.'s Inc. 108*l*; Pop. 227.) Formerly Lieut. in H.M. 10th Infantry. Author, *A Brief Treatise on Geology*, 1839; *A Word on the Divine Promises as to the Restoration of the Jews to their own Land*; *Of the Author and First Cause of Evil, with Final Deliverance of Christ's Kingdom from it*; *The Watchman's Daily Prayer Union for Israel*; *Prayer for the House of Israel*; *Scripture Teachings with Brief Notes on the Coming Glory of Christ and His Kingdom*, 1862. Editor, *The World in which I live*, 1856, 7*s* 6*d*; *My Country, the History of the British Isles*, 5 parts, 1*s* each; *The Story of Papal Rome*, 2*s*; and *Houghton and the Walpoles*, 1866, 2*s* 6*d*. [19]

BROOME, John William, *Haslingden Grane, near Manchester.*—Sid. Coll. Cam. Scho. and Exhib. of, B.A. 1858; Deac. 1858 and Pr. 1860 by Bp of Man. C in sole charge of district of Haslingden Grane 1861. Formerly C. of Chipping 1858–61. [20]

BROOME, Louis George Francis, *Whittlebury, Towcester, Northants.*—Literate; Deac. 1847 and Pr. 1848 by Bp of Pet. P. C. of Whittlebury, with Silverstone, Dio. Pet. 1853. (Patron, the Crown; P. C.'s Inc. 468*l* and Ho; Pop. Whittlebury 487, Silverstone 1166.) Dom. Chap. to Lord Southampton 1853. Formerly Lieut. in H.M. 30th Regt. 1844–47. [21]

BROTHERS, James, *Brabourne, Ashford, Kent.*—Corpus Coll. Cam. B.A. 1839; Deac. 1840, Pr. 1841. V. of Brabourne with Monk's Horton R. Dio. Cant. 1846. (Patron, Abp of Cant; Brabourne, Tithe—App. 613*l* 0*s* 6*d*, V. 270*l* 3*s* 6*d*; Glebe, 2 acres; Monk's Horton, Tithe, 142*l* 4*s*; Glebe, 15¼ acres; V.'s Inc. 450*l* and Ho; Pop. Brabourne 743, Monk's Horton 153.) [22]

BROUGHAM, Matthew Nixon, *Cury, Helston, Cornwall.*—Ex. Coll. Ox. B.A. 1854; Deac. 1854 and Pr. 1855 by Bp of Ex. P. C. of Cury and Gunwalloe, Dio. Ex. 1864. Formerly C. of Germoe. [23]

BROUGHTON, Clement Francis, *Norbury, Ashbourn, Derbyshire.*—Emman. Coll. Cam. B.A. 1828, M.A. 1832; Deac. 1829 and Pr. 1830 by Bp of Lich. R. of Norbury with Snelston C. Dio. Lich. 1834. (Patron, the present R; Tithe—Norbury, 216*l*; Glebe, 108 acres; Tithe—Snelston, 350*l*; R.'s Inc. 850*l* and Ho; Pop. Norbury 476, Snelston 371.) Formerly V. of Uttoxeter, Staffs, 1830–54. [24]

BROUGHTON, Delves, *Doddington, Nantwich, Cheshire.*—Caius Coll. Cam. B.A. 1837; Deac. 1838, Pr. 1839. P. C. of Doddington, Dio. Ches. (Patron, Sir Henry Delves Broughton, Bart; Tithe—App. 55*l*; P. C.'s Inc. 150*l*; Pop. 566.) Chap. of the D. of Broughton, Eccleshall, Staffs, Dio. Lich. (Patron, Sir Henry D. Broughton, Bart; Tithe—App. 48*l* 10*s*; Chap.'s Inc. 120*l*.) [25]

BROUGHTON, Henry Vivian, *Wellingborough, Northants.*—St. Peter's Coll. Cam. B.A. 1841. M.A. 1844; Deac. 1841, Pr. 1842. V. of Wellingborough, Dio. Pet. 1842. (Patron, L. Vivian, Esq; Tithe, 38*l*; V.'s Inc. 400*l*; Pop. 6382.) [1]

BROUGHTON, William Latham, *The Cottage, Belmont, Durham.*—Bp Hat. Hall, Dur. Licen. Theol; Deac. 1850 and Pr. 1851 by Bp of Dur. C. of Belmont. Formerly C. of St. Andrew's, Deptford, 1850–55, and St. Hilda's, Hartlepool, 1856. [2]

BROWELL, James, *Muswell hill, Middlesex, N.*—Ex. Coll. Ox. B.A. 1836, M.A. 1839; Deac. 1837 and Pr. 1838 by Bp of Salis. P. C. of St. James's, Muswell-hill, Dio. Lon. 1846. (Patron, Bp of Lon; P. C.'s Inc. 280*l* and Ho; Pop. 921.) Formerly C. of Warminster 1837, Twickenham 1841, Fulham 1844. [3]

BROWN, Abner Edmund, *Isham, Wellingborough.*—C. of Isham. [4]

BROWN, Abner William, *Gretton, Rockingham, Northants.*—Queens' Coll. Cam. B.A. 1831, M.A. 1846. V. of Gretton, Dio. Pet. 1851. (Patron, Bp of Pet; V.'s Inc. 400*l* and Ho; Pop. 909.) One of the Rural Deans of Weldon; Hon. Can. of Pet. Cathl. 1851. [5]

BROWN, Alfred, *Calverley Vicarage, Leeds.*—Queen's Coll. Ox. 4th cl. Lit. Hum. and B.A. 1838, M.A. 1841; Deac. 1839 and Pr. 1840 by Bp of Rip. V. of Calverley, Dio. Rip. 1845. (Patron, Ld Chan; Tithe—App. 7*l*, Imp. 837*l* 12*s* 1*d*, V. 150*l*; Glebe, 10 acres; V.'s Inc. 240*l* and Ho; Pop. 3379.) Surrogate for Dios. of York and Rip. Formerly P. C. of Cross-stone, near Halifax, 1841–45. [6]

BROWN, Arthur, *Wetherden Rectory, Stowmarket.*—St. John's Coll. Cam. 24th Sen. Opt. and B.A 1849; Deac. 1849 and Pr. 1850 by Bp of Nor. C. of Wetherden 1866. Formerly C. of Bergh Apton, Norwich, 1849–52, Cheshunt, Herts, 1852–65. Author, *Cheshunt in Olden Times*, 1863, 2*s*; *Wetherden Hall*, 1867, 1*s*. [7]

BROWN, Arthur Thomas, *Croydon, S.*—St. John's Coll. Ox. B.A. 1851; Deac. 1854 and Pr. 1856 by Bp of Pet. Formerly C. of St. Edmund's, Northampton, 1854–57, Ch. Ch. Croydon, 1857–67. [8]

BROWN, Dixon, *Unthank Hall, Haltwhistle.*—Ex. Coll. Ox. B.A. 1848, M.A. 1853; Deac. 1849 and Pr. 1850 by Bp of Ches. Formerly R. of Howick, Dio. Dur. 1854, and Sec. to the Alnwick and Bamburgh Branch, S.P.C.K. [9]

BROWN, Edgar, *Cadney, Brigg, Lincolnshire.*—St. Bees; Deac. 1847 and Pr. 1848 by Bp of Lich. C. of Cadney and Howsham 1852. Formerly C. of Longton, Staffs, 1847–49, Ropsley, Lincs, 1849–52. [10]

BROWN, Edward, *Addingham, Penrith.*—V. of Addingham, Dio. Carl. 1855. (Patrons, D. and C. of Carl; V.'s Inc. 300*l* and Ho; Pop. 754.) [11]

BROWN, Edward William, *Sketty, Swansea.*—Trin. Coll. Cam. Jun. Opt. B.A. 1863, M.A. 1867; Deac 1864 and Pr. 1865 by Bp of St. D. P. C. of Sketty, Dio. St. D. 1865. (Patron, H. H. Vivian, Esq; P. C.'s Inc. 220*l*; Pop. 1312.) Formerly Vice-Prin. of South Wales Training College 1863–65. [12]

BROWN, Felix, *Stopham, Petworth, Sussex.*—Magd. Coll. Cam. B.A. 1838, M.A. 1842; Deac. 1840, Pr. 1841. R. of Stopham, Dio. Chich. 1843. (Patron, George Barttelot, Esq; Tithe, 153*l*; Glebe, 28 acres; R.'s Inc. 173*l* and Ho; Pop. 130.) [13]

BROWN, Frederick, *Barnard Castle, Durham.*—V. of Barnard Castle, Dio. Dur. 1865. (Patron, Trin. Coll. Cam; V.'s Inc. 600*l* and Ho; Pop. 4477.) Fell. of Trin. Coll. Cam. [14]

BROWN, Frederick, *Nailsea Rectory, near Bristol.*—Ex. Coll. Ox. B.A. 1836, M.A. 1839; Deac. 1838 and Pr. 1839 by Bp of B. and W. R. of Nailsea, Dio. B. and W. 1839. (Patron, the present R; Tithe, 430*l*; Glebe, 2 acres; R.'s Inc. 432*l* and Ho; Pop. 1323.) Formerly C. of Flax-Bourton, Somerset, 1838. [15]

BROWN, George, *Redmarshall, Stockton-on-Tees.*—Univ. of Dur. Licen. Theol. 1838; Deac. 1837 and Pr. 1838 by Bp of Dur. R. of Redmarshall, Dio. Dur. 1856. (Patron, the Crown; Tithe—Imp. 56*l* 16*s* 8*d*, R. 378*l* 10*s*; Glebe, 8 acres; R.'s Inc. 378*l* and Ho; Pop. 228.) Formerly P. C. of St. John's, Darlington, 1844–56. Author, *The Volume of Creation*; *Gleanings in Natural Theology*; *A Manual of Divinity*. [16]

BROWN, G., *Elton, Bury, Lancashire.*—C. of Elton. [17]

BROWN, George James, *Bladon, Woodstock, Oxon.*—Ch. Ch. Ox. B.A. 1854, M.A. 1857; Deac. 1855 and Pr. 1858 by Bp of Ox. Dom. Chap. to the Duke of Marlborough 1858; C. of Bladon 1862. Author, *Lectures on the Gospel according to St. John, forming a Continuous Commentary*, 2 vols, 1863, 24*s*. [18]

BROWN, George Richard, *Kirkham, Lancashire.*—Ch. Ch. Ox. 2nd cl. Lit. Hum. 3rd cl. Math. et Phy. and B.A. 1838, M.A. 1841; Deac. 1846 and Pr. 1847 by Bp of Ox. V. of Kirkham, Dio. Man. 1862. (Patron, Ch. Ch. Ox; Tithe, 1033*l*; Glebe, 2 acres; V.'s Inc. 1130*l* and Ho; Pop. 4017.) Surrogate. Formerly P. C. of Maiden Bradley, Wilts, 1851–62. [19]

BROWN, Henry, *The Rectory, Woolwich.*—Ball. Coll. Ox. B.A. 1826, M.A. 1830; Deac. 1827, Pr. 1828. R. of Woolwich, Dio. Lon. 1851. (Patron, Bp of Roch; Tithe, comm. 180*l*; R.'s Inc. 800*l* and Ho; Pop. 35,237.) [20]

BROWN, Henry, *Burwell, Cambridge.*—Caius Coll. Cam. 13th Wrang. B.A. 1860, 2nd cl. Theol. Trip. 1861, M.A. 1863; Deac. 1861 and Pr. 1862 by Bp of Ely. C. of Burwell 1866. Formerly C. of Knapwell, Hunts, 1861–66. [21]

BROWN, the Venerable James, *Perth, Western Australia.*—Trin. Coll. Cam. M.A. 1852; Deac. 1844 and Pr. 1845 by Bp of Rip. Archd. of York, W. Australia. Formerly C. of Lockwood, Yorks, and Narberth, Pembrokeshire. [22]

BROWN, James Landy, *The Grove, Chapel Field, Norwich.*—St. John's Coll. Cam. B A. 1837, M.A. 1840; Deac. 1837 and Pr. 1838 by Bp of Nor. Chap. of the Castle, Norwich. [23]

BROWN, James Mellor, *Isham, Wellingborough.*—R. of Isham, Dio. Pet. 1839. (Patron, Bp of Pet; R.'s Inc. 400*l* and Ho; Pop. 433.) [24]

BROWN, James Richard, *Knighton, Radnorshire.*—Emman. Coll. Cam. B.A. 1830, M.A. 1833; Deac. 1831 and Pr. 1832 by Bp of Herf. P. C. of Knighton, Dio. Herf. (Patron, Earl of Powis; Tithe—Imp. 290*l* and 9 acres of Glebe; P. C.'s Inc. 155*l* and Ho; Pop. 1853.) R. of Bedstone, Salop, Dio. Herf. 1841. (Patron, E. Rogers, Esq; Tithe, 110*l*; R.'s Inc. 230*l* and Ho; Pop. 164.) [25]

BROWN, James Smith, *Wisbech, Cambs.*—St. Cath. Coll. Cam. B.A. 1848, M.A. 1851; Deac. 1850 and Pr. 1851 by Bp of Lin. C. of St. Peter's, Wisbech. [26]

BROWN, James Taylor, *Winckley-square, Preston.*—Ch. Coll. Cam. Jun. Opt. 2nd cl. Cl. Trip. and B.A. 1852, M.A. 1855; Deac. 1854 and Pr. 1856 by Bp of Man. P. C. of Trinity, Preston, Dio. Man. 1867. (Patrons, V. of Preston and Trustees alt; P. C.'s Inc. 150*l*; Pop. 4287.) Formerly C. of St. George's, Bolton-le-Moors, 1854–60, Trinity, Preston, 1860, Trinity, Marylebone, 1860–63; P. C. of Nayland, Suffolk, 1863–67. [27]

BROWN, James William, *St. Paul's-terrace, Wolverhampton.*—New Inn Hall, Ox. B.A. 1846; Deac. 1847, Pr. 1848. Chap. of the South Staffordshire Hospital. [28]

BROWN, James Wilson Davy, *Hinton Martell, Wimborne, Dorset.*—Caius Coll. Cam. B.A. 1862; Deac. 1862 and Pr. 1863 by Bp of Pet. C. of Hinton Martell 1865. Formerly C. of All Saints', Northampton, 1862–65. [29]

BROWN, John, *Batcombe, Evercreech, Bath.*—Ex. Coll. Ox. B.A. 1827; Deac. 1828 and Pr. 1829 by Bp of Lon. R. of Batcombe with Upton-Noble P. C. Dio. B. and W. 1841. (Patron, the present R; Tithe, 869*l*; Glebe, 90 acres, 220*l*; R.'s Inc. 1039*l* and Ho; Pop. Batcombe 713, Upton-Noble 217.) Formerly C. of Great Dunmow 1828–29, Maldon 1830–32, Broxted 1832–39, all in Essex. [30]

BROWN, John, *Shutlanger, Towcester.*—Brasen. Coll. Ox. B.A. 1862, M.A. 1865; Deac. 1862 and Pr. 1863 by Bp of Pet. C. of Stoke Bruerne 1862. [31]

BROWN, John, *Kirk-Andrews-on-Eden, Carlisle.*—Trin. Coll. Cam. Jun. Opt. and B.A. 1827; Deac. 1828 and Pr. 1829 by Bp of Carl. R. of Beaumont with Kirk-Andrews-on-Eden, Dio. Carl. 1852. (Patron, Earl of Lonsdale; Tithe, 191*l*; Glebe, 92 acres; R.'s Inc. 255*l* and Ho; Pop. Beaumont 287, Kirk-Andrews 120.) Formerly C. of Bowness, Carlisle, 1828–52. [1]

BROWN, John Henry, *Middleton-in-Teasdale, Barnard Castle, Durham.*—R. of Middleton-in-Teasdale with Forest C. and Harwood C. Dio. Dur. (Patron, the Crown; Middleton-in-Teasdale, Tithe, 135*l*; Forest, Tithe, 150*l*; R.'s Inc. 500*l* and Ho; Pop. 3769.) [2]

BROWN, John Henry, *North Holme, Newark.*—Late Scho. of Trin. Coll. Cam. Prizeman, 1830, 1831, 1832, 12th Wrang. 2nd cl. Cl. Trip. and B.A. 1833, M.A. 1836; Deac. 1837 and Pr. 1838 by Abp of York. V. of North Holme with Langford P. C. Dio. Lin. 1860. (Patron, Trin. Coll. Cam; V.'s Inc. 100*l*; Pop. 282.) [3]

BROWN, John James, *Dalton-le-Dale, Durham.*—C. of Dalton le-Dale. [4]

BROWN, John Jones, *Harlech, Merionethshire.*—Jesus Coll. Ox. B.A. 1836, M.A. 1837; Deac. and Pr. 1838 by Bp of Ban. R. of Llandanwg with Llanbedr, near Harlech, Dio. Ban. 1846. (Patron, Bp of Llan; Llandanwg, Tithe, 102*l*; Llanbedr, Tithe, 111*l*; Glebe, 4 acres; R.'s Inc. 217*l*; Pop. Llandanwg 732, Llanbedr 370) Rural Dean. Formerly C. of Llandegfan with Beaumaris 1838-46. [5]

BROWN, John Morgan, 19, *North Brink, Wisbech.*—Wor. Coll. Ox. B.A. 1853, M.A. 1857; Deac. and Pr. 1853 by Bp of Wor. C. of Elm, near Wisbech, 1866. [6]

BROWN, John Mortlock, *Christ Church Rectory, Blackfriars-road, London, S.*—St. Edm. Hall, Ox. B.A. 1858, M.A. 1863; Deac. 1858 and Pr. 1859 by Abp of York. C. of Ch. Ch. Southwark, 1866. Formerly C. of St. Saviour's, York, 1858–60; Miss. of Ch. Miss. Soc. Panjab, India, 1860–66. Author, *Remember God Now*, 1859; *Abigail's Death*, 1860; *Unveiled Face*, 1860, all Sermons. [7]

BROWN, John Wills, *Trent Vale, Stoke-upon-Trent.*—Dub. A.B. 1845, A.M. 1854; Deac. 1845 by Bp of Elphin, Pr. 1846 by Bp of Kilmore and Ardagh. P. C. of Trent Vale, Dio. Lich. 1854. (Patron, R. of Stoke-upon-Trent; P. C.'s Inc. 165*l*; Pop. 2183.) [8]

BROWN, Joseph Humphrey, *Dalton-le-Dale, Fence-Houses, Durham.*—Deac. 1817 and Pr. 1819 by Bp of Dur. V. of Dalton-le-Dale, Dio. Dur. 1832. (Patrons, D. and C. of Dur; Tithe—App. 112*l* 10*s*, Eccles. Commis. 90*l*, V. 127*l*; Glebe, 25½ acres; V.'s Inc. 215*l* and Ho; Pop. 2295.) [9]

BROWN, Joseph Thomas, *Datchet Vicarage, Windsor.*—Corpus Coll. Cam. M.A. 1850; Deac. 1846 and Pr. 1847 by Bp of Wor. R. of St. Paul's, Wokingham, Dio. Ox. 1867. (Patron, J. Walter, Esq; R.'s Inc. 190*l*; Pop. 1600.) Formerly C. of St. Nicholas', Warwick, and St. Mary's, Marylebone; P. C. of Ch. Ch. Nailsea; C. of Shenfield, Essex; V. of Cookham, Berks; C. of Datchet, Bucks. [10]

BROWN, Lancelot Robert, *Saxmundham, Suffolk.*—St. John's Coll. Cam. B.A. 1808, M.A. 1819. R. of Saxmundham, Dio. Nor. 1826. (Patron, W. Long, Esq; Tithe, 286*l*; Glebe, 29½ acres; R.'s Inc. 326*l* and Ho; Pop. 1222.) R. of Kelsale with Carlton R. near Saxmundham, Dio. Nor. 1826. (Patron, Col. Bence; Kelsale, Tithe, 717*l* 6*s*; Glebe, 70 acres; Carlton, Tithe, 137*l* 14*s*; Glebe, 2½ acres; R.'s Inc. 942*l* and Ho; Pop. Kelsale 1084, Carlton 116.) [11]

BROWN, Langton Edward, *Dormington, Herefordshire.*—Trin. Coll. Cam. B.A. 1832; Deac. 1832, Pr. 1833. V. of Dormington with Bartestree P. C. Dio. Herf. 1844. (Patrons, Exors. of the late E. F. Foley, Esq; Dormington, Tithe, 149*l* 19*s* 6*d*; Glebe, 6 acres; Bartestree, Tithe, 90*l*; V.'s Inc. 284*l* and Ho; Pop. Dormington 77, Bartestree 61.) [12]

BROWN, Laurence Lawson, *Orari, New Zealand.*—Trin. Coll. Cam. B.A. 1844; Deac. 1844, Pr. 1845. Orari, New Zealand. Formerly P. C. of Witton-le-Wear, near Darlington. [13]

BROWN, Meredith, *Bishop's Canning, Devizes.*—P. C. of Chittoe, Dio. Salis. 1846. (Patron, Bp of Salis; P. C.'s Inc. 100*l*; Pop. 382.) [14]

BROWN, Michael, *Kimberworth, Rotherham.*—C. of Kimberworth. [15]

BROWN, Richard, *Holgate Parsonage, High-lane, near Stockport.*—Ch. Coll. Cam. B.A. 1855, M.A. 1858; Deac. 1855, Pr. 1856. P. C. of High Lane, Dio. Ches. 1860. (Patron, R. of Stockport; P. C.'s Inc. 135*l* and Ho; Pop. 1250.) [16]

BROWN, Richard Neil Duguid, 2, *Willow-walk, Bermondsey, London, S.E.*—Trin. Coll. Ox. B.A. 1841; Deac. 1842 by Bp of G. and B. Pr. 1843 by Bp of Llan. P. C. of St. James's, Bermondsey, Dio. Lon. 1851. (Patron, R. of Bermondsey; P. C.'s Inc. 212*l*; Pop. 19,339.) [17]

BROWN, R. Lewis, M.A., Dom. Chap. to Marquis of Downshire. [18]

BROWN, Robert, *Vicarage, Evesham.*—St. Mary Hall, Ox; Deac. 1865 by Bp of G. and B. Pr. 1866 by Bp of Wor. C. of Evesham 1866. Formerly C. of Sudeley and Chap. of the Winchcomb Union, Glouc. 1865–66. Compiler of *Supplemental Hymn and Tune Book*, Novello; and Composer of several musical works. [19]

BROWN, Samuel Christmas, *Haughley, Stowmarket, Suffolk.*—St. John's Coll. Cam. B.A. 1842; Deac. 1842, Pr. 1843. Formerly C. of Marshfield, Chippenham. [20]

BROWN, Silvanus, *Porlock, Minehead, Somerset.*—Pemb. Coll. Ox. B.A. 1825, M.A. 1827; Deac. 1825 and Pr. 1827 by Bp of Ex. R. of Porlock, Dio. B. and W. 1838. (Patron, Ld Chan; Tithe, 420*l*; Glebe, 1½ acres; R.'s Inc. 488*l* and Ho; Pop. 835.) [21]

BROWN, Stephen, *Strawberry-hill, Haverfordwest.*—Queen's Coll. Ox. S.C.L. 1853; Deac. 1854 and Pr. 1855 by Bp of St. D. R. of Hasguard, Dio. St. D. 1856. (Patron, Ld Chan; Tithe, 168*l* 0*s* 6*d*; R.'s Inc. 174*l*; Pop. 145.) Formerly C. of Steynton 1854–56. [22]

BROWN, Stephen, *East Shefford, Hungerford, Berks.*—Jesus Coll. Cam. B.A. 1838, M.A. 1841; Deac. 1842 and Pr. 1843 by Bp of Ex. R. of East Shefford, Dio. Ox. 1846. (Patron, the present R; Tithe, 371*l*; Glebe, 17 acres; R.'s Inc. 400*l* and Ho; Pop. 70.) Formerly C. of North Molton, Devon, 1842–44, Shipton-le-Moyne, Bristol, 1844–46. [23]

BROWN, Thomas, *Petworth, Sussex.*—Chap. to the Gaol, Petworth; R. of Barlavington, Dio. Chich. 1853. (Patron, T. Biddulph, Esq; R.'s Inc. 68*l*; Pop. 136.) [24]

BROWN, Thomas, *Hemingston Rectory, Needham-Market, Suffolk.*—Pemb. Coll. Cam. B.A. 1822; Deac. 1823 and Pr. 1824 by Bp of Nor. R. of Hemingston, Dio. Nor. 1824. (Patron, Sir G. N. B. Middleton; Tithe, 369*l*; Glebe, 66 acres; R.'s Inc. 480*l* and Ho Pop. 395.) [25]

BROWN, Thomas, *St. Asaph, Flintshire.*—Hebrew Scho. of Lampeter 1840, B.D. 1855; Deac. 1841, Pr. 1842. Choral V. of St. Asaph Cathl. 1855 (Value 250*l*; Patron, Bp of St. A.). Surrogate. [26]

BROWN, Thomas, *Prebendal House, Chichester.*—Magd. Hall, Ox. B.A. 1826, M.A. 1829; Deac. 1830, Pr. 1831. P. C. of St. Paul's, Chichester, Dio. Chich. 1836. (Patrons, D. and C. of Chich; P. C.'s Inc. 230*l*; Pop. 3232.) R. of St. Peter the Less, Chichester, Dio. Chich. 1836. (Patron, Dean of Chich; R.'s Inc. 45*l*; Pop. 344.) Preb. of Highley in Chich. Cathl. 1840; Surrogate. [27]

BROWN, Thomas Bentley, *Normanton Rectory, Stamford.*—Emman. Coll. Cam. B.A. 1855, M.A. 1858; Deac. 1857 and Pr. 1858 by Bp of Pet. R. of Pilton, Dio. Pet. 1858. (Patron, Lord Aveland; Tithe, 89*l*; Glebe, 22 acres; R.'s Inc. 135*l* and Ho; Pop. 70.) R. of Normanton, Dio. Pet. 1863. (Patron, Lord Aveland; Tithe, 84*l*; Glebe, 18 acres; R.'s Inc. 109*l* and Ho; Pop. 59.) Dom. Chap. to Lord Aveland; Surrogate. Formerly C. of Uppingham 1857, Pilton 1857, Normanton 1859. [28]

BROWN, Thomas Charles, 48, *Cadogan-place, London, S.W.*—Jesus Coll. Cam. B.A. 1822; Deac. 1820 and Pr. 1823 by Bp of Nor. R. of Exhall and Wixford, Warwick, Dio. Wor. 1855. (Patron, Ld Chan; R.'s Inc. 420*l*; Pop. 325.) Formerly Chap. for 6 years to Huntingdon Gaol, and Min. of St. Peter's, Pimlico, for 16 years. [1]

BROWN, Thomas Edward, *Clifton College, Bristol.*—Ch. Ch. Ox. Servitor 1849, 1st cl. Lit. Hum. 1st cl. Modern Hist. and B.A. 1853, M.A. 1856; Deac. 1856 and Pr. 1857 by Bp of Ox. Fell. of Oriel Coll. 1854. 2nd Mast. of Clifton Coll. [2]

BROWN, Thomas James, *Sydling Vicarage, Dorchester.*—New Coll. Ox. B.A. 1837, M.A. 1840; Deac. 1838 and Pr. 1839 by Bp of Ox. V. of Sydling, Dio. Salis. 1846. (Patrons, Warden and Fellows of Win. Coll; Tithe, comm. 112*l*; Glebe, 7 acres; V.'s Inc. 290*l* and Ho; Pop. 692.) P. C. of Nether Cerne, Dorset, Dio. Salis. 1853. (Patron, R. B. Sheridan, Esq; Tithe—Imp. 148*l*; P. C.'s Inc. 60*l*; Pop. 95.) Late Fell. of New Coll. Ox; C. of Enstone 1838, Portsmouth 1840. [3]

BROWN, Thomas Kenworthy, *Lisbon.*—Ch. Coll. Cam. B.A. 1843, M.A. 1846; Deac. 1844 by Abp of York, Pr. 1846 by Bp of Rip. British Chap. at Lisbon. Formerly Chap. to the English residents at Madeira. [4]

BROWN, Thomas Medlicott, *Osborne House, Southampton.*—St. Cath. Coll. Cam. B.A. 1860; Deac. 1861 and Pr. 1862 by Bp of Ely. C. of All Saints', Southampton, 1863. Formerly C. of March, Cambs, 1861–63. [5]

BROWN, Thomas Richard, *Southwick Vicarage, Oundle, Northants.*—V. of Southwick, Dio. Pet. 1834. (Patron, G. Capron, Esq; V.'s Inc. 110*l* and Ho; Pop. 136.) [6]

BROWN, William, *Little Hormead, Buntingford, Herts.*—St. John's Coll. Cam. B.A. 1843, M.A. 1846. R. of Little Hormead, Dio. Roch, 1852. (Patron, St. John's Coll. Cam.; Tithe, 279*l* 5*s*; Glebe, 67 acres; R.'s Inc. 349*l* and Ho; Pop. 103.) [7]

BROWN, William, *Blaydon Rectory, near Newcastle-upon-Tyne.*—Univ. Coll. Dur. B.A. 1842, M.A. 1859; Deac. 1842 and Pr. 1843 by Bp of Dur. P. C. of St. Cuthbert Stella, Dio. Dur. 1845. (Patrons, the Crown and Bp of Dur. alt; P. C.'s Inc. 300*l* and Ho; Pop. 3751.) [8]

BROWN, William Haig, *Charter House, London, E.C.*—Pemb. Coll. Cam. Jun. Opt. 1st cl. Cl. Trip. and B.A. 1846, M.A. 1849; Deac. 1852, Pr. 1853; Fell. of Pemb. Coll. Cam. 1848, Jun. Tut. 1852, Dean 1853. Head Mast. of Charter House Sch. [9]

BROWN, William Henry, *Wheatacre Rectory, Beccles, Suffolk.*—Late Scho. Exhib. and Fell. of Caius Coll. Cam. 10th Wrang. 1st cl. Nat. Sci. Trip. and B.A. 1854, M.A. 1858; Deac. 1854 and Pr. 1855, by Bp of Ely. R. of Wheatacre, Dio. Nor. 1858. (Patron, Caius Coll. Cam.; Tithe, 224*l*; Glebe, 70 acres; R.'s Inc. 300*l* and Ho; Pop. 160.) Formerly C. of Brandsby, Yorks, 1855–58. [10]

BROWN, W. R. H., *South Cove, Southwold, Suffolk.*—C. of South Cove. [11]

BROWN, Wilse, *Whitstone, near Exeter.*—Late Scho. of Emman. Coll. Cam. Sen. Opt. and B.A. 1833; Deac. 1834 by Bp of G. and B. Pr. 1835 by Bp of Ex. R. of Whitstone, Dio. Ex. 1857. (Patron, the present R; R.'s Inc. 670*l* and Ho; Pop. 571.) [12]

BROWNE, Alfred, *Flitton, near Silsoe, Beds.*—Ch. Ch. Ox. 2nd cl. Lit. Hum. and B.A. 1826, M.A. 1829; Deac. 1827 and Pr. 1828 by Bp of Ox. V. of Flitton, Dio. Ely, 1834. (Patron, Ch. Ch. Ox; Land in lieu of Tithe—Imp. 242 acres; V. 184 acres; V.'s Inc. 310*l* and Ho; Pop. 597.) Surrogate. Author, Translations of 2nd and 3rd Vols. of *Heeren's Ideen über den Handel, die Politik, u. s. f.* (Asiatic Nations), Oxford, 1833. [13]

BROWNE, Alfred Tilleman, *Maidstone.*—Ch. Ch. Ox. 2nd cl. Nat. Sci. and B.A. 1858, M.A. 1862; Deac. 1863 and Pr. 1864 by Bp of Roch. C. of Trinity, Maidstone, 1866. Formerly C. of Walkern, Herts. [14]

BROWNE, Arthur, *Marham, Downham Market, Suffolk.*—St. John's Coll. Cam. 6th Wrang. and B.A. 1819, M.A. 1823; Deac. 1821 and Pr. 1822 by Bp of Nor. V. of Marham, Dio. Nor. 1827. (Patron, St. John's Coll. Cam; Tithe—Imp. 645*l* 15*s* 2*d*, V. 360*l* 2*s* 2*d*; Glebe, 22 acres, and 41 acres of land in Rockland All Saints and Rockland St. Peter's; V.'s Inc. 460*l* and Ho; Pop. 870.) Author, *A Short Treatise on the Differential Calculus*, 1823. [15]

BROWNE, Augustus, *The Rectory, Drayton-Bassett, Tamworth, Staffs.*—King's Coll. Lon. Theol. Assoc. 1849; Deac. 1850 and Pr. 1851 by Bp of Lich. R. of Drayton-Bassett, Dio. Lich. 1857. (Patron, Ld Chan; Tithe, 212*l* 12*s* 9*d*; Glebe, 23 acres; R.'s Inc. 290*l* and Ho; Pop. 441.) Formerly C. of Drayton-Bassett 1850–57. [16]

BROWNE, Barry Charles, 6, *York-buildings, Gloucester.*—Dub. A.B; Deac. 1840 by Bp of Killaloe, Pr. 1840 by Abp of Dub. R. of St. John the Baptist's, Gloucester, Dio. G. and B. 1854. (Patron, Ld Chan; R.'s Inc. 158*l*; Pop. 2332.) [17]

BROWNE, Benjamin Hayward Hudlestone, *Aston Sandford, Thame.*—Deac. 1843, Pr. 1844. R. of Aston Sandford, Bucks, Dio. Ox. 1862. (Patrons, John and William Dover, Esqrs; R.'s Inc. 155*l* and Ho; Pop. 70.) [18]

BROWNE, Charles Chapman, *Minchin Hampton, Gloucester.*—Univ. Coll. Ox. B.A. 1863, M.A. 1866; Deac. 1864 and Pr. 1865 by Bp of G. and B. C. of Minchin Hampton 1866. Formerly C. of Cirencester 1864. [19]

BROWNE, Charles Henry, *Worcester College, Oxford.*—Wor. Coll. Ox. 3rd cl. Math. et Phy. and B.A. 1840, M.A. 1843. Fell. of Wor. Coll. Ox. [20]

BROWNE, Edward Slater, *St. Katherine's Parsonage, Savernake Forest, Hungerford.*—Wor. Coll. Ox. B.A. 1852, M.A. 1855; Deac. 1854 and Pr. 1855 by Bp of Roch. P. C. of the District of St. Katherine's, Savernake Forest, Dio. Salis. 1864. (Patron, the Marquis of Ailesbury; Pop. 504.) Formerly Asst. C. of Holy Trinity, Halstead; Asst. C. of Newton-on-Ouse, York; P. C. of St. John Baptist's, Purbrook, Hants; and Sen. C. of Warminster, Wilts. [21]

BROWNE, George, *Lenton, Notts.*—Dub. A.B. 1826; Deac. 1826, Pr. 1827. V. of Lenton, Dio. Lin. 1840. (Patrons, Trustees; Glebe, 42 acres; V.'s Inc. 300*l* and Ho; Pop. 4982.) [22]

BROWNE, G., *Kildwick, Leeds.*—C. of Kildwick. [23]

BROWNE, George Forrest, *St. Catherine's College, Cambridge.*—St. Cath. Coll. Cam. Math. and Theol. Tripos, Maitland Prizeman, B.A. 1856, M.A. 1863; Deac. 1858 and Pr. 1859 by Bp of Ox. Chap. and Lect. of St. Cath. Coll. Cam. 1863. Formerly Theol. Tut. in Trin. Coll. Glenalmond, and Bell Lect. in the Scottish Episcopal Church. Author, *Ice Caves of France and Switzerland*, Longmans, 1865, 12*s* 6*d*. [24]

BROWNE, George Osborne, *Tor-Mohun, Torquay.*—Jesus Coll. Cam. Jun. Opt. B.A. 1855, M.A. 1859; Deac. 1856 by Bp of Carl. Pr. 1857 by Abp of York. C. of Tor-Mohun 1867. Formerly C. of Skipsea, Yorks, 1856–57, Trinity, Hull, 1857–67; Chap. to Earl of Lucan. [25]

BROWNE, Harvey Atkyns, *Stow Maries, Maldon, Essex.*—Queen's Coll. Ox. B.A. 1823, M.A. 1824; Deac. 1823 by Bp of Salis. Pr. 1824 by Bp. of Lon. R. of Stow Maries, Dio. Roch. 1836. (Patron, Rev. James Coling; Tithe, 675*l*; Glebe, 40 acres; R.'s Inc. 720*l* and Ho; Pop. 265.) [26]

BROWNE, Henry, *Neatishead Vicarage, near Norwich.*—Trin. Coll. Cam. B.A. 1834, M.A. 1839; Deac. 1835 by Bp of Carl. Pr. 1836 by Bp of G. and B. V. of Neatishead, Dio. Nor. 1859. (Patron, Bp of Nor; Tithe, 186*l*; Glebe, 46 acres; V.'s Inc. 271*l* and Ho; Pop. 620.) Formerly C. of Bedingham, Norfolk, 1835, Freethorpe and Wickhampton, Norfolk, 1838, Nettlesbed, Kent, 1841, Eastbourne, Sussex, 1846, Nonington and Ore 1847, King's Lynn 1848, Neatishead 1850. [27]

BROWNE, Henry, *Pevensey Vicarage, Eastbourne, Sussex.*—Corpus Coll. Cam. Bell's Univ. Scho. 1823, B.A. 1826, M.A. 1829; Deac. 1827 by Bp of Nor. Pr. 1831 by Bp of Chich. V. of Pevensey, Dio. Chich. 1854. (Patron, Bp of Chich; Tithe—App. 30*l*. and 80 acres of Glebe; V. 1153*l*; Glebe, 10 acres; V.'s Inc. 1153*l*; Pop. 385.) Preb. of Waltham, in Chich. Cathl. 1842; Exam. Chap. to the Bp of Chich. 1843. Formerly V. of Rudgwick 1831–33; R. of Earnley with Almodington 1833–54; Rural Dean of Manhood, 1838–45; Prin. of Chich. Dioc. Theol. Coll. 1842–47; P. C. of St. Bartholomew's, Chich. 1850–54. Author, *Ordo Sæclorum, a Treatise on the Chronology of the Holy Scriptures*, 1854, 20*s*; St. Augustine's *Short Treatises* (part), 1847; St. Augustine's *Homilies on St. John*, Vol. I. 1848, Vol. II. 1849; St. Chrysostom's *Homilies on the Acts*, Vol. I. 1851, Vol. II. 1852, Edited with Reformation of the Text, Re-Translation and Notes, all published in *The Library of the Fathers*; *A Handbook of Hebrew Antiquities*, 1851, 3*s* 6*d*; Sophocles, *Œdipus Tyrannus*, *Œdipus Coloneus*, and *Antigone* (from Schneidewin), 4*s* each; Euripides, *Bacchæ Iphigenia in Tauris* (from Schöne), 3*s* each; Xenophon's *Anabasis* (from Hertlein), 6*s* 6*d*; Madvig's *Greek Syntax, with Appendix on the Particles*, 8*s* 6*d*; Cicero, *On Old Age*, 2*s* 6*d*; Sallust, *Jugurtha*, 3*s* 6*d*; Tacitus, *Annals*, Vol. I. 5*s*, Vol. II. 6*s*; *The Second Hebrew Book* (Notes on the Book of Genesis, completed from Chap. xviii.), 1853, 9*s*, all published in T. K. Arnold's *School and College Books*, Rivingtons, 1851–55; Papers on Egyptian Chronology, and on various subjects of Biblical Interpretation and Historical Theology in Arnold's *Theological Critic*, 1851–52; and in Kitto's *Cyclopædia of Biblical Literature*, 1863, etc; *Remarks on Mr. Greswell's Fasti Catholici*, 1852, 1*s* 6*d*; *A Copious Phraseological English-Greek Lexicon* (commenced by T. K. Arnold, in conjunction with Dr. Fräderadorff), 1855, 20*s*. [1]

BROWNE, Henry, *Letheringsett, Holt, Norfolk.*—Lin. Coll. Ox. B.A. 1824, M.A. 1825; Deac. 1828 and Pr. 1829 by Bp of Salis. R. of Letheringsett, Dio. Nor. 1861. (Patron, the present R; Tithe, 262*l*; Glebe, 27 acres; R.'s Inc. 322*l* and Ho; Pop. 320.) [2]

BROWNE, Henry, *Eastham, Tenbury, Worcestershire.*—Trin. Coll. Ox. B.A. 1847; Deac. and Pr. 1848 by Bp of Herf. R. of Eastham with Hanley William R. Hanley Child C. and Orleton C. Dio. Herf. 1853. (Patron, the present R; Eastham, Tithe, 474*l* 13*s* 7*d*; Hanley William, Tithe, 161*l*; Hanley Child, Tithe, 144*l* 10*s*; Orleton, Tithe, 130*l*; Glebe, 200 acres; R.'s Inc. 948*l* and Ho; Pop. Eastham 347, Hanley William 120, Hanley Child 199, Orleton 99.) Surrogate. [3]

BROWNE, Henry Albert, *Toft next-Newton, Market-Rasen, Lincolnshire.*—Queen's Coll. Ox. B.A. 1822, M.A. 1824. R. of Newton-by-Toft, Dio. Lin. 1832. (Patron, Lieut.-Gen. Wilkinson; Tithe, 180*l*; R.'s Inc. 230*l*; Pop. 81.) R. of Toft-next-Newton, Dio. Lin. 1834. (Patron, Ld Chan; Tithe, 240*l*; R.'s Inc. 270*l*. and Ho; Pop. 85.) [4]

BROWNE, Henry Joy, *Southgate-street, Bury St. Edmunds.*—Caius Coll. Cam. B.A. 1862; Deac. 1864 and Pr. 1866 by Bp of Ely. C. of St. Mary's, Bury St. Edmunds, 1864. [5]

BROWNE, James Caulfield, *Vicarage, Dudley.*—St. John's Coll. Cam. B.A. 1827, M.A. 1840, D.C.L. incorporated 1845 at St. John's Coll. Ox.; Deac. 1827 and Pr. 1829 by Bp of Ely. V. of Dudley, Dio. Wor. 1845. (Patron, Earl of Dudley; Glebe, 2 farms in Staffs; V.'s Inc. 1050*l* and Ho; Pop. 18,197.) Formerly C. of Great Berkhampstead 1829–42; R. of Compton-Martin 1840–45. [6]

BROWNE, James Francis, *Moulton, near Richmond, Yorks.*—Lond. Coll. of Div; Deac. 1866 by Bp of Rip. Asst. C. of Middleton-Tyas 1866. [7]

BROWNE, James Thomas, *St. Edmund's, Northampton.*—Dub. A.B. 1826, A.M. 1832, *ad eund.* Cam. 1840; Deac. and Pr. 1827. P. C. of St. Edmund's, Northampton, Dio. Pet. 1846. (Patrons, the Crown and Bp of Pet. alt; P. C.'s Inc. 150*l*; Pop. 6445.) Chap. to the Northampton Union 1854. [8]

BROWNE, James William, *Much Hadham, Ware.*—New Inn Hall, Ox. B.A. 1846, M.A. 1858; Deac. 1846 and Pr. 1847 by Bp of Roch. C. of Much Hadham. Formerly C. of Coggeshall 1846–48, and again 1859–63; 2nd Mast. in Exmouth Sch. Devon, 1838–46, and 2nd Mast. in Twyford Sch. Winchester, 1848–58; C. of Greenstead Green, Essex, 1863. [9]

BROWNE, John, *Cassington, Oxford.*—C. of Cassington. [10]

BROWNE, John, *Towersey, Thame, Bucks.*—C. of Towersey. [11]

BROWNE, John, *Limber-Magna, Ulceby Junction, Lincolnshire.*—Late Scho. of St. John's Coll. Cam. B.A. 1830, M.A. 1833, *ad eund.* Ox. 1848; Deac. 1830 and Pr. 1831 by Abp of York. V. of Limber-Magna, Dio. Lin. 1849. (Patron, Ld Chan; Corn Rent in lieu of Tithe—V. 472*l* 2*s*; Glebe, 132 acres; V.'s Inc. 649*l* and Ho; Pop. 514.) J.P. for the Counties of Westmoreland and Lincolnshire. Formerly R. of Barming, Kent. [12]

BROWNE, John, *Weston Begard, Hereford.*—Queen's Coll. Ox. B.A. 1822, M.A. 1864; Deac. 1824, Pr. 1825. C. of Weston Begard. Formerly P. C. of Milton, Hants, 1834–40; V. of Compton Chamberlayn, Wilts, 1840–49. [13]

BROWNE, John Carter, *Horncastle, Lincolnshire.*—Emman. Coll. Cam. Sen. Opt. 1859; Deac. 1860 by Bp of Nor. Pr. 1863 by Bp of Ox. 2nd Mast. of Horncastle Gr. Sch. and C. in sole charge of Mareham-on-the-Hill and High Toynton 1866. [14]

BROWNE, John Geoffrey, *Kiddington, Woodstock, Oxon.*—Dub. A.B. 1818; Deac. and Pr. 1822. R. of Kiddington, Dio. Ox. 1823. (Patron, Viscount Dillon; Tithe, 403*l* 4*s*; R.'s Inc. 426*l*; Pop. 305.) [15]

BROWNE, John George Colton, *Dudley.*—Corpus Coll. Cam. B.A. 1858; Deac. 1858 and Pr. 1859 by Bp of Wor. P. C. of St. James's, Dudley, 1866. (Patron, V. of Dudley; P. C.'s Inc. 300*l*; Pop. 6745.) Formerly C. of Dudley 1858–66. [16]

BROWNE, John Henry, *Lowdham, near Nottingham.*—V. of Lowdham, Dio. Lin. 1842. (Patron, Earl Manvers; Tithe—Imp. 26*l* 9*s* 4*d*, V. 14*l* 6*s* 4*d*; Glebe, 104½ acres; V.'s Inc. 294*l* and Ho; Pop. 1503.) [17]

BROWNE, John Thomas, *Haigh, Wigan.*—Dub. A.B. 1831; Deac. 1835 and Pr. 1836 by Bp of Ches. Dom. Chap. to the Earl of Crawford and Balcarres 1847. Formerly P. C. of Haigh, Wigan, 1838–63. [18]

BROWNE, Philip, *Edgbaston, Birmingham.*—Corpus Coll. Cam. B.A. 1842, M.A. 1856; Deac. 1842, Pr. 1843. P. C. of St. James's, Edgbaston, Dio. Wor. 1852. (Patron, Lord Calthorpe; P. C.'s Inc. 230*l*; Pop. 4694.) Formerly C. of All Saints', Derby, 1842–49, St. George's, Edgbaston, 1849–52. [19]

BROWNE, P., *Sheffield.*—C. of Dyer's Hill, Sheffield. [20]

BROWNE, Ralph Charles, 36, *Parkgate-street, Dublin.*—Univ. Coll. Dur. Licen. Theol. 1854; Deac. 1854 and Pr. 1856 by Bp of Ex. Chap. to H M. Forces 1862. Formerly C. of King's Teignton, Devon, 1854–56, Honiton 1856–62. [21]

BROWNE, Robert, *Bickley, Kent, S.E.*—Dub. A.B. 1858; Deac. 1858 by Bp of Win. Pr. 1859 by Abp of Cant. R. of Lullingstone, Dio. Cant. 1866. (Patron, Sir P. H. Dyke, Bart; Tithe, 330*l*; Glebe, 20 acres; R.'s Inc. 360*l*; Pop. 63.) Dom. Chap. to Marquis of Sligo. Formerly C. of St. John's, Margate, 1858–62, St. Matthew's, Denmark Hill, 1862–64, St. Mary's, Islington, 1864–66. [22]

BROWNE, Robert Henry Nisbett, 36, *Inverness-road, Bayswater, London, W.*—Wor. Coll. Ox. B.A. 1852; Deac. 1852, Pr. 1854. Formerly C. of Northfield, Birmingham. [23]

BROWNE, The Ven. Robert William, *Rectory, Weston-super-Mare.*—St. John's Coll. Ox. Double 1st cl. and B.A. 1831, M.A. 1834; Deac. 1833, Pr. 1834. R. of Weston-super-Mare, Dio. B. and W. 1862. (Patron, Bp of B. and W; R.'s Inc. 300*l* and Ho; Pop. 1507.) Archd. of Bath 1860; Canon Res. of Wells 1863; Exam. Chap. to Bp of B. and W.; Surrogate. Formerly Preb. of Newington, in St. Paul's Cathl.

1845, and of St. Decuman's, in Wells, 1858; Prof. Cl. Lit. in King's Coll. Lond. 1835; Chap. to H.M. Forces in Lond; Chap. to the Bp of Lich; Fell. of St. John's Coll. Ox. 1830, Tut. 1831; Select Preacher at Ox. 1842–43; Fell. of the Geological Soc. Author, *Histories of Greece and Rome* (Gleig's School Series), S.P.C.K; *Histories of Greek and Roman Classical Literature*; *Ethics of Aristotle translated, with Notes and Introduction*; *King's College Examination Questions*; *Latin Grammar for Ladies*; *Tracts for Soldiers*, S.P.C.K.; *Sermons on the Daily Service*; *The Christian Ministry* (a Charge delivered at Visitation). [1]

BROWNE, Rupert Montague, *Upper Norwood, Surrey, S.*—St. Bees; Deac. 1855, Pr. 1856. C. of All Saints', Upper Norwood, 1855. [2]

BROWNE, Sidney Spanswick, 7, *Richmond-terrace, Mare-street, Hackney, N.E.*—St. Bees; Deac. 1856 and Pr. 1858 by Bp of Lich. C. of St. Mary's, Haggerston, and Precentor of the Choir. Formerly C. of St. John's, Wolverhampton,' St. Paul's, Pendleton, St. Luke's, King's Cross, and West Hackney, London. Author, *Words of 232 Anthems, with Introits*, 1863. [3]

BROWNE, S. B., *Hope-Mansell, Mitcheldean, Herefordshire.*—R. of Hope-Mansell, Dio. Herf. 1865. (Patron, Ld Chan; R.'s Inc. 250*l* and Ho; Pop. 205.) [4]

BROWNE, Thomas, *Carleton in Cleveland, Northallerton, Yorks.*—St. Bees; Deac. 1817 and Pr. 1820 by Abp of York. P. C. of Carleton, Dio. York, 1823. (Patron, J. R. Reeve, Esq; Modus, 6*l* 19*s*; Glebe, 14 acres; P. C.'s Inc. 52*l* and Ho; Pop. 243.) Formerly P. C. of Faceby 1823–66. [5]

BROWNE, Thomas, *Idsworth, Horndean, Hants.*—C. of Idsworth. [6]

BROWNE, Thomas Birch Llewelyn, *Bodvari, Denbigh.*—Late Scho. of Jesus Coll. Ox. B.A. 1831, M.A. 1833; Deac. 1832 by Bp of Ox. Pr. 1833 by Bp of Ban. R. of Bodvari, Dio. St. A. 1850. (Patron, Bp of Llan; Tithe, 320*l*; Glebe, 16 acres; R.'s Inc. 336*l* and Ho; Pop. 813.) Formerly C. of Mold 1834–40; P. C. of Flint 1840–50. [7]

BROWNE, Thomas Briarly, *East Acklam Rectory, York.*—Dub. A.B. 1840, A.M. 1856; Deac. 1841 and Pr. 1842 by Bp of Rip. R. of East Acklam, Dio. York, 1864. (Patron, Abp of York; Tithe, 163*l*; Glebe, 56 acres; R.'s Inc. 321*l* 4*s* 10*d* and Ho; Pop. 781.) Formerly C. of Wortley, Leeds, 1841, Ross 1843; R. of Hilston 1858. Author, *Full Age*, a sermon, Hull, 1867, 6*d*. [8]

BROWNE, Thomas Cooper, 59, *High-street, Oxford.*—Trin. Coll. Cam. B.A. 1836, M.A. 1839; Deac. 1837, Pr. 1838. Formerly P. C. of Headington Quarry, near Oxford, 1852–56. [9]

BROWNE, Thomas Murray, *Almondsbury, Bristol.*—V. of Almondsbury, Dio. G. and B. 1864. (Patron, Bp of G. and B.; V.'s Inc. 1000*l*; Pop. 1864.) Formerly V. of Standish, Glouc. 1839–64. [10]

BROWNE, Walter Elliott, *Great Bealings, near Woodbridge.*—Univ. of Lon. 1860; Deac. 1861 and Pr. 1862 by Bp of Nor. C. of Great Bealings 1863. Formerly C. of Playford 1861–63. [11]

BROWNE, W., *Dilham, Smallburgh, Norfolk.*—C. of Dilham with Honing. [12]

BROWNE, William, *Worcester College, Oxford*—Fell. of Wor. Coll. Ox. [13]

BROWNE, William James Caulfield, *Kittisford Rectory, Wellington, Somerset.*—St. John's Coll. Ox. M.A. R. of Kittisford, Dio. B. and W. 1862. (Patrons, Trustees; R.'s Inc. 280*l* and Ho; Pop. 133.) [14]

BROWNE, William Pulsford, *North Somercotes Vicarage, Louth, Lincolnshire.*—Queens' Coll. Cam. B.A. 1850; Deac. 1850 and Pr. 1852 by Bp of Ex. V. of North Somercotes, Dio. Lin. 1865. (Patron, Chan. of Duchy of Lancaster; V.'s Inc. 510*l* and Ho; Pop. 1100.) Formerly C. of Kingsbridge, with Churchstow, Devon, 1850, Twerton, Somerset, 1852, East and West Anstey, Devon, 1854. [15]

BROWNE, William Sainsbury, *Stanton Prior, Bristol.*—Pemb. Coll. Ox. Hon. 4th cl. Lit. Hum. and B.A. 1851, M.A. 1854; Deac. 1852 by Bp of Madras, Pr. 1853 by Bp of Ox. R. of Stanton Prior, Dio. B. and W. 1866. (Patron, W. H. P. Gore Langton, Esq; Tithe, 192*l*; Glebe, 19½ acres; R.'s Inc. 250*l* and Ho; Pop. 136.) Formerly C. of Isle Abbotts, Somerset, 1852–55, Dittisham, Devon, 1855–59, Curland, Somerset, 1859–62, Orchard Portman, 1862–66. [16]

BROWNING, Henry Bailey, *St. Martin's, Stamford, Lincolnshire.*—Queens' Coll. Cam. 3rd Sen. Opt. B.A. 1855, M.A. 1858; Deac. 1855 and Pr. 1856 by Bp of Pet. R. of St. George with St. Paul's, Stamford, Dio. Lin. 1862. (Patron, Marquis of Exeter; Tithe, 90*l*; Glebe, rent 72*l*; R.'s Inc. 213*l*; Pop. 1881). Chap. of Stamford Borough Gaol. Author, *The Rules of Algebra Extended to Incommensurable Ratio*, 1851, 3*s*; *A Theory of the Negative Sign*, 1852, 3*s*; *Aids to Pastoral Visitation*, 2nd ed. 1862, 3*s* 6*d*; *Fatherhood of God*, 3rd ed. 1863, 1*s*; *Questions on the Apostles' Creed and Answers*, 1864, 3*d*; *Questions and Answers on the Creed, the Lord's Prayer, Confirmation, and the Sacraments*, 1864, 3*d*. [17]

BROWNING, Thomas Peak, *Shipton, Market Weighton.*—Stud. of Chich. Theol. Coll; Deac. 1853 and Pr. 1854 by Abp of York. C. of Market Weighton with Shipton 1866. Formerly C. of Alne 1853–61, Newton-upon-Ouse 1861–66. Author, Prize Essay, *Freedom of Worship*, Rivingtons, 1865, 6*d*. [18]

BROWNING, William Thomas, *Thorp Mandeville, Banbury.*—Ex. Coll. Ox. B.A. 1846; Deac. 1847 and Pr. 1848 by Bp of Pet. [19]

BROWNJOHN, Joshua, *Wroxham, Norwich.*—King's Coll. Lond. Theol. Assoc. 1857; Deac. 1857 and Pr. 1859 by Bp of Nor. C. of Wroxham 1866. Formerly C. of Walton with Felixstowe 1857, St. Clement's, Ipswich, 1861. [20]

BROWNJOHN, S. D., *Ickworth, Bury St. Edmunds.*—C. of Ickworth and Horringer. [21]

BROWNLOW, William, *Wilmslow, near Manchester.*—Pemb. Coll. Ox. B.A. 1822, M.A. 1825; Deac. 1824 and Pr. 1825 by Bp of Lin. R. of Wilmslow, Dio. Ches. 1829. (Patron, Sir T. J. Trafford, Bart; Tithe, 1071*l* 16*s*; Glebe, 85 acres; R.'s Inc. 1140*l* and Ho; Pop. 6616.) Author, *A Visitation Sermon*, 1829; *A Solution of Cubic Equations*, 1841; *Sermon on the Death of the Duke of Wellington*, 1852. [22]

BROWNRIGG, Edmund, *Wolsingham, Darlington.*—Univ. Coll. Dur. B.A. 1848, M.A. 1850; Deac. 1848 and Pr. 1850 by Bp of Dur. C. of Wolsingham. [23]

BROWNRIGG, John Studholme, *Christ Church Parsonage, Broad Town, Wootton Basset.*—Magd. Coll. Cam. Scho. of, 3rd cl. in Theol. Hons. Reading Prize, B.A. 1864; Deac. 1864 by Bp of Pet. for Bp of Roch. Pr. 1865 by Bp of Roch. P. C. of Broad Town, Dio. Salis. 1866. (Patron, V. of Clyffe Pypard; Glebe, 2 acres; P. C.'s Inc. 124*l* and Ho; Pop. 473.) Dom. Chap. to Duke of St. Albans. Formerly C. of Wenden Lofts, Essex. [24]

BROWNRIGG, Thomas Richard, *St. Jude's Parsonage, Southsea, Portsea.*—Dub. A.B; Deac. 1847 and Pr. 1848 by Bp of Win. P. C. of St. Jude's, Southsea, 1851. (Patroness, Mrs. T. R. Brownrigg; P. C.'s Inc. 450*l* and Ho; Pop. 6301.) Surrogate. [25]

BRUCE, David, *Merrington Vicarage, Bishop Auckland.*—Jesus Coll. Cam. B.A. 1835, M.A. 1838; Deac. 1837 and Pr. 1838 by Bp of Rip. V. of Merrington, Dio. Dur. 1864. (Patrons, D. and C. of Dur; V.'s Inc. 454*l* and Ho; Pop. 1300.) Hon. Can. of Dur. Formerly P. C. of St. Luke's, Ferry-hill, Durham, 1845–64. [26]

BRUCE, James Andrew, *King's Sutton, Banbury.*—Deac. 1857 and Pr. 1858 by Bp of Wor. V. of King's Sutton, Dio. Pet. 1864. (Patroness, Mrs. Willes; Tithe, 50*l*; Glebe, 82 acres; V.'s Inc. 200*l* and Ho; Pop. 1350.) [27]

BRUCE, Lloyd Stewart, *Barton-in-Fabis, Nottingham.*—Dub. A.B. 1852, A.M. 1854, M.A. Ox. 1856; Deac. 1852 and Pr. 1853 by Bp of S. and M. R. of Barton-in-Fabis, Dio. Lin. 1863. (Patron, Abp of

York; R.'s Inc. 420*l* and Ho; Pop. 295.) Chap. to Abp of York. Formerly R. of Hale, Hants, 1862–65. [1]

BRUCE, Theophilus Robert, *Carlton, Yeadon, Leeds.*—St. Bees; Deac. 1856 and Pr. 1859 by Bp of Rip. Chap. of the Poorhouse and C. of Carlton. [2]

BRUCE, Thomas Charles, *Jesus College, Cambridge.*—Fell. of Jesus Coll. Cam. [3]

BRUCE, William, *St. Nicholas, near Cardiff.*—Oriel Coll. Ox. B.A. 1839, M.A. 1841; Deac. 1839, Pr. 1840. R. of St. Nicholas, Dio. Llan. 1840. (Patron, J. Bruce Pryce, Esq; Tithe, 210*l*; Glebe, 60 acres; R.'s Inc. 280*l* and Ho; Pop. 354.) Proctor for D. and C. of Llan; Can. Res. of Llan; Rural Dean; Chap. to Bps of St. A. and Ban. [4]

BRUCE, William, *St. James's Parsonage, Bristol.*—Queens' Coll. Cam. B.A. 1839, M.A. 1841. P. C. of St. James's, Bristol, Dio. G. and B. 1851. (Patrons, Trustees; P. C.'s Inc. 250*l*; Pop. 6951.) [5]

BRUCE, William Henry, *Strood, Kent.*—Lampeter, B.A. 1866; Deac. 1866 by Bp of Roch. C. of Strood 1866. [6]

BRUCE, William Samuel.—Caius Coll. Cam. Wrang. and B.A. 1859, M.A. 1863; Deac. 1860 and Pr. 1861 by Bp of Lon. C. of St. Margaret's, Westminster, 1864. Formerly C. of St. Mark's, Upper Holloway, 1860–62, Ch. Ch. Clevedon, 1862-64. [7]

BRUMELL, Edward, *Holt, Thetford, Norfolk.* St. John's Coll. Cam. 3rd Wrang. 2nd Smith's Prizeman, and B.A. 1837, M.A. 1840, B.D. 1847; Deac. 1844 and Pr. 1845 by Bp of Ely. R. of Holt, Dio. Nor. 1853. (Patron, St. John's Coll. Cam; Tithe, 585*l*; Glebe, 57 acres; R.'s Inc. 676*l* and Ho; Pop. 1635.) Rural Dean. Formerly Fell. Tut. and President of St. John's Coll. Cam. [8]

BRUNTON, William Alexander Whannell Hewitt.—St. Peter's Coll. Cam. B.A. 1846. Dom. Chap. to Marquis of Dalhousie. Formerly R. of Chadwell, Essex, 1859–66. [9]

BRUNWIN, Peter Maxey, *Bradwell, Braintree, Essex.*—St. Peter's Coll. Cam. B.A. 1843; Deac. 1844, Pr. 1845. R. of Bradwell, Dio. Roch. 1845. (Patron, M. P. C. Brunwin, Esq; Tithe, 345*l*; Glebe, 31 acres; R.'s Inc. 390*l* and Ho; Pop. 273.) [10]

BRUNYEE, Nathaniel, *Belton Rectory, Bawtry.*—Clare Coll. Cam. B A. 1857, M.A. 1860; Deac. 1858 and Pr. 1859 by Abp of York. C. in sole charge of Belton 1862. Formerly C. in sole charge of Adlingfleet, Yorks, 1858–59. [11]

BRUTON, Walter Meddon, *West Worlington, Morchard Bishop, Devon.*—St. Peter's Coll. Cam. S.C.L. 1841, B.C.L. 1843; Deac. 1842 and Pr. 1843 by Bp of Ex. R. of West Worlington, Dio. Ex. 1846. (Patron, Sir G. S Stucley, Bart; Tithe, 160*l*; Glebe, 84 acres; R.'s Inc. 200*l*; Pop. 193.) [12]

BRUTON, William, *Sidlesham, near Chichester.* Ex. Coll. Ox. B.A. 1843; Deac. 1844 and Pr. 1845 by Bp of Salis. V. of Sidlesham, Dio. Chich. 1849. (Patron, Bp of Chich; Tithe, 182*l* 10*s*; Glebe, 36*l*; V.'s Inc. 218*l* 10*s*; Pop. 960.) Formerly C. of Northmore Green 1844–45, Sidlesham 1845–49. [13]

BRUTTON, Thomas, *Newcastle-on-Tyne.*—Theol. Coll. Wells, 1849, Pemb. Coll. Ox. B.A. 1848, M.A. 1851; Deac. 1850 by Bp of Roch. Pr. 1851 by Bp of Ex. C. and Sunday Even. Lect. of St. Nicholas', Newcastle; Surrogate. [14]

BRUXNER, George Edward, *Thurlaston, near Leicester.*—Ch. Ch. Ox. B.A. 1836, M A. 1838; Deac. 1837, Pr. 1838. R. of Thurlaston, Dio. Pet. 1845. (Patron, the Rev. J. Arkwright; R.'s Inc. 440*l* and Ho; Pop. 698.) [15]

BRYAN, George, *Mumby, Alford, Lincolnshire.*—St. John's Coll. Cam. B.A. 1823, M.A. 1826. P. C. of St. Leonard's, Mumby, Dio. Lin. 1826. (Patron, V. of Mumby; P C.'s Inc. 70*l*.) V. of Huttoft, near Alford, Dio. Lin. 1833. (Patron, Bp of Lin; V.'s Inc. 80*l*; Pop. 710.) [16]

BRYAN, Guy, *Woodham-Walter, Maldon, Essex.*—St. Peter's Coll. Cam. B.A. 1803, M.A. 1807; Deac. 1804, Pr. 1805. R. of Woodham-Walter, Dio. Roch. 1819. (Patroness, Mrs. Coles; Tithe, 506*l*; R.'s Inc. 524*l* and Ho; Pop. 598.) [17]

BRYAN, Guy, Jun., *Swanton-Novers, Briningham, Thetford.*—St. Peter's Coll. Cam. B.A. 1837, M.A. 1841; Deac. 1841, Pr. 1842. C. of Swanton-Novers. [18]

BRYAN, Hugh, *Pinchbeck, Spalding, Lincolnshire.*—Clare Coll. Cam. LL.B. 1859, M.L. 1863; Deac. 1859 and Pr. 1860 by Bp of Pet. C. of East Pinchbeck 1866. Formerly C. of St. Margaret's, Leicester, 1859, Oakham 1862. [19]

BRYAN, Joseph W., *Cliddesden, Basingstoke, Hants.*—R. of Cliddesden with Farleigh-Wallop R. Dio. Win. 1840. (Patron, Earl of Portsmouth; Cliddesden, Tithe, 553*l*; Glebe, 10 acres; Farleigh-Wallop, Tithe, 342*l* 10*s*; Glebe, 9 acres; R.'s Inc. 924*l* and Ho; Pop. Cliddesden 320, Farleigh-Wallop 118.) [20]

BRYAN, Percival Wilmot, *Charlton-Adam, Somerton.*—St. Bees; Deac. 1843, Pr. 1845. V. of Charlton-Adam, Dio. B. and W. 1861. (Patron, Rev. Guy Bryan; Tithe, 57*l* 2*s* 1*d*; Glebe, 24 acres; V.'s Inc. 100*l*; Pop. 530.) Author, *Stammering Considered with Relation to the Management of the Breath*, 1847; *The Mind, the Breath, and Speech*, 1848. [21]

BRYAN, Reginald Guy, *Fosbury, Hungerford, Wilts.*—Trin. Coll. Cam. 23rd Wrang. and B.A. 1842, M.A. 1847; Deac. 1842 and Pr. 1843 by Bp of Pet. P. C. of Fosbury, Dio. Salis. 1856. (Patron, R. C. L. Bevan, Esq; P. C.'s Inc. 150*l*; Pop. 336.) [22]

BRYAN, Richard Syndercombe, *East Worlington, West Morchard, Devon.*—Caius Coll. Cam. B.A. 1832; Deac. 1833 and Pr. 1844 by Bp of Ex. R. of Cheldon, Devon, Dio. Ex. 1845. (Patron, Earl of Portsmouth; Tithe, 73*l*; Glebe, 30 acres; R.'s Inc. 118*l*; Pop. 97.) R. of East Worlington, Dio. Ex. 1852. (Patron, Earl of Portsmouth; Tithe, 195*l*; Glebe, 70 acres; R.'s Inc. 290*l* and Ho; Pop. 284.) Chap. to Earl of Portsmouth. [23]

BRYAN, William Bryan, *Rodington Rectory, near Shrewsbury.*—Wor. Coll. Ox. B.A. 1857, M.A. 1860; Deac. 1858 and Pr. 1859 by Bp of Ches. R. of Rodington, Dio. Lich. 1860. (Patron, Ld Chan; Tithe—Imp. 35*s*; R. 294*l* 16*s* 6*d*; Glebe, 30 acres; R.'s Inc. 320*l* and Ho; Pop. 481.) Dom. Chap. to Earl of Crawford and Balcarres. Formerly C. of Haigh, Lancashire. [24]

BRYAN, Wilmot Guy, *London-road, Ipswich.*—St. Peter's Coll. Cam. B.A. 1846, M.A. 1850; Deac. 1846 and Pr. 1847 by Bp of Roch. Formerly C. of Freston, Suffolk, 1849, Trimingham, Norfolk, 1852, Rodmarton, Glouc. 1855; P. C. of Leavenheath, Suffolk, 1859–65. [25]

BRYANS, Francis, *Backford, near Chester.*—St. Edm. Hall Ox. B.A. and M.A. 1823; Deac. 1823 and Pr. 1824 by Bp of Ches. V. of Backford, Dio. Ches. 1838. (Patron, Bp of Ches; Glebe, 20 acres; V.'s Inc. 230*l* and Ho; Pop. 525.) [26]

BRYANS, Francis Richard, *Rode, Lawton, Cheshire.*—Brasen. Coll. Ox. B.A. 1858; Deac. 1859 and Pr. 1860 by Bp of Ches. C. of Rode 1863. Formerly C. of Duddon 1859. Author, *A First Step to Sight Singing*, 1*s*; *A Morning and Evening Service*, 1866, 1*s*. [27]

BRYANS, Richard, *Ampthill, near Bedford.*—Brasen. Coll. Ox. B.A. 1853, M.A. 1856; Deac. 1854 and Pr. 1855 by Bp of Lin. Late C. of Bawtry and Austerfield, Yorks. [28]

BRYANS, Richard, Jun., *Holmrook, Whitehaven.*—Ch. Coll. Cam. B.A. 1857, M.A. 1861; Deac. 1858 and Pr. 1860 by Bp of Carl. C. of Irton, Cumberland, 1858. [29]

BRYANS, William, *Tarvin, near Chester.*—Trin. Coll. Cam. B.A. 1845, M.A. 1848; Deac. 1846, Pr. 1847. V. of Tarvin, Dio. Ches. 1852. (Patron, Bp of Lich; Tithe—App. 855*l* 16*s* 9*d*, V. 627*l* 18*s* 3*d*; Glebe, 2 acres; V.'s Inc. 584*l* and Ho; Pop. 2693.) [30]

BRYANT, Francis John, *North Brentor, Tavistock, Devon.*—Wad. Coll. Ox. B.A. 1850, Deac. 1855 and Pr. 1856 by Bp of Ex. P. C. of Brentor, Dio. Ex.

1858. (Patron, Duke of Bedford; P. C.'s Inc. 60*l*; Pop. 128.) Formerly C. of Lamerton, Devon. [1]

BRYANT, George, *Sheerness, Kent.*—Emman. Coll. Cam. B.A. 1840, M.A. 1844; Deac. 1842, Pr. 1843. P. C. of Sheerness, Dio. Cant. 1844. (Patron, P. C. of Minster; P. C.'s Inc. 300*l*; Pop. 18,186.) C. of Warden, Sheppy, 1850; Surrogate. [2]

BRYANT, James Henry, *Temple House, Nuneaton.*—St. John's Coll. Cam. Hulsean Prizeman, B.D. 1867; Deac. 1854 and Pr. 1855 by Bp of Wor. P. C. of Astley, Warw. Dio. Wor. 1856. (Patron, C. N. Newdegate, Esq. M.P; Glebe, 53 acres; P. C.'s Inc. 120*l*; Pop. 315.) Formerly C. of Chilvers Cotton. Author, *Mutual Influence of Christianity and the Stoic School* (Hulsean Prize 1867.) Macmillans. [3]

BRYANT, John Barker, *North Dalton, Great Driffield.*—P. C. of North Dalton, Dio. York, 1863. (Patron, James Walker, Esq; P. C.'s Inc. 84*l*; Pop. 486.) [4]

BUBB, Charles De Lannoy Hammond. —St. John's Coll. Cam. B.D. 1861; Deac. 1859 by Bp of Wor. Pr. 1860 by Bp of Lon. Formerly C of Reddal Hill, Staffs, 1859, Sanderstead, Surrey, 1862. [5]

BUBB, Henry, *Duntisbourne-Rouse, Cirencester.* —Pemb. Coll. Ox. B.A. 1836, M A. 1838; Deac. 1840 and Pr. 1841 by Bp of G. and B. C. of Baunton 1861. Formerly C. of Duntisbourne-Rouse. [6]

BUCHANAN, Alexander Henry, *Hales Hall, Sheriff-Hales, Salop.*—P. C. of Hales, Dio. Lich. 1856. (Patron, the present P. C; P. C.'s Inc. 120*l*; Pop. 318.) [7]

BUCHANAN, James Robert, *Herne, Kent.*—King's Coll. Lon. Theol. Assoc. 1853; Deac. 1853, Pr. 1854. V. of Herne, Dio. Cant. 1866. (Patron, Abp of Cant; V.'s Inc. 400*l* and Ho; Pop. 1644.) Formerly P. C. of Ch. Ch. Herne Bay. [8]

BUCHANAN, Thomas Boughton, *Wishford Magna, Salisbury.*—Ex. Coll. Ox. 1st cl. in Mods. B.A. 1856, M.A. 1858; Deac. 1857 and Pr. 1859 by Bp of Salis. R. of Wishford Magna, Dio. Salis. 1863. (Patron, Earl of Pembroke; R.'s Inc. 342*l* and Ho; Pop. 381.) Formerly C. of Wilton and Chap. to Lord Herbert of Lea. Author, *A Plain Ash-Wednesday Sermon*, 1861. [9]

BUCK, Richard Hugh Keats, *St. Dominick, Callington, Cornwall.*—Sid. Coll Cam. B.A. 1837; Deac. 1838 and Pr. 1839 by Bp of Ex. R. of St. Dominick, Dio. Ex. 1853. (Patron, Rev. F. L. Bazeley; Tithe, 380*l*; Glebe, 106 acres; R.'s Inc. 490*l* and Ho; Pop. 862.) [10]

BUCK, W. H. Meade, *Sutton, Seaford, Sussex.* —V. of Sutton with Seaford V. Dio. Chich. 1864. (Patron, Ld Chan; V.'s Inc. 216*l*; Pop. 1084.) [11]

BUCKBY, Richard, *Begelly, Tenby, Pembrokeshire.*—R. of Begelly with Williamston C. Dio. St. D. 1839. (Patron, Lord Milford; Tithe, 255*l* 9*s* 8*d*; R.'s Inc. 260*l* and Ho; Pop. 1301.) [12]

BUCKE, Benjamin Walter, *Trinity Parsonage, Lee, Kent.*—King's Coll. Lon. and St. John's Coll. Cam; M.A. by Abp of Cant; Deac. 1850 and Pr. 1852 by Bp of Nor. P. C. of Holy Trinity, Lee, Dio. Lon. 1863. (Patron, L. Glenton, Esq; P. C.'s Inc. 1000*l* and Ho; Pop. 1100.) Dom. Chap. to the Marquis of Westmeath. Formerly C. of Rendlesham, Suffolk, St. James's, Paddington; Preacher at the Magdalen Hospital, Lond. [13]

BUCKERFIELD, Francis Henchman, *Collingbourne-Ducis, Marlborough, Wilts.*—Magd. Hall, Ox. B.A. 1827, M.A. 1831; Deac. 1827 and Pr. 1829 by Bp of Salis. R. of Collingbourne-Ducis, Dio. Salis. 1862. (Patron, Marquis of Ailesbury; R.'s Inc. 716*l*; Pop. 553.) Rural Dean; Surrogate. Formerly V. of Little Bedwyn, Wilts, 1843–62. [14]

BUCKERIDGE, Alfred, *St. James's Parsonage, Exeter.*—Trin. Coll. Cam. B.A. 1851; Deac. 1851 and Pr. 1852 by Bp of Ex. P. C. of St. James's, City and Dio. of Ex. 1856. (Patron, V. of Heavitree, near Exeter; P. C.'s Inc. 190*l* and Ho; Pop. 4200.) Rural Dean 1866. Formerly Asst. C. and Chap. to the Liverydole Almshouses, Heavitree 1851, Asst. C. of St. Sidwell's, Exeter. [15]

BUCKHAM, John, *Bishop's Wood, Brewood, Staffs.*—St. John's Coll. Cam. B.A. 1841, M.A. 1844; Deac. 1841, Pr. 1842. P. C. of Bishop's Wood, Dio. Lich. 1851. (Patron, V. of Brewood; Tithe, 80*l*; Glebe, 1 acre; P. C.'s Inc. 225*l* and Ho; Pop. 588.) [16]

BUCKINGHAM, James, *Doddiscombsleigh, Chudleigh, Devon.*—Wad. Coll. Ox. B.C.L. 1836. R. of Doddiscombsleigh, Dio. Ex. 1856. (Patron, the present R; R.'s Inc. 346*l* and Ho; Pop. 348.) [17]

BUCKINGHAMSHIRE, The Right Hon, Augustus Edward HOBART, sixth Earl of, *Richmond Lodge, Sidmouth, Devon.*—Brasen. Coll. Ox. B.A. 1815, M.A. 1818; Deac. 1816, Pr. 1817. Preb. of Kinvaston in the Coll. Ch. of Wolverhampton (Value 18*l*.) [18]

BUCKLAND, Matthew Harvey, *Laleham, near Chertsey, Surrey.*—Corpus Coll. Ox. B.A. 1844, M.A. 1847; Deac. 1846 and Pr. 1847 by Bp of Lon. Formerly C. of Laleham. [19]

BUCKLAND, Samuel, *Great Torrington, Devon* —Ch. Ch. Ox. 3rd cl. Lit. Hum. 3rd cl. Math. et Phy. and B.A. 1838, M.A. 1841; Deac. 1841 and Pr. 1842 by Bp of Ox. V. of Great Torrington, Dio. Ex. 1849. (Patron, Ch. Ch. Ox; Tithe—App. 493*l* 12*s*, V. 12*l* 5*s*; V.'s Inc. 160*l* and Ho; Pop. 3298.) Surrogate; Dom. Chap. to Lord Harris. [20]

BUCKLAND, William John, *Hankerton Vicarage, Malmesbury, Wilts* —Wor. Coll. Ox. B.A. 1860, M.A. 1861; Deac. 1860 and Pr. 1861 by Bp of Ex. V. of Hankerton, Dio. G. and B. 1864. (Patron, R. of Crudwell; V.'s Inc. 280*l* and Ho; Pop. 393.) Formerly C. of Camborne, Cornwall, and Stawell and Sutton Mallett, Somerset. [21]

BUCKLE, Edward Valentine, *Banstead, Epsom, Surrey.*—Lin. Coll. Ox. B A. 1853, M.A. 1855, Theol. Coll. Wells 1853; Deac. 1854 and Pr. 1855 by Bp of Ox. V. of Banstead, Dio. Win. 1865. (Patron, Earl of Egmont; Tithe, 330*l*; Glebe, 1 acre, V.'s Inc. 300*l* and Ho; Pop. 900.) Formerly C. of Tadmarton, Oxon, and Isleworth, Middlesex. [22]

BUCKLE, George, *Twerton, near Bath.*—Late Scho. of Corpus Coll. Ox. 2nd cl. Lit. Hum. 1st cl. Math. et Phy. and B.A. 1842, M.A. 1845; Deac. 1846 and Pr. 1848 by Bp of Ox. V. of Twerton, Dio. B. and W. 1852. (Patron, Oriel Coll. Ox; Tithe—App. 2*l* 10*s*, Imp. 82*l* 10*s*, V. 251*l* 0*s* 6*d*; Glebe, 51½ acres; V.'s Inc. 380*l* and Ho; Pop. 3102.) Late Fell. of Oriel Coll. Ox. 1843; Tut. Math. Exam. 1846; Exam. in Responsions, 1850. [23]

BUCKLE, George Manley, *Parsonage, East Molesey, Surrey.*—King's Coll. Cam. Fell. of, 2nd cl. Cl. Trip. B.A. 1859, M.A. 1862; Theol. Coll. Salisbury; Deac. 1863 and Pr. 1864 by Bp of Win. P. C. of East Molesey, Dio. Win. 1866. (Patron, King's Coll. Cam; Glebe, 37 acres; P. C.'s Inc. 200*l* and Ho; Pop. 800.) Formerly C. of Thames Ditton 1863–65. [24]

BUCKLE, John, *Ashperton Parsonage, Ledbury, Herefordshire.*—St. Mary Hall, Ox. 3rd cl. Lit. Hum. 1843, B.A. 1844, M.A. 1847; Deac. 1844 and Pr. 1845 by Bp of Herf. V. of Stretton-Grandison with the Chapelry of Ashperton, Dio. Herf. 1859. (Patron, Rev. John Hopton; Tithe, 351*l*; Glebe, 160 acres; V.'s Inc. 620*l* and Ho; Pop. Stretton-Grandison 130, Ashperton 534.) Formerly C. of Coddington 1845–48, Purleigh 1848–51, Ashperton 1851–59. [25]

BUCKLE, Matthew Hughes George, *Edlingham, Alnwick, Northumberland.*—Wad. Coll. Ox. 2nd cl. Lit. Hum. and B.A. 1824, M.A. 1831; Deac. 1825, Pr. 1827. V. of Edlingham, Dio. Dur. 1839. (Patrons, D. and C. of Dur; Tithe—App. 682*l* 7*s* 4*d*, V. 282*l* 4*s* 8*d*; Glebe, 130 acres; V.'s Inc. 482*l* and Ho; Pop. 676.) Late Fell. and Tut. of Wad. Coll. Ox. [26]

BUCKLE, The Ven. Robert Bentley, *Upway, Dorchester.*—Sid. Coll. Cam. 4th Wrang. and B.A. 1824, M.A. 1827; Deac. 1827, Pr. 1828. R. of Upway, Dio. Salis. 1837. (Patron, Bp of Salis; Tithe, 380*l*; Glebe, 36½ acres; R.'s Inc. 430*l* and Ho; Pop. 646.) Preb. of Stratton in Salis. Cathl. 1841. Formerly Fell. and Math. Lect. of Sid. Coll. Cam; Archd. of Dorset 1836–63. [27]

BUCKLE, William, *Stretton-Grandison, Ledbury.* —C. of Stretton-Grandison. [1]

BUCKLER, Josiah Fell, *Tinsley, Rotherham.* —Caius Coll. Cam. B.A. 1855; Deac. 1855 and Pr. 1856 by Bp. of Ches. V. of Tinsley, Dio. York, 1862. (Patron, Earl Fitzwilliam; V.'s Inc. 139*l*; Pop. 697.) Formerly C. of St. Paul's, Macclesfield, 1855–60, Wentworth, Rotherham, 1860–62. [2]

BUCKLER, William, *Ilchester, Somerset.*—Magd. Coll. Ox. B.A. 1832. M.A. 1838; Deac. 1833 and Pr. 1835 by Bp of B. and W. R. of Ilchester, Dio. B. and W. 1837. (Patron, Bp of Lon; Tithe—App. 3*l* 9*s* 6*d*; R. 51*l* 10*s*; Glebe, 46 acres; R.'s Inc. 150*l* and Ho; Pop. 781.) [3]

BUCKLEY, Felix John, *Stanton St. Quintin, Chippenham.*—Mert. Coll. Ox. M.A. 1858; Deac. 1858 and Pr. 1859 by Bp of Ex. R. of Stanton St. Quintin, Dio. G. and B. 1867. (Patron, Earl of Radnor; Glebe, 400 acres; R.'s Inc. 400*l* and Ho; Pop. 338.) Formerly C. of Buckland-Monachorum, Devon, 1858, Rownhams. Hants, 1861, Nunton, Wilts, 1863. [4]

BUCKLEY, Henry William, *Hartshorne (Derbyshire), near Burton-upon-Trent.*—Mert. Coll. Ox. 2nd cl. Lit. Hum. and B.A. 1820, M.A. 1822; Deac. 1823 and Pr. 1824 by Bp of Ox. R. of Hartshorne, Dio. Lich. 1833. (Patrons, Earl of Chesterfield and W. Blake, Esq; Glebe, 392 acres; R.'s Inc. 540*l* and Ho; Pop. 1040.) [5]

BUCKLEY, John Wall, 1, *St. Mary's-terrace, Paddington-green, London, W.*—Magd. Coll. Cam. B.A. 1837, M.A. 1840; Deac. 1839, Pr. 1839. P. C. of St. Mary's, Paddington, Dio. Lon. 1843. (Patron, Bp of Lon; P. C.'s Inc. 500*l* and Ho; Pop. 10,646.) [6]

BUCKLEY, Joseph, *Sopworth, Chippenham.*—Magd. Coll. Cam. B.A. 1835, M.A. 1839; Deac. 1836, Pr. 1837. V. of Badminton, Dio. G. and B. 1840. (Patron, Duke of Beaufort; V.'s Inc. 40*l* and Ho; Pop. 524.) R. of Sopworth, Wilts, Dio. G. and B. 1853. (Patron, Duke of Beaufort; Tithe, 174*l*; Glebe, 101 acres; R.'s Inc. 300*l* and Ho; Pop. 214.) Dom. Chap. to the Duke of Beaufort 1841. [7]

BUCKLEY, William Edward, *Middleton-Cheney, near Banbury.*— Brasen. Coll. Ox. 1st cl. Lit. Hum. and B.A. 1839, M.A. 1842; Deac. 1847 and Pr. 1850 by Bp of Ox. R. of Middleton-Cheney, Dio. Pet. 1853. (Patron, Brasen. Coll. Ox; Glebe, 318 acres; R.'s Inc. 460*l* and Ho; Pop. 1250.) Rural Dean. Formerly Fell. and Tut. of Brasen. Coll. Ox.; Prof. of Anglo-Saxon in the Univ. of Ox. 1844–50; Prof. of Cl. Lit. East India Coll. Haileybury, 1850–53. Editor, *The Old English Version of Partonope of Blois*, edited for the Roxburghe Club, London, 1862, 4to; Burton Robert, *Philosophaster Comœdia nunc primum in lucem producta, Poemata nunc in unum collecta*; Hertfordiæ typis Stephani Austin, 1862, edited and presented to the members of the Roxburghe Club. [8]

BUCKLEY, William Louis, *Ashbury, Hatherleigh, Devon.*—Dub. A.B. 1853. R. of Ashbury, Dio. Ex. 1861. (Patron, Ld Chan; Tithe, 73*l* 10*s* 6*d*; Glebe, 70 acres; R.'s Inc. 123*l* and Ho; Pop. 80.) [9]

BUCKMASTER, John, *Wandsworth, Surrey.*—V. of Wandsworth, Dio. Win. 1856. (Patroness, Mrs. Buckmaster; Tithe—Imp. 525*l*, V. 640*l*; Glebe 260 acres; V.'s Inc. 660*l* and Ho; Pop. 4813.) [10]

BUCKMASTER, Ralph Nevile, 16, *Holland-street, Kensington, London, W.*—Ch. Ch. Ox. B.A. 1841; Deac. 1841, Pr. 1842. C. of St. James's Norland, Notting-hill. [11]

BUCKNER, Charles, *Wyke House, Chichester.*—Wad. Coll. Ox. B.A. 1828, M.A. 1831, B.D. 1842; Deac. 1830 and Pr. 1831 by Bp of Chich. R. of West Stoke, Sussex, Dio. Chich. 1849. (Patron, Ld Chan; Tithe, 161*l*; Glebe, 14 acres; R.'s Inc. 180*l* and Ho; Pop. 94.) [12]

BUCKNER, John, *Bapchild, Sittingbourne, Kent.* —St. John's Coll. Cam. B.A. 1840, M.A. 1843; Deac. 1840 and Pr. 1841 by Abp of Cant. V. of Bapchild, Dio. Cant. 1855. (Patrons, D. and C. of Chich; Tithe—App. 437*l* 2*s* 3*d*, and 5 acres of Glebe, V. 167*l* 7*s* 9*d*; Glebe, 28 acres; V.'s Inc. 190*l*; Pop. 389.) [13]

H

BUCKNILL, George, *High Ercall, Wellington, Salop.*—Trin. Coll. Ox. 3rd cl. Lit. Hum. and B.A. 1842, M.A. 1844; Deac. and Pr. 1843 by Bp. of Pet. V. of High Ercall, Dio. Lich. 1859. (Patron, Duke of Cleveland; Tithe, 441*l* 8*s* 9*d*; Glebe, 29 acres; V.'s Inc. 509*l* 8*s* 9*d* and Ho; Pop. 1250.) [14]

BUCKNILL, William Samuel, *Nuneaton, Warwickshire.*—Trin. Coll. Cam. B.A. 1834; Deac. 1835 and Pr. 1836 by Bp of Lich. P. C. of Burton-Hastings, Dio. Wor. 1844. (Patron, the present P. C; P. C.'s Inc. 108*l*; Pop. 199.) Sinecure R. of Stretton-Baskerville (no Ch.) Dio. Wor. 1850. (Patron, the Crown; Tithe, 100*l*; R.'s Inc. 100*l*; Pop. 74.) Head Mast. of King Edward VI.'s Gr. Sch. Nuneaton; Chap. to Nuneaton Union. [15]

BUCKOLL, Henry James, *Rugby School, Warwickshire.*—Queen's Coll. Ox. B.A. 1826, M.A. 1829. Asst. Mast. in Rugby Sch. [16]

BUCKSTON, Henry, *Lichfield.*—St. John's Coll. Cam. B.A. 1856, M.A. 1859; Deac. 1857 and Pr. 1858 by Bp of Lich. C. of St. Mary's, Lichfield, 1866. Formerly C. of Rugeley, Staffs. 1857. [17]

BUCKSTON, Rowland German, *Sutton-on-the-Hill, Derby.*—Brasen. Coll. Ox. B.A. 1850, M.A. 1853; Deac. 1853 and Pr. 1854 by Bp of Lich. V. of Sutton-on-the-Hill, Dio. Lich. 1861. (Patron, the present V; V.'s Inc. 200*l* and Ho; Pop. 310.) Formerly C. of Eccleshall, Staffs. 1853, Bradbourne, Derbyshire, 1855. [18]

BUCKWELL, William Blackwall, *Littleover, Derby.*—Wad. Coll. Ox. B.A. 1863, M.A. 1864; Deac. 1864 by Bp. of Ches. Pr. 1864 by Bp of Lich. C. in sole charge of Littleover 1864. [19]

BUCKWORTH, Thomas Everard, *Norbury, (Staffs.), near Newport.*—Dub. 1838, A B. 1842; Deac. 1847 and Pr. 1848 by Bp of Nor. R. of Norbury, Dio. Lich. 1849. (Patron, Earl of Lichfield; Tithe, 430*l*; Glebe, 58 acres; R.'s Inc. 620*l* and Ho; Pop. 364.) [20]

BUDD, Joseph, *Westbrook House, Farringdon, Berks.*—Cuddesdon Theol. Coll; Deac. 1855 and Pr. 1857 by Bp of Ox. C. of Littleworth 1855; Chap. of the Farringdon Union Workhouse 1861. [21]

BUDD, William B., *St. Gabriel's, Fenchurch-street, London, E.C.*— C. of St. Gabriel's, Fenchurch-street, with St. Margaret Pattens, London. [22]

BUDDICOM, Robert Joseph, *Morton, Gainsborough.*—Brasen. Coll. Ox. 2nd cl. Lit. Hum. and B.A. 1837, M.A. 1860; Deac. 1838 and Pr. 1839 by Bp of Lin. P. C. of Morton, Dio. Lin. 1862. (Patron, Bp of Lin; P. C.'s Inc. 92*l*; Pop. 616.) Formerly C. of Horley, Oxon, 1838–42; R. of Smethcote, Salop, 1842–62. Author, *Translation of Sallust*, several Tracts, and Two Assize Sermons. [23]

BUDGE, Henry Simcoe, *Westcott, Dorking.*—Dub. A.B. 1862; Deac. 1864, Pr. 1865. C. of Westcott 1867. Formerly Asst. Mast. in Bath Proprietary Coll. 1862–64; C. of Ormskirk 1864–66. [24]

BULKELEY, Henry John, *Sulham, Reading.* —Lin. Coll. Ox. B.A. 1864, M.A. 1866; Deac. 1866 by Bp of Ox. C. of Sulham 1866. [25]

BULKELEY, R. G., *Stoke-upon-Trent.*—C. of Stoke. [26]

BULKELEY-OWEN, Thomas Mainwaring Bulkeley, *Welsh-Hampton, Ellesmere, Salop.*—Ch. Ch. Ox. B.A. 1848; Deac. 1850 and Pr. 1851 by Bp of Lich. P. C. of Welsh-Hampton, Dio. Lich. 1863. (Patrons, Guardians of S. K. Mainwaring, Esq; P. C.'s Inc. 180*l*; Pop. 550.) Formerly C. of Tibberton. [27]

BULKLEY, Edward, *Ashford Hill, Reading.*—Lin. Coll. Ox. 2nd cl. Lit. Hum. B.A. 1856, M.A. 1859; Deac. 1856 by Bp of Lon. Pr. 1860 by Bp of Down and Connor. P. C. of Woodlands, Kingsclere, Dio. Win. 1862. (Patron, V. of Kingsclere; Glebe, 4 acres; P. C.'s Inc. 120*l* with Ho; Pop. 1175.) Formerly Tut. in St. Columba's Coll. Dub. 1857–61; Asst. C. of Grange-Gorman, Dio. Dub. 1860–61. [28]

BULL, Alfred Ernest, 3, *St. John's-terrace, Southall Green, Middlesex.*—Emman. Coll. Cam. Scho. of,

B.A. 1861; Deac. 1862 and Pr. 1865 by Bp of Lon. London Dioc. Home Missionary to the Brickmakers of Southall and Heston. Formerly C. of St. Luke's, King's Cross, 1862; Asst. Mast. at Kensington Proprietary Gr. Sch. 1864. [1]

BULL, Alfred Nicholas, *Woollavington, Bridgwater, Somerset.*—Sid. Coll. Cam. B.A. 1834, M.A. 1851; Deac. 1834 by Bp of Carl. Pr. 1838 by Bp of Ely. V. of Woollavington with Puriton, Dio. B. and W. 1851. (Patrons, D. and C. of Windsor; Woollavington, Tithe—App. 50*l*, V. 200*l*; Glebe, 31 acres; Puriton, Tithe—App. 118*l* 18*s* 7*d*, V. 75*l*; Glebe, 6 acres; V.'s Inc. 375*l* and Ho; Pop. Woollavington 415, Puriton 604) Author, *Brief Memoir of the Rev. Nicholas Bull, LL.B. Vicar of Saffron Walden, Essex, and of Ickleton, Cambridgeshire, with Selections from his Poetical and other Writings*, 1847; *Two Letters to Rev. C. S. Grueber, on his Misquotation and Perversion of Bishop Jewell*, 1857. [2]

BULL, Augustine Howie, *Cerne Abbas, Dorchester.*—Trin. Coll. Cam. Jun. Opt. 1st cl. Cl. Trip. and B.A. 1849, M.A. 1852; Deac. 1850 and Pr. 1851 by Bp of Herf. P. C. of Cerne Abbas, Dio. Salis. 1866. (Patron, Lord Rivers; Glebe, 2 acres; P. C.'s Inc. 100*l* and Ho; Pop. 1100.) Formerly P. C. of Toft, Cheshire; and Chap. to the Bp of Sydney; C. in sole charge of Market Drayton. Author, *The Atonement*, a pamphlet; *Jesus and the Twelve, or the Training of Christ's Disciples*, Parkers, 1868. [3]

BULL, Charles, *Stanley, Falkland Islands.*—Deac. 1851 by Bp of Cape Town. Pr. 1856 by Bp of Win. Colonial Chap. Stanley, Falkland Islands. Formerly C. of St. Anne's, Soho, St. Michael's, Burleigh-street, Strand, Ch. Ch. Endell-street, St. Giles's, and Miss. of the S.P.G. at Plettenburgh Bay and Schoomberg, South Africa. [4]

BULL, Charles Cary, *St. Helier's, Jersey.*—Deac. 1861 and Pr. 1862 by Bp of Lich. Min. of St. Andrew's Chapel, St. Helier's, 1865. Formerly C. of Riddings and Somercotes, Derbyshire, 1861–64, Bicester, Oxon, 1864–65. [5]

BULL, Edward, *Pentlow (Essex), near Sudbury.*—M.A. by Abp of Cant; Deac. 1826 by Abp of York, Pr. 1828 by Bp of Nor. R. of Pentlow, Dio. Roch. 1834. (Patron, the present R; Tithe, 518*l*; Glebe, 27½ acres; R.'s Inc. 583*l* and Ho; Pop. 397.) [6]

BULL, Elijah Serle, *Colchester.*—Queens' Coll. Cam. B.A. 1831; Deac. 1832 and Pr. 1833. Formerly Min. of St. Botolph's, Colchester, 1838–44. [7]

BULL, George Tippet, *Treslothan, Camborne, Cornwall.*—Dub. A.B. 1839; Deac. 1839 and Pr. 1841 by Bp of Ex. P. C. of the District Chapelry of St. John, Treslothan, Dio. Ex. 1846. (Patron, Mrs. Pendarves; P. C.'s Inc. 130*l* and Ho; Pop. 1804.) [8]

BULL, Henry, *Lathbury, Newport-Pagnell, Bucks.*—Ch. Ch. Ox. B.A. 1819, M.A. 1821; Deac. 1819 and Pr. 1820. P. C. of Lathbury, Dio. Ox. 1838. (Patron, Ch. Ch. Ox; Tithe—App. 59*l* 1*s*, P. C. 290*l* 16*s* 7½*d*; P. C.'s Inc. 300*l* and Ho; Pop. 147.) Rural Dean. [9]

BULL, Henry Charles, *St. James's, Wigan.*—Jesus Coll. Cam. M.A; Deac. 1858, Pr. 1859. P. C. of St. James's, Wigan, Dio. Man. 1863. (Patron, N. Eckersley, Esq; P. C.'s Inc. 160*l*; Pop. 3750.) Formerly C of Golborne 1858–60, Carisbrooke 1860–64. [10]

BULL, Henry Edward Marriott, *Stoke-Ash Rectory, Stonham, Suffolk.*—St. Cath. Coll. Cam. B.A. 1856; Deac. 1857 and Pr. 1858 by Abp of York. R. of Stoke-Ash, Dio. Nor. 1861. (Patron, the present R; Tithe, comm 363*l*; Glebe, 15 acres; R.'s Inc. 363*l* and Ho; Pop. 371.) [11]

BULL, Henry Dawson Ellis, *Borley, Sudbury.*—Wad. Coll. Ox. M.A. 1858; Deac. 1858 and Pr. 1859 by Bp of Ely. R. of Borley, Dio. Roch. 1862. (Patron, Rev. Ed. Bull, R. of Pentlow; Tithe, 280*l*; Glebe, 10 acres; R.'s Inc. 300*l* and Ho; Pop. 190.) [12]

BULL, Henry John, *Barnstaple, Devon.*—St. John's Coll. Cam. 9th Wrang. and B.A. 1841, M.A. 1844; Deac. 1844 and Pr. 1845 by Bp of Lon. P. C. of St. Mary Magdalene's, Barnstaple, Dio. Ex. 1856. (Patrons, Crown and Bp alt; P. C.'s Inc. 165*l*; Pop. 2540.) Formerly C. of St. James the Great, Bethnal-green, 1845–46, Ledbury, Herf. 1847–51, Axminster 1852–54, Lower Norwood, Surrey, 1855. [13]

BULL, Richard, *Harwich, Essex.*—St. John's Coll. Cam. B.A. 1839, M.A. 1843; Deac. and Pr. 1841. V. of Dovercourt with P. C. of Harwich, Dio. Roch. 1852. (Patron, Ld Chan; Dovercourt, Tithe, 134*l* 2*s* 9*d*; Rent from Glebe, 80*l*; V.'s Inc. 242*l* 13*s* 4½*d*; Harwich, Tithe, 18*l*; P. C.'s Inc. 82*l* 3*s* 3*d*; Pop. Dovercourt 1231, Harwich 3839.) Surrogate. Formerly C. of Dovercourt with Harwich 1841–52. [14]

BULL, Robert Cooke, *Midhurst, Sussex.*—Emman. Coll. Cam. 2nd cl. Cl. Trip. B.A. 1858, M.A. 1862; Deac. 1859 and Pr. 1860 by Bp of Ely. R. of Lynch, Dio. Chich. 1862. (Patron, Earl of Egmont; Tithe, 38*l*; no Glebe nor Ho; R.'s Inc. 81*l*; Pop. 111.) Formerly C. of St. Andrew's, Cambridge, 1859–61. [15]

BULL, Thomas, *Sibbertoft Vicarage, near Market Harborough.*—St. Cath. Coll. Cam. B.A. 1834, M.A. 1842; Deac. 1834 and Pr. 1835 by Bp of Pet. V. of Sibbertoft, Dio. Pet. 1863. (Patron, Bp of Pet; Tithe, 330*l*; Glebe, 70*l*; V.'s Inc. 400*l* and Ho; Pop. 394.) Formerly C. of Haselbeech, Northants, 1834, Corby 1842. [16]

BULL, Thomas, *Great Oakley, Kettering.*—Chap. of D. of Great Oakley, Dio. Pet. 1845. (Patron, Sir A. Brooke; Chap's Inc. 65*l*; Pop. 195.) [17]

BULL, William, *Ramsey, Harwich.*—V. of Ramsey, Dio. Roch, 1852. (Patron, Ld Chan; Tithe—Imp. 973*l* 14*s*, V. 301*l* 8*s* 9*d*; V.'s Inc. 310*l* and Ho; Pop. 605.) [18]

BULL, William Edge Elijah Mason, *Over Vicarage, near Winsford, Cheshire.*—Queens' Coll. Cam. B.A. 1861; Deac. 1863 and Pr. 1864 by Bp of Ches. C. of Over St. Chads 1863. [19]

BULL, William Howie, *Billinghurst Vicarage, Horsham, Sussex.*—St. John's Coll. Cam. 12th Sen. Opt. B.A. 1819, M.A. 1825; Deac. 1819, Pr. 1820. V. of Billinghurst, Dio. Chich. 1860. (Patron, Sir Charles Goring, Bart; Tithe, 200*l* 15*s*; Glebe, 13 acres; V.'s Inc. 260*l*; Pop. 1495.) Formerly C. of Sheffield 1822–27; P. C. of Sowerby, near Halifax, for 22 years; and V. of Old Newton, Suffolk, for 11 years. [20]

BULL, William Lownds, *St. John's Bowling, Bradford, Yorks.*—St. John's Coll. Cam. B.A. 1861; Deac. 1863 and Pr. 1864. C. of St. John's Bowling 1863. [21]

BULLEN, Abraham William, *Vineyards, Great Baddow, Chelmsford.*—Trin. Coll. Cam. B.A. 1841, M.A. 1848; Deac. 1843 by Bp of Wor. Pr. 1844 by Bp of G. and B. V. of Great Baddow, Dio. Roch. 1846. (Patron, the present V; Tithe—Imp. 641*l* 5*s*, V. 448*l*; Glebe, 2 acres; V.'s Inc. 462*l* and Ho; Pop. 2061.) Formerly C. of Filleigh, with East Buckland, Devon, 1843–45. [22]

BULLEN, Edward, *Eastwell, Melton Mowbray.*—Trin. Hall. Cam. S.C.L. 1818; Deac. and Pr. 1819 by Bp of Lin. R. of Eastwell, Dio. Pet. 1831. (Patron, Ld Chan; Tithe, 348*l* 12*s*; Glebe, 40 acres; R.'s Inc. 390*l* and Ho; Pop. 160.) [23]

BULLEN, John, *Bevois Hill, Southampton.*—Dub. A.B. 1850; Deac. 1850, Pr. 1851. P. C. of St. Matthew's, Southampton, Dio. Win. 1866. (Patron, Bp of Win; P. C.'s Inc. 400*l*; Pop. 3000.) Formerly C. of Ch. Ch. Tunbridge Wells, and Folkestone. Author, *The Death of a Christian Soldier*; *Notes on the Canticles*, etc. [24]

BULLEN, J. G., *St. Mary Church, Torquay.*—C. of St. Mary Church. [25]

BULLER, Antony, *Tavy St. Mary, Tavistock, Devon.*—Oriel Coll. Ox. B.A. 1831, M.A. 1834; Deac. 1832 and Pr. 1833 by Bp of Ex. R. of Tavy St. Mary, Dio. Ex. 1833. (Patron, John Buller, Esq; Tithe, 207*l* 10*s*; Glebe, 30 acres; R.'s Inc. 246*l* and Ho; Pop. 1202.) [26]

BULLER, Henry John, *West Parley Rectory, Wimborne, Dorset.*—Trin. Coll. Ox. M.A. 1833; Deac. 1836, Pr. 1837. R. of West Parley, Dio. Salis. 1839. (Patroness, Mrs. Buller; Tithe—App. 44*l*, R. 250*l*; Glebe,

25 acres; R.'s Inc. 284*l* and Ho; Pop. 268.) Formerly C. of East Allington 1836, Landrake 1838. [1]

BULLER, Reginald J., *Troston Rectory, Bury St. Edmunds.*—R. of Troston, Dio. Ely, 1841. (Patron, Ld Chan; R.'s Inc. 400*l* and Ho; Pop. 322.) [2]

BULLER, Richard, *Lanreath, Liskeard.*—Oriel Coll. Ox. B.A. 1826, M.A. 1829; Deac. 1828 by Bp of Ex. Pr. 1829 by Bp of B. and W. R. of Lanreath, Dio. Ex. 1829. (Patron, John Francis Buller, Esq; Tithe, 502*l* 11*s*; Glebe, 94 acres; R.'s Inc. 605*l* and Ho; Pop. 553.) Formerly P. C. of Herodsfoot. [3]

BULLER, William Edmund, *Over Stowey, Bridgwater, Somerset.*—Ex. Coll. Ox. B.A. 1853, M.A. 1856, Stud. of Wells Theol. Coll; Deac. 1855 by Bp of Ox. Pr. 1856 by Bp of B. and W. V. of Over Stowey, Dio. B. and W. 1856. (Patron, Lord Taunton; Tithe—Imp. 133*l* 1*s*, V. 165*l*; Glebe, 1 acre; V.'s Inc. 183*l* and Ho; Pop. 613.) Rural Dean of Bridgwater 1857; Commissary in England to Bishop Tozer. Formerly C. of Buckland Newton, Dorset. [4]

BULLEY, Frederick, *Magdalen College, Oxford.*—Magd. Coll. Ox. 3rd cl. Lit. Hum. and B.A. 1829, M.A. 1832, B.D. 1840, D.D. 1856; Deac. 1833 and Pr. 1834 by Bp of Ox. President of Magd. Coll. Ox. 1855. [5]

BULLICK, Charles A., *Walsall, Staffs.*—C. of Walsall. Formerly C. of St. John's, Ipswich. [6]

BULLINGER, Ethelbert William, 24, *Horbury-crescent, Kensington-park, London, W.*—King's Coll. Lon. Theol. Assoc; Deac. 1861 and Pr. 1862 by Bp of Win. C. of St. Peter's, Notting-hill, 1866. Formerly C. of Bermondsey, Surrey, 1861–63, Tittleshall, Norfolk, 1863–66. [7]

BULLIVANT, Charles, *East Leake Parsonage, Loughborough.*—Deac. 1857 and Pr. 1858 by Bp of Lich. C. in sole charge of East Leake 1866. Formerly C. of Cheadle 1857, and Checkley, Staffs, 1858–66. [8]

BULLIVANT, Henry, *Lower Whitley, Dewsbury, Yorks.*—Sid. Coll. Cam. B.A. 1838. P. C. of Lower Whitley, Dio. Rip. 1846. (Patron, Bp of Rip; Tithe—App. 101*l*; P. C.'s Inc. 280*l*.) [9]

BULLIVANT, Henry Everard, *Lubenham, Market Harborough.*—St. Cath. Coll. Cam. B.A. 1841, M.A. 1845; Deac. 1841, Pr. 1842. V. of Lubenham, Dio. Pet. 1842. (Patron, Thomas Paget, Esq; Tithe—Imp. 249*l* 19*s* 6*d*; V.'s Inc. 130*l*; Pop. 640.) Surrogate. [10]

BULLIVANT, John Hamilton, *Pytchley, Kettering.*—Queens' Coll. Cam. B.A. 1843; Deac. 1843 by Bp of Ely, Pr. 1844 by Bp of Lich. V. of Pytchley, Dio. Pet. 1851. (Patron, Bp of Lich; Tithe—App. 737*l* 2*s*; V.'s Inc. 99*l* and Ho; Pop. 536.) [11]

BULLIVANT, John Henry, *Ashton, Newton-le-Willows, Lancashire.*—St. Bees; Deac. 1861 and Pr. 1862 by Bp of Lich. C. of St. Thomas's in Ashton in Makerfield, 1863. Formerly C. of Northwood, Stoke-upon-Trent, 1861–63, Bradford, Yorks, 1863. [12]

BULLOCK, Charles, *St. Nicholas Rectory, Worcester.*—St. Bees, Sen. Librarian; Deac. 1855 by Abp of York, Pr. 1856 by Bp of Carl. R. of St. Nicholas', City and Dio. of Worcester. (Patron, Bp of Wor; Pop. 1933.) Chap. of the General Infirmary. Formerly C. of Rotherham, Yorks; Luton, Beds. Author, *God's Kingdom* and *National Responsibility* (two Sermons on the Fall of Sebastopol), 1*s*; *The Way Home, or the Gospel in the Parable*, 1*s* 6*d*; *Sin and its Cure, or the Syrian Leper*, 2*s* 6*d* and 1*s* 6*d*; *Infant Baptism and the Fatherhood of God*, 2*d*; *Essays and Reviews*, 6*d*; *Bible Inspiration, What it is, and What it is Not*, 1*s*; *Loyalty to Christ*; *Dorcas*; and other single Sermons; *The Key of the Controversy, or Faith's View of the Second Advent*, 2*d*; *Heart Cheer for Home Sorrow*, 1*s* 6*d*; *The Homes of Scripture*, 1*s* 6*d*; *Hymns, Chiefly Modern*, 1*s* 6*d*; all published by W. Macintosh, London. Editor, *Our Own Fireside, a Magazine of Home Literature for the Christian Family*, 6*d* monthly, vols i, ii and iii. 7*s* 6*d* each. [13]

BULLOCK, Frederick, *Colaton-Raleigh, Ottery St. Mary, Devon.*—Ex. Coll. Ox. B.A. 1853; Deac. 1854 and Pr. 1856 by Bp of Lich. V. of Colaton-Raleigh, Dio. Ex. 1857. (Patron, Dean of Ex; Tithe—App. 324*l*, V. 295*l*; Glebe, 43 acres; V.'s Inc. 378*l* and Ho; Pop. 748.) [14]

BULLOCK, George Frederick, *Bovey Tracey, South Devon.*—Queen's Coll. Ox. B.A. 1849, M.A. 1852; Deac. 1858 and Pr. 1859 by Bp of Ex. Sen. C. of Bovey Tracey. Formerly C. of Widdecombe-in-the-Moor, 1858–59; V. of Buckfastleigh 1859–61; C. of Torwood 1861–63; St. John's, Torquay, 1863. [15]

BULLOCK, George Martin, *Chalfont, Slough, Bucks.*—St. John's Coll. Ox. B.A. 1837, M.A. 1841, B.D. 1846; Deac. 1839 and Pr. 1840 by Bp of Ox. V. of Chalfont St. Peter, Dio. Ox. 1863. (Patron, St. John's Coll. Ox; V.'s Inc. 800*l* and Ho; Pop. 1344.) [16]

BULLOCK, James George, 5, *Louvain-road, New Wandsworth, S.W.*—Caius Coll. Cam. B.A. 1860, M.A. 1864; Deac. 1860 and Pr. 1861 by Bp of Roch. C. of Ch. Ch. Battersea 1864. Formerly C. of Saffron Walden 1860–63, Bootle with Linacre, Liverpool, 1863–64. [17]

BULLOCK, John Frederic, *Radwinter, Braintree, Essex.*—Clare Hall Cam. B.A. 1831, M.A. 1834; Deac. 1832, Pr. 1833. R. of Radwinter, Dio. Roch. 1844. (Patrons, Lord Maynard and Rev. W. T. Bullock; Tithe, 700*l*; Glebe, 62 acres; R.'s Inc. 760*l* and Ho; Pop. 946.) Rural Dean. [18]

BULLOCK, Mitford, *Skirpenbeck, Stamford-bridge, Yorks.*—Corpus Coll. Cam. B.A. 1834; Deac. 1835, Pr. 1836. R. of Skirpenbeck, Dio. York, 1840. (Patron, Ld Chan; Tithe, 9*s*; Glebe, 134 acres; R.'s Inc. 224*l*; Pop. 198.) [19]

BULLOCK, Richard, *Barrow-on-Humber, Lincoln.*—Oriel Coll. Ox. B.A. 1861, M.A. 1864; Deac. 1863 and Pr. 1864 by Bp of Lin. V. of Barrow-on-Humber, Dio. Lin. 1866. (Patron, Ld Chan; Tithe, 250*l*; Glebe, 35 acres; V.'s Inc. 300*l* and Ho; Pop. 2500.) Formerly C. of Barton-on-Humber 1863–66. [20]

BULLOCK, R., *Wakefield.*—Asst. Chap. of the Prison, Wakefield. [21]

BULLOCK, Walter, *Faulkbourn Hall, Witham, Essex.*—Caius Coll. Cam. Scho. Jun. Opt. B.A. 1843, M.A. 1846; Deac. 1846 by Bp of Lon. Pr. 1847 by Bp of Roch. Formerly C. of Little Horkesley, Essex, 1846–47; R. of Faulkbourn 1847–53. [22]

BULLOCK, William, *Colney Hatch, Middlesex, N.*—St. Mary Hall, Ox. B.A. 1846; Deac. 1847, Pr. 1848. Chap. of the Colney Hatch Asylum. [23]

BULLOCK, William Greenway, *Clough Hill, Rotherham.*—St. John's Coll. Cam. B.A. 1863; Deac. 1863 and Pr. 1864 by Bp of Lon. C. of St. John's, Masbrough, 1866. Formerly C. of All Saints', Notting-hill, 1863, Wapping 1865. [24]

BULLOCK, William Thomas, 5, *Park-place, St James's-street, London, S.W.*—Magd Hall, Ox. B.A. 1847, M.A. 1850; Deac. 1847, Pr. 1848. Asst. Sec. to the S.P.G. 1850, and Sec. 1864. Formerly C. of St. Anne's, Westminster, 1847–50. Author, various articles in Dr. Smith's *Dictionary of the Bible*, Murray, 1861–63. [25]

BULLOCKE, Henry Bawden, *The Rectory, Truro.*—Ex. Coll. Ox. B.A. 1836, M.A. 1848; Deac. 1837 and Pr. 1839 by Bp of Ex. R. of St. Mary's, Truro, Dio. Ex. 1865. (Patrons, Trustees of late Prebendary Harvey; Tithe, 30*l*; R.'s Inc. 130*l* and Ho; Pop. 3200.) Formerly C. of St. Mary's, and Prin. of the Exeter Dio. Female Training Coll. Truro; V. of Mullion, Cornwall, 1853–65. [26]

BULLOCKE, Henry, *Oxford.*—C. of St. Paul's, Oxford. [27]

BULMAN, George Robert, *Old Elvet, Durham.*—Univ. Coll. Dur. B.A. 1858, M.A. 1861; Deac. 1858 and Pr. 1859 by Bp of Dur. Chap. of Durham County Prisons. Formerly C. of Chester-le-Street, Durham, Eckington, Derbyshire. [28]

BULMAN, Job George, *Houghton-le-Spring, Fence Houses, Durham.*—Univ. Coll. Dur. Theo. Licen. and B.A. 1856, M.A. 1865; Deac. 1856 by Bp of Man. Pr. 1857 by Bp of Dur. Formerly C. of Bishop Auckland, 1856; Reader at the Rolls Chapel, London, 1861; C of Chiswick 1865. [29]

BULMER, Charles Henry, *Credenhill, Hereford.*—Magd. Coll. Cam. M.A.; Deac. 1856 and Pr. 1857 by Bp of Herf. R. of Credenhill, Dio. Herf. 1861. (Patron, Trustees of the late Rev. J. Eckley; Tithe, 362*l*; Glebe, 28 acres; R.'s Inc. 450*l* and Ho; Pop. 199.) Formerly C. of Westhide, near Hereford. [1]

BULMER, Edward, *Ailstone-hill, Hereford.*—St. John's Coll. Cam. B.A. 1819, M.A. 1822; Deac. 1819, Pr. 1820. R. of Moreton-on-Lugg, Herf. Dio. Herf. 1839. (Patron, Preb. of Moreton-Magna in Herf. Cathl; Tithe—App. 18*l* 4*s*, R. 212*l* 8*s* 4*d*; R.'s Inc. 220*l* and Ho; Pop. 77.) Min. Can. of Herf. Cathl. 1820. (Value, 19*l*.) [2]

BULMER, Edward, *The Close, Norwich.*—St. Peter's Coll. Cam. Scho. 1852, B.A. 1855, M.A. 1858; Deac. 1855 and Pr. 1856 by Bp of Herf. Min. Can. of Nor. Cathl. Formerly C. of Moreton-on-Lugg, Herefordshire. [3]

BULMER, Richard William, *Oakham, Rutland.*—St. Aidan's; Deac. 1858 and Pr. 1859 by Abp of York. C. of Burley-on-the-Hill, Rutland, 1861. Formerly C. of St. Matthew's, Sheffield, 1858. [4]

BULMER, Robert John, *Houghton-le-Spring, Durham.*—St. John's Coll. Cam. B.A. 1843, M.A. 1846. 2nd Mast. of Houghton-le Spring Gr. Sch. Durham. [5]

BULMER, William, *Radstock, near Bath.*—Univ. Coll. Dur. B.A. 1854, M.A. 1857; Deac. 1856 by Bp of Pet. Pr. 1857 by Bp of Dur. C. in sole charge of Radstock 1865. Formerly C. of Barnack, Northants, Shildon, Durham, Acton, Middlesex, and St. Lawrence, Isle of Wight. [6]

BULMER, William, *Brotherton, Normanton, Yorks.*—Magd. Coll. Cam. B.A. 1801, M.A. 1804; Deac. 1801, Pr. 1802. V. of Ferry-Fryston, Dio. York, 1852. (Patrons, Sub-Chanter and Vicars-Choral of York Cathl; Tithe—App. 405*l* 5*s*, and 64½ acres of Glebe, V. 192*l* 5*s* 10*d*; Glebe, 75½ acres; V.'s Inc. 288*l*; Pop. 904.) Formerly Deputy V. Choral of York Minster 1801, Probationary V. 1801, Member of the Coll. of Vicars-Choral 1802, Succentor Vicariorum 1851–53; V. of St. Martin's, Coney-street, York, 1803–29; P. C. of St. Sampson's, York, 1821–52; V. of St. Mary's, Bishophill, 1829–52. [7]

BULMER, William Henry Philip, *St. Andrew's Parsonage, Deptford, Sunderland.*—St. Bees; Deac. 1829, Pr. 1830. P. C. of Deptford, Dio. Dur. 1843. (Patron, Bp of Ches; P. C.'s Inc. 350*l* and Ho; Pop. 10,908.) [8]

BULSTRODE, George, *Ely.*—C. of Trinity, Ely. [9]

BULTEEL, Courtenay James Cooper, *Holbeton, Erme-Bridge, Modbury, Devon.*—Ball. Coll. Ox. B.A. 1828, M.A. 1831; Deac. 1828 and Pr. 1831 by Bp of B. and W. V. of Holbeton, Dio. Ex. 1831. (Patron, the Crown; Tithe—Imp. 494*l* 5*s*, V. 340*l*; V.'s Inc. 345*l*; Pop. 965.) V. of Ermington with Kingston C. Devon, Dio. Ex. 1834. (Patrons, the Crown and Rev. W. J. and Mrs. Pinwell; Ermington, Tithe—Imp. 287*l*, Sinecure R. 270*l*, V. 308*l*; Kingston, Tithe—App. 113*l* 6*s* 3*d*, Imp. 111*l*, V. 109*l*; Glebe, 22 acres; V.'s Inc. 441*l* and Ho; Pop. Ermington 761, Kingston 451.) [10]

BULWER, Henry Earle, *Erpingham Rectory, Aylsham, Norfolk.*—Pemb. Coll. Cam. B.A. 1862, M.A. 1866; Deac. 1864 and Pr. 1865 by Bp of Ely. C. of Erpingham 1867. Formerly C. of Litlington, Cambs, 1864. Roydon, Norfolk, 1866. [11]

BULWER, James, *Hunworth, Holt, Norfolk.*—Jesus Coll. Cam. B.A. 1818, M.A. 1823; Deac. 1818 by Bp of Nor. Pr. 1822 by Bp of Kilmore. R. of Stody with Hunworth R. Dio. Nor. 1848. (Patroness, Lady Suffield; Stody, Tithe, 237*l*; Glebe, 31 acres; Hunworth, Tithe, 152*l* 10*s*; Glebe, 27 acres; R.'s Inc. 458*l*; Pop. Stody 160, Hunworth 206.) Formerly P. C. of Booterstown, Dublin, 1823–33, Min. of York Chapel, and C. of St. James's, Westminster, 1833–48. Author, *Views of Madeira*, 1825–26; *Views of Cintra, in Portugal*; *Views in the West of England.* [12]

BUMPSTED, Thomas Jeffery, *Dinder Rectory, Wells, Somerset.*—Queen's Coll. Ox. B.A. 1820; Deac. 1822 by Bp of Ely, Pr. 1823 by Bp of Ches. R. of Dinder, Dio. B. and W. 1862. (Patron, Bp of B. and W; Tithe, 190*l* 5*s*; Glebe, 15 acres; R.'s Inc. 200*l*; Pop. 244.) Hon. Preb. of Wells. Formerly C. of Berkeley, near Frome, 1822–34, Burrington, near Bristol, 1834–62. [13]

BUMSTEAD, James, *Glodwick, Oldham.*—Wor. Coll. Ox. B.A. 1846, M.A. 1850; Deac. 1846 and Pr. 1847 by Bp of Lon. P. C. of Glodwick, Dio. Man. 1851. (Patrons, the Crown and Bp of Man. alt; P. C.'s Inc. 165*l*; Pop. 7200.) Late C. of Trin. Ch. Stepney, and Chap. to the Tower Hamlets Cemetery. [14]

BUNBURY, Thomas Edwin George, *H.M.S. "Esk."*—St. John's Coll. Ox. B.A. 1860; Deac. 1860 by Bp of B. and W. Chap. of H.M.S. "Esk." [15]

BUNBURY, Thomas Henry, *Great Warley, Brentwood, Essex.*—Dub. A.B. 1831; Deac. 1831 and Pr. 1832 by Bp of Ches. P. C. of Ch. Ch. Great Warley, Dio. Roch. 1855. (Patrons, Trustees; P. C.'s Inc. 215*l* and Ho; Pop. 1734.) Formerly C. of Birkenhead 1831, Whitwick 1839; P. C. of Sighill 1846. [16]

BUNCH, Robert James, *Emmanuel Rectory, Loughborough.*—Emman. Coll. Cam. B.A. 1827, M.A. 1830, B.D. 1837; Deac. 1830, Pr. 1831. R. of Emmanuel, Loughborough, Dio. Pet. 1848. (Patron, Emman. Coll. Cam; Tithe, 428*l*; Glebe, 154 acres; R.'s Inc. 784*l* and Ho; Pop. 4554.) Hon. Can. of Pet. Cathl. 1850; Surrogate; Rural Dean. Late Fell. of Emman. Coll. Cam. 1829. Author *A Visitation Sermon*, preached before the Archdeacon of Leicester and Clergy, 1851. [17]

BUNCOMBE, Charles Joseph, 40, *Holgate-road, York.*—Literate; Deac. 1855 and Pr. 1856 by Abp of York. V. of St. Mary's, Bishophill Junior, City and Dio. York. 1857. (Patrons, D. and C. of York; Tithe, 70*l*; Glebe, 35 acres; V.'s Inc. 140*l*; Pop. 2213.) Formerly C. of St. Lawrence, York, 1855–57. [18]

BUNN, Henry, *Tosside, Settle, Yorks.*—St. Bees; Deac. 1848 and Pr. 1849 by Bp of Man. P. C. of Tosside, Dio. Rip. 1855. (Patron, V. of Gisburn; P. C.'s Inc. 90*l* and Ho; Pop. 96.) Formerly C. of All Saints', Islington; P. C. of Houghton, Yorks. Author, *A Treatise on Purgatory*, 1849, 2*s* 6*d*; *Letters on National Education, &c.*; *A Voice from Many Lands, or the Missionary Enterprise*, 1851, 5*s*; *The Vampire of Christendom, a Book for the Times*, 1855, 3*s* 6*d*; etc. [19]

BUNSEN, Henry George de, *Lilleshall, Newport, Salop.*—Oriel Coll. Ox. 2nd cl. Lit. Hum. and B.A. 1840, M.A. 1843; Deac. 1841 by Bp of Chich. Pr. 1842 by Bp of Wor. V. of Lilleshall, Dio. Lich. 1847. (Patron, Duke of Sutherland; Tithe—Imp. 2*l* 17*s* 6*d*, V. 279*l*; Glebe, 38½ acres; V.'s Inc. 350*l* and Ho; Pop. 1391.) Dom. Chap. to the Duke of Sutherland; Chap. to the Bp of Man; Rural Dean. Formerly C. of Dunchurch, Warwickshire, 1841–42. [20]

BUNTING, Anthony, *The Crescent, Leicester.*—Dub. A.B. 1853; Deac. 1854 and Pr. 1855 by Bp of Ox. C. of a Conventional District, Leicester. Formerly C. of Mulsoe, Bucks, and Cranfield, Beds. [21]

BURBIDGE, Edward, *Aldbourne, Wilts.*—Emman. Coll. Cam. B.A. 1862; Deac. 1863 and Pr. 1864 by Bp of Salis. C. of Aldbourne. [22]

BURBIDGE, Frederick William, *The Schools, Shrewsbury.*—Ch. Coll. Cam. 5th Sen. Opt. 7th in 1st cl. Cl. Trip. B.A. 1862, M.A. 1865; Deac. 1865 and Pr. 1866 by Bp of Ely. Fell. of Ch. Coll. Cam. and Asst. Mast. in Shrewsbury Sch. [23]

BURBIDGE, John, *St. Stephen's Parsonage, Sheffield.*—Literate; Deac. 1855 and Pr. 1856 by Bp of Lich. P. C. of St. Stephen's, Sheffield, 1858. (Patron, Henry Wilson, Esq. Westbrook; P. C.'s Inc. 400*l*; Pop. 4097.) Formerly C of Chesterfield 1856–57. [24]

BURBIDGE, Thomas, *Hexton, Silsoe, Herts.*—Trin. Coll. Cam. B.A. 1842. V of Hexton, Dio. Roch. 1858. (Patroness, Mrs. Young De Lantour; V.'s Inc. 100*l*; Pop. 234.) Author, *Hours and Days* (Devotional Poems), 1851; *School Life* (Sermons preached in the Chapel of Leamington Coll.) 1854. [25]

BURD, Alfred, *Clifton.*—St. Alban Hall, Ox. B.A. 1852, M.A. 1854; Deac. 1852 and Pr. 1854 by Bp of Lich. Formerly C. of Harley, Salop, 1852, Bockleton, Hereford, 1863, Frome-hill, Hereford, 1864. [1]

BURD, Charles, *Wortham, Shrewsbury.* — St. John's Coll. Cam. B.A. 1856, M.A. 1859; Deac. 1857 and Pr. 1858 by Bp of Lich. C. of Wortham 1865. Formerly C. of Leebrockhurst, Salop, 1857, Lapworth, Warwickshire, 1860, Denton, Norfolk, 1863. [2]

BURD, Frederick, *Cressage, Shrewsbury.*—Ch. Ch. Ox. Careswell Exhib. B.A. 1849, M.A. 1852; Deac. 1850 by Bp of Ches. Pr. 1851 by Bp of Wor. P. C. of Cressage, Dio. Lich. 1864. (Patron, Rev. H. Thursby Pelham; Tithe, 208*l*; Glebe, 20 acres; P. C.'s Inc. 248*l*; Pop. 350.) Formerly C. of Lymm, Cheshire, 1850, Leighton, Salop, 1851, Shawbury 1853, Cressage 1853–64. [3]

BURD, John, *Chirbury Vicarage, near Shrewsbury.* —Ch. Ch. Ox. Fell. Exhib. 3rd cl. Lit. Hum. and B.A. 1850, M.A. 1853; Deac. 1852 and Pr. 1853 by Bp of Nor. V. of Chirbury, Dio. Herf. 1863. (Patrons, Trustees; Tithe—Imp. 1003*l* 3*s* 2*d*; V.'s Inc. 200*l* and Ho; Pop. 620.) Formerly C. of Parham with Hacheston, Suffolk, 1852–55, Middle, Salop, 1855–63. [4]

BURD, Percy, *Tidenham Vicarage, Chepstow.*— Dur. Univ. Licen. in Theol; Deac. 1857 and Pr. 1858 by Bp of Lich. V. of Tidenham, Dio. G. and B. 1862. (Patron, D. Higford Burr, Esq; Tithe, 359*l*; Glebe, 110 acres; V.'s Inc. 441*l*; Pop. 1473.) [5]

BURD, William Stevens, *Preston-Gubbalds, Salop.*—Ch. Ch. Ox. B.A. 1841, M.A. 1847; Deac. 1841 by Bp of Lich. Pr. 1842 by Bp of Herf. P. C. of Preston-Gubbalds, Dio. Lich. 1849. (Patron, Sir Henry Tyrwhitt, Bart; Glebe, 58 acres; P. C.'s Inc. 150*l*; Pop. 337.) Formerly C. of Shawbury 1841–46, Meole Brace 1847–49, both in Salop. [6]

BURDEKIN, James, *Croxall, Tamworth.*—Deac. 1860, Pr. 1861. C. of Croxall 1866. Formerly C of Tamworth 1860–66. [7]

BURDER, Alfred, *Oakley Vicarage, Bishops Stortford.*—Magd. Hall, Ox. B.A. 1842, M.A. 1844; Deac. 1842 and Pr. 1843 by Bp of Lon. V. of Oakley, Dio. Roch. 1846. (Patron, Christ's Hospital, London; Tithe, 100*l*; Glebe, 15 acres; V.'s Inc. 202*l* and Ho; Pop. 405.) Surrogate. Formerly C. of St. Mary's, Islington, 1842–46. [8]

BURDER, Charles Sumner, *Ham Rectory, Hungerford, Wilts.*—St. Mary Hall, Ox. B.A. 1853, M.A. 1857; Deac. 1854 and Pr. 1856 by Bp of Win. R. of Ham. Dio. Salis. 1863. (Patron, Bp of Win; R.'s Inc. 457*l*; Pop. 249.) Formerly C. of Privett, Hants. [9]

BURDER, Frederick Gouldsmith, *Child's Ercall, Market Drayton.*—C. of Child's Ercall. [10]

BURDETT, William, *North Molton, South Molton, Devon.*—Queens' Coll. Cam. B.A. 1838, M.A. 1845; Deac. 1838 and Pr. 1839 by Bp of Ches. V. of North Molton with Twitchen P. C. Dio. Ex. 1840. (Patron, Lord Poltimore; North Molton, Tithe—Imp. 1292*l* 17*s* and 6½ acres of Glebe; Glebe, 5 acres; Twitchen, Tithe—Imp. 210*l* 17*s* 6*d*; V.'s Inc. 170*l* and Ho; Pop. North Molton 1842, Twitchen 227.) Author, *Selection of Psalms and Hymns*; *Pastoral Addresses.* [11]

BURDETT, W. J., *Basingstoke, Hants.*—St. Edm. Hall, Ox. B.A. 1864; Deac. 1865 and Pr. 1867 by Bp of Win. C. of Basingstoke 1865. [12]

BURDON, John, *English Bicknor, Coleford, Glouc.* —Univ. Coll. Ox. 1st cl. Math et Phy. and B.A. 1833, Queen's Coll. M.A. 1836; Deac. 1835 by Bp of Carl. Pr. 1836 by Bp of Dur. R. of English Bicknor, Dio. G. and B. 1844. (Patron, Queen's Coll. Ox; Tithe 392*l*; Glebe, 9 acres; R.'s Inc. 401*l* and Ho; Pop. 461.) R. of Welsh Bicknor, Dio. Herf. 1850. (Patron, Ld Chan; Tithe, 155*l*; Glebe, 17 acres; R.'s Inc. 175*l* and Ho; Pop. 80.) Late Michel Fell. of Queen's Coll. Ox. [13]

BURDON, Richard, *Haselbury-Bryan, Blandford, Dorset.*—R. of Haselbury-Bryan, Dio. Salis. 1859. (Patron, Duke of Northumberland; R.'s Inc. 500*l* and Ho; Pop. 761.) [14]

BURDON, William James, *South Ormsby, Alford, Lincolnshire.* — C. of South Ormsby with Ketsby. [15]

BURFIELD, Henry John, *St. James's Parsonage, Bradford, Yorks.*—Lin. Coll. Ox. B.A. 1851, M.A. 1854; Deac. 1851 and Pr. 1852 by Bp of Wor. P. C. of St. James's, Bradford, Dio. Rip. 1852. (Patron, J. Wood, Esq; Glebe, ½ acre; P. C.'s Inc. 300*l* and Ho; Pop. 1981.) Hon. Can. of Ripon. Formerly C. of St. Thomas's, Birmingham, 1851. Author, *The District Visitor's Record*, 1853, 8*d*; *The Present Crisis* (a Sermon), 1853; *The Ministry and its Hindrances* (a Visitation Sermon), 1857; *Angelic Guardianship* (a sermon preached at St. Michael's College, Tenbury), 1864. Editor of *Ripon Diocesan Calendar*, published annually. [16]

BURGES, Frank, *Winterbourne Rectory, Bristol.* —St. John's Coll. Ox. B.A. 1835, M.A. 1839, B.D. 1844; late Fell. of St. John's Coll. Ox. R. of Winterbourne, Dio. G. and B. 1863. (Patron, St. John's Coll. Ox; R.'s. Inc. 600*l* and Ho; Pop. 1280.) [17]

BURGES, John Hart, *Bishop Ryder's Parsonage, Birmingham.*—Dub. Vice-Chan. Prizeman and A.B. 1850, A.M. 1858, B.D. and D.D. 1867; Deac. 1850 and Pr. 1851 by Bp of Dur. P. C. of Bp Ryder's Ch. Birmingham, Dio. Wor. 1857. (Patrons, Trustees; P. C.'s Inc. 300*l* and Ho; Pop. 9346.) Formerly P. C. of West Hartlepool 1853–57. Author, *A Sermon*; *Loss of the Dapper* (a Tract). [18]

BURGES, Richard Bennett, *Waddesdon, near Aylesbury, Bucks.*—Dub. A.B. 1851; Deac. 1851 and Pr. 1852. R. of Waddesdon, third portion, Dio. Ox. 1860. (Patron, Duke of Marlborough; R.'s Inc. 175*l*; Pop. 1786.) Formerly C. of Norton Durham, and Steeple Claydon, Bucks. [19]

BURGESS, Bryant, *Latimer Rectory, Chesham, Bucks.*—Ex. Coll. Ox. B.A. 1841, M.A. 1845; Deac. 1843 and Pr. 1844 by Bp of Lin. R. of Latimer, Dio. Ox. 1857. (Patron, Hon. C. C. Cavendish; Tithe, 125*l*; Glebe, 5 acres; R.'s Inc. 126*l* and Ho; Pop. 170) V. of Flaunden, Herts, Dio. Roch. 1857. (Patron, Hon. C. C. Cavendish; Tithe, 50*l*, Qu. Anne's Bounty, 55*l*; Glebe, 3 acres; V.'s Inc. 108*l*; Pop 244.) Surrogate. [20]

BURGESS, Henry, *Whittlesey Vicarage, Cambs.* —Univ. of Göttingen, A.M. and Ph.D. LL.D. of Glasgow; Deac. 1850 and Pr. 1851 by Bp of Man. V. of St. Andrew's, Whittlesey, Dio. Ely, 1861. (Patron, Ld Chan; Tithe—Imp. 3954*l* 8*s* 6½*d*, V. 451*l* 10*s* 5*d*; Glebe, 56*l*; V.'s Inc. 530*l* and Ho, subject to repayment of 1350*l* with interest to Queen Anne's Bounty.) Author, *Select Metrical Hymns and Homilies of Ephraem Syrus*, translated from the Syriac, with Introduction and Notes; *The Repentance of Nineveh, by Ephraem Syrus*, with Introduction and Notes; *The Festal Letters of Athanasius* (translated from the Syriac, and edited for the "Library of the Fathers," by the Rev. H. G. Williams); *The Power of Personal Godliness in Evangelising Mankind*; *The Bible and Lord Shaftesbury, a Letter to Dr. Macbride*; *The Amateur Gardener's Year-Book*; *Poems on Various Subjects*; Editor of *The Clerical Journal.* Late Editor of *The Journal of Sacred Literature.* [21]

BURGESS, Henry Martyn, *Aldingham Hall, Ulverston.*—Dub. A.B. 1860; Deac. 1862 by Bp of Ox. Pr. 1863 by Bp of Tasmania. Formerly C. of St. Nicholas', Newbury, 1862. [22]

BURGESS, John Hugh, *Burford Vicarage, Oxon.*—V. of Burford with Fulbrook P. C. Dio. Ox. 1860. (Patron, Bp of Ox; V.'s Inc. 350*l* and Ho; Pop. 2041.) [23

BURGESS, Richard, 69, *Cadogan-place, Chelsea, London, S.W.*—St. John's Coll. Cam. B. D. 1835; Deac. 1820 and Pr. 1823 by Abp of York. R. of Upper Chelsea, Dio. Lon. 1836. (Patron, Earl Cadogan; R.'s Inc. 850*l*; Pop. 6150.) Preb. of Tottenhall in St Paul's Cathl. 1850 (Value, 7*l*.) Formerly Hon. Sec. to the London Diocesan Board of Education for 8 years. Hon. Member of the Royal Institute of British Architects, and Member-Correspondent of the Pontifical Archæological Academy in Rome. Author, *A Treatise on the Ludi Circenses*, 1828, 7*s* 6*d*; *Topography and Antiquities of*

Rome, 2 vols. 1831, 63s; *Greece and the Levant*, 2 vols. 12s. 1835; *Lectures delivered in the English Chapel at Rome, during Lent*, 1831; various Pamphlets on Education, Sermons, etc. [1]

BURGESS, Robert, *Radcliffe-on-Trent, Notts.*—Ch. Coll. Cam. B.A. 1841, M.A. 1844; Deac. 1843, Pr. 1844. V. of Radcliffe-on-Trent, Dio. Lin. 1845. (Patron, Earl Manvers; Glebe, 70 acres; V.'s Inc. 170*l* and Ho; Pop. 1371.) [2]

BURGESS, Robert Burdett, *Chickney, Thaxted, Essex.*—Queens' Coll. Cam. B.A. 1831, M.A. 1834; Deac. 1832, Pr. 1833. R. of Chickney, Dio. Roch. 1858. (Patron, Capt. H. Byng, R.N; Tithe, 170*l*; Glebe, 40½ acres; R.'s Inc. 210*l*; Pop. 76.) [3]

BURGESS, Samuel, *Stony Stratford, Bucks.*—St. John's Coll. Cam. B.A. 1864; Deac. 1864 and Pr. 1867 by Bp of Ox. C. of Stony Stratford 1866. [4]

BURGESS, William Johnson, *Lacy Green, Prince's Risborough, Bucks.*—Ex. Coll. Ox. Hon. 4th cl. and B.A. 1837, M.A. 1840; Deac. 1838, Pr. 1839. P. C. of Lacy Green, Dio. Ox. 1848. (Patron, P. C. of Prince's Risborough; Glebe, 63 acres; P. C.'s Inc. 120*l* and Ho; Pop. 1050.) Chap. of Wycombe Union 1853. Formerly C. of Warbledon, Sussex, 1838–40, Great Missenden, Bucks, 1840–44, Aston Clinton, Bucks, 1844–48. Author, *Buckinghamshire Antiquities*, and other Papers, in *Records of Buckinghamshire* by the Bucks Archæological and Antiquarian Society. [5]

BURGESS, William Roscoe, *Latchford, near Warrington.*—Caius Coll. Cam. B.A. 1859; Deac. 1860 and Pr. 1861 by Bp of Ches. P. C. of Ch. Ch. Latchford, Dio. Ches. 1866. (Patron, R. of Grappenhall; P. C.'s Inc. 100*l*; Pop. 906.) Formerly P. C. of Horton with Piddington, Northants, 1863; C. of St. Andrew's, Whittlesey, 1864–66. [6]

BURGON, John William, *Oriel College, Oxford.*—Wor. Coll. Ox. 2nd cl. Lit. Hum. and B.A. 1848, Oriel Coll. Ox. M.A. 1848, Newdigate Prize Poem 1845, Ellerton Theol. Essay 1847, Denyer Theol. Essay 1851; Deac. 1848 and Pr. 1849 by Bp of Ox. Fell. of Oriel Coll; V. of St. Mary the Virgin, City and Dio. Ox. 1863. (Patron, Oriel Coll. Ox; V.'s Inc. 40*l*; Pop. 382.) Author, *Mémoire sur les Vases Panathenaïques, par Le Chevalier P. O. Bröndsted, traduit de l'Anglais*, 4to, Paris, 1833; *The Life and Times of Sir Thomas Gresham, compiled chiefly from his Correspondence in the State Paper Office*, 2 vols. 1839; *Petra, a Poem to which a few short Poems are now added*, 1846; *Some Remarks on Art, with reference to the Studies of the University*, 1846; *Oxford Reformers, a Letter to Endemus and Eodemus*, 1854; *A Century of Verses in Memory of the Reverend the President of Magdalen College* (Dr. Routh), 4to. 1855; *A Plain Commentary on the Four Holy Gospels, intended chiefly for Devotional Reading*, 8 vols. 1855; *Ninety short Sermons for Family Reading, following the course of the Christian Seasons*, 2 vols. 1st series, 1855 Editor, jointly with the Rev. H. J. Rose, of *Fifty Cottage Prints from Sacred Subjects, intended chiefly for distribution among the Poor*, 1851; *Thirty-six Cottage-wall Prints*, fol. 1853; *The Picture Bible* (Part I.) 4to. 1854; *The History of Our Lord Jesus Christ* (with 72 Engravings), 1855. Author, *Historical Notices of the Colleges of Oxford*, 4to. 1857; *Portrait of a Christian Gentleman, a Memoir of Patrick Fraser Tytler, Esq.* 1859; *Inspiration and Interpretation, Seven Sermons preached before the University of Oxford, being an Answer to Essays and Reviews*, 1861; *Letters from Rome to Friends in England*, 1862; *A Treatise on the Pastoral Office, addressed chiefly to Candidates for Holy Orders or to those who have recently undertaken the Cure of Souls*, 1864; *Ninety-one Short Sermons*, 2 vols. 2nd series, 1867. [7]

BURKE, John William, *Brampton-park, Hants.*—Queens' Coll. Cam. B.A. 1845; Deac. 1842. Lect. of Huntingdon; Chap. to the Earl of Tankerville. [8]

BURKE, Joshua Ingham, *Batheaston, Bath.*—C. of Batheaston. [9]

BURKE, Thomas James, *Cucklington, Wincanton, Somerset.*—Deac. 1849 and Pr. 1850 by Bp of Nor. R. of Cucklington with Stoke Trister and Bayford R. Dio. B. and W. 1862. (Patron, W. Phelips, Esq; R.'s Inc. 700*l* and Ho; Pop. 675.) [10]

BURKITT, William, *Leeds Parsonage, Maidstone.*—St. Edm. Hall, Ox. B.A. 1821, M.A. 1824; Deac. 1821 and Pr. 1822 by Bp of Bristol. P. C. of Leeds with Broomfield, Dio. Cant. 1843. (Patron, Abp of Cant; Leeds, Tithe—App. 623*l* 2*s* 9*d*; Broomfield, Tithe—App. 241*l* 15*s* 7*d*; P. C.'s Inc. 165*l*; Pop. Leeds 656, Broomfield 150.) [11]

BURKITT, William Esdaile, *Charlton, Salisbury.*—Ex. Coll. Ox. B.A. 1857; Deac. 1856 and Pr. 1857 by Bp of Llan. P. C. of Charlton, Dio. Salis. 1860. (Patron, V. of Downton; Glebe, ¾ of an acre; P. C.'s Inc. 83*l* and Ho; Pop. 303.) Chap. to Earl Nelson 1859. Formerly C. of Caldicot, Monmouthshire, 1856–59. [12]

BURLAND, Charles Isherwood, *Arreton Vicarage, Isle of Wight.*—Lin. Coll. Ox. B.A. 1853, M.A. 1856; Deac. 1854 by Bp of Rip. Pr. 1855 by Abp of York. C. of Arreton 1857. [13]

BURLTON, Henry Beaumont, *Farway Rectory, Honiton, Devon.*—Oriel Coll. Ox. B.A. 1848; Deac. 1850, Pr. 1852. R. of Farway, Dio. Ex. 1854. (Patron, Richard Marker, Esq; Tithe, 290*l*; Glebe, 24 acres; R.'s Inc. 320*l* and Ho; Pop. 368.) [14]

BURMESTER, Alfred, *Mickleham, Dorking, Surrey.*—Trin. Coll. Cam. B.A. 1810, M.A. 1813; Deac. 1810 and Pr. 1811 by Bp of Ely. R. of Mickleham, Dio. Win. 1813. (Patron, the present R; Tithe, 435*l*; Glebe, 35½ acres; R.'s Inc. 508*l* and Ho; Pop. 694.) [15]

BURMESTER, George, *Little Oakley, Harwich.*—Ball. Coll. Ox. B.A. 1817, M.A. 1821; Deac. 1828, Pr. 1829. R. of Little Oakley, Dio. Roch. (Patron, the present R; Tithe, 415*l*; Glebe, 30½ acres; R.'s Inc. 428*l* and Ho; Pop. 306.) Surrogate. [16]

BURN, Andrew, *Kinnersley, near Wellington, Salop.*—Queens' Coll. Cam. B.A. 1817, M.A. 1820; Deac. 1817, Pr. 1818. R. of Kinnersley, Dio. Lich. 1841. (Patron, Duke of Sutherland; Tithe, 340*l*; Glebe, 82¾ acres; R.'s Inc. 480*l* and Ho; Pop. 208.) [17]

BURN, George, *Hatfield Broad Oak, Harlow, Essex.*—Trin. Coll. Cam. 1st cl. Cl. Trip. Sen. Opt. Chan. Medallist, B.A. 1851, M.A. 1854; Deac. 1854 by Bp of Ely, Pr. 1855 by Bp of Lich. V. of Hatfield Broad Oak, Dio. Roch. 1858. (Patron, Trin. Coll. Cam; V.'s Inc. 180*l* and Ho; Pop. 928.) Formerly C. of Lilleshall, Salop; Fell. of Trin. Coll. Cam. [18]

BURN, Henry, *Rishangels, Eye, Suffolk.*—Can. of Brecon; R. of Rishangels, Dio. Nor. 1849. (Patron, the present R; Tithe, 206*l* 12*s* 10*d*; R.'s Inc. 350*l* and Ho; Pop. 229.) [19]

BURN, Robert, *Trinity College, Cambridge.*—Trin. Coll. Cam. Bracketed Sen. Classic 1852, 2nd Jun. Opt. 1852, 2nd cl. Nat. Sci. 1852, B.A. 1852, M.A. 1855; Deac. 1860 by Bp of Lich. Pr. 1862 by Bp of Ely. Fell. and Tut. of Trin. Coll. Cam. [20]

BURN-MURDOCH, James McGibbon, *Riverhead Parsonage, Sevenoaks.*—Downing Coll. Cam. B.A. 1859, M.A. 1863; Deac. 1861 and Pr. 1862 by Abp of Cant. P. C. of Riverhead, Dio. Cant. 1863. (Patron, R. of Sevenoaks; Glebe, 8*l*; P. C.'s Inc. 90*l* and Ho; Pop. 1100.) [21]

BURNABY, Gustavus Andrew, *Somerby Vicarage, Oakham.*—Emman. Coll. Cam. B.A. 1811, M.A. 1828; Deac. 1826, Pr. 1827. V. of Somerby, Leicestershire, Dio. Pet. 1866. (Patron, the present V; V.'s Inc. 246*l* and Ho; Pop. 506.) Can. of St. Ninian's in the Coll. Ch. of Middleham, Yorks, 1842; Surrogate; Chap. to H.R.H the Duke of Cambridge. Formerly R. of St. Peter's, Bedford, 1835–66. [22]

BURNABY, Henry Fowke, *King's College, Cambridge*, and *New University Club, St. James's-street, London, S. W.*—King's Coll. Cam. B.A. 1858, M.A. 1861; Deac. 1859 and Pr. 1860 by Bp of Lin. Fell. of King's Coll. Cam; C. of St. Mary's the Less, Cambridge, 1867. Formerly C. of Birch, Essex, 1861. [23]

BURNABY, Robert William, 8, *Lincoln-street, Leicester.*—New Coll. Ox. B.A. 1863; Deac. 1865 and Pr. 1866 by Bp of Pet. C. of St. George's, Leicester, 1865. [1]

BURNABY, Sherrard Beaumont.—Ch. Coll. Cam. Sen. Opt. B.A. 1854, M.A. 1857; Deac. 1857 by Bp of Lon. Dom. Chap. to Earl Fortescue. Formerly C. of Trinity, Stepney, 1857. [2]

BURNABY, Thomas, *Stonton-Wyville Rectory, Market Harborough.*—Trin. Coll. Cam. B.A. 1843; Deac. 1847 and Pr. 1848 by Bp of Pet. R. of Stonton-Wyville, Dio. Pet. 1860. (Patron, Earl of Cardigan; Tithe, 7*l* 7*s*; Glebe, 96 acres; R.'s Inc. 240*l* and Ho; Pop. 102.) Formerly C. of Badby with Newnham, Northants, 1847–51. [3]

BURNE, John Butler, *Aldermaston, Reading.*—Ch. Ch. Ox. 4th cl. Lit. Hum. and B.A. 1850; Deac. 1851 and Pr. 1852. P. C. of Aldermaston, Dio. Ox. 1854. (Patron, Higford D. Burr, Esq; P. C.'s Inc. 150*l*; Pop. 585.) [4]

BURNE, Thomas, *Moreton, Newport, Salop.*—Magd. Coll. Cam; Deac. 1847, Pr. 1849. P. C. of Moreton, Dio. Lich. 1850. (Patron, P. C. of Gnossall; P. C.'s Inc. 60*l* and Ho; Pop. 679.) [5]

BURNELL, Samuel, *Winwick, Newton-le-Willows.*—Late Scho. of Queens' Coll. Cam. Math. Prizeman, Sen. Opt. and B.A. 1826, M.A. 1830; Deac. 1828 and Pr. 1829 by Bp of Chich. Head Mast. of the Winwick Gr. Sch. 1851. (Patron, W. J. Legh, Esq., M.P., Lyme Hall, Cheshire.) [6]

BURNET, John, LL.D., *The Vicarage, Bradford, Yorks.*—V. of Bradford, Dio. Rip. 1846. (Patrons, Simeon's Trustees; Tithe—Imp. 569*l* 0*s* 3*d*, V. 323*l*; V.'s Inc. 650*l* and Ho; Pop. 51,419.) Chap. to the Bradford Union; Rural Dean; Surrogate. [7]

BURNET, John Eccleston, *Lowmoor, Bradford, Yorks.*—Oriel Coll. Ox. B.A. 1850; Deac. 1850, Pr. 1851. P. C. of Wibsey, Low Moor, Dio. Rip. 1865. (Patron, V. of Bradford; P. C.'s Inc. 350*l* and Ho; Pop. about 4000.) Formerly P. C. of Wilsden 1863–65. [8]

BURNET, Richard, *Lewes, Sussex.*—Late Scho. of Trin. Coll. Dub. A.B; Deac. 1830, Pr. 1832. Chap. to the East Sussex County Prisons, 1838; Surrogate. Author, *Easy Catechism for Ignorant Adults, &c.* 3*d*; *Short Notes on the Prayer Book Psalms*, 1*s*; Sermons, etc. [9]

BURNET, Thomas, 13, *Finsbury-square, London, E.C.*—Univ. Edin. and Ch. Coll. Cam. B.D. 1822, D.D. 1831, *ad eund.* Ox. 1853; Deac. 1810 and Pr. 1811 by Bp of Llan. R. and Lect. of St. James's, Garlickhithe, City and Dio. Lon. 1837. (Patron, by Bp of Lon; Tithe, 200*l*, Lect. 100*l*; R.'s Inc. 350*l* and Ho; Pop. 461.) Fell. of the Royal Society. Author, various Sermons and pieces of Poetry. [10]

BURNET, W. R., *Newcastle-on-Tyne.*—Min. of St. Thomas's Chap. Newcastle. [11]

BURNET, William, 34, *Albion-grove West, Barnsbury, London, N.*—Dub. A.B. 1856, A.M. 1860; Deac. 1856 and Pr. 1857 by Bp of Man. C. in sole Charge of St. Andrew's, Islington, 1866. Formerly C. of Wilton, Blackburn, 1856–59, St. Luke's, Blackburn, 1859–61, St. John's, Lewes, 1861–63, Ch. Ch. Birmingham 1863–64, Walsall, 1864–66. Author, *The Unchangeable Saviour*, and *The Gospel Triumph*, both sermons; and *Aids to Catechising.* [12]

BURNETT, Arthur Bernard, *Morestead Rectory, Winchester.*—St. John's Coll. Cam. B.A. 1842; Deac. 1845 and Pr. 1846 by Bp of Salis. C. of Morestead 1864. Formerly C. of Alderbury, near Salisbury, 1845–47; Incumb. of St. Stephen's, Willunga, South Australia, 1849–56; P. C. of Freefolk, Hants, 1857–61. [13]

BURNETT, George, *Scotby, Carlisle.*—Dub. A.B. 1845; Deac. 1850 by Bp of Ossory, Pr. 1851 by Bp of Cashel. P. C. of Scotby, Dio. Carl. 1865. (Patrons, G. H. Head and D. Hodgson, Esqrs; P. C.'s Inc, 67*l*; Pop. 520.) Formerly Min. of St. James's, Birkenhead. [14]

BURNETT, John Castle, *St. Michael's Rectory, Bath.*—St. John's Coll. Cam. B.A. 1829, M.A. 1833; Deac. 1831, Pr. 1831. R. of St. Michael's, Bath, Dio. B. and W. 1857. (Patrons, Simeon's Trustees; R.'s Inc. 107*l* and Ho; Pop. 2951.) Formerly V. of Berrow, Somerset, 1841–45; V. of North Curry with West Hatch P. C. Somerset, 1845–57. [15]

BURNETT, Richard Parry, *Stanwell Vicarage, Staines, Middlesex.*—Deac. 1835 and Pr. 1836 by Bp of B. and W. V. of Stanwell, Dio. Lon. 1858. (Patron, Ld Chan; Tithe—Imp. 620*l*, V. 280*l*; Glebe, 6 acres; V.'s Inc. 290*l* and Ho; Pop. 1203.) Formerly C. of Christian-Malford, Wilts, 1835–38, Membury near Axminster, 1838–58. [16]

BURNETT, William, *Boxgrove Vicarage, Chichester.*—New Coll. Ox. B.A. 1837, M.A. 1841, Deac. 1841 and Pr. 1842 by Bp of Ox. V. of Boxgrove, Dio. Chich. 1858. (Patron, Duke of Richmond; Tithe, 902*l*; Glebe, 7 acres; V.'s Inc. 910*l* and Ho; Pop. 680.) Formerly Fell. of New Coll. Ox; C. of Laindon, Essex, 1843–46; R. of Tangmere, Sussex, 1847–58. [17]

BURNEY, Alexander D'Arblay, *Gaer Hill, Maiden Broadley, Bath.*—Trin. Coll. Cam. Jun. Opt. B.A. 1861, M.A. 1864; Deac. 1862, Pr. 1863. C. of Marston-Bigot 1866. Formerly C. of Walmersley 1862, and Heywood, Lancashire, 1865. [18]

BURNEY, Charles, *The Rectory, Wickham Bishops, Essex.*—Magd. Coll. Ox. B.A. 1837, M.A. 1840; Deac. 1838 and Pr. 1839 by Bp of Lon. R. of Wickham Bishops, Dio. Roch. 1864. (Patron, Bp of Roch; Tithe, 476*l*; Glebe, 80 acres; R.'s Inc. 536*l* and Ho; Pop. 616.) Chap. to Bp of Roch. 1849; Surrogate; Rural Dean; Hon. Can. of Roch. Formerly V. of Halstead, Essex, 1850–64. [19]

BURNEY, Edward, *Gosport, Hants.*—Magd. Hall, Ox. B.A. 1838, M.A. 1841. Head Mast. of the Royal Naval and Military Academy, and C. of Trinity, Gosport. [20]

BURNEY, Edward Kaye, *Thornham, Maidstone.*—Madg. Coll. Ox. B A. 1839, M.A. 1842; Deac. 1840. Pr. 1841. V. of Thornham with Allingham R. Dio. Cant. 1850. (Patron, the present V; Thornham, Tithe—App. 6*l* 8*s*, Imp. 513*l* 4*s*, V. 513*l* 5*s* 6*d*; V.'s Inc. 600*l* and Ho; Pop. 531.) [21]

BURNEY, Henry, *Wavendon, Woburn, Beds.*—Ex. Coll. Ox. B.A. 1836; Deac. 1839 and Pr. 1840 by Bp of B. and W. R. of Wavendon, Dio. Ox. 1847. (Patron, Henry Arthur Hoare, Esq; Tithe, 702*l* 11*s* 5*d*; Glebe, 83 acres; R.'s Inc. 850*l* and Ho; Pop. 879.) Rural Dean. [22]

BURNEY, Henry Bannerman, *Norton St. Philip, Bath.*—Oriel Coll. Ox. B.A. 1841, M.A. 1845; Deac. 1842, Pr. 1843. V. of Norton St. Philip, Dio. B. and W. 1866. (Patron, Bp of B. and W; Tithe, 120*l*; Glebe, 4 acres; V.'s Inc. 130*l* and Ho; Pop. 650.) Preb. of Wells. Formerly Chap. at Calcutta. [23]

BURNHAM, Charles Havey, *Cogenhoe Rectory, Northampton.*—Brasen. Coll. Ox. Hulme Exhib. B.A. 1854, M.A. 1857; Deac. 1855 and Pr. 1856 by Bp of Pet. R. of Cogenhoe, Dio. Pet. 1864. (Patron, G. Burnham, Esq; R.'s Inc. 400*l* and Ho; Pop. 360.) Formerly C. of Bozeat with Strixton, Northants, 1855, Sandy, Beds, 1859. [24]

BURNINGHAM, George Nowell, *Old Windsor, Berks.*—Ex. Coll. Ox. B.A. 1864; Deac. 1866 by Bp of Ox. C. of Old Windsor 1866. [25]

BURNINGHAM, Thomas, *Charlwood (Surrey), Crawley, Sussex.*—Trin. Coll. Ox. B.A. 1830, M.A. 1861; Deac. 1832, Pr. 1833. R. of Charlwood, Dio. Win. 1856. (Patron, H. C. Wise, Esq; R.'s Inc. 550*l* and Ho; Pop. 1542.) Formerly C. of Brunstead, Norfolk, Burston, Surrey, and Milbrook, Hants. [26]

BURNS, William, *Blackpool.*—St. Bees and St. John's Coll. Cam. M.A. 1849; Deac. 1833 and Pr. 1835 by Bp of Ches. Formerly V. of Farnworth with Kersley, Lancashire, 1836–66. [27]

BURNS, William Henry, 74, *Grosvenor-street, Chorlton-on-Medlock, Manchester.*—Bp Hat. Hall, Dur. Scho. of, B.A. 1859, Licen. Theol. 1860, M.A. 1863; Deac. 1861 and Pr. 1862 by Bp of Man. C. of St. Philip's, Hulme, 1866. Formerly C. of Farnworth with Kersley 1862. [28]

BURNSIDE, John Charles, *New London-road, Chelmsford.*—King's Coll. Lon. Theol. Assoc. 1857; Deac. 1857 and Pr. 1858 by Bp of Lich. Sen. C. of St. John's, Moulsham, Chelmsford. [1]

BURNSIDE, William, *Plumtree, Nottingham.*—St. John's Coll. Cam. B.A. 1840, M.A. 1844; Deac. 1841 and Pr. 1842 by Bp of Lin. R. of Plumtree, Dio. Lin. 1865. (Patron, W. S. Burnside, Esq; R.'s Inc. 1100*l* and Ho; Pop. 600.) Formerly R. of Broxholme, Lincoln, 1847–65. [2]

BURRELL, John, *West Stockwith Vicarage, near Gainsborough.*—Univ. Coll. Dur. Licen. Theol. 1841; Deac. 1842 and Pr. 1843 by Bp of Dur. P. C. of West Stockwith, Dio. Lin. 1859. (Patrons, Trustees of W. Huntingdon; Glebe, 86 acres; V.'s Inc. 270*l* and Ho; Pop. 738.) Formerly P. C. of Byrness, Northumberland, 1843–59. [3]

BURRELL, John Fletcher, *Ipswich.*—King's Coll. Lon. Theol. Assoc; Deac. 1857 and Pr. 1858 by Bp of Nor. P. C. of St. Mary-at-Elms, Ipswich, Dio. Nor. 1863. (Patrons, Parishioners; P. C.'s Inc. 100*l*; Pop 1178.) [4]

BURRELL, Matthew, *Chatton, near Belford, Northumberland.*—Corpus Coll. Ox. B.A. 1834, M.A. 1837; Deac. 1838, Pr. 1839. V. of Chatton, Dio. Dur. 1844. (Patron, Duke of Northumberland; Tithe—Imp. 669*l* 16*s* 4*d*, V. 543*l* 2*s* 1*d*; V.'s Inc. 544*l* and Ho; Pop. 1651.) [5]

BURRELL, Richard, *Stanley, Wakefield.*—Ch. Coll. Cam. B.A. 1848, M.A. 1854; Deac. 1848 and Pr. 1849 by Bp of Rip. P. C. of Stanley, Dio. Rip. 1851. (Patron, V. of Wakefield; Glebe, 50 acres; P. C.'s Inc. 230*l* and Ho; Pop. 3084.) Surrogate. [6]

BURRIDGE, Edward, *Westley-Waterless, Newmarket.*—Ex. Coll. Ox; Deac. 1837, Pr. 1839. R. of Westley-Waterless, Cambs, Dio. Ely, 1850. (Patron, the present R; R.'s Inc. 400*l* and Ho; Pop. 213.) [7]

BURRIDGE, Thomas Waters, *Bradford, near Taunton.*—Magd. Hall. Ox. B.A. 1848, M.A. 1850; Deac. 1848 and Pr. 1849 by Bp of Ox. Chap. to the Forces 1861. Formerly C. of Speen 1848–51; P. C. of Stockcross 1851–58; V. of Bradford, Somerset, 1858–61. [8]

BURROUGH, James Waldron, *Totnes, Devon.*—Queen's Coll. Ox. B.A. 1832, M.A. 1836; Deac. 1835 and Pr. 1836 by Bp of Ex. V. of Totnes, Dio. Ex. 1838. (Patron, Ld Chan; V.'s Inc. 168*l* and Ho; Pop. 3409.) Surrogate. [9]

BURROUGH, John, *The Carrs, Kirkham, Preston.*—Queen's Coll. Ox. M.A. 1859; Deac. 1857 and Pr. 1858 by Bp of Herf. Head Mast. of Kirkham Gr. Sch. (Patron, the Drapers' Company.) Formerly C. of Kingsland, Heref; 2nd Mast. of Lucton Gr. Sch. Heref. [10]

BURROUGH, J. Ashton, B.A.—Chap. Royal Navy. [11]

BURROUGHES, Jeremiah, *Lingwood Lodge, Norwich.*—Emman. Coll. Cam. B.A. 1817, M.A. 1819; Deac. and Pr. 1819 by Bp of Nor. R. of Burlingham St. Andrew with St. Edmund R. Norfolk, Dio. Nor. 1819. (Patron, H. N. Burroughes Esq; St. Andrew, Tithe, 296*l* 15*s*; Glebe, 9 acres; St. Edmund, Tithe, 287*l* 11*s*; Glebe, 10¾ acres; R.'s Inc. 619*l*; Pop. St. Andrew 186, St. Edmund 85.) R. of Burlingham St. Peter, Norfolk, Dio. Nor. 1830. (Patron, H. N. Burroughes, Esq; Tithe, 148*l* 13*s*; Glebe, 10 acres; R.'s Inc. 166*l*; Pop. 80.) Rural Dean. [12]

BURROUGHES, R., *Pencombe, Bromyard, Herefordshire.*—C. of Pencombe. [13]

BURROW, Henry Hurst, *Drigg, Cumberland.*—Magd. Hall, Ox. B.A. 1852; Deac. 1853 and Pr. 1854; by Bp of Ches. C. of Drigg 1866. Formerly C. of Severn Stoke, Worcester. [14]

BURROW, James, *Hampton Vicarage, Middlesex, S.W.*—Queen's Coll. Ox. Scho. of, B.A. 1841, M.A. 1844; Deac. 1842 and Pr. 1843 by Bp of Dur. V. of Hampton, Dio. Lon. 1862. (Patron, Ld Chan; V.'s Inc. 700*l* and Ho; Pop. 3391.) Formerly P. C. of Ashford 1852–61, and Chap. to the Bakewell Union. [15]

BURROW, John, *Ilfracombe, Devon.*—St. Peter's Coll. Cam. B.D. 1867; Deac. 1844 and Pr. 1846 by Bp of Gibraltar. Formerly Asst. Civil Chap. Gibraltar 1844, Govt. Chap. 1852; Sen. C. of St. Stephen's, Camden Town, London, 1848, Ditcheat, Somerset, 1851. [16]

BURROW, Robert John, *Caton, near Lancaster.*—St. John's Coll. Cam. 16th Jun. Opt. B.A. 1855, M.A. 1858; Deac. 1857 and Pr. 1858 by Bp of Man. C. of Littledale 1862. Formerly C. of Tatham Fell, Lancashire, 1857–62. [17]

BURROWES, E. D., M.A., LL.D., *Kimmeridge, Corfe Castle, Dorset.*—Chap. of D. of Kimmeridge, Dio. Salis. 1862. (Patron, Lieut.-Col. Mansel; Chap.'s Inc. 100*l* and Ho; Pop. 185.) [18]

BURROWES, Henry, *Waterloo, near Liverpool.*—Dub. A.B. 1858, A.M. 1861; Deac. 1858 and Pr. 1859 by Bp of Meath. C. of Waterloo 1867. Formerly C. of Baddanstown and Sullamore, Meath; Sen. C. of St. Peter's, Regent's-square, Lond. 1860–63; C. of Trinity, Dover, 1863–67. [19]

BURROWES, Thomas Robert, *Hutton, Weston-super-Mare.*—Dub. A.B. 1840; Deac. 1841 by Bp of B. and W. Pr. 1842 by Bp of Ely. R. of Hutton, Dio. B. and W. 1856. (Patron, G. Gibbs, Esq; Tithe, 327*l* 19*s* 2*d*; Glebe, 65 acres; R.'s Inc. 454*l* and Ho; Pop. 349.) Formerly C. of the Abbey, Bath. [20]

BURROWS, Charles Herbert, *Wilton, Wilts.*—C. of Wilton and Netherhampton. [21]

BURROWS, Charles Hubert, *Freemantle, near Southampton.*—C. of Freemantle. [22]

BURROWS, Henry William, 3, *Chester-place, Regent's-park, London, N.W.*—St. John's Coll. Ox. B.A. 1837, M.A. 1840, B.D. 1845; Deac. 1839 and Pr. 1840. P. C. of Ch. Ch. St. Pancras, Dio. Lon. 1851. (Patron, Bp of Lon; P. C.'s Inc. uncertain; Ho; Pop. 9867.) Author, *Parochial Sermons*, 5*s*. [23]

BURROWS, John, *Dunham Massey, Bowdon, Cheshire.*—Dub. A.B. 1862; Deac. 1862 and Pr. 1863 by Bp of Ches. Min. of St. Mark's Chapel, Dunham Massey, 1864. Formerly C. of St. Simon's, Liverpool, 1862–64. [24]

BURROWS, Leonard Francis, *Rugby.*—Wad. Coll. Ox. Vinerian Scho. 1st cl. Lit. Hum. B.A. 1843, M.A. 1849; Deac. 1849 and Pr. 1850 by Bp of Ox. Asst. Mast. Rugby Sch. 1850; Fell. of Wad. Coll. Ox. [25]

BURROWS, William Francis, *Christchurch, Hants.*—Magd. Hall. Ox; Deac. 1821 and Pr. 1822 by Bp of Win. V. of Christchurch with Holdenhurst C. Dio. Win. 1830. (Patrons, D. and C. of Win; Tithe—Imp. 3200*l* 15*s* 6*d*; V.'s Inc. 316*l* and Ho; Pop. Christchurch 6352, Holdenhurst 781.) Surrogate 1831. Author, *Catechism on Confirmation*, 1834; *Sermons*, vol. 1, 1842, vol. 2, 1845, 10*s*. each; *Pastoral Advice to Young Christians*, 1845, 4*s*; *Help to Family Prayers*, 1854. [26]

BURT, John, *The Cottage, Upway, Dorchester.*—C. of Bincombe. [27]

BURT, John Thomas, *Broadmoor Asylum, Wokingham, Berks.*—Trin. Coll. Cam. B.A. 1838; Deac. 1838 by Bp of Lich. Pr. 1839 by Abp of Cant. Chap. to the Broadmoor Criminal Lunatic Asylum 1863. Formerly Chap. to Hanwell Lunatic Asylum 1842; Asst. Chap. at Pentonville Prison 1845; Chap. to the Birmingham Gaol 1854. Author, *Results of the System of Separate Confinement*, 1852; *A Sermon on behalf of the Birmingham Discharged Prisoners' Aid Society*; *Irish Facts and Wakefield Figures in Relation to Convict Discipline in Ireland Investigated*; *Convict Discipline in Ireland.* [28]

BURT, John Toll, *Seething, near Norwich.*—Caius Coll. Cam. 18th Sen. Opt. and B.A. 1822, M.A. 1825; Deac. 1823, Pr. 1824. P. C. of Seething, Dio. Nor. 1837. (Patrons, Trustees of Norwich Hospital; Tithe—Imp. 458*l* and ½ acre of Glebe; P. C.'s Inc. 125*l* and Ho; Pop. 431.) P. C. of Mundham, Norfolk, Dio. Nor. 1837. (Patrons, Trustees of Norwich Hospital; Tithe—Imp. 442*l* and 2¼ acres of Glebe; P. C.'s Inc. 125*l*; Pop. 282.) [29]

BURT, Robert Gascoyne, *St. Mary's Rectory, Hoo, near Rochester.*—Ex. Coll. Ox. B.A. 1814, M.A. 1818; Deac. 1815, Pr. 1816. R. of St. Mary's, Hoo,

Dio. Roch. 1816. (Patron, the present R; Tithe—App. 74l 13s, R. 602l; Glebe, 11 acres; R.'s Inc. 613l and Ho; Pop. 264.) R. of High Halstow, Kent, Dio. Roch. 1823. (Patron, the present R; Tithe, 759l; Glebe, 5 acres; R.'s Inc. 764l and Ho; Pop. 363.) [1]

BURTON, Alexander Bradly, *Holy Trinity Parsonage, Southampton.*—Trin. Coll. Cam. B.A. 1847, M.A. 1850; Deac. 1847 by Bp of Nor. Pr. 1848 by Abp of York. P. C. of Holy Trin. Southampton, Dio. Win. 1857. (Patrons, Trustees; P. C.'s Inc. 300l; Pop. 5421.) Hon. Chap. to the Hampshire Female Penitentiary. Formerly C. of Trin. Ch. Sheffield, 1847–48; P. C. of Ch. Ch. Luton, Chatham, 1848–51; Assoc. Sec. to the Ch. Pastoral Aid Soc. 1851–57. [2]

BURTON, Charles Henry, *St. Philip's Parsonage, Liverpool.*—Corpus Coll. Cam. B.A. 1839, M.A. 1843; Deac. and Pr. 1840. P. C. of St. Philip's, Liverpool, Dio. Ches. 1846. (Patron, John Fernihough, Esq; P. C.'s Inc. 400l.) Surrogate. Author, *Ye see the Distress we are in* (a Sermon, published during the Commercial Panic in Liverpool), 1847, 1s; *The Royal Supremacy* (a Sermon), 6d; *Concurrent Festivals*, 1850, 6d; *War* (a Sermon), 1854, 6d; etc. [3]

BURTON, Charles James, *Shadwell Lodge, Carlisle.*—Queen's Coll. Ox. B.A. 1813, M.A. 1816; Deac. 1815 by Bp of Lich. Pr. 1816 by Bp of Salis. V. of Lydd, Dio. Cant. 1821. (Patron, Abp of Cant; Tithe, 1609l; Glebe, 28 acres; V.'s Inc. 1650l and Ho; Pop. 1667.) Chan of the Dio. of Carl. 1855; Hon. Can. of Carl. Cathl. 1857. Formerly Michel Fell. of Queen's Coll. Ox. 1816–18; P. C. of Ash-next-Sandwich and Nonington with Womenswould, Kent, 1817–21. Author, *View of the Creation of the World*, 1836, 9s; *Lectures on Archbishop Cranmer*, 1861, 3s 6d; *Charges to the Clergy*, 1863–65–66; *Hints on National Education*, 1816; *Short Inquiry into the Character and Designs of the British and Foreign Bible Society*, 1817; *A Sermon suited to the Times*, 1819; *Revelation Vindicated in two Sermons*, 1820; *The Church on the Sacrament of Baptism*, 1865, 4d; *The Church on the Sacrament of the Holy Supper*, 1865, 4d. [4]

BURTON, Clarke Watkins, *Cliburn, Penrith.*—Clare Coll. Cam. B.A. 1850, M.A. 1854; Deac. 1856 and Pr. 1857 by Bp of Carl. R. of Cliburn, Dio. Carl. 1858. (Patron, Bp of Carl; Tithe, 56l 13s. 7d; Glebe, 218 acres; R.'s Inc. 288l and Ho; Pop. 367.) Formerly C. of Dalston. [5]

BURTON, Gustavus Matthews, 104, *Bloomsbury, Chorlton-on-Medlock, Manchester.*—M. of Royal Coll. of Surgeons, Lond. 1848; St. Andrew's, M.D. 1852; St. Aidan's 1858; Deac. 1853 and Pr. 1854 by Bp of Ches. R. of All Saints', Chorlton-on-Medlock, Dio. Man. 1867. (Patrons, Trustees of late Rev. Thomas Burton; R.'s Inc. 300l; Pop. 13,000.) Formerly C. of St. Helen's, 1853, St. John the Baptist's, Toxteth-park, Liverpool, 1856; P. C. of St. Matthew's, Liverpool, 1860–67. Author, *The British Choir Book*, 4to, 1861, 10s. [6]

BURTON, Henry, *Atcham, near Shrewsbury.*—Ch. Ch. Ox. B.A. 1826, M.A. 1831; Deac. 1826, Pr. 1827. R. of Upton Cressett, Salop, Dio. Herf. 1829. (Patron, Rev. H. T. Pelham; Tithe, 191l 7s; Glebe, 3¾ acres; R.'s Inc. 148l; Pop. 72.) V. of Atcham, Dio. Lich. 1831. (Patron, R. Burton, Esq; Tithe—Imp. 568l 18s, V. 240; Glebe, 31 acres; V.'s Inc. 310; Pop. 406.) Rural Dean 1853. [7]

BURTON, John.—Asst Mast. of Proprietary Sch. Birkenhead. [8]

BURTON, Langhorne Burton, *Somersby, Horncastle, Lincolnshire.*—Trin. Coll. Cam. B.A. 1831; Deac. 1835 and Pr. 1836 by Bp of Lin. R. of Bag-Enderby, Lincolnshire, Dio. Lin. 1836. (Patron, the present R; Tithe, 210l; Glebe, 84½ acres; R.'s Inc. 250l; Pop. 81.) R. of Somersby, Dio. Lin. 1837. (Patron, the present R; Tithe, 202l; Glebe, 12 acres; R.'s Inc. 220l and Ho; Pop. 72.) [9]

BURTON, Richard, *Rothley, Loughborough.*—Lin. Coll. Ox. B.A. 1853, M.A. 1856; Deac. 1854 and Pr. 1855 by Bp of Roch. C. of Rothley 1858. Formerly C. of Colne-Engaine, Essex. [10]

BURTON, Richard John, *Woodcott, Newbury.*—Ch. Coll. Cam. 15th Wrang. B.A. 1849, M.A. 1852; Deac. 1850 and Pr. 1851 by Bp of Win. P. C. of Woodcott, Dio. Win. 1856. (Patron, Earl of Carnarvon; P. C.'s Inc. 80l; Pop. 80.) Formerly C. of Hurstbourne Priors 1850–56; Fell. of Ch. Coll. Cambridge 1850–60; Dom. Chap. to Earl of Portsmouth 1854–56. [11]

BURTON, Robert Clerke, *Taverham, Norfolk.*—Clare Coll. Cam. B.A. 1825, M.A. 1828; Deac. 1826 by Bp of Lich. Pr. 1826 by Bp of Ches. R. of Taverham, Dio. Nor. 1850. (Patrons, Bp of Nor. and Rev. J. N. Micklethwait; Tithe, 329l 9s; Glebe, 42 acres; R.'s Inc. 346l; Pop. 212.) Author, *Sermons*, 1834, 6s 6d. Editor of *Monthly Record of S.P.G. Missions.* [12]

BURTON, Robert Lingen, *Abbey House, Shrewsbury.*—Ch. Ch. Ox. B.A. 1824, M.A. 1827; Deac. 1825 and Pr. 1826 by Bp of Lich. Chap. of St. Giles', Shrewsbury, Dio. Lich. 1826. (Patron, Ld Chan; Chap.'s Inc. 80l; Pop. 575.) [13]

BURTON, Roger Taylor, *Soberton, Bishops Waltham, Hants.*—St. John's Coll. Cam. B.A. 1844, M.A. 1845; Deac. 1844, Pr. 1845. Formerly P. C. of St. John's, Newhall, Derbyshire, 1845–58. [14]

BURY, J. M., *Tickhill, Rotherham.*—V. of Tickhill, Dio. York, 1863. (Patron, G. S. Foljambe, Esq; V.'s Inc. 261l and Ho; Pop. 1980.) [15]

BURY, Thomas William, *Bramcote Vicarage, near Nottingham.*—Emman. Coll. Cam. B.A. 1856, M.A. 1859; Deac. 1859 and Pr. 1860 by Bp of Lich. V. of Attenborough with Bramcote C. Dio. Lin. 1861. (Patron, G. S. Foljambe, Esq; Tithe, 300l; Glebe, 27 acres; V.'s Inc. 410l and Ho; Pop. Bramcote 691, Attenborough 1110.) Formerly C. of Smalley, near Derby, 1859–60. [16]

BURY, William, *Chapel House, Kilnsey, Skipton, Yorks.*—St. John's Coll. Cam. 1st cl. Cl. Trip. B.A. 1833, M.A. 1837; Deac. 1837 and Pr. 1838 by Bp of Lin. R. of Burnsall, Dio. Rip. 1839. (Patron, Earl Craven; Tithe, 602l 14s 4d; Glebe, 51 acres; R.'s Inc. 680l and Ho; Pop. 1225.) Formerly C. of Barton-upon-Humber, Lincolnshire, 1838–39. [17]

BURY, William, *Pimperne Rectory, Blandford.*—R. of Pimperne, Dio. Salis. 1862. (Patron, Lord Portman; R.'s Inc. 500l and Ho; Pop. 495.) R. of Fifehead Neville, Dio. Salis. 1866. (Patron, Lord Rivers; R.'s Inc. 230l and Ho; Pop. 87.) Formerly C. of Tickhill, Rotherham. [18]

BUSFEILD, William, *Keighley, Yorks.*—Univ. Coll. Ox. B.A. 1823, M.A. 1826; Deac. 1825, Pr. 1826. R. of Keighley, Dio. Rip. 1840. (Patron, Duke of Devonshire; Tithe, 226l 12s 11d; Glebe, 59 acres; R.'s Inc. 420l and Ho; Pop. 11,749.) Rural Dean. [19]

BUSFIELD, T. R.—C. of All Souls', Manchester. [20]

BUSH, James, *Ousby Rectory, Penrith.*—St. Mary Hall, Ox. B.A. 1846, M.A. 1848; Deac. 1846 and Pr. 1847 by Bp of Carl. R. of Ousby, Cumberland, Dio. Carl. 1854. (Patron, Bp of Carl; Tithe, 315l; Glebe, 32 acres; R.'s Inc. 396l and Ho; Pop. 294.) [21]

BUSH, James Ward, *Crewkerne, Somerset.*—Queen's Coll. Ox. B.A. 1866; Deac. 1866 and Pr. 1867 by Bp of B. and W. C. of Crewkerne 1866. [22]

BUSH, Joseph, *Ormskirk, Lancashire.*—Wad. Coll. Ox. B.A. 1834, M.A. 1853; Deac. 1836 and Pr. 1837 by Bp of B. and W. V. of Ormskirk with Scarisbrick C. Dio. Ches. 1853. (Patron, Earl of Derby; Tithe—App. 94l, Imp. 4138l 19s; Glebe, 21 acres; V.'s Inc. 289l and Ho; Pop. 7824.) [23]

BUSH, Paul, *Duloe, Liskeard.*—St. Mary Hall, Ox. B.A. 1843, M.A 1847, *ad eund.* Cam. 1848; Deac. 1846 by Bp of Ely, Pr. 1846 by Bp of Carl. R. of Duloe, Dio. Ex. 1840. (Patron, Ball. Coll. Ox; Tithe, 620l; Glebe, 50 acres; R.'s Inc. 690l and Ho; Pop. 797.) [24]

BUSH, Robert Wheler, F.R.G.S., 1, *Milner-square, Islington, London, N.*—Wor. Coll. and Mert. Coll. Ox. Scho. of, 2nd cl. Lit. Hum. 1842, Univ. Theol. Prize Essayist 1844 and 1845, B.A. 1842, M.A. 1844; Deac. 1844 and Pr. 1845 by Bp of Ches. Head Mast. of the Proprietary Sch. Islington; Lect. at St. Swithin's,

Strand. Select Preacher at Oxford 1849 and 1850. Formerly Sen. Cl. Mast. at Rossall Sch; Morning Preacher at St. Marylebone, 1853–55: Asst. Min. at St. Peter's, Vere-street, and St. Mary's, Hornsey. Author, *England's Two Great Military Captains, Marlborough and Wellington* (a Lecture delivered to the Members of the Church of England Young Men's Society at Islington, 1852), 1853, 1s 6d; *A Sermon on the Death of Dr. Spry*, Rector of St. Marylebone, 1854, 6d; etc. [1]

BUSH, Thomas Henry, *Burton, Christchurch, Hants.*—St. John's Coll. Cam. 15th Wrang. Tyrwhitt's Hebrew Prize, B.A. 1859, M.A. 1862; Deac. 1861 and Pr. 1862 by Bp of Win. C. in sole charge of Burton 1862. Formerly Math. Mast. and Chap. Clapham Gr. Sch. 1860. [2]

BUSHBY, Edward, *Impington, near Cambridge.*—St. John's Coll. Cam. B.A. 1816, M.A. 1819, B.D. 1827; Deac. 1818 and Pr. 1820 by Bp of Ely. V. of Impington, Dio. Ely, 1832. (Patrons, D. and C. of Ely; Glebe, 58 acres; V.'s Inc. 138l; Pop. 335.) Fell. of St. John's Coll. Cam. [3]

BUSHELL, Christopher Josiah, *Barkisland, Halifax.*—St. Bees; Deac. 1851 and Pr. 1853 by Bp of Rip. P. C. of Barkisland, Dio. Rip. 1856. (Patron, V. of Halifax; P. C.'s Inc. 75l; Pop. 1374.) Formerly C. of St. John's, Dewsbury Moor. [4]

BUSHELL, William Done, *Harrow School, Harrow.*—St. John's Coll. Cam. 7th Wrang. 2nd cl. Cl. Trip. B.A. 1861, M.A. 1864; Deac. 1864 and Pr. 1866 by Bp of Ely. Asst. Mast. at Harrow Sch. 1866. Late Fell. of St. John's Coll. Cam. [5]

BUSHNELL, John Hext, *Partyseal, Grosmont, near Hereford.*—Wor. Coll. Ox. B.A. 1836, M.A. 1845; Deac. 1837, Pr. 1839. [6]

BUSHNELL, R. S., *Hatcham, Kent.*—C. of St. James's, Hatcham. [7]

BUSHNELL, Thomas Hext, *Beenham-Valence, Reading.*—Pemb. Coll. Ox. B.A. 1846, M.A. 1851; Deac. 1848, Pr. 1849. V. of Beenham-Valence, Dio. Ox. 1855. (Patroness, Mrs Bushnell; V.'s Inc. 250l and Ho; Pop. 505.) Dom. Chap. to the Earl of Romney 1851. Late C. of Langley, Kent, 1848–50. [8]

BUSS, Alfred Joseph, 19, *Bartholomew Villas, Kentish Town, London, N.W.*—King's Coll. Lon. Theol. Assoc. 1854, B.A. 1858; Deac. 1854 and Pr. 1855 by Bp of Lon. Chap. of St. Marylebone Infirmary and Workhouse 1866; Hon. Sec. of Home for Gentlemen, Queen-square. Formerly C. of St. John the Evangelist's, Limehouse, 1854, Trinity, St. Pancras, 1856, St. Olave's, Hart-street, 1858, St. Stephen's, St. John's-wood, 1861. Author, *Death the Christian's True Birthday* (a Sermon on the Death of the Rev. D. Laing), 1860. [9]

BUSS, Septimus, 14, *Camden-street, Camden-town, London, N.W.*—King's Coll. Lon. B.A. 1858, LL.B. 1863; Deac. 1860 and Pr. 1861 by Bp of Lon. Chap. of St. Pancras Workhouse; Lect. at St. Andrew's, Haverstock-hill. Formerly C. of St. Peter's, Regent square, 1860; Sen. C. of Trinity, Haverstock-hill, 1862. [10]

BUSSELL, Barton T., *Golcar, near Huddersfield.*—C. of St. John's, Golcar. [11]

BUSSELL, John Garrett, *Newark, Notts.*—Trin. Coll. Ox. B.A. 1829. V. of Newark, Dio. Lin. 1835. (Patron, the Crown; Tithe—App. 147l 2s 10d, Imp. 367l 17s 2d, V. 209l 19s 6d; V.'s Inc. 440l and Ho; Pop. 7832.) Preb. of Carlton-cum-Thirlby in Lin. Cathl. 1859; Rural Dean; Surrogate. [12]

BUSSELL, John William, *Neyland, South Wales.*—Wor. Coll. Ox. B.A. 1844, M.A. 1866; Deac. 1846 and Pr. 1847 by Abp of Cant. Chap. Pembroke Dockyard 1866. Formerly C. of Great Mongeham, Kent; Chap. in H.M.'s Ships "Caledonia," "London," "Calcutta," "Blenheim," and "Liffey." [13]

BUSSELL, William James, *Kingston-on-Thames.*—Pemb. Coll. Ox. B.A. 1826, M.A. 1830; Deac. 1827 and Pr. 1828 by Bp of Ex. [14]

BUSTON, Roger, *Twyford, near Winchester.*—Emman. Coll. Cam. Wrang. and B.A. 1830, M.A. 1833, B.D. 1840; Deac. and Pr. 1835. V. of Twyford, Dio. Win. 1849. (Patron, Emman. Coll. Cam; Tithe—Imp. 700l, V. 300l; V.'s Inc. 274l and Ho; Pop. 926.) Formerly Fell. and Tut. of Emman. Coll. Cam. 1840–50. [15]

BUSWELL, William, *Widford Rectory, Chelmsford.*—Queens' Coll. Cam. 6th Jun. Opt. and B.A. 1834; Deac. 1836 and Pr. 1837 by Bp of Lon. R. of Widford, Dio. Roch. 1840. (Patron, Arthur Pryor, Esq; Tithe, 257l; Glebe, 20 acres; R.'s Inc. 302l and Ho; Pop. 257.) Chap. to the Chelmsford Union 1842. Formerly Evg. Lect. St. Peter's, St. Albans, Herts. Author, *Plain Parochial Sermons on Important Subjects*, 1842, 6s; *An Immediate and Serious Consideration of our Latter End an Imperative Duty*, 1843; *Israel's Conversion and Restoration, God's Predestined Purpose of Mercy and Love*, 1849. [16]

BUSWELL, William, *Naughton, Bildeston, Suffolk.*—Queens' Coll. Cam. 2nd cl. Cl. Trip. B.A. 1864; Deac. 1866 by Bp of Ely. C. of Nedging 1866 [17]

BUTCHER, Charles Henry, *Shanghai, China.*—Bp Hat. Hall, Dur. Fell. of, B.A. 1858; Deac. 1858 by Bp of Lon. Chap. at Shanghai 1864. Formerly C. of St. Paul's, Hammersmith. [18]

BUTCHER, Edmund Lyde, *Westoe, South Shields.*—Bp Hat. Hall, Dur. Licen. in Theol. 1854; Deac. 1854 by Bp of Dur. Pr. 1855 by Bp of Man. P. C. of Westoe, Dio. Dur. 1865. (Patrons, Trustees; P. C.'s Inc. 150l.) Formerly C. of Gainford, near Darlington, 1854–63. [19]

BUTCHER, James Hornby, *Ramsbottom, Manchester.*—St. Bees, Librarian; Deac. 1842 and Pr. 1843 by Bp of Ches. P. C. of Ramsbottom, Dio. Man. 1844. (Patrons, the Crown and Bp of Man. alt; P. C.'s Inc. 170l; Pop. 5000.) [20]

BUTCHER, Robert, *Shareshill, Wolverhampton.* Queen's Coll. Birmingham; Deac. 1863 and Pr. 1864 by Bp of Lich. C. of Shareshill 1867. Formerly C. of St. Mark's, Wolverhampton, 1863. [21]

BUTCHER, Samuel John, *St. Helen Auckland, Durham.*—Dub. A.B. 1859, A.M. 1864; Deac. 1861 and Pr. 1862 by Bp of Dur. C. of St. Helen Auckland 1865. Formerly C. of Jarrow 1861–64. [22]

BUTLER, Alfred Stokes, *Markfield Rectory, Leicester.*—Deac. 1847 and Pr. 1849 by Bp of Pet. R. of Markfield, Dio. Pet. 1860. (Patron, Marquis of Hastings; Tithe, 163l; Glebe, 170 acres; R.'s Inc. 500l and Ho; Pop. 1297.) Formerly P. C. of Penn-street, Bucks. Author, *The Church Catechism Scripturally Explained.* [23]

BUTLER, Arthur Gray, *Haileybury College, Hertford.*—Oriel Coll. Ox. 1st cl. Lit. Hum. Ireland Scho. M.A. 1853; Deac. 1861 and Pr. 1862 by Bp of Ox. Head Mast. of Haileybury Coll; Fell. of Oriel Coll. Ox. [24]

BUTLER, Charles Robert, *The Vicarage, Porchester, Fareham, Hants.*—Wor. Coll. Ox. B.A. 1827, M.A. 1831; Deac. 1829 and Pr. 1831 by Bp of Win. V. of Porchester, Dio. Win. 1857. (Patron, Thomas Thistlethwayte, Esq; Tithe, 160l; Glebe, 12 acres; V.'s Inc. 230l and Ho; Pop. 766.) Formerly C. of Christchurch, Hants, 1829, Catherington, Hants, 1831. Author, *Address to Singers in Country Churches*, 6d. [25]

BUTLER, Daniel, *Great Chart, Ashford, Kent.*—Lin. Coll. Ox. Hon. 4th cl. Lit. Hum. and B.A. 1835, M.A. 1837; Deac. 1837 and Pr. 1838 by Bp of Lon. R. of Great Chart, Dio. Cant. 1866. (Patron, Abp of Cant; R.'s Inc. 750l and Ho; Pop. 806.) Formerly Head Mast. of the Clergy Orphan School, Canterbury. [26]

BUTLER, Frederick Brisbane, *Helidon, Daventry.*—Mert. Coll. Ox. Scho. of, 1859, 2nd cl. Lit. Hum. 1863, B.A. 1864, M.A. 1866; Deac. 1865 by Bp of Pet. C. of Helidon 1865. [27]

BUTLER, George, *Liverpool.*—Ex. Coll. Ox. Univ. Scho. 1841, 1st cl. Lit. Hum. and B.A. 1845, M.A. 1846; Deac. 1854 and Pr. 1855 by Bp of Ox. Prin. of Liverpool Coll. Formerly Vice-Prin. of Cheltenham Coll; Cl. Examiner to H. M. Sec. of State for War 1855; Examiner for the Hon. E. I. C.'s Civil Service 1856. Author, *Principles of Imitative Art*, 1852; *Descriptio Antiqui Codicis Virgiliani* (privately printed), 1854; *Essay on the Raphael Drawings in the University*

Galleries ("Oxford Essays"), 1856; *Village Sermons*, 1856; *Prayers based on Select Psalms*, 1857; etc. [1]

BUTLER, George Ambrose, *Harlington, Dunstable, Beds.*—Tylney Exhib. of Queen's Coll. Ox. B.A. 1839; Deac. 1840 and Pr. 1841 by Bp of Ox. V. of Harlington, Dio. Ely, 1858. (Patron, Major Cooper; V.'s Inc. 170*l* and Ho; Pop. 529.) Formerly C. of St. Marylebone, London. [2]

BUTLER, Henry Montagu, *Harrow, Middlesex.*—Trin. Coll. Cam. B.A. 1855, M.A. 1858; Deac. and Pr. 1859 by Bp of Lich. Head Mast. of Harrow Sch. 1859. Formerly Fell. of Trin. Coll. Cam. 1856–59. [3]

BUTLER, James, *Burnley, Lancashire.*—All Souls Coll. Ox. B.A. 1836, M.A. 1839, D.C.L. 1865; Deac. 1837 and Pr. 1838 by Abp of York. Head Mast. of the Burnley Gr. Sch; Surrogate. [4]

BUTLER, James Edward, 125, *New Kent-road, London, S.E.*—Dub. A.B. 1861; Deac. and Pr. 1861 by Bp of Kilmore. C. in sole charge of Locks Fields Mission, Walworth, 1864. Formerly C. of Boyle and Warrington. [5]

BUTLER, John, *Inkpen, near Hungerford, Berks.*—R. of Inkpen, Dio. Ox. 1850. (Patron, J. Butler, Esq; Tithe, 617*l* 10*s*; Glebe, 12 acres; R.'s Inc. 629*l* and Ho; Pop. 748.) [6]

BUTLER, John B. M., *Langton, Speldhurst, Kent.*—Trin. Coll. Cam. Sen. Opt. B.A. 1862, M.A. 1865; Deac. 1862 and Pr. 1863 by Bp of Chich. C. of Langton 1865. Formerly C. of St. Mary Magdalen's, St. Leonards-on-Sea, 1862–65. [7]

BUTLER, Piers, *Ulcome, Staplehurst, Kent.*—R. of Ulcome, Dio. Cant. 1861. (Patron, Hon. C. B. C. Wandesford; R.'s Inc. 440*l* and Ho; Pop. 621.) [8]

BUTLER, Richard, 25, *Burgess-terrace, Hyde-road, Ardwick, Manchester.*—Dub. A.B. 1840, A.M. 1846; Deac. 1841, Pr. 1842. P. C. of St. Silas', Higher Ardwick, Dio. Man. 1842. (Patrons, Trustees; P. C.'s Inc. 180*l*; Pop. 10,375.) [9]

BUTLER, Samuel Johnson, *Penrith.*—New Coll. Ox. B.A. 1845, M.A. 1850; Deac. 1846 and Pr. 1847 by Bp of Ches. V. of Penrith, Dio. Carl. 1853. (Patron, Bp of Carl; Tithe, 24*l*; Glebe, 40 acres; V.'s Inc. 300*l* and Ho; Pop. 5148.) Surrogate. [10]

BUTLER, Thomas, *Theale, Reading.*—Magd. Coll. Ox. B.A. 1834, M.A. 1836, B.D. 1845; Deac. 1835, Pr. 1836. R. of Theale, Dio. Ox. (Patron, Magd. Coll. Ox; Tithe, 573*l*; Glebe, 140 acres; R.'s Inc. 774*l* and Ho; Pop. 700.) Late Fell. of Magd. Coll. Ox. [11]

BUTLER, Thomas, *Langar, Elton, Notts.*—St. John's Coll. Cam. 20th Sen. Opt. 7th in 1st cl. Cl. Trip. and B.A. 1829, M.A. 1832; Deac. 1829 and Pr. 1830 by Bp of Herf. R. of Langar with Barnston C. Dio. Lin. 1834. (Patron, J. Wright, Esq; Langar, Tithe, 2*l* 6*s*; Glebe, 342 acres; Barnston, Tithe—App. 1*l* 16*s*, R. 17*l* 12*s*; Glebe, 9 acres; R.'s Inc. 420*l* and Ho; Pop. 320.) Rural Dean 1854. Formerly C. of Meole Brace, Dio. Herf. 1829–34. [12]

BUTLER, Thomas, D.D., *Alexton, Uppingham.*—R. of Alexton, Dio. Pet. 1862. (Patron, Lord Berners; R.'s Inc. 160*l* and Ho; Pop. 67.) [13]

BUTLER, Thomas Lapp, *Wellington, Salop.*—Dub. A.B. 1848; Deac. 1848, Pr. 1849. Min. of Ch. Ch. Wellington, Dio. Lich. 1852. (Patron, V. of Wellington; Min.'s Inc. 150*l* and Ho.) [14]

BUTLER, William, *Great Sandall, Wakefield.*—Ox. 2nd cl. Lit. Hum. M.A. 1833. V. of Great Sandall, Dio. Rip. 1860. (Patron, Ld Chan; V.'s Inc. 280*l* and Ho; Pop. 2061.) Formerly Head Mast. of Gr. Sch. Nottingham, 1833–60. [15]

BUTLER, William James, *Appleton, Abingdon, Berks.*—Magd. Coll. Ox. B.A. 1824, M.A. 1827, B.D. 1838. R. of Appleton, Dio. Ox. 1844. (Patron, Magd. Coll. Ox; Tithe, 465*l*; Glebe, 27 acres; R.'s Inc. 515*l* and Ho; Pop. 549.) R. of Tubney, Berks, Dio. Ox. 1844. (Patron, Magd. Coll. Ox; Tithe, 148*l*; Glebe, 10 acres; R.'s Inc. 152*l*; Pop. 180.) Rural Dean. [16]

BUTLER, William John, *Wantage, Berks.*—Late Scho. of Trin. Coll. Cam. B.A. 1840, M.A. 1844; Deac. 1841, Pr. 1842. V. of Wantage, Dio. Ox. 1846. (Patrons, D. and C. of Windsor; Tithe—App. 1390*l*, V. 750*l*; Glebe, 5 acres; V.'s Inc. 755*l* and Ho; Pop. 3385.) Surrogate 1847; Diocesan Inspector of Schools 1849; Rural Dean 1853. Formerly C. of Dogmersfield, Hants, 1841, Puttenham, Surrey, 1843; P. C. of Wareside, Herts, 1844. Author, *Sermons for Working Men.* [17]

BUTLER, William Joseph, *Thwing, Bridlington, Yorks.*—St. John's Coll. Cam. B.A. 1820, M.A. 1824; Deac. 1823 by Bp of Lin. Pr. 1825 by Abp of York. R. of Thwing, Dio. York, 1828. (Patron, Ld Chan; Tithe, 47*l*, R.'s Inc. 600*l* and Ho; Pop. 416.) [18]

BUTLIN, William, *St. Sepulchre's Vicarage, Northampton.*—V. of St. Sepulchre's, Northampton, Dio. Pet. 1840. (Patroness, Miss Butlin; V.'s Inc. 150*l* and Ho; Pop. 6538.) [19]

BUTLIN, William Heygate, *Fisherton Anger, Salisbury.*—Corpus Coll. Cam. B.A. 1860; Deac. 1864 and Pr. 1865 by Bp of G. and B. C. of Fisherton Anger 1866. Formerly C. of Stroud 1864–65. [20]

BUTLIN, William Wright, *Penponds, Camborne, Cornwall.*—Sid. Coll. Cam. B.A. 1836; Deac. 1837 and Pr. 1838 by Bp of Lich. P. C. of Penponds, Dio. Ex. 1850. (Patrons, the Crown and Bp of Ex. alt; P. C.'s Inc. 150*l*; Pop. 2012.) [21]

BUTT, George, *Chesterfield.*—Ch. Ch. Ox. Hon. 4th cl. Lit. Hum. and B.A. 1838, M.A. 1841; Deac. 1838 and Pr. 1839 by Bp of Ox. V. and Aft. Lect. of Chesterfield, Dio. Lich. 1851. (Patron, Bp of Lich; Tithe—Eccl. Comm. 1050*l*, V. 357*l* 15*s*; Glebe, 3 acres; V.'s Inc. 410*l* and Ho; Pop. 10,720.) Surrogate. Formerly Chap. of Ch. Ch. Ox. 1838–42. [22]

BUTT, James Acton, *Three Counties Asylum, Arlesey, Baldock, Beds.*—Wor. Coll. Ox. B.A. 1854, M.A. 1859; Deac. 1855 by Bp of Win. Pr. 1856 by Bp of G. and B. Chap. to the Three Counties Asylum, near Arlesey, 1860. Formerly C. of Droxford, Hants, 1855, Newent, Glouc. 1856, Skeyton, Norfolk, 1858. [23]

BUTT, John Henry, *Buntingford, Herts.*—Caius Coll. Cam. B.A. 1851; Deac. 1852, Pr. 1853. V. of Layston with Buntingford, Dio. Roch. 1853. (Patron, Wm. Butt, Esq; V.'s Inc. 167*l*; Pop. 998.) [24]

BUTT, John Martin, *Wingrave, Aylesbury, Bucks.*—Magd. Hall, Ox. B.A. 1828, M.A. 1831. V. of Wingrave, Dio. Ox. 1850. (Patron, Earl Brownlow; V.'s Inc. 126*l* and Ho; Pop. 863.) [25]

BUTT, Phelpes John, *Freiburg, Baden.*—Lin. Coll. Ox. B.A. 1820, M.A. 1823; Deac. 1821, Pr. 1822. Chap. at Freiburg; Chap. to the Earl of Besborough. [26]

BUTTANSHAW, Francis, 19, *Lee Park, London, S.E.*—Univ. Coll. Ox. 2nd cl. Lit. Hum. and B.A. 1822, M.A. 1825; Deac. 1824 and Pr. 1825. Formerly C. of Barming 1824–32, West Peckham 1832–38; Chap. to the Kent Lunatic Asylum 1833–61. [27]

BUTTANSHAW, Francis, *Chinnor, Tetsworth, Oxon.*—Univ. Coll. Ox. B.A. 1851, M.A. 1854; Deac. 1851 and Pr. 1852 by Bp of Lon. C. of Chinnor 1855. Formerly C. of Harmondsworth and West Drayton, Middlesex, 1851–53, Fobbing, Essex, 1853–55. [28]

BUTTANSHAW, George, *Hitchin, Herts.*—St. John's Coll. Ox. B.A. 1861; Deac. 1862 and Pr 1863 by Bp of Roch. C. of Hitchin. [29]

BUTTANSHAW, Henry, *Edworth Rectory, near Baldock, Herts.*—Oriel Coll. Ox. B.A. 1853, M.A. 1860; Deac. 1854 and Pr. 1855 by Abp of Cant. R. of Edworth, Dio. Ely, 1861. (Patron, C. C. Hale, Esq; Tithe, 240*l*; Glebe, 8 acres; R.'s Inc. 255*l*; Pop. 99.) Chap. of Biggleswade Union, 1866 (Val. 40*l*.) Formerly C. of Dymchurch and St. Mary's in the Marsh 1854–56, Hitchin 1856–57, Clifton, Beds, 1857–58, Biggleswade 1858–59, Redgrave, Suffolk, 1859–60. [30]

BUTTANSHAW, John, 13, *Russell-street, Bath.*—Corpus Coll. Ox. Scho, 1847, Fell. 1856–64, B.A. 1851, M.A. 1854; Deac. 1854 and Pr. 1855 by Abp of Cant. C. of the Abbey, Bath, 1865. Formerly C. of Eastry, Kent, 1854, Corn-street Chapel, Bath, 1860. [31]

BUTTEMER, Archdall, *Farncombe, Godalming, Surrey.*—Emman. Coll. Cam. B.A. 1850, M.A. 1853; Deac. 1850, Pr. 1851. P. C. of Shackleford, Dio. Win. 1866. (Patron, Bp of Win; Tithe, 289*l*; Glebe, 4 acres; P. C.'s. Inc. 384*l*; Pop. 500.) Formerly C. of Farncombe 1859–66. [1]

BUTTEMER, Robert Durant, *Millbrook, near Southampton.*—Clare Coll. Cam. B.A. 1834, M.A. 1837; Deac. 1835 and Pr. 1836 by Bp of Win. Formerly R. of Easton, near Winchester, 1846–58. [2]

BUTTERFIELD, Henry, *Fulmer, Gerrard's Cross, Bucks.*—Ch. Coll. Cam. B.A. 1824, M.A. 1837; Deac. 1825 and Pr. 1826 by Bp of Chich. Min. Can. of St. George's Collegiate Chapel, Windsor, 1828. (Value 100*l* and Res.) R. of Fulmer, Dio. Ox. 1842. (Patrons, D. and C. of Windsor; Tithe, 298*l* 13*s* 11*d*; Glebe, 3 acres; R.'s Inc. 300*l* and Ho; Pop. 351.) [3]

BUTTERFIELD, J., *Longney, Gloucester.*—C. of Longney and Elmore. [4]

BUTTERFIELD, William, *Alphington, Exeter.*—St. Edm. Hall, Ox. B.A. 1827, M.A. 1834; Deac. 1827, Pr. 1828. R. of Alphington, Dio. Ex. 1851. (Patron, the present R; Tithe, 794*l* 16*s* 4*d*; Glebe, 24¾ acres; R.'s Inc. 900*l* and Ho; Pop. 1250.) Rural Dean. [5]

BUTTERWORTH, Albert Nelson, *Kettleshulme, Stockport.*—St. John's Coll. Cam. B.A. 1850; Deac. 1850 by Bp of Nor. Pr. 1852 by Bp of Salis. P. C. of Saltersford with Kettleshulme, Dio. Ches. 1864. (Patron, V. of Prestbury; P. C.'s Inc. 70*l*; Pop. 507.) [6]

BUTTERWORTH, George, *Deerhurst, Tewkesbury, Gloucestershire.*—Ball. Coll. Ox. B.A. 1845, M.A. 1846; Deac. 1846, Pr. 1847. P. C. of Deerhurst with Apperley, Dio. G. and B. 1856. (Patron, Bp of G. and B; P. C.'s Inc. 130*l* and Ho; Pop. 930.) Formerly C. of Henbury, near Bristol. [7]

BUTTERWORTH, Joseph Henry, *Stapleton, near Bristol.*—Ex. Coll. Ox. 2nd cl. Lit. Hum. 2nd cl. Math. et Phy. and B.A. 1836, M.A. 1838; Deac. 1838 and Pr. 1839 by Bp of Win. P. C. of Stapleton, Dio. G. and B. 1846. (Patron, Sir J. H. G. Smyth; Tithe—Imp. 298*l* 12*s*; Glebe, 27 acres; P. C.'s Inc. 160*l* and Ho; Pop. 4607.) [8]

BUTTON, John Viny, *Blofield, near Norwich.*—Queens' Coll. Cam. 3rd Sen. Opt. and B.A. 1810, M.A. 1813; Deac. 1814, Pr. 1815. C. of Blofield. Late Fell. of Queens' Coll. Cam. [9]

BUTTRESS, Allen, *Newark, Notts.*—Pemb. Col. Cam. B.A. 1864, M.A. 1867; Deac. 1865. C. of Farndon, Notts, 1865. [10]

BUXTON, Harry John Wilmot, *Alderney.*—Brasen Coll. Ox. 2nd cl. Law and Mod. Hist. B.A. 1866; Deac. 1866 by Bp of Win. C. of Alderney 1866. [11]

BUXTON, Thomas, *Blackburn.*—Corpus Coll. Cam. Univ. Prizeman, B.A. 1855, M.A. 1858; Deac. 1858 and Pr. 1859 by Bp of Ely. [12]

BYAM, Richard Burgh, *Petersham, Richmond, Surrey.*—King's Coll. Cam. B.A. 1808, M.A. 1811; Deac. 1814 by Bp of Nor. Pr. 1815 by Bp of Lon. V. of Kew with Petersham C. Dio. Win. 1828. (Patron, King's Coll. Cam; V.'s Inc. 520*l*; Pop. Kew 1099, Petersham 637.) Formerly Dean of Divinity and Tut. of King's Coll. Cam. 1821–28; Cl. Exam. 1827–28; Chap. to H.R.H. the late Duke of Sussex; one of the Univ. Preachers at Whitehall; R. of Sampford-Courtney, Devon, 1827–28. [13]

BYERS, James Broff, *Lamphey, near Pembroke.*—Queens' Coll. Cam; Deac. 1819 by Bp of Nor. Pr. 1820 by Bp of St. D. V. of Lamphey, Dio. St. D. 1824. (Patron, Bp of St. D; Tithe—App. 60*l*, V. 74*l* 15*s*; Glebe, 24 acres; V.'s Inc. 115*l*; Pop. 365.) R. of Newchurch, Radnor, Dio. St. D. 1828. (Patron, Bp of St D; Tithe, 148*l* 12*s* 8*d*; Glebe, 3 acres; R.'s Inc. 187*l* and Ho; Pop. 132.) [14]

BYERS, Octavius Bathurst, *Broad-green, Croydon, Surrey.*—Queens' Coll. Cam. B.A. 1846, M.A. 1851; Deac. 1847, Pr. 1848. P. C. of Ch. Ch. Croydon, Dio. Cant. 1852. (Patron, Trustees of Abp Sumner; P. C.'s Inc. 400*l* and Ho; Pop. 5160.) [15]

BYERS, Sparks Beaumont, *North-end, Fulham, S.W.*—Late Scho. of St. Peter's Coll. Cam. B.A. 1844; Deac. 1844 and Pr. 1845 by Bp of Lon. P. C. of St. Mary's Chapel, North-end, Dio. Lon. 1856. (Patrons, present P. C. and Major Byers; P. C.'s Inc. 200*l*; Pop. 3702.) Chap. to Earl of Errol. Formerly C. of St. John's, Walham-green, Fulham. [16]

BYERS, Timothy, *Leake Vicarage, Boston.*—Scho. of Ch. Coll. Cam. Sen. Opt. 2nd cl. Univ. Member's Prizeman and B.A. 1844, M.A. 1847; B.D. 1860; Deac. 1845 and Pr. 1846 by Bp of Pet. V. of Leake, Dio. Lin. 1865. (Patrons, Govs. of Oakham and Uppingham Schs. and Hospitals; V.'s Inc. 200*l* and Ho; Pop. 1959.) Formerly 2nd Mast. of Oakham Sch. 1844–64; Chap. of Rutland County Gaol 1848–65. Author, *The Objective Character of Christian Faith* (a Sermon preached before the Univ. of Cam.), 1860. [17]

BYERS, William, *Greasbrough, near Rotherham.*—St. Bees; Deac. 1847 and Pr. 1848 by Bp of Rip. P. C. of Greasbrough, Dio. York, 1856. (Patron, Earl Fitzwilliam; P. C.'s Inc. 179*l*; Pop. 2987.) Formerly C. of Kilnhurst, near Rotherham, 1854–56. [18]

BYNG, The Hon. Francis E. C.—Ch. Ch. Ox. B.A. 1856, M.A. 1858; Deac. 1858 and Pr. 1859. P. C. of St. Peter's, Onslow-gardens, Dio. Lon. 1867. Formerly P. C. of Trinity, Twickenham, 1862–67. [19]

BYNG, John, *Boxford Rectory (Suffolk), near Colchester.*—Mert. Coll. Ox. B.A. 1834, M.A. 1838; Deac. 1835 by Bp of Roch. Pr. 1836 by Bp of Chich. R. of Boxford, Dio. Ely, 1850. (Patron, the Crown; Tithe, 658*l* 10*s*; Glebe, 38 acres; R.'s Inc. 728*l* and Ho; Pop. 986.) [20]

BYRD, William, *Badsey, Evesham, Worcestershire.*—Magd. Hall, Ox. B.A. 1824, M.A. 1826; Deac. and Pr. 1826 by Bp of Wor. [21]

BYRDE, Frederick Louis, *Woking, Surrey.*—Queen's Coll. Ox. B.A. 1863; Deac. 1865 and Pr. 1866 by Bp of G. and B. C. of Woking 1867. Formerly C. of St. James's, Bristol, 1865–67. [22]

BYRNE, Henry Barnes, *Milford Vicarage, Lymington, Hants.*—Queen's Coll. Ox. Hert. Lat. Scho. 1845, 2nd cl. Lit. Hum. 1847, B.A. 1847, M.A. 1850; Deac. 1850 and Pr. 1851 by Bp of Wor. V. of Milford, Dio. Win. 1863. (Patron, Queen's Coll. Ox; Tithe, 279*l*; Glebe, 20 acres; V.'s Inc. 310*l*; Pop. 1050.) Chap. to Abp of York. Late Fell. Tut. and Dean of Queen's Coll. Ox; and Scho. of Oriel. [23]

BYRNE, John Rice, 22, *Upper Seymour street, Portman-square, W. and Council Office, Downing-street, London, S.W.*—Late Scho. of Univ. Coll. Ox. B.A. 1850, M.A. 1852; Deac. 1852, Pr. 1856. One of H.M. Inspectors of Schools. [24]

BYRON, The Hon. Augustus, *Kirkby-Mallory, Hinckley, Leicestershire.*—Mert. Coll. Ox. B.A. 1849, M.A. 1852; Deac. 1851 and Pr. 1852 by Bp of Lich. R. of Kirkby-Mallory, Dio. Pet. 1861. (Patrons, Trustees; R.'s Inc. 400*l* and Ho; Pop. 216.) [25]

BYRON, John, *Killingholme, Ulceby, Lincolnshire.*—Brasen. Coll. Ox. 3rd cl. Lit. Hum. and B.A. 1839, M.A. 1841; Deac. 1840, Pr. 1841. V. of Killingholme with Habrough, Dio. Lin. 1842. (Patron, Earl of Yarborough; Killingholme, Tithe—Imp. 12*s*; Glebe, 135 acres; Habrough, Glebe, 197 acres; V.'s Inc. 350*l*; Pop. Killingholme 736, Habrough 364.) Rural Dean. [26]

BYRON, John, *Elmstone Hardwick, near Cheltenham.*—Ex. Coll. Ox. B.A. 1826, M.A. 1830; Deac. 1828 and Pr. 1829 by Bp of Lin. V. of Elmstone Hardwick, Dio. G. and B. 1833. (Patron, Ld Chan; Tithe—Imp. 709*l* 5*s*, V. 219*l* 10*s*; Glebe, 10 acres; V.'s Inc. 233*l* and Ho; Pop. 440.) Chap. to the Duke of Sutherland. [27]

BYRON, The Hon. William, *Stoke-Talmage, Tetsworth, Oxon.*—Ball. Coll. Ox. B.A. 1852; Deac. 1854 and Pr. 1855 by Bp of Ox. R. of Stoke Talmage, Dio. Ox. 1857. (Patron, Earl of Macclesfield; Tithe, 57*l* 15*s*; Glebe, 50*l* 5*s*; R.'s Inc. 250*l* and Ho; Pop. 113.) Formerly V. of Lewknor, Oxon. 1855–57; Fell. of All Souls Coll. Ox. [28]

BYRTH, Henry Stewart, *Bardsley Parsonage, near Ashton-under-Lyne.*—Brasen. Coll. Ox. 2nd cl. Math. Ellerton Theol. Prize Essay 1856, B.A. 1854, M.A. 1856; Deac. 1856 and Pr. 1858 by Bp of Lon. P. C. of Bardsley, Dio. Man. 1862. (Patrons, Hulme's Trustees; P. C.'s Inc. 145*l* and Ho; Pop. 2758.) Formerly Asst. C. of Bow, Middlesex, 1856, Newton-le-Willows 1859. [1]

BYRTH, Stewart, *Seacombe, Birkenhead.*—Bp Hatfield's Hall, Dur. 2nd cl. Cl. and B.A. 1853, M.A. 1858; Deac. 1853 and Pr. 1854 by Abp of York. P. C. of Seacombe, Dio. Ches. 1864. [2]

CACHEMAILLE, Alfred Julius James, *Pamplemousses, Mauritius.*—Caius Coll. Cam. B.A. 1864; Deac. 1865 and Pr. 1866 by Bp of Win. Chap of Pamplemousses. Formerly C. of St. Michael's, Stockwell, 1865–66. [3]

CACHEMAILLE, Ernest Peter, 33, *Euston-square, London, N.W.*—Caius Coll. Cam. Sen. Opt. B.A. 1860; Deac. 1860 and Pr. 1861 by Bp of Win. C. of St. Pancras 1864. Formerly C. of Christchurch, Camberwell, 1860–63. [4]

CACHEMAILLE, James Louis Victor, *Island of Serk, near Guernsey.*—Literate; Deac. 1834 and Pr. 1835 by Bp of Win. P. C. of Serk, Dio. Win. 1834. (Patron, Lord of Serk; P. C.'s Inc. 80*l*; Pop. 583.) Author, Tracts in French, *Essai sur la Résurrection*, 1850; *Le Palais de Cristal*, 1852; *Quelques Signes des Derniers, Temps*, 1853; *Le Salut par Grace*, 1853; *Quelques Idées sur la Parabole des Dix Vierges*, 1853; *Sécurité du Peuple de Dieu*, 1854; *Une Croix la Marque Visible de la Bête*, 1854; *Aimer Marque Visible des Disciples de Christ*, 1854; *Qui est Gog?* 1854; *Seigneur-Jésus viens*, 1855 (from 2*d* to 5*d* each); *Sur le Serviteurs et sur les Domestiques*, Toulouse, 1854, 1*d*; *Aujourd'hui*, 1854. [5]

CADDELL, Henry, *St. Peter's Vicarage, Colchester.*—Scho. Corpus Coll. Cam. B.A. 1834, M.A. 1839; Deac. 1834 and Pr. 1835 by Bp of Ex. V. of St. Peter's, Colchester, Dio. Roch. 1854. (Patrons, Simeon's Trustees; Tithe, 19*l* 15*s* 3*d*; V.'s Inc. 280*l* and Ho; Pop. 2127.) Surrogate. Author, *Sermons*, 1843, 7*s* 6*d*. [6]

CADMAN, William, 5, *Upper Harley-street, London, W.*—St. Cath. Hall, Cam. B.A. 1839, M.A. 1842; Deac. 1839 and Pr. 1840 by Bp of Ely. R. of Trinity, St. Marylebone, Dio. Lon. 1859. (Patron, the Crown; R.'s Inc. 1030*l*; Pop. 13,951.) Formerly R. of St. George the Martyr's, Southwark, 1852–59. [7]

CADOGAN, Edward, *Walton D'Eivile, Warwick.*—P. C. of Walton D'Eivile, Dio. Wor. 1860. (Patron, Sir C. Mordaunt, Bart; P. C.'s Inc. 156*l*.) [8]

CADWALLADER, James, *Usk, Monmouthshire.*—Jesus Coll. Ox. B.A; Deac. 1838 and Pr. 1839 by Bp of Ox. Chap of the County Prison, Usk, 1860. [9]

CAFFIN, Benjamin Charles, *Grammar School, Durham.*—Wor. Coll. Ox. 1st cl. Lit. Hum. B.A. 1850, M.A. 1852; Deac. 1851, Pr. 1852. Fell. and Tut. of Wor. Coll. 1852. 2nd Mast. of Dur. Cathl. Gr. Sch. [10]

CAFFIN, Charles Smart, *Broadway, Worcestershire.*—Caius Coll. Cam. B.A. 1841, M.A. 1844; Deac. 1841 and Pr. 1842 by Bp of Roch. V. of Broadway, Dio. Wor. 1862. (Patrons, Trustees; V.'s Inc. 240*l* and Ho; Pop. 1566.) Formerly V. of Milton-next-Sittingbourne, Kent, 1852–62. [11]

CAFFIN, George Benjamin, *Brimpton, Reading.*—St. John's Coll. Ox. B.A. 1832. V. of Brimpton, Dio. Ox. 1858. (Patron, the present V; Tithe, 326*l*; V.'s Inc. 385*l*; Pop. 462.) Surrogate. Formerly V. of Chislet, Canterbury, 1855–58. [12]

CAFFIN, G. C., *St. Ives, Cornwall.*—C. of St. Ives. [13]

CAINE, Thomas, *Kirk-Lonan Vicarage, Douglas, Isle of Man.*—Literate; Deac. 1835 and Pr. 1836 by Bp of S. and M. V. of Kirk-Lonan, Dio. S. and M. 1853. (Patron, the Crown; Tithe, 125*l*; Glebe, 13 acres; V.'s Inc. 140*l* and Ho; Pop. 2909.) Formerly Chap. of St. Luke's, Braddan, Isle of Man, 1836–53. [14]

CAINE, William, *Moss Side Grove, Greenheys, Manchester.*—Dub. Erasmus Smith's Exhib. and A.B. 1850, A.M. 1853; Deac. 1855 and Pr. 1856 by Bp of Man. Formerly C of Ch. Ch. Moss-side, near Manchester, 1855–57; for some years Tut. and Res. Mast. in Dub. Univ. Author, *Biographical Notices of 100 Temperance Reformers*. 1860, 2*s* 6*d*; *Teetotalism in Harmony with the Bible*, 2*d*; *The Traffic in Intoxicating Drinks on the Lord's Day*, 1*d*; and contributions to various Theological and Temperance Periodicals. [15]

CAKEBREAD, William.—C. of Trinity, Whitehaven. [16]

CALCOTT, John William Calcott Berkeley, 5, *St. John's-villas, Blackheath, London, S.E.*—Dub. A.B 1844; Deac. and Pr. 1845 by Bp of Lich. Formerly V of Flitwick, Beds, 1850–55. [17]

CALCRAFT, John Neville, *Haceby Rectory, Folkingham, Lincolnshire.*—Clare Hall, Cam. B A. 1824, M.A. 1828; Deac. 1825, Pr. 1826. R. of Haceby, Dio. Lin. 1832. (Patron, Sir G. E. Welby, Denton Hall; Tithe, 139*l*; Glebe, 54 acres; R.'s Inc. 219*l* and Ho; Pop. 61.) C. of Dembleby, near Folkingham, 1832. [18]

CALDER, Frederick, *Grammar School, Chesterfield.*—St. John's Coll. Cam. B.A. 1840, M.A. 1853; Deac. 1842, Pr. 1844. Head Mast. of Chesterfield Gr. Sch. 1846. Author, *Arithmetic, Part I.* 1850, 2*s*. *Part II.* 1851, 4*s* 6*d*; *Supplement on Decimal Coinage*, 1854, 6*d*. [19]

CALDER, William, *Bromley, Kent.*—St. John's Coll. Cam. B.A. 1853; Deac. 1855 and Pr. 1856 by Bp of Lich. C. of Bromley 1866. Formerly C. of St. Werburgh's, Derby, 1855, St. Andrew's, Liverpool, 1857, Heaton Mersey, Manchester, 1859, Wandsworth, Surrey, 1862. [20]

CALDER, William, *Fairfield, Walton-on-the-Hill, Liverpool.*—P. C. of Fairfield, Walton-on-the-Hill, 1853. (Patrons, the Bushby family; Pop. 4289.) [21]

CALDICOTT, John William, *Grammar School, Bristol.*—Jesus Coll. Ox. B.A. 1851, M.A. 1854; Deac. 1852, Pr. 1853. Head Mast. of Bristol Gr. Sch. Formerly Tut. of Jesus Coll. Ox. [22]

CALDWELL, Charles, *St. Martin's-at-Oak, Norwich.*—P. C. of St. Martin's-at-Oak 1858. (Patrons, D. and C. of Nor; P. C.'s Inc. 102*l*; Pop. 2516.) Chap. of the Borough Asylum, St. Augustine's Gates, Norwich. [23]

CALEY, George Augustus, *Bilderston, Ipswich.*—St. John's Coll. Cam. B.A. 1854, M.A. 1857; Deac. 1854 and Pr. 1855 by Bp of Wor. C. of Hitcham 1863; Chap. of Cosford Union, Suffolk. Formerly C. of Cradley, Worc. 1854–56, Tredington, Worc. 1856–58, Swafield, Norfolk, 1858–59, Great Bricet, Suffolk, 1859–63. [24]

CALLENDAR, Hugh, *Hatherop Rectory, Fairford.*—St. John's Coll. Cam. 4th Wrang. B.A. 1851, Fell. of St. John's and Fell. of Magd. 1853, M.A. 1854, Tut. of Magd. 1857–60; Deac. 1853 and Pr 1854 by Bp of Ely. R. of Hatherop, Dio. G. and B 1860. (Patron, His Highness the Maharajah Duleep Singh; Glebe, 339 acres; R.'s Inc. 302*l* and Ho; Pop. 323.) [25]

CALLENDAR, William, *Blackmore, Ingatestone, Essex.*—Magd. Hall, Ox. B.A. 1842; Deac. 1843, Pr. 1844. P. C. of Blackmore, Dio. Roch. 1853. (Patron, Exors. of C. A. Crickett, Esq; P. C.'s Inc. 85*l*; Pop. 644.) [26]

CALLENDER, Henry Sealy, 12, *Langham-street, London, W.*—St. John's Coll. Ox. B.A. 1861, M.A. 1864; Deac. 1861 and Pr. 1862 by Bp of Carl. C. of All Souls, Marylebone, 1866. Formerly C. of Ambleside 1861–66. [27]

CALLENDER, Richard C., *Portswood, Southampton.*—Caius Coll. Cam. B.A. 1863; Deac. 1864 and Pr. 1865 by Bp of Win. C. of Portswood 1864. [28]

CALLEY, Charles Benet, *Steeple-Bumstead, Haverhill, Essex.*—V. of Steeple-Bumstead, Dio. Roch 1865. (Patron, Ld Chan; Tithe, 400*l* 2*s* 5*d*; Glebe

3 acres; V.'s Inc. 405*l* and Ho; Pop. 1158.) Formerly C. of Ditcheat, Somerset. [1]

CALLIPHRONAS, Demetrius P., *Walpole Vicarage, Wisbeach.*—Trin. Coll. Cam. B.A. 1838, M.A. 1841; Deac. 1842 by Bp of Lin. Pr. 1848 by Bp of Nor. V. of Walpole St. Andrew, Dio. Nor. 1863. (Patron, Rev. C. Hare Townshend; V.'s Inc. 1259*l*; Pop. 800.) Formerly C. of Burgh, Lincolnshire, 1842, Southery, Norfolk, 1843; R. of West Walton-Lewes, Norfolk, 1848–63. [2]

CALLIS, John, *Berners-street, Ipswich.*—St. Cath. Coll. Cam. 2nd cl. Nat. Sci. Trip. B.A. 1865; Deac. 1865 and Pr. 1866 by Bp of Nor. C. of St. Margaret's, Ipswich, 1865. [3]

CALLIS, William.—C. of Slaidburn, Clitheroe. [4]

CALTHROP, F. J.—C. of Wellingborough. [5]

CALTHROP, Gordon, *Highbury New Park, London, N.*—Trin. Coll. Cam. 1st cl. Cl. Trip. B.A. 1847, M.A. 1852; Deac. 1851 and Pr. 1853 by Bp of Ox. P. C. of St. Augustine's, Highbury, Dio. Lon. 1864. Formerly Scho. and Chap. of Trin. Coll. Cam; and Min. of Trin. Chap. Cheltenham, 1858–64. Author, *Temptation of Christ*, 1861; *Passion Week Lectures*, 1862; and *Lectures to the Working Classes*, 1863. [6]

CALTHROP, Henry, *Great Braxted Rectory, Witham, Essex.*—Corpus Coll. Cam. B.A. 1825, M.A. 1828, B.D. 1835; Deac. 1827 by Bp of Ely, Pr. 1827 by Bp of Lich. Preb. of Longdon in Lich. Cathl. 1841; R. of Great Braxted, Dio. Roch. 1841. (Patron, Corpus Coll. Cam; Tithe, 618*l*; Glebe, 67 acres; R.'s Inc. 738*l* and Ho; Pop. 384.) Formerly Fell. and Tut. of Corpus Coll. Cam; Exam. Chap. to the Bp of Lich. Author, *A Sermon at the Consecration of James, Bishop of Sodor and Man*, 1838. [7]

CALTHROP, Robert Gordon, *Irton Parsonage, Whitehaven.*—Wor. Coll. Ox. B.A. 1851, M.A. 1854; Deac. 1851 and Pr. 1853 by Bp of Dur. P. C. of Irton, Dio. Carl. 1851. (Patron, S. Irton, Esq; Tithe—Imp. 194*l* 2*s* 1¾*d*; P. C.'s Inc. 100*l*; Pop. 555.) P. C. of Drigg, near Ravenglass, Dio. Carl. 1856. (Patron, S. Irton, Esq; P. C.'s Inc. 88*l*; Pop. 440.) Formerly C. of Newburn, Northumberland, Stamfordham, Northumberland, St. Peter's, Leeds. Author, *Hints on the Cholera to the Parishioners of Stamfordham*; *A Few Words to the Parishioners of Irton*; *A Few Words to the Parishioners of Irton and Drigg.* [8]

CALVERLEY, Henry, *South Stoke Vicarage, Bath.*—Trin. Coll. Cam. B.A. 1815, M.A. 1819; Deac. and Pr. 1819 by Bp of Ex. V. of South Stoke, Dio. B. and W. 1839. (Patron, the present V; Tithe, 168*l* 15*s*; Glebe, 15 acres; V.'s Inc. 200*l* and Ho; Pop. 375.) Preb. of Wells. [9]

CALVERLEY, Henry Calverley, *Corpus Christi College, Oxford.*—Corpus Coll. Ox. B.A. 1848, M.A. 1851; Deac. 1853 and Pr. 1854 by Bp of Ox. Fell. of Corpus Coll. Ox. Formerly C. of St. Mary's, Reading, 1853, St. Mary's, Aylesbury, 1861. [10]

CALVERT, Arthur, *Crediton, Devon.*—Head Mast. of Crediton Gr. Sch. [11]

CALVERT, Charles G., *Upwell, near Downham Market*—Jesus Coll. Cam. B.A. 1856; Deac. 1857 and Pr. 1859 by Bp of Ely. C. of Upwell 1865. Formerly C. of Thetford 1863. [12]

CALVERT, N. R., *Childerley, Cambs.*—R. of Childerley, Dio. Ely, 1832. (Patron, N. Calvert, Esq; R.'s Inc. 20*l*; Pop. 50.) [13]

CALVERT, Thomas, *Dinnington Vicarage, Newcastle-on-Tyne.*—V. of Dinnington, Dio. Dur. 1864. (Patron, M. Bell, Esq; V.'s Inc. 190*l* and Ho; Pop. 774.) [14]

CALVERT, Thomas Bainbridge, *Darley Parsonage, Ripley, Yorks.*—St. Aidan's; Deac. 1850 by Bp of Ches. Pr. 1851 by Abp of York. P. C. of Thornthwaite, Dio. Rip. 1856. (Patron, V. of Hampsthwaite; P. C.'s Inc. 138*l*; Pop. 930.) [15]

CALVERT, William, *The Parsonage, Kentish-town, London, N.W.*—Pemb. Coll. Cam. B.A. 1842, M.A. 1852; Deac. 1842 and Pr. 1844 by Bp of Wor. P. C. of St. John the Baptist's, Kentish-town, Dio. Lon. 1858. (Patron, V. of St. Pancras; P. C.'s Inc. 300*l* and Ho; Pop. 11,595.) Min. Can. of St. Paul's 1848. Formerly C. of Longdon, Worc. 1842, Merstham, Surrey, 1846, Shilbottle, Northumb. 1847; R. of St. Antholine, Lond. 1849–58. Author, *The Wife's Manual*; *Prayers, Thoughts, and Songs on Several Occasions of a Matron's Life*; *The Wandering Soul, a Parable in Rhyme*, 4to 10*s* 6*d*; *A Sermon delivered before the 29th Volunteers* 1860. [16]

CALVERT, W.—C. of St. Mary Magdalen's, Peckham. [17]

CALVERT, William Bainbridge, *Vicarage, Huddersfield.*—Pemb. Coll. Cam. B.A. 1843, M.A. 1848; Deac. 1843 by Bp of Lin. Pr. 1844 by Abp of York. V. of Huddersfield, Dio. Rip, 1866. (Patron, Sir. J. W. Ramsden, Bart; Tithe, 125*l*; Glebe, 70*l*; V.'s Inc. 500*l* and Ho; Pop. 9362.) Surrogate. Formerly C. of Cottingham, Yorks, 1843–47, Frome Selwood 1847–52, St. John's, Clapham, 1852–55, St. Michael's, Stockwell, 1855–57; P. C. of St. Paul's, Dorking, 1857–66. [18]

CAMBRIDGE, Edward Pickard, *Warmwell Rectory, near Dorchester.*—Trin. Hall. Cam. Jun. Opt. and B.A. 1845, M.A. 1848; Deac. 1846, Pr. 1847. R. of Warmwell with Poxwell R. Dio. Salis. 1849. (Patron, John T. Trinchard, Esq; Warmwell, Tithe, 128*l*; Glebe, 50 acres; Poxwell, Tithe, 161*l* 7*s* 6*d*; Glebe, 30½ acres; R.'s Inc. 370*l* and Ho; Pop. Warmwell 148, Poxwell 82.) [19]

CAMBRIDGE, George Pickard, *Bloxworth Rectory, Wareham, Dorset.*—Mert. Coll. Ox. B.A. 1812, M.A. 1815; Deac. 1815 by Bp of Ex. Pr. 1815 by Bp of Salis. R. of Winterbourne-Thompson, near Blandford, Dio. Salis. 1822. (Patron, G. E. Bankes, Esq; Tithe, 80*l*; Glebe, ½ acre; R.'s Inc. 80*l*; Pop. 39.) R. of Bloxworth, Dio. Salis. 1850. (Patron, the present R; Tithe, 280*l*; Glebe, 50 acres; R.'s Inc. 330*l* and Ho; Pop. 264.) [20]

CAMBRIDGE, Octavius Pickard, *Bloxworth, Dorset.*—Dur. Theol. Licen. 1857, B.A. 1858, M.A. 1859; Deac. 1858 and Pr. 1859 by Bp of Ches. C. of Bloxworth and Winterbourne-Thompson. Formerly C. of Scarisbrick, Lancashire. [21]

CAMERON, Archibald Allen, *Hurst, Reading.*—Pemb. Coll. Ox. B.A. 1831, M.A. 1833; Deac. 1832, Pr. 1833. P. C. of Hurst, Dio. Ox. 1833. (Patron, Bp of Ox; Tithe—App. 1540*l*; P. C.'s Inc. 160*l*; Pop. 1915.) [22]

CAMERON, Donald, *Snitterfield Vicarage, near Stratford-upon-Avon.*—Wad. Coll. Ox. B.A. 1818, M.A. 1825; Deac. 1819 and Pr. 1820 by Bp of Ox. V. of Snitterfield, Dio. Wor. 1840. (Patron, Bp of Wor; Tithe—Imp. 109*l* 10*s*, V. 55*l*; Glebe, 238 acres; V.'s Inc. 284*l* and Ho; Pop. 881.) Formerly Fell. of Wad. Coll. Ox. 1821. [23]

CAMERON, Donald, jun., *Daventry, Northants.*—St. Mary Hall, Ox. B.A. 1853, M.A. 1855; Theol. Coll. Wells, 1854; Deac. 1855 and Pr. 1856 by Bp of B. and W. C. of Daventry. Formerly C. of Cirencester 1858. [24]

CAMERON, Francis, *Charlton, Kent.*—Deac. 1842, Pr. 1843. R. of Charlton, Dio. Lon. 1862. (Patron, Sir T. M. Wilson, Bart; R.'s Inc. 350*l* and Ho; Pop. 3667.) [25]

CAMERON, Francis Marten, *Bonnington Rectory, Hythe, Kent.*—Ch. Ch. Ox. B.A. 1846, M.A. 1849, 2nd cl. Math; Deac. 1847 and Pr. 1848 by Bp of Lin. R. of Bonnington, Kent, Dio. Cant. 1861. (Patron, T. Papillon, Esq; Tithe, 212*l*; Glebe, 30 acres; R.'s Inc. 256*l*; Pop. 187.) P. C. of Bilsington, Kent, Dio. Cant. 1861. (Patron, W. H. Cosway, Esq; Glebe Land (not in Parish) 20*l*; P. C.'s Inc. 60*l*; Pop. 350.) Formerly C. of Swaby 1847; P. C. of Brookham 1849; R. of Crowhurst, Sussex, 1859. [26]

CAMERON, George Thomas, *Heckington, Sleaford, Lincolnshire.*—Ch. Ch. Ox. 3rd cl. Lit. Hum. and B.A. 1843, M.A. 1846; Deac. 1844 and Pr. 1845 by Bp of Lon. V. of Heckington, Dio. Lin. 1861. (Patron, W. Allison, Esq; V.'s Inc. 340*l* and Ho; Pop.

1725.) Formerly C. of St. Peter's, Saffron-hill, London, 1844; Iclesham, Sussex, 1846, St. Ebbe's, Oxford, 1847; R. of Bonnington and P. C. of Bilsington, Kent, 1860. [1]

CAMERON, Jonathan Henry Lovett, *Shoreham, Kent.*—Trin. Coll. Cam. B.A. 1831, M.A. 1834; Deac. 1836, Pr. 1837. V. of Shoreham, Kent, Dio. Cant. 1860. (Patrons, D. and C. of Westminster; V.'s Inc. 371*l* and Ho; Pop. 1146.) Formerly R. of Buckhorn Weston 1852–60. [2]

CAMERON, William, 2, *Church Villas, St. James's-road, Croydon.*—Queens' Coll. Cam. B.A. 1856, M.A. 1860; Deac. 1858 and Pr. 1859 by Bp of Lon. P. C. of St. Saviour's, Croydon, Dio. Cant. 1867. Formerly C. of St. Stephen's, Camden-town, 1858, St. Andrew's, Croydon, 1862. [3]

CAMIDGE, Charles Edward, *Wakefield.*—Wad. Coll. Ox. B.A. 1859, M.A. 1861; Deac. 1860 and Pr. 1861 by Abp of York. C. of Wakefield 1861; Hon. Chap. to Ancient Order of Foresters for the West Riding 1865. Formerly C. of Sheffield 1860. Author, *Sermon preached at Wakefield to the Foresters*; *Sermon on Wakefield Industrial and Fine Art Exhibition*, 1865; *Sermon on Lay Help*, 1867; *A History of Wakefield and its Industrial and Fine Art Exhibition*, 1866, 3*s*. [4]

CAMIDGE, Charles Joseph, *The Vicarage, Wakefield.*—St. Cath. Coll. Cam. Scho. and Prizeman 1821, B.A. 1824; Deac. 1824, Pr. 1825. Hon. Can. of Rip. V. of Wakefield, Dio. Rip. 1855. (Patron, Ld Chan; V.'s Inc. 350*l* and Ho; Pop. 8437.) Formerly P. C. of Nether Poppleton, Yorks, 1826–55; Chap. to the York Union 1849; Even. Lect. at St. Margaret's, York. Author, *The Christian, an Example*, 1846. [5]

CAMILLERI, Michael Angelo, *Lyford Parsonage, Wantage, Berks.*—Malta Univ. Theol. Coll. 1834; Deac. and Pr. 1836 by Bp of Malta. P. C. of Lyford, Dio. Ox. 1863. (Patron, Wor. Coll. Ox; P. C.'s Inc. 150*l* and Ho; Pop. 140.) Formerly C. of Goosey with Stanford-in-the-Vale, Berks, 1858. Translator of the *New Testament* and the *Book of Common Prayer* into Maltese. Editor of *The Indicators* of Malta, 1846–47. [6]

CAMM, John Brooke Maher, *Horsham, Sussex*—Magd. Hall, Ox. B.A. 1865; Deac. 1866 by Bp of Chich. C. of Horsham 1866. Formerly Cornet in the 12th Royal Lancers, 1863–64. [7]

CAMMACK, John Caparn, *Newbottle, Fence Houses, Durham.*—Dur. Found. Scho. 1863, Barry Scho. 1865, Licen. in Theol. 1865; Deac. 1865 and Pr. 1866 by Bp of Dur. C. of Newbottle with Herrington 1865. Formerly Asst. Mast. in Heath Gr. Sch. Halifax, 1863–65. [8]

CAMPBELL, Alexander Burrowes, *The Downwood, Blandford.*—Dub. A.B. 1830, Ch. Ch. Ox. M.A. Chap. to Earl Cowley 1858. Formerly P. C. of Great Redisham, Suffolk. Author, *Sermons on the Death of William III*; *On the Scottish Episcopacy*; *A Humiliation Sermon*, etc. [9]

CAMPBELL, Andrew Ramsay, *Aston Rectory, Rotherham.*—Ball. Coll. Ox. 2nd cl. Lit. Hum. and B.A. 1835, M.A. 1838; Deac. 1839, Pr. 1840. R. of Aston, Dio. York, 1853. (Patron, Duke of Leeds; Glebe, 30 acres; R.'s Inc. 798 and Ho; Pop. 995.) Chap. to Bp of Lon. Author, Two Sermons, *The Limits of Allowable Difference in Questions of Doctrine*; *Baptismal Regeneration*, 1850; *Building on the Foundation* (a Sermon), 1851; etc. [10]

CAMPBELL, The Hon. Archibald George, *Knipton Rectory, Grantham.*—Ball. Coll. Ox. B.A. 1848, M.A. 1850; Deac. 1850, Pr. 1851. R. of Knipton, Dio. Pet. 1853. (Patron, Duke of Rutland; Tithe, 189*l*; Glebe, 50 acres; R.'s Inc. 280*l* and Ho; Pop. 300.) [11]

CAMPBELL, Augustus, *Childwall Vicarage, near Liverpool.*—Trin. Coll. Cam. B.A. 1807, M.A. 1812; Deac. 1811, Pr. 1812. R. of Liverpool, Dio. Ches. 1829. (Patron, J. Stewart, Esq; Tithe, 400*l* and Fees; R.'s Inc. 1200*l*.) V. of Childwall, Lancashire, Dio. Ches. 1829. (Patron, Bp of Ches; Tithe—App. 1931*l* 17*s* 7*d*; Imp. 2*s* 6*d*, V. 412*l* 10*s* 10*d*; V.'s Inc. 500*l* and Ho.) Author, *Rights of the English Clergy asserted, and the Probable Amount of their Incomes estimated*; *An Appeal to the Gentlemen of England on behalf of the Church of England*; *Reply to an Article* On Church Establishments *in* Edinburgh Review; *Letter on Convocation*; Three *Visitation Sermons*, etc. [12]

CAMPBELL, Charles, *Beechamwell, Swaffham, Norfolk.*—R. of Beechamwell All Saints with Shingham R. Dio. Nor. 1822. (Patron, Ld Chan; Beechamwell, Tithe, 123*l* 15*s*; Shingham, Tithe, 108*l*; Glebe, 24 acres; R.'s Inc 232*l*; Pop. 62.) V. of Weasenham All Saints with Weasenham St. Peter's V. Dio. Nor. 1822. (Patron, Ld Chan; Weasenham All Saints, Tithe—Imp. 350*l* and 17 acres of Glebe, V. 226*l* 15*s*, Weasenham St. Peter's, Tithe—App. 6*l* 10*s*, Imp. 222*l*, V. 151*l* 10*s*; V.'s Inc. 378*l*; Pop. Weasenham All Saints 360, Weasenham St. Peter's 320.) [13]

CAMPBELL, Colin, *St. Thomas's Parsonage, Lancaster.*—Trin. Coll. Cam. B.A. 1857, M.A. 1860; Deac. 1857 and Pr. 1858 by Bp of Man. P. C. of St. Thomas's, Lancaster, Dio. Man. 1858. (Patron, the present P. C.; P. C.'s Inc. 170*l* and Ho; Pop. 2908.) [14]

CAMPBELL, David.—C. of St. Mary's, Newington, Surrey. [15]

CAMPBELL, Donald, *Upper Lewisham-road, London, S.E.*—Trin. Coll. Cam. 3rd cl. Math. Trip. B.A. 1864; Deac. 1865, Pr. 1866. C. of St. John's, Deptford, 1865. [16]

CAMPBELL, Duncan, *Pentridge, Cranborne, Dorset.*—Edin. and Aberdeen; M.A. 1843 by Abp of Cant; Deac. 1834 and Pr. 1835 by Bp of Ches. R. of Pentridge, Dio. Salis. 1849. (Patron, Ld Chan; Tithe, 215*l* 7*s* 9*d*; Glebe, 48 acres; R.'s Inc. 260*l* and Ho; Pop. 295.) Formerly C. of Poulton-le-Fylde, Lancashire, 1835; P. C. of Crossens, Lancashire, 1838; C. of St. Peter's, Worcester, 1839, Newbold-on-Avon 1843; P. C. of Berron, Worc. 1845. [17]

CAMPBELL, Edward Augustus Pitcairn, *Childwall Vicarage, Liverpool.*—Trin. Coll. Cam. B.A. 1843, M.A. 1846; Deac. 1844, Pr. 1845. C. of Childwall. [18]

CAMPBELL, George, *New Swindon Parsonage, Wilts.*—P. C. of St. Mark's, New Swindon, Dio. G. and B. 1852. (Patron, Bp of G. and B; Glebe, 1 acre; P. C.'s Inc. 206*l* and Ho; Pop. 4167.) [19]

CAMPBELL, James William, *Palgrave Rectory, Diss, Suffolk.*—Trin. Coll. Cam. B.A. 1833, M.A. 1836. R. of Palgrave, Dio. Nor. 1864. (Patron, Sir Edward Kerrison, Bart; R.'s Inc. 530*l* and Ho; Pop. 739.) Formerly V. of Eye, Suffolk, 1838–64. [20]

CAMPBELL, James William, 6, *White-street, Coventry.*—Pemb. Coll. Ox. B.A. 1866; Deac. and Pr. 1866 by Bp of Wor. C. of St. Michael's, Coventry, 1866. [21]

CAMPBELL, J.—C. of Holcombe, near Bury, Lancashire. [22]

CAMPBELL, John Archibald Legh, *Helpston, Market Deeping, Northants.*—Oriel Coll. Ox. B.A. 1847, M.A. 1852, and Theol. Coll. Wells; Deac. 1848, Pr. 1853. V. of Helpston, Dio. Pet. 1855. (Patron, Hon. G. W. Fitzwilliam; Glebe, 35 acres; V.'s Inc. 110*l* and Ho; Pop. 763.) [23]

CAMPBELL, John James, *Great Tew, Enstone, Oxon.*—Ball. Coll. Ox. B.A. 1836, M.A. 1839; Deac. 1837, Pr. 1838. V. of Great Tew, Dio. Ox. 1844. (Patron, M. P. W. Boulton, Esq; Rent Charge, 44*l*; Glebe, 20 acres; V.'s Inc. 124*l* and Ho; Pop. 454.) Surrogate. [24]

CAMPBELL, John Usher, *South Pickenham, Swaffham, Norfolk.*—R. of South Pickenham, Dio. Nor. 1865. (Patron, E. Applethwaite, Esq; R.'s Inc. 390*l*; Pop. 159.) Formerly Chap. of Dockyard, Pembroke. [25]

CAMPBELL, Lewis, *St. Andrews, Scotland.*—Ball. Coll. Ox. B.A. 1853, M.A. 1857; Deac. 1856 and Pr. 1857 by Bp of Ox. Prof. of Greek in Univ. of St. Andrews. Formerly Tut. of Queen's Coll. Ox. 1856–58; V. of Milford with Hordle, Hants, 1858–64. Author, *The Theætetus of Plato, with Revised Text and English Notes*, 1861, 9*s*; *A Lecture on Socrates*, 1858; a Pamphlet on the Oxfordshire Examinations, 1857. [26]

CAMPBELL, Straton Charles, *Cockley-Cley, Swaffham, Norfolk.*—Corpus Coll. Cam. B.A. 1846, M.A. 1849; Deac. 1847, Pr. 1848. R. of Cockley-Cley, Dio. Nor. 1850. (Patron, T. R. Backworth, Esq; Tithe, 180*l*; Glebe, 100 acres; R.'s Inc. 210*l*; Pop. 263.) [1]

CAMPBELL, S. D.—C. of Nuneaton, Warwickshire. [2]

CAMPBELL, Thomas, *Boston.*—St. Bees; Deac. 1857 and Pr 1858 by Abp of York. P. C. of Brothertoft, Dio. Lin. 1864. (Patron, Thomas Gee, Esq; P. C.'s Inc. 150*l*; Pop. 110.) Formerly C. of Barton-Agnes 1857, Brandsby 1859. Author, *England's Duty to the Orphans of her Slain*, 1859, 1*s*; *Are we Christians?* 1859, 1*s*; *On the Signs of the Times*, 1860, 6*d*; *The Cattle Plague Viewed in its Relation to Second Causes*, 1866, 6*d*. [3]

CAMPBELL, William, *Privy Council Office, Downing-street, London, S.W.*—Ch. Coll. Cam. B.A. 1848, M.A. 1867; Deac. 1848, Pr. 1851. One of H.M. Inspectors of Schools. [4]

CAMPBELL, William, *Uppingham, Rutland.*—Emman. Coll. Cam. Sen. Opt. B.A. 1858, M.A. 1864; Deac. 1858 and Pr. 1859 by Bp of Lin. Asst. Mast. of Uppingham Sch. 1863. Formerly C. of Hyson Green, Nottingham, 1858–61; a Cl. Mast. in Cheltenham Coll. [5]

CAMPBELL, William Adderley, *Madrid.*—Wor. Coll. Ox. B.A. 1860; Deac. 1860 by Bp of Win. British Chap. at Madrid. Formerly C. of All Saints', Clapham, 1860. [6]

CAMPBELL, William Fraser, *Hungerford, Berks.*—Ch. Ch. Ox. B.A. 1866; Deac. 1866 by Bp of Ox. C. of Hungerford 1866. [7]

CAMPBELL, William Pitcairn Alexander, *Almeley Vicarage, Letton, Hereford.*—Queens' Coll. Cam Sen. Opt. and B.A. 1848, M.A. 1852; Deac. 1850 and Pr. 1851 by Bp of Salis. V. of Almeley, Dio. Herf. 1865. (Patron, Bp. of Wor; Tithe, 207; Glebe, 60 acres; V.'s Inc. 360*l* and Ho; Pop. 637.) Formerly C. of Bitton, Glouc. and Beaudesert, Warw. [8]

CAMPBELL, William Walter.—Chap. of H.M.S. "Royal George." Formerly Chap. and Naval Instructor of H.M.S. "Iris." 1857. [9]

CAMPBELL-COLQUHOUN, John Erskine, *Crockham Parsonage, Edenbridge, Kent.*—P. C. of Crockham, Dio. Cant. 1865. (Patroness, Mrs. W. St. John Mildmay; P. C.'s Inc. 140*l* and Ho; Pop. 542.) [10]

CAMPE, Charles.—Deac. 1846, Pr. 1847. P. C. of Ch. Chapel, St. John's Wood, London, 1863. (Patrons, Trustees.) Formerly P. C. of St. Mark's, Norwich. Author, *Sermons on the Temptation of Christ*, 1853, 2*s*. [11]

CAMPION, Charles Heathcote, *Westmeston Rectory, Hurstpierpoint, Sussex.*—Ch. Ch. Ox. B.A. 1836; Deac. 1840, Pr. 1841. R. of Westmeston with Chiltington, Dio. Chich. 1848. (Patron, W. J. Campion, Esq; Tithe, 590*l*; Glebe, 30 acres; R.'s Inc. 630*l* and Ho; Pop. Westmeston 288, Chiltington 281.) [12]

CAMPION, John. *Doncaster.*—M.A. by Abp of Cant. P. C. of St. James's, Doncaster, Dio. York, 1864. (Patrons, E. Denison and E. B. Denison, Esqs; P. C.'s Inc. 160*l*; Pop. 800.) Formerly C. of Ch. Ch. Doncaster; V. of East Acklam, Yorks, 1847–64. [13]

CAMPION, J. G. C.—C. of Great Wakering, Essex. [14]

CAMPION, William Magan, *Queens' College, Cambridge.*—Queens' Coll. Cam. 4th Wrang. and B.A. 1849, M.A. 1852; Deac. 1851 and Pr. 1855 by Bp of Ely; Fell. of Queens' Coll. Cam. 1850, Tut. 1853; R. of St. Botolph's, Cambridge, Dio. Ely, 1862. (Patron, Queens' Coll. Cam; R.'s Inc. 122*l*; Pop. 758.) Whitehall Preacher 1862–64. Author, *Nature and Grace* (Sermons preached in Chapel Royal, Whitehall), Deighton's, Cambridge, 1864, 6*s* 6*d*. Joint-Editor of *The Prayer-Book interleaved*, Rivington's, 1866, 7*s* 6*d*. [15]

CANCELLOR, John Henry, *Ash Rectory, Farnboro' Station.*—Trin. Coll. Cam. B.A. 1856, M.A. 1859; Deac. 1857 and Pr. 1858 by Bp of Lich. C. of Ash 1863. Formerly C. of Breaston. [16]

CANDY, Charles, *Shottermill Parsonage, Haslemere, Surrey.*—Lin. Coll. Ox. 2nd cl. Math. 3rd cl. Lit. Hum. B.A. 1822, M.A. 1824; Deac. 1824, Pr. 1825. P. C. of the District of Shottermill, Dio. Win. 1850. (Patron, Archd. of Surrey; P. C.'s Inc. 76*l* and Ho; Pop. 579.) Formerly C. of Midhurst, Sussex, 1825–33. [17]

CANDY, George, *South Newington, Banbury.*—V. of South Newington; Dio. Ox. 1864. (Patron, Ex. Coll. Ox; V.'s Inc. 320*l* and Ho; Pop. 400.) [18]

CANDY, Henry Houston, *Burnham, near Maldon, Essex.*—Trin. Coll. Cam. B.A. 1852; Deac. 1853 and Pr. 1854 by Bp of Wor. R. of Burnham, Essex, Dio. Roch. 1862 (R.'s Inc. 558*l*; Pop. 1870.) Formerly R. of Cricksea with Althorne V. Dio. Roch. 1860–62. [19]

CANDY, Herbert, *Pydel Trenthide Vicarage, Dorchester.*—Lin. Coll. Ox. B.A. 1857, M.A. 1859; Deac. 1857 by Bp of Lich. Pr. 1859 by Bp of Nor. C. of Pydel Trenthide (sole charge) 1863. Formerly C. of Morston, Norfolk, 1858–59, Buckland-Newton, Dorset, 1860–61, Bradford-on-Avon 1861–63. [20]

CANDY, Thomas Henry, *High-street, Huntingdon.*—Sid. Coll. Cam. 28th Wrang. 3rd cl. Theol. B.A. 1856, M.A. 1859; Deac. 1857 and Pr. 1858 by Bp of Ely. Fell. of Sid. Coll. Cam. 1856; C. of Conington, Hunts, 1865. Author, *The Antidote*, 1861, 1*s*; *Internal Evidence of the Truth of the Mosaic History*, 1863, 3*s*; *Critical Greek Testament*, 1867, 14*s*; *School Greek Testament*, Rivington's, 1866, 4*s* 6*d*. [21]

CANE, Alfred Granger, *Broadgate, Lincoln.*—St. John's Coll. Cam. B.A. 1866; Deac. 1867 by Bp of Lin. C. of St. Swithin's, Lincoln, 1867. [22]

CANE, John Brettle, *Weston Rectory, Newark.*—St. John's Coll. Cam. B.A. 1851, M.A. 1854; Deac. 1852 and Pr. 1853 by Bp of Pet. R. of Weston, Dio. Lin. 1862. (Patron, Earl Manvers; Glebe, 311 acres, of which 302 acres are let for 499*l* 11*s*; R.'s Inc. 520*l*; Pop. 380.) Formerly C. of Asfordby, Leicestershire, 1852–54, Bury, Lancashire, 1854–55; P. C. of Perlethorpe, Notts, 1855–62. [23]

CANE, Thomas Coats, *Southwell, Notts.*—St. John's Coll. Cam. B.A. 1823, M.A. 1826; Deac. 1824 by Bp of Ches. Pr. 1824 by Abp of York. P. C. of Kirklington, Notts, Dio. Lin. 1838. (Patron, Chap. of Southwell Coll. Ch; Tithe—App. 500*l*; P. C.'s Inc. 152*l* and Ho; Pop. 241.) Formerly P. C. of Halloughton, Notts, 1840–67. [24]

CANHAM, Henry, *Waldringfield, Woodbridge, Suffolk.*—Trin. Hall. Cam. LL.B. 1852; Deac. 1852 and Pr. 1853 by Bp of G. and B. P. C. of Ramsholt, Dio. Nor. 1854. (Patron, Bp of Nor; P. C.'s Inc. 70*l*; Pop. 186.) Chap. of Woodbridge Union 1856. [25]

CANN, Henry Foster, *Friars Lodge, Exeter.*—Ch. Coll. Cam. B.A. 1850, M.A. 1853; Deac. 1850 and Pr. 1851 by Bp of Ches. R. of St. Kerrian with St. Petrock, Dio. Ex. 1856. (Patrons, D. and C. of Ex; R.'s Inc. 210*l*; Pop. St. Kerrian 479, St. Petrock 220.) Formerly C. of Holy Trinity, Exeter; one of the City Bodleian Lecturers. [26]

CANN, Ponsford, *Virginstowe, Launceston, Cornwall.*—Pemb. Coll. Camb. B.A. 1827; Deac. 1828, Pr. 1829. R. of Virginstowe, Dio. Ex. 1842. (Patron, Ld Chan; Tithe, 119*l*; Glebe, 40 acres; R.'s Inc. 149*l* and Ho; Pop. 141.) P. C. of Broadwoodwigger, Dio. Ex. 1842. (Patrons, D. and C. of Bristol; Tithe—App. 410*l*; P. C.'s Inc. 90*l*; Pop. 1170.) [27]

CANNELL, John, *Auckland-terrace, Douglas, Isle of Man.*—Deac. 1824 and Pr. 1827 by Bp of S. and M. P. C. of St. Matthew's, Douglas, Dio. S. and M. 1835. (Patron, Bp of S. and M; P. C.'s Inc. 73; Pop. 2794.) Surrogate. [28]

CANNING, Thomas, *Tupsley, Hampton Bishop, Hereford.*—Emman. Coll. Cam. B.A. 1849, M.A. 1852; Deac. 1850 and Pr. 1851 by Bp of Wor. P. C. of Tupsley, Dio. Herf. 1864. (Patron, Bp of Herf; P. C.'s Inc. 120*l*; Pop. 803.) [29]

CANTERBURY, The Rt. Hon. and Most Rev. Charles LONGLEY, Lord Archbishop of Canterbury, Primate of all England and Metropolitan, *Lambeth Palace, London, S. and Addington Park, Croydon, Surrey.*—Ch. Ch. Ox. 1st cl. Lit. Hum. and B.A. 1815, M.A. 1818, B.D. and D.D. 1829; Deac. 1818 and Pr. 1819 by Bp of Ox. Consecrated First Bp of Ripon 1836, translated to Durham 1856, to York 1860, to Canterbury 1862. (Episcopal Jurisdiction, the greater part of the County of Kent; Inc. of See, 15,000*l*; Pop. 474,603; acres, 914,170; Deaneries, 14; Benefices, 352; Curates, 166; Church Sittings, 167,792.) His Grace is one of the Lords of Her Majesty's Most Honourable Privy Council; Extraordinary Visitor of Eton College; Visitor of All Souls and Mert. Colls. Ox. King's Coll. Lond. Dulwich Coll. St. Augustine's Coll. Cant. and of Harrow Sch. in conjunction with the Bp of Lon; President of the S.P.C.K. the S.P.G. and the National Society; a Principal Trustee of the British Museum; a Governor of the Charter House. His Grace was formerly one of the Examiners in Lit. Hum. at Oxford, 1825; Proctor of the University 1827; P. C. of Cowley, Oxon, 1825; R. of West Tytherley, Hants, 1828; subsequently Head Mast. of Harrow Sch. Author, *Charges* (to the Clergy of Dio. of Rip), 1838, 1841, 1844, 1847, 1850, 1853; *A Sermon* (for the S.P.C.K. printed in the report), 1842; *A Sermon* (on the Consecration of Holy Trin. Ch. Wakefield), 1844; *The Danger of Neglecting Religious Privileges* (a Sermon), 1845; *A Pastoral Letter to the Clergy of the Diocese of Ripon*, 1850; *A Letter to the Parishioners of St. Saviour's, Leeds, with an Appendix*, 1851; various other Sermons and Episcopal Charges. [1]

CANTRELL, William H., M.A., *Bulwell Rectory, Nottingham.*—R. of Bulwell, Dio. Lin. 1865. (Patron, Rev. A. Padley; R.'s Inc. 370*l* and Ho; Pop. 3660.) Formerly V. of Atteuborough, Notts, 1859–65. [2]

CAPARN, William Barton, *Draycot, Wells, Somerset.*—Brasen. Coll. Ox. B.A. 1843, M.A. 1846; Deac. 1843 and Pr. 1845 by Bp of Rip. P. C. of Draycot, Somerset, Dio. B. and W. 1861. (Patrons, V. of Cheddar and R. of Stoke, alt; P. C.'s Inc. 60*l*; Pop. 618.) Formerly V. of West Torrington, Dio. Lin. 1847–61. [3]

CAPARN, William John, *Christ Church Parsonage, Cubitt Town, Isle of Dogs, London, E.*—St. Aidan's; Deac. 1852 and Pr. 1853 by Abp of York. P. C. of Ch. Ch. Poplar, Dio. Lon. 1856. (Patron, Bp of Lon; P. C.'s Inc. 300*l* and Ho; Pop. 8579.) Formerly C. of Trinity, Wicker, Sheffield, 1852, St. Mary's, Sheffield, 1853, Episcopal Chapel, Gray's-inn-Lane, Lond. 1855–56; Chap. of the Training Ship "Worcester." [4]

CAPE, Jonathan, *Croydon, Surrey.*—Trin. Coll. Cam. 5th Wrang. and B.A. 1816, M.A. 1819; Deac. 1817 by Bp of Herf. Pr. 1818 by Bp of Salis. Sen. Prof. Addiscombe Coll. 1823, F.R.S., and F.R.A.S. Author, *A Course of Mathematics*, 5th edit. 2 vols. 1856, 32*s*; *Mathematical Tables*, ib. 10*s* 6*d*. [5]

CAPE, William, *Peterborough.*—Corpus Coll. Cam. B.A. 1827, M.A. 1830; Deac. 1828 and Pr. 1829 by Bp of Pet. Hon. Can. of Pet. 1864; V. of Bringhurst with Great Easton V. Leicestershire, Dio. Pet. 1833. (Patrons, D. and C. of Pet; Land in lieu of Tithe, 132 acres; V.'s Inc. 280*l*; Pop. 825.) Formerly Head Mast. of the Pet. Cathl. Gr. Sch. [6]

CAPEL, Arthur Douglas, *St. John's College, Cambridge.*—Bishop's Coll. Lennoxville, Canada East, B.A. 1861; Deac. 1863 and Pr. 1864 by Bp of Salis. Formerly Tut. in Mathematics, Bishop's Coll. Lennoxville, and 2nd Mast. in Junior Department of same College 1857–63; C. of Trinity, Wareham, Dorset, 1863. [7]

CAPEL, Bury, *Abergavenny, Monmouthshire.*—Ch. Coll. Cam. B.A. 1850, M.A. 1853; Deac. 1852 and Pr. 1853 by Bp of Ely. V. of Abergavenny, Dio. Llan. 1863. (Patron, Sir Ivor Guest, Bart; Tithe, comm. 502*l*; V.'s Inc. 502*l*; Pop. 6086.) Surrogate. [8]

CAPEL, Henry Martyn, 11, *Carpenter-road, Birmingham.*—St. John's Coll. Cam. 8th Sen. Opt. and B.A. 1854, M.A. 1858; Deac. 1855 and Pr. 1856 by Bp of Salis. One of H.M. Asst. Inspectors of Schs. 1857; Inspector 1863. Formerly C. of Wareham, Dorset, 1855–57. [9]

CAPEL, Samuel Richard, *Wareham, Dorset.*—Wad. Coll. Ox. B.A. 1824, M.A. 1827; Deac. and Pr. 1827. R. of Wareham, with St. Martin's and St. Mary's R.'s and the C. of Arne, Dio. Salis. 1841. (Patron, J. H. Calcraft, Esq; Holy Trinity, Tithe—App. 11*l*; Imp. 2*l*, R. 90*l*; Glebe, 6 acres; St. Martin's, R. 212*l*; Glebe, 2 acres; St. Mary's, Imp. 94*l*, R. 103*l* 0*s* 1*d*; Glebe, 2 acres; Arne, Tithe, 104*l*; R.'s Inc. 509*l* and Ho; Pop. Wareham 3076, Arne 180.) Chap. Wareham and Purbeck Union 1841; Surrogate. [10]

CAPEL, William Forbes, *Cranley, near Guildford, Surrey.*—Theol. Assoc. King's Coll. Lond. 1854; Deac. 1854 by Bp of Lon. Pr. 1855 by Bp of Colombo. Formerly Asst. C. of Camden-town, Lond., and C. of Cranley. [11]

CAPEL, William Rawlins, *Bickenhill Vicarage, near Birmingham.*—Ch. Coll. Cam. B.A. 1851, M.A. 1854; Deac. 1851 by Bp of Wor. Pr. 1852 by Bp of Lich. V. of Bickenhill, Dio. Wor. 1863. (Patron, Earl of Aylesford; Tithe, 324*l*; Glebe, 20 acres; V.'s Inc. 400*l* and Ho; Pop. 744.) Formerly C. of Yoxall, Staffs. 1852–54; Chap. in H.M. Madras Service, 1854–61. [12]

CAPES, W. W.—C. of Abbott's Ann, Hants. [13]

CAPPER, Daniel, *Lyston, Llanwarne, Ross.*—Queens' Coll. Cam. B.A. 1828, M.A. 1832; Deac. 1830, Pr. 1831. Formerly R. of Huntley, near Gloucester, 1839–66. Author, *Practical Results of the Workhouse System*, 2 edits. 1834, 2*s* 6*d*; *A Sermon*, 1835. [14]

CAPRON, C. H. W., *Warmington, Oundle, Northants.*—C. of Warmington. [15]

CAPRON, George Halliley, *Stoke Doyle, Oundle.*—St. John's Coll. Cam. B.A. 1839; Deac. 1840 and Pr. 1841 by Bp of Pet. R. of Stoke Doyle, Dio. Pet. 1841. (Patron, George Capron, Esq; Tithe, 89*l*; Glebe, 33 acres; R.'s Inc. 150*l* and Ho; Pop. 180.) Rural Dean. Formerly C. of Stoke Doyle. [16]

CARDALE, Edward Thomas, *Uckfield, Sussex.*—Literate; Member of Hon. Soc. of Gray's Inn; Deac. 1847 and Pr. 1848 by Bp of Rip. R. of Uckfield, Dio. Chich. 1863. (Patron, Abp of Cant; Tithe, 335*l* 2*s* 6*d*; Glebe, 1 acre; R.'s Inc. 335*l* 2*s* 6*d*; Pop. 1740.) Formerly V. of Podington, Beds, 1849–54; P. C. of Flax-Bourton 1854–60. Author, *The Sin of Doubting the Presence of Christ in His Church* (a Sermon), 1850, 6*d*; *God's Dealings with us Nationally and their Object* (a Sermon for the Fast Day on account of the Russian War in *The Church of England Magazine*, 1855); *The Minister's Object is the Salvation of his People* (a Sermon), 1863; *The Inspiration of Holy Scripture as taught in the Church of England*, 1864, 8*d*; *An Order of Service to be used on the Ministration of Public Baptism of Infants at the same time as the reception into Church of Infants privately Baptized*, Rivingtons, 1866, 1*s*. [17]

CARDALE, George Carter, *Dalwood, Honiton, Devon.*—St. Peter's Coll. Cam. B.A. 1822, M.A. 1825. C. of Dalwood 1864. Formerly C. of Wood Walton, Hunts, 12 years, Rothersthorpe, Northants, 3 years, Cawnby and Burgh-on-Bain, Linc. each 4 years. [18]

CARDALL, William.—St. Peter's Coll. Cam. B.A. 1837, M.A. 1849; Deac. 1838 and Pr. 1839 by Bp of Ches. P. C. of Ch. Ch. Mayfair, Lond. Dio. Lon. 1865. (Patron, Bp of Lon.) Formerly V. of Budbrooke, Warwickshire, 1848–56; C. of St. George's, Hanover-square, Lond. Author, *Sermons preached at Lancaster*, 1843; *Israel's Journeys and Stations in the Wilderness*, 1848, 5*s* 6*d*; *Stand Fast* (a Sermon), 6*d*. [19]

CARDEN, A.—C. of St. Peter's, Plymouth. [20]

CARDEN, James, 20, *New Finchley-road, St. John's Wood, London, N.W.*—Mert. Coll. Ox. M.A. 1843;

Deac. 1845 by Bp of G. and B. Formerly C. of Oddington, near Stow-on-the-Wold, East Brent 1845–46. [1]

CARDEN, Robert Augustus, *Sunderland.*—Ex. Coll. Ox. B.A. 1859, M.A. 1862; Deac. 1859 and Pr. 1860 by Bp of Ox. Chap. of Missions to Seamen, Sunderland. Formerly C. of Shiplake, Oxon. [2]

CARDEW, George, *Helmingham, Stonham, Suffolk.*—Ex. Coll. Ox. 1st cl. Phy. et Math. 2nd cl. Lit. Hum. B.A. 1833, M A. 1836; Deac. 1835 and Pr. 1836 by Bp of Salis. R. of Helmingham, Dio. Nor. 1861. (Patron, Ld Chan; Tithe, comm. 540*l*; Glebe, 37 acres; R.'s Inc. 600*l* and Ho; Pop. 320.) Formerly C. of East and West Knoyle, Dio. Salis. 1835–41; Min. of All Saints' Chapel, Bath, 1842–43; C. of West Teignmouth 1844, Old Alresford, Hunts, 1845; P. C. of Kingsclere, Woodlands, Dio. Win. 1845–61. [3]

CARDEW, James Walter, *West Knoyle, Mere, Wilts.*—St. John's Coll. Cam. B.A. 1833, M.A. 1837. R. and V. of Knoyle Oderon, *alias* Little, or West Knoyle, Dio. Salis. 1843. (Patrons, Rev. J. S. Stockwell and Lord Pembroke; Tithe, 428*l*; Glebe, 51 acres; R. and V.'s Inc. 469*l*; Pop. 187.) [4]

CARDEW, John Haydon, *Cheltenham* — Ex. Coll. Ox. B.A 1847; Deac. 1847, Pr. 1848. Chap. of the General Hospital, Cheltenham. Formerly C. of St. Paul's, Forest of Dean, Cleeve Prior, Worcestershire [5]

CARDWELL, J. H.—C. of St. James's, Clerkenwell, Lond. [6]

CAREW, John Warrington, *Clatworthy Rectory, Wiveliscombe, Somerset.*—Trin. Coll. Cam. LL.B. 1860; Deac. 1860 and Pr. 1861 by Bp of Wor. R. of Clatworthy, Dio. B. and W. 1861. (Patron, G. H. W. Carew, Esq; Tithe, 283*l*; Glebe, 93 acres; R.'s Inc. 400*l* and Ho; Pop. 310.) Formerly C. of Shrawley, Worcester, 1860–61. [7]

CAREW, Robert Baker, *Bickleigh Rectory, near Tiverton, Devon.*—Ch. Ch. Ox. B.A. 1846, M.A. 1849; Deac. 1847 and Pr. 1848 by Bp of Ex. R. of Bickleigh, Dio. Ex. 1849. (Patron, Sir W. P. Carew, Bart; Tithe, 359*l*; Glebe, 51 acres; R.'s gross Inc. 460*l* and Ho; Pop. 254.) Chap. to the Bp of Ex. 1850. [8]

CAREW, Robert Palk, *Rattery Vicarage, Totnes, Devon.* — Downing Coll. Cam. B.A. 1843, M.A. 1846; Deac. 1844 and Pr. 1845 by Bp of Ex. V. of Rattery, Dio. Ex. 1845. (Patron, Lady Carew; Tithe, 200*l*; V.'s Inc. 219*l* and Ho; Pop. 396.) [9]

CAREY, Adolphus Frederick, *Brixham, Devon.*—Wad. Coll. Ox. B.A. 1845, M.A. 1848; Deac. 1847 and Pr. 1848 by Bp of Pet. V. of Brixham with Chapelry of Churston Ferrars, Dio. Ex. 1861. (Patron, the Crown; V.'s Inc. 494*l* and Ho; Pop. Brixham 1398, Churston Ferrars 766.) Formerly Asst. Min. of St. Matthew's Chapel, Spring Gardens, Lond. 1859; British Chap. at Lugano, Switzerland, 1858–59. [10]

CAREY, Alfred Henry, *Owston Parsonage, Oakham.*—Ex. Coll. Ox. B.A. 1853, M.A. 1856; Deac. 1854 and Pr. 1855 by Bp of Ex. R. of Withcote, Dio. Pet. 1866. (Patron, F. Palmer, Esq; Glebe, 16 acres; P. C.'s Inc. 74*l* and Ho; Pop. 169.) P. C. of Owston, Dio. Pet. 1866. (Patron, F. Palmer, Esq; P. C.'s Inc. 72*l* and Ho; Pop. 169.) Formerly C. of Downe St. Mary, Devon, and Braughton and Waddenhoe, Northants. [11]

CAREY, A. Dobree, M.A., *Bawtry, Worksop, Yorks.*—P. C. of Bawtry with Austerfield, Dio. Lin. 1859. (Patron, Trin. Coll. Cam; Pop. Bawtry 389, Austerfield 1011.) [12]

CAREY, Charles, *Kingweston Rectory, Somerton, Somerset.*—Oriel Coll. Ox. B.A. 1838, M.A. 1841; Deac. 1840 and Pr. 1841 by Bp of Ox. R. of Kingweston, Dio. B. and W. 1859. (Patron, F. H. Dickinson, Esq; Tithe, 156*l*; Glebe, 29 acres; R.'s Inc. 195*l* and Ho; Pop. 172.) Formerly C. of Greinton, Somerset, and Spelsbury, Oxon. [13]

CAREY, Edmund Theodore, 2, *Hove Villas, Hove, Brighton.*—Trin. Coll. Cam. B.A. 1862, M.A. 1865; Deac. 1865 and Pr. 1866 by Bp of Chich. C. of Preston with Hove 1865. [14]

CAREY, Frederick Charles, *Guernsey.*—Wor. Coll. Ox. B.A. 1842; Deac. 1843, Pr. 1845. R. of St. Mary Câtel, Guernsey, Dio. Win. 1860. (Patron, the Governor; R.'s Inc. 150*l* and Ho; Pop. 2071.) Formerly C. of St. Martin's, Guernsey. [15]

CAREY, George, *Bridlington.*—Dub. A.B. 1846, Dur. Licen. Theol. 1848; Deac. 1848 and Pr. 1849 by Bp of Dur. P. C. of Lowthorpe with Ruston Parva P. C. Dio. York, 1853. (Patron, Colonel St. Quintin; P. C.'s Inc. 145*l*; Pop. Lowthorpe 171, Ruston Parva 161.) Formerly C. of Bishopwearmouth 1848, Stockton-on-Tees 1849. [16]

CAREY, Henry, *North Waltham, Micheldever, Hants.*—Wor. Coll. Ox. B.A. 1831, M.A. 1836; Deac. 1832, Pr. 1833. R. of North Waltham, Hants, Dio. Win. 1863. (Patron, Bp of Win; R.'s Inc. 379*l* and Ho; Pop. 484.) Surrogate. Formerly R. of All Saints', Southampton, 1855. [17]

CAREY, James Gaspard Le Marchant, *Snodland Rectory, near Rochester.*—Trin. Coll. Cam. 1st cl. Cl. Trip. Sen. Opt. and B.A. 1853, M.A. 1856; Deac. 1853 by Bp of Ox. Pr. 1854 by Bp of B. and W. R. of Snodland, Dio. Roch. 1866. (Patron, Bp. of Roch; Tithe, 406*l*; Glebe, 19 acres; R.'s Inc. 436*l* and Ho; Pop. 1600.) Formerly C. of Charlcombe, Somerset, 1853–56, Henny, Essex, 1856–66. [18]

CAREY, John Peter, *Rothersthorpe Vicarage, near Northampton.*—Dub. A.B. 1836; Deac. 1846 by Bp of Lich. Pr. 1846 by Bp. of Herf. V. of Rothersthorpe, Dio. Pet. 1849. (Patron, W. L. W. Samwells, Esq; Glebe, 65 acres; V.'s Inc. 113*l* and Ho; Pop. 289.) [19]

CAREY, J. D., *Sutton, Surrey.*—Chap. to the Poor Law Institution, Sutton, Surrey. [20]

CAREY, Osmond, B.A., *St. Matthew's, Guernsey.*—P. C. of St. Matthew's, Guernsey, Dio. Win. 1862. (Patron, the R. of St. Mary Câtel; P. C.'s Inc. 80*l*.) [21]

CAREY, Peter, *St. Saviour's, Guernsey.*—Trin. Coll. Cam. B.A. 1830, M.A. 1833, Deac. 1833, Pr. 1834. R. of St. Saviour's, Guernsey, Dio. Win. 1843. (Patron, the Governor; R.'s Inc. 150*l* and Ho; Pop. 942.) [22]

CAREY, Tupper, *Fifield Bavant, Salisbury.*—Ch. Ch. Ox. B.A. 1846, M.A. 1852; Deac. 1847 by Bp of B. and W. Pr. 1848 by Bp of Salis. R. of Fifield Bavant, Dio. Salis. 1861. (Patron, Marquis of Bath; Tithe, 146*l*; Glebe, 20 acres; R.'s Inc. 130*l*; Pop. 85.) P. C. of Ebbesborne Wake 1861. (Patron, Bp of Salis; P. C.'s Inc. 80*l*; Pop. 326.) Rural Dean. Formerly C. of Longbridge Deverill, 1847–59, East Harnham 1859–61. [23]

CARGILL, Clement, *Haigh, Wigan.*—C. of Haigh. [24]

CARGILL, James Dudley, *Southwell, Notts.*—St. John's Coll. Cam. B.D. 1860; Deac. 1851 by Bp of Llan. Pr. 1852 by Bp of G. and B. Head Mast. of Southwell Coll. Sch. 1863. Formerly 3rd Mast. of Bishop's Coll. Bristol, 1850; C. of St. Michael's, Bristol, 1851; 2nd Mast. and Chap. of Bishop's Coll. Bristol 1854; C. of Fretherne 1856. [25]

CARGILL, John, *Shirbrook, Pleasley (Derbyshire), near Mansfield.*—P. C. of Shirbrook, Pleasley, Dio. Lich. 1854. (Patron, R. of Pleasley; P. C.'s Inc. 35*l*; Pop 342.) [26]

CARGILL, Robert John, *Alrewas, near Lichfield.*—St. John's Coll. Cam. B.A. 1861; Deac. 1862 and Pr. 1863 by Bp of Pet. C. of Alrewas 1864. Formerly C. of Cotterstock 1862. [27]

CARLETON, Edward Crofton Ellis, *Bolton-road, Over Darwen, Lancashire.*—St. John's Coll. Cam. B.A. 1866; Deac. 1866. C. of St. John's, Over Darwen, 1866. [28]

CARLETON, the Hon. R., *Nateley-Scures, Basingstoke, Hants.*—R. of Nateley-Scures, Dio. Win. 1819. (Patron, Lord Dorchester; R.'s Inc. 200*l* and Ho; Pop. 271.) [29]

CARLETON, William, *The Cottage, Piltown, Kilkenny.*—Dom. Chap. to Lord Dorchester. [30]

CARLISLE, The Hon. and Right Rev. Samuel WALDEGRAVE, Lord Bishop of Carlisle, *Rose Castle, Carlisle.*—Ball. and All Souls Colls. Ox. 1st cl. Lit. Hum. 1st cl. Maths. and B.A. 1839, M.A. 1842, D.D. 1860; Deac. 1841 and Pr. 1842 by Bp of Ox. Consecrated Bp of Carlisle 1860. (Episcopal Jurisdiction, Cumberland, Westmoreland, and parts of Lancashire; Inc. of See, 4500*l* and residence; Pop. 266,591; acres, 1,563,726; Deaneries, 7; Benefices, 262; Curates, 47; Church Sittings, 48,472.) His Lordship was formerly Fell. of All Souls Coll. Ox. 1839; Public Exam. 1846; Select Preacher 1846; Bampton Lect. 1854; C. of St. Ebbe's, Oxford, 1841–44; R. of Barford St. Martin, Wilts, 1844–60; Can. Res. Treas. and Preb. of Calne in Salis. Cathl. 1857–60. Author, *Way of Peace, or Teaching of Scripture concerning Justification, Sanctification, and Assurance* (set forth in four sermons preached before the Univ. of Ox. in 1847–48), 3rd ed. 1861; *The Bible in Italy in* 1851 (a speech delivered before the Bedford Auxiliary Bible Soc.) 2nd edit. 1852, 3*d*; *Grieve not the Holy Spirit of God, and Christ Crucified the Christ for this and every Age* (two sermons before the Univ. of Ox.); *New Testament Millenarianism, or the Kingdom and Coming of Christ, as taught by Himself and his Apostles* (set forth in eight sermons preached before the Univ. of Ox. being the Bampton Lectures for 1854); *Words of Eternal Life* (sermons preached in Salisbury Cathl.) 1864; *Charge delivered in* 1861, London, W. Hunt and Co. [1]

CARLISLE, Charles Henry, *Hollinsclough, near Buxton.*—King's Coll. Lond. Associate, 1859; Deac. 1859 and Pr. 1860 by Bp of Lich. P. C. of Quarnford, Dio. Lich. 1863. (Patron, Sir J. H. Crewe, Bart; P. C.'s Inc. 96*l*; Pop. 525.) C. of Hollinsclough 1859. Formerly C. of Reapsmoor and Newtown. [2]

CARLISLE, John Herdman, *Southport.*—Wad. Coll. Ox. B.A. 1853, M.A. 1858; Deac. 1853 and Pr. 1854 by Bp of Ches. Formerly P. C. of St. Luke's, Formby, 1856–59. [3]

CARLON, Cecil Baylis.—Trin. Coll. Cam. Sen. Opt. B.A. 1854, M.A. 1859; Deac. 1856 and Pr. 1857 by Bp of Win. C. of Trinity, Marylebone, Lond. Formerly C. of Bishop's Sutton 1856–60, and Tichborne, Hants, 1860. [4]

CARLYLE, Thomas Fairfax, *Wray Parsonage, Melling, Lancashire.*—P. C. of Wray, Dio. Man. 1845. (Patrons, Trustees; P. C.'s Inc. 200*l* and Ho; Pop. 878.) [5]

CARLYON, Clement Winstanley, *St. Just Rectory, near St. Mawes, Cornwall.*—Clare Coll. Cam. B.A. 1833; R. of St. Just-in-Roseland, Dio. Ex. 1836. (Patron, J. Hawkins, Esq; R.'s Inc. 456*l* and Ho; Pop. 1546.) Chap. of Donative of St. Anthony-in-Roseland, Dio. Ex. 1849. (Patron, Sir S. T. Spry; Pop. 169.) Rural Dean. [6]

CARLYON, Edward, *Dibden Rectory, Southampton.*—Ex. Coll. Ox. B.A. 1830; Deac. 1831, Pr. 1832. R. of Dibden, Dio. Win. 1860. (Patron, E. N. Harvey, Esq; Tithe, 415*l*; Glebe, 7 acres; R.'s Inc. 400*l* and Ho; Pop. 513.) Formerly V. of Lamerton, Dio. Ex. 1840–60. [7]

CARLYON, Frederick, *Teversham Rectory, Cambridge.*—Pemb. Coll. Cam. B.A. 1837, M.A. 1863; Deac. 1839 and Pr. 1840 by Bp of G. and B. R. of Teversham, Dio. Ely, 1867. (Patron, Bp of Ely; R.'s Inc. 370*l* and Ho; Pop. 231.) Chap. to Bp of Ely. Formerly C. of Bitton 1839, Mevagissey 1842–49; R. of Stellenbosch, South Africa and Colonial Chap. 1849–62; C. of Hildersham and Great Abington, Cambs. 1862. [8]

CARLYON, John, *St. Merryn Vicarage, Padstow, Cornwall.*—Pemb. Coll. Cam. B.A. 1831; Deac. 1833 by Bp of Ex. Pr. 1834 by Bp of B. and W. V. of St. Merryn, Dio. Ex. 1857. (Patron, Bp. of Ex; Tithe—Imp. 510*l*, V. 250*l* 10*s*; V.'s Inc. 300*l* and Ho; Pop. [illegible].) Formerly C. of St. Merryn 1833–57. Author, *Family Sermons.* [9]

CARLYON, Philip, *Widdecombe Vicarage, Ashburton, Devon.*—Emman. Coll. Cam; 2nd Sen. Opt. and B.A. 1834, 1st Tyrwhitt's Heb. Scho. 1836, M.A. 1837; Deac. 1836, Pr. 1837. V. of Widdecombe-in-the-Moor, Devon, Dio. Ex. 1861. (Patron, D. and C. of Ex; Tithe, 280*l*; Glebe, 58 acres; P. C.'s Inc. 320*l*; Pop. 450.) Formerly P. C. of Revelstoke, Dio. Ex. 1856–61, St. James's, Exeter, 1842–56. Author, *A Catechism on the Distinctive Marks of the Church, and on Confirmation.* [10]

CARLYON, Thomas Stackhouse, *Glenfield Rectory, near Leicester.*—Pemb. Coll. Cam. Sen. Opt. and B.A. 1823, M.A. 1828; Deac. 1825 and Pr. 1826 by Bp of Ex. R. of Glenfield with Braunston and Kirkby, Dio. Pet. 1849. (Patron, J. B. Winstanley, Esq; Tithe, 150*l*; R.'s Inc. 800*l* and Ho; Pop. 1234.) [11]

CARNE, John James, *Eglos-Merther, Probus, Cornwall.*—Trin. Coll. Cam. Jun. Opt. and B.A. 1847, M.A. 1850; Deac. 1850 and Pr. 1851 by Bp of Roch. V. of Merther, Dio. Ex. 1862. (Patron, V. of Probus; V.'s Inc. 32*l*; Pop. 384.) Formerly C. of Brent Pelham, Herts, 1850–52, Illogan, Cornwall, 1853–56, Moreleigh, Devon, 1857–61. Author, *An Order of Metrical Psalms for Sundays and other Holy days, with Rules for the use of the Collects and Lessons,* Mozley, 1856; *An Attempt to identify the Domesday Manors in Cornwall,* 1865; *The Bishopric of Cornwall, Saxon Period,* 1867; and other Papers in *Journal of the Royal Institution of Cornwall.* [12]

CARNEGIE, John Hemery, *Cranbourne Vicarage, Dorset.*—St. Cath. Hall, Cam. B.A. 1836, M.A. 1839; Deac. 1837, Pr. 1838. V. of Cranbourne, Dio. Salis. 1842. (Patron, Marquis of Salisbury; Tithe—Imp. 520*l* 16*s* 3*d*, V. 86*l*; V.'s Inc. 151*l* and Ho; Pop. 1948.) Rural Dean; Surrogate. [13]

CARNSEW, Thomas Stone, *Poughill, Bude, Cornwall.*—St. John's Coll. Cam. B.A. 1855; Deac. 1855 by Bp of Lich. Pr. 1856 by Bp of Ex. V. of Poughill, Dio. Ex. 1857. (Patron, Ld Chan; Tithe, 124*l*; Glebe, 3½ acres; V.'s Inc. 136*l* and Ho; Pop. 363.) Formerly C. and Lect. of St. Peter's, Derby, 1855 and Poughill 1856. [14]

CARPENDALE, William Henry, *Cheltenham.*—Literate; Deac. 1857 and Pr. 1858 by Bp of Rip. C. of Trinity Chapel, Cheltenham. Formerly C. of South Brent, Somerset, and St. Andrew's, Leeds; Lieut. in the East Indian Navy. [15]

CARPENTER, Charles Thomas, *Kensie, Launceston, Cornwall.*—Sid. Coll. Cam. B.A. 1825; Deac. 1832 by Bp of Ex. Pr. 1834 by Bp of B. and W. Chap. to Lord Beaumont. Formerly C. of Week, St. German's, Devon, 1842. [16]

CARPENTER, George, *Christchurch, New Zealand.*—St. John's Coll. Cam. Jun. Opt. and B.A. 1843, M.A. 1846; Deac. 1844 and Pr. 1845 by Bp of Lon. Formerly V. of Stapleford, Wilts, 1854–65. [17]

CARPENTER, John.—C. of North and South Stoke, Lincolnshire. [18]

CARPENTER, Thomas, *Adlington Parsonage, Chorley, Lancashire.*—Dub. A.B. 1837; Deac. 1839 and Pr. 1840 by Bp of Ches. P. C. of Adlington, Dio. Man. 1839. (Patron, the R. of Standish; P. C.'s Inc. 145*l* and Ho; Pop. 3331.) [19]

CARPENTER, Thomas, *Syderstone, Fakenham, Norfolk.*—Sid. Coll. Cam. B.A. 1862, M.A. 1865; Deac. 1862 by Bp of Ches. Pr. 1864 by Bp of Win. C. of Syderstone 1866. Formerly C. of Ch. Ch. Southwark. Author, *Memoir of Rev. Dr. Carpenter.* [20]

CARPENTER, William, 3, *Burney-street, Greenwich, S.E.*—Sid. Coll. Cam. B.A. 1863; Deac. 1863 and Pr. 1864 by Bp of Ely. Mission District, Ch. Ch. Poplar (Stipend, 200*l*.) Formerly C. of Tydd St. Giles, Cambs. 1863–66. [21]

CARR, Arthur, *Wellington College, Wokingham, Berks.*—Corpus Coll. Ox. Open. Exhib. 1856, B.A. 1860, M.A. 1863, 2nd cl. Lit. Hum. 1860, Ellerton Theol. Prize 1862; Deac. 1861 and Pr. 1863 by Bp of Ox. Tut. and Asst. Mast. at Wellington Coll. [22]

CARR, Charles, *Whitworth, near Durham.*—Ex. Coll. Ox. B.A. 1835; Deac. 1837, Pr. 1838. P. C. of Whitworth, Dio. Dur. 1848. (Patrons, D. and C. of Dur; Tithe, 309*l*; Glebe, 20 acres; P. C.'s Inc. 340*l* and Ho; Pop. 3629.) [1]

CARR, Charles Heathcote, *St. John's Parsonage, Limehouse, London, E.*—Dub. A.B. 1850, A.M. 1860; Deac. 1849 and Pr. 1850 by Bp of Lich. P. C. of St. John's, Limehouse, Dio. Lon. 1853. (Patron, Bp of Lon; P. C.'s Inc. 324*l* and Ho; Pop. 9531.) Formerly C. of St. John's, Derby, 1849, St. Anne's, Limehouse, 1851. [2]

CARR, Cuthbert John, *Witton-Gilbert, Durham.*—Dur. B.A. 1841, Theol. Licen. 1842, M.A. 1843; Deac. 1842, Pr. 1843. P. C. of Witton-Gilbert with Kimblesworth R. Dio. Dur. 1850. (Patrons, D. and C. of Dur; Witton-Gilbert, Tithe, 301*l*; Glebe, 25 acres; P. C.'s Inc. 335*l* and Ho; Pop. Witton-Gilbert 948, Kimblesworth 37.) [3]

CARR, Edmund, *Dalston, near Carlisle.*—St. John's Coll. Cam. Lady Margaret Scho. and Wrang. B.A. 1848, M.A. 1851; Deac. 1849 and Pr. 1850 by Bp of Salis. V. of Dalston, Dio. Carl. 1866. (Patron, Bp of Carl; V.'s Inc. 400*l* and Ho; Pop. 2442.) Ex. Chap. to the Bp of Carl. Formerly C. of Barford St. Martin, near Salisbury, 1849 56; R. of Bonchurch, Isle of Wight, 1856–61; P. C. of Casterton, Westmoreland, 1861–66. Author, *A Pastor's Parting Words of Affectionate Counsel to his Flock*, 1861, 1*s*. [4]

CARR, Edmund Donald, *Woolstaston Rectory, Leebotwood, Shrewsbury.*—Emman. Coll. Cam. B.A. 1852; Deac. 1853 by Bp of Lich. Pr. 1855 by Bp of Herf. R. of Woolstaston, Dio. Herf. 1865. (Patron, Rev. F. H. Wolryche-Whitmore; Tithe, 144*l*; Glebe, 6 acres; R.'s Inc. 147*l* and Ho; Pop. 84.) Formerly P. C. of Ratlinghope 1857–65. Author, *A Night in the Snow—a Struggle for Life*, 1*s*. [5]

CARR, Edward.—Dub. A.B. 1853; Deac. 1853, Pr. 1854 by Bp of Lich. Formerly C. of Baslow, Derbyshire, 1853–55, East Grinstead, Sussex, All Souls', Langham-place, and All Saints', Gordon-square, Lond. [6]

CARR, Edward, *St. Helen's Parsonage, Lancashire.*—Dub. A.B. 1831, LL.B. and LL.D. 1852; Deac. 1832, Pr. 1833. P. C. of St. Helen's, Dio. Ches. 1846. (Patrons, Trustees; Tithe, 50*l*; Glebe, 4 acres; P. C.'s Inc. 500*l* and Ho; Pop. 16,026.) Dom. Chap. to Lord Dunsany; Surrogate. Author, *Sermons*; *A Sermon on Unity*, 1847; *A Sermon on the Intercession of Christ*; *A Visitation Sermon*; *Family Liturgy*; etc. [7]

CARR, Edwin Trevor Septimus, *St. Catherine's College, Cambridge.*—Ch. Coll. Cam. Scho. of, 1858, Bell's Scho. 1859, 1st cl. in Cl. Trip. 1862, Fell. of St. Cath. Coll. 1862; Deac. 1864 and Pr. 1866 by Bp of Ely. Tut. of St. Cath. Coll. 1867. Formerly Asst. Mast. at Shrewsbury Sch. 1862; Asst. Tut. at St. Cath. Coll. Cam. 1862. [8]

CARR, Henry Byne, *Whickham Rectory, Gateshead, Durham.*—Univ. Coll. Ox. B.A. 1833, M.A. 1836; Deac. 1836, Pr. 1838. R. of Whickham, Dio. Dur. 1846. (Patron, Ld Chan; Tithe, 464*l* 10*s*; Glebe, 200 acres; R.'s Inc. 737*l* and Ho; Pop. 6101.) Formerly C. of Tynemouth 1836, Northallerton 1838, Alnwick 1839. [9]

CARR, James, *Sherburn Hospital, Durham.*—Deac. 1820, Pr. 1821. Hon. Can. in Dur. Cathl. 1860; Mast. of Sherburn Hosp. 1862. (Patron, Bp of Dur; Master's Inc. 500*l*.) Formerly P. C. of St. Hilda's, South Shields, 1831. [10]

CARR, James Haslewood, *Broadstairs, Kent.* Dur. Fell. of, 1853, B.A. 1852, M.A. 1855; Deac. 1854 and Pr. 1856 by Bp. of B. and W. P. C. of Broadstairs, Dio. Cant. 1866. (Patron, V. of St. Peter's; P. C.'s Inc. 250*l*; Pop. 1459.) Formerly C. of Kelston, near Bath, Hurworth, near Darlington, St. John's, Edinburgh, and St. Mary's, Kilburn, Lond. [11]

CARR, John Anby, *Shipton-Oliffe, Andoversford, Cheltenham.*—New Inn Hall, Ox. B.A. 1843; Deac. 1844 and Pr. 1845 by Bp of Pet. R. of Shipton-Oliffe with Shipton-Sollars, Dio. G. and B. 1862. (Patron, W. B. Peachy, Esq; R.'s Inc. 450*l* and Ho; Pop. Shipton-Oliffe 255, Shipton-Sollars 80.) Formerly C. of Belshford. [12]

CARR, Thomas Arnold, *Cranbrook Vicarage, Kent.*—Brasen. Coll. Ox. B.A. 1851, M.A. 1854; Deac. 1852 and Pr. 1853 by Abp of Cant. V. of Cranbrook, Dio. Cant. 1858. (Patron, Abp of Cant; Tithe—App. 1000*l* and 65 acres of Glebe, V. 66*l* 6*s*; Glebe, 1 acre; V.'s Inc. 250*l* and Ho; Pop. 2995.) Formerly C. of Maidstone 1854–58, Folkestone 1852-55. [13]

CARR, Thomas William, *Barming Rectory, Maidstone.*—Wad. Coll. Ox. Hon. 4th cl. Lit. Hum. and B.A. 1853, M.A. 1857; Deac. 1856 and Pr. 1857 by Abp of Cant. R. of Barming, Dio. Cant. 1865. (Patron, Ld Chan; Tithe, 380*l*; Glebe, 69 acres; R.'s Inc. 610*l* and Ho; Pop. 589.) Formerly C. of St. Peter's with Holy Cross, Canterbury, 1856–57; R. of Loddington, Northants, 1857–65. [14]

CARR, Walter Raleigh, *Ware, Herts.*—Pemb. Coll. Ox. B.A. 1866; Deac. 1866 by Bp of Roch. C. of Ware 1866. [15]

CARRICK, John Lowry, *Witham Friary, Frome, Somerset.*—Queen's Coll. Ox. 4th cl. Lit. Hum. and B.A. 1849, M.A. 1852; Deac. 1851 by Bp of B. and W. Pr. 1852 by Bp of Ex. P. C. of Witham Friary, Dio. B. and W. 1858. (Patron, Duke of Somerset; P. C.'s Inc. 106*l* and Ho; Pop. 576.) Formerly C. of Witham Friary. [16]

CARRINGTON, The Very Rev. Henry, *Deanery, Bocking, Braintree, Essex.*—Caius Coll. Cam. B.A. 1837, M.A. 1840; Deac. 1838, Pr. 1839. Dean and R. of Bocking, Dio. Roch. 1845. (Patron, Abp of Cant; Tithe, 1267*l*; Glebe, 113 acres; R.'s Inc. 1407*l* and Ho; Pop. 3555.) [17]

CARRINGTON, Robert, *Barnes, Surrey.*—Corpus Coll. Cam. Scho. of, B.A. 1859, M.A. 1862; Deac. 1859 and Pr. 1860 by Bp of Win. C. of Barnes 1863. Formerly C. of Camden Ch. Camberwell, 1859. [18]

CARROLL, Frederick, *Tallington, Stamford, Lincolnshire.*—Ch. Coll. Cam. B.A. 1850, M.A. 1854; Deac. 1851 and Pr. 1852 by Bp of Ox. V. of Tallington, Dio. Lin. 1861. (Patron, Earl of Lindsey; V.'s Inc. 220*l* and Ho; Pop. 246.) Formerly C. of Dinder, Aldridge, Staffs. [19]

CARROLL, Thomas, *Oddington, Chipping Norton.*—Trin. Coll. Cam. B.A. 1863, M.A. 1866; Deac. 1866 and Pr. 1867 by Bp of G. and B. C. of Oddington 1867. Formerly C. of Stroud 1866. [20]

CARROW, Harry, 4, *St. Leonard's-terrace, Maida-hill, London, W.*—Trin. Coll. Cam. M.A; Deac. 1837 and Pr. 1838 by Bp of B. and W. Formerly R. of Loxton, Somerset, 1850–65. [21]

CARSON, Gustavus, *Liverpool.*—Assoc. Sec. of the Irish Society. [22]

CARSON, Thomas, *Scarning Rectory, East Dereham, Norfolk.*—St. Peter's Coll. Cam. B.A. and M.A; Deac. 1843 by Bp of Lich. Pr. 1844 by Bp of Lin. R. and V. of Scarning, Dio. Nor. 1848. (Patron, Chas. Lombe, Esq; Tithe—Imp. 260*l*, R. 496*l*; R.'s Inc. 500*l* and Ho; Pop. 693.) Surrogate. [23]

CARTE, Edward, *Gentleshaw, near Rugeley, Staffs.*—Dub. A.B. 1830; Deac. 1831 and Pr. 1832 by Bp of Lich. P. C. of Gentleshaw, Dio. Lich. 1837. (Patrons, Bp and D. and C. of Lich. alt; P. C.'s Inc. 100*l* and Ho; Pop. 625.) P. C. of Farewell, Staffs, Dio. Lich. 1838. (Patron, Marquis of Anglesey; Tithe, 129*l* 5*s* 3*d*; P. C.'s Inc. 50*l*; Pop. 189.) Dom. Chap. to the Marquis of Anglesey. [24]

CARTE, Thomas Sampson, M.A., *King's College, London, W.C.*—Asst. Mast. King's Coll. Sch. Lond. [25]

CARTER, Arthur Richard, 1, *Warwick-terrace, Upper Clapton, London, N.E.*—Queen's Coll. Ox. B.A. 1860, M.A. 1862; Deac. and Pr. 1860 by Bp of Dur. C. of St. Thomas's, Upper Clapton, 1866. Formerly C. of Whitworth and St. Paul's, Spennymoor, Durham, 1860, and Farrington Gurney and Stone Easton, Somerset, 1864. [26]

CARTER, Eccles James, *Kingston Vicarage, Taunton, Somerset.*—Ex. Colls. Ox. B.A. 1834, M.A.

1838; Deac. 1835, Pr. 1836. V. of Kingston, Dio. B. and W. 1851. (Patrons, D. and C. of Bristol; Tithe—App. 398*l* 5*s*, V. 200*l* 10*s*; Glebe, 2¾ acres; V.'s Inc. 218*l* and Ho; Pop. 892.) [1]

CARTER, Edward Nicholl, *Heckmondwike, Normanton.*—St. Bees 1821; Deac. 1825 and Pr. 1826 by Bp of York. P. C. of Heckmondwike, Dio. Rip. 1842. (Patron, V. of Birstal; P. C. Inc. 300*l* and Ho; Pop. 6344.) Formerly C. of Batley 1825–27, Mirfield 1827–38; P. C. of Lottersdale 1838–42. [2]

CARTER, George, *Compton-Beauchamp, Farringdon, Berks.*—St. John's Coll. Ox. 4th cl. Lit. Hum. and B.A. 1836; Deac. 1836, Pr. 1837. R. of Compton-Beauchamp, Dio. Ox. 1849. (Patron, Earl Craven; Tithe, 338*l*; Glebe, 22¾ acres; R.'s Inc. 368*l* and Ho; Pop. 128.) Dom. Chap. to Earl Craven. [3]

CARTER, George, *Falkingham, Lincolnshire.*—Emman. Coll. Cam. LL.B. 1853; Deac. 1850 by Bp of Ely, Pr. 1851 by Bp of Lin. R. of Falkingham with Laughton V. Dio. Lin. 1861. (Patron, Lord Aveland; R.'s Inc. 511*l*; Pop. 721.) Formerly C. of Coningsby 1852–61. [4]

CARTER, Henry James, *Duxford Vicarage, near Cambridge.*—Clare Coll. Cam. B.A. 1855, M.A. 1865; Deac. 1855 by Bp of Nor. Pr. 1856 by Bp of Ely. V. of St. John's, Duxford, Dio. Ely, 1865. (Patron, Clare Coll. Cam; V.'s Inc. 200*l* and Ho; Pop. 387.) Formerly C. of Trinity, Ely, 1855, Wisbeach 1858, Littleport 1860. [5]

CARTER, James, *Bridekirk Vicarage, Cockermouth.*—St. Bees, Librarian; Deac. 1833 and Pr. 1834 by Bp of Ches. V. of Bridekirk, Dio. Carl. 1851. (Patroness, Mrs. Dykes; Tithe—Imp. 291*l*; V. 58*l*; Glebe, 217 acres; V.'s Inc. 220*l* and Ho; Pop. 995.) Rural Dean of Cockermouth. Author, various Tracts. [6]

CARTER, James Henry, *Weaste, Manchester.*—Trin. Coll. Ox. B.A. 1849, M.A. 1865; Deac. 1849 and Pr. 1850 by Abp of York. P. C. of Weaste, Dio. Man. 1865. (Patrons, Five Trustees; P. C.'s Inc. 400*l* and Ho; Pop. 2000.) Formerly C. of Helmsley, Yorks, 1849–52, Waghen, Yorks, 1852–59, Eccles, Lancashire, 1859–65. [7]

CARTER, James Wray, 7, *Avenue-road, Bow-road, E.*—Literate; Deac. 1861, Pr. 1862. P. C. of Ch. Ch. Stratford, West Ham, Essex, 1864. (Patrons, Trustees; P. C.'s Inc. 135*l*; Pop. 4000.) Formerly C. of Wellington, Staffs, 1861–62, St. Peter's, Saffron-hill, London, 1863–64, Asst. Chap. at Tower Hamlets Cemetery 1863–66. [8]

CARTER, John, *Saxton Parsonage, Tadcaster, Yorks.*—St. John's Coll. Cam. B.A. 1824, M.A. 1827, S.T.P. 1840; Deac. 1825 and Pr. 1826 by Abp of York. P. C. of Saxton, Dio. York, 1832. (Patrons, Lord and Lady Ashtown; Tithe—Imp. 543*l* 7*s* 6*d*; Glebe, 3½ acres; P. C.'s Inc. 76*l* 10*s* and Ho; Pop. 461.) Formerly Head Mast. of Queen Elizabeth's Gr. Sch. Wakefield; C. of Aberford 1825–31. [9]

CARTER, John, *Frenchay Rectory, near Bristol.*—St. John's Coll. Ox. B.A. 1830, M.A. 1834, B.D. 1839; Deac. 1831 by Bp of Ox. Pr. 1832 by Bp of Roch. R. of Frenchay, Dio. G. and B. 1840. (Patron, St. John's Coll. Ox; Tithe, 153*l*; Glebe, 290 acres; R.'s Inc. 480*l* and Ho; Pop. 1446.) Formerly Fell. of St. John's Coll. Ox. [10]

CARTER, John, *York.*—R. of St. Michael's, Spurriergate, York, Dio. York, 1858. (Patron, Ld Chan; R.'s Inc. 91*l*; Pop. 486.) [11]

CARTER, John, *Sutton St. James, Hull.*—P. C. of Sutton St. James, Dio. York, 1865. (Patron, H. Broadley, Esq; P. C.'s Inc. 110*l*; Pop. 1176.) [12]

CARTER, John Edward, *Luddington Rectory, Goole, Yorks.*—Ex. Coll. Ox. B.A. 1841; Deac. 1842 and Pr. 1843 by Bp of Lin. R. of Luddington, Dio. Lin. 1865. (Patron, J. M. Carter, Esq; R.'s Inc. 510*l* and Ho; Pop. 900.) Formerly R. of Mistley with Bradfield, 1845. [13]

CARTER, L. M.—C. of St. John the Baptist's, Toxteth-park, Liverpool. [14]

CARTER, Richard Foster, *Rowner Rectory, Fareham, Hants.*—St. John's Coll. Cam. B.A. 1833; Deac. 1833 and Pr. 1834 by Bp of Win. R. of Rowner, Dio. Win. 1837. (Patron, Rev. C. P. Brune; Tithe, 402*l*; Glebe, 7 acres; R.'s Inc. 412*l* and Ho; Pop. 147.) [15]

CARTER, Robert Oliver, *Colwall-green, near Malvern, Herefordshire.*—Oriel Coll. Ox. B.A. 1859, M.A. 1861, 3rd cl. Lit. Hum; Deac. 1860 and Pr. 1861 by Bp of Wor. Head Mast. of the Gr. Sch. Colwall, and Private Tut. Formerly C. of Trinity, Coventry, 1860–61; Head. Mast of Merchant Taylors' Sch. Gt. Crosby, 1861–63. [16]

CARTER, Samuel Robert, *Brantham Rectory, Manningtree, Suffolk.*—Emman. Coll. Cam. B.A. 1842, M.A. 1845, B.D. 1852. R. of Brantham, Dio. Nor. 1855. (Patron, Emman. Coll. Cam; Tithe, 507*l*; Glebe, 22 acres; R.'s Inc. 550*l* and Ho; Pop. 445.) [17]

CARTER, Thomas, *Burnham Vicarage (Bucks), near Maidenhead.*—King's Coll. Cam. B.A. 1798, M.A. 1802; Deac. and Pr. 1802 by Bp of Salis. V. of Burnham with Boveney C. Dio. Ox. 1833. (Patron, Eton Coll; Tithe—Imp. 871*l*, V. 666*l* 10*s*; Glebe, 24¼ acres; V.'s Inc. 714*l* and Ho; Pop. 2233.) Vice-Provost of Eton Coll; Rural Dean. [18]

CARTER, Thomas, *Walton-on-the-Hill, Liverpool.*—Wor. Coll. Ox. 4th cl. Lit. Hum. and B.A. 1832, M.A. 1835; Deac. and Pr. 1833 by Bp of Ches. Chap. of the Borough Gaol, Liverpool. [19]

CARTER, Thomas, *Littleborough, Manchester.*—Queen's Coll. Ox. 3rd cl. Lit. Hum. B.A. 1853, M.A. 1857; Deac. 1855 by Bp of Ox. Pr. 1857 by Bp of Man. V. of Littleborough, Dio. Man. 1864. (Patron, V. of Rochdale; V.'s Inc. 300*l* and Ho; Pop. 5922.) Formerly C. of St. Andrew's, Bradfield, Berks, Garstang, St. Mary's, Ulverston, and St. Chad's, Rochdale. [20]

CARTER, Thomas Garden, *Linton Vicarage, Staplehurst, Kent.*—Trin. Coll. Cam. B.A. 1847, M.A. 1851; Deac. 1847 and Pr. 1848 by Bp of Roch. V. of Linton, Dio. Cant. 1859. (Patrons, Trustees of the late Earl Cornwallis; Tithe, 325*l*; Glebe, 1 acre; V.'s Inc. 270*l* and Ho; Pop. 625.) Formerly C. of Standon, Herts, and Littlebury, Essex, 1847–52; V. of St. Nicholas', Warwick, 1853–59. [21]

CARTER, Thomas Thellusson, *Clewer Rectory, near Windsor.*—Ch. Ch. Ox. 1st cl. Lit. Hum. and B.A. 1831, M.A. 1832; Deac. 1832 by Bp of Salis. Pr. 1833 by Bp of Lin. R. of Clewer, Dio. Ox. 1844. (Patron, Eton Coll; Tithe, 458*l* 19*s* 9*d*; Glebe, 24¼ acres; R.'s Inc. 520*l* and Ho; Pop. 3363.) [22]

CARTER, William, *Slingsby Rectory, near York.*—Queens' Coll. Cam. Jun. Opt. and B.A. 1830, M.A. 1833; Deac. 1830 and Pr. 1831 by Bp of Lin. R. of Slingsby, Dio. York. 1856. (Patron, Earl of Carlisle; Tithe, 419*l*; Glebe, 96 acres; R.'s Inc. 516*l* and Ho; Pop. 707.) [23]

CARTER, William Adolphus, *Eton College, Bucks.*—King's Coll. Cam. B.A. 1838, M.A. 1841. 2nd Mast. Eton Coll; Fell. of King's Coll. Cam. [24]

CARTER, William David, *Radcliffe, near Manchester.*—Queens' Coll. Cam. B.A. 1859, M.A. 1862; Deac. 1859 and Pr. 1860 by Bp of Man. P. C. of St. John's, Stand-lane, Dio. Man. 1866. (Patrons, Bp of Man. Earl Derby, and R. of Stand; P. C.'s Inc. 90*l*.) Formerly C. of Walmersley 1859, Radcliffe 1862, Stand 1864. [25]

CARTER, William Edward Dickson, *Shipton-under-Wychwood, near Chipping-Norton, Oxon.*—New Coll. Ox. late Fell. of, B.A. 1844, M.A. 1847; Deac. 1844, Pr. 1845. V. of Shipton-under-Wychwood, Dio. Ox. 1852. (Patron, Bp of Ox; Tithe—Imp. 760*l* and 75¾ acres of Glebe, V. 223*l* 17*s* 6*d*; Glebe, 85 acres; V.'s Inc. 402*l* and Ho; Pop. 1954.) Surrogate; a Magistrate for the Co. of Oxon. [26]

CARTER-SQUIRE, John Abraham, *Healey Parsonage, Bedale, Yorks.*—Ch. Coll. Cam. B.A. 1846, M.A. 1849; Deac. 1847 and Pr. 1848 by Bp of Rip. P. C. of Healey, Dio. Rip. 1849. (Patron, V. of Masham; P. C.'s Inc. 182*l* and Ho; Pop. 900.) [27]

CARTHEW, James, *Spa, Germany.*—Ex. Coll. Ox. 4th cl. Lit. Hum. and B.A. 1838, M.A. 1840; Deac. 1840, Pr. 1841. Chap. at Spa. Formerly C. of Northfleet, near Gravesend. [1]

CARTHEW, W. H. M.—C. of Brough, Westmoreland. [2]

CARTLEDGE, William Ashforth, *Holgate-terrace, York.*—St. John's Coll. Cam. B.A. 1843, M.A. 1847; Deac. 1843 and Pr. 1844 by Bp of Ches. R. of St. Paul's, City and Dio. York, 1856. (Patrons, Trustees; Inc. uncertain; Pop. 2409.) Formerly R. of Dalby, Yorks, 1848–56. [3]

CARTMAN, John, *Skipton-in-Craven, Yorks.*—Trin. Coll. Cam. B.A. 1832, M.A. 1847; Deac. 1845 and Pr. 1846 by Bp of Nor. 2nd Mast. of Skipton Gr. Sch. [4]

CARTMAN, William, *Skipton-in-Craven, Yorks.*—Literate; Deac. 1823 and Pr. 1824 by Abp of York. Head Mast. of Skipton Gr. Sch. Formerly C. of Bingley-Skipton, and of Thirsk, Yorks. [5]

CARTMELL, James, *Christ's College, Cambridge.*—Emman. Coll. Cam. 7th Wrang. B.A. 1833, M.A. 1836, B.D. 1846, D.D. 1849; Deac. 1833 by Bp of Lin. Pr. 1835 by Bp of Carl. Mast. of Ch. Coll. 1849; Chap. in Ordinary to the Queen 1851. Formerly Fell. and Tut. of Ch. Coll. [6]

CARTMELL, John, *Ashfordby, Melton Mowbray.*—Pemb. Coll. Cam. Sen. Opt. and B.A. 1843, M.A. 1846; Deac. 1845 and Pr. 1846 by Bp of Pet. R. of Ashfordby, Dio. Pet. 1857. (Patron, Rev. F. G. Burnaby; Tithe, 2*l* 2*s*; Glebe, 252 acres; R.'s Inc. 455*l*; Pop. 485.) Formerly C. of Barkestone and Plungar, Leicestershire. [7]

CARTWRIGHT, Anson William Henry.—Queens' Coll. Cam. B.A. 1856, M.A. 1866; Deac. 1859 by Bp of Wor. Pr. 1860 by Bp of Salis. C. of St. Peter's, Stepney, 1867. Formerly C. of St. Michael's, East Teignmouth, 1859–60, St. John's, Hammersmith, 1860–63, St. Paul's, Bow Common, 1863–67. Author, *Sermons on Subjects*, Bosworth, 1866, 2s 6d. [8]

CARTWRIGHT, Charles Johnson, *Bradfield, Bury St. Edmunds.*—R. of Bradfield with Rushbrook, Dio. Ely, 1858. (Patron, Marquis of Bristol; Tithe—App. 7*l*, R. 430*l* 7*s*; Rushbrook, Tithe, 263*l* 10*s* 6*d*; R.'s Inc. 693*l*; Pop. Bradfield 427, Rushbrook 185.) [9]

CARTWRIGHT, Frederick William, *Aynhoe, Banbury, Northants.*—Ch. Ch. Ox. 1841. R. of Aynhoe, Dio. Pet. 1862. (Patron, W. C. Cartwright, Esq; R.'s Inc. 550*l* and Ho; Pop. 595.) [10]

CARTWRIGHT, George Leopold, *Brislington, near Bristol.*—Ex. Coll. Ox. B.A. 1837, M.A. 1839; Deac. 1838, Pr. 1839. C. of Brislington 1839; Chap. to the Keynsham Union 1845. [11]

CARTWRIGHT, John, *Bury St. Edmunds.* [12]

CARTWRIGHT, John, 22, *Old Elvet, Durham.*—Ch. Coll. Cam. B.A. 1827, M.A. 1830; Deac. 1827, Pr. 1828. Min. Can. of Dur. Cathl. 1834. Formerly P. C. of Ferryhill 1843–44, Wilton-Gilbert 1849–51. Author, *Translations from Goethe and Euripides.* [13]

CARTWRIGHT, John Hockin, *Winterbourne-Dantsey, Marlborough, Wilts.*—Ex. Coll. Ox. B.A. 1828; Deac. 1829 by Bp of G. Pr. 1831 by Bp of B. and W. P. C. of Winterbourne-Dantsey, Dio. Salis. 1844. (Patron, Bp of Salis; Tithe—App. 245*l*; P. C.'s Inc. 80*l*; Pop. 171.) P. C. of Winterbourne-Earls, Dio. Salis. 1851. (Patron, Bp of Salis; Tithe—App. 490*l*; Glebe, 137 acres; P. C.'s Inc. 160*l*; Pop. 276.) [14]

CARTWRIGHT, Robert, *Ellingham Rectory, Bungay, Suffolk.*—Ch. Coll. Cam. B.A. 1825; Deac. 1825, Pr. 1827. R. of Ellingham, Dio. Nor. 1848. (Patrons, Trustees; Tithe, 339*l*; Glebe, 114*l*; R.'s Inc. 453 and Ho; Pop. 386.) Formerly R. of Thwaite, Norfolk, 1838–66. [15]

CARTWRIGHT, Theodore John, *Preston-Bagot, Henley-in-Arden, Warwickshire.*—Univ. Coll. Ox. 1st cl. Math. et Phy. 1827, B.A. 1828, M.A. 1829; Deac. 1829, Pr. 1830. R. of Preston-Bagot, Dio. Wor. 1831. (Patron, the present R; Tithe, 342*l*; Glebe, 20 acres; R.'s Inc. 380*l* and Ho; Pop. 220.) [16]

CARTWRIGHT, T. E., *Braintree, Essex.*—V. of Braintree, Dio. Roch. 1865. (Patron, Rev. C. J. Cartwright; V.'s Inc. 360*l* and Ho; Pop. 4620.) [17]

CARTWRIGHT, William, *Westbury-upon-Trym, near Bristol.*—P. C. of Westbury-upon-Trym with Redland C. Dio. G. and B. 1847. (Patron, Rev. Charles Vivian; P. C.'s Inc. 650*l* and Ho; Pop. 5290.) [18]

CARTWRIGHT, William Henry, *Butcombe, Wrington, Somerset.*—Trin. Coll. Ox. B.A. 1821, M.A. 1826. R. of Butcombe, Dio. B. and W. 1848. (Patron, the present R; Tithe, 210*l*; R.'s Inc. 250*l*; Pop. 223.) [19]

CARTWRIGHT, William Lyster, *Whitstable, Kent.*—St. Edm. Hall, Ox. B.A. 1861, M.A. 1862; Deac. 1862 by Bp of St. A. Pr. 1866 by Abp of Cant. C. of Whitstable and Seasalter 1866. Formerly C. of Llandrinio 1862; 3rd Mast. Oswestry Gr. Sch; Head Mast. St. Ann's, Streatham Hill, 1863. [20]

CARUS, William, *The Close, Winchester.*—Trin. Coll. Cam. Wrang. 1st cl. Cl. Trip. and B.A. 1827, M.A. 1830; Deac. 1828 by Bp of Ely, Pr. 1830 by Bp of Lich. Can. Res. of Win. Cathl. 1851 (Value, 755*l* and Res.) P. C. of Ch. Ch. Winchester, Dio. Win. 1860. (Patrons, Trustees; P. C.'s Inc. 68*l*; Pop. 700.) Rural Dean. Formerly C. of St. Michael's, Cambridge, 1828; Lect. of Trin. Ch. Cambridge, 1832; C. of St. Mary's, Cambridge, 1833; P. C. of Trinity 1837; P. C. of St. Mary's 1842; V. of Romsey 1851; R. of St. Maurice's, Winchester, 1854. Late Fell. of Trin. Coll. Cam. 1829, Sen. Dean 1836, Sen. Fell. 1850; Select Preacher to Univ. 1854, '59, and '66. Author, *Simeon's Memoirs*, 8vo. 1847, 14*s*, 12mo. Hatchards, 1848, 7*s*; Visitation, Ordination, Cathedral, and University Sermons. [21]

CARUS-WILSON, Charles, *Ramsgate.*—Corpus Coll. Cam. B.A. 1847, M.A. 1850; Deac. 1848 and Pr. 1849 by Bp of Man. V. of Ramsgate, Dio. Cant. 1867. (Patron, Abp of Cant; V.'s Inc. 480*l* and Ho; Pop. 9243.) Formerly V. of Eastry, Kent, 1854–67. [22]

CARVER, Alfred James, *Dulwich College, London, S.*—Trin. Coll. Cam. Bell's Univ. Scho. Sen. Opt. 1st cl. Cl. Trip. and B.A. 1849, M.A. 1852; Deac. 1853 by Bp of Ely, Pr. 1854 by Bp of Lon. Mast. of Dulwich Coll. and Head Mast. of Upper Sch. in Dulwich Coll. 1858. Formerly C. of St. Olave's, Old Jewry, Lond; 2nd Mast. of St. Paul's Sch. Lond. 1852; Fell. and Cl. Lect. of Queens' Coll. Cam. [23]

CARVER, Charles, *Walton-le-Soken, Colchester.*—Corpus Coll. Cam. B.A. 1840; Deac. 1840 and Pr. 1841 by Bp of Pet. V. of Walton-le-Soken, Dio. Roch. 1862. (Patroness, Elizabeth Burgess; Tithe, 133*l*; Glebe, 1 acre; V.'s Inc. 143*l* and Ho; Pop. 697.) Formerly C. of Farthingstone, Northants, 1840–41. [24]

CARVER, David, *Parsonage, Hyson-green, Nottingham.*—Caius Coll. Cam. B.A. 1845; Deac. 1845, Pr. 1846. P. C. of the Consolidated District Chapelry of St. Paul's, Hyson-green, Notts, Dio. Lin. 1852. (Patrons, Trustees; P. C.'s Inc. 212*l* and Ho; Pop. 2858.) [25]

CARVER, Jeremiah W., *St. John's Parsonage, Finchingfield, Braintree, Essex.*—Caius Coll. Cam. B.A. 1834; Deac. 1835 by Bp of Lon. Pr. 1836 by Bp of Chich. P. C. of St. John's, Finchingfield, Dio. Lon. 1849. (Patron, Bp of Win; P. C.'s Inc. 100*l* and Ho; Pop. 722.) [26]

CARVER, Jonathan, *Thursford Parsonage, Walsingham, Norfolk.*—St. Bees; Deac. 1847 and Pr. 1849 by Bp of Nor. C. of Great Snoring and Thursford 1850. Formerly C. of Wells-next-the-Sea 1847–50. [27]

CARVER, W. J., *Winfarthing, Diss, Norfolk.*—R. of Winfarthing, Dio. Nor. 1816. (Patron, Earl of Albemarle; Pop. 615.) [28]

CARWARDINE, Henry Alexander, *Tolleshunt-Major, Maldon, Essex.*—St. John's Coll. Cam. B.A. 1853, M.A. 1856. V. of Tolleshunt-Major, Dio. Roch. 1856. (Patron, Rev. C. W. Carwardine; Tithe, 158*l*; Glebe, 20 acres; R.'s Inc. 186*l*; Pop. 438.) [29]

CARWARDINE, John Bryan, *St. Lawrence, Maldon, Essex.*—Emman. Coll. Cam. B.A. 1818, M.A.

1822; Deac. 1818, Pr. 1820. R. of St. Lawrence, Newland, Dio. Roch. 1829. (Patron, Ld Chan; Tithe, 550*l*; Glebe, 6 acres; R.'s Inc. 556*l* and Ho; Pop. 184.) [1]

CARWARDINE, Thomas William, *Cavenham, near Mildenhall, Suffolk.*—St. John's Coll. Cam. B.A. 1841, M.A. 1844; Deac. 1844, Pr. 1845. V of Cavenham, Dio. Ely, 1845. (Patron, Ld Chan; Glebe, 300 acres; V.'s Inc. 113*l*; Pop. 229.) [2]

CARWITHEN, George W. T., *Ashprington, Totnes, Devon.*—Oriel Coll. Ox. B.A. 1832, M.A. 1835; Deac. 1833, Pr. 1834. R. of Ashprington, Dio. Ex. 1859. (Patron, the present R; R.'s Inc. 537*l*; Pop. 537.) Formerly P. C. of Frithelstock, Devon, 1841–56. [3]

CARWITHEN, George E.—Chap. of H.M.S. "Hibernia." [4]

CARWITHEN, John Charles, *Stokenham, Kingsbridge.*—Ex. Coll. Ox. 1833, B.A. 1837; Deac. 1840, Pr. 1841. V. of Stokenham with C. of Chivelstone, and C. of Sherford, Dio. Ex. 1861. (Patron, the Crown; Stokenham, Tithe, 360*l* 5*s*, Glebe, 1 acre; Chivelstone, Tithe, 164*l* 10*s*; Sherford, Tithe, 171*l* 5*s*; V.'s Inc. 841*l* and Ho; Pop. Stokenham 1566, Chivelstone 523, Sherford 404.) Dom. Chap. to Earl Fortescue; Rural Dean. Formerly R. of Challacombe 1848–61. [5]

CARWITHEN, William Henry, *Aylesbeare Vicarage, near Exeter.*—Wor. Coll. Ox. Hon. 4th cl. Lit. Hum. B.A. 1834, M.A. 1837; Deac. 1836, Pr. 1837. V. of Aylesbeare with Newton Poppleford C. Dio. Ex. 1848. (Patron, the present R; Tithe, 143*l* 15*s* 2*d*; Glebe, 59 acres; V.'s Inc. 210*l* and Ho; Pop. Aylesbeare 418, Newton Poppleford 661.) Surrogate. [6]

CARY, Charles Thomas, *Kingsbury, near Birmingham.*—Magd. Hall, Ox. B.A. 1829, M.A. 1832. V. of Kingsbury, Dio. Wor. 1832. (Patron, Ld Chan; Tithe, 44*l* 16*s* 1½*d*; V.'s Inc. 125*l*; Pop. 1428.) [7]

CARY, James Walter, *Southampton.*—Magd. Hall, Ox. B.A. 1824, M.A. 1828, B.D. and D.D. 1846. P. C. of St. Paul's, Southampton, Dio. Win. 1862. [8]

CARY, Lucius Ormsby, *Old Romney, Kent.*—Trin. Coll. Cam. B.A. 1860; Deac. 1860. C. of Old Romney. Formerly C. of St. Mary's Extra, Southampton. [9]

CARY, Offley Henry, *Warrington.*—Ch. Ch. Ox. B.A. 1860, M.A. 1862; Deac. 1861 and Pr. 1862 by Bp of Ox. Head Mast. of the Gr. Sch. Warrington, 1863. Formerly C. of Dry Sandford, near Oxford, 1862–63 [10]

CASBORNE, Walter John Spring, *Newhouse, Pakenham, Bury St. Edmunds.*—Trin. Coll. Cam. B.A. 1812, M.A. 1819; Deac. 1813, Pr. 1814. Formerly C. of Thurston, near Bury St. Edmunds. [11]

CASE, Thomas, *Horton Vicarage, Wimborne, Dorset.*—Wor. Coll. Ox. B.A. 1831; Deac. 1832 by Bp of Roch. Pr. 1833 by Bp of G. and B. V. of Horton with Woodlands, Dio. Salis. 1839. (Patron, Earl of Shaftesbury; Tithe, Horton, 73*l* 2*s* 6*d*, Woodlands, 78*l* 17*s* 6*d*; Glebe, 3 acres; V.'s Inc. 152*l* and Ho; Pop Horton 431, Woodlands 496.) [12]

CASEY, Henry Ernest.—C. of Upton with Chalvey, Bucks. [13]

CASHEL, Frederick, *Oswestry, Salop.*—Dub. A.B. 1842; Deac. 1843 by Bp of Meath, Pr. 1843 by Abp of Armagh. P. C. of Trinity, Oswestry, Dio. St. A. 1851. (Patron, V. of Oswestry; P. C.'s Inc. 150*l*; Pop. 2683.) [14]

CASHER, Charles Edward, *Albert street, Blandford, Dorset.*—Caius Coll. Cam. Jun. Opt. Coll. Exhib. B.A. 1855, M.A. 1858; Deac. 1858 and Pr. 1859 by Bp of Win. C. of Durweston with Bryanston, Dorset, 1864. Formerly C. of Ch. Ch. North Brixton, Surrey, 1858–64. [15]

CASHMAN, George Grey, 1, *Mid Portland-terrace, Southampton.*—Dub. A.B. 1842, A.M. 1849; Deac. 1842 and Pr. 1843 by Bp. of Ches. Formerly C. of St. Paul's, Bury, 1842–44, St. Mark's, Bath, 1844–47, All Saints', Southampton, 1847–50, Holy Rood, Southampton, 1850–52 and 1861–66, St. Michael's, Southampton, 1856–59. [16]

CASS, Charles William, *Telham House, near Battle, Sussex.*—Emman. Coll. Cam. B.A. 1848, M.A. 1851; Deac. 1849 and Pr. 1850 by Bp of Herf. Formerly C. of Hope-under-Dinmore, Herefordshire, 1849–51, Bexhill, Sussex, 1851–52; V. of Harlington, Sussex, 1852–62. [17]

CASS, Frederick Charles, *The Rectory, Monken Hadley, Middlesex.*—Ball. Coll. Ox. B.A. 1846, M.A. 1849; Deac. 1850 and Pr. 1851 by Bp of Chich. R. of Monken Hadley, Dio. Lon. 1860. (Patron, the present R; R.'s Inc. 200*l* and Ho; Pop. 1053.) Formerly C. of Hove, Sussex, 1850, Penshurst, Kent, 1853, St. Mary's, Dover, 1858. [18]

CASS, George Grainger, *Middlesmoor, near Pateley Bridge, Yorks.*—Wad. Coll. Ox. B.A. 1858; Deac. 1859 and Pr. 1860 by Bp of Rip. P. C. of Middlesmoor, Dio. Rip. 1864. (Patron, V. of Kirkby Malzeard; Glebe, 20 acres; P. C.'s Inc. 127*l* and Ho; Pop. 666.) Formerly C. of St. John's, Huddersfield, and Whitkirk, near Leeds. [19]

CASS, William Anthony, *Westgate Common, Wakefield.*—Deac. 1854 and Pr. 1855 by Bp of Rip. P. C. of Westgate Common, Wakefield, Dio. Rip. 1861. (Patron, P. C. of Alverthorpe; P. C.'s Inc. 164*l*.) Formerly C. of Horbury 1854–61. [20]

CASSELS, Andrew, *Staincliffe Hall, near Dewsbury.*—St. John's Coll. Cam. B.A. 1829, M.A. 1833; Deac. 1830 and Pr. 1831 by Bp of Ches. V. of Batley, Dio. Rip. 1839. (Patrons, Earl Cardigan and Earl Wilton alt; Tithe, 130*l*; Glebe, 39½ acres; V.'s Inc. 300*l* and Ho; Pop. 14,173.) Surrogate. Formerly P. C. of St. Peter's, Morley, near Leeds, 1831–39; C. of St. Philip's, Salford, Manchester, 1830–31. [21]

CASSIDI, William, *Grindon, Stockton-on-Tees.*—Dub. A.B. 1836; Deac. 1837 and Pr. 1838 by Bp of Dur. V. of Grindon, Dio. Dur. 1841. (Patron, Earl Vane; Tithe, 100*l*; Glebe, 85 acres; V.'s Inc. 250*l* and Ho; Pop. 830.) Formerly P. C. of St. Giles', Durham, 1839–41. [22]

CASSIN, Burman, *Battersea, Nine Elms, Surrey.*—Trin. Coll. Cam. B.A. 1858; Deac. 1858 by Bp of Win. P. C. of St. George's, Battersea, Dio. Win. 1860. (Patron, V. of Battersea; P. C.'s Inc. 158*l* and Ho; Pop. 3697.) Formerly C. of Merton. [23]

CASSON, George, *Wold Rectory, near Northampton.*—Brasen. Coll. Ox. 2nd cl. Lit. Hum. and B.A. 1831; Deac. 1834 by Bp of Ox. Pr. 1835 by Bp of Lon. R. of Wold *alias* Old, Dio. Pet. 1842. (Patron, Brasen. Coll. Ox; Glebe, 340 acres; R.'s Inc. 478*l* and Ho; Pop. 472.) Formerly Fell. of Brasen. Coll. Ox. [24]

CASSON, Henry Crozier, *Thetford, Ely.*—Ch. Coll. Cam. B.A. 1862; Deac. 1862 by Bp of Ely, Pr. 1863 by Bp of Lich. C. of Stretham with Thetford 1864. Formerly C. of Long Eaton 1862–64. [25]

CASSON, John, *Ironville, Alfreton, Derbyshire.*—Deac. 1823, Pr. 1824. P. C. of Ironville, Dio. Lich. 1850. (Patron, Francis Wright, Esq. Osmaston Manor; P. C.'s Inc. 185*l* and Ho; Pop. 2293.) [26]

CASTLEDEN, George, *Ramsgate.*—Queens' Coll. Cam. B.A. 1865; Deac. 1866 by Abp of Cant. C. of Ch. Ch. Ramsgate, 1866. [27]

CASTLEHOW, William, *North Cadbury, Castle Carey, Somerset.*—Emman. Coll. Cam. 14th Wrang. and B.A. 1842, M.A. 1845, B.D. 1852; Deac. 1845, Pr. 1846. R. of North Cadbury, Dio. B. and W. 1861 (Patron, Emman. Coll. Cam; Tithe, 489*l* 12*s* 2½*d*; Glebe, 144½ acres; R.'s Inc. 780*l* and Ho; Pop. 997.) Fell and Hebrew Lect. of Emman. Coll. Cam. [28]

CASTLEMAN, William Henry.—Trin. Coll. Cam. B.A. 1859; Deac. 1860 by Bp of Win. C. of Deane and Ash, Whitchurch, Hants. Formerly C. of Crawley 1860. [29]

CASTLEY, Elias.—St. Bees; Deac. 1858 and Pr. 1859 by Abp of York. C. of Skelton with Brotton, Redcar, Yorks. Formerly C. of St. John's, Darlington, 1860, Hinderwell, Yorks. 1858–60. [30]

CASTLEY, Joseph, *Pembroke College, Cambridge.*—Pemb. Coll. Cam. 1st cl. in Cl. Trip. B.A. 1859. M.A. 1862; Deac. 1861 and Pr. 1862 by Bp of Wor. Fell and Dean of Pemb. Col. Formerly Asst. Mast. at Rossal Sch. and 2nd Mast. of Leamington Coll. [1]

CASWALL, Henry, *Figheldean Vicarage, near Amesbury, Wilts.*—Kenyon Coll. Ohio, U.S. M.A. 1834, Trin. Coll. Hartford, Connecticut, U.S. D.D. 1854; Deac. 1831 by Bp of Ohio, Pr. 1837 by Bp of Indiana. V. of Figheldean, Dio. Salis. 1848. (Patron, Bp of Salis; Tithe, App. 670*l* 10*s*, Imp. 201*l* 15*s*, V. 180*l*; Glebe, 2¾ acres; V.'s Inc. 350*l* and Ho; Pop. 472.) Preb. of Bedminster and Redcliffe, in Salis. Cathl. Formerly held two R.'s in the United States. Author, *America and the American Church*, 2 edits. 7*s* 6*d*; *Prophet of the Nineteenth Century*, 1843, 7*s* 6*d*; *City of the Mormons*, 2 edits. 1842–43, 1*s* 6*d*; *Jerusalem Chamber*, 1850, 1*s* 6*d*; *Pilgrimage to Canterbury*, 1852, 6*d*; *Scotland and the Scottish Church*, 1853, 5*s*; *Western World Revisited*, 1854, 5*s*; *The Martyr of the Pongas*, 1858, 5*s*. 6*d*. [2]

CASWALL, Robert Clarke, *Figheldean, near Amesbury, Wilts.*—St. Edm. Hall, Ox. B.A. 1861; Deac. 1862 and Pr. 1863 by Bp of Salis. C. of Figheldean. [3]

CATCHPOLE, James, *Clanville, Andover, Hants.*—C. of Weyhill, Hants. [4]

CATHCART, Nassau, *Trinity Parsonage, Guernsey.*—Dub. A.B. 1848, A.M. 1865; Deac. and Pr. 1852 by Bp of Down. P. C. of Trinity, Guernsey, Dio. Win. 1861. (Patrons, Trustees; P. C.'s Inc. 300*l*; Pop. 4000.) Formerly C. of St. Anne's and St. George's, Belfast; P. C. of St. Thomas's, Dugort, Achill. [5]

CATLOW, J. S., M.A., *St. John's College, Oxford.*—Fell. of St. John's Coll. Ox. [6]

CATO, Thomas Ensor, *Wye, Ashford, Kent.*—Oriel Coll. Ox. B.A. 1860, M.A. 1864; Deac. 1862, Pr. 1863. P. C. of Wye, Dio. Cant. 1866. (Patron, Earl of Winchelsea; P. C.'s Inc. 70*l* and Ho; Pop. 1594.) Formerly C. of Ashford. [7]

CATOR, Charles, *Stokesley Rectory, Yorks.*—Brasen. Coll. Ox. B.A. 1809, M.A. 1812; Deac. 1810 and Pr. 1811 by Abp of York. R of Stokesley, Dio. York, 1835. (Patron, Abp of York; Tithe, 1206*l* 6*s* 4*d*; Glebe, 90 acres; R.'s Inc. 1400*l* and Ho; Pop. 2401.) Author, *Division Dangerous to the Church of Christ in England*, 1826; *The Work of an Evangelist*, 1833; *The Necessity of a National Church*, Letter to Sir R. Peel, 3 edits. 1835–36; *Doctrine and Ritual of the Church of England*, Letter to the Abp of Cant. 1836; etc. [8]

CATOR, William Albemarle Bertie, *Carshalton Rectory, Surrey.*—Mert. Coll. Ox. B.A. 1843; Deac. 1844, Pr. 1845. R. of Carshalton, Dio. Win. 1845. (Patron, John Cator, Esq; Tithe, 875*l*; Glebe, 11 acres; R.'s Inc. 920*l* and Ho; Pop. 2538.) [9]

CATOR, William Lumley Bertie, *Wragby, Lincolnshire.*—Trin. Coll. Cam. B.A. 1856; Deac. 1858 by Bp of Salis. C. of Wragby. Formerly C. of Wilton, Wilts. [10]

CATTLE, John William, *Dewlish, Dorchester.*—Magd. Coll. Ox. B.A. 1854, M.A. 1859; Deac. 1856 and Pr. 1858 by Bp of Wor. C. of Dewlish. Formerly C. of Ledbury and of Stoke Prior, Worc. [11]

CATTLEY, Henry Thomas, *Fulford, near York.*—St. John's Coll. Ox. B.A. 1849, M.A. 1861; Deac. 1850 and Pr. 1851 by Abp of York. C. of Fulford 1866. Formerly C. of St. Paul's, Hull, 1850–57; P. C. of Sutton St. James-in-Holderness 1857–65. [12]

CATTLEY, Richard, *Worcester.*—Wor. Coll. Ox. B.A. 1848, M.A. 1851; Deac. 1849, Pr. 1850. Min. Can. of Wor. Cathl. 1855 (Value 150*l*). Surrogate. [13]

CATTLEY, Stephen Reed, *Clapham-rise, London, S.W.*—Queens' Coll. Cam. B.A. 1830, M.A. 1833; Deac. 1830, Pr. 1831. P. C. of St. John's, Clapham, Dio. Win. 1857. (Patron, R. of Clapham; Pop. 2543.) Chap. to the Earl of Scarborough 1835; Chap. to the Female Orphan Asylum, Lambeth, 1842. Formerly R. of Bagthorpe, Dio. Nor. 1832–57. Author, *The First Stone of a New Building, or Remarks upon Discharged Prisoners' Treatment* (a Sermon preached before the Court of Aldermen, &c.), 1849; *Camels that bear Spices* (a Sermon preached to the Grocers' Co.); etc. [14]

CAUDWELL, Francis, *Carnmenellis, Redruth, Cornwall.*—Magd. Hall Ox; Deac. 1854 by Bp. of G. and B. Pr. 1857 by Bp of Wor. P. C. of Carnmenellis, Dio. Ex. 1858. (Patroness, Mrs. Broadley; Glebe, 3 acres; P. C.'s Inc. 184*l* and Ho; Pop. 3094.) Formerly C. of Chaddesley-Corbett and Oldswinford; Chap. to Price's Candle Co. [15]

CAUNTER, Richard McDonald, *Drayton, Banbury.*—Sid. Coll. Cam. Scho. 1st. cl. LL.B.; Deac. 1824 and Pr. 1825 by Bp of Lon. R. of Drayton, Dio. Ox. 1862. (Patron, Earl Delawarr; Tithe, 84*l* 8*s* 10*d*; Glebe, 76 acres; R.'s Inc. 480*l* and Ho; Pop. 152.) Formerly P. C. of Highclere, Hants, 1840, Woodcote, Hants, 1852, Hanwell, Oxon, 1860. Author, *Attila and other Poems*, Boone, 1832, 10*s* 6*d*. [16]

CAUSTON, Charles, *Lasham Rectory, Alton, Hants.*—R. of Lasham, Dio. Win. 1865. (Patron, F. G. E. Jervoise, Esq; R.'s Inc. 390*l* and Ho; Pop. 235.) [17]

CAUSTON, Charles, *Stretton-on-Fosse, Moreton-in-the-Marsh, Gloucestershire.*—Trin. Coll. Ox. B.A. 1824, M.A. 1827; Deac. 1824, Pr. 1825. R. of Stretton-on-Fosse with Ditchford B. Warw, Dio. Wor. 1839. (Patroness, Mrs. Fitzgerald; Tithe, Stretton, 184*l*; Glebe, 240 acres; R.'s Inc. 350*l* and Ho; Pop. 435.) [18]

CAUSTON, Edward Atherton, *Lymington, Hants.*—St. John's Coll. Cam. B.A. 1862; Deac. 1862 and Pr. 1863 by Bp of Lich. C. of Boldre, near Lymington, 1865. Formerly C. of Trinity, Burton-on-Trent. [19]

CAUSTON, Thomas Lilford Neil, 43, *Parsons Mead, Croydon, Surrey, S.*—St. John's Coll. Cam. B.A. 1859. M.A. 1862; Deac. 1860, Pr. 1861. P. C. of St. Matthew's, Croydon, Dio. Cant. 1866. (Patron, V. of Croydon; Pop. 300.) Formerly C. of Ch. Ch. Croydon. [20]

CAUTLEY, Edmund Harling, *Kildale Rectory, North Allerton.*—Emman. Coll. Cam. B.A. 1850, M.A. 1853; Deac. 1850 and Pr. 1851 by Bp of Ox. R. of Kildale, Dio. York, 1867. (Patron, Rev. C. P. Cleaver; R.'s Inc. 150*l*; Pop. 221.) Formerly C. of Bradwell, Oxon, and Thirkleby, Yorks. [21]

CAUTLEY, George Spencer, *Nettleden (Bucks), near Tring, Herts.*—Pemb. Coll. Cam. B.A. 1829; Deac. 1831, Pr. 1832. P. C. of Nettleden, Dio. Ox. 1857. (Patron, Earl Brownlow; P. C.'s Inc. 60*l*.) [22]

CAUTLEY, Joshua, *Thorney, near Peterborough.*—Jesus Coll. Cam. B.A. 1834; Deac. 1834 and Pr. 1835 by Bp. of Lin. Chap. of the Don. of Thorney Abbey, Dio. Ely, 1853. (Patron, Duke of Bedford; Chap.'s Inc. 230*l*; Pop. 2219.) [23]

CAVAN, Samuel, *Rainford, Prescot, Lancashire.*—Deac. 1840, Pr. 1841. P. C. of Rainford, Dio. Ches. 1855. (Patron, V. of Prescot; P. C.'s Inc. 135*l* and Ho; Pop. 2784.) [24]

CAVAN, Samuel, *Mansfield, Notts.*—St. Bees; Deac. 1855, Pr. 1856. C. of Mansfield 1865. Formerly C. of Pinxton, St. Peter's, Nottingham, and Trinity, Calne. Author, *Some Forcible Quotations and Plain Remarks about the Lord's Supper*, 1866, 6*d*; *Confession, Absolution, Baptismal Regeneration*, etc. 1867, 4*d*. [25]

CAVE, Robert Haynes, *Lydgate Rectory, Newmarket.*—Ex. Coll. Ox. B.A. 1853; Deac. 1853 and Pr. 1855 by Bp of Lich. R. of Lydgate, Dio. Ely, 1858. (Patron, the present R; Tithe, 310*l*; Glebe, 33 acres; R.'s Inc. 370*l* and Ho; Pop. 443.) [26]

CAVE-BROWNE, William Henry, *Dunmore, by Stirling.*—Ch. Ch. Ox. B.A. 1850, M.A. 1857; Deac. 1850 by Bp of Salis. Pr. 1851 by Bp of Roch. Incumb. of St. Andrew's, Dunmore, Dio. Edin. 1862. Formerly C. of East Grafton, Dio. Salis. 1851, Great Baddow, Dio. Roch. 1852–54, St. Mary's the Less, Lambeth, 1854–58, Ludgershall, Dio. Salis. 1858–62. [27]

CAVE-BROWNE-CAVE, Ambrose Sneyd, *Stretton-en-le-Field, Ashby-de-la-Zouch.*—Corpus Ch. Coll. Ox. B.A. 1856; Deac. 1857 and Pr. 1859 by Bp of Ox. R. of Stretton-en-le-Field, Dio. Lich. 1860. (Patron, Sir Mylles C. B. Cave, Bart; Tithe, 307*l*; Glebe, 51 acres;

R.'s Inc. 432*l* and Ho; Pop. 108.) Formerly C. of Deddington, Dio. Ox. 1857; R. of Strensham, Dio. Wor. 1859. [1]

CAVE-BROWNE-CAVE, Edward Farsyde, *Moor Critchel, Wimborne.*—Jesus Coll. Cam. Cl. Prizeman, 2nd cl. in Cl. Trip. and B.A. 1856, M.A. 1859; Deac. 1857 and Pr. 1858 by Bp of Man. C. of Moor Crichel and Long Crichel 1866. Formerly C. of Penwortham 1857–58, Hugglescote and Donington (sole charge) 1858–64; Min. of Lound Chapel, near Retford, 1865–66. [2]

CAVE-BROWNE-CAVE, Fitzherbert Astley, *Cockerham, Lancaster.*—Brasen. Coll. Ox. B.A. 1863, M.A. 1866; Deac. 1865 and Pr. 1866 by Bp of Man. C. of Cockerham. [3]

CAVE-BROWNE-CAVE, William Cecil, *Ashfield, Sydney.*—Magd. Hall, Ox. M.A. 1860. Incumb. of St. John's, Ashfield. Formerly C. of Ch. Ch. Salford. [4]

CAVELL, Frederick, *Swardeston, Norfolk.*—King's Coll. Lond. Theol. Assoc; Deac. 1851 and Pr. 1852 by Bp of Nor. V. of Swardeston, Dio. Nor. 1863. (Patron, John Steward, Esq; Tithe, 145*l*; Glebe, 90*l*; V.'s Inc. 220*l*; Pop. 400.) Formerly Chap. to the Royal Sea-Bathing Infirmary, Margate; C. of Garlinge, Isle of Thanet, East Carleton, Norfolk, and St. Mary's and St. Mark's, Islington, 1860–63. [5]

CAVELL, Henry Theodore, 4, *Stoneleigh Villas, Bath.*—Deac. 1849 and Pr. 1850 by Bp of Nor. P. C. of St. James's, Bath, Dio. B. and W. 1861. (Patrons, Simeon's Trustees; P. C.'s Inc. 278*l*; Pop. 5788.) Formerly C. of St. Clements, Ipswich, 1849, St. Helen's, Ipswich, 1851, St. Michael's, Stockwell, 1857. [6]

CAVELL, Robert Corry, *Binham, near Wells, Norfolk.*—Deac. 1849 and Pr. 1850 by Bp of Ches. V. of Binham, Dio. Nor. 1865. (Patron, T. T. Clarke, Esq; Title, 100*l*; Glebe, 53*l*; V.'s Inc. 155*l* and Ho; Pop. 810.) Formerly C. of St. Saviour's, Norwich; R. of St. Swithin's, Norwich, 1857–65. Author, *Lectures on the Lord's Supper; Family Prayers.* [7]

CAVIE, Alexander Joseph Lyon, *Seckington, near Tamworth, Staffs.*—St. John's Coll. Cam. B.A. 1825; Deac. 1825, Pr. 1826. P. C. of Shuttington, Warw. Dio. Wor. 1845. (Patron, Earl of Essex; Glebe, 174 acres; P. C.'s Inc. 300*l*; Pop. 194.) Formerly C. of Seckington. [8]

CAVILL, George, *Pulborough, Petworth, Sussex.*—Jesus Coll. Cam. M.A. 1865; Deac. 1862 and Pr. 1864 by Bp of St. D. C. of Pulborough 1866. Formerly C. of Swansea 1862, Trinity, Southampton, 1864. [9]

CAWLEY, Thomas, *Harwood, Bolton-le-Moors.*—Wad. Coll. Ox. B.A. 1860; Deac. 1860 and Pr. 1861 by Bp of Pet. P. C. of Harwood, Dio. Man. 1866. (Patrons, Trustees; P. C.'s Inc. 100*l* and Ho; Pop. 1525.) Formerly C. of Naseby and Castor. [10]

CAWOOD, John, *Pensax Parsonage, Tenbury.*—St. Edm. Hall, Ox. B.A. 1844, M.A. 1847; Deac. 1845 and Pr. 1846 by Bp of Herf. P. C. of Pensax, Dio. Herf. 1847. (Patron, V. of Lindridge; P. C.'s Inc. 108*l* and Ho; Pop. 503.) [11]

CAWSTON, John.—Chaplain of H. M. S. "Sutlej." [12]

CAY, Alfred.—King's Coll. Lond. Theol. Assoc, Deac. 1857 by Bp of Win. C. of St. Mary's, Newington, Surrey. Formerly C. of Ch. Ch. Brixton. [13]

CAY, Christopher, *Coney Weston, Ixworth, Suffolk.*—Emman. Coll. Cam. LL.B. 1860; Deac. 1860 by Bp of Win. Pr. 1862 by Bp of Roch. C. in sole charge of Coney Weston 1865. Formerly C. in sole charge of St. John's, Higham, Kent, 1862–65. [14]

CAYLEY, Edward, *South Leverton, Retford.*—St. John's Coll. Cam. B.A. 1855, M.A. 1858; Deac. 1855 and Pr. 1856 by Bp of Pet. V. of South Leverton with Cottam C. Dio. Lin. 1867. (Patron, Bp of Lin; V.'s Inc. 360*l* and Ho; Pop. South Leverton 408, Cotton 86.) Formerly P. C. of Brinsley 1862–67. [15]

CAYLEY, Reginald Arthur, *Scampton, Lincolnshire.*—Mert. Coll. Ox. B.A. 1860, M.A. 1863; Deac. 1863 by Bp of Lich. Pr. 1863 by Bp of Lin. R. of Scampton, Dio. Lin. 1863. (Patron, Sir Digby Cayley, Bart; Tithe, 300*l*; Glebe, 1½ acres; R.'s Inc. 310*l* and Ho; Pop. 250.) Formerly C. of Eckrington, near Chesterfield, 1862–63. [16]

CAZALET, William Wahab, 28, *Southampton-street, Strand, London, W.C.* and *Watford, Herts.*—Trin. Coll. Cam. B.A. 1833, M.A. 1837; Deac. 1834 and Pr. 1836 by Bp of G. and B. Chap. to the Watford Union; Teacher of Elocution. Author, *On the Musical Department of the Great Exhibition* (a Lecture delivered before the Society of Arts, 1852); *On the Right Management of the Voice in Speaking and Reading*, 1855, 3rd edit. 1860; *Stammering, its Cause and Cure*, 1858, 3rd edit. 1860; *The Art of Singing*, 1861, 2nd edit. 1865, 2*s* 6*d*; *On the Reading of the Church Liturgy*, 1*s* 6*d*. [17]

CAZENOVE, Arthur, *St. Mark's Parsonage, Reigate, Surrey.*—Ex. Coll. Ox. 3rd cl. Hist. and Law, B.A. 1853, M.A. 1856; Deac. 1857 and Pr. 1858 by Abp of Cant. P. C. of St. Mark's, Reigate, Dio. Win. 1859. (Patron, Bp of Win; P. C.'s Inc. 420*l* and Ho.; Pop. 2500.) Formerly C. of Woodchurch and Frittenden. Author, *A Defence of Lord Strafford*; *Inaugural Sermon at St. Mark's, Reigate.* [18]

CAZENOVE, John Gibson, *The College, Isle of Cumbrae, Greenock, Scotland.*—Brasen. Coll. Ox. 2nd cl. Lit. Hum. Math. et Phy, and B.A. 1843. M.A. 1846; Deac. 1846, Pr. 1848. Vice-Provost of Cumbrae Coll. 1854, Provost 1867. Author, *Mahommedanism*, in the 8th edition of *Encyclopædia Britannica*; Sermons, *Possibilities of Union*, Mozley, 1865; *Inconsistency*, Rivingtons, 1866. [19]

CECIL, William, *Longstanton St. Michael, near Cambridge*—Magd. Coll. Cam. Bell's Univ. Scho. 1811, Wrang. and B.A. 1814, M.A. 1817; Deac. 1819, Pr. 1820. R. of Longstanton St. Michael, Dio. Ely, 1823. (Patron, Magd. Coll. Cam.; Tithe, 250*l*; Glebe, 78 acres; R.'s Inc. 318*l* and Ho; Pop. 145.) Author, *Two Mechanical Papers in Proceedings of Cambridge Philosophical Society*; *Hints on Confirmation*, 1833, 4*d*; *Visitation Sermon at Cambridge*, 1*s*; *Church Choir Organ-book*, fol. 21*s* (Three Vocal Parts detached, 4*s* each); *Church Choir Hymn-book*, 2*s* 6*d*; *The Child's Progress from Birth to Glory, illustrated in a Selection of Poetical Pieces, adapted to Music*, fol. 12*s*; *Recollections for Solemn Seasons*; *Rachel's Tears* and *Spanish Metres illustrated* in Music and English verse, one vol. folio, 1866, 4*s* 6*d*. [20]

CERJAT, Henry Sigismund, *West Horsley Rectory, Ripley, Surrey.*—Trin. Coll. Cam. B.A. 1835; Deac. 1836 by Bp of Ely, Pr. 1837 by Bp of Nor. R. of West Horsley, Dio. Win. 1841. (Patron, Henry Weston, Esq; Tithe, 310*l*; Glebe, 100 acres; R.'s Inc. 396*l* and Ho; Pop. 706.) [21]

CHADWICK, Edward, *Thornhill Lees, near Dewsbury, Yorks.*—St. John's Coll. Cam. M.A. P. C. of Thornhill Lees, Dio. Rip. 1860. (Patron, Bp of Rip; P. C.'s Inc. 158*l* and Ho; Pop. 1553.) [22]

CHADWICK, James, *Kedleston, near Derby.*—Corpus Coll. Cam. B.A. 1837, M.A. 1842; Deac. 1837, Pr. 1838 by Bp of Ches. C. of Kedleston 1861. Formerly C. of Eccles 1837, Chesterfield 1847, Sheffield 1857. [23]

CHADWICK, James, *Tatham Chapel, Bentham, near Lancaster.*—Queens' Coll. Cam. B.A. 1848; Deac. 1848 and Pr. 1850 by Bp of Ches. P. C. of Tatham Chapel, Dio. Man. 1862. (Patron, R. of Tatham; Glebe, 140*l*; P. C.'s Inc. 152*l*; Pop. 284.) Formerly C. of St. John's, Dukinfield, 1848, Slaidburn, Yorks, 1857. [24]

CHADWICK, Joseph William, *Dorking, Surrey.*—Queen's Coll. Ox. B.A. 1863, M.A. 1866; Deac. 1863 and Pr. 1864 by Abp of York. C. of Dorking 1867. Formerly C. of Dunnington 1863–67. [25]

CHADWICK, Robert, *Christ Church Parsonage, Lofthouse, Wakefield.*—St. Bees; Deac. 1842, Pr. 1843. P. C. of Ch. Ch. Lofthouse, Dio. Rip. 1844. (Patron, V. of Rothwell; P. C.'s Inc. 112*l* and Ho; Pop. 2099.) Formerly Asst. C. of Rothwell 1842-44. [26]

CHAFY, William Lucas, *Bath.*—Sid. Coll. Cam. B.A. 1829, M.A. 1832; Deac. 1830, Pr. 1831. Formerly Fell. of Dulwich Coll. 1836–37. [1]

CHALK, Richard Gregory, *Wilden Rectory, near Bedford.*—Trin. Coll. Cam. B.A. 1846; Deac. 1848 and Pr. 1849 by Bp of Ely. R. of Wilden, Dio. Ely, 1849. (Patroness, Mrs. Chalk; Glebe, 472 acres; R.'s Inc. 465*l* and Ho; Pop. 591.) [2]

CHALK, Thomas, *Quainton Rectory, Winslow, Bucks.*—St. Peter's Coll. Cam. B.A. 1862; Deac. 1862, Pr. 1863. R. of Quainton, Dio. Ox. 1867. (Patron, A. R. Chalk, Esq; R.'s Inc. 543*l* and Ho; Pop. 929.) Formerly C. of Loddiswell with Buckland Tout Saints 1863–64, V. of same 1864–67. [3]

CHALKER, Alfred Ball, *North Benfleet, Chelmsford.*—Emman. Coll. Cam. B.A. 1851, M.A. 1854; Deac. 1852. Pr. 1854. R. of Benfleet, Dio. Roch. 1863. (Patron, Emman. Coll. Cam; R.'s Inc. 706*l* and Ho; Pop. 285.) Formerly C. of St. Giles's and St. Peter's, Cambridge; late Fell. and Asst. Tut. of Emman. Coll. 1852; Jun. Proctor of the Univ. 1857–58. [4]

CHALKER, Frederick, *Ridgway, Plympton, Devon.*—Corpus Coll. Ox. B.A. 1847, M.A. 1850; Deac. 1852 and Pr. 1853 by Bp of Ox. Fell. of Corpus Coll. Ox. [5]

CHALLIS, James, 13, *Trumpington-street, Cambridge.*—Trin. Coll. Cam. 1st Smith's Prizeman, Sen. Wrang. and B.A. 1825, M.A. 1828; Deac. 1830 by Bp of Lich. Pr. 1830 by Bp of Pet. Plumian Prof. of Astronomy 1836. Author, *Astronomical Observations made at the Cambridge Observatory in the Years* 1836–60, Deighton, Bell and Co, 1837–64; *Creation in Plan and in Progress*, Macmillan, 1861. [6]

CHALLIS, James Law, *Papworth Everard, St. Ives, Hunts.*—Trin. Coll. Cam. B.A. 1856, M.A. 1859; Deac. 1858 and Pr. 1859 by Bp of Ely. R. of Papworth Everard, Dio. Ely, 1860. (Patron, Trin. Coll. Cam; Tithe, comm. 187*l* 10*s*; Glebe, 22 acres; R.'s Inc. 220*l* 10*s* and Ho; Pop. 133.) Formerly C. of Arrington, Cambs. 1858–59; Asst. C. of All Saints and St. John's, Huntingdon, 1859–60. [7]

CHALLIS, Nathan, *Groby Parsonage, Leicestershire.*—St. Bees; Deac. 1855 and Pr. 1856 by Bp of Pet. C. of Ratby 1866. Formerly C. of Ch. Ch. Leicester, 1855–58, Thame, Oxon, 1858–66. [8]

CHALMER, Edward Boteler, *Whitely-wood Hall, near Sheffield.*—Dub. A.B. 1840, A.M. 1846; Deac. and Pr. 1840 by Bp of Ches. P. C. of Fullwood, Sheffield, Dio. York, 1844. (Patroness, Miss Silcock; Glebe, 1 acre; P. C.'s Inc. 140*l*; Pop. 1801.) Chap. to the Ecclesall-Bierlowe Union. Formerly P. C. of Great Crosby 1840. [9]

CHALMER, Edmund Boteler, *Broughton-terrace, Lower Broughton, Manchester.*—Dub. A.B. 1851, A.M. 1856, *ad eund.* Ox. 1857; Deac. 1851 and Pr. 1852 by Bp of Ches. R. of St. Matthias', Salford, Dio. Man. 1857. (Patrons, Trustees; R.'s Inc. 300*l*; Pop. 7194.) Formerly C. of Tintwistle; Assoc. Sec. of Colonial Ch. and Sch. Soc; C. of St. James's, Manchester and Afternoon Lect. at St. Saviour's. Author, *The Lord, my Shepherd* (a Sermon), 1851, 6*d*; *Mormonism a Delusion* (a Lecture), 1852, 6*d*; *The Death of Jesus a Propitiation for the Sins of all Mankind* (a Sermon on Good Friday), Hatchard, 1858, 6*d*; *The Parson, the Parish, and the Working Men* (account of the first Working Men's Club in England), Nisbet, 1859, 1*s*; *Daily Calendar of the New Testament*, 1866. [10]

CHALMERS, Frederick Skene Courtenay, *Beckenham, Kent.*—St. Cath. Coll. Cam. B.D. 1858. R. of Beckenham, 1851. (Patron, J. Cator, Esq; Tithe, 842*l*; Glebe, 14 acres; R.'s Inc. 900*l* and Ho; Pop. 2124.) Chap. to the Earl of Carnwath 1849. Author, *The Christian Home*, 1*s* 6*d*. [11]

CHALMERS, John, *Scamblesby Grove, Horncastle, Lincolnshire.*—King's Coll. Lond. M.A. by Abp of Cant; Deac. 1850 and Pr. 1851 by Bp of Herf. R. of Oxcombe, Dio. Lin. 1863. (Patron, D. Briggs, Esq; Tithe, 204*l*; Glebe, 4½ acres; R.'s Inc. 220*l* and Ho; Pop. 27.) Formerly P. C. of St. Stephen's, Brighton, 1857–61, and of Leonards-on-Sea 1856–57. [12]

CHALONER, John William, *Newton-Kyme Rectory, Tadcaster, Yorks.*—Magd. Coll. Cam. B.A. 1836, M.A. 1851; Deac. 1838 by Bp of Rip. Pr. 1838 by Abp of York. R. of Newton-Kyme, Dio. York, 1851. (Patron, T.W.C. Fairfax, Esq; Tithe, Imp. 30*l*, R. 385*l*; Glebe, 37 acres; R.'s Inc. 422*l* and Ho; Pop. 162.) [13]

CHAMBERLAIN, Cator.—C. of North Chapel, Petworth. [14]

CHAMBERLAIN, Frederick Townshend, *Hawarden, Chester.*—Dub. A.B. 1856, A.M. 1859; Deac. 1853 and Pr. 1854 by Bp of Ches. C. of Hawarden 1865. Formerly C. of St. Philip's and St. Thomas's, Liverpool, Trinity, Chester, and Whitchurch, Salop. [15]

CHAMBERLAIN, George William, *Cheltenham.*—Wad. Coll. Ox. B.A. 1837, M.A. 1848; Deac. 1839 and Pr. 1840 by Bp. of Barbados. P. C. of St. James's, Suffolk-square, Cheltenham, Dio. G. and B. 1857. (Patrons, Trustees; P. C.'s Inc. 250*l*.) Formerly Chap. to late Bp and to the present Bp of Barbados; R. of Port of Spain, and Rural Dean of the Island of Trinidad; P. C. of St. Matthew's, Birmingham, 1848–57. [16]

CHAMBERLAIN, Robert, *The Grange, Bexhill, near Hastings.*—St. Peter's Coll. Cam. 29th Sen. Opt. B.A. 1836, M.A. 1839; Deac. 1837 and Pr. 1838 by Bp of Lin. Formerly C. of Barbage 1837–39, Hinckley 1839–43, Woodstone 1843–59. [17]

CHAMBERLAIN, Thomas, *Oxford.*—Ch. Ch. Ox. Stud. of, 3rd cl. Lit. Hum. and B.A. 1831, M.A. 1834; Deac. 1832 and Pr. 1833 by Bp of Ox. V. of St. Thomas's, City and Dio. of Ox. 1842. (Patron, Ch. Ch. Ox; V.'s Inc. 120*l*; Pop. 2820.) Sec. of the Dioc. Board of Education 1839; Rural Dean 1844. Author, *Dissenters Recalled*; *Restitution to the Church*; *Letter to the Bishop of Oxford*; *Theory of Christian Worship*, 2nd edit. 1855, 4*s* 6*d*; *The Seven Ages of the Church*, 1858, 3*s*. [18]

CHAMBERLAIN, Thomas Ffoster, *Rufford, Ormskirk, Lancashire.*—Ch. Coll. Cam. B.A. 1841, M.A. 1842; Deac 1842 and Pr. 1843 by Bp of Ches. R. of Rufford, Dio. Man. 1848. (Patrons, Reps. of the late L. G. N. Starkie, Esq; Tithe, 580*l*; Glebe, 14 acres; R.'s Inc. 600*l*; Pop. 865.) Hon. Can. of Man. Cathl. 1859; Surrogate. [19]

CHAMBERLAIN, Walter, *Goodwin House, Bolton-le-Moors.*—Corpus Coll. Cam. B.A. 1844, M.A. 1848; Deac. 1844 and Pr. 1845 by Bp of Ches. P. C. of St. John's, Little Bolton, Dio. Man. 1846. (Patrons, the Crown and Bp of Man. alt. P. C.'s Inc. 156*l*; Pop. 5233.) Author, *Notes on the Restoration and Conversion of Israel*, 1854, 14*s*. [20]

CHAMBERLAINE, S.—C. of Maddington, Wilts. [21]

CHAMBERLAYNE, Edward Francis, *Aston-Magna (Worcestershire), near Moreton-in-Marsh.*—St. John's Coll. Cam. B.A. 1829, M.A. 1833; Deac. 1830, Pr. 1883. P. C. of Aston-Magna, Dio. Wor. 1847. (Patron, Ld Redesdale; Glebe, 5 acres; P. C.'s Inc. 248*l* and Ho; Pop. 259.) [22]

CHAMBERLAYNE, John, *Estwick (Herts), near Harlow.*—Jesus Coll. Cam. B.A. 1813, M.A. 1816; Deac. 1815, Pr. 1816. R. of Estwick, Dio. Roch. 1825. (Tithe, 204*l*; Glebe, 50 acres; R.'s Inc. 268*l* and Ho; Pop. 116.) [23]

CHAMBERLIN, Thomas Chamberlin Bigsby, *West Deeping, Market Deeping.*—Emman. Coll. Cam. B.A. 1858, M.A. 1866; Deac. 1860 and Pr. 1863 by Bp of Lin. C. of West Deeping 1863. Formerly C. of Kirton in Lindsey and Northorpe 1860, Osbournby 1862. [24]

CHAMBERS, George, *Rochester.*—St. John's Coll. Cam. B.D. 1849; Deac. 1839 and Pr. 1840 by Bp of B. and W. Formerly C. of Midsomer Norton 1839–43, Binegar 1843–47, Burnham 1847–52, Chatham 1852–58; Chap. of Medway Union 1855–59. [25]

CHAMBERS, John, M.A., *Grammar School, Ely.*—Head Mast. of Gr. Sch. Ely. [26]

CHAMBERS, John Charles, 1, *Greek-street, Soho-square, London, W.*—Emman. Coll. Cam. Sen. Opt. 2nd cl. Cl. Trip. and B.A. 1840, Tyrwhitt's Hebr. Scho. 1842, M.A. 1843; Deac. 1842 and Pr. 1846 by Bp of Rip. P. C. of St. Mary-the-Virgin's, Crown-street, Soho, Dio. Lon. 1856. (Patron, Rev. Nugent Wade; P. C.'s Inc. 300*l* and Ho; Pop. 6003.) Warden of the House of Charity, Greek-street, Soho, 1856; Hon. Chap. to the Newport Market Refuge. Formerly Can. and Chan. of St. Ninian's Cathl. Perth, 1850; P. C. of St. Mary Magdalen's, Harlow, 1853. Author, *Sermons preached at Perth and other parts of Scotland*, Masters; *Communion in the Prayers*, Palmer; *Union of the Natural and Supernatural Substances in the Holy Eucharist*, Masters; *Reformation not Deformation*, etc. [1]

CHAMBERS, Oswald Lyttelton, *Hook Hall, near Howden, Yorks.*—Univ. Coll. Ox. B.A. 1843, M.A. 1848; Deac. 1844, Pr. 1846. P. C. of Hook, Dio. York, 1863. (Patron, Right Hon. T. H. S. Estcourt. M.P; Tithe, 30*l* 8*s* 7*d*; Glebe, 49*l*; P. C.'s Inc. 137*l*; Pop. 415.) Formerly C. of St. John's, Leeds, and of Tetbury. [2]

CHAMBERS, R.—C. of Knill, Herefordshire. [3]

CHAMBERS, Richard Franklin, *Merston, Chichester.*—Dub. A.B. 1824; Deac. 1826 by Abp of Dub. Pr. 1827 by Bp of Meath. R. of Merston, Dio. Chich. 1858. (Patron, Ld Chan; Tithe, 263*l*; Glebe, 7 acres; R.'s Inc. 230*l*; Pop. 79*l*.) Formerly P. C. of Summers-town, Dio. Win. 1848–58. [4]

CHAMBERS, Thomas, *Halewood, Liverpool.*—Magd. Hall, Ox. B.A. 1850, M.A. 1858; Deac. 1852 and Pr. 1853 by Bp of Ches. P. C. of Halewood, Dio. Ches. 1864. (Patron, V. of Childwall.) Formerly C. of Halewood and Childwall. [5]

CHAMBERS, Thomas, D.D., *Royal Naval School, New-cross, Deptford, London, S.E.*—Head Mast. of the Royal Naval School, New-cross. [6]

CHAMBERS, William, *West Ilsley, Berks.*—Wor. Coll. Ox. 2nd cl. Lit. Hum. and B.A. 1850; Deac. 1851 and Pr. 1852 by Bp of Ox. Fell. and Div. Lect. of Wor. Coll. 1851; Tut. of Wor. Coll. 1857; Sen. Proctor, 1863. C. of West Ilsley 1866. Editor, *Select Orations of Cicero with English Notes*, Rivingtons, 1866. [7]

CHAMBERS, William Frederic, *North Kelsey Vicarage, Kirton-in-Lindsey, Lincolnshire.*—Trin. Coll. Cam. B.A. 1852, M.A. 1856; Deac. 1853 by Bp of Herf. Pr. 1854 by Bp of Lin. V. of North Kelsey, Dio. Lin. 1854. (Patron, Preb. of North Kelsey in Lin. Cathl; V.'s Inc. 260*l* and Ho; Pop. 870.) [8]

CHAMBERS, William Hampton, 16, *Yonge Park, Holloway, London, N.*—Dur. Theol. Licen. 1859, B.A. 1862, M.A. 1865; Deac. 1859 and Pr. 1860 by Bp of Lon. Min. of St. Anne's, temporary church, Holloway, 1867. Formerly C. of St. Matthias', Bethnal-green, 1859, Moorside, Lancashire, 1861–64; London Dioc. Home Missionary 1864–67. [9]

CHAMNEY, Robert Mascall, *Cheltenham.*—St. Peter's Coll. Cam. Scho. of, B.A. 1844; Deac. 1845 and Pr. 1846 by Bp of B. and W. Prin. of the Training Coll. Cheltenham, 1864. Formerly C. of Hatch Beauchamp 1845, Watton, Herts, 1851–64. [10]

CHAMPERNOWNE, Richard, *Dartington, Totnes, Devon.*—Ch. Ch. Ox. B.A. 1839, M.A. 1842. R. of Dartington, Dio. Ex. 1859. (Patron, H. Champernowne, Esq; R.'s Inc. 924*l*; Pop. 626.) Formerly C. of Dartington. [11]

CHAMPION, John, *Edale, Derbyshire.* [12]

CHAMPNESS, Edward Thomas.—Formerly V. of Upton with Chalvey, Bucks, 1844–67. [13]

CHAMPNEYS, Charles Francis, *Wendover Vicarage, Bucks.*—St. Bees; Deac. 1846, Pr. 1847. V. of Wendover, Dio. Ox. 1850. (Patron, Ld Chan; V.'s Inc. 270*l* and Ho; Pop. 1932.) [14]

CHAMPNEYS, Maximilian Hugh Stanley, *Epperstone Rectory, Southwell, Notts.*—Brasen. Coll. Ox. B.A. 1838, M.A. 1841; Deac. 1841 by Bp of Lich. Pr. 1842 by Bp of Herf. R. of Epperstone, Dio. Lin. 1853. (Patrons, Hulme's Trustees; Tithe, 20*l* 6*s* 6*d*; Glebe, 266 acres; R.'s Inc. 340*l* and Ho: Pop. 518.) [15]

CHAMPNEYS, Thomas Phipps Amian, *Badsworth, Pontefract.*—Mert. Coll. Ox. B.A. 1830, M.A. 1833. R. of Badsworth, Dio. York, 1859. (Patron, Earl of Derby; Tithe, 517*l*; Glebe, 168 acres; R.'s Inc. 696*l*; Pop. 744.) Formerly V. of Owston, Dio. York, 1850–59. [16]

CHAMPNEYS, Weldon, *Wendover Vicarage, Tring.*—Brasen. Coll. Ox. B.A. 1861, M.A. 1864; Deac. 1862 and Pr. 1863 by Bp of Ox. C. of Wendover, Bucks, 1862. [17]

CHAMPNEYS, William Weldon, 31, *Gordon-square, London, W.C.*—Brasen. Coll. Ox. Fell. of 1831, 2nd cl. Lit. Hum. and B.A. 1828, M.A. 1831; Deac. and Pr. 1831 by Bp of Ox. Can. Res. of St. Paul's Cathl. 1851 (Value 1000*l*.) V. of St. Pancras, Dio. Lon. 1860. (Patrons, D. and C. of St. Paul's Cathl; V.'s Inc. 1150*l* and Ho; Pop. 13,000.) Rural Dean. Formerly C. of Dorchester, Oxon, 1831; C. in sole charge of St. Ebbe's, Oxford, 1831; R. of Whitechapel, London, 1837–60. Author, *Sermons on the Liturgy*, on *Images*, on *Spirit in the Word*; *Facts and Fragments*; *Parish Work*; etc. published by Seeleys. [18]

CHANCELLOR, James, *St. John's Parsonage, Derby.*—Dub. A.B. 1852, A.M. 1855; Deac. 1853 and Pr. 1854 by Bp of Lich. P. C. of St. John's, Derby, Dio. Lich. 1857. (Patron, V. of St. Werburgh's; P. C.'s Inc. 300*l* and Ho; Pop. 6228.) Formerly C. of St. John's, Derby, 1853–57. [19]

CHANDLER, Henry Christian David, *The Rectory, Narberth.*—Caius Coll. Cam. B.A. 1859, Deac. 1860 and Pr. 1861 by Bp of St. D. R. of Narberth, Dio. St. D. 1863. (Patron, the Crown; Tithe, 510*l*; Glebe, 176*l*; R.'s Inc. 690*l* and Ho; Pop. 2948.) [20]

CHANDLER, John, *Witley Vicarage, Godalming, Surrey.*—Corpus Coll. Ox. B.A. 1827, M.A. 1830; Deac. 1831 and Pr. 1832 by Bp of Ox. V. of Witley, Dio. Win. 1839. (Patron, the present V; Tithe, 200*l* 5*s*; Glebe, ½ acre; V.'s Inc. 210*l* and Ho; Pop. 836.) Rural Dean. Author, *Translation of Primitive Hymns*; Tracts. [21]

CHANTER, John Mill, *Ilfracombe Vicarage, Devon.*—Oriel Coll. Ox. B.A. 1831, M.A. 1834. V. of Ilfracombe with Lee C. Dio. Ex. 1836. (Patron, the Preb. of Ilfracombe in Salis. Cathl; V.'s Inc. 150*l* and Ho; Pop. 2560.) [22]

CHAPELHOW, Joseph, *Musgrave Rectory, Brough, Westmoreland.*—Deac. 1819 and Pr. 1821 by Bp of Carl. R. of Great Musgrave, Dio. Carl. 1846. (Patron, Bp of Carl; Tithe, 126*l*; Glebe, 104 acres; R.'s Inc. 200*l* and Ho; Pop. 192.) Formerly C. of Kirkland, Penrith, 1819–45; V. of Newton Reigney, Penrith, 1845–46. [23]

CHAPLIN, Ayrton, *Carshalton, Surrey.*—Corpus Coll Cam. 3rd cl. Cl. Trip. 1866; Deac. 1866 by Bp of Win. C. of Carshalton 1866. [24]

CHAPLIN, Edward Morland, *Chilton, Steventon, Berks.*—Magd. Hall, Ox. B.A. 1854; Deac. 1854 and Pr. 1855 by Bp of Ex. R. of Chilton, Dio. Ox. 1857. (Patron, G. B. Morland, Esq; Tithe—Imp. 60*l* 8*s*, R. 438*l* 19*s* 1*d*; R.'s Inc. 460*l*; Pop. 315.) Formerly C. of Harberton, Devon. [25]

CHAPLIN, William, *Staveley, near Kendal, Westmoreland.*—Emman. Coll. Cam. B.D; St. Bees, Divinity Prize and Librarian, 1850; Deac. 1850, Pr. 1851. P. C. of Staveley, Dio. Carl. 1858. (Patron, V. of Kendal; P. C.'s Inc. 125*l*; Pop. 1064.) Formerly C. of Kendal 1850–58. [26]

CHAPLYN, George Robert, *St. Thomas, West Indies.*—Trin. Coll. Cam. B.A. 1850, M.A. 1858; Deac. 1852 and Pr. 1853 by Bp of Rip. Formerly C. of Worplesdon. [27]

CHAPMAN, Arthur Thomas, *Emmanuel College, Cambridge.*—Emman. Coll. Cam. Fell. of, 1862; Deac. 1863, Pr. 1864. [28]

CHAPMAN, Benjamin, *Leatherhead, Surrey.*—V. of Leatherhead, Dio. Win. (Patrons, D. and C. of Roch; Tithe, 270*l* 5*s* 9*d*; V.'s Inc. 300*l* and Ho: Pop. 2079.) [29]

CHAPMAN, Charles, *Acrise Rectory, Elham, Canterbury.*—Corpus Coll. Cam. 24th Wrang. and B.A. 1830, M.A. 1833; Deac. 1831, Pr. 1832. R. of Acrise, Dio. Cant. 1846. (Patron, W. A. Mackinnon, Esq; Tithe, 226*l*; Glebe, 44 acres; R.'s Inc. 246*l* and Ho; Pop. 173.) [1]

CHAPMAN, Charles, B.A.—British Chap. at Bilboa, Spain. [2]

CHAPMAN, Charles.—Chap. of H.M.S. "Gladiator." [3]

CHAPMAN, Dawson Francis, *St. Peter's Parsonage, Preston.*—Dub. A.B. 1856, A.M. 1859; Deac. 1856 and Pr. 1857 by Bp of Man. P. C. of St. Peter's, Preston, Dio. Man. 1862. (Patron, V. of Preston; P. C.'s Inc. 300*l* and Ho; Pop. 13,550.) Formerly C. of Preston, 1859, Trinity, Blackburn, 1856–59. Author, *A New Year's-Eve Sermon*, Blackburn, 1856; *Morning and Evening Prayer for Persons much employed*, Preston, 1858; *Questions and Answers on the Principles of an Established Church*, 1862; *Lectures on the English Liturgy*, Preston, 1866. [4]

CHAPMAN, Edward Martin, *Low Toynton, Horncastle, Linc.*—Lin. Coll. Ox. B.A. 1847; Deac. 1848, Pr. 1850. V. of Low Toynton, Dio Lin. 1862. (Patron, Lord Willoughby D'Eresby; Tithe, 5*l* 2*s*; Glebe, 180 acres; V.'s Inc. 300*l* and Ho; Pop. 155.) Chap. to Horncastle Union 1864. Formerly V. of Swinstead, near Bourne, Dio. Lin. 1850. [5]

CHAPMAN, Edward William, 71, *Frenchgate, Doncaster.*—Trin. Coll. Cam. B.A. 1864; Deac. 1866, Pr. 1867. C. of Doncaster 1866. [6]

CHAPMAN, Frank Robert, *Bury St. Edmunds.*—Ex. Coll. Ox. B.A. 1852, M.A. 1855; Deac. 1854 and Pr. 1855 by Bp of Rip. P. C. of St. James's, Bury St. Edmunds, Dio. Ely, 1865. (Patron, H. Wilson, Esq; Pop. 3222.) Formerly C. of St. Mary Abbott, Kensington, and of Leeds; P. C. of Walsham-le-Willows, Dio. Ely, 1860–65. [7]

CHAPMAN, The Right Rev. James, *Wootton Courtney Rectory, Dunster, Taunton.*—King's Coll. Cam. B.A. 1823, M.A. 1826, D.D. 1845; Deac. 1824 by Bp of Ely, Pr. 1825 by Bp of Chich. Fell. of Eton Coll. 1862; R. of Wootton Courtney, Dio. B. and W. 1863. (Patron, Eton Coll; Tithe, Rent Charge, 270*l*; Glebe, 112 acres; R.'s Inc. 430*l* and Ho; Pop. 410.) Formerly Asst. Mast. at Eton and Even. Lect. at Windsor; R. of Dunton Waylett, Essex, 1834–45; Bishop of Colombo from 1845 to 1861. Author, Occasional Charges, Sermons, and Journals. [8]

CHAPMAN, John, *Milton Rectory, Cambridge.*—King's Coll. Cam. Fell. of, B.A. 1827, M.A. 1830; Deac. 1827, Pr. 1828. R. of Milton, Dio. Ely, 1841. (Patron, King's Coll. Cam; R.'s Inc. 625*l* and Ho; Pop. 494.) Formerly C. of Haslemere, Surrey, 1827–41, Ampthill, Beds, 1841–46. [9]

CHAPMAN, John, *Newport, Bishops Stortford.*—Dub. A.B. 1839, A.M. 1845; Deac. 1842 and Pr. 1843 by Bp of Win. V. of Newport, Dio. Roch. 1850. (Patron, Bp of Roch; Tithe—Imp. 283*l*, V. 115*l*; Glebe, 24 acres; V.'s Inc. 280*l* and Ho; Pop. 886.) Formerly P. C. of Bothamsall, Notts, and Dom. Chap. to Duke of Newcastle. [10]

CHAPMAN, John, *Thornton Rust, Bedale, Yorks.* [11]

CHAPMAN, John, *The Schools, Shrewsbury.*—Emman. Coll. Cam. 2nd cl. in Cl. Trip. B.A. 1856; Deac. 1863 and Pr. 1865 by Bp of Lich. Asst. Mast. in Shrewsbury Sch. [12]

CHAPMAN, John Mitchel, *Tendring Rectory, Colchester.*—Ex. Coll. Ox. 2nd cl. Lit. Hum. and B.A. 1821; Deac. and Pr. 1824. R. of Tendring, Dio. Roch. 1838. (Patron, Ball. Coll. Ox; Tithe, 840*l*; Glebe, 108½ acres; R.'s Inc. 970*l* and Ho; Pop. 715.) Formerly Fell. and Tut. of Ball. Coll. Ox. 1824; Mast. of the Schs. 1826 and 1827. Author, *Occasional Sermons*; *Reminiscences of the Author of the Christian Year* (printed for private circulation). [13]

CHAPMAN, Justice, *Elksley, Retford, Notts.*—St. Cath. Coll. Cam. B.A. 1850, M.A. 1853; Deac. 1851, Pr. 1852. V. of Elksley, Dio. Lin. 1861. (Patron, Duke of Newcastle; Tithe, Rent Charge 80*l*; Glebe, 13 acres; V.'s Inc. 130*l* and Ho; Pop. 362.) Formerly C. of Clarborough, Notts, 1851; P. C. of New Bolingbroke, Dio. Lin. 1854–61. [14]

CHAPMAN, Richard, *Normanton Rectory, Grantham, Lincolnshire.*—St. John's Coll. Cam. B.A. 1828, M.A. 1839; Deac. 1835, Pr. 1836. R. of Normanton, Dio. Lin. 1854. (Patron, Marquis of Bristol; Tithe, 70*l*; Glebe, 12 acres; R.'s Inc. 94*l* and Ho; Pop. 172.) Author, *A Greek Harmony of the Gospels, with Notes and Verbal Parallelisms*, 4to, 1835, 21*s*. [15]

CHAPMAN, Roger, *Burton-in-Lonsdale (Yorks), near Lancaster.*—Deac. 1826, Pr. 1827. Formerly P. C. of Burton-in-Lonsdale 1831–66. [16]

CHAPMAN, William Edward, *Stanhope, Durham.*—Ch. Miss. Coll. Lon; Deac. 1864 and Pr. 1865 by Bp of Rip. C. in sole charge of Eastgate, near Stanhope, 1866. Formerly C. of Honley with Brockholes, near Huddersfield, 1864–66. [17]

CHAPMAN, William Hay, *Doveridge Vicarage, Uttoxeter.*—Trin. Coll. Cam. Jun. Opt. B.A. 1856, M.A. 1859; Deac. 1856 and Pr. 1858 by Bp of Nor. V. of Doveridge, Dio. Lich. 1867. (Patron, Duke of Devonshire; V.'s Inc. 650*l* and Ho; Pop. 750.) Formerly P. C. of High Cross, Herts, 1861; P. C. of Southwold, Suffolk, 1864–67. [18]

CHAPMAN, William James, 9, *Highbury-terrace, London, N.*—Dub. A.M. 1861; Deac. 1859 and Pr. 1860 by Bp of Carl. P. C. of Ch. Ch. Highbury, Dio. Lon. 1863. (Patrons, Trustees; P. C.'s Inc. 550*l*; Pop. 3229.) Formerly C. of Barbon, Westmoreland, 1859; P. C. of Arlecdon, Cumberland, 1860; C. of St. Giles', Camberwell, 1860, St. Mary's, Islington, 1862. [19]

CHAPPEL, Eldon Vaughan, *East Orchard, Shaftesbury.*—Trin Coll. Cam. B.A. 1853, M.A. 1856; Deac. 1853 and Pr. 1854 by Bp of Rip. V. of East Orchard, Dio. Salis. 1863. (Patron, V. of Iwerne Minster; Tithe, 100*l*; Rent from Glebe, 4*l*; V.'s Inc. 164*l* and Ho; Pop. 300.) Formerly C. of Rothwell, Yorkshire, 1853, Burgh with Winthorpe, Linc. 1860. [20]

CHAPPEL, William Pester, *Camborne Rectory, Cornwall.*—Wor. Coll. Ox. B.A. 1850, M.A. 1854; Deac. 1851 and Pr. 1852 by Bp of Rip. R. of Camborne, Dio. Ex. 1858. (Patron, J. F. Bassett, Esq; Tithe, Imp. 8*l*, R. 800*l*; Glebe, 55 acres; R.'s Inc. 885*l* and Ho; Pop. 7610.) Surrogate. Formerly Sen. C. of Hampstead, Middlesex. [21]

CHARGE, John, *Copgrove Rectory, Boroughbridge, Yorks.*—R. of Copgrove, Dio. Rip. 1813. (Patron, Thomas Duncombe, Esq; Tithe, 175*l*; Glebe, 25 acres; R.'s Inc. 209*l* and Ho; Pop. 68.) Rural Dean. [22]

CHARLES, George.—C. of Holy Cross and of Broughton, Worcestershire. [23]

CHARLES, Samuel, *Harvington, Evesham.*—Trin. Coll. Cam. B.A. 1842, M.A. 1845; Deac. 1842, Pr. 1844. [24]

CHARLES, Thomas, *Llanedwen, near Bangor.*—Lampeter; Deac. 1852 and Pr. 1853 by Bp of Ban. C. of Llanidan, Anglesey. [25]

CHARLESWORTH, Beedam, 1, *Paragon, Clifton, Bristol.*—Trin. Coll. Cam. Scho. of, 17th Wrang. B.A. 1827, M.A. 1830; Deac. 1830 by Bp of Roch. Pr. 1830 by Bp of Lon. C. in charge of the Henderson Memorial Church, Clifton. Formerly V. of Darfield, Dio. York, 1830–62. Author, *An Address on Confirmation*; *The Holy Spirit the Giver, and Light, and Comfort to Believers*, 1859; etc. [26]

CHARLESWORTH, Edward Gomersall, *Vicarage, Acklam, Middlesbro'.*—St. Bees 1852; Deac. 1853 by Abp of York, Pr. 1854 by Bp of Rip. V. of West Acklam, Dio. York, 1865. (Patron, Thomas Hustler, Esq; Tithe, 60*l*; Glebe, 20*l*; V.'s Inc. 200*l* and Ho; Pop. 300*l*.) Formerly C. of St. Mark's, Old-street, Lond. 1859–60, Kirby-on-the Moor, and Scammonden, Yorks, and Trinity, Darlington. Author, *The Ministry of the Bible*, Macintosh; *The Word in the Heart*, Seeleys; *Poems* (private circulation). [27]

CHARLESWORTH, Joseph Rhodes, *Elstead, Godalming, Surrey.*—St. John's Coll. Cam. 19th Sen. Opt. B.A. 1847, M.A. 1850; Deac. 1847 and Pr. 1848 by Abp of York. P. C. of Elstead, Dio. Win. 1854. (Patron, Wm. Stephenson, Esq; Tithe—App. 330*l*; Glebe, 5 acres; P. C.'s Inc. 47*l* and Ho; Pop. 818.) [1]

CHARLESWORTH, Joseph William, *Heacham, Lynn.*—St. Peter's Coll. Cam. B.A. 1831; Deac. 1832, Pr. 1833. V. of Heacham, Dio. Nor. 1853. (Patron, C. F. Neville Rolfe, Esq; Tithe, 263*l* 12*s* 8*d*; Glebe, 7¾ acres; V.'s Inc. 240*l*; Pop. 990.) [2]

CHARLESWORTH, Samuel, *Limpsfield Rectory, Godstone, Surrey.*—St. Bees; Deac. 1853 and Pr. 1854 by Bp of Win. R. of Limpsfield, Dio. Win. 1856. (Patron, Wm. Granville Leveson Gower, Esq; Tithe, 699*l* 18*s* 1*d*; Glebe, 28½ acres; R.'s Inc. 769*l* and Ho; Pop. 1216.) [3]

CHARLETON, John Kynaston, *Elberton, Vicarage, Almondsbury, Gloucestershire.*—Queen's Coll. Ox. B.A. 1826; Deac. 1826 and Pr. 1827 by Bp of Bristol. V. of Elberton, Dio. G. and B. 1828. (Patron, Bp of G. and B; Tithe—App. 81*l* 10*s*; Imp. 8*l*; V. 204*l* 10*s*; Glebe, 34 acres; V.'s Inc. 263*l* and Ho; Pop. 180.) [4]

CHARLEWOOD, Thomas, *Kinoulton, near Nottingham.*—St. Alban Hall, Ox. B.A. 1846; Deac. 1847, Pr. 1848. V. of Kinoulton, Dio. Lin. 1848. (Patron, Bp of Ches; Tithe—App. 462*l*, V. 238*l*; V.'s Inc. 240*l*; Pop. 430.) [5]

CHARLTON, Charles, *St. Paul's Parsonage, Alnwick.*—St. John's Coll. Cam. B.A. 1841, M.A. 1844; Deac. 1842 and Pr. 1843 by Bp of Pet. P. C. of St. Paul's, Alnwick, Dio. Dur. 1846. (Patron, Duke of Northumberland; P. C.'s Inc. 200*l* and Ho; Pop. 3277.) Formerly C. of Slipton, Northants, 1842–43, Cranford, Northants, 1843–44. [6]

CHARLTON, Charles Dennis, 33, *St. Mary's-terrace, Hastings.*—St. John's Coll. Cam. B.A. 1831, M.A. 1835; Deac. and Pr. 1832 by Bp of Chich. V. of Laughton, Dio. Chich. 1845. (Patron, Earl of Chichester; Tithe, 243*l*; Glebe, 6 acres; V.'s Inc. 253*l* and Ho; Pop. 742.) [7]

CHARLTON, James Allen, *Gosforth, Newcastle-on-Tyne.*—Dur. B.A. 1849, Licen. Theol. 1850, M.A. 1853; Deac. 1850 and Pr. 1851 by Bp of Dur. C. of Gosforth. [8]

CHARLTON, John Kynaston, *Longford Rectory, Newport, Salop.*—Ch. Ch. Ox. B.A. 1833, M.A. 1836; Deac. 1835, Pr. 1836. R. of Longford, Dio. Lich. 1844. (Patron, R. M. Leeke, Esq; Tithe, 144*l* 16*s* 6*d*; Glebe, 52 acres; R.'s Inc. 620*l* and Ho; Pop. 214.) [9]

CHARLTON, Robert, *Althorpe, near Doncaster.*—Queens' Coll. Cam. B.A. 1849; Deac. and Pr. 1849 by Bp of Ox. R. of Althorpe, Dio. Lin. 1862. (Patron, the Crown; Tithe—Imp. 5*l*, R. 320*l*; Glebe, 24 acres; R.'s Inc. 400*l* and Ho; Pop. 844.) Formerly P. C. of Kingsdown, Dio. Cant. 1850–62. [10]

CHARLTON, Samuel, *Fridaybridge Parsonage, Elm, Cambs.*—St. John's Coll. Cam. B.A. 1847, M.A. 1850; Deac. 1848 and Pr. 1849 by Bp of Ely. P. C. of Fridaybridge, Dio. Ely, 1860. (Patron, Bp of Ely; Tithe, 300*l*; Glebe, 8 acres and Ho; Pop. 869.) Formerly C. of Coveney 1848–52, temporarily of Isleham, Hemingford Gray, and St. Michael's, Coventry, 1852, Gazeley and Kentford 1852–56, Bottisham with Bottisham Lode 1856–60. Author, an *English Grammar*; *Letters on Popery*; etc. [11]

CHARLTON, William Henry, *Easton Rectory, Stamford.*—Trin. Coll. Cam. B.A. 1837, M.A. 1841; Deac. 1838 by Bp of Roch, Pr. 1839 by Bp of Pet. R. of Easton, Dio. Pet. 1848. (Patron, Marquis of Exeter; R.'s Inc. 480*l* and Ho; Pop. 984.) Dom. Chap. to the Marquis of Exeter 1846. Author, *A Life of the Lord-Treasurer Burghley*; *A Guide to Burghley House.* [12]

CHARRINGTON, Nicholas George, *Hawkley Parsonage, Petersfield.*—Oriel Coll. Ox. B.A. 1843, M.A. 1846; Deac. 1845, Pr. 1846. P. C. of Hawkley, Dio. Win. 1865. (Patron, J. J. Maberley, Esq; P. C.'s Inc. 150*l* and Ho; Pop 312.) [13]

CHARSLEY, Robert Harvey, *St. John's Lodge, Iffley-road, Oxford.*—St. Mary Hall, Ox. B.A. 1853, M.A. 1856; Deac. 1853, Pr. 1855. Chap. of the Radcliffe Infirmary. [14]

CHARTER, J.—C. of Shelton, Staffs. [15]

CHARTERS, Robert Henry, *Gainsborough.*—St. John's Coll. Cam. 27th Wrang. B.A. 1853; Deac. 1853 and Pr. 1855 by Bp of Rip. Mast. of the Gainsborough Gr. Sch. 1858. Formerly Asst. Mast. in Sedberg Gr. Sch; and 2nd Mast. of Walsall Gr. Sch. [16]

CHASE, Charles Frederic, *St. Anne's Rectory, St. Andrew's Hill, London, E.C.*—Trin. Hall, Cam. B.A. 1845, M.A. 1849; Deac. 1845 and Pr. 1846 by Bp of Pet. R. of St. Andrew-by-the-Wardrobe with St. Anne's, Blackfriars, City and Dio. Lon. 1852. (Patrons, Ld Chan. and Parishioners alt; Tithe, 233*l* 6*s* 8*d*; R.'s Inc. 260*l* and Ho; Pop. St. Andrew's 682, St. Anne's 2615.) [17]

CHASE, Drummond Percy, *St. Mary Hall, Oxford.*—Oriel Coll. Ox. 1st cl. Lit. Hum. and B.A. 1841, M.A. 1844; Deac 1844 and Pr. 1849 by Bp of Ox. Fell. of Oriel Coll. Ox. 1842; Principal of St. Mary Hall, Ox. 1857. Author, *Translation of Aristotle's Ethics*, 1847; etc. [18]

CHASE, Henry John Neale, *Twyning, Tewkesbury.*—King's Coll. Lond. Assoc. 1855; Deac. 1855 and Pr. 1856 by Abp of Cant. C. in sole charge of Twyning 1865. Formerly C. of Patrixbourne with Bridge 1855, Ch. Ch. Dover, 1856, Bourton-on-the-Hill 1857, St. John's, Cheltenham, 1865. [19]

CHASE, Temple Hamilton, *Cosgrove, Stony Stratford, Northants.*—Trin. Coll. Ox. 1837, Michel Scho. of Queen's Coll. Ox. 1840, 3rd cl. Lit. Hum. and B.A. 1841, M.A. 1844; Deac. 1842, Pr. 1843. Michel Fell. of Queen's Coll. Ox. 1843; C. of Cosgrove. Formerly P. C. of Lydbrook, Glouc. 1853–66. [20]

CHATAWAY, James, *Heckfield Vicarage, Winchfield.*—Clare Coll. Cam. B.A. 1851, M.A. 1854; Deac. 1852 and Pr. 1853 by Bp of Wor. C. of Heckfield 1866. Formerly V. of Wartling, Sussex, 1856–66. [21]

CHATAWAY, Thomas Eagle, *Peckleton Rectory, Hinckley.*—Emman. Coll. Cam. B.A. 1852, M.A. 1855; Deac. 1854 and Pr. 1855 by Bp of Wor. R. of Peckleton, Dio. Pet. 1864. (Patron, the present R; Tithe, 400*l*; Glebe, 80 acres; R.'s Inc. 460*l* and Ho; Pop. 376.) Formerly C. of Malvern Link 1854, Ecton 1857. [22]

CHATER, Andrew Fuller, *Nantwich Rectory, Cheshire.*—Dub. A.B. 1842, A.M. 1845; Deac. 1844, Pr. 1845. R. of Nantwich, Dio. Ches. 1846. (Patron, Lord Crewe; Tithe—Imp. 72*l* 3*s* 0½*d*, R. 117*l* 17*s* 9*d*; Glebe, 5 acres; R.'s Inc. 330*l* and Ho; Pop. 6546.) Chap. to Nantwich Union 1851; Surrogate 1847; Rural Dean of Nantwich 1865. Formerly C. of Drumcondra 1844, St. Thomas's, Dublin, 1845. [23]

CHATER, Daniel Sutcliffe, *Blackawton Vicarage, South Devon.*—Dub. A.B. 1845; Deac. 1845 and Pr 1846 by Bp of Ches. V. of Blackawton, Dio. Ex. 1861. (Patron, Henry Gibbon, Esq; Tithe, 75*l*; Glebe, 9¼ acres; V.'s Inc. 118*l* and Ho; Pop. 1234.) Formerly C. of Nantwich 1845–47; Head Mast. of Acton Gr. Sch. Cheshire, 1848–61. [24]

CHATFIELD, Allen William, *Much Marcle Vicarage (Herefordshire), near Dymock, Gloucestershire.*—Trin. Coll. Cam. Bell's Univ. Scho. Prizeman, 1st cl. Cl. Trip. and B.A. 1831, M.A. 1836; Deac. 1832 and Pr. 1833 by Bp of Roch. V. of Much Marcle with Yatton C. Dio. Herf. 1848. (Patron, W. M. Kyrle, Esq; Much Marcle, Tithe—App. 431*l* 12*s*, V. 45*l*; Glebe, 21 acres; Yatton, Tithe, 288*l* 10*s*; Glebe, 5 acres; V.'s Inc. 900*l* and Ho; Pop. Much Marcle 984, Yatton 225.) Rural Dean of Ross 1850. Formerly V. of Stotfold, Beds, 1833–48. Author, *An Assize Sermon*, 1835; *A Sermon in Aid of the S.P.C.K. and S.P.G.* 1850; *Three Sermons on the War*, 1854–55. [25]

CHATFIELD, Robert Money, *Woodford Vicarage, Salisbury.*—Trin. Coll. Cam. Jun. Opt. 5th in 1st cl. Cl. Trip. and B.A. 1827, M.A. 1831; Deac. 1828 and Pr. 1829 by Bp of S. and M. V. of Woodford with Wilsford-cum-Lake, Dio. Salis. 1830. (Patron, Bp of Salis; Woodford, Tithe—App. 640*l*, V. 189*l*; Glebe, 2¾ acres; Wilsford, Tithe—App. 52*l*, V. 52*l* 10*s*; V.'s Inc. 439*l* 10*s* and Ho; Pop. Woodford, 500, Wilsford-cum-Lake 140.) Rural Dean. Author, *A Memoir*; *Visitation Sermon*; *Catechism and Tract on Discipline*; etc. [1]

CHAVASSE, Ludovick Thomas, *Rushall Vicarage, Walsall, Staffs.*—St. Peter's Coll. Cam. B.A. 1851, M.A. 1854; Deac. 1852 by Bp of Man. Pr. 1853 by Bp of Wor. V. of Rushall, Dio. Lich. 1842. (Patrons, George Mellish, Esq, and H. Gurdon, Esq; Tithe—Imp. 14*l* 9*s* 6*d*, V. 175*l*; Glebe, 9½ acres; V.'s Inc. 330*l* and Ho; Pop. 3500.) Formerly C. of Ch. Ch. Birmingham, Wendover, Bucks, St. Peter's, Coventry, St. Matthew's, Denmark-hill, Lond. [2]

CHAVE, Edward William Tanner, *St. Anne's Vicarage, Wandsworth, S.W.*—Wor. Coll. Ox. S.C.L. 1840, B.A. 1841, M.A. 1844, B.D. and D.D. 1859; Deac. 1841 and Pr. 1842 by Bp of Ex. V. of St. Anne's, Wandsworth, Dio. Win. 1866. (Patroness, Miss Du Buisson; Tithe, 390*l*; Glebe, 3 acres; V.'s Inc. 800*l* and Ho; Pop. 7613.) Formerly R. of St. Pancras', Exeter, 1845–60; V. of Collumpton, Devon, 1861–64. [3]

CHAWNER, Charles Fox, *Blechingley Rectory, Reigate, Surrey.*—Corpus Coll. Cam. B.A. 1830, M.A. 1834. R. of Blechingley, Dio. Win. 1841. (Patron, Henry Chawner, Esq; Tithe, 1200*l*; Glebe, 100 acres; R.'s Inc. 1280*l* and Ho; Pop. 1691.) [4]

CHAWNER, Darwin Frank, *Fulbeck, Grantham.*—St. Peter's Coll. Cam. B.A. 1858, M.A. 1861; Deac. 1858 and Pr. 1859 by Bp of Ely. C. of Fulbeck. Formerly C. of Bolnhurst, Beds, 1863. [5]

CHAWNER, William, *Crich Vicarage, near Derby.*—St. John's Coll. Cam. B.A. 1844; Deac. 1843 and Pr. 1844 by Bp of Ches. V. of Crich, Dio. Lich. 1855. (Patrons, Trustees; V.'s Inc. 290*l*; Pop. 2839.) Formerly Chap. of the Liverpool Infirmary 1844–45; P. C. of Hurdsfield 1845–49, P. C. of Hollingsclough, 1849–50, P. C. of Quarnford 1850–55. [6]

CHAYTOR, Henry, *Croxdale, Durham.*—St. Mary Hall, Ox. B.A. 1827; Deac. 1832 by Bp of Roch. Pr. 1833 by Bp of Ches. R. of Croxdale, Dio. Dur. 1841. (Patrons, D. and C. of Dur; Tithe, 90*l* 15*s*; R.'s Inc. 280*l* and Ho; Pop. 478.) Formerly C. of Croxdale 1832–37. [7]

CHEALES, Alan Benjamin, *Brockham, Reigate, Surrey.*—Ch. Coll. Cam. Sen. Opt. and B.A. 1850, M.A. 1853; Deac. 1853 by Bp of G. and B. Pr. 1855 by Bp of Ox. P. C. of Brockham Green, Dio. Win. 1859. (Patron, Col. Goulburn; P. C.'s Inc. 190*l* and Ho; Pop. 761.) Formerly C. of Wargrave; Travelling Bachelor of the Univ. of Cam. 1850–53. [8]

CHEALES, John, *Skendleby, Spilsby, Lincolnshire.*—Brasen. Coll. Ox. B.A. 1822, M.A. 1825. V. of Skendleby, Dio. Lin. 1840. (Patron, Lord Willoughby D'Eresby; Tithe, 132*l* 10*s* 10*d*; Glebe, 23 acres; V.'s Inc. 190*l*; Pop. 299.) [9]

CHEEL, James, *St. Helens, Lancashire.*—Theol. Assoc. King's Coll. Lond; Deac. 1854 and Pr. 1855 by Abp of York. P. C. of Trinity, St. Helens, Dio. Ches. 1864. (Patron, P. C. of St. Helens; Pop. 4150.) Formerly C. of St. Mary's, Hull. [10]

CHEERE, Edward, *Little Drayton Parsonage, Market Drayton, Salop.*—King's Coll. Lond. Assoc. 1836; Deac. 1846 Pr. 1847. P. C. of Little Drayton, Dio. Lich. 1848. (Patron, V. of Drayton-in-Hales; P. C.'s Inc. 180*l* and Ho.; Pop. 2162.) Formerly C. of Drayton-in-Hales 1846–47. Author, *Church Catechism Explained*, 1861, 2*s* 6*d*. [11]

CHEERE, Frederick, *Ingham Rectory, Bury St. Edmunds.*—St. John's Coll. Cam. B.A. 1827, M.A. 1830; Deac. 1830 and Pr. 1831 by Bp of Lon. C. of Ingham. [12]

CHEESE, Edward, *Rectory, Haughton-le-Skerne, Darlington.*—Ball. Coll. Ox. B.A. 1856, M.A. 1858, M.A. Dur. 1862; Deac. 1857 and Pr. 1858 by Bp of Carl. R. of Haughton-le-Skerne, Dio. Dur. 1862. (Patron, Bp of Dur; Tithe, 700*l*; Glebe, 200*l*; R.'s Inc. 900*l* and Ho; Pop. 1100.) Chap to Bp of Dur. 1862. Formerly Chap. to Bp of Carl. 1857; Chap. to Bp Villiers of Dur. 1860; P. C. of Raughton Head, Cumberland, 1858–60. Author, *Pastoral Addresses at Raughton Head*, Carlisle, 1856–59; *Address on Restoration of Chapel at Coatham*, Darlington, 1865; *The Love of Life and the Love of God* (a Sermon on the Death of W. Bewick), Darlington, 1866. [13]

CHEESE, James Albert, *Gosforth Rectory, near Whitehaven.*—St. John's Coll. Cam. 9th Jun. Opt. B.A. 1851, M.A. 1854; Deac. 1852 and Pr. 1853 by Bp of Pet. R. of Gosforth, Dio. Carl. 1861. (Patron, Earl of Lonsdale; Glebe, 200 acres; R.'s Inc. 111*l* and Ho; Pop. 1146.) Formerly C. of Crick 1852–61. Author, *The Work of the Christian Ministry, its Manner and Reward*, 1863, 1*s*. [14]

CHEESE, John Edmund, *Bosbury Vicarage, Ledbury.*—Literate; Cl. Prizeman and Scho. Lampeter 1848; Deac. 1851 and Pr. 1852 by Bp. of St. D. V. of Bosbury Dio. Herf. 1866. (Patron, Bp of Herf; Tithe, 400*l*; V.'s Inc. 400*l* and Ho; Pop. 1100.) Formerly Asst. Cl. Mast. Coll. Institution, Llandovery, 1848–53; C. of St. Peter's, Hereford, 1853–56, Sutton St. Nicholas 1856–63; Presteign and Surrogate 1863-66. Author, *Parochial Sermons*, Macintosh, 1856; etc. [15]

CHEETHAM, Henry, *Quarndon, Derby.*—Ch. Coll. Cam. Scho. B.A. 1856, M.A. 1859; Deac. 1856 and Pr. 1857 by Bp of Roch. P. C. of Quarndon, Dio. Lich. 1858. (Patron, Lord Scarsdale; P. C.'s Inc. 114*l* and Ho; Pop. 496.) Formerly C. of Saffron Walden 1856–58. [16]

CHEETHAM, Samuel, 6, *Alleyn-road, Norwood, S.*—Ch. Coll. Cam. 6th Sen. Opt. 8th in 1st cl. Cl. Trip. B.A. 1850, M.A. 1853; Deac. 1851 and Pr. 1852 by Bp of Ches. Prof. of Pastoral Theology in King's Coll. Lond. 1863; Chap. of Dulwich Coll. (Val. 300*l* a-year and Ho.) 1866. Late Fell. and Asst. Tut. of Ch. Coll. Cam; Vice-Prin. of Coll. Institution, Liverpool; C. of Hitchin, Herts; Vice-Prin. of the Theol. Coll. and C. of St. Bartholomew's, Chichester. Author, *The Law of the Land and the Law of the Mind*, Macmillans, 1866; articles in *Contemporary Review*; etc. [17]

CHELL, George Russell, *Kneesall Vicarage, Newark.*—St. John's Coll. Cam. B.A. 1859; Deac. 1861 and Pr. 1862 by Abp of Cant. V. of Kneesall, Dio. Lin. 1868. (Patron, Chap. of Southwell; V.'s Inc. 300*l* and Ho; Pop. 553.) Formerly C. of Tenterden 1861, Hoveringham 1862. [18]

CHELL, James, *Bury, Lancashire.*—St. Bees; Deac. 1854. P. C. of St. Paul's, Bury, Dio. Man. 1862. (Patrons, Trustees; P. C.'s Inc. 300*l* and Ho; Pop. 10,808.) Formerly C. of St. Barnabas', Manchester. [19]

CHEPMELL, Havilland Le Mesurier, *Royal Military College, Sandhurst.*—Pemb. Coll. Ox. 1st cl. Lit. Hum. and B.A. 1833, M.A. 1836, B.D. and D.D. 1851; Deac. 1834 and Pr. 1835 by Bp of Ox. Chap. to the Royal Military College, Sandhurst, 1841. Author, *A Short Course of History*, 9th edit. Whittaker, 1867, 5*s*; *A Short Course of History*, 2nd series, 2 vols. 1857, 12*s*. [20]

CHEPMELL, William Henry, *Jesus College, Oxford.*—Magd. Hall, Ox. B.A. 1841, Jesus Coll. Ox. M.A. 1843; Deac. 1842, Pr. 1843. Fell. of Jesus Coll. Ox. Formerly C. of St. Peter-le-Bayley, Oxford. [21]

CHERRILL, Alfred King, *London-road, Worcester.*—St. John's Coll. Cam. 31st Wrang. 1st cl. Moral Sci. Trip. B.A. 1862, M.A. 1865; Deac. 1863 and Pr. 1864 by Bp of Win. C. of St. Helen's and St. Alban's, and 3rd. Mast in Cathl. Sch. Worcester, 1866. Formerly C. of Godstone, Surrey, 1863, Trinity, Greenwich, 1865. [22]

CHERRY, Benjamin Newman, *Hallow, near Worcester.*—Clare Coll. Cam. Scho. of, Jun. Opt. B.A. 1862; Deac. 1863 and Pr. 1864 by Bp of Wor. C. of Grimley with Hallow 1863. [23]

CHESHIRE, Henry Freeman, *Wyke, near Guildford, Surrey.*—Ox. B.A. 1832, M.A. 1843; Deac. 1835 and Pr. 1836 by Bp of B. and W. P. C. of Wyke,

Dio. Win. 1850. (Patron, Eton Coll; P. C.'s Inc. 181*l* and Ho; Pop. 521.) [1]

CHESSHIRE, Humphrey Pountney, *Stratton Vicarage, Swindon, Wilts.*—St. Peter's Coll. Cam. B.A. 1850, M.A. 1853; Deac. 1850, Pr. 1851. V. of Stratton St. Margaret, Dio. G. and B. 1864. (Patron, Mert. Coll. Ox. on nom. of Bp of G. and B; V.'s Inc. 280*l* and Ho; Pop. 1642.) Chap. of the Highworth and Swindon Union. Formerly C. of Headon with Upton, Notts; V. of same 1858–64. [2]

CHESSHIRE, J. S.—C. of St. George's, Kidderminster. [3]

CHESTER, The Right Rev. William JACOBSON, Lord Bishop of Chester, *The Palace, Chester.*—Lin. Coll. Ox. B.A. 1827, M.A. 1829, D.D. by decree of Convocation 1848; Deac. 1830, Pr. 1831. Consecrated Bp of Ches. 1865. (Episcopal Jurisdiction, the County Palatine of Chester and a portion of Lancashire; Inc. of See, 4500*l*; Pop. 1,248,416; Acres, 968,312; Deaneries, 8; Benefices, 360; Curates, 193; Church Sittings, 288,694.) His Lordship is Clerk of the Closet to the Queen. His Lordship was formerly Fell. of Ex. Coll. 1829; Vice-Prin. of Magd. Hall 1832; Select Preacher 1833 and 1842; Public Orator 1842; P. C. of Iffley 1839–40; R. of Ewelme, Dio. Ox. 1848–65; Regius Prof. of Divinity, Univ. of Ox. 1848–65; Can. of Ch. Ch. Ox. 1848–65. Author, *Clerical Duties* (an Ordination Sermon), 1836; New Editions of *Nowell's Catechism* (Univ. Press, 1835 and 1844); *S. Clementis Romani, S. Ignatii, S. Polycarpi, Patrum Apostolicorum quæ supersunt*, 2 vols. ib. 1838 (reprinted 1840 and 1847); *Sermons preached at Iffley*, 1840, reprinted in 1846; *Sermon on the Queen's Accession*, 1847; New Edition of *The Oxford Paraphrase and Annotations on the Epistles of St. Paul*, Univ. Press, 1852; *The Collected Works of Bishop Sanderson*, 6 vols. ib. 1854. [4]

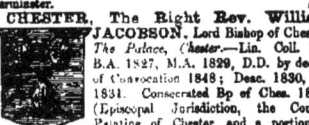

CHESTER, Greville John.—Queen's Coll. Ox. B.A. 1853, and Theol. Coll. Wells; Deac. 1855 by Abp of York, Pr. 1856 by Bp of Carl. Formerly P. C. of St. Jude's, Moorfields, Sheffield, 1858; C. of Crayke, Durham, 1855–58. Author, *Poems*, 1856, 3*s* 6*d*; *Statute Fairs, their Evils and their Remedy*; various Sermons. [5]

CHESTER, Matthew, *St. Helen's Auckland, Bishops Auckland.*—Deac. 1817, Pr. 1818. P. C. of St. Helen's Auckland, Dio. Dur. 1822. (Patron, Bp of Dur; Tithe—Imp. 119*l* 1*s* 6*d*; P. C. 6*l* 7*s* Glebe, 30 acres; P. C.'s Inc. 286*l*; Pop. 2843.) [6]

CHESTER, Thomas Henry, *Parsonage, South Shields.*—Dur. B.A. 1850, M.A. 1857; Deac. 1851 and Pr. 1852 by Bp of Dur. P. C. of South Shields, Dio. Dur. 1862. (Patrons, D. and C. of Dur; Glebe, 50 acres; P. C.'s Inc. 500*l* and Ho; Pop. 6000.) Surrogate. Formerly C. of Jarrow 1851–59, St. Helen's Auckland 1859–60; P. C. of Jarrow 1860–62. [7]

CHETTLE, William Walker, *Brook House, Ash-road, Aldershot.*—St. Aidan's; Deac. 1866 by Bp of Win. C. of Aldershot 1866. [8]

CHETWODE, George, *Ashton-under-Lyne Rectory, Lancashire.*—Brasen. Coll. Ox. B.A. 1814, M.A. 1815. R. of Ashton-under Lyne, Dio. Man. 1816. (Patron, Earl of Stamford and Warrington; R.'s Inc. 1000*l* and Ho; Pop. 25,363.) P. C. of Chilton, Bucks, Dio. Ox. 1829. (Patron, C. S. Ricketts, Esq; P.C.'s Inc. 69*l*; Pop. 364.) [9]

CHEVALLIER, Charles Henry, *Aspall, Debenham, Suffolk.*—Trin. Coll. Ox. 3rd cl. Lit. Hum. and B.A. 1847, M.A. 1852; Deac. 1848, Pr. 1849. P. C. of Aspall, Dio. Nor. 1849. (Patron, the present P. C; Tithe—Imp. 251*l* 13*s*; Glebe, 25 acres; P. C.'s Inc. 280*l*; Pop. 156.) Magistrate for the Co. of Suffolk. [10]

CHEVALLIER, Temple, *The College, Durham.*—Pemb. Coll. and St. Cath. Coll. Cam. Bell's Univ. Scho. 1814, 2nd Wrang. 2nd Smith's Prizeman and B.A. 1817, M.A. 1820, B.D. 1833; Deac. 1820 and Pr. 1821 by Bp of Ely. P. C. of Esh, Dio. Dur. 1835. (Patron, Bp of Dur; P. C.'s Inc. 206*l* and Ho; Pop. 942.) Hon. Can. of Dur. Cathl. 1846; Prof. of Mathematics and Astronomy in the Univ. of Dur. 1835; Registrar of the Univ. of Dur. 1835; Rural Dean. Formerly Fell. of Pemb. Coll. Cam. and Fell. and Tut. of St. Cath. Coll. Cam; Hulsean Lecturer 1826–27. Author, *Hulsean Lectures*, 1826–27; Translator of the *Epistles of Clement of Rome, Polycarp, and Ignatius, and of the Apologies of Justin Martyr and Tertullian*, 1 vol. 1833, 2nd edit. 1851; *Sermons*, 1 vol. 1835. [11]

CHEYNE, Thomas Kelly, *St. Edmund Hall, Oxford.*—Wor. Coll. Ox. B.A. 1862, Kennicott Hebrew Scho. 1863, Johnson, Theol. Scho. 1863, Ellerton Theol. Prize 1863; Pusey and Ellerton Hebrew Scho. 1864, Chan's English Essay 1864, M.A. 1865; Deac. 1864 and Pr. 1865 by Bp of Ox. Chap. and Div. Lect. of St. Edm. Hall 1864. [12]

CHICHESTER, The Right Rev. Ashhurst Turner GILBERT, Lord Bishop of Chichester, 31, *Queen Anne-street, Cavendish-square, London, W.* and *The Palace, Chichester, Sussex.*—Brasen. Coll. Ox. 1st cl. Lit. Hum. 1808, B.A. 1809, M.A. 1811, B.D. 1817, D.D. 1822. Consecrated Bp of Chich. 1842. (Episcopal Jurisdiction, the County of Sussex; Inc. of See, 4200*l*; Pop. 363,735; Acres, 934,851; Deaneries, 12; Benefices, 330; Curates, 104; Church Sittings, 133,512.) His Lordship was formerly Examiner in Lit. Hum. Ox. 1816; Fell. of Brasen. Coll; Principal of Brasen. Coll. Ox. 1822–42. Author, *Anniversary Sermon for the S.P.G.* (printed in the Society's Report), 1847; *God's Blessing the only Security against National Want*, 1847; *Jacob and Israel Contrasted*, 1847; *Sermon on the Consecration of St. Paul's Church, Brighton*, 1849; *Pictorial Crucifixes* (a Pamphlet), 1852; *Self-Sacrifice for Christ and his Gospel*, 1854; *The Knowledge of a Future Life under the Old Testament and under the New*, 1859; various single Sermons and Episcopal Charges. [13]

CHICHESTER, A. Manners.—C. of Ramsgate, Kent. [14]

CHICHESTER, James Hamilton John, *Arlington, Barnstaple.*—Magd. Coll. Cam. B.A. 1822, M.A. 1825; Deac. 1824, Pr. 1825. R. of Loxhore, Dio. Ex. 1825. (Patron, Sir Bluro Chichester, Bart; Tithe, 175*l*; Glebe, 50 acres; R.'s Inc. 354; Pop. 126.) R. of Arlington, Devon, Dio. Ex. 1824. (Patron, Sir Bluro Chichester; Tithe, 275*l*; Glebe, 110 acres; R.'s Inc. 320*l*; Pop. 219.) [15]

CHICHESTER, James John, *Clovelly Rectory, Bideford, Devon.*—Magd. Hall, Ox. B.A. 1848; Deac. 1849 and Pr. 1850 by Bp of St. D. R. of Clovelly, Dio. Ex. 1856. (Patroness, Mrs. Hamlyn Fane; Tithe, 213*l* 10*s*; Glebe, 100 acres; R.'s Inc. 310*l* and Ho; Pop. 925.) [16]

CHICHESTER, J. C. B.—C. of Bothal, Northumberland. [17]

CHIDLOW, Charles, 24, *Elizabeth-street, Pembroke-place, Liverpool.*—Jesus Coll. Ox. 3rd cl. in Law and Mod. History and B.A. 1860; Deac. 1866 by Bp of Ches. C. of St. Mary Magdalene's, Liverpool, 1866. [18]

CHILD, Alfred, *Rotherfield, near Tunbridge Wells.*—R. of Rotherfield, Dio. Chich. 1865. (Patron, Earl of Abergavenny; R.'s Inc. 1500*l* and Ho; Pop. 3031.) [19]

CHILD, Alfred, *Compton Dando, Bristol.*—Emman. Coll. Cam. B.A. 1862; Deac. 1863 and Pr. 1864 by Bp of Salis. C. of Compton Dando 1866. Formerly C. of Amesbury and Allington, near Salisbury, 1863–66. [20]

CHILD, John.—C. of Jarrow, Durham. [21]

CHILD, Thomas, *Upper Clatford, Andover, Hants.*—Queen's Coll. Ox. B.A. 1828, M.A. 1835; Deac. 1831 by Bp of Lich, Pr. 1838 by Bp of Win. R. of Upper Clatford, Dio. Win. 1868. (Patron, the present R; Tithe, 525*l*; Glebe, 38 acres; R.'s Inc. 680*l* and Ho; Pop. 706.) Formerly C. of Appleshaw. [22]

CHILD, Vicesimus Knox, *Little Easton Rectory, Dunmow, Essex.*—Sid. Coll. Cam. B.A. 1829, M.A. 1832; Deac. 1829 and Pr. 1830 by Bp of Lin. R. of

Little Easton, Dio. Roch. 1855. (Patron, Viscount Maynard; Tithe, 316*l*; Glebe, 58 acres; R.'s Inc. 360*l* and Ho; Pop. 357.) [1]

CHILDE, Arthur, *Edwin Ralph Rectory, Bromyard, Herefordshire.*—Trin. Coll Cam. B.A. 1840, M.A. 1843; Deac. 1845 and Pr. 1846 by Bp of Ches. R. of Edwin Ralph with Collington R. Dio. Herf. 1847. (Patron, W. Childe, Esq; Tithe, 260*l* 5*s*; Glebe, 17 acres; Collington, Tithe, 146*l* 16*s*; Glebe, 43 acres; R.'s Inc. 435*l* and Ho; Pop. Edwin Ralph 165, Collington 150.) [2]

CHILDE, Charles Frederick, *Holbrook Rectory, Ipswich.*—Emman. Coll. Cam. B.A. 1832, M.A. 1837. R. of Holbrook, Dio. Nor. 1858. (Patron, Rev. John Brewster Wilkinson; Tithe, 488*l*; Glebe, 7 acres; R.'s Inc. 500*l* and Ho; Pop. 903.) Formerly Prin. of the Church Miss. Coll. and Sunday Even. Lect. at St. Mary's, Islington. [3]

CHILDE, Edward George, *Kinlet Hall (Salop), Bewdley.*—Trin. Coll. Cam. B.A. 1843, M.A. 1846; Deac. 1845, Pr. 1846. V. of Kinlet, Dio. Herf. 1846. (Patron, W. L. Childe, Esq; Tithe, 7*s* 6*d*, V. 320*l*; Glebe, 45 acres; V.'s Inc. 410*l* and Ho; Pop. 424.) V. of Cleobury Mortimer, Salop, Dio. Herf. 1847. (Patron, W. L. Childe, Esq; Tithe—Imp. 12*s* 6*d*; App. 18*s* 6*d* and 6 acres of Glebe, V. 552*l*; V.'s Inc. 560*l* and Ho; Pop. 1397.) [4]

CHILDERS, Charles. — British Chap. at Nice. [5]

CHILDS, Henry Horatio.—C. of Caxton, Cambs. [6]

CHILDS, John Glynn, *St. Dennis, St. Austell, Cornwall.*—Trin. Coll. Cam. B.A. 1833; Deac. 1833 by Bp of Carl. Pr. 1834 by Bp of Ex. R. of St. Dennis, Dio. Ex. 1852. (Patron, Hon. G. M. Fortescue; Tithe, 253*l* 10*s*; Glebe, 5 acres; R.'s Inc. 254*l*; Pop. 993.) Formerly C. of Lydford, Devon, 1833, Woolfardisworthy 1835, Tregony 1837, St. Blazey 1839, Perran-Arworthal, Cornwall, 1842; P. C. of St. Paul's, East Stonehouse, Devon, 1844; C. of Hatfield, Herts, 1847. [7]

CHILDS, Thomas Cave, *Nympton St. George, South Molton, Devon.*—Sid. Coll. Cam. M.A; Deac. 1844, Pr. 1845. R. of Nympton St. George, Dio. Ex. 1857. (Patron, Sir T. D. Acland, Bart; R.'s Inc. 310*l* and Ho; Pop. 258.) Formerly P. C. of St. Mary's, Devonport, 1846. [8]

CHILDS, William Linington, *Carrington, Boston, Linc.*—Magd. Hall, Ox. B.A. 1851; Deac. 1851 and Pr. 1852 by Bp of Lin. P. C. of Carrington, Dio. Lin. 1862. (Patrons, Trustees; P. C.'s Inc. 86*l*; Pop. 347.) P. C. of Frithville, Boston, Dio. Lin. 1862. (Patrons, Trustees; P. C.'s Inc. 82*l*; Pop. 317.) Formerly C. of Boston 1851, St. Margaret's, King's Lynn, 1854, Thurgarton with Hoveringham 1856. [9]

CHILMAN, William G.—C. of Wetwang, Yorks. [10]

CHILTON, George Robert Comyn.—Ch. Ch. Ox. B.A. 1848, M.A. 1852; Deac. 1853 and Pr. 1854 by Bp of Nor. Formerly C. of Harleston, Norfolk, 1853–54, Puttenham 1856–59, and Wanborough, Surrey, 1861. [11]

CHILTON, Robert, *Slapton Rectory, Leighton Buzzard.*—Trin. Coll. Cam. Wrang. and B.A. 1848, M.A. 1851; Deac. 1849 and Pr. 1851 by Bp of G. and B. C. in sole charge of Slapton 1867. Formerly C. of Westbury and Hungerford. [12]

CHINNERY, Sir Nicholas, Bart., 18, *Hyde-park-square, London, W.*—Queens' Coll. Cam. B.A. 1825, M.A. 1829; Deac. 1827 and Pr. 1828 by Bp of Lich. Formerly C. of Charlton, Dio. Lich. 1827, Ch. Ch. Gloucester, 1829, Ardingly, Sussex, 1830, Trinity Chapel, Conduit-street, Lond. 1855. Author, *The Coming of Christ in His Millennial Glory*, 1829; *The Duty of Contending for the Faith*, 1862; *Anglican Formalism*, 1862; *The Design of Heresies*, 1867. [13]

CHIPPINDALL, John, *St. Luke's Rectory, Cheetham Hill, Manchester.*—Wor. Coll. Ox. B.A. 1848, M.A. 1850; Deac. 1848 and Pr. 1849 by Bp of Roch. R. of St. Luke's, Cheetham, Dio. Man. 1863. (Patrons, Trustees; R.'s Inc. 750*l* and Ho; Pop. 4719.) Formerly C. of St. Peter's, St. Albans, 1848–51; P. C. of Rocester, Staffs, 1851–55; P. C. of Warslow with Elkstone, Staffs, 1855–63. [14]

CHITTENDEN, Charles Grant, *Boddesdon, Herts.*—B.A. 1851; Deac. 1851, Pr. 1852. Formerly C. of Bishops Hatfield. [15]

CHITTENDEN, John, D.D., 10, *Linden-grove, Nunhead, Peckham, S.E.* [16]

CHITTENDEN, Thomas Knapp, *Kirtlington Vicarage, near Oxford.*—St. John's Coll. Ox. B.A. 1840, M.A. 1844, B.D. 1849; Deac. 1842 and Pr. 1843 by Bp of Ox. V. of Kirtlington, Dio. Ox. 1858. (Patron, St. John's Coll. Ox; 226½ acres in lieu of Tithes; Glebe, 3 acres; V.'s Inc. 431*l* and Ho; Pop. 710.) Formerly C. of Bix, near Henley-on-Thames; Fell. of St. John's Coll. Ox. [17]

CHOLMELEY, Charles Humphrey, *Magdalen College, Oxford.*—Magd. Coll. Ox. B.A. 1851, M.A. 1853; Deac. 1857 and Pr. 1858 by Bp of Ox. Fell. of Magd. Coll. Ox. Formerly R. of Sherborne St. John, Hants, 1864–65. [18]

CHOLMELEY, James, *Swaby, near Alford.*—Emman. Coll. Cam. Scho. of, 2nd Sen. Opt. and B.A. 1856, Ox. M.A. 1860; Deac. 1860 and Pr. 1862 by Bp of Ox. R. of Swaby, Dio. Lin. 1865. (Patron, Magd. Coll. Ox; Glebe, 327 acres; R.'s Inc. 480*l* and Ho; Pop. 497.) Formerly Math. Mast. of Gr. Sch. Bath 1857; Fell. of Magd. Coll. Ox. 1857; Math. Lect. of Magd. Coll. 1859–64; C. of Forest-hill, Oxon, 1860–64; V. of Abbotskerswell, Devon, 1864–65. [19]

CHOLMELEY, John, *The Rectory, Carleton-Rode, Attleborough.*—St. Cath. Coll. Cam. Scho. B.A. 1850, M.A. 1853; Deac. 1851 and Pr. 1852 by Bp of Lin. R. of Carleton-Rode, Dio. Nor. 1859. (Patron, Sir R. J. Buxton; Tithe, 921*l*; Glebe, 50 acres; R.'s Inc. 968*l* and Ho; Pop. 905.) Formerly P. C. of Wainflete St. Mary, Linc. 1852–59. [20]

CHOLMELEY, Robert, D.D., *Findon, Shoreham, Sussex.*—Wad. Corpus and Magd. Colls. Ox. B.A. 1840, M.A. 1843; Deac. 1841 by Bp of Ox. V. of Findon, Dio. Chich. 1860. (Patron, Magd. Coll. Ox; V.'s Inc. 500*l* and Ho; Pop. 655.) Fell. of Magd. Coll. Ox. 1843; Sen. Proctor 1854; Vice-President of Magd. Coll. Ox. 1856. [21]

CHOLMELEY, Waldo, *St. Mary's Vicarage, South Walsham, Blofield, Norwich.*—St. Bees; Deac. 1856 and Pr. 1857 by Bp of Man. V. of South Walsham, Dio. Nor. 1865. (Patrons, Trustees of Norwich Hospital; Tithe, 160*l*; Glebe, 26 acres; V.'s Inc. 230*l* and Ho; Pop. 360.) P. C. of Hemblington, Dio. Nor. 1866. (Patrons, D. and C. of Nor; P. C.'s Inc. 80*l*; Pop. 220.) Formerly C. of Church Kirk 1856–58, Hambledon 1858–61, South Kelsey 1863–65. [22]

CHOLMONDELEY, The Hon. Henry Pitt, *Adlestrop Rectory, Chipping Norton.*—Ch. Ch. Ox. B.A. 1840, M.A. 1845; Deac. 1845 and Pr. 1846 by Bp of Ox. R. of Broadwell with Adlestrop, Dio. G. and B. 1852. (Patron, Lord Leigh; Glebe, 500 acres; R.'s Inc. 715*l* and Ho; Pop. Broadwell 398, Adlestrop 184.) Rural Dean. Formerly Fell. of All Souls', Ox. and R. of Hamstall-Ridware, Staffs, 1848–52. Author, *Parish Sermons*, Shrimpton, Oxford, 1856, 5*s*. [23]

CHOLMONDELEY, George James, *Canterbury, New Zealand.*—St. Aidan's, 1858; Deac. 1858 by Bp of Nor. Pr. 1859 by Bp of G. and B. Formerly C. of Lydney with Aylburton, Glouc. 1858–60. [24]

CHOLMONDELEY, Richard Hugh, *Leaton Parsonage, Shrewsbury.*—Trin. Coll. Cam. B.A. 1851, M.A; Deac. 1852, Pr. 1853. P. C. of Leaton, Dio. Lich. 1865. (Patrons, C. S. and A. Lloyd, Esqs; P. C.'s Inc. 110*l* and Ho; Pop. 434.) Formerly C. of Hodnet, Salop, and Farnborough, Warwickshire. [25]

CHOPE, Richard Robert, *Wilton House, Hereford-square, South Kensington, London, S.W.*—Ex. Coll. Ox. B.A. 1855; Deac. 1856 and Pr. 1857 by Bp of G. and B. P. C. of St. Augustine's, Hereford-square (a new district). Formerly C. of Stapleton 1856, Sherborne 1858, Upton Scudamore 1859, Brompton 1861. Author,

Hymn and Tune Book, Simpkin, Marshall and Co; *Hymn and Tune Book*, Mackenzie; *Prayer-Book Noted and Pointed, Canticles and Psalms separately*, Mackenzie; *The Catechist*, Simpkin, Marshall and Co; *Choral Communion Office*, Rivingtons. [1]

CHOPE, Thomas How, *Hartland, Bideford, Devon.*—P. C. of Hartland, Dio. Ex. 1859. (Patrons, Govs. of Charter-house, Lond; P. C.'s Inc. 97*l* and Ho; Pop. 1916.) Formerly C. of Hawkesbury. [2]

CHORLEY, Francis W.—P. C. of St. Luke's, Leeds, Dio. Rip. 1864. (Patron, V. of Leeds; P. C.'s Inc. 136*l* and Ho; Pop. 5000.) [3]

CHORLTON, Samuel, *Brook-villa, Brook-hill, Sheffield.*—Dub. A.B. 1861, A.M. 1865; Deac. 1866 and Pr. 1867 by Abp of York. 2nd Mast. of Gr. Sch. and C. of St. James's, Sheffield. [4]

CHOWNE, James Henry, *Slape House, Beaminster, Dorset.*—St. Peter's Coll. Cam. B.A. 1847, M.A. 1851; Deac. 1847 and Pr. 1848 by Bp of Wor. Formerly C. of Pershore 1848, Netherbury 1854; Travelling Sec. of S.P.G. 1858–65; previously an Officer in the Bengal Army. [5]

CHRETIEN, Charles Peter, *Cholderton, Salisbury.*—Brasen. Coll. Ox. 1st cl. Lit. Hum. and B A. 1841, M.A. 1844; Deac. 1844, Pr. 1846. R. of Cholderton, Dio. Salis. 1860. (Patron, Oriel Coll. Ox; Tithe, 265*l*; Glebe, 7 acres; R.'s Inc. 300*l* and Ho; Pop. 191.) Formerly Fell. Dean and Tut. of Oriel Coll. Author, *An Essay on a Logical Method*, 1848; *Lectures on the Study of Theology*, 1851; *The Letter and the Spirit* (University Sermons) Macmillan, 1861. [6]

CHRISTIAN, Frederick White, *South Wingfield, Alfreton, Derbyshire.*—Trin. Hall, Cam. B.A. 1859; Deac. 1859 and Pr. 1860 by Bp of Pet. C. of South Wingfield. Formerly C. of Tinwell and Stubton. [7]

CHRISTIE, Campbell Manning, *The Parsonage, Morpeth-street, Bethnal-green, London, N.E.*—St. Bees; Deac. 1841 and Pr. 1842 by Bp of Ches. P. C. of St. Simon Zelotes', Bethnal-green, Dio. Lon. 1857. (Patron, Bp of Lon; P. C.'s Inc. 300*l* and Ho; Pop. 6216.) Formerly C. of St. Nicholas', Whitehaven, 1841–44; P. C. of Thornthwaite, Cumberland, 1844–51, P. C. of Stony Stratford, Bucks, 1851–57. [8]

CHRISTIE, Charles H.—C. of All Saints', Margaret-street, Marylebone, Lond. [9]

CHRISTIE, James John, *Rotherham.*—St. John's Coll. Cam. B.A. 1855, M.A. 1858; Deac. 1856 and Pr. 1857 by Bp of Lon. Head Mast. of Rotherham Gr. Sch. 1865. Formerly Math. Lect. at the Training Coll. Highbury, Lond. 1855–57; 2nd Mast. of East Retford Gr. Sch. 1860–65; C. of Waterford, near Hertford, 1859–60, Lound, near East Retford, 1861–64. [10]

CHRISTIE, Richard Cooper, *Castle-Combe, Chippenham, Wilts.*—Trin. Hall, Cam. Scho. of, LL.B. 1828. R. of Castle-Combe, Dio. G. and B. 1851. (Patron, G. P. Scrope, Esq. M.P; Tithe, 383*l*; Glebe, 25 acres; R.'s Inc. 400*l*; Pop. 534.) [11]

CHRISTOPHER, Alfred Millard William, *St. Aldate's, Oxford.*—Jesus Coll. Cam. 19th Wrang. and B.A. 1843, M.A. 1849; Deac. 1849 and Pr. 1850 by Bp of Win. R. of St. Aldate's, City and Dio. Ox. 1859. (Patrons, Simeon's Trustees; Tithe, 124*l* 14*s* 11*d*; Glebe, 12 acres; R.'s Inc. 237*l*; Pop. 1834.) Formerly Assoc. Sec. to the Ch. Miss. Soc; Prin. of La Martinière, Calcutta; C. of St John's, Richmond. Author, *Look and Live* (a Tract), 6*d*. Editor of the *Life of the Rev. J. J. Weitbrecht, Church Missionary at Burdwan, in Bengal*, 7*s* 6*d*. [12]

CHRISTOPHERSON, Arthur, *Caton Parsonage, near Lancaster.*—St. John's Coll. Cam. 10th Sen. Opt. and B.A. 1836, M.A. 1839; Deac. 1840 and Pr. 1841 by Bp of Ches. P. C. of Caton, Dio. Man. 1852. (Patron, V. of Lancaster; Tithe—Imp. 184*l* 13*s* 4*d*, P. C. 48*l*; Glebe, 70 acres; P. C.'s Inc. 160*l* and Ho; Pop. 1067.) [13]

CHRISTOPHERSON, Brian, *Batley, Leeds.*—St. John's Coll. Cam. B.A. 1862, M.A. 1865; Deac. 1863 and Pr. 1864 by Bp of Rip. Head Mast. of Batley Gr. Sch. 1864. Formerly C. of St. James's, Thornes, 1863. [14]

CHRISTOPHERSON, Henry.—Deac. 1867 by Bp of Lon. C. of St. Clement's, Notting-hill. [15]

CHRISTOPHERSON, John, *Westmoreland-street, High Harrogate.*—Queens' Coll. Cam. B.A. 1839; Deac. 1841, Pr. 1842. Assoc. Sec. of Soc. for Evangelisation of Jews. [16]

CHRITCHLEY, John Martyn, *Chester.*—Dub. A.B. 1858; Deac. 1859 by Bp of Chich. Vice-Prin. of Training Coll. Chester. [17]

CHUDLEIGH, Nicholas Ford, *St. Columb Minor Parsonage, St. Columb, Cornwall.*—Magd. Hall, Ox. B.A. 1833; Deac. 1833 and Pr. 1834 by Bp of Ex. P. C. of St. Columb Minor, Dio. Ex. 1841. (Patron, Lord Churston; Glebe, 28 acres; P. C.'s Inc. 155*l* and Ho; Pop. 2067.) [18]

CHURCH, Alfred John, *Merchant Taylors' School, 6, Suffolk-lane, Cannon-street, London, E.C.*—Lin. Coll. Ox. B.A. 1851, M.A. 1853; Deac. 1853, Pr. 1854. Fourth Mast. in Merchant Taylors' Sch. and C. of St. Peter's, Marylebone. Formerly C. of Westport St. Mary, Wilts. [19]

CHURCH, Charles Marcus, *Theological College, Wells.*—Oriel Coll. Ox. 2nd cl. Lit. Hum. and B.A. 1845, M.A. 1850; Deac. 1850 and Pr. 1851 by Bp of B. and W. Prin of the Theol. Coll. Wells; Sub-Dean and Preb. of Wells Cathl. [20]

CHURCH, George Lemon, *Chacewater Parsonage, Truro, Cornwall.*—St. John's Coll. Cam. B.A. 1846; Deac. 1846 and Pr. 1847 by Bp of Ex. P. C. of Chacewater, Dio. Ex. 1848. (Patron, V. of Kenwyn; P. C.'s Inc. 140*l* and Ho; Pop. 4629.) [21]

CHURCH, Richard William, *Whatley Rectory, Frome, Somerset.*—R. of Whatley, Dio. B. and W. 1853. (Patron, Rev. J. S. H. Horner; Tithe, 226*l*; Glebe, 17 acres; R.'s Inc. 232*l* and Ho; Pop. 221.) [22]

CHURCH, William Montagu Higginson, *Hunstanton Vicarage, King's Lynn, Norfolk.*—Dur. Licen. in Theol. 1842; Deac. and Pr. 1842 by Bp of Dur. V. of Hunstanton, Dio. Nor. 1861. (Patron, H. S. Le Strange, Esq; Tithe, 299*l* 13*s*; Glebe, 18 acres; V.'s Inc. 330*l* and Ho; Pop. 630.) Formerly C. of Wooler, Northumberland, 1842–43; V. of Geddington with Newton, Dio. Pet. 1844–61. Author, *Do you love Christ?* (a Tract). [23]

CHURCHILL, Benjamin, *Bearley, near Stratford-on-Avon.*—Queen's Coll. Ox. B.C.L. 1846; Deac. 1846 and Pr 1847 by Bp of Wor. P. C. of Bearley, Dio. Wor. 1865. (Patron, King's Coll. Cam; Tithe, 6*l*; Glebe, 25 acres; P.C.'s Inc. 71*l*; Pop. 238.) Formerly C. of Gaydon 1846–52, Wolverton 1852–64. [24]

CHURCHILL, E. B. C., M.A., *Portsea, Hants.*—P. C. of All Saints', Portsea, Dio. Win. 1861. (Patron, the V. of Portsea; P. C.'s Inc. 301*l*; Pop. 18,478.) Surrogate. [25]

CHURCHILL, Smith, *Boughton Rectory, Stoke Ferry, Norfolk.*—Pemb. Coll. Cam. B.A. 1835; Deac. 1840 by Bp of Nor. Pr. 1842 by Bp of Ely. R. of Boughton, Dio. Nor. 1853. (Patron, Sir W. J. H. B. Folkes, Bart; Tithe, 418*l*; Glebe, 29 acres; R.'s Inc. 458*l* and Ho; Pop. 238.) [26]

CHURCHILL, William, *Winterbourne Stickland Rectory, Blandford, Dorset.*—Wor. Coll. Ox. B.A. 1825; Deac. 1827 by Bp of Llan. Pr. 1827 by Bp of Ely. R. of Winterbourne Stickland, Dio. Salis. 1828. (Patron, Baron Hamboro; Tithe, 326*l* 10*s* 4*d*; R.'s Inc. 350*l* and Ho; Pop. 444.) Author, *Questions on the Church Catechism.* [27]

CHURTON, Bernard, *Wheathill Rectory, Bridgnorth, Salop.*—St. John's Coll. Cam. B.A. 1833; Deac. 1834 and Pr. 1835 by Bp of Herf. R. of Wheathill, Dio. Herf. 1849. (Patron, the present R; Tithe, 215*l*; Glebe, 93 acres; R.'s Inc. 300*l* and Ho; Pop. 123.) Chap. to Viscount Boyne. [28]

CHURTON, The Venerable Edward, *Crayke Rectory, near York.*—Ch. Ch. Ox. B.A. 1821, M.A. 1824; Deac. 1826 and Pr. 1827 by Bp of Lon. R. of Crayke, Dio. York, 1835. (Patron, Bp of Dur; Tithe,

686*l*; R.'s Inc. 700*l* and Ho; Pop. 585.) Preb. of Knaresborough in York Cathl. 1841; Archd. of Cleveland 1846 (Value, 206*l*.) Author, *The Cleveland Psalter*; *Gongora, or, a Historical and Critical Essay on the Age of Philip III. and IV. of Spain, with Translations from the Works of Gongora*, 2 vols. Murray, 1863. [1]

CHURTON, Henry Burgess Whitaker, *Icklesham Vicarage, Rye, Sussex.*—Ball. Coll. Ox. B.A. 1831, M.A. 1835; Deac. 1835 and Pr. 1836 by Bp of Ox. V. of Icklesham with Rye Harbour C. Dio. Chich. 1844. (Patron, Bp of Ox; Tithe—App. 471*l* 13*s* 8*d*, V. 735*l* 3*s*; Glebe, 4½ acres; V.'s Inc. 800*l* and Ho; Pop. 816.) Preb. of Colworth in Chich. Cathl. 1842; Exam. Chap. to the Bp of Chich; Preacher at the Charterhouse, 1842–44. Author, *Land of the Morning*, 1851, 10*s* 6*d*; *Gerhard's Meditations* (Translated and Edited jointly with the Rev. H. Highton, of Rugby), 1840, 3*s* 6*d*; *Texts for Students*, Parts I. and II. 1840–41, 1*s*. [2]

CHURTON, William Ralph, *King's College, Cambridge.*—King's Coll. Cam. 15th Wrang. 1860, Hulsean Prize 1860, 1st cl. Theol. Ex. 1860, B.A. 1860, M.A. 1863; Deac. 1860 and Pr. 1861 by Bp of Lin. Fell. Dean and Tut. of King's Coll. and C. of Great St. Mary's, Cambridge, 1864; Exam. Chap. to Bp of Roch. 1867. Formerly C. of St. George's, Kidderminster, 1860–64. Author, *The Influence of the Septuagint Version of the Old Testament upon the Progress of Christianity*, Macmillans, 1861, 3*s* 6*d*. [3]

CHUTE, Devereux W., *Sherborne St. John, Basingstoke.*—Univ. Coll. Ox. B.A. 1862, M.A. 1865; Deac. 1863 and Pr. 1864 by Bp of G. and B. R. of Sherborne St. John, Dio. Win. 1865. (Patron, W. Chute, Esq; Tithe, 596*l*; Glebe, 75 acres; R.'s Inc. 660*l* and Ho; Pop. 675.) Formerly C. of Cirencester 1864–65. [4]

CHUTE, George, *Drayton-in-Hales, Market-Drayton, Salop.*—V. of Drayton-in-Hales, Dio. Lich. 1856. (Patron, Richard Corbett, Esq; Tithe, Imp. 785*l* 18*s* 2*d*, V. 250*l*; Glebe, 3 acres; V.'s Inc. 280*l* and Ho; Pop. 2762.) [5]

CHUTE, John, 11, *Edmund-street, Bradford, Yorks.*—Dub. A.B. 1864, A.M. 1867; Deac. 1866 and Pr. 1867 by Bp of Rip. C. of St. John's, Bradford, 1866. [6]

CLACK, William Courtenay, *Moreton-Hampstead, Devon.*—R. of Moreton-Hampstead, Dio. Ex. 1865. (Patron, Earl of Devon; Tithe, 780*l*; Glebe, 60 acres; R.'s Inc. 840*l* and Ho; Pop. 1468.) [7]

CLAPCOTT, John William, *Thrigby, Norwich.*—Lin. Coll. Ox. B.A. 1842; Deac. 1843, Pr. 1844. R. of Thrigby, Dio. Nor. 1862. (Patron, T. Brown, Esq; Tithe, 212*l* 13*s*; Glebe, 6½ acres; R.'s Inc. 221*l* and Ho; Pop. 45.) Formerly C. of Frostenden. [8]

CLAPIN, Alfred Charles, *Sherborne, Dorset.*—St. John's Coll. Cam. Sen. Opt. and B.A. 1849, M.A. 1862; Bachelier-ès-lettres, Univ. of France, 1843; Deac. 1852 and Pr. 1862 by Bp of Salis. Asst. Mast. at the King's Sch. Sherborne. Author, *A Treatise on Optical Problems*, 1850, 4*s*; *French Grammar for Public Schools*, 1866, 2nd ed. 1867, Bell and Daldy, 2*s* 6*d*. [9]

CLAPP, Thomas, *Stratton, near Cirencester.*—Ex. Coll. Ox. Exhib. and B.A. 1859, M.A. 1862; Deac. 1860 and Pr. 1861 by Bp of Lich. C. of Stratton 1865. [10]

CLARE, George Thomas, *Bainton Rectory, Great Driffield, Yorks.*—St. John's Coll. Ox. B.A. 1833, M.A. 1836; Deac. 1833 and Pr. 1834 by Bp of Ox. R. of Bainton, Dio. York, 1840. (Patron, St. John's Coll. Ox; R.'s Inc. 760*l* and Ho; Pop. 465.) Rural Dean. [11]

CLARE, Hamilton John.—C. of St. John's, Kensal-green. [12]

CLARK, Charles, *Kendal.*—Chap. to the Kendal House of Correction. [13]

CLARK, E. L.—C. of Asby, Westmoreland. [14]

CLARK, Francis Storer.—St. John's Coll. Cam. B.A. 1858, M.A. 1861; Deac. 1859 and Pr. 1860 by Bp of Nor. Formerly C. of St. Margaret's, Ipswich. [15]

CLARK, George, *Gedney Hill, near Wisbech, Cambs.*—St. John's Coll. Cam. B.A. 1855; Deac. 1855 and Pr. 1856 by Bp of B. and W. C. of Gedney Hill. Formerly C. of Dunkerton, Somerset. [16]

CLARK, The Venerable George, *Robeston Wathen, near Narberth.*—Univ. Coll. Ox. 2nd cl. Lit. Hum. and B.A. 1831, M.A. 1833; Deac. and Pr. 1834 by Abp of Cant. Archd. and Preb. of St. David's (Val. 290*l* and Res.) Preb. of Moreton and Whaddon in Herf. Cathl. 1848; Exam. Chap. to the Bp of Herf. 1848; Surrogate. Formerly C. of St. Dunstan's-in-the-East, Lond. 1834, Alton, Hants, 1835, All Saints' and St. Clements', Hastings, 1842, Tawstock, Devon, 1843; V. of Cautley, Yorks, 1845; R. of Tenby 1854–67. Author, *Primary Charge at Archdeacon's Visitation*, Rivingtons, 1865, 1*s*. [17]

CLARK, George Frederick, *Ufton, Rugby.*—Trin. Hall, Cam. B.A. 1855, M.A. 1858; Deac. and Pr. 1856 by Bp. of Lich. R. of Ufton, Dio. Wor. 1869. (Patron, Bp of Wor; V.'s Inc. 200*l* and Ho; Pop. 201.) Formerly Sen. C. of St. Paul's, Stafford. Author, various Papers in *Quarterly Journal of the Chemical Society*. [18]

CLARK, George Nesse, *Saxelby, Melton Mowbray.*—Corpus Coll. Cam. B.A. 1844; Deac. 1846 and Pr. 1847 by Bp of Pet. R. of Saxelby, Dio. Pet. 1852. (Patron, Earl of Aylesford; Glebe, 156 acres; R.'s Inc. 250*l* and Ho; Pop. 120.) Formerly C. of Nether Seale 1846–48, North Luffenham 1848–51. [19]

CLARK, Henry, *Stoke-next-Guildford, Surrey.*—Trin. Coll. Cam. B.A. 1860, M.A. 1864; Deac. 1861 and Pr. 1863 by Bp of Rip. C. of Stoke-next-Guildford 1864. Formerly C. of Wortley, Yorks, 1861. [20]

CLARK, James, *Bempton, Burlington.*—Dub. A.B. 1845; Deac. 1846 and Pr. 1847 by Bp of Pet. P. C. of Bempton, Dio. York, 1862. (Patron, Harrison Broadley, Esq; P. C.'s Inc. 90*l*; Pop. 346.) P. C. of Speeton, Dio. York, 1862. (Patron, Lord Londesborough; P. C.'s Inc. 60*l*; Pop. 140.) Formerly C. of Wyfordby, Burton-Lazars and Cadney; P. C. of Ripley. [21]

CLARK, James.—C. of Rotherham. [22]

CLARK, James Ord, *Beltingham, Haydonbridge, Northumberland.*—Literate; Deac. 1836, Pr. 1837. P. C. of Beltingham with Greenhead, Dio. Dur. 1845. (Patron, V. of Haltwhistle: P. C.'s Inc. 130*l* and Ho.) [23]

CLARK, John.—Queens' Coll. Cam. B.A. 1836, M.A. 1839; Deac. 1837 and Pr. 1839 by Bp of Ches. Dom. Chap. to Lord Howden. Formerly V. of Hunslet, Dio. Rip. 1841. [24]

CLARK, John C., B.D., *Chertsey, Surrey.* [25]

CLARK, John Dixon, *Belford Hall, Belford, Northumberland.*—Univ. Coll. Ox. 4th cl. Lit. Hum. and B.A. 1833, M.A. 1836; Deac. 1835 by Bp of Carl. Pr. 1837 by Bp of Dur. [26]

CLARK, John Holdenby, *Hilgay, Market Downham, Norfolk.*—St. John's Coll. Cam. B.A. 1861, M.A. 1865; Deac. 1862 and Pr. 1863 by Abp of York. C. of Hilgay 1867. Formerly C. of Barmby Moor and Fangloss 1862–64, Cubley and Marston Montgomery 1864–67. [27]

CLARK, John Meek, *Magdalene College, Cambridge,* and *Oxford and Cambridge University Club, Pall-mall, London.*—Magd. Coll. Cam. B.A. 1856, M.A. 1859; Deac. 1857, Pr. 1859. Fell. and Lect. of Magd. Coll. Cam. [28]

CLARK, Joseph, *Kegworth Rectory, Derby.*—Ch. Coll. Cam. Wrang. Fell. of Ch. Coll. 1838, B.A. 1838, M.A. 1841; Deac. 1839 and Pr. 1840 by Bp of Ely. R. of Kegworth with Chapelry of Isley Walton, Dio. Pet. 1853. (Patron, Ch. Coll. Cam; R.'s Inc. from 400 acres, and Tithe 126*l* 5*s*; Ho; Pop. Kegworth 1773, Isley Walton 46.) [29]

CLARK, Joseph, *Parsonage, Great Crosby, near Liverpool.*—Deac. 1821 and Pr. 1823 by Bp of Carl. P. C. of Great Crosby, Dio. Ches. 1855. (Patron, R. of Sefton; Glebe 18 acres; P. C.'s Inc. 250*l* and Ho; Pop. 3794.) Formerly C. of Watermillock, Cumberland, 1821, Great Crosby 1825, Sefton 1829. [30]

CLARK, Joseph.—C. of Woodford, Essex. [31]

CLARK, Joseph, *Little Bytham, Stamford, Linc.*—Magd. Hall, Ox. B.A. 1850; Deac. 1850, Pr. 1851.

R. of Little Bytham, Dio. Lin. 1859. (Patron, Bp of Lin. alt. with D. and C. of Lin; R.'s Inc. 329*l* and Ho; Pop. 362.) Formerly C. of Chalfont St. Giles. [1]

CLARK, J. P.—Precentor and Minor Can. of Gloucester Cathl. [2]

CLARK, Samuel, *Bredwardine, Hereford.*—Magd. Hall, Ox. B.A. 1845, M.A. 1845; Deac. 1846 by Bp of Pet. Pr. 1847 by Bp of Lon. V. of Bredwardine with Brobury R. Dio. Herf. 1862. (Patrons, Exors. of Rev. N. H. Newton; Tithe, 300*l*; Glebe, 80 acres; V.'s Inc. 380*l* and Ho; Pop. Bredwardine 420, Brobury 76.) Formerly Vice-Prin. of St. Mark's Coll. Chelsea, 1846–51; Prin. of the National Society's Training Coll. Battersea, 1851–63. Author, Articles in *Smith's Dictionary of the Bible* on the Hebrew Festivals and other subjects, 1860–63; *British Geography*, folio, Nat. Soc. 1850; *The School Physical Atlas*, 1852; *The Bible Atlas with Notes and Dissertations*, S.P.C.K. 1867. [3]

CLARK, Samuel, *Shiffnal, Salop.*—Dub. and Queen's Coll. Birmingham; Warneford Theol. Prize; Deac. 1866 and Pr. 1867 by Bp of Lich. Asst. C. of Shiffnal 1866. Formerly Head Mast. of Shiffnal Gr. Sch. 1856. [4]

CLARK, Thomas, *Gedney Hill Parsonage, Holbeach, Lincolnshire.*—Literate; Deac. 1809 and Pr. 1818 by Bp of Ches. P. C. of Gedney Hill, Dio. Lin. 1812. (Patron, the present P. C; P. C.'s Inc. 100*l* and Ho; Pop. 466.) [5]

CLARK, Thomas, *Vicarage, Poulton-le-Fylde, Lancashire.*—Queens' Coll. Cam. B.A. 1826, M.A. 1829; Deac. 1827 and Pr. 1828 by Bp of Lin. V. of Poulton-le-Fylde, Dio. Man. 1864. (Patron, Rev. C. Hesketh; Tithe, 214*l*; Glebe, 29 acres; V.'s Inc. 275*l* and Ho; Pop. 1890.) Rural Dean; Surrogate. Formerly Min. of Ch. Ch. Preston, 1836. Author, *Questions on the Articles of Religion with Scripture Proofs*, Skeffington, 4th ed. 6d. [6]

CLARK, Thomas Henry, 4, *Chandos-place, Clifton.*—Brasen. Coll. Ox. B.A. 1857, M.A. 1860; Deac. 1857 and Pr. 1858 by Bp of Win. C. of Clifton 1865. Formerly C. of Brockham, Surrey, 1857, Bucklebury, Reading, 1859; P. C. of St. Philip's, Stepney, 1861; C. of Davenham 1862, C. of Ch. Ch. Derby, 1863. [7]

CLARK, Thomas Humphris.—C. of Dursley, Gloucestershire. [8]

CLARK, Walter, *Derby.*—Head Mast. of Derby Gr. Sch. [9]

CLARK, William, *Cleator Moor, Whitehaven.*—St. Bees; Deac. 1865 by Bp of Carl. C. of Cleator 1865. [10]

CLARK, William, M.D., *Trinity College, Cambridge.* [11]

CLARK, William George, *Trinity College, Cambridge.*—Trin. Coll. Cam. 1st cl. Cl. Trip. and B A. 1844, M.A. 1847; Deac. 1853 and Pr. 1854 by Bp of Ely. Fell. of Trin. Coll. 1844; Tut. of Trin. Coll. 1856; Public Orator of the Univ. 1857. Author, *Gazpacho: Summer Months in Spain*, 1850; *Peloponnesus: Notes of Study and Travel*, 1858. [12]

CLARK, William Robinson, *The Vicarage, Taunton.*—King's Coll. Aberdeen, and Magd. Hall, Ox. M.A; Deac. 1857 and Pr. 1858 by Bp of Wor. V. of St. Mary Magdalene's, Taunton, Dio. B. and W. 1859. (Patrons, Trustees; Tithe, 50*l*; Glebe, 100*l*; V.'s Inc. 400*l* and Ho; Pop. 5695.) Formerly C. of St. Matthias', Birmingham, 1857, St. Mary Magdalene's, Taunton, 1858. Author, *Doctrine of Christian Baptism*, Longmans, 1859, 1s 6d; *The Parable of the Prodigal Son*, Bell and Daldy, 1860, 2s 6d; *Four Advent Sermons*, Longmans, 1861, 1s 6d; *The Redeemer* (14 Sermons), Bell and Daldy, 1863, 5s; *The Comforter* (12 Sermons), Rivingtons, 1864, 4s; *Two Advent Sermons*, 1864, 6d; *The Four Temperaments* (6 Sermons), 1865, 2s; etc. [13]

CLARKE, Adam, *Longton Rectory, Stoke-on-Trent, Staffs.*—Ex. Coll. Ox. B.A. 1854; Deac. 1856 and Pr. 1857 by Bp of Ely. R. of Longton, Dio. Lich. 1862. (Patron, J. Carey, Esq; Glebe, ½ acre; R.'s Inc. 400*l* and Ho; Pop. 12,706.) Formerly C. of St. Neot's, Hunts, 1856–58, Long Preston, Yorks, 1861–63. [14]

CLARKE, Alured James, *Elvington Rectory, York.*—Wad. Coll. Ox. B.A. 1854, M.A. 1857; Deac. 1854 and Pr. 1856 by Bp of Wor. R. of Elvington, Dio. York, 1865. (Patron, Rev. J. E. Clarke; R.'s Inc. 340*l* and Ho; Pop. 429.) Formerly C. of Dunchurch, Warwickshire, 1854–56. [15]

CLARKE, Andrew Brooke, *Collyhurst Rectory, Manchester.*—Dub. A.B. 1840; Deac. and Pr. 1842. R. of Collyhurst, Dio. Man. 1860. (Patrons, Trustees; R.'s Inc. 350*l* and Ho; Pop. 4000.) Formerly P. C. of Embleton, Cumberland, 1858; C. of Wythop, near Cockermouth. Author, *The Church Catechism, broken into Questions and explained*, 1s; *The Thirty-nine Articles explained*, 6d. [16]

CLARKE, Beaumarice Stracey, *Witham, Essex.*—St Bees; Deac. 1840 and Pr. 1841 by Bp of Ches. R. of Little Braxted, Dio. Roch. 1863. (Patrons, Trustees of Sir W. B. Rush; Tithe, 155*l*; Glebe, 7 acres; R.'s Inc. 180*l*; Pop. 111.) Formerly C. of Denton, near Manchester, 1840–42; Chap. in the H. E. I. Co.'s service, Madras, 1843. Author, *An Essay towards the Interpretation of the Apocalypse*, 1864, 8s. [17]

CLARKE, Benjamin Philpot, *St Jude's, Kirk Andreas, Isle of Man.*—Dub. A.B. 1855; Deac. 1855 and Pr. 1856 by Bp of S. and M. P. C. of St. Jude's, Dio. S. and M. 1865. (Patron, Archdeacon Moore; P. C.'s Inc. 100*l*.) Formerly C. of Port St. Mary. [18]

CLARKE, Benjamin Strettell, *Houghton-street, Southport, Lancashire.*—Dub. A.B. 1845, A.M. 1856; Deac. 1846 and Pr. 1847 by Bp of Ches. P. C. of Ch. Ch. Southport, Dio. Ches 1849. (Patron, Rev. C. Hesketh; Glebe, 2 acres; P. C.'s Inc. 350*l*.) Surrogate. [19]

CLARKE, Cecil Jervis, *Huddersfield.*—Dub. A.B. 1852, A.M. 1860; Deac. 1853 and Pr. 1854 by Bp of Ches. P. C. of Ch. Ch. Mold Green, Huddersfield, Dio. Rip. 1864. (Patron, R. of Kirkheaton; P. C.'s Inc. 110*l*; Pop. 5000.) Formerly C. of Newton-in-Makerfield, The Abbey, Shrewsbury, St. John's, Broughton, Manchester. [20]

CLARKE, Sir Charles, Bart.—Trin. Coll. Cam. B.A. 1835, M.A. 1838; Deac. 1836 by Bp of Ely, Pr. 1837 by Bp of Win. Formerly R. of Hanwell, Dio. Lon. 1847–64. [21]

CLARKE, Charles John.—C. of Tisbury, Wiltshire. [22]

CLARKE, Charles Leopold Stanley, *Lodsworth, Petworth, Sussex.*—New Coll. Ox. B.C.L. 1844; Deac. 1841 and Pr. 1845 by Bp of Ox. P. C. of Lodsworth, Dio. Chich. 1846. (Patron, Earl of Egmont; Tithe—App. 90*l*; Imp 110*l*; Glebe, 2 acres; P. C.'s Inc. 65*l* and Ho; Pop. 629.) Fell. of New Coll. Ox; Dom. Chap. to the Earl of Egmont; Rural Dean and Preb. of Chich. 1858. [23]

CLARKE, C. P.—C. of St Martin's-in-the-Fields, Lond. [24]

CLARKE, Charles Whitley, *Bridestow Rectory, Crediton, Devon.*—Trin. Coll. Cam. B.A. 1845, M.A. 1849; Deac. 1846, Pr. 1847. R. of Bridestow with Sourton, Dio. Ex. 1858. (Patron, Bp. of Ex; Tithe, Bridestow, 317*l* 5*s*, Sourton, 258*l*; R.'s Inc. 624*l* and Ho; Pop. Bridestow 832, Sourton 543.) Dom. Chap. to Lord Ashburton. Formerly C. of Moccas, Herf. 1846–48, Rickling, Essex, 1848–50, St. Margaret's, Westminster, 1850–52, Kensington, Lond. 1852–57; Min. of Bedford Chapel, Bloomsbury, Lond. 1857–58. [25]

CLARKE, Edwin W.—C. of Wicker, Sheffield. [26]

CLARKE, Frederick James, *Reddal-hill, Dudley.*—Dub. A.B. 1841; Deac. 1841, Pr. 1842. P. C. of Reddal-hill, Staffs, Dio. Wor. 1845. (Patrons, Crown and Bp alt; P. C.'s Inc. 300*l*; Pop. 10,349.) [27]

CLARKE, Frederick Kent, *School House, Stafford.*—Univ. Lond. and Clare Coll. Cam. 3rd Sen. Opt. B.A. 1855, M.A. 1858; Deac. 1856 and Pr. 1857 by Bp of Ex. Head Mast. of King Edward's Sch. Stafford, 1860 (Inc. 104*l* 5*s*.) P. C. of St. Chad's, Stafford, Dio. Lich. 1866. (Patron, Preb. in Lich.

Cathl; P. C.'s Inc. 85*l*.) Formerly 2nd Mast. of Queen Mary's Sch. Walsall, 1858–60. [1]

CLARKE, George Pettman, *Repton, Burton-upon-Trent.*—St. John's Coll. Cam. Wrang. 3rd cl. Cl. Trip. and B.A. 1849, M.A. 1852; Deac. 1855 and Pr. 1856 by Bp of Lich. Math. Mast. of Repton Sch. 1852. [2]

CLARKE, Henry, *Northfield Rectory (Worcestershire), near Birmingham.*—Dub. A.B. 1825, A.M. 1835, *ad eund.* Ox. 1839; Deac. 1828 by Bp of Lich. Pr. 1829 by Bp of Wor. R. of Northfield with C. of Bartley Green Dio. Wor. 1834. (Patrons, Rev. Edward William Fenwicke and others; Northfield, Tithe, 805*l*; Glebe, 44½ acres; R.'s Inc. 1280*l* and Ho; Pop. Northfield 1647, Bartley Green 172.) [3]

CLARKE, Henry, *Marchington Woodlands, Uttoxeter.*—Bp Hat. Hall, Dur. B.A. 1856, M.A. 1859; Deac. 1856 by Bp of Man. Pr. 1857 by Bp of Dur. P. C. of Marchington Woodlands, Dio. Lich. 1866. (Patron, Thomas Webb, Esq; P. C.'s Inc. 95*l*; Pop. 339.) Formerly C. of Somersall Herbert. [4]

CLARKE, Henry William.—C. of St. Matthew's, Marylebone, Lond. [5]

CLARKE, James Sanderson, *Goudhurst Vicarage, Cranbrook, Kent.*—V. of Goudhurst, Dio. Cant. 1864. (Patrons, D. and C. of Roch; V.'s Inc. 580*l* and Ho; Pop. 1874.) Formerly C. of Lewisham; P. C. of All Saints', Blackheath, 1858–64. [6]

CLARKE, James William, *Shipston-on-Stour, Worcestershire.*—St. Cath. Hall, Cam. B.A. 1854, M.A. 1857; Deac. 1854 and Pr. 1855 by Bp of Wor. P. C. of Lower Lemington, Glouc. Dio. G. and B. 1855. (Patron, Lord Redesdale; P. C.'s Inc. 80*l*; Pop. 57.) Chap. to the Shipston Union 1854. Formerly C. of Idlicote, Warwickshire. [7]

CLARKE, John, *Soudon, Brixham, Devon.*—Ex. Coll. Ox. B.A. 1827; Deac. 1829, Pr. 1835. [8]

CLARKE, John, *Meerbrook Parsonage, Leek, Staffs.*—Rostock, M.A. Ph. D. 1862; St. Aidan's; Deac. 1854 and Pr. 1855 by Abp of York. P. C. of Meerbrook, Dio. Lich. 1863. (Patron, the V. of Leek; P. C.'s Inc. 120*l*; Pop. 560.) Author, *Do Well to Thyself*, 1855; *Antidote to Infidelity*, 1860; *A Happy World, or the Power of Influence Practically Considered*, 1861; *We Pray for England's Widowed Queen*, set to music. [9]

CLARKE, John Erskine, *St. Michael's Vicarage, Derby.*—Wad. Coll. Ox. B.A. 1850, M.A. 1853; Deac. 1851 and Pr. 1852 by Bp of Rip. V. of St. Michael's, Derby, Dio. Lich. 1856. (Patron, Ld Chan; V.'s Inc. 126*l* and Ho; Pop. 1961.) P. C. of St. Andrew's, Derby, Dio. Lich. 1866. (Patron, Bp of Lich; P. C.'s Inc. 200*l*; Pop. 6000.) Formerly C. of St. Mary's, Lichfield. Author, *Plain Papers on Social Economy of the People*; *Heart-Music, a Poetry Book for Working People*; *Hearty Staves, a Song-book for Workmen*; *Children at Church.* Editor of the *Parish Magazine.* [10]

CLARKE, John F., *Falmouth.*—Queen's Coll. Cork, B.A. 1858, *ad eund.* Dur. Licen. Theol. 1860; Deac. 1860 by Bp of Dur. C. of Falmouth 1863. Formerly C. of Winlaton, Durham. [11]

CLARKE, John Michell, *Forest-hill, Sydenham, Kent.*—St. John's Coll. Cam. B.A. 1846, M.A. 1850; Deac. 1847, Pr. 1848. P. C. of Ch. Ch. Forest-hill, Dio. Lon. 1854. (Patron, Lord Dartmouth; P. C.'s Inc. 400*l*; Pop. 4640.) [12]

CLARKE, John Thomas, *Cumbrane, Llanvrechra, Monmouth.*—Jesus Coll. Ox. B.A. 1851; Deac. 1852 by Bp of Win. Pr. 1854 by Bp of Llan. C. of Cumbrane. [13]

CLARKE, John William, *Compton-Basset, Calne, Wilts.*—R. of Compton-Basset, Dio. Salis. 1866. (Patron, Bp of Salis; R.'s Inc. 600*l* and Ho; Pop. 369.) [14]

CLARKE, Joshua, *Uldale Rectory, Wigton, Cumberland.*—St. Bees; Deac. 1821 and Pr. 1822 by Bp of Ches. R. of Uldale, Dio. Carl. 1833. (Patron, Rev. J. Cape; Tithe—App. 1*l*, R. 130*l*; Glebe, 22 acres; R.'s Inc. 151*l* and Ho; Pop. 294.) P. C. of Ireby, Dio. Carl. 1843. (Patrons, D. and C. of Carl; Tithe—App. 154*l*; Glebe, 27 acres; P. C.'s Inc. 50*l* and Ho; Pop. 465.) [15]

CLARKE, Lewis.—Pemb. Coll. Ox. B.A. 1857; Deac. 1857 and Pr. 1858 by Bp of G. and B. C. of Patrixbourne with Bridge, Canterbury. Formerly C. of Tewkesbury and Walton-Cardiff, Glouc. [16]

CLARKE, Moses.—Dub. A.B. 1863; Deac. 1863 and Pr. 1864 by Bp of Win. C. of St. John's, Horsleydown, Southwark. Formerly C. of St. Andrew's, Lambeth. [17]

CLARKE, Richard Frederick, *St. John's College, Oxford.*—St. John's Coll. Ox. B.A. 1860, M.A. 1864; Deac. 1862 and Pr. 1864 by Bp. of Ox. Fell. of St. John's. Formerly C. of St. Giles's, Oxford, 1863. [18]

CLARKE, Robert John, *Towcester Vicarage, Northants.*—V. of Towcester, Dio. Pet. 1855. (Patron, Bp of Lich; Tithe—App. 75*l*, Imp. 6*s*, V. 5*l* 5*s*; V.'s Inc. 250*l* and Ho; Pop. 2715.) Surrogate. [19]

CLARKE, Samuel, *Sambrook, Newport, Salop.*—St. John's Coll. Ox. B.A. 1840, M.A. 1841; Deac. 1841, Pr. 1842. P. C. of Sambrook, Dio. Lich. 1856. (Patron, J. C. Borough, Esq; P. C.'s Inc. 120*l* and Ho; Pop. 552.) Author, *The Perils of Peace*; *An Address to the Parishioners of Ken, on the Life of Bishop Ken.* [20]

CLARKE, Samuel Childs, *Grammar School House, Launceston.*—St. Mary Hall, Ox. B.A. 1844, M.A. 1846; Deac. 1844 and Pr. 1845 by Bp of Ely. P. C. of St. Thomas's, Launceston, Dio. Ex. 1848. (Patrons, Inhabitants; Endow. 120*l*; P. C.'s Inc. 110*l*; Pop. 887.) Head Mast. of the Launceston Gr. Sch. 1849; Surrogate. Author, *Thoughts in Verse from a Village Churchman's Note Book*, 1848, 3*s* 6*d*. [21]

CLARKE, Samuel Thomas, *Kent's Bank, Newton-in-Cartmel, Lancashire.*—St. John's Coll. Cam. B.A. 1847, M.A. 1851; Deac. and Pr. 1848 by Bp of Ches. Formerly P. C. of Colton-in-Furness 1848–66. [22]

CLARKE, Theophilus, *Tadcaster, Yorks.*—Corpus Coll. Cam. Scho. 1829, Prizeman 1830, B.A. 1832; Deac. 1835 by Bp of Lin. Pr. 1836 by Abp of York. C. of Tadcaster. Formerly Head Mast. of the Bodmin Gr. Sch. Cornwall. [23]

CLARKE, Thomas, 2, *North-terrace, Wandsworth, S.W.*—C. of St. Ann's, Wandsworth. [24]

CLARKE, Thomas, *Llandilo-tal-y-bont, Swansea.*—Literate; Deac. 1821 and Pr. 1822 by Bp of St. D. V. of Llandilo-tal-y-bont, Dio. St. D. 1845. (Patron, Howell Gwyn, Esq; Tithe—Imp. 173*l* 5*s* 8*d*, V. 143*l* 9*s*; Glebe, 28 acres; V.'s Inc. 174*l* and Ho; Pop. 1331.) [25]

CLARKE, Thomas, *Micheldever, Hants.*—Dub. Div. Prizeman, 1812, A.B. 1814; Deac. 1814, Pr. 1815. V. of Micheldever with Stratton C. Dio. Win. 1816. (Patron, Lord Northbrook; V.'s Inc. 315*l* and Ho; Pop. Micheldever 1041, Stratton 365.) [26]

CLARKE, Thomas, *Brixham, Devon.*—Queen's Coll. Ox. B.A. 1836; Deac. 1835 and Pr. 1836 by Bp of Ex. Formerly C. of Ashprington. [27]

CLARKE, Thomas, *Ormside Rectory, Appleby, Westmoreland.*—Queens' Coll. Cam. B.A. 1846; Deac. 1846 and Pr. 1847 by Bp of Ches. R. of Ormside, Dio. Carl. 1856. (Patron, Bp of Carl; Tithe, 76*l*; Rent from Glebe, 130*l*; R.'s Inc. 206*l* and Ho; Pop. 188.) Formerly C. of Bacup, Rochdale, 1846, St. Mary's, Sheffield, 1848, St. George's, Sheffield, 1850, St. George's, Bloomsbury, Lond. 1854; Chap. to the late Dr. Villiers, Bp of Carlisle, 1856. Author, *Letters on Education.* [28]

CLARKE, Thomas Ambrose, *Chippenham, Wilts.*—Lin. Coll. Ox. B.A. 1837, M.A. 1840. R. of Kellaways, Dio. G. and B. 1857; Chap. to the Chippenham Union. [29]

CLARKE, Thomas Foster, *Denton Parsonage, Otley.*—Deac. 1865 and Pr. 1866 by Bp of Lich. P. C. of Denton, Dio. Rip. 1867. (Patron, M. Wyvill, jun. Esq. M.P; P. C.'s Inc. 100*l* and Ho; Pop. 120.) Formerly C. of Marchington, Staffs. [30]

CLARKE, Thomas Grey, *Odiham Vicarage, Winchfield, Hants.*—Queen's Coll. Ox. 2nd cl. Lit. Hum. and B.A. 1839, M.A. 1842; Deac. 1841 by Bp of Chich. Pr. 1842 by Bp of Salis. R. of Odiham with Greywell V. Dio. Win. 1858. (Patron, Bp of Win; Tithe, 530*l*; R.'s Inc.

640*l* and Ho; Pop. 3131.) Rural Dean and Surrogate. Formerly P. C. of Woodmancote, Hants. Author, *Memoir of Anna Maria Clarke*, 1853, 8*s* 6*d*; *Scripture References*, 1*s* 6*d*. [1]

CLARKE, Thomas Joseph, *Southport, Lancashire.*—Trin. Coll. Cam. Sen. Opt. in Math. Trip. B.A. 1859; Deac. 1859 and Pr. 1860 by Bp of Ches. P. C. of St. Paul's, Southport, Dio. Ches. 1864. (Patrons, Trustees; P. C.'s Inc. 300*l*; Pop. 3500.) Formerly C. of Ch. Ch. Southport, 1859. Author, *The Cross of Christ*, 1864. [2]

CLARKE, Walrond, *North Petherton, Bridgwater.*—Emman. Coll. Cam. 1860; Deac. 1864 and Pr. 1865 by Bp of B. and W. C. of North Petherton 1864. [3]

CLARKE, Walter John, *Swinderby Vicarage, Newark.*—Ball. Coll. Ox. B.A. 1834, M.A. 1838; Deac. 1836 by Bp of Ban. Pr. 1837 by Bp of Lich. V. of Swinderby, Dio. Lin. 1848. (Patron, the present V; Tithe—Imp. 73*l* 2*s*, V. 15*l* 17*s* 9*d*; Glebe, 150 acres; V.'s Inc. 260*l* and Ho; Pop. 572.) V. of Eagle, Dio. Lin. 1853. (Patron, T. B. Colton, Esq; Tithe, 5*l* 2*s* 11*d*; Glebe, 90 acres; V.'s Inc. 110*l*; Pop. 533.) Rural Dean. [4]

CLARKE, William, *Wingham, Sandwich, Kent.*—Queen's Coll. Ox. B.A. 1845, M.A. 1848; Deac. 1846, Pr. 1849. P. C. of Wingham, Dio. Cant. 1859. (Patron, Nathaniel Bridges, Esq; Tithe—Imp. 1368*l*; P. C.'s Inc. 115*l*; Pop. 1060.) Formerly C. of Icklesham, Sussex, 1846–52, St. Stephen's, Brighton, 1852–56; Chap. at Hyères, France, 1856–59. Author, *A Few Thoughts for Young Persons of the Educated Classes*, 1857. [5]

CLARKE, William, *Firbank, Kendal.*—St. John's Coll. Cam. M.A. 1832; Deac. 1830 and Pr. 1831. P. C. of Firbank, Dio. Carl. 1849. (Patron, V. of Kirkby Lonsdale; P. C.'s Inc. 80*l*; Pop. 345.) [6]

CLARKE, W.—C. of Roehampton, Surrey. [7]

CLARKE, William Graset, *Charlton-Abbots, Winchcombe, Glouc.*—Oriel Coll. Ox. B.A. 1844, M.A. 1846; Deac. 1845, Pr. 1846. P. C. of Charlton-Abbots, Dio. G. and B. 1859. (Patron, J. C. Chamberlayne, Esq; P. C.'s Inc. 42*l*; Pop. 109.) Formerly C. of Icomb, Glouc. [8]

CLARKE, William Henry, *Cold Higham Rectory, Towcester, Northants.*—Ex. Coll. Ox; 2nd cl. Math. et Phy. and B.A. 1814, M.A. 1817. R. of Cold Higham, Dio. Pet. 1817. (Patron, Earl of Pomfret; Glebe, 250 acres; R.'s Inc. 372*l* and Ho; Pop. 349.) [9]

CLARKE, William Wilcox, *North Wootton Rectory, Lynn, Norfolk.*—Wad. Coll. Ox. 2nd cl. Lit. Hum. and B.A. 1829, M.A. 1833; Deac. 1832, Pr. 1833. R. of North Wootton, Dio. Nor. 1834. (Patroness, Hon. Mary Greville Howard; Tithe, 200*l*; Glebe, 4 acres; R.'s Inc. 240*l* and Ho; Pop. 247.) [10]

CLARKSON, Christopher, 7, *Hyde Park-terrace, Plymouth.*—R. of Holsworthy, Dio. Ex. 1859. (Patron, the present R; Tithe, 725*l*; Glebe, 50 acres; R.'s Inc. 1000*l* and Ho; Pop. 1724.) Surrogate. [11]

CLARKSON, George Arthur, *Amberley Vicarage, Arundel, Sussex.*—Jesus Coll. Cam. 47th Wrang. and B.A. 1837; Deac. 1839 by Bp of Chich. Pr. 1840 by Bp of Roch. V. of Amberley with Houghton Chapelry, Dio. Chich. 1840. (Patron, Bp of Chich; Amberley, Tithe—App. 384*l* 9*s* 3*d*, V. 6*l* 6*s*; Glebe, 136 acres; Houghton, Tithe, Imp. 2*l* 14*s*; V.'s Inc. 288*l* and Ho; Pop. Amberley 650, Houghton 165.) [12]

CLARKSON, Lewis Furnell, *Molesworth (Hunts), near Thrapstone.*—Emman. Coll. Cam. B.A. 1846, M.A. 1852; Deac. 1847, Pr. 1848. R. of Molesworth, Dio. Ely, 1854. (Patron, Bp of Ches; Tithe, 33*l* 14*s* 6*d*; Glebe, 294 acres; R.'s Inc. 312*l* and Ho; Pop. 256.) [13]

CLARKSON, Thomas, *Wyverstone Rectory, Stowmarket, Suffolk.*—St. John's Coll. Cam. Sen. Opt. B.A. 1837, M.A. 1840; Deac. 1840 and Pr. 1841 by Bp of Ely. R. of Wyverstone, Dio. Nor. 1855. (Patron, J. Moseley, Esq; Tithe, 354*l*; Glebe, 15 acres; R.'s Inc. 354*l* and Ho; Pop. 302.) Formerly R. of Chillenden, Kent, 1852–55. [14]

CLARKSON, Thomas Bayley, *Wakefield.*—Deac. 1824 and Pr. 1825 by Abp of York. Chap. to the West York County Asylum 1843. (Patrons, Visiting Magistrates; Stip. 250*l*.) Formerly P. C. of Chapelthorpe 1827-43. Author, *Strictures on Female Education in the Higher and Middle Ranks of English Society*, 1825. [15]

CLARKSON, Townley Lebeg, *Elmham, near Halesworth, Suffolk.*—Ch. Coll. Cam. B.A. 1832, M.A. 1835; Deac. 1832, Pr. 1833. R. of South Elmham, Dio. Nor. 1855. (Patron, Sir Robert Shafto Adair, Bart; Tithe, App. 5*l*, R. 377*l*; Glebe, 9¾ acres; R.'s Inc. 400*l*; Pop. 240.) Formerly R. of Beyton, Suffolk. Author, *The True Channel of Christian Charity*. [16]

CLAXTON, Donald Maclean, *Brougham Villa, Coronation-road, Bristol.*—St. Edm. Hall, Ox. B.A. 1865, M.A. 1866; Deac. 1865 and Pr. 1866 by Bp of G. and B. C. of St. Mary's Redcliff, Bristol, 1865. [17]

CLAXTON, Joseph Dickson, 13, *Pembroke-road, Kensington, London, W.*—Trin. Coll. Cam. B.A. 1850, M.A. 1853; Deac. 1852 by Bp of Ches. Pr. 1853 by Bp of Lich. P. C. of St. Philip's, Kensington, Dio. Lon. 1857. (Patron, the present P. C; P. C.'s Inc. 150*l*; Pop. 5264.) Formerly C. of Butterton, Staffs, and St. Barnabas', Kensington. [18]

CLAY, Edmund, *Brighton.*—Trin. Coll. Cam. B.A. 1847. Min. of St. Margaret's Chapel, Brighton. Formerly P. C. of St. Luke's Chapel, Leamington. Author, *Commentary on Song of Solomon*. [19]

CLAY, Edward K.—C. of Tankersley, Yorks. [20]

CLAY, George Hollis, *Kington, Herefordshire.*—Clare Coll. Cam. B.A. 1860; Deac. 1860 by Bp of Dur. C. of Kington. [21]

CLAY, John, *Stapenhill (Derbyshire), Burton-on-Trent.*—Deac. 1835 and Pr. 1836 by Bp of Lich. V. of Stapenhill, Dio. Lich. 1837. (Patron, Marquis of Anglesey; Tithe, 147*l*; Glebe, 86 acres; V.'s Inc. 300*l*; Pop. 831.) [22]

CLAY, Pelham Fellowes, *Chawleigh Rectory, Chumleigh, Devon.*—Sid. Coll. Cam. Prizeman, B.A. 1819; Deac. 1820 and Pr. 1821 by Bp of Ex. R. of Chawleigh, Dio. Ex. 1821. (Patron, Earl of Portsmouth; Tithe, 470*l* 5*s* 10*d*; R.'s Inc. 470*l* and Ho; Pop. 801.) R. of Eggesford, near Chumleigh, Dio. Ex. 1821. (Patron, Earl of Portsmouth; Tithe, 61*l* 16*s* 6*d*; R.'s Inc. 130*l* and Ho; Pop. 126.) [23]

CLAY, Walter Lowe, 30, *Harewood-square, London, N.W.*—Emman. Coll. Cam. Sen. Opt. B.A. 1855, M.A. 1858; Deac. 1855 and Pr. 1856 by Bp. of Pet. C. of Ch. Ch. Marylebone, 1864. Formerly C. of Blisworth, Kenilworth, and Trinity, Coventry. Author, *The Prison Chaplain*, Macmillan, 1861; *Our Convict Systems*, ib. 1862; *The Power of the Keys*, ib. 1864 [24]

CLAY, William French.—Magd. Coll. Cam. B.A. 1858; Deac. 1858 by Bp of S. and M. Chap. at Pau. Formerly C. of Lezayre, Isle of Man. Assoc. Sec. of Ch. Miss. Soc. [25]

CLAYDON, Edmund Augustus, 4, *Church-terrace, Lee, London, S.E.*—St. John's Coll. Cam. Scho. of, Wrang. and B.A. 1851, M.A. 1854; Deac. 1853 and Pr. 1854 by Bp of Pet. Private Tutor for the Universities and the Army. Formerly Math. Mast. at Sedbergh, Yorks, 1851–52; C. of Marholm, near Peterborough, 1853–54; Chap. and Sen. Mast. of Ordnance Sch. at Carshalton. [26]

CLAYDON, Octavius, *Addlethorpe, Boston.*—New Inn Hall, Ox. B.A. 1848; Deac. 1848 and Pr. 1849 by Bp of Lich. C. of Addlethorpe. Formerly C. of South Scarle and Silk Willoughby. [27]

CLAYFORTH, Henry, *Wombwell, Barnsley.*—Dub. A.B. 1857; Deac. 1857 and Pr. 1858 by Abp of York. R. of Wombwell, Dio. York, 1864. (Patron, R. of Darfield, one turn; Trin. Coll. Cam. two turns; Tithe, 170*l*; Glebe, 2 acres; R.'s Inc. 260*l* and Ho; Pop. 3737.) Formerly C. of Darfield 1857–64. [28]

CLAYTON, A. P., *Fyfield House, Maidenhead, Berks.*—Caius Coll. Cam. M.A. [29]

CLAYTON, Charles, *Stanhope Rectory, Durham.*—Caius Coll. Cam. Browne's Medallist 1833–34, Wrang. 1st cl. Cl. Trip. B.A. 1836, M.A. 1839; Deac. 1837 and

Pr. 1836 by Bp of Roch. R. of Stanhope, Dio. Dur. 1865. (Patron, Bp of Rip; Tithe, 700*l*; Glebe, 32*l*; R.'s Inc. 1650*l* and Ho; Pop. 2000.) Hon. Can. of Rip; Exam. Chap. to Bp of Rip. Formerly Asst. Min. of St. John's, Chatham, 1837–48; Sec. of Ch. Pastoral Aid Soc. 1845–47; Fell. and Hon. Tut. of Caius Coll. Cam. 1848–65; Min. of Trinity, Cambridge, 1851–65. Author, *Parochial Sermons*, 4th ed. 5*s*; *Occasional Sermons*, 4th ed. 5*s*; *Cambridge Sermons*, 1st series, 2nd ed. 5*s*; 2nd series, 5*s*; etc. [1]

CLAYTON, Edward, *Astbury, Congleton, Cheshire.*—Ch. Ch. Ox. 3rd cl. Lit. Hum. M.A. 1842; Deac. 1841, Pr. 1842. R. of Astbury, Dio. Ches. 1858. (Patron, Lord Crewe; Tithe, 2049*l*; R.'s Inc. 2229*l* and Ho; Pop. 1442.) Rural Dean; Proctor for Archdeaconry of Chester. Formerly Stud. of Ch. Ch; P. C. of Stratton Audley, Oxon; Miss. to the Kafirs under Bp Armstrong. [2]

CLAYTON, Edward ffarington, *Ludlow.*—St. John's Coll. Cam. B.A. 1853, M.A. 1856; Deac. 1854 and Pr. 1855 by Bp of G. and B. R. of Ludlow, Dio. Herf. 1867 (Patroness, Lady Mary Windsor-Clive; Tithe, 28*l*; Glebe, 55 acres; R.'s Inc. 290*l* and Ho; Pop. 5200.) Formerly C. of Putney. [3]

CLAYTON, John Henry, *Milland, Liphook.*—Wor. Coll. Ox. B.A. 1832; Deac. 1833 and Pr. 1834 by Bp of Ches. P. C. of Milland, Dio. Chich. 1868. (Patron, Rev. J. M. Meath; P. C.'s Inc. 60*l* and Ho.) [4]

CLAYTON, Lewis, 64, *Mare Fair, Northampton.*—Emman. Coll. Cam. B.A. 1860, M.A. 1863; Deac. 1861 and Pr. 1862 by Bp of Roch. C. of St. James's End, Northampton, 1866. Formerly C. of Halstead, Essex, 1861–64, Hanbury, Worc. 1865-66. [5]

CLEARY, Augustus Castle.—St. Aidan's; Deac. 1863 and Pr. 1864 by Bp of Dur. C. of St. Mark's, Birmingham. Formerly C. of Shincliffe 1863. [6]

CLEATHER, George Ellis, *Churton, Devizes, Wilts.*—Ex. Coll. Ox. B.A. 1846; Deac. 1847, Pr. 1848. V. of Churton, Dio. Salis. 1862. (Patron, Ld Chan; V.'s Inc. 180*l*; Pop. 332.) [7]

CLEATHER, George Parker, *Aldbourne Vicarage, Hungerford, Wilts.*—Ex. Coll. Ox. B.A. 1820, M.A. 1824; Deac. and Pr. 1822. V. of Aldbourne, Dio. Salis. 1852. (Patron, Bp of Salis; Tithe—App. 1475*l* and 119 acres of Glebe, V. 212*l*; Glebe, 3 acres; V.'s Inc. 484*l* and Ho; Pop. 1539.) [8]

CLEAVE, William Oke, *Jersey.*—Prin. of Victoria Coll. Jersey. Formerly V. of Hinxton, Cambs, 1862–65. [9]

CLEAVER, Charles Pierrepont, *Appleton-le-Street, Malton, Yorks.*—Magd. Coll. Cam. B.A. 1852; Deac. 1852 and Pr. 1853 by Bp of Lin. V. of Appleton-le Street, Dio. York, 1854. (Patrons, Trustees; Tithe—App. 148*l* 15*s*, Imp. 361*l* 8*s* 2½*d*, V. 209*l* 8*s* 4*d*; Glebe, 273 acres; V.'s Inc. 606*l* and Ho; Pop. 967.) [10]

CLEAVER, Euseby Digby.—Ch. Ch. Ox. B.A. 1854; Deac. 1854 and Pr. 1855 by Bp of Ox. Formerly C. of Ducklington, Oxon, and St. Barnabas', Pimlico. [11]

CLEAVER, William Henry, 28, *Delamere-terrace, London, W.*—Ch. Ch. Ox. B.A. 1856, M.A. 1859; Deac. 1863 and Pr. 1864 by Bp of Pet. C. of St. Mary Magdalene's, Paddington, 1865. Formerly C. of Kibworth, Leicester, 1863. [12]

CLEEVE, Charles William, 1, *Clairmont-hill, St. Heliers, Jersey.*—St. Alban Hall, Ox. B.A. 1823; Deac. 1824 and Pr. 1826 by Bp of Ex. Min. of the Prop. Chap. of St. Paul's, St. Heliers, Jersey, 1861. Formerly C. of St. George's, Exeter, High Harrogate, Yorks, Clifton Campville, Staffs, Ashton, Devon, 5 years; Missionary in Demerara, 9 years; Chap. at Vevey, Switzerland, 3 years; Chap. at Palermo, Sicily, 3 years; C. of St. Pancras, Chichester; and Min. of St. Andrew's, Jersey, 4 years. Author, *Influence* (a Lecture), 6*d*, *Romanism and Ritualism*, 1867, 6*d*. [13]

CLEGG, John, *Toddington Rectory, Beds.*—Magd. Hall, Ox. B.A. 1859, M.A. 1861; Deac. 1860 by Bp of B. and W. Pr. 1862 by Bp of Wor. R. of Toddington, Dio. Ely, 1862. (Patron, John Clegg, Esq; R.'s Inc. 700*l* and Ho; Pop. 2433.) Formerly C. of Claines, near Worcester, 1861–62. [14]

CLEMENGER, George.—Dub. A.B. 1848; Deac. 1851 and Pr. 1852 by Bp of Lich. Chap. of H.M.S. "Frederick William." [15]

CLEMENGER, Robert Parsons, *St. Thomas's Parsonage, Elm-road, Camden-square, London, N.W.*—Dub. A.B. 1844, A.M. 1855; Deac. 1844 and Pr. 1845 by Bp of Lin. P. C. of St. Thomas's, Agar-town, Dio. Lon. 1851. (Patrons, Crown and Bp alt; P. C.'s Inc. 500*l* and Ho; Pop. 6000.) Formerly C. of St. Mary's, Nottingham, 1844, Ballyshannon 1846, Loxley, Warwickshire, 1847, Old St. Pancras, Lond. 1850; Chap. to Grove Hall Asylum, Bow, 1857–66. [16]

CLEMENT, Benjamin Prowting, *Winchester.*—Ex. Coll. Ox. B.A. 1837, M.A. 1841; Deac. 1837 and Pr. 1838 by Bp of Win. Min. Can. of Win. Cathl. 1839. [17]

CLEMENT, George, *St. Ouen, St. Heliers, Jersey.*—St. Peter's Coll. Cam. B.A. 1850, M.A. 1853; Deac. 1850 and Pr. 1851 by Bp of Win. R. of St. Ouen, Dio. Win. 1861. (Patron, Gov. of Jersey; R.'s Inc. 120*l* and Ho; Pop. 2320.) Formerly C. of St. Heliers. [18]

CLEMENT, T., *Empshot Vicarage, Alton, Hants.*—V. of Empshot, Dio. Win. 1864. (Patron, J. Eldridge, Esq; V.'s Inc. 120*l* and Ho; Pop. 167.) [19]

CLEMENTS, Dalston, *Warleggan Rectory, Bodmin, Cornwall.*—Queens' Coll. Cam. B.A. 1827; Deac. 1827 and Pr. 1828 by Bp of Ex. R. of Warleggan, Dio. Ex. 1834. (Patron, G. W. F. Gregor, Esq; Tithe, 170*l*; Glebe, 19 acres; R.'s Inc. 200*l* and Ho; Pop. 295.) P. C. of Temple (no church), Cornwall, Dio. Ex. 1840. (Patron, Sir B. Wrey, Bart; Tithe, 21*l*; P. C.'s Inc. 36*l*; Pop. 12.) [20]

CLEMENTS, The Hon. Francis Nathaniel, *Norton Vicarage, Stockton-on-Tees, Durham.*—Oriel Coll. Ox. B.A. 1836; Deac. 1836, Pr. 1837. V. of Norton, Dio. Dur. 1849. (Patron, Bp of Dur; Tithe—Imp. 317*l* 10*s*, V. 80*l*; Glebe, 256 acres; V.'s Inc. 380*l* and Ho; Pop. 2317.) Hon. Can. of Dur. [21]

CLEMENTS, George Cowdell, *Haslingfield, Cambs.*—Emman. Coll. Cam. B.A. 1851, M.A. 1854; Deac. 1852, Pr. 1853. V. of Haslingfield, Dio. Ely, 1863. (Patron, John Mitchell, Esq; Tithe—Imp. 272*l*, 1½ acres of Glebe; V. 651*l*; Glebe, 6½ acres; V.'s Inc. 660*l* and Ho; Pop. 762.) Formerly C. of West Caistor, Sidestrand, Norfolk. [22]

CLEMENTS, Henry George John, *Vicarage, Sidmouth, Devon.*—Ch. Ch. Ox. B.A. 1852, M.A. 1856; Deac. 1854 and Pr. 1856 by Bp of Ex. V. of Sidmouth, Dio. Ex. 1855. (Patroness, Mrs. Jenkins; Tithe, 276*l*, Glebe, 24 acres; V.'s Inc. 460*l* and Ho; Pop. 3354.) Formerly C. of Sidmouth 1854–60, and St. Mark's, Torquay; P. C. of Ashfield, Coote Hill, Cavan, Ireland. Author, *Holy Places of Palestine*; *Lord Macaulay: His Life and Writings*; etc. [23]

CLEMENTS, Jacob, *Vicarage, Gainsborough.*—Oriel Coll. Ox. Hon. 4th cl. Lit. Hum. B.A. 1842, M.A. 1845; Deac. 1843 and Pr. 1844 by Bp of G. and B. V. of Gainsborough, Dio. Lin. 1859. (Patron, Bp of Lin; V.'s Inc. 550*l* and Ho; Pop. 3909.) Preb. of Corringham in Lin. Cathl. 1859; Surrogate. Formerly C. of Upton St. Leonard's, near Gloucester, 1843–46; P. C. of same, 1846–49. Author, *The Farmer's Case, with regard to Education, plainly stated*, 6*d*; *Three Sermons preached at Cuddesdon*, Parker, 1859, 1*s* 6*d*; *The Apostles' Prayer for the Ephesians* (a Farewell Sermon), 1860, 6*d*; *The Danger of Keepers of Vineyards* (an Ordination Sermon), 1861, 6*d*; *Lessons and Duties from the late Royal Death*, 1861, 6*d*; *Wealth, its Danger and Blessedness*, 1862, 6*d*; *The Wearied Prophet and his Word from God* (a Visitation Sermon), 1863, 6*d*—all published by E. Nest, Gloucester. [24]

CLEMENTS, William, 5, *Buckingham-terrace, Victoria-park, London, N.E.*—Deac. 1864 and Pr. 1865 by Bp of Lon. Missionary C. of a Dist. in Whitechapel 1867. Formerly C. of All Saints', Stepney, 1864. [25]

CLEMENTS, William Frederick, *Chorley Wood, Rickmansworth.*—King's Coll. Lon. Assoc. 1860;

Deac. 1860 and Pr. 1861 by Bp of Roch. C. in sole charge of Charley Wood 1864. Formerly C. of St. Peter's, Colchester, 1860, St. James's, Isle of Grain, Kent, 1862, St. Mary's, Hoo, Kent, 1863. [1]

CLEMENTSON, Alfred, *Hanley, Upton-on-Severn.*—Emman. Coll. Cam. B.A. 1860, M.A. 1863; Deac. 1862 and Pr. 1863 by Bp of Lin. C. of Hanley Castle; Fell. of Emman. Coll. Cam. 1867. Formerly C. of Brocklesby, Linc. 1862-64, Ashburton, Canterbury, New Zealand, 1865–66. [2]

CLEMENTSON, William, *St. Michael's Parsonage, Toxteth-park, Liverpool.*—Dub. A.B. 1844, A.M. 1847, *ad eund.* M.A. Ox. 1847; Deac. 1844, Pr. 1845. P. C. of St. Michael's, Toxteth-park, Dio. Ches. 1857. (Patron, W. Jones, Esq; P. C.'s Inc. 210*l*.) Surrogate. Formerly Superintendent of the Special Mission to Roman Catholics in Great Britain, conducted by the Protestant Reformation Society, 1852. Author, Pamphlets, *The Church of England and her Calumniators*, 1847; *The Persecuting Principles of the Church of Rome*, 1853. [3]

CLERE, Henry, *Tickenham Vicarage, Clevedon.*—Queens' Coll. Cam. B.A. 1847, M.A. 1858; Deac. 1847 and Pr. 1848 by Bp of Ches. V. of Tickenham, Dio. B. and W. 1865. (Patron, Bp of Wor; V.'s Inc. 160*l* 16*s* 8*d* and Ho; Pop. 400.) Formerly C. of Newton-in-Mottram, Cheshire, 1847, St. Mary's Rochdale, 1848; P. C. of Walsden, Lancashire, 1854–65. Author, *Sermons, Doctrinal and Practical*, 1853, 8*s*; *The Death of Clement Royds, Esq. High Sheriff of Lancashire*, 1850 (a Sermon), 1854, 1*s*; joint author of *Clere and Shaw's Grammar*, Longmans, 1864, 9*d*; etc. [4]

CLERK, David Malcolm, *Kingstone-Deverill, Warminster, Wilts.*—St. John's Coll. Cam. B.C.L. 1829; Deac. 1831 and Pr. 1832 by Bp of B. and W. Preb. of Warminster in Wells Cathl. 1840; R. of Kingstone-Deverill, Dio. Salis. 1846. (Patron, Marquis of Bath; Glebe, 349 acres; R.'s Inc. 316*l*; Pop. 376.) [5]

CLERK, Henry Thompson.—Deac. 1854 and Pr. 1855 by Abp of Cant. Formerly Chap. Royal Navy. [6]

CLERKE, The Ven. Charles Carr, *Milton Rectory, Abingdon, Berks.*—Ch. Ch. Ox. B.A. 1818, M.A. 1821, B.D. 1830, D.D. 1847; Deac. 1822, Pr. 1823. Archd. of Ox. 1830, with Canonry of Ch. Ch. annexed (value 500*l*); Sub-Dean of Ch. Ch; R. of Milton, Dio. Ox. (Patron, Ch. Ch. Ox; Tithe, 560*l*; Glebe, 3 acres; R.'s Inc. 563*l* and Ho; Pop. 429.) Chap. to the Bp of Ox. Author, *An Ordination Sermon*, 1816; *The Order of Consecration of Churches, Chapels and Churchyards*; several *Archidiaconal Charges*. [7]

CLEVELAND, Henry, *Romaldkirk Rectory, Barnard Castle.*—St. John's Coll. Cam. B.A. 1825, M.A. 1828; Deac. 1826, Pr. 1827. R. of Romaldkirk, Dio. Rip. 1850. (Patron, J. Bowes, Esq; Tithe, 240*l* 12*s*; Glebe, 600 acres; R.'s Inc. 850*l* and Ho; Pop. 1364.) Surrogate. Formerly R. of Barkstone, Linc. 1829–50. [8]

CLEVELAND, William Henry, *Tathwell, Louth, Lincolnshire.*—Sid. Coll. Cam. B.A. 1854; Deac. 1855, Pr. 1856. C. of Tathwell. [9]

CLIFF, Benjamin, *Macclesfield.*—St. John's Coll. Cam. B.A. 1862; Deac. 1862 and Pr. 1863 by Bp of Ches. C. of Ch. Ch. Macclesfield 1864. Formerly C. of St. George's, Sutton, Macclesfield, 1862–64. [10]

CLIFFE, Allen Robert, M.A.—Dom. Chap. to Lord Carew. [11]

CLIFFE, Loftus Anthony.—St. John's Coll. Cam. B.A. 1821; Deac. 1821, Pr. 1822. [12]

CLIFFORD, Edmund, *Frethorne, Stonehouse, Glouc.*—Trin. Coll. Cam. B.A. 1843; Deac. 1845 and Pr. 1846 by Bp of G. and B. C. of Frethorne. [13]

CLIFFORD, Henry Marcus, *Deighton Grove, York.*—Wad. Coll. Ox. B.A. 1856, M.A. 1866; Deac. 1858 and Pr. 1859 by Abp of York. P. C. of Fulford, York, Dio. York, 1864. (Patron, W. H. Key, Esq; P. C.'s Inc. 97*l*; Pop. 2478.) Chap. to the Forces, York, 1866. Formerly C. of Oswald Kirk, Yorks, 1858-59 Searby, near Brigg, Lincolnshire, 1859–62. [14]

CLIFFORD, John, *Alderton, near Malmesbury, Wilts.*—Trin. Coll. Cam. B.A. 1847, M.A. 1852; Deac. 1848 and Pr. 1849 by Bp of Ox. P. C. of Alderton, Dio. G. and B. 1864. (Patron, Sir J. Neald, Bart; P. C.'s Inc. 80*l* and Ho; Pop. 188.) Formerly P. C. of Chipping Sodbury 1859. [15]

CLIFFORD, John Bryant, *Highbury-place, Cotham, Bristol.*—St. Cath. Coll. Cam. B.A. 1831, M.A. 1832; Deac. 1831, Pr. 1832. P. C. of St. Matthew's, Kingsdown, Dio. G. and B. 1838. (Patrons, Trustees; P. C.'s Inc. 400*l*.) [16]

CLIFTON, Alfred, *Yardley Wood, Birmingham.*—Lin. Coll. Ox. B.A. 1840, M.A. 1843; Deac. 1841 and Pr. 1842 by Bp of Wor. P. C. of Yardley Wood, Dio. Wor. 1849. (Patrons, Trustees; P. C.'s Inc. 180*l* and Ho; Pop. 687.) [17]

CLIFTON, Charles Rede, *North-Aston, Woodstock, Oxon.*—Mert. Coll. Ox. B.A. 1841, M.A. 1848. V. of North-Aston, Dio. Ox. 1848. (Patron, J. Wills, Esq; Tithe—Imp. 50*l* 12*s* 2*d*, V. 187*l* 7*s* 1*d*; V.'s Inc. 206*l*; Pop. 296.) Formerly C. of Somerton, Oxon. [18]

CLIFTON, George Hill, *Ripple Rectory (Tewkesbury), Worcestershire*—Wor. Coll. Ox. B.A. 1829, M.A. 1833; Deac. 1830 and Pr. 1831 by Bp of Wor. R. of Ripple with Queenhill, Dio. Wor. 1838. (Patron, Bp of Wor; R.'s Inc. 1020*l* and Ho; Pop Ripple 106, Queenhill 939.) Late Fell. of Wor. Coll. Ox. [19]

CLIFTON, P. R.—Asst. Mast. in the King's Sch. Sherborne, Dorset. [20]

CLIMENSON, John, *Shiplake Vicarage, Henley-on-Thames.*—V. of Shiplake, Dio. Ox. 1866. (Patrons, D. and C. of Windsor; V.'s Inc. 150*l* and Ho; Pop. 582.) [21]

CLINT, Leonidas, *Brockhampton, Ross.*—Trin. Coll. Cam. Sen. Opt. B.A. 1853, M.A. 1859; Deac. 1859 and Pr. 1861 by Bp of St. D. P. C. of Brockhampton, Dio. Herf. 1865. (Patrons, D. and C. of Herf; Tithe, 63*l* 10*s*; Glebe, 24*l*; P. C.'s Inc. 95*l*; Pop. 147.) Off. Min. of Fawley Chapel 1865. Formerly C. of Lamphey, Pembrokeshire, All Saints', Hereford, and Presteign, Radnor. [22]

CLINTON, Charles John Fynes, 39, *Bedford-square, London, W.C.*—Oriel Coll. Ox. B.A. 1822, M.A. 1825; Deac. 1823, Pr. 1824. R. of Cromwell, Notts, Dio. Lin. 1828. (Patron, Duke of Newcastle; Glebe, 248 acres; R.'s Inc. 420*l* and Ho; Pop. 162.) Formerly V. of Strensall and V. of Osbaldwick, York, 1824–27; V. of Orton with Scarrington, Notts, 1827–35. Author, *An Address to all Classes on the First Visitation of the Cholera in* 1832; *Plain Doctrinal and Practical Sermons*, 1842, 6*s*. Editor of *Clinton's Epitome of Chronology of Rome and Constantinople*, 1853, 6*s* 6*d*; *Literary Remains of Henry Fynes Clinton*, 1854, 9*s* 6*d*. [23]

CLINTON, Henry Fiennes, *Bothamsall, Ollerton, Notts.*—Dur. Univ. Coll. Jun. Hebr. Prizeman, 1846, B.A. 1848, M.A. 1852; Deac. 1849, Pr. 1850. P. C. of Bothamsall, Dio. Lin. 1850. (Patron, Duke of Newcastle; Tithe—Imp. 300*l*, P. C. 50*l*; P. C.'s Inc. 50*l*; Pop. 296.) Dom. Chap. to the Duke of Newcastle 1850. [24]

CLINTON, Osbert Fynes, *Leyland, Preston.*—St. John's Coll. Cam. Wrang. B.A. 1862, M.A. 1866; Deac. 1862 and Pr. 1864 by Abp of Cant. P. C. of St. James's, Leyland, Dio. Man. 1864. (Patroness, Miss Ffarington; P. C.'s Inc. 220*l* and Ho; Pop. 1427.) Formerly C. of Ramsgate 1862–64. [25]

CLISSOLD, Augustus, *Stoke Newington, London, N.*—Ex. Coll. Ox. B.A. 1819; Deac. and Pr. 1823 by Bp of Salis. Author, *Letter to the Abp of Dublin on the Practical Nature of Swedenborg's Theological Works*; *The End of the Church*; *Review of the Principles of Apocalyptical Interpretation*, 2 vols; *Spiritual Exposition of the Apocalypse, in which Swedenborg's Interpretations of the Apocalypse are Confirmed by the Writings of the Fathers*, 4 vols; *Swedenborg's Writings and Catholic Teaching*; *Letter to the Vice-Chancellor of Oxford on the Present State of Theology*; various Tracts, etc. Translator of Swedenborg's *Principia*, 2 vols; Swedenborg's *Economy of the Animal Kingdom*, 2 vols. [26]

CLISSOLD, Edward Mortimer, *Wrentham Rectory, Wangford, Suffolk.*—Ex. Coll. Ox. B.A. 1852; Deac. 1852, Pr. 1853. R. of Wrentham, Dio. Nor.

1854. (Patron, Sir E. S. Gooch, Bart; Tithe, 580*l*; Glebe, 23 acres; R.'s Inc. 650*l* and Ho; Pop. 1051.) [1]

CLISSOLD, Henry Bayley, 4, *James-street, Westbourne-terrace, London, W.*—Oriel Coll. Ox. 4th cl. Math. B.A. 1850, M.A. 1854; Deac. 1851 and Pr. 1852 by Bp of Lon. Sec. to the Trinitarian Bible Soc; C. of All Saints', Woodridings, Pinner, Middlesex. Formerly C. of St. Mark's, Old-street-road, 1851–54; St. George-the-Martyr's, Queen-square, 1854–56. [2]

CLIVE, Archer, 66, *Grosvenor-street, London, W.* and *Whitfield, Hereford.*—Brasen. Coll. Ox. 2nd cl. Lit. Hum. and B.A. 1821, M.A. 1823; Deac. 1825 and Pr. 1826 by Bp of Herf. Preb. of Pyon Parva in Herf. Cathl. Formerly R. of Solihull, Warw. 1829–47. Author, *A Few Words on the Poor Law.* [3]

CLIVE, George Arthur, *Shrawardine Rectory, near Shrewsbury.*—R. of Shrawardine, Dio. Lich. 1840. (Patron, Earl of Powis; Tithe, 388*l*; R.'s Inc. 400*l* and Ho; Pop. 161.) V. of Montford, near Shrewsbury, Dio. Lich. 1840. (Patron, Earl of Powis; Tithe—Imp. 20*l*, V. 247*l*; Glebe, 40 acres; V.'s Inc. 304*l*; Pop. 468.) [4]

CLIVE, The Venerable William, *Blymhill Rectory, Shiffnal, Staffs.*—St. John's Coll. Cam. B.A. 1817, M.A. 1820; Deac. 1818, Pr. 1819. R. of Blymhill, Dio. Lich. 1865. (Patron, Earl of Bradford; Tithe, 530*l*; Glebe, 50*l*; R.'s Inc. 600*l* and Ho; Pop. 501.) Formerly Chap. to late Duke of Northumberland 1824; Hon. Can. of St. Asaph 1849; Archd. of Montgomery, resigned; V. of Welshpool 1819–65. [5]

CLOSE, The Very Rev. Francis, D.D., *The Deanery, Carlisle.*—St. John's Coll. Cam. B.A. 1820, M.A. 1826, Scho. of St. John's; Deac. 1820 and Pr. 1821 by Bp of Lich. Dean of Carlisle 1856 (Value 1400*l* and Ho.) P. C. of St. Mary's, Carlisle, 1865. (Patrons, D. and C. of Carl; P. C.'s Inc. 300*l* and Ho; Pop. 8041.) Formerly C. of Church Lawford, Warw. 1820, Willesden and Kingsbury, Lond. 1822, Trin. Ch. Cheltenham, 1824; R. of Cheltenham 1826–56. P. C. of Ch. Ch. Carlisle, 1861–65. Author, *Nine Sermons on the Liturgy*; *Miscellaneous Sermons*, 2 vols. 10*s*. each; *Historical Discourses*, 10*s*; Sermons on Types, Parables, etc; *Eighty Sketches of Sermons and Essay*, 1861, 5*s* 6*d*; *The Footsteps of Error*, 1863, 9*s*. [6]

CLOSE, Henry Charles, *Puttenham Rectory, Tring, Herts.*—Queens' Coll. Cam. B.A. 1838; Deac. 1839, Pr. 1841. R. of Puttenham, Dio. Roch. 1858. (Patron, Bp of Pet; Glebe, 190 acres; R.'s Inc. 260*l* and Ho; Pop. 135.) Formerly C. of Breedon-on-the-Hill and Worthington, Leicestershire. [7]

CLOSE, Richard.—C. of St. Mary's, Preston. [8]

CLOSE, Robert Shaw, *Kirkby Ravensworth, Richmond, Yorks.*—Dub. A.B. 1838; Deac. 1838, Pr. 1840. P. C. of Kirkby Ravensworth, Dio. Rip. 1865. (Patron, Bp of Rip; P. C.'s Inc. 160*l* and Ho; Pop. 1248.) Formerly C. of Patrick Brompton, Yorks. [9]

CLOUGH, Alfred Butler, *Braunston Rectory, near Daventry, Northants.*—Jesus Coll. Ox. B.A. 1818, M.A. 1821, B.D. 1829. R. of Braunston, Dio. Pet. 1838. (Patron, Jesus Coll. Ox; Tithe, 252*l*; R.'s Inc. 848*l* and Ho; Pop. 1228.) Rural Dean. Formerly Fell. and Tut. of Jesus Coll. Ox. 1817–20. [10]

CLOWES, Albert.—C. of Northfield, Worcestershire. [11]

CLOWES, George, *Oak Hill, Surbiton, Surrey.*—Trin. Coll. Cam. B.A. 1862, M.A. 1866; Deac. 1864 and Pr. 1865 by Bp of Win. C. of Ch. Ch. Surbiton, 1864. [12]

CLOWES, James Aaron, *Westleton, Yoxford, Suffolk.*—Deac. 1851 and Pr. 1852 by Bp of Melbourne. V. of Westleton, Dio. Nor. 1861. (Patron, Rev. E. Hollond; V.'s Inc. 325*l*; Pop. 940.) Formerly C. of Westleton 1858; Incumb. of St. Mark's, Collingwood, Australia, 1852. [13]

CLUBBE, Charles Whishaw, *Hughenden Vicarage, High Wycombe, Bucks.*—St. John's Coll. Cam. 21st Wrang. and B.A. 1845, M.A. 1848; Deac. 1847 and Pr. 1848 by Bp of Nor. V. of Hughenden, Dio. Ox. 1851. (Patron, Right Hon. B. Disraeli; Tithe—Imp. 330*l*, V. 337*l*; Glebe, 3½ acres; V.'s Inc. 380*l* and Ho; Pop. 917.) Surrogate. Formerly C. of Palgrave, Suffolk, 1847–51. [14]

CLUBBE, James Henchman, *Igborough, Brandon, Norfolk.*—St. John's Coll. Cam. B.A. 1842, M.A. 1845; Deac. 1842 and Pr. 1844 by Bp of Nor. C. of Igborough. Formerly C. of Roydon, Norfolk. [15]

CLUFF, Samuel O'Malley.—C. of Quarry Bank, Brierley Hill, Staffs. [16]

CLUTTERBUCK, Arthur, *Great Yarmouth*—Ex. Coll. Ox. B.A. 1864; Deac. 1866 by Bp of Nor. Asst. C. of Great Yarmouth. [17]

CLUTTERBUCK, Charles Francis, *Newark Park, Wotton-under-Edge, Glouc.*—Queen's Coll. Ox. 1845; Lampeter; Deac. and Pr. 1852 by Bp of Llan. R. of Ozleworth, *alias* Wozleworth, Dio. G. and B. 1852. (Patron, L. Clutterbuck, Esq; Tithe, 116*l* 10*s* 8*d*; Glebe, 23 acres; R.'s Inc. 160*l* and Ho; Pop. 130.) [18]

CLUTTERBUCK, Henry, *Buckland-Dinham, Frome, Somerset.*—St. Peter's Coll. Cam. Scho. of, B.A. 1831, M.A. 1836; Deac. 1834 by Bp of Chich. Pr. 1834 by Bp of Lin. V. of Buckland-Dinham, Dio. B. and W. 1846. (Patron, Bp of B. and W; Tithe, 150*l*; Glebe, 27 acres; V.'s Inc. 250*l* and Ho; Pop. 459.) [19]

CLUTTERBUCK, James Charles, *Long Wittenham Vicarage, Abingdon, Berks.*—Ex. Coll. Ox. B.A. 1826, M.A. 1829; Deac. and Pr. 1825 by Bp of Ox. V. of Long Wittenham, *alias* Wittenham Earls, Dio. Ox. 1830. (Patron, Ex. Coll. Ox; Glebe, 111 acres; V.'s Inc. 200*l* and Ho; Pop. 583.) Formerly Fell. of Ex. Coll. Ox. [20]

CLUTTERBUCK, John Balfour, *Leighterton Rectory, Wotton-under-Edge, Glouc.*—St. Peter's Coll. Cam. B.A. 1855; Deac. 1856, Pr. 1857. R. of Boxwell with Leighterton, Dio. G. and B. 1857. (Patrons, Trustees of late R. T. Huntley, Esq; Glebe, 80 acres; R.'s Inc. 325*l* and Ho; Pop. 255.) Formerly C. of Tresham, Glouc. 1856–57. [21]

CLUTTERBUCK, J. C.—Asst. Chap. Chelsea Hospital. Formerly C. of St. Mary's, West Brompton. [22]

CLUTTERBUCK, Lewis Balfour, *Dynton Rectory, Bath.*—Wad. Coll. Ox. B.A. 1844; Deac. 1845, Pr. 1846. R. of Dynton, Dio. G. and B. 1847. (Patron, Ld Chan; Tithe, 340*l*; Glebe, 93 acres; R.'s Inc. 445*l* and Ho; Pop. 499.) [23]

CLUTTERBUCK, Lorenzo, *Bredon, Tewkesbury.*—Dub. A.B. 1855, A.M. 1858; Deac. 1857 and Pr. 1858 by Bp of Wor. C. of Bredon 1863. Formerly C. of Bidford 1857–59, Exhall with Wixford 1858–63. [24]

CLUTTERBUCK, Robert Hawley.—King's Coll. Lond. Theol. Assoc. 1862; Deac. 1862 by Bp of Lich. Pr. 1864 by Bp of Lon. P. C. of St. Philip's, Clerkenwell, Dio. Lon. 1867. (Patron, P. C. of St. Mark's, Clerkenwell; P. C.'s Inc. 250*l*; Pop. 9000.) Formerly C. of Plaistow, Essex, 1864–66, and St. Mark's, Clerkenwell, 1866. [25]

CLUTTON, John, *Hereford.*—Wor. Coll. Ox. B.A. 1826, M.A. 1829; Deac. 1826, Pr. 1827. Preb. of Norton in Herf. Cathl. 1831 (Value, 20*l*.) [26]

CLUTTON, Ralph, *Saffron Walden, Essex.*—Emman. Coll. Cam. B.A. 1826, M.A. 1829, B.D. 1836; Deac. and Pr. 1828 by Bp of Ely. V. of Saffron Walden, Dio. Lon. 1844. (Patron, Lord Braybrooke; Tithe—Imp. 761*l* 8*s*, V. 300*l*; Glebe, 5 acres; V.'s Inc. 314*l* and Ho; Pop. 5474.) Surrogate; Rural Dean. Formerly Fell. of Emman. Coll. Cam. [27]

CLYDE, James Burdon, *Bradworthy Vicarage, Holsworthy, Devon.*—St. John's Coll. Cam. B.A. 1831; Deac. 1833 and Pr. 1834 by Bp of Ex. V. of Bradworthy with Pancras Wyke, Dio. Ex. 1845. (Patron, the Crown; Bradworthy, Tithe—Imp. 485*l* 10*s*, V. 195*l*; Glebe, 26 acres; Pancras Wyke, Tithe—Imp. 260*l*, V. 100*l*; Glebe, 8 acres; V.'s Inc. 346*l* and Ho; Pop. Bradworthy 981, Pancras Wyke 378.) [28]

COAR, Charles John, *Canterbury.*—Ball. Coll. Ox. B.A; Deac. 1856 and Pr. 1857 by Bp of Herf. Chap. to H. M.'s Forces, Canterbury. [29]

COATES, Arthur, *Pemberton, Wigan.*—Dub. A.B. 1846; Deac. 1846, Pr. 1848. P. C. of Pemberton,

Dio. Ches. 1849. (Patron, R. of Wigan; P. C.'s Inc. 200*l*; Pop. 8358.) Surrogate. [1]

COATES, Arthur Tomline, *Percy Parsonage, Newcastle-on-Tyne.*—Dur. B.A. 1857; Deac. 1857 and Pr. 1858 by Bp of Dur. P. C. of Percy, Dio. Dur. 1865. (Patron, Duke of Northumberland; P. C.'s Inc. 200*l* and Ho; Pop. 4000.) Formerly C. of St. John's, Ryton, 1857–60, Lee, Hexham, 1860–63, Lamesley 1863–65. [2]

COATES, James, *Chelmorton Parsonage, Bakewell, Derbyshire.*—Literate; Deac. 1811 and Pr. 1812 by Abp of York. P. C. of Sheldon, Bakewell, Dio. Lich. 1814. (Patron, V. of Bakewell; Tithe—App. 7*l*, Imp. 15*l* 15*s*; Glebe, 60 acres; P. C.'s Inc. 90*l*; Pop. 178.) P. C. of Chelmorton, Dio. Lich. 1815. (Patron, V. of Bakewell; Glebe, 60 acres; P. C.'s Inc. 70*l* and Ho; Pop. 229.) [3]

COATES, Robert Patch, *Darenth Vicarage, Dartford, Kent.*—St. John's Coll. Cam. Sen. Opt. 1st cl. Cl. Trip. and B.A. 1834, M.A. 1837; Deac. 1835 and Pr. 1836 by Bp of Chich. V. of Darenth, Dio. Roch. 1863. (Patrons, D. and C. of Roch; V.'s Inc. 350*l* and Ho; Pop. 626.) Surrogate. Formerly Even. Lect. at Frindsbury; 2nd Mast. of the Roch. Cathl. Gr. Sch. 1853; Fell. of St. John's Coll. Cam. [4]

COATES, Samuel, *Sowerby, Thirsk, Yorks.*—Jesus Coll. Cam. Jun. Opt. 2nd cl. Cl. Trip. B.A. 1830, M.A. 1833; Deac. 1830 by Bp of Ches. Pr. 1831 by Abp of York. Preb. of York Cathl. 1843. Formerly P. C. of Sowerby 1843–65. [5]

COATES, William Hodgson, *Tilston, Malpas, Cheshire.*—C. of Tilston. Formerly C. of West Kirby, Bolton-le-Moors. [6]

COATES, William Unett, *Rockhampton Rectory, Thornbury, Glouc.*—Pemb. Coll. Cam. B.A. 1853, M.A. 1856; Deac. 1853 and Pr. 1854 by Bp of Wor. R. of Rockhampton, Dio. G. and B. 1859. (Patroness, Mrs. Coates, Clifton; Tithe, 289*l* 2*s*; Glebe, 15 acres; R.'s Inc. 325*l* and Ho; Pop. 248.) Formerly C. of Stoke Lacy, Hereford. [7]

COBB, Benjamin, *Vicarage, Lydd, Kent.*—Corpus Coll. Cam. 30th Sen. Opt. B.A. 1842, M.A. 1845; Deac. 1843 and Pr. 1844 by Abp of Cant. C. of Lydd 1855. Formerly C. of Old Romney 1843, East Sutton 1845, and Cranbrook 1848. [8]

COBB, Charles, *Dymchurch, Folkestone, Kent.*—Ch. Coll. Cam. Sch. Sen. Opt. 1850, B.A. 1850, M.A. 1853; Deac. 1853 and Pr. 1854 by Bp of Roch. R. of Dymchurch, Dio. Cant. 1860. (Patron, Ld Chan; Tithe, 138*l* 4*s*; Glebe, 10 acres; R.'s Inc. 150*l* and Ho; Pop. 721.) Sinecure R. of Blackmanstone, Dio. Cant. 1860. (Patron, Abp of Cant; Tithe, 13*l* 16*s*; Glebe, 11 acres; R.'s Inc. 44*l*; Pop. 8.) Formerly C. of Halstead, Essex, 1853–55, St. Nicholas-at-Wade 1855–57, Lambeth 1857–58, Sheppey 1858–60. [9]

COBB, Clement Francis, *Barnsley, Yorks.*—Trin. Coll. Cam. 3rd cl. Cl. Trip. B.A. 1850, M.A. 1856; Deac. 1850 and Pr. 1851 by Bp of Win. P. C. of St. George's, Barnsley, Dio. Rip. 1861. (Patron, Bp of Rip; P. C.'s Inc. 300*l* and Ho; Pop. 5945.) Hon. Chap. to Bp of Rip. Formerly Prin. of the Ch. Miss. Soc. Coll. *alias* Jay Narain's Coll. Benares. [10]

COBB, John William, *Norwich.*—Queens' Coll. Cam. B.A. 1835; Deac. 1834, Pr. 1835. R. of St. Margaret's, Norwich, Dio. Nor. 1848. (Patron, Bp of Nor; R.'s Inc. 80*l*; Pop. 1604.) Chap. of the City Gaol. [11]

COBB, John Wolstenholme, *Kidmore End, Henley-on-Thames.*—Brasen. Coll. Ox. B.A. 1850, M.A. 1853; Deac. 1853 and Pr. 1854 by Bp of Roch. P. C. of Kidmore End, Dio. Ox. 1863. (Patron, Bp of Ox; P. C.'s Inc. 80*l* and Ho; Pop. 605.) Formerly C. of Northchurch. [12]

COBB, Robert, *Deptling Vicarage, Maidstone.*—Caius Coll. Cam. B.A. 1819, M.A. 1822; Deac. 1820, Pr. 1821. R. of Burmarsh, Kent, Dio. Cant. 1825. (Patron, the Crown; Tithe, 269*l* 5*s* 3*d*; Glebe, 7 acres; R.'s Inc. 270*l*; Pop. 170.) V. of Debtling, *alias* Deptling, Dio. Cant. 1831. (Patron, Abp of Cant; Tithe—App. 166*l* 2*s* 6*d*, and 24 acres of Glebe, with Ho, V. 121*l* 19*s* 6*d*; Glebe, 10 acres, with Ho; V.'s Inc. 255*l* and Ho; Pop. 344.) [13]

COBB, Thomas, *Rochester.*—Sid. Coll. Cam. Sen. Opt. and B.A. 1849, M.A. 1853; Deac. 1852 and Pr. 1853 by Bp of Lon. Head Mast. of Sir Joseph Williamson's Free Sch. Rochester. Formerly C. of Greenwich 1852–61. [14]

COBB, William, *Shoulden, Deal, Kent.*—Ch. Ch. Ox. B.A. 1841, M.A. 1844; Deac. 1842 and Pr. 1844 by Bp of Lon. P. C. of Shoulden, Dio. Cant. 1855. (Patron, Abp of Cant; Tithe, 280*l*; P. C.'s Inc. 230*l* and Ho; Pop. 407.) Formerly V. of Appledore with Ebony C. Dio. Cant. 1844–55. [15]

COBB, William Francis, *Nettlestead, Maidstone.*—Emman. Coll. Cam. B.A. 1854; Deac. 1855, Pr. 1856. R. of Nettlestead with West Barming R. Dio. Cant. 1862. (Patron, the present R; R.'s Inc. 600*l* and Ho; Pop. Nettlestead 535, West Barming 24.) Formerly C. of Nettlestead. [16]

COBBE, Henry, *Milton Bryant Rectory, Woburn, Beds.*—Oriel Coll. Ox. B.A. 1840, M.A. 1843; Deac. 1842 by Bp of Kilmore, Pr. 1843 by Bp of Meath. R. of Milton Bryant, Dio. Ely, 1866. (Patron, Ld Chan; Tithe, 233*l*; Glebe, 6 acres; R.'s Inc. 252*l* and Ho; Pop. 300.) Formerly C. of Kilmore, Armagh, 1842; Incumb. of Grange, Armagh, 1846. [17]

COBBETT, R. S.—C. of St. Mark's, Old-street-road, Lond. [18]

COBBOLD, E. A.—C. of Wickhambreux, Kent. [19]

COBBOLD, Richard, *Wortham Rectory (Suffolk), near Diss.*—Caius Coll. Cam. B.A. 1820, M.A. 1823; Deac. 1821, Pr. 1822. R. of Wortham, Dio. Nor. 1825. (Patron, the present R; Tithe, 860*l*; Glebe, 40 acres; R.'s Inc. 921*l* and Ho; Pop. 1060.) Rural Dean. Author, *Valentine Verses*, 100 original Sketches, 1827; *Serious and Religious Poetry*, 1828; *A Catechism for the Second Advent*, 1829, 3*d*; *The Spirit of the Litany*, 1833, 6*d*; *Margaret Catchpole*, 1845; *Mary Ann Wellington*, 1846; *Zenon the Martyr*, 1847; *Friston Tower*, 1848; *A Voice from the Mount*, 1848; *Character of Woman*, 1848; *The Young Man's Home*, 1849; *Regeneration* (a Pamphlet), 1850; *The Comforter*, 1850; *A Father's Legacy to his Children*, 1851; *Provident Society Sermon*, 1851; *Death-bed Canticles*, 1854; *A Sermon*, for the benefit of the St. Anne Society, Lond; *The Union Child's Belief*, 1855; various Sermons, Pamphlets, and Addresses; *Canticles of Life*, 1860, 2*s* 6*d*; *Norfolk Mid-Night Tale*, 1867; *The Lord's Prayer, a Private Prayer*; *The Beatitudes*, 1867. [20]

COBBOLD, Richard Wilkie Waller, *Hollesley Rectory, Woodbridge, Suffolk.*—Caius Coll. Cam. B.A. 1846, M.A. 1849; Deac. 1847 and Pr. 1848 by Bp of Nor. R. of Hollesley, Dio. Nor. 1857. (Patroness, Mrs. Waller; Tithe, 940*l*; Glebe, 30 acres; R.'s Inc. 970*l* and Ho; Pop. 603.) Formerly C. of Thelveton and Scole, Norfolk. [21]

COBBOLD, The Ven. Robert Henry, *Broseley Rectory, Salop.*—St. Peter's Coll. Cam. Sen. Opt. 2nd cl. Math. Trip. 2nd cl. Cl. Trip. B.A. 1843, M.A. 1846; Deac. 1844 and Pr. 1845 by Bp of Nor. R. of Broseley with Lindley R. Dio. Herf. 1859. (Patron, Lord Forester; Glebe, 12 acres; R.'s Inc. 480*l*; Pop. 3318.) Formerly V. of Field Dalling, Norfolk, 1858–59; Archd. of Ningpo, Victoria, 1856–58. Author, *Questions on the Collects*; *The Chinese at Home, or, Pictures of the Chinese*, 1859; *England's Reception of Denmark's Daughter* (a Sermon). [22]

COBHAM, Jonathan Blenman, *Dingley Rectory, Market Harborough, Northants.*—Oriel Coll. Ox. 2nd cl. Lit. Hum. and B.A. 1823, M.A. 1825; Deac. 1828 and Pr. 1829 by Bp. of Nor. R. of Dingley, Dio. Pet. 1854. (Patron, H. H. H. Hungerford, Esq; Tithe, 342*l*; Glebe, 54 acres; R.'s Inc. 437*l* and Ho; Pop. 97.) Formerly C. of Mattishall, Norfolk, 1828, Windlesham, Surrey, 1831, Walton, Somerset, 1834; V. of Edwinstowe, Notts, 1843. [23]

COCHRANE, Barton, *Hundleby, Spilsby, Lincolnshire.*—V. of Hundleby, Dio. Lin. 1863. (Patron, Lord Willoughby De Eresby; V.'s Inc. 135*l*; Pop. 704.) [24]

COCHRANE, David Crawford, *Etwall Lodge, Derby.*—Dub. A.B. 1856, A.M. 1860, M.A. Ox. *com. caus.* 1861; Deac. 1859 and Pr. 1860 by Bp of Lich. Mast. of Sir John Porte's Hospital at Etwall 1866 (Stip. 200*l* a year). Formerly C. of Trinity, Burton-on-Trent, 1859–61; Chap. in Mauritius 1861–66. [1]

COCHRANE, James Henry Dickson, *Cheadle Hulme Parsonage, Stockport.*—Dub. A.B. 1854, A.M. 1862; Deac. 1857 and Pr. 1859 by Bp of G. and B. C. in sole charge of All Saints', Cheadle Hulme, 1863. [2]

COCHRANE, Thomas, M.A., *Warwick.*—Mast. of Lord Leycester's Hospital, Warwick. [3]

COOK, Thomas Astley, 18, *Rodney-street, Pentonville, London, N.*—Trin. Coll. Cam. 27th Wrang. and B.A. 1834, M.A. 1839; Deac. 1839 by Bp of Lon. Math. Lect. King's Coll. Lond. and Prof. of Math. and Nat. Phil. in Queen's Coll. Lond. [4]

COCKAYNE, Thomas Oswald, 17, *Montague-street, Russell-square, London, W.C.*—St. John's Coll. Cam. Wrang. B.A. 1828, M.A. 1834; Deac. 1832 and Pr. 1833 by Bp of B. and W. Mast. King's Coll. Sch. Formerly C. of Keynsham 1832. Author, *Greek Syntax; Life of Turenne; Outlines of History of Jews; Outlines of History of France; Outlines of History of Ireland;* Papers in the Transactions of the Philological Society—*Saxon Narratiunculæ, Saxon Leechdoms, St. Margaret, in old English.* [5]

COCKBURN, George Alexander, *Pickering Vicarage, Yorks.*—Sid. Coll. Cam. B.A. 1828, M.A. 1832; Deac. 1829 and Pr. 1830 by Abp of York. V. of Pickering with Newton-upon-Rawcliffe P. C. Dio. York, 1858. (Patron, Dean of York; Tithe, 160*l* 6*s* 2*d*; Glebe, 40 acres; V.'s Inc. 150*l* and Ho; Pop. Pickering 3740, Newton-upon-Rawcliffe 1243.) Author, *First Chapters in the Church*; etc. [6]

COCKELL, Thomas Whitehead.—Wad. Coll. Ox. B.A. 1816, M.A. 1823; Deac. 1817 by Bp of B. and W. Pr. 1818 by Bp of Salis. Formerly C. of All Cannings, Devizes. [7]

COCKERELL, George William, *Kingston-upon-Thames, Surrey.*—Queen's Coll. Ox. B.A. 1840, M.A. 1841; Deac. 1839, Pr. 1840. P. C. of St. John the Baptist's, Kingston Vale, Dio. Win. 1850. (Patron, Bp of Win; P. C.'s Inc. 100*l*; Pop. 270.) [8]

COCKERELL, Henry, *North Weald, Epping Essex.*—Trin. Coll. Ox. B.A. 1823, M.A. 1827; Deac. 1824, Pr. 1825. V. of North Weald, Dio. Roch. 1827. (Patrons, Bp of Roch. and R. P. Ward, Esq. alt; Tithe—Imp. 431*l* 10*s*, V. 451*l* 10*s*; Glebe, 2 acres; V.'s Inc. 507*l* and Ho; Pop. 842.) [9]

COCKERELL, Louis Arthur, *North Weald, Epping, Essex.*—Ball. Coll. Ox. B.A. 1861; Deac. 1863 by Bp of Roch. C. of North Weald 1863. [10]

COCKERHAM, Joseph, *Denstone, Cheadle, Staffs.*—Deac. and Pr. 1849. P. C. of Denstone, Dio. Lich. 1860. (Patron, T. P. Heywood, Esq; P. C.'s Inc. 150*l*.) Formerly C. of Norbury with Snelston 1850. [11]

COCKETT, Francis John, *Denton, Northampton.*—St. Aidan's; Deac. 1860 by Bp of Pet. C. of Denton. Formerly C. of Yardley-Hastings 1860. [12]

COCKETT, William, *Upperby Parsonage, Carlisle.*—Dub. A.B. 1843, A.M. 1847, *ad eund.* Ox. M.A. 1856; Deac. 1843 and Pr. 1844 by Bp of Rip. P. C. of Upperby, Dio. Carl. 1846. (Patrons, D. and C. of Carl; Glebe, 1 acre; P. C.'s Inc. 150*l* and Ho; Pop. 1898.) Formerly Mast. of Knaresborough Gr. Sch. and C. of Knaresborough. Author, *A Sermon on the Union of Church and State,* 1849; *The Anglican and Romish Churches, their Origin and Merits respectively considered,* 1850; *Education as it is required at the Present Time,* 1854; *Sermons for the Times,* 1859. [13]

COCKEY, Edward, *Hockley Vicarage, Chelmsford.*—Wad. Coll. Ox. B.A. 1830, M.A. 1834; Deac. 1835 and Pr. 1836 by Bp of Ox. V. of Hockley, Essex, Dio. Roch. 1846. (Patron, Wad. Coll. Ox; Tithe—Imp. 938*l*, V. 312*l*; Glebe, 8 acres; V.'s Inc. 320*l* and Ho; Pop. 798.) Formerly C. of Dowry Chapel, Clifton, 1855–65; Rural Dean of Rochford 1849–60. [14]

COCKIN, William, *Bishopwearmouth Rectory, Sunderland.*—Brasen. Coll. Ox. 2nd cl. Lit. Hum. and B.A. 1835, M.A. 1841; Deac. 1835, Pr. 1836. R. of Bishopwearmouth, Dio. Dur. 1863. (Patron, Bp. of Dur; Tithe, 1192*l*; Glebe, 90 acres; R.'s Inc. 1900*l*; Pop. 16,462.) Rural Dean; Exam. Chap. to Bp of Dur. Formerly R. of St. George's, Birmingham, 1851; Head Mast. of the Kidderminster Gr. Sch. 1843–51. Author, *A Visitation Sermon,* 1864, 1*s*. [15]

COCKIN, William, jun., *Bishopwearmouth, Sunderland.*—C. of Bishopwearmouth. Formerly C. of St. Matthias', Birmingham. [16]

COCKS, Charles Richard Somers, *Neen Savage Vicarage (Salop), near Bewdley.*—Ch. Ch. Ox. B.A. 1836, M.A. 1840; Deac. 1837 by Bp of Herf. Pr. 1838 by Bp of Wor. V. of Wolverley, Dio. Wor. 1838. (Patrons, D. and C. of Wor; Tithe—App. 811*l*, V. 39*l* 0*s* 6*d*; Land, in lieu of Tithe, 210 acres; Glebe, 8 acres; V.'s Inc. 290*l* and Ho; Pop. 1451.) V. of Neen Savage, Dio. Herf. 1843. (Patron, Ld Chan; Tithe—Imp. 76*l*, V. 220*l*; Glebe, 9 acres; V.'s Inc. 400*l* and Ho; Pop. 452.) Dom. Chap. to Earl Somers. [17]

COCKS, Henry Bromley, *Leigh Rectory, Worcester.*—Ex. Coll. Ox. B.A. 1854, M.A. 1856; Deac. 1855 by Abp of Cant. Pr. 1857 by Bp of Wor. R. of Leigh, Dio. Wor. 1857, with Chapelry of Bransford annexed. (Patron, Earl Somers; Tithe, 330*l*; Glebe, 20 acres; R.'s Inc. 350*l*; Pop. Leigh 992, Bransford 260.) Formerly C. of Ide Hill, Kent. [18]

COCKSHOTT, George, *St. Helens.*—Dur. B.A. 1864; Deac. 1863 and Pr. 1864 by Bp of Lich. C. of St. Helens 1866. Formerly C. of St. Werburgh's, Derby, 1864–65. [19]

COCKSHOTT, John William, *Burwell Vicarage, Newmarket.*—St. Cath. Coll. Cam. Sen. Opt. B.A. 1849, M.A. 1853; Deac. 1849 and Pr. 1851 by Bp of Rip. V. of Burwell, Dio. Ely, 1857. (Patron, Univ. of Cam; V.'s Inc. 335*l*; Pop. 1987.) Rural Dean; Surrogate. Formerly C. of Soham. [20]

CODD, Alfred, *Beaminster, Dorset.*—St. John's Coll. Cam. B.A. 1849; Deac. 1850, Pr. 1851. V. of Beaminster with Trinity C. Dio. Salis. 1857. (Patron, Bp of Salis; Tithe, 333*l* 15*s*; Glebe, 2 acres; V.'s Inc. 461*l* and Ho; Pop. 2614.) Surrogate. Formerly R. of Hawridge 1853–57. Author, *Eight Lectures on Isaiah liii.*, Rivingtons, 1864, 3*s* 6*d*; *Church Missions* (a Sermon), 1866; *A Revision of the Rubrics,* Parker, 1857, 1*s*. [21]

CODD, Edward Thornton, *Tachbrooke Vicarage, Leamington.*—St. John's Coll. Cam. 11th Wrang. and B.A. 1839, M.A. 1842; Deac. 1840 and Pr. 1841 by Bp of G. and B. Select Preacher before the University in 1851 and 1864. V. of Bishop's Tachbrooke, Dio. Wor. 1859. (Patron, Bp of Lich; Glebe, 7 acres; V.'s Inc. 343*l* and Ho; Pop. 620.) Formerly C. of Minchinhampton 1840, St. Giles's, Cambridge, 1841; P. C. of Cotes Heath, Staffs, 1844–59. Author, *Sermons preached in the Parish Church of St. Giles's, Cambridge,* 1846, 6*s* 6*d*; *Sermons addressed to a Country Congregation, with Three preached before the University of Cambridge,* 1852, 6*s*; *A Letter to the Bishop of Lichfield on Diocesan Theological Colleges,* 1853, 1*s*; *Sermons addressed to a Country Congregation,* 2nd series, 1855, 6*s* 6*d*; *Twenty-five Chants, Single and Double,* 1858, 6*d*; *Music to Advent Hymn,* 3*d*. [22]

CODD, Samuel, *Kingsbury, near Tamworth.*—St. Bees; Deac. 1859 and Pr. 1860 by Bp of Lich. C. of Kingsbury with Dosthill 1866. [23]

CODDINGTON, Henry Hallet, *Hockerill, Bishops Stortford, Herts.*—Trin. Coll. Cam. Jun. Opt. Goldsmith's Exhib. B.A. 1862, M.A. 1865; Deac. 1864 and Pr. 1865 by Bp of Roch. C. of Hockerill 1864. [24]

CODRINGTON, Henry, *Goathurst, Bridgwater, Somerset.*—St. John's Coll. Cam. B.A. 1832; Deac. 1832 and Pr. 1833 by Bp of B. and W. C. of Goathurst. Author, *Family Prayers,* 1845. [25]

CODRINGTON, John Edward.—C. of Lambeth. Formerly C. of Sutton Coldfield. [26]

CODRINGTON, Richard Chute, *Combe St. Nicholas, Somerset.*—Jesus Coll. Cam. Scho. of, LL.B. 1833; Deac. 1831 and Pr. 1832 by Bp of B. and W. Formerly C. of Thorn St. Margaret, Somerset, and Clayhidon, Devon, 1831–33, Donyatt, Somerset, 1834–36. Author, *Church Reform*, 1838, 2s 6d; *Remarks on the Currency*, 1839, 2s 6d; *The Age we Live in*, 1863. [1]

CODRINGTON, Richard Gibson, *Gibraltar.*—Dub. A.B. 1857; Deac. 1857 and Pr. 1858 by Bp of B. and W. Chap. to the Forces, Gibraltar. Formerly C. of Runnington, Wellington. [2]

CODRINGTON, Robert Henry, *Auckland, New Zealand.*—Wad. Coll. Ox. B.A. 1852, M.A. 1857; Deac. 1856 and Pr. 1858 by Bp of Ox. Melanesian Mission, Auckland; Fell. of Wad. Coll. Ox. Formerly C. of St. Peter's-in-the-East, Oxford. [3]

COGAN, Henry, *East Dean Vicarage, Chichester.*—St. John's Coll. Cam. B.A. 1837, M.A. 1841; Deac. 1838, Pr. 1839. V. of East Dean, Dio. Chich. 1850. (Patron, the present V; V.'s Inc. 120l and Ho; Pop. 343.) R. of Up-Waltham, Sussex, Dio. Chich. 1850. (Patron, Lord Leconfield; Tithe, 128l 3s 10d; Glebe, 7 acres; R.'s Inc. 138l and Ho; Pop. 71.) [4]

COGHLAN, James Henry, 35, *York-street, Oldham.*—St. Aidan's; Deac. 1858 and Pr. 1859 by Bp of Rip. C. of Oldham and of St. Andrew's District. Formerly C. of Elland 1858, Creagh, Cork, 1861, St. James's, Liverpool, 1862, St. Thomas's, Preston, 1863. [5]

COGHLAN, John Armstrong, 7, *Douglas-road, Canonbury-park, Islington, N.*—Dub. A.M. P. C. of St. Paul's, Ball's Pond, Dio. Lon. 1861. (Patrons, Trustees; P. C.'s Inc. 550l; Pop. 11,789.) Formerly C. of Wendy with Shingay, Cambs; P. C. of St. James's, Jersey. [6]

COGHLAN, William, *Grove-street, Ardwick, Manchester.*—St. Bees; Deac. 1861 and Pr. 1862 by Bp of Ches. C. of St. Jude's, Manchester, 1866. Formerly C. of St. Matthew's, Liverpool, 1861, St. James's, West Derby, 1862, St. Stephen's, Liverpool, 1863. [7]

COGHLAN, William Boyle, 367, *Portland-terrace, Oxford-road, Manchester.*—Dub. A.B. 1852, A.M. 1855; Deac. 1853 and Pr. 1854 by Bp of Herf. Formerly C. of Cherbury, Salop, 1853–57. [8]

COGSWELL, Norris, *Keelby, Ulceby, Lincolnshire.*—St. John's Coll. Cam. B.A. 1827, M.A. 1831; Deac. and Pr. 1827. V. of Holton-le-Clay, Dio. Lin. 1833. (Patron, Ld Chan; Tithe—Imp. 4l, V. 12l; Glebe, 95 acres; V.'s Inc. 182l; Pop. 297.) V. of Immingham, Dio. Lin. 1837. (Patrons, Earl of Yarborough and others; Tithe—Imp. 56l 14s 3d, V. 162l 11s 3d; Glebe, 12 acres; V.'s Inc. 175l; Pop. 261.) [9]

COHEN, James, *Rectory, Whitechapel, London, E.*—Pemb. Coll. Cam. M.A. 1842; Deac. 1842, Pr. 1843. R. of St. Mary's, Whitechapel, Dio. Lon. 1860. (Patron, Bp of Lon; R.'s Inc. 800l and Ho; Pop. 15,476.) Formerly Mast. in Christ's Hospital, 1842; C. of Cheshunt 1843; C. of St. Dunstan's West, Lond. 1846, and Chap. City Prison, 1847. [10]

COKE, Edward Francis, 190, *Bethnal-green-road, London, N.E.,* and *West-green, Tottenham.*—Brasen. Coll. Ox. Hulmian Exhib. B.A. 1840, M.A. 1845; Deac. 1840 and Pr. 1841 by Bp of Herf. P. C. of St. James's the Great, Bethnal-green, Dio. Lon. 1852. (Patron, Bp of Lon; P. C.'s Inc. 292l and Ho; Pop. 4269.) Formerly C. of All Saints', Hereford, 1840; P. C. of Plymstock, Devon, 1843. [11]

COKE, George Francis, *Le Moor, Eardisley, Herefordshire.*—Ex. Coll. Ox. 4th cl. Lit. Hum. and B.A. 1854; Deac. 1854, Pr. 1855. Formerly C. of Piddle-Hinton. [12]

COKE, John Henry, *Ropsley Rectory, Grantham, Lincolnshire.*—Pemb. Coll. Ox. B.A. 1835. R. of Ropsley, Dio. Lin. 1846. (Patron, Duke of Rutland; R.'s Inc. 940l and Ho; Pop. 845.) [13]

COKE, William, *Marstow, Ross, Herefordshire.*—P. C. of Marstow with Pencoyd P. C. Dio. Herf. 1831. (Patron, V. of Sellack; Marstow, Tithe—App. 8l 10s, P. C. 194l 4s; Pencoyd, Tithe—App. 154l 18s 5d, P. C. 68l 9s 10d; P. C.'s Inc. 269l; Pop. Marstow 142, Pencoyd 219.) [14]

COKER, Cadwallader, *Shalstone Rectory, Bucks.*—New Coll. Ox. B.A. 1848, M.A. 1852; Deac. 1848, Pr. 1849. R. of Shalstone, Dio. Ox. 1854. (Patroness, Mrs. Fitzgerald; Tithe, 140l; Glebe, 44 acres; R.'s Inc. 225l and Ho; Pop. 243.) Rural Dean. [15]

COKER, John, *Tingewick, Bucks.*—New Coll. Ox. B.A. 1842, M.A. 1847; Deac. 1844, Pr. 1845. R. of Tingewick, Dio. Ox. 1855. (Patron, New Coll. Ox; R.'s Inc. 359l; Pop. 914.) Fell. of New Coll. Ox. [16]

COLBECK, John Abernethy, *Brighton.*—King's Coll. Lond. Theol. Assoc. 1864; Deac. 1864 and Pr. 1865 by Bp of Lon. C. of Brighton 1867. Formerly C. of St. Philip's, Earl's Court, Kensington, 1864. [17]

COLBECK, William Royde, *Fressingfield Vicarage, near Harlestone, Suffolk.*—Emman. Coll. Cam. B.A. 1827, M.A. 1830, B.D. 1836; Deac. 1829, Pr. 1830. V. of Fressingfield with Withersdale R. Dio. Nor. 1846. (Patron, Emman. Coll. Cam; Fressingfield, Tithe—Imp. 919l, V. 399l 17s; Glebe, 25 acres; Withersdale, Tithe, 221l 10s; Glebe, 42 acres; V.'s Inc. 579l and Ho; Pop. Fressingfield 1325, Withersdale 225.) Hon. Can. of Nor. Formerly Fell. of Emman. Coll. Cam. 1829. [18]

COLBORNE, Hon. Graham, *Dittisham Rectory, Totnes, Devon.*—St. John's Coll. Ox. B.A. 1844, M.A. 1848; Deac. 1848 and Pr. 1852 by Bp of G. and B. R. of Dittisham, Dio. Ex. 1853. (Patron, Earl of Mount Edgcumbe; Tithe, 465l; Glebe, 85 acres; R.'s Inc. 530l and Ho; Pop. 762.) [19]

COLBOURNE, John, *Hinckley, Leicestershire.*—St. Peter's Coll. Cam. B.A. 1852; Deac. 1852, Pr. 1853. V. of Hinckley, Dio. Pet. 1865. (Patrons, D. and C. of Westminster; V.'s Inc. 550l and Ho; Pop. 4599.) Formerly P. C. of St. Matthias', Bethnal-green, Lond. 1854–65. [20]

COLBY, Edmund Reynolds.—Emman. Coll. Cam. 1854, Ex. Coll. Ox. B.A. 1856; Deac. 1857 by Bp of Ex. Pr. 1857 by Bp of B. and W. Formerly Chap. of H.M.S. "Madagascar," 1858; C. of St. Mary's and St. Martin's, Isles of Scilly, and St. Paul's, Exeter. [21]

COLBY, Frederic Thomas, *Exeter College, Oxford.*—Ex. Coll. Ox. 2nd cl. Lit. Hum. 1849, B.A. 1852, M.A. 1853; Deac. 1850 and Pr. 1852 by Bp of Ox. Fell. and Bursar of Ex. Coll. [22]

COLBY, James, *Meldreth, Royston.*—Sid. Coll. Cam. B.A. 1863; Deac. 1863 by Bp of Ely. C. of Meldreth 1863. [23]

COLBY, Robert, *Ansford Rectory, Castle Carey, Somerset.*—R. of Ansford, Dio. B. and W. 1838. (Patron, F. Woodford, Esq; R.'s Inc. 310l and Ho; Pop. 306.) Formerly C. of Ansford. [24]

COLDHAM, George, *Glemsford Rectory, Sudbury, Suffolk.*—Caius Coll. Cam. B.A. 1825, M.A. 1828; Deac. and Pr. 1827 by Bp of Nor. V. of East Walton with Gayton-Thorpe R. Dio. Nor. 1831. (Patron, A Hamond, Esq; Tithe—App. 230l, V. 178l 1s; Gayton-Thorpe, Tithe—Imp. 2l 6s 8d, R. 312l 15s; Glebe, ½ acre; V.'s Inc. 490l and Ho; Pop. East Walton 175, Gayton-Thorpe 169.) R. of Glemsford, Suffolk, Dio. Ely, 1833. (Patron, Bp of Ely; Tithe, 826l; Glebe, 75¼ acres; R.'s Inc. 920l and Ho; Pop. 1932.) [25]

COLDHAM, James Charles, *East Walton Vicarage, Lynn, Norfolk.*—King's Coll. Cam. B.A. 1858, M.A. 1860; Deac. 1861 and Pr. 1862 by Bp of Lin. C. of East Walton and Gayton-Thorpe, Norfolk; Fell. of King's Coll. Cam. [26]

COLDHAM, John, *Snettisham Vicarage, Lynn, Norfolk.*—V. of Snettisham, Dio. Nor. 1812. (Patron, H. L. S. Le Strange, Esq; V.'s Inc. 110l and Ho; Pop. 1173.) R. of Anmer, Castle Rising, Dio. Nor. 1816. (Patron, H. Coldham, Esq; Tithe, 200l; Glebe, 70 acres; R.'s Inc. 256l; Pop. 142.) R. of Stockton, Dio. Nor. 1816. (Patron, Duke of Norfolk; Tithe, 259l 18s; R.'s Inc. 280l; Pop. 129.) Rural Dean. [27]

COLDWELL, Charles Simeon, 14, *Bloomsbury-street, London, W.C.*—Brasen. Coll. Ox. Hulmian. Exhib. B.A. 1861; Deac. 1865 and Pr. 1866 by Bp of Lon. C. of St. John's, Drury-lane, 1865. Formerly

Asst. Mast. of Rossall Sch. 1861–62; Fell. and Tut. of Bishop's Coll. Cape of Good Hope, 1862–64. [1]

COLDWELL, Clement Leigh, *Hopton Congeford, Ludlow.*—Pemb. Coll. Ox. B.A. 1856, M.A. 1859; Deac. 1857 and Pr. 1858 by Bp of Lich. P. C. of Clee St. Margaret's, Dio. Herf. 1864. (Patron, Rev. H. Thursby Pelham; P. C.'s Inc. 164*l* 10*s*; Pop. 281.) P. C. of Hopton Congeford, Dio. Herf. 1865. (Patron, Sir C. Rouse Boughton, Bart; P. C.'s Inc. 74*l* and Ho; Pop. 30.) Formerly C. of Wem, Salop, 1857–61; Astbury, Cheshire, 1861–64. [2]

COLDWELL, Thomas, *Green's Norton, Towcester, Northants.*—Deac. 1827, Pr. 1829. R. of Green's Norton, Dio. Pet. 1853. (Patron, the Crown; Tithe, 16*l*; Glebe, 300 acres; R.'s Inc. 749*l* and Ho; Pop. 903.) Chap. to the Duke of Grafton. [3]

COLDWELL, William Edward, *Sandon Vicarage, Stone, Staffs.*—Ch. Ch. Ox. 3rd cl. Lit. Hum. and B.A. 1848; Deac. 1849 and Pr. 1850 by Bp of Ox. V. of Sandon, Dio. Lich. 1867. (Patron, Earl of Harrowby; Tithe, 340*l*; Glebe, 12*l*; V.'s Inc. 355*l* and Ho; Pop. 570.) Dom. Chap. to Duke of Marlborough. Formerly C. of Sandon. [4]

COLE, A. R.—C. of St. Luke's, Newtown, Southampton. [5]

COLE, Charles, *Greenock, Scotland.*—Clare Hall, Cam. B.A. 1817; Deac. and Pr. 1819 by Bp of Lon. Incumb. of St. John's Episcopal Ch. Greenock. (Patron, Sir M. R. Shaw Stewart, Bart; Incumb.'s Inc. 300*l*.) [6]

COLE, Edward, *Great Plumstead, near Norwich.*—St. John's Coll. Cam. B.A. 1826, M.A. 1829; Deac. 1826 and Pr. 1827 by Bp of Nor. P. C. of Great Plumstead, Dio. Nor. 1833. (Patrons. D. and C. of Nor; Tithe—App. 502*l* 14*s* 6*d*, and 44¾ acres of Glebe, P. C.'s Inc. 100*l*; Pop. 342.) Chap. to the County Lunatic Asylum, 1834; Hon. Sec. to the Norfolk and Norwich Savings Bank 1828. Formerly Acting Hon. Sec. to the Norfolk and Norwich Nat. Sch. Soc. 1830. [7]

COLE, Edward Maule, *Wetwang, Driffield.*—Oriel Coll. Ox. B.A. 1857; Deac. 1858 and Pr. 1859 by Abp of York. V. of Wetwang with Fimber C. Dio. York, 1865. (Patron, Abp of York; V.'s Inc. 300*l* and Ho; Pop. 827.) Formerly P. C. of Whitwood Mere, Yorks. Author, *Noah's Flood*, 6*d*. [8]

COLE, Francis, *St. Issey, Padstow, Cornwall.*—Ex. Coll. Ox. B.A. 1810; Deac. 1810, Pr. 1813. V. of St. Issey, Dio. Ex. 1844. (Patrons, D. and C. of Ex; Tithe—App. 459*l*, V. 223*l* 1*s* 2*d*; Glebe, 40 acres; V.'s Inc. 279*l*; Pop. 756.) [9]

COLE, Francis Charles, *Odiham, Hants.*—Wad. Coll. Ox. M.A. 1859, Deac. 1861 and Pr. 1862 by Bp of Win. P. C. of Long Sutton, Dio. Win. 1863. (Patron, St. Cross Hospital; P. C.'s Inc. 73*l*; Pop. 320.) Formerly C. of St. Luke's, Southampton, 1861. [10]

COLE, Francis Edward Baston, *Pelynt Vicarage, Liskeard, Cornwall.*—St. Edm. Hall, Ox. B.A. 1842; Deac. 1842 and Pr. 1843 by Bp of Ex. V. of Pelynt, Dio. Ex. 1858. (Patron, J. H. Buller, Esq; Tithe, 235*l*; Glebe, 71 acres; V.'s Inc. 350*l* and Ho; Pop. 729.) Formerly C. of Oakhampton 1842, Pilaton 1846. Author, *The Methodistic Theory of Conversion Antagonistic to the Theory of the Church*, Parkers, 1*s*. [11]

COLE, George, *Bethersden Vicarage, Tenterden.*—Corpus Coll. Cam. B A; Deac. 1829, Pr. 1830. V. of Bethersden, Dio. Cant. 1866. (Patron, Abp of Cant; Tithe, 98*l*; Glebe, 22*l*; V.'s Inc. 261*l* 18*s* and Ho; Pop. 1125.) Formerly C. of Rainham. Author, *I am a Christian—What then?* 5*s*; *The Decision of Ruth, addressed to Candidates for Confirmation*, 1*s*; *The Threefold Cord, or Justification by the Grace of God, the Blood of Christ, and the Faith of Man*, 1*s*; *Tracts on Important Questions*; *Tracts on the Prayer Book*, 1*s* 6*d*; various other Tracts. [12]

COLE, George Edward, *Quinton, Northants.*—St. Mary Hall, Ox. B.A. 1839, M.A. 1847; Deac. 1842 by Bp of Win. Pr. 1844 by Bp of Salis. R. of Quinton, Dio. Pet. 1862. (Patron, Ld Chan; Tithe, 2*l* 12*s*; R.'s Inc. 295*l*; Pop. 119.) Formerly Prof. of History and Latin at the Royal Military Coll. Farnborough, 1846; one of the Board of Examiners for Army Commissions 1849–57. [13]

COLE, George Lamont, *Wellisford House, Wellington, Somerset.*—St. John's Coll. Cam. B.A. 1848, M.A. 1851; Deac. 1849, Pr. 1850. V. of Thorn St. Margaret, Taunton, Dio. B. and W. 1857. (Patron, Archd. of Taunton; Tithe—App. 108*l*; V. 54*l*; V.'s Inc. 125*l*; Pop. 144.) [14]

COLE, George William, *Redditch, Worcestershire.*—Downing Coll. Cam. B.A. 1864; Deac. 1866 by Bp of Wor. C. of Redditch 1866. [15]

COLE, Henry Hearle, *Harlyn Lodge Cotham Brow, Bristol.*—St. John's Coll. Cam. B.A. 1847; Deac. 1847 and Pr. 1848 by Bp of Wor. C. of St. Matthias', Bristol, 1861. Formerly C. of Charles the Martyr, Plymouth, 1851, Romsey, Hants, 1855, St. Jude's, Bristol, 1857. [16]

COLE, John, 1, *Silver-terrace, Exeter.*—St. John's Coll. Cam. Sen. Opt. B.A. 1843, M.A. 1846; Deac. 1845 and Pr. 1846 by Bp of Ex. R. of St. Pancras, Exeter, Dio. Ex. 1861. (Patrons, D. and C. of Ex; Glebe, 13 acres; R.'s Inc. 66*l*; Pop. 345.) Formerly C. of Sampford-Spiney 1845, Bridestow 1847, Callington 1847, Tong 1855, Sourton 1857, Marlborough 1859–61. Author, *Parochial Sermons*, 1858, 4*s* 6*d*; *Christ's Address to Prostrate Jerusalem* (a Sermon), 1862; *The Shortness and Uncertainty of Life* (a Sermon), 1862; *The Observation of Nature too much Neglected with Regard to Religion* (a Sermon), 1866. [17]

COLE, John Francis, *Kirdford Vicarage, Petworth, Sussex.*—Wor. Coll. Ox. B.A. 1826; Deac. 1827, Pr. 1829. V. of Kirdford with Plastow Chapelry, Dio. Chich. 1839. (Patron, Lord Leconfield; Tithe—Imp. 694*l* 4*s*, V. 501*l* 1*s*; V.'s Inc. 500*l* and Ho; Pop. 1784.) [18]

COLE, Robert, *Greenlaw, Edinburgh.*—Chap. to the Military Prison, Greenlaw; Dom. Chap. to the Earl of Rosslyn. Formerly P. C. of Tidcombe, Dio. Salis. [19]

COLE, Robert Eden George, *Doddington Rectory, Lincoln.*—Univ. Coll. Ox. B.A. 1854, M.A. 1857; Deac. 1854 and Pr. 1856 by Bp of Lin. R. of Doddington, Dio. Lin. 1861. (Patron, G. K. Jarvis, Esq. Doddington Hall; R.'s Inc. 260*l* and Ho; Pop. 270.) Formerly C. of Doddington 1855–56, Langar, with Barnston, Notts, 1856–61. [20]

COLE, Thomas Henry, *Parkhurst, Isle of Wight.*—Ex. Coll. Ox. B.A. 1858, M.A. 1861; Deac. 1858 and Pr. 1859 by Bp of Chich. Chap. to the Forces, Parkhurst. Formerly C. of Preston with Hove, Sussex, 1858, Frittenden 1859–61, St. Mary's, Dover, 1861–62; Chap. to the Forces at Aldershot 1862–63, Portsmouth 1863–65, Woolwich, Limerick, and Parkhurst, 1865–67. [21]

COLE, William, *The Litten, Newbury.*—Mert. Coll. Ox. 2nd cl. Maths. 4th cl. Lit. Hum. M.A. 1847; Deac. 1847 and Pr. 1848 by Bp of Wor. R. of Padworth, Dio. Ox. 1865. (Patron, Ld Chan; Glebe, 27 acres; R.'s Inc. 290*l* and Ho; Pop. 298.) Formerly Mast. of Newbury Gr. Sch. [22]

COLE, W. Alston, *Malpas, Newport, Monmouthshire.*—C. of Malpas. [23]

COLE, W. Barry, 57, *Montpelier-road, Brighton.*—Caius Coll. Cam. B.A. 1853; Deac. 1855 and Pr. 1856 by Bp of Win. [24]

COLE, William Gordon, *Trinity College, Oxford.*—Trin. Coll. Ox. B.A. 1858, M.A. 1861; Deac. 1865 by Bp of Salis. Pr. 1866 by Bp of Ox. Fell. of Trin. Coll. 1859. [25]

COLE, William Sibthorpe, *Ryther Rectory, Tadcaster, Yorks.*—Wor. Coll. Ox. 2nd cl. Lit. Hum. B.A. 1820, M.A. 1822; Deac. 1822 and Pr. 1823 by Bp of Ox. R. of Ryther with Ossendyke, Dio. York, 1846. (Patron, Ld Chan; Tithe, comm. 618*l* 16*s* 4*d*; Glebe, 12 acres; R.'s Inc. 658*l* and Ho; Pop. 372.) Formerly C. of St. Margaret's-at-Cliffe, Dover, 1828; Even. Lect. at St. Mary's Dover, 1828; V. of Westcliffe, Dover, 1830; Min. of Trin. Ch. Dover, 1835; Chap. to the Lord Warden of the Cinque Ports 1837. Author, *Two Sermons on the Pastoral Office preached before the Univ. of Ox.* 1833. [26]

COLE, W. S, *South Brent Vicarage, Ashburton, Devon.*—V. of South Brent, Dio. Ex. 1866. (Patron, Rev. N. Cole; V.'s Inc. 890*l* and Ho; Pop. 1205.) [1]

COLEBY, George, *Colby Rectory, North Walsham, Norfolk.*—Corpus Coll. Cam. B.A. 1817; Deac. 1817 Pr. 1820. R. of Colby, Dio. Nor. 1842. (Patron, Lord Suffield; Tithe, 361*l* 16*s*; Glebe, 7 acres; R.'s Inc. 366*l* and Ho; Pop. 269.) [2]

COLEMAN, Charles Handley, 2, *George-street, Edgbaston, Birmingham.*—St. Bees; Deac. 1847 and Pr. 1848 by Bp of Lich. P. C. of Immanuel Ch. Birmingham, Dio. Wor. 1865. (Patrons, Trustees; P. C.'s Inc. 340*l*; Pop. 10,000.) Author, *The Best Day the Neglected Day*, 1852; *Fifteen Important Questions for those who only attend the Public Services of God's House occasionally*; *A true Wesleyan*; *Excessive Ritualism*, 1867. [3]

COLEMAN, Henry John, *Sloley, Norwich.*—Corpus Coll. Cam. B.A. 1849, M.A. 1853; Deac. 1850 and Pr. 1851 by Bp of Nor. C. of Sloley. Formerly C. of Worstead 1850, and Swanton Abbotts, Norfolk, 1853. [4]

COLEMAN, James, *Allerton, Weston-super-Mare.*—Oriel Coll. Ox. B.A. 1853, M.A. 1856; Deac. 1855 and Pr. 1856 by Bp of B. and W. R. of Allerton, Dio. B. and W. 1858. (Patrons, D. and C. of Wells; R.'s Inc. 223*l*; Pop. 292.) [5]

COLEMAN, John Charles, *Clare Vicarage, Suffolk.*—Dub. A.B. 1836; Deac. 1837 and Pr. 1838 by Bp of Ches. V. of Clare, Dio. Ely, 1854. (Patron, Duchy of Lancaster; Tithe—App. 343*l*, Imp. 34*l* 7*s* 8*d*, V. 237*l* 18*s* 8*d*; Glebe, 25 acres; V.'s Inc. 296*l* and Ho; Pop. 1657.) Formerly P. C. of St. James's, Standard-hill, Nottingham. [6]

COLEMAN, John Noble, 5, *The Terrace, Ryde, Isle of Wight.*—Queen's Coll. Ox. M.A; Deac. 1814 by Bp of B. and W. Pr. 1815 by Bp of Glouc. Surrogate. Formerly P. C. of Ventnor 1837–55. Author, *Psalterium Messianicum Davidis Regis et Prophetæ*, 12*s*; *Memoir of Rev. Richard Davis*, 1865, 7*s* 6*d*; *A New Translation of Ecclesiastes, with Notes.* [7]

COLERIDGE, Alfred James, *Bromham Vicarage, near Bedford.*—Univ. Coll. and Demy of Magd. Coll. Ox. B.A. 1855; Deac. 1856 and Pr. 1857 by Bp of Ox. V. of Bromham with Oakley V. Dio. Ely, 1866. (Patron, Eton Coll; Bromham—Tithe, Imp. 350*l* 11*s* 9*d*, V. 220*l*; Glebe, 19 acres; Oakley, Glebe, 64 acres; V.'s Inc. 400*l* and Ho; Pop. Bromham 353, Oakley 457.) Formerly C. of Great and Little Haseley, Oxon, 1857–61; R. of Rokeby, Yorks, 1861–66. [8]

COLERIDGE, Derwent, *Hanwell Rectory, Middlesex.*—St. John's Coll. Cam. B.A. 1824, M.A. 1830; Deac. 1826 and Pr. 1827 by Bp of Ex. R. of Hanwell, Dio. Lon. 1864. (Patron, Bp of Lon; Tithe, 400*l*; Glebe, 25 acres; R.'s Inc. 436*l* and Ho; Pop. 2687.) Preb. of Islington in St. Paul's Cathl. 1846 (Value 2*l*). Formerly Prin. of St. Mark's Coll. Chelsea, 1841–64. Author, *Advent Sermon*, 1831, 1*s*; *Scriptural Character of the English Church*, 1840, 12*s*; *Farewell Sermon*, 1841, 1*s*; *Letter on the National Schools and Training College, Stanley Grove*, 1842; *A Second Letter*, 1842; *The Teachers of the People* (a Sermon), 1843; several Pamphlets on Educational Subjects. Editor of the *Works of Hartley Coleridge*, with *Memoir*; *Poems of W. M. Praed*, with *Memoir*. [9]

COLERIDGE, Edward, *Maple-Durham, Reading.*—Ex. and Corpus Colls. Ox. B.A. 1822, M.A. 1825. V. of Maple-Durham, Dio. Ox. 1862. (Patron, Eton Coll; Tithe—App. 59*l* 14*s* 3*d*, V. 851*l* 5*s* 9*d*; Glebe, 52¼ acres; R.'s Inc. 881*l* and Ho; Pop. 486.) Fell of Eton Coll. [10]

COLERIDGE, Edwin Ellis, *Buckerell Vicarage, Honiton, Devon.*—Trin. Coll. Ox. B.A. 1825; Deac. 1826 and Pr. 1827 by Bp of Ex. V. of Buckerell, Dio. Ex. 1829. (Patrons, D. and C. of Ex; Tithe—App. 183*l*, V. 135*l*; Glebe, 2 acres; V.'s Inc. 155*l* and Ho; Pop. 312.) [11]

COLERIDGE, Frederick John, *Cadbury Vicarage, Tiverton, Devon.*—Ox. B.A. 1850, M.A. 1853; Deac. 1851 and Pr. 1852 by Bp of Ex. V. of Cadbury, Dio. Ex. 1855. (Patron, the present V; Tithe—Imp. 95*l* 13*s* 7*d*, V. 172*l* 10*s*; Glebe, 5 acres; V.'s Inc. 194*l* and Ho; Pop. 230.) Formerly C. of Mawgan and St. Martin 1851, Ottery St. Mary 1852. [12]

COLES, Edward Norman, *Pottesgrove Rectory, Woburn, Beds.*—Deac. 1848 and Pr. 1849 by Bp of Wor. R. of Battlesden with Pottesgrove, Dio. Ely, 1858. (Patrons, Trustees of the late Sir G. Page Turner; Tithe, 450*l*; Glebe, 2 acres; R.'s Inc. 500*l* and Ho; Pop. 441.) Formerly C. of Hardwick and Weedon, Bucks. [13]

COLES, Henry Apreece, *Marnham, near Newark, Notts.*—St. John's Coll. Cam. B.A. 1829; Deac. 1830, Pr. 1831. V. of Marnham, Dio. Lin. 1844. (Patron, Hon. Chas. Henry Cust; Tithe—Imp. 31*l* 18*s* 4*d*, V. 261*l* 1*s*; Glebe, 62 acres; V.'s Inc. 392*l* and Ho; Pop. 348.) [14]

COLES, James Stratton, *Shepton-Beauchamp Rectory, Ilminster, Somerset.*—Emman. Coll. Cam. B.A. 1831, M.A. 1834; Deac. 1834 and Pr. 1835 by Bp of B. and W. R. of Shepton-Beauchamp, Dio. B. and W. 1836. (Patron, Rev. P. Smith; Tithe, 373*l*; Glebe, 16 acres; R.'s Inc. 390*l* and Ho; Pop. 658.) P. C. of Barrington, Somerset, Dio. B. and W. 1848. (Patrons, D. and C. of Bristol; Tithe—App. 396*l* 6*s*; P. C.'s Inc. 75*l*; Pop. 563.) Preb. of Timberscombe in Wells Cathl. 1848; Rural Dean of Crewkerne. [15]

COLES, Jefferis William, *Long Ashton, Somerset.*—Wor. Coll. Ox. B.A. 1845; Deac. 1846 and Pr. 1847 by Bp of G. and B. Chap. to the Bedminster Union 1848. [16]

COLES, Richard Edward, *Petersfield.*—Pemb. Coll. Ox. B.A. 1862; Deac. 1863, Pr. 1864. Asst. C. of Petersfield, and Chap. of Petersfield Union 1863. [17]

COLES, Thomas Henry, *Honington, Grantham.*—Clare Coll. Cam. Jun. Opt. and B.A. 1803, M.A. 1806, D.D. 1818; Deac. 1803, Pr. 1805. V. of Honington, Dio. Lin. 1805. (Patron, Sir T. G. Apreece; Tithe, 200*l* 1*s*; Glebe, 1 acre; V.'s Inc. 215*l*; Pop. 157.) [18]

COLES, Thomas Stirling, *Framlingham, Suffolk.*—Corpus Coll. Cam. Sen. Opt. and B.A. 1836, M.A. 1840; Deac. 1838 and Pr. 1839 by Bp of Ches. Formerly C. of St. Matthew's, Islington; P. C. of St. George's, Manchester; C. of Stowmarket, Suffolk. [19]

COLEY, James, *Barrackpore, Bengal.*—Ch. Ch. Ox. Scho. of, B.A. 1838, M.A. 1839; Deac. 1840 by Bp of Wor. Pr. 1842 by Bp of Ely. Chap. at Barrackpore. Formerly East India Chaplaincy 1842; C. of St. Cross, Oxford, 1863. Author, *The Honble. Company's Ecclesiastical Establishment*, an article in *Calcutta Review*, Sept. 1852; *Journal of the Sutlej Campaign*, in *Calcutta Christian Intelligencer*, 1846; *The Study of the Bible, of the Prayer-Book, of Church History by the People*, and *Church Congresses*, in *Oxford Magazine*, 1863. [20]

COLING, James, *Badby, Daventry, Northants.*—St. John's Coll. Cam. B.A. 1850; Deac. 1850 and Pr. 1851 by Bp of Lich. C. of Badby with Newnham. Formerly C. of St. Mark's, Wolverhampton, 1850; P. C. of Stockingford, Nuneaton, 1853; C. of Astley, Salop, 1860; Miss C. of a district in St. Chad's, Shrewsbury, 1861. [21]

COLLARD, Edwin Curwen, *Alton Pancras, near Dorchester.*—Deac. 1853. Pr. 1854. V. of Alton Pancras, Dio. Salis. 1864. (Patrons, D. and C. of Salis; V.'s Inc. 208*l* and Ho; Pop. 270.) Formerly Chap. and Lect. to the Training Sch. Salisbury; C. of Combe Bissett, Salisbury. [22]

COLLES, Goddard-Richards Purefoy, *Sutton, Beckingham, Newark.*—Dub. A.B. 1860, L.L.B. 1863, L.L.D. 1866; Deac. 1862 and Pr. 1863 by Bp of Lich. C. of Fenton with Stragglethorpe, Beckingham, 1865. Formerly C. of Norbury 1862–65. [23]

COLLES, William Morris, *Melton Mowbray Vicarage, Leicestershire.*—Dub. Hons. in Science 1841 Prizes in Science and Hebrew 1842, A.B. 1843, A.M. 1854; Deac. 1843 and Pr. 1844 by Bp of Ches. V. of Melton Mowbray with Freeby C. Burton Lazars C. Sysonby C. and Welby C. Dio. Pet. 1866. (Patron, Thomas Frewen, Esq; Glebe, 2 acres; V.'s Inc. 620*l* and Ho; Pop. 4936.) Surrogate, 1850. Formerly C.

of St. George's, Manchester, 1843–45, Preston 1845, Ch. Ch. Salford, 1847–49, Melton-Mowbray 1849–66. Author, *Wherefore Serveth the Law*, 1d; *The Doctrines, Dangers, and Duties of Churchmen*, 9d; *Sisters of Mercy, Sisters of Misery*, 6d; *Romanism Refuted*, 4d; *The Great Question Answered* (a Sermon) 6d. [1]

COLLETT, Anthony, *Dover.*—Trin. Coll. Cam. B.A. 1859; Deac. 1859 and Pr. 1860 by Abp of Cant. C. of St. Mary's, Dover, 1860. [2]

COLLETT, Henry Pyemont, *Islington Vicarage, King's Lynn.*—Trin, Hall, Cam. B.A 1854; Deac. 1859 and Pr. 1861 by Bp of Nor. V. of Islington, Dio. Nor. 1867. (Patron, the Crown; Tithe, 100*l*; Glebe, 5 acres; V.'s Inc. 104*l* and Ho; Pop. 300.) Formerly C. of Kesgrave with Brightwell, Suffolk, 1859–62, Shenton, Leic. 1862–63; P. C. of Fordham, Norfolk, 1863–67. [3]

COLLETT, William, *Hawstead Rectory, Bury St. Edmunds.*—R. of Hawstead, Dio. Ely, 1852. (Patron, Sir T. G. Cullum; Tithe, 581*l*; Glebe, 37 acres; R.'s Inc. 637*l* and Ho; Pop. 446.) Chap. to H.R.H. the Duke of Cambridge. [4]

COLLETT, William Lloyd, *St. Stephen's Parsonage, Shepherd's Bush, Hammersmith, W.*—Queen's Coll. Ox. B.A. 1842, M.A. 1845; Deac. 1842, Pr. 1843. P. C. of St. Stephen's, Hammersmith, Dio. Lon. 1856. (Patron, Bp of Lon; Endow. 190*l*; Pew rents 210*l* P. C.'s Inc. 425*l* and Ho; Pop. 6268.) [5]

COLLETT, William Michael, *Oriel College, Oxford.*—Trin. Coll. Ox. B.A. 1862, M.A. 1864; Deac. 1864 and Pr. 1865 by Bp of Ox. Fell. and Tut. of Oriel Coll. Ox. Formerly Tut. and Asst. Mast. in Wellington Coll. 1863–65. [6]

COLLETT, William Reynolds, *Hethersett Rectory, Wymondham, Norfolk.*—Caius Coll. Cam. 13th Wrang. and B.A. 1845, M.A. 1848; Deac. 1846 and Pr. 1849 by Bp of Ely. R. of Hethersett with Canteleff R. Dio. Nor. 1856. (Patron, Caius Coll. Cam; Tithe, 855*l* 3*s* 6*d*; Glebe, 58 acres; R's Inc. 905*l* and Ho; Pop. 1169.) Fell. of Caius Coll. Cam. [7]

COLLETT, W. S., M.A., *Clare College, Cambridge.*—Sen. Fell. of Clare Coll. Cam. [8]

COLLETT, Woodthorpe, *Brightwell, Ipswich.*—St. Cath. Coll. Cam. B.A. 1820, M.A. 1825; Deac. 1821 and Pr. 1822 by Bp of Lin. P. C. of Brightwell with Foxhall and Kesgrave, Dio. Nor. 1854. (Patron, Sir J. K. Shaw, Bart; Brightwell, Tithe—Imp. 8*l* 15*s*; Glebe, 7 acres; Foxhall, Tithe—Imp. 70*l*; Kesgrave, Tithe—Imp. 42*l* 2*s* 6*d*; P. C.'s Inc. 120*l*; Pop. 365.) Surrogate. [9]

COLLEY, James, *Shrewsbury.*—St. John's Coll. Cam. B.A. 1830, M.A. 1833; Deac. 1831, Pr. 1832. P. C. of St. Julian's, Shrewsbury, Dio. Lich. 1862. (Patron, Earl of Tankerville; P. C.'s Inc. 130*l*; Pop. 1762.) Surrogate. Author, *The Christian's Creed, set forth chiefly in the Words of Scripture*, 6d; *A Visitation Sermon*, 1842; *Baptismal Regeneration, explained in Extracts from various Divines*, 3d; *Haweis's Communicant's Companion, with Additional Prayers, &c.*, 1s 6d. [10]

COLLIER, Charles, *Training College, Winchester.*—Dub. A.B. 1850, A.M. 1854, *ad eund.* Ox. 1856; Deac. 1853 and Pr. 1854 by Abp of York. Prin. of Training Coll. and Chap. of St. John's Hospital, Winchester; Hon. Chap. of the 15th Hants Volunteer Rifle Corps. Formerly Asst. C. of Sheffield, and 2nd Mast. of Sheffield Gr. Sch. Author, *Wolvesey Palace* (a Lecture), 6d; *St. Swithun* (a Sermon) 6d. [11]

COLLIER, C. J., B.C.L., *Fairfield, Rye, Kent.*—P. C. of Fairfield, Kent, Dio. Cant. 1850. (Patron, Earl of Guilford; P. C.'s Inc. 57*l*; Pop. 69.) [12]

COLLIER, Henry N., *Trinity Clergy House, Great Portland-street, London, W.*—Ch. Coll. Cam. 2nd cl. Cl. Trip. B.A. 1859, M.A. 1862; Deac. 1859 and Pr. 1860 by Bp of Carl. C. of Trinity, Marylebone, 1863. Formerly C. of Kendal 1859–62. [13]

COLLIN, John, *Rickling Vicarage, Bishops Stortford, Essex.*—Emman. Coll. Cam. 22nd Sen. Opt. and B.A. 1828, M.A. 1831; Deac. 1829 and Pr. 1831 by Bp of Lon. V. of Rickling, Dio. Roch. 1834. (Patron, Bp of Roch; Tithe—Imp. 278*l* 16*s* 6*d*, V. 127*l* 5*s* 6*d*; Glebe, 7 acres; V.'s Inc. 281*l* and Ho; Pop. 502.) Formerly C. of Rickling; R. of Heydon with Little Chishall, Essex, 1844–51. [14]

COLLIN, Joseph, *Elmdon, near Royston, Herts.*—Literate; Deac. 1853 by Bp of Ex. Pr. 1856 by Bp of Roch. R. of Streethall, Essex, Dio. Roch. 1856. (Patrons, Exors. of the late Archd. Raymond; Tithe, 151*l*; Rent from Glebe, 100*l*; R.'s Inc. 251*l*; Pop. 45.) Formerly C. of Bodmin, Cornwall. [15]

COLLING, Thomas Adams, *Buckland Brewer, Bideford, Devon.*—Lin. Coll. Ox. B.A. 1825; Deac. 1825 and Pr. 1826 by Bp of Ex. V. of Buckland Brewer with East Putford and Bulkworthy C. Dio. Ex. 1836. (Patron, the Crown; Buckland Brewer, Tithe—Imp. 240*l*, V. 235*l* 10*s*; Glebe, 9 acres; East Putford Tithe—Imp. 65*l* 10*s*; V. 55*l*; Bulkworthy, Tithe—Imp. 37*l* 10*s*, V. 36*l*; V.'s Inc. 326*l* and Ho; Pop. Buckland Brewer 922, East Putford 190, Bulkworthy 128.) [16]

COLLINGWOOD, Charles Edward Stuart, *Southwick Rectory, Sunderland.*—Dur. Van-Mildert Scho. 1852, Hebr. Prizeman and B A. 1853, Theol. Prizeman 1854, M.A. 1856; Deac. 1854 and Pr. 1855 by Abp of York. R. of Southwick, Dio. Dur. 1863. (Patron, D. and C. of Dur; Tithe, 112*l*; Rent from Glebe, 80*l*; R.'s Inc. 440*l* and Ho; Pop. 4683.) Formerly C. of Northallerton 1854–56, Hendon, Bishopwearmouth, 1856–63; Fell. of Univ. Coll. Dur. [17]

COLLINS, Caleb, *Stedham Rectory, Midhurst, Sussex.*—St. John's Coll. Cam. B.A. 1823, M.A. 1826; Deac. 1823, Pr. 1824. R. of Stedham with Heyshot R. Dio. Chich. 1826. (Patroness, The Hon. Mrs. V. Harcourt; Tithe—Imp. 2*l* 5*s*, R. 291*l*; Heyshot, Tithe, 318*l*; R.'s Inc. 720*l* and Ho; Pop. Stedham 530, Heyshot 396.) [18]

COLLINS, Charles Creaghe, 9, *Mecklenburgh-square, London, W.C.*—Ch. Coll. Cam. B.A. 1850, M.A. 1853; Deac. 1850 Pr. 1851. P. C. of St. Mary's, Aldermanbury, City and Dio. Lon. 1854. (Patrons, the Parishioners; Tithe, 150*l*; P. C.'s Inc. 255*l*; Pop. 443.) [19]

COLLINS, Charles Matthew Edward, *Trewardale, Blisland, Bodmin, Cornwall.*—Ex. Coll. Ox. 2nd cl. Lit. Hum. and B.A. 1836, M.A. 1839; Deac. and Pr. 1840 by Bp of Wor. Local Inspector of Schools for East and West Cornwall; one of H.M. Justices of the Peace for Cornwall. Formerly Dioc. Inspector of Schools for the Deanery of Trigg. [20]

COLLINS, Ebenezer, *Cowslip Green, Wrington, Somerset.*—C. of Ch. Ch. Redhill, Wrington, 1863. [21]

COLLINS, George, *The Parsonage, Laister-Dyke, Bradford, Yorks.*—St. Cath. Coll. Cam. Scho. 16th Sen. Opt. B.A. 1855, M.A. 1858, *ad eund.* Ox. 1861; Deac 1857, Pr. 1858. P. C. of St. Mary's, Bradford, Dio. Rip. 1861. (Patrons, Simeon's Trustees; P. C.'s Inc. 300*l* and Ho; Pop. 8000.) Formerly C. of St. Maurice's, Winchester, 1857–59, St. Aldate's, Oxford, 1860–61, Trinity, Cambridge, 1861. Author, various Sermons published by John Dale and Co., Bradford. [22]

COLLINS, Henry, *Wincanton, Somerset.*—Dub. A.B. 1823, A.M. 1830; Deac. 1824, Pr. 1825. P. C. of Wincanton, Dio. B. and W. 1838. (Patrons, U. and G. Messiter; Tithe, Imp. 490*l*; P. C.'s Inc. 130*l*; Pop. 2450.) [23]

COLLINS, Henry, *Scammonden, Huddersfield.*—St. John's Coll. Cam. 24th Wrang. Scho. B.A. 1859, M.A. 1862; Deac. 1861 and Pr. 1862 by Bp of Rip. P. C. of Scammonden, or Deanhead, Dio. Rip. 1865. (Patron, V. of Huddersfield; P. C.'s Inc. 197*l* and Ho; Pop. 1011.) Formerly C. of Calverley with Bolton 1861–65. [24]

COLLINS, Henry, *Knaresborough, Yorks.*—Formerly Chap. of the Carlton Union, Gainsley, Yorks. [25]

COLLINS, John, *Shepley Parsonage, Huddersfield.*—St. Cath. Coll. Cam. Scho. of, B.A. 1855, M.A. 1858. P. C. of Shepley, Dio. Rip. 1858. (Patron, V. of Kirkburton; P. C.'s Inc. 100*l* and Ho; Pop. 1432.) Formerly C. of Kirkburton. [1]

COLLINS, John Argyle Welsh, *Waikato, Auckland, New Zealand.*—St. John's Coll. Cam. Scho. of, 1853–58, B.A. 1856; Deac. 1857 and Pr. 1859 by Bp of Ex. Chap. to the Forces 1861. Formerly C. of Millbrook, Devon. [2]

COLLINS, John Coombes, *St. John's Parsonage, Eastover, Bridgwater.*—St. John's Coll. Cam. B.A. 1826, M.A. 1848; Deac. 1829, Pr. 1830. P. C. of St. John the Baptist's, Eastover, Dio. B. and W. 1846. (Patrons, the Crown and Bp of B. and W. alt; P. C.'s Inc. 175*l* and Ho; Pop. 4792.) Surrogate. [3]

COLLINS, John Ferdinando, *Highworth, Wilts.*—Corpus Coll. Ox. B.A. 1859, M.A. 1863; Deac. 1861 and Pr. 1862 by Bp of Ox. C. of Highworth 1863. Formerly C. of Shirburn, Oxon, 1861–63. [4]

COLLINS, Joseph William, *Stogursey, near Bridgwater.*—Dub. A.B. 1859; Deac. 1860 and Pr. 1861 by Bp of Ches. C. of Stogursey. [5]

COLLINS, Richard, *Kirkburton Vicarage, Huddersfield.*—V. of Kirkburton, Dio. Rip. 1843. (Patron, Ld Chan; Tithe—Imp. 20*l* 12*s* 8*d*; V.'s Inc. 310*l* and Ho; Pop. 9728.) [6]

COLLINS, Richard, *Cottayam, near Allepie, S. India.*—St. John's Coll. Cam. B.A. 1851, M.A. 1854; Deac. 1851 and Pr. 1853 by Bp of Rip. Prin. of the Ch. Miss. Coll. Cottayam. [7]

COLLINS, Richard, *St. Saviour's Vicarage, Leeds.*—Univ. Coll. Ox. S.C.L. 1848, B.A. 1857, M.A. 1858; Deac. 1851, Pr. 1858. V. of St. Saviour's, Leeds, Dio. Rip. 1859. (Patrons, Trustees; V.'s Inc. 280*l*; Pop. 6881.) [8]

COLLINS, Robert Cave Wood, *Harefield Parsonage, Uxbridge.*—Ex. Coll. Ox. 2nd cl. Lit. Hum. and B.A. 1833, M.A. 1841; Deac. 1839 and Pr. 1840. by Bp of Lon. Chap. of D. of Harefield, Dio. Lon. 1864. (Patron, C. N. Newdegate, Esq; Chap's Inc. 75*l* and Ho; Pop. 1567.) Formerly C. of Harefield. [9]

COLLINS, Robert Codrington, *Towcester, Northants.*—Dur. Licen. Theol. 1851; Deac. 1851 and Pr. 1852 by Bp of Pet. V. of Easton Neston, Dio. Pet. 1861. (Patron, Earl of Pomfret; V.'s Inc. 250*l*; Pop. 170.) Formerly C. of Towcester 1851–55. [10]

COLLINS, Thomas, *Farnham, Knaresborough, Yorks.*—Univ. Coll. Ox. B.A. 1801, M.A. 1804, B.D. 1811; Deac. 1803 and Pr. 1804 by Bp of Ox. P. C. of Farnham, Dio. Rip. 1818. (Patrons, the present P. C. and — Shann, Esq; P. C.'s Inc. 138*l*; Pop. 572.) Formerly Fell. of Magd. Coll. Ox. 1804; Public Examiner at Oxford 1813–15; R. of Horsington, Linc. 1815–16; R. of Barningham, Yorks, 1816–29. [11]

COLLINS, Thomas, *Marr, near Doncaster.*—Sid. Coll. Cam. B.A. 1856; Deac. 1859 and Pr. 1860 by Bp of Lich. C. of Marr. Formerly C. of St. George's, Newcastle-under-Lyme, 1859; 2nd Mast. of Newcastle Gr. Sch. [12]

COLLINS, Thomas Farmer, *New Bilton, Rugby.*—Brasen. Coll. Ox. Hulme Exhib. B.A. 1859, M.A. 1862; Deac. 1861 and Pr. 1862 by Bp of Pet. C. of Bilton 1863. Formerly C. of Geddington, Northants, 1861, Tring, Herts, 1862. [13]

COLLINS, William, *King's Lynn, Norfolk.*—St. Cath. Coll. Cam. Sen. Opt. B.A. 1858, M.A. 1861; Deac. 1859 and Pr. 1860 by Bp of Nor. C. of St. Nicholas', King's Lynn, 1866. Formerly C. of St. Mary's and Chap. of the Hospital, Woodbridge, 1859–61; Missionary Chap. of the Colonial and Continental Ch. Soc. at Cochin, Malabar Coast, India, 1861–65. [14]

COLLINS, William, *St. Mary's Parsonage, Ramsey, Hunts.*—Ex. Coll. Ox. B.A. 1852, M.A. 1859; Deac. 1853 and Pr. 1854 by Bp of G. and B. P. C. of St. Mary's, Ramsey, Dio. Ely, 1859. (Patron, Edward Fellowes, Esq; Tithe Rent Charge, 150*l*, P. C.'s Inc. 150*l* and Ho; Pop. 1068.) Formerly C. of Highworth, Wilts, 1853–55, Hes-well, Yorks, 1855–60. [15]

COLLINS, William Lucas, *Kilsby Vicarage, Rugby.*—Jesus Coll. Ox. 2nd cl. Lit. Hum. B.A. 1838, M.A. 1841; Deac. 1840 by Bp of Ox. Pr. 1841 by Bp of St. D. V. of Kilsby, Dio. Pet. 1867. (Patron, Bp of Pet; Tithe, 4*l*; Glebe, 84 acres; V.'s Inc. 300*l* and Ho; Pop. 539.) Formerly C. of Great Houghton, Northants, 1853–62, Brafield-on-the-Green 1862–67; R. of Cheriton, Glamorganshire, 1841–67. [16]

COLLINSON, Henry King, *Stannington Vicarage, Morpeth, Northumberland.*—Queen's Coll. Ox. B.A. 1827, M.A. 1833; Deac. 1827, Pr. 1828. V. of Stannington, Dio. Dur. 1845. (Patron, Bp of Dur; Tithe—Imp. 700*l* 18*s* 11*d*, V. 342*l* 3*s* 10½*d*; Glebe, 21 acres; V.'s Inc. 379*l* and Ho; Pop. 1058.) [17]

COLLIS, George, *Margate.*—King's Coll. Lond. Theol. Assoc. 1863; Deac. 1864 and Pr. 1865 by Bp of Salis. C. of Margate 1865. Formerly C. of Calne, Wilts, 1864–65. [18]

COLLIS, Henry, *St. Philip's Parsonage, Maidstone.*—Caius Coll. Cam. B.A. 1858, M.A. 1861; Deac. 1858 and Pr. 1859 by Bp of Ely. P. C. of St. Philip's, Maidstone, Dio. Cant. 1862. (Patron, P. C. of All Saints', Maidstone; P. C.'s Inc. 73*l* and Ho; Pop. 2500.) Formerly C. of St. Andrew's the Less, Cambridge, 1858–62. [19]

COLLIS, John Day, *Bromsgrove Grammar School, Worcestershire.*—Wor. Coll. Ox. 1st cl. Lit. Hum. and B.A. 1838, Kennicott Hebr. Scho. 1839, Pusey and Ellerton Heb. Scho. and M.A. 1841, D.D. 1860; Deac. 1839 and Pr. 1842 by Bp of Ox. Head Mast. of Edward VI. Gr. Sch. Bromsgrove, 1843; Hon. Can. of Wor. Cathl. 1853; Grinfield Lecturer on the Septuagint, Ox. 1863. Formerly Fell. of Wor. Coll. Ox. Author, *Praxis Græca, Part I. Etymology,* 6th ed. 2*s* 6*d*; *Part II. Syntax,* 3rd ed. 6*s*; *Part III. Accentuation,* 6th ed. 3*s*; *Praxis Latina, Part I. for Beginners,* 5th ed. 2*s* 6*d*; *Part II. for Advanced Pupils,* 3rd ed. 3*s*; *Praxis Latina, Part I, adapted to the Public School Latin Primer,* 2*s* 6*d*; *The Chief Tenses of Irregular Latin Verbs, tabularly arranged,* 11th ed. 1*s*; *Greek Verbs,* do. 1*s*; *Praxis Iambica, Elementary and Progressive Exercises in Greek Tragic Senarii,* 5th ed. 4*s* 6*d*; *Tirocinium Gallicum* (A Short French Grammar for Classical Schools), 3rd ed. 3*s* 6*d*; *Pontes Classici, Greek and Latin,* 6th ed. 3*s* 6*d* each; *Ponticulus Græcus et Latinus,* 1*s* each; *History of Bromsgrove School,* 5*s* 6*d*. [20]

COLLIS, T. W., *Brighton.*—Dub. A.B. 1858; Deac. by Bp of Cashel, and Pr. 1860 by Bp of Ely. C. of St. Paul's, Brighton. Formerly C. of Luton and Leighton Buzzard. [21]

COLLISON, Frederick William Portlock, *Marwood Rectory, Barnstaple, Devon.*—St. John's Coll. Cam. 6th Wrang. and B.A. 1836, M.A. 1839, B.D. 1846; Deac. 1838 and Pr. 1839 by Bp of Ely. R. of Marwood, Dio. Ex. 1853. (Patron, St. John's Coll. Cam; Tithe, 635*l* 14*s* 2*d*; Glebe, 26 acres; R.'s Inc. 655*l* and Ho; Pop. 1009.) [22]

COLLISON, George Vaux, *Bacton, Hereford.*—Lampeter; Deac. 1864 and Pr. 1865 by Bp of Herf. C. of Newton-in-Clodock, and Chap. to the Dore Union, Herefordshire, 1864. [23]

COLLISON, Henry, *Litcham, Norfolk.*—Pemb. Coll. Cam. B.A. 1816, M.A. 1819. R. of East Bilney with Beetley, Dio. Nor. 1833. (Patron, W. Collison, Esq; East Bilney, Tithe, 118*l*; Glebe, 20 acres; Beetley, Tithe—App. 14*s* 6*d*, R. 500*l* 6*s* 6*d*; R.'s Inc. 550*l* and Ho; Pop. East Bilney 198, Beetley 363.) Formerly Chap. to the King's Bench Prison; Chap. of the Marshalsea and of the Court of Her Majesty's Palace of Westminster; Military Chap. at the Cape of Good Hope. [24]

COLLISON, Henry, *Heworth, Gateshead.*—Pemb. Coll. Cam. B.A. 1860, M.A. 1866; Deac. 1862 and Pr. 1864 by Bp. of Dur. C. of Heworth 1862. [25]

COLLS, John Flowerdew, *Laindon Rectory, Essex.*—Trin. Coll. Cam. B.D. 1834, D.D. 1842; Deac. 1830, Pr. 1831. R. of Laindon with Basildon, Dio. Roch. 1858. (Patron, Bp of Roch; Tithe, Laindon, 520*l*; Glebe, 30 acres; Basildon, Tithe, 280*l*; Glebe, 23 acres; R.'s Inc. 800*l* and Ho; Pop. 586.) Author, *Vindication of Infant Baptism,* 10*s*; *Utilitarianism Unmasked,* 1*s* 6*d*. [26]

COLLUM, H. R., *Hythe, Kent.*—C. of Hythe. [27]

COLLYER, Robert, *Warham Wells, Norfolk.*—R. of Warham All Saints with St. Mary R. Dio. Nor. 1844. (Patron, Earl of Leicester; Tithe, Warham All Saints, 247*l*; Glebe, 8 acres; Warham St. Mary, Tithe, 373*l* 10*s*; R.'s Inc. 628*l*; Pop. Warham All Saints 318, Warham St. Mary 74.) Hon. Can. of Nor. 1856. [1]

COLLYER, Thomas, *Gislingham Rectory, Eye, Suffolk.*—R. of Gislingham, Dio. Nor. 1851. (Patron, the present R; Tithe, 651*l*; Glebe, 54 acres; R.'s Inc. 721*l* and Ho; Pop. 623.) [2]

COLLYNS, Charles Henry, *Wirksworth, Derbyshire.*—Ch. Ch. Ox. Stud. Fell. and Exhib. of, B.A. 1841, M.A. 1844; Deac. 1843 and Pr. 1844 by Bp of Ox. Head Mast. of Wirksworth Gr. Sch. 1867. Formerly C. of St. Mary Magdalene's, Oxford, 1844–45, Swanswick, near Bath, 1866–67. Translator of *Works of St. Pacian* (Library of the Fathers), 1844. Author, *School Prayers*; *Short Prayers for Family Use*; *My Children's First Reading Book.* [3]

COLLYNS, John Edward, *Mariansleigh, South Molton, Devon.*—King's Coll. Lond. Theol. Assoc; Deac. 1851 and Pr. 1853 by Bp of Ex. P. C. of Mariansleigh, Dio. Ex. 1856. (Patrons, Trustees of Davey's Charity; Tithe—Imp. 165*l* 10*s*; P. C.'s Inc. 150*l*; Pop. 281*l*.) Formerly C. of Honiton, Devon. [4]

§ **COLLYNS, John Martyn,** *Bensington, alias Benson, near Wallingford, Oxon.*—Ch. Ch. Ox. Stud. 1846, 2nd cl. Lit. Hum. and B.A. 1848, M.A. 1851; Deac. 1850 and Pr. 1851 by Bp of Ox. P. C. of Bensington, or Benson, Dio. Ox. 1858. (Patron, Ch. Ch. Ox; Tithe—App. 1046*l*, and 17½ acres of Glebe, P. C. 157*l* 10*s*; Glebe, 2½ acres; P. C.'s Inc. 200*l*; Pop. 1169.) Formerly P. C. of St. Leonard's, Drayton, Dio. Ox. 1855–58. [5]

COLLYNS, John Martyn, *Sancreed Vicarage, Penzance, Cornwall.*—Ex. Coll. Ox. B.A. 1814, M.A. 1817; Deac. 1815, Pr. 1816. V. of Sancreed, Dio. Ex. 1851. (Patrons, D. and C. of Ex; Tithe—App. 170*l*, V. 352*l* 12*s* 8*d*; Glebe, 5 acres; V.'s Inc. 365*l* and Ho; Pop. 1233.) [6]

COLPOYS, James Adair Griffith, *Droxford Rectory, Bishops Waltham, Hants.*—Ex. Coll. Ox. B.A. 1824, M.A. 1824; Deac. 1825 by Bp of Herf. Pr. 1826 by Bp of Salis. R. of Droxford, Dio. Win. 1831. (Patron, Bp of Win; Tithe, 1015*l* 17*s* 8*d*; Glebe, 23 acres; R.'s Inc. 1050*l* and Ho; Pop. 513.) [7]

COLQUHOUN, Robert, *Rochester.*—C. of St. Peter's, Rochester. [8]

COLSON, Charles, *Great Hormead Vicarage, Buntingford, Herts.*—St. John's Coll. Cam. 3rd Wrang. and B.A. 1839, M.A. 1842; Deac. 1841, Pr. 1842. V. of Great Hormead, Dio. Roch. 1842. (Patron, St. John's Coll. Cam; Land in lieu of Tithe, 120 acres; V.'s Inc. 134*l* and Ho; Pop. 660.) Surrogate. Formerly Fell. of St. John's Coll. Cam. 1840. [9]

COLT, Sir Edward Harry Vaughan, Bart., *Hill Vicarage, near Berkeley, Glouc.*—Queen's Coll. Ox. B.A. 1836; Deac. 1838, Pr. 1839. V. of Hill, Dio. G. and B. 1839. (Patrons, Reps. of Dr. Herbert Jenner; Tithe—App. 179*l* 15*s* 9*d*, and 33 perches of Glebe, V. 250*l*; V.'s Inc. 250*l* and Ho; Pop. 216.) [10]

COLTMAN, George, *Stickney Rectory, Boston, Lincolnshire.*—Brasen. Coll. Ox. B.A. 1833; Deac. 1834 and Pr. 1835 by Bp of Lin. R. of Stickney, Dio. Lin. 1835. (Patron, the present R; Glebe, 178 acres; R.'s Inc. 370*l* and Ho; Pop. 851.) P. C. of Hagnaby, Dio. Lin. 1845. (Patron, T. Coltman, Esq; Corn Rent, 10*l*; Glebe, 32 acres; P. C.'s Inc. 80*l*; Pop. 93.) Rural Dean. One of H.M. J.P. for the parts of Lindsey, and also for the parts of Holland. co. Lin. [11]

COLTON, William Charles, *Leaden-Roding, Chipping Ongar, Essex.*—Queen's Coll. Ox. B.A. 1836. R. of Leaden-Roding, Dio. Roch. 1864. (Patron, Ld Chan; R.'s Inc. 250*l*; Pop. 207.) [12]

COLVILE, Frederick Leigh, *Leek Wotton Vicarage, near Warwick.*—Trin. Coll. Ox. B.A. 1840, M.A. 1843; Deac. and Pr. 1841. V. of Leek Wotton, Dio. Wor. 1842. (Patron, Lord Leigh; Tithe, 4*l* 19*s*; Glebe, 150 acres; V.'s Inc. 370*l* and Ho; Pop. 389.) Chap. of Stoneleigh Abbey 1853; Dom. Chap. to Lord Leigh. Formerly Rural Dean of Coventry. Author, *Catechism of the Liturgy of the Church of England*, 9th ed. 1850, 6*d*; *A Few Words respecting the Church of England, being Plain Reading for Plain People*, 4*d*; *A Few Observations on Education, addressed to Parochial Teachers*, 1858, 3*d*, published by Rivingtons. [13]

COLVILE, Robert Acton, 12, *Newbie-terrace, Belmont-road, Liverpool.*—Ch. Coll. Cam. B.A. 1857; Deac. 1857 and Pr. 1858 by Bp of Ely. Formerly C. of Great and Little Livermere 1857–59, Dilhorne 1859–60, North and South Lopham 1861–62. [14]

• **COLVILL, John Burleigh,** *Reading.*—Dub. A.B. 1847; Deac. 1847 by Bp of Ches. Pr. 1848 by Bp of B. and W. Chap. of the County Gaol, Reading. Formerly C. of St. Mary's, Reading. [15]

COLVIN, John William, *Great Yarmouth.*—Corpus Coll. Ox. B.A. 1862, M.A. 1865; Deac. 1863 and Pr. 1864 by Bp of Nor. Asst. C. of Great Yarmouth 1863; Even. Lect. at St. George's, Great Yarmouth. [16]

COLWILL, James, *Buckland Brewer, near Bideford.*—Magd. Coll. Cam. Scho. 1856, B.A. 1859; Deac. 1859 and Pr. 1860 by Bp of B. and W. C. of Buckland Brewer 1867. Formerly C. of Lyncombe 1859. [17]

COLYER, John Edmeades, *Fenny Drayton Rectory, near Nuneaton.*—St. Peter's Coll. Cam. B.A. 1855; Deac. 1855 and Pr. 1856 by Bp of Man. R. of Fenny Drayton, Dio. Pet. 1857. (Patron, V. A. Eyre, Esq; Land in lieu of Tithe, 200 acres; R.'s Inc. 520*l* and Ho; Pop. 134.) Formerly C. of St. Clement's, Spotland, Lancashire. [18]

COMBER, Charles Thomas.—Jesus Coll. Cam. B.A. 1849; Deac. 1850, Pr. 1851. Chap. R.N. [19]

COMBER, Henry George Wandesford, *Oswaldkirk Rectory, near York.*—Jesus Coll. Cam. B.A. 1821; Deac. 1822, Pr. 1824. R. of Oswaldkirk, Dio. York, 1835. (Patrons, Trustees of the Rev. T. Comber; Tithe, 409*l* 10*s*; Glebe, 297 acres; R.'s Inc. 720*l* and Ho; Pop. 524.) [20]

COMINS, John, *North Huish, Ivy Bridge, Devon.*—Queen's Coll. Ox. B.A. 1843; Deac. and Pr. by Bp of Ex. R. of North Huish, Dio. Ex. 1860. (Patron, the present R; R.'s Inc. 550*l* and Ho; Pop. 432.) Preb. of Endellion. Formerly C. of Colyton. [21]

COMPSON, Edward Bate, *Hillesley, Wotton-under-Edge, Glouc.*—Queen's Coll. Ox. B.A. 1835; Deac. 1835 by Bp of Win. Pr. 1836 by Bp of Ely. P. C. of Hillesley, Dio. G. and B. 1856. (Patron, Bp of G. and B; P. C.'s Inc. 71*l* and Ho; Pop. 574.) Formerly C. of Wotton-under-Edge. [22]

COMPSON, John, *Great Wyrley, Walsall, Staffs.*—P. C. of Great Wyrley Dio. Lich. 1850. (Patron, P. C. of Cannock; P. C.'s Inc. 163*l*; Pop. 2067.) [23]

COMPTON, The Right Hon. Lord Alwyne, *Chadstone, Northants.*—Trin. Coll. Cam. Wrang. and M.A. 1848; Deac. 1850, Pr. 1851. R. of Castle Ashby, Northants, Dio. Pet. 1852. (Patron, Marquis of Northampton; Tithe, 237*l*; Glebe, 120 acres; R.'s Inc. 420*l* and Ho; Pop. 183.) Hon. Can. of Pet. 1856. [24]

COMPTON, Berdmore, *Rectory*, 7, *Henrietta-street, Covent-garden, London, W.C.*—Mert. Coll. Ox. 1838, 1st cl. Math. 3rd cl. Lit. Hum. and B.A. 1841, M.A. 1843; Deac. 1853, Pr. 1857. R. of St. Paul's, Covent-garden, Dio. Lon. 1865. (Patron, Duke of Bedford; R.'s Inc. 500*l* and Ho; Pop. 5150.) Formerly R. of Barford, near Warwick, 1857–65. [25]

COMPTON, Daniel Goddard, *Wroxton, near Banbury.*—Ex. Coll. Ox. B.A. 1861, M.A. 1864; Deac. 1862 and Pr. 1863 by Bp of B. and W. V. of Wroxton with Balscott, Dio. Ox. 1864. (Patron, Col. J. S. North, M.P; Glebe, 2 acres; V.'s Inc. 135*l*; Pop. Wroxton 570, Balscott 230.) Formerly C. of South Petherton 1862. [26]

COMPTON, John, *Minestead Parsonage, Lyndhurst, Hants.*—Mert. Coll. Ox. 1st cl. Math. et Phy. 1840; Deac. 1840, Pr. 1841. R. of Minestead with Lyndhurst Chapelry annexed, Dio. Win. 1842. (Patron, H. Compton, Esq; Tithe, 626*l*; Glebe, 9 acres; R.'s Inc.

650*l* and Ho; Pop. Minestead 905, Lyndhurst 1022.) Rural Dean of East Fordingbridge; Surrogate. [1]

COMPTON, John, *Workhouse, Westminster, S.W.*—Chap. of the Workhouse, St. James's. [2]

COMPTON, Paulet Mildmay, *Mapperton Rectory, Beaminster, Dorset.*—Trin. Coll. Cam. B.A. 1846; Deac. 1847 and Pr. 1848 by Bp of Win. R. of Mapperton, Dio. Salis, 1848. (Patron, H. C. Compton, Esq; Glebe, 51 acres: R.'s Inc. 270*l* and Ho; Pop. 91.) R. of the Sinecure R. of Wytherstone, Dorset, Dio. Salis. 1849. (Patron, H. C. Compton, Esq; R.'s Inc. 100*l*.) Formerly C. of Milford, Dio. Win. 1847–48, Hooke, Dio. Salis. 1851–63. [3]

COMPTON, Thomas Hoyle, *Froome-Selwood, Somerset.*—Corpus Coll. Cam. Jun. Opt. B.A. 1848, M.A. 1851: Deac. 1850 by Bp of Man. Pr. 1851 by Bp of Ox. C. of Froome-Selwood 1862. Formerly C. of St. John's Longsight, Manchester, 1850; P. C. of Kidmore End, Oxon. 1851; C. of Calbourne with Newton, Isle of Wight, 1858. [4]

COMYN, Horatio Nelson William, *Brunstead Rectory, Stalham, Norfolk.*—Caius Coll. Cam. B.A. 1829; Deac. 1830, Pr. 1831. R. of Brunstead, Dio. Nor. 1841. (Patron, Earl of Abergavenny; Tithe 240*l*, Glebe, 22¾ acres; R.'s Inc. 286*l* and Ho; Pop. 99.) P. C. of Walcott, Dio. Nor. 1850. (Patron, Bp of Nor; Tithe—App. 347*l* and 3½ acres of Glebe; P. C.'s Inc. 45*l*; Pop. 141.) Surrogate. [5]

COMYNS, George Thomas, *Sidbury Vicarage, Sidmouth.*—Wad. Coll. Ox. B.A. 1830; Deac. 1831 and Pr. 1833 by Bp of Ex. V. of Sidbury, Dio. Ex. 1864. (Patrons, D. and C. of Ex; Tithe, 616*l*; Glebe, 6 acres; V.'s Inc. 625*l* and Ho; Pop. 1670.) Formerly C. of Axmouth; V. of Axmouth 1858–64. [6]

COMYNS, George Younge, 9, *Eastgate, Louth.*—St. John's Coll. Ox. B.A. 1865; Deac. 1867 by Bp of Lin. C. of Louth 1867. [7]

CONDER, Alfred, *Middleton, Bognor.*—Queens' Coll. Cam. Sen. Opt. B.A. 1861, M.A. 1864; Deac. 1863 and Pr. 1864 by Bp of Lon. R. of Middleton, Dio. Chich. 1866. (Patron, G. H. Roe, Esq; Tithe, 128*l*; R.'s Inc. 173*l*; Pop. 89.) Formerly C. of Ch. Ch. St. George's-in-the-East, Lond. 1863–65. [8]

CONEY, Charles Baring, *Fleet, near Weymouth, Dorset.*—Corpus Coll. Cam. B.A. 1841, M.A. 1844; Deac. 1843 and Pr. 1844 by Bp of Salis. R. of Fleet, Dio. Salis. 1863. (Patron, Rev. C. Goodden; R.'s Inc. 66*l*; Pop. 160*l*.) Chap. to the Bp of Dur. Formerly R. of St. Aldate's, Gloucester, 1858–63. [9]

CONEY, Edward Cecil, *Burtle, Bridgwater.*—Ch. Ch. Ox. B.A. 1860; Deac. 1861 and Pr. 1862 by Bp of B. and W. P. C. of Burtle, Dio. B. and W. 1864. (Patron, G. S. Poole, Esq; P. C.'s Inc. 300*l*; Pop. 248.) Formerly C. of St. Mary's, Bridgwater, and Bovey Tracey, Devon. [10]

CONEY, Thomas, *Woolwich.*—Univ. Coll. Ox. B.A. 1849, M.A. 1853; Deac. 1850 by Bp of G. and B. Pr. 1851 by Bp of Llan. Chap. to the Forces, Woolwich. Formerly C. of Wick and Abson, Glouc. 1850–56. [11]

CONEY, Thomas Boucher, *Pucklechurch, Bristol.*—Ball. Coll. Ox. B.A. 1821; Deac. 1823, Pr. 1824. V. of Pucklechurch with the Chapelries of Westerleigh, Wick and Abson annexed, Dio. G. and B. 1840. (Patrons, D. and C. of Wells; Tithe—App. 103*l*, V. 765*l* 16*s* 6*d*; Glebe, 50 acres; V.'s Inc. 845*l* and Ho; Pop. Pucklechurch 265, Westerleigh 674, Wick and Abson 833.) Rural Dean of Hawkesbury; Hon. Can. of Bristol 1851. [12]

CONGREVE, Ralph, *Grammar School, Burton, near Neston, Cheshire.*—Corpus Coll. Cam. B.A. 1839, M.A. 1849; Deac. 1840 and Pr. 1841 by Abp of Cant. Head Mast. of Gr. Sch. Burton Formerly P. C. of Burton 1841. [13]

CONINGTON, John, *Southwell, Notts.*—Jesus Coll. Cam. B.A. 1821; Deac. 1821, Pr. 1822. P. C. of Trinity, Southwell, Dio. Lin. 1846. (Patrons, Trustees; P. C.'s Inc. arising from Pew Rents, about 100*l* and Ho; Pop. 852.) [14]

CONNELL, Arthur, *Gorton, Manchester.*—Aidan's; Deac. 1856 and Pr. 1857 by Bp of Down and Connor. R. of St. Mark's, Gorton, Dio. Man. 1865. (Patron, R. of Gorton, Pop. 4305.) Formerly C. of Lurgan, co. Down. [15]

CONNELL, James, *Hammersmith, Middlesex, W.*—Ball. Coll. Ox. 2nd cl. Lit. Hum. 2nd cl. Math. et Phy. and B.A. 1836, M.A. 1838; Deac. 1836, Pr. 1837. V. of Hammersmith, Dio. Lon. 1860. (Patron, Bp of Lon; V.'s Inc. 546*l* and Ho; Pop. 8794.) Formerly P. C. of St. Barnabas', Lond. 1857. [16]

CONNELL, R. L., *Barton-upon-Irwell, Eccles, Lancashire.*—P. C. of Barton-upon-Irwell, Dio. Man. 1862. (Patrons, Bp of Man. and others; P. C.'s Inc. 150*l* and Ho; Pop. 14,216.) [17]

CONNOLY, James Charles, *Woolwich, Kent.*—Chap. of Royal Dockyard, Woolwich, 1854. (Chap.'s Inc. 182*l* 10*s*.) [18]

CONNOR, George Henry, *Newport, Isle of Wight.*—Dub. A.B. 1845, A.M. 1851; Deac. 1846 by Bp of Down and Connor, Pr. 1847 by Bp of Lin. P. C. of Newport, Dio. Win. 1857. (Patron, Queen's Coll. Ox; P. C.'s Inc. 150*l*; Pop. 3819.) Surrogate for the Isle of Wight. Formerly Min. of St. Thomas's, Newport. [19]

CONNOR, Richard George, *Pratt-street, Camden-town, London, N.W.*—Chap. to the Workhouse and Almshouses, St. Martin-in-the-Fields, Westminster. [20]

CONOR, John Richard, *St. Simon's, Liverpool.* Dub. A.B. 1833, A.M. 1837; Deac. 1834, Pr. 1835. P. C. of St. Simon's, Liverpool, Dio. Ches. 1839. (Patrons, the Crown and Bp of Ches. alt; Pop. 5716.) Surrogate. [21]

CONSIDINE, Robert Augustus Wellesley, *Alveley, Bridgnorth, Salop.*—St. John's Coll. Cam. Wrang. 3rd cl. Cl. Trip. and B.A. 1832, M.A. 1835; Deac. 1836, Pr. 1837. P. C. of Alveley, Dio. Herf. 1837. (Patroness, Mrs. Wakeman; Tithe, Imp. 578*l* 16*s* 8*d*; Glebe, 1¼ acres; P. C.'s Inc. 109*l*; Pop. 1018) Author, *The Christian's Gratitude for the Mercies of the Past Year* (a Sermon), 1848, 1*s*. [22]

CONSTABLE, John, *Royal Agricultural College, Cirencester.*—Trin. Coll. Cam. B.A. 1848, M.A. 1854; Deac. 1848 and Pr. 1849 by Bp of Rip. Prin. of the Royal Agricult. Coll. Cirencester, 1859. Formerly Mast. of the Gr. Sch. Clapham, Surrey; C. of Thorner, Yorks, Upleadon, Glouc. and Upham, Hants. Author, *Agricultural Education*, Longman, 1864, 3*s* 6*d*; *Practice with Science*, ib. 1866, 5*s*. [23]

CONSTABLE, J. P. Goulton, *Cottesbach Rectory, Lutterworth.*—R. of Cottesbach, Dio. Pet. 1844. (Patron, Rev. R. Marriott; R.'s Inc. 340*l* and Ho; Pop. 125.) [24]

CONSTABLE, William John Rawson, *Donington, Spalding, Lincolnshire.*—Clare Coll. Cam. Prizeman, 1842–44, Wrang. and B.A. 1845; Deac. and Pr. 1848 by Bp of Ches. Head Mast. of Donington Gr. Sch. 1853. [25]

CONSTERDINE, James Whitworth, *Alderley Edge, near Manchester.*—Trin. Coll. Cam. B.A. 1849, M.A. 1852; Deac. 1849 and Pr. 1850 by Bp of Man. P. C. of St. Philip's, Chorley, Dio. Ches. 1853. (Patrons, Five Trustees; P. C.'s Inc. 380*l* and Ho; Pop. 2000.) Formerly C. of Ch. Ch. Salford, 1849–52. [26]

CONWAY, Robert, *Morden-terrace, Rochester.*—Trin. Coll. Cam. B.A. 1853, M.A. 1857; Deac. 1853 and Pr. 1854 by Bp of Roch. Chap. of Fort Clarence Military Prison, and Military Hospital at Fort Pitt, Rochester. Formerly C. of St. Nicholas', Rochester. [27]

CONWAY, William, *St. Margaret's Rectory, Westminster, S.W.*—Trin. Coll. Cam. B.A. 1836, M.A. 1839; Deac. 1840 and Pr. 1841 by Bp of Roch. Canon of Westminster 1864; R. of St. Margaret's, Westminster, Dio. Lon. 1864. (Patron, the Crown; R.'s Inc. 500*l* and Ho; Pop. 8697.) Rural Dean. Formerly V. of St. Nicholas', Rochester, 1852–64. [28]

CONWAY, William Augustus, *Heywood, Lancashire.*—Deac. 1845, Pr. 1846. P. C. of Heap Heywood, Dio. Man. 1853. (Patron, Bp of Ches; P. C.'s Inc. 150*l*; Pop. 7633.) [29]

CONYBEARE, Charles Ranken, *Itchin-Stoke, Alresford, Hants.*—Ch. Ch. Ox. B.A. 1843, M.A. 1846; Deac. 1844 and Pr. 1851 by Bp of Ox. V. of Itchin-Stoke with Abbotston, Dio. Win. 1857. (Patron, Lord Ashburton; V.'s Inc. 260*l* and Ho; Pop. 295.) Formerly V. of Pyrton, Oxon, 1852–57; Tut. of Ch. Ch. Ox. and Select Preacher before the Univ. 1855–56. [1]

CONYNGHAM, John, *Weston Rectory, near Norwich.*—New Coll. Ox. B.C.L. 1830; Deac. 1830, Pr. 1831. R. of Weston-Longville, Dio. Nor. 1839. (Patron, New Coll. Ox; Tithe, 680*l*; Glebe, 46 acres; R.'s Inc. 750*l* and Ho; Pop. 471.) Formerly Fell. of New Coll. Ox. [2]

COOK, Bell, *Heigham, Norwich.*—Deac. 1820 and Pr. 1821 by Bp of Nor. R. of St. Paul's, Norwich, Dio. Nor. 1826. (Patrons, D. and C. of Nor; R.'s Inc. 140*l*; Pop. 2907.) [3]

COOK, Charles, *Trinity Parsonage, Swansea, Glamorganshire.*—St. Bees; Deac. 1844 and Pr. 1846 by Bp of Ches. P. C. of Trinity, Swansea, Dio. St. D. 1854. (Patron, Church Patronage Society; P. C.'s Inc. 220*l* and Ho; Pop. 4305.) Surrogate. Formerly C. of Bacup, Lancashire, 1845; Min. of Mariners' Ch. Hull, 1846. [4]

COOK, Christopher, *Mamhilad Vicarage, Pontypool.*—Lampeter; Deac. 1850 and Pr. 1851 by Bp of Llan. P. C. of Llanvihangel-Ponty-Moile, Dio. Llan. 1851. (Patron, C. H. Leigh, Esq; P. C.'s Inc. 96*l*; Pop. 205.) P. C. of Mamhilad, Dio. Llan. 1855. (Patrons, D. and C. of Llan; Glebe, 20 acres; P. C.'s Inc. 76*l* and Ho; Pop. 297.) Formerly C. of Llanvihangel-Ponty-Moile and Llantheny-Vach. [5]

COOK, Edward Wilson, *Stevington Vicarage, near Bedford.*—St. John's Coll. Cam. Wrang. and B.A. 1842, M.A. 1845, *ad eund.* Ox. 1855; Deac. 1844 and Pr. 1845 by Bp of Rip. V. of Stevington, Dio. Ely, 1862. (Patron, Duke of Bedford; Glebe, 97 acres; V.'s Inc. 230*l* and Ho; Pop. 606.) Author, *Death and its Issues* (Sermon on the death of Francis, 7th Duke of Bedford, K.G.), 2 eds. 1861, 6*d*; and other Sermons. [6]

COOK, Flavel Smith, *Liskeard, Cornwall.*—Dub. A.B. 1853; Deac. 1853 and Pr. 1854 by Bp of Ex. V. of Liskeard, Dio. Ex. 1863. (Patrons, Heirs of the Rev. J. H. Todd; Tithe, 500*l*; Glebe, ¾ acre; V.'s Inc. 500*l* and Ho; Pop. 6504.) Formerly C. of Millbrook 1853–55, and P. C. of same 1855–63. [7]

COOK, Frederic Charles, 17, *Orsett-terrace, Westbourne-terrace, Paddington, London, W.*—St. John's Coll. Cam. 1st cl. Cl. Trip. and B.A. 1828, M.A. 1840; Deac. 1839 and Pr. 1840 by Bp of Lon. Chap. and Preacher to the Hon. Soc. of Lincoln's Inn 1860; Canon of Exeter 1864; Chap. in Ordinary to the Queen. Author, *Acts of the Apostles with Commentary.* [8]

COOK, James, *Peopleton, Pershore,* and 47, *Portland-place, London, W.*—Magd. Coll. Cam. S.C.L. 1847, LL.B. 1850, M.L.L. 1860, Deac. 1850 and Pr. 1852 by Abp of Cant. R. of Peopleton, Dio. Wor. 1855. (Patron, the present R; Tithe, 250*l*; Glebe, 30 acres; R.'s Inc. 300*l*; Pop. 326.) [9]

COOK, Robert Keningale, *The Vicarage, Smallbridge, Rochdale.*—Corpus Coll. Cam. 2nd Jun. Opt. and B.A. 1837, M.A. 1841; Deac. 1837 and Pr. 1838 by Bp of Ches. V. of Smallbridge, Dio. Man. 1839. (Patron, V. of Rochdale; V.'s Inc. 420*l* and Ho; Pop. 5644.) Surrogate. [10]

COOKE, Charles, *Withycombe Rectory, Dunster, Somerset.*—St. Cath. Hall, Cam. B.A. 1842; Deac. and Pr. 1844 by Abp of York. R. of Withycombe, Dio. B. and W. 1844. (Patron, T. Hutton, Esq; Tithe—App 3*l* 3*s*, R. 241*l* 1*s*; Glebe, 7 acres; R.'s Inc. 255*l* and Ho; Pop. 349.) [11]

COOKE, Charles John Rashleigh, *Chesterton Rectory, Peterborough.*—Oriel Coll. Ox. B.A. 1852, M.A. 1856; 3rd cl. in Lit. Hum. et Math; Deac. 1854 and Pr. 1855 by Bp of Win. R. of Chesterton with Haddon, Dio. Ely, 1863. (Patron, Marquis of Huntly; R.'s Inc. 700*l* and Ho; Pop. Chesterton 129, Haddon 146.) Formerly C. of Headley, near Epsom, 1854–56, Orton-Longueville 1856–57; R. of Orton-Longueville, Dio. Ely, 1857–63. [12]

COOKE, Charles Russell, *Haveringland, Norwich.*—Clare Coll. Cam. B.A. 1859, M.A. 1862; Deac. 1859 and Pr. 1860 by Bp of Ely. P. C. of Haveringland, Dio. Nor. 1864. (Patron, Edward Fellowes, Esq. M.P; P. C.'s Inc. 103*l*; Pop. 130.) [13]

COOKE, Christopher Flood, *Diseworth Vicarage, Loughborough.*—Magd. Hall, Ox. B.A. 1842; Deac. 1842 and Pr. 1843 by Bp of Win. V. of Diseworth, Dio. Pet. 1852. (Patrons, Haberdashers' Co. and Christ's Hospital alt; Glebe, 108 acres; V.'s Inc. 220*l* and Ho; Pop. 567.) Chap. of Shardlow Union 1865. Formerly C. of Godalming, Surrey, 1842–45, Chelmondiston, Suffolk, 1845–46; P. C. of Berden, Essex, 1846–52. [14]

COOKE, Daniel, *Brompton, Chatham.*—Deac. and Pr. 1839 by Bp of Lich. P. C. of Brompton, Dio. Roch. 1847. (Patrons, Rev. W. and Miss Conway; P. C.'s Inc. 280*l*; Pop. 8119.) [15]

COOKE, E. H., *Flixton, Manchester.*—C. of Flixton. [16]

COOKE, George Frederic, *Orchard Portman, near Taunton.*—New Coll. Ox. 3rd cl. Lit. Hum. B.A. 1859, M.A. 1862; Deac. 1859 and Pr. 1860 by Bp of B. and W. C. of Orchard Portman 1866. Formerly C. of St. Mary's, Taunton, 1859, St. Mary's, Redcliff, Bristol, 1864. [17]

COOKE, George Harris, *Thorpe Hamlet, near Norwich.*—Wad. Coll. Ox. 2nd cl. Lit. Hum. and B.A. 1849, M.A. 1852; Deac. 1850 and Pr. 1851 by Bp of Wor. P. C. of St. Matthew's, Thorpe Hamlet, Dio. Nor. 1858. (Patron, R. of Thorpe; P. C.'s Inc. 99*l* and Ho.) Formerly 2nd Mast. of Leamington Coll. [18]

COOKE, George Robert Davies, *Skellow Hall, Doncaster.*—Ch. Ch. Ox. B.A. 1859; Deac. 1860 and Pr. 1861 by Abp of York. V. of Owston, Dio. York, 1862. (Patron, P. B. Davies Cooke, Esq; Tithe, 100*l*; Glebe, 42 acres; V.'s Inc. 166*l* and Ho; Pop. 454.) Formerly C. of Stillingfleet 1860–62; Chap. to Earl of Scarborough 1862. [19]

COOKE, George Theophilus, *Beckley, near Oxford.*—Magd. Coll. Ox. M.A. 1846, B.D. 1855; Deac. 1844, Pr. 1845. P. C. of Beckley, Dio. Ox. 1847. (Patroness, Mrs. Anne Cooke; P. C.'s Inc. 104*l*; Pop. 749.) [20]

COOKE, Henry Bowen, *Darfield Rectory, Barnsley.*—Trin. Hall, Cam. LL.B. 1821; Deac. 1821 and Pr. 1822 by Abp of York. R. of the 1st Mediety of Darfield, Dio. York, 1833. (Patron, the present R; Tithe—Imp. 1304*l* 0*s* 3½*d* and 27½ acres of Glebe, R. 1304*l* 0*s* 3½*d*; Glebe, 55½ acres; R.'s Inc. 1600*l* and Ho; Pop. 5078.) [21]

COOKE, Henry Pennant, *Nuneham Courtenay Rectory, Oxford.*—Emman. Coll. Cam. B.A. 1847, M.A. 1850; Deac. and Pr. 1848. R. of Nuneham Courtenay, Dio. Ox. 1855. (Patron, G. G. Harcourt, Esq; Tithe, 463*l*; Glebe, 52 acres; R.'s Inc. 500*l* and Ho; Pop. 314.) Formerly C. of Whitburn, Sunderland. [22]

COOKE, James Young, *Semer, near Ipswich.*—Clare Coll. Cam. M.A. R. of Semer, Dio. Ely, 1838. (Patron, the present R; Tithe, 370*l*; Glebe, 67 acres; R.'s Inc. 450*l* and Ho; Pop. 429.) [23]

COOKE, John, M.A., *East Wittering, Chichester.*—R. of East Wittering, Dio. Chich. 1861. (Patron, Bp of Lon; Tithe—App. 133*l* 12*s* 11*d*, R. 290*l* 9*s* 4*d*; R.'s Inc. 240*l* and Ho; Pop. 223.) [24]

COOKE, John Russel, *Preston, near Faversham, Kent.*—Ox. B.A. 1857. C. of Preston 1862. [25]

COOKE, J. T., *Ramsgate.*—C. of Trinity, Ramsgate. [26]

COOKE, Robert Bryan, *Bryn Alyn, Mold, Flints.*—Ch. Ch. Ox. 1st cl. Lit. Hum. and B.A. 1823; Deac. 1824, Pr. 1825. Formerly R. of Wheldrake, Yorks, 1834. [27]

COOKE, Robert Herbert, *Malvern Lodge, Lansdown, Cheltenham.*—Sid. Coll. Cam. 31st Wrang. and B.A. 1845, M.A. 1848, B.D. 1855; Deac 1847, Pr. 1848. Fell. of Sid. Coll. Cam. 1849. Formerly Dean of Sid. Coll. [28]

COOKE, Samuel, *Langton St. Andrew Parsonage, Horncastle, Lincolnshire.*—St. Mary Hall, Ox. B.A. 1848, M.A. 1850; Deac. 1849 and Pr. 1850 by Bp of Lin. P. C. of Langton St. Andrew, Dio. Lin. 1850. (Patron, Bp of Lin; Glebe, 10 acres; P. C.'s Inc. 70*l* and Ho; Pop. 610.) Chap. of the D. of Kirkstead, Lincolnshire, Dio. Lin. 1850. (Patron, Rev. J. B. Holden; Chap.'s Inc. 40*l*; Pop. 153.) [1]

COOKE, Samuel Hay, *Great Budworth, Northwich, Cheshire.*—Ch. Ch. Ox. B.A. 1840, M.A. 1843; Deac. 1842 and Pr. 1844 by Bp of Ox. V. of Great Budworth, Dio. Ches. 1858. (Patron, Ch. Ch. Ox; V.'s Inc. 626*l* and Ho; Pop. 3765.) Formerly P. C. of Benson, Oxon, 1850. [2]

COOKE, Thomas, 12, *St. George's-place, Brighton.*—Oriel Coll. Ox. 1st cl. Lit. Hum. and B.A. 1813, M.A. 1817; Deac. and Pr. 1817 by Bp of G. V. of Brigstock with Stanion C. Northants, Dio. Pet. 1824. (Patron, Duke of Cleveland; V.'s Inc. 244*l*; Pop. Brigstock 1159, Stanion 351.) P. C. of St. Peter's, Brighton, Dio. Chich. 1828. (Patron, V. of Brighton; P. C.'s Inc. 200*l*.) Dom. Chap. to the Earl of Malmesbury; Surrogate. Author, *A Sermon on Friendly Societies*; *Letter on the Wild or Whistling Swan.* [3]

COOKE, William, *University Club, Suffolk-street, Pall-Mall, London, S.W.*—Trin. Hall, Cam. Jun. Opt. 3rd cl. Cl. Trip. and B.A. 1843, M.A. 1847; Deac. 1844 and Pr. 1845 by Bp of Lon. Hon. Can. of Chester 1854. Formerly P. C. of St. John's, Charlotte-street, Fitzroy-square, Lond. 1848–50, P. C. of St. Stephen's, Hammersmith, 1850–56; V. of Gazeley, Suffolk, 1856–66; Exam. Chap. to Bp of Ches. 1849–57; Select Preacher of Univ. of Cam. 1850. Author, *The Power of the Priesthood in Absolution*, Parkers; and various sermons. [4]

COOKE, William Harris, *Norwich.*—Corpus Coll. Cam. B.A. 1852; Deac. 1852, Pr. 1853. P. C. of St. Saviour's, City and Dio. Nor. 1854. (Patrons, D. and C. of Nor; P. C.'s Inc. 90*l*; Pop. 1532.) Formerly C. of Caston, Norfolk. [5]

COOKES, Henry Winford, *Astley Rectory, Stourport, Worcestershire.*—Wor. Coll. Ox. B.A. 1840; Deac. and Pr. 1841. R. of Astley, Dio. Wor. 1842. (Patrons, Trustees of the Rev. D. J. J. Cookes; Tithe, 750*l*; Glebe, 18 acres; R.'s Inc. 775*l* and Ho; Pop. 864.) [6]

COOKES, Thomas Horace, *Worcester College, Oxford.*—Wor. Coll. Ox. B.A. 1844, M.A. 1847. Fell. of Wor. Coll. Ox. [7]

COOKESLEY, Henry Parker, *Wimborne Minster, Dorset.*—Trin. Coll. Cam. 1830, Bell's Scho. 1830, B.A. 1831; Deac. 1837, Pr. 1839. One of the Priests of the Royal Peculiar Collegiate Church of Wimborne Minster, Dio. Salis. 1849. (Patrons, the Govs. of Queen Elizabeth's Gr. Sch; Pr.'s Inc. 250*l*.) [8]

COOKESLEY, Thomas Murray, *Draughton Rectory, Northampton.*—R. of Draughton, Dio. Pet. 1866. (Patron, H. H. Hungerford, Esq; R.'s Inc. 400*l* and Ho; Pop. 190.) Formerly C. of Macclesfield. [9]

COOKESLEY, William Gifford, *Hammersmith, Middlesex, W.*—King's Coll. Cam. B.A. 1825, M.A. 1827; Deac. 1827 by Bp of Ely, Pr. 1835 by Bp of Roch. P. C. of St. Peter's, Hammersmith, Dio. Lon. 1860. (Patron, Bp of Lon; P. C.'s Inc. 500*l*; Pop. 5415.) Chap. to Lord Ravensworth. Formerly V. of Hayton, Yorks, 1857–60; Asst. Mast. of Eton Coll. [10]

COOKSON, Charles, *Maxey Vicarage, near Market Deeping.*—St. John's Coll. Cam. B.A. 1833; Deac. 1833, Pr. 1834. V. of Maxey, Dio. Pet. 1850. (Patrons, D. and C. of Pet; Glebe, 156 acres; V.'s Inc. 394*l* and Ho; Pop. 643.) Surrogate. Formerly Min. Can. of Pet. Cathl. 1833; Chap. to Peterborough Gaol for 16 years. [11]

COOKSON, Christopher, *Dallington, Northampton.*—St. John's Coll. Ox. B.A. 1846; Deac. 1847, Pr. 1850. V. of Dallington, Dio. Pet. 1863. (Patron, J. Beddell, Esq; Tithe—Imp. 2*l* 5*s*, V. 21*l* 1*s* 6*d*; V.'s Inc. 180*l* and Ho; Pop. 636.) [12]

COOKSON, Edward, *Kirkby Thore Rectory, Penrith.*—Univ. Coll. Ox. B.A. 1831, M.A. 1835; Deac. 1833 by Bp of Dur. Pr. 1834 by Abp of York. R. of Kirkby Thore, Dio. Carl. 1852. (Patron, Sir R. Tufton, Bart; Tithe, 255*l*; Glebe, 650 acres; R's Inc. 755*l* and Ho; Pop. 455.) [13]

COOKSON, Frederick, *Stowupland, Stowmarket, Suffolk.*—Corpus Coll. Cam B.A. 1831; Deac. 1832 by Abp of York, Pr. 1834 by Bp of Lin. P. C. of Trin. Ch. Stowupland, Dio. Nor. 1862. (Patron, V. of Stowmarket; Tithe, 30*l*; P. C.'s Inc. 93*l*; Pop. 750.) Formerly C. of Kirk-Ella, Yorks, 1832–33, Easton Magna, Leic. 1833–46, Wilby and Hargham, Norfolk, 1846–52, Combs, Suffolk, 1855–62. [14]

COOKSON, Henry Wilkinson, *St. Peter's College Lodge, Cambridge.*—St. Peter's Coll. Cam. 7th Wrang. and B.A. 1832, M.A. 1835, D.D. 1848; Deac. 1837, Pr. 1847. Mast. of St. Peter's Coll. Cam. 1847. Formerly R. of Glaston, Rutland, 1847. [15]

COOKSON, James, *Marton Parsonage, Blackpool, Lancashire.*—Dub. A.B. 1841, A.M. 1864; Deac. 1841 and Pr. 1842 by Bp of Ches. P. C. of Marton, Dio. Man. 1843. (Patron, V. of Poulton-le-Fylde; P. C.'s Inc. 160*l* and Ho; Pop. 1691.) Formerly C. of Marton. [16]

COOKSON, O., *Shoreham, Sussex.*—Asst. Mast. of St. Saviour's, Sch. Shoreham; C. of Hangleton. [17]

COOKWORTHY, Urquhart, *Sandford Orcas, near Sherborne, Dorset.*—Ch. Coll. Cam. B.A. 1847; Deac. 1847 by Bp of Ches. Pr. 1848 by Bp of Man. C. in sole charge of Sandford Orcas. Formerly C. of Bures St. Mary, Suffolk, and Fowey, Cornwall. [18]

COOLEY, William Lake Johnson, *Rennington Parsonage, Alnwick, Northumberland.*—Bp Hat. Hall, Dur. B.A. 1857, M.A. 1860; Deac. 1856 and Pr. 1857 by Abp of Cant. P. C. of Rennington with Rock P. C. 1860. (Patron, V. of Embleton; Glebe, 4 acres; P. C.'s Inc. 200*l* and Ho; Pop. Rennington 263, Rock 250.) Formerly C. of St. Mary, Romney Marsh, Kent, 1856–57, Dymchurch, Kent, 1857–58, Newburn, Newcastle-on-Tyne, 1858–60. [19]

COOMBE, Alexander Bain, *The Hermitage, Petworth, Sussex.*—Univ. Coll. Ox. B.A. 1860, M.A. 1862; Deac. 1860 and Pr. 1861 by Bp of Win. Chap. of the West Sussex County Prison. Formerly C. of Ch. Ch. Bermondsey, 1860–62, Trinity, Haverstock Hill, 1863, St. Paul's, Maidstone, 1863–66. [20]

COOMBE, Charles George, *Crookes Parsonage, Sheffield.*—St. Peter's Coll. Cam. B A. 1846, M.A. 1849; Deac. 1847 and Pr. 1848 by Bp of Ely. P. C. of St. Thomas's, Crookes, Dio. York, 1855. (Patrons, Five Trustees; P. C.'s Inc. 300*l* and Ho; Pop. 3452.) Surrogate. Formerly Math. Mast. of the Proprietary School, Islington; Asst. Min. of the Chapel of Ease, Holloway; Fell. of St. Peter's Coll. Cam. [21]

COOMBE, John Adams, *Alburgh, Harleston, Norfolk.*—St. John's Coll. Cam. 4th Wrang, and B.A. 1840, M.A. 1843; Deac. 1841, Pr. 1842. R. of Alburgh, Dio. Nor. 1846. (Patron, St. John's Coll. Cam; Tithe—App. 10*l* 15*s*, R. 461*l* 5*s* 11*d*; R.'s Inc. 478*l* and Ho; Pop. 587.) Formerly Fell. of St. John's Coll. Cam. Author, *Solutions of the Cambridge Problems.* [22]

COOMBE, John Henry, *Cleasby Parsonage, near Darlington.*—Deac. 1846 and Pr. 1847 by Bp of Ches. C. in sole charge of Cleasby 1854. Formerly C. of Preston Patrick, Westmoreland, 1846; Morning Lect. St. Michael-le-Belfry, York, 1849; C. of All Saints', York, 1850; P. C. of Egton and Newland, Lancashire, 1848. [23]

COOMBE, Thomas, 2, *Compton-terrace, Clifton-road, Brighton.*—Trin. Coll. Cam. 16th Wrang. and B.A. 1843, M.A. 1846; Deac. 1844 by Bp of Wor. Pr. 1846 by Bp of Chich. P. C. of All Saints', Brighton, Dio. Chich. 1852. (Patron, V. of Brighton; P. C.'s Inc. from pew rents about 200*l*; Pop. 5000.) Surrogate. Formerly C. of Brighton 1844–52. [24]

COOMBES, Edwin, *Moorlands, Parkstone, Poole.*—Dub. A.B. 1862, A.M. 1865; King's Coll. Lond. 1864; Deac. 1864 and Pr. 1865 by Bp of Salis. C. of Great Canford, Dorset, 1864. [25]

COOMBES, Jeremiah, *Portwood, Stockport.*—Deac. 1859 and Pr. 1860 by Bp of Ches. P. C. of Portwood, Dio. Ches. 1862. (Patrons, Crown and Bp alt; P. C.'s Inc. 300*l*; Pop. 5346.) Formerly C. of Stockport Greatmoor 1860–62; Asst. Mast. of Stockport Gr. Sch. 1854–62. [1]

COOMBES, Josiah, *Wiggenhall St. Peter's Vicarage, near Lynn, Norfolk.*—St. Bees; Deac. 1841 and Pr. 1843 by Bp of Carl. V. of Wiggenhall St. Peter, Dio. Nor. 1853. (Patron, Ld Chan; Tithe—Imp. 115*l* 8*s* 9*d*, V. 120*l*; Glebe, 2 acres; V.'s Inc. 125*l*; Pop. 153.) [2]

COOMBS, Charles, 12, *South Devon-place, Plymouth.*—Dub. A.B. 1855, A.M. 1858; Deac. 1855 and Pr. 1856 by Bp of Ex. P. C. of Sutton-on-Plym, Dio. Ex. 1866. (Patrons, Bp and Crown alt; P. C.'s Inc. 300*l*; Pop. 6237.) Formerly C. of St. Peter's, Plymouth, 1855–66. [3]

COOMBS, William, *The Priory, Titley, Herefordshire.*—St. John's Coll. Cam. Sen. Opt. Scho. and Prizeman, B.A. 1837, M.A. 1840; Deac. 1838 and Pr. 1839 by Bp of Ches. C. in sole charge of Titley 1866. Formerly C. of Prescot 1838–41; P. C. of St. Catherine's, Wigan, 1841–58; Chap. of Featherstone Castle, Northumberland, 1858–60; C. in sole charge of Stanstead Abbotts, Herts, 1860–66. [4]

COOPE, Joseph Richard, *Bucknell Vicarage, Salop.*—Ch. Ch. Ox. B.A. 1833, M.A. 1835; Deac. 1834 and Pr. 1835 by Bp of Lon. V. of Bucknell, Salop, with Buckton, Herf. Dio. Herf. 1836. (Patron, Grocers' Company, Lond; Tithe—App. 95*l*, V. 312*l* 15*s* 2*d*; Glebe, 240 acres; V.'s Inc. 400*l* and Ho; Pop. 790.) [5]

COOPE, William John, *Falmouth.*—St. Mary Hall, Ox. B.A. 1831, M.A. 1834. R. of Falmouth, Dio. Ex. 1838. (Patron, the present R; Tithe—Imp. 45*l*, R. 140*l*; R.'s Inc. 694*l*; Pop. 9392.) [6]

COOPER, Alfred, *Brighton.*—St. John's Coll. Ox. B.A. 1843, M.A. 1846; Deac. 1845 and Pr. 1846 by Bp of Lon. P. C. of St. Ann's, Brighton, Dio. Chich. 1863. (Patron, V. of Brighton.) Formerly C. of Hampstead 1845–47, Newchurch 1848–61, Brighton 1861–63. Author, *Political Features of the Papal Usurpation*, 1850; *Victory by Prayer*, 1854; *Prayer and Practice*, 1855; *Thanksgiving for Success in Battle, a Fearful Proof of Human Degradation, yet strictly according to Scripture* (a Sermon), 1855; *Lessons from the Harvest Field*, 1866. [7]

COOPER, Alfred, *Sigglesthorne, Hull.*—Dur. B.A. 1861; Deac. 1863 and Pr. 1864 by Abp of York. Asst. C. of Sigglesthorne 1863. [8]

COOPER, Arthur Henry, *South Ockendon, Romford, Essex.*—Trin. Coll. Cam. B.A. 1859, M.A. 1864; Deac. 1860 and Pr. 1861 by Bp of Lin. C. of South Ockendon 1866. Formerly C. of North Carlton and Saxilby 1860, South Carlton and Riseholme 1861–63, Ch. Ch. Hornsey, Lond. 1863–65, Wanstead, Essex, 1865; St. Michael's Islington, Lond. 1865–66. [9]

COOPER, Augustus, *Sylcham Hall, Harleston, Suffolk.*—Pemb. Coll. Cam. B.A. 1810; Deac. 1812 and Pr. 1813 by Bp of Nor. R. of Billingford with Little Thorpe R. Norfolk, Dio. Nor. 1823. (Patron, G. Wilson, Esq; Billingford, Tithe, 287*l* 10*s*; Glebe, 30 acres; Little Thorpe, Tithe, 26*l*; R.'s Inc. 364*l*; Pop. Billingford 199, Little Thorpe 21.) P. C. of Sylcham, Dio. Nor. 1833. (Patron, L. Press, Esq; Tithe, Imp. 403*l* 10*s* 11½*d*; Glebe, 10 acres; P. C.'s Inc. 63*l* and Ho; Pop. 357.) [10]

COOPER, Charles Beauchamp, *Morley Rectory, near Wymondham, Norfolk.*—Univ. Coll. Ox. B.A. 1824, M.A. 1827; Deac. 1826, Pr. 1827. R. of Morley St. Botolph with the Chapelry of Morley St. Peter annexed, Dio. Nor. 1832. (Patron, the present R; Tithe, 580*l*; Glebe, 43 acres; R.'s Inc. 650*l* and Ho; Pop. St. Botolph 278, St. Peter 147.) Rural Dean of Hingham, 1844–58. [11]

COOPER, David, *Redfield House, St. George's, near Bristol.*—Dub. A.B. 1837, A.M. 1843; Deac. and Pr. 1837. P. C. of Trinity, Bristol, Dio. G. and B. 1850. (Patrons, Trustees; P. C.'s Inc. 345*l* and Ho; Pop. 12,735.) [12]

COOPER, Edward, 32, *Richmond-terrace, Clifton.*—Queen's Coll. Ox. 4th cl. Math. et Phy. and B.A. 1846, M.A. 1853; Deac. 1853 and Pr. 1854 by Bp of G. and B. Formerly C. of Stoke Gifford 1853, Melksham 1855, Tilton 1857. [13]

COOPER, Edward, *Zeal Monachorum, Exeter.*—Trin. Hall, Cam. B.C.L. 1835; Deac. 1834 and Pr. 1835 by Bp of Llan. R. of Zeal Monachorum, Dio. Ex. 1856. (Patron, the present R; R.'s Inc. 388*l*; Pop. 549.) Formerly C. of Zeal Monachorum. [14]

COOPER, Edward Henry.—Dur. Theol. Licen. 1857; Deac. 1858 and Pr. 1859 by Bp of Nor. C. of St. Martin's-in-the-Fields, Lond. Formerly C. of Coddenham, Suffolk. [15]

COOPER, Francis, *St. Paul's, Southport.*—St. John's Coll. Cam. B.A. 1864; Deac. 1864 and Pr. 1865 by Bp of Ches. C. of St. Paul's, Southport, 1864. [16]

COOPER, George Miles, *Wilmington Vicarage, Hurst-green, Sussex.*—St. John's Coll. Cam. 2nd Smith's Prizeman, 2nd Wrang. and B.A. 1819, M.A. 1822; Deac. 1820, Pr. 1821. V. of Wilmington, Dio. Chich. 1835. (Patron, Duke of Devonshire; Tithe—Imp. 65*l*, V. 51*l* 16*s*; Glebe, 4 acres; V.'s Inc. 116*l* and Ho; Pop. 250.) R. of West Dean, Sussex, Dio. Chich. 1839. (Patron, Duke of Devonshire; Tithe—Eccles. Commis. 218*l*, R. 165*l*; Glebe, 6 acres; R.'s Inc. 171*l*; Pop. 153.) Preb. of Hova Villa in Chich. Cathl. 1849; Dom. Chap. to Duke of Devonshire. Formerly Fell. and Asst. Tut. of St. John's Coll. Cam. [17]

COOPER, Henry, *Nunnington, Oswaldkirk, Yorks.*—R. of Nunnington, Dio. York, 1857. (Patron, Ld Chan; R.'s Inc. 284*l* and Ho; Pop. 423.) [18]

COOPER, Henry, *Stoke Prior Parsonage, Leominster, Herefordshire.*—St. John's Coll. Cam. Prizeman, B.A. 1845, King's Coll. Lond. Prizeman; Deac. 1846 by Bp of B. and W. Pr. 1847 by Bp of Rip. P. C. of Stoke Prior with Docklow P. C. Dio. Herf. 1853. (Patron, V. of Leominster; Stoke Prior, Tithe—App. 142*l* 8*s* 6¾*d*; Glebe, 23 acres; Docklow, Tithe—App. 35*l* 16*s* 1½*d*, P. C. 1*l* 12*s* 6*d*; P. C.'s Inc. 160*l* and Ho; Pop. Stoke Prior 448, Docklow 185.) P. C. of Marston-Stannett, Dio. Herf. 1860. (Patron, R. of Pencombe; P. C.'s Inc. 100*l*.) Formerly C. of Cudworth, Somerset, 1846, Huddersfield 1847. Author, *Greek Plays, translated with Critical Notes*; various Sermons and Lectures. [19]

COOPER, Henry Gisborne, *Barton-under-Needwood, Burton-on-Trent, Staffs.*—St. John's Coll. Ox. B.A. 1824, M.A. 1839. P. C. of Barton-under-Needwood, Dio. Lich. 1838. (Patron, D. of Lich; Glebe, 19 acres; P. C.'s Inc. 145*l* and Ho; Pop. 1589.) [20]

COOPER, Henry Law, *Shipley, Horsham.*—St. John's Coll. Cam. B.A. 1849, M.A. 1852; Deac. 1850 and Pr. 1851 by Bp of Chich. P. C. of Shipley, Dio. Chich. 1859. (Patroness, Hon. Mrs. V. Harcourt; Glebe, 5 acres; P. C.'s Inc. 230*l* and Ho; Pop. 1091.) Formerly P. C. of The Dicker Church, Dio. Chich. 1852–59. [21]

COOPER, James Hughes, *The Rectory, Tarporley, Cheshire.*—Trin. Coll. Cam. Jun. Opt. B.A. 1855, M.A. 1858; Deac. 1855 and Pr. 1856 by Bp of Chich. R. of Tarporley, Dio. Ches. 1865. (Patrons, Lord and Lady Binning and Hon. Miss Arden; Tithe, 700*l*; Glebe, 12 acres; R.'s Inc. 720*l* and Ho; Pop. 2577.) Formerly C. of Cuckfield 1855, St. Mary Magdalen's, Brighton, 1860; P. C. of Ottershaw, Chertsey. [22]

COOPER, John, *Wadham College, Oxford.*—Wad. Coll. Ox. B.A. 1837, M.A. 1842; Deac. 1843. Fell. and Sub-Warden of Wad. Coll. Ox. [23]

COOPER, The Ven. John, *Kendal Vicarage, Westmoreland.*—Trin. Coll. Cam. Wrang. 1st cl. Cl. Trip. and B.A. 1835, M.A. 1838; Deac. 1837, Pr. 1838. V. of Kendal, Dio. Carl. 1858. (Patron, Trin. Coll. Cam; V.'s Inc. 580*l* and Ho; Pop. 7210.) Archd. of Westmoreland 1865; Hon. Can. of Carl; Rural Dean; Surrogate. Formerly V. of St. Andrew's the Great, Cambridge, 1843–58; Fell. of Trin. Coll. Cam. 1837, Tut. 1845. [24]

COOPER, John Edward, *Forncett St. Mary, Long Stratton, Norfolk.*—St. John's Coll. Cam. 9th Wrang.

and B.A. 1846, M.A. 1849; Deac. 1849 and Pr. 1853 by Bp of Ely. R. of Forncett St. Mary, Dio. Nor. 1853. (Patron, Earl of Effingham; Tithe, 515*l*; Glebe, 8 acres; R.'s Inc. 600*l* and Ho; Pop. 299.) Formerly Fell. of St. John's Coll. Cam. 1846–53; Asst. Mast. of the Repton Sch. 1846–48. Author, *The Nature of Reprobation, and the Preacher's Liability to it*, a Visitation Sermon with Notes and Appendix, 1859, 1*s*; *Train up a Child in the Way he should Go, or the Principles and Practice of Church Education*, 1863, 3*d*. [1]

COOPER, Mark, *The Deanery, Southampton.*—St. John's Coll. Cam. Prizeman, B.A. 1828, M.A. 1831; Deac. 1828 and Pr. 1829 by Abp of York. R. of St. Mary's, Southampton, Dio. Win. 1860. (Patron, Bp of Win; R's Inc. 1000*l* and Ho; Pop. 10,561.) Surrogate. Formerly V. of Bramshaw, Hants, 1840–60. Author, *Three Tracts on Confirmation*; various Tracts and Sermons. [2]

COOPER, Nathaniel, *Oxon Parsonage, Shrewsbury.*—Magd. Coll. Cam. B.A. 1847, M.A. 1851; Deac. 1849 and Pr. 1850 by Bp of Rip. P. C. of Oxon and Shelton, Dio. Lich. 1864. (Patron, V. of St. Chad's, Shrewsbury; P. C.'s Inc. 114*l* and Ho; Pop. 450.) Formerly C. of Bradford 1849–51, Ruyton XI. Towns, Salop, 1851–60, Montford, Salop, 1860–64. [3]

COOPER, Philip Arden, *Orton-on-the-Hill (Leicestershire), Atherstone.*—Oriel Coll. Ox. B.A. 1824, M.A. 1826; Deac. 1828, Pr. 1829. V. of Orton-on-the-Hill, Dio. Pet. 1834. (Patron, Bp of Pet; Land in lieu of Tithe, 156 acres; V.'s Inc. 230*l* and Ho; Pop. 334.) [4]

COOPER, Richard, *Congresbury, Somerset.*—P. C. of St. Ann's, Congresbury, Dio. B. and W. 1864. (Patron, Bp of B. and W.) Formerly Head Mast. of Weston-super-Mare Coll. [5]

COOPER, Robert Jermyn, *West Chiltington Rectory, Petworth, Sussex.*—Ch. Ch. Ox. B.A. 1816, M.A. 1820. R. of West Chiltington, Dio. Chich. 1835. (Patron, Earl of Abergavenny; Tithe—App. 18*l* 10*s*, Imp. 6*l*, R. 770*l*; Glebe, 12 acres; R.'s Inc. 788*l* and Ho; Pop. 668). Author, *Letter to Lord John Russell on the Repeal of the Test and Corporation Acts*, 1828; *Address to the Members of the Bible Society*, 1829; *Letter to Earl Ducie on the Reform Bill*, 1831; *Letter on Catholic Emancipation*, 1839; *On the Sabbath Question*, 1857; *On Reform and the Irish Church*, 1866; *On Capital Punishment*, 1867; *On the Successive and Distinctive Divine Covenants.* [6]

COOPER, Robert Jermyn, jun., *Fylingdales, Whitby.*—Ch. Ch. Ox. B.A. 1853; Deac. 1854 and Pr. 1856 by Abp of York. P. C. of Fylingdales, Dio. York, 1859. (Patron, Abp of York; P. C.'s Inc. 300*l*; Pop. 1721.) Surrogate. Formerly C. of Scalby and Ashby-de-la-Zouch. [7]

COOPER, Rowland Helme, *Eastleach, Lechlade, Glouc.*—St. Edm. Hall, Ox. B.A. 1818, M.A. 1820; Deac. 1819, Pr. 1820. P. C. of Eastleach-Turnville, Dio. G. and B. 1851. (Patrons, D. and C. of Glouc; P. C.'s Inc. 64*l*; Pop. 506.) R. of Eastleach-Martin, Dio. G. and B. 1858. (Patron, Ld Chan; P. C.'s Inc. 150*l*; Pop. 216.) [8]

COOPER, Samuel Lovick Astley, *Gawcott, near Buckingham.*—Brasen. Coll. Ox. B.A. 1849, M.A. 1852; Deac. 1850 and Pr. 1851 by Bp of Win. P. C. of Gawcott, Dio. Ox. 1864. (Patrons, Trustees; Glebe, 11 acres; P. C.'s Inc. 140*l* and Ho; Pop. 602.) Formerly C. of Gilling, Yorks, 1856–62, Padbury and Hillesden, Bucks, 1862–64. [9]

COOPER, Thomas, *The Parsonage, Clayton-le-Moors, Accrington.*—Ch. Coll. Cam. Scho. Theol. Prizeman and Gold Medallist of Ch. Coll. Sen. Opt. in Math. Hon. 1860, B.A. 1860, M.A. 1863; Deac. 1860 and Pr. 1861 by Bp of Man. C. in sole charge of Clayton-le-Moors 1863. Formerly Sen. C. of St. Peter's, Blackburn, 1860–63. [10]

COOPER, Thomas Jarratt, *Marlingford Rectory, Norwich.*—St. John's Coll. Cam. 13th Jun. Opt. and B.A. 1855, M.A. 1858; Deac. 1855 and Pr. 1856 by Bp of Ches. R. of Marlingford, Dio. Nor. 1866. (Patron, Rev. Thomas Greene; Tithe, 162*l* 2*s*; Glebe, 35 acres; R.'s Inc. 211*l* and Ho; Pop. 224.) Formerly C. of Runcorn, Cheshire, 1855–58, Thornham, Norfolk, 1858–66. [11]

COOPER, Thomas John, *Staveley, Newton-in-Cartmel.*—Univ. Coll. Ox. B.A. 1860, M.A. 1863; Deac. 1860 and Pr. 1861 by Bp of Lich. P. C. of Staveley-in-Cartmel, Lanc. Dio. Carl. 1864. (Patron, Duke of Devonshire; Glebe, 12 acres; P. C.'s Inc. 105*l*; Pop. 409.) Formerly C. of Fenton, Staffs, 1860, St. Mary's, Applethwaite, 1862. [12]

COOPER, Thomas Lovick, *Empingham Vicarage (Rutland), near Stamford.*—Magd. Coll. Cam. B.A. 1824, M.A. 1826; Deac. 1825 and Pr. 1826 by Bp of Nor. V. of Empingham, Dio. Pet. 1831. (Patron, Bp of Pet; Tithe and Endow. 255*l*; Glebe, 53 acres; V.'s Inc. 405*l* and Ho; Pop. 921.) R. of Mablethorpe with Stane, Linc. Dio. Lin. 1831. (Patron, the present R; Mablethorpe, Tithe, 419*l*; Stane, Tithe, 78*l*; Glebe, 97 acres; R.'s Inc. 700*l*; Pop. 336.) Formerly R. and Patron of Ingoldesthorpe, Norfolk, and of Hawkeshead, Lancashire. [13]

COOPER, William, *Clifton.*—Queen's Coll. Ox. B.A. 1855, M.A. 1858; Deac. 1859 and Pr. 1860 by Bp of G. and B. Formerly C. of Stoke Gifford, near Bristol, 1859, St. Mary's, Scarborough, 1863. [14]

COOPER, William, *Melcombe Regis, Dorset.*—C. of Melcombe Regis. [15]

COOPER, William, *Rippingale Rectory, Bourne, Lincolnshire.*—Trin. Coll. Cam. B.A. 1838; Deac. 1840 and Pr. 1842 by Bp of Win. R. of Rippingale, Dio. Lin. 1853. (Patron, Lord Aveland; Glebe, 557 acres; R.'s Inc. 873*l* and Ho; Pop. 569.) [16]

COOPER, W. Waldo, *West Rasen, Market Rasen, Lincolnshire.*—R. of West Rasen, Dio. Lin. 1856. (Patron, the present R; R.'s Inc. 543*l*; Pop. 245.) [17]

COOPER, William Rickford Astley, *Froyle Vicarage, Alton, Hants.*—Univ. Coll. Ox. B.A. 1846, M.A. 1847; Deac. 1850 and Pr. 1851 by Bp of Ox. V. of Froyle, Dio. Win. 1864. (Patron, Sir C. Miller, Bart; V.'s Inc. 290*l* and Ho; Pop. 766.) [18]

COOPLAND, George, 11, *Tanner-row, York.*—Deac. 1821 and Pr. 1822 by Bp of York. R. of St. Margaret's with St. Peter-le-Willows R. York, Dio. York, 1838. (Patron, Ld Chan; Glebe, 13 acres; R.'s Inc. 130*l*; Pop. St. Margaret 1704, St. Peter-le-Willows 526.) Chap. to the York House of Correction 1824. Author, *The Faithful Fulfilment of the Christian Ministry*, 1843, 1*s*. [19]

COOPLAND, Thomas Paul, *Scawby, Brigg, Lincolnshire.*—St. Cath. Coll. Cam. B.A. 1857; Deac. 1858 by Bp of Rip. C. of Scawby. Formerly C. of Thurstonland 1858. [20]

COOTE, Algernon, *Nonington Parsonage, Wingham, Kent.*—Brasen Coll. Ox. 2nd cl. Lit. Hum. and B.A. 1840, M.A. 1840; Deac. 1841 and Pr. 1842 by Bp of Ches. P. C. of Nonington, Dio. Cant. 1856. (Patron, Abp of Cant; P. C.'s Inc. 176*l* and Ho; Pop. 895.) Formerly R. of Marsh Gibbon, Bucks, 1844–56. [21]

COPE, Charles Henry, *Auckland, Durham.*—C. of St. Andrew's, Auckland. [22]

COPE, Edward Meredith, *Trinity College, Cambridge.*—Trin. Coll. Cam. B.A. 1841, M.A. 1844; Deac. 1843, Pr. 1844. Fell. of Trin. Coll. Cam. [23]

COPE, Francis Haden, *Wilmslow, Manchester.*—St. John's Coll. Cam. B.A. 1851, M.A. 1854; Deac. 1851, Pr. 1852. C. of Wilmslow; Surrogate. Formerly C. of Windermere. [24]

COPE, Russell, *St. Mark's Parsonage, Nottingham.*—St. Bees 1843; Deac. 1843, Pr. 1844. P. C. of St. Mark's, Nottingham, Dio. Lin. 1856. (Patrons, Trustees; P. C.'s Inc. 160*l*; Pop. 12,119.) Formerly C. of St. Peter's, Chester. [25]

COPE, Sir William Henry, Bart., *Bramshill, Hartfordbridge, Hants.*—Magd. Hall, Ox. M.A. 1840; Deac. 1840. Formerly Min. Can. of St. Peter's, Westminster Abbey, 1842–53; Chap. to the Westminster Hospital 1843–51. Author, in conjunction with the Rev. H. Stretton, of *Visitatio Infirmorum*, 1848, 3rd ed. 1854. Editor of *Sir Anthony Cope's Meditations on Twenty Select Psalms*, 1848. [26]

COPE, William Rogers, *Hartshill, Atherstone, Warwickshire.*—Theol. Assoc. King's Coll. Lond; Deac. 1850, Pr. 1851. P. C. of Hartshill, Dio. Wor. 1859. (Patron, V. of Mancetter; P. C.'s Inc. 155*l* and Ho; Pop. 1129.) Formerly P. C. of Baslow 1854–59. [1]

COPELAND, George Dale, *St. Stephen's Parsonage, Westmorland-road, Walworth, London, S.*—St. Bees; Deac. 1859 and Pr. 1860 by Bp of Ches. Min. of St. Stephen's, Walworth. Formerly C. of St. Thomas's, Wigan, and St. Jude's, Manchester. [2]

COPELAND, William John, *Farnham Rectory, Bishops Stortford, Essex.*—Trin. Coll. Ox. B.A. 1829; M.A. 1831, B.D. 1840. R. of Farnham, Dio. Roch. 1849. (Patron, Trin. Coll. Ox; Tithe, 615*l*; Glebe, 23 acres; R.'s Inc. 645*l* and Ho; Pop. 556.) Rural Dean. Formerly Fell. of Trin. Coll. Ox. [3]

COPEMAN, Arthur Charles, *St. Andrew's Parsonage, Norwich.*—King's Coll. Lond. Univ. Gold Medal in Anatomy and Physiology, M.B. 1848, M.R.C.S.E. 1845 and L.A.C. 1845; Deac. and Pr. 1851 by Bp of Wor. P. C. of St. Andrew's, City and Dio. Nor. 1856. (Patrons, the Parishioners; P. C.'s Inc. 100*l* and Ho; Pop. 978.) Formerly C. of St. Nicholas', Warwick, St. James's, Bury St. Edmunds; Sen. C. of Wisbeach, Cambs. [4]

COPEMAN, Frederick J., *Durham.*—Cl. Tut. of Durham University. [5]

COPLESTON, John Gay, *Offwell Rectory, Honiton, Devon.*—Oriel Coll. Ox. B.A. 1824, M.A. 1827; Deac. 1825, Pr. 1826. R. of Offwell, Dio. Ex. 1841. (Patron, the present R; Tithe, 270*l*; Glebe, 83 acres; R.'s Inc. 395*l* and Ho; Pop. 303.) [6]

COPLESTON, Reginald Edward, *Vicarage, Edmonton, Middlesex.*—Ex. Coll. Ox. 2nd cl. Lit. Hum. and B.A. 1832, M.A. 1835; Deac. 1834, Pr. 1835. V. of Edmonton, Dio. Lon. 1863. (Patrons, D. and C. of St. Paul's; Tithe, 950*l*; Glebe, 23 acres; V.'s Inc. 1150*l* and Ho; Pop. 4085.) Formerly V. of Barnes, Surrey, 1840–63; Fell. of Ex. Coll. Ox. [7]

COPLESTON, William James, *Cromhall, Chipping Sodbury, Glouc.*—Oriel Coll. Ox. B.A. 1825; Deac. 1828 and Pr. 1829 by Bp of Ox. R. of Cromhall, Dio. G. and B. 1839. (Patron, Oriel Coll. Ox; Tithe, 452*l* 5*s*; Glebe, 79 acres; R.'s Inc. 570*l* and Ho; Pop. 681.) Rural Dean. Author, *Memoir of Edward Copleston, D.D. Bishop of Llandaff,* 1851, 10*s*. [8]

COPNER, James, *Frithelstock, Torrington, North Devon.*—St. Mary Hall, Ox. B.A. 1850, M.A. 1853; Deac. 1851 by Bp of G. and B. Pr. 1852 by Bp of Ex. P. C. of Frithelstock, Dio. Ex. 1860. (Patron, Francis T. Johns, Esq; P. C.'s Inc. 116*l*; Pop. 632.) Formerly C. of Ilfracombe, 1851, St. Mary's the Less, Lambeth, 1853, Hartland 1855, Devizes 1857. Author, *Sermons,* 1856, 3*s* 6*d*; *Hints on the Education of Childhood,* 1860, 1*s* 6*d*; *How to be Happy, or an Elixir for Ennui,* 1863, 5*s*. [9]

COPPARD, William Isaac, *Plympton St. Mary, Devon.*—Emman. Coll. Cam. B.A. 1809, M.A. 1815; Deac. 1810 and Pr. 1811 by Bp of Rich. Dom. Chap. to the Earl of Morley 1840; Rural Dean 1841; Hon. Local Sec. to the Archæological Institute, and to the Exeter Diocesan Architectural Society. Formerly P. C. of Plympton St. Mary 1817–65. Author, *Cottage Scenes during the Cholera,* 1848, 3*s* 6*d*. [10]

CORBET, Athelstan, *Adderley Rectory, Market Drayton, Salop.*—Magd. Coll. Cam. 1859; Deac. 1861 and Pr. 1862 by Bp of B. and W. R. of Adderley, Dio. Lich. 1863. (Patron, R. Corbet, Esq; Tithe, 666*l*; Glebe, 19 acres and Ho; Pop. 428.) Formerly C. of Swainswick, Somerset. [11]

CORBET, Rowland William, *Headington-hill, Oxford.*—Trin. Coll. Cam. B.A. 1860; Deac. 1862 and Pr. 1864 by Bp of G. and B. Formerly C. of Bedminster. [12]

CORBETT, Elijah Bagott, *Shere, Guildford.*—King's Coll. Lond; Deac. 1862 and Pr. 1863 by Bp of Win. C. of Shere 1862. [13]

CORBETT, James Wortley, *Wigginton Rectory, near York.*—Mert. Coll. Ox. B.A. 1838; Deac. 1838 and Pr. 1839 by Abp of York. R. of Wigginton, Dio. York, 1845. (Patron, Ld Chan; Tithe, 179*l* 16*s* 3*d*; Glebe, 26 acres; R.'s Inc. 262*l* and Ho; Pop. 349.) [14]

CORBETT Lionel, *Longnor, Shrewsbury.*—Ch. Ch. Ox. B.A. 1854, M.A. 1858; Deac. 1855 and Pr. 1856 by Bp of Herf. R. of Pontesbury, 3rd Portion, Dio. Herf. 1867. (Patron, Reginald Cholmondeley, Esq; Tithe, 370*l*; Glebe, 59 acres; R.'s Inc. 500*l* and Ho; Pop. 950.) Formerly P. C. of Leebotwood with Longnor, 1856–67. [15]

CORBOULD, Edward James, *Wood-Speen House, near Newbury, Berks.*—Wad. Coll. Ox. B.A. 1851, M.A. 1854; Deac. 1853 and Pr. 1854 by Bp of Lich. Afternoon Lect. at Mary's Church, Speenhamland. Formerly C. of Buxton, Derby, 1853–57, Barcheston, Warw. 1857–60. [16]

CORBOULD, Thomas, *Tacolneston, Wymondham, Norfolk.*—Corpus Coll. Cam. B.A. 1818; Deac. 1819 and Pr. 1820 by Bp of Nor. R. of Tacolneston, Dio. Nor. 1858. (Patroness, Mrs. Warren; Tithe, 555*l*; R.'s Inc. 560*l*; Pop. 452.) [17]

CORBOULD, William Henry, *Rhodes, Middleton, Lancashire.*—King's Coll. Lond. Theol. Assoc. 1858; Deac. 1858 and Pr. 1859 by Bp of Lon. P. C. of Rhodes, Dio. Man. 1864. (Patron, R. of Middleton; P. C.'s Inc. 105*l* and Ho; Pop. 1700.) Formerly C. of St. Barnabas', King's-square, Lond. 1858–59, St. Stephen's, Camden Town, 1859–61, St. Leonard's, Middleton, 1861–64. [18]

CORDEAUX, Henry Taylor, *West Wickham, Kent.*—St. John's Coll. Cam. B.A. 1857, M.A. 1867; Deac. 1857 by Bp of Roch. Pr. 1858 by Bp of Ely. C. of West Wickham 1866. Formerly C. of Luton, Beds, Chevening, Kent, and Croydon, Surrey. [19]

CORDEAUX, John, *Hoyland Parsonage, Barnsley.*—St. Cath. Coll. Cam. B.A. 1828, M.A. 1841; Deac. 1828 and Pr. 1829 by Bp of Lin. P. C. of Hoyland, Dio. York, 1850. (Patron, Earl Fitzwilliam; Glebe, 91 acres; P. C.'s Inc. 404*l* and Ho; Pop. 3645.) [20]

CORDEAUX, Richard Dymoke Cawdron, *Paull Vicarage, near Hull.*—St. Cath. Coll. Cam. B.A. 1857; Deac. 1858 and Pr. 1859 by Bp of Ches. V. of Paull with Thorngambald, Dio. York, 1866. (Patron, Earl of Effingham; Glebe, 65 acres; V.'s Inc. 230*l* and Ho; Pop. 884.) Formerly C. of Halton, Cheshire, Woodhorn, Northumberland, Blandford, Dorset, Winterbourne, Stickland, Dorset, and Tredington, Worcestershire. [21]

CORDEAUX, William Henry, *Leamington, Warwickshire.*—St. Bees 1857; Deac. 1858 and Pr. 1859 by Bp of Lich. C. of St. Mary's, Leamington. Formerly C. of Marston, Montgomery, 1858. [22]

CORDEUX, Godfrey Pigott, *New Malton, Yorks.*—Magd. Hall, Ox. Lusby Scho. 1847, Scho. of Wor. Coll. Ox. 1849, 2nd cl. Lit. Hum. and B.A. 1850, M.A. 1853; Deac. 1852, Pr. 1853. Formerly Mast. of the Proprietary Sch. Cheltenham; P. C. of St. Leonard's, New Malton, Yorks, 1855; C. of Trinity, Micklegate, York; Fell. of Wor. Coll. Ox. 1852. [23]

CORFE, Joseph, *The Close, Exeter.*—Magd. Coll. Ox. 1st cl. Lit. Hum. and B.A. 1827, M.A. 1828; Deac. 1828 and Pr. 1829 by Bp of Ox. Pr. Vicar of Ex. Cathl. 1836. Formerly R. of Allhallows-on-the-Walls 1836; R. of St. Kerrian with St. Petrock R. City and Dio. Ex. 1844; Rural Dean. 1851. [24]

CORFE, Nelson Benjamin, *Ashbrittle, Wellington, Somerset.*—Wor. Coll. Ox. B.A. 1860; Deac. 1860 and Pr. 1862 by Bp of G. and B. C. of Ashbrittle. Formerly C. of Awre, Glouc. 1860. [25]

CORFIELD, Frederick, *Heanor Vicarage, Derby.*—Deac. 1840 by Bp of Lon. Pr. 1842 by Bp of Win. V. of Heanor, Dio. Lich. 1866. (Patron, F. Wright, Esq; V.'s Inc. 300*l* and Ho; Pop. 4084.) Dom. Chap. to Lord Clermont. Formerly R. of Templecrone, Donegal, 1842–66. [26]

CORFIELD, Thomas, *Bedminster, Bristol.*—C. of St. John's, Bedminster. [27]

CORFIELD, William, *Llangattock, Abergavenny, Monmouthshire.*—Ch. Coll. Cam. B.A. 1833; Deac. 1833 and Pr. 1834 by Bp of Lich. R. of Llangattock, near Usk, Dio. Llan. 1863. Patron, Earl of Abergavenny;

Tithe, 233*l*; Glebe, 100 acres; R.'s Inc. 400*l* and Ho; Pop. 252.) Formerly R. of Llanfeist 1850–63. [1]

CORFIELD, William Booth, *Llangattock, Abergavenny.*—Trin. Coll. Cam. B.A. 1861, M.A. 1865; Deac. 1863 and Pr. 1864 by Bp of Lich. C. of Llangattock and Llansantffraed. Formerly C. of High Ercal, Salop, 1863–65. [2]

CORK, Joseph Duncan, *Bickleigh Vicarage, Plymouth.*—Ex. Coll. Ox. B.A. 1834, M.A. 1836; Deac. 1836 and Pr. 1838 by Bp. of Ex. V. of Bickleigh with Sheepstor C. Dio. Ex. 1848. (Patron, Sir R. Lopes, Bart; Bickleigh, Tithe—App. 437*l*; Sheepstor, Tithe—Imp. 31*l* 7*s*, V. 61*l* 3*s*; V.'s Inc. 286*l* and Ho; Pop. Bickleigh 402, Sheepstor 98.) Rural Dean 1854. [3]

CORKER, George William, *Fenny Stratford, Bucks.*—Trin. Coll. Cam. B.A. 1848, M.A. 1851. P. C. of Fenny Stratford, Dio. Ox. 1864. (Patron, Henry Hoare, Esq; P. C.'s Inc. 110*l*; Pop. 1199) Chap. to Earl of Romney. [4]

CORLES, Harry, *Langham Rectory, Bury St. Edmunds.*—R. of Langham, Dio. Ely, 1852. (Patron, Ld Chan; Tithe, 268*l*; Glebe, 52 acres; R.'s Inc. 338*l* and Ho; Pop. 242.) [5]

CORLETT, John, *Peel, Isle of Man.*—St. Bees; Deac. 1855 and Pr. 1856 by Bp of Rip. P. C. of St. John's, Peel, Dio. S. and M. 1866. (Patron, the Crown; P. C.'s Inc. 67*l* and Ho.) Formerly C. of St. Stephen's, Selby, 1858, St. Matthew's, Leeds; P. C. of Cronk y Voddee, Peel, 1859–66. [6]

CORNALL, Richard, *Bristol.*—St. Bees; Deac. 1859 and Pr. 1860 by Bp of Ches. P. C. of Emmanuel Ch. Bristol, Dio. G. and B. 1862. (Patrons, Trustees.) Formerly C. of Ch. Ch. Everton, 1859–62. [7]

CORNFORD, Arthur, *Lowestoft, Suffolk.*—Deac. 1860 and Pr. 1861 by Bp. of Lich. C. of St. John's, Lowestoft, 1864. Formerly C. of St. Peter's, Belper, 1860–62, St. Mary's, Bury St. Edmunds, 1862–64. [8]

CORNFORD, Edward, *Cam, Dursley.*—St. John's Coll. Cam. B.A. 1855, M.A. 1863; Deac. 1856 by Bp of Ex. Pr. 1857 by Bp of Grahamstown. V. of Cam, Dio. G. and B. 1862. (Patron, Bp of G. and B; Tithe, none; Glebe, 6 acres; V.'s Inc. 150*l* and Ho; Pop. 1500.) Dioc. Inspector of Schs. Formerly C. of Loxbeer 1857; Chap. to Bp of Grahamstown 1858–59; C. of Stroud 1860–63. [9]

CORNFORD, James, *Norbiton, near Kingston, Surrey.*—Trin. Coll. Cam. B.A. 1862; Deac. 1862 and Pr. 1864 by Bp of Win. C. of Norbiton. [10]

CORNFORD, Nathaniel, *Newland, near Coleford, Gloucestershire.*—Emman. Coll. Cam. B.A. 1860, M.A. 1864; Deac. 1861 and Pr. 1862 by Bp of G. and B. C. of Newland. Formerly C. of St. James's, Bristol, 1861. [11]

CORNISH, Charles, *Narberth, South Wales.*—Pemb. Coll. Ox. B.A. 1849, M.A. 1852; Deac. 1850 by Bp of Ex. Pr. 1851 by Bp of Salis. R. of Ludchurch, Dio. St. D. 1857. (Patron, Ld Chan; Tithe, 85*l*; Glebe, 9*l*; R.'s Inc. 94*l*; Pop. 264.) P. C. of Templeton, Dio. St. D. 1863. (Patron, the Crown; Tithe, 182*l*; P. C.'s Inc. 182*l*; Pop. 650.) Formerly C. of Wotton Dorset, 1850, Yerbeston, Pembrokeshire, 1855. [12]

CORNISH, Charles John, *Debenham Vicarage, Suffolk.*—Corpus Coll. Ox. B.A. 1856; Deac. 1858 by Bp of Ex. Pr. 1859 by Bp of Nor. V. of Debenham, Dio. Nor. 1859. (Patron, Lord Henniker; Tithe, 282*l*; V.'s Inc. 300*l* and Ho; Pop. 1488.) Formerly C. of Sidbury, Devon, 1858–59. [13]

CORNISH, Charles Lewis, *Compton-Dando, near Bristol.*—Ex. Coll. Ox. 1st cl. in Lit. Hum. 1831, Fell. 1830–42, Tut. 1834–42, M.A. 1834; Deac. 1832 by Bp of Roch. Pr. 1833 by Bp of Ox. V. of Compton-Dando, Dio. B. and W. 1859. (Patron, Bp of B. and W; Tithe, 144*l*; Glebe, 50 acres; V.'s Inc. 200*l* and Ho; Pop. 347.) [14]

CORNISH, Frank Fortescue, *Marine-terrace, Victoria Docks, London, E.*—Ex. Coll. Ox. 2nd cl. Lit. Hum. 1860, B.A. 1861, M.A. 1863; Deac. 1863 by Bp of Lon. C. of St. Mark's, Victoria Docks, 1863. [15]

CORNISH, H. H., *New Inn Hall, Oxford.*—Prin. of New Inn Hall. [16]

CORNISH, Hubert Kestell, *Bakewell Vicarage, Derbyshire.*—Ex. Coll. Ox. 2nd cl. Lit. Hum. and B.A. 1825, M.A. 1828; Deac. 1826 and Pr. 1827 by Bp of Ex. V. of Bakewell, Dio. Lich. 1840. (Patrons, D. and C. of Lich; Tithe—App. 554*l* 2*s* 4*d*, Imp. 867*l* 18*s* 4*d*, V. 94*l*; V.'s Inc. 500*l* and Ho; Pop. 3225.) Rural Dean. Formerly Fell. of Ex. Coll. Ox. 1828. Author, *Fourteen Sermons on the Lord's Supper*, 1834; *Family and Private Prayers*, 1839; *Translation of part of St. Chrysostom's Epist. I. to the Corinthians*, in *Library of the Fathers*, etc. [17]

CORNISH, John Rundle, *Sidney College, Cambridge.*—Sid. Coll. Cam. B.A. 1859, M.A. 1862; Deac. 1863 and Pr. 1864 by Bp of Ely. Fell. of Sid. Coll. [18]

CORNISH, Robert Kestell, *Landkey Rectory, Barnstaple, Devon.*—Corpus Coll. Ox. B.A. 1846, M.A. 1849; Deac. 1847 and Pr. 1849 by Bp of Chich. R. of Landkey, Dio. Ex. 1866. (Patron, Bp of Ex; R.'s Inc. 300*l* and Ho; Pop. 700.) Formerly V. of Coleridge 1856–61; R. of Revelstoke, Devon, 1861–66. [19]

CORNISH, Sydney William, *The Vicarage, Ottery St. Mary, Devon.*—Ex. Coll. Ox. 2nd cl. Lit. Hum. and B.A. 1822, M.A. 1825, B.D. and D.D. 1836; Deac. 1824 and Pr. 1825 by Bp of Ox. V. of Ottery St. Mary, Dio. Ex. 1841. (Patron, Ld Chan; Tithe—App. 995*l* 15*s*, Imp. 250*l* 12*s* 10*d*; V.'s Inc. 162*l* and Ho; Pop. 4340.) Surrogate 1841. Formerly Fell. of Ex. Coll. Ox. 1822–27; Head Master of the King's Sch. Ottery St. Mary, 1824–63. Author, *Frequent Communion* (a Sermon), Masters, 1841; *Faith in the Efficacy of the Means of Grace* (Visitation Sermon), 1842. [20]

CORNISH, Thomas Brooking, *Westbrook, Macclesfield.*—Oriel Coll. Ox. 1st cl. Lit. Hum. B.A. 1837, M.A. 1840; Deac. 1841 and Pr. 1842 by Bp of Ox. Head Mast. of King Edward's Sch. Macclesfield. Formerly Fell. of Oriel Coll. Ox. [21]

CORNISH, William Floyer, *Marston, Oxford.*—Lin. Coll. Ox. B.A. 1857, M.A. 1860; Deac. 1860 and Pr. 1861 by Bp of Ox. C. of Marston 1862. Formerly Asst. C. of All Saints', Oxford, 1860–62. [22]

CORNWALL, Alan Gardner, *Ashcroft House, Wotton-under-Edge, Glouc.*—Trin. Coll. Cam. B.A. 1821, M.A. 1824; Deac. 1821 and Pr. 1822 by Bp of Win. R. of Newington Bagpath with Owlpen, Dio. G. and B. 1827. (Patron, Col. Kingscote, C.B., M.P; Tithe, 300*l*; Glebe, 50 acres; R.'s Inc. 420*l*; Pop. Bagpath 242, Owlpen 91.) R. of Beverstone with Kingscote C. Dio. G. and B. 1839. (Patron, the Crown; Tithe, 549; Glebe, 104 acres; R.'s Inc. 650*l* and Ho; Pop. Beverstone 170, Kingscote 311.) Chap. in Ordinary to the Queen. Formerly C. of Elvetham, Hants, 1821–27; V. of Stansted-Mountfichet, Essex, 1826–27. Author, single Sermons, and Annual Christmas Addresses to the Parishioners of both Parishes since 1832. [23]

CORNWALL, Alan Kingscote, *Bencombe, Dursley.*—Trin. Coll. Cam; Deac. 1856 and Pr. 1857 by Abp of Cant. C. of Newington Bagpath with Owlpen 1858. Formerly C. of Sandridge, Kent. [24]

CORNWALL, Albert P., *Burnham, near Chichester.*—Dur. Licen. Theol. 1851; Deac. 1851 and Pr. 1853 by Bp of Chich. V. of Barnham, Dio. Chich. 1860. (Patron, Bp of Chich; V.'s Inc. 80*l*; Pop. 149.) Formerly C. of Lower Beeding, Horsham, and Flimwell, Sussex. [25]

CORNWALL, Arthur Walton, *Midhurst, Sussex.*—Dur. Licen. in Theol. 1851; Deac. 1851 and Pr. 1853 by Bp of Chich. Chap. of Midhurst Union 1861. Formerly Asst. C. of Midhurst 1865. [26]

CORNWALL, George, *Earnley, Chichester, Sussex.*—R. of Earnley with Almodington, Dio. Chich. 1854. (Patrons, Bp of Chich. 2 turns, Duke of Norfolk, 1 turn; Tithe, 433*l*; Glebe, 7 acres; R.'s Inc. 444*l*; Pop. 116.) [27]

CORNWALL, Richard Nevill, *Eynesford Vicarage, Dartford, Kent.*—V. of Eynesford, Dio. Cant. 1852. (Patron, Abp of Cant; Tithe—Sinecure R. 600*l*,

V. 481*l* 0*s* 8*d*; V.'s Inc. 491*l* and Ho; Pop. 1117.) Dom. Chap. to the Marquis of Conyngham. [1]

CORNWALL, William Augustus, *Moccas, Hereford.*—Dub. A.B. 1844; Deac. 1847, Pr. 1849. R. of Moccas, Dio. Herf. 1861. (Patron, Sir George Cornwall, Bart; R.'s Inc. 186*l*; Pop. 196.) Formerly C. of St. Paul's, Kersall. [2]

CORNWALL, William Augustus, 9, *Sergeants' Inn, Fleet-street, London, E.C.*—Assoc. Sec. of the Colonial and Continental Ch. Miss. Soc. [3]

CORNWELL, Thomas Charles Brand, *Geddington Vicarage, Kettering, Northants.*—Emman. Coll. Cam. Wrang. and B.A. 1849, M.A. 1852; Deac. 1851 and Pr. 1852 by Bp of Pet. V. of Geddington with Newton D. Dio. Pet. 1861. (Patron, Duke of Buccleuch; V.'s Inc. 135*l* and Ho; Pop. Geddington 885, Newton 85.) Formerly C. of Stanwick 1851–53, Lawhitton 1853–54, Standford-in-the-Vale, Berks, 1854–56, Geddington 1856–61. [4]

CORNWELL, William, *Crossens Parsonage, Southport, Lancashire.*—King's Coll. Lond. Theol. Assoc; Deac. 1850 by Bp of Lon. Pr. 1852 by Bp of Ches. P. C. of Crossens, Dio. Ches. 1852. (Patrons, Trustees; Pop. 756.) [5]

CORRANCE, Charles Thomas, *Parham Vicarage, Wickham Market, Suffolk.*—Trin. Coll. Ox. B.A. 1845, M.A. 1848; Deac. 1849 by Bp of Chich. Pr. 1850 by Bp of Nor. V. of Parham with Hacheston, Dio. Nor. 1850. (Patron, F. Corrance, Esq; Parham, Tithe—Imp. 168*l*, V. 177*l*; Glebe, 4 acres; Hacheston, Tithe—Imp. 278*l*, V. 169*l*; Glebe, 3 acres; V.'s Inc. 346*l* and Ho; Pop. Parham 470, Hacheston 426.) Author, *What the Church is*, 1853, 6*d*; *Our Christian Pledge*, 1854, 3*d*; *Episcopacy, its Origin, Claims, and present Position in the Church of England*, 1867, 6*d*. [6]

CORRANCE, Henry Francis, *Arkley, Chipping Barnet, Herts.*—Clare Hall, Cam. B.A. 1837, M.A. 1847; Deac. and Pr. 1840 by Bp of Pet. C. of Arkley 1861. Formerly C. of Shoreham. [7]

CORRIE, Edgar Siritt, *Great Maplestead, Halstead, Essex.*—Emman. Coll. Cam. B.A. 1848, M.A. 1856; Deac. 1849 and Pr. 1850 by Bp of Herf. V. of Great Maplestead, Dio. Roch. 1858. (Patron, Rev. D. Fraser; V.'s Inc. 204*l*; Pop. 462.) Formerly C. of Braxted, Essex. [8]

CORRIE, George Elwes, *Jesus College, Cambridge.*—St. Cath. Coll. Cam. Wrang. and B.A. 1817, M.A. 1820, B.D. 1831 and D.D. 1852. Mast. of Jesus Coll. Cam. 1849; R. of Newton, Isle of Ely, Dio. Ely, 1851. (Patron, Bp of Ely; Tithe, 710*l*; Glebe, 176 acres; R.'s Inc. 1130*l* and Ho; Pop. 431.) Rural Dean 1851; Exam. Chap. to the late Bp of Ely. Formerly Norrisian Prof. of Divinity of the University of Cam. 1838–54. Author, *Historical Notices of the Interferences of the Crown* [illegible]*th the English Universities*, 1833; *Burnet's History of the* [illegible]*eformation*, edited for the use of Students, 1847; *Twysden's Historical Vindication of the Church of England*, edited for the University Press, 1847; *The Homilies, with the various readings and the quotations from Patristical Writers*, edited for the University Press, 1850; *Wheatley* [illegible]*n the Book of Common Prayer, with the additional notes*, edited for the University Press, 1858. [9]

CORSER, George James, *Burrington Vicarage, near Ludlow.*—Brasen. Coll. Ox. B.A. 1851, M.A. 1853; Deac. 1853 and Pr. 1854 by Bp of Lich. V. of Burrington, Dio. Herf. 1866. (Patron, Ld Chan; V.'s Inc. 150*l* and Ho; Pop. 231.) Formerly C. of Norton, Northants, and Woore, Salop; V. of Wolfhamcote 1863–66; Head. Mast. of Daventry Gr. Sch. 1863–66. [10]

CORSER, Richard Kidston, 11, *Pembury-grove, Hackney, London, N.E.*—Corpus Coll. Cam. M.A. 1863; Deac. 1858, Pr. 1860. C. of St. John's, Hackney, 1863. [11]

CORSER, Thomas, *Stand Rectory, near Manchester.*—Ball Coll. Ox. B.A. 1815, M.A. 1818. R. of Stand, Dio. Man. 1826. (Patron, Earl of Wilton; R.'s Inc. 270*l* and Ho; Pop. 8758.) V. of Norton-by-Daventry, Northants. Dio. Pet. 1828. (Patron, Beriah Botfield, Esq; Tithe, App. 119*l* 17*s* 1*d*, Imp. 7*l* 14*s* 6*d*, V. 229*l* 11*s*; V.'s Inc. 280*l*; Pop. 480.) Rural Dean; Surrogate. [12]

CORT, Jonathan Johnson, *Sale (Cheshire), near Manchester.*—St. John's Coll. Cam. 5th Wrang. 2nd cl. Cl. Trip. and B.A. 1850, M.A. 1853; Deac. 1850 and Pr. 1851 by Bp of Wor. P. C. of St. Anne's, Sale, Dio. Ches. 1856. (Patrons, Trustees; P. C.'s Inc. 520*l*; Pop. 3031.) Fell. of St. John's Coll. Cam. 1851. Formerly Asst. Mast. in King Edward's Sch. Birmingham 1850. Author, *Sermon on the War with Russia*, 1854, 6*d*; *Sermon on the Bible Society*, 1859, 4*d*; etc. [13]

CORY, Edward William, *Meldreth, Royston, Cambs.*—St. Peter's Coll. Cam. 5th Sen. Opt. Div. Prizeman, B.A. 1854, M.A. 1857; Deac. 1853 and Pr. 1854 by Bp of Chich. V. of Meldreth, Dio. Ely, 1864. (Patrons, D. and C. of Ely; 120 acres in lieu of tithe; Glebe, 3 acres; V.'s Inc. 230*l* and Ho; Pop. 735.) Formerly C. of Peasmarsh 1854, Stretham 1859. [14]

CORY, Henry Cory, 11, *Buckingham street, London, W.C.*—St. John's Coll. Cam. B.A. 1849, M.A. 1852; Deac. 1849 and Pr. 1850 by Bp of Win. Missionary Sec. to the Irish Church Missions. [15]

CORY, Robert, *Stanground, Peterborough.*—Emman. Coll. Cam. B.A. 1823, M.A. 1826, B.D. 1833; Deac. 1825 and Pr. 1826 by Bp of Ely. V. of Stanground with Farcet C. Dio. Ely, 1842. (Patron, Emman. Coll. Cam; Tithe, 800*l*; Glebe, 233 acres; V.'s Inc. 1232*l* and Ho; Pop. Stanground 1100, Farcet 778.) Formerly Fell. of Emman. Coll. Cam. 1835–42. [16]

CORY, Robert Woolmer, *Blundeston, Lowestoft, Suffolk.*—Pemb. Coll. Cam. Sen. Opt. and B.A. 1834, M.A. 1840; Deac. 1835 by Bp of Roch. Pr. 1835 by Bp of Chich. R. of Blundeston with Flixton, Dio. Nor. 1865. (Patrons, Exors. of T. Morse, Esq; R.'s Inc. 700*l* and Ho; Pop. Blundeston 664, Flixton 37.) Formerly V. of Horsey, Norfolk, 1853–57; C. of Blundeston 1857. [17]

CORYTON, Granville, *St. Mellion Rectory, Plymouth.*—Oriel Coll. Ox. B.A. 1840; Deac. 1840 and Pr. 1841 by Bp of Ex. R. of St. Mellion, Dio. Ex. 1841. (Patron, A. Coryton, Esq; Tithe, 232*l*; Glebe, 68 acres; R.'s Inc. 297*l* and Ho; Pop. 299.) [18]

COSENS, Edward Hyde Frowd, *Shepton Mallet, Somerset.*—St. Mary Hall, Ox. B.A. 1856, M.A. 1858; Deac. 1857 and Pr. 1858 by Bp of Lin. Chap. of the County Gaol, Shepton Mallet, 1859. Formerly C. of North and South Carlton, Linc. 1857–59. [19]

COSENS, Robert, *Longburton Vicarage, Sherborne, Dorset.*—Pemb. Coll. Ox. B.A. 1840; Deac. 1841 and Pr. 1842 by Bp of Salis. V. of Longburton with Holnest Chapelry, Dio. Salis. 1842. (Patron, the present V; Longburton, Tithe—Imp. 123*l*, V. 103*l*; Holnest, Tithe—Imp. 140*l*, V. 110*l*; Glebe, Longburton, 20 acres, Holnest, 13 acres; V.'s Inc. 275*l* and Ho; Pop. Longburton 336, Holnest 147.) [20]

COSENS, William Reyner, *Holy Trinity Parsonage, Westminster, S.W.*—Magd. Hall, Ox. Huish, Lucy, and Meeke Scho. B.A. 1852, M.A. 1855; Deac. 1853 and Pr. 1854 by Bp of Salis. P. C. of Trinity, Westminster, Dio. Lon. 1864. (Patrons, D. and C. of Westminster; P. C.'s Inc. 600*l* and Ho; Pop. 6365.) Formerly C. of Warminster, Wilts, 1853, Laverstock, Wilts (sole charge), 1854; R. of St. Andrew's, Chichester, and Min. Can. of Chich. Cathl. 1855–57; Sec. to Additional Curates Society 1857–65. Author, *Family Prayers*, 1854; *The Fall of Judas, a Warning to Christians*, 1856; *Church Reformation, a Sermon*, 1858; *Home Responsibilities, a Sermon*, 1860; *Occasional Sermons*, 1861; *London Dens and Mission Work among them*, 1863; *Faithful Preaching of the Word, and Holy Life and Sound Doctrine* (Sermons), 1865. [21]

COSSER, Walter Maude, *Titchfield Vicarage, Fareham, Hants.*—Trin. Coll. Ox. B A. 1838, M.A. 1841; Deac. 1840, Pr. 1841. V. of Titchfield, Dio. Win. 1852. (Patrons, D. and C. of Win; Tithe—App. 2708*l*, V. 83*l*; Glebe, 3 acres; V.'s Inc. 230*l* and Ho; Pop. 2637.) [22]

COSSERAT, George Peloquin Graham, *Winfrith Rectory, Dorchester.*—Ex. Coll. Ox. B.A. 1839, M.A. 1844; Deac. 1839, Pr. 1840. R. of Winfrith-Newburg with Burton C. Dio. Salis. 1851. (Patron, Bp of Salis; Tithe—App. 490*l* 10*s*, R. 483*l* 6*s*; Glebe, 95 acres; R.'s Inc. 700*l* and Ho; Pop. Winfrith-Newburg with Burton 1020.) Author, *Baptismal Regeneration* (a Sermon), 1845; *Public, Family and Private Worship* (a Sermon), 1846; *Letter to the Bishop of Exeter on Catechising*, 1850. [1]

COSTOBADIE, Hugh Palliser, *King's Norton Vicarage, near Leicester.*—St. John's Coll. Cam. B.A. 1828; Deac. 1829, Pr. 1830. V. of King's Norton with Little Stretton C. Dio. Pet. 1858. (Patron, Henry Green, Esq; Tithe—Imp. 7*s* 6*d*, App. 10*s*, V. 95*l*; Glebe, 10 acres; V.'s Inc. 120*l* and Ho; Pop. 154.) [2]

COSWAY, Samuel, *Chute Vicarage, Andover, Wilts.*—V. of Chute, Dio. Salis. 1838. (Patron, Bp of Salis; Tithe—App. 350*l*, V. 302*l*; V.'s Inc. 328*l* and Ho; Pop. 538.) [3]

COTES, Digby Octavius, *Purton, Swindon, Wilts.*—Univ. Coll. Ox. 4th cl. Lit. Hum. 1st cl. Math. et Phy. and B.A. 1836, M.A. 1840; Deac. 1838 and Pr. 1839 by Bp of Ox. C. of Purton. [4]

COTES, D. H., *Worcester.*—R. of St. Alban's and St. Helen's, Worcester, Dio. Wor. 1863. (Patron, Bp of Wor; R.'s Inc. 154*l* and Ho; Pop. 1807.) [5]

COTES, Septimus, *Newington Rectory, Wallingford.*—Wad. Coll. Ox. B.A. 1829, M.A. 1830; Deac. and Pr. 1833. R. of Newington with Britwell C. Dio. Ox. 1845. (Patron, Bp of Ox; Newington, Tithe, 228*l*; Britwell, Tithe, 129*l*; R.'s Inc. 357*l* and Ho; Pop. Newington 403, Britwell 43.) [6]

COTESWORTH, Henry, *Tempsford Rectory (Beds), near St. Neot's.*—St. Peter's Coll. Cam. Wrang. and B.A. 1832, M.A. 1835; Deac. 1834, Pr. 1835. R. of Tempsford, Dio. Ely, 1847. (Patron, the Crown; Glebe, 334 acres; R.'s Inc. 300*l*; Pop. 566.) Formerly Gisborne Fell. of St. Peter's Coll. Cam. [7]

COTHAM, George Toulson, 148, *Walworth-road, London, S.*—Dub. A.B. 1846; Deac. 1847 and Pr. 1848 by Bp of Rip. P. C. of St. John's, Walworth, Dio. Lon. 1859. (Patrons, Trustees.) [8]

COTTAM, Henry, *Fern Bank, Old Trafford, Manchester.*—Pemb. Coll. Cam. B.A. 1860; Deac. 1861 and Pr. 1862 by Bp of Man. C. of Whalley Range; Lect. at Owen's Coll. Manchester. Formerly Math. Mast. of the Manchester Sch. [9]

COTTER, Charles Purcell, *Stantonbury Vicarage, Stony-Stratford.*—Dub. A.B. 1845, A.M. 1860; Deac. 1849 by Bp of Cork, Pr. 1850 by Bp of Salis. V. of Stantonbury with New Bradwell, Dio. Ox. 1857. (Patron, Earl Spencer; Tithe, 60*l*; Glebe, 2 acres; V.'s Inc. 180*l* and Ho; Pop. 1207.) Formerly C. of Donoughmore, Cloyne, 1849, Hadlow, Kent, 1853, Tincleton, Dorset, 1850. [10]

COTTER, James Laurence, *The Parsonage, Lydiate, Ormskirk.*—Dub. A.B. 1845, M.B. 1847; M.R.C.S. Lond. 1847; Deac. 1854 by Bp of Pet. Pr. 1835 by Bp of Kilmore. P. C. of Lydiate, Dio. Ches. 1861. (Patron, R. of Halsall; P. C.'s Inc. 150*l* and Ho; Pop. 1853.) Formerly C. of Castor 1854, Killyon and Kilroran, Ireland (sole charge), 1856, St. Peter's, Dublin, 1857, Greetland, Halifax, 1857, St. Stephen the Martyr's, Liverpool, 1859. [11]

COTTER, J. G., *Winterbourne, Whitchurch, Dorset.*—C. of Winterbourne. [12]

COTTER, Joseph Rogerson, *Houghton Rectory, Blandford, Dorset.*—Dub. A.B. 1845; Deac. 1845 by Bp of Kilmore, Pr. 1846 by Bp of Killaloe. R. of Winterborne Houghton, Dio. Salis. 1857. (Patroness, Mrs. Michel; Tithe, 180*l*; Glebe, 118 acres; R.'s Inc. 270*l* and Ho; Pop. 284.) Formerly C. of Winterborne Houghton. [13]

COTTINGHAM, Henry, *Heath, Chesterfield.*—Magd. Coll. Cam. B.A. 1838, M.A. 1841; Deac. 1839, Pr. 1840. V. of Heath, Dio. Lich. 1859. (Patron, Duke of Devonshire; Tithe, 230*l*; Glebe, 5 acres; V.'s Inc. 235*l* and Ho; Pop. 369.) V. of Ault-Hucknall, Derbyshire, Dio. Lich. 1850. (Patron, Duke of Devonshire; Tithe—Imp. 33*l* 19*s* 6*d*, V. 105*l*; Glebe, 27½ acres; V.'s Inc. 125*l*; Pop. 686.) Formerly V. of Hathersaye 1847–59. [14]

COTTINGHAM, James, *Shotwick, Chester.*—Clare Coll. Camb. 3rd cl. Cl. Trip. Jun. Opt. and B.A. 1827; Deac. 1827 and Pr. 1828 by Bp of Ches. P. C. of Shotwick, Dio. Ches. 1831. (Patrons, D. and C. of Ches; Glebe, 24 acres; P. C.'s Inc. 115*l* and Ho; Pop. 800.) Formerly C. of Ribchester, Lancashire, 1827–29, Swavesey, Cambs. 1829–31. [15]

COTTLE, Henry Wyatt, *Harford Rectory, Ivybridge, Devon.*—Sid. Coll. Cam. B.A. 1826; Deac. 1826 and Pr. 1827 by Bp of Salis. R. of Harford, Dio. Ex. 1854. (Patroness, Lady Rogers; Tithe, 185*l*; Glebe, 40 acres; R.'s Inc. 255*l* and Ho; Pop. 158.) In New Zealand at present. [16]

COTTLE, Thomas, *Shalfleet, Yarmouth, Isle of Wight.*—Pemb. Coll. Ox. B.A. 1827 M.A. 1829; Deac. 1832, Pr. 1833. V. of Shalfleet, Dio. Win. 1849. (Patron, Ld Chan; Tithe—Imp. 981*l* 4*s* 11*d*, V. 210*l*; Glebe, 5 acres; V.'s Inc. 210*l* and Ho; Pop. 1196.) [17]

COTTON, Arthur Benjamin, *St. Paul's Parsonage, Bow-common, London, E.*—Ch. Ch. Ox. B A. 1854; Deac. 1856 and Pr. 1857 by Bp of Ox. P. C. of St. Paul's, Bow-common, Dio. Lon. 1858. (Patron, the present P. C; P. C.'s Inc. 287*l* and Ho; Pop. 6500.) [18]

COTTON, Benjamin, *Rockford Rectory, Essex.*—Trin. Coll. Cam. B.A. 1859; Deac. 1851 and Pr. 1852 by Bp of Win. R. of Rochford, Dio. Roch. 1862. (Patron, Earl of Mornington; Tithe, 585*l*; Glebe, 54 acres; R.'s Inc. 665*l* and Ho; Pop. 1696.) Formerly V. of Shipton Bellinger 1858–62. [19]

COTTON, Henry James, *Dalbury Rectory, Derbyshire.*—Wor. Coll. Ox. B.A. 1835; Deac. 1837 and Pr. 1838 by Bp. of Win. R. of Dalbury, Dio. Lich. 1857. (Patroness, Mrs. Eliz. Cotton; Tithe, 184*l*; Glebe, 47 acres; R.'s Inc. 305*l* and Ho; Pop. 263.) [20]

COTTON, Richard Lynch, *Worcester College, Oxford.*—Wor. Coll. Ox. Scho. 1815, 2nd cl. Lit. Hum. and B.A. 1815, M.A. 1818, D.D. 1839; Deac. 1817, Pr. 1818. Provost of Wor. Coll. Ox. 1839. Formerly Select Preacher of the Univ. of Ox. 1840, Vice-Chancellor of the Univ. 1852–55; V. of Denchworth, Berks, 1823–39; Chap. to the Earl of St. Germans 1824. Author, *The Way of Salvation* (Sermons); *Lectures on the Lord's Supper.* [21]

COTTON, William Charles, *Frodsham Vicarage, Cheshire.*—Ch. Ch. Ox. Newcastle Scho. 1832, B.A. 1835, M.A. 1837; Deac. 1837 and Pr. 1839 by Bp of Ox. V. of Frodsham, Dio. Ches. 1857. (Patron, Ch. Ch. Ox; Tithe—App. 800*l*, V. 572*l*; Glebe, 60 acres; V.'s Inc. 600*l* and Ho; Pop. 3701.) Formerly C. of St. Mary's Redcliffe, Bristol. [22]

COUCHMAN, Henry, *Haileybury College, Hertford.*—Trin. Coll. Ox. B.A. 1862, M.A. 1864; Deac. 1865 and Pr. 1866 by Bp of Roch. C. of Great Amwell, near Ware, 1865. [23]

COUCHMAN, John, *Thornby, Northants.*—Clare Coll. Cam. B.A. 1833, M.A. 1837; Deac. 1836 and Pr. 1837 by Bp of Wor. R. of Thornby, Dio. Pet. 1847. (Patron, the present R; Tithe, 320*l*; Glebe, 46 acres; R.'s Inc. 380*l* and Ho; Pop. 252.) [24]

COULCHER, William Bedell, *Diss, Norfolk.*—Emman. Coll. Cam; Deac. 1818 and Pr. 1820 by Bp of Nor. R. of Wattisfield, Suffolk, Dio. Ely, 1863. (Patrons, Trustees; Tithe, 379*l* 15*s* 10*d*; Glebe, 30 acres; R.'s Inc. 420*l* and Ho; Pop. 615.) Formerly P. C. of Bradninch, Devon, 1853–63. [25]

COULSON, A. B., *Bothal, near Morpeth.*—C. of Bothal and Hebburn. [26]

COULSON, John, *South Shields.*—Dur. B.A. 1863; Deac. 1863 and Pr. 1864 by Bp of Dur. Fell. of Dur. Univ; C. of South Shields. [27]

COULSON, John Edmond, *Long Preston Vicarage, Skipton, Yorks.*—Ch. Ch. Ox. B.A. 1847, M.A. 1849; Deac. 1848, Pr. 1851. V. of Long Preston, Dio. Rip. 1858. (Patron, Ch. Ch. Ox; V.'s Inc. 315*l* and Ho; Pop. 1168.) Dom. Chap. to Duke of Marlborough. Formerly C. of Walton and Weston in Gordano, Somerset. [1]

COULSON, Thomas Borlase, *St. Burian, Penzance.*—Trin. Coll. Cam. B.A. 1854, M.A. 1857, Sen. Opt; Deac. 1855 by Bp of Lon. Pr. 1856 by Bp of Win. R. of St. Burian, Dio. Ex. 1864. (Patron, the Prince of Wales as Duke of Cornwall; Tithe, 570*l*; Glebe, 3¼ acres; R.'s Inc. 690*l* and Ho; Pop. 1428.) Formerly C. of St. Clement's Danes, Lond; V. of Skipsea, Yorks, 1862–64. [2]

COULTHARD, Robert, *Sulhamstead Rectory, Reading.*—Queen's Coll. Ox. B.A. 1820, M.A. 1823; Deac. and Pr. 1823. R. of Sulhamstead-Abbas with Sulhamstead-Banister, Dio. Ox. 1845. (Patron, Queen's Coll. Ox, Tithe, 668*l*; Glebe, 26 acres; R.'s Inc. 683*l* and Ho; Pop. Sulhamstead-Abbas 285, Sulhamstead-Banister 147.) Formerly Fell. of Queen's Coll. Ox. [3]

COULTHARD, Thomas, *Plymstock, Devon.*—Queen's Coll. Ox. B.A. 1841; Deac. 1841, Pr. 1842. P. C. of Plymstock, Dio. Ex. 1855. (Patrons, D. and C. of Windsor; Tithe, App. 781*l* 3*s* 6*d*; P. C.'s Inc. 174*l*; Pop. 1915.) [4]

COULTHURST, William Henry, *Giggleswick, Settle, Yorks.*—Magd. Coll. Cam. LL.B. 1852; Deac. 1852, Pr. 1853. V. of Giggleswick, Dio. Rip. 1853. (Patrons, J. C. Coulthurst and J. Hartley, Esqrs; Tithe—Imp. 75*l* 5*s* 1*d*, V. 550*l*; V.'s Inc. 560*l*; Pop. 690.) [5]

COULTON, Richard, *West Bromwich, Staffs.*—C. of Ch. Ch. West Bromwich. [6]

COUPLAND, Edward, *Northmoor, Witney.*—St. John's Coll. Ox. B.A. 1850, M.A. 1852, B.D. P. C. of Northmoor, Dio. Ox. 1858. (Patron, St. John's Coll. Ox; Tithe, Imp. 504*l* 3*s*; Glebe, 40 acres; P. C.'s Inc. 115*l*; Pop. 364.) Fell of St. John's Coll. Ox. [7]

COURT, James Charles Lett, *Widdington, Bishops Stortford, Essex.*—Ex. Coll. Ox. B.A. 1848, M.A. 1853; Deac. 1850 and Pr. 1851 by Bp of Ox. R. of Widdington, Dio. Roch. 1862. (Patron, Major M. H. Court; Tithe, 580*l*; Glebe, 42 acres; R.'s Inc. 640*l* and Ho; Pop. 409.) Formerly C. at Rotherfield Greys 1850, Little Brickhill, Bucks, 1852–56; P. C. of Little Brickhill 1856–60. [8]

COURTENAY, Anthony Lefroy, 22, *Claremont-square, Pentonville, London, N.*—Dub. A.M. and D.D. P. C. of St. James's, Pentonville, Dio. Lon. 1854. (Patron, the P. C. of Clerkenwell; P. C.'s Inc. 300*l*; Pop. 11,974.) Dom. Chap. to Earl Hardwicke. [9]

COURTENAY, The Hon. Charles Leslie. *Bovey-Tracey Vicarage, Newton-Abbott, Devon.*—Ch. Ch. Ox. B.A. 1837, M.A. 1838; Deac. 1840 by Bp of Ox. Pr. 1842 by Bp of Salis. V. of Bovey-Tracey, Dio. Ex. 1849. (Patron, the Crown; Tithe—Imp. 222*l* 17*s*, V. 450*l*; Glebe, 7 acres; V.'s Inc. 490*l* and Ho; Pop. 208.) Canon of Windsor, and Chap. in Ordinary to the Queen, 1849. [10]

COURTENAY, The Hon. Henry Hugh, *Mamhead Rectory, near Exeter.*—Mert. Coll. Ox. B.A. 1833, M.A. 1844; Deac. 1835, Pr. 1836. R. of Mamhead, Dio. Ex. 1845. (Patron, Sir L. Newman, Bart; Tithe, 145*l*; Glebe, 20 acres; R.'s Inc. 175*l* and Ho; Pop. 218.) [11]

COURTENAY, John Brownlee, 121, *New Kent-road, Southwark, London, S.*—Dub. Scho. A B. 1853, A.M. 1857; Deac. 1853 by Abp of Dub. Pr. 1854, by Bp of Cork. Formerly C. of St. Luke's, Dublin, 1853, St. Peter's, Holborn, Lond. 1855, St. Mary's, Whitechapel, 1856, St. Stephen's, Southwark (sole charge), 1860. [12]

COURTENAY, John Polkinghorne, 2. *Brackley Cottages, Upper Lewisham-road, London, S.E.*—King's Coll. Lond. 1st cl. Theol. Assoc. 1857; M.A. by Abp of Cant. 1867; Deac. 1857 and Pr. 1858 by Bp of Lon. P. C. of Ch. Ch. Deptford, Dio. Roch. 1864. (Patrons, Bp of Lon. and others; Pop. 10,000.) Formerly C. of St. John's, Deptford. Author, *Weep ye not for the Dead, Parental Love, God is Merciful,* and other Tracts. [13]

COURTIER, Frederick William Hall, *Grendon, Northampton.*—Clare Coll. Cam. B.A. 1865; Deac. 1867 by Bp of Pet. C. of Grendon 1867. [14]

COURTNEY, Frederick, *Plymouth.*—P. C. of Charles Chapel, Plymouth, Dio. Ex. 1865. (Patrons, Trustees; P. C.'s Inc. 100*l*.) [15]

COURTNEY, Henry Courtney, *Wolverton, Stratford-on-Avon.*—R. of Wolverton, Dio. Wor. 1868. (Patron, Rev. B. Winthrop; R.'s Inc. 400*l* and Ho; Pop. 159.) [16]

COUSENS, Rowland Richard.—Ch. Coll. Cam. B.A. 1857; Deac. 1857 and Pr. 1858 by Bp of Bombay. Assoc. Sec. of Ch. Pastoral Aid Soc. Formerly Min. of Trin. Chap. Bombay, 1857–60; Asst. Chap. at Smyrna 1860–63; P. C. of New Buckenham, Norfolk, 1863–66. [17]

COUSINS, Dennis Louis, *Bristol.*—St. Peter's Coll. Cam. Scho. Sen. Cl. Prizeman 1835, B.A. 1836, M.A. 1840; Deac. 1839 and Pr. 1840 by Bp of G. and B. P. C. of St. Simon's, Bristol, Dio. G. and B. 1865. (Patrons, Crown and Bp alt; P. C.'s Inc. 150*l*; Pop. 1932.) Formerly C. of Cheltenham 1839, Welland 1843, Eckington 1846, Halford 1851, Abbot's Leigh 1852, Bristol 1853; P. C. of Kingswood 1856–65. Author, *Diary of Workhouse Chaplain,* 1847, 6*s*; *Letter to Sir George Grey,* 1849, 1*s*; *Practical Sermons on the Holy Communion,* 1863, 2*s* 6*d*. [18]

COUTTS, Charles Frederick, *Roehampton, Surrey, S.W.*—C. of Roehampton. [19]

COVE, Edward, *Thoresway Rectory, Caistor, Lincolnshire.*—Wor. Coll. Ox. B.A. 1825; Deac. 1830, Pr. 1831. R. of Thoresway, Dio. Lin. 1831. (Patron, Ld Chan; Glebe, 696 acres; R.'s Inc. 493*l* and Ho; Pop. 196.) [20]

COVENTRY, Henry William, *Woolstone Rectory, Cheltenham.*—Pemb. Coll. Ox. B.A. 1852; Deac. 1853 and Pr. 1854 by Bp of Wor. R. of Woolstone, Dio. G. and B. 1854. (Patron, Earl of Coventry; Tithe, 161*l*; Glebe, 36 acres; R.'s Inc. 235*l* and Ho; Pop. 81.) P. C. of Oxenton, Dio. G. and B. 1855. (Patron, Earl of Coventry; Glebe, 25 acres; P. C.'s Inc. 85*l*; Pop. 136.) [21]

COVENTRY, The Hon. Thomas Henry, *Severn-Stoke Rectory, near Worcester.*—Ch. Ch. Ox. B.A. 1814, M.A. 1817; Deac. and Pr. 1816. R. of Croome Hill, Dio. Wor. 1826. (Patron, Ld Chan; Tithe, 115*l*; Glebe, 60¾ acres; R.'s Inc. 240*l* and Ho; Pop. 198.) R. of Severn-Stoke, Dio. Wor. 1833. (Patron, Earl of Coventry; Tithe, 768*l* 12*s*; R.'s Inc. 890*l* and Ho; Pop. 679.) [22]

COVEY, Charles, *Alderton Rectory, Cheltenham.*—St. John's Coll. Cam. B.A. 1819, M.A. 1822; Deac. 1821, Pr. 1822. R. of Alderton, Dio. G. and B. (Patron, the present R; Tithe, 150*l* for the Hamlet of Dixton, Land in lieu of Tithe, 260 acres; Glebe, 30 acres; R.'s Inc. 500*l* and Ho; Pop. 487.) R. of Great Washbourne, Dio. G. and B. 1837. (Patron, the present R; a small Modus in lieu of Tithe; Glebe, 38 acres; R.'s Inc. 84*l*; Pop. 83.) [23]

COVEY, Charles Rogers, *Ermington Vicarage, Ivybridge, Devon.*—St. Peter's Coll. Cam. S.C.L. 1857, LL.B. 1859; Deac. 1858 and Pr. 1860 by Bp of Ex. C. of Ermington 1865. Formerly C. of Buckfastleigh and Kingston, Devon. [24]

COWAN, Ernest, *St. Paul's Vicarage, Wolverhampton.*—Caius Coll. Cam. B.A. 1858; Deac. 1859 and Pr. 1860 by Bp of Win. V. of St. Paul's, Wolverhampton, Dio. Lich. 1866. (Patron, Rev. W. Dalton; V.'s Inc. 300*l* and Ho; Pop. 5959.) Formerly C. of Havant, Hants, 1859–62, St. Mary's, Brighton, 1863; Assoc. Sec. Colonial and Continental Ch. Soc. 1863–66. [25]

COWAN, James Galloway, *St. John's Parsonage, Hammersmith, W.*—Literate; M.A. by Abp of Cant. 1863; Deac. 1852 and Pr. 1853 by Bp of Lon. P. C. of St. John's, Hammersmith, Dio. Lon. 1863. (Patron, the V; P. C.'s Inc. 350*l* and Ho; Pop. 5000.) Commissary to the Bp of Orange Free State. Formerly C. of Barnes 1852–53; C. and Even. Lect. of St. James's, Westminster, 1854–56; P. C. of Abp Tenison's Chapel, Lond. 1856–63. Author, *Christian Marriage Indissoluble* (Sermon), 1857; *Plain Sermons,* 1st. Ser. 1859,

3s 6d, 2nd Ser. 1860, 5s, 3rd Ser. 1860, 5s; *Prayers for Sunday Schools*, 1863, 2d. [1]

COWAN, Thomas, 16, *St. Domingo-grove, Everton, Liverpool.*—Dub. A.B. 1830, A.M. 1854; Deac. 1842 and Pr. 1843 by Bp of Ches. P. C. of St Chrysostom's, Everton, Dio. Ches. 1861. (Patrons, Five Trustees; P. C.'s Inc. 420*l*; Pop. 9453.) Surrogate. Formerly C. of Christchurch, Liverpool, 1842–46; P. C. of St. Thomas's, Toxteth, 1846–51, St. Andrew's, Liverpool, 1851-62. [2]

COWARD, James, *Langdale Parsonage, Ambleside.*—St. Bees; Deac. 1844 and Pr. 1846 by Bp of Rip. P. C. of Langdale, Dio. Carl. 1860. (Patron, R. of Grasmere; P. C.'s Inc. 160*l* and Ho; Pop. 534.) Formerly Sen. C. of Timberland, Linc. [3]

COWARD, John Henry, *Residentiary Houses, Amen-corner, Paternoster-row, London, E.C.*—Pemb. Coll. Cam. B.A. 1843, M.A. 1848; Deac. 1844 and Pr. 1845 by Abp of Cant. Min. Can. of St. Paul's 1847 (Value 150*l*.); R. of St. Benet with St. Peter, Paul's-wharf, City and Dio. Lon. 1852. (Patrons, D. and C. of St. Paul's; Fire Act Comm. R. 200*l*; R.'s Inc. 272*l*; Pop. 947.) Almoner and Gr. Mast. of the Choristers of St. Paul's; Chap. to the Vintners' Company. [4]

COWARD, Ralph John, *Mevagissey, Cornwall.* Brasen. Coll. Ox. B.A. 1849, M.A. 1853; Deac. 1853 by Bp of Man. Pr. 1854 by Bp of Chich. V. of Mevagissey, Dio. Ex. 1862. (Patrons, Exors. of J. Benbow, Esq; Tithe, 161*l*; Glebe, 23 acres; V.'s Inc. 220*l* and Ho; Pop. 1904.) Formerly C. of Lower Beeding, Sussex; Chap. to the Midhurst Union. [5]

COWDELL, Henry, *Cold-Weston, Ludlow, Salop.*—Wor. Coll. Ox. B.A. 1816. R. of Cold-Weston, Dio. Herf. 1816. (Patron, F. H. Cornwall, Esq; Tithe, 42*l* 10*s*; R.'s Inc. 100*l*; Pop. 36.) [6]

COWELL, George, *Lydgate Vicarage, Lees, Manchester.*—St. Bees; Deac. 1829, Pr. 1830. V. of Lydgate, Dio. Man. 1835. (Patron, V. of Rochdale; Glebe, 3 acres; V.'s Inc. 300*l* and Ho; Pop. 6124.) [7]

COWELL, Henry Von-der-Heyde, *Clifton Villa, Ford-street, Coventry.*—King's Coll. Lond. B.A. 1861; Deac. 1866 by Bp of Wor. C. of St. Michael's, Coventry, 1866. *The Theory of Vision Vindicated and Explained by the Right Rev. G. Berkeley, D.D.*, edited, with Annotations, Macmillan, 1860, 4s 6d. [8]

COWELL, M. B., *Ash Bocking, Needham, Suffolk.*—V. of Ash Bocking, Dio. Nor. 1862. (Patron, Ld Chan; Tithe—App. 3*l*, V. 375*l*; Glebe, 26¾ acres; V.'s Inc. 419*l* and Ho; Pop. 324.) [9]

COWIE, Benjamin Morgan, *Stoke House, Stoke d'Abernon, near Cobham, Surrey.*—St. John's Coll. Cam. Sen. Wrang. and B.A. 1839, M.A. 1842, B.D. 1855; Deac. 1841 and Pr. 1842 by Bp of Ely. Gresham Prof. of Geometry 1854; V. of St. Lawrence's, Jewry, with St. Mary Magdalen's, Milk-st. R. City and Dio. Lon. 1857. (Patrons, Ball. Coll. Ox. and D. and C. of St. Paul's, alt; V.'s Inc. 300*l*; Pop. 535.) Min. Can. of St. Paul's 1856; Chap. in Ordinary to the Queen; Warburtonian Lect. at Lincoln's-inn; one of H.M. Sch. Inspectors. Formerly Fell. of St. John's Coll. 1839; Moderator 1843; Principal of the Engineers' Coll. Putney, 1844–51; Select Preacher 1852; Hulsean Lecturer 1853–54. Author, *Catalogue of MSS. and Source Books in St. John's Coll. Cam. Library*, 4to, Parker, 1842; *Scripture Difficulties* (Hulsean Lecture for 1853, and 2nd Series, 1854), 2 vols. [10]

COWLARD, W., *Beaulieu, Southampton.*—C. of Beaulieu. [11]

COWPLAND, Robert, *Weeford Parsonage, Lichfield, Staffs.*—Dub. A.B. 1834, A.M. 1839; Deac. 1834 and Pr. 1835 by Bp of Lich. P. C. of Weeford with Hints P. C. Dio. Lich. 1844. (Patron, Bp of Lich; Weeford, Tithe, 903*l* 12*s* 9*d*; Glebe, 3 acres; Hints, Tithe—Eccles. Com. 522*l* 10*s*; P. C.'s. Inc. 198*l*; Pop. Weeford 399, Hints 290.) Formerly C. of Weeford and Hints 1834–44. [12]

COX, Charles William, *Malpas, Cheshire.*—Trin. Coll. Cam. B.A. 1852, M.A. 1855; Deac. 1854 and Pr. 1855 by Bp of Carl. R. of the Lower Mediety of Malpas, Dio. Ches. 1862. (Patron, T. T. Drake, Esq; Joint R.'s Tithe, 1632 2s 10d; Glebe, 31 acres; R.'s Inc. of Lower Med. 900*l* and Ho; Pop. 3370.) Formerly R. of Croxton, Dio. Lin. 1858–62; Chap. to the Forces at Sheffield, Portsmouth and Colchester, 1855–58. [13]

COX, Edward, *Luccombe Rectory, Minehead, Somerset.*—R. of Luccombe, Dio. B. and W. 1839. (Patron, Sir Thomas Dyke Acland, Bart; Tithe, 365*l*; Glebe, 60 acres; R.'s Inc. 470*l* and Ho; Pop. 474.) [14]

COX, Frederick, *Marlowes, Hemel Hempstead, Herts.*—Lin. Coll. Ox. B.A. 1818, M.A. 1819; Deac. 1819 and Pr. 1820 by Abp of Cant. P. C. of Upper Winchendon, Bucks, Dio. Ox. 1821. (Patron, Duke of Marlborough; Tithe, Imp. 351*l* 5*s*; P. C.'s Inc. 60*l*; Pop. 220.) Formerly Head Mast. of Aylesbury Free Gr. Sch. [15]

COX, Frederick, *Watford, Herts.*—Wad. Coll. Ox. B.A. 1852; Deac. 1853, Pr. 1855. P. C. of St. Andrew's, Watford, Dio. Roch. 1856. (Patrons, Trustees; Pop. 946.) Formerly C. of Woburn, Beds. [16]

COX, Frederic, 37, *Hurman-street, Kingsland-road, London, N.E.*—King's Coll. Lond. Theol. Assoc. 1866; Deac. 1866 and Pr. 1867 by Bp of Lon. C. of St. Stephen's, Spitalfields, 1866. [17]

COX, George William, *The Knoll, Cambridge Town, Farnborough Station.*—Trin. Coll. Ox. S.C.L. 1849, B.A. and M.A. 1859; Deac. 1850 by Bp of Ox. Pr. 1851 by Bp of Ex. Formerly C. of Salcombe Regis, Devon, 1850–51, St. Paul's, Exeter, 1854–57; Mast. in Cheltenham College 1860–61. Author, *Poems, Legendary, and Historical*, 1850; *Tales from Greek Mythology*, 1861; *The Great Persian War*, 1861; *Tales of the Gods and Heroes*, 1862; *Tales of Thebes and Argos*, 1864; Editor with Professor Brande of *Dictionary of Science, Literature, and Art*, all published by Longmans. [18]

COX, James, *Colchester.*—R. of Virley, near Colchester, Dio. Roch. 1840. (Patron, Rev. C. S. Coxwell; Tithe, 160*l* 10*s*; Glebe, 18 acres; R.'s Inc. 180*l*; Pop. 67.) C. of Salcott, Essex. [19]

COX, James, *Liverpool.*—Head Mast. of the Middle Sch. Liverpool. [20]

COX, James, *Halton Parsonage, Runcorn, Cheshire.*—Dub. A.B. 1836, A.M. 1846, *ad eund.* Ox. 1852; Deac. 1837, Pr. 1838. P. C. of Halton, Dio. Ches. 1850. (Patron, Sir R. Brooke; Tithe, App. 82*l* 16*s* 4*d*; P. C.'s Inc. 200*l* and Ho; Pop. 1541.) Surrogate. [21]

COX, James Septimus, *Litton Cheney, near Dorchester.*—Corpus Coll. Cam. Sen. Opt. and B.A. 1829, M.A. 1833; Deac. 1830 and Pr. 1831 by Bp of Lin. R. of Litton Cheney, Dio. Salis. 1833. (Patron, Ex. Coll. Ox; Tithe, 675*l*; Glebe, 120 acres; R.'s Inc. 800*l* and Ho; Pop. 501.) Formerly P. C. of Harpswell, Lincolnshire, 1830–33. [22]

COX, John, *Walgrave, near Northampton.*—St. Mary Hall, Ox. B.A. 1825, M.A. 1828; Deac. 1827, Pr. 1828. C. of Walgrave and Hannington, Northants. [23]

COX, John, *The Rectory, Wickerley, Yorks.*—Trin. Coll. Cam. B.A. 1858, M.A. 1861; Deac. 1861 and Pr. 1862 by Bp of Ches. R. of Wickerley, Dio. York, 1863. (Patron, the present R; Tithe, none; Glebe, 289 acres; R.'s Inc. 400*l* and Ho; Pop. 799.) Formerly C. of St. Mary's, Birkenhead, 1861, Woodchurch 1861-62; Asst. Min. and Lect. St. James's, Birkenhead, 1862–63. [24]

COX, J. Charles, *Paris.*—Dom. Chap. to Earl Cowley and Chap. of H.M.'s Embassy at Paris. [25]

COX, John Cooke, *Chilworthy House, Chard, Somerset.*—Trin. Coll. Cam. S.C.L. and B.C.L. 1838; Deac. 1839 and Pr. 1840 by Bp of B. and W. R. of Stocklinch Magdalen, Somerset, Dio. B. and W. 1848. (Patron, Rev. C. J. Allen; Tithe, 100*l* 8*s*; R.'s Inc. 143*l*; Pop. 116.) [26]

COX, John Edmund, F.S.A., 24, *Talbot-terrace, Westbourne-park, London, W.*—All Souls Coll. Ox. B.A. 1836, M.A. 1840; Deac. 1836, Pr. 1837. V. of St. Helen's, Bishopsgate, Dio. Lon. 1849. (Patrons, D. and C. of St. Paul's; V.'s Inc. 40*l*; Pop. 558.) Chairman of the Clergy Relief Society; Hon. Chap. to the West Middlesex Volunteers. Author, *Principles of the Reformation*; *Life of Archbishop Cranmer*; *Life of Luther*, R.T.S; *England's Danger and England's Duty* (a Sermon), 1850, 1*s*; various Sermons, Pamphlets, etc. Editor of *James's Bellam Papale*, 3*s* 6*d*; *James's Treatise of the Corruption of Scripture, Councils and Fathers, &c. for Maintenance of Popery, &c.* 12*s*; *Works of Archbishop Cranmer*, 2 vols. Parker Soc; *Townsend's Accusations of History against the Church of Rome*, 3*s* 6*d*; *Protestanism contrasted with Romanism*, 2 vols. 28*s*. [1]

COX, John Miles, *Misterton, Crewkerne, Somerset.*—Wor. Coll. Ox. B.A. 1839, M.A. 1844; Deac. and Pr. 1840 by Bp of Pet. V. of Misterton, Dio. B. and W. 1853. (Patrons, D. and C. of Win; Tithe—Imp. 205*l*, V. 17*l* 10*s*; Glebe, 43 acres; V.'s Inc. 180*l*; Pop. 588.) [2]

COX, John Sheffield, *Sibson, Atherstone, Leicestershire.*—Pemb. Coll. Ox. B.A. 1820, M.A. 1822. R. of Sibson, Dio. Pet. 1859. (Patron, Pemb. Coll. Ox; Tithe, 420*l* 2*s*; R.'s Inc. 1000*l* and Ho; Pop. 480.) Formerly Fell. of Pemb. Coll. Ox. [3]

COX, Joseph Mason, *Bishop's Tawton, Barnstaple.*—Lin. Coll. Ox. B.A. 1848, M.A. 1851; Deac. 1848, Pr. 1850. V. of Bishop's Tawton, Dio. Ex. 1866. (Patron, Bp of Ex; V.'s Inc. 500*l* and Ho; Pop. 830.) Formerly Head Mast. of Taunton Coll. Sch. and Asst. C. of Trinity, Taunton; Sub-Warden of St. Peter's Coll. Radley, 1853; C. of Rotherfield-Peppard 1850, Bradfield 1851; Vice-Prin. of the Theol. Coll. St. Mary Church, Devon, 1852 [4]

COX, Richardson, *Tickenhall, near Derby.*—Corpus Coll. Cam. Scho. of, M.A 1832; Deac. 1831 by Bp of Lich. Pr. 1832 by Bp of Nor. P. C. of Tickenhall, Dio. Lich. 1838. (Patron, Sir John Harper Crewe, Bart; Tithe, 50*l*; Glebe, 70 acres; P. C.'s Inc. 300*l*; Pop. 1068.) Chap. of the D. of Caulk, Derby, Dio. Lich. 1845. (Patron, Sir John Harper Crewe, Bart; Chap.'s Inc. 56*l*; Pop. 78.) [5]

COX, Robert Henry, *Hardingstone, Northampton.*—Dub. A.B. 1848; Deac. 1848 and Pr. 1849 by Bp of Rip. V. of Hardingstone, Dio. Pet. 1863. (Patron, Ld Chan; V.'s Inc. 555*l* and Ho; Pop. 1915.) Formerly V. of Duston, Dio. Pet. 1851–63. [6]

COX, Thomas, *Kimcote Rectory, Lutterworth, Leicestershire.*—Wor. Coll. Ox. B.A. 1825; Deac. 1826, Pr. 1827. R. of Kimcote, Dio. Pet. 1834. (Patron, Lord Willoughby de Broke; R.'s Inc. 566*l* and Ho; Pop. 501.) [7]

COX, Thomas, *Atherstone-upon-Stour, Stratford-on-Avon.*—Trin. Coll. Ox. B.A. 1811, M.A. 1813, D.D. 1824; Deac. 1811 and Pr. 1812 by Bp of Lich. R. of Atherstone-upon-Stour, Dio. Wor. 1814. (Patron, the present R; Tithe—App. 15*l*, R. 253*l*; Glebe, 11¾ acres; R.'s Inc. 290*l* and Ho; Pop. 90.) Formerly R. of Oxhill 1824–62. [8]

COX, Thomas, *The Heath, Halifax.*—St. John's Coll. Cam. Sen. Opt. 1st cl. Cl. Trip. B.A. 1845, M.A. 1848; Deac. 1855 and Pr. 1856 by Bp of Man. Mast. of Queen Elizabeth's Gr. Sch. Heath, 1861. Formerly Asst. Mast. of the Gr. Sch. Preston, 1850–55, and 2nd Mast. of same, 1855–58; Prin. of Avenham Sch. Preston, 1858–61. [9]

COX, Thomas, *Threapwood Parsonage, Wrexham.*—Deac. 1852 and Pr. 1853 by Bp of Ches. P. C. of Threapwood, Dio. St. A. 1854. (Patron, Bp of Ches; Glebe, 4 acres; P. C.'s Inc. 73*l* and Ho; Pop. 328.) Formerly C. of Waverton, Chester, 1852–55. [10]

COX, Thomas, *Monksilver Rectory, Taunton.*—Trin. Coll. Cam. B.A. 1846, M.A. 1850; Deac. 1850 by Bp of B. and W. Pr. 1851 by Bp of Salis. R. of Monksilver, Dio. B. and W. 1863. (Patrons, D. and C. of Windsor; Tithe, 210*l*; Glebe, 34 acres; R.'s Inc. 270*l* and Ho; Pop. 310.) Formerly C. of Timberscombe, Somerset, 1850, Farleigh Castle 1853; P. C. of Broomfield 1856; C. of West Ilsey, Berks, 1858; P. C. of Mollington, Oxon, 1861. [11]

COX, Thomas, 5, *Brixton Rise, Surrey, S.*—King's Coll. Lond. Theol. Assoc; Deac. 1860 and Pr. 1861 by Bp of Wor. C. of All Saints', Clapham Park, 1866. Formerly C. of Stockwell Chapel 1860; Asst. C. of St. Stephen's, South Lambeth, 1863. [12]

COX, William Hayward, *Eaton Bishop, Herefordshire.*—Pemb. Coll. Ox. 1st cl. Lit. Hum. 2nd cl. Math. and B.A. 1825, M.A. 1829; Deac. 1826 by Abp of Cashel. Pr. 1827 by Bp of Ox. R. of Eaton Bishop, Dio. Herf, 1854. (Patron, Bp of Herf; Tithe, 476*l* 18*s* 10*d*; Glebe, 35 acres; R.'s Inc. 450*l* and Ho; Pop. 463.) Rural Dean; Exam. Chap. to Bp of Herf. 1848; Preb. of Inkberrow in Herf. Cathl. 1854; Proctor in Convocation for the Dio. of St. D. 1853–55. Formerly R. of Carfax, Ox. 1839–52; Oxford Corporation Lect. 1849; R. of Tenby 1852–54; Vice-Prin. of St. Mary Hall, Ox. 1836; Public Cl. Examiner, Ox. 1831, 1834, 1835, 1836; Theol. Examiner 1842. Author, *The Propositions attributed by Prof. Pusey to Dr. Hampden compared with the Text of the Bampton Lectures*, 1836. [13]

COX, William Lamb, *Cautley, Sedbergh, Yorks.*—Magd. Hall. Ox. B.A. 1833, M.A. 1836; Deac. 1837, Pr. 1838. P. C. of Cautley with Dowbiggin, Dio. Rip. 1864. (Patron, V. of Sedbergh; P. C.'s Inc. 90*l*; Pop. 276.) Formerly P. C. of Heywood, Wilts, 1854; P. C. of Quarry Bank, Staffs, 1845–54; P. C. of Ashfield, Norfolk, 1862–64. [14]

COXE, Henry Octavius, 14, *Beaumont-street, Oxford.*—Corpus Coll. Ox. B.A. 1833, M.A. 1836; Deac. 1835, Pr. 1836. Librarian of the Bodleian Library, 1838; Chap. of Corpus Coll. Ox. 1845; C. of Wytham, Berks. Editor, *Rogeri de Wendover Chronica*, sumptibus Societat. Hist. Anglic. 5 vols. 1841–44; *Metrical Life of Edward the Black Prince, in French, by the Chandos Herald, with Translation and Notes*, 4to. Roxburghe Club, 1842; *Joh. Goweri "Vox Clamantis,"* 4to. ib. 1854. Author, *Catalogus Codd. MSS. Coll. et Aul. Oxon.* 2 vols. 4to. Univ. Press, 1852; *Catalogus Codd. MSS. Græcorum in Bibl. Bodl.* 4to. Univ. Press, 1853; *Catalogus Codd. MSS. Canonicorum Bibl. Bodl.* 4to. ib. 1854. [15]

COXHEAD, John James, *Fulham, S.W.*—Corpus Coll. Ox. 3rd cl. Lit. Hum. B.A. 1860, M.A. 1864; Deac. 1860 and Pr. 1861 by Bp of Lon. C. of Fulham 1863. Formerly C. of St. Clement's Danes, Westminster, 1860–63. [16]

COXHEAD, William Langston, *Kirby Vicarage, Colchester.*—Trin. Coll. Cam. B.A. 1836, M.A. 1839; Deac. 1836 by Bp of G. and B. Pr. 1837 by Bp of B. and W. V. of Kirby-le-Soken, Dio. Roch. 1862. (Patrons, Trustees; Tithe, comm. 230*l*; Glebe, 4 acres; V.'s Inc. 260*l* and Ho; Pop. 875.) Formerly C. of Ilfracombe 1836, Okehampton 1838, Kirby 1842. [17]

COXON, Mark, *Heswall Rectory, Neston, Cheshire.*—St. Bees; Deac. 1832 and Pr. 1833 by Bp of Ches. R. of Heswall, Dio. Ches. 1839. (Patrons, A. H. Davenport, Esq. and Richard Barker, Esq. alt; Tithe, 280*l*; Glebe, 30*l*; R.'s Inc. 310*l* and Ho; Pop. 778.) [18]

COXWELL, Charles Smith, *East Chinnock Rectory, Yeovil, Somerset.*—St. Bees; Deac. 1821 and Pr. 1822 by Bp of Ches. R. of East Chinnock, Dio. B. and W. 1839. (Patron, Ld Chan; Tithe, 147*l* 10*s*; Glebe, 43 acres; R.'s Inc. 200*l* and Ho; Pop. 552.) Formerly C. of Brigg, Cumberland, 1821–24, Yetminster, Dorset, 1824–27, Evershot, Dorset, 1827–40. [19]

COYTE, James, *Polstead Rectory (Suffolk), near Colchester.*—Caius Coll. Cam. B.A. 1818, M.A. 1821; Deac. 1819, Pr. 1820. R. of Polstead, Dio. Ely, 1840. (Patron, St. John's Coll. Ox; Tithe, 875*l*; Glebe, 17 acres; R.'s Inc. 940*l* and Ho; Pop. 922.) Surrogate. [20]

CRABBE, George.—Trin. Coll. Cam. B.A. 1807, M.A. 1811; Deac. 1808, Pr. 1809. Formerly R. of Bredfield with Lowdham, Suffolk, 1820–58. Author, *Life of the Rev. George Crabbe.* [21]

CRABBE, George, *Merton Rectory, Watton, Norfolk.*—Queens' Coll. Cam. B.A. 1842; Deac. 1842, Pr. 1843. R. of Merton, Dio. Nor. 1851. (Patron, Lord Walsingham; Tithe, 201*l* 14*s*; Glebe, 25¼ acres; R.'s Inc. 284*l* and Ho; Pop. 194.) Dom. Chap. to Lord Walsingham [22]

CRABTREE, Ely Willcox, *Museum-street, York.*—St. Cath. Coll. Cam. 8th Wrang. and B.A. 1858, M.A. 1862; Deac. 1861 and Pr. 1862 by Bp of Ely. H.M. Inspector of Schools 1867. Formerly Pres. Dean and Fell. of St. Cath. Coll. Cambridge. [1]

CRACROFT, Robert Wentworth, *Harrington, Spilsby, Lincolnshire.*—Ball Coll. Ox. B.A. 1846; Deac. 1849, Pr. 1850. R. of Harrington, Dio. Lin. 1850. (Patron, Rev. Sir H. J. Ingilby, Bart; Tithe, 243*l*; Glebe, 40½ acres; R.'s Inc. 310*l* and Ho; Pop. 104.) R. of Brinkhill, Dio. Lin. 1850. (Patron, Rev. Sir H. J. Ingilby, Bart; R.'s Inc. 155*l*; Pop. 175.) [2]

CRADOCK, Edward Hartopp, *Brasenose College, Oxford.*—Brasen. Coll. Ox. B.A. 1831, M.A. 1834, B.D. and D.D. 1854; Deac. 1834 and Pr. 1835 by Bp of Ox. Prin. of Brasen. Coll. Ox. 1853. [3]

CRADOCK, L., *Lynn Regis.*—C. of St. Margaret's, Lynn Regis. [4]

CRAGG, Stephen, *Coventry.*—Magd. Hall, Ox. B.A. 1826, M.A. 1828. P. C. of St. Thomas's, Coventry, Dio. Wor. 1846. (Patrons, the Crown and Bp of Wor. alt; P. C.'s Inc. 300*l*; Pop. 5496.) [5]

CRAIG, Allen Tudor, *Bordighera, North Italy.*—Wad. Coll. Ox. B.A. 1858; Deac. 1859 and Pr. 1860 by Bp of Lon. English Chap. at Bordighera. Formerly C. of Morcott, Rutland. [6]

CRAIG, Bernard Riccarton.—Magd. Hall, Ox. B.A. 1861, M.A. 1864; Deac. 1863 by Bp of Win. Formerly C. of Sholing 1862, and Bitterne, Hants, 1863. [7]

CRAIG, Herbert Tudor, *Aldershot.*—Magd. Hall, Ox. B.A. 1855; Deac. 1855 and Pr. 1856 by Abp of Cant. Chap. to the Forces, Aldershot. Formerly C. of Ch. Ch. Southampton, 1857–59, Folkestone 1855–57, Trinity, Dover, 1859–65. [8]

CRAIG, James, *Albrighton, Shrewsbury.*—Magd. Hall, Ox. B.A. 1851, M.A. 1855; Deac. 1851 and Pr. 1852. P. C. of Albrighton, Dio. Lich. 1863. (Patron, W. Sparrier, Esq; P. C.'s Inc. 52*l* and Ho; Pop. 78.) [9]

CRAIG, John, *Leamington.*—Dub. A.B. 1827, A.M. 1832, *ad eund* Cam. 1834; Deac. 1829 and Pr. 1830 by Bp. of Elphin. V. of Leamington Priors, Dio. Wor. 1839. (Patroness, Mrs. Eliz. Wise; Tithe, 39*l* 17*s* 6*d*; Glebe, 23 acres; V.'s Inc. 500*l*; Pop. 13,421.) Formerly R. of Fetcham, Surrey, 1836–39. Author, *Comforts for Mourners,* a vol. of Sermons; *The Pathway of Resignation,* 4 eds; *Astral Wonders*; *Things in Heaven, and Things on the Earth, and Things in the Waters under the Earth*; various Letters, Sermons, Tracts, etc. [10]

CRAIG, John Kershaw, *Burley, Ringwood, Hants.*—Magd. Hall, Ox. B.A. 1828. P. C. of Burley, Dio. Win. (Patron, Bp of Win; P. C.'s Inc. 120*l*; Pop. 672.) [11]

CRAIG, Stewart Baillie, *St. Mark's Parsonage, Hull.*—Dub. A.B. 1849; Deac. 1850 by Bp of Limerick, Pr. 1851 by Bp of Cork. P. C. of St. Mark's, Hull, Dio. York, 1866. (Patrons, Crown and Abp of York alt; P. C.'s Inc. 300*l* and Ho; Pop 7172.) Formerly C. of St. Munchin's, Limerick, 1850, St. John's, Hull, 1852; Min. of Mariners' Ch. Hull, 1856. [12]

CRAKANTHORP, Charles Churchill, *Castle-Bytham, Stamford.*—Lin. Coll. Ox. B.A. 1845, M.A. 1848; Deac. 1845 and Pr. 1846 by Bp of Win. V. of Castle-Bytham, Dio. Lin. 1858. (Patrons, D. and C. of Lin; V.'s Inc. 200*l*; Pop. 875.) Formerly C. of Navenby, Linc. Author, *Three Tracts to the Parishioners of Navenby*; *A Club Sermon.* [13]

CRAKE, The Very Rev. Edward Neville, *The Deanery, Battle, Sussex.*—Trin. Coll. Cam. B.A. 1848, M.A. 1851; Deac. 1850 and Pr. 1851 by Bp of Lon. Dean and V. of Battle, Dio. Chich. 1863. (Patron, Duke of Cleveland; Tithe, comm. 450*l*, Modus on town, 220*l*; Rent from Glebe, 68*l* 14*s* 10*d*; V.'s Inc. 738*l* 14*s* 10*d*; Pop. 2793.) Formerly C. of All Saints, Knightsbridge, Lond. 1850–61. [14]

CRALLAN, Thomas Edward, *Warminster, Wilts.*—Emman. Coll. Cam. B.A. 1849, M.A. 1857; Deac. 1849 and Pr. 1850 by Bp of Chich. Head Mast. of Lord Weymouth's Sch. Warminster, 1857. Formerly 2nd Mast. of Lewes Gr. Sch. 1849–51; C. of Newick, Sussex, 1851–57. [15]

CRANBROOK, James, *Wolverhampton.*—C. of St. Mary's, Wolverhampton. [16]

CRANMER, H. Gordon, *Bothal, Morpeth.*—C. of Bothal. [17]

CRASS, William, *Northchurch, Berkhampstead, Herts.*—Dur. B.A. and Licen. in Theol. 1858; Deac. 1858 and Pr. 1859 by Bp of Dur. C. of Northchurch. Formerly C. of Bedlington, Northumberland, 1858, Kettering 1864. [18]

CRASTER, Thomas Henry, *Gainsborough.*—Univ. Coll. Ox. B.A. 1857, M.A. 1860; Deac. 1860 and Pr. 1861 by Bp of Lin. C. of Gainsborough. Formerly C. of St. John's, Mansfield, 1860. [19]

CRAUFURD, Charles Henry, *Old Swinford Rectory, Stourbridge, Worcestershire.*—Magd. Hall, Ox. B.A. 1831, M.A. 1833; Deac. 1830 and Pr. 1831 by Bp of Lich. R. of Old Swinford, Dio. Wor. 1835. (Patron, Earl of Dudley; Tithe, 220*l*; Glebe, 350 acres; R.'s Inc. 980*l* and Ho; Pop. 2749.) [20]

CRAUFURD, Sir George William, Bart., *Burgh Hall, Spilsby, Lincolnshire.*—Queens' Coll. Cam. B.A. 1819, M.A. 1831; Deac. 1820 by Bp of Glouc. Pr. 1822 by Bp of B. and W. R. of Scremby, Linc. Dio. Lin. 1862. (Patron, Rev. H. Brackenbury; Corn Rent, 150*l*; Glebe, 33 acres; R.'s Inc. 199*l*; Pop. 184.) Formerly Chap. to the Hon. E.I.C. on the Bengal Establishment 1822–33; Div. Lect. in King's Coll. Cam. 1831–38; V. of Burgh 1838–45. Author, *Examination Questions on Butler's Analogy*; Similar Works designed as Helps to Students in Divinity Examinations at the University. [21]

CRAVEN, Charles, *Spexhall Rectory, Haselworth, Suffolk.*—St. John's Coll. Cam. Wrang. and B.A. 1819, M.A. 1825; Deac. 1820, Pr. 1822. R. of Spexhall, Dio. Nor. 1847. (Patron, Ld Chan; Tithe, 297*l* 4*s*; Glebe, 45½ acres; R.'s Inc. 360*l* and Ho; Pop. 181.) Formerly Sen. Prof. of Bishop's Coll. Calcutta. Author, Sermons on several occasions; *The Present State and Future Prospects of Christianity,* 1830; *The Providential Preservation of our Most Gracious Queen from the late Traitorous Attempt upon Her Life,* 1842; *Church Extension,* 1843. [22]

CRAVEN, Charles Audley Assheton, *Sheffield.*—St. Peter's Coll. Cam. B.A. 1852, M.A. 1857; Deac. 1852 and Pr. 1853 by Bp of Nor. Chap. to the Forces, Sheffield. Formerly Asst. Chap. to the Forces in the Crimea, 1855–56; C. of Carlton, Suffolk, 1852–55. Author, *Adventures of a Gentleman in Search of the Church of England*; *The Rite of Holy Baptism.* [23]

CRAVEN, Dacre, *Isleworth, W.*—St. John's Coll. Ox. Craven Scho. (Founder's Kin) B.A. 1855, M.A. 1857; Deac. 1855 and Pr. 1856 by Bp of Lon. C. of Isleworth 1866. Formerly C. of St. Thomas's, Bethnal-green, 1855; P. C. of Chantry, Somerset, 1859. [24]

CRAVEN, Samuel, *Heckington, near Sleaford.* Sid. Coll. Cam. B.A. 1855, M.A. 1863; Deac. 1855 and Pr. 1856 by Bp of Wor. C. of Heckington 1863. Formerly C. of Stourport 1½ years, Walsall 5½ years. [25]

CRAWFORD, Charles John, *Woodmansterne Rectory, near Epsom, Surrey.*—Wad. Coll. Ox. B.A. 1832, M.A. 1834, B.D. and D.D. 1847; Deac. 1832, Pr. 1833. R. of Woodmansterne, Dio. Win. 1834. (Patron, Ld Chan; Tithe, 377*l* 5*s* 1½*d*; Glebe, 13 acres; R.'s Inc. 460*l* and Ho; Pop. 271.) Author, *Against the Marriage of a Widower with his deceased Wife's Sister* (a Pamphlet), 1849. [26]

CRAWFORD, William Andrew, *Shalden Rectory, near Alton, Hants.*—Ex. Coll. Ox. B.A. 1853, M.A. 1856; Deac. 1855 and Pr. 1856 by Bp of Win. R. of Shalden, Dio. Win. 1859. (Patron, Ld Chan; Tithe, 335*l*; Glebe, 23 acres; R.'s Inc. 360*l* and Ho; Pop. 185.) Formerly C. of All Saints', Southampton, 1856–57, Hamble-le-Rice 1857–59. [27]

CRAWFORD, William H., *St. Peter's College, Cambridge.*—Fell. of St. Peter's Coll. [28]

CRAWFURD, Charles Walter Payne, *East Court, East Grinstead, Sussex.*—Brasen. Coll. Ox. B.A. 1847, M.A. 1850; Deac. 1850, Pr. 1851. Formerly C. of Bourton-on-Water, 1858, Snettisham, Norfolk, Chievely, Berks, Great Chart, Kent, Westbury-on-Severn, Glouc. [1]

CRAWHALL, Septimus J., *Watford, Herts.* Magd. Coll. Ox. B.A. 1862; Deac. 1862, Pr. 1863. C. of Watford 1866. Formerly C. of Trinity, Gainsborough, 1863–64, St. Mary's, West Brompton, 1865. [2]

CRAWLEY, Charles David.—Ch. Ch. Ox. B.A. 1858, M.A. 1865; Deac. 1860 and Pr. 1862 by Bp of Salis. Formerly C. of Warminster 1860–67. [3]

CRAWLEY, Charles Yonge, *Grey Friars, Gloucester.*—Oriel Coll. Ox. B.A. 1835, M.A. 1848; Deac. 1837, Pr. 1838. R. of Taynton, Dio. G. and B. 1864. (Patrons, D. and C. of Glouc; Tithe—App. 27*l*, R. 444*l* 19*s* 4*d*; Glebe, 22 acres; R.'s Inc. 460*l*; Pop. 689.) Min. Can. of Glouc. Cathl. 1841 (Value, 150*l*). Chap. to the Glouc. Infirmary 1845; Surrogate 1853. [4]

CRAWLEY, Edmund Jones, *Moncton-Combe, near Bath.*—Jesus Coll. Ox. B.A. 1813, M.A. 1818; Deac. 1814 and Pr. 1815 by Bp of Ex. Preb. of Taunton in Wells Cathl. 1840. [5]

CRAWLEY, Henry, *Stow-Nine-Churches Rectory, Weedon, Northants.*—Ball. Coll. Ox. B.A. 1831, M.A. 1834. R. of Stow-Nine-Churches, Dio. Pet. 1849. (Patron, W. Gibbs, Esq; Tithe—Imp. 133*l* 0*s* 4*d*, R. 500*l* 7*s*; Glebe, 97 acres; R.'s Inc. 720*l* and Ho; Pop. 353.) [6]

CRAWLEY, Henry Owen, *Semington, Trowbridge.*—St. John's Coll. Cam. B.A. 1844; Deac. 1845 by Bp of B. and W. Pr. 1846 by Bp of Llan. C. of Semington; Chap. of the Melksham Union. Formerly C. of St. Helen's, Abingdon, 1856; Wigglesworth Lect. Abingdon, 1857; C. of Monksilver, Somerset. [7]

CRAWLEY, Richard, *Steeple Ashton, Trowbridge, Wilts.*—Trin. Coll. Cam. 1st sen. Opt. and B.A. 1814, M.A. Magd. Coll. 1817; Deac. 1815 and Pr. 1816 by Bp of Ely. V. of Steeple Ashton with Semington C. 1828. (Patron, the Mast. of Magd. Coll. Cam; Tithe—App. 21*l* 17*s*, Imp. 673*l* 10*s*, V. 820*l*; Glebe, 18 acres; V.'s Inc. 846*l*; Pop. Ashton Steeple 964, Semington 489.) Preb. of Ruscomb Southbury in Salis. Cathl. 1843. Formerly Fell. and Tut. of Magd. Coll. Cam. 1815–28; Preacher at Whitehall 1827–28; Rural Dean of Potterne 1838–54. [8]

CRAWLEY, Robert Evans, *Potterspury Vicarage, Stony Stratford, Northants.*—Magd. Hall, Ox. B.A. 1844, M.A. 1848; Deac. 1844 and Pr. 1845 by Bp of Salis. V. of Potterspury, Dio. Pet. 1852. (Patron, Earl of Bathurst; Tithe, Imp. 42*l* 6*s* 8*d*; Glebe, 46 acres; V.'s Inc. 114*l* and Ho; Pop. 1710.) C. of Furthoe, Northants; Surrogate. [9]

CRAWLEY, Robert Townsend, *Cressing, Braintree, Essex.*—Ch. Ch. Coll. Ox. B.A. 1855, Stud. at Wells Theol. Coll. 1855, M.A. 1858; Deac. 1855 and Pr. 1856 by Bp of B. and W. V. of Cressing, Dio. Roch. 1866. (Patron, V. of Witham; V.'s Inc. 250*l* and Ho; Pop. 582.) Formerly C. of Huntspill 1856, Witham 1857–63, Cressing 1864 66. [10]

CRAWLEY, Thomas William, *Heyford, Weedon, Northants.*—Magd. Hall, Ox. B.A. 1848, M.A. 1851; Deac. 1849 by Bp of Dur. Pr. 1851 by Bp of Pet. R. of Heyford, Dio. Pet. 1851. (Patron, the present R; Tithe, 150*l*; Glebe, 50 acres; R.'s Inc. 315*l* and Ho; Pop. 807.) Formerly Asst. C. of Houghton-le-Spring 1849. [11]

CRAWLEY, The Ven. William, *Bryngwyn Rectory, Newport, Monmouthshire.*—Magd. Coll. Cam. Wrang. and B.A. 1824, M.A. 1827; Deac. 1825 and Pr. 1826 by Bp of Ely. R. of Bryngwyn, Dio. Llan. 1834. (Patron, Earl of Abergavenny; Tithe—Imp. 66*l*, R. 171*l* 10*s*; Glebe, 49 acres; R.'s Inc. 211*l* and Ho; Pop. 313.) Archd. of Monmouth 1844 (Val. 32*l*). Can. of Llandaff 1858 (Val. 350*l*). Formerly R. of Llanvihangel Yaterne Llewerne, Monmouthshire, 1831–58. Author, Charges, 1847, 1849, 1852, 1853; Sermons, etc. [12]

CREE, Edward David, *Upper Tooting, Surrey.*—Oriel Coll. Ox. B.A. 1849. M.A. 1852; Deac. 1850, Pr. 1851. P. C. of Trinity, Upper Tooting, Dio. Win. 1855. (Patron, R. of Streatham; P. C.'s Inc. 250*l*; Pop. 1055.) Author, *Dr. Tye's Motlets for Four Voices; Church Psalm Tunes, exclusively from ancient sources*, 2*s*; *The Threshold of the Sanctuary, a Devotional Manual for Candidates for Holy Orders, containing Offices for each day in Ember-week, with an Appendix of Appropriate Readings*, 2*s*. [13]

CREE, James, *Ower Moigne, near Dorchester.*—Corpus Coll. Cam. B.C.L; Deac. 1840, Pr. 1841. V. of Chaldon-Herring, Dorset, Dio. Salis. 1844. (Patron, Edward Weld, Esq; Lulworth Castle; Tithe—Imp. 170*l* and 115 acres of Glebe, V. 9*l*; Glebe, 2 acres; V.'s Inc. 63*l*; Pop. 341.) [14]

CREE, John Adams, *Great Marlow.*—Magd. Coll. Ox. Fell. of, 2nd cl. Cl. 1st cl. Math. et Phy. and B.A. 1847, M.A. 1849; Deac. 1848 and Pr. 1849 by Bp of Win. V. of Great Marlow with Trinity C. Dio. Ox. 1867. (Patron, Bp of Ox; V.'s Inc. 300*l* and Ho; Pop. 4198.) Formerly C. of St Mary's, Dover, 1852, Upton with Chalvey 1858. [15]

CREE, John Robert, *Ower Moigne, Dorchester.* [16]

CREED, Henry Keyworth, *Chedburgh Rectory, Bury St. Edmunds.*—Ch. Coll. Cam. B.A. 1853; Deac. 1854 by Bp of Down and Connor, Pr. 1855 by Bp of Nor. R. of Chedburgh, Dio. Ely, 1864. (Patron, Marquis of Bristol; Glebe, 49 acres; R.'s Inc. 198*l* and Ho; Pop. 300.) Formerly C. of Carlton Colville 1854; P. C. of Derwent 1856; C. of Great Saxham 1858, Monewden 1862. [17]

CREEK, Edward Basnett, *Swanmore Parsonage, Bishops Waltham.*—Dub. A.B. 1838, A.M. 1845; Deac. 1838 and Pr. 1839 by Bp of Ches. P. C. of Swanmore, Dio. Win. 1847. (Patron, the R. of Droxford; Tithe, 50*l*; Glebe, 12*l* 10*s*; P. C.'s Inc. 160*l* and Ho; Pop. 849.) Formerly C. of Preston Patrick 1838–39, Paignton 1842–43, Kings Kerswell 1844–46. [18]

CREENY, William Frederick, *St. Helena.*—St. John's Coll. Cam. B.A. 1853; Deac. 1853 by Bp of Ely, Pr. 1854 by Bp of Nor. Chap. to Bp of St. Helena. Formerly Sen. C. of Wellingborough, and St. Mark's, Lakenham, Norfolk. [19]

CREESER, John, *Redlynch, Bruton, Somerset.*—C. of Redlynch. [20]

CREIGHTON, Archibald, *Great Grimsby, Lincolnshire.*—Lin. Coll. Ox. 2nd cl. Lit. Hum. and B.A. 1810, M.A. 1817; Deac. 1812 and Pr. 1814 by Bp of Lich. V. of Stallingborough, Co. and Dio. Lin. 1836. (Patron, Bp of Lin; Tithe—App. 68*l* 6*s* 9*d*, Imp. 167*l* 15*s* 6*d*; V.'s Inc. 120*l*; Pop. 433.) [21]

CREIGHTON, George, *Arkendale Parsonage, Knaresborough.*—St. Bees; Deac. 1844 and Pr. 1845 by Bp of Ches. P. C. of Arkendale, Dio. Rip. 1845. (Patron, V. of Knaresborough; P. C.'s Inc. 199*l* and Ho; Pop. 242.) [22]

CREMER, Cremer, *Beeston, Cromer, Norfolk.*—R. of Beeston-Regis, Dio. Nor. 1832. (Patron, the Duchy of Lancaster; Tithe, 136*l*; Glebe, 4 acres; R.'s Inc. 139*l*; Pop. 196.) [23]

CREMER, Robert Marler, *North Barningham, North Walsham.*—Corpus Coll. Cam. B.A. 1822; Deac. 1823, Pr. 1824. R. of North Barningham, Dio. Nor. 1844. (Patron, W. H. Windham, Esq; Tithe, 164*l* 9*s* 2*d*; Glebe, 14 acres; R.'s Inc. 185*l* and Ho; Pop. 30.) [24]

CRESER, John, *St. Colan Vicarage, near St. Columb, Cornwall.*—St. Bees; Deac. 1821 and Pr. 1822 by Abp of York. V. of St. Colan, Dio. Ex. 1837. (Patron, Bp. of Ex; Tithe—Imp. 110*l*, V. 145*l*; Glebe, 15 acres; V.'s Inc. 165*l* and Ho; Pop. 255.) [25]

CRESSWELL, George Sackville, *Posbury, Crediton.*—P. C. of Posbury, Devon, Dio. Ex. (Patron, J. H. Hipperley, Esq.) Formerly C. of Winkleigh, North Devon. [26]

CRESSWELL, Oswald Joseph, *Hanworth Rectory, Hounslow, Middlesex.*—Corpus Coll. Ox. M.A. 1827; Deac. 1826, Pr. 1827. R. of Hanworth, Dio. Lon.

1846. (Patron, Algernon Perkins, Esq; Glebe, 276 acres; R.'s Inc. 545l and Ho; Pop. 763.) [1]

CRESSWELL, Thomas Trenham, *Steeple Vicarage, Maldon, Essex.*—Trin. Coll Cam. B.A. 1824; Deac. 1825 by Bp of Chich. Pr. 1827 by Bp of Lon. V. of Steeple with Stangate, Dio. Roch. 1838. (Patrons, Sir B. W. Bridges, Bart, and I. T. Hunt, Esq. alt; Tithe—Imp. 387l 9s 11d, V. 160l 11s 3d; Glebe, 30 acres; V.'s Inc. 180l and Ho; Pop. 539.) [2]

CRESSWELL, William Francis, *St. Arvan's, Chepstow, Monmouthshire.*—Pemb. Coll. Ox. Exhib. of, 1834, B.A. 1838, M.A. 1840; Deac. 1840, Pr. 1841. P. C. of St. Arvan's, Dio. Llan. 1842. (Patron, Duke of Beaufort; Tithe—Imp. 22l 1s 4d, App. 55l 9s; Glebe, from Queen Anne's Bounty, 38 acres; P. C.'s Inc. 54l; Pop. 379.) [3]

CRESWELL, Henry, *Clun, Shrewsbury.*—St. Cath. Coll. Cam. B.A. 1846; Deac. 1848 and Pr. 1849 by Bp of Ox. P. C. of Newcastle, Clun, Dio. Herf. 1855. (Patron, Earl Powis; Tithe, 117l 4s 9d; Glebe, 2 acres; P. C.'s Inc. 122l; Pop. 580.) Formerly C. of Cookham-Dean, Berks. [4]

CRESWELL, Richard H., *Stockport.*—P. C. of St. Peter's, Stockport, Dio. Ches. 1842. (Patron, Rev. H. Wright; P. C.'s Inc. 250l; Pop. 4455.) [5]

CRESWELL, Samuel, *Vicarage, Radford, Notts.*—St. John's Coll. Cam. B.A. 1827, M.A. 1830; Deac. 1828 and Pr. 1829 by Abp of York. V. of Radford, Dio. Lin. 1840. (Patron, Ld Chan; Glebe, 57 acres; V.'s Inc. 300l; Pop. 6338.) Surrogate. [6]

CRESWELL, Samuel Francis, F.R.G.S., F.R.A.S., *Grammar School, Dartford, Kent.*—St. John's Coll. Cam. Sen. Opt. and B.A. 1859, M.A. 1862; Deac. 1860 and Pr. 1861 by Abp of Cant. Head Mast. of Dartford Gr. Sch. and Chap. of Kent County Penitentiary 1866. Formerly Mast. of Tonbridge Gr. Sch. and C. of Hildenborough 1859–62; Sen. Math. Mast. of Cathl. Sch. Durham 1862–65; Acting Mast. of Lancaster Gr. Sch. and C. in sole charge of Ch. Ch. Lancaster, 1865–66. Author, *Collections towards the History of Printing in Nottinghamshire*, 1863, 4to, 2s. Contributor to *Annals of Nottinghamshire*, 4 vols, 1853; *Notes on the Early Typography of Nottinghamshire* in Allen's *Illustrated Hand-Book*, 1866. [7]

CREWDSON, G.—C. of All Saints', Mile-end, Stepney, Middlesex. [8]

CREWE Henry Harpur, *Drayton-Beauchamp, Tring, Bucks.*—Trin. Coll. Cam. B.A. 1851, M.A. 1855; Deac. 1856 and Pr. 1857 by Bp. of Nor. R. of Drayton-Beauchamp, Dio. Ox. 1860. (Patrons, S. W. Jenney and A. H. Jenney, Esqs; R.'s Inc. about 300l; Pop. 268.) Formerly C. of Drinkstone and Greeting St. Peter's. [9]

CREYKE, Robert, *Edlington, Doncaster.*—R. of Edlington, Dio. York, 1844. (Patron, W. B. Wrightson, Esq; Tithe, 268l 12s; Glebe, 51 acres; R.'s Inc. 335l; Pop. 149.) [10]

CREYKE, The Ven. Stephen, *Bolton Percy Tadcaster.*—Corpus Coll. Ox. 1st cl. Lit. Hum. and B.A. 1816, M.A. 1819; Deac. 1820 and Pr. 1821 by Abp of York. R. of Bolton Percy, Dio. York, 1865. (Patron, Abp of York; R.'s Inc. 1500l and Ho; Pop. 1200.) Can. Res. of York 1857. Formerly R. of Beeford, Yorks, 1844–65; Archd. of York 1847–67. [11]

CRICHLOW, Henry McIntosh, *Alfington, Honiton, Devon.*—Trin. Coll. Cam. B.A. 1827, M.A. 1834; Deac. 1833 by Bp of Ex. Pr. 1834 by Bp of B. and W. C. of St. James's, Ottery St. Mary, 1862. Formerly C. of Radipole, Dorset, 1841–50, Puddletown, Dorset, 1858–60. [12]

CRICK, Frederic Charles, *Little Thurlow Rectory (Suffolk), near Newmarket.*—St. John's Coll. Cam. B.A. 1830, M.A. 1833; Deac. 1830 and Pr. 1831 by Bp of Nor. R. of Little Thurlow, Dio. Ely, 1848. (Patroness, Mrs. Soame; Tithe, 402l 8s 9d; Glebe, 80 acres; R.'s Inc. 500l and Ho; Pop. 369.) [13]

CRICK, Thomas, *Staplehurst Rectory, Cranbrook, Kent.*—R. of Staplehurst, Dio. Cant. 1843. (Patron, St. John's Coll. Cam; Tithe, 1200l; Glebe, 1 acre; R.'s Inc. 1202l and Ho; Pop. 1695.) [14]

CRICKMER, William Burton, *Beverley, Yorks.*—St. Edm. Hall, Ox. B.A. 1855, M.A. 1858; Deac. 1855 and Pr. 1856 by Bp of Lon. P. C. of Beverley-Minster, Dio. York, 1864. (Patrons, Simeon's Trustees.) C. of St. John's Chapel, Beverley. Formerly C. of St. John's, Deptford, 1855–57, St. Marylebone 1857–58; Missionary (the Pioneer) in British Columbia 1858–62; Assoc. Sec. Colonial and Continental Ch. Soc. 1862–64. Author, *The Ecclesiastical History of Beverley-Minster* (a Paper read before the Yorkshire Architectural Society), 1865. [15]

CRIDGE, Edward, *Vancouver's Island.*—St. Peter's Coll. Cam. B.A. 1848; Deac. 1848, Pr. 1849. Chap. to the Hudson's Bay Co; Chap. at Vancouver's Island 1854. Formerly C. of North Walsham, Norfolk, 1848, West Ham 1851; P. C. of Ch. Ch. West Ham, 1852. [16]

CRIDLAND, Alexander, *Hensall Parsonage, Snaith, Yorks.*—P. C. of Hensall with Heck, Dio. York, 1853. (Patron, Viscount Downe; P. C.'s Inc. 125l and Ho; Pop. 633.) [17]

CRIPPS, Charles, *Stone Parsonage, Berkeley, Glouc.*—Magd. Hall, Ox. 4th cl. Lit. Hum. B.A. 1842, M.A. 1852; Deac. 1842 and Pr. 1843 by Bp of G. and B. P. C. of Stone, Dio. G. and B. 1848. (Patron, V. of Berkeley; Glebe, 8 acres; P. C.'s Inc. 80l and Ho; Pop. 277.) [18]

CRIPPS, John Marten, *Great Yeldham Rectory, Halstead, Essex.*—R. of Great Yeldham, Dio. Roch. 1843. (Patrons, Exors. of Sir W. B. Rush; Tithe, 507l 6s; Glebe, 41 acres; R.'s Inc. 561l and Ho; Pop. 696.) [19]

CRIPPS, William Richard, *Lenton, Nottingham.*—Ch. Coll. Cam. Jun. Opt B.A. 1860; Deac. 1860 and Pr. 1861 by Bp of Ches. C. of Lenton 1867. Formerly C. of Little St. John's, Chester, 1860–64, Clifton, Derbyshire, 1864–67. [20]

CRISFORD, Alexander Thomas, *Great Shelford Vicarage, Cambs.*—Trin. Coll. Cam. Jun. Opt. and B.A. 1845, M.A. 1848; Deac. 1846 and Pr. 1848 by Bp of Ely. V. of Great Shelford, Dio. Ely, 1852. (Patron, Bp of Ely; Glebe, 1 acre; V.'s Inc. 90l and Ho; Pop. 1006.) [21]

CRISPIN, James Vaughan, *Nantwich, Cheshire.*—King's Coll. Lond. Gen Assoc. 1859, Theol. Assoc. 1860, 1st cl. Royal Coll. of Preceptors 1857; Deac. 1863 and Pr. 1864 by Bp of Ches. Head Mast. of Nantwich Gr. Sch. 1866. Formerly C. of Crewe 1863. [22]

CROCKER, James, *Felsted, Essex.*—Trin. Coll. Cam. Sen. Opt. B A. 1825, M.A. 1828; Deac. 1825 and Pr. 1826 by Bp of Lon. Formerly 2nd Mast. of Felsted Sch. 1826. Author, *Essentials of Hebrew Grammar*, 1s 6d; *Theory, &c., of the Latin Subjunctive Mode*; *Exercises for the Latin Subjunctive Mode*, 3s 6d; *A New Proposal for a Geographical System of Measures and Weights conveniently introducible generally by retaining familiar notions and familiar names, to which are added Remarks on Systems of Coinage*, Lond. 1864. [23]

CROCKER, William Foord, *Brandon Ferry Rectory, Brandon, Suffolk.*—Trin. Hall, Cam. B.A. 1856, M.A. 1859; Deac. 1858 and Pr. 1859 by Bp of Ex. R. of Brandon Ferry with Wangford, Dio. Ely, 1865. (Patron, T. E. Cartwright, Esq; R.'s Inc. 570l and Ho; Pop. Brandon Ferry 2218, Wangford 50.) Formerly C. of Sidmouth, Devon, 1858–61, Chardstock All Saints, Dorset, 1861–65. [24]

CROCKETT, Herbert Frederick, *Poulshot, Devizes.*—Trin. Coll. Ox. B.A. 1851; Deac. 1852 and Pr. 1854 by Bp of Llan. C. of Poulshot 1864. Formerly C. of Codford St. Mary and Mappowder. [25]

CROCKETT, John Molyneux, *Withernwick Vicarage, Hull.*—Deac. and Pr. 1841. V. of Withernwick, Dio. York, 1864. (Patron, Dean of Lich; Tithe, 47l; Glebe, 96 acres; V.'s Inc. 210l and Ho; Pop. 499.) Surrogate. Formerly C. of Tattenhill, Staffs, 1843–64. [26]

CROCKETT, Robert Princep, *Eccleston Parsonage, Prescot, Lancashire.*—Brasen. Coll. Ox. B.A. 1837; Deac. and Pr. 1838. P. C. of Ch. Ch. Eccleston,

Dio. Ches. 1838. (Patron, S. Taylor, Esq; Tithe, Imp. 192*l*; P. C.'s Inc. 110*l* and Ho; Pop. 2328.) [1]

CROFT, The Ven. James, *Saltwood Rectory, Hythe, Kent.*—St. John's Coll. Cam. B.A. 1807, M.A. 1808; Deac. 1810, Pr. 1811. R. of Saltwood, Dio. Cant. 1812. (Patron, Abp of Cant; Tithe, 685*l*; Glebe, 60 acres; R.'s Inc. 760*l* and Ho; Pop. 643.) R. of Cliffe-at-Hoo, Kent, Dio. Roch. 1818. (Patron, Abp of Cant; Tithe, 1383*l* 5*s* 11*d*; Glebe, 8 acres; R.'s Inc. 1399*l* and Ho; Pop. 980.) Can. Res. of Cant. Cathl. 1822, annexed to Archd. (Value, 900*l* and Res.) Archd. of Cant. 1825 (Value, 146*l* 15*s*.) [2]

CROFT, James Halls, *Timberscombe Vicarage, Dunster, Somerset.*—V. of Timberscombe, Dio. B. and W. 1853. (Patron, Bp of B. and W; Tithe—App. 174*l* 8*s* 2*d*, V. 146*l*; V.'s Inc. 175*l* and Ho; Pop. 434.) [3]

CROFT, John, *Catterick Vicarage, Yorks.*—Trin. Coll. Cam. 11th Wrang. and B.A. 1814, M.A. 1817; Deac. 1818, Pr. 1819. V. of Catterick, Dio. Rip. 1841. (Patron, Bp of Rip; Tithe—App. 114*l*, Imp. 1421*l* 5*s* 5*d*, V. 767*l* 3*s* 6*d*; V.'s Inc. 800*l* and Ho; Pop. 2914.) Formerly Fell. of Ch. Coll. Cam. 1816. [4]

CROFT, Percy James, *Kingstone Rectory, Canterbury.*—Trin. Coll. Cam B.A. 1842, M.A. 1862; Deac. 1843 and Pr. 1844 by Abp of Cant. R. of Kingstone, Dio. Cant. 1861. (Patrons, Trustees of Sir J. Brydges, Bart; Tithe, 491*l* 13*s* 8*d*; Glebe, 15 acres; R.'s Inc. 521*l* and Ho; Pop. 310.) Dom. Chap. to Duke of Northumberland. Formerly C. of Saltwood 1843, Tachbrook 1847; V. of Exning 1848; R. of Kirton 1854. Author, *A Farewell Sermon*, 1861. [5]

CROFT, Ralph Calvert Williams, *Walmsley, Bolton-le-Moors.*—Dub. A.B. 1855; Deac. 1855 and Pr. 1856 by Bp of Ches. P. C. of Walmsley, Dio. Man. 1860. (Patron, V. of Bolton; V.'s Inc. 145*l* and Ho; Pop. 3412.) Formerly C. of Bolton-le-Moors 1858–60, Cherry-Burton, Yorks. [6]

CROFT Richard, *Hillingdon, Uxbridge, Middlesex.*—Ball. Coll. Ox. Scho. and Fell. of Ex. Coll. 2nd cl. Lit. Hum. and B.A. 1829, M.A. 1832; Deac. 1836 and Pr. 1837 by Bp of Ox. V. of Hillingdon, Dio. Lon. 1856. (Patron, Bp of Lon; Tithe, none; Glebe, 600*l*; V.'s Inc. 660*l* and Ho; Pop. 6224.) Rural Dean. Formerly V. of Hartburn, Dio. Dur. 1845. [7]

CROFT, Stephen, *St. Mary Stoke Rectory, Ipswich.*—Trin. Coll. Cam. B.A. 1817, M.A. 1821; Deac. 1820 by Bp of Ely, Pr. 1820 by Bp of Nor. R. of St. Mary Stoke, Dio. Nor. 1820. (Patrons, D. and C. of Ely; Tithe—App. 471*l*, Imp. 42*l*; Glebe, 45 acres; R.'s Inc. 440*l* and Ho; Pop. 2518.) [8]

CROFT, Thomas, *Holme Parsonage, Burton, Westmoreland.*—Ch. Coll. Cam. B.A. 1847, M.A. 1851; Deac. 1847 and Pr. 1848 by Bp of Ches. P. C. of Holme, Dio. Carl. 1860. (Patron, V. of Burton; P. C.'s Inc. 150*l* and Ho; Pop. 750.) Formerly Asst. C. of Casterton, near Kirkby Lonsdale; Head Mast. of the Kirkby Lonsdale Gr. Sch. [9]

CROFT, Thomas Charles Henry, *Caius College, Cambridge.*—Caius Coll. Cam. B.A. 1854, M.A. 1857; Deac. 1855 and Pr. 1857 by Bp of Ely. Sen. Fell. of Caius Coll. Cam. [10]

CROFT, Thomas Hutton, *Hutton-Bushel Vicarage, Sherborne, Yorks.*—Trin. Coll. Cam. B.A. 1822, M.A. 1826; Deac. 1822 by Abp of York, Pr. 1822 by Bp of Ox. V. of Stillington, Yorks, Dio. York, 1822. (Patron, Preb. of Stillington in York Cathl; Tithe—Imp. 6*l*, V. 42*l*; Glebe, 8½ acres; V.'s Inc. 178*l* and Ho; Pop. 738.) V. of Hutton-Bushel, Dio. York, 1826. (Patron, Earl Fitzwilliam; Tithe, 160*l*; Glebe, 200 acres; V.'s Inc. 400*l* and Ho; Pop. 912.) Preb. of Stillington in York Cathl. 1831 (Value, 62*l*.) [11]

CROFT, William Llewellyn, *Stokesley, Yorks.*—Deac. 1850 and Pr. 1851 by Bp of Nor. C. of Stokesley. Formerly C. of Easingwold, Yorks. [12]

CROFTS, Charles Daniel, *Caythorpe Rectory, Grantham.*—St. John's Coll. Cam. B.A. 1845; Deac. 1845 and Pr. 1846 by Bp of Chich. R. of Caythorpe with Fristo, Dio. Lin. 1847. (Patron, G. Hussey Roche, Esq; Tithe, 1090*l* 15*s* 4*d*; Glebe, 14 acres; R.'s Inc. 1111*l* and Ho; Pop. 822.) [13]

CROFTS, Christopher, *Sevenoaks, Kent.*—Magd. Hall, Ox. B.A. 1828, M.A. 1830; Deac. and Pr. 1828. Head Mast. of Queen Elizabeth's Gr. Sch. Sevenoaks, 1854. Formerly Head Mast. of the Camberwell Coll. Sch. in union with King's Coll. Lond. [14]

CROFTS, John David Macbride, *Newland, Glouc.*—Wor. Coll. Ox. 3rd cl. Lit. Hum. and B.A. 1851, M.A. 1854; Deac. 1854 and Pr. 1855 by Bp of Chich. Head Mast. of Newland Gr. Sch. 1858. Formerly Res. Cl. Mast. of the Coll. Armagh. [15]

CROFTS, William, *Dunston, Lincolnshire.*—Emman. Coll. Cam. B.A. 1850. V. of Dunston, Dio. Lin. 1856. (Patron, Bp of Lin; V.'s Inc. 172*l*; Pop. 575.) [16]

CROISDALE, John, *East Rainton, Durham.*—P. C. of East Rainton, Dio. Dur. 1866. (Patrons, D. and C. of Dur; P. C.'s Inc. 300*l*.) [17]

CROKER, J., *Brailsford, Derby.*—R. of Brailsford, Dio. Lich. 1860. (Patron, Earl Ferrars; Tithe, 500*l*; Glebe, 67 acres and Ho; R.'s Inc. 673*l*; Pop. 732.) [18]

CROKER, Joseph Morrison, *Lavenham, Suffolk.*—Caius Coll. Cam. B.A. 1840; Deac. 1846 and Pr. 1849 by Bp of Ely. R. of Lavenham, Dio. Ely, 1855. (Patron, Caius Coll. Cam; Tithe, 894*l*; R.'s Inc. 900*l* and Ho; Pop. 1823.) Formerly Fell. of Caius Coll. Cam. [19]

CROKER, Richard.—Dub. A.B. 1837; Deac. 1838 and Pr. 1839 by Abp of York. Chap. of H.M.S. "Liverpool." Formerly Superintendent and Chap. of the Indust. Sch. Feltham. [20]

CROLY, Richard, *Dunkeswell Parsonage, Honiton, Devon.*—Dub. A.M. *ad eund.* Ox. P. C. of Dunkeswell, Dio. Ex. 1852. (Patroness, Mrs. M. Graves; Tithe—Imp. 130*l*; P. C.'s Inc. 60*l* and Ho; Pop. 418.) P. C. of Dunkeswell Abbey, Dio. Ex. 1852. (Patroness, Mrs. E. P. Simcoe; P. C.'s Inc. 50*l*; Pop. 224.) [21]

CROMPTON, Benjamin, *Unsworth Parsonage, Bury, Lancashire.*—P. C. of Unsworth, Dio. Man. 1844. (Patron, R. of Prestwich; P. C.'s Inc. 150*l* and Ho.) [22]

CROMPTON, Samuel Gilbert, *Carlton, Selby, Yorks.*—Jesus Coll. Cam. B.A. 1813; Deac. 1814, Pr. 1816. P. C. of Carlton-in-Snaith, Dio. York, 1839. (Patron, Rev. Wilmot Ware; P. C.'s Inc. 220*l* and Ho; Pop. 752.) [23]

CROMWELL, John Gabriel, *St. Mark's College, Chelsea, S.W.*—Brasen. Coll. Ox. B.A. 1846, M.A. 1849; Deac. 1850 and Pr. 1853 by Bp of Dur. Prin. of St. Mark's Coll. Chelsea; Hon. Can. of Dur. 1856. Formerly Prin. of the Dioc. Training Sch. for Schoolmasters, Durham, 1849; R. of St. Mary's the Less, Durham, 1858. [24]

CRONSHAW, Christopher, *Brougham-terrace, Arkwright-street, Bolton.*—St. Bees; Deac. 1862 and Pr. 1863 by Bp of Man. C. of St. George's, Bolton, 1864. Formerly C. of St. Barnabas', Manchester, 1862–63. [25]

CRONSHAW, James, *Wigan.*—St. Bees; Deac. 1852, Pr. 1853. P. C. of St. Thomas's, Wigan, Dio. Ches. 1854. (Patron, R. of Wigan; P. C.'s Inc. 300*l*; Pop. 6788.) [26]

CROOK, Henry Simon Charles, *Uphaven Vicarage, Marlborough, Wilts.*—Lin. Coll. Ox. B.A. 1828, M.A. 1832; Deac. 1828 and Pr. 1829 by Bp of B. and W. V. of Uphaven, Dio. Salis. 1840. (Patron, Ld Chan; Tithe—Imp. 594*l* 18*s* and 1½ acres of Glebe, V. 145*l* 12*s*; Glebe, 2 acres; V.'s Inc. 125*l* and Ho; Pop. 508.) Rural Dean 1860; Dioc. Inspector of Schs. 1860; Surrogate. [27]

CROOK, James Sutcliffe, *Stourport, Worcestershire.*—Dur. B.A; Deac. 1855 and Pr. 1856 by Bp of Wor. C. of Lower Mitton 1862. Formerly C. of St. Matthew's, Smethwick, and Rowley Regis, Staffs. [28]

CROOKE, Cornelius Hargreave, *Wantage, Berks.*—St. John's Coll. Cam. B.A. 1850; Deac. 1852 and Pr. 1854 by Bp of Ox. Head Mast. of the Wantage Gr. Sch. 1856. Formerly C. of Challow, Berks. [29]

CROOKSHANK, Gerrard Alexander, 21, *Bedford-street, Strand, London, W.C.*—Dub. A.B. 1852,

A.M. 1860; Deac. 1853 and Pr. 1854 by Bp of Lich. London Dioc. Home Missionary 1867. Formerly C. of Basildon, Berks, 1855–58, St. Paul's, Covent-garden, 1859–66. [1]

CROOME, Thomas Boys, *Siston Rectory, Bristol.*—Trin. Coll. Ox. B.A. 1837, M.A. 1841; Deac. 1839, Pr. 1840. R. of Siston, Dio. G. and B. 1847. (Patron, F. B. N. Dickenson, Esq; Tithe, 360*l*; Glebe, 14 acres; R.'s Inc. 380*l* and Ho; Pop. 343.) [2]

CROOME, William, *Iron-Acton, Glouc.*—Literate; Deac. 1841 by Bp of Wor. Pr. 1842 by Bp of Lin. C. of Iron-Acton 1857. Formerly C. of St. Thomas's, Birmingham, 1842, Wainfleet St. Mary, Lincolnshire, 1843, Avening, Glouc. 1853, Chipping Sodbury 1855. Author, *The Memorial, being the Substance of Conversations with Dissenters on their Chief Objections to the Church of England,* 1843, 2*s* 6*d*; *Baptismal Suretyship,* 1843. [3]

CROSBY, Joseph, *Lawrence-street, York.*—Deac. 1828 and Pr. 1829 by Abp of York. R. of St. Crux, York, Dio. York, 1838. (Patron, Ld Chan; R.'s. Inc. 90*l*; Pop. 905.) P. C. of St. Paul's, Heslington, Dio. York, 1851. (Patron, Abp of York; P. C.'s Inc. 60*l*; Pop. 290.) [4]

CROSLAND, John, *Grainthorpe Parsonage, Louth, Lincolnshire.*—Magd. Coll. Cam. Jun. Opt. and B.A. 1824, M.A. 1827; Deac. 1824 by Bp of St. D. Pr. 1825 by Bp of Ely. P. C. of Grainthorpe, Dio. Lin. 1830. (Patron, Magd. Coll. Cam; Tithe, Imp. 900*l*; P. C.'s Inc. 170*l* and Ho; Pop. 738.) Formerly Fell. of Magd. Coll. Cam. [5]

CROSLAND, Jonathan, *Pocklington, near York.*—Dur. Licen. Theol. 1859; Deac. 1859 and Pr. 1860 by Bp of B. and W. C. of Pocklington with Yapham and Meltonby 1866. Formerly C. of Berkley 1859–61, Wetwang 1861–66. [6]

CROSS, Edgar Herman, *Canterbury.*—C. of St. Martin's and St. Paul's, Canterbury. [7]

CROSS, John, *Mursley, Winslow, Bucks.*—King's Coll. Lond. Theol. Assoc; Deac. 1853 and Pr. 1854 by Bp of Rip. R. of Mursley, Dio. Ox. 1860. (Patron, William Selby Lowndes, Esq; R.'s Inc. 480*l* and Ho; Pop. 476.) Formerly C. of Chipping Norton, Oxon. [8]

CROSS, John Edward, *Appleby, near Brigg, Lincolnshire.*—Ch. Ch. Ox. 2nd cl. Lit. Hum. Math. and Phy. B.A. 1843, M.A. 1846; Deac. 1846 by Bp of Ches. Pr. 1847 by Bp of Man. V. of Appleby, Dio. Lin. 1856. (Patron, C. Winn, Esq; Tithe, 210*l*; Glebe, 9 acres; V.'s Inc. 225*l*; Pop. 581.) Formerly C. of Bolton-le-Moors 1846–49. [9]

CROSS, Silas, *Glebe Farm House, Hanbury, Bromsgrove.*—St. Peter's Coll. Cam. B.A. Lich. Theol. Coll; Deac. 1861 and Pr. 1863 by Bp of Lich. C. of Hanbury 1864. Formerly C. of Ashbourne, Derbyshire, 1861–64. [10]

CROSSE, Arthur Bayly, *Kessingland Rectory, Wangford, Suffolk.*—Caius Coll. Cam. B.A. 1853, M.A. 1860; Deac. 1853 by Bp of Ely, Pr. 1854 by Bp of Nor. R. of Kessingland, Dio. Nor. 1865. (Patron, Bp of Nor; Tithe, 420*l*; Glebe, 58 acres; R.'s Inc. 500*l* and Ho; Pop. 872.) Formerly C. of Trimingham 1853; R. of same 1858; C. of St. John's, Great Yarmouth, 1860. [11]

CROSSE, Charles Henry, *Wistanstow, near Shrewsbury.*—Caius Coll. Cam. B.A. 1851, M.A. 1854; Deac. 1854 and Pr. 1855 by Bp of Ely. C. of Wistanstow. Formerly C. of Stow-with-Quay, Cambs. Author, *Analysis of Paley's Evidences of Christianity.* [12]

CROSSE, James, *Lydeard St. Lawrence, Taunton.* St. Alban Hall, Ox. B.A. 1816, M.A. 1820; Deac. 1815 by Bp of Ches. Pr. 1819 by Bp of B. and W. R. of Lydeard St. Lawrence, Dio. B. and W. 1833. (Patron, Robert Harvey, Esq; Tithe, comm. 400*l*; Glebe, 69 acres; R.'s Inc. 500*l* and Ho; Pop. 670.) R. of Tolland, Dio. B. and W. 1835. (Patron, Ld Chan; Tithe, comm. 140*l*; Glebe, 42 acres; R.'s Inc. 224*l* and Ho; Pop. 130.) Formerly C. of Lydeard St. Lawrence 1821. [13]

CROSSE, John Dudley Oland, *Pawlet Vicarage, Bridgwater, Somerset.*—Ex. Coll. Ox. B.A. 1826, M.A. 1830; Deac. and Pr. 1827 by Bp of B. and W. V. of Pawlet, Dio. B. and W. 1827. (Patron, Ld Chan; Tithe, Imp. 200*l*; V. 350*l* 10*s*; Glebe, 9 acres; V.'s Inc. 370*l* and Ho; Pop. 555.) Author, *A Selection of Verses from the Psalms of David, with a Short Account of each Psalm, derived chiefly from Bishop Horne, by a Country Clergyman,* 1849. [14]

CROSSE, Marlboro, *Newhall, Burton-on-Trent.*—P. C. of St. John's, Newhall, Dio. Lich. 1863. (Patrons, Trustees; P. C.'s Inc. 162*l*; Pop. 2246.) [15]

CROSSE, Robert, *Ockham Rectory, Ripley, Surrey.*—Ball. Coll. Ox. B.A. 1835; Deac. 1835 and Pr. 1837 by Bp of B. and W. R. of Ockham, Dio. Win. 1852. (Patron, Earl of Lovelace; Tithe, 292*l*; Glebe, 139 acres; R.'s Inc. 390*l* and Ho; Pop. 682.) Dom. Chap. to the late Duke of Cambridge 1837. [16]

CROSSE, T. F., D.C.L., *Hastings.*—P. C. of Trinity, Hastings, Dio. Chich. 1859. (Pop. 1683.) Rural Dean. [17]

CROSSLAND, Thomas, *Milford, Derby.*—Sid. Coll. Cam. B.A. 1843, M.A. 1848; P. C. of Milford, Dio. Lich. 1858. (Patrons, Crown and Bp of Lich. alt; P. C.'s Inc. 150*l* and Ho; Pop. 1770.) Formerly P. C. of St. Thomas's, Hyde, Dio. Ches. 1850–58. [18]

CROSSLEY, Thomas, *Leigh, Cheadle, Staffs.*—C. of Leigh. [19]

CROSSMAN, Charles Danvers, *Godolphin School, Hammersmith, W.*—Wor. Coll. Ox. Scho. of, B.A. 1859, M.A. 1861; Deac. 1860 by Bp of Ox. Pr. 1862 by Bp of Pet. 2nd Mast. of Godolphin Sch. [20]

CROSSMAN, Thomas, *Belmont, Durham.*—Dur. B.A. 1848; Deac. 1848, Pr. 1849. P. C. of Belmont, Dio. Dur. 1852. (Patrons, the Crown and Bp of Dur. alt; Tithe—Imp. 517*l*; Glebe, 2 acres; P. C.'s Inc. 150*l*; Pop. 4000.) [21]

CROSSWELL, Robert James, *South Petherton, Ilminster.*—Oriel Coll. Ox. 3rd cl. Lit. Hum. B.A. 1859, M.A. 1862. C. of South Petherton 1865. Formerly C. of Steeple with Tyneham, Dorset, 1861–63. [22]

CROSTHWAITE, Benjamin, *St. Andrew's Vicarage, Leeds.*—Dub. A.B. 1831, A.M. 1838; Deac. 1831 and Pr. 1833 by Bp of B. and W. V. of St. Andrew's, Leeds, Dio. Rip. 1845. (Patrons, Trustees; Tithe, 3*l* 11*s*, V.'s Inc. 190*l* and Ho; Pop. 5725.) Surrogate. [23]

CROSTHWAITE, John Clarke, *Church-passage, St. Mary-at-hill, London, E.C.*—R. of St. Mary-at-hill with St. Andrew Hubbard R. City and Dio. Lon. 1844. (Patrons, the Parishioners and Duke of Northumberland alt; R.'s Inc. 420*l* and Ho; Pop. St. Mary-at-hill 738, St. Andrew Hubbard 205.) [24]

CROSSTHWAITE, Robert Jarratt, *Bishopthorpe, York.*—Trin. Coll. Cam. Bracketed 8th Wrang. B.A. 1860, M.A. 1863; Deac. 1862 by Bp of Ely, Pr. 1863 by Abp of York. C. of Bishopthorpe 1866; Private Sec. to Abp of York; Fell. of Trin. Coll. 1862. Formerly C. of North Cave, Yorks, 1862. [25]

CROUCH, James Frederick, *Pembridge Rectory, Leominster.*—Corpus Coll. Ox. B.A. 1830, M.A. 1833, B.D. 1841. R. of Pembridge, Dio. Herf. 1849. (Patron, Corpus Coll. Ox; Tithe, 1007*l* 5*s*; R.'s Inc. 1020*l* and Ho; Pop. 1500.) Formerly Fell. of Corpus Coll. Ox. [26]

CROUCH, William, *Frome, Somerset.*—Ex. Coll. Ox. B.A. 1836, M.A. 1847; Deac. and Pr. 1838. C. of Trinity, and Chap. of the Union, Frome. [27]

CROUGHTON, Robert Fleetwood, *Newmarket.*—Jesus Coll. Cam. B.A. 1822, M.A. 1854; Deac. 1822 and Pr. 1823 by Bp of Lin. Chap. to Newmarket Union 1850. Formerly C. of Letchworth 1822. [28]

CROW, Edward, *Creaton Rectory, Northampton.*—St. Cath. Hall, Cam. Sen. Opt. and B.A. 1836, M.A. 1839; Deac. 1836, Pr. 1837. R. of Creaton, Dio. Pet. 1850. (Patron, Rev. E. F. Beynon; Glebe, 147 acres; R.'s Inc. 294*l* and Ho; Pop. 510.) Author, *Plain Sermons,* 3*s.* [29]

CROW, Frederick Alfred, *Alcester Rectory, Bromsgrove, Warwickshire.*—Ch. Coll. Cam. B.A. 1835, M.A. 1838; Deac. 1835, Pr. 1836. R. of Alcester, Dio. Wor. 1844. (Patron, Marquis of Hertford; Tithe, 7*l*;

Glebe, 84½ acres; R.'s Inc. 304*l* and Ho; Pop. 2128.) Surrogate. [1]

CROWDEN, Charles, *Cranbrook, Kent.*—Lin. Coll. Ox. 2nd cl. Lit. Hum. B.A. 1859, M.A. 1861; Deac. 1860 and Pr. 1861 by Bp of Lon. Head Mast. of Cranbrook Gr. Sch. Formerly Asst. Mast. at Merchant Taylors' Sch. Lond. 1860; C. of St. Margaret's, Lothbury, Lond. 1861; Sec. to the Columbia Mission 1863. [2]

CROWDER, John Hutton, *Rome.*—Mert. Coll. Ox. B.A. 1841, M.A. 1844; Deac. 1843 and Pr. 1844 by Bp of Ches. Chap. to the English Residents at Rome. Formerly C. of St. George's, Everton, Liverpool, 1843–45, St. George's, Bloomsbury, Lond. 1846–48; P. C. of Whalley Range, Manchester, 1849–54; Min. of Octagon Chapel, Bath, 1860–64. Author, *Truth and Love,* 1860, 5*s*; *Hopes of Italy,* 1864, 1*s*. [3]

CROWDY, Anthony, *Titsey Rectory, near Godstone, Surrey.*—Brasen. Coll. Ox. 3rd cl. Lit. Hum. B.A. 1823, M.A. 1826; Deac. 1827 and Pr. 1828 by Bp of Salis. R. of Titsey, Dio. Win. 1861. (Patron, Granville Leveson Gower, Esq; Tithe, 290*l* 13*s* 3*d*; Glebe, 30 acres; R.'s Inc. 350*l* and Ho.; Pop. 167.) Formerly C. of Castle Eaton, Wilts, 1827; V. of King's Sombourne, Hants, 1829; C. of Longstock, Hants, 1831; P. C. of Aldershot, Hants, 1837; R. of Winnal, Winchester, 1841. Author, *Church of England Village Dialogues,* 3rd ed. 1842; *Christian Villager's Guide Book,* 2nd ed. 1857; and various Sermons and Tracts published by Nisbet and Co. [4]

CROWE, Robert, *Woodhouse Parsonage, Huddersfield.*—Dub. A.B. 1847, A.M. 1852; Deac. 1847, Pr. 1848. P. C. of Ch. Ch. Woodhouse, Dio. Rip. 1851. (Patron, Bp. of Rip; P. C.'s Inc. 150*l* and Ho; Pop. 3324.) [5]

CROWFOOT, John Rustat, *Wangford Parsonage, Suffolk.*—Caius Coll. Cam. 12th Wrang. and B.A. 1839, M.A. 1842, B.D. 1849; Deac. 1840 and Pr. 1842 by Bp of Ely. P. C. of Wangford with Henham, and V. of Reydon, Dio. Nor. 1860. (Patron, Earl of Stradbroke; Tithe, 218*l*; Glebe, 4 acres; Gross Inc. 270*l* and Ho; Pop. 1156.) Formerly C. of Eynesbury, Hunts, 1840–41; P. C. of Southwold 1854–60; Fell. Divinity and Hebrew Lect. of Caius Coll. and Divinity Lect. of King's Coll. Cam. Author, *College Tuition by a "Fellow of a College,"* 1845; *Remarks on some Questions of Economy and Finance affecting the University of Cambridge,* 1848; *Academic Notes on the Holy Scriptures* (1st Series), 1850, 2*s* 6*d*; *Bishop Pearson's Five Lectures on the Acts of the Apostles and Annals of St. Paul* (edited in English), *with Notes,* 1851, 4*s* 6*d*; *Plea for a Colonial and Missionary College at Cambridge,* 1854. [6]

CROWLEY, James Campbell, *St. John's Rectory, Devonport.*—Wad. Coll. Ox. B.A. 1828; Deac. 1829 by Bp of Ex. Pr. 1831 by Bp of B. and W. R. of St. John's, Cornwall, Dio. Ex. 1844. (Patron, W. H. Pole Carew, Esq; Tithe, 116*l*; Glebe, 80 acres; R.'s Inc. 245*l* and Ho; Pop. 213.) [7]

CROWTHER, Francis Riddell, *Bradford, Yorks.*—Caius Coll. Cam. 12th Sen. Opt. B.A. 1839, M.A. 1843; Deac. 1840, Pr. 1842. C. of All Saints', Little Horton, Bradford, 1865. Formerly C. of St. Paul's, Leeds, 1856–64, Batley 1864–65. [8]

CROWTHER, John Browne, *Longnor, near Buxton.*—Queens' Coll. Cam. B.A. 1853; Deac. 1858 by Bp of Down, Pr. 1860 by Bp of Rip. P. C. of Longnor, Dio. Lich. 1863. (Patron, V. of Alstonfield; P. C.'s Inc. 190*l*; Pop. 2500.) [9]

CROWTHER, Samuel Bryan, *Christiana.*—Clare Coll. Cam. B.A. 1852; Deac. 1853 and Pr. 1854 by Bp of Wor. Consular Chap. at Christiana. Formerly C. of Welwyn. [10]

CROWTHER, William, *Claines, Worcester.*—St. Cath. Coll. Cam. Scho. of, B.A. 1853, M.A. 1864; Deac. 1853 and Pr. 1854 by Bp of Man. P. C. of Claines, Dio. Wor. 1855. (Patron, Sir O. P. Wakeman; Tithe—App. 107*l*, Imp. 1024*l* 12*s* 10*d*. P. C.'s Inc. 180*l* and Ho; Pop. 4337.) [11]

CROZIER, James Alexander, *Netley, Southampton.*—Dub. A.B. 1843, A.M. 1846; Deac. 1844 by Bp of Llan. Pr. 1845 by Abp of Dub. Chap. to H.M. Forces—Went to the Crimea in Jan. 1855, at Corfu, Sept. 1856, at Gibraltar, Nov. 1856, at Pembroke Dock, April, 1861, at Royal Victoria Hospital, Netley, March, 1863. Formerly C. of Rathdrum, Ireland, 1844; R. of Kilkenny West 1847. [12]

CRUDDAS, George, *Warden Vicarage, Hexham.*—Lin. Coll. Ox. B.A 1851, M.A. 1854; Deac. 1852 and Pr. 1853 by Abp of York. V. of Warden with Newbrough C. and Haydon Bridge C. Dio. Dur. 1867. (Patron, the present V; V.'s Inc. 620*l* and Ho; Pop. Warden 716, Newbrough 703, Haydon Bridge 2221.) Formerly C. of St. Matthew's, Helmsley, and Waghen, Yorks. [13]

CRUICKSHANK, E. R., *Pewsey, Wilts.*—C. of Pewsey. [14]

CRUMP, Chivers Henry, *Wellington, Salop.*—St. Bees; Deac. 1866 and Pr. 1867 by Bp of Lich. C. of All Saints', Wellington. Formerly C. of St. John's, Wolverhampton. [15]

CRUMP, John, *Bootle, Liverpool.*—P. C. of Bootle, Dio. Ches. 1850. (Patron, W. S. Millar, Esq; Tithe, 285*l*; P. C.'s Inc. 160*l*; Pop. 6414.) [16]

CRUMP, J. B., *Barnsley.*—C. of St. Mary's, Barnsley. [17]

CRUSE, Francis, *Christ Church Parsonage, Worthing.*—St. Edm. Hall, Ox. B.A. 1851; Deac. 1851 and Pr. 1852 by Bp of Salis. P. C. of Ch. Ch. Worthing, Dio. Chich. 1864. (Patron, R. of Broadwater; Tithe, 32*l*; P. C.'s Inc. 550*l* and Ho; Pop. 4000.) Formerly C. of Earlstoke, Wilts, 1851–52, Great Warley, Essex, 1852–56; P. C. of St. Jude's, Southwark, 1856–64. Author, *Village Sermons,* 1855, 5*s*; *The Real Teaching of the Church of England on the Sacrament of Baptism* (in reply to Mr. Spurgeon), 4th ed. 1864, 4*d*; *Newness of Life, or a Vindication of the High Standard of Spiritual Fitness required by the Church of England in Candidates for Confirmation,* 4*d*; *"Son, Remember," or a Scene in the Life of a Lost Spirit,* 2*d*; *Christ Crucified,* 2*d*. [18]

CRUSO, Henry Edmund Tilsley, *Vines Gate, Brasted, Sevenoaks.*—Wor. Coll. Ox. 2nd cl. Lit. Hum. B.A. 1864, M.A. 1867; Deac. 1865 and Pr. 1866 by Abp of Cant. C. of Brasted 1867. Formerly Asst. Cl. Mast. at the King's Sch. and C. of St. Andrew's, Canterbury. [19]

CRUTCH, Stephen Spicer, *Lee (Tring), Bucks.*—St. Cath. Coll. Cam. B.A. 1847; Deac. 1847, Pr. 1848. P. C. of Lee, Dio. Ox. 1854. (Patron, J. Deering, Esq; P. C.'s Inc. 75*l*; Pop. 116.) [20]

CRUTTENDEN, G. W., *Little Kimble, Tring.*—R. of Little Kimble, Dio. Ox. 1862. (Patrons, Trustees of Mrs. Cruttenden; R.'s Inc. 200*l* and Ho; Pop. 182.) [21]

CRUWYS, George, *Cruwys Morchard Court, Tiverton, Devon.*—St. John's Coll. Cam. B.A. 1824, M.A. 1829; Deac. 1826 by Bp of Ex. Pr. 1829 by Bp of G. and B. R. of Cruwys Morchard, Dio. Ex. 1835. (Patron, the present R; Tithe, 524*l*; Glebe, 135 acres; R.'s Inc. 659*l* and Ho; Pop. 685.) [22]

CUBITT, Benjamin Lucas, *Catfield Rectory, Stalham, Norfolk.*—Ex. Coll. Ox. B.A. 1832; Deac. 1833 and Pr. 1834 by Bp of Nor. R. of Catfield, Dio. Nor. 1851. (Patrons, Bp of Nor. and the present R. alt; Tithe, 606*l*; Glebe, 18 acres; R.'s Inc. 636*l* and Ho; Pop. 666.) [23]

CUBITT, Charles, *Great Bourton, Banbury.*—Trin. Coll. Cam. B.A. 1864, M.A. 1867; Deac. 1866 by Bp of Ox. C. of Great Bourton 1866. [24]

CUBITT, Francis William, *Fritton, Lowestoft, Suffolk.*—St. John's Coll. Cam. B.A. 1821; Deac. 1824, Pr. 1825. R. of Fritton St. Edmund, Dio. Nor. 1832. (Patron, the present R; Tithe, 270*l*; Glebe, 14 acres; R.'s Inc. 300*l*; Pop 200.) [25]

CUBITT, Spencer Henry, *Bradford, Yorks.*—St Aidan's; Deac. 1863, Pr. 1864. C. of Bradford. Formerly C. of Drypool, Hull, 1863. [26]

CUFF, George, *Tynemouth.*—C. of Tynemouth. [27]

CUMBERLEGE, John, *Tilsworth Lodge, Hastings.*—Lampeter, B.D. 1853; Deac. 1838 by Bp of St. D.

Pr. 1839 by Abp of York. P. C. of St. Matthew's, Silver-hill, St. Leonards, Dio. Chich. 1864. (Patron, present P. C; P. C.'s Inc. 110*l*.) Formerly P. C. of Egginton 1843; V. of Tilsworth 1845. [1]

CUMBERLEGE, Samuel Francis, *Woburn Parsonage, Beds.*—Ch. Coll. Cam. B A. 1835, M A. 1838; Deac. 1835 and Pr. 1836 by Bp of Lin. P. C. of Woburn, Dio. Ely, 1856. (Patron, Duke of Bedford; P. C.'s Inc. 250*l* and Ho; Pop. 1764.) [2]

CUMBY, Anthony, *Scorton, Catterick, Yorks.*—Corpus Coll. Cam. B.A. 1827, M.A. 1830. P. C. of Bolton-on-Swale, Dio. Rip. 1836. (Patron, V. of Catterick; Tithe—App. 54*l*; P. C.'s Inc. 155*l*.) Mast. of the Gr. Sch. Scorton. [3]

CUMBY, William, *Beadnell, Chat-hill, Northumberland.*—Univ. Coll. Ox. B.A. 1845, M.A. 1848; Deac. 1845 and Pr. 1846 by Bp of Rip. P. C. of Beadnell, Dio. Dur. 1853. (Patron, P. C. of Bambrough; Tithe—Imp. 40*l* 14*s*; Glebe, 3 acres; P. C.'s Inc. 96*l* and Ho; Pop. 577.) Formerly C. of Bellerby, Yorks, 1845–53. [4]

CUMMING, John Partridge.—Ch. Coll. Cam. B.A. 1848; Deac. 1850 and Pr. 1851 by Abp of Cant. Formerly C. of Lydd, Kent, 1853. [5]

CUMMING, Joseph George, *St. John's Parsonage, Victoria-park-square, Bethnal-green, London, N.E.*—Emman. Coll. Cam. Sen. Opt. B.A. 1834, M.A. 1837; Deac. 1835 by Bp of Pet. Pr. 1856 by Bp of Roch. P. C. of St. John's, Bethnal-green, Dio. Lon. 1867. (Patron, Bp of Lon; P. C.'s Inc. 320*l* and Ho; Pop. 14,000.) Formerly C. of North Runcton, Norfolk, 1835; Cl. Mast. West Riding Proprietary School 1838; Vice-Prin. King William's Coll. Isle of Man, 1841; Head Mast. of King Edward VI.'s Gr. Sch. Lichfield, 1855; Warden, Prof. of Cl. Lit and Prof. of Geol. Queen's Coll. Birmingham, 1858; R. of Mellis, Suffolk, 1861–67. Author, *The Isle of Man, its History, Physical, Ecclesiastical, Civil and Legendary*, 1848; *The Excellency of the Liturgy of the Church of England*, 1848; *Chronology of Ancient, Sacred and Profane History*, 1853; *The Story of Rushen Castle and Rushen Abbey*, 1857; *The Runic and other Monumental Remains of the Isle of Man*, 4to, 1857; *Guide to the Isle of Man*, 1861. Editor of *Sacheverell's Survey of the Isle of Man* and *Chaloner's Description of the Isle of Man* (Vols. I. and X. of the Manx Society); *The Crucified Man* (a Sermon by Robert Harris in 1852), 1862. Author of Memoirs in *Quarterly Journal of the Geological Society of London*, in *Edinburgh New Philosophical Journal*, in *British Association Reports*, in *Journal of the Archæological Institute*, etc. [6]

CUMMING, J. J., *East Carleton, Norwich.*—R. of East Carleton, Dio. Nor. 1860. (Patron, Peter Day, Esq; R.'s Inc. 176*l*; Pop. 244.) [7]

CUMMING, Samuel, *Stopsley, Luton.*—Pemb. Coll. Cam. 11th Sen. Opt. Exhib. B.A. 1841, M.A. 1846; Deac. 1843 and Pr. 1844 by Abp of Cant. P. C. of Stopsley, Dio. Ely, 1861. (Patron, Col. Sowerby; P. C.'s Inc. 203*l*; Pop. 842.) Formerly C. of Milton, Kent, All Saints', Lambeth, Trinity, Stepney, and Wye, Kent. [8]

CUMMINGS, Charles James, *Cheadle Rectory, Cheshire.*—Brasen. Coll. Ox. B.A. 1844, M.A. 1847; Deac. 1844 and Pr. 1845 by Bp of Ex. R. of Cheadle, Dio. Ches. 1847. (Patron, Rev. Sir Henry Delves Broughton, Bart; Tithe, 658*l* 5*s* 5*d*; R.'s Inc. 659*l* and Ho; Pop. 5860.) Surrogate. [9]

CUMMINS, E. R. King, *Flax Bourton, Bristol.*—C. of Flax Bourton. [10]

CUMMINS, Henry Irwin, *St. Alban's Rectory, Wood-street, Cheapside, London, E.C.*—Caius Coll. Cam. B.A. 1847, M.A. 1852; Deac. 1847 and Pr. 1848 by Bp of Lon. R. of St Alban's, Wood-street, with St. Olave's, Silver-street, City and Dio. Lon. 1854. (Patrons, D. and C. of St. Paul's and Eton Coll. alt; R.'s Inc. 330*l* and Ho; Pop. St. Alban's 276, St. Olave's 527.) [11]

CUMMINS, Richard Swete, *St. James's Rectory, Colchester.*—Ch. Coll. Cam. B.A. 1851, M.A. 1855; Deac. 1851, Pr. 1852. R. of St. James's, Colchester, Dio. Roch. 1857. (Patron, Ld Chan; Tithe—App. 3*l* 6*s*, R. 75*l* 14*s* 4*d*; R.'s Inc. 180*l* and Ho; Pop. 1959.) Formerly C. of All Souls', Marylebone. [12]

CUNDILL, James John, *Muggleswick, Gateshead.*—P. C. of Muggleswick, Dio. Dur. 1855. (Patrons, D. and C. of Dur; P. C.'s Inc. 300*l* and Ho; Pop. 788.) [13]

CUNDILL, John, *Durham.*—Dur. Univ. Fell. of, 1839, B.A. 1837, M.A. 1840, B.D. 1850; Deac. 1838, Pr. 1839. P. C. of St. Margaret's, Durham, Dio. Dur. 1842. (Patrons, D. and C. of Dur; Tithe—App. 84*l*, P. C. 277*l*; Glebe, 20 acres; P. C.'s Inc. 330*l* and Ho; Pop. 3430.) Surrogate and Deputy-Judge of the Dio. of Dur. 1858; Theol. Examiner 1855–56; Proctor in Convocation of York. [14]

CUNLIFFE, George, *Wrexham, Denbighshire.*—Ball. Coll. Ox. B.A. 1817, M.A. 1822; Deac. 1819 and Pr. 1820 by Bp of St. A. V. of Wrexham, Dio. St. A. 1826. (Patron, Bp of St. A; Tithe—Imp. 2374*l* 3*s* 9*d*; V. 630*l* 19*s* 9*d*; Glebe, 9 acres; V.'s Inc. 688*l* and Ho; Pop. 12,354.) Hon. Can. of St. A. 1855. [15]

CUNLIFFE, Henry, *Shiffnal, Salop.*—Ball. Coll. Ox. B.A. 1848, M.A. 1850; Deac. 1849 and Pr. 1850 by Bp of Lich. V. of Shiffnal, Dio. Lich. 1852. (Patron, Rev. John Brooke; Tithe—Imp. 1634*l*, V. 307*l*; Glebe, 60 acres; V.'s Inc. 400*l* and Ho; Pop. 3157.) Chap. to the Duchess of St. Albans 1852; Rural Dean of Shiffnal 1853. [16]

CUNNICK, John, *Ystradyfodwg, Pontypridd, Glamorganshire.*—C. of Ystradyfodwg. [17]

CUNNINGHAM, Albert Henry, *Basing, Basingstoke, Hants.*—Queen's Coll Ox. B.A. 1860; Deac. 1861 and Pr. 1862 by Bp of Ox. C. of Basing 1866. Formerly C. of Hanney, Berks, 1861–63, Combe St. Nicholas, Somerset, 1863–66. [18]

CUNNINGHAM, Edward, *Arthingworth, Northampton.*—Brasen Coll. Ox. B.A. 1861, M.A. 1864, C. of Arthingworth. [19]

CUNNINGHAM, Francis Macaulay, *Witney.*—Trin. Coll. Cam. B.A. 1838, M.A. 1845; Deac. 1839, Pr. 1840. R. of Witney, Dio. Ox. 1864. (Patron, Bp of Win; R.'s Inc. 1450*l* and Ho; Pop. 3611.) Formerly R. of East Tisted. [20]

CUNNYNGHAME, Hugh Robert, *The Crescent, Ripon.*—Dur. B.A. 1845, M.A. 1847; Deac. 1845 and Pr. 1846 by Bp of Dur. Chap. of the Ripon Ho. of Correction 1867. Formerly C. of Washington 1845, St. Andrew Auckland 1849, Sedgfield 1851; Incumb. of St. James's, Muthil, Scotland, 1856. [21]

CUNYNGHAME, James Joseph Myrton, *Little Wigborough, near Colchester.*—St. John's Coll. Ox. B.A. 1854, M.A. 1857; Deac. 1856 by Bp of Lin. Pr. by Abp of York. R. of Little Wigborough, Dio. Roch. 1866. (Patrons, Govs. of Charterhouse; Tithe, 225*l* 10*s*; Glebe, 20 acres; R.'s Inc 250*l*; Pop. 92.) Formerly C. of Beckingham 1856, Elton 1862, Knaresborough 1863. [22]

CUPISS, Thomas, *Edlaston Rectory, Ashbourne, Derbyshire.*—Queens' Coll. Cam. B.A. 1829, M.A. 1832; Deac. 1829 by Bp of Lon. Pr. 1830 by Abp of York. R. of Edlaston, Dio. Lich. 1854. (Patron, Bp of Lich; Tithe, 165*l* 4*s* 4*d*; Glebe, 41 acres; R.'s Inc. 234*l* 15*s* 4*d* and Ho; Pop. 207.) [23]

CURE, Edward Capel, *Bloomsbury, London, W.C.*—Ball. Coll. Ox. 2nd cl. Lit. Hum. B.A. 1851, M.A. 1854; Deac. 1855 and Pr. 1856 by Bp of Ox. R. of St. George's, Bloomsbury, Dio. Lon. 1867. (Patron, Ld Chan; R.'s Inc. 800*l* and Ho; Pop. 17,392.) Formerly Fell. of Mert. Coll. Ox; V. of St. Peter's-in-the-East, Oxford, 1858–67. [24]

CURE, Lawrence Capel, *Roding-Abbess, Chipping Ongar, Essex.*—R. of Roding-Abbess, Dio. Roch. 1858. (Patron, Capel Cure, Esq; R.'s Inc. 323*l* and Ho; Pop. 220.) [24]

CURGENVEN, Francis Henry, 24, *East Southernhay, Exeter.*—Corpus Coll. Ox. 2nd cl. Lit. Hum. B.A. 1859, M.A. 1861; Deac. 1861 by Bp of Ox. Pr. 1862 by Bp of Ex. Fell. of Corpus Coll. Ox. and Pr. Vicar of Exeter Cathl 1864. Formerly C. of Plympton St. Mary, Devon, 1861 64. [25]

CURGENVEN, John, *Lyme Regis.*—Jesus Coll. Cam. B.A. 1860; Deac. 1861 and Pr. 1862 by Bp of Salis. C. of Lyme Regis 1864. Formerly 2nd Mast. of Dorchester Gr. Sch. 1860–62; C. of Nether-Cerne 1861–62, Wootton Bassett 1863–64. [1]

CURLING, William, *China-terrace, Lambeth, S.*—Wad. Coll. Ox. B.A. 1827, M.A. 1832; Deac. 1828, Pr. 1829. Preacher at the Asylum for Female Orphans, Lambeth, 1829; Chap. and Even. Preacher at St. Saviour's, Southwark, 1833; Surrogate. Author, *The Churches of England and Rome Contrasted* (17 Sermons), 1840; *A Letter to Cardinal Wiseman on his Illegal Assumption of Archiepiscopal Authority in England*; *A Letter to Mr. Mayhew, in Reply to his Address to the Working Classes on the Opening of the Crystal Palace on the Lord's Day*, 1853; *Remarks on the Cholera*; *Sermon before the Univ. of Oxford*; etc. [2]

CURME, Thomas, *Sandford Vicarage, Woodstock, Oxon.*—Wor. Coll. Ox. B.A. 1828. V. of Sandford, Dio. Ox. 1841. (Patrons, Duke of Marlborough, 1 turn, Rev. E. Marshall, 2 turns; Tithe—Imp. 71*l*, V. 50*l* 8*s*; V.'s Inc. 210*l* and Ho; Pop. 476.) Dom. Chap. to the Duke of Marlborough. [3]

CURPHEY, William Thomas, *Loders Vicarage, Bridport.*—Trin. Coll. Cam. B.A. 1854, M.A. 1857; Deac. 1854 and Pr. 1856 by Bp of Lin. V. and R. of Loders, Dio. Salis. 1859. (Patrons, Ld Chan and Sir M. H. Nepean, Bart. alt; Tithe—V. 200*l*, R. 115*l*; Glebe, 3 acres; R.'s Inc. 340*l*; Pop. 1060.) Formerly C. of Dorrington and Morton, Linc. and Ch. Ch. Liverpool. [4]

CURREY, George, *The Charterhouse, London, E.C.*—Preacher at the Charterhouse. [5]

CURREY, Robert Arthur, *Markham House, Wyke Regis, Dorset.*—St. John's Coll. Ox. B A. 1844, M.A. 1848; Deac. 1845 and Pr. 1846 by Bp of Herf. R. of West Chickerell, Dio. Salis. 1864. (Patrons, Duchess Dow. of Cleveland and Lord Sandwich; Tithe, 280*l*; Glebe, 46 acres; R.'s Inc. 440*l* and Ho; Pop. 660.) Formerly Chap. and Can. Capetown. [6]

CURRIE, Archibald.—C. of St. Andrew's, Silchester-road, Kensington. [7]

CURRIE, Charles, *Tilney Vicarage, Lynn, Norfolk.*—Pemb. Coll. Cam. 19th Wrang. and B.A. 1823; M.A. 1826; Deac. 1824, Pr. 1825. V. of Tilney All Saints with St. Lawrence, Dio. Nor. 1835. (Patron, Pemb. Coll. Cam; Tithe—Imp. 1298*l* 11*s*, V. 307*l* 6*s*; Glebe, 58 acres; V.'s Inc. 374*l* and Ho; Pop. All Saints 510, St. Lawrence 855.) [8]

CURRIE, Frederick Hill, *Flaunden, Chesham, Bucks.*—Wad. Coll. Ox. B.A. 1858, M.A. 1863; Deac. 1858 and Pr. 1859 by Bp of B. and W. C. of Flaunden 1867. Formerly C. of Kingsbury Episcopi 1858, Bridgwater 1859, Elm 1859–66. [9]

CURRIE, Frederick Larkins, *Bright Waltham, Wantage, Berks.*—Ch. Coll. Cam. B.A. 1846, M.A. 1849; Deac. 1848 and Pr. 1849 by Bp of Nor. C. of Bright Waltham 1861. Formerly C. of Clenchwharton, Lynn. [10]

CURRIE, James, *Dearham, Maryport, Cumberland.*—Deac. 1823, Pr. 1824. V. of Dearham, Dio. Carl. 1839. (Patron, J. Christian, Esq; Tithe—App. 542*l* 2*s* 5*d*, Imp. 230*l* 0*s* 9*d*, V. 12*l*; V.'s Inc. 96*l* and Ho; Pop. 2595.) [11]

CURRIE, James, *Wellington Heath, Ledbury.*—P. C. of Wellington Heath, Dio. Herf. 1857. (Patron, Bp of Herf; P. C.'s Inc. 100*l* and Ho; Pop. 500.) [12]

CURRIE, James, *West Lavington, Midhurst, Sussex.*—Univ. Coll. Ox. B.A. 1824, M.A. 1827; Deac. 1826, Pr. 1827. P. C. of West Lavington, Dio. Chich. 1850. (Patron, Bp of Ox; P. C.'s Inc. 40*l* and Ho; Pop. 172.) [13]

CURRIE, Maynard Wodehouse, *Mentmore Vicarage, Leighton Buzzard.*—Trin. Coll. Cam. Jun. Opt. B.A. 1851, M.A. 1854; Deac. 1852, Pr. 1854. V. of Mentmore, Dio. Ox. 1859. (Patron, Baron M. A. de Rothschild, M.P; Tithe, 190*l*; V.'s Inc. 199*l* 10*s*. and Ho; Pop 399.) Rural Dean of Murnley 1862. Formerly C. of Banbury 1852–54, Saltwood, Kent, 1854–58, Longworth, Bucks, 1858–59. [14]

CURRIE, Thomas, *Bridgham Rectory, East Harling, Norfolk.*—Emman. Coll. Cam. B.A. 1826; Deac. 1826, Pr. 1827. R. of Bridgham 1839. (Patron, Ld Chan; Tithe, 372*l*; Glebe, 15 acres; R.'s Inc. 400*l* and Ho; Pop. 328.) V. of Roudham, Norfolk. 1841. (Patron, Sir T. S. Sebright, Bart; Tithe, 87*l*; V.'s Inc. 115*l*; Glebe, 8 acres; Pop. 132.) [15]

CURSHAM, Curzon, *Hartwell, near Northampton.*—Caius Coll. Cam. B.A. 1836. P. C. of Hartwell, Dio. Pet. 1845. (Patron, H. Castleman, Esq; Tithe—App. 2*l* 5*s*; P. C.'s Inc. 100*l*; Pop. 542.) [16]

CURSHAM, Francis Lambert, *Lyddington, Uppingham.*—Ch. Coll. Cam. 18th Sen. Opt. and B.A. 1845; Deac. 1848 and Pr. 1849 by Bp of Pet. V. of Horninghold, Leicestershire, Dio. Pet. 1854. (Patron, T. Chamberlayne, Esq; Tithe—Imp. 10*l*, V. 23*l*; V.'s Inc. 94*l*; Pop. 105.) C. of Lyddington, Rutland, 1866. [17]

CURSHAM, Thomas Leeson, *Mansfield Vicarage, Notts.*—Lin. Coll. Ox. B.A. 1807, M.A. 1813, D.C.L. 1826; Deac. 1808 and Pr. 1809 by Abp of York. V. of Mansfield, Dio. Lin. 1813. (Patron, Bp of Lin; Tithe—App. 800*l*, V. 200*l*; V.'s Inc. 200*l* and Ho; Pop. 6033.) V. of Blackwell, Derbyshire, Dio. Lich. 1825. (Patron, Duke of Devonshire; Tithe—Imp. 170*l* 2*s* 6*d*, V. 101*l* 2*s* 6*d*; Glebe, 1 acre; V.'s Inc. 102*l*; Pop. 517.) [18]

CURSHAM, W. S., *Blackwell, Alfreton, Derbyshire.*—C. of Blackwell. [19]

CURTEIS, George Herbert, *Lichfield.*—Univ. Coll. Ox. B.A. 1846, M.A. 1849; Fell. of Ex. Coll. 1847; Deac. 1848 by Bp of Ox. Pr. 1859 by Abp of Cant. Prin. of Lich. Theol. Coll. 1857; Preb. of Lich. 1858. Formerly C. of Minster, Thanet, 1848; Fell. of St. Augustine's Miss. Coll. Cant. 1851; Tut. and Sub. R. of Ex. Coll. Ox. 1855; Select Preacher 1857 and 1866. Author, *Spiritual Progress*, Sermons preached in Ex. Coll. Chapel, 1855; *The Evangelisation of India* (Sermon), 1857; *Cathedral Restoration* (Sermons), 1860. [20]

CURTEIS, Jeremiah, *Shelton Rectory, Long Stratton.*—St. John's Coll. Cam; Deac. 1834 by Bp of Lin. Pr. 1835 by Bp of Roch. R. of Shelton with Hardwick, Dio. Nor. 1835. (Patron, F. Bacon Frank, Esq; Tithe, 640*l*; Glebe, 30 acres; R.'s Inc. 726*l* and Ho; Pop. 460*l*.) Formerly V. of Rushall, Norfolk. [21]

CURTEIS, T. Spencer, *Rostherne, Knutsford, Cheshire.*—C. of Rostherne. [22]

CURTIS, Charles George, *Constantinople.*—Mert. Coll. Ox. B.A. 1844, M.A. 1852; Deac. 1845, Pr. 1846. Chap. at Constantinople. Formerly Asst. Mast. of the Charterhouse Sch. Lond. [23]

CURTIS, Edward, *Huggate, Pocklington, Yorks.*—R. of Huggate, Dio. York, 1863. (Patron, Ld Chan; R.'s. Inc. 500*l* and Ho; Pop. 589.) [24]

CURTIS, Edward, *Beaulieu, Southampton.*—St. Alban Hall, Ox. and Theol. Coll. Chich; Deac. 1864 and Pr. 1865 by Bp of Chich. C. of Beaulieu 1865. Formerly C. of Rye, Sussex, 1864. [25]

CURTIS, Francis, *All Saints' Rectory, Colchester.*—Ball. Coll. Ox. B.A. 1833, M.A. 1839; Deac. 1834 and Pr. 1835 by Abp of Cant. R. of All Saints', Colchester, Dio. Roch. 1861. (Patron, Ball. Coll. Ox; Tithe, 288*l*; Rent from Glebe, 25*l*; R.'s Inc. 320*l* and Ho; Pop. 680.) Formerly C. of Cranbrook, Kent, 1834, St. Clement and All Saints', Hastings, 1838; R. of St. Leonard's, Colchester, 1839. [26]

CURTIS, F. H., *Liverpool College, Liverpool.*—Mast. in Upper Sch. of Liverpool Coll. [27]

CURTIS, George James, *Coddington Rectory, near Ledbury.*—Wor. Coll. Ox. B.A. 1848, M.A. 1850; Deac. 1848 by Bp of Herf. Pr. 1850 by Bp of Roch. R. of Coddington, Dio. Herf. 1860. (Patron, Bp of Herf; Tithe, comm. 186*l*; Glebe, 36 acres; R.'s Inc. 170*l* and Ho; Pop. 168.) Formerly R. of Farndish, Beds, 1850–60. [28]

CURTIS, Henry Eldridge, *Gosport.*—St. John's Coll. Cam. B.A. 1863; Deac. 1864 and Pr. 1865 by Bp of Chich. C. of Trinity, Gosport, 1867. Formerly C. of All Saints' and Southover, Lewes, 1864–66, Kencott, Oxon, 1866. [1]

CURTIS, James Burrell, 24, *Fitzwilliam-street, Cambridge.*—St. Cath. Coll. Cam; 1st cl. Hon. in Theol. 1st cl. Tyrwhitt Heb. Scho. B.A. 1858, M.A. 1861; Deac. 1861 and Pr. 1862 by Bp of Ely. Chap. of St. Cath. Coll. 1862. Formerly C. of St. Andrew's the Great, Cambridge. [2]

CURTIS, John, *Bay View-terrace, Jersey.* [3]

CURTIS, John, 8, *Bryanston-terrace, Brighton.*—St. John's Coll. Cam. B.A. 1835; Deac. 1839 and Pr. 1840 by Bp of Ex. [4]

CURTLER, Thomas Gale, *Bevere Knoll, Worcester.*—Wad. Coll. Ox. B.A. 1848, M.A. 1856; Deac. 1849 and Pr. 1850 by Bp of Nor. P. C. of Barbourne, Dio. Wor. 1862. (Patroness, Mrs. J. M. Gutch; P. C.'s Inc. 75*l*; Pop. 1500.) Formerly C. of Aslacton 1849–52; R. of Doverdale 1852–57; P. C. of Aslacton 1857–61. [5]

CURTLER, William Henry, *Lympstone Rectory, near Exeter.*—Trin. Coll. Ox. 1st cl. Lit. Hum. and B.A. 1850, M.A. 1857; Deac. 1852 and Pr. 1853 by Bp of Ox. R. of Lympstone, Dio. Ex. 1858. (Patron, T. G. Curtler, Esq; Tithe, 264*l*; Glebe, 13 acres; R.'s Inc. 300*l* and Ho; Pop. 1111.) Formerly R. of Abbess-Roding, Essex, 1853–58; Fell. of Trin. Coll. Ox. [6]

CURTOIS, Atwill, *Branston Rectory, near Lincoln.*—Lin. Coll. Ox. B.A. 1833. R. of Branston, Dio. Lin. 1847. (Patron, Rev. P. Curtois; Tithe, 224*l* 10*s* 3*d*; R.'s Inc. 680*l* and Ho; Pop. 1469.) [7]

CURTOIS, Peregrine, *Hemingford-Grey Vicarage, St. Ives, Hunts.*—Trin. Hall, Cam. S.C.L. 1829, B.C.L. 1849; Deac. 1829 by Bp of Lin. Pr. 1831 by Bp of Nor. V. of Hemingford-Grey, Dio. Ely, 1849. (Patron, Trin. Hall, Cam; Glebe, 76 acres; V.'s Inc. 211*l* and Ho; Pop. 1103.) [8]

CURTOIS, Peregrine Edward, *Hollesley, Woodbridge, Suffolk.*—Sid. Coll. Cam. B.A. 1861, M.A. 1864; Deac. 1861 and Pr. 1862 by Bp of Ely. C. of Hollesley 1865. Formerly C. of Hemingford-Grey, Hunts, 1861–62, Market Deeping, Linc. 1862–65. [9]

CURWEN, Alfred Francis, *Harrington, Workington, Cumberland.*—R. of Harrington, Dio. Carl. 1862. (Patron, E. S. Curwen, Esq; R.'s Inc. 250*l* and Ho; Pop. 1788.) [10]

CURWEN, Henry, *Workington Rectory, Cumberland.*—R. of Workington, Dio. Carl. (Patron, H. Curwen, Esq; R.'s Inc. 975*l* and Ho; Pop. 4139.) Surrogate. [11]

CURZON, The Hon. Frederic Emmanuel, *Mickleover, Derby.*—Magd. Coll. Cam. M.A. 1820; Deac. and Pr. 1820. V. of Mickleover with Littleover C. and Findern C. Dio. Lich. 1820. (Patrons, Lord and Dowager Lady Scarsdale; Tithe—Imp. 178*l*, V. 22*l* 3*s*; Glebe, 192 acres; Littleover, Glebe, 64 acres; Findern, Glebe, 70 acres; V.'s Inc. 510*l* and Ho; Pop. Mickleover 1101, Littleover 604, Findern 399.) Formerly R. of Kedleston, Dio. Lich. 1850. [12]

CUSINS, Frederick Teeling, *Nottingham.*—Sid. Coll. Cam. B.A. 1849, M.A. 1852; Deac. 1853, Pr. 1854. Head Mast. of the Gr. Sch. Nottingham. Formerly 2nd Mast. of Boteler's Free Gr. Sch. Warrington. [13]

CUSSONS, John, *Felstead, Chelmsford.*—St. Cath. Coll. Cam. B.A. 1867; Deac. 1867 by Bp of Roch. C. of Felstead 1867. [14]

CUST, Arthur Perceval, *Reading.*—Brasen. Coll. Ox. B.A. 1850, M.A. 1854; Deac. 1851 by Bp of Ox. Pr. 1852 by Bp of Roch. V. of St. Mary's, Reading, Dio. Ox. 1861. (Patron, Bp of Ox; Tithe, 701*l*; Glebe, 1½ acres; V.'s Inc. 706*l* and Ho; Pop. 10,940.) Rural Dean 1858. Formerly R. of Cheddington 1853–61; Fell. of All Souls Coll. Ox. [15]

CUST, Daniel Mitford, *Seaham Harbour, Fence House, Durham.*—Ch. Coll. Cam. 30th Wrang. and B.A. 1845, M.A. 1848; Deac. 1846 and Pr. 1847 by Bp of Ely. P. C. of Seaham Harbour, Dio. Dur. 1863. (Patron, Earl Vane; P. C.'s Inc. 300*l* and Ho; Pop. 4137.) Formerly P. C. of Netherwitton, Dio. Dur. 1847–63; C. of Whitburn, Durham. [16]

CUST, Edwards, *Danby-hill, Northallerton, Yorks.*—St. John's Coll. Cam. Fell. of, 11th Wrang. and B.A. 1827; Deac. 1829, Pr. 1830. R. of Danby-Wiske with Yafforth, Dio. Rip. 1840. (Patron, the present R; Danby-Wiske, Tithe—App. 6*l* 10*s*, Imp. 84*l* 1*s*; Glebe, 419 acres; Yafforth, Tithe—Imp. 53*l* 11*s*; R.'s Inc. 445*l*; Pop. Danby-Wiske 353, Yafforth 204.) P. C. of Hutton-Bonville, Northallerton, Dio. York, 1852. (Patroness, Mrs. Mary A. Pierse; V.'s Inc. 58*l*; Pop. 129.) Hon. Can. of Rip; Rural Dean 1855. [17]

CUSTANCE, Charles William Neville.—Corpus Coll. Cam. B.A. 1858, M.A. 1861; Deac. 1859 and Pr. 1860 by Bp of Lon. Formerly C. of Uxbridge 1859–61, Maulden 1862; R. of Brampton, Norfolk, 1864–67. [18]

CUSTANCE, Frederick, *Colwall Rectory (Herefordshire), Great Malvern.*—Trin. Coll. Cam. 27th Sen. Opt. and B.A. 1825, M.A. 1839; Deac. 1825 by Bp of B. and W. Pr. 1826 by Bp of Ches. R. of Colwall, Dio. Herf. 1841. (Patron, Bp of Herf; Tithe, 454*l*; R.'s Inc. 530*l* and Ho; Pop. 1537.) Preb. of Herf; Rural Dean. Author, Two Sermons for the S.P.G. and S.P.C.K. [19]

CUSTANCE, G. M., *Blackmarston, Hereford.*—Min. Can. of Hereford 1865; C. of Blackmarston. [20]

CUSTANCE, John, *Blickling Rectory, Aylesham, Norfolk.*—R. of Blickling with Erpingham R. Dio. Nor. 1839. (Patroness, Dowager Lady Suffield; Blickling, Tithe, 404; Glebe, 17 acres; Erpingham, Tithe, 478*l*; Glebe, 18 acres; R.'s Inc. 920*l* and Ho; Pop. Blickling 392, Erpingham 423.) [21]

CUTHBERT, George, *Oswestry, Salop.*—Dub. A.B. 1836; Deac. 1839 by Bp of Londonderry, Pr. 1839 by Bp of Kildare. C. of Oswestry 1853; Surrogate, and Chap. of Poorhouse. [22]

CUTHBERT, George Seignelay, *Bradpole, Bridport.*—C. of Bradpole. [23]

CUTLER, Charles Septimus, *Hathersage Vicarage, Sheffield.*—St. John's Coll. Cam. Scho. 1854, B.A. 1856; Deac. 1858 and Pr. 1860 by Bp of Lich. V. of Hathersage, Derbyshire, Dio. Lich. 1865. (Patron, Duke of Devonshire; V.'s Inc. 200*l* and Ho; Pop. 974.) Formerly C. of Darley 1858. [24]

CUTLER, Henry George Gervase, *St. John's Common, Burgess Hill, Sussex.*—St. John's Coll. Ox. B.A. 1852; Deac. 1853 and Pr. 1854 by Bp of Roch. Formerly C. of Ch. Ch. Brighton, 1860, Mortlake, Surrey, and East Donyland, Essex. [25]

CUTTING, John Henry, *Barnsley.*—St. John's Coll. Cam. B.A. 1864; Deac. 1865 by Bp of Rip. C. of St. Mary's, Barnsley, 1865. [26]

CUTTING, William Aubrey, *Trimingham, North Walsham, Norfolk.*—Corpus Coll. Cam. Jun. Opt. 3rd cl. Cl. Trip. and B.A. 1856, M.A. 1859; Deac. 1857 and Pr. 1858 by Bp of Nor. R. of Trimingham, Dio. Nor. 1861. (Patron, Duchy of Lanc; Tithe, 133*l*; Glebe, 3 acres; R.'s Inc. 146*l*; Pop. 451.) Formerly C. of St. Martin's, Norwich, 1857, Lower Sheringham-with-Weybourne 1858–61. [27]

CUTTS, Edward Lewes, 7, *Whitehall, London, S.W.*—Queens' Coll. Cam. 4th Sen. Opt. B.A. 1848; Deac. and Pr. 1848 by Abp of Cant. Chief Sec. of Soc. for Promoting the Employment of Additional Curates in Populous Places; Commissary of Bp of Honolulu. Formerly C. of Kelvedon, Coggeshall, Essex; P. C. of Billericay, Essex, 1859–65. Author, *Manual of Sepulchral Slabs and Crosses,* 1849, 12*s*; *Colchester Castle not a Roman Temple,* 1854, 2*s* 6*d*; *Church Furniture and Decoration,* 1854, 5*s*; *Essay on the Christmas Decoration of Churches, &c.* 2nd ed. 5*s*; *The Villa of Claudius,* S.P.C.K. 1*s* 6*d*; *Home Missions and Church Extension,* 6*d*; *Church Extension and New Endowments,* 6*d*; *The Pastor's Address to his District Visitors,* 1861, 2*d*, etc. [28]

CUXSON, George Appleby, *Dinton Vicarage, Aylesbury.*—Magd. Hall, Ox. B.A. 1842, M.A. 1843; Deac. 1843 and Pr. 1844 by Bp of Pet. R. of Dinton, Dio. Ox. 1865. (Patron, Ld Chan; R.'s Inc. 500*l* and Ho; Pop. 814.) Formerly R. of Halton, Bucks, 1857–65. [29]

DACRE, William, *Irthington, Carlisle.*—V. of Irthington, Dio. Carl. 1852. (Patron, Joseph Dacre, Esq; Tithe, Imp. 2*l* 15*s*; V.'s Inc. 300*l*; Pop. 977.) [1]

DACRE, George, *Preston.*—Chap. to the Forces, Preston. [2]

D'AETH, Charles John Hughes, *Wickhambreux Rectory, Wingham, Kent.*—Wad. Coll. Ox. B.A. 1849; Deac. 1850 and Pr. 1851 by Bp of Wor. R. of Wickhambreux, Dio. Cant. 1862. (Patron, Admiral Hughes D'Aeth; Tithe, 749*l* 11*s* 6*d*; Glebe, 20½ acres; R.'s Inc. 725*l* and Ho; Pop. 461.) Formerly R. of Knowlton, Kent, 1851–62. [3]

D'AETH, Cloudesley Hughes, *Knowlton, Wingham, Kent.*—R. of Knowlton, Dio. Cant. 1862. (Patron, Admiral H. D'Aeth; Tithe, 120*l*; Glebe, 13½ acres; R.'s Inc. 174*l*; Pop. 31.) [4]

D'AETH, Wyndham C. H. Hughes, *Arborfield, Reading.*—C. of Arborfield. [5]

DAINTRY, John, *North Rode, Congleton, Cheshire.*—Trin. Coll. Cam. B.A. 1818, M.A. 1821; Deac. 1828 and Pr. 1829 by Bp of Win. Formerly P. C. of North Rode (of which he is Patron) 1849–63. [6]

DAINTY, Thomas, *Lichfield.*—St. Cath. Coll. Cam. B.A. 1830, M.A. 1839; Deac. 1830 and Pr. 1831 by Bp of Lin. Head Mast. of the Lich. Dio. Training Sch. 1839; Preb. of Lich. 1849; Sacristy of Lich. Cathl. [7]

DAKYNS, John Horsley, *Holy Island, Berwick.*—Trin. Coll. Cam. S.C.L. 1821, Hon. D.D. 1844; Deac. 1822, Pr. 1823. Priest in Ordinary of Her Majesty's Chapels-Royal; Chap. to H.M. the King of Hanover; C. of Holy Island. Author, *Guide to Herne Church, Kent.* [8]

DALBY, Robert, *Belton Vicarage, Loughborough.*—St. John's Coll. Cam. B.A. 1832, M.A. 1837; Deac. 1833 and Pr. 1834 by Bp of Lin. V. of Belton, Dio. Pet. 1840. (Patron, Marquis of Hastings; Tithe—Imp. 2*l* 10*s*, V. 10*l* 10*s*; Glebe, 112 acres; V.'s Inc. 161*l* and Ho; Pop. 781.) Rural Dean 1852. [9]

DALBY, William Ballard, *Hinton St. George, Ilminster.*—St. John's Coll. Cam. B.A. 1850; Deac. 1850 and Pr. 1851 by Bp. of Pet. R. of Hinton St. George, Dio. B. and W. 1865. (Patron, Earl Powlett; R.'s Inc. 200*l* and Ho; Pop. 701.) Formerly C. of Hoby with Rotherby 1850–51; V. of Wiggenhall, Norfolk, 1851–65. [10]

DALE, B., *Eccles, Manchester.*—C. of Eccles. [11]

DALE, C., *Ham, Sandwich, Kent.*—R. of Ham, Dio. Cant. 1859. (Patron, Ld Chan; R.'s Inc. 200*l*; Pop. 47.) [12]

DALE, Frederick Spencer, *St. Luke's, Birmingham.*—Trin. Coll. Cam. 14th Sen. Opt. and B.A. 1848, M.A. 1859; Deac. 1850 by Bp of Roch. Pr. 1851 by Bp of Wor. P. C. of St. Luke's, Birmingham, Dio. Wor. 1860. (Patrons, Trustees; P. C.'s Inc. 380*l*; Pop. 19,623.) Formerly C. of Hales Owen, St. John's, Ladywood, and St. Martin's, Birmingham. [13]

DALE, Henry, *Wilby Rectory, Northants.*—Magd. Coll. Ox. Demy, 1st cl. Lit. Hum. and B.A. 1834, M.A. 1836; Deac. 1838, Pr. 1839. R. of Wilby, Dio. Pet. 1853. (Patron, H. M. Stockdale, Esq; Glebe, 247 acres; R.'s Inc. 315*l* and Ho; Pop. 456.) Formerly V. of East Stoke 1851–53. Author, *Translation of Thucydides* (Bohn's Cl. Lib), 2 vols. 1848, 7*s*; and part of *Xenophon's Hellenics*, 1854. [14]

DALE, Lawford William Torriano, *Chiswick, W.*—Trin. Coll. Cam. B.A. 1848, M.A. 1852; Deac. 1849, Pr. 1850. V. of Chiswick, Dio. Lon. 1857. (Patrons, D. and C. of St. Paul's; V.'s Inc. 615*l* and Ho; Pop. 3882.) Formerly C. of St. Pancras, Lond. Author, *A Sermon on Reformatory Schools*, 1853. [15]

DALE, Peter Steele, *Hollinfare, Warrington.*—P. C. of Hollinfare, Dio. Ches. 1829. (Patron, R. of Warrington; P. C.'s Inc. 150*l*; Pop. 752.) [16]

DALE, Samuel, *Eccles, Manchester.*—C. of ecles. [17]

DALE, Thomas, *Therfield Rectory, Royston, Herts*, and 2, *Amen-court, London, E.C.*—Corpus Coll. Cam. B.A. 1821, M.A. 1825; Deac. 1821 and Pr. 1822 by Bp of Lon. R. of Therfield Dio. Roch. 1860. (Patrons, D. and C. of St. Paul's; Tithe, 937*l*; Glebe, 50 acres; R.'s Inc. 994*l* and Ho; Pop. 972.) Can. Res. of St. Paul's 1843 (Value, 1000*l*). Formerly V. of St. Bride's, Lond. 1835; Tuesday Morn. Lect. of St. Margaret's, Lothbury, 1837; Preb. of St. Paul's 1842; V. of St. Pancras 1846–59; Prof. of English Literature in Univ. Coll. Lond. 1829; in King's Coll. 1836; Select Preacher before the Univ. of Cam. in 1832, 1835, and 1862. Author, *Widow of Nain and other Poems*, 1819; *Outlaw of Taurus*, 1821; *Irad and Adah, a Tale of the Flood*, 1822; *Translation of the Tragedies of Sophocles*, 1824; *Sermons preached at St. Bride's, Fleet-street*, 1831; *Five Discourses preached before the University of Cambridge*, 1832; *Introductory Lecture on the Study of the English Language and Literature*, 1828; *Introductory Lecture to the Study of Theology and the Greek Testament*, 1829; *Sermons before the University of Cambridge*, 1835–36; *The Philosopher entering into the Kingdom of Heaven*, 1837; *National Religion conducive to the Prosperity of the State*, 1837; *Faithfulness in the Stewardship of the Mysteries of God* (Visitation Sermon published by command of the Bishop), 1842; *The Sabbath Companion—Essays on Christian Faith and Practice*, 1844; *The Good Shepherd, a Commentary on Psalm xxiii.* 1845; *The Golden Psalm*, 1847; *The Domestic Liturgy and Family Chaplain*, 1848; *Five Years of Church Extension in St. Pancras*, 1852; *The Lamentation of the Church on the Removal of a Faithful Minister* (Rev. H. Hughes), 1852; *Wondrous and Fearful Mechanism of Man* (a Sermon preached on behalf of the Univ. Coll. Hospital), 1852; *God's Providential Care of Children* (a Sermon on behalf of the Infant Orphan Asylum), 1854; *A Martyr's Testimony*, preached in St. Paul's Cathl. on Feb. 4, 1855, being the Tercentenary of the Martyrdom of John Bradford. [18]

DALE, Thomas Pelham, 14, *Torrington-square, London W.C.*—Sid Coll. Cam. 25th Wrang. and B.A. 1845, M.A. 1848; Deac. 1845 and Pr. 1846 by Bp of Win. R. of St. Vedast's, Foster-lane, with St. Michael-le-Querne, City and Dio. Lond. 1847. (Patrons, Abp of Cant. and D. and C. of St. Paul's alt; R.'s Inc. 330*l*; Pop. St. Vedast 278, St. Michael-le-Querne 74.) Lect. at St. Pancras', Lond. Late Fell. of Sid. Coll. Cam. [19]

DALISON, John Beauvoir, *Manton Rectory, Kirton-in-Lindsey, Lincolnshire.*—Mert. Coll. Ox. B.A. 1844, M.A. 1849; Deac. 1845 and Pr. 1847 by Bp of Chich. R. of Manton, Dio. Lin. 1852. (Patron, W. Dalison, Esq; Tithe, 210*l*; Glebe, 118 acres; R.'s Inc. 280*l* and Ho; Pop. 281.) [20]

DALLAS, Augustus Robert Charles, *Wonston Rectory, Micheldever Station, Hants.*—Deac. and Pr. 1821 by Bp of Salis. R. of Wonston, Dio. Win. 1828. (Patron, Bp of Win; Tithe, 967*l*; Glebe, 20 acres; R.'s Inc. 1150*l* and Ho; Pop. 706.) Chap. to the Bp of Win. [21]

DALLAS, C. R., *Furncombe, near Godalming, Surrey.*—P. C. of Farncombe, Dio. Win. 1859. (Patron, Bp of Win; P. C.'s Inc. 150*l*; Pop. 2084.) [22]

DALLAS, John, *Laxfield Vicarage, Woodbridge, Suffolk.*—Deac. 1821 by Bp of Glouc. Pr. 1822 by Bp of Ches. V. of Laxfield, Dio. Nor. 1851. (Patron, Rev. E. Holland; Tithe—Imp. 617*l* 10*s*, V. 220*l*; Glebe, 13¾ acres; V.'s Inc. 258*l* and Ho; Pop 1031.) [23]

D'ALMAINE, Henry Norman, 20, *Great Marlborough-street, London, W.*—Queens' Coll. Cam. B.A. 1860, M.A. 1863; Deac. 1861 and Pr. 1862 by Bp of Lon. C. of St. James's, Piccadilly, 1867. Formerly C. of St. Luke's, Berwick-street, Soho, 1861–67. [24]

DALTON, Arthur, *Springfield, Chelmsford.*—Queens' Coll. Cam. B.A. 1852; Deac. 1852, Pr. 1853. C. of Springfield; Surrogate. Formerly C. of Tamworth and Chelmsford. [25]

DALTON, Cecil, *Grewelthorpe, Ripon.*—P. C. of Grewelthorpe, Dio. Rip. 1856. (Patron, V. of Masham; P. C.'s Inc. 120*l*; Pop. 483.) [26]

DALTON, Charles Browne, *Highgate, N.*—Wad. Coll. Ox. 2nd cl. Lit. Hum. 2nd cl. Math et Phy. B.A. 1833, M.A. 1836; Deac. 1835 and Pr. 1836 by Bp of Ox. Preb. of St. Paul's 1845; P. C. of Highgate, Dio.

Lon. 1854. (Patron, Bp of Lon; P. C.'s Inc. 650*l*; Pop. 4547.) Late Exam. Chap. to Bp of Lon; late Fell. of Wad. Coll; Chap. of Lincoln's-inn 1837–46; Select Preacher 1848; R. of Lambeth 1846–54; Rural Dean of Southwark. [1]

DALTON, Henry.—Dub. A.B. 1825, A.M. 1845, *ad eund.* Ox; Deac. 1826, Pr. 1827. Chap. to the Earl of Leinster. Formerly P. C. of Frithelstock, Devon, 1856–60. Author, *Our Dangers*; *Lectures on the First and Second Advent*; *Brief Remarks on the Irish National Education Plan*; *A Few Thoughts on the Bishop of Exeter's Last Charge*; *Body, Soul, and Spirit*; etc. [2]

DALTON, James, *St. Issel's Rectory, near Tenby.*—Literate; Deac. 1828 and Pr. 1829 by Bp of St. D. R. of St. Issel's, Dio. St. D. 1839. (Patrons, D. and C. of St. D; Tithe—App. 140*l* 11*s* 6*d*, R. 105*l* 8*s* 6*d*; Glebe, 10 acres; R.'s Inc. 137*l* and Ho; Pop. 2022.) [3]

DALTON, James Edward, *Seagrave Rectory, Loughborough.*—Queens' Coll. Cam. 10th Wrang. Fell. 1832–52, B.A. 1830, M.A. 1833, B.D. 1842; Deac. 1831, Pr. 1832. R. of Seagrave, Dio. Pet. 1851. (Patron, Queens' Coll. Cam; R.'s Inc. 450*l* and Ho; Pop. 443.) [4]

DALTON, John, *The Elms, Kelsall, near Chester.*—Deac. 1842 and Pr. 1843 by Bp of Ches. P. C. of Kelsall, Dio. Ches. 1844. (Patron, V. of Tarvin; Tithe—App. 190*l*; P. C.'s Inc. 200*l*; Pop. 693.) [5]

DALTON, J., *West Kirby, Cheshire.*—C. of West Kirby. [6]

DALTON, J. B.—C. of St. Philip's, Earl's-court, Kensington. [7]

DALTON, John Neale, *Milton Keynes, near Newport Pagnell.*—Caius Coll. Cam. Wrang. B.A. 1834, M.A. 1837; Deac. 1834 by Bp of Nor. Pr. 1835 by Bp of Carl. R. of Milton Keynes, Dio. Ox. 1857. (Patron, G. Finch, Esq. Burley-on-the-Hill, Rutland; Tithe, 480*l*; Glebe, 48 acres; R.'s Inc. 600*l* and Ho; Pop. 346.) Surrogate. Formerly C. of Beeston-Regis 1834–36, Suffield 1836–37, Walthamstow 1837–44; Even. Lect. of Christ Church, Spitalfields, 1844; V. of Greetham, Rutland, 1844–57. [8]

DALTON, John Neale, Jun., *Cambridge.*—C. of St. Edward's, Cambridge. [9]

DALTON, Richard, *Kelmarsh Rectory, near Northampton.*—Univ. Coll. Ox. B.A. 1836, M.A. 1845; Deac. 1838 and Pr. 1839 by Bp of Win. R. of Kelmarsh, Dio. Pet. 1862. (Patron, Lord Bateman; R.'s Inc. 700*l* and Ho; Pop. 167.) Formerly C. of Kelmarsh. [10]

DALTON, Samuel Neale, *Foulness Rectory, Rochford, Essex.*—Caius Coll. Cam. Wrang. and Crosse Theol. Scho. 1837, B.A. 1837, M.A. 1840; Deac. 1837 by Bp of Win. Pr. 1840 by Bp of Roch. R. of Foulness, Dio. Roch. 1848. (Patron, G. Finch, Esq; Tithe, 41*l* 9*s* 4*d*; Glebe, 12 acres; R.'s Inc. 300*l* and Ho; Pop. 681.) [11]

DALTON, Thomas, *Whitehaven, Cumberland.*—St. John's Coll. Cam. B.D. 1849; Deac. 1832 and Pr. 1833 by Bp of Ches. P. C. of Trinity, Whitehaven, Dio. Carl. 1840. (Patron, Earl of Lonsdale; P. C.'s Inc. 250*l*; Pop. 5088.) Surrogate; Hon. Can. of Carl; Rural Dean. [12]

DALTON, Thomas, *Eton College, Windsor.*—Caius Coll. Cam. 21st Wrang. 3rd cl. Cl. Trip; Deac 1862 and Pr. 1863 by Bp of Ox. Asst. Mast. at Eton. [13]

DALTON, William, *The Lloyd, Wolverhampton.*—P. C. of St. Philip's, Penn, Dio. Lich. 1859. (Patron, the present P. C; P. C.'s Inc. 100*l*; Pop. 852.) Preb. of Sandiacre in Lich. Cathl. 1856. Formerly V. of St. Paul's, Wolverhampton, 1856–63. [14]

DALTON, William Browne, *Little Burstead, Billericay, Essex.*—Pemb. Coll. Cam. Sen. Opt. and 2nd cl. Cl. Trip. B.A. 1830, M.A. 1834; Deac. 1830 and Pr. 1831 by Bp of Lon. R. of Little Burstead, Dio. Roch. 1843. (Tithe, 356*l*; Glebe, 32 acres; R.'s Inc. 400*l* and Ho; Pop. 186.) Rural Dean; Surrogate. Formerly C. of Hadleigh, Suffolk, 1830–32, Inworth, Essex, 1832–43. [15]

DALTON, William Henry, *Southborough, Tunbridge Wells.*—C. of Southborough. [16]

DALTRY, John William, *Madeley Vicarage, Newcastle-under-Lyme.*—Trin. Coll. Cam. B.A. 1828, M.A. 1831; Deac. 1831 and Pr. 1832. V. of Madeley, Dio. Lich. 1853. (Patroness, Hon. Mrs. C. Offley; Tithe,—Imp. 333*l* 8*s*. 5*d*, V. 192*l*; Glebe, 12 acres; V.'s Inc. 275*l* and Ho; Pop. 1940.) [17]

DALTRY, Thomas William, *Hambledon, Horndean, Hants.*—Trin. Coll. Cam. B.A. 1855, M.A. 1859; Deac. 1858 by Bp of Chich. Formerly C. of Petworth, Sussex, 1858–59, Hambledon 1859–62. [18]

DALY, Michael Smith, *Gomersal, Leeds.*—Dub. A.B. 1839; Deac. 1840 and Pr. 1841 by Bp of Rip. P. C. of Gomersal, Dio. Rip. 1848. (Patrons, the Crown and Bp of Rip. alt; Glebe, 1 acre; P. C.'s Inc. 148*l*; Pop. 3502.) [19]

DAMAN, Charles, *Oriel College, Oxford.*—Magd. Coll. Ox. 1st cl. Lit. Hum. and B.A. 1834, M.A. 1837; Deac. 1837 by Bp of Win. Pr. 1853 by Bp of Ox. Fell. of Oriel Coll. 1836; Tut. 1837. [20]

DAMER, L. W. D., *Cheddington Rectory, Tring, Bucks.*—R. of Cheddington, Dio. Ox. 1862. (Patron, Earl Brownlow; R.'s Inc. 250*l* and Ho; Pop. 628.) [21]

DAMES, Arthur Longworth, *Kenton Vicarage, Exeter.*—Dub. A.B; Deac. and Pr. 1830 by Bp of Kildare, V. of Kenton, Dio. Ex. 1836. (Patrons, D. and C. of Salis; Tithe, 380*l*; Glebe, ½ acre; V.'s Inc. 400*l* and Ho; Pop. 1121.) Formerly C. of Pewsey, Wilts, 1830. [22]

DAMPIER, Augustus, 2, *St. Katherine's, Regent's-park, London, N.W.*—St. John's Coll. Ox. B.A. 1857, M.A. 1864; Deac. 1859 and Pr. 1860 by Bp of Win. Formerly C. of Egham, Surrey, 1859–61. [23]

DAMPIER, William James, *Coggeshall Vicarage, Kelvedon, Essex.*—Ch. Coll. Cam. B.A. 1829, M.A. 1832; Deac. and Pr. 1830. V. of Coggeshall, Dio. Roch. 1841. (Patron, C. Du Cane, Esq; V.'s Inc. 300*l* and Ho; Pop. 4108.) R. of Markshall, Dio. Roch. 1866. (Patron, W. Honywood, Esq; R.'s Inc. 170*l* and Ho; Pop. 42.) Surrogate. [24]

DANBY, Samuel, *Weston-by-Welland, Market Harborough.*—Deac. 1841 by Bp of Lin. Pr. 1842 by Abp of York. V. of Weston-by-Welland with Sutton Basset V. Dio. Pet. 1862. (Patron, Rev. H. Nicholson; V.'s Inc. 300*l* and Ho; Pop. 351.) Formerly C. of Malton, Yorks, 1841–43, Huddersfield 1843–47; P. C. of St. Paul's, King's-cross, Halifax, 1847–59; Chap. of the Belper Union 1859; P. C. of Ch. Ch. Belper, 1859–62. [25]

DAND, James John, *Chevington, Acklington, Northumberland.*—Ch. Coll. Cam. Jun. Opt. in Math. Trip. Kepyer Scho. and B.A. 1856, M.A. 1859; Deac. 1857 and Pr. 1858 by Bp of Carl. P. C. of Chevington, Dio. Dur. 1863. (Patron, Bp of Dur; Pop. 635.) Formerly C. of Kirby Thore, Carlisle, 1857, Tynemouth 1859, Ancroft 1862. [26]

DAND, Thomas, *Bleckingdon Rectory, near Oxford.*—Queen's Coll. Ox. B.A. 1832, M.A. 1836. R. of Bleckingdon, Dio. Ox. 1846. (Patron, Queen's Coll. Ox; Tithe, 332*l* 8*s* 4d; Glebe, 209 acres; R.'s Inc. 648*l* and Ho; Pop. 659.) Late Fell. of Queen's Coll. Ox. [27]

DANDSDAY, John Henry, 4, *Jersey Villas, Bath-road, Hounslow, W.*—King's Coll. Lond. Deac. 1858 and Pr. 1859 by Bp of Lon. C. of Heston 1862. Formerly C. of St. Philip's, Dalston. [28]

DANDY Richard, *Brunswick-terrace, North Shore, Liverpool.*—St. Bees; Deac. 1853 and Pr. 1854 by Bp of Ches. P. C. of St. Aidan's, Liverpool. (Patron, R. of St. Nicholas', Liverpool.) [29]

DANGAR, J. G., *Boyton, Launceston.*—P. C. of Boyton, Dio. Ex. 1866. (Patron, Rev. G. Prideaux; P. C.'s Inc. 120*l* and Ho; Pop. 476.) [30]

DANGERFIELD, John Howell, 2, *Moorfield-place, Hereford.*—St. Mary Hall, Ox. B.A. 1851; Deac. 1852, Pr. 1853. [31]

DANIEL, Alfred, *Trinity Parsonage, Frome-Selwood, Somerset.*—Ex. Coll. Ox. 3rd cl. Lit. Hum. and B.A. 1830, M.A. 1833; Deac. 1833 by Bp of Bristol, Pr. 1834 by Bp of Roch. P. C. of Trinity, Frome, Dio. B. and W. 1838. (Patron, V. of Frome-Selwood; P. C.'s

Inc. 230*l* and Ho; Pop. 3819.) Surrogate. Formerly C. of Wareham, Dorset, 1833–38. [1]

DANIEL, Alfred Edwin, *Ulverston, Lancashire.*—C. of Ulverston. [2]

DANIEL, Charles Henry Olive, *Worcester College, Oxford.*—Fell. and Tut. of Wor. Coll. Ox. [3]

DANIEL, Charles John, *Hope Vicarage, Castleton, Derbyshire.*—Dub. A.B. 1831, A.M. 1836; Deac. 1836 and Pr. 1837 by Bp of Ches. V. of Hope, Dio. Lich. 1856. (Patrons, D. and C. of Lich; Tithe—App. 580*l* 5*s*, Imp. 608*l* 10*s*, V. 116*l* 15*s*; Glebe, 10 acres; V.'s Inc. 250*l* and Ho; Pop. 4032.) Editor, *Prayers for Holy Communion*; *Godly Sayings of Old Fathers*; *Prayers and Hints for District Visitors.* [4]

DANIEL, Edwin Swann, *Sawston, near Cambridge.*—Corpus Coll. Cam. B.A. 1847; Deac. 1851 and Pr. 1852 by Bp of Nor. V. of Sawston, Dio. Ely, 1855. (Patrons, Ferdinand Huddleston and John Gosling, Esqs; Glebe, 100 acres; V.'s Inc. 188*l* 10*s*; Pop. 1363.) Formerly C. of Tilney St. Lawrence 1851–53, Hartfield 1853–55. [5]

DANIEL, Evan, *Battersea, S.W.*—Prin. of the Training College, Battersea. [6]

DANIEL, George, *Mountnessing, near Brentwood, Essex.*—C. of Mountnessing. Formerly Incumb. of Southwell, S. Africa, 1857–61. [7]

DANIEL, Henry Arthur, *Stockland-Bristol, Bridgwater.*—St. John's Coll. Ox. B.A. 1852, M.A. 1855; Deac. 1854 and Pr. 1855 by Bp of Win. V. of Stockland-Bristol, Dio. B. and W. 1857. (Patron, Thomas Daniel, Esq; Tithe—Imp. 60*l*, V. 153*l* 18*s*; Glebe, 22 acres; V.'s Inc. 240*l* and Ho; Pop. 142.) Formerly C. of West Tisted, Hants. [8]

DANIEL, Henry Townley, *Treswell Rectory, East Retford, Notts.*—St. Peter's Coll. Cam. B.A. 1833, M.A. 1836; Deac. 1834 and Pr. 1835 by Bp of B. and W. R. of Treswell, Dio. Lin. 1837. (Patrons, D. and C. of York; Tithe, 266*l*; Glebe, 43 acres; R.'s Inc. 350*l*; Pop. 270.) [9]

DANIEL, John, *East Ardsley Parsonage, near Wakefield.*—St. John's Coll. Cam. 2nd Sen. Opt. and B A. 1832; Deac. 1833 by Bp of Ex. Pr. 1834 by Bp of B. and W. P. C. of East Ardsley, Dio. Rip. 1843. (Patron, Earl of Cardigan; Glebe, 80 acres; P. C.'s Inc. 370*l* and Ho; Pop. 1069.) Author, *Farewell Sermon at St. Levan,* 1838, 3*s* 6*d.* [10]

DANIEL, John Edge, *Ipswich.*—Chap. to the County Gaol, Ipswich. [11]

DANIEL, Robert, *Park place, York.*—St. John's Coll. Cam. B.D. 1853. V. of Osbaldwick, near York, Dio. York, 1846. (Patron, Abp of York; Tithe, 95*l*; V.'s Inc. 108*l*; Pop. 342.) Head Mast. of Abp Holgate's Gr. Sch. York. [12]

DANIEL, Rowland, *Goodwick, Fishguard, Haverfordwest.*—Lampeter; Deac. 1832, Pr. 1833. V. of Granston with St. Nicholas, Pembrokeshire, Dio. St. D. 1845. (Patron, Bp of St. D; Granston, Tithe—Imp. 50*l*, V. 50*l*; St. Nicholas, Tithe—App. 102*l*, V. 51*l*; Glebe, 25 acres; V.'s Inc. 110*l*; Pop. 440.) [13]

DANIEL, William Coxon, *St. John's Parsonage, Boothroyd, Dewsbury.*—Magd. Hall, Ox. M.A. 1855; Deac. 1855 and Pr. 1857 by Bp of Rip. V. of Dewsbury Moor, Dio. Rip. 1858. (Patron, V. of Dewsbury; V.'s Inc. 150*l* and Ho; Pop. 3256.) Formerly C. of Sandal Magna 1855–57, Dewsbury 1857–58. [14]

DANIEL, William Eustace.—C. of St. Mark's, Whitechapel, Lond. [15]

DANIEL, W. Mayou, *Little Wakering, Prittlewell, Essex.*—Wad. Coll. Ox. B.A. 1860; Deac. 1861 and Pr. 1862 by Bp of G. and B. V. of Little Wakering, Dio. Roch. 1866. (Patron, Bartholomew's Hospital, Lond; Tithe, 230*l*; Glebe, 2 acres; V.'s Inc. 230*l*; Pop. 283.) [16]

DANIELL, Edward Hansford, *Upper Bullinghope, near Hereford.*—Ch. Coll. Cam. B.A. 1831, M.A. 1840; Deac. 1835, Pr. 1836. V. of Upper Bullinghope (or Bullingham) with Lower Bullinghope and Grafton, Dio. Herf. 1854. (Patron, Bp of Herf; Tithe, 213*l* 16*s*; Glebe, 70 acres; V.'s Inc. 300*l* and Ho; Pop. 431.) [17]

DANIELL, Egerton Frederic, *Kinson, Wimborne, Dorset.*—Ch. Ch. Ox. B.A. 1856; Deac. 1857 and Pr. 1859 by Bp of Ox. P. C. of Kinson. Formerly C. of Canford Magna with Kinson 1858. [18]

DANIELL, George Frederic, *Aldingbourne, Chichester.*—Magd. Coll. Cam. B.A. 1841, M.A. 1844; Deac. 1841 by Bp of B. and W. Pr. 1842 by Bp of Chich. V. of Aldingbourne, Dio. Chich. 1852. (Patron, Bp of Chich; Tithe, 245*l*; Glebe, 42 acres; V.'s Inc. 350*l* and Ho; Pop. 772.) Formerly C. of Dennington, near Chichester. 1841–53. [19]

DANIELL, George Warwick Bampfylde, *Martin Parsonage, near Salisbury.*—Caius Coll. Cam. B.A. 1823, M.A 1826; Deac. 1822 by Bp of G. Pr. 1826 by Bp of B. and W. P. C. of Martin, Dio. Salis. 1854. (Patron, V. of Damerham; Glebe, 3½ acres; P. C.'s Inc. 64*l* and Ho; Pop. 574.) [20]

DANIELL, John Jeremiah, *Langley Fitzurse, Chippenham, Wilts.*—Literate; Deac. 1848 by Bp of Man. Pr. 1850 by Bp of Ex. V. of Langley Fitzurse, Dio. G. and B. 1865. (Patron, V. of Kington St. Michael; Tithe, 100*l*; Glebe, ½ acre; V.'s Inc. 126*l*; Pop 549.) Formerly C. of St. Peter's Chapel, Kington-Langley, 1858. Author, *Life of Mrs. Godolphin*; *Geography of Cornwall*; *Book of Prayers for Young People*; *Lays of the English Cavaliers*; etc. [21]

DANIELL, Raymond Samuel, *Dalston, London, N.E.*—Magd. Hall, Ox. B.A. 1844, M.A. 1851; Deac. 1844, Pr. 1845. C. of St. Philip's, Dalston. [22]

DANIELS, Thomas, 11, *Chorlton-road, Hulme, Manchester.*—Queens' Coll. Cam. B.A. 1850, M.A. 1853; Deac. and Pr. 1850. P. C. of St. Paul's, Hulme, Dio. Man. 1853. (Patron, Sir Benjamin Heywood, Bart; P. C.'s Inc. 150*l*; Pop. 6375.) [23]

DANSEY, Edward, *Kenwith Lodge, near Bideford.*—Downing Coll. Cam. B.A. 1832, M.A. 1836; Deac. 1833 and Pr. 1834 by Bp of Bristol. V. of Abbotsham, near Bideford, Dio. Ex. 1851. (Patron, E. U. Vidal, Esq; Tithe, 120*l*; Glebe, 37 acres; V.'s Inc. 206*l* and Ho; Pop. 365.) Formerly C. of Shapwick, Dorset, 1833, Gussage All Saints 1834–41, Winterbourne Zelston 1841–51. [24]

DARBY, Edwin Armitage, *Leeds.*—Emman. Coll. Cam. late Scho. of, Sen. Opt. and B.A. 1845, M.A. 1848; Deac. 1853 and Pr. 1857 by Bp of Man. C. of St. Mary's, Leeds, 1866. Formerly C. of Farnham, Yorks. 1858. [25]

DARBY, Edward George, *Kinoulton, near Nottingham.*—St. John's Coll. Cam. B.A. 1859; Deac. 1860 and Pr. 1861 by Bp of Lin. C. of Kinoulton 1860. [26]

DARBY, George William, *Fersfield Rectory, Diss, Norfolk.*—R. of Fersfield, Dio. Nor. 1851. (Patron, Charles S. M. Kyrle, Esq; Tithe, 375*l*; R.'s Inc. 400*l* and Ho; Pop. 295.) [27]

DARBY, John Clere Scott, *Warbleton, Hurst Green, Sussex.*—Ch. Ch. Ox. B.A. 1852, M.A. 1863; Deac. 1854 by Bp of Wor. Pr. 1855 by Bp of Chich. C. of Warbleton 1861. Formerly C. of East Chiltington, Hurstpierpoint, 1854–61. [28]

DARBY, John Lionel, *Newburgh, Ormskirk, Lancashire.*—Dub. A.B. 1854, A.M. 1865; Deac. 1856 and Pr. 1857 by Bp of Ches. P. C. of Newburgh, Dio. Ches. 1859. (Patron, Earl of Derby; P. C.'s Inc. 90*l*; Pop. 900.) Exam. Chap. to Bp of Ches. [29]

DARBY, John T., *Oxford.*—R. of St. Clement's, Oxford, Dio. Ox. 1861. (Patron, Ld Chan; R.'s Inc. 120*l*; Pop. 2286.) [30]

DARBY, Martin Baylie, *Hingham, Norfolk.*—St. John's Coll. Cam. 11th Wrang. and B.A. 1825; Deac. 1825, Pr. 1828. R. of Hackford, near Hingham. Dio. Nor. 1838. (Patron, T. T. Gurdon, Esq; Tithe, 220*l*; Glebe, 23 acres; R.'s Inc. 260*l*; Pop. 222.) [31]

DARBY, Thomas, *Warrington House, Audley, Staffs.*—St. John's Coll. Cam. B.A. 1855; Deac. 1856 and Pr. 1857 by Bp of Lich. Head Mast. of Audley Gr. Sch. 1858. (Patrons, 19 Trustees.) Formerly C. of Chesterton, Staffs, 1856–58. [32]

DARBY, Wareyn William, *Shottisham Rectory, Woodbridge.*—Trin. Coll. Cam. B.A. 1862; Deac. 1864 and Pr. 1865 by Bp of Nor. R. of Shottisham, Dio. Nor. 1866. (Patrons, Rev. W. and Rev. M. B. Darby; Tithe, 230*l*; Glebe, 25 acres; R.'s Inc. 279*l* and Ho; Pop. 317.) Formerly C. of Wangford, Suffolk. [1]

DARBY, William, *Riddlesworth, Thetford, Norfolk.*—St. Peter's Coll. Cam. B.A. 1829, M.A. 1832; Deac. 1829 Pr. 1830. R. of the United R.'s of Riddlesworth, Gasthorpe and Knettishall, Dio. Nor. 1839. (Patron, T. Thornhill, Esq; Tithe, 354*l*; Glebe, 63 acres; R.'s Inc. 425*l*; Pop. Riddlesworth 97, Gasthorpe 87, Knettishall 84.) [2]

DARBY, William Arthur, *St. Luke's Rectory, Chorlton-on-Medlock, Manchester.*—M.A. by Abp of Cant; Deac. 1848 and Pr. 1849 by Bp of Cashel. R. of St. Luke's, Chorlton-on-Medlock, Dio. Man. 1857. (Patron, Sebastian Bazley, Esq; R.'s Inc. 300*l* and Ho; Pop. 7380;) F.R.A.S. Formerly C. of Ch. Ch. Salford. Author, a Series of Pamphlets on the Roman Catholic controversy—*The Canon of Holy Scripture*; *Notes and Queries on the Immaculate Conception*; *The Mother of God*; *Mary Ever Virgin*; *St. Peter never at Rome*; *Romish Frauds*, etc; *Church Establishments* versus *Voluntaryism*; *Church Vestments, an Examination, Scriptural, Historical, Ecclesiastical*; *The Astronomical Observer, a Hand-book to the Observatory*, Hardwicke, 7*s* 6*d*. [3]

D'ARCY, Anthony R., *Morningside, Nailsworth.*—St. Aidan's; Deac. 1859 and Pr. 1860 by Bp of Lich. Min. of Inchbrook Chapel, Dio. G. and B. 1864. (Patrons, Proprietors; Min.'s Inc. 175*l*.) Formerly C. of Edlaston, Derbyshire, 1859, Tenby 1861, and Forest Green in Avening 1864. [4]

DARELL, Sir William Lionel, Bart., *Fretherne Rectory, Stonehouse, Glouc.*—Ch. Ch. Ox. B.A. 1839, M.A. 1842; Deac. 1840 by Bp of Chich. Pr. 1841 by Bp. of Wor. R. of Fretherne, Dio. G. and B. 1844. (Patron, the present R; Tithe, 155*l* 6*s*; Glebe, 20 acres; R.'s Inc. 290*l* and Ho; Pop. 201.) [5]

DARLING, Frederick, *The Ridge, Hartfield, Tunbridge-wells.*—Oriel Coll. and New Inn Hall, Ox. B.A. 1843, M.A. 1851; Deac. 1845 and Pr. 1846 by Bp of G. and B. [6]

DARLING, James, *Bampton Vicarage, Penrith.*—King's Coll. Lond. Theol. Assoc. 1849, M.A. and Ph. D. of Rostock 1862; Deac. 1849 and Pr. 1851 by Bp of Lich. V. of Bampton, Dio. Carl. 1862. (Patron, Ld Chan; Tithe, 27*l* 16*s*; Glebe, 75 acres; V.'s Inc. 135*l* and Ho; Pop. 541.) Formerly C. of Longnor, Staffs, 1849–62, St. Paul's, Bristol, 1852–54; Incumb. of St. John's, Melbourne, 1854–61. Author, *Letters, Doctrinal and Practical*, 3 vols. Seeleys, 1851–53; etc. [7]

DARLING, James George, *Eyke, Woodbridge, Suffolk.*—Trin. Coll. Cam. B.A. 1849, M.A. 1854; Deac. 1849 and Pr. 1850 by Abp of Cant. R. of Eyke, Dio. Nor. 1857. (Patron, Earl of Stradbroke; R.'s Inc. 440*l*; Pop. 486.) Formerly R. of Lowton, Lanc. [8]

DARLING, Thomas, 6, *Russell-square, London, W.C.*—R. of St. Michael-Royal with St. Martin Vintry R. City and Dio. Lon. 1848. (Patrons, D. and C. of Cant. and Bp of Wor. alt; Tithe, 140*l*; R.'s Inc. 248*l*; Pop. St. Michael-Royal 169, St. Martin-Vintry 244.) [9]

DARNBROUGH, John Whitton, *South Otterington, Thirsk, Yorks.*—Lin. Coll. Ox. B.A. 1845; Deac. 1845 and Pr. 1846 by Abp of York. R. of South Otterington, Dio. York. (Patron, T. Darnbrough, Esq; Tithe, 270*l*; Glebe, 50 acres; R.'s Inc. 330*l* and Ho; Pop. 412.) [10]

DARNELL, Daniel, *Welton Vicarage, near Daventry.*—Trin. Coll. Cam. B.A. 1834, M.A. 1843; Deac. 1837, Pr. 1838. V. of Welton, Dio. Pet. 1846. (Patron, Ld Chan; V.'s Inc. 210*l* and Ho; Pop. 592.) Formerly Head Mast. of the King's Coll. Sch. and R. of St. Matthew's, New Providence, Bahamas. [11]

DARNELL, D. C. W.—*Welton, near Daventry.*—C. of Welton. [12]

DARNELL, James, *Tunbridge Wells.* [13]

DARNELL, William, *Bamburgh Glebe, Belford, Northumberland.*—Corpus Coll. Ox. 4th cl. Lit. Hum. and B.A. 1838, M.A. 1843; Deac. 1839, Pr. 1840. V. of Bamburgh, Dio. Dur. 1841. (Patrons, Trustees of the late Lord Crewe, Bp of Dur; Tithe, 46*l*; V.'s Inc. 350*l* and Ho; Pop. 2069.) Chap. to the Duke of Buccleuch 1839. [14]

DARTNELL, Richard Waller, *Stogursey Vicarage, Bridgwater.*—Dub. A.B. 1847; Deac. 1848 and Pr. 1849 by Bp of G. and B. C. of Stogursey 1860. Formerly C. of New Swindon, Wilts, 1848–50; V. of Rodbourne Cheney, Wilts, 1850–57; C. of St. Paul's, Tiverton, 1856–58, Winsham, Somerset, 1858–60. Author, *The Apostacy*, a Tract. [15]

DARWALL, Leicester, *Criggion Parsonage (near Shrewsbury), Montgomeryshire.*—Trin. Coll. Cam. B.A. 1835, M.A. 1838; Deac. 1836, Pr. 1837. P. C. of Criggion, Dio. Herf. 1838. (Patron, V. Vickers, Esq; Glebe, 14½ acres; P. C.'s Inc. 106*l* and Ho; Pop. 187.) Author, *Christ's Ministers to give Attendance to Reading, to Exhortation, to Doctrine* (a Visitation Sermon), 1841, 2*s* 6*d*; *Outline of the Ecclesiastical Transactions and Government of the English Romanists, &c.* 1842, 1*s*; *The Catholic Church, or the Romish Schism, Which?* 1851, 1*s*; *The Church of England a True Branch of the Holy Catholic Church*, 1853, 6*s*. [16]

DASENT, Charles Underwood, *Alford, Lincolnshire.*—Trin. Coll. Cam. Jun. Opt. 3rd cl. Cl. Trip. and B.A. 1848, M.A. 1851; Deac. 1850 and Pr. 1851 by Abp of Armagh. Head Mast. of the Gr. Sch. Alford, and C. of Anderby. Formerly Mast. of 5th cl. in King's Coll. Sch. Lond. [17]

DASHWOOD, Charles John, *Billingford Rectory, Elmham, Thetford, Norfolk.*—Corpus Coll. Cam. B.A. 1834, M.A. 1840; Deac. 1835 by Bp of Chich. Pr. 1836 by Bp of Ely. R. of Billingford, Dio. Nor. 1850. (Patron, Earl of Leicester; Tithe, 360*l*; Glebe, 18 acres; R.'s Inc. 385*l* and Ho; Pop. 354.) [18]

DASHWOOD, George Henry, *Stow Bardolph Vicarage, Downham Market, Norfolk.*—Lin. Coll. Ox. B.A. 1824, M.A. 1825, Deac. and Pr. 1825 by Bp of Ox. V. of Stow Bardolph with Wimbotsham R. Dio. Nor. 1852. (Patron, Sir T. Hare; Stow Bardolph, Tithe—Imp. 362*l* 4*s* 8*d*, V. 158*l* 19*s*; Wimbotsham, Tithe—App. 6*l*, R. 380*l* 11*s*; V.'s Inc. 530*l* and Ho; Pop. Stow Bardolph 1090, Wimbotsham 608.) Author, *Vicecomites Norfolciæ*, quarto, 1843; *Sigilla Antiqua*, folio and quarto, 1847; 2nd Series, 1862; all privately printed. [19]

DASHWOOD, Samuel Vere, *Stanford-on-Soar, Loughborough.*—Brasen. Coll. Ox. B.A. 1826; Deac. 1829 by Bp of Roch. Pr. 1829 by Bp of Lon. R. of Stanford-on-Soar, Dio. Lin. 1829. (Patron, the present R; Tithe, 420*l*; R.'s Inc. 460*l* and Ho; Pop. 140.) [20]

DAUBENY, Edward Andrew, *Ampney Crucis Vicarage, Cirencester.*—Corpus Coll. Ox. B.A. 1807, M.A. 1810; Deac. and Pr. 1807 by Bp of G. and B. R. of Hampnett, with Stowell R. Glouc. Dio. G. and B. 1819. (Patrons, Heirs of Lord Stowell; Hampnett, Tithe, 320*l*; Glebe, 40 acres; Stowel, Tithe, 170*l*; R.'s Inc. 536*l*; Pop. Hampnett 156, Stowel 41.) P. C. of Ampney St. Peter, Dio. G. and B. 1820. (Patron, Bp of G. and B; Tithe—App. 32*l* 7*s*. P. C. 1*l*; P. C.'s Inc. 50*l*; Pop. 188.) Formerly V. of Ampney Crucis 1829–64. [21]

DAUBENY, Edmund Thomas, *Bedhampton Rectory, Havant, Hants.*—Magd. Coll. Ox. B.A. 1864; Deac. 1864 by Bp of Llan. Pr. 1865 by Bp of Win. R. of Bedhampton, Dio. Win. 1865. (Patron, E. J. Daubeny, Esq; Tithe, 330*l*; Glebe, 26 acres; R.'s Inc. 400*l* and Ho; Pop. 576.) Formerly C. of Usk and Monkswood 1864–65. [22]

DAUBENY, Francis, *Mepal Rectory, near Ely.*—Jesus Coll. Cam. B.A. 1841; Deac. 1841, Pr. 1842. R. of Mepal, Dio. Ely, 1844. (Patrons, D. and C. of Ely; Tithe, 280*l*; Glebe, 42 acres; R.'s Inc. 332*l* and Ho; Pop. 510.) [23]

DAUBENY, G., *Liddiard-Tregoz, Swindon, Wilts.*—R. of Liddiard-Tregoz, Dio. G. and B. 1839. (Patroness, Mrs. Collins; R.'s Inc. 680*l* and Ho; Pop. 795.) [24]

DAUBENY, Henry Jones, *Tewin, near Hertford.*—Jesus Coll. Cam. B.A. 1836, M.A. 1839; Deac. 1837 and Pr. 1838 by Bp of Ely. R. of Tewin, Dio. Roch. 1843. (Patron, Jesus Coll. Cam; Tithe, 470*l* 10*s*; Glebe, 42 acres; R.'s Inc. 524*l* and Ho; Pop. 547.) Late Fell. of Jesus Coll. Cam. [1]

DAUBENY, John, *Salisbury.*—Ex. Coll. Ox. B.A. 1857, M.A. 1858; Deac. and Pr. by Bp of Ox. Dom. Chap. to Bp of Salis; Succentor of Salis. Cathl. [2]

DAUBENY, Thomas, *Woodeaton Rectory, near Oxford.*—St. Mary Hall, Ox. M.A. 1855; Deac. 1856 by Bp of Ox. Pr. 1857 by Bp of G. and B. R. of Woodeaton, Dio. Ox. 1864. (Patron, Richard Weyland, Esq; Tithe, 150*l*; Glebe, 9 acres; R.'s Inc. 170*l* and Ho; Pop 90.) Formerly C. of Ducklington with Cokethorpe, Oxon, 1856–57, Ampney Crucis, Glouc. 1857–64. [3]

DAUBUZ, John, *Killiow, Truro.*—Ex. Coll. Ox. B.A. 1825; Deac. 1827 and Pr. 1828 by Bp of B. and W. Formerly R. of Creed, Cornwall, 1829–57. [4]

DAUNT, Edward Synge Townsend, *St. Stephen's-by-Launceston.*—Dub. A.B. 1845, A.M. 1852; Deac. 1847 by Bp of Tuam, Pr. 1848 by Bp of Killaloe. V. of St. Stephen's, Dio. Ex. 1853. (Patrons, Ratepayers and Feoffees; V.'s Inc. 137*l* 7*s* 6*d*; Pop. 873.) [5]

DAUNT, Robert, *Darcy Lever, Bolton, Lancashire.*—Dub. A B. 1862, A.M. 1865; Deac. 1863 and Pr. 1864 by Bp of Man. C. of Lever Bridge 1865. Formerly C. of Farnworth, Bolton, 1863–64. [6]

DAVENEY, Henry, *Colton, Norwich.*—Deac. 1847, Pr. 1848. C. of Colton. [7]

DAVENEY, Thomas Beevor, 2, *St. Paul's-road, Bow Common, E.*—Lin. Coll. Ox. 3rd cl. Lit. Hum. B.A. 1858, M.A. 1861; Deac. 1863 and Pr. 1864 by Bp of Ely. C. of St. Paul's, Bow Common, 1867 Formerly C. of Apsley Guise, Beds, 1863–64; P. C of Soulbury, Bucks, 1864–66; C. of St. Saviour's, Pimlico, 1866–67. Author, *Sermon on Death of Rev. J. Vaux Moore,* 1864. [8]

DAVENPORT, Francis William, *Great Malvern.*—Deac. 1860 and Pr. 1861 by Bp of Nor. C. of Great Malvern 1863. Formerly C. of Beccles, Suffolk, 1860–63. [9]

DAVENPORT, George, *St. James's, Hampstead-road, London, N.W.*—Queen's Theol. Coll. Birmingham; Deac. 1857, Pr. 1858. C. of St. James's, Hampstead-road. Formerly C. of Tamworth 1857–58, St. Luke's, Birmingham, 1858 62, St. George's, Newcastle-under-Lyme 1862–63, Calne 1863–66. [10]

DAVENPORT, G. H., *Yazor, Hereford.*—V. of Yazor, Dio. Herf. 1863. (Patron, the present V; V.'s Inc. 280*l*; Pop. 287.) [11]

DAVENPORT, James, *Welford Rectory, Stratford-on-Avon.*—St. John's Coll. Ox. B.A. 1845, M.A. 1848; Deac. 1847, Pr. 1849. V. of Weston-on-Avon, Glouc. Dio. G. and B. 1849. (Patroness, Countess De La Warr; Glebe, 37 acres; V.'s Inc. 84*l*; Pop. 137.) R. of Welford, Dio. G. and B. 1865. (Patroness, Countess De La Warr; Tithe, comm. 300*l*; Glebe, 107 acres; R.'s Inc. 450*l* and Ho; Pop. 659.) [12]

DAVENPORT, John Charles, *Skeffington Rectory, near Leicester.*—Wad. Coll. Ox. B.A. 1827; Deac. 1829 and Pr. 1830 by Bp of Lin. R. of Skeffington, Dio. Pet. 1836. (Patron, the present R; Tithe, 193*l*; Glebe, 238 acres; R.'s Inc. 665*l* and Ho; Pop. 244.) Chap. of Noseley. (Patron, Sir A. G. Hazlerigg, Bart; Value, 60*l*.) [13]

DAVEY, Henry Mahony, *Funtington, Chichester.*—Emman. Coll. Cam. B.A. 1860, M.A. 1863; Deac. 1861 and Pr. 1862 by Bp of Chich. C. of Funtington 1866. Formerly C. of Steyning 1861–66. [14]

DAVEY, John, *Hertford.*—Queens' Coll. Cam. Scho. and Prizeman, B.A. 1861, M.A. 1866; Deac. 1862 and Pr. 1863 by Bp of B. and W. Head Mast. of Hertford Gr. Sch. 1864. Formerly Asst. C. of Redlynch 1862–64, and 2nd Mast. of King's Sch. Bruton, Somerset, 1856–64. [15]

DAVEY, William Harrison, *Vicarage, Aston Rowant, Tetsworth.*—Lin. Coll. Ox. Scho. 1844, 2nd cl. Lit. Hum. 2nd cl. Lit. Math. and B.A. 1847, M.A. 1850, Mrs. Denyer's Theol. Prize 1851; Deac. 1850 and Pr. 1851 by Bp of Roch. V. of Aston Rowant, Dio. Ox. 1864. (Patron, Bp of Ox; Tithe, 85*l* 2*s*; Glebe, 64 acres; V.'s Inc. 190*l* and Ho; Pop. 884.) Formerly C. of Halstead, Essex, 1850, C. and P. C. of Appledram, Sussex, 1852–59; Vice-Prin. of Chich. Theol. Coll. 1852–59; Vice-Prin. of Cuddesdon Theol. Coll. 1859–64. Author, *On the Divinity of the Holy Ghost* (Mrs. Denyer's Theol. Prize Essay, Oxford, 1851), 1851, 1*s* 6*d*; *Articuli Ecclesiæ Anglicanæ, or the Several Editions of the Articles during the Reigns of Edward VI. and Elizabeth Compared,* Parkers, Oxford, 1861, 2*s* 6*d*. [16]

DAVID, E. M., *Kempsey, Worcester.*—C. of Kempsey. [17]

DAVID, William, *St. Fagan's Rectory, Cardiff.*—Jesus Coll. Ox. B.A. 1846, M.A. 1850; Deac. 1846 by Bp of Ox. Pr. 1848 by Bp of Herf. R. of St. Fagan's, Dio. Llan. 1857. (Patroness, Dow. Countess Amherst; R.'s Inc. 465*l* and Ho; Pop. 656.) Formerly Colonial Travelling Fell. of Jesus Coll. Ox. 1845–55; C. of St. George's, Kingston, Canada. [18]

DAVID, William, *Training College, Exeter.*—Deac. 1852 and Pr. 1854 by Bp of Ex. Principal of the Exeter Training Coll. for Schoolmasters 1851. [19]

DAVIDSON, Arthur A., *Bawtry, Notts.*—C. of Bawtry with Austerfield. [20]

DAVIDSON, Arthur, *Weymouth.*—Ch. Miss. Coll. Islington; Deac. 1853 by Abp of Cant. Pr. 1855 by Bp of Bombay. C. of Melcombe Regis 1866. Miss. of C.M. Soc. in West India 1853–66. [21]

DAVIDSON, Francis, *Milton-road, Woolston, Southampton.*—Deac. 1861 by Bp of Ely, Pr. 1862 by Bp of Wor. P. C. of St. Mary's, Scholing, Dio. Win. 1866. (Patron, Bp of Win; P. C.'s Inc. 120*l*; Pop. 1200.) Formerly C. of St. James's, Ashted, Birmingham, 1861–63, Canning Town, West Ham, Essex (sole charge), 1864, Fareham, Hants, 1864–65, Bittern, Southampton, 1865–66. [22]

DAVIDSON, George, *Colne, Lancashire.*—Dub. A.B. 1862; Deac. 1863 and Pr. 1865 by Bp of Man. C. of Colne 1863. [23]

DAVIDSON, Hugh Coleman, *Bowling Green House, Castletown, Isle of Man.*—Deac. 1851, Pr. 1854. Formerly C. of St. Mary's, Castletown; Mast. of King William's Coll. Isle of Man. [24]

DAVIDSON, James, *Nafferton Vicarage, Great Driffield, Yorks.*—Deac. and Pr. 1843 by Bp of Rip. V. of Nafferton, Dio. York. 1854. (Patron, Abp of York; V.'s Inc. 130*l* and Ho; Pop. 1535.) Surrogate; Hon. Sec. to the Additional Curates' Soc. East Riding of York. [25]

DAVIDSON, John Wright, *Broughton-in-Furness.*—Glasgow and St. Bees; Deac. 1865 by Bp of Carl. C. of Broughton-in-Furness 1865. Author, *The Arguments reviewed in Bland's Angels of Scripture,* Glasgow, 1858. [26]

DAVIDSON, J., *Halliwell, Bolton, Lancashire.*—C. of St. Paul's, Halliwell. [27]

DAVIDSON, Jonas Pascal Fitzwilliam, *Chipping Sodbury, Gloucestershire.*—Lin. Coll. Ox. 3rd cl. Lit. Hum. and B.A. 1853, M.A. 1854; Deac. 1856 and Pr. 1857 by Bp of Salis. P. C. of Chipping Sodbury, Dio. G. and B. 1866. (Patron, Rev. R. S. Nash; P. C.'s Inc. 170*l* and Ho; Pop. 1100.) Formerly C. of All Saints', Dorchester; V. of Frampton, Dorset, 1862–66. [28]

DAVIDSON, Thomas, *Hambleton Vicarage, near Oakham, Rutland.*—Queens' Coll. Cam. B.A. 1825; Deac. 1825 and Pr. 1826 by Bp of Nor. V. of Hambleton with Bramston, Dio. Pet. 1856. (Patrons, D. and C. of Lin; V.'s Inc. 170*l* and Ho; Pop. 721.) Formerly C. of St. Mary Quay, Ipswich, 1825–29, St. Helen's, Ipswich, 1829–40; R. of St. Stephen's, Ipswich, 1851–56. Author, *So we Preach* (a Sermon), 1851. [29]

DAVIDSON, Thomas, *Fontmell, Shaftesbury.*—Corpus Coll. Cam. B.A. 1859; Deac. 1860 and Pr. 1861 by Abp of Cant. R. and V. of Fontmell Magna with West Orchard C. Dio. Salis. 1866. (Patron, George Carr Glyn, Esq. M.P; Tithe, Fontmell, 520*l*, West Orchard 150*l*; Glebe, 30 acres; R.'s Inc. 750*l* and Ho; Pop. Fontmell 875, West Orchard 103.) Formerly C. of Bexley, Kent, 1860, Ewell, Surrey, 1863. [1]

DAVIE, Charles Robert Ferguson, *Yelverton Rectory, Norwich.*—Trin. Hall, Cam. M.A. 1861; Deac. 1860 and Pr. 1861 by Bp of B. and W. R. of Yelverton with Alpington R. Dio. Nor. 1865. (Patron, Ld Chan; Tithe, 408*l*; Glebe, 15 acres; R.'s Inc. 450*l* and Ho; Pop. 260.) Formerly C. and then P. C. of Wythiel Florey, Somerset; R. of Exhall and Wixford 1863–65. [2]

DAVIE, George John, *Market Bosworth.*—Ex. Coll. Ox. B.A. 1840, M.A. 1843; Deac. 1840, Pr. 1841. Head Mast. of the Gr. Sch. Market Bosworth. Formerly C. of Whitwell, near York. [3]

DAVIE, Philip Gibbs, *St. Leonard's, Exeter.* [4]

DAVIE, William Cufaude, *Cringleford Hall, Norwich.*—St. John's Coll. Cam. Sen. Opt. B.A. 1844, M.A. 1847; Deac. 1845 by Bp of Lin. Pr. 1847 by Bp of Nor. Chap. of the Diocesan Female Training Institution, Norwich; C. in sole charge of Intwood with Keswick 1852. Formerly Asst. Math. Mast. Eton Coll. 1844; Head Mast. of Yarmouth Gr. Sch. 1846; Chap. to Military Lunatic Asylum, Yarmouth, 1849. [5]

DAVIES, A, *Rookhope, Darlington.*—P. C. of Rookhope, Dio. Dur. 1866. (Patron, Bp of Rip; P. C.'s Inc. 400*l*.) [6]

DAVIES, Alfred, *Norwich.*—P. C. of St. Michael at Thorn, Norwich, Dio. Nor. 1865. (Patron, Marquis of Lothian; P. C.'s Inc. 100*l*; Pop. 2121.) [7]

DAVIES, Arthur Morgan, *Brancepeth, Durham.*—Jesus Coll. Ox. Scho. of, 3rd cl. Lit. Hum. B.A. 1866; Deac. 1866 by Bp of Dur. C. of Brancepeth 1866. [8]

DAVIES, Charles, *Trinity Parsonage, St. Ann's-street, Liverpool.*—P. C. of Trin. Ch. Liverpool, Dio. Ches. 1847. (Patron, Rev. N. Lovaine; P. C.'s Inc. 250*l*.) [9]

DAVIES, Charles Greenall, *The Vicarage, Tewkesbury.*—St. Mary Hall, Ox. 3rd cl. Lit. Hum. and B.A. 1828, M.A. 1833; Deac. 1828 and Pr. 1830 by Bp of Chich. V. of Tewkesbury, Dio. G. and B. 1846. (Patron, Ld Chan; Tithe, 90*l*; Glebe, 280 acres; R.'s Inc. 480*l* and Ho; Pop. 5876.) P. C. of Walton Cardiffe, Glouc. Dio. G. and B. 1847. (Patron, All Souls Coll. Ox; P. C.'s Inc. 68*l*; Pop. 71.) Hon. Can. Glouc. 1854; Rural Dean. Author, *Sermons*, Seeleys, 1840; various Tracts; *Educational Difficulties*, Hatchards; *Thoughts on the Reform Bill*, 1859; single Sermons. [10]

DAVIES, Charles Maurice, 155, *Queen's-road, Bayswater, London, W.*—Univ. Coll. Dur. B.A. 1849, M.A. 1852, B.D. 1864, D.D. 1864; Deac. 1851 by Bp of Ex. Pr. 1852 by Bp of Salis. Fell. of the Univ. of Dur; 1850–56. Head Mast. of West London College 1861. Formerly C. of Huish Champflower, Somerset, 1851–52, St. Matthew's, City-road, Lond. 1853–55, St. Paul's, Kensington, 1864–66. [11]

DAVIES, Charles Tizard, *The Rectory, Ecton, Northants.*—Queens' Coll. Cam. B.A, 1840; Deac. 1842 and Pr. 1843 by Abp of Cant. R. of Ecton, Dio. Pet. 1849. (Patron, the Crown; R.'s Inc. 700*l* and Ho; Pop. 641.) [12]

DAVIES, Charles William, *West Ham, Essex.*—St. Edm. Hall, Ox. B A. 1845; Deac. 1846 and Pr. 1847 by Bp of Salis. Chap. of the West Ham Union. [13]

DAVIES, Daniel, *Kinnersley, Weobley, Herefordshire.*—C. of Kinnersley. [14]

DAVIES, Daniel Owen, *Trevethin, Pontypool.*—Lampeter; Deac. 1864 and Pr. 1865 by Bp of St. D. C. of Trevethin 1867. Formerly C. of St. Ishmael's with Llansaint, Carmarthenshire, 1864–67. [15]

DAVIES, David, *Castle Caereinion Rectory, Welshpool, Montgomeryshire.*—Deac. 1825, Pr. 1826. R. of Castle Caereinion, Dio. St. A. 1847. (Patron, Bp of St. A; Tithe, 628*l*; Glebe, 16 acres; R.'s Inc. 656*l* and Ho; Pop. 882.) Author, *Anerchiad Eglwysydd* (a Tract on Confirmation, in Welsh), 1847, 3*d*. [16]

DAVIES, David, *Llantillio-Crosseny Vicarage, near Monmouth.*—V. of Llantillio-Crosseny, Dio. Llan. 1846. (Patrons, D. and C. of Llan; Tithe—App. 230*l* 15*s* 10*d*, Imp. 29*l* 11*s*, V. 213*l* 10*s*; V.'s Inc. 275*l* and Ho; Pop. 748.) [17]

DAVIES, David, *Bayton Vicarage, Bewdley, Worcestershire.*—Wor. Coll. Ox. B.A. 1814, M.A. 1816; Deac. 1815, Pr. 1816. V. of Mamble with Bayton, Dio. Herf. 1845. (Patron, Ld Chan; Mamble, Tithe—Imp. 235*l*, V. 179*l* 18*s*; Glebe, ½ acre; Bayton, Glebe, 183 acres; V.'s Inc. 409*l* and Ho; Pop. Mamble 307, Bayton 447.) Formerly Mast. of the Rock Gr. Sch. Worc. [18]

DAVIES, David, *Pennal, Aberdovey, Merionethshire.*—Deac. 1814, Pr. 1815. P. C. of Pennal, Dio. Ban. 1819. (Patron, Bp of Ban; P. C.'s Inc. 80*l*; Pop. 588.) [19]

DAVIES, David, *Dylife, Machynlleth, North Wales.*—Lampeter, Hannah More Scho. 1848; Deac. 1848 and Pr. 1849 by Bp of Ban. P. C. of Dylife, Dio. St. A. 1856. (Patron, Bp of St. A; Tithe, App. 215*l*; Glebe, ½ acre; P. C.'s Inc. 200*l* and Ho; Pop. 858.) Chap. of Caersws Union 1850. Formerly C. of Llanwnog, Montgomeryshire, 1848. Translator of *Dr. Slyman on Cholera into the Welsh Language*, 1849. [20]

DAVIES, David, *Gwenddwr, Erwood, Hereford.*—Lampeter 1st cl. and Scho. 1846; Deac. 1849 by Bp of Man. Pr. 1850 by Bp of St. D. P. C. of Gwenddwr, Dio. St. D. 1860. (Patron, Sir Joseph Russell Bailey, Bart; Tithe, Imp. 250*l*; P. C.'s Inc. 140*l*; Pop. 528.) C. of Crickadarn 1862. Formerly C. of Gwynvai, Llanddausant. [21]

DAVIES, David, *Gwytherin, Llanrwst.*—St. Bees; Deac. 1861 and Pr. 1862 by Bp of St. A. R. of Gwytherin, Dio. St. A. 1865. (Patron, Bp of St. A; Tithe, 170*l*; Glebe, 29 acres; R.'s Inc. 200*l* and Ho; Pop. 450.) Formerly C. of Llansannan 1861, Rhyl 1862, Tremeirchion 1865. [22]

DAVIES, David, *Gellygaer, Glamorganshire.*—C. of Gellygaer. [23]

DAVIES, David, *Yspytty-Cenfyn, Aberystwyth, Cardiganshire.*—Deac. 1825 and Pr. 1826 by Bp of St. D. P. C. of Yspytty-Cenfyn, Dio. St. D. 1837. (Patrons, Landowners; P. C.'s Inc. 120*l*.) [24]

DAVIES, David, *Llangunllo Vicarage, Knighton, Radnorshire.*—Deac. 1822 and Pr. 1823 by Bp of St. D. V. of Llangunllo, Dio. St. D. 1843. (Patron, Bp of St. D. Tithe—App. 300*l*, V. 100*l*; Glebe, 6 acres; V.'s Inc. 102*l* and Ho; Pop. 599.) V. of Pilleth, Dio. St. D. 1843. (Patron, Bp of St. D; Tithe—App. 69*l* 1*s*; V. 23*l* 0*s* 4*d*; V.'s Inc. 65*l*; Pop. 104.) Rural Dean 1855. [25]

DAVIES, David, *Risca, Newport, Monmouthshire.*—Deac. 1822, Pr. 1823. P. C. of Llanvihangel-Llantarnam, Monmouthshire, Dio. Llan. 1827. (Patron, Edward Blewitt, Esq; Tithe—Imp. 90*l*, P. C. 100*l* 12*s*; Glebe, 21 acres; P. C.'s Inc. 135*l*; Pop. 1301.) P. C. of Risca, Dio. Llan. 1836. (Patron, V. of Bassaleg; Tithe—App. 80*l*, P. C. 54*l* 14*s*; Glebe, 62 acres; P. C.'s Inc. 120*l*; Pop. 2744.) [26]

DAVIES, David, *Llansantffraid Rectory, Conway.*—Lampeter 1844; Deac. 1845 and Pr. 1846 by Bp of Herf. R. of Llansantffraid Glan, Dio. St. A. 1867. (Patron, Bp of St. A; Tithe, 273*l* 9*s* 3*d*; Glebe, 14 acres; R.'s Inc. 306*l* and Ho; Pop. 304.) Formerly P. C. of Trenddyn, Mold, 1849–67. [27]

DAVIES, David, *Wenalet, Nevern (Pembrokeshire), near Cardigan.*—Literate; Deac. 1821, Pr. 1822. R. of Meline, Pembrokeshire, Dio. St. D. 1841. (Patron, Rev. D. Protheroe; Tithe, 160*l*; Glebe, 6 acres; R.'s Inc. 170*l*; Pop. 414.) [28]

DAVIES, D., *Llandeveisant, Carmarthenshire.*—Lampeter 1846; Deac. 1849, Pr. 1850. C. of Llandeveisant. [29]

DAVIES, D., *Belgrave-villa, Victoria-road, Bristol.*—St. Edm. Hall, Ox. B.A. 1824, M.A. 1865; Deac. and Pr. 1824 by Bp of Nor. Formerly C. of St. Clement's, Ipswich, 1824, St. John's, Weston, near Bath, 1840–44; R. of Claverton 1847–52. Author, *A Manual of Inter-*

cessory Prayer, 1828; *Instruction in the Romish Controversy, founded on the Best Authorities*, 1856. [1]

DAVIES, David, *Aberdare, Glamorganshire.*—Literate; Deac. 1857 by Bp of Llan. C. of the Welsh Church, Aberdare. [2]

DAVIES, D. Bernard, *Blackrod, Bolton-le-Moors.*—Dub. A.B. 1863; Deac. 1863 by Bp of Rip. Pr. by Bp of Man. 1865. C. of Blackrod. Formerly C. of St. James's, Halifax, and Birkenshaw, Leeds. [3]

DAVIES, D. Hamilton.—C. of St. Saviour's, Paddington, Lond. [4]

DAVIES, David Henry, *Mumbles, near Swansea.*—Lampeter; Deac. 1864. C. of Oystermouth 1865. Formerly C. of Llanboidy 1864. [5]

DAVIES, David Watkin, *Llanfairpwllgwyngyll, Bangor.*—Jesus Coll. Ox. B.A. 1849; Deac. 1850, Pr. 1851. R. of Llanfairpwllgwyngyll with Llandysilio, Dio. Ban. 1866. (Patron, Bp of Ban; Tithe, 233*l*; Glebe, 10 acres; R.'s Inc. 233*l* and Ho; Pop. 2054.) Formerly P. C. of Llanelltyd, Merionethshire, 1854–66. [6]

DAVIES, Edward, *Brington, Kimbolton, Hunts.*—C. of Brington. [7]

DAVIES, Edward, *Himley Rectory near Dudley.*—Trin. Coll. Cam. B.A. 1825, M.A. 1828; Deac. 1825 and Pr. 1826 by Bp of Lich. R. of Himley, Dio. Lich. 1845. (Patron, Earl of Dudley; Tithe, 312*l*; Glebe, 13 acres; R.'s Inc. 341*l* and Ho; Pop. 367.) Formerly C. of Prior's Lee, Salop, 1825–27, Kingswinford, Staffs. 1827–45. [8]

DAVIES, Edward, *Park-row, Nottingham.*—St Aidan's; Deac. 1852 and Pr. 1854 by Bp of Rip. Chap. to the firm of Thos. Adams and Co. Lace Merchants, Nottingham. Formerly C. of Honley, near Huddersfield. [9]

DAVIES, Edward Acton, *Malvern Link Parsonage, Great Malvern.*—St. John's Coll. Ox. B.A. 1828, M.A. 1833; Deac. 1829 and Pr. 1830. P. C. of Malvern Link, Dio. Wor. 1853. (Patron, Earl Beauchamp; Tithe, 120*l*; P. C.'s Inc. 300*l* and Ho; Pop. 1670.) [10]

DAVIES, Edward Hugh, *Dwygyvylchi, Conway.*—V. of Dwygyvylchi, Dio. Ban. 1865. (Patron, L. Eyton, Esq; V.'s Inc. 125*l* and Ho; Pop. 1386.) [11]

DAVIES, Edward Lloyd, *Golborne, Warrington.*—C. of Golborne. [12]

DAVIES, Edward Lutwyche, *Little Thurrock, Grays, Essex.*—Jesus Coll. Ox. B.A. 1826, M.A. 1828; Deac. 1826 and Pr. 1827 by Bp of Herf. R. of Little Thurrock, Dio. Roch. 1860. (Patrons, Trustees of late Rev. E. Bowlby; Tithe, comm. 523*l* 10*s* 6*d*; Glebe, 8½ acres; R.'s Inc. 505*l* and Ho; Pop. 294.) Formerly P. C. of Kenderchurch 1828, P. C. of Kilpech 1835. [13]

DAVIES, Edward Reed, *Cathedine Cottage, Crickhowell.*—Pemb. Coll. Ox. B.A. 1850, M.A. 1853; Deac. 1851 and Pr. 1852 by Bp of G. and B. R. of Cathedine, Dio. St. D. 1865. (Patron, Archd of Brecon; Tithe, comm. 160*l*; R.'s Inc. 180*l*; Pop. 191.) Surrogate. [14]

DAVIES, Edward William Lewis, *Adlingfleet Vicarage, Goole, Yorks.*—Jesus Coll. Ox. Univ. Scho. 1833, B.A. 1836, M.A. 1839; Deac. and Pr. 1837. V. of Adlingfleet, Dio. York, 1852. (Patron, Ld Chan; Tithe, Imp. 345*l* 6*s*; Glebe, 70 acres; V.'s Inc. 350*l* and Ho; Pop. 390.) Rural Dean 1855. Author, *Algiers in* 1857. [15]

DAVIES, Edwin, 35, *Vicarage road, Camberwell, S.*—Deac. 1866 by Bp of Win. C. of Emmanuel Ch. Camberwell, 1866. Author, *Our Heavenly Home*, 3*s* 6*d*; *Life at Bethany*, 3*s*; *The Hope of the Bereaved*, 1*s* 6*d*; *Key to Bunyan's Pilgrim's Progress*, 3*s* 6*d*; *Children in Heaven*, 1*s* 6*d*; *Rahab*, 6*d*; *Our Angel Companions*, 3*s* 6*d*. Editor, *Henry Smith's Sermons*, 2 vols. 8*s*; etc. [16]

DAVIES, Enoch William, *Glanwern House, Talsarn, Carmarthen.*—Lampeter, B.A. 1864; Deac. 1864 and Pr. 1865 by Bp of St. D. C. of Dihewyd and Llanayron 1864. Author, many Tracts and Sermons. [17]

DAVIES, Evan, *Heneglwys, Anglesey.*—Deac. 1865 and Pr. 1866 by Bp of Man. C. of Heneglwys 1867. Formerly C. of Little Marsden, Lancashire, 1865. [18]

DAVIES, Evan, *Felinfoel, Llanelly, Carmarthenshire.*—Lampeter; Deac. 1859 and Pr. 1861 by Bp of St. D. C. of Trinity, Felinfoel, 1861. Formerly C. of Llangyndeyrn 1859. [19]

DAVIES, Evan Lewis, *Newmarket, Rhyl, Flintshire.*—Jesus Coll. Ox. B.A. 1842, M.A. 1844; Deac. 1843 by Bp of St. A. Pr. 1845 by Bp of Herf. P. C. of Newmarket, Dio. St. A. 1859. (Patron, Bp of St. A; P. C.'s Inc. 100*l*; Pop. 520.) [20]

DAVIES, E. L., *Cefnceido Hall, Rhayader, Radnor.*—Trin. Coll. Cam. M.A. R. of Stanfield, Norfolk, Dio. Nor. 1864. (Patron, the present R; R.'s Inc. 360*l* and Ho; Pop. 195.) Formerly C. of Burton Abbots, Berks. [21]

DAVIES, E., *Wilford Rectory, Nottingham.*—R. of Wilford, Dio. Lin. 1864. (Patron, Sir J. Clifton, Bart; R.'s Inc. 600*l* and Ho; Pop. 604.) [22]

DAVIES, Evan James, *Parsonage, Upper Machen, Newport, Monmouthshire.*—Clare Coll. Cam. B.A. 1857; Deac. 1858 and Pr. 1859 by Bp of Llan. C. of Machen 1864. Formerly C. of Monmouth 1858–61, Dixton 1861–63; Chap. under Missions to Seamen. Ryde, Isle of Wight. [23]

DAVIES, E. J., *Llandilo-Vawr, Llandilo, Carmarthenshire.*—C. of Llandilo-Vawr. [24]

DAVIES, Evan William, *Holyhead, Anglesey.*—St. Bees and Lampeter; Deac. 1856 and Pr. 1857 by Bp of Llan. C. of Holyhead 1861. Formerly C. of Newcastle and Bettws 1856–58, Rhymney 1858–61. [25]

DAVIES, Frederick, *Wiggenhall St. Mary Magdalen, King's Lynn.*—Caius Coll. Cam. B.A. 1854; Deac. 1855, Pr. 1861. V. of Wiggenhall St. Mary Magdalen, Dio. Nor. 1865. (Patron, Rev. W. B. Darby; Tithe, 254*l*; Glebe, 3½ acres; V.'s Inc. 279*l* 10*s*; Pop. 954.) Dom. Chap. to Earl Powlett. Formerly R. of Hinton St. George, Somerset, 1861–65. [26]

DAVIES, Frederick.—Chap. of H.M.S. "Pallas." [27]

DAVIES, George Jennings, *Ringwell House, Ditcheat, Castle Carey, Somerset.*—Ex. Coll. Ox. B.A. 1847; Deac. 1848, Pr. 1849. Formerly C. of Kemsing with Seal, Kent. Author, *The Completeness of Wellington as a National Character*, 1*s*; *Two Sermons to Benefit Clubs* (1st series), 2*s*; *Four Sermons to Benefit Clubs* (2nd series), 3*s* 6*d*; *The Order of Confirmation Explained for the Use of Candidates*, 6*d*. [28]

DAVIES, H., *Emsworth, Hants.*—C. of Emsworth. [29]

DAVIES, Henry, *Thomas Town, Merthyr Tydfil.*—Literate; Deac. 1866 by Bp of Llan. C. of St. Tydfil's Well, Merthyr Tydfil. [30]

DAVIES, Henry B. C., *Whitton Rectory, Presteign, Radnorshire.*—Lampeter, late scho. of; Deac. 1858 and Pr. 1859 by Bp of Llan. C. in sole charge of Whitton. [31]

DAVIES, Henry Harris, 3, *Raglan-street, Beaumaris, Anglesey.*—Lampeter, Giessen, M.A. and Ph. D. 1848; Deac. 1848 and Pr. 1849 by Bp of St. D. P. C. of Llangoed with Llaniestyn C. and Llanfihangel-Tyn-Sylwy C. Dio. Ban. 1851. (Patron, R. J. Hughes, Esq; Llangoed, Tithe, Imp. 210*l*; Llaniestyn, Tithe, Imp. 188*l*; Llanfihangel-Tyn-Sylwy, Tithe, Imp. 106*l*; P. C.'s Inc. 150*l*; Pop. Llangoed 618, Llaniestyn 212, Llanfihangel-Tyn-Sylwy 54.) Author, *Welsh Sermon*, 1854, 3*s*; *Welsh Letters, on Heresy and Schism*, 1859; *A Prize Essay on the Effect of Heat, Light, Air, and Water on Vegetation*, 1861; *The Beaumaris Cemetery, an Elegy*, 1863. [32]

DAVIES, Henry Lewis, *Kenarth Vicarage, Newcastle Emlyn, Carmarthenshire.*—Lampeter; Deac. 1823, Pr. 1824. V. of Kenarth, Dio. St. D. 1852. (Patron, Bp of St. D; Tithe—Imp. 266*l* 13*s* 4*d*, V. 133*l* 6*s* 8*d*; Glebe, 4 acres; V.'s Inc. 210*l* and Ho; Pop. 464.) [33]

DAVIES, Henry Robert, *Church-street, Leominster.*—Wor. Coll. Ox. B.A. 1851; Deac. 1852 by Bp of Lin. Pr. 1853 by Bp of B. and W. P. C. of Llanelwedd, Radnor, Dio. St. D. 1862. (Patron, E. D. Thomas Esq; Glebe, 1 acre; P. C.'s Inc. 100*l* and Ho; Pop. 102.) Formerly C. of Wellington 1853–57, Bexhill 1857–58. [1]

DAVIES, Henry William, *Chepstow.*—Lampeter, B.A. 1866; Deac. 1866 by Bp of Llan. C. of Chepstow 1866. [2]

DAVIES, Huson Sylvester, *Egham, Surrey.*—C. of Egham. [3]

DAVIES, James, *Moor Court, Kington, Herefordshire.*—Lin. Coll. Ox. Scho. B.A. 1844, M.A. 1846; Deac. 1845 and Pr. 1846 by Bp of G. and B. Inspector of Schools, Dio. Herf. and Hon. Sec. of the Church Building Society, Salop Archdeaconry 1852. Formerly Head Mast. of King Edward's Sch. Ludlow; P. C. of Ch. Ch. Dean Forest, Glouc. Translator, *Alcestis of Euripides into English Verse,* Longmans, 1849, 1s 6*d*; *Theocritus, Bion, Moschus, &c.* Bohn, 1853; *Hesiod, Callimachus' Theognis,* Bohn; *Terence, with Notes critical and explanatory,* Weale, 1858–60; *Plato's Apology, Crito and Phædon, with Notes critical, &c.* Weale, 1861; *The Prometheus, Vinctus of Æschylus, with Notes critical, &c.* Weale, 1862; *Septem contra Thebas of Æschylus,* Weale, 1864; *The Fables of Babrius in two parts, translated into English Verse from the text of Sir G. Cornewall Lewis,* Lockwood, 1860. Author, *Nugæ, Original and Translated Poems,* Hardwicke, 1854. Mr. Davies assumed the surname of Davies instead of Banks, by Royal Licence, in 1858. [4]

DAVIES, James, *Abbenhall Rectory, near Ross.*—Oriel Coll. Ox. 2nd cl. Lit. Hum. B.A. 1808, M.A. 1811; Deac. and Pr. 1810 by Bp of G. and B. R. of Abbenhall, Dio. G. and B. 1837. (Patron, J. F. Sevier, Esq; Tithe, 140*l*; Glebe, 24 acres; R.'s Inc. 164*l* and Ho; Pop. 228.) Rural Dean; Chap. to Lord Sherborne. Author, *Case of Constance Kent; Ritual and Common Sense,* and other Tracts. [5]

DAVIES, James, *Braishfield House, Romsey, Hants.*—Mert. Coll. Ox. B.A. 1817, M.A. 1819; Deac. 1820 and Pr. 1821 by Bp of Win. P. C. of Chilworth, Hants, Dio. Win. 1840. (Patron, J. Fleming, Esq; P. C.'s Inc. 7*l*; Pop. 176.) P. C. of Baddesley North, Hants, Dio. Win. 1842. (Patron, T. Chamberlayne, Esq; P. C.'s Inc. 112*l*; Pop. 189.) [6]

DAVIES, James, *Llanfrothen, Portmadoc, Merionethshire.*—Lampeter 1858–61; Deac. 1861 and Pr. 1862 by Bp of St. D. R. of Llanfrothen, Dio. Ban. 1865. (Patron, Bp of Ban; R.'s Inc. 120*l* and Ho; Pop. 681.) Formerly Asst. C. of Llandefeilog and Llangendeirne 1861–62, V. of Llandfeilog 1862–65. [7]

DAVIES, James Melbourne, *St. Woolos, Newport, Monmouthshire.*—Pemb. Coll. Cam. B.A. 1863, M.A. 1867; Deac. 1866 and Pr. 1867 by Bp of Llan. C. of St. Woolos, Newport, 1866. [8]

DAVIES, Jemson, *St Nicholas', Leicester.*—Clare Coll. Cam. B.A. 1818, M.A. 1821; Deac. 1818 and Pr. 1819 by Bp of Lin. V. of St. Nicholas', Leicester, Dio. Pet. 1841. (Patron, Ld Chan; Tithe, 2*l* 6*s* 6*d*; V.'s Inc. 150*l*; Pop. 3200.) Formerly C. of St. Nicholas', 1818–41. [9]

DAVIES, Jenkin, *Mold Vicarage, Flintshire.*—Lampeter B.A. 1852, M.A. 1855; Deac. 1843 by Bp of Llan. Pr. 1844 by Bp of St. A. V. of Mold, Dio. St. A. 1854. (Patron, Bp of St. A; Tithe—App. 107*l* 4*s* 2½*d*, Imp. 2178*l* 12*s* 4*d*, V. 370*l*; Glebe, 4 acres; V.'s Inc. 402*l* and Ho; Pop. 4881.) Surrogate. [10]

DAVIES, John, *Clydey, Newcastle in Emlyn, Pembrokeshire.*—C. of Clydey. [11]

DAVIES, John, *Reynoldston, Swansea.*—R. of Reynoldston, Dio. St. D. 1834. (Patron, C. R. M. Talbot, Esq; R.'s Inc. 150*l*; Pop. 270.) Surrogate. [12]

DAVIES, John, *Llanychaiarn, Aberystwith.*—Pemb. Coll. Cam. B.A. 1854, M.A. 1857; Deac. 1854 and Pr. 1855 by Bp of Llan. P. C. of Llanychaiarn, Dio. St. D. 1863. (Patron, Sir A. P. B. Chichester, Bart; P. C.'s Inc. 110*l*; Pop. 580.) Formerly C. of Aberpergwm and St. Fagan's, Aberdare, 1862. [13]

DAVIES, John, *Dudley.*—Trin. Coll. Cam. B.A. 1832, M.A. 1835; Deac. 1832 and Pr. 1833. P. C. of St. Edmund's, Dudley, Dio. Wor. 1844. (Patron, V. of Dudley; P. C.'s Inc. 300*l*; Pop. 3213.) Chap. to the Dudley Union. [14]

DAVIES, John, *Eglwys-Rhos, Conway.*—Dub. A.B 1835, A.M. 1838; Deac. 1836 and Pr. 1837 by Bp of St. A. P. C. of Eglwys-Rhos, Dio. St. A. 1846. (Patron, Bp of St. A; Tithe, App. 489*l* 19*s*; P. C.'s Inc. 168*l*; Pop. 832.) [15]

DAVIES, John, *Llanddulas, Rhyl.*—R. of Llanddulas, Dio. St. A. 1865. (Patron, Bp of St. A; R.'s Inc. 186*l* and Ho; Pop. 619.) [16]

DAVIES, J., *Yscybor-y-Coed, Cardigan.*—P. C. of Yscybor-y-Coed, Dio. St. D. (Patroness, Mrs. Jane Davis; P. C.'s Inc. 90*l*; Pop. 546.) [17]

DAVIES, John, *Trenddyn Parsonage, Mold, Flintshire.*—St. Bees; Deac. 1862 and Pr. 1863 by Bp of St. A. P. C. of Trenddyn, Dio. St. A. 1867. (Patron, Bp of St. A.; Tithe, 63*l* 14*s*; Glebe, 32 acres; P. C.'s Inc. 140*l* and Ho: Pop. 1525.) Formerly C. of Cwm, Flints, 1862–67. [18]

DAVIES, John, *Walsoken Rectory, Wisbech.*—St. John's Coll. Cam. Wrang. 1842 and Hulsean Prize Essay 1842; Deac. and Pr. 1843 by Bp of Lon. R. of Walsoken, Dio. Nor. 1857. (Patron, the present R; Tithe, 1232*l* 17*s* 3*d*; Glebe, 30 acres; R.'s Inc. 1298*l* and Ho; Pop. 2685.) Formerly P. C. of Smallwood, Cheshire, 1853–57. Author, *On the Relation of the Moral Precepts of the Old and New Testament to each other* (Hulsean Prize, 1843), 3*s* 6*d*; sundry Papers in the London Philological Society since 1853. [19]

DAVIES, John, *Llanrwst, Denbighshire.*—Lampeter, Sen. Scho. Deac. 1858 and Pr. 1859 by Bp of St. D. C. of Llanrwst 1861. Formerly C. of Yspytty Ystwyth 1858–60, Felinfoel, Llanelly, 1860–61. [20]

DAVIES, John, *St. David's, Festiniog, near Carnarvon.*—Lampeter, Eldon Welsh Scho. and Reading Prizeman 1856; Deac. 1857 and Pr. 1858 by Bp of St. D. P. C. of St. David's, Festiniog, Dio. Ban. 1865. (Patroness, Mrs. Oakeley; P. C.'s Inc. 180*l* and Ho; Pop. 4000.) Formerly C. of Llanfair-ar-ybryn, Carmarthen, 1857–58, Waunfaur, Carnarvon, 1858–61; P. C. of Llannwchllyn 1861–65. [21]

DAVIES, John, *Pennant Llanfyllin, Montgomeryshire.*—C. of Pennant with Penybont. [22]

DAVIES, John, *Dewsbury, Yorks.*—C. of Dewsbury. [23]

DAVIES, John Bayley, *Waters Upton Rectory, Wellington, Salop.*—St. John's Coll. Cam. B.A. 1862, M.A. 1866; Deac. 1864 and Pr. 1865 by Bp of Lin. R. of Waters Upton, Dio. Lich. 1866. (Patron, the present R; Tithe, 141*l*; Glebe, 33 acres; R.'s Inc. 330*l* and Ho; Pop. 206.) Formerly C. of Morton, Lincolnshire, 1864–66. [24]

DAVIES, John Clement, *Derwen Rectory, Ruthin, Denbighshire.*—Trin. Coll. Cam. B.A. 1835; Deac. 1836 and Pr. 1837 by Bp of Ban. R. of Derwen, Dio. St. A. 1859. (Patron, Bp of St. D; R.'s Inc. 480*l* and Ho; Pop. 573.) Formerly C. of Barmouth 1837, Dolgellau 1841, Carnarvon 1844; R. of Llanvair, Barmouth, 1846–59. [25]

DAVIES, John Cynon, *Rheola, Neath, Glamorganshire.*—Deac. 1865 and Pr. 1866 by Bp of Llan. Chap. to N. V. E. Vaughan, Esq; Rheola 1866; Head Mast. of Cadoxton and Neath Gr. Sch. 1866. Formerly C. of Newton Nottage 1865–66. [26]

DAVIES, John David, *Llanmadock, Swansea.*—Dub. A.B. 1855, A.M. 1859; Deac. 1855 and Pr. 1856 by Bp of St. D. R. of Llanmadock, Dio. St. D. 1860. (Patron, Ld Chan; R.'s Inc. 120*l*; Pop. 225.) [27]

DAVIES, John Evan, *Llangelynin Rectory, near Dolgelly.*—Jesus Coll. Ox. B.A. 1848, M.A. 1851; Deac. and Pr. 1849 by Bp of St. A. R. of Llangelynin, Dio. Ban. 1865. (Patron, R. Ll. Jones-Parry, Esq; Tithe, 400*l*; Glebe, 1 acre; R.'s Inc. 400*l*; Pop. 1600.) Formerly P. C. of Rhos-y-cal 1849–51; P. C. of St. Mary's, Llanrwst, 1852–60; P. C. of Trevor 1861–65. [28]

DAVIES, J. Griffith, *Ystalyfera, near Swansea.*—Formerly C. of Llanrhidian and Penclawdd. [29]

DAVIES, John Hamilton, *Dale Villa, Leamington Priors.*—Univ. of Glasgow 1841–43, Sen. Hebr. and Div. Stud. B.A. 1843, Old Coll. Univ. of Leyden 1843–48; Deac. and Pr. by Bp of Wor. C. of Leamington Priors 1858. Formerly serving English Ref. Ch. Rotterdam; C. of Leamington Priors 1856, Holy Trinity, Coventry, 1857. Author, *Life and Times of Sir Walter Raleigh*, 1849; reviews and articles in many periodicals. Editor of 5th ed. of *Geology and Scripture*, Bohn, 1852. [1]

DAVIES, John Hart, *Gisburn Vicarage, Skipton.*—Trin. Coll. Cam. 22nd Wrang. B.A. 1863, M.A. 1866; Deac. 1863 and Pr. 1864 by Abp of Cant. V. of Gisburn, Dio. Rip. 1867. (Patron, Ld Chan; V.'s Inc. 400*l* and Ho; Pop. 1756.) Formerly C. of Ch. Ch. Ramsgate, 1863, St. Michael's, Pimlico, 1866. [2]

DAVIES, John Lane, *Rectory, Talachddu, Brecon.*—St. Aidan's; Deac. 1849 and Pr. 1860 by Abp of Cant. P. C. of Llanthew, Dio. St. D. 1862. (Patron, Archd. of Brecon; Tithe, App. 300*l*; Glebe, 8 acres; P. C.'s Inc. 97*l*; Pop. 292.) P. C. of Battle, Dio. St. D. 1862. (Patrons, Messrs. Lloyd and Watkins; Tithe, Imp. 135*l*; P. C.'s Inc. 94*l*; Pop. 151.) Formerly C. of Appledore, Kent, 1859, Neath 1861, Talachddw 1864. Author, various musical compositions published by Novello. [3]

DAVIES, John Llewellyn, 18, *Blandford-square, London, N.W.*—Trin. Coll. Cam. Bell's Univ. Scho. 1845, B.A. 1848, M.A. 1851; Deac. 1851 and Pr. 1852 by Bp of Dur. R. of Ch. Ch. Marylebone, Dio. Lon. 1856. (Patron, the Crown; R.'s Inc. 550*l*; Pop. 30,000.) Formerly Fell. and Coll. Preacher of Trin. Coll. Cam; P. C. of St. Mark's, Whitechapel, Lond. 1853–56. Author, *Sermons on the Manifestation of the Son of God, with a Preface addressed to Laymen on the present Position of the Clergy of the Church of England; and an Appendix on the Testimony of Scripture and the Church as to the Possibility of Pardon in the Future State*, 6s 6d; *St. Paul and Modern Thought, Remarks on some of the Views advanced in Professor Jowett's Commentary on St. Paul*, 2s 6d; *The Work of Christ; or the World Reconciled to God, Sermons Preached in Christ Church, St. Marylebone, with a Preface on the Atonement Controversy*, 6s; *Baptism, Confirmation, and the Lord's Supper, as interpreted by their outward signs, three Expository Addresses for Parochial Use*, 1s 6d; in *Tracts for Priests and People*—No. IV. *The Signs of the Kingdom of Heaven, an Appeal to Scripture on the Question of Miracles*, 1s; No. XI. *The Spirit Giveth Life*, 1s; and No. XIII. *A Review of the Bishop of Gloucester and Bristol's Essay in "Aids to Faith,"* in conjunction with the Rev. Francis Garden, M.A. 1s. all published by Macmillan and Co. [4]

DAVIES, John Peter, *Llangeitho, Lampeter, Cardiganshire.*—St. Aidan's; Deac. 1851 and Pr. 1852 by Bp of Ches. P. C. of Bettws-Leiky, Cardiganshire, Dio. St. D. 1853. (Patron, Edward Evans, Esq; Tithe, App. 110*l*; Glebe, 85 acres; P. C.'s Inc. 61*l*; Pop. 349.) [5]

DAVIES, John Silvester, *Woolston, Southampton.*—Pemb. Coll. Ox. 4th cl. Math et Phy. 1852, B.A. 1853, M.A. 1856; Deac. 1853 by Bp of Ox. Pr. 1856 by Bp of Win. P. C. of St. Mark's, Woolston, Dio. Win. 1864. (Patron, Bp of Win; Tithe, 150*l*; P. C.'s Inc. 200*l*; Pop. 1200.) Formerly C. of St. Aldate's, Oxford, 1853–55; P. C. of Jesus Chapel, Southampton, 1856–60; Asst. Chap. at Alexandria 1860–61; C. of St. Peter's, Southampton, 1862–63. Editor, *An English Chronicle*, etc. *with Appendix and Additions from the Eulogium, Camden Society*, 4to. 1856. Author, *Patriotism* (a Sermon), Parkers, 1860. [6]

DAVIES, Lewis, *Temple Druid, Maenclochog, Haverfordwest.*—Deac. 1825 and Pr. 1827 by Bp of St. D. P. C. of Llan-y-Keran, Pemb. Dio. St. D. 1845. (Patron, Lord Milford; Tithe, Imp. 187*l* 9*s*; P. C.'s Inc. 56*l*; Pop. 416.) P. C. of Ford, Dio. St. D. 1838. (Patron, W. E. Tucker, Esq; Tithe—Imp. 46*l* 14*s*, P. C. 1*l*; P. C.'s Inc. 74*l*; Pop. 41.) [7]

DAVIES, Lewis Charles Connemara, *Charlton-Musgrove, Wincanton, Somerset.*—Wad. Coll. Ox. B.A; Pr. 1828 by Bp of Lich. R. of Charlton-Musgrove, Dio. B. and W. 1864. (Patron, Rev. W. Marriott Leir; Tithe, comm. 463*l*; Glebe, 52 acres; R.'s Inc. 563*l* and Ho; Pop. 418.) Formerly C. of Eckington with Killamarsh, Derbyshire, 1828–39. [8]

DAVIES, Matthew, *Bednall, Staffs.*—Brasen. Coll. Ox. M.A. 1814; Deac. 1814 and Pr. 1815 by Bp of Lich. P. C. of Acton Trussell with Bednall, Dio. Lich. 1841. (Patrons, Hulme's Trustees; Tithe, comm. 118*l*; P. C.'s Inc. 234*l*; Pop. 617.) [9]

DAVIES, Matthew Watkin, *Maids Moreton, Buckingham.*—Ch. Ch. Ox. B A. 1849, M.A. 1852; Deac. 1850 and Pr. 1851 by Bp of Ches. C. of Maids Moreton 1857. Formerly C. of Aldborough, Yorks, and Gravely, Cambs. [10]

DAVIES, Mercer, 19, *Queen's-square, Westminster, London, S.W.*—Trin. Coll. Cam. Sen. Opt. and B.A. 1844, M.A. 1847; Deac. 1845 and Pr. 1846 by Bp of Lon. C. of St. Mary's, Vincent-square, Westminster, 1864. Formerly C. of St. Margaret's, Westminster. [11]

DAVIES, Morgan, *Llanrwst Rectory, Denbighshire.*—Wad. Coll. Ox. B.A. 1826, M.A. 1834; Deac. 1828 and Pr. 1829 by Bp of St. A. R. of Llanrwst, Dio. St. A. 1852. (Patron, Bp of St. A; Tithe—Imp. 85*l*, R. 916*l* 19*s* 2*d*; Glebe, 1 acre; R.'s Inc. 918*l* and Ho; Pop. 3993.) Cursal Can. of Galfridus Ruthin in St. A. Cathl. 1854; Rural Dean and Surrogate; Chap. to Bp of St. A. [12]

DAVIES, Nathaniel, *West Lexham Rectory, Litcham, Swaffham, Norfolk.*—Pemb. Coll. Ox. 2nd cl. Lit. Hum. and B.A. 1834, M.A. 1846; Deac. 1835 and Pr. 1836 by Bp of Ches. Preb. of St. D. Cathl. 1842. R. of West Lexham, Dio. Nor. 1854. (Patron, the present R; Tithe, 195*l* 10*s*; Glebe, 58 acres; R.'s Inc. 250*l* and Ho; Pop. 152.) Formerly C. of Grappenhall, Cheshire, 1835–36; Steynton with Johnston, Pembrokeshire, 1836–40; Min. Can. and Mast. of the Chapter Sch. St. David's 1840–54. Author, *Notes on the Cathedral of St. David; Manual of Ancient Geography.* [13]

DAVIES, Octavius, *Aberystwith.*—Magd. Coll. Cam. B.A. 1864; Deac. 1865 and Pr. 1866 by Bp of St. D. C. of Aberystwith 1865. [14]

DAVIES, Philip, *Bloxwich, near Walsall.*—C. of Bloxwich. [15]

DAVIES, Reed, *Llangunider, Brecon.*—C. of Llangunider. [16]

DAVIES, Richard, *Storridge, Malvern.*—Dub. A.M. 1826; Deac. 1828 and Pr. 1829 by Bp of Cloyne. P. C. of St. John the Evangelist's, Storridge, Cradley, Dio. Herf. 1856. (Patron, R. of Cradley; Glebe, 6 acres; P. C.'s Inc. 150*l* and Ho; Pop. 375.) [17]

DAVIES, Richard, *Holmer Vicarage, Hereford.*—St. John's Coll. Cam. Shrewsbury Sch. Exhib. and St. John's Coll. Exhib. B.A. 1855, M.A. 1858; Deac. 1856 by Bp of B. and W. Pr. 1857 by Bp of G. and B. C. of Holmer 1865. Formerly C. of Lydney, Glouc. 1856–58, All Saints', Hereford, 1859, Kington, Herf. 1860–62; P. C. of Brockhampton 1863–65. [18]

DAVIES, Richard, *Llawr-y-Bettws, Corwen, N. Wales.*—St. Bees; Deac. 1860, Pr. 1862. P. C. of Llawr-y-Bettws, Dio. St. A. 1864. (Patron, Bp of St. A; P. C.'s Inc. 120*l*; Pop. 450.) Formerly C. of Llandderfell. [19]

DAVIES, The Venerable Richard William Payne, *Court-y-Gollen, Crickhowell, Breconshire.*—Wor. Coll. Ox. B.A. 1829, M.A. 1853; Deac. 1830, Pr. 1832. R. of Llangasty Tallylln, Breconshire, Dio. St. D. 1833. (Patron, the present R; Tithe, 262*l*; Glebe, 12 acres; R.'s Inc. 240*l*; Pop. 200.) Archd. of Brecon, and Cursal Preb. in St. D. Cathl. 1859. Author, *Charges*, 1861, '62, '64, '65, '67, Parkers, Oxford. [20]

DAVIES, Robert, *East Drayton, East Retford, Notts.*—V. of East Drayton-cum-Membris, with Askham V. and Stokeham R. Dio. Lin. 1845. (Patrons, D. and C. of York; East Drayton, Tithe—App. 300*l*, V. 67*l* 3*s* 11½*d*; Glebe, 5 acres; Askham, Tithe—App. 201*l* 10*s*, V. 59*l* 3*s* 11*d*; Glebe, ½ acre; Stokeham, Tithe, 123*l*; Glebe, 20 acres; V.'s Inc. 290*l*; Pop. East Drayton, 263, Askham 287, Stokeham 53.) [21]

DAVIES, Robert Hedges Eyre, *Leigh Sinton, Malvern.*—Trin. Coll. Cam. B.A. 1861, M.A. 1864; Deac. 1862 and Pr. 1868 by Bp of Wor. C. of Leigh and Bransford 1862. [1]

DAVIES, Robert Henry, 178, *Oakley-street, Chelsea, S.W.*—Dub. A.B. 1844; Deac. and Pr. 1846. P. C. of the Old Church, Chelsea, Dio. Lon. 1855. (Patron, the R. of Chelsea; P. C.'s Inc. 250*l*.) Author, *The Contrast*, 1853; various Tracts; *Three Tests for Christian Professors*, Macintosh, 1867. [2]

DAVIES, Robert Pritchard, *St. Mary's, Hertford.*—Corpus Coll. Cam. Wrang. and B A. 1845, M.A. 1848; Deac. 1846, Pr. 1847. P. C. of St. Mary's, Hatfield, Herts, Dio. Roch. 1849. (Patroness, Miss Mills; P. C.'s Inc. 100*l* and Ho.) [3]

DAVIES, Septimus Russell, 10, *Lee-terrace, Lee, S.E.*—Queens' Coll. Cam. M.A. P. C. of St. Stephen's, Lewisham, Dio. Roch. 1865. (Patron, the present P. C; Pop. 2500.) [4]

DAVIES, Thomas, *Llanwrin Rectory, Machynlleth, Montgomeryshire.*—Lampeter, 1st cl. Scho; Deac. 1837 and Pr. 1838 by Bp of St. D. R. of Llanwrin, Dio. Ban. 1862. (Patron, Bp of Ban; Glebe, 1 acre; R.'s Inc. 365*l* and Ho; Pop. 650.) Formerly C. of Holyhead 1840. [5]

DAVIES, Thomas, *Llanddoget, Llanrwst, Denbighshire.*—Jesus Coll. Ox. B A. 1820, M.A. 1823; Deac. 1821, Pr. 1822. R. of Llanddoget, Dio. St A. 1825. (Patron, Bp of St. A; Tithe, 174*l*; Glebe, 14 acres; R.'s Inc. 212*l* and Ho; Pop. 276.) [6]

DAVIES, Thomas, *Treberwedd, Dehewyd, Talsarn, viâ Carmarthen.*—Magd. Hall, Ox. B.A. 1815, M.A. 1818; Deac. 1815 by Bp of B. and W. Pr. 1816 by Bp of St. D. P. C. of Llanychaëron with Dehewyd, Dio. St. D. 1853. (Patron, Major Lewis; P. C.'s Inc. 180*l*; Pop. Llanychaëron 228, Dehewyd 454.) [7]

DAVIES, Thomas, *Abernant Solva, Haverfordwest, Pembrokeshire.*—Deac. 1832 and Pr. 1833 by Bp of St. D. V. of Brawdy with Hays Castle V. of Pembrokeshire, Dio. St. D. 1839. (Tithe—Brawdy, App. 203*l* 15*s*, V. 70*l*; Hays Castle—App. 21*l*, Imp. 129*l*, V. 30*l*; V.'s Inc. 174*l*; Pop. Brawdy 644, Hays Castle 297.) [8]

DAVIES, Thomas, *Brymbo, Wrexham.*—St. Bees; Deac. 1865 and Pr. 1866 by Bp of St. A. C. of Brymbo 1865. [9]

DAVIES, Thomas, *Llanfyllin, Montgomery.*—Chap. of the Union, Llanfyllin. [10]

DAVIES, Thomas, *Abercrose, Ystradgunlais, near Swansea.*—Lampeter; Deac. 1865 and Pr. 1867 by Bp of St. D. C. of Ystradgunlais 1865. [11]

DAVIES, The Ven. Thomas Hart Francis Penrose, *Ramsgate.*—Trin. Hall, Cam. B.A. 1837, M.A. 1841; Deac. 1837 and Pr. 1838 by Bp of Nor. P.C. of Ch. Ch. Ramsgate, Dio. Cant. 1853. (Patrons, Trustees; P. C.'s Inc. various from pew rents; Pop. 2622.) Formerly C. of Knaresborough 1839–41; P. C. of Trinity, Nottingham, 1841–51; Archd. of Melbourne, Australia, 1851–53. [12]

DAVIES, Thomas Howell, *Llangullo Rectory, Cardiganshire.*—Lampeter; Deac. 1831 and Pr. 1832 by Bp of St. D. R. of Llangullo, Dio. St. D. 1833. (Patrons, Freeholders; Tithe, 175*l*; Glebe, 120 acres; R.'s Inc. 235*l* and Ho; Pop. 599.) [13]

DAVIES, Thomas Lewis, *Aberavon, Glamorganshire.*—St. Bees; Deac. 1865 by Bp of Llan. C. of Aberavon 1866. Formerly C. of Gellygaer 1865–66. [14]

DAVIES, Thomas Lewis Owen, *Pear Tree Parsonage, Southampton.*—Ex. Coll. Ox. B.A. 1856, M.A. 1860; Deac. 1857 and Pr. 1860 by Bp of Win. P.C. of St. Mary's Extra, Southampton, Dio. Win. 1860. (Patroness, Mrs. Davies; Glebe, 40*l*; P. C.'s Inc. 200*l* and Ho; Pop. 950.) [15]

DAVIES, Thomas Morgan, *Llanilid Rectory, Cowbridge, Glamorganshire.*—Jesus Coll. Ox. B.A. 1844, M.A. 1847. R. of Llanilid with Llanharran. C. Dio. Llan. 1848. (Patron, Ld Ohan; Llanilid, Tithe, 136*l* 5*s*; Llanharran, Tithe, 193*l* 17*s*; R.'s Inc. 340*l* and Ho; Pop. Llanilid 150, Llanharran 299.) [16]

DAVIES, Thomas Zephaniah, *Whitford Vicarage, Holywell.*—Jesus Coll. Ox. 4th cl. Lit. Hum. and B.A. 1843, M.A. 1849; Deac. 1843, Pr. 1844. V. of Whitford, Dio. St. A. 1865. (Patron, Bp of St. A; V.'s Inc. 390*l* and Ho; Pop. 1488.) Formerly R. of Llanddulas 1858–65. [17]

DAVIES, Uriah, 3, *Willow Bridge-road, Canonbury, London, N.*—St. John's Coll. Cam. Scho. Sen. Opt. B.A. 1847, M.A. 1863; Deac. 1847 and Pr. 1848 by Abp of York. P. C. of St. Matthew's, Islington, Dio. Lon. 1861. (Patron, P. C. of St. Paul's, Ball's-pond; P. C.'s Inc. 400*l*; Pop. 6791.) Formerly C. of St. John's 1847–48, and St. Mark's, Hull, 1848–49; Chap. in India, Madras Dioc. Additional Clergy Soc. 1849–59. [18]

DAVIES, Watkin, *Maid's Moreton, Buckingham.* [19]

DAVIES, William, *Llanwonno Parsonage, Pontypridd, Glamorganshire.*—Deac. 1848 and Pr. 1849 by Bp of Herf. P. C. of Llanwonno with St. David's C. Dio. Llan. 1850. (Patron, V. of Llantrissent; Glebe, 1 acre; P. C.'s Inc. 356*l* and Ho; Pop. 8720.) Surrogate. Formerly C. of Llanfabon 1849. [20]

DAVIES, William, *Fishguard, Pembrokeshire.*—Lampeter; Deac. 1849 and Pr. 1850 by Bp of St. D. R. of Llanychaer, Dio. St. D. 1866. (Patrons, Exors. of late Rev. J. W. James; R.'s Inc 79*l*; Pop. 194.) R. of Puncheston, Dio. St. D. 1866. (Patrons, Exors. of late Rev. J. W. James; R.'s Inc. 135*l* and Ho; Pop. 231.) Formerly C. of Llanychaer and Puncheston 1849–66. [21]

DAVIES, William, *Llangendeirn, Carmarthen.*—P. C. of Llangendeirn with Pontyates C. Dio. St. D. 1862. (Patron, Rees G. Thomas, Esq; P. C.'s Inc. 100*l*; Pop. 2355.) [22]

DAVIES, William, *Merthyr Tydvil.*—C. of Merthyr Tydvil. [23]

DAVIES, William, *Wrexham.*—Queens' Coll. Cam. B.A. 1845; Deac. 1844, Pr. 1847. C. of Wrexham 1849. Formerly C of Flint and of St. Paul's, Liverpool, 1844–47; P. C. of Minera 1847–49. [24]

DAVIES, William Gabriel, *Cemmaes Rectory, Montgomeryshire.*—Lampeter; Deac. 1843 and Pr. 1844 by Bp of Llan. R. of Cemmaes, Dio. Ban. 1856. (Patron, Bp of Ban; Tithe, 340*l*; Glebe, 5 acres; R.'s Inc. 350*l* and Ho; Pop. 840.) Formerly C. of Cadoxton juxta Neath 1843–44; P. C. of Brymbo, Denbighshire, 1846–56, and Chap. to the Union House 1849–56. [25]

DAVIES, William George, *Abergavenny, Monmouthshire.*—Lampeter, B.D. 1866; Deac. 1850 and Pr. 1851 by Bp of Llan. Chap. to the Joint Counties Asylum, Abergavenny, 1852 (Stipend 200*l*.) Formerly C. of Chepstow 1850, Govilon 1853. Author, *Consciousness the Standard of Truth, or Peerings into the Logic of the Future*, Williams and Norgate, 1861, 3*s* 6*d*. [26]

DAVIES, William Henry, 1, *St. George's-place, Hyde-park-corner, London, W.*—Chap. of St. George's Hospital. [27]

DAVIES, William Rees, *Radford-Semele, Leamington.*—Wor. Coll. Ox. B.A. 1818, M.A. 1826; Deac. 1819 and Pr. 1820 by Bp of Ox. V. of Radford-Semele, Dio. Wor. 1862. (Patrons, Messrs. Williams; Tithe, 120*l*; Glebe, 45 acres; V.'s Inc. 250*l* and Ho; Pop. 527.) Formerly P.C. of Knighton-on-Teme, 1844–61. [28]

DAVIS, Benjamin, *Claines, near Worcester.*—Queen's Coll. Ox. B.A. 1832, M.A. 1835. Min. of St. George's, Claines, Dio. Wor. (Patron, P. C. of Claines; Min.'s Inc. 130*l*.) [29]

DAVIS, Charles Henry, *Cainscross, near Stroud.*—Wad. Coll. Ox. Hon. 4th cl. 1843, B.A. 1844, M.A. 1847; Deac. 1846 and Pr. 1847 by Bp of G. and B. Chap. of Stroud Union Workhouse 1851 (Stipend, 60*l* a year); Surrogate. Formerly Chap. of Chavenage Chapel, Horsley, 1846–51; C. of Horsley 1846–49. Author, *A Practical Defence of the Evangelical Clergy, or the Prayer Book's reputedly Popish portions really Protestant, Dissenters themselves being Witnesses*, 1864; *The Protestant Rite of Confirmation*, 2*d*; *Bible Inspiration and Church Absolution*, 1*s*; *Anti-Essays, or the Essays and Reviews of* 1860 *Fallacious and Futile*, 3*s* 6*d*; *The Bible, on what Ground, and to what Extent, can we believe the Canonical Books of Scripture to be Inspired?* 6*d*; *Prayer-Book Difficulties Explained*, 2*s* 6*d*; *The Convocation's Problem* *of Liturgical Revision Solved*, 2s; *A School-room Lecture Liturgy, and Aid at Family Prayer*, 1s 6d; *Justification by Faith only*, 1s; *Liturgical Revision advocated and illustrated on Orthodox Principles*, 2s 6d; etc. [1]

DAVIS, Daniel Thomas, *Dany Graig, Pontypridd, Glamorganshire.*—Jesus Coll. Ox. M.A; Deac. and Pr. by Bp of Llan. C. of Pontypridd. Formerly C. of Eglwys Drindod. [2]

DAVIS, Edmund, *Longtown, near Hereford.*—Lexington Coll. United States, M.A. 1834; Deac. 1834 by Bp of Kentucky, Pr. 1839 by Bp of St. D. P. C. of Longtown, Dio. Herf. 1849. (Patron, V. of Clodock; P. C.'s Inc. 90l; Pop. 892.) P. C. of Llanfaino, Dio. Herf. 1849. (Patron, V. of Clodock; P. C.'s Inc. 86l; Pop. 283.) [3]

DAVIS, Edwin John, *Alexandria.*—Magd. Hall, Ox. B.A. 1851; Deac. 1860 and Pr. 1861 by Bp of Lon. British Chap. at Alexandria. [4]

DAVIS, Frederick, *Charlton Marshall, Blandford.*—St. Bees; Deac. 1851 and Pr. 1852 by Bp of Rip. C. of Spetisbury with Charlton Marshall, Dorset. [5]

DAVIS, Frederick, *Woodside, South Norwood, S.*—C. of St. James's, Croydon. [6]

DAVIS, Frederick, *Manor House, Northfleet, Gravesend.* [7]

DAVIS, Frederick Whylock, 6, *Grove-street, Ardwick, Manchester.*—R. N. Coll. Portsmouth; M.A. by Abp of Cant; Deac. 1848 and Pr. 1849 by Bp of Rip. R. of St. Peter's, Oldham-road, Manchester, Dio. Man. 1856. (Patrons, Five Trustees; R.'s Inc. 300l; Pop. 11,128.) Formerly a Lieut. in the Royal Artillery; C. and P. C. of Shepley, Yorks, 1848–52; C. of West Ham, Essex, 1852–56. Author, *A Retrospect*, 1851, 1s; several Sermons and Addresses. [8]

DAVIS, Henry Jones, *Cayo Vicarage, near Llandovery, Carmarthenshire.*—Lampeter; Deac. 1848 and Pr. 1849 by Bp of St. D. V. of Conwill-gaio *alias* Cayo with Llansawel V. Dio. St. D. 1851. (Patron, Prince of Wales; Conwill-gaio, Tithe—Imp. 400l, V. 142l 10s; Llansawel, Tithe—Imp. 232l, V. 102l 5s; Glebe, 56 acres; V.'s Inc. 320l and Ho; Pop. Conwill-gaio 2251, Llansawel 1003.) Surrogate 1854; a Magistrate for the Co. of Carmarthen. Author, several Welsh treatises; etc. [9]

DAVIS, James Wallworth, *Slinfold, Horsham, Sussex.*—St. Bees; Deac. 1864 and Pr. 1865 by Bp of Pet. C. of Slinfold 1866. Formerly C. of Kegworth, Leic. 1864–65. [10]

DAVIS, John, *Ashwick, Oakhill, Bath.*—Trin. Hall, Cam. LL.B. 1822; Deac. 1816 and Pr. 1817 by Bp of B. and W. P. C. of Ashwick, Dio. B. and W. 1826. (Patron, V. of Kilmersdon; P. C.'s Inc. 122l; Pop. 778.) [11]

DAVIS, John, *Ffynnondewi-fawr, Solva, Haverfordwest, Pembrokeshire.*—Lampeter, Eldon, Scho. 1844, B.D. 1853; Deac. 1846 and Pr. 1847 by Bp. of St. D. V. of Llandeloy with Llanhowell, Pembrokeshire, Dio. St. D. 1848. (Patrons, D. and C. of St. D; Tithe, 86l; Glebe, 87 acres; V.'s Inc. 150l; Pop. Llandeloy 208, Llanhowell 184.) Author, *The Creation* (Prize Essay), 1849. Contributor to *Yr Haul*; *Y Protestant*; the old *Gwron Cymreig*; *Y Cymro*; *Yr Eglwysydd.* Editor of *Yr Addysgydd* (a Welsh Educational Journal), 1851–52. [12]

DAVIS, John, *Maendu, Cardiff.*—Magd. Hall, Ox. B.A. 1858, M.A. 1864; Deac. 1863 and Pr. 1864 by Bp of Llan. C. of Maendu. Formerly C. of St. David's, Merthyr Tydvil, 1863. [13]

DAVIS, John, *Outwood, Blechingley, Redhill, Surrey.*—King's Coll. Lond. Assoc. 1856; Deac. 1856 and Pr. 1857 by Bp of Lich. Formerly C. of Newcastle, Staffs, 1856–58, Nutfield, Surrey, 1858–65. [14]

DAVIS, John Gerrard, *Dorchester.*—Ch. Coll. Cam. B.A. 1857; Deac. 1857 and Pr. 1858 by Bp of Salis. Chap. of the Dorset Co. Hospital and C. of Trinity, Dorchester. [15]

DAVIS, John Westley, *Tamworth.*—Head. Mast. of Tamworth Gr. Sch. [16]

DAVIS, John William, *Loppington Vicarage, Shrewsbury.*—Wor. Coll. Ox. late Fell. B.A. 1840, M.A. 1846; Deac. 1840 and Pr. 1841 by Bp of Herf. V. of Loppington, Dio. Lich. 1853. (Patron, Ld Chan; Tithe, 175l; Glebe, 40l; V.'s Inc. 215l and Ho; Pop. 575.) Formerly C. of Wolborough, Devon, 1844–51. [17]

DAVIS, Lewis, *Henry's Moat, Pembrokeshire.*—P. C. of Pontvaen, Dio. St. D. 1831. (Patron, R. F. Gower, Esq; Tithe, Imp. 46l 14s; P. C. 1l; P. C.'s Inc. 75l; Pop. 32.) C. of Henry's Moat. [18]

DAVIS, Samuel, *Burrington Vicarage, Chumleigh, Devon.*—Ch. Coll. Cam. Wrang. and B.A. 1835; Deac. 1835 and Pr. 1837 by Bp of Ely. V. of Burrington, Dio. Ex. 1852. (Patron, Rev. J. Buckingham; Tithe—Imp. 301l 10s, V. 252l 10s; Glebe, 105 acres; V.'s Inc. 362l and Ho; Pop. 939.) [19]

DAVIS, S. C.—C. of St. Paul's, Ball's-pond, Islington, Lond. [20]

DAVIS, Thomas, *Roundhay Parsonage, near Leeds.*—Queen's Coll. Ox. B.A. 1833, M.A. 1837; Deac. and Pr. 1833 by Bp of Wor. P. C. of Roundhay, Dio. Rip. 1839. (Patron, William Nicholson, Esq; P. C.'s Inc. 225l and Ho; Pop. 620.) Formerly C. of All Saints', Worcester, 1833–39. Author, *Devotional Verse for a Month and other Brief Pieces*, 3s; *Excuses for Neglecting Church Answered*, 2d, 4 edits; *Hints to Sunday School Teachers*, 2d, 2 eds; *The Voter's Duty*, 2d, 4 eds; *A Hundred Epitaphs in Verse for Churchyards and Cemeteries*, 6d; *Songs for the Suffering*, 4s 6d; *Hymns Old and New, for Church and Home, and for Travel by Land or Sea*, 1864, 1s 6d. [21]

DAVIS, Thomas.—St. John's Coll. Cam. B.A. 1850; Deac. 1850 and Pr. 1851 by Bp of Win. Formerly Chap. R.N. [22]

DAVIS, Thomas, *Hexham, Northumberland.*—C. of Hexham. [23]

DAVIS, Thomas John, *Fisherton Delamere, Heytesbury, Wilts.*—Emman. Coll. Cam. B.C.L. 1850; Deac. and Pr. 1852 by Bp of Wor. V. of Fisherton Delamere, Dio. Salis. 1854. (Patron, J. Davis, Esq; Tithe, 140l; Glebe, 22 acres; V.'s Inc. 150l and Ho; Pop. 370.) Formerly C. of Stratford-on-Avon 1852. [24]

DAVIS, Weston Brocklesby, *Torquay.*—St. John's Coll. Cam. B.A. 1851, M.A. 1854; Deac. 1856 and Pr. 1858 by Bp of Ex. Prin. of Torquay Preparatory Coll. Formerly C. of St. Mary Magdalen and Upton Torquay. [25]

DAVIS, William Smith, *Tonge Parsonage, near Middleton, Lancashire.*—Corpus Coll. Cam. B.A. 1859, M.A. 1862; Deac. 1859 and Pr. 1860 by Bp of Man. P. C. of Tonge with Alkrington, Dio. Man. 1860. (Patron, R. of Prestwich; P. C.'s Inc. 300l and Ho; Pop. 5600.) Formerly C. of Prestwich 1859–60. [26]

DAVISON, Charles Henry, *Harlington Rectory, near Hounslow.*—Licen. Theol. Univ. Coll. Dur. 1852; Deac. 1852 and Pr. 1853 by Bp of Dur. R. of Harlington, Dio. Lon. 1856. (Patron, the present R; R.'s Inc. 500l and Ho; Pop. 1159.) [27]

DAVISON, John Robert, *Moseley Parsonage, Birmingham.*—Corpus Coll. Ox. B.A. 1845, M.A. 1847; Deac. 1846 and Pr. 1847 by Bp of Wor. P. C. of Moseley, Dio. Wor. 1852. (Patron, V. of Bromsgrove; P. C.'s Inc. 153l and Ho; Pop. 2591.) [28]

DAVY, Charles Raikes, *Tracy Park, near Bath.*—Ball. Coll. Ox. B.A. 1840, M.A. 1843; Deac. 1840 and Pr. 1841 by Bp of G. and B. Formerly R. of Adel, near Leeds, 1854–57. [29]

DAVY, Thomas, *East Knottingley, Pontefract.*—St. Cath. Coll. Cam. B.A. 1845; Deac. 1845 and Pr. 1846 by Bp of Lich. P. C. of East Knottingley, Dio. York, 1848. (Patrons, the Crown and Abp of York alt; P. C.'s Inc. 150l; Pop. 2181.) [30]

DAVY, Thomas Gibson, *North Creake, Fakenham, Norfolk.*—King's Coll. Lond. Theol. Assoc. 1862; Deac. 1862 and Pr. 1863 by Bp of Nor. C. of North Creake 1862. [31]

DAVY, William Tanner, *Stoke Cannon, Exeter.*—Ex Coll. Ox. P. C. of Stoke Cannon, Dio. Ex. 1866. (Patrons, D. and C. of Ex; P. C.'s Inc. 200l and Ho; Pop. 452.) Formerly C. of Chumleigh; P. C. of Lynton with Countesbury, Devon, 1861–66. [32]

DAVYS, Edmund, *Leicester.*—St. John's Coll. Cam. 16th Wrang. and B.A. 1845, M.A. 1848; Deac. 1846 and Pr. 1847 by Bp of Pet. P. C. of Trinity, Leicester, Dio. Pet. 1865. (Patron, T. Frewen, Esq; P. C.'s Inc. 600*l*.) Surrogate. Formerly V. of St. John Baptist's, Peterborough, 1850–65. Author, *District Visitor's Companion*, 8d. [1]

DAVYS, The Ven. Owen, *The Precincts, Peterborough.*—St. John's Coll. Cam. B.A. 1817, M.A. 1820; Deac. 1817 and Pr. 1818 by Abp of York. Archd. of Northampton with Canonry of Pet. annexed 1842. (Value Archd. 88*l*; Canonry, 500*l* and Res.) R. of Fiskerton, Linc. Dio. Lin. 1846. (Patrons, D. and C. of Pet; Tithe, 152*l* 4*s* 8*d*; Glebe, 245 acres; R.'s Inc. 470*l* and Ho; Pop. 524.) [2]

DAVYS, Owen William, *Wheathampstead Rectory, near St. Albans.*—St. John's Coll. Cam. B.A. 1851, M.A. 1854; Deac. 1852 and Pr. 1853 by Bp of Pet. R. of Wheathampstead, Dio. Roch. 1859. (Patron, Bp of Pet; Tithe, 782*l*; Glebe, 40 acres; R.'s Inc. 860*l* and Ho; Pop. 2017.) Formerly R. of Stilton, Hunts, 1853–59. Author, *An Architectural and Historical Guide to Peterborough Cathedral*, 3rd ed. 1863, 1*s*. [3]

DAW, Charles Henry Thomas Wyer, *Otterham Rectory, Camelford.*—St. Cath. Coll. Cam. B.A. 1858, M.A. 1861; Deac. 1860 and Pr. 1861 by Bp of Ely. R. of Otterham, Dio. Ex. 1861. (Patron, C. H. Daw, Esq; Tithe, 174*l*; Rent from Glebe of 68 acres, 26*l*; R.'s Inc. 200*l* and Ho; Pop. 160.) Formerly C. of Trinity, Ely, 1860. [4]

DAWE, Alfred.—C. of Trinity, St. Pancras, Lond. [5]

DAWE, Charles J. S.—Asst. Chap. at St. Mark's Coll. Chelsea. [6]

DAWES, Arthur Longworth, *Kenton Vicarage, Exeter.*—Dub. A.B. 1829, A.M. 1832; Deac. 1830 by Bp of Kildare, Pr. 1830 by Bp of Killaloe. V. of Kenton, Dio. Ex. 1836. (Patrons, D. and C. of Salis; Tithe—App. 461*l*, V. 380*l*; Glebe, ½ acre; V.'s Inc. 396*l* and Ho; Pop. 1121.) [7]

DAWES, George Ash, *Martock, Somerset.*—Dub. and Dur. B.A. 1855; Deac. 1856 and Pr. 1857 by Bp of S. and M. P. C. of Ash, Dio. B. and W. 1865. (Patron, V. of Martock; P. C.'s Inc. 70*l*; Pop. 543.) Formerly Chap. of St. Luke's, Baldwin, Isle of Man, 1856–58; C. of Breaston, Derby, 1859–65. [8]

DAWES, Henry John, *Gillingham, near Chatham.*—St. Edm. Hall Ox. M.A. 1822; Pr. 1823 by Bp of Ox. [9]

DAWES, Henry Pelham, *Asheldam Vicarage, Maldon, Essex.*—Trin. Coll. Cam. B.A. 1841; Deac. 1842 and Pr. 1843 by Bp of Roch. V. of Asheldam, Dio. Roch. 1859. (Patron, Bp of Roch; Tithe, comm. 420*l*; Glebe, 46 acres; V.'s Inc. 500*l* and Ho; Pop. 212.) Formerly Chap. to the Witham Union, Essex; C. of Prittlewell, Essex. [10]

DAWES, John Samuel, *Newton House, Surbiton, Surrey, S. W.*—Dub. A.M. Berlin, Halle, and Jena, Ph. D; Deac. 1851 and Pr. 1855 by Bp of Guiana. C. of Petersham, Surrey, 1864. Formerly C. of New Amsterdam, Berbice, 1853, Cathedral, Georgetown, Demerara, 1854; Garrison Chap. and Vice-Prin. of Queen's Coll. Georgetown, 1854–56; Episcopal Min. at Harrisburgh, Pennsylvania, 1856–57; C. of St. Paul's, Dalston, Lond. 1860, Tattenhall, Cheshire, 1861. Author, *A Plea for the Clergy of the Church of England*, 1866. [11]

DAWES, Septimus, *Long Sutton, Holbeach, Lincolnshire.*—P. C. of St. James's, Long Sutton, Dio. Lin. 1830. (Patron, V. of Long Sutton; P. C.'s Inc. 65*l*; Pop. 526.) Formerly C. of St. Nicholas', Long Sutton. [12]

DAWES, Thomas, *Canon-Pyon, near Hereford.*—Corpus Coll. Cam. 2nd Sen. Opt. 3rd cl. Cl. Trip. and B.A. 1831, M.A. 1836; Deac. 1839, Pr. 1840. V. of Canon-Pyon, Dio. Herf. 1853. (Patrons, D. and C. of Herf; Glebe, 10 acres; V.'s Inc. 340*l*; Pop. 768.) [13]

DAWES, William, *Rotherfield, Tunbridge-wells.*—Emman. Coll. Cam. B.A. 1845, M.A. 1848; Deac. 1845 by Abp of Cant. Pr. 1847 by Bp of Roch. C. of Rotherfield. [14]

DAWKINS, J. A., *Farmington, Northleach, Glouc.*—R. of Farmington, Dio. G. and B. 1858. (Patron, H. E. Waller, Esq; R.'s Inc. 140*l* and Ho; Pop. 284.) [15]

DAWKINS, J. C., *Widmerpool, near Melton Mowbray.*—C. of Widmerpool. [16]

DAWSON, Ambrose Pudsey, *Bolton Abbey, Skipton.*—Trin. Coll. Cam. B.A. 1865; Deac. 1866 by Bp of Rip. C. of Bolton Abbey. [17]

DAWSON, Arthur, 8, *Dawson-street, Dublin.*—Dub. A.B. 1855, A.M. 1864; Deac. 1855 and Pr. 1857 by Bp of Salis. Incumb. of St. Bartholomew's, Dublin, Dio. Dub. 1864. (Patron, Archd. of Dub; Inc. 50*l*; Pop. 2000.) Chap. to Abp of Dub. 1864; Organizing Sec. for Ireland to S.P.G. 1862. Formerly C. of Bremhill, Wilts, 1855, St. Gabriel's, Pimlico, Lond. 1860. Author, *A Call to Missionary Work*, 1862; *Christian Union a Condition of Missionary Success*, 1864; *Free Parish Churches*, 1865. [18]

DAWSON, Benjamin Smith, *Yazor, Hereford.*—Ex. Coll. Ox. Scho. of, B.A. 1857, M.A. 1860; Deac. 1859 and Pr. 1860 by Bp of Ex. C. of Yazor 1865. Formerly C. of St. Teath, Cornwall, 1859–64. [19]

DAWSON, Edward Goodall, *Otton Belchamp Rectory, Sudbury, Suffolk.*—King's Coll. Lond. Theol. Assoc; Deac. 1862 and Pr. 1863 by Bp of Pet. R. of Otton Belchamp, Dio. Roch. 1864. (Patrons, Trustees of the late Rev. E. H. Dawson; Tithe, comm. 446*l*; Glebe, 1 acre; R.'s Inc. 450*l* and Ho; Pop. 375.) Formerly C. of Billesden with Goadby and Rolleston, Leic. [20]

DAWSON, Frederic Akers, *Buscot Rectory, Berks.*—Brasen Coll Ox. 2nd cl. Lit. Hum. and B.A. 1818, M.A. 1820; Deac. 1829 and Pr. 1830 by Bp of Ox. R. of Buscot, Dio. Ox. 1854. (Patron, R. Campbell, Esq; Tithe, 535*l*; Glebe, 64 acres; R.'s Inc. 619*l* and Ho; Pop 428.) Formerly Chap. to the Hon. E.I.C. 1835–54. [21]

DAWSON, George, *Woodleigh, Totnes, Devon.*—Ex. Coll. Ox. 1st cl. Math. 3rd cl. Lit. Hum. and B.A. 1826, M.A. 1829; Deac. 1838 and Pr. 1839 by Bp of Ox. R. of Woodleigh, Dio. Ex. 1841. (Patron, Ex. Coll. Ox; Tithe, 340*l*; Glebe, 85 acres, with cottages; R.'s Inc. 460*l* and Ho; Pop. 213.) Late Fell. of Ex. Coll. Ox. [22]

DAWSON, G., *Colne, Whalley, Lancashire.*—C. of Colne. [23]

DAWSON, Henry, *St. John's, Wakefield.*—St. Cath. Hall, Cam. B.A. 1831, M.A. 1834; Deac. 1831, Pr. 1832. [24]

DAWSON, Henry, *Hopton Rectory, East Harling, Suffolk.*—Oriel Coll. Ox. B.A. 1815, M.A. 1818, Deac. 1816 by Bp of Lon. Pr. 1817 by Abp of Cant. R. of Hopton, Dio. Ely, 1827. (Patron, Ld Chan; Tithe, comm. 307*l* 10*s*; Glebe, 32 acres; R.'s Inc. 355*l*. and Ho; Pop. 643.) R. of Bunwell, Attleborough, Norfolk, Dio. Nor. 1821. (Patron, Sir R. J. Buxton, Bart; Tithe, 744*l*; Glebe, 52 acres; R.'s Inc. 828*l* and Ho; Pop. 940.) [25]

DAWSON, John, *Stonegate Parsonage, Hurstgreen, Sussex.*—Pemb. Coll. Cam. B.A. 1848; Deac. and Pr. 1849 by Bp of Win. P. C. of Stonegate, Dio. Chich. 1857. (Patron, G. C. Courthope, Esq; Glebe, 2 acres; P. C.'s Inc. 170*l* and Ho; Pop. 444.) Formerly C. of Ewell, Surrey. Author, *Weekly Communion*, 1866. [26]

DAWSON, John Frederick, *Toynton, Spilsby, Lincolnshire.*—R. of St. Peter's, Toynton, Dio. Lin. 1827. (Patron, Lord Willoughby D'Eresby; R.'s Inc. 200*l*; Pop. 433.) P. C. of All Saints', Toynton, Dio. Lin. 1827. (Patron, Lord Willoughby D'Eresby; P. C.'s Inc. 250*l*; Pop. 471.) [27]

DAWSON, Richard, *Sutton-Benger, Chippenham.*—Brasen Coll. Ox. B.A. 1850, M.A. 1853; Deac. 1854 and Pr. 1855 by Bp of Chich. V. of Sutton-Benger, Dio. G. and B. 1862. (Patrons, D. and C. of Salis; Tithe, 280*l*; Glebe, 60*l*; V.'s Inc. 340*l* and Ho; Pop. 406.) Formerly C. of Midhurst 1854, Stockport 1856; P. C. of Marple 1858–62. [28]

DAWSON, William, *Mission House, Havelock-road, Great Yarmouth.*—Ex. Coll. Ox. 1st cl. Law and

Modern Hist. 1859, B.A. 1859, M.A. 1863; Deac. 1859 and Pr. 1862 by Bp of Ely. C. of St. James's Mission Ch. Great Yarmouth, 1862. Formerly C. of Hopton, Suffolk, 1859–62. Author, *The Mark to press forward to* (a Sermon), 1861; *A Tract for Churchgoers, A Suffolk Village, An Advent Message, Thoughts for Lent,* and *The Soberness of True Religion,* Bury St. Edmunds. [1]

DAWSON, William, *Moor Allerton Vicarage, Leeds.*—Deac. 1845 and Pr. 1846 by Bp of Rip. V. of Moor Allerton, Dio. Rip. 1854. (Patrons, Trustees; V.'s Inc. 160*l* and Ho; Pop. 700.) Surrogate; Organizing Sec. of National Soc. Formerly C. of Long Preston and St. Paul's, Leeds; P. C. of Brewery Field, Holbeck. Author, *Moor-Allerton Tracts.* [2]

DAWSON, William, *Eynesbury, Hants.*—Ch. Coll. Cam. B.A. 1859, M.A. 1863; Deac. 1863 and Pr. 1864 by Bp of Ely. C. of Eynesbury. [3]

DAWSON, William Vaucrosson, 77, *Windsor-road, Holloway, London, N.*—St. Mary Hall, Ox. B.A. 1849, M.A. 1853; Deac. 1850 by Bp of Ex. Pr. 1853 by Abp of Cant. Formerly C. of Botus Fleming, Cornwall, 1850–51, Hadlow, Kent, 1852–53, Cooling, Kent, 1853–58, Alfrick and Lulsley, Worc. 1859–61, all sole charges; P. C. of Muker, Yorks, 1863, and resigned through ill-health 1864. Author, *Analysis of the XXXIX. Articles, according to the Text of Bishop Beveridge, for the Use of Students for Holy Orders, with appropriate Headings to each Article, Quotations from the Fathers and Scripture Proofs,* 1855. [4]

DAWSON-DUFFIELD, Count Roger Dawson, *Sefton Rectory, Liverpool,* and *Coverham, near Bedale, Yorks.*—Corpus and Downing Colls. Cam. Scho. of Corpus, B.A. 1838, M.A. 1841, LL.D. 1842; Deac. 1839 by Bp of Rip. Pr. 1841 by Bp of Pet. R. of Sephton or Sefton, Dio. Ches. 1863. (Patron, Marquis De Rothwell; Tithe, comm. 1824*l* 10*s*; Glebe, 11 acres; R.'s Inc. 1967*l* and Ho; Pop. 4319.) Sinecure R. of Calcethorpe, Linc. Dio. Lin. 1852. (Patron, Wastell Briscoe, Esq; Tithe, 60*l*; R.'s Inc. 60*l*.) Formerly V. of Great Eversden, Dio. Ely, 1854–63; Chap. to H.R.H. the late Duke of Cambridge; Surrogate. Author, Articles on Heraldic, Genealogical and Antiquarian Subjects; *Remarks on Foreign Titles,* 1858; *Wesleyan Methodism* (a Tract), 1842; *A Sermon preached at East Cowton, Yorkshire,* 1840; *A Sermon preached at Lamarsh, Essex, on the Death of H.R.H. the Duke of Cambridge,* 1850; *A Sermon preached at Coverham, Yorkshire, on the Death of Harriet E. A. De C. Dawson-Duffield,* 1862; *A Sermon preached at Sephton, Lancashire,* 1863; *A Sermon preached at Carlton, Yorkshire,* 1864; *A Sermon on the Death of Rev. Canon Dawson-Duffield,* 1866; Joint-Contributor of two articles published in Part V. *Monumental Brasses* by the Cambridge Camden Soc. signed R.D.D; etc. [5]

DAY, Alfred Bloxsome, *Thirsk.*—Queen's Coll. Ox. M.A. 1857; Deac. 1859 and Pr. 1860 by Bp of Wor. C. of Thirsk 1866. Formerly C. of Misterton, Lutterworth, 1861, Pontefract 1865. [6]

DAY, Alfred George, *Caius College, Cambridge.*—Caius Coll. Cam. B.A. 1847, M.A. 1850; Deac. 1851, Pr. 1853. Sen. Fell. of Caius Coll. Cam. 1847. [7]

DAY, Arthur Benjamin, *Bristol.*—Wor. Coll. Ox. B.A. 1851 M.A. 1853; Deac. 1852, Pr. 1853. P. C. of St. Luke's, Bristol, Dio. G. and B. 1859. (Patron, V. of St. Philip and St. Jacob's; P. C.'s Inc. 250*l*; Pop. 2989.) Formerly C. of St. Philip and St. Jacob's, and Olveston. [8]

DAY, C., *Hollym, Hull.*—V. of Hollym with Withernsea C. Dio. York, 1864. (Patron, Rev. C. G. Hegge; V.'s Inc. 500*l*; Pop. Hollym 423, Withernsea 202.) [9]

DAY, Charles, *Mucking, Romford, Essex.*—St. John's Coll. Cam. LL.B. 1824; Deac. 1823 and Pr. 1824 by Bp of Lin. V. of Mucking Dio. Roch. 1842. (Patrons, D. and C. of St. Paul's; Tithe—App. 400*l*, V. 200*l*; Glebe, 29 acres; V.'s Inc. 232*l*; Pop. 253.) Formerly V. of Rushmere; P. C. of Theale; Min. of Trinity Chapel, St. George's-in-the-East, Lond; Chap. of City of London Union. Author, *Collection of Sacred Songs, composed and arranged for three and four voices;* various Pamphlets. [10]

DAY, Edmund, *Norton, Malton, Yorks.*—Sid. Coll. Cam. B.D. 1832; Deac. 1813, Pr. 1814. P. C. of Norton, Dio. York, 1834. (Patron, the present P. C; P. C.'s Inc. 100*l*; Pop. 2983.) V. of Willerby, Yorks, Dio. York, 1836. (Patron, Ld Chan; Glebe, 180 acres; V.'s Inc. 158*l*; Pop. 468.) [11]

DAY, Edward, *Kirby Bedon Rectory, Norwich.*—Trin. Coll. Ox. B.A. 1812; Deac. 1814 and Pr. 1815 by Bp of Nor. R. of Kirby Bedon, Dio. Nor. 1822. (Patron, Rev. H. J. Muskett; Tithe, 259*l*; Glebe, 5 acres; R.'s Inc. 311*l* and Ho; Pop. 277.) [12]

DAY, Edward, *St. Mark's, Old-street-road, London, E.C.*—Dub. A.B. 1848; Deac. 1849, Pr. 1850. P. C. of St. Mark's, Dio. Lon. 1865. (Patron, Bp of Lon; P. C.'s Inc. 450*l* and Ho; Pop. 5479.) Formerly C. of St. Anne's, Limehouse, 1851. [13]

DAY, Edwin, *Ely.*—Trin. Coll. Cam. B.A. 1848, M.A. 1851; Deac. 1849 and Pr. 1850 by Bp of Ex. C. of Trinity, Ely, 1865. Formerly Prin. of Cleveland House Sch. Brixton Hill, Surrey. [14]

DAY, Frederick, *Heighington, Lincoln.*—St. John's Coll. Cam. 11th Sen. Opt. and B.A. 1849, M.A. 1852; Deac. 1850 and Pr. 1851 by Bp of Pet. Head Mast. of Heighington Gr. Sch. 1855; C. of Washingborough with Heighington 1866. Formerly Vice-Prin. of Coll. Sch. Huddersfield, 1849; C. of All Saints', Northampton, 1850. [15]

DAY, George, *Leyburn, Bedale, Yorks.*—Magd. Coll. Ox. B.A. 1858, M.A. 1862; Deac. 1859 and Pr. 1860 by Bp of Lin. C. of Wensley 1862. Formerly C. of Barton-on-Humber 1859–62. [16]

DAY, George, *Baldwyn-Brightwell, Tetsworth, Oxon.*—Ch. Ch. Ox. B.A. 1834, M.A. 1835; Deac. 1834, Pr. 1835. R. of Baldwyn-Brightwell, Dio. Ox. 1841. (Patron, W. F. L. Stone, Esq; R.'s Inc. 400*l* and Ho; Pop. 277.) [17]

DAY, Henry George, *Sedbergh.*—St. John's Coll. Cam. 5th Wrang. 9th in 1st cl. Cl. Trip. B.A. 1854, M.A. 1857; Deac. 1859 and Pr. 1861 by Bp of Ely. Head Mast. of Sedbergh Free Gr. Sch. 1861. (Patron, St. John's Coll. Cam.) Formerly Fell. of St. John's Coll. Cam; Asst. Mast. at Brighton College 1859. [18]

DAY, Henry Josiah, *The Rectory, Barnsley.*—St. Cath. Coll. Cam. 3rd cl. Cl. Trip. and B.A. 1856, M.A. 1859; Deac. 1858 and Pr. 1859 by Bp of Lon. R. of Barnsley, Dio. Rip. 1863. (Patron, Bp of Rip; Glebe, 72 acres; R.'s Inc. 460*l* and Ho; Pop. 7710.) Formerly P. C. of St. Leonard's, Bucks, 1861–63; previously C. of St. Botolph's, Aldgate, Lond. 1858–60, St. Paul's, Walworth, 1860–61. [19]

DAY, Henry Y., *Burton-on-Trent.*—Trin. Hall. Cam. LL.B. 1854, LL.D. 1864; Deac. 1851 and Pr. 1852 by Bp of Nor. Head Mast. of Barton Gr. Sch. [20]

DAY, Hermitage Charles, *Bredhurst, Chatham.*—Brasen. Coll. Ox. M.A. 1857; Deac. 1856, Pr. 1857. V. of Bredhurst, Dio. Cant. 1864. (Patron, Abp of Cant; V.'s Inc. 130*l*; Pop. 240.) Formerly C. of Battlefield, Salop, 1856, Bishopstone, Wilts, 1860, Uffington, Salop, 1861. [21]

DAY, John, *Naseby Vicarage, Welford.*—St. John's Coll. Cam. B.A. 1842, M.A. 1845; Deac. 1843 by Bp of Lin. Pr. 1844 by Abp of York. V. of Naseby, Dio. Pet. 1866. (Patron, George Ashby Ashby, Esq; V.'s Inc. 83*l* and Ho; Pop. 811.) Formerly C. of Pitsford. [22]

DAY, John Josiah, *St. Cuthbert's Parsonage, Bensham, Gateshead.*—Corpus Coll. Cam. B.A. 1837, M.A. 1844; Deac. 1841 and Pr. 1842 by Bp of Salis. P. C. of St. Cuthbert's, Bensham, Dio. Dur. 1865. (Patron, Bp of Dur; P. C.'s Inc. 440*l* and Ho; Pop. 4000.) Formerly Head Mast. at King's Sch. Sherborne, Dorset; 2nd Mast. Blackheath Proprietary Sch; P. C. of Beverley-Minster 1855–64. [23]

DAY, John Tomlinson, *Bletsoe Rectory, near Bedford.*—Corpus Coll. Cam. B.A. 1830, M.A. 1833; Deac. 1830 and Pr. 1831 by Bp of Lin. R. of Bletsoe, Dio. Ely, 1832. (Patron, Lord St. John; Tithe,

343*l* 18*s* 9*d*; Glebe, 38 acres; R.'s Inc. 400*l* and Ho; Pop. 412.) [1]

DAY, Maurice, *Worcester.*—Ex. and Univ. Colls. Ox. Hertford Scho. 1847, Ireland Scho. 1849, B.A. 1851, M.A. 1855; Deac. 1852 by Bp of Salis. Head Mast. of the Coll. Sch. Worcester; R. of St. Swithin's, Worcester; Dio. Wor. 1865. (Patrons, D. and C. of Wor; R.'s Inc. 190*l* and Ho; Pop. 764.) [2]

DAY, Russell, *Eton, near Windsor.*—King's Coll. Cam. Craven Univ. Scho. B.A. 1850, M.A. 1853; Deac. 1857. Asst. Mast. at Eton Coll. Formerly Fell. of King's Coll. Cam. [3]

DAY, Theodore Henry, *Feltwell, Brandon, Norfolk.*—Caius Coll. Cam. B.A. 1857; Deac. 1857 and Pr. 1858 by Bp of Nor. C. of Feltwell. Formerly C. of Reedham. [4]

DAY, Vaughan Campbell, *Ash Priors, Taunton.*—New Inn Hall, Ox. B.A. 1842, M.A. 1844. P. C. of Ash Priors, Dio. B. and W. 1855. (Patron, Sir T. B. Lethbridge, Bart; Tithe, Imp. 110*l*; P. C.'s Inc. 75*l*; Pop. 207.) [5]

DAYKIN, W. Y., *Stoke Fleming, Dartmouth.*—R. of Stoke Fleming, Dio. Ex. 1859. (Patron, Rev. W. Farwell; R.'s Inc. 700*l* and Ho; Pop. 861.) [6]

DAYMAN, Edward Arthur, *Shillingstone Rectory, Blandford, Dorset.*—Ex. Coll. Ox. 1st cl. Lit. Hum. 1829, B.A. 1830, M.A. 1831, B.D. 1841; Deac. 1835 and Pr. 1836 by Bp of Ox. R. of Shilling-Okeford, *alias* Shillingstone, Dio. Salis. 1842. (Patron, Ex. Coll. Ox; Tithe, 370*l*; Glebe, 71½ acres; R.'s Inc. 470*l* and Ho; Pop. 509.) Rural Dean 1849; Preb. of Salis. 1862. Late Fell. and Tut. of Ex. Coll. Ox. 1828, Pro Proctor, 1835; Exam. in Lit. Hum. 1838, 1839, 1841, 1843; Exam. to the Hertford Sch. 1838; Sen. Proctor 1840. [7]

DAYMAN, John, *Skelton Rectory, Penrith.*—Corpus Coll. Ox. 1819, 1st cl. Lit. Hum. and B.A. 1823, M.A. 1826; Deac. 1828 and Pr. 1829 by Bp of Ox. R. of Skelton, Dio. Carl. 1831. (Patron, Corpus Coll. Ox; Tithe, 110*l*; Ancient Allotment of Common, 320 acres; Glebe, 33 acres; R.'s Inc. 300*l* and Ho; Pop. 719.) Rural Dean. Author, *Dante's Divina Commedia, translated in terza rima,* 1865; *Suggestions to the Laity of Cumberland on Church Reform* (a Tract), 1851; *The Word of God compared with Man's Traditions* (a Tract on Liturgical Revision), 1854. [8]

DAYMAN, Phillips Donnithorne, *Poundstock Vicarage, Stratton, Cornwall.*—Ball. Coll. Ox. B.A. 1833, M.A. 1836. V. of Poundstock, Dio. Ex. 1841. (Patron, J. Dayman, Esq; Tithe—Imp. 378*l* 10*s*, V. 202*l*; Glebe, 25 acres; P. C.'s Inc. 275*l*; Pop. 534.) [9]

DAYMOND, Albert Cooke, *Framlingham, Suffolk.*—Literate; Deac. 1862 and Pr. 1863 by Bp of Lon. Head Mast. Albert Middle Class Coll. Framlingham. Formerly Asst. Chap. St. Mark's Coll. Chelsea. [10]

DAYMOND, Charles, *Training College, Peterborough.*—M.A. by Abp of Cant. 1862; Deac. 1851, Pr. 1852. Prin. of the Training Coll. Peterborough, 1858; Min. Can. and Sacristan of Pet. Cathl. 1865. Formerly Normal Mastership of St. Mark's Coll. Chelsea, 1850–58. [11]

DAYRELL, Robert William, *Monk-Hopton, Bridgnorth, Salop.*—Magd. Coll. Cam. B.A. 1836, M.A. 1837; Deac. 1838 by Abp of York, Pr. 1841 by Bp of Herf. P. C. of Monk-Hopton, Dio. Herf. 1841. (Patron, Lord Wenlock; Tithe, Imp. 115*l* 18*s*; P. C.'s Inc. 88*l*; Pop. 175.) [12]

DEACLE, Edward Leathes Young, *Abbey Court, Chester.*—Sid. Coll. Cam. B.A. 1851, M.A. 1859; Deac. 1851, Pr. 1852. Precentor and Sacristan of Chester Cathl. 1866. Formerly C. of Buxton and of Stevenage. [13]

DEACLE, Hicks, *Coltishall, near Norwich.*—Emman. Coll. Cam. B.A. 1820; Deac. 1820 and Pr. 1822 by Bp of Bristol. V. of Dilham with Honing V. Norfolk, Dio. Nor. 1833. (Patron, Bp of Nor; Dilham, Tithe—App. 315*l* 9*s* 3*d*, V. 168*l* 6*s* 9*d*; Glebe, 2 acres; Honing, Tithe—App. 283*l* 4*s* 6*d*, V. 145*l* 2*s* 3*d*; Glebe, 7 acres; V.'s Inc. 380*l*; Pop. Dilham 425, Honing 304.) [14]

DEACLE, Thomas Hicks, *Bawburgh Vicarage, Norwich.*—St. John's Coll. Cam. Sen. Opt. Math. Trip. B.A. 1840, M.A. 1844; Deac. 1841 and Pr. 1842 by Bp of Nor. V. of Bawburgh, Dio. Nor. 1860. (Patrons, D. and C. of Nor; Tithe, comm. 109*l*; V.'s Inc. 120*l* and Ho; Pop. 430.) Formerly C. of Hetherset, Norwich, and Trinity, Bungay. [15]

DEACON, George Edward, *Leek, Staffs.*—Corpus Coll. Ox. B.A. 1831, M.A. 1834; Deac. 1834 and Pr. 1835 by Bp of Ox. V. of Leek, Dio. Lich. 1860. (Patron, Bp of Lich; V.'s Inc. 300*l* and Ho; Pop. 5507.) Formerly C. of St. Giles', Oxford, 1836–38, St. Lawrence's, Exeter, 1839–40, Rawmarsh, Yorks, 1840–42, Ottery St. Mary, Devon, 1842–53, Sidmouth 1853–57. Author, *The Church Catholic,* the 48th in Series *Sermons for Sundays, &c.,* edited by the Rev. A. Watson, 1846; *Baptismal Regeneration not left an Open Question by the Church of England,* 1850; *Beautiful Churches, a Partial Realisation of the Earnest Expectation of the Creature,* 1859. [16]

DEACON, John Charles Hall, *Alfreton Vicarage, Derbyshire.*—Queens' Coll. Cam. 26th Wrang. and B.A. 1848, M.A. 1852; Deac. 1852 and Pr. 1853 by Bp of Lich. V. of Alfreton, Dio. Lich. 1856. (Patron, C. R. P. Morewood, Esq; Tithe—Imp. 742*l* 12*s* 6*d*, V. 15*l*; Glebe, 74 acres; V.'s Inc. 174*l* and Ho; Pop. 8800.) Surrogate; Rural Dean. Formerly C. of Ilkeston 1852–55, St. Giles', Cripplegate, Lond. 1855–56. [17]

DEAKIN, Benjamin, *Corringham, Romford, Essex.*—Queen's Coll. Birmingham; Deac. 1860, Pr. 1861. C. of Corringham 1862. Formerly C. of Bloxwich, Staffs, 1860–62. [18]

DEAN, Charles Kilshaw, *Over Tabley, Knutsford, Cheshire.*—Queen's Coll. Ox. B.A. 1840, M.A. 1841; Deac. 1841 and Pr. 1842 by Bp of Ches. P. C. of Over Tabley, Dio. Ches. 1860. (Patron, T. J. Langford Brooke, Esq. and Bp of Ches. alt; Glebe, 1 acre; P. C.'s Inc. 130*l*; Pop. 792.) Formerly C. of South Shore, Blackpool. [19]

DEAN, Edmund, *Bussage, near Stroud.*—P. C. of Bussage, Dio. G. and B. 1861. (Patron, Bp of G. and B; P. C.'s Inc. 30*l* and Ho; Pop. 312.) [20]

DEAN, Edward, *Barlby Parsonage, Selby, Yorks.*—P. C. of Barlby, Dio. York, 1848. (Patron, V. of Hemingborough; P. C.'s Inc. 165*l* and Ho; Pop. 470.) [21]

DEAN, G. F., *Tranmere, Birkenhead.*—P. C. of St. Paul's, Tranmere, Dio. Ches. 1862. (Patron, John Orred, Esq; P.'s C. Inc. 200*l* and Ho; Pop. 3936.) [22]

DEAN, Thomas, *Warton Vicarage, Lancaster.* Deac. and Pr. 1819 by Bp of Salis. V. of Warton, Dio. Man. 1844. (Patrons, D. and C. of Wor; V.'s Inc. 230*l* and Ho; Pop. 1386.) Surrogate 1844; Rural Dean 1854. Formerly Mast. of Colwall Gr. Sch. and P. C. of Berrow and Little Malvern. [23]

DEAN, Thomas Cuming, *Redbourn Vicarage, Kirton-in-Lindsey, Lincolnshire.*—Theol. Assoc. King's Coll. Lond. 1853; Deac. 1853 and Pr. 1854 by Bp of Win. V. of Redbourn, Dio. Lin. 1866. (Patron, Duke of St. Albans; V.'s Inc. 360*l* and Ho; Pop. 2043.) Formerly C. of Boldre, Hants, and Hornchurch, Essex. [24]

DEANE, Arthur Mackreth, *Heywood, Lancashire.*—Emman. Coll. Cam. 8th Sen. Opt. and B.A. 1859, M.A. 1862; Deac. 1860 by Abp of Cant. Pr. 1861 by Bp of Lich. C. of Heywood 1866. Formerly C. of St. Dunstan's, Canterbury, 1860–61, St. Mary's, Stafford, 1861–63; St. Luke's, Leek, 1863–66. [25]

DEANE, Charles Henry, *Cannanore, Madras.*—Magd. Coll. Ox. B.A. 1855, M.A. 1857; Deac. 1856 and Pr. 1857 by Bp of Ox. Formerly P. C. of West Tisted, Hants, 1860; Fell. of Magd. Coll. Ox. [26]

DEANE, Francis Hugh, *Stainton-le-Vale Rectory, Caistor, Lincolnshire.*—Magd. Coll. Ox. late Fell. of, B.A. 1842, M.A. 1845, B.D; Deac. 1844 and Pr. 1846 by Bp of Lich. R. of Stainton-le-Vale, Dio. Lin. 1864. (Patron, Lieut.-Gen. Angerstein; R.'s Inc. 100*l*; Pop. 191.) Formerly C. of Wirksworth, Derbyshire, 1844 46, Hillmorton, Warw. 1847–49; P. C. of

Lower Beeding, Sussex, 1855–61; C. in sole charge of Stainton-le-Vale 1861–64. [1]

DEANE, George, *Bighton Rectory, Alresford, Hants.*—St. Mary Hall, Ox. B.A. and M.A. 1823; Deac. and Pr. 1823 by Bp of Herf. R. of Bighton, Dio. Win. 1827. (Patron, Rev. J. T. Maine; Tithe, 400*l*; Glebe, 21 acres; R.'s Inc. 420*l* and Ho; Pop. 299.) [2]

DEANE, Henry, *Hintlesham Rectory, Ipswich.*—Ex. Coll. Ox. B.A. 1829, M.A. 1834; Deac. 1830 and Pr. 1831 by Bp of Nor. R. of Hintlesham, Dio. Nor. 1855. (Patroness, Mrs. Deane; Tithe, 582*l*; Glebe, 44½ acres; R.'s Inc. 640*l* and Ho; Pop. 613.) Formerly Chap. H.E.I.C. [3]

DEANE, Henry, *St. John's College, Oxford.*—St. John's Coll. Ox. B.A. 1860, M.A. 1864; Deac. 1863 by Bp of Ox. Pr. 1866 by Bp of Salis. Math. Lect. of St. John's Coll. 1867; also 1861–63; C. of St. Giles', Oxford, 1867. Formerly C. of St. Thomas', Salisbury, 1863–67. [4]

DEANE, Henry, *Gillingham Vicarage (Dorset), near Wincanton.*—New Coll. Ox. B.C.L. 1826. V. of Gillingham with East Stower C. West Stower C. Enmore Green C. and Motcomb C. Dio. Salis. 1832. (Patron, Bp of Salis; Gillingham, Tithe—App. 1001*l* 5*s*, Imp. 206*l* 6*s*, V. 680*l* 10*s*; East Stower, Tithe—Imp. 146*l* 10*s*, V. 273*l* 12*s*; West Stower, Tithe—Imp. 92*l*, V. 183*l*; Motcombe, Tithe, V. 700*l* 2*s*; V.'s Inc. 1500*l* and Ho; Pop. Gillingham 3036, East Stower 426, West Stower 215, Motcombe 1433.) Preb. of Salis. 1842; Rural Dean. [5]

DEANE, John Bathurst, *St. Martin's Outwich Rectory, London, E.C.*—Pemb. Coll. Cam. Sen. Opt. and B.A. 1820, M.A. 1823; Deac. 1821 by Bp of Ex. Pr. 1823 by Bp of Lon. R. of St. Martin's Outwich, City and Dio. Lon. 1855. (Patron, Merchant Taylors' Company; R.'s Inc. about 650*l* and Ho; Pop. 165.) Fell. of the Society of Antiquaries. Late Mast. of Merchant Taylors' Sch. 1836–55. Author, *The Worship of the Serpent traced throughout the World, and its Traditions referred to the Events in Paradise*, 2nd ed. Rivingtons, 1833, 12*s*; *The Church and the Chapters*, 1840; *The Campaign of* 1708 *in Flanders*, 1846; Articles in *The Archæologia*, vols. 25, 26. [6]

DEANE, John Williams, *Riby, Great Grimsby, Lincolnshire.*—St. John's Coll. Ox. B.A. 1839, M.A. 1845. V. of Riby, Dio. Lin. 1847. (Patron, George Tomline, Esq; Tithe, 130*l*; Glebe, 1 rood; V.'s Inc. 160*l*; Pop. 242.) [7]

DEANE, Richard Wallace, *Turville Vicarage, Henley-on-Thames.*—Ex. Coll. Ox. B.A. 1841, M.A. 1846; Deac. 1843 and Pr. 1844 by Bp of Ely. V. of Turville, Dio. Ox. 1861. (Patrons, Lord Camoys, Sir J. R. Bailey, and R. Ovey, Esq. each in turn; V.'s Inc. 107*l* and Ho; Pop. 437.) Formerly Chap. of the Bedford Infirmary and Union 1852–61. [8]

DEANE, Robert Henry, *St. Luke's Parsonage, Sheffield.*—Dub. A.B. 1842; Deac. 1844 by Bp of Ches. Pr. 1846 by Abp of York. P. C. of Holliscroft, Sheffield, Dio. York, 1848. (Patrons, the Crown and Abp of York, alt; P. C.'s Inc. 300*l* and Ho; Pop. 6229.) [9]

DEANE, William Edward, 11, *Charrington-street, Oakley-square, London, N.W.*—Magd. Hall, Ox. B.A. 1864; Deac. 1866 by Bp of Ox. Pr. 1867 by Bp of Lon. C. of Old St. Pancras, Lond. 1867. Formerly Vice-Prin. of Culham Training Coll. Oxford, 1866. [10]

DEANE, William John, *Ashen Rectory, Sudbury.* Oriel Coll. Ox. B.A. 1847; Deac. 1847 and Pr. 1849 by Bp of Wor. R. of Ashen, Dio. Roch. 1853. (Patron, Chan. of Duchy of Lancaster; Tithe, 395*l*; Glebe, 24 acres; R.'s Inc. 420*l* and Ho; Pop. 344.) Formerly Asst. C. of Rugby, 1847; C. of Wyck Rissington 1849; R. of South Thoresby, Linc. 1852. Author, *Lyra Sanctorum, Lays for the Minor Festivals of the English Church*, 1850, 3*s* 6*d*; *Catechism of the Holy Days*, 1850, 2nd ed. 1860, 6*d*; *Manual of Household Prayer*, 1857, 1*s* 6*d*; *The Proper Lessons from the Old Testament, with a plain Commentary*, 1864; Pamphlets, etc. [11]

DEANS, James, *Exminster, Devon.*—St. John's Coll. Cam. B.A. 1833, M.A. 1836; Deac. 1833 by Bp of Roch. Pr. 1833 by Bp of Lin. V. of Exminster, Dio. Ex. 1863. (Patrons, Govs. of Crediton Ch. Corp. Trust; V.'s Inc. 300*l* and Ho; Pop. 1780.) Surrogate. Formerly C. of Attercliffe, Sheffield, 1833–34, Wadworth, Doncaster, 1834–37; Lect. of Rotherham, Yorks, 1836–37; Chap. of Coll. Ch. of Crediton, 1837–63. [12]

DEANS, Joseph, *Melbourne Vicarage, near Derby.*—Ch. Coll. Cam. Sen. Opt. and B.A. 1827; Deac. 1827, Pr. 1829. P. C. of Chellaston, near Derby, Dio. Lich. 1830. (Patron, Bp of Lich; Tithe, Imp. 77*l* 2*s* 6*d*; Glebe, 52 acres; P. C.'s Inc. 120*l*; Pop. 484.) V. of Melbourne, Dio. Lich. 1831. (Patron, Bp of Lich; Tithe, 14*s* 8*d*; Glebe, 78 acres; V.'s Inc. 236*l* and Ho; Pop. 2621.) Author, *History of Melbourne Church.* [13]

DEAR, Robert, 6, *Grove, Blackheath, S.E.*—Dub. A.B. 1837, A.M. 1842; Deac. 1838 and Pr. 1839 by Bp of Win. R. of the United Parishes of St. Mary Woolnoth with St. Mary Woolchurch R. City and Dio. Lon. 1848. (Patrons, the Crown and Sir George Middleton Broke, Bart. alt; Tithe, comm. 265*l* 13*s* 4*d*; R.'s Inc. 340*l*; Pop. St. Mary Woolnoth 291, St. Mary Woolchurch 102) Lect. of St. Mary Woolnoth 1837 (Value 70*l*.) Author, *Sermon* (in Aid of the Funds of the Watermen's Almshouses, Penge), 1848, 1*s*; Sermons in *London Pulpit.* [14]

DEAR, William Smith, *Albourne Rectory, Hurstpierpoint, Sussex.*—R. of Albourne, Dio. Chich. 1850. (Patron, John Goring, Esq; Tithe, 310*l*; Glebe, 10 acres; R.'s Inc. 326*l* and Ho; Pop. 341.) [15]

DEARDEN, G. F., *Birkenhead.*—C. of Trinity, Birkenhead. [16]

DEARDEN, Henry Woodhouse, *St. Paul's Parsonage, Maidstone.*—Dub. A.B. 1851, A.M. 1856; Deac. 1853 and Pr. 1854 by Abp of Cant. P. C. of St. Paul's, Maidstone, Dio. Cant. 1861. (Patron, Abp of Cant; P. C.'s Inc. 300*l* and Ho; Pop. 5000.) Formerly C. of Platt and of Loose, Kent. [17]

DEARSLEY, William Augustus St. John, *Bodlestreet Green Rectory, Hurst Green, Sussex.*—Caius Coll. Cam. B.A. 1861; Deac. 1862 and Pr. 1863 by Bp of Chich. R. of Bodlestreet Green, Dio. Chich. 1864. (Patron, Dr. Wellesley; Tithe, 140*l*; R.'s Inc. 140*l* and Ho; Pop. 800.) [18]

DEARSLY, C. H., *St. Albans, Herts.*—C. of St. Michael's, St. Albans. [19]

DEARSLY, William Henry, *Nettlestone House, Ryde, Isle of Wight.*—Sid. Coll. Cam. B.A. 1835; Deac. 1835, Pr. 1836. P. C. of St. Helen's, Isle of Wight, Dio. Win. 1845. (Patron, the Provost of Eton Coll; P. C.'s Inc. 130*l*; Pop. 1039.) Author, *Tale of the Southern Isle*; *Sermons*, 1867, 5*s*. [20]

DEBARY, Thomas, 35, *Mount-street, London, W.*—Lin. Coll. Ox. M.A. 1852; Deac. 1850 and Pr. 1851 by Bp of G. and B. Formerly C. of Clapham, Sussex. Author, *Notes of a Residence in the Canary Islands*, Rivingtons, 1851. [21]

DE BENTLEY, W., *Bayston Hill, Shrewsbury.*—C. of Bayston Hill. [22]

DE BOINVILLE, William Chastel, *Burton Vicarage, Westmorland.*—Trin. Coll. Ox. Deac. 1848 and Pr. 1850 by Bp of G. and B. V. of Burton-in-Kendal, Dio. Carl. 1866. (Patrons, Simeon's Trustees; V.'s Inc. 240*l* and Ho; Pop. 800.) Formerly C. of Avening, Glouc. 1848; and Stoke, Surrey, 1863. [23]

DE BOUDRY, Daniel, *Salesbury, Blackburn.*—Magd. Hall, Ox. B.A. 1832; Deac. 1832 by Bp of Lin. Pr. 1833 by Bp of Bristol. P. C. of Salesbury, Dio. Man. 1850. (Patron, V. of Blackburn; P. C.'s Inc. 150*l*; Pop. 1292.) [24]

DE BRISAY, Henry Delacour, *Tettenhall Parsonage, Wolverhampton.*—Univ. Coll. Ox. 2nd cl. in Sci. Nat. B.A. 1855, M.A. 1857; Deac. 1855 by Bp of Colombo, Pr. 1856 by Bp of Lon. P. C. of Tettenhall, Dio. Lich. 1862. (Patron, Lord Wrottesley; Glebe, 52 acres; P. C.'s Inc. 178*l* and Ho; Pop. 3716.) Formerly C. of Barnes, Surrey, 1856–62. [25]

DE BURGH, Robert Sill, *West Drayton, Uxbridge, Middlesex.*—St. John's Coll. Cam. B.A. 1823; Deac. and Pr. 1824. V. of Harmondsworth with West

Drayton, Dio. Lon. 1844. (Patron, H. De Burgh, Esq; Glebe, 165 acres; V.'s Inc. 620*l* and Ho; Pop. Harmondsworth 1385, West Drayton 951.) [1]

DE CASTRO, Francis William, *Arley, Coventry.*—Caius Coll. Cam. B.A. 1858, M.A. 1861; Deac. 1858 and Pr. 1859 by Bp of Ely. R. of Arley, Dio. Wor. 1863. (Patron, Rev. R. R. Vaughton; R.'s Inc. 351*l* and Ho; Pop. 230.) Formerly Asst. C. of Stretham, Isle of Ely, 1858–59; C. of St. Edwards's, Cambridge, 1859–60, Westborough, Linc. 1860–63. [2]

DE CHAIR, Frederick Blackett, *Morley, near Wymondham, Norfolk.*—Jesus Coll. Cam. B.A. 1860, M.A. 1864; Deac. 1861, Pr. 1862. C. of Morley 1863. Formerly C. of Hingham, Norfolk, 1861. [3]

DECK, Alfred, *Royal Military College, Sandhurst, Farnborough, Hants.*—Trin. Coll. Cam B.A. 1852, M.A. 1855; Deac. 1852 and Pr. 1853 by Bp of Win. Prof. of Mathematics in the Royal Military Coll. Sandhurst 1855. Fell. of Geological Soc. [4]

DECK, Henry, *Hampsthwaite, Ripley, Yorks.*—Corpus Coll. Cam. B.A. 1841, M.A. 1844; Deac. 1841 and Pr. 1842 by Abp of York. V. of Hampsthwaite, Dio. Rip. 1862. (Patrons, Heirs of the late T. Shann, Esq; V.'s Inc. 300*l* and Ho; Pop. 1484.) Formerly P. C. of St. Stephen's, Islington, Lond. 1852–62. [5]

DECK, John, *St. Stephen's Parsonage, Hull.*—Ch. Coll. Cam. B.A. 1837, Norrisian Prizeman 1837, M.A. 1840; Deac. 1838 and Pr. 1839 by Abp of York. P. C. of St. Stephen's, Hull, Dio. York, 1844. (Patron, V. of Hull; P. C.'s Inc. 380*l* and Ho; Pop. 11,551.) Formerly C. of St. John's, Hull, 1838–44. Author, *The Style and Composition of the Writings of the New Testament no way inconsistent with the Belief that the Writers of them were Divinely Inspired* (Norrisian Prize Essay), 1837, 3*s*; *Infant Baptism*, 1*s*; *Priestly Eucharistic Vestments, ignored for 300 years in the Church of England, Are they now desirable? Canonical? Legal?*; "*Contend for the Faith*," and other Sermons. [6]

DE COETLOGON, Charles F. J., *Aix-la-Chapelle.*—British Chap. at Aix-la-Chapelle. [7]

DE COETLOGON, Charles Prescott, *Brattleby, Lincoln.*—Ex. Coll Ox. B.A. 1860, M.A. 1864; Deac. 1860 by Bp of Lon. Pr. 1863 by Bp of Wor. C. of Brattleby. Formerly C. of Chesterton, Warwick, 1860–63. [8]

DE CRESPIGNY, Frederick John Champion, *Hampton-Wick, Middlesex.*—Magd. Coll. Cam. B.A. 1844; Deac. 1847 and Pr. 1848 by Bp. of Lin. P. C. of Hampton-Wick, Dio. Lon. 1858. (Patron, Ld Chan; P. C.'s Inc. 160*l* and Ho; Pop. 1994.) Dom. Chap. to Lord Rodney. Formerly P. C. of Emman. Ch. Camberwell, 1850–58. [9]

DEEDES, Charles, *Bengeo Rectory, Hertford.*—Mert. Coll. Ox. B.A. 1831; Deac. 1832 and Pr. 1833 by Abp of Cant. R. of Bengeo, Dio. Roch. 1847. (Patron, Abel Smith, Esq. M.P; Tithe, 620*l*; Glebe, 6 acres; R.'s Inc. 629*l* and Ho; Pop. 1850.) Rural Dean 1864. Formerly R. of Hinxhill, Kent, 1833–35; R. of West Camel, Somerset, 1835–47. [10]

DEEDES, Gordon Frederic, *Haydor Vicarage, Sleaford, Lincolnshire.*—Wad. Coll. Ox. B.A. 1836, M.A. 1841; Deac. 1837 and Pr. 1838 by Bp of Lon. V. of Haydor with Kelby C. and Culverthorpe C. Dio. Lin. 1856. (Patron, John Archer Houblon, Esq; Land in lieu of Tithe, 500 acres; V.'s Inc. 600*l* and Ho; Pop. Haydor 346, Kelby 99, Culverthorpe 120.) Formerly R. of Willingale-Doe, Essex, 1845–56. [11]

DEEDES, Julius, *Marden Vicarage, Staplehurst, Kent.*—Trin. Coll. Ox. B.A. 1819, M.A. 1821; Deac. 1823 and Pr. 1824 by Abp of Cant. V. of Marden, Dio. Cant. 1847. (Patron, Abp of Cant; Tithe—App. 1254*l* 12*s* 9*d*, V. 937*l* 10*s*; V.'s Inc. 950*l* and Ho; Pop. 2395.) Rural Dean. [12]

DEEDES, Lewis, *Braintfield Rectory, Hertford.*—Emman. Coll. Cam. B.A. 1839, M.A. 1843; Deac. and Pr. 1839. R. of Braintfield, Dio. Roch. 1840. (Patron, Abel Smith, Esq; Tithe, 332*l* 19*s* 6*d*; Glebe, 32 acres; R.'s Inc. 360*l* and Ho; Pop. 220.) [13]

DEERR, George Patton Theophilus, *Wadhurst, Hurst Green, Sussex.*—Caius Coll. Cam. B.A. 1858; Deac. 1858 by Bp of Lon. C. of Wadhurst. Formerly C. of St. Mary's, Whitechapel, Lond. [14]

DEEY, Alfred William, *Alton, Hants.*—Mert. Coll. Ox. B.A. 1860, M.A. 1863; Deac. 1861 and Pr. 1862 by Bp of B. and W. C. of Alton 1863. Formerly 2nd Mast. of Crewkerne Gr. Sch. and C. of Chaffcombe, Somerset, 1860–63. Author, *The Christian Sanctuary*, 1864. [15]

DEEY, William, 7, *St. Thomas's-street, Southwark, S.E.*—P. C. of St. Thomas's, Southwark, Dio. Win. 1839. (Patrons, the Governors of St. Thomas's Hospital; P. C.'s Inc. 225*l*; Pop. 1466.) [16]

DE FONTAINE, Lewis H., *St. Jude's, Gray's Inn-road, London, W.C.*—C. of St. Jude's. [17]

DE GEX, George Frederick, *Christ Church Parsonage, Frome Selwood.*—Pemb. Coll. Cam. Scho. of, 13th Sen. Opt. B.A. 1843, M.A. 1846; Deac. 1843 and Pr. 1845 by Bp of Dur. P. C. of Ch. Ch. Frome, Dio. B. and W. 1856. (Patron, V. of Frome-Selwood; Glebe, 50 acres let for 76*l*; P. C.'s Inc. 110*l* and Ho; Pop. 2885.) Chap. to the Marquis of Bath 1857. Formerly C. of Heworth, Durham, 1843, St. Barnabas', Pimlico, Lond. 1849, Frome-Selwood 1852, West Buckland 1855. Author, *Warnings without Fruit*; *The Harvest, The End of the World.* [18]

DE GREY, The Hon. Frederick, *Copdock Rectory, Ipswich.*—St. John's Coll. Cam. M.A. 1836; Deac. 1836 by Abp of York, Pr. 1837 by Bp of Nor. R. of Copdock with Washbrook V. Dio. Nor. 1837. (Patron, Lord Walsingham; Copdock, Tithe, 308*l*; Glebe, 28 acres; Washbrook, Tithe—Imp. 191*l* 10*s*, V. 224*l* 10*s*; R.'s Inc. 675*l* and Ho; Pop. Copdock 341, Washbrook 451.) [19]

DE GRUCHY, George, *Little Bealings, Woodbridge, Suffolk.*—Ex. Coll. Ox. B.A. 1840; Deac. 1842 and Pr. 1843 by Bp of Win. R. of Little Bealings, Dio. Nor. 1854. (Patron, Rev. W. T. Smythies; Tithe—Imp. 5*s*, R. 164*l*; Glebe, 7 acres; R.'s Inc. 168*l* and Ho; Pop. 278.) [20]

DE HAVILLAND, Charles Richard, 26, *Limes Grove, Lewisham, S.E.*—Oriel Coll. Ox. B.A. 1846, M.A. 1850; Deac. 1846, Pr. 1847. Chap. of the Thames Ch. Mission; Dom. Chap. to Viscount Molesworth. Formerly P. C. of Downside, near Bath, 1847–52; V. of Great Toller 1852–56; Min. of Laura Chapel, Bath, 1857–58; Chap. at Memel and Konigsberg 1860–65, Author, *Rome's Outworks*, 1850; *Sermon at the Opening of the English Church at Memel*, 1863. [21]

DE HERIZ, Forbes Smith, *Aston-Bottrell Rectory, Bridgnorth, Salop.*—Dub. A.B. 1838; Deac. 1838, Pr. 1839. R. of Aston-Bottrell, Dio. Herf. 1849. (Patron, Duke of Cleveland; Tithe, 345*l*; Glebe, 70 acres; R.'s Inc. 420*l* and Ho; Pop. 171.) [22]

DE JERSEY, Peter Rivers, *Aslacton, Long Stratton, Norfolk.*—Trin Coll. Ox. B.A. 1850; Deac. and Pr. 1853. P. C. of Aslacton, Dio. Nor. 1865. (Patron, Rev. T. G. Curtler; P. C.'s Inc. 60*l*; Pop. 356.) Formerly C. of Moulsham, Essex, and Doddington, Cambs. [23]

DELAFELD, The Count John, 18, *Princes-terrace, Knightsbridge, London, S.W.*—Can. of St. Cuthbert's in the Collegiate Church of Middleham, Yorks, 1842; Dom. Chap. to the Earl of Limerick. [24]

DELAFONS, John Thomas Harcourt, *Tiffield Rectory, near Towcester, Northants.*—Corpus Coll. Cam. B.A. 1848; Deac. 1849 and Pr. 1850 by Bp of Ex. R. of Tiffield, Dio. Pet. 1858. (Patron, Lord Southampton; R.'s Inc. 300*l* and Ho; Pop. 214.) Chap. of Towcester Union 1867. Formerly C. of Silverstone, Northants. [25]

DELAFOSSE, Augustus Newland, *Town Close, Norwich.*—Oriel Coll. Ox. B.A. 1847, M.A. 1851; Deac. 1848 and Pr. 1849 by Bp of Win. Formerly P. C. of St. Martha's, Guildford, 1849–52; C. of Broadwinsor, Dorset, and St. James's, Southampton; C. in sole charge of Aylsham, Norfolk, 1862–67. Author, *Sermon on the Death of the Prince Consort*, 2 eds. Southampton. [26]

DE LA HOOKE, James, *Bridgwater, Somerset.*—Jesus Coll. Cam. B.A. 1821; Deac. 1822, Pr. 1823. P. C. of Trinity, Bridgwater, Dio. B. and W. 1845. (Patron, V. of Bridgwater; P. C.'s Inc. 250*l*; Pop. 3201.) Formerly R. of Lower Gravenhurst, Beds. [1]

DE LA MARE, Abraham, *Woolwich-common, Kent.*—Caius Coll. Cam. B.A. 1831, M.A. 1834; Deac. and Pr. 1832 by Bp of Lich. R. of St. Thomas's, Woolwich, Dio. Lon. 1845. (Patron, Sir Thomas Maryon Wilson, Bart; R.'s Inc. 511*l*; Pop. 8263.) [2]

DELAMERE, John Henry, *Failsworth, near Manchester.*—Dub. Prizeman in Cl. and Science, A.B. 1836; Deac. and Pr. 1838. P. C. of Failsworth, Dio. Man. 1844. (Patrons, the Crown and Bp of Man. alt; P. C.'s Inc. 300*l*; Pop. 5113.) [3]

DELAP, A. B., *Canning-town, E.*—King's Coll. Lond. Assoc; Deac. 1862 and Pr. 1863 by Bp of Lich. Miss. C. of Canning-town 1866. [4]

DE LEVANTE, Edward, 14, *Milner-street, Chelsea, London, S.W.*—King's Coll. Lond. Theol. Assoc; Deac. 1854 and Pr. 1855 by Bp of Lon. Formerly C. of St. Saviour's, Upper Chelsea. [5]

DE LISLE, George Walter, *Marlborough College, Wilts.*—Trin. Coll. Cam. 34th Wrang. and B.A. 1850, M.A. 1853; Deac. 1851, Pr. 1852. Asst. Mast. of Marlborough Coll. 1854. [6]

DELMAR, Jackson, *Swalcliffe Rectory, near Canterbury.*—Corpus Coll. Cam. B.A. 1826; Deac. 1828, Pr. 1829. R. of Swalcliffe, Dio. Cant. 1839. (Patron, Earl Cowper; Tithe, 315*l*; Glebe, 9½ acres; R.'s Inc. 327*l* and Ho; Pop. 168.) [7]

DELMAR, William Baldock, *Elmstone Rectory, Wingham, Kent.*—St. John's Coll. Cam. B.A. 1837; Deac. 1838 and Pr. 1839 by Abp of Cant. R. of Elmstone, Dio. Cant. 1839. (Patron, W. Delmar, Esq; Tithe, 267*l* 8*s*; Glebe, 11 acres; R.'s Inc. 285*l* and Ho; Pop. 75.) P. C. of Trinity, Ash, Dio. Cant. 1861. (Patron, Abp of Cant; P. C.'s Inc. 50*l*.) [8]

DEMAIN, Henry, *Hertford.*—Queen's Coll. Ox. B.A. 1826, M.A. 1828; Deac. 1826, Pr. 1827. Chap. of Herts County Gaol and Ho. of Correction 1838. [9]

DEMANS, R.—C. of St. Luke's, Chelsea. [10]

DE MOLEYNS, William Bishop, *Wrington Rectory, near Bristol.*—Dub. A.B. 1844, A.M. 1864, *ad eund.* Cam. 1866; Deac. 1844 and Pr. 1845 by Bp of Salis. C. in sole charge of Wrington 1853; Dom. Chap. to Lord Ventry 1845; Decanal Inspector of Schs. 1859; Hon. Chap. to 27th Vale of Wrington Volunteer Rifle Corps 1861. Formerly C. of Trowbridge 1844, Redruth 1846, Westbury-on-Trym 1847. Author, *National Judgments the Fruit of National Sins* (Fast-day Sermon), 1849, 1*s*; *Where was your Church before Luther?* 6*d*; *Scripture the Sole Rule of Faith*, 4*d*; *Sermons on Papal Aggression*; *Living Peaceably with all Men* (Sermon to Volunteers), 1861. [11]

DE MOWBRAY, J. H. T. M., *Caistor, Lincolnshire.*—C. of Caistor. [12]

DENDY, Arthur, *Albrighton, Shrewsbury.*—Wad. Coll. Ox. B.A. 1846, M.A. 1851; Deac. 1848 and Pr. 1849 by Bp of Nor. P. C. of Albrighton, Dio. Lich. 1866. (Patron, W. Sparrow, Esq; P. C.'s Inc. 56*l* and Ho; Pop. 78.) Formerly P. C. of Southwater, Sussex, 1853–57; P. C. of Longcross, Surrey, 1857–61. [13]

DENE, Arthur, *Horwood House, Bideford, Devon.*—Ex. Coll. Ox. B.A. 1834, M.A. 1836; Deac. 1835 and Pr. 1836 by Bp of Ex. R. of Horwood, Dio. Ex. 1858. (Patron, Rev. O. Dene; Tithe, 127*l*; R.'s Inc. 180*l* and Ho; Pop. 109.) R. of Newton-Tracy, Bideford, Dio. Ex. 1861. (Patron, Ld Chan; R.'s Inc. 80*l*; Pop. 136.) [14]

DENE, Octavius, *Madras.*—Sid. Coll. Cam. B.A. 1848; Deac. 1850 and Pr. 1852 by Bp of Ex. Formerly R. of Newton-Tracey, Devon, 1858–61. [15]

DENHAM, Augustus Frederic, *Westhide, Hereford.*—Dub. A.B. 1857; Deac. 1857 and Pr. 1858 by Abp of York. C. of Westhide 1861. Formerly C. of Barmston, York, 1857–59, Mablethorpe, Linc. 1860–61. [16]

DENISON, The Ven. George Anthony, *Brent Vicarage, Weston-super-Mare, Somerset.*—Ch. Ch. Ox. 1st cl. Lit. Hum. and B.A. 1826, M.A. Fell. of Oriel and Latin Essayist 1828, English Essayist 1829; Deac. and Pr. 1832. V. of East Brent, Dio. B. and W. 1845. (Patron, Bp of B. and W; Tithe—App. 89*l* and 3 acres of Glebe, V. 690*l*; Glebe, 80 acres; V.'s Inc. 930*l* and Ho; Pop. 797.) Archd. of Taunton 1851. (Inc. of Archd. 150*l*.) Author, *National Education* (Letter to Rt. Hon. W. E. Gladstone), 1847, 1*s*; *Correspondence with Sir J. Kay Shuttleworth*, 1847, 1*s*; *Letter to the Bishop of Bath and Wells*, 1848, 1*s* 6*d*; *Proposal for a Church School Fund*, 1848, 1*s*; *Statement addressed to the Committee of the National Society*, 1849, 1*s*; *Outline of a Plan for combining State Assistance with Safety of Church Education*, 1850; *Why should the Bishops sit in the House of Lords?* 3rd ed. 1851, 1*s*; *The Position and Prospects of the National Society*, 1853, 1*s*; *Correspondence with the late Bishop of Bath and Wells*, 1854, 6*d*; *The Catechism of the Church of England the Basis of all Teaching in Parish Schools* (a Charge), 2nd ed. 1853, 1*s* 6*d*; *Seravia on the Holy Eucharist* (translated and now first printed from the MS. in Brit. Mus.), 1855, 7*s* 6*d*; numerous Charges, Sermons, Tracts, and Pamphlets. [17]

DENMAN, John, *Castleton, near Yarm, Yorks.*—Formerly P. C. of Knottingley, Yorks, 1852–63; C. in sole charge of Barnard Castle, Durham, 1863–67. [18]

DENMAN, The Hon. Lewis William, *Willian Rectory, Hitchin, Herts.*—Magd. Coll. Cam. 3rd cl. Cl. Trip. 8th on the Poll, and B.A. 1844, M.A. 1844; Deac. 1844 and Pr. 1845 by Bp of Dur. R. of Willian, Dio. Roch. 1861. (Patron, Francis Pym, Esq; R.'s Inc. 600*l* and Ho; Pop. 281.) Formerly R. of Washington, Durham, 1848–61. [19]

DENMAN, William Joel, *Stoke Parsonage, Sudbury.*—St. Cath. Coll. Cam. B.A. 1847; Deac. 1847 and Pr. 1850 by Bp of Nor. P. C. of Stoke-by-Clare, Dio. Ely, 1863. (Patroness, Mrs. Rush, Elsenham Hall, Essex; Tithe, Imp. 737*l* 1*s* 6*d*; P. C.'s Inc. 80*l* and Ho; Pop. 863.) Chap. of Stoke Coll. (Salary, 30*l*.) Formerly C. of Brantham 1848–55, Stoke-by-Clare 1855–63. Author, *The Lord our Portion, an Address to Young Persons lately confirmed*, 2*d*; *School Pieces with Reference to Music*, 3*d*. [20]

DENNETT, James, *Cheltenham.*—Theol. Assoc. King's Coll. Lond. C. of Cheltenham. Formerly P. C. of Aldershot, Hants, 1853–66. [21]

DENNETT, Richard, *Valparaiso.*—British Chap. at Valparaiso. [22]

DENNEY, John, *Hitchin, Herts.*—St. John's Coll. Cam. B.A. 1861, M.A. 1864; Deac. 1862 and Pr. 1863 by Bp of Man. C. of Hitchin 1865. Formerly C. of Trinity, Over Darwen, Lancashire, 1862–64, Edenham, Lincolnshire, 1864–65. [23]

DENNING, James, *Shrewsbury.*—Dub. A.B. 1842; Deac. 1842 and Pr. 1843. Chap. to the County Prison, Shrewsbury, 1853. [24]

DENNING, Stephen Poyntz, *St. Andrew's College, Bradfield, Reading.*—Univ. Coll. Dur. Found. Scho. 1846, Van Mildert Scho. 1848, Fell. 1849, B.A. 1848, M.A. 1851; Deac. 1851 by Bp of Dur. Pr. 1852 by Bp of Wor. Head Mast of St. Andrew's College, Bradfield. Formerly Head Mast. of Wor. Cathl. Sch. 1852–56. [25]

DENNIS, George T., *Springfield, Chelmsford.*—C. of Springfield. [26]

DENNIS, Mark Gretton, *Witham, Essex.*—Corpus Coll. Cam. B.A. 1818; Deac. 1820, Pr. 1821. V. of Great Totham, Essex, Dio. Roch. 1850. (Patrons, Trustees of late W. P. Honywood, Esq; Tithe—Imp. 700*l*, V. 178*l*; Glebe, 2 acres; V.'s Inc. 180*l* and Ho; Pop. 812.) [27]

DENNIS, Philip Gretton, *North Luffenham Rectory, Stamford.*—Emman. Coll. Cam. 24th Wrang. and B.A. 1845, B.D. R. of North Luffenham, Dio. Pet. 1862. (Patron, Emman. Coll. Cam; Tithe, 624*l*; R.'s Inc. 624*l* and Ho; Pop. 491.) Fell. of Emman. Coll. Cam. [28]

DENNIS, Robert Nathaniel, *Blatchingdon, near Seaford, Sussex.*—Clare Coll. Cam. B.A. 1840; Deac. 1840, Pr. 1841. R. of East Blatchingdon, Dio. Chich. 1844. (Patrons, the Exors. of the late John King,

Esq; Tithe, 200*l* 1*s* 10*d*; R.'s Inc. 250*l* and Ho; Pop. 128.) [1]

DENNIS, Thomas Morris, *Blackborough Rectory, Collumpton, Devon.*—Deac. 1851 and Pr. 1852 by Bp of Lin. R. of Blackborough, Dio. Ex. 1857. (Patron, Earl of Egremont; Tithe, 80*l*; Glebe, 74 acres; R.'s Inc. 162*l* and Ho; Pop. 76.) [2]

DENNY, Alexander, 40, *St. James's-place, London, S.W.* [3]

DENNY, John C., *Rhayader, Radnorshire.*—St. Bees; Deac. 1858 and Pr. 1859 by Bp of Lich. C. in sole charge of Rhayader 1865. Formerly C. of Riddings, Derbyshire, 1858, Wellington, Salop, 1860, Ch. Ch. West Bromwich, 1863. [4]

DENNY, Richard, *Ingleton, near Lancaster.*—Dub. A.B. 1836; Deac. 1837 and Pr. 1838 by Bp of Ches. P. C. of Ingleton, Dio. Rip. 1844. (Patron, R. of Bentham; Tithe, App. 438*l* 5*s* 11½*d*; Glebe, 17 acres; P. C.'s Inc. 120*l*; Pop. 1081.) [5]

DENNY, W. H., *Fulham, London, S.W.*—C. of St. John's, Fulham. [6]

DENNYS, Nicholas Belfield, *Forton, near Gosport, Hants.*—Queens' Coll. Cam. B.A. 1835; Deac. 1836, Pr. 1837. Chap. to Military Prison, Gosport, 1855; Surrogate 1849. Formerly C. of Walton, Suffolk, 1836, Downton, Wilts, 1838; P. C. of Trinity, Portsea. [7]

DENSHAM, John Cox, *Ringshall Rectory, Stowmarket, Suffolk.*—St. Cath. Coll. Cam. B.A. 1854, M.A. 1862; Deac. 1856 and Pr. 1857 by Bp of Ely. C. in sole charge of Ringshall 1866. Formerly C. of Hilton, Hunts, 1856, Fawkham, Kent, 1858, Bromley, Kent, 1862. [8]

DENT, Charles, *South Shields.*—Trin. Coll. Cam. B.A. 1863, M.A. 1866; Deac. 1863 and Pr. 1864 by Bp of Ox. C. of St. Hilda's, South Shields, 1866. Formerly C. of Great Bourton, Oxon, 1864–65. [9]

DENT, Joseph Jonathan, *Hunsingore, Wetherby, Yorks.*—Trin. Coll. Cam. B.A. 1851, M.A. 1855; Deac. 1852 and Pr. 1853 by Bp of Win. C. of Hunsingore 1855. Formerly C. of Richmond, Surrey, 1852–55. [10]

DENT, Richard Frankland, *Coverham Parsonage, Bedale, Yorks.*—St. Cath. Coll. Cam. Scho. and Div. Prizeman; B.A. 1864, M.A. 1867; Deac. 1864 by Bp of Ches, Pr. 1865 by Bp of St. A. P. C. of Coverham with Horsehouse, Dio. Rip. 1867. (Patron, Thomas Topham, Esq; Tithe, 100*l*; Glebe, 150 acres; P. C.'s Inc. 275*l* and Ho; Pop. 1231.) Formerly C. of Sefton 1864, St. Mary Magdalen's, Liverpool, 1865, Coverham with Horsehouse (sole charge) 1866. [11]

DENT, Thomas Robinson, *St. Jude's Vicarage, Pottery Field, Leeds.*—Bp Hat. Hall, Dur. Licen. in Theol. 1848, M.A. by Abp of Cant. 1863; Deac. 1848 and Pr. 1849 by Bp of Rip. V. of St. Jude's, Pottery Field, Dio. Rip. 1851. (Patrons, Crown and Bp alt; V.'s Inc. 300*l* and Ho; Pop. 6043.) Formerly C. of Hunslet 1848–51. Author, *Sermon on the Death of the Prince Consort*, Leeds, 3*d*. [12]

DENT, William, *Market Deeping, Lincolnshire.*—C. of Market Deeping. [13]

DENT, William, *Lassington, near Gloucester.*—R. of Lassington, Dio. G. and B. 1830. (Patrons, Sir J. W. Guise and the Bp of G. and B; Tithe, 119*l*; Glebe, 6 acres; R.'s Inc. 131*l*; Pop. 73.) [14]

DENT, William, *Long Sleddale, Kendal.*—P. C. of Long Sleddale, Dio. Carl. 1862. (Patron, V. of Kendal; P. C.'s Inc. 80*l* and Ho; Pop. 137.) [15]

DENTON, Charles Jones, *Askham Richard, near York.*—Ch. Coll. Cam. B.A. 1821, M.A. 1825; Deac. 1821 by Bp of Ches. Pr. 1822 by Abp of York. V. of Askham Richard, Dio. York, 1862. (Patron, the present V; V.'s Inc. 294*l* and Ho; Pop. 234.) Formerly C. of West Deeping, Linc. and East Walton, Norfolk. [16]

DENTON, Douglas Demetrius, *Aycliffe, Durham.*—C. of Aycliffe. [17]

DENTON, John, *Trinity Parsonage, Ashby-de-la-Zouch.*—St. John's Coll. Cam. Scho. of, Prizeman 1849 and 1850, Jun. Opt. B.A. 1852, M.A. 1855; Deac. 1853 and Pr. 1854 by Bp of Pet. P. C. of Trinity, Ashby-de-la-Zouch, Dio. Pet. 1856. (Patron, V. of Ashby-de-la-Zouch; P. C.'s Inc. 200*l* and Ho; Pop. 2270.) P. C. of Willesley, Dio. Lich. 1866. (Patroness, Lady Edith Maud Abney-Hastings; P. C.'s Inc. 73*l*; Pop. 45.) Surrogate. Formerly C. of All Saints', Northampton, 1853–54, Ashby-de-la-Zouch 1854–56. [18]

DENTON, Nathaniel, *North Stoke (Oxon), near Wallingford.*—Ch. Miss. Coll. Islington; Deac. and Pr. 1843 by Bp of Lon. C. of North Stoke with Newnham Murren. [19]

DENTON, William, 48, *Finsbury-circus, London, E.C.*—Wor. Coll. Ox. B.A. 1844, M.A. 1848; Deac. 1844 by Bp of Salis. Pr. 1845 by Bp of Ox. P. C. of St. Bartholomew's, Cripplegate, Dio. Lon. 1850. (Patron, the Crown; Tithe, 256*l*; P. C.'s Inc. 534*l*; Pop. 4216.) Formerly C. of Bradfield, Oxon, 1844, Barking, Essex, 1845, Shoreditch, Lond. 1847–50. Author, *The Supremacy of St. Peter*, Masters, 1857, 6*d*; *The Displacement of the Poor by Metropolitan Railways*, 1861; *Commentary on Sundays and Saints Day Gospels*, 3 vols. Bell & Daldy, 1860–63, 42*s*; *Servia and the Servians*, 1862, 9*s* 6*d*; *The Christians in Turkey*, 1863, 1*s*; *Commentary on the Lord's Prayer*, Rivingtons, 1864, 5*s*. [20]

DE PARAVICINI, Francis, *Avening Rectory, Stroud.*—R. of Avening, Dio. G. and B. 1857. (Patron, the present R; Tithe, 767*l* 5*s*; Glebe, 104 acres; R.'s Inc. 870*l* and Ho; Pop. 2070.) Formerly V. of South Scarle, Notts, 1846–57. [21]

DE PLEDGE, George, *Sheffield.*—C. of Sheffield. [22]

DE PLEDGE, Joseph Price, *Lamesley Vicarage, Chester-le-street, Durham.*—Univ. Coll. Dur; Deac. 1850, Pr. 1851. V. of Lamesley, Dio. Dur. 1865. (Patron, Lord Ravensworth; V.'s Inc. 150*l* and Ho; Pop. 2234.) Formerly C. of Chester-le-street. [23]

DE PUTRON, Henry Bertram, *Ombersley, near Droitwich.*—Caius Coll. Cam. B.A. 1862; Deac. 1864 and Pr. 1865 by Bp of Pet. C. of Ombersley 1867. Formerly C. of Redmile, Leic. 1864. [24]

DE PUTRON, Pierre, *Rodmell Rectory, Lewes, Sussex.*—Pemb. Coll. Ox. B.A. 1848, M.A. 1851; Deac. 1849 and Pr. 1850 by Bp of Lon. R. of Rodmell, Dio. Chich. 1858. (Patron, Bp of Chich; R.'s Inc. 400*l* and Ho; Pop. 292.) Formerly C. of Rodmell. [25]

DE QUETTEVILLE, Philip, *Stodmarsh, near Canterbury.*—St. Peter's Coll. Cam. 5th Sen. Opt. B.A. 1853, M.A. 1856; Deac. 1855 and Pr. 1858 by Bp of Ches. C. of Stodmarsh. [26]

DE QUETTEVILLE, William, *Brinkworth Rectory, Chippenham.*—Pemb. Coll. Ox. 3rd cl. Math. et Phy. and B.A. 1852, M.A. 1854; Deac. 1853 by Bp of Ox. Pr. 1854 by Bp of Win. R. of Brinkworth, Dio. G. and B. 1861. (Patron, Pemb. Coll. Ox; R.'s Inc. 900*l* and Ho; Pop. 1273.) Formerly Fell. of Pemb. Coll. Ox; C. of Studley. [27]

DE RENZI, George Binks, *The Penitentiary, Millbank, London, S.W.*—Dub. A.B. 1844; Deac. 1844 and Pr. 1845 by Bp of Dur. Chap. of Penitentiary, Millbank, 1858. Formerly Chap. of Leeds Borough Gaol. [28]

DE ROMESTIN, Augustus Henry Eugene, *St. John's College, Oxford.*—St. John's Coll. Ox. B.A. 1852, M.A. 1854; Deac. 1853, Pr. 1854. Formerly C. of St. Thomas the Martyr's, Oxford; Chap. of the Floating Chapel. [29]

DERRIG, Hugh, *Stanwix, Carlisle.*—C. of Stanwix. [30]

DE SALIS, Henry Jerome Augustine Fane, *Fringford Rectory, Bicester.*—Ex. Coll. Ox. B.A. 1850, M.A. 1853; Deac. 1850, Pr. 1852. R. of Fringford, Dio. Ox. 1852. (Patron, Ld Chan; Tithe, 187*l*; R.'s Inc. 200*l* and Ho; Pop. 401.) [31]

DE SAUSMAREZ, Havilland, *St. Peter's Rectory, Northampton.*—Caius Coll. Cam. Wrang. and B.A. 1835; Deac. 1837, Pr. 1838. R. of St. Peter's with Upton C. Dio. Pet. 1850. (Patron, St. Katherine's Hospital, Lond; R.'s Inc. 390*l* and Ho; Pop. St. Peter's 1216, Upton 36.) Late Fell. of Pemb. Coll. Ox. 1850. [32]

DESBOROUGH, Henry John, *Therfield, near Royston.*—Wad. Coll. Ox. B A. 1855, M.A. 1858; Deac. 1856 and Pr. 1858 by Bp of Win. C. of Therfield. Formerly C. of Effingham 1859. [1]

DESHON, Henry Charles, *East Coulston, Westbury, Wilts.*—St. Bees; Deac. 1851, Pr. 1852. R. of East Coulston, Dio. Salis. 1858. (Patron, Ld Chan; Tithe, 160*l* 10*s*; Glebe, 28 acres; R.'s Inc. 190*l* and Ho; Pop. 119.) Late C. of West Ashton, Wilts; previously a Member of the College of Surgeons. [2]

DE SOYRES, Francis, 9, *Baring-crescent, Exeter.*—Mert. Coll Ox. B.A. [3]

DESPARD, George, 80, *Belsize-road, London, N.W.*—Dub. A.B. 1851, A.M. 1863; Deac. 1853 and Pr. 1854 by Bp of Lin. P. C. of Trinity, Kilburn, Dio. Lon. 1863. (Patrons, Trustees; P. C.'s Inc. 750*l*; Pop. 7000.) Formerly C. of Lenton, Notts, 1853–56; Sec. to Church of England Young Men's Society 1857; Sec. to Pastoral Aid Society 1858–63. Author, *The Mystery of Affliction*; *Care and what to do with it*; *Ritualism*; etc. [4]

DESPARD, George Pakenham, *Melbourne, Victoria.*—King's Coll. Windsor, Nova Scotia, B.A. 1832, Magd. Coll. Cam. B.A. 1836; Deac. and Pr. 1837. Formerly Chap. of the Clifton Union, Glouc; Sec. of the Patagonian Miss. Soc. and of the Bristol and Clifton Clerical Assoc. Author, *Hope Deferred not Lost*, 1853, 5*s*. [5]

DESPREZ, Philip S., *Alvediston Vicarage, Salisbury.*—V. of Alvediston, Dio. Salis. 1862. (Patron, V. of Broad Chalke; V.'s Inc. 100*l* and Ho; Pop. 267.) Author, *The Apocalypse fulfilled in the Consummation of the Mosaic Economy*, 3rd ed. 1861. [6]

DE ST. CROIX, Henry Charles, *Longbridge, Deverill, Wilts.*—Corpus Coll. Cam. 20th Sen. Opt. and B.A. 1854; Deac. 1854 and Pr. 1855 by Bp of Ex. C. of Longbridge. Formerly C. of North Molton, Devon, Chantry, Somerset. [7]

DE ST. CROIX, William, *Glynde, Lewes, Sussex.*—St. John's Coll. Cam. B.A. 1842, M.A. 1858; Deac. 1843, Pr. 1844. V. of Glynde, Dio. Chich. 1844. (Patrons, D. and C. of Windsor; Tithe, 122*l*; Glebe, 10 acres; V.'s Inc. 150*l* and Ho; Pop. 321.) Chap. to the Westfirle Union. Author, *A Few Words to Parents who have Children at School*, 1845; various Sermons. [8]

DE TEISSIER, George Frederick, *Church Brampton Rectory, near Northampton.*—Corpus Coll. Ox. Scho. 1838, 1st cl. Lit. Hum. and B.A. 1842, M.A. 1845, B.D. 1853, Cl. Moderator 1853–54; Deac. 1845 and Pr. 1846 by Bp of Ox. R. of Church and Chapel Brampton, Dio. Pet. 1856. (Patron, Corpus Coll. Ox. Land in lieu of Tithe, 267 acres; Glebe, 51 acres; R.'s Inc. 430*l* and Ho; Pop. 328.) Rural Dean. Formerly Fell. and Tut. of Corpus Coll. Ox. 1847–48; C. of St. Peter-le-Bailey, Oxford, 1855–56. Author, *Outlines of the Christian Faith*, 1846; *Some Plain Words on the Lord's Supper*, 1852; *A Companion to the Lord's Supper*, 1853; *Village Sermons*, 1st Series, 1863, 2nd Series, 1865, Macmillans; *House of Prayer*, ib. 1866; *Clergy and Laity*, a Tract, ib. 1867. [9]

DE TEISSIER, Philip Antoine, *Church Brampton, Northampton.*—Corpus Coll. Ox. 4th cl. Lit. Hum. B A. 1841, M.A. 1844; Deac. 1842 by Bp of Salis. Pr. 1843 by Bp of Lon. Author, *Short Forms of Prayer*, 1851; *Sunshine in Sorrow*, 1866. [10]

DE VEAR, Walter, *Tovil Parsonage, Maidstone.*—Queens' Coll. Cam. B.A. 1851, M.A. 1854; Deac. 1851 and Pr. 1852 by Abp of Cant. P. C. of Tovil, Dio. Cant. 1857. (Patrons, Abp of Cant, and Mrs. Charlton, alt; P. C.'s Inc. 75*l* and Ho; Pop. 897.) Formerly C. of Goudhurst, Kent. [11]

D'EVELYN, C. James, *Berwick-on-Tweed.*—C. of Berwick. [12]

D'EVELYN, John William, *Armoy Rectory, Ballymoney, Ireland.*—Cam. and Dub. A.B. 1843, A.M. 1846; Deac. 1843 and Pr. 1844 by Bp of Nor. R. of Armoy, Dio. Connor, 1851. Formerly V. of Stanford and Tottington, Norfolk, 1845–51. [13]

DEVENISH, Charles Weston, *Publow, near Bristol.*—Trin. Coll. Cam. 36th Wrang. and B.A. 1855; Deac. 1855 and Pr. 1856 by Bp of Chich. P. C. of Publow, Dio. B. and W. 1864. (Patron, Bp of B. and W; P. C.'s Inc. 25*l*; Pop. 643.) Formerly C. of Battle, and Chap. of the Battle Union, Sussex. [14]

DEVEREUX, Nicholas Jessop, 29, *Shaw-street, Liverpool.*—Dub. A.B. 1863; Deac. 1865, Pr. 1866. C. of St. Silas', Liverpool, 1865. [15]

DEVEREUX-QUICK, Adrian G., *Broughton, near Brigg, Lincolnshire.*—Corpus Coll. Cam. B.A. 1859; Deac. 1859 and Pr. 1860 by Bp of Ely. C. of Broughton 1861. Formerly C. of Steeple Morden, Cambs, 1859–61. [16]

DEVEY, Henry Edwin, *Evesham, Worcestershire.*—Pemb. Coll. Ox. B.A. 1840, M.A. 1848; Deac. 1841 by Bp of Lich. Pr. 1842 by Bp of Herf. Formerly C. of Fladbury 1855–58, V. of All Saints', Evesham, 1858–65. [17]

DE VITRE, George Edward Denis, *Weston Vicarage, Stevenage, Herts.*—Trin. Coll. Cam. B.A. 1856; Deac. 1857 and Pr. 1858 by Bp of Lon. V. of Weston, Dio. Roch. 1864. (Patron, C. C. Hale, Esq; V.'s Inc. 228*l* and Ho; Pop. 1196.) Formerly C. of Trinity, Twickenham, and Cookham Dean, Berks. [18]

DEVON, Edward Beachcroft, *North Moor, Witney.*—St. John's Coll. Ox. B.A. 1837, M.A. 1863; Deac. 1860 and Pr. 1861 by Bp of B. and W. Fell. of St. John's Coll. Ox; P. C. of Northmoor, Dio. Ox. 1867. (Patron, St. John's Coll Ox; P. C.'s Inc. 115*l*; Pop. 375.) Formerly C. of Barrington and Shepton-Beauchamp 1860, Newbury, Berks, 1863. [19]

DEW, Croft Worgan, *Calcutta.*—Jesus Coll. Cam. B.A. 1852, M.A. 1855; Deac. 1852 and Pr. 1853 by Bp of Carl. Formerly D. and C.'s Lect. of St. Cuthbert's, Carlisle, 1855; Chap. to the Carlisle and Cumberland Infirmary 1855; Asst. Military Chap. of the Garrison, Carlisle Castle, 1855. [20]

DEW, Edward Parker, *Great Berkhamsted, Herts.*—Ex. Coll. Ox. B.A. 1861, M.A. 1864; Wells Theol. Coll. 1864–65; Deac. by Bp of Roch. 1865. C. of Great Berkhamsted 1865. [21]

DEW, George Platt, *Wolves-Newton, Usk, Monmouthshire.*—Jesus Coll. Cam. B.A. 1856; Deac. 1857 and Pr. 1858 by Bp of Llan. R. of Wolves-Newton, Dio. Llan. 1863. (Patron, Bp of Llan; R's Inc. 300*l* and Ho; Pop. 193.) Dom. Chap. to Lord Raglan 1858. Formerly C. of Llandenny, near Newport, 1857–63. [22]

DEW, Henry, *Whitney Rectory, near Hereford.*—Jesus Coll. Cam. B.A. 1842; Deac. 1842 and Pr. 1843 by Bp of Herf. R. of Whitney, Dio. Herf. 1843. (Patron, Tomkyns Dew, Esq; Tithe, 234*l*; Glebe, 17 acres; R.'s Inc. 260*l* and Ho; Pop. 260.) [23]

DEWDNEY, George, *Gussage Rectory, Salisbury.*—Queen's Coll. Ox. B.A. 1822, M.A. 1824. R. of Gussage, Dorset, Dio. Salis, 1830. (Patron, Lord Portman; Tithe—Imp. 114*l* 3*s*, R. 404*l*; R.'s Inc. 410*l* and Ho; Pop. 311.) [24]

DEWE, George Downing, *Dickleburgh, Scole, Norfolk.*—St. Cath. Coll. Cam. B.A. 1862; Deac. 1863 and Pr. 1864 by Bp of Nor. C. of Dickleburgh 1866. Formerly C. of Drayton 1864, and Rockland St. Mary, Norfolk, 1865. [25]

DEWE, Samuel, *Kingsdown, near Dartford, Kent.*—R. of Kingsdown with Mapiscombe C. Dio. Roch. 1836. (Patrons, D. and C. of Roch; R.'s Inc. 420*l*; Pop. 428.) [26]

DEWES, Alfred, *Pendlebury, Lancashire.*—Queens' Coll. Cam. B.A. 1848, M.A. 1851; Deac. 1849, Pr. 1850. P. C. of Ch. Ch. Pendlebury, Dio. Man. 1860. (Patron, Bp of Man; P. C.'s Inc. 250*l*; Pop. 3170.) Formerly C. of St. John's, Pendlebury. Author, *A Plea for a New Translation of the Scriptures*, Longmans, 1866, 3*s*. [27]

DEWHURST, John Heyliger, *Layer-de-la-Haye Parsonage, Colchester.*—Wor. Coll. Ox. B.A. 1831, M.A. 1834. P. C. of Layer-de-la-Haye, Dio. Roch. 1845. (Patron, Sir G. H. Smyth, Bart; Tithe, Imp. 680*l*; P. C.'s Inc. 110*l* and Ho; Pop. 807.) P. C. of

Bere-Church, Colchester, Dio. Roch. 1845. (Patron, Thomas White, Esq; P. C.'s Inc. 110*l*; Pop. 112.) [1]

DEWING, James, *Dodbrooke Rectory, Kingsbridge, Devon.*—Trin. Coll. Cam, B.A. 1837; Deac. 1837, Pr. 1838. R. of Dodbrooke, Dio. Ex. 1850. (Patron, the present R; Tithe, 104*l* 18*s* 4*d*; Glebe, 42 acres; R.'s Inc. 240*l* and Ho; Pop. 1183.) [2]

DE WINTON, Henry, *Boughrood Rectory, Hay, Radnor.*—Trin. Coll. Cam Sen. Opt. 3rd in 1st cl. Cl. Trip. Sir W. Browne's medal for Greek Ode, B.A. 1846, M.A. 1849; Deac. 1848 and Pr. 1849 by Bp of St. D. R. of Boughrood, Dio. St. D. 1849. (Patron, Bp of St. D; Tithe, 247*l*; Glebe, 4½ acres; R.'s Inc. 256*l* and Ho; Pop. 292.) [3]

DIBDIN, Robert William, 62, *Torrington-square, London, W.C.*—St. John's Coll. Cam. B.A. 1833, M.A. 1838; Deac. 1834 and Pr. 1835 by Bp of Ches. Min. of West-street Chapel, St. Giles-in-the-Fields, Dio. Lon. (Min.'s Inc. derived from Pew-rents.) Formerly C. of Middlewich, Cheshire, 1834–38; St. George's, Bloomsbury, 1841–42. Author, Three vols. of Sermons, 1838, 1840, 1850; *Life of Edward* VI. 1842; *Ought the Prayer-Book to be revised?* 1864, 1*s*; *History of West-street Chapel,* 1*s*; *The Village Rectory, or Truth in Fiction,* 5*s*; *England Warned and Counselled,* 1851; and various Sermons and Tracts all published by Nisbets. [4]

DICKEN, Alldersey, *Norton Rectory, near Bury St. Edmunds.*—St. Peter's Coll. Cam. B.A. 1815, M.A. 1818, D.D. 1833; Deac. and Pr. 1817. R. of Norton, Dio. Ely, 1831. (Patron, St. Peter's Coll. Cam; Tithe, 611*l* 10*s*; Glebe, 21 acres; R.'s Inc. 575*l* and Ho; Pop. 948.) Formerly Head Mast. of Blundell's, Sch. Tiverton, Devon, 1823–34. Author, *Deborah* (Seatonian Prize Poem), 1818, 2*s* 6*d*; *Sermons before the University of Cambridge,* 1823, 2*s* 6*d*; *Remarks on the Marginal Notes and References in the Authorised Version of the Holy Scriptures,* 1847, 2*s* 6*d*. [5]

DICKEN, Charles Rowland, *Balsham Rectory, Linton, Cambs.*—Corpus Coll. Cam. B.A. 1822, M.A. 1825; Deac. 1835 and Pr. 1837 by Bp of Lon. R. of Balsham, Dio. Ely, 1861. (Patrons, Govs. of Charterhouse, Lond; R.'s Inc. 1250*l* and Ho; Pop. 1162.) Formerly Reader and Librarian of the Charterhouse, 1838; Lect. of St. Benet's, Paul's-wharf, Thames-street, 1841. [6]

DICKER, Hamilton Eustace, *Dunkirk.*—Theol. Coll. Chich. 1854–55; Deac. 1855 and Pr. 1856 by Bp of Chich. British Chap. at Dunkirk. Formerly C. of Warminster. [7]

DICKIN, Richard Parkes, *Stainton, near Rotherham.*—Ch. Ch. Ox; Deac. 1859 and Pr. 1860 by Bp of Rip. C. of Stainton 1863. Formerly C. of New Wortley, Leeds, 1859–60, Tarporley, Cheshire, 1861. [8]

DICKINS, Charles Allan, *Tardebigge, Vicarage, near Bromsgrove, Worcestershire.*—Univ. Coll. Ox. B.A. 1852, M.A. 1855; Deac. 1853 and Pr. 1854 by Bp of Wor. V. of Tardebigge, Dio. Wor. 1855. (Patroness, Lady Windsor; Tithe—Imp. 1260*l* 11*s* 9*d*, V. 466*l*; Glebe, 41 acres; V.'s Inc. 624*l* and Ho; Pop. 1117.) [9]

DICKINS, Henry Compton, *The College, Winchester.*—New Coll. Ox. 1st cl. Law and Mod. Hist. B.A. 1860, M.A. 1864; Deac. 1865 and Pr. 1867 by Bp of Win. Fell. of New Coll. Ox; Tut. of Winchester Coll. 1861. [10]

DICKINS, Thomas Bourne, *All Saints' Parsonage, Warwick.*—Jesus Coll. Cam. S.C.L. 1855; Deac. 1855 and Pr. 1856 by Bp of Ches. P. C. of All Saints', Warwick, Dio. Wor. 1861. (Patron, V. of St. Nicholas', Warwick; P. C.'s Inc. 100*l*; Pop. 2000.) Chap. to County Lunatic Asylum 1860. Formerly C. of Thurstaston, Cheshire, 1855–56, St. Nicholas', Warwick, 1857–61; Prov. Grand Chap. of the Freemasons of Warwickshire, 1860–62. [11]

DICKINSON, Alfred Albert, *Knowstone, South Molton, Devon.*—Queen's Coll. Ox. B.A. 1863, M.A. 1866; Deac. 1863 and Pr. 1866 by Bp of Ex. C. in sole charge of Knowstone with Molland 1867. Formerly C. of North Molton 1863–66. [12]

DICKINSON, Charles Septimus, 186, *Edgware-road, London, W.*—Mast. in Maida Hill Gr. Sch. [13]

DICKINSON, Frederick Binley, 6, *Lansdowne-crescent, Leamington.*—Brasen. Coll. Ox. Hulmian Exhib. B.A. 1855. M.A. 1858; Deac. 1857 by Bp of Wor. Pr. 1858 by Bp of Ex. C. of Lillington, near Leamington, 1865. Formerly C. of Dawlish 1857–58, Tavistock 1858–61, St. Martin's-in-the-Fields, Lond. 1861–65; Morning Reader at Westminster Abbey 1864–65. [14]

DICKINSON, George Charles, *Winterton Vicarage, Brigg, Lincolnshire.*—St. Aidan's; Deac. 1860 and Pr. 1861 by Abp of York. V. of Winterton, Dio. Lin. 1863. (Patron, Ld Chan; Tithe, 82*l* 10*s*; Glebe, 122*l* 2*s*; V.'s Inc. 204*l* 12*s* and Ho; Pop. 1780.) Formerly C. of the Mariners' Ch. Hull, 1860-63. [15]

DICKINSON, George Cockburn.—Deac. 1863 by Bp of Pet. Pr. 1864 by Bp of Man. C. of Kensington. Formerly C. in sole charge of Ellenbrook, Lancashire. [16]

DICKINSON, Henry Strahan, *Chattisham Vicarage, Ipswich.*—Trin. Coll. Cam. B.A. 1832, M.A. 1835; Deac. 1836, Pr. 1837. V. of Chattisham, Dio. Nor. 1840. (Patron, Eton Coll; Tithe, 142*l* 10*s*; Glebe, 21 acres; V.'s Inc. 179*l* and Ho; Pop. 192.) [17]

DICKINSON, Thomas Rutherford, 22, *Sussex-road, Holloway, London, N.*—Magd. Coll. Cam. and Queen's Coll. Ox. B.A. 1833, M.A. 1841; Deac. 1834 and Pr. 1836 by Bp of Ches. Sunday Even. Lect. at St. James's, Aldgate, Lond. Formerly C. of Ribchester 1834–38, South Shields 1838–41; P. C. of Quernmoore 1841–42; P. C. of Salesbury 1842–46; C. of St. Thomas's, Exeter, 1846–50; R. of Nymet Rowland 1850–52; C. of St. Simon's, Salford, 1852-56, Mossley 1856–60, St. Thomas's, Lambeth, 1860, Ch. Ch. Battersea, 1860; Sunday Even. Lect. of St. James's, Bethnal Green, 1861; C. of Walkern, Herts, 1861–63, Tooting, Surrey, 1863, Pentonville 1863–65, Ch. Ch. Blackfriars-road 1866. Author, several pamphlets on the Factory Question in prose and verse 1827–28; various tracts, 1830–66. [18]

DICKINSON, William Henry, *St. Catherine Colman Rectory,* 68, *Fenchurch-street, London, E.C.*—Ch. Coll. Cam. LL.B. 1822. R. of St. Catherine Colman, City and Dio. Lon. 1847. (Patron, Bp of Lon; R.'s Inc. 590*l* and Ho; Pop. 444.) [19]

DICKINSON, Willoughby Willey, *Wolferton, Lynn, Norfolk.*—Brasen. Coll. Ox. B.A. 1838, M.A. 1841; Deac. 1841 and Pr. 1842 by Bp of Nor. R. of Wolferton, Dio. Nor. 1862. (Patron, Bp of Nor; R.'s Inc. 250*l*; Pop. 179.) Formerly P.C. of Playford, near Ipswich, 1848–58; R. of Martlesham, Suffolk, 1859–61. [20]

DICKSON, David, *Sundon Vicarage, Dunstable.*—Dub. A.B. 1838, A.M. 1846; Deac. and Pr. 1847. V. of Sundon with Streatley V. Dio. Ely, 1857. (Patron, Sir E. H. P. Turner, Bart; V.'s Inc. 200*l* and Ho; Pop. 791.) [21]

DICKSON, Edward Henry Wathen, *Little Ouseburn, Yorks.*—Trin. Coll. Cam. B.A. 1861, M.A. 1865; Deac. 1861 and Pr. 1862 by Bp of Ox. V. of Little Ouseburn, Dio. Rip. 1866. (Patron, Bp of Rip; V.'s Inc. 250*l* and Ho; Pop. 550.) Formerly C. of Waddesdon, Bucks, and Westbourne, Sussex. [22]

DICKSON, George David William.—Ex. Coll. Ox. B.A. 1843, M.A. 1849; Deac. 1845, Pr. 1846. P. C. of St. James' the Less, Westminster, Dio. Lon. 1861. (Patrons, D. and C. of Westminster; P. C.'s Inc. 300*l*; Pop. 6365.) Formerly C. of St. Michael's, Chester-square, Pimlico. [23]

DICKSON, Robert Bruce, *Coleshill, Amersham, Bucks.*—Trin. Coll. Cam. B.A. 1864; Deac. 1865 by Bp of Lon. Pr. 1866 by Bp of Ox. C. of Coleshill 1866. Formerly C. of Trinity, Brompton, Middlesex, 1865–66. [24]

DICKSON, Thomas Briggs, *Eastchurch Rectory, Queenborough, Kent.*—Emman. Coll. Cam. Fell. of, 4th Sen. Opt. and B.A. 1828, M.A. 1831, B.D. 1835; Deac. 1831 and Pr. 1832 by Bp of Ches. R. of Eastchurch, Dio. Cant. 1858. (Patron, John Swainson, Esq;

R.'s Inc. 1668*l* 14*s* 6*d* and Ho; Pop. 996.) Formerly P. C. of Whittle-le-Woods, Lancashire, 1831–38; P. C. of Marple, Cheshire, 1842–58. [1]

DICKSON, Thomas Miller, 54, *Castle-street, Cambridge.*—Edinburgh Univ. Prize Essayist 1843, Clare Hall, Cam. B.A. 1848, M.A. 1851; Deac. 1851 and Pr. 1852 by Bp of Lon. C. of St. Giles's, with St. Peter's, Cambridge. Formerly Head Mast. of Berwick-upon-Tweed Gr. Sch. [2]

DICKSON, William Edward, *The College, Ely.*—Corpus Coll. Cam. B.A. 1846, M.A. 1851; Deac. 1846 and Pr. 1847 by Bp of Lich. Precentor and Sacristan of Ely Cathl. 1858. (Value, 200*l* and Ho.) Formerly P. C. of Goostrey, Cheshire, 1848–58. Author, *Papers on Parochial Subjects*; *Railways and Locomotion*; *Our Workshops*, S.P.C.K; *Storm and Sunshine*, 1857; *Singing in Parish Churches*, 1858. [3]

DICKSON, William Richard, *Woodlands St. Mary, Hungerford, Berks.*—Trin. Coll. Ox. 2nd cl. Lit. Hum. B.A. 1850, M.A. 1851; Deac. 1850, Pr. 1851. P. C. of Woodlands St. Mary, Dio. Ox. 1864. (Patron, J. Aldridge, Esq; Glebe, 9 acres; P. C.'s Inc. 200*l* and Ho; Pop. 350*l*.) Formerly C. of Churchstoke 1850–52, Walford 1854–64. [4]

DIDHAM, Richard Cunningham, *Lea Fields, Abbots Bromley, Staffs.*—Emman. Coll. Cam. B.A. 1846, M.A. 1849; Deac. 1846, Pr. 1847. Author, *Sacrilege—The Majority of the Bishops of the Church of England proved under the Wrath of God, and Obnoxious to His Curse, with reference to their Sanction of the late Alienation of the Clergy Reserves in Canada*, 1853, 1*s*. [5]

DIGBY, George, *Clifton.*—Dub. A.B. 1830, A.M. 1833; Deac. 1830 by Bp of Killaloe, Pr. 1833 by Bp of Ches. P. C. of Low Harrogate, Dio. Rip. 1838. (Patron, V. of Pannall; P. C.'s Inc. 120*l* and Ho; Pop. 998.) [6]

DIGBY, Kenelm Henry, *Tittleshall Rectory, Litcham, Norfolk.*—Ch. Ch. Ox. B.A. 1833; Deac. 1834 by Bp of Roch. Pr. 1835 by Bp of Wor. R. of Tittleshall with Wellingham R. Dio. Nor. 1855. (Patron, Earl of Leicester; Tittleshall, Tithe, 681*l*; Glebe, 58 acres; Wellingham, Tithe—App. 16*s*, Imp. 1*l* 12*s*, R. 266*l*; Glebe, 3¾ acres; R.'s Inc. 1009*l* and Ho; Pop. Tittleshall 544, Wellingham 145.) Hon. Ca., of Nor. [7]

DIGBY, Richard Henry Wingfield, *Thornford Rectory, Sherborne, Dorset.*—R. of Thornford, Dio. Salis. 1863. (Patron, G. D. W. Digby, Esq; R.'s Inc. 248*l* and Ho; Pop. 415.) [8]

DIGHTON, Charles E., *Mitcheldean Rectory, Glouc.*—R. of Mitcheldean, Dio. G. and B. 1857. (Patron, M. Colchester, Esq; Tithe, 176*l* 13*s*; Glebe, 5 acres; R.'s Inc. 190*l* and Ho; Pop. 689.) J.P. for co. of Gloucester. Formerly C. of Hazleton, Glouc. [9]

DIGHTON, James Lister, *Dixton Vicarage, Monmouth.*—Ex. Coll. Ox. B.A. 1820, M.A. 1822; Deac. 1821 and Pr. 1824 by Bp of Glouc. V. of Dixton, Dio. Llan. 1833. (Patron, the present V; Tithe—Imp. 211*l* 4*s* 2*d*, V. 222*l* 3*s*; Glebe, 12 acres; V.'s Inc. 250*l* and Ho; Pop. 758.) Rural Dean. [10]

DIGWEED, John, *Steventon Overton, Hants.* [11]

DILLON, E. W., *Berne.*—British Chap. at *Berne.* [12]

DIMOCK, James Francis, *Barnborough Rectory, Doncaster.*—St. John's Coll. Cam. Bell's Scho. 1830, 29th Wrang. and B.A. 1833, M.A. 1837; Deac. 1836, Pr. 1837. R. of Barnborough, Dio. York, 1863. (Patron, Southwell Coll. Ch; Tithe, 534*l*; Glebe, 96 acres; R.'s Inc. 680*l* and Ho; Pop. 462.) Formerly Min. Can. of Southwell 1846; Chap. to the Notts House of Correction. Author, *Explanation of the XXXIX Articles* 1843, 1845; *The Holy Communion* (a Sermon), 1844; *Architectural History of Southwell Church* (in *Archæological Journal*), 1853. [13]

DIMOCK, Nathaniel, *Larkfield Cottage, near Maidstone.*—St. John's Coll. Ox. B.A. 1847; Deac. 1848 by Bp of Nor. Pr. 1850 by Abp of Cant. C. of East Malling, Kent. Author, *Conversion, Six plain Sermons*, Rivingtons, 1856, 2*s* 6*d*; *Thoughts about Miracles*, 2*d*; *Surly Sam*, 2*d*; *Remember*; *A New Heart for a New Year.* [14]

DIMOND-CHURCHWARD, Marcus Dimond, 10, *Lower Durnford-street, Stonehouse, Plymouth.*—Ch. Coll. Cam. B.A. 1859, M.A. 1863; Deac. 1860 by Bp of B. and W. Pr. 1862 by Bp of Ex. P. C. of St. Paul's, Stonehouse, Dio. Ex. 1865. Formerly C. of St. John's, Kenwyn, Cornwall, 1860. [15]

DIMONT, Charles Harding, 7, *Cavendish-road, Wandsworth road, London, S.W.*—Literate; Deac. 1859 and Pr. 1860 by Bp of Lich. Min. of Mission Ch. and C. of St. Barnabas', South Kennington. Formerly C. of Ch. Ch. Stone, 1859. [16]

DINGLE, James, *Whitby.*—St. Aidan's; Deac. 1855 and Pr. 1856 by Abp of York. C. of Whitby. [17]

DINGLE, John, *Lanchester Parsonage, Durham.*—Corpus Coll. Cam. B.A. 1840, M.A. 1862; Deac. 1840 and Pr. 1841 by Bp of Lich. P. C. of Lanchester, Dio. Dur. 1855. (Patron, Bp of Dur; Glebe, 9 acres; P. C.'s Inc. 320*l* and Ho; Pop. 1200.) Formerly P. C. of Withington, Salop, 1849–56; Mast of the High Ercall Gr. Sch. Author, *The Divine Obligation of the Sabbath Demonstrated*, 1849, 1*s*; *The Harmony of Revelation and Science*, 1863, 6*s*. [18]

DINGLEY, Richard Samuel, *Costock, Lowboro', Yorks.*—Ex. Coll. Ox. B.A. 1857; Deac. 1858 and Pr. 1860. Formerly C. of Nunton 1859, Bishopstone 1863. [19]

DINNIS, Francis Henry, *St. John's College, Cambridge.*—St. John's Coll. Cam. B.A. 1862, 14th Wrang. Scho. of St. John's; Deac. 1862 and Pr. 1863 by Bp of Ches. Formerly Vice-Prin. of Chester Dioc. Training Coll. 1862–63. [20]

DINSDALE, Charles Waterland, *Priddy, Wells.*—Dub. A.B. 1845; Deac. 1846 and Pr. 1847 by Bp of Man. P. C. of Priddy, Dio. B. and W. 1862. (Patron, Bp of B. and W; Tithe, comm. 43*l*; Glebe, 7 acres; P. C.'s Inc. 300*l* and Ho; Pop. 251.) [21]

DISBROWE, Henry John, *Wellbourne, Grantham.*—All Souls Coll. Ox. B.C.L. 1816; Deac. 1819, Pr. 1820. R. of Wellbourne, Dio. Lin. 1820. (Patroness, Countess of Buckingham; R.'s Inc. 511*l* and Ho; Pop. 664.) Late Fell. of All Souls Coll. Ox. 1816. [22]

DISNEY, James William King, *St. Saviour's Vicarage, Clareborough, Retford, Notts.*—Dub. A.B. 1836; Deac. 1837 and Pr. 1838 by Abp of Dub. V. of Clareborough with St. Saviour's C. Dio. Lin. 1859. (Patrons, Simeon's Trustees; Tithe, 116*l*; Glebe, 43*l*; V.'s Inc. 800*l* and two Hos; Pop. 2412.) Formerly P. C. of Ch. Ch. Newark, 1844–59. Author, *The Work of God*, 1*s*; *Invitation to the Lord's Supper*, R.T.S. 1*d*; *Garments for the Body and the Soul*, 2*d*; etc. [23]

DISTIN, Henry Lewis.—Caius Coll. Cam. B.A. 1841; Deac. 1841 and Pr. 1842 by Bp of Rip. Formerly C. of High Harrogate 1841–43, Bythorne, Hunts, 1843–65. [24]

DISTIN, John William Brookfield, *Paignton, Torquay.* [25]

DITCHER, Joseph, *South Brent Vicarage, Weston-super-Mare.*—Queens' Coll. Cam; M.A. 1817 by Abp of Cant; Deac. and Pr. 1818 by Bp of Lon. V. of South Brent, Dio. B. and W. 1841. (Patron, Archd. of Wells; Tithe—App. 91*l*, V. 689*l*; Glebe, ½ acre; V.'s Inc. 690*l* and Ho; Pop. 905.) Surrogate. Formerly Chap. to H M. Superintendent and Commandant at Honduras 1819–21; P. C. of Holy Trinity, Bitton, 1821–35; C. of Hutton 1835–36; Prin. Acting Surrogate of the Dio. and Judge of the Consistorial Episcopal Court of B. and W. 1836–41. Author, *A Statement of the Proceedings in the Case of Ditcher v. Denison.* [26]

DIX, Edward, *The College, Epsom.*—Ex. Coll. Ox. B.A. 1858; Deac. 1859 and Pr. 1861 by Bp of Ex. Asst. Mast. of the College, Epsom, 1863. Formerly Asst. C. of St. Andrew's Chapel, Plymouth, and 2nd Mast. of Plymouth New Gr. Sch. 1859–60; Asst. C. of St. Neelyn, Cornwall, 1861–62. [27]

DIX, Joshua, 29, *St. Paul's-road, Camden-town, London, N.W.*—All Souls Coll. Ox. B.A. 1833, M.A. 1839; Deac. 1835 by Bp of Lon. Pr. 1836 by Abp of

Cant. R. of Allhallows, Bread-street, with St. John the Evangelist R. City and Dio. Lon. 1851. (Patrons, Abp and D. and C. of Cant. alt; Tithe, comm. 233*l* 6*s* 8*d*; R.'s Inc. 283*l*; Pop. Allhallows 95, St. John's 27.) [1]

DIX, Thomas, *Thwaite Rectory, Hanworth, Norwich.*—Ch. Ch. Ox. B.A. 1826; Deac. 1828 Pr. 1829. R. of Thwaite All Saints', Dio. Nor. 1850. (Patron, Bp of Nor; Tithe, 202*l* 16*s*; Glebe, 7 acres; R.'s Inc. 185*l*; Pop. 147.) [2]

DIX, Thomas Woodrow, *Manley, Frodsham, Cheshire.*—Ch. Ch. Ox. B.A. 1857, M.A. 1864; Deac. 1858 and Pr. 1859 by Bp of Nor. C. of Manley and Helsby 1860. Formerly C. of South Lopham, Norfolk. [3]

DIXON, Alexander, *Higham Ferrers, Northants.*—Lin. Coll. Ox. B.A. 1849; Deac. 1850, Pr. 1851. C. of Higham Ferrers. [4]

DIXON, Arthur, *Devonport*—Bp Hat. Hall, Dur. 1850, Licen. Theol. and B.A. 1851, M.A. 1856; Deac. 1851 and Pr. 1852 by Bp. of Ex. P. C. of St. Stephen's, Devonport, Dio. Ex. 1863. (Patrons, Crown and Bp alt; P. C.'s Inc. 156*l*; Pop. 3306.) Formerly C. of Stoke Damerel. [5]

DIXON, Edmund Saul, *Intwood Rectory, near Norwich.*—Corpus Coll. Cam. B.A. 1831, M.A. 1834; Deac. 1831, Pr. 1832. R. of Intwood with Keswick R. Dio. Nor. 1842. (Patron, C. W. Unthank, Esq; Intwood, Tithe, 146*l* 8*s* 4*d*; Glebe, 16 acres; Keswick, Tithe, 228*l* 14*s* 3*d*; R.'s Inc. 387*l* and Ho; Pop. Intwood 68, Keswick 154.) [6]

DIXON, George, *Egton Bridge, Grosmont, Whitby.*—Deac. 1822 and Pr. 1823 by Abp of York. P. C. of Egton, Dio. York, 1847. (Patron, Abp of York; Tithe, App. 175*l*; P. C.'s Inc. 135*l*; Pop. 870.) [7]

DIXON, George, *Helmsley, Yorks.*—St. Cath. Hall, Cam. B.A. 1816, M.A. 1819; Deac. 1816, Pr. 1817. V. of Waghen, *alias* Wawne, Yorks, Dio. York, 1827. (Patron, Abp of York; Tithe—App. 810*l*, V. 125*l*; Glebe, ¾ acre; V.'s Inc. 300*l* and Ho; Pop. 408.) V. of Helmsley with Pockley C. Dio. York, 1830. (Patron, Lord Feversham; Tithe—Imp. 27*l* 12*s*, V. 405*l*; Glebe, 30 acres; V.'s Inc. 565*l* and Ho; Pop. Helmsley 2045, Pockley 199.) Preb. of York 1846; Rural Dean and Surrogate. Author, Sermons, *Public Thanksgiving*, 1849; *The Papal Aggression*, 1851; *The Eucharist*, 1854. [8]

DIXON, Henry, *Ferring Vicarage, Worthing, Sussex.*—Brasen. Coll. Ox. B.A. 1820, M.A. 1822; Deac. 1821, Pr. 1822. V. of Ferring with Kingston R. and East Preston V. (annexed), Dio. Chich. 1832. (Patron, Bp of Chich; Ferring, Tithe—App. 292*l* 5*s* 1*d*, and 7½ acres of Glebe, V. 89*l* 5*s*; Glebe, 21 acres; Kingston, Tithe—App. 92*l*, V. 18*l* 1*s* 6*d*; Glebe, 1¼ acres; East Preston, Tithe—App. 209*l* 16*s* 4*d*, V. 40*l*; Glebe, 9½ acres; V.'s Inc. 500*l* and Ho; Pop. Ferring 253, Kingston 45, East Preston 320.) [9]

DIXON, Henry Augustus.—C. of St. John's, Waterloo-road, Lambeth. [10]

DIXON, Henry John, *St. Mary Hall, Oxford.*—St. Mary Hall, Ox. B.A. 1840, M.A. 1857; Deac. 1841, Pr. 1842. Formerly C. of Largashall, Sussex. [11]

DIXON, James, *Wrexham, Denbighshire.*—C. of Wrexham. [12]

DIXON, James Murray, *Trinity Rectory, Bath.*—St. Edm. Hall, Ox, B.A. 1838, M.A. 1844; Deac. 1839 and Pr. 1840 by Bp of Roch. R. of Trinity, Bath, Dio. B. and W. 1852. (Patrons, Trustees; Tithe, 16*l*; R.'s Inc. 310*l*; Pop. 7555.) Surrogate. [13]

DIXON, John, *Letheringham Parsonage, Wickham Market.*—St. John's Coll. Cam. B.A. 1847, M.A. 1851; Deac. 1847 and Pr. 1848 by Bp of Pet. P. C. of Hoo with Letheringham, Dio. Nor. 1863. (Patrons, Trustees; Tithe—Hoo, Imp. 287*l* 8*s*, Letheringham, Imp. 151*l* 2*s*; Glebe, 60 acres; P. C.'s Inc. 110*l* and Ho; Pop. Hoo 195, Letheringham 206.) Formerly C. of St. Nicholas', Leicester, 1847 and 1858–60; St. Mary's, Leicester, 1848–58. Author, *Practical Exposition of the Sacraments*, 6*d*; and various Sermons. [14]

DIXON, John Gilbert, *St. Mary's Parsonage, Church-passage, Spital-square, N.E.*—Caius Coll. Cam. Jun. Opt. Math. Trip. B.A. 1863; Deac. 1863 and Pr. 1864 by Bp of Lon. P. C. of St. Mary's, Spital-square, Dio. Lon. 1866. (Patrons, Trustees of Hyndman's Bounty; P. C.'s Inc. 150*l* and Ho; Pop. 4041.) Formerly C. of St. Thomas's, Portman-square, 1863–65, Clare Market Mission Chapel 1865–66. [15]

DIXON, John Holmes, *Linkenholt Rectory, Hungerford.*—Queen's Coll. Ox. B.A. 1851, M.A. 1852; Deac. 1852 and Pr. 1853. R. of Linkenholt, Dio. Win. 1864. (Patrons, Exors. of late Rev. J. M. Colson; Tithe, 168*l*; Glebe, 40 acres; R.'s Inc. 208*l* and Ho; Pop. 88.) C. of Buttermere, Wilts, 1859. Formerly C. of Vernham Dean 1852–53; Asst. Mast. of St. Bees Sch. 1854–57. [16]

DIXON, John Jones, *Ivy Cottage, Hindley, Wigan.*—Magd. Coll. Cam. B.A. 1839, Pr. 1840. P. C. of Abrams, Wigan, Dio. Ches. 1839. (Patron, R. of Wigan; Tithe, App. 242*l*; Glebe, ½ acre; P. C.'s Inc. 150*l*; Pop. 1544.) [17]

DIXON, Richard Watson, 1, *Albert-street, Carlisle.*—Pemb. Coll. Ox. M.A. 1860, Arnold Prize Essay 1858, Cramer Prize (Sacred Poem) 1863; Deac. 1858 and Pr. 1859 by Bp of Win. 2nd Mast. of High Sch. Carlisle. Author, *Christ's Company and other Poems*, 1861, 5*s*; *Historical Odes*, 4*s*; and numerous articles in periodicals. [18]

DIXON, Robert, *St. Matthew's Parsonage, Rugby.*—St. Cath. Coll. Cam. B.A. 1828, M.A. 1831, D.D. 1852; Deac. 1832 and Pr. 1833 by Bp of S. and M. P. C. of St. Matthew's, Rugby, Dio. Wor. 1866. (Patrons, Trustees; Pop. 2919.) Formerly Prin. of King William's Coll. Isle of Man. [19]

DIXON, Robert, 1, *Richmond-place, Hereford.*—St. John's Coll. Cam. 5th Sen. Opt. 3rd in 2nd cl. Cl. Trip. B.A. 1857, M.A. 1860; Deac. 1859 and Pr. 1860 by Bp of Herf. C. of St. Nicholas', Hereford, 1866; 2nd Mast. of the Cathl. Sch. Hereford. Formerly C. of St. John's, 1859–60, and of St. Nicholas', Hereford, 1860–61. [20]

DIXON, Thomas, *Bingley, near Leeds.*—St. John's Coll. Cam. 5th Wrang. and B.A. 1844, M.A. 1847; Deac. 1845, Pr. 1846. Head Mast. of Bingley Gr. Sch. 1851. Formerly Fell. of Jesus Coll. Cam. 1845; Math. Lect. 1845; Head Math. 2nd Cl. and Hebrew Mast. of the Liverpool Coll. Sch. 1846–51. [21]

DIXON, Thomas, *Stockleigh-English, Crediton, Devon.*—Deac. 1818, Pr. 1819. R. of Stockleigh-English. Dio. Ex. 1844. (Patron, Ld Chan; Tithe, 154*l* 18*s*; Glebe, 31 acres; R.'s Inc 215*l* and Ho; Pop. 114.) [22]

DIXON, Thomas, *Trinity Parsonage, South Shields.*—Downing Coll. Cam. M.A; Deac. 1823 and Pr. 1824 by Abp of York. P. C. of Trinity, South Shields, Dio. Dur. 1833. (Patrons, D. and C. of Dur; Tithe, 249*l*; Glebe, 1 acre; P. C.'s Inc. 460*l* and Ho; Pop. 14,500.) Surrogate; Rural Dean. [23]

DIXON, Thomas Baker, *Albemarle-terrace, Ashton-under-Lyne.*—St. Bees; Deac. 1859 and Pr. 1860 by Bp of Ches. P. C. of St. James's, Hurst Brook, Ashton, Dio. Man. 1866. (Patrons, Trustees; P. C.'s Inc. 105*l*; Pop. 5580.) Formerly C. of St. John's, Dukinfield, 1859, Ch. Ch. Ashton, 1860. [24]

DIXON, Thomas Carpenter, *Quarry Bank Parsonage (Staffs), near Stourbridge.*—Dub. A.B. 1830, A.M. 1836, LL.B. and LL.D. 1850; Deac. 1830, Pr. 1832. P. C. of Quarry Bank, Dio. Lich. 1854. (Patrons, the Crown and Bp of Lich. alt; P. C.'s Inc. 300*l* and Ho; Pop. 4790.) Chap. of the Stourbridge Union. [25]

DIXON, Thomas Harrison, *Guisborough, Yorks.*—Univ. Coll. Dur. Licen. Theol. and B.A. 1848, M.A. 1851; Deac. 1848 by Bp of Rip. Pr. 1849 by Abp of York. P. C. of Upleatham, Yorks, Dio. York, 1856. (Patron, Abp of York; P. C.'s Inc. 85*l* 10*s*; Pop. 521.) Mast. of Guisborough Gr. Sch. [26]

DIXON, Thomas Morrison, 36, *Esplanade, Nottingham.*—St. Bees; Deac. 1860 by Bp of Carl. Pr. 1862 by Bp of Dur. C. of St. Paul's, Nottingham, 1867. Formerly C. of Gateshead. [27]

DIXON, William, *Broughton Parsonage, Preston.*—Deac. 1813 and Pr. 1814 by Bp of Ches. P. C. of Broughton, Dio. Man. 1817. (Patron, Sir H. B. Hoghton,

Bart; Tithe—App. 12*l* 12*s*, Imp. 157*l* 10*s*; Glebe, 8 acres; P. C.'s Inc. 120*l* and Ho; Pop. 841.) [1]

DIXON, William Francis, *Syston, Leicester.*—St. John's Coll. Cam. B.A. 1860; Deac. 1861 by Bp of Roch. Pr. 1863 by Abp of Cant. C. of Syston 1867. Formerly C. of Wimbish, Essex, 1861–63, Syleham, Suffolk with Billingford, Norfolk (sole charge), 1865–67. [2]

DIXON, William Taylor, *Chilthorne-Domer, near Yeovil, Somerset.*—St. Cath. Coll. Cam. B.A. 1846, M.A. 1850; Deac. 1846, Pr. 1847. V. of Chilthorne-Domer, Dio. B. and W. 1860. (Patron, Rev. J. Baily; V.'s Inc. 250*l* and Ho; Pop. 242.) Formerly P. C. of Buslingthorp, Yorks, 1849–60; Head Mast. and Chap. of the Training Sch. Leeds. [3]

DOBBIN, Abraham Joseph Lockett, *Ruddington Vicarage, near Nottingham.*—Dub. A.B. 1859; Deac. 1861 and Pr. 1862 by Bp of Man. C. of Ruddington, and St. James's, Nottingham, 1866. Formerly C. of St. John's, Chadderton, 1861, and St. Matthew's, Chadderton, Lancashire, 1864. [4]

DOBIE, John, *Heidelberg.*—Corpus Coll. Cam. B.A. 1839, M.A. 1842; Deac. 1839, Pr. 1840. Chap. to the British Residents, Heidelberg. Formerly Chap. to the Dartmoor Prison 1850. [5]

DOBINSON, Logan, *Lockington Rectory, Beverley, Yorks.*—Wad. Coll. Ox. B.A. 1843; Deac. 1844, Pr. 1845. R. of Lockington, Dio. York, 1853. (Patron, James Walker, Esq; Tithe, 120*l*; Glebe, 260 acres; R.'s Inc. 600*l* and Ho; Pop. 486.) [6]

DOBREE, Daniel, *Forest Rectory, St. Peter's Port, Guernsey.* -Pemb. Coll. Ox. B.A. 1828, M.A. 1829; Deac. 1830 and Pr. 1834 by Bp of G. and B. R. of the united Parishes of the Forest and Torteval, Guernsey, Dio. Win. 1836. (Patron, the Lieut.-Governor; R.'s Inc. 170*l* and Ho; Pop. 977.) Formerly Cl. Mast. of Elizabeth Coll. Guernsey. Author, *Translation of the Articles of the Church of England into French, with Notes,* Guernsey. [7]

DOBREE, De Lisle De Beauvoir, *Ashmore, Salisbury.*—St. Peter's Coll. Cam. B.A. 1850; Deac. 1850, Pr. 1851. C. of Ashmore. Formerly C. of Alderney and of St. Matthew's, Guernsey. [8]

DOBREE, George, *Cockfield, Sudbury, Suffolk.*—Dub. A.B. 1853; Deac. 1854, Pr. 1855. C. of Cockfield. Formerly C. of St. Barnabas', Liverpool. [9]

DOBREE, James Bonamy, *Grundisburgh, Woodbridge, Suffolk.*—Corpus Coll. Cam. B.A. 1857, M.A. 1860; Deac. 1858 by Bp of Ex. Pr. 1860 by Bp of Chich. C. of Grundisburgh 1861. Formerly C. of Washfield, Devon, 1858–59, Battle, Sussex, 1860–61. [10]

DOBREE, John Gale, *Holton St. Mary (Suffolk), Colchester.*—Pemb. Coll. Cam. Sen. Opt. and B.A. 1818, M.A. 1821; Deac. 1819 by Bp of Lon. Pr. 1820 by Bp of Nor. R. of Holton St. Mary, Dio. Nor. 1855. (Patron, Sir C. Rowley, Bart; Tithe, 220*l*; Glebe, 36 acres; R.'s Inc. 279*l* and Ho; Pop. 167.) Formerly R. of Newbourne, Suffolk. [11]

DOBREE, Osmond, *Knypersley, Congleton.*—Dub. A.B; Deac. 1856 and Pr. 1857 by Bp of Lin. C. of Biddulph 1863; Min. of Knypersley. Formerly C. of St. Mary's, Nottingham, and St. John's, Guernsey. Author, *Separation from Evil not God's principle of Unity,* 1862, 6*d.* [12]

DOBREE, Peter Stephens, *Roncevul, Guernsey.*—Trin. Coll. Cam. B.A. 1847, M.A. 1852; Deac. 1849 and Pr. 1850 by Bp of B. and W. Garrison Chap. at Guernsey 1857. [13]

DOBSON, Frederick, *Stratfield-Mortimer, near Reading.*—Mert. Coll. Ox. B.A. 1823, M.A. 1828; Deac. and Pr. 1827 by Bp of Salis. [14]

DOBSON, John Ralph, *Elsworth Rectory, St. Ives, Hunts.*—Lin. Coll. Ox. B.A. 1834; Deac. 1835 by Bp of Ches. Pr. 1836 by Abp of York. R. of Elsworth, Dio. Ely, 1853. (Patron, Duke of Portland; Tithe, comm. for land; Glebe, 667 acres; R.'s Inc. 500*l* and Ho; Pop. 787.) Dom. Chap. to Duke of Portland 1851. [15]

DOBSON, Robert Steward, *Brook House, Bradfield-Saling, Braintree, Essex.*—St. John's Coll. Cam. B.A. 1834, M.A. 1836; Deac. 1834 and Pr. 1835 by Bp of Nor. Chap. of D. of Bradfield-Saling, Dio. Roch. 1841. (Patron, W. Sandle, Esq; Tithe—Imp. 270*l*, Chap. 100*l*; Glebe, 1½ acres; Chap.'s Inc. 107*l*; Pop. 356.) Chap to the Braintree Union 1841. [16]

DOBSON, William, *Cheltenham.*—Trin. Coll. Cam. 3rd in 1st cl. Cl. Trip. and B.A. 1832, M.A. 1835; Deac. 1839, Pr. 1840. Late Prin. of Cheltenham Coll; Fell. of Trin. Coll. Cam. 1834. Author, *Schleiermacher's Introduction to Dialogues of Plato, translated,* 1834. [17]

DOD, Joseph Yates, *Edge Hall, Malpas.*—Trin. Coll. Cam. B.A. 1825, M.A. 1832; Deac. 1825 by Bp of Lich. Pr. 1827 by Bp of Ches. Formerly Chap. of the Tower of London. [18]

DOD, Philip Hayman, *Lichfield.*—Wor. Coll. Ox. B.A. 1839, M.A. 1846; Deac. 1841, Pr. 1842. Min. Can. of Lich. Cathl. 1842 (Value 120*l*); Mast. and Warder of St. John's Hospital, Lichfield; Hon. Sec. to the Lichfield Dioc. Board of Education. [19]

DODD, Edward, *Magdalen College, Cambridge.*—Magd. Coll. Cam. B.A. 1828, M.A. 1830. V. of St. Giles's with St. Peter's P. C. Cambridge, Dio. Ely, 1844. (Patron, Bp of Ely; V.'s Inc. 170*l*; Pop. St. Giles's 2119, St. Peter's 569.) Fell. of Magd. Coll. Cam. [20]

DODD, F. S., *Chalfont St. Peter, Slough, Bucks.*—C. of Chalfont St. Peter. [21]

DODD, Henry Alison, *Sparsholt Vicarage, Wantage, Berks.*—Queen's Coll. Ox. B.A. 1819, M.A. 1822; Deac. 1825, Pr. 1826. V. of Sparsholt with Kingston Lisle, Dio. Ox. 1841. (Patron, Queen's Coll. Ox; Tithe—App. 466*l* and 35 acres of Glebe, V. 321*l* 12*s*; Glebe, 12 acres and Ho; Pop. 863.) Surrogate. Late Chap. Fell. Dean, Librarian, and Bursar of Queen's Coll. Ox; Sen. Proctor of the Univ. 1833; Delegate of Accounts. [22]

DODD, Henry Philip, *Ramsgate.*—Pemb. Coll. Ox. B.A. 1851, M.A. 1854; Deac. 1852 and Pr. 1853 by Abp of Cant. [23]

DODD, Henry Russell, *Warrington.*—C. of Warrington 1866. Formerly Sen. Asst. Mast. Charterhouse, Lond. [24]

DODD, John, *Lumley Parsonage, Fence Houses, Durham.*—Univ. Coll. Dur. B.A. 1850, M.A. 1851; Deac. 1852 and Pr. 1853 by Bp of Dur. P. C. of Lumley, Dio. Dur. 1862. (Patron, Bp of Dur; P. C.'s Inc. 300*l* and Ho; Pop. 1928.) Chap. to Duck's Hospital. Formerly C. of Lumley 1852. Author, *History of Chester-le-Street Church,* 10*s*; *The Pitman's Daughter, or Struggles for Education.* [25]

DODD, Joseph, *Hampton-Poyle Rectory, near Oxford.*—Queen's Coll. Ox. 2nd cl. Lit. Hum. and B.A. 1833; Deac. 1837 and Pr. 1838 by Bp of Ox. R. of Hampton-Poyle, Dio. Ox. 1840. (Patron, Queen's Coll. Ox; Glebe, 25 acres; R.'s Inc. £90*l* and Ho; Pop. 125.) [26]

DODD, Thomas Forster, *Bishop Hatfield's Hall, Durham.*—Univ. Coll. Dur. B.A. 1857, Fell. 1858, M.A. 1859; Deac. 1860 and Pr. 1861 by Bp of Nor. C. of St. Margaret's, Durham, and Vice-Prin. of Hatfield Hall 1865. [27]

DODDS, George, *Corringham, Vicarage, Gainsborough, Lincolnshire.*—Pemb. Coll. Cam. B.D. 1833, D.D. 1839; Deac. 1822 and Pr. 1823 by Abp of York. V. of Corringham, Dio. Lin. 1831. (Patron, Bp of Lin; Tithe, App. 710*l* 11*s* 8*d*; Glebe, 15 acres; V.'s Inc. 300*l* and Ho; Pop. 717.) P. C. of Harpswell, Dio. Lin 1844. (Patrons, Whichcot Family; P. C.'s Inc. 52*l*; Pop. 104.) Formerly C. of Skipwith 1822, Ledsham 1823, Rochdale 1827. Author, *On Minerals and Fossils in the Ledstone Museum,* 4to; *On the Curiosities of the Ledstone Museum,* 4to; *On China and Earthenware in the Ledstone Museum,* 4to. 1828; various Antiquarian papers in *Gentleman's Magazine.* [28]

DODDS, Henry Luke, *Great Glen, Leicester.*—Ch. Ch. Ox. M.A. 1838; Deac. 1838 and Pr. 1839 by Bp of Win. V. of Glen-Magna with Stretton-Magna C. Dio. Pet. 1855. (Patron, C. W. Packe, Esq. M.P; Tithe, 140*l* 7*s* 3*d*; Glebe, 38 acres; V.'s Inc. 237*l* and Ho; Pop. Glen-Magna 786, Stretton-Magna 38.) [29]

DODGSON, The Venerable Charles, *Croft Rectory, Darlington.*—Ch. Ch. Ox. Double 1st cl. 1821, B.A. 1822, M.A. 1824; Deac. 1823, Pr. 1824. R. of Croft, Dio. Rip. 1843. (Patron, the Crown; Tithe, 923*l*; Glebe, 23 acres; R.'s Inc. 900*l* and Ho; Pop. 761.) Can. Res. of Rip. Cathl. 1852; Archd. of Richmond 1854; Chap. to Abp of Cant. [1]

DODGSON, Charles Lutwidge, *Christ Church, Oxford.*—Ch. Ch. Ox. 3rd cl. Lit. Hum. 1st cl. Math. B.A. 1854, M.A. 1857; Deac. 1861 by Bp of Ox. Stud and Math. Lect. of Ch. Ch. Ox. Author, *Notes on Euclid, Books I. and II. for Responsions*; *Notes on Algebra for Responsions*; *The Formulæ of Plane Trigonometry, printed with Symbols instead of Words to express Goniometrical Ratios*, 1861; *A Syllabus of Plane Algebraical Geometry, Part I., including the Point, Straight Line, and Circle*; *A Guide to the Mathematical Student in reading, reviewing, and working examples*; *Part I. Pure Mathematics*, 1864, all published by Parkers; *The Dynamics of a Particle with an Excursus on the New Method of Evaluation*, Vincent, Oxford; *The Elements of Determinants with their Application to simultaneous Linear Equations and Algebraical Geometry*, Macmillans, 1867. [2]

DODGSON, Isaac, *Lanercost Priory, near Brampton, Cumberland.*—St. Peter's Coll. Cam. 5th Jun. Opt. B.A. 1843, M.A. 1846; Deac. 1844 and Pr. 1845 by Bp of Carl. V. of Lanercost, Dio. Carl. 1845. (Patron, Earl of Carlisle; Tithe—Imp. 20*l*, P. C. 3*l*; V.'s Inc. 178*l* and Ho; Pop. 1295.) Formerly C. of Beaumont and Kirk-Andrews-on-Eden 1844–45; P. C. of Upper Denton, Cumberland, 1845–59. [3]

DODGSON, Skeffington H., *Croft, near Darlington.*—C. of Croft. [4]

DODGSON, Thomas, *Swettenham Rectory, Congleton, Cheshire.*—Bp Hat. Hall, Dur. B.A. 1858, M.A. 1862, Licen. in Theol. 1859; Deac. 1859 and Pr. 1861 by Bp of Dur. C. in sole charge of Swettenham 1863. Formerly C. of Hetton-le-Hole 1859–63. [5]

DODINGTON, Henry Phelps Marriott, *Bere Regis, Blandford.*—Trin. Coll. Cam. B.A. 1864; Deac. 1866 by Bp of Salis. C. of Bere Regis 1866. [6]

DODINGTON [late MARRIOTT], Thomas, *Bowden, Henstridge, Somerset.*—Ch. Coll. Cam. B.A. 1827; Deac. and Pr. 1827. R. of Stowell, Somerset, Dio. B. and W. 1828. (Patron, H. M. Dodington, Esq; Tithe, 169*l*; Glebe, 27¾ acres; R.'s Inc. 220*l*; Pop. 133.) [7]

DODSON, Christopher, *Penton-Mewsey Rectory, Andover, Hants.*—Univ. Coll. Ox. B.A. 1813, M.A. 1817. R. of Grateley, near Andover, Dio. Win. 1819. (Patron, Rev. J. Constable; Tithe, 273*l* 5*s*; Glebe, 20 acres; R.'s Inc. 299*l*; Pop. 176.) R. of Penton-Mewsey, Dio. Win. 1832. (Patron, Rev. J. Constable; Tithe, 286*l*; Glebe, 40 acres; R.'s Inc. 326*l* and Ho; Pop. 277.) [8]

DODSON, Edward, *Great Wakering, Rochford, Essex.*—Trin. Coll. Cam. B.A. 1817; Deac. 1818, Pr. 1820. V. of Great Wakering, Dio. Roch. 1839. (Patron, Bp of Roch; Tithe—Imp. 640*l* and 60 acres of Glebe, V. 290*l*; Glebe, 2 acres; V.'s Inc. 264*l*; Pop. 1018.) [9]

DODSON, Paul Augustus, *Burgh, Boston, Lincolnshire.*—Wor. Coll. Ox. B.A. 1844, M.A. 1847; Deac. 1844 and Pr. 1845 by Bp of Lin. P. C. of Haugh, near Alford, Dio. Lin. 1847. (Patron, Charles Horsfall Bell, Esq; Tithe, 6*l* 13*s* 4*d*; P. C.'s Inc. 75*l*; Pop. 18.) Formerly C. of Sutterby, Linc. [10]

DODSWORTH, George, *Gravesend, Kent.*—St. Cath. Coll. Cam. B.D. 1833, D.D. 1839, *ad eund.* Ox. 1844; Deac. 1823 and Pr. 1824 by Bp of Ches. Chap. to Viscount Ranelagh. Formerly Missionary and Chap. to H.M.'s Forces in Newfoundland; C. of Harewood, Yorks, 1849–54. Author, *Sermon on the Queen's Accession* (preached in the Chapel Royal, Windsor Park, 1838.) [11]

DODSWORTH, Joseph, *Bourne, Lincolnshire.*—Lin. Coll. Ox. B.A. 1819; Deac. 1820 and Pr. 1821 by Bp of Lin. V. of Bourne, Dio. Lin. 1842. (Patrons, Exors. of the late J. L. Ostler, Esq; Tithe—Imp. 12*l*, V. 20*l*; Glebe, 205 acres; V.'s Inc. 600*l* and Ho; Pop. 3771.) Head Mast. of Bourne Gr. Sch; Rural Dean; Surrogate. [12]

DOE, John Hall, *Dewsbury.*—Trin. Coll. Cam. B.A. 1864; Deac. 1865 and Pr. 1867 by Bp of Rip. C. of Dewsbury 1865. [13]

DOHERTY, Charles William, *Hampton Court Palace, Middlesex, S.W.*—Dub. A.M. 1852; Deac. 1852, Pr. 1853. Formerly Min. of Brompton Chapel, Kensington, 1857; R. of Pilham, Linc. 1853–57; Chap. to the Marquis of Ely 1853; previously an Officer in the Prince Consort's Own Rifle Brigade, serving in North America. [14]

DOKE, Richard, *Great Addington Rectory, Thrapston.*—St. Aidan's, Deac. 1861; Pr. 1862 by Abp of Cant. R. of Great Addington, Dio. Pet. 1863. (Patron, the present R; R.'s Inc. 450*l*, derived from rent of 327 acres of land and Ho; Pop. 307.) Formerly C. of Buckland with Guston, near Dover, 1861–63. [15]

DOLAN, John Alexander, *Gambia Settlement, Africa.*—Dub. A.B. 1845, A.M. 1848; Deac. and Pr. 1847 by Bp of Dur. Formerly C. of Paddington, Lond. [16]

DOLBÉ, Charles Vincent.—C. of St. Thomas's, Charterhouse, Lond. [17]

DOLBEN, Charles, *Ipsley Rectory (Warwickshire), near Redditch.*—Trin. Coll. Ox. B.A. 1841; Deac. 1841 and Pr. 1842. R. of Spernall, near Studley, Dio. Wor. 1843. (Patron, C. Chambers, Esq; Tithe, 167*l* 2*s*; Glebe, 35 acres; R.'s Inc. 197*l* and Ho; Pop. 91.) R. of Ipsley, near Redditch, Dio. Wor. 1843. (Patron, the present R; Tithe, 699*l* 10*s*; Glebe, 45 acres; R.'s Inc. 799*l* and Ho; Pop. 344.) [18]

DOLBY, John Smith, *Howell Rectory, Sleaford, Lincolnshire.*—Lin. Coll. Ox. B.A. 1831, M.A. 1834; Deac. 1833, Pr. 1834. R. of Howell, Dio. Lin. 1864. (Patrons, Trustees; R.'s Inc. 150*l* and Ho; Pop. 72.) Formerly P. C. of All Saints, Stanway, Essex, 1845-64. [19]

DOLIGNON, J. W., *East Looe, Cornwall.*—P. C. of East and West Looe, Dio. Ex. 1858. (Patron, Bp of Ex; P. C.'s Inc. 85*l*; Pop. 1860.) [20]

DOLLING, James Radclyffe, *Sharrington, Holt, Norfolk.*—Wor. Coll. Ox. B.A. 1859, M.A. 1862; Deac. 1859 and Pr. 1860 by Bp of Nor. R. of Sharrington, Dio. Nor. 1861. (Patron, Rev. Sir E. R. Jodrell, Bart; Tithe, 302*l*; Glebe, 1½ acres; R.'s Inc. 302*l* and Ho; Pop. 257.) Formerly C. of Sharrington, 1859-61. [21]

DOLLING, Robert James Todd, *Wormshill Rectory, Sittingbourne, Kent.*—Pemb. Coll. Cam. B.A. 1831, M.A. 1834; Deac. 1832 and Pr. 1833 by Abp of Cant. R. of Wormshill, Dio. Cant. 1835. (Patron, Christ's Hospital, Lond; Tithe, 266*l*; Glebe, 30 acres; R.'s Inc. 311*l* and Ho; Pop. 253.) C. of Bicknor 1865. Formerly C. of Old Romney and St. Mary's, Kent, 1832–35. [22]

DOLPHIN, John, *Antingham Rectory, North Walsham, Norfolk.*—Trin. Coll. Cam. B.A. 1828; Deac. 1828 and Pr 1829 by Bp of Lon. R. of Antingham St. Mary with Thorpe-Market V. and Bradfield D. Dio. Nor. 1831. (Patron, Lord Suffield; Antingham, Tithe—App. 28*l* 10*s*, R. 340*l*; Glebe, 42 acres; Thorpe-Market, Tithe—Imp. 155*l* 10*s*, V. 80*l* 10*s* 6*d*; Bradfield, Tithe—App. 160*l*, and 2½ acres of Glebe, V. 55*l*; R.'s Inc. 475*l* and Ho; Pop. Antingham St. Mary 227, Thorpe Market 215.) [23]

DOLPHIN, John Maximilian, *Coddington Parsonage, Newark.*—Oriel Coll. Ox. B.A. 1860; Deac. 1860 and Pr 1861 by Bp of Lin. P. C. of Coddington, Dio. Lin. 1863. (Patron, Bp of Lin; Glebe, 37 acres; P. C.'s Inc. 95*l* and Ho; Pop. 510.) Formerly C. of North Carlton, Dio. Lin. 1860-63. [24]

DOMAN, John George, 118, *Manchester-road, Bolton-le-Moors.*—Emman. Coll. Cam. 1st Sen. Opt. and B.A. 1852, M.A. 1860; Deac. 1853 and Pr. 1854. P. C. of St. Mark's, Bolton, Dio. Man. 1866. (Patrons, Trustees; P. C.'s Inc. 170*l*; Pop. 5000.) Formerly C. of Shap, 1855, and Head Mast. of the Lowther Gr. Sch. Westmoreland, 1854. [25]

DOMBRAIN, Henry, *Framilode Rectory, Stonehouse, Gloucestershire.*—R. of Framilode, Dio. G. and B. 1867. (Patron, Bp of G. and B; R.'s Inc. 88*l* and Ho; Pop. 635.) Formerly C. of Chippenham. [1]

DOMBRAIN, Henry Honeywood, *Deal.*—Dub. A.B. 1839; Deac. 1841 by Bp of Meath, Pr. 1842 by Bp of Kilmore. P. C. of St. George's, Deal, Dio. Cant. 1849. (Patron, Abp of Cant; P. C.'s Inc. 280*l*; Pop. 2731.) Formerly C. of Bray, Ireland, 1841–47, Ch. Ch. Ramsgate, 1847–49. Author, *The Sacrifice of the Lord Jesus in Type and Fulfilment*, 1859; *Little Edward, Breakers Ahead*, and other tracts. [2]

DOMBRAIN, James, *Northumberland House, Dereham-road, Norwich.*—Deac. 1864 and Pr. 1865 by Abp of Cant. P. C. of St. Benedict's, Norwich, Dio. Nor. 1865. (Patrons, Parishioners; P. C.'s Inc. 115*l*; Pop. 1500.) Hon. Sec. of Soc. for Promoting Christianity among the Jews. Formerly C. of St. Peter's with Holy Cross, Westgate, Canterbury, 1864. [3]

DOMVILE, Charles Compton, *Nettleton Rectory, Chippenham.*—Wad. Coll. Ox. 4th cl. Lit. Hum. B.A. 1838, M.A. 1843; Deac. 1840, Pr. 1841. R. of Nettleton, Dio. G. and B. 1850. (Patron, the present R; Tithe, comm. 443*l*; Glebe, 14 acres; R.'s Inc. 473*l* and Ho; Pop. 632.) Author, Letters in *The Morning Post* in favour of the Divorce Act. [4]

DONAGAN, Henry Robert, *St. Andrew's Villas, Bradford, Yorks.*—Literate; Deac. 1858 and Pr. 1860 by Bp of Rip. P. C. of St. Thomas's, Bradford, Dio. Rip. 1862. (Patron, Bp of Rip; P. C.'s Inc. 300*l*; Pop. 8150.) Formerly C. of Ch. Ch. Bradford, 1858–62. [5]

DONALDSON, Augustus Blair, *St. John's Clergy House, 67, Marton-road, Middlesborough, Yorks.*—Oriel Coll. Ox. Robinson Exhib. of, 2nd cl. Lit. Hum. B.A. 1864, M.A. 1866; Deac. 1865 and Pr. 1866 by Abp of York. C. of St. John's, Middlesborough. [6]

DONALDSON, George, 8, *Robinson-street, Sunderland.*—St. Aidan's; Deac. 1859 and Pr. 1860 by Bp of Tuam. Chap. to Seamen, Sunderland, 1866. Formerly Clerical Missionary, Clifden, Dio. Tuam. 1859. [7]

DONNE, Charles Edward, *Faversham, Kent.*—Trin. Coll. Cam. B.A. 1857, M.A. 1862; Deac 1858 and Pr. 1859 by Bp of Pet. V. of Faversham, Dio. Cant. 1866. (Patrons, D. and C. of Cant; V.'s Inc. 400*l* and Ho; Pop. 6383.) Surrogate; Dom. Chap. to Viscount Sydney. Formerly C. of St. Edmund's, Northampton, 1858–60, Trinity, Paddington, 1860–66. Author, *Thoughts on Repentance*, 1861, etc. [8]

DONNE, Nathaniel Kemp.—Queens' Coll. Cam. B.A. 1853, M.A. 1857; Deac. 1854 and Pr. 1855 by Bp of Roch. Formerly C. of Merville and Aston 1864, Little Faringdon 1865. [9]

DONNER, James Hales, *Pleshey, near Chelmsford.*—King's Coll. Lond. Theol. Assoc. 1853; Deac. 1853 by Bp of Wie. Pr. 1854 by Bp of Lich. P. C. of Pleshey, Dio. Roch. 1867. (Patron, T. T. Tufnell, Esq; Glebe, 20 acres; P. C.'s Inc. 145*l* and Ho; Pop. 351.) Formerly C. of Chesterton 1853, Talk o' th' Hill 1855, St. Mary's, Stafford, 1858, Stratton, Wilts, 1861, Thurlby 1863, Weobly 1865. Author, *The Benefits and Management of Literary Institutions*, 6d. [10]

DONNISON, James Watson Stote, *Mendham, near Harleston, Norfolk.*—Univ. Coll. Ox. Scho. B.A. 1830, M.A 1835; Deac. 1831 and Pr. 1832 by Bp of Lon. [11]

DONOVAN, D.—Chap. to the Forces. [12]

DONOVAN, Joseph, *Barrington House, Dorking.* [13]

DORAN, John Wilberforce.—St. John's Coll. Cam. Scho. of, 1855, B.A. 1857; Deac. 1857 by Bp of Ely, Pr. 1858 by Bp of Roch. Formerly Min. of St. Thomas's, Bethnal-green, 1859; C. of St. Alban's, Holborn, 1863. [14]

DORIA, Andrew, *Brook Cottage, Alderley Edge.*—Pemb. Coll. Cam. B.A. 1856, M.A. 1866; Deac. 1856 and Pr. 1857 by Bp of Man. C. of Lindow District, Alderley Edge, 1864. Formerly C. of Harpurhey 1856–58, Blackley, Manchester, 1858–64. [15]

DORIA, Samuel, *Wigan.*—St. John's Coll. Cam. Scho. 1826, Sen. Opt. 3rd cl. Cl. Trip. and B.A. 1829, M.A. 1844; Deac. 1841, Pr. 1842. Head Mast. of Wigan Gr. Sch. 1848. Author, *Compendium of Ancient Geography for the use of Schools*, 1849, 4s; *Exegetical and Historical Exposition of Church Catechism in Question and Answer for the use of Schools*, 1850, 1s 6d; *The Sunday School* (a Poem), 1851, 2s; *The Grammar Schools of Britain* (a Poem), 1852, 3s 6d; *An Ode on the Inauguration of the Crystal Palace*, 1854, 1s 6d. [16]

DORNFORD, Joseph, *Plymtree Rectory, Collumpton, Devon.*—Trin. Coll. Cam. 1811, Scho. 1812, B.A. 1816, M.A. 1821; Wad. Coll. Ox. Queen's Scho. 1816, Fell. of Oriel, 1819; Deac. 1821 and Pr. 1822 by Bp of Ox. R. of Plymtree, Dio. Ex. 1832. (Patron, Oriel Coll. Ox; Tithe, 285*l*; Glebe, 42 acres; R.'s Inc. 360*l* and Ho; Pop. 462.) Preb. of Ex. 1844. [17]

D'ORSEY, Alexander James Donald, *Corpus Christi College, Cambridge, and 9, Upper Seymour-street West, Hyde Park, London, W.*—Glasgow and Cam. Chan.'s English Medallist at Cam. Cl. Hons. and Prizes for History, Prose, and Poetry at Glasgow; Corpus Coll. Cam. B.D. 1860; Deac. 1846 and Pr. 1847 by Bp of Glasgow. Lect. on Elocution in King's Coll. Lond. 1864; Asst. Min of St. George's, Albemarle-street, Lond. Formerly Mast. in the High Sch. of Glasgow 1834–54, Incumb. of St. John's, Anderston, Glasgow, 1847, Chap. in Madeira 1856, Chap. to Bp of Gibraltar 1859, Chancellor's English Medallist 1860, Lect. in History and English at Corpus Coll. Cam. 1860, Lect. at Royal Institution 1862, Lect. at St. Augustine's, Canterbury, 1862. Author, *Introduction to Composition, English Grammar*, 2 vols; *Spelling by Dictation*; *Portuguese Grammar*; *Portuguese Dialogues*; *The Great Comet of 1858* (a Cambridge Prize Poem); *The Study of the English Language*; *Letters to the Archbishop of Canterbury, Lord Brougham*; *The Duty of the Church of England to her own Children in Foreign Parts*; etc. [18]

DOUDNEY, David Alfred, Jun., *St. James's Parsonage, Carlisle.*—Dub. A.B. 1861, A.M. 1864; Deac. 1861 and Pr. 1862 by Bp of Carl. P. C. of St. James's, Carlisle, Dio. Carl. 1863. (Patrons, Five Trustees; P. C.'s Inc. 150; Pop. 3000.) Afternoon Lect. at St. Cuthbert's, Carlisle. (Patrons, D. and C. of Carl.) Chap. to the Bp of Carl. Formerly C. of Stanwix 1861–63. [19]

DOUDNEY, David Alfred, D.D., *Bedminster, Bristol.*—Deac. and Pr. 1847 by Bp of Cashel. P. C. of St. Luke's, Bedminster, Dio. G. and B. 1859. (Patrons, Trustees; P. C.'s Inc. 420*l*; Pop. 6020.) Editor of *The Gospel Magazine* and *Old Jonathan*, both monthly, Author, *Heart Breathings*; *Musings*; *Sympathy*; *Bible Lives and Bible Lessons*, etc. [20]

DOUGHTY, Ernest George, *Martlesham Rectory, Woodbridge, Suffolk.*—Trin. Coll. Cam. B.A. 1859, M.A. 1862; Deac. 1859 and Pr. 1860 by Bp of Carl. R. of Martlesham, Dio. Nor. 1861. (Patron, F. G. Doughty, Esq; Tithe, 423*l*; Glebe, 13 acres; R.'s Inc. 455*l* and Ho; Pop. 465.) Formerly C. of St. Michael's, Appleby, 1859–61. [21]

DOUGHTY, Thomas, *Walsoken, Norfolk.*—St. Bees; Deac. 1860, Pr. 1861. C. of Walsoken 1866. [22]

DOUGLAS, Archibald James, *Mathon, Malvern.*—V. of Mathon, Dio. Wor. 1848. (Patrons, D. and C. of Westminster; Tithe, Appr. 139*l* 16*s* 11*d*; V.'s Inc. 166*l*; Pop. 475.) [23]

DOUGLAS, The Hon. Arthur Gascoigne, *Scaldwell Rectory, near Northampton.*—Univ. Coll. Dur. B.A. 1849, Licen. Theol. and M.A. 1850; Deac. 1850 by Bp of Dur. Pr. 1851 by Bp of Wor. R. of Scaldwell, Dio. Pet. 1856. (Patron, Duke of Buccleuch; Tithe, 13*l* 10*s*; Glebe, 135 acres; R.'s Inc. 380*l* and Ho; Pop. 396.) Formerly C. of Kidderminster 1850–53; R. of St. Olave's, Southwark, 1855–58. [24]

DOUGLAS, Charles, *The Vicarage, Pembroke.*—Deac. 1849, Pr. 1850. V. of Pembroke, Dio. St. D.

1854. (Patron, M. A. Saurin, Esq; V.'s Inc. 500*l* and Ho; Pop. 5578.) Surrogate 1854. [1]

DOUGLAS, The Hon. Henry, *Hanbury Rectory, Bromsgrove, Worcestershire.*—Univ. Coll. Dur. B.A. 1845, Licen. Theol. 1846; M.A. 1846; Deac. 1846 and Pr. 1847 by Bp of Wor. R. of Hanbury, Dio. Wor. 1855. (Patron, H. F. Vernon, Esq; Tithe, 1150*l*; Glebe, 162 acres; R.'s Inc. 1212*l* and Ho; Pop. 1044.) Hon. Can. of Cunbrae, Scotland, 1865. Formerly Chap. to the Bp of Capetown, and Min. of St. John's, Capetown, 1847–54. [2]

DOUGLAS, Herman, *Newborough, Peterborough.* P. C. of Newborough, Dio. Pet. 1863. (Patron, the Crown; P. C.'s Inc. 280*l*; Pop. 806.) [3]

DOUGLAS, James John, *St. Mary's Parsonage, Kirriemuir, Scotland.*—Lampeter, B.D. 1853; Deac. 1844 and Pr. 1845 by Abp of York. Dom. Chap. to the Earl of Airlie; Incumb. of St. Mary's, Kirriemuir. Author, *Points of Difference between the Church and the Sects,* 1851. [4]

DOUGLAS, Philip Henry, *Thrumpton, Derby.*—P. C. of Thrumpton, Notts. Dio. Lin. 1868. (Patron, J. E. Wescomb, Esq; P. C.'s Inc. 87*l*; Pop. 144*l*.) [5]

DOUGLAS, Robert, *Stratford-place, Spring-lane, Sheffield.*—Dub. A.B. 1861; Deac. 1862 and Pr. 1863 by Bp of Ches. C. of St. George's, Sheffield, 1865. Formerly C. of Bowden, Cheshire, 1862. Author, *Pastoral Words for the Times,* 1866, 6*d.* [6]

DOUGLAS, Stair, *Chichester.*—Ball. Coll. Ox. B.A. 1826, M.A. 1830; Deac. 1827, Pr. 1829. Preb. of Chich. 1854; P. C. of Funtington, near Chichester, Dio. Chich. 1856. (Patrons, D. and C. of Chich; Tithe, App. 980*l*; P. C.'s Inc. 80*l* and Ho; Pop. 1099.) Rural Dean. Formerly R. of Fishbourne, Sussex, 1850–56; Dom. Chap. to the Marquis of Queensberry. [7]

DOUGLAS, Thomas, *Overton (Flintshire), near Ellesmere, Salop.*—Deac. 1856, Pr. 1857. C. of Overton. Formerly C. of St. James's, Accrington. [8]

DOUGLAS, William, *Clifton, Bristol.*—Ex. Coll. Ox. B.A. 1855, M.A. 1858; Deac. 1857 and Pr. 1858 by Bp of Man. Formerly C. of Whalley, Lancashire. [9]

DOUGLAS, William Frederick, *Scrayingham, Yorks.*—Ch. Coll. Cam. B.A. 1838, M.A. 1842; Deac. 1838 and Pr. 1839 by Bp of G. and B. R. of Scrayingham, Dio. York, 1845. (Patron, the Crown; Tithe, 410*l*; Glebe, 262 acres; R.'s Inc. 760*l* and Ho; Pop. 480.) Rural Dean of West Buckrose 1847. [10]

DOUGLAS, William Willoughby, *Salwarpe Rectory, Droitwich.*—St. John's Coll. Cam. B.A. 1847, M.A. 1852; Deac. 1848, Pr. 1849. R. of Salwarpe, Dio. Wor. 1849. (Patron, the present R; R.'s Inc. 530*l* and Ho; Pop. 442.) Rural Dean; Hon. Can. of Wor. [11]

DOUGLASS, Arthur, B.A.—Dom. Chap. to the Marquis of Westmeath. [12]

DOUGLASS, Charles Edward, 14, *Clifton-terrace, Brighton.*—Trin. Coll. Cam. B.A. 1846, M.A. 1836; also M.A. of Kenyon Coll. Ohio, U.S; Deac. 1846, Pr. 1848. P. C. of St. Stephen's, Brighton, Dio. Chich. 1861. (Patron, V. of Brighton; P. C.'s Inc. about 450*l*, variable, from pew-rents exclusively.) Formerly C. of Brighton 1861. Author, *The One Fold of Christ, or Practical and Spiritual Unity,* 2*s*; *The Doctrine of Holy Baptism practically explained in Three Discourses,* 1*s* 6*d*; *An Outline of the Principles of Public Worship,* Parkers, 3*s*. [13]

DOUTON, Charles George, *Biggleswade Vicarage, Beds.*—Ch. Ch. Ox. B.A. 1844, M.A. 1847; Deac. 1844 and Pr. 1846 by Bp of Ely. V. of Biggleswade, Dio. Ely, 1855. (Patron, Bp of Ely; Tithe—App. 987*l* 10*s*, V. 312*l* 10*s*; V.'s Inc. 370*l* and Ho; Pop. 4631.) Surrogate. [14]

DOVE, J. T., *Cowbitt, Spalding, Lincolnshire.*—Caius Coll. Cam. M.A. P. C. of Cowbitt, Dio. Lin. 1862. (Patrons, Certain Feoffees; P. C.'s Inc. 625*l* and Ho; Pop. 649.) [15]

DOVER, John William, *St. Mary's College, Harlow, Essex.*—Jesus Coll. Cam. Sen. Opt. Scho. and Prizeman, B.A. 1861; Deac. 1862 and Pr. 1863 by Bp of Nor. Vice-President of St. Mary's Coll. Harlow. Formerly C. of Hunstanton, Norfolk, 1862–64. [16]

DOVETON, Frederick, *South Normanton Rectory, Alfreton, Derbyshire.*—Corpus Coll. Ox. B.A. 1809, M.A. 1813. R. of South Normanton, Dio. Lich. 1819. (Patron, Rev. John Bird; Tithe, 290*l* 12*s* 6*d*; R.'s Inc. 395*l* and Ho; Pop. 1808.) [17]

DOVETON, John Bazett, *Burnett, Pensford, Somerset.*—R. of Burnett, Dio. B. and W. 1846. (Patron, the present R; Tithe, 92*l* 8*s*; Glebe, 29 acres; R.'s Inc. 141*l*; Pop. 98.) [18]

DOVETON, William Blake, *Corston Vicarage, Bath.*—Trin. Coll. Ox. B.A. 1844, M.A. 1847; Deac. 1847 and Pr. 1848 by Bp of B. and W. V. of Corston, Dio. B. and W. 1862. (Patron, Bp of B. and W; V.'s Inc. 170*l* and Ho; Pop. 472.) Formerly R. of Sampford Peverell, Devon, 1854–57; V. of Spreyton, Devon, 1857–62. [19]

DOWDING, Benjamin Charles, *South Broom Parsonage, Devizes, Wilts.*—Trin. Coll. Ox. B.A. 1834, M.A. 1838; Deac. 1836 and Pr. 1837 by Bp of Salis. P. C. of South Broom, Dio. Salis. 1838. (Patron, V. of Cannings Episcopi; P. C.'s Inc. 200*l* and Ho; Pop. 2007.) Rural Dean; Surrogate. [20]

DOWDING, Townley Ward, *Marlborough, Wilts.*—Caius Coll. Cam. B.A. 1842, M.A. 1846; Deac. 1844 and Pr. 1845 by Bp of Salis. R. of St. Peter's, Marlborough, Dio. Salis. 1859. (Patron, Bp of Salis; R.'s Inc. 150*l*; Pop. 1781.) Surrogate. Formerly V. of Preshute, Wilts, 1849–59. [21]

DOWDING, William, *Idmiston, Salisbury.*—Mert. Coll Ox. B.A. 1838, M.A. 1842; Deac. and Pr. 1841. V. of Idmiston with Porton, Dio. Salis. 1862. (Patron, Bp of Salis; V.'s Inc. 300*l*; Pop. 542.) Formerly C. of Verwood, Dorset, 1856. [22]

DOWDING, William Charles, *Great Eccleston, Garstang, Lancashire.*—Ex. Coll. Ox. B.A. 1841, M.A. 1850; Deac. 1841 by Bp of Lich. Pr. 1842 by Bp of Herf. P. C. of Great Eccleston with Elswick and Larbrick P. C. Dio. Man. 1864. (Patron, V. of St. Michael-on-Wyre; Glebe, 26 acres; P. C.'s Inc. 180*l* and Ho; Pop. 1140.) Formerly P. C. of Langrove, Herefordshire. Author, *Romanism not Catholic,* 1843; *Africa in the West,* 1852; *Revival of Bishop Berkeley's Bermuda College,* 1853; *Religious Partizanship,* 1854; "*Limited Liability,*" *in things Religious,* 1862; *Life of George Calixtus,* 1863; *The Church and the Country in reference to the Education Question,* 1865; *Jottings from German Theology,* 1864; *Jottings from Danish Theology,* 1867. [23]

DOWE, Philip, *Barnet, Middlesex.*—Dub. A.B; Deac. 1844, Pr. 1845. C. of Ch. Ch. Barnet. Formerly P. C. of Knypersley, Cheshire, 1851–58. Author, *Judæa Rediviva, or the Restoration of the Jews.* [24]

DOWELL, Edward William, *Dunton, Norfolk.*—Jesus Coll. Cam. B.A. 1846; Deac. 1847, Pr. 1848. V. of Dunton, Dio. Nor. 1855. (Patron, Ld Chan; Tithe—Imp. 350*l*, V. 177*l*; V.'s Inc. 177*l*; Pop. 126.) [25]

DOWELL, George, *Gladestry, Kington, Radnor.*—Trin. Coll. Ox. B.A. 1827, M.A. 1830; Deac. 1831 and Pr. 1833 by Bp of B. and W. R. of Gladestry, Dio. St. D. 1860. (Patron, Ld Chan; R.'s Inc. 380*l*; Pop. 350.) Formerly V. of Llanigon, Brecknock, 1852–60. [26]

DOWELL, Stephen Wilkinson, *Gosfield, Halstead, Essex.*—Wor. Coll. Ox. B.A. 1824; Deac. 1825, Pr. 1826. V. of Gosfield, Dio. Roch. 1848. (Patron, S. Courtauld, Esq; Tithe—Imp. 161*l* 16*s* 3*d*, V. 257*l* 16*s*; Glebe, 60 acres; V.'s Inc. 345*l* and Ho; Pop. 620.) Author, *Catechism on the Services of the Church of England, compiled chiefly from the Notes of Bishop Mant's Book of Common Prayer, Pearson on the Creed, &c.* Rivingtons, 1852. [27]

DOWLAND, Edmund, *Salisbury.*—St. John's Coll. Cam. B.A. 1857, M.A. 1859; Deac. 1859 and Pr. 1860 by Bp of Chich. Mast. of the Cathl. Sch. Salisbury. [28]

DOWLE, Thomas, 55, *Philpot-street, Commercial-road, London, E.*—Emman. Coll. Cam. B.A. 1859; Deac.

1861 and Pr. 1863 by Bp of Man. Min. of St. Augustine's Chapel, Stepney, Dio. Lon. 1863. (Min.'s Inc. 200*l*; Pop. 6000.) Formerly C. of Glodwick, Lanc. 1861. Author, *The Bishop of London's Fund: What it has done for Eastern London*, 2*d*. Editor, *St. Augustine's District Magazine*, 1*d*. Monthly. [1]

DOWLER, Henry Turner, *Aldeburgh Vicarage, Suffolk*.—Magd. Coll. Cam. B.A. 1838, M.A. 1842; Deac. 1837 and Pr. 1838 by Bp of Chich. V. of Aldeburgh, and Lord of the Vicarage Manor with Hazlewood V. Dio. Nor. 1839. (Patron, F. J. V. Wentworth, Esq; Tithe, 265*l*; Glebe, 15 acres; V.'s Inc. 385*l* and Ho; Pop. 1812.) Rural Dean of Orford 1839. [2]

DOWLING, Barre Beresford, *Brown Candover, Micheldever Station, Hants*.—Dub. A.B. 1849; Deac. 1852 and Pr. 1853 by Bp of Lich. R. of Brown Candover with Chilton Candover R. Dio. Win. 1864. (Patron, Lord Ashburton; R.'s Inc. 600*l* and Ho; Pop. 464.) Formerly C. of St. Thomas's, Winchester. [3]

DOWLING, Edward, *Timperley Parsonage, Altrincham, Cheshire*.—Dub. A.B. 1845, A.M. 1850; Deac. 1846 by Bp of Ches. Pr. 1848 by Bp of Man. P. C. of Ch. Ch. Timperley, Dio. Ches. 1849. (Patrons, Trustees; Tithe, App. 274*l* 17*s*; P. C.'s Inc. 210*l* and Ho; Pop. 2392.) [4]

DOWLING, Thomas, *Lucton, Kingsland, Herefordshire*.—Wad. Coll. Ox. 1st cl. in Nat. Sci. B A. 1859, M.A. 1861; Deac. 1864 by Bp of Herf. Pr. 1866 by Bp of G. and B. for Bp of Herf. Asst. C. of Lucton 1864. [5]

DOWN, Charles John, *Hemington Rectory, Radstock, Bath*.—Ex. Coll. Ox. B.A. 1848; Deac. 1848, Pr. 1850. R. of Hemington with Hardington R. Dio. B. and W. 1862. (Patron, Lord Poltimore; R.'s Inc. 700*l* and Ho; Pop. Hemington 459, Hardington 22.) Formerly C. of Semington and Chap. to the Melksham Union, Wilts. [6]

DOWNALL, The Venerable John, *Okehampton Vicarage, Devon*.—Magd. Hall, Ox. Exhib. and Scho. B.A. 1826, M.A. 1829; Deac. 1826 by Bp of Lich. Pr. 1829 by Bp of Ches. V. of Okehampton, Dio. Ex. 1850. (Patron, A. B. Savile, Esq; Tithe—Imp. 271*l*, V. 355*l*; Glebe, 230 acres; V.'s Inc. 600*l* and Ho; Pop. 1929.) Archd. of Totnes 1859; Preb. of Ex. 1855; Chap. to the Duke of Devonshire; Surrogate. Justice of the Peace for the County of Devon. Formerly C. of St. Mark's, Liverpool, and of Blidworth and Oxton, Notts, 1831–43; P. C. of St. George's, Kidderminster, 1843–49. Author, *Laying on of Hands, or Plain Letters on Confirmation*, 1840, 3rd ed. 1859; *Address after Confirmation*, 3rd ed. 1845, 5th ed. 1859; *A Charge to the Clergy and Churchwardens of the Archdeaconry of Totnes*, 1859; etc. [7]

DOWNE, George Edward, *Rushden Rectory, Higham Ferrers, Northants*.—Corpus Coll. Cam. B.A. 1839; Deac. and Pr. 1840 by Abp of Cant. R. of Rushden, Dio. Pet. 1843. (Patron, Ld Chan; Glebe, 350 acres; R.'s Inc. 450*l* and Ho; Pop. 1748.) [8]

DOWNES, G. B.—C. of Heap St. James, near Manchester. [9]

DOWNES, James, *Stonnall, Walsall, Staffs*.—New Inn Hall, Ox. B.A. 1835; Deac. 1836, Pr. 1837. P. C. of Stonnall, Dio. Lich. 1840. (Patron, V. of Shenstone: P. C.'s Inc. 120*l* and Ho; Pop. 966.) [10]

DOWNES, John, *Hannington, Northampton*.—R of Hannington, Dio. Pet. 1866. [11]

DOWNES, William Edward, *Baylham, Ipswich*.—Wad. Coll. Ox. B.A. 1850, M.A. 1853; Deac. 1851, Pr. 1852. R. of Baylham, Dio. Nor. 1859. (Patron, W. Downes, Esq; R.'s Inc. 300*l*; Pop. 327.) Formerly C. of Palgrave, Diss. [12]

DOWNES, William Henry, *Llansannor Rectory, Cowbridge, Glamorganshire*.—Wor. Coll. Ox. B.A. 1851; Deac. 1851 and Pr. 1852 by Bp of St. D. R. of Llansannor, Dio. Llan. 1855. (Patron, Sir J. Bailey, Bart; Tithe, 191*l* 6*s*; R.'s Inc. 176*l*; Pop. 197.) [13]

DOWNING, Henry, *Kingswinford, Dudley*.—Trin. Coll. Ox. Hon. 4th cl. Lit. Hum. and B.A. 1838, M.A. 1840; Deac. and Pr. 1840. P. C. of St. Mary's, Kingswinford, Dio. Lich. 1846. (Patron, Earl of Dudley; P. C.'s Inc. 450*l*; Pop. 4029.) [14]

DOWNING, Henry Edward, *Wells, Norfolk*.—Ch. Ch. Coll. Ox. Magd. Exhib. of, and S.C.L. 1856; Deac. 1857 and Pr. 1859 by Bp of Rip. R. of Wells, Dio. Nor. 1864. (Patron, Rev. J. R. Hopper; R.'s Inc. 800*l* and Ho; Pop. 3464.) Formerly C. of St. John's, Golcar. [15]

DOWNING, Josiah, *Leeds*.—Corpus Coll. Cam. B.A. 1845; Deac. 1845 and Pr. 1846 by Bp of Dur. Chap. to the Leeds Workhouse and Industrial Schs. 1860. (Patrons, Leeds Board of Guardians; Salary, 200*l*.) Formerly C. of Edmondbyers, Durham, 1845, Ponsonby, Cumberland, 1846, Rostherne, Cheshire, 1850, St. George's, Sheffield, 1854. [16]

DOWNING, Samuel Penrose, *Sutton Waldron, Shaftesbury, Dorset*.—Caius Coll. Cam. B.A. 1849; Deac. 1850 and Pr. 1851 by Bp of Nor. C. of Sutton Waldron. Formerly P. C. of Rumburgh, Suffolk, 1851–58. [17]

DOWNTON, Henry, *Geneva*.—Trin. Coll. Cam. B.A. 1840, M.A. 1843; Deac. 1843, Pr. 1844. British Chap. at Geneva. Formerly P. C. of St. John's, Chatham, 1849–57; Dom. Chap. to Lord Monson. [18]

DOWNWARD, Peter, *Hodnet, Salop*.—Queen's Coll. Ox. B.A. 1846, M.A. 1848; Deac. 1846, Pr. 1847. C. of Hodnet. Formerly C. of Lebotwood and Longnor, Salop. [19]

DOWSON, Charles, *Lound Rectory, Lowestoft, Suffolk*.—Ex. Coll. Ox. S.C.L. 1848; Deac. 1850, Pr. 1851. R. of Lound, Dio. Nor. 1859. (Patron, Benjamin Dowson, Esq; Tithe, 415*l*; Glebe, 22 acres; R.'s Inc. 460*l* and Ho; Pop. 466.) Formerly V. of Lesbury, Northumberland, 1854–58; R. of Morborne, Hunts, 1858–59. [20]

DOWTY, George, *St. Leonard's, Shoreditch, London, N.E.*—Sen. C. of St. Leonard's, Shoreditch. [21]

DOYLE, Bentinck, J. F., *Chipping Warden, Banbury*.—R. of Chipping Warden, Dio. Pet. 1864. (Patroness, Rt. Hon. Lady S. North; R.'s Inc. 300*l* and Ho; Pop. 489.) [22]

DOYLE, James B., *Douglas, Isle of Man*.—C. of St. Barnabas', Douglas. [23]

DOYLE, William, *Old Trafford, Manchester*.—Dub. A.B. 1846; Deac. 1847 by Bp of Ches. Pr. 1848 by Bp of Man. R. of Old Trafford, Dio. Man. 1865. (Patron, Bp of Man; R.'s Inc. 560*l*; Pop. 2184.) Formerly R. of St. Stephen's, Chorlton-upon-Medlock, 1854–65. [24]

DOXEY, J. S., *Milnrow, near Rochdale*.—C. of Milnrow. [25]

D'OYLY, Charles John, 15, *Gloucester-place, Portman-square, London, W.*—Trin. Coll. Cam. Jun. Opt. and B.A. 1843, M.A. 1845; Deac. 1844 and Pr. 1845 by Bp of Lich. Chap. to Lincoln's-inn 1860. Formerly Min. of St. John's, Broad-court, St. Martin's-in-the-Fields, Lond. 1855–60. Author, *The True Faith of a Christian*, 1856, 2*s* 6*d*; *A Few Words upon Election*, 1858. [26]

DRABBLE, Peter B., *Ealing, Middlesex, W.*—P. C. of St. Paul's, Ealing, Dio. Lon. 1864. (Patrons, Crown and Bp of Lon. alt; P. C.'s Inc. 200*l*; Pop. 4409.) [27]

DRAGE, Charles, *Westerfield, Ipswich*.—Emman. Coll. Cam. B.A. 1811, M.A. 1814; Deac. 1811 and Pr. 1812 by Bp of Lon. R. of Westerfield, Dio. Nor. 1835. (Patron, Bp of Nor; Tithe, 350*l*; Glebe, 2 acres; R.'s Inc. 352*l* and Ho; Pop. 325.) [28]

DRAGE, William Henry, *Rochester*.—V. of St. Margaret's, Rochester, Dio. Roch. 1832. (Patrons, D. and C. of Roch; V.'s Inc. 450*l* and Ho; Pop. 3769.) [29]

DRAKE, Charles Digby Mackworth, *Huntshaw Rectory, Great Torrington, Devon*.—St. John's Coll. Cam. B.A. 1824, M.A. 1827; Deac. 1825, Pr. 1826. R. of Huntshaw, Dio. Ex. 1834. (Patron, Lord Clinton; Tithe, 197*l* 10*s*; Glebe, 36 acres; R.'s Inc. 243*l* and Ho; Pop. 233.) [30]

DRAKE, C. Mackworth, *Seaton Vicarage, Axminster.*—V. of Seaton with Beer C. Dio. Ex. 1867. (Patrons, Heirs of Lord Rolle; V.'s Inc. 250*l* and Ho; Pop. 1966.) V. of Chittlehampton, Dio. Ex. 1864. (Patrons, Heirs of Lord Rolle; V.'s Inc. 500*l* and Ho; Pop. 1343.) [1]

DRAKE, Edward Tyrwhitt, *Amersham, Bucks.*—Magd. Coll. Cam. B.A. 1857, M.A. 1860; Deac. 1860 and Pr. 1861 by Bp of Ox. R. of Amersham with Coleshill C. Dio. Ox. 1864. (Patron, T. T Drake, Esq; R.'s Inc. 1500*l* and Ho; Pop. 3550.) Formerly C. of Chalfont St. Giles. [2]

DRAKE, Francis Charles, *Puddletown, Dorset.*—Jesus Coll. Cam. Cl. Scho. and Prizeman, Jun. Opt. B.A. 1850; Deac. 1854 by Bp of B. and W. Pr. 1856 by Bp of Nor. V. of Puddleton, Dio. Salis. 1866. (Patron, Marquis of Hastings; Tithe, 506*l*; Glebe, 10½ acres; V.'s Inc. 522*l* and Ho; Pop. 1241.) Formerly C. of West Monkton, Somerset, 1854, Hollesley, Suffolk, 1856; P. C. of Willesley, Derbyshire, 1860. [3]

DRAKE, Frederick Edward Tyrwhitt, *Bedfield Rectory, Wickham Market, Suffolk.*—Pemb. Coll. Ox. M.A; Deac. 1852 and Pr. 1853 by Bp of Ches. R. of Bedfield, Dio. Nor. 1866. (Patron, Earl of Stradbroke; R.'s Inc. 310*l* and Ho; Pop. 400.) Formerly P. C. of High Legh 1853–56; R. of Little Wigborough 1856–66. [4]

DRAKE, James Thomas, *Dicker, Arlington, Sussex.*—P. C. of Dicker, Dio. Chich. 1863. (Patron, Bp of Chich; P. C.'s Inc. 140*l* and Ho; Pop. 550.) [5]

DRAKE, John, *Great Wratting Rectory, Haverhill, Suffolk.*—Trin. Coll. Cam. B.A. 1859; Deac. 1859 and Pr. 1860 by Bp of B. and W. R. of Great and Little Wratting, Dio. Ely 1864. (Patron, F. Drake, Esq; Tithe, 615*l*; Glebe, 96 acres; R.'s Inc. 700*l* and Ho; Pop. 616.) Formerly C. of Ch. Ch. Frome, 1859, Northill, Beds, 1862, Crookham with Ewshott 1863. [6]

DRAKE, John Alexander, *Brockley, Bury St. Edmunds.*—Magd. Hall, Ox. B.A. 1858, M.A. 1862; Deac. 1862 and Pr. 1864 by Abp of Cant. R. of Brockley, Dio. Ely, 1865. (Patron, the present R; Tithe, 458*l*; Glebe, 27 acres; R.'s Inc. 510*l* and Ho; Pop. 340.) Formerly C. of Bethersden 1862; Incumb. of Smallhythe 1865. [7]

DRAKE, John Tyrwhitt, *Cottesbrooke Rectory, Northampton.*—Trin. Hall, Cam. B.C.L. 1851; Deac. and Pr. 1845 by Bp of Lin. R. of Cottesbrooke, Dio. Pet. 1865. (Patron, Sir J. H. Langham, Bart; R.'s Inc. 520*l* and Ho; Pop. 201.) Formerly R. of Malpas, Cheshire, 1845–62; R. of Croxton, Lincolnshire, 1862–65. [8]

DRAKE, Nathan Richard.—Trin. Coll. Cam. B.A. 1831; Deac. 1832, Pr. 1833. Formerly C. of Earls Colne, Essex. [9]

DRAKE, Richard, *Stourmouth, Canterbury.*—R. of Stourmouth, Dio. Cant. 1840. (Patron, Bp of Wor; Tithe, 425*l*; Glebe, 12 acres; R.'s Inc. 457*l* and Ho; Pop. 300.) [10]

DRAKE, Thomas, *Barrow-on-Soar, Loughborough.*—St. John's Coll. Cam. 13th Wrang. B.A. 1838, M.A. 1845; Deac. 1840, Pr. 1841. P. C. of Mountsorrel, Dio. Pet. 1861. (Patron, V. of Barrow-on-Soar; P. C.'s Inc. 260*l*; Pop. 857.) Head Mast. of the Barrow-on-Soar Gr. Sch. 1846. Author, *A Few Thoughts on the Cosmos*; *The Mosaic Account of Creation distinguished from Geology.* [11]

DRAKE, Thomas Rumpf, *Fittleworth, Petworth.*—Corpus Coll. Cam. Jun. Opt. B.A. 1840, M.A. 1844; Deac. and Pr. 1849 by Bp of S. and M. V. of Fittleworth, Dio. Chich. 1860. (Patron, Bp of Chich; Tithe, comm. 450*l*; Rent from Glebe, 12*l* 10*s*; V.'s Inc. 462*l* 10*s* and Ho; Pop. 681.) Formerly Asst. Min. St. John's, Chichester, 1844–48; R. of All Saints', Chichester, 1848–60; V. of West Hampnett 1850–60; Chap. to Chichester Poorhouse 1858–60; Even. Lect. St. Pancras, Chichester, 1856–60. Author, *Ordination Sermon*, 1854. [12]

DRAKE, Walter, *Moulsoe Rectory, Newport Pagnell, Bucks.*—Ch. Coll. Cam. B.A. 1829, M.A. 1835; Deac. 1831, Pr. 1832. V. of Bradwell, Bucks, Dio. Ox. 1833. (Patron, Ld Chan; Tithe, 250*l*; Glebe, 6 acres; V.'s Inc. 256*l* and Ho; Pop. 479.) R. of Moulsoe, Dio. Ox. 1842. (Patron, Lord Carrington; R.'s Inc. 300*l* and Ho; Pop. 234.) [13]

DRAKE, William, *Sedgebrook Rectory, Grantham.*—St. John's Coll. Cam. 15th Sen. Opt. 4th in 2nd cl. Cl. Trip. B.A. 1835, M.A. 1838; Deac. 1837 by Bp of Lin. Pr. 1838 by Bp of Nor. R. of Sedgebrook with East Allington C. Dio. Lin. 1864. (Patron, Ld Chan; R.'s Inc. 750*l* and Ho; Pop. Sedgebrook 269, East Allington 275.) Hon. Can. of Worcester 1861; Hon. Chap. in Ordinary to the Queen 1867; Rural Dean; Surrogate. Late Fell. of St. John's Coll. Cam; Hebrew Examiner in the Univ. of Lond; 2nd Mast. of Gr. Sch. and Lect. of St. John-the-Baptist, Coventry, 1841–57; V. of Trinity, Coventry, 1857–64. Author, *The Rule of Faith* (a Sermon), 1840; *The Treasure and its Keepers*, 1841; *An Address to the Members of the Leicester Mechanics' Institute on the Study of Natural History*, 1841; *The Evils of our Social Condition, a Call to Repentance and Prayer* (University Sermon), 1844; *Fasciculus Primus Historiæ Britannicæ, with Notes, for the use of Schools*, 1845, 3*s* 6*d*; *Fast-day Sermons*, 1849; *What shall we do unto the Child that shall be Born?* (Sermon) 1850; *Notes, Critical and Explanatory, on Jonah and Hosea*, 1853, 9*s*; *Thirty Sermons on Jonah, Amos, and Hosea*, 1853, 7*s* 6*d*; *A Plea for the Enforcement of a Knowledge of Hebrew upon Candidates for Holy Orders* (Pamphlet), 1853; *Words on the War* (2 Sermons), 1854; *Life for Life* (a Sermon referring to the execution of Wm. Palmer), 1856; etc. [14]

DRAKE, William, *West Coker, Yeovil, Somerset.*—Dub. A.B. 1844; Deac. 1845 by Bp of Lich. Pr. 1846 by Bp of Ossory. C. of West Coker. [15]

DRAKE, William Fitt, *West Halton Rectory, Brigg, Lincolnshire.*—Corpus Coll. Cam. B.A. 1811, M.A. 1823; Deac. and Pr. 1810. R. of West Halton, Dio. Lin. 1835. (Patron, Bp of Nor; Tithe, 253*l* 12*s*; Glebe, 335 acres; R.'s Inc. 890*l* and Ho; Pop. 220.) Formerly Min. Can. of Nor. and V. of St. Stephen's, Norwich, 1811–35; Exam. Chap. to Dr. Bathurst, late Bp of Nor. [16]

DRAKE, William Hinton, *St. Ives, Cornwall.*—Sid. Coll. Cam. B.A. 1843; Deac. 1845, Pr. 1846. P. C. of Halsetown, Cornwall, Dio. Ex. 1846. (Patrons, Crown and Bp of Ex. alt; Glebe, 2 acres; P. C.'s Inc. 180*l* and Ho; Pop. 1940.) Author, *The Christian Ministry* (a Visitation Sermon), 1852. [17]

DRAKEFORD, David James, *Soberton, Bishop's Waltham, Hants.*—C. of Soberton. [18]

DRAPER, Joseph Busby, *Saltley, near Birmingham.*—Cheltenham Coll; Deac. 1861 and Pr. 1862 by Bp of Wor. Vice-Prin. of Worcester, Lichfield, and Hereford Training College, Saltley, 1860. [19]

DRAPER, William Henry, *Bromyard, Herefordshire.*—Wor. Coll. Ox; Deac. 1860, Pr. 1861. C. of Bromyard 1860. [20]

DRAWBRIDGE, Thomas Oben, *Rodmersham, Sittingbourne, Kent.*—Queens' Coll. Cam. B.A. 1830, M.A. 1843; Deac. 1830 and Pr. 1832 by Bp of Lich. V. of Rodmersham, Dio. Cant. 1846. (Patron, P. Panton, Esq. M.D; Tithe—Imp. 413*l* 17*s*, V. 136*l* 3*s*; Glebe, 20 acres; V.'s Inc. 156*l*; Pop. 294.) [21]

DRAWBRIDGE, William Barker, *Nagode, Bundelcund, India.*—Caius Coll. Cam. LL.B. 1857; Deac. 1855 and Pr. 1856 by Abp of York. Chap. at Nagode. Formerly C. of St. Margaret's, Rochester. [22]

DREAPER, John, *Northampton.*—Dub. A.B. 1840; Deac. and Pr. 1846 by Bp of Wor. Chap. of the County Gaol, Northampton. Formerly Asst. Chap. to the Convict Prison, Wakefield; C. of St. Thomas's, Birmingham, 1846–47, Saddington, Leicestershire, 1847–52. [23]

DREAPER, J. Jestin, *Warrington.*—Dub. A.B. 1859; Deac. 1863, Pr. 1864. Miss. C. of Golborne, near Warrington. [24]

DREW, Andrew Augustus Wild, 5, *Park-road Villas, Forest-hill, London, S.E.*—Trin. Coll. Cam. B.A. 1859, M.A. 1863; Deac. 1860 and Pr. 1861 by Abp of Cant. Min. of St. Michael's, Nunhead, 1865.

Formerly C. of Benenden, Kent, 1860, Ewhurst, Sussex, 1862, Ch. Ch. Forest Hill, 1863. [1]

DREW, Francis Robert, *Malvern College, Worcestershire.*—Sid. Coll. Cam. Wrang. B.A. 1859, M.A. 1862; Deac. 1864 and Pr. 1865 by Bp of Wor. Sen. Math. Mast. of Malvern Coll. Formerly Vice-Prin. of Chelmsford Sch; Math. Lect. at Cholmondeley Sch. Author, *Six Sermons for Boys*, Simpkin, Marshall and Co. 1865. [2]

DREW, George Smith, *St. Barnabas', South Kennington, London, S.*—St. John's Coll. Cam. Scho. Wrang. and B.A. 1843, M.A. 1847; Deac. 1843 and Pr. 1844 by Bp of Lon. P. C. of St. Barnabas', Kennington, Dio. Win. 1858. (Patron, P. C. of St. Mark's, Kennington; P. C.'s Inc. 350*l*; Pop. 9722.) Formerly V. of Pulloxhill, Beds, 1844-58. Author, *Sermons*, Rivingtons, 1845; *Distinctive Excellences of the Book of Common Prayer*, 1845; *Scripture Studies*, 1852; *Lectures on Evening Classes*, Darling, 1852; *Scripture Lands in Connexion with their History*, Smith and Elder, 1860; *Reasons of Faith, or the Scripture Argument Explained and Developed*, 1862; *Colenso's Examination of the Pentateuch Examined*, Bell and Daldy, 1863; *Ritualism in some recent Developments*; articles in *Fairbairn's Imperial Bible Dictionary*; etc. [3]

DREW, Heriot Stambanks, *Comberton, Cambridge.*—St. John's Coll. Cam. Sen. Opt. and B.A. 1834; Deac. 1839 and Pr. 1840 by Bp of Nor. C. of Comberton and Harlton. Formerly C. of Pettistree, Suffolk. [4]

DREW, James, *Ilfracombe.*—St. John's Coll. Cam. B.A. 1854, M.A. 1857; Deac. 1860 and Pr. 1861 by Bp of B. and W. C. of Ilfracombe 1865. Formerly C. of Westbury, Wilts, and Symondsbury, Dorset. [5]

DREW, Josias Henry, *Speen, Newbury.*—Ex. Coll. Ox. B.A. 1852, M.A. 1860; Deac. 1853 and Pr. 1854 by Bp of Ex. C. of St. Mary's, Speenhamland, Berks, 1865. Formerly C. of Gwennap and Budock, Cornwall. [6]

DREW, W. H., *Blackheath, Kent, S.E.*—Math. Mast. Proprietary Sch. Blackheath; C. of Crockenhill, Dartford. [7]

DREWE, William Ball, *Longstock Vicarage, near Stockbridge, Hants.*—St. Mary Hall, Ox. Dyke Scho. B.A. 1846, M.A. 1852; Deac. 1847 and Pr. 1849 by Bp of Nor. V. of Longstock, Dio. Win. 1849. (Patroness, Lady Barker Mill; Tithe, comm. 315*l*; Glebe, 5 acres; V.'s Inc. 315*l* and Ho; Pop. 445.) Formerly C. of Foulsham, Norfolk, 1847–49. [8]

DRIFFIELD, George Townshend, *Bow Rectory, Middlesex.*—Brasen. Coll. Ox. B.A. 1839, M.A. 1842; Deac. 1840 and Pr. 1841 by Bp of Ox. R. of Bow, *alias* St. Mary Stratford Bow, Dio. Lon. 1844. (Patron, Bp of Lon; Tithe, App. 40*l*; Glebe, ½ acre; R.'s Inc. 297*l* and Ho; Pop. 4432.) Formerly Fell. of Brasen. Coll. Ox. 1839–45; C. of St. Clement's, Oxford, 1841, Prescot, Lancashire, 1842, Richmond, Yorks, 1843; P. C. of St. Philip's, Stepney, 1844. [9]

DRIFFIELD, Joseph Charles, *Tolleshunt d'Arcy, Maldon, Essex.*—Clare Hall, Cam. B.A. 1819; Deac. 1814, Pr. 1817. V. of Tolleshunt d'Arcy, Dio. Roch. 1819. (Patron, J. G. Rebow, Esq; Tithe—Imp. 351*l*, V. 250*l*; Glebe, 3 acres; V.'s Inc. 296*l*; Pop. 794.) [10]

DRISCOLL, Charles, *Edenderry, King's Co., Ireland.*—Dub. A.B. 1825; Deac. 1826 by Bp of Kilmore, Pr. 1828 by Bp of Meath. R. of Ballymacwilliam, Kildare, 1830. Formerly C. of St. Mary's, Lichfield; Lect. of Bow, Middlesex; C. of St. Luke's, Chelsea, St. Clement Danes, Strand, and St. Marylebone, Lond. [11]

DROSIER, Thomas, *Colebrooke, near Copplestone, N. Devon.*—Sid. Coll. Cam. B.A. 1828; Deac. 1837 by Bp of Chich. Pr. 1838 by Bp of Nor. V. of Colebrooke, Dio. Ox. 1848. (Patrons, D. and C. of Ex; Tithe—App. 435*l* 10*s*, V. 168*l* 8*s*; Glebe, 15 acres; V.'s Inc. 176*l* and Ho; Pop. 802.) Formerly C. of Boughton 1837, Wells 1846, Warham All Saints 1846, Barnham Westgate 1847, all in Norfolk. [12]

DROUGHT, Adolphus, *Shirley, Hants.*—Dub. A.M. 1832; Deac. 1828, Pr. 1831. C. of Shirley 1864. Formerly C. of Castletown 1829, Castlepollard 1832; R. of Aghancon 1841; C. of Ardrapan 1851; R. of Clonterskert 1855, all in Ireland. Author, *Book of Family Prayers*, Dublin, 1846, 6*d*. [13]

DROUGHT, Charles Bristow, *Ilkley, near Otley, Yorks.*—Dub. A.B. 1830, A.M. 1833; Deac. 1831 by Bp of Clonfert, Pr. 1832 by Bp of Cloyne. Formerly C. of Ilkley. [14]

DROUGHT, Henry, *Walker, Newcastle-on-Tyne.*—Literate; Deac. 1859 and Pr. 1860 by Bp of Dur. C. of Walker 1859. [15]

DRUCE, Arthur John, *Ryde, Isle of Wight.*—St. John's Coll. Cam. 1852, 2nd cl. Cl. Trip. and B.A. 1853, M.A. 1856; Deac. 1854 and Pr. 1855 by Bp of St. A. C. of St. Thomas's, Ryde. Formerly C. of Gresford, Denbigh, 1854–58. [16]

DRUCE, Gerald William, 3, *Fortess-terrace West, Kentish-town, London, N.W.*—Ex. Coll. Ox. B.A. 1859, M.A. 1862; Deac. 1860 and Pr. 1861 by Bp of Win. C. of St. John's, Kentish-town, 1864. Formerly C. of Chertsey 1860, Huntley 1862. Author, *Four Christmas Carols*, music and words, 6*d*. [17]

DRUITT, William, *Crawley, Winchester.*—King's Coll. Lond. Assoc. 1859; Deac. 1859 and Pr. 1860 by Bp of Win. C. of Crawley 1862. Formerly C. of Chilcombe, Winchester, 1859-62. [18]

DRUMMOND, David Thomas Kerr, *Edinburgh.*—Wor. Coll. Ox; Deac. 1830 by Bp of Llan. Pr. 1831 by Bp of Bristol. Min. of St. Thomas's English Episcopal Chap. Edinburgh. Formerly C. of Henbury and Compton, Glouc. 1830–32. Author, *Exposition of St. John's Gospel*; *The Gospel in the Parables*; etc. [19]

DRUMMOND, Heneage, *Leckhamsted Rectory, near Buckingham.*—Ball. Coll. Ox. B.A. 1833, M.A. 1834; Deac. 1834 and Pr. 1835 by Bp of Lin. R. of Leckhamsted, Dio. Ox. 1835. (Patron, H. W. Beauclerk, Esq; Tithe, 517*l*; Glebe, 79½ acres; R.'s Inc. 480*l* and Ho; Pop. 482.) [20]

DRUMMOND, James, *Gaulby, Leicester.*—Ch. Ch. Ox. B.A. 1822, M.A. 1824; Deac. 1824 by Bp of Lin. Pr. 1826 by Bp of Lon. R. of Gaulby, Dio. Pet. 1859. (R.'s Inc. 300*l* and Ho; Pop. 98.) Hon. Can. of Pet. 1853. [21]

DRUMMOND, Morton, *Exmoor, South Molton.*—P. C. of Exmoor, Dio. B. and W. 1861. (Patron, the Crown; P. C.'s Inc. 180*l* and Ho; Pop. 323.) [22]

DRUMMOND, Robert, *St. Catherine Court, Bath.*—Trin. Coll. Cam. B.A. 1827, M.A. 1830; Deac. 1827 and Pr. 1828 by Bp of Lin. Formerly V. of Feering, Essex, 1829–66. [23]

DRUMMOND, Spencer Rodney, *Brighton.*—Ch. Ch. Ox. B.A. 1813, M.A. 1815; Deac. 1813, Pr. 1815. Formerly P. C. of St. John's, Brighton, 1843–62. Author, *Elements of Christian Religion*, 1845, 3*s* 6*d*; *Letter to the Archbishop of Canterbury on Self-supporting Schools*, 1*s*; etc. [24]

DRUMMOND-HAY, Frederic, *Rollestone Vicarage, Newark-on-Trent.*—Magd. Coll. Ox. B.A. 1863; Deac. and Pr. 1864 by Bp of Ox. V. of Rollestone, Dio. Lin. 1865. (Patron, Coll. Ch. Southwell; V.'s Inc. 300*l* and Ho; Pop. 587.) Formerly C. of Wantage, Berks. [25]

DRURY, Benjamin Heath, *Caius College, Cambridge.*—Caius Coll. Cam. B.A. 1840, M.A. 1843; Deac. 1841, Pr. 1842. Sen. Fell. and Tut. of Caius Coll. Cam. Late Mast. in Harrow Sch. [26]

DRURY, Benjamin Joseph, *Rudgwick, near Horsham.*—V. of Rudgwick, Dio. Chich. 1865. (Patron, Bp of Chich; V.'s Inc. 300*l* and Ho; Pop. 1068.) [27]

DRURY, Charles, *Pontesbury Rectory, near Shrewsbury.*—Oriel Coll. Ox. 2nd cl. Lit. Hum. and B.A. 1809, Queen's Coll. M.A. 1810; Deac. 1812, Pr. 1813. R. of Pontesbury, 2nd portion, with Cruckton Chapelry, Dio. Herf. 1824. (Patron, Queen's Coll Ox; Tithe—Imp. 127*l* 9*s*, R. 2nd portion, 837*l*; Glebe, 58½ acres; R.'s Inc. 851*l* and Ho; Pop. 3466.) Preb. of Warham in Herf. Cathl. 1842. Late Michel Fell. of Queen's Coll. Ox. 1811. [28]

DRURY, Charles Roua, *Madras.*—St. John's Coll. Cam. B.A. 1845; Deac. 1846, Pr. 1847. Formerly V. of Leominster 1852–56. [1]

DRURY, F. W.—Dom. Chap. to Lord Lilford. [2]

DRURY, George, *Claydon Rectory, Ipswich.*—Ch. Coll. Cam. B.A. 1841; Deac. 1843 and Pr. 1845 by Bp of Nor. R. of Claydon with Akenham R. Dio. Nor. 1846. (Patroness, Miss E. Drury; Claydon, Tithe—App. 3*l* 11*s*, R. 246*l* 9*s*; Glebe, 31 acres; Akenham, Tithe, 260*l*; Glebe, 20 acres; R.'s Inc. 590*l* and Ho; Pop. Claydon 501, Akenham 94.) [3]

DRURY, George, *Thorpe, near Chertsey, Surrey.*—All Souls' Coll. Ox. B.A. 1853, M.A. 1860; Deac. 1856 and Pr. 1857 by Bp of Win. C. of Thorpe 1862. Formerly C. of Paper-Harrow 1856–62. [4]

DRURY, Henry John, *West-Down Vicarage, Ilfracombe, Devon.*—Wor. Coll. Ox. B.A. 1840; Deac. 1841 and Pr. 1842 by Bp of Ex. V. of West-Down, Dio. Ex. 1845. (Patron, Bp of Ex; Tithe—Imp. 163*l* 3*s*, V. 255*l*; V.'s Inc. 270*l* and Ho; Pop. 554.) [5]

DRURY, J.—Assoc. Sec. to the London Society for Promoting Christianity among the Jews. [6]

DRURY, William, *Kirk Braddan Vicarage, Douglas, Isle of Man.*—Deac. 1832 and Pr. 1833 by Bp of S. and M. V. of Kirk Braddan, Dio. S. and M. 1847. (Patron, Bp of S. and M; Tithe, 140*l*; Glebe, 27 acres; V.'s Inc. 220*l* and Ho; Pop. 2794.) [7]

DRURY, William J. J., *Brussels.*—British Chap. at Brussels, and Chap. to H.M. the King of the Belgians. [8]

DRY, Thomas, *North Walsham, Norfolk.*—Mert. Coll. Ox. Jackson's Scho. 1825, 3rd cl. Lit. Hum. and Maths. 1828, B.A. 1829, M.A. 1832; Deac. 1832 and Pr. 1833 by Bp of Lon. C. of Worstead 1856; Head Mast. of the North Walsham Gr. Sch. 1843. Formerly Head Mast. of Forest Proprietary Sch. 1834; Min. of St. Paul's, Walthamstow, 1840. [9]

DRY, William, M.A., 15, *Abbotsford Park, Edinburgh.*—Caius Coll. Cam. B.A. 1842, M.A. 1850; Deac. 1843 by Bp of Lon. Pr. 1845 by Bp of Tasmania. [10]

DRY, William, *Whitchurch Rectory, near Monmouth.*—Brasen. Coll. Ox. B.A. 1845, M.A. 1848; Deac. 1846 and Pr. 1847 by Bp of Ches. R. of Whitchurch, Dio. Herf. 1862. (Patron, William Dry, Esq; Tithe, 280*l*; Glebe, 6 acres; R.'s Inc. 300*l* and Ho; Pop. 860.) Formerly C. of Burton Abbotts, Oxon. [11]

DRY, William John, *Weston-on-the-Green Vicarage, Bicester.*—Wad. Coll. Ox. B.A. 1844, M.A. 1848; Deac. 1844, Pr. 1851. V. of Weston-on-the-Green, Dio. Ox. 1844. (Patron, Hon. P. Bertie; Tithe—Imp. 304*l*, V. 230*l*; Glebe, 4 acres; V.'s Inc. 234*l* and Ho; Pop. 549.) Surrogate 1855. [12]

DRYBURGH, Joseph Andrew, *Mylor, Falmouth.*—C. of Mylor. [13]

DU ANE, D. W.—Formerly C. of All Saints', Birmingham. [14]

DUBERLY, Charles, *Wolsingham Rectory, Darlington.*—Ch. Ch. Ox. B.A. 1838; Deac. 1836 and Pr. 1837 by Bp of Lin. R. of Wolsingham, Dio. Dur. 1856. (Patron, Bp of Ches; Tithe, 900*l*; Glebe, 10 acres; R.'s Inc. 910*l* and Ho; Pop. 2267.) Formerly P. C. of Cowsden 1844–56. [15]

DU BOULAY, Francis, *Lawhitton Rectory, Launceston.*—R. of Lawhitton, Dio. Ex. 1839. (Patron, Bp of Ex; R.'s Inc. 500*l* and Ho. Pop. 435.) [16]

DU BOULAY, Francis Houssemayne, *Heddington Rectory, Calne, Wilts.*—Ex. Coll. Ox. B.A. 1849, M.A. 1851; Deac. 1851 and Pr. 1852 by Bp of Salis. R. of Heddington, Dio. Salis. 1853. (Patron, the present R; Tithe, comm. 268*l*; Glebe, 15 acres; R.'s Inc. 300*l* and Ho; Pop. 358.) Rural Dean. [17]

DU BOULAY, Henry Houssemayne, *Babbacombe, Torquay.*—Ex. Coll. Ox. B.A. 1863; Deac. 1864 and Pr. 1865 by Bp of Ex. Dom. Chap. and Sec. to Bp of Ex. Formerly C. of St. Mary Church 1864–67. [18]

DU BOULAY, James Thomas Houssemayne, *Southgate Hill, Winchester.*—Ex. Coll. Ox. Hon. 4th cl. Lit. Hum. Law and Mod. Hist. 1854, B.A. 1854, M.A. 1856; Deac. 1860 and Pr. 1861 by Bp of Ox. Asst. Mast. of Win. Coll. 1862. Late Fell. and Tut. of Ex. Coll. Ox. 1856–62. [19]

DU BOULAY, William Thomas, 12, *Palace-gardens-terrace, Kensington. London, W.*—Trin. Coll. Cam. Sen. Opt. B.A. 1855, M.A. 1861; Deac. 1856 and Pr 1857 by Bp of Ely. C. of Kensington 1861. Formerly C. of Shillington, Beds, 1856–59, Pluckley, Kent, 1859–61. [20]

DU BUISSON, Edmund, *Breinton, Hereford.*—Oriel Coll. Ox. M.A. 1848; Deac. 1846 by Bp of Salis. Pr. 1848 by Bp of G. and B. V. of Breinton, Dio. Herf. 1854. (Patron, Bp of Herf; Tithe, comm. 185*l*; Grant from Eccles. Commis. 121*l*; V.'s Inc. 256*l* and Ho; Pop. 400.) [21]

DU CANE, Alfred Richard, *Rostherne Vicarage, Knutsford, Cheshire.*—Trin. Coll. Cam. B.A. 1857, M.A. 1860; Deac. 1858, Pr. 1859. V. of Rostherne, Dio. Ches. 1862. (Patron, Lord Egerton; R.'s Inc. 350*l* and Ho; Pop. 2473.) Formerly C. of Oakmoor 1858–62. [22]

DUCK, John Hare, *Upper Tean, Tean, Staffs.*—Dub. A.B. 1845, A.M. 1847; Deac. 1845 and Pr. 1846 by Abp of Dub. P. C. of Tean, Dio. Lich. 1857. (Patron, R. of Checkley; P. C.'s Inc. 180*l* and Ho; Pop. 1171.) Formerly Chap. to the Royal Infirmary, Lunatic Asylum, and Lock Hospital, Liverpool. [23]

DUCKER, John, *Wardle, near Rochdale.*—Brasen. Coll. Ox. B.A. 1844, M.A. 1847; Deac. 1846 by Bp of Ches. Pr. 1848 by Bp of Man. V. of Wardle, Dio. Man. 1858. (Patron, V. of Smallbridge; V.'s Inc. 200*l* and Ho; Pop. 2176.) [24]

DUCKETT, William, *Branksea, Poole, Dorset.*—P. C. of Branksea, Dio. Salis. 1863. (P. C.'s Inc. 70*l*; Pop. 123.) [25]

DUCKWORTH, Robinson, *Windsor Castle, Berks,* and *Athenæum Club, London, S.W.*—Univ. Coll. Ox. Scho. 1853, 1st cl. Lit. Hum. B.A. 1857, M.A. 1859; Deac. 1858 and Pr. 1859 by Bp of Salis. Instructor to H.R.H. Prince Leopold 1866, and Governor 1867. Formerly Asst. Mast. at Marlborough Coll. Wilts, 1858–60; Fell. and Tut. of Trin. Coll. Ox. 1860–66. [26]

DUCKWORTH, William Arthur, *Puttenham, Guildford.*—Trin. Coll. Cam. B.A. 1852, M.A. 1855; Deac. 1854 by Bp of Rip. Pr. 1855 by Bp of Lich. R. of Puttenham, Dio. Win. 1859. (Patron, Ld Chan; R.'s Inc. 375*l* and Ho; Pop. 402.) [27]

DUDDING, Horatio Nelson, *St. Peter's Vicarage, St. Albans, Herts.*—Ex. Coll. Ox. 1st cl. Lit. Hum. and B.A. 1830, M.A. 1831; Deac. 1836 and Pr. 1837 by Bp of Ox. V. of St. Peter's, Dio. Roch. 1842. (Patron, the Crown; Tithe—App. 830*l* 16*s*, Imp. 462*l* 2*s* 7*d*, V. 300*l*; V.'s Inc. 397*l* and Ho; Pop. 3183.) [28]

DUDDING, Henry Swan, *Stanton Rectory, Ixworth, Suffolk.*—Magd. Hall, Ox. B.A. 1854, M.A. 1857; Deac. 1855 and Pr. 1856 by Bp of Nor. R. of Stanton All Saints' with Stanton St. John R. 1865. (Patron, Rev. R. E. Lofft; Tithe, 983*l*; Glebe, 31 acres; R.'s Inc. 1050*l* and Ho; Pop. 1045.) Formerly C. of Burnham, Sutton and Overy, Norfolk, and Hurworth, Durham. [29]

DUDDING, John, *Washingborough Rectory, Lincoln.*—Trin. Hall, Cam. LL.B. 1859, LL.M. 1862; Deac. 1860 and Pr. 1861 by Bp of Ely. R. of Washingborough, Dio. Lin. 1866. (Patron, the present R; R.'s Inc. 1600*l* and Ho; Pop. 1200.) Formerly C. of Naughton, Suffolk, 1860. [30]

DUDDING, Richard, *Bennington, Boston, Lincolnshire.*—St. Aidan's; Deac. 1851, Pr. 1852. C. of Bennington. [31]

DUDGEON, Michael Fox.—Chap. to Lord Keane. [32]

DUDLEY, Joseph, *Sarnesfield Rectory, Kington, Herefordshire.*—Wor. Coll. Ox. B.A. 1830; Deac. 1832 by Bp of Wor. Pr. 1833 by Bp of Herf. R. of Sarnesfield,

Dio. Herf. 1846. (Patron, Thos. Monington, Esq; Tithe, 180*l*; Glebe, 50 acres; R.'s Inc. 250*l* and Ho; Pop. 120.) Formerly C. of Broadwas 1832–33, Edwin-Ralph 1833–37; P. C. of Marston, Hereford, 1837–43; C. of Cubert, Cornwall, 1843–46. [1]

DUDLEY, S., *Portland, Dorset.*—C. of Portland. [2]

DUDLEY, Samuel George, *Barton Stacey, Hants.*—Jesus Coll. Ox. B.A. 1837, M.A 1840; Deac. 1838 and Pr. 1839 by Bp of Ox. C. of Barton Stacey. Formerly C. of St. John's, Winchester. [3]

DUDLEY, William Charles, *Weaverham, Northwich, Cheshire.*—Queens' Coll. Cam. B.A. 1838, M.A. 1858, *ad eund.* Ox. M.A. 1859; Deac. 1838 and Pr. 1839 by Bp of Ches. C. of Weaverham 1863. Formerly C. of Wharton, Cheshire, 1838–40; P. C. of Trinity, Sheerness, 1840–41; Missionary to New Zealand 1841–55; C. of Henley on Thames, while on leave of absence from N. Z. 1850–51; C. of Clifton Reynes, Bucks, 1855, Over, Cheshire, 1857–63. [4]

DUDLEY, William Mason, *Whitchurch Vicarage, Hants.*—St. Cath. Coll. Cam. B.A. 1830, M.A. 1846; Deac. and Pr. 1830. V. of Whitchurch, Dio. Win. 1844. (Patron, Bp of Win; Tithe—App. 1436*l* 6*s* 10*d*, V. 19*l* 12*s*; Glebe, 180 acres; V.'s Inc. 260*l* and Ho; Pop. 1962.) R. of Laverstoke, Dio. Win. 1846. (Patron, Melville Portal, Esq; Tithe, 180*l*; Glebe, 107 acres; R.'s Inc. 180*l*; Pop. 122.) Surrogate. Author, *Sermons on Church and State.* [5]

DUDMAN, Lumsden Shirreff, *Pitney Rectory, Langport, Somerset.*—Wad. Coll. Ox. B.A. 1842; Deac. 1844 by Bp of Lon. Pr. 1845 by Abp of Cant. R. of Pitney, Dio. B. and W. 1851. (Patron, Capt. J. Dudman; Tithe—App. 67*l* 17*s* 7*d*, R. 78*l* 8*s* 4*d*; Glebe, 18 acres; R.'s Inc. 200*l* and Ho; Pop. 374.) [6]

DUELL, Thomas, *Barton Parsonage, Preston.*—St. Bees; Deac. and Pr. 1831 by Bp of Ches. P. C. of Barton, Dio. Man. 1832. (Patrons, C. R. Jacson and G. Marton, Esqrs. alt; Tithe—App. 9*l*, Imp. 96*l* 2*s* 5*d*; P. C.'s Inc. 125*l* and Ho; Pop. 886.) Head Mast. of Billsborough Gr. Sch. [7]

DUFFIELD, H. G., *Oswaldtwistle, Accrington.*—C. of Oswaldtwistle. [8]

DUFFIN, John, *Barnby-upon-Don, Doncaster.*—St. John's Coll. Cam. B.A. 1848; Deac. 1849 and Pr. 1850 by Bp of Roch. V. of Barnby-upon-Don, Dio. York, 1856. (Patron, John Newsome, Esq; Glebe, 70 acres; V.'s Inc. 123*l*; Pop. 644.) [9]

DUFTON, John, *Bredfield, Woodbridge, Suffolk.*—Dub. A.B. 1826, A.M. 1829; Deac. and Pr. 1827. R. of Bredfield with Lowdham and Pettistree V. Dio. Nor. 1858. (Patron, Ld Chan; Tithe, Bredfield, 325*l*; Glebe, 27 acres; Lowdham and Pettistree—Imp. 220*l*, V. 96*l*; Glebe, 1 acre; R. and V.'s Inc. 350*l*; Pop. 454.) Formerly R. of Warehorne, Kent, 1838–58; Dom. Chap. to Marquis of Normanby 1830. Author, *The Present State of the Church of England*, 1841, 1*s*; *National Education, What it is, and What it should be*, 1847, 2*s* 6*d*; *The Prison and the School*, 1848, 1*s* 6*d*; *Lectures delivered before Mechanics' Institutions.* [10]

DUGDALE, Richard, *Crosby, Maryport, Cumberland.*—Dub. A.B. 1839; Deac. 1839, Pr. 1840. P. C. of Cross Canonby, Dio. Carl. 1853. (Patrons, D. and C. of Carl; P. C.'s Inc. 160*l*; Pop. 750.) [11]

DUGGAN, Motherwell, *Cornforth Ferryhill, Durham.*—Dub. A.B. 1849; Deac. 1850, Pr. 1851. P. C. of Cornforth, Dio. Dur. 1865. (Patrons, the Crown and Bp of Dur. alt; P. C.'s Inc. 200*l*; Pop. 1618.) Formerly C. of Harworth 1850–54, Trinity, Darlington, 1854–60, Eston 1860–62, Cornforth 1862–65. [12]

DUGMORE, Henry, *Pensthorpe, Fakenham, Norfolk.*—R. of Pensthorpe, Dio. Nor. 1832. (Patrons, Trustees; Tithe, 170*l*; R.'s Inc. 170*l*; Pop. 12; no church.) [13]

DU HEAUME, William, *Trinity Rectory, Jersey.*—Jesus Coll. Cam. B.A. 1847, M.A. 1850; Deac. 1847 by Bp of Ox. Pr. 1848 by Bp of Win. R. of Trinity, Jersey, Dio. Win. 1850. (Patron, the Governor; Tithe, Imp. 130*l*; Glebe, 6 acres; R.'s Inc. 180*l* and Ho; Pop. 2273.) [14]

DUKE, Edward, *Lake House, near Salisbury.*—Ex. Coll. Ox. B.A. 1836, M.A. 1858; Deac. 1839 and Pr. 1840 by Bp of Salis. C. of Wilsford, Wilts. Formerly C. of St. Edmund's, Salisbury, 1839–49. [15]

DUKE, Francis, *The Curacy, Stanhope, Darlington.*—St. John's Coll. Cam. B.A. 1862, M.A. 1865; Deac. 1862 by Bp of Roch. Pr. 1864 by Bp of Ely. C. of Stanhope with Ho. 1866; Surrogate. Formerly C. of Trinity, Cambridge, 1862–66. [16]

DUKE, Henry Hinxman, *Westbury, Wilts.*—St. Mary Hall, Ox. B.A. 1838; Deac. 1839, Pr. 1840. V. of Westbury with Chapelry of Dilton, Dio. Salis. 1850. (Patron, Bp of Salis; Tithe—App. 2428*l* 19*s* 6*d*, V. 235*l* 0*s* 6*d*; Glebe, 30½ acres; V.'s Inc. 550*l* and Ho; Pop. 3674.) Surrogate; Patron of the P. C. of Bratton. Author, *Analysis of Bishop Butler's Analogy, &c. so far as relates to Natural Religion, with Considerations on certain Arguments therein advanced*, 4*s* 6*d*. [17]

DUKE, Rashleigh, *Church Eaton, near Stafford.*—Queen's Coll. Ox. 4th cl. Lit. Hum. B.A. 1849; Deac. 1849, Pr. 1853. C. of Church Eaton 1854. [18]

DUKE, Robert Richard, *Netherfield, near Battle, Sussex.*—Caius Coll. Cam. LL.B. 1859; Deac. 1859 and Pr. 1860 by Bp of Chich. P. C. of Netherfield, Dio. Chich. 1862. (Patron, Bp of Chich; P. C.'s Inc. 60*l* and Ho; Pop. 500.) [19]

DUKE, William H., *St. Mary's Vale, Brompton, Chatham.*—Chap. of H.M. Prison, Chatham. Formerly C. of Stoke-upon-Trent; Chap. of Millbank Penitentiary; Chap. H.M. Prison, Dartmoor. [20]

DULLEY, David Morton, *Mutford, Beccles, Suffolk.*—Caius Coll. Cam. 14th Wrang. and B.A. 1853, M.A. 1856; Deac. 1855 and Pr. 1856 by Bp of Ely. Fell. of Caius Coll. Cam. 1854. V. of Mutford with Barnby, Dio. Nor. 1858. (Patron, Caius Coll. Cam; V.'s Inc. 150*l*; Pop. Mutford 386, Barnby 270.) Formerly C. of St. Peter's, St. Albans, 1855–58. [21]

DUMBLETON, Edgar Norris, *Brecon, S. Wales.*—Ex. Coll. Ox. B.A. 1853; Deac. 1854 by Bp of Ox. Pr. 1855 by Bp of B. and W. Formerly C. of St. Mary the Virgin's, Oxford, 1854–56; P. C. of St. Edmund's, Wells, Somerset, 1856–57; C. of Chislehurst, Kent, 1858–60; P. C. of St. Michael's, Ryde, 1860–66. Author, *A Plea for Religious Societies in Parishes*, 1857; *Five Sermons on the Daily Services*, 1859. [22]

DUMERGUE, Walter Scott, *Fareham Vicarage, Hants.*—Corpus Coll. Cam. 22nd Wrang. and B.A. 1842, M.A. 1845; Deac. 1842 and Pr. 1843 by Abp of York. V. of Fareham, Dio. Win. 1852. (Patron, Bp of Win; Glebe, 4 acres; V.'s Inc. 500*l* and Ho; Pop. 3889.) [23]

DUN, James, *Todmorden, Lancashire.*—Univ. Coll. Dur. B.A. 1862; Deac. 1864 by Bp of Rip. Formerly C. of St. Mary's, Leeds, 1864–66. [24]

DUNBAR, Sir William, Bart., *Walwyn's Castle Rectory, Haverfordwest.*—Magd. Hall, Ox. S.C.L; Deac. 1831 and Pr. 1832 by Bp of B. and W. R. of Walwyn's Castle, Dio. St. D. 1862. (Patron, Ld Chan; Tithe, 270*l*; Glebe, 45 acres; R.'s Inc. 350*l* and Ho; Pop. 351.) Formerly C. of Upton, Somerset, 1831, Stoke-upon-Trent 1832; Min. of the Floating Church, and Chap. to the Sailors' Home, Lond. 1839; Min. of St. Paul's Chapel, Aberdeen, 1842; Min. of St. Paul's, Camden Town, 1855; C. of Kew 1856. Author, *Pulpit Recollections*, 1841, 6*s*. [25]

DUNCAN, Francis, *West Chelborough Rectory, Dorchester.*—Trin. Coll. Cam. B.A. 1830, M.A. 1834; Deac. 1831 and Pr. 1835 by Bp of Wor. R. of West Chelborough, Dio. Salis. 1839. (Patron, G. Bullock, Esq; Tithe, 82*l*; Glebe, 29 acres; R.'s Inc. 122*l* and Ho; Pop. 73.) Formerly C. of Alcester, Great Toller, and West Compton. [26]

DUNCAN, James, *Alverstoke, Hants.*—Marischal Coll. Aberdeen, M.A. 1858; Deac. 1862 and Pr. 1863 by Bp of Win. C. of Alverstoke 1862. [27]

DUNCAN, James Irwin, *Bristol.*—Dub; Deac. 1854 by Bp of Gibraltar, Pr. 1855 by Bp of Meath.

C. of St. Michael's, Bristol. Formerly Asst. Mast. of Malta Protestant Coll. 1852; C. of Drunconrath, Ireland, 1855, St. Thomas's, Kendal, 1863. [1]

DUNCAN, John, *Calne, Wilts.*—V. of Calne, Dio. Salis. 1865. (Patron, Bp of Salis; V.'s Inc. 800*l* and Ho; Pop. 4591.) Formerly P. C. of Lyneham, Wilts, 1859–65. [2]

DUNCAN, William Robert, *St. Peter's Parsonage, Liverpool.*—Edinburgh Univ. and St. Bees; Deac. 1844 and Pr. 1845 by Bp of Ches. Sen. C. of St. Peter's, Liverpool, and Surrogate 1854. Formerly P. C. of Matterdale, Cumberland. [3]

DUNCOMBE, The Very Rev. and Hon. Augustus, *The Deanery, York,* and *Calwick Ashbourne, Derbyshire.*—Wor. Coll. Ox. B.A. 1836, M.A. 1850; Deac. 1837 and Pr. 1838 by Abp of York. Dean of York 1858 (Value, 2000*l* and Res). [4]

DUNCOMBE, Edward, *Barthomley Rectory, Crewe, Cheshire.*—Brasen. Coll. Ox. B.A. 1823; Deac. 1825 and Pr. 1826 by Abp of York. R. of Barthomley, Dio. Ches. 1851. (Patrons, Trustees of the late Lord Crewe; Tithe, 711*l*; Glebe, 75 acres; R.'s Inc. 833*l* and Ho; Pop. 697.) Author, *Church Reform* (a Visitation Sermon), York, 1832; etc. [5]

DUNCOMBE, Henry John, *Kirby Sigston Rectory, Northallerton.*—R. of Kirby-Sigston, Dio. York. (Patron, the present R; Tithe, 652*l* 4*s* 8*d*; R.'s Inc. 750*l*; Pop. 257.) [6]

DUNCOMBE, William, *Crowle Vicarage (Lincolnshire), near Bawtry.*—Queens' Coll. Cam. B.A. 1843, M.A. 1846; Deac. 1843, Pr. 1844. V. of Crowle, Dio. Lin. 1844. (Patron, the present R; Glebe, 500 acres; V.'s Inc. 804*l* and Ho; Pop. 2648.) [7]

DUNCOMBE, William Duncombe Van der Horst, 47, *York-crescent, Clifton* and *The College, Hereford.*—Brasen. Coll. Ox. B.A. 1856, M.A. 1857; Deac. 1858 and Pr. 1859 by Bp of Herf. Asst. Vicar Choral in Hereford Cathl. 1867. Formerly C. of Bishopstone 1858–59, Allensmore 1862–67. [8]

DUNDAS, The Hon. Charles, *Epworth Rectory, Bawtry, Lincolnshire.*—Trin. Coll. Cam. M.A. 1826; Deac. 1830 and Pr. 1831. R. of Epworth, Dio. Lin. 1843. (Patron, the Crown; Tithe—Imp. 16*l*, R. 935*l*; Glebe, 44 acres; R.'s Inc. 988*l* and Ho; Pop. 2097.) Rural Dean. [9]

DUNDAS, George, *St. Matthew's Parsonage, Nottingham.*—Univ. Coll. Dur. Licen. Theol; Deac. 1845, Pr. 1846. P. C. of St. Matthew's, Nottingham, Dio. Lin. 1855. (Patrons, Trustees; P. C.'s Inc. 400*l*; Pop. 5455.) Formerly C. of St. Alkmund's, Shrewsbury. [10]

DUNDAS, James Whitley Deans, *Kintbury Vicarage, Hungerford, Berks.*—Magd. Coll. Cam. B.A. 1834, M.A. 1837; Deac. 1835 and Pr. 1836 by Bp of Nor. V. of Kintbury, Dio. Ox. 1840. (Patron, Admiral Dundas; Tithe—Imp. 402*l* 12*s* 3*d*, V. 803*l*; Glebe, 2 acres; V.'s Inc. 813*l* and Ho; Pop. 1725.) [11]

DUNDAS, Robert Bruce, *Harpole Rectory, near Northampton.*—Trin. Coll. Cam. 1844. R. of Harpole, Dio. Pet. 1848. (Patron, Earl Fitzwilliam; R.'s Inc. 570*l* and Ho; Pop. 833.) [12]

DUNDAS, Robert James, *King-street, Chelmsford.*—Ex. Coll. Ox. B.A. 1856, M.A. 1859; Deac. 1858 and Pr. 1859 by Bp of Nor. Sen. C. of Chelmsford 1866. Formerly C. of Great Yarmouth 1858; R. of St. John's, Victoria, Vancouver Island, and Chap. to Bp of Columbia 1859. [13]

DUNDAS, Thomas Henry, *Warton Parsonage, Kirkham, Lancashire.*—Dub. A.B. P. C. of Warton with Freckleton, Dio. Man. (Patron, Ch. Ch. Ox; Tithe, App. 1193*l* 10*s*; P. C.'s Inc. 360*l* and Ho; Pop. 1325.) Formerly Dom. Chap. to Lord Cloncurry. [14]

DUNDERDALE, Robert, *Leck Parsonage, near Kirkby Lonsdale, Westmoreland.*—St. John's Coll. Cam. 2nd Jun. Opt. 2nd in 2nd cl. Cl. Trip. and B.A. 1824, M.A. 1827; Deac. 1824, Pr. 1825. P. C. of Leck, Lancashire, Dio. Man. 1837. (Patron, V. of Tunstall; Tithe—App. 73*l* 9*s* 9*d*, Imp. 66*l*; P. C.'s Inc. 77*l* and Ho; Pop. 324.) Author, *Poems on Religious and Moral Subjects,* 1829, 6*s*; *Redemption and other Poems,* 1834; *A Sermon,* 1846; *Poems on Lake Scenery,* 1847; *Two Sermons,* 1852. [15]

DUNFORD, William.—Min. of Brompton Chap. Kensington, Lond. [16]

DUNINGHAM, John, *St. Mary-at-the-Quay, Ipswich.*—St. Peter's Coll. Cam. Wrang B.A. 1825, M.A. 1828; Deac. 1827 and Pr. 1828 by Bp of Nor. P. C. of St. Mary-at-the-Quay, Dio. Nor. 1851. (Patrons, the Parishioners; P. C.'s Inc. 116*l* and Ho; Pop. 974.) Chap. of Borough Gaol, Ipswich, 1851; Surrogate. Formerly 2nd Mast. of Hackney Sch. 1830–33; Head Mast. of Colchester Gr. Sch. 1839–51. [17]

DUNKLEY, John, *Wesley-street, Toxteth-park, Liverpool.*—Literate; Deac. 1848, Pr. 1849. Chap. of the Workhouse, Toxteth-park, Liverpool (Stipend, 130*l*.) Formerly Chap. of the General Hospital, Birmingham. [18]

DUNLAP, Arthur Philip, *Bardwell Rectory, Bury St. Edmunds.*—St. John's Coll. Ox. B.A. 1831, M.A. 1835, B.D. 1840; Deac. 1832 and Pr. 1833 by Bp of Ox. R. of Bardwell, Dio. Ely, 1852. (Patron, St. John's Coll. Ox; Tithe, 788*l*; Glebe, 36 acres; R.'s Inc. 812*l* and Ho; Pop. 882.) Late Fell. of St. John's Coll. Ox. [19]

DUNN, Andrew Hunter.—C. of St. Mark's, Notting-hill, Lond. [20]

DUNN, Arthur, *Sevenoaks, Kent.*—Ch. Coll. Cam. B.A. 1857; Deac. 1859 and Pr. 1860 by Bp of Man. C. of Sevenoaks 1863. Formerly C. of St. Andrew's, Manchester, 1859, Hillingdon, Middlesex, 1862. [21]

DUNN, James, *Milverton, Wellington, Somerset.*—Brasen. Coll. Ox. B.A. 1865; Deac. 1865 and Pr. 1866 by Bp of B. and W. C. of Milverton 1865. [22]

DUNN, James Charles Tracy, *Jevington Rectory, Eastbourne, Sussex.*—Queens' Coll. Cam. B.A. 1828; Deac. 1831 and Pr. 1842 by Bp of Chich. C. of Jevington 1852. Formerly C. of Lindfield 1833–39, Newhaven 1839–47, Hooe 1847–52. [23]

DUNN, John, *Todmorden, Rochdale.*—C. of Todmorden. [24]

DUNN, John Woodham, *Warkworth, Alnwick.*—Queens' Coll. Cam. B.A. 1836, M.A. 1866; Deac. 1836, Pr. 1837. V. of Warkworth, Dio. Dur. 1853. (Patron, Bp of Carl; Tithe—App. 1924*l* 18*s* 10½*d*, Imp. 25*l*, V. 533*l* 2*s* 8*d*; V.'s Inc. 533*l* and Ho; Pop. 4669.) [25]

DUNN, Robert, *Gatcombe Rectory, Isle of Wight.*—Ch. Coll. Cam. Jun. Opt. Math. Trip. B.A. 1862, M.A. 1865; Deac. 1864 and Pr. 1865 by Bp of Lich. C. in sole charge of Gatcombe 1867. Formerly 2nd Mast. of Wolverhampton Gr. Sch. 1862–67; Asst C. of Coll. Ch. Wolverhampton 1864–67. [26]

DUNN, Robert, *Honiton, Devon.*—C. of Honiton. [27]

DUNN, Robert James, *Huntsham Rectory, Bampton, Devon.*—Ex. Coll. Ox. B.A. 1832, M.A. 1837; Deac. 1833 and Pr. 1834 by Bp of Win. R. of Huntsham, Dio. Ex. 1854. (Patron, A. H. D. Troyte, Esq; Tithe, 180*l*; Glebe, 61 acres; R.'s Inc. 241*l* and Ho; Pop. 248.) [28]

DUNN, Thomas, 6, *Rosamond-street, Manchester.*—Wor. Coll. Ox. B.A. 1856, M.A. 1858; Deac. 1857 and Pr. 1858 by Bp of Rip. C. of St. Philip's, Hulme, Manchester, 1865. Formerly C. of Thorner, Leeds, 1857, St. John the Baptist's, Hulme, 1859. [29]

DUNN, Thomas, *Cringleford, near Norwich.*—Deac. 1849 by Bp of Newfoundland, Pr. 1852 by Bp of Nova Scotia. P. C. of Cringleford, Dio. Nor. 1862. (Patrons, Trustees of the Great Hospital, Norwich; P. C.'s Inc. 100*l* and Ho; Pop. 205.) Formerly Sup. of British N. America School Soc. in Newfoundland; Corresponding Sec. of the Colonial Ch. and Sch. Soc. Nova Scotia; Miss. at Stewiacke, Nova Scotia; C. of Monk Soham, Suffolk, 1858, Boxhall, Suffolk, 1858-61. [30]

DUNN, Thomas Higgon, *Tenby, Pembrokeshire.*—Lampeter; Deac. 1844 and Pr. 1845 by Bp of St. D. Formerly C. of Glascomb with Colva 1844–45, St. Mary's, Leicester, 1845–46, Mitcham, Surrey, 1846-48. [31]

DUNNE, James Robert, *Chadderton, near Manchester.*—Dub. A.B. 1843; Deac. 1843 and Pr. 1844 by Abp of Cant. P. C. of St. Matthew's, Chadderton, Dio. Man. 1844. (Patrons, the Crown and Bp of Man. alt; P. C.'s Inc. 180*l*; Pop. 4273.) [1]

DUNNE, Joseph, *Nottingham.*—Chap. of the Union, Nottingham. [2]

DUNNING, Richard, *Rock House, Torpoint, Devonport.*—Queens' Coll. Cam. B.A. 1824, M.A. 1827; Deac. 1824 by Bp of Lich. Pr. 1825 by Bp of Ex. P. C. of Torpoint, Dio. Ex. 1835. (Patron, V. of Antony; Endow. 2149*l* 18*s* 7*d*, 3 per Cents; P. C.'s Inc. 124*l*; Pop. 2000.) Dom. Chap. to Lord Lisle 1840. Formerly C. of Ruan, Cornwall, 1824-35. [3]

DUNNING, William Beatson, *Boston.*—C. of Wyberton, Boston. Formerly C. of Tydd St. Mary Wisbech. [4]

DUNSTER, Henry Peter, *Wood Bastwick Vicarage, near Norwich.*—Magd. Hall, Ox. B.A. 1837, M.A. 1838; Deac. 1837 and Pr. 1838 by Bp of Lon. V. of Wood Bastwick with Panxworth R. Dio. Nor. 1848. (Patron, John Cator, Esq; Wood Bastwick, Tithe—Imp. 292*l* 3*s* 10*d*, V. 145*l* 6*s* 11*d*; Glebe, 26 acres; Panxworth, Tithe, 143*l* 16*s* 9*d*; Glebe, 31 acres; V.'s Inc. 403*l* and Ho; Pop. Wood Bastwick 294, Panxworth 62) Author, *Fragments of History*; *Froissart's Chronicles condensed*; *Stories from Froissart*; *Drexelius on Eternity*; *True Stories of the Times of Richard II*; *Historical Tales of Lancastrian Times*, Griffith and Farran. [5]

DUPONT, Hubert Napoleon, *Southampton.*—Min. of St. Julian's French Church, Southampton. (Patrons, Trustees; Min.'s Inc. 75*l*.) [6]

DU PORT, Charles Durrell, *Bombay.*—Caius Coll. Cam. B.A. 1859; Deac. 1860 by Bp of Lon. Formerly C. of Trinity, Marylebone, Lond. 1860. [7]

DUPORT, James Mourant, *Mattishall Vicarage, East Dereham, Norfolk.*—Caius. Coll. Cam. B.A. 1855, M.A. 1858; Deac. 1855 and Pr. 1856 by Bp of Ely. Fell. of Caius Coll. Cam; V. of Mattishall with Pattesley R. Dio. Nor. 1861. (Patron, Caius Coll. Cam; V.'s Inc. 500*l* and Ho; Pop. 971.) [8]

DU PRE, Edward, *King's Cliffe Rectory, Wansford, Northants.*—Queens' Coll. Cam. B.A. 1846; Deac. 1847 and Pr. 1848 by Bp of Wor. R. of King's Cliffe, Dio. Pet. 1863. (R.'s Inc. 750*l* and Ho; Pop. 1360.) Formerly P. C. of Temple Guiting, Glouc. 1849-63. [9]

DU PRE, Henry Ramus, *Shellingford Rectory, Faringdon, Berks.*—Ex. Coll. Ox. B.A. 1840; Deac. 1841 and Pr. 1842 by Bp of Chich. R. of Shellingford, Dio. Ox. 1848. (Patron, T. M. Goodlake, Esq; Tithe, 516*l* 13*s* 3*d*; R.'s Inc. 540*l* and Ho; Pop. 308.) [10]

DU PRE, Michael Thomas, *Walsham-le-Willows, Bury St. Edmunds.*—Lin. Coll. Ox. B.A. 1833. P. C. of Walsham-le-Willows, Dio. Ely, 1865. (Patron, S. Golding, Esq; P. C.'s Inc. 100*l*; Pop. 1290.) Formerly P. C. of Riston with Roxham, Norfolk, 1848-59, V. of Lower Guiting with Farmcote, Gloucestershire, 1859-65. [11]

DU PRE, Samuel, *Highley Vicarage, Bridgnorth.*—V. of Highley, Dio. Herf. 1843. (Patron, J. Perry, Esq; Tithe—Imp. 109*l* 11*s*, V. 115*l* 10*s*; Glebe, 89 acres; V.'s Inc. 340*l* and Ho; Pop. 407.) [12]

DUPUIS, Charles Sanders Skelton, *Binton Rectory, Stratford-on-Avon.*—Pemb. Coll. Ox. B.A. 1818, M.A. 1821; Deac. 1821 and Pr. 1822. R. of Binton, Dio. Wor. 1836. (Patron, Marquis of Hertford; Tithe, 10*s*; Glebe, 16 acres; R.'s Inc. 180*l* and Ho; Pop. 230.) [13]

DUPUIS, George John, *Worplesdon Rectory, Guildford.*—King's Coll. Cam. B.A. 1819, M.A. 1822; Deac. 1824, Pr. 1831. Fell. of Eton Coll. 1838. R. of Worplesdon, Dio. Win. 1862. (Patron, Eton Coll; R.'s Inc. 800*l* and Ho; Pop. 1563.) Formerly R. of Hemingby, Lincolnshire, 1831-40; Lower Mast. of Eton Coll. 1834-38; R. of Creeting, Suffolk, 1840-62. [14]

DUPUIS, George Richard, *Manor House, Eton College.*—King's Coll. Cam. B.A. 1858, M.A. 1861; Deac. 1860 and Pr. 1861 by Bp of Ox. Asst. Upper Mast. in Eton Sch. [15]

DUPUIS, Theodore Crane, *Vicarage, Burnham, Somerset.*—Pemb. Coll. Ox. 2nd cl. Lit. Hum. 1852 and 1854, B.A. 1854, M.A. 1856; Deac. 1860 and Pr. 1862 by Bp of B. and W. V. of Burnham, Dio. B. and W. 1867. (Patrons, D. and C. of Wells; V.'s Inc. 635*l* and Ho; Pop. 1709.) Formerly C. of Twerton, Bath, 1861-62, St. Cuthbert's, Wells, 1862-67. [16]

DURBIN, Frederic Jeanes, *Harston, Cambridge.*—Trin. Coll. Cam. B.A. 1838, M.A. 1855; Deac. 1840, Pr. 1841. V. of Harston, Dio. Ely, 1848. (Patron, Bp of Ely; Glebe, 103 acres; V.'s Inc. 200*l* and Ho; Pop. 782.) [17]

DURDIN, Alexander Warham, *St. George's Colegate, Norwich.*—Dub. A.B. 1834, A.M. 1865; Deac. 1835, Pr. 1836. P. C. of St. George's, Colegate, City and Dio. Nor. 1852. (Patrons, D. and C. of Nor; P. C.'s Inc. 90*l*; Pop. 1607.) [18]

DURELL, John Durell, *Marchwood, Southampton.*—New Inn Hall, Ox. B.A. 1840; Deac. and Pr. 1841. P. C. of Marchwood, Dio. Win. 1860. (Patron, H. Holloway, Esq; P. C.'s Inc. 140*l* and Ho; Pop. 1185.) [19]

DURELL, J. P., *Eccleshall, Staffs.*—C. of Eccleshall. [20]

DURELL, John Vavasor, *St. John's College, Cambridge.*—St. John's Coll. Cam. Fell. of, 4th Wrang. B.A. 1860, M.A. 1863; Deac. 1863 and Pr. 1864 by Bp of Ely. Fell. and Tut. of St. John's Coll. [21]

DURELL, Thomas Vavasor, *Mongewell, near Wallingford.*—Ch. Ch. Ox. B.A. 1821, M.A. 1824; Deac. 1822, Pr. 1823. R. of Mongewell, Dio. Ox. 1852. (Patrons, Trustees; Tithe, 370*l*; Glebe, 6 acres; R.'s Inc. 376*l* and Ho; Pop. 133.) [22]

DURHAM, The Right Rev. Charles BARING, Lord Bishop of Durham, *Auckland Castle, Bishop's Auckland, Durham.*—Ch. Ch. Ox. Double 1st cl. and B.A 1829, M.A. 1832, D.D. 1856; Select Preacher 1845 and 1852. Consecrated Bp of Gloucester and Bristol 1856; translated to Durham 1861. (Episcopal Jurisdiction, the Counties of Durham, Northumberland and Hexhamshire; Inc. of See, 8000*l*; Pop. 858,095; Acres, 1,906,835; Deaneries, 13; Benefices, 245; Curates, 106; Church Sittings, 126,099.) His Lordship is Count Palatine, and Custos Rotulorum of the Principality of Durham; a Senator of the Lond. Univ. and Visitor of the Univ. of Dur. His Lordship was formerly R. of All Souls', St. Marylebone, and R. of Limpsfield, Surrey, 1855-56; Chap. in Ordinary to the Queen 1851-56. [23]

DURHAM, Thomas Charles, *Chatsworth-place, Carlisle.*—Jesus Coll. Cam. late Fell. of, Wrang. 3rd cl. Cl. Trip. B.A. 1849, M.A. 1852; Deac. 1852 and Pr. 1853 by Bp of Dur. Head Mast. of Cathl. Sch. Carlisle, 1861. Formerly Math. Mast. of Durham Gr. Sch. 1850; Head Mast. of Berwick Gr. Sch. 1856-61. [24]

DURNFORD, Arthur Gifford, *Hindolveston Vicarage, Guist, Norfolk.*—St. John's Coll. Cam. B.A. 1835, M.A. 1839; Deac. 1836 and Pr. 1837 by Bp of Lon. V. of Hindolveston, Dio. Nor. 1848. (Patrons, D. and C. of Nor; Tithe—App. 434*l*, V. 50*l*; Glebe, 16 acres; V.'s Inc. 220*l* and Ho; Pop. 705.) [25]

DURNFORD, Edmund, *Monxton, Andover, Hants.*—King's Coll. Cam. B.A. 1832, M.A. 1835; Deac. 1832, Pr. 1834. R. of Monxton, Dio. Win. 1846. (Patron, King's Coll. Cam; Tithe, 340*l*; Glebe, 69 acres; R.'s Inc. 407*l* and Ho; Pop. 275.) [26]

DURNFORD, Francis Edward, *Eton College.*—King's Coll. Cam. B.A. 1840, M.A. 1843; Deac. 1842. Lower Mast. in Eton Coll. Late Fell. of King's Coll. Cam. [27]

DURNFORD, Richard, *Middleton Rectory, Manchester.*—Magd. Coll. Ox. 1st cl. Lit. Hum. and B.A. 1826, M.A. 1829; Deac. 1830, Pr. 1831. R. of Middleton, Dio. Man. 1835. (Patron, W. Wagstaff, Esq; Tithe, 439*l* 19*s* 6*d*; R.'s Inc. 950*l* and Ho; Pop. 10,028.) Hon. Can. of Man. 1854; Surrogate; Rural Dean. Late Fell. of Magd. Coll. Ox. [28]

DURRANT, Isaac, *Thornton Parsonage, Fleetwood, Lancashire.*—Queens' Coll. Cam. B.A. 1845, M.A. 1848; Deac. and Pr. 1845 by Bp of Ches. P. C. of

Thornton, Dio. Man. 1853. (Patrons, Trustees; P. C.'s Inc. 110*l* and Ho; Pop. 826.) [1]

DURRANT, John, *Braishfield, Romsey.*—Queens' Coll. Cam. B.A. 1854, M.A. 1860; Deac. 1854 and Pr. 1855 by Bp of Ches. P. C. of Braishfield, Dio. Win. 1861. (Patron, R. of Mitchelmersh; P. C.'s Inc. 50*l* and Ho; Pop. 452.) [2]

DURRANT, Reginald Norman, *South Elmham Hall, Bungay, Suffolk.*—Emman. Coll. Cam. Sen. Opt. and B.A. 1850, M.A. 1853; Deac. 1851 and Pr. 1852 by Bp of Nor. P. C. of Rumburgh with St. Michael, Dio. Nor. 1855. (Patron, G. Durrant, Esq; Rumburgh, Tithe, Imp. 200*l*; St. Michael, Tithe—App. 4*l* 8*s* 6*d*, Imp. 40*l* and 3 roods of Glebe; P. C.'s Inc. 136*l*; Pop. Rumburgh 405, St. Michael 156.) [3]

DURST, John, *Norwich.*—Caius Coll. Cam. B.A. 1859, M.A. 1862; Deac. 1859 and Pr. 1860 by Bp of Nor. P. C. of St. Peter's Mountergate, Norwich, Dio. Nor. 1862. (Patrons, D. and C. of Nor; P. C.'s Inc. 78*l*; Pop. 2868.) Formerly C. of St. Stephen's, Norwich, 1859, Mattishall 1861. [4]

DURST, William, *Penshurst, Tonbridge, Kent.*—Emman. Coll. Cam. B.A. 1861; Deac. 1861 and Pr. 1862 by Bp of Wor. C. of Penshurst. Formerly C. of St. John's Ladywood, Birmingham, 1861–63. [5]

DURY, Edwin Alexander, *Bishop Thornton, Ripley, Yorks.*—Emman. Coll. Cam. Jun. Opt. B.A. 1852, M.A. 1855; Deac. 1854 and Pr. 1855 by Bp of Rip. P. C. of Bishop Thornton, Dio. Rip. 1859. (Patrons, D. and C. of Rip; P. C.'s Inc. 100*l* and Ho; Pop. 541.) Formerly C. of Knaresborough 1854, Bilton, 1856, Manningham 1859. [6]

DU SAUTOY, Francis Peter, *Ockley Rectory, Dorking.*—St. John's Coll. Cam. 1850, 7th Wrang. and B.A. 1851, M.A. 1854; Deac. 1853 by Bp of Pet. Pr. 1855 by Bp of Ely. Fell. of Clare Hall 1854; R. of Ockley, Dio. Win. 1865. (Patron, Clare Coll. Cam; R.'s Inc. 600*l* and Ho; Pop. 564.) [7]

DU SAUTOY, Frederic, *Mark Parsonage, near Bridgwater.*—Queens' Coll. Cam. 19th Wrang. late Scho. B.A. 1828, M.A. 1831; Deac. 1830 and Pr. 1831 by Bp of Lich. P. C. of Mark, Dio. B. and W. 1860. (Patrons, Eccles. Commis; Rent from Glebe, 70*l*; P. C.'s Inc. 300*l* and Ho; Pop. 1217.) Formerly C. of Haselbury Plucknett 1836–60; Fell. of Queens' Coll. 1830–35. Author, *Self-Delusion*, 1832, 2*s* 6*d*; *Sermons*, 1836, 5*s*; *Haselbury Tracts*, 1840; *Via Media, an Ecclesiastical Chart*, 1840; *The Jews* (25 lectures), 1843; *Twenty Sermons on Book of Common Prayer*, 1845, 6*s*. 6*d*; Scientific Lectures on *Geology*, *Nature's Chemistry*, etc, 1850; *Memorial Fragments*, 1856, 2*s* 6*d*; and many single Sermons and Pamphlets. [8]

DU SAUTOY, William, *Taunton.*—Sid. Coll. Cam. B.A. 1834. P. C. of Trinity, Taunton, Dio. B. and W. 1856. (Patron, Bp of B. and W; P. C.'s Inc. 165*l*; Pop. 2786.) Formerly P. C. of Trinity, Richmond, Yorks, 1845–56. [9]

DUTHIE, Charles James, *Walmersley, Bolton, Lancashire.*—C. of Walmersley. [10]

DUTHY, William, *Sudborough Rectory, Thrapstone, Northants.*—Queen's Coll. Ox. B.A. 1819, M.A. 1824; Deac. 1820 by Bp of Lon. Pr. 1821 by Bp of Herf. R. of Sudborough, Dio. Pet. 1823. (Patron, Bp of Pet; Tithe, 378*l*; Glebe, 30 acres; R.'s Inc. 436*l* and Ho; Pop. 321.) Rural Dean. [11]

DUTTON, Alfred, *Catcott, Bridgwater.*—Queens' Coll. Cam. S.C.L. 1854, LL.B. 1856; Deac. 1855 and Pr. 1856 by Bp of B. and W. Chap. of Don. of Catcott, Dio. B. and W. 1864. (Patron, A. Henniker, Esq; Chap.'s Inc. 120*l*; Pop. 740.) Formerly C. of Trinity, Walcot, Bath, and St. Michael's, Coventry. [12]

DWARRIS, Brereton Edward, *Bywell St. Peter's Vicarage (Northumberland), near Gateshead.*—Univ. Coll. Dur. B.A. 1839, M.A. 1842; Deac. 1840, Pr. 1841. V. of Bywell St. Peter's, Dio. Dur. 1845. (Patrons, D. and C. of Dur; Tithe, App. 1361*l* 2*s* 7*d*; Glebe, 7 acres; V.'s Inc. 330*l* and Ho; Pop. 1355.) Late Fell. and Tut. of the Univ. of Dur. [13]

DYCE, Alexander, 9, *Gray's-inn-square, London, W.C.*—Ex. Coll. Ox. B.A. 1819; Deac. 1819, Pr. 1820. Formerly C. of Lanteglos, Cornwall, 1821–25, Nayland, Suffolk, 1825–27. Author, *Specimens of British Poetesses*, 1827; *Translations from Quintus Smyrnæus*, 1831; *The Works of William Shakespeare*, 6 vols. 1850–58; numerous editions of British and Latin Classics. [14]

DYER, Charles James, *Stamford Baron, Lincolnshire.*—Queen's Coll. Ox. B.A. 1856, M.A. 1859; Deac. 1856 and Pr. 1857. C. in sole charge of Stamford Baron; Surrogate; Dom. Chap. to the Marquis of Exeter 1861. Formerly C. of St. Matthias', Bethual-green, 1856–57; Dioc. Inspector of Schools and Asst. Min. of St. Mary's, Park-street, Lond. 1857–61. Author, *Letter to the Bishop of London on the State of Education in the Diocese of London*, 1860, published by the London Dioc. Board of Education. [15]

DYER, Frederick T. Stewart, *Heckmondwike, near Leeds.*—C. of Heckmondwike. [16]

DYER, James Hardwicke, *Great Waltham Vicarage, Chelmsford.*—Trin. Coll. Ox. 1st cl. Math. et Phy. and B.A. 1820, M.A. 1825, B.D. 1835; Deac. 1825 and Pr. 1827 by Bp of G. and B. V. of Great Waltham, Dio. Roch. 1837. (Patron, Trin. Coll. Ox; Tithe—Imp. 1800*l* and 124 acres of Glebe, V. 400*l*; Glebe, 3 acres; V.'s Inc. 410*l* and Ho; Pop. 2380.) [17]

DYER, J. N., *Gwennap, Redruth, Cornwall.*—C. of Gwennap. [18]

DYER, William.—Jesus Coll. Ox. B.A. 1830, M.A. 1838; Deac. 1831 and Pr. 1832 by Bp of Salis. Formerly P. C. of Imber, Wilts, 1841–65. [19]

DYKE, E. F., *Crayford, Kent.*—C. of Crayford. [20]

DYKE, Henry, *Greatworth Rectory, Brackley, Northants.*—Wad. Coll. Ox. B.A. 1829. R. of Greatworth, Dio. Pet. 1848. (Patron, Mr. Beechy; Tithe, 280*l*; R.'s Inc. 305*l* and Ho; Pop. 157.) [21]

DYKE, John Dixon, 3, *Charles-street, Berkeley-square, London, W.*—Ch. Ch. Ox. B.A. 1859, M.A. 1862; Deac. 1860 by Bp of Lon. Pr. 1861 by Bp of Roch. Asst. Min. of Grosvenor Chapel, South Audley-street, Lond. Formerly C. of Chatham 1860–62, Charlton by Blackheath 1862–63. [22]

DYKE, Percival Hart, *Kirk Sandall, Doncaster.*—Ch. Ch. Ox. B.A. 1861, M.A. 1862; Deac. 1862, Pr. 1863. C. of Kirk Sandall. Formerly C. of Vobster, Somerset, 1862. [23]

DYKE, William, *Badgington Rectory, near Cirencester.*—Jesus Coll. Ox; B.A. 1835, M.A. 1837, B.D. 1845; Deac. 1837 by Bp of Ox. Pr. 1838 by Bp of Herf. R. of Badgington, Dio. G. and B. 1861. (Patron, Jesus Coll. Ox; Tithe, 220*l*; Glebe, 78 acres; R.'s Inc. 300*l* and Ho; Pop. 175.) Formerly C. of Cradley, Herf. 1837–44; Fell. and Tut. of Jesus Coll. Ox. 1845–61. [24]

DYKES, Joseph Backhouse, *St. Oswald's Vicarage, Durham.*—St. Cath. Coll. Cam. B.A. 1847, M.A. 1850; Deac. 1847 and Pr. 1848 by Abp of York. V. of St. Oswald's, City and Dio. Dur. 1862. (Patrons, D. and C. of Dur; V.'s Inc. 450*l* and Ho; Pop. 5040.) Formerly Precentor of Dur. Cathl. 1849. [25]

DYKES, Joseph Balantine, *Headley Rectory, Liphook, Hants.*—Queen's Coll. Ox. B.A. 1822, M.A. 1826. R. of Headley, Dio. Win. 1848. (Patron, Queen's Coll. Ox; Tithe, 848*l* 3*s* 4*d*; R.'s Inc. 860*l* and Ho; Pop. 1320.) Late Fell. of Queen's Coll. Ox. [26]

DYKES, Lawson Peter, *Keyworth, near Nottingham.*—Queen's Coll. Ox. 3rd cl. Lit. Hum. and B.A. 1833, M.A. 1837. C. of Keyworth; Fell. of Queen's Coll. Ox. [27]

DYMOCK, F., *Worcester.*—C. of St. Alban's and St. Helen's, Worcester. [28]

DYMOKE, John, *Roughton Rectory, Horncastle, Lincolnshire.*—R. of Roughton with Haltham-upon-Bain R. Dio. Lin. 1829. (Patron, H. Dymoke, Esq; R.'s Inc. 416*l* and Ho; Pop. Roughton 131, Haltham-upon-Bain 215.) R. of Scrivelsby with Dalderby R. near Horncastle, Dio. Lin. 1829. (Patron, Sir H. Dymoke, Bart; Tithe,

700*l*; R.'s Inc. 710*l*; Pop. Scrivelsby 168, Dalderby 40.) [1]

DYNE, John Bradley, *Highgate School, Middlesex.*—Wad. Coll. Ox. 1827, 2nd cl. Lit. Hum. and B.A. 1830, M.A. 1834, D.D. 1858; Deac. 1835 and Pr. 1836 by Bp of Ox. Head Mast. of the Highgate Sch. 1838. Late Fell. of Wad. Coll. Ox. 1832, Div. Lect. 1837; Mast. of the Schools, Ox. 1836–38. [2]

DYOTT, William Herrick, *Austrey Vicarage, Atherstone, Warwickshire.*—Trin. Coll. Cam. B.A 1832, M.A. 1836; Deac. 1834 and Pr. 1835 by Bp of Lin. V. of Austrey, Dio. Wor. 1844. (Patron, Ld Chan; Tithe—Imp. 74*l* 4*s*, V. 100*l*; Glebe, 100 acres; V.'s Inc. 300*l* and Ho; Pop. 557.) Dom. Chap. to Viscount Combermere. [3]

DYSON, Edwin, *Ashton-under-Lyne.*—St. Bees; C. of Ch. Ch. Ashton. Formerly C. of Miles Platting, and St. John's, Dukinfield. [4]

DYSON, Francis, *Cricklade Vicarage, Wilts.*—New Inn Hall, Ox. B.A. 1841, M.A. 1842; Deac. 1843 and Pr. 1844 by Bp of Salis. V. of Cricklade, Dio. G. and B. 1849. (Patrons, D. and C. of Salis; Tithe—App. 481*l*, Imp. 4*l* 8*s*; V. 473*l* 19*s* 6*d*; Glebe, 6 acres; V.'s Inc. 488*l* and Ho; Pop. 1453.) [5]

DYSON, Henry Marsden, *Farcet, Peterborough.*—Emman. Coll. Cam. Fell. of, B.A. 1856, M.A. 1859, B.D. 1866; Deac. 1857 and Pr. 1858 by Bp of Ely. C. of Farcet, Hunts, 1859. Formerly C. of New Radford, Nottingham, 1858. [6]

DYSON, W. H., *Maidstone.*—C. of St. Paul's, Maidstone. [7]

EADE, John Davie, *Aycliffe Vicarage, Darlington.*—Caius Coll. Cam. B.A. 1827, M.A. 1830; Deac. 1828 by Bp of Lon. Pr. 1829 by Abp of York. V. of Aycliffe, Dio. Dur. 1835. (Patrons, D. and C. of Dur; Tithe—App. 262*l* 3*s* 6*d*, V. 84*l* 19*s* 6*d*; Glebe, 7 acres; V.'s Inc. 350*l* and Ho; Pop. 1458.) Hon. Can. of Dur. 1847; Rural Dean; Sec. to the Dioc. Ch. Building Soc. Formerly C. of Moor Monkton, York; P. C. of Witton-le-Wear, Durham. [8]

EADE, William, *Wolviston, Stockton-on-Tees.*—Sid. Coll. Cam. B.A. 1839, M.A. 1843; Deac. 1840 and Pr. 1841 by Bp of Nor. R. of Wolviston, Dio. Dur. 1865. (Patrons, D. and C. of Dur; R.'s Inc. 400*l* and Ho; Pop. 787.) Formerly C. of Aycliffe. [9]

EADON, John Eadon, *Dringhouses, York.*—Trin. Coll. Ox. B.A. 1855, M.A. 1857; Deac. 1857 by Bp of Roch. C. of Dringhouses. [10]

EAGAR, Thomas Thompson, *Audenshaw, near Manchester.*—Dub. A.B. 1836, A.M. 1841; Deac. 1841 and Pr. 1842 by Abp of Cant. P. C. of Audenshaw, Dio. Man. 1844. (Patrons, the Crown and Bp of Man. alt; Glebe, 1 acre; P. C.'s Inc. 200*l* and Ho; Pop. 5185.) Author, *Church Property, the Origin of Tithes, the Establishment of the Church in Britain, her early Independence of Rome, the Origin, Sources and Amount of her Revenues, with Historical and Documentary Proofs*, 4*s*. [11]

EAGLES, Charles Lionel, *Longtown Vicarage, Abergavenny.*—Wad. Coll. Ox. B.A. 1848; Deac. 1848 and Pr. 1849 by Bp of St. D. P. C. of Craswall, Herf. Dio. Herf. 1851. (Patron, V. of Clodock; Glebe, 25 acres; P. C.'s Inc. 65*l*; Pop. 356.) C of Clodock, Hereford. [12]

EAGLES, James, 118, *Bloomsbury, Birmingham.*—Corpus Coll. Cam. B.A. 1847, M.A. 1850; Deac. 1847 and Pr. 1848 by Bp of Wor. P. C. of St. Bartholomew's, Birmingham, Dio. Wor. 1851. (Patron, R. of St. Martin's, Birmingham; P. C.'s Inc. 250*l*; Pop. 10,281.) [13]

EAGLES, John King, *Hill Farrance, Taunton.*—Trin. Coll. Cam. B.A. 1831; Deac. 1832, Pr. 1833. C. of Hill Farrance. [14]

EAGLETON, Charles James, *Largs, Scotland.*—Queen's Coll. Ox. B.A. 1852, M.A. 1857; Deac. 1853 by Bp of Chich. Pr. 1855 by Bp of Lon. Incumb. of St. Columba's, Largs. (Patron, the Hon. G. F. Boyle.) Formerly Chap. at the Office of H.M.'s Printers, Lond. [15]

EAGLETON, John William, *Swayfield Rectory, Grantham.*—Magd. Hall, Ox. B.A. 1852; Deac. 1851 and Pr. 1852 by Bp of Pet. R. of Swayfield, Dio. Lin. 1856. (Patron, Ld Chan; Tithe, 222*l* 9*s* 10*d*; Glebe, 50 acres; R.'s Inc. 300*l* and Ho; Pop. 263.) Formerly C. of Wardley with Belton 1851–56. [16]

EALES, Samuel John, *Grammar School, Halstead, Essex.*—Theol. Coll. Chich; Deac. 1862 by Bp of Lon. Pr. 1863 by Bp of Roch. Head Mast. of Halstead Gr. Sch. Formerly C. of St. Mary's, Tothill Fields, Lond. 1862–63. [17]

EALES, William Thomas Huxham, *Yealmpton, Devon.*—Trin. Coll. Cam. B.A. 1834; Deac. 1835 and Pr. 1836 by Bp of Ex. V. of Yealmpton, Dio. Ex. 1857. (Patron, Bp of Ex; Tithe, 355*l*; Glebe, ½ acre; V.'s Inc. 355*l* and Ho; Pop. 1035.) Surrogate. Formerly C. of Ashburton with Bickington 1835, St. Breoke, Cornwall, 1844, Wolborough, Devon, 1851. [18]

EARDLEY, Stenton, *Streatham, Surrey.*—P. C. of Emmanuel, Streatham, Dio. Win. 1854. (Patrons, the Hamilton family and R; P. C.'s Inc. 365*l*; Pop. 1247.) [19]

EARDLEY, William, *Rampton Vicarage, Newark, Notts.*—Queen's Coll. Birmingham, 1853; Deac. 1855 and Pr. 1856 by Bp of Ches. V. of Rampton, Dio. Lin. 1867. (Patron, Bp of Rip; V.'s Inc. 310*l* and Ho; Pop. 496.) Formerly C. of St. Mark's, Dukinfield, 1855–56, Ironbridge 1856–57, Madeley 1857–58; P. C. of Ironbridge 1858–67. [20]

EARDLEY-WILMOT, Edward Revell, 10, *Chandos-street, Cavendish-square, London, W.*—Trin. Hall, Cam. B.A. 1840, M.A. 1847; Deac. 1840, Pr. 1841. R. of All Souls', Marylebone, Dio. Lon. 1855. (Patron, the Crown; R.'s Inc. 800*l*; Pop. 15,268.) Formerly V. of Kenilworth, Warw. 1843–55; Hon. Can. of Wor. 1850. [21]

EAREE, William.—St. Bees; Deac. 1847 by Bp of Dur. Pr. 1848 by Bp of Ches. Formerly P. C. of Setmurthy, Cumberland, 1851–56. [22]

EARLE, Alfred, *West Alvington, Kingsbridge, Devon.*—Magd. Hall, Ox. Lusby Scho. and B.A. 1854, M.A. 1855; Deac. 1858 and Pr. 1859 by Bp of Salis. V. of West Alvington with South Huish C. Marlborough C. and South Milton C. Dio. Ex. 1865. (Patrons, D. and C. of Salis; V.'s Inc. 1000*l*; Pop. 2364.) Formerly C. of St. Edmund's, Salisbury; R. of Monkton Farleigh, Wilts, 1863–65. [23]

EARLE, Francis, *Whorlton, Northallerton.*—Dub. A.B. and A.M. 1844; Deac. 1848, Pr. 1849. P. C. of Whorlton, Cleveland, Dio. York, 1855. (Patron, Marquis of Ailesbury; Tithe—Imp. 390*l* 6*s* 6*d*, P. C. 25*l* 0*s* 9*d*; Glebe, 22 acres; P. C.'s Inc. 95*l*; Pop. 844.) [24]

EARLE, Henry John, *High Ongar Rectory, Chipping Ongar.*—St. John's Coll. Cam; Deac. 1822, Pr. 1823. R. of High Ongar, Dio. Roch. 1823. (Patron, the present R; Tithe, 1382*l* 2*s* 3*d*; Glebe, 92 acres; R.'s Inc. 1500*l* and Ho; Pop. 1177.) [25]

EARLE, John, *Swanswick Rectory, Bath, and Oriel College, Oxford.*—Magd. Coll. Ox. 1st cl. Lit. Hum. and B.A. 1845, M.A. 1849. Fell. and Tut. of Oriel Coll; R. of Swanswick, Dio. B. and W. 1857. (Patron, Oriel Coll. Ox; Tithe—Imp. 55*l* 19*s*, R. 190*l*; Glebe, 18¾ acres; R.'s Inc. 233*l* and Ho; Pop. 632.) Anglo-Saxon Prof. at Oriel Coll. Ox. 1849. [26]

EARLE, J. Henry, *Minster-Lovell, Witney, Oxon.*—C. of Minster-Lovell. [27]

EARLE, Leonard Harcourt, *St. Paul's, Shadwell, E.*—Queens' Coll. Cam. B.A. 1857, M.A. 1865; Deac. 1857 by Bp of Win. Pr. 1858 by Bp of Salis. Dioc. Home Missionary 1864. Formerly C. of Shrivenham 1857–58, Stower Provost 1858–60, Charlton, Dover, 1861–64. [28]

EARLE, Richard Bethell, *Southwell, Notts.*—Deac. and Pr. 1852 by Abp of Cant. P. C. of Edingley, near Southwell, Dio. Lin. 1854. (Patron, the Chap. of Southwell; P. C.'s Inc. 250*l*; Pop. 389.) Chap. to Southwell Union. Formerly C. of Knockholt, Kent, 1852. [29]

EARLE, Robert, *Wateringbury, Kent.*—V. of Minster-Lovell, Dio. Ox. 1818. (Patron, Eton Coll; Tithe—Imp. 119*l* 3*s* 5*d*, V. 119*l* 3*s* 5*d*; Glebe, 62 acres; V.'s Inc. 219*l*; Pop. 586.) [1]

EARLE, Walter, *Uppingham, Rutland.*—Asst. Mast. in Uppingham Gr. Sch. [2]

EARLE, William, *Grange Court, Chigwell, Essex.*—Prin. of the Grange Sch. Chigwell. Formerly Head Mast. of the Tunbridge Wells Sch. 1845–55. [3]

EARLE, William James, *Uppingham, Rutland.*—St. John's Coll. Cam. Wrang. and B.A. 1849, M.A. 1853; Deac. 1850, Pr. 1851. 2nd Mast. of Uppingham Gr. Sch. 1849. Formerly C. of Ayston, Rutland. [4]

EARLY, John Bush, *St. John's Grove, Richmond, S.W.*—Wor. Coll. Ox. B.A. 1860, M.A. 1863; Deac. 1861 and Pr. 1862 by Bp of G. and B. C. of St. John's, Richmond, 1866. Formerly C. of St. Mark's, Cheltenham, 1861. [5]

EARNSHAW, John, *Rock Ferry, Cheshire.*—Sec. to S.P.G. for Archdeaconry of Liverpool. [6]

EARNSHAW, John William, *Birkenshaw, near Leeds.*—St. Cath. Coll. Cam. 16th Sen. Opt. B.A. 1857, M.A. 1862; Deac. 1859 and Pr. 1860 by Bp of Rip. P. C. of Birkenshaw with Hunsworth, Dio. Rip. 1863. (Patron, V. of Birstal; Glebe, 3 acres; P. C.'s Inc. 150*l* and Ho; Pop. 3633.) Formerly 2nd Mast. of Queen Eliz. Gr. Sch. Halifax, 1857–58; C. of Birstal 1859–63. [7]

EARNSHAW, Samuel, *Broomfield, Sheffield.*—St. John's Coll. Cam. 1st Smith's Prizeman, Sen. Wrang. and B.A. 1831, M.A. 1834; Deac. 1834, Pr. 1846. Chap. on Queen Mary's Foundation in the Church and Parish of Sheffield, Dio. York, 1847. (Patrons, the Church Burgesses; Value, 400*l*.) Author, *Treatise on Statics*, 10*s*; *Treatise on Dynamics*, 14*s*; Several Mathematical Tracts; Papers in *Philosophical Transactions*, *Philosophical Magazine*, etc. [8]

EARNSHAW, Samuel Walter, *Nether Whitacre, Coleshill.*—St. John's Coll. Cam. B.A. 1857; Deac. 1857 and Pr. 1858 by Bp of Lon. C. of Nether Whitacre 1862. Formerly C. of Bromley St. Leonards, Middlesex, 1857, St. Thomas's, Birmingham, 1859. [9]

EARNSHAW, T. G., *Collyhurst, Manchester.*—C. of Collyhurst. [10]

EAST, Edward, *Hounslow Parsonage, Middlesex.*—Magd. Hall, Ox. B.A. 1842, M.A. 1846; Deac. 1842, Pr. 1844. P. C. of Hounslow, Dio. Lon. 1851. (Patron, Bp of Lon; P. C.'s Inc. 280*l* and Ho; Pop. 5201.) [11]

EAST, Rowland Baldwin, *St. Andrew's Parsonage, Newcastle-upon-Tyne.*—St. Aidan's; M.A. 1858 by Abp of Cant; Deac. 1853, Pr. 1855. P. C. of St. Andrew's, Dio. Dur. 1857. (Patron, the V. of Newcastle-upon-Tyne; P. C.'s Inc. 300*l* and Ho; Pop. 11,418.) Chap. to the Troops at Newcastle; Surrogate. Formerly C. of St. Michael's, Madeley, Salop; Member of the Faculty of Physicians and Surgeons of Glasgow, 1839, and Licentiate of Apothecaries' Hall, 1840. [12]

EAST, Sydney, *Northover, near Ilchester.*—St. Peter's Coll. Cam. B.A. 1850; Deac. 1850, Pr. 1851. V. of Northover, Dio. B. and W. 1865. (Patron, J. H. Chichester, Esq; V.'s Inc. 130*l* and Ho; Pop. 122.) [13]

EASTBURN, Charles Fryer, *St. Mark's College, Chelsea, London, S.W.*—St. John's Coll. Cam. Fell. of, B.A. 1851, M.A. 1855; Deac. 1852, Pr. 1853. Vice-Prin. of St. Mark's Coll. Chelsea. Formerly Math. Lect. at St. Mark's Coll. [14]

EASTERBY, Richard Dalby; *Lastingham, Pickering.*—Dur; Deac. 1836 and Pr. 1837 by Abp of York. V. of Lastingham with Farndale C. Dio. York, 1850. (Patron, Ld Chan; Tithe—App. 468*l* 19*s*, V. 261*l* 18*s* 6*d*; Glebe, 73 acres; V's Inc. 330*l* and Ho; Pop. 1597.) [15]

EASTHER, Alfred, *Almondbury, Huddersfield.*—Emman. Coll. Cam. B.A. 1841, M.A. 1845; Deac. 1846, Pr. 1847. Head Mast of King James's Sch. Almondbury, 1848. [16]

EASTHER Charles, *Beverley.*—St. John's Coll. Cam. B A. 1839, M.A. 1843; Deac. 1840 and Pr. 1841 by Bp of Rip. Head Mast. of Beverley Gr. Sch. 1845; Chap. to the Beverley Union 1856. Formerly Head Mast. of Kirkby-Ravensworth Gr. Sch. [17]

EASTMAN, George, *Clapham, Surrey, S.*—P. C. of St. Stephen's, Clapham-park, Dio. Win. 1867. Formerly C. of St. George's, Hanover-square, Lond. [18]

EASTMAN, George, *Draycot-Foliatt, Swindon, Wilts.*—St. John's Coll. Cam. B.A. 1848, B.D. 1862; Deac. 1849 and Pr. 1850 by Abp of York. R. of Draycot-Foliatt, Dio. Salis. 1858. (Patron, A. Goddard, Esq; Tithe, comm. 180*l*; R.'s Inc. 172*l*; Pop. 27.) Formerly C. of Brixton, Surrey. [19]

EASTMAN, William Samuel, *Stafford.*—King's Coll. Lond. Theol. Assoc; Deac. 1859 and Pr. 1860 by Bp of Lich. Asst. Chap. of the County Gaol, Stafford; C. of Ch. Ch. Stafford, 1859. [20]

EASTWICK, James, *Stamford.*—St. Cath. Coll. Cam. B.A. 1820, M.A. 1823. Formerly C. of Duddington and Collyweston, Northants. [21]

EATON, Henry.—C. of St. Andrew's, Hoxton, Lond. [22]

EATON, H. Knight, *Armidale Villa, Redland, Bristol.*—Literate; Deac. 1865 and Pr. 1867 by Bp of St. D. C. of St. Paul's, Clifton. Formerly C. of Swansea. [23]

EATON, John, *Shardlow, near Derby.*—Trin. Coll. Cam. B.A. 1847, M.A. 1852; Deac. 1847, Pr. 1848. R. of Shardlow, Dio. Lich. 1851. (Patron, James Sutton, Esq; R.'s Inc. 300*l*; Pop. 945.) [24]

EATON, John Richard Turner, *Lapworth Rectory, Birmingham.*—Mert. Coll. Ox. 1st cl. Lit. Hum. B.A. 1845, M.A. 1848; Deac. 1848 and Pr. 1850 by Bp of Ox. R. of Lapworth, Dio. Wor. 1864. (Patron, Mert. Coll. Ox; Tithe, 347*l*; Glebe, 32 acres; R.'s Inc. 428*l* and Ho; Pop. 560.) Late Fell. and Tut. of Mert. Coll. Ox; Public Examiner in Lit. Hum. 1852, '60, '63; Select Preacher 1863. Author, *The Politics of Aristotle with English Notes*, 1855. [25]

EATON, Thomas, *West Kirby, Upton, Birkenhead.*—Trin. Coll. Cam. B.A. 1829, M.A. 1843; Deac. 1831 and Pr. 1833 by Bp of Ches. Can. Res. of Ches. Cathl. 1843 (Value, 500*l* and Res.) R. of West Kirby, Dio. Ches. 1860. (Patrons, D. and C. of Ches; Tithe, 656*l* 13*s* 5*d*; Glebe, 47 acres; R.'s Inc. 711*l* and Ho; Pop. 1042.) Formerly V. of Eastham 1847; Rural Dean of Wirral. [26]

EATON, Thomas Ray, *Fishtoft, Boston, Lincolnshire.*—C. of Fishtoft. [27]

EATON, Walter.—Mert. Coll. Ox. B.A. 1844, M.A. 1847; Deac. 1844 and Pr. 1845 by Bp of Wor. Formerly Head Mast. of Uffculme Gr. Sch. [28]

EATON, William Ray, *Oulton, Aylesham, Norfolk.*—Corpus Coll. Cam. B.A. 1852; Deac. 1852 by Bp of Nor. Pr. 1853 by Bp of Ely. C. of Oulton. Formerly C. of Mileham, Norfolk. [29]

EATON, W. F., *Millbrook, Southampton.*—C. of Millbrook. [30]

EBDEN, James Collett, *Great Stukeley Vicarage, near Huntingdon.*—Caius Coll. Cam. 6th Wrang. and B.A. 1816, Trin. Hall, M.A. 1819; Deac. 1817 and Pr. 1818 by Bp of Nor. V. of Great Stukeley, Dio. Ely, 1838. (Patron, Trin. Hall, Cam; Land in lieu of Tithe, 75 acres; V.'s Inc. 145*l* and Ho; Pop. 416.) R. of King's Ripton, Hunts, Dio. Ely, 1842. (Patron, Ld Chan; Tithe, 10*s* 6*d*; Land in lieu of Tithe, 206 acres; R's Inc. 230*l*; Pop. 267.) Formerly Fell. of Caius Coll. Cam. 1816; Fell. and Tut. of Trin. Hall, 1818; Head Mast. of Queen Eliz. Sch. Ipswich, 1832; Official to Archd. of Huntingdon. Author, *Sermon on Occasion of the Queen being fired at*, 1840, 1*s*; *Parochial Lectures on the Church Catechism*, 1841, 3*s*; *Arnold and Riddle's Latin Dictionary Abridged*, 4to. 1853, 10*s* 6*d*; *Selections from Ovid's Metamorphoses*, in *Arnold's School Classics*. [31]

EBSWORTH, George Searl, *Croxton-Kerrial, Grantham.*—Clare Hall, Cam. Wrang. and B.A. 1837, M.A. 1840; Deac. 1838 and Pr. 1839 by Bp of Lon. V. of Croxton-Kerrial, Dio. Pet. 1863. (Patron, Duke of Rutland; V.'s Inc. 247*l* and Ho; Pop. 594.) Formerly V. of Ilkeston 1842–63. [32]

EBSWORTH, John Joseph, *St. Paul's Parsonage, Forest of Dean.*—St. Edm. Hall, Ox. B.A. 1845, M.A. 1848. P. C. of St. Paul's, Forest of Dean, Dio. G. and B. 1858. (Patron, Bp of G. and B; P. C.'s Inc. 160*l* and Ho; Pop. 4909.) Formerly C. of Temple, Bristol. [1]

EBSWORTH, Joseph Woodfall, *Weighton, Yorks.*—C. of Market Weighton. [2]

ECHALAZ, John Manuel, *Appleby Rectory, Atherstone, Leicestershire.*—Trin. Coll. Ox. 2nd cl. Lit. Hum. and B.A. 1822, M.A. 1824; Deac. 1823 by Bp of Lon. Pr. 1830 by Bp of Lin. R. of Appleby, Dio. Pet. 1830. (Patron, George Moore, Esq; Glebe, 430 acres; R.'s Inc. 800*l* and Ho; Pop. 1070.) Hon. Can. of Pet; Rural Dean of Sparkenhoe 1838; one of H.M. Justices of the Peace for Leic. Formerly Fell. and Tut. of Trin. Coll. Ox. [3]

EDDIE, Richard, *Broughton-Sulney Rectory, Melton Mowbray.*—Brasen. Coll. Ox. 3rd cl. Lit. Hum. and B.A. 1839, M.A. 1842; Deac. 1841 and Pr. 1842 by Bp of Lin. R. of Broughton-Sulney, Dio. Lin. 1858. (Patron, Sir J. Radcliffe; Glebe, 245 acres; R.'s Inc. 409*l* and Ho; Pop. 406.) [4]

EDDOWES, Edmund, *Hartford, Northwich, Cheshire.*—Jesus Coll. Cam. B.A. 1858, M.A. 1860; Deac 1859, Pr. 1860. P. C. of Hartford, Dio. Ches. 1863. (Patrons, Trustees; P. C.'s Inc. 120*l*; Pop. 967.) Formerly C. of St. Thomas's, Stockport, 1859. [5]

EDDOWES, John, *St. Jude's Parsonage, Bradford, Yorks.*—Magd. Coll. Cam. B.A. 1850, M.A. 1853; Deac. and Pr 1850. P. C. of St. Jude's, Bradford, Dio. Rip. 1857. (Patron, V. of Bradford; P. C.'s Inc. 350*l* and Ho; Pop. 5861.) Formerly C. of Loppington 1850–52; V. of Garton-upon-the-Wolds 1852–57. Author, *The Agricultural Labourer as he really is*, 6*d*; *Martinmas Musings, or Thoughts about the Hiring Day*, 2*d*; *Leisure Hours* (a Lecture); *Why has all this befallen us?* (Fast-day Sermon), 1855; *The Union of Church and State—What is it? The Church of England, the Poor Man's Church*; *The Church's Sacramental Teaching*; other Sermons and Tracts. [6]

EDDRUP, Edward Paroissien, *Salisbury.*—Wad. Coll. Ox. 2nd cl. Lit. Hum. and B.A. 1845, M.A. 1847; Deac. 1846, Pr. 1847. Chan. of Salis. Cathl; Prin. of the Theol. Coll. Salisbury. Formerly C. of St. Gabriel's, Pimlico. Author, *The Papal Aggression* (a Sermon), 1850; *The Thugs*, S.P.C.K; *Parochial Sermons*, 1860; *Scripture and Science*, 1865. [7]

EDDY, Charles, *Queen's College, Oxford.*—Fell. of Queen's Coll. and Lect. at Trinity Coll. Ox. [8]

EDDY, John, *Elworthy Rectory, Taunton.*—Trin. Coll. Ox. B.A. 1824, M.A. 1827. R. of Elworthy, Dio. B. and W. 1844. (Patron, the present R; Tithe—App. 3*l* 3*s*, R. 230*l* 12*s*; Glebe, 66 acres; R.'s Inc. 310*l* and Ho; Pop. 197.) [9]

EDDY, Stephen Ray, *Buxton Parsonage, Derbyshire.*—Ch. Coll. Cam. B.A. 1858, M.A. 1861; Deac. 1856 and Pr. 1859 by Bp of Rip. P. C. of Buxton, Dio. Lich. 1865. (Patron, Duke of Devonshire; P. C.'s Inc. 400*l* and Ho; Pop. 1875.) Formerly C. of Coley 1858–60, St. Thomas's, Huddersfield, 1860; V. of Youlgreave 1860–65. [10]

EDEN, Arthur, *Ticehurst, Hurst-green, Sussex.*—Queen's Coll. Ox. B.A. 1847, M.A. 1856; Deac. 1848 and Pr. 1849 by Abp of Cant. V. of Ticehurst, Dio. Chich. 1851. (Patrons, D. and C. of Cant; Tithe—App. 457*l* 13*s* 4*d*, Imp. 64*l* 4*s*, V. 868*l* 1*s* 4*d*; Glebe, 14 acres; V.'s Inc. 820*l* 18*s* 6*d* and Ho; Pop. 1758.) [11]

EDEN, Charles Page, *Aberford Vicarage, South Milford, Yorks.*—Oriel Coll. Ox. 1st cl. Lit. Hum. and B.A. 1830, M.A. 1833; Deac. 1833 and Pr. 1834 by Bp of Ox. V. of Aberford, Dio. York, 1850. (Patron, Oriel Coll. Ox; Tithe—Imp. 482*l*, V. 290*l*; Glebe, 45 acres; V.'s Inc. 364*l* and Ho; Pop. 1009.) Formerly Examiner in Lit. Hum. Ox. 1840–42; V. of St. Mary-the-Virgin's, Ox. 1843–50; Select Preacher, Ox. 1838 and 1853. Author, *Sermons*, preached at St. Mary's, Oxford, 1855. [12]

EDEN, John Patrick, *Sedgfield Rectory, Durham.*—St. John's Coll. Cam. B.A. 1836, M.A. 1840; Deac. 1836, Pr. 1837. R. of Sedgfield, Dio. Dur. 1863. (Patron, Bp of Dur; Tithe, 1547*l* 16*s* 2*d*; Glebe, 385 acres; R.'s Inc. 1800*l* and Ho; Pop. 2656.) Hon. Can. of Dur. 1847; Rural Dean. Formerly R. of Bishopwearmouth 1848–63. [13]

EDEN, Robert, *The Vicarage, Wymondham, Norfolk.*—Corpus Coll. Ox. B.A. 1825, M.A. 1827; Deac. 1827, Pr. 1828. V. of Wymondham, Dio. Nor. 1854. (Patron, Bp of Nor; Tithe—App. 2192*l* 15*s* 4*d*, V. 799*l* 4*s* 8*d*; Glebe, 10,613 acres; V.'s Inc. 761*l* and Ho; Pop. 4952.) Chap. to Bp of Nor. 1849; Hon. Can. of Nor. 1852; Dioc. Inspector of Schools; Surrogate; Examiner, under the Board of Control, of Candidates for the East India College, Haileybury, 1839. Formerly Fell. of Corpus Coll. and Mast. of the Schools, Ox. 1828–29; V. of North Walsham, Norfolk, 1851–54; Min of St. Mary's, Lambeth; Head Mast. of Hackney and Camberwell Collegiate Schools; and C. of St. Mark's, Kennington. Author, *The Churchman's Theological Dictionary*, 2 eds. 5*s*; *The Confession of Christ before Men* (a Sermon for the Church Missionary Society), 1834; *The Unity of the Church in her Communion and Ministry* (Two Sermons preached before the University of Oxford), 1836; *Religious Declension* (a Sermon before the University of Oxford), 1838; *The Examinations and Writings of Archdeacon Philpot, with a Biographical Notice*, Parker Society, 1842. Editor of Bishop Wilson's *Perpetual Government of Christ's Church, with a Notice of the Work and its Author*, Oxford Univ. Press, 1843; *The Moderation of the Church of England, by Timothy Puller, D.D.* a new edition, *with an Introductory Preface*; Dean Stanley's *Faith and Practice of a Church-of-England-Man, with Notes, and an Introductory Essay on the Leading Principles of the Church of England*; *Some Thoughts on the Inspiration of the Holy Scriptures.* [14]

EDEN, Robert, *Eydon, Banbury.*—Oriel Coll. Ox. B.A. 1859, M.A. 1864; Deac. 1861 and Pr. 1862 by Bp of Pet. Chap. of Don. of Canons Ashby, Dio. Pet. 1863. (Patron, Sir H. E. Leigh Dryden, Bart; Pop. 55.) Formerly C. of Eydon, 1862. [15]

EDGAR, Joseph Haythorne, *Putney, Surrey, S.W.*—Wad. Coll. Ox. B.A. 1856, M.A. 1858; Deac. 1860 and Pr. 1861 by Bp of Lon. C. of Putney. Formerly Lieut. Royal Artillery 1856–59; Lect. on Mechanical Drawing at the Royal Sch. of Mines, Lond; Lect. on Geometrical Drawing at King's Coll. Lond. [16]

EDGCOMBE, William, *Thornbury Rectory, Brandis-corner, North Devon.*—Pemb. Coll. Ox. B.A. 1838; Deac. 1839 and Pr. 1840 by Bp of Ex. R. of Thornbury St. Peter, Dio. Ex. 1840. (Patroness, Mrs. Edgcombe; Tithe, 225*l*; Glebe, 100 acres; R.'s Inc. 275*l* and Ho; Pop. 365.) Surrogate. [17]

EDGCOME, George, *Penwerris, Falmouth.*—St. John's Coll. Cam. B.A. 1854, M.A. 1861; Deac. 1855 and Pr. 1856 by Bp of Ex. P. C. of Penwerris, Dio. Ex. 1861. (Patron, the Ven. Chan. Phillpotts; P. C.'s Inc. 150*l*; Pop. 800.) Formerly C. of St. Ive 1855–58, St. Gluvias 1858–61. [18]

EDGE, Charles Fane, *Naughton Rectory, Bildeston, Suffolk.*—St. John's Coll. Cam. B.A. 1843, M.A. 1846. Formerly British Chap. at Bahia. [19]

EDGE, Francis, *Cubbington Vicarage, Leamington.*—Ch. Coll. Cam. B.A. 1857, M.A. 1862; Deac. 1857 by Bp of Dur. Pr. 1858 by Bp of Wor. V. of Cubbington, Dio. Wor. 1865. (Patron, the present V; V.'s Inc. 316*l* and Ho; Pop. 964.) Formerly C. of Stourport 1857, Essington 1860, Ecton (sole charge) 1864. [20]

EDGE, William, *Nedging Hall, Bildeston, Suffolk.*—Emman. Coll. Cam. Sen. Thorpe Scho. B.A. 1809; Deac. 1809 and Pr. 1810 by Bp of Nor. R. of Naughton, Bildeston, Dio. Ely, 1810. (Patron, the present R; Tithe, 202*l* 17*s* 9*d*; Glebe, 56 acres; R.'s Inc. 259*l* and Ho; Pop. 155.) R. of Nedging, Dio. Ely, 1822. (Patron, the present R; Tithe, 195*l*; Glebe, 30 acres; R.'s Inc. 225*l* and Ho; Pop. 171.) [21]

EDGE, William John, *Benenden Vicarage, Staplehurst, Kent.*—Emman. Coll. Cam. B.A. 1834, M.A.

1837; Deac. 1836 and Pr. 1837 by Bp of Lon. V. of Benenden, Dio. Cant. 1858. (Patron, Right Hon. Gathorne Hardy, M.P; Tithe—Imp. 500*l*, V. 151*l* 8*s*; Glebe, 1 acre; V.'s Inc. 215*l* and Ho; Pop. 1662.) Chap. to the Earl of Westmoreland 1838. Formerly Select Preacher before the Univ. of Cam. 1855; Rural Dean and R. of Waldringfield, Suffolk, 1838–48; P. C. of Hartshill, Warw. 1848–54; R. of St. Aldate's, Gloucester, 1854–58. Author, *The Vision of Peace, or Thoughts in Verse on the late Secessions to Rome*, 1847, 1*s* 6*d*; *A Lecture on Infidelity*, 1849, 1*s* 6*d*; *A Letter to Lord Ashley on the alleged Romanistic Tendencies of the Younger Clergy*, 1850, 1*s*; *An Essay towards Union, being a Treatise on Election and Final Perseverance*, 1850, 4*d*; *Plain Remarks on Infant Baptism, Confirmation, and the Three Orders of the Christian Ministry, with Answers to Objections to the Burial Service* (a Tract), 4th ed. 1850, 3*d*; *The Second Adam, a Course of Lectures designed to illustrate the Divinity of our Lord, and the Union of the Divine and Human Natures in His Sacred Person*, 1853, 10*s* 6*d*; sundry occasional Sermons. [1]

EDGELL, Charles William, *Chapmanslade, Westbury, Wilts.*—Oriel Coll. Ox. B.A. 1846; Deac. 1847, Pr. 1848. P. C. of Rodden, Frome, Dio. B. and W. 1860. (Patron, Rev. E. Edgell; P. C.'s Inc. 220*l*; Pop. 234.) [2]

EDGELL, Edward Betenson, *Bromham Rectory, Chippenham.*—Ball. Coll. Ox. B.A. 1840; Deac. 1842 by Bp of Ely, Pr. 1843 by Bp of Salis. R. of Bromham, Dio. Salis. 1857. (Patron, the present R; Tithe, comm. 820*l*; Glebe, 60 acres; R.'s Inc. 940*l* and Ho; Pop. 1189.) Formerly C. of Champflower, Somerset, 1842–43, Bromham 1843–57. [3]

EDGELL, Harry, *Nacton Rectory, Ipswich.*—St. John's Coll. Cam. B.A. 1831, M.A. 1836; Deac. 1833, Pr. 1834. R. of Nacton and Levington. Dio. Nor. 1835. (Patroness, Lady Harland; Tithe, 525*l*; Glebe, 22 acres; R.'s Inc. 563*l* and Ho; Pop. Nacton 580, Levington 228.) Rural Dean. [4]

EDGELL, Henry Ffolkes.—Oriel Coll. Ox. B.A. 1842; Deac. and Pr. 1843 by Bp of Salis. Retired Chap. R.N. [5]

EDGELL, Michael Seymour, *Swanley Parsonage, Dartford, Kent.*—Oriel Coll. Ox. B.A. 1844; Deac. 1845, Pr. 1846. P. C. of Swanley, Dio. Cant. 1861. (Patron, the Rev. J. H. Hotham.) Formerly C. of Rodden, Somerset, St. John's, Waterloo-road, Lambeth; V. of St. Margaret's Leicester; C. of St. Giles', Camberwell. [6]

EDGELL, William Charles, *Uggeshall, Wangford, Suffolk.*—St. John's Coll. Ox. B.A. 1835, M.A. 1838; Deac. and Pr. 1837. R. of Uggeshall with Sotherton, Dio. Nor. 1842. (Patron, Earl of Stradbroke; Tithe, Uggeshall, 392*l*; Glebe, 43 acres; Sotherton, 275*l*; Glebe, 12 acres; R.'s Inc. 742*l*; Pop. Uggeshall 272, Sotherton 187.) Formerly C. of Charlton, Oxon, 1837, Stanwell, Middlesex, 1839, Hungerford, Berks, 1841, [7]

EDGHILL, John Cox, *Halifax, Nova Scotia.*—King's Coll. Lond. Theol. Assoc; Deac. 1858 by Bp of Lon. Chap. to the Forces, Halifax. Formerly C. of St. Mark's Whitechapel, Lond. [8]

EDGINGTON, C. N., *St. Leonards-on-Sea, Sussex.*—C. of St. Mary Magdalen's, St. Leonards. [9]

EDISON, Edward John, *Stock Rectory, Ingatestone, Essex.*—Ch. Coll. Cam. B.A. 1825, M.A. 1828; Deac. 1826 and Pr. 1827 by Bp of Lon. R. of Stock-Harward with Ramsden-Bellhouse R. Dio. Roch. 1840. (Patron, J. Edison, Esq; Stock-Harward, Tithe, 435*l*; Glebe, 24 acres; Ramsden-Bellhouse, Tithe, 455*l*; Glebe, 20 acres; R.'s Inc. 934*l* and Ho; Pop. Stock-Harward 657, Ramsden-Bellhouse 492.) [10]

EDLESTON, Joseph, *Gainford, Darlington.*—Trin. Coll. Cam. Member's Prizeman, 1839, 1840, 15th Wrang. and B.A. 1838, M.A. 1841; LL.D. 1863; Deac. 1847 and Pr. 1848 by Bp of Ely. Sen. Fell. and Bursar of Trin. Coll. Cam; Sen. Proctor 1854–55. V. of Gainford, Dio. Dur. 1862. (Patron, Trin. Coll. Cam; V.'s Inc. 801*l* and Ho; Pop. 2384.) Editor of the *Correspondence of Sir Isaac Newton and Professor Coates*, 1850. [11]

EDLIN, Vernon, *Burlington House, Westbourne Park, London, W.*—Trin. Coll. Cam. B.A. 1855; Deac. 1860 by Abp of Cant. C. of Bedford Chapel, Bloomsbury, 1865. Formerly Mast. in Cheltenham Coll. 1856; C. of Upton Warren, near Bromsgrove, 1860. [12]

EDLIN, William James, *Trinity College, Cambridge.*—Trin. Coll. Cam. Wrang. and B.A. 1847, M.A. 1850; Deac. 1848, Pr. 1849. Chap. of Trin. Coll. Cam. Formerly C. of St. John's, Leicester. [13]

EDMAN, Edward Hudson, *Sutton, Isle of Ely.*—St. John's Coll. Cam. B.A. 1845, M.A. 1848; Deac. 1846 and Pr. 1847 by Bp of Lin. P. C. of Muker, Dio. Rip. 1864. (Patron, V. of Grinton; Glebe, 130 acres; P. C.'s Inc. 130*l* and Ho; Pop. 1004.) Formerly C. of Addlethorpe 1846–64, and Ingoldmells 1846–59. Author, *The Immortal Destiny of Man* (a Sermon), 1848. [14]

EDMEADES, M. R., *Ramsbury, Wilts.*—C. of Ramsbury. [15]

EDMEADES, William Henry, *Nurstead Court, Gravesend, Kent.*—Mert. Coll. Ox. B.A. 1826, M.A. 1830; Deac. 1826 and Pr. 1827 by Bp of Roch. R. of Nurstead, Dio. Roch. 1827. (Patron, the present R; Tithe, 173*l* 8*s* 6*d*; Glebe, 37 acres; R.'s Inc. 230*l*; Pop. 57.) [16]

EDMONDES, C. G., *Newcastle, Bridgend, Glamorganshire.*—C. of Newcastle. [17]

EDMONDES, Charles, *Lampeter.*—Prof. of Latin in St. David's Coll. Lampeter. [18]

EDMONDES, Frederick William, *Saleston, Bridgend, Glamorganshire.*—Jesus Coll. Ox. B.A. 1862, M.A. 1865; Deac. 1864 and Pr. 1865 by Bp of Llan. C. of Newcastle, Bridgend, 1864. [19]

EDMONDES, Thomas, *Cowbridge, Glamorganshire.*—Jesus Coll. Ox. B.A. 1829, M.A. 1832; Deac. 1829, Pr. 1830. V. of Llanblethian with Cowbridge and Welsh St. Donats, Dio. Llan. 1835. (Patrons, D. and C. of Glouc; Llanblethian, Tithe—App. 271*l* 6*s* 5*d*, V. 141*l*; Glebe, 55 acres; Cowbridge, Tithe, 17*l* 3*s*; Welsh St. Donats, Tithe—App. 116*l* 9*s* 11*d*, V. 50*l*; V.'s Inc. 298*l*; Pop. Llanblethian 753, Cowbridge 1094, Welsh St. Donats 275.) Rural Dean 1844. [20]

EDMONDS, George, *Little Wenlock, Salop.*—Ch. Ch. Ox. R. of Little Wenlock, Dio. Herf. 1841. (Patron, Lord Forester; Tithe, 551*l* 13*s*; Glebe, 12 acres; R.'s Inc. 564*l*; Pop. 988.) Formerly V. of Madeley, Salop. [21]

EDMONDS, James Hamilton, *Cronk ÿ Voddée, Isle of Man.*—B.A. 1836. P. C. of Cronk ÿ Voddée, Dio. S. and M. 1866. (Patroness, Mrs. Cecil Hall; P. C.'s Inc. 65*l* and Ho; Pop. 360.) Formerly C. of St. Dunstan's, Stepney, Lond. 1853, Miningsby, Lincolnshire (sole charge), 1861. [22]

EDMONSTONE, Charles Welland, *Hornsey-lane, Highgate-hill, N.*—Ch. Ch. Ox. 1st cl. Lit. Hum. B.A. 1833, M.A. 1838; Deac. 1834 by Bp of Nor. Pr. 1835 by Bp of Carl. P. C. of St. John's, Holloway, Dio. Lon. 1847. (Patrons, Trustees; P. C.'s Inc. 600*l*; Pop. 7286.) [23]

EDMUNDS, John, *Kyloe Parsonage, Berwick on-Tweed.*—Dur. B.A. 1843, M.A. 1847; Deac. 1837 and Pr. 1838 by Bp of Dur. P. C. of Kyloe, Dio. Dur. 1851. (Patrons, D. and C. of Dur; Tithe, Imp. 200*l*; P. C.'s Inc. 307*l* and Ho; Pop. 1004.) Author, *Village Sermons* (1st and 2nd series); *Lent Lectures*; *A Commentary on St. Paul's Epistles to the Thessalonians.* [24]

EDMUNDS, William, *Lampeter.*—Lampeter; Deac. 1851, Pr. 1854. R. of Rhôstie, Dio. St. D. 1863. (Patron, Bp of St. D; R.'s Inc. 101*l*; Pop. 122.) Mast. of Lampeter Gr. Sch. Formerly Asst. C. of Lampeter. Editor, *Hanes y Ffydd.* [25]

EDOUART, Augustin Gaspard, *The Vicarage, Leominster.*—St. John's Coll. Cam. B.A. 1840, M.A. 1850; Deac. 1840 and Pr. 1841 by Bp of Ches. V. of Leominster, Dio. Herf. 1862. (Patron, Ld Chan; Tithe, 144*l*; Glebe, 22*l* 10*s*; V.'s Inc. 300*l* and Ho; Pop. 4908.) Surrogate. Formerly C. of Deane, Bolton-le-Moors, 1840–41; P. C. of St. Paul's, Blackburn, 1841–50; P. C. of St. Michael's, Burleigh-street, Lond. and Chap. of

Charing Cross Hospital 1850–62. Author, *Correspondence with the Bishop of London on the Exeter Hall Services*, 1858; and several Sermons. [1]

EDRIDGE, Henry Percival, *Stone, Rye.*—Emman. Coll. Cam. Prizeman, 1853-55, Scho. Wrang. 1856, B.A. 1856, M.A. 1859; Deac. 1858, Pr. 1859. V. of Stone, Dio. Cant. 1862. (Patrons, D. and C. of Cant; Glebe, 4 acres; V.'s Inc. 447*l* and Ho; Pop. 422.) Formerly C. of Tidworth, Hants, 1858, Enborne and Hampstead-Marshall, Berks, 1859, Saltwood, Kent, 1860. [2]

EDWARDES, David Edward, *Laugharne, Carmarthenshire.*—Glasgow, M.A. 1865; Deac. 1866 by Bp of St. D. C. of Laugharne 1866. [3]

EDWARDES, Frederick Francis, *Gileston Manor, Cowbridge, Glamorganshire.*—Corpus Coll. Ox. B.A. 1823, M.A. 1826, B.D. 1833; Deac. 1826, Pr. 1827. R. of Gileston, Dio. Llan. 1847. (Patron, the present R; Tithe, 77*l*; Glebe, 13½ acres; R.'s Inc. 117*l*; Pop. 70.) Formerly Fell. of Corpus Coll. Ox. [4]

EDWARDES, H. C., *Llanwrda, Bangor.*—C. of Llanwrda. [5]

EDWARDES, St. Leger Frederick Hope, *Greet Rectory, Tenbury.*—Trin. Coll. Cam. 1st cl. Cl. Trip. B.A. 1862; Deac. 1864 and Pr. 1865 by Bp of Herf. R. of Greet, Dio. Herf. 1865. (Patron, T. H. Hope Edwardes, Esq; Tithe, 151*l*; Glebe, 38 acres; R.'s Inc. 189*l* and Ho; Pop. 150.) Formerly C. of Greet 1864. [6]

EDWARDES, Stephen, *Merton College, Oxford.*—Mert. Coll. Ox. 1st cl. Maths. 2nd cl. Lit. Hum. B.A. 1848, M.A. 1851, Moderator 1852–53; Deac. 1852 and Pr. 1854 by Bp of Ox. P. C. of Woolvercott, Dio. Ox. 1853. (Patron, Mert. Coll. Ox; Glebe, 35 acres; P. C.'s Inc. 190*l*; Pop. 617.) Fell. and Math. Lect. of Mert. Coll. Ox. [7]

EDWARDES, The Hon. Thomas, *Belshford, Horncastle.*—Trin. Coll. Cam. M.A. 1844; Deac. 1845, Pr. 1846. R. of Belshford, Dio. Lin. 1863. (Patron, Ld Chan; R.'s Inc. 425*l*; Pop. 638.) Formerly R. of Brougham, Westmoreland, 1846–63. [8]

EDWARDS, Allen Thomas, 5, *Kennington-terrace, S.*—St. Cath. Coll. Cam. M.A. P. C. of St. Philip's, Lambeth, Dio. Win. 1863. (Patron, R. of Lambeth; P. C.'s Inc. 300*l*.) Formerly V. of St. Paul's, Chatham, 1858–63; Chap. to Trinity Almshouses, Mile-end; Metropolitan Dist. Sec. to British and Foreign Bible Soc. 1854–58; P. C. of St. Matthias', Bethnal Green, 1849-54. [9]

EDWARDS, Allen Thomas, Jun., *St. Stephen's Parsonage, South Lambeth, S.*—Corpus Coll. Cam. B.A. 1866; Deac. 1866 by Bp of Win. C. of St. Stephen's, South Lambeth, 1866. [10]

EDWARDS, Anderson, *Temple Sowerby, near Penrith.*—C. of Temple Sowerby. [11]

EDWARDS, Andrew, *Magdalen College, Oxford.*—Magd. Coll. Ox. B.A. 1816, M.A. 1818, B.D. 1828; Deac. 1816, Pr. 1817. Fell. of Magd. Coll. Ox. [12]

EDWARDS, Anthony Ambrose, *All Saints' Vicarage, Leeds.*—Dub; Deac. 1845, Pr. 1847. V. of All Saints', Leeds, Dio. Rip. 1854. (Patrons, the Crown and Bp of Rip. alt; Tithe, 10*l*; V.'s Inc. 170*l* and Ho; Pop. 10,288.) [13]

EDWARDS, Bartholomew, *Ashill Rectory, Watton, Norfolk.*—St. John's Coll. Cam. 7th Sen. Opt. and B.A. 1811, M.A. 1814; Deac. 1812, and Pr. 1813 by Bp of Nor. R. of Ashill, Dio. Nor. 1813. (Patron, the present R; Tithe—App. 21*l*, R. 987*l*; Glebe, 30 acres; R.'s Inc. 1017*l* and Ho; Pop. 696.) Rural Dean of Breckles. [14]

EDWARDS, B., *Chirk, Denbighshire.*—C. of Chirk. [15]

EDWARDS, Charles, *Hill Side Villas, Bradford, Yorks.*—Caius Coll. Cam. B.A. 1860, M.A. 1863; Deac. 1860 and Pr. 1862 by Bp of Rip. P. C. of Trinity, Bradford, Dio. Rip. 1864. (Patrons, Five Trustees; P. C.'s Inc. 233*l*; Pop. 9520.) Formerly C. of Trinity, Low Moor, 1860-64, St. Mark's, Low Moor (sole charge), 1864. [16]

EDWARDS, David, *North Nibley, Dursley.*—Ch. Ch. Ox. Stud. of, 3 cl. Lit. Hum. B.A. 1851, M.A. 1853; Deac. 1853 and Pr. 1856 by Bp of Ox. P. C. of North Nibley, Dio. G. and B. 1857. (Patron, Ch. Ch. Ox; P. C.'s Inc. 170*l* and Ho; Pop. 1020.) [17]

EDWARDS, David, *Ffestiniog Rectory, Tany-Bwlch, Merioneth.*—Deac. 1840, Pr. 1841. R. of Ffestiniog and Maentwrog, Dio. Ban. 1851. (Patron, Bp of Ban; Ffestiniog, Tithe, 141*l* 18*s*; Glebe, 3 acres; Maentwrog, Tithe, 100*l*; R.'s Inc. 242*l* and Ho; Pop. Ffestiniog 4553, Maentwrog 883.) Surrogate 1851. Author, *A Vindication of the Established Church*, 1850, translated into Welsh, 1851; *An Essay on Godliness* (in Welsh), 1852. [18]

EDWARDS, Ebenezer, *Mallwyd Rectory, Montgomeryshire.*—Lampeter, B.D. 1854; Deac. 1843 and Pr. 1844 by Bp of St. A. R. of Mallwyd, Dio. Ban. 1852. (Patron, Bp of Ban; Tithe, 340*l*; Glebe, 2 acres; R.'s Inc. 360*l* and Ho; Pop. 1400.) Formerly Chap. of Welsh Church, Ely-place, Lond. 1843–56. [19]

EDWARDS, Ebenezer Wood, *Ruabon Vicarage, Denbighshire.*—Jesus Coll. Ox. Scho. 3rd cl. Lit. Hum. B.A. 1852, M.A. 1855; Deac. 1853 and Pr. 1854 by Bp of St. A. V. of Ruabon, Dio. St. A. 1862. (Patron, Bp of St. A; Tithe, 606*l*; Glebe, 28 acres; V.'s Inc. 660*l* and Ho; Pop. 2418.) Formerly C. of Llangollen; V. of Nantglyn. [20]

EDWARDS, Edward, *Llanstephan, Carmarthen.*—C. of Llanstephan with Llangunnock. [21]

EDWARDS, Edward, *Eglwys Fach, Cardigan.*—P. C. of Elgwys Fach, Dio. St. D. 1865. (Patron, Rev. L. C. Davies; P. C.'s Inc. 90*l*.) [22]

EDWARDS, Edward, *Penegoes Rectory, Machynlleth, Montgomeryshire.*—Deac. 1821 and Pr. 1822 by Abp of York. R. of Penegoes, Dio. St. A. 1849. (Patron, Bp of Llan; Tithe, 250*l*; Glebe, 16 acres; R.'s Inc. 300*l* and Ho; Pop. 930.) Formerly P. C. of Marsden, Yorks, 1823. Author, *Pastoral Recollections*, by Presbyter, 1836, 2*s*; *Twenty-one Sermons*, 1838, 6*s* 6*d*; *Letter to the London Union on the Evil Tendency of Tractarianism*, 1851, 1*s* 6*d*; *Christianity the Foundation of National Education*, 1856; and several Tracts on Church subjects. Editor of Heylin's *Right of the Bishops to Sit and Vote in the House of Peers*, 1835. [23]

EDWARDS, Edward Frank, *Middlewich, Cheshire.*—St. Aidan's; Deac. 1865 by Bp of St. A. Pr. 1866 by Bp of Ches. C. of Middlewich 1865. [24]

EDWARDS, Edward Justin, *Trentham Parsonage, Newcastle-under-Lyme, Staffs.*—P. C. of Trentham, Dio. Lich. (Patron, Duke of Sutherland; Tithe, Imp. 52*l* 2*s* 6*d*; P. C.'s Inc. 120*l* and Ho; Pop. 832.) Preb. of Lichfield. [25]

EDWARDS, George, *Blackley, Manchester.*—St. John's Coll. Cam. B.A. 1864, M.A. 1867; Deac. 1864 and Pr. 1865 by Bp of Man. C. of Blackley 1864. [26]

EDWARDS, George, *Bolton, Lancashire.*—C. of Emmanuel's, Bolton. [27]

EDWARDS, G. J. S., *Skirlaugh, Hull.*—C. of Swine with Skirlaugh. [28]

EDWARDS, George Robertson, *Shawbury Vicarage, Shrewsbury.*—Brasen. Coll. Ox. B.A. 1830; Deac. 1830 and Pr. 1831 by Bp of St. A. V. of Shawbury, Dio. Lich. 1854. (Patron, Sir Vincent Rowland Corbet, Bart; Tithe—Imp. 440*l* 8*s*, V. 394*l* 12*s*; Glebe, 35 acres; V.'s Inc. 460*l* and Ho; Pop. 1027.) [29]

EDWARDS, Griffith, *Llangadfan Rectory, Welshpool.*—Dub. A.B. 1843, A.M. 1846; Deac. 1843 by Bp of Pet. Pr. 1843 by Bp of St. A. R. of Llangadfan, Dio. St. A. 1863. (Patron, Bp of St. A; Tithe, 308*l*; Glebe, 26 acres; R.'s Inc. 332*l* and Ho; Pop. 657.) Formerly C. of Llangollen 1843; P. C. of Minera, Wrexham, 1849–63. Author, *Sylw ar Gatecism*, 1843, 8*d*; *Prize Poems, in Welsh, and others in Welsh and English*, 1846, 3*s*; *The Inundation of Cantre 'r Gwaelod*, 1849, 1*s*; *Literary Remains of the late Rev. J. Blackwell* (Welsh and English), 1851, 5*s*; *Thirty Welsh Sermons*, 1854, 5*s*; *Our New Church* translated into

Welsh, S.P.C.K. Editor of *Y Protestant* (a Welsh Church of England Journal), 1840-43. [1]

EDWARDS, Henry, *Wiggenhall St. Germans, Lynn, Norfolk.*—St Bees; 1st cl. and Prizeman, 1845; Deac. 1846 and Pr. 1847 by Bp of Nor. V. of Wiggenhall St. Germans, Dio. Nor. 1850. (Patrons, D. and C. of Nor; Tithe, 134*l* 19*s*; Glebe, 12 acres; V.'s Inc. 160*l* 10*s* 6*d*; Pop. 633.) C. of North Runcton and Setchey 1863. Author, *Lectures on Jonah*, 1837, 7*s*; *Analysis of the Revelation of St. John on a Plan entirely New*, 1863, 1*s*. [2]

EDWARDS, Henry, *Churchstanton Rectory, Honiton, Devon.*—Lin. Coll. Ox. B.A. 1843; Deac. 1842 by Bp of Ex. Pr. 1843 by Bp of G. and B. R. of Churchstanton, Dio. Ex. 1846. (Patron, the present R; Tithe, 310*l*; Glebe, 122 acres; R.'s Inc. 470*l* and Ho; Pop. 961.) R. of Wambrook, Dorset, Dio. Salis. 1850. (Patron, the Rev. H. H. A. Smith; Tithe, 264*l*; Glebe, 27 acres; R.'s Inc. 336*l* and Ho; Pop. 286.) Rural Dean. [3]

EDWARDS, Henry Grey, *Llandinorwig Parsonage, Carnarvon.*—Lampeter; Deac. 1845 by Bp of Nor. Pr. 1846 by Bp of Ban. P. C. of Llandinorwig, Dio. St. D. 1856. (Patron, G. D. A. Smith, Esq; Glebe, 12 acres; P. C.'s Inc. 200*l* and Ho; Pop. 3346.) Surrogate. Formerly C. of Longnor 1845; P. C. of Beddgelert 1846-48; C. of Llanbeblig and Carnarvon 1848-56. [4]

EDWARDS, Henry Thomas, *Vicarage, Aberdare.*—Jesus Coll. Ox. B.A. 1860; Deac. 1861 by Bp of St. D. Pr. 1861 by Bp of St. A. V. of Aberdare, Dio. Llan. 1866. (Patron, Marquis of Bute; V.'s Inc. 284*l* and Ho; Pop. 28,559.) Author, *Eight Days in the Camp* (a Sermon), Rivingtons, 1865; *Church Extension in Aberdare*, 1867. [5]

EDWARDS, Howell Powell, *The Vicarage, Caerleon.*—Jesus Coll. Ox. Scho. B.A. 1848, M.A. 1851; Deac. 1850 and Pr. 1851 by Bp of Llan. V. of Llangattock, Dio. Llan. 1857. (Patrons, D. and C. of Llan; Tithe, 229*l* 9*s*; Glebe, 100*l*; R.'s Inc. 335*l* and Ho; Pop. 1544.) Rural Dean 1853. Formerly C. of Newcastle 1850, Margam 1851; P. C. of Llanddeurfach 1852-57. [6]

EDWARDS, Isaac, *Swansea.*—C. of Swansea. [7]

EDWARDS, James, *Barningham Rectory, Ixworth, Suffolk.*—Downing Coll. Cam. B.A. 1846, M.A. 1849. R. of Barningham with Coney Weston R. Dio. Ely, 1850. (Patron, R. Hunt, Esq; Tithe, 976*l* 16*s* 5*d*; Glebe, 26 acres; R.'s Inc. 1050*l* and Ho; Pop. Barningham 489, Coney Weston 254.) [8]

EDWARDS, John, *The Rectory, Bradford-cum-Beswick, Manchester.*—St. Aidan's; M.A. by Abp of Cant. 1866; Deac. 1855 and Pr. 1856 by Abp of York. R. of Bradford-cum-Beswick, Dio. Man. 1861. (Patron, Bp of Man; R.'s Inc. 300*l* and Ho; Pop. 7000.) Formerly C. of Whitby 1855-57. [9]

EDWARDS, John, *The Vicarage, Minety, near Malmesbury.*—St. John's Coll. Cam. 14th Wrang. and B.A. 1849, M.A. 1852; Deac. 1850 and Pr. 1851 by Bp of Wor. V. of Minety, Dio. G. and B. 1858. (Patron, Archd. of Wilts; Tithe, 330*l* 5*s* 6*d*; Glebe, 15 acres; V.'s Inc. 350*l* and Ho; Pop. 812.) Formerly C. of St. Andrew's, Worcester, 1850, Sheriffhales, Salop, 1853-59. [10]

EDWARDS, John, *Newtown Rectory, Montgomeryshire.*—St. Peter's Coll. Cam. B.A. 1832, M.A. 1841; Deac. and Pr. 1832. R. of Newtown, Dio. St. A. 1844. (Patron, Bp of St. A; Tithe, 510*l*; Glebe, 3½ acres; R.'s Inc. 535*l* and Ho; Pop. 3692.) Author, *The Corn Laws* (a Pamphlet); *The Death of the Righteous the Monitor of the Living* (a Funeral Sermon); *The Men of Nineveh and the Men of England* (Fast-Day Sermon), 1855. [11]

EDWARDS, John, *Prestbury Vicarage, Cheltenham.*—St. Mary Hall, Ox. B.A. 1856, M.A. 1857; Deac. 1856 by Bp of Lich. Pr. 1857 by Bp of Ox. V. of Prestbury, Dio. G. and B. 1860. (Patron, the Rev. John Edwards; V.'s Inc. 320*l* and Ho; Pop. 1297.) Formerly C. of Harlaston, Chipping Norton, and St. Paul's, Knightsbridge. [12]

EDWARDS, John Cox, *Bolnhurst Rectory, Bedford.*—Emman. Coll. Cam. Jun. Opt. B.A. 1861, M.A. 1864; Deac. 1863 and Pr. 1864 by Bp of Pet. C. in sole charge of Bolnhurst 1866. Formerly C. of Hinckley 1863-65, Colmworth 1865-67. [13]

EDWARDS, John David, *Rhosymedre Parsonage, Ruabon, Denbighshire.*—Jesus Coll. Ox. B.A. 1830; Deac. 1832, Pr. 1833. P. C. of Rhosymedre, Dio. St. A. 1843. (Patron, Sir W. W. Wynn; P. C.'s Inc. 50*l*; Pop. 5305.) Author, *Sacred Music*, 2 vols. 1st vol. 1836, 2nd vol. 1843. [14]

EDWARDS, John Robert, *Holt Parsonage, Wrexham, Denbighshire.*—Pemb. Coll. Ox. B.A. 1813, M.A. 1815; Deac. 1815, Pr. 1816. P. C. of Holt, Dio. St. A. 1825. (Patrons, D. and C. of Win; P. C.'s Inc. 187*l* and Ho; Pop. 1029.) Formerly Fell. of Pemb. Coll. Ox. [15]

EDWARDS, John Wilkinson, *Baddiley, Nantwich, Cheshire.*—Brasen. Coll. Ox. 3rd cl. Lit. Hum. and B.A. 1834; Deac. 1835, Pr. 1836. R. of Baddiley, Dio. Ches. 1839. (Patron, J. Tollemache, Esq; Tithe, 195*l*; Glebe, 9 acres; R.'s Inc. 195*l*; Pop. 272.) P. C. of Woodhay, Dio. Ches. 1843. (Patron, J. Tollemache, Esq; P. C.'s Inc. 102*l* and Ho; Pop. 254.) [16]

EDWARDS, J., *Aberdare.*—C. of Aberdare. Formerly C. of Dowlais. [17]

EDWARDS, Joseph, *Barrow-on-Trent Vicarage, Derbyshire.*—Trin Coll. Cam. Sen. Opt. 3rd cl. Cl. Trip. and B.A. 1824, M.A. 1834; Deac. and Pr. 1824 by Bp of Lon. V. of Barrow-on-Trent with Twyford C. Dio. Lich. 1855. (Patron, A. Moore, Esq; V.'s Inc. 147*l*; Pop. 526.) Chap. to the Dowager Duchess of Norfolk. Formerly P. C. of Wattisham and Brice, Suffolk; 2nd Mast. of King's Coll. Sch. (22 years); Cl. Exam. at Christ's Hospital (20 years); Chap. to the Fishmongers' Company, and Even. Lect. at St. Mary-le-Strand, Lond. (14 years). Author, *Sermons*, 1827; *Catiline and Jugurtha of Sallust*; *Latin Lyrics*; *Latin Elegiacs*; *Initia Latina*; *Oral Exercises in Latin*; *Latin Exercises for Middle Forms*; *English Exercises*; *The Andromache of Euripides, with Notes*; *A Practical Exposition of the Book of Psalms*; etc. [18]

EDWARDS, Joseph, *Croft Rectory, Leominster.*—Ex. Coll. Ox. B.A. 1835; Deac. 1837, Pr. 1839. R. of Croft with Yarpole V. Dio. Herf. 1839. (Patron, E. H. K. Davies, Esq; Croft, Tithe, 120*l*; Glebe, 71 acres; Yarpole, Tithe—Imp. 273*l*, R. 27*l* 4*s* 2*d*; Glebe, 22 acres; R.'s Inc. 300*l* and Ho; Pop. Croft 155, Yarpole 630.) Rural Dean. [19]

EDWARDS, Joseph Charles, *Ingoldmells Rectory, Boston, Lincolnshire.*—M.A. and LL.D; Fell. of Royal Soc. of Lit; formerly Fell. Clare Hall Cam; M.A. Glasgow 1844, St. Aidan's 1847; Deac. 1850 by Bp of Wor. Pr. 1859 by Bp of Dur. R. of Ingoldmells, Dio. Lin. 1864. (Patron, Rev. Dr. Dodsworth; Tithe, 120*l*; Glebe, 16¾ acres; R.'s Inc. 183*l* and Ho; Pop. 319.) Formerly C. of St. Nicholas', Warwick, 1850, Keyingham and Burton, Yorks, 1852, Goadsby and Rollestone, Leic. 1854-56; Afternoon Preacher, Berkeley Chapel, Lond. 1856; Even. Preacher, St. Thomas's, Stepney, 1857; C. of Birley, Northumberland, 1858, Irthlingborough, Northants, 1860, Burrington, Devon, 1862; Min. of Catcott, Somerset, 1863. Author, *Sermons*; *Essays, Tales and Poems*; *The Spiritual Temple* (Sermon); *Sunday Morning* (a Sacred Duet); *Origin and Influence of Poetry* (Lecture); *Sabbath Eve Song*; *Can a Jew sit in Parliament?* (Pamphlet); *Church, Queen, and Constitution* (an Essay); *The Village Church* (a Song); *Five Sacred Songs*; *Harvest Home* (a Song); *My Heart can Trust no more* (a Song); *Psalms and Hymns, Old and New, designed for Congregational Worship and Private Devotion*; *Manual of School Teaching*; *The Cambrian Sacred Minstrel* (a Collection of Welsh Tunes adapted to English Words); *Stepping Stone to Vocal Music, or the Art of Singing at Sight*; *Millenarianism Examined* (Pamphlet); *The Dishonesty of Infidelity* (a Letter to Bishop Colenso); *Man's Devices and God's Counsel* (Sermon preached on the Fast-day, March 21, 1855); *The Gospel of Christ the Power of God* (Sermon); *The Deluge and*

Noah's Faith (Sermon); *The Sacrifice of Abel* (Sermon); *The Law of Retribution* (Sermon); *The Eternal Results of Faithful Preaching* (Sermon); *The Language and Literature of Wales* (Essay read at the University of Göttingen); *The English Language and Literature* (Essay); *Letters on Political and Ecclesiastical Matters, by an Obscure Man*; *The Fading Nature of Man and the Eternity of God's Word* (Sermon); *Paul before Felix* (Sermon); *The Brazen Serpent* (Sermon); *The Desire of Angels* (Sermon); *The Christian Warrior* (Sermon preached on the Death of General Havelock); *The Lincoln Diocesan Architectural Society and the Rector of Ingoldmells*, 1865, 1s; *The Rector's Dream and the Reform Bill*, 1867; various other Pamphlets, Essays, Poems, &c., in English and Welsh. [1]

EDWARDS, Lambart Campbell, *Harrow Park, Harrow-on-the-Hill, N.W.*—Trin. Coll. Cam. B.A. 1844, M.A. 1852; Scho. of Trin. Coll. Cam. 1848, 34th Wrang; Deac. 1848 and Pr. 1849 by Bp of Wor. V. of Dorney, Dio. Ox. 1856. (Patron, Rev. H. Palmer; Tithe—Imp. 53*l* 9*s* 6*d*, V. 67*l*; Glebe, 20 acres; V.'s Inc. 117*l* and Ho; Pop. 367.) Formerly Asst. Mast. in Sir Roger Cholmley's Sch. Highgate, 1851. [2]

EDWARDS, N. W., *Easton-in-Gordano, Bristol.*—C. of Easton-in-Gordano. [3]

EDWARDS, Reginald Campbell, *Speen, Newbury, Berks.*—Wad. Coll. Ox. B.A. 1853, M.A. 1856; Deac. 1855 by Bp of Wor. Pr. 1856 by Bp of Chich. C. of Speen. Formerly C. of Hurstpierpoint. [4]

EDWARDS, Richard, *Mitton Vicarage, near Clitheroe.*—V. of Mitton, Dio. Rip. 1848. (Patron, John Aspinall, Esq; Tithe, Imp. 462*l* 0*s* 8*d*; V.'s Inc. 155*l* and Ho; Pop. 724.) Surrogate. [5]

EDWARDS, Robert Wynne, *Meifod, Welshpool.*—Brasen. Coll. Ox. Vaughan Exhib. 1842, 3rd cl. Lit. Hum. and B.A. 1846; Deac. and Pr. 1848 by Bp of St. A. V. of Meifod, Dio. St. A. 1860. (Patron, Bp of St. A; Tithe—App. 597*l* 17*s* 3*d*, V. 490*l* 5*s* 6*d*; Glebe, 7 acres; V.'s Inc. 510*l* 5*s* 6*d* and Ho; Pop. 1010.) Preb. of Meliden in St. A. Cathl; Chap. to Bp of St. A. Formerly R. of Llanfihangel-yn-Gwynfa 1858–60; P. C. of Gwersylit, Denbighshire, 1852–58; Dioc. Inspector of Schs. 1854–58. [6]

EDWARDS, Roger, *Llanfechell Rectory, Amlwch, Anglesey.*—Jesus Coll. Ox. B.A. 1813; Deac. and Pr. 1814 by Bp of Ban. R. of Llanfechell, Dio. Ban. 1836. (Patron, Bp of Ban; Tithe, 438*l* 10*s*; Glebe, 20 acres; R.'s Inc. 458*l* and Ho; Pop. 958.) Author, *A Collection of Psalms and Hymns*, 1824; *A Treatise on the Sacrament*, in Welsh, 1824. [7]

EDWARDS, Samuel, *Viney-hill, Forest of Dean.*—St. Bees; Deac. 1853 and Pr. 1854 by Bp of Lich. P. C. of All Saints', Viney-hill, Dio. G. and B. 1866. (Patron, Rev. W. H. Bathurst; Glebe, 5 acres; P. C.'s Inc. 150*l*; Pop. 1200.) Formerly C. of Fenton, Staffs, 1853, Burton Latimer, Northants, 1854–57, Ch. Ch. Clifton, 1857–59, Mangotsfield 1859–66. Author, *Scripture Questions*, 1848; *Seven Asian Churches*; *The Bicentenary*, a Dialogue. [8]

EDWARDS, Samuel Valentine, *St. Vincent Lodge, Hanwell, Middlesex.*—Trin. Coll. Ox. B A. 1830; Deac. 1830, Pr. 1831. Formerly Chap. to the Central District School, Hanwell, 1853–58. Author, *A Tract on Clothing Clubs*; *A Sermon on the Death of the Rev. W. W. Pym*; *A Sermon on the Conversion and Restoration of the Jews*; *The Rise and Progress of the Norwich School*; *The Coming of Jesus*; etc. [9]

EDWARDS, Thomas, *Yerbeston, Narberth.*—Lampeter, Scho. and Prizeman; Deac. 1862 and Pr. 1863 by Bp of Llan. C. of Yerbeston 1865. Formerly C. of Coychurch 1862. [10]

EDWARDS, Thomas, *Llanwyddelan Rectory, Berriew.*—Lampeter; Deac. 1850 and Pr. 1852 by Bp of St. D. R. of Llanwyddelan, Dio. St. A. 1862. (Patron, Bp of Llan; Tithe, 254*l*; Glebe, 50 acres; R.'s Inc. 320*l* and Ho; Pop. 476.) Formerly C. of Landisilio-Gogo and Llanyranog 1851 62. [11]

EDWARDS, Thomas Hawley, *Bishopswood Parsonage, Ross, Herefordshire.*—St. John's Coll. Cam. B.A. 1846; Deac. 1846 by Bp of Lich. Pr. 1850 by Bp of Herf. P. C. of All Saints', Bishopswood, Dio. Herf. 1857. (Patron, J. Partridge, Esq; Glebe, 6 acres; P. C.'s Inc. 80*l* and Ho; Pop. 403.) Formerly C. of St. Alkmund's, Shrewsbury, 2 years; C. in sole charge of Benthall, Much Wenlock, 7 years. [12]

EDWARDS, Thomas Hyne, *Llandewyrcwm, Builth.*—Formerly Chap. at Adlington Hall and at Mottram Hall, Cheshire. [13]

EDWARDS, Thomas Wynne, *St. Asaph, Flintshire.*—Vicar-Choral of St. A. Cathl. 1828 (Value, 250*l*.) V. of Rhuddlan, near Rhyl, Flintshire, Dio. St. A. 1827. (Patron, Bp of St. A; Tithe—App. 729*l*, V. 264*l* 2*s* 10*d*; Glebe, 12 acres; V.'s Inc. 288 and Ho; Pop. 1432.) [14]

EDWARDS, William, *Llangollen Vicarage, Denbighshire.*—Deac. 1825, Pr. 1826. V. of Llangollen, Dio. St. A. 1849. (Patron, Bp of St. A; Tithe—Imp. 1051*l* 6*s* 9*d*, V. 486*l*; Glebe, 9 acres; V.'s Inc 445*l* and Ho; Pop. 4300.) Surrogate. [15]

EDWARDS, William Christopher, *Tan-y-graig, Llangefni, Anglesey.*—Jesus Coll. Ox. B.A. 1851, M.A. 1853; Deac. 1853 by Bp of Ban. Pr. 1854 by Bp of Llan. C. of Llangefni with Tregayan 1864. Formerly C. of Llanfechell 1853, Coyty 1854, Llanwnog 1855–56; Chap. of Newtown and Llanidloes Union 1854–55. [16]

EDWARDS, William Edward, *Orleton Vicarage, near Ludlow.*—Brasen. Coll. Ox. B.A. 1846, M.A. 1849; Deac. 1847 and Pr. 1848 by Bp of Dur. V. of Orleton, Dio. Herf. 1853. (Patrons, the Governors of Lucton Free Sch; Tithe—Imp. 145*l* 16*s* 1½*d*, V. 129*l* 19*s* 4½*d*; Glebe, 1 acre; V.'s Inc. 159*l* and Ho; Pop. 600.) [17]

EDWARDS, William Henry, *Hickling Rectory, Notts.*—Queens' Coll. Cam. 15th Wrang. and B.A. 1841, Fell. of Queens' Coll. 1841, M.A. 1844, B.D. 1853. R. of Hickling, Dio. Lin. 1857. (Patron, Queens' Coll. Cam; Glebe, 490 acres; R.'s Inc. 420*l* and Ho; Pop. 642.) Formerly R. of St. Botolph's, Cambridge, 1853–57. [18]

EDWARDS, William James Fussell, *Stoke St. Michael, near Oakhill, Bath.*—Queens' Coll. Cam. B.A. 1832, M.A. 1842; Deac. 1832 and Pr. 1834 by Bp of B. and W. P. C. of Stoke St. Michael, *alias* Stokelane, Dio. B. and W. 1834. (Patron, V. of Doulting; Tithe—Imp. 75*l*, P. C. 75*l*; P. C.'s Inc. 170*l*; Pop. 734.) [19]

EDWARDS, W. J., *Llandow, Cowbridge, Glamorganshire.*—R. of Llandow, Dio. Llan. 1858. (Patron, Jesus Coll. Ox; R.'s Inc. 266*l* and Ho; Pop. 138.) P. C. of Monknash, Dio. Llan. 1863. (Patron, J. Bruce Pryce, Esq; P. C.'s Inc. 76*l*; Pop. 121.) [20]

EDWARDS, William Owen, *Lampeter.*—Lampeter, Scho. and Prizeman; Deac. 1860 and Pr. 1861 by Bp of Llan. C. of Lampeter 1862. Formerly C. of Newcastle, Bridgend, 1860–62. [21]

EDWARDS, William Walter, 38, *Bury-street, St. James's, London, S.W.*—St. Peter's Coll. Cam. 2nd cl. Theol. Trip. B.A. 1859, M.A. 1866; Deac. 1860 and Pr. 1861 by Bp of Lon. P. C. of St. John the Baptist's, Piccadilly, Dio. Lon. 1865. (Patron, R. of St. James's; P. C.'s Inc. 150*l*; Pop. 5455.) Formerly C. of Hanover Chapel, Regent-street, 1860; V. of Loddiswell, Devon, 1862. [22]

EDWARDS, Zachary James, *Axminster, Devon.*—Wad. Coll. Ox. 2nd cl. Lit. Hum. 2nd cl. Math. et Phy. and B.A. 1821, M.A. 1827; Deac. 1822 by Bp of Ex. Pr. 1823 by Bp of Bristol. R. of Combe-Pyne, Dio. Ex. 1840. (Patron, H. Knight, Esq; Tithe, 115*l*; Glebe, 28 acres; R.'s Inc. 130*l*; Pop. 118.) Chap. to the Axminster Union. Formerly Fell. of Wad. Coll. Ox. Author, *The Ferns of the Axe*, Hamilton, Adams, and Co. 2*s* 6*d*. [23]

EEDLE, Edward, *South Bersted Vicarage, Bognor, Sussex.*—Ch. Ch. Ox. 1st cl. Math. et Phy. 2nd cl Lit. Hum. 1816, B.A. 1817, M.A. 1820; Deac. and Pr. 1820 by Bp of Salis. V. of South Bersted, Dio. Chich. 1824. (Patron, Abp of Cant; Tithe—App. 810*l*, V. 400*l*; Glebe, 1 acre; V.'s Inc. 420*l* and Ho; Pop. 605.) Rural

Dean 1852; Preb. Chich. 1855. Author, *Sermon in Aid of Chichester Infirmary*, 1843; *Visitation Sermon*, 1847. [1]

EGAN, John Cruice, 3, *St. Agnes-terrace, Victoria Park-road, South Hackney, N.E.*—Glasgow, M.D. 1842, M.R.I.A. 1845; Deac. 1859 by Bp of Lon. Pr. 1861 by Abp of Cant. C. of South Hackney 1863. Formerly C. of St. Peter's, Maidstone, 1861–63. Author, various works on Medical Science. [2]

EGERTON, C. Cadwallader, *New College, Oxford.*—Fell. of New Coll. Ox. [3]

EGERTON, George Henry, *Middle Rectory, Salop.*—Brasen. Coll. Ox. B.A. 1844, M.A. 1847; Deac. 1845, Pr. 1846. R. of Middle, Dio. Lich. 1847. (Patron, Earl Brownlow; Tithe, 1100*l*; Glebe, 3 acres; R.'s Inc. 1100*l* and Ho; Pop. 802.) Preb. of Lich. 1862; Rural Dean of Wem 1867. [4]

EGERTON, John Coker, *Burwash Rectory, Hurst Green, Sussex.*—Brasen. Coll. Ox. 3rd cl. Lit. Hum. B.A. 1852, M.A. 1854; Deac. 1854 and Pr. 1856 by Bp of Salis. R. and V. of Burwash, Dio. Chich. 1867. (Patron, Rev. J. Egerton; Tithe, 1015*l*; Glebe, 82 acres; R.'s Inc. 1115*l* and Ho; Pop. 2142.) Formerly C. of Nunton, Wilts, 1854–57, Burwash 1857–62, and 1865–67, St. Andrew's Undershaft, Lond. 1862–65. [5]

EGERTON, Philip R., *Bloxham, Oxon.*—Fell. of New Coll. Ox; Mast of All Saints' Sch. Bloxham. [6]

EGERTON, William Henry, *Whitchurch Rectory, Salop.*—Brasen. Coll. Ox. B.A. 1834, M.A. 1835; Deac. 1835, Pr. 1837. R. of Whitchurch with Marbury R. Dio. Lich. 1846. (Patron, Earl Brownlow; Whitchurch, Tithe, 1350*l*; Glebe, 35 acres; Marbury, Tithe, 328*l*; Glebe, 11 acres; R.'s Inc. 1678*l* and Ho; Pop. Whitchurch 4947, Marbury 779.) Rural Dean; Chap. to the Earl of Enniskillen 1840. Formerly Fell. of Brasen. Coll. Ox. 1836. Author, *The Pew System* (an Address delivered at Holnet), Simpkin, Marshall and Co. 1862; *The Prayers* (a Sermon), 1866. [7]

EGLES, Edward Henry, *Enfield, Middlesex.*—Emman. Coll. Cam. B.A. 1857; Deac. 1857 and Pr. 1858 by Bp of Ely. C. of St. Andrew's, Enfield, 1859. Formerly C. of Litlington, Cambs. 1857. [8]

EGREMONT, Edward, *Wroxeter Vicarage, Shrewsbury.*—Trin. Coll. Cam. B.A. 1824, M.A. 1826; Deac. 1824 by Bp of Kilmore, Pr. 1826 by Bp of Lich. V. of Wroxeter, Dio. Lich. 1829. (Patron, Duke of Cleveland; Tithe—Imp. 606*l* 6*s*, V. 270*l*; Glebe, 26½ acres; V.'s Inc. 334*l* and Ho; Pop. 616.) [9]

EKINS, Jeffery, *Little Sampford Rectory, Braintree, Essex.*—New Coll. Ox. B.C.L; Deac. and Pr. 1831. R. of Little Sampford, Dio. Roch. 1842. (Patron, New Coll. Ox; Tithe, 715*l*; R.'s Inc. 858*l* and Ho; Pop. 477.) [10]

ELAND, Henry George, *Bedminster, near Bristol.*—Magd. Hall, Ox. B A. 1837, M.A. 1840. V. of Bedminster, Dio. G. and B. 1852. (Patron, Bp of G. and B; Tithe—App. 90*l*, Imp. 5*s*, V. 400*l*; V.'s Inc. 410*l*; Pop. 3911.) Surrogate. [11]

ELD, Francis John, *Worcester.*—St. John's Coll. Ox. 3rd cl. Lit. Hum. B.A. 1852, M.A. 1855; Deac. 1857 and Pr. 1858 by Bp of Wor. Head Mast. of Wor. Gr. Sch. 1860; R. of Spetchley, Dio. Wor. 1865. (Patron, R. Berkeley, Esq; R.'s Inc. 120*l*; Pop. 140.) Formerly Asst. Mast. at Rossall Sch. 1854–57; C. of Rugby 1857–59. [12]

ELD, James Henry, *St. John's College, Oxford.*—St. John's Coll. Ox. 4th cl. Lit. Hum. and B.A. 1845, M.A. 1849, B.D. 1854; Deac. 1846 and Pr. 1847 by Bp of Rip. Fell. of St. John's Coll. Ox; P. C. of Fyfield, Berks, Dio. Ox. 1863. (Patron, St. John's Coll. Ox; P. C.'s Inc. 125*l*; Pop. 439.) [13]

ELDRIDGE, John Adams, *Bishop Wilton Vicarage, near Pocklington.*—Wor. Coll. Ox. B.A. 1841, M.A. 1851; Deac. 1841, Pr. 1842. V. of Bishop Wilton, Dio. York, 1857. (Patron, Sir T. Sykes, Bart; V.'s Inc. 180*l* and Ho; Pop. 919.) Formerly P. C. of St. James's, Sutton, near Hull, 1847–57. [14]

ELERS, Edward Henry, *Fovant, Salisbury.*—Univ. Coll. Ox. M.A; Deac. and Pr. 1860 by Bp of Salis. C. in sole charge of Fovant 1862. [15]

ELEY, Henry, 9, *Bloomsbury-place, Brighton.*—St. Peter's Coll. Cam. B.A. 1830, M.A. 1836; Deac. and Pr. 1830. Formerly V. of Coggeshall 1838; P. C. of St. Paul's, High Beech, 1842; V. of Broomfield, Essex, 1843–61. Author, *The Burial Rites of the Church the Privilege of the Baptized* (a Sermon), 1840; *Geology in the Garden*, 1859, 6*s*. [16]

ELGER, James Wentworth, *Newport, Isle o Wight.*—Queens' Coll. Cam. B.A. 1845; Deac. 1845 and Pr. 1846 by Bp of Lich. Chap. of the Poorhouse, Newport, 1853. Formerly C. of Coxley, Staffs, 1845, Birmingham 1848, Banbury 1850. [17]

ELGIE, Walter Francis, *Midhurst, Sussex.*—St. Edm. Hall, Ox. B.A. 1859; M.A. 1864; Deac. 1861 and Pr. 1862 by Bp of Chich. C. of West Lavington, Sussex, 1863. Formerly Asst. C. of Lodsworth, Sussex, 1861–63. [18]

ELGOOD, John Charles, *Hull.*—C. of St. Luke's, Hull. Formerly C. of Skegness, Lincolnshire. [19]

ELIAS, Alfred, *Whitchurch, near Cardiff.*—Deac. 1862, Pr. 1863. C. of Whitchurch 1866. Formerly C. of Aberystruth. [20]

ELIOT, Charles John, *Alnwick.*—Corpus Coll. Cam. B.A. 1860, Deac. 1860 by Bp of Win. Pr. 1861 by Bp of Chich. C. of Alnwick 1864. Formerly C. of Wilmington and West Dean, Sussex, 1860–62, Blandford, Dorset, 1862–64. [21]

ELIOT, Edward, *The Vicarage, Norton Bavant, Warminster.*—New Coll. Ox. Scho. 1845, Fell. 1847, 3rd cl. Lit. Hum. 1849, S.C.L. 1848, B.C.L 1853; Deac. 1853 and Pr. 1854 by Bp of Ox. V. of Norton Bavant, Dio. Salis. 1863. (Patron, Ld Chan; Tithe, 138*l*; Glebe, 40 acres; V.'s Inc. 228*l* and Ho; Pop. 261.) Formerly C. of Tredington, Worc. 1853–56, and again, 1859–60, Norton Bavant, Wilts, 1856–57, Sutton-under-Brailes, Glouc. 1858–59; P. C. of Sibford, Oxon. 1860–63. [22]

ELIOT, Philip Frank, 8, *Richmond Hill, Bath.*—Trin. Coll. Ox. 2nd cl. Lit. Hum. and B.A. 1857, M.A. 1858; Deac. 1858 by Bp of Win. Pr. 1860 by Abp of Cant. C. in sole charge of St. Stephen's, Lansdown, Bath. Formerly C. of St. Michael's, Winchester; Chap. at Cally Gatehouse, Scotland; C. of Walcot, Bath. Author, *The Fall of Man* (Five Sermons), 1*s*; *God's Gift to Man* (a Christmas Tract), 1*d*. [23]

ELIOT, William, *Compton Abbas, Shaftesbury.*—Wad. Coll. Ox B.A. 1853, M.A. 1855; Deac. 1855 by Bp of G. and B. Pr. 1856 by Bp of B. and W. R. of Compton Abbas, Dio. Salis. 1866. (Patron, Sir R. G. Glyn, Bart; Tithe, 340*l*; R.'s Inc. 340*l* and Ho; Pop. 456.) Formerly C. of Minchinhampton 1855–62; V. of Mayfield, Staffs, 1862–66. [24]

ELIOT, William Lawrence, *Creeting All Saints, Needham, Suffolk.*—King's Coll. Cam. B.A. 1834, M.A. 1837; Deac. 1841, Pr. 1842. R. of Creeting All Saints, with St. Mary and St. Olave R. Dio. Nor. 1862. (Patron, Eton Coll; Tithe, 750*l*; Glebe, 80 acres; R.'s Inc. 867*l* and Ho; Pop. All Saints 333, St. Mary 202, St. Olave 41.) Fell. of Eton Coll. Formerly Asst. Mast. of Eton Sch. [25]

ELLABY, James Watts, *Woodstone, Peterborough.*—C. of Woodstone. [26]

ELLACOMBE, Henry Nicholson, *Bitton Vicarage, near Bristol.*—Oriel Coll. Ox. B.A. 1844, M.A. 1848; Deac. and Pr. 1847 by Bp of Lich. V. of Bitton, Dio. G. and B. 1850. (Patron, Bp of G. and B; Tithe—App. 310*l* and 20 acres of Glebe, V. 265*l*; Glebe, 6 acres; V.'s Inc. 277*l* and Ho; Pop. 621.) Surrogate. [27]

ELLACOMBE, Henry Thomas, *Clyst St. George Rectory, Devon.*—Oriel Coll. Ox. B.A. 1812, M.A. 1816; Deac. 1816 by Bp of Ex. Pr. 1817 by Bp of Glouc. R. of Clyst St. George, Dio. Ex. 1850. (Patron, W. Gibbs, Esq; Tithe, 325*l*; Glebe, 6 acres; R.'s Inc. 340*l* and Ho; Pop. 300.) Dom. Chap. to Earl of Harrington. Formerly C. of Cricklade 1816–17, Bitton 1817–35; V. of Bitton 1835–50. Author, *Practical Remarks on Belfries and Ringers*, 1850, 1*s*; *The Bells of the Church* (a Sermon), 1864, 1*s*; *History of Clyst St. George*, 4to. Exeter, 1861, 12*s*; *History of the Manor of*

Bitton, 1867; *The Bells of Devonshire*, 4to. Bell and Daldy, 1867, 30*s*. [1]

ELLAM, John, *Drypool Parsonage, Hull.*—St. Bees; Deac. 1858 and Pr. 1859 by Abp of York. P. C. of Drypool, Dio. York, 1863. (Patrons, Simeon's Trustees; P. C.'s Inc. 300*l* and Ho; Pop. 9000.) Formerly C. of St. James's, Hull, 1858–62, Cheltenham 1862–63. [2]

ELLER, George, *West Winch Rectory, Lynn Regis, Norfolk.*—Queens' Coll. Cam. B.A. 1840, M.A. 1844; Deac. 1840 and Pr. 1841 by Bp of Nor. R. of West Winch, Dio. Nor. 1846. (Patron, Ld Chan; Tithe, 338*l* 10*s*; Glebe, 29 acres; R.'s Inc 430*l* and Ho; Pop. 470.) Dom. Chap. to Marquis Cholmondeley. Author, *Pastoral Address to Proprietors and Parishioners*, 1847 and 1853. [3]

ELLER, Irvin, *Faldingworth Rectory, Wragby, Lincolnshire.*—R. of Faldingworth, Dio. Lin. 1848. (Patron, Hon. C. H. Cust; Tithe, 191*l*; Glebe, 87 acres; R.'s Inc. 284*l* and Ho; Pop. 365.) Rural Dean. Formerly R. of St. Peter's, Saltfleetby, 1841–48; Sec. of the Lincolnshire Architectural Society. Author, *Plain Words to Plain People on the Duty of Christian Unity, and on the Proper Exercise of the Right of Private Judgment*, 1839; *The History of Belvoir Castle*, 1841; various Papers as Sec. of the Lincolnshire Architectural Society. [4]

ELLERBECK, Jonathan, *Houghton, Settle.*—St. Bees; Deac. 1860, Pr. 1862. P. C. of Houghton, Dio. Rip. 1864. (Patron, V. of Gisburn; P. C.'s Inc. 108*l* and Ho; Pop. 500.) [5]

ELLERSHAW, Henry, *Millington, Pocklington.*—Literate; Deac. 1819 and Pr. 1820 by Abp of York. V. of Millington with Great Givendale V. Dio. York, 1862. (Patron, Abp of York; Tithe, 30*l*; Glebe, 215 acres; V.'s Inc. 300*l* and Ho; Pop. Millington 275, Great Givendale 86.) Formerly C. of Tinsley 1820, Braithwell with Bramley 1823, Firbeck and Letwell 1836, Conisbrough 1839, Edlington 1841, Hooton Roberts 1851–61. [6]

ELLERSHAW, Henry, Jun., *Mexborough Vicarage, Rotherham.*—Bp Hatfield's Hall, Dur. B.A. 1858; Deac. 1858 and Pr. 1860 by Bp of Dur. V. of Mexborough, Dio. York, 1860. (Patron, Archd. of York; Tithe, App. 677*l*; Glebe, 38 acres; V.'s Inc. 300*l* and Ho; Pop. 2665.) Surrogate. Formerly Asst. C. of Berwick-on-Tweed 1858–60. [7]

ELLERSHAW, J.—C. of St. Stephen's, Westminster. [8]

ELLERTON, George Mouat Keith, 34, *Approach-road, Victoria Park, London, N.E.*—Brasen. Coll. Ox. Scho. and Hulme Exhib. B.A. 1840, M.A. 1843; Deac. 1841 by Abp of Cant. Pr. 1842 by Bp of Salis. C. of St. Bartholomew's, Bethnal-green, 1863. Formerly C. of Ifield, Kent, 1841–43, Milton-Clevedon 1843–54, St. Michael's, Stockwell, 1858-59, All Saints', Northampton, 1859–62, Syston, Leicester, 1862–63. [9]

ELLERTON, John, *Crewe Green, Crewe, Cheshire.*—Trin. Coll. Cam. B.A. 1849, M.A. 1854; Deac. 1850 and Pr. 1851 by Bp of Chich. P. C. of Crewe Green, Dio. Ches. 1860. (Patron, Lord Crewe; Tithe, 180*l*; Glebe, 7 acres; P. C.'s Inc. 185*l* and Ho; Pop. 387.) Formerly C. of Easebourne 1850, Brighton, and Lect. of St. Peter's, Brighton, 1852. [10]

ELLICOTT, Charles Spencer, *Whitwell, near Stamford.*—Trin. Hall, Cam. LL.B. 1821; Deac. 1817 and Pr. 1818 by Bp of Lin. R. of Whitwell, Dio. Pet. 1818. (Patron, Earl of Gainsborough; Tithe, 140*l*; Glebe, 54 acres; R.'s Inc. 325*l* and Ho; Pop. 104.) V. of Threckingham, Dio. Lin. 1829. (Patron, Arthur Heathcote, Esq; Tithe, 55*l*; Glebe, 53 acres; V.'s Inc. 155*l*; Pop. 180.) Rural Dean of Oakham 1848. [11]

ELLIOT, Frederick Ebrington, *Ongar, Essex.*—Chap. of the Union, Ongar. [12]

ELLIOT, Frederick Roberts, *Tor, Torquay.*—Ex. Coll. Ox. B.A. 1862, M.A. 1865: Deac. 1864 and Pr. 1865 by Bp of Salis. C. of Tor Mohun 1866. [13]

ELLIOT, George, *Southwell School, Notts.*—Pemb. Coll. Cam. B.A. 1833, M.A. 1843; Deac. 1836 and Pr. 1837 by Bp of Carl. Mast. of Southwell Sch. [14]

ELLIOT, The Very Rev. Gilbert, *The Deanery, Bristol.*—St. John's Coll. Cam. B.A. 1822, M.A. 1824, D.D. 1850; Deac. 1823, Pr. 1824. Dean of Bristol 1850. Author, *Sermons*, 1850; occasional Sermons and Tracts. [15]

ELLIOT, John Elphinstone, *Whalton, Newcastle-upon-Tyne.*—St. Cath. Coll. Cam. B.A. 1841, M.A. 1846; Deac. 1840, Pr. 1841. R. of Whalton, Dio. Dur. 1843. (Patron, R. Bates, Esq; Tithe, 624*l* 5*s* 9½*d*; Glebe, 127 acres; R.'s Inc. 764*l* and Ho; Pop. 495.) [16]

ELLIOT, Robert William, *St. Leonard's Parsonage, New Malton, Yorks.*—Corpus Coll. Cam. B.A. 1853, M.A. 1856; Deac. 1857 and Pr. 1858 by Abp of York. P. C. of St. Leonard's, New Malton, Dio. York, 1863. (Patron, Earl Fitzwilliam; P. C.'s Inc. 195*l* and Ho; Pop. 2221.) Formerly C. of Etton, Yorks, 1857, Barton-le-Street 1859, Sewerby with Malton and Grindale 1860, St. Leonard's, New Malton, 1861–63. [17]

ELLIOT, William, *Cardington Vicarage, Salop.*—Magd. Coll. Cam. 2nd cl. Cl. Trip. Sen. Opt. and B.A. 1854; Deac. 1854 and Pr. 1855 by Bp of Lich. V. of Cardington, Dio. Herf. 1866. (Patron, Rowland Hunt, Esq; Tithe, 47*l*; Glebe, 360 acres; V.'s Inc. 315*l* and Ho; Pop. 768.) Formerly Fell. of Magd. Coll. Cam. 1854–58; C. of Montford 1854, Chetwynd 1857. R. of Easthope 1864. [18]

ELLIOT, William Henry, *Worsall Hall, Yarm, Yorks.*—Dur. B.A. 1838, M.A. 1841, Licen. Theol. 1840; Deac. 1841 and Pr. 1842 by Abp of York. V. of Stockburn, Dio. Dur. 1847. (Patron, Mast. of Sherburn Hospital; Tithe—Imp. 343*l* 18*s*, V. 116*l* 4*s* 8*d*; Glebe, 3 acres; V.'s Inc. 250*l*; Pop. 231.) P. C. of Worsall, Dio. York, 1865. (Patron, V. of Northallerton; P. C.'s Inc. 80*l*; Pop. 130.) [19]

ELLIOTT, Charles Boileau, *Tattingstone Rectory, near Ipswich.*—Queens' Coll. Cam. B.A. 1833, M.A. 1836; Deac. 1833, Pr. 1834. R. of Tattingstone, Dio. Nor. 1838. (Patron, C. Elliott, Esq; Tithe, 402*l*; Glebe, 38¾ acres; R.'s Inc. 457*l* and Ho; Pop. 426.) Formerly of the Bengal Civil Service; V. of Godalming, Surrey, 1833–38. Fell. of the Royal and of the Royal Geological Societies. Author, *On the Influence of Climate on National Character*, 1821; *On the Abolition of Suttees*, and *The Admission of Natives of India to Situations under Government*, 1828; *Letters from the North of Europe, or Travels in Holland, Denmark, Norway, Sweden, Finland, Russia, Prussia, and Saxony*, 1832, 15*s*; *Travels in the Three Great Empires of Austria, Russia, and Turkey*, 2 vols. 1838, 30*s*; *A Sermon on the Vicissitudes of Life*, 1838. [20]

ELLIOTT, Charles John, *Winkfield Vicarage, near Windsor.*—St. Cath. Coll. Cam. Crosse Univ. Scho. and B.A. 1840, 1st cl. Tyrwhitt Univ. Scho. 1842, M.A. 1843; Deac. 1842 and Pr. 1843 by Bp of Lon. V. of Winkfield, Dio. Ox. 1844. (Patrons, D. and C. of Salis; Tithe—App. 668*l* 12*s* 5*d* and 18¾ acres of Glebe, V. 570*l* 12*s* 2*d*; Glebe, 13½ acres; V.'s Inc. 600*l* and Ho; Pop. 830.) Formerly C. of St. John's, Holloway, 1842–44. Author, *A Visitation Sermon*, 1845; and other Sermons; *Enquiry into the Doctrine of the Church of England on Private Confession and Absolution*, 1859; *The North Side of the Table, an Examination of certain modern interpretations of the Rubrics*, Parkers. [21]

ELLIOTT, Edward Bishop, *Lewes-crescent, Brighton.*—Trin. Coll. Cam. 4th Sen. Opt. and B.A. 1816, M.A. 1819, Seatonian Prizeman 1820 and 1822; Deac. 1821 by Bp of Ely, Pr. 1822 by Bp of Nor. Preb. of Hill Deverill in Heytesbury Coll. Ch. 1826; Min. of St. Mark's Chapel, Kemptown, Brighton, Dio. Chich. 1853. (Patrons, Trustees of St. Mary's Hall; Min.'s Inc. 500*l*.) Formerly Fell. of Trin. Coll. Cam. 1817–24; V. of Tuxford, Notts, 1824–40. Author, *Sermons*, 1838; *Horæ Apocalypticæ*, 1st ed. 3 vols. 1844, 5th ed. 4 vols. 1862; *Vindiciæ Horariæ*, 1848; *Replies to Arnold and Candlish*; *Seatonian Prize Poems*; *Warburton Lectures for 1849–53*, 1856; various Sermons and Pamphlets. Editor, *Memoir of Lord Haddo, 5th Earl of Aberdeen*, 1867. [22]

ELLIOTT, Edward King, *Broadwater Rectory, Worthing.*—Trin. Coll. Cam. 8th Sen. Opt. B.A. 1852, M.A. 1856; Deac. 1852, Pr. 1853. R. of Broadwater, Dio. Chich. 1853. (Patron, the present R; Tithe, 800*l*; Glebe, 40 acres; R.'s Inc. 850*l* and Ho; Pop. 3246.) Assoc. Sec. for Irish Ch. Mission in West Sussex. Author, *A Visit to the Scenes of the Irish Revival*, 1*s* 6*d*; etc. [1]

ELLIOTT, George, *Church House, Merton, S.*—Univ. and King's Colls. Lond. B.A. and Theol. Assoc; Deac. 1866 by Bp of Win. C. of Merton; Prin. of Merton Coll. [2]

ELLIOTT, James, *Pitminster Lodge, Taunton.*—Corpus Coll. Cam. B.A. 1830, M.A. 1833; Deac. 1830 by Bp of Lich. Pr. 1831 by Bp of Chich. [3]

ELLIOTT, John, *Randwick Parsonage, Stroud.*—St. Edm. Hall, Ox. B.A. 1818, M.A. 1821; Deac. and Pr. 1818 by Bp of Glouc. P. C. of Randwick, Dio. G. and B. 1819. (Patron, V. of Standish; Tithe—Imp. 88*l*, P. C. 72*l*; Glebe, 55 acres; P. C.'s Inc. 150*l* and Ho; Pop. 645.) [4]

ELLIOTT, John, *Rockbeare, Devonshire.* [5]

ELLIOTT, Joseph Davenport, *Hendford, Yeovil.*—P. C. of Hendford, Dio. B. and W. 1854. (Patrons, the Crown and Bp of B. and W. alt; P. C.'s Inc. 150*l*; Pop. 3997.) [6]

ELLIOTT, Julius Marshall, *Brighton.*—P. C. of St. Mary's, Brighton, Dio. Chich. 1866. (Patron, the present P. C; P. C.'s Inc. 100*l*.) [7]

ELLIOTT, William, *Tranmere, Bebington, Birkenhead.*—P. C. of St. Catherine's, Tranmere, Dio. Ches. 1860. (Patron, R. of Bebington; P. C.'s Inc. 150*l* and Ho; Pop. 5672.) Formerly R. of All Saints', Worcester, 1834–60. [8]

ELLIOTT, William Foster, *East Dulwich, S.E.*—St. Bees; M.A. by Abp of Cant. 1866; Deac. 1846 and Pr. 1847 by Bp of Ches. P. C. of St. John's, East Dulwich, Dio. Win. 1865. (Patrons, Trustees; P. C.'s Inc. 600*l* and Ho; Pop. 2000.) Formerly C. of Whitewell, 1846, Ch. Ch. Bolton, 1847, Cranfield, Beds, 1848–58; Min. of East Dulwich Chapel 1858–65. [9]

ELLIS, Alfred B., *Woore, near Market Drayton.*—P. C. of Woore, Dio. Lich. 1865. (Patron, G. Kenrick, Esq; P. C.'s Inc. 96*l* and Ho; Pop. 839.) [10]

ELLIS, Arthur, *Llangwyllog, Llangefni, Anglesey.*—Dub. A.B. 1838; Deac. 1838 and Pr. 1839 by Bp of Ban. P. C. of Llangwyllog, Dio. Ban. 1850. (Patron, Sir R. W. B. Bulkeley, Bart; Tithe, Imp. 110*l*; P. C.'s Inc. 150*l* and Ho; Pop. 207.) C. of Coedana. [11]

ELLIS, Arthur Ayres, *Stotfold Vicarage, Baldock.*—Trin. Coll. Cam. Fell. 1854, Jun. Opt. in Math. 1st cl. Cl. and Moral Trip. Whewell's Moral Phil. Prizeman, Carus Prizeman, B.A. 1852, M.A. 1855; Deac. 1855 and Pr. 1856 by Bp of Man. V. of Stotfold, Dio. Ely, 1860. (Patron, Trin. Coll. Cam; V.'s Inc. 242*l* and Ho; Pop. 2071.) Formerly Sen. Cl. Mast. Liverpool Coll. 1853–57; Jun. Dean of Trin. Coll. Cam. and Divinity Lect. in Ch. Coll. 1859–60. Author, *Bentleii Critica Sacra*, 1862. [12]

ELLIS, Conyngham, *Cranbourne Vicarage, Windsor.*—Dub. A.B. 1838, A.M. 1841; Deac. 1849 and Pr. 1850 by Bp of Ox. V. of Cranbourne St. Peter, Dio. Ox. 1850. (Patron, Bp of Ox; Glebe, 10 acres; V.'s Inc. 130*l* and Ho; Pop. 900.) Formerly C. of Holy Trinity, Sunningdale, 1849. Author, *Weekly Communion*, 1862; *From the Font to the Altar*, 1863. [13]

ELLIS, David Henry, *Roydon, Lynn, Norfolk.*—C. of Roydon. [14]

ELLIS, Edmund, *Wimborne, Dorset.* [15]

ELLIS, Edward, *Wharram-in-the-Street, New Malton, Yorks.*—V. of Wharram-in-the-Street, Dio. York, 1832. (Patron, Lord Middleton; Tithe, 157*l* 10*s*; Glebe, 3 acres; V.'s Inc. 162*l*; Pop. 140.) [16]

ELLIS, Edward, *Leamington.*—Assoc. Sec. to Irish Church Missions; R. of Oranmore, Ireland. [17]

ELLIS, Edward Chauncy, *Langham Rectory, Colchester.*—Trin. Coll. Cam. B.A. 1832, M.A. 1835; Deac. 1836, Pr. 1836. R. of Langham, Dio. Roch. 1847. (Patron, Duchy of Lancaster; Tithe, comm. 640*l*; Glebe, 68 acres; R.'s Inc. 692*l* and Ho; Pop. 862.) Surrogate. Formerly C. of White Colne, Essex, 1835; V. of Dedham, Essex, 1839. [18]

ELLIS, James Francis, *Pocklington Vicarage, Yorks.*—Literate; Deac. 1832 and Pr. 1833 by Abp of York. V. of Pocklington with Yapham C. Ousethorpe C. and Meltonby C. Dio. York, 1840. (Patron, Abp of York; Tithe—App. 436*l*, V. 52*l* 3*s* 6*d*; V.'s Inc. 107*l* and Ho; Pop. 2688.) [19]

ELLIS, John, *Ebberston Vicarage, Heslerton, York.*—St. Bees; Deac. and Pr. 1829 by Abp of York. V. of Ebberston with Allerston C. Dio. York, 1836. (Patron, Abp of York; V.'s Inc. 445*l* and Ho; Pop. Ebberston 572, Allerston 413.) Formerly C. of Seainton 1829, Barton-le-street 1830, Snaith, with Gr. Sch. 1833. Author, *A Sermon preached at Snaith before the Society of Odd Fellows*, 1836, 1*s*; *An Abridgment of Murray's Grammar, in Question and Answer*, 1837, 1*s*; *A Sermon before the Odd Fellows at Ebberston*, 1840, 1*s*; *A Sermon on the Hartley Pit Disaster*, 1862; *A Sermon on the Lancashire Distress*, 1862. [20]

ELLIS, John, *St. Eval Vicarage, St. Columb, Cornwall.*—V. of St. Eval, Dio. Ex. 1865. (Patron, Bp of Ex; V.'s Inc. 180*l* and Ho; Pop. 295.) [21]

ELLIS, John, *Weymouth.*—St. John's Coll. Cam. Scho. 7th Sen. Opt. and B.A. 1852, M.A. 1855; Deac. 1852 and Pr. 1853 by Bp of Salis. Head Mast. of the Weymouth Gr. Sch. 1863. Formerly Asst Mast. Marlborough Coll. 1852–56; Head Mast. of the Cathl. Gr. Sch. Salisbury, 1856–63. [22]

ELLIS, John Clough Williams, *Sidney-Sussex College, Cambridge.*—Sid. Coll. Cam. 3rd Wrang. B.A. 1856, M.A. 1859; Deac. 1858 by Bp of Ely. Fell. and Tut. of Sid. Coll. Cam; V. of Madingley, Dio. Ely, 1865. (Patron, Bp of Ely; Glebe, 9 acres; V.'s Inc. 120*l*; Pop. 279.) [23]

ELLIS, John Henry, *Brill Parsonage, Thame.*—Trin. Coll. Cam. Sen. Opt. B.A. 1862, M.A. 1865; Deac. 1863 and Pr. 1864 by Abp of Cant. P. C. of Brill with Boarstall, Dio. Ox. 1866. (Patroness, Mrs. Ricketts; P. C.'s Inc. 105*l* and Ho; Pop. Brill 1450, Boarstall 230.) Formerly C. of Lyminge, Kent, 1863–65, Leyton, Essex, 1866. [24]

ELLIS, John Joseph, *Hangleton, Portslade, Sussex.*—C. of Hangleton, and St. Andrew's, Portslade. [25]

ELLIS, John Rathbone, *Westerdale Vicarage, Yarm, York.*—St. Aidan's; Deac. and Pr. 1852 by Abp of York. V. of Westerdale, Dio. York, 1858. (Patron, Abp of York; V.'s Inc. 276*l* and Ho; Pop. 279.) Formerly C. of Westerdale 1852–58. Author, *Lectures on the History of the English Bible*; occasional Sermons. [26]

ELLIS, John Smith, *Wilton-le-Wear, Bishop's Auckland, Durham.*—St. Cath. Coll. Cam. B.A. 1836; Deac. 1836 by Abp of Cant. Pr. 1837 by Abp of York. P. C. of Wilton-le-Wear, Dio. Dur. 1860. (Patron, H. Chaytor, Esq. and Crown alt; P. C.'s Inc. 300*l* and Ho; Pop. 1366.) Formerly V. of Llantrisent with Pertholey V. 1857. [27]

ELLIS, John Williams, *Glasfryn, Pwllheli, Carnarvonshire.*—St. John's Coll. Cam. B.A. 1831; Deac. 1836 and Pr. 1837 by Bp of Ban. R. of Llanaelhairn, near Pwllheli, Dio. Ban. 1844. (Patron, Bp of Ban; Tithe, 195*l*; R.'s Inc. 220*l*; Pop. 736.) [28]

ELLIS, Joseph, *Wilsden Parsonage, Bingley.*—St. John's Coll. Cam. B.A. 1858; Deac. 1858 and Pr. 1859 by Bp of Rip. P. C. of Wilsden with Allerton, Dio. Rip. 1865. (Patron, V. of Bradford; P. C.'s Inc. 150*l* and Ho; Pop. 6000.) [29]

ELLIS, Philip Constable, *Rectory, Llanfairfechan, Bangor.*—Jesus Coll. Ox. B.A. 1843, M.A. 1845; Deac. 1846 and Pr. 1847 by Bp of Ban. R. of Llanfairfechan, Dio. Ban. 1862. (Patron, Bp of Ban; Tithe, comm. 360*l*; Glebe, 9 acres; R.'s Inc. 419*l* 5*s* and Ho; Pop. 1199.) Rural Dean; Exam. Chap. to Bp of Ban. Formerly C. of Holyhead 1847–50; P. C. of Llanfaes and Penmon 1850–62. Author, *Letters to a Dissenting Minister*; and *Three Sermons.* [30]

ELLIS, Robert, *Birdsall, New Malton, Yorks.*—P. C. of Birdsall, Dio. York, 1831. (Patron, Marquis of

Hertford; Tithe—Imp. 672*l* and 542 acres of Glebe; P. C.'s Inc. 40*l*; Pop. 355.) V. of Wharram-Percy, New Malton, Yorks, Dio. York, 1832. (Patron, Lord Middleton; Tithe, Imp. 96*l*; V.'s Inc. 60*l*; Pop. 484.) P. C. of Acaster-Malbis, Dio. York, 1819. (Patron, F. Lawley, Esq; P. C.'s Inc. 66*l*; Pop. 270.) [1]

ELLIS, Robert, *St. John's College, Cambridge.*—St. John's Coll. Cam. B.A. 1840, M.A. 1843. Sen. Fell. of St. John's Coll. Cam. [2]

ELLIS, R. S., *Copenhagen.*—British Chap. at Copenhagen. [3]

ELLIS, Rowland, *Gresford, Wrexham.*—Jesus Coll. Ox. B.A. 1863; Deac. 1864 and Pr. 1865 by Bp of St. A. C. of Gresford 1864. [4]

ELLIS, Samuel Adcock, *Long Itchington Vicarage, Rugby.*—St. John's Coll. Cam. Sen. Opt. B.A. 1838, M.A. 1841; Deac. 1841 by Bp. of Lich. Pr. 1842 by Bp of Ex. V. of Long Itchington, Dio. Wor. 1864. (Patrons, I. D. Ellis, Esq. and Lord Leigh; Tithe, 14*l* 18*s*; Glebe, 120 acres; V.'s Inc. 280*l* and Ho; Pop. 1150.) Formerly C. of Teigngrace, Devon, 1841–42; P. C. of St. Ives 1843–50; Mast. in Cheltenham Coll. 1850–64. [5]

ELLIS, Thomas Roberts, *Conway, Carnarvonshire.*—Dub. A.B. 1836; Deac. 1838, Pr. 1839. R. of Gyffin, Dio. Ban. 1852. (Patron, Bp of Ban; Tithe, 386*l*; Glebe, 10 acres; R.'s Inc. 386*l* and Ho; Pop. 715.) Formerly C. of Caerhun 1838–52. [6]

ELLIS, William.—Queen's Coll. Birmingham; Deac. 1861, Pr. 1862. C. of St. Mathias', Bethnal Green. Formerly C. of Ashby Magna 1863, St. Matthew's, Rugby, 1861. [7]

ELLIS, The Hon. William Charles, *Sheepwash, Morpeth.*—Ball. Coll. Ox. B.A. 1858, M.A. 1860, 2nd cl. in Law and Mod. Hist; Deac. 1859 and Pr. 1860 by Bp of Man. R. of Bothal with Sheepwash R. and Hebburn Chap. Dio. Dur. 1861. (Patron, Duke of Portland; Tithe, 1357*l*; Glebe, 106 acres; R.'s Inc. 1477*l* and Ho; Pop. 1828.) Formerly C. of Prestwich 1859–62. [8]

ELLIS, William Webb, *Laver Magdalen, Chipping Ongar, Essex.*—Brasen. Coll. Ox. B.A. 1829, M.A. 1831. R. of Laver Magdalen, Dio. Roch. 1855. (Patron, Rev. S. C. Mason; Tithe, 310*l*; R.'s Inc. 315*l*; Pop. 213.) Formerly Min. of St. George's, Albemarle-st., Lond. [9]

ELLISON, Charles Christopher, *Bracebridge Vicarage, Lincoln.*—Trin. Coll. Cam. B.A. 1857, M.A. 1860; Deac. 1858 and Pr. 1859 by Bp of Lin. V. of Bracebridge, Dio. Lin. 1863. (Patron, present V; Tithe, Imp. 153*l* 19*s* 5*d*, V. 258*l* 4*s* 6*d*; V.'s Inc. 290*l* and Ho; Pop. 836.) C. of Boultham 1862. Formerly C. of Newark 1858-60, Wrawby 1862. [10]

ELLISON, Henry, *Melsonby Rectory, Darlington.*—Univ. Coll. Ox. 2nd cl. Lit. Hum. and B.A. 1842, M.A. 1844; Deac. 1844, Pr. 1846. R. of Melsonby, Dio. Rip. 1852. (Patron, Univ. Coll. Ox; Tithe—Imp. 9*l* 6*s* 6*d*, R. 716*l* 14*s* 9*d*; Glebe, 94 acres; R.'s Inc. 817*l* and Ho; Pop. 471.) Formerly Fell. of Univ. Coll. Ox. [11]

ELLISON, Henry John, *Windsor.*—Trin. Coll. Cam. Jun. Opt. 3rd cl. Cl. Trip. B.A. 1835, M.A. 1838; Deac. 1838 and Pr. 1839 by Bp of Ely. V. of New Windsor, Dio. Ox. 1855. (Patron, Ld. Chan; Tithe—App. 693*l* 6*s* 11*d*, Imp 103*l*, V. 394*l* 9*s* 7*d*; V.'s Inc. 930*l* and Ho; Pop. 6728.) Chap. to the Duke of Devonshire; Preb. of Lich. 1854; Reader to the Queen at Windsor Castle, 1856. Formerly P. C. of All Souls', Brighton, 1840–43; V. of Edensor, Derbyshire, 1845–55. Author, *Sermons on Married Life*, 2nd ed. Rivingtons, 1859, 2*s* 6*d*; *The Temperance Reformation Movement in the Church of England*, 2nd ed. Partridge, 1*s*; etc. [12]

ELLISON, John, *Sowerby Bridge, Halifax.*—St. Bees 1850; M.A. 1860; Deac. 1852 and Pr. 1853 by Bp of Ches. P. C. of Sowerby Bridge, Dio. Rip. 1863. (Patron, V. of Halifax; P. C.'s Inc. 300*l* and Ho; Pop. 7000.) Surrogate. Formerly Chap. to the New Farnley Iron Company 1857; C. of St. Bartholomew's, Liverpool, 1852–53; Sen. C. of Wellingborough 1853–57. Author, *Life of Moses and Journeys of Israel*, 4 eds. 1*s* 6*d*; *Sermons for Children*, 1*s* 6*d*; *Children's Prayers*; various Tracts on the Bible and the Church. [13]

ELLISON, J., Chap. to Railway Labourers in the North of London. [14]

ELLISON, Joseph Rowland, *Collyhurst, Manchester.*—Literate; Deac. 1856 and Pr. 1857 by Bp of Lich. R. of the Albert Memorial Church, Manchester, 1864. Formerly C. of Longnor, Salop, 1856, North Meols, Lanc. 1859, St. George's, Manchester, 1861. Author, *The Penny Hymn-Book and Liturgy for Sunday Schools.* [15]

ELLISON, William, *Bishop's Cleeve, Cheltenham.*—Dub. A.B. 1847; Deac. 1847 by Bp of Ches. Pr. 1851 by Bp of G. and B. C. of Bishop's Cleeve 1859. Formerly Sen. C. of Stroud. [16]

ELLISON, William John, *Gottenburg, Sweden.*—Wad. Coll. Ox. B.A. 1849. Chap. to the English Residents at Gottenburg. Formerly C. of All Saints', Fulham. [17]

ELLISS, Henry Christopher, *St. Saviour's, Nottingham.*—St. Aidan's; Deac. 1859 and Pr. 1860 by Abp of York. P. C. of St. Saviour's, Nottingham, Dio. Lin. 1865. (Patrons, Trustees; P. C.'s Inc. 300*l* and Ho; Pop. 6000.) Formerly C. of Thorganby 1859, St. Mary's, Nottingham, 1862. [18]

ELLMAN, Edward Boys, *Berwick Rectory, Lewes, Sussex.*—Wad. Coll. Ox. 1st cl. Math. et. Phy. 4th cl. Lit. Hum. and B.A. 1837, M.A. 1840; Deac. 1838 by Bp of Lin. Pr. 1840 by Bp of Chich. R. of Berwick, Dio. Chich. 1846. (Patrons, Trustees; Tithe, 387*l* 10*s*; Glebe, 31 acres; R.'s Inc. 430*l* and Ho; Pop. 169.) Formerly C. of Berwick 1838–44; V. of Wartling 1844–46. [19]

ELLWOOD, Robert G., *Thornbury, Gloucestershire.*—C. of Thornbury. [20]

ELLWOOD, Thomas, *Torver, Coniston, Lancashire.*—St. Bees 1860; Deac. 1861 and Pr. 1862 by Bp of Carl. P. C. of Torver, Dio. Carl. 1864. (Patron, disputed; Glebe, 5*l*; P. C.'s Inc. 59*l*; Pop. 200.) Formerly C. of Torver; Mast. in the Gr. Sch. St. Bees. [21]

ELLWOOD, William, *Hargrave, Chester.*—Chap. of Don. of Hargrave, Dio. Ches. 1839. (Patrons, Trustees; Chap's Inc. 100*l*.) [22]

ELMER, Frederick, *Golden Hill, Stoke-upon-Trent.*—St. Bees; Deac. 1852 and Pr. 1853 by Abp of York. P. C. of Golden Hill, Dio. Lich. 1858. (Patron, Bp of Lich; P. C.'s Inc. 203*l*; Pop. 2675.) Formerly P. C. of St. Paul's, Over Tabley, Cheshire. [23]

ELMHIRST, Edward, *Shawell Rectory, Rugby.* Trin. Coll. Cam. B.A. 1835; Deac. 1835, Pr. 1836. R. of Shawell, Dio. Pet. 1841. (Patron. Ld Chan; Tithe, 359*l*; Glebe, 70 acres; R.'s Inc. 450*l* and Ho; Pop. 205.) J.P. for the County of Leicester. [24]

ELMHIRST, R., *Brearton, near Knaresborough.* P. C. of Brearton, Dio. Rip. 1866. (Patron, V. of Knaresborough; P. C.'s Inc. 100*l*; Pop. 275.) [25]

ELMHIRST, William, *Elmhirst, near Barnsley.*—Trin. Coll. Ox. B.A. 1849, M.A. 1853; Deac. 1850 and Pr. 1851 by Bp of Lin. Chap. of Don. of Stainborough 1862. (Patron, F. W. T. Vernon Wentworth, Esq; Glebe, 80 acres; Chap.'s Inc. 80*l*; Pop. 471.) Formerly C. of Gainsborough 1850-60, Wigtoft and Quadring 1860–62. [26]

ELRINGTON, Charles Richard, *Roydon Rectory, Diss.*—Dub. A.B. 1850, A.M. 1865; Deac. 1851 by Bp of Pet. Pr. 1853 by Bp of B. and W. R. of Roydon, Dio Nor. 1859. (Patron, George Edward Frere, Esq; Tithe, 456*l*; Glebe, 46 acres; R.'s Inc. 506*l* and Ho; Pop. 619.) Formerly C. of Wellingborough 1851–52, Stokecourcy, Somerset, 1853–59. [27]

ELRINGTON, Robert Bisset Fenwick, *The Vicarage, Lower Brixham, Devon.*—Dub. A.B. 1846, A.M. 1859; Deac. 1848 and Pr. 1849 by Bp of Pet. V. of Lower Brixham, Dio. Ex. 1855. (Patron, the Crown; Glebe, 8 acres; V.'s Inc. 280*l* and Ho; Pop. 4586.) Surrogate. Formerly C. of Finedon, Northants, 1849, Stokecourcy, Somerset, 1855. [28]

ELRINGTON, Thomas William, *Saling Vicarage, Braintree, Essex.*—Dur. Licen. Theol. 1850; Deac. 1850 and Pr. 1851 by Bp of Ox. V. of Great Saling, Dio. Roch. 1856. (Patron, Wm. Villiers Fowke, Esq; Tithe—V. 142*l*, 35*l* to V. of Felstead, 34*l* 4*s* to Guy's Hospital, and 305*l* 18*s* Imp; Glebe, 7¾ acres; V.'s Inc. 148*l* and Ho; Pop. 361.) [1]

ELRINGTON, William Frederick, *Great Haywood, Stafford.*—Dub. A.B. and St. Bees; Deac. 1851, Pr. 1852. P. C. of Great Haywood, Dio. Lich. 1854. (Patron, Earl of Lichfield; P. C.'s Inc. 110*l* and Ho; Pop. 904.) [2]

ELSDALE, Daniel, 96, *Lothian-road, Camberwell New-road, S.*—Brasen. Coll. Ox. B.A. 1860, M.A. 1862; Deac. 1860 and Pr. 1861 by Bp of Lin. Missionary C. of St. John's District, Kennington, 1867. Formerly C. of Great Grimsby 1862–64; Chap. of Cuddesdon Theol. Coll. 1864–66. [3]

ELSE, John Edward, *Twywell Rectory, Thrapstone, Northants.*—Dub. A.B. 1852, A.M. 1854; Deac. 1854, Pr. 1855. V. of Slipton, Dio. Pet. 1860. (Patrons, W. B. Stopford, Esq. and Mrs. Stopford; Glebe, 107 acres; V.'s Inc. 107*l*; Pop. 144.) C. of Twywell 1854. Formerly C. of The Harrowdens, Northants, 1854. [4]

ELSEE, Charles, *Rugby.*—Asst. Mast. Rugby Sch. [5]

ELSWORTH, J. W., *Bowling, Bradford, Yorks.*—C. of St. John's, Bowling. [6]

ELTON, Charles Allen, *Holt, Norfolk.*—Sid. Coll. Cam. Blundell Fell. and Lect. B.A. 1843, M.A. 1846, B.D. 1853; Deac. 1846 by Bp of Ely, Pr. 1848 by Bp of Ex. Head Mast. of the Gresham Gr. Sch. Holt, 1858. Formerly C. of Willingham, Hunts, 1852–58; Blundell Fell. of Sid. Coll. Cam. [7]

ELTON, Edward, *Wheatley Parsonage, Oxon.*—Ball. Coll. Ox. Hon. 4th cl. Lit. Hum. and B.A. 1837, M.A. 1841; Deac. 1839 by Bp of Ex. Pr. 1841 by Bp of Salis. P. C. of Wheatley, Dio. Ox. 1849. (Patron, Bp of Ox; Glebe, 55 acres; P. C.'s Inc. 260*l* and Ho; Pop. 1031.) Formerly C. of Erchfont and Stanton St. Bernard, Wilts, 1839–47, Bierton with Buckland and Stoke Mandeville, Bucks, 1847–51. [8]

ELTON, George, *Iver Heath, Uxbridge.*—King's Coll. Lond. Theol. Assoc; Deac. 1853 and Pr. 1854 by Bp of Lich. P. C. of St. Margaret's, Iver Heath, Dio. Ox. 1862. (Patron, C. Meeking, Esq; P. C.'s Inc. 100*l* and Ho; Pop. 575.) Formerly C. of Winford, Bristol, and Audley, Staffs. [9]

ELTON, Henry George Tierney, *Downham, near Ely.*—Literate; Deac. 1853 by Bp of Ox. Pr. 1854 by Bp of B. and W. C. of Downham. Formerly C. of Farnham, Dorset. [10]

ELTON, William Tierney, *White Stanton, Chard, Somerset.*—Wor. Coll. Ox. B.A. 1825; Deac. 1826 and Pr. 1827 by Bp of B. and W. R. of White Stanton, Dio. B. and W. 1827. (Patron, Isaac Elton, Esq; Tithe, 222*l*; Glebe, 51 acres; R.'s Inc. 280*l*; Pop. 259.) [11]

ELVY, John Miller, *Manchester.*—St. Peter's Coll. Cam. B.A. 1856, M.A. 1860; Deac. 1857, Pr. 1858. C. of the Cathl. Manchester. Formerly C. of St. Mary's Platt, 1857, St. Andrew's, Ancoats, 1861. [12]

ELWELL, Alfred Odell, *Long Ashton, near Bristol.*—Wor. Coll. Ox. B.A. 1857, M.A. 1860; Deac. 1858 and Pr. 1860 by Bp of G. and B. C. of Long Ashton 1866. Formerly C. of Sherborne with Windrush, Glouc. 1858–63, Redmarley d'Abitot, Worc. 1863–66. [13]

ELWELL, William Edward, *Dauntsey Rectory, Malmesbury.*—Univ. Coll. Ox. 3rd cl. Lit. Hum. and B.A. 1832, M.A. 1834; Deac. 1834 and Pr. 1835 by Bp of Lich. R. of Dauntsey, Dio. G. and B. 1859. (Patron, the present R; R.'s Inc. 344*l* and Ho; Pop. 578.) Formerly C. of Terrington, Norfolk. [14]

ELWES, Frederick, *Wixoe, near Halstead, Essex.*—R. of Wixoe, Dio. Ely, 1831. (Patron, J. E. H. Elwes, Esq; Tithe, 200*l*; R.'s Inc. 233*l* 15*s* and Ho; Pop. 145.) Sinecure R. (1846) and V. (1849) of Gestingthorpe, Essex, Dio. Roch. (Patron, J. E. H. Elwes, Esq; Rectorial rent charge, 520*l*, Vicarial 183*l*; Pop. 769.) [15]

ELWIN, Fountain, *Walcot-parade, Bath.*—St. Edm. Hall, Ox. B.A. 1809; Deac. 1810 by Bp of Bristol, Pr. 1811 by Bp of Salis. V. of Temple Church, Bristol, Dio. G. and B. 1816. (Patrons, J. S. Harford, Esq. and others; V.'s Inc. 300*l*; Pop. 5592.) Formerly Min. of Octagon Chapel, Bath. Author, *Practical Sermons*, 2 vols. 5*s* each; *Lectures on Gideon*, 4*s*; *Lectures on Ephraim*, 4*s*; occasional Sermons. [16]

ELWIN, George, *Mitcham, Surrey, S.*—Corpus Coll. Ox. 1st cl. Law and Modern History, B.A. 1860; Deac. 1861 and Pr. 1862 by Bp of Win. C. of Mitcham 1865. Formerly C. of St. Michael's, Winchester, 1861. [17]

ELWIN, George Saunders, *Folkestone.*—St. Cath. Hall, Cam. B.A. 1836, M.A. 1839; Deac. 1837, Pr. 1838. R. of Hawkinge, Kent, Dio. Cant. 1851. (Patron, Abp of Cant; Tithe, 138*l*; R.'s Inc. 140*l*; Pop. 133.) [18]

ELWIN, Peter James, *Itteringham, Aylsham, Norfolk.*—Deac. 1849, Pr. 1850. R. of Itteringham with Mannington R. Dio. Nor. 1856. (Patron, Earl of Orford; Itteringham, Tithe, 351*l* 10*s*; Glebe, 25 acres; Mannington, Tithe, 5*l* 5*s*; R.'s Inc. 378*l*; Pop. 370.) Formerly C. of Itteringham. [19]

ELWIN, Whitwell, *Booton Rectory, Norwich.*—Caius Coll. Cam. B.A. 1839; Deac. 1839 and Pr. 1840 by Bp of B. and W. R. of Booton, Dio. Nor. 1849. (Patron, H. Elwin, Esq; Tithe, 294*l* 10*s*; Glebe, 23 acres; R.'s Inc. 323*l* and Ho; Pop. 246.) [20]

ELWYN, Richard, *Clifton, near York.*—Trin. Coll. Cam. Fell. 1850, Bell and Craven Scho. Members' Prizeman, B.A. 1849, M.A. 1852; Deac. 1858 and Pr. 1859 by Bp of Lon. Head Mast. of St. Peter's Sch. Clifton. Formerly 2nd Mast. of Charterhouse Sch. 1855; Head Mast. of same 1858–63. [21]

ELWYN, William Maundy Harvey, *Waresley Vicarage, Hunts.*—Pemb. Coll. Cam. 17th Wrang. and B.A. 1837, M.A. 1840; Deac. 1840 and Pr. 1841 by Bp of Ely. V. of Waresley, Dio. Ely, 1848. (Patron, Pemb. Coll. Cam; Tithe—Imp. 362*l*, V. 188*l*; Glebe, 98 acres; V.'s Inc. 308*l* and Ho; Pop. 292.) [22]

ELY, The Right Rev. Edward Harold BROWNE, Lord Bishop of Ely, *Ely House, Dover-street, London, W.* and *The Palace, Ely.*—Emman. Coll. Cam. Wrang. Crosse Theol. Scho. 1st Tyrwhitt Heb. Scho. Norrisian Prize, B.A. 1832, M.A. 1835, B.D. 1855, D.D. 1864; Deac. 1836 and Pr. 1837 by Bp of Ely. Consecrated Bp of Ely 1864. (Income of See, 5500*l*; Episcopal Jurisdiction, the counties of Bedford, Cambridge and Huntingdon, and part of Suffolk; Pop. 480,716; Acres, 1,357,765; Deaneries, 26; Benefices, 531.) His Lordship is Visitor of St. Peter's, Jesus and St. John's Colls. and Visitor to the Master of Trinity Coll. Cam. His Lordship was Formerly Fell. and Tut. of Emman. Coll. 1837; P. C. of St. Sidwell's, Exeter, 1841; Vice-Prin. and Prof. of Hebrew at St. David's Coll. Lampeter, 1843; Preb. of St. David's 1848; V. of Kenwyn and Preb. of Exeter 1849; Norrisian Prof. of Divinity at Cambridge 1854; V. of Heavitree 1857; Can. of Exeter 1857. Author, *An Exposition of the XXXIX. Articles*, 2 vols. 1850–53, 22*s* 6*d*, 7th ed. in one vol. 1866, 16*s*; *Sermons on the Atonement and Other Subjects*, 1859, 5*s*; *Messiah Foretold and Expected*, 1862, 4*s*; *The Pentateuch and the Elohistic Psalms in Reply to Bishop Colenso*, 1863, 2*s*; Contributions to *Aids to Faith*, Smith's *Dictionary of the Bible*, and various Sermons and Pamphlets. [23]

ELY, Anthony, *Whitminster, Stonehouse, Glouc.*—St. John's Coll. Cam. B.A. 1827; Deac. 1827 and Pr. 1828 by Bp of Lich. P. C. of Wheatenhurst, *alias* Whitminster, Dio G. and B. 1834. (Patron, John Bengough, Esq; P. C.'s Inc. 142*l*; Pop. 409.) Surrogate 1854. Formerly C. of Blymhill, Staffs, 1827–29, St. Michael's, Gloucester, 1829–33, Abenhall 1833–34. [24]

ELY, Edwyn Anthony, *Gloucester.*—St. John's Coll. Cam. B.A. 1861; Deac. 1863 and Pr. 1864 by Bp of Lich. R. of Lassington, Dio. G. and B. 1867. (Patrons, Sir William V. Guise, Bart. 2 turns and Bp of G. and B. one turn; Tithe, 119*l*; Glebe, 6½ acres; R.'s Inc. 130*l*;

Pop. 72.) Formerly C. of North Harborne 1863, St. Mary de Lode, Gloucester, 1866–67. [1]

EMERIS, John, *St. James's Parsonage, Gloucester.*—Univ. Coll. Ox. B.A. 1839, M.A. 1842; Deac. 1840 and Pr. 1841 by Bp of Lin. P. C. of St. James's, Gloucester, Dio. G. and B. 1848. (Patron, Bp of G. and B.; P. C.'s Inc. 180*l* and Ho; Pop. 5498.) [2]

EMERSON, Titus, *Allendale Rectory, Haydonbridge, Northumberland.*—Dur. Licen. Theol. 1850; Deac. 1850 and Pr. 1851 by Bp of Dur. R. of Allendale, Dio. Dur. 1853. (Patron, W. B. Beaumont, Esq; Tithe, 112*l* 3*s*; Glebe, 30 acres; R.'s Inc. 250*l* and Ho; Pop. 2400.) Formerly C. of Shildon, Durham, 1850, Madeley, Salop, 1852. [3]

EMERTON, James Alexander, *Hanwell College, Bishopstown, W.*—Magd. Hall, Ox. B.A. 1832, M.A. 1835, B.D. 1843, D.D. 1843; Deac. 1834, Pr. 1835. Formerly C. of Hanwell 1834–47; P. C. of New Brentford 1847. Author, *Five Sermons on Church Extension*, 5*s*; *The Discipline of the Church in the Choice of her Ministers* (a Sermon), 1*s*; *The National Education of the Poor* (two Sermons), 1*s*; *Hobbyn's Charity*, 1*s*; *Voluntary Tithes*; *On the Death of the Duke of Wellington*, 1*s*; *Peace, the Christian's Duty*, 1*s*; *A Letter to Lord John Russell on University Reform*, 1*s*; *A Presidential Address to the Members of the Hanwell Mutual Improvement Society*, 6*d*; *An Address on Higher and Middle-class Education* (written for the Social Science Congress, York); *The Public Schools Crib* (an Address on the inauguration of the Cobden Memorial); various other Sermons and Pamphlets. [4]

EMERY, The Ven. William, *Corpus Christi College, Cambridge.*—Corpus Coll. Cam. B.A. 1847, M.A. 1850; Deac. 1849, Pr. 1850. Sen. Fell. Bursar and Tut. of Corpus Coll. Cam; Archd. of Ely 1864. [5]

EMLY, Frederick Septimus, *Kirkby Underwood, Bourne, Lincolnshire.*—Wad. Coll. Ox. B.A. 1823, M.A. 1826; Deac. 1831 and Pr. 1832 by Bp of Pet. R. of Kirkby-Underwood, Dio. Lin. 1838. (Patron, Bp of Lin; Land in lieu of Tithe and Glebe, 200 acres; R.'s Inc. 210*l*; Pop. 189.) Chap. to the Folkingham Ho. of Correction. [6]

EMPSON, Arthur John, *Eydon Rectory, Banbury.*—Downing Coll. Cam. B.A. 1852, M.A. 1861; Deac. 1852 by Bp of Rip. Pr. 1853 by Bp of Pet. R. of Eydon, Dio. Pet. 1853. (Patron, Ld Chan; Tithe, 14*l*; Rent from Glebe, 400*l*; R.'s Inc. 414*l* and Ho; Pop. 575.) [7]

EMPSON, Chappell May, *Kennerleigh, Crediton, Devon.*—King's Coll. Lond. 1847; Deac. 1851 by Bp of Ex. Pr. 1854 by Bp of Lich. R. of Kennerleigh, Dio. Ex. 1860. (Patrons, Govs. of Crediton Charity; Tithe, 95*l*; Glebe, 40 acres; R.'s Inc. 145*l* and Ho; Pop. 106.) Formerly C. of St. Endellion and Gnosall; M.R.C.S.E., L.A.C. 1847–50. [8]

EMPSON, William Henry, *Wellow Vicarage, Romsey, Hants.*—Trin. Coll. Cam. B.A. 1840, M.A. 1844; Deac. 1841 and Pr. 1842 by Abp of York. V. of Wellow, Dio. Win. 1844. (Patron, W. E. Nightingale, Esq; Tithe—Imp. 320*l* 16*s* 4*d*, V. 245*l* 5*s*; Glebe, 26 acres; V.'s Inc. 268*l* and Ho; Pop. East Wellow 332, West Wellow 408.) [9]

EMRA, John, *Biddestone, Chippenham.*—Ball. Coll. Ox. B.A. 1828, M.A. 1831; Deac. 1830 and Pr. 1831 by Bp of G. and B. R. and V. of Biddestone with Slaughterford P. C. Dio. G. and B. 1864. (Patron, Win. Coll; Glebe, 4½ acres; R.'s Inc. 206*l* 7*s* 9*d* and Ho; Pop. Biddestone 441, Slaughterford 141.) Formerly P. C. of Redlynch, Dio. Salis. 1838–64. Author, *Prayers for the Pulpit*, 1838; *The Truth Spoken in Love* (a Sermon); *The Second Temple* (a Dramatic Poem), 1844. [10]

ENGLAND, James, *Queen's College, Liverpool.*—Prof. in Queen's College. [11]

ENGLAND, Thomas, *North Lew Rectory, Exbourne, Devon.*—Pemb. Coll. Cam. 1826, Prizeman 1828, 1st cl. Math. Trip. and B.A. 1830, M.A. 1833; Deac. 1831, Pr. 1832. R. of North Lew, Dio. Ex. 1847. (Patron, the Crown; Tithe, 370*l*; Glebe, 500 acres; R.'s Inc. 500*l* and Ho; Pop. 930.) [12]

ENGLEHEART, H., *Bedfont Lodge, Middlesex.* [13]

ENGLISH, John Francis Hawker, *Brentwood, Essex.*—Ch. Coll. Cam. LL.B. 1847, LL.D. 1853; Deac. 1847 and Pr. 1848 by Bp of Wor. P. C of Brentwood, Dio. Roch. 1854. (Patron, C. T. Tower, Esq; P. C.'s Inc. 130*l* and Ho; Pop. 3093.) Surrogate. [14]

ENGLISH, William, *Milton, Sittingbourne, Kent.*—V. of Milton, Dio. Cant. 1862. (Patrons, D. and C. of Cant; V.'s Inc. 400*l* and Ho; Pop. 2731.) Surrogate. Formerly V. of Broadway 1858–62; R. of 1st Mediety of Bradfield, Norfolk, 1855–58. [15]

ENGLISH, William Watson, *South Tawton Vicarage, Devon.*—Magd. Hall, Ox. and Univ. of Glasgow, M.A; Deac. 1860 and Pr. 1862 by Bp of Roch. C. in sole charge of South Tawton, Devon, 1864. Formerly C. of Laugharne, South Wales, and Abbot's Langley, Herts. Author, *Man Considered in respect of Freedom, Dependence, and a State of Probation, with Remarks on Romans* viii.-xi, 1863, 2*s*; *Infant Baptism practised in the Jewish Church, in the Times of the Apostles, and in all Ages of the Christian Church, with some Remarks on the Origin of the Sect of Anabaptists, and an Explanation and Defence of the Doctrinal Teaching of the Prayer Book*, 1864, 2nd ed. 4*d*; *The Church, what and how broad is it?—being Lectures on the Origin, Rationale and Breadth of the Church of God*, 1864, 2*s* 6*d*; *An Elementary Treatise on Moral Philosophy for Students, and specially adapted for use in Theological Colleges*, Rivingtons, 1865, 4*s* 6*d*; *On Miracles, their compatibility with philosophical principles* (reprinted from the *Journal of Transactions of the Victoria Institute*), 1866. [16]

ENGSTROM, Charles Robert Lloyd, *The Priory, Croydon, S.*—Pemb. Coll. Ox. B.A. 1866; Deac. 1866 by Abp of Cant. C. of Croydon 1866. [17]

ENRAGHT, Matthew, *Lyminster, Arundel.*—Dub. A.B. 1826, A.M. 1832; Deac. 1834 and Pr. 1835 by Abp of Armagh. V. of Lyminster, Dio. Chich. 1856. (Patron, Bp of Lon; Tithe—Imp. 375*l* and 5¾ acres of Glebe, V. 351*l* and ¾ acre of Glebe; V.'s Inc. 351*l* and Ho; Pop. 908.) Formerly P. C. of Nonington, Kent, 1852–56. [18]

ENRAGHT, Richard William, *Wrawby, Brigg, Lincolnshire.*—Dub. A.B. 1859; Deac. 1861 and Pr. 1862 by Bp of G. and B. C. of Wrawby. Formerly C. of Corsham, Wilts, 1861. [19]

ENSOR, Frederick, *Lustleigh, Newton Abbot, Devon.*—Downing Coll. Cam. B.A. 1838; Deac. 1838, Pr. 1840. R. of Lustleigh, Dio. Ex. 1847. (Patron, the present R; Tithe, 200*l*; Glebe, 36 acres; R.'s Inc. 236*l* and Ho; Pop. 322.) [20]

ERCK, John Caillard, 2, *Alma Villas, Bath.*—Dub. A.B. 1851, A.M. 1859; Deac. 1857 and Pr. 1859 by Bp of Ches. Min. of Octagon Chapel, Bath, 1865. Formerly C. of St. Jude's, Liverpool, 1857–59; P. C. of Kilbride, Bray, Ireland, 1859–61; C. of Octagon Chapel, Bath, 1864. Author, *Absolution—Apostolical and Ministerial*, Simpkin, Marshall and Co. 6*d*; *The Christian Altar* (a Sermon), 1866. [21]

ERLE, Christopher, *Hardwicke Rectory, Aylesbury.*—New Coll. Ox. B.A. 1812, M.A. 1815; Deac. 1818, Pr. 1819. R. of Hardwicke, Dio. Ox. 1833. (Patron, New Coll. Ox; Glebe, 477 acres; R.'s Inc. 735*l* and Ho; Pop. 708.) Formerly Fell. of New Coll. Ox. [22]

ERLE, Walter, *Gillingham, Shaftesbury.* [23]

ERRINGTON, John Launcelot, *Berechurch, Essex.*—Brasen. Coll. Ox. B.A. 1851; Deac. 1852, Pr. 1853. C. of Berechurch. Formerly C. of Ashbourne. [24]

ERRINGTON, John Richard, *Ashbourne Vicarage, Derbyshire.*—Wor. Coll. Ox. B.A. 1831, M.A. 1839. V. of Ashbourne with Mapleton R. Dio. Lich. 1850. (Patron, Bp of Lich; Ashbourne; Tithe—App. 622*l* 2*s* 6*d*, V. 41*l*; Mapleton, Tithe, 38*l* 16*s* 8*d*; V.'s Inc. 374*l* and Ho; Pop. Ashbourne 3860, Mapleton 185.) Rural Dean. [25]

ERSKINE, H. M., *Aspley Guise, Woburn, Beds.*—R. of Aspley Guise, Dio. Ely, 1865. (Patron, Duke of Bedford, R.'s Inc. 280*l* and Ho; Pop. 1437.) [26]

ERSKINE, John.—Dub. A.B. 1854, A.M. 1857; Deac. 1855 by Bp of Down and Connor, Pr. 1856 by Bp of Derry and Raphoe. Chap. of H.M.S. "Revenge." Formerly C. of St. Clement's, Bristol. [1]

ERSKINE, Thomas, *Alderley Rectory, Congleton.*—Trin. Coll. Cam. 2nd cl. Cl. Trip. B.A. 1851, M.A. 1854; Deac. 1852 and Pr. 1853 by Bp of Ox. R. of Alderley, Dio. Ches. 1864. (Patron, Lord Stanley of Alderley; Tithe, 750*l*; R.'s Inc. 750*l* and Ho; Pop. 1418.) Formerly C. of St. Mary's, Reading, 1852; R. of Steppingly, Beds, 1853–64. [2]

ESCHELBACH, Albert, *Dollar, Stirling, Scotland.*—Gottingen; Deac. 1865 by Bp of Dur. Pr. 1866 by Bp of Edinburgh. [3]

ESCOTT, Charles Sweet, *Tillingham, Maldon, Essex.*—Ex. Coll. Ox. B.A. 1832; Deac. 1833 by Bp of G. and B. Pr. 1834 by Bp of Win. V. of Tillingham, Dio. Roch. 1859. (Patrons, D. and C. of St. Paul's; V.'s Inc. 314*l* and Ho; Pop. 1040.) Formerly V. of Wednesbury 1855–59. [4]

ESCOTT, George Sweet, *Barnwood, Gloucester.*—Lin. Coll. Ox. B.A. 1828, M.A. 1831. V. of Barnwood, Dio. G. and B. 1844. (Patrons, D. and C. of Glouc; Tithe—App. 350*l*, V. 176*l*, Glebe, 1 rood; V.'s Inc. 177*l*; Pop. 507.) [5]

ESCOTT, Hay Sweet, *Somersetshire College, Bath.*—Ball. Coll. Ox. 3rd cl. Lit. Hum. and B.A. 1839, M.A. 1858; Deac. 1840, Pr. 1859. Head Mast. of Somersetshire Coll. Bath. Author, *Chief Events of Ancient History Synchronistically arranged*; *A Letter to a Friend in Doubt on Christian Evidences*, Bell and Daldy, 1860. [6]

ESCOTT, W. Sweet, *Carlton, Bedford.*—New Coll. Ox. Fell. of. R. of Carlton with Chellington R. Dio. Ely, 1863. (Patron, Lord Dynevor; R.'s Inc. 375*l*; Pop. Carlton 470, Chellington 136.) [7]

ESCOTT, William Sweet, *Great Barford, St. Neots.*—Dub. A.B. 1864; Deac. 1865 by Bp of Roch. Pr. 1865 by Bp of Ely. C. of Roxton with Barford Magna 1865. [8]

ESCREET, John, *Grosvenor-place, Clifton.*—Wor. Coll. Ox. B.A. 1848, M.A. 1852; Deac. 1849 and Pr. 1850 by Bp of Win. Formerly C. of St. Paul's, Herne Hill, 1849–51, St. Stephen's, Camden Town, 1851–54; Chap. to the Army in the Crimea. [9]

ESPIN, John, *Precincts, Rochester.*—Mert. Coll. Ox. Post Master of, Ox. 1st cl. Math. B.A. 1860, M.A. 1862; Deac. 1860 and Pr. 1862 by Bp of Lon. 2nd Mast. of Cathl. Sch. Rochester, 1863; Surrogate. Formerly 2nd Mast. of St. John's Foundation Sch. and Asst. C. of St. James's, Clapton, 1860–63. [10]

ESPIN, Thomas Espinell, *Hadleigh Rectory, Chelmsford.*—Lin. Coll. Ox. 1st cl. Lit. Hum. and B.A. 1846, M.A. and Fell. of Lin. Coll. 1849, Tut. of Lin. Coll. 1852, Denyer Theol. Prize Essayist 1852 and 1853, B.D. 1859; Select Preacher 1864 and 1865; Deac. 1849, Pr. 1850. R. of Hadleigh, Essex, Dio. Roch. 1853. (Patron, Lin. Coll. Ox; Tithe, 440*l*; Glebe, 70 acres; R.'s Inc. 458*l* and Ho; Pop. 451.) Prof. of Theol. Queen's Coll. Birmingham, 1853, and Warden of, 1865; Exam. Chap. to Bp of Ches; Rural Dean. Author, *Our Want of Clergy* (a Sermon), Parkers, 1863; *Critical Essays*, Rivingtons, 1864; etc. [11]

ESPINASSE, Richard, *Surbiton, Surrey.*—Ch. Ch. Ox. B.A. 1854, M.A. 1858; Deac. 1855 and Pr. 1856 by Bp of Roch. C. of Surbiton 1865. Formerly C. of Bishops Hatfield, Herts, 1855, Wickham Bishops, Essex, 1856–65. [12]

ESSINGTON, Robert William, *Shenstone Vicarage, Lichfield.*—King's Coll. Cam. B.A. 1841, M.A. 1844, Seatonian Prizeman 1846; Deac. 1842 and Pr. 1843 by Bp of Lin. V. of Shenstone, Dio. Lich. 1848. (Patron, the Rev. J. Peel, D.D; Tithe, 385*l*; Glebe, 37 acres; V.'s Inc. 440*l* and Ho; Pop. 1060.) Rural Dean. [13]

ESTCOURT, Edmund Hiley Bucknall, *Eckington Rectory, Chesterfield.*—Ball. Coll. Ox. B.A. 1825, Mert. Coll. Ox. M.A. 1827; Deac. 1827 and Pr. 1828 by Bp of Ox. R. of Eckington, Dio. Lich. 1843. (Patron, the Crown; Tithe, 330*l*; Glebe, 350 acres; R.'s Inc. 780*l* and Ho; Pop. 4319.) [14]

ESTCOURT, William John Bucknall, *Long Newnton Rectory, Tetbury, Wilts.*—Ball. Coll. Ox. B.A. 1834, M.A. 1838; Deac. 1839, Pr. 1841. R. of Long Newnton, Dio. G. and B. 1856. (Patron, Right Hon. T. H. Sotheron Estcourt; Tithe, 365*l*; R.'s Inc. 400*l* and Ho; Pop. 277.) Hon. Can. of Glouc; Rural Dean. Formerly C. of Bishops Cannings 1839, Penselwood, Somerset, 1846; V. of Sedgeford, Norfolk, 1849–56. [15]

ESTRIDGE, Henry, *Ramsgate.*—Trin. Coll. Ox. 1st cl. Lit. Hum. 1854, B.A. 1855, M.A. 1858; Deac. 1856 and Pr. 1857 by Abp of Cant. C. of Ch. Ch. Ramsgate. Formerly Tutor to the Maharajah Duleep Singh 1855–56. Author, *Reminiscences of School Life*; *Highland Sports.* [16]

ESTRIDGE, John Julius, *Puncknowle Rectory, Bridport, Dorset.*—St. John's Coll. Cam. B.A. 1822, M.A. 1840; Deac. 1822, Pr 1824. R. of Puncknowle, Dio. Salis. 1845. (Patrons, W. K. Tynte, Esq. and Mrs. M. G. Mansel, Puncknowle; Tithe, 257*l*; Glebe, 34 acres; R.'s Inc. 307*l* and Ho; Pop. 502.) Formerly C. of Stratford Turgis, Hants, 1822, Winterbourne-Clenston, Dorset, 1826. [17]

ETCHES, William Haigh, *Longborough Vicarage, Stow-on-the-Wold.*—Brasen. Coll. Ox. B.A. 1850, M.A. 1854; Deac. 1851 and Pr. 1853 by Bp of Wor. V. of Longborough with Seasoncote R. Dio. G. and B. 1867. (Patrons, Lord Leigh and Sir C. Cockrell; V.'s Inc 250*l* and Ho; Pop. 736.) Formerly C. of St. Michael's, Coventry, 1851–58; R. of Hamstall Ridware 1858–61; C. (sole charge) St. Stephen's, Bath, 1861–64; Min. of St. Saviour's temporary Church, Tollington Park, Lond. [18]

ETHELSTON, Charles Wicksted, *Uplyme Rectory, Lyme-Regis.*—Trin. Coll. Cam. B.A. 1822, M.A. 1825; Deac. 1824 and Pr. 1825 by Bp of Ex. R. of Uplyme, Dio. Ex. 1842. (Patron, the present R; Tithe, 450*l*; Glebe, 36 acres; R.'s Inc. 528*l* and Ho; Pop. 877.) [19]

ETHELSTON, Hart, *George-street, Cheetham Hill, near Manchester.*—Brasen. Coll. Ox. B.A. 1830, M.A. 1839; Deac. 1830 and Pr. 1833 by Bp of Ches. R. of St. Mark's, Cheetham, Dio. Man. 1831. (Patrons, the D. and C. of Man; R.'s Inc. 360*l*; Pop. 2377.) [20]

ETHERIDGE, John Hebgin.—Caius Coll. Cam. B.A. 1855, M.A. 1859; Deac. 1861 and Pr. 1862 by Abp of Cant. Formerly C. of St. Paul's, Maidstone, 1861–63. [21]

ETHERIDGE, Sanders, *Hinton Rectory, Alresford, Hants.*—Caius Coll. Cam. B.A. 1859, M.A. 1862; Deac. 1859 and Pr. 1860 by Bp of Pet. C. in sole charge of Hinton Ampner 1867. Formerly C. of Kettering 1859–62; St. Paul's, Clapham, 1862–66, Farnham 1866–67. [22]

ETTY, A. H., *Sedgefield, Durham.*—C. of Sedgefield. [23]

ETTY, Simeon James, *Wanborough, Shrivenham.*—New Coll. Ox. B.A. 1829, M.A. 1832; Deac. 1831 by Bp of Win. Pr. 1832 by Bp of Ox. V. of Wanborough, Dio. G. and B. 1841. (Patrons, D. and C. of Win; Tithe, 125*l*; Glebe, 250*l*; V.'s Inc. 375*l* and Ho; Pop. 963.) Formerly V. of Wootton St. Lawrence and Min. Can. of Winchester, 1834–41. [24]

EUSTACE, George, *Heptonstall Parsonage, near Manchester.*—Literate; Deac. 1859 and Pr. 1860 by Bp of Rip. P. C. of Heptonstall, Dio. Rip. 1861. (Patron, V. of Halifax; P. C.'s Inc. 300*l* and Ho; Pop. 6000.) Formerly C. of St Peter's, Sowerby, Halifax, 1859–60. [25]

EUSTACE, Robert Henry, *Sampford, Braintree, Essex.*—St. Peter's Coll. Cam. B.A. 1848, M.A. 1851; Deac. 1849, Pr. 1850. V. of Great Sampford with Hempstead 1850. (Patron, Sir W. Eustace; V.'s Inc. 300*l*; Pop. Sampford 865, Hempstead 797.) [26]

EVANS, Albert Eubule, *Windsor.*—St. Mary Hall, Ox. B.A; Deac. 1864, Pr. 1866. C. of Windsor 1866. Formerly C. of Slough, and Private Tut. at Eton Coll. Author, *Pietas Puerilis*, Masters, 1865, 2*s* 6*d.* [27]

EVANS, Alfred Bowen, *St. Mary-le-Strand, Westminster, W.C.*—D.D. 1864 by Abp of Cant. R. of St. Mary-le-Strand, Dio. Lon. 1861. Patron, Ld Chan; R.'s Inc. 266*l*; Pop. 2072.) Lect. of St. Andrew's, Marylebone. Formerly C. of Enfield. Author, *Dissent and its Inconsistencies*, 1841; *Lectures on the Return of Jesus Christ to our Earth*, 1843; *Christianity in its Homely Aspects*, 2 vols. Masters, 1850; *Lectures on the Book of Job*, Bosworth, 1856; *The Future of the Human Race*; *Morning and Evening Services for Households*, Skeffington, 1864; etc. [1]

EVANS, Arthur, *Little Somerford, Malmesbury, Wilts.*—Pemb. Coll. Ox. B.A. 1834, M.A. 1838; Deac. 1836, Pr. 1837. R. of Bremilham, Wilts, Dio. G. and B. 1840. (Patron, Hon. and Rev. R. Bowles; Tithe, 140*l*; R.'s Inc. 146*l*; Pop. 29.) R. of Somerford-Parva, Dio. G. and B. 1847. (Patron, Earl of Ilchester; Tithe, 262*l*; Glebe, 32 acres; R.'s Inc. 320*l*; Pop. 335.) [2]

EVANS, Arthur R., *Clifton Hampden, Abingdon.*—C. of Clifton Hampden. [3]

EVANS, Benjamin, *Llanstephan Parsonage, Carmarthenshire.*—Lampeter; Deac. 1822 and Pr. 1823 by Bp of St. D. P. C. of Llanstephan with Llangynnog P. C. Dio. St. D. 1843. (Patrons, Messrs. Morris and W. Lloyd; P. C.'s Inc. 110*l* and Ho; Pop. Llanstephan 1229, Llangynnog 717.) [4]

EVANS, Charles, *King Edward's School, Birmingham.*—Trin. Coll. Cam. Craven Univ. Scho. 1846, Sen. Chancellor's Medallist, Sen. Opt. æq. 1st in 1st cl. Cl. Trip. and B.A. 1847; Deac. 1852, Pr. 1854. Head Mast. of King Edward's Sch. Formerly Asst. Mast. of Rugby Sch; Fell. of Trin. Coll. Cam. [5]

EVANS, Charles, *Blackwell, Wirksworth.*—St. John's Coll. Cam. B.A. 1832, M.A. 1836; Deac. 1833 and Pr. 1834 by Bp of Lich. P. C. of Trinity, Matlock Bath, Dio. Lich. 1865. (Patrons, Trustees; P. C.'s Inc. 130*l* and Ho; Pop. 1258.) Formerly P. C. of Ch. Ch. Halland, Derbyshire, 1838–55; R. of St. Clement's, Worcester, 1858–65. [6]

EVANS, Charles John, *Ovington Rectory, Thetford, Norfolk.*—King's Coll. Cam. 2nd cl. Cl. Trip. and B.A. 1854, M.A. 1857; Deac. 1855 and Pr. 1856 by Bp of Lin. R. of Ovington, Dio. Nor. 1865. (Patron, Univ. of Cam; Tithe, 410*l*; Glebe, 22 acres; R.'s Inc. 436*l* and Ho; Pop. 291.) Formerly Fell. of King's Coll. Cam. 1853–66; C. of Denton, Norfolk, 1855–60, St. Edward's, Cambridge, 1864–65. [7]

EVANS, Daniel, *Bangor Vicarage, Carnarvonshire.*—V. of Bangor with Pentir C. Dio. Ban. 1858. (Patron, Bp of Ban; V.'s Inc. 450*l* and Ho; Pop. 10,662.) Formerly C. of Bangor. [8]

EVANS, Daniel, *Glyncorrwg, Neath, Glamorganshire.*—C. of Glyncorrwg and Spelter Works, Maesteg. [9]

EVANS, Daniel, *Corris, Machynlleth, North Wales.*—St. Bees; Deac. 1856 and Pr. 1857 by Bp of Llan. P. C. of Corris, Dio. Ban. 1859. (Patron, Earl Vane; P. C.'s Inc. 120*l*; Pop. 1050.) Formerly C. of Mynydyslwyn, Monmouth; Trvedyrhew, Merthyr-Tydfil. [10]

EVANS, Daniel, *Bridgend, Glamorganshire.*—V. of Pyle and Kenvig, Bridgend, Dio. Llan. 1863. (Patron, Bp of Llan; V.'s Inc. 110*l*; Pop. Pyle 1192, Kenvig 278.) [11]

EVANS, Daniel Silvan, *Llanymawddwy Rectory, Dinas Mawddwy, Merionethshire.*—Lampeter; Deac. 1848 and Pr. 1849 by Bp of Ban. R. of Llanymawddwy, Dio. Ban. 1862. (Patron, Bp of Ban; Tithe, 235*l*; Glebe, 10 acres; R.'s Inc. 246*l* and Ho; Pop. 595.) Formerly Welsh Lect. of Lampeter; C. of Llandegwining and Penllech 1848–52, Llangian and Llanvihangel Bachellaeth 1852–62. Author, *Emynau* (Hymns), 1840; *Blodau Ieuainc* (Prose and Verse), 1843; *Telynegion* (Lyrics), 1846; *Elfenau Gallofyddiaeth* (Elements of Mechanics), 1850; *Elfenau Seryddiaeth* (Elements of Astronomy), 1851; *English and Welsh Dictionary*, 2 vols. 1852–58, 31*s* 6*d*; *A New Edition of the Bardd Cwsg, with Notes and Life of the Author*, 1853; A New Edition of Samuel's Welsh Translation of Grotius *De Veritate, with a Biographical Preface*, 1854; Translation of Dr. Adam Clarke's *Commentary on the Pentateuch*, 1855; *Pregeth ar Farwolaeth y Cadben R. Lloyd Edwards*, 1855; *Llythyraeth yr Iaith Gymraeg* (Welsh Orthography), 1861, 2*s*. Editor of *Y Brython* (a Welsh Literary Magazine), 1858–60; *Y Marchog Crwydrad* (a legend of the 17th Century), 1864. [12]

EVANS, Daniel Warren, *Child-Okeford, Blandford, Dorset.*—St. John's Coll. Cam. B.A. 1830; Deac. 1830 and Pr. 1831 by Bp of G. and B. R. of Child-Okeford, Dio. Salis. 1868. (Patron, Rev. C. E. North; Tithe, 270*l*; Glebe, 70 acres; R.'s Inc. 370*l* and Ho; Pop. 773.) Formerly C. of Child-Okeford. [13]

EVANS, David, *Kilgerran Rectory, Pembroke.*—R. of Kilgerran, Dio. St. D. 1844. (Patron, Ld Chan; Tithe, 191*l*; Glebe, 9 acres; R.'s Inc. 201*l* and Ho; Pop. 1236.) [14]

EVANS, David, *Llanllwchaiarn Rectory, New Quay.*—Queens' Coll. Cam. B.D. 1830; Deac. 1820 and Pr. 1821 by Bp of Win. R. of Llanllwchaiarn, Dio. St. D. 1838. (Patron, Bp of St. D; Tithe, 236*l*; Glebe, 8*l*; R.'s Inc. 256*l* and Ho; Pop. 1976.) [15]

EVANS, David, *Llansantffraid Glyn Dyfrdwy, Corwen, Merionethshire.*—R. of Llansantffraid Glyn Dyfrdwy, Dio. St. A. 1862. (Patron, Bp of St. A; Tithe, 86*l*; R.'s Inc. 100*l* and Ho; Pop. 161.) [16]

EVANS, David, *Llanycil Rectory, Bala.*—St. Bees; Deac. 1856 and Pr. 1858 by Bp of St. A. R. of Llanycil and Ch. Ch. Bala, Dio. St. A. 1867. (Patron, Bp of St. A; Tithe, 320*l*; Glebe, 8 acres; R.'s Inc. 360*l* and Ho; Pop. 3000.) Formerly C. of Nantglyn, Denbigh, 1856, Llanrhaiadr-yn-Mochnant, Oswestry, 1857; P. C. of St. Mark's, Bala, 1858–59; P. C. of Pontblyddyn, Mold, 1859–67. [17]

EVANS, David, *Ford, Arundel, Sussex.*—R. of Ford, Dio. Chich. 1855. (Patron, Bp of Chich; Tithe, 235*l* 8*s*; Glebe, 1 acre; R.'s Inc. 237*l*; Pop. 106.) C. of Climping, Arundel. [18]

EVANS, David, *Vicarage, Morriston, Swansea.*—Lampeter, Math. Prizeman 1831, 2nd cl. Hons; Deac. 1833 by Bp of St. D. Pr. 1834 by Bp of Llan. V. of Llangyfelach with Gorseinon C. Glamorgan, Dio. St. D. 1845. (Patron, Bp of St. D; Tithe—App. 845*l*, V. 205*l*; V.'s Inc. 300*l* and Ho; Pop. 11,500. P. C. of Morriston, Dio. St. D. 1850. (Patron, Sir John Morris, Bart; P. C.'s Inc. 85*l*.) Surrogate 1855. [19]

EVANS, David, *Llangathen, Llandilo-Vawr, Carmarthenshire.*—V. of Llangathen, Dio. St. D. 1849. (Patron, Bp of St. D; V.'s Inc. 180*l*; Pop. 977.) [20]

EVANS, Edward, *Llanddewi-Brevi, Lampeter, Cardiganshire.*—St. Cath. Hall, Cam. B.A. 1829; Deac. and Pr. 1831 by Bp of Ban. P. C. of Llanddewi-Brevi with Llanbadarn-Odwyn C. Dio. St. D. 1830. (Patrons, Earl of Lisburne and Mr. Price, alt; Tithe—App. 7*l* 13*s* 4*d*, Imp. 999*l* 6*s* 8*d*, P. C. 67*l*; Bounty Land, 450 acres; P. C.'s Inc. 218*l*; Pop. Llanddewi-Brevi 1756, Llanbadarn-Odwyn 527.) P. C. of Gartheli, Dio. St. D. 1852. (Patron, P. C. of Llanddewi; P. C.'s Inc. 104*l*; Pop. 296.) [21]

EVANS, Edward, *Halkyn Rectory, Holywell.*—Dub. A.B. 1834, A.M. 1837; Deac. 1823 by Bp of Salis. Pr. 1824 by Bp of Bristol. R. of Halkyn, Dio. St. A. 1851. (Patron, Bp of St. A; Tithe, 380*l* 10*s*; Glebe, 1½ acres; R.'s Inc. 384*l* and Ho; Pop. 1334.) Formerly C. of Gwaenysecor, Flints, 1827; P. C. of Newmarket. [22]

EVANS, Edward, *Belper.*—Caius Coll. Cam. Jun. Opt. B.A. 1865; Deac. 1865 and Pr. 1866 by Bp of Lich. C. of Belper 1865. [23]

EVANS, Edward, *Llanmihangel Rectory, Cowbridge.*—Literate; Deac. 1845 and Pr. 1846 by Bp of Llan. R. of Llanmihangel, Dio. Llan. 1859. (Patroness, Dowager Countess of Dunraven; Tithe, 130*l*; Glebe, 41 acres and Ho; Pop. 29.) Formerly C. of Llandy-fodwg; P. C. of Monknash. [24]

EVANS, Edward, *Llanfihangel Rectory, Oswestry.*—Jesus Coll. Ox. B.A. 1836; Deac. 1837 and Pr. 1838 by Bp of St. A. R. of Llanfihangel yng Nghwnfa, Dio. St. A. 1860. (Patron, Ld Chan; Tithe, 401*l*; Glebe, 1 acre; R.'s Inc. 402*l* and Ho; Pop. 546.) [25]

EVANS, Edward Arthur, *Pembridge, Leominster.*—Trin. Coll. Cam. B.A. 1862; Deac. 1864 and Pr. 1865 by Bp of Herf. C. of Pembridge 1866. Formerly C. of Little Hereford 1864. [1]

EVANS, Edward Charles, *Downham Rectory, Billericay, Essex.*—Oriel Coll. Ox. B.A. 1837, M.A. 1838; Deac. 1837 and Pr. 1838 by Bp of Herf. R. of Downham, Dio. Roch. 1867. (Patron, R. B. Berens, Esq; R.'s Inc. 500*l* and Ho; Pop. 247.) Formerly P. C. of Eyton, Herefordshire, 1851–67. [2]

EVANS, Eleazer, *Llanegwad, near Carmarthen.*—Literate; Deac. 1816 by Bp of B. and W. Pr. 1818 by Bp of Lin. V. of Llanegwad, Dio. St. D. 1844. (Patron, Bp of St. D; Tithe—Imp. 400*l* 16*s* 8*d*, V. 299*l* 5*s* 4*d*; V.'s Inc. 299*l*; Pop. 1920.) Author, *A Farewell Sermon,* 1828. [3]

EVANS, Erasmus, *Morriston, Swansea.*—Lampeter; Deac. 1866 by Bp of St. D. C. of Llangyfelach with Morriston 1866. [4]

EVANS, Evan, *Glyndyfrdwy, Corwen.*—P. C. of Glyndyfrdwy, Dio. St. A. 1865. [5]

EVANS, Evan, *Pembroke College, Oxford.*—Pemb. Coll. Ox. B.A. 1835, M.A. 1838. Can. of Gloucester and Mast of Pemb. Coll. 1864. [6]

EVANS, Evan, *Hafod, Talsarn, Carmarthen.*—Lampeter, Scho. of, 1848; Deac. 1849 and Pr. 1850 by Bp of St. D. R. of Llangeitho, Dio. St. D. 1852. (Patron, Bp of St. D; Tithe, 117*l* 10*s*; Glebe, 20 acres; R.'s Inc. 164*l*; Pop. 453.) P. C. of Bettws-Leiki, Dio. St. D. 1860. (Patron, P. C. of Llanddewi-Brevi; P. C.'s Inc. 50*l*; Pop. 349.) Formerly C. of Trefilan 1849; P. C. of Blaenpenal 1851. [7]

EVANS, Evan, *Court, near Lampeter.*—Lampeter; Deac. and Pr. 1844. V. of Llantownlle, Cardiganshire, Dio. St. D. 1845. (Patron, Bp of St. D; Tithe—App. 117*l* 3*s* 4*d*, V. 58*l* 11*s* 8*d*; Glebe, 4 acres; V.'s Inc. 160*l*; Pop. 803.) [8]

EVANS, Francis, *Salisbury.*—St. John's Coll. Cam. B.A. 1815, M.A. 1818; Deac. 1817, Pr. 1819. [9]

EVANS, Frederic John Morgan, *Hinderclay Rectory, Botesdale, Suffolk.*—St. Peter's Coll. Cam. B.A. 1849; Deac. and Pr. 1851 by Bp of Wor. C. of Hinderclay 1865. Formerly C. of St. Michael's, Worcester, and Warnden 1851; Chap. R.N; R. of Smith and Hamilton Parishes, Bermuda. [10]

EVANS, Frederic Rawlins, *Hagley, near Stourbridge.*—Ex. Coll. Ox. B.A. 1864; Deac. 1866 and Pr. 1867 by Bp of Wor. C. of Hagley 1866. [11]

EVANS, Frederick, *Linstead Magna, Halesworth, Suffolk.*—P. C. of Linstead Magna, Dio. Nor. 1862. (Patron, Lord Huntingfield; P. C.'s Inc. 97*l*; Pop. 115.) P. C. of Linstead Parva, Dio. Nor. 1862. (Patron, Lord Huntingfield; P. C.'s Inc. 78*l*; Pop. 227.) [12]

EVANS, George Henry, *Woodchester Rectory, Stroud.*—Dub. A.B 1827, A.M. 1830; Deac. 1831 and Pr. 1831 by Bp of Elphin. R. of Woodchester, Dio. G. and B. 1858. (Patron, C. Hooper, Esq; Tithe, 265*l*; Glebe, 30 acres; R.'s Inc. 295*l* and Ho; Pop. 816.) [13]

EVANS, George William Davis, *Reculver, Canterbury.*—St. John's Coll. Cam. B.A. 1818, M.A. 1821. V. of Reculver with Heath C. Dio. Cant. 1832. (Patron, Abp of Cant; Reculver, Tithe—App. 535*l*, V. 130*l*; Glebe, 3 acres; Heath, Tithe—App. 230*l*, V. 105*l*; V.'s Inc. 240*l*; Pop. Reculver 254, Heath 348.) [14]

EVANS, Griffith, *Llandyvriog, Newcastle Emlyn, Cardiganshire.*—Lampeter; Deac. 1831 and Pr. 1832 by Bp of St. D. V. of Llandyvriog with Llanvair-Trelygen R. Dio. St. D. 1862. (Patron, Bp of St. D; R.'s Inc. 147*l*; Pop. Llandyvriog 249, Llanvair-Trelygen 81.) Formerly P. C. of Tremaen, near Cardigan, 1844–62. [15]

EVANS, Henry, *Standish, Wigan.*—Dub. A.B. 1857; Deac. 1857 and Pr. 1858 by Bp of Ches. C. of Standish 1865. Formerly C. of Walton Breck 1857–58; Math. Mast. in Liverpool Coll. 1851–60; Mast. of Gr. Sch. Chorley, 1860–65. [16]

EVANS, Henry, *Pembrey, Llanelly.*—C. of St. Ishmael's, Carmarthenshire. [17]

EVANS, Henry George, *Stradishall Rectory, Newmarket, Suffolk.*—R. of Stradishall, Dio. Ely, 1859. (Patron, Sir R. Harland; R.'s Inc. 325*l* and Ho; Pop. 425.) Formerly C. of Manningtree, Essex; R. of Freystrop, Pembrokeshire. [18]

EVANS, Henry Griffith, *Crediton, Devon.*—Corpus Coll. Cam. 30th Wrang. and B.A. 1860, 2nd cl. Theol. Trip. 1861, M.A. 1863; Deac. 1861 and Pr. 1862 by Bp of Lon. 2nd Mast. of Crediton Gr. Sch. Formerly C. of St. Thomas's, Charterhouse, Lond. 1862–63. [19]

EVANS, Henry James, *Charterhouse, London, E.C.*—Pemb. Coll. Cam. Scho. of, 1st in 2nd cl. Cl. Trip. B.A. 1857, M.A. 1861; Deac. 1861, and Pr. 1862 by Bp of Lon. Asst. Mast. in Charterhouse Sch. [20]

EVANS, Hugh, *Scremerston Parsonage, near Berwick-on-Tweed.*—Dur. B.A. 1842, M.A. 1845; Deac. 1838 by Bp of Dur. Pr. 1840 by Bp of Rip. P. C. of Scremerston, Dio. Dur. 1850. (Patrons, D. and C. of Dur; P. C.'s Inc. 230*l* and Ho; Pop. 1227.) [21]

EVANS, J. M.—C. of St. Mary Magdalen's, Southwark. [22]

EVANS, James, *Llanddeiniol, Aberystwith.*—St. Bees; Deac. 1852 and Pr. 1853 by Bp. of Llan. P. C. of Llanddeiniol, Dio. St. D. 1859. (Patrons, R. Price, Esq. M.P. and Capt. Vaughan; P. C.'s Inc. 113*l*; Pop. 270.) Formerly C. of Trevathin 1852, Maesty 1853–59. Author, *A Welsh Pamphlet on the Two Thousand*; *A Welsh Treatise in Defence of the Historical Truth of the Five Books of Moses,* 1864. [23]

EVANS, James, *Llangower, Bala.*—R. of Llangower, Dio. St. A. 1861. (Patron, Bp of St. A; R.'s Inc. 136*l* and Ho; Pop. 345.) [24]

EVANS, J. B., *Roch, Haverfordwest.*—V. of Roch, Dio. St. D. 1865. (Patron, Ld Chan; V.'s Inc. 150*l*; Pop. 679.) [25]

EVANS, James Higgon, *Corfe Castle, Wareham, Dorset.*—Lampeter 1839, B.D. 1854; Deac. 1844, Pr. 1845. V. of Merriott, Somerset, Dio. B. and W. 1856. (Patrons, D. and C. of Bristol; V.'s Inc. 440*l* and Ho; Pop. 1413.) [26]

EVANS, James John, *Nantmel, Rhayader, Radnorshire.*—P. C. of Llanvihangel-Helygen 1848 with Llanyre P. C. 1858, Dio. St. D. (Patrons, Bp of St. D and V. of Nantmel, alt; P. C.'s Inc. Llanvihangel, 100*l*; Pop. 110; Llanyre, 150*l*; Pop. 744.) Surrogate. Formerly C. of Nantmel. [27]

EVANS, J. J., *Cantreff, Brecon.*—R. of Cantreff, Dio. St. D. 1866. (Patron, Rev. T. Powell; Pop. 126.) [28]

EVANS, James Joyce, 7, *St. Mark's square, Regent's-park, London, N.W.*—Trin. Coll. Cam. B.A. 1837, M.A. 1841; Deac. 1842, Pr. 1844. Chap. of the Home and Colonial Training Sch. Gray's-inn-road, 1846. Editor of *Life and Remains of the Rev. J. H. Evans,* 2 eds. 1855, 7*s* 6*d*. [29]

EVANS, James Williams, *Bassingthorpe, Corby, Lincolnshire.*—V. of Bassingthorpe with Westby, Dio. Lin. 1818. (Patron, Earl of Dysart; V.'s Inc. 250*l*; Pop. 154.) P. C. of Costessey, Dio. Nor. 1845. (Patron, Corporation of Norwich; Pop. 1047.) [30]

EVANS, J., *Bridge Sollers, Hereford.*—C. of Bridge Sollers. [31]

EVANS, J.—C. of St. Mark's, Leeds. [32]

EVANS, John, M.A., *Society for Promoting Christian Knowledge, Great Queen-street, Lincoln's-Inn-Fields, London, W.C.*—Sec. to the S.P.C.K. [33]

EVANS, John, *St. Clear's Vicarage, Carmarthenshire.*—Deac. 1821 and Pr. 1822 by Bp of St. D. V. of St. Clears, Dio. St. D. 1831. (Patron, C. G. Phillips, Esq; Tithe—Imp. 187*l* 15*s* 4*d*, V. 93*l* 17*s* 8*d*; Glebe, 9 acres; V.'s Inc. 104*l* and Ho; Pop. 1129.) V. of Llangan, St. Clears, Dio. St. D. 1831. (Patron, Bp of St. D; Tithe—App. 156*l* 8*s*, Imp. 25*l* 8*s*, V. 78*l* 4*s*; V.'s Inc. 90*l*; Pop. 641.) C. of Llanginning. [34]

EVANS, John, *Kenchester, Hereford.*—Magd. Coll. Cam. B.A. 1824, M.A. 1827; Deac. and Pr. 1825 by Bp of Herf. R. of Kenchester, Dio. Herf. 1836. (Patron, Ld Chan; Tithe, 143*l* 14*s*; R.'s Inc. 195*l*; Pop. 100.) [35]

EVANS, John, 11, *Bartlett's-buildings, Holborn, London, W.C.*—Lampeter; Deac. 1850 by Bp of Llan. Pr. 1851 by Bp of St. D. Min. of the Metropolitan Welsh Ch. Ely-place, Holborn, Dio. Lon. 1852. (Patrons, Trustees; P. C.'s Inc. 250*l*.) [1]

EVANS, John, *Bryndulas, Llanidloes, Montgomeryshire.*—Lampeter; Deac. 1828 and Pr. 1829 by Bp of St. D. V. of Llangurig, Montgomery. Dio. Ban. 1852. (Patron, Ld Chan; Tithe—Imp. 420*l*, V. 177*l*; Glebe, 4 acres; V.'s Inc. 310*l*; Pop. 1641.) [2]

EVANS, John, *Edengale, Lichfield.*—Lin. Coll. Ox. 2nd cl. Lit. Hum. and B.A. 1811, M.A. 1814; Deac. 1812, Pr. 1813. P. C. of Edengale, Dio. Lich. 1824. (Patron, Preb. of Weeford in Lich. Cathl; Glebe, 46 acres; P. C.'s Inc. 80*l* and Ho; Pop. 208.) [3]

EVANS, John, *Crickhowell, Brecknock.*—Lampeter, B.D. 1853; Deac. 1829, Pr. 1830. V. 1837, and R. 1851, of Crickhowell, Dio. St. D. (Patron, Duke of Beaufort; Tithe—Imp. 93*l* 0*s* 6*d*, V. 50*l* 11*s* and ¾ acre of Glebe, R. 101*l* 2*s* and 1¾ acres of Glebe; V. and R.'s Inc. 226*l* and Ho; Pop. 1516.) Surrogate; Chap. to the Crickhowell Union. Author, *Thanksgiving Sermon on the late Chartist Insurrection*, 1840. [4]

EVANS, John, *Whixall, Whitchurch, Shropshire.*—Ch. Ch. Ox. 2nd cl. Lit. Hum. 2nd cl. Math. et Phy. B.A. 1818, M.A. 1821; Deac. 1824, Pr. 1828. P. C. of Whixall, Dio Lich. 1844. (Patron, V. of Prees; Tithe, App. 385*l*; Glebe, 44 acres; P. C.'s Inc. 130*l* and Ho; Pop. 938.) Dom. Chap. to F. M. Viscount Combermere; Surrogate, for the Peculiar of Prees. Author, *Compendious View of the Authenticity and Inspiration of the Old and New Testaments*, 1828, 3*s*; *Appendix to Watts' Scripture History*, 1830, 1*s*; *Synopsis of Aldrich's Logic*, 1*s* 6*d*; *Solution of Simple and Quadratic Equations*, 1835, 1*s* 6*d*; *Narrative of the Fires near Whitchurch, Shropshire*, 3*s*; *Fundamental Doctrines of the Church of England*, 1838, 3 eds. 3*d*; *Poems*, 1839, 2*s* 6*d*; *Statutes of the 4th General Council of the Lateran*, 1843, 4*s* 6*d*; *The Persecuting Spirit of Rome*, 1851; *Origin and Progress of Mariolatry*, 1852, 6*d*; *Papal Aggressions and Concessions to Rome*, 3*d*; *The Principles of the Working of Vulgar and Decimal Fractions and Duodecimals familiarly explained*, 3 eds. 1*s*; *Questions on Pearson on the Creed*, Rivingtons, 1863, 1*s* 6*d*; *Dwellings of the Poor*, Hardwicke, 3*d*; etc. [5]

EVANS, John, *Grassendale, near Liverpool.*—Dub. A.B. 1844, A.M. 1853, *ad eund.* Ox. 1853; Deac. 1844 by Bp of Kildare, Pr. 1845 by Abp of Armagh. P. C. of St. Mary's, Grassendale, Dio. Ches. 1854. (Patrons, Trustees; P. C.'s Inc. from Pew Rents, 350*l*; Pop. 912.) Author, *A Sermon on the Sin of Cruelty to Animals*, 1851, 6*d*; *A Sermon on the Death of the Rev. Edward Tottenham, B.D.* 1853. [6]

EVANS, the Ven. John, *Llanllechid Rectory, Bangor.*—Dub. A.B. 1841, A.M. 1862; Deac. 1841 and Pr 1842 by Bp of Ban. R. of Llanllechid, Dio. Ban. 1862. (Patron, Bp of Ban; Tithe, 465*l*; Glebe, 18 acres; R.'s Inc. 483*l* and Ho; Pop. 2724.) Archd. of Merioneth and Can. Res. of Ban. 1866; Rural Dean. Formerly C. of Llanbedr y Cennin 1841; P. C. of Pentrevoelas 1844–57; R. of Machynlleth 1857. [7]

EVANS, John, *Alltmawr, Builth, Brecknock.*—Deac. 1818 by Bp of Ely, Pr. 1818 by Bp of Ches. P. C. of Alltmawr, Dio. St. D. (Patron, V. of Llanavanfawr; Tithe, App. 50*l* 13*s* 4*d*; P. C.'s Inc. 50*l*; Pop. 45.) [8]

EVANS, John David, *Eton College, Bucks.*—St. John's Coll. Cam. 1st cl. Cl. Trip. B.A. 1862, M.A. 1865; Deac. 1866. Asst. C. of Trinity, Windsor, 1866. [9]

EVANS, John Harrison.—St. John's Coll. Cam. 3rd Wrang. 1st cl. Cl. Trip. and B.A. 1828, M.A. 1831; Deac. 1833, Pr. 1834. Formerly Fell. and Asst. Tut. of St. John's Coll. Cam; Head Mast. of Sedberg Sch. 1838; Chap. of Mission to Seamen, Sunderland. Author, *First Three, and Ninth and Eleventh Sections of Newton's Principia*, 4th ed. [10]

EVANS, John Myddelton, *Pitsford Rectory, Northampton.*—Ex. Coll. Ox. B.A. 1859, M.A., 1862; Wells Theol. Coll; Deac. 1860 and Pr 1861 by Bp of B. and W. C. of Pitsford 1866. Formerly C. of Ilminster 1860, Rockingham 1864. [11]

EVANS, John Pugh, *Efenechtyd Rectory, Ruthin.*—St. Bees; Deac. 1856 and Pr. 1857 by Bp. of St. A. R. of Efenechtyd, Dio. St. A. 1865. (Patron, Bp of St. A; Tithe, 200*l*; Glebe, 10 acres; R.'s Inc. 210*l* and Ho; Pop. 211.) Formerly C. of Llandderfel 1858. [12]

EVANS, John Williams, *St. Melon's, Cardiff.*—Jesus Coll. Ox. 1st cl. Law and Modern History and B.A. 1860, M.A. 1862; Deac. 1860 and Pr. 1862 by Bp of Llan. V. of St. Melon's with Llanedarn, Dio. Llan. 1864. (Patron, Bp. of Llan; Tithe, 171*l*; Glebe, 49 acres; V.'s Inc. 250*l* and Ho; Pop. 977.) Formerly C. of Cowbridge and Llanblethian 1860–64. [13]

EVANS, Jonah Bowen, *St. Harmon, Rhayader, Radnorshire.*—Lampeter, Creaton Prizeman, B.D; Deac. 1829 and Pr. 1830 by Bp of St. D. V. of St. Harmon, Dio. St. D. 1845. (Patron, Bp of St. D; Tithe—App. 152*l* 10*s* 9*d*, V. 152*l* 10*s* 9*d*; Glebe, ½ acre; V.'s Inc. 194*l*; Pop. 902.) Author, *Prize Essays*, *The History of the Lords Marchers*, 1837; *The Canals, Tramroads, and Railways of Gwent and Morgannog*, 1838; *The Border Wars of Radnorshire*, 1838; *The Inestimable Blessing to the World in General by the Restoration of the Jews*, 1839. [14]

EVANS, Joseph Glover, *Rudford Rectory, near Gloucester.*—Pemb. Coll. Ox. B.A. 1851, M.A. 1864; Deac. 1856 and Pr. 1857 by Bp of Roch. R. of Rudford, Dio. G. and B. 1866. (Patrons, D. and C. of Glouc; Tithe, comm. 332*l*: Glebe, 5 acres; R.'s Inc. 336*l* and Ho; Pop. 210.) Formerly C. of Maldon 1856, Dunton 1857, Southminster 1859, and St. George's, Gravesend, 1862. [15]

EVANS, Joshua, *Llanover Vicarage, Abergavenny, Monmouthshire.*—Deac. 1819 by Bp of Ox. Pr. 1819 by Bp of Ches. V. of Llanover, Dio. Llan. 1843. (Patrons, D. and C. of Llan; Tithe—App. 146*l* 10*s*, V. 250*l*; V.'s Inc. 591*l* and Ho; Pop. 474.) [16]

EVANS, Lewis, *Sandbach, Cheshire.*—Wad. Coll. Ox. 3rd cl. Lit. Hum. 3rd cl. Math. et. Phy. and B.A. 1836, M.A. 1842; Deac. 1843 and Pr. 1844 by Bp of Ox. Head Mast. of the Sandbach Free Gr. Sch. 1850. Formerly Fell. and Jun. Bursar of Wad. Coll. Ox. 1840. Editor of *Marshall's Penitential Discipline*; *Bishop Beveridge's Sermons*, 8 vols. Parker. Translator of *Juvenal, Persius, and Lucilius.* Joint Editor of *Notes on Thucydides.* [17]

EVANS, Lewis, *Ystrad Meurig, near Tregaron.*—Lampeter, and Oriel Coll. Ox. B.A. 1833; Deac. 1834 and Pr. 1835 by Bp of Glouc. R. of Yspyth Ystwyth with Ystrad Meurig, Dio. St. D. 1859. (Patron, Earl of Lisburne; R.'s Inc. 120*l*; Pop. Yspyth 850, Ystrad Meurig, 150.) Formerly C. of Stinchcombe 1834; V. of Llanvihangel-Creuddyn 1835. [18]

EVANS, Morgan, *Llangwyryvon, Aberystwith.*—P. C. of Llangwyryvon, Dio. St. D. 1849. (Patron, J. P. B. Chichester, Esq; P. C.'s Inc. 180*l*; Pop. 557.) [19]

EVANS, Rees, *Llandebie Vicarage, Llanelly, Carmarthenshire.*—Lampeter, late Scho; Deac. 1847 by Bp of Llan. Pr. 1848 by Bp of St. D. V. of Llandebie, Dio. St. D. 1861. (Patron, Bp of St. D; Tithe—App. 350*l*, V. 175*l*; V.'s Inc. 180*l* and Ho; Pop. 2828.) Formerly C. of Llandilofawr 1850–61. [20]

EVANS, Richard, *Hales Parsonage, Drayton-in-Hales.*—Wor. Coll. Ox. B.A. 1852; Deac. 1853 and Pr. 1854 by Bp of Pet. C. of Hales 1859. Formerly C. of Packington with Swibston 1853, Drayton-in-Hales 1855, Honingham with Tuddenham 1856, Quidenham and Snetterton 1857. [21]

EVANS, Richard Davies, *Kingsland, Leominster.*—Deac. 1828, Pr. 1829. R. of Kingsland, Dio. Herf. 1841. (Patron, Rev. R. D. Evans; Tithe—Imp. 55*l*, R. 785*l*; Glebe, 66½ acres; R.'s Inc. 883*l* and Ho; Pop. 1150.) [22]

EVANS, Samuel, *Marshfield Vicarage, Newport, Monmouthshire.*—Lampeter; Deac. 1846 by Bp of Ely, Pr. 1847 by Bp of Llan. V. of Marshfield, Dio. Llan. 1855. (Patrons, D. and C. of Bristol; Tithe—App. 177*l* 13*s* 8*d*,

V. 50*l* 3*s* 4*d*; Glebe, 35 acres; V.'s Inc. 91*l* and Ho; Pop. 509.) P. C. of Peterstone-Wentloge 1854. [1]

EVANS, Samuel, *Christ Church Parsonage, Pontblyddyn, Mold.*—Lampeter, Eldon Welsh Scho. B.A. 1865; Deac. 1865 and Pr. 1866 by Bp of St. A. P. C. of Pontblyddyn, Dio. St. A. 1867. (Patron, V. of Mold; P. C.'s Inc. 90*l* and Ho; Pop. 1378.) Formerly C. of Ruabon 1865–67. [2]

EVANS, Samuel, *Llangan Rectory, Cowbridge, Glamorganshire.*—R. of Llangan, Dio. Llan. 1857. (Patrons, Earls of Clarendon and Dunraven; R.'s Inc. 280*l* and Ho; Pop. 23.) V. of St. Mary Hill, Dio. Llan. (Patron, Sir T. D. Aubrey, Bart; V.'s Inc. 90*l*; Pop. 252.) [3]

EVANS, Thomas, *Brockley Hill, Lewisham, Kent.*—C. of St. Saviour's, Brockley-hill. [4]

EVANS, Thomas, *Broughton-in-Craven, Skipton.*—Ch. Ch. Ox. Careswell Exhib. B.A. 1853, M.A. 1856; Deac. 1854 and Pr. 1856 by Bp of Ox. V. of Broughton, Dio. Rip. 1861. (Patron, Ch. Ch. Ox; Tithe, 94*l*; Glebe, 101 acres; V.'s Inc. 250*l* and Ho; Pop. 274.) Formerly Asst. Mast. of Magd. Coll. Sch. 1854–58; Head Mast. of Ch. Ch. Sch. 1859–61. [5]

EVANS, Thomas, *Llanvalteg Rectory, Narberth, Pembrokeshire.*—Jesus Coll. Ox. B.A. 1834, M.A. 1837; Deac. 1836 and Pr. 1837 by Bp of St. D. R. of Llanvalteg, Dio. St. D. 1856. (Patron, Bp of St. D; R.'s Inc. 220*l*; Pop. 353.) Formerly C. of Penboyr, Carmarthenshire. [6]

EVANS, Thomas, *Maesgwynne, Carmarthenshire.*—Lampeter; Deac. 1827 and Pr. 1828 by Bp of St. D. Formerly C. of Llangybre, and Lect. at Llanstephan, Carmarthen. [7]

EVANS, Thomas, *Eglwyswrw Vicarage, Newport, near Cardigan.*—Lampeter; Deac. 1839 and Pr. 1840 by Bp of St. D. V. of Eglwyswrw, Dio. St. D. 1856. (Patron, Ld Chan; Tithe—Imp. 170*l* and 30 acres of Glebe, V. 80*l*; Glebe, 25 acres; V.'s Inc. 120*l* and Ho; Pop. 490.) P. C. of Llanvair-Nantgwyn, Dio. St. D. 1866. (Patron, J. W. Bowen, Esq; P. C.'s Inc. 100*l*; Pop. 189.) [8]

EVANS, Thomas, *Carew, Pembrokeshire.*—Lampeter; Deac. 1866 by Bp of St. D. C. of Carew and Rhydberth 1866. [9]

EVANS, T., *Llanrhystid, Aberystwith.*—V. of Llanrhystid, Dio. St. D. 1863. (Patron, Bp of St. D; Tithe, 63*l*; Glebe, 46 acres; R.'s Inc. 118*l*; Pop. 1533.) [10]

EVANS, Thomas, *Goytre, Abergavenny.*—R. of Goytre, Dio. Llan. (Patron, Earl of Abergavenny; Tithe, 295*l*; Glebe, 3 acres; R.'s Inc. 297*l*; Pop. 668.) [11]

EVANS, Thomas David, *Cwm Avon, Taibach.* Deac. 1858 and Pr. 1865 by Bp of Llan. C. of Michaelstone-super-Avon 1861. Formerly C. of Coy Church 1858, Aberavon with Baglan 1859. [12]

EVANS, Thomas Henry, *Llandegla, Ruthin, Denbighshire.*—C. of Llandegla. [13]

EVANS, Thomas Howel, *Cadeby, Hinckley, Leicestershire.*—St. Aidan's; Deac. 1856 and Pr. 1857 by Bp of Pet. C. of Cadeby 1859. Formerly C. of Little Missenden, Bucks, Packington, Leicestershire. [14]

EVANS, Thomas Saunders, *Durham.*—St. John's Coll. Cam. Porson Prizeman 1838, B.A. 1839, M.A. 1845; Deac. 1844, Pr. 1846. Can. of Dur. and Prof. of Greek in Dur. Univ. Formerly Asst. Mast. in Rugby Sch. [15]

EVANS, Thomas Simpson, *Stoke Newington Common, N.*—St. Alban's Hall, Ox. 2nd cl. Lit. Hum. B.A. 1822, M.A. 1825; Deac. and Pr. 1822 by Bp of Glouc. V. of St. Leonard's, Shoreditch, Dio. Lon. 1841. (Patron, Archd. of Lon; V.'s Inc. 797*l*; Pop. 14,058.) Formerly C. and Lect. of Kensington 1824. Author, Sermons; Tracts on *Tithes, Observance of Ascension,* etc. [16]

EVANS, Turberville.—Ex. Coll. Ox. B.A. 1863; Deac. 1863 and Pr. 1864 by Bp of Roch. P. C. of St. James's, Curtain-road, Dio. Lon. 1867. (Patron, V. of Shoreditch; P. C.'s Inc. 500*l* and Ho; Pop. 11,249.) Formerly C. of Witham, Essex, 1863–67. [17]

EVANS, William, *Rhymney, Newport, Monmouthshire.*—P. C. of Rhymney, Dio. Llan. 1856. (Pop. 7650.) [18]

EVANS, William, *Shipston-upon-Stour Rectory, Worcestershire.*—Jesus Coll. Ox. B.A. 1817, M.A. 1820, B.D. 1825; Deac. 1817 and Pr. 1818 by Bp of Ox. R. of Shipston-upon-Stour with Tidmington, Dio. Wor. 1827. (Patrons, Jesus Coll. Ox. 2 turns, and D. and C. of Wor. 1 turn; Shipston-upon-Stour, Tithe, 522*l* 0*s* 8*d*; Tidmington, Tithe, 216*l*; Glebe, 45 acres; R.'s Inc. 810*l* and Ho; Pop. Shipston-upon-Stour 1760, Tidmington 69.) [19]

EVANS, William, *Silian Vicarage, Lampeter.*—Lampeter; Deac. 1849 by Bp of St. D. Pr. 1851 by Bp of Llan. V. of Llanwnen with Silian C. Dio. St. D. 1854. (Patron, Bp of St. D; Llanwnen, Tithe—App. 1*l*, V. 50*l*; Silian, Tithe—App. 62*l* 17*s* 5*d*, Imp. 7*l* 14*s* 9*d*, V. 31*l* 8*s* 8½*d*; Glebe, 41 acres; V.'s Inc. 130*l* and Ho; Pop. Llanwnen 344, Silian 341.) [20]

EVANS, William, *Bryncock, Cadoxton-by-Neath, Glamorganshire.*—C. of Bryncock and Dur-y-Felin, Cadoxton. [21]

EVANS, William, *Henfynyw, Aberayron.*—Lampeter; Deac. 1865 by Bp of St. D. C. of Henfynyw 1865. [22]

EVANS, W., *St. Bride's Minor, Bridgend, Glamorganshire.*—V. of St. Bride's Minor, Dio. Llan. 1863. (Patron, Earl of Dunraven; Tithe, 155*l* 6*s* 5*d*; R.'s Inc. 180*l* and Ho; Pop. 879.) [23]

EVANS, William Cornwallis, *Campsall Vicarage, Doncaster.*—Deac. 1847 and Pr. 1848 by Bp of Ches. V. of Campsall, Dio. York, 1853. (Patron, George Cooke Yarborough, Esq; Tithe—Imp. 65*l*, V. 16*l* 13*s* 4*d*; Glebe, 80 acres; V.'s Inc. 135*l* and Ho; Pop. 1083.) Formerly P. C. of Skelbrooke, Yorks, 1855–67. [24]

EVANS, William Edward, *Burton Court, Leominster, Herefordshire.*—Clare Hall, Cam. B.A. 1823, M.A. 1826; Deac. 1824 by Bp of Pet. Pr. 1825 by Bp of St. A. Prælector of Herf. Cathl. 1845. (Value, 40*l*.) Can. of Hereford; V. of Madley with Tibberton C. Dio. Herf. 1850. (Patrons, D. and C. of Herf; Tithe—App. 762*l*, V. 566*l*; V.'s Inc. 640*l* and Ho; Pop. Madley 970, Tibberton 153.) Author, *An Order of Family Prayers,* 1844; *Songs of the Birds,* 1845; *Sermons on Genesis, &c.,* 1849. [25]

EVANS, William Howell, *Llandyssil, Montgomery.*—Jesus Coll. Ox. B.A. 1856, M.A. 1859; Deac. 1858 and Pr. 1859 by Bp of Roch. C. of Llandyssil. Formerly C. of Frating with Thorington 1858. [26]

EVANS, W. S., *York.*—Travelling Sec. of Missions to Seamen; P. C. of Ulley, Dio. York, 1867. (Patron, Viscount Halifax; P.C.'s Inc. 50*l* and Ho; Pop. 165.) [27]

EVANSON, Charles, *Montpelier, Bristol.*—St. Edm. Hall, Ox. B.A. 1834, M.A. 1838; Deac. 1834 and Pr. 1835 by Bp of Salis. P. C. of St. Andrew's, Montpelier, Bristol, Dio. G. and B. 1845. (Patron, Bp of G. and B; P. C.'s Inc. 270*l*; Pop. 5591.) Author, *The Church, the Pillar and Ground of the Truth* (a Visitation Sermon), 1846. [28]

EVANSON, Richard Macdonnell, *Llansoy Rectory, Usk, Monmouthshire.*—Oriel Coll. Ox. B.A. 1847; Deac. 1847 and Pr. 1848 by Bp of G. and B. R. of Llansoy, Dio. Llan. 1849. (Patron, Duke of Beaufort; Tithe, 190*l*; Glebe, 17 acres; R.'s Inc. 206*l* and Ho; Pop. 168.) Rural Dean. Editor of *John Evelyn's History of Religion,* 2 vols. [29]

EVANSON, Robert Macdonnell, *Ainsworth Parsonage, near Bolton.*—Dub. A.B. 1846, A.M. 1849, *ad eund.* Ox. 1849; Deac. 1845, Pr. 1846. P. C. of Ainsworth, *alias* Cockey, Dio. Man. 1857. (Patron, R. of Middleton; Tithe, App. 48*l*; P. C.'s Inc. 185*l* and Ho; Pop. 1803.) Formerly C. of St. Luke's, Heywood, near Manchester. [30]

EVE, Henry, *South Ockendon Rectory, Romford, Essex.*—R. of South Ockendon, Dio. Roch. 1819. (Patron, J. Cliffe, Esq; Tithe, 833*l* 0*s* 6*d*; R.'s Inc. 843*l* and Ho; Pop. 1267.) [31]

EVELYN, Edmund B., *Wotton, Surrey.*—R. of Wotton, Dio. Win. 1857. (Patron, W. J. Evelyn, Esq;

Tithe, 525*l*; Glebe, 129 acres; R.'s Inc. 666*l* and Ho; Pop. 433.) [1]

EVERARD, Edward Browne, *Burnham-Thorpe Rectory, Burnham-Westgate, Norfolk.*—Ball. Coll. Ox. B.A. 1823, M.A. 1829; Deac. 1825, Pr. 1826. R. of Burnham-Thorpe, Dio. Nor. 1853. (Patron, Earl of Orford; Tithe—App. 8*l* 15*s*, R. 704*l*; Glebe, 30 acres; R.'s Inc. 734*l* and Ho; Pop. 427.) [2]

EVERARD, Edward John, *Didmarton Rectory, Chippenham, Wilts.*—St. John's Coll. Cam. Lady Margaret's Scho. B.A. 1836; Deac. 1837 and Pr. 1840 by Bp of G. and B. R. of Oldbury-on-the-hill with Didmarton R. Dio. G. and B. 1840. (Patron, Duke of Beaufort; Oldbury, Tithe, 245*l*; Didmarton, Tithe, 141*l* 13*s*; Glebe, 34 acres, R.'s Inc. 420*l*; Pop. Oldbury 440, Didmarton 92.) [3]

EVERARD, George, *Framsden Vicarage, Stonham, Suffolk.*—St. John's Coll. Cam. B.A. 1851, M.A. 1854; Deac. and Pr. 1852. V. of Framsden, Dio. Nor. 1858. (Patron, J. Tollemache, Esq. M.P; Tithe—Imp. 567*l*, V. 344; Glebe, 43½ acres; V.'s Inc. 375*l* and Ho; Pop. 811.) Formerly C. of Trinity, Marylebone, and St. Mary's, Hastings. Author, *Day by Day, or Counsels for Christians*, W. Hunt and Co. 1865, 3*s*; *Not your own, or Counsels for Young Christians*, ib. 1866, 1*s*; etc. [4]

EVERARD, Salisbury, *Swaffham Vicarage, Norfolk.*—Ball. Coll. Ox. B.A. 1831, M.A. 1835; Deac. 1832, Pr. 1833. V. of Swaffham with Threxton R. Dio. Nor. 1844. (Patron, Bp of Nor; Swaffham, Tithe—App. 1159*l* 10*s* and 110 acres of Glebe, V. 564*l* 15*s* 8*d*; Glebe, 38 acres; Threxton, Tithe, 171*l* 2*s* 8*d*; Glebe, ½ acre; V.'s Inc. 789*l* and Ho; Pop. Swaffham 3559, Threxton 80.) Hon. Can. of Norwich 1863; Rural Dean. [5]

EVERED, Charles William Henry, *Otterhampton, Bridgwater.*—R. of Otterhampton, Dio. B. and W. (Patron, the present R; R.'s Inc. 240*l* and Ho; Pop. 235.) Formerly R. of Exton 1833. [6]

EVERED, Elwin Everard John, *Bishopton, Stratford-on-Avon.*—St. John's Coll. Cam. B.A. 1854; Deac. 1855 and Pr. 1856 by Bp of Rip. P. C. of Bishopton, Dio. Wor. 1862. (Patron, V. of Stratford.) C. of Stratford-on-Avon. Formerly C. of Fladbury, Wyre-Piddle, Wilsford, and Cross-Stone. Author, *Have you been Baptized? Are you a Communicant? The Sin of Schism as exemplified in the Rebellion of Korah, Dathan and Abiram*; *The Close of the Year*; *The Festival of Shakespeare*; *The Cattle Plague*; all published by Masters. [7]

EVERED, Everard Robert Fountain, *South Darley, Matlock, Derbyshire.*—St. Peter's Coll. Cam. Cl. and Math. Prizeman 1853, B.A. 1855, M.A. 1860; Deac. 1855 and Pr. 1856 by Bp of Man. P. C. of St. Mary's, Cross Green, South Darley, Dio. Lich. 1864. (Patron, R. of North Darley; P. C.'s Inc. 100*l* and Ho; Pop. 582.) Formerly C. of Madeley, St. George's, Chorley, Lane; P. C. of Tharlby, Notts, 1859–64. [8]

EVEREST, William Frederick, *Bodmin.*—Magd. Hall, Ox. B.A. 1842; Deac. 1841, Pr. 1842. Chap. of the Cornwall County Gaol 1858. Formerly P. C. of Laneast, Launceston, 1844. [9]

EVERETT, Arthur Joseph, *Berry-Pomeroy Vicarage, Totnes, Devon.*—Clare Coll. Cam. Jun. Opt. B.A. 1860; Deac. 1860 and Pr. 1861 by Bp of B. and W. V. of Berry-Pomeroy, Dio. Ex. 1861. (Patron, Duke of Somerset; Tithe, 420*l*; Glebe, 2 acres; V.'s Inc. 450*l*; Pop. 1065.) Formerly C. of Wells 1860–61. [10]

EVERETT, Charles Dundas, *Besselsleigh Rectory, Abingdon.*—Queen's Coll. Ox. B.A. 1849; Deac. 1841, Pr. 1842. R. of Besselsleigh, Dio. Ox. 1858. (Patron, K. J. W. Lenthall, Esq; R.'s Inc. 300*l* and Ho; Pop. 92.) Formerly C. of Alton-Barnes, Wilts; Chap. R.N. Author, *Note-book in the Mediterranean, Corfu, Albania, &c.* [11]

EVERETT, Charles Henry, *Tangley, Andover.*—Ball. Coll. Ox. B.A. 1856; Deac. 1857 and Pr. 1858 by Bp of Ox. R. of Faccombe with Tangley C. Hants, Dio. Win. 1858. (Patron, the Rev. G. F. Everett; Faccombe, Tithe—App. 6*s*; R. 420*l*; Glebe, 66 acres; Tangley, Tithe, 330*l*; Glebe, 1½ acres; R.'s Inc. 817*l* and Ho; Pop. Faccombe 243, Tangley 270.) [12]

EVERETT, C. W., *Woolhampton, Berks.*—St. John's Coll. Cam. B.A. 1832; Deac. 1832 and Pr. 1833 by Bp of Salis. R. of Woolhampton, Dio. Ox. 1859. (Patron, the present R; R.'s Inc. 202*l* and Ho; Pop. 559.) [13]

EVERETT, Edward, *Manningford Abbotts Rectory, Pewsey, Wilts.*—St. John's Coll. Cam. B.A. 1839; Deac. 1841 and Pr. 1842 by Bp of Pet. R. of Manningford Abbotts, Dio. Salis. 1857. (Patron, Sir. F. Astley, Bart; Tithe, 315*l*; R.'s Inc. 320*l* and Ho; Pop. 139.) Formerly C. of Wilsford, Wilts. [14]

EVERETT, Edward Dawley.—St. Aidan's; Deac. 1863 by Bp of Ches. Formerly C. of Parr, St. Helens. [15]

EVERETT, George Blake, *Ashfield, Debenham, Suffolk.*—Deac. 1851 and Pr. 1852 by Bp of Nor. P. C. of Ashfield, Dio. Nor. 1864. (Patron, Lord Henniker; P. C.'s Inc. 53*l*; Pop. 306.) Formerly R. of St. Edmund's, Norwich, 1856; C. of St. Swithin's, Norwich. [16]

EVERETT, George Frederick, *Shaw Rectory, near Newbury.*—Ball. Coll. Ox. 1st cl. in Lit. Hum. 1813, B.A. 1814, M.A. 1816; Deac. 1816 and Pr. 1817 by Bp of Salis. V. of Shaw with Dennington 1847. (Patron, Henry Richard Eyre, Esq; Tithe, 621*l*; Glebe, 28 acres; R.'s Inc. 550*l* and Ho; Pop. 680.) [17]

EVERETT, Henry, 27, *Trafalgar-place, Devonport.*—Ex. Coll. Ox. B.A. 1859, M.A. 1863; Deac. 1860, Pr. 1862. P. C. of St. John's, Devonport, Dio. Ex. 1863. (Patron, R. of Stoke.) Formerly C. of Tor-Mohun 1860, Newton St. Cyres 1862, Stoke 1863. [18]

EVERETT, Thomas Ellis, *Gibraltar Cottage, Monmouth.*—St. Aidan's; Deac. 1853 and Pr. 1854 by Abp of Cant. V. of Rockfield, Dio. Llan. 1858. (Patron, Sir John Harding; Tithe, 20*l*; Glebe, 29 acres; V.'s Inc. 79*l*; Pop. 260.) Formerly C. of Halstead, Kent, 1853, Pailton and Copston, Warwickshire, 1854. [19]

EVERS, Edwin, 2, *Caroline-place, Charles-street, Hull.*—St. Cath. Coll. Cam. B.A. 1865; Deac. 1867 by Abp of York. C. of St. Paul's, Sculcoates, 1867. [20]

EVERSFIELD, S., *Sneyd, Burslem.*—P. C. of Sneyd, Dio. Lich. 1866. (Patrons, Crown and Bp of Lich. alt; P. C.'s Inc. 150*l* and Ho; Pop. 3071.) [21]

EVERY, John James.—Jesus Coll. Cam. B.A. 1852; Deac. 1853. Chap. of H.M.S. "Clio." [22]

EVERY, Nicholas Thomas, *St. Kew Vicarage, Wadebridge, Cornwall.*—Clare Hall Cam. B.A. 1850; Deac. 1851, Pr. 1852. V. of St. Kew, Dio. Ex. 1851. (Patroness, Mrs. Every; Tithe, 520*l*; Glebe, 31 acres; V.'s Inc. 601*l* and Ho; Pop. 1182.) [23]

EVETTS, Thomas, *Monks Risborough Rectory, Tring.*—Corpus Coll. Ox. B.A. 1842, M.A. 1844; Deac. 1843, Pr. 1844. R. of Monks Risborough, Dio. Ox. 1863. (Patron, Bp of Ox; Glebe, 430 acres; R.'s Inc. 760*l* and Ho; Pop. 979.) Surrogate 1852; Rural Dean 1853. Formerly C. of Clifton Reynes 1843–48; P. C. of Holy Trin. Dist. Prestwood, 1849–63. [24]

EVILL, Alfred, *Mayfield, Ashbourne.*—Lin. Coll. Ox. B.A. 1855, M.A. 1858; Deac. 1857 and Pr. 1858 by Bp of Lon. V. of Mayfield, Dio. Lich. 1866. (Patroness, Mrs. Greaves; Tithe, 70*l*; Glebe, 25 acres; V's Inc. 180*l* and Ho; Pop. 1006.) Formerly C. of Bloomsbury, Lond. 1857–59, Middle Claydon 1859, Claydon Steeple, Bucks, 1860. [25]

EVORS, Charles Robert, *Kington, Pershore, Worcestershire.*—St. Aidan's; Deac. 1854 and Pr. 1855 by Bp of Ches. R. of Kington, Dio. Wor. 1859. (Patron, W. Laslett, Esq; Tithe, 97*l*; Glebe, 20 acres; R.'s Inc. 117*l*; Pop. 172.) C. of Grafton Flyford. Formerly P. C. of Saltersford 1855–58. [26]

EWALD, Ferdinand Charles, LL.D., 8, *Palestine-place, Cambridge-road, London, N.E.*—Lect. of the Jews' Episcopal Chapel, Lond; Chap. to Bp Gobat of Jerusalem. [27]

EWALD, W. H., *Constantinople.*—Asst. Chap. at Constantinople. Formerly C. of Assington, Suffolk. [28]

EWART, William, *Vicarage, Bishops-Cannings, Devizes.*—Ex. Coll. Ox. B.A. 1842, M.A. 1844; Deac. 1842 by Bp of Pet. Pr. 1843 by Bp of Wor. V. of Bishops-Cannings, Dio. Salis. 1862. (Patrons, D. and C.

of Salis; Tithe, 500*l*; Rent from Glebe, 36*l*; V.'s Inc. 536*l* and Ho; Pop. 1109.) Formerly C. of Pimperne 1844. Author, *Lessons for Writing from Dictation, for the Use of Schools*, 1849; *Anchurus and other Poems*, 1851. [1]

EWBANK, George, 4, *Belvedere-terrace, Brighton.*—Caius Coll. Cam. 1st Sen. Opt. and B.A. 1847, M.A. 1854; Deac. 1848 and Pr. 1849 by Bp of Win. Formerly C. of St. Margaret's, Brighton. [2]

EWBANK, Henry, *St. John's, Ryde, Isle of Wight.*—Brasen. Coll. Ox. B.A. 1852, M.A. 1856; Deac. 1851 and Pr. 1852 by Abp of Cant. P. C. of St. John's, near Ryde, Dio. Win. 1867. (Patron, Rev. W. H. Dearsley; P. C.'s Inc. from pew-rents.) Formerly P. C. of St. James's, Ryde, 1856–67. [3]

EWEN, Edward, *Stanway, Colchester.*—St. Peter's Coll. Cam. B.A. 1853. C. of Stanway. Formerly C. of Belchamp-Otton, Essex. [4]

EWEN, Henry L'Estrange, *Chatham.*—St. John's Coll. Cam. B.A. 1855, M.A. 1858; Deac. 1865 and Pr. 1866 by Bp of Roch. C. of St. John's, Chatham, 1865. [5]

EWEN, W. H. L., *Bishops Lydeard, Somerset.*—C. of Bishops Lydeard.

EWING, Alexander, *Bishopwearmouth, Durham.*—C. of Bishopwearmouth. [6]

EWING, Alexander, 30, *Argyll-road, Mile End, London, E.*—Deac. 1863 and Pr. 1864 by Abp of Cant. C. of Bethnal Green 1867. Formerly C. of Westmill, Herts, 1863–65, St. Peter's, Stepney, 1865–66. [7]

EWING, John Aiken, *Westmill Rectory, Buntingford.*—St. John's Coll. Ox. B.A. 1847, M.A. 1848; Deac. 1848 by Bp of Ox. Pr. 1849 by Bp of Wor. R. of Westmill, Dio. Roch. 1851. (Patroness, Countess of Mexborough; Tithe, comm. 540*l*; Glebe, 40 acres; R.'s Inc. 570*l* and Ho; Pop. 353.) Rural Dean 1861; Diocesan Inspector of Schools 1863. [8]

EWING, John Gordon, 42, *Hockley Hill, Birmingham.*—Queen's Coll. Birmingham; Deac. 1866 by Bp of Wor. C. of St. George's, Birmingham, 1866. [9]

EWING, William, *North Pickenham, Swaffham, Norfolk.*—Lin. Coll. Ox. B.A. 1839, M.A. 1843; Deac. 1841 and Pr. 1842 by Bp of Nor. R. of North Pickenham with Houghton-on-the-Hill R. Dio. Nor. 1855. (Patron, Edmund Farrer, Esq; Tithe, 499*l*; Glebe, 111 acres; R.'s Inc. 660*l* and Ho; Pop. North Pickenham 287, Houghton-on-the-Hill 49.) [10]

EXETER, The Right Rev. Henry PHILLPOTTS, Lord Bp of Exeter, *The Palace, Exeter*, and *Bishopstowe, Torquay, Devon.*—Corpus Coll. Ox. Chancellor's Bachelor's Prize Essay 1795, Magd. Coll. Ox. B.A. 1795, M.A. 1798, B.D. and D.D. 1821; Deac. 1802 by Bp of Lon. Pr. 1804 by Bp of Ban. Can. of Dur. Cathl. 1831. Consecrated Bp of Ex. 1831 (also Treasurer of Ex. Cathl. heretofore annexed, and included in the net value of the See, from which they will be severed at the next avoidance, when the Inc. of the See will be raised to 5000*l*; Net Value of See 2700*l*; Jurisdiction, the Counties of Devonshire, Cornwall, and the Scilly Isles; Pop. 953,763; Acres, 2,530,780; Deaneries, 32; Benefices, 657; Curates, 268; Church sittings, 323,037.) His Lordship was formerly Visitor of Ex. Coll. Ox. 1831; a Fell. of Magd. Coll. Ox. 1795. Author, *Sermons before the University of Oxford*, 4to. 1804; *Sermons for the Sons of the Clergy*, 4to. 1815; *Letter to Right Hon. W. S. Browne on a Bill to amend the Laws respecting the Settlement of the Poor*, 1819; *Letter to the Freeholders of the County of Durham*, 1819; *Remarks on an Article in* "The Edinburgh Review" (No. 64), 1820; *Remarks on a Note in* "The Edinburgh Review" (No. 65), 1820; *Letter to Earl Grey on certain Charges advanced by him against the Clergy of the County of Durham*, 3 eds. 1821; *Letter to Jeffrey on an Article entitled* "*Durham Case, Clerical Abuses*," *in* "The Edinburgh Review," 1823; *Letters to Charles Butler, Esq.* 1825; *Supplementary Letter to Charles Butler, Esq.* 1826; *A Letter to the Right Hon. George Canning on the Catholic Question*, 1827; *A Letter to the Right Hon. George Canning, on the Catholic Bill*, 1827; *A Letter to an English Layman on the Coronation Oath*, 1828; *Speech on the Second Reading of the Reform Bill*, 1832; *Speech on New Plan of National Education in Ireland*, 1833; *A Charge*, 2 eds. 1833; *Speech on a Petition of certain Members of the Senate of Cambridge*, 1834; *Speech on Moving for a Select Committee on National Education in Ireland*, 1836; *A Charge*, 1836; *Speech in the House of Lords, on the Church Discipline Bill*, 1838; *A Charge*, 1839; *Speech on Socialism*, 1840; *Correspondence between the Bishop of Exeter and the Ecclesiastical Inquiry Commissioners*, 1841; *A Charge*, 1842; *A Letter to the Clergy of the Diocese of Exeter on the Use of the Offertory*, 1843; *A Sermon preached at a General Ordination*, 1843; *The Widow's Mite* (a Sermon), *and a Pastoral Letter to the Inhabitants of Plymouth*, 1844; *Report of the Proceedings under the Bishop of Exeter's Commission to inquire into the Complaint against the Rev. W. Blunt*, 1844; *Letter to the Clergy of the Diocese of Exeter on Observance of the Rubric*, 1844; *Letter to the Dean of Exeter on a Memorial from him, and certain Residentiaries, to the Archbishop of Canterbury*, 1844; *A Charge*, 1845; *Reply to Lord John Russell's Letter on the Remonstrance of the Bishops against the Appointment of Dr. Hampden*, 2 eds. 1847; *Letters to the Archdeacons of the Diocese of Exeter on Scripture Readers*, 1847; *Sermon for the General Fast-day*, 1847; *A Charge*, 1848; *Sermon Preached for the Devonport and Plymouth Spiritual Destitution Relief Fund*, 1849; *The Case of the Rev. Mr. Shore, a Letter to the Archbishop of Canterbury*, 4 eds. 1849; *Protest of the Bishop of Exeter (in the Arches Court); on the Institution of Mr. Gorham*, 1850; *Reply to the Addresses of the Clergy on the Romish Aggression*, 1850; *Letter to the Archbishop of Canterbury on the Decision of the Privy Council in the Gorham Case*, 1850; *Letter to the Churchwardens of Brampford Speke*, 1850; *Pastoral Letter to the Clergy of Exeter on the State of the Church*, 8 eds. 1851; *Speech in the House of Lords on the Prohibited Affinity Marriage Bill*, 1851; *Letter to the Clergy of the Diocese of Exeter on Certain Statements in a Charge made by the Archdeacon of Middlesex*, 1851; *Letter to Sir R. Inglis on certain Statements in No.* 139 of "The Edinburgh Review," entitled "Bishop Phillpotts," 3 eds. 1852; *Confession and Absolution, a Letter to the Dean of Exeter*, 1852, *A Letter to the Clergy of the Archdeaconry of Totnes, in answer to an Address on the Necessity of Episcopal Ordination*, 2 eds. 1852; *A Letter to Miss Sellon*, 1852; *Pastoral Letter to the Clergy of the Diocese of Exeter*; *A Pastoral Letter to the Clergy of his Diocese, before his Triennial Visitation, in* 1854; *Confirmation, its Duties and Privileges*, 1856; *Answer to Addresses from Clergymen of the Diocese of Exeter on the Judgment of the Court of Bath, in Ditcher v. the Archdeacon of Taunton*, 2 eds. 1856; *Speech delivered on the Motion of the Lord Chancellor, that the Church Discipline Bill be read a second time*, 1856; *Letter to the Right Hon. Dr. Lushington, on his Judgment in the Case of Westerton v. Liddell (Clerk)*; *A Pastoral Letter to the Clergy*, 1857; *Correspondence between the Bishop of Exeter and the Right Hon. T. B. Macaulay on certain Statements respecting the Church of England*, 1860; *Letter to the Bishop of Lichfield on the claim of his Lordship's authority in favour of the Bill Legalising Marriage with the Sister of a deceased Wife*, 1860; *Addresses delivered to the Clergy of the Diocese of Exeter at his 11th Visitation*, 1863; Various other Sermons, Charges, Pamphlets, &c. [11]

EXTON, Francis, *Filby, near Norwich.*—St. John's Coll. Cam. Sen. Opt. 3rd cl. Lit. Hum. Burney Prize 1856, B.A. 1856, M.A. 1859; Deac. 1857 and Pr. 1858 by Bp of Nor. C. of Filby 1857. Author, *The Church of England on the Fourth Commandment, and the Word of God on a Seventh Day Sabbath*, 1860, 2*s*; *A Plain Help to Public Worship*; *Questions and Answers on the Order for Morning and Evening Prayer*, 1863, 2*s*. Joint Author of *More about Farm Lads*, 1865, 2*s* 6*d*. [12]

EXTON, Richard, *Hemley Rectory, Woodbridge, Suffolk.*—Literate; Deac. 1834 by Bp of Nor. Pr. 1835 by Bp of Pet. R. of Hemley, Dio. Nor. 1844. (Patron, Ld Chan; Tithe, 201*l* 1*s* 7*d*; Glebe, 34 acres; R.'s Inc. 250*l* and Ho; Pop. 63.) [1]

EYRE, Charles James Phipps, 20, *Upper Wimpole-street, London, W.*—R. of St. Marylebone, Dio. Lon. 1857. (Patron, the Crown; R.'s Inc. 1270*l*; Pop. 29,098.) Rural Dean. Formerly P. C. of St. James's, Bury St. Edmunds, 1842–57; Chap. to Lord Methuen. [2]

EYRE, Daniel James, *The Close, Salisbury.*—Oriel Coll. Ox. B A. 1824, M.A. 1827; Deac. 1826 and Pr. 1827 by Bp of Salis. Sub-Dean of Salis. Cathl. 1846. Author, *The Rite of Confirmation Explained*, 4th ed. 1852. [3]

EYRE, Francis John, *Englefield Rectory, Reading.*—Trin. Coll. Cam. B.A. 1834; Deac. 1835, Pr. 1836. R. of Englefield, Dio. Ox. 1855. (Patron, R. B. De Beauvoir, Esq; Tithe, 409*l*; Glebe, 33 acres; R.'s Inc. 450*l* and Ho; Pop. 392.) [4]

EYRE, Frederick Drought, 13, *College-terrace, Hammersmith, W.*—Ch. Coll. Cam. B.A. 1828, M.A. 1834; Deac. 1832 and Pr. 1834 by Bp of Lich. [5]

EYRE, Frederick Kinneer, *Mudeford, Christchurch, Hants.*—St. John's Coll. Ox. B.A. 1826, M.A. 1837; Deac. 1835, Pr. 1836. P. C. of Hinton Admiral, Dio. Win. 1862. (Patron, Sir G. Gervis, Bart; P. C.'s Inc. 72*l*.) Formerly C. of Hinton Admiral. [6]

EYRE, Henry Samuel, *Newington Vicarage, Sittingbourne.*—Ch. Ch. Ox. B.A. 1838, M.A. 1840. V. of Newington, Dio. Cant. 1862. (Patron, Eton Coll; Tithe—Imp. 605*l*, V. 338*l*; V.'s Inc. 340*l* and Ho; Pop. 854.) [7]

EYRE, John Francis Nash, *Denholme, Bradford, Yorks.*—St. Bees, 1854; Deac. 1854. P. C. of Denholme, Dio. Rip. 1861. (Patrons, Crown and Bp alt; P. C.'s Inc. 150*l* and Ho; Pop. 2816.) Surrogate. Formerly C. of Kirkby-Misperton, Great Habton, Little Habton, Great Barugh, and Little Barugh, Yorks, 1854–58. [8]

EYRE, William Leigh Williamson, *Woodcote, Newport, Salop.*—Lich. Theol. Coll; Deac. 1865 and Pr. 1866 by Bp of Lich. C. of Sheriff Hales with Woodcote 1865. [9]

EYRE, William Thomas, *Padbury, Bucks*, and *Rosebank, Sidmouth.*—Brasen. Coll. Ox. 2nd cl. Lit. Hum. B.A. 1816, M.A. 1819; Deac. 1818, Pr. 1819. V. of Padbury, Dio. Ox. 1830. (Patron, the Crown; Modus of 6*s* 8*d*; Glebe, 72 acres; V.'s Inc. 140*l*; Pop. 550.) P. C. of Hillesden, Dio. Ox. 1830. (Patrons, D. and C. of Ch. Ch. Ox; App. Glebe, 286 acres; P. C.'s Inc. 210*l*; Pop. 251.) Formerly C. of Winslow, Bucks, Owre, Newnham, Glouc. and Blockley, Worc. Author, single Sermons, *The Constitutional Ascendency of the United Church of England and Ireland Maintained*, 1828; *Visitation Sermon before the Bishop of Lincoln, at Buckingham*, 1830; *The Reformed Church of England*, 1850; *The Prayer of Faith shall save the Sick*, 1853; *A Guide to Blockley*; *Extracts of Examples of the Sin of Drunkenness with the warnings of Holy Scripture annexed*, 2nd ed. for gratuitous distribution. [10]

EYRES, Charles, *Melton Rectory, Norwich.*—Caius Coll. Cam. B.A. 1832, Norrisian Prizeman 1833, M.A. 1835; Deac. 1833, Pr. 1834. R. of Great Melton with St. Mary and All Saints, Dio. Nor. 1851. (Patron, Caius Coll. Cam; Tithe—App. 6*l* 10*s*, R. 748*l* 10*s*; Glebe, 22 acres; R.'s Inc. 770*l* and Ho; Pop. 368.) Formerly Fell. of Caius Coll. Cam. 1851. Author, *Norrisian Prize Essay*, 1834; *An Assise Sermon*, 1837; *Observations on University Reform*, 1850. [11]

EYTON, Charles Watkin Wynne, *Aston-Clinton, near Tring.*—Jesus Coll. Ox. B.A. 1822, M.A. 1824, B.D. 1834; Deac. 1822, Pr. 1823. R. of Aston-Clinton, Dio. Ox. 1848. (Patron, Jesus Coll. Ox; Land in lieu of Tithe, 514 acres; R.'s Inc. 506*l* and Ho; Pop. 1108.) Formerly Fell. of Jesus Coll. Ox. [12]

FABER, Arthur Henry, *Malvern, Worcestershire.*—New Coll. Ox. M.A. 1853. Fell. and Tut. of New Coll. Ox. Head Mast. of the Malvern Proprietary Sch. [13]

FABER, Francis Atkinson, *Saunderton Rectory, Tring, Herts.*—Univ. Coll. Ox. Scho. 1822, 2nd cl. Lit. Hum. and B.A. 1826, M.A. 1828, Magd. Coll. B.D. 1836; Deac. 1827 by Bp of Dur. Pr. 1828 by Abp of York. R. of Saunderton, Dio. Ox. 1845. (Patron, Magd. Coll. Ox; Tithe, 2*l* 5*s*; Glebe, 404 acres; R.'s Inc. 400*l* and Ho; Pop. 232.) Formerly Fell. of Magd. Coll. Ox. 1833; Select Preacher 1834; Tut. of Magd. Coll. Ox. 1835; C. of Grindon, Durham, 1828–30, Whitworth, Durham, 1831–33. Author, *Memoir of the Rev. G. S. Faber* (prefixed to the 2nd ed. of *Many Mansions in the House of the Father*) Royston, 1854. [14]

FABER, John Cooke, *Chicklade Rectory, Hindon, Wilts.*—Ch. Ch. Ox. 3rd cl. Lit. Hum. and B.A. 1834. R. of Chicklade, Dio. Salis. 1839. (Patron, Marquis of Bath; Tithe, 205*l*; R.'s Inc. 235*l* and Ho; Pop. 143.) [15]

FAGAN, Feltrim, *Guernsey.*—P. C. of All Saints', Guernsey, Dio. Win. 1865. (Patron, John James, Esq; P. C.'s Inc. 150*l*.) [16]

FAGAN, George Hickson Urquhart, *Stoke-Rodney Rectory, Wells.*—Oriel Coll. Ox. 3rd cl. Lit. Hum. B.A. 1838, M.A. 1841; Deac. 1840, Pr. 1841. R. of Stoke-Rodney, Dio. B. and W. 1859. (Patron, Bp of B. and W; Tithe, 334*l*; R.'s Inc. 350*l* and Ho; Pop. 323.) Preb. of Combe the 3rd, Wells Cathl. 1853; Rural Dean; Hon. Chap. to the Duke of Buccleuch; Hon. Sec. of the B. and W. Diocesan Society. Formerly R. of Kingweston, Somerset, 1849–59. [17]

FAGAN, Henry Stuart, *Broad-street, Bath.*—Pemb. Coll. Ox. 2nd cl. Lit. Hum. 1st cl. Math. et Phy. and B.A. 1850, M.A. 1853; Deac. 1850 by Bp of Ox. Pr. 1852 by Bp of Lich. Head Mast. of the Bath Gr. Sch; R. of Charlcombe, Dio. B. and W. 1858. (Patrons, Trustees of the Bath Charities; R.'s Inc. 230*l* and Ho; Pop. 378.) Formerly Head Mast. of the Burton-on-Trent Gr. Sch. 1851; Asst. Mast. of King Edward's Sch. Birmingham, 1851–55; Head Mast. of the Market Bosworth Gr. Sch. 1855–58. [18]

FAGGE, John Frederick, *Aston Cantlow Vicarage, Henley-in-Arden, Warwickshire.*—Univ. Coll. Ox. B.A. 1835; Deac. 1841 and Pr. 1842 by Bp of Nor. V. of Aston Cantlow, Dio. Wor. 1849. (Patron, Rev. E. B. K. Fortescue; Glebe, 4 acres; V.'s Inc. 80*l* and Ho; Pop. 618.) [19]

FAIRBAIRN, Adam H., *Knowl Hill, Twyford, Berks.*—Trin. Coll. Cam. B.A. 1859, M.A. 1862; Deac. 1860 and Pr. 1861 by Bp of Ox. P. C. of Knowl Hill, Dio. Ox. 1864. (Patrons, Trustees; P. C.'s Inc. 90*l* and Ho; Pop. 850.) Formerly C. of Wargrave 1860, Wilton 1863. [20]

FAIRBANKS, Joseph Henry, *Luton Rectory, Chatham.*—Clare Coll. Cam. B.A. 1846, M.A. 1850; Deac. 1846, Pr. 1847. R. of Ch. Ch. Luton, Dio. Roch. 1852. (Patron, R. of Chatham; R.'s Inc. 200*l* and Ho; Pop. 2730.) [21]

FAIRCLOUGH, Richard John, 44, *Irvine-street, Liverpool.*—Ch. Coll. Cam. Scho. B.A. 1862, M.A. 1866; Deac. 1862 and Pr. 1863 by Bp of Carl. C. of Liverpool 1865. Formerly C. of Aspatria, Cumberland, 1862. [22]

FAIRLES, Septimus, *Lurgashall Rectory, Petworth, Sussex.*—R. of Lurgashall, Dio. Chich. 1851. (Patron, Lord Leconfield; Tithe, 463*l*; Glebe, 10 acres; R.'s Inc. 473*l* and Ho; Pop. 727.) [23]

FAITHFULL, Ferdinand, *Headley Rectory, Leatherhead, Surrey.*—R. of Headley, Dio. Win. 1830. (Patrons, Heirs of late Hon. Col. Howard; Tithe, 211*l*; Glebe, 15½ acres; R.'s Inc. 237*l* and Ho; Pop. 322.) [24]

FAITHFULL, George, *Llanwenarth, near Abergavenny.*—Caius Coll. Cam. B.A. 1852; Deac. 1852, Pr. 1853. R. of Llanwenarth, Dio. Llan. 1865. (Patron, Earl of Abergavenny; R.'s Inc. 300*l* and Ho; Pop. 119.) Formerly C. of Horsmonden, Kent. [25]

FAITHFULL, James Grantham, 23, *Oxford-terrace, Edgware-road, London, W.*—Ex. Coll. Ox. B.A. 1838, M.A. 1842; Deac. 1842 and Pr. 1843 by Bp of Lin. V. of Cheshunt, Dio. Roch. 1858. (Patron, Marquis of Salisbury; Tithe, 454*l*; Glebe, 26 acres; V.'s Inc. 750*l* and Ho; Pop. 4563.) Formerly V. of North Mimms, Herts, 1854–56; R. of Clothall, Herts, 1856–58. Author, *Justification by Faith*; *Wayside Thoughts*; *Confirmation Hymns*; *Address to Students of Cheshunt College*, etc. [1]

FAITHFULL, Valentine Grantham, 23, *Royal Circus, Edinburgh.*—Corpus Coll. Cam. B.A. 1842, M.A. 1845; Deac. 1845, Pr. 1846. Incumb. of Trinity Chapel, Dean Bridge, Edinburgh, 1853. Formerly C. of Hatfield, Herts. [2]

FALCON, J., *Lenham, Maidstone.*—C. of Lenham. [3]

FALCON, Robert Steward, *Queen's College, Oxford.*—Queen's Coll. Ox. 1st cl. Lit. Hum. and B.A. 1851, M.A. 1854; Deac. 1852, Pr. 1853. Fell. of Queen's Coll. Ox. [4]

FALCON, Thomas William, *Queen's College, Oxford.*—Queen's Coll. Ox. 1st cl. Lit. Hum. 3rd cl. Math. et. Phy. and B.A. 1853, M.A. 1856; Deac. 1850 by Bp of Ox. Fell. and Tut. of Queen's Coll. Ox; R. of Charlton-upon-Otmoor, Dio. Ox. 1862. (Patron, Queen's Coll. Ox; Pop. 687.) [5]

FALCONER, David Richard, *The Vicarage, Hartlepool.*—Univ. Coll. Dur. Licen. Theol. 1855; Deac. 1855 and Pr. 1856 by Bp of Man. V. of Hartlepool, Dio. Dur. 1867. (Patron, V. of Hart; Tithe, 14*l*; Glebe, 130 acres; V.'s Inc. 300*l* and Ho; Pop. 7300.) Formerly C. of Bishopwearmouth 1855–63; P. C. of Shotton with Haswell 1863–67. [6]

FALCONER, William, *Bushey, Watford, Herts.*—Oriel Coll. Ox. 1st cl. Math. 2nd cl. Lit. Hum. and B.A. 1824, Ex. Coll M.A. 1827; Deac. 1837, Pr. 1839. R. of Bushey, Dio. Roch. 1839. (Patron, Ex. Coll. Ox; Tithe, 765*l*; Glebe, 35 acres; R.'s Inc. 835*l* and Ho; Pop. 3159.) Formerly Fell. of Ex. Coll. Ox. 1827–39; Public Examiner 1832–33 1836–38. Translator of *The Geography of Strabo* (Bohn's Classical Library), 3 vols. 1857. [7]

FALKNER, Francis Bancks, *Appleby Magna, Leicestershire.*—St. John's Coll. Cam. 12th Wrang. and B.A. 1854, M.A. 1859; Deac. 1857, Pr. 1858. Head Mast. of the Gr. Sch. Appleby Magna, 1864. Formerly 2nd Mast. of Aldenham Gr. Sch. 1854–59; C. of Aldenham 1858; Head Mast. of Brackley Gr. Sch. 1859–64. [8]

FALKNER, Thomas, *York.*—Caius Coll. Cam. B.A. 1853; Deac. 1853 and Pr. 1854 by Bp of Salis. Vicar-Choral and Librarian of York Minster; P. C. of Dringhouses, Dio. York, 1867. (Patron, Dr Wilkinson; P. C.'s Inc. 100*l*; Pop. 400.) [9]

FALKNER, Thomas Alexander, *Dorchester.*—C. of Holy Trinity, Dorchester. [10]

FALKNER, Trueman Tully, *Kelstern, Louth.*—V. of Kelstern, Dio. Lin. 1866. (Patron, Right Hon. J. E. Denison; V.'s Inc. 150*l*; Pop. 196.) [11]

FALLE, Edward, *St. Brelade's Rectory, Jersey.*—Pemb. Coll. Ox. B.A. 1823, M.A. 1827; Deac. 1826, Pr. 1827. R. of St. Brelade's, Jersey, Dio. Win. 1829. (Patron, Governor of Jersey; R.'s Inc. 150*l* and Ho; Pop. 2354.) [12]

FALLOON, Hugh, *Woodborough-road, Nottingham.*—Ch. Coll. Cam. B.A. 1864; Deac. 1865, Pr. 1866. C. of St. Ann's, Nottingham. [13]

FALLOON, William Marcus, 24, *Percy-street, Liverpool.*—Dub. Scho. A.M. 1837, A.B. 1859; Deac. and Pr. 1838. P. C. of St. Bride's, Liverpool, Dio. Ches. 1851. (Patrons, Trustees; P. C.'s Inc. 500*l*; Pop. 3954.) Surrogate. Formerly P. C. of St. John's, Liverpool; previously C. of St. Jude's, Liverpool, 1839–43. Author, *Drops from the Well of Living Water*; *Links of Gold from the Chain of Grace*; *Hymns for Sunday and Day Schools*; *More and More, a Word to My Flock*, 1854; *Six Addresses to the Congregation of St. John's, Liverpool*; *A Pastor's Warning, and Pastor's Word in Season*; *Consider what I say*; *Remember and Repent*; *Beware and be Stedfast*; *Believe and be Sure*; *Be not Deceived*; *Sunday-School Teachers, their Position, Qualifications, and Responsibilities*, 2 eds. [14]

FALLS, John, *Brockenhurst, near Lymington.*—Dub. A.B. 1830. V. of Brockenhurst, Dio. Win. 1862. (Patron, J. Morant, Esq; Tithe, 75*l*; V.'s Inc. 120*l* and Ho; Pop. 1082.) Formerly Chap. in the Royal Navy; C. of Brockenhurst. [15]

FALLS, Richard, 5, *Blackheath-terrace, S.E.*—Dub. A.B. 1864; Deac. 1866. Formerly C. of St. Paul's, Bury, Lancashire. [16]

FANE, Arthur, *Fulbeck Rectory, Grantham.*—Ex. Coll. Ox. B.A. 1829; Deac. 1836, Pr. 1837. R. of Fulbeck, Dio. Lin. 1863. (Patron, Col. Henry Fane; Glebe, 33 acres; R.'s Inc. 534*l* and Ho; Pop. 728.) Dom. Chap. to the Earl of Westmoreland 1841; Preb. of Yatesbury in Salis. Cathl. 1854. Formerly V. of Warminster 1841–63. [17]

FANE, Frederick Adrian Scroop, *Priors, Brentwood, Essex.*—Trin. Coll. Ox. B.A. 1832; Deac. 1834 and Pr. 1835 by Bp of Ox. P. C. of Norton-Mandeville, Essex, Dio. Roch. 1854. (Patron, C. Cure, Esq; Tithe—Imp. 193*l* 18*s* 6*d*, and 23 acres of Glebe; Glebe, 40 acres; P. C.'s Inc. 93*l*; Pop. 129.) [18]

FANSHAWE, Arthur Adolphus, *Bubbenhall, Kenilworth.*—New Coll. Ox. S.C.L. 1851, B.C.L. and M.A. 1856; Deac. 1854 and Pr. 1856 by Bp of Ox. P. C. of Bubbenhall, Dio. Wor. 1862. (Patron, Bp of Wor; P. C.'s Inc. 240*l* and Ho; Pop. 346.) Fell. of New Coll. Ox. [19]

FANSHAWE, Charles Simon Faithfull, *Upham Rectory, Bishops Waltham, Hants.*—Magd. Coll. Ox. B.A. 1827, M.A. 1830; Deac. 1829 and Pr. 1830 by Bp of Ox. R. of Upham, Dio. Win. 1855. (Patron, Bp of Win; Tithe, 420*l* 10*s*; Glebe, 2 acres; R.'s Inc. 450*l* and Ho; Pop. 589.) [20]

FANSHAWE, Frederick, *The Grammar School, Bedford.*—Ball. Coll. Ox. 1st cl. Lit. Hum. 3rd cl. Math. et Phy. and B.A. 1842, Ex. Coll. M.A. 1844; Deac. 1844, Pr. 1845. Fell. of Ex. Coll. Ox. 1842. Head Mast. of Bedford Gr. Sch. 1855. Formerly Tut. Heb. Lect. and Sen. Bursar of Ex. Coll. Ox. Author, *Vis per Angliam Ferro Strata* (Latin Prize Poem), 1841. [21]

FANSHAWE, Henry Leighton, *South Weston Rectory, Tetsworth, Oxon.*—New Coll. Ox. M.A. 1853; Deac. 1855 and Pr. 1856 by Bp of Ox. Fell. of New Coll. Ox. R. of Adwell with South Weston, Dio. Ox. 1866. (Patron, H. Birch Reynardson, Esq; Tithe, 196*l*; Glebe, 23 acres; R.'s Inc. 365*l* and Ho; Pop. 160.) Formerly C. of Shipton-under-Wychwood 1855, Clifton Hampden, Oxon, 1857. [22]

FANSHAWE, John Faithfull, *Withington, near Shrewsbury.*—P. C. of Withington, Dio. Lich. 1856. (Patron, R. of Upton Magna; P. C.'s Inc. 200*l*; Pop. 232.) [23]

FARBRACE, George Henry Teale, *Eythorne Rectory, Dover.*—Ch. Coll. Cam. B.A. 1808, M.A. 1824. R. of Eythorne, Dio. Cant. 1809. (Patrons, Earl of Guilford and T. Papillon, Esq. alt; Tithe, 502*l* 14*s* 2*d*; R.'s Inc. 510*l* and Ho; Pop. 461.) [24]

FARBROTHER, Alfred, *Spotland, Rochdale.*—St. John's Coll. Cam. 3rd cl. Cl. Trip. B.A. 1866; Deac. 1866. C. of Spotland. [25]

FARDELL, Henry William King, *Friesthorpe, Lincolnshire.*—Queens' Coll. Cam. B.A. 1854, M.A. 1857; Deac. 1854 and Pr. 1855 by Bp of Ely. R. of Friesthorpe with Snarford, Dio. Lin. 1866. (Patrons, Bp of Lin. and D. and C. alt; R.'s Inc. 340*l* and Ho; Pop. 150.) [26]

FARDELL, John George, *Banham Rectory, Attleborough, Norfolk.*—Ch. Coll. Cam. B.A. 1833, M.A. 1836; Deac. 1833, Pr. 1835. R. of Banham, Dio. Nor. 1856. (Patron, Ld Chan; Tithe, 1261*l*; Glebe, 35 acres; R.'s Inc. 1326*l* and Ho; Pop. 1163.) Formerly R. of Sprotborough, Yorks, 1837–56. [27]

FAREBROTHER, Charles, *Corby Vicarage, Colsterworth, Lincolnshire.*—Trin. Coll. Ox. B.C.L. 1844; Pr. 1846 by Bp. of Wor. R. of Irnham with Corby V.

Dio. Lin. 1851. (Patron, W. H. Woodhouse, Esq; Irnham, Tithe, 600*l*; Glebe, ½ acre; Corby, Tithe—Imp. 100*l*, V. 126*l*; Glebe, 82 acres; R.'s Inc. 800*l* and Ho; Pop. Irnham, 347, Corby 818.) Formerly C. of Ch. Ch. Worthing 1848–53; Chap. to the late Duke of Cambridge, and to the Lord Mayor of London 1846. Author, *The Election of the Lord Mayor of London* (a Sermon), 1846. [1]

FAREBROTHER, Henry William, *Arlington Vicarage, Hurst Green, Sussex.*—New Inn Hall, Ox. S.C.L. 1847; Deac. and Pr. 1848. V. of Arlington, Dio. Chich. 1862. (Patron, Bp of Lon; V.'s Inc. 200*l* and Ho; Pop. 427.) [2]

FAREBROTHER, Thomas, *New Walk, Leicester.*—Queen's Coll. Ox. B.A. 1829, M.A. 1834; Deac. 1830 and Pr. 1831 by Bp of Lich. Formerly C. of Stockton, Warwickshire, 1830–36; Brampton by Dingley 1836–42; P. C. of Ward-End, Aston, Birmingham 1842–54; C. of Weston-on-Trent, Derby, 1857–63. [3]

FARLEY, George, 4, *Clifton Wood, Bristol.*—Trin. Coll. Cam. B.A. 1822, M.A. 1825; Deac. 1822 and Pr. 1823 by Bp of Win. Formerly P. C. of Cherhill, Wilts, 1844–60. [4]

FARLEY, Thomas, *Ducklington Rectory, near Witney.*—Magd. Coll. Ox. B.A. 1818, M.A. 1821, B.D. 1828, D.D. 1852; Deac. 1819 by Bp of Ox. Pr. 1820 by Bp of Win. R. of Ducklington with Cokethorpe Chapel, Dio. Ox. 1836. (Patron, Magd. Coll. Ox; Tithe, 475*l*; Glebe, 37 acres; R.'s Inc. 610*l* and Ho; Pop. 606.) Formerly Fell. of Magd. Coll. Ox. [5]

FARLEY, William Meymott, *Cretingham, Wickham Market, Suffolk.*—St. Bees; Deac. 1840, Pr. 1841. V. of Cretingham, Dio. Nor. 1863. (Patron, Ld Chan; V.'s Inc. 173*l* and Ho; Pop. 343.) Formerly C. of Mottram-in-Longendale 1840, Trinity, Salford, 1841, Baldock, Herts, 1842, Saffron Walden 1843, Haddenham, Bucks, 1845, Bexley, Kent, 1857, Erith 1859. Author, *On Regeneration*, 1*s*. [6]

FARMAN, Samuel, *Layer-Marney Rectory, Kelvedon, Essex.*—Literate; Deac. 1834, Pr. 1838. R. of Layer-Marney, Dio. Roch. 1844. (Patrons, the Trustees of the late Quintin Dick, Esq. M.P; Tithe, 466*l*; Glebe, 3 acres; R.'s Inc. 473*l* and Ho; Pop. 276.) Author, *Part of the Hebrew-Spanish Scripture*, Vienna; *Il futuro Destino d'Israele*, Malta; *Constantinople and Damascus in Connection with the present War*, 1856. [7]

FARMAN, Samuel, *Layer-Marney, Kelvedon, Essex.*—St. John's Coll. Cam. B.A. 1859; Deac. 1860 and Pr. 1861 by Bp of Roch. C. of Layer-Marney 1860. [8]

FARMBROUGH, James Cooper, *Spernall Rectory, near Redditch, Warwickshire.*—St. Mary Magd. Hall, Ox. S.C.L. 1854; Deac. 1857 and Pr. 1860 by Bp of Ox. C. of Spernall 1860. Formerly C. of Weston Underwood, Bucks, 1857, Holwell, Oxon, 1859. [9]

FARMER, James, *Croft Rectory, near Hinckley, Leicestershire.*—Trin. Hall Cam. S.C.L. 1851; Deac. 1852, Pr. 1853 by Bp of Pet. C. of Croft 1854. Formerly C. of Billesdon 1852; Broughton Astley 1853. [10]

FARMER, John, *Dagenham Vicarage, Romford, Essex.*—V. of Dagenham, Dio. Roch. 1861. (Patron, the present R; Tithe—App. 1036*l*, V. 851*l* 2*s* 6*d*; Glebe, 4½ acres; V.'s Inc. 864*l* and Ho; Pop. 2708.) [11]

FARMER, J. Prior.—C. of Berkeley Chapel, May Fair, Lond. [12]

FARMER, J., *Babworth, East Retford.*—C. of Babworth 1867. [13]

FARMER, Richard Cotton, *Barlaston, near Stone.*—St. John's Coll. Cam. B.A. 1863; Deac. 1864, Pr. 1865 by Bp of Lich. C. of Barlaston 1866. Formerly C. of Pensnett, near Dudley, 1864. [14]

FARQUHAR, Edward Mainwaring, *Gainsborough, Lincolnshire.*—Ex. Coll. Ox; B.A. 1865, M.A. 1867; Deac. 1866, Pr. 1867 by Bp of Lin. C. of Gainsborough. [15]

FARQUHAR, James, *Llanthewy Skirrid Rectory, Abergavenny, Monmouthshire.*—Jesus Coll. Ox. B.A. 1836, M.A. 1839; Deac. 1836 and Pr. 1837 by Bp of Llan. R. of Llanthewy-Skirrid, Dio. Llan. 1852. (Patroness, Mrs. M. H. Jones; Tithe, 147*l*; Glebe, 109½ acres; R.'s Inc. 235*l*; Pop. 88.) [16]

FARQUHARSON, Robert, *Blandford, Dorset.*—Ch. Ch. Ox. B.A. 1833, M.A. 1841; Deac. 1833 Pr. 1834. R. of Long-Langton, Dio. Salis. 1855. (Patron, J. J. Farquharson, Esq; Tithe, 379*l*; Glebe, 73 acres; R.'s Inc. 452*l*; Pop. 174.) Preb. of Salis. [17]

FARRANT, John Quillin, *Cheddar, Somerset.*—C. of Cheddar. [18]

FARRAR, Adam Storey, *Durham.*—St. Mary Hall, Ox. 1st cl. Lit. Hum. 2nd cl. Math. Arnold History Prize, Denyer's Theol. Prizes, B.A. 1850, M.A. 1852; B.D. and D.D. 1864; Deac. 1852 and Pr. 1853 by Bp of Ox. Prof. of Div. and Eccles. Hist. in the Univ. of Dur. 1864. (Patron, Bp of Dur.) Formerly Fell. of Queen's Coll. Ox. 1852–63; Tut. of Wad. Coll. 1855–64; Preacher at Whitehall 1858–60. Author, *Hints to Students in Classical Honours in the University of Oxford*, 1856, 1*s* 6*d*; *Science in Theology* (University Sermons), Murray, 1859, 9*s*; *Critical History of Free Thought* (Bampton Lectures for 1862), Murray, 1862, 16*s*. [19]

FARRAR, Frederic William, *Harrow-on-the-Hill, Middlesex.*—Trin. Coll. Cam. and the Univ. of Lond; Chan.'s Engl. Medal 1852, Le Bas Prize 1856, Norrisian Prize 1857, Univ. Scho. of the Univ. of Lond. 1852, Hon. Fell. of King's Coll. Lond. 1862; B.A. 1855, M.A. 1857; Deac. 1854 by Bp of Salis. Pr. 1855 by Bp of Ely. Asst. Mast. of Harrow Sch; Fell. of Trin. Coll. Cam. Author, *The Arctic Regions* (Prize Poem); *Christian Doctrine of the Atonement*, 1857; *Eric, or Little by Little, a Tale of School Life*, 1857; *Julian Home*, 1859; *The Origin of Language*, 1860; *St. Winifred or the World of School*, 1862; *Chapters on Language*, 1865; *Greek Grammar Rules*, 1866; *Greek Syntax*, 1867; Lectures and Sermons. [20]

FARRAR, James, *St. John's Parsonage, near Mytholmroyd, viâ Manchester.*—Trin. Coll. Cam. B.A. 1854; Deac. 1856 and Pr. 1857 by Bp of Pet. P. C. of St. John's in the Wilderness, Halifax, Dio. Rip. 1859. (Patron, V. of Halifax; P. C.'s Inc. 133*l* with pew rents and Ho; Pop. 1667.) Formerly C. of Passenham, Northants, 1856–58, St. Mary's, Sowerby, 1859. [21]

FARRAR, John Martindale, 46, *Upper Brunswick-place, Brighton.*—M.A. Ox; Deac. 1851 and Pr. 1852 by Bp of Ches. Formerly C. of Hurdsfield, Cheshire, 1851–53, Croydon, Surrey, 1853–56; V. of Burgh with Winthorpe, Linc. 1856–57; Min. of the Temporary Ch. Hampstead, 1857–59; P. C. of St. Paul's, Hampstead, 1859–60; R. of Broughton-Pogis-with-Filkins, Oxon, 1861–67. [22]

FARRAR, Wesley, *Castleside, Gateshead.*—New Inn Hall, Ox. B.A. 1844, M.A. 1847; Deac. 1850, Pr. 1851. P. C. of Castleside, 1864. (Patron, Crown and Bp alt; Glebe, 7 acres; P. C.'s Inc. 300*l* and Ho.) Formerly C. of Lanchester 1850, Hilgay, Norfolk, 1853–56, Sydney, Australia, 1857–60, Wicker, Sheffield, 1860–64. [23]

FARRELL, Maurice, *Woughton-on-the-Green Rectory (Bucks), near Fenny Stratford.*—R. of Woughton-on-the-Green, Dio. Ox. 1855. (Patron, the present R; R.'s Inc. 280*l* and Ho; Pop. 314.) [24]

FARRER, C. P., *Sidcup, Bromley, Kent.*—P. C. of Sidcup, Dio. Cant. 1861. (Patron, Bp of Wor; P. C.'s Inc. 160*l* and Ho; Pop. 976.) [25]

FARRER, Frederic, *The Rectory, Bigbury, Ivybridge, Devon.*—St. John's Coll. Ox. B.A. 1849, M.A. 1861; Deac. 1849 by Bp of Lon. Pr. 1851 by Bp of Ely. R. of Bigbury, Dio. Ex. 1861. (Patrons, the Duke of Cleveland and Earl of Sandwich; Tithe, 500*l*; Glebe, 100 acres; R.'s Inc. 640*l* and Ho; Pop. 497.) Formerly C. of St. Michael's, Chester-square, Lond. 1850, Euston and Barnham, Suffolk, 1851; Asst. Chap. in Bengal 1852–60. [26]

FARRER, Matthew Thomas, *Shirley, Croydon, Surrey.*—Trin. Coll. Cam. B.A. 1838, M.A. 1841; Deac. 1840 and Pr. 1841 by Abp of Cant. P. C. of Shirley, Dio. Cant. 1841. (Patron, Abp of Cant; P. C.'s Inc. 60*l* and Ho; Pop. 642.) V. of Addington, Dio. Cant. 1843. (Patron, Abp of Cant; V.'s Inc. 266*l*; Pop. 639.) [27]

FARRINGTON, Edward Holmes, *Landcross Rectory, near Bideford, Devon.*—Magd. Coll. Cam. B.A. 1835; Deac. and Pr. 1836. R. of Landcross, Dio. Ex. 1847. (Patrons, Heirs of Lord Rolle; Tithe, 63*l*; Glebe, 8 acres; R.'s Inc. 100*l* and Ho; Pop. 109.) [1]

FARROW, Charles, *Tong Parsonage, Leeds.*—Bp Hat. Hall, Dur. B.A. 1857, Ellerton Scho; Deac. 1858 and Pr. 1859 by Bp of Lich. V. of Tong, near Leeds, Dio. Rip. 1866. (Patron, Col. Tempest; V.'s Inc. 380*l* and Ho; Pop. 3200.) Dom. Chap. to Lord Middleton 1862. Formerly C. of Mucklestone, Staffs, 1856, Birdsall, Yorks, 1862. [2]

FARROW, Henry, *Calverley, Leeds.*—St. Aidan's; Deac. 1865, Pr. 1866 by Bp of Rip. C. of Calverley. [3]

FARROW, John, *Upper Helmsley Rectory, near York.*—St. Bees; Deac. 1820, Pr. 1821. R. of Upper Helmsley, Dio. York, 1828. (Patron, Ld Chan; R.'s Inc. 126*l* and Ho; Pop. 78.) V. of Gate Helmsley, Dio. York, 1851. (Patron, Abp of York; V.'s Inc. 130*l*; Pop. 200.) [4]

FARROW, John Rotherford, *Riccall Vicarage, York.*—St. Cath. Coll. Cam. B.A. 1846; Deac. 1847, Pr. 1848. V. of Riccall, Dio. York, 1863. (Patron, Abp of York; V.'s Inc. 325*l* and Ho; Pop. 783.) Formerly C. of Riccall. [5]

FARTHING, George Lax, 1, *York-terrace, Southampton.*—St. John's Coll. Cam. B.A. 1855, M.A. 1856; Deac. 1863, Pr. 1865 by Bp of Salis. C. of St. Peter's, Southampton. Formerly C. of Atworth and Chalfield Magna 1863. [6]

FARTHING, Thomas Newham, *Denton, Manchester.*—R. of Ch. Ch. Denton. Dio. Man. 1846. (Patrons, the Crown and Bp of Man. alt; R.'s Inc. 165*l*; Pop. 3579.) [7]

FARWELL, William, *St. Martin's Rectory, East Looe, Cornwall.*—Trin. Coll. Ox. B.A. 1828; Deac. 1829, Pr. 1830. R. of St. Martin's, Dio. Ex. 1830. (Patrons, Dowager Countess of Sandwich and Duke of Cleveland alt; Tithe, 369*l*; Glebe, 108 acres; R.'s Inc. 520*l* and Ho; Pop. 343.) [8]

FAUGHT, Frederick Le Clerc.—Clare Coll. Cam. B.A. 1854; Deac. 1855 by Bp of Ely, Pr. 1856 by Bp of Lich. [9]

FAUGHT, George S., *Bradfield St. Clare, Bury St. Edmunds.*—C. of Bradfield St. Clare. [10]

FAULKENER Henry B., *Westgate House, Long Melford, Suffolk.*—Brasen. Coll. Ox. 2nd cl Lit. Hum. B.A. 1815, M.A. 1818; Deac. 1823 by Bp of Salis. [11]

FAULKNER, Charles.—British Chap. at Roobaix and Croix. [12]

FAULKNER, Edwyn, *Worcester.*—St. Peter's Coll. Cam. B.A. 1821, M.A. 1824; Deac. 1822, Pr. 1823. Chap. to the Berkeley Hospital and City Gaol, Worcester; Surrogate. [13]

FAULKNER, Henry Bayntun, *Budbrooke Vicarage, near Warwick.*—Caius Coll. Cam. B.A. 1847; Deac. 1847 and Pr. 1848 by Bp of Wor. V. of Budbrooke, Dio. Wor. 1856. (Patron, W. E. Wood, Esq; Tithe—Imp. 426*l* 18*s*, V. 322*l*; V.'s Inc. 500*l* and Ho; Pop. 492.) Formerly C. of Weston-on-Avon, Glouc. and Chap. to the Stratford-on-Avon Union. [14]

FAULKNER, Henry Martyn, *Buenos Ayres, South America.*—Brasen. Coll. Ox. 2nd cl. Lit. Hum. and B.A. 1815, M.A. 1818; Deac. 1822, Pr. 1823. British Chap. at Buenos Ayres. [15]

FAULKNER, Richard Rowland, *Havering-atte-Bower, Romford, Essex.*—St. John's Coll. Cam. B.D. 1826; Deac. 1813, Pr. 1814. V. of the Holy Sepulchre, Cambridge, Dio. Ely, 1825. (Patrons, the Parishioners; Glebe, 36 acres; V.'s Inc. 60*l*; Pop. 547.) P. C. of Havering-atte-Bower, Dio. Roch. 1834. (Patron, W. P. Barnes, Esq; Tithe—App. 5*l*, Imp. 1515*l* 17*s* 11*d*; Glebe, 72 acres; P. C.'s Inc. 80*l* and Ho; Pop. 429.) [16]

FAULKNER, Thomas, *West Britton, Wakefield.*—King's Coll. Lond. Theol. Assoc. 1858; Deac. 1858 and Pr. 1859 by Bp of Nor. P. C. of West Britton, Dio. Rip. 1865. (Patron, W. B. Beaumont, Esq. M.P; P. C.'s Inc. 100*l* and Ho; Pop. 400.) Formerly C. of Corton and Gunton, Suffolk, 1858, St. Mark's, Peterborough, 1860, Darton, Barnsley, 1862. [17]

FAULKNER, William Andrew, *Churchill Rectory, Worcester.*—Magd. Hall, Ox. B.A. 1839; Deac. 1840, Pr. 1841. R. of Churchill, Dio. Wor. 1863. (Patron, Robert Berkeley, Esq; Land in lieu of Tithe; R.'s Inc. 200*l* and Ho; Pop. 78.) Formerly C. of Beaudesert. [18]

FAULKNER, William Cloudesley, *Beckford, Tewkesbury, Gloucestershire.*—St. Peter's Coll. Cam. B.A. 1821, M.A. 1824; Deac. and Pr. 1821. C. of Alston, Teddington and Washbourne, Worc. [19]

FAULKNER, William Elisha, *Little Steeping, Spilsby, Lincolnshire.*—Wor. Coll. Ox. B.A. 1854; Deac. 1855 and Pr. 1856 by Bp of Ex. C. of Little Steeping. Formerly C. of St. Paul's, Birmingham. [20]

FAUNTHORPE, John Pincher, *St. John's College, Battersea.*—Lond. Univ. B.A. 1865; Deac. 1867 by Bp of Win. Vice-Prin. of St. John's Training Coll. Battersea. Author of an *Elementary Physical Atlas*, 3*s*. Stanford, 1867. [21]

FAUQUIER, George Lille Wodehouse, *West Haddon Vicarage, Daventry, Northants.*—Pemb. Coll. Cam. Sen. Opt. and B.A. 1821; Deac. 1822 and Pr. 1823 by Bp of Nor. V. of West Haddon, Dio. Pet. 1854. (Patron, the present V; Glebe, 160 acres; V.'s Inc. 265*l* and Ho; Pop. 963.) [22]

FAUSSET, Andrew Robert, *St. Cuthbert's Rectory, Heworth, York.*—Dub. A.B. 1843, A.M. 1846; Deac. 1847 and Pr. 1848 by Bp of Dur. R. of St. Cuthbert's, City and Dio. York, 1859. (Patron, Ld Chan; Tithe, comm. 177*l* 7*s* 6*d*; Glebe, 64*l* 4*s*; R.'s Inc. 241*l* 11*s* 6*d*; Eccles. Commis. Grant 90*l*; Pop. 2911.) Author, *Terence, with Critical Notes*, 1844, 5*s*; *Homer's Iliad*, B. I. to VIII. 1846, 7*s* 6*d*; *Livy*, B. I. to III. 1849, 7*s* 6*d*; *Hecuba translated*, 1850, 1*s* 6*d*; *Medea translated*, 1851, 1*s* 6*d*; *The Written Word the Infallible Judge of the Church, not the Church of the Word*, 1852, 4*d*; *Ireland and the Irish*, 1854, 6*d*; *Scripture and the Prayer Book in Harmony*, 1854, 3*s* 6*d*; *Vinet's Homiletics, or the Theory of Preaching with Notes*, 1856; *The Faculties of The Lower Animals, and their Claims on Man* (a Lecture before the Durham Athenæum), 1858; *The Gnomon of the New Testament by Bengel edited in English*, 5 vols. Clark, Edinburgh, 1857, 31*s* 6*d*; *The Critical and Explanatory Pocket Bible*, 4 vols. Collins, Glasgow, 1862, 14*s*; the 2nd, 3rd, part of the 5th and 6th vols. of *The Critical, Experimental, and Practical Commentary*, 6 vols. Collins, Glasgow, 3*l* 3*s*. [23]

FAUSSETT, Godfrey.—Corpus Coll. Cam. and Magd. Coll. Ox. B.A. 1836, M.A. 1838, B.D. 1849. Formerly R. of Edgeworth, Dio. G. and B. 1860–64. [24]

FAUSSETT, Henry Godfrey, *Littleton Parsonage, near Evesham.*—Ch. Ch. Ox. 4th cl. Lit. Hum. and B.A. 1845, M.A. 1848; Deac. 1850, Pr. 1851. P. C. of South Littleton with North and Middle Littleton, Dio. Wor. 1854. (Patrons, D. and C. of Ch. Ch. Ox; South Littleton, Tithe, App. 93*l* 3*s* 3*d*; P. C.'s Inc. 266*l* and Ho; Pop. South Littleton, 294, North and Middle Littleton 303) Rural Dean of Evesham 1864. [25]

FAUSSETT, Robert, *Christ Church, Oxford.*—Ch. Ch. Ox. 1st cl. Math. et Phy. B.A. 1849, M.A. 1852, Stud. of Ch. Ch. 1845, Math. Lect. of Ch. Ch. 1850–55, Math. Moderator 1860, Math. Exam. 1864; Deac. 1858 by Bp of Ox. Pr. 1859 by Abp of Cant. Formerly C. of Halfway Street, Bexley, 1858–62. Editor of *Faussett's Sacred Chronology*, 1855. [26]

FAUVEL, Thomas.—Dub. A.B. 1854; Deac. 1855 and Pr. 1856 by Bp of Ches. Formerly Asst. C. of Carrington, Cheshire. [27]

FAWCETT, Christopher, *Somerford-Keynes, Cricklade, Wilts.*—Univ. Coll. Ox. 2nd cl. Lit. Hum. 1823, B.A. 1824, M.A. 1829; Deac. 1825, Pr. 1826. V. of Somerford Keynes, Dio. G. and B. 1852. (Patron, Rev. C. Fawcett; Glebe, 47 acres; V.'s Inc. 200*l* and Ho; Pop. 386.) [28]

FAWCETT, Henry, 27, *St. Peter's-road, Mile End, E.*—Clare Coll. Cam. B.A. 1859, M.A. 1862; Deac.

1859 and Pr. 1860 by Bp of Carl. Miss. C. of St. Peter's Mission, Stepney, 1865. Formerly C. of Stanwix, Carlisle, 1859–61, Chelmsford 1861–65. [1]

FAWCETT, James, *Knaresborough Vicarage, Yorks.*—Clare Coll. Cam. B.A. 1821, M.A. 1824; Deac. 1821 by Bp of Ches. Pr. 1822 by Abp of York. V. of Knaresborough, Dio. Rip. 1851. (Patron, Bp of Rip; V.'s Inc. 380*l* and Ho; Pop. 6308.) Surrogate. Author, *Early Records of the Church of England*, 1848, 1*s*. [2]

FAWCETT, John Morris, *Liverpool.*—Magd. Coll. Cam. B.A. 1851; Deac. 1851 and Pr. 1852 by Bp of Rip. C. of St. Martin's, Liverpool. [3]

FAWCETT, John Turner Colman, *Kildwick Vicarage, Leeds.*—Ch. Ch. Ox. B.A. 1826, M.A. 1829; Deac. 1827, Pr. 1829. V. of Kildwick in Craven, Dio. Rip. 1843. (Patron, Ch. Ch. Ox; Tithe—App. 530*l* 17*s* 7*d*, V. 256*l* 8*s* 6*d*; Glebe, 220 acres; V.'s Inc. 370*l* and Ho; Pop. 6389.) Author, *Address to the Inhabitants of Cowling*; *Remarks on Kildwick Church*; *Sermon to Lead Miners*; *Observations on Certain Trials at York Assizes*, 1855. [4]

FAWCETT, Joshua, *Low Moor, Bradford, Yorks.*—Trin. Coll. Cam. B.A. 1829, M.A. 1836; Deac. 1830, Pr. 1831. Chap. to Lord Dunsany 1842. Formerly P. C. of Wibsey, Bradford, 1833–65. Author, *Lyra Ecclesiastica*, fol; *Churches of York*, fol; *History of St. Mary's, Scarborough*; *Church Rides round Scarborough*; *Visitation Sermon*; *Pastoral Addresses*; *A Sermon on the Holmfirth Flood, &c*; *History of the Church of St. Peter's, Bradford*; *History of the Church of St. Thomas-à-Becket, Heptonstall*; *The Church Rambler in Craven*; *Ancient and Modern Burial Rites*; *Memorial of a Beloved Child*; *Memorial of the Church of St. Mary-the-Virgin, Oxenhope.* Editor of *The Village Churchman.* [5]

FAWCETT, Stephen Glas, *Willoughby, Spilsby, Lincolnshire*, and 7, *Boltons, London, S.W.*—Magd. Coll. Cam. Wrang. and B.A. 1833, M.A. 1836; Deac. 1835 by Bp of Carl. Pr. 1837 by Bp of Ely. R. of Willoughby, Dio. Lin. 1867. (Patron, Lord Willoughby de Eresby; Tithe, 1050*l*; Glebe, 60 acres; R.'s Inc. 1200*l* and Ho.) Formerly V. of Eaton-Socon, Beds, 1845–61; P. C. of Edenham, Linc. 1861–67. Late Fell. and Tut. of Magd. Coll. Cam. [6]

FAWCETT, William, *Morton, Bingley, Yorks.*—Lin. Coll. Ox. 3rd cl. Lit. Hum. B.A. 1838; Deac. 1839 and Pr. 1840 by Bp of Lin. P. C. of Morton with Riddlesden C. Dio. Rip. 1845. (Patrons, Crown and Bp alt; P. C.'s Inc. 157*l* and Ho; Pop. 2432.) Formerly C. of Fenton with Stragglethorpe 1839–41, Keighley 1841–44, Calverley 1845. [7]

FAWKES, Ayscough, *Leathley, Otley, Yorks.*—Brasen. Coll. Ox. B.A. 1828. R. of Leathley, Dio. Rip. 1837. (Patron, Ld Chan; Tithe—Imp. 110*l* 17*s* 6*d*, R. 164*l* 15*s* 5*d*; R.'s Inc. 318*l*; Pop. 272.) Rural Dean. [8]

FAWKES, Frederick.—Univ. Coll. Dur. B.A. 1856; Deac. 1857 and Pr. 1858 by Bp of Lich. Formerly C. of St. Peter's, Derby. [9]

FAWKES, F. F., *Upton Park, Slough.*—P. C. of Great and Little Hampton, Evesham, Dio. Wor. 1839. (Patron, Ch. Ch. Ox; P. C.'s Inc. 98*l*; Pop. 513.) [10]

FAWNS, J. A., *Richmond, Yorkshire.*—C. of Richmond. [11]

FAWSETT, Thomas, *East Stoke Vicarage, near Newark, Notts.*—Clare Coll. Cam. B.A. 1819, M.A. 1822; Deac. 1819 by Bp of Ches. Pr. 1821 by Bp of Lin. V. of East Stoke with Syreston C. and Elston C. Dio. Lin. 1854. (Patron, Bp of Lin; V.'s Inc. 308*l* and Ho; Pop. East Stoke 204, Syreston 220, Elston 270.) [12]

FAWSSETT, John, *Baumber Vicarage, Horncastle, Lincolnshire.*—Jesus Coll. Cam. B.A. 1831, M.A. 1834; Deac. 1835, Pr. 1836. R. of Waddingworth, Dio. Lin. 1843. (Patron, Ld Chan; Tithe, 137*l* 10*s*; Glebe, 25 acres; R.'s Inc. 143*l*; Pop. 82.) V. of Great Sturton with Baumber, Dio. Lin. 1849. (Patron, Ld Chan; Glebe, 250 acres; V.'s Inc. 115*l*; Pop. 179.) [13]

FAWSSETT, J. B., *Longworth, Berks.*—C. of Longworth. [14]

FAWSSETT, Richard *Smeeton Westerby, Kibworth Beauchamp, Leicestershire.*—Lin. Coll. Ox. B.A. 1829, M.A. 1831. Deac. 1830, Pr. 1831; R. of Westerby, Dio. Pet. 1852. (Patron, R. of Kibworth-Beauchamp; P. C.'s Inc. 160*l*; Pop. 533.) Formerly C. of St. Margaret's, Leicester, 1835–39; P. C. of Ch. Ch. Leicester, 1839–52. [15]

FAYLE, Richard, *Torquay, Devon.*—St. Mary Hall, Ox. B.A. 1846, M.A. 1847. Min. of Trin. Chapel, Torquay, Dio. Ex. 1838. (Patron, the present Min; Min.'s Inc. 200*l*.) [16]

FEACHEM, Algernon.—Trin. Coll. Cam. B.A. 1833, M.A. 1836; Deac. 1838 and Pr. 1839 by Bp of St. A. Formerly R. of East Horsley, Surrey, 1846-65. [17]

FEACHEM, George Henry, *Oakwood, Dorking, Surrey.*—Trin. Coll. Cam. B.A. 1829, M.A. 1837; Deac. and Pr. 1829 by Bp of Win. P. C. of Oakwood, Dio. Win. 1851. (Patron, W. J. Evelyn, Esq; P. C.'s Inc. 340*l*; Pop. 703.) [18]

FEARNE, Thomas Gleadow, *Richmond, Port Natal, South Africa.*—St. Cath. Hall, Cam. B.A. 1840, M.A. 1845; Deac. 1839 and Pr. 1841 by Bp of Ches. Canon of St. Peter's, Moritz Bay, 1859; Archd. of D'Urban; Missionary of the S.P.G. [19]

FEARNLEY, John, *Lincoln's inn-fields, London, W.C.*—Trin. Coll. Cam. B.A. 1825, M.A. 1829; Deac. and Pr. 1826 by Bp of Lon. 2nd Mast. of King's Coll. Sch. Lond. [20]

FEARNLEY, Matthew, *Moreton, Birkenhead.*—St. John's Coll. Cam. 19th Wrang. B.A. 1847, M.A. 1850; Deac. 1850 and Pr. 1851 by Abp of York. R. of Ch. Ch. Moreton, Dio. Ches. 1863. (Patron, William Inman, Esq: Tithe, 208*l* 6*s* 1*d*; R.'s Inc. 208*l* 6*s* 1*d*; Pop. 563.) Formerly C. of Darfield, Barnsley, 1850–54; Miss. in China 1855–59; C. of St. Anne's, Birkenhead, 1860–63. [21]

FEARNSIDES, William, *Harley Wood, Todmorden, Yorks.*—Deac. 1858 and Pr. 1859 by Bp of Rip. P. C. of All Saints', Harley Wood, Todmorden, Dio. Rip. 1865. (Patron, V. of Halifax; P. C.'s Inc. 300*l*; Pop. 7500.) Formerly C. of St. John's, Bradford, 1858–65. [22]

FEARON, Daniel Rose.—St. John's Coll. Cam. 21st Sen. Opt. and B.A. 1826, M.A. 1829; Deac. 1827 and Pr. 1828 by Bp of Nor. Formerly V. of Assington, Suffolk, 1844–61. [23]

FEARON, The Ven. Henry, *Loughborough Rectory, Leicestershire.*—Emman. Coll. Cam. Sen. Opt. and B.A. 1824, M.A. 1827; Deac. 1826 and Pr. 1827 by Bp of Chich. R. of Loughborough, Dio. Pet. 1848. (Patron, Emman. Coll. Cam; Tithe, 22*l*; Glebe, 300 acres; R.'s Inc. 1050*l* and Ho; Pop. 6401.) Archd. of Leicester; Hon. Can. of Pet. Cathl. 1849. Formerly Fell. of Emman. Coll. Cam. Author, *What to Learn and What to Unlearn*; *Sermons on Public Occasions*, 1859. [24]

FEARON, John, *Holme Bridge Parsonage, Huddersfield.*—Queen's Coll. Ox. 4th cl. Lit. Hum. and B.A. 1838; Deac. 1839 and Pr. 1840 by Bp of Rip. P. C. of Holme Bridge, Dio. Rip. 1847. (Patron, V. of Almondbury; Tithe, App. 7*l*, Imp. 4*l*; Glebe, 4½ acres; P. C.'s Inc. 190*l* and Ho; Pop. 2708.) [25]

FEARON, Samuel Hall, *Weston, Harewood, Leeds.*—Queen's Coll. Ox. 3rd cl. Lit. Hum. and B.A. 1848, M.A. 1851; Deac. 1849 and Pr. 1851 by Bp of Ches. P. C. of Weston, Harewood, Dio. Rip. 1866. (Patron, R. of Harewood; P. C.'s Inc. 100*l* and Ho; Pop. 317.) Formerly C. of Harewood, Leeds. [26]

FEATHER, George, *York-place, Newton Heath, Manchester.*—Deac. 1864; Pr. 1865 by Bp of Ches. C. of Newton Heath 1866. Formerly C. of Warrington 1864–66. [27]

FEATHERSTON, Robert Nicholson, *Accrington.*—Jesus Coll. Cam. B.A. 1842; Deac. 1842, Pr. 1843. P. C. of Ch. Ch. Accrington, Dio. Man. 1851. (Patrons, Trustees; P. C.'s Inc. 300*l*; Pop. 5322.) [28]

FEATHERSTONE, Thomas, *Priory Parsonage, Tynemouth.*—St. Aidan's; Deac. 1857 and Pr. 1858 by Bp of Dur. P. C. of Holy Saviour's, Tynemouth, Dio. Dur. 1861. (Patron, Duke of Northumberland; P. C.'s Inc. 200*l* and Ho; Pop. 5000.) Chap. to H.M. Forces; Surrogate. Formerly C. of Holy Trinity, S. Shields, 1857–60; Chap. to Sailors' Home, N. Shields, 1860–61. [1]

FEATHERSTONHAUGH, Walker, *Edmondbyers Rectory, Gateshead, Durham.*—Univ. Coll. Dur. B.A. 1843, M.A. 1845; Deac. 1845 and Pr. 1847 by Bp of Dur. R. of Edmondbyers, Dio. Dur. 1856. (Patrons, D. and C. of Dur; Tithe, 143*l*; Glebe, 114 acres; R.'s Inc. 305*l* and Ho; Pop. 455.) Formerly Fell. of Univ. Coll. Dur. 1843. [2]

FEETHAM, William, *Penrhôs, Monmouth.*—St. John's Coll. Ox. B.A. 1846, M.A. 1848; Deac. 1847, Pr. 1848. V. of Penrhôs, Dio. Llan. 1865. (Patrons, D. and C. of Llan; Tithe, 96*l*; Glebe, 44 acres; V.'s Inc. 150*l* and Ho; Pop. 376.) Formerly C. of St. Woolos, Mon. 1847, Bremhill, Wilts, 1861. [3]

FEILD, James Meyrick, *Ashwater, Launceston.*—Wor. Coll. Ox. B.A. 1847; Deac. 1848 and Pr. 1849 by Bp of Ex. R. of Ashwater, Dio. Ex. 1864. (Patron, W. W. Melhuish, Esq; Tithe, 569*l*; Glebe, 94 acres; R.'s Inc. 700*l* and Ho; Pop. 940.) Formerly Asst. C. of Sheepwash 1848, Highampton 1855, Hatherleigh 1853, Ashwater 1862. [4]

FEILD, Samuel Hands, *Hurdsfield, Macclesfield.*—Wor. Coll. Ox. B.A. 1830, M.A. 1833; Deac. 1833, Pr. 1834. P. C. of Hurdsfield, Dio. Ches. 1838. (Patrons, Hyndman's Trustees; P. C.'s Inc. 130*l* and Ho; Pop. 3836.) Formerly P. C. of Trinity, Ramsgate, 1850–58. [5]

FEILDEN, George Ramsay, *Bebington Rectory, Birkenhead.*—Ch. Ch. Ox. B.A. 1850, M.A. 1853; Deac. 1853 and Pr. 1854 by Bp of Ox. R. of Bebington, Dio. Ches. 1862. (Patron, the present R; Tithe, 720*l* 3*s* 6*d*; Glebe, 3 acres; R.'s Inc. 770*l* and Ho; Pop. 3411.) [6]

FEILDEN, Henry Arbuthnot.—St. Alban Hall Ox. 3rd cl. Lit. Hum. and B.A. 1851; Deac. 1852 and Pr. 1853 by Bp of Ely. Formerly P. C. of Smallwood, Cheshire, 1857–62. [7]

FEILDEN, Henry James, *Kirk-Langley Rectory, Derbyshire.*—Brasen. Coll. Ox. 2nd cl. Lit. Hum. 1817, B.A. 1818, M.A. 1820; Deac. and Pr. 1820. R. of Kirk-Langley, Dio. Lich. 1820. (Patron, G. Meynell, Esq; Tithe, 222*l*; R.'s Inc. 420*l* and Ho; Pop. 648.) [8]

FEILDEN, John Robert, *Baconsthorpe, Holt, Norfolk.*—Ch. Ch. Ox. 1848, B.A. 1849, M.A. 1852; Deac. 1851, Pr. 1852. R. of Baconsthorpe, Dio. Nor. 1861. (Patron, J. T. Mott, Esq; Pop. 328.) Dom. Chap. to the Marquis of Cholmondeley. [9]

FEILDEN, Oswald, *Field House, Markington, Uttoxeter.*—Brasen. Coll. Ox. B.A. 1818, M.A. 1831; Deac. 1821, Pr. 1822. Formerly R. of Weston-under-Lizard, Staffs, 1833–59. [10]

FEILDEN, Oswald Mosley, *Whittington, Oswestry.*—Ch. Ch. Ox. B.A. 1859, M.A. 1863; Deac. 1861 and Pr. 1862 by Bp of St. A. P. C. of Welsh Frankton, Dio. St. A. 1865. (Patrons, R. of Whittington and Earl Brownlow, alt; P. C.'s Inc. 180*l*; Pop. 533.) Formerly C. of Whittington 1861. [11]

FEILDEN, William Leyland, *Knowsley, Prescot, Lancashire.*—Ch. Ch. Ox. B.A. 1847, M.A. 1849; Deac. 1848 and Pr. 1849 by Bp of G. and B. P. C. of Knowsley, Dio. Ches. 1855. (Patron, Earl of Derby; Tithe—App. 280*l*, Imp. 300*l*; P. C.'s Inc. 350*l*; Pop. 1349.) Chap. to the Marquis of Cholmondeley. [12]

FEILDING, The Hon. C. W. A., *Stapleton Rectory, Salop.*—Trin. Coll. Cam. M.A. 1856; Deac. 1858, Pr. 1859. R. of Stapleton, Dio. Lich. 1863. (Patron, Hon. H. W. Powys; Tithe, 609*l*; Glebe, 12 acres; R.'s Inc. 609*l* and Ho; Pop. 281.) Formerly C. of Clayton with Keymer, Sussex, 1858–60, Kirkby-Mallory, Leicestershire, 1860, Chilton-Foliat, Wilts, 1861–63. [13]

FELIX, Hugh, *Llanybyther Vicarage, Lampeter, Cardiganshire.*—V. of Llanwenog, near Lampeter, Dio. St. D. 1845. (Patron, Bp of St. D; Tithe—Imp. 412*l* 5*s* 11¾*d*, V. 147*l* 14*s* 0½*d*; V.'s Inc. 150*l*; Pop. 1521.) V. of Llanybyther, Dio. St. D. 1847. (Patron, Ld Chan; Tithe—Imp. 160*l*, V. 70*l*; Glebe, 7½ acres; V.'s Inc. 118*l* and Ho; Pop. 1131.) [14]

FELIX, John, *Llanfihangel-Lledrod, Aberystwith, Cardiganshire.*—P. C. of Llanfihangel-Lledrod, Dio. S. D. 1828. (Patron, Bp of St. D; P. C.'s Inc. 115*l*; Pop. 1125.) [15]

FELIX, John, *Great Blakenham, Ipswich.*—C. of Great Blakenham. [16]

FELIX, Peter, *Easton-Neston, Towcester, Northants.*—Trin. Coll. Cam. B.D. 1830; Deac. 1814 and Pr. 1815 by Bp of Ches. V. of Easton-Neston, Northants, Dio. Pet. 1825. (Patron, Earl of Pomfret; Tithe, Imp. 482*l* 1*s* 9*d*; V.'s Inc. 160*l* and Ho; Pop. 160.) [17]

FELL, George Hunter, *East Worldham, Alton, Hants.*—Magd. Coll. Ox. B.A. 1843, M.A. 1845, B.D. 1855, D.D. 1858; Deac. 1843 and Pr. 1844 by Bp of Ox. V. of East Worldham, Dio. Win. 1861. (Patron, Magd. Coll. Ox; V.'s Inc. 150*l*; Pop. 235.) Fell. of Magd. Coll. Ox. Formerly R. of Horsington, Lincolnshire, 1855–58; Chap. to Lady Croke 1855. [18]

FELL, James Alexander, *Penkridge Parsonage, Staffs.*—Corpus Coll. Cam. B.A. 1847, M.A. 1850; Deac. 1847 and Pr. 1848 by Bp of Pet. P. C. of Penkridge, Dio. Lich. 1851. (Patron, Lord Hatherton; Tithe, Imp. 1500*l*; Glebe, 3 acres; P. C.'s Inc. 290*l* and Ho; Pop. 2510.) Rural Dean of Penkridge 1853. Formerly C. of Cossington, Leic. 1847, and St. Mary's, Lichfield, 1850. [19]

FELL, John, *Grammar School, Huntingdon.*—Trin. Coll. Cam. B.A. 1818, M.A. 1821; Deac. 1817 by Bp of Ches. Pr. 1818 by Bp of Lin. V. of St. Mary's, with St. Benedict's, Huntingdon, Dio. Ely, 1861. (Patron, Ld Chan; V.'s Inc. 180*l* and Ho; Pop. 1924.) Head Mast. of the Huntingdon Gr. Sch. 1823; Chap. of the Huntingdon Union. Formerly P. C. of Wilburton, Isle of Ely, 1822–61. [20]

FELL, John Edwin, *Acton Vicarage, Sudbury, Suffolk.*—St. John's Coll. Cam. B.A. 1837, M.A. 1840; Deac. 1837, Pr. 1838. V. of Acton, Dio. Ely, 1850. (Patron, Earl Howe; Tithe—Imp. 375*l*, V. 375*l*, Glebe, 1 acre; V.'s Inc. 375*l* and Ho; Pop. 558.) [21]

FELL, Samuel Irton.—Queen's Coll. Ox. B.A. 1825, M.A. 1832; Deac. 1830, Pr. 1831. Formerly P. C. of Ambleside, Westmoreland, 1846–60. [22]

FELL, Thomas, *Sheepy, Atherstone, Leicestershire.*—R. of Sheepy Magna and Parva with Ratcliffe Culey C. Dio. Pet. 1856. (Patron, the present R.; R.'s Inc. 1100*l*; Pop. 761.) Hon. Can. of Pet.; Rural Dean. [23]

FELL, William Henry.—Trin. Coll. Cam. B.A. 1852, M.A. 1855; Deac. 1854 by Bp of Man. Pr. 1855 by Bp of St. A. Formerly P. C. of New Fens, Flints, 1858–60. [24]

FELLOWES, Charles, *Shottesham Rectory, Norwich.*—St. John's Coll. Cam. Sen. Opt. 2nd cl. Cl Trip and B.A. 1836; Deac. 1836 by Bp of Ely, Pr. 1838 by Bp of Nor. R. and V. of Shottesham All Saints with St. Mary V. Dio. Nor. 1838. (Patron, R. Fellowes, Esq; Tithe—App. 10*l* 12*s* 6*d*, Imp. 441*l* 4*s* 6d, R. and V. 564*l* 10*s*; Glebe, 74½ acres; R. and V.'s Inc. 604*l* and Ho; Pop. Shottesham All Saints 484, Shottesham St. Mary 369.) R. of Mautby, Norfolk, Dio. Nor. 1838. (Patron, R. Fellowes, Esq; Tithe, 600*l*; Glebe, 46½ acres; R.'s Inc. 669*l* 15*s* and Ho; Pop. 68.) [25]

FELLOWES, Edmund Fearon Burrell Bourke, *Kilham Vicarage, Driffield, Yorks*—St. John's Coll. Cam. B.A. 1831; Deac. 1832, Pr. 1833. V. of Kilham, Dio. York, 1845. (Patron, Abp of York; Tithe, App. 21*l*; Glebe, 84 acres; V.'s Inc. 300*l* and Ho; Pop. 1260.) Formerly C. of Euborne 1832–39; New Radnor 1839–41; Newport, Barnstaple, 1841. [26]

FELLOWES, Henry John, *Over-Wallop Rectory, Stockbridge, Hants.*—St. John's Coll. Ox. B.A. 1834, M.A. 1838; Deac. 1838, Pr. 1839. R. of Over-Wallop, Dio. Win. 1852. (Patron, Earl of Portsmouth; Tithe—Imp. 100*l* 10*s*, R. 820*l*; Glebe, 6 acres; R.'s Inc. 826*l* and Ho; Pop. 508.) [27]

FELLOWES, Thomas Lyon, *Beighton Rectory, Acle, Norfolk.*—Ch. Ch. Ox. B.A. 1840; Deac. 1841 and Pr. 1842 by Bp of Nor. R. of Beighton, Dio. Nor. 1844. (Patron, R. Fellowes, Esq; Tithe—App. 1*l* 3*s*, R. 420*l*; Glebe, $8\frac{1}{4}$ acres; R.'s Inc. 436*l* and Ho; Pop. 365.) Author, *A New Analysis of Aristotle's Rhetoric.* [1]

FELLOWS, Edward, *Derby.*—C. of St. Peter's with Normanton, Derby. [2]

FELLOWS, Edward Thomas, *Felbridge Parsonage, East Grinstead.*—Brasen. Coll. Ox, M.A. 1861; Deac. 1858 by Bp of Ely, Pr. 1861 by Bp of Chich. P. C. of Felbridge, Dio. Win. 1865. (Patron, C. H. Gatty, Esq: Glebe, 3 acres; P. C.'s Inc. 100*l* and Ho; Pop. 400.) [3]

FELLOWS, Spencer, *Zeal's Green, Mere, Wilts.*—P. C. of Zeal's Green, Dio. Salis. 1865. (Patron, V. of Mere; P. C.'s Inc. 360*l* and Ho; Pop. 559.) [4]

FELTON, William, 31, *Esplanade, Nottingham.*—St. Aidan's; Deac. 1862 and Pr. 1863 by Abp of York. Chap. of the Borough Gaol, Nottingham, 1865. Formerly C. of Chapel Town, near Sheffield, 1862–64; P. C. of Byley with Yatehouse, Ches. 1864. [5]

FENDALL, Charles Bathurst, *Woodcote House, Windlesham, near Farnborough.*—Jesus Coll. Cam. Scho. of, Jun. Opt. B.A. 1857, M.A. 1865; Deac. 1859 and Pr. 1860 by Bp of Win. Head Mast. of Woodcote House School. [6]

FENDALL, Henry, *New Zealand.*—Emman. Coll. Cam. B.A. 1816; Deac. 1819, Pr. 1820. Formerly V. of Crambe, Yorks, 1839–61. [7]

FENN, Anthony Cox, *Henny Rectory, Sudbury, Suffolk.*—St. John's Coll. Cam. B.A. 1858; Deac. 1859 and Pr. 1860 by Bp of B. and W. C. of Great and Little Henny, Sudbury, 1865. Formerly C. of Ilchester, Somerset, 1859–62, Colne Engaine 1862–65. [8]

FENN, Joseph, *Blackheath-park, Lewisham, S.E.*—Min. of Blackheath-park Chapel, Dio. Roch. (Patron, A. Cator, Esq; Min.'s Inc. 250*l*.) [9]

FENN, Joseph Finch, *Cheltenham.*—Trin. Coll. Cam. B.A. 1842, M.A. 1845; Deac. 1845, Pr. 1846. P. C. of Ch. Ch. Lansdown, Cheltenham, Dio. G. and B. 1860. (Patrons, Trustees; P. C.'s Inc. 450*l*.) Formerly Fell. of Trin. Coll. Cam. 1844–47; V. of Stotfield, Beds, 1847–60. [10]

FENN, Patrick, *Wrabness Rectory, near Manningtree, Essex.*—St. John's Coll. Cam. 2nd Jun. Opt. 1822; Deac. 1823 and Pr. 1824 by Bp of Lon. R. of Wrabness, Dio. Roch. 1847. (Patron, Ld Chan; Tithe, 344*l*; Glebe, $58\frac{1}{2}$ acres; R.'s Inc. 426*l* and Ho; Pop. 226.) Author, *An Introductory Sermon, addressed to the Parishioners of Wrabness,* 1848. [11]

FENN, Thomas Ford, *Derby.*—Trin. Coll. Cam. M.A. Head Mast. of Trent Coll. near Derby. Formerly C. of Wootton, Isle of Wight. [12]

FENN, W. M., *Tankersley, Barnsley, Yorks.*—R. of Tankersley, Dio. York, 1864. (Patron, Earl Fitzwilliam; R.'s Inc. 474*l* and Ho; Pop. 1403.) [13]

FENNELL, George Keith, *Enford, Pewsey, Wilts.*—Trin. Coll. Cam; Deac. 1840, Pr. 1840. C. of Enford. Formerly Head Mast. of the Temple Gr. Sch. Brighton, 1836–46; R. of Chalvington, Sussex, 1850–54. Author, *The Rule of Church Charity,* London and Paris, 1856. [14]

FENNER, Thomas Paris, M.A.—Dom. Chap. to Viscount Arbuthnot. [15]

FENTON, Charles, *Birkenhead.*—St. Aidan's; Deac. 1853 and Pr. 1854 by Bp of Ches. C. of Holy Trinity, Birkenhead. Formerly C. of Middlewich 1853–61. [16]

FENTON, George Livingstone.—Dub. A.B. 1836; Deac. 1837 by Bp of Limerick, Pr. 1837 by Bp of Lich. Formerly V. of Lilleshall, Salop. [17]

FENTON, John Albert, *Ripon, Yorks.*—Corpus Coll. Cam. B.A 1843, M.A. 1846; Deac. 1844, Pr. 1845 by Bp of Lich. Commissary of Bp of Christchurch, New Zealand. Formerly C. of Norton, Derbyshire, 1844–51; Incumb. of St. Paul's, Dunedin, N.Z. 1851–59; Incumb. of St John's, Waikouati, and Rural Dean of Otago and Southland 1859–63. Author, *Cottage Lectures on the Seven Churches of Asia Minor* 1*s*, 1857, Mackintosh. [18]

FENTON, John Kirkby, *Caldecote Rectory, Nuneaton.*—R. of Caldecote, Dio. Wor. 1862. (Patron, K. Fenton, Esq; R.'s Inc. 180*l* and Ho; Pop. 130.) [19]

FENTON, Samuel, *Wavertree, Liverpool.*—Ch. Ch. Ox. B.A. 1817, M.A. 1821; Deac. 1818 by Bp of Glouc. Pr. 1820 by Bp of Ox. P. C. of St. Mary's, Wavertree, Dio. Ches. 1853. (Patron, Bp of Ches; P. C.'s Inc. 170*l*; Pop. 1897.) Author, *A Treatise on Salted Brandy; A Guide to the United States of America.* [20]

FENTON, Theophilus J., *Tunstall, Staffs.*—C. of Tunstall. [21]

FENTON, Thomas, *Ings Parsonage, Kendal.*—Dub. A.B. 1850, A M. 1859; Deac. 1849 and Pr. 1850 by Bp of S. and M. P. C. of Ings, *alias* Hugil, Dio. Carl. 1854. (Patron, V. of Kendal; Tithe, 70*l*; P. C.'s Inc. 93*l* and Ho; Pop. 391.) Author, *Three Plain Answers to the Question, Why are you a Member of the Church of England?* 7th ed. with Appendix, Simpkin & Co. [22]

FENTRELL, C., *Rotherham.*—Head Mast. of the Free Gr. Sch. Rotherham. [23]

FENWICK, Charles Bisset, *Pillaton Rectory, St. Mellion, Cornwall.*—Dub. A.B. 1852; Deac. 1851 by Bp of Cork, Pr. 1852 by Bp of Down and Connor. R. of Pillaton, Dio. Ex. 1861. (Patron, Edward Collins, Esq; Tithe, comm. 200*l*; Glebe, 85 acres; R.'s Inc. 293*l* and Ho; Pop. 349.) [24]

FENWICK, Edward William, *Craythorne, Burton-on-Trent.*—Ch. Coll. Cam. B.A. 1849, M.A. 1852; Deac. 1851 and Pr. 1853 by Bp of Lich. Formerly C. of Batterton, Staffs, 1851, Eriswell, Suffolk, 1852, Egginton, Derby, 1853–56, and Wimbledon 1856–57. [25]

FENWICK, John, *Thurning Rectory, Thetford, Norfolk.*—Corpus Coll. Cam. 9th Wrang. B.A. 1842, M.A. 1845, B.D. 1852; Deac. 1842 and Pr. 1845 by Bp of Herf. R. of Thurning, Dio. Nor. 1858. (Patron, Corpus Coll. Cam; Tithe, comm. 370*l*; Glebe, 23 acres; R.'s Inc. 415*l* 15*s* 2*d* and Ho; Pop. 178.) Formerly Head Mast. of Ipswich Gr. Sch. 1843–50. Late Fell. and Tut. of Corpus Coll. Cam. [26]

FENWICK, John Edward Addison, *Needwood Parsonage, Burton-on-Trent.*—P. C. of Needwood, Dio. Lich. 1853. (Patron, Duchy of Lancaster; P. C.'s Inc. 170*l* and Ho) [27]

FENWICK, W., *Deptford, Durham.*—C. of Deptford. [28]

FENWICK, W. G. N., *Castle Cary, Somerset.*—C. of Castle Cary. [29]

FENWICKE, Gerard Charles, *Blaston Rectory (Leicestershire), near Uppingham.*—Wor. Coll. Ox. B.A. 1841; Deac. 1844 and Pr. 1845 by Bp of Pet. R. of Stockerston, Leicestershire, Dio. Pet. 1845. (Patrons, T. Walker and G. Bellairs, Esqs; Tithe, 202*l*; Glebe, $37\frac{1}{2}$ acres; R.'s Inc. 232*l*; Pop. 50.) R. of Blaston St. Giles, Dio. Pet. 1850. (Patron, Rev. G. O. Fenwicke; Tithe, 168*l* 17*s* 4*d*; Glebe, $32\frac{1}{2}$ acres; R.'s Inc. 229*l* and Ho; Pop. 25.) [30]

FEREMAN, George, *Brize-Norton Vicarage, Faringdon, Berks.*—Ch. Ch. and All Souls Coll. Ox. Hon. 4th cl. Math. et Phy. and B.A. 1846, M.A. 1849; Deac. 1847 and Pr. 1848 by Bp of Ox. V. of Brize-Norton, Dio. Ox. 1859. (Patron, Ch. Ch. Ox; R.'s Inc. 300*l* and Ho; Pop. 721.) Surrogate. Formerly Chap. of Ch. Ch. Cathl. Ox. 1847–58; Chap. of All Souls Coll. Ox. 1850–59; Junior Proctor of the Univ. of Ox. 1855–56. [31]

FERGIE, Thomas Francis, *Ince, near Wigan.*—Queens' Coll. Cam. B.D. 1865; Deac. 1859 and Pr. 1860 by Bp of Ches. P. C. of Ince, Dio. Ches. 1862. (Patrons, Simeon's Trustees; P. C.'s Inc. 300*l*; Pop. 11,000.) Formerly C. of St. Catherine's, Wigan, 1859. Author, *Elementary School Grammar; Analysis of the Church Catechism; The Church of England before Augustine.* [32]

FERGUSON, Douglas, *Walkington Rectory, Beverley.*—R. of Walkington, Dio. York, 1860. (Patron, the present R; Tithe, 537*l*; Glebe, 237 acres; R.'s Inc.

785*l* and Ho; Pop. 676.) Dom. Chap. to the Duke of Cleveland. [1]

FERGUSON, Richard, *Smethwick, near Birmingham.*—Pemb. Coll. Cam. B.A. 1839, M.A. 1842. P. C. of St. Matthew's, Smethwick, Dio. Lich. 1859. (Patron, P. C. of Smethwick; P. C.'s Inc. 91*l* including pew rents; Pop. 3935.) Late Fell. of Pemb. Coll. Cam. [2]

FERGUSON, Richard William, *Llandogo Parsonage (Monmouthshire), near Coleford.*—Queen's Coll. Ox. B.A. 1850, Deac. 1850, Pr. 1851. P. C. of Llandogo with Whitebrook C. Dio. Llan. 1853. (Patron, Bp of Llan; Tithe, App. 151*l* 13*s* 5*d*; Glebe, 8½ acres; P. C.'s Inc. 107*l* and Ho; Pop. 648.) Author, *The Divine Authority of Holy Scripture*, 1858, Hatchard; *Salus Mundi summa Lex and other Essays on the Aims of the Mosaic Law, &c.*, Macintosh, 1866. [3]

FERGUSON, Thomas Pattinson, *Shenfield Rectory, Brentwood, Essex.*—Trin. Coll. Cam. Wrang. and B.A. 1839, M.A. 1842; Deac. 1840 and Pr. 1841 by Bp of Lich. R. of Shenfield, Dio. Roch. 1864. (Patroness, Countess Cowper; R.'s Inc. 513*l* and Ho; Pop. 978.) [4]

FERNIE, John, *Yeldon Rectory, Higham-Ferrers, Beds.*—Caius Coll. Cam. B.A. 1825, M.A. 1840; Deac. 1826 by Bp of Lin. Pr. 1827 by Bp of Ely. R. of Yelden, Dio. Ely, 1849. (Patron, P. C. Bunting, Esq; Tithe, 356*l*; Glebe, 60 acres; R.'s Inc. 440*l* and Ho; Pop. 286.) Fell. of Caius Coll. Cam. 1827. [5]

FERNIE, John, *Lynn Regis, Norfolk.*—Emman. Coll. Cam. B.A. 1853, M.A. 1857; Deac. 1854, Pr. 1855. P. C. of St. John's, Lynn, Dio. Nor. 1860. (Patron, Bp of Nor; P. C.'s Inc. 170*l*; Pop. 8867.) [6]

FERRALL, C. W., *Thorpe Arnold, Leicestershire.*—C. of Thorpe Arnold. [7]

FERRERS, Norman Macleod, *Caius College, Cambridge.*—Caius Coll. Cam. Sen. Wrang. and 1st Smith's Prize 1851, B.A. 1851, M.A. 1854; Deac. 1859 and Pr. 1860 by Bp of Ely. Sen. Fell. of Caius Coll. Cam. [8]

FERRIER, Edward, *Castletown, Isle of Man.*—Pemb. Coll. Cam. Jun. Opt. and B.A. 1850, M.A. 1853; Deac. 1850 and Pr. 1851 by Bp of Lon. P. C. of St. Mary's, Castletown, Dio. S. and M. 1855. (Patron, the Governor; P. C.'s Inc. 60*l*; Pop. 5065.) Chap. to the Forces and to the Gaol, Castletown, 1855. Formerly C. of St. James's, Southampton. [9]

FERRIER, Henry William.—Corpus Coll. Cam. B.A. 1846, M.A. 1850; Deac. 1848 and Pr. 1849. Formerly C. of Baschurch, Shrewsbury. [10]

FERRIS, Alfred Harry.—Magd. Hall, Ox. B.A. 1847; Deac. 1858 by Bp of Roch. Formerly C. of Tring 1858. [11]

FERRIS, Thomas Boys, *Guiseley Rectory, Leeds.*—Trin. Coll. Ox. B.A. 1833, M.A. 1839. R. of Guiseley, Dio. Rip. 1859. (Patrons, G. L. Fox, Esq. for 2 turns and Trin. Coll. Cam. for 1 turn; R.'s Inc. 790*l* and Ho; Pop. 2758.) Surrogate. Formerly R. of Corscombe, Dorset, 1851–59. [12]

FERRY, William, *Hoo St. Mary's, Kent.*—King's Coll. Lond. Theol. Assoc; Deac. 1863 and Pr. 1864 by Bp of Roch. C. of Hoo St. Mary's 1866. Formerly Asst. C. of Stebbing 1863–66. [13]

FERRYMAN, Edward Augustus.—Univ. Coll. Ox. B.A. 1841; Deac. 1842 and Pr. 1843. C. of Privett, Hants. [14]

FESSEY, George Frederick, *Redditch Vicarage, Worcestershire.*—Lin. Coll. Ox. B.A. 1828, M.A. 1845; Deac. 1831, Pr. 1832. V. of Redditch, Dio. Wor. 1841. (Patroness, Lady Windsor; V.'s Inc. 330*l* and Ho; Pop 5441.) [15]

FESTING, George Arthur, *Clifton Parsonage, Ashburne, Lichfield.*—St. John's Coll. Cam. B.A. 1857, M.A. 1860; Deac. 1857 and Pr. 1858. P. C. of Clifton by Ashburne, Dio. Lich. 1867. (Patron, V. of Ashburne; P. C.'s Inc. 80*l* and Ho; Pop. 500.) Formerly C. of Eccleshall, Staffs, 1858–59, Ashburne 1860–67. [16]

FESTING, John Wogan, 1, *Queen-square Place, Westminster, London, S.W.*—Trin. Coll. Cam. B.A. 1860, M.A. 1863; Deac. 1860 and Pr. 1861 by Bp of Lon. C. of Ch. Ch. Broadway, Westminster, 1860. [17]

FEW, Charles Edward, *Seal, Sevenoaks, Kent.*—Ch. Ch. Ox. B.A. 1864; Deac. 1865 and Pr. 1866 by Abp of Cant. C. of Seal. [18]

FEW, William Jebb, 4, *Castle-crescent, Reading.*—Ch. Ch. Ox. B A. 1857, M.A. 1860; Deac. 1858 and Pr. 1859 by Bp of Ox. C. of St. Mary's, Reading, 1862. Formerly C. of Henley-on-Thames 1858–60, Alverstoke 1860–61. [19]

FFENNEL, W. J., *Crayford, Kent.*—C. of Crayford. [20]

FFINCH, Benjamin Sanderson, *St. Paul's Rectory, Deptford, Kent.*—Trin. Coll. Cam. B.A. 1827, M.A. 1830; Deac. 1827 and Pr. 1828 by Bp of Roch. R. of St. Paul's, Deptford, Dio. Lon. 1834. (Patron, W. W. Drake, Esq; R.'s Inc. 450*l* and Ho; Pop. 20,321.) Lect. of St. Paul's, Deptford, 1847; Chap. to Trin. Ho. 1847; Dom. Chap. to the Earl of Buchan 1842. [21]

FFINCH, Matthew Mortimer, *Ludwell Parsonage, Salisbury.*—Oriel Coll. Ox. B.A. 1861; Deac. 1862 and Pr. 1863 by Bp of Salis. C. of Donhead St. Mary, Wilts, 1863. Formerly C. of Holy Trinity and St. Peter's, Shaftesbury, 1862–63. [22]

FFOLKES, Henry Edward Browne, *Hillington Rectory, Lynn, Norfolk.*—Univ. Coll. Ox. B.A. 1846, M.A. 1849; Deac. 1847 and Pr. 1848 by Bp of Roch. R. of Hillington, Dio. Nor. 1853. (Patron, Sir W. J. H. B. Ffolkes, Bart; Tithe, 449*l*; Glebe, 50 acres; R.'s Inc. 449*l* and Ho; Pop. 330.) [23]

FFOLLIOTT, Francis, *Wishaw Rectory, Birmingham.*—St. John's Coll. Cam. B.A. 1823, M.A. 1824; Deac. 1825 and Pr. 1826 by Bp of Pet. R. of Wishaw, Dio. Wor. 1857. (Patron, John Ffolliott, Esq; Tithe, 320*l*; Glebe, 58 acres; R.'s Inc. 413*l* and Ho; Pop. 216.) [24]

FFOLLIOTT, James Robert, *Douglas, Isle of Man.*—Dub. A.B. 1858, A.M. 1863; Deac. 1858 and Pr. 1859 by Bp of Down and Connor. C. of St Barnabas', Kirk Braddon, 1863. [25]

FFOLLIOTT, William, *Yew Tree House, Kirkheaton, Huddersfield.*—Dub. A.B. 1847; Deac. 1848 and Pr. 1849 by Bp of Man. C. of Kirkheaton. Formerly C. of St. Michael's and Chap. of Missions to Seamen, Liverpool. Author, *The Christian's Dream*, 1853, 1*s* 6*d*; *Cartmel Church, and Sermons preached therein*, 1854, 2*s* 6*d*; *Cartmeltonia*, 1854, 1*s*. [26]

FFOULKES, The Ven. Henry Powell, *Llandyssil, Montgomery.*—Ball. Coll. Ox. 4th cl. Lit. Hum. B.A. 1837, M.A. 1840; Deac. 1839, Pr. 1840. Archd. of Montgomery 1861; Can. Res. of St. Asaph 1861 (Value, 350*l*); R. of Llandyssil, Dio. St. A. 1857. (Patron, Bp of Llan; R.'s Inc. 500*l*; Pop. 790.) Formerly C. of Halkin 1839; Stip. C. of St. Matthew's, Buckley, Hawarden, 1840–57. [27]

FFRENCH, Frederick, *Oxton, Southwell, Notts.*—V. of Oxton, Dio. Lin. 1858. (Patron, Bp of Rip; Tithe—Imp. 404*l* 7*s*, V. 177*l* 17*s* 3*d*; Glebe, 2 acres; V.'s Inc. 330*l* and Ho; Pop. 738.) [28]

FFRENCH, James Frederick Metge, *Havant, Hants.*—St. Aidan's; Deac. 1866. C. of Havant. [29]

FFRENCH, W. S., *Taunton, Somerset.*—C. of St. Mary's, Taunton. [30]

FIDLER, Isaac, *Easington Rectory, Tetsworth, Oxon.*—New Inn Hall, Ox. B.A. 1840; Deac. 1817 and Pr. 1819 by Bp of Ches. R. of Easington, Dio. Ox. 1842. (Patron, Bp of Ox; Tithe, 73*l* 14*s*; Glebe, 5 acres; R.'s Inc. 96*l*; Pop. 26.) Author, *Observations on the United States and Canada*, 1833; *The Travels in England of Nicander Nucius in the Reign of Henry VIII.* (Transcribed from a Greek MS. in the Bodleian Library), Camden Soc. [31]

FIELD, Arthur Thomas, *The Parsonage, Peak Forest, Derbyshire.*—St. John's Coll. Cam. B.A. 1859; Deac. 1859 by Bp of Nor. Pr. 1860 by Abp of York. P. C. of Peak Forest, Dio. Lich. 1865. (Patron, the Duke of Devonshire; Glebe, 1½ acres; P. C.'s Inc. 145*l* and Ho;

Pop. 542.) Formerly C. of Holbrook, near Ipswich, 1859–60, Bossall 1860–62, Settrington 1862–65. [1]

FIELD, Augustus, *Pool Quay, Welshpool, Montgomery.*—Clare Hall, Cam. B A. 1853, M.A. 1856; Deac. 1853 and Pr. 1854 by Bp of St A. P. C. of Pool Quay, Dio. St. A 1863. (Patron, Earl of Powis; P. C.'s Inc. 218*l* 16*s*; Pop. 600.) Formerly C. of Tregynon, Montgomery, 1853–62. [2]

FIELD, Crispin, *Dudley, Worc.*—C. of St. John's, Dudley. [3]

FIELD, Edmund, *Lancing College, Sussex.*—Ex. Coll. B.A. 1847, M.A. 1849; Deac. 1848 by Bp of Salis. Pr. 1849 by Bp of Ex. Fell. and Sen. Chap. of St. Nicholas' Coll. Lancing, 1854. Formerly Asst. C. of Lower Brixham 1848–53. [4]

FIELD, Edward B., B.C.L.—Dom. Chap. to the Earl of Rosebery, Edinburgh. [5]

FIELD, Frederick.—Trin. Coll. Cam. Tyrwhitt's Hebrew Scho. and B.A. 1823, M.A. 1826; Deac. 1828 by Bp of Lin. Pr. 1828 by Bp of Ely. Formerly R. of Reepham, Norfolk, 1842–63; Fell of Trin. Coll. Cam. 1824–43. Editor of *S. Joannis Chrysostomi Homiliæ in Matthæum* (the Greek Text Revised, with Various Readings of MSS. collated for this Edition, and Critical Notes), 3 vols. Cam. Univ. Press (for the Editor), 1839; *S. Joannis Chrysostomi Interpretatio Omnium Epistolarum Paulinarum per Homilias facta* (on the same plan as the former, forming part of the "Bibliotheca Patrum Ecclesiæ Catholicæ"), Vol. I. 1849, Vol. II. 1847, Vol. III. 1845, Vol. IV. 1852, Vol. V. 1855, Vol. VI. 1858; *Barrow's Treatise on the Pope's Supremacy* (new ed. revised from the Original MS. for the S.P.C.K.), 1851; *Vetus Testamentum ex Versione Septuaginta Interpretum secundum Codicem Alexandrinum* (Grabe's Text, revised and re-arranged for the Foreign Translation Committee of the S.P.C.K.) Univ. Press, Ox; *Psalterium juxta LXX. Interpretes* (extracted from the above), 1857. [6]

FIELD, John, *West Rounton Rectory, Northallerton, Yorks.*—Magd. Hall, Ox. B.A. 1834, M.A. 1837; Deac. 1836, Pr. 1837. R. of West Rounton, Dio. York, 1858. (Patron, Ld Chan; R.'s Inc. 350*l* and Ho; Pop. 222.) Late Chap. to the Berks Gaol, Reading, 1840–58. Author, *Prison Discipline*, 2 vols. 1848, 20*s*; *Life of Howard*, 1850, 12*s*; *University and other Sermons*, 1853, 8*s* 6*d*; S.P.C.K. Tract No. 640, *A Chaplain's Word at Parting*; No. 686, *Friendly Advice to a Prisoner*; *Observations on Convict Discipline*, 1855; *Correspondence of John Howard*, 1856; *Remarks on the Lord's Prayer*, 1857. [7]

FIELD, John, *Oldbury-on-Severn, Thornbury, Bristol.*—Literate; Deac. 1849 and Pr. 1851 by Bp of St. D. R. of Oldbury, Dio. G. and B. 1864. (Patrons, D. and C. of Ch. Ch. Ox; Glebe, 2½ acres; Tithe, 209*l*; R.'s Inc. 260*l* and Ho; Pop. 1000.) Formerly Chap. of Training Coll. Carmar, 1849; C. of Carmar 1849; Mast. of Gr. Sch. 1851; Lect. of Thornbury 1853; Chap. of Thornbury Union 1855. [8]

FIELD, John Edward, *Morpeth.*—Wor. Coll. Ox. B.A. 1862 and Pr. 1865, by Bp of Dur. C. of Morpeth 1864. [9]

FIELD, Samuel Pryer, *Sawbridgeworth, Herts.*—Pemb. Coll. Cam. B.A. 1839, M.A. 1843; Deac. 1840, Pr. 1841. V. of Sawbridgeworth, Dio. Roch. (Patron, Bp of Roch; V.'s Inc. 400*l* and Ho; Pop. 1631.) Formerly R. of Boulge with Debach, Suffolk, 1850-62 [10]

FIELD, Thomas, *Pampisford Vicarage, Cambridge.*—St. John's Coll. Cam. Bell's Univ. Scho. 1841, 1st cl. Cl. Trip. 1844, B.A. 1844, M.A. 1847, B.D. 1854. Fell. and Asst. Tut. of St. John's 1847–58; Univ. Cl. Trip. Exam. 1856, '57, '59 and '60; Deac. 1850 and Pr. 1853 by Bp of Ely. V. of Pampisford, Dio. Ely, 1863. (Patron, E. J. Mortlock, Esq; Tithe, comm. for 43 acres of Glebe; V.'s Inc. 86*l* and Ho; Pop. 347.) Formerly V. of Madingley, Cambs, 1858–62. [11]

FIELD, Walter, *Godmersham Vicarage, Canterbury.*—Wor. Coll. Ox. B.A. 1848, M.A. 1850; Deac. 1849 and Pr. 1851 by Abp of York. V. of Godmersham with Challock C. Dio. Cant. 1864. (Patron, Abp of Cant; Tithe, 315*l*; Glebe, 4 acres; V.'s Inc. 325*l* and Ho; Pop. 761.) Formerly C. of St. Paul's, Hull, 1849, All Saints', Hull, 1851, St. Leonard's, Streatham, Surrey, 1852, St. Edward's, Romford, 1856. [12]

FIELDING, Allen, 2, *Lansdowne Villas, Maidstone-road, Rochester.*—Corpus Coll. Cam. B.A. 1823, M.A. 1828; Deac. and Pr. 1827. Chap. R.N. 1834. Formerly Chap. to the Royal Dockyard, Chatham, 1851. [13]

FIELDING, George, *North Ockendon, Romford, Essex.*—St. John's Coll. Cam. B.A. 1811, M.A. 1818; Deac. 1816, Pr. 1817. R. of North Ockenden, Dio. Roch. 1845. (Patron, R. B. De Beauvoir, Esq; Tithe, 500*l*; Glebe, 30 acres; R.'s Inc. 550*l* and Ho; Pop. 341.) [14]

FIELDING, George, *St. James's Parsonage, Clitheroe, Lancashire.*—St. Bees; Deac. and Pr. 1851. P. C. of St. James's, Clitheroe, Dio. Man. 1852. (Patrons, Five Trustees; Tithe—Imp. 143*l* 1*s* 2*d*, P. C. 1*l* 10*s* 8*d*; P. C.'s Inc. 86*l* and Ho; Pop. 2895.) Author, *Dialogue on Sunday Schools*, 2*d*; *Two Addresses on Sunday Schools*, 4*d*; *Funeral Sermon on the Death of the Rev. W. P. Powell, D.C.L.* 6*d*. [15]

FIELDING, George Hanbury, *North Ockendon, Romford, Essex.*—Lin. Coll. Ox. B.A. 1852, Wells Theol. Coll; Deac. 1854, Pr. 1855. Formerly R. of Tredunnoc, Monmouthshire, 1855. [16]

FIELDING, Henry, *Salmonby Rectory, Horncastle, Lincolnshire.*—Emman. Coll. Cam. B.A. 1820, M.A. 1823; Deac. 1820 and Pr. 1821 by Bp of Ches. R. of Salmonby, Dio. Lin. 1840. (Patron, the present R; Tithe, 300*l*; Glebe, 12 acres; R.'s Inc. 315*l*; Pop. 101.) C. of Ashby-Puerorum, Lincolnshire, 1844. [17]

FIENNES, The Hon. Cecil, *Ashow, Kenilworth.*—New Coll. Ox. M.A. R. of Ashow, Dio. Wor. 1866. (Patron, Lord Leigh; R.'s Inc. 300*l* and Ho; Glebe, 12 acres; Pop. 149.) [18]

FIENNES, The Hon. Wingfield, *Silchester, Hants.*—R. of Silchester, Dio. Win. 1865. (Patron, Duke of Wellington; R.'s Inc. 308*l* and Ho; Pop. 480.) Formerly C. of Ashow, Warw. [19]

FIGGINS, John Leighton, 201, *York-street, Cheetham, Manchester.*—Queens' Coll. Cam. B.A. 1832; Deac. 1833 and Pr. 1835 by Bp of Ches. R. of St. James's, Manchester, Dio. Man. 1866. (Patrons, D. and C. of Man; R.'s Inc. 240*l*; Pop. 4075.) Chap. of Harpurhey Cemetery 1856. Formerly C. of Lymm with Warburton 1833; P. C. of Linthwaite 1835, St. Matthew's, Liverpool, 1837, St. Clement's, Manchester, 1843. Author, *The Power of the Keys* (a Sermon). [20]

FILLEUL, Philip, *St. Helier's, Jersey.*—R. of St. Helier's, Dio. Win. 1850. (Patron, the Crown; R.'s Inc. 650*l* and Ho.) [21]

FILLEUL, Philip Valpy Mourant, *Biddesham Rectory, Weston-super-Mare.*—Wad. Coll. Ox. B.A. 1847, M.A. 1853. R. of Biddesham, Dio. B. and W. 1858. (Patron, Bp of Lon; R.'s Inc. 151*l*; Pop. 147.) Late Warden of Ch. Coll. Tasmania, 1853–58. Author, *English Bookkeeper*, Rivingtons, 1857. [22]

FINCH, George, *West Dereham, Stoke Ferry, Norfolk.*—Univ. Coll. Ox. B.A. 1857, M.A. 1862; Deac. 1859 and Pr. 1861 by Bp of Nor. Formerly C. of West Dereham 1859–62, St. Stephen's, St. Albans, Herts, 1862–64. [23]

FINCH, Matthew Isaac, *North Ferriby, Brough, Yorks.*—St. Cath. Hall, Cam. B.A. 1842, M.A. 1845; Deac. 1842 and Pr. 1843 by Bp of Ches. Formerly C. of Ch. Ch. Hull. [24]

FINCH, Robert, *Pangbourne Rectory, Reading.*—Trin. Coll. Cam. B.A. 1851, M.A. 1854; Deac. 1852, Pr. 1853. R. of Pangbourne, Dio. Ox. 1857. (Patron, E. A. Breedon, Esq; R.'s Inc. 450*l* and Ho; Pop. 753.) Formerly C. of Wittersham and Brenzett. [25]

FINCH, Thomas, *Morpeth, Northumberland.*—Magd. Coll. Cam. B.A. 1824; Deac. 1824, Pr. 1825. Chap. to the Northumberland County Gaol 1841 and County Asylum 1859; Surrogate. [26]

FINCH, Thomas Ross, *Sonning, Reading.*—Wad. Coll. Ox. B.A. 1861, M.A. 1864; Deac. 1862 and

Pr. 1863 by Bp of Man. C. of Sonning. Formerly C. of Penwortham 1862–65. [1]

FINCH, William, *Warboys Rectory, Huntingdon.*—R. of Warboys, Dio. Ely, 1828. (Patron, T. Daniel, Esq; R.'s Inc. 1300*l* and Ho; Pop. 1911.) [2]

FINCH, William, *Burmington Parsonage, Shipston-on-Stour.*—St. John's Coll. Cam. Sen. Opt. and B.A. 1858, M.A. 1861; Deac. 1858 and Pr. 1859 by Bp of Ches. C. of Burmington 1864; Dom. Chap. to Lord Lisle 1860. Formerly C. of Sandbach 1858–61, Fareham 1861–63. [3]

FINCH, William Stafford, *Englefield House, 55, Downham-road, London, N.*—St. Edm. Hall, Ox. B.A. 1847, M.A. 1850; Deac. 1847 and Pr. 1848 by Bp of Lon. P. C. of St. Peter's, De Beauvoir Town, Dio. Lon. 1861. (Patron, Richard Benyon, Esq. M.P.) Formerly C. of St. James's, Curtain Road, Lond. 1847, West Hackney 1851. Author, *Prize Essay on the Church of England Self-supporting Village,* 1850, 1*s*; *Sermon on Confirmation,* 1852; *Sermon on the Funeral of the Duke of Wellington,* 1852; *Sermons* (preached at West Hackney), Masters, 7*s* 6*d*; *Lectures on the English Reformation,* 2*s* 6*d*; *Sermon on the Death of Lord Macaulay,* 1860; *Plea for the Preservation of the City Churches* 1860; *The Theory of Miracles,* Batty, 1863. [4]

FINCHER, Joseph Guillemard, *Hursley, Hants.*—Literate; Deac. 1857 and Pr. 1858 by Bp of Lon. C. of Hursley. Formerly C. of St. Gabriel's, Pimlico; Head Mast. of St. George's Gr. Sch. Pimlico. [5]

FINDEN, George Sketchley, *Newport-Pagnel, Bucks.*—King's Coll. Lond. Assoc. 1859; Deac. 1860 and Pr. 1861 by Bp of Ox. C. of Moulsoe, Bucks, 1863. Formerly C. of Monks Risborough, Bucks, 1860, Newport-Pagnel 1861–62. [6]

FINDLAY, William, *Willington, near Burton-on-Trent.*—V. of Willington, Dio. Lich. 1855. (Patrons, Corporation of Etwall Hospital and Repton Sch; V.'s Inc. 85*l*; Pop. 477.) [7]

FINDLAY, William Benjamin, *Etherley Rectory, Bishop Auckland.*—Ch. Ch. Ox. B.A. 1848, M.A. 1858; Deac. 1848 and Pr. 1849 by Bp of Ches. R. of Etherley, Dio. Dur. 1866. (Patron, Bp of Man; Tithe, 2*l* 15*s*; Glebe, 72 acres; R.'s Inc. 300*l* and Ho; Pop. 1712.) Formerly C. of Hindley 1848–54, Atherton 1854–66. [8]

FINLAY, Edward Bullock, *Cheltenham.*—Wor. Coll. Ox. 2nd cl. Lit. Hum. and B.A. 1849, M.A. 1854; Deac. 1854 by Bp of Down and Connor, Pr. 1855 by Bp of Nor. Formerly 2nd Mast. of Queen Elizabeth's Gr. Sch. Dedham, 1853–54; C. of Stratford St. Mary, Suffolk, 1854–57, Frittenden, Kent, 1859, Gazeley 1859–60. [9]

FINLEY, John, *Aveley Vicarage, near Romford, Essex.*—Trin. Coll. Cam. B.A. 1831, M.A. 1834; Deac. 1831 and Pr. 1333 by Bp of Lich. V. of Aveley, Dio. Roch. 1865. (Patron, Bp of Roch; Tithe, 317*l*; Glebe, 8 acres; V.'s Inc. 329*l* and Ho; Pop. 930.) Formerly C. of Ch. Ch. Birmingham, 1831–32, Colwich, Staffs, 1832–34, Milwich, Staffs, 1834–36, Dudley 1836–37; V. of Studley 1837–54; C. of Ingestre, Staffs, 1854–57; R. of St. Michael Bassishaw, Lond. 1857–65. [10]

FINNY, Henry Maturin, *The Cottage, Gotham, Kegworth, Derby.*—Dub. A.B. 1851; Deac. 1853 and Pr. 1854 by Bp of Win. C. of Gotham and Ratcliffe-on-Soar 1863. Formerly C. of Lymington, Hants, 1853–58; Sec. in Ireland to the Colonial and Continental Ch. Soc. 1858–63. [11]

FIRMIN, John Palmer, *Dane Bank House, near Congleton, Cheshire.*—Queens' Coll. Cam. B.A. 1842, M.A. 1845; Deac. 1842 and Pr. 1843 by Bp of Ches. P. C. of Ch. Ch. Eaton, Cheshire, Dio. Ches. 1857. (Patron, G. C. Antrobus, Esq; P. C.'s Inc. 70*l*; Pop. 485.) P. C of Marton, Dio. Ches. 1858. (Patrons, Trustees of Hyndman's Charity; P. C.'s Inc. 130*l*; Pop. 3836.) Formerly P. C. of Trinity Chapel, Odd Rode, Cheshire, 1847–57. [12]

FIRMIN, Robert, *Yoxford, near Saxmundham, Suffolk.*—Clare Coll. Cam. B.A. 1823, M.A. 1846; Deac. 1823 and Pr. 1825 by Bp of Llan. V. of Yoxford, Dio. Nor. 1846. (Patron, the present V; Tithe—Imp. 284*l*, V. 194*l*; Glebe, 5 acres; V.'s Inc. 240*l*; Pop. 1111.) Surrogate 1854. [13]

FIRMSTONE, Edward, *Hyde Abbey School, Winchester.*—Lin. Coll. Ox. 2nd cl. Lit. Hum. and B.A. 1846, M.A. 1849; Deac. 1847 and Pr. 1848 by Bp of Ox. Head Mast. of Hyde Abbey Sch. Formerly Head Mast. of Queen Elizabeth's Free Gr. Sch. Hartlebury, Worcestershire, 1852–55. [14]

FIRTH, George Arthur, *St. Michael's Parsonage, New Malton, Yorks.*—Ch. Ch. Ox. 2nd cl. Lit. Hum. and B.A. 1851; Deac. 1852 and Pr. 1853 by Abp of York. P. C. of St. Michael's, New Malton, Dio. York, 1855. (Patron, Earl Fitzwilliam; P. C.'s Inc. 210*l* and Ho; Pop. 1566.) [15]

FIRTH, Raywood, *93, Fishergate-hill, Preston.*—St. Aidan's and Dub. A.B. 1861, A.M. 1864; Deac. 1858 and Pr. 1859 by Bp of Ches. P. C. of Ch. Ch. Preston, Dio. Man. 1864. (Patrons, Trustees; P.C.'s Inc. 325*l*; Pop. 5600.) Formerly C. of St. Anne's, Birkenhead, 1858–60; Assoc. Sec. to C. M. Soc. 1861–64. [16]

FISH, George, *Erpingham, Aylsham, Norfolk.*—Trin. Coll. Cam. B.A. 1834; Deac. 1834 and Pr. 1835 by Bp of Roch. R. of Ingworth, near Aylsham, Dio. Nor. 1835. (Patron, Admiral Windham; Tithe, 170*l*; Glebe, 13 acres; R.'s Inc. 190*l*; Pop. 153.) [17]

FISH, Ishmael, *Whitby.*—St. Bees 1864; Deac. 1856 and Pr. 1857 by Abp of York. P. C. of Egton, Dio. Carl. 1867. (Patron, Abp of York; P. C.'s Inc. 300*l*, and Grant of Eccles. Comm. 1400*l* for building; Pop. 800.) Formerly Superintendent of Castle Howard Reformatory 1856. Author, *The Stranger's Tale, a Story of Humble Life,* 1855, 1*s*; Various Papers relating to Reformatories; *Government of the Household* (a Sermon), 3*d*. [18]

FISH, John, *Egremont, Whitehaven.*—Dub. A.B. 1855, A.M. 1858; Deac. 1860 and Pr. 1861 by Bp of Tuam. C. of Egremont 1867. Formerly C. of St. Mark's, Hull, 1862, Atwick 1865. [19]

FISH, John Dent.—Caius Coll. Cam. B.A. 1850, M.A. 1853; Deac. 1851 and Pr. 1852 by Bp of Lich. Formerly C. of Brereton, near Rugeley, 1852–53. [20]

FISH, J. L., *19, Little Tower-street, London, E.C.*—R. of St. Gabriel Fenchurch with St. Margaret Pattens R. City and Dio. Lon. 1867. (Patrons, Ld Chan. and Corporation of Lond. alt; Tithe, comm. 129*l*; R.'s Inc. 264*l* and Ho; Pop. St. Gabriel 178, St. Margaret Pattens 103) [21]

FISH, Richard George, *Stillington, York.*—C. of Stillington. [22]

FISHER, Andrew.—Univ. Coll. Dur. Theol. Licen. 1858; Deac. 1855 and Pr. 1856 by Bp of Man. Formerly C. of St. Peter's, Preston. [23]

FISHER, C. E., *Grantham, Lincolnshire.*—R. of North and South Stoke, Dio. Lin. 1865. (Patron, Preb. of South Grantham; R.'s Inc. 785*l* and Ho; Pop. 394.) [24]

FISHER, Charles John, *Ovington Clare Rectory, Halstead, Essex.*—Jesus Coll. Cam. B.A. 1841, M.A. 1844; Deac. 1842 and Pr. 1843 by Bp of Lon. R. of Ovington with Tilbury-juxta-Clare R. and Allbrights C. Dio. Roch. 1843. (Patron, the present R; Ovington, Tithe, 214*l*; Glebe, 22 acres; Tilbury, Tithe—App. 12*l*, R. 265*l* 15*s*; Glebe, 16 acres; R.'s Inc. 569*l* and Ho; Pop. Ovington 145, Tilbury 236.) [25]

FISHER, Edmund, *Chipping-Ongar Rectory, Essex.*—St. Peter's Coll. Cam. 7th Wrang. and B.A. 1823, M.A. 1826; Deac. 1825 by Bp of Ely, Pr. 1826 by Bp of Lin. R. of Chipping-Ongar, Dio. Roch. 1832. (Patron, Admiral Swinbourne; Tithe, 144*l* 6*s* 3*d*; Glebe, 4½ acres; R.'s Inc. 168*l* and Ho; Pop. 867.) [26]

FISHER, Edmund Henry, *Fulham Palace, S.W.*—Trin. Coll. Cam. Fell. of, B.A. 1858, M.A. 1861; Deac. 1864 and Pr. 1865 by Bp of Salis. Dom. Chap. to Bp of Lon. Author, *The Goth and the Saracen,* Macmillan. [27]

FISHER, Edward Robert, *West Malling, Kent.*—Bp Hat. Hall, Dur. B.A. 1856, M.A. 1859; Deac. 1856 by Bp of Man. Pr. 1857 by Bp of Dur. C. of West Malling. [28]

FISHER, Francis, *Downham, Cambs.*—Emman. Coll. Cam. Sen. Opt. and B.A. 1844; Deac. 1845, Pr. 1846. R. of Downham, Dio. Ely, 1863. (Patron, Bp of Ely; Tithe, 1110*l* 10*s*; Glebe, 131 acres; R.'s Inc 1150*l* and Ho; Pop. 2158.) Formerly C. of Downham. [1]

FISHER, Frederick, *Maiden-Newton, Dorchester.*—Literate; Deac. 1847 by Bp of New Zealand, Pr. 1853 by Bp of Salis. C. of Maiden-Newton. Formerly Miss. at Howick, New Zealand, under the S.P.G. [2]

FISHER, Frederick Colborne, *Walton-on-Trent, Burton, Derbyshire.*—St. Mary Hall, Ox. B.A. 1850, M.A. 1852; Deac. 1850, Pr. 1851. R. of Walton-on-Trent, Dio. Lich. 1860. (Patron, P. H. Fisher, Esq; R.'s Inc. 818*l* and Ho; Pop. 430.) [3]

FISHER, George, *Rugby.*—St. Cath. Coll. Cam. Sen. Opt. B.A. 1821, M.A. 1825; Deac. 1821, Pr. 1827. Formerly Astronomer in the Expedition to the North Pole 1818 and 1821–23. C. of Stanstead, Essex, 1825, Ampthill, Beds, 1827; Prin. and Chap. to the Royal Hosp. Schs. Greenwich. [4]

FISHER, George Henry, *Willenhall, Walsall, Staffs.*—Min. of Willenhall, Dio. Lich. (Patrons, the Inhabitants; Tithe, Imp. 640*l*; Min.'s Inc. 300*l*; Pop. 3923.) [5]

FISHER, Harry Charrington, *Sustead Parsonage, near Norwich.*—Jesus Coll. Cam. M.A. 1863. Deac. 1864 by Bp of Pet. Pr. 1865 by Bp of Roch. R. of Bessingham, Dio Nor. 1866. (Patron, Rev. H. C. Fisher; Tithe, 131*l*; Glebe, 30 acres; R.'s Inc. 187*l*; Pop. 138.) P. C. of Sustead, Norfolk. Formerly C. of Kirby-le Soken 1864–66. [6]

FISHER, Henry, *Leamington.*—St. Aidan's; Deac. 1850 and Pr. 1851 by Bp of Ches. Min. of St. Luke's, Leamington, 1856. Formerly C. of Boughton, Chester, 1850, Kirkheaton, Yorks, 1852, St. Andrew's, Birmingham. [7]

FISHER, Henry, *Higham-on-the-Hill, Hinckley.*—Jesus Coll. Cam. Scho. Sen. Opt. and B.A. 1860, M.A. 1863; Deac. 1861 by Bp of Pet. Pr. 1862 by Bp of Wor. C. of Higham 1867. Formerly Asst. Mast. of King Edward's Sch. Bromsgrove, 1861–62; C. of Hales-Owen 1862–64, Blockley 1864–66. [8]

FISHER, James, *The Rectory, Dorchester.*—Wor. Coll. Ox. B.A. 1847, M.A. 1851; Deac. 1847 and Pr. 1848 by Bp of G. and B. R. of Holy Trinity, Dorchester, with Frome Whitfield R. Dio. Salis. 1855. (Patrons, Trustees of the Free School Almshouses; R.'s Inc. 500*l* and Ho; Pop. 1601.) [9]

FISHER, John, *Heapey Parsonage, Chorley, Lancashire.*—Literate; Deac. 1822 and Pr. 1823 by Abp of York. P. C. of Heapey, Leyland, Dio. Man. 1832. (Patron, V. of Leyland; Tithe—App. 63*l*, Imp. 32*l*, P. C. 50*l*; Glebe, 13 acres; P. C.'s Inc. 160*l* and Ho; Pop. 396.) Author, *The Wisdom of Winning Souls* (a Sermon); The *Blessedness of having God for our Father and the Guide of our Youth* (a Sermon addressed to Young Persons). [10]

FISHER, John, *Higham-on-the-Hill, Hinckley, Leicestershire.*—Sid. Coll. Cam. B.A. 1819, M.A. 1820; Deac. 1821, Pr. 1822. R. of Higham-on-the Hill, Dio. Pet. 1832. (Patron, the present R; Glebe, 368 acres; R.'s Inc. 586*l* and Ho; Pop. 559.) [11]

FISHER, John, *Magdalen College, Oxford.*—Brasen. Coll. Ox. B.A. 1831, Magd. Coll. M.A. 1836, B.D. and D.D. 1844. Fell. of Magd. Coll. Ox. [12]

FISHER, John Turner, *Hessenford, St. Germans, Cornwall.*—Univ. Coll. Ox. B.A. 1844; Deac. 1845, Pr. 1847. P. C. of Hessenford, Dio. Ex. 1851. (Patron, P. C. of St. Germans; P. C.'s Inc. 100*l* and Ho; Pop. 963.) [13]

FISHER, Osmond, *Harleton Rectory, Cambridge.*—Jesus Coll. Cam. Fell 1845, 18th Wrang. and B.A. 1841, M.A. 1844, F.G.S. F.C.P.S; Deac. 1844 and Pr. 1845 by Bp of Salis. R. of Harleton, Dio. Ely, 1867. (Patron, Jesus Coll. Cam; Glebe, 304 acres, R.'s Inc. 313*l* and Ho; Pop. 302.) Formerly C. of Writhlington, Somerset, 1844, All Saints, Dorchester, 1846; V. of Elmstead, Essex, 1857–67; Tut. of Jesus Coll. Cam. 1853. Author, *The Institution of the Ministry* (a Sermon) 1846; *The Office of Sponsors not to be refused*, 1847; *Digest of the Correspondence on the Management Clauses* 1849; *Two Sermons with Notes on the Present Crisis*, 1850; *A Plea for Precious Lives* (a Sanitary Tract), 1*d*. [14]

FISHER, Robert, *Accrington, Lancashire.*—Brasen. Coll. Ox. B.A. 1847, M.A. 1849; Deac. 1848 and Pr. 1849 by Bp of Lin. C. of Ch. Ch. Accrington, 1865. Formerly C. of Shaw and Littleborough 1860–65. [15]

FISHER, Robert, *Dent, Sedbergh, Yorks.*—C. of Dent. [16]

FISHER, Thomas Ruggles, *Liston Rectory, (Essex), near Sudbury.*—King's Coll. Lond; Deac. 1853, Pr. 1854. R. of Liston, Dio. Roch. 1855. (Patron, R. Lambert, Esq; Tithe, 205*l*; Glebe, 18 acres; R.'s Inc. 241*l* and Ho; Pop. 95.) [17]

FISHER, Wilfred, *Westwell Rectory, Burford, Oxon.*—Ch. Ch. Ox. B.A. 1855, M.A. 1858; Deac. 1858 by Bp of Ox. R. of Westwell, Dio. Ox. 1861. (Patron, Ch. Ch. Ox; R.'s Inc. 180*l* and Ho; Pop. 169.) [18]

FISHER, William, *Poulshot Rectory, Devizes, Wilts.*—Ch. Ch. Ox. B.A. 1819, M.A. 1821. R. of Poulshot, Dio. Salis. 1823. (Patron, Bp of Salis; Tithe, 380*l*; Glebe, 80 acres; R.'s Inc. 580*l* and Ho; Pop. 334.) Can. Res. of Salis. Cathl. with Prebendal Stall of Ilfracombe annexed, 1834. (Value, 800*l* and Res.) [19]

FISHER, William, 33, *Hamilton-terrace, Milford.*—King's Coll. Lond. Theol. Assoc. 1839, Caius Coll. Cam. B.A. 1846, M.A. 1850; Deac. 1857, Pr. 1858 by Bp of Ches. Chap. of Missions to Seamen. Formerly V. of Hartlip, Kent, 1852–58. C. of Hindley 1859, St. Matthew's, Bristol, 1859–67. [20]

FISHER, William Frederick, *Wootton, Isle of Wight.*—Trin. Coll. Cam. B.A. 1850, M.A. 1853; Deac. 1852, Pr. 1853. C. of Wootton 1866. [21]

FISHLAKE, John Roles, *Little Cheverel Rectory, Devizes, Wilts.*—Wad. Coll. Ox. 1st cl. Lit. Hum. and B.A. 1810, M.A. 1814; Deac. 1813, Pr. 1814. R. of Little Cheverel, Dio. Salis. 1823. (Patron, Earl of Radnor; Land in lieu of Tithe, 190 acres; R.'s Inc. 405*l*; and Ho; Pop. 234.) Late Fell. of Wad. Coll. Ox. Author, *Translation of Buttman's Lexilogus* 1836; 3rd ed. 1846; *Translation of Buttman's Catalogue of Irregular Greek Verbs*, 1837, 2nd ed. 1844. [22]

FISK, George, *Great Malvern Vicarage, Worcestershire.*—Corpus Coll. Cam. B.C.L. 1832; Deac. 1832 by Bp of Roch. Pr. 1833 by Bp of Carl. Preb. of Freeford in Lich. Cathl. 1843; V. of Great Malvern, Dio. Wor. 1856. (Patroness, Lady Emily Foley; V.'s Inc. 350*l* and Ho; Pop. 6054.) Formerly C. of St. Botolph's, Cambridge, 1832; R. of Darlaston 1835; V. of Walsall 1837; P. C. of Ch. Chapel, Maida Hill, 1846. Author, *Sermons* (preached at St. Botolph's, Cam.), 1835, 12*s*; *A Pastor's Memorial of the Holy Land*, 6th ed. 7*s* 6*d*; *A Sevenfold Aspect of Popery*, 1852, 4*s* 6*d*; *Twelve Aspects of Christ*, 1854, 4*s*; *An Orphan Tale told in Rhyme*, 2*s* 6*d*; etc. [23]

FISKE, John Robert, *Kettlebaston Rectory, Bildeston, Suffolk.*—St. Cath. Hall, Cam. B.A. 1828; Deac. 1828 and Pr. 1831 by Bp of Nor. R. of Kettlebaston, Dio. Ely, 1839. (Patron, Rev. Thomas Fiske; Tithe—App. 3*l* 5*s*, R. 300*l*; Glebe, 17 acres; R.'s Inc. 321*l* and Ho; Pop. 198.) [24]

FISKE, Robert White, *North Leigh, Witney.*—Trin. Coll. Cam. 2nd cl. Cl. Trip. and B.A. 1845, M.A. 1849; Deac. 1851 and Pr. 1852 by Bp of Roch. V. of North Leigh, Dio. Ox. 1861. (Patron, Ld Chan; V.'s Inc. 160*l* and Ho; Pop. 738.) [25]

FITCH, Adam, *Thornton Steward Vicarage, Bedale, Yorks.*—Ch. Coll. Cam. B.A. 1830, M.A. 1833; Deac. 1832 by Bp of Roch. Pr. 1837 by Bp of Ely. V. of Thornton Steward, Dio. Rip. 1849. (Patron, Bp of Rip; Tithe—App. 135*l* 8*s* 6*d*, and 8½ acres of Glebe, V. 1[illegible]; Glebe, 52 acres; V.'s Inc. 238*l* and Ho; Pop. 283.) [26]

FITCH, Edward Henry, *Bridekirk, near Cockermouth.*—St. Bees; Deac. 1867 by Bp of Carl. C. of Bridekirk. [27]

FITCH, Frederick, *Cromer, Norfolk.*—Ch. Coll. Cam. B.A. 1843, M.A. 1846; Deac. 1843, Pr. 1845. V. of Cromer, Dio. Nor. 1852. (Patron, Bp of Nor;

Tithe—App. 166*l* 2*s* 6*d*, V. 74*l*; V.'s Inc. 102*l*; Pop. 1367.) Surrogate. [1]

FITCH, Samuel Edward, *Aylmerton, Cromer, Norfolk.*—C. of Aylmerton with Runton. [2]

FITTON, Frederick Chambers, *Bagshot, Surrey.*—Emman. Coll. Cam. M.A; Deac. 1858 and Pr. 1859 by Bp of Win. C. of Bagshot 1868. Formerly C. of Freshwater, Isle of Wight, 1858–61, Richmond, Surrey, 1862. [3]

FITZ-GERALD, The Ven. Augustus Otway, *Charlton Mackerel, Taunton, Somerset.*—Ball. Coll Ox. B.A. 1835, M.A. 1841; Deac. 1836 and Pr. 1837 by Bp of B. and W. R. of Charlton Mackerel, Dio. B. and W. 1853. (Patron, John Brymer, Esq; Tithe, 264*l*; Glebe, 151 acres; R.'s Inc. 480*l* and Ho; Pop. 367.) Archd. of Wells 1863. Formerly R. of Fledborough, Notts, 1837–53. Author, *Lectures on the Church Catechism,* 1845, 6*s*. [4]

FITZ-GERALD, Frederick A. H., *Weybread Vicarage, Harleston.*—Deac. 1859 and Pr. 1860 by Bp of Pet. V. of Weybread, Dio. Nor. 1863. (Patroness, Mrs. Fitz-Gerald; Tithe, 126*l*; Glebe, 10 acres; V.'s Inc. 139*l* and Ho; Pop. 713.) Formerly C. of Little Dalby, Melton-Mowbray, 1859–63. [5]

FITZ-GERALD, Gerald Stephen, *Wanstead Rectory.*—Dub. A.B. 1848, A.M. 1850; Deac. 1848, Pr. 1849 by Bp of Win. R. of Wanstead, Dio. Lon. 1864. (Patron, Earl Cowley; Tithe, 402*l*; Glebe, 200 acres; R.'s Inc. 616*l* and Ho; Pop. 2800.) [6]

FITZ-GERALD, John, *The Parsonage, Pratt-street, Camden-town, London, N.W.*—Univ. Coll. Ox. B.A. 1853, M.A. 1863; Deac. 1853 and Pr. 1854 by Abp of Cant. P. C. of Camden-town, Dio. Lon. 1857. (Patron, V. of St. Pancras, Lond; P. C.'s Inc. 300*l* and Ho; Pop. 15,850.) Formerly V. of Borden, Kent, 1855–57. Author, *What is the Faith of the Essayists and Reviewers?* J. H. Parker, 1861. Editor of *Hymns and Anthems* for the Services of the Church, J. and C. Mozley, 1860. [7]

FITZ-GERALD, Richard, *Winslade Rectory, Basingstoke, Hants.*—Ex. Coll. Ox. B.A. 1837; Deac. 1838 and Pr. 1839 by Bp of Win. R. of Winslade, Dio. Win. 1850. (Patron, Lord Bolton; Tithe, 207*l* 2*s* 6*d*; Glebe, 12 acres; R.'s Inc. 219*l* and Ho; Pop. 183.) [8]

FITZ-GERALD, William George, *Bridgwater, Somerset.*—King's Coll. Lond. and St. John's Coll. Cam. V. of Bridgwater with Chilton, Dio. B. and W. 1864. (Patron, Ld Chan; R.'s Inc. 325*l* and Ho; Pop. 4167.) [9]

FITZGERALD, Henry, *Bredon Rectory, (Worcestershire), near Tewkesbury.*—Dub. A.B. 1848, A.M. 1831; Deac. and Pr. 1850 by Bp of Kildare. R. of Bredon with Norton C. and Cutsdean C. Dio. Wor. 1853. (Patron, Duke of Portland; R.'s Inc. 2300*l* and Ho; Pop. Bredon 1156, Norton 243, Cutsdean 162.) [10]

FITZHERBERT, Thomas, *Marston-Magna Rectory, Yeovil, Somerset.*—R. of Ashington, near Ilchester, Somerset, Dio. B. and W. (Tithe, 125*l*; Glebe, 25 acres; R.'s Inc. 172*l* and Ho; Pop. 57.) R. of Marston-Magna, Dio. B. and W. 1842. (Patron, Capt. James Maurice Shipton, R.N; Tithe, 305*l*; Glebe, 87 acres; R.'s Inc. 407*l* and Ho; Pop. 379.) [11]

FITZ-HUGH, William Anthony, *Street Rectory, Hurstpierpoint, Sussex.*—R. of Street, Dio. Chich. 1831. (Patron, H. C. Lane, Esq; Tithe, 205*l*; Glebe, 31 acres; R.'s Inc. 238*l* and Ho; Pop. 190.) Preb. of Middleton in Chich. Cathl. 1860. [12]

FITZPATRICK, Richard William, *Bedford.*—St. Peter's Coll. Cam. B.A. 1841, M.A. 1844; Deac. 1850, Pr. 1851. P. C. of Trinity, Bedford, Dio. Ely, 1858. (Patron, V. of St. Paul's, Bedford; P. C.'s Inc. 196*l*; Pop. 3044.) [13]

FITZROY, Augustus, *Ramsgate, Kent.*—Trin. Coll. Cam. B.A. 1828, M.A. 1831; Deac. 1829 by Bp of Pet. Pr. 1830 by Bp of Nor. Formerly R. of Fakenham Magna, Suffolk, 1835–57; P. C. of Sapiston, Suffolk, 1834-57. [14]

FITZ-WYGRAM, Fitzroy John, *New Hampton, Middlesex.*—Trin. Coll. Cam. B.A. 1849, M.A. 1852; Deac. 1850, Pr. 1851. P. C. of St. James's, New Hampton, Dio. Lon. 1863. [15]

FIXSEN, John Frederick, *Merton, Surrey.*—Trin. Coll. Cam. B.A. 1852, M.A. 1855; Deac. 1853 and Pr. 1858 by Bp of Ox. P. C. of Merton, Dio. Win. 1863. (Patroness, Mrs. Edelman; Glebe, 2½ acres; P. C.'s Inc. 150*l* and Ho; Pop. 1822.) [16]

FLAMSTEED, Alvery Richard Dodsley, *Lambley Rectory, Nottingham.*—Ex. Coll. Ox. B.A. 1859, M.A. 1863; Deac. 1860 and Pr. 1861 by Bp of Pet. R of Lambley, Dio. Lin. 1861. (Patron, the present R; Tithe, 600*l*; Glebe, 92 acres; R.'s Inc. 600*l* and Ho; Pop. 836.) Formerly C. of Birstall, near Leicester, 1860–61. [17]

FLATHER, Alfred John, 37, *Burton-crescent, London, W.C.*—St. John's Coll. Cam. Jun. Opt. B.A. 1861, M.A. 1864; Deac. 1861 and Pr. 1862 by Bp of Lon. C. of St. Peter's, Regent-square, St. Pancras, Lond. 1864. Formerly C. of St. Mary Somerset with St. Mary Mounthaw, Lond. 1861, and Aft. Lect. 1863–64. [18]

FLAVELL, John Webb, *Ridlington, Smallburgh, Norfolk.*—Dub. A.B. 1834; Deac. 1835, Pr. 1836. R. of Ridlington with East Ruston V. Dio. Nor. 1836. (Patrons, Lord Wodehouse and D. and C. of Windsor alt; Ridlington, Tithe—App. 32*l* 10*s*, R. 184*l* 7*s* 2*d*; Glebe, ¾ acre; East Ruston, Tithe, App. 941*l* 5*s*; Glebe, 11 acres; R.'s Inc. 218*l*; Pop. Ridlington 236, East Ruston 757.) [19]

FLEAY, Frederick Gard, *Grammar School, Leeds.*—Trin. Coll. Cam. B.A. 1853, M.A. 1856; Deac. 1856 and Pr 1857 by Bp of Ox. Mast. of Commercial Dep. Gr. Sch. Leeds. Formerly Vice-Prin. of the Oxford Dioc. Training Coll. 1856. Author, *Almond Blossoms* (Lyrics), 5*s*; *English Grammar,* 1*s*; *Hints on Preaching,* 6*d*. [20]

FLEETWOOD, Peter L. Hesketh, *Ryarsh, Maidstone.*—C. of Ryarsh. [21]

FLEETWOOD, William, *Swaffham Bulbeck Vicarage, Cambs.*—V. of Swaffham Bulbeck, Dio. Ely, 1854. (Patron, Bp of Ely; V.'s Inc. 220*l* and Ho; Pop. 873.) [22]

FLEMING, Arthur Willis.—Dom. Chap. to Lord Heytesbury. [23]

FLEMING, David, *Coxhoe, Ferry Hill, Durham.* Glasgow Univ. B.A. 1856; Deac. 1858 and Pr. 1859 by Bp of Rip. P. C. of Coxhoe, Dio. Dur. 1867. (Patrons, Crown and Bp alt; P. C.'s Inc. 200*l*; Pop. 2600.) Formerly C. of St. Saviour's, Leeds, 1858–59, Grosmont, Yorks, 1859–63, West Hartlepool 1863–66. [24]

FLEMING, H. R., *Friezland, Yorks.*—C. of Friezland. [25]

FLEMING, James, 161, *Camberwell Grove, Surrey.*—Magd. Coll. Cam. Travelling Bachelor to the Univ. B.A. 1853, M.A. 1856, B.D. 1865; Deac. 1853 and Pr. 1854 by Bp of Nor. P. C. of Camden Ch. Camberwell, Dio. Win. 1866. (Patrons, Trustees; P. C.'s Inc. 900*l*; Pop. 5170.) Prof. of English Literature and Elocution at the Somersetshire Coll. Formerly C. of St. Stephen's, Ipswich, 1853–55, St. Stephen's, Bath, 1855–56, and Min. of All Saints Chapel, Bath, 1856–58. Author, *Are you Happy?* 2*d*; *Where is your Christianity?* Ipswich, 2*d*; *Bath Penny Readings*; *Select Readings,* Peach, Bath. [26]

FLEMING, John, *Saitisham Hall, near Lynn, Norfolk.*—St. John's Coll. Cam. B.A. 1842, M.A. 1845; Deac. 1842 and Pr. 1843 by Bp of Nor. V. of St. Mary the Virgin's, Wiggenhall, Dio. Nor. 1852. (Patron, Ld Chan; Tithe, 92*l*; Glebe, 1½ acres; V.'s Inc. 140*l* and Ho; Pop. 307.) Chap. of Lynn Gaol. [27]

FLEMING, J. R., *Strensall, Yorks.*—C. of Strensall. [28]

FLEMING, Sydney Hall, 1, *Belfield-terrace, Weymouth.*—Assoc. King's Coll. Lond. C. of Trinity, Weymouth. [29]

FLEMING, Thomas, *Pembroke College, Cambridge.*—Pemb. Coll. Cam. B.A. 1831, M.A. 1834. Abp Grindall's Fell. of Pemb. Coll. Cam. [30]

FLEMING, Thomas S., 1, *Roscoe-place, Sheepscar, Leeds.*—Ch. Miss. Coll. Islington; Deac. 1859 by

Abp of Cant. Pr. 1860 by Bp of Victoria. P. C. of St. Clement's, Leeds, Dio. Rip. 1866. (Patron, Bp of Rip; P. C.'s Inc. 250*l*; Pop. 4000.) Formerly Assoc. Sec. of Ch. Miss. Soc. for Notts, Lincolnshire and Rutland 1864, and Derbyshire 1865; Miss. to Ningpo, China, 1859–63. [1]

FLEMING, William, *Hornsey, London, N.*—St. Cath. Coll. Cam. LL.B. 1859; Deac. 1857 and Pr. 1858 by Bp of Chich. P. C. of Ch. Ch. Crouch End, Hornsey, Dio. Lon 1862. (Patron, Bp of Lon; Pop. 1200.) Formerly Jun. Chap. to the Home and Colonial Training Institution 1858. [2]

FLEMYNG, Francis Patrick, *Glenfeulan, Helensburgh, Dumbartonshire.*—Magd. Coll. Cam. B.A. 1847, M.A. 1852, LL.D. 1867; Deac. 1847 by Bp of Ches. Pr. 1847 by Bp of Pet. Formerly C. of St. Mary's, Chester, 1847; Mil. Chap. Weedon 1848, Cape of Good Hope 1849, Mauritius 1854; P. C. of Kidmore, Oxon, 1858. Author, *Kaffraria*, Smith and Elder, 1852, 6*s*; *South Africa*, Hall and Virtue, 1855, 10*s*; *Mauritius*, S.P.C.K. 1862, 2*s* 6*d*. [3]

FLETCHER, George Henry, *Charles, Plymouth.*—Corpus Coll. Cam. B.A. 1848, M.A. 1851; Deac. 1850, Pr. 1851. C. of Charles. Formerly Incumb. of Laura Chapel, Bath. [4]

FLETCHER, Henry, *Trinity Parsonage, Shrewsbury.*—Brasen. Coll. Ox. B.A. 1844, M.A. 1846; Deac. 1844 and Pr. 1845 by Bp of Lin. P. C. of Holy Trinity, Coleham, Shrewsbury, Dio. Lich. 1862. (Patron, Earl of Tankerville; P. C.'s Inc. 40*l* and pew rents; Pop. 2774.) Formerly C. of Horncastle 1844, St. Chads 1846, and Holy Cross, Shrewsbury, 1851; P. C. of Betton Strange, Shrewsbury, 1856. [5]

FLETCHER, Henry Mordaunt, *Derry Hill, Calne, Wilts.*—Ball. Coll. Ox. B.A. 1847; Deac. 1847, Pr. 1848. P. C. of Ch. Ch. Derry Hill, Dio. Salis. 1856. (Patron, V. of Calne; P. C.'s Inc. 300*l*; Pop. 1388.) Formerly R. of North Stoke 1853–56. [6]

FLETCHER, Henry Thomas, *Bicker Vicarage, Spalding, Lincolnshire.*—Deac. 1844 and Pr. 1845 by Bp of Ches. V. of Bicker, Dio. Lin. 1853. (Patrons, D. and C. of Lin; Glebe, 280 acres; V.'s Inc. 500*l* and Ho; Pop. 832.) Dom. Chap. to the Duke of St. Albans 1849. Formerly P. C. of St. George's, Chorley, 1845–60. Author, *Strange Children* (a Visitation Sermon), 1853, 6*d*. [7]

FLETCHER, Horatio Samuel, *Bilston Parsonage, Staffs.*—Queen's Coll, Ox. B.A. 1829; Deac. 1822, Pr. 1823. P. C. of Bilston, Dio. Lich. 1836. (Patrons, Resident Householders; P. C.'s Inc. 635*l* and Ho; Pop. 7457.) Formerly V. of St. Mary's, Bilston, 1830–36. [8]

FLETCHER, Isaac, *Burwell, Cambridgeshire.*—C. of Burwell. [9]

FLETCHER, James, *Birkenhead, Cheshire.*—Ball. Coll. Ox. B.A. 1849, M.A. 1852; Deac. 1851, Pr. 1852. Formerly V. of Cubington, Warwick. [10]

FLETCHER, James Phillips, 4, *Provost-road, Haverstock-hill, London, N.W.*—St. John's Coll. Cam. B.D. 1856; Deac. 1845, Pr. 1847. P. C. of St. Saviour's, Hampstead, Dio. Lon. 1856. (Patron, the P. C. of Hampstead; P. C.'s Inc. 300*l*; Pop. 2945.) Author, *Notes from Nineveh*, 1851, 21*s*; *Rambles in the East*, S.P.C.K; *Autobiography of a Missionary*, 1853, 21*s*; *History of India*, S.P.C.K. 1855; etc. [11]

FLETCHER, John.—St. Mary Hall, Ox. Blundell's Exhib. B.A. 1840, M.A. 1842, B.D. 1854; Deac. 1841 by Bp of Ex. Pr. 1842 by Bp of Lon. Formerly Prin. of King's Coll. Nassau; C. of St. Giles', Reading. [12]

FLETCHER, John Waltham, *Welford-road, Leicester.*—Brasen. Coll. Ox. B.A. 1842, M.A. 1845; Deac. 1842 and Pr. 1843 by Bp of Wor. Chap. to the Leicester County Gaol. [13]

FLETCHER, Joseph, *Dowles Rectory, Bewdley, Salop.*—St. Edm. Hall, Ox. B.A. 1812, M.A. 1814; Deac. and Pr. 1812 by Bp of Salis. R. of Dowles, Dio. Herf, 1818. (Patrons, J. Taylor and others; Tithe, 130*l* 8*s*; Glebe, 1½ acres; R.'s Inc. 166*l* and Ho; Pop. 98.) Chap. to the Earl of Huntingdon. [14]

FLETCHER, Matthew, *Tarleton Rectory, near Preston.*—Dub. A.B. 1844, B.A. St. Edm. Hall, Ox. 1844; Deac. 1845 and Pr. 1848 by Bp of Ches. R. of Tarleton, Dio. Man. 1864. (Patron, the present R; Tithe, 764*l*; Glebe, 84 acres; R.'s Inc. 960*l* and Ho; Pop. 1987.) Formerly Government Chap. to the New Convict Establishment in Western Australia 1850–52; C. of Tarleton 1853–64. [15]

FLETCHER, Richard, *Grove Bank, Highgate, N.*—Wad. Coll. Ox. 2nd. cl. Lit. Hum. B.A. 1859, M.A. 1864; Deac. 1866 and Pr. 1867 by Bp of Lon. Asst. Mast. and Chap. of Sir R. Cholmeley's Sch. Highgate. [16]

FLETCHER, Robert, *Radcliffe, Manchester.*—Brasen. Coll. Ox. M.A. 1844; Deac. 1842, Pr. 1844. P. C. of St. Thomas's, Radcliffe, Dio. Man. 1844. (Patron, Earl of Wilton; Glebe, 4 acres; P. C.'s Inc. 180*l* and Ho; Pop. 5115.) [17]

FLETCHER, Thomas, *Clifton, Bristol.*—Dub. A.B. 1856; Deac. 1856 and Pr. 1857. C. of Ch. Ch. Clifton. [18]

FLETCHER, Thomas Woodcock, *St. Stephen's Vicarage, Willenhall, Wolverhampton.*—Dub. A.B. 1840, A.M. 1843; Deac. 1845 and Pr. 1846 by Bp of Lich. V. of St. Stephen's, Willenhall, Dio. Lich. 1848. (Patrons, the Crown and Bp. of Lich. alt; Endow, 150*l*; V.'s Inc. 210*l* and Ho; Pop. 6168.) Surrogate 1855. [19]

FLETCHER, William, *Wimborne Minster, Dorset.*—Brasen. Coll. Ox. 1st cl. Lit. Hum. and B.A. 1833, M.A. 1836, D.D. 1846; Deac. 1834 by Bp of Ox. Pr. 1835 by Bp of Lich. Head Mast. of Queen Elizabeth's Sch. Wimborne; Chap. to the Wimborne Union 1859. [20]

FLETCHER, William Mellor, *Dixton Rectory, Monmouth.*—St. Bees; Deac, 1855, Pr. 1856. Formerly C. of Thorndon, Suffolk, 1855, Narburgh with Narford, Norfolk, 1856–59. [21]

FLINDT, Gustavus, *St. Jude's Parsonage, Glasgow.*—King's Coll. Lond; Deac. 1853 and Pr. 1856 by Bp of Win. Incumb. of St. Jude's, Glasgow, 1857. Formerly C. of Keynsham, Somerset. [22]

FLINT, Charles Ramsay, 3, *Lansdowne-terrace-west, Brighton.*—St. Peter's Coll. Cam. S.C.L. 1831; Deac. 1831 and Pr. 1833 by Abp of York. V. of Glentworth, Dio. Lin. 1852. (Patron, Earl of Scarborough; Tithe—Imp. 510*l*, V. 340*l*; Glebe, 6 acres; V.'s Inc. 340*l* and Ho; Pop. 340.) Dom. Chap. to the late Marquis of Thomond 1851. [23]

FLINT, William Charles Raffles, *Sunningdale Parsonage, Staines.*—Trin. Coll. Cam. B.A. 1841, M.A. 1844; Deac. 1843 and Pr. 1844 by Bp of Win. P. C. of Sunningdale, Dio. Ox. 1857. (Patron, Bp of Ox; P. C.'s Inc. 90*l* and Ho; Pop. 750.) Formerly C. of Idsworth, Hants, 1843–45, Morden, Surrey, 1845–50, Great Rollright, Oxon, 1851–55. [24]

FLINTOFF, Theodore Nevins, *Shelsley Walsh, Worcester.*—Emman. Coll. Cam. 3rd cl. Cl. Trip. B.A. 1859, M.A. 1863; Deac. 1862 and Pr. 1863 by Bp of Roch. R. of Shelsley Walsh, Dio. Herf. 1864. (Patron, Earl of Dudley; R.'s Inc. 100*l*; Pop. 57.) Chap. and Manager of the Woodbury Hill Reformatory. Formerly C. of Gosfield, Essex, 1862–63. [25]

FLOOD, Frederick, *Buckfastleigh, Ashburton, Devon.*—Dub. A.B. 1857; Deac. 1857 and Pr. 1858 by Bp of Ex. Head Mast. of the Gr. Sch, Ashburton, 1859. Formerly C. of Buckfastleigh 1857–59. [26]

FLOOD, James C., M.A.—British Chap. at Frankfort-on-the-Maine. [27]

FLOOD, Samuel, *St. Matthew's Vicarage, Leeds.*—Queens' Coll. Cam. B.D. 1856; Deac. 1846 and Pr. 1847 by Bp of Lich. V. of St. Matthew's, Leeds, Dio. Rip. 1852. (Patrons, the Crown and Bp of Rip. alt; Tithe, 10*l*; V.'s Inc. 160*l* and Ho; Pop. 5500.) Formerly C. of Repton 1846; V. of Beaminster 1848. Author, *The Christian Watchman*; *The Christian's Treasure*; *Beneficence the Duty of the Rich*; *The Spirit's Voice to the Church* (Lectures on the Epistles to the Seven Churches). [28]

FLOUD, Thomas, *Overton Rectory, Hants.*—Wad. Coll. Ox. B.A. 1834, M.A. 1837; Deac. 1837 and Pr.

1838 by Bp of B. and W. R. of Overton with Tadley, Dio. Win. 1864. (Patron, Bp of Win; Tithe, 557*l*; Glebe, 2 acres; R.'s Inc. 620*l* and Ho; Pop. 1460.) Formerly C. of Buckland Dinham, Somerset, 1837, Liss, Hants, 1840, Ewell, Surrey, 1847, Steep, Hants, 1851. [1]

FLOWER, Walker, 10, *Cambridge-terrace, Dover.*—Ex. Coll. Ox. B.A. 1866; Deac. 1866 by Abp of Cant. C. of St. Mary's, Dover. [2]

FLOWER, William, *Upperthong Parsonage, Almondbury, Yorks.*—Dub; Deac. 1851, Pr. 1852. P. C. of Upperthong, Dio. Rip. 1856. (Patrons, the Crown and Bp of Rip. alt; P. C.'s Inc. 175*l* and Ho; Pop. 2690.) Formerly C. of St. Paul's, Huddersfield. [3]

FLOWER, William Balmborough.—Magd. Coll. Cam. B.A. 1843; Deac. 1843 and Pr. 1845 by Bp of Ches. Formerly R. of Crawley, Sussex, 1855–56. Author, *Sunday Evening Musings, and other Poems*; *Stray Leaves from the German*; *Practical English Grammar*; *Translation of St. Vincent of Lerins*; *Translation of Select Epistles of St. Cyprian*; *Translation of Thomas à Kempis' Soliloquy*; *Reading Lessons for Diocesan Schools*; *Classical Tales and Legends*; *Tales of Faith and Providence*; *Henry of Eichenfels*; *Lucy Ashcroft, the Manufacturer's Daughter*; various Tales for Children; *A Litany and Prayers for use during the Cholera*; *Non-Episcopal Orders* (a letter to the Rev. W. Goode, M.A); *The Church and the Sacraments*; *The Church and the Ministry*; *Old Church of England Principles no New Faith*; *The Prayers to be Said or Sung?* *What shall be done to regain the Lost?* (a Letter to the Bishop of Exeter); Sermons, *Love One Another*; *Reverence to Christ*; *Choral Service the Sacrifice of Prayer*; *Stand Fast in the Faith*; *The Glories of the Church of Christ*; *The Works of the Lord are Great*; *Choral Services and Ritual Observances, with an Address to his Parishioners.* Editor of *The Churchman's Companion*, 18 vols. Masters. [4]

FLOWERS, Field, *Tealby, Market-Rasen, Lincolnshire.*—Lin. Coll. Ox. B.A. 1827; Deac. 1827 and Pr. 1828 by Bp of Lin. V. of Tealby, Dio. Lin. 1835. (Patron, Rt Hon. C. Tennyson D'Eyncourt; Tithe, 100*l*; Glebe, 12 acres; V.'s Inc. 125*l*; Pop. 221.) V. of Legsby, near Market-Rasen, Dio. Lin. 1842. (Patron, Sir J. Nelthorpe; Tithe—Imp. 114*l*, V. 156*l*; Glebe, 60 acres; V.'s Inc. 221*l*; Pop. 365.) Formerly C. of Bradley 1827–28, North Thoresby and Grainsby 1828–35. Author, *Dying Hours of a Young Villager*, 2*d*; *Plan for Increasing the Usefulness of Parish Clerks*, 6*d*. [5]

FLOWERS, Octavius Henry, *Sheriff Hutton, near York.*—Queens' Coll. Cam. B.A. 1842; Deac. 1842 by Bp of Lon. Pr. 1843 by Abp of York. V. of Sheriff Hutton, Dio. York, 1857. (Patron, Abp of York; V.'s Inc. 205*l*; Pop. 1223.) Formerly C. of Nunnington, Yorks. Author, *Essentials of Dutch Grammar*, Amsterdam. [6]

FLOWERS, William Henry, *Ulceby, North Lincolnshire.*—Jesus Coll. Cam. B.A. 1831; Deac. 1831, Pr. 1832. V. of Ulceby, Dio. Lin. 1844. (Patron, Ld Chan; Glebe, 121 acres; V.'s Inc. 321*l* and Ho; Pop. 1048.) [7]

FLOYD, C. G., *South Runcton, near Downham, Norfolk.*—Ch. Ch. Ox. R. of South Runcton, with Holme R. and Wallington R. Dio. Nor. 1866. (Patron, R. Peel, Esq; R.'s Inc. 650*l*; Pop. 481.) Formerly C. of the Higher Mediety of Malpas. [8]

FLOYD, George, *Galleyden, Galleywood, Chelmsford.*—Caius Coll. Cam. B.A. 1856, M.A. 1859; Deac. 1857 and Pr. 1858 by Bp of Nor. C. of Great Baddow, Essex, 1862. Formerly C. of Briston, Norfolk, and King's Sutton, Northants. [9]

FLOYD, Thomas, *Castle Hall, Staleybridge, Cheshire.*—Dub A.B. 1845, A.M. 1850; Deac. 1845 and Pr. 1846 by Bp of Rip. P. C. of Castle Hall, Dio. Ches. 1847. (Patrons, Trustees; P. C.'s Inc. 300*l*; Pop. 7612.) Formerly C. of St. Paul's, Buttershaw, Bradford, Yorks, 1845–47. [10]

FLOYER, Aysooghe, *Marshchapel, Grimsby, Lincolnshire.*—Wad. Coll. Ox. B.A. 1844, M.A. 1847; Deac. 1845, Pr. 1846. P. C. of Marshchapel, Dio. Lin. 1846. (Patron, the present P. C; Tithe, Imp. 637*l* 10*s*; Glebe, 6 acres; P. C.'s Inc. 226*l*; Pop. 671.) [11]

FLOYER, Charles, M.A.—Chap. to Lord Sudeley. [12]

FLUDYER, John Henry, *Ayston Rectory, Uppingham, Rutland.*—B.A. 1826, Deac. 1827. R. of Ayston, Dio. Pet. 1834. (Patron, G. Fludyer, Esq; Tithe, 52*l*; R.'s Inc. 210*l* and Ho; Pop. 85.) R. of Thistleton, Rutland, Dio. Pet. 1834. (Patron, Major-Gen. Fludyer; R.'s Inc. 196*l* and Ho; Pop. 142.) [13]

FLYNN, Edward H.—C. of St. Anne's, Soho, Lond. [14]

FLYNN, Thomas Henry, 10, *St. James's-square, Bradford, Yorks.*—St. Aidan's; Deac. 1857 and Pr. 1858 by Bp of Ches. P. C. of St. Luke's, Bradford, Dio. Rip. 1862. (Patron, Bp of Rip; R.'s Inc. 300*l* and Ho; Pop. 10,356.) Formerly C. of Liverpool 1857–59, Brighouse 1859–62. Author, *The Threefold Blessing*, 2 Cor. xiii. 14 (a Farewell Sermon in Brighouse Church). [15]

FOGG, P. P., *Highgate, N.*—Jesus Coll. Ox. B.A. 1859, M.A. 1862; Deac. 1860; Pr. 1862. C. of St. Michael's, Highgate 1864. Formerly C. of St. Mary's the Less, Lambeth, 1860–62. [16]

FOLEY, Edward Walwyn, *All Saints' Parsonage, Derby.*—Wad. Coll. Ox. 3rd cl. Lit. Hum. and B.A. 1831, M.A. 1836; Deac. 1833 by Bp of Ox. Pr. 1834 by Bp of Wor. P. C. of All Saints', Derby, Dio. Lich. 1849. (Patrons, Simeon's Trustees; P. C.'s Inc. 220*l* and Ho; Pop. 3342.) Chap. to Lord Waterpark. Late Fell. of Wad. Coll. Ox. Author, *Twelve Sermons on the Liturgy*, 1847, 2 eds. [17]

FOLEY, John, *Wadhurst Vicarage (Sussex), near Tunbridge Wells.*—Wad. Coll. Ox. 3rd cl. Lit. Hum. and B.A. 1825, M.A. 1831, B.D. 1842; Deac. and Pr. 1829 by Bp of Wor. V. of Wadhurst, Dio. Chich. 1846. (Patron, Wad. Coll. Ox; Tithe—Imp. 699*l* 15*s* and 2 acres of Glebe; V. 914*l* 15*s*; Glebe, 12 acres; V.'s Inc. 820*l* and Ho; Pop. 2044.) Late Fell. of Wad. Coll. Ox. [18]

FOLLETT, Richard Francis, *Winscombe Vicarage, Weston-super-Mare.*—St. John's Coll. Cam. and Theol. Coll. Wells, B.A. 1854, M.A. 1857; Deac. 1857 and Pr. 1858 by Bp of B. and W. V. of Winscombe, Dio. B. and W. 1863. (Patrons, D. and C. of Wells; V.'s Inc. 210*l*; Pop. 1326.) Formerly C. of East Pennard, Somerset, 1857–60, Hemyock, Devon, 1860–63. [19]

FOLLETT, William Webb, *Malvern Wells, Worc.*—C. of Malvern Wells. [20]

FOLLIOTT, James, 1, *Egerton Villas, Douglas-road, Canonbury, London, N.*—Pemb. Coll. Ox. B.A. 1822, M.A. 1825; Deac. 1823 and Pr. 1824 by Bp of Ches. [21]

FONTANE, W., *Hurst, Ashton-under-Lyne.*—C. of Hurst. [22]

FOOKES, William.—Caius Coll. Cam. B.A. 1853, and Chich. Theol. Coll; Deac. 1855 and Pr. 1856 by Bp of Ely. C. of Stoke Gifford, Gloucestershire. Formerly C. of Polloxill, Beds. [23]

FOOKS, Thomas Broadley, *Thame, Oxon.*—New Coll. Ox. B.A. 1833, B.C.L. and D.C.L. 1841. Head Mast. of Thame Gr. Sch. and Dom. Chap. to Baroness Wenman. [24]

FOORD, Richard Henry, *Foxholes, Malton, Yorks.*—Trin. Coll. Cam. B.A. 1848; Deac. 1848, Pr. 1849. R. of Foxholes, Dio. York, 1850. (Patron, B. Sykes, Esq; Tithe, 389*l*; Glebe, 418 acres; R.'s Inc. 581*l* and Ho; Pop. 319.) [25]

FOOT, Cunningham Noel, *Dogmersfield Rectory, Winchfield, Hants.*—Trin. Coll. Cam. B.A. 1856; Deac. 1856 and Pr. 1857 by Bp of Lon. R. of Dogmersfield, Dio. Win. 1860. (Patron, Sir H. B. P. St. John Mildmay, Bart; Tithe, 331*l*; Glebe, 6 acres; R.'s Inc. 345*l* and Ho; Pop. 251.) [26]

FOOT, Jeffry Robert, *Hanbury Vicarage, Burton-upon-Trent, Staffs.*—Sid. Coll. Cam. Scho. and Lovett's Exhib. B.A. 1843; Deac. 1843 and Pr. 1844 by Bp of

Win. V. of Hanbury, Dio. Lich. 1860. (Patron, Bp of Lich; V.'s Inc. 400*l* and Ho; Pop. 1027.) Formerly C. of Hanbury 1854–60. [1]

FOOT, Lundy, *Long Bredy Rectory, Dorchester.*—Dub. A.B. 1815, A.M. 1818; Deac. 1823, Pr. 1824. R. of Long Bredy with Little Bredy Chap. Dio. Salis. 1829. (Patron, R. Williams, Esq; Long Bredy, Tithe, 460*l*; Glebe, 75 acres; Little Bredy, Tithe, 225*l*; R.'s Inc. 685*l* and Ho; Pop. Long Bredy 250, Little Bredy 199.) Rural Dean 1832; Preb. of Netherbury-in-Terra in Salis. Cathl. 1854. [2]

FOOT, Richard Gorges, *Horton Rectory, Slough, Bucks.*—Dub. A.B. 1847, A.M. 1859; Deac. 1847 and Pr. 1848 by Bp of Win. R. of Horton, Dio. Ox. 1853. (Patrons, Mrs. Swire, and J. S. Swire, Esq; Land in lieu of Tithe, 235½ acres; Glebe, 8 acres; R.'s Inc. 460*l* and Ho; Pop. 385.) Formerly C. of Rotherhithe 1847–50; R. of Little Birch, Hereford, 1852–54. [3]

FOOTE, John Andrews, 26, *Fulham-place, Harrow-road, London, W.*—King's Coll. Lond. M.A. 1864, Theol. Assoc. 1852; Deac. 1852, Pr. 1853. C. of St. Mary's, Paddington. [4]

FOOTTIT, Edward Walker, *Gonalston Rectory, near Lowdham, Notts.*—Emman. Coll. Cam. B.A. 1836; Deac. 1836, Pr. 1837. R. of Gonalston, Dio. Lin. 1842. (Patron, John L. Francklin, Esq; Glebe, 150 acres; R.'s Inc. 400*l* and Ho; Pop. 107.) [5]

FOOTTIT, James, *Bitchfield, Corby, Lincolnshire.*—Ex. Coll. Ox. B.A. 1831; Deac. 1832, Pr. 1833. V. of Bitchfield, Dio. Lin. 1863. (Patron, Bp of Lin; Tithe—App. 200*l* and 169 acres of Glebe, V. 150*l*; Glebe, 5 acres; V.'s Inc. 185*l*; Pop. 159.) Formerly C. of Stragglethorpe. [6]

FORBES, Charles, *South Banbury, Oxon.*—Univ. of Edinburgh, M.A. 1839; Deac. 1840 and Pr. 1841 by Bp of Dur. V. of South Banbury, Dio. Ox. 1846. (Patron, Bp of Ox; Tithe, 19*l*; Glebe, 4½ acres; P. C.'s Inc. 200*l*; Pop. 4043.) Dom. Chap. to the late Earl Grey 1840; Chap. to the Banbury Union 1849. [7]

FORBES, Edward, 45, *Rue de Penthieu, Paris.*—Deac. 1840, Pr. 1841. Chap. of the English Church, Rue d'Aguesseau, Paris. Formerly P. C. of St. George's, Douglas, Isle of Man, 1847–58. Author, *A Pastoral Address; A Visitation Sermon; An Address on Missions to the Heathen.* [8]

FORBES, Granville Hamilton, *Broughton Rectory, Kettering.*—Downing Coll. Cam. B.A. and Burney Prizeman 1847; Deac. 1848, Pr. 1849. R. of Broughton St. Andrew's, Dio. Pet. 1849. (Patron, Duke of Buccleuch; Glebe, 300 acres; R.'s Inc. 500*l* and Ho; Pop. 800.) Formerly C. of Warndon, Worc. 1848. Author, *Burney Prize Essay,* 1847, Macmillan; *The Voice of God in the Psalms,* Macmillan, 1865; Sermons, etc. [9]

FORBES, John, *New Wortley, Leeds.*—C. of St. Simon's, New Wortley. [10]

FORD, Adam, 24, *Upper Warwick-street, Liverpool.*—St. Aidan's; Deac. 1857, Pr. 1858 by Bp of Ches. Chap. to Seamen. Formerly C. of Macclesfield, 1857, St. Anne's, Liverpool, 1859. [11]

FORD, Alfred William.—King's Coll. Lond. Deac. 1866, and Pr. 1867 by Bp of Roch. C. of St. Mary's, Chatham, 1866. [12]

FORD, Charles Henry, *Bishopton Vicarage, Stockton-on-Tees.*—Univ. Coll. Dur. B.A. 1845, Licen. Theol. 1846, M.A. 1850; Deac. 1846 and Pr. 1847 by Bp of Dur. V. of Bishopton, Dio. Dur. 1858. (Patron, Bp of Dur; V.'s Inc. 250*l* and Ho; Pop. 448.) Formerly C. of Sedgefield, Durham. [13]

FORD, Edward, *The Parsonage, King's Sterndale, Buxton.*—St. John's Coll. Cam. B.A. 1853; Deac. 1853, Pr. 1864. P. C. of King's Sterndale, Dio. Lich. 1865. (Patron, Rev. E. Pickford; P. C.'s Inc. 78*l* and Ho; Pop. 200.) Formerly C. of Harrow, Middlesex, and Wambrook, Dorset. [14]

FORD, Frederick, *Chester.*—Trin. Coll. Cam. B.A. 1825, M.A. 1830; Deac. 1827 and Pr. 1828 by Bp of Ches. R. of St. Peter's, City and Dio. Ches. 1861. (Patron, Bp of Ches; Glebe, 22½ acres; R.'s Inc. 250*l*; Pop. 798.) Formerly Chap. at Heidelberg; R. of St. Peter's, Chester, 1846, resigned through ill-health 1855, and re-elected 1861. [15]

FORD, James, *Hirondelle, Torquay.*—Oriel Coll. Ox. 1814, 3rd cl. Lit. Hum. and B.A. 1818, M.A. 1822; Deac. 1822 and Pr. 1823 by Bp of Pet. Preb. in Ex. Cathl. 1849. Author, *Twelve Sermons,* 1838; *The Gospels Illustrated (chiefly in the Doctrinal and Moral Sense), from Ancient and Modern Authors,* 4 vols. 1848–52; *Prayer-book Rhymes, or the Order for Morning Prayer explained in Verse,* 1853; six occasional Sermons; and seven Religious Tracts. [16]

FORD, James, *Somerton Rectory, Bury St. Edmunds.*—Dub. A.B. 1835; Deac. 1835 and Pr. 1836. R. of Somerton, Dio. Ely, 1853. (Patroness, Dowager Marchioness of Downshire; Tithe, 300*l*; Glebe, 39 acres; R.'s Inc. 352*l* and Ho; Pop. 158.) [17]

FORD, J., *Kingswinford, Staffs.*—C. of Kingswinford. [18]

FORD, John, *Old Romney Rectory, Kent.*—Queens' Coll. Cam. B.A. 1849; Deac. 1848 and Pr. 1849 by Abp of Cant. R. of Old Romney, Dio. Cant. 1853. (Patron, Abp of Cant; Tithe—App. 37*l* 13*s* 3*d*, R. 200*l*; Glebe, 25 acres; R.'s Inc. 284*l* and Ho; Pop. 151.) [19]

FORD, John, *Christ Church Parsonage, Stone, Staffs.*—Deac. 1848, Pr. 1849. P. C. of Ch. Ch. Stone, Dio. Lich. 1853. (Patrons, Simeon's Trustees; Glebe, 5 acres; P. C.'s Inc. 226*l* and Ho; Pop. 4629.) Surrogate. [20]

FORD, John Chubb, *Buenos Ayres.*—British Chap. at Buenos Ayres. Formerly Vice-Prin. of the York Dioc. Training Sch. [21]

FORD, Mortimer William, *Yarcombe, Devon.*—V. of Yarcombe, Dio. Ex. 1866. (Patron, the Crown; V.'s Inc. 486*l*; Pop. 815.) Formerly C. of Hilton, Hunts. [22]

FORD, Richard Robert, 156, *Cambridge-street, Pimlico, London, S.W.*—Queens' Coll. Cam. B.A. 1828, M.A. 1842; Deac. 1840 and Pr. 1841 by Bp of Lin. Formerly C. of St. James's, Clerkenwell, Lond. [23]

FORD, William, *Lane End Parsonage, Stoke-upon-Trent.*—Magd. Coll. Cam. Shrewsbury Scho. and Univ. Askew Prizeman, B.A. 1824, M.A. 1827; Deac. 1825 by Bp of Lich. Pr. 1827 by Bp of Ely. P. C. of St. John's, Lane End, Longton, Dio. Lich. 1839. (Patrons, Trustees; Glebe, 18 acres; P. C.'s Inc. 280*l* and Ho; Pop. 7000.) Surrogate. Formerly C. of Tydd St. Giles, Cambs, 1827, Stoke-upon-Trent 1836. [24]

FORDE, Arthur Frederick, *Twigworth, Gloucester.*—Wad. Coll. Ox. B.A. 1847; Deac. 1849 by Bp of Wor. Pr. 1850 by Bp of G. and B. P. C. of St. Matthew's, Twigworth, Dio. G. and B. 1857. (Patron, Bp of G. and B; P. C.'s Inc. 100*l*; Pop. 552.) [25]

FOREMAN, Edward B., *Houghton, Arundel.*—P C. of North Stoke, Dio. Chich. 1856. (Patron, Lord Leconfield; P. C.'s Inc. 57*l*; Pop. 60.) Formerly C. of Eastergate, Chichester, 1853–55, Amberley-cum-Houghton 1856–61. [26]

FORESTER, The Hon. Orlando Watkin Weld, *Gedling, Notts.*—Trin. Coll. Cam. M.A. 1836; Deac. 1836, Pr. 1837. R. and V. of Gedling, Dio. Lin. 1867. (Patron, Earl of Chesterfield; R.'s and V.'s Inc. 1075*l*; Pop. 3130.) Preb. of Bullinghope in Herf. Cathl. 1847. Formerly R. of Brosely, Salop, 1841–59; R. of Doveridge, Uttoxeter, 1859. Author, Pamphlet on *Bishop of Hereford's Appointment*; *Baptism* (a Tract), 1850; *Visitation Sermon,* 1853. [27]

FORGE, Christopher, *Mapleton, Skirlaugh, near Hull.*—Jesus Coll. Cam. B.A. 1819, M.A. 1824; Deac. 1819 and Pr. 1820 by Abp of York. P. C. of Mapleton, Dio. York, 1821. (Patron, Abp of York; Tithe—App. 417*l* 17*s* and 132¾ acres of Glebe, P. C. 29*l* 5*s*; Glebe, 5½ acres; P. C.'s Inc. 60*l* and Ho; Pop. 475.) R. of Goxhill, Beverley, Dio. York, 1845. (Patron, Rev. C. Constable; Tithe, 175*l* 13*s*; Glebe, 39½ acres; R.'s Inc. 320*l*; Pop. 68.) [28]

FORMBY, James, *Frindsbury, Rochester.*—Brasen. Coll. Ox. B.A. 1819, M.A. 1822. V. of Frindsbury, Dio. Roch. 1826. (Patron, Bp of Roch; Tithe—

App. 700*l*, V. 413*l* 15*s*; Glebe, 25 acres; V.'s Inc. 450*l*; Pop. 2219.) [1]

FORMBY, Lonsdale, *Formby, near Liverpool.*—St. Cath. Coll. Cam. B.A. 1842; Deac. 1843, Pr. 1845. P. C. of Formby, Dio. Ches. 1847. (Patron, R. of Walton-on-the-Hill; Tithe—App. 247*l* 17*s*; P. C.'s Inc. 125*l*; Pop. 1780.) [2]

FORMBY, Richard Edward, *Latchingdon Rectory, Maldon, Essex.*—Brasen Coll. Ox. B.A. 1846; Deac. 1846 and Pr. 1847 by Bp of Lich. R. of Latchingdon, Dio. Roch. 1859. (Patron, Abp of Cant; Glebe, 49 acres; R.'s Inc. 730*l* and Ho; Pop. 430.) Formerly P. C. of Hythe, Kent, 1854–59. [3]

FORREST, R. W.—Chap. of the Lock Hospital, Paddington, Lond. Formerly P. C. of St. Andrew's, Liverpool, 1862. [4]

FORREST, Thomas Guest.—St. Peter's Coll. Cam. B.A. 1848; Deac. 1849 by Bp of Man. Pr. 1851 by Bp of Wor. C. of Dovoran, near Truro. Formerly C. of Portsea. [5]

FORRESTER, George.—C. of Upper Chelsea. [6]

FORSHAW, Charles James, *Stocklinch-Ottersey Rectory, Ilminster, Somerset.*—Dur; Deac. 1850 and Pr. 1853 by Bp of Man. R. of Cricket-Malherbie, Somerset, Dio. B. and W. 1855. (Patroness, Mrs. Elizabeth Pitt; Tithe, 54*l* 0*s* 10*d*; Glebe, 26 acres; R.'s Inc. 108*l*; Pop. 21.) P. C. of Cudworth, Somerset, Dio. B. and W. 1856. (Patron, Bp of B. and W; P. C.'s Inc. 60*l*; Pop. 151.) C. of Stocklinch-Ottersey. Formerly C. of Ilminster. [7]

FORSHAW, Thurstan, *Newchapel Parsonage, Tunstall, Staffs.*—St. Bees; Deac. and Pr. 1836. P. C. of Newchapel, Dio. Lich. 1841. (Patrons, Ralph Sneyd, Esq. and others; P. C.'s Inc. 110*l* and Ho; Pop. 3440.) [8]

FORSS, Francis Stephen, *Limpley Stoke, Bradford-on-Avon.*—King's Coll. Lond. Theol. Assoc. 1857; Deac. 1857 and Pr. 1858 by Bp of Salis. P. C. of Winsley with Limpley Stoke P. C. Dio. Salis. 1862. (Patrons, D. and C. of Bristol; P. C.'s Inc. 160*l*; Pop. 965.) Formerly C. of Limpley Stoke. [9]

FORSTER, Bennet, *Meldreth, near Royston.*—Ch. Coll. Cam. B.A. 1861, M.A. 1864; Deac. 1865 by Bp of Ely. C. of Meldreth 1865. [10]

FORSTER, Charles, *Stisted Rectory, Braintree, Essex.*—R. of Stisted, Dio. Roch. (Patron, Abp of Cant; Tithe, 750*l*; Glebe, 153 acres; R.'s Inc. 965*l* and Ho; Pop. 821.) One of the Six Preachers of Cant. Cathl. [11]

FORSTER, Charles Thornton, *Hinxton Vicarage, Saffron Walden.*—Jesus Coll. Cam. 1st cl. Cl. Trip. 1859, B.A. 1859, M.A. 1862 Fell. 1863,; Deac. 1862 and Pr. 1864 by Bp of Ely. V. of Hinxton, 1865. (Patron, Jesus Coll. Cam; R.'s Inc. 350*l* and Ho; Pop. 499.) [12]

FORSTER, Francis.—St. Cath. Hall, Cam. Sen. Opt. 1st cl. Cl. Trip. B.A. 1832, M.A. 1835; Deac. and Pr. 1840 by Bp of Ely. Formerly Fell. of St. Cath. Hall, Cam; V. of Ridgwell, Essex, 1840–62. [13]

FORSTER, Francis, *West Ayton, Yorks.*—Queen's Coll. Ox. B.A. 1851, M.A. 1854; Deac. 1851 and Pr. 1853 by Bp of Salis. C. of Hutton Buscel, 1863. [14]

FORSTER, Henry Brookes, *Coln-Rogers Rectory, Northleach, Glouc.*—Corpus Coll. Cam. B.A. 1833, M.A. 1836; Deac. 1834 and Pr. 1835 by Bp of G. and B. R. of Coln-Rogers, Dio. G. and B. 1841. (Patrons, D. and C. of Glouc; Tithe, 248*l* 12*s*; Glebe, 40 acres; R.'s Inc. 282*l* and Ho; Pop. 116.) Hon. Can. of Glouc. 1866; Rural Dean of Cirencester 1855. Formerly C. of Duntsbourne Abbotts 1834, Northchurch, Herts, 1836, Stratton 1856. [15]

FORSTER, John, *Stambourne Rectory, near Halstead, Essex.*—Magd. Coll. and Corpus Coll. Cam. B.A. 1834, M.A. 1838; Deac. 1836, by Bp of G. and B. Pr. 1836 by Bp of Lon. R. of Stambourne, Dio. Roch. 1858. (Patroness, the Queen as Duchess of Lancaster; Tithe, 566*l*; Glebe, 20 acres; R.'s Inc. 528*l* and Ho; Pop. 537.) Formerly Chap. of the Savoy, Strand, Lond. 1838–58. Author, *The Churchman's Guide*, 1840; *The Gospel Narrative* (Dedicated, by special permission, to the Queen), 1845, 4th ed. 1847; various Sermons. [16]

FORSTER, John Jebb, *West Malling, Maidstone.*—St. John's Coll. Cam. 37th Wrang. B.A. 1857; Deac. 1857 and Pr. 1858 by Abp of Cant. C. of West Malling. Formerly C. of Chilham with Molash, Kent. [17]

FORSTER, Thomas, *Lowton Rectory, near Warrington.*—Dub. A.B. 1849, A.M. 1852; Deac. 1850 and Pr. 1851 by Bp of Ches. R of Lowton, Dio. Ches. 1856. (Patron, Earl of Derby; Tithe, App. 107*l*; Glebe, 56 acres; R.'s Inc. 250*l* and Ho; Pop. 1519.) [18]

FORSTER, Thomas, *Cassington, near Oxford.*—New Coll. Ox. B.A. 1815, M.A. 1818. V. of Cassington, Dio. Ox. 1824. (Patron, Ch. Ch. Ox; V.'s Inc. 170*l*; Pop. 433.) [19]

FORSTER, William, *Horton Parsonage, Leek, Staffs.*—P. C. of Horton, Dio. Lich. (Patron, J. C. Antrobus, Esq; Tithe, App. 1*l* 4*s*, Imp. 237*l* 15*s* 6*d*, P. C. 2*l*; P. C.'s Inc. 115*l* and Ho; Pop. 1046.) [20]

FORT, Charles, *Heyford, Oxon.*—Corpus Coll. Ox. B.A. 1849, M.A. 1851; Deac. 1852 and Pr. 1854 by Bp of Ox. Fell. and Sen. Bursar of Corpus Coll. Ox. R. of Heyford, Oxon, 1866. (Patron, Corpus Coll. Ox; R.'s Inc. 496*l*; Pop. 625.) Formerly C. of Begbroke, near Oxford. [21]

FORT, Richard, *Coopersale Parsonage, Epping, Essex.*—St. John's Coll. Ox. B.A. 1848, M.A. 1851; Deac. 1849, Pr. 1852. P. C. of Coopersale, Dio. Roch. 1854. (Patroness, Miss A. Houblon; P. C.'s Inc. 126*l* and Ho; Pop. 539.) [22]

FORTESCUE, Henry Raymundo, *East Allington Rectory, Totnes, Devon.*—Ex. Coll. Ox. B.A. 1842; Deac. 1843 and Pr. 1844 by Bp of Salis. R. of East Allington, Dio. Ex. 1844. (Patron, W. B. Fortescue, Esq; Tithe, 500*l*; Glebe, 113 acres; R.'s Inc. 620*l* and Ho; Pop. 521.) [23]

FORTESCUE, The Hon. John, *Poltimore Rectory, near Exeter.*—Magd. Coll. Cam. M.A. 1816; Deac. 1819 by Bp of Salis. Pr. 1820 by Bp of Ches. Can. Res. of Wor. Cathl. 1834 (Value 800*l* and Res.). R. of Poltimore with Huxham R. Dio. Ex. 1835. (Patron, Lord Poltimore; Poltimore, Tithe, 306*l*; Glebe, 66 acres; Huxham, Tithe, 124*l*; Glebe, 22 acres; R.'s Inc. 591*l* and Ho; Pop. Poltimore 348, Huxham 134.) Mast. of St. Oswald's Hospital, Worcester. [24]

FORTESCUE John, *Bewdley, Worcestershire.*—St. Edm. Hall. Ox. B.A. 1846, M.A. 1849; Deac, 1846 and Pr. 1848 by Bp of Herf. P. C. of Bewdley, Dio. Herf. 1853. (Patron, R. of Ribbesford; Pop. 1143.) Surrogate 1854. [25]

FORTESCUE, Robert Henry, *Stockleigh Pomeroy, Crediton, Devon.*—Ex. Coll. Ox. 3rd cl. Lit. Hum. and B.A. 1834, M.A. 1837; Deac. 1835 by Bp of Win. Pr. 1836 by Bp of Ex. R. of Stockleigh Pomeroy, Dio. Ex. 1854. (Patron, Bp of Ex; Tithe, 180*l*; Glebe, 42 acres; R.'s Inc. 270*l* and Ho; Pop. 168.) Formerly C. of Revelstoke 1835, Bideford 1844, Bigbury 1848; Chap. to Bp of Colombo 1845. Author, *The Duty of Conforming to the Rubrics* (a Sermon); *A Clergyman's Address to his Parishioners on the Duty of Contributing in Aid of the S.P.G.* 1839; *The Tudor Supremacy in Jurisdiction unlimited* (a Visitation Sermon), 1850, 1*s*; *A Correspondence with Dr. Pusey on Auricular Confession*, 1854, 1*s*; A Letter to Archdeacon Freeman, *Is weekly Communion of Divine Obligation?* 1866, Rivingtons, 1*s*. [26]

FORTESCUE, William Fraine, *Chesterton Vicarage, Bicester.*—New Coll. Ox. B.A. 1831, M.A. 1835; Deac. 1832, Pr. 1833. V. of Chesterton, Dio. Ox. 1849. (Patron, New Coll. Ox; Glebe, 215 acres; V.'s Inc. 220*l* and Ho; Pop. 884.) [27]

FORWARD, Edward.—St. John's Coll. Cam. B.A. 1856; Deac. 1856 and Pr. 1857 by Bp of Salis. C. of Hazelbury Bryan, Dorset, 1863. Formerly C. of Bettiscombe 1856. [28]

FOSBERY, George William, *Bawby, Retford, Notts.*—Caius Coll. Cam. B.A. 1858; Deac. 1858 and Pr. 1859 by Bp of Ches. P. C. of Scofton, Notts, Dio. Lin. 1864. (Patron, G. S. Foljambe, Esq; R.'s Inc. 150*l* and

Ho.) V. of Selston, Notts, Dio. Lin. 1864. (Patrons, Heirs of Sir W. Dixie, Bart; V.'s Inc. 175*l* and Ho; Pop. 2541.) Formerly C. of Worksop and Scofton. [1]

FOSBERY, Thomas Vincent, M.A., *St. Giles's Vicarage, Reading.*—Deac. 1831 and Pr. 1832 by Bp of Salis. V. of St. Giles's, Reading, Dio. Ox. 1857. (Patron, Bp of Ox; Tithe, 512*l*; V.'s Inc. 600*l* and Ho; Pop. 10,200.) Surrogate; Chap. to Bp of Ox. Formerly P. C. of Sunningdale, Berks, 1847–57. [2]

FOSTER, Sir Cavendish Hervey, Bart., *Thoydon-Garnon, Epping, Essex.*—Magd. Coll. Cam. B.A. 1840; Deac. 1841, Pr. 1842. R. of Thoydon-Garnon, Dio. Roch. 1843. (Patron, Sir T. N. Abdy, Bart; Tithe, 650*l*; Glebe, 64 acres; R.'s Inc. 690*l* and Ho; Pop. 556.) [3]

FOSTER, Charles, *St. John's Parsonage, Dudley-hill, near Bradford, Yorks.*—St. Aidan's; Deac. 1857, Pr. 1859. P. C. of Tong Street, Dio. Rip. 1860. (Patron, Col. Tempest; P. C.'s Inc. 35*l* and Ho. without cure of souls.) Formerly Sen. C. of Tong 1857–60. [4]

FOSTER, Charles, *Compton Martin, Somerset.*—R. of Compton Martin, Dio. B. and W. 1865. (Patrons, Trustees; R.'s Inc. 305*l* and Ho; Pop. 560.) [5]

FOSTER, Charles George, *St. David's-hill, Exeter.*—Magd. Hall, Ox. 3rd cl. Lit. Hum. 2nd cl. Math. Lusby Scho. B.A. 1859, M.A. 1862; Deac. 1859 by Bp of Ex. Pr. 1860 by Bp of B. and W. C. of St. David's, Exeter, 1862. Formerly C. of Allhallows, Exeter, 1859–61. [6]

FOSTER, Charles William, *Dalton, Rotherham.*—Ch. Coll. Cam. B.A. 1849, M.A. 1852; Deac. 1849 and Pr. 1851 by Abp of York. P. C. of Dalton, Dio. York, 1858. (Patron, G. S. Foljambe, Esq; P. C.'s Inc. 170*l* and Ho; Pop. 369.) [7]

FOSTER, Francis, *Haverfordwest.*—Dub. A.B. 1858, A.M. 1861; Deac. 1858 and Pr. 1859 by Bp of G. and B. R. of Prendergast, Dio. St. D. 1862. (Patron, Ld Chan; R.'s Inc. 200*l*; Pop. 1540.) Formerly C. of St. Michael's, and Chap. of the Asylum for the Blind, Bristol. [8]

FOSTER, Frederic Adolphus La Trobe, *Little Munden Rectory, Ware, Herts.*—Oriel Coll. Ox. 4th cl. Lit. Hum. and B.A. 1842, M.A. 1845; Deac. 1844 and Pr. 1845 by Bp of Ches. R. of Little Munden, Dio. Roch. 1867. (Patron, Lt-Col. Loyd; Tithe, comm. 592*l*; Glebe, 72 acres and Ho; Pop. 601.) [9]

FOSTER, Frederic William, *Grammar School, Leeds.*—Trin. Coll. Ox. B.A. 1849, M.A. 1854; Deac. 1851, Pr. 1852. Asst Mast. Gr. Sch. Leeds. [10]

FOSTER, George.—St. Bees; Deac. 1853 and Pr. 1855 by Bp of Rip. Formerly C. of Kirkburton, Huddersfield. [11]

FOSTER, Henry, *Selsey Rectory, Chichester.*—St. John's Coll. Cam. B.A. 1838, M.A. 1841; Deac. 1838 and Pr. 1839 by Bp of Lon. R. and V. of Selsey, Dio. Chich. 1863. (Patron, Bp of Chich; Tithe, 690*l*; Glebe, 40 acres; R.'s Inc. 720*l* and Ho; Pop. 900.) Preb. of Selsey in Chich. Cathl. 1860; Rural Dean 1866. Formerly Asst. Min. of Margaret Chapel, Lond. 1838–39; Sen. C. of Ch. Ch. St. Pancras, Lond. 1839; Sequestrator of Appledram, Sussex, and Prin. of Dioc. Training Coll. Chichester, 1840–42; C. of Lurgashall, Sussex, 1842–47; V. of Selmeston and Alceston, Sussex, 1847–63; Chap. and Sec. to Dioc. Training Coll. Brighton, 1847–63. [12]

FOSTER, John, *Foxearth Rectory (Essex), near Sudbury.*—St. Mary Hall, Ox. B.A. 1843, M.A. 1846; Deac. 1842 and Pr. 1843 by Bp of Ox. R. of Foxearth, Dio. Roch. 1845. (Patron, the present R; Tithe—Imp. 68*l* 16*s*, R. 443*l*; Glebe, 23 acres; R.'s Inc. 463*l* and Ho; Pop. 400.) Dom. Chap. to the Earl of Sefton. [13]

FOSTER, John, *Oaks Parsonage, Ashby-de-la-Zouch.*—P. C. of Oaks and Copt Oak P. C. Charnwood Forest, Dio. Pet. 1856. (Patrons, Lords of Six Manors on the Forest; P. C.'s Inc. 180*l* and Ho; Pop. Oaks 702, Copt Oak 393.) [14]

FOSTER, John Smith, *Wivelsfield, Hurstpierpoint, Sussex.*—Pemb. Coll. Cam. and Theol. Coll. Wells; Deac. 1841, Pr. 1842. P. C. of Wivelsfield, Dio. Chich. 1864. (Patroness, Miss J. Tanner; P. C.'s Inc. 126*l*; Pop. 1162.) Formerly C. of South Cerney with Cerney Wick. [15]

FOSTER, Jonathan, *Kettlewell, Skipton, Yorks.*—St. Bees; Deac. 1820, Pr. 1821. V. of Kettlewell, Dio. Rip. 1822. (Patron, R. Foster, Esq; Tithe—Imp. 87*l* 4*s* 8*d*, V. 19*l* 16*s* 1*d*; Glebe, 53 acres; V.'s Inc. 123*l*; Pop. 646.) [16]

FOSTER, Joseph, *Greatham Rectory, Hants.*—Ch. Coll. Cam. Jun. Opt. B.A. 1857, M.A. 1860; Deac. 1860 by Bp of G. and B. Pr. 1862 by Bp of B. and W. C. of Greatham 1866. Formerly C. of Lydney, Glouc. 1860, Nailsea 1862. [17]

FOSTER, Joseph, *Leintwardine, Salop.*—Dub. A.B. 1858; Deac. 1859 and Pr. 1860 by Bp of Pet. C. of Leintwardine 1862. Formerly C. of Ashby Magna, Leicester, 1859–61. [18]

FOSTER, Kingsman, *Dowsby Rectory, Folkingham, Lincolnshire.*—St. John's Coll. Cam. 7th Sen. Opt. and B.A. 1806, M.A. 1810; Deac. and Pr. 1807. R. of Dowsby, Dio. Lin. 1807. (Patron, the present R; Tithe, 279*l* 12*s*; Glebe, 116 acres; R.'s Inc. 480*l* and Ho; Pop. 195.) [19]

FOSTER, Kingsman Baskett, *Dowsby, Folkingham, Lincolnshire.*—C. of Dowsby. Formerly C. of Frampton, Dorset. [20]

FOSTER, Richard, *Choppington, Northumberland.*—Dur; Deac. 1859 and Pr. 1860 by Bp of Lich. P. C. of Choppington, Dio. Dur. 1863. (Patrons, D. and C. of Dur; P. C.'s Inc. 300*l* and Ho; Pop. 3000.) Formerly C. of Wellington, Staffs, 1859–60, Croxdale, Durham, 1861, Kelloe, Durham, 1862. [21]

FOSTER, Robert, *Burpham, Arundel.*—Corpus Coll. Cam. B.A. 1842, M.A. 1845; Deac. 1845 and Pr. 1846 by Bp of Chich. V. of Burpham, Dio. Chich. 1855. (Patrons, D. and C. of Chich; Tithe, 150*l*; Glebe, 10 acres; V.'s Inc. 206*l*; Pop. 256.) [22]

FOSTER, Thomas, *Falstone Rectory, Hexham, Northumberland.*—Emman. Coll. Cam. B.A. 1821, M.A. 1834; Deac. 1822 and Pr. 1823 by Bp of Salis. R. of Falstone, Dio. Dur. 1839. (Patrons, Governors of Greenwich Hospital; Tithe, 228*l*; Glebe, 204 acres; R.'s Inc. 290*l* and Ho; Pop. 1016.) Formerly Chap. R.N. 1825–34; V. of Alston Moor, Cumberland, 1834–1839. [23]

FOSTER, William, *Hilston, Roos, Hull.*—Magd. Coll. Cam. Jun. Opt. 2nd cl. Cl. Trip. and B.A. 1834, M.A. 1837; Deac. 1835. Fell. of Magd. Coll. Cam. 1834. [24]

FOTHERGILL, Ernest Henry, *Clevedon, Somerset.*—Dub. A.B. 1853; Deac. 1854 and Pr. 1855 by Bp of Roch. C. of Clevedon 1858. Formerly Chap. of R.N. [25]

FOTHERGILL, Henry George, *Belstone Rectory, Okehampton, Devon.*—St. Bees; Deac. 1834 and Pr. 1835 by Abp of York. R. of Belstone, Dio. Ex. 1836. (Patron, the present R; Tithe, 110*l*; Glebe, 101 acres; R.'s Inc. 196*l* and Ho; Pop. 181.) [26]

FOTHERGILL, Henry John Arundell, *Antron Lodge, Helstone, Cornwall.*—St. Bees; Deac. 1855 and Pr. 1856 by Bp of Nor. C. of Sithney, near Helstone. Formerly C. of St. Peter's, Thetford, Norfolk. [27]

FOTHERGILL, Percival Alfred, *Watford Vicarage, Rugby.*—Dub. A.B. 1853; Deac. 1858 and Pr. 1859 by Bp of Chich. V. of Watford, Dio. Pet. 1866. (Patron, Ld Chan; Tithe, 191*l*; Glebe, 43 acres; V.'s Inc. 306*l* and Ho; Pop. 450.) Formerly Chap. and Naval Instructor, R.N.; R. of South Heighton with Tarring Neville 1861–66. [28]

FOULIS, Sir Henry, Bart., *Great Brickhill Rectory, Bletchley, Bucks.*—St. John's Coll. Cam. B.A. 1817, M.A. 1820; Deac. 1823 and Pr. 1824 by Bp of Lin. R. of Great Brickhill, Dio. Ox. 1835. (Patron, Sir P. D. P. Duncombe, Bart; Tithe, 80*l*; Glebe, 271 acres; R.'s Inc. 425*l* and Ho; Pop. 590.) Preb. of Walton Westhall with Gorehall in Lin. Cathl. 1844. [29]

FOULKES, Francis B., *Harworth, Notts.*—Chap. of St. Mary's Hospital, Harworth. [30]

FOULKES, Thomas Brown, *Llanyblodwell Vicarage, Oswestry, Salop.*—Queens' Coll. Cam. B.A. 1840, M.A. 1846; Deac. 1840 and Pr. 1843 by Bp of St. A. V. of Llanyblodwell, Dio. St. A. 1860. (Patron, Bp of St A; Tithe, 200*l*; Glebe, 30*l*; V.'s Inc. 250*l* and Ho; Pop. 930.) Formerly C. of Knockin, Salop, 1843–60. [1]

FOUNTAINE, John, *Southacre Rectory, Swaffham, Norfolk.*—Deac. 1840, Pr. 1841. R. of Southacre, Dio. Nor. 1846. (Patron, A. Fountaine, Esq; Tithe, 510*l*; Glebe, 44½ acres; R.'s Inc. 556*l* and Ho; Pop. 92.) [2]

FOWELL, Richard Drake, *New Brighton, Birkenhead.*—P. C. of New Brighton, Dio. Ches. 1856. (Patron, Bp of Ches; P. C.'s Inc. 450*l* and Ho; Pop. 3000.) [3]

FOWERAKER, E. T., *Exeter.*—C. of St. Mary's Major, Exeter. [4]

FOWKE, Francis.—St. Peter's Coll. Cam. B.A. 1830, M.A. 1843; Deac. 1840, Pr. 1841. Formerly P. C. of Pensnett, Staffs, 1844–58. [5]

FOWKE, William Lyme, *Barkestone Vicarage, Bottesford, Notts.*—Queens' Coll. Cam. B.A. 1842; Deac. 1842 and Pr. 1843 by Bp of Pet. V. of Barkestone, Dio. Pet. 1860. (Patron, Duke of Rutland; V.'s Inc. 125*l* and Ho; Pop. 411.) Formerly V. of Eaton, Leic. 1845–60. [6]

FOWLE, Edmund, *Shipton Bellinger, Marlborough, Wilts.*—St. Bees 1854–56; Deac. 1856 and Pr. 1857 by Bp of Salis. V. of Shipton Bellinger, Dio. Win. 1862. (Patron, G. Sloane Stanley, Esq; Tithe, 169*l*; Glebe, 2 acres; V.'s Inc. 169*l*; Pop. 270.) Formerly C. of Allington and Asst. C. of Amesbury 1856–62. [7]

FOWLE, Fulwar William, *Amesbury, Wilts.*—Mert. Coll. Ox. B.A. 1813, M.A. 1844; Deac. 1814, Pr. 1815. R. of Allington, Dio. Salis. 1816. (Patron, Earl of Craven; Tithe—App. 257*l* 10*s*, R. 220*l*; Glebe, 37 acres; R.'s Inc. 270*l*; Pop. 93.) P. C. of Amesbury, Dio. Salis. 1817. (Patrons, D. and C. of Windsor; Tithe—App. 955*l*, P. C. 1*l*; P. C.'s Inc. 133*l* 8*s* and Ho; Pop. 1138.) Chap. to the Amesbury Union 1837; Preb. Salis. Cathl. 1841. Author, *Plain Sermons*, Vol. I. 1835; Vol. II. 1836, 5*s* 6*d*; *Sermons, chiefly designed to show the Practical Working of Faith*, 1845, 4*s* 6*d*; *Two Sad Deaths in one Sabbath*, 2*d*; *Short Lectures from the Bible*, 4*d*; *Conviction without Conversion*, 4th ed. 2*d*; etc. [8]

FOWLE, James, *Pebworth, Chipping Campden, Glouc.*—Wad. Coll. Ox. B.A. 1818, M.A. 1823. V. of Pebworth, Dio. G. and B. 1825. (Patrons, Miss Miller, and T. Skekell, Esq; V.'s Inc. 100*l*; Pop. 736.) R. of Quinton, near Chipping Campden, Dio. G. and B. 1826. (Patrons, D. and C. of Wor; Tithe—App. 63*l*, R. 10*s*; R.'s Inc. 70*l*; Pop. 557.) [9]

FOWLE, Thomas Welbank, *Holy Trinity Parsonage, Hoxton, London, N.*—Oriel Coll. Ox. B.A. 1858, M.A. 1861; Deac. 1859 and Pr. 1860 by Bp of Lon. C. (sole charge) of Holy Trinity, Hoxton, 1863. Formerly C. of Staines 1859–63. Author, *Types of Christ in Nature, being Nine Sermons preached at Staines*, 1864, 2*s* 6*d*. [10]

FOWLE, William Cecil, *Brinsop Vicarage, near Hereford.*—Wad. Coll. Ox. B.A. 1835, M.A. 1838; Deac. 1837 and Pr. 1838 by Bp of Wor. V. of Brinsop, Dio. Herf. 1866. (Patron, Bp of Herf; Tithe, App. 107*l*; Glebe, 120 acres; V.'s Inc. 160*l* and Ho; Pop. 150.) Formerly V. of Ewyas Harold 1845–66. [11]

FOWLE, William Henry, *Langford Budville, Wellington, Somerset.*—Trin. Coll. Ox. B.A. 1846; Deac. 1846 and Pr. 1848 by Bp of B. and W. P. C. of Langford-Budville, Dio. B. and W. (Patron, Archd. of Taunton; P. C.'s Inc. 150*l* and Ho; Pop. 420.) Formerly C. of East Brent 1852 and 1863–66; Chap. Cape of Good Hope 1853–58. Author, *The Bible and the Church*, etc. [12]

FOWLER, Alfred Enoch, *Saffron Walden Grammar School, Essex.*—Queens' Coll. Cam. B.A. 1843; Deac. 1843, Pr. 1844. Head Mast. of the Saffron Walden Gr. Sch. [13]

FOWLER, Charles Augustus, *Bartonfields, Canterbury.*—Oriel Coll. Ox. B.A. 1840, M.A. 1841; Deac. 1841 and Pr. 1842 by Bp of Lich. R. of St. Margaret's, Canterbury, Dio. Cant. 1863. (Patron Archd. of Cant; Tithe, 40*l*; R.'s Inc. 67*l* and Ho; Pop. 660.) Formerly C. of Buxton, Derbyshire, 1841; P. C. of St. Bartholomew's, Chichester; C. of Bradfield, Berks, and Modley, Hereford; R. of Crawley, Sussex; P. C. of Kingskerswell, Devon; P. C. of Sarisbury, Hants. Author, *Parochial Sermons*, Masters, 3*s* 6*d*. [14]

FOWLER, Edward Thomas Straton, *Cotmanhay Parsonage, Ilkeston, Derbyshire.*—Jesus Coll. Cam. B.A. 1853, M.A. 1855; Deac. 1853 and Pr. 1855 by Bp of Lin. P. C. of Cotmanhay, Dio. Lich. 1858. (Patrons, the Crown and Bp alt; P. C.'s Inc. 150*l* and Ho; Pop. 2800.) Formerly C. of St. James's, Nottingham, and Attenborough, Notts. [15]

FOWLER, Francis William, *Bathwick, near Bath.*—St. John's Coll. Cam. B.A. 1844; Deac. 1849, Pr. 1850. C. of Bathwick 1853. Formerly C. of West Littleton, Glouc. 1849–53. Author, *Answer to the Bishop of Natal.* [16]

FOWLER, Frederic Cook, *Corton, near Lowestoft.*—Jesus Coll. Cam. B.A. 1825; Deac. 1825. Pr. 1827. V. of Corton, Dio. Nor. 1837. (Patron, Ld Chan; Tithe—Imp. 242*l*, V. 120*l*; Glebe, 30 acres; V.'s Inc. 158*l*; Pop. 530.) R. of Gunton, Suffolk, Dio. Nor. 1837. (Patrons, Trustees; Tithe, 133*l* 10*s*; Glebe, 9 acres; R.'s Inc. 147*l*; Pop. 73.) Author, *Scripture Proportions, or the Danger of Imbibing Error at the Fountain of Truth*, 2*s*. [17]

FOWLER, Henry, *Dinton, Salisbury.*—Ex. Coll. Ox. B.A. 1850, M.A. 1852; Deac. 1852 by Bp of Wor. Pr. 1853 by Bp of Salis. C. of Dinton with Teffont-Magna, Wilts. Formerly Asst. C. of Upton Scudamore. [18]

FOWLER, Hugh, *College Gardens, Gloucester.*—Sid. Coll. Cam. Jun. Opt. 2nd cl. Cl. Trip. B.A. 1838, M.A. 1841; Deac. 1840, Pr. 1841 by Bp of Ex. Head Mast. of the Cathl. Gr. Sch. Gloucester, 1854. Formerly Mast. of Helston Gr. Sch. 1847; Mast. of Bideford Gr. Sch. 1849. Author, *Christian Education* (a Sermon); *Auxilia Græca*, Bell and Daldy, 1856, 8*s* 6*d*. [19]

FOWLER, John, *School House, Lincoln.*—Queens' Coll. Cam. Jun. Opt. 2nd cl. Cl. Trip. and B.A. 1849, M.A. 1851; Deac. 1850 and Pr. 1852 by Bp of Salis. Head Mast. of Lin. Gr. Sch. 1857; Chap. Warden of St. Anne's, Bedehouses, Lincoln, 1864. (Stipend 100*l* a year.) Formerly Asst. Mast. in Marlborough Coll. 1849–57; C. of Boultham, near Lincoln, 1857–61. [20]

FOWLER, John Kenning, *East Lambrook Rectory, Ilminster, Somerset.*—Queens' Coll. Cam. B.A. 1837; Deac. 1837 and Pr. 1838 by Bp of Lin. R. of East Lambrook in Kingsbury Episcopi, Dio. B. and W. 1859. (Patrons, D. and C. of Wells; R.'s Inc. 210*l* and Ho.) Chap. of the Union, Langport, Somerset, 1857. [21]

FOWLER, John Nottingham, *Skerne, near Driffield, Yorks.*—Magd. Coll. Cam. B.A. 1842, M.A. 1845; Deac. 1843, Pr. 1844. P. C. of Skerne, Dio. York, 1853. (Patron, Lord Londesborough; Tithe, Imp. 30*l* 11*s* 8*d*; Glebe, 27 acres; P. C.'s Inc. 71*l*; Pop. 207.) [22]

FOWLER, Joseph Thomas, *The College, Hurstpierpoint.*—Bp Hat. Hall, Dur; B.A. 1861, M.A. 1864; Deac. 1861, and Pr. 1863 by Bp of G. and B. Chap. of St. John's Middle Sch. Hurstpierpoint, 1863. (Patron, Provost of St. Nicholas' Coll. Lancing; Chap.'s Inc. 150*l*; Pop. 350.) Formerly C. of Houghton-le-Spring, Durham, 1861. [23]

FOWLER, Newell Vicary, *Sidney-Sussex College, Cambridge.*—Sid. Coll. Cam. Sen. Opt. 3rd cl. Cl. Trip. and B.A. 1852; Deac. 1853 and Pr. 1854 by Bp of Ex. Fell. of Sid. Coll. Cam. Formerly C. of Towednack, Cornwall. [24]

FOWLER, Robert, *Grosvenor House, Tunbridge Wells.*—Ch. Coll. Cam. late Fell. 16th Wrang. B.A. 1853, M.A. 1856; Deac. 1853 by Bp of Ches. Pr. 1854 by Bp of Ely. Formerly C. of West Lavington, Wilts, 1855. Author, *Solutions of Questions on Mixed Mathematics*, 1863, 3*s* 6*d*; *Treatise on Algebra*, 1860, 6*s*. [25]

FOWLER, Robert, *Wavertree, Liverpool.*—Emman. Coll. Cam. B.A. 1859, M.A. 1867; Deac. 1863 and Pr. 1864 by Bp of Nor. C. of Wavertree 1865. Formerly C. of Dickleburgh, Norfolk, 1863–65. [1]

FOWLER, Robert Rodney, *Brodwas Rectory, Worcester.*—Sid. Coll. Cam. Prizeman, Jun. Opt. and B.A. 1853; Deac. 1853 and Pr. 1854 by Abp of York. R. of Brodwas, Dio. Wor. 1862. (Patrons, D. and C. of Wor; R.'s Inc. 300*l* and Ho; Pop. 311.) Formerly Min. Can. and Sacrist. of Wor. Cathl. 1854 and Head Mast. of the Choristers' Sch. 1857. [2]

FOWLER, Thomas, *Lincoln College, Oxford.*—Mert. Coll. Ox. 1st cl. Math. and Lit. Hum. B.A. 1854, M.A. 1856, Denyer Theol. Essay 1858; Deac. 1855 and Pr. 1857 by Bp of Ox. Fell. and Tut. of Lin. Coll. Ox. 1855; Proctor 1862; Public Examiner 1864–67. Author, *The Elements of Deductive Logic*, Oxford, Clarendon Press, 1867, Macmillan and Co. 3*s* 6*d*. [3]

FOWLER, William, *Liversedge, Normanton.*—Ch. Coll. Cam. B.A. 1857, M.A. 1860; Deac. 1859 and Pr. 1860 by Bp of Rip. P. C. of Liversedge, Dio. Rip. 1864. (Patron, V. of Birstal; P. C.'s Inc. 300*l* and Ho; Pop. 6500.) Formerly C. of St. John's, Cleckheaton, 1859. [4]

FOWNES, J. E., *St. Albans, Herts.*—C. of St. Alban's. [5]

FOX, Charles James, 12, *Hill-street, Liverpool.*—Queen's Coll. Birmingham; Deac. 1865, Pr. 1867. C. of St. Bartholomew's, Liverpool, 1867. Formerly C. of St. John's, Liverpool. [6]

FOX, Edward, *The Vicarage, Romford, Essex*—New Coll. Ox. B.A. 1848, M.A. 1852; Deac. 1849 and Pr. 1850 by Abp of Armagh. V. of Romford with Noak Hill. C. Dio. Roch. 1863. (Patron, New Coll. Ox; No endowment, but a yearly stipend of 700*l* with Ho. and 1½ acres of land allowed by the Patrons; Pop. 4304.) Formerly Asst. Mast. of Royal School, Armagh, 1849–52; C. of Powerstock, Dorset, 1853–56; Lect. and Tut. of New College, Ox. 1859–63. [7]

FOX, Edward Walton.—Wad. Coll. Ox. B.A. 1847; Deac. 1848, Pr. 1849. Chap. of H.M.S. "Canopus." Formerly Chap. R.N. 1851; Chap. to H.M.S. "St. Jean D'Acre," Black Sea, 1855–56. [8]

FOX, Edwin, *South-parade, York.*—Queens' Coll. Cam. B.A. 1846, M.A. 1850; Deac. 1846 by Bp of Ches. Pr. 1847 by Abp of York. P. C. of St. John's, Micklegate, City and Dio. York. 1851. (Patrons, D. and C. of York; P. C.'s Inc. 210*l*; Pop. 872.) [9]

FOX, George Edmund, *Hale Parsonage, Farnham, Surrey.*—Dub. and King's Coll. Lond; Deac. 1854 and Pr. 1855 by Bp of Rip. P. C. of Hale, Dio. Win. 1863. (Patron, V. of Farnham; P. C.'s Inc. 340*l*; Pop. 3200.) Chap. to Farnham Union. Formerly C. of Sowerby, near Halifax, 1854, Camden Ch. Camberwell, 1859, St. Peter's, Hereford, 1860, Lowestoft 1861, Stoke-next-Guildford 1862. [10]

FOX, George Townshend, *Durham.*—Trin. Coll. Cam. B.A. 1845, M.A. 1851; Deac. 1848 by Abp of Cant. Pr. 1848 by Bp of Ches. P. C. of St. Nicholas', City and Dio. Dur. 1856. (Patroness, Marchioness of Londonderry; P. C.'s Inc. 284*l*; Pop. 2606.) Author, *Memoir of the Rev. Henry Watson Fox, Missionary to the Teloogoo People, South India*, 1850; *The Bible the Sole Rule of Faith, and a few Plain Words about Popery and Tractarianism* (Two Sermons), 1850; *Ten Sermons, with a Prefatory Letter to Bishop M'Ilvaine, New York*, 1851; *Priestly Celibacy Exposed* (a Lecture), 1854. [11]

FOX, Henry, *Allington, Bridport, Dorset.*—Ball. Coll. Ox. 2nd cl. Lit. Hum. and B.A. 1814, M.A. 1817; Deac. 1814 by Bp of Salis. Pr. 1815 by Bp of B. and W. P. C. of Allington, Dio. Salis. 1819. (Patron, the present P. C; Tithe, Imp. 190*l*; P. C.'s Inc. 133*l*. and Ho; Pop. 1915.) R. of Pilsdon, Dorset, Dio. Salis. 1830. (Patroness, Mrs. Bower; Tithe, 68*l* 2*s* 8*d*; Glebe, 21 acres; R.'s Inc. 104*l*; Pop. 86.) [12]

FOX, Henry, *The Lawn, Rugby.*—St. John's Coll. Cam. B.A. 1826, M.A. 1829; Deac. 1829 and Pr. 1830 by Bp of Lin. Formerly R. of Cooling, Kent, 1858. [13]

FOX, Joseph, *Heptonstall, near Manchester.*—St. Bees; Deac. 1866 and Pr. 1867 by Bp of Rip. C. of Heptonstall 1866. [14]

FOX, Joseph Hamilton, *Padiham Parsonage, near Burnley, Lancashire.*—King's Coll. Lond. and Queen's Coll. Birmingham; Deac. 1859 and Pr. 1860 by Abp of York. P. C. of Padiham, Dio. Man. 1865. (Patron, Le G. N. Starkie, Esq; P. C.'s Inc. 205*l* and Ho; Pop. 10,000.) Formerly C. of Oversilton, Yorks, 1859, Wilmslow, Ches. 1862. [15]

FOX, Octavius, *Knightwick Rectory, near Worcester.*—Lin. Coll. Ox. B.A. 1834, M.A. 1837. R. of Knightwick with Doddenham C. Dio. Wor. 1852. (Patrons, D. and C. of Wor; Knightwick, Tithe, 151*l* 11*s* 9*d*; Glebe, 20 acres; Doddenham, Tithe, 141*l* 7*s* 6*d*; Glebe, 18 acres; R.'s Inc. 362*l* and Ho; Pop. Knightwick 166, Doddenham 278.) [16]

FOX, Peter, *Whittle-le-Woods, Leyland, Preston.*—Dub. A.B. 1850, A.M. 1854; Deac. 1850, Pr. 1851. P. C. of Whittle-le-Woods, Dio. Man. 1860. (Patron, V. of Leyland; P. C.'s Inc. 160*l* and Ho; Pop. 3000.) Formerly C. of Leyland. [17]

FOX, Richard James Lord, *Woodchurch, Birkenhead.*—St. Aidan's; Deac. 1858 and Pr. 1859 by Bp of Ches. C. of Woodchurch. Formerly C. of Tintwistle 1858. [18]

FOX, Samuel, *Morley Rectory, near Derby.*—Pemb. Coll. Ox. B.A. 1825, M.A. 1828; Deac. 1826 and Pr. 1827 by Bp of Lich. V. of Horsley, Derbyshire, Dio. Lich 1837. (Patron, E. D. Sitwell, Esq; Tithe—Imp. 545*l* 15*s*, V. 172*l* 2*s*; V.'s Inc. 210*l* and Ho; Pop. 2250.) R. of Morley Dio. Lich. 1844. (Patrons, Trustees and E. D. Sitwell, Esq. alt; Tithe, 663*l* 18*s* 4*d*; Glebe, 139 acres; R.'s Inc. 898*l* and Ho; Pop. 951.) Surrogate. Author, *Translation of Poetical Calendar of the Anglo-Saxons*; *Translation of the Metres and Prose of Boethius*; *History of English Monachism*; *Visitation Sermon*; etc. [19]

FOX, Samuel, *Pilgwenlly, Newport, Monmouthshire.*—P. C. of Pilgwenlly, Dio. Llan. 1864. (Patron, Bp of Llan; P. C.'s Inc. 300*l*; Pop. 7000.) [20]

FOX, Samuel William Darwin, *Halifax.*—Wad. Coll. Ox. B.A. 1864; Deac. and Pr. 1865 by Bp of Rip. C. of St. James's, Halifax, 1867. Formerly C. of St. Paul's, Manningham, Bradford, Yorkshire, 1865. [21]

FOX, Thomas, *Abbas Combe, Wincanton, Somerset.*—Wad. Coll. Ox. B.A. 1839; Deac. 1840 and Pr. 1842 by Bp of B. and W. R. of Abbas Combe, Dio. B. and W. 1860. (Patron, the present R; R.'s Inc. 420*l* and Ho; Pop. 487.) Formerly C. of Belchalwell and Fifehead Neville, Dorset, 1845. [22]

FOX, Vaughan Simpson, *Horsley Vicarage, Nailsworth.*—Ball. Coll. Ox. B.A. 1855, M.A. 1858; Deac. 1857 and Pr. 1858 by Bp of G. and B. V. of Horsley, Dio. G. and B. 1862. (Patron, Bp of G. and B; V.'s Inc. 200*l* and Ho; Pop. 2558.) Chap. of Chavenage, Dio. G. and B. 1852. (Patron, Lord of Manor; Chap.'s Inc. 30*l*.) Formerly C. of Leonard's Stanley, near Stonehouse. [23]

FOX, William, *Brixton, Isle of Wight.*—C. of Brixton. [24]

FOX, William Charles, *The Grange, Frampton Cotterell, Bristol.*—St. John's Coll. Cam. M.B. 1849; Deac. 1856 and Pr. 1857 by Bp of Lich. C. of Frampton Cotterell. Formerly C. of St. Mary's, Shrewsbury. [25]

FOX, William Darwin, *Delamere Rectory, Northwich, Cheshire.*—Ch. Coll. Cam. B.A. 1829, M.A. 1833. R. of Delamere, Dio. Ches. 1838. (Patron, the Crown; Land in lieu of Tithe, 102 acres; Glebe, 40 acres; R.'s Inc. 200*l* and Ho; Pop. 1146.) [26]

FOX, William Henry, *Shelford, Nottingham.*—Sid. Coll. Cam. 10th Sen. Opt. and B.A. 1854, M.A. 1857; Deac. 1855 and Pr. 1856 by Bp of Lin. C. of Shelford 1867. Formerly C. of Beeston and Radcliffe-on-Trent. [27]

FOXLEY, Joseph, *Market Weighton, Yorks.*—St. John's Coll. Cam. Sen. Opt. 1st cl. Cl. Trip. Browne's Medal, Member's Prize, Burney Prize, B.A. 1854, M.A. 1857; Deac. 1855 by Abp of York, Pr. 1856 by Bp of

Carl. V. of Market Weighton with Shipton C. Dio. York, 1857. (Patron, Abp of York; V.'s Inc. 300*l* and Ho. with an allowance of 120*l* from Eccles. Commis. for a Curate; Pop. Weighton 2178, Shipton 411.) Surrogate; Rural Dean of Weighton. Formerly Asst. Mast. St. Peter's Sch. York, 1834; Fell. of St. John's Coll. Cam. and Clerical Sec. to Abp Musgrave 1856. Author, *Burney Prize Essay*, 1854, 1*s*. [1]

FOXTON, George Lardner, *Kempsey, near Worcester.*—Ch. Coll. Cam. M.A. 1826; Deac. and Pr. 1818. V. of Kempsey, Dio. Wor. 1852. (Patrons, D. and C. of Wor; Tithe, App. 553*l* and 187½ acres of Glebe, V. 230*l*; Glebe, 1 acre; V.'s Inc. 277*l* and Ho; Pop. 1433.) [2]

FOY, John.—Travelling Sec. of the Additional Curates' Society. [3]

FOY, William Henry, *Belsize Park, Hampstead, Middlesex, N.W.*—Prin. of the Indian Civil Service and Military Coll. Belsize Park, Hampstead. [4]

FOYSTER, George Alfred, *All Saints'-street, Hastings.*—Trin. Coll. Cam. Jun. Opt. B.A. 1859, M.A. 1862; Deac. 1861 and Pr. 1862 by Abp of Cant. R. of All Saints', Hastings, Dio. Chich. 1862. (Patron, the present R; Tithe, 131*l* 15*s* 6*d*; Rent from Glebe, 85*l*; R.'s Inc. 274*l* 16*s* 4*d*; Pop. 3486.) Formerly C. of Ryarsh, Kent, 1861–62. [5]

FOYSTER, Henry Brereton, *St. Clement's Rectory, Hastings.*—Trin. Coll. Cam. 2nd cl. Cl. Trip. 2nd cl. Theol. Trip. B.A. 1857, M.A. 1860; Deac. 1858 and Pr. 1860 by Bp of Roch. R. of St. Clement's, Hastings, Dio. Chich. 1861. (Patron, the present R; R.'s Inc. 160*l* and Ho; Pop. 3038.) Formerly C. of All Saints', Hockerill, 1858–61. [6]

FRAMPTON, Charles Thomas, *Chichester.*—Clare Coll. Cam. B.A. 1844, M.A. 1847; Deac. 1847, Pr. 1848. C. of St. Peter's-the-Less, Chichester. Formerly P. C. of Leverstock Green, Herts, 1851–61. [7]

FRAMPTON, John, *Tetbury Vicarage, Glouc.*—Ex. Coll. Ox. B.A. 1820, M.A. 1822. V. of Tetbury with St. Saviour's C. Dio. G. and B. 1828. (Patron, C. Stanton, Esq; Tithe—App. 246*l* 15*s*, V. 807*l* 17*s*; Glebe, 67 acres; V.'s Inc. 880*l* and Ho; Pop. 3274.) Hon. Can. of Glouc. Cathl. 1848. [8]

FRAMPTON, Richard George Davis Frampton, *Stapenhill, Derbyshire.*—St. Aidan's; Deac. 1858 and Pr. 1860 by Bp of G. and B. C. of Stapenhill. [9]

FRAMPTON, William Charlton, *Moreton Rectory, Dorchester.*—Trin. Coll. Cam. B.A. 1833, M.A. 1834; Deac. 1839 and Pr. 1840 by Bp of Salis. R. of Moreton, Dio. Salis. 1840. (Patron, J. Frampton, Esq; Tithe, 217*l*; Glebe, 38 acres; R.'s Inc. 269*l* and Ho; Pop. 293.) [10]

FRAMPTON, William Jenner.—Magd. Hall, Ox. B.A. 1855; Deac. 1855 and Pr. 1856 by Bp of Lich. Formerly C. of St. John's, Leicester. [11]

FRANCE, George, *Brockdish Rectory, Scole, Norfolk.*—Ex. Coll. Ox. 2nd cl. Math. et Phy. 4th cl. Lit. Hum. and B.A. 1837, M.A. 1838; Deac. 1839 and Pr. 1840 by Bp of Lon. R. of Brockdish, Dio. Nor. 1842. (Patron, the present R; Tithe, 350*l*; Glebe, 25 acres; R.'s Inc. 400*l* and Ho; Pop. 544.) [12]

FRANCE, Thomas, *Davenham Rectory, Northwich, Cheshire.*—Trin. Coll. Cam. 3rd Wrang. and B.A. 1824, M.A. 1830; Deac. 1832, Pr. 1833. R. of Davenham, Dio. Ches. 1839. (Patron, James F. France, Esq; Tithe, comm. 778*l* 14*s* 3*d*; Glebe, 18*a*. 2*r*. 24*p*; Pop. 2300.) [13]

FRANCE, Thomas William Hamilton, *Ambleside, Westmoreland.*—Trin. Coll. Cam. B.A. 1863, M.A. 1867; Deac. 1864 and Pr. 1865 by Abp of York. C. of Ambleside 1866. Formerly C. of Balby with Exthorpe 1864–66. [14]

FRANCES, Sandys, *Dormston, Feckenham, Worcestershire.*—P. C. of Dormston, Dio. Wor. 1864. (Patron, W. Laslett, Esq; P. C.'s Inc. 53*l*; Pop. 97.) [15]

FRANCIS, Albert Edward, *Shenfield, Brentwood, Essex.*—Jesus Coll. Cam. B.A. 1864, Deac. 1866 by Bp of Roch. C. of Shenfield 1866. [16]

FRANCIS, Christopher Dunkin, *Tysoe Vicarage, Kineton, Warwickshire.*—Ex. Coll. Ox. 3rd cl. Lit. Hum. and B.A. 1836, M.A. 1840; Deac. 1837, Pr. 1838. V. of Tysoe with Compton-Wynyates R. Dio. Wor. 1852. (Patron, Marquis of Northampton; Tysoe, Tithe, 2*l* 19*s*; Glebe, 119 acres; Compton-Wynyates, Tithe, 200*l* 14*s*; V.'s Inc. 386*l*; Pop. Tysoe 1035, Compton-Wynyates 37.) [17]

FRANCIS, Herbert O., *Bridport, Dorset.*—Emman Coll. Cam. B.A. 1860, M.A. 1864; Deac. 1862 and Pr. 1863 by Bp of Salis. C. of St. Andrew's, Bradpole, 1866. Formerly C. of Canford Magna, Dorset, 1862, Weymouth 1864. [18]

FRANCIS, James, *Milbank Prison, Westminster.*—St. John's Coll. Cam. B.A. 1862; Deac. 1863 and Pr. 1865 by Bp of Rip. Asst. Chap. of Milbank Prison 1866. Formerly C. of St. Mary's, Leeds, 1863, Halton Gill, Craven, 1864; Asst. Chap. of Wakefield Prison 1865. [19]

FRANCIS, James, *Waltham Abbey, Essex.*—Ch. Coll. Cam. B.A. 1838; Deac. 1841, Pr. 1842. Chap. of Don. of Waltham Holy Cross, *alias* Waltham Abbey, Dio. Roch. 1846. (Patrons, Trustees of the Earl of Norwich; Tithe, Imp. 1419*l*; Glebe, ½ acre; Chap.'s Inc. 200*l*; Pop. 4513.) [20]

FRANCIS, John, *Bishop Otter's College, Chichester.*—St. John's Coll. Cam. Jun. Opt. B.A. 1861, M.A. 1864; Deac. 1861 and Pr. 1862 by Bp of Chich. C. of Westhampnett 1861 and C. of Eartham (sole charge) 1865. Author, *The Exercise of the Active Virtues such as Courage and Patriotism is entirely Consistent with the Spirit of the Gospel* (the Burney Prize Essay 1863). Cambridge, 1864, 2*s*. [21]

FRANCIS, Philip, *Stibbard, Guist, Norfolk.*—Corpus Coll. Cam. B.A. 1820, M.A. 1828; Deac. 1820, Pr. 1822. [22]

FRANCIS, Robert, 18, *St. James's-street, Newcastle-upon-Tyne.*—St. Bees; Deac. 1864 and Pr. 1866 by Bp of Dur. C. of St. Andrews, Newcastle-upon-Tyne, 1864. [23]

FRANCIS, Robert John, *Upper Mary-street, Norwich.*—Corpus Coll. Cam. Sen. Opt. B.A. 1797; Deac. and Pr. 1801. R. of Billesby, Dio. Nor. 1860. (Patron, B. P. Nunes, Esq; R.'s Inc. 648*l* and Ho; Glebe, 3 acres; Pop 531.) [24]

FRANCIS, William, *Newcastle-under-Lyme.*—St. John's Coll. Cam. B.A. 1829; Deac. by Bp of Herf. Pr. 1839 by Bp of Lich. Chap. of the Union, Newcastle-under-Lyme. Formerly C. of Ruyton in XI. Towns, Salop, 1838–39, Audley 1839–48. Author, *Argument and Sauce to Curb the rough, reckless, backbiting Tongue*, 1862. [25]

FRANCIS, William Adderley, *Little Tey Rectory, Kelvedon, Essex.*—Ch. Coll. Cam. B.A. 1839, M.A. 1842; Deac. 1841, Pr. 1842. R. of Little Tey, Dio. Roch. 1857. (Patron, Bp of Roch; R.'s Inc 140*l* and Ho; Pop. 63.) Dom. Chap. to the Earl of Meath. Formerly C. of Paglesham, Essex. [26]

FRANCIS, W. F., *Great Saxham, Bury St. Edmunds.*—C. of Great Saxham. [27]

FRANCKEN, Charles William, *Wicken, Soham, Cambs.*—St. Cath. Hall, Cam. B.A. 1841; Deac. 1843 and Pr. 1844 by Bp of Nor. P. C. of Wicken, Dio. Ely, 1858. (Patroness, Miss Hatch; P. C.'s Inc. 56*l*; Pop. 995.) [28]

FRANCKLIN, John Fairfax, *Whaplode, Spalding, Lincolnshire.*—Clare Coll. Cam. late Fell. M.A. 1833; Deac. 1827, Pr. 1828. V. of Whaplode, Dio. Lin. 1859. (Patron, Ld Chan; Tithe, comm. 553*l* 4*s*; Glebe, 7 acres; V.'s Inc. 600*l* and Ho; Pop. 1818.) Chap. to the 16th Lincolnshire Rifle Volunteers. Formerly P. C. of New Buckenham, Norfolk; R. of West Newton, Norfolk. Author, *Unitarianism not Christianity*; *An Exposition of the 10th and 17th Articles of the Church, Free-Will and Predestination Explained*, 1857; *The Indivisibility of Christ's Church* (a Sermon) 1857; *Scriptural Authority for National Armaments* (a Sermon), 1860. [29]

FRANEY, John.—St. John's Coll. Cam. B.A. 1854; Deac. 1855 by Bp of Llan. Pr. 1856 by Bp of Nor. Formerly C. of Hellesdon, Norwich. [30]

FRANKLING, William, *Hexham, Northumberland.*—St. Bees; Deac. 1842, Pr. 1843. C. of Hexham. [1]

FRANKLYN, James H., *Bournemouth, Hants.*—Chap. of the Sanatorium, Bournemouth. [2]

FRANKLYN, Thomas Ward, 55, *Onslow-square, South Kensington, London, S.W.*—St. John's Coll. Cam. B.A. 1823, M.A. 1826; Deac. 1824 and Pr. 1826 by Bp of G. and B. Formerly P. C. of Ch. Ch. Tunbridge Wells, 1857. [3]

FRANKS, Edward Robert, *Downham Market, Norfolk.*—Trin. Coll. Cam. B.A. 1846; Deac. 1849, Pr. 1850. R. of Downham Market, Dio. Nor. 1850. (Patron, the present R; Tithe—App. 10*l* 17*s* 6*d*, R. 500*l*; Glebe, 29 acres; R.'s Inc. 564*l* and Ho; Pop. 3133.) [4]

FRANKS, George Henry, *Misterton Rectory, Lutterworth, Leicestershire.*—Ex. Coll. Ox. B.A. 1832; Deac. and Pr. 1835. R. of Misterton, Dio. Pet. 1835. (Patron, J. H. Franks, Esq; Tithe, 619*l* 15*s*; Glebe, 13 acres; R.'s Inc. 930*l* and Ho; Pop. 554.) [5]

FRANKS, John Firth, *Park-terrace, Croydon.*—Trin. Hall, Cam. 14th Sen. Opt. B.A. 1854, M.A. 1857: Deac. 1855 and Pr. 1856 by Bp of Ches. P. C. of St. Andrew's, Croydon, Dio. Cant. 1864. (Patron, Rev. J. H. Randolph, Sanderstead; P. C.'s Inc. 150*l*; Pop. 2800.) Formerly C. of Bebbington, Cheshire, 1855–59, Hillingdon, Middlesex, 1859–61, Croydon 1861–64. [6]

FRASER, Alexander Charles, *Woolwich, Kent.*—Deac. 1840, Pr. 1841. Chap. of the Royal Military Academy, Woolwich, 1847; C. of Greenwich; Dom. Chap. to the Marquis of Anglesey. [7]

FRASER, Duncan, *Halstead Parsonage, Essex.*—Trin. Coll. Cam. B.A. 1837, M.A. 1840; P. C. of Holy Trinity, Halstead, Dio. Roch. 1845. (Patron, Bp of Roch; Glebe, ½ acre; P. C.'s Inc. 150*l* and Ho; Pop. 2890.) Rural Dean and Surrogate. [8]

FRASER, George, *St. Mary's Vicarage, Wolverhampton.*—Queens' Coll. Cam. B.D. 1853; Deac. 1840 and Pr. 1841 by Bp of Chich. V. of St. Mary's, Wolverhampton, Dio. Lich. 1842. (Patroness, Miss Hinckes; V.'s Inc. 250*l* and Ho; Pop. 8413.) Rural Dean. [9]

FRASER, James, *Ufton Rectory, near Reading.*—Ox. B.A. Lin. Coll. 1840, Fell. of Oriel 1840, M.A. Oriel Coll. 1842, 1st cl. Lit. Hum. and Ireland Scho. 1839; Deac. 1846 and Pr. 1847 by Bp of Ox. R. of Ufton-Nervet, Dio. Ox. 1860. (Patron, Oriel Coll. Ox; Tithe, 479*l*; Glebe, 60 acres; R.'s Inc. 529*l* and Ho; Pop. 368.) Inspector of Schs. in Oxford Dio; Preb. of Salis. Cathl; Chap. to Bp of Salis. Formerly Tut. of Oriel Coll. 1842–47; R. of Cholderton, Wilts, 1847–60; Chan. of Salis. Cathl. 1858–60; Select Preacher in Univ. Oxford, 1854 and 1862. Author, *Six Sermons preached before the University of Oxford*, 1856; *Report on Education*, presented to Royal Commissioners on Education, 1860; *Report on Education in the United States of Canada*, presented to the Schools' Inquiry Commission, 1867; occasional Sermons and Pamphlets. [10]

FRASER, Lewis.—Jesus Coll. Cam. 2nd cl. Cl. Trip. B.A. 1862; Deac. 1863 and Pr. 1864 by Bp of Lon Central African Mission. Formerly C. of Holy Trinity, Tottenham, 1863. [11]

FRASER, Thomas Southworth, *King's Buildings, Chester.*—Deac. 1865 by Bp of Ches. C. of Ch. Ch. Chester, 1865. [12]

FRASER, William, *Alton Vicarage, Cheadle, Staffs.*—Wor. Coll. Ox. 3rd cl. Lit. Hum. B.A. 1845, M.A. and B.C.L. 1848, D.C.L. 1861; Deac. 1848 and Pr. 1849 by Bp of Lich. V. of Alton, Dio. Lich. 1858. (Patron, Earl of Shrewsbury; Tithe, 250*l*; Glebe, 4 acres; V.'s Inc. 260*l* and Ho; Pop. 1563.) P. C. of Cotton, Dio. Lich. 1862. (Patron, V. of Alton; Glebe, 50 acres; P. C.'s Inc. 50*l*; Pop. 446.) Dom. Chap. to the Earl of Shrewsbury and Talbot; Proctor in Convocation for the Dio. of Lich. 1865. Formerly C. of Uttoxeter 1848–50, Hordley 1850–51, Tor-Mohun 1851–53, Alton 1853–58. Author, *Holy Confirmation* (a Sermon), 1849; *The Constitutional Nature of the Convocations of the Church of England*, 1852; *A Letter to a Convocation Man*, 1853; *Parish Sermons*, 1st Series, 1855; do. 2nd Series, 1860; *The Old Week's Preparation for the Holy Sacrament of the Lord's Supper* (edited), 1855; *A Plain Commentary on the Book of Psalms, chiefly founded on the Fathers*, 2 vols. 1857; *The Veracity of Holy Scripture implied in the Fatherhood of God* (a University Sermon), 1863; *Thoughts on Convocational Reform*, 1863; *A Confirmation Register*, 1863, S.P.C.K; Contributor to the *Sermons and Tracts for the Christian Seasons* and other periodicals. [13]

FRASER, William, *Oswaldtwistle, Lancashire.*—Dub. A.B. 1865; Deac. 1866 by Bp of Man. C. of Oswaldtwistle 1866 [14]

FRASER, William Francis, *Stisted, Braintree, Essex.*—Emman. Coll. Cam. B.A. 1856; Deac. 1857 and Pr. 1858 by Bp of Roch. C. of Stisted 1860. Formerly C. of Coggeshall 1857–59. [15]

FRASER, William Frederick Chambers Sugden, *Chaplain's House, County Prison, Maidstone.*—St. Mary Hall, Ox. 1858; Deac. 1861 and Pr. 1863 by Bp of Dur. Chap. to Kent County Prison 1866. Formerly C. of Norham 1861–64; Chap. of North Eastern Reformatory and C. of Stannington, Northumberland, 1864–65; Asst. Chap. of West Riding Prison, Wakefield, and Hon. Chap. of West Riding Home for Female Penitents, 1865–66. [16]

FRAZELL, Richard Howard, *South Normanton Rectory, Derbyshire.*—Dub. A.B. 1827; Deac. 1828 by Bp of Ex. Pr. 1834 by Bp of Lich. P. C. of Annesley, Notts, Dio. Lin. 1848. (Patron, J. Chaworth Musters, Esq; P. C.'s Inc. 88*l*; Pop. 288.) C. of South Normanton, Derbyshire. [17]

FRAZER, Arthur Bruce, *Haversham Rectory, Newport Pagnell, Bucks.*—Trin. Coll. Cam. B.A. 1847, M.A. 1851; Deac. 1851 and Pr. 1852 by Bp of Chich. R. of Haversham, Dio. Ox. 1856. (Patron, the present R; R.'s Inc. 195*l* and Ho; Pop. 280.) Formerly C. of St. John's, Brighton, 1851–54. [18]

FRAZER, John, *Towednack, St. Ives, Cornwall.*—Dub. A.B. 1833, A.M. 1837; Deac. 1838 by Bp of Kildare, Pr. 1838 by Abp of Dub. C. of Towednack. Formerly P. C. of Emman. Ch. Bolton, 1839–41; Head Mast. of the Liskeard Gr. Sch. 1841–47; C. of St. Wenn 1847–53; Asst. Chap. of Woolwich Dockyard 1853–60; C. of St. Neot's 1860–62. [19]

FREEBORN, John William, *Llanrwst, Carnarvonshire.*—Wor. Coll. Ox. 2nd cl. Math. et Phy. and B.A. 1846, M.A. 1849; Deac. 1847, Pr. 1849. Head Mast. of the Llanrwst Gr. Sch. 1851. [20]

FREELING, George Noel, *Winterslow, Salisbury.*—Mert. Coll. Ox. 3rd cl. Lit. Hum. and B.A. 1852; Deac. 1854, Pr. 1855 by Bp of Ox. Fell. of Mert. Coll. 1852; C. of Winterslow 1854. [21]

FREELING, James Robert.—Ex. Coll. Ox. B.A. 1850, M.A. 1861; Deac. 1852 by Bp of Ely, Pr. 1853 by Bp of Salis. British Chap. at Chantilly. Formerly C. of Farley and Pitton, Wilts; P. C. of Burcombe, Salisbury, 1855, Sharnbrook, Beds. 1861. [22]

FREEMAN, Alfred, *Pillerton Vicarage, Kineton, Warwick.*—Trin. Coll. Ox. B.A. 1856, M.A. 1859; Deac. 1858 and Pr. 1864 by Bp of Wor. V. of Pillerton Hersey with Pillerton Priors, Dio. Wor. 1864. (Patron, Rev. H. Mills; Glebe, 62 acres; V.'s Inc. 130*l* and Ho; Pop. Pillerton Hersey 242, Pillerton Priors 190.) Formerly C. of Pillerton 1858–64. [23]

FREEMAN, Allan Davidson, *Montpellier House, Montpellier-road, Brighton.*—Literate; Deac. 1862 and Pr. 1863 by Bp of Limerick. Vice-Prin. of the Western Coll. Brighton, 1867. Formerly C. of Kilflynn, Dio. Ardfert, 1862–63; C. and Precentor of St. Martin's-on-the-Hill, Scarborough, 1864–67. [24]

FREEMAN, Charles Earle, *The Parsonage, West Malvern.*—Magd. Hall, Ox. B.A. 1848, M.A. 1851; Deac. 1847 and Pr. 1848 by Bp of Dur. P. C. of St. James's, West Malvern, Dio. Wor. 1856. (Patrons, D. and C. of Westminster; Glebe, 2 acres; P. C.'s Inc. 230*l* and Ho; Pop. 1417.) Author, *The Weekly Offertory*, two Sermons with Preface, 1863, 1*s*. [25]

FREEMAN, Francis Alton, *Shadforth, Durham.*—Dub. A.B. 1858, A.M. 1860; Deac. 1858 and Pr.

1859 by Bp of Dur. C. of Shadforth. Formerly C. of Southwick, near Sunderland, 1858–63, Reepham St. Mary with Kerdiston 1863. [1]

FREEMAN, Frederic, *Lancaster.*—Dur. B.A. 1862; Deac. 1862 and Pr. 1863 by Abp of York. C. of St. Mary's, Lancaster. Formerly C. of Market Weighton with Shipton 1862. [2]

FREEMAN, Frederick Earle, *West Lydford Rectory, Somerton, Somerset.*—Ex. Coll. Ox. B.A. 1852, M.A. 1854; Deac. 1854 and Pr. 1855 by Bp of G. and B. R. of West Lydford, Dio. B. and W. 1858. (Patrons, Heirs of the late Mrs. Colston; Glebe, 212 acres; R.'s Inc. 350*l* and Ho; Pop. 300.) Formerly C. of Lydbrook, Glouc. 1854–58. [3]

FREEMAN, Gage Earle, *Wild Boar Clough, near Macclesfield.*—St. John's Coll. Cam. B.A. 1845, M.A. 1850; Deac. 1846 and Pr. 1847 by Bp of Pet. P. C. of Macclesfield Forest with Clough, Dio. Ches. 1856. (Patron, Earl of Derby; P. C.'s. Inc. 150*l* and Ho; Pop. 300.) Formerly P. C. of Emman. Ch. Bolton-le-Moors, 1854–56. Author, *Falconry, its Claims, History, and Practice,* 1859; *Mount Carmel,* a Story of Modern English Life, Bentley, 1867; Essays, etc. [4]

FREEMAN, George John, *Bruntingthorpe, Lutterworth, Leicestershire.*—Trin. Hall, Cam. B.A. 1811; Deac. 1811, Pr. 1812. R. of Bruntingthorpe, Dio. Pet. 1834. (Patron, the present R. during his life, afterwards reverting to the Bridges family; Glebe, 286 acres; R.'s Inc. 387*l*; Pop. 413.) Author, *Sketches in Wales,* 1826, 21*s*. [5]

FREEMAN, Henry Frere, *Snelston, Derbyshire.*—Brasen. Coll. Ox. B.A. 1860, M.A. 1863; Deac. 1862 and Pr. 1863 by Bp of Wor. C. of Norbury and Snelston 1866. [6]

FREEMAN, John, *Ashwicken Rectory, Lynn, Norfolk.*—St. Peter's Coll. Cam. B.A. 1837, M.A. 1840; Deac. 1838 and Pr. 1840 by Bp of Nor. R. of Ashwicken with Leziate R. (no Ch.) Dio. Nor. 1841. (Patron, the present R; Ashwicken, Tithe, 240*l*; Glebe, 10 acres; Leziate, Tithe, 280*l* 10*s* 5*d*; Glebe, 3 acres; R.'s Inc. 540*l* and Ho; Pop. Ashwicken 108, Leziate 197.) Rural Dean 1846. Author, *Life of Kirby, the Entomologist,* 1852, 15*s*. [7]

FREEMAN, John Deane, M.A.—Dom. Chap. to Viscount Doneraile. [8]

FREEMAN, The Ven. Philip, *Thorverton Vicarage, Collumpton, Devon.*—Trin Coll. Cam. B.A. 1839, M.A. 1842; Deac. 1842, Pr. 1844. V. of Thorverton, Dio. Ex. 1858. (Patrons, D. and C. of Ex; V.'s Inc. 510*l* and Ho; Pop. 1211.) Can. of Ex. 1864; Archd. of Ex. 1865; Exam. Chap. to Bp of Ex. Formerly Prin. of Theol. Coll. Chich. 1846–58. Author, *Thoughts on the proposed Dissolution of the C.C.S.* 1845; *Proportion in Gothic Architecture,* 1848; *Plea for the Education of the Clergy,* 1851, 1*s* 6*d*; *Plain Directions for using the Morning and Evening Prayer,* 1854, 3*d*; *The Principles of Divine Service, an Inquiry into the Order for Morning and Evening Prayer, and for the Holy Communion,* 2 vols 1855. [9]

FREEMAN, Robert Marriott, *High Leigh Parsonage, Knutsford.*—Ch. Ch. Ox. B.A. 1859; Deac 1860 and Pr. 1861 by Bp of Roch. P. C. of High Leigh, Dio. Ches. 1863. (Patron, E. Leigh, Esq; P. C.'s Inc. 160*l*; Pop. 1004.) Formerly C. of Stevenage 1860–63. [10]

FREEMAN, Thomas Matthew, *Mellor, near Stockport.*—Dur. Licen. in Theol. 1854; Deac. 1854 by Bp of Win. Pr. 1855 by Bp of Lich. P. C. of Mellor, Dio. Lich. 1859. (Patron, Rev. Thomas M. Freeman; Glebe, 42 acres; P. C.'s Inc. 120*l*; Pop. 3378.) Surrogate. Formerly C. of Whitfield, Derbyshire, 1856; St. Paul's, Paddington-in-Pendleton, Lancashire, 1857, Mellor 1858. [11]

FREEMAN, William Henry, *Saxted, Wickham Market.*—Caius Coll. Cam. B.A. 1856, M.A. 1858; Deac. 1858 and Pr. 1859 by Bp of Nor. C. of Dennington, Suffolk, 1858. [12]

FREER, Henry Leftwich, *Mansergh, Westmoreland.*—Deac. 1863 and Pr. 1864 by Abp of York. P. C. of Mansergh, Dio. Carl. 1864. (Patron, V. of Kirkby Lonsdale; Glebe, 120 acres; P. C.'s Inc. 130*l* and Ho; Pop. 190.) Formerly C. of Wath-upon-Dearne 1863–64. [13]

FREER, Thomas Henry, *Wellington College, Wokingham, Berks.*—Trin. Coll. Cam. 1st cl. Cl. Trip. Sen. Moralist, B.A. 1856, M.A. 1860; Deac. 1861 and Pr. 1863 by Bp of Ox. Tut. and Asst. Mast. at Wellington Coll. [14]

FREER, William Haughton, *Seckington Rectory, Tamworth.*—Trin. Coll. Cam. B.A. 1853, M.A. 1856; Deac. 1853 and Pr. 1854 by Bp of Lich. R. of Seckington, Dio. Wor. 1863. (Patron, Sir R. Burdett, Bart; Tithe, 212*l* 14*s* 9*d*; Glebe, 27 acres; R.'s Inc. 252*l* 14*s* 9*d* and Ho; Pop. 128.) Formerly C. of Colwich, Staffs, 1853–55, Cubley with Marston Montgomery 1855–58; P. C. of Marchington 1860–63. [15]

FREER, William Thomas, *Houghton-on-the-Hill Rectory, Leicester.*—Trin. Coll. Ox. B A. 1848, M.A. 1851; Deac. 1850 and Pr. 1851 by Bp of Pet. R. of Houghton-on-the-Hill, Dio. Pet. 1855. (Patron, W. Freer, Esq; R.'s Inc. 262*l* and Ho; Pop. 462.) [16]

FREETH, Frederick Harvey, *The Parsonage, Lyss, near Petersfield, Hants.*—Dur. B.A. 1845, M.A. 1848; Deac. 1845 and Pr. 1846 by Abp of Cant. P. C. of Lyss, Dio. Win. 1858. (Patron, Bp of Win; Tithe, App. 383*l*; Glebe, 6¾ acres; P. C.'s Inc. 395*l*; Pop. 806.) Formerly C. of Old Romney with St. Mary's, Kent, 1845; C. of Lyminge, Kent, 1849; Canon of Coll. Ch. Isle of Cumbrae, Scotland, 1851; C. of Frome Selwood, Somerset, 1853, Albury, Surrey, 1855. [17]

FREETH, Thomas Jacob, *Fotherby, near Louth, Lincolnshire.*—Ch. Coll. Cam. B.A. 1849, Voluntary Theo. Examination 1849, M.A. 1853; Univ. Lond. LL.D. 1841, 1st cl. and Hons. LL.B. 1843; Deac. 1849 by Bp of Salis. Pr. 1849 by Bp of Lich. V. of Fotherby, Dio. Lin. 1857. (Patron, Ld Chan; Glebe, 72 acres; V.'s Inc. 150*l*; Pop. 267.) Formerly C. of St. Peter's, Wolverhampton, 1849–54; Asst. Chap. to the Crimean Army 1854–56; C. of Holy Trinity, Clapham, 1856, Great Tey, Essex, 1857. Formerly an Attorney and Solicitor. [18]

FREMANTLE, William Henry.—All Souls Coll. Ox. 1st. cl. Lit. Hum. and B.A. 1853, M.A. 1855; Deac 1855 and Pr. 1856 by Bp of Ox. R. of St. Mary's, Marylebone, Lond. Dio. Lon. 1865. (Patron, Crown; Pop. 17,678.) Hon. Chap. to Bp of Lon. Late Fell. of All Souls Coll. Ox; Formerly V. of Lewknor, Oxon, 1857, and C. of Middle Claydon, Bucks. Author, *The Influence of Commerce on Christianity* (Prize Essay), 1854; *Ecclesiastical Judgments of the Privy Council, with Preface by Bishop of London,* 1865, Murray. [19]

FREMANTLE, William Robert, *Claydon Rectory, Winslow, Bucks.*—Ch. Ch. Ox. Magd. Coll. B.A. 1829, M.A. 1832; Deac. 1833, Pr. 1834. R. of Middle Claydon, Dio. Ox. 1841. (Patron, Sir H. Verney, Bart; Tithe, 540*l*; R.'s Inc. 550*l* and Ho; Pop. 146.) V. of East Claydon with Steeple Claydon, Dio. Ox. 1841. (Patron, Sir H. Verney, Bart; East Claydon, Tithe 20*l*; V.'s Inc. 300*l* and Ho; Pop. East Claydon 385, Steeple Claydon 946.) Rural Dean. Author, *Eastern Churches,* 1*s* 6*d*; *Memoir of the Rev. Spencer Thornton,* 4th ed. 5*s*; *Light from the New Testament,* 6*s*; *Sermon at the first Triennial Visitation of the Bishop of Oxford.* [20]

FRENCH, Frederic, *Worlingworth Rectory, Woodbridge, Suffolk.*—St. Peter's Coll. Cam. B.A. 1847, M.A. 1850; Deac. 1848, Pr. 1850. R. of Worlingworth with Southolt C. Dio. Nor. 1853. (Patron, Lord Henniker; Worlingworth, Tithe, 680*l*; Glebe, 52 acres; Southolt, Tithe, 237*l* 10*s*; Glebe, 1½ acres; R.'s Inc. 987*l* and Ho; Pop. Worlingworth 740, Southolt 193.) [21]

FRENCH, G., *Derby.*—Dub. A.B. 1858; Deac. 1858 and Pr. 1860 by Bp of Tuam. C. of Trinity, Derby, 1861. Formerly C. of Skreen, Ireland, 1858–60. Author *The Kingdom of Heaven is at Hand,* 1862, 1*s*, Macintosh; Pamphlets and Lectures. [22]

FRENCH George, *Heworth, York.*—H.M. Inspector of Schools. Formerly C. of St. Mary-Woolnoth, Lond; 2nd Mast. of St. Saviour's Gr. Sch. Southwark. [1]

FRENCH, George, *Everton, Liverpool.*—Dub. A.B. 1848, A M. 1858; Deac. 1851 by Bp of Killaloe, Pr. 1852 by Bp of Cork. C. of St. Peter's, Everton, 1861. [2]

FRENCH, Henry Day, *Ringwood, Hants.*—Emman. Coll. Cam. B.A. 1864, M.A. 1867; 7th Jun. Opt. Johnson's Scho; Deac. 1865 and Pr. 1866, by Bp of Win. C. of Ringwood. [3]

FRENCH, John, *Bodmin, Cornwall.*—Univ. Coll. Ox. M.A. Formerly C. of Lanivet. [4]

FRENCH, Mark Dyer, *West Allington, Grantham.*—Brasen. Coll. Ox. B.A. 1837, M.A. 1840; Deac. 1837 by Abp of York, Pr. 1838 by Bp of Lin. R. of West Allington, Dio. Lin. 1867. (Patron, Ld Chan; R.'s Inc. 245*l*; Pop. 135.) Formerly C. of St. George's, Hanover-square, Lond. W. 1845-47; St. John's, Paddington, 1847. [5]

FRENCH, Peter, *Burton-on-Trent, Staffs.*—Queen's Coll. Ox. B.A. 1822, M.A. 1824; Deac. 1822 and Pr. 1823 by Bp of Salis. P. C. of Holy Trinity with Stretton, Burton-on-Trent, Dio. Lich. 1824. (Patron, Marquis of Anglesey; Pop. 5465.) Chap. to the Burton Union. [6]

FRENCH, Robert Jackson, *Flockton, near Wakefield.*—St. Bees; Deac. 1852, Pr. 1854. P. C. of Flockton with Denby Grange, Dio. Rip. 1859. (Patrons, Trustees; P. C.'s Inc. 100*l* and Ho; Pop. 2057.) Formerly C. of Whitley, Yorks, 1855. Author, *An Examination of Conscience, by the Rule of God's Commandments,* 1863, 9*d*, Bell and Daldy. [7]

FRENCH, Thomas De Freyne.—Jesus Coll. Ox. B.A. 1832, M.A. 1836; Deac. 1833 by Bp of Roch. Pr. 1834 by Bp of Wor. Formerly C. of Swynshed. [8]

FRENCH, Thomas Lee, *Thrandeston (Suffolk), near Scole.*—Emman. Coll. Cam. B.A. 1844, M.A. 1847; Deac. 1845, Pr. 1846. R. of Thrandeston, Dio. Nor. 1845. (Patron, Sir E. Kerrison, Bart; Tithe—App. 4*l* R. 465*l*; R.'s Inc. 475*l* and Ho: Pop. 364.) [9]

FRENCH, Thomas Valpy, *Cheltenham.*—Univ. Coll. Ox. 1843, 1st cl. Lit. Hum. and B.A. 1846, Latin Essayist 1848; Deac. 1848, Pr. 1849. P. C. of St. Paul's, Cheltenham, Dio. G. and B. 1864. (Patron, R. of Cheltenham; P. C.'s Inc. 300*l*; Pop. 6000.) [10]

FREND, William Henry, *Canterbury.*—Univ. Coll. Dur. Licen. Theol. 1854; Deac. 1854 and Pr. 1855 by Bp of Lich. Formerly C. of Wellington, Salop, and P. C. of Tiptree Heath, Essex, 1856. [11]

FRERE, Constantine, *Finningham Rectory, Stowmarket, Suffolk.*—Corpus Coll. Cam. B.A. 1843, M.A. 1846, Sen. Opt. 1st cl. Cl; Deac. 1845 and Pr. 1846 by Bp of Glouc. R. of Finningham, Dio. Nor. 1847. (Patron, G. E. Frere, Esq; Tithe—App. 12*s* 6*d*, R. 450*l*; Glebe, 26 acres; R.'s Inc. 500*l* and Ho; Pop. 542.) [12]

FRERE, Edward Hanbury, *Horham Rectory, Wickham Market, Suffolk.*—Caius Coll. Cam. Sen. Opt. and B.A. 1849, M.A. 1852; Deac. 1850, Pr. 1851. R. of Horham, Dio. Nor. 1852. (Patron, the present R; Tithe, 452*l* 10*s*; Glebe, 23 acres; R.'s Inc. 487*l* and Ho; Pop. 396.) [13]

FRERE, Henry Temple, *Burston Rectory, Diss, Norfolk.*—Corpus Coll. Cam. B.A. 1845, M.A. 1850; Deac. 1845 and Pr. 1846 by Bp of Nor. R. of Burston, Dio. Nor. 1854. (Patron, Ld Chan; Tithe, 470*l*; Glebe, 76 acres; R.'s Inc. 584*l* and Ho; Pop. 419.) [14]

FRERE, John Alexander, *Shillington Vicarage, Hitchin, Beds.*—Trin. Coll. Cam. B.A. 1838, M A. 1841; Deac. 1842 and Pr. 1843 by Bp of Ely. V. of Shillington, Dio. Ely, 1853. (Patron, Trin. Coll. Cam; Glebe, 45 acres; V.'s Inc. 128*l* and Ho; Pop. 1788.) Formerly Whitehall Preacher 1847–48; Christian Advocate of the Univ. of Cam. 1848–50; Fell. Tut. and Sen. Dean. of Trin. Coll. 1840-47. Author, *Inspiration of Scripture,* 1850; *Inconsistencies of the Rationalistic Mode of Treating the Contents of the Sacred Scriptures,* 1851; *Idea of the Incarnation not derived from Jewish or Greek Speculation,* 1852; *The Testimony of the Spirit to the Incarnation,* 1853. [15]

FRESHFIELD, John Minet, *Stanton by-Dale-Abbey, Derby.*—Ball. Coll. Ox. B.A. 1857; Deac. 1858 by Bp of Nor. R. of Stanton-by-Dale-Abbey, Dio. Lich. 1862. (Patron, Earl Stanhope; R.'s Inc. 300*l* and Ho; Pop. 499.) Formerly C. of St. Nicholas', Great Yarmouth. [16]

FRESHNEY, Frederick, *Skidbrooke Vicarage, Louth, Lincolnshire.*—Ch. Coll. Cam. B.A. 1859, M.A. 1862; Deac. 1859 and Pr. 1860 by Abp of York. V. of Skidbrooke-with-Saltfleet Haven, Dio. Lin. 1862. (Patron, the present V; Tithe, comm. 377*l* 13*s* 6*d*; Glebe, 17*l* 4*s*; V.'s Inc. 394*l* 17*s* 6*d* and Ho; Pop. 361.) Formerly C. of Scalby, Yorks, 1859, Skidbrooke-with-Saltfleet Haven 1861. [17]

FREUER, Edward, *Cratfield, Halesworth, Suffolk.*—Ch. Coll. Cam. B.A. 1835; Deac. 1838 and Pr. 1840 by Bp of Nor. V. of Cratfield, Dio. Nor. 1862. (Patron, Rev. E. Hollond; Tithe, 110*l*; Glebe, 15½ acres; V.'s Inc. 140*l* and Ho; Pop. 604.) Formerly C. of Stow Bedow 1838, Southolt 1843, Bedfield 1845, Rattlesden 1846, Bedfield 1847. [18]

FREWER, George, *Eton College, Bucks.*—St. John's Coll. Cam. Sen. Opt. and B.A. 1844, M.A. 1847; Deac. 1845 by Bp of Lin. Pr. 1847 by Bp of Ox. Asst. Math. Mast. Eton Coll. 1844; Div. Lect. of St. George's Chapel, Windsor, 1854. [19]

FREWER, Henry, 3, *Clifton Wood, Clifton.*—Jesus Coll. Ox. 4th cl. Lit. Hum. B.A. 1854, M.A. 1857; Deac. 1861 and Pr. 1862 by Bp of Ex. Sen. Asst. Clas. Mast. of the Gr. Sch. Bristol, 1864. Formerly C. of St. Paul, near Penzance, 1861. C. of St. Austell, Cornwall, 1862. Second Mast. of the Gr. Sch. Ashby-de-la-Zouch, 1863. [20]

FRIEL, T. H.—C. of St. John's, Hoxton, Lond. [21]

FRIEL, W. J., *Birkdale, Southport, Lancashire.*—C. of Birkdale. [22]

FRIPP, Charles Spencer, *Portishead, Somerset.*—Magd. Hall Ox. and Theol. Assoc. of King's Coll. Lond. 1849; Deac. 1849 and Pr. 1850 by Bp of B. and W. C. of Portishead. Formerly P. C. of Ch. Ch. Nailsea. [23]

FRITCHE, George Cheslyn, *The Rectory, Newton Regis, Tamworth.*—Dur. B.A. 1856; Deac. 1853, Pr. 1854. R. of Newton-in-the-Thistles, or Newton Regis, Dio. Wor. 1863. (Patron, George Fritche, Esq; R.'s Inc. 300*l* and Ho; Pop. 442.) Formerly C. of Littleover and Findern, Derbyshire, and Chap. to the Derby County Lunatic Asylum. [24]

FRITH, Edward Blackstone Cokayne, *Marldon, Devon.*—Ch. Ch. Ox. B.A. 1852; Deac. 1853 and Pr. 1855 by Bp of Ox. C. of Marldon. Formerly P. C. of of King's Sterndale, Derbyshire, 1858–63, and C. of Cranmore, Somerset. [25]

FRITH, James, *Bisley, Stroud.*—Ch. Ch. Ox. B.A. 1844, M.A. 1848; Deac. 1845 and Pr. 1846 by Bp of Wor. C. of Bisley. Formerly C. of South Moreton, Berks. [26]

FRITH, Marischal Keith Smith, *Allestree Parsonage, near Derby.*—Ex. Coll. Ox. B.A. 1841, M.A 1842; Deac. 1842, Pr. 1843. P. C. of Allestree, Dio. Lich. 1864. (Patron, T. W. Evans, Esq, M.P; P. C.'s Inc. 44*l* and Ho; Pop. 529.) Formerly C. of Puttenham, Herts, 1842–43; R. of Puget and Warwick, Bermuda, 1845–64. [27]

FRITH, William Armetriding, *Gainsborough, Lincolnshire.*—Wor. Coll. Ox. B.A. 1849, M.A. 1852; Deac. 1850, Pr. 1851. P. C. of Holy Trinity, Gainsborough, Dio. Lin. 1854. (Patron, Bp of Lin; P. C.'s Inc. 140*l* and Ho; Pop. 2436.) [28]

FROST, Charles, *Purton, near Swindon, Wilts.*—C. of Purton. [29]

FROST, George, 28, *Kensington-square, London, W.*—2nd Mast. of Kensington Proprietary Sch; Chap. of the Kensington Workhouse. [30]

FROST, John Dixon, *Winchmore-hill, Edmonton, Middlesex.*—St. Cath. Coll. Cam. B.A. 1831, M.A. 1834, B.D. 1842; Deac. 1831 by Bp of Lon. Pr. 1832 by Abp of York. P. C. of St. Paul's, Winchmore-hill, Dio. Lon.

1843. (Patron, V. of Edmonton; P. C.'s Inc. 100*l*; Pop. 1674.) [1]

FROST, J. Loxdale, *Bowling, Bradford, Yorks.*—Magd. Coll. Cam. M.A. 1841; P. C. of St. John's, Bowling, Dio. Rip. 1842. (Patron, V. of Bradford; Tithe, App. 20*l*, Imp. 23*l* 9*s* 3½*d*; P. C.'s Inc. 180*l*; Pop. 3488.) Surrogate. [2]

FROST, Percival, 11, *Sussex-square, Brighton.*—St. John's Coll. Cam. Sen. Opt. 1st cl. Cl. Trip. and B.A. 1848, M.A. 1851; Deac. 1848 and Pr. 1849 by Bp of Win. Late Chap. of the Gr. Sch. Clapham, Surrey. Author, *Tables of Greek Accidence*, 1851; *Materials for Latin and Greek Prose*, 1852; *Thucydides Sicilian Expedition*, 1867; *Eclogæ Latinæ of Analecta Græca, &c.* [3]

FROST, Richard George, *Sproughton Cottage, Ipswich.*—Trin. Coll. Cam. B.A. 1861; Deac. 1862 and Pr. 1863 by Bp of Roch. C. of Sproughton 1866. Formerly C. of Ardleigh, Essex, 1864. [4]

FROST, Robert Myers, *High-street, Poplar, London, E.*—Pemb. Coll. Cam. B.A. 1844; Deac. and Pr. 1845. C. of Poplar. Formerly C. of Hambledon, Hants. [5]

FROST, William, *The Oaks, Thorpe, near Norwich.*—Clare Coll. Cam. B.A. 1821; Deac. 1822 and Pr. 1823 by Bp of Nor. [6]

FROST, William Mumford.—Queens' Coll. Cam. B.A. 1850; Deac. 1852 and Pr. 1853. Formerly C. of Tring, Herts. [7]

FRY, William, *Hanham, near Bristol.*—Dub. A.B. 1843; Deac. 1843 and Pr. 1844 by Bp of B. and W. P. C. of Hanham with Ch. Ch. C. Dio. G. and B. 1845. (Patron, V. of Bitton; P. C.'s Inc. 130*l* and Ho; Pop. 1271.) Formerly C. of Banwell, Somerset, 1843–45. [8]

FRY, William, M.A., *Leicester.*—Hon. Can. of Pet; Hon. Sec. to the Leicester Archidiaconal Board of Education and County National School Society. [9]

FRY, William Baker, 13, *Mecklenburgh-square, London, W.C.*—Dub. A.B. 1852; Deac. 1852 by Bp of Cork, Pr. 1853 by Bp of Meath. C. of St. Bartholomew's, Gray's inn-road, Lond. 1863. Formerly C. of Toomna 1852, Castlerea 1853. [10]

FRY, William Targett, *Grantham, Lincolnshire.*—Ex. Coll. Ox. B.A. 1864, M.A. 1867; Deac. 1865 and Pr. 1866 by Bp of Lin. C. of Grantham 1865. [11]

FRYER, Charles Gulliver, 53, *Pembridge-villas, Hyde-park, London, W.*—St. John's Coll. Cam. M.A. 1827; Deac. 1830, Pr. 1831. V. of Eltham, Kent, Dio. Lon. 1841. (Patrons, Trustees of the late Sir G. Page Turner, Bart; Tithe—Imp. 987*l* 13*s* 2*d*, V. 435*l*; Glebe, 40 acres; V.'s Inc. 550*l* and Ho; Pop. 3009.) [12]

FRYER, F. W., *St. Edward's School, Oxford.*—St. Edm. Hall, Ox. B.A. 1860, M.A. 1863; Deac. 1861 by Bp of Ches. Pr. 1862 by Bp of Lich. Head Mast. of St. Mary's Sch. Ox. 1863; C. of St. Thomas the Martyr's, Ox. Formerly C. of St. Mary's, Stafford. [13]

FRYER, Henry Edmund.—Pemb. Coll. Ox. B.A. 1826, M.A. 1829; Deac. 1826 by Bp of Ely, Pr. 1827 by Bp of Bristol. Dom. Chap. to the Duke of Richmond. Formerly R. of Battlesden, Beds, 1850–58. [14]

FRYER, William, *Medbourne, near Market Harboro'.*—Ch. Coll. Cam. B.A. 1846; Deac. 1846 and Pr. 1847 by Bp of Rip. C. of Medbourne with Holt 1866. Formerly P. C. of St. Matthew's, West Town, Dewsbury, 1848–51; P. C. of St. Paul's, Hanging Heaton, Dewsbury, 1852–55; C. of Great Creaton, Northants, 1862–66. [15]

FUGE, James, *Over Peover Parsonage, Knutsford, Cheshire.*—Magd. Hall, Ox. 3rd cl. Lit. Hum. and B.A. 1838, M.A. 1839; Deac. 1843, Pr. 1844. P. C. of Over Peover, Dio. Ches. 1852. (Patron, Sir H. Mainwaring, Bart; Glebe, 51 acres; P. C.'s Inc. 185*l* and Ho; Pop. 750.) [16]

FULCHER, Thomas, *Old Buckenham, Attleborough, Norfolk.*—Sid. Coll. Cam. B.A. 1824; Deac. 1824 and Pr. 1825 by Bp of Nor. P. C. of Old Buckenham, Dio. Nor. 1850. (Patrons, certain Feoffees; Tithe—Imp. 1522*l* 4*s* 1*d*, P. C. 16*l* 13*s* 4*d*; Glebe, 25 acres; P. C.'s Inc. 98*l*; Pop. 1214.) [17]

FULFORD, John Loveland, *Woodbury Parsonage, Exeter.*—Trin. Coll. Cam. B.A. 1837, M.A. 1843; Deac. 1837, Pr. 1838. P. C. of Woodbury, Dio. Ex. 1846. (Patrons, Vicars Choral of Ex. Cathl; Tithe, Apps. 1070*l* 14*s* 2*d*; P. C.'s Inc. 150*l* and Ho; Pop. 1550.) Author, Papers in *The Transactions of the Exeter Diocesan Architectural Society*; *A Letter to my Parishioners.* [18]

FULFORD, John Loveland Langdon, *Combe Keynes, Wareham, Dorset.*—St. Mary Hall, Ox. Dyke Scho. B.A. 1864, M.A. 1867; Deac. 1865 and Pr. 1866 by Bp of Salis. C. of Combe Keynes, 1867. Formerly C. of Symondsbury 1865–67. [19]

FULFORD, William.—C. of St. Andrew's, Kensington, W. [20]

FULLAGAR, Hugh Scales, *Packington, Coventry.*—Caius Coll. Cam. B.A. 1858, M.A. 1863; Deac. 1860 and Pr. 1862 by Bp of Ox. C. of Great and Little Packington 1863; Chap. to the Earl of Aylesford. Formerly C. of Over Winchendon, Aylesbury, etc. [21]

FULLER, Alfred, *West Itchenor, Sussex.*—St. John's Coll. Cam. Jun. Opt. B.A. 1856; Deac. 1857 and Pr. 1858 by Bp of Lich. R. of West Itchenor, Dio. Chich. 1865. (Patron, Ld Chan; R.'s Inc. 151*l*.) Formerly C. of Kirk Hallam, Derbyshire, Stoughton, Hants, etc. [22]

FULLER, Charles James, *Longworth, Faringdon.*—St. Mary Hall, Ox. B.A. 1848, M.A. 1851; Deac. 1849 and Pr. 1850 by Bp of Wor. C. of Longworth with Charney, Berks. Formerly C. of Leek Wooton, Warwick. [23]

FULLER, Ernest Adolphus, *Cirencester.*—Emman. Coll. Cam. B.A. 1853, M.A. 1857; Deac. 1853 and Pr. 1854 by Bp of G. and B. C. of Cirencester 1864. Formerly C. of Colesbourne, Cheltenham. [24]

FULLER, Harry Albert, *Walton Vicarage, Stafford.*—Dub. A.B. 1857, A.M. 1861; Deac. 1858 and Pr. 1859 by Abp of Cant. C. of Berkswick, near Stafford, 1866. Formerly C. of St. Peter's with Holy Cross, Canterbury, 1858, Woolavington with Graffham, Petworth, Sussex, 1864. [25]

FULLER, Henry, *Thornhaugh Rectory, Wansford, Northants.*—St. Alban Hall, Ox. B A. 1823; Deac. and Pr. 1827 by Bp of Chich. R. of Thornhaugh with Wansford, Dio. Pet. 1858. (Patron, Duke of Bedford; R.'s Inc. 500*l* and Ho; Pop. 423.) Formerly V. of Willington, near Bedford, 1834–58. [26]

FULLER, John, *Thurcaston Rectory, Loughborough.*—Emman. Coll. Cam. 5th Wrang. and B.A. 1846, M.A. 1849, B.D. 1856; Deac. 1849 and Pr. 1850 by Bp of Ely. R. of Thurcaston, Dio. Pet. 1864. (Patron, Emman. Coll. Cam; R.'s Inc. 760*l* and Ho; Pop. 360.) Formerly Fell. of Emman. Coll. 1848, Tut. 1850–64. [27]

FULLER, John Mee, 25, *Ebury-street, London, S.W.*—St. John's Coll. Cam. Jun. Opt. Crosse Univ. Scho. and B.A. 1856, 1st cl. Theol, Trip. 1859, Tyrwhitt's Univ. Scho. 1860, M.A. 1862; Kaye Univ. Prize 1863; Deac. 1860 and Pr 1861 by Bp of Lon. C. of St. Peter's, Pimlico, 1863. Formerly C. of Ch. Ch. Ealing, 1860–62, Grosvenor Chapel, South Audley-street, Lond. 1862–63. Author, *An Essay on the Authenticity of the Book of Daniel* (Kaye Univ. Prize), Cambridge, 1864, 6*s*. [28]

FULLER, Joseph.—Clare Hall, Cam. Sen. Opt. and B.A. 1848; Deac. 1848, Pr. 1850. Formerly C. of Newton St. Loe. [29]

FULLER, Morris J., *Prince Town, Dartmoor, Devon.*—Queens' Coll. Cam. B.A. 1855; Deac. 1856 by Bp of B. and W. Pr. 1856 by Bp of Ex. P. C. of Prince Town, Dartmoor, Dio. Ex. 1863. [30]

FULLER, Thomas, 1, *Eaton-place, Belgrave-square, London, S.W.*—St. John's Coll. Cam. 6th Wrang. and B.A. 1812, Hulsean Prizeman and M A. 1815; Deac. 1813 and Pr. 1814 by Bp of Ely. P. C. of St. Peter's, Pimlico, Dio. Lon. 1827. (Patron, Bp of Lon; P. C.'s Inc. 1000*l*; Pop. 14,328.) Late Fell. of St. John's Coll. Cam. 1812. Author, *On the Comparative Value of Miracles* *and Prophecy as Evidences of Christianity* (Hulsean Prize), 1815. [1]

FULLER, Trayton, *Chalvington Rectory, Hurst Green, Sussex.*—Brasen. Coll. Ox. B.A. 1851, M.A. 1854; Deac. 1853 and Pr. 1854 by Bp of Chich. R. of Chalvington, Dio. Chich. 1854. (Patron, Owen Fuller Meyrick, Esq; Tithe, 200*l*; Glebe, 28 acres; R.'s Inc. 190*l* and Ho; Pop. 149.) [2]

FULLERTON, Arthur, *Thriberg Rectory, Rotherham, Yorks.*—Emman, Coll. Cam. B.A. 1834; Deac. 1836 by Abp of York, Pr. 1837 by Bp of Rip. R. of Thriberg, Dio. York, 1843. (Patron, J. Fullerton, Esq; Tithe, 220*l*; Glebe, 111 acres; R.'s Inc. 380*l* and Ho, Pop. 238.) [3]

FULLERTON, Charles Garth, *Boothby Graffoe, Lincoln.*—Emman. Coll. Cam. B.A. 1860; Deac. 1861 by Bp of Down and Connor, Pr. 1862 by Bp of Meath. R. of Boothby Graffoe, Dio. Lin. 1863. (Patron, J. Fullerton, Esq; Tithe, 126*l*; Glebe, 303 acres; R.'s Inc. 626*l* and Ho; Pop. 218.) [4]

FURLONG, Charles Joseph, *Capecure, Boulogne-sur-Mer, France.*—Sid. Coll. Cam. Jun. Opt. 2nd cl. Cl. Trip. and B.A. 1824, M.A. 1843; Deac. 1828 by Bp of Salis. Pr. 1831 by Bp of B. and W. Min. of Trin. Ch. Boulogne, 1847. Formerly V. of Warfield, Berks, 1834–60. Author, *Sermons, chiefly practical,* 1836, 8*s*; *The Times of the End* (Five Sermons on the Apocalypse), 1st ed. 1848, 2nd ed. 1849, 1*s* 6*d*; *Who is the Supreme Head of the Catholic Church?* (Four Lectures), 1851, 1*s* 6*d*; *The Christian Soldier* (a Sermon preached at the H.E.I.C.'s Military Chapel of Warley Barracks), 1855, 2*d*; *Sermons, Practical and Doctrinal, preached to an English Congregation on the Continent,* 6*s*; numerous single Sermons. [5]

FURLONG, Thomas, *Bath.*—Queens' Coll. Cam. B.A. 1825, M.A. 1834; Deac. 1825 by Bp of Raphoe, Pr. 1826 by Abp of Tuam. C. of Trinity, Bath. Formerly C. of Anaduff 1825–33, Tuam Cathl. 1833–35, Delgany 1835–49, Sissinghurst, Kent, 1849–52, Ch. Ch. Tonbridge Wells, 1852–56; Chap. of Bath Penitentiary 1856. Author, *Our Little Study, or Conversations on Law of Matter, Law of Instinct, Law of Mind,* 1850, 3*s* 6*d*. [6]

FURNEAUX, Alan, *St. Germans Parsonage, Cornwall.*—Ball. Coll. Ox. B.A. 1862, M.A. 1865; Deac. 1864 and Pr. 1865 by Bp of Ex. C. of St. German's 1864. [7]

FURNEAUX, Henry, *Corpus Christi College, Oxford.*—Corpus Coll. Ox. 1st cl. Lit. Hum. and B.A. 1851, M.A. 1854; Deac. 1856 and Pr. 1857 by Bp of Ox. Fell. and Tut. of Corpus Coll. Ox. [8]

FURNEAUX, Tobias, *St. Germans Parsonage, Cornwall.*—Magd. Hall. Ox. B.A. 1824, M.A. 1832; Deac. 1823, Pr. 1824 by Bp of Ex. P. C. of St. Germans, Dio. Ex. 1827. (Patrons, D. and C. of Windsor; Tithe, App. 1649*l*; Glebe, 3 acres; P. C.'s Inc. 150*l* and Ho; Pop. 966.) Surrogate 1828. Formerly C. of Liskeard 1823–26. [9]

FURNEAUX, William Duckworth, *Berkley Rectory, Frome, Somerset*—Ex. Coll. Ox. Scho. 1835, 2nd cl. Lit. Hum. B.A. 1837, M.A. 1840; Deac. 1840 and Pr. 1841 by Abp of Cant. R. of Berkley, Dio. B. and W. 1860. (Patron, Sir Charles Mordaunt, Bart. M.P. Walton, Warwick; Tithe, comm. 340*l*; Glebe, 56 acres; R.'s Inc. 420*l* and Ho; Pop. 386.) Formerly C. of Barnes, Surrey, 1840–42; P. C. of Walton, Warwickshire, 1842–60. [10]

FURNIVAL, James, *Escot, Ottery St. Mary, Devon.*—Queens' Coll. Cam. B.A. 1822, M.A. 1826; Deac. 1823 and Pr. 1825 by Bp of Wor. P. C. of Escott, Dio. Ex. 1855. (Patron, Sir John Kennaway, Bart; Glebe, 4 acres; P. C.'s Inc. 75*l* and Ho; Pop. 534.) [11]

FURNIVAL, James, Jun., *Hamworthy, Poole, Dorset.*—Brasen. Coll. Ox. Hulmeian Exhib. B.A. 1856, M.A. 1863; Deac. 1857 and Pr. 1858 by Bp. of Salis. P. C. of Hamworthy, Dio. Salis. 1863. (Patron, Eton Coll; Tithe, 65*l*; P. C.'s Inc. 110*l*; Pop. 393.) Formerly C. of Wimborne Minster, Dorset, 1857; British Chap. at Heidelberg 1860. [12]

FURSDON, Edward, *Fursdon, Tiverton.*—Oriel Coll. Ox. 3rd cl. Lit. Hum. B.A. 1833, M.A. 1836; Deac. 1834 and Pr. 1835 by Bp of Ex. [13]

FURSDON, Walter, *Berry Narbor, Ilfracombe, Devon.*—K.S. from Eton Coll. Pemb. Coll. Ox. B.A. 1856; Deac. 1857 and Pr. 1858 by Bp of Win. R. of Berry Narbor, Dio. Ex. 1860 (Patrons, Devisees of the late G. Sydenham Fursdon, Esq. and others; Tithe, 560*l*; Glebe, 130 acres; R.'s Inc. 700*l* and Ho; Pop. 775.) Formerly C. of Chessington, near Kingston-on-Thames, 1857–60. [14]

FURSE, Charles Wellington, *Vicarage, Staines,* and *Halsdon House, Crediton, Devon.*—Ball. Coll. Ox. M.A; Deac. 1848 and Pr. 1849 by Bp of Ox. V. of Staines, Dio. Lon. 1863. (Patron, Ld Chan; V.'s Inc. 800*l* and Ho; Pop. 2749.) Formerly C. of Clewer, Berks; Lect. of St. George's Chapel, Windsor; C. of Ch. Ch. St. Pancras, Lond. Author, *Sermons,* 6*s*. [15]

FUSSELL, James George Curry, 18, *Cadogan-place, Sloane-street, London, S.W.*—Trin. Coll. Cam. Jun. Opt. 2nd cl. Cl. Trip. and B.A. 1845, M.A. 1848; Deac. 1845 by Bp of Salis. Pr. 1846 by Bp of B. and W. One of H.M. Inspectors of Schools 1852. [16]

FUSSELL, John Thomas Richardson, *Mells, near Frome, Somerset*—Trin. Coll. Cam. B.A. 1848, M.A. 1851; Deac. 1848 and Pr. 1849 by Bp of Chich. Formerly P. C. of Holy Trinity, Chantry, Somerset, 1852–58. [17]

FYFFE, Henry, *Wortley House, Worthing, Sussex.*—New Inn Hall, Ox. B.A. 1843, M.A. 1847; Deac. 1842, Pr. 1843. [18]

FYLER, James, *Woodlands, Bagshot, Surrey.*—Ball. Coll. Ox. B.A. 1842; Deac. 1843 and Pr. 1844 by Bp of Salis. R. of Windlesham with Bagshot, Dio. Win. 1861. (Patron, Ld Chan; Tithe, rent charge, 400*l* 2*s*; Glebe, 90 acres; R.'s Inc. 550*l* and Ho; Pop. 2000.) Formerly R. of Sutton Bonnington 1848–54, Siddington, Gloucestershire, 1855–61. [19]

FYLER, Samuel Arnot, *Cornhill, near Coldstream, Northumberland.*—Trin. Coll. Ox. B.A. 1825, M.A. 1839; Deac. 1827 by Bp of Dur. Pr. 1828 by Abp of York. P. C. of St. Giles's, Durham. (Patrons, Marquess and Marchioness of Londonderry; P. C.'s Inc. 180*l*; Pop. 2798.) V. of Cornhill, Dio. Dur. 1834. (Patrons, D. and C. of Dur; Tithe—App. 163*l*; Glebe, 6 acres; P. C.'s Inc. 300*l*; Pop. 853.) Formerly C. of Brompton, near Northallerton, 1831. Author, *History of Church-rates,* 1858. [20]

FYSON, Nicholas Isaac Hill, *Downham, Ely.*—Wor. Coll. Ox. B.A. 1865, M.A. 1866; Deac. 1865 and Pr. 1866 by Bp of Herf. C. of Downham 1867. Formerly C. of Cradley, Great Malvern. [21]

GABB, Baker, *Llanvihangel-ystern-Llewern, Monmouth.*—R. of Llanvihangel-ystern-Llewern, Dio. Llan. 1858. (Patron, Earl of Abergavenny; R.'s Inc. 211*l*; Pop. 183.) [22]

GABB, James, *Bulmer, New Malton, Yorks.*—Caius Coll. Cam. Wrang. B.A. 1854; Deac. 1854 and Pr. 1855 by Abp of York. R. of Bulmer, Dio. York, 1867. (Patron, Earl Fitzwilliam; Tithe, 83*l*; Glebe, 210 acres; R.'s Inc. 395*l* and Ho; Pop. 1077.) Dom. Chap. to the Earl of Carlisle at Castle Howard 1855. Formerly C. of Barton-le-Street 1854, Bulmer 1864. Author, *Steps to the Throne, or Meditations and Prayers in Verse,* Nisbet and Co. cloth, 2*s* 6*d*. [23]

GABB, James Frederic Secretan, *Charlton Kings Parsonage, near Cheltenham.*—Jesus Coll. Ox. B.A. 1831, M.A. 1833; Deac. 1832, Pr. 1833. P. C. of Charlton Kings, Dio. G. and B. 1834. (Patron, Jesus Coll. Ox; Tithe—Imp. 771*l* 8*s* 5*d*; P. C.'s Inc. 180*l* and Ho; Pop. 3443.) [24]

GABRIEL, Edward, *St. George's Parsonage, Kendal, Westmoreland.*—Corpus Coll. Cam. B.A. 1852; Deac. 1852, Pr. 1853 by Bp of Wor. P. C. of St. George's, Kendal, Dio. Carl. 1856. (Patron, V. of Kendal; Glebe, 70 acres; P. C.'s Inc. 216*l* and Ho; Pop. 3500)

Chap. of Kendal House of Correction; Surrogate. Formerly C. of St. George's, Kendal, Ch. Ch. Birmingham, 1852, St. James's, Liverpool, 1854. [1]

GABRIEL, John Bath, *All Saints' Rectory, Birmingham.*—St. Edm. Hall, Ox. Hon. 4th cl. Lit. Hum. B.A. 1840, M.A. 1843; Deac. 1840 and Pr. 1841 by Bp of G. and B. R. of All Saints', Birmingham, Dio. Wor. 1856. (Patrons, Trustees; R.'s Inc. 450*l* and Ho; Pop. 11,469.) Formerly V. of Chepstow 1845–56. [2]

GACE, F. A., M.A., *Barling, Ingatestone, Essex.*—V. of Barling, Dio. Roch. 1863. (Patrons, D. and C. of St. Paul's; Tithe—Imp. 350*l*, V. 176*l*; Glebe, 27 acres; V.'s Inc. 236*l*; Pop. 354.) [3]

GADSBY, Caventry Cawpian John, *South Shoebury, Essex.*—Caius Coll. Cam. Math. Trip. B.A. 1863, M.A. 1866; Deac. 1866 by Bp of Roch. C. of Great Wakering 1866. [4]

GAINSFORD, George, *Woodside, Hitchin, Herts.*—Pemb. Coll. Ox. B A. 1851, M.A. 1854; Deac. 1852 by Bp of Wor. Pr. 1854 by Bp of Roch. P. C. of Holy Saviour's, Hitchin, Dio. Roch. 1865. (Patron, Rev. G. Gainsford; Pop. 1200.) Formerly C. of Hitchin, 1852, Walmer, Kent, 1854; V. of Rostherne, Cheshire, 1858–62. [5]

GAISFORD, George, *Tangmere, Chichester.*—Ch. Ch. Ox; formerly Stud. B.A. 1849, M.A. 1852; Deac. 1850 by Bp of Ox. Pr. 1851 by Bp of Lon. R. of Tangmere, Dio. Chich. 1858. (Patron, Duke of Richmond; Tithe, 278*l*; Glebe, 18 acres; R.'s Inc. 312*l* and Ho; Pop. 201.) Formerly P. C. of Wigginton, Herts, 1854–58. [6]

GAISFORD, Stephen Henry, *Clifford, Tadcaster, Yorks.*—Dub. Heb. Prize 1833; A.B. 1839, A.M. 1846; Deac. 1844 and Pr. 1845 by Abp of York. P. C. of Clifford, Dio. York, 1861. (Patron, G. Lane Fox, Esq; Tithe, 27*l*; P. C.'s Inc. 105*l* and Ho; Pop. 1030.) Formerly C. of Saxton 1844, South Milford 1846, Bramham 1849, Gayton 1852, Kirk Deighton 1853, Clifford 1861. [7]

GAISFORD, T. A., *Abingdon, Berks.*—C. of Abingdon. [8]

GAITSKELL, Isaac, *Whitworth, Rochdale.*—Trin. Coll. Cam. Sen. Opt. and B.A. 1825, M.A. 1837; Deac. 1825 by Bp of Lin. Pr. 1830 by Bp of Ches. V. of Whitworth, Dio. Man. 1842. (Patrons, Trustees; Glebe, 190 acres; P. C.'s Inc. 310*l*; Pop. 8324.) [9]

GAITSKELL, John, M.A., 1, *Church-street, Kensington, London, W.* [10]

GALAHER, George Fitzgerald, *St. Mark's, Horselydown, Southwark, S.E.*—Dub. A.B. 1839; Deac. 1839 and Pr. 1840 by Abp of Cant. P. C. of St. Mark's, Horselydown, Southwark, Dio. Win. 1845. (Patrons, the Crown and Bp of Win. alt; P. C.'s Inc. 100*l*; Pop. 2336.) Formerly C. of Weaverham, Ches; P. C. of Compstall Bridge, near Stockport; P. C. of St. Paul's, Jersey; Sec. to Lond. Irish Soc. Author, *Simple Sermons, after the Fashion of the Reformers*; *Popery the Tyrant of the Human Race*; *The Origin and History of Auricular Confession*, 1850, etc. [11]

GALBRAITH, J., *Stockport, Cheshire.*—C. of St. Mary's, Stockport. [12]

GALE, Henry, *Treborough Rectory, Taunton, Somerset.*—Trin. Hall, Cam. 1st cl. Civil Law, B.C.L. 1836; Deac. 1850 by Abp of Cant. Pr. 1851 by Bp of Wor. R. of Treborough, Dio. B. and W. 1857. (Patron, Sir Walter C. Trevelyan, Bart; Glebe, 28 acres; R.'s Inc. 160*l* and Ho; Pop. 183.) Formerly P. C. of Nether Ham, Somerset, 1855–57. Author, *Religion, Rights, and Revenue, by the Shade of Sir Robert Peel*; *Apostolic Temperance* (a Reply to Dr. Cumming). [13]

GALE, Isaac Sadler, *Clifton, Bristol.*—Wad. Coll. Ox. 3rd cl. Lit. Hum. and B.A. 1848, M.A. 1851; Deac. 1849, Pr. 1850. R. of St. John the Baptist, Bristol, Dio. G. and B. 1855. (Patrons, Trustees; R.'s Inc. 229*l*; Pop. 960.) Formerly C. of Harrow on-the Hill. [14]

GALE, James *Urswick, Ulverstone.*—V. of Urswick, Dio. Carl. 1861. (Patrons, the Landowners; Tithe, 200*l*; Glebe, 10 acres; V.'s Inc. 240*l* and Ho; Pop. 808.) [15]

GALE, John Henry, *Milton Lilbourne, Pewsey, Wilts.*—Wad. Coll. Ox. B.A. 1843. V. of Milton Lilbourne, Dio. Salis. 1846. (Tithe—Imp. 744*l*, V. 139*l* 10*s*; V.'s Inc. 140*l*; Pop. 697.) [16]

GALE, J. A. E., *Tinwell, Stamford.*—C. of Tinwell. [17]

GALE, Knight, *St. Andrew's Parsonage, Bradford, Yorks.*—King's Coll. Lond; Deac. 1850, Pr. 1851. P. C. of St. Andrew's, Horton, Bradford, Dio. Rip. 1853. (Patrons, Simeon's Trustees; P. C.'s Inc. 235*l* and Ho) [18]

GALE, W. B., *Willersey, Chipping Campden, Gloucestershire.*—R. of Willersey, Dio Glouc. 1863. (Patron, Rev. J. H. Worgan; R.'s Inc. 162*l* and Ho; Pop. 373.) Formerly C. of Great Snoring, Norfolk. [19]

GALE, W. H., *Horrington, Wells, Somerset.*—C. of Horrington. [20]

GALE, William Wilkins, *Forscote, near Bath.*—C. of Forscote. [21]

GALINDO, Philemon Alfred, *Bradshaw, Bolton, Lancashire.*—Dub. A.B. 1838; Deac. 1839 and Pr. 1840 by Bp of Ches. P. C. of Bradshaw, Dio. Man. 1844. (Patron, V. of Bolton-le-Moors; P. C.'s Inc. 160*l*; Pop. 1968.) [22]

GALL, Francis Herbert, *Cottesbrooke, Northampton.*—Trin. Coll. Cam. B.A. 1846, M.A. 1849; Deac. 1846 and Pr. 1847 by Bp of Roch. C. of Cottesbrooke 1860. Formerly C. of Rushden, Herts, 1846–59; R. of Letchworth, Herts, 1853–59; C. of Wallington, Herts, 1859–60. [23]

GALL, Samuel, 2, *Idol lane, Great Tower-street, London, E.C.*—Queens' Coll. Cam. B.A. 1838, M.A. 1852; Deac. and Pr. 1843 by Bp of Lon. Classical Mast. of Christ's Hospital Lond. 1846; Lecturer of St. Dunstan's-in-the-East, Lond. 1858. [24]

GALLACHER, William Robert, 14, *Clough-street, Bury, Lancashire.*—St. Bees; Deac. 1864 and Pr. 1865 by Bp of Carl. C. of St. Paul's, Bury. Formerly C. of Christ Ch. Whitehaven, 1864, St. Michael's, Manchester, 1866. [25]

GALLAHER, Alexander, *Blackburn.*—Dub. A.B. 1859, A.M. 1862; Deac. 1859 and Pr. 1860 by Bp of Man. C. in sole charge of St. Luke's, Blackburn, 1861. Formerly C. of Oswaldtwistle 1859–61. [26]

GALLAND, Basil A., *Bream, near Lydney, Gloucestershire.*—Lin. Coll. Ox. B.A. 1865; Deac. 1866 by Bp of G. and B. C. of Bream 1866. [27]

GALLICHAN, James.—St. John's Coll. Cam. Jun. Opt. and B.A. 1832; Deac. 1834, Pr. 1835. [28]

GALLOWAY, James, *Spaxton, Bridgwater, Somerset.*—Ex. Coll. Ox. B.A. 1821, M.A. 1824; Deac. and Pr. 1826. R of Spaxton, Dio. B. and W. 1846. (Patron, the present R; Tithe, 663*l*; Glebe, 66 acres; R.'s Inc. 750*l* and Ho; Pop. 1057.) [29]

GALLOWAY, William Brown, 21, *St. Mark's-crescent, Regent's-park, London, N.W.*—P. C. of St. Mark's, Albert-road, Regent's-park, Dio. Lon. 1849. (Patrons, D. and C. of St. Paul's; P. C.'s Inc. 350*l*; Pop. 6986.) [30]

GALLWEY, Thomas Gifford, *Leicester.*—St. John's Coll. Cam. B.A. 1836, M.A. 1850; Deac. 1837 and Pr. 1838 by Bp of Lin. Formerly Chap. R.N; C. of Wigton Magna, Leicestershire, and St. Andrew's, Leicester. [31]

GALTON, John Lincoln, *Colleton-crescent, Exeter.*—St. Edm. Hall, Ox. B.A. 1831, M.A. 1834; Deac. 1831 by Bp of Lich. Pr. 1833 by Bp of Lin. P. C. of St. Sidwell's, Exeter, Dio. Ex. 1851. (Patron, V. of Heavitree; Tithe, App. 65*l*; P. C. 18*l* 6*s* 3*d*, and 47*l* 10*s* 4*d* from Qu. A. Bounty; 33*l* from Eccl. Commis; P. C.'s Inc. 300*l*; Pop. 6278.) Chap. to the Earl of Roden 1832. Author, *Notes of Lectures on Song of Solomon*, 1859; and on *Book of Revelation*, 1859. [32]

GAMAN, John, *Boughton, Cheshire.*—St. Cath. Hall, Cam. B.A. 1838; Deac. 1838, Pr. 1839. P. C. of St. Paul's, Chester, Dio. Ches. 1842. (Patron, V. of

St. John's, Chester; P. C.'s Inc. 80*l* and Interest of 800*l* in lieu of Ho; Pop. 3002.) [1]

GAMBIER, Charles Gore Gambier.—St. John's Coll. Ox. B.A. 1845; Deac. 1847, Pr. 1848. [2]

GAMBLE, Henry, *Clifton Parsonage, near Ashbourne, Derbyshire.*—Ex. Coll. Ox. 2nd cl. Lit. Hum. and B.A. 1815; Deac. 1816 by Bp of Ches. Pr. 1817 by Bp of Ex. P. C. of Clifton, Dio. Lich. 1846. (Patron, V. of Ashbourne; Tithe, App. 12*l*, Eccles. Commis. 156*l*; P. C.'s Inc. 85*l* and Ho; Pop. 503.) Div. Lect. of Ashbourne. [3]

GAMLEN, Charles, *The Firs, Shareshill, Wolverhampton.*—Wad. Coll. Ox. B.A. 1866; Deac. 1867 by Bp of Ches. C. of St. Peter's, Wolverhampton, 1867. [4]

GAMMAGE, James, *Belbroughton, Stourbridge, Worcestershire.*—St. Bees; Deac. 1857, and Pr. 1858 by Bp of Ches; C. of Belbroughton 1866. Formerly C. of St. Mary's, Newton, Hyde, 1857-58; British Columbia, S.P.G. 1858-64; C. of St. Paul's, Bury, Lanc. 1864-66. [5]

GAMMELL, James Stewart, *Outwood, Wakefield.*—Jesus Coll. Cam. 1st. Sen. Opt. B.A. 1851, M.A. 1854; Deac. 1852 and Pr. 1853 by Bp of St. A. P. C. of Outwood, Dio. Rip. 1860. (Patron, P. C. of Stanley; P. C.'s Inc. 96*l* and Ho; Pop. 2385.) Formerly Stip. C. of Dolvor, Montgomery, 1852, St. Paul's, Hammersmith, 1857, St. Paul's, Vauxhall, 1858. [6]

GAMSON, Robert, *Normanton-on-Trent, Newark, Notts.*—St. Cath. Hall, Cam. B.A. 1832, M.A. 1835; Deac. 1833 and Pr. 1834 by Bp of Lin. V. of Normanton-on-Trent, Dio. Lin. (Patron, the present V; Glebe, 85 acres; V.'s Inc. 185*l*; Pop. 462.) [7]

GANDELL, Robert, *Holywell Lodge, Oxford.*—Queen's Coll. Ox. Michel Scho. 2nd cl. Lit. Hum. and B.A. 1843, Kennicott Scho. 1844, Pusey and Ellerton Scho. 1845, M.A. 1846; Deac. 1846 and Pr. 1847 by Bp of Ox. City Lect. at St. Martin's Carfax, Oxford, 1856; Chap. of Corpus Coll. Ox. 1853. Formerly Fell. of Queen's Coll. Ox. 1845; Asst. Tut. of Magdalen Hall, Ox. 1848; Select Preacher 1859; Grinfield Lect. on the Septuagint 1859; Senior Proctor 1860-61; and Laudian Prof. of Arabic 1861. Author, *The Prophecy of Joel, in Hebrew, poetically arranged*; *Jehovah Goalenu* (a Sermon), *The Greater Glory of the Second Temple* (a Sermon); and Editor of *Lightfoot's Horæ Hebraicæ et Talmudicæ*, 4 vols. Univ. Press. 1859. [8]

GANDY, James Hunter, *Stanwick, Higham Ferrers, Northants.*—Trin. Coll. Cam. B.A. 1848, M.A. 1853; Deac. 1848 and Pr. 1850 by Bp of B. and W. R. of Stanwick, Dio. Pet. 1862. (Patron, Ld Chan; Glebe, 32 acres; R.'s Inc. 410*l* and Ho; Pop. 669.) Formerly P. C. of Upton 1858; V. of Old Cleeve, Somerset, 1851-58. [9]

GANE, Brisco Morland, *Noke, near Oxford.*—Magd. Hall, Ox. B.A. 1840; Deac. 1841 and Pr. 1842 by Bp of Ex. R. of Noke, Dio. Ox. 1864. (Patron, Duke of Marlborough; Tithe, 60*l*; Glebe, 29 acres; R.'s Inc. 100*l* and Ho; Pop. 116.) Formerly C. of Ottery St. Mary 1841, Honiton 1841, Felstead 1856, Stanford-le-Hope 1860; Chap. of Orsett Union 1863. [10]

GANTILLON, Peter John Francis, *Cheltenham.*—St. John's Coll. Cam. 2nd cl. Lit. Hum. and B.A. 1851, M.A. 1854; Deac. 1856 and Pr. 1857 by Bp of Pet. Cl. Mast. in Cheltenham Coll. Formerly C. of St. John's, Leicester; 2nd Mast. of the Coll. Sch. Leicester. [11]

GAPE, Charles, *Sibsey Vicarage, Boston, Lincolnshire.*—V. of Sibsey, Dio. Lin. 1827. (Patron, Ld Chan; V.'s Inc. 315*l* and Ho; Pop. 1297.) V. of Willoughton, near Kirton-in-Lindsey, Dio. Lin. 1837. (Patrons, King's Coll. Cam. and the Earl of Scarborough alt; V.'s Inc. 195*l*; Pop. 620.) [12]

GAPE, Charles, *Rushall Vicarage, Scole, Norfolk.*—Corpus Coll. Cam. B.A. 1859, M.A. 1862; Deac. 1860 and Pr. 1861 by Bp of Ches. V. of Rushall, Dio. Nor. 1866. (Patron, Rev. William Tattersall; Tithe—Imp. 300*l* and 69 acres of Glebe; Glebe, 8½ acres; V.'s Inc. 143*l* and Ho; Pop. 242.) Formerly C. of Waterloo, Liverpool, 1860, St. Michael's, Toxteth Park, 1861, Ashby, with Oby, and Thirne, Norfolk, 1862-64, and West Somerton, near Great Yarmouth, 1864-66. [13]

GARBETT, Edward, *Surbiton, Kingston-on-Thames.*—Brasen. Coll. Ox. 2nd cl. Lit. Hum. and B.A. 1841, M.A. 1844; Deac. 1841, Pr. 1842. P. C. of Ch. Ch. Surbiton, Dio. Win. 1863. (Patron, W. H. Stone, Esq; Pop. 1400.) Formerly P. C. of St. Bartholomew's, Gray's-inn-road, Lond. 1850; Min. of the Episcopal Chapel, Gray's-inn-road, Lond. 1854. Author, *The Soul's Life*, 1852; *Sermons for Children*, 1854; etc. [14]

GARBETT, The Ven. James, *Clayton, near Hurstpierpoint, Sussex.*—Brasen. Coll. Ox. 1st cl. Lit. Hum. and B.A. 1822, M.A. 1825; Deac. 1827, Pr. 1828. R. of Clayton with Keymer C. Dio. Chich. 1835. (Patron, Brasen. Coll. Ox; Clayton, Tithe—Imp. 39*l* 2*s*, R. 400*l*; Glebe, 23½ acres; Keymer, Tithe—Imp. 261*l* 6*s* 3*d*, R. 340*l*; Glebe, 14 acres; R.'s Inc. 780*l*; Pop. Clayton 863, Keymer 1612.) Archd. of Chich. 1851 (Value, 200*l*.) Formerly Michel Fell. of Queen's Coll Ox; Fell. of Brasen. Coll; Public Examiner 1829; Bampton Lect. 1842; Prof. of Poetry 1842-52; Preb. of Bracklesham in Chich. Cathl. 1843 Author, various Sermons, Pamphlets, and Latin Lectures. [15]

GARDE, John Fry, *Kirkpatrick, Isle of Man.*—Dub. A.B. 1850, A.M. 1853; Deac. 1842, Pr. 1844. V. of Kirk Patrick, Dio. S. and M. (Patron, Bp of S. and M. V.'s Inc. 180*l* and Ho; Pop. 2778.) Formerly Chap. of St. John's, Kirk German 1845. [16]

GARDE, Richard, *Harrold Vicarage, Beds.*—Dub. A.B. 1837; Deac. 1838 by Bp of Lin. Pr. 1839 by Bp of Pet. V. of Harrold, Dio. Ely, 1845. (Patroness, Countess Cowper; V.'s Inc. 200*l* and Ho; Pop. 1119.) [17]

GARDEN, Francis, 67, *Victoria-street, Westminster*, and *Oxford and Cambridge Club, Pall-Mall, London, S. W.*—Trin. Coll. Cam. Hulsean Prizeman 1832, B.A. 1833, M.A. 1836; Deac. and Pr. 1836. Sub-Dean of H.M. Chapels Royal, Lond. 1859; Prof. of Theology and Moral Philosophy, Queen's Coll. Lond. and C. of St. Stephen's, Westminster. Formerly Jun. Incumb. of St. Paul's Episcopal Chapel, Edinburgh; Asst. to the English Chap. at Rome 1851-52. Author, *Hulsean Prize Essay for* 1832-33; *Nature and Benefits of Holy Baptism*; *Letter to Lord Bishop of Cashel*, 1846; *Vindication of Scottish Episcopate*, 1847; *Discourses on Heavenly Knowledge and Heavenly Love*, 1848; *Lectures on the Beatitudes*, 1853; *Four Sermons* (preached at Rome), 1854. [18]

GARDINER, Alexander, *Eccles New Road, Manchester.*—Dub. A.B. 1844, M.A. 1850; Deac. 1847 and Pr. 1848 by Bp of Rip. C. of the Salford Union 1849. Formerly C. of Dewsbury and Hartshead, Yorks, 1845-46. Author, *An Ode to the Queen*, 1837. [19]

GARDINER, E. J., B.A., *Buckingham.*—Sen. C. of Buckingham. Formerly C. of St. Mary's, Taunton. [20]

GARDINER, Frederick Augustus, *Chatham.*—Dub. and Ox. B.A. 1858, M.A. 1865; Deac. 1858 and Pr. 1860 by Bp of Rip. Asst. Chap. of Chatham Prison, 1867. Formerly C. of Lydgate (sole charge) and C. of St. John's, Wakefield (sole charge), 1862-67. Author, *Sermon on the Marriage of their Royal Highnesses the Prince and Princess of Wales*, Hicks and Allen, Wakefield, 1*s*. [21]

GARDINER, Gainsborough, *Warndon, Worcester.*—C. of Warndon. [22]

GARDINER, George Edward, *The Vicarage, Farnham, Surrey.*—Brasen. Coll. Ox. B.A. 1864, M.A. 1867; Deac. 1866 by Bp of Win. C. of Farnham 1866. [23]

GARDINER, George Gregory, *Paris.*—Ex. Coll. Ox. B.A. 1827, M.A. 1830; Deac. 1829 and Pr. 1831 by Bp of B. and W. British Chap. at Paris. Formerly Chap. to the British residents in Bonn; Min. of the Octagon Chapel, Bath. [24]

GARDINER, Robert, 17, *Goodham-hill, Burnley.*—Dub. A.B. 1865; Deac. 1866 by Bp of Man. C. of St. James's, Burnley, 1866. [25]

GARDINER, R. E., *Roche, St. Austell, Cornwall.*—R. of Roche, Dio. Ex. 1863. (Patrons, Trustees of the late J. Thornton, Esq. and J. Rashleigh, Esq; Tithe, 474*l* 14*s* 3*d*; Glebe, 34½ acres; R.'s Inc. 600*l* and Ho; Pop. 1882.) [1]

GARDINER, R. G. W., *Axminster, Devon.*—C. of Axminster. [2]

GARDNER, Herbert, *Bottisham Lode Parsonage, near Cambridge.*—Corpus Coll. Cam. B.A. 1861, M.A. 1865; Deac. 1861 and Pr. 1862 by Bp of Ely. P. C. of St. James's, Bottisham Lode, and Long Meadow, Dio. Ely, 1867. (Patron, Trin. Coll. Cam; P. C.'s Inc. 70*l* and Ho; Pop. 750.) Formerly C. of Caddington, Beds, 1861–62, Lutterworth 1863–66, and Chipping Campden 1866–67. [3]

GARDNER, Hilton, *Stanley, West Derby, Liverpool.*—Caius Coll. Cam. B.A. 1859; Deac. 1860 by Bp of Ches. C. of Stanley. Formerly C. of St. Paul's, Warrington, 1860. [4]

GARDNER, James Cardwell, *Bunbury, near Tarporley, Cheshire.*—Emman. Coll. Cam. B.A. 1857; M.A. 1860; Deac. 1859 and Pr. 1864 by Bp of Ches. Asst. C. of Hollingfare 1859–60, Walton-le-Dale 1861–4, Bunbury 1864. [5]

GARDNER, John, *Skelton Rectory, Redcar, Yorks.*—Trin. Coll. Cam. LL.B. 1847, LL.D. 1853; Deac. 1854 and Pr. 1855 by Abp of York. R. of Skelton with Brotton, Dio. York, 1857. (Patron, Abp of York; R.'s Inc. 450*l* and Ho; Pop. Skelton 1457, Brotton 509.) Formerly C. of Etton, near Beverley, Yorks. [6]

GARDNER, John Ludford, *Tunstall, Stoke-on-Trent.*—St. Bees and Wor. Coll. Ox; Deac. 1857 and Pr. 1858 by Bp of Pet. Sen. C. of Tunstall 1864. Formerly C. of Rotherhithe 1859–61, Halliwell 1861–4; Chap. to 23rd Surrey Rifle Volunteers. [7]

GARDNER, Richard, 10, *St. Michael's-terrace, Stoke Damerel, Devonport.*—St. Edm. Hall, Ox. B.A. 1835, M.A. 1841: Deac. 1835 and Pr. 1836 by Bp of Lin. Min. of the Chapel of Ease of St. Michael's, Stoke Damerel, Dio. Ex. 1845. (Patron, R. of Stoke Damerel; Inc. uncertain, wholly derived from pew rents.) [8]

GARDNER, Samuel Wright, *The Lodge, near Usk, Monmouthshire.*—Deac. 1837, Pr. 1838. R. of Llanvihangel Gobion, Dio. Llan. 1866. (Patron, Sir Samuel Fludyer, Bart; Tithe, Imp. 82*l* 12*s*; Glebe, 40*l*; R.'s Inc. 122*l* 12*s*; Pop. 190.) Formerly P. C. of Trostrey, 1843, Kemeys-Commander, Usk, 1857. [9]

GARDNER, Thomas, *St. Anne's, Stanley Parsonage, West Derby, Liverpool.*—Queens' Coll. Cam. B.A. 1831, M.A. 1842; Deac. 1831, Pr. 1832. P. C. of St. Anne's, Stanley, Dio. Ches. 1831. (Patron, the present P. C; P. C.'s Inc. 150*l* and Ho.) Surrogate 1844. [10]

GARDNER, Thomas Woodward, *Dorton, Thame, Bucks.*—Ch. Ch. Ox. B.A. 1822; Deac. 1823 and Pr. 1825 by Bp of Lin. P. C. of Ashendon with Dorton P. C. Dio. Ox. 1845. (Patron, Ch. Ch. Ox; Tithe, Ashendon, App. 300*l* 17*s* 9*d*; Glebe, 97 acres; Tithe, Dorton, App. 330*l*; Glebe, 45 acres; P. C.'s Inc. 180*l*; Pop. Ashendon 325, Dorton 137.) [11]

GARDNER, Tobias Edward, *Leamington.*—St. John's Coll. Ox. B.A. 1859; Deac. 1860 by Bp of Win. Asst. Min. of Trinity Chapel, Leamington. Formerly C. of St. Matthew's, Brixton, 1860. [12]

GARDNER, Townley, 115, *Queen's-road, Bayswater, W.*—Dur. B.A. 1861; Deac. and Pr. 1862 by Bp of Lich. C. of St. Matthew's, Bayswater, 1866. Formerly C. of Ilkestone, Derbyshire, 1862, St. Michael's, Islington, 1864. [13]

GARDNER, William, *Coalville Parsonage, Leicestershire.*—Deac. 1842 and Pr. 1843, by Bp of Pet. P. C. of Ch. Ch. Coalville, Dio. Pet. 1848. (Patron, Rev. Thomas Webb Minton; P. C.'s Inc. 186*l* and Ho; Pop. 2000.) [14]

GARDNER, William, *Orpington, Kent.*—V. of Orpington with St. Mary-Cray, Dio. Cant. 1866. (Patron, Abp of Cant; R.'s Inc. 372*l*; Pop. 3130.) [15]

GARFIT, Arthur, *Richmond, Surrey.*—Trin. Coll. Cam. B.A. 1847, M.A. 1850; Deac. 1847 and Pr. 1848 by Bp of Lich. C. of Richmond 1852. Formerly C. of St. Mary's, Lichfield, 1847, Yarmouth 1850. Author, *The Education Question*, 1862, 4*s*; *The Ecclesiastical Commission*, 1864, 1*s*; etc. [16]

GARFIT, Edward, *Harlaxton Rectory, near Grantham.*—St. John's Coll. Cam. B.A. 1835, M.A. 1854; Deac. 1835 and Pr. 1836 by Bp of Lin. R. of Harlaxton, Dio. Lin. 1867. (Patron, Bp of Lin; R.'s Inc. 598*l* and Ho; Pop. 488.) P. C. of North Carlton, Linc. Dio. Lin. 1847. (Patrons, J. B. and S. Slater, Esqrs; Tithe—App. 410*l*, Imp. 2*l*; P. C.'s Inc. 76*l*; Pop. 163.) Rural Dean of Lawress 1855. Author, single Sermons. [17]

GARFIT, Mark, *Coningsby Rectory, Boston.*—Trin. Coll. Cam. B.A. 1837; Deac. and Pr. 1838 by Bp of Lin. R. of Coningsby, Dio. Lin. 1863. (Patron, Lord Aveland; R.'s Inc. 661*l* and Ho; Pop. 1938.) Formerly R. of Stretton 1842. [18]

GARLAND, Arthur George, *Southgate-street, Winchester.*—St. Peter's Coll. Cam. B.A. 1850, M.A. 1854; Deac. 1854, Pr. 1855. C. of Ch. Ch. Winchester. Formerly C. of St. Michael's, Winchester. [19]

GARLAND, George Vallis, *The Rectory, Langton Matravers, Wareham, Dorset.*—Trin. Coll. Cam. B.A. 1847, M.A. 1852; Deac. 1850 and Pr. 1851 by Bp of Lin. R. of Langton Matravers, Dio. Salis. 1852. (Patron, J. Bingley Garland, Esq; Tithe, 385*l*; Glebe, 18 acres; R.'s Inc. 400*l* and Ho; Pop. 735.) Formerly C. of Crowle, Linc. 1850–52. Author, *Plain Possible Solutions of the Objections of the Right Rev. J. W. Colenso, Bishop of Natal*, 1863. [20]

GARLAND, John, *Mordiford Rectory, Herefordshire.*—St. John's Coll. Cam. 3rd cl. Cl. Trip. and B.A. 1851, M.A. 1854; Deac. 1851 by Abp of York, Pr. 1852 by Bp of Wor. R. of Mordiford, Dio. Herf. 1855. (Patroness, Lady Emily Foley; Tithe, 310*l*; Glebe, 13¾ acres; R.'s Inc. 360*l* and Ho; Pop. 691.) Formerly C. of the Abbey Church, Great Malvern. [21]

GARLAND, John Nibbs, *Shipham, Somerset.*—Deac. 1833, Pr. 1834. R. of Shipham, Dio. B. and W. 1865. (Patrons, D. and C. of Wells; R.'s Inc. 148*l* and Ho; Pop. 520.) Formerly C. of St. John's, Weston. [22]

GARLAND, Nathaniel Arthur, *Parsonage House, Lower Tulse-hill, Brixton, London, S.*—Ch. Ch. Ox. B.A. 1838, M.A. 1856; Deac. 1840 by Bp of Herf. Pr. 1843 by Bp of Chich. P. C. of St. Matthew's, Brixton, Dio. Win. 1855. (Patron, Abp of Cant; P. C.'s Inc. 750*l* and Ho; Pop. 10,305.) Formerly V. of Sibertswold and Colsbred 1851–53; R. of Deal, Kent, 1853–55. Author, *A Visitation Sermon.* [23]

GARLAND, Richard, *Sunderland*—Corpus Coll. Cam. 1st cl. S.C.L. 1852; Deac. 1853, Pr. 1854. C. of St. John's, Sunderland. Formerly C. of King's-hill, Wednesbury, and St. John's, Darlington. [24]

GARLAND, Thomas Bloom, *Barningham Rectory, Barnard Castle.*—Magd. Coll. Cam. B.A. 1859, M.A. 1862; Deac. 1859 by Bp of Wor. Pr. 1860 by Bp of Lon. C. in sole charge of Barningham 1867. Formerly C. of Netherton, Dudley, 1859–62, Tettenhall, Wolverhampton, 1863–66. [25]

GARLAND, Trevor Lorance, *Little Eaton, Derby.*—St. John's Coll. Cam. 14th Jun. Opt. B.A. 1843, M.A. 1846: Deac. 1855 and Pr. 1856 by Bp of Lich. C. of Little Eaton 1855. [26]

GARNET, Henry Eli, *Friarmere, Rochdale.*—V. of Friarmere, Dio. Man. 1864. (Patron, V. of Rochdale; V.'s Inc. 300*l*; Pop. 2229.) Formerly C. of Rochdale. [27]

GARNETT, Thomas, *Bank House, Barbon, Kirkby Lonsdale, Westmoreland.*—Fell. of Dur. Univ. 1839; Deac. 1840, Pr. 1841. [28]

GARNIER, The Very Rev. Thomas, *The Deanery, Winchester.*—All Souls' Coll. Ox. B.C.L. 1800, D.C.L. 1850. Dean of Win. 1840. (Dean's Inc. 1515*l* and Res.) R. of Bishopstoke Dio. Win. 1807. (Patron, Bp of Win; Tithe, 617*l* 10*s*; Glebe, 21 acres; R.'s Inc. 645*l* and Ho; Pop. 1890.) [29]

GARNON, William, *Rawtenstall, Manchester.*—St. Bees. Deac. 1867 by Bp of Man. C. of Rawtenstall 1867. [30]

GARNSEY, Henry Edward Fowler, *Ledsham, Yorks.*—Magd. Coll. Ox. 4th cl. Lit. Hum. and B.A. 1848. Gloucestershire Fell. of Magd. Coll. Ox. [1]

GARRARD, Castell, *Wickham Skeith, Stonham, Suffolk.*—Corpus Coll. Cam. B.A. 1842, M.A. 1846; Deac. 1843, Pr. 1844. V. of Wickham Skeith, Dio. Nor. 1844. (Patron, the present V; Tithe—Imp. 422*l* 5*s*, V. 129*l* 10*s*; Glebe, 9¾ acres; V.'s Inc. 143*l*; Pop. 564.) [2]

GARRARD, Charles James, *Ryde, Isle of Wight.*—Queens' Coll. Cam. B.A. 1849, M.A. 1852; Deac. 1848, Pr. 1849. P. C. of St. John's, Oakfield, Ryde, Dio. Win. 1855. (Patron, P. C. of St. Helens; P. C.'s Inc. 100*l*; Pop. 1547.) [3]

GARRARD, Samuel, *Salford Priors, Warwickshire*—V. of Salford Priors, Dio. Wor. 1860. (Patron, Rev. S. Garrard; V.'s Inc. 111*l*; Pop. 858.) [4]

GARRARD, Thomas, *St. John's College, Oxford.*—St. John's Coll. Ox. B.A. 1840, M A. 1844, B.D. Fell. of St. John's Coll. Ox. [5]

GARRATT, Charles Foster, *Little Tew Parsonage, Enstone, Oxon.*—Oriel. Coll. Ox. B.A. 1856, M.A. 1857; Deac. 1855 and Pr. 1856 by Abp of York. P. C. of Little Tew, Dio. Ox. 1858. (Patron, Bp of Ox; Glebe, 28 acres; P. C.'s Inc. 106*l* and Ho; Pop. 275.) Formerly C. of Ledsham-cum-Fairburn, Yorks. [6]

GARRATT, Samuel, *Ipswich.*—Trin. Coll. Cam. B.A. 1839; Deac. 1840, Pr. 1841. P. C. of St. Margaret's, Ipswich, Dio. Nor. 1867. (Patrons, Simeon's Trustees; P. C.'s Inc. 300*l* and Ho; Pop. 8108.) Formerly P. C. of Trinity, Lincoln's-inn-fields, Lond. 1850–67. Author, *Dawn of Life*, 3*s* 6*d*; *Scripture Symbolism*, 3*s* 6*d*; *Children of God*, 4*d*; *Missionary's Grave, England's Sin, and God's Warning*, 6*d*; *Our Father, or Jesus Teaching to Pray*, 2*s* 6*d*; *The Irish in London*, 4*d*. [7]

GARRATT, Sudlow, *Merifield, Torpoint, Cornwall.*—Oriel Coll. Ox. B.A. 1848; Deac. 1849 and Pr. 1850 by Bp of Lich. C. of Antony. [8]

GARRATT, William.—Trin. Coll. Cam. Coll. Prizeman, B.A. 1838, M.A. 1842; Deac. 1839 by Bp of Lich. Pr. 1840 by Bp of G. and B. Formerly P. C. of St. John's, Fulham, 1845. [9]

GARRATT, W. F. Henry, *Pennington, near Lymington.*—Trin. Coll. Cam. B.A. 1864; Deac. 1867 by Bp of Win. C. of Pennington 1867. [10]

GARRETT, Frank.—Wor. Coll. Ox. B.A. 1858; Deac. 1860 by Bp of St. D. Formerly Asst. C. of St. David's, Carmarthen, 1860; 2nd Mast. of Carmarthen Gr. Sch; Hon. Chap. to the 2nd Carmarthenshire Rifle Volunteers. [11]

GARRETT, Henry Godden.—New Coll. Ox. S.C.L. 1853; Deac. 1854 and Pr. 1855 by Bp of Llan. Formerly C. of St. Mary's, Cardiff, and Roath, Glamorgan. [12]

GARRETT, Henry Webb, *Kingsbury, Tamworth.*—St. Cath. Hall, Cam. B.A. 1848, M.A. 1855; Deac. 1849 and Pr. 1850 by Bp of Man. C. of All Saints', Birmingham, 1867. Formerly C. of the Priory Church, Christchurch, Hants; C. of Kingsbury. [13]

GARRETT, John, *Moss Side, Manchester.*—Dub. A.M; Deac. 1845 by Bp of Tuam, Pr. 1846 by Abp of York. R. of Moss Side, Dio. Man. 1864. (Patron, R. Gardner, Esq; R.'s Inc. 600*l*; Pop. 6114.) Formerly C. of St. Mark's, Hull, St. Mary's, Beverley, Wheatley, Oxon; Chap. and Mast. of Strood's Charity at Egham; R. of Biscathorpe, Linc; V. of St. Paul, Cornwall; Commissary to the Bp of Columbia (3 years); Hon. Sec. in Eng. to the West Connaught Church Endow. Fund. Author, *Address on Education to the Archdeacon of the East Riding*, 1849; Several Reports on the Columbia Mission; *Good News from Ireland*, 1*s* 6*d*. [14]

GARRETT, J. F., *Elton, Matlock, Derbyshire.*—R. of Elton, Dio. Lich. 1836. (Patrons, The Inhabitants; R.'s Inc. 105*l* and Ho; Pop. 491.) C. of Stanton and Rowtor, Dio. Lich. [15]

GARRETT, Thomas, *Carlton-crescent, Southampton.*—Queen's Coll. Ox. B.A. 1831; Deac. 1831 and Pr. 1832 by Bp of B. and W. C. of Holy Rhood, Southampton, 1867. Formerly V. of East Pennard with West Bradley 1839–45, Martock with Long Load 1845–59; C. of Wellington, Somerset, 1831–37, Weston-super-Mare 1837–38, Abbey Church, Bath, 1838–39. [16]

GARRETT, William Thomas.—Dub. A.B. 1842, A.M. 1854; Deac. 1848 and Pr. 1849 by Bp of Rip. Formerly C. of East Witton. [17]

GARRETT, W. W., B.A.—Chap. and Naval Instructor of H.M.S. "Valorous." [18]

GARRICK, James Percy, 35, *Devonshire-street, Portland-place, London, W.*—Caius Coll. Cam. 9th Wrang. and B.A. 1858; Deac. 1858 by Bp of Ely. C. of St. Marylebone, Lond. 1858; Fell. of Caius Coll. Cam. [19]

GARROD, Henry John, *Royal Infirmary, Liverpool.*—Dub. A.B. 1854; Deac. 1849 and Pr. 1850 by Bp of Pet. Chap. of the Liverpool Royal Infirmary. Formerly C. of Trinity Church, Liverpool. [20]

GARROULD, W. J., B.A., *Halesworth, Suffolk.*—Asst. C. of Halesworth with Chediston. [21]

GARROW, Edward William, *Dowdswell, near Cheltenham.*—Brasen. Coll. Ox. B.A. 1837, M.A. 1841; Deac. 1837, Pr. 1840. P. C. of Compton-Abdale, Glouc. Dio. G. and B. 1847. (Patrons, D. and C. of Bristol; Tithe, App. 406*l* 10*s*; P. C.'s Inc. 79*l*; Pop. 258.) [22]

GARRY, Nicholas Thomas, *St. Mark's Parsonage, Lakenham, Norwich.*—Queen's Coll. Ox. 3rd cl. Lit. Hum, B.A. 1852, M.A. 1856; Deac. 1854 and Pr. 1855 by Bp of Nor. P. C. of St. Mark's, Lakenham, Dio. Nor. 1861. (Patrons, D. and C. of Nor; P. C.'s Inc. 200*l* and Ho; Pop. 3808.) Formerly C. of Great Yarmouth 1854–57, St. Michael's, Handsworth (sole charge), 1857–60, St. Mary's, Aylesbury, 1860–61. Author, Visitation Sermon preached at Long Stratton, 1866, *Jerusalem Destroyed and yet Triumphant*, 6*d*, Rivingtons. [23]

GARTON, George John, *Alfriston, Lewes, Sussex.*—St. Cath. Coll. Cam. Starne Scho. B.A. 1848; Deac. 1843 by Bp of Ely, Pr. 1844 by Bp of Lich. C. of Alfriston. Formerly C. of Market-Stainton, Linc. and Kirkheaton, Yorks. Author, various Sermons. [24]

GARVEN, Edward Dakin, *Runcorn, Cheshire.*—Brasen. Coll. Ox. B.A. 1858; Deac. 1859 and Pr. 1860 by Bp of Ches. Chap. to the Earl of Ellesmere's Floating Chapel, Runcorn, 1860. Formerly C. of Runcorn 1859–60. [25]

GARVEY, Charles, *Manthorpe Parsonage, Grantham, Lincolnshire.*—Ex. Coll. Ox. B.A. 1845, M.A. 1848; Deac. 1845 and Pr. 1847 by Bp of Lin. P. C. of Manthorpe with Londonthorpe P. C. Dio. Lin. 1851. (Patron, Earl Brownlow; P. C.'s Inc. 200*l* and Ho; Pop. Manthorpe 206, Londonthorpe 228.) [26]

GARVEY, Edward, 36, *Park Parade, Ashton-under-Lyne.*—St. Bees; Deac 1861 and Pr. 1862 by Bp of Ches. C. of Ashton-under-Lyne 1865. Formerly C. of St. Thomas's, Hyde, near Manchester, 1861. [27]

GARVEY, James, *Ashby Rectory, Great Grimsby.*—Ch. Coll. Cam. B.A. 1840, M.A. 1843; Deac. 1843 by Bp of Lich. Pr. 1844 by Bp of Herf. R. of Ashby with Fenby, Dio. Lin. 1850. (Patron, Ld Chan; Tithe—App. 5*l* 16*s* 6*d*, R. 300*l*; Glebe, 44 acres; R.'s Inc. 375*l* and Ho; Pop. 274.) R. of Brigsley, Dio. Lin. 1856. (Patron, Coll. Ch. Southwell; R.'s Inc. 60*l*; Pop. 152.) [28]

GARVEY, Richard, *Snelland, Wragby, Lincolnshire.*—Emman. Coll. Cam. B.A. 1835, M.A. 1838; Deac. 1835 by Bp of Lin. Pr. 1838 by Bp of Rip. R. of Snelland, Dio. Lin. 1861. (Patron, Hon. C. H. Cust; Tithe, 258*l*; Glebe, 43 acres; R.'s Inc. 301*l*; Pop. 1387.) C. of Stainton by Langworth, Linc. Formerly R. of Saltfleetby St. Clements, 1848. [29]

GARWOOD, John, 88, *Red Lion-square, London, W.C.*—Magd. Hall, Ox. B.A. 1831, M.A. 1834; Deac. 1831 and Pr. 1832 by Bp of Lin. Clerical Sec. to the Lond. City Mission 1837. Formerly P. C. of St. Mary, Spital-square, Lond. 1832–46. Author, *The Million-peopled City*, 4*s* 6*d*. [30]

GARWOOD, Octavius Appleby, *Willingham-by-Stow, Lincolnshire.*—Wor. Coll. Ox. B.A. 1866. C. of Willingham-by-Stow and Coates 1861. [31]

GARWOOD, William, *4, Sea-view, Burlington Quay, Yorks.*—Wor. Coll. Ox. B.A. 1858, M.A. 1860; Deac. 1859 and Pr. 1860 by Abp of York. Formerly C. of Cottingham 1859–61. [1]

GASCOIGN, T. H., *Spondon House, near Derby.*—Formerly P. C. of Grange, Keswick, 1862–64. [2]

GASCOYNE, Richard, *Bath.*—Deac. 1825, Pr. 1826. Formerly C. of Mickleton, Worc. Author, *The Jews of Old*, 1852, 1s; *The Ten-horned Beast of Daniel and St. John*, 6d; *A New Solution of the Revelation of St. John*, 2nd ed. 5s. [3]

GASELEE, John, *Little Yeldham, Halstead, Essex.*—St. John's Coll. Ox. B.A. 1828, M.A. 1831; Deac. 1828, Pr. 1829. R. of Little Yeldham, Dio. Roch. 1837. (Patron, Ld Chan; Tithe, 276*l*; Glebe, 2 acres; R's Inc. 280*l* and Ho; Pop. 307.) Rural Dean 1846. [4]

GASKARTH, Isaac, *Lowick Hall, Ulverstone, Lancashire.*—St. Bees 1830; Deac. 1831 and Pr. 1832 by Bp of Ches. P. C. of Lowick, Ulverstone, Dio. Carl. 1846. (Patrons, Mrs. Gaskarth, Miss Everard, and John Montagu, Esq; Tithe, 18*l*; Glebe, 16 acres; P. C.'s Inc. 115*l* and Ho; Pop. 574.) Formerly C. of Ireleth 1831, Greystoke 1833, Brindle 1837; P. C. of Haverthwaite 1839. [5]

GASKELL, Thomas Kynaston, *Buckingham.*—C. of Buckingham. [6]

GASKILL, John, *Spennymoor, Ferryhill, Durham.*—Deac. by Bp of Ex. Pr. by Bp of Dur. C. of Whitworth with Spennymoor. Formerly C. of Ringmore, Devon. [7]

GASTER, Thomas Joseph, *St. John's School Church, Blenheim-grove, Peckham, S.E.*—Ch. Miss. Coll. Islington; Deac. 1856 by Bp of Lon. Pr. 1857 by Bp of Calcutta. Miss. C. of St. John's Sch. Church, Peckham. Formerly Ch. Miss. 1856–62; C. of St. Giles's, Camberwell, and Sen. C. of Clapham. [8]

GATENBY, Andrew, *Winston Vicarage, Stoneham, Suffolk.*—St. John's Coll. Cam. B.A. 1824. V. of Winston, Dio. Nor. 1857. (Patrons, D. and C. of Ely; V.'s Inc. 180*l* and Ho; Pop. 352.) Formerly C. of Littleport, near Ely. [9]

GATHERCOLE, Michael Augustus, *Chatteris Vicarage, Cambs.*—Literate; Deac. 1832 by Bp of Lich. Pr. 1833 by Abp of York. V. of Chatteris, Dio. Ely, 1845. (Patron, W. Hawkins, Esq; Tithe, Imp. 42*l* 10*s*; V.'s Inc. 1420*l* and Ho; Pop. 4731.) Formerly C. of Burnsall, Yorks, 1833–36, Cleasby, Yorks, 1836–39. Author, *Letters to a Dissenting Minister*, 5 eds. 4*s* 6*d*. Editor of *The Church Magazine*, 6 vols. 1839-44. [10]

GATRILL, James Matcham, *Horbury Parsonage, Wakefield.*—Deac. 1860 and Pr. 1861 by Bp of Rip. C. of Horbury Bridge Miss. Chapel, 1867. Formerly C. of Whitechapel, Cleckheaton, 1860, St. Peter's, Bradford, 1862, St. Barnabas, Leeds, 1865. [11]

GATTEY, Joseph, *Harpford Vicarage, Ottery St. Mary, Devon.*—Sid. Coll. Cam. B.A. 1827, M.A. 1830; Deac. 1828, Pr. 1829. V. of Harpford with Ven Ottery R. Dio. Ex. 1852. (Patrons, Lord Clinton and others; Harpford, Tithe, Imp. 130*l*, V. 133*l*; Glebe, 8 acres; Ven Ottery, Tithe, 116*l*; Glebe, 16 acres; V.'s Inc. 249*l* and Ho; Pop. Harpford 243, Ven Ottery 101.) [12]

GATTY, Alfred, *Ecclesfield Vicarage, Sheffield.*—Ex. Coll. Ox. B.A. 1836, M.A. 1839, B.D. and D.D. 1860; Deac. 1837 and Pr. 1838 by Bp of Rip. V. of Ecclesfield, Dio. York, 1839. (Patron, Duke of Norfolk; V.'s Inc. 600*l* and Ho; Pop. 4825.) Sub-Dean of York Cathl; Rural Dean. Formerly C. of Bellerby, Yorks 1837–39. Author, *Sermons*, 1846, 2nd ed. 1847, 8*s*; *Sermons*, 2nd Series, 8*s*, 1848; *The Bell, its Origin, History and Uses*, 2nd ed. 1848, 3*s*; *The Vicar and his Duties*, 1853, 2*s* 6*d*; *Twenty Plain Sermons*, 1858, 5*s*; *Baptism Misunderstood*, and other Pamphlets. Co-Editor of Dr. Wolff's *Travels and Adventures*, and Joint-Author of *Old Folks from Home*. Editor of a new and enlarged edition of Hunter's Hallamshire. [13]

GATTY, Robert Henry.—Trin. Coll. Ox. B.A. 1850, M.A. 1853; Deac. 1851 and Pr. 1852 by Bp of Nor. Formerly C. of Clapton 1859, Abbot's Kerswell, Devon. [14]

GAULT, Archibald, *The Cottage, Cushendall, co. Antrim, Ireland.*—Dub. A.B. 1852; Deac. 1853; Pr. 1854. Missionary of the Irish Ch. Mission Soc. Formerly C. of Trinity, Pilgwenlly, Newport, Monmouthshire. [15]

GAUNTLETT, John George, *Northampton-terrace, Swansea.*—Wor. Coll. Ox. 3rd cl. Math. et Phy. and Lit. Hum. B.A. 1856, M.A. 1858; Deac. 1857 and Pr. 1858 by Bp of St. D. C. of Trinity, and Prin. of Collegiate Sch. Swansea, 1867. [16]

GAUSSEN, James Charles, *Lyons, France.*—British Chap. at Lyons. [17]

GAUSSEN, John Ash.—Dub. A.B. 1847, A.M. 1850; Deac. and Pr. 1848 by Abp of York. R. of Waltham, Dio. Lin. 1865. (Patron, Southwell Coll. Sch; R.'s Inc. 331*l* and Ho; Pop. 856.) Formerly V. of Rolleston, Notts. [18]

GAWN, John Douglas, *Chew Magna, Somerset.*—Dub. A.B. 1859; Deac. 1862 and Pr. 1863 by Bp of Salis. C. of Chew Magna. [19]

GAWNE, R. Murray, *Coxley, Somerset.*—C. of Coxley. [20]

GAWTHROP, Thomas, *Todwick, Rotherham, Yorks.*—Dub. A.B. 1841; Deac. 1841 by Bp of Lich. Pr. 1843 by Bp of Herf. C. of Todwick. Formerly C. of Kilham, Yorks. [21]

GAY, Alfred, *Guildford.*—Trin. Coll. Cam. B.A. 1858; Deac. 1859 and Pr. 1860 by Abp of Cant. C. of St. Nicholas', Guildford. Formerly C. of Ch. Ch. Folkestone, 1859. [22]

GAY, William, M.A., *Penn, Wolverhampton.*—C. of St. Philip's, Penn. [23]

GAYE, Charles Hicks, *St. Matthew's Rectory, Ipswich.*—St. John's Coll. Cam. 8th Sen. Opt. and B.A. 1825, M.A. 1830; Deac. 1829, Pr. 1830 by Bp of Pet. R. of St. Matthew's, Ipswich, Dio. Nor. 1847. (Patron, Ld Chan; Tithe, Imp. 80*l*; R.'s Inc. 302*l* and Ho; Pop 7000.) Surrogate. Author, single Sermons. [24]

GAYER, H. W., *Cucklington, Somerset.*—C. of Cucklington. [25]

GAZE, John Pellew, *Brooke, Newport, Isle of Wight.*—R. of Brooke, Dio. Win. 1859. (Patroness, Mrs. Gaze; R.'s Inc. 250*l*; Pop. 156.) C. of Mottistone, Isle of Wight. Formerly C. of Brooke. [26]

GAZELEY, Robert Court, *Wayford, Crewkerne, Somerset.*—Ch. Coll. Cam. B.A. 1837, M.A. 1840; Deac. 1837, Pr. 1838. R. of Wayford, Dio. B. and W. 1857. (Patron, J. Alexander, Esq; R.'s Inc. 160*l*; Pop. 191.) [27]

GEAKE, E. H. A., *Willington, near Newcastle-on-Tyne.*—Dub. A.B. 1856; Deac. 1857 and Pr. 1858 by Bp of Ches. R. of Willington, Dio. Dur. 1859. (Patrons, the Crown and Bp of Dur. alt; Tithe, 197*l* 9*s* 2*d*; R.'s Inc. 220*l*; Pop. 795.) [28]

GEARY, Henry, *Herne Bay, Kent.*—Corpus Coll. Cam. B.A. 1861, M.A 1864; 3rd cl. Cl. Scho. of Corpus Coll; Deac. 1861 and Pr. 1862 by Bp of Lon. P. C. of Ch. Ch. Herne Bay, Dio. Cant. 1864. (Patrons, Exors. of late Rev. H. Geary; P. C.'s Inc. 350*l* and Ho; Pop. 1650.) Formerly C. of All Saints', Dalston, 1862, St. James's, Piccadilly, 1863. [29]

GEDDES, Alexander, *Barkstone, Grantham.*—St. Peter's Coll. Cam. 24th Sen. Opt. Scho. and Prizeman, B.A. 1850, M.A. 1854; Deac. 1854 and Pr. 1856 by Bp of Lin. C. of Barkstone. Formerly C. of Ownby, and Ropsley [30]

GEDGE, Augustus, *Ludborough Rectory, Louth, Lincolnshire.*—Ch. Coll. Cam. B.A. 1851; Deac. 1852, Pr. 1853. R. of Ludborough, Dio. Lin. 1854. (Patron, Richard Thorold, Esq; Tithe, 2*l* 2*s*; Glebe, 380 acres; R.'s Inc. 580*l*; Pop. 401.) [31]

GEDGE, Henry Erskine, *Barrowden, near Stamford, Lincolnshire.*—Caius Coll. Cam. B.A. 1856, M.A. 1864; 1st cl. Theo. Trip. 1857; Deac. and Pr. 1857 by Bp of Lich. C. of Barrowden 1867. Formerly C. of Brewood, Staffs, 1857–60, Blatherwycke, Northants, 1864; Afternoon Lect. Melton Mowbray, 1866–7. [32]

GEDGE, John Wycliffe, 354, *Gray's-inn-road, W.C.*—Trin. Coll. Cam. B.A. 1859; Deac. 1859 and Pr. 1860 by Bp of Lon. Chap. of the Home and Colonial Training Coll. Gray's-inn-road, Lond. 1865; C. of St. Lawrence Jewry, 1867. Formerly C. of Trinity, Cheltenham 1859; Prin. of Otaki Training Coll. New Zealand 1860–62; Chap. of Refuge for Destitute, Dalston, 1862–65; Even. Lect. St. Mary, Hornsey Rise, N. 1865–7; C. of St. Jude's, Gray's-inn-road, 1865–7. [1]

GEDGE, Johnson Hall, 4, *North Park-road, Harrogate.*—Trin. Coll. Cam. Scho. of, 1852, Bell Univ. Scho. 1851, 18th Wrang. 1853; Deac. 1854 and Pr. 1855 by Bp of Lich. Assoc. Sec. Ch. Miss. Soc. for Yorkshire, 1864. Formerly C. of Holbrooke, Derby, 1855–7, Wimbledon 1857–9, St. Michael's, Chester-square, Pimlico, 1861–3. Author of *Sermons preached at Wimbledon*, 1860. [2]

GEDGE, Joseph, *Bildeston, Ipswich.*—Jesus Coll. Cam. 8th Sen. Opt. and 1st Math. Prizeman, B.A. 1820, M.A. 1823; Deac. and Pr. 1823 by Bp of G. and B. R. of Bildeston, Dio. Ely, 1849. (Patron, the present R; Tithe, 430*l*; Glebe, 50 acres; R.'s Inc. 500*l* and Ho; Pop. 788.) [3]

GEDGE, Sydney, *All Saints' Vicarage, Northampton.*—St. Cath. Hall, Cam. 14th Wrang. 7th in 1st cl. Cl. Trip. and B.A. 1824, M.A. 1827; Deac. 1826 by Bp of Nor. Pr. 1826 by Bp of Ely. V. of All Saints', Northampton, Dio. Pet. 1859. (Patron, Lord Overstone; Tithe, comm. 100*l*; Glebe, 2½ acres; V.'s Inc. 200*l* and Ho; Pop. 6400.) Formerly Fell. of St. Cath. Coll. Cam. 1825–27; 2nd Mast of King Edward's Sch. Birmingham, 1835–59. [4]

GEDGE, William Wilberforce.—Caius Coll. Cam. 2nd cl. Cl. Trip. B.A. 1857; Deac. 1858 and Pr. 1859 by Bp of Wor. Head Mast. of the Juvenile Prop. Sch. Cheltenham. Formerly Mast. of King Edward's Sch. Birmingham. [5]

GEE, Richard, *Abbots-Langley Vicarage, Watford, Herts.*—Wad. Coll. Ox. 3rd cl. Lit. Hum. and B.A. 1840, M.A. 1844; Deac. 1840 and Pr. 1841 by Bp of Lon. V. of Abbots-Langley, Dio. Roch. 1844. (Patron, W. Jones Loyd, Esq; Tithe, Imp. 856*l* 17*s* 6*d*; V. 315*l*; Glebe, 7 acres; V.'s Inc. 315*l* and Ho; Pop. 2000.) Rural Dean; Hor. Can. of Roch. Author, *Visitation Sermons*, 1845 and 1848; Architectural Papers, &c. [6]

GEE, William, *East Coker Vicarage, Yeovil.*—St. John's Coll. Cam. Jun Opt. 3rd cl. Cl. Trip. and B.A. 1849; Deac. 1850 and Pr. 1851 by Bp of Ex. V. of East Coker, Dio. B. and W. 1864. (Patrons, D. and C. of Ex; Tithe, 267*l*; Glebe, 7 acres; V.'s Inc. 279*l* and Ho; Pop. 1186.) Formerly C. of Marldon, Devon; Priest-V. of Ex. Cathl. 1852–64; R. of St. Martin's, Exeter, 1854–64. [7]

GEER, Henry Isaac, *Cotham, Redcar.*—King's Coll. Lond. Theol. Assoc; Deac. 1864 by Abp of York. C. of Ch. Ch. Cotham, 1864. [8]

GEGG, Joseph, *Wandsworth-common, Surrey.*—Literate; Deac. 1845 and Pr. 1847 by Bp of Jamaica. Asst. Chap. to the House of Correction, Wandsworth-common, 1857 (Stipend, 210*l*). Formerly Chap. to H.M. troops in Honduras 1847–55; C. of Old Weston, Hunts, 1855–57. [9]

GELDART, George Cooke.—St. Peter's Coll. Cam. B.A. 1843; Deac. 1843 and Pr. 1844 by Bp of Nor. [10]

GELDART, Henry, *Hellingly Vicarage, Hurst Green, Sussex.*—Clare Coll. Cam. B.A. 1854, M.A. 1861; Deac. 1854 and Pr. 1856 by Bp of Pet. V. of Hellingly, Dio. Chich. 1866. (Patrons, Trustees of the Warneford Lunatic Asylum; Tithe, 670*l*; Glebe, 7½ acres; V.'s Inc. 425*l* and Ho; Pop. 1606.) Formerly C. of Little Billing, Northants, St. Mary-in-the-Castle, Hastings, and St. Jude's, Chelsea. [11]

GELDART, James, *Podington Vicarage, Wellingborough.*—Trin. Hall. Cam. Jun. Opt. B.A. 1846, M.A. 1849; Deac. 1847 and Pr. 1848 by Bp of Pet. V. of Podington, Dio. Ely, 1854. (Patron, R. L. Orlebar, Esq; Hinwick House; Glebe, 150 acres; V.'s Inc. 200*l* and Ho; Pop. 643.) Formerly C. of Little Billing, Northants, 1847, Shepton Mallet, Somerset, 1848–54. [12]

GELDART, James William, *The Rectory, Kirk-Deighton, Wetherby, Yorks.*—LL.B. 1806, LL.D. 1814; Deac. and Pr. 1809 by Bp of Ely. R. of Kirk-Deighton, Dio. Rip. 1840. (Patron, the present R; Tithe, 758*l*; Glebe, 76 acres; R.'s Inc. 901*l* and Ho; Pop. 485.) Formerly Fell. of St. Cath. Hall; Reg. Prof. of Civil Law in Univ. Cam. 1814–47; Fell. and Tut. of Trin. Hall. Cam. 1809–20. Editor of Bp Halifax's *Analysis of the Civil Law*, 1836, Maxwell. [13]

GELDART, James William, *Kirk-Deighton, Wetherby, Yorks.*—Trin. Hall, Cam. LL.B. 1859, LL.M. 1863; Deac. 1860 and Pr. 1861 by Bp. of Ox. C. of Kirk-Deighton 1862. Formerly C. of Wheatley 1860. [14]

GELDART, Richard John, *The Rectory, Little Billing, Northampton.*—St. Cath. Coll. Cam. late Fell. Jun. Opt. B.A. 1809, M.A. 1812, D.D. 1842; Deac. 1809 and Pr. 1810 by Abp of York. R. of Little Billing, Dio. Pet. 1817. (Patron, Earl Brownlow; Tithe, 349*l*; Glebe, 8 acres; R.'s Inc. 420*l* and Ho; Pop. 76.) [15]

GELDART, Richard William, *Clyst St. Lawrence Rectory, Cullompton, Devon.*—Clare Hall, Cam. Jun. Opt. and B.A. 1844; Deac. 1845, Pr. 1849 by Bp of Pet. R. of Clyst St. Lawrence, Dio. Ex. 1866. (Patron, Rev. D. Geldart; Tithe, 270*l*; Glebe, 47½ acres; R.'s Inc. 299*l* and Ho; Pop. 160.) Formerly C. of Longney and Elmore, Glouc. [16]

GELL, Francis, *Shaftesbury, Dorset.*—R. of Trinity, Shaftesbury with St. Peter's R. Dio. Salis. (Patron, Earl of Shaftesbury; R.'s Inc. 100*l* and Ho; Pop. 2029.) Formerly Chap. in India. [17]

GELL, John Philip, 1, *Lansdowne-crescent, Kensington-park, London, W.*—Trin. Coll. Cam. B.A. and M.A. 1839; Deac. 1843 and Pr. 1844 by Bp of Tasmania. P.C. of St. John's, Notting-hill 1854. (Patron, Bp of Lon; Net Val. 430*l*; Pop. 6000.) Formerly Chap. to the Bp of Tasmania 1844; Warden of Ch. Coll. Tasmania, 1846–48. [18]

GELL, Philip, *Friar Gate, Derby.*—Trin. Coll. Cam. B.A. 1805, M.A. 1808; Deac. 1806 and Pr. 1807 by Bp of Lich. Formerly Min. of St. John's, Derby, 1829; Asst. Lect. of All Saints, Derby, 1850; Rural Dean 1837. Author, *Observations on the Hebrew Idiom*, 1821; *An Essay on Spiritual Baptism and Communion*, 1847; *Essay on Sacramental Baptism*, 1864; *The Revelation Historically and Critically Interpreted.* [19]

GELL, Robert, *Kirk Ireton, Wirksworth, Derbyshire.*—Queens' Coll. Cam. B.A. 1817, M.A. 1820; Deac. and Pr. 1817 by Bp of Glouc. R. of Kirk Ireton, Dio. Lich. 1854. (Patron, Bp of Lich; Tithe, 286*l* 11*s* 1*d*; Glebe, 70 acres; R.'s Inc. 409*l* and Ho; Pop. 515.) [20]

GEM, Arthur, *Foleshill Vicarage, Coventry.*—V. of Foleshill, Dio. Wor. 1853. (Patron, Ld Chan; Tithe—Imp. 75*l*, V. 353*l* 14*s*; Glebe, 37 acres; V.'s Inc. 390*l* and Ho; Pop. 4909.) [21]

GEM, C. H., *Dudley, Worcestershire.*—C. of Dudley. [22]

GEM, S. Harvey, *Malvern Wells, Worcestershire.*—C. of Malvern Wells. [23]

GENT, Robert Abraham, *South Molton, Devon.*—St. Bees 1851; Deac. 1851 and Pr. 1852 by Bp of Man. C. of South Molton 1866. Formerly C. of St. Paul's, Prince's-park, Liverpool. [24]

GEOGHEGAN, Edward, *Bardsea, near Ulverstone.*—Dub. A.B. 1842, A.M. 1845; Deac. 1851 and Pr. 1852 by Bp of Ches. P. C. of Bardsea, Dio. Carl. 1865. (Patrons, G. Swainson, and J. Hockin, Esqs; P. C.'s Inc. 140*l*; Pop. 272.) Formerly C. of Nantwich 1851–65. [25]

GEORGE, David John, *Trelough, Wormbridge, near Hereford.*—Jesus Coll. Ox. 3rd cl. Lit. Hum. and B.A. 1829, M.A. 1832; Deac. 1830 and Pr. 1831 by Bp of Ox. R. of the United Benefices of Wormbridge D. 1834 with St. Devereux R. 1837, Dio. Herf. (Patron, Rev. Archer Clive; Wormbridge, Tithe, Imp. 100*l*; St. Devereux, Tithe, 166*l*; Glebe, 58 acres; R.'s Inc. 291*l* and Ho; Pop. Wormbridge 91, St. Devereux 242.) [26]

GEORGE, James, *The Vicarage, Sutton Maddock, Salop.*—St. Bees; Deac. 1860, Pr. 1861. C. of Sutton Maddock 1863. Formerly C. of Marston Montgomery, 1860–63. [1]

GEORGE, John, *Deeping St. James, Market Deeping, Lincolnshire.*—Emman. Coll. Cam. B.A. 1840, M.A. 1843; Deac. 1840 and Pr. 1841 by Bp of Lin. V. of Deeping St. James, Dio. Lin. 1841. (Patron, Sir Thomas Whichcote, Bart; Glebe, 75 acres; V.'s Inc. 170*l* and Ho; Pop. 1763.) [2]

GEORGE, John, *Aberpergwm, Neath, Glamorgan.*—Lampeter; Deac. 1855 and Pr. 1856 by Bp of Llan. P. C. of Aberpergwm, Dio. Llan. 1862. (Patron, Rees Williams, Esq; P. C.'s Inc. 119*l* and Ho; Pop. 2000.) Formerly C. of Glyncorrwg 1857. [3]

GEORGE, John Picton, *Maes-y-velin, Bridell, Cardigan.*—Deac. 1814, Pr. 1815. R. of Bridell, Dio. St. D. 1833. (Patrons, Freeholders of Parish; Tithe, 180*l*; R.'s Inc. 180*l*; Pop. 326.) P. C. of Abbey-cwm-hir, Dio. St. D. 1818. (Patron, F. Phillips, Esq; P. C.'s Inc. 61*l*; Pop. 537.) Formerly C. (temporarily) of Whitechurch, Pembrokeshire. [4]

GEORGE, Philip Edward, *Combe Hay Rectory, Bath.*—Trin. Coll. Ox. B.A. 1850, M.A. 1852; Deac. 1851 by Bp of Ex. Pr. 1852 by Bp of G. and B. R. of Combe Hay, Dio. B. and W. 1857. (Patron, S. Butler, Esq; Tithe, 257*l*; Glebe, 40 acres; R.'s Inc. 307*l* and Ho; Pop. 258.) Formerly C. of Abbenhall 1851–53, Puttenham 1854–56, Westbury, Wilts, 1856–57. [5]

GEPP, Edward Francis, *High Easter Vicarage, Chelmsford.*—Wad. Coll. Ox. B.A. 1841, M.A. 1848; Deac. 1846 by Bp of Ely, Pr. 1846 by Bp of Roch. V. of High Easter with Good Easter, Dio. Roch. 1849. (Patrons, D. and C. of St. Paul's; Tithe, High Easter, 177*l*, Good Easter, 120*l*; Glebe, High Easter, 1½ acres, Good Easter, 1½ acres; V.'s Inc. 350*l* and Ho; Pop. High Easter 947, Good Easter 539.) Chap. to High Sheriff of Essex 1859. Formerly C. of Rainham 1846, and Upminster, Essex, 1847–49. [6]

GEPP, George Edward, *Ashbourne Grammar School, Derbyshire.*—Wad. Coll. Ox. 2nd cl. Lit. Hum. and B.A. 1830, M.A. 1833; Deac. 1832 by Bp of Roch. Pr. 1833 by Bp of Ox. Head Mast. of Ashbourne Gr. Sch. 1836. Formerly Asst. Mast. of Harrow Sch. 1832–36. [7]

GEPP, Henry John, *Broughton Banbury.*—New Coll. Ox. B.A. 1857, M.A. 1860; Deac. 1860 by Bp of Ox. Fell. of New Coll. Ox. C. of Broughton, Banbury. [8]

GERMON, Nicholas, *The Elms, Greenheys, Manchester.*—Oriel Coll. Ox. 2nd cl. Lit. Hum. and B.A. 1821, M.A. 1825; Deac. 1822 and Pr. 1823 by Bp of Ches. R. of St. Peter's, City and Dio. Man. 1825. (Patrons, twenty-one trustees; R.'s Inc. 240*l*; Pop. 2904.) Surrogate. Formerly Head Master of Manchester Sch. [9]

GERMON, Nicholas, *Broomfield Parsonage, Bridgwater, Somerset.*—Oriel Coll. Ox. B.A. 1838, M.A. 1845; Deac. 1840 and Pr. 1841 by Bp of Lon. P. C. of Broomfield, Dio. B. and W. 1858. (Patron, J. Hamilton, Esq; P. C.'s Inc. 100*l* and Ho; Pop. 500.) Formerly C. of Bishops-Hull, Somerset. [10]

GERMON, Nicholas Medland, *Newchurch-in-Pendle, Burnley.*—Brasen. Coll. Ox. Hulme Exhib. B.A. 1850, M.A. 1853; Deac. 1853 and Pr. 1854 by Bp of Lin. P. C. of Newchurch-in-Pendle, Dio. Man. 1865. (Patrons, Hulme trustees; P. C.'s Inc. 192*l*; Pop. 1300.) Formerly C. of Kirk Smeaton; and Mast. of the Lower Sch. Manchester. Author, Sermons, &c. [11]

GERTY, H. L., *Worcester.*—C. of St. Martin's, Worcester. [12]

GERY, Hugh Wade, *Bolnhurst Rectory, St. Neots, Beds.*—Emman. Coll. Cam. B.A. 1819, M.A. 1821; Deac. 1821, Pr. 1822. R. of Bolnhurst, Dio. Ely, 1828. (Patron, — Harvey, Esq; Tithe—Imp. 65*l* 3*s*, R. 101*l* 16*s*; Glebe, 108 acres; R.'s Inc. 204*l* and Ho; Pop. 348.) [13]

GERY, Robert Wade, *Colmworth Rectory, St. Neots, Beds.*—Emman. Coll. Cam. B.A. 1824, M.A. 1827; Deac. 1825, Pr. 1826. R. of Colmworth, Dio. Ely, 1830. (Patron, the present R; Glebe, 423 acres; R.'s Inc. 358*l* and Ho; Pop. 523.) [14]

GIBBENS, Frederick.—Chap. of H.M.S. "Arethusa." [15]

GIBBENS, William, *Chignal-Smealy, Essex.*—Corpus Coll. Cam; Deac. 1847 and Pr. 1848 by Bp of Lich. R. of Chignal-Smealy, Dio. Roch. 1864. (Patron, Major Spitty; R.'s Inc. 120*l*; Pop. 70.) Formerly C. of Bridestow and Sourton, Devon. [16]

GIBBES, Heneage, *Sidmouth, Devon.*—Downing Coll. Cam. M.B. 1826, M.L. 1829. P. C. of All Saints', Sidmouth, Dio. Ex. (Patrons, Sir J. Kennaway and others.) [17]

GIBBON, Charles Iliffe, *Lutton Rectory, Oundle, Northants.*—Dub. A.B. 1841, Sen. Mod. and Gold Medallist 1841, Bp Law's Math. Prizeman 1842, A.M. 1846; Deac. 1846, Pr. 1848. R. of Lutton with Washingley, Dio. Pet. 1854. (Patron, Earl Fitzwilliam; Lutton, Tithe, 220*l* 2*s*; Glebe, 30 acres; Washingley, Tithe, 6*l* 13*s* 4*d*; Glebe, 9 acres; R.'s Inc. 260*l*; Pop. Lutton 196, Washingley 75.) [18]

GIBBON, George, *Shepscombe, Painswick, Glouc.*—St. Cath. Coll. Cam. B.A. 1838, M.A. 1842; Deac. 1839, Pr. 1840. P. C. of Shepscombe, Dio. G. and B. (Patron, V. of Painswick; P. C.'s Inc. 130*l* and Ho; Pop. 510.) Formerly P. C. of Hartshill, Warwickshire, 1852–59. [19]

GIBBON, James Harries, *Kerry, Newtown, N. Wales.*—St. David's Lampeter; B.A. 1866; Deac. 1866 by Bp of St. Asaph. C. of Kerry, Montgomeryshire. [20]

GIBBON, William Lloyd, *Wallingford.*—St. John's Coll. Cam. B.A. 1822, M.A. 1828; Deac. 1825 and Pr. 1826 by Bp of Nor. Chap. to the Wallingford Union. Formerly Pres. of Devon Coll. Bermuda, 1830; Miss. in Bermuda from S.P.G. 1835–40, Tasmania 1840; Chap. of Trinity, Launceston, 1843–47; C. of St. John's, Hoxton, and Chap. to Shoreditch Workhouse; C. of Wilmington 1852; Chap. to Dartford Union, Kent, 1853–64. [21]

GIBBON, William Wynter, *Wapley Vicarage, Chipping Sodbury, Glouc.*—Ch. Coll. Cam. B.A. 1846, M.A. 1850; Deac. 1846 by Bp of Wor. Pr. 1848 by Bp of G. and B. V. of Wapley, Dio. G. and B. 1862. (Patrons, D. and C. of Bristol; V.'s Inc. 340*l* and Ho; Pop. 358.) Min. Can. of Bristol Cathl. 1852 (Value, 150*l*). Formerly C. of Clifton 1848. [22]

GIBBONS, Benjamin, *Mitton Vicarage, Stourport.*—Wad. Coll. Ox. B.A. 1846, M.A. 1850; Deac. 1849 by Bp of Lon. Pr. 1850 by Bp of Wor. V. of Lower Mitton, Dio. Wor. 1861. (Patron, V. of Kidderminster; Tithe, 92*l*; V.'s Inc. 188*l* and Ho; Pop. 2958.) Formerly C. of St. Stephen's, Portland Town, Lond. 1849, St. George's, Kidderminster, 1850–53, St. Mary's, Kidderminster, 1854–57, with Trimpley, 1857–61. Author, *Notes and Suggestions for a History of Kidderminster*, 1859; *The Scriptural Account of Disease*, 1861; *A Review of the Year*, 1862; *The Holy City*, 1864; Sermons. [23]

GIBBONS, George, *Witton Parsonage, Northwich, Cheshire.*—Sid. Coll. Cam. B.A. 1824, M.A. 1828; Deac. 1824, Pr. 1825. P. C. of Witton, Dio. Ches. 1842. (Patron, Rev. R. Greenhall; Glebe, 45 acres; P. C.'s Inc. 168*l* and Ho; Pop. 4867.) [24]

GIBBONS, George Buckmaster, *Laneast, Launceston, Cornwall.*—St. John's Coll. Cam. B.A. 1835; Deac. 1835 and Pr. 1836 by Bp of Ex. P. C. of Laneast, Launceston, Dio. Ex. 1866. (Patron, J. C. Lethbridge, Esq; P. C.'s Inc. 101*l*; Pop. 240.) Formerly P. C. of Launceston. [25]

GIBBONS, Robert, *Handley, near Salisbury.*—Wad. Coll. Ox. B.A. 1849, M.A. 1865; Deac. 1851 and Pr. 1852 by Bp of Lin. P. C. of Handley-cum-Gussage St. Andrew, Dio. Salis. 1867. (Patrons, D. and C. of Windsor; Glebe, 20 acres; P. C.'s Inc. 112*l* and Ho; Pop. 1302.) Formerly C. of Caister and Mark's Hall 1855–58, Bulkington 1860–63. [26]

GIBBONS, Thomas, *St. Peter Tavy Rectory, Tavistock, Devon.*—Pemb. Coll. Cam. Sen. Opt. and B.A.

1838; Deac. 1838 by Bp of Win. Pr. 1840 by Bp of Ex. R. of St. Peter Tavy, Dio. Ex. 1855 (Patron, Bp of Ex; R.'s Inc. 200*l* and Ho; Pop. 469.) Formerly Asst. C. and Sunday Even. Lect. of Tavistock. Author, sundry Pamphlets. [1]

GIBBS, John Lomax, *Clifton Hampden, Abingdon.*—Ex. Coll. Ox. B.A. 1853, M.A. 1856; Deac. 1859, Pr. 1860. P. C. of Clifton Hampden, Dio. Ox. 1864. (Patron, H. H. Gibbs, Esq; Glebe, 9 acres; P. C.'s Inc. 290*l* and Ho; Pop. 350.) Formerly C. of St. Mark's, Torwood, Torquay, 1859. [2]

GIBBS, Joseph Games, *Pontefract.*—Trin. Coll. Cam. B.A. 1861, M.A. 1866; Deac. 1863 and Pr. 1864 by Abp of York. R. of Whitwood Mere, Dio. York, 1867. (Patron, Abp of York; Tithe, 120*l*; Glebe, 1 acre; R.'s Inc. 180*l*; Pop. 1000.) Formerly C. in sole charge of Doncaster 1863, Kirk Sandall 1864–65, Conisbro', 1866. [3]

GIBBS, Michael, 7, *King Edward-street, London, E.C.*—Caius Coll. Cam. 10th Wrang. B.A. 1835, M.A. 1838; Deac. 1836 by Bp of Roch. Pr. 1837 by Bp of Ely. V. of Ch. Ch. Newgate, with the united R. of St. Leonard's, Dio. Lon. 1841. (Patrons, Governors of St. Bartholomew's Hospital and D. and C. of Westminster alt; V.'s Inc. 465*l*; Pop. Ch. Ch. 1975, St. Leonard's 297.) First Sec. to the Cambridge Board of Education; elected Proctor in Convocation for the Dio. of Lon. 1855–59 and 1865; Hon. Preb. of St. Paul's 1856; Rural Dean 1864. Formerly Fell. of Caius Coll. Cam. Author, various Sermons. [4]

GIBBS, Thomas Crook, *Coates Rectory, Cirencester.*—Trin. Coll. Ox. B.A. 1842, M.A. 1845; Deac. 1843, Pr. 1844. R. of Coates, Dio. G. and B. 1848. (Patron, Rev. William Dewe; Glebe, 483 acres; R.'s Inc. 430*l* and Ho; Pop. 417.) [5]

GIBNEY, John Somerville, *Minor Canons' Houses, Lincoln Cathedral.*—Min. Can. of Lin. Cathl. (Value, 42*l* 14*s* 9*d*.) P. C. of St. Michael's, City and Dio. Lin. 1845. (Patron, Precentor of Lin. Cathl; P. C.'s Inc. 126*l*; Pop. 1296.) Sequestrator of St. Mark's P. C. City and Dio. Lin. 1845. (Patron, Precentor of Lin. Cathl; Tithe, 7*l* 15*s*; P. C.'s Inc. 80*l*; Pop. 722.) [6]

GIBSON, Alfred Augustus, *Stanley, Derbyshire.*—P. C. of Stanley, Dio. Lich. 1851. (Patron, Sir H. Wilmot, Bart; P. C.'s Inc. 64*l*; Pop. 534) [7]

GIBSON, Arthur, *Chedworth, Northleach, Glouc.*—Queen's Coll. Ox. B.A. 1804, M.A. 1808; Deac. 1808, Pr. 1809. V. of Chedworth, Dio. G. and B. 1828. (Patron, Queen's Coll. Ox; Tithe—App. 556*l* 13*s* 4*d*, and 118¼ acres of Glebe, V. 278*l* 6*s* 8*d*; Glebe, 109¾ acres; V.'s Inc. 377*l* and Ho; Pop. 954.) Author, *Club Sermons*, 3 eds. 1844, 1847, 1854, 4*s*; *Sermons on various subjects*, 1853, 6*s*, 2nd Series, 1865, 5*s*. [8]

GIBSON, Charles Henry, *Batley, Yorkshire.*—Ch. Coll. Cam. B.A. 1857; Deac. 1858 and Pr. 1859 by Bp of Roch. C. of Batley 1865. Formerly C. of Gillingham, Kent, and Bolton-le-Sands. [9]

GIBSON, Christopher Mends, *St. Clement's, Truro, Cornwall.*—Jesus Coll. Cam. B.A. 1837; Deac. and Pr. 1828. V. of St. Clement's with St. Paul's C. Dio. Ex. 1839. (Patron, Ld Chan; Tithe, Imp. 340*l*; Glebe, ¾ acre; V.'s Inc. 350*l* and Ho; Pop. 500.) Formerly C. of Inwardleigh 1828, Charles Ch. Plymouth, 1829; P. C. of Chacewater 1831. Author, *The Prophecies, showing their particular Fulfilment respecting the Church of Rome*, 1842; *The Present Times* (a Tract), 1851; etc. [10]

GIBSON, Henry, *Fyfield Rectory, near Ongar, Essex.*—Ch. Coll. Cam. 2nd Sen. Opt. B.A. 1830; Deac. 1831 and Pr. 1832 by Bp of Ches. R. of Fyfield, Dio. Roch. 1833. (Patroness, Lady Cowley; Tithe, 741*l*; Glebe, 63 acres; R.'s Inc. 805*l* and Ho; Pop. 629.) Formerly C. of Caton, near Lancaster, 1831–33. Author, *The Occasional Offices of the Book of Common Prayer in their Connection with Baptism*, 1854, 3*d*. [11]

GIBSON, Henry Atkinson, *Linslade, Leighton Buzzard.*—Wad. Coll. Ox. B.A. 1856, M.A. 1859; Deac. 1857 and Pr. 1859 by Bp of G. and B. P. C. of Linslade, Dio. Ox. 1861. (Patron, Bp of Ox; P. C.'s Inc. 130*l* and Ho; Pop. 1511.) Surrogate. Formerly C. of Bibury, Glouc. 1857–60. [12]

GIBSON, John, *Acton Round, Bridgnorth, Salop.*—Dub. A.B. 1845; Deac. 1846 by Bp of Lin. Pr. 1847 by Bp of Limerick. P. C. of Acton Round, Dio. Herf. 1853. (Patron, Sir F. R. E. Acton, Bart; Tithe—Imp. 46*l* 2*s*; P. C.'s Inc. 90*l*; Pop. 168.) C. of Upton Cressett, Salop. [13]

GIBSON, John, *Blanchland Parsonage, Gateshead.*—Dur. B.A. 1837, M.A. 1838; Deac. 1838 and Pr. 1839 by Bp of Dur. P. C. of Blanchland, Dio. Dur. 1855. (Patrons, Trustees of the late Lord Crewe, Bp of Dur; Glebe, 50 acres; P. C.'s Inc. 200*l* and Ho; Pop. 474.) [14]

GIBSON, John, *Garston, near Liverpool.*—Dub. A.B. 1817; Deac. 1816 and Pr. 1817 by Bp of B. and W. P. C. of Garston, Dio. Ches. (Patron, Richard Watt, Esq; Tithe—App. 195*l*, P. C. 8*l*; Glebe, 16 acres; P. C.'s Inc. 190*l* and Ho; Pop. 2016.) Surrogate 1855. [15]

GIBSON, John, *King's Stanley Rectory, Stonehouse, Glouc.*—Jesus Coll. Cam. Wrang. and B.A. 1840, M.A. 1843; Deac. 1843 and Pr. 1846 by Bp of Ely. R. of King's Stanley, Dio. G. and B. 1857. (Patron, Jesus Coll. Cam; R.'s Inc. 340*l* and Ho; Pop. 1488.) Formerly Tut. and Fell. of Jesus Coll. Cam. 1842–57. [16]

GIBSON, John Dawson, *Worksop.*—Trin. Coll. Cam. B.A. 1845, M.A. 1848; Deac. 1845 and Pr. 1846 by Bp of Win. P. C. of Brinsley, Notts, Dio. Lin. 1867. (Patron, Duke of Newcastle; P. C.'s Inc. 150*l* and Ho; Pop. 1200.) C. of Worksop. Formerly C. of Ham, Surrey, 1846–7; Chap. of H.M.'s Bombay Estab. 1848–65. [17]

GIBSON, John Henry Ashley, 4, *Clarence-street, Brighton.*—Clare Coll. Cam. late Scho. of, B.A. 1852, M.A. 1858; Deac. 1853 and Pr. 1854 by Bp of Ches. C. of St. Paul's, Brighton. Formerly C. of St. Barnabas', Pimlico, Lond. and Wymering, Hants. [18]

GIBSON, J. Summer, *Corley, near Coventry.*—C. of Corley. [19]

GIBSON, Jonathan, *Newbold Pacey Vicarage, Kineton, Warwickshire.*—Queen's Coll. Ox. B.A. 1807, M.A. 1810. V. of Newbold Pacey, Dio. Wor. 1848. (Patron, Queen's Coll. Ox; Tithe, Imp. 266*l* 14*s*; V. 118*l* 6*s*; V.'s Inc. 639*l* and Ho; Pop. 360.) [20]

GIBSON, Marsden, 40, *Elizabeth-street, Chester-square, S.W.*—Trin. Coll. Cam. B.A. 1865; Deac. 1865 and Pr. 1866 by Bp of S. and M. C. of St. Michael's, Chester-square, 1867. Formerly C. of Rushen, Isle of Man. 1865–7. [21]

GIBSON, Nicholas William, *The Polygon, Ardwick, Manchester.*—Trin. Coll. Cam. Wrang. B.A. 1824, Tyrwhitt's Heb. Scho. 1826, M.A. 1827; Deac. 1826 and Pr. 1827 by Bp of Ches. R. of St. Thomas's, Ardwick, Dio. Man. 1831. (Patrons, D. and C. of Man; R.'s Inc. 254*l*; Pop. 10,147.) Can. of Manchester 1861; (Value, 600*l*.) Rural Dean. Formerly Chap. of Trin. Coll. Cam. [22]

GIBSON, Richard Hudson, *East Cowes, Isle of Wight.*—Trin. Coll. Cam; B.A. 1849. P. C. of East Cowes, Dio. Win. 1864. (Patron, R. of Whippingham; P. C.'s Inc. 150*l* and Ho; Pop. 1954.) Formerly C. of Rickinghall. [23]

GIBSON, Robert, *Bolton-le-Sands, Lancaster.*—Pemb. Coll. Cam. B.A. 1818, M.A. 1821; Deac. 1819, Pr. 1820. V. of Bolton-le-Sands, Dio. Man. 1824. (Patron, Bp of Man; Tithe—App. 810*l*, V. 101*l*; V.'s Inc. 195*l* and Ho; Pop. 1288.) [24]

GIBSON, Robert Bowness, *Rectory House, Sherborne-lane, London, E.C.*—R. of St. Mary Abchurch with St. Lawrence Pountney P. C. City and Dio. Lon. 1844. (Patron, Corpus Coll. Cam; Tithe, 120*l*; R.'s Inc. 256*l*; Pop. St. Mary Abchurch 264, St. Lawrence Pountney 233.) [25]

GIBSON, Robert Christopher, *Weston Lullingfield Parsonage, near Shrewsbury.*—Dur; Deac. and Pr. 1849 by Bp of Salis. P. C. of Weston Lullingfield, Dio. Lich. 1857. (Patroness, Miss C. Barrett; P. C.'s Inc. 280*l* and Ho; Pop. 319.) [26]

GIBSON, Stanley Taylor, *Sandon Rectory, near Chelmsford, Essex.*—Queens' Coll. Cam. 13th Wrang. and B.A. 1848, M.A. 1851, B.D. 1860; Deac. 1852 and Pr. 1854 by Bp of Ely. R. of Sandon, Dio. Roch. 1862. (Patron, Queens' Coll. Cam; Tithe, comm. 707*l*; Glebe, 28 acres; R.'s Inc. 730*l* and Ho; Pop. 512.) Formerly R. of St. Botolph's, Cambridge, 1857; C. of Whittlesford, Cambs, All Saints', Paddington, Lond. and St. George the Martyr's, Queen-square, Lond; Fell. of Queens' Coll. Cam. [1]

GIBSON, William, *Tilty Parsonage, near Dunmow, Essex.*—St. John's Coll. Cam. B.A. 1849; Deac. 1849 by Bp of Roch. Pr. 1851 by Bp of Pet. P. C. of Tilty, Dio. Roch. 1859. (Patron, Viscount Maynard; P. C.'s Inc. 120*l* and Ho; Pop. 83.) Formerly C. of Exton, Rutland, 1850–59. [2]

GIBSON, William Greeme, *Hollingbourne, Maidstone.*—Wor. Coll. Ox. B.A. 1844, M.A. 1846; Deac. 1845, Pr. 1846. V. of Hollingbourne with Huckinge V. Dio. Cant. 1866. (Patron, Abp of Cant; V.'s Inc. 480*l* and Ho; Pop. 1300.) Formerly P. C. of St. Peter's, Drypool, Yorks, 1851–57; V. of North Curry, Somerset, 1857. [3]

GIBSON, William Lewis, *Darnall, Sheffield.*—P. C. of Darnall, Dio. York, 1845. (Patrons, Trustees; P. C.'s Inc. 150*l*; Pop. 2403.) [4]

GIBSONE, Burford Waring, *Proprietary School, Eaton-square, London, S.W.*—Trin. Coll. Cam. 9th Wrang. 3rd cl. Cl. Trip. B.A. 1853, M.A. 1861; Deac. 1854 by Abp of Cant. Pr. 1856 by Bp of Wor. Head Mast. of Proprietary Sch. Eaton-square, F.C.S., F.G.S. Formerly C. of All Saints', Norwood, 1854; Chap. of Queen's Hosp. Birmingham, 1855–57; Head Mast. of Grosvenor Coll. Bath, 1857–62; Second Mast. in Mercers' Sch. Lond. 1862–66. Author, *Sermon on Crimean War; Spring Flora of Bath; Chemical Addenda.* [5]

GIFFARD, Jervis Trigge, *Long Ditton Rectory, Kingston on-Thames.*—New Coll. Ox. B.A. 1826, M.A. 1829; Deac. 1828 by Bp of Herf. Pr. 1829 by Bp of Win. R. of Long Ditton, Dio. Win. 1838. (Patron, New Coll. Ox; Tithe, 535*l*; Glebe, 20 acres; R.'s Inc. 550*l* and Ho; Pop. 1445.) Formerly C. of Old Alresford, Hants, 1828; V. of East Wellon 1834. [6]

GIFFORD, Edwin Hamilton, *Walgrave Rectory, Northampton.*—St. John's Coll. Cam. 15th Wrang. Sen. Cl. Sen. Medallist, and B.A. 1843, M.A. 1846; Deac. 1844 and Pr. 1845 by Bp of Lich. R. of Walgrave, Dio. Pet. 1866. (Patron, Bp of Pet; R.'s Inc. 600*l* and Ho; Pop. 650.) Head Mast. of King Edward's Sch. Birmingham, 1848; Hon. Can. of Wor. Cathl. 1853, Exam. Chap. to Bp of Pet. Formerly Fell. of St. John's Coll. Cam. [7]

GIFFORD, Francis Osbern, *Hartley Wintney, Hartford-bridge, Hants.*—St. John's Coll. Ox. B.A. 1845; Deac. 1845 and Pr. 1846 by Bp of Win. V. of Hartley Wintney, Dio. Win. 1850. (Patroness, Lady St. John Mildmay; Tithe—Imp. 397*l* 1*s* 3*d*, V. 175*l* 11*s* 6*d*; Glebe, 4½ acres; V.'s Inc. 180*l*; Pop. 1746.) [8]

GIFFORD, The Hon. George Robert, *Rackenford Rectory, Tiverton.*—Caius Coll. Cam. Jun. Opt. and B.A. 1849. R. of Rackenford, Dio. Ex. 1867. (Patron, Rev. G. Porter; R.'s Inc. 360*l* and Ho; Pop. 486.) Formerly R. of Littleton, Middlesex, 1856–67. [9]

GIFFORD, The Hon. John, *Siddington, Glouc.*—Emman. Coll. Cam. Jun. Opt. and Hon. M.A. 1844; Deac. and Pr. 1845 by Bp of Wor. R. of Siddington, Dio. G. and B. 1862. (Patron Ld Chan; Tithe, 30*l*; Glebe, 300 acres; R.'s Inc. 440*l* and Ho; Pop. 474.) Formerly R. of Widworthy 1855; V. of Shelford 1846-55; P. C. of St. Martha's, Chilworth, 1853–55; Chap. to late Lord Lyndhurst. [10]

GIFFORD Joseph, *The Parsonage, Newport, Barnstaple, Devon.*—Ch. Coll. Cam. Schol. 1849, Heb. Priseman, 1850, B.A. 1852, M.A. 1856; Deac. 1852 by Bp of Lich. Pr. 1853 by Bp of Ex. P. C. of Newport, Dio. Ex. 1853. (Patron, V. of Bishop's Tawton; P. C.'s Inc. 300*l* and Ho; Pop. 1027.) Formerly C. of Boningale, Salop, 1852–53. [11]

GIFFORD, J., 12, *Lincoln's-inn-fields, London.*—Formerly C. of Holdenhurst. [12]

GILBANKS, George, *Wollaston, Stourbridge.*—P. C. of Wollaston, Dio. Wor. 1860. (Patron, W. O. Foster, Esq; P. C.'s Inc. 200*l*; Pop. 2041.) [13]

GILBANKS, George F., *Beeston, near Leeds.*—Clare Coll. Cam. B.A. 1849, M.A. 1853; Deac. 1849 by Bp of Carl Pr. 1851 by Bp of Lich. P. C. of Beeston, Dio. Rip. 1859. (Patron V. of Leeds; Tithe—App. 114*l* 1*s* 4*d*; Glebe, 80 acres; P. C.'s Inc. 216*l*; Pop. 2547.) Formerly C. of St. Matthew's, Smethwick, Birmingham. [14]

GILBERT, Edward Wiles, *Farnworth, Manchester.*—Jesus Coll. Cam. B.A. 1850, M.A. 1853; Deac. 1852, Pr. 1854. C. of Farnworth. Formerly C. of Bishopwearmouth, and St. Mary's, Swansea. [15]

GILBERT, George, *Syston, Grantham.*—Corpus Coll. Cam. B.A. 1819, M.A. 1822; Deac. 1820 by Bp of Pet. Pr. 1822 by Bp of Lin. V. of Syston, Dio. Lin. 1830. (Patron, Sir John Charles Thorold, Bart; V.'s Inc. 83*l* and Ho; Pop. 238.) Preb. of All Saints Thorngate in Lin. Cathl. 1863; Surrogate for Dios. of Lin. and Pet. Formerly C. of Grantham 1821–22, 2nd Mast. of Grantham Sch. 1820–51. [16]

GILBERT, George, *Claxton Grange, Norwich.*—Emman. Coll. Ox. Exhib. and B.A. 1849, M.A. 1852; Deac. 1849 by Bp of Nor. Pr. 1851 by Bp of Roch. V. of Claxton, Dio. Nor. 1862. (Patrons, Representatives of Sir C. H. J. Rich, Bart; Tithe, 57*l*; Glebe, 9 acres; R.'s Inc. 75*l*; Pop. 202.) Formerly C. of Ware 1849–51, Horningham 1851–53, Claxton 1853–62. [17]

GILBERT, Henry Abraham, *Tiverton, Devon.*—Ex. Coll. Ox. B.A. 1831; Deac. 1833, Pr. 1834. R. of Clare Portion with Withley C. Tiverton, Dio. Ex. 1855. (Patrons, Earl of Harrowby and others; R.'s Inc. 473*l*.) Formerly C. of Tiverton. [18]

GILBERT, John Bellamy, *Cantley Rectory, near Norwich.*—Emman. Coll. Cam. B A. 1857, M.A. 1866; Deac. 1859 and Pr. 1860 by Bp of Ely. R. of Cantley, Dio. Nor. 1860. (Patron, W. A. Gilbert, Esq; Tithe, 300*l*; Glebe, 43½ acres; R.'s Inc. 336*l* and Ho; Pop. 235.) Formerly C. of Hadleigh, Suffolk, 1859–60. [19]

GILBERT, John Denny, *Manor House, Chedgrave, Norwich.*—St. John's Coll. Cam. Sen. Opt. and B.A. 1836, M.A. 1839; Deac. 1838, Pr. 1839 by Bp of Nor. R. of Hellington, Norfolk, Dio. Nor. 1840. (Patron, Sir C. Rich, Bart; Tithe, 120*l*; Glebe, 12 acres; R.'s Inc. 149*l* 15*s*; Pop. 98.) Formerly R. of Cantley. [20]

GILBERT, Philip Parker, *St. Giles's Vicarage, Wells-street, Cripplegate, London, E.C.*—Magd. Coll. Cam. B.A. 1835, M.A. 1839; Deac. 1835 by Bp of Lon. Pr. 1836 by Bp of G. and B. V. of St. Giles's, Cripplegate, Dio. Lon. 1857. (Patrons, D. and C. of St. Paul's; Tithe, 1509*l*; V.'s Inc. 1700*l*; Pop. 9000.) Formerly R. of St. Augustine's with St. Faith's, City and Dio. Lon. 1853–57. Author, various Sermons, etc. [21]

GILBERT, Richard, *Guestwick Vicarage, Thetford.*—St. Cath. Hall, Cam. B.A. 1849, M.A. 1852; Deac. 1849 and Pr. 1851 by Bp of Nor. V. of Guestwick, Dio. Nor. 1861. (Patron, W. E. L. Bulwer, Esq; Tithe, 88*l*; Glebe, 22½ acres; V.'s Inc. 120*l* and Ho; Pop. 203.) Formerly C. of Reepham with Kerdiston. [22]

GILBERT, Thomas Morrell, *Heversham, near Milnthorpe.*—Trin. Coll. Cam. 12 Wrang. 3rd cl. Cl. Trip. B.A. 1857, M.A. 1860; Deac. 1861 and Pr. 1862 by Bp of Chich. V. of Haversham, Dio. Carl. 1866. (Patron, Trin. Coll. Cam; V.'s Inc. 700*l* and Ho; Pop. 1100.) Formerly Fell. of Trin. Coll. Cam. 1859; C. of Hurstpierpoint 1861, St. Bartholomew's, Chichester, 1863. P. C. of St. Bartholomew's Chichester, 1864; Vice-Prin. of Theol. Coll. Chichester, 1863. [23]

GILBERT, William, *Chearsley, Bucks.*—St. Aidan's; Deac. 1852 and Pr 1853 by Bp of Ches. P. C. of Chearsley, Dio. Ox. 1867. (Patron, Bp of Ox; P. C.'s Inc. 85*l*; Pop. 290.) Formerly C. of Blackburn, Piddington, and St. George's, Wigan. Author, *Tract on Confirmation.* [24]

GILBERT, William Henry Long, 5, *Warwick Gardens, East, Kensington, W.*—Brasen. Coll. Ox. B.A.

1852, M.A. 1864; Deac. 1853 and Pr. 1854 by Bp of Pet. Sen. C. of St. Philip's, Earls Court, Kensington, 1866. Formerly C. of Hungerton with Twyford, Leic. 1853–55, Barlavington, Sussex, 1856–57, Leighton Buzzard 1857–60, St. Paul's, Bedminster, 1860–63, Greenham, Newbury, 1863–66. [1]

GILBERTSON, Lewis, *Jesus College, Oxford.*—Jesus Coll. Ox. 3rd cl. Lit. Hum. B.A. 1836, M.A. 1839, B.D. 1847; Deac. 1837 and Pr. 1838 by Bp of G. and B. Fell. and Lect. of Jesus Coll. Ox. Formerly P. C. of Llangorwen 1841–52. [2]

GILBY, Francis Duncan, *Whittington, Gloucestershire.*—Clare Coll. Cam. B.A. 1827, M.A. 1830; Deac. 1828 and Pr. 1829 by Abp of York. R. of Whittington, Dio. G. and B. 1866. (Patron, H. Wright, Esq; R.'s Inc. 279*l* and Ho; Pop. 217.) Formerly P. C. of St. James's, Cheltenham, 1834. [3]

GILDEA, William, *West Lulworth, Wareham, Dorset.*—Ex. Coll. Cam. 4th cl. Lit. Hum; B.A. 1856, M.A. 1858; Deac. 1856 and Pr. 1858 by Bp of Salis. P. C. of West Lulworth, Dio. Salis. 1862. (Patron, Bp of Salis; Tithe, 120*l*; Glebe, 4 acres; P. C.'s Inc. 120*l* and Ho; Pop. 446.) Formerly C. of Compton Valence 1856–61. [4]

GILDER, Edward, *St. Dunstan's, Canterbury.*—St. John's Coll. Cam. B.A. 1850, M.A. 1853; Deac. 1851 and Pr. 1852 by Abp of Cant. V. of St. Dunstan's, City and Dio. Cant. 1861. (Patron, Abp of Cant; Tithe, 93*l*; Glebe, 10 acres; V.'s Inc. 182*l*; Pop. 1521.) Rural Dean 1863. Formerly C. of St. Martin's and St. Paul's, Canterbury. [5]

GILDER, Horace, *St. Peter's Rectory, Sandwich, Kent.*—St. John's Coll. Cam. B.A. 1846, M.A. 1849; Deac. 1847 by Bp of Rip. Pr. 1848 by Abp of York. R. of St. Peter's, Sandwich, Dio. Cant. 1851. (Patrons, Ld Chan. and W. Tringham, Esq. alt; Tithe, 7*l*; Glebe, 24 acres; R.'s Inc. 85*l* and Ho; Pop. 1085.) [6]

GILDER, William, *Mackworth Vicarage, Derby.*—St. John's Coll. Cam. B.A. 1845, M.A. 1848; Deac. 1846 and Pr. 1847 by Bp of G. and B. V. of Mackworth, Dio. Lich. 1850. (Patron, F. Mundy, Esq; V.'s Inc. 175*l* and Ho; Pop. 525.) Formerly C. of Tickenham. [7]

GILDERDALE, John Smith, *Forest School, Walthamstow, Essex.*—Oriel Coll. Ox. B.A. 1851, M.A. 1852, Denyer's Theol. Prize Essay 1855, Deac. 1852 and Pr. 1853 by Bp of Lon. Second Mast. of Forest Sch. Walthamstow. Author, *Disciplina Rediviva, or Hints and Helps for Youths leaving School*, 1856, Bell and Daldy. [8]

GILES, Charles William, *Milton Hall, Cambridge.*—St. John's Coll. Cam. B.A. 1847, M.A. 1850, D.D. 1865; Deac. 1847 by Bp of Nor. Pr. 1848 by Abp of York. [9]

GILES, Edwin, M.A., *Hewelsfield, Coleford, Glouc.*—P. C. of Hewelsfield, Dio. G. and B. 1862. (Patrons, D. and C. of Herf; P. C.'s Inc. 131*l*; Pop. 417.) [10]

GILES, John Allen, *Cranford, Hounslow, Middlesex.*—Corpus Coll. Ox. 1824, B.A. 1828, Double 1st cl. Vinerian Scho. 1831, M.A. 1831, Fell. of Corpus Coll. 1833, D.C.L. 1838. Formerly C. of Bampton 1845–54, Perivale (sole charge) 1857–61; Head Mast. of Camberwell Coll. Sch. 1834–36; Head Mast. City of Lond. Sch. 1836–40. Author, *Scriptores Græci Minores, Sappho, &c.* 2 vols; *Terentii Comœdiæ*; *Antimachii Colophonii Reliquiæ*; *Quinti Enni Reliquiæ*; *Severi Sancti Carmen*; *Rufi Festi Avieni Opera*; *Maximiani Opera*, 8vo; *Germanici Opera*; *Codex Apocryphus Novi Testam.* 2 vols; *Adhelmi, Episc. Shireburn Opera*; *Bedæ Venerabilis Opera*, 12 vols; *Anecdota Bedæ, Lanfranci, &c*; *Bonifacii Mogunt. Opera*, 2 vols; *Lanfranci Opera*, 2 vols; *Sancti Thomæ Cantuar.* (Becket) *Vita*, 2 vols; *Sancti Thomæ Cantuar. variis Scriptoribus Epistolæ*, 2 vols; *Herberti de Bosham Opera*, 2 vols; *Gilberti Foliot Opera*, 2 vols; *Arnulfi Lexoviensis Opera*; *Joannis Saresber. Opera*, 5 vols; *Petri Blesensis Opera*, 4 vols; *Benedicti Pet. Vita et Mir S. Thomæ*; *Scriptores de Reb. Gest. Will. I.*; *W. Abbatis Dervensis Epistolæ*; *Galfridi Monum. Hist. Briton*; *Roberti Grosseteste Carmina*; *Radulphi Nigri Chronica*; *Chronicon Angl. Petrib*; *Geoffrey Gaimar, Estorie des Angles*; *Belisarii Carmen*; *Chronica Trium Regum Lancast*; *Galfridi le Baker de Swinbroke Chronicon*; *Incerti Auct. Chron. de Bello Sancto*; *Herbert de Losinga Epistolæ*; *Vita quorundam Anglo-Saxon*; *Carmen de Belisario*; *Locke's and Shaftesbury's Letters*; *Rev. G. Herbert's Works*, 2 vols; *Rev. Dr. Hole's Works*, 3 vols; *Barker's Literary Anecdotes*; *Whole Works of Roger Ascham, with Life*, 4 vols; English Translation of Chronicles, &c; *Anglo-Saxon Chronicle and Bede's History*; *Six Old Chronicles, Gildas, &c*; *William of Malmesbury's History*; *Chronicles of the Crusades*; *Roger of Wendover's Chronicle*, 2 vols; *Matthew Paris's English History*, 3 vols; *Venerable Bede's Minor Historical Works*; *Works of King Alfred the Great*, 3 vols; Original Historical Works; *History of the Ancient Britons*, 2 vols; *Life and Times of Alfred the Great*; *Life and Letters of Thomas à Becket*, 2 vols; *History of Bampton*; *History of Witney*; *Hebrew Records*; *Christian Records*; *Heathen Records*; Educational Works: *Greek Lexicon*; *Greek Grammar*; *Latin Grammar for Colleges*, 3rd edit; the previous work, abridged; *Bland's Verses and Key, revised*, 8vo; *Murray's English Grammar*; *Enfield's Speaker*; School Edit. of *Sallust and Phædrus*; *Lecteur Français*; *French Grammar*; *Il Lettore Italiano*; *Italian Grammar*; *First Lessons in Bible, Grecian, Roman, English, Scottish, Irish, American*, and *French Histories*, 8 vols; *First Lessons on Common Subjects, Class Book*; *English Grammar, Geography, Arithmetic, Logic, Classical Mythology, Astronomy, Optics, Natural Philosophy, Moral Philosophy, Chronology*, 13 vols; *Historical Questions on the Old and New Testament*; *Story-Book of English History*; *Keys to the Classics*, 36 vols. [11]

GILES, John Harold, *Bedminster.*—Magd. Coll. Cam. B.A. 1864, 30th Wrang. 1864; Deac. 1865 and Pr. 1866 by Bp of G. and B. C. of St. Paul's, Bedminster, 1865. [12]

GILES, Robert, *Partney Rectory, Spilsby, Lincolnshire.*—Ex. Coll. Ox. B.A. 1852; Deac. 1852, Pr. 1853. R. of Partney, Dio. Lin. 1854. (Patron, Lord Willoughby d'Eresby; Tithe, 211*l* 2*s* 6*d*; Glebe, 3 acres; R.'s Inc. 220*l*; Pop. 487.) Formerly C. of Partney 1852–54. [13]

GILES, William Theophilus, *Netherleigh House, near Chester.*—Dub. A.B. 1858, A.M. 1861; Deac. 1859 and Pr. 1860 by Bp of Ches. C. of St. Mary's-on-the Hill, Chester, 1859. [14]

GILL, Dugald Campbell, M.A., *Midgham Cottage, Newbury.* [15]

GILL, Francis Turner, *Warfield Vicarage, Bracknell.*—Downing Coll. Cam. B.A. 1852, M.A. 1857; Deac. 1854 and Pr. 1855 by Bp of Wor. V. of Warfield, Dio. Ox. 1860. (Patrons, Trustees of late Rev. R. Faithfull; Tithe—Imp. 668*l* 11*s* 10*d*, V. 200*l*; Glebe, 16 acres; V.'s Inc. 250*l*; Pop. 828.) Formerly P. C. of Bishopton, Stratford on-Avon, 1856–59. [16]

GILL, Hugh Stowell, *Rushen Vicarage, Castletown, Isle of Man.*—Dub. A.B. 1853; Deac. 1853 and Pr. 1854 by Bp of S. and M. V. of Kirk-Christ-Rushen, Dio. S. and M. 1859. (Patron, the Crown; V.'s Inc. 180*l* and Ho; Pop. 3300.) Formerly Chap. of St. Luke's, Baldwin, Isle of Man, 1853–56; Chap. of Ch. Ch. Laxey, 1856–59. [17]

GILL, Jeremiah C., *Lee, Kent.*—Magd. Hall, Ox. 3rd cl. Lit. Hum. Deac. 1854 and Pr. 1856 by Bp of Wor. [18]

GILL, John, *Holne Vicarage, Ashburton.*—Trin. Coll. Cam. B.A. 1851, M.A. 1854; Deac. 1852 and Pr. 1854 by Bp of Ex. V. of Holne, Dio. Ex. 1858. (Patron, Rev. S. Lane; Tithe, 190*l*; Glebe, 25 acres; V.'s Inc. 220*l* and Ho; Pop. 348.) Formerly C. of Ch. Ch. Plymouth, 1852–54, Woodhouse Eaves, Loughborough, 1854–57, Holne 1857–58. [19]

GILL, Thomas Howard, 5, *Hyde-road, Manchester.*—Trin. Coll. Cam. Sen. Opt. B.A. 1859; Deac. 1859 and Pr. 1860 by Bp of S. and M. R. of St. Jude's, Man. 1865. (Patrons, Five Trustees; R.'s Inc. 300*l*; Pop. 12,268.) Formerly C. of Malew 1859; Chap. of St. Mark's, Isle of Man, 1863. [20]

GILL, William, *Sandsend, Whitby.*—Dur. Div. Scho. Barry Scho. Theol. Prizeman and Licen. in Theol. 1861; Deac. 1861 and Pr. 1862 by Abp of York. C. of Lythe with Ugthorpe 1861. [1]

GILL, William, *Stannington Parsonage, Ecclesfield, Sheffield.*—Deac. 1829 and Pr. 1830 by Abp of York. P. C. of Stannington, Dio. York, 1846. (Patron, V. of Ecclesfield; P. C.'s Inc. 129*l* and Ho; Pop. 2909.) [2]

GILL, William, *Kirk-Mallew, Ballasalla, Isle of Man.*—Deac. 1820, Pr. 1821. V. of Kirk-Mallew, Dio. S. and M. 1828. (Patron, the Crown; V.'s Inc. 185*l* and Ho; Pop. 5065.) Surrogate 1847; Diocesan Inspector of Schools 1850. Proctor of Clergy in York Convocation 1859; Re-elected 1865. [3]

GILL, William, *Venn, Tavistock, Devon.*—Magd. Hall, Ox. B.A. 1839; Deac. 1840 and Pr. 1841 by Bp of Win. [4]

GILL, William, *Hertingfordbury.*—Corpus Coll. Cam; Deac. 1849. R. of Hertingfordbury, Dio. Roch. 1865. (Patron, the Crown; Tithe and Glebe land 600*l* and Ho; Pop. 900.) Formerly P. C. of St. John's, Fitzroy-square, Lond. and R. of Barton, Beds. Author, *The Forethought of Wisdom*, 1858; *Thoughts for the Times*, 1859, Nisbet. [5]

GILLAM, C. M. de P., *Milborne Port, Somerset.*—V. of Milborne Port. [6]

GILLAM, John, *Combeinteignhead, Devon.*—C. of Combeinteignhead. [7]

GILLAM, T. H., *Culham, Abingdon.*—Pemb. Coll. Ox. M.A. V. of Culham, Dio. Ox. 1862. (Patron, Bp of Ox; Tithe, App. 29*l* 5*s* 9*d*; Glebe, 60 acres; V.'s Inc. 100*l* and Ho; Pop. 474.) Chap. to Bp of Chester; Surrogate. [8]

GILLAN, J. H., *Guernsey.*—C. of St. John's, Guernsey. [9]

GILLARD, John, *Davidstow Vicarage, Boscastle, Cornwall.*—Oriel Coll. Ox. B A. 1820; Deac. 1821 and Pr. 1824 by Bp of Ex. V. of Davidstow, Dio. Ex. 1864. (Patron, H.R.H. Prince of Wales, Duke of Cornwall; Tithe, 241*l* 6*s* 8*d*; Glebe, 26 acres; V.'s Inc. 270*l* and Ho; Pop. 394.) Formerly C. of Treneglos and Warbston 1823, St. Clether and St. Juliot, 1825. R. of Sydenham Damerel, Devon, 1832, C. of Davidstow, 1836. [10]

GILLETT, Daniel, *Geldeston Rectory, Beccles.*—Magd. Coll. Cam. B.A. 1839, M.A. 1844; Deac. 1840 and Pr. 1841 by Bp of Nor. R. of Geldeston, Dio Nor. 1857. (Patron, Ld. Chan; Tithe, 170*l* 6*s*; Glebe, 32 acres; R.'s Inc. 220*l* and Ho; Pop. 345.) C. of Stockton 1848. Formerly C. of Bixley with Earl-Framingham 1840–48. [11]

GILLETT, Edward, *Runham Vicarage, Filby, Norwich.*—Emman. Coll. Cam. 1839, Exhib. 1841, 13th Sen. Opt. B.A. 1842, M A. 1845; Deac. 1843 and Pr. 1844 by Bp of Nor. V. of Runham, Dio. Nor. 1852. (Patron, Bp of Nor; Tithe—App. 255*l* 0*s* 9*d*, V. 145*l* 5*s* 10*d*; Glebe, 36 acres; V.'s Inc. 212*l* and Ho; Pop. 396.) [12]

GILLETT, Gabriel Edwards, *Waltham Rectory, Melton Mowbray, Leicestershire.*—Oriel Coll. Ox. 2nd Lit. Hum. 2nd cl. Math. et Phy. and B.A. 1820, M.A. 1823; Deac. 1822, Pr. 1823. R. of Waltham-on-the-Wolds, Dio. Pet. 1831. (Patron, Duke of Rutland; Glebe, 420 acres; R.'s Inc. 506*l* and Ho; Pop. 672.) Rural Dean; Proctor in Convocation for Dio. Pet. 1850; Hon, Can. of Pet. 1867. [13]

GILLETT, Hugh Hodgson, *Waltham, Melton Mowbray.*—Ex. Coll. Ox. B.A. 1857, M.A. 1860; Deac. 1859 and Pr. 1860 by Bp of Ox. C. of Waltham 1867. Formerly C. of Wantage with Charlton 1859, Finedon, Higham Ferrers, 1862, Compton Guildford, 1865 7. [14]

GILLETT, J., *Compton, Surrey.*—C. of Compton. [15]

GILLETT, Jesse, *Worlingham Rectory, Beccles, Suffolk.*—St. Bees; Deac. 1862 by Bp of Ches. Pr. 1863 by Bp of Lich. C. of Worlingham 1867. Formerly C. of Crewe, Cheshire, 1862–3, Ellastone and Stanton, Staffs, 1863–7. [16]

GILLHAM, Thomas Wheeler, *Caldecot Vicarage, Rockingham.*—Corpus Coll. Cam. B.A. 1823, M.A. 1826; Deac. and Pr. 1825. V. of Liddington with Caldecote, Dio. Pet. 1835. (Patron, Bp of Pet; Liddington, Tithe—App. 4*l*, V. 5*l*; Glebe, 84 acres; Caldecote, Tithe—App. 1*l* 6*s* 4*d*, V. 13*s* 4*d*; Glebe, 47 acres; V.'s Inc. 310*l*; Pop. Liddington 618, Caldecote 346.) [17]

GILLING, George Robert, *Halse, Taunton.*—P. C. of Fitzhead, Dio. B. and W. 1861. (Patron, V. of Wiveliscombe; P. C.'s Inc. 200*l* and Ho; Pop. 300.) [18]

GILLING, John Charles, *St. Mark's Parsonage, Rosherville, Northfleet, Kent.*—Wor. Coll. Ox. B.A. 1851, M.A. 1854; Deac. 1851 and Pr. 1852 by Bp of G. and B. P. C. of St. Mark's, Rosherville, Dio. Roch. 1858. (Patron, G. Rosher, Esq; P. C.'s Inc. 300*l* and Ho; Pop. 1750.) Formerly C. of Sudeley and Gretton, Glouc. [19]

GILLINGTON, John Maurice, *Audlem, Nantwich.*—Dub. A.B. 1851, A.M. 1857; Deac. 1851 by Bp of Meath, Pr. 1852 by Bp of Cork. C. of Audlem 1860. Formerly C. of Clara, Meath, 1851, St. Peter's, Athlone, 1853, Neston, Cheshire, 1856. [20]

GILLMOR, Clotworthy, *Bow, Crediton.*—St. John's Coll. Cam. M.A. 1845; Deac. 1840 and Pr. 1841 by Bp of B. and W. R. of Bow, *alias* Nymet-Tracey with Broad-Nymet, Dio. Ex. 1856. (Patron, F. Vandermeulen, Esq; R.'s Inc. 600*l*; Pop. 904.) Formerly V. of Dartford, Kent, 1844–56; C. of Herscham, Surrey. Author, *Reply to the Hon Baptist Noel*, 2nd ed. [21]

GILLMOR, William, *Illingworth Parsonage, Halifax.*—Dub. A.B. 1826, A.M. 1830; Deac. and Pr. 1829. P. C. of Illingworth, Dio. Rip. 1836. (Patron, V. of Halifax; Tithe, Imp. 57*l*; Glebe, 64 acres; P. C.'s Inc. 210*l* and Ho; Pop. 8896) Surrogate 1862. Formerly C. of Halifax. Author, *Christian Loyalty, a Sermon*, 1833; *Church-rates Voluntary and Compulsory*, 1837; *Church Establishments Lawful, but Church-rates not Expedient*, 1837; *A Pastoral Address to the Inhabitants of Illingworth*, 1839; *The Unity of the Church*, 1840; *The Pew System*, 1843; *National Sin the Cause of National Judgment*, 1847; *The Church of England, Scriptural, Efficient and Indestructible*, 1849; *Convocation*, 1853; *A Letter to the Parishioners of Illingworth*, 1853; *Submission under the Divine Chastisement*, 1855; *Twenty and Five Years*, 1861; *The Voyage of Life*, 1867; and various other Sermons, Pamphlets and Articles on Religious and Political affairs. [22]

GILLSON, Edward, *Mount Sorrel, Loughborough, Leicestershire.*—Trin. Hall, Cam. B.A. 1835, M.A. 1853; Deac. 1835 and Pr. 1836 by Bp of Ely. P. C. of Ch. Ch. Mount Sorrel, Dio. Pet. 1858. (Patron, Rev. C. Kemble; P. C.'s Inc. 150*l* and Ho; Pop. 897.) Formerly V. of High Littleton 1855–58. Author, *The Coming of the Lord to Judge the Earth, Doctrinally and Practically Considered*, 1845, 2*s* 6*d*; *The Relapsed Demoniac, a Warning to England against the Return of Popery*, 1854, 1*s*; *A Pastor's Parting Token of Affection to a beloved and loving People* (the substance of Ten Sermons), 1845, 3*s* 6*d*; *Table Talking Disclosures of Satanic Wonders and Prophetic Signs*, 3*d*; *A Watchman's Appeal, with special reference to the Wonders of the Age*, 4*d*; *A Farewell Address*, 4*d*; *An Earthly Blight with a Heavenly Hope*, 2*d*. [23]

GILLSON, Septimus, *Mugginton, Derby.*—Sid. Coll. Cam. B.A. 1863; Deac. 1863 by Bp of Pet. C. of Mugginton 1867. Formerly C. of Castle Donington 1863–65, Christ Church, Worthing, 1866. [24]

GILLUM, Sidney George, *Tongham, Farnham, Surrey.*—St. Peter's Coll. Cam. 1st cl. Theol. Trip. 1859, B.A. 1858, M.A. 1863; Deac. 1859 and Pr. 1860 by Bp of Win. P. C. of St. Paul's, Tongham, Dio. Win. 1866. (Patron, Archd. of Surrey; P. C.'s Inc. 100*l*; Pop. 735.) Formerly C. of Vernham Dean, Hants, 1859–62, Brightwell, Berks, 1864, Old Alresford, Hants, 1865. [25]

GILMORE, John, *Ramsgate, Kent.*—Caius Coll. Cam. B.A. 1853, M.A. 1856; Deac. 1854 and Pr. 1856 by Bp of Ches. P. C. of Trinity, St. Lawrence, Ramsgate, Dio. Cant. 1858. (Patron, V. of St. Lawrence, Ramsgate; P. C.'s Inc. 150*l*; Pop. 1351.) Author, *The*

Sailor Lad's Cry of Victory, 3s ; *The Death of the Fisherman*, 2s. [1]

GILSON, Samuel, *Rectory, Gratwich, Uttoxeter.*—Magd. Hall, Ox. B.A. 1847, M.A. 1848; Deac. 1846, Pr. 1847. R. of Gratwich, Dio. Lich. 1861. (Patron, Earl of Shrewsbury; Tithe, 100*l* 3*s*; Glebe 20 acres; R.'s Inc. 121*l* and Ho; Pop. 101.) P. C. of Kingstone, Staffs, Dio. Lich. 1861. (Patron, Earl of Shrewsbury; Tithe—App. 4*l*, Imp. 121*l* 11*s* 8*d*; P. C.'s Inc. 72*l*; Pop. 312.) Formerly C. of St. Mary's, Stafford, 1847; P. C. of St. Chad's, Stafford, and 2nd Mast. of Gr. Sch. Stafford, 1840-54; Archd. of Montreal, Canada, 1854–61, Vancouver Island, British Columbia, 1864–7. [2]

GINN, Frederick G., M.A., *Bunwell, Harling, Norfolk.*—C. of Bunwell. [3]

GIPPS, Frederick, *Corbridge-on-Tyne, Northumberland.*—Univ. Coll. Ox. B.A. 1849, M.A. 1853; Deac. 1851, Pr. 1852 by Bp of Lich. V. of Corbridge with Halton C. Dio. Dur. 1853. (Patrons, D. and C. of Carl; Tithe—App. 480*l* 2*s* 4*d*, Imp. 6*l* 18*s*, V. 111*l* 0*s* 6*d*; Glebe, 30 acres; V.'s Inc. 560*l* and Ho; Pop. 2170.) [4]

GIPPS, Henry, *The Abbey, Carlisle.*—Wor. Coll. Ox. 1st cl. Lit. Hum. and B.A. 1819, M.A. 1822; Deac. 1821, Pr. 1822. Can. Res. of Carl Cathl. 1845; V. of Crosthwaite, Cumberland, Dio. Carl. 1855. (Patron, Bp of Carl; Tithe—Imp. 385*l* 13*s* 11*d*, V. 432*l* 13*s* 2*d*; Pop. 1583.) Surrogate. Formerly Fell. of Wor. Coll. Ox; Exam. Chap. to the Bp of Carl. 1827. [5]

GIRARDOT, John Chancourt, *Car-Colston Vicarage, Bingham, Notts.*—Brasen. Coll. Ox. B.A. 1821, M.A. 1824; Deac. 1821 and Pr. 1822 by Bp of Lin. R. of Screveton, Notts, Dio. Lin. 1824. (Patron, T. Dickinson Hall, Esq; R.'s Inc. 275*l*; Pop. 241.) V. of Car-Colston, Notts, Dio. Lin. 1838. (Patron, the present V; Tithe, 153*l*; Glebe, 20 acres; V.'s Inc. 230*l* and Ho; Pop. 299.) [6]

GIRARDOT, William Lewis, *Hinton Charterhouse, Bath.*—Emman. Coll. Cam. B.A. 1832, M.A. 1835; Deac. 1835 and Pr. 1836 by Bp of Lon. P. C. of Hinton Charterhouse, Dio. B. and W. 1848. (Patron, V. of Norton St. Philip; P. C.'s Inc. 125*l*; Pop. 615.) [7]

GIRAUD, Edward Augustus, 10, *Northgate-street, Bury St. Edmunds.*—St. John's Coll. Cam. Wrang. and B.A. 1822, M.A. 1825; Deac. 1823 and Pr. 1824 by Bp of Ely. Fell. of Dulwich Coll. 1834. R. of Stanningfield, Bury St. Edmunds, Dio. Ely, 1856. (Patron, Sir Edward Rokewode Gage, Bart; Tithe, 345*l*; Glebe, 44 acres; R.'s Inc. 395*l*; Pop. 351.) [8]

GIRAUD, Henry Arthur, 28, *Gloucester-street, Pimlico, London, S.W.*—Mert. Coll. Ox. Scho. of Wor. Coll. 1st cl. Lit. Hum. and B.A. 1839, M.A. 1843; Deac. 1841 by Abp of Cant. Pr. 1842 by Abp of York. Chap. of King's Coll. Hospital, Lond. Formerly C. of Trinity, Tottenham, 1849. [9]

GIRDLESTONE, Charles, *Kingswinford Rectory, Stourbridge,* and *Holywell House, Weston-super-Mare.*—Wad. Coll. Ox. 1st cl. Lit. Hum. 2nd cl. Math. et Phy. and B.A. 1818, Ball. Coll. Ox. M.A. 1821; Deac. 1820, Pr. 1821. R. of Kingswinford, Dio. Lich. 1847. (Patron, Earl of Dudley; Tithe, 663*l*; Glebe, 150 acres; R.'s Inc. 950*l* and Ho; Pop. 5200.) Formerly Fell. of Ball. Coll. Ox; Examiner in Lit. Hum. 1825; Select Preacher 1825 and 1829; C. of Hastings 1822, Ferry Hincksey, Berks, 1824; V. of Sedgley, Staffs, 1826; R. of Alderley, Cheshire, 1837–47. Author, *The Holy Bible, with a Family Commentary*, 6 vols. 1832–42, 63*s*; *Seven Sermons on Christian Life*, 1823, 3 eds. 2*s* 6*d*; *Seven Sermons on Social Conduct*, 1825, 3 eds. 2*s* 6*d*; *Twenty Parochial Sermons, with an Appendix containing Parochial Papers*, 1829, 3 eds. (First Series), 5*s*; *Seven Sermons in the Time of Cholera*, 1832, 2 eds. 2*s* 6*d*; *Seven Sermons on the Lord's Supper*, 1833, 2 eds. 1*s*; *Seven Sermons on the Church Catechism*, 1833, 2*s* 6*d*; *Twenty Parochial Sermons, with an Appendix containing Helps for Family Devotion* (Second Series), 1833, 2 eds. 5*s*; *A Course of Sermons for each Sunday in the Year*, 2 vols. 1834, 14*s*; *A Concordance of the Prayer-book Translation of the Psalms*, 1834, 4*s* 6*d*; *Devotions for Private Use*, 1835, 2*s*; *Devotions for Family Use*, 1835, 2*s*; *Collection of Hymns for Private and Public Use*, 1835, 2*s*; *Scripture Writing Copies*, 1835, 3*d*; *The Book of Psalms, according to the Two Authorised Translations, in parallel columns, with Marginal Notes*, 1836, 4*s* 6*d*; *Twenty Parochial Sermons, on particular occasions, with an Appendix of Notes and Illustrations* (Third Series), 1836, 2 eds. 5*s*; *Farewell Sermons on leaving the Charge of Sedgley Parish*, 1837, 4*s* 6*d*; *Sedgley Church Tracts*, 28 in number, 1831–36; *Three Letters on Church Reform*, 1832–3–4, 1*s*; *Letters on the Unhealthy Condition of Dwellings*, 2 eds. 1854, 1*s* 6*d*; *Palingenesia*, 1850, 2*d*; *Sanitary Reform* (a Lecture), 1853, 3*d*; *Lectures on the Four Gospels*, 1853, 15*s*; the following single Sermons on Church Rates, published by Rivingtons, 6*d* each: *God's Word and Ministers*, 1838; *The Judgment of Solomon*, 1843; *The Right of Private Judgment*, 1847; *The Messiah Pierced*, 1850; *Scripture Politics*, 1851; also, single *Sermons*, 1*s* a dozen; *How to Live Happily*, 1838; *The Increase of Mankind a Blessing*, 1842; *The Cause and Cure of Abject Poverty*, 1847; *The Nature and Value of Good Government*, 1848; *Testimony against Romanism*, 1850; *The Signs of the Times*, 1853; *The Questions of the Day, by the Creature of an Hour*, 1857; *Mahomet versus the Pope*; *Negative Theology, an Argument for Liturgical Revision*, 1861; *Black Bartholomew's Day*, 1862; *Letter to Bishop of London*, 1863; *An Appeal to Evangelical Churchmen*, 1864. Editor, conjointly with Rev. W. A. Osborne, of the *Works of Horace for Young Persons*, Longmans, 7*s* 6*d*. [10]

GIRDLESTONE, Edward, *Halberton, Tiverton,* and *Canon's House, Bristol.*—Ball. Coll. Ox. 2nd cl. Lit. Hum. and B.A. 1826, M.A. 1829; Deac. 1828, Pr. 1830. Can. Res. of Bristol, 1854; V. of Halberton, Dio. Ex. 1862. (Patrons, D. and C. of Bristol; Tithe, 682*l*; Glebe, 40 acres; V.'s Inc. 690*l* and Ho; Pop. 1663.) Formerly V. of Wapley 1858–62; V. of St. Nicholas with St. Leonard's, Bristol, 1855–58. Author, *Sermons*, 1 vol; *Reflected Truth*, Mackintosh; and many occasional Sermons. [11]

GIRDLESTONE, Edward Deacon.—Wad. Coll. Ox. B.A. 1851; Deac. 1853. Formerly C. of Reedham, Norfolk. Author, *Heart Impropriation* (a Sermon), 1856. [12]

GIRDLESTONE, F. G., *Landford, Salisbury.*—C. of Landford. [13]

GIRDLESTONE, Francis Paddon, *Chaplain's Lodge, Hawkestone, Shrewsbury.*—Ch. Coll. Cam. B.A. 1856, M.A. 1864; Deac. 1861 by Bp of Dur. Pr. 1863 by Bp of Win. Dom. Chap. to Viscount Hill. Formerly C. of Heathery Cleugh, Durham, Normanton, Yorks, and Freemantle, Southampton. Author, Sermons and Tracts. [14]

GIRDLESTONE, Henry, *Landford Rectory, near Salisbury.*—St. Cath. Hall, Cam. B.A. 1809; Deac. 1808 and Pr. 1812 by Bp of Nor. R. of Colton, Norfolk, Dio. Nor. 1815. (Patron, Ld Chan; Tithe, 305*l*; Glebe, 25 acres; R.'s Inc. 384*l*; Pop. 228.) R. of Landford, Dio. Salis. 1833. (Patron, Earl Nelson; Tithe, 210*l*; Glebe, 43¾ acres; R.'s Inc. 285*l* and Ho; Pop. 278.) Author, various Sermons and Tracts, 1818–32; *The Hope of Israel*, 1842; *Notes on the Apocalypse, an Inquiry relative to the Chronology and Geography of the Apocalypse*, 1847. [15]

GIRDLESTONE, Henry, *Bath.*—Emman. Coll. Cam. B.A. 1854; Deac. 1856, Pr. 1857. V. of Bathampton, Dio. B. and W. 1866. (Patrons, D. and C. of Bristol; Tithe, 130*l*; V.'s Inc. 170*l*; Pop. 350.) Formerly C. of Kingswinford 1856, Penkridge 1859, Westbury-on-Trym 1865. [16]

GIRDLESTONE, John Gay, *Kelling Rectory, Holt, Norfolk.*—R. of Kelling with Salthouse R. Dio. Nor. 1840. (Patroness, Mrs. Girdlestone; Kelling, Tithe, 300*l*; Glebe, 14 acres; Salthouse, Tithe, 220*l*; Glebe, 1½ acres; R.'s Inc. 541*l* and Ho; Pop. Kelling 211, Salthouse 268.) [17]

GIRDLESTONE, Robert Baker, *Clapham, S.*—Ch. Ch. Ox. B.A. 1859, M.A. 1861; Deac. 1860 and Pr.

1861 by Bp of Chich. C. of St. James's, Clapham. Formerly C. of Worthing. [1]

GIRDLESTONE, W. Harding, *Ryde, Isle of Wight.*—Ch. Coll. Cam. M.A. V. of Ryde, Dio. Win. 1863. (Patron, Bp of G. and B; Tithe, 120l; V.'s Inc. 120l; Pop. 6000.) Surrogate. [2]

GIRLING, John Charles, *Great Hautbois, Coltishall, Norfolk.*—R. of Great Hautbois, Dio. Nor. 1859. (Patron, Samuel Bignold, Esq; P. C.'s Inc. 169l; Pop. 195.) Formerly C. of Cromer. [3]

GIRLING, William Henry, *Newton-Solney, Burton-on-Trent.*—St. Aidan's 1856; Deac. 1857 and Pr. 1858 by Bp of Rip. Chap. of Don. of Newton-Solney, Burton-on-Trent, Dio. Lich. 1864. (Patron, Sir Henry Every, Bart; Chap.'s Inc. 150l; Pop. 406.) Formerly C. of Slaithwaite 1857–60, Rashcliffe-Lockwood 1860–64. [4]

GISBORNE, James, *Croxall Vicarage, Burton-on-Trent.*—V. of Croxall, Dio. Lich. 1838. (Patron, Ld Chan; Tithe, 218l; V.'s Inc. 490l and Ho; Pop. 247.) [5]

GLADSTONE, David Thomas, *Loddington Rectory, near Kettering.*—Wad. Coll. Ox. 2nd cl. Math. et Phy. B.A. 1845, M.A. 1849; Deac. 1847 and Pr. 1848 by Bp of Rip. R. of Loddington, Dio. Pet. 1865. (Patron, Ld Chan; Tithe, 384l 14s; Glebe, 115l 6s; R.'s Inc. 500l and Ho; Pop. 290.) Formerly C. of Leeds 1847–51; P. C. of St. Thomas's, Leeds, 1851–54; C. of Guiseley 1855–59, Kirkby Malzeard 1859–65. [6]

GLADSTONE, John, *Stoke-upon-Terne Rectory, Hodnet, Salop.*—Brasen. Coll. Ox. B.A. 1823, M.A. 1826; Deac. 1826 and Pr. 1827 by Bp of Ches. R. of Stoke-upon-Terne, Dio. Lich. 1846. (Patron, Richard Corbett, Esq; Tithe, 949l 10s; Glebe, 50 acres; R.'s Inc. 1049l and Ho; Pop. 961.) [7]

GLADSTONE, John Eddowes, *Elm Cottage, Wraxall, Somerset.*—Magd. Hall, Ox. B.A. 1845; Deac. 1845 and Pr. 1846 by Bp of Nor. C. of Tickenham. Formerly C. of St. Clement's, Norwich, 1845; P. C. of St. Mark's, New Lakenham, Norfolk, 1846–51. [8]

GLADWIN, Charles, *Woolley, Kimbolton.*—Jesus Coll. Cam. B.A. 1834, M.A. 1862; Deac. 1834 by Bp of Ches. Pr. 1835 by Bp of Lin. R. of Woolley, Dio. Ely, 1860. (Patron, J. Cockerell, Esq; Tithe, 2l 8s; Glebe, 170 acres; V.'s Inc. 132l 8s; Pop. 90.) Formerly C. of Great Linford, Leckhamstead, and Cholesbury, Bucks. [9]

GLAISTER, William, *Southwell, Notts.*—Univ. Coll. Ox. B.A. 1865; Deac. 1865 and Pr. 1866 by Bp of Lin. C. of Southwell 1865. [10]

GLANVILLE, Edward Fanshawe, *Clevedon House, Oxford.*—Ex. Coll. Ox. B.A. 1828, M.A. 1830; Deac. 1831, Pr. 1833. Formerly P. C. of St. Luke's, Tideford, a district Chapelry of St. Germans, Cornwall, 1854–56; R. of Wheatfield, Oxon, 1836–52. [11]

GLANVILLE, Henry Carew, *Sheviocke Rectory, Devonport.*—Ex. Coll. Ox. Fell. of, 3rd cl. Lit. Hum. M.A. 1852; Deac. 1853, Pr. 1855. R. of Sheviocke, Dio. Ex. 1855. (Patron, W. H. P. Carew, Esq; Tithe, 347l; Glebe, 100 acres; R.'s Inc. 447l and Ho; Pop. 671.) [12]

GLANVILLE, James Gordon, *Ellingham Vicarage, near Ringwood, Hants.*—Dub. A.B. 1837; Deac. 1843, Pr. 1846. V. of Ellingham, Dio. Win. 1858. (Patron, Eton Coll; V.'s Inc. 170l and Ho; Pop. 306.) Formerly C. of Whiteparish, Wilts, 1847–58. [13]

GLASCODINE, Richard W., *Litlington, Royston, Herts.*—C. of Litlington. [14]

GLASCOTT, Cholmeley Cradock, 32, *Rue Satory, Versailles, near Paris.*—Ball. Coll. Ox. 3rd cl. Lit. Hum. B.A. 1847; Deac. 1849 and Pr. 1850 by Bp of Lon. British Chap. at Versailles 1856. [15]

GLASCOTT, Thomas, *Rodborough Rectory, Gloucestershire.*—Ball. Coll. Ox. B.A. 1814, M.A. 1820; Deac. 1815 and Pr. 1816 by Bp of Ex. R. of Rodborough, Dio. G. and B. 1840. (Patron, D. Ricardo, Esq; Tithe, 186l 12s; Glebe, 74l; R.'s Inc. 300l and Ho; Pop. 1756.) Formerly C. of Stockleigh Pomeroy 1815–18, Rodborough 1818–40. [16]

GLASSON, Henry.—St. John's Coll. Cam. B.A. 1852; Deac. 1852, Pr. 1853. Chap. of H.M.S. "St. George." [17]

GLAZEBROOK, James Kirkland, *Lower Darwen Parsonage, Blackburn, Lancashire.*—Magd. Hall, Ox. B.A. 1831, M.A. 1837; Deac. 1831 and Pr. 1832 by Bp of Ches. P. C. of Lower Darwen, Dio. Man. 1841. (Patron, V. of Blackburn; Tithe, Imp. 117l 18s 6d; Glebe, 5 acres; P. C.'s Inc. 150l and Ho; Pop. 2081.) Author, *Socialism* (a Sermon), 1839; *Puseyism, or Remarks on Portions of the 13th Chapter of Newman on Justification*, 1839; *Table Talking a Fraud, or Godfrey's Cordial for the Satanic Agency School*, 1854. [18]

GLAZEBROOK, John Kirkland, *Melling Parsonage, Ormskirk, Lancashire.*—Magd. Hall, Ox. B.A. 1846, M.A. 1848; Deac. 1847, Pr. 1849. P. C. of Melling, Dio. Ches. 1849. (Patron, R. of Halsall; P. C.'s Inc. 110l and Ho; Pop. 728.) [19]

GLEADALL, John William, 11, *Regent-square, London, W.C.*—St. Cath Coll. Cam. B.A. 1823, M.A. 1827; Deac. 1826, Pr. 1827. Morning Preacher at the Foundling Hospital; Lect. of St. Mary-at-Hill, City of Lond; Fell. of St. Cath. Coll. Cam. Author, *Lectures on the Apostacy*; *Lectures on the Inspiration of Holy Scripture*; *Lectures on the Sabbath*; *Lectures on Christianity*; various single Sermons. [20]

GLEADHILL, Andrew Clarke.—C. of St. Titus', Liverpool. [21]

GLEADOWE, Richard William, *Neston Vicarage, Cheshire.*—Caius Coll. Cam. B.A. 1834, M.A. 1837; Deac. 1835 and Pr. 1836 by Bp of Lich. V. of Neston, Dio. Ches. 1853. (Patrons, D. and C. of Ches; Glebe, 12 acres; V.'s Inc. 750l and Ho; Pop. 3956.) Surrogate. Formerly Head Mast. of the Chester Gr. Sch; Min. Can. and Sacrist. of Chester Cathl. [22]

GLEADOWE, Thomas Littlewood, *Frodesley Rectory, near Shrewsbury.*—Ch. Coll. Cam. B.A. 1831, M.A. 1835; Deac. 1832 and Pr. 1833 by Bp of Lich. R. of Frodesley, Dio. Lich. 1842. (Patron, the present R; Tithe, 400l; Glebe, 21 acres; R.'s Inc. 450l and Ho; Pop. 256.) Author, *Daily Prayers for Christian Households*, 1853. [23]

GLEDHILL, Joseph, *Ripponden, Halifax.*—Dur. Theol. Licen. 1859; Deac. 1859 and Pr. 1861 by Bp of Rip. C. of Ripponden 1859. [24]

GLEIG, George Robert, 8, *Warwick-square, Pimlico, London, S.W.*—Ball. Coll. Ox. B.A. 1819, M.A. 1851; Deac. 1819 and Pr. 1820 by Abp of Cant. R. of Ivychurch, Kent, Dio. Cant. 1822. (Patron, Abp of Cant; Tithe, 450l; R.'s Inc. 460l and Ho; Pop. 273.) Chaplain-General of the Forces 1845; Inspector-General of Military Schools 1846; Preb. of Willesden in St. Paul's Cathl. 1848 (Value, 2l). Formerly P. C. of Ash, Kent, 1821–22; Chap. of Chelsea Hospital 1834-65. Author, *Life of Arthur Duke of Wellington*, 1864; *Life of Sir Thomas Monroe*, 3 vols. 1830; *Life of Lord Clive*; *Life of Warren Hastings*, 3 vols; *India and its Army*, 1857; *Continuation of the Late Marquis of Londonderry's History of the Peninsular War*, 1857; *Germany, Bohemia and Hungary visited in* 1857, 1859; *Sketch of the Military History of Great Britain*, 1845; *Sale's Brigade in Afghanistan*, 1846; *Campaigns of the British Army at Washington*, 1847; *History of India*, 4 vols; *Story of the Battle of Waterloo*; *The Leipsic Campaign*; *The National Library* (14 Nos.), 1830–32; *Lectures before the Church of England Young Men's Society*, 1853; *Essays, Historical, Biographical, and Miscellaneous*, 2 vols. 1858; *Sacred History* and *History of the British Colonies* (*Gleig's School Series* in progress); Fiction—*The Subaltern*, 1826; *The Chelsea Pensioners*, 1829; *The Country Curate*, 1830; *Allan Breck*, 1834; *Chelsea Hospital* 3 vols. 1838; *Catherine Randolph*; *The Light Dragoon*, 1851; *The Only Daughter*, 3 vols; *Waltham, or Chronicles of a Country Village*; *Things Old and New, a sequel to Waltham*; Theology—*A Guide to the Holy Sacrament of the Lord's Supper*, 1835; *Religion in the Ranks*; *The Soldier's Help to Divine Truth*; *The Soldier's Manual of Devotion*; *History of the Bible*, 2 vols; *Sermons Doctrinal and Practical*, 1829; *Sermons for the*

Seasons of Advent, Christmas and Epiphany, 1844; *A Letter to Sir E. Knatchbull*, 1823; *A Letter to the Bishop of London on Church Reform*, 1833; *Some Observations on the Constitution and Tendency of the Church Missionary Society.* [1]

GLEN, William, *Stewkley, Leighton Buzzard.*—Emman. Coll. Cam. Wrang. and B.A. 1856, M.A. 1859; Deac. 1857 and Pr. 1858 by Bp of Ches. C. of Stewkley, Bucks, 1862. Formerly C. of Bunbury, Cheshire, 1857, Marsh Gibbon, Bucks, 1861. [2]

GLENCROSS, James, M.A., *Liskeard, Cornwall.* [3]

GLENCROSS, James Hickes, *Helland, Bodmin.*—Ch. Coll. Cam. B.A. 1853; Deac. 1853 and Pr. 1855 by Bp of Ex. R. of Helland, Dio. Ex. 1859. (Patron, W. Morshead, Esq; Tithe, 218*l* 10*s*; Glebe, 22 acres; R.'s Inc. 258*l* and Ho; Pop. 224.) Formerly C. of Bodmin. [4]

GLENNIE, Alfred Henry, *Kirkby Lonsdale, Westmoreland.*—Trin. Coll. Cam. Jun. Opt. B.A. 1866; Deac. 1866. C. of Kirkby Lonsdale. [5]

GLENNIE, John David, *Blore Rectory, near Ashbourne.*—Ch. Coll. Cam. B.A. 1848, M.A. 1852; Deac. 1849 and Pr. 1850 by Abp of Cant. C. in sole charge of Blore Ray, Staffs, 1861. Formerly C. of Postling, Kent, 1849–51, Lyminge, Kent, 1851–53; Lond. Dioc. Inspector of Schools 1853–57; H.M. Asst. Inspector of Schools, London and Middlesex, 1857–58, Norfolk, Suffolk and Essex, 1858–60. Author, *Hints from an Inspector of Schools*, Stanford, 1858, 1*s*. [6]

GLENNIE, John David, 51, *Green-street, Grosvenor-square, London, W.*—Trin. Coll. Cam. B.A. 1819, M.A. 1823; Deac. 1822 by Bp of Nor. Pr. 1822 by Bp of Lin. Sec. of the S.P.C.K. Formerly Sec. of the Clergy Orphan Corporation; Treasurer of the French Protestant Ecclesiastical Committee; P. C. of Sandgate, Kent, 1822; Min. of St. Mary's Chapel, Park-street, Grosvenor-square, Lond. 1835. [7]

GLOSSOP, Charles, *Wolverton Rectory, Beckington, Somerset.*—R. of Road with Wolverton, Dio. B. and W. 1812. (Patron, G. Goldney, Esq; Tithe, 455*l*; Glebe, 85 acres; R.'s Inc. 556*l* and Ho; Pop. Road 663, Wolverton 171.) [8]

GLOSSOP, George Goodwin Pownall, *Twickenham, S.W.*—Trin. Coll. Cam. B.A. 1849, M.A. 1851; Deac. 1852 and Pr. 1853 by Bp of Ox. V. of Twickenham, Dio. Lon. 1865. (Patrons, D. and C. of Windsor; Tithe, comm. 634*l*; Glebe, 9 acres; V.'s Inc. 800*l* and Ho; Pop. 4800.) Formerly C. at Isleworth and Windsor; R. of West Dean, Wilts, 1861–65. [9]

GLOSSOP, Henry, *Silver Hall, Isleworth, Middlesex.*—Corpus Coll. Cam. B.A. 1804, M.A. 1807; Deac. and Pr. 1804 by Bp of Lon. Formerly V. of Isleworth. [10]

GLOUCESTER and BRISTOL, The Right Rev. Charles John ELLICOTT, Lord Bp of Gloucester and Bristol, *The Palace, Gloucester*, and *Athenæum, Pall-mall.*—St. John's Coll. Cam. Bell's Univ. Prizeman and Hulsean Prizeman 1843, Sen. Opt. and 2nd cl. Cl. Trip. and B.A. 1841, M.A. 1844; Deac. 1846 and Pr. 1847 by Bp of Ely. Consecrated Bp of Gloucester and Bristol 1863. (Income of See, 5000*l* and Res; Jurisdiction, the County of Gloucester, the City and Deaneries of Bristol, of Bedminster and of Abbot's Leigh, Somerset, and the Deaneries of Malmesbury and Cricklade, Wilts; Pop. 568,574; Acres, 1,010,503; Deaneries, 13; Benefices, 443; Curates, 189; Church Sittings, 197,568.) His Lordship was formerly Fell. of St. John's Coll. Cam; R. of Pilton, Rutlandshire, 1841–48; Prof. of Divinity in King's Coll. Lond. 1848–61; Dean of Exeter 1861–63. Author, *Treatise on Analytical Statics*, 1851; *Obligation of the Sabbath* (Hulsean Prize Essay), 1843; *Critical and Grammatical Commentary on the Galatians*, 1854; *Critical and Grammatical Commentary on the Ephesians*, 1855; *Critical and Grammatical Commentary on Philippians and Colossians*; *on Thessalonians*; *on the Pastoral Epistles*, 1858; *Lectures on the Life of Our Lord*; *The Broad and the Narrow Way*; *Primary Charge for* 1864. [11]

GLOVER, Edward, *Capetown.*—Jesus Coll. Cam. Sen. Opt. B.A. 1849, M.A. 1852; Deac. 1851 and Pr. 1852 by Bp of Wor. Warden of Native College, Dio. of Capetown, 1859; Chap. to Bp of Capetown. Formerly C. of Frankley, Worc. 1851; R. of Schoonberg, Dio. Capetown, 1856. [12]

GLOVER, Frederick Augustus, *Shadforth, Durham.*—St. Bees; Deac. 1866 by Bp of Dur. C. of Shadforth 1866. [13]

GLOVER, George, *Enmore Green, Shaftesbury.*—Ch. Coll. Cam. Sch. Sen. Opt. B.A. 1857, M.A. 1860; Deac. 1858 and Pr. 1859 by Bp of Roch. C. of Enmore Green 1861. Formerly C. of Benfleet 1858, Tisbury 1860. [14]

GLOVER, Henry, *Croydon, S.*—St. Bees; Deac. 1857 and Pr. 1858 by Abp of Cant. C. of St. Matthew's, Croydon. Formerly C. of Trinity, Maidstone, and Ch. Ch. Dover. [15]

GLOVER, John, *Brading, Ryde, Isle of Wight.*—Trin. Coll. Cam. Wrang. 2nd cl. Cl. Trip. and B.A. 1846, M.A. 1849; Deac. 1849 by Bp of Win. Pr. 1850 by Bp of Cork. V. of Brading, Dio. Win. 1862. (Patron, Trin. Coll. Cam; Tithe—Imp. 1319*l* 3*s* 6*d* and Glebe, 16½ acres, V. 331*l* 12*s* 6*d* and Glebe, 5 acres; V.'s Inc. 350*l* and Ho; Pop. 1183.) Formerly C. of Hollymount, co. Down, 1849, and Trumpington, Cambs, 1853; Librarian of Trin. Coll. Cam. 1858. [16]

GLOVER, John Hulbert, 3, *St. Katharine's, Regent's-park, London, N.W.*—Clare Coll. Cam. 5th in 1st cl. Cl. Trip. 3rd Jun. Opt. and B.A. 1843, M.A. 1846; Deac. 1849 and Pr. 1851 by Bp of Ely. P. C. of Kingsthorpe, Northants, Dio. Pet. 1856. (Patron, St. Katharine's Hospital; Glebe, 270 acres; P. C.'s Inc. 650*l* and Ho; Pop. 1906.) Brother of St. Katharine's Hospital, Regent's-park, 1854. Formerly Fell. of Clare Coll. Cam. [17]

GLOVER, Josephus, *Lansdowne-crescent, Bath.*—St. John's Coll. Cam. Prizeman in Moral Philos. 6th Wrang. and B.A. 1848, M.A. 1851, B.D. 1860, D.D. 1866; Deac. 1853 by Bp of Ely, Pr. 1854 by Bp of B. and W. Prin. of the Univ. Sch. Bath. [18]

GLOVER, Octavius, *Emmanuel College, Cambridge.*—Emman. Coll. Cam. 13th Wrang. Crosse and 2nd Tyrrwhit Scho. B.A. 1854, M.A. 1857, B.D. 1864. Formerly Chap. of H.M.S. "Clio;" Vice-Prin. of the Coll. Sch. Vancouver's Island, 1860–63. Author, *A Life of Christ from Ewald*, 1865, 9*s*; *A Short Treatise on Sin*, Masters, 1866, 3*s* 6*d*; *The Person of Christ, an Historical Treatise*, Deighton, Bell and Co., 1867, 3*s*. [19]

GLOVER, Richard, *Christ Church Parsonage, Dover.*—Dur. Barry Theol. Scho. Licen. in Theol. 1851, M.A. 1862; Deac 1851 and Pr. 1852 by Abp of Cant. P. C. of Ch. Ch. Dover, Dio. Cant. 1862. (Patrons, Trustees; P. C.'s Inc. from pew rents; Pop. 1803.) Surrogate. Formerly C. of Folkestone 1851–54; P. C. of Holy Trinity, Maidstone, 1854–62. Author, *By the Waters of Babylon*, a series of Sermons to Young Men, 1857, 3*s* 6*d*; *The Light of the World, or Holman Hunt's Great Allegorical Picture translated into Words*, 1862, 2nd ed. 1863, 2*s* 6*d*; *The Finding of Christ in the Temple* (on Holman Hunt's Picture) 1866, 4*s*; various single Sermons; etc. [20]

GLOVER, William Henry, *Thornden, Eye.*—Ex. Coll. Ox. B.A. 1839; Deac. 1849 and Pr. 1850. R. of Thornden, Dio. Nor. 1861. (Patron, Rev. T. C. E. Warcup; Tithe, 370*l*; Glebe, 79½ acres; R.'s Inc. 850*l* and Ho; Pop 764.) Formerly Chap. of the Donative of St. Mary's, Bungay, 1850. [21]

GLUBB, John Matthew, *Shermanbury Rectory, near Hurstpierpoint, Sussex.*—Ex. Coll. Ox. 2nd cl. Lit. Hum. and B.A. 1814, M.A. 1829; Deac. 1814 and Pr. 1815 by Bp of Ex. R. of Shermanbury, Dio. Chich. 1836. (Patroness, Mrs. Hunt; Tithe, 387*l*; Glebe, 15 acres; R.'s Inc. 405*l* and Ho; Pop. 464.) Rural Dean 1855; Surrogate; Dioc. Inspector of Schools 1855. [22]

GLUBB, Peter Southmead, *St. Anthony-in-Meneage Vicarage, Helston, Cornwall.*—Sid. Coll. Cam. B.D. 1857; Deac. 1848 and Pr. 1849 by Bp of Ex. V. of St. Anthony-in-Meneage, Dio. Ex. 1858. (Patron, Ld Chan; Tithe—Imp. 210*l*, V. 140*l*; Glebe, 2 acres; V.'s Inc. 150*l* and Ho; Pop. 252.) Formerly C. of Saltash, Cornwall. [1]

GLYN, Carr John, *Witchampton, Wimborne, Dorset.*—Ch. Ch. Ox. M.A. 1824; Deac. 1828, Pr. 1829. R. of Witchampton, Dio. Salis. 1830. (Patron, H. G. Sturt, Esq. M.P; Tithe, 269*l* 10*s* 9*d*; Glebe, 19½ acres; R.'s Inc. 326*l* and Ho; Pop. 588.) R. of Little Hinton, Dorset, Dio. Salis. 1830. (Patron, Sir R. G. Glyn, Bart; Tithe, 77*l*; Glebe, 31¼ acres; R.'s Inc. 126*l*; Pop. 54.) Formerly Chap. to Lord de Mauley. Author, *The Bible Society and its Deep Importance and Usefulness for Fifty Years.* [2]

GLYN, Charles Thomas, *Wycliffe Rectory, Greta-bridge, Yorks.*—Trin. Coll. Cam. B.A. 1843; Deac. 1844 and Pr. 1845 by Bp of Pet. R. of Wycliffe, Dio. Rip. 1854. (Patron, Sir C. Constable; Tithe, 427*l* 17*s* 6*d*; Glebe, 40 acres; R.'s Inc. 490*l* and Ho; Pop. 162.) [3]

GLYN, Sir George Lewen, Bart., *Ewell, Epsom, Surrey.*—Ch. Ch. Ox. M.A. 1828; Deac. and Pr. 1831 by Bp of Win. V. of Ewell, Dio. Win. 1831. (Patron, the present V; Tithe, 236*l*; Glebe, 7 acres; V.'s Inc. 290*l*; Pop. 1922.) Chap. to the Earl of Shaftesbury. Author, *Life of Elisha, in Eleven Plain and Practical Discourses*, 1857, 2*s*. [4]

GLYN, Henry Thomas, *Melbury-Abbas Rectory, Shaftesbury, Dorset.*—New Inn Hall, Ox. B.A. 1845; Deac. 1846 and Pr. 1847 by Bp of Nor. R. of Melbury-Abbas, Dio. Salis. 1847. (Patron, Sir Richard G. Glyn, Bart; Tithe, 380*l*; Glebe, 1½ acres; R.'s Inc. 380*l* and Ho; Pop. 412.) Rural Dean 1853. [5]

GLYNN, Albert, 73, *Seel-street, Liverpool.*—St. Peter's Coll. Cam. 16th Wrang. and B.A. 1853, M.A. 1858; Deac. 1855 by Bp of Ely. Bye-Fell. of St. Peter's Coll. Cam; 2nd Mast. at the Royal Institution, Liverpool. [6]

GLYNN, Charles, *Wolvey Vicarage, near Hinckley.*—Trin. Coll. Cam. B.A. 1851, M.A. 1854; Deac. 1851 by Bp of Llan. Pr. 1852 by Bp of G. and B. V. of Wolvey, Dio. Wor. 1859. (Patrons, Bp of Wor. and J. W. Smith, Esq. alt; Tithe—Imp. 7*l* 6*s*, V. 9*l* 2*s* 6*d*; V.'s Inc. 250*l* and Ho; Pop. 958.) Formerly C. of Grimley, Worcester, and Bromesberrow, Glouc. [7]

GLYNNE, Henry, *Hawarden Rectory, Chester.*—Ch. Ch. Ox. B.A 1833, M.A. 1835; Deac. and Pr. 1834 by Bp of Ox. R. of Hawarden, Flintshire, Dio. St. A. 1834. (Patron, Sir Stephen Glynne, Bart; Tithe, 2871*l* 4*s* 5*d*; Glebe, 100 acres; R.'s Inc. 3000*l* and Ho; Pop. 7014.) Rural Dean 1851; Hon. Can. of St. A. 1855. [8]

GOALEN, Alexander, 49, *Holywell-street, Oxford.*—Brasen. Coll. and New Inn Hall, Ox. B.A. 1857; Deac. 1858 and Pr. 1859 by Bp of Ox. Lect. in Nat. Sci. at New Inn Hall, Ox. and C. of Abingdon. Formerly C. of Culham; and Hon. Chap. to the Central Dioc. Sch. Thame. Author, *Four Sermons on the Comfortable Words in the Office for the Holy Communion.* [9]

GOBAT, Samuel Benoni, *Parsonage, Is-y-Coed, Wrexham.*—Trin. Coll. Ox. B.A. 1860; Deac. 1860 by Bp of Win. P. C. of Is-y-Coed, Dio. St. A. 1862. (Patrons, D. and C. of Win; P. C.'s Inc. 79*l* and Ho; Pop. 482.) Formerly C. of Romsey 1860–62. [10]

GODBER, William, *Abberton, Essex.*—King's Coll. Lond. Assoc. 1862; Deac. 1862 and Pr. 1863 by Bp of Roch. C. of Abberton. [11]

GODBY, Charles Henry, *Henley-on-Thames, Oxon.*—Lin. Coll. Ox. 2nd cl. Lit. Hum. and B.A. 1843, M.A. 1846; Deac. 1844, Pr. 1845. Head Mast. of the Henley-on-Thames Gr. Sch. 1844. [12]

GODDARD, Daniel Ward, *Holwell, Burford, Oxon.*—Ex. Coll. Ox. B.A. 1833, M.A. 1835; Deac. 1834, Pr. 1835. P. C. of Holwell, Dio. Ox. 1860. (Patron, Col. Bagot Lane; P. C.'s Inc. 100*l*; Pop. 193.) [13]

GODDARD, Edward, *Eartham, Chichester.*—V. of Eartham, Dio. Chich. 1828. (Patron, the Preb. of Eartham; Tithe, 192*l* 12*s*; Glebe, 19 acres; V.'s Inc. 214*l*; Pop. 121.) [14]

GODDARD, Francis, *Hillmarton Vicarage, Calne.*—Brasen. Coll. Ox. B.A. 1836, M.A. 1839; Deac. 1837 and Pr. 1838 by Bp of Salis. V. of Hillmarton, Dio. Salis. 1858. (Patron, the Crown; Tithe, 400*l*; Glebe, 5 acres; V.'s Inc. 445*l* and Ho; Pop. 787.) Rural Dean; Surrogate. Formerly C. of Winterbourne Bassett, Wilts, 1837, Writhlington, Somerset, 1845; P. C. of Alderton, Wilts, 1849–58. [15]

GODDARD, Francis Aspinwall, *Milford House, Sutton Coldfield, Warwickshire.*—St. John's Coll. Ox. B.A. 1861, M.A. 1865; Deac. 1864 by Abp of Cant. Pr. 1865 by Bp of Roch. C. of Sutton Coldfield 1866; 2nd Mast. of Sutton Coldfield Gr. Sch. Formerly C. of Mistley, Essex, 1864–66; Asst. Mast. at Dedham Gr. Sch. Essex, 1863–66. [16]

GODDARD, George Frederick, *Southfleet Rectory, Gravesend, Kent.*—Magd. Coll. Ox. B.A. 1839. R. of Southfleet, Dio. Roch. 1854. (Patron, Bp of Roch; Tithe, 875*l*; Glebe, 6 acres; R.'s Inc. 887*l* and Ho; Pop. 717.) Hon. Can. of Roch. [17]

GODDARD, Thomas, *Rectory, Kingsley, Cheadle, Staffs.*—Sid. Coll. Cam. B.A. 1846, M.A. 1859; Deac. 1847 by Bp of Pet. Pr. 1848 by Bp of Lich. R. of Kingsley, Dio. Lich. 1859. (Patron, James Beech, Esq; R.'s Inc. 340*l* and Ho; Pop. 2640.) Formerly P. C. of Forsbrooke 1852–59. [18]

GODDARD, William Ward, *Wittersham, Staplehurst, Kent.*—Ex. Coll. Ox. B.A. 1864; Deac. 1866 by Abp of Cant. C. of Wittersham 1866. [19]

GODDEN, William Worcester, *Brighton.*—Wor. Coll. Ox. B.A. 1847, M.A. 1851; Deac. 1849 and Pr. 1850 by Bp of Chich. Sen. C. of Brighton 1860. Formerly C. of Brighton 1849, Petworth 1851. [20]

GODDING, John, *Homerton, London, N.E.*—Magd. Hall, Ox. B.A. 1856, M.A. 1857; Deac. 1856 and Pr. 1857 by Bp of Carl. P. C. of St. Barnabas', Homerton, Dio. Lon. 1860. (Patron, Bp of Lon; P. C.'s Inc. 300*l* and Ho; Pop. 8663.) Formerly C. of St. Mary's, Carlisle, 1856–58, Barkingside with Aldboro' Hatch 1858–60. [21]

GODFERY, William, *Martin-Hussingtree Rectory, Worcestershire.*—St. John's Coll. Cam. B.A. 1819, M.A. 1822; Deac. 1819 by Bp of Nor. Pr. 1820 by Bp of Lon. R. of Martin-Hussingtree, Dio. Wor. 1853. (Patrons, D. and C. of Wor; Tithe, 248*l* 8*s*; Glebe, 2 acres; R.'s Inc. 255*l* and Ho; Pop. 170.) Formerly R. of Bredicot-cum-Tibberton, Worc. 1841–53. [22]

GODFRAY, Frederick, *St. Heliers, Jersey.*—Wad. Coll Ox. B.A 1844, M.A. 1847; Deac. 1846. Dom. Chap. to the Earl of Limerick. [23]

GODFREY, Daniel Race, *Grosvenor College, Bath.*—Queen's Coll. Ox. Grand Compounder, 2nd cl. Lit. Hum. and B.A. 1810, M.A. 1817, B.D. and D.D. 1841; Deac. 1810 by Bp of B. and W. Pr. 1811 by Bp of Salis. Prin. of Grosvenor Coll. Bath; R. of Elm, Somerset, Dio. B. and W. 1866. (Patron, Rev. C. T. Griffith; R.'s Inc. 200*l* and Ho; Pop. 323.) [24]

GODFREY, Daniel Race, jun., *Stow-Bedon, Attleborough.*—Queen's Coll. Ox. 1st cl. Lit. Hum. and B.A. 1834, M.A. 1837; Deac. 1838 and Pr. 1839 by Bp of B. and W. R. of Stow-Bedon, Dio. Nor. 1859. (Patron, the present R; Tithe, 336*l* 10*s*; Glebe, 10 acres; R.'s Inc. 350*l* and Ho; Pop. 343.) Formerly Prin. of the Coll. Sch. Weston-super-Mare. [25]

GODFREY, Frederick, *Wenhaston, Halesworth, Suffolk.*—V. of Wenhaston, Dio. Nor. 1864. (Patron, Ld Chan; V's Inc. 120*l*; Pop. 948.) [26]

GODFREY, George, *Roxby, Brigg, Lincolnshire.*—Queen's Coll. Ox. B.A. 1864, M.A. 1865; Deac. 1864 and Pr. 1865 by Abp of York. C. in sole charge of Roxby with Risby 1866. Formerly C. of St. Mary's, Sheffield, 1864. [27]

GODFREY, Nathaniel Stedman, *Portsea, Hants.*—P. C. of St. Bartholomew's, Portsea, Dio. Win. 1863. (Patron, Bp of Win.) Formerly P. C. of Wortley,

Yorks, Dio. Rip. 1850–62. Author, *The Conflict and the Triumph*, 1855, 6s 6d. [1]

GODFREY, William, *Studley, Bromsgrove.*—Queens' Coll. Cam. B.A. 1824, M.A. 1828; Deac. and Pr. 1823. V. of Studley, Dio. Wor. 1860. (Patron, R. Knight, Esq; Tithe—Imp. 1098*l* 5*s* 4*d*, V. 2*l* 13*s*; Glebe, 10 acres; V.'s Inc. 148*l*; Pop. 2230.) Formerly V. of Ravenstone 1823; P. C. of Weston Underwood 1827. [2]

GODFREY, William, *Kennett Hall, near Newmarket.*—R. of Kennett, Dio. Ely, 1835. (Patron, the present R; Tithe, 200*l*; R.'s Inc. 225*l*; Pop. 207.) [3]

GODLEY, James, B.A., *Exeter College, Oxford.* [4]

GODSELL, George, 8, *Park-road, Plaistow, Essex.*—Magd. Hall, Ox. B.A. 1856, M.A. 1861; Deac. 1857 and Pr. 1859 by Bp of Lon. Miss. C. of St. Andrew's Mission Church, Plaistow, 1862. Formerly C. of St. Bartholomew's, Bethnal-green, 1857–62. [5]

GODSON, Arthur Richard, 12, *Gordon-street, Gordon-square, London, W.C.*—St. John's Coll. Ox. B.A. 1853, M.A. 1859; Deac. 1854 and Pr. 1855 by Bp of Wor. P. C. of All Saints', Gordon-square, Dio. Lon. 1862. (Patron, Bp of Lon; P. C.'s Inc. 300*l*; Pop. 6780.) Formerly C. of St. Luke's, Birmingham, 1854–56, All Souls', Langham-place, Lond. 1856–62. [6]

GODSON, Edwin, *Croscombe, Wells.*—C. of Croscombe; Chap. of the Somerset County Lunatic Asylum. Formerly C. of Shepton Mallett. [7]

GODSON, George St. A., *Shenley, Herts.*—Pemb. Coll. Cam. Sen. Opt. and 2nd cl. Moral Sci. Trip. B.A. 1856, M.A. 1863; Deac. 1857 and Pr. 1858 by Abp of Cant. C. of Shenley 1860. Formerly C. of St. Alphage's, Canterbury, 1857, St. John the Evangelist's, St. Pancras, Lond. 1858. [8]

GODSON, John, *The Parsonage, Coldhurst, Oldham.*—St. Cath. Hall, Cam. B.A. P. C. of Coldhurst, Dio. Man. 1845. (Patrons, the Crown and Bp of Man. alt; P. C.'s Inc. 150*l*; Pop. 3046.) [9]

GODSON, John, jun., *Warrington.*—St. Cath. Coll. Cam. B.A. 1859, M.A. 1867; Deac. 1859 and Pr. 1860 by Bp of Man. C. of St. Paul's, Warrington, 1866. Formerly C. of Colne, Lancashire, and Halifax, Yorks. [10]

GODSON, John, *Shipton-on-Cherwell, Kidlington, Oxford.*—Queen's Coll. Birmingham; Deac. 1859 and Pr. 1860 by Bp of Wor. C. in sole charge of Shipton-on-Cherwell 1866. Formerly C. of St. Martin's, Worcester, 1859, Hadleigh, Essex, 1860, Boyne Hill 1864, Bampton 1865. Author, *Daily Prayers for Family and Private Use*, Rivingtons, 1866, 1*s* 6*d*. [11]

GOE, Field Flowers, 27, *Albion-street, Hull.*—Magd. Hall, Ox. 3rd cl. Lit. Hum. B.A. 1857, M.A. 1860; Deac. and Pr. 1858 by Abp of York. P. C. of Ch. Ch. Hull, Dio. York, 1858. (Patrons, V. of Sculcoates and eight trustees; P. C.'s Inc. 370*l*; Pop. 15,000.) Formerly C. of Ch. Ch. Hull, 1858. [12]

GOGGIN, James Frederick, *Luckington Rectory, Chippenham.*—Deac. 1862 and Pr. 1863 by Bp of Ches. R. of Luckington, Dio. G. and B. 1864. (Patron, the present R; Tithe, comm. 292*l* 15*s*; Glebe, 44 acres; R.'s Inc. 382*l* and Ho; Pop. 316.) Formerly C. of Wigan. [13]

GOING, John, *St. Paul's Parsonage, Walworth, London, S.*—Dub. A.B. 1847, A.M. 1858; Deac. 1849 and Pr. 1850 by Bp of Win. P. C. of St. Paul's, Walworth, Dio. Lon. 1859. (Patrons, D. and C. of Cant; P. C.'s Inc. 300*l* and Ho; Pop. 11,770.) Formerly Min. of the Factory Chapel of Price's Patent Candle Company, Vauxhall, Lond. 1850–58. [14]

GOLDBERG, J. B., *Constantinople.*—Missionary at Constantinople. [15]

GOLDHAM, Richard, *Newnham Vicarage, Baldock, Herts.*—Corpus Coll. Cam. B.A. 1842; Deac. 1841 and Pr. 1842 by Bp of Lich. R. of Caldecote, Dio. Roch. 1853. (Patron, C. C. Hale, Esq; Tithe, 73*l*; Glebe, 14 acres; R.'s Inc. 90*l*; Pop. 44.) V. of Newnham, Dio. Roch. 1853. (Patron, J. Remington Mills, Esq; Tithe—Imp. 14*l* 15*s*, V. 62*l* 0*s* 6*d*; Glebe, 24 acres; V.'s Inc. 115*l* and Ho; Pop. 135.) [16]

GOLDHAWK, Thomas Woods, *Sheldwich, Faversham.*—Wor. Coll. Ox. B.A. 1835, M.A. 1843; Deac. 1835 and Pr. 1836 by Bp of G. and B. V. of Sheldwich, Dio. Cant. 1850. (Patrons, D. and C. of Cant; Tithe—App. 530*l* 6*s*, and 2 acres of Glebe, V. 200*l* 6*s*; Glebe, 1 acre; V.'s Inc. 201*l*; Pop. 616.) [17]

GOLDIE, Charles Dashwood, *St. Ives, Hunts.*—St. John's Coll. Cam. 2nd Sen. Opt. B.A. 1847, M.A. 1850; Deac. 1848 and Pr. 1849 by Bp of Lin. V. of St. Ives with Old Hurst C. and Woodhurst C. Dio. Ely, 1866. (Patrons, J. Ansley, Esq. and Trustees; Pop. St. Ives 3395, Old Hurst 174, Woodhurst 554.) Asst. Sec. of S.P.G. Formerly P. C. of St. Thomas's, Colnbrook, Bucks, 1852–66. [18]

GOLDIE, George, *Corston, Chippenham.*—Dub. Vice-Chan.'s Prizes, A.B. 1855, A.M. 1862; Deac. 1857 and Pr. 1858 by Bp of G. and B. C. of Malmesbury (with Corston and Rodbourne, sole charge) 1866. Formerly C. of Stanton St. Quintin. [19]

GOLDING, Benjamin Bass, *Skelton, Yorks.*—Trin. Coll. Cam. B.A. 1815, M.A. 1818. R. of Skelton, Dio. York, 1846. (Patron, J. Hepworth, Esq; Glebe, 108 acres; R.'s Inc. 120*l* and Ho; Pop. 61.) [20]

GOLDING, Henry, *The Rectory, Stratford St. Mary, Colchester.*—Trin. Coll. Cam. B.A. 1838; Deac. 1842 and Pr. 1843 by Bp of Nor. R. of Stratford St. Mary, Dio. Nor. 1844. (Patron, Duchy of Lancaster; Tithe, 325*l*; Glebe, 18¾ acres; R.'s Inc. 360*l* and Ho; Pop. 654.) [21]

GOLDING, Josiah Edward, *The Vicarage, Griston, near Watton, Norfolk.*—Queens' Coll. Cam. Sen. Opt. Math. and Theol. Prizeman, B.A. 1831, M.A. 1834; Deac. 1833 and Pr. 1834 by Bp of Lin. V. of Griston, Dio. Nor. 1860. (Patron, Bp of Ely.) Formerly C. of Hinderclay. Author of *Explanatory and Practical Notes on the Prayer-Book*, 1860, 5*s*. [22]

GOLDING, Samuel, *Martindale Parsonage, Penrith.*—P. C. of Martindale, Dio. Carl. 1858. (Patron, J. De Whelpdale, Esq; P. C.'s Inc. 50*l* and Ho; Pop. 174.) Formerly Asst. C. of Frating with Thorington, Essex. [23]

GOLDNEY, Adam, *East Pennard, Shepton Mallett.*—Trin. Coll. Cam. B.A. 1832, M.A. 1837; Deac. 1832, Pr. 1833. V. of East Pennard with West Bradley C. Dio. B. and W. 1845. (Patron, Bp of B. and W; East Pennard, Tithe—App. 125*l* 18*s* 8*d*, V. 128*l* 1*s* 4*d*; Glebe, 22 acres; West Bradley, Tithe—App. 30*l*, V. 50*l*; Glebe, 12½ acres; V.'s Inc. 355*l* and Ho; Pop. East Pennard 531, West Bradley 136.) [24]

GOLDNEY, George, *King's College, Cambridge.*—Fell. of King's Coll. Cam. [25]

GOLDNEY, John Kellow.—St. John's Coll. Ox. B.A. 1821, M.A. 1824; Deac. 1822 by Bp of G. and B. Pr. 1823 by Bp of Ches. Formerly Chap. R.N. 1824; Chap. to Royal Dockyard at Bermuda 1835–38; Chap. of Greenwich Hospital 1838–65. [26]

GOLDSMITH, Edmund, *Hinton-on-the-Green Rectory (Glouc.), near Evesham.*—Deac. 1822 by Bp of Ches. Pr. 1823 by Abp of York. R. of Hinton-on-the Green, Dio. G. and B. 1849. (Patroness, Mrs. Baker Cresswell; Tithe—App. 234*l*, R. 237*l*; Glebe, 30 acres; R.'s Inc. 258*l* and Ho; Pop. 176.) [27]

GOLDSMITH, Edmund Hubert, *Duntsbourne Rouse, near Cirencester.*—Corpus Coll. Ox. B.A. 1851, M.A. 1854; Deac. 1857 by Bp of Ox. Pr. 1859 by Bp of Dur. R. of Duntsbourne Rouse, Dio. G. and B. 1859. (Patron, Corpus Coll. Ox; Glebe, 230 acres; R.'s Inc. 320*l* and Ho; Pop. 126.) Formerly Asst. Mast. of the Gr. Sch. Durham. [28]

GOLIGHTLY, Charles Portales, *Marston, Oxford.*—Oriel Coll. Ox. 3rd cl. Lit. Hum. and B.A. 1828, M.A. 1830; Deac. 1830, Pr. 1831. C. of Marston. Formerly C. of Headington, Oxon. [29]

GOLIGHTLY, Thomas Gildart, *Shipton-Moyne Rectory, Tetbury, Glouc.*—Brasen. Coll. Ox. M.A. 1851; Deac. 1852 and Pr. 1853 by Bp of Pet. R. of Shipton-Moyne, Dio. G. and B. 1856. (Patron, Right Hon. T. H. S. Estcourt; Tithe, 370*l*; Glebe, 173 acres; R.'s Inc. 460*l* and Ho; Pop. 407.) Rural Dean. [30]

GOMPERTZ, Solomon, *Luton St. John, Teignmouth, Devon.*—St. John's Coll. Cam. B.A. 1829; Deac. 1828 and Pr. 1830 by Bp of Lon. V. of Luton St. John, Dio. Ex. 1867. (Patron, Rev. W. R. Ogle; Tithe, 20*l*; V.'s Inc. 70*l*; Pop. 220.) Formerly P. C. of Chalford, Glouc. 1839–64. Author, *Faith and Practice* (Sermons), 1839, 7*s*; *Psalms and Hymns, with Devotional Prefaces*; *Sword of the Spirit* (printed and published by Parishioners of Chalford), 1850; *Heresy of Swedenborg* (two Pamphlets exposing the fallacies of Swedenborg's Theology); Visitation Sermon. [1]

GOOCH, Charles John, *Toppesfield Rectory, Halstead, Essex.*—Ch. Ch. Ox. B.A. 1821, M.A. 1824; Deac. 1826 and Pr. 1827 by Bp of Nor. R. of South Cove, Suffolk, Dio. Nor. 1828. (Patron, Sir T. S. Gooch, Bart; Tithe, 267*l* 10*s*; Glebe, 13 acres; R.'s Inc. 298*l* and Ho; Pop. 187.) R. of Toppesfield, Dio. Roch. 1829. (Patron, the Crown; Tithe, 1100*l*; Glebe, 20 acres; R.'s Inc. 1120*l* and Ho; Pop. 1045.) [2]

GOOCH, Francis Harcourt, *Hambledon, Godalming, Surrey.*—Mert. Coll. Ox. B.A. 1865; Deac. 1865 and Pr. 1866 by Bp of Win. C. of Hambledon 1865. [3]

GOOCH, Frederick, *Baginton Rectory, Coventry.*—Ch. Ch. Ox. B.A. 1826, M.A. 1828, D.C.L. 1837; Deac. 1828 by Bp of Roch. Pr. 1829 by Bp of Ox. R. of Baginton, Dio. Wor. 1833. (Patron, W. Davenport Bromley, Esq; Tithe, 355*l*; Glebe, 19 acres; R.'s Inc. 376*l* and Ho; Pop. 211.) Rural Dean 1838. Formerly Fell. of All Souls Coll. Ox. 1828–53. [4]

GOOCH, John, *Grammar School, Reigate.*—Caius Coll. Cam. B.A. 1841, M.A. 1844; Deac. 1843. Head Mast. of the Gr. Sch. Reigate. Formerly 2nd Mast. of Wolverhampton Gr. Sch. 1846. [5]

GOOCH, Philip Sherlock, *Cookley, Halesworth, Suffolk.*—Mert. Coll. Ox. B.A. 1860; Deac. 1864 and Pr. 1865 by Bp of Nor. C. of Huntingfield and Cookley 1864. [6]

GOOCH, Richard, *North Cove, Beccles, Suffolk.*—R. of Frostenden, Dio. Nor. 1806. (Patron, Thomas Barne, Esq; R.'s Inc. 360*l*; Pop. 409.) R. of North Cove with Willingham R. Dio. Nor. 1810. (Patron, Ld Chan; R.'s Inc. 380*l*; Pop. North Cove 200, Willingham 142.) [7]

GOOCH, William, *Stainton Vicarage, Middlesborough, Yorks.*—R. of Benacre with Easton Bavents R. and North Hales V. near Southwold, Suffolk, Dio. Nor. 1823. (Patron, Sir T. S. Gooch, Bart; Benacre, Tithe, 359*l* 0*s* 4*d*; Easton Bavents, Tithe, 321*l* 5*s*; R.'s Inc. 703*l*; Pop. Benacre 212, Easton Bavents 7, North Hales 192.) V. of Stainton, Dio. York, 1835. (Patron, Abp of York; Tithe—App. 1070*l* 14*s*, Imp. 98*l* 10*s*, V. 205*l*; V.'s Inc. 333*l* and Ho; Pop. 732.) Rural Dean; Preb. of York 1845. [8]

GOOCH, W. H.—C. of Lee, Kent. [9]

GOOD, Charles Patten, *Eccleshall Vicarage, Staffs.*—Ex. Coll. Ox. B.A. 1844, M.A. 1847; Deac. 1845 and Pr. 1846 by Bp of Lich. V. of Eccleshall, Dio. Lich. 1856. (Patron, Bp of Lich; V.'s Inc. 254*l* and Ho; Pop. 2844.) Rural Dean; Chap. to 38th Company of 1st Battalion Staffordshire Rifle Volunteers; Patron of Cotes Heath P. C. Formerly P. C. of St. James's, Handsworth, 1854–56. [10]

GOOD, Edward.—Chap. of H.M.S. "Achilles." [11]

GOOD, Henry, *Wimborne Minster, Dorset.*—Trin. Hall, Cam. LL.B. 1826; Deac. 1823, Pr. 1824. Senior Min. of the Royal Peculiar Coll. Ch. of Wimborne Minster, Dio. Salis. 1841. (Patron, the Corporation; Tithes, 2500*l* on 11,966 acres; Rent-charge, 2416*l*; Annual Stipend of the Three Clergymen, 250*l* each; Pop. including the Chapelry of Holt, 4807.) Surrogate. [12]

GOOD, Philip Henry, *St. George's-square, Portsea.*—Dub. A.B. 1863, A.M. 1866; Deac. 1864 and Pr. 1865 by Bp of Man. C. of St. John's, Portsea, 1866. Formerly C. of St. Peter's, Manchester, 1864. [13]

GOOD, William Fulford, *Poole-park, Highweek, Devon.*—Trin. Coll. Cam. B.A. 1835; Deac. 1835, Pr. 1836. Chap. of Newton Abbott Union, Devon. Author, *Arithmetical Rules and Questions*, 1844, 2*s*; *Miscellaneous Questions in Arithmetic*, 1844, 1*s* 4*d*; *Answers to Arithmetical and Miscellaneous Questions*, 1844, 1*s* 6*d*. [14]

GOODACRE, Francis Burges, *Wilby Rectory, Attleborough, Norfolk.*—St. John's Coll. Cam. M.B. 1852, L.M. 1858, M.D. 1860; Deac. 1858 and Pr. 1859 by Bp of Ex. R. of Wilby with Hargham, Dio. Nor. 1863. (Patron, John Goodacre, of Rugby (Minor); R.'s Inc. 390*l* and Ho; Pop. Wilby 98, Hargham 88.) Formerly C. of Penzance 1858, Peatling Parva 1861. [15]

GOODACRE, Frederick William, *Lutterworth.*—Emman. Coll. Cam. B.A. 1858, Deac. 1859 by Bp of Man. Pr. 1860 by Bp of Pet. Chap. to the Union, Lutterworth, and C. of Cottesbach 1867. Formerly C. of Little Ashby, 1859, Daventry 1863. [16]

GOODACRE, Robert Henry, *Ipstones Parsonage, Cheadle, Staffs.*—Literate; Deac. 1839 and Pr. 1840 by Bp of Lin. P. C. of Ipstones, Dio. Lich. 1861. (Patrons, the Freeholders; P. C.'s Inc. 183*l* and Ho; Pop. 1632.) Formerly C. of Mansfield Woodhouse, Notts, 1839–44, Leek, Staffs, 1844–50; P. C. of Waterfall, Staffs, 1850–51; Chap. to Staffs. County Gaol 1850–59. Author, *The Fruits of Sin*, 1860, 2*s*; and other Sermons. [17]

GOODALL, William, *Bournemouth.*—St. Cath. Coll. Cam. B.A. 1837, M.A. 1840; Deac. 1837, Pr. 1838. C. of Holdenhurst, Hants. Formerly C. of Isle Abbotts and Isle Brewers 1837–39, Calne 1839–42; Chap. in Bombay 1842–63. [18]

GOODAY, Robert Septimus, *St. James's Parsonage, Oldham.*—Ex. Coll. Ox. B.A. 1848, M.A. 1858; Deac. 1850 and Pr. 1851 by Bp of Wor. P. C. of St. James's, Oldham, Dio. Man. 1864. (Patron, R. of Prestwich; P. C.'s Inc. 400*l* and Ho; Pop. 18,000.) Surrogate. Formerly C. of Eccles and Prestwich. [19]

GOODCHILD, Thomas Oliver, *Hackney Rectory, Church-street, Hackney, London, N.E.*—Ex. Coll. Ox. B.A. 1822, M.A. 1825; Deac. 1824, Pr. 1825. R. of Hackney, Dio. Lon. 1839. (Patron, W. G. T. Tyssen Amherst, Esq; Tithe, 981*l* 10*s*; R.'s Inc. 990*l* and Ho; Pop. 10,581.) [20]

GOODCHILD, William George, *East Tilbury Vicarage, Romford, Essex.*—Sid. Coll. Cam. B.A. 1841, M.A. 1845; Deac. 1841, Pr. 1842. V. of East Tilbury, Dio. Roch. 1844. (Patron, Ld Chan; Tithe—Imp. 382*l*; Glebe, 28 acres; V. 244*l*; V.'s Inc. 244*l* and Ho; Pop. 403.) [21]

GOODDAY, James, *Romford, Essex.*—Queens' Coll. Cam. B.A. 1848, M.A. 1853; Deac. and Pr. 1849 by Bp of Roch. Chap. to the Romford Union. [22]

GOODDAY, Septimus, *Ipswich.*—Pemb. Coll. Cam. B.A. 1832, M.A. 1835; Deac. 1833 and Pr. 1834 by Bp of Lon. [23]

GOODDEN, Charles Culliford, *Montacute Vicarage, Ilminster.*—Ex. Coll. Ox. B.A. 1839, M.A. 1840; Deac. 1841 by Bp of Ely, Pr. 1842 by Bp of B. and W. V. of Montacute, Dio. B. and W. 1843. (Patron, W. Phelips, Esq; Tithe, 190*l*; Glebe, 5 acres; V.'s Inc. 200*l* and Ho; Pop. 992.) [24]

GOODDEN, George, *North Barrow Rectory, Castle Carey, Somerset.*—R. of North Barrow, Dio. B. and W. 1831. (Patron, Lord Portman; Tithe, 120*l*; Glebe, 40 acres; R.'s Inc. 165*l* and Ho; Pop. 114.) P. C. of South Barrow, Dio. B. and W. 1836. (Patroness, Mrs. Toogood; Tithe—Imp. 144*l*; P. C.'s Inc. 85*l*; Pop. 140.) [25]

GOODDEN, Wyndham Jeane, *Nether Compton, Sherborne, Dorset.*—Oriel Coll. Ox. B.A. 1822, M.A. 1832; Deac. 1823 by Bp of Bristol, Pr. 1824 by Bp of Ches. R. of Nether Compton with Over Compton R. Dio. Salis. 1824. (Patron, John Goodden, Esq; Nether Compton, Tithe, 250*l*; Glebe, 22 acres; Over Compton, Tithe, 87*l* 3*s* 1*d*; Glebe, 52 acres; R.'s Inc. 460*l*; Pop. Nether Compton 376, Over Compton 149.) [26]

GOODE, Alfred Juan, *Newbury, Berks.*—Clare Coll. Cam. B.A. 1857, M.A. 1861; Deac. 1862 and Pr. 1863 by Bp of Ely. C. of Enborne and Hampstead Marshall, Berks, 1865. Formerly C. of Withersfield 1862–64, Little Thurlow 1864–65. [27]

GOODE, The Very Rev. William, *The Deanery, Ripon.*—Trin. Coll. Cam. 1st cl. Cl. Trip. 1822,

B.A. 1825, M.A. 1828; Deac. and Pr. 1825. Dean of Ripon 1860 (Dean's Inc. 1000*l* and Res). Formerly C. of Ch. Ch. Newgate-street, Lond. 1825–35; R. of St. Antholin's, Lond. 1835–49; R. of Allhallows, 1849–56; R. of St. Margaret Lothbury with St. Christopher le-Stocks and St. Bartholomew Exchange, Lond. 1856–60; Warburtonian Lect. 1853–57. Author, *The Divine Rule of Faith and Practice; or, a Defence of the Catholic Doctrine that Holy Scripture has been, since the times of the Apostles, the sole Divine Rule of Faith and Practice to the Church; against the Dangerous Errors of the Authors of the Tracts for the Times, and the Romanists; as, particularly, that the Rule of Faith is "made up of Scripture and Tradition together," &c; in which also the Doctrines of the Apostolical Succession, the Eucharistic Sacrifice, &c., are fully discussed*, 3 vols. 2nd ed. revised and enlarged; *A Memoir of the late Rev. W. Goode, M.A Rector of St. Andrew, Wardrobe, and St. Ann, Blackfriars*, 2nd ed. *with Appendix of Select Letters*, 9*s*; *The Modern Claims to the Possession of the Extraordinary Gifts of the Spirit, stated and examined, and compared with the most remarkable cases of a similar kind that have occurred in the Christian Church; with some General Observations on the subject*, 2nd ed. *with numerous Additions; and an Appendix on the Heresy with which the Claims are connected*, 10*s* 6*d*; *An Answer to a Letter addressed to the Lord Chancellor on the Case of the Dissenters, in a Letter to the Same, by a Clergyman*, 2nd ed. 1*s*; *A Reply to the Letters on the Voluntary Principle by a "Quiet Looker-on," in Two Letters by Philalethes*, 1*s* (1) Tracts on Church Rates, viz., *A Brief History of Church Rates, proving the liability of a parish to them to be a common-law liability; including a Reply to the Statements on that subject in Sir John Campbell's Letter to the Right Hon. Lord Stanley, on the Law of Church Rates*, 2nd ed. considerably enlarged; (2) *A Reply to the Article on Church Rates in the* "Edinburgh Review," No. 143; (3) *A Reply to the Answer of the* "Edinburgh Review," *to the two following Publications*: 1. *A Brief History of Church Rates.* 2. *A Reply to the Article on Church Rates in the* "Edinburgh Review", No. 143, *in Two Letters to the Editor*; (4) *A Final Reply to the Answer of the Author of the Articles on Church Rates in the* "Edinburgh Review," *in a Letter to the Editor*; the above four tracts in one vol., 7*s* 6*d*; *Some Difficulties in the late Charge of the Bishop of Oxford respectfully pointed out in a Letter to his Lordship*, 2nd ed. 1*s*; *Two Treatises on the Church; the First by Thomas Jackson, D.D., commended by Dr. Pusey as "one of the best and greatest minds our Church has nurtured;" the Second by Robert Sanderson, D.D. formerly Lord Bishop of Lincoln; to which is added a Letter of Bishop Cosin on the Validity of the Orders of the Foreign Reformed Churches, edited with Introductory Remarks*, 5*s*; *The Case as it Is; or a Reply to the Letter of Dr. Pusey to the Archbishop of Canterbury; including a Compendious Statement of the Doctrines and Views of the Tractators as expressed by themselves*, 3rd ed. 1*s*; *Altars Prohibited by the Church of England, in two parts*, 2*s* 6*d*; *A Letter to a Lay Friend in Answer to Inquiries respecting the state of things in the Church, and the Course which the present Crisis demands from those who tender its Welfare*, 2nd ed. 1*s*; *Tract* 90 *Historically Refuted; or, a Reply to a Work by the Rev. F. Oakeley, entitled "The Subject of Tract* 90 *historically examined,"* 5*s*; *A few Remarks on the Religious Opinions Relief Bill, and the Oath of Supremacy*, 6*d*; *Remarks on the Clergy Offences Bill, as proposed to Parliament in* 1847, *and re-introduced, with a few alterations, in* 1848, *reprinted from the* "Christian Observer" *for September*, 1847, *and March*, 1848, 6*d*; *Remarks on Attempted Restorations of Popish Fittings in Churches, &c., reprinted from the* "Christian Observer" *for April*, 1848, 6*d*; *A Defence of the Thirty-nine Articles as the Legal and Canonical Test of Doctrine in the Church of England in all points treated of in them; being a Reply to the Bishop of Exeter's Remarks upon a clause proposed for insertion in the Clergy Offences Bill*, 2nd ed. 1*s*; *A Vindication of the "Defence of the Thirty-nine Articles," in reply to the recent Charge of the Bishop of Exeter*, 2nd ed., *to which is added an Appendix, containing additional Remarks, &c.* 2*s* 6*d*; *Review of the Judgment of Sir H. J. Fust, Kt., in the case of Gorham v. the Bishop of Exeter, reprinted from the* "Christian Observer" *for December*, 1849, 1*s*; *The Doctrine of the Church of England as to the Effects of Baptism in the Case of Infants, with an Appendix, containing the Baptismal Services of Luther and the Nuremberg and Cologne Liturgies*, 2nd ed. 15*s*; *An Unpublished Letter of Peter Martyr, Reg. Div. Prof. Oxford, to Henry Bullinger, written from Oxford just after the completion of the Second Prayer Book of Edward VI., in which he testifies his satisfaction with it; maintains, at the same time, that grace is not conferred by virtue of the Sacraments; and gives an account of a Controversy at that period on the subject, in our Church, which delayed the publication of the Articles; affording additional proof of the meaning of the Articles, with Remarks*, 1*s*; *A Letter to the Bishop of Exeter, containing an Examination of his Letter to the Archbishop of Canterbury*, seventh thousand, 3*s*; *Reply to the Letter and Declaration respecting the Royal Supremacy, received from Archdeacons Manning and Wilberforce, and Professor Mill*, 3rd ed., *with Appendix containing the Letter and Declaration replied to, and a Correspondence with Archdeacon Manning*, 1*s*; *Address delivered at a Public Meeting of the Inhabitants of Allhallows the Great and Less, London, convened for the purpose of considering the propriety of presenting an Address to the Crown on the recent act of papal aggression*, Nov. 15, 1850, printed at the request of the parishioners, 6*d*; *Aids for determining some disputed Points in the Ceremonial of the Church of England*, 2nd ed. 4*s*; *A Vindication of the Doctrine of the Church of England on the Validity of the Orders of the Scotch and Foreign Non-Episcopal Churches; in three Pamphlets on the subject containing* (1) *A General Review of the subject.* (2) *A Reply to Archdeacon Churton and Chancellor Harrington*, 2nd ed. (3) *A Reply to the Bishop of Exeter's Letter to the Archdeacon of Totnes*, 3rd ed. *to which is appended an Answer to his Defenders, the Rev. Messrs. Scott and Flower*, 5*s*; *A Letter to Sir W. P. Wood, Q.C., M.P., on his Charge against some of the Clergy of giving a non-natural interpretation to the Prayer-book, inconsistent with their retention of preferment in the Church*, 2nd ed. *to which are added the Answer of Sir W. P. Wood, and the Author's Reply, &c.*, 1*s*; *The Case of Archdeacon Wilberforce compared with that of the Rev. G. C. Gorham, in Reply to some Remarks in the recent Charge of Archdeacon Wilberforce*, 6*d*; *Reply to a Pamphlet entitled "A Few Words to the Rev. W. Goode, on the Hypothetical Principle of Interpreting the Prayer-book, by a Lay Churchman," including a few Remarks on "A Letter to the Right Hon. Lord J. Russell by a Member of the Middle Temple,"* 6*d*; *The Nature of Christ's Presence in the Eucharist, or, the true Doctrine of the Real Presence vindicated in opposition to the fictitious real presence asserted by Archdeacon Denison, Mr. (late Archdeacon) Wilberforce, and Dr. Pusey; with a full proof of the real character of the attempt made by those authors to represent their doctrine as that of the Church of England and her divines*, 2 vols. 24*s*; *A Supplement to his Work on the Eucharist, containing Two Letters of Bishop Geste (one hitherto unknown) from the State Paper Office, illustrating the history and meaning of the 28th and 29th Articles, together with a Reply to Dr. Pusey's Answer, and a few remarks on the attempts made by Archdeacon Denison and others to discredit that work without answering it*, 2*s*; *Is the Reformation a Blessing? If it is, shall we leave unnoticed the 17th of November*, 1858, *the three hundredth anniversary of its permanent establishment in this country by the accession of Queen Elizabeth?* fourth thousand, 6*d*; *The Blessings of the Reformation* (a Sermon on the tercentenary of its first permanent establishment in this country by the accession of Queen Elizabeth on Nov. 17, 1558,) 6*d*; *Brotherly Communion with the Foreign Protestant Churches desired and cultivated by the highest and best of the Divines of the Church of England* (an Address, delivered at Cambridge at a private Meeting of some of the Senior Members of the University, and published at their request), 2s; *A Sermon on the lamented Death of His Royal Highness the late Prince Consort, Preached in Ripon Cathedral, on the day of his Funeral,* Dec. 23, 1861, *published at the request of the Mayor and Corporation, and others present,* 2nd ed. price 6d; *Holy Scripture the Sole Authoritative Expositor of the Faith, and its Subjection to Church-Authority the Proved Pathway to the Church of Rome,* a Sermon on Acts xvii. 11, 12, preached at Ripon Cathedral, March 30, 1862, *with notes further illustrative of the subject, and of the present doctrine and spirit of the Church of Rome, published by request,* 2nd ed. 1s; *Fulfilled Prophecy a proof of the Truth of Revealed Religion, being the Warburtonian Lectures for* 1854–58, *with an Appendix of Notes, including a full investigation of Daniel's Prophecy of the Seventy Weeks,* 9s; *Rome's Tactics, or a Lesson for England from the Past,* 2s; etc; all published by Hatchards. [1]

GOODE, William Peckham, *Earsham Rectory, Norfolk.*—Ch. Coll. Cam. B.A. 1845, M.A. 1848; Deac. 1845 and Pr. 1846 by Abp of Cant. R. of Earsham, Dio. Nor. 1855. (Patron, Sir William Windham Dalling, Bart; Tithe—App. 16*l* 8*s*, R. 493*l* 10*s*; Glebe, 46½ acres; R.'s Inc. 587*l* and Ho; Pop. 697.) [2]

GOODE, Wollaston, *St. Giles's Rectory, Colchester, Essex.*—Trin Hall. Cam. Scho. of, B.A. 1846, M.A. 1850; Deac. 1849 and Pr. 1850 by Bp of Roch. R. of St. Giles', Colchester, Dio. Roch. 1857. (Patron, T. M. Gepp, Esq; Tithe, 200*l*; R.'s Inc. 250*l* and Ho; Pop. 2736.) Formerly C. of East Donyland, Essex, 1849, St. Giles'-in the-Fields, Lond. 1852, St. James's, Croydon Common, 1854. [3]

GOODENOUGH, Robert William, *Whittingham Vicarage, Alnwick.*—Ch. Ch. Ox. 1826, B.A. 1830, M.A. 1832; Deac. 1832 by Bp of Roch. Pr. 1833 by Abp of York. V. of Whittingham, Dio. Dur. 1835. (Patrons, D. and C. of Carl; Tithe—App. 1260*l* 3*s* 4*d*, Imp. 10*s*, V. 605*l* 18*s* 8*d*; Glebe, 44 acres; V.'s Inc. 675*l* and Ho; Pop. 1923.) [4]

GOODFORD, Charles Old, *Eton College, Bucks.*—King's Coll. Cam. B.A. 1836, M.A. 1839, B.D. and D.D. 1848. Provost of Eton Coll; R. of Chilton-Canteloe, Yeovil, Dio. B. and W. 1848. (Patron, H. Goodford, Esq; Tithe, 225*l*; R.'s Inc. 268*l* and Ho; Pop. 112.) [5]

GOODHART, Charles Joseph, 1, *Hollywood-grove, West Brompton, London, S.W.*—Trin. Coll. Cam. 22nd Wrang. 4th in 2nd cl. Cl. Trip, B.A. 1826, M.A. 1831; Deac. 1827 and Pr. 1828 by Bp of Bristol. Min. of Park Chapel, Chelsea, Dio. Lon. 1852. (Patrons, Trustees.) Clerical Sec. of the London Society for Promoting Christianity amongst the Jews 1853. Formerly C. of Haselbury Bryan, Dorset, 1827–30, Broad Chalke, Wilts, 1830–36; Min. of St. Mary's Chapel, Reading, 1836–52. Author, *A Week's Prayers for the Children of the Poor,* 3d; *A Week's Prayers for Grown up Persons among the Poor; Christian Consistency the Foundation of Christian Fellowship* (a Sermon), 1835; *The Beloved Physician* (Two Sermons on the Death of T. King, Esq; M.D. of Reading), 1840, 1s 6d; *Restoration of the Jews* (a Sermon), 1848; *Divine Authority, &c. of the Lord's Day* (a Sermon), 1850; *The Jews our Creditors* (a Lecture to Young Men), 1850; *Appeal to Faithful Protestants* (a Sermon), 1850; *Abraham and his Seed* (a Sermon), 3d; *The Pre-millennial Advent* (a Sermon); Prophetical Sermons: *Covenant with David,* 1842; *Old Testament on the Second Advent,* 1843; *Established Holiness of the Church at the Lord's Advent,* 1845; *Special Object of our Lord's Ministry,* 1846; *Different Degrees of Glory,* 1847; *Messiah's Triumphant Reign the Reward of His Sufferings,* 1848; *The Powers of the World to Come,* 1849; *Divine Grace in Jewish Ordinances,* 1850; *Prophetical Significance of Balaam,* 1851; *The Removal of the Curse,* 1852; *The Recovery of a Lost World,* 1833; *The State of the Jews before the Lord's Second Coming,* 1854; *The Kingship and Glory of the Saints,* 1855; *Religious and Moral Aspects of the Jews in the last Days,* 1856; *Glimpses of Grace and Glory* (Sermons), 3s 6d, 1859; *What a Man Soweth he must Reap* (Sermon), 1d, 1858; *The Holy Spirit the Author and Giver of Life; The Indwelling of the Holy Spirit in the Children of God* (two Sermons), 1860. Editor of *The Book of Family Prayer,* 1844. [6]

GOODLAKE, Thomas William, *Swindon Rectory, near Cheltenham.*—Pemb. Coll. Ox. 3rd cl. Lit. Hum. and B.A. 1834, M.A. 1836, *ad eund.* Cam. 1843; Deac. 1834 and Pr. 1835 by Bp of Ox. R. of Swindon, near Cheltenham, Dio. G and B. 1861. (Patron, J. Surman Surman, Esq; Glebe, 32 acres; R.'s Inc. 450*l* and Ho; Pop. 227.) Surrogate. Formerly Fell. and Bursar of Pemb. Coll. Ox. 1841; V. of Bradwell, Ox. 1845; R. of Broughton with Filkins, Ox. 1855–61; Dioc. Inspector of Schools 1847–61. Author, *A Letter to his Parishioners on Cheltenham Anti-Ritualist Lectures,* 1867. [7]

GOODMAN, Godfrey, *Bishop Stortford.*—King's Coll. Lond. Theol. Assoc; Deac. and Pr. 1849 by Bp of Roch. Head Mast. of the High Sch. Bishop Stortford, 1850; Chap. to the Bishop Stortford Union 1849. [8]

GOODMAN, John Parsons, *Keystone, Thrapstone.*—Emman. Coll. Cam. Scho. of, 1840, B.A. 1842, M.A. 1846; Deac. 1843, and Pr. 1844 by Bp of Pet. R. of Keystone, Dio. Ely, 1848. (Patron, Earl Fitzwilliam; Tithe, 350*l*; Glebe, 25 acres; R.'s Inc. 356*l* and Ho; Pop. 199.) Hon. Organising Sec. for S.P.G. for Archdeaconry of Huntingdon; Chap. of the Thrapstone Union, Northants. Formerly C. of Castor, Northants, 1843–48. [9]

GOODRICH, Bartlet George, *Hardmead, Newport Pagnell.*—Univ. Coll. Ox. B.A. 1848; Deac. 1849 and Pr. 1850 by Bp of Win. R. of Hardmead, Dio. Ox. 1856. (Patrons, Exors. of the late R. Shedden, Esq; R.'s Inc. 200*l*; Pop. 91.) Formerly C. of Enborne and Hamstead Marshall, Berks. [10]

GOODRICH, Octavius, *Humber Rectory, Leominster.*—Oriel Coll. Ox. B.A. 1838; Deac. 1838, Pr. 1839. R. of Humber, Dio. Herf. 1854. (Patron, Ld Chan; Tithe—App. 82*l* 9*s*, R. 107*l*; R.'s Inc. 170*l* and Ho; Pop. 251.) [11]

GOODRICK, John Gray, *Bix, Henley-on-Thames.*—St. Cath. Hall, Cam. B.A. 1845; Deac. 1845 and Pr. 1847 by Bp of Ches. C. of Bix 1865. Formerly C. of Durston 1856; Asst. C. of Oldham 1845–51, Meole Brace, Shrewsbury, 1851–56. [12]

GOODRIDGE, Henry Painter, *Cosham, Hants.* St. Alb. Hall, Ox. B.A. 1865; Deac. 1864 and Pr. 1866 by Bp of Ox. C. of Widley, with Wymering, Hants. Formerly C. of St. Thomas's, Oxford, 1864–66. [13]

GOODWIN, Frederick George, *Thurlton Rectory, Loddon, Norfolk.*—Corpus Coll. Cam. B.A. 1839, M.A. 1842; Deac. 1840 and Pr. 1841 by Bp of Nor. R. of Thurlton, Dio. Nor. 1845. (Patrons, Trustees; Tithe, 221*l*; Glebe, 23 acres; R.'s Inc. 263*l* and Ho; Pop. 405.) P. C. of Raveningham, Dio. Nor. 1851. (Patron, Sir Hickman Bacon, Bart; Tithe—Imp. 519*l* 2*s* 10*d*, and 2 acres of Glebe, P. C. 6 acres of Glebe; P. C.'s Inc. 85*l*; Pop. 264.) Surrogate. [14]

GOODWIN, George Septimus, *Hardley, Loddon, Norfolk.*—Ch. Coll. Cam. 14th Sen. Opt. and B.A. 1846, M.A. 1849; Deac. 1848 and Pr. 1849 by Bp of Nor. P. C. of Hardley, Dio. Nor. 1862. (Patrons, Trustees of Gt. Hospital, Norwich; P. C.'s Inc. 150*l*; Pop. 271.) Formerly C. of Weston, Suffolk. [15]

GOODWIN, The Very Rev. Harvey, *The Deanery, Ely.*—Caius Coll. Cam. 2nd Wrang. Smith's Prizeman and B.A. 1840, M.A. 1843, D.D. 1858; Deac. 1842 and Pr. 1844 by Bp of Ely. Dean of Ely 1858 (Value, 717*l* 10*s* 7*d* and Res). Formerly Fell. of Caius Coll. Cam; Hulsean Lect. 1855–57; Min. of St. Edward's, Cambridge, 1848–58. Author, *Parish Sermons,* 5 vols; *University Sermons,* 1853, 1855; *Lectures on the Church Catechism; Short Sermons on the Lord's Supper; A Guide to the Parish Church; Confirmation Day;* a variety of Mathematical Works, etc. [16]

GOODWIN, Henry, *Twyning, Tewkesbury, Glouc.*—Ch. Ch. Ox. 4th cl. Lit. Hum. and B.A. 1842, M.A. 1845; Deac. 1843 and Pr. 1844 by Bp of B. and W. V. of

Twyning, Dio. G. and B. 1844. (Patron, Ch. Ch. Ox; Tithe —App. 900*l*, Imp. 45*l*; V.'s Inc. 183*l*; Pop. 992.) [1]

GOODWIN, Henry, *Middlewich, Cheshire.*—Deac. 1863 and Pr. 1864 by Bp of Ches. V. of Middlewich, Dio. Ches. 1864. (Patron, J. Moreton Wood, Esq; V.'s Inc. 160*l*; Pop. 4000.) Formerly C. of Middlewich. [2]

GOODWIN, Henry Albert, *Westhall, Wangford, Suffolk.*—Corpus Coll. Cam. 11th Wrang. B.A. 1843; M.A. 1846; Deac. and Pr. 1844. V. of Westhall, Dio. Nor. 1857. (Patrons, D. and C. of Nor; V.'s Inc. 200*l*; Pop. 468.) Surrogate. Formerly C. of Saham Toney, Norfolk. [3]

GOODWIN, James, *Lambourne Rectory, Essex.*—Corpus Coll. Cam. 12th Wrang. and B.A. 1828, M.A. 1831, B.D. 1838; Deac. 1829, Pr. 1831. R. of Lambourne, Dio. Roch. 1847. (Patron, Corpus Coll. Cam; Tithe, 610*l*; Glebe, 34 acres; R.'s Inc. 620*l* and Ho; Pop. 890.) Rural Dean 1854; Surrogate. Late Sen. Fell. Bursar and Tut. of Corpus Coll. Cam; Select Preacher at Cam. 1851. Author, *Account of the Rites and Ceremonies used at the Consecration of Archbishop Parker*; *Evangelia Augustini Gregoriana*, Antiq. Soc; One of the Sermons in *Sermons by Thirty-nine Living Divines*, 1840; *Gospel of St. Matthew translated by Sir John Cheke*, 1843, 7*s* 6*d*; *The Shadow and the Substance* (a Poem), 1*s*; Articles VI. and VII. in the Rev. J. J. Smith's *College Plate*, Cam. Antiq. Soc. 1845; *Sermons on the Cretan Church, its Doctrine and Religious Discipline as set forth in the Epistle of St. Paul to Titus*, 1860; *Harvest Sermon* in 1860 and 1862; *Sermon on National Education*, 1863; *The Christian Minister's Sufficient Maintenance* (a Sermon with Notes in aid of the Fund for providing the Augmentation of Small Livings), Ongar, 1*s*; and other Sermons. Editor of No. L. of the Percy Society's Publications. [4]

GOODWIN, John, *Lickey Parsonage, Bromsgrove, Worcestershire.*—St. Cath. Coll. Cam. Scho. 1849–51, 11th Sen. Opt. and B.A. 1851, M.A. 1856; Deac. 1851 and Pr. 1852 by Bp of Lich. P. C. of The Lickey, Dio. Wor. 1853. (Patron, V. of Bromsgrove; P. C.'s Inc. 200*l* and Ho; Pop. 1361.) Formerly Librarian of St. Cath. Coll. Cam. 1849–51; C. of Burslem 1851–53. [5]

GOODWIN, Robert, *Hildersham Rectory, near Cambridge.*—Clare Hall, Cam. B.A. 1839, M.A. 1842; Deac. 1839 and Pr. 1840 by Bp of Ely. V. of Abington Magna, Dio. Ely, 1845. (Patron, Thomas Mortlock, Esq; V.'s Inc. 120*l*; Pop. 330.) R. of Hildersham, Dio. Ely, 1847. (Patron, the present R; Tithe, 407*l*; Glebe, 70 acres; R.'s Inc. 482*l* and Ho; Pop. 227.) [6]

GOODY, Charles James, 13, *Beaumont-street, Marylebone, London, W.*—Caius Coll. Cam. Sen Opt. Wortley Exhib. B.A. 1858, M.A. 1861; Deac. 1858 by Bp of Win. Incumb. of the Parish Chapel, Marylebone, Dio. Lon. 1866. (Patron, R. of Marylebone; Incumb.'s Inc. 200*l*.) Formerly C. of Trinity, Southampton, and St. Marylebone. [7]

GORDON, Adam Charles, *Dodleston Rectory, Wrexham.*—St. John's Coll. Cam. Sen. Opt. B.A. 1856, M.A. 1860; Deac. 1857 and Pr. 1859 by Bp of Wor. R. of Dodleston, Dio. Ches. 1867. (Patrons, D. and C. of Ches; R.'s Inc. 700*l* and Ho; Pop. 814.) Formerly C. of Trinity, Coventry, 1857–59, Plemstall, near Chester, 1859–60, Dodleston 1861–67. [8]

GORDON, Adam S., *Chelsfield, Bromley, Kent.*—Oriel Coll. Ox. M.A. 1856; Deac. 1855 and Pr. 1856 by Abp of Cant. C. of Chelsfield 1855. [9]

GORDON, Alexander, 19, *Sutton-place, Hackney, London, N.E.*—Magd. Hall, Ox. B.A. 1842, M.A. 1847; Deac. 1842 and Pr. 1843 by Bp of Lon. P. C. of St. Philip's, Dalston, Dio. Lon. (Patron, R. of Hackney; P. C.'s Inc. 350*l*; Pop. 10,247.) Formerly C. of Hackney. [10]

GORDON, Arthur P., *Newtimber Rectory, Hurstpierpoint, Sussex.*—Ch. Ch. Ox. B.A. 1859, M.A. 1862; Deac. 1861 and Pr. 1862 by Bp of Salis. R. of Newtimber, Dio. Chich. 1863. (Patrons, Trustees of the late C. Gordon, Esq; Pop. 162.) Formerly Asst. C. of Pitton and Farley, Wilts. [11]

GORDON, Cosmo Reid, 2, *Campden-hill-terrace, Kensington, W.*—Edin. Univ. M.A. 1853; Deac. 1857 and Pr. 1858 by Bp of Rip. Head Mast. of the Bayswater and Notting-hill Proprietary Sch; Min. of St. Mary's, Park-street, Park-lane, Lond. Formerly C. of St. John's, Bradford, and Mast. of Bradford High Sch. 1857–58; Sen. C. of Ch. Ch. Salford, 1858–59; C. in sole charge of Ch. Ch. Moss Side, Manchester, 1859–64; Asst. Min. of St. Paul's, Onslow-square, Kensington, 1864–67. Author, *Thoughts on the Eternal*, Longmans, 1864, 6*s*; Sermons, Reviews, etc. [12]

GORDON, Cosmo Spenser, *Messing Vicarage, near Kelvedon.*—Ex. Coll. Ox. B.A. 1841; Deac. 1843 and Pr. 1844 by Bp of Pet. V. of Messing, Dio. Roch. 1861. (Patron, Earl of Verulam; Tithe, 433*l*; Glebe, 36 acres; V.'s Inc. 480*l* and Ho; Pop. 813.) Formerly C. of St. Martin's, Leicester, 1843, Harpole, Northants. 1844, Stanford Rivers, Essex, 1845–49, St. Mark's, North Audley-street, Lond. 1849–51, Amersham, Bucks, 1851–56, Ongar, Essex, 1858–59, Sunningdale, Berks, 1861. [13]

GORDON, The Hon. Douglas, *Salisbury.*—Trin. Coll. Cam. M.A. 1846; Deac. 1847, Pr. 1848. Can. of Salis. 1860; (Value 500*l* and Res.) Chap. in Ordinary to the Queen. Formerly R. of Great Stanmore 1848–60. [14]

GORDON, Edward, *Kildale, Stokesley, Yorks.*—Corpus Coll. Cam. B.A. 1853; Deac. 1855 by Abp of York, Pr. 1856 by Bp of Carl. R. of Kildale, Dio. York, 1860. (Patroness, Mrs. Livesey; R.'s Inc. 120*l*; Pop. 221.) Formerly C. of Fritwell, Kilnwicke and Aike, Yorks. [15]

GORDON, Francis, *Christ Church Rectory, Biddulph Moor, Congleton, Cheshire.*—Emman. Coll. Cam. B.A. 1851, M.A. 1858; Deac. 1851 and Pr. 1852 by Bp of Win. R. of Biddulph Moor, Dio. Lich. 1863. (Patron, James Bateman, Esq; Tithe, 56*l* 7*s* 11*d*; R.'s Inc. 150*l* 10*s* 3*d* and Ho; Pop. 1200.) Formerly C. of Ch. Ch. Camberwell, 1851–61, St. Paul's, Dalston, Lond. 1862. [16]

GORDON, George, *Whittington Rectory, Chesterfield, Derbyshire.*—Brasen. Coll. Ox. B.A. 1814, M.A. 1818. R. of Whittington, Dio. Lich. 1816. (Patron, Bp of Lich; R.'s Inc. 305*l* and Ho; Pop. 2636.) R. of Muston, Melton Mowbray, Dio. Pet. 1822. (Patron, Ld Chan; Tithe, 426*l* 14*s*; R.'s Inc. 436*l* and Ho; Pop. 360.) [17]

GORDON, Henry Doddridge, *Harting, Petersfield, Sussex.*—New Coll. Ox. 2nd cl. Lit. Hum. B A. 1856, M.A. 1858; Deac. 1858 and Pr. 1859 by Bp of Ox. R. and V. of Harting, Sussex, 1864. (Patroness, Lady Featherstonhaugh; V.'s Inc. 250*l* and Ho; Pop. 1247.) Formerly C. of Lamorbey, Kent, 1856, Adderbury, Oxon, 1858–64. [18]

GORDON, John George, 23, *Notting-hill-terrace, London, W.*—Dub. A.B. 1841; Sid. Coll. Cam. M.A. 1844, LL.D. Dub. 1853; Deac. 1844 and Pr. 1845 by Bp of G. and B. Prin. of the Collegiate Institution, Notting-hill-terrace. Formerly Head Mast. of Loughborough Gr. Sch. 1852. [19]

GORDON, Michael, *Nunney, Frome Selwood, Somerset.*—Dub. A.B. 1829, A.M. 1832; Deac. 1842 by Bp of Derry, Pr. 1843 by Bp of Down. C. of Nunney 1865. Author, *Nature Pictures* in *Dublin University Magazine*, 1859–61; Prize Poem at Trin. Coll. Dub. republished, 1862; etc. [20]

GORDON, Osborne, *Easthampstead, Bracknell, Berks.*—Ch. Ch. Ox. B.A. 1836, M.A. 1839, B.D. 1847; Deac. 1839, Pr. 1840. R. of Easthampstead, Dio. Ox. 1861. (Patron, Ch. Ch. Ox; Tithe, 511*l*; Glebe, 92 acres; R.'s Inc. 588*l* and Ho; Pop. 789.) Formerly Stud. and Censor of Ch. Ch; Proctor of the Univ. Ox. 1846–47; Member of the Hebdomadal Council 1854 and 1857. Author, *University Education and Extension* (a Pamphlet). 1847. [21]

GORDON, Richard, *Elsfield Vicarage, near Oxford.*—V. of Elsfield, Dio. Ox. 1832. (Patron, Col. J. Sidney North; Tithe, 186*l*; Glebe, 2 acres; V.'s Inc. 220*l* and Ho; Pop. 179.) V. of Marston, near Oxford,

Dio. Ox. 1849. (Patron, Rev. T. H. Whorwood; Tithe—Imp. 280*l* 13*s* 6*d*, V. 200*l*; V.'s Inc. 210*l*; Pop. 452.) Rural Dean; Surrogate. [1]

GORDON, Robert, *Hammerwich, near Lichfield.*—Ch. Coll. Cam. B.A. 1854, M.A. 1857; Deac. 1854 and Pr. 1856 by Bp of Lich. P. C. of Hammerwich, Dio. Lich. 1858. (Patrons, Trustees; Tithe, 196*l* 16*s* 7*d*; P. C.'s Inc. 250*l*; Pop. 530.) Formerly C. of Speen and Lect. of Speenhamland, near Newbury. [2]

GORDON, Robert Augustus, *Barley Rectory, near Royston.*—Pemb. Coll. Cam. B.A. 1837, M.A. 1840; Deac. 1839, Pr. 1840. R. of Barley, Dio. Roch. 1853. (Patron, the Crown; Tithe—App. 5*l* 8*s* 3*d*, R. 581*l*; Glebe, 32 acres; R.'s Inc. 630*l* and Ho; Pop. 809.) Rural Dean 1854. [3]

GORDON, R. Wake, *Woodhouse, Leeds.*—Wad. Coll. Ox. B.A. 1861, M.A. 1863; Deac. 1865 and Pr. 1866 by Bp of Rip. C. of St. Mark's, Woodhouse, 1865. [4]

GORE, Hon. Annesley Henry, *Withcall Rectory, Louth, Lincolnshire.*—Dub. A.B. 1829; Deac. and Pr. 1833 by Bp of Kildare. R. of Withcall, Dio. Lin. 1844. (Patron, Ld. Chan; R.'s Inc. 516*l* and Ho; Pop. 121.) [5]

GORE, Arthur, 68, *Hope-street, Liverpool.*—Dub. Univ. Scho. in Cl. and Gold Medal in Math. and Phy. A.B. 1853, A.M. 1858; Deac. 1855 and Pr. 1856 by Bp of Derry. P. C. of St. Luke's, Liverpool, Dio. Ches. 1861. (Patrons, Reps. of C. Lawrence, Esq; P. C.'s Inc. 400*l* and Ho.) [6]

GORE, Arthur Lewis, *Broadheath, near Worcester.*—Jesus Coll. Cam. Cl. and Eng. Prizeman, B.A. 1859; Deac. 1861 and Pr. 1862 by Bp of Wor. Asst. C. of St. John's-in-Bedwardine, Worcester. Formerly C of Grays, Essex. [7]

GORE, Charles Frederick, *Edenbridge Vicarage, Kent.*—St. John's Coll. Ox. B.A. 1853, M.A. 1857; Deac. 1853 and Pr. 1854 by Bp of Lon. V. of Edenbridge, Dio. Cant. 1859. (Patron, Fred. Robt. Gore, Esq; Tithe—Imp. 785*l*, V. 436*l*; V.'s Inc. 436*l* and Ho; Pop. 1737.) Formerly C. of Hampstead, Middlesex, 1853–55. [8]

GORE, George, *Newton St. Loe Rectory, near Bath.*—R. of Newton St. Loe, Dio. B. and W. 1841. (Patron, W. Gore Langton, Esq; Tithe, 410*l*; Glebe, 48 acres; R.'s Inc. 490*l* and Ho; Pop. 401.) [9]

GORE, Henry James, *Rusper Rectory, Horsham, Sussex.*—Mert. Coll. Ox. B.A. 1835, M.A. 1845; Deac. 1837, Pr. 1838. R. of Rusper, Dio. Chich. 1853. (Patron, H. Rideout, Esq; Tithe, 296*l* 9*s* 11*d*; Glebe, 40 acres; R.'s Inc. 316*l* and Ho; Pop. 590.) [10]

GORE, John, *Shalbourne, Hungerford, Berks.*—Caius Coll. Cam. B.A. 1824; Deac. 1828 and Pr. 1829 by Bp of Lin. Min. Can. of Windsor 1829; V. of Shalbourne, Dio. Ox. 1842. (Patrons, D. and C. of Windsor; Glebe, 10 acres; V.'s Inc. 445*l* and Ho; Pop. 1011.) Author, *Scripture Narratives in Verse, with Psalms, Hymns, and Spiritual Songs,* 1853, 3*s* 6*d*. [11]

GORHAM, George Martyn, *Walkeringham Vicarage (Notts), near Gainsborough.*—Trin. Coll. Cam. Crown Scho. 1851, Burney Essay 1851, Hulsean Essay 1853, 14th Wrang. 2nd cl. Cl. Trip. 1st cl. Moral Sci. B.A. 1851, M.A. 1854; Deac. 1853 and Pr. 1854 by Bp of Ox. V. of Walkeringham, Dio. Lin. 1855. (Patron, Trin. Coll. Cam; Glebe, 157 acres; V.'s Inc. 214*l* and Ho; Pop. 633.) Dioc. Inspector of Schools; Organising Sec. for S.P.G. in Notts, and for A.C.S. in Dio. Lin. Formerly Fell. of Trin. Coll. Cam. Author, *On Future Punishment,* 1851, 3*s* 6*d*; *Primitive Episcopacy* (Hulsean Prize), 1854, 3*s* 6*d*. Editor of *Xenophon's Cyropædia, with English Notes,* 1856. [12]

GORING, John, *Wiston, near Steyning.* [13]

GORLE, James, *Whatcote Rectory, Shipston-on-Stour.*—Clare Coll. Cam. B.A. 1828, Tyrwhitt Heb. Scho. 1st cl. Cl. Trip. 1829, M.A. 1832, 2nd Seatonian Prizeman 1835; Deac. 1830 by Bp of G. and B. Pr. 1831 by Bp of Wor. R. of Whatcote, Dio. Wor. 1842. (Patron, Sir A. Dalrymple, Bart; Glebe, 218 acres; R.'s Inc. 270*l* and Ho; Pop. 180.) Author, *Fables in Verse, from Ancients and Moderns,* 1838, 3*s*; *Sacred Poems,* 1841, 5*s*; A Sermon, in *Sermons by Dignitaries and other Clergymen,* 1845; *Analysis of Pearson on the Creed, with Examination Questions,* 1855, 4*s*; *Analysis of Butler's Analogy,* 1855, 3*s*; *Examination Questions on Professor Browne's Exposition of the Articles,* 1857, 3*s* 6*d*; *Analysis of Hooker's Ecclesiastical Polity,* Bk. 5, 1858, 4*s*. [14]

GORMAN, Robert Johnson, *Milburne, Penrith.*—P. C. of Milburne, Dio. Carl. 1865. (Patron, Sir R. Tufton, Bart; P. C.'s Inc. 95*l*; Pop. 324.) Formerly P. C. of St. John's, Murton, Appleby. [15]

GORMAN, Thomas Murray, 13, *Campden-grove, Kensington, W.*—Magd. Hall Ox. B.A. 1863, M.A. 1865; Deac. 1863 and Pr. 1864 by Bp of Lon. Asst. C. of St. Mary Abbotts, Kensington, 1866. Formerly C. of Ch. Ch. Marylebone 1863. [16]

GORNALL, James, *St. John's, Oldham.*—St. Bees 1st cl. Prizeman and Librarian; Deac. 1854 and Pr. 1855 by Bp of Ches. P. C. of St. John's, Chadderton, Oldham, Dio. Man. 1864. (Patrons, Crown and Bp of Man. alt; P. C.'s Inc. 300*l*; Pop. 6081.) Formerly Head Mast. of Slaidburn Gr. Sch. and Min. of St. James's Chapel, Dalehead, Slaidburn, 1857. [17]

GORST, Peter Freeland, *Saxby Rectory, Melton Mowbray.*—St. John's Coll. Cam. B.A. 1863, M.A. 1867; Deac. 1862 by Abp of York, Pr. 1864 by Bp of Pet. C. of Saxby with Stapleford 1864. [18]

GORTON, Frederick Robert, *Kelsa's, Saxmundham.*—St. John's Coll. Cam. B.A. 1853; Deac. 1853, Pr. 1854. C. of Carlton, Kelsale, Suffolk. Formerly C. of Badingham, Carlton, Suffolk, Gunthorpe, Norfolk. [19]

GORTON, Robert, *Badingham, Saxmundham.*—Jesus Coll. Cam. B.A. 1821, M.A. 1825; Deac. 1831, Pr. 1832. R. of Badingham, Dio. Nor. 1831. (Patron, the present R; Tithe, 883*l*; R.'s Inc. 940*l* and Ho; Pop. 749.) [20]

GORTON, Robert Gregson, *Padworth, near Reading.*—St. John's Coll. Cam. B.A. 1847, M.A. 1855; Deac. 1847 and Pr. 1848 by Bp of Nor. Formerly P. C. of Peter's Marland, Devon, 1852–57; R. of Great Stanmore, Middlesex, 1857–61. [21]

GORTON, William Henry, *Portisham Vicarage, Dorchester.*—Trin. Coll. Cam. B.A. 1828; Deac. 1829 and Pr. 1830 by Bp of Bristol. V. of Portisham, Dio. Salis. 1837. (Patron, W. Manfield, Esq; Glebe, 3¾ acres; V.'s Inc. 36*l* and Ho; Pop. 719.) Formerly C. of Chickerell 1830, Radipole and Buckland-Ripers 1831-36. [22]

GOSLETT, E. M.—C. of Chorlton-on-Medlock, Manchester. [23]

GOSLING, Edward Johnson, *Monk-street, Monmouth.*—Magd. Hall, Ox. B.A. 1832, M.A. 1835; Deac. 1833, Pr. 1834. Chap. to the Monmouth County Gaol 1836. [24]

GOSLING, Francis, *Burghclere, Hants.*—C. of Burghclere. [25]

GOSLING, John Frederick, *Cirencester.*—C. of Watermoor, Cirencester. Formerly C. of Cirencester. [26]

GOSS, John, *The College, Hereford.*—Ex. Coll. Ox. B.A. 1848, M.A. 1850; Deac. 1850 and Pr. 1851 by Bp of Herf. Succentor and Vicar Choral of Herf. Cathl. 1853; V. of St. John Baptist's, Hereford, 1859. (Patrons, D. and C. of Herf; V.'s Inc. 300*l* and Ho; Pop. 1419.) Formerly Asst. Mast. Herf. Cathl. Sch. 1852–57. [27]

GOSS, Thomas, *Stapleton Rectory, Carlisle.*—Queen's Coll. Ox. B.A; Deac. 1864 and Pr. 1865 by Bp of Carl. R. of Stapleton, Dio. Carl. 1867. (Patron, Earl of Carlisle; R.'s Inc. 100*l* and Ho; Pop. 984.) Formerly C. of Brampton, Cumberland, 1864–65, and Sen. C. of same 1865–67. [28]

GOSSE, Henry, *Red-hill, Reigate, Surrey.*—Ex. Coll. Ox. B.A. 1838, M.A. 1841; Deac. 1839, Pr. 1840. P. C. of St. John's, Red-hill, with St. Matthew's C. Dio. Win. 1846. (Patron, Bp of Win.) [29]

GOSSET, Clement Hammond, *Rectory, Langton Herring, Weymouth.*—Trin. Coll. Cam. Sen. Opt. and B.A. 1849, M.A. 1852; Deac. 1851 and Pr. 1852 by Bp of Win. R. of Langton Herring, Dio. Salis. 1860.

(Patron, W. Sparks, Esq; Tithe, 86*l*; Glebe, 33 acres; R.'s Inc. 135*l* and Ho; Pop. 241.) Formerly C. of St. Luke's, Jersey, 1851–54, Faringdon, Hants, 1854–57, West Tisted 1857, Harbridge 1858, Greywell 1859–60. [1]

GOSSET, Isaac Henry, *Northam Vicarage, Bideford, Devon.*—Ex. Coll. Ox. 4th cl. Lit. Hum. and B.A. 1837, M.A. 1839; Deac. 1840, Pr. 1841. V. of Northam, Dio. Ex. 1844. (Patrons, D. and Cans. of Windsor; Tithe, App. 525*l* and 60 acres of Glebe; Glebe, 2 acres; V.'s Inc. 270*l* and Ho; Pop. 1477.) Rural Dean. [2]

GOTT, John, *Bramley Parsonage, Leeds.*—Brasen. Coll. Ox. B.A. 1853, M.A. 1854; Deac. 1857 and Pr. 1858 by Bp of Nor. P. C. of Bramley, Dio. Rip. 1866. (Patron, V. of Leeds; P. C.'s Inc. 280*l* and Ho; Pop. 8100.) Formerly C. of St. Nicholas', Great Yarmouth; Min. of St. Andrew's, Yarmouth. [3]

GOUGH, Edmund, *Warslow Parsonage, Ashborne, Staffs.*—P. C. of Elkstone and Warslow P. C. Dio. Lich. 1866. (Patron, V. of Alstonfield; P. C.'s Inc. 180*l* and Ho; Pop. 689.) [4]

GOUGH, John, *Long Load, Ilminster.*—St. John's Coll. Cam. B.A. 1859; Deac. 1861 and Pr. 1862 by Bp of G. and B. Min. of Long Load, Somerset. Formerly C. of St. Paul's, Cheltenham, 1861. Author, *Sermons*, 1863, 1*s* 6*d*. [5]

GOUGH, R. H. L., *Oldham.*—C. of St. Mary's, Oldham. [6]

GOUGH, W. Hensell, *Widley, Portsmouth.*—C. of Widley with Wymering. Formerly C. of Ch. Ch. Clapham, Surrey. [7]

GOULBURN, The Very Rev. Edward Meyrick, *Norwich.*—Ball. Coll. Ox. 1st cl. Lit. Hum. and B.A. 1839, Mert. Coll. Ox. M.A. 1842, D.C.L. 1850, D.D. 1856; Deac. 1842 and Pr. 1843 by Bp of Ox. Dean of Norwich 1866. Formerly C. of Quebec Chapel, Lond; Head Mast. of Rugby Sch. 1850; Fell. and Tut. of Mert. Coll. Ox. 1839–41; P. C. of Holywell 1841; P. C. of St. John's, Paddington, Lond. 1859–67. Author, *The Resurrection of the Body* (Bampton Lectures), 10*s* 6*d*; *Parochial Sermons*, 10*s*; *On the Devotional Study of Holy Scripture*, 3*s* 6*d*; *Short Devotional Forms*, 1*s*; *Rudimentary Essay on the Philosophy of Grammar*, 2*s*; *Thoughts on Personal Religion*; *The Idle Word*; *The Office of the Holy Communion in the Book of Common Prayer*; *The Inspiration of Holy Scripture*; *Occasional Sermons during the last Twenty Years*, 2 vols; *An Address to the Sisters of St. Peter's House, Brompton-square*; *Family Prayers in the Liturgical Form*; numerous detached Sermons, Lectures and Tracts. [8]

GOULD, Alfred Benjamin, *St. Mark's Vicarage, Wolverhampton.*—V. of St. Mark's, Wolverhampton, Dio. Lich. 1864. (Patrons, the Crown and Bp of Lich. alt; V's Inc. 150*l* and Ho; Pop. 6282.) [9]

GOULD, Charles Baring, *Lew Trenchard Rectory, Lew Down, Devonshire.*—Magd. Coll. Cam. B.A. 1831; Deac. 1831 and Pr. 1832 by Bp of Ex. R. of Lew Trenchard, Dio. Ex. 1833. (Patron, E. B. Gould, Esq; Tithe, 265*l*; Glebe, 56 acres; R.'s Inc. 310*l* and Ho; Pop. 353.) [10]

GOULD, George, *Cropwell-Bishop, Bingham, Notts.*—Univ. Coll. Ox. B.A. 1821, M.A. 1824; Deac. and Pr. 1822. V. of Cropwell-Bishop, Dio. Lin. 1840. (Patron, Bp of Rip. and Bp of Man. alt; Land in lieu of Tithe, 60 acres; V.'s Inc. 300*l* and Ho; Pop. 638.) [11]

GOULD, George Masters, *Grammar School, Maidstone, Kent.*—Head Mast. of the Maidstone Gr. Sch. Formerly Mast. of the Ilminster Gr. Sch; P. C. of Chillington, Somerset, 1851–61. [12]

GOULD, James Aubrey, *Bodicote Parsonage, Banbury, Oxon.*—New Coll. Ox. B.C.L. 1850; Deac. 1850 and Pr. 1851 by Bp of Ox. P. C. of Bodicote, Dio. Ox. 1856. (Patron, New Coll. Ox; P. C.'s Inc. 100*l* and Ho; Pop. 626.) [13]

GOULD, John Nutcombe, *Stokeinteignhead Rectory, Teignmouth.*—Wad. Coll. Ox. B.A. 1827. R. of Stokeinteignhead, Dio. Ex. 1847. (Patron, Bp of Ex; Tithe, 429*l*; R.'s Inc. 470*l* and Ho; Pop. 628.) [14]

GOULD, R. Freke, *Stoke Pero, Minehead, Somerset.*—R. of Stoke Pero, Dio. B. and W. 1857. (Patron, J. Quick, Esq; R.'s Inc. 92*l*; Pop. 51.) [15]

GOULD, Robert John, *Stratfield Mortimer, Reading.*—Wad. Coll. Ox. M.A. 1831; Deac. 1833 and Pr. 1834 by Bp of Lin. V. of Stratfield Mortimer, Dio. Ox. 1860. (Patron, Eton Coll; Tithe, 274*l* 3*s*; Glebe, 32 acres; V.'s Inc. 286*l* and Ho; Pop. 1419.) Formerly C. of New Windsor 1844–54; P. C. of Trull, Somerset, 1857–58. [16]

GOULD, William, *Hatch Beauchamp, Taunton.*—Ball. Coll. Ox. 3rd cl. Lit. Hum. and B.A. 1829, M.A. 1832; Deac. 1830, Pr. 1831. R. of Hatch Beauchamp, Dio. B. and W. 1854. (Patron, Rev. T. F. Dymock; Tithe, 119*l*; Glebe, 42 acres; R.'s Inc. 168*l* and Ho; Pop. 234.) [17]

GOULDEN, Alfred, B., 63, *Upper Kennington-lane, Vauxhall, S.*—C. of St. Peter's, Vauxhall. Formerly C. of Batcombe, Dorset. [18]

GOVER, William, *Diocesan Training College, Saltley, near Birmingham.*—Corpus Coll. Cam. B.A. 1841, M.A. 1845; Deac. 1843, Pr. 1844. Prin. of the Worcester, Lichfield, and Hereford Training Coll. 1852; Hon. Can. of Wor. 1867; Chap. to the Earl of Annesley 1851. Formerly C. of St. Paul's Birmingham, 1843, St. Thomas's, Birmingham, 1848, St. Andrew's, Holborn, Lond. 1849, St. Pancras', Lond. 1850. Author, *Justification* (two Sermons), 1848; *A Sermon for Scripture Readers' Association*, 1849; *Our Work* (a paper on Education read before the Social Science Congress), 1857; *Remarks on Clerical Subscription*, 1863; *Patronage, or Representative Trusts for New Churches, in large Towns*, 1865; *The Conscience Clause*, 1865; *Day-school Education in Birmingham*, 1867; *Rural Schools, Hints on the Extension of Aid to small Schools*, 1867. [19]

GOVETT, Decimus Storry.—Wad. Coll. Ox. B A. 1855, M A. 1859; Deac. 1851 and Pr. 1853 by Bp of Lon. Formerly C. of Wymering, Middlesex, and Drayton, Norfolk. Author, *On the Evils of the Pew System*. [20]

GOVETT, John Clement, *Pontesbright, Kelvedon, Essex.*—P. C. of Pontesbright, Dio. Roch. 1866. (Patrons, the Parishioners; P. C.'s Inc. 70*l*; Pop. 370.) Formerly C. of Staines, and Mark's Tey. [21]

GOVETT, Thomas Romaine, *Alby Rectory, Hanworth, Norfolk.*—Deac. 1848 and Pr. 1849 by Bp of Ches. R. of Alby, Dio. Nor. 1853. (Patron, Earl of Orford; Tithe, 196*l*; Glebe, 15½ acres; R.'s Inc. 200*l* and Ho; Pop. 231.) Author, *Illustrations of Scripture, by an Eye-witness*. [22]

GOWER, Anthony Hesketh, *Ridge Vicarage, Barnet, Herts.*—Ch. Ch. Ox. B.A. 1821; Deac. 1825 and Pr. 1826 by Bp of Lon. C. of Ridge 1839. Formerly C. of Dengie, Essex, 1825, Aldworth, Berks, 1829, Little Warley, Essex, 1834, Ayott St. Peter, Herts, 1837. [23]

GOWER, Herbert, *Clevedon, near Bath.*—Ch. Ch. Ox. B.A. 1821, M.A. 1825; Deac. 1822, Pr. 1823. [24]

GOWER, Stephen Stock, *Wandsworth, Surrey, S.W.*—St. John's Coll. Cam. Sen. Opt. and B.A. 1839, M.A. 1842; Deac. 1840 and Pr. 1841 by Bp of Win. C. of All Saints', Wandsworth. Formerly C. of Kingston-on-Thames 1844–52. [25]

GOWRING, George James, *Ilminster.*—Magd. Hall, Ox. 2nd cl. Lit. Hum. 4th cl. Math. et Phy. and B.A. 1850, M.A. 1852; Deac. 1851 and Pr. 1852 by Bp. of Ox. Head Mast. of the Ilminster Gr. Sch; P. C. of Kingston, Dio. B. and W. 1859. (Patron, John Lee Lee, Esq; P. C.'s Inc. 60*l*; Pop. 276.) Formerly C. of Banbury. Author, *Sermons on the Lord's Day, and some Prominent Points of Christian Doctrine and Practice*, 1855, 5*s*. [26]

GOWRING, John William.—Trin. Coll. Cam. 11th Wrang. and B.A. 1833; Deac. 1833 by Bp of Ches. Pr. 1835 by Bp of Nor. Lect. at St. John's, Horselydown, and St. Giles', Cripplegate, Lond. [27]

GOYNE, Richard Morgan, *Tredegar, Monmouthshire.*—Literate; Deac. 1860 and Pr. 1865 by Bp of

Llan. Home Miss. to the Miners and Colliers. Formerly C. of Ebbw Vale, Tredegar, 1860. [1]

GRABHAM, Thomas, *High Halstow Rectory, Rochester.*—St. John's Coll. Cam. Wrang. B.A. 1854, M.A. 1857; Deac. 1856 and Pr. 1857 by Abp of Cant. R. of High Halstow, Dio. Roch. 1867. (Patron, T. Briggs, Esq; R.'s Inc. 700*l* and Ho; Pop. 363.) Formerly P. C. of Trinity, Sittingbourne. [2]

GRACE, Henry Thomas, *Westham Vicarage, Eastbourne, Sussex.*—Pemb. Coll. Cam. 1st Sen. Opt. and B.A. 1811, M.A. 1814; Deac. 1812 by Bp of Lon. Pr. 1812 by Bp of Ely. R. of Jevington, Dio. Chich. 1812. (Patron, Duke of Devonshire; Tithe, 465*l*; Glebe, 17 acres; R.'s Inc. 485*l* and Ho; Pop. 263.) V. of Westham, Dio. Chich. 1820. (Patron, Duke of Devonshire; Tithe —Imp. 1082*l*, V. 570*l*; Glebe, 1½ acres; V.'s Inc. 575*l* and Ho; Pop. 833.) Rural Dean. Formerly Bye Fell. of Pemb. Coll. Cam. [3]

GRACE, Oliver James, *Lacey Green, Risborough, Tring.*—Jesus Coll. Cam. B.A. 1856, M.A. 1859; Deac. 1856 and Pr. 1858 by Bp of Ox. C. of Saunderton. [4]

GRAFTON, Augustus William, *Wells, Somerset.*—Trin. Hall, Cam. Scho. of, 1st cl. Theol. Trip. and B.A. 1858, M.A. 1861; Deac. 1859 and Pr. 1860 by Abp of Cant. Vice-Prin. of the Wells Theol. Coll. Formerly C. of St. Martin's with St. Paul's, Canterbury; St. Edward's, Cambridge. [5]

GRAHAM, A., *Great Bromley Rectory, Essex.*—R. of Great Bromley, Dio. Roch. 1860. (Patron, W. Graham, Esq; Tithe, 858*l* 13*s* 6*d*; R.'s Inc. 880*l* and Ho; Pop. 758.) [6]

GRAHAM, A. D.—C. of St. Paul's, Covent-garden, Lond. [7]

GRAHAM, Charles Ryves, *Kirkby-Ireleth, Ulverston.*—V. of Kirkby-Ireleth, Dio. Ches. 1832. (Patrons, D. and C. of York; Tithe—App. 84*l* and 42 acres of Glebe, V. 22*l*; Glebe, 4 acres; V.'s Inc. 125*l*; Pop. 1512.) [8]

GRAHAM, Christopher, *Bidstone Parsonage, Birkenhead, Cheshire.*—P. C. of Bidstone, Dio. Ches. 1851. (Patron, Bp of Ches; Tithe—App. 455*l* 2*s* 2*d*, and ½ an acre of Glebe; P. C.'s Inc. 100*l* and Ho; Pop. 2154.) [9]

GRAHAM, George, 34, *Claremont-square, London, N.*—Corpus Coll. Cam. Scho. of, 1st cl. Theol. Trip. and B.A. 1867; Deac. 1867 by Bp of Lon. C. of St. Michael's, Islington. [10]

GRAHAM, Henry John, *Pudsey Parsonage, near Leeds.*—Deac. 1842 and Pr. 1843 by Abp of York. P. C. of Pudsey, Dio. Rip. 1854. (Patron, V. of Calverley; P. C.'s Inc. 300*l* and Ho; Pop. 10,936.) Formerly C. of Whitby 1842; P. C. of Eyton and Goatland 1844; Chap. of the Infirmary, Sheffield, 1847. [11]

GRAHAM, James John George, *Much Cowarne, Bromyard, Herefordshire.*—Queen's Coll. Ox. B.A. 1845; M.A. 1848; Deac. 1846 and Pr. 1847 by Bp of G. and B. V. of Much Cowarne, Dio. Herf. 1861. (Patron, Bp of Wor; Tithe, 241*l* 5*s* 4*d*; Glebe, 9 acres; V.'s Inc. 300*l* and Ho; Pop. 568.) Formerly Sen. C. of Trinity, Coventry. [12]

GRAHAM, John, *Lichfield.*—Dub. Vice-Chan's Prizeman, B.A. 1844, M.A. 1849 *ad eund.* Ox; Deac. 1844 and Pr. 1845 by Bp of Dur. R. of St. Chad's, Lichfield, Dio. Lich. 1861. (Patron, V. of St. Mary's, Lichfield; R.'s Inc. 320*l*; Pop. 1659; St. Chad's was constituted a Rectory by annexing rectorial tithes in 1861.) Formerly C. of Castle Eden, Durham, 1844, Tintern Abbey 1847; Afternoon Lect. Trinity, Margate, 1851; P. C. of St. Chad's, Lichfield, 1853–61. Author, *The Way of Salvation, or Salvation—What is it? How is it? Why is it?* [13]

GRAHAM, John, *Cosgrove Rectory, Stony Stratford.*—Queens' Coll. Cam. Wrang. and B.A. 1825, M.A. 1828; Deac. and Pr. 1827 by Bp of Ely. R. of Cosgrove, Dio. Pet. 1835. (Patroness, Mrs. H. Mansell; Tithe, 33*l* 8*s*; R.'s Inc. 370*l* and Ho; Pop. 776.) Formerly Fell. of Queens' Coll. Cam. 1826–30. [14]

GRAHAM, John, *Chester.*—Ch. Coll. Cam. LL.B. 1859, LL.M. 1862; Deac. 1860, Pr. 1861. P. C. of Little St. John's, Chester, 1864. (Patrons, Charity Trustees; P. C.'s Inc 289*l*; Pop. 61.) Formerly C. of Wallasey, Cheshire, 1860–64. [15]

GRAHAM, John, *Painsthorpe, Wakefield.*—Jesus Coll. Cam. B.A. 1864; Deac. 1867 by Bp of Rip. C. of Painsthorpe 1867. [16]

GRAHAM, M. Reginald, M.A., *Arthuret Rectory, Longtown, Cumberland.*—R. of Arthuret, Dio. Carl. 1863. (Patron, Sir F. M. Graham, Bart; Tithe, 840*l* 19*s* 6*d*; Glebe, 32 acres; R.'s Inc. 1209*l* and Ho; Pop. 3714.) [17]

GRAHAM, Philip, B.A., *Over Darwen Parsonage, Blackburn.*—P. C. of St. James's, Over Darwen, Dio. Man. 1864. (Patron, V. of Blackburn; Glebe, 45 acres; P. C.'s Inc. 229*l* and Ho; Pop. 1795.) [18]

GRAHAM, Reuben, *Plaistow, Bromley, Kent.*—Dub. A.B. 1855; Deac. 1856 by Bp of Rip. P. C. of St. Mary's, Plaistow, Dio. Cant. 1863. (Patron, the present P. C. Pop. 2000.) Formerly C. of Coley. [19]

GRAHAM, Thomas.—C. of St. Margaret's, Westminster. [20]

GRAHAM, William Henry.—St. Aidan's; Deac. 1854 and Pr. 1855 by Bp of Pet. P. C. of St. Paul's, Upper Penge, Dio. Win. 1866. [21]

GRAHAM, William Paley, *Blyborough Rectory, Kirton-in-Lindsey, Lincolnshire.*—Queen's Coll. Ox. B.A. 1839, M.A. 1843. R. of Blyborough, Dio. Lin. 1847. (Patron, Ld Chan; Tithe, 557*l*; R.'s Inc. 565*l* and Ho; Pop. 209.) [22]

GRAIN, Charles, *Wacton Rectory, Long Stratton, Norfolk.*—Pemb. Coll. Cam. B.A. 1837, M.A. 1842; Deac. 1839 and Pr. 1840 by Bp of Ely. R. of Wacton Magna with Wacton Parva Sinecure R. Dio. Nor. 1846. (Patron, the present R; Tithe, 323*l* 4*s*; Glebe, 31 acres; R.'s Inc. 353*l* and Ho; Pop. 244.) [23]

GRAINGER, George William, *Luppitt Vicarage, Honiton.*—V. of Luppitt, Dio. Ex. 1856. (Patroness, Mrs. Bernard; Tithe—Imp. 198*l* 2*s*, V. 140*l* 0*s* 8*d*; V.'s Inc. 150*l* and Ho; Pop 714.) [24]

GRAINGER, John, *Penn Vicarage, Amersham, Bucks.*—Caius Coll. Cam. B.A. 1848, M.A. 1851; Deac. 1848 and Pr. 1849 by Bp of Lon. V. of Penn. Dio. Ox. 1860. (Patron, Earl Howe; Tithe, 338*l* 6*s* 7*d*; Glebe, 42 acres; V.'s Inc. 406*l* and Ho; Pop. 500.) Formerly Tut. Ch. Miss. Coll. Islington, 1848–51; Asst. Math. Mast. Eton Coll. 1851–60. [25]

GRAINGER, John Cecil, 1, *Margaret-grove, Canonbury, London, N.*—Univ. Coll. Ox. B.A. 1860, M.A. 1866; Deac. 1866 by Bp of Lon. C. of St. Augustine's, Highbury, 1866. [26]

GRANE, John Willis, *Hope-under-Dinmore, Leominster, Herefordshire.*—Ex. Coll. Ox. B.A. 1842, M.A. 1844; Deac. and Pr. 1843. P. C. of Hope-under-Dinmore, Dio. Herf. 1858. (Patron, I. H. Arkwright, Esq; Glebe, 12 acres; P. C.'s Inc. 133*l* and Ho; Pop. 662.) Formerly P. C. of Ch. Ch. Northam, Southampton, 1851–58. [27]

GRANGE, James Demain, 5, *Union-road, Rotherhithe, S.E.*—King's Coll. Lond. Assoc. 1864; Deac. 1865 and Pr. 1866 by Bp of Win. C. of Ch. Ch. Rotherhithe, Surrey, 1865. [28]

GRANT, Alexander, *Manningford-Bruce Rectory, Pewsey, Wilts.*—R. of Manningford-Bruce, Dio. Salis. 1845. (Patrons, Trustees; Tithe, 310*l* 5*s*; Glebe, 1¾ acres; R.'s Inc. 316*l* 5*s* and Ho; Pop. 252.) Rural Dean. [29]

GRANT, Alexander Ronald, *Hitcham Rectory, Bildeston, Suffolk.*—Trin. Coll. Cam. 7th Wrang. and B.A. 1845, M.A. 1848; Deac. 1849 and Pr. 1850 by Bp of Ely. R. of Hitcham, Dio. Ely, 1861. (Patron, the Crown; Tithe, 1159*l*; Glebe, 37 acres; R.'s Inc. 1200*l* and Ho; Pop. 991.) Rural Dean 1864. Formerly V. of Helion-Bumpstead, Essex, 1850–53; P. C. of St. Michael's, Cambridge, 1853–55; Asst. Inspector of Schools 1855–61; Fell. of Trin. Coll. Cam. 1847–55. Author, *Introductory Treatise on Plane Astronomy*, 1850, 6*s*. [30]

GRANT, The Ven. Anthony, *Aylesford Vicarage, Maidstone.*—New Coll. Ox. B.C.L. 1829, Chancellor's (Latin) Prize Essay 1830, Theol. Prize Essay 1832, D.C.L. 1842; Deac. 1834 by Bp of Ox. Pr. 1836 by Bp of Lon. V. of Aylesford, Dio. Roch. 1862. (Patrons, D. and C. of Roch; Tithe—App. 650*l* 13*s* 5*d*, V. 597*l* 11*s* 3*d*; V.'s Inc. 687*l* and Ho; Pop. 2057.) Archd. of Rochester, and of St. Albans 1846; Can. of Roch. 1860; Chap. to the Bp of Roch. Formerly V. of Romford 1838–62; Fell. of New Coll. Ox; Bampton Lecturer 1843; Select Preacher 1854. Author, *Missions* (The Bampton Lectures), 1843; *Ramsden Sermon*, 1852; *Historical Sketch of the Crimea*, 1855. [1]

GRANT, Charles, *Threlkeld Parsonage, Penrith.*—P. C. of Threlkeld, Dio. Carl. 1866. (Patron, Earl of Lonsdale; P. C.'s Inc. 60*l* and Ho; Pop. 380.) Formerly C. of Threlkeld. [2]

GRANT, E. P., M.A., *Bishop's Caundle, Sherborne, Dorset.*—R. of Bishop's Caundle, Dio. Salis. 1862. (Patron, G. D. W. Digby, Esq; Tithe, 250*l*; R.'s Inc. 260*l* and Ho; Pop. 371.) [3]

GRANT, Francis Basett, *Cullompton Vicarage, Devon.*—Ch. Ch. Ox. M.A. 1818; Deac. 1819, Pr. 1820. V. of Cullompton, Dio. Ex. 1864. (Patron, Rev. J. Oldham; Glebe, 12 acres; V.'s Inc. 460*l* and Ho; Pop. 3185.) Formerly R. of Shelton, Staffs, 1845–64. [4]

GRANT, F. Cecil Hope, *West Kirby, Upton, Cheshire.*—C. of West Kirby. [5]

GRANT, Henry Carmichael, *Sutton, Surrey.*—Jesus Coll. Cam. B.A. 1858; Deac. 1860 by Bp of Ches. C. of Sutton; Surrogate. Formerly C. of Bollington 1860. [6]

GRANT, Joseph Brett, *Oxenhope Parsonage, Bradford, Yorks.*—Emman. Coll. Cam. B.A. 1843; Deac. 1843 by Bp of Ches. Pr. 1845 by Bp of Rip. P. C. of Oxenhope, Dio. Rip. 1845. (Patrons, the Crown and Bp of Rip. alt; P. C.'s Inc. 150*l* and Ho; Pop. 2880.) Author, *A Brief Account of Diocesan Synods*, 1852; *There is one Body* (a Sermon), 1853, 2*d*; *A Letter to Working Men on the Existence of God*, 1854; *The Knowledge of Common Things* (a Lecture.) [7]

GRANT, Robert, *Bradford-Abbas, Sherborne, Dorset.*—New Coll. Ox. B.C.L. 1822; Deac. 1819, Pr. 1820. V. of Bradford-Abbas with Clifton-Maybank, Dio. Salis. 1828. (Patron, Win. Coll; Bradford-Abbas, Tithe, —Imp. 238*l* 17*s* 11*d* and $8\frac{3}{4}$ acres of Glebe, V. 156*l* 6*s* 3*d*; Glebe, $9\frac{1}{2}$ acres; Clifton-Maybank, Tithe, 245*l*; Glebe, 30 acres; V.'s Inc. 480*l* and Ho; Pop. Bradford-Abbas 585, Clifton-Maybank 73.) Preb. of Beaminster Secunda in Salis. Cathl. 1845; Rural Dean; Fell. of Win. Coll. 1828. Author, *Lectures on the Parable of the Prodigal Son*, 1830; *Kapiolani and other Poems*, 1848. [8]

GRANTHAM, George Peirce, *Hotham, Brough, Yorks.*—King's Coll. Lond. B.A. 1861; Deac. 1859 and Pr. 1862 by Bp of Ex. C. of Hotham 1865. Formerly C. of All Hallows East, Exeter, 1859–61, Rame, Cornwall, 1861–65. Author, *Name this Child, or a Few Words to Parents and Sponsors concerning the selection of suitable and correct names for Children*, Masters, 1864, 6*d*; *The Three Kings of Orient* (a Christmas Carol), Novello, 1865, 2*d*; *Holy Songs*, Ib. 1866, 1*s* 6*d*. [9]

GRANVILLE, Augustus Kerr Bozzi, *Hatcham Parsonage, Deptford, Kent.*—Corpus Coll. Cam. B.A. 1838, M.A. 1841; Deac. 1839 and Pr. 1840 by Bp of B. and W. P. C. of St. James's, Hatcham, Dio. Lon. 1845. (Patrons, the Crown and Bp of Lon. alt; P. C.'s Inc. 200*l* and Ho; Pop. 9887.) Dom. Chap. to the Earl of Ripon. Author, various Sermons; *Form of Preparation for Holy Communion*; *How to Settle the Church-rate Question*, 1856. [10]

GRANVILLE, Court, *Alnwick Parsonage, Northumberland.*—Trin. Coll. Cam. B.A. 1831, M.A. 1834; Deac. 1835 by Bp of Lich. Pr. 1837 by Bp of Wor. P. C. of Alnwick, Dio. Dur. 1859. (Patron, Duke of Northumberland; P. C.'s Inc. 200*l* and Ho; Pop. 3965.) Hon. Can. of Dur. Cathl. 1851; Rural Dean; Dom. Chap. to the Duke of Northumberland 1847. Formerly V. of Thaxted, Essex, 1854–59; P. C. of Alnwick 1846–54. [11]

GRANVILLE, Granville John, *Pleasley Rectory, Mansfield.*—Deac. 1837, Pr. 1838. R. of Pleasley, Derbyshire, Dio. Lich. 1867. (Patron, W. P. Thornhill, Esq; Tithe, 650*l*; Glebe, 55 acres; R.'s Inc. 710*l* and Ho; Pop. 271.) Formerly V. of Stratford-on-Avon, 1855–67. [12]

GRASETT, James, *Edwin Loach Rectory, Bromyard.*—Univ. Coll. Ox. B.A. 1821, M.A. 1824; Deac. 1823 by Bp of Glouc. Pr. 1824 by Bp of Bristol. R. of the United R.'s of Edwin Loach (Wor.) with Tedstone Wafer (Herf.) Dio. Herf. 1842. (Patron, E Higginson, Esq; Edwin Loach, Tithe, 71*l* 16*s*; Glebe, 34 acres; Tedstone Wafer, Tithe, 80*l* 5*s*; Glebe, $\frac{1}{2}$ acre; R.'s Inc. 200*l* and Ho; Pop. Edwin Loach 53, Tedstone Wafer 74.) [13]

GRASETT, James Elliot, *Knighton-on-Teme Parsonage, Tenbury.*—Dur. Deac. 1857 and Pr. 1858 by Bp of Herf. P. C. of Knighton-on-Teme, Dio. Herf. (Patron, V. of Lindridge; P. C.'s Inc. 100*l*; Pop. 563.) Formerly C. of Lindridge. [14]

GRATRIX, James, *Armitage Bridge Parsonage, Huddersfield.*—St. John's Coll. Cam. 11th Wrang. B.A. 1828, M.A. 1832; Deac. and Pr. 1828 by Bp of Lich. P. C. of Armitage Bridge, Dio. Rip. 1862. (Patrons, John Brooke, Esq. and V. of Almondsbury; P. C.'s Inc. 195*l* and Ho; Pop. 2446.) Formerly C. of Hayfield, Preston, Great Snoring, Halifax; P. C. of St. James's, Halifax, 1834; V. of Kensworth 1854. Author, *Sermons*, 10*s*. Halifax, 1843; *Sermon on the Little Horn, Dan.* vii. 8, 1853; *Exposition of the Church Catechism*, 3 eds. [15]

GRAVES, Charles Edward, 2, *Trumpington-street, Cambridge.*—St. John's Coll. Cam. Porson Prizeman 1861, 2nd in 1st cl. Cl. Trip. 1862, B.A. 1862, M.A. 1865; Deac. 1866 and Pr. 1867 by Bp of Ely. C. of Chesterton, Cambridge, 1866. [16]

GRAVES, John, *Cheltenham College.*—Ch. Coll. Cam. Scho. 1852, 2nd cl. Cl. Trip. and B.A. 1855, M.A. 1858; Deac. 1859 by Abp of Cant. Pr. 1860 by Bp of Win. Cl. Mast. in Cheltenham Coll. Formerly Lect. in History at Training Coll. Battersea, 1857–59; Mast. in Kensington Sch. 1859–61. [17]

GRAVES, John, *Bradenham, High Wycombe.*—R. of Bradenham, Dio. Ox. 1865. (Patron, the present R; R.'s Inc. 260*l* and Ho; Pop. 185.) Formerly C. of Bradenham. [18]

GRAVES, John, *Underbarrow Parsonage, Kendal.*—St. Bees, Librarian; Deac. 1835 and Pr. 1836 by Bp of Ches. P. C. of Underbarrow, Dio. Ches. 1839. (Patron, V. of Kendal; Glebe, 12 acres; P. C.'s Inc. 90*l* and Ho.) [19]

GRAVES, John, jun., *Underbarrow, Kendal.*—C. of Underbarrow. [20]

GRAVES, Richard Drought, *Hanford, Stoke-upon-Trent.*—St. John's Coll. Cam. B.A. 1855; Deac. 1858 and Pr. 1859 by Bp of Ely. P. C. of Hanford, Dio. Lich. 1865. (Patron, Duke of Sutherland; P. C.'s Inc. 140*l*; Pop. 900*l*.) Formerly C. of Hitcham, Suffolk, and Mitcham, Surrey. [21]

GRAY, Arthur, *Orcop, near Ross, Herefordshire.*—Univ. Coll. Ox. B.A. 1846, M.A. 1849; Deac. 1847 and Pr. 1848 by Bp of Dur. Chap. of Donative of Orcop, Dio. Herf. 1859. (Patron, the present Chap; Chap.'s Inc. 31*l*; Pop. 583.) Formerly C. of Holy Trinity, Stockton-on-Tees, 1847; Gainford, Durham, 1852. [22]

GRAY, Charles, *East Retford.*—Trin. Coll. Cam. 9th Wrang. 1855, M.A. 1858; Deac. 1861 by Bp of Lich. Pr. 1863 by Bp of Ely. V. of East Retford, Dio. Lin. 1866. (Patron, Sir J. Sutton, Bart; V.'s Inc. 135*l* and Ho; Pop. 2900.) Chap. to Bp of Ely; Rural Dean; Fell. of Trin. Coll. Cam. Formerly Asst. Tut. of Trin. Coll. Cam. 1857–66. [23]

GRAY, C., *Northwood, Hanley, Staffs.*—C. of Northwood. [24]

GRAY, Charles Edward, *Skipwith, Selby.*—Brasen. Coll. Ox. B.A. 1837, M.A. 1840. V. of Skipwith, Dio. York, 1863. (Patron, Ld Chan; Tithe—Imp. 113*l* 15*s*, V. 150*l*; Glebe, 3 roods; V.'s Inc. 151*l*;

Pop. 769.) Formerly P. C. of Princes Risborough 1845–63. [1]

GRAY, Charles Norris, *Kidderminster.*—Univ. Coll. Ox. B.A. 1864; Deac. 1864 by Bp of Ox. Pr. 1866 by Bp of Wor. C. of Kidderminster 1864. [2]

GRAY, Edmund, *Sharow Parsonage, Ripon.*—Dur. B.A. 1848, M.A. 1851; Deac. 1849 and Pr. 1850 by Bp of Rip. P. C. of Sharow, Dio. Rip. 1852. (Patrons, D. and C. of Rip; Tithe—App. 35*l* 15*s*, Imp. 155*l* 18*s*; Ripon Charities, 4*l* 15*s*; Glebe, 10 acres; P. C.'s Inc. 155*l* and Ho; Pop. 738.) Formerly C. of Dacre Banks 1849–50; P. C. of same 1850–52. Author, *Lessons on the Book of Common Prayer*, 1861–62; *Notes and Questions on the Epistles for Sundays in the Christian Year*, both published in *Pleasant Hours*, Nat. Soc; etc. [3]

GRAY, Edward, *Alwalton Rectory, Peterborough.*—Ex. Coll. Ox. B.A. 1849, M.A. 1852; Deac. 1850 and Pr. 1851 by Bp of Chich. R. of Alwalton, Dio. Ely, 1853. (Patrons, D. and C. of Pet; Glebe, 185 acres; R.'s Inc. 200*l* and Ho; Pop. 342.) [4]

GRAY, E. K.—C. of St. Peter's, Bayswater, Lond. [5]

GRAY, Frederick Henry, *Westley Rectory, near Newmarket.*—Lin. Coll. Ox. B.A. 1852, M.A. 1855 *ad eund.* Cam. 1859; Deac. 1853 and Pr. 1854 by Bp of Roch. C. in sole charge of Westley Waterless. Formerly C. of Halstead, Essex, 1853–55, Borley, Essex, 1855–59, Brinkley, Cambs, 1859–61; Chap. of King's Coll. Cambridge, 1861–66. Joint-Editor of *The Oxford and Cambridge Psalter*, Rivingtons. [6]

GRAY, George Robert, *Inkberrow Vicarage, Alcester, Worcestershire.*—V. of Inkberrow, Dio. Wor. 1830. (Patron, Earl of Abergavenny; Tithe, 800*l*; Glebe, 89½ acres, V.'s Inc. 950*l* and Ho; Pop. 1573.) [7]

GRAY, Henry Richard, *Crawley Down, Crawley, Sussex.*—P. C. of Crawley Down, Dio. Chich. 1861. (Patron, R. of Worth; Tithe, 100*l*; P. C.'s Inc. 155*l* and Ho; Pop. 1400.) [8]

GRAY, Horace Faithful, *Pilton Vicarage, near Shepton Mallett, Somerset.*—Corpus Coll. Ox. 2nd cl. Lit. Hum. and B.A. 1837, M.A. 1840; Deac. 1837 by Bp of Win. Pr. 1838 by Bp of Ely. V. of Pilton, Dio. B. and W. 1841. (Patron, Bp of B. and W; Tithe—App. 245*l* and 1 acre of Glebe, V. 185*l*; Glebe, 28½ acres; V.'s Inc. 336*l* and Ho; Pop. 1202.) Hon. Can. of Wells Cathl. 1842; Rural Dean 1845; Chap. to the 15th Somerset Rifle Volunteers. Formerly Dioc. Inspector of Schs. 1841–44; Warden and Prof. of Pastoral Theology, Queen's Coll. Birmingham, 1849–52. Author, *New Year's Address*, 1848; *Speech on Education*, ib; *Sermon against Rebellion*, ib; *Inaugural Address at Queen's College, Birmingham*, 1849; *Discourse on the Death of the Prince Consort*, 1862; *The Gospel of Peace; A Sermon to the Volunteers*, 1863. [9]

GRAY, James Black, *Oxford.*—Fell. of St. John's Coll. Ox; P. C. of St. Philip and St. James's, City and Dio. Ox. 1862. (Patron, St. John's Coll; Pop. 1620.) [10]

GRAY, John Durbin, *Abbotsley Vicarage, St. Neots, Hunts.*—Ball. Coll. Ox. B.A. 1843, M.A. 1846; Deac. 1845 by Bp of G. and B, Pr. 1846 by Bp of Ex. V. of Abbotsley, Dio. Ely, 1856. (Patron, Ball. Coll. Ox; V.'s Inc. 130*l* and Ho; Pop. 486.) [11]

GRAY, John Edward, *Wembley-park, Middlesex.*—Oriel Coll. Ox. B.A. 1821, M.A. 1824; Deac. 1822 and Pr. 1823 by Bp of Pet. [12]

GRAY, Joseph Henry, *Douglas, Isle of Man.*—Dub. A.B. 1835, A M. 1838; Deac. 1837, Pr. 1838. P. C. of St. Barnabas', Douglas, Dio. S. and M. 1852. (Patrons, Trustees; P. C.'s Inc. 240*l* and Ho.) Formerly Prin. of the Ch. Miss. Coll. Madras, 1838–48. Author, *Two Lectures on Mormonism*, 1851, 6*d*; *Principles and Practices of the Mormons*, 1853; *The Dying Saint*, 1853; *Address before Confirmation*, 1855, 4*d*; *Grace All Sufficient*, 1862; *Our Lord's Portrait*, 1862; etc. [13]

GRAY, Loftus, *Sedgeberrow Rectory, Evesham.*—R. of Sedgeberrow, Dio. Wor. 1866. (Patron, D. and C. of Wor; R.'s Inc. 280*l* and Ho; Pop. 354.) Formerly C. of Montgomery. [14]

GRAY, Robert Henry, *Kirkby Parsonage, Walton-on-the-Hill, Lancashire.*—Ch. Ch. Ox. 3rd cl. Lit. Hum. and 3rd cl. Math. et Phy. 1839, B.A. 1840, Johnson's Theol. Scho. 1841; Deac. 1840, Pr. 1841. P. C. of Kirkby, Dio. Ches. 1850. (Patron, Earl of Sefton; Tithe—App. 465*l* and 1¾ acres of Glebe; P. C.'s Inc. 250*l*; Pop. 1815.) Exam. Chap. to the Bp of S. and M. [15]

GRAY, Samuel, *Pateley Bridge, Leeds.*—St. John's Coll. Cam. B.A. 1844, M.A. 1847; Deac. 1844 and Pr. 1845 by Bp of Dur. P. C. of Pateley Bridge, Dio. Rip. 1864. (Patrons, D. and C. of Rip; P. C.'s Inc. 300*l* and Ho; Pop. 2752.) Formerly P. C. of Cundall, Yorks, 1861–64. [16]

GRAY, Thomas D., 24, *Carey-street, Lincoln's Inn, London, W.C.*—Queens' Coll. Cam. Wrang. B.A. 1865; Deac. 1866 and Pr. 1867 by Bp of Lon. C. of St. Clement Danes, Westminster, 1866. [17]

GRAY, Walter Augustus, *Arksey Vicarage, Doncaster.*—Trin. Coll. Cam. Jun. Opt. B.A. 1853, M.A. 1857, *ad eund.* Ox. 1858; Deac. 1853 and Pr. 1854 by Bp of Win. V. of Arksey, Dio. York, 1866. (Patron, Sir W. R. C. Cooke, Bart; Tithe, 100*l*; Glebe, 5 acres; V.'s Inc. 120*l* and Ho; Pop. 1100.) Formerly C. of Alverstoke 1853–54, Almondsbury 1854–58, Cranborne 1859–61, Water Moor, Cirencester, 1861–63, Almondsbury 1863–66. [18]

GRAY, William, *Jewish Operative Institution, Palestine-place, Bethnal-green, N.E.*—Dub. A.B. 1839; Deac. 1840 by Bp of Lich. Pr. 1841 by Abp of Armagh. Formerly Miss. of S.P.G. 1843; R. of St. Ann's, New Providence, Bahamas, 1845; R. of St. Thomas's, Turk Island, 1848; R. of St. Mathew's, New Providence, 1850; Chap. at Moscow 1853; Asst. Sec. of the Patagonian Miss. Soc. 1858. [19]

GRAY, William, *Upton Lovell, Heytesbury, Wilts.*—St. Bees; Deac. 1826, Pr. 1827. R. of Upton Lovell, Dio. Salis. 1842. (Patron, Ld Chan; Tithe, 320*l*; Glebe, 26 acres; R.'s Inc. 390*l* and Ho; Pop. 210.) Author, *A Village Clergyman's Address to his Parishioners on Confirmation*, S.P.C.K. 1848. [20]

GRAY, William Francis, *Faringdon Rectory, Topsham, Devon.*—Wad. Coll. Ox. B.A. 1846, M.A. 1848. R. of Faringdon, Dio. Ex. 1862. (Patron, Bp of Ex; Tithe, 450*l*; Glebe, 59 acres; P. C.'s Inc. 580*l* and Ho; Pop. 331.) Chap. to the Bp of Ex. Formerly V. of Cornwood 1852–62. [21]

GRAYSON, William, *The Parsonage, Toynton St. Peter's, Spilsby.*—St. Cath. Coll. Cam. Scho. and Prizeman, B.A. 1859; Deac. 1860 by Bp of Man. Pr. 1861 by Bp of Ely. C. of Toynton All Saints with Toynton St. Peter's 1867. Formerly C. of Hurst, Ashton-under-Lyne, 1860, Leighton Buzzard 1863. [22]

GRAYSTONE, Arthur Conrad, *Sutton-upon-Trent, Newark.*—St. John's Coll. Cam. LL.B. 1858, M.L. 1862; Deac. 1859 and Pr. 1861 by Bp of Lich. V. of Sutton, Dio. Lin. 1867. (Patron, the present V; Tithe, 77*l*; Glebe, 196*l*; V.'s Inc. 289*l*; Pop. 1147.) Formerly C. of Clay Cross 1859–61, Beckingham, near Gainsborough, 1861–63, Sherfield English, Hants, 1863–67. [23]

GREAM, Nevill, *Springfield Dukes, near Chelmsford.*—Magd. Coll. Cam. B.A. 1843, M.A. 1846; Deac. 1843 and Pr. 1844 by Bp of Chich. H.M. Inspector of Schs. for Essex 1865. Formerly C. of Blackawton, Devon, and Tetbury, Glouc; Inspector of Schs. for Lancashire 1859. [24]

GREAR, William Theophilus, 1, *Cornwall-terrace, Penzance.*—Deac. 1852 and Pr. 1853 by Bp of Rip. P. C. of Godolphin, Dio. Ex. 1865. (Patron, the Crown and Bp of Ex. alt; P. C.'s Inc. 150*l*; Pop. 1884.) Formerly C. of Daisy Hill, Bradford, 1852–55, Bramley, near Leeds, 1855–59, St. Mark's, Woodhouse, Leeds, 1859–61; V. of Hemingborough 1861; C. of St. John's, Portland, Dorset, 1863–65. [25]

GREATHEED, John, *Penistone, near Sheffield.*—Trin. Coll. Cam. Scho. of, B.A. 1864; Deac. 1865, Pr. 1867. C. of Penistone. [26]

GREATHEED, Samuel Stephenson, *Corringham, Romford, Essex.*—Trin. Coll. Cam. 4th Wrang. and B.A. 1835, M.A. 1838; Deac. 1838 by Bp of Ely, Pr. 1840 by Bp of Lon. R. of Corringham, Dio. Roch. 1862. (Patron, the present R; Tithe, 838*l*; Glebe, 29 acres; R.'s Inc. 867*l* and Ho; Pop. 229.) Formerly Fell. of Trin. Coll. Cam. 1837; C. of West Drayton, Middlesex, 1840; one of the original Editors of *The Cambridge Mathematical Journal*; Composer of several Pieces of Sacred Music. [1]

GREATHEED, Stephenson, *Cuckfield, Sussex.*—Corpus Coll. Cam. 2nd cl. Cl. Trip. B.A. 1862, M.A. 1865; Deac. 1863 and Pr. 1864 by Bp of Lich. C. of St. Wilfrid's, Cuckfield, 1866. Formerly C. of St. Thomas's, Brampton, Derbyshire, 1863–64. [2]

GREATOREX, Dan, *St. Paul's Parsonage, Whitechapel, London, E.*—St. Bees; Deac. 1856 and Pr. 1857 by Bp of Lich. P. C. of St. Paul's, Whitechapel, Dio. Lon. 1862. (Patrons, Trustees.) Chap. to the Sailors' Home, Wells-street, Lond. Formerly C. of St. Mary's, Bilston, Staffs; Chap. to the Thames Church Mission. [3]

GREATOREX, Edward, *Bishop Cosin's Library, Durham.*—Pemb. Coll. Ox. B.A. 1845, M.A. 1847; Deac. 1847, Pr. 1848. Librarian of Bp Cosin's Lib; Precentor of Durham Cathl. 1849 (Value, 250*l*). Author, *A Book of Family Prayers collected from the Public Liturgy of the Church of England*, 1854, 3*s* 6*d*. [4]

GREATREX, Charles Butler, *Halberton, Tiverton, Devon.*—King's Coll. Lond; Deac. 1855 and Pr. 1856 by Bp of Lich. Formerly C. of Stanton-upon-Hine, Loppington, and Much Wenlock, Salop. [5]

GREAVES, Henry Addington, 6, *Bedford-terrace, Plymouth.*—Corpus Coll. Cam. 2nd cl. Cl. Trip. 1st Sen. Opt. B.A. 1824, M.A. 1827; Deac. 1826 and Pr. 1831 by Bp of Ex. V. of Charles with Compton Gifford C. Plymouth, Dio. Ex. 1846. (Patrons, Executors of the late Sir C. Bisshopp, Bart; Tithe, Imp. 6*l* 10*s*, V. 525*l*; V.'s Inc. 660*l*; Pop. Charles 17,153, Compton Gifford 880.) Surrogate. Formerly P. C. of East Stonehouse 1836–46. [6]

GREAVES, John William, *Ranworth, Blofield, Norfolk.*—Deac. 1836 by Bp of Nor. Pr. 1838 by Bp of Ely. V. of Ranworth with Upton Dio. Nor. 1843. (Patron, Bp of Nor; Ranworth, Tithe—App. 225*l*, V. 131*l*; Glebe, 11 acres; Upton, Tithe—App. 286*l* 16*s* and ¾ acre of Glebe, Imp. 4*l* 5*s*, V. 160*l* 13*s*; Glebe, 20¼ acres, V.'s Inc. 320*l* and Ho; Pop. Ranworth 282, Upton 601.) [7]

GREAVES, J. W., *Horsford, Norwich.*—C. of Horsford and Horsham, Norfolk. [8]

GREAVES, Joshua, *Great Missenden Vicarage, Bucks.*—Trin. Coll. Cam. B.A. 1843, M.A. 1846; Deac. 1844 and Pr. 1845 by Bp of Wor. V. of Great Missenden, Dio. Ox. 1852. (Patrons, Trustees of J. O. Oldham, Esq; Tithe—Imp. 515*l* 15*s* 11*d*, V. 337*l* 10*s*; Glebe, 1 acre; V.'s Inc. 338*l* and Ho; Pop. 1803.) Formerly C. of St. George's, and P. C. of St. Peter's, Birmingham. [9]

GREAVES, Richard, *Pitville Parade, Cheltenham.*—Wad. Coll. Ox. B.A. 1816, M.A. 1820; Deac. 1818, Pr. 1819. [10]

GREAVES, Richard Wilson, *Tooting Rectory, Surrey.*—Wad. Coll. Ox. B.A. 1840, M.A. 1843; Deac. 1842 by Bp of Herf. Pr. 1843 by Bp of Lich. R. of Tooting, Dio. Win. 1844. (Patron, the present R; Tithe, 230*l*; Glebe, 31 acres; R.'s Inc. 410*l* and Ho; Pop 2055.) [11]

GREAVES, Talbot Aden Ley, *Melcombe Regis Rectory, Weymouth, Dorset.*—St. John's Coll. Cam. B.A. 1850, M.A. 1853; Deac. and Pr. 1850 by Bp of Lich. R. of Melcombe Regis with Radipole C. Dio. Salis. 1856. (Patron, Rev. Ed. Hollond; Tithe, 288*l*; Glebe, 3 acres; R.'s Inc. 300*l* and Ho; Pop. 6127.) Formerly V. of Mayfield 1850–54. [12]

GREEN, A. J. M., *St. David's.*—Min. Can. of St. D. 1867; Mast. of Coll. Sch. St. David's, 1867. Formerly C. of Llanelly. [13]

GREEN, Charles, *Bishop Auckland.*—Deac. 1860 and Pr. 1861 by Bp of Dur. C. of St. Andrew's, Bishop Auckland, 1864. Formerly C. of Seaham Harbour 1860–63. [14]

GREEN, Charles, *Malta.*—Ch. Coll. Cam. Sen. Opt. and B.A. 1836; Deac. 1837 and Pr. 1838 by Abp of Cant. Chap. to the Forces, Malta. Formerly Chap. to the Forces at Chatham 1846. [15]

GREEN, Charles Edward Maddison, *Lyonshall Vicarage, near Kington.*—Emman. Coll. Cam. B.A. 1859; Deac. 1859 and Pr. 1860 by Bp of Lin. V. of Lyonshall, Dio. Herf. 1866. (Patron, Bp of Wor; Tithe, 356*l*; Glebe, 14 acres; V.'s Inc. 400*l* and Ho; Pop. 960.) Formerly C. of Tydd St. Mary 1859; Pr. Chap. of St. Mary's, Warwick, 1861–66. [16]

GREEN, Conrad Samuel, *Helme, Huddersfield.*—Deac. 1862 and Pr. 1863 by Bp of Rip. C. of Helme 1864. Formerly C. of Kirkburton 1862. [17]

GREEN, E. A., *Cardiff.*—C. of St. Mary's, Cardiff. [18]

GREEN, Edmund H., *Great Bedwyn, Marlborough.*—C. of Great Bedwyn. [19]

GREEN, Edward, *Uley, Dursley, Gloucestershire.* C. of Uley. [20]

GREEN, Edward Dyer, *Bromborough Rectory, Cheshire.*—Queens' Coll. Cam. and Univ. Coll. Lond. M.A. 1855 by Abp of Cant; Deac. 1844 and Pr. 1845 by Bp of Salis. P. C. of Bromborough, Dio. Ches. 1860. (Patrons D. and C. of Ches; Tithe, Imp. 302*l* 19*s*, P. C. 50*l* 1*s*; Glebe, 6 acres; P. C.'s Inc. 196*l* and Ho; Pop. 1271.) Surrogate 1863. Formerly C. of Pitney 1844–46. Middlezoy 1846–50, Trelystan 1850–54, St. Oswald's, Chester, 1855–60; Head Mast of Langport Gr. Sch. 1842–46. Editor of the *Chester Diocesan Calendar*, Hon. Sec. and Treas. of the Pearson Memorial Fund. [21]

GREEN, Edward Freer, *Duddington Parsonage, Stamford.*—Emman. Coll. Cam. LL.B. 1859, L.M. 1866; Deac. 1857 and Pr. 1858 by Bp of Ches. P. C. of Duddington, Dio. Pet. 1863. (Patron, Bp of Pet; Glebe, 36 acres; P. C.'s Inc. 152*l* and Ho; Pop. 393.) Formerly C. of St. Silas and of St. Mary's, Edge Hill, Liverpool, Chalford, Glouc. and Kegworth, near Derby. [22]

GREEN, Edward Jonathan, *Leintwardine Vicarage, Ludlow.*—V. of Leintwardine, Dio. Herf. 1853. (Patron, Earl of Oxford; Tithe—App. 198*l* 2*s* 5*d*, Imp. 685*l* 6*s* 10*d*, V. 1400*l*; Glebe, 2 roods; V.'s Inc. 415*l* and Ho; Pop. 1812.) [23]

GREEN, Edward Kennedy, *Sedbergh, near Kendal.*—St. John's Coll. Cam. Fell. of, 8th in 1st cl. Cl. Trip. B.A. 1856, M.A. 1860; Deac. 1861 and Pr. 1862 by Bp of Man. P. C. of Cautley, with Dowbiggin, Dio. Rip. 1867. (Patron, V. of Sedbergh; P. C.'s Inc. 93*l*; Pop. 276.) Formerly Asst. Mast. at Rossall Sch. 1857–63; Asst. Mast. at Brighton Coll. 1864; C. of Sedbergh 1865–66, Grange, Lancashire, 1866–67. [24]

GREEN, Edward Kent, *West Derby, Liverpool.*—C. of West Derby. [25]

GREEN, Edward Peter, *Weare Vicarage, Weston super-Mare.*—Ex. Coll. Ox. B.A. 1848, M.A. 1849, Wells Theol. Coll; Deac. 1849 and Pr. 1850 by Bp of B. and W. C. of Weare 1866. Formerly C. of Allerton 1849; Min. of Queenstown, S. Africa, 1854–63; C. of St. Peter's, Southampton, 1864–66. Author, *Confirmation, What it is not and what it is*, Grahamstown. [26]

GREEN, Eldred, *Thornton-le-Street, Yorks.*—Queen's Coll. Ox. B.A. 1845; Deac. 1846 and Pr. 1847 by Bp of Ex. V. of Thornton-le-Street, Dio. York, 1866. (Patrons, D. and C. of Ch. Ch. Ox; Tithe, 59*l* 10*s*; Glebe, 45*l*; V.'s Inc. 154*l* 10*s*; Pop. 231.) Formerly C. of Cubert 1846, St. Ervan 1848, St. Breock 1851, all in Cornwall; P. C. of Loweswater, Cumberland, 1858–66. [27]

GREEN, Frederick Septimus, *Finchley Parsonage, Middlesex.*—Caius Coll. Cam. B.A. 1838; Deac. and Pr. 1839. P. C. of Trinity, Finchley, Dio. Lon. 1846. (Patron, Bp of Lon; P. C.'s Inc. 240*l* and Ho; Pop. 1944.) Chap. of Marylebone Cemetery. [28]

GREEN, George Clark, *Modbury Vicarage, Devon.*—King's Coll. Cam. B.A. 1852, M.A. 1856; Deac. 1854 by Bp of Lin. Pr. 1855 by Bp of Pet. V. of Modbury, Dio. Ex. 1859. (Patron, Eton Coll; Tithe—

Imp. 780*l*, V. 406*l* 15*s*; Glebe, 9 acres; V.'s Inc. 440*l* and Ho; Pop. 1621.) Formerly P. C. of Hamworthy, Dorset, 1858–59; C. of Everdon, Northampton; Fell. of Eton Coll. and Fell. of King's Coll. Cam. [1]

GREEN, George Edward, *Boldon Rectory, Gateshead.*—Dur. B.A. 1845; Deac. 1847 and Pr. 1848. Hon. Can. of Dur; R. of Boldon, Dio. Dur. 1863. (Patron, Bp of Dur; R.'s Inc. 700*l* and Ho; Pop. 1024.) Surrogate. Formerly P. C. of Auckland St. Andrew, Durham. [2]

GREEN, G. W., *Court Henry, Carmarthen.* [3]

GREEN, Henry, *Gloucester.*—R. of St. Aldate's, Gloucester, Dio. G. and B. 1863. (Patron, Bp of G. and B; R.'s Inc. 210*l*; Pop. 710.) Dom. Chap. to the Bp of G. and B. [4]

GREEN, H. S., *Llanstadwell, Milford Haven.*—V. of Llanstadwell, Dio. St. D. 1866. (Patron, Lewis Child, Esq; V.'s Inc. 94*l*; Pop. 1745.) [5]

GREEN, Isaac, *Sedbergh, Yorks.*—Queens' Coll. Cam. B.A. 1830, M.A. 1834; Deac. 1831 and Pr. 1833 by Bp of Ches. P. C. of Howgill, Yorks, Dio. Rip. 1836. (Patron, V. of Sedbergh; P. C.'s Inc. 100*l*.) 2nd Mast. of Sedbergh Gr. Sch. [6]

GREEN, James, *St. John's-in-Weardale, Stanhope, Darlington.*—Deac. 1818 and Pr. 1819 by Bp of Dur. P. C. of Weardale, Dio. Dur. 1865. (Patron, Bp of Dur; P. C.'s Inc. 400*l* and Ho; Pop. 4600.) Formerly C. of Weardale 1830–65. [7]

GREEN, James Spurgeon, *Witton Rectory, Norwich.*—Ch. Coll. Cam. B.A. 1847, M.A. 1851; Deac. 1848, Pr. 1849. R. of Witton with Brundall, Dio. Nor. 1854. (Patron, the present R; Witton, Tithe—App. 2*l* 2*s*, R. 245*l*; Glebe, 36½ acres; Brundall, Tithe—App. 7*s*, R. 155*l* 16*s* 6*d*; Glebe, 9½ acres; R.'s Inc. 494*l* and Ho; Pop. Witton 144, Brundall 104.) [8]

GREEN, James Wastie, *The Rectory, Presteign, Radnorshire.*—Ball. Coll. Ox. 2nd cl. Lit. Hum. and B.A. 1846, M.A. 1851; Deac. 1850 and Pr. 1851 by Bp of Lon. C. in sole charge of Presteign 1867. Formerly Head Mast. of the Camberwell Coll. Sch. Lond. 1854–59; C. of Kington 1859; Chap of Dinmore 1860–66. [9]

GREEN, J., *Seaham Harbour, Durham.*—C. of Seaham Harbour. [10]

GREEN, John, 9, *Lonsdale-square, Islington, N.*—Trin. Coll. Cam. B.A. 1848, M.A. 1851; Deac. 1848 and Pr. 1849 by Bp of Win. C. of St. Mary's, Islington, 1866. Formerly C. of West Tytherly, Hants, 1848, Trinity, Marylebone, 1849, Tamworth 1855, St. Bartholomew's, Gray's-inn-road, Lond. 1857, St. Peter's, Notting Hill, 1863. [11]

GREEN, John, *Eyam, Derbyshire.*—R. of Eyam, Dio. Lich. 1862. (Patrons, the Dukes of Devonshire and Buckingham alt; Tithe, 187*l* 2*s*; Glebe, 57 acres; R.'s Inc. 273*l* and Ho; Pop. 1673.) [12]

GREEN, John, *Little Leighs, Chelmsford.*—Emman. Coll. Cam. B.D. 1835. R. of Little Leighs, Dio. Roch. 1851. (Patron, Rev. J. C. Green; Tithe, 385*l* 5*s*; Glebe, 16 acres; R.'s Inc. 403*l* and Ho; Pop. 171.) [13]

GREEN, John Fowler, *Erdington, Birmingham.*—St. Peter's Coll. Cam. B.A. 1849, M.A. 1852; Deac. 1849 and Pr. 1850 by Bp of Wor. P. C. of Ward-End, Aston, Dio. Wor. 1854. (Patron, V. of Aston; P. C.'s Inc. 75*l*.) [14]

GREEN, John Henry Bakewell, *Normanton, Ashby-de-la-Zouch.*—Jesus Coll. Cam. 2nd cl. Cl. Trip. and B.A. 1839, M.A. 1842; Deac. 1840, Pr. 1841. P. C. of Normanton-le-Heath, Dio. Pet. 1852. (Patron, the Crown; P. C.'s Inc. 286*l* and Ho; Pop. 178.) [15]

GREEN, John Richard, *Stepney, London, E.*—Jesus Coll. Ox. B.A. 1860; Deac. 1860 by Bp of Lon. P. C. of St. Philip's, Stepney, Dio. Lon. 1866. (Patron, Bp of Lon; P. C.'s Inc. 300*l*; Pop. 14,805.) Formerly C. of St. Barnabas', King's-square, and Trinity, Hoxton, Lond. [16]

GREEN, John Samuel, *Wooler Vicarage, Northumberland.*—Ch. Coll. Cam. Sen. Opt. and B.A. 1838, M.A. 1841, *ad eund.* Dur. 1842; Deac. and Pr. 1840 by Bp of Lin. V. of Wooler with Fenton, Dio. Dur. 1843. (Patron, Bp of Ches; Tithe—Imp. 54*l* 1*s*, V. 404*l*; Glebe, 56 acres; V.'s Inc. 532*l* and Ho; Pop. 1697.) [17]

GREEN, Joseph, *Owmby Rectory, Market Rasen.*—Corpus Coll. Cam. B.A. 1830, M.A. 1836; Deac. 1831 and Pr. 1832 by Bp of Lin. R. of Owmby, Dio. Lin. 1841. (Patron, Duchy of Lancaster; Glebe, 240 acres; R.'s Inc. 360*l* and Ho; Pop. 314.) V. of Cameringham, Dio. Lin. 1842. (Patron, Lord Monson; Tithe, 90*l*; Glebe, 58 acres; V.'s Inc. 162*l*; Pop. 137.) Formerly C. of Saxby and Glentworth 1831, Owmby and Cameringham 1839. [18]

GREEN, Josephus Henry, *Southwell, Notts.*—Dur. B.A. 1859, M.A. 1863; Deac. 1857 and Pr. 1859 by Bp of Lich. Chap. to Notts. Co. House of Correction 1864 (Stipend 150*l*). Formerly C. of Ilkeston, Derbyshire, 1857–59, Stannington, Northumberland, 1859–63; Chap. to North Eastern Reformatory Sch. Northumberland, 1859–64. [19]

GREEN, Martin Johnson, *Steepleton Rectory, near Dorchester.*—Lin. Coll. Ox. B.A. 1836, M.A. 1838; B.D. 1848; Deac. 1838, Pr. 1839. R. of Winterbourne Abbas with Winterbourne Steepleton R. Dio. Salis. 1848. (Patron, Lin. Coll. Ox; Winterbourne Abbas, Tithe, 240*l*; Glebe, 88¾ acres; Winterbourne Steepleton, Tithe, 178*l*; Glebe, 28 acres; R.'s Inc. 487*l* and Ho; Pop. Winterbourne Abbas 205, Winterbourne Steepleton 191.) Formerly Fell. of Lin. Coll. Ox. 1837; Junior Proctor 1847; Chap. of St. Michael's, Oxford, 1846–48. [20]

GREEN, Robert, *Long Horsley Vicarage, Morpeth, Northumberland.*—V. of Long Horsley, Dio. Dur. 1824. (Patron, Ld Chan; Tithe—Imp. 527*l* 10*s* 1*d*, V. 249*l* 10*s*; V.'s Inc. 336*l* and Ho; Pop. 964.) [21]

GREEN, Robert Charles, *Loughton, near Stony Stratford.*—Trin. Coll. Cam. Fell. of, 1st cl. Cl. Trip. 1857, M.A. 1861; Deac. 1861 by Bp of Ely, Pr. 1862 by Bp of Lich. R. of Loughton, Dio. Ox. 1864. (Patron, Trin. Coll. Cam; Glebe, 300 acres; R.'s Inc. 420*l* and Ho; Pop. 400.) Formerly C. of St. Peter's, Belper, 1861–64. [22]

GREEN, Robert Gambier, *Ampthill, Beds.*—C. of Ampthill. [23]

GREEN, Sidney Faithhorn, *Swinton Parsonage, Manchester.*—Trin. Coll. Cam. B.A. 1863; Deac. 1865, Pr. 1866. C. of Swinton 1865. [24]

GREEN, Thomas, *Stowe, Knighton, Salop.*—R. of Stowe, Dio. Herf. 1841. (Patron, Ld Chan; Tithe—Imp. 48*l*, R. 205*l*; R.'s Inc. 210*l*; Pop. 161.) C. of Bedstone and Hopesay, Salop. [25]

GREEN, Thomas, *Church Missionary College, Islington, London, N.*—Brasen. Coll. Ox. 2nd cl. Lit. Hum. and B.A. 1841, M.A. 1844; Deac. 1843 and Pr. 1844 by Bp of Ches. Prin. of the Ch. Miss. Coll. Islington, 1858; Min. of St. John Baptist's Chapel, Gloucester-road, Islington. Formerly P. C. of Friezland, near Manchester, 1849–58. [26]

GREEN, Thomas, *Holbeach, Lincolnshire.*—St. John's Coll. Cam. B.A. 1863, M.A. 1867; Deac. 1863 and Pr. 1865 by Bp of Lin. C. of Holbeach 1863. [27]

GREEN, Thomas, *Badby Vicarage, Daventry, Northants.*—Ch. Ch. Ox. B.A. 1809, M.A. 1811; Deac. 1811 by Bp of Ox. Pr. 1812 by Abp of Cant. V. of Badby with Newnham V. Dio. Pet. 1816. (Patron, Ch. Ch. Ox; Glebe, 163 acres; V.'s Inc. 306*l* and Ho; Pop. Badby 618, Newnham 514.) Rural Dean. [28]

GREEN, Thomas Fordham, *Graveley, Stevenage, Herts.*—Ch. Coll. Cam. B.A. 1818, M.A. 1821; Deac. and Pr. 1819. R. of Graveley with Chesfield R. (no Church), Dio. Roch. 1820. (Patron, the present R; Tithe, 446*l*; Glebe, 37 acres; R.'s Inc. 478*l* and Ho; Pop. 422.) [29]

GREEN, Thomas Lingard, *Sudbury, Suffolk.*—Trin. Coll. Ox. B.A. 1854, M.A. 1856; Deac. 1855 and Pr. 1856 by Bp of Pet. C. of St. Gregory and St. Peter's, Sudbury, 1857. Formerly C. of Oundle 1855–57. [30]

GREEN, Thomas Robinson, *Newcastle-on-Tyne.*—Lin. Coll. Ox. B.A. 1842, M.A. 1846; Deac. 1843 by Bp of Pet. Pr. 1844 by Bp of Dur. P. C. of Byker, Dio. Dur. 1845. (Patrons, the Crown and Bp of Dur. alt; P. C.'s Inc. 300*l*; Pop. 10,388.) Chap. to John

Bowes, Esq., Gibside; Chap. to the Trinity House, Newcastle. [1]

GREEN, Thomas Sheldon, *Ashby-de-la-Zouch, Leicestershire.*—Ch. Coll. Cam. B.A. 1826, M.A. 1829; Deac. and Pr. 1830 by Bp of Lin. Head Mast. of the Ashby-de-la-Zouch Gr. Sch; Chap. to the Union, Ashby-de-la-Zouch. Author, *A Treatise on the Grammar of the New Testament*, 1842, new ed. 1862; *A Course of Developed Criticism*, 1856; *The Twofold New Testament*, 1866; *Critical Notes, Supplementary to the Grammar of the New Testament*, 1867. [2]

GREEN, Valentine, *Birkin Rectory, near Knottingley.*—St. John's Coll. Cam. B.A. 1822, M.A. 1825; Deac. 1823 and Pr. 1824 by Bp of Lin. R. of Birkin with Haddesley C. Dio. York, 1835. (Patron, Rev. T. Hill; Tithe, 626*l*; Glebe, 310 acres; R.'s Inc. 1050*l* and Ho; Pop. 821.) Formerly C. of Aylestone, Leic. 1823; V. of Barkstone and of Plungar, Leic. 1826; R. of Knipton, Leic. 1831. [3]

GREEN, V. T., *Bloxham, Banbury.*—C. of Bloxham. [4]

GREEN, W., *Pentrebach, Merthyr-Tydvil.*—P. C. of Pont-y-Rhun or Pentrebach, Dio. Llan. 1862. (Patron, Anthony Hill, Esq; P. C.'s Inc. 65*l*; Pop. 5288.) [5]

GREEN, William, *Steeple-Barton, Woodstock, Oxon.*—Queens' Coll. Cam. 1st Math. Prizeman, Sen. Opt. and B.A. 1820, M.A. 1824; Deac. 1821 by Bp of Glouc. Pr. 1822 by Bp of Lin. V. of Steeple-Barton, Dio. Ox. 1855. (Patrons, Duke of Marlborough and Henry Hall, Esq. alt; Tithe—Imp. 422*l*, V. 50*l*; Glebe, 70 acres; V.'s Inc. 112*l*; Pop. 859.) Author, *A Funeral Sermon on the Death of Henry Dobbs, Esq.* Editor of the *Pocket Prayer-Book*, 11th ed. 1839, 2*s*. [6]

GREEN, William, *Filey.*—Deac. 1815 and Pr. 1816 by Abp of York. V. of Muston, Dio. York, 1834. (Patron, Admiral Mitford; V.'s Inc. 250*l*; Pop. 391.) [7]

GREEN, William, *Little Clacton Vicarage, near Colchester.*—Pemb. Coll. Ox. M.A. 1847; Deac. 1845, Pr. 1846. V. of Little Clacton, Dio. Roch. 1850. (Patrons, Exors. of late F. Nassau, Esq; Tithe—Imp. 612*l* 10*s*, V. 156*l*; V.'s Inc. 150*l* and Ho; Pop. 584.) [8]

GREEN, William, *Hexthorpe, Doncaster.*—Corpus Coll. Cam. B.A. 1829; Deac. 1829, Pr. 1830. P. C. of Balby with Hexthorpe, Dio. York, 1847. (Patron, Rev. R. J. Banks; P. C.'s Inc. 165*l*; Pop. 707.) [9]

GREEN, William, *Penshurst Rectory, Tunbridge, Kent.*—R. of Penshurst with St. Peter's C. Dio. Cant. 1852. (Patron, Lord de Lisle and Dudley; Glebe, 42 acres; R.'s Inc. 820*l* and Ho; Pop. 1698.) [10]

GREEN, William, *Winterton Rectory, Great Yarmouth.*—Trin. Coll. Cam. B.A. 1844, M.A. 1847; Deac. 1856 and Pr. 1857 by Bp of Pet. R. of Winterton, with East Somerton, Dio. Nor. 1867. (Patrons, Trustees to Rev. W. Green; Tithe, 544*l*; Glebe, 30 acres; R.'s Inc. 556*l* and Ho; Pop. Winterton 682, East Somerton 62.) Formerly C. of Goadby, Leic. 1856–63, Guist, Norfolk, 1863–67. [11]

GREEN, William Edward, 3, *China-terrace, Lambeth, S.*—Wor. Coll. Ox. B.A. 1851, M.A. 1854; Deac. 1851 and Pr. 1852 by Bp of Ox. P. C. of Trinity, Lambeth, Dio. Win. 1859. (Patron, R. of Lambeth; P. C.'s Inc. 300*l*; Pop. 7079) Formerly C. of Marsh Gibbon, Bucks, 1851, Lee, Kent, 1854. Author, *Memorials of the Rev. C. Green*, Rivingtons. [12]

GREENALL, the Ven. Richard, *Wilton House, Northwich, Cheshire.*—Brasen. Coll. Ox. B.A. 1828, M.A. 1831; Deac. 1829 and Pr. 1830 by Bp of Ches. Archd. of Chester 1866. P. C. of Stretton, Dio. Ches. 1831. (Patron, T. H. Lyon, Esq; Tithe—App. 91*l*, Imp. 6*l*; P. C.'s Inc. 180*l*; Pop. 833.) Rural Dean 1839; Hon. Can. of Ches. 1865. Author, *The Servant of Christ*; *A Conscience Void of Offence* (Visitation Sermons); and other occasional Sermons. [13]

GREENALL, Richard, *Hawkshead, Windermere.*—Brasen. Coll. Ox. B.A. 1852, M.A. 1855; Deac. 1853 and Pr. 1854 by Bp of Ches. V. of Hawkshead, Dio. Carl. 1865. (Patron, Chan. of Duchy of Lancaster; Tithe, 20*l*; Glebe, 25 acres; V.'s Inc. 190*l* and Ho; Pop. 1302.) Surrogate. Formerly C. of Grappenhall, Cheshire; P. C. of St. Thomas's, Eccleston, 1858; C. of Ch. Ch. Latchford, 1860–65. [14]

GREENALL, Thomas, *Grappenhall Rectory, Warrington.*—Brasen. Coll. Ox. B.A. 1845, M.A. 1848. R. of Grappenhall, Dio. Ches. 1848. (Patron, the present R; R.'s Inc. 550*l* and Ho; Pop. 3586.) [15]

GREENE, E., *East Witton, Yorks.*—C. of East Witton. [16]

GREENE, Edward, *Newmarket, Suffolk.*—C. of St. Mary's, Newmarket. [17]

GREENE, Edward, *Bramshot, Liphook, Hants.*—Magd. Coll. Ox. B.A. 1830, M.A. 1833, B.D. 1842, D.D. 1844. Fell. of Magd. Coll. Ox. C. of Bramshot. Formerly C. of Tuxlith. [18]

GREENE, Henry.—British Chap. at Pisa and Baths of Lucca. [19]

GREENE, Henry Burnaby, *Longparish, Whitchurch, Hants.*—Corpus Coll. Cam. B.A. 1817, M.A. 1822; Deac. 1818 and Pr. 1819 by Bp of Salis. V. of Longparish, Dio. Win. 1821. (Patron, Rev. H. Woodcock; Tithe, Imp. 754*l* 3*s* 7*d*, V. 250*l*; Glebe, 10 acres; V.'s Inc. 250*l*; Pop. 803.) [20]

GREENE, Henry Haddon, *Rogate, Petersfield, Hants.*—Wor. Coll. Ox. B.A. 1824, M.A. 1826; Deac. 1824 and Pr. 1825 by Bp of Chich. V. of Rogate, Dio. Chich. 1841. (Patron, Ld Chan; Tithe—Imp. 398*l* 12*s* 11*d*, V. 302*l*; Glebe, 18 acres; V.'s Inc. 330*l*; Pop. 990.) [21]

GREENE, Joseph, *Cubley Rectory, Sudbury, Derby.*—Dub. B.A. 1845, M.A. 1848; Deac. 1848 and Pr. 1849 by Abp of York. R. of Cubley with Marston Montgomery R. Dio. Lich. 1858. (Patron, the present R; Tithe, Cubley, 381*l*; Glebe, 5 acres; Marston Montgomery, Tithe, 140*l*; R.'s Inc. 520*l* and Ho; Pop. Cubley, 383, Marston Montgomery 405.) Rural Dean. Formerly C. of Scarborough 1848–49, Guiting, Glouc. and Halton, Bucks. Author, *Insect Hunter's Companion*; etc. [22]

GREENE, Richard, *Tunbridge Wells.*—Emman. Coll. Cam. Sen. Opt. and B.A. 1824; Deac. 1826 and Pr. 1827 by Bp of Chich. [23]

GREENE, Thomas, *Fulmodestone, Guist, Thetford, Norfolk.*—Corpus Coll. Cam. B.A. 1812, M.A. 1815, B.D. 1823; Deac. 1813, Pr. 1814. R. of Fulmodestone with Croxton R. Dio. Nor. 1835. (Patron, Corpus Coll. Cam; Tithe, 558*l*; Glebe, 64 acres; R.'s Inc. 638*l* and Ho; Pop. 400.) Can. of Nor; Rural Dean. [24]

GREENE, Thomas Huntley, *Marsh Gibbon Rectory, Bicester.*—Ball. Coll. Ox. B.A. 1847, M.A. 1849; Deac. 1847, Pr. 1848. R. of Marsh Gibbon, Dio. Ox. 1856. (Patron, Bp of Ox; Tithe, comm. 500*l*; Glebe, 127 acres; R.'s Inc. 650*l* and Ho; Pop. 858.) Formerly C. of St. John's, Bedwardine, Worcester, 1847; Chap. to Bp of Gibraltar 1848; Chap. to Hon. Soc. of Gray's Inn 1850; Chap. to Blomfield, late Bp of Lon. 1853. [25]

GREENE, William Clayton, *Clare Mount, Wallasea, Birkenhead.*—Clare Hall, Cam. Sen. Opt. 3rd cl. Cl. Trip. and B.A. 1840, M.A. 1845; Deac. 1843, Pr. 1844. Head Mast. of Clare Mount Sch. [26]

GREENE, William Graham, *Tower of London, E.*—P. C. of Trinity, Minories, Dio. Lon. 1865. (Patron, Ld Chan; P. C.'s Inc. 69*l*; Pop. 420.) Chap. of the Tower of London 1866. [27]

GREENFIELD, John, *Packington, Leicestershire.*—C. of Packington. [28]

GREENFIELD, William Frederick, *Dulwich College, S.*—Pemb. Coll. Cam. Wrang. and B.A. 1849, M.A. 1852; Deac. 1851, Pr. 1852. Head Mast. of the Lower Sch. Dulwich Coll. 1858. Formerly C. of Copdock, Suffolk, and 2nd Mast. of Queen Elizabeth's Sch. Ipswich, 1850–58. [29]

GREENHAM, William, *Harley, Much Wenlock, Salop.*—Magd. Hall, Ox. B.A. 1849; Deac. 1849, Pr. 1850. R. of Harley, Dio. Lich. 1859. (Patron, Duke of Cleveland; R.'s Inc. 276*l* and Ho; Pop. 220.) Formerly P. C. of Norley 1849–59. [30]

GREENHOW, Edward, *Nether Poppleton, York.*—Deac. 1825 and Pr. 1826 by Bp of Ches. P. C. of Nether Poppleton with Upper Poppleton. P. C. Dio. York, 1864. (Patron, Abp of York; Glebe, 49 acres; P. C.'s Inc. 300*l* and Ho; Pop. 706.) Formerly C. of Nun Monkton 1825, Great Ouseburn 1832; P. C. of Nun Monkton 1844; P. C. of Copmanthorpe 1846. [1]

GREENHOW, Edward, jun., *Newton-upon-Ouse, Yorks.*—St. Bees; Deac. 1851 and Pr. 1852 by Bp of Man. P. C. of Newton-upon-Ouse, Dio. York, 1854. (Patron, Hon. P. Dawnay; Tithe, 40*l*; Glebe, 250 acres; P. C.'s Inc. 420*l* and Ho; Pop. 931.) Formerly C. of Bacup, Manchester, and Newton-upon-Ouse. [2]

GREENLAND, Thomas, *Raithby, Spilsby, Lincolnshire.*—Corpus Coll. Cam. B.A. 1848; Deac. 1849, Pr. 1850. R. of Raithby, Dio. Lin. 1864. (Patron, Ld Chan; R.'s Inc. 301*l*; Pop. 200.) Formerly V. of Wenhaston 1852–64. [3]

GREENLY, J. Prosser, *Laverstock, Wilts.*—C. of Laverstock. [4]

GREENSLADE, William, *Stoke-sub-Hambden, Ilminster.*—Trin. Coll. Cam. B.A. 1833, M.A. 1839; Deac. 1834 and Pr. 1835 by Bp of Win. P. C. of Stoke-sub-Hambden, Dio. B. and W. 1852. (Patron, T. Hawkesworth, Esq; Tithe, Imp. 447*l* 10*s*; Glebe, 151 acres; P. C.'s Inc. 104*l*; Pop. 1395.) [5]

GREENSTREET, Frederick Waters, *Winterbourne Down, Glouc.*—Trin. Coll. Cam. B.A. 1849, M.A. 1852; Deac. 1849 and Pr. 1850 by Bp of Herf. P. C. of All Saints', Winterbourne, Dio. G. and B. 1861. (Patron, St. John's Coll. Ox; P. C.'s Inc. 96*l* and Ho.) Formerly C. of All Saints', Winterbourne-Down. [6]

GREENSTREET, Octavius Pechell, *Winterbourne, near Bristol.*—Trin. Coll. Cam. B.A. 1856, and Cuddesdon; Deac. 1857 and Pr. 1858 by Bp of Ex. [7]

GREENSTREET, William George, *Pattingham Vicarage, Wolverhampton.*—Ch. Coll. Cam. B.A. 1836, M.A. 1839; Deac. 1837, Pr. 1838. V. of Pattingham, Dio. Lich. 1847. (Patron, Earl of Dartmouth; Tithe, 342*l* 2*s*; Glebe, 1½ acres; V.'s Inc. 355*l* and Ho; Pop. 1126.) P. C. of Patshull, Staffs, Dio. Lich. 1847. (Patron, Earl of Dartmouth; Glebe, 53 acres; P. C.'s Inc. 80*l*; Pop. 194.) [8]

GREENWAY, Charles, *Over Darwen, Blackburn.*—Dur. B.A. 1847, Licen. Theol. 1848, M.A. 1849; Deac. 1848 and Pr. 1849 by Bp of Man. P. C. of St. James's Chapel, Over Darwen, Dio. Man. 1851. (Patron, V. of Blackburn; Glebe, 45 acres; P. C.'s Inc. 189*l* 17*s* 6*d* and Ho; Pop. 1795.) [9]

GREENWAY, William Whitmore, *Newbold-de-Verdun Rectory, Market Bosworth.*—Trin. Hall, Cam. LL.B. 1825; Deac. 1821, Pr. 1822. R. of Newbold-de-Verdun, Dio. Pet. 1822. (Patron, the present R; Glebe, 330 acres; R.'s Inc. 560*l* and Ho; Pop. 700.) Rural Dean. Formerly R. of Hardwicke, Northants, 1841–66. [10]

GREENWELL, Alan, *Haydock, Warrington.*—Dur. B.A. 1845, M.A. 1846; Deac. 1848, Pr. 1849. P. C. of St. James's, Haydock, Dio. Ches. 1865. (Patron, R. of Ashton-in-Makerfield; Pop. 3754.) Formerly Chap. to Durham Gaol 1854. [11]

GREENWELL, Nicholas, *St. Barnabas' Vicarage, Holbeck, Leeds.*—Dur. B.A. 1847, Licen. Theol. 1848; Deac. 1848 and Pr. 1852 by Bp of Rip. V. of St. Barnabas', Leeds, Dio. Rip. 1854. (Patrons, the Crown and Bp of Rip. alt; V.'s Inc. 313*l* and Ho; Pop. 6869.) Formerly C. of Holbeck 1848 51, Aston, Worc, 1852. Leeds 1852–53. [12]

GREENWELL, William, *Horton Vicarage, Blyth, Northumberland.*—Dur. B.A. 1851, M.A. 1860, Licen. Theol. 1853; Deac. 1853 and Pr. 1854 by Bp of Dur. V. of Horton, Dio. Dur. 1855. (Patron, V. of Woodhorn; Tithe, 2*l* 10*s*; Glebe, 30 acres; V.'s Inc. 300*l* and Ho; Pop. 6787.) Formerly C. of Escomb, Durham, 1853–55, Tynemouth 1855–56; Sunday Even. Lect. at Blyth 1857–60; Chap. of Don. of Blyth 1860–66. [13]

GREENWELL, William, M.A., *Durham.*—Chap. of Bp Cosin's Hall, Durham; Min. Can. of Dur; R. of St. Mary's-the-Less, Durham, Dio. Dur. 1865. (Patron, Ld Chan; R.'s Inc. 120*l*; Pop. 106.) [14]

GREENWELL, William, *Clifton, York.*—St. John's Coll. Cam. B.A. 1843; Deac. 1844 and Pr. 1845 by Abp of York. C. of St. Michael's, Spurriergate, York, 1866. Formerly C. of Market Weighton 1844. [15]

GREENWOOD, George, *St. Thomas's Hospital, Surrey Gardens, S.*—Trin. Coll. Cam. Wrang. and 3rd cl. Cl. Trip. B.A. 1850, M.A. 1852; Deac. 1851 and Pr. 1853 by Bp of Roch. Hospitaller of St. Thomas's Hospital 1860. (Patrons, the Governors; Hosp.'s Inc. 325*l*.) Formerly C. of Colne-Engaine, Essex, 1851–54; Lect. of St. John's, Southwark, 1855–59; Asst. Hosp. of St. Thomas's 1855–60; Chap. of Bethlehem Hospital 1859–60. [16]

GREENWOOD, Henry, *Beelsby, Caistor, Lincolnshire.*—R. of Beelsby, Dio. Lin. 1865. (Patron, Coll. Ch. of Southwell; R.'s Inc. 500*l*; Pop. 181.) [17]

GREENWOOD, Henry Barwel, *Sutton-upon-Derwent, York.*—St. Cath. Coll. Cam. B.A. 1845. R. of Sutton-upon-Derwent, Dio. York, 1865. (Patron, Viscount St. Vincent; R.'s Inc. 580*l* and Ho; Pop. 385.) Formerly P. C. of St. Saviour's, Ashton, Staffs, 1846–58; V. of Caverswall, Staffs, 1858–65. [18]

GREENWOOD, Jabez, *The Rectory, Middleton St. George, Darlington.*—St. Bees; Ten years Man, St. John's Coll. Cam; Deac. 1861 and Pr. 1862 by Bp of Dur. R. of Middleton St. George, Dio. Dur. 1865. (Patron, H. A. W. Cox, Esq; Tithe, 79*l*; Glebe, 16*l*; R.'s Inc. 100*l*; Pop. 350.) Formerly C. of Crook, Durham, 1861–63, Eston, Middlesbro', 1863–65. [19]

GREENWOOD, John, *Grammar School, Ely.*—Dub. A.B. 1858, A.M. 1861. 2nd Mast. of the Ely Gr. Sch. [20]

GREENWOOD, John Henry, *Hurst, Ashton-under-Lyne.*—Literate; Deac. 1835 by Abp of York, Pr. 1838 by Bp of Rip. P. C. of Hurst, Dio. Man. 1846. (Patrons, the Crown and Bp of Man. alt; P. C.'s Inc. 290*l* and Ho; Pop. 6214.) [21]

GREET, Alexander, *Wheat-hill, Somerton, Somerset.*—Caius Coll. Cam. B.A. 1859; Deac. 1859 and Pr. 1860 by Bp of B. and W. R. of Wheathill, Dio. B. and W. 1865. (Patroness, Mrs. Milles; R.'s Inc. 120*l* and Ho; Pop. 38.) Formerly C. of Stoke St. Gregory and Milverton. [22]

GREEVES, Henry, *Caton Green, Lancaster.*—St. Bees; Deac. 1858 and Pr. 1859 by Abp of York. C. of Caton 1865. Formerly C. of Selby, Yorks, 1858. [23]

GREGG, Henry, *Melton Mowbray.*—King's Coll. Lond. Assoc; Deac. 1853 and Pr. 1854 by Abp of Cant. R. of Brooksby, Leic. Dio. Pet. 1860. (Patron, Lord Alfred Paget; R.'s Inc. 300*l*; Pop. 44.) Formerly C. of Shipborne, Kent. [24]

GREGG, John Robert, *Bagendon, Cirencester.*—Dub. Scho. of, A.B. 1854, A.M. 1862; Deac. 1854 and Pr. 1855 by Bp of Lich. C. of North Cerney, Cirencester, 1866. Formerly C. of Burton-on-Trent, Staffs, St. Lawrence's, Reading, and Sandon, Essex. [25]

GREGG, Thomas Husband, *Cradley, Brierley Hill, Staffs.*—Dub. A.B. 1861, A.M. 1867; Deac. 1863 and Pr. 1864 by Bp of Salis. C. of Cradley 1866. Formerly C. of Portland 1863–64, Winterbourne Houghton 1865; Chap. to South Staffordshire Hospital, and Asst. C. of St. Paul's, Wolverhampton, 1865–66. Author, *The Everlasting Covenant: What is it?* 1864; *Two Hundred Scripture Questions*, 1864, 2*d*, *Key to same*, 2*d*; *Fitness for Heaven*, 1865; *By Grace*, 1866; *In the Book*, 1865. Editor, *Gilead*, 1d monthly, Freeman. [26]

GREGORY, Arthur Thomas, *Trusham Rectory, Bovey Tracey, Devon.*—Lin. Coll. Ox. B.A. 1831; Deac. 1840 and Pr. 1841 by Bp of Lich. R. of Trusham, Dio. Ex. 1863. (Patron, Sir J. G. R. de la Pole; R.'s Inc. 200*l* and Ho; Pop. 223.) Formerly P. C. of Flixton, Manchester, 1843–63. [27]

GREGORY, Arthur Tighe, *Bawdsey Vicarage, Woodbridge, Suffolk.*—Dub. LL.B. and A.M; Deac. 1843 and Pr. 1844 by Bp of Nor. V. of Bawdsey, Dio. Nor. 1847. (Patron, Ld Chan; Tithe—Imp. 304*l* 16*s* 6*d*, V. 193*l* 0*s* 3*d*; Glebe, 2 acres; V.'s Inc. 248*l* and Ho; Pop. 426.) [28]

GREGORY, Arthur William, *Corley, Coventry.*—Trin. Coll. Ox. B.A. 1823, M.A. 1823; Deac. 1832, Pr. 1824. V. of Corley, Dio. Wor. 1824. (Patron, A. F. Gregory, Esq; Tithe, 397*l* 15*s* 4*d*; R.'s Inc. 400*l*; Pop 397.) P. C. of Stivichall, Dio. Wor. 1824. (Patron, A. F. Gregory, Esq; P. C.'s Inc. 90*l*; Pop. 72.) [1]

GREGORY, Charles, *Sandford, Crediton, Devon.*—Wad. Coll. Ox. B.A. 1825, M.A. 1853; Deac. 1826, Pr. 1827. P. C. of Sandford, Dio. Ex. 1836. (Patrons, Three Governors and Inhabitants; P. C.'s Inc. 314*l* and Ho; Pop. 1842.) Author, *Sermons,* 1839. [2]

GREGORY, Edmund Ironside, *Clifton.*—Emman. Coll. Cam. 21st Sen. Opt. Thorpe Scho. B.A. 1858, M.A. 1861; Deac. 1859 and Pr. 1860 by Bp of Nor. Min. Can. of Bristol 1862; C. of St. Peter's, Bristol. Formerly C. of All Saints', South Lynn, 1859, Hilgay, Norfolk, 1861. [3]

GREGORY, Francis Maundy, *Devizes, Wilts.*—C. of Devizes. [4]

GREGORY, Francis Thomas, *St. Mary's Platt, Sevenoaks, Kent.*—Univ. Coll. Ox. B.A. 1823, M.A. 1825; Deac. 1829 by Abp of Cant. Pr. 1830 by Bp of Lon. P. C. of St. Mary's Platt, Dio. Cant. 1854. (Patron, Abp of Cant; Glebe, 5 acres; P. C.'s Inc. 00*l* and Ho; Pop. 1023.) [5]

GREGORY, Henry, *Witney.*—Ch. Ch. Ox B.A. 1822, M.A. 1834; Deac. 1825, Pr. 1826. V. of Asthall, Dio. Ox. 1834. (Patron, Eton Coll; V.'s Inc. 90*l*, Pop. 424.) Head Mast. of the Witney Gr. Sch. 1834. Formerly C. of Caggs, Oxon. [6]

GREGORY, James.—C. of St. Mary's, West Brompton, Lond. [7]

GREGORY, John George, *The Rectory, Bonchurch, Isle of Wight.*—Caius Coll. Cam. B.A. 1853, M.A. 1854; Deac. 1853 and Pr. 1854 by Bp of Wor. R. of Bonchurch, Dio. Win. 1862. (Patron, H. B. Leeson, Esq. M.A. M.D. F.R.S; Tithe, 60*l*; Glebe, 70 acres; R.'s Inc. 200*l* and Ho; Pop. 544.) Formerly C. of Trinity, Coventry, 1853–56. All Saints', Lambeth, 1856–57, Trinity, Islington, 1857–59; P. C. of St. Clement's Nechells, Birmingham, 1859–62. Author, *Earth's Eventide,* 1863, 4*s*. [8]

GREGORY, Lewis, *Oadby, Leicester.*—Trin. Coll. Cam. B.A. 1833; Deac. 1833 and Pr. 1835 by Bp of Ex. V. of Oadby, Dio. Pet. 1856. (Tithe, 38*l* 7*s* 9*d*; Glebe, 110 acres; V.'s Inc. 300*l*; Pop. 1254.) [9]

GREGORY, Maze William, *Wisborough Green Vicarage, Horsham.*—Wad. Coll. Ox. 4th cl. Math. et Phy. and B.A. 1846, M.A. 1849; Deac. 1848 and Pr. 1849 by Bp of Ches. V. of Wisborough Green with Loxwood C. Dio. Chich. 1866. (Patron, Bp of Lon; Tithe, 441*l*; Glebe, 5 acres; V.'s Inc. 500*l* and Ho; Pop. 1682.) Formerly V. of Roade, Northants, 1858–66. Author, *The Sins and Punishment of our Members,* Rivingtons, 1867, 1*s*. [10]

GREGORY, Robert, *Parsonage-house, Prince's-road, Kennington-cross, London, S.*—Ch. Ch. Ox. B.A. 1843, M.A. 1846; Deac. 1843, Pr. 1844. P. C. of St. Mary's-the-Less, Prince's-road, Lambeth, Dio. Win. 1853. (Patron, R. of Lambeth; P. C.'s Inc. 300*l* and Ho; Pop. 9805.) Author, *Plea for Small Parishes,* 1849, 1*s*; *The Difficulties and Organization of a poor Metropolitan Parish,* 1866. [11]

GREGSON, William, *Elvaston, Derby.*—St. Bees; Deac. 1864 by Bp of Herf. Pr. 1866 by Bp of Lich. C. of Elvaston 1866. Formerly C. of St. Martin's, Hereford, 1864. [12]

GREIG, George.—St. Edm. Hall. Ox B.A. 1833, M.A. 1838; Deac. 1834 by Bp of Lich. Pr. 1835 by Bp of Lin. C. of South Lambeth Union, Surrey. Formerly C. of Warnford, Hants, and Kennington, Surrey, 1847–58. [13]

GREIVE, William Thomas, *Colnbrook Parsonage, Bucks.*—Edin. Univ. and Trin. Coll. Glenalmond; Deac. 1850, Pr. 1851. P. C. of Colnbrook, Dio. Ox. 1866. (Patron, Bp of Ox; Glebe, 4 acres; P. C.'s Inc. 68*l* 10*s* and Ho; Pop. 1500.) Formerly C. of Clewer, and Sub-Warden of the House of Mercy, Clewer, 1861–65. [14]

GRENFELL, Algernon Sydney, *Mostyn House, Parkgate, Chester.*—Ball. Coll. Ox. B.A 1859, M.A. 1862; Deac. 1861 by Bp of Lich. Formerly Asst. Mast. at Repton Sch. 1860–62. [15]

GRENSIDE, Charles, *Great Massingham Rectory, Swaffham, Norfolk.*—R. of Great Massingham, Dio. Nor. 1816. (Patron, Marquis of Cholmondeley; Tithe, 900*l*; Glebe, 101 acres; R.'s Inc. 1000*l* and Ho; Pop. 934.) [16]

GRENSIDE, Christopher, *Old Malton, Malton, Yorks.*—St. Peter's Coll. Cam. B.A. 1841, M.A. 1854; Deac. 1841, Pr. 1842. P. C. of Old Malton, Dio. York, 1864. (Patron, Earl Fitzwilliam; P. C.'s Inc. 170*l*; Pop. 1302.) Formerly C. of St. Mark's, Lyncombe, Rochford, Essex, 1854–57; British Chap. at Archangel 1843–47, at Moscow, 1847–53; C. of Sheffield 1863. [17]

GRENSIDE, John Doughty, *Donington Vicarage, near Spalding, Lincolnshire.*—Ex. Coll. Ox. B.A. 1843, M.A. 1845; Deac. 1844 and Pr. 1845 by Bp of Ex. V. of Donington, Dio. Lin. 1851. (Patron, Rev. J. Wilson; Tithe, 100*l*; Glebe, 12 acres; V.'s Inc. 175*l* and Ho; Pop. 1690.) Formerly C. of North Molton and Twitchen, Devon, 1844–46, Quadring, Lincoln, 1846–48, Donington and Surfleet 1848–51. [18]

GRENSIDE, Ralph, *Over Whitacre, Coleshill, Warwickshire.*—Univ. Coll. Ox. B.A. 1827, M.A. 1831; Deac. 1828 by Bp of Lond. Pr. 1829 by Abp of York. P. C. of Over Whitacre, Dio. Wor. 1846. (Patron, G. D. W. Digby, Esq; Tithe—Imp. 98*l* 4*s* 9*d*, P. C. 118*l* 11*s* 11*d*; P. C.'s Inc. 186*l*; Pop. 284.) [19]

GRENSIDE, Ralph, *Crathorne Rectory, Yarm, Yorks.*—Univ. Coll. Ox. B.A. 1825, M.A. 1830. P. C. of Seamer, near Stokesley, Yorks, Dio. York, 1825. (Patron, Lord Leconfield; Tithe—Imp. 367*l* 13*s* 8*d*, P. C. 19*l* 8*s* 8*d*; P. C.'s Inc. 65*l* and Ho; Pop. 260.) R. of Crathorne, Dio. York, 1827. (Patron, H. Dugdale, Esq; Tithe, 84*l*; R.'s Inc. 210*l* and Ho; Pop. 256.) [20]

GRENSIDE, William Bent, *Melling Vicarage, near Lancaster.*—Trin. Coll. Cam. B.A. 1846, M.A. 1849; Deac. 1846 and Pr. 1847 by Bp of Ches. V. of Melling, Dio. Man. 1855. (Patron, Ld Chan; Tithe, 45*l*; V.'s Inc. 150*l* and Ho; Pop. 349.) Formerly C. of Claughton, Lancashire. [21]

GRESLEY, Nigel, *Nether Seale, Ashby-de-la-Zouch.*—Trin. Coll. Cam. B.A. 1858; Deac. 1859 and Pr. 1860 by Bp of B. and W. R. of Nether Seale and Over Seale, Dio. Pet. 1860. (Patron, Sir Thomas Gresley, Bart; Tithe, 950*l*; Glebe, 72 acres; R.'s Inc. 1082*l*; Pop. 1260.) Formerly Asst. C. of Chewton-Mendip, Somerset, 1859–60. [22]

GRESLEY, William, *Boyne Hill, Maidenhead, Berks.*—Ch. Ch. Ox. 2nd cl. Lit. Hum. and B.A. 1822, M.A. 1823; Deac. 1825 and Pr. 1826 by Bp of Ox. Preb. of Lich. 1840; P. C. of Boyne Hill, Dio. Ox. 1857. (Patron, Bp. of Ox.; P. C.'s Inc. 120*l* and Ho; Pop. 1071.) Formerly C. of St. Paul's, Brighton. Author, *Ecclesiastes Anglicanus, Portrait of an English Churchman; Short Treatise on the Church; Ordinances of Confession;* various Books, Tracts, Sermons, etc. [23]

GRESSON, John George, M.A., *Richmond House, Worthing, Sussex.*—Ex. Coll. Ox. 2nd cl. Lit. Hum; Deac. 1858 and Pr. 1859 by Bp of Ox. [24]

GRESWELL, Clement, *Tortworth Rectory, Wotton-under-Edge, Glouc.*—Corpus Coll. Ox. afterwards Oriel Coll. 1st cl. Lit. Hum. and B.A. 1827, M.A. 1830; Deac. 1836 and Pr. 1837 by Bp of Ox. R. of Tortworth, Dio. G. and B. 1840. (Patrons, Oriel Coll. Ox; Tithe, 348*l* 9*s*; Glebe, 58 acres; R.'s Inc. 426*l* and Ho; Pop. 235.) Formerly Fell. of Oriel Coll. Ox. 1830, Tut. 1832. [25]

GRESWELL, Edward, *Corpus Christi College, Oxford.*—Brasen. Coll. Ox. B.A. 1819, M.A. 1822, B.D. 1830; Deac. 1825 and Pr. 1826 by Bp of Ox. Vice-Pres. and Fell. of Corpus Coll. Ox. Author, *An Exposition of the Parables and of other Parts of the Gospels,* 5 vols. 1835, 63*s*; *Dissertations upon the Principles and Arrangements of a Harmony of the Gospels,* 4 vols. 2nd ed. Univ. Press, 1837, 63*s*; *Harmonia Evangelica, sive quatuor*

Evangelia atque Actus Apostolorum, Græce, pro temporis et rerum serie in partes sex distributi, ed. quinta Oxonii e Prelo Academico, 1855, 9s 6d; *Prolegomena ad Harmoniam Evangelicam, sive de Primariis nonnullis ad Chronologiam Evangelicam spectantibus Dissertationes quatuor; Accedunt Kalendarii Anni Sacri ab anno* A.C.N. 1511, *usque ab* A.D. 94 *in annis expansis Tabulæ* LXXXV. *&c.* ib. 1840, 9s 6d; *Joannis Miltoni Fabulæ Samson Agonistes et Comus, Græce*, 1832, 5s; *Fasti Temporis Catholici* and *Origines Kalendariæ*, 4 vols; *General Tables of the Fasti Catholici, or Fasti Temporis Perpetui from* B.C. 4004 *to* A.D. 2000, 4to; *Introduction to the Tables of the Fasti Catholici, both the General and Supplementary*, Oxon. Univ. Press, 1852, 65s; *Origines Kalendariæ Italicæ, Nundinal Calendars of Ancient Italy; Nundinal Calendar of Romulus, Calendar of Numa Pompilius, Calendar of the Decemvirs, Irregular Roman Calendar, and Julian Correction; Tables of the Roman Calendar from* U.C. 4 *of Varro* (B.C. 750) *to* U.C. 1108 (A.D. 355), 4 vols. 1854, 2l 2s; *Preliminary Address of the Origines Kalendariæ Italicæ*, etc. 2s; *Origines Kalendariæ Hellenicæ, or the History of the Primitive Calendar among the Greeks before and after the Legislation of Solon*, 6 vols. 1862, 84s; *The Three Witnesses, and the Threefold Cord, being the Testimony of the Natural Measures of Time of the Primitive Calendar, and of Antediluvian and Postdiluvian Tradition, on the principal questions of fact in sacred or profane Antiquity*, London, Rivington, 1862, 7s 6d; *The Objections to the Historical Character of the Pentateuch in Part 1 of Dr. Colenso's "Pentateuch" considered, &c.* London, Rivington, 5s. [1]

GRESWELL, William, *Kilve Rectory, Bridgwater, Somerset.*—Brasen. Coll. Ox. 1st cl. Lit. Hum. B.A. 1817, M.A. 1820; Deac. 1821, Pr. 1822. R. of Kilve with Stringston V. Dio. B. and W. 1837. (Patron, Ball. Coll. Ox; Kilve, Tithe, 200l; Glebe, 87 acres; Stringston, Tithe, 180l; Glebe, 45 acres; R.'s Inc. 500l and Ho; Pop. Kilve 226, Stringston 144.) Formerly Fell. of Ball. Coll. Ox. Author, *The Mosaic Ritual; The Burial Service*, 2 vols. [2]

GRETTON, Frederic Edward, *Stamford, Lincolnshire.*—St. John's Coll. Cam. Sen. Opt. 1st cl. Cl. Trip. and B.A. 1826, M.A. 1829, B.D. 1836; Deac. 1827, Pr. 1828. Head Mast. of the Stamford Gr. Sch. Formerly R. of St. Mary's, Stamford, 1847–64. Author, *Elmsleiana Critica*, 1833, 7s 6d; *Introduction to the Translation of English Poetry into Latin Elegiacs and Hexameters*, 1838, 3s; *Parochial Sermons*, 1843, 6s; *Classical Parallels*, 1847, 2s 6d; *Five Sermons on Romanism*, 1851, 4s; *Reddenda, or Passages for Translation into Latin Prose and Verse*, 1853, 4s 6d; occasional Sermons. [3]

GRETTON, William Henry, *Goodrich, Ross, Herefordshire.*—Pemb. Coll. Ox. B.A. 1851, M.A. 1853; Deac. 1851 and Pr. 1852 by Bp of Lich. C. of Goodrich. Formerly C. of Hampton Bishop. [4]

GREVILLE, Eden Septimus, *St. Paul's, Clapham, S.W.*—Clare Coll. Cam. B.A. 1832; Deac. and Pr. 1832. P. C. of St. Paul's, Clapham, Dio. Lon. 1861. (Patron, R. of Clapham; P. C.'s Inc. 300l.) Formerly R. of Bonsall 1833–61. [5]

GREY, E. J., *Harworth, Bawtry, Notts.*—C. of Harworth. [6]

GREY, George, *Woodbury-Salterton, Exeter.*—Magd. Hall, Ox. B.A. 1854, M.A. 1857; Deac. 1853, Pr. 1854. P.C. of Woodbury-Salterton, Dio. Ex. 1863. (Patroness, Mrs. Thornycraft; P. C.'s Inc. 100l; Pop. 498.) Formerly V. of Stanford, Norfolk. [7]

GREY, The Hon. Francis Richard, *The Rectory, Morpeth.*—Trin. Coll. Cam. M.A. 1834. Rural Dean; R. of Morpeth with Ulgham P. C. Dio. Dur. 1842. (Patron, Earl of Carlisle; Tithe—Imp. 12l 3s 10d, R. 147l 2s 6d; R.'s Inc. 1625l and Ho; Pop. Morpeth 5612, Ulgham 362.) Hon. Can. of Dur. [8]

GREY, The Hon. John, *Houghton-le-Spring, Fence Houses, Durham.*—Trin. Coll. Cam. 1st cl. Cl. Trip. and M.A. 1832; Deac. 1835 by Bp of Lin. Pr. 1836 by Bp of Roch. R. of Houghton-le-Spring, Dio. Dur. 1847. (Patron, Bp of Dur; Tithe, 950l; Glebe, 343 acres; R.'s Inc. 1600l and Ho; Pop. 8530.) Hon. Can. of Dur. [9]

GREY, William, *Torquay.*—Formerly P. C. of Milford, Surrey, 1860–65. [10]

GREY, William Hewett Charles, *North Sherwood-street, Nottingham.*—St. John's Coll. Cam. B.A. 1822, M.A. 1825; Deac. 1822 and Pr. 1823 by Abp of York. Formerly C. of Kirton, Tuxford, Notts, 1822–24. [11]

GRIBBLE, Charles Besley, *Constantinople.*—Ch. Coll. Cam. B.A. 1839, M.A. 1847; Deac. 1839 and Pr. 1840 by Bp of Lin. British Chap. at Constantinople. Formerly P. C. of St. Paul's (Mariner's Ch.), Dio. Lon. 1847; Chap. to the Sailors' Home and Destitute Sailors' Asylum 1847; C. of Olney, Bucks; Miss. in Canada. [12]

GRICE, Joseph Hill, *Upton-on-Severn, Worcestershire.*—Ch. Ch. Ox. B.A. 1831, M.A. 1833; Deac. 1832 and Pr. 1833 by Bp of Wor. C. of Ripple, near Upton-on-Severn. Formerly C. of Queenhill, Worc. [13]

GRICE, William, *Tothill Rectory, Alford, Lincolnshire.*—Queens' Coll. Cam. B.A. 1827; Deac. 1827, Pr. 1828. R. of Tothill, Dio. Lin. 1851. (Patron, Lord Willoughby de Broke; Tithe, 137l 10s; Glebe, 68 acres; R.'s Inc. 183l and Ho; Pop. 61.) [14]

GRICE, William, *Lillington, near Leamington.*—Univ. Coll. Ox. B.A. 1834, M.A. 1837; Deac. 1837 by Bp of Lin. Pr. 1838 by Bp of Wor. P. C. of Sherborne, Dio. Wor. 1848. (Patroness, Miss Ryland; Glebe, 82 acres; P. C.'s Inc. 135l; Pop. 167.) Chap. of Broughton, Dio. Lich. 1863. (Patron, Sir H. Delves Broughton, Bart; Glebe, 67 acres; Chap.'s Inc. 110l.) Formerly C. of Hatton, near Warwick, 1837–39; Chap. of Wroxhall, Warwick, 1837–54. [15]

GRIER, Frederick, *Douglas, Isle of Man.*—Dub. A.B. 1859; Deac. 1859 and Pr. 1860 by Bp of Lich. Asst. C. of St. Thomas's, Douglas, 1864. Formerly C. of Heath and Hault Hucknall 1859, Enfield 1862. [16]

GRIER, Richard Macgregor, *The Vicarage, Rugeley.*—Pemb. Coll. Ox. B.A. 1857; Deac. 1858 and Pr. 1859 by Bp of Lich. V. of Rugeley, Dio. Lich. 1865. (Patrons, D. and C. of Lich; Tithe, 315l; V.'s Inc. 500l and Ho; Pop. 3003.) Formerly C. of Trinity, Burton-on-Trent, 1852–62, St. Heliar's, Jersey, 1862, St. Mary's, Lichfield, 1862–65. [17]

GRIFFIN, The Hon. Cornelius, *Haselor, Alcester, Warwickshire.*—Deac. 1818 by Bp of Salis. Pr. 1818 by Bp of Lon. V. of Haselor, Dio. Wor. 1846. (Patrons, Ld Chan; V.'s Inc. 42l; Pop. 355.) [18]

GRIFFIN, Edward, *Stoke Albany Rectory, Rockingham, Northants.*—P. C. of Great Bowden, Market Harborough, Dio. Pet. 1814. (Patron, Ch. Ch. Ox; Tithe—App. 9l 7s 5d; P. C.'s Inc. 86l; Pop. 1395.) R. of Stoke Albany, Dio. Pet. 1831. (Patron, G. L. Watson, Esq; Tithe—Imp. 30l, R. 30l; R.'s Inc. 216l and Ho; Pop. 344.) V. of Wilbarston, Dio. Pet. 1831. (Patron, G. L. Watson, Esq; V.'s Inc. 187l; Pop. 721.) [19]

GRIFFIN, William Nathaniel, *Ospringe Vicarage, Faversham, Kent.*—St. John's Coll. Cam. B.A. 1837, M.A. 1840, S.T.B. 1847; Deac. 1841, Pr. 1842. V. of Ospringe, Dio. Cant. 1848. (Patron, St. John's Coll. Cam; Tithe—Imp. 832l 5s and 185½ acres of Glebe. V. 305l; Glebe, 29 acres; V.'s Inc. 364l and Ho; Pop. 1111.) Rural Dean. Formerly Fell. and Tut. of St. John's Coll. Cam. 1837; Public Exam. in Math. et Phy. 1848. Author, *Treatise on Optics*, 1842; *The Theory of Double Refraction*, 1842; *Treatise on the Motion of a Rigid Body*, 1847; *The Elements of Mensuration*, 1852. [20]

GRIFFINHOOFE, Thomas John, *Arkesden Vicarage, Bishops Stortford.*—Pemb. Coll. Ox. B.A. 1844, M.A. 1847; Deac. 1844 and Pr. 1845 by Bp of Lon. V. of Arkesden, Dio. Roch. (Patron, Rev. W. B. Wolfe; V.'s Inc. 181l and Ho; Pop. 596.) Formerly C. of Arkesden. [21]

GRIFFITH, Charles, *Glyn Celyn, Brecon.*—Ch. Ch. Ox. B.A. 1827, M.A. 1830; Deac. 1828, Pr. 1829. R. of Talachddu, Dio. St. D. (Patroness, Mrs. A. Griffith; Tithe, 135l; Glebe, 40 acres; R.'s Inc. 175l and Ho; Pop. 193.) Preb. of St. D; Rural Dean and Surrogate. [1]

GRIFFITH, Charles, B.A., *Cadoxton, near Neath, Glamorganshire.*—C. of Cadoxton. [2]

GRIFFITH, Charles Arthur, *Berwick St. John, Salisbury.*—New Coll. Ox. B.A. 1838, M.A. 1842; Deac. 1839 and Pr. 1841 by Bp of Ox. R. of Berwick St. John, Dio. Salis. 1855. (Patron, New Coll. Ox; Tithe, 518*l*; Glebe, 52½ acres; R.'s Inc. 575*l* and Ho; Pop. 499.) [3]

GRIFFITH, Charles Higman, *Stratfield Turgis, Winchfield, Hants.*—Literate; Deac. 1852 and Pr. 1853 by Bp of Win. R. of Stratfield Turgis, Dio. Win. 1862. (Patron, Duke of Wellington; R.'s Inc. 500*l* and Ho; Pop. 195.) Formerly C. of St. George's, Wrotham, Kent, 1853–57, Stratfield Turgis 1858–62. [4]

GRIFFITH, D., *Beaumaris, Anglesey.*—Chap. of the Anglesey Gaol, Beaumaris. [5]

GRIFFITH, David Hanmer, *Cadoxton Vicarage, Neath, Glamorganshire.*—Jesus Coll. Ox. B.A. 1836, M.A. 1837; Deac. 1836 by Bp of Ely, Pr. 1837 by Bp of G. and B. V. of Cadoxton-juxta-Neath with Aberpergwm and Crynant C. Dio. Llan. 1837. (Patron, R. H. Myers, Esq; Tithe—Imp. 739*l* 3*s* 8*d*, V. 450*l*; Glebe, 13 acres; V.'s Inc. 500*l* and Ho; Pop. 2664.) Rural Dean 1855; Surrogate; Magistrate for the Counties of Glamorgan and Brecon. [6]

GRIFFITH, Edward, *Barbon, Kirby Lonsdale, Westmoreland.*—C. of Barbon. [7]

GRIFFITH, Edward, M.A., *Quatford Castle, Bridgnorth, Salop.* [8]

GRIFFITH, Edward, *St. Keverne Vicarage, Helston, Cornwall.*—Ex. Coll. Ox. B.A. 1821, M.A. 1827; Deac. 1826 and Pr. 1827 by Bp of Ex. V. of St. Keverne, Dio. Ex. 1854. (Patroness, Mrs. Griffith; Tithe—Imp. 1163*l* 10*s*, V. 512*l*; V.'s Inc. 544*l* and Ho; Pop. 1892.) [9]

GRIFFITH, Edward George, *Winterbourne Cherborough, Salisbury.*—Trin. Coll. Cam. B.A. 1841, M.A. 1845; Deac. 1849 and Pr. 1850 by Bp of Roch. R. of Winterbourne Cherborough, Dio. Salis. 1853. (Patron, Ld Chan; Tithe, 219*l* 6*s* 6*d*; Glebe, 11 acres; R.'s Inc. 235*l* and Ho; Pop. 150.) [10]

GRIFFITH, G., *Rectory, Machynlleth, Montgomeryshire.*—R. of Machynlleth, Dio. Ban. 1862. (Patron, Bp of Ban; Tithe, 400*l* 10*s*; Glebe, 3½ acres; R.'s Inc. 400*l* and Ho; Pop. 2396.) [11]

GRIFFITH, George Sandham, *Bampton-Aston Vicarage, Faringdon, Berks.*—Clare Coll. Cam. B.A. 1854, M.A. 1857; Deac. 1855 and Pr. 1856 by Bp of Chich. C. in sole charge of Bampton-Aston 1858, and also of Yelford 1863. Formerly Asst. C. of Steyning, Sussex, 1855–57. [12]

GRIFFITH, Henry, 17, *White Friars, Chester.*—Jesus Coll. Ox. B.A. 1824, M.A. 1827; Deac. 1827 and Pr. 1828 by Bp of Ox. Formerly P. C. of Llandrygarn and Bodwrog, Anglesey, 1829–62. Translator into Welsh of Watkins' *Catechism of the Figurative Language of Scripture*; Mason's *Crumbs from the Master's Table*; Bishop Horne's *Commentary on the Psalms.* [13]

GRIFFITH, Henry Thomas, *North Walsham.*—Pemb. Coll. Ox. B.A. 1850; Deac. 1852 and Pr. 1853 by Abp of York. V. of Felmingham, Dio. Nor. 1866. (Patron, Bp of Nor; Tithe, 145*l*; Glebe, 14 acres; V.'s Inc. 200*l*; Pop. 432.) Formerly C. of St. Stephen's, Hull, 1852–56, Hanworth, Norfolk, 1856–64; P. C. of Sustead, and C. of Bessingham, Norfolk, 1864–66. [14]

GRIFFITH, James, *Flaxton, York.*—Queens' Coll. Cam. B.A. 1840; Deac. 1840 and Pr. 1841 by Bp of Lin. P. C. of Flaxton, Dio. York, 1861. (Patrons, D. and C. of Dur; Glebe, 69 acres; P. C.'s Inc. 250*l* and Ho; Pop. 367.) Formerly C. of Ancaster, Linc. 1840 42, Sand Hutton, York, 1842–61. [15]

GRIFFITH, John, *The Precincts, Rochester.*—Scho. of Trin. Coll. Cam. 1809, Bell's Univ. Scho. 1810, Wrang. and B.A. 1812, M.A. 1815, B.D. 1822, D.D. 1831. Can. of Roch. 1827. Formerly Fell. of Emman. Coll. Cam. [16]

GRIFFITH, John, *Llanynys Vicarage, Denbighshire.*—Jesus Coll. Ox. B.A. 1828, M.A. 1830; Deac. 1829 and Pr. 1831 by Bp of Ban. V. of Llanynys with Chapelry of Gyffylliog, Dio. Ban. 1850. (Patron, Bp of Ban; Tithe—App. 845*l* 5*s*, V. 422*l* 12*s* 8*d*; Glebe, 3 acres; V.'s Inc. 422*l* 12*s* 8*d* and Ho; Pop. Llanynys 723, Gyffylliog 567.) Rural Dean 1862; Surrogate 1851. Formerly C. of Llangelynin, Carmarthenshire, 1829–32, Llanerchymedd, Anglesey, 1832–50. Contributor to several Welsh periodicals. [17]

GRIFFITH, John, *The College, Brighton.*—St. John's Coll. Cam. 10th Wrang. and 2nd cl. Cl. Trip. B.A. 1840, M.A. 1843; Deac. 1843, Pr. 1844. Prin. of the Brighton Coll. Formerly P. C. of Trinity Chapel, Brighton. [18]

GRIFFITH, John, *Rectory, Merthyr-Tydvil.*—Queens' Coll. Cam. B.A. 1841, M.A. 1844; Deac. and Pr. 1842. R. of Merthyr-Tydvil, Dio. Llan. 1859. (Patron, Marquis of Bute; R.'s Inc. 675*l* and Ho; Pop. 21,028.) Surrogate; Rural Dean. Formerly V. of Aberdare with St. Elvan's P. C. 1846. Author, *The Church in Wales*; *Education in Wales* (a Reply to Mr. Bright's Speech in the House of Commons), 1848; *Protest against Inducting English Incumbents into Livings where Welsh only is Spoken*; *Rowlands, the Founder of Welsh Methodism, defended from the Attack of the "Quarterly Review,"* 1852. [19]

GRIFFITH, John, *Rectory, Neath, Glamorganshire.*—Lampeter, Scho. 1838; Deac. 1843 and Pr. 1844 by Bp of Llan. R. of Neath with Llantwit, Dio. Llan. 1855. (Patron, Marquis of Bute; Tithe, 365*l*; Rent from Glebe, 75*l*; R.'s Inc. 440*l* and Ho; Pop. Neath 6734, Llantwit 1470.) Formerly C. of Aberustruth 1843; P. C. of Nantyglo 1844; R. of Llansannor 1846; V. of St. Mary Hill 1848. Head Mast. of the Cardigan Gr. Sch. 1839–41. [20]

GRIFFITH, J. Pugh.—C. of Ely Chapel, Lond. [21]

GRIFFITH, Joseph William, *Bettws-y-Coed, Llanrwst, Carnarvonshire.*—Jesus Coll. Ox. B.A. 1852; Deac. 1853 and Pr. 1854 by Bp of Ban. P. C. of Bettws-y-Coed, Dio. Ban. 1861. (Patron, Bp of Ban; P. C.'s Inc. 84*l*; Pop. 509.) P. C. of Dolwydelan, Dio. Ban. 1861. (Patron, Lord Willoughby D'Eresby; P. C.'s Inc. 112*l*; Pop. 811.) Formerly V. of Trefylwys, Montgomeryshire, 1855–61. [22]

GRIFFITH, L., *Rectory, Deal.*—R. of Deal, Dio. Cant. 1862. (Patron, Abp of Cant; Tithe—Imp. 80*l*, R. 464*l* 10*s* 10*d*; R.'s Inc. 472*l* and Ho; Pop. 1982.) [23]

GRIFFITH, Richard Williams, *Llanfairisgaer, Bangor.*—Jesus Coll. Ox. B.A. 1854, M.A. 1856; Deac. 1855 by Bp of Ches. Pr. 1856 by Bp of Ban. P. C. of Llanfairisgaer, Dio. Ban. 1860. (Patron, Bp of Ban; P. C.'s Inc. 109*l*; Pop. 1060*l*.) Formerly C. of Holyhead 1855–59, Llanfairisgaer 1859–60. [24]

GRIFFITH, Samuel Young Nayler, *St. Ebbe's, Rectory, Oxford.*—Ex. Coll. Ox. B.A. 1846, M.A. 1853; Deac. 1848 and Pr. 1849 by Bp of Rip. C. in sole charge of St. Ebbe's, Oxford, 1860. Formerly C. in sole charge of Waterleigh, Glouc. 1850; C. of St. Luke's Dist. Leeds, 1848. [25]

GRIFFITH, Thomas, 8, *Clapton-square, Hackney, London, N.E.*—St. John's Coll. Cam. B.A. 1822, M.A. 1832; Deac. 1821, Pr. 1822. Min. of Ram's Episc. Chapel, Homerton, Dio. Lond. 1830. (Patrons, Trustees; Min.'s Inc. *uncertain*, arising from Pew-rents.) Preb. of St. Paul's 1862. Author, *Sermons*, 1830, 2nd ed. 1838; *Life a Pilgrimage*, 1833; *Leading Idea of Christianity*, 1833, 2nd ed. 1838; *Present for the Afflicted*, 1834; *The Spiritual Life*, 1834, 8th ed. 1856; *On Confirmation*, 1835, 4th ed. 1850; *Christian Loyalty*, 1836; *Confirmation Tract*, 1837, 7th ed. 1864; *The Christian Church*, 1837; *On the Lord's Supper*, 1838, 3rd ed. 1846; *On the Lord's Prayer*, 1839, 2nd ed. 1840; *Live while you Live*, 1841, 7th ed. 1857; *Our Baptismal Standing*, 1850; *Practical Hints for Communicants*, 1850; *Why we should protest against the Church of Rome*, 2nd ed. 1850; *The Duty of Defence*, 3rd ed. 1854; *The Fatherhood of God*,

1862; *Plea for Holy Scripture*, 1864; *Faith grounded on Reason*, 1864; *Ministers not Masters*, 1866. [1]

GRIFFITH, Thomas, *Cwm Vicarage, St. Asaph, Flintshire.*—Queens' Coll. Cam. B.A. 1825, M.A. 1828; Deac. 1825 and Pr. 1826 by Bp of St. A. V. of Cwm, Dio. St. A. 1858. (Patron, Bp of Llan; Tithe, 340*l*; Glebe, 9 acres; V.'s Inc. 350*l* and Ho; Pop. 495.) Formerly V. of Llanfawr, Merionethshire, 1843–58. [2]

GRIFFITH, Thomas Henry, *Hornchurch Vicarage, Essex.*—New Coll. Ox. B.A. 1851, B.C.L. 1856; Deac. 1856 and Pr. 1857 by Bp of Ox. V. of Hornchurch, Dio. Roch. 1863. (Patron, New Coll. Ox; V.'s Inc. 740*l* and Ho; Pop. 2224.) [3]

GRIFFITH, Thomas Thompson, 2, *Minor Canon-row, Rochester.*—Clare Coll. Cam. B.A. 1850, M.A. 1856; Deac. 1851 by Bp of Roch. Pr. 1854 by Abp of York. Min. Can. of Roch. 1859; Precentor of Roch. Cathl. 1863. [4]

GRIFFITH, William, *Mill-street, Crewe.*—St. Bees; Deac. 1866 by Bp of Ches. C. of Ch. Ch. Monk's Coppenhall. [5]

GRIFFITH, W. W., *Heyope, Knighton, Radnorshire.*—R. of Heyope, Dio. St. D. 1856. (Patron, Bp of St. D; R.'s Inc. 120*l*; Pop. 283.) [6]

GRIFFITHS, Arthur, *Llanelly, Breconshire.*—Deac. 1848, Pr. 1849. P. C. of Llanelly Dio. St. D. 1851. (Patron, Duke of Beaufort; Pop. 9603.) [7]

GRIFFITHS, David, *Resolven Vicarage, Neath, Glamorganshire.*—Jesus Coll. Cam. Ox. S.C.L. 1852, B.A. 1856; Deac. 1852 and Pr. 1853 by Bp of Llan. V. of Resolven, Dio. Llan. 1860. (Patron, Marquis of Bute; V.'s Inc. 88*l* and Ho; Pop. 762.) P. C. of Glyncorrwg with Blaengwrach, Dio. Llan. 1860. (Patron, N. V. E. Vaughan, Esq; P. C.'s Inc. 100*l*; Pop. Glyncorrwg 322, Blaengwrach 280.) Formerly C. of Aberdare 1852–58; P. C. of Ystradyfodwg 1858–60. [8]

GRIFFITHS, David, *Carmarthen-street, Llandilo Vawr, Carmarthen.*—Lampeter; Deac. 1864 by Bp of St. D. C. of Llandilo Vawr. [9]

GRIFFITHS, Edward, *Llanmartin Rectory, Newport, Monmouthshire.*—Deac. 1837 and Pr. 1838 by Bp of Llan. R. of Llanmartin with Wilcrick, Dio. Llan. 1857. (Patron, W. P. Herrick, Esq; Tithe, 150*l*; Glebe, 20 acres; R.'s Inc. 230*l* and Ho; Pop. 209.) Formerly P. C. of the Oaks Ch. Charnwood Forest, 1852–57, St. Peter's, Copt Oak, Charnwood Forest, 1853–57. [10]

GRIFFITHS, Edward Meredith, *Aberdare.*—Queen's Coll. Birmingham; Deac. 1852 by Bp of Llan. C. of Aberdare 1854. Formerly C. of Llanwonno 1852–54. [11]

GRIFFITHS, Frederick Pelham, *Lewisham, Kent, S.E.*—Literate; Deac. 1863 by Bp of Ches. Formerly C. of Hollinfare, Lancashire, 1863. [12]

GRIFFITHS, George Pruen, *Hillfield, Cheltenham.*—Wad. Coll. Ox. B.A. 1849, M.A. 1851; Deac. 1850 and Pr. 1851 by Bp of G. and B. P. C. of St. Mark's, Cheltenham, Dio. G. and B. 1862. (Patrons, Trustees; P. C.'s Inc. 250*l*; Pop. 1450.) Formerly C. of Tewkesbury 1850, St. Peter's, Cheltenham, 1857. [13]

GRIFFITHS, James, *Llanllwchaiarn, New Quay, Carmarthen.*—Lampeter, B.A. 1866; Deac. 1867 by Bp of St. D. C. of Llanllwchaiarn. [14]

GRIFFITHS, James Richard, *Llangeler Vicarage, Newcastle-Emlyn, Carmarthenshire.*—Deac. 1832 and Pr. 1833 by Bp of St. D. V. of Llangeler, Dio. St. D. 1853. (Patron, Bp of St. D; Tithe—Imp. 64*l*, Sinecure R. 244*l* and ½ acre Glebe, V. 122*l*; Glebe, 44 acres; V.'s Inc. 180*l* and Ho; Pop. 1573.) [15]

GRIFFITHS, John, *Wadham College, Oxford.*—Wad. Coll. Ox. B.A. 1827, M.A. 1833; Deac. 1828, Pr. 1829. Keeper of the Archives, Oxford. [16]

GRIFFITHS, John, *Cwmavon, Taibach, Glamorganshire.*—Lampeter, Sen. Scho; Deac. 1850 by Bp of Llan. Pr. 1851 by Bp of St. D. P. C. of Michaelstone-super-Avon, Dio. Llan. 1863. (Patrons, the English Copper Company; P. C.'s Inc. 154*l* and Ho; Pop. 7000.) Formerly C. of Llanelly 1850, Llanmon and Llanddarog 1856, Kilvey, Swansea, 1861. [17]

GRIFFITHS, John, *The Parsonage, Mynyddyslwyn, Newport, Monmouthshire.*—St. Augustine's Coll. Canterbury; Deac. 1852 and Pr. 1853 by Bp of Nova Scotia. P. C. of Mynyddyslwyn, Dio. Llan. 1860. (Patron, Bp of Llan; Glebe, 35 acres; P. C.'s Inc. 182*l* and Ho; Pop. 4191.) Formerly Miss. of the S.P.G. 1852 and 1857; C. of Cynwyl Elfed and St. David's, Carmarthen, 1855, Neath 1859, Languick 1860. Author, *Journal of Missionary Labours in Nova Scotia*, 1856, 6*d*; *The Conversation that becometh the Gospel of Christ*, 1863, 3*d*. [18]

GRIFFITHS, John, *Glyntaf Parsonage, near Cardiff.*—P. C. of Glyntaf, Dio. Llan. 1849. (Patron, Bp of Llan; P. C.'s Inc. 250*l* and Ho; Pop. 7443.) [19]

GRIFFITHS, John, *Llandilo Vawr, Carmarthen.*—Lampeter B.D. 1854; Deac. 1829 and Pr. 1830 by Bp of St. D. V. of Llandilo Vawr, Dio. St. D. 1852. (Patron, Bp of St. D; Tithe—Imp. 1024*l* 8*s*, V. 512*l* 4*s*; V.'s Inc. 524*l*; Pop. 4283.) Rural Dean of Llandilo 1852. Author, Welsh Sermons. [20]

GRIFFITHS, J. Frederick, *Brancepeth, Durham.*—C. of Brancepeth. [21]

GRIFFITHS, Rees, *Penhenrin, Llanwinio, Carmarthenshire.*—Deac. 1845, Pr. 1846. P. C. of Llanwinio, Dio. St. D. 1845. (Patron, W. P. Howell, Esq; P. C.'s Inc. 94*l*; Pop. 944.) [22]

GRIFFITHS, Thomas, *Bridge-street, Kidwelly, Carmarthenshire.*—Deac. 1825, Pr. 1826. V. of Kidwelly, Dio. St. D. 1840. (Patron, Ld Chan; Tithe—Imp. 386*l*, V. 103*l* 17*s*; Glebe, 3½ acres; V.'s Inc. 117*l*; Pop. 1652.) [23]

GRIFFITHS, Walter, *St. Lythan's, Glamorganshire.*—V. of St. Lythan's, Dio. Llan. 1863. (Patron, Archd. of Llan; Tithe, 140*l*; Glebe, 40 acres; V.'s Inc. 190*l* and Ho; Pop. 136.) [24]

GRIFFITHS, William D., *Kimbolton, Hunts.*—C. of Kimbolton. [25]

GRIGG, Thomas Nattle, *St. George Vicarage, near Bristol.*—St. Peter's Coll. Cam. Scho. of, B.A. 1835; Deac. 1838 and Pr. 1840 by Bp of Nor. V. of St. George, near Bristol, Dio. G. and B. 1857. (Patron, the present V; Tithe, 290*l*; Glebe, 38 acres; V.'s Inc. 580*l* and Ho; Pop. 3600.) [26]

GRIGNON, Robert Scarlett, *Lewes, Sussex.*—Trin. Coll. Cam. B.A. 1843; Deac. 1846 by Bp of Nor. Pr. 1847 by Bp of Llan. R. of St. John-sub-Castro, Lewes, Dio. Chich. 1851. (Patron, the present R; Tithe—Imp. 42*l*, R. 250*l*; Glebe, 2¾ acres; R.'s Inc. 320*l*; Pop. 2308.) Formerly V. of Dedham, Essex, 1847–49; V. of Long Bennington, Linc. 1849–51. [27]

GRIGNON, William Stanford, *Felstead Grammar School, Essex.*—Trin. Coll. Cam. B.A. 1846, M.A. 1849; Deac. 1850 by Bp of Chich. Pr. 1853 by Bp of B. and W. Head Mast. of Felstead Gr. Sch. 1855. Formerly Prin. of Sheffield Coll. Sch. 1853–55. [28]

GRIGSON, William, *Whinburgh Rectory, East Dereham, Norfolk.*—Corpus Coll. Cam. B.A. 1833, M.A. 1836; Deac. 1833 by Bp of Nor. Pr. 1834 by Bp of Roch. R. of Whinburgh with Westfield R. Dio. Nor. 1843. (Patron, the present R; Tithe—App. 5*l* 5*s*; R. 325*l* 7*s*; Glebe, 43¾ acres; R.'s Inc. 400*l* and Ho; Pop. Whinburgh 220, Westfield 124.) [29]

GRIMALDI, Alexander B., *New Seaham, Sunderland.*—C. of New Seaham. [30]

GRIMALDI, Henry Beaufort, *The Parsonage, Guildford, Western Australia.*—St. John's Coll. Ox. and King's Coll. Lond; Deac. 1858 and Pr. 1859 by Bp of Lich. Formerly C. of Nonington 1860, Darlaston 1858–60. [31]

GRIMES, Joseph William.—Chap. of H.M.S. "Excellent." [32]

GRIMLEY, Horatio Nelson, *Grammar School, Helston, Cornwall.*—Univ. Coll. Lond. 3rd in Math. Hons. B.A. 1863, St. Peter's Coll. Cam. 12th Wrang. B.A. 1865; Deac. 1865 and Pr. 1866 by Bp of Ex. C. of Helston 1865; Head Mast. of Helston Gr. Sch. [33]

GRIMSTON, A., *Lund Vicarage, Beverley.*—V. of Lund. Dio. York, 1863. (Patron, C. Grimston, Esq;

Tithe, 8*s*; Glebe, 149 acres; V.'s Inc. 188*l*; Pop. 503.) [1]

GRIMSTON, The Hon. Edward Harbottle, *Pebmarsh Rectory, Halstead, Essex.*—Ch. Ch. Ox. B.A. 1831, All Souls' Coll. M.A. 1838; Deac. 1842 and Pr. 1843 by Bp of Ox. R. of Pebmarsh, Dio. Roch. 1841. (Patron, Earl of Verulam; Tithe, 592*l*; Glebe, 26 acres; R.'s Inc. 625*l* and Ho; Pop. 653.) R. of Great Henny, Essex, Dio. Roch. 1845. (Patron, Earl of Verulam; Tithe, 375*l*; Glebe, 60 acres; R.'s Inc. 469*l* and Ho; Pop. 363) Formerly Fell. of All Souls' Coll. Ox. [2]

GRINDLE, Edmund Samuel, *Cuckfield, Sussex.*—Queen's Coll. Ox. Scho. of, 1858, Hon. 4th cl. Lit. Hum. 1861, 3rd cl. Maths. 1862, B.A. 1862, M.A. 1865; Deac. 1864 and Pr. 1865 by Abp of York. C. of Cuckfield 1867. Formerly C. of Bolton Percy and Siggiesthorne, Yorks. [3]

GRINDLE, Henry Augustus Louis, *Devizes, Wilts.*—St. Mary Hall, Ox. B.A. 1858, M.A. 1861; Deac. 1858 and Pr. 1859 by Bp of Nor. Chap. of St. Peter's Rowde, Devizes, 1866. Formerly C. of Burnham Overy 1858–63; Bishops Cannings 1863–64; Vice Prin. of York Dioc. Training Coll. for Masters 1864–65; C. of South Broom, Devizes, 1865–66. [4]

GRINDLE, Walter Smith, 26, *Bessborough-street, Pimlico, S.W.*—King's Coll. Lond. Assoc; Deac. 1866. Asst. C. of Trinity, Westminster, 1866. [5]

GRINDROD, William, *Chester.*—Trin. Coll. Cam. Jun. Opt. and B.A. 1855, M.A. 1858; Deac. 1856 and Pr. 1857 by Bp of Man. Min. Can. and C of St. Oswald's, Chester. Formerly Asst. C. of Standish, Lancashire, 1856–57; C. of Kirkby, Lancashire, 1857–59, St. Mary's, Shrewsbury, 1859–60. [6]

GRINFIELD, Thomas, *Shirland Rectory, near Derby.*—R. of Shirland, Dio. Lich. 1827. (Patrons, Sir R. Tufton, Bart. and others; Tithe—App. 19*l*. R. 183*l*; Glebe, 61 acres; R.'s Inc. 274*l* and Ho; Pop. 1426.) [7]

GRINSTEAD, Charles, *Torella, Torquay.*—St. Cath. Coll. Cam. B.A; Deac. 1860 by Bp of Ex. Pr. 1864 by Bp of Ely. Sen. C. of Tor Mohun 1865. Formerly C. of St. Michael's, East Teignmouth, 1860–62, Great St. Andrew's, Cambridge, 1862–65. [8]

GRISDALE, John, *Arncliffe, near Skipton, Yorks.*—St. Bees; Deac. 1855 by Abp of York, Pr. 1860 by Bp of Man. P. C. of Halton Gill, Dio. Rip. 1866. (Patron, V. of Arncliffe; P. C.'s Inc. 150*l*; Pop. 70.) C. of Arncliffe 1866. Formerly C. in sole charge of Burnsall, Yorks. [9]

GRISDALE, Joseph, *Wymondham, Norfolk.*—Emman. Coll. Cam. B.A. 1828; Deac. 1840 and Pr. 1841 by Bp of Nor. Head Mast. of Wymondham Free Gr. Sch. Formerly P. C. of Burton-Hastings; Sub-Mast. of Norwich Gr. Sch. [10]

GRIST, William, *Bewdley, Staffs.*—St. John's, Coll. Cam. B.A. 1860; Deac. 1861 and Pr. 1862 by Bp of Win. Head Mast. of Bewdley Gr. Sch. 1864. [11]

GRIX, William Bevern, *Grammar School, Congleton, Cheshire.*—Queens' Coll. Cam. B.A. 1852 M.A. 1856; Deac. 1855 and Pr. 1856 by Bp of Ches. Head Mast. of the Congleton Gr. Sch. 1856; Chap. to Sir C. W. Shakerley, Bart. 1863. [12]

GROGAN, George William, *Somerton Vicarage, Somerset.*—Dub. A.B. 1848; Deac. 1849, Pr. 1850. V. of Somerton, Dio. B. and W. 1867. (Patron, Earl of Ilchester; Tithe, 259*l*; Glebe, 108*l*; V.'s Inc. 460*l* and Ho; Pop. 2206.) Formerly P. C. of St. Matthew's-in-Thorpe, Hamlet, Norwich, 1851–58. C. 1859–65, and R. of Clenchwarton, Norfolk, 1865–67. Author, *The Seven Churches.* [13]

GRONOW, R. G., *Fanshawe, Congleton, Cheshire.*—Ch. Coll. Cam. B.A. 1864; Deac. 1865 by Bp of St. A. Pr. 1867 by Bp of Ches. P. C. of Capesthorne with Siddington P. C. Dio. Ches. 1867. (Patron, Arthur Henry Davenport, Esq; P. C.'s Inc. 310*l* and Ho; Pop. Capesthorne 114, Siddington 433.) Formerly C. of Steyning, Sussex. [14]

GRONOW, Thomas, 8, *Clarence-crescent, Windsor,* and *Ash Hall, South Wales.*—Brasen. Coll. Ox. B.A. 1819, M.A. 1822; Deac. 1820 by Bp of Llan. Pr. 1821 by Bp of Bristol. Dom. Chap. to the Earl of Lisburne. [15]

GROOM, John, *St. Margaret's Rectory, Whalley-range, Manchester.*—Wad. Coll. Ox. B.A. 1841, M.A. 1846; Deac. 1852 and Pr. 1854 by Bp of Ches. R of Whalley-range, Dio. Man. 1852. (Patrons, Trustees; R.'s Inc. 400*l* and Ho; Pop. 4200.) Formerly C. of Padiham 1842, St. John's, Liverpool, 1845; P. C. of Rainford 1847–52. [16]

GROOME, John Hindes, *Earl Soham Rectory, near Framlingham, Suffolk.*—R. of Earl-Soham, Dio. Nor. 1845. (Patron, the present R; Tithe, 607*l*; Glebe, 9 acres; R.'s Inc. 623*l* and Ho; Pop. 745.) [17]

GROOME, Robert Hindes, *Monk Soham Rectory, Woodbridge, Suffolk.*—Caius Coll. Cam. B.A. 1832, M.A. 1835; Deac. 1833 and Pr. 1834 by Bp of Nor. R. of Monk-Soham, Dio. Nor. 1845. (Patron, the present R; Tithe, 445*l*; Glebe, 90 acres; R.'s Inc. 620*l* and Ho; Pop. 442.) Hon. Can. of Nor. [18]

GROOMES, John, *Shalford Vicarage, Braintree, Essex.*—Queens' Coll. Cam. B.A. 1834, M.A. 1837; Deac. 1834 and Pr. 1835 by Bp of Lich. V. of Shalford, Dio. Roch. 1848. (Patron, Bp of B. and W; Tithe, 203*l*; V.'s Inc. 327*l* and Ho; Pop. 760.) [19]

GROSE, Thomas, 137, *Fenchurch-street, London, E.C.*—Clare Hall, Cam. Sen. Opt. and B.A. 1827, M.A. 1830; Deac. 1832 by Bp of Ox. Pr. 1833 by Bp of Lon. R. of St. Peter's, Cornhill, Dio. Lon. 1866. (Patron, Corporation of Lond; Pop. 533.) Formerly Lect. of St. John's, Wapping, 1833; Chap. of the Stepney Union 1838; C. of St. Peter's, Cornhill, 1839. Author, *Answer to Tiptaft on the Discipline of the Church of England,* 1832; *Reply to American Anti-Theistical Catechism,* 1834; *Illustrations of the Brazen Tablet in St. Peter's, Cornhill,* 1840; *Sermon* (published by request of the parishioners), 1854. [20]

GROSVENOR, F. J., *Brentwood, Essex.*—C. of Brentwood. [21]

GROVE, Charles, *Odstock Rectory, near Salisbury.*—R. of Odstock, Dio. Salis. 1817. (Patron, Earl of Radnor; R.'s Inc. 285*l* and Ho; Pop. 184.) Preb. of Salis. 1828; Rural Dean. [22]

GROVE, Charles Henry, *Sedgehill, near Shaftesbury.*—Univ. Coll. Ox. B.A. 1816, M.A. 1824; Deac. 1818, Pr. 1819. R. of Berwick St. Leonard with Sedgehill Chap. Dio. Salis. 1826. (Patron, Marquis of Westminster; Tithe, 250*l*; Glebe, 110 acres; R.'s Inc. 330*l*; Pop. Berwick St. Leonard 40, Sedgehill 194.) [23]

GROVE, George, *Llanwenarth, Abergavenny.*—P. C. of Llanwenarth Ultra or Govilon, Dio. Llan. (Patron, R. of Llanwenarth Citra; P. C.'s Inc. 300*l*; Pop. 1547.) [24]

GROVE, John, *Burrington, Wrington, Somerset.*—C. of Burrington. [25]

GROVE, W. H., *Littleport, Ely.*—C. of Littleport 1867. [26]

GROVER, J., *Atherstone, Warwickshire.*—Math. Mast. of Atherstone, Gr. Sch. [27]

GROVER, Thomas Chester, *Wilnecote, Tamworth.*—Emman. Coll. Cam. B.A. 1838, M.A. 1841; Deac. 1838, Pr. 1839. P. C. of Wilnecote, Dio. Lich. 1861. (Patron, V. of Tamworth; P. C.'s Inc. 147*l*; Pop. 1650.) Formerly C. of Warsop. [28]

GROVES, John, *Upper Poppleton, near York.*—King's Coll. Lond. Theol. Assoc. 1864; Deac. 1864 and Pr. 1865 by Abp of York. C. of Upper and Nether Poppleton 1866. Formerly C. of St. Paul's, York, 1864. [29]

GROVES, William Kynaston, *Boulogne sur-Mer, France.*—Ch. Coll. Cam. Latin Prizeman and B.A. 1827, M.A. 1834; Deac. 1833 by Bp of Nor. Pr. 1834 by Bp of Roch. Min. of the Lower British Ch. Boulogne, 1842. [30]

GRUBB, the Ven. Charles Septimus, *Maritzburg, Natal, South Africa.*—Jesus Coll. Cam. B.A. 1854; Deac. 1854 and Pr. 1855 by Bp of Ox. Archd. of Maritzburg. Formerly C. of Bledlow and St. John's, Lacey Green, Bucks, 1855–59. [31]

GRUEBER, Charles Stephen, *Hambridge Parsonage, Curry Rivell, Somerset.*—Magd. Hall, Ox. B.A. 1839; Deac. 1840 and Pr. 1841 by Bp of Win. P. C. of St. James's, Hambridge, Dio. B. and W. 1844. (Patron, Bp of B. and W; P. C.'s Inc. 160*l* and Ho; Pop. 536.) Author, *On the Judgment of the Privy Council in the case of Gorham v. Bishop of Exeter with Appendix on Baptism,* 6*d*; *Holy Baptism, a Complete Statement of the Church's Doctrine, with an Explanatory Comment upon Fifty Passages of Holy Scripture,* 1*s* 6*d*; *The One Faith* (a Sermon), 1*s*; *Article XXIX. considered in Reference to the Three Sermons of the Archdeacon of Taunton,* 6 eds. 1855, 6*d*; *Dr. Lushington's Judgment, in the Case of Westerton v. Liddell, upon Ornaments of the Church. considered by a Parish Priest, who has not in use the Articles complained of,* 2 eds. 1856, 6*d*. [1]

GRUGGEN, Frederick James, *Pocklington, Yorks.*—St. John's Coll. Cam. 6th Wrang. and B.A. 1843, Hulsean Prizeman 1844, M.A. 1846; Deac. 1846 by Bp of Chich. Pr. 1847 by Bp of Ely. Head Mast. of Pocklington Gr. Sch. 1848. (Patron, St. John's Coll. Cam.) Formerly Fell. of St. John's Coll. Cam; Vice-Prin. and Tutor of St. Bees 1847–48. Author, *The Hulsean Prize Essay for* 1844, 3*s* 6*d*. [2]

GRUGGEN, George Septimus, 42, *Leazes-terrace, Newcastle-on-Tyne.*—St. John's Coll. Cam. 22nd Wrang. B.A. 1858, M.A. 1861; Deac. 1858 and Pr. 1859 by Bp of Rip. Asst. Chap. of St. Thomas's, Newcastle-on-Tyne. Formerly C. of Yafforth, Northallerton, 1858–60. Bradfield, Reading, 1861–62. [3]

GRUNDY, George Docker, *Lees Parsonage, near Oldham.*—Brasen. Coll. Ox. B.A. 1829, M.A. 1832; Deac. 1830 and Pr. 1831 by Bp of Lin. P. C. of St. John's, Lees, Dio. Man. 1838. (Patron, R. of Ashton-under-Lyne; P. C.'s Inc. 150*l* and Ho.) Author, several Sermons; *An Exposition of the Church Catechism.* [4]

GRUNDY, George, Frederick, *Liscard, Cheshire.*—Brasen. Coll. Ox. Colquitt Clerical Exhibitioner Double Hon. 4th cl. and S.C.L. 1852, B.A. 1857, M.A. 1867; Deac. 1857, Pr. 1858. Head Mast. of Tower Sch. Liscard. Formerly C. of St. Catherine's, Liverpool, 1857–59. [5]

GRUNDY, Thomas Richard, *Styal, Handforth, near Manchester.*—Brasen. Coll. Ox. B.A. 1860, M.A. 1863; Deac. 1861 and Pr. 1862 by Bp of Pet. C. of Styal Chapel, Wilmslow, Cheshire, 1866. Formerly C. of Wardeley with Belton, Rutland, and Ightham, Kent. [6]

GRUNDY, William James, *St. James the Less Parsonage, Victoria-park, Bethnal-green, London, N.E.*—Literate; Deac. 1851, Pr. 1852. P. C. of St. James's the Less, Dio. Lon. 1839. (Patron, Bp of Lon; P. C.'s Inc. 200*l*; Pop. 6000.) Formerly R. of Kilvington, Notts. [7]

GRYLLS, Charles, *Lanhydrock, Bodmin, Cornwall.*—Trin. Coll. Cam. B.A. 1833; Deac. 1835 by Bp of B. and W. Pr. 1836 by Bp of Ex. P. C. of Lanhydrock, Dio. Ex. 1844. (Patron, T. J. Agar-Robartes, Esq. M.P; Pop. 197.) Preb. of Endellion 1844. Formerly C. of Illogan 1835, Bodmin 1841; Chap. to County Lunatic Asylum 1842. [8]

GUARD, John, *Langtree Rectory, Torrington, Devon.*—Oriel Coll. Ox. B.A. 1828, M.A. 1831; Deac. 1830 and Pr. 1831 by Bp of Ex. R. of Langtree, Dio. Ex. 1839. (Patron, the Hon. Mark Rolle; Tithe, 470*l*; Glebe, 67 acres; R.'s Inc. 520*l* and Ho; Pop. 887.) Organising Sec. of S.P.G. for the Archdeaconry of Barnstaple 1860. Formerly C. of Dunchideock 1830–31; P. C. of St. Giles, Torrington, 1832–39; Lect. of Great Torrington 1837–38–39. Author, *A Christian Scholar's Manual,* 1834; *A Visitation Sermon,* 1836; *A Sermon preached at the Anniversary of the Exeter Free Grammar School, In Memoriam C. H. Collyns, D.D.* 1862. [9]

GUBBINS, Richard Shard, *Upham, Bishop Waltham.*—St. John's Coll. Cam. B.A. 1850, M.A. 1853; Deac. 1852 and Pr. 1853 by Bp of Win. C. of Upham, Hants, 1859. Formerly C. of Crawley, Hants, 1852, Brightwell, Berks, 1858. [10]

GUERRITZ, Mamerto, *The Vicarage, Colyton, Devon.*—St. Edm. Hall, Ox. B.A. 1848; Deac. 1848 and Pr. 1849 by Bp of B. and W. V. of Colyton, Dio. Ex. 1860. (Patrons, D. and C. of Exeter; Tithe—Imp. 800*l*, V. 460*l*; Glebe, 5 acres; V.'s Inc. 520*l* and Ho; Pop. 2446.) Formerly C. of Bigbury 1854–57, Penzance 1857–60. Editor and Translator of various Spanish Works. [11]

GUEST, Charles, *Burton-on-Trent.*—St. Aidan's; Deac. 1857 and Pr. 1858 by Bp of Ches. P. C. of Ch. Ch. Burton-on-Trent, Dio. Lich. 1864. (Patron, P. C. of Burton; P. C.'s Inc. 300*l* and Ho; Pop. 10,000.) Formerly C. of St. Clement's, Windsor, Liverpool, St. Thomas's, Liverpool, Tamworth, and Bicester; Chap. of Don. of Newton Solney. Author, *Sunday, the Lord's Day,* 1867. [12]

GUEST, George William, *York.*—St. John's Coll. Cam. B.A. 1853, M.A. 1857; Deac. 1854 and Pr. 1855 by Bp of Man. Min. Can. of York Cathl. 1862 (Inc. 280*l*); R. of All Saints', North-street, York, 1864. (Patron, Ld Chan; R.'s Inc. 165*l*; Pop. 1417.) Formerly C. of St. Stephen's, Salford, 1854, Sutton-on-the-Hill 1856; P. C. of Derwent 1859. [13]

GUEST, Thomas Hill, *Hightown, Manchester.*—Ch. Coll. Cam. Scho. and Prizeman, 3rd cl. Cl. Trip. 28th Wrang. B.A. 1862, M.A. 1865; Deac. 1864 and Pr. 1865 by Bp of Man. C. of St. Luke's, Cheetham, Manchester, 1866. Formerly C. of St. Philip's, Bradford-road, Manchester, 1864–66. [14]

GUILDING, John Melville, *Sowerby, Thirsk.*—King's Coll. Lond; Deac. 1852 and Pr. 1853 by Abp of York. V. of Sowerby, Dio. York, 1865. (Patron, Abp of York; Tithe, 270*l*; V.'s Inc. 320*l* and Ho; Pop. 1267.) Formerly C. of Crayke, Yorks, 1852, All Souls', Langham-place, Lond. 1854; Gov. Chap. Bermuda, 1856; C. of Thirsk, Yorks, 1863. [15]

GUILLE, Charles Sydney, *St. Peter Port, Guernsey.*—Wad. Coll. Ox. B.A. 1854, M.A. 1856; Deac. 1855 and Pr. 1856 by Bp of Lich. C. of St. Peter Port, Guernsey. Formerly Asst. C. of Sheriff Hales, Salop. [16]

GUILLE, Edward, *St. Luke's House, St. Luke's New Parish, Jersey.*—St. John's Coll. Cam. B.A. 1831; Deac. 1831, Pr. 1832. P. C. of St. Luke's, Dio. Win. 1846. (Patrons, the Crown and Bp of Win. alt; Endow. 150*l*; P. C.'s Inc. 230*l*.) [17]

GUILLE, George De Carteret, *Little Torrington Rectory, Devon.*—Pemb. Coll. Ox. B.A. 1839, M.A. 1843; Deac. 1840 and Pr. 1841 by Bp of Win. R. of Little Torrington, Dio. Ex. 1853. (Patrons, Lord Rolle and others; Tithe, 460*l*; Glebe, 44 acres; R.'s Inc. 506*l* and Ho; Pop 563.) [18]

GUILLE, Philip, *St. Martin's Rectory, St. Heliers, Jersey.*—R. of St. Martin's, Dio. Win. 1838. (Patron, the Governor; R.'s Inc. 210*l* and Ho; Pop. 3558.) [19]

GUILLE, The Very Rev. William, *St. Peter Port Rectory, Guernsey.*—Oriel Coll. Ox. 1st cl. Lit. Hum. and B.A. 1814, M.A. 1817; Deac. 1816, Pr. 1817. R. of St. Peter Port, Dio. Win. 1858. (Patron, the Governor; R.'s Inc. 860*l* and Ho.) Dean of Guernsey. Formerly R. of St. Andrew's, Guernsey, 1837–58. [20]

GUILLEBAUD, Henry Lea, *Thurgarton, Southwell, Notts.*—Trin. Coll. Cam. 15th Wrang. and B.A. 1839, M.A. 1842; Deac. 1841 and Pr. 1842 by Bp of Ely. P. C. of Thurgarton with Hoveringham, Dio. Lin. 1848. (Patron, Trin. Coll. Cam; Thurgarton, Glebe, 3 acres; Hoveringham, Tithe—Imp. 36*l* 16*s*; P. C.'s Inc. 168*l*; Pop. Thurgarton 361, Hoveringham 367.) Formerly Fell. of Trin. Coll. Cam. [21]

GUILLEMARD, William Henry, *Royal College, Armagh, Ireland.*—Pemb. Coll. Cam. 6th in 1st cl. Cl. Trip. 28th Wrang. Crosse Scho. 1838, B.A. 1838, Tyrwhitt Heb. Scho. 1841, M.A. 1842, B.D. 1849; Deac. 1841 by Bp of Ely, Pr. 1843 by Bp of Bristol. Head Mast. of the Royal Coll. Armagh, 1848. (Patron, Abp of Armagh.) Fell. of Pemb. Coll. Cam. [22]

GUINNESS, Frederick William, *Manchester.*—St. John's Coll. Cam. B.A. 1862; Deac. 1862 by

Abp of York. Formerly C. of Attercliffe, Sheffield, 1863. [1]

GUINNESS, Robert, *Wantage, Berks.*—Queen's Coll. Ox. B.A. 1863; Deac. 1864 by Bp of Ox. C. of Wantage. [2]

GUINNESS, Robert Wyndham, *Vicarage, Guiting Power, Winchcomb, Gloucestershire.*—St. John's Coll. Cam. 2nd cl. Nat. Sci. Trip. B.A. 1862, M.A. 1866; Deac. 1863 and Pr. 1864 by Bp of G. and B. C. in sole charge of Guiting Power with Farmcote 1867. Formerly C. of St. James's, Bristol, and Chap. to the Bristol Penitentiary 1863; C. of Cheltenham 1864. [3]

GUISE, Frederick Charles, M.A., *Longhope Vicarage, Gloucester.*—V. of Longhope, Dio. G. and B. 1861. (Patron, Sir J. W. Guise; Tithe, 400*l*; Glebe, 20 acres; V.'s Inc. 420*l* and Ho; Pop. 1104.) [4]

GUISE, George Clifford, *Pulverbatch Rectory, Shrewsbury.*—Dur. B.A. 1841, M.A. 1843; Deac. 1841 and Pr. 1842 by Bp of G. and B. R. of Pulverbatch, Dio. Herf. 1848. (Patroness, Miss Webb; Tithe, 530*l*; Glebe, 45 acres; R.'s Inc. 575*l* and Ho; Pop. 534.) [5]

GULL, George Eckford, *Rusthall, Tunbridge Wells.*—Lond. Hons. in Physiology, B.A. 1858; Deac. and Pr. 1864 by Abp of Cant. Formerly C. of St Paul's, Rusthall, 1864–66. [6]

GUMLEY, William.—C. of St. Stephen's, Old Ford, Bow, Middlesex. [7]

GUNN, John, *Barton-Turf Vicarage, Neatishead, Norfolk.*—Ex. Coll. Ox. B.A. 1824, M.A. 1827; Deac. 1829 by Bp of Nor. Pr. 1829 by Bp of Pet. V. of Barton-Turf with Irstead R. Dio. Nor. 1829. (Patron, Bp of Nor; Barton-Turf. Tithe—App. 295*l* 19*s* and 2 roods of Glebe, V. 171*l* 1*s*; Glebe, 34 acres; Irstead, Tithe, 202*l*; Glebe, 13 acres; V.'s Inc. 451*l* and Ho; Pop. Barton-Turf 379, Irstead 149.) Rural Dean of Waxham 1842. [8]

GUNNER, Edward, *Great Cheverel Rectory, Devizes, Wilts.*—Trin. Coll. Ox. B.A. 1846, M.A. 1847; Deac. 1846 by Abp. of York, Pr. 1847 by Bp of Rip. R. of Cheverel Magna, Dio. Salis. 1865. (Patron, the present R; Glebe, 305 acres; R.'s Inc. 400*l* and Ho; Pop. 561.) Formerly C. of Whiston, Yorks, 1846–49, Hambledon, Hants, 1849–51, Waltham St. Lawrence, Berks, 1858–65. [9]

GUNNERY, Reginald, *Upper Hornsey Rise, London, N.*— St. John's Coll. Cam. B.A. 1847, M.A. 1850; Deac. and Pr. 1848 by Abp of York. P. C. of St. Mary's, Hornsey Rise, Dio. Lon. 1861.) (Patrons, Trustees; P. C.'s Inc. 400*l*; Pop. 3500.) Formerly C. of St. Mary's, Hull, 1848–53; Sec. to the Ch. of England Education Society 1854. [10]

GUNNING, Sir Henry John, *Horton, Northampton.*—Ball. Coll. Ox. B.A. 1820, M.A. 1822; Deac. 1821, Pr. 1822. Formerly R. of Knockin 1822–25; P. C. of Horton 1826–33; R. of Wigan 1833–64. Author, *Tract upon Self-Examination*, 1830; *The Observance of the Sabbath* (a Tract), 1835; *Relative Duties at the present Crisis* (a Sermon), 1842. [11]

GUNNING, Joseph Wiat, *East Boldre, Beaulieu, Southampton.*—Queens' Coll. Cam. Jun. Opt. B.A. 1840, King's Coll. Lond. Hebrew Prize 1836; Deac. 1841 and Pr. 1842 by Bp of G. and B. P. C. of East Boldre, Dio. Win. 1842. (Patron, Bp of Win; Glebe, ½ acre; P. C.'s Inc. 102*l* and Ho; Pop. 690.) Formerly C. of Swindon, Wilts, 1841–42. [12]

GUNNING, Peter, *Inwardleigh Rectory, Exbourne, Devon.*—Deac. 1837, Pr. 1839. R. of Inwardleigh, Dio. Ex. 1845. (Patrons, Trustees; Tithe, 250*l* 1*s*; Glebe, 230 acres; R.'s Inc. 360*l* and Ho; Pop. 535.) [13]

GUNSON, William Mandell, *Christ's College, Cambridge.*—Ch. Coll. Cam. Wrang. 1st cl. Cl. Trip. and B.A. 1847, M.A. 1850; Deac. and Pr. 1849 by Bp of Ely. Fell. and Tut. of Ch. Coll. Cam. 1851. [14]

GUNTER, W.—Chap. of H.M.S. "Egmont." [15]

GUNTON, John, *Marsham Rectory, Norwich.*—Ch. Coll. Cam. Sen. Opt. and B.A. 1828; Deac. 1829 and Pr. 1830 by Bp of Nor. R. of Marsham, Dio. Nor. 1844. (Patron, Earl of Lichfield; Tithe, comm. 344*l*; Glebe, 66 acres; R.'s Inc. 400*l* 10*s* and Ho; Pop. 630.) [16]

GURDEN, William, *Westbury Vicarage, Buckingham.*—Lin. Coll. Ox. B.A. 1814. V. of Westbury, Dio. Ox. 1817. (Patron, Hon. P. Barrington; Tithe—Imp. 5*l*, V. 64*l* 18*s*; V.'s Inc. 109*l* and Ho; Pop. 379.) [17]

GURDON, Edward, *Barnham Broom, Wymondham, Norfolk.*—Trin. Coll. Cam. B.A. 1835, M.A. 1838; Deac. 1839 and Pr. 1841 by Bp of Nor. R. of Barnham Broom with Bixton R. and Kimberley V. Dio. Nor. 1848. (Patron, Earl of Kimberley; Tithe, 604*l*; Glebe, 126 acres; R.'s Inc. 800*l* and Ho; Pop. Barnham Broom 481, Kimberley 112.) Rural Dean. Formerly C. of Hackford 1839–40, Reymerston 1841–48. [18]

GURDON, Philip, *Cranworth, Shipdham, Norfolk.*—R. of Reymerstone, Dio. Nor. 1825. (Patron, B. Gurdon, Esq; Tithe—App. 8*l* 15*s*, R. 469*l* 10*s* 6*d*; Glebe, 18¾ acres; R.'s Inc. 493*l* and Ho; Pop. 321. R. of South-Burgh, near Watton, Dio. Nor. 1828. (Patron, B. Gurdon, Esq; R.'s Inc. 249*l*; Pop. 317.) R. of Cranworth with Letton R. near Shipdham, Dio. Nor. 1832. (Patron, B. Gurdon, Esq; Cranworth, Tithe, 214*l* 8*s*; Glebe, 28 acres; Letton, Tithe, 200*l*; R.'s Inc. 449*l* and Ho; Pop. Cranworth 264, Letton 111.) [19]

GURLEY, George Mathews, *Warkworth, Alnwick, Northumberland.*—C. of Warkworth. [20]

GURNEY, Archer, *Paris.*—Deac. 1849, Pr. 1850. Formerly Sen. C. of Buckingham. Author, *King Charles I.* (Dramatic Poem); *Spring Songs of the Present*; etc. [21]

GURNEY, Augustus William, *Wribbenhall, Stourport.*—P. C. of Wribbenhall, Dio. Wor. 1864. (Patron, V. of Kidderminster; P. C.'s Inc. 150*l*; Pop. 1057.) [22]

GURNEY, Frederick, *Torwood, Devon.*—C. of Torwood. [23]

GURNEY, H. F. S., *Chadderton, Oldham.*—C. of St. Matthew's, Chadderton. [24]

GURNEY, Henry Peter, *Uffington Vicarage, Faringdon, Berks.*—St. John's Coll. Cam. B.A. 1848; Deac. and Pr. 1850. V. of Uffington, Dio. Ox. 1855. (Patron, C. Eyre, Esq; V.'s Inc. 350*l* and Ho; Pop. 644) Formerly R. of Tregony with Cuby, Cornwall, 1850–55. [25]

GURNEY, John Langton, *Castle Hill, Lincoln.*—St. Bees; Deac. 1862 and Pr. 1863 by Bp of Lich. C. of Riseholme and South Carlton 1865. Formerly C. of Tamworth 1862. [26]

GURNEY, John Phillips, *Great Canfield Vicarage, Great Dunmow, Essex.*—Queens' Coll. Cam. B.A. 1823, M.A. 1834; Deac. 1822 by Bp of Ely, Pr. 1822 by Bp of Lon. V. of Great Canfield, Dio. Roch. 1822. (Patron, J. M. Wilson, Esq; Tithe—Imp. 592*l* 3*s*, V. 132*l* 8*s*; Glebe, ¾ acres; V.'s Inc. 140*l* and Ho; Pop. 468.) Formerly Chap. of Black Chapel, Great Waltham, Essex. Author, *The Death and Resurrection of the Two Witnesses*, 1849, 6*d*; *The Woman and the Dragon, or the Conflict between Christianity and Paganism, being an Exposition of the 12th Chapter of the Apocalypse* (a Tract), 1851, 1*s*; *The Question, Are you a True Christian? considered, or a few Remarks addressed to Every One*, 1854, 4*d*; *The Approaching Fall of Rome*, 1857. [27]

GURNEY, Thomas William Henry, *Clavering Vicarage, Essex.*—St. John's Coll. Cam. late Scho. Wrang. B.A. 1837, M.A. 1851; Deac. 1838 and Pr. 1839 by Bp of Lon. V. of Clavering with Langley C. Dio. Roch. 1862. (Patrons, the Governors of Christ's Hospital; Tithe, Clavering—Imp. 504*l*, V. 466*l* 1*s* 8*d*, Langley—Imp. 152*l*, V. 153*l*; Glebe, Clavering, 7 acres, Langley, 43 acres; V.'s Inc. 679*l* and Ho; Pop. Clavering 1047, Langley 410.) Formerly Mast. of Mr. Travers's Sch. Christ's Hospital and Lect. on Sir Wolstan Dixie's Foundation at St. Michael's Bassishaw, Lond. [28]

GURNEY, William, *Doncaster.*—Emman. Coll. Cam. Wrang. and B.A. 1847, M.A. 1853; Deac. 1848 and Pr. 1853 by Bp of Ches. Head Mast. of the Gr. Sch. Doncaster, 1862. Formerly Head Mast. of the Goldsmiths' Gr. Sch. Stockport, 1847. [29]

GURNEY, William Hay, *North Runcton Rectory, King's Lynn, Norfolk.*—Trin. Coll. Cam. B.A. 1850, M.A. 1858; Deac. 1851 and Pr. 1852 by Bp of Pet. R. of North Runcton with Hardwick R. and Setchy R. Dio. Nor. 1861. (Patron, D. Gurney, Esq; Tithe, 738*l* 18*s*: Glebe, 23 acres; R.'s Inc. 870*l* and Ho; Pop. 395.) Formerly C. of St. Nicholas', Leicester, 1851–52, North Runcton 1852–61. [1]

GURNEY, William Walter, *Roborough Rectory, Torrington, Devon.*—R. of Roborough, Dio. Ex. 1837. (Patron, Rev. Thomas May; Tithe, 280*l* 8*s*; R.'s Inc. 304*l* and Ho; Pop. 478.) [2]

GURNEY, William Warren, *Lightcliffe, Todmorden, Yorks.*—P. C. of Lightcliffe, Dio. Rip. 1840. (Patron, V. of Halifax; P. C.'s Inc. 150*l*; Pop. 2347.) [3]

GURNHILL, James, 45, *George-street, Hull.*—Emman. Coll. Cam. B.A. 1862; Deac. 1862 and Pr. 1863 by Abp of York. C. of Trinity, Hull, 1862. Author, *English Retraced*, Bell and Daldy, 5*s*. [4]

GUTCH, Charles, 39, *Upper Park-place, Dorset-square, London, N.W.*—Sid. Coll. Cam. B.A. 1844, M.A. 1847, B.D. 1854; Deac. 1845 and Pr. 1847 by Bp of Ely. Fell. of Sid. Coll. Cam; P. C. of St. Cyprian's, Marylebone, Dio. Lon. 1866. (Patrons, Trustees; P. C.'s Inc. 152*l*; Pop. 3000.) Formerly C. of All Saints', Marylebone. Author, *The Work and Will of God* (a Sermon), Masters; *The Way to resist Roman and State Aggression* (a Sermon), ib; *Sound an Alarm, or the Consequences of altering the Prayer Book* (a Sermon), Leicester, 1850; *The sure Judgment of God on the Rich for Neglect of the Poor* (a Sermon), Leeds; *The Stained Glass Window in the Parish Church* (a Sermon), Masters; *The Will of God our Sanctification*, Hayes; "*Give ye them to Eat*," Church Press; *The Profaneness of Pharaoh*, Rivingtons. [5]

GUTTERES, Frederick Edward.—Chap. of H.M.S. "Narcissus." [6]

GUY, Frederic Barlow, *Forest School, Walthamstow, Essex.*—Lin. Coll. Ox. 1844, B.A. 1848, M.A. 1850, D.D. 1866; Deac. 1848 and Pr. 1851 by Bp of Ox. Head Mast. of the Forest Sch. Walthamstow, 1856. Formerly Head Mast. of St. Andrew's Coll. Bradfield, 1850–52. [7]

GUY, Henry, *Asby Rectory, Appleby, Westmoreland.*—St. Bees; Deac. 1821 and Pr. 1822 by Bp of Carl. R. of Asby, Dio. Carl. 1834. (Patroness, Miss Hill; Tithe, 224*l*; Glebe, 5½ acres; R.'s Inc. 236*l* and Ho; Pop. 440.) [8]

GUY, Henry Wills, *Winterbourne-Clenstone Rectory, Blandford, Dorset.*—Ex. Coll. Ox. B.A. 1840. R. of Winterbourne-Clenstone, Dio. Salis. 1845. (Patron, the Pleydell and Damer Families alt; Tithe, 190*l*; Glebe, 2½ acres; R.'s Inc. 195*l* and Ho; Pop. 106.) [9]

GUYON, Charles Langford, *Lamyat Rectory, Evercreech, near Bath.*—Wad. Coll. Ox. B.A. 1833, M.A. 1836; Deac. 1833 and Pr. 1834 by Bp of Ex. R. of Lamyat, Dio. B. and W. 1841. (Patrons, Trustees; Tithe, 210*l*; Glebe, 43 acres; R.'s Inc. 291*l* and Ho; Pop. 240.) [10]

GWATKIN, Thomas, *Dulwich College, S.*—St. John's Coll. Cam. 1st cl. Cl. Trip. B.A. 1862, M.A. 1865; Deac. 1865 and Pr. 1866 by Bp of Ely. Fell. of St. John's Coll. Cam; Asst. Mast. at Dulwich Coll. [11]

GWILLYM, Richard, *Stockbridge House, Ulverston.*—Brasen. Coll. Ox. B.A. 1825, M.A. 1827; Deac. 1827 and Pr. 1829 by Bp of Ches. P. C. of Ulverston, Dio. Carl. 1835. (Patron, Rev. Alfred Peache; Glebe, 121 acres; P. C.'s Inc. 163*l*; Pop. 5938.) Surrogate; Rural Dean 1837; Dep. Chancellor of Carlisle 1862; Hon. Can. of Carlisle 1864; Dom. Chap. to Lord Harrowby 1836. Formerly C. of West Derby, Liverpool, 1827, St. Stephen's, Exeter, 1833. [12]

GWILT, Robert, *Icklingham Rectory, Mildenhall, Suffolk.*—Caius Coll. Cam. B.A. and M.A. 1836; Deac. 1836 and Pr. 1838 by Bp of Ely. R. of Icklingham St. James with Icklingham All Saints, Dio. Ely, 1857. (Patron, the present R; Tithe, comm. 560*l*; Glebe, 34 acres; R.'s Inc. 600*l* and Ho; Pop. 625.) [13]

GWYN, James Bevan, *Merthyr Mawr, Bridgend, Glamorganshire.*—Jesus Coll. Ox. Hon. 4th cl. in Law and Mod. Hist. B.A. 1854, M.A. 1857; Deac. 1857 and Pr. 1858 by Bp of Llan. P. C. of Merthyr Mawr, Dio. Llan. 1863. (Patroness, Mrs. Nicholl; P. C.'s Inc. 92*l*; Pop. 174.) Formerly C. of Cowbridge 1857–59; P. C. of Monknash 1859–63. [14]

GWYN, P. Preston, *Little Brandon, Norfolk.*—R. of Little Brandon, Dio. Nor. 1862. (Patron, Isaac Preston, Esq; R.'s Inc. 300*l*; Pop. 208.) [15]

GWYN, Richard, *The Elms, Shrewsbury.*—Magd. Coll. Cam. B.A. 1848; Deac. 1848 and Pr. 1850 by Bp of Ches. Formerly C. of Marton, Chester, 1849–50, Prees, Salop, 1851–52, Stanton, Salop, 1853–54, Fradswell, Staffs, 1855–56. [16]

GWYN, Richard Hamond, *South Repps, Norwich.*—Ex. Coll. Ox. B.A. 1835; Deac. 1839 and Pr. 1840 by Bp of Nor. R. of South Repps, Dio. Nor. 1862. (Patron, Duchy of Lancaster; R.'s Inc. 700*l* and Ho; Pop. 816.) Formerly V. of Roughton, Norwich, 1855–62. [17]

GWYNN, Thomas, *Marlow Place, Great Marlow.*—Ch. Ch. Ox. B.A. 1847, M.A. 1850; Deac. 1849 and Pr. 1850 by Bp of Ox. Formerly Chap. of Ch. Ch. 1849–51; Asst. Mast. in Marlborough Coll. 1851–57; Head Mast. of Aylesbury Gr. Sch. 1857–61. [18]

GWYNNE, G. F. J. G. E., *Bettws, Newtown, Montgomeryshire.*—C. of Bettws. [19]

GWYTHER, Henry, *Yardley Vicarage, Birmingham.*—Trin. Coll. Cam. B.A. 1817, M.A. 1820; Deac. 1817, Pr. 1819. V. of Yardley, Dio. Wor. 1821. (Patron, J. M. Severne, Esq; Glebe, 322 acres; V.'s Inc. 600*l* and Ho; Pop. 3354.) Author, *The Psalmist*; *Cottager's Week*; *Joshua*; Sermons; etc. [20]

GWYTHER, John, *Fewston Vicarage, Otley, Yorks.*—St. John's Coll. Cam. B.A. 1827; Deac. 1828, Pr. 1829. V. of Fewston with Thurcross C. and West End C. Dio. Rip. 1844. (Patron, Ld Chan; Allotment in lieu of Tithes, 750 acres; Glebe, 20 acres; V.'s Inc. 150*l* and Ho; Pop. 1485.) [21]

GYLES, Edwin, *All Saints' Parsonage, Nottingham.*—St. John's, Coll. Cam. Sen. Opt. B.A. 1856, M.A. 1864; Deac. 1856 and Pr. 1857 by Bp of Ches. P. C. of All Saints', Nottingham, Dio. Lin. 1864. (Patrons, W. Windley, Esq. and others; P. C.'s Inc. 400*l* and Ho; Pop. 6000.) Formerly C. of St. John's, Lowestoft, 1857; V. of Laughton with Wildsworth, Lincolnshire, 1860.) [22]

HACKMAN, Adolphus, *Epsom, Surrey.*—Brasen. Coll. Ox. B.A. 1849, M.A. 1852; Deac. 1854. Asst. Mast. at the College, Epsom. [23]

HACKMAN, Alfred, *Christ Church, Oxford.*—Ch. Ch. Ox. Hon. 4th cl. Lit. Hum. and B.A. 1837, M.A. 1840; Deac. 1837 and Pr. 1839 by Bp of Ox. Precentor of Ch. Ch. Cathl. Ox. 1841. (Value, 75*l* and Res.) P. C. of St. Paul's, Oxford, Dio. Ox. 1844. (Patron, Bp of Ox; P. C.'s Inc. 150*l*; Pop. 2915.) [24]

HACON, Henry, *Purfleet, Romford, Essex.*—St. Bees, Rupert's Land Prizeman; Deac. 1862 and Pr. 1863 by Bp of Roch. Formerly C. of Fairstead, 1862, and West Thurrock with Purfleet 1864. [25]

HACON, James, *Crosby Ravensworth, Westmoreland.*—St. Bees; Deac. 1861 and Pr. 1862 by Bp of Carl C. of Crosby Ravensworth 1863. Formerly C. of St. Michael's, Appleby, 1861–63; P. C. of Hilton with Murton, Westmoreland, 1862–63. [26]

HADATH, Edward Evans, *Spalding, Lincolnshire.*—Dub. A.B. 1858, A.M. 1861, M.A. *com. causâ*, Ox. 1865; Deac. 1861 and Pr. 1863 by Bp of Rip. C. of Spalding 1866. Formerly C. of Little Holbeck, Leeds, 1861, Ossett with Gawthorpe 1863, Wath-on-Dearne 1866. [27]

HADDAN, Alfred Smethurst, *Clay Cross, Chesterfield.*—St. Edm. Hall, Ox. B.A. 1861; Deac. 1863 and Pr. 1864 by Bp of B. and W. C. of Clay Cross 1867. Formerly C. of Compton Dando, Somerset, 1863–65. [28]

HADDAN, Arthur West, *Barton-on-the-Heath, Warwickshire.*—Trin. Coll. Ox. 1st cl. Lit. Hum. 2nd cl. Math. et Phy. and B.A. 1837, M.A. 1840 B.D. 1847; Deac. 1840 and Pr. 1842 by Bp of Ox. R. of Barton-on-the-Heath, Dio. Wor. 1857. (Patron, Trin. Coll. Ox; R.'s Inc. 380*l* and Ho; Pop. 184.) Fell. of Trin. Coll. Ox; Public Examiner in Lit. Hum. 1848. [1]

HADDOCK, Jeremiah William, 1, *Windsor-terrace, Bedford.*—Clare Coll. Cam. B.A. 1849, M.A. 1853; Deac. 1850 and Pr. 1851 by Bp of Ely. V. of Clapham, Beds. Dio. Ely, 1861. (Patron, Rev. Lord J. Thynne; Tithe, 157*l* 9*s* 10*d*; Glebe, 75 acres; V.'s Inc. 300*l*; Pop. 582.) Formerly C. of Kempston 1850-55, Northill, 1857-58, Campton with Shefford 1858-61, all three in Beds. [2]

HADDOCK, Joseph, *Thorpe-by-Ixworth, Bury St. Edmunds.*—Chap. of the D. of Thorpe-by-Ixworth, Dio. Ely, 1824. (Patron, Sir Charles Lamb, Bart; Chap.'s Inc. 23*l*; Pop. 139.) [3]

HADDON, Thomas Cornfield, *Frethorpe, Acle, Norfolk.*—St. John's Coll. Cam. LL.B. 1831; Deac. 1830 by Bp of Lin. Pr. 1837 by Bp of Roch. P. C. of Tunstall, Norfolk, Dio. Nor. 1840. (Patron, Bp of Nor; Tithe, Imp. 389*l* 12*s*; Glebe, 33 acres; P. C.'s Inc. 75*l*; Pop. 112.) [4]

HADEN, John Clarke, *Hutton Rectory, Brentwood, Essex,* and 4, *Dean's Yard, Westminster, London, S.W.*—Corpus Coll. Cam. B.A. 1827, M.A. 1830; Deac. 1828, Pr. 1829. Priest in Ordinary to the Queen 1834 (Value, 78*l*.) R. of Hutton, Dio. Roch. 1839. (Patrons, D. and C. of St. Paul's; Tithe, 360*l*; Glebe, 22 acres; R.'s Inc. 413*l* and Ho; Pop. 400.) Precentor of Westminster Abbey 1846. (Value, 300*l* and Ho.) Formerly Min. Can. of St. Paul's. [5]

HADFIELD, Alfred, *Silverdale Parsonage, near Lancaster.*—St. Mary Hall, Ox. B.A. 1829, M.A. 1832; Deac. 1829 and Pr. 1831 by Bp of Lich. P. C. of Silverdale, Warton, Dio. Man. 1850. (Patron, V. of Warton; Tithe—App. 88*l*; P. C.'s Inc. 96*l* and Ho; Pop. 294.) Formerly P. C. of Trinity, Bolton-le-Moors, 1838–49. [6]

HADFIELD, James, *Witchampton, Wimborne, Dorset.*—St. John's Coll. Cam. B.A. 1850, M.A. 1853; Deac. 1850, Pr. 1851. C. of Witchampton and Hinton Parva. [7]

HADLEY, James, *Bagthorpe, Rougham, Norfolk.*—R. of Bagthorpe, Dio. Nor. 1860. (Patron, Rev. S. R. Cattley; R.'s Inc. 130*l*; Pop. 69.) [8]

HADOW, Charles Edward, *East Barnet, Herts.*—Trin. Coll. Ox. B.A. 1851; Deac. 1852, Pr. 1853. R. of East Barnett, Dio. Roch. 1866. (Patron, the Crown; R.'s Inc. 700*l* and Ho; Pop. 651.) Formerly Chap. in Bengal. [9]

HADOW, George, *Tidcombe Rectory, Tiverton, Devon.*—Ball. Coll. Ox. B.A. 1839, M.A. 1840; Deac. 1840, Pr. 1841. R. of Tidcombe Portion with Chevithorne, C. Dio. Ex. 1865. (Patron, Earl of Harrowby and others; R.'s Inc. 780*l* and Ho.) Formerly V. of St. Just-in-Penwith, Cornwall, 1855–65. [10]

HADOW, William Elliot, *Ebrington Vicarage, Moreton-in-Marsh.*—Ch. Coll. Cam. Found. Scho. and Porteous Gold Medallist, Jun. Opt. and B.A. 1849, M.A. 1852; Deac. 1851 and Pr. 1852 by Bp of Ex. V. of Ebrington, Dio. G. and B. 1865. (Patron, Ld Chan; Glebe, 44 acres; V.'s Inc. 126*l* and Ho; Pop. 576.) Formerly Asst. C. of Tavistock and Brent Tor, Devon, 1854–57; Even. Lect. of Tavistock 1855–57; C. of St. Mary Tavy, Devon, 1857–58, Ebrington, Glouc. 1858–65. [11]

HAGGARD, Christopher, *Barnstaple, Devon.*—Ch. Ch. Ox. B.A. 1851, M.A. 1854; Deac. 1852 and Pr. 1853 by Bp of Win. P. C. of Trinity, Barnstaple, Dio. Ex. 1862. (Patron, Bp of Ex; P. C.'s Inc. 110*l* and Ho; Pop. 1655.) Formerly C. of St. Anne's, Wandsworth, Surrey. [12]

HAGUE, Samuel, *Queen's Park, Chester.*—Dur. Licen. in Theol. 1856; Deac. 1856 and Pr. 1857 by Bp of Dur. C. of Waverton 1867. Formerly C. of Trinity, Sunderland, 1856, All Saints', Manchester, 1860, Trinity, Hulme, 1864. [13]

HAIGH, Daniel, *Buckden Vicarage, Hunts.*—St. Cath. Hall, Cam. 1st Jun. Opt. and B.A. 1834, M.A. 1838; Deac. 1836, Pr. 1837. V. of Buckden, Dio. Ely, 1850. (Patron, Bp of Pet; Glebe, 64 acres; V.'s Inc. 234*l* and Ho; Pop. 1699.) Surrogate 1850. [14]

HAIGH, John, *Shirley Parsonage, Southampton.*—Queen's Coll. Ox. Hon. 4th cl. B.A. 1838, M.A. 1846; Deac. 1838 and Pr. 1839 by Bp of Rip. P. C. of Shirley, Dio. Win. 1862. (Patron, Rev. G. G. Lawrence; P. C.'s Inc. 480*l* and Ho; Pop. 4941.) Formerly P. C. of St. Paul's, Huddersfield, 1844–62. [15]

HAIGH, Henry, *Petersfield, Hants.*—Trin. Coll. Cam. B.A. 1859, M.A. 1863; Deac. 1861 and Pr. 1862 by Bp of Win. C. of Petersfield. [16]

HAILSTONE, John, *Bottisham, Newmarket, Cambs.*—Trin. Coll. Cam. B.A. 1832, M.A. 1835; Deac. 1833 and Pr. 1834 by Bp of Ely. Formerly V. of Bottisham 1837–61; Rural Dean. [17]

HAINES, Herbert, *Hampden House, Gloucester.*—Ex. Coll. Ox. B.A. 1848, M.A. 1851; Deac. 1849 by Bp of Ches. Pr. 1850 by Bp of G. and B. 2nd Mast. of the Glouc. Coll. Sch. 1850; Chap. to the County Lunatic Asylum 1854. Author, *A Manual for the Study of Monumental Brasses,* for the Architectural Society, 1848, 10*s* 6*d*; *Rules for the Gender of Latin Nouns, and the Perfects and Supines of Verbs, with Hints on Latin Construing, &c.,* 1855, 1*s* 6*d*; *A Manual of Monumental Brasses, and List of those remaining in the British Isles, with 200 Illustrations,* 1861, 21*s*; *St. Paul, a Witness to the Resurrection* (a Sermon before the Univ. of Ox.), 1867, 1*s*; *A Guide to the Cathedral Church of Gloucester,* 1867, 1*s* 6*d*. [18]

HAINES, Samuel Charles, *Northampton.*—Chap. to Northampton Lunatic Asylum 1864. Formerly C. of Ingersoll, Canada West, 1859; Incumb. of Durham, C.W. 1860, Sheetsville, C.W. 1863. [19]

HAINS, Philip F. J. B., *Wigan.*—P. C. of St. George's, Wigan, Dio. Ches. 1864. (Patron, R. of Wigan; P. C.'s Inc. 300*l*; Pop. 10,782.) [20]

HAKE, Robert, *The Precincts, Canterbury.*—St. Edm. Hall, Ox. 4th cl. Lit. Hum. Boden Sanscrit Scho. and B.A. 1845, Pusey and Ellerton Scho. Theol. Examination and M.A. 1847; Deac. 1847, Pr. 1848. Precentor of Cathl. 1864; R. of George the Martyr's with St. Mary Magdalen's R. Canterbury, Dio. Cant. 1866. (Patrons, D. and C. of Cant; Glebe, 1 acre; R.'s Inc. 93*l* and Ho; Pop. St. George's 1254, St. Mary Magdalen's 429.) Min. Can. of Cant. 1854. Formerly Chap. of New Coll. Ox. 1847–54. Author, *Holy Matrimony,* 1855. [21]

HAKE, Thomas Gordon, 3, *Old Steyne, Brighton.*—King's Coll. Lond. Assoc; Deac. 1866 and Pr. 1867 by Bp of Chich. C. of St. Stephen's, Brighton. [22]

HAKING, Richard, *Rodbourne-Cheney, Swindon, Wilts.*—V. of Rodbourne-Cheney, Dio. G. and B. 1862. (Patron, the present V; Tithe—Imp. 41*l*, V. 30*l*; V.'s Inc. 120*l* and Ho; Pop. 670.) [23]

HALCOMB, Thomas Robert, *Lincoln College, Oxford.*—Brasen. Coll. Ox. B.A. 1856, M.A. 1858; Deac. 1858 and Pr. 1859 by Bp of Win. Fell. of Lin. Coll. Ox. Formerly C. of Adderstone 1858. [24]

HALCOMBE, John Joseph, *Charterhouse, London, E.C.*—Magd. Coll. Cam. Scho. of, B.A. 1856, M.A. 1860; Reader at the Charterhouse, Lond. 1862. (Patrons, Governors of Charterhouse; Reader's Inc. 150*l*.) Hon. Sec. to the Curates' Augmentation Fund. Formerly C. of Highgate. Author, *The Indian Mutiny* (two Sermons), 2nd ed. 1*s*; *The Speaker at Home, or Papers on Reading and Extempore Speaking,* 2nd ed. 3*s* 6*d*. [25]

HALDANE-CHINNERY, Alexander, *Calne.*—Trin. Coll. Cam. LL.B. 1864; Deac. 1865 by Bp of Salis. C. of Calne 1866. [26]

HALE, Edward, *Eton College, Bucks.*—Emman. Coll. Cam. B.A. 1850, M.A. 1853; Deac. 1851, Pr. 1852. Asst. Math. Mast. of Eton Coll. [27]

HALE, George, *Sydney College, Cambridge.*—Tayler Lect. of Sydney Coll. [28]

HALE, George Carpenter, 48, *Belsize-square, Hampstead, N.W.*—Trin. Coll. Cam. B.A. 1829, M.A. 1832; Deac. 1830, Pr. 1831. Formerly V. of Hayes, near Uxbridge, Middlesex, 1844–57. [1]

HALE, John Godwin, *The Vicarage, Tottenham, Middlesex, N.*—Oriel Coll. Ox. B.A. 1852, M.A. 1855, Wells Theol. Coll; Deac. 1854 and Pr. 1855 by Bp of Roch. V. of Tottenham, Dio. Lon. 1862. (Patrons, D. and C. of St. Paul's; Tithe—App. 885*l* 10*s* and 90 acres of Glebe, V. 800*l* and 6 acres of Glebe; V.'s Inc. 840*l* and Ho; Pop. 4914.) Formerly C. of St. Michael's, St. Albans, and Hawkwell and South Ockendon, Essex. [2]

HALE, Philip, *Daventry.*—St. John's Coll. Cam. B.A. 1840; Deac. 1841 and Pr. 1842 by Bp of Lon. V. of Wolfhamcote, Dio. Wor. 1866. (Patroness, Viscountess Hood; V.'s Inc. 73*l*; Pop. 444.) Mast. of Daventry Gr. Sch. Formerly Head Mast. of Abp Tenison's Gr. Sch. St. Martin's-in-the-Fields, Lond. 1844–56; V. of Burrington, Herefordshire, 1856–66. Author, *The Conditions of National Prosperity* (a Sermon), 1847; *Marriage with a Deceased Wife's Sister contrary to Christian Practice and repugnant to Christian Feeling*, 1848; *Plea for Archbishop Tenison's Library*, 1851; *Cost, an Element of Sacrifice*, 1852; *Selene* (a Christian Fairy Tale), 1855; *Apology for the Sign of the Cross*, 1857; *The Cross and Lighted Candles in Churches, a Dialogue*, 1858. [3]

HALE, Robert, *Thorpe-Bassett, New Malton, Yorks.*—Brasen. Coll. Ox. B.A. 1838, M.A. 1840. R. of Thorpe-Bassett, Dio. York, 1856. (Patron, Earl Fitzwilliam; Tithe, 338*l* 12*s* 2*d*; R.'s Inc. 373*l*; Pop. 219.) [4]

HALE, Thomas, *Christ Church Parsonage, Belper.*—Dur. Theol. Priseman, Licen. in Theol. and M.A; Deac. 1853 and Pr. 1854 by Bp of Lich P. C. of Bridge Hill, Belper, Dio. Lich. 1862. (Patrons, Crown and Bp alt; P. C.'s Inc. 190*l* and Ho; Pop. 2839.) [5]

HALE, William, *Claverton Rectory, Bath.*—Magd. Hall, Ox. B.A. 1827, M.A. 1829. R. of Claverton, Dio. B. and W. 1851. (Patron, G. Vivian, Esq; Tithe, 162*l* 11*s*; Glebe, 34½ acres; R.'s Inc. 200*l* and Ho; Pop. 213.) [6]

HALE, The Ven. William Hale, *Master's Lodge, Charterhouse, London, E.C.*—Oriel Coll. Ox. 2nd cl. Lit. Hum. 2nd cl. Math. et Phy. and B.A. 1817, M.A. 1820; Deac. 1818 and Pr. 1819 by Bp of Lon. Archd. of Lon. with Can. of St. Paul's annexed, 1842 (Value 670*l*). Mast. of the Charterhouse. Formerly V. of St. Giles's, Cripplegate, Lond. 1847–57; Archd. of Middlesex 1840–47. Author, *An Ordination Sermon*, 1824; *Observations on Clerical Funds* (A Letter to the Bp of Ches.), 1826; *An Essay on the Supposed Existence of a Quadripartite and Tripartite Division of Tithes in England, for the Clergy, the Poor, and the Fabric of the Church*, Part I. 1832, Part II. 1833; *some Remarks on the Probable Consequences of Establishing a General Registry of Births, and Legalising the Registration of Dissenters' Baptisms*, 1834; *Remarks on two Bills, now before Parliament, for Registering Births and Deaths in England, &c.* 1836; *Bishop Jeremy Taylor's "Doctrine and Practice of Repentance," extracted and abridged*, 1836; *The Antiquity of the Church-rate System Considered*, printed for the Reform Association, 1837; *The Pontifical Law on the Subject of the Utensils and Repairs of Churches* as set forth by Fabius Alberti in his "De Sacris Utensilibus," *translated by W. H. H.* (privately printed) 1838; *Institutiones Piæ, or Meditations and Devotions* (originally collected and published by H. I. and afterwards ascribed to Bishop Andrews), *edited and arranged* 1839; *Epistles of Bishop Hall, a Selection, especially adapted for the Time of Trouble*, 1840; *A Charge* (to the Clergy of the Archdeaconry of St. Albans), 1840; *Precedents in Causes of Office against Churchwardens and others, &c., Illustrative of the Law of Church Rates* (Extracts from the Act Books of the Consistory Court of Lond.), 1841; *A Sermon* (for the Sons of the Clergy), 1841; *A Sermon* (at the Consecration of the Bishop of Lich.), 1843; *Proposals for establishing Colleges for Examining the Qualifications of National, Commercial and Classical Schoolmasters, and granting Certificates of Qualification* (a Letter to the Archbishop of Canterbury), printed in compliance with his Grace's desire, not published, 1843; *The Case of Obedience to Rulers in Things Indifferent, and the Power of the Offertory as a Means of Church Extension* (a Charge), 1843; *Bishop Jeremy Taylor's Holy Living and Dying, revised, abridged, and adapted to general use.* 2nd ed. 1845; *The Approaching Contest with Romanism* (a Charge), 1845; *A Series of Precedents and Proceedings in Criminal Causes, extending from 1475 to 1640, extracted from the Law Books of Ecclesiastical Courts in the Dio. of Lon. illustrative of the Discipline of the Church of England, to which is prefixed an Introductory Essay* (*on the Ecclesiastical Law*), 1847; *The Connection of the Government Scheme of Education with the Interests of the Established Church* (a Charge), 1847; *The Sick Man's Guide* (being Prayers, extracted from Bishop Taylor's "Holy Living and Dying"), 2nd ed. 1848; *The Four Gospels, with Annotations* (by the Right Rev. John Lonsdale, D.D. Bishop of Lich. and the Ven. W. H. Hale), 4to. 1849; *A Charge* (to the Clergy of the Archdeacon of Lon.), 1849; *The Duties of the Deacons and Priests in the Church of England compared, with Suggestions for the Extension of the Order of Deacons, and the Establishment of an Order of Sub-Deacons*, 1850; *A Charge* (to the Clergy of the Archdeaconry of Lon.), 1851; *Suggestions for the Extension of the Ministry and the Revival of the Order of Sub-Deacons*, 1852; *Suggestions for the Extension of the Ministry by the Revival of the Lesser Orders of Ministers* (a Charge), 1853; *Some Account of the Past History and Present Condition of the Charterhouse*, privately printed, 1854; *Some Account of the Hospital of King Edward VI. called Christ's Hospital, its past and present condition*, 1855; *Intrà-Mural Burial in England not injurious to Public Health, its Abolition injurious to Religion and Morals* (a Charge), 1855; *The Domesday of St. Paul's of the year* 1222, 4to. 1858 (reprinted for the Camden Society); *Registrum Pr. Mariæ Wigorniensis* (printed for the Camden Society), 1864; On the list of the S.P.C.K.—*A Method of Preparation for Confirmation*; *A Churchman's Answer to the Question, Why do you bring your Child to be Baptized? Bishop Ken's "Winchester Manual" adapted to general use*; *The Pious Christian's Daily Preparation for Death and Eternity* (from "Hele's Devotion"); Articles in The Encyclopædia Metropolitana, *Baptism*; *Baptist*; *Bishop*, Vol. XV; *Confirmation*, Vol. XVII; *History of the Jews*, Chap. 15, Vol. IX; *An Inquiry into the Legal History of the Supremacy of the Crown in Matters of Religion, with especial reference to the Church in the Colonies*, Rivingtons, 1867; *The Queen's Supremacy the Constitutional Bond of Union between the Church of England and her Branches in the Colonies*, Rivingtons, 1867. [7]

HALES, George, *Birstwith Parsonage, Ripley, Yorks.*—Ch. Coll. Cam. LL.B. 1852; Deac. 1850 and Pr. 1852 by Bp of Man. P. C. of Birstwith, Dio. Rip. 1857. (Patron, John Greenwood, Esq; P. C.'s Inc. 233*l* and Ho; Pop. 640.) Formerly C. of Middleton, Lancashire, 1850–53, Bolton by Bolland, Yorks, 1853; P. C. of Birch-in-Middleton, Lancashire, 1853–57. [8]

HALES, John Dixon, *St. John's Parsonage, Richmond, Surrey, S.W.*—Trin. Coll. Cam. Scho. of, 6th Sen. Opt. B.A. 1826; Deac. 1828 and Pr. 1829 by Bp of B. and W. P. C. of St. John's, Richmond, Dio. Win. 1837. (Patron, V. of Richmond; P. C.'s Inc. 300*l* and Ho; Pop. 4721.) Formerly C. of Portlebury, Bristol, 1828; R. of Charmouth, Dorset, 1832. Author, *The Supremacy of Truth*, 1851; *Roman Versions of the Bible*; *A Protest against the Circulation of the Papal Latin Vulgate and its Versions by the British and Foreign Bible Society*; *The Bible or the Bible Society*; pamphlets published by Wertheim and Co. [9]

HALES, Richard Cox, *Woodmancote Rectory, Hurstpierpoint, Sussex,* and *Magdalen Hall, Oxford.*—Magd. Coll. Cam. Scho. of, 1838, Jun. Opt. and B.A. 1840, M.A. 1843, *ad eund.* Magd. Hall, Ox. M.A. 1850; Deac. 1841 and Pr. 1842 by Bp of Win. R. of Woodmancote, Dio. Chich. 1860. (Patron, Ld Chan; Tithe, 485*l*; Glebe, 24 acres; R.'s Inc. 400*l* and Ho; Pop. 331.) City Lect. at St. Martin Carfax, Oxford, 1850; Surrogate of Archd. of Oxford. Formerly C. of Itchen Stoke, Hants, 1841-43, St. Peter-le-Bailey, Oxford; R. of Carfax, Oxford, 1852–60. Author, *Six Sermons at St. Peter-le-Bailey, Oxford, with Prayers for particular Occasions*, 1852, 3s; *Series of Tales for Children translated from the German of Christoph Von Schmid*, 2nd ed. 1859, 1s 6d; *Farewell Address to Parishioners of St. Martin Carfax*, 1860; and various single Sermons. [1]

HALES, William Atherstone, *St. John's Parsonage, St. John's Wood, N.W.,* and *Cavendish Club, Regent-street, London, W.*—Caius Coll. Cam. B.A. 1855, M.A. 1864; Deac. 1855 and Pr. 1856 by Bp of Wor. Asst. Preacher at St. John's Chapel, St. John's Wood, 1867. Formerly C. of St. Peter's, Birmingham, 1855; Lect. of St. Andrew's, Holborn, Lond. 1856; Chap. to the King of Hanover 1857; C. in sole charge of Ickham 1859; C. of Boxley 1860; R. of St. Margaret's, Canterbury, 1861; Min. of Trinity Chapel, and Sen. C. of All Saints', Wandsworth, 1864. [2]

HALFORD, John Frederick, *Wistow, Leicester.*—Trin. Coll. Cam. B.A. 1852, M.A. 1858; Deac. 1853, Pr. 1854. V. of Wistow with C. of Newton Harcourt, Leic. Dio. Pet. 1867. (Patron, Sir Henry Halford, Bart; Glebe, 76 acres; V.'s Inc. 100*l*; Pop. 247.) P. C. of Kilby, Leic. Dio. Pet. 1867. (Patron, Sir Henry Halford, Bart; P.C.'s Inc. 80*l* and Ho; Pop. 362.) Formerly C. of Corsington 1853–55. [3]

HALKE, J. T., *Waters-Upton, Wellington, Salop.*—C. of Waters-Upton. [4]

HALKETT, Dunbar Stuart, *Little Bookham Rectory, Leatherhead, Surrey.*—R. of Little Bookham, Dio. Win. 1848. (Patrons, Exors. of the Rev. G. B. P. Pollen; Tithe—App. 10*l*, R. 162*l*; Glebe, 41½ acres; R.'s Inc. 204*l* and Ho; Pop. 172.) [5]

HALL, Alfred, *The Brooms, Sheffield.*—Sid. Coll. Cam. B.A. 1851; Deac. 1855 and Pr. 1856 by Abp of York. Formerly C. of St. George's, Sheffield, and Horwich, Bolton-le-Moors; P. C. of Ulley, Yorks, 1860–67. [6]

HALL, Ambrose William, *Debden Rectory, Saffron Walden, Essex.*—St. Peter's Coll. Cam. B.A. 1841, M.A. 1844; Deac. 1841 and Pr. 1842 by Bp of Nor. R. of Debden, Dio. Roch. 1858. (Patron, Sir F. Vincent, Bart; Tithe, 965*l* 4*s* 1¾*d*; R.'s Inc. 836*l* and Ho; Pop. 942.) Formerly P. C. of Ch. Ch. Long Cross, Surrey, 1846–58. [7]

HALL, Bracebridge Heming, *Stapleford Vicarage, near Salisbury.*—St. John's Coll. Cam. B.A. 1856, M.A. 1859; Deac. 1858 and Pr. 1859 by Bp of Lich. V. of Stapleford, Dio. Salis. 1864. (Patrons, D. and C. of Windsor; Glebe, 1½ acres; V.'s Inc. 114*l* and Ho; Pop. 274.) Patron of Weddington R. near Nuneaton. Formerly C. of Barlaston, Staffs, and West Lulworth and Burton, Dorset. [8]

HALL, Carter, *North Curry Vicarage, Taunton.*—V. of North Curry, Dio. B. and W. 1866. (Patrons, D. and C. of Wells; V.'s Inc. 500*l* and Ho; Pop. 1839.) Formerly V. of Hollingbourn, Kent. 1855–66. [9]

HALL, Charles, *Kirkby Green, Sleaford, Lincolnshire.*—V. of Kirkby Green, Dio. Lin. 1866. (Patron, Ld Chan; V.'s Inc. 200*l*; Pop. 175.) [10]

HALL, Charles Antin, *Denham Rectory (Bucks), near Uxbridge.*—R. of Denham, Dio. Ox. 1846. (Patron, the present R; Tithe, 980*l*; Glebe, 62 acres; R.'s Inc. 1080*l* and Ho; Pop. 1068.) [11]

HALL, Charles Ranken, *Shire-Newton Rectory, Chepstow, Monmouthshire.*—Ch. Ch. Ox. B.A. 1836, M.A. 1839; Deac. 1836 and Pr. 1838 by Bp of B. and W. R. of Shire-Newton, Dio. Llan. 1856. (Patron, Bp of Llan; R.'s Inc. 320*l* and Ho; Pop. 886.) [12]

HALL, Edmund, *Myland Rectory, Colchester.*—Emman. Coll. Cam. Scho. B.A. 1852, M.A. 1856; Deac. 1852 and Pr. 1853 by Bp of Lon. R. of Myland, Dio. Roch. 1855. (Patroness, Countess Cowper; Tithe, 576*l* 10*s*; Glebe, 30 acres; R.'s Inc. 700*l* and Ho; Pop. 880.) Formerly C. of St. John's, Notting-hill, Lond. 1852. [13]

HALL, Edmund, *Swanwick, Alfreton, Derbyshire.*—St. Peter's Coll. Cam. LL.B. 1855; Deac. 1855 by Bp of Wor. Pr. 1858 by Bp of Chich. P. C. of Swanwick, Dio. Lich. 1867. (Patrons, Trustees; P. C.'s Inc. 300*l* and Ho; Pop. 1800.) Formerly C. of St. Margaret's, Brighton, 1857–59; Mast. in King Edward's Gr. Sch. Stourbridge; C. of St. Giles', Norwich, 1859–67. [14]

HALL, Edward Duncan, *Coln St. Dennis Rectory, Northleach, Glouc.*—Pemb. Coll. Ox. B.A. 1848, M.A. 1851; Deac. 1849, Pr. 1850. R. of Coln St. Dennis, near Northleach, Dio. G. and B. 1860. (Patron, Pemb. Coll. Ox; Tithe, 298*l*; Glebe, 65 acres; R.'s Inc. 400*l*; Pop. 206.) Late Fell. of Pemb. Coll. Ox. 1848. [15]

HALL, Edward Vine, 9, *Powis Grove, Brighton.*—Magd. Coll. Ox. B.A. 1859, M.A. 1862; Deac. 1861 by Bp of Ox. Pr. 1863 by Bp of Chich. Min. of Trinity Chapel, Brighton, 1866. Formerly C. of Brighton, and Hurst, near Reading. Author, *An Evening Chant Service for Country Choirs*; *The Silver Sequence*, Hayes. Editor, *The Oxford Psalter, according to the Pointing long in use at Magdalen College, Oxford*, University Press, Oxford. [16]

HALL, Frederick, *Egham, Surrey.*—Jesus Coll. Cam. Jun. Opt. B.A. 1862, M.A. 1865; Deac. 1863 and Pr. 1864 by Bp of Lich. C. of Egham 1866. Formerly C. of St. Mary's, Wolverhampton, 1863. Author, *A Short Historical Account of the Collegiate Church of St. Peter, Wolverhampton*, Wolverhampton, 1865, 3*s* 6*d*; *A Simple Service Book for Children*, Egham, 1866, 3*d*. [17]

HALL, George, *Chapel-en-le-Frith, near Stockport.*—Ch. Coll. Cam. Scho. of, Sen. Opt. B.A. 1835; Deac. 1835 and Pr. 1836 by Bp of Ches. P. C. of Chapel-en-le-Frith, Dio. Lich. 1836. (Patrons, the Parishioners; Tithe, 14*l*; Glebe, 75 acres; P. C.'s Inc. 210*l* and Ho; Pop. 3651.) Rural Dean of Castleton 1850. [18]

HALL, George, *Ely.*—St. Cath. Hall, Cam. 35th Wrang. and B.A. 1839, M.A. 1842; Deac. 1841, Pr. 1842. Min. Can. of Ely 1852; P. C. of Chettisham, near Ely, Dio. Ely, 1852. (Patrons, D. and C. of Ely; P. C.'s Inc. 79*l*.) [19]

HALL, George Charles, *Churcham Vicarage, near Gloucester.*—Magd. Coll. Ox. 3rd cl. Lit. Hum. and B.A. 1833, M.A. 1834; Deac. 1834, Pr. 1835. V. of Churcham with Bulley C. Dio. G. and B. 1837. (Patrons, D. and C. of Glouc; Churcham, Tithe, 240*l* 1*s*; Glebe, 107 acres; Bulley, Tithe—App. 300*l*, V. 39*l*; V.'s Inc. 300*l* and Ho; Pop. Churcham 645, Bulley 226.) Select Preacher before the Univ. of Ox. 1845–46. [20]

HALL, G. P., *Norham, Berwick-on-Tweed.*—C. of Norham. [21]

HALL, George Rome, *Chipchase Park House, Hexham.*—St. Bees 1858; Deac. 1858 and Pr. 1859 by Abp of York. Chap. of Chipchase Castle Chapel. (Patron, Hugh Tayler, Esq; Chap.'s Inc. 100*l*.) C. in sole charge of Birtley 1860. Formerly C. of Goole, Yorks, 1858. Author, *Memoir on the Aboriginal Occupation of Western Northumberland* (read before the British Association 1863); and other papers contributed to the Ethnological Society and the Antiquarian and Naturalist's Societies of Newcastle-on-Tyne. [22]

HALL, George Thomas, *Hempnall, Long Stratton, Norfolk.*—V. of Hempnall, Dio. Nor. 1852. (Patron, T. T. Mott, Esq; Tithe—Imp. 611*l* 15*s*, V. 388*l* 5*s*; Glebe, 46 acres; V.'s Inc. 457*l*; Pop. 1094.) [23]

HALL, Henry, *Semley Rectory, Shaftesbury, Wilts.*—Ch. Ch. Ox. Stud. of, B.A. 1835, M.A. 1837; Deac. 1840 and Pr. 1841 by Bp of Ox. R. of Semley, Dio. Salis. 1856. (Patron, Ch. Ch. Ox; Tithe, 516*l*; Glebe, 98 acres; R.'s Inc. 600*l* and Ho; Pop. 699.) Formerly C. of Warminster. [24]

HALL, Henry, *Cambridge.*—Magd. Coll. Cam. 14th Wrang. and B.A. 1841, M.A. 1844; Deac. 1842, Pr. 1845. Dom. Chap. to Lord Monson 1842; P. C. of St. Paul's, Cambridge, Dio. Ely, 1862. (Patrons, Trustees; P. C.'s Inc. 125*l* and Ho; Pop. 3229.) Formerly Head Mast. of Gr. Sch. St. Alban's, 1845–62; Fell. of Magd. Coll. Cam. 1841–45. [25]

HALL, Henry, *Earls Colne, Essex.*—St. John's Coll. Cam. B.A. 1863, M.A. 1867; Deac. 1864 and Pr. 1865 by Bp of G. and B. C. of Earls Colne 1867. Formerly C. of Marshfield, Glouc. 1864–67. [26]

HALL, Henry Banks, *Risley, Nottingham.*—Trin. Hall, Cam. LL.B; Deac. 1830, Pr. 1831. P. C. of Risley with Breaston, Dio. Lich. 1835. (Patron, Bp of Lich; Tithe—Imp. 650*l*; Glebe, 33 acres; P. C.'s Inc. 300*l* and Ho; Pop. Risley 203, Breaston 709.) [1]

HALL, Henry Francis Udney, *Datchet, Vicarage, Windsor.*—Dub. A.B. 1844; Deac. 1845, Pr. 1846. V. of Datchet, Dio. Ox. 1853. (Patrons, D. and C. of Windsor; V.'s Inc. 155*l* and Ho; Pop. 932.) [2]

HALL, Hilkiah Bedford, *Halifax.*—Univ. Coll. Dur. B.A. 1845, M.A. 1848, B.C.L. 1859; Deac. 1848 and Pr. 1849 by Bp of Dur. Aft. Lect. of the Parish Church, Halifax, 1861. Formerly C. of Long Benton 1848, Darlington 1852, St. James' Bradford, 1858; V. of Russagh 1858. Author, *A Companion to the Authorised Version of the New Testament*, 1856, 3*s* 6d; *Sodom* (a Sermon), 1860, 1*s*; *A New Translation of St. Paul's Epistle to the Colossians*, 1860, 6*d*; *The Manifestation of Christ, a Course of Epiphany Lectures*, 1863, 2*s*; *John Baptist, a Course of Advent Sermons*, 1864, 1*s*; all published by Bell and Daldy, London. [3]

HALL, Humphrey Farran, *The Parsonage, High Legh, Knutsford, Cheshire.*—St. Peter's Coll. Cam. B.A. 1861; Deac. 1863 by Bp of Roch. Pr. 1864 by Bp of Pet. Chap. of High Legh, Dio. Ches. 1866. (Patron, G. Cornwall Legh, Esq. M.P; Chap.'s Inc. 105*l*; Pop. 700.) Formerly C. of Debden, Essex, 1865-66. [4]

HALL, Isaac, *Shap, Westmoreland.*—Literate; Deac. 1816, Pr. 1817. P. C. of High Toynton with Mareham-on-the-Hill, Dio. Lin. 1855. (Patron, Bp of Carl; P. C.'s Inc. 160*l*; Pop. 420.) [5]

HALL, James, *West Tanfield, Bedale, Yorks.*—Wad. Coll. Ox. B.A. 1817, M.A. 1819; Deac. 1820 by Bp of Ely, Pr. 1820 by Bp of Salis. R. of West Tanfield, Dio. Rip. 1826. (Patron, Marquis of Ailesbury; Tithe, 400*l*; Glebe, 62 acres; R.'s Inc. 416*l* and Ho; Pop. 623.) Dom. Chap. to the Marquis of Ailesbury 1822. Formerly C. of Little Bedwin and Froxfield 1820; V. of Great Bedwin, Wilts, 1822–26. [6]

HALL, John, *York-place, Clifton, Bristol.*—St. Edm. Hall, Ox. B.A. 1813, M.A. 1816, B.D. 1823; Deac. 1811, Pr. 1812. R. of St. Werburgh's, Bristol, Dio. G. and B. 1832. (Patron, Ld Chan; R.'s Inc. 65*l*; Pop. 40.) Hon. Can. of Bristol 1846. Author, *Parochial Discourses on the Thirty-nine Articles*, Bristol, 1825, Bagster, 1828; *Expository Discourses on the Gospels, for Sundays and principal Festivals*, 2 vols, 1831; *Explanatory Discourses on the Epistles for Sundays and the principal Festivals*, 2 vols. 1838; *Scriptural Sermons on the Liturgy, Morning and Evening Prayer, and Holy Communion*, 2 vols. 1849; Occasional Sermons, chiefly funeral, 1838–47; *Family Prayers for Two Weeks*, 5th ed. 1850. [7]

HALL, JOHN, M.A., *Seaforth, Liverpool.* [8]

HALL, John, 6, *Eltham-place, Foxley-road, Vassal-road, Brixton, S.*—Edin. Univ; Deac. 1865, Pr. 1866. P. C. of St. Mark's, Walworth, Dio. Lon. 1865. (Patron, Bp of Lon; Pop. 6094.) Author, various Sermons and Pamphlets. [9]

HALL, John Robert, *Hunton Rectory, Staplehurst, Kent.*—Ch. Ch. Ox. B.A. 1830, M.A. 1833; Deac. 1832 and Pr. 1833 by Bp of Ox. R. of Hunton, Dio. Cant. 1865. (Patron, Abp of Cant; Tithe, 907*l* 10*s*; Glebe, 25 acres; R.'s Inc. 1057*l* and Ho; Pop. 935.) Exam. Chap. to Abp of Cant. Formerly V. of St. Mary Magdalen's, Oxford, 1838-44, Frodsham, Cheshire, 1844–57; R. of Boldon, Durham, 1857–63; Preb. of York 1860–63; R. of Coulsdon, Surrey, 1863–65. [10]

HALL, John Slater, *Whenby, Easingwold, Yorks.*—Lin. Coll. Ox. B.A. 1846, M.A. 1849; Deac. 1848, Pr. 1849. C. of Whenby. Formerly C. of Draughton, Northants. [11]

HALL, John Stephen, *Dalby Rectory, York.*—Deac. 1847 by Bp of Rip. Pr. 1848 by Abp of York. R. of Dalby, Dio. York, 1856. (Patron, the present R; Tithe, 261*l*; Glebe, 4½ acres; R.'s Inc. 261*l* and Ho; Pop. 149.) Formerly C. of Kirkstall, Leeds, 1847; *Locum Tenens* of Brafferton 1848; C. of Wath, Ripon, 1849-50, Dalby, York, 1851–56. [12]

HALL, John William, *Woolley, near Wakefield.*—Trin. Coll. Cam. Scho. and Latin Verse Prizeman, B.A. 1835, M.A. 1838; Deac. 1840 and Pr. 1841 by Bp of Lich. C. of Woolley 1849. Formerly C. of West and South Hanningfield, Essex, 1846; previously Mast. in Cheltenham Coll. 1844; Mast. in Shrewsbury Sch. 1838. [13]

HALL, Joseph, *Horncastle, Lincolnshire.*—Stud. of Trin. Coll. Dub; Deac. 1858 and Pr. 1861 by Bp of Lich. C. of Horncastle 1866. Formerly C. of Edensor 1858, Dresden 1860, St. John's, Hull, 1862, Gedling, 1863. [14]

HALL, Joseph, *Sowerby Bridge, Yorks.*—B.A. Lond. 1860; Deac. 1862 by Bp of Ches. Pr. 1863 by Bp of Rip. C. of Sowerby Bridge 1863. Formerly C. of Norbury, Cheshire, 1862. [15]

HALL, Joseph, *Edensor, near Bakewell, Derbyshire.*—Chap. of the Don. of Edensor, Dio. Lich. 1855. (Patron, Duke of Devonshire; Tithe—Imp. 5*l* 10*s*; Chap.'s Inc. 300*l*; Pop. 645.) [16]

HALL, Joseph, *Knockholt Rectory, Sevenoaks, Kent.*—Corpus Coll. Cam. B A. 1844, M.A. 1847; Deac. and Pr. 1844 by Bp of Lich. R. of Knockholt, Dio. Cant. 1855. (Patron, Abp of Cant; Tithe—App. 250*l* 10*s* 6*d*, R. 140*l* 10*s* 6*d*; Glebe, 3 acres; R.'s Inc. 150*l* and Ho; Pop. 617.) Author, *What is the good of Confirmation?* Macintosh, 2nd ed. 1865, 3*d*; and other Tracts. [17]

HALL, J. E., *Cleveland-terrace, Hyde-park, London, W.* [18]

HALL, Lewis Duval, *Riverhead, Sevenoaks, Kent.*—C. of Riverhead. [19]

HALL, Robert, *Lewisham, Kent.*—Ch. Coll. Cam. B.A. 1850, M.A. 1854; Deac. 1855 by Bp of Wor. C. of Dartmouth Chapel, Lewisham. [20]

HALL, Robert Edward, *Congerstone Rectory, (Leicestershire), near Atherstone.*—Emman. Coll. Cam. B.A. 1832, M.A. 1837; Deac. 1832, Pr. 1833. V. of Shackerstone, Dio. Pet. 1836. (Patron, Earl Howe; V.'s Inc. 185*l*; Pop. 462.) R. of Congerstone, Dio. Pet. 1842. (Patron, Earl Howe; R.'s Inc. 258*l* and Ho; Pop. 250.) Dom. Chap. to Earl Howe 1842. Formerly C. of Swepston and Snareston 1832, Ashby-de-la-Zouch 1832, Clifton Campville, Staffs, 1833. [21]

HALL, R. S. B. H., *Winfrith Newburgh, Dorchester.*—C. of Winfrith Newburgh. [22]

HALL, Tansley, *Boylstone, Uttoxeter, Derbyshire.*—R. of Boylstone, Dio. Lich. 1861. (Patron, the present R; Tithe, 10*l*; Glebe, 154 acres; R.'s Inc. 420*l* and Ho; Pop. 268.) Formerly C. of Boylstone. [23]

HALL, Thomas Grainger, *East Hill, Wandsworth, S.W.*—Magd. Coll. Cam. 5th Wrang. and B.A. 1824, M.A. 1827; Deac. 1827 and Pr. 1828 by Bp of Ely. Prof. of Mathematics in King's Coll. Lond; Preb. of Wenlocksbarn in St. Paul's Cathl. 1845; Chap. to the Bp of Lich. Late Fell. and Tut. of Magd. Coll. Cam. [24]

HALL, Thomas Hepworth, *Purstone Hall, Pontefract.*—St. John's Coll. Cam. B.A. 1849, M.A. 1852; Deac. 1849 and Pr. 1850 by Bp of Rip. Formerly Lect. of Halifax 1855–58; C. of Edmonton 1852–55. [25]

HALL, Thomas Owen, *East Carlton, Rockingham, Northants.*—Lin. Coll. Ox. B.A. 1852; Deac. 1853, Pr. 1854. C. of East Carlton 1864. Formerly C. of Hawkley, Hants, 1853–56, Penn, Bucks, 1856–60, Bringhurst with Great Easton, Northants, 1860–64. [26]

HALL, W., *Durham.*—C. of St. Nicholas', Durham. [27]

HALL, William, *The Park, Sheffield.*—Ox. 3rd cl. Lit. Hum. and 4th cl. Math. B.A. 1834, M.A. 1844; Deac. 1835, Pr. 1836. P. C. of Dyer's Hill, Sheffield, Dio. York, 1849. (Patrons, the Crown and Abp of York alt; P. C.'s Inc. 150*l*; Pop. 7717.) [28]

HALL, William, *Little Saxham, Bury St Edmunds.*—R. of Little Saxham, Dio. Ely, 1852. (Patron, Marquis of Bristol; R.'s Inc. 350*l* and Ho; Pop. 171.) [29]

HALL, William Cradock, *Pilton Parsonage, Barnstaple.*—Queen's Coll. Ox. B.A. 1823, M.A. 1825; Deac. 1828 by Bp of Lon. Pr. 1828 by Bp of Chich.

P. C. of Pilton, Dio. Ex. 1850. (Patron, W. C. Hodge, Esq; P. C.'s Inc. 120*l* and Ho; Pop. 1860.) [1]

HALL, William David, *The Lea, Glouc.*—New Coll. Ox. B.A. 1838, M.A. 1843; Deac. 1839 and Pr. 1841 by Bp of Ox. P. C. of Lea, Dio. G. and B. 1853. (Patron, V. of Linton; Tithe—App. 176*l* 16*s* 6*d*; Glebe, 2 acres; P. C.'s Inc. 70*l*; Pop. 226.) Fell. of New Coll. Ox. Formerly Chap. R.N. 1841–43. [2]

HALL, William John, *Tottenham, N.*—Trin. Coll. Cam. B.A. 1853, M.A. 1857; Deac. 1853 and Pr. 1854 by Bp of G. and B. R. of St. Clement's, Eastcheap with St. Martin Orgar R. City and Dio. Lon. 1865. (Patrons, Bp of Lon. and D. and C. of St. Paul's alt; R.'s Inc. 340*l*; Pop. 494.) Min. Can. of St. Paul's 1862. Formerly P. C. of Trinity, Tottenham, 1861–65. [3]

HALLAM, John Winfield, *Kirton-in-Lindsey, Lincolnshire.*—Deac. 1850 and Pr. 1852 by Bp of Ex. Chap. of the Gaol, Kirton-in-Lindsey. Formerly C. of St. James's the Great, Devonport, and Chap. of the Devonport Borough Gaol 1852. [4]

HALLEN, Arthur Washington, *Alloa, Scotland.*—St. John's Coll. Cam. B.A. 1858; Deac. 1858 and Pr. 1859 by Bp of Wor. Formerly C. of Redmarley-d'Abitot, Worc. 1858. [5]

HALLEN, William, *Holywell Vicarage, near Guilsborough, Northants.*—Ch. Coll. Cam. B.A. 1823; Deac. 1824, Pr. 1825. V. of Holywell, Dio. Pet. 1850. (Patron, R. Hichens, Esq; Tithe, 60*l*; Glebe, 28 acres; V.'s Inc. 158*l* and Ho; Pop. 266.) [6]

HALLET, Abraham Vernon Hughes, *Bruges.*—Emman. Coll. Cam. B.A. 1843, M.A. 1847; Deac. 1844 and Pr. 1845 by Bp of Salis. British Chap. at Bruges. Formerly V. of Stradsett, Norfolk, 1847–58. [7]

HALLETT, Gerard Ludlow.—Trin. Hall. Cam. LL.B 1860, LL.M. 1863, B.C.L. Ox; Deac. 1860 and Pr. 1861 by Bp of Lon. Lect. of St. Benet and St. Peter, Paul's-wharf, Lond; Chap. of Kissingen, Bavaria. Formerly C. of Trinity, Sloane-street, Chelsea. [8]

HALLETT, James Hughes, *Waltham Vicarage, near Canterbury.*—Oriel Coll. Ox. B.A. 1829, M.A. 1832. R. of Bircholt, near Ashford, Dio. Cant. 1836. (Patron, Sir N. J. Knatchbull, Bart; Tithe, 60*l*; R.'s Inc. 75*l*; Church in ruins; Pop. 30.) V. of Waltham with Petham V. Dio. Cant. 1837. (Patrons, Abp of Cant. and Sir J. E. Honywood, Bart, alt; Waltham, Tithe—App. 400*l* and 82½ acres of Glebe, V. 320*l* and 1½ acres of Glebe; Petham, Tithe—App. 30*l* 7*s* 6*d*, Imp. 450*l* 0*s* 1*d*, and ½ acre of Glebe, V. 440*l* 10*s* 6*d*; Glebe, 2½ acres; V.'s Inc. 760*l* and Ho; Pop. Waltham 608, Petham 596.) [9]

HALLETT, John Henry Hughes, *Westbere, near Canterbury.*—Caius Coll. Cam. B.A. 1843, M.A. 1846; Deac. 1842, Pr. 1843. C. of Westbere. [10]

HALLETT, John Thomas, *Priors Hardwick, Daventry.*—V. of Priors Hardwick, Dio. Wor. 1861. (Patron, Earl Spencer; Tithe—Imp. 46*l* 17*s*, V. 40*l*; V.'s Inc. 250*l* and Ho; Pop. 323.) [11]

HALLEWELL, John, *Stroud.*—Ch. Coll. Cam. Wrang. and B.A. 1818, M.A. 1821; Deac. 1819 and Pr. 1821 by Bp of Lin. Formerly Fell. of Ch. Coll. Cam; Chap. of H.E.I. Co. Madras, 1823–39; R. of Chillenden, Kent, 1844–52. [12]

HALLIFAX, John, *Breane Rectory, Axbridge, Somerset.*—R. of Breane, Dio. B. and W. 1859. (Patron, W. Willes, Esq; R.'s Inc. 230*l* and Ho; Pop. 145) [13]

HALLIFAX, John Savile, *Groton, Boxford, Suffolk.*—R. of Groton, Dio. Ely, 1837. (Patrons, J. W. Willett, Esq, and others; Pop. 554. [14]

HALLIFAX, Joseph, *Kirkbride Rectory, Wigton, Cumberland.*—Queen's Coll. Ox. B.A. 1851, M.A. 1854; Deac. 1852 and Pr. 1853 by Bp of Ox. R. of Kirkbride, Dio. Carl. 1855. (Patron, the present R. R.'s Inc. 242*l* and Ho; Pop. 311.) Formerly C. of Briza-Norton, Oxon, 1852–55. [15]

HALLIWELL, Thomas, *Walpole-road, Brighton.*—New Inn Hall, Ox. B.A. 1837, M.A. 1840; Deac. 1838 and Pr. 1839 by Bp of Nor. C. of St. Andrew's, Hove, Sussex, 1866. Formerly P. C. of Ch. Ch. Wrington, Somerset, 1844. [16]

HALLORAN, Edward James Pearce, *Beaworthy, Launceston.*—St. John's Coll. Cam. B.A. 1856; Deac. 1855 and Pr. 1857 by Bp of Ex. R. of Beaworthy, Devon, Dio. Ex. 1862. (Patron, Edwin Force, Esq; Tithe, 145*l*; Glebe, 68 acres; R.'s Inc. 185*l* and Ho; Pop. 298.) Formerly C. of Trinity Chapel, Knackersknowle, near Plymouth, 1857, St. Andrew's, Plymouth; Prin. of the South Devon Coll. Sch. Plymouth. [17]

HALLOWES, Brabazon, *Kilken Vicarage, Mold, Flintshire.*—Lin. Coll. Ox. B.A. 1841, M.A. 1844; Deac. 1842, Pr. 1843. V. of Kilken, Dio. St. A. 1851. (Patron, Bp of G. and B; Tithe, 343*l*; Glebe, 20 acres; V.'s Inc. 363*l* and Ho; Pop. 650.) [18]

HALLS, George, *Clent Vicarage, Stourbridge.*—Queens' Coll. Cam. B.A. 1841, M.A. 1844. V. of Clent, Dio. Wor. 1860. (Patron, Ld Chan; Tithe, 315*l*; Glebe, 33 acres; V.'s Inc. 400*l* and Ho; Pop. 966.) Formerly V. of Long-Bennington, Linc. 1851–60. [19]

HALLWARD, John Leslie.—Wor. Coll. Ox. B.A. 1845, M.A. 1848; Deac. 1846 and Pr. 1847 by Bp of Pet. Formerly C. of Swepstone and Snarestone, Leic. 1846–54, Fawkham, Kent, 1855–57; R. of Caldecote, Warw. 1857–61; C. of Kelmarsh, Northants, 1861, Clifton Hampden, Bucks, 1862. [20]

HALLWARD, John William, *Wandsworth, Surrey, S.W.*—King's Coll. Lond; Deac. 1851, Pr. 1852. Chap. to the House of Correction, Wandsworth, 1860. (Patron, Secretary of State for the Home Office; Chap.'s Inc. 250*l*.) Formerly C. of St. Stephen's, Hammersmith, 1853–60. [21]

HALLWARD, Nathaniel William, *Milden Rectory, Bildestone, Suffolk.*—Wor. Coll. Ox. B.A. 1817, M.A. 1820; Deac. 1820 and Pr. 1821 by Bp. of Nor. R. of Milden, Dio. Ely, 1827. (Patron, Gurdon Family; Tithe, 340*l*; Glebe, 22 acres; R.'s Inc. 360*l* and Ho; Pop. 159.) Chap. to Viscount Lorton. Formerly Chap. at Caen 1842–47. [22]

HALLWARD, Thomas William Onslow, *Lexden, near Colchester.*—Univ. Coll. Ox. B.A. 1850, M.A. 1853; Deac. 1851, Pr. 1853. C. of Lexden. Chap. to the Army Works Corps, Crimea, 1855–56. [23]

HALMSHAW, Charles, *Yeadon, Leeds.*—St. Bees; Deac. 1866 by Bp of Rip. C. of Yeadon, 1866. [24]

HALPIN, Robert.—Dub. A.B. 1843; Deac. 1844 by Bp of G. and B. Pr. 1845 by Abp of Dub. Chap. to H.R.H. the Duke of Cambridge; Chap. to the Forces, London. [25]

HALSTEAD, Thomas Daniel, *Greenwich, S.E.*—Dub. A.B. 1846; Deac. 1846, Pr. 1847. P. C. of St. Paul's, Greenwich, Dio. Lon. 1864. (Patrons, Trustees; P. C.'s Inc. 300*l*; Pop. 10,000.) Formerly Chap. of St. Thomas's Hospital, Newcastle-on-Tyne. [26]

HALSTED, O. P., *Scott Willoughby, Folkingham, Lincolnshire.*—R. of Scott Willoughby, Dio. Lin. 1860. (Patron, Earl Brownlow; R.'s Inc. 140*l*; Pop. 19.) [27]

HALTON, Immanuel, *Langwith Rectory, Mansfield, Derbyshire.*—Dub. A B. 1810, ad eund. Trin. Coll. Ox. 1812. V. of South Wingfield, near Alfreton, Dio. Lich. 1815. (Patron, Duke of Devonshire; Tithe—Imp. 50*l*, V. 195*l* 4*s* 6*d*; V.'s Inc. 328*l*; Pop. 1241.) R. of Langwith, Dio. Lich. 1819. (Patron, Duke of Devonshire; Tithe, 202*l*; Glebe, 44½ acres; R.'s Inc. 242*l* and Ho; Pop. 183.) [28]

HALTON, L. M., *Thruxton Rectory, Andover, Hants.*—R. of Thruxton, Dio. Win. 1832. (Patron, Rev. D. Baynes; R.'s Inc. 430*l* and Ho; Pop. 247.) [29]

HALY, John Billing, *Tavistock.*—St. John's Coll. Cam. B.A. 1859; Deac. 1859 and Pr. 1860 by Bp of Ex. C. of Tavistock 1862. Formerly C. of Ch. Ch. Plymouth, 1859–62. [30]

HALY, Nicholas, *Harford Rectory, Ivybridge, Devon.*—Literate; Deac. 1855 and Pr. 1857 by Bp of Ex. C. of Harford 1863. Formerly C. of St. Gluvias 1855, Tresco, Scilly Islands, 1857, Camborne St. Breake 1858, St. Erth 1859. Author, *A Sermon at St. Erth*, 1860. [31]

HAMBLETON, George, *Theydon-Bois Vicarage, Epping, Essex.*—Deac. 1837, Pr. 1839. V. of

Theydon-Bois, Dio. Roch. 1842. (Patroness, Mrs. Hall Dare; Glebe, 5 acres; V.'s Inc. 166*l* and Ho; Pop. 610.) [1]

HAMERTON, Chisnall, *Eastrington Vicarage, Howden, Yorks.*—Trin. Coll. Cam. B.A. 1829; Deac. 1831, Pr. 1833. V. of Eastrington, Dio. York, 1841. (Patron, Ld Chan; Tithe—Imp. 212*l* 6*s* 5*d*, V. 82*l* 13*s* 6½*d*; V.'s Inc. 200*l* and Ho; Pop. 1906.) [2]

HAMERTON, Samuel Collingwood, *The North Gate, Warwick.*—Univ. Coll. Ox. Scho. and Math. Exhib. 2nd cl. Lit. Hum. 3rd cl. Maths. B.A. 1856, M.A. 1861; Deac. and Pr 1857 by Bp of Dur. P. C. of St. Paul's, Warwick, Dio. Wor. 1866. (Patron, V. of St. Mary's, Warwick; P. C.'s Inc. 170*l* and Ho; Pop. 2700.) Formerly C. of Morpeth, Stoke-upon-Trent, St. Mary's, Lichfield; P. C. of Cotes Heath and Cannock. Author, *Harvest Hymn* and *Christmas Carol* with Music, London Masters and Novello. [3]

HAMES, Hayter George, *Chagford Rectory, near Exeter.*—Ch. Ch. Ox. B.A. 1848, M.A. 1853; Deac. 1850, Pr. 1851. R. of Chagford, Dio. Ex. 1852. (Patron, the present R; Tithe, 539*l* 10*s* 11*d*; Glebe, 100 acres; R.'s Inc. 650*l* and Ho; Pop. 1379.) [4]

HAMILTON, Archibald Robert, *Greenham, Newbury, Berks.*—Dub. A.B. 1850, A.M. 1854; Deac. 1854 by Abp of Armagh. Pr. 1855 by Bp of Raphoe. V. of Greenham, Dio. Ox. 1859. (Patron, Bp of Ox; Tithe—Imp. 422*l*, V. 130*l*; V.'s Inc. 130*l*; Pop. 590.) [5]

HAMILTON, Arthur Hayne, *Heavitree, Exeter.*—St. John's Coll. Ox. 3rd cl. Lit. Hum. and B.A. 1854; Deac. 1848 and Pr. 1849 by Bp of Ex. R. of St. Mary Arches, Exeter, Dio. Ex. 1866. (Patron, Bp of Ex; Tithe, 10*l*; Glebe, 102 acres; R.'s Inc. 158*l* and Ho; Pop. 652.) Formerly C. of Callington, Cornwall, 1860–64. [6]

HAMILTON, Charles James, *Kimberworth Parsonage, near Rotherham.*—Dub. A.B. 1838, A.M. 1863; Deac. 1839 and Pr. 1840 by Bp of Ches. P. C. of Kimberworth, Dio. York, 1860. (Patron, V. of Rotherham; P. C.'s Inc. 200*l* and Ho; Pop. 3848.) Formerly P. C. of St. John's, Birkenhead, 1858. [7]

HAMILTON, Charles James, 47, *Chester-square, London, S.W.*—Trin. Coll. Cam. B.A. 1863, M.A. 1866; Deac. 1864 and Pr. 1865 by Bp of Nor. C. of St. Michael's, Chester-square, 1866. Formerly C. of Southwold, Suffolk, 1864–66. [8]

HAMILTON, George, 32, *Burton-crescent, Bloomsbury, London, W.C.*—Min. of Ch. Ch. Woburn-square, Bloomsbury, Dio. Lon. 1833. (Patron, R. of Bloomsbury; Min's Inc. 300*l*.) [9]

HAMILTON, George Burton, *Springfield, Chelmsford.*—Corpus Coll. Ox. M.A. 1828; Deac. 1828 and Pr. 1829 by Bp of Lon. Chap. to the Gaol, Chelmsford, 1848. Author, *The Scriptural and Protestant Character of the English Liturgy as contemplated by its Compilers*, Longmans. [10]

HAMILTON, The Ven. George Hans, *Eglingham Vicarage, Alnwick.*—Dub. A.B. 1845, A.M. 1851, *ad eund.* Univ. of Dur. 1852, *ad eund.* Ox. 1858; Deac. 1846 and Pr. 1847 by Bp of Nor. Archd. of Lindisfarne with V. of Eglingham annexed, Dio. Dur. 1865. (Patron, Bp of Dur; Tithe, 800*l*; Glebe, 130 acres; V.'s Inc. 1000*l* and Ho; Pop. 1845.) Surrogate; Hon. Chap. to the Berwick-on-Tweed Artillery Volunteers; J.P. for Northumberland. Formerly Hon. Can. of Dur. 1863; Rural Dean; V. of Berwick-on-Tweed 1854; Chap. to the Gaol, Berwick, 1854; Chap. to the Durham County Prisons 1848–54; C. of Sunderland 1846–48. Author, *Annual Reports on Durham County Gaol and House of Correction, as Chaplain*, 1849–53, 6*d* each; *An Account of the Reformatory Institution for Juvenile Offenders at Mettray, in France, from the Pamphlet of M. Augustin Cochin, LL.D, with Two Illustrations and Introduction*, 1855, 1*s*. [11]

HAMILTON, Hans Frederick, *Combe St. Nicholas, Chard, Somerset.*—B.N. Coll. Ox. B.A. 1852, M.A. 1856; Deac. 1853 and Pr. 1855 by Bp of Chich. V. of Combe St. Nicholas, Dio. B. and W. 1861. (Patron, Bp of B. and W; V.'s Inc. 470*l* and Ho; Pop. 1228.) Formerly R. of Langton Herring, Dorset, 1856–57; V. of Sidmouth, Devon, 1857–61. [12]

HAMILTON, The Very Rev. Henry Parr, *The Deanery, Salisbury.*—Trin. Coll. Cam. 9th Wrang. B.A. 1816, M.A. 1819. Dean of Salis. 1850. (Inc. 1000*l*.) Fell. of the Royal Soc. and of the Royal Geological Soc. Late Fell. of Trin. Coll. Cam. Author, *Principles of Analytical Geometry*; *An Analytical System of Conic Sections*, 5th ed; *The Education of the Lower Classes* (a Sermon, with Notes), 2nd ed. 1841; *Practical Remarks on Popular Education in England and Wales*; *The Church and the Education Question* (a Letter to the Bishop of Ripon); *The Privy Council and the National Society*; *The Question concerning the Management of Church of England Schools Stated and Examined*; *The Difficulties of the Believer and the Objections of the Sceptic* (a Visitation Sermon), 1843; *The Present Position of the Church of England* (a Sermon preached at the Bishop of Ripon's Visitation, 1844). [13]

HAMILTON, Hugh Staples, *Manston Parsonage, Leeds.*—Dub; Queen's Scho. A.B. 1842; Deac. 1843 by Bp of Lin. Pr. 1844 by Bp of Tuam. P. C. of Manston, Dio. Rip. 1847. (Patron, the R. of Barwick-in-Elmet; P. C.'s Inc. 180*l* and Ho; Pop. 606.) Formerly C. of Kilowen, Dio. Derry, 1843, Ballintra, Dio. Raphoe, 1845; C. in sole charge of Donaghadee 1845. [14]

HAMILTON, James, *Ballymacool, Dunboyne,* and *Sackville-street Club, Dublin.*—Ch. Coll. Cam. B.A. 1847, M.A. 1850; Deac. 1847 and Pr. 1848 by Bp of Pet. Sec. to Irish Auxiliary of the Colonial and Continental Ch. Soc. [15]

HAMILTON, James, *Doulting Vicarage, Shepton Mallet, Somerset.*—V. of Doulting with East Cranmore C. West Cranmore C. and Downhead C. Dio. B. and W. 1867. (Patron, Col. Horner; V.'s Inc. 700*l* and Ho; Pop. 1278.) Formerly P. C. of St. Barnabas', Bristol, 1866. [16]

HAMILTON, James Milne, *Chalgrave Vicarage, Leighton Buzzard.*—Trin. Coll. Cam. B.A. 1856, M.A. 1860; Deac. 1857 and Pr. 1858 by Bp of Ches. V. of Chalgrave, Dio. Ely, 1861. (Patron, the present V; Glebe, 53 acres; V.'s Inc. 150*l*; Pop. 961.) Formerly C. of Hollinfare 1857–59, East Ravendale 1860–61. [17]

HAMILTON, John, *Lynsted, Sittingbourne, Kent.*—Brasen. Coll. Ox. B.A. 1828, M.A. 1832; Deac. 1829 and Pr. 1830 by Bp of Lon. V. of Lynsted, Dio. Cant. 1839. (Patron, Archd. of Cant; Tithe—App. 627*l* 1*s* 4½*d*, V. 247*l* 15*s*; Glebe, 3 acres; V.'s Inc. 275*l* and Ho; Pop. 1029.) [18]

HAMILTON, John Vesey, *Little Chart Rectory, Charing, Kent.*—Magd. Hall, Ox. B.A. 1818, M.A. 1824. R. of Little Chart, Dio. Cant. 1838. (Patron, Abp of Cant; Tithe, 414*l* 17*s* 10*d*; R.'s Inc. 420*l* and Ho; Pop. 304.) [19]

HAMILTON, Joseph Harriman, 47, *Chester-square, Pimlico, London, S.W.*—Trin. Coll. Cam. Wrang. and B.A. 1822, M.A. 1825; Deac. 1824, Pr. 1825. P. C. of St. Michael's, Chester-square, Dio. Lon. 1848. (Patron, Marquis of Westminster; Pop. 10,371.) Preb. of St. Paul's 1859. Formerly Chap. of Trin. Coll. Cam. [20]

HAMILTON, Leveson Russell, 3, *Alma Villas, Bath.*—Ch. Ch. Ox. B.A. 1845, M.A. 1850; Deac. 1846 and Pr. 1847 by Bp of B. and W. Formerly C. of Lovington and Castle Cary, Bicknoller, and North Cadbury. [21]

HAMILTON, Richard Hugh, *Oulton Parsonage, Leeds.*—Dub. A.B. 1841; Deac. 1846 and Pr. 1847 by Abp of York. P. C. of Oulton, Dio. Rip. 1848. (Patron, John Calverley, Esq; P. C.'s Inc. 200*l* and Ho; Pop. 1851.) [22]

HAMILTON, Thomas Robert.—Dub. A.B. 1848; Deac. 1849 by Bp of Down and Connor, Pr. 1853 by Abp of Armagh. Chap. to the Bp of Carl; Chap. R.N. [23]

HAMILTON, Walter, *Waldershare, Dover.*—Trin. Coll. Cam. B.A. 1850, M.A. 1853; Deac. 1850 and Pr. 1851 by Abp of Cant. V. of Waldershare with Ashley, Dio. Cant. 1856. (Patron, Abp of Cant; Tithe—App. 143*l* 11*s* 11*d*, V. 233*l* 2*s* 6*d*; V.'s Inc. 245*l*; Pop. 104.) V. of Whitfield, *alias* Beauxfield, Dover, Dio. Cant. 1856. (Patron, Abp of Cant; Tithe—App. 234*l* 13*s* 7*d*, V. 98*l* 16*s* 5*d*; V.'s Inc. 150*l*; Pop. 264.) [1]

HAMILTON, William Henry, *Marton, Skipton, Yorks.*—Dub. A.B. 1848, A.M. 1856; Deac. 1848, Pr. 1849. R. of Marton, Dio. Rip. 1857. (Patron, Rev. D. R. Roundell; R.'s Inc. 240*l* and Ho; Pop. 286.) Formerly C. of Witton, Northwich, Cheshire, 1848–49, Marton 1849–57. [2]

HAMILTON, William Jennings, *Ivinghoe Vicarage, near Tring, Bucks.*—Pemb. Coll. Ox. B.A. 1825, M.A. 1828; Deac. 1826 and Pr. 1827 by Bp of Lin. V. of Ivinghoe, Dio. Ox. 1845. (Patron, Earl Brownlow; Tithe—Imp. 9*l* 9*s* 6*d*, V. 14*l* 12*s*; Glebe, 194 acres; V.'s Inc. 300*l* and Ho; Pop. 1849.) Formerly P. C. of Nettleden, Bucks, 1834–57. [3]

HAMILTON-GORDON, The Hon. Douglas, *Northolt, Harrow, London, N.W.*—Trin. Coll. Cam. M.A. 1845; Deac. 1847 by Bp of Lon. Pr. 1848 by Bp of Lin. V. of Northolt, Dio. Lon. 1860. (Patron, Brasen. Coll. Ox; Tithe, 600*l*; Glebe, 80*l*; V.'s Inc. 682*l* and Ho; Pop. 658.) Chap. to the Queen 1857; Can. of Salis. 1860. Formerly C. of Addington, Surrey, 1847; R. of Gt. Stanmore, Middlesex, 1848; Dom. Chap. to Abp Howley. [4]

HAMMICK, St. Vincent Love, *Milton Abbott Vicarage, Tavistock, Devon.*—Ex. Coll. Ox. 2nd cl. Lit. Hum. 2nd cl. Math. et Phy. and B.A. 1828, M.A. 1830; Deac. 1829 and Pr. 1830 by Bp of Ox. V. of Milton-Abbott, Dio. Ex. 1836. (Patron, Duke of Bedford; Tithe—Imp. 384*l*, V. 416*l*; Glebe, 87 acres; V.'s Inc. 640*l* and Ho; Pop. 1062.) Formerly Fell. of Ex. Coll. Ox. [5]

HAMMOND, Baldwin, *Stourton, Bath.*—Magd. Hall, Ox. M.A. 1865. C. of Stourton 1865. [6]

HAMMOND, Charles Edward, *Exeter College, Oxford.*—Ex. Coll. Ox. 3rd cl. Lit. Hum. and 1st cl. Math. B.A. 1858, M.A. 1861; Deac. 1861 and Pr. 1862 by Bp of Ox. Fell. and Tut. of Ex. Coll. Ox. Math. Moderator 1862 and 1863. [7]

HAMMOND, Egerton Douglas, *Sundridge, Sevenoaks, Kent.*—Mert. Coll. Ox. B.A. 1854; Deac. 1845, Pr. 1846. R. of Sundridge, Dio. Cant. 1859. (Patron, Abp of Cant; R.'s Inc. 630*l* and Ho; Pop. 893.) Formerly V. of Northbourne, Kent, 1852–59. [8]

HAMMOND, Henry A.—Mert. Coll. Ox. B.A. 1852, M.A. 1553; Deac. 1853 and Pr. 1854 by Bp of Ox. Formerly C. of Middle Claydon, Bucks, 1853, East Claydon 1854, Southborough, Kent, 1858; P. C. of Trinity, Dover, 1863–67. Author, *National Temperance Hymn and Song Book, with Recitations for Adults and Children*, Tweedie, 1862, 1*s*. [9]

HAMMOND, James Nicholas, *Victoria College, Jersey.*—Trin. Coll. Cam. B.A. 1848, M.A. 1851; Deac. 1849, Pr. 1850. Prof. of English Literature, Victoria Coll. Formerly C. of Redenhall and Harleston, Norfolk. [10]

HAMMOND, John William, *Codford St. Mary, Heytesbury, Wilts.*—St. John's Coll. Ox. B.A. 1850, M.A. 1853; Fell. of St. John's. R. of Codford St. Mary, Dio. Salis. 1861. (Patron, St. John's Coll. Ox; R.'s Inc. 325*l* and Ho; Pop. 404.) Formerly Chap. and Asst. Cl. Mast. at the Royal Naval Sch. New Cross. [11]

HAMMOND, Joseph, *Chapel-Allerton, near Leeds.*—Univ. and King's Coll. Lond. B.A. 1858, LL.B. 1860; Deac. 1864 and Pr. 1865 by Bp of Rip. C. of St. Paul's, Leeds, 1865. Formerly C. of St. James's, Leeds, 1864. Author, *The Apostolic Rule of Prayer* (a Sermon), Leeds, 1864. [12]

HAMMOND, Robert, *Brighton.*—Jesus Coll. Cam. B.A. 1852, M.A. 1855; Deac. 1852 by Bp of Nor. Pr. 1853 by Bp of Ely. C. of St. Paul's, Brighton, 1866. Formerly C. of Riddlesworth and Knettishall, Norfolk, 1852–54; Asst. Mast. at St. Andrew's Coll. Bradfield, Reading, 1856–63; Chap. of St. Saviour's Sch. Shoreham, 1863–66. [13]

HAMMOND, William, *Hadstock Rectory, Linton, Cambs.*—Queens' Coll. Cam. B.A. 1825, M.A. 1828; Deac. 1825 by Bp of Lin. Pr. 1826 by Bp of Lon. C. of Hadstock, Essex, 1864. Formerly C. of Balsham, Essex, 1825–26, Burnham, Essex, 1826–58. [14]

HAMMOND, William, *North Harborne, Smethwick, Birmingham.*—Lichfield Theol. Coll; Deac. 1865 and Pr. 1866 by Bp of Lich. C. of North Harborne 1865. [15]

HAMOND, Henry, *Widford Rectory, Ware, Herts.*—St. John's Coll. Cam. B.A. 1831; Deac. 1833 and Pr. 1834 by Bp of Lon. R. of Widford, Dio. Roch. 1834. (Patron, W. Parker Hamond, Esq; Tithe, 290*l*; Glebe, 23 acres; R.'s Inc. 324*l* and Ho; Pop. 486.) [16]

HAMPDEN, Edward Renn, *Cradley Rectory (Herefordshire), near Malvern.*—R. of Cradley, Dio. Herf. 1854. (Patron, Bp of Herf; Tithe, 1090*l*; Glebe, 100 acres; R.'s Inc. 1173*l* and Ho; Pop. 1077.) Chap. to Bp of Herf; Preb. of Hereford 1867. [17]

HAMPSHIRE, William Knowlton, *Bournemouth, Hants.*—Pemb. Coll. Cam. B.A. 1859, M.A. 1864; Deac. 1860, Pr. 1861. Asst. C. of Bournemouth 1866. Formerly C. of Clayton with Keymer 1860, Lower Beeding, 1863. [18]

HAMPSON, Edward, *Bromborough, Birkenhead.*—St. John's Coll. Ox. B.C.L. 1813, D.C.L. 1815. Formerly C. of Bromborough. [19]

HAMPSON, William Seymour, *Stubton Rectory, Newark.*—Ch. Ch. Ox. B.A. 1853, M.A. 1856; Deac. 1854, Pr. 1856. R. of Stubton, Dio. Lin. 1857. (Patron, George Nevile, Esq; Tithe, 268*l* 12*s*; Glebe, 44 acres; R.'s Inc. 300*l*; Pop. 157.) Formerly C. of Okehampton, Devon, 1854–57. [20]

HAMPTON, Henry, *Wolverhampton.*—Magd. Coll. Cam. M.A. 1845; Deac. 1829, Pr. 1830. V. of St. John's, Wolverhampton, Dio. Lich. 1862. (Patron, Earl of Stamford; V.'s Inc. 300*l* and Ho; Pop. 7988.) Surrogate. Formerly P. C. of St. Luke's, Holloway, Lond 1855–62. [21]

HAMPTON, John, *Tenbury.*—Queens' Coll. Cam. Scho. of, Divinity Prizeman, B.A. 1862; Deac. 1862 by Bp of Win. Pr. 1863 by Bp of Herf. Fell. and Choirmaster of St. Michael's Coll. Tenbury. [22]

HANBURY, Arthur, *Bures (Suffolk), near Colchester.*—Trin. Coll. Cam. B.A. 1823, M.A. 1827; Deac. and Pr. 1828. V. of Bures St. Mary with Bures Hamlet annexed, Essex, Dio. Ely, 1828. (Patron, O. Hanbury, Esq; Bures St. Mary; Tithe—App. 8*l*, Imp. 574*l*, V. 246*l*; Glebe, 2 acres; Bures Hamlet, Tithe—Imp. 387*l*, V. 81*l*; Glebe, 11 acres; V.'s Inc. 390*l*; Pop. 1659.) [23]

HANBURY, Arthur, jun., *Bures, near Colchester.*—Trin. Coll. Cam. B.A. 1855; Deac. 1855 and Pr. 1856 by Bp of Nor. C. of Bures. Formerly C. of Campsey-Ash, Suffolk. [24]

HANBURY, The Hon. Arthur Allen Bateman, *Shobdon, Leominster.*—Ch. Ch. Ox. Fell. of, Exhib. 1850, B.A. 1851 Deac. and Pr. 1853. R. of Shobdon, Dio. Herf. 1853. (Patron, Lord Bateman; Tithe, 610*l*; Glebe, 60 acres; R.'s Inc. 670*l* and Ho; Pop. 503.) Preb. of Hereford 1866; Dom. Chap. to Lord Bateman. [25]

HANBURY, Hubert Henry, *Ticehurst, Hurst Green, Sussex.*—Clare Coll. Cam. 2nd cl. Cl. Trip. B.A. 1863, M.A. 1866; Deac. 1864 and Pr. 1865 by Bp of Chich. C. of Ticehurst 1866. Formerly C. of Selsey 1864–66. [26]

HANBURY, John Chapel, *Palace Yard, Hereford.*—Wad. Coll. Ox. B.A. 1857, M.A. 1859; Deac. 1858 and Pr. 1859 by Bp of Herf. C. of Pipe, near Hereford; 2nd Cl. Mast. in Herf. Cathl. Sch. 1858. [27]

HANBURY, Thomas, *Church-Langton, Kibworth, Leicester.*—St. Edm. Hall, Ox. B.A. 1846, M.A. 1866; Deac. 1846, and Pr. 1847 by Bp of Lin. R. of Church-Langton, Dio. Pet. 1848. (Patron, Rev. W. Hanbury; Glebe, 50 acres; R.'s Inc 945*l* and Ho; Pop. 831.) [28]

HANBURY, William, *Harborough-Magna Rectory, Rugby.*—Ch. Ch. Ox. B.A. 1806, M.A. 1809. R. of Harborough-Magna, Dio. Wor. 1809. (Patron,

J. W. Boughton Leigh, Esq; Tithe, 67*l* 10*s*; R.'s Inc. 298*l* and Ho; Pop. 295.) R. of St. Ebbe's, City and Dio. Ox. 1816. (Patron, Ld Chan; R.'s Inc. 111*l* and Ho; Pop. 2300.) [1]

HANCOCK, John, *Haslebury Plucknett, Crewkerne, Somerset.*—Trin. Coll. Cam. Sen. Opt. and B.A. 1846; Deac. 1846 and Pr. 1847 by Bp of B. and W. C. of Haslebury Plucknett. Formerly C. of Pimperne, Dorset. [2]

HANCOCK, Richard Andrew, 1, *Newcastle-street, Cubitt-town, London, E.*—King's Coll. Lond. Theol. Assoc. 1866; Deac. 1867. C. of Ch. Ch. Poplar, 1866. [3]

HANCOCK, Robert, *Bathford Vicarage, Bath.*—Corpus Coll. Cam. B.A. 1839; Deac. 1840 and Pr. 1841 by Abp of York. V. of Bathford with Bathampton, Dio. B. and W. 1856. (Patrons, D. and C. of Bristol; Bathford, Tithe—Imp. 114*l*, V. 160*l*; Glebe, 52 acres; Bathampton, Tithe—Imp. 120*l*, V. 130*l*; V.'s Inc. 360*l* and Ho; Pop. 892.) [4]

HAND, Henry George, *Hepworth Rectory, Ixworth, Suffolk.*—King's Coll. Cam. B.A. 1833, M.A. 1836; Deac. 1835, Pr. 1836. R. of Hepworth, Dio. Ely, 1851. (Patron, King's Coll. Cam; Tithe—App. 8*l*; R. 530*l*; Glebe, 40 acres; R.'s Inc. 570*l* and Ho; Pop. 594.) Formerly Fell. of King's Coll. Cam. [5]

HAND, John, *Handsworth Rectory, Sheffield.*—Trin. Hall, Cam. LL.B. 1826; Deac. 1826, Pr. 1828. R. of Handsworth, Dio. York, 1830. (Patron, Duke of Norfolk; R.'s Inc. 666*l* and Ho; Pop. 3951.) [6]

HANDBOROUGH, Windsor, *Evenload Rectory, Moreton-in-the-Marsh, Worcestershire.*—Ex. Coll. Ox. B.A. 1854, M.A. 1857; Deac. 1856, Pr. 1857. R. of Evenload, Dio. Wor. 1857. (Patrons, Reps. of late Mrs. Ann James; R.'s Inc. 400*l* and Ho; Pop. 276.) [7]

HANDCOCK, John Harward Jessop, *Woodlands Parsonage, near Sevenoaks.*—St. Aidan's; Deac. 1858 and Pr. 1859 by Bp of Ches; P. C of Woodlands, Dio. Cant. 1860. (Patroness, Mrs. E. M. Vincent; Glebe, 3 acres; P. C.'s Inc. 65*l* and Ho; Pop. 164.) Formerly C. of St. Helens, Lancashire, 1858–60. [8]

HANDCOCK, Richard George, *Hucclecote Parsonage, Gloucester.*—Ch. Coll. Cam. Sen. Opt. and B.A. 1852, M.A. 1855; Deac. 1853 and Pr. 1854 by Bp of Ches. P. C. of Hucclecote, Dio. G. and B. 1861. (Patron, Bp of G. and B; P. C.'s Inc. 30*l* and Ho; Pop. 359.) Formerly C. of St. Luke's, Cheltenham, 1857–60. [9]

HANDCOCK, William Fraser, *Tivoli, Cheltenham.*—Deac. 1845, Pr. 1846. P. C. of St. Luke's, Cheltenham, Dio. G. and B. 1854. (Patron, R. of Cheltenham; P. C.'s Inc. 350*l*; Pop. 2961.) [10]

HANDFORD, James George, *Shereford, Fakenham, Norfolk.*—R. of Shereford, Dio. Nor. 1864. (Patron, Marquis of Townshend; Tithe, 192*l*; Glebe, 58½ acres; R.'s Inc. 250*l*; Pop. 62.) Formerly C. of Tunbridge, Kent. [11]

HANDLEY, Augustus Bernard, *Fisherton Rectory, Salisbury.*—Queen's Coll. Ox. B.A. 1824; Deac. 1839 by Bp of B. and W. Pr. 1839 by Bp of Herf. R. of Fisherton-Anger, Dio. Salis. 1864. (Patrons, Trustees; Tithe, 162*l*; Glebe, 56*l*; R.'s Inc. 284*l* and Ho; Pop. 2500.) Formerly P. C. of West Fordington 1846–59; V. of Alton Pancras, Dorset, 1859–64. [12]

HANDLEY, Edward, *Great Marlow, Bucks.*—C. of Great Marlow. [13]

HANDLEY, William, *Winthorpe Rectory, Newark, Notts.*—St. John's Coll. Cam. B.A. 1834, M.A. 1837; Deac. 1834, Pr. 1836. R. of Winthorpe, Dio. Lin. 1836. (Patron, John Handley, Esq; Tithe, 1*l* 8*s*; R.'s Inc. 170*l*; Pop. 269.) [14]

HANHAM, Abdiel, *Lowestoft, Suffolk.*—King's Coll. Lond. Assoc; Deac. 1858 and Pr. 1859 by Bp of Lon. C. of Lowestoft 1863. Formerly C. of Ch. Ch. Poplar, Lond. 1858–60. Wareham, Dorset, 1860 63. [15]

HANKEY, Montagu, *Ramsgate.*—C. of Ramsgate. [16]

HANKIN, D. B., *Ware, Herts.*—P. C. of Ch. Ch. Ware, Dio. Roch. 1864. (Patron, R. Hanbury, Esq; P. C.'s Inc. 150*l*; Pop. 1690.) [17]

HANKINS, Thomas Frederick Paull, *Hereford.*—Queen's Coll. Ox. B.A. 1819; Deac. 1820, Pr. 1821. Chap. of the Union, Hereford. [18]

HANKINSON, Edward Francis Edwards, *King's Lynn, Norfolk.*—Trin. Coll. Cam. B.A. 1833, M.A. 1836; Deac. 1835, Pr. 1836. Hon. Can. of Nor. 1863. Formerly P. C. of St. John's, King's Lynn, 1846–60; R. of North Lynn 1860–66. [19]

HANKINSON, The Ven. Robert Edwards, *North Creake Rectory, Fakenham, Norfolk.*—Corpus Coll. Cam. B.A. 1820, M.A. 1824; Deac. 1821 and Pr. 1822 by Bp of Nor. Archd. of Norwich 1857. (Value, 200*l*.) R. of North Creake, Dio. Nor. 1863. (Patrons, Earl Spencer and Bp of Nor. alt; Tithe, comm. 1025*l*; Glebe, 187 acres; R.'s Inc. 1268*l* and Ho; Pop. 708.) Formerly R. of Halesworth, Suffolk, 1850–63. [20]

HANMER, Henry, *Grendon Rectory, Atherstone, Warwickshire.*—New Inn Hall, Ox. B.A. 1842, M.A. 1844; Deac. 1842, Pr. 1844. R. of Grendon, Dio. Wor. 1844. (Patron, Sir G. Chetwynd; Tithe, 558*l*; Glebe, 27 acres; R.'s Inc. 585*l* and Ho; Pop. 561.) Rural Dean. [21]

HANMER, Thomas Walden, *Simpson Rectory (Bucks), near Fenny Stratford.*—Brasen. Coll. Ox. B.A. 1803, M.A. 1807. V. of Little Missenden, Amersham, Bucks, Dio. Ox. 1810. (Patron, Earl Howe; Tithe—Imp. 309*l* 10*s*, V. 280*l* 6*s* 4*d*; V.'s Inc. 285*l*; Pop. 647.) R. of Simpson, Dio. Ox. 1845. (Patron, Sir J. Hanmer, Bart; R.'s Inc. 330*l* and Ho; Pop. 353.) [22]

HANNAH, John, *Trinity College, Glenalmond, Perthshire.*—Corpus Coll. Ox. 1837, 1st cl. Lit. Hum. and B.A. 1840, Lin. Coll. M.A. 1843, D.C.L. 1853; Deac. 1841 and Pr. 1842 by Bp of Ox. Warden of Trin. Coll. and Pantonian Prof. of Theology, Glenalmond. Late Fell. of Lin. Coll. Ox; Bampton Lect. 1863. Author, *Discourses on the Fall and its Results*, Rivingtons, 1857, 5*s*; *The Relation between the Divine and Human Elements in Holy Scripture*, 1863, Murray, 10*s* 6*d*. Editor *Poems and Psalms of Henry King, D.D*, Macpherson, Oxford, 1843; *Poems by Sir Henry Wotton, Sir Walter Raleigh, and others*, Pickering, 1845. [23]

HANNAM, Edward Pett, *East Grinstead, Sussex.*—St. John's Coll. Cam. B.A. 1824, M.A. 1827; Deac. 1824 by Bp of Nor. Pr. 1826 by Bp of Lon. V. of Borden, Dio. Cant. 1857. (Patron, Rev. G. M. Musgrave; Tithe, 270*l*; Glebe, 15*l*; V.'s Inc. 290*l* and Ho; Pop. 1023.) Formerly C. of St. Pancras, Middlesex, 1829; Chap. to H.M. Household Brigade of Cavalry, 1825; P. C. of St. Stephen's, Camden-town, Middlesex, 1836. Author, *The Hospital Manual, or Soldier's Guide in Sickness*, 1830; *The Family Monitor*, 1831; *The Invalid's Help to Prayer and Meditation*, 1834; *Prayers, &c. for Wives and Mothers*, 1835; *Questions for Young Persons about to be Confirmed*, 1850; now on List of S.P.C.K. Nos. 106, 414, 515, and 814; *The Weekly Offertory, its Nature and Advantages*, 1844. [24]

HANNAY, James, *Ashley Rectory, Stockbridge, Hants.*—Wor. Coll. Ox. 1831, B.A. 1834, M.A. 1837; Deac. and Pr. 1837. R. of Ashley, Dio. Win. 1843. (Patron, the present R; Tithe, 365*l*; Glebe, 37 acres; R.'s Inc. 490*l* and Ho; Pop. 104.) Fell. of Wor. Coll. Ox. [25]

HANNINGTON, Henry, *King's College, Cambridge.*—King's Coll. Cam. B.A. 1822, M.A. 1825. Sen. Fell. of King's Coll. Cam. [26]

HANSARD, Septimus Holmes, *The Rectory, Bethnal Green, London, N.E.*—Univ. Coll. Ox. B.A. 1846, M.A. 1849; Deac. 1846, Pr. 1847. R. of Bethnal Green, Dio. Lon. 1864. (Patron, Bp of Lon; R.'s Inc. 614*l* and Ho; Pop. 9360.) Formerly C. of St. Mary's, Bryanston-square, Lond. 1848. [27]

HANSELL, Edward Halifax, *High-street, Oxford.*—Magd. Coll. Ox. 2nd cl. Lit. Hum. and B.A. 1836, M.A. 1838, B.D. 1847; Deac. 1839 and Pr. 1843 by Bp of Ox. Prælector of Theology, Magd. Coll. Ox. 1852; R. of East Ilsley, Berks, Dio. Ox. 1866. (Patron, Magd. Coll. Ox; Tithe, 700*l*; Glebe, 63¼ acres; R.'s Inc. 800*l* and Ho; Pop. 746.) Formerly Mast. of the Schools 1841–45, Examiner in Classics 1842–43, in Theology

1850, in Mathematics 1851–52, in Modern History 1855; Fell. Tut. and Math. Lect. of Magd. Coll. Ox; Tut. of Mert. Coll. 1845–49; Select Preacher, Univ. of Ox. 1846–47. [1]

HANSELL, Henry, *Magdalen College, Oxford.*—Magd. Coll. Ox. B.A. 1852, M.A. 1855; Deac. 1854 by Bp of Ox. Pr. 1855 by Bp of Lin. Fell. of Magd. Coll. Ox. Formerly C. of Halton Holegate, Linc. [2]

HANSELL, Peter, *Kingsdon Rectory, Somerton, Somerset.*—Univ. Coll. Ox. B.A. 1826, M.A. 1829. R. of Kingsdon, Dio. B. and W. 1835. (Patron, Univ. Coll. Ox; Tithe, 342*l*; Glebe, 61½ acres; R.'s Inc. 435*l* and Ho; Pop. 472.) British Chap. at Caen. [3]

HANSON, Charles Constantine, *Constantinople.*—St. Aidan's; Deac. 1862 and Pr. 1864 by Bp of Win. Chap. to the English residents at Constantinople. Formerly C. of Albury, Surrey, 1862, Odiham, Hants, 1864. [4]

HANSON, Edward Kington.—Pemb. Coll. Ox. B.A. 1861, M.A. 1864; Deac. 1863, Pr. 1864. Formerly C. of Crewkerne 1863. [5]

HANSON, George Lowdon, *Great Burstead Vicarage, Billericay, Essex.*—Queen's Coll. Ox. B.A. 1823, M.A. 1825; Deac. 1825 and Pr. 1826 by Bp of Win. V. of Great Burstead, Dio. Roch. 1856. (Patron, Lord Petre; Tithe, 171*l* 12*s* 2*d*; Glebe, 6 acres; V.'s Inc. 200*l* and Ho; Pop. 715.) [6]

HANSON, John William, *Cold Ashby, Welford, Northants.*—King's Coll. Lond. Assoc; Deac. 1861 and Pr. 1862 by Bp of Win. C. of Cold Ashby. Formerly C. of St. James's, Southampton, 1861, St. Matthew's, Brixton, Surrey, 1862, Winslow, Bucks, 1863. [7]

HANSON, Stephen, *Westing Rectory, Brandon, Suffolk.*—Caius Coll. Cam. 10th Wrang. and B.A. 1848, M.A. 1851; Deac. 1851 and Pr. 1852 by Bp of Ely. R. of Westing All Saints with Westing St. Mary R. Dio. Nor. 1857. (Patron, Caius Coll. Cam; Tithe, comm. 517*l*; Glebe, 150 acres; R.'s Inc. 560*l* and Ho; Pop. 365.) Late Fell. of Caius Coll. Cam. [8]

HARBIN, Charles, *Teston Rectory, Maidstone.*—Wad. Coll. Ox. B.A. 1822, M.A. 1826; Deac. 1823 by Bp of Ox. Pr. 1824 by Bp of B. and W. R. of Teston, Dio. Cant. 1854. (Patron, Earl of Gainsborough; Tithe, 241*l* 2*s*; Glebe, 24 acres; R.'s Inc. 265*l* and Ho; Pop. 267.) [9]

HARBIN, Wadham, *Esher, Surrey.*—Wad. Coll. Ox. B.A. 1817, M.A. 1820; Deac. 1819, Pr. 1820. R. of Esher, Dio. Win. 1828. (Patron, H. J. Pye, Esq; Tithe, 500*l*; Glebe, ½ acre; R.'s Inc. 502*l*; Pop. 146.) [10]

HARBORD, Charles Hodgson.—Corpus Coll. Cam. B.A. 1860; Deac. 1862 and Pr. 1863 by Bp of Roch. Chap. of H.M.S. "Princess Royal." Formerly C. of Writtle, Essex, and West Hackney, Lond. Author, *Lord Clive, a Poem*, 1864, 6*d*. [11]

HARBORD, The Hon. John, *Morden College, Blackheath, S.E.*—Magd. Coll. Cam. M.A. 1854; Deac. 1856 and Pr. 1857 by Bp of Nor. Chap. of Morden Coll. Blackheath, Dio. Roch. 1865. (Patrons, Trustees; Salary, 58*l*; Rents, 750*l*; Chap.'s Inc. 800*l* and Ho; 40 members of Coll.) Formerly C. of Gayton 1856; R. of West Harling 1860; R. of Gunton with Hanworth, Norfolk, 1864. [12]

HARBORD, John Bradley.—Chap. of H.M.S. "Boscawen." [13]

HARCOURT, Charles Granville Vernon, *Rothbury Rectory, Northumberland.*—R. of Rothbury, Dio. Dur. 1824. (Patron, Bp. of Carl; Tithe, 914*l* 17*s* 10*d*; R.'s Inc. 1106*l* and Ho; Pop. 2387.) Can. Res. of Carlisle 1837. (Value, 1000*l* and Res.) [14]

HARCOURT, William Vernon, *Residentiary Houses, York Minster.*—Can. Res. of York with the Preb. Stall of North Newbald annexed, 1823. (Value, 975*l* and Res.) Sinecure R. of Kirby-in-Cleveland, Dio. York, 1823. (Patron, Abp of York; Value, 558*l*.) Formerly R. of Bolton Percy, York, 1837–65. [15]

HARDEN, Henry William, *Hemsby, near Yarmouth.*—Magd. Coll. Cam. Sen. Opt. 1st cl. Nat. Sci. Trip. B.A. 1851; Deac. 1853 by Bp of Nor. Pr. 1854 by Bp of Win. V. of Hemsby, Dio. Nor. 1864. (Patron, Robert Copeman, Esq; Tithe, 185*l*; Glebe, 28 acres; V.'s Inc. 200*l* and Ho; Pop. 664.) Formerly C. of Charlwood 1854–64. Author, *Conscience and its Rights* (two Sermons.) [16]

HARDEN, John William, *Condover Vicarage, near Shrewsbury.*—St. John's Coll. Cam. B.A. 1829, M.A. 1832; Deac and Pr. by Bp of Ches. V. of Condover, Dio. Lich. 1842. (Patron, E. W. S. Owen, Esq; Tithe—Imp. 1092*l*, V. 211*l* 5*s*; Glebe, 6½ acres; V.'s Inc. 268*l* and Ho; Pop. 1181.) Author, *Scripture Proofs on Leading Doctrines of the Gospel*, 2*d*; *Scripture Proofs on Relative Duties of Christians*, 3*d*; *Questions for Scripture Classes*, 2*d*, etc. [17]

HARDING, David, 26, *Milton-terrace, Wandsworth-road, S.*—Ex. Coll. Ox. 4th cl. Math. et Phy. and B.A. 1850, M.A. 1862; Deac. 1851 and Pr. 1854 by Bp of Roch. C. of Clapham 1865. Formerly C. of Lee, Kent. [18]

HARDING, Derisley, *Caldecott Vicarage, Caxton, Cambridge.*—Pemb. Coll. Cam. B.A. 1813, M.A. 1816; Deac. 1816 and Pr. 1829. V. of Barton, Cambs, Dio. Ely, 1835. (Patron, Bp of Pet; Tithe—Imp. 400*l*, V. 138*l*; Glebe, 36 acres; V.'s Inc. 193*l*; Pop. 324.) [19]

HARDING, George Shipton, *Cheswardine Vicarage, Market Drayton.*—Brasen. Coll. Ox. B.A. 1839, M.A. 1842; Deac. 1841 and Pr. 1843 by Bp of Lich. V. of Cheswardine, Dio. Lich. 1867. (Patron, Egerton W. Harding, Esq; Tithe, 209*l*; Glebe, 20 acres; V.'s Inc. 295*l* and Ho; Pop. 993.) Formerly C. of Broughton, Staffs, 1841–43; V. of Tong, Salop, 1843–54; C. of Cheswardine 1854–67. [20]

HARDING, George Thomas, *Hinstock, Market Drayton.*—Wad. Coll. Ox. B.A. 1865; Deac. 1866 and Pr. 1867 by Bp of Lich. C. of Hinstock, Salop, 1866. [21]

HARDING, Henry, *Tilston Parsonage, near Tarporley, Cheshire.*—Univ. Coll. Ox. M.B. 1838, M.D. 1846; Deac. 1847 and Pr. 1848 by Bp of Wor. P. C. of Tilston, Dio. Carl. 1850. (Patron, J. Tollemache, Esq; P. C.'s Inc. 95*l* and Ho; Pop. 1407.) [22]

HARDING, John, *Goodleigh, Barnstaple, Devon.*—Ball. Coll. Ox. 3rd cl. Lit. Hum. and B.A. 1823, M.A. 1827; Deac. 1824 by Bp of Lin. Pr. 1825 by Bp of Ex. R. of Goodleigh, Dio. Ex. 1831. (Patron, the present R; Tithe, 203*l*; Glebe, 30 acres; R.'s Inc. 260*l* and Ho; Pop. 294.) Rural Dean 1835. [23]

HARDING, John, *Walkern Rectory, Buntingford, Herts.*—King's Coll. Cam. B.A. 1819, M.A. 1823; Deac. 1819, Pr. 1823. R. of Walkern, Dio. Roch. 1839. (Patron, King's Coll. Cam; Tithe—Imp. 75*l* 7*s*, and 100½ acres of Glebe, R. 588*l* 13*s*; Glebe, 26 acres; R.'s Inc. 630*l* and Ho; Pop. 823.) Rural Dean 1851; one of H.M. Justices of the Peace for the County of Hertford 1854. Formerly Morning Reader, Dean of Divinity, and Sen. Fell. of King's Coll. Cam; Proctor 1830; Scrutator 1831. [24]

HARDING, John, *Ayott St. Lawrence, Welwyn, Herts.*—Ch. Miss. Coll. Islington; Deac. 1846 and Pr. 1847 by Bp of Lon. C. of Ayott St. Lawrence 1860. Formerly Miss. in Travancore, India; C. of Hockley, Essex, and Marylebone, Lond. Author, *Peace unto the Heathen*, 2*s* 6*d*; *God's Word, its Purpose and Accomplishment*, 3*d*; *Providing for our Own*, 3*d*; *Mercy for Israel*, Mackintosh, 3*d*. [25]

HARDING, John, *Hook Norton, Chipping Norton, Oxon.*—Brasen. Coll. Ox. B.A. 1864, M.A. 1867; Deac. 1866 and Pr. 1867 by Bp of Ox. C. of Hook Norton 1866. [26]

HARDING, John Richard, *Hingham, Norfolk.*—St. John's Coll. Cam. B.A. 1846, M.A. 1849; Deac. 1848 and Pr. 1849 by Bp of Rip. C. in sole charge of Hingham, Norfolk, 1861. Formerly C. of St. Paul's, Huddersfield, 1848–50, Sedbergh 1850–59, Dallington, Northants, 1860–61. [27]

HARDING, John T., *Stratton, near Cirencester.*—C. of Stratton. [28]

HARDING, Joseph Lymebear, *Littleham Rectory, Bideford, Devon.*—Ex. Coll. Ox. B.A. 1842; Deac. 1842 and Pr. 1843 by Bp of Ex. R. of Littleham, Dio. Ex. 1843. (Patron, G. Anthony, Esq; Tithe, 190*l*; Glebe, 93 acres; R.'s Inc. 287*l* and Ho; Pop. 406.) Rural Dean. [1]

HARDING, Joseph Wingfield, *Tong Parsonage, Shiffnall, Salop.*—P. C. of Tong, Dio. Lich. 1856. (Patron, Earl of Bradford; Tithe—Imp. 391*l* 9*s* 10*d*, and 2 acres of Glebe; P. C.'s Inc. 88*l* and Ho; Pop. 532.) [2]

HARDING, Thomas, *Bexley Vicarage, Kent.*—Wor. Coll. Ox. 2nd cl. Lit. Hum. and B.A. 1826, M.A. 1828; Deac. 1828 and Pr. 1829 by Bp of Lon. V. of Bexley, Dio. Cant. 1833. (Patron, Viscount Sidney; Tithe—Imp. 1046*l*, V. 702*l* 6*s* 10*d*; V.'s Inc. 680*l* and Ho; Pop. 2000.) Rural Dean. Formerly Chap. of Bethlehem Hospital 1831–36. Author, Sermons:—*Hezekiah's Appeal to Isaiah, a Lesson for the Times*, 1840; *Boast not thyself of To-morrow*, 1842; *The Signs of the Times*, 1848; *A Thankful Review of the Year*, 1846–49; *True Sorrow in Affliction*, 1849; *God's Predestination, the Confidence of His Saints*, 1850; *Feed my Sheep*, 1850; *The Battle of Armageddon*, 1851; *The other Gospel of Rome*, 1852; *The Law of the Sabbath*, 1852; *The faithful Pastor to be remembered*, 1853; *England's Stability and Salvation*, 1853; *An Appeal in Behalf of the Waldensian Church*, 1855; *Caution and Encouragement to the Holy Communion*, 1856; *The Faithful Branch Purged*, 1863; *Naomi changed into Mara*, 1860; *The Pastor strengthened in the Brother bereaved*, 1857; *A Pastor's Farewell*, 1866. Editor of *Bullinger's Decades*, for the Parker Society, 4 vols. 1849–52. [3]

HARDING, William, *Sulgrave (Northants), near Banbury.*—Univ. Coll. Ox. B.A. 1828, M.A. 1832; Deac. 1828, Pr. 1830. V. of Sulgrave, Dio. Pet. 1829. (Patron, the present V; V.'s Inc. 246*l* and Ho; Pop. 565.) [4]

HARDING, William, *Watford, Herts.*—Wad. Coll. Ox. B.A. 1864; Deac. 1865 and Pr. 1866 by Bp of Roch. C. of St. Andrew's, Watford, 1865. [5]

HARDINGE, Thomas Hartshorne, *Ashley Rectory, Market-Drayton.*—Wad. Coll. Ox. D.D; Deac. 1823 and Pr. 1824 by Bp of Lich. R. of Ashley, Dio. Lich. 1836. (Patrons, H. C. Meynell Ingram, Esq, and Rev. A. H. R. Hebden; R.'s Inc. 360*l* and Ho; Pop. 870.) Chap. to the Earl of Shrewsbury and Talbot. [6]

HARDINGHAM, Charles Hugh, 47, *Great Dover-street, Southwark, London, S.*—Trin. Coll. Cam. B.A. 1854; Deac. 1859 and Pr. 1860 by Bp of Win. 2nd Mast. of Queen Elizabeth's Gr. Sch. St. Olave's, Southwark, Lond. [7]

HARDISTY, William Lane, *Eton College, Windsor.*—St. John's Coll. Cam. Scho. of, 1840, B.A. in Hons. 1843, M.A. 1846; Deac. 1844, Pr. 1845. Asst. Mast. of Eton Coll. 1852. Formerly C. of St. Giles-in-the-Fields, Lond. [8]

HARDMAN, Joseph William, *St. Katharine's, Felton-hill, Winford, Bristol.*—Dub. A.B. 1855, A.M. 1858; Deac. 1857 by Bp of Cork, Pr. 1858 by Bp of Down and Connor. P. C. of St. Katharine's, Winford, 1866. Formerly P. C. of St. John's, Upper Studley, Wilts, 1859–61; Chap. of Don. of Barrow Gurney, Somerset, 1861–64. [9]

HARDMAN, Richard Peers, *Armyn, near Goole, Yorks.*—King's Coll. Lond. Theol. Assoc. 1859; Deac. 1859 and Pr. 1860 by Abp of York. P. C. of Armyn, Dio. York, 1862. (Patron, A. C. Heber Percy, Esq. and Mr. Yarburgh; P. C.'s Inc. 100*l* and Ho; Pop. 557.) Formerly C. of St. Stephen's, Hull, 1859–62. [10]

HARDWICH, T. F., *Easington, Durham.*—C. of Easington. Formerly C. of Shildon. [11]

HARDWICK, Charles, *St. Michael's Rectory, Gloucester.*—Univ. Coll. Ox. B.A. 1821, M.A. 1824; Deac. 1821, Pr. 1822. R. of St. Michael's with St. Mary-de-Grace P. C. Gloucester, Dio. G. and B. 1839. (Patron, Ld Chan; St. Michael, Tithe, 16*s* 3*d*; R.'s Inc. 220*l* and Ho; Pop. St. Michael 1755, St. Mary-de-Grace 251.) [12]

HARDY, Arthur, *Armitage Bridge, Huddersfield.*—Magd. Coll. Cam. B.A. 1859; Deac. 1860 and Pr. 1861 by Bp of Ely. C. in sole charge of Armitage Bridge 1866. Formerly C. of Dunstable 1860, St. George's, Leeds, 1865. [13]

HARDY, Arthur Octavius, *Calcutta.*—Trin. Coll. Ox. B.A. 1861, M.A. 1864; Deac. 1862 and Pr. 1864 by Bp of Ox. Bengal Chaplaincy 1864. Formerly Tut. and Asst. Mast. Wellington Coll. 1861–64. [14]

HARDY, Charles, *Hilborough Rectory, near Brandon, Norfolk.*—Pemb. Coll. Cam. 2nd Sen. Opt. and B.A. 1816, M.A. 1819; Deac. 1816 and Pr. 1817 by Bp of Nor. R. of Hilborough, Dio. Nor. 1857. (Patron, Rev. John Burrough; Tithe, 460*l*; Glebe, 62 acres; R.'s Inc. 400*l* and Ho; Pop. 365.) Formerly V. of St. Paul's, Walden, Herts, 1835–57. [15]

HARDY, Charles, *Hayling, Havant, Hants.*—Ch. Coll. Cam. B.A. 1826; Deac. 1826 and Pr. 1827 by Bp of Chich. V. of Hayling, Dio. Win. 1832. (Patroness, Miss Padwick; Tithe—Imp. 829*l* 6*s* 2*d*, V. 185*l* 6*s* 2*d*; Glebe, 34 acres; V.'s Inc. 230*l*; Pop. 1039.) Formerly C. of Sub-Deanery, Chichester, 1827. [16]

HARDY, Edward Creek, *Longdon-upon-Tern, Wellington, Salop.*—Dub. A.B. 1849; Deac. 1850 and Pr. 1851 by Abp of Armagh. P. C. of Longdon-upon-Tern, Dio. Lich. 1865. (Patron, Duke of Sutherland; Tithe, 210*l*; P. C.'s Inc. 220*l*; Pop. 92.) Formerly C. of Kilmore, Armagh; C. in sole charge of Great Bolas, Salop, 1864. [17]

HARDY, Henry, *Jurby, Ramsey, Isle of Man.*—St. John's Coll. Cam; Deac. 1850 and Pr. 1851 by Bp of B. and W. V. of Jurby, Dio. S. and M. 1858. (Patron, Bp of S. and M; V.'s Inc. 180*l* and Ho; Pop. 911.) Formerly C. of Jurby; Dioc. Inspector of Schools. [18]

HARDY, Henry Haistwell, *Horfield Parsonage, Bristol.*—Univ. Coll. Ox. B.A. 1848, M.A. 1851; Deac. 1850 by Bp of Wor. Pr. 1851 by Bp of G. and B; P. C. of Horfield, Dio. G. and B. 1864. (Patron, Bp of G. and B; P. C.'s Inc. 220*l* and Ho; Pop. 963.) Formerly V. of Preston, Somerset, 1855–64. [19]

HARDY, John Frederick, *Sidney-Sussex College, Cambridge.*—Sid. Coll. Cam. B.A. 1848. Fishmongers' Fell. of Sid. Coll. Cam. [20]

HARDY, Thomas William, *Malaga, Spain.*—Trin. Coll. Cam. 6th Wrang. 2nd cl. Cl. Trip. B.A. 1856; Deac. 1857 and Pr. 1858 by Bp of Ely. British Chap. at Malaga. Formerly V. of Shudy-Camps, Cambs, 1858–63; R. of St. Stephen's, Exeter, 1863–65. [21]

HARE, E. Montague, *Little Dunham, Swaffham, Norfolk.*—R. of Little Dunham, Dio. Nor. 1866. (Patrons, Reps of late Rev. J. Nelson; R.'s Inc. 500*l* and Ho; Pop. 327.) [22]

HARE, Frederick John, *Edgbaston Grammar School, Birmingham.*—Mast. in Edgbaston Gr. Sch. [23]

HARE, Henry, *Halwell, Totnes, Devon.*—Ex. Coll. Ox. B.A. 1817; Deac. 1818 by Bp of Ches. Pr. 1819 by Bp of Ex. P. C. of Halwell, Dio. Ex. 1847. (Patrons, D. and C. of Ex; Tithe—App. 235*l*, V. 182*l*; P. C.'s Inc. 160*l*; Pop. 357.) [24]

HARE, Henry Bassano, *Fiddington, near Bridgwater.*—Trin. Coll. Ox. B.A. 1849, M.A. 1851; Deac. 1852 and Pr. 1853 by Bp of Salis. R. of Fiddington, Dio. B. and W. 1859. (Patron, Sholto V. Hare, Esq; Tithe, 200*l*; Glebe, 40 acres; R.'s Inc. 280*l*; Pop. 213.) Formerly C. of Westwood, Wilts, and Chap. to Bradford Union 1852–59. [25]

HARE, Henry George, *Halwell, Totnes, Devon.*—Ex. Coll. Ox. B.A. 1851; Deac. 1853 and Pr. 1854 by Bp of Ex. C. of Halwell 1855. Formerly C. of Sticklepath, Devon, 1853–55. [26]

HARE, Hugh James, *Docking Vicarage, Rougham, Norfolk.*—Queen's Coll. Ox. B.A. 1851, M.A. 1855; Deac. 1852 and Pr. 1853 by Bp of Nor. C. of Docking, and Chap. of the Union. [27]

HARE, John, *Repton, Burton-on-Trent.*—Ch. Ch. Ox. 1812; Deac. and Pr. 1812. Formerly Chap. of Newton Solney, Derbyshire, 1814–61. [28]

HARE, John David, 19, *Park-village East, Regent's-park, London, N.W.*—Dub. A.B. 1829, A.M.

1831, LL.B. 1837, LL.D. 1845, D.C.L. Ox. 1846; Deac. 1840 by Abp of Cant. Pr. 1841 by Bp of Lin. Chap. to Middlesex Hospital. [1]

HARE, William, *Winchester.*—Dub. A.B. 1826; Deac. 1826 by Abp of Dub. Pr. 1828 by Bp of Kildare. Chap. to the Forces, Winchester. [2]

HARE, William, *Owersby Vicarage, Market Rasen, Lincolnshire.*—V. of Owersby with Kirkby-Osgodby, Dio. Lin. 1865. (Patron, W. Angerstein, Esq; V.'s Inc. 320*l* and Ho; Pop. 974.) [3]

HARFORD, Edward John, *Henbury, near Bristol.*—Oriel Coll. Ox. B.A. 1854; Deac. 1857 by Bp of Win. Pr. 1860 by Bp of G. and B. C. of Henbury 1860. Formerly C. of Deal, Kent. [4]

HARFORD, Frederick Kill.—Min. Can. of Westminster. [5]

HARGRAVE, Benjamin Langwith, *Tunbridge Wells.*—Deac. 1838 and Pr. 1839 by Abp of York. C. of Frant, Sussex, 1859. Formerly C. of Croft, Yorks, 1838, Lowdham, Notts, 1840, Lenton, Notts, 1841, Hartfield, Sussex, 1842–59. [6]

HARGREAVES, James, *West Tilbury Rectory, Grays Thurrock, Essex.*—R. of West Tilbury, Dio. Roch. 1847. (Patron, Ld Chan; Tithe, 561*l*; Glebe, 47½ acres; R.'s Inc 618*l* and Ho; Pop. 385.) [7]

HARINGTON, Charles, *The Rectory, Stoke Lacy, Bromyard.*—Ch. Ch. Ox. B.A. 1861, M.A. 1863; Deac. 1863 and Pr. 1864 by Bp of Roch. R. of Stoke Lacy, Dio. Herf. 1865 (Patrons, Mrs. Cotton and the present R; Tithe, comm. 320*l*; Glebe, 19 acres; R.'s Inc. 350*l* and Ho; Pop. 348.) Formerly C. of Cold Norton, Essex, 1863–65. [8]

HARINGTON, Edward Charles, *The Close, Exeter.*—Wor. Coll. Ox. B.A. 1826, M.A. 1833; Deac. 1828 and Pr. 1829 by Bp of Ex. Chan. and Can. of Exeter 1856. (Value, 976*l* and Res.) Chap. to the Troops, Exeter. Author, *The Object, Importance, and Antiquity of the Rite of Consecration of Churches,* 7*s*; *On the Reconsecration and Reconciliation of Churches,* 3*s*; *Two Ordination Sermons* (published at the request of the Bishop of Exeter), 2 eds. 3*s* each; *Brief Notes on the Church of Scotland,* 4*s*; *The Reformers of the Anglican Church, and Mr. Macaulay's History of England,* 2 eds. 3*s* 6*d*; *The Bull of Pope Pius IX. and the Ancient British Church,* 1*s* 6*d*; *The Fifty-fifth Canon and the Kirk of Scotland,* 3*s* 6*d*; *A Few Words in Reply to the Rev. W. Goode on the Fifty-fifth Canon,* 1*s*; *The Purity of the Church of England, and the Corruptions of the Church of Rome,* 2*s*; *Rome's Pretensions Tested,* 1*s* 6*d*; *Pope Pius IV. and the Book of Common Prayer,* 1*s*; *Bradford the Martyr and Sir John Harrington*; a series of papers in *The British Magazine* on Romish Errors. [9]

HARINGTON, Edward Templer, *Vicarage, Axmouth, Devon.*—Wor. Coll. Ox. B.A. 1851, M.A. 1854; Deac. 1855 and Pr. 1856 by Bp of Ox. V. of Axmouth, Dio. Ex. 1864. (Patron, W. T. Hallett, Esq; Tithe, comm. 242*l*; Glebe, 41 acres; V.'s Inc. 302*l* and Ho; Pop. 662.) Formerly C. of Sibford, Oxon, 1855, Bridestowe, Devon, 1859; P. C. of Bickington, Devon, 1861. [10]

HARINGTON, Henry Duke, *Knossington, near Oakham.*—Ex. Coll. Ox. B.A. 1827, M.A. 1830; Deac. 1830 and Pr. 1831 by Bp of Ox. R. of Knossington, Dio. Pet. 1864. (Patron, Thomas Frewen, Esq; Tithe, 255*l* 3*s* 6*d*; Glebe, 42 acres; R.'s Inc. 321*l* and Ho; Pop. 251.) Late Fell. of Ex. Coll. Ox. and Hebrew Lect; C. of Kidlington, Oxon, 1833; V. of South Newington, Oxon, 1836–64. Author, *A Manual for the Use of Sponsors,* 6*d*. [11]

HARKE, Frederic Martyn, *Edgehill, Liverpool.*—Dub. A.B. 1840, A.M. 1849; Deac. 1843 and Pr. 1845 by Bp of Ches. P. C. of St. Mary's, Edgehill, Dio. Ches. 1854. (Patron, J. Stewart, Esq; P. C.'s Inc. 300*l*.) [12]

HARKE, William Henry, 10, *Addiscombe-villas Croydon, S.*—Dub. A.B. 1856, A.M. 1860; Deac. 1856 and Pr. 1857 by Bp of Ches. C. of St. James's, Croydon. Formerly P. C. of Newhall, Derbyshire, 1858–63. [13]

HARKER, William, *Emmanuel Vicarage, Camberwell, London, S.*—St. Cath. Coll. Cam. B.A. 1839, M.A. 1844, and M.A. of Magd. Coll. Ox. 1844; Deac. 1839 by Bp of Ches. Pr. 1840 by Bp of Lin. V. of Emmanuel, Camberwell, Dio. Win. 1863. (Patron, the present V; V.'s Inc. 450*l* and Ho; Pop. 8923.) Formerly P. C. of St. Barnabas', South Kennington, 1849–58; V. of Pulloxhill, Beds, 1858–61; P. C. of St. Paul's, Worcester, 1861–63. Author, *The Common Lot* (a Sermon on Death), 1857; *The Marriage Bond* (a Sermon on the Marriage of the Princess Royal of England), 1858; *A Marriage Memorial* (two Sermons on the Marriage of the Prince of Wales), 1863; *Ministerial Review and Parting Exhortations,* 1858; *True Wisdom Triumphant,* 1858; *Christian Responsibility,* 1859; *Completeness in Christ,* 1862; *Fourteen New Years' Addresses,* 1849–63; *Lectures on the Second Advent of our Lord Jesus Christ,* 1862; and numerous Tracts. [14]

HARKNESS, George Law, *St. James's Rectory, Shaftesbury, Dorset.*—St. John's Coll. Cam. B.A. 1847, M.A. 1851; Deac. 1849 and Pr. 1850 by Bp of B. and W. R. of St. James's, Shaftesbury, Dio. Salis. 1859. (Patron, Earl of Shaftesbury; Tithe, 400*l*; R.'s Inc. 425*l* and Ho; Pop. 931.) [15]

HARKNESS, Henry Law, *Great Malvern.*—St. John's Coll. Cam. B.A. 1849, M.A. 1854; Deac. 1852 and Pr. 1853 by Bp of Wor. C. of Trinity, North Malvern, 1854. Author, *Lectures on Egypt and the Holy Land,* 1*s* 6*d*. [16]

HARKNESS, Robert, *Wimborne St. Giles, Dorset.*—St. John's Coll. Cam. B.A. 1848, M.A. 1851; Deac. 1849, Pr. 1851. R. of Wimborne St. Giles, Dio. Salis. 1865. (Patron, Earl of Shaftesbury; Tithe, comm. 545*l*; Glebe, 155 acres; R.'s Inc. 745*l* and Ho; Pop. 436.) Formerly P. C. of Trinity, North Malvern, 1855–62; R. of Sternfield, Suffolk, 1862–65. [17]

HARLAND, Edward, *Colwich Vicarage, Staffs.*—Wad. Coll. Ox. B.A. 1831, M.A. 1833; Deac. 1833 and Pr. 1834 by Bp of Lich. V. of Colwich, Dio. Lich, 1851. (Patron, Bp of Lich; Tithe, 515*l*; Glebe, 8 acres; V.'s Inc. 555*l* and Ho; Pop. 829.) Surrogate; Chap. to the Earl of Harrowby. Formerly C. of Newborough 1833–36, Sandon 1836–51. Author, *Index Sermonum,* 1858, 7*s* 6*d*; *Church Psalter and Hymnal,* Routledge, 4*d*. [18]

HARLEY, William, *Turweston, Brackley, Bucks.*—Magd. Coll. Cam. B.A. 1848, M.A. 1851; Deac. 1848, Pr. 1849. R. of Turweston, Dio. Ox. 1862. (Patrons, D. and C. of Westminster; R.'s Inc. 326*l*; Pop. 335.) Formerly V. of Steventon, Berks, 1851–62. [19]

HARLOCK, Alfred King, *Westhorpe Rectory, Stowmarket, Suffolk.*—St. Peter's Coll. Cam. B.A. 1855, M.A. 1858; Deac. 1856 and Pr. 1857 by Bp of Ely. R. of Westhorpe, Dio. Nor. 1858. (Patron, the present R; Tithe, comm. 350*l*; Glebe, 16 acres; R.'s Inc. 350*l* and Ho; Pop. 227.) Formerly C. of Hadleigh, Suffolk, 1856–58. [20]

HARMAN, Edward, *Scaleby Rectory, Carlisle.*—Caius Coll. Cam. Jun. Opt. 3rd cl. Cl. Trip. B.A. 1850. M.A. 1853; Deac. 1853 and Pr. 1854 by Bp of Roch. R. of Scaleby, Dio. Carl. 1866. (Patron, Bp of Carl; Tithe, 31*l* 10*s*; Glebe, 40 acres; R.'s Inc. 115*l* and Ho; Pop. 548.) Formerly C. of Hempstead, Essex, 1853, Eastbourne, Sussex, 1856; R. of North Stoke, Somerset, 1857; R. of Bonsall, Derbyshire, 1862; C. of Droxford, Hants, 1865. [21]

HARMAN, John, *Enfield, Middlesex.*—Clare Coll. Cam. B.A. 1837, M.A. 1842; Deac. 1837, Pr. 1839, P. C. of St. James's, Enfield, Dio. Lon. 1854. (Patron, V. of Enfield; P. C.'s Inc. 220*l*; Pop. 4954.) Chap. to Royal Small Arms Manufactory, Enfield-lock. [22]

HARMER, George, *Maisemore Parsonage, near Gloucester.*—St. John's Coll. Ox. B.A. 1850, M.A. 1852; Deac. 1851, Pr. 1852. P. C. of Maisemore, Dio. G. and B. 1857. (Patron, Bp of G. and B; P. C.'s Inc. 95*l* and Ho; Pop. 516.) Formerly C. of Limpsfield, Surrey. [23]

HARMER, Henry Marven, *Paddington, Eccles, Manchester.*—Dub. A.B. 1845, A.M. 1854; Deac. 1845, Pr. 1846. P. C. of Paddington, Dio. Man. 1863.

(Patrons, Crown and Bp alt; P. C.'s Inc. 160*l*; Pop. 6488.) Formerly C. of Royton, Lanc. 1845–47, St. Paul's, Manchester, 1847–51. St. Thomas's, Pendleton, 1851–54, St. George's, Pendleton, 1854–58; P. C. of Charleston, Eccles, 1858–63. [1]

HARNESS, William, 3, *Hyde-park-terrace, Kensington Gore, W.*—Ch. Coll. Cam. B.A. 1812, M.A. 1815; Deac. 1813 by Bp of Salis. Pr. 1814 by Bp of Ely. P. C. of All Saints', Knightsbridge, Dio. Lon. 1849. (Patron, R. of St. Margaret's, Westminster; P. C.'s Inc. 500*l*; Pop. 7041.) Preb. of St. Paul's. Formerly C. of Kilmeston, Hants, 1812, Dorking 1814–16, Preacher Conduit-street Chapel, Lond. several years, Hampstead 1823–26, Regent-square Ch. 1826–46, Knightsbridge 1846. Author, *Connection of Christianity with Human Happiness* (Boyle Lectures), 1823; *Parochial Sermons*, 1838; *Sermons on Education*, 1840; *Cambridge Sermons* (as Select Preacher), 1841; *Claims of the Church of Rome* (six Sermons), 1851; Two Dramatic Poems, privately printed; etc. [2]

HARNETT, Francis William, *Wolverton, Stony Stratford.*—King's Coll. Lond. B.A. 1848, Theol. Assoc. 1851; Deac. 1851 and Pr. 1852 by Bp of Lich. P. C. of St. George the Martyr's, Wolverton, Dio. Ox. 1860. (Patrons, Trustees of late Dr. Radcliffe; P. C.'s Inc. 150*l* and Ho; Pop. 1793.) Formerly C. of Watford, Herts, 1855–60. [3]

HARNEY, C. L., *Lingfield, Surrey.*—C. of Lingfield. [4]

HARPER, Edmund Tristram Horatio, *Abingdon, Berks.*—Pemb. Coll. Ox. B.A. 1845, M.A. 1849; Deac. 1852, Pr. 1853. 2nd Mast. of Abingdon Gr. Sch. 1855; Chap. of the Union, and C. and Lect. at Abingdon. [5]

HARPER, Ephraim, 31, *Bury New-road, Manchester.*—Dub. A.B. 1836; Deac. 1838 by Bp of Elphin. Pr. 1839 by Bp of Kildare. R. of St. Simon's, Salford, Dio. Man. 1846. (Patrons, the Crown and Bp of Man. alt; R.'s Inc. 300*l*; Pop. 6957.) Formerly C. of Philipstower, King's Co. 1836. Author, *Lives of Cranmer, Latimer and Hooper*, Manchester; and various Sermons. [6]

HARPER, Francis Whaley, *Selby Parsonage, Yorks.*—St. John's Coll. Cam. 1st cl. Cl. Trip. and B.A. 1837, M.A. 1840; Deac. 1844, Pr. 1846. P. C. of the Abbey Church, Selby, Dio. York, 1850. (Patron, Abp of York; Glebe, 31 acres; P. C.'s Inc. 300*l* and Ho; Pop. 5424.) Rural Dean 1861. Formerly Fell. of St. John's Coll. Cam; Cl. Lect. of Sid. Coll; Public Exam. for Cl. Hons. in the Univ. of Cam. 1847–48. Author, *Powers of the Greek Tenses, and other Papers*; *Sermons preached before the University of Cambridge*, 1847–48; *The Incomes of the Clergy, what they ought to be, and how to make them so*, 1856; *Dialogues on National Church and National Church Rate*, 1861. [7]

HARPER, Hugo Daniel, *Sherborne, Dorset.*—Jesus Coll. Ox. Fell. of, Johnson's Scho. Math. Scho. 2nd cl. Lit. Hum. 1st cl. Math. et Phy. B.A. 1845, M.A. 1847; Deac. 1846 by Bp of Ox. Pr. 1854 by Bp of Salis. Head Mast. of Sherborne Sch. [8]

HARPER, Latimer, *Burton Latimer, Kettering, Northants.*—Emman. Coll. Cam. B.A. 1823; Deac. 1824, Pr. 1825. R. of Catthorpe, Leic. Dio. Pet. 1825. (Patron, the present R; Tithe, 181*l* 7*s* 6*d*; R.'s Inc. 260*l* and Ho; Pop. 146.) [9]

HARPER, Philip Gregson, *Pelsall Vicarage, Wolverhampton.*—Wad. Coll. Ox. B.A. 1820, M.A. 1822; Deac. 1821, Pr. 1822. V. of Pelsall, Dio. Lich. 1859. (Patron, Bp of Lich; V.'s Inc. 160*l* and Ho; Pop. 1892.) Formerly C. of Pelsall; P. C. of Walsall Wood, Staffs, 1838–59. [10]

HARPER, Robert, *Dudley.*—Corpus Coll. Cam. 15th Wrang. and B.A. 1850, M.A. 1853; Deac. 1854 and Pr. 1859 by Bp of Wor. Head Mast. of Dudley Gr. Sch. 1854; C. of Dudley, 1859. [11]

HARPLEY, William, *Clayhanger Rectory, Tiverton.*—St. John's Coll. Cam. 11th Wrang. B.A. 1856, M.A. 1860; Deac. 1858, and Pr. 1861 by Bp of Ex. R. of Clayhanger, Dio. Ex. 1866. (Patron, W. N. Row, Esq; Tithe, 244*l*; Glebe, 42 acres; R.'s Inc. 325*l* and Ho; Pop. 274.) P. C. of Petton Chapel 1867. Formerly Head Mast. of Plymouth Gr. Sch. 1858–66; Asst. C. of St. Andrew's Chapel 1859–61. [12]

HARPUR, George, *North Clifton, Notts.*—Dub. A.B. 1855; Deac. 1856 and Pr. 1857 by Bp of Lin. C. of North Clifton. Formerly C. of South Collingham. Author, *Christ in the Psalms*, 1862, 6*s*. [13]

HARRIES, George, *Maenclochog, Haverfordwest, Pembrokeshire.*—Deac. 1819, Pr. 1820. V. of Llangolman with Llandilo, Pemb. Dio. St D. (Patron, H. W. Bowen, Esq; Llangolman, Tithe—Imp. 76*l* 6*s* 8*d*, V. 33*l* 13*s* 4*d*; Llandilo, Tithe—Imp. 22*l*, V. 11*l*; V.'s Inc. 98*l*; Pop. Llangolman 282, Llandilo 126.) Formerly V. of Maenclochog, Pemb. 1841–63. [14]

HARRIES, Gilbert Charles Frederick, *Gelligaer Rectory, Newport, Monmouthshire.*—Jesus Coll. Ox. B.A. 1849, M.A. 1852; Deac. 1851 and Pr. 1852 by Bp of Llan. R. of Gelligaer with Brithdir C. Glamorgan, Dio. Llan. 1862. (Patrons, Marquis of Bute's Trustees; Tithe, 669*l*; Glebe, 9 acres; R.'s Inc. 690*l* and Ho; Pop. Gelligaer 1899, Brithdir 3879.) Rural Dean and Surrogate; and Hon. Sec. to the Brecon Archidiaconal Education Board. Formerly C. of St. David's, Merthyr-Tydfil, 1851–53, St. Mary's, Brecon, 1853–55; R. of Llandefarlegfach, Brecon, 1855–62. [15]

HARRIES, John, *Trallong, Brecon.*—Lampeter; Deac. 1852, Pr. 1854. P. C. of Trallong, Dio. St. D. 1859. (Patron, Bp of St. D; P. C.'s Inc. 59*l*; Pop. 278.) C. of Llywell. [16]

HARRIES, Thomas, *Llandissilio (Carmarthenshire), near Narberth.*—Deac. 1841, Pr. 1842. V. of Llandissilio, Dio. St. D. 1850. (Patron, Bp of St. D; Tithe—App. 242*l* 18*s*, Imp. 9*l* 12*s*, V. 132*l* 10*s*; V.'s Inc. 135*l*; Pop. 1036.) P. C. of Egremont, Carmarthenshire, Dio. St. D. 1850. (Patron, R. Mansell, Esq; Tithe, Imp. 85*l*; P. C.'s Inc. 50*l*; Pop. 124.) [17]

HARRIES, William, *Malins Lee, Dawley, near Wellington, Salop.*—Lampeter; Deac. 1831 and Pr. 1832 by Bp of St. D. P. C. of Malins Lee, Dio. Lich. 1843. (Patron, P. C. of Great Dawley; P. C.'s Inc. 150*l* and Ho; Pop. 4512.) Author, *Sermon on Matt.* xxiv. 1, 2, 1848; *Conversation on the Burial Service*, 1849. [18]

HARRIES, William, *Marlais, Milford, Pembrokeshire.*—V. of Marlais, Dio. St. D. (Patron, Ld Chan; V.'s Inc. 80*l*; Pop. 443.) C. of St. Bride's, Pembrokeshire. [19]

HARRIES, William Ware, *Knebworth, Stevenage, Herts.*—Jesus Coll. Cam. B.A. 1861, M.A. 1865; Deac. 1862 and Pr. 1863 by Bp of Roch. C of Knebworth 1864. Formerly C. of Codicote 1862–64. [20]

HARRIS, Alfred Edward Ormonde, *Stoke Vicarage, Rochester.*—King's Coll. Lond. Theol. Assoc. Deac. 1855 by Bp of Lon. Pr. 1856 by Bp of Roch. V. of Stoke, Dio. Roch. 1856. (Patron, J. Pearson, Esq; Tithe—App. 145*l* 15*s*, Imp. 573*l* 0*s* 5*d*, V. 160*l* 12*s*; Glebe, 44½ acres; V.'s Inc. 282*l* and Ho; Pop. 557.) [21]

HARRIS, Charles, *St. Mary's Parsonage, Summers-Town, near Tooting, Surrey, S.*—Wad. Coll. Ox. B.A. 1844, M.A. 1847; Deac. 1845 and Pr. 1846 by Bp of Herf. P. C. of St. Mary's, Summers-Town, Dio. Win. 1859. (Patrons, Trustees; Glebe, 5 acres; P. C.'s Inc. 225*l* and Ho; Pop. 920.) Chap. to St. Clement's Danes Almshouses, Streatham (Value, 50*l*.) Formerly C. of Clun, Salop, 1845–46, Trinity, Cheltenham, 1847–55. [22]

HARRIS, The Ven. and Hon. Charles Amyand, *Bremhill Vicarage, Chippenham.*—Oriel Coll Ox. B.A. 1835, All Souls, M.A. 1837; Deac. 1836 by Bp of Ox. Pr. 1837 by Bp of Lon. Archd. of Wilts 1863. (Value, 200*l*.) V. of Bremhill with Highway, Dio. Salis. 1863. (Patron, Bp of Salis; V.'s Inc. 525*l* and Ho; Pop. 1293.) Chap. to Bp of Salis. Formerly Fell. of All Souls, Ox; Preb. of Chardstock in Salis. Cathl. 1841; P. C. of Rownhams, Southampton, 1855–63. [23]

HARRIS, Charles Butler, *Dunstable.*—Queens' Coll. Cam. B.A. 1845, M.A. 1865; Deac. and Pr. 1845. Dunstable Coll. and Commercial Sch. Formerly P. C. of Helsingtoo, Westmoreland, 1851–60. [24]

HARRIS, Charles Sumpter, *Littleport, Ely.*—Trin. Hall, Cam. S.C.L. 1856, B.C.L. 1859, M.A. 1861; Deac. 1856 and Pr. 1857 by Bp of Ely. P. C. of Little Ouse, Norfolk, Dio. Ely, 1866. (Patron, Bp of Ely; Tithe, 210*l*; Glebe, 85 acres; P. C.'s Inc. 280*l*; Pop. 800.) Formerly C. of Swavesey, Cambs; P. C. of Bottisham, Cambs. 1863–66. [1]

HARRIS, Edward, *Swanton-Abbott, Norwich.*—Ex. Coll. B.A. 1852, and Wells Theol. Coll; Deac. 1853 and Pr. 1854 by Bp of Salis. R. of Swanton-Abbott, Dio. Nor. 1863. (Patron, W. L. J. Jex-Blake, Esq; Tithe, 275*l*; Glebe, 10 acres; R.'s Inc. 300*l*; Pop. 523.) Formerly C. of Southbroom, Wilts. [2]

HARRIS, F., *Chipping Norton, Oxon.*—V. of Chipping Norton, Dio. Ox. 1866. (Patron, D. and C. of Glouc; V.'s Inc. 180*l* and Ho; Pop. 3510.) [3]

HARRIS, Frederic William, *Medmenham Vicarage, near Great Marlow, Bucks.*—Trin. Coll. Cam. B.A. 1837, M.A. 1840; Deac. 1838 and Pr. 1839 by Bp of Ches. V. of Medmenham, Dio. Ox. 1855. (Patron, C. R. Scott Murray, Esq; Tithe—Imp. 10*l*, V. 200*l* 15*s*; Glebe, 2 acres; V.'s Inc. 200*l* and Ho; Pop. 380.) [4]

HARRIS, Frederick William, *Summers-Town, near Tooting, Surrey, S.*—C. of Summers-Town. [5]

HARRIS, George Collyer, *Torquay.*—Ex. Coll. Ox. B.A. 1856, M.A. 1858; Deac. 1857 and Pr. 1858 by Bp of G. and B. Min. of St. Luke's, Chapel of Ease, Torquay, Dio. Ex. 1862. (Patron, P. C. of Tor Mohun; Min.'s Inc. 280*l*.) Preb. of Ex. 1865. Formerly C. of Chipping Campden 1859, Tor Mohun 1859. Author, *Lessons from St. Peter's Life*, Rivingtons, 1865; *Church Seasons and Present Times*, Ib. 1867, 5*s*. [6]

HARRIS, George Hemington, *Tunstead, Norwich.*—Ex. Coll. Ox. B.A. 1849, M.A. 1852, Theol. Coll. Wells; Deac. 1850, Pr. 1851. V. of Tunstead with South Ruston, Dio. Nor. 1863. (Patroness, Mrs. Mack; V.'s Inc. 340*l*; Pop. 507.) Formerly C. of Downton and Nunton, Salisbury. [7]

HARRIS, George Poulett, *Bangor Monachorum, near Wrexham.*—Trin. Coll. Cam. Sen. Opt. 2nd cl. Cl. Trip. and B.A. 1844, M.A. 1854; Deac. 1845, Pr. 1847. C. of Bangor 1866. Formerly Head Mast. of the Ch. of Eng. Endow. Sch. St. John's, Newfoundland, 1855–64. [8]

HARRIS, Henry, *Winterbourne Bassett, Swindon, Wilts.*—Magd. Coll. Ox. B.A. 1841, M.A. 1843, B.D. 1858; Deac. 1842, Pr. 1853. R. of Winterbourne Bassett, Dio. Salis. 1858. (Patron, Magd. Coll. Ox; Tithe, 687*l* 15*s* 6*d*; Glebe, 41 acres; R.'s Inc. 708*l*; Pop. 249.) Formerly P. C. of Horspath, Oxon, 1853–58. [9]

HARRIS, Henry, *Horbling Vicarage, Folkingham, Lincolnshire.*—St. Cath. Hall, Cam. B.A. 1841; Deac. 1841, Pr. 1842. V. of Horbling, Dio. Lin. 1845. (Patron, Bp of Lin; Tithe, 10*l*; Glebe, 262 acres; V.'s Inc. 272*l* and Ho; Pop. 546.) [10]

HARRIS, Henry Hibbert, *Allhallows Parsonage, Wigton, Cumberland.*—St. Bees; Deac. 1857 and Pr. 1859 by Bp of Carl. P. C. of Allhallows, Dio. Carl. 1859. (Patron, Bp of Carl; P. C.'s Inc. 100*l* and Ho; Pop. 256.) [11]

HARRIS, Henry Thomas, *Llangunider Rectory, Crickhowell.*—New Inn Hall Ox. R. of Llangunider, Dio. St. D. 1862. (Patron, Duke of Beaufort; R.'s Inc. 450*l* and Ho; Pop. 3133.) [12]

HARRIS, Henry Truman, *Grey Friar's Green, Coventry.*—Queen's Coll. Cam. B.A. 1831; Deac. 1832 and Pr. 1833 by Abp of York. Min. of Ch. Ch. Chapel of Ease, in the parish of St. Michael's, Coventry, Dio. Wor. 1845. (Patron, V. of St. Michael's, Coventry; Min.'s Inc. derived solely from Pew Rents, 179*l*.) [13]

HARRIS, Herbert, *Whitchurch, Salop.*—St. John's Coll. Ox. B.A. 1842, M.A. 1846; Deac. 1844 and Pr. 1845 by Abp of Cant. 2nd Mast. of the Gr. Sch. Whitchurch. [14]

HARRIS, J., *Greenwich, S.E.*—Chap. of the "Dreadnought" Hospital Ship, Greenwich. [15]

HARRIS, J. O., 19, *Stainsley-road, Limehouse, E.*—St. Cath. Coll. Cam. B.A. 1858; Deac. 1858 and Pr. 1859 by Bp of Ex. C. of St. Matthew's Mission District, Limehouse. [16]

HARRIS, James, *Chester.*—Head Mast. of the Cathl. Sch. Chester. Author, *Exercises in English Grammar and Composition*, 2nd ed. 1*s*; *Graduated Exercises in Arithmetic and Mensuration*, Longmans, 2*s* 6*d*. [17]

HARRIS, James, *Paglesham Rectory, Rochford, Essex.*—Pemb. Coll. Ox. Scho of, B.A. 1842, M.A. 1844; Deac. 1842 and Pr. 1843 by Bp of Ex. R. of Paglesham, Dio. Roch. 1860. (Patron, Bp of Pet; Tithe, comm. 560*l*; Glebe, 18 acres; R.'s Inc. 554*l* and Ho; Pop. 447.) Formerly C. of Yarnscombe and Sunday Even. Lect. at Barnstaple 1842; C. of Tawstock 1846, St. Mary's, Southampton, 1853. Author, *Don't Chance It*, 8th thousand, Wertheim and Mackintosh, 1859; *An Alphabetical Prayer for a Little Child*, 1852. [18]

HARRIS, James Henry Beresford, *Cannon Gate House, near Hythe.*—Sid. Coll. Cam. LL.B. 1851; Deac. 1853 and Pr. 1855 by Bp of Wor. Chap. to the Forces 1855. Patron of West Stoke R. Sussex. [19]

HARRIS, John, *Buildwas, Ironbridge, Salop.* [20]

HARRIS, John, *Madeley, Wellington, Salop.*—C. of Madeley. [21]

HARRIS, Joseph, 2, *Fulham-place, Paddington, London, W.*—Pemb. Coll. Cam. 24th Wrang. and B.A. 1840, M.A. 1845; Deac. 1844, Pr. 1845. Asst. Mast. of the City of Lond. Sch. 1841; C. of St. Philip's Chapel, Paddington. [22]

HARRIS, Joseph, M.A., *Westcotes, Leicester.* [23]

HARRIS, Joseph Hemington, *Kanescombe, Torquay.*—Clare Coll. Cam. 5th Wrang. and B.A. 1822, M.A. 1825, D.D. 1829; Deac. 1824, Pr. 1825. P. C. of Tor-Mohun with Cockington, Dio. Ex. 1848. (Patron, C. H. Mallock, Esq; Tithe—Imp. 267*l* 10*s*; P. C.'s Inc. 270*l*; Pop. Tor-Mohun 4217, Cockington 210.) Formerly Fell. of Clare Coll. Cam; Prin. of Upper Canada Coll. Toronto. [24]

HARRIS, Percy Bysshe, *Corby Rectory, Thrapstone, Northants.*—Clare Coll. Cam. B.A. 1829, M.A. 1834; Deac. 1829 and Pr. 1830 by Bp of Pet. R. of Corby, Dio. Pet. 1834. (Patron, Earl of Cardigan; Tithe, 62*l* 2*s* 5*d*; R.'s Inc. 339*l* and Ho; Pop. 850.) R. of Deene, Northants, Dio. Pet. 1834. (Patron, Earl of Cardigan; Tithe, 428*l* 2*s* and 94 acres of Land; R.'s Inc. 570*l* and Ho; Pop. 540.) [25]

HARRIS, P. S., *Budbrooke, near Warwick.*—C. of Budbrooke. [26]

HARRIS, Richard Deodatus, *Hobart Town, Tasmania.*—Trin. Coll. Cam. B.A. 1843, M.A. 1852; Deac. and Pr. 1847. Head Mast. of the High Sch. Hobart Town, 1858. Formerly Cl. Mast. of the Blackheath Sch. 1849–58; 2nd Mast. of the Sheffield Coll. Sch. 1843; Vice-Prin. of the Huddersfield Coll. 1844; C. of Longsight, Manchester, 1847. [27]

HARRIS, Robert, *Ipplepen Vicarage, Newton Abbott, Devon.*—Trin. Coll. Cam. Exhib. B.A. 1833, M.A. 1837; Deac. 1832 and Pr. 1833 by Bp of Lich. V. of Ipplepen, Dio. Ex. 1862. (Patrons, D. and C. of Windsor; Tithe, 72*l* 10*s*; Glebe, 18 acres; V.'s Inc. 130*l* and Ho; Pop. 977.) Formerly C. of Wolverhampton 1833; P. C. of Brierly Hill, Staffs, to 1856; R. of Bradfield, Norfolk, to 1859; P. C. of St. Mark's, Hull, to 1862. [28]

HARRIS, Samuel Bache, *Florence.*—Clare Coll. Cam. Sen. Opt. Scho. and Prizeman of Coll. B.A. 1851, M.A. 1854; Deac. 1853 and Pr. 1854 by Bp of Wor. Chap. to the English Embassy at Florence. Formerly C. of Great Malvern 1853, St. Marylebone 1855, Ewell 1857; P. C. of St. Martin's-at-Palace, Norwich, 1859–66. [29]

HARRIS, Samuel George, *Highweek, Newton Abbott, Devon.*—Ex. Coll. Ox. 4th cl. Lit. Hum. B.A. 1848, M.A. 1857; Deac. 1848 by Bp of B. and W. Pr. 1850 by Bp of Ex. R. of Highweek, Dio. Ex. 1864. (Patron, Bp of Ex; Tithe, 378*l*, with reservation of 60*l* to the present V. of Kingsteignton; Glebe, 13½ acres; R.'s Inc. 350*l* and Ho; Pop. 1571.) Formerly C. of Cornworthy 1848-51, Diptford 1851-52, Membeniot 1853-56, Churston-Ferrers 1856-61, Highweek 1861-64. [1]

HARRIS, Stanford, 61, *Higher Ardwick, Manchester.*—St. Edm. Hall, Ox. B.A. 1847, M.A. 1850; Deac. 1847 and Pr. 1848 by Bp of Ches. P. C. of St. Barnabas', Manchester, Dio. Man. 1852. (Patrons, Trustees; P. C.'s Inc. 300*l*; Pop. 8232.) Formerly C. of North Meols, Lancashire, 1847; Chap. of Debtors' Gaol and Union Workhouse, Halifax, 1850; C. of Brighouse, Yorks, 1852. [2]

HARRIS, T.—Min. of the District of Kilvey, Llansamlet, Glamorganshire. [3]

HARRIS, Thomas, *Swerford, Enstone, Oxon.*—Magd. Coll. Ox. B.A. 1844. R. of Swerford, Dio. Ox. 1849. (Patron, Magd. Coll. Ox; Tithe, 188*l* 8*s* 11*d*; R.'s Inc. 540*l* and Ho; Pop. 402.) Formerly Fell. of Magd. Coll. Ox. [4]

HARRIS, Thomas, *Kirkhenton Hall, Newcastle-on-Tyne.*—Jesus Coll. Cam. B.A. 1863, M A. 1867; Deac. 1864 and Pr. 1865 by Bp of Rip. Chap. of Don. of Kirkheaton, Dio. Dur. 1865. (Patron, C. Bewicke, Esq; Pop. 160.) Formerly C. of St. Mary's, Barnsley, 1864-65. Author, *The Kingship of Christ in His Church, the only Security for the Faith* (a Sermon), 1864. [5]

HARRIS, W. C., *Brasenose College, Oxford.*—Scho. of Brasen. Coll. Ox. [6]

HARRIS, William, *Seaton, Devon.*—Pemb. Coll. Ox. B.A. 1855, M.A. 1858; Deac. 1857 and Pr. 1858 by Bp of Ex. C. of Seaton and Beer 1857. Author, *The Day of Judgment* (an Advent Sermon), 1860, 1*s*. [7]

HARRIS, William, *Llanarthney, Llandilo-Fawr, Carmarthenshire.*—Lampeter; Deac. 1830, Pr. 1831. V. of Llanarthney, Dio. St. D. 1852. (Patron, Bp of St. D; Tithe—App. 666*l* 13*s* 4*d*; V. 333*l* 6*s* 8*d*; Glebe, 1 acre; V.'s Inc. 333*l*; Pop. 2001.) [8]

HARRIS, William Henry, *North Pickenham, Swaffham, Norfolk.*—Pemb. Coll. Ox. B.A. 1854, M.A. 1857; Deac. 1854 and Pr. 1855 by Bp of Lich. C. of St. Andrew's, North Pickenham with St. Mary the Virgin's, Houghton-on-the-Hill, 1862. Formerly C. of St. Peter's with Normanton, Derby, 1854, St. Peter's and St. Paul's, Swaffham with Threxton, 1857. [9]

HARRISON, Alfred, 132, *Albany-street, Regent's Park, N.W.*—Caius Coll. Cam. B.A. 1857; Deac. 1859 and Pr. 1860 by Bp of Lich. C. of Ch. Ch. St. Pancras, Lond. 1865. Formerly C. of Hope, Derbyshire, 1859-63, Digby, Lincolnshire, 1863-65. [10]

HARRISON, The Ven. Benjamin, *Precincts, Canterbury.*—Ch. Ch. Ox. 1st cl. Lit. Hum. 2nd cl. Math. et Phy. and B.A. 1830, M.A. 1833; Deac. 1832 by Bp of Roch. Pr. 1833 by Bp of Ox. Archd. of Maidstone with Canonry in Cant. Cathl. annexed, 1845. (Value of Archdeaconry and Canonry, 900*l* and Res.) Formerly Dom. Chap. to the Abp of Cant. 1838-48; one of the Six Preachers in Cant. Cathl. 1842-45. Author, *An Historical Inquiry into the True Interpretation of the Rubrics respecting the Sermon and the Communion Service,* 1845; *Charge to the Clergy of the Archdeaconry of Maidstone, at his Primary Visitation,* 1846; *The Religious Care of the Church's Sanctuaries, and the Religious Education of her Children* (a Charge), 1847; *The Remembrance of a Departed Guide and Ruler in the Church of God* (a Charge) 1848; *Prophetic Outlines of the Christian Church and the Anti-Christian Power, as traced in the Visions of Daniel and St. John* (Warburtonian Lectures), 1849; *Privileges, Duties and Perils in the English Branch of the Church of Christ at the present Time* (Six Sermons preached in Canterbury Cathedral), 1850; *The Church the Guardian of her Children, her Guide the Oracles of God* (a Charge), 1850; *The present Position of the Church of England and the consequent Duties of her Ministers* (a Charge), 1851; *The Church's Sons brought back to her from far* (Funeral Sermon for Bishop Broughton, preached in Canterbury Cathedral), 1853; *The Church-rate Question and the Principles involved in it* (a Charge) 1854; *Church-rate Abolition in its latest Form* (a Charge), 1855; *All Things referred to God* (Funeral Sermon for the Right Hon. Sir Robert Harry Inglis, Bart., preached at Milton Bryan), 1855. [11]

HARRISON, Bowyer, *Maughold, Ramsey, Isle of Man.*—Deac. 1815, Pr. 1816. V. of Maughold, Dio. S. and M. 1818. (Patron, the Crown; V.'s Inc. 175*l* and Ho; Pop. 4545.) [12]

HARRISON, Christopher Robert, *Peldon Rectory, Colchester.*—All Souls Coll. Ox. 2nd cl. Lit. Hum. B.C.L. 1845; Deac. 1844 and Pr. 1845 by Bp of Roch. R. of Peldon, Dio. Roch. 1855. (Patroness, the Countess Waldegrave; Tithe, 582*l* 10*s*; Glebe, 24 acres; R.'s Inc. 609*l* and Ho; Pop. 501.) Formerly R. of Leigh, Essex, 1852-55. [13]

HARRISON, Charles Sawkins, *Cottisford Rectory, Brackley.*—Univ. Coll. Dur. B.A. 1837, M A. 1840; Deac. 1838 and Pr. 1839 by Bp of Ches. R. of Cottisford, Dio. Ox. 1853. (Patron, Eton Coll; Tithe, 302*l*; Glebe, 62 acres; R.'s Inc. 400*l* and Ho; Pop. 269.) [14]

HARRISON, David John, *The Rectory, Ludgvan, Penzance.*—Pemb. Coll. Ox. B.A. 1846, M.A. 1849; Deac. 1848 and Pr. 1849 by Bp of Lon. R. of Ludgvan, Dio. Ex. 1862. (Patrons, Duke of Cleveland and Earl of Sandwich alt; Tithe, 808*l*; Glebe, 23 acres; R.'s Inc. 820*l* and Ho; Pop. 3480.) Formerly C. of Tottenham 1848, St. Peter's, Walworth, 1852; P. C. of St. Paul's, Tottenham, 1855-62. [15]

HARRISON, Edward Henry, 3, *Suffolk-square, Cheltenham.*—Caius Coll. Cam. B.A. 1864; Deac. 1865 by Bp of St. A. Pr. 1866 by Bp of Ches. C. of Leckhampton, Glouc. 1867. Formerly C. of Trinity, Southport, 1865-66, St. John's, Chester, 1867. [16]

HARRISON, Francis, *North Wraxall, Chippenham.*—Queens' Coll. Ox. Bridgman Exhib. 1847, 3rd cl. Lit. Hum. 1st cl. Math. et Phy. and B.A. 1850, M.A. 1853, Sen. Math. Scho. 1852; Public Examiner 1855, 1867; Moderator 1856, 57, 62, and 63; Proctor of the University 1864-65. R. of North Wraxall, Wilts, Dio. G. and B. 1866. (Patron, Oriel Coll. Ox; Tithe, 375*l*; Glebe, 87 acres; R.'s Inc. 500*l* and Ho; Pop. 466.) Late Fell. Math. Lect. Tut. and Dean of Oriel Coll. 1852-67. Author, *The Cloud of Witnesses* (a Sermon) 1859. [17]

HARRISON, Francis Lupton, *South Muskham, Newark, Notts.*—Caius Coll. Cam. B.A. 1856, M.A. 1859; Deac. 1857 and Pr. 1858 by Bp of Rip. V. of South Muskham, Dio. Lin. 1864. (Patron, Bp of Rip; V.'s Inc. 150*l*; Pop. 277.) Formerly C. of St. Andrew's, Leeds. [18]

HARRISON, Frederic, *Newent, Glouc.*—C. of Newent. [19]

HARRISON, Frederick Standen, *Woolwich.*—C. of Woolwich. [20]

HARRISON, George, *Rainow Parsonage, Macclesfield.*—Lin. Coll. Ox. B.A. 1825, M.A. 1828; Deac. 1826 and Pr. 1827 by Bp of Lin. P. C. of Rainow, Dio. Ches. 1843. (Patron, V. of Prestbury; Tithe, Imp. 165*l* 2*s* 2*d*; P. C.'s Inc. 120*l* and Ho; Pop. 1550.) [21]

HARRISON, George, *Sutcombe Rectory, Holsworthy, Devon.*—St. Cath. Coll. Cam. B.A. 1830, M.A. 1837; Deac. 1830 and Pr. 1831 by Bp of Lich. R. of Sutcombe, Dio. Ex. 1853. (Patron, W. B. Coham, Esq; Tithe, 300*l*; Glebe, 62 acres; R.'s Inc. 340*l* and Ho; Pop. 441.) Formerly V. of New Brentford, Middlesex, 1842-53; P. C. of Elstead, Surrey, 1841-42. [22]

HARRISON, Goodeve, *Oliocio, near Colchester.*—Jesus Coll. Cam. B.A. 1819, M.A. 1822; Deac. 1820, Pr. 1821. [23]

HARRISON, Henry, *The Parsonage, Idle, near Leeds.*—Dur. Licen. Theol; Deac. 1850, Pr. 1851. P. C. of Idle, Dio. Rip. 1857. (Patron, V. of Calverley; P. C.'s Inc. 300*l* and Ho; Pop. 9155.) Formerly C. of Ch. Ch. Salford, 1854-57. Author, *Memoirs of James Wilson,* 1858. [24]

HARRISON, Henry, *Kilndown Parsonage, Goudhurst, Kent.*—Trin. Coll. Cam. Jun. Opt. and B.A. 1835, M.A. 1838; Deac. 1836 and Pr. 1837 by Abp of Cant. P. C. of Kilndown, Dio. Cant. 1840. (Patron, A. J. Beresford Hope, Esq; Glebe, 2½ acres; P. C.'s Inc. 350*l* and Ho; Pop. 904.) Dom. Chap. to Viscount Beresford 1843. Formerly C. of Goudhurst 1835. Author, *Addresses to the Parishioners of Kilndown on the Fast-day for the Cholera*, 1849; *Prayers for the Sick, Wounded, and Dying in the Time of War.* [1]

HARRISON, H.A., *Witney.*—C. of Witney. [2]

HARRISON, J., *Beckford Vicarage, Tewkesbury.*—V. of Beckford with Aston-under Hill C. Dio. G. and B. 1865. (Patron, R. Timbrill, Esq; V.'s Inc. 390*l* and Ho; Pop. 884.) [3]

HARRISON, J., *Birkenshaw, Leeds.*—C. of Birkenshaw. [4]

HARRISON, James Harwood, sen., M.A., —*Bugbrooke, Weedon, Northants.* [5]

HARRISON, James Harwood, jun., *Bugbrooke Parsonage, Weedon, Northants.*—Magd. Coll. Ox. B.A. 1857, M.A. 1865; Deac. 1857 by Bp of Pet. Pr. 1858 by Bp of Man. R. of Bugbrooke, Dio. Pet. 1859. (Patron, Rev. J. H. Harrison, sen; Tithe, 50*l*; Glebe, 410 acres; R.'s Inc. 850*l* and Ho; Pop. 935.) [6]

HARRISON, James Knowles, *Lowther Cottages, Holloway, London, N.*—Deac. 1845 and Pr. 1846 by Abp of Cant. P. C. of St. Clement's, Barnsbury-park, Islington, Dio. Lon. 1858. (Patron, V. of Islington; P. C.'s Inc. 150*l*; Pop. 5000.) Formerly P. C. of Ford, Herefordshire, 1852–58. [7]

HARRISON, Jasper Nicolls, *Laugharne Vicarage, St. Clear's, Carmarthenshire.*—Wor. Coll. Ox. 2nd cl. Lit. Hum. and B.A. 1830, M.A. 1835; Deac. 1831, Pr. 1832. V. of Laugharne with Llansadurnen R. Dio. St. D. 1834. (Patrons, D. and C. of Win; Laugharne, Tithe—Imp. 739*l* 14*s* 9*d*, V. 215*l* 11*s* 3*d*; Llansadurnen, Tithe, 200*l*; Glebe, 23 acres; V.'s Inc. 456*l* and Ho; Pop. Laugharne 1868, Llansadurnen 194.) Formerly Fell. and Tut. of Wor. Coll. Ox. [8]

HARRISON, John, *Andover, Hants.*—Dub. A.B. 1835, A.M. 1838; Deac. 1840 and Pr. 1841 by Bp of Ches. Head Mast. of the Andover Gr. Sch; Chap. to the Andover Union; C. of Penton Mewsey 1857. [9]

HARRISON, John, *Cowley Hill, St. Helens.*—Dub. A.B. 1862, LL.B. 1863; Deac. 1863, Pr. 1864. C. of St. Thomas's, Eccleston, 1863. [10]

HARRISON, John, *Bishopstone, Seaford, Sussex.*—V. of Bishopstone, Dio. Chich. 1846. (Patron, Bp of Lon; V.'s Inc. 88*l*; Pop. 322.) [11]

HARRISON, John, *Aughton Vicarage, York.*—V. of Aughton with Cottingwith C. Dio. York, 1860. (Patron, A. J. Fletcher, Esq; V.'s Inc. 140*l* and Ho; Pop. 633.) [12]

HARRISON, John, *Askern, near Doncaster.*—Deac. 1854 and Pr. 1855 by Bp of Lich. P. C. of Fenwick, Dio. York, 1867. (Patron, Abp of York; P. C.'s Inc. 100*l*; Pop. 486.) Formerly C. of Burslem 1854–58, Rotherham 1858–60, Sheffield 1860–63, Pitsmoor, Sheffield, 1863–67. Author, *The Scriptural Doctrine of Justification*, Nisbet, 6*d*; *An Antidote to the Teaching of certain Anglo-Catholics concerning Worshipping Eastward, Altar Adoration, Clerical Sacerdotalism, Baptism and the Real Presence, with an Exposure of their Assumption that their Religion is the Bible interpreted by the Church*, Longmans, 1*s* 6*d*; *Whose are the Father's? or the Teaching of certain Anglo-Catholics on the Church and its Ministry contrary alike to the Holy Scripture, to the Fathers of the First Six Centuries, and to those of the Reformed Church of England; with a Catena Patrum of the First Six Centuries, and of the English Church of the Latter Half of the Sixteenth Century*, Longmans, 1866, 16*s*. [13]

HARRISON, John Branfill, *Walmer, Kent.*—Trin. Coll. Cam. B.A. 1845, M.A. 1848; Deac. 1846, Pr. 1847. V. of Walmer, Dio. Cant. 1854. (Patron, Abp of Cant; Tithe—App. 233*l* 2*s* 6*d*, P. C. 113*l*; Glebe, 7 acres; P. C.'s Inc. 280*l*; Pop. 3275.) Formerly P. C. of Stapleford, Notts, 1848; C. of Maidstone 1849. Author, *Reasons for not submitting to the Romish Church, in Answer to a Letter by H. W. Wilberforce to his late Parishioners at East Farleigh* (a Pamphlet), 1851, 4*d*. [14]

HARRISON, John Brownrigg, *Plumpton Parsonage, Penrith.*—Deac. 1829 and Pr. 1830 by Bp of Carl. P. C. of Plumpton, Dio. Carl. 1839. (Patron, Mr. Dixon; Glebe, 25 acres; P. C.'s Inc. 64*l* and Ho; Pop. 333.) Formerly C. of Culgaith 1829–37. [15]

HARRISON, John Butler, *Evenley Vicarage, Brackley, Northants.*—Magd. Coll. Ox. B.A. 1811, M.A. 1814, B.D. 1821; Deac. and Pr. 1814 by Bp of Glouc. V. of Evenley, Dio. Pet. 1832. (Patron, Magd. Coll. Ox; Tithe—Imp. 218*l*, V. 67*l*; Glebe, 119 acres; V.'s Inc. 180*l* and Ho; Pop. 525.) [16]

HARRISON, John Butler, jun., *Evenley, Brackley, Northants.*—New Coll. Ox. B.A. 1858, M.A. 1861; Deac. 1864 and Pr. 1866 by Bp of Ox. C. of Evenley 1864; Fell. of New Coll. Ox. [17]

HARRISON, John James, B.A.—Chap. of H.M.S. "Victory." [18]

HARRISON, John Newman, *Reigate Vicarage, Surrey.*—V. of Reigate, Dio. Win. 1847. (Patron, the present R; Tithe—Imp. 1066*l* 14*s* 10*d*, V. 380*l*; V.'s Inc. 478*l* and Ho; Pop. 9975.) Surrogate. [19]

HARRISON, Michael, *Steeple-Langford, Heytesbury, Wilts.*—Corpus Coll. Ox. B.A. 1837, M.A. 1840, B.D. 1847; Deac. 1840 and Pr. 1841 by Bp of Ox; R. of Steeple-Langford, Dio. Salis. 1853. (Patron, Corpus Coll. Ox; Tithe—Imp. 42*l*, R. 668*l*; Glebe, 49½ acres; R.'s Inc. 720*l* and Ho; Pop. 628.) Formerly Fell. of Corpus Coll. Ox. [20]

HARRISON, Octavius Swale, *Thorn Falcon Rectory, Taunton.*—Queen's Coll. Ox. B.A. 1828, M.A. 1830; Deac. 1829, Pr. 1830. R. of Thorn Falcon, Dio. B. and W. 1842. (Patron, J. Batten, Esq; Tithe, 140*l*; Glebe, 73½ acres; R.'s Inc. 240*l* and Ho; Pop. 296.) Formerly Chap. R.N. [21]

HARRISON, Richard Hopkins, *Builth, Brecon.*—Trin. Coll. Ox. B.A. 1828, M.A. 1834; Deac. 1829 by Bp of Herf. Pr. 1830 by Bp of Ox. P. C. of Builth, *alias* Llanvair-yn-Muallt, Dio. St. D. 1844. (Patron, Thomas Thomas, Esq; Tithe—Imp. 84*l* and 50 acres of Glebe; P. C.'s Inc. 113*l*; Pop. 1110.) P. C. of Llanddewi-'r-Cwm, near Builth, Dio. St. D. 1845. (Patrons, R. B. Price and V. Pocock, Esqs. alt; Tithe—Imp. 121*l* 4*s*; P. C.'s Inc. 77*l*; Pop. 215.) [22]

HARRISON, Robert John, *Forden, Welshpool, Montgomeryshire.*—Emman. Coll. Cam. B.A. 1836, M.A. 1840; Deac. 1836, Pr. 1837. P. C. of Forden, Dio. Herf. 1844. (Patrons, Grocers' Company; Tithe, Imp. 462*l* 13*s* 3*d*; P. C.'s Inc. 138*l* and Ho; Pop. 926.) [23]

HARRISON, Thomas, *Christ Church Parsonage, Stafford.*—Dub. A.B. 1829, A.M. 1832; Deac. 1829 by Bp of Herf. Pr. 1830 by Bp of Ches. P. C. of Ch. Ch. Stafford, Dio. Lich. 1839. (Patron, R. of Stafford; P. C.'s Inc. 300*l* and Ho; Pop. 5423.) Sinecure R. of Creswell, Staffs, Dio. Lich. 1852. (Patron, Capt. Whitby; Tithe, 20*l*; Sinecure R.'s Inc. 20*l*; Pop. 12.) [24]

HARRISON, Thomas, *Barham, near Canterbury.*—P. C. of Womenswould, Canterbury, Dio. Cant. 1845. (Patron, Abp of Cant; Tithe, 53*l* 18*s* 6*d*; Glebe, 2 acres; P. C.'s Inc. 87*l*; Pop. 276.) [25]

HARRISON, Thomas, *Rackheath Rectory, near Norwich.*—Emman. Coll. Cam. Sen. Opt. B.A. 1849, M.A. 1852; Deac. 1850 and Pr. 1851 by Abp of York. R. of Rackheath, Dio. Nor. 1864. (Patron, Sir H. J. Stracey, Bart; Tithe, 456*l*; Glebe, 23 acres; R.'s Inc. 474*l* and Ho; Pop. 271.) Formerly C. of Leven, near Beverley, 1850–52, Bembridge, Isle of Wight, 1852–61; P. C. of Aslacton, Norfolk, 1861–64. [26]

HARRISON, Thomas, *Newchurch, New Romney, Kent.*—R. and V. of Newchurch, Dio. Cant. 1854. (Patron Abp of Cant; Tithe, R. and V. 632*l*; Glebe, 3 acres; R. and V.'s Inc. 636*l*; Pop. 332.) [27]

HARRISON, Thomas Dalton, *Mickley, Ripon.*—Deac. 1839 and Pr. 1840 by Abp of York. P. C. of Mickley, Dio. Rip. 1858. (Patron, V. of Masham; P. C.'s Inc. 80*l* and Ho; Pop. 210.) Formerly C. of Cawood, 1839–41, Kirklington 1842, Ripley 1842–48; V. of Upton, Lincolnshire, 1848–58. [28]

HARRISON, Thomas Thomas, *Thorp Morieux Rectory, Bildeston, Suffolk.*—R. of Thorp

Morieux, Dio. Ely, 1848. (Patron, J. H. Harrison, Esq; Tithe, 620*l*; R.'s Inc. 656*l* and Ho; Pop. 447.) [1]

HARRISON, Thomas Wayne, *Compton Dundon, Somerton, Somerset.*—Ch. Coll. Cam. B.A. 1832; Deac. 1833, Pr. 1834. V. of Compton Dundon, Dio. B. and W. 1863. (Patrons, Bp of Lon. and Bp of B. and W. alt; V.'s Inc. 300*l* and Ho; Pop. 662.) Formerly C. of Compton Dundon. [2]

HARRISON, William, *Chester.*—Ch. Ch. Ox. 2nd cl. Lit. Hum. 2nd cl. Math. et Phy. and B.A. 1820, M.A. 1823; Deac. 1820, Pr. 1821. V. of St. Oswald's with Bruera C. Chester, Dio. Ches. 1827. (Patrons, D. and C. of Ches; Tithe—App. 480*l* 5*s* 6*d*, V. 141*l*; Glebe, 19 acres; V.'s Inc. 204*l* Pop. 4680.) Min. Can. of Ches 1839; Surrogate. Formerly Mast of the King's Sch. Chester. Author, *Sermons*, 1859, 5*s*. [3]

HARRISON, William, *Warmington Rectory. Banbury.*—Ch. Ch. Ox. 1818; Deac. 1823, Pr. 1825, R. of Warmington, Dio. Wor. 1831. (Patrons, Hulme's Trustees; Tithe, 187*l*; Glebe, 189 acres; R.'s Inc. 460*l* and Ho; Pop. 452.) Formerly Usher in Westminster Sch. 1822. [4]

HARRISON, William, *Grimsargh, near Preston.*—Dub. A.B. 1832, A.M. 1843; Deac. 1836 and Pr. 1837 by Bp of Ches. P. C. of Grimsargh, Dio. Man. 1865. (Patron, V. of Preston; P. C.'s Inc. 92*l* and Ho; Pop. 353.) Formerly C. of Penwortham 1836, Waddington 1853. [5]

HARRISON, William, *Combe Hay, Bath.*—Brasen. Coll. Ox. B.A. 1846, M.A. 1849; Deac. 1846 and Pr. 1847 by Bp of Ches. R. of Pontesbury, First Portion, Dio. Herf. 1847. (Patron, the present R; Tithe, 785*l* 6*s*; Glebe, 22 acres; R.'s Inc. 835*l* and Ho; Pop. 1660.) Surrogate. Formerly C. of Ch. Ch. Macclesfield, 1846–47. [6]

HARRISON, William, *Birch Rectory, Colchester.*—Brasen. Coll. Ox. 3rd cl. Lit. Hum. and B.A. 1832, M.A. 1835; Deac. 1834, Pr. 1835. R. of Birch, Dio. Roch. 1848. (Patrons, Bp of Roch. and C. G. Round, Esq. alt; Tithe, 720*l*; Glebe, 72 acres; R.'s Inc. 770*l* and Ho; Pop. 940.) Dom. Chap. to H.R.H. the Duchess of Cambridge. Author, *Greek Grammar*, 1840; *Tongue of Time*, 1842; *Consecrated Thoughts*, 1843; *Sermons on the Decalogue*, 1844; *Shepherd and his Sheep*, 1844; *Light of the Forge*, 1852. [7]

HARRISON, William Anthony, 11, *Lawn-place, South Lambeth-road, London, S.*—Caius Coll. Cam. 1st cl. Moral Sci. Trip. and B.A. 1856, M.A. 1863; Deac. 1856 and Pr. 1857 by Bp of Ox. C. of St Mary's the Less, Lambeth, 1864. Formerly C. of Witney 1856–64. [8]

HARRISON, William Bagshaw, *Gayton-le-Marsh Rectory, Alford, Lincolnshire.*—Sid. Coll. Cam. B.A. 1826, M.A. 1829; Deac. 1826 and Pr. 1827 by Bp of Lon. R. of Gayton-le-Marsh, Dio. Lin. 1833. (Patron, Ld Chan; Tithe, 457*l* 10*s*; Glebe, 73 acres; R.'s Inc. 537*l* and Ho; Pop. 331.) Formerly C. of Folkestone 1827, Maidstone 1828. [9]

HARRISON, William Dann, *South Stoneham Vicarage, Southampton.*—Wor. Coll. Ox. B.A. 1826, M.A. 1828; Deac. 1826, Pr. 1827. V. of Crondall, Hants, Dio. Win. 1833. (Patron, St. Cross Hospital, Winchester; Tithe—Imp. 1963*l* 3*s* 6*d*, V. 592*l* 4*s* 9*d*; V.'s Inc. 593*l*; Pop. 1481.) V. of South Stoneham, Dio. Win. 1835. (Patron, R. of St. Mary's, Southampton; Tithe—App. 1430*l*, V. 500*l*; V.'s Inc. 500*l* and Ho; Pop. 736.) [10]

HARRISON, William Estcourt, *St. Peter's School House, York.*—St. Cath. Coll. Cam. B.A. 1832, M.A. 1840. Mast. in St. Peter's Sch. York. [11]

HARRISON, William Gorst, *Hart, Ferryhill, Durham.*—Trin. Coll. Cam. B.A. 1828, M.A. 1834; Deac. 1829 by Abp of York, Pr. 1831 by Bp of Dur. V. of Hart, Dio. Dur. 1845. (Patron, Ld Chan; Tithe—App. 15*l*, Imp. 331*l* 10*s*, V. 163*l* 15*s* 6*d*; Glebe, 75 acres; V.'s Inc. 238*l* and Ho; Pop. 736.) [12]

HARRISON, William Henry, *Victoria Cottage, Devizes.*—Lampeter, Philip's Scho. B.A. 1865; Deac. 1864 and Pr. 1865 by Bp of Salis. C. of St. John's and St. Mary's, Devizes, 1866. Formerly C. of Keevil with Bulkington, Wilts, 1864. [13]

HARRISON, William T., *St. John's, Great Yarmouth.*—Trin. Coll. Cam. 2nd cl. Cl. Trip. B.A. 1860, M.A. 1863; Deac. 1861, Pr. 1862. Min. of St. John's, Great Yarmouth, Dio. Nor. 1864. (Min.'s Inc. 198*l*.) Formerly C. of Great Yarmouth 1861–64. [14]

HARRISON, Robert Everson, *Hannington Rectory (Hants), Newbury.*—Ch. Coll. Cam. B.A. 1841, M.A. 1844; Deac. 1841 and Pr. 1842 by Bp of Lin. R. of Hannington, Dio. Win. 1857. (Patron, Bp of Win; Tithe, 410*l*; Glebe, 16 acres; R.'s Inc. 440*l* and Ho; Pop. 264.) Formerly C. of Allington and Sedgebrook, Lincolnshire, 1841–44, Fawley, Hants, 1844–57. [15]

HARSTON, Edward, *Sherborne Vicarage, Dorset.*—V. of Sherborne, Dio. Salis. 1854. (Patron, the Crown; Tithe—Imp. 1735*l*, V. 200*l*; V.'s Inc. 260*l* and Ho; Pop. 5793.) Chap. of Bp Neville's Hospital, Sherborne; Surrogate. [16]

HART, Cornelius, *Lingen, Presteign, Herefordshire.*—Corpus Coll. Cam. M.A. 1841. P. C. of Lingen, Dio. Herf. 1862. (Patron, Bp of Herf; P. C.'s Inc. 70*l*; Pop. 287.) Formerly P. C. of St. Pancras Old Church, Lond. 1850–62. [17]

HART, Dudley, *Downham Parsonage, Clitheroe.*—Dub. A.M; King's Coll. Lond. Theol. Assoc; Deac. 1854 and Pr. 1855 by Bp of Lon. P. C. of Langho, Dio. Man. 1859. (Patron, V. of Blackburn; P. C.'s Inc. 140*l*; Pop. 1038.) C. of Downham. Formerly C. of St. Mark's, Old-street, Lond. 1854–59. [18]

HART, Edgar Oswald, 45, *Charlotte-street, Hull.*—St. Aidan's; Deac. 1860 and Pr. 1861 by Abp of York. Min. of the Mariners' Ch. Hull, Dio. York, 1866. (Patrons, Trustees; Min.'s Inc. 200*l*.) Formerly C. of Drypool 1861, Walton with Felixstowe 1862–65, Mariners' Ch. Hull, 1865–66. [19]

HART, George Augustus Frederick, *Arundel, Sussex.*—Ch. Coll. Cam. B.A. 1820, M.A. 1823; Deac. 1823 and Pr. 1824 by Bp of Nor. V. of Arundel, Dio. Chich. 1844. (Patron, Earl of Albemarle; Tithe—Imp. 160*l*, V. 222*l* 7*s* 11*d*; Glebe, 1 rood, 12 perches; V.'s Inc. 230*l*; Pop. 2498.) Chap. in Ordinary to the Queen 1848; Surrogate. [20]

HART, H. M., *Gillingham, Chatham.*—C. of Gillingham. [21]

HART, Henry Cornelius, *Bradenham, near High Wycombe.*—Trin. Coll Cam. B.A. 1835, M.A. 1838; Deac. 1839, Pr. 1841. Dom. Chap. to the Duke of Argyll 1847. [22]

HART, John, *Adstock Rectory, Buckingham.*—St. John's Coll. Cam. Scho. of, B.A. 1846, M.A. 1850; Deac. 1846 and Pr. 1847 by Bp of Ox. C. in sole charge of Adstock 1861. Formerly C. of Soulbury, Bucks, 1846, Wardington, Oxon, 1848, Marsley, Bucks, 1852. [23]

HART, John, *Alphington, near Exeter.*—Ex. Coll. Ox. B.A. 1827. [24]

HART, Richard, *Catton, near Norwich.*—Dub. A.B. 1827; Deac. 1828 and Pr. 1829 by Bp of Nor. V. of Catton, Dio. Nor. 1837. (Patrons, D. and C. of Nor; Tithe, 160*l*; Glebe, 13¾ acres; V.'s Inc. 200*l*; Pop. 646.) Author, *Medulla Conciliorum*, 1833; *Materialism Refuted*, 1835; *Ecclesiastical Records*, 1836, 2nd ed. 1846; etc. [25]

HART, Richard Haworth, 16, *Fulham-place, Harrow-road, W.*—Emman. Coll. Cam. B.A. 1853, M.A. 1857; Deac. 1854 and Pr. 1855 by Bp of Lon. P. C. of St. Barnabas', Marylebone, Dio. Lon. 1866. (Patron, the Crown; P. C.'s Inc. 200*l*; Pop. 8664.) Formerly C. of St. Luke's, Berwick-street, Lond. Blackburn and Whalley, Lancashire, and Ch. Ch. Marylebone. [26]

HART, Robert, *Guestingthorpe Vicarage, near Halstead, Essex.*—Corpus Coll. Cam. Jun. Opt. B.A. 1860, M.A. 1863; Deac. and Pr. 1860 by Bp of Roch. C. in sole charge of Guestingthorpe 1861. Formerly C. of Brent and Furneux Pelham, Herts, 1860–61. [27]

HART, Robert Slater, *Colton, Newton-in-Cartmel.*—Deac. 1863 and Pr. 1865 by Bp of Carl. P. C. of Colton, Dio. Carl. 1866. (Patrons, 70 landowners; Tithe, 78*l* 10*s* 6*d*; P. C.'s Inc. 96*l* and Ho; Pop. 1076.) Formerly C. of Hawkshead 1863. [1]

HART, William, *Bungay, Suffolk.*—St. John's Coll. Cam. B.A. 1866; Deac. 1866 by Bp of Man. Head Mast. of the Bungay Gr. Sch; C. of Ellingham. Formerly C. of Walton-le-Dale, Lancashire, 1866–67. [2]

HARTE, E. J.—Chap. of H.M.S. "Gibraltar." [3]

HARTE, Joseph William, *Marston, Yardley, Birmingham.*—Chap. of the Don. of Marston, Dio. Wor. 1847. (Patrons, Trustees; Chap's Inc. 75*l*.) [4]

HARTLEY, Alfred Octavius, *St. Mary's, Beccles, Suffolk.*—Magd. Coll. Cam. Jun. Opt. 1st in 2nd cl. Cl. Trip. and B.A. 1849, M.A. 1852; Deac. 1849 and Pr. 1850 by Bp of Ely. Head Mast. of Beccles Gr. Sch. 1853. Formerly Fell. of Magd. Coll. Cam. [5]

HARTLEY, Arthur Robert, *Ryde, Isle of Wight.*—C. of St. Thomas's, Ryde. [6]

HARTLEY, Charles, *Stocking-Pelham, Buntingford, Herts.*—St. John's Coll. Ox. 3rd cl. Lit. Hum. and B.A. 1845, M.A. 1848; Deac. 1845 and Pr. 1846 by Bp of Ex. R. of Stocking-Pelham, Dio. Roch. 1851. (Patron, A. P. Welch, Esq; Tithe, 159*l*; Glebe, 30 acres; R.'s Inc. 188*l* 18*s* and Ho; Pop. 126.) Formerly C. of Mabe 1846; P. C. of Porthleven 1847–51. [7]

HARTLEY, Henry Robert, *Wetherby, Yorks.*—C. of Wetherby. [8]

HARTLEY, James Bishop, *Staveley Rectory, Boroughbridge, Yorks.*—Jesus Coll. Cam. B.A. 1835; Deac. 1835, Pr. 1838. R. of Staniley, *alias* Staveley, Dio. Rip. 1847. (Patron, the present R; Tithe, 5*s*; Glebe, 286 acres; R.'s Inc. 350*l* and Ho; Pop. 343.) [9]

HARTLEY, John, *Child's Wickham, Broadway, Glouc.*—V. of Child's Wickham, Dio. G. and B. 1861. (Patrons, Trustees; Tithe, 125*l*; V.'s Inc. 300*l* and Ho; Pop. 440.) [10]

HARTLEY, Richard Fleming, *Thorpe Salvin, Worksop.*—Queens' Coll. Cam. B.A. 1828, M.A. 1832. P. C. of Wales, near Worksop, Dio. York. 1835. (Patron, Abp of York; P. C.'s Inc. 190*l*; Pop. 305.) P. C. of Thorpe Salvin, Dio. York, 1835. (Patron, Abp of York; Tithe, 380*l*; P. C.'s Inc. 380*l* and Ho; Pop. 387.) [11]

HARTLEY, Thomas, *Raskelfe, Easingwold, Yorks.*—Dub. A.B. 1830, A.M. 1833; Deac. 1830 by Abp of York, Pr. 1831 by Bp of Ches. P. C. of Raskelfe, Dio. York, 1845. (Patron, Bp of Ches; Tithe, 191*l* 14*s* 8*d*; Glebe, 35 acres; P. C.'s Inc. 318*l* 14*s* 8*d* and Ho; Pop. 577.) Formerly C. of Hutton, Yorks, 1830; P. C. of Lowick, Lanc 1831, Blawith, Lanc. 1841. Author, *Visitation Sermon at Ulverston*, 1844; *Vegetation and the Bible*, Mackintosh, 1865, 1*s*; *The Rock and the Keys*, 1867, 6*d*. [12]

HARTLEY, Thomas Shakespeare, *Doulting, Shepton-Mallet, Somerset.*—Theol. Assoc King's Coll. Lond. 1st cl. 1850; Deac. 1851, Pr. 1852. C. of Doulting and Downhead. [13]

HARTLEY, William Samuel, *Laughton-en-le-Morthen Vicarage, Rotherham.*—Queens' Coll. Cam. B.A. 1835; Deac. 1835, Pr. 1836. V. of Laughton-en-le-Morthen with St. John's P. C. Dio. York, 1840. (Patron, Preb. of Laughton in York Cathl; Tithe—App. 481*l*, V. 50*l*; Glebe, 5 acres; V.'s Inc. 307*l* and Ho; Pop. 894.) [14]

HARTSHORNE, Charles Kerrich, *Norden, near Rochdale.*—Ch. Ch. Ox. B.A. 1853, M.A. 1856; Deac. 1854 by Bp of Ox. Pr. 1857 by Bp of Rip. V. of St. Paul's, Norden, Dio. Man. 1865. (Patron, Bp of Man; V.'s Inc. 300*l*; Pop. 2662.) Formerly C. of St. Clements', Spotland, Rochdale. [15]

HARTSHORNE, John Ashford, *Christ Church, Oxford.*—Ch. Ch. Ox. B.A. 1861, M.A. 1864; Deac. 1863 and Pr. 1864 by Bp of Ches. Chap. of Ch. Ch. Ox; C. of South Hinksey, Berks, 1865. Formerly C. of Daddon, Cheshire, 1863. [16]

HARVEY, Charles Gilbert, *Fleetwood, Lancashire.*—Asst. Mast. of Rossall Sch. Fleetwood. [17]

HARVEY, Charles Musgrave, *Hampstead, Middlesex, N.W.*—Ch. Ch. Ox. B.A. 1859; Deac. 1860 by Bp of Roch. C. of Hampstead 1864. Formerly C. of Halstead, Essex, 1860. [18]

HARVEY, E. George, *Truro.*—R. of St. Mary's, Truro, Dio. Ex. 1860. (Patron, Rev. W. W. Harvey; R.'s Inc. 150*l* and Ho; Pop. 3117.) [19]

HARVEY, Frederick Burn, *Great Berkhampstead, Herts.*—Magd. Hall, Ox. S.C.L. 1854; Deac. 1854 and Pr. 1855 by Bp of Roch. 2nd Mast. of the Gr. Sch. Great Berkhampstead, 1847. [20]

HARVEY, George Gayton, *Hailsham Vicarage, Hurst Green, Sussex.*—St. John's Coll. Cam. B.A. 1825; Deac. 1826 by Bp of Lich. Pr. 1826 by Abp of York. V. of Hailsham, Dio. Chich. 1846. (Patron, Mr. Sheppard; Tithe—Imp. 420*l*, V. 599*l* 10*s*; V.'s Inc. 600*l* and Ho; Pop. 2098.) Author, *Helps and Hints towards Effectual Fervent Prayer, or a Weekly Course of Subjects for the Throne of Grace*, 1845. [21]

HARVEY, George Ludford, *Yate Rectory, Chipping-Sodbury, Glouc.*—Sid. Coll. Cam. B.A. 1822; Deac. 1823 and Pr. 1824 by Bp of Glouc. R. of Yate, Dio. G. and B. 1843. (Patron, the present R; Tithe, 717*l* 10*s*; Glebe, 154 acres; R.'s Inc 1017*l* and Ho; Pop. 1188.) Formerly V. of Diseworth, Leic. [22]

HARVEY, George Tyson, *Lincoln.*—Ch. Coll. Cam. 11th Sen. Opt. B.A. 1860, M.A. 1865; Deac. 1861 and Pr. 1862 by Bp of Lin. Min. Can. of Lin. 1865; C. of St. Mary Magdalene's, Lincoln, 1861. Formerly Math. Mast. of Lincoln Gr. Sch. [23]

HARVEY, Gilmour, *Santon Vicarage, Castletown, Isle of Man.*—Deac. and Pr. by Bp of S. and M. V. of Kirk St. Ann, Dio. S. and M. 1865. (Patron, the Crown; V.'s Inc. 150*l* and Ho; Pop. 693.) Formerly C. of Malew, Isle of Man, 1840–55; Bursar and Chap. of King William's Coll. Castletown, 1855–65. [24]

HARVEY, Henry Auber, *Tring, Herts.*—Ch. Ch. Ox. Hon. 4th cl. Lit. Hum. B.A. 1846, M.A. 1849; Deac. 1849 and Pr. 1850 by Bp of G. and B. P. C. of Tring, Dio. Roch. 1856. (Patron, Ch. Ch. Ox; P. C.'s Inc. 300*l* and Ho; Pop. 4841.) Formerly C. of Tewkesbury 1849-51, Olveston, Glouc. 1851–56. [25]

HARVEY, Henry B., *Newbald, Brough, Yorks.*—Clare Coll. Cam. B.A. 1831; Deac. 1840 and Pr. 1841 by Bp of Lich. V. of Newbald, Dio. York, 1863. (Patrons, D. and C. of York; V.'s Inc. 300*l* and Ho; Pop. 910*l*.) Formerly C. of Aston, Rotherham, 1842–53, Bolton-Percy, Tadcaster, 1853–63. [26]

HARVEY, Herbert, *The Parsonage, Betley, Crewe.*—Ch. Ch. Ox. B.A. 1857, M.A. 1863; Deac. 1859 and Pr. 1860 by Bp of Ches. P. C. of Betley, Dio. Lich. 1862. (Patron, C. Wicksted, Esq; Tithe, 60*l*; Rent from Glebe, 100*l*; P. C.'s Inc. 150*l* and Ho; Pop. 884.) Formerly C. of Bebbington, Cheshire, 1859–61, Langar, Notts, 1861-62. [27]

HARVEY, John Ridout, *Winchcomb Vicarage, Glouc.*—St. Alban Hall, Ox. B.A. 1832. V. of Winchcomb with Gretton C. Dio. G. and B. 1834. (Patron, Lord Sudeley; Tithe—App. 40*l*, Imp. 10*l* 7*s* 6*d*, V. 18*l* 6*s*; V.'s Inc. 134*l* and Ho; Pop. 2937.) R. of Sudeley Manor, Winchcomb, Dio. G. and B. 1834. (Patron, J. Dent, Esq; Tithe—App. 18*l* 6*s* 6*d*, Imp. 10*l* 7*s* 6*d*, R. 40*l*; R.'s Inc. 45*l*; Pop. 98*l*.) [28]

HARVEY, Richard, *Hornsey Rectory, Middlesex, N.,* and *College Green, Gloucester.*—St. Cath. Coll. Cam. 6th Sen. Opt. B.A. 1818, M.A. 1821; Deac. 1821 and Pr. 1822 by Bp of Nor. R. of Hornsey, Dio. Lon. 1829. (Patron, Bp of Lon; Modus, 35*l*; Glebe, 44 acres; R.'s Inc. 430*l* and Ho; Pop. 2300.) Preb. of St. Paul's 1843; Chap. in Ordinary to the Queen 1847; Chap. to Abp of York; Can. of Gloucester 1858. Formerly C. of St. Botolph's, Bishopsgate, Lond. 1823. Author, *The Christian entitled to Legal Protection in the Observance of the Lord's Day*, Parker, 1836; *Hymns*, 1837; *Two Sermons*, 1850; *Suspense*, 1854; *The Sabbath, or Rest the Right of every Man*, 1855, Groombridge. Editor, *A Song to David by Christopher Smart*, 1819. [29]

HARVEY, Richard, *Sarisbury, Southampton.*—P. C. of Sarisbury, Dio. Win. 1862. (Patron, V. of Titchfield; P. C.'s Inc. 120*l* and Ho; Pop. 1406.) [30]

HARVEY, Samuel, *Fordingbridge, Hants.*—Corpus Coll. Cam. B.A. 1843; Deac. 1844 and Pr. 1845 by Bp of Lich. C. of Fordingbridge. [1]

HARVEY, Spencer Philip, *Cuxton, near Rochester.*—Trin. Hall, Cam. B.A. 1863, M.A. 1867; Deac. 1865 and Pr. 1866 by Bp of Roch. C. of Cuxton 1865. [2]

HARVEY, Thomas, *Cowden Rectory, Edenbridge, Kent.*—Pemb. Coll. Cam. B.A. 1816, M.A. 1818; Deac. 1819 by Bp of Nor. Pr. 1821 by Bp of Lon. R. of Cowden, Dio. Cant. 1835. (Patron, the present R; Tithe, 583*l* 17*s* 6*d*; Glebe, 4 acres; R.'s Inc. 587*l* 17*s* 6*d* and Ho; Pop. 565.) [3]

HARVEY, Thomas.—King's Coll. Lond. Assoc; Deac. 1863 and Pr. 1864. C. of St. John's, Battersea, Surrey. [4]

HARVEY, William Maundy, *Sutton-by-Dover.*—Wad. Coll. Ox. B.A. 1827, M.A. 1831. R. of Little Mongeham, Deal, Kent, Dio. Cant. 1835. (Patron, Abp of Cant; Tithe—App. 102*l* 16*s*, R. 329*l* 13*s* 6*d*; R's Inc. 350*l*; Pop. 138.) P. C. of Sutton-by-Dover, Dio. Cant. 1835. (Patron, Abp of Cant; P. C.'s Inc. 107*l*; Pop. 141.) Surrogate. [5]

HARVEY, William Wigan, *Buckland Rectory, near Buntingford, Herts.*—King's Coll. Cam. B.A. 1832, 1st cl. Tyrwhitt's Heb. Schs. 1833, M.A. 1836, B.D. 1855; Deac. 1833 by Abp of Cant. Pr. 1834 by Bp of Lin. R. of Buckland, Dio. Roch. 1844. (Patron, King's Coll. Cam; Tithe—App. 49*l* 15*s* 6*d*, R. 330*l* 13*s* 6*d*; Glebe, 31 acres; R.'s Inc. 374*l* 10*s* and Ho; Pop. 385.) Surrogate. Formerly Fell. and Divinity Lect. of King's Coll. Cam. 1832–44. Author, *Address to the Provost and Fellows of King's College on the B.A. Degree*, 1837; *Ecclesiæ Anglicanæ Vindex Catholicus*, 3 vols. 1842; *Prælectio Academica in Prov.* viii. 22, 1848; *University and Visitation Sermons*, 1853; *History and Theology of the Three Creeds*, 1854; *S. Irenæi quæ supersunt Opera*, 1857; *Sermons*, 1 vol. 1859; *On the Rating of Tithe Rent Charge*, Bell and Daldy. [6]

HARWARD, Edwin Cuthbert, *Market Rasen, Lincolnshire.*—Trin. Coll. Ox. B.A. 1857, M.A. 1860; Deac. 1858 and Pr. 1859 by Bp of Lin. V. of Market Rasen, Dio. Lin. 1866. (Patron, Ld Chan; V.'s Inc. 260*l* and Ho; Pop. 2563.) Formerly C. of St. Nicholas', Lincoln, and Louth. [7]

HARWARD, John Frederic, *Little Maplestead, Halstead, Essex.*—St. John's Coll. Cam. B.A. 1842, M.A. 1846; Deac. 1843 by Bp of Herf. Pr. 1844 by Bp of Lich. P. C. of Little Maplestead, Dio. Roch. 1855. (Patrons, Proprietors of Hall Farm, Little Maplestead; Tithe—Imp. 205*l*; Glebe, 20 acres; P. C.'s Inc. 72*l*; Pop. 325.) [8]

HARWOOD, Reynold, 5, *St. Ann's-terrace, Lewes.*—Theol. Coll. Chich; Deac. and Pr. 1859. C. of Hamsey, Lewes, 1864. Formerly C. of Appledram, Sussex, and Ormesby St. Margaret, Norfolk. [9]

HARWOOD, Thomas Eustace, *Old Windsor, Berks.*—Ch. Ch. Ox. 3rd cl. Lit. Hum. M.A. 1863; Deac. 1860 and Pr. 1861 by Bp of Pet. C. of Old Windsor 1862. Formerly Asst. C. of Whitwick, Leic. 1860–62. [10]

HASKER, George Henry, *St. Leonards-on-Sea, Sussex.*—Ex. Coll. Ox. B.A. 1817; Deac. 1819, Pr. 1820. [11]

HASKINS, Charles, *Burleigh House, Val Plaisant, Jersey.*—Dub. A.B. 1825, A.M. 1829; Deac. 1830 by Bp of Kildare, Pr. 1833 by Bp of Ches. [12]

HASKINS, Edmund Henry, *Stow Parsonage, Gainsborough.*—Queen's Coll. Ox. B.A. 1839, M.A. 1843; Deac. 1840 by Bp of Rip. Pr. 1842 by Bp of Ox. P. C. of Stow, Dio. Lin. 1865. (Patron, Bp of Lin; Glebe, 15 acres; P. C.'s Inc. 300*l* and Ho; Pop. 1071.) Formerly C. of Cromwell, Notts. Author, *Protestant's Guide to Church Catechism*, 1851. [13]

HASKOLL, Joseph, *East Barkwith Rectory, Wragby, Lincolnshire.*—Clare Coll. Cam. B.A. 1843, M.A. 1847; Deac. 1843 by Bp of Pet. Pr. 1843 by Abp of Cant. R. of East Barkwith, Dio. Lin. 1854. (Patron, G. F. Heneage, Esq; Glebe, 215 acres; R.'s Inc. 270*l* and Ho; Pop. 387. Formerly C. of St. Peter's, Walworth, 1843–47, Leigh-on-Mendip, Somerset, 1847–48; Can. of St. Ninian's, Perth, Scotland, 1850–56; Incumb. of St. Lawrence, Lawrence Kirk, 1853–54. Author, *History of Sunday Schools* in the *Encyclopædia Metropolitana*, 1840; *Life of Cervantes*, 1846; *Life of Shakespere and Notes to Select Plays*, 1846; *History of France for Children*, 1855; *Memoir of Rev. C. F. Erskine*, prefixed to Erskine's *Sermons*, 1864. [14]

HASLAM, Charles Edward, *Kirk Ella, Hull.*—St. John's Coll. Cam. B.A. 1865; Deac. 1866 and Pr. 1867 by Abp of York. C. of Kirk Ella, Yorks, 1866. [15]

HASLAM, Michael, *Waberthwaite, Whitehaven.*—St. Bees; Deac. 1863 and Pr. 1864 by Bp of Carl. C. of Waberthwaite, Cumberland. [16]

HASLAM, William, *Buckenham Rectory, Norwich.*—R. of Buckenham with Hassingham R. Dio. Nor. 1863. (Patron, Sir T. B. Proctor Beauchamp, Bart; Buckenham, Tithe, 137*l*; Glebe, 39 acres; Hassingham, Tithe, 102*l*; Glebe, 8 acres; R.'s Inc. 300*l* and Ho; Pop. 167.) [17]

HASLAM, William, *Starkies, Bury.*—St. John's Coll. Cam. B.A. 1852; Deac. 1854 and Pr. 1855 by Bp of Man. Garrison Chap. Wellington Barracks, Bury, Dio. Man. 1857; 2nd Mast. Bury Gr. Sch. 1863. [18]

HASLEGRAVE, Joseph, 18, *Colebrook-row, Islington, London, N.*—P. C. of St. Peter's, Islington, Dio. Lon. 1835. (Patrons, Trustees; P. C.'s Inc. 350*l* and Ho; Pop. 13,509.) [19]

HASLEHURST, Richard Kay, *Alrewas Vicarage, Lichfield.*—Trin. Coll. Cam. B.A. 1842, M.A. 1847; Deac. 1844, Pr. 1845. V. of Alrewas, Dio. Lich. 1851. (Patron, Preb. of Alrewas in Lich. Cathl; Tithe—App. 450*l*, V. 250*l*; Glebe, 34 acres; V.'s Inc. 320*l* and Ho; Pop. 1633.) [20]

HASLEWOOD, Ashby Blair, *Maidstone.*—Ch. Coll. Cam. B.A. 1834; Deac. 1834 and Pr. 1835 by Abp of Cant. P. C. of Trinity, Maidstone, Dio. Cant. 1866. (Patron, Abp of Cant; P. C.'s Inc. 510*l* and Ho; Pop. 8720.) Surrogate. Formerly C. of Hackney 1839, Greenwich 1841; Morn. Preacher at Abp Tenison's Chap. Regent-street, and Even. Lect. at St. James's, Piccadilly, 1845; P. C. of St. Mark's, Hamilton-terrace, Lond. 1845–64; V. of St. Michael's, Coventry, 1864–66. [21]

HASLEWOOD, Boulby, *Oswaldtwistle Parsonage, Accrington.*—St. John's Coll. Cam. B.A. 1852; Deac. 1854 by Bp of Ches. Pr. 1854 by Bp of Dur. P. C. of Oswaldtwistle, Dio. Man. 1857. (Patrons, Bp and Chan. of Chester and three lay Trustees; P. C.'s Inc. 320*l* and Ho; Pop. 6103.) Formerly C. of Easington, Durham, 1854, Blackburn 1856; Chap. to R. E. Egerton Warburton, Esq. 1857. Author, *Sermons for the Times*; *Dialogue on Confirmation*, 1859. [22]

HASLEWOOD, Boulby Thomas, *Ribchester Vicarage, Blackburn.*—St. Peter's Coll. Cam. Sen. Opt. B.A. 1818; Deac. 1819 by Abp of York, Pr. 1820 by Bp of Ox. V. of Ribchester with Stidd P. C. Dio. Man. 1829. (Patron, Bp of Man; Tithe—App. 165*l* and 173 acres of Glebe, V. 30*l*; V.'s Inc. 200*l* and Ho; Pop. 1828.) [23]

HASLEWOOD, Dickens, *Kettlewell, Skipton.*—St. John's Coll. Cam. Jun. Opt. and B.A. 1846, M.A. 1850; Deac. 1846 and Pr. 1847 by Bp of Ches. V. of Kettlewell, Dio. Rip. 1867. (Patroness, Miss Belland, Settle; Tithe, 10*l*; Glebe, 140*l*; V.'s Inc. 160*l*; Pop. 600.) Formerly C. of Settle, Yorks, 1859, Richmond 1860, West Hartlepool 1864; P. C. of Coxhoe, Durham, 1866. [24]

HASLEWOOD, Francis.—King's Coll. Lond. Theol. Assoc. 1863; Deac. 1863 and Pr. 1864 by Bp of Lon. C. of St. Luke's, Marylebone, Lond. 1866. Formerly C. of St. Peter's ad Vincula, the Tower, Lond. 1863, St. Mary's, Bryanston-square, Lond. 1864. Author, *The Antiquities of Smarden, Kent, with Illustrations*, 1866, two eds. 8vo, 10*s* 6*d*, 4to, 12*s* 6*d*. [25]

HASLEWOOD, Frederick Fitzherbert, *Smarden Rectory, Staplehurst, Kent.*—St. John's Coll. Cam. 1824, 5th Sen. Opt. and B.A. 1827, M.A. 1830

Deac. 1827, Pr. 1828. R. of Smarden, Dio. Cant. 1857. (Patron, Abp of Cant; R.'s Inc. 510*l* and Ho; Pop. 1130.) Formerly C. of Smarden. [1]

HASLEWOOD, Frederick George, *St. Lawrence, Ramsgate.*—Clare Coll. Cam. Scho. and six times Priseman, Sen. in Civil Law Trip. 1857, and in Moral Sci. Trip. 1858, LL.B. 1859, *ad eund.* Ox. B.C.L. 1860, LL.M. 1862; Deac. 1858 by Bp of Lon. Pr. 1859 by Abp of Cant. C. of St. Lawrence, Thanet, 1858. [2]

HASLEWOOD, Thomas, *West Hartlepool.*—Literate; Deac. 1864 and Pr. 1866 by Bp of Dur. C. of West Hartlepool 1864. [3]

HASLEWOOD, William Maude, *The Parsonage, Great Harwood, Accrington.*—St. John's Coll. Cam. B.A. 1851; Deac. 1851 and Pr. 1853 by Bp of Man. P. C. of Great Harwood, Dio. Man. 1861. (Patron, V. of Blackburn; P. C.'s Inc. 300*l* and Ho; Pop. 4070.) Formerly C. of Ribchester 1851, St. Mary's, Preston, 1851–56, Slaidburn 1856–57; P. C. of Tockholes 1857–61. [4]

HASLEWOOD, William Philip, *Ardingley Rectory, Cuckfield, Sussex.*—Trin. Coll. Cam. B.A. 1839, M.A. 1842; Deac. 1840, Pr. 1841. R. of Ardingley, Dio. Chich. 1844. (Patron, J. W. H. Peyton, Esq; Tithe, 588*l*; R.'s Inc. 590*l* and Ho; Pop. 626.) [5]

HASLUCK, James George Edward, *Little Sodbury Rectory, Chipping Sodbury.*—Pemb. Coll. Ox. B.A. 1841, M.A. 1843; Deac. 1842 and Pr. 1843 by Bp of G. and B. R. of Little Sodbury, Dio. G. and B. 1851. (Patron, W. H. H. Hartley, Esq; Tithe, 200*l*; Glebe, 30 acres; R.'s Inc. 241*l* and Ho; Pop. 143.) [6]

HASSALL, James, 302, *Park-road, Toxteth-park, near Liverpool.*—Trin. Coll. Cam. B.A. 1829, M.A. 1832; Deac. 1830 and Pr. 1831 by Bp of Ches. P. C. of St. John Baptist's, Toxteth Park, Dio. Ches. 1832. (Patron, Rev. Dr. Hardman; Pop. 17,534.) Formerly C. of Eastham, Chester, 1830. [7]

HASSALL, John Thomas, *Wattisfield, Scole, Norfolk.*—Univ. Coll. Dur. Theol. Licen; Deac. 1857 and Pr. 1858 by Bp of Lich. C. in sole charge of Wattisfield 1867. Formerly C. of Alfreton, Derbyshire, 1857, Yalding, Kent, 1859. [8]

HASSALL, Thomas, *Rearsby Rectory, near Leicester.*—R. of Rearsby, Dio. Lin. 1857. (Patron, Rev. N. Morgan; Tithe, 5*l* 19*s* 3*d*; R.'s Inc. 650*l* and Ho; Pop. 645.) Formerly P. C. of Shelford, Notts. [9]

HASTED, Henry, *Pitsea Rectory, Rayleigh, Essex.*—Magd. Coll. Cam. B.A. 1856; Deac. 1857 and Pr. 1858 by Bp of Carl. R. of Pitsea, Dio. Roch. 1861. (Patrons, Hon. L. F. C. Dawnay and Rev. R. Heathcote alt; Tithe—Imp. 170*l* 10*s*, R. 420*l*; R.'s Inc. 430*l* and Ho; Pop. 263.) Formerly R. of Bradfield-Combust, Suffolk, 1858–61. [10]

HASTED, Henry John, *Sproughton Rectory, Ipswich.*—Magd. Coll. Cam. B.A. 1831, M.A. 1834; Deac. 1831 by Bp of Roch. Pr. 1832 by Bp of Pet. R. of Sproughton, Dio. Nor. 1849. (Patron, Marquis of Bristol; Tithe, 527*l*; Glebe, 13 acres; R.'s Inc. 579*l* and Ho; Pop. 598.) Rural Dean. Formerly R. of Bradneld-Combust and Welnethan Parva 1832–49. [11]

HASTIE, Henry Hepburn, *Great Chishall Vicarage (Essex), near Royston.*—Pemb. Coll. Cam. B.A. 1838; Deac. 1839 and Pr. 1840 by Bp of Chich. V. of Great Chishall, Dio. Roch. 1844. (Patron, Rev. R. Wilkes; Glebe, 137 acres; V.'s Inc. 160*l* and Ho; Pop. 473.) Formerly C. of East Grinstead, Sussex, 1839, Hartfield, Sussex, 1840, Debden, Essex, 1841–45. [12]

HASTINGS, Henry James, *Martley Rectory, near Worcester.*—Trin. Coll. Cam. Sen. Opt. B.A. 1819, M.A. 1822; Deac. 1820 and Pr. 1821 by Bp of Wor. R. of Martley, Dio. Wor. 1856. (Patron, the present R; Tithe, 800*l*; Glebe, 85 acres; R.'s Inc. 1100*l* and Ho; Pop. 1140.) Rural Dean 1847; Hon. Can. of Worcester 1848. Formerly C. of Martley 1820–31 and again 1851–56; R. of Areley Kings, near Stourport, 1831–56. Author, *Cause of the Irish Pleaded* (a Sermon), 1822, 1*s*; *The Pillar and Ground of the Truth* (a Visitation Sermon), 1833, 1*s*; *The Ministry in the Lord and How to Fulfil it* (Ordination Sermon), 1848, 1*s*; *Reasons for not Signing the Proposed Address to the Bishop of Worcester, and Remarks on the late Decision in Gorham v. Exeter*, 1850, 1*s*; *Parochial Sermons from Advent to Trinity Sunday*, 1845, 12*s*; *Parochial Sermons from Trinity Sunday to Advent*, 1846, 12*s*; *The Whole Armour of God, Four Sermons before the University of Cambridge*, 1848, 3*s* 6*d*; *East Indian Mutiny* (a Sermon), 1857, 6*d*; *Readiness for the Coming of the Son of Man* (a Sermon), 1*s*. [13]

HASTINGS, John David, *Trowbridge Rectory, Wilts.*—Dub. A.B. 1823, A.M. 1826; Deac. 1826, Pr. 1827. R. of Trowbridge, Wilts, Dio. Salis. 1841. (Patron, Duke of Rutland; Tithe—Imp. 21*l* 17*s*, R. 625*l* 14*s* 10*d*; Glebe, 67 acres; R.'s Inc. 900*l* and Ho; Pop. 7204.) Preb. of Salis. 1860; Rural Dean of Pottern 1848; Surrogate 1850. Author, *The Touchstone of Truth*, 1*s*; *The Church Restored*, 21*s*; *The Faithfulness of the Clergy the Safety of the Church*, 2nd ed; *A Visitation Sermon*, 1*s*; *The Trinity* (a Sermon preached 1836), 1*s*; *The Resurrection* (a Funeral Sermon), 1*s*; *Brotherly Love* (a Sermon), 6*d*; *The Absolution of the Church of Rome not the Absolution of the Church of England*, 1*s*; *A Form of Service adapted to the Ceremony of laying the First Stone of Churches and Chapels in connection with the Established Church*, 3*d* or 20*s* per hundred. Editor of the *Rev. George Crabbe's Posthumous Sermons, with Dedicatory Preface, by permission, to H.R.H. Prince Albert.* [14]

HASTINGS, John Parsons, *Areley Regis Rectory, near Stourport, Worcestershire.*—Trin Coll. Cam. Jun. Opt. 2nd cl. Cl. Trip. and B.A. 1846, M.A. 1849; Deac. 1845 and Pr. 1847 by Bp of Wor. R. of Areley Regis, Dio. Wor. 1856. (Patron, Rev. H. J. Hastings; Tithe—Imp. 3*l* 9*s*, R. 345*l* 12*s*; Glebe, 42 acres; R.'s Inc. 450*l* and Ho; Pop. 564.) Formerly C. of Areley Regis 1851–56; Chap. to the Bp of Llan. 1850–56; Chap. of Trin. Coll. Cam. 1848–51. Author, *Rural Education* (an Address delivered before the Social Science Congress at Birmingham 1857). [15]

HASTINGS, Samuel, *Gloucester.*—C. of St. Mary de Crypt, Gloucester. Formerly C. of St. John's, Preston. [16]

HASTINGS, Warren Burrows, *Ludford Market Rasen, Lincolnshire.*—Trin. Coll. Cam. B.A. 1848, M.A. 1851; Deac. 1848 and Pr. 1849 by Bp of Lon. V. of Ludford-Magna with Ludford-Parva R. Dio. Lin. 1859. (Patrons, E. Heneage, Esq. M.P. and A. Boucherett, Esq; V.'s Inc. 292*l* and Ho; Pop. 807.) Formerly C. of Hampstead 1848–52, Wolverley 1852–55, Ludford 1855–59. [17]

HATCH, Charles, *Fordingbridge, Hants.*—King's Coll. Cam. B.A. 1819; Deac. 1819 by Bp of Ely, Pr. 1823 by Bp of Nor. V. of Fordingbridge with Ibsley R. Dio. Win. 1840. (Patron, King's Coll. Cam; Fordingbridge, Tithe—Imp. 1250*l*, V. 670*l*; Glebe, 7½ acres; Ibsley, Tithe, 295*l*; V.'s Inc. 972*l* and Ho; Pop. Fordingbridge 2088, Ibsley 286.) Surrogate. [18]

HATCH, Edwin, *Toronto, Canada.*—Pemb. Coll. Ox; Deac. 1858 by Bp of Lon. Cl. Prof. in the Univ. of Toronto. Formerly C. of St. Thomas's, Charterhouse, Lond. [19]

HATCH, Henry John, *Stone House, Linton, Staplehurst, Kent.*—Magd. Coll. B.A. 1849, M.A. 1852; Deac. 1848, Pr. 1849. Chap. to the Maidstone Union Workhouse 1866. Formerly Chap. to the Wandsworth House of Correction 1851. Late Proprietor and Editor of *The Philanthropist*. Author, *John Mildred, or Love one another*, Tweedie, 1862, 2*s* 6*d*. [20]

HATCHARD, John, *St. Andrew's Vicarage, Plymouth.*—Magd. Coll. Cam. B.A. 1816, M.A. 1820; Deac. 1816, Pr. 1817. V. of St. Andrew's, Plymouth, Dio. Ex. 1824. (Patron, Church Patron. Society; Tithe—Imp. 2*l*; V.'s Inc. 877*l* and Ho; Pop. 18,243.) Author, *National Mercies deserve National Thanksgivings* (a Sermon) 1820, 1*s* 6*d*; *The Prediction and Promises of God Respecting Israel* (a Sermon), 1825, 1*s* 6*d*; *Two Sermons, on National Sins*, 1831, 1*s* 6*d*; *Brief Memoir of a Clergyman's Daughter*, 1830, 4*d*. [21]

HATCHARD, Thomas Goodwin, *St. Nicholas' Rectory, Guildford, Surrey.*—Brasen. Coll. Ox. B.A. 1841, M.A. 1845; Deac. 1840 and Pr. 1841 by Bp of Win.

R. of St. Nicholas', Guildford, Dio. Win. 1856. (Patron, Bp of Win; R.'s Inc. 600*l* and Ho; Pop. 2005.) Surrogate; Rural Dean; Dom. Chap. to the Marquis of Conyngham. Formerly R. of Havant, Hants, 1846–56. Author, *Feed my Lambs* (a Sermon in Monosyllables), 7th thousand; *Harvest Blessings* (a Sermon); *Thanks-offering* (a Harvest Sermon); *The German Tree for Children*; *Food for my Flock* (a volume of Parochial Sermons); *The Floweret Gathered* (a Memoir.) [1]

HATFIELD, John Hanson, *Manchester.*—Emman. Coll. Cam. B.A. 1849, M.A. 1852; Deac 1849, Pr. 1850. Chap. of the Chorlton Union, Manchester. [2]

HATHAWAY, Edward Penrose, 139, *The Grove, Camberwell, S.*—Queen's Coll. Ox. B.A. 1839, M.A. 1844; Deac. 1864 and Pr. 1866 by Bp of Lon. C. in sole charge of Camberwell 1867. Formerly Missionary of Seven Dials district 1865–66; C. of St. Giles'-in-the-Fields, Lond. 1866–67. [3]

HATHAWAY, Manton, *St. George's Parsonage, Darlaston, Wednesbury, Staffs.*—Trin. Coll. Cam. B.A. 1845; Deac. and Pr. 1846 by Abp of York. P. C. of St. George's, Darlaston, Dio. Lich. 1850. (Patrons, the Crown and Bp of Lich. alt; P. C.'s Inc. 180*l*; Pop. 3972.) Chap. of Walsall Union 1853, Chap. at Rough Hay Works, Darlaston, 1858. [4]

HATHERELL, James Williams, *The Lodge, Westend, Southampton.*—Brasen. Coll. Ox. 1820, B.A. 1823, M.A. 1826, B.D. and D.D. 1841; Deac. 1824 by Bp of Lich. Pr. 1826 by Bp of Wor. P. C. of St. James's, Westend, Southampton, Dio. Win. 1843. (Patron, V. of South Stoneham; P. C.'s Inc. 230*l*; Pop. 2141.) [5]

HATHORNTHWAITE, Thomas, *Lancaster.*—Dub. A.B. 1835, LL.D, 1861; Deac. 1835 and Pr. 1836 by Bp of Ches. P. C. of St. Ann's, Lancaster, Dio. Man. 1864. (Patron, V. of Lancaster; P. C.'s Inc. 220*l* and Ho; Pop. 3032.) Formerly Asst. C. of St. Ann's, Lancaster, 1835–36; C. of Caton, Lancaster, 1837–40; P. C. of Great Eccleston, Lancashire, 1841–61. Author, *Poems, Latin and English*, 1848; various tracts on the Lord's Day, Dissent; etc. [6]

HATHWAY, Robert Callow, *Kewstoke Vicarage, Weston-super-Mare.*—Jesus Coll. Ox. B.A. 1822, M.A. 1826; Deac. and Pr. 1824. V. of Kewstoke, Dio. B. and W. 1835. (Patron, Ld Chan; Tithe, 321*l*; Glebe, 30 acres; V.'s Inc. 402*l* and Ho; Pop. 560.) [7]

HATHWAY, William Joseph, 22, *St. Botolph's-place, Lincoln.*—Wor. Coll. Ox. B.A. 1851; Deac. 1853 by Bp of Madras, Pr. 1854 by Bp of B. and W. P. C. of St. Botolph's, Lincoln, Dio. Lin. 1860. (Patron, Bp of Lin; P. C.'s Inc. 150*l*; Pop. 1027.) Formerly Asst. C. of Locking, Somerset, Horncastle 1859–60. Author, *Meditationes Sacræ*, 1*s*; *Fragments in Verse*, 1*s*; *Dark November Fog*, 2*d*; *She hath done what she could*, 3*d*; etc. [8]

HATTON, John Leigh Smeathman, *Ulles-thorpe Villa, Scarborough.*—Wor. Coll. Ox. B.A. 1860; Deac. 1860 and Pr. 1861 by Bp of Lin. P. C. of Butterwick, Dio. York, 1865. (Patron, R. of Foxholes; Glebe, 10 acres; P. C.'s Inc. 65*l*; Pop. 120.) Asst. Chap. Scarborough Borough Gaol 1867; Patron of Rothersthorpe, Northants. Formerly C. of Orston 1861, Monks Kirby, Rugby, 1863. [9]

HAUGHTON, G. D., *Bath.* [10]

HAUGHTON, William, *South Wootton Rectory, King's Lynn, Norfolk.*—Deac. 1835, Pr. 1836. R. of South Wootton, Dio. Nor. 1842. (Patron, Ld Chan; Tithe, 270*l*; Glebe, 8 acres; R.'s Inc. 290*l* and Ho; Pop. 150.) [11]

HAUTENVILLE, Rawdon William, *Walton Rectory, Clevedon, Somerset.*—Univ. Coll. Ox. B.A. 1846, M.A. 1849; Deac. 1847 by Bp of B. and W. Pr. 1848 by Bp of St. D. R. of Walton with Weston-in-Gordano, Dio. B. and W. 1866. (Patron, Sir W. Miles, Bart. Tithe, 300*l*; Glebe, 51 acres; R.'s Inc. 380*l* and Ho; Pop. 370.) Formerly C. of Hay, Brecon, 1847–49, Woolavington, Somerset, 1850–51, Milverton 1851–56, R. of Yatton Keynell, Wilts, 1857–66; C. of Weston-in-Gordano 1857 66. Author, *The Character of the Church of England as opposed to Romanism and Puritanism* (a Visitation Sermon), 1855. [12]

HAVERFIELD, William Robert, *Bathwick, Bath.*—Corpus Coll. Ox. B.A. 1849, M.A. 1852; Deac. 1850 and Pr. 1852. C. of St. John Baptist's, Bathwick. Formerly C. of Batheaston. [13]

HAVERGAL, Francis Tebbs, *The College, Hereford.*—New Coll. Ox. B.A. 1852, M.A. 1856; Deac. 1852 and Pr. 1853 by Bp of Herf. Vicar Choral and Min. Can. 1853, Sub-Treasurer of Herf. Cathl. 1866; V. of Pipe and Lyde, Dio. Herf. 1861. (Patrons, D. and C. of Herf; Glebe, 12½ acres; V.'s Inc. 290*l* and Ho; Pop. 210.) Author, *Visitor's Handyside and Ground Plan of Hereford Cathedral*, 1863–65. Editor, *Diocesan Calendar*, 1865–66; *Fasti Herefordenses*, 4to. 1868. [14]

HAVERGAL, Henry East, *Cople, near Bedford.*—New Coll. Ox. B.A. 1842, M.A. 1845; Deac. and Pr. 1844 by Bp of Ox. V. of Cople, Dio. Ely, 1847. (Patron, Ch. Ch. Ox; Tithe—App. 535*l*, V. 215*l*; Glebe, 13 acres; V.'s Inc. 227*l* and Ho; Pop. 565.) Editor of two editions of *George Wither's Hymns of the Church* (1623), 16mo. Ox. 1846; *Preces of Tallis* (never before printed), Ox. 1847; various other musical works. [15]

HAVERGAL, William Henry, *Shareshill, near Wolverhampton.*—St. Edm. Hall, Ox. B.A. 1815, M.A. 1819; Deac. 1816 by Bp of B. and W. Pr. 1817 by Bp of Lich. P. C. of Shareshill, Dio. Lich. 1860. (Patron, Lord Hatherton; Glebe, 4 acres; P. C.'s Inc. 143*l*; Pop. 530.) Hon. Can. of Wor. 1845. Formerly R. of Astley, Worc. 1829–42; R. of St. Nicholas', Worc. 1845–60. Author, *Four Sermons*, on different occasions, *Ordination Sermon*, 1845; *Death for Murder* (Assize Sermon), 1847; *Historical Sermons*, 2 vols. Hatchards, 1853; Musical Works; *Gresham Prize Service*, 1836; *Gresham Prize Anthem*, 1845. Editor of Ravencroft's Psalter (1611), 1847; *Old Church Psalmody*, 1849; *History of the Old Hundredth Psalm*, 1854; and above fifty Musical Compositions published by Shepherd and Novello. [16]

HAVILAND, Arthur Coles, *St. John's College, Cambridge.*—St. John's Coll. Cam. 1852, 39th Wrang. and B.A. 1853; Deac. 1855 and Pr. 1857 by Bp of Ox. P. C. of Horningsey, Dio. Ely, 1864. (Patron, St. John's Coll. Cam; Pop. 402.) Fell. of St. John's Coll. Cam. 1853. Formerly C. of Colnbrook, Bucks; P. C. of St. John's, Bodle-street Green, Sussex, 1858–64. [17]

HAVILAND, George Edward, *Warbleton Rectory, Hurst Green, Sussex.*—St. John's Coll. Cam. 6th Sen. Opt. B.A. 1846, M.A. 1849; Deac. 1847 and Pr. 1848 by Bp of Win. R. of Warbleton, Dio. Chich. 1850. (Patron, the present R; Tithe, 830*l*; Glebe, 38 acres; R.'s Inc. 880*l* and Ho; Pop. 958.) Formerly C. of Odiham, Hants, 1847–50. Author *Christ's Presence the Encouragement of His Ministers in the Visitation of the Sick* (a Visitation Sermon), 1855. [18]

HAVILAND, John, *Fladbury Rectory, Pershore, Worcestershire.*—St. John's Coll. Cam. B.A. 1843, M.A. 1846, Norrisian Prize Essay 1848; Deac. 1844 and Pr. 1845 by Bp of Ex. R. of Fladbury, Dio. Wor. 1863. (Patron, Bp of Wor; R.'s Inc. 778*l* and Ho; Pop. 1204.) Formerly V. of Pampisford, Cambridge, 1845–63. [19]

HAWEIS, Hugh Reginald, 24, *Welbeck-street, Cavendish-square, London, W.*—Trin. Coll. Cam. M.A; P. C. of St. James's, Marylebone, Dio. Lon. 1866. (Patron, the Crown.) [20]

HAWEIS, John Oliver Willyams, *Colwood, Slaugham, near Crawley.*—Queen's Coll. Ox. B.A. 1828, M.A. 1830; Deac. 1829 and Pr. 1830 by Bp of Lon. Author, *Sketches of the Reformation and Elizabethan Age*, 1844; *Sermons* at the Magdalen Hospital, 5*s*; *On the Death of the Duke of Wellington*, 6*d*; *Three Sermons on Various Occasions*; *Light Sown for the Righteous* (a Sermon), privately printed, 1855. [21]

HAWES, James, 6, *Park-terrace, Oxford.*—Magd. Hall. Ox. B.A. 1858; Deac. 1859 by Bp of Carl. Pr. 1862 by Bp of Lon. Formerly C. of Preston Patrick, Westmoreland, 1859; Vice-Prin. of the Metropolitan Training Coll. Highbury, Lond; Sen. Mast. Ch. Mis.

sionaries Children's Home. Author, *Critical English Testament*, 3 vols. Strahan, 1866–67. [1]

HAWES, Robert, *Tunstall Parsonage, Staffs.*—St. John's Coll. Cam. B D; Deac. 1840 and Pr. 1841 by Bp of Lon. P. C. of Tunstall, Dio. Lich. 1853. (Patron, R. Sneyd, Esq; P. C.'s Inc. 260*l* and Ho; Pop. 11,150.) Surrogate; Dom. Chap. to the Earl of Shrewsbury. Formerly Miss. and Chap. at Jaunpur, N. India, 1841–49; C. of Walsall, Staffs, 1849–53. [2]

HAWES, Thomas Henry, *Burgh Castle Rectory, Great Yarmouth.*—Magd. Hall, Ox. 1824, B.A. 1828, M.A. 1834, B.D. 1839; Deac. 1829 by Bp of Chich. Pr. 1830 by Bp of Ox. R. of Burgh Castle, Dio. Nor. 1857. (Patron, Ld Chan; R.'s Inc. 400*l* and Ho; Pop. 458.) Dom. Chap. to the Duke of Argyll. Late Chap. of New Coll. Ox. 1829–37. Composer, *Two Penitential Anthems*, 4*s*; *Morning and Communion Service in A*, 4*s*; *Congregational Psalmody*, 5*s* (Voice Parts, 2*s* each); *Chants*, 1*s*; *Three Short Devotional Anthems*, 4*s*; etc. [3]

HAWKE, Edward Henry Julius, *Willingham Rectory, Gainsborough.*—St. Cath. Coll. Cam. B.A. 1839, M.A. 1843. R. of Willingham, Dio. Lin. 1854. (Patron, B. E. Hawke, Esq; Tithe, 30*l*; Glebe, 312 acres; R.'s Inc. 352*l* and Ho; Pop. 520.) V. of Coates, Dio. Lin. 1865. (Patron, Sir John Ramsden; V.'s Inc. 70*l*; Pop. 50.) [4]

HAWKER, Isaac, *The Vicarage, Faringdon, Berks.*—St. Aidan's; Deac. 1859 and Pr. 1860 by Bp of Dur. C. of Faringdon with Little Coxwell 1866. Formerly C. of South Shields 1859, Charles, Plymouth. 1863–66. [5]

HAWKER, John Manley, *Ideford Rectory, Chudleigh, Devon.*—Ball. Coll. Ox. 3rd cl. Lit. Hum. and B.A. 1842, M.A. 1845; Deac. 1843, Pr. 1844. R. of Ideford, Dio. Ex. 1856. (Patron, the present R; Tithe, 255*l*; Glebe, 65 acres; R.'s Inc. 360*l* and Ho; Pop. 358.) Formerly C. of Modbury 1843; P. C. of Tipton St. John 1844; C. of Horley with Hornton 1844, Earley, Berks, 1849. [6]

HAWKER, Robert Stephen, *Morwenstow, Stratton, Cornwall.*—Magd. Hall, Ox. B.A. 1828, M.A. 1836; Deac. 1829 by Bp of Ex. Pr. 1831 by Bp of B. and W. V. of Morwenstow, Dio. Ex. 1834. (Patron, Bp of Ex; Tithe—Imp. 390*l*, V. 365*l*; Glebe, 72 acres; V.'s Inc. 448*l*; Pop. 868.) Formerly C. of Wellcombe, Devon. Author, *Pompeii* (Newdigate Prize Poem), 1827; *Records of the Western Shores*, 1832, second series, 1836; *Ecclesia*, 1841; *Reeds Shaken with the Wind*, 1842, second cluster, 1843; *Echoes of Old Cornwall*, 1845. [7]

HAWKES, Abiathar, *Rushton Rectory, Kettering, Northants.*—Wad. Coll. Ox. B.A. 1836, M.A. 1846; Deac. 1836, Pr. 1837. R. of Rushton, Dio. Pet. 1858. (Patron, W. C. Thornhill, Esq; Tithe, 650*l*; Glebe, 104 acres; R.'s Inc. 754*l* and Ho; Pop. 484.) Dom. Chap. to the Earl of Essex. Formerly C. of Barcombe, Sussex. [8]

HAWKES, Richard Henry, *St. Leonards-on-Sea, Sussex.*—Pemb. Coll. Ox. B.A. 1853, M.A. 1858; Deac. 1854 and Pr. 1856 by Bp of Ex. C. of Ch. Ch. St. Leonards, 1865. Formerly C. of Buckfastleigh, Devon, 1854, Shepton Beauchamp and Bonnington, Somerset, 1856, Grimley, Worcestershire, 1859. [9]

HAWKES, Samuel John, *Guildford.*—Queen's Coll. Ox. Fell. of. C. of St. Nicholas', Guildford, Surrey. [10]

HAWKINS, Bradford Denne, *Rivenhal Rectory, Witham, Essex.*—Pemb. Coll. Ox. B.A. 1820, M.A. 1822; Deac. 1823, Pr. 1824. R. of Rivenhall, Dio. Roch. 1853. (Patrons, Heirs of Lord Western; Tithe, 950*l*; Glebe, 136 acres; R.'s Inc 1154*l* and Ho; Pop. 719.) Formerly Fell. of Pemb. Coll. Ox. [11]

HAWKINS, Charles, *Christ's Hospital, London, E.C.*—Ch. Ch. Ox. Fell. Scho. of, 2nd cl. Lit. Hum. and S.C.L. 1842, B.C.L. 1846; Deac. 1846 by Bp of Lon. Pr. 1847 by Bp of Roch. Asst. Upper Mast. of Christ's Hospital, Lond. Formerly 2nd Mast. of Christ's Hospital, Hertford. Author, *The Andromache of Euripides*, Bentley, 1852; *Anthon's Cæsar Revised*, Longmans, 1855. [12]

HAWKINS, C. H., *Winchester.*—Chap. of Winchester Coll. [13]

HAWKINS, Charles Frederick, *Great Bedwyn, Hungerford, Wilts.*—Trin. Coll. Cam. B.A. 1863, M.A. 1867; Deac. 1864 and Pr. 1865 by Bp of Salis. Asst. C. of Bedwyn Magna 1864. [14]

HAWKINS, Edward, *St. Woolos Vicarage, Newport, Monmouthshire.*—Pemb. Coll. Ox. B.A. 1822, M.A. 1825; Deac. 1823 and Pr. 1824 by Bp of G. and B. V. of St. Woolos with Bettws C. Dio. Llan. 1843. (Patron, Bp of G. and B; St. Woolos, Tithe—App. 287*l* 18*s* 5*d*, V. 203*l* 12*s* 7*d*; Bettws, Tithe—App. 82*l* 10*s*, Imp. 4*l* 16*s* 1*d*, V. 42*l*; V.'s Inc. 286*l* and Ho; Pop. St. Woolos 11,877, Bettws 84.) Can. Res. of Llan. 1862; Rural Dean; Surrogate; Proctor for the Clergy of Dio. Llan. 1865. [15]

HAWKINS, Edward, *Oriel College, Oxford.*—St. John's Coll. Ox. Double 1st cl. and B.A. 1811, M.A. 1814, B.D. and D.D. 1828; Deac. 1816 and Pr. 1817 by Bp of Ox. Provost of Oriel Coll. Ox. with a Canonry in Roch. Cathl. (Value, 600*l* and Res.) R. of Purleigh, Essex, Dio. Roch. 1828. (Tithe, 1704*l*; R.'s Inc. 1720*l* and Ho; Pop. 1095.) Formerly Tut. of St. John's Coll. Ox. 1812; Fell of Oriel Coll. Ox. 1813; Tut. of Oriel 1819; V. of St. Mary's the Virgin, Oxford, 1823; Whitehall Preacher 1827; Select Preacher 1820, 1824, 1830, and 1842; Bampton Lect. 1840; Dean Ireland's Prof. of the Exegesis of Holy Scripture 1847–61; Member of the Hebdomadal Council of the Univ. of Oxford. Author, *Sermons on Scriptural Types and Sacraments, with Observations upon some Recent Theories* (preached before the Univ. of Ox.), 6*s*; *Sermons on the Church* (preached before the Univ. of Ox.), 7*s*; *Discourses upon some of the Principal Objects and Uses of the Historical Scriptures of the Old Testament* (preached before the Univ. of Ox.), 6*s*; *An Inquiry into the Connected Uses of the Principal Means of attaining Christian Truth* (the Bampton Lectures for 1840), 2 eds. 10*s* 6*d*; *A Dissertation on the Use of Unauthoritative Tradition*, 2 eds. 1*s* 6*d*; *An Inaugural Lecture, upon the Foundation of Dean Ireland's Professorship*, 1*s* 6*d*; *A Manual for Christians, Designed for their Use at any Time after Confirmation*, 7 eds. J. H. Parker, 6*d*; *The Poetical Works of John Milton* (with Notes, &c.), 4 vols. 30*s*; Occasional Sermons, *The Duty of Private Judgment*, 3 eds. 1*s*; *The Apostolical Succession*, 2 eds. 1*s* 6*d*; *The Nature and Obligation of Apostolic Order*, 1*s*; *The Presence of God in the Church by the Holy Spirit*, 1*s*; *The Ministry of Men in the Economy of Grace, and the Danger of Overvaluing it*, 1*s* 6*d*; *Christianity not the Religion either of the Bible only or of the Church*, 1*s*; *Systematic Preaching*, 1*s*; *The Way of Salvation*, 1*s*; *The Duty and Means of Promoting Christian Knowledge without impairing Christian Unity*, 6*d*; *Church Extension in England and Wales*, 6*d*; *The Duty of Moral Courage*, 6*d*; *Christ our Example*, 6*d*; *Christian Unity*, 6*d*; *The Province of Private Judgment*, 1*s*; *Liberty of Private Judgment*, 1*s* 6*d*; *Notes upon Subscription, Academical and Clerical*, 1*s* 6*d*; and various other Pamphlets. [16]

HAWKINS, Edward William, *Huddersfield.*—Pemb. Coll. Ox. B.A. 1856, M.A. 1859; Deac. 1857 and Pr. 1858 by Bp of Ex. C. of St. Thomas's, Huddersfield 1862; Fell. of Pemb. Coll. Ox. Formerly C. of St. Erme 1857–59, St. Ives, Cornwall, 1860–62. [17]

HAWKINS, E. C., *Clapton, London, N.E.*—Head Mast. of St. John's Foundation Sch. Clapton. [18]

HAWKINS, Ernest, 20, *Dean's Yard, Westminster, S.W.*—Ball. Coll. Ox. B.A. 1824, M.A. 1827, Fell. of Ex. Coll. Ox. 1831, B.D. 1839. Can. of Westminster 1864; Min. of Curzon Chapel, Mayfair, 1850. (Patron, Earl Howe; Min's Inc. 400*l*.) Preb. of St. Paul's 1844. Late Sec. to the S.P.G; Hon. Sec. to the Colonial Bishoprics' Fund. Author, *Historical Notices of the Missions of the Church of England in the North American Colonies, previous to the Independence of the United States*, 1845; *Annals of the Dioceses of Fredericton, Quebec and Toronto*, 1848; *A Book of Family Prayer*, 1856; *Ramsden Sermon*, Oxford, 1861; *The Book of Psalms, with Explanatory Notes*, 1857. [19]

HAWKINS, George Cæsar, *Honington Rectory, Ixworth, Suffolk.*—Oriel Coll. Ox. B.A. 1829; Deac. 1832, Pr. 1833. R. of Honington, Dio. Ely, 1844. (Patron, Ld Chan; Tithe, 336*l*; Glebe, 30 acres; R.'s Inc. 400*l*; Pop. 363.) [1]

HAWKINS, Henry, *Cuckfield, Sussex.*—Ex. Coll. Ox. B.A. 1848, M.A. 1859; Deac. 1849 and Pr. 1851 by Bp of Roch. Chap. to the Cuckfield Union 1854; Chap. of the Sussex County Lunatic Asylum 1859. [2]

HAWKINS, Henry Annesley, *Topcliffe Vicarage, Thirsk, Yorks.*—Trin. Coll. Cam. B.A. 1836; Deac. 1836, Pr. 1837. V. of Topcliffe, Dio. York, 1838. (Patrons, D. and C. of York; Tithe—App. 1153*l* 17*s* 6*d*, Imp. 1040*l*, V. 538*l* 12*s* 8*d*; Glebe, 6 acres; V.'s Inc. 600*l* and Ho; Pop. 1234.) [3]

HAWKINS, Henry Cæsar Hankins, *Edington Parsonage, Bridgwater.*—Ch. Ch. Ox. B.A. 1821. P. C. of Chilton-on-Polden with Edington P. C. Dio. B. and W. 1842. (Patron, the V. of Moorlinch; Chilton-on-Polden, Tithe—App. 78*l* 4*s*; Imp. 80*l*; Edington, Tithe—App. 111*l* 5*s*, Imp. 90*l*; P. C.'s Inc. 128*l* and Ho; Pop. Chilton-on-Polden 427, Edington 268.) [4]

HAWKINS, Herbert Samuel, *Beyton Rectory, Bury St. Edmunds.*—Jesus Coll. Ox. B.A. 1842, M.A. 1844; Deac. 1843 and Pr. 1844 by Bp of Dur. R. of Beyton, Dio. Ely, 1855. (Patron, Ld Chan; Tithe, 210*l*; Glebe, 10 acres; R.'s Inc. 225*l* and Ho; Pop. 360.) [5]

HAWKINS, James Benjamin Head, 4, *Park-street, Taunton.*—Mert. Coll. Ox. Postmaster of, 2nd cl. Lit. Hum. B.A. 1856, M.A. 1859; Deac. 1858 and Pr. 1859 by Bp of B. and W. Formerly Mast. of Taunton Coll. Sch. 1856-59, C. of Bishops Hull 1858-59, and Norton Fitzwarren, Somerset, 1859-64. [6]

HAWKINS, Sir John Cæsar, Bart., *St. Albans.*—Oriel Coll. Ox. Ellerton Theol. Essay 1859, B.A. 1853, M.A. 1861; Deac. 1860 and Pr. 1861 by Bp of Roch. R. of St. Albans, Dio. Roch. 1866. (Patron, Bp of Roch; R.'s Inc. 180*l* and Ho; Pop. 3671.) Surrogate. Formerly C. of St. Margaret's, Rochester, 1860-62; P. C. of St. Paul's, Chatham, 1863-64; P. C. of Westcott, Surrey, 1864-66. [7]

HAWKINS, John Cunningham Calland Bennett Popkin, *Ramsbury Vicarage, Hungerford, Wilts.*—Pemb. Coll. Ox. B.A. 1814, M.A. 1823; Deac. 1817, Pr. 1818. V. of Ramsbury, Dio. Salis. 1840. (Patron, Ld Chan; Tithe—Imp. 373*l* 14*s* 8*d*, V. 125*l*; Glebe, 66 acres; V.'s Inc. 270*l* and Ho; Pop. 2533.) Surrogate. [8]

HAWKINS, Joseph Beaumont, 16, *Rue des Princes, Marseilles.*—Consular Chap. at Marseilles. [9]

HAWKINS, Robert, *Lamberhurst Vicarage, Kent.*—Pemb. Coll. Ox. B.A. 1827, M.A. 1830. V. of Lamberhurst, Dio. Cant. 1834. (Patrons, D. and C. of Roch; Tithe—App. 375*l* 5*s*, V. 638*l* 5*s* 6*d*; V.'s Inc. 666*l* and Ho; Pop. 1605.) Dom. Chap. to the Marquis of Camden. [10]

HAWKINS, R. Macleod, *Leyton, Essex.*—C. of All Saints', Leyton, 1867. Formerly C. of Beckenham, Kent. [11]

HAWKINS, William Bentinck Lethem, 23, *Great Marlborough-street, Regent-street, London, W.*—Ex. Coll. Ox. B.A. 1824, M.A. 1827. Chap. to H.R.H. the Duke of Cambridge. [12]

HAWKS, William, *Saltash, Cornwall.*—Trin. Hall, Cam. LL.B. 1822; Deac. and Pr. 1824. P. C. of Saltash, Dio. Ex. 1846. (Patrons, Exors. of Sir R. S. Hawks; P. C.'s Inc. 100*l* and Ho; Pop. 1900.) [13]

HAWKSHAW, Edward Burdett, *Weston-under-Penyard, near Ross, Herefordshire.*—Oriel Coll. Ox. B.A. 1835; Deac. 1841 and Pr. 1843 by Bp of Herf. R. of Weston-under-Penyard, Dio. Herf. 1855. (Patron, Bp of Herf; R.'s Inc. 600*l* and Ho; Pop. 828.) Chap. to the Earl of Erne 1842. Formerly R. of Brampton Abbotts, Herefordshire, 1849-55. [14]

HAWKSLEY, John, 16, *Richmond-terrace, Clifton.*—St. Edm. Hall, Ox. B.A. 1839; Deac. 1839 by Bp of Lich. Pr. 1841 by Bp of Win. Formerly C. of Kingston, Devon. [15]

HAWKSLEY, John Webster, *Redruth, Cornwall.*—R. of Redruth, Dio. Ex. 1835. (Patron, J. F. Basset, Esq; R.'s Inc. 450*l*; Pop. 9155.) [16]

HAWKSLEY, John Webster, *Bodmin, Cornwall.*—Dub. A.B. 1857; Deac. 1857 and Pr. 1859 by Bp of Ex. C. of Bodmin. [17]

HAWKSWORTH, John, *The Grove, Wem, Salop.*—Dub. A.B. 1812, A.M. 1816; Deac. 1830 and Pr. 1831 by Bp of Lich. P. C. of Broughton, Salop, Dio. Lich. 1864. (Patron, Viscount Hill; P. C.'s Inc. 65*l*; Pop. 140.) Formerly Barrister-at-Law of Lincoln's Inn, Lond. 1819-29; P. C. of Woore, Salop, 1830-64. Author, *Parochial Lectures*, 1854, 5*s*; *Warning against Idolatry*, 1865, 3*d*. [18]

HAWLEY, Edward, *Shire Oaks, Worksop, Notts.*—Sid. Coll. Cam. B.A. 1854; Deac. 1854. Min of Shire Oaks Chapel, Dio. Lin. 1863. (Patron, Duke of Newcastle; Min.'s Inc. 90*l*.) [19]

HAWLEY, Henry Charles, *Leybourne Rectory, Maidstone.*—Trin. Coll. Cam. B.A. 1846; Deac. 1847, Pr. 1848. R. of Leybourne, Dio. Cant. 1849. (Patron, Sir J. Hawley, Bart; Tithe, 329*l* 12*s*; Glebe, 194 acres; R.'s Inc. 530*l* and Ho; Pop. 289.) [20]

HAWLEY, James, *Norton Rectory, Faversham, Kent.*—R. of Norton, Dio. Cant. (Patron, Bp of Wor; R.'s Inc. 350*l* and Ho; Pop. 134.) [21]

HAWLEY, William, *Douglas, Isle of Man.*—Literate; Deac. 1847 and Pr. 1849 by Bp of S. and M. P. C. of St. George's, Douglas, Dio. S. and M. 1859. (Patron, Bp of S. and M; P. C.'s Inc. 250*l*.) [22]

HAWORTH, A., *St. Catherine's, Manchester.*—R. of St. Catherine's, Manchester, Dio. Man. 1859. (Patrons, Trustees; R.'s Inc. 200*l*, Pop. 7618.) [23]

HAWORTH, Henry, *Rawtenstall, Manchester.*—Queens' Coll. Cam. 1st Sen. Opt. B.A. 1837; Deac. 1837 and Pr. 1838 by Bp of Ches. P. C. of Rawtenstall, Dio. Man. 1847. (Patrons, the present P. C. and Rev. W. Whitworth; P. C.'s Inc. 300*l*; Pop. 7823.) Surrogate. Formerly C. of Salesbury 1837; P. C. of Goodshaw 1839. [24]

HAWORTH, James, *Chester.*—P. C. of St. Michael's with St. Olave's, City and Dio. Ches. 1850. (Patron, Bp of Ches; Tithe—App. 89*l*; P. C.'s Inc. 175*l*; Pop. St. Michael's 922, St. Olave's 480*l*.) [25]

HAWORTH, John Gorell, *Tunstead Parsonage, Stacksteads, Manchester.*—St. Aidan's; Deac. 1849, Pr. 1850. P. C. of Tunstead, Dio. Man. 1851. (Patrons, Trustees; P. C.'s Inc. 95*l* and Ho; Pop. 4681.) [26]

HAWORTH, Samuel, *Salehouse Vicarage, Wroxham, Norwich.*—St. John's Coll. Cam. B.A. 1848; Deac. and Pr. 1848 by Bp of Ches. V. of Wroxham with Salehouse V. Dio. Nor. 1857. (Patron, W. H. Trafford, Esq; Tithe, 324*l* 10*s*; Glebe, 46*l*; V.'s Inc. 380*l* and Ho; Pop. Wroxham 409, Salehouse 686.) Formerly C. of Stalmine, Lancashire. [27]

HAWORTH, William, *Staveley, near Chesterfield.*—St. Mark's Coll. Chelsea; Deac. 1859 by Bp of Wor. Pr. 1863 by Bp of Ex. C. of Stavely. Formerly C. of Camborne, Cornwall, and St. Mary's, Barnsley. [28]

HAWORTH, William, *Fence, Burnley.*—St. John's Coll. Cam. B.A. 1835, M.A. 1837; Deac. 1836, Pr. 1837. P. C. of Fence, Dio. Man. 1837. (Patron, W. Holden, Esq; P C.'s Inc. 73*l* and Ho; Pop. 1331.) [29]

HAWTAYNE, William Gambier, *Whitton, Middlesex, W.*—Magd. Hall, Ox. M.A; Deac. 1839, Pr. 1840. P. C. of Whitton, Dio. Lon. 1862. (Patron, V. of Twickenham; Tithe, 51*l*; P. C.'s Inc. 130*l* and Ho; Pop. 700.) [30]

HAWTHORN, Robert, *Stapleford Vicarage, Cambs.*—St. Peter's Coll. Cam. B.A. 1830, M.A. 1833; Deac. 1831, Pr. 1832. V. of Stapleford, Dio. Ely, 1845. (Patrons, D. and C. of Ely; V.'s Inc. 185*l* and Ho; Pop. 465.) [31]

HAWTHORN, Roscoe, *Barking, Essex.*—Trin. Coll. Cam. B.A. 1862; Deac. 1864 by Bp of Pet. Pr.

1865 by Bp of Win. C. of Barking 1867. Formerly C. of Whitwell, Isle of Wight, 1865. [1]

HAWTREY, Henry Courtenay, *Church House, Windsor.*—Emman. Coll. Cam. B.A. 1844, M.A. 1847; Deac. 1844, Pr. 1845. R. of Trinity, Windsor, Dio. Ox. 1852. (Patron, Ld Chan; Tithe, 35*l*; P. C.'s Inc. 35*l*; Pop. 3055.) Acting Chap. to H.M. Household Troops in Garrison at Windsor. (Salary, 120*l*.) [2]

HAWTREY, John William, *Eton College, Windsor.*—King's Coll. Cam. Scho. 1837, Fell. 1840, B.A. 1841, M.A. 1845; Deac. 1843 by Bp of Lin. Asst. Mast. of Eton Coll. 1842. [3]

HAWTREY, Montague John Gregg, *Rimpton Rectory, near Sherborne.*—Trin. Coll. Cam. 3rd Sen. Opt. 2nd in 2nd cl. Cl. Trip. and B A. 1829, M.A. 1832; Deac. 1833 and Pr. 1834 by Bp of Ches. R. of Rimpton, Dio. B. and W. 1841. (Patron, Bp of Win; Tithe, 221*l*; Glebe, 50 acres; R.'s Inc. 340*l* and Ho; Pop. 282.) Preb. of Wells 1860; Rural Dean. Formerly R. of Chilton-Cantelo, Somerset, 1848–57. Author, *Sponsors for the Poor*, 1840; Γίνου γρηγορῶν, καὶ στήριξον τὰ λοιπὰ ἃ μέλλει ἀποθανεῖν. Rev. iii. 2; *Earnest Address to New Zealand Colonists, with reference to their intercourse with the Native Inhabitants*, 1840; *Justice to New Zealand*, 1860; Articles in the new edition of Kitto's Cyclopædia. [4]

HAWTREY, Stephen Thomas, *Eton College, Windsor.*—Trin. Coll. Cam. B.A. 1832, M.A. 1835; Deac. and Pr. 1835. Head Math. Mast. of Eton. Coll. Formerly P. C, of Trinity, Windsor, 1844–51. [5]

HAY, Charles Rae, *Ridlington Rectory, Uppingham, Rutland.*—Mert. Coll. Ox. B.A. 1840, M.A. 1843; Deac. 1842 and Pr. 1843 by Bp of Win. R. of Ridlington, Dio. Pet. 1858. (Patron, Earl of Gainsborough; Tithe, 351*l*; Glebe, 40 acres; R.'s Inc. 421*l* and Ho; Pop. 316.) Formerly V. of Thundridge, Herts, 1853–55; V. of Kirby Moorside, Yorks, 1856–58. [6]

HAY, The Right Hon. Lord Thomas, *Rendlesham Rectory, Suffolk.*—Trin. Coll. Cam. M.A. 1823. R. of Rendlesham, Dio. Nor. 1830. (Patron, the Crown; Tithe, 505*l*; Glebe, 53 acres; R.'s Inc. 588*l* and Ho; Pop. 359.) Rural Dean. [7]

HAYCROFT, Isaac, *Chipping Barnet, Herts.*—C. of Chipping Barnet. [8]

HAYDEN, Charles Frederick, *Helmdon Rectory, Brackley, Northants.*—Corpus Coll Ox. B.A. 1846, M.A. 1849; Deac. 1849 and Pr. 1850 by Bp of Ox. R. of Helmdon, Dio. Pet. 1855. (Patron, Corpus Coll. Ox; Tithe, 35*l*; Glebe, 60 acres; R.'s Inc. 276*l* and Ho; Pop. 602.) R. of Stotsbury, (no ch.) Northants, Dio. Pet. 1855. (Patron, Univ. of Ox; R.'s Inc. 5*l*; Pop. 23.) Formerly Chap. of the Don. of Catcott, Somerset, 1850–55; Fell. of Corpus Coll. Ox. [9]

HAYDEN, Frederick William.—Dub. A.B. 1840; Deac. 1841, Pr. 1842. Chap. of the Pauper Lunatic Asylum for the N. and E. Ridings of York. (Salary, 140*l*.) [10]

HAYDEN, Henry G., *Ealing, Middlesex, W.* [11]

HAYDON, William, *Midhurst, Sussex.*—Univ. Coll. Ox. B.A. 1845, M.A. 1849; Deac. 1847, Pr. 1848. P. C. of Midhurst, Dio. Chich. 1860. (Patron, Earl of Egmont; P. C.'s Inc. 147*l* 15*s*; Pop. 1340.) Formerly C. of Lodsworth, Sussex, 1847–51; R. of Wotton, Surrey, 1851–57; C. of Langley, Kent, 1857–59; Beddington, Surrey 1859–60. [12]

HAYES, Charles, *Brampton Bierlow, Rotherham, Yorks.*—Magd. Hall, Ox. B.A. 1834; Deac. 1835 by Bp of Carl. Pr. 1836 by Bp of Dur. P. C. of Brampton Bierlow, Dio. York, 1855. (Patron, V. of Wath-upon-Dearne; P. C.'s Inc. 150*l*; Pop. 1733) Author, *Sermons* (preached in the Parish Churches of Rotherham and Wath-upon-Dearne), 1846. [13]

HAYES, Edward, 30, *Greenhill-street, Greenheys, Manchester.*—St. Alban Hall, Ox. 3rd cl. Lit. Hum, B.A. 1861, M.A. 1863; Deac. 1861 and Pr. 1862 by Bp of Lin. C. of St. John Baptist's, Hulme, 1866. Formerly C. of Coleby 1861, Hundleby, Linc. 1862, St. Margaret's, Leicester, with Knighton, 1863, St. Mary Magdalene's, Paddington, Lond. 1864. [14]

HAYES, Henry, *Denshanger, near Stony Stratford, Bucks.*—King's Coll. Lond. Assoc. 1867; Deac. 1867. C. of Passenham with Denshanger, 1867. Author, *What is Baptism?* 3*d*; *The Ministry of the Clergy and Laity*, 2*d*. [15]

HAYES, John, *Coalbrookdale Parsonage, near Wellington, Salop.*—Magd. Hall, Ox. B.A. 1838, M.A. 1841; Deac. 1838 and Pr. 1840 by Bp of Ches. P. C. of Coalbrookdale, Dio. Herf. 1854. (Patron, A. Darby, Esq; P. C.'s Inc. 230*l* and Ho; Pop. 1551.) Formerly P. C. of Harpurhey, near Manchester, 1840–54. [16]

HAYES, Sir John Warren, Bart., *Arborfield Rectory, Reading.*—Wad. Coll. Ox. B.A. 1821, M.A. 1824; Deac. 1822, Pr. 1823. R. of Arborfield, Dio. Ox. 1839. (Patron, Lord Braybrooke; Tithe, 398*l*; Glebe, 2 acres; R.'s Inc. 350*l* and Ho; Pop. 286.) [17]

HAYES, Robert, *Woodhouse Eaves, near Loughborough.*—St. Bees; Deac. 1861 and Pr. 1862 by Bp of Pet. C. of Woodhouse Eaves 1863. Formerly C. of St. John's, Leicester, 1861–63. [18]

HAYES, Thomas, *Duntsbourn-Abbots, Cirencester.*—St. John's Coll. Cam. B.A. 1834, M.A. 1838; Deac. 1838, Pr. 1839. R. of Duntsbourne-Abbots, Dio. G. and B. 1861. (Patron, the present R; R.'s Inc. 300*l* and Ho; Pop. 354.) Formerly C. of Duntsbourn-Abbots. [19]

HAYES, Thomas, *Bracewell, Skipton, Yorks.*—St. John's Coll. Cam. Sen. Opt. and B.A. 1825; Deac. 1825, Pr. 1827. V. of Bracewell, Dio. Rip. 1842. (Patron, J. T. Hopwood, Esq; V.'s Inc. 117*l*; Pop. 140.) [20]

HAYES, Thomas, *Hulme, Manchester.*—C. of Trinity, Hulme. [21]

HAYES, William, 6, *St. Katharine's, Regent's-park, London, N.W.*—Trin. Coll. Cam. B.A. 1839. Asst. Mast. of King's Coll. Sch. Lond; Chap. to St. Katharine's Hospital, Regent's-park. [22]

HAYES, William, *Stockton Heath Parsonage, near Warrington.*—Deac. 1843 and Pr. 1844 by Bp of Ches. P. C. of Stockton Heath or Wilderspool, Dio. Ches. 1852. (Patrons, Gilbert and Edward Greenall, Esqrs. and Rev. Thomas Greenall; Glebe, 2 acres; Inc. 140*l* and Ho; Pop. 1763.) [23]

HAYGARTH, Henry William, *Wimbledon, Surrey, S.W.*—Ex. Coll. Ox. B.A. 1851, M.A. 1854; Deac. and Pr. 1853 by Bp of Roch. P. C. of Wimbledon, Dio. Lon. 1859. (Patrons, D. and C. of Wor; P. C.'s Inc. 400*l*; Pop. 4644.) Formerly C. of Chigwell 1853–55, and of Chingford, Essex, 1855–59. [24]

HAYLEY, Burrell, *Catsfield Rectory, Battle, Sussex.*—Wor. Coll. Ox. B.A. 1832, M.A. 1833; Deac. 1831 and Pr. 1833 by Bp of Chich. R. of Catsfield, Dio. Chich. 1843. (Patron, Earl of Ashburnham; Tithe, 370*l*; Glebe, 34 acres; R.'s Inc. 395*l* and Ho; Pop. 584.) [25]

HAYLEY, John Burrell, *Brightling Rectory, Hurst Green, Sussex.*—Wor. Coll. Ox. B.A. 1845, M.A. 1847; Deac. 1845, Pr. 1846. R. of Brightling, Dio. Chich. 1850. (Patron, Rev. Burrell Hayley; Tithe, 642*l*; R.'s Inc. 600*l* and Ho; Pop. 661.) Surrogate. [26]

HAYLEY, Thomas, 7, *Osnaburgh-terrace, Regent's-park, London, N.W.*—Ex. Coll. Ox. B.A. 1855, M.A. 1857; Deac. 1855 by Bp of B. and W. Pr. 1856 by Bp of G. and B. C. of Ch. Ch. St. Pancras, Lond. Formerly C. of Westbury-on-Severn, Glouc. [27]

HAYMAN, Henry, *Grammar School House, Cheltenham.*—St. John's Coll. Ox. 2nd cl. Lit. Hum. 2nd cl. Math. et Phy. and B.A. 1845, M.A. 1851, B.D. 1854; Deac. 1847 and Pr. 1848 by Bp of Lon. Head Mast. of Cheltenham Gr. Sch. 1859. (Patron, Corpus Coll. Ox.) Formerly Head Mast. of Qu. Elizabeth's Free Gr. Sch. Southwark, and Asst. Preacher at the Temple Ch. Lond. Author, *A Pamphlet in connexion with the Question of Marriage with a Deceased Wife's Sister*; *Dialogues of the Early Church*; *Retail Mammon* (a Tale); *Latin and Greek Verse Translation Exercises*, 1865; *Letter to Professor Mansell condemning the Public Schools Latin Primer*, 1867. Editor, *The Odyssey of Homer*, 1866. [28]

HAYMES, Robert Evered, *Hopesay, Salop.*—C. of Hopesay. [1]

HAYNE, John, *Stawley Rectory, Wellington, Somerset.*—Trin. Coll. Cam. B.A. 1835; Deac. 1837, Pr. 1838. R. of Stawley, Dio. B. and W. 1842. (Patron, the present R; Tithe, 140*l*; R.'s Inc. 150*l* and Ho; Pop. 188.) R. of Raddington, Somerset, Dio. B. and W. 1845. (Patron, Rev. O. Trevelyan; Tithe, 143*l*; R.'s Inc. 200*l* and Ho; Pop. 121.) [2]

HAYNE, Leighton George, *Helston, Cornwall.*—V. of Helston, Dio. Ex. 1866. (Patron, Queen's Coll. Ox; V.'s Inc. 500*l* and Ho; Pop. 3841.) Coryphæus of the Univ. of Ox. [3]

HAYNE, Richard, *Mistley Rectory, Manningtree, Essex.*—St. Peter's Coll. Cam. B.D. 1840, D.D. 1845. R. of Mistley with Bradfield V. Dio. Roch. 1861. (Patron, the present R; Mistley, Tithe, 668*l*; Bradfield, Tithe, 193*l*; Glebe, 40 acres; R.'s Inc. 986*l* and Ho; Pop. Mistley 1539, Bradfield 914.) [4]

HAYNE, Richard James, *Buckland Monachorum Vicarage, Plymouth.*—Ex. Coll. Ox. B.A. 1846, M.A. 1851; Deac. 1847 and Pr. 1849 by Bp of Ex. V. of Buckland Monachorum, Dio. Ex. 1855. (Patron, Rev. Dr. Hayne; Tithe—Imp. 174*l*, V. 304*l*; Glebe, 49 acres; V.'s Inc. 430*l* and Ho; Pop. 1489.) [5]

HAYNE, Thomas, *Rastrick Parsonage, Huddersfield.*—Deac. 1832, Pr. 1833. P. C. of Rastrick, Dio. Rip. 1837. (Patron, V. of Halifax; P. C.'s Inc. 150*l* and Ho; Pop. 4516.) [6]

HAYNES, Edward Cragg, *Empson Villa, Goole, Yorks.*—Trin. Coll. Cam. B.A. 1849; Deac. 1849, Pr. 1850. Formerly C. of Drayton Beauchamp, Bucks. [7]

HAYNES, Edward Joseph, *Albert-terrace, Fulwood Park, near Preston.*—King's Coll. Lond. Theol. Assoc. 1857; Deac. 1857 and Pr. 1858 by Bp of Chich. P. C. of Fulwood, Dio. Man. 1863. (Patron, V. of Lancaster; P. C.'s Inc. 180*l*; Pop. 1200.) Formerly C. of Slindon with Binstead, Sussex, 1857, Ch. Ch. Preston, 1860 Fulwood 1863. [8]

HAYNES, Robert, *Stowey Vicarage, near Bristol.*—Pemb. Coll. Ox. B.A. 1830, M A. 1831; Deac 1833 and Pr. 1834 by Bp of Lich. V. of Stowey, Dio. B. and W. 1858. (Patron, Bp of B. and W; Tithe, 171*l* 9*s* 10*d*; Glebe, 33 acres; V.'s Inc. 200*l* and Ho; Pop. 181.) Formerly C. of Podymore Milton, Somerset. [9]

HAYNES, Robert James, 12, *Hart-street, Bloomsbury, London, W.C.*—Caius Coll. Cam. B.A. 1855, M.A. 1858; Deac. 1855 by Bp of Pet. Pr. 1858 by Bp of G. and B. Min. of Brill Chapel, St. Pancras, Dio. Lon. 1864. (Patron, Bp of Lon; Min.'s Inc. 200*l*; Pop. 7000.) Formerly C. of St. George's, Bloomsbury, 1861–63. [10]

HAYS, John, *Leeds.*—Ch. Coll. Cam. 12th Wrang. B.A. 1845. M.A. 1848; Deac. 1847 and Pr. 1848 by Bp of Ely. Fell. of Ch. Coll. Cam; C. of Leeds 1864. Formerly C. of Fen Drayton, Cambs, 1849–50; Tut. of Ch. Coll. Cam. 1851. [11]

HAYTER, Charles Frederick, *East Mersea Rectory, Colchester.*—Magd. Hall, Ox. B.A. 1852, M.A. 1858; Deac. 1853 by Bp of Wor. Pr. 1854 by Bp of Guiana. R. of East Mersea, *alias* East Mersey, Dio. Roch. 1857. (Patron, the Crown; Tithe, 427*l*; Glebe, 25 acres; R.'s Inc. 467*l* 5*s* and Ho; Pop. 305.) Formerly C. of Chitworthy 1853, Stiffkey and Morston 1854, Kirtlington 1855, Stoke Talmage 1856. Author, *Keeping Saints Days* (a Tract). Masters, 1865; etc. [12]

HAYTER, George Goodenough, *Burnham Sutton Rectory, Lynn, Norfolk.*—Oriel Coll. Ox. 1838, 2nd cl. Lit. Hum. and B.A. 1841, M.A. 1845; Deac. 1843, Pr. 1844. R. of Burnham Sutton with the Medieties of Burnham-Ulph R. and Burnham-Norton R. and V. of Burnham-Overy, Dio. Nor. 1854. (Patron, Ld Chan; Burnham-Sutton and Burnham-Ulph, Tithe—App. 1*l*, R. 418*l* 5*s*; Glebe, 14 acres; Burnham-Norton, Tithe—R.'s Moiety, 130*l* 17*s* 6*d*; R.'s Moiety of Glebe, 16 acres; Burnham-Overy, Tithe—App. 3*l*, Imp. 244*l*, V. 155*l*; Glebe, 18 acres; R.'s and V.'s Inc. 785*l*; Pop. Burnham-Sutton 368, Burnham-Ulph 338, Burnham-Norton 172, Burnham-Overy 648.) [13]

X

HAYTER, Thomas Miller, *Shepton Mallett, Somerset.*—Emman. Coll. Cam. B.A. 1861, M.A. 1865; Deac. 1862 and Pr. 1863 by Bp of B. and W. C. of Shepton Mallett 1865. Formerly C. of Midsomer-Norton, Somerset, 1862–65. [14]

HAYTHORNE, Joseph, *Congresbury Vicarage, near Bristol.*—St. Mary Hall, Ox. B.A 1820, M.A. 1822. V. of Congresbury with Wick St. Lawrence C. Dio. B. and W. 1825. (Patron, R. Hunt, Esq; Congresbury, Tithe—App. 191*l* and 10½ acres of Glebe, V. 531*l*; Glebe, 11 acres; Wick St. Lawrence, Tithe, V. 250*l*; Glebe, 1 acre; V.'s Inc 855*l* and Ho; Pop. Congresbury 1190, Wick St. Lawrence 270.) [15]

HAYTON, Edward Josiah, *Bradborne, Wirksworth, Derbyshire.*—Univ. Coll. Dur. B.A. 1846, M.A. 1849; Deac. 1849 and Pr. 1850 by Bp of Dur. V. of Bradborne with Ballidon C. Dio. Lich. 1861. (Patron, Duke of Devonshire; V.'s Inc. 120*l*; Pop. 340.) [16]

HAYTON, George, *Niton Rectory, Newport, Isle of Wight.*—Queen's Coll. Ox. 2nd cl. Lit. Hum. 2nd cl. Math. et Phy. and B.A. 1853, M.A. 1856; Deac. 1855 and Pr. 1856 by Bp of Ox R. of Niton, Dio. Win. 1858. (Patron, Queen's Coll. Ox; Tithe, 378*l*; Glebe, 19 acres; R.'s Inc. 680*l* and Ho; Pop. 700.) Formerly R. of South Weston, Oxon, 1856–58; Fell. of Queen's Coll. Ox. 1855–58. [17]

HAYTON, Gerard, *Kentmere Parsonage, Kendal.*—St. Bees; Deac. 1833 and Pr. 1835 by Bp of Ches. P. C. of Kentmere, Dio. Ches. 1845. (Patron, V. of Kendal; Glebe, 24½ acres; P. C.'s Inc. 80*l* and Ho; Pop. 186.) [18]

HAYTON, Thomas, *Long Crendon, Thame.*—Queen's Coll. Ox. 2nd cl. Lit. Hum. 1818, B.A. 1819; Deac. 1818, Pr. 1820. P. C. of Long Crendon, Dio. Ox. 1821. (Patron, Lord Churchill; Glebe, 148 acres; P. C.'s Inc. 210*l* and Ho; Pop. 1570.) [19]

HAYWARD, Frederick Lawson, *Tunstall Rectory, Wickham Market, Suffolk.*—Corpus Coll. Cam. B.C.L. 1859; Deac. 1859 and Pr. 1860 by Bp of Chich. R. of Tunstall with Dunningworth R. Dio. Nor. 1862. (Patron, the present R; Tithe, 541*l* 4*s*; R.'s Inc. 550*l* and Ho; Pop. 701.) [20]

HAYWARD, George Anstice, *Lexden House, Reigate, Surrey.*—St. John's Coll. Cam. B.A. 1850, M.A. 1853; Deac. 1851 by Bp of Ely, Pr. 1854 by Abp of Cant. [21]

HAYWARD, Henry Rudge, *Lydiard Millicent, Swindon, Wilts.*—Pemb. Coll. Ox. Fell. of, 4th cl. Lit. Hum. and B.A. 1853, M.A. 1856; Deac. 1855 and Pr. 1856 by Bp of Ox. R. of Lydiard Millicent, Dio. G. and B. 1864. (Patron, Pemb. Coll. Ox; Tithe, 508*l*; R.'s Inc. 520*l*; Pop. 588.) [22]

HAYWARD, John Wheeler, *Granborough, Winslow, Bucks.*—Trin. Coll. Cam. B.A. 1847, M.A. 1848; Deac. 1849 and Pr. 1851 by Bp of Ox. V. of Granborough, Dio. Ox. 1855. (Patron, Ld Chan; Tithe, 75*l*; Glebe, 25 acres; V.'s Inc. 120*l* and Ho; Pop. 374.) [23]

HAYWARD, William, *Shildon, Bishop's Auckland, Durham.*—C. of Shildon. [24]

HAZEL, William, *St. Peter's Rectory, Wallingford, Berks.*—Ch. Ch. Ox. B.A. 1825, M.A. 1828; Deac. 1826 and Pr. 1827 by Bp of Ox. R. of St. Peter's, Wallingford, Dio. Ox. 1855. (Patron, Bp of Ox; Tithe, 12*l* 10*s* 8*d*; R.'s Inc. 100*l* and Ho; Pop. 472.) Formerly Head Mast. of Portsmouth Gr. Sch. 1830–55. [25]

HAZELL, James Henry, 16, *Park-road, Peckham, S.E.*—Corpus Coll. Cam. B.A. 1859, M.A. 1862; Deac. 1859 and Pr. 1860 by Bp of Ox. P. C. of St. Andrew's, Peckham, Dio. Win. 1866. (Patron, P. C. of Camden Ch. Camberwell; P. C.'s Inc. 300*l*; Pop. 6000.) Formerly C. of Olney, Bucks, 1859–61, Camden Ch. Camberwell, 1861–65. [26]

HAZLEDINE, William, *Kingsdon, Taunton.*—St. Aidan's; Deac. 1852, Pr. 1853. C. in sole charge of Kingsdon, Somerset, 1860. Formerly C. of Broseley, Salop, 1852–53, Lindfield, Sussex, 1854–55; Chap. H.E.I.C. service, Bengal, 1855–59; Chap. of Toungoo, Burmah. [27]

HEACOCK, William, *Newton in-the-Thistles, Tamworth.*—Wor. Coll. Ox. B.A. 1792. R. of Newton-in-the-Thistles, Dio. Wor. (Patrons, Sir R. Burdett and W. P. Inge, Esq; R.'s Inc. 306*l* and Ho; Pop. 442.) [1]

HEAD, G., *Aston Somerville, Evesham.*—Trin. Coll Cam. B.A. 1844, M.A. 1847; Deac. 1845 and Pr. 1846 by Abp of York. R. of Aston Somerville, Dio. G. and B. 1847. (Patron, Lord Somerville; Tithe, 230*l*; Glebe, 40 acres; R.'s Inc. 330*l* and Ho; Pop. 101.) Formerly C. of Doncaster 1845. [2]

HEAD, George Frederick, *Brunswick-street, Carlisle.*—Caius Coll. Cam. B.A. 1860, M.A. 1864; Deac. 1861 and Pr. 1862 by Bp of Man. P. C. of St. John's, Carlisle, Dio. Carl. 1867. (Patrons, Dean of Carl. and others; P. C.'s Inc. 310*l*; Pop. 4000) Formerly C. of St. Thomas's, Lancaster, 1861–65, St. Helen's, Ipswich, 1865–67. Author, *Lost! Lost!* R. T. S. [3]

HEAD, George Quintrell, 8, *Albert-street, Mornington-crescent, London, N. W*—Corpus Coll. Cam. Scho. of, 29th Wrang. B.A. 1850, M.A. 1853; Deac. 1851 and Pr. 1853 by Bp of Chich. C. of St. Matthew's, Oakley-square, Camden-town, 1866. Formerly C. of Ninfield, Sussex, and Trinity, Gray's-inn-road, Lond. [4]

HEADEACH, Albert Workman, *Over Darwen, Lancashire.*—Wad. Coll. Ox. M.A; Deac. 1865 by Bp of Man. C. of Trinity, Over Darwen, 1865. [5]

HEADLAM, Arthur William, *Whorlton, Darlington.*—Trin. Coll. Cam. 29th Wrang. 10th in 1st cl. Cl. Trip. B.A. 1849, M.A. 1852; Deac. 1849 and Pr. 1851 by Bp of Roch. P. C. of Whorlton, Dio. Dur. 1854. (Patron, V. of Gainford; Tithe, 75*l*; Glebe, 60 acres; P. C.'s Inc. 140*l*; Pop. 292.) Formerly C. of Knebworth, Herts, 1851–52, Wycliffe, Yorks, 1853. [6]

HEADLAM, James Garnett, 2, *York terrace, Tunbridge Wells.*—Brasen. Coll. Ox. 3rd cl. Lit Hum. B.A. 1830, M.A. 1833; Deac. 1833 and Pr. 1834 by Bp of G. and B. Formerly C. of Windrush 1833-38, Liverpool 1838–58. [7]

HEADLAND, Edward, *Broadway Rectory, Dorchester.*—Caius Coll. Cam. Fell. of, 14th Wrang. 3rd cl. Cl. Trip; Deac. 1855 and Pr. 1856 by Bp of Ely. R. of Bincombe-with Broadway, Dio. Salis. 1861. (Patron, Caius Coll. Cam; R.'s Inc. 500*l* and Ho; Pop. 808) Formerly C. of St. Mary's, Bury St. Edmunds, 1855–57; Sen. C. of St. Marylebone, Lond. 1857–61. Author, *The Happy Sufferer* (a Tract); joint-author with Rev. H. B. Swete of *The Epistles of St. Paul to the Thessalonians, with Introductions, Notes, Practical Thoughts, &c.*, 1863, and *The Epistle of St. Paul to the Galatians, with an Introduction, Notes, Practical Thoughts, &c.* Hatchards, 1866. [8]

HEADLEY, Alexander, *Hardenhuish Rectory, Chippenham, Wilts.*—Corpus Coll. Cam. and St. Bees; Deac. 1852 and Pr. 1853 by Bp of Chich. R. of Hardenhuish, Dio. G. and B. 1837. (Patrons, Trustees of E. L. Clutterbuck, Esq; Tithe, 90*l*; Glebe, 5 acres; R.'s Inc. 100*l* and Ho; Pop. 103.) Surrogate. Formerly C. of Christian Malford, Wilts. [9]

HEAFIELD, Richard Jewsbury, *St. Luke's Vicarage, Bilston, Staffs.*—St. Cath. Coll. Cam. B.A. 1845, M.A. 1848; Deac. 1845 by Bp of Ches. Pr. 1845 by Bp of Lich. V. of St. Luke's, Bilston, Dio. Lich. 1846. (Patrons, the Crown and Bp of Lich. alt; V.'s Inc. 210*l* and Ho; Pop. 4902.) [10]

HEALD, William Margetson, *Birstal Vicarage, near Leeds.*—Trin. Coll. Cam. 8th in 1st cl. Cl. Trip. 8th Sen. Opt. Members' Prizeman 1827, B.A. 1826, M A. 1829; Deac. 1826 and Pr. 1827 by Abp of York. V. of Birstal, Dio. Rip. 1836. (Patron, Bp of Rip; Tithe—App. 15*l*, Imp. 530*l* 5*s*, V. 378*l* 2*s*; Glebe, 1½ acres; V.'s Inc. 400*l* and Ho; Pop. 5121.) Hon. Can. of Rip; Rural Dean. Formerly Chap. of Trin. Coll. Cam. 1829–44. [11]

HEALE, Edmund Markham, *Yelling Rectory, near Huntingdon.*—Queen's Coll. Ox. Boden Sanskrit Scho. 1844, B.A. 1847, M.A. 1850; Deac. 1848 by Bp of Chich. Pr. 1849 by Bp of Salis. R. of Yelling, Dio. Ely, 1860. (Patron, Ld Chan; Tithe, 290*l*; Glebe, 37 acres; R.'s Inc. 327*l* 10*s* and Ho; Pop. 414.) Formerly C. of West Lulworth 1848, Chilfrome 1849-51; Prof. of Classics in R. M. Coll. Sandhurst, 1851–59; C. of Woolavington 1859–60. Author, *Manual of Geography for the Use of Military Students*, 1853, 4*s* 6*d*, 3rd ed. 1856. [12]

HEALE, Edward, 14, *Parade road, St. Heliers, Jersey.*—Corpus Coll. Cam; Deac. 1847, Pr. 1848. P. C. of All Saints', St. Heliers, Dio. Win. 1847. (Patron, R. of St. Heliers; P. C.'s Inc. 120*l*.) [13]

HEALE, James Newton, *Woodbury Salterton, near Exeter.*—Trin. Coll. Cam. 3rd cl. Cl. Trip. B.A. 1860, M.A. 1863; Deac. 1861 and Pr. 1862 by Bp of Lich. C. of Woodbury Salterton 1866. Formerly C. of Wombourn, Wolverhampton, 1861. [14]

HEALE, John, *Poyntington, Somerset.*—Queens' Coll. Cam. Scho. of, B.A. 1840; Deac. and Pr. 1840 by Bp of Ches. R. of Poyntington, Dio. B. and W. 1842. (Patron, Lord Willoughby de Broke; Tithe, 200*l*; Glebe, 26 acres; R.'s Inc. 240*l* and Ho; Pop. 174.) Member of the Board of Education, Wells, 1867. [15]

HEALE, William James, *Wombourn Vicarage, Wolverhampton.*—Wad. Coll. Ox. B.A. 1831, M.A. 1834; Deac. 1833, Pr. 1834. V. of Wombourn with Trysull V. Dio. Lich. 1849. (Patrons, Trustees; Tithe—Imp. 456*l* 2*s* 10*d*, V. 196*l* 6*s* 8*d*; Glebe, 580 acres; V.'s Inc. 600*l* and Ho; Pop. 1700.) [16]

HEALY, Edward, *Bishop Auckland, Durham.*—Trin. Coll. Cam. B.A. 1847; Deac. 1851 by Bp of Rip. Pr. 1854 by Bp of Dur. Head Mast. of Gr. Sch. Bishop Auckland, 1853. [17]

HEALY, John, *Redmile Rectory (Leicestershire), near Bottesford.*—Caius Coll. Cam. B.A. 1826; Deac. 1827, Pr. 1828. R. of Redmile, Dio. Pet. 1853. (Patron, Duke of Rutland; Glebe, 315 acres; R.'s Inc. 486*l* and Ho; Pop. 521.) Author, *Treatise on an Established Church*, 1835. [18]

HEALY, John Brasby, *Studley, Ripon.*—Emman. Coll. Cam. Sen. Opt. B.A. 1853; Deac. 1856 and Pr. 1857 by Bp of Lon. P. C. of Aldfield with Studley, Dio. Rip. 1863. (Patron, Earl de Grey and Ripon; P. C.'s Inc. 55*l*; Pop. 360.) Formerly C. of Ch. Ch. Marylebone 1856, Great Waldingfield 1858, St. Luke's, Chelsea, 1860, Clapham, Surrey, 1862. [19]

HEANEY, James, *Swinfleet Parsonage, Goole, Yorks.*—King's Coll. Lond; Deac. 1848, Pr. 1849. P. C. of Swinfleet, Dio. York, 1852. (Patron, V. of Whitgift; Tithe—Imp. 415*l* 16*s* 4*d*; Glebe, 19½ acres; P. C.'s Inc. 180*l*; Pop. 1149.) [20]

HEAP, Richard Henry, *Thornton Parsonage, Bradford, Yorks.*—Dur. Licen. Theol. 1851; Deac. 1851 and Pr. 1853 by Bp of Rip. P. C. of Thornton, Dio. Rip. 1855, (Patron, V. of Bradford; P. C.'s Inc. 300*l* and Ho; Pop. 4814.) Formerly C. of Great Horton, near Bradford, 1851–55. [21]

HEAP, Robert, *Walthamstow, Essex.*—Literate; Deac. 1829, Pr. 1830. Formerly P. C. of St. James's, Walthamstow, 1849–65. [22]

HEAPS, George Walter, *Shincliffe, Durham.*—Dur. Scho. 1864, B.A. 1866, Licen. in Theol. 1865; Deac 1866 by Bp of Dur. C. of Shincliffe 1866. [23]

HEARD, James Neville, *Chiddingfold, Godalming, Surrey.*—C. of Chiddingfold; Dom. Chap. to Earl of Winterton. [24]

HEARD, John B., *Bilton, Harrogate, Yorks.*—P. C. of Bilton, Dio. Rip. 1864. (Patron, W. Sheepshanks, Esq; P. C.'s Inc. 160*l*; Pop. 407.) [25]

HEARD, Thomas James, *Beedon Vicarage, Newbury, Berks.*—Wor. Coll. Ox. B.A. 1853, M.A. 1856; Deac. 1854 and Pr. 1855 by Bp of B. and W. C. of Beedon 1856. Formerly C. of St. James's, Taunton, 1854–56. [26]

HEARN, Edward Maurice, *Hurst Green Parsonage, Blackburn.*—Dub. A.B. 1827, A.M. 1831; Deac. 1827 by Bp of Ferns, Pr. 1828 by Bp of Kildare. P. C. of Hurst Green, Dio. Rip. 1838. (Patrons, Five Trustees; Glebe, 1 acre; P. C.'s Inc. 32*l* and Ho; Pop. 1430.) Formerly C. of Coolbanagher, 1827–34, and of Killiegh, Ireland, 1834–38. Author, *Man of Sin*, 3*s* 6*d*; *The Succession of Popes in Milner's Apostolic Tree*, 9*d*;

Litany of Loretto Examined, Reformation Struggles; etc. [1]

HEARN, Henry Thomas, *West-street, Wareham, Dorset.*—Dub. A.B. 1851; Deac. 1852, Pr. 1853. C. of Wareham with Arne 1867. Formerly C. of North Strand Chapel, Dublin, 1852, St. James's, Burnley, Lancashire, 1854, St. James's, Accrington, 1862, Bossal, York, 1865. Author, *An Address to Sheriff Hutton Free Gift Society*, York, 1866, 6d. [2]

HEARN, Michael Elijah, *Martin, Horncastle.*—Trin. Coll. Ox. B.A. 1838; Deac. 1838 and Pr. 1839 by Bp of Ex. R. of Martin, Dio. Lin. 1861. (Patrons, Messrs. Oldham and Slater; R.'s Inc. 150*l*; Pop. 56.) [3]

HEARN, Thomas John, *Roxwell Vicarage, Chelmsford.*—New Coll. Ox. 3rd cl. Lit. Hum. and B.A. 1847, M.A. 1850; Deac. 1850 by Bp of Ox. Pr. 1851 by Bp of Wor. V. of Roxwell, Dio. Roch. 1851. (Patron, New Coll. Ox; Tithe—App. 1029*l* and 28 acres of Glebe, Imp. 66*l* 12*s*; V.'s Inc. 250*l* and Ho; Pop. 986.) Formerly Fell. of New Coll. Ox. 1842–52; Assist. Mast. in Winchester Coll. 1847–51. [4]

HEARTLEY, Charles Tebbott, *Swansea.*—St. Cath. Hall, Cam. B.A. 1849, M.A. 1853; Deac. 1849, Pr. 1853. Head Mast. of the Gr. Sch. Swansea. [5]

HEASTIE, Edward, *Union House, Wolverhampton.*—Dub. Hons. in Logic and Maths. Primate's Hebrew Prizeman, A.B. 1837; Deac. 1851 and Pr. 1852 by Bp of Ches. Chap. of the Wolverhampton Union 1858 (Salary, 160*l*.) Formerly Lect. in Hebrew at St. Aidan's; C. of Ch. Ch. Crewe, St. Martin's, Tipton, and St. James's, Wolverhampton. [6]

HEATH, Charles, *Ward End, Aston, Birmingham.*—P. C. of Ward End, Dio. Wor. 1865. (Patron, V. of Aston; P. C.'s Inc. 70*l*.) [7]

HEATH, Charles Harbord, *Bucknall Rectory, near Bagnall, Staffs.*—Ch. Coll. Cam. Coll. Prizeman, 1848, B.A. 1850; Deac. 1850 and Pr. 1851 by Bp of Win. R. of Bucknall with Bagnall, Dio. Lich. 1852. (Patron, Rev. E. Powys; Tithe, 530*l*; Glebe, 80 acres; R.'s Inc. 695*l*; Pop. Bucknall 1746, Bagnall 424.) [8]

HEATH, Christopher, 4, *Balmoral-terrace, St. Heliers, Jersey.*—Jesus Coll. Cam. Sen. Opt. B.A. 1839; Deac. 1840 by Bp of Jamaica, Pr. 1841 by Bp of Win. C. of St. Mark's, St. Heliers, Dio. Win. 1847. (Patron, R. of St. Heliers; C.'s Inc. 200*l*.) [9]

HEATH, Dunbar Isidore, *Esher, Surrey.*—Trin. Coll. Cam. 5th Wrang. and B.A. 1838, M.A. 1841; Deac. 1843, Pr. 1844. Formerly V. of Brading, Isle of Wight, 1846–62. Author, *Future Human Kingdom of Christ*, Vol. I. 1852, 10*s*, Vol. II. 1853, 6*s*; *The Exodus Papyri*, 1855, 5*s*; *A Record of the Patriarchal Age, or the Proverbs of Aphobis, B.C.* 1900, *now first translated from the Egyptian*, 1858; *Sermons on Important Subjects* 1859, 3*s*. [10]

HEATH, Frank, *Northolt, Harrow, Middlesex.*—Trin. Hall, Cam. M.A. Formerly C. of Northolt. [11]

HEATH, George, *Canewdon Vicarage, Rochford, Essex.*—Corpus Coll. Cam. B.A. 1829; Deac. 1830, Pr. 1831. V. of Canewdon, Dio. Roch. 1847. (Patron, Bp of Pet; Tithe—Imp. 980*l*, V. 575*l*; Glebe, 60 acres; V.'s Inc. 560*l* and Ho; Pop. 661.) [12]

HEATH, John Moore, *Enfield Vicarage, Middlesex.*—Trin. Coll. Cam. B.A. 1830, M.A. 1833. V. of Enfield, Dio. Lon. 1844. (Patron, Trin. Coll. Cam; V.'s Inc. 1170*l* and Ho; Pop. 6543.) Formerly Fell. and Tut. of Trin. Coll. Cam. [13]

HEATH, Joseph, *New Bolingbroke, Boston.*—Corpus Coll. Cam. B.A. 1848, M.A. 1851; Deac. 1849 and Pr. 1852 by Bp of G. and B. P. C. of New Bolingbroke, Dio. Lin, 1862. (Patrons, Trustees of Fen Chapels; P. C.'s Inc. 100*l* and Ho; Pop. 947.) Formerly C. of Almondsbury, Glouc. 1849–55, Croughton, Northants, 1855–56, Highclere, Hants, 1856–57, Rippingale, Linc. 1858–61. [14]

HEATH, William Mortimer, *Lytchett Matravers Rectory, Poole, Dorset.*—Ex. Coll. Ox. B.A. 1844, M.A. 1847; Deac. 1846 and Pr. 1847 by Bp of Salis. R. of Lychett Matravers, Dio. Salis. 1850. (Patron, Wad. Coll. Ox; Tithe, comm. 422*l*; Glebe, 121 acres; R.'s Inc. 510*l* and Ho; Pop. 855.) Formerly C. of Newton Toney 1846–48, Corfe Castle 1848–50; Grand Chap. to Dorset Freemasons 1865–66. Author, *The Masons' Light* (Sermon before Grand Lodge of Dorset), Poole, 1865. [15]

HEATHCOTE, Charles John, *Upper Clapton, London, N.E.*—Trin. Coll. Cam. B.A 1817, M.A. 1822; Deac. 1823 by Bp of Ches. Pr. 1825 by Bp of Ox. Formerly P. C. of St. Thomas's, Stamford-hill, Middlesex, 1827–61. [16]

HEATHCOTE, George, *Conington Rectory, Peterborough.*—St. John's Coll. Cam. 26th Wrang. 1833, M.A. by Abp of Cant. 1834; Deac. 1834 and Pr. 1835 by Bp of Lin. R. of Conington, Dio. Ely, 1835. (Patron, J. Moyer Heathcote, Esq; Tithe, 450*l*; Glebe, 28 acres; R.'s Inc. 500*l* and Ho; Pop. 301.) Rural Dean. [17]

HEATHCOTE, Gilbert, *Colerne, Chippenham.*—Trin. Coll. Cam. B.A. 1838; Deac. 1839, Pr. 1840. V. of Colerne, Dio. G. and B. 1846. (Patron, Warden of New Coll. Ox; V.'s Inc. 120*l* and Ho; Pop. 1040.) [18]

HEATHCOTE, Gilbert Vyvyan, *West Deeping Rectory, Market Deeping.*—Ball. Coll. Ox. afterwards in the Indian Army; Deac. 1858 and Pr. 1860 by Bp of Ex. R. of West Deeping, Dio. Lin. 1867. (Patron, Ld Chan; Glebe, 200 acres; R.'s Inc. 400*l* and Ho; Pop. 340.) Formerly C. of Chittlehampton 1858–60, Boyton 1860–61, Rushall, Wilts, 1861–62; P. C. of Hopton Congeford, Salop, 1862–65; C. of Ch. Ch. and St. John's, St. Leonards-on Sea, 1865–67. Author, *Seven Sermons preached on the Sundays in Lent and Easter Day*, 1862, 2*s* 6*d*; *Sermons*, J. H. and J. Parker, 1865, 5*s*. [19]

HEATHCOTE, Gilbert Wall, *Ash, Farnham, Surrey.*—New Coll. Ox. B.C.L. 1832; Deac. 1829, Pr. 1830. R. of Ash, Dio. Win. 1838. (Patron, Winchester Coll; Tithe, 415*l* 19*s*; Glebe, 9 acres; R.'s Inc. 460*l* and Ho; Pop. 1148.) Fell. of Win. Coll. [20]

HEATHCOTE, Samuel John, *Williton, Taunton.*—Magd. Coll. Cam. B.A. 1846; Deac. 1846 and Pr. 1847 by Bp of Salis. P. C. of Williton, Dio. B. and W. 1854. (Patron, V. of St. Decuman's; Glebe, 3 acres; P. C.'s Inc. 64*l* 12*s* and Ho.) Surrogate. Formerly C. of Bower-Chalk and Alvediston 1846–49, Hordle 1850–54. [21]

HEATHCOTE, Thomas, *Lavington Vicarage, Grantham.*—St. Cath. Coll. Cam. B.A. 1833. V. of Lavington, *alias* Lenton, with Hanby V. Dio. Lin. 1835. (Patron, Lord Aveland; Lavington, Tithe, 231*l* 16*s* 10*d*; Hanby, Tithe, 135*l*; V.'s Inc. 519*l* and Ho; Pop. 330.) [22]

HEATHCOTE, William Neston, *Ditteridge, Chippenham.*—R. of Ditteridge, Dio. G. and B. 1857. (Patron, Col. W. B. Northey, Esq; Tithe, 86*l* 14*s*; Glebe, 26½ acres; R.'s Inc. 125*l*; Pop. 110.) [23]

HEATHER, George Frederick, *Royal Naval School, New Cross, S.E.* and 5, *Nettleton road, New Cross.*—Dub. A.B. 1860; Deac. 1861 and Pr. 1862 by Bp of Lon. Second Classical Mast. and Asst. Chap. of the Royal Naval Sch; C. of St. Michael's, Wood-street, Lond. Formerly C. of St. James's, Hatcham, S.E. [24]

HEATHER, William, *Dilwyn Vicarage, Leominster.*—Corpus Coll. Cam. 2nd cl. Law Trip. 1853, 2nd cl. Moral Sci. Trip. 1854, S.C.L. 1853, LL.B. 1856, LL.D. 1865; Deac. 1856 by Bp of Carl. Pr. 1857 by Abp of York. V. of Dilwyn, Dio. Herf. 1864. (Patron, Bp of Herf; Tithe, 440*l*; Glebe, 45 acres; V.'s Inc. 535*l* and Ho; Pop. 1069.) Sec. of the Hereford Ch. Building Soc. and Organising Sec. for the Dio. of Herf. to the Incorporated Ch. Building Soc. Formerly C. of St. John's, Sheffield, 1856–57, Holmes, near Hereford (sole charge), 1858. Author, *Hereford Cathedral, its History and Restoration*, 1863; *Church Restoration*, 1864; *Sermons on various Occasions*, 1867; Lectures, etc. [25]

HEATHFIELD, John, 27, *Mount Preston, Leeds.*—Trin. Coll. Cam. B.A. 1860; Deac. 1862 and Pr. 1863 by Bp of Rip. C. of St. George's, Leeds, 1862. [26]

HEATHMAN, William Grendon, *Exeter.*—St. Cath. Coll. Cam. B.A. 1829; Deac. 1830 by Bp of B. and W. Pr. 1831 by Bp of Ex. R. of St. Lawrence's, City and Dio. Ex. 1848. (Patron, Ld Chan; Glebe, 30 acres; R.'s Inc. 140*l*; Pop. 561.) Author, *Switzerland in* 1855, 10*s*; *The Jews*; numerous Sermons and Tracts. [1]

HEATON, Arthur Frederick, *Axminster, Devon.*—Clare Coll. Cam. B.A. 1863, Deac. 1865 by Bp of Ex; Pr. 1866 by Bp of Salis. [2]

HEATON, Charles Wilson, *Jesus College, Oxford.*—Jesus Coll. Ox. B.A. 1841, M.A. 1844, B.D. 1852; Deac. 1843 by Bp of Ches. Pr. 1844 by Bp of St. A. R. of Plumpton, Dio. Pet. 1856. (Patron, Jesus Coll. Ox; R.'s Inc. 75*l*; Pop. 42.) Fell. of Jesus Coll. Ox. 1844. [3]

HEATON, George.—St. Cath. Hall, Cam. B.A. 1831, M.A. 1834; Deac. 1831 and Pr. 1833 by Abp of York. Formerly P. C. of St. Mary's, Cheltenham, 1852. Author, *Reply to R. M. Beverley, Esq.* 1831; *Opus Operandum*, 1851; *A Defence of the Queen's Supremacy*, 1851; etc. [4]

HEATON, Henry Howard, *Wylye, Wilts.*—Corpus Coll. Cam. B.A. 1859, M.A. 1862; Deac. 1861, Pr. 1862. C. of Wylye 1867. Formerly C. of Easton-in-Gordano 1861, Tockenham 1865. [5]

HEATON, Hugh Edward, *Bettws-yn Rhos, Abergele, Denbighshire.*—Jesus Coll. Ox. B.A. 1844, M.A. 1847; Deac. 1845 by Bp of Ox. Pr. 1846 by Bp of Herf. V. of Bettws-yn-Rhos, Dio. St. A. 1859. (Patron, Bp of St. A; Tithe, 399*l* 6*s* 2*d*; Glebe, 6 acres; V.'s Inc. 400*l* and Ho; Pop. 838.) Formerly C. of Mold, Flints, 1845–52; P. C. of Llangedwin, Oswestry, 1852 59. [6]

HEAVEN, C., *Bordesley, Warwickshire.*—C. of St. Andrew's, Bordesley. [7]

HEAVEN, Hudson Grosett.—Trin. Coll. Ox. 3rd cl. Lit. Hum. 4th cl. Math. et Phy. and B.A. 1851, M.A. 1852; Deac. 1852 and Pr. 1854 by Bp of B. and W. Formerly Mast. of the Taunton Coll. Sch. 1855. [8]

HEAVEN, William Henry, *Netheravon, Amesbury, Wilts.*—Trin. Coll. Cam. Jun. Opt. B.A. 1848, M.A. 1851; Deac. 1849 by Bp of B. and W. Pr. 1851 by Bp of Ex. C. of Netheravon 1856. Late C. of Whitchurch, Somerset, 1853–56; previously C. of Pilton, Somerset, 1849–53. [9]

HEAVISIDE, James William Lucas, *Norwich.*—Sid. Coll. Cam. B.A. 1830, M.A. 1833, 2nd Wrang. and Smith's Prizeman 1830; Deac. 1832 and Pr. 1833 by Bp of Roch. Can. Res. of Norwich 1860. Formerly Prof. of Math. at the Hon. E.I Co.'s Coll. Haileybury, 1838; Exam. in Math. and Nat. Phil. for the Univ. of Lond. 1843, and for the Council of Military Education, 1858. Formerly Fell. and Tut. of Sid. Coll. Cam. [10]

HEAVYSIDE, John, *Grahamstown, Cape of Good Hope.*—St. Bees; Deac. 1829 by Bp of Lon. Pr. 1830 by Bp of Madras. Chap. at Grahamstown 1833. (Stipend, 400*l* and Ho.) [11]

HEAWOOD, Edward Browne, *Allington Rectory, Maidstone.*—Ch. Ch. Ox. B.A. 1843, M.A. 1845; Deac. 1844 and Pr. 1845 by Abp of Cant. R. of Allington, Dio. Cant. 1852. (Patron, Earl of Romney; Tithe, 145*l*; Glebe, 5½ acres; R.'s Inc. 151*l* and Ho; Pop. 66.) Dom. Chap. to Dow. Countess of Romney. [12]

HEAWOOD, John Richard, *Combs, Stowmarket.*—All Souls Coll. Ox. B.A. 1846; Deac. 1853 and Pr. 1855 by Bp of Chich. R. of Combs, Dio. Nor. 1864. (Patron, Earl of Ashburnham; R.'s Inc. 880*l* and Ho; Pop. 1243.) Formerly C. of Woodcote, Salop, and 2nd Mast. of the Newport Gr. Sch. [13]

HEBDEN, Arthur Henry Ramsgate.—Trin. Coll. Cam. B.A. 1855, M.A. 1859; Deac. 1856 and Pr. 1857 by Abp of Cant. C of East Farleigh 1866. Formerly C. of Pembury, Kent. [14]

HEBDON, Jeffry, *Preston Patrick, Burton, Westmoreland.*—Deac. 1817, Pr. 1819. P. C. of Preston Patrick, Dio. Ches. 1829. (Patron, the Earl of Lonsdale; Tithe—App. 35*l*; P. C.'s Inc. 150*l* and Ho; Pop. 488.) [15]

HEBERDEN, Frederick, *Wilmington Vicarage, Dartford, Kent.*—St. John's Coll. Cam. B.A. 1832, M.A. 1835; Deac. 1833 by Bp of Glouc. Pr. 1834 by Bp of Roch. V. of Wilmington, Dio. Cant. 1840. (Patrons, D. and C. of Roch; Tithe—App. 331*l*, V. 360*l*; Glebe, 11 acres; V.'s Inc. 331*l* and Ho; Pop. 1058.) Formerly C. of West Thurrock, Essex. 1838–63. [16]

HEBERDEN, George, *Ranmore Parsonage, Dorking, Surrey.*—Oriel Coll. Ox. B.A. 1856, M.A. 1859. P. C. of Ranmore, Dio. Win. 1860. (Patron, Geo. Cubitt, Esq; P. C.'s Inc. 150*l* and Ho; Pop. 275.) Formerly C. of Wraxall, Somerset, 1857–58, Great Bookham, Surrey, 1858–60. [17]

HEBERDEN, Henry Buller, *Uffculme, Cullompton, Devon.*—Ex. Coll. Ox; 3rd cl. Law and Mod. Hist. B.A. 1862, M.A. 1865; Deac. 1864 and Pr. 1865 by Bp of Lin. C. of Uffculme 1866. Formerly C. of Gainsborough 1864–66. [18]

HEBERDEN, John, *Great Bookham, Leatherhead, Surrey.*—Jesus Coll. Cam. B.A. 1859, M.A. 1862; Deac. 1859 and Pr. 1860 by Bp of Win. C. of Great Bookham 1860. Formerly C. of St. Mary's, Southampton, 1859. [19]

HEBERDEN, William, *Great Bookham Vicarage, Leatherhead, Surrey.*—V. of Great Bookham, Dio. Win. 1821. (Patron, Viscount Downe; Tithe—Imp. 232*l* 15*s* 4*d*, V. 374*l* 14*s* 4*d*; V.'s Inc. 607*l* 9*s* 8*d* and Ho; Pop. 1012.) [20]

HEBERDEN, William, *Broadhembury Vicarage, Honiton, Devon*—Oriel Coll. Ox. B.A. 1825, Ex. Coll. Ox. M.A. 1828; Deac. 1827 by Bp of B. and W. Pr. 1828 by Bp of Ex. V. of Broadhembury. Dio. Ex. 1829. (Patrons, D. and C. of Ex; Tithe—App. 330*l*, V. 250*l*; Glebe, 6 acres; V.'s Inc. 310*l* and Ho; Pop. 817.) [21]

HEBERT, Charles, *Lowestoft.*—Trin. Coll. Cam. Wrang. 1st cl. Cl. Trip. and B.A. 1831, M.A. 1834; Deac. and Pr. 1834. V. of Lowestoft, Dio. Nor. 1862. (Patron, Bp of Nor; Tithe, 320*l*; Glebe rent, 10*l*; V.'s Inc. 380*l* and Ho; Pop. 6705.) Formerly C. of Longborough 1833; V. of Grendon 1834; C. of Cheltenham 1835, St. James's, Clapham, 1839; V. of Lechlade 1844; R. of Burslem 1851–62. Author, *Atonement by Propitiation*, 1860, 6*d*; *Neology not True, and Truth not New*, 1861, 2*s* 6*d*; *On Clerical Subscription*, 1862, 7*s* 6*d*; *The Soul led to Jesus in Confirmation*, 1863; *Confirmation, Six Papers of Questions, &c.* 1863. [22]

HEBERT, Henry Venn, *Bury St. Edmunds.*—Trin. Coll. Cam. B.A. 1864, M.A. 1867; Deac. 1863 by Bp of Nor. Pr. 1866 by Bp of Ely. C. of St. Mary's, Bury St. Edmunds, 1866. Formerly C. of Swanton Morley with Worthing 1863–66. [23]

HECKER, H. T., *Aigburth, Liverpool.*—Trin. Coll. Ox; Deac. 1830 by Bp of Herf. Pr. 1831 by Bp of G. and B. P. C. of Aigburth, Dio. Ches. 1852. (Patrons, Trustees; P. C.'s Inc. 400*l*; Pop. 1994.) Formerly C. of New Radnor 1830–39, Sevenoaks 1839–44, Wheathampstead 1844–52. [24]

HECKFORD, J. D., *Ruskington, Lincolnshire.*—V. of Ruskington (2nd Mediety), Dio. Lin. 1845. (Patron, Ld Chan; V.'s Inc. 102*l*; Pop. 1089.) [25]

HEDGELAND, John White, *Exeter.*—Emman. Coll. Cam. B.A. 1852, M.A. 1855; Deac. 1852 and Pr. 1853 by Bp of Ex. R. of St. Martin's and St. Stephen's, Exeter, Dio. Ex. St. Martin's 1864, St. Stephen's 1865. (Patrons, Bp and D. and C. of Ex; R.'s Inc. St. Martin's, 77*l*; Pop. 207; St. Stephen's, 54*l*; Pop. 407.) Formerly C. of Kenwyn, Cornwall. [26]

HEDGELAND, Philip, *Penzance.*—Pemb. Coll. Ox. B.A. 1849, M.A. 1858; Deac. 1849 and Pr. 1850 by Bp of Ex. P. C. of Penzance, Dio. Ex. 1860. (Patron, Bp of Ex. with consent of V. of Madron; Glebe, 3 acres; P. C.'s Inc. 300*l*; Pop. 8000.) Formerly C. of Bridestow with Sourton 1849–54, Madron 1854–60. Author, *The Pastor's Charge* (a Visitation Sermon), 1863; and other occasional sermons. [27]

HEDGES, Edward, *Pau, France.*—Queens' Coll. Cam. B.A. 1833, M.A. 1836; Deac. 1834, Pr. 1835. British Chap. at Pau. [28]

HEDLEY, Matthew, *Whalley, Lancashire.*—Pem. Coll. Cam. M.A. 1863; Deac. 1864 and Pr. 1866 by Bp of Man. C. of Langho, Lancashire, 1864. [29]

HEDLEY, Thomas, *Masham Vicarage, Bedale, Ripon.*—Trin. Coll. Cam. B.A. 1844, M.A. 1847. V. of Masham with Kirby Malzeard V. Dio. Rip. 1856. (Patron, Trin. Coll. Cam; Masham, Tithe—Imp. 931*l*, V. 246*l*; Glebe, 9½ acres; Kirby Malzeard, Tithe—App. 5*l*, Imp. 220*l* 16*s*, V. 45*l*; V.'s Inc. 400*l* and Ho; Pop. Masham, 1538, Kirby Malzeard 1917.) Hon. Can. of Rip. 1865. Late Fell. of Trin. Coll. Cam. [1]

HEDLEY, William, *Beckley Rectory, Staplehurst.*—Queen's Coll. Ox. Double 1st cl. and B.A 1841, M.A. 1844; Deac. 1846 and Pr. 1848 by Bp of Ox. R. of Beckley, Sussex, Dio. Chich. 1861. (Patron, Univ. Coll. Ox; Tithe, 875*l*; Glebe, 25 acres; R.'s Inc. 915*l* and Ho; Pop. 1252.) Formerly Fell. and Tut. of Univ. Coll. Ox; Public Exam. in Math. et Phy. 1848; in Lit. Hum. 1851 and 1856; Select Preacher 1859. [2]

HEELIS, Edward, *Long Marton Rectory, Appleby, Westmoreland.*—Emman. Coll. Cam. B.A. 1819, M.A. 1822; Deac. 1819, Pr. 1821. R. of Long Marton, Dio. Carl. 1833. (Patron, Sir Richard Tufton, Bart; Tithe, 165*l*; Glebe, 572 acres; R.'s Inc. 480*l* and Ho; Pop. 762.) Rural Dean of Appleby, and Hon. Can. of Carlisle. [3]

HEELIS, John, *Long Marton, Appleby.*—Queen's Coll. Ox. Hon. 4th cl. Lit. Hum. and B.A. 1848, M.A. 1852; Deac. 1849 and Pr. 1851 by Bp of Carl. C. of Long Marton. Author, *An Assize Sermon*, Longmans, 1860. [4]

HEFFILL, William, *St. Mark's Parsonage, Dukinfield, Stockport.*—P. C. of St. Mark's, Dukinfield, Dio. Ches. 1846. (Patrons, Crown and Bp of Ches. alt; P. C.'s Inc. 160*l* and Ho; Pop. 8127.) [5]

HEIGHAM, Arthur L. C., *Newport-Pagnell, Bucks.*—Magd. Coll. Cam. B.A. 1860; Deac. 1861 and Pr. 1862 by Bp of Ox. V. of Newport-Pagnell, Dio. Ox. 1866. (Patron, Bp of Ox; V.'s Inc. 245*l*; Pop. 3823.) Formerly C. of St. Giles', Reading, 1861–63, Totternhoe, Beds, 1864–66. [6]

HEISCH, John Gottfried, *Church Missionary College, Islington, N.*—Trin. Coll. Cam. B.A. 1835, M.A. 1858; Deac. 1839, Pr. 1840. Vice-Prin. of Miss. Coll. Formerly C. of St. Mary's, Islington, 1839–41. [7]

HELDER, Francis William, *Enfield Highway, Middlesex, N.*—King's Coll. Lond. Assoc. 1853; Deac. 1853 and Pr. 1854 by Bp of Lon. C. of St. James's, Enfield Highway, 1863. Formerly C. of Kensington 1854–58, Walworth 1859–63. [8]

HELE, Fitz-Henry, *Little Hempston Rectory, Totnes, Devon.*—Queen's Coll. Ox. B.A. 1828, M.A. 1830; Deac. 1829 and Pr. 1831 by Bp of Ex. R. of Little Hempston, *alias* Hempston Arundel, Dio. Ex. 1837. (Patron, the Crown; Tithe, 207*l*; Glebe, 58 acres; R.'s Inc. 300*l* and Ho; Pop. 244.) Chap. of the Union, Totnes. [9]

HELE, George Selby, *Keillos, Bishopsteignton, Teignmouth, Devon.*—St. Peter's Coll. Cam. B.A. 1823, M.A. 1826; Deac. 1823 by Bp of Salis. Pr. 1825 by Bp of Chich. Formerly V. of Grays Thurrock, Essex, 1826–29; C. of Patcham, Sussex, 1829–35. [10]

HELLICAR, Arthur Gresley, *Bromley, Kent.*—Wad. Coll. Ox. 3rd cl. Lit. Hum. B.A. 1858, M.A. 1860; Deac. 1859 and Pr. 1860 by Bp of B. and W. P. C. of Bromley, Kent, 1865. (Patron, Bp of Wor; Tithe—App. 1220*l* 16*s*; Glebe, 71 acres; P. C.'s Inc. 300*l*; Pop. 3500.) Formerly C. of Wraxall, near Bristol, 1859, Bromley 1861–65. [11]

HELLIER, John Shaw, *Lester Place, Tower-street, Dudley.*—Lin. Coll. Ox. B.A. 1861, M.A. 1862; Deac. 1862 and Pr. 1863 by Bp of G. and B. C. of Dudley 1866; Chap. of the Holly Hall Schools 1866. Formerly C. of Tormarton with West Littleton 1862, Dursley 1864–66. [12]

HELLIER, Thomas Shaw, *Weston Bampfylde Rectory, Ilchester, Somerset.*—Lin. Coll. Ox. B.A. 1825, M.A. 1826; Deac. 1825, Pr. 1826. R. of Weston Bampfylde, Dio. B. and W. 1857. (Patron, the present R; Tithe, 173*l* 14*s*; Glebe, 22 acres; R.'s Inc. 208*l* and Ho; Pop. 146.) Formerly P. C. of Little Compton, Glouc. 1842–56. [13]

HELLINS, Charles Tertius, 9, *Mount Beacon, Bath.*—King's Coll. Lond. 1st cl. Theol. Assoc. 1856; Deac. 1856 and Pr. 1857 by Bp of B. and W. C. of Walcot, Bath. Formerly C. of Holy Trinity, Bath. [14]

HELLINS, John, *Chaplain's House, County Prison, Exeter.*—All Souls Coll. Ox. 4th cl. Lit. Hum. and B.A. 1851, M.A. 1857; Deac. 1852 and Pr. 1854 by Bp of Ex. Chap. of the Devon County Prison, Exeter, 1859. [15]

HELME, Robert, *Leverstock Green, Hemel Hempstead.*—Trin. Coll. Cam. 6th Sen. Opt. and B.A. 1853, M.A. 1856; Deac. 1854 and Pr. 1855 by Bp of Roch. P. C. of Leverstock Green, Dio. Roch. 1861. (Patron, Earl of Verulam; Glebe, 3½ acres; P. C.'s Inc. 95*l*; Pop. 1247.) Formerly C. of St. Andrew's, Halstead, 1854–56, Hillingdon 1856–57, Chelmsford 1859–61. [16]

HELMORE, Thomas, 6, *Cheyne-walk, Chelsea, London, S.W.*—Magd. Hall, Ox. B.A. 1840, M.A. 1845; Deac. 1840 and Pr. 1841 by Bp of Lich. Precentor of St. Mark's Coll. Chelsea. (Value, 100*l*.) Mast. of the Children of Her Majesty's Chapels-Royal, 1846. (Value, 77*l*.) Priest in Ordinary of her Majesty's Chapels-Royal, 1847. (Value 80*l*.) Hon. Precentor of the Motett Choir. Formerly Pr.-Vic. of Lich. Cathl.; Vice-Prin. of St. Mark's Coll. Chelsea. Author and Editor, *The Psalter Noted*; *The Canticles Noted*; *A Brief Directory of the Plain Song*; *A Manual of Plain Song*; *A Hymnal Noted*; *Carols for Christmas*; *Carols for Easter* (these works are in numerous editions and sizes); Translation of *Fétis On Choir and Chorus Singing*; *Music of Three Hymns of the Eastern Church*; *The St. Mark's Chant-book*; *The Canticles Accented*; *Two Settings of the "Te Deum" from Baini and Alfieri*; *Hymn in Time of Cattle Plague*; all published by Novello and Masters. [17]

HELYAR, Henry, *Pendomer Rectory, Yeovil, Somerset.*—Pemb. Coll. Ox. B.A. 1838; Deac. 1839 and Pr. 1840 by Bp of B. and W. R. of Pendomer, Dio. B. and W. 1856. (Patron, William Helyar, Esq; Tithe, 193*l*; Glebe, 73½ acres; R.'s Inc. 252*l* and Ho; Pop. 96.) [18]

HELYAR, Hugh Welman, *Sutton Bingham, Yeovil, Somerset.*—St. John's Coll. Cam. 1819, M.A. 1822; Deac. 1820, Pr. 1821. R. of Sutton Bingham, Dio. B. and W. 1820. (Patron, W. Helyar, Esq; Tithe, 113*l*; Glebe, 76¼ acres; R.'s Inc. 190*l* and Ho; Pop. 67.) R. of Beerhacket, Dorset, Dio. Salis. 1825. (Patrons, Sir J. Mudden and W. Helyar, Esq; Tithe, 164*l*; Glebe, 38½ acres; R.'s Inc. 228*l*; Pop. 96.) [19]

HELYAR, Wyndham Hugh, *Thorne Coffin, Yeovil, Somerset.*—Trin. Coll. Ox. B.A. 1851; Deac. 1853 and Pr. 1856 by Bp of B. and W. R. of Thorne Coffin, Dio. B. and W. 1856. (Patron, Rev. W. Sabine; Tithe, 138*l*; Glebe, 8 acres; R.'s Inc. 200*l* and Ho; Pop. 100.) [20]

HEMING, Henry, *East Farndon Rectory, near Northampton.*—St. John's Coll. Ox. B.A. 1834, M.A. 1838, B.D. 1843; Deac. 1835 and Pr. 1836 by Bp of Ox. R. of East Farndon, Dio. Pet. 1855. (Patron, St. John's Coll. Ox; R.'s Inc. 500*l* and Ho; Pop. 242.) Formerly P. C. of Northmoor, near Witney, 1843–55; Fell. of St. John's Coll. Ox. [21]

HEMMANS, Fielder, *Tetney Vicarage, Grimsby, Lincolnshire.*—St. Peter's Coll. Cam. 29th Wrang. and B.A. 1851, M.A. 1854; Deac. 1851 and Pr. 1852 by Bp of Lin. V. of Tetney, Dio. Lin. 1860. (Patron, Bp of Lin; Glebe, 144 acres; V.'s Inc. 300*l* and Ho; Pop. 917.) Bye Fell. of St. Peter's Coll. Cam. Formerly C. of All Saints', Wragby, Lincolnshire. [22]

HEMMING, Benjamin, *Pershore, Worcestershire.*—Magd. Hall, Ox. B.A. 1830, M.A. 1832; Deac. and Pr. 1831. P. C. of Wick, near Pershore, Dio. Wor. 1848. (Patron, V. of Pershore; P. C.'s Inc. 105*l*; Pop. 318.) Chap. to the Pershore Union 1850; C. of Bricklehampton, near Pershore. [23]

HEMMING, B. F., *Peopleton, Worcestershire.*—C. of Peopleton. [24]

HEMMING, George, *Little Parndon Rectory, Harlow, Essex.*—Mert. Coll. Ox. B.A. 1819, M.A. 1822. R. of Thundersley, Dio. Roch. 1822. (Patron, the present

R; Tithe, 584*l*; Glebe, 40 acres; R.'s Inc. 650*l* and Ho; Pop. 531.) R. of Little Parndon, Harlow, Essex, Dio. Roch. 1829. (Patron, the present R; Tithe, 186*l* 11*s* 2*d*; R.'s Inc. 215*l* and Ho; Pop. 71.) [1]

HEMMING, William Spence, *Rayne Rectory, Braintree, Essex.*—Ch. Coll. Cam. Sen. Opt. Deac. 1850, Pr. 1851 by Bp of Roch. B.A. 1849. R. of Rayne, Dio. Roch. 1855. (Patron, Earl of Essex; Tithe, 500*l*; Glebe, 27 acres; R.'s Inc. 524*l* and Ho; Pop. 401.) [2]

HEMSTED, John, *Ickford Rectory, Wheatley.*—Magd. Hall, Ox. B.A. 1841, M.A. 1844; Deac. 1841, Pr. 1842. R. of Ickford, Dio. Ox. 1861. (Patron, Rev. J. C. Townsend; Tithe, 434*l* 14*s*; R.'s Inc. 441*l* and Ho; Pop. 437.) Formerly R. of Gratwick, Staffs, 1854–61; P. C. of Kingstone, Staffs, 1854–61. [3]

HEMSWORTH, Addison Browne, *Rockland All Saints' Rectory, Attleborough, Norfolk.*—Pemb. Coll. Cam. B.A. 1845, M.A. 1848; Deac. 1846 and Pr. 1847 by Bp of Nor. R. of Rockland All Saints with Rockland St. Andrew, Dio. Nor. 1850. (Patron, the present R; Tithe, 498*l*; Glebe, 32 acres; R.'s Inc. 550*l* and Ho; Pop. Rockland All Saints 300, Rockland St. Andrew 111.) Surrogate. Ex-Diocesan Inspector of Schools. Author, Public Lectures on *The East, Crimea, Russia, Australia, and New Zealand.* [4]

HEMSWORTH, Augustus Barker, *Ashfield House, Bury St Edmunds, Suffolk.*—Trin. Coll. Cam. B.A. 1844, M.A. 1849; Deac. 1845 and Pr. 1846 by Bp of Nor. R. of Bacton, Suffolk, Dio. Nor. 1858. (Patron, the present R; Tithe, 750*l*; Glebe, 53 acres; R.'s Inc. 900*l* and Ho; Pop. 733.) Formerly P. C. of Thompson, Norfolk, 1850–58; C. of Great Ryburgh and Little Ryburgh, Norfolk. [5]

HENDERSON, Henry Glass, *Court House, Tetbury, Glouc.*—King's Coll. Lond. 1852; Deac. 1852 and Pr. 1853 by Bp of Lon. Formerly C. of Romford, Essex. [6]

HENDERSON, James, *Ancroft, Berwick-on-Tweed.*—Univ. Coll. Dur. 1st cl. Cl. Van Mildert Scho. Fell. Univ. Theol. Prizeman; Deac. 1863 and Pr. 1865 by Bp of Dur. P. C. of Ancroft, Dio. Dur. 1866. (Patrons, D. and C. of Dur; Tithe, 275*l*; Glebe, 40 acres; P. C.'s Inc. 315*l* and Ho; Pop. 1100. (Formerly C. of Newcastle-on-Tyne 1843–45, Hurworth-on-Tees, 1845–46. [7]

HENDERSON, James Armstrong, *Ingoldsby, Grantham.*—Queen's Coll. Ox. 4th cl. Lit. Hum. B.A. 1852, M.A. 1859; Deac. 1853, Pr. 1854 by Abp of York. C. of Ingoldsby. Formerly C. of St. John's, Sheffield, Huntspill, Somerset, and Bickenhall, Somerset. [8]

HENDERSON, James Henry, *The College, Ely.*—Trin. Coll. Cam. B.A. 1842, M.A. 1846; Deac. 1842, Pr. 1843. P. C. of Holy Trinity, City and Dio. Ely, 1855. (Patrons, D. and C. of Ely; P. C.'s Inc. 170*l*; Pop. 5185.) Min. Can. of Ely; Chap. to the Ely House of Correction. Formerly Sen. C. of Hull. [9]

HENDERSON, John, *Colne Parsonage, Lancashire.*—Deac. 1817, Pr. 1818. P. C. of Colne, Dio. Man. 1821. (Patrons, Hulme's Trustees; Tithe—Imp. 36*l*; P. C. 19*l*; P. C.'s Inc. 180*l* and Ho; Pop. 5089.) Surrogate. [10]

HENDERSON, Joseph Rawlins, *Dufton Rectory, Appleby, Westmoreland.*—Trin. Coll. Ox. B.A. 1805, M.A. 1808. R. of Dufton, Dio. Carl. 1849. (Patron, Sir Richard Tufton, Bart; Tithe, 148*l*; R.'s Inc. 175*l* and Ho; Pop. 495.) [11]

HENDERSON, Robert, *Brompton Ralph Rectory, Wiveliscombe, Somerset.*—Dub. A.B. 1822, M.A. 1852; Deac. 1824 and Pr. 1825 by Bp of Derry. R. of Brompton Ralph, Dio. B. and W. 1854. (Patrons, John Blommart, Esq. and Miss Escott; Tithe, 410*l*; Glebe, 113 acres; R.'s Inc. 554*l* and Ho; Pop. 436.) [12]

HENDERSON, Samuel Roden, *Wanstrow, Somerset.*—St. Bees; Deac. 1858, Pr. 1859. C of Wanstrow. Formerly C. of Malpas, Cheshire, 1858, North Harborne, Birmingham, 1861, Wheaton Aston 1864. [13]

HENDERSON, Thomas Julius, *South Benfleet Vicarage, Rayleigh, Essex.*—Wad. Coll. Ox. B.A. 1849, M.A. 1852; Deac. 1850 and Pr. 1851 by Bp of Roch. V. of South Benfleet, Dio. Roch. 1859. (Patrons, D. and C. of Westminster; V.'s Inc. 260*l* and Ho; Pop. 573.) P. C. of Canvey-Island, Dio. Roch. (Patron, Bp of Roch; P. C.'s Inc. 180*l*; Pop. 200.) Formerly Min. of St. Swithin's Chapel, Kennington, Berks, 1856–59. [14]

HENDERSON, William George, *Grammar School, Leeds.*—Magd. Coll. Ox. 1st cl. Lit. Hum. 2nd cl. Math. and B.A. 1840, M.A. 1843, D.C.L. 1853. Head Mast. of the Leeds Gr. Sch. Formerly Prin. of Victoria Coll. Jersey. [15]

HENDRICKSON, William, *Chorlton, near Newcastle, Staffs.*—P. C. of Chapel Chorlton, Dio. Lich. 1854. (Patron, Bp of Lich; Tithe—App. 244*l* 1*s* 4*d*; P. C.'s Inc. 150*l* and Ho; Pop. 484.) [16]

HENDY, Francis Paul James, *St. Neot's Vicarage, Liskeard.*—V. of St. Neot's, Dio. Ex. 1862. (Patron, Rev. R. G. Grylls; V.'s Inc. 380*l* and Ho; Pop. 1423.) [17]

HENHAM, James Larkin, *Kenn, Devon.*—Ch. Coll. Cam. B.A. 1859; Deac. 1860 by Abp of York. C. of Kenn. Formerly C. of Scalby, Yorks. [18]

HENLEY, F. G., *Cumnor, Abingdon.*—V. of Cumnor, Dio. Ox. 1861. (Patron, Earl of Abingdon; V.'s Inc. 300*l* and Ho; Pop. 1021.) [19]

HENLEY, The Hon. Robert, *Putney, Surrey, S.W.*—Ball. Coll. Ox. 2nd cl. Lit. Hum. 1852, B.A. 1853, M A. 1856; Theol. Coll. Wells; Deac. and Pr. 1854 by Bp of Chich. P. C. of Putney with St. John's C. Dio. Lon. 1861. (Patrons, D. and C. of Wor; Tithe—App. 620*l*; P. C.'s Inc. 400*l*; Pop. 5507.) Formerly C. of St. Mark's, Horsham. Author, *The Great High Priest,* 1858, 1*s* 6*d*; *Saintliness,* 1864, 6*s*. [20]

HENLEY, T. C., *Sidmouth, Devon.*—C. of Sidmouth. [21]

HENLY, John, *Ruscombe, Berks.*—P. C. of Ruscombe, 1864. (Patron, Bp of Ox; P. C.'s Inc. 200*l*; Pop. 265.) [22]

HENN, John, *Old Trafford, Manchester.*—King's Coll. Lond. B.A. 1857; Deac. 1858 and Pr. 1859 by Bp of Man. Head Mast. of the Manchester Commercial Schs. 1855. Formerly C. of St. John's, Manchester. Author, *A New System of Teaching the Fundamental Rules of Arithmetic*; *Formulæ for Parsing in the English, Latin, French and German Languages*; *Arithmetical Tables*; *Ministerial Responsibility* (a Sermon). [23]

HENNAH, William Veale, *East Stoke, Wareham.*—Ex. Coll. Ox. B.A. 1822, M.A. 1865; Deac. 1822 and Pr. 1823 by Bp of Ex. R. of East Stoke, 1864. (Patron, Sir H. Oglander, Bart; Glebe, 7 acres; R.'s Inc. 404*l* and Ho; Pop. 594.) Formerly Dom. Chap. to Earl Radnor; Chap. to Royal Navy; P. C. of East Cowes, Isle of Wight. [24]

HENN-GENNYS, Edmund John, *Whitley Hall, near Plymouth.*—St. Aidan's; Deac. 1860 and Pr. 1861 by Abp of Cant. C. of Tamerton-Folliott, near Plymouth, 1867. Formerly C. of Veryan, Cornwall, 1863, Ide Hill, Sevenoaks, Kent, 1861. [25]

HENNIKER, Douglas H. C., *Shrewsbury, Salop.*—Trin. Coll. Cam. B.A. 1861, M.A. 1864; Deac. 1863 and Pr. 1864 by Bp of Lich. C. of Shrewsbury. [26]

HENNIKER, Robert, *South Charlton, Chathill, Northumberland.*—Trin. Coll. Ox. 1st cl. Lit. Hum. 2nd cl. Nat. Sci. Johnson Theol. Scho. B.A. 1856, M.A. 1860; Deac. 1857 and Pr. 1858 by Bp of Roch. P. C. of South Charlton, Dio. Dur. 1860. (Patron, Duke of Northumberland; P. C.'s Inc. 174*l* and Ho; Pop. 261.) Formerly C. of Thaxtead 1857, St. Michael's, Alnwick, 1858–60. Author, *Trifles for Travellers,* Murray, 1864. [27]

HENNIKER, Rowland, *Cauldon Parsonage, Leek, Staffs.*—P. C. of Cauldon, Dio. Lich. 1860. (Patron, A. Henniker, Esq; Tithe, 80*l*; P. C.'s Inc. 88*l*; Pop. 400.) P. C. of Waterfall, Leek, Dio. Lich. 1860. (Patron, A. Henniker, Esq; Glebe, 53 acres; P. C.'s Inc. 60*l*; Pop. 533.) [28]

HENNING, Edward Nares, *Sherborne, Dorset.*—Wor. Coll. Ox. B.A. 1825; Deac. 1826 and Pr. 1827 by Bp of B and W. P. C. of Hilfield, Dorset, Dio. Salis. 1852. (Patron, V. of Sydling; Tithe—App. 10*l*, Imp. 56*l* 19*s* 6*d*; P. C.'s Inc. 90*l*; Pop. 111.) [29]

HENREY, Thomas, *Lezayre Vicarage, Isle of Man.*—Deac. and Pr. 1850. V. of Lezayre, Dio. S. and M. 1863. (Patron, the Crown; V.'s Inc. 240*l* and Ho; Pop. 2520.) Formerly P. C. of St. Day, Cornwall, 1854–57; P. C. of Ch. Ch. Belper, 1857–63. [1]

HENRY, Joseph.—British Chap. at Lima. [2]

HENSHAW, Robert Ibbetson Bazett, *Lydlinch Rectory, Blandford, Dorset.*—Queen's Coll. Ox. B.A. 1819, M.A. 1823; Deac. and Pr. 1823. R. of Lydlinch, Dio. Salis. 1848. (Patron, F. W. Fane, Esq; Tithe, 440*l*; Glebe, 60½ acres; R.'s Inc. 550*l* and Ho; Pop. 404.) Surrogate. [3]

HENSLEY, Alfred, *Grove, East Retford, Notts.*—Wor. Coll. Ox. B.A. 1846, M.A. 1848; Deac. 1847, Pr. 1848. R. of Grove, Dio. Lin. 1859. (Patron, G. H. Vernon, Esq; R.'s Inc. 220*l* and Ho; Pop. 113.) Formerly C. of Kerry, Montgomery. [4]

HENSLEY, Charles, *Cabourne Vicarage, near Caistor, Lincolnshire.*—St. Cath. Coll. Cam. B.A. 1827, M.A. 1833; Deac. 1827 and Pr. 1828 by Bp of Lin. V. of Cabourne, Dio. Lin. 1854. (Patron, Earl of Yarborough; Glebe, 280 acres; V.'s Inc. 340*l* and Ho; Pop. 171.) Formerly P. C. of Trinity, Gainsborough, 1843–54. [5]

HENSLEY, Lewis, *Hitchin Vicarage, Herts.*—Trin. Coll. Cam. 1st Smith's Prizeman, Sen. Wrang. and B.A. 1846, M.A. 1849; Deac. 1851 by Bp of Ely, Pr. 1852 by Bp of Ox. V. of Hitchin, Dio. Roch. 1856. (Patron, Trin. Coll. Cam; V.'s Inc. 700*l* and Ho; Pop. 7000.) Rural Dean 1867. Formerly C. of Upton with Chalvey, Bucks, 1852–56; V. of Ippollitts with Great Wymondham, 1856; Fell. and Asst. Tut. of Trin. Coll. Cam. 1846–52. Author, *Household Devotions, or Family Prayers for the Church Seasons*, 1864, 6*s* 6*d*; *Shorter Household Devotions*, 1*s*; *Hymns for the Sundays after Trinity*, 1864, 1*s*; *Hymns for the Minor Sundays from Advent to Whitsuntide*, 1867, 1*s*; published by Bell and Daldy. [6]

HENSLOW, George, 10, *South Crescent, Bedford-square, London, W.C.*—Deac. 1859 and Pr. 1861 by Bp of Chich. Head Mast. of the Gr. Sch. South Crescent, Bedford-square, 1865. Formerly C. of Steyning, Sussex, 1859–61; Head Mast. of Hampton-Lucy Gr. Sch. Hampton-Lucy, Warwickshire, 1861–64. [7]

HENSLOW, Leonard Ramsey, *Pulham St. Mary Magdalene, Harleston, Norfolk.*—St. John's Coll. Cam. B.A. 1854, M.A. 1857; Deac. 1854 and Pr. 1855 by Bp of Ely. R. of Pulham St. Mary Magdalene, Dio. Nor. 1863. (Patron, the Crown; Tithe, 646*l*; P. C.'s Inc. 646*l* and Ho; Pop. 1279.) Formerly C. of Hitcham 1854, Bargor Monachorum 1856, Great Chart, Kent, 1860. [8]

HENSLOWE, Edward Pering, *Huish-Episcopi Vicarage, Langport, Somerset.*—Deac. 1823, Pr. 1825. V. of Huish-Episcopi with Langport C. Dio. B. and W. 1839. (Patron, Archd. of Wells; Huish-Episcopi, Tithe—App. 4*l* 17*s* 6*d*, V. 2*l* 5*s* 6*d*; Langport, Tithe—App. 15*l*, V. 70*l*; V.'s Inc. 130*l* and Ho; Pop. Huish-Episcopi 679, Langport 1133.) [9]

HENSLOWE, J. L. B., *Thorne Falcon, Somersetshire.*—C. of Thorne Falcon. [10]

HENSLOWE, William Henry, *Tottenhill, Lynn, Norfolk.*—Jesus Coll. Cam. B.A. 1827, M.A. 1830; Deac. 1827 and Pr. 1828 by Bp of Lon. P. C. of Tottenhill, Dio. Nor. 1840. (Patron, Bp of Nor; P. C.'s Inc. 62*l*; Pop. 342.) P. C. of Wormegay, Norfolk, Dio. Nor. 1840. (Patron, Bp. of Nor; Tithe—Imp. 350*l*; and 3 acres of Glebe; P. C.'s Inc. 45*l*; Pop. 423.) Hon. Member of the African Institute at Paris. Author, *Eight Sermons addressed to the Royal Regiment of Artillery*, 1836, 7*s*; *The Phonarthron, or Natural System of the Sounds of Speech for all Languages, with Application to English, French, Hebrew, Music, Arithmetic*, 1840, 12*s*; *The Moral of the Beard, or Shaving Denounced*, 4*d*; *The Bishop Blighted.* [11]

HENVILLE, Edward, *Attercliffe, Sheffield.*—Dur. A.B. 1860; 1st cl. Lit. Hum. 1850, 1st cl. Logic and Maths; Fell. of the Royal Astronom. Soc. and Fell. of the Royal Asiatic Soc; Deac. 1863 and Pr. 1864 by Bp of Rip. C. of Attercliffe 1867. Formerly Head Mast. of Fishlake Gr. Sch. Doncaster, 1858–62; C. of Emley 1863, St. Mark's, Hull, and Lastingham, Yorks. [12]

HEPBURN, Francis Robert, *Chailey Parsonage, Lewes.*—Ch. Ch. Ox. B.A. 1847, M.A. 1854; Deac. and Pr. 1849. R. of Chailey, Dio. Chich. 1852. (Patronesses, Mrs. Hepburn and Mrs. Blencowe; Tithe, 684*l*; Glebe, 5 acres; R.'s Inc. 727*l* and Ho; Pop. 1344.) [13]

HEPHER, John, *Newtown, Leeds.*—St. Mark's Coll. Chelsea; Deac. 1853, Pr. 1857 by Bp of Ox. P. C. of St. John the Baptist, Newtown, Leeds, Dio. Rip. 1867. (Patrons, Bp of Rip. V. of Leeds, and Incumb. of St. Mary's; P. C.'s Inc. 200*l*; Pop. 7000.) Formerly C. of Crosby, Ravensworth, near Penrith, Goosey, near Farringdon, Pinchbeck, near Spalding. Author, *A Few Hints for the Bereaved*, No. 1169 List of S.P.C.K., 4*s* per 100; *Slander and Tittle Tattle*, 1*s* 6*d* per 100, Edmonson, Lancaster. [14]

HEPPENSTALL, Frederic.—St. John's Coll. Cam. B.A. 1858; Deac. 1860 by Bp of Lon. Head Mast. of Perse Sch. Cambridge. Formerly Asst. Mast. in King Edward's Sch. Birmingham, 1859; Asst. Mast. in Univ. Coll. Sch. Lond. 1858–59. [15]

HEPWORTH, John Watson, *Marthall Parsonage, near Knutsford, Cheshire.*—St. John's Coll. Cam. B.A. 1840; Deac. and Pr. 1842. P. C. of Marthall, Dio. Ches. 1849. (Patron, Lord Egerton; P. C.'s Inc. 125*l*; Pop. 525.) Chap. to the Altrincham Union 1854. [16]

HEPWORTH, Robert, *Cheltenham.*—St. Edm. Hall, Ox. B.A. 1823; Deac. 1824, Pr. 1825. Formerly P. C. of Treddington, Glouc. 1829–57. [17]

HEPWORTH, William Henry Francklin, 5, *Easthrook-villas, Dover.*—Magd. Coll. Cam. B.A. 1855, M.A. 1859. C. of St. James's, Dover. [18]

HERBERT, David William, *Tremain, Cardigan.*—St. Mary Hall, Ox. B.A. 1853; Deac. 1854 and Pr. 1855 by Bp of Llan. P. C. of Blaen-Porth, Dio. St. D. 1862. (Patrons, Hon. G. Vaughan and Capt. S. Jones Penny, alt; P. C.'s Inc. 119*l*; Pop. 752.) P. C. of Tremain, Dio. St. D. 1862. (Patron, Rev. R. Miles; P. C.'s Inc. 83*l* and Ho; Pop. 282.) [19]

HERBERT, Edward, *Llandyfrydog Rectory, Llannerchymedd, Anglesey.*—Jesus Coll. Ox. B.A. 1827; Deac. 1828 and Pr. 1829 by Bp of Ban. R. of Llandyfrydog-with-Llanvihangel-Tre-'r-Beirdd. C. Dio. Ban. 1849. (Patron, Bp of Ban; Tithe, 530*l* 3*s*; Glebe, 3 acres; R.'s Inc. 533*l* and Ho; Pop. Llandyfrydog 706, Llanvihangel-Tre-'r-Beirdd 356.) [20]

HERBERT, E. Otway, *Withyam, Tunbridge Wells.*—St. Aidan's; Deac. 1865, Pr. 1866. P. C. of the District Chapelry of St. John's, Withyam, 1867. (Patron, Lord De la Warr; P. C.'s Inc. varies; House; Pop. 800.) Formerly C. of Acton, near Nantwich, 1865–66, All Saints', Warrington, 1866–67. [21]

HERBERT, George, *Bidford, Alcester.*—Wad. Coll. Ox. B.A. 1858; Deac. 1866 and Pr. 1867 by Bp of Wor. C. of Bidford 1866. [22]

HERBERT, The Hon. George, *Clun Vicarage, Ludlow.*—St. John's Coll. Cam. M.A. 1848; Deac. 1850 and Pr. 1851 by Bp of Wor. V. of Clun-with-Chapel-Lawn C. Dio. Herf. 1855. (Patron, Earl of Powis; Tithe—Imp. 415*l*, V. 802*l* 2*s*; V.'s Inc. 824*l* and Ho; Pop. 1758.) Preb. of Herf. Formerly C. of Kidderminster 1850–55. [23]

HERBERT, George William.—Ex. Coll. Ox. B.A. 1852, M.A. 1854; Deac. 1855 and Pr. 1856 by Bp of Wor. P. C. of St. Peter's, Vauxhall, Lambeth, Dio. Win. 1860. (Patrons, Trustees; P. C.'s Inc. 300*l* and Ho.) Formerly C. of St. Mary-the-Virgin's, Tothill-fields, Westminster. [24]

HERBERT, Henry, *Carno, Newtown, Montgomeryshire.*—Ball. Coll. Ox. B.A. 1833. P. C. of Carno, Dio. Ban. 1838. (Patron, Sir Watkin Williams Wynn, Bart; Tithe—App. 101*l* 6*s*, Imp. 197*l* 8*s*, P. C. 27*l*; P. C.'s Inc. 100*l*; Pop. 969.) [25]

HERBERT, Henry, *Seer Green, Beaconsfield, Bucks.*—P. C. of Seer Green, Dio. Ox. 1858. (Patron, Eton Coll; P. C.'s Inc. 100*l* and Ho; Pop. 334.) [26]

HERBERT, Henry Alfred, *Staverton, near Cheltenham.*—Dub. A.B. 1826; Deac. 1827 and Pr 1828 by Bp of Lich. [1]

HERBERT, James Bankes, *Kilrhedyn, near Newcastle-Emlyn, Carmarthenshire.*—Jesus Coll. Ox. B.A. 1849, M.A. 1852; Deac. 1850 and Pr. 1851 by Bp of Ban. R. of Kilrhedyn, Dio. St. D. 1856. (Patron, Ld Chan; R.'s Inc. 400*l* and Ho; Pop. 1074.) Formerly C. of Llanidan, Anglesey. [2]

HERBERT, John, *Walkden Parsonage, Worsley, Manchester.*—St. John's Coll. Cam. B.A. 1835, M.A. 1840; Deac. 1836 by Bp of Lon. Pr. 1837 by Bp of Wor. P. C. of Walkden Moor, Dio. Man. 1860. (Patron, Earl of Ellesmere; P. C.'s Inc. 180*l* and Ho; Pop. 3500.) [3]

HERBERT, John Arthur, *Glan Hafern, Newtown, Montgomeryshire.*—Univ. Coll. Ox. B.A. 1831, M.A. Ox. 1834, M.A. Cam. 1867; Deac. 1830 and Pr. 1831 by Bp of St. A. R. of Penstrowed, Montgomeryshire, Dio. Ban. 1834. (Patron, Bp of Ban; Tithe, 110*l*; Glebe, 15 acres; R.'s Inc. 115*l* and Ho; Pop. 142.) Rural Dean; Hon. Can. of Bangor; Diocesan Inspector of Schools; Surrogate. Formerly C. of Llanllwchaiarn, near Newtown. [4]

HERBERT, Samuel Asher, 2, *Woodbine-place, Gateshead.*—Dub. Heb. Prizeman 1846, A.B. 1848; Deac. 1847 and Pr. 1848 by Bp of Dur. R. of St. James's, Gateshead, Dio. Dur. 1864. (Patron, Bp of Dur; Tithe, 120*l*; P. C.'s Inc. 320*l* and Ho; Pop. 4500.) Formerly C. of Sunderland 1847–49, Gateshead 1849–58, Clerkenwell, Lond. 1858–62, Gateshead 1862–64. Author, *The Apostle Paul, a Model for Sunday-school Teachers.* 1862. [5]

HERBERT, Thomas William, *Southend, Essex.*—P. C. of Southend, Dio. Roch. 1862. (Patrons, Three Trustees; P. C.'s Inc. 50*l*; Pop. 1716.) Surrogate. [6]

HERBERT, William, *Dolecle-lan, Llansantffread, Aberystwith, Cardiganshire.*—Deac. 1820, Pr. 1821 by Bp of St. D. V. of Llansantffread, Dio. St. D. 1836. (Patron, Bp of St. D; Tithe—App. and Imp. 350*l*, Imp. 38*l*, V. 92*l*; V.'s Inc. 106*l*; Pop. 1360.) P. C. of the Chapelry of Rhydybriew, in the Parish of Llywel, Brecon, Dio. St. D. 1836. (Patron, V. of Llywel; P. C.'s Inc. 150*l*; Pop. 305.) Formerly C. of Llanbadarn 1820, Glasbury 1827. [7]

HEREFORD, The Right Rev. Renn Dickson HAMPDEN, Lord Bishop of Hereford, 107, *Eaton-place, London, S.W.* and *The Palace, Hereford.*—Oriel Coll. Ox. 1st cl. Lit. Hum. et Math. B.A. 1814, M.A. 1817, B.D. and D.D. 1833. Consecrated Bp of Herf. 1848. (Episcopal Jurisdiction, the County of Hereford, with parts of the adjoining counties of Worcester, Salop, Radnorshire, and Montgomeryshire; Inc. of See, 4200*l*; Pop. 232,401; Acres, 986,244; Deaneries, 13; Benefices, 358; Curates, 98; Church Sittings, 102,685.) His Lordship was formerly Bampton Lect. 1832; Prof. of Moral Philosophy and Regius Prof. of Divinity and Can. of Ch. Ch. Ox. 1836–48. Author, *De Ephororum apud Lacedæmonios Magistratu* (Chancellor's Prize for Latin Essay), 1814; *Inaugural Lecture read before the University of Oxford in the Divinity School*, 2 eds. 1836; *Parochial Sermons*, 1836; *The Scholastic Philosophy considered in its Relation to Christian Theology* (Bampton Lectures), 3 eds; *Lectures Introductory to Study of Moral Philosophy*; *A Lecture on Tradition* (read before the University in the Divinity School), 4 eds. 1841; *The Philosophical Evidence of Christianity*; *A Letter to the Right Hon. Lord John Russell*; *Sermons* (preached before the Univ. of Oxford, from 1836 to 1847), 1848; *Charges* (delivered at several successive Visitations). [8]

HEREFORD, R., *Sutton St. Nicholas, Herefordshire.*—C. of Sutton St. Nicholas. [9]

HERIOT, George, *Newcastle-on-Tyne.*—Univ. Coll. Dur. B.A. 1837, M.A. 1840; Deac. 1840 and Pr. 1841 by Bp of Dur. P. C. of St. Ann's, Newcastle-on-Tyne, Dio. Dur. 1842. (Patron, the V. of Newcastle-on-Tyne; P. C.'s Inc. 150*l*; Pop. 4537.) Chap. to the Infirmary. [10]

HERKLOTS, Gerard Andreas, *Frognal Cottage, Hampstead, London, N.W.*—Ex. Coll. Ox. B.A. 1856; Deac. 1859 by Bp of Lon. C. of Hampstead 1859. [11]

HERNAMAN, John William Duncombe, *Hampton Park, Hereford.*—St. John's Coll. Cam. 28th Wrang. B.A. 1848, M.A. 1851; Deac. 1850 and Pr. 1851 by Abp of York. One of H.M. Inspectors of Schools. [12]

HERON, George, *Carrington, Ashton-on Mersey, Cheshire.*—Brasen. Coll. Ox. B.A. 1826, M.A. 1829; Deac. 1828, Pr. 1829. P. C. of Carrington, Dio. Ches. 1831. (Patron, Earl of Stamford and Warrington; Tithe—App. 130*l*; P. C.'s Inc. 400*l*; Pop. 521.) [13]

HERON, Michael Maxwell, *Heddon-on-the-Wall, Newcastle on Tyne.*—V. of Heddon-on-the-Wall, Dio. Dur. 1849. (Patron, Ld Chan; V.'s Inc. 252*l* and Ho; Pop. 744.) Dom. Chap. to the Earl of Stair. [14]

HERRING, Armine Styleman, 45, *Colebrooke-row, London, N.*—Corpus Coll. Cam. B.A. 1856; Deac. 1858 and Pr. 1859 by Bp of Herf. P. C. of St. Paul's, Clerkenwell, 1865. (Patrons, Crown and Bp of Lon. alt; P. C.'s Inc. 200*l*; Pop. 8000.) Formerly C. of Eardisley, Herefordshire, and Chap. to Kington Workhouse, 1858–59, Ventnor 1859–60; Sen. C. of St. Luke's, King's-cross, Lond. 1860–62; Sen. C. of St. James's, Clerkenwell, 1862–65. Author, several Tracts, etc. [15]

HERRING, William Harvey, *Fordham Rectory, Colchester, Essex.*—Trin. Coll. Cam. B.A. 1835; Deac. 1836 and Pr. 1837. R. of Fordham, Dio. Roch. 1839. (Patrons, O. S. Onley, Esq. and Countess Cowper; Tithe, 760*l*; Glebe, 25 acres; R.'s Inc. 760*l* and Ho; Pop. 800.) [16]

HERRINGHAM, William Walton, *Hawksworth Rectory, Bingham, Notts.*—St. Peter's Coll. Cam. B.A. 1847, M.A. 1850; Deac. 1848 by Bp of Nor. Pr. 1849 by Bp of Roch. R. of Hawksworth, Dio. Lin. 1859. (Patron, the present R; Glebe, 149 acres; R.'s Inc. 340*l* and Ho; Pop. 176.) Formerly C. of Borley, Essex, 1848–53, St. Nicholas', Guildford, 1854–56; R. of Chadwell St. Mary's, Essex, 1856–59. Author, *Catechism on the first three Chapters of Genesis*, 1865, Macintosh. [17]

HERVEY, The Ven. and Right Hon. Lord Arthur Charles, *Ickworth Park, Bury St. Edmunds.*—Trin. Coll. Cam. 1st cl. Cl. Trip. and M.A. 1830; Deac. 1832 by Bp of Nor. Pr. 1832 by Bp of Pet. R. of the united R.'s of Ickworth with Hornings-heath, *alias* Horringer, Dio. Ely, 1832 and 1852. (Patron, the Marquis of Bristol; Tithe—Ickworth, 192*l* 1*s* 6*d*; Glebe, 5 acres; Hornings-heath, Tithe, 575*l*; Glebe, 15 acres; R.'s Inc. 810*l* and Ho; Pop. Ickworth 65 Hornings-heath 670.) Archd. of Sudbury 1862. Author, *Hints on Infant Baptism* (a Tract), 1838, 6*d*; *Thanksgiving Sermons for Victories over the Sikhs*, 1846; *Parochial Sermons*, 2 vols. 1850; *Missionary Sermons in Ely Cathedral*, 1851; *Genealogies of our Lord and Saviour Jesus Christ reconciled*, Macmillans, 1853, 10*s* 6*d*; *Inspiration of Holy Scripture* (Four Sermons preached before Cam. Univ.), Macmillans, 1855; various other Sermons and Lectures. [18]

HERVEY, The Right Hon. Lord Charles Amelius, *Great Chesterford Vicarage, Saffron Walden, Essex.*—Trin. Coll. Cam. Honorary M.A. 1836; Deac. 1838 by Bp of Ely, Pr. 1839 by Bp of Lon. V. of Great Chesterford with Little Chesterford R. Dio. Roch. 1839. (Patron, Marquis of Bristol; Glebe, 13 acres; V.'s Inc. 570*l* and Ho; Pop. Great Chesterford 1027, Little Chesterford 276.) [19]

HERVEY, George, 3, *Lansdowne-terrace, London Fields, London, N.E.*—Clare Coll. Cam. 12th Sen. Opt. B.A. 1848, M.A. 1851; Deac. 1849 and Pr. 1850 by Bp of Ely. P. C. of St. Augustine's, Haggerston, Dio. Lon. 1863. (Patrons, Trustees; P. C.'s Inc. 300*l*; Pop. 9000.) Formerly Asst. Math. Mast. King Edward VI. Sch. Bury St. Edmunds, 1848–51. C. of West Hackney, 1851–62. [20]

HERVEY, John Frederick Arthur, *Shotley Rectory, Ipswich.*—Trin. Coll. Cam. 2nd cl. Cl. Trip.

B.A. 1863, M.A. 1866; Deac. 1864 and Pr. 1865 by Bp of Ox. R. of Shotley, Dio. Nor. 1866. (Patron, Marquis of Bristol; Tithe, 585*l*; Glebe, 69 acres; R.'s Inc. 658*l*; Pop. 550.) Formerly C. of Aylesbury, Bucks. 1864–66. [1]

HERVEY, Thomas, *Colmer Rectory, Alton, Hants.*—Clare Coll. Cam. Sen. Opt. Greene's Prize, B.A. 1840, M.A. 1843; Deac. 1841 and Pr. 1842 by Bp of Rip. R. of Colmer with Priors Dean R. Dio. Win. 1852. (Patroness, Mrs. Hervey; Tithe, 500*l*; Glebe, 30 acres; R.'s Inc. 530*l* and Ho; Pop. Colmer 151, Priors Dean 129.) Formerly C. of Woodhouse, Leeds, 1841–45; Hawkhurst and Newenden, Kent, 1845–52. Editor of *Winchester Diocesan Calendar*, annual. [2]

HESELRIGE, Charles Maynard, *Carlton-Curliew Rectory, near Burton Overy, Leicestershire.*—Queens' Coll. Cam. B.A. 1828, M.A. 1831; Deac. and Pr. 1828 by Bp of Herf. R. of Carlton-Curliew, Dio. Pet. 1846. (Patron, Sir J. H. Palmer, Bart; Tithe, 143*l* 10*s*; R.'s Inc. 245*l*; Pop. 308) [3]

HESELRIGE, Charles Maynard, jun., *Carlton-Curliew, near Burton Overy, Leicestershire.*—C. of Carlton-Curliew. [4]

HESKETH, Charles, *North Meols Rectory, Southport, Lancashire.*—Trin. Coll. Ox. B.A. 1827, M.A. 1830; Deac. 1827 and Pr. 1828 by Bp of Ches. R. of North Meols, Dio. Ches. 1835. (Patron, the present R; Tithe, 888*l* 12*s* 6*d*; Glebe, 15½ acres; R.'s Inc. 908*l* and Ho; Pop. 15,191.) Rural Dean. Proctor for the Archdeaconry of Liverpool. [5]

HESLOP, Edward William, *Thornton Dale Rectory, Pickering, Yorks.*—Queen's Coll. Ox. B.A. 1851, M.A. 1855; Deac. 1852 and Pr. 1853 by Abp of York. R. of Thornton Dale, Dio. York, 1857. (Patron, Rev. J. R. Hill; Tithe, 171*l* 13*s*; R.'s Inc. 380*l* and Ho; Pop. 893.) [6]

HESLOP, George Henry, *St. Bees, Whitehaven.*—Queen's Coll. Ox. 1st cl. Lit. Hum. and B.A. 1846, M.A. 1848; Deac. 1848 and Pr. 1850 by Bp of Ox. Head Mast. of St. Bees Gr. Sch. 1854. Late Fell. and Asst. Tut. of Queen's Coll. Ox. [7]

HESLOP, Gordon, *Cossal, near Nottingham.*—Queen's Coll. Ox. B.A. 1851, M.A. 1855; Deac. 1851 and Pr. 1852 by Abp of York. C. of Cossal. [8]

HESLOP, John Wallis, *Weaverthorpe Vicarage, near Ganton, Yorks*—Deac. 1842 and Pr. 1843 by Abp of York. V. of Weaverthorpe, Dio. York, 1856. (Patrons, D. and C. of York; V.'s Inc. 200*l*; Pop. 1033.) Formerly C. of Felskirk, Yorks. [9]

HESLOP, Richard, 2, *Victoria-road, St. Albans, Herts.*—Deac. and Pr. 1826 by Abp of York. P. C. of St. John's, Park, Sheffield, Dio. York, 1855. (Patrons, Trustees; P. C.'s Inc. 300*l* and Ho; Pop. 9014.) C. of St. Peter's, St. Albans, Herts, 1866. Formerly P. C. of Otterford, Somerset, 1851–55, Ainsworth, Manchester, 1836–51, Birch-in-Middleton, Lanc. 1834–36, Slaley, Northumberland, 1831–48; C. of High Hoyland, Yorks, 1826–32, Ilton, Somerset, 1846–53, Creaton, Northants, 1858–59, Kentchurch, Hereford, 1864, Skirbeck, Boston, 1864–65, Orby 1865–66, and St. Mary's, Harrogate, 1866; Chap. to High Sheriff of Westmoreland, 1828–29. Author, *Farewell Sermon at Ilton*, 1853; *Spiritual Nursery*, 1860; *Parting Advice*, 1861; *Sermons*, 1841, 10*s* 6*d*; *An Assize Sermon at Appleby*, 1828. [10]

HESLOP, William, *East Witton Vicarage, Bedale, Yorks.*—Queens' Coll. Cam. B.A. 1834. V. of East Witton, Dio. Rip. 1838. (Patron, Marquis of Ailesbury; Tithe—Imp. 42*l* 16*s*; V.'s Inc. 95*l* and Ho; Pop. 621.) Surrogate. [11]

HESSE, Frederick Legrew, *Rowberrow Rectory, Axbridge, Somerset.*—Trin. Hall, Cam. LL.B. 1827. R. of Rowberrow, Dio. B. and W. 1829. (Patron, Bp of Wor; Tithe, 74*l* 5*s*; R.'s Inc. 134*l* and Ho; Pop. 241.) P. C. of Puxton, Axbridge, Somerset, Dio. B. and W. 1849. (Patrons, D. and C. of Bristol; Tithe—App. 170*l* and 23½ acres of Glebe; P. C.'s Inc. 65*l*; Pop. 147.) [12]

HESSE, George John, *Haslemere, Surrey.*—C. of Haslemere. [13]

HESSE, Legrew James, *Haslemere Rectory, Surrey.*—Trin. Coll. Ox. B.A. 1825, M.A. 1829. R. of Chiddingfold with Haslemere C. Dio. Win. 1838. (Patron, Bp of Win; Chiddingfold, Tithe, 634*l*; Glebe, 13½ acres; Haslemere, Tithe, 240*l*; R.'s Inc. 894*l* and Ho; Pop. Chiddingfold 1167, Haslemere 952.) [14]

HESSEY, Francis, *St. Barnabas' Parsonage, Addison-road, London, W.*—St. John's Coll. Ox. S.C.L. 1837, B.C.L. 1839, D.C.L. 1843; Deac. 1839 and Pr. 1840 by Bp of Ox. P. C. of St. Barnabas', Kensington, Dio. Lon. 1853. (Patron, V. of Kensington; P. C.'s Inc. from Pew Rents; Pop. 5000.) Formerly Fell. of St. John's Coll. Ox; C. of Kentish-town 1839–40; Prin. of Huddersfield Coll. Sch. 1840–43; Head Mast. of Kensington Sch. 1843 53. Author, *The Extension of the Home Episcopate*, Cundall, 1865; *The Establishment of a Native Ministry, the Object of Christian Missions* (Sermons), 1864; *Public Catechising the Means of attaching the People to the Church*, 1866; *Catechetical Lessons on the Parables, on the Miracles, on the Prayer Book*, Parker, 1854, 1867; various Sermons, Papers, &c. [15]

HESSEY, James Augustus, 10, *Leinster-gardens, Hyde Park, W., Merchant Taylors' School, Suffolk-lane, City, E.C.,* and *Gray's Inn, London, W.C.*—St. John's Coll. Ox. 1st cl. Lit. Hum. B.A. 1836, M.A. 1840, D.C.L. 1846; Deac. 1837, Pr. 1838. Head Mast. of Merchant Taylors' Sch. 1845; Preacher to the Hon. Soc. of Gray's Inn 1850; Preb. of St. Paul's Cathl. 1860; Fell. of St. John's Coll. Ox. 1832–46; Public Examiner, Ox. 1842–44; Grinfield Professor of the Septuagint 1865–67; Select Preacher 1850; Bampton Lect. 1860. Author, *Schemata Rhetorica*, Oxford, 1845; *A Scripture Argument against permitting Marriage with a Wife's Sister* (in a Clergyman's Letter to a Friend), 1849, 2nd ed. 1850, 3rd ed. 1855; *God's Guardianship of the Church of England against Rome*. 1850; *Offending in one Point*, 1856; *The Defenced City a Ruin*, 1855; *Early will I seek Thee* (on the Death of the Rev. W. H. Hart), 1861; and *The Restoration of Holy Places*, 1862; being five Sermons preached at Gray's Inn; *Middle Class Education*, 1862; *Christ's Tenderness for the Sinner* (Sermon at the Foundling), 1862; *Sunday, its Origin, History, and present Obligation considered* (eight Sermons preached as Bampton Lecturer), 1860, 2nd ed. 1861 with a copious index; *The Public School Boy* (an Address at Walthamstow School), 1864, 3rd ed. 1866; *Biographies of the Kings of Judah* (Lectures preached in Lent), 1864; various Tracts for the Marriage Law Defence Society; Sermons in the *Tracts for Christian Seasons*, 3rd series, 1863–64. [16]

HESSEY, Robert Falkner, *Basing Vicarage, Basingstoke.*—Magd. Coll. Ox. 1st cl. Lit. Hum. Latin Verse Prize and B.A. 1848, M.A. 1851; Deac. 1855 and Pr. 1857 by Bp of Ox. V. of Basing with Upper Nately, Dio. Win. 1864. (Patron, Magd. Coll. Ox; V.'s Inc. 725*l*; Pop. 1140.) Fell. and Tut. of Magd. Coll. Ox. 1853. [17]

HETHERINGTON, John, 85, *Upper Stanhope-street, Liverpool.*—St. Bees; Deac. 1862 and Pr. 1863 by Bp of Ches. Chap. to the "Mersey Mission Afloat," 1867. Formerly C. of Edge-hill, Liverpool, 1862–66; Broseley, Salop, 1866–67. [18]

HETHERINGTON, Joseph, *Clifton, Workington, Cumberland.*—Queen's Coll. Ox. B.A. 1833, M.A. 1835; Deac. 1835 and Pr. 1836 by Bp of Wor. P. C. of Clifton, Dio. Carl. 1850. (Patron, R. of Workington; Glebe, 34 acres; P. C.'s Inc. 100*l*; Pop. 1085.) [19]

HETLING, Frederick Thomas, *Testerton, Norwich.*—Oriel Coll. Ox. B.A. 1859; Deac. 1863 and Pr. 1864 by Bp of B. and W. R. of Testerton, Dio. Nor. 1867. (Patron, J. H. Morse-Boycott, Esq; R's Inc. 13*l* 13*s*; Pop. 11.) Formerly C. of Marston Bigot 1863. [20]

HETLING, George Hilhouse, *Woodlands, Frome-Selwood, Somerset.*—Literate; Deac. 1849 and Pr. 1852 by Bp of Ex. Asst. C. of Woodlands. [21]

HEURTLEY, Charles Abel, *Christ Church, Oxford.*—Corpus Coll. Ox. Fell. of, Ellerton Theol. Prizeman, 1st cl. Math. B.A. 1827, D.D. 1853; Deac. 1831, Pr. 1832. R. of Fenny Compton, Warw. Dio. Wor. 1840.

(Patron, Corpus Coll. Ox; Glebe, 400 acres; R.'s Inc. 600*l* and Ho; Pop. 638.) Margaret Prof. of Divinity, Ox. 1853; Can. of Ch. Ch. Ox. 1853. Formerly C. of Wardington and Claydon, Oxon, 1831–40; Select Preacher of Univ. Ox. 1834, 1838 and 1851; Bampton Lect. 1845; Hon. Can. of Wor. Cathl. 1848. Author, *Plain Words about Prayer*, 1833; *University Sermons*, 1837, 6*s*; *University Sermons on the Union between Christ and His People*, 2 eds. 1842, 1851, 5*s* 6*d*; *Lectures on Justification* (Bampton Lectures for 1845), 2 eds. 9*s*; *Parochial Sermons*, 1st Series, 2 eds. 1849 and 1851; 2nd Series, 1850; 3rd Series, 1852, 5*s* 6*d* each; *Mutual Dependence the Link of Society* (Visitation Sermon); *Delay in returning to God* (Lenten Sermon), 1857; *The Repentance of Judas* (Lenten Sermon), 1858; *Harmonia Symbolica, a Collection of Creeds belonging to the Ancient Western Church*, Oxford University Press, 1858; *The Form of Sound Words and other Sermons preached before the University of Oxford* 7*s* 6*d*; *De Fide et Symbolo Tractatus Tres*, 1864, 2*s* 6*d*; Essay on Miracles in *Replies to Essays and Reviews*, J. H. and J. Parker, 1862; *The Doctrine of the Eucharist: Christ present by Spirit and Grace*, 1867; *An Inquiry into the Scriptural Warrant for addressing Prayer to Christ*, 1867. [1]

HEWET, Philip, *Binstead, Ryde, Isle of Wight.*—St. John's Coll. Cam. B.A. 1822; Deac. 1823, Pr. 1824. R. of Binstead, Dio. Win. 1833. (Patron, Bp of Win; Tithe, 70*l*; Glebe, 7 acres; R.'s Inc. 80*l*; Pop. 486.) [2]

HEWETSON, John, *Measham Parsonage, Atherston.*—Corpus Coll. Cam. B.A. 1847, M.A. 1850; Deac. and Pr. by Abp of York. P. C. of Measham, Dio. Lich. 1852. (Patron, Marquis of Hastings; P. C.'s Inc. 97*l* and Ho; Pop. 1569.) [3]

HEWETT, John, *Babbicombe, Torquay.*—Clare Coll. Cam. B.A. 1853, M A. 1856; Deac. 1855 by Bp of Chich. Pr. 1856 by Bp of Pet. Asst. C. of St. Mary Church, Devon; C. in sole charge of Babbicombe 1865. Formerly C. of Battle, Sussex, 1855; R. of Compton Martin, Somerset, 1857. [4]

HEWETT, John Prowse, *Norton Fitzwarren Rectory, Taunton.*—Pemb. Coll. Ox. B.A. 1853, M.A. 1855; Deac. 1854 by Bp of G. and B. Pr. 1855 by Bp of Ex. R. of Norton, Dio. B. and W. 1864. (Patroness, Mrs. Hewett; Tithe—App. 288*l* 15*s*; Glebe, 8 acres; R.'s Inc. 327*l* and Ho—the manor of Wooney, of which the R. is Lord, is appendant to the R; Pop. 634.) Formerly C. of St. James's, Hambridge, Taunton, Combe, Raleigh and Sheldon, Devon; C. of Bicknoller, near Taunton, 1859. [5]

HEWETT, John William, *Croft House, Tutbury, Staffs.*—Trin. Coll. Cam. B.A. 1849, M.A. 1852; Deac. 1849 and Pr. 1850 by Bp of Chich. C. in sole charge of Scropton, Derbyshire, 1866. Formerly Fell. and Tut. of St. Nicolas' Coll. Shoreham, 1849–52; C. of Bloxham and Head Mast. of Bloxham Gr. Sch. 1853–56; C. of St. George's, Whitwick, Leic. 1857. Author, *History and Description of Exeter Cathedral*; *History and Description of Ely Cathedral*; single Sermons and Letters; *Verses by a Country Curate*; Papers in the *Exeter* and *North Oxfordshire Architectural Societies' Transactions*; Editor of *The Sealed Copy of the Prayer Book*, Masters; *Liber Precum*, J. W. Parker; *Bibliotheca Sacra Parvulorum*, Rivingtons; *From Advent to Advent*, Bemrose, Derby; etc. [6]

HEWETT, William Henry, *Yarburgh Rectory, near Louth, Lincolnshire.*—Magd. Hall Ox. B.A. 1854, M.A. 1856; Deac. 1854 and Pr. 1855 by Bp of Ox. R. of Yarburgh, Dio. Lin. 1863. (Patron, G. J. Yarburgh, Esq; Glebe, 230 acres; R.'s Inc. 300*l* and Ho; Pop. 279.) Formerly C. of Little Tew 1854, and Banbury, Oxon, 1857, Milton, Berks, 1859; Min. Can. and Precentor of Carlisle Cathl. 1861. [7]

HEWISON, George Henry, *Portland-street, York.*—St. John's Coll. Cam. Sen. Opt. B.A. 1859; Deac. 1860 and Pr. 1861 by Abp of York. 2nd Mast. of Abp Holgate's Sch. York. Formerly C. of Osbaldwick, Yorks. [8]

HEWITT, George, 22, *Red Roch-street West, Derby-road, Liverpool.*—St. Bees; Deac. 1865 and Pr. 1866 by Bp of Ches. Missionary C. of St. Clement's Liverpool. Formerly C. of St. John's, Liverpool, 1866. [9]

HEWITT, James John, *Madeira.*—Dub. A.B. 1854; Deac. 1855 and Pr. 1856 by Bp of Salis. British Consular Chap. at Madeira. Formerly C. of Tincleton, Dorset, and Trinity, Haverstock-hill, Lond. [10]

HEWITT, Thomas, *Emmanuel College, Cambridge*, and *Rottingdean, Brighton.*—Emman. Coll. Cam. B.A. 1858, M.A. 1861; Deac. 1859 and Pr. 1860 by Bp of Ely. Fell. and Bursar of Emman. Coll; Proctor for University 1867. [11]

HEWITT, Thomas Swinton, *Leysters, Tenbury, Herefordshire.*—Wor. Coll. Ox. B.A. 1841. M.A. 1845; Deac. 1841, Pr. 1842. P. C. of Leysters, Dio. Herf. 1858. (Patron, Richard Prescott Deal, Esq; Tithe, 254*l* 18*s* 10*d*; Glebe, 90 acres; P. C.'s Inc. 344*l* 13*s* 10*d* and Ho; Pop. 267.) Formerly R. of North Marden, Sussex, 1851–58. [12]

HEWLETT, Alfred, *Astley Parsonage, near Manchester.*—Magd. Hall, Ox. B.A. 1831, M.A. 1837, B.D. and D.D. 1865; Deac. and Pr. 1831. P. C. of Astley, Dio. Man. 1840. (Patron, V. of Leigh; Tithe—Imp. 132*l* 13*s* 2*d*; P. C.'s Inc. 270*l* and Ho; Pop. 2109.) Surrogate for the Dios. of Man. and Ches. Author, *The End of the World*, 1832, 1*s*; *Thirteen Plain Sermons*, 1839, 2*d* each; *Life of George Marsh*, 2*s* 6*d*; *Our Sunday School*, 2*s* 6*d*; *Christian Cottagers' Magazine*, in Monthly Parts, from 1845 to 1852, 2*d*; *The Millennium* (Seven Lectures), 1854, 1*s* 6*d*; *The District Visitor*, a periodical, 1854, 1*d*. [13]

HEWLETT, Ebenezer, *St. Paul's Rectory, Brunswick-street, Manchester.*—King's Coll. Lond. Assoc. 1852, M.A. by Abp of Cant. 1865; Deac. 1852 and Pr. 1853 by Bp of Lon. R. of St. Paul's, Chorlton-on-Medlock, Manchester, 1862. (Patrons, Trustees; Pop. 4500.) Formerly C. of St. John's, Bethnal-green, Lond. 1853–55; Calne, Wilts, and Chap. of Calne Union Workhouse, 1855–57; Min. of St. Saviour's Sch. Ch. and Lect. of St. Saviour's, Manchester, 1857–62. Author, *Twelve Sermons*; *Notes of a Union Chaplain*, 1st and 2nd Series; *My Dark Days*; *Good-bye*; *The Bereaved Mother*; *Fulness of Joy*; *The Blunted Weapon and the Silenced Tongue*; and other Sermons and Tracts. [14]

HEWLETT, J. H., *Codicote, Herts.*—C. of Codicote. [15]

HEWLETT, James Philip, *Tredington, Tewkesbury.*—C. of Tredington. [16]

HEWLETT, Jesse, *Milwall, Middlesex, E.*—King's Coll. Lond; Deac 1864 and Pr. 1865 by Bp of Lon. Missionary C. of St. Luke's, Millwall. Formerly C. of Ch. Ch. Poplar, 1864–66. [17]

HEWSON, Joseph, *City Gaol, Chester.*—Chap. of the City Gaol, Chester; Chap. of the Chester Cemetery, and C. of St. Michael's, Chester. [18]

HEWSON, Robert.—Dub. A.B. 1837, A.M. 1840; Deac. 1840 by Bp of Killaloe, Pr. 1840 by Bp of Limerick. Formerly C. of St. Mary's, St. George's-in-the East, Lond. [19]

HEWSON, William, 1, *St. Hilda's-terrace, Whitby.*—St. John's Coll. Cam. B.A. 1830, M.A. 1833; Deac. 1830 by Bp of Lon. Pr. 1831 by Abp of York. P. C. of Goatland, near Whitby, Dio. York, 1847. (Patron, Abp of York; P. C.'s Inc. 53*l*; Pop. 319.) Author, *The Christian's Bible*; *The Oblation and Temple of Ezekiel's Prophetic Visions*, 1858, 4*s*. [20]

HEXT, George, *St. Veep, Cornwall.*—Corpus Coll. Ox. 1st cl. Lit. Hum. and B.A. 1840, M.A. 1843, D.D. 1851; Deac. 1843, Pr. 1844. V. of St. Veep, Dio. Ex. 1857. (Patron, F. Howell, Esq; Tithe—Imp. 322*l* 10*s*, V. 233*l* 14*s* 6*d*; Glebe, 18 acres; V.'s Inc. 250*l* and Ho; Pop. 628.) Rural Dean. Formerly Fell. Tut. and Bursar of Corpus Coll. Ox. [21]

HEXT, John Hawkins, *Teignton Regis Vicarage, Newton Abbey, Devon.*—Ex. Coll. Ox. B.A. 1831, M.A. 1834; Deac. and Pr. 1833. V. of Teignton Regis with Highweek P. C. Dio. Ex. 1858. (Patron, Bp of Ex; V.'s Inc. 410*l* and Ho; Pop. Teignton Regis 1632, Highweek 1571.) Surrogate. Formerly V. of Morval, Cornwall, 1843–58. [22]

HEXTER, William.—King's Coll. Lond. Theol. Assoc; Deac. 1855 and Pr. 1856 by Abp of Cant. C. of Selworthy, Somersetshire. Formerly C. of High Halden, Kent, and St. Thomas's, Lambeth. [1]

HEY, Charles Edward, *Winchester.*—Caius Coll. Cam. B.A. 1858; Deac. 1858 by Bp of Lin. Min. Can. of Win. Cathl. 1862. Formerly C. of North Wheatley, Notts. [2]

HEY, Robert, *Belper, Derbyshire.*—St. John's Coll. Cam. Sen. Opt. Exhib. B.A. 1842, M.A. 1845; Deac. 1842, Pr. 1843. P. C. of Belper, Dio. Lich. 1845. (Patron, V. of Duffield; Tithe—App. 20*l*, Imp. 477*l* 9*s*; Glebe, 1 acre; P. C.'s Inc. 200*l* and Ho; Pop. 6106.) Surrogate; Preb. of Lich; Rural Dean of Alfreton 1854. Formerly C. of Shirley 1842, Ashbourne 1844. [3]

HEY, Samuel, *Sawley, Derbyshire.*—Corpus Coll. Cam. B.A. 1827, M.A. 1830; Deac. 1828, Pr. 1829. V. of Sawley with Long Eaton C. Dio. Lich. 1844. (Patron, Bp of Lich; Glebe, 9 acres; V.'s Inc. 290*l* and Ho; Pop. Sawley 1082, Long Eaton 1551.) Rural Dean 1851. [4]

HEY, William, *York.*—St. John's Coll. Cam. 12th Wrang. and 2nd in 3rd cl. Cl. Trip. B.A. 1834, M.A. 1837; Deac. 1837 by Bp of Ely, Pr. 1838 by Abp of York. V. of St. Helen's, City and Dio. York, 1854. (Patron, Ld Chan; Glebe, 27 acres; V.'s Inc. 105*l*; Pop. 547.) Can. of York 1864; Preb. of Weighton in York Cathl. 1854. Formerly Fell. of St. John's Coll. Cam. and Head Mast. of St. Peter's Sch. York. [5]

HEYCOCK, Charles, *Oakham.*—St. John's Coll. Cam. B.A. 1818, M.A. 1826; Deac. 1818, Pr. 1819. Formerly P. C. of Owston, Leic. 1827–57; also R. of Whitcote, Leic. 1827–57. Author, *The Prophetic Period of Papal Domination* (Two Sermons), 1853, 1*s*; *Linguæ Anglicanæ Clavis* (an English Grammar), 1854, 2*s* 6*d*. [6]

HEYCOCK, Thomas, *Somersham, St. Ives, Hunts.*—St. John's Coll. Cam. B.A. 1854, M.A. 1857; Deac. 1855 and Pr. 1856 by Bp of Lin. C. of Pidley 1857. Formerly C. of Llandenny, Monmouth, 1855–57. [7]

HEYGATE, Thomas Edmund, *Sheen, near Ashbourne, Staffs.*—Queens' Coll. Cam. B.A. 1849, M.A. 1852. P. C. of Sheen, Dio. Lich. 1862. (Patron, A. J. Beresford Hope, Esq; P. C.'s Inc. 63*l* and Ho; Pop. 427.) Formerly C. of Sheen. [8]

HEYGATE, William Edward, *Southend Rochford, Essex.*—St. John's Coll. Ox. 3rd cl. Lit. Hum. and B.A. 1839, M.A. 1842; Deac. and Pr. 1840. C. of Leigh, Essex, 1857. Formerly C. of Great Wakering, Essex, Hadleigh, Essex, and Gerrans, Cornwall. Author, *The Manual, a Book of Devotions chiefly intended for the Poor*, 1*s*; *William Blake, or the English Farmer*, 3*s* 6*d*; *Godfrey Davenant at School*, 2*s* 6*d*; *Ellen Meyrick, or False Excuses*, 2*s* 6*d*; *Probatio Clerica, or Aids in Self-Examination to Candidates for Holy Orders*, 1845; *Pierre Poussin, or Thoughts of Christ's Presence*, 1851; *The Wedding Gift*, 1856; *Ember Hours*, 2*s* 6*d*—all published by Masters; *Care of the Soul*, 3*s* 6*d*; *The Good Shepherd*, 8*s*, published by Rivingtons; *Scholar and Trooper*, 5*s*, J. H. and J. Parker; *Evening of Life*, Masters, 1856; *Catholic Antidotes*, 1856, Masters. [9]

HEYSHAM, John, *Lazonby Vicarage, Penrith.*—St. John's, Coll. Cam. B.A. 1815, M.A. 1818; Deac. 1816, Pr. 1817. V. of Lazonby, Dio. Carl. 1846. (Patron, Bp of Carl; Tithe—Imp. 329*l*, V. 454*l*; Glebe, 60 acres; V.'s Inc. 543*l* and Ho; Pop. 570.) Surrogate 1827; Hon. Sec. and Treasurer to the Clergy Widows and Orphans' Relief Society, 1823. Formerly P. C. of Hayton 1820–21; P. C. of Sebergham 1821–46. [10]

HEYWOOD, Henry Robinson, *Swinton Park, near Manchester.*—Trin. Coll. Cam. B.A. 1856, M.A. 1860; Deac. 1857 and Pr. 1858 by Bp of Wor. P. C. of Swinton, Dio. Man. 1864. (Patron, V. of Eccles; Glebe, 50 acres; P. C.'s Inc. 240*l* and Ho; Pop. 6000.) Formerly C. of Southam, Warwick, 1857–59, St. John's, Pendlebury, Manchester, 1859–64. [11]

HEYWOOD, James John, 22, *Bedford-place, Russell-square, London, W.C.*—Trin. Coll. Cam. Wrangham Prizeman, 33rd Wrang. 9th in 1st cl. Cl. Trip. and B.A. 1850, M.A. 1853; Deac. 1853 and Pr. 1854 by Bp of Lon. Mast. of the Lower Sixth Form in King's Coll. Sch. Lon. 1853. [12]

HEYWOOD, Nathaniel, *St. Mark's Parsonage, Easton, Bristol.*—Trin. Coll. Cam. Sen. Opt. B.A. 1851, M.A. 1856; Deac. 1852 and Pr. 1853 by Bp of Wor. P. C. of Lower Easton, Dio. G. and B. 1858. (Patron, Bp of G. and B; P. C.'s Inc. 170*l* and Ho; Pop. 2939.) [13]

HEYWOOD, Oliver, *Oakridge Parsonage, Bisley, Glouc.*—Dub. A B. 1856, A.M. 1860; Deac. 1856 and Pr. 1857 by Bp of Man. P. C. of Oakridge, Dio. G. and B. 1860. (Patron, Bp of G. and B; P. C.'s Inc. 90*l* and Ho; Pop. 873.) [14]

HEYWORTH, James, *Henbury Hill, near Bristol.*—Trin. Coll. Cam. B.A. 1830, M.A. 1832; Deac. 1833 by Abp of York. [15]

HIBBIT, Arthur, *Little Ilford Rectory, Essex.*—St. Cath. Coll. Cam. B.A. 1841; Deac. and Pr. 1842. R. of Little Ilford, Dio. Lon. 1847. (Patron, John Wight Wight, Esq; Tithe, 328*l*; Glebe, 40 acres; R.'s Inc. 404*l* and Ho; Pop. 594.) [16]

HIBBS, Richard, *Beverstone Rectory, Nailsworth, Gloucester.*—St. John's Coll. Cam. B.A. 1841, M.A. 1844; Deac. 1841 and Pr. 1842 by Bp of Lin. C. of Beverstone (sole charge), 1865. Formerly Min. of Ch. of England in Edinburgh. Author, various Pamphlets. [17]

HICHENS, Baron, *Ottershaw, near Chertsey, Surrey.*—C. of Ottershaw. [18]

HICHENS, Frederick H., *Speldhurst, Kent.*—Ex. Coll. Ox. C. of Speldhurst. [19]

HICHENS, Richard, *St. John's Parsonage, Colchester.*—Ex. Coll. Ox. 3rd cl. Cl, 4th cl. Math. B.A. 1851, M.A. 1854; Deac. 1851 and Pr. 1852 by Bp of Dur. P. C. of St. John's, Colchester, Dio. Roch. 1863. (Patron, Archd. of Colchester; P. C.'s Inc. 256*l* and Ho; Pop. 600.) Formerly C. of St. Stephen's, Westminster, 1860, Rowley, Yorks, 1861. [20]

HICHENS, T. S., *Guilsborough, Northants.*—V. of Guilsborough, Dio. Pet. 1864. (Patron, R. Hichens, Esq; V.'s Inc. 500*l*; Pop. 730.) [21]

HICK, James Watson, *Byer's Green, Bishop Auckland, Durham.*—Univ. Coll. Dur. B.A. 1836, M.A. 1837, B.D. 1850. P. C. of Byer's Green, Dio. Dur. 1845. (Patron, Bp of Dur; Tithe—App. 77*l* 12*s*, Imp. 56*l* 16*s* 10½*d*; Glebe, 82 acres; P. C.'s Inc. 300*l*; Pop. 2691.) Organizing Sec. in the Dio. of Dur. to the S.P.G. [22]

HICKES, Heathfield Weston, *Cranford Rectory, Hounslow, Middlesex.*—Pemb. Coll. Ox. B.A. 1825, M.A. 1829. R. of Cranford, Dio. Lon. 1837. (Patron, Earl Fitzhardinge; Tithe, 251*l* 6*s*; Glebe, 13 acres; R.'s Inc. 268*l* and Ho; Pop. 530.) [23]

HICKLEY, John George, *Walton, near Glastonbury.*—Trin. Coll. Ox. 1834, 2nd cl. Lit. Hum. and B.A. 1837, M.A. 1841, B.D. 1843; Deac. 1843, Pr. 1845. R. of Street with Walton C. Somerset, Dio. B. and W. 1850. (Patron, Marquis of Bath; Street, Tithe—App. 3*s*, R. 489*l* 14*s*; Glebe, 8 acres; Walton, Tithe—App. 6*s*, R. 385*l*; Glebe, 18½ acres; R.'s Inc. 880*l* and Ho; Pop. Street 1898, Walton 731.) Late Fell. of Trin. Coll. Ox. 1843. [24]

HICKLING, Edmund L., *Halesworth, Suffolk.* [25]

HICKMAN, Richard, *Bodington Rectory, Leamington.*—Emman. Coll. Cam. B.A. 1842, M.A. 1845; Deac. 1843 and Pr. 1844 by Bp of Wor. C. of Bodington (sole charge) 1861. Formerly C. of Kingswinford, Staffs, 1847–59. [26]

HICKMAN, Thomas Greene, *Bury St. Edmunds.*—Trin. Coll. Cam. B.A. 1816, M.A. 1819; Deac. 1816 and Pr. 1817 by Bp of Pet. Chap. to the Suffolk General Hosp. and Bury Union and Asylum. [27]

HICKMAN, W., *Warminster, Wilts.*—C. of Warminster. [28]

HICKMAN, Walter B., *West Harling, Norfolk.*—R. of West Harling, Dio. Nor. 1864. (Patroness, Lady Nugent; R.'s Inc. 160*l* and Ho; Pop. 124.) [29]

HICKS, George Grisdale, *Cubberley, near Cheltenham.*—Ex. Coll. Ox. B.A. 1859; Deac. 1859 and Pr. 1860 by Bp of G. and B. C. of Cubberley 1859. [1]

HICKS, Herbert Sawyer, *St. Peter's Parsonage, Tynemouth.*—St. Cath. Coll. Cam. B.A. 1855, M.A. 1862; Deac. 1858 and Pr. 1859 by Bp of Man. P. C. of St. Peter's, Tynemouth, Dio. Dur. 1860. (Patron, Duke of Northumberland; P. C.'s Inc. 200*l* and Ho; Pop. 7516.) Formerly C. of St. Peter's, Halliwell, Bolton-le-Moors, 1858–60, Wixoe, Suffolk, 1860. [2]

HICKS, James, *Piddle-Trenthide, near Dorchester.*—Oriel Coll. Ox. B.A. 1834; Deac. 1835 and Pr. 1836 by Bp of G. and B. V. of Piddle-Trenthide, Dio. Salis. 1845. (Patrons, D. and C. of Win; Tithe—App. 420*l*, V. 88*l*; Glebe, 198 acres; V.'s Inc. 251*l* and Ho; Pop. 800.) Chap. to the Cerne Union. [3]

HICKS, John Champion, *Kirklington, Ripon.*—Caius Coll. Cam. B.A. 1864; Deac. 1865 and Pr. 1866 by Bp of Rip. C. of Kirklington 1866. Formerly C. of Hornby, Catterick, 1865. [4]

HICKS, John Thomas Forbes, *Ampleforth, York.*—V. of Ampleforth, Dio. York, 1853. (Patron, Abp of York; V.'s Inc. 280*l* and Ho; Pop. 450.) Formerly C. of Cherry-Burton and Leconfield, Yorks. [5]

HICKS, R. W. S., *Kirk Smeaton, Yorks.*—R. of Kirk Smeaton, Dio. York, 1865. (Patron, Earl Fitzwilliam; R.'s Inc. 370*l*; Pop. 333.) [6]

HICKS, Thomas Nash, *Torquay.*—C. of Upton, Torquay. [7]

HICKS, William, *Sturmer Rectory, Halstead, Essex.*—Magd. Coll. Cam. B.A. 1823, M.A. 1826; Deac. 1823 and Pr. 1829. R. of Sturmer, Dio. Roch. 1829. (Patron, Rev. G. H. Fletcher; Tithe, 267*l*; Glebe, 18¾ acres; R.'s Inc. 300*l* and Ho; Pop. 340.) Surrogate. Chap. to the Risbridge Union 1836. Formerly C. of Caxton 1823, Wendy 1824. [8]

HIDES, William, *Gayton Parsonage, Stafford.*—St. John's Coll. Cam. B.A. 1839, M.A. 1863; Deac. 1839, Pr. 1840. P. C. of Gayton, Dio. Lich. 1843. (Patroness, Mrs. Cave Browne; Tithe—Imp. 222*l* 13*s*; Glebe, 1 acre; P. C.'s Inc. 53*l* and Ho; Pop. 249.) P. C. of Stowe, Staffs, Dio. Lich. 1843. (Patroness, Mrs. Cave Browne; Tithe—Imp. 508*l* 15*s*; P. C.'s Inc. 87*l*; Pop. 432.) Surrogate. Formerly C. of Selston, Linc. 1839–43. [9]

HIGGENS, Robert, *Wareside Parsonage, Ware, Herts.*—Wor. Coll. Ox; Deac. 1847 by Bp of Roch. Pr. 1848 by Bp of Ely. P. C. of Wareside, Dio. Roch. 1855. (Patron, V. of Ware; P. C.'s Inc. 150*l* and Ho; Pop. 7011.) [10]

HIGGINS, Edward, *Bosbury House, Hereford.*—Brasen. Coll. Ox. B A. 1825, M.A. 1827; Deac. 1826, Pr. 1827. [11]

HIGGINS, Henry Hugh, *Rainhill, Prescot, Lancashire.*—Corpus Coll. Cam. Sen. Opt. and B.A. 1836, M.A. 1840; Deac. 1838, Pr. 1839. Chap. to the West Derby Lunatic Asylum 1853. [12]

HIGGINS, Thomas, 4, *York-street, Portman-square, London, W.* and *Rose Wood, Pangbourne, Reading.*—Brasen. Coll. Ox. 2nd cl. Lit. Hum. and B.A. 1818, M.A. 1820; Deac. 1819, Pr. 1820. [13]

HIGGINSON, George Noel, *Trinity Parsonage, Ipswich.*—C. (sole charge) of Trinity, Ipswich, 1866. Formerly R. of Grace Ch. Waterdown, Canada, 1860; Sen. C. of St. Mary Redcliff, Bristol, 1866. [14]

HIGGINSON, John, *Thormanby Rectory, Easingwold, Yorks.*—Queen's Coll. Ox. B.A. 1834, M.A. 1836; Deac. 1835 by Bp of Ches. Pr. 1836 by Abp of Cant. R. of Thormanby, Dio. York, 1836. (Patrons, Viscount Downe and Sir G. Cayley alt; Tithe, 246*l*; Glebe, 38½ acres; R.'s Inc. 284*l* and Ho; Pop. 147.) [15]

HIGGON, W. Henry, *West Robeston, Milford.*—R. of West Robeston, Dio. St. D. 1859. (Patron, Prince of Wales; R.'s Inc. 180*l*; Pop. 159.) [16]

HIGGS, Richard William, *Handborough Rectory, Enham, Oxon.*—St. John's Coll. Ox. B C.L. 1836, D.C.L. 1841; Deac. 1837, Pr. 1838. R. of Handborough, Dio. Ox. 1854. (Patron, St. John's Coll. Ox; R.'s Inc. 420*l* and Ho; Pop. 1059.) Late Fell. of St. John's Coll. Ox. [17]

HIGHAM, Thomas, *St. Catherine's Parsonage, Wigan.*—St. John's Coll. Cam. B.A. 1857; Deac. 1857 and Pr. 1858 by Bp of Ches. P. C. of St. Catherine's, Wigan, Dio. Ches. 1863. (Patron, R. of Wigan; P. C.'s Inc. 300*l* and Ho; Pop. 7909.) Formerly C. of St. Mary's, Chester, and All Saints', Wigan. Author, *Sermons*; *Jehovah the Believer's Confidence.* [18]

HIGHMORE, Frederick Nathaniel, *Thurlestone Grange, Elvaston, Derbyshire.*—St. John's Coll. Cam. B.A. 1834, M.A. 1838; Deac. 1837, Pr. 1838. V. of Elvaston, Dio. Lich. 1841. (Patron, Earl of Harrington; Tithe, 241*l* 17*s* 5*d*; Glebe, 47 acres; V.'s Inc. 380*l*; Pop. 499.) Formerly Head Mast. of the Royal Gr. Sch. Burnley, 1839–41. [19]

HIGHTON, Alfred, *Podimore Rectory, near Ilchester, Somerset.*—St. John's Coll. Cam. Sen. Opt. and B A. 1853, M.A. 1856; Deac. 1856 and Pr. 1858 by Bp of B. and W. C. of Milton Podimore. [20]

HIGHTON, Henry, 11, *Sussex-square, Brighton.*—Queen's Coll. Ox. 1st cl. Lit. Hum. 2nd cl. Math. Michel Fell. B.A. 1837, M.A. 1840; Deac. 1839, Pr. 1840. Formerly Asst. Mast. of Rugby School 1842–59; Prin. of Cheltenham Coll. 1859–62. Author, *Religious Teachings at Rugby.* 1850; *Revised Translation of New Testament,* Bagster, 1863; various Pamphlets. [21]

HIGNETT, George Edward, *Kidsgrove, Staffordshire.*—Brasen. Coll. Ox. 4th cl. (Hon.) Law and Hist. B.A. 1863, M.A. 1867; Deac. 1865 by Bp of Man. Pr. 1866 by Bp of Lich. C. of Kidsgrove 1866; C. of St. Luke's, Liverpool, 1865–66. Author, *Selection of Additional Hymns for Public Worship,* Wardle, Kidsgrove. [22]

HIGNETT, Harry Alfred, *Ringway Parsonage, Altrincham, Cheshire.*—Oriel Coll. Ox. B.A. 1861, M.A. 1864; Deac. 1862 and Pr. 1863 by Bp of Ches. P. C. of Ringway, Dio. Ches. 1864. (Patron, Lord Egerton of Tatton; Glebe, 36 acres; P. C.'s Inc. 140*l* and Ho; Pop. 560.) Formerly C. of Rostherne 1862, Astbury 1864. [23]

HILDEBRAND, James Slessor, *Colombo, Ceylon.*—Emman. Coll. Cam. B A. 1847; Deac. 1848. Head Mast. of the Gr. Sch. Colombo. [24]

HILDEBRAND, John B., *Kibworth, near Market Harborough.*—Dub. A.B. 1823; Deac. 1824 and Pr. 1825 by Bp of Lin. R. of Saxby with Stapleford V. Dio. Pet. 1834. (Patron, Earl of Harborough; R.'s Inc. 168*l* and Ho; Pop. Saxby 117, Stapleford 109.) Head Mast. of the Gr. Sch. and Lect. of Kibworth. [25]

HILDEBRAND, William, *Little Carlton, Louth.*—Clare Coll. Cam. B.A. 1843; Deac. 1843 and Pr. 1844 by Bp of Pet. R. of Little Carlton and Castle Carlton, Dio. Lin. 1865. (Patron, J. Forster, Esq; R.'s Inc. of Little Carlton, 159*l* and Ho; Pop. 181; Castle Carlton, 69*l*; Pop. 45.) Formerly R. of Millbrook, Beds. [26]

HILDYARD, Alexander Grant, *St. Martin's, Stamford.*—Pemb. Coll. Cam. Bell's Univ. Scho. 1834, B.A. 1837, M.A. 1840; Deac. 1841 and Pr. 1842 by Bp of Pet. Dom. Chap. to Lord Nelson; C. of Easton-on-the-Hill 1866. Formerly V. of Madingley, Cambs. 1855–57. [27]

HILDYARD, Charles Frederic, *Grammar Schoolhouse, Bury, Lancashire.*—Wor. Coll. Ox. 4th cl. Lit. Hum. and B.A. 1849; Deac. 1852 and Pr. 1854 by Bp of Lin. Mast. of the Gr. Sch. Bury, 1858. Formerly 2nd Mast. of King Edward VI.'s Free Gr. Sch. Grantham, 1852–58. [28]

HILDYARD, Frederick, *Swanington Rectory, near Norwich.*—Trin. Coll. Cam. B.A. 1825, M.A. 1828; Deac 1832, Pr. 1833. R. of Swanington with Wood Dalling V. Dio. Nor. 1840. (Patron, Trin. Hall, Cam; Swanington, Tithe, 403*l* 17*s*; Glebe, 13 acres; Wood Dalling, Tithe—Imp. 400*l* and 112 acres of Glebe, V. 38*l* 9*s* 6¾*d*; Glebe, 56½ acres; R.'s Inc. 530*l* and Ho; Pop. Swanington 385, Wood Dalling 508.) Late Fell. and Tut. of Trin. Hall, Cam. [29]

HILDYARD, Henry Charles Thoroton, *Rowley Rectory, Brough, Yorks.*—Mert. Coll. Ox. B.A. 1846; Deac. 1847, Pr. 1848. R. of Rowley, Dio. York,

1852. (Patron, T. B. T. Hildyard, Esq; Tithe, 1050*l*; Glebe, 185 acres; R.'s Inc. 1281*l* and Ho; Pop. 476.) [1]

HILDYARD, Horatio Samuel, *Loftus Rectory, Redcar, Yorks.*—St. Peter's Coll. Cam. 23rd Sen. Opt. 5th in 1st cl. Cl. Trip. Latin Essay Prize, B.A. 1829, M.A. 1832; Deac. and Pr. 1831. R. of Loftus, Dio. York, 1842. (Patron, Ld Chan; Tithe, 463*l*; Glebe, 50 acres; R.'s Inc. 550*l* and Ho; Pop. 1103.) Rural Dean of Cleveland 1850. Late Fell. of St. Peter's Coll. Cam. [2]

HILDYARD, James, *Ingoldsby Rectory, near Grantham, Lincolnshire.*—Ch. Coll. Cam. Six Browne's Gold Medals, Chan.'s Medal, Battie's Univ. Sch., Two Members' Prizes, 2nd in 1st Cl. Trip. Sen. Opt. B.A. 1833, M.A. 1836, B.D. 1845; Deac. 1833 and Pr 1834 by Bp of Lin. R. of Ingoldsby, Dio. Lin. 1846. (Patron, Ch. Coll. Cam; Tithe, commuted at 550*l*; Glebe, 66 acres; R.'s Inc. 650*l* and Ho; Pop. 427.) Formerly Fell. and Tut. of Ch. Coll. Cam; Sen. Proctor; University Preacher; Preacher at Whitehall. Author, *The Menæchmei and Aulularia of Plautus, with Latin Notes and Copious Glossary*, 2nd ed. Parkers, 1846; *Five Sermons before the University, with a Plan for establishing a Voluntary Theological Examination*, Parkers, 1841, 5*s*; *The Obligation of the University* (a Commemoration Sermon), 1841, 1*s*; *The University System of Private Tuition Examined in a Moral, Intellectual, and Pecuniary point of View*, 1844, 1*s* 6*d*; *Mission to China*, 1843. 1*s*; *Further Consideration of the University System of Education*, 1845, 1*s* 6*d*; *Three Sermons on the Present Position of the Church*, Rivingtons, 1843; *Sermons, chiefly Practical, preached at Whitehall in* 1843–44, Parkers, 10*s* 6*d*; *Abridgment of the Sunday Morning Service, in a Letter to Bishop Tarton*, 2nd ed. 1856; *How is it to be Done?* 1856; *The People's Call for a Revision of the Liturgy, in a Letter to Lord Palmerston*, 1857, 1*s*; *Occasional Reflections on Men and Things*, 1861; *The Ingoldsby Letters, in Reply to the Bishops on the Revision of the Book of Common Prayer*, 2 vols. 3rd ed. Routledges, 12*s*; *Notes upon the Ecclesiastical Commission*, Ridgway, 1863, 1*s*. [3]

HILDYARD, Richard, *Lewcombe Rectory, Melbury, Osmond, Dorchester.*—Trin. Hall Cam. B.A. 1838, M.A. 1841; Deac. 1838 and Pr. 1839 by Abp of York. R. of East Chelborough *alias* Lewcombe, Dio. Salis. 1857. (Patroness, Miss C. F. Hildyard; Tithe, 180*l*; Glebe, 114 acres; R.'s Inc. 340*l* and Ho; Pop. 93.) Formerly C. and R. of Winestead, Yorks, 1838–49. [4]

HILDYARD, William, *Market-Deeping, Lincolnshire.*—Trin. Coll. Cam. B.A. 1817, M.A. 1820; Deac. 1819 by Bp of Nor. Pr. 1820 by Bp of G. and B. R. of Market-Deeping, Dio. Lin. 1830. (Patron, Ld Chan; Land in lieu of Tithe, 273 acres; R.'s Inc. 647*l* and Ho; Pop. 1337.) Late Fell. and Tut. of Trin. Hall, Cam. 1824–30. [5]

HILDYARD, William, *Beverley.*—Asst. P. C. of Beverley Minster, Dio. York, 1820. [6]

HILES, Robert, *Olveston, Bristol.*—St. John's Coll. Cam. B.A. 1859, M.A. 1863; Deac. 1861 and Pr. 1862 by Bp of Ely. C. of Olveston 1864. Formerly C. of Layham, Suffolk, 1861–63. [7]

HILEY, Richard William, *Thorparch Grange, Tadcaster.*—St. Mary Hall, Ox. 3rd cl. Lit. Hum. Exhib. B.A. 1852, M.A. 1853; Deac. 1853 and Pr. 1854 by Bp of Ches. V. of Wighill, near Tadcaster, Dio. York, 1863. (Patron, Andrew Montagu, Esq; V.'s Inc. 150*l*; Pop. 280.) Formerly for nine years 2nd Mast. in The College, Liverpool, and C. to the Ven. J. Jones, Archd. of Liverpool. Author, *Scripture Questions*, 1*s* 6*d*, Longman. [8]

HILEY, Simeon, *St. John's College, Cambridge.*—St. John's Coll. Cam. 11th Wrang. and B A. 1844, M.A. 1847, B.D. 1854; Deac. 1844, Pr. 1845. Fell. of St. John's Coll. Cam. [9]

HILEY, Walter, 7, *Rothesay Villas, Richmond, Surrey.*—Wad. Coll. Ox. 3rd cl. Lit. Hum. 2nd cl. Mod. B.A. 1857, M.A. 1862; Deac. 1858 and Pr. 1859 by Abp of York. Travelling Clerical Sec. to the Curates' Augmentation Fund. Formerly C. of Wighill, Yorks, 1858, St. James's, Cheltenham, 1861, St. Luke's, Cheltenham, 1862, Trinity, Upper Chelsea, 1865. [10]

HILL, Abraham, *Leicester.*—St. John's Coll. Cam. Prizeman, Wrang. and B.A. 1839; Deac. 1840, Pr. 1841. P. C. of St. George's, Leicester, Dio. Pet. 1863. (Patron, Preb. of Lin; P. C.'s Inc. 300*l*; Pop. 10,333.) Formerly Head Mast. of the Coll. Sch. Leicester. Author, *Greek Accidence*, 1854, 3*s*. [11]

HILL, Arthur, *Portland.*—Asst. Chap. of the Convict Establishment, Portland. [12]

HILL, Arthur, *Charfield Rectory, Wotton-under-edge, Glouc.*—Dub. A.B. 1851; called to the Bar 1826; Deac. 1829 by Bp of Glouc. Pr. 1830 by Bp of Chich. R. of Charfield, Dio. G. and B. 1853. (Patron, Sir J. Neeld, Bart; Tithe, 323*l*; Glebe, 40 acres; R.'s Inc. 395*l* and Ho; Pop. 629.) [13]

HILL, Benjamin, *Norton, Presteign, Radnor.*—V. of Norton, Dio. Herf. 1860. (Patron, R. G. Price, Esq; V.'s Inc. 150*l*; Pop. 313.) [14]

HILL, Charles, *Dalby Parsonage, Isle of Man.*—Lin. Coll. Ox. B.A. 1843, M.A. 1847; Deac. 1844, Pr. 1846. P. C. of St. James's, Dalby, Dio. S. and M. 1858. (Patron, Bp of S. and M; P. C.'s Inc. 60*l*.) Formerly C. of Thenford, Northants, 1844-46, Great Rollright, Oxon, 1846–47, Staverton, Northants, 1848–53. P. C. of Piddington, Oxon, 1853. Author, *Moral and Religious Poems*, 1 vol. [15]

HILL, Charles, *Culworth Rectory, near Banbury.*—Ch. Coll. Cam. B.A. 1845, M.A. 1848; Deac. 1846 and Pr. 1847 by Bp of Lich. R. and V. of Culworth, Northants, Dio. Pet. 1854. (Patron, William Wilson, Esq; Tithe—R. 509*l*, V. 167*l*; Glebe, 28 acres; R. and V.'s Inc. 732*l* and Ho; Pop. 652.) Formerly C. of Wolstanton, Staffs, 1846-48, Newington next Sittingbourne, Kent, 1848–52, Appledore, Kent, 1852–53, Minster, Isle of Sheppey, and Chap. to the Minster Union, 1853–54. [16]

HILL, Charles Grey, *Great Stanmore, Middlesex.*—C. of Great Stanmore. [17]

HILL, Copinger, *Buxhall Rectory, Stowmarket, Suffolk.*—Corpus Coll. Cam. 12th Wrang. and B.A. 1822, M.A. 1825; Deac. 1822 by Bp of Bristol, Pr. 1827 by Bp of Ely. R. of Buxhall, Dio. Nor. 1852. (Patron, the present R; Tithe, 680*l*; Glebe, 39 acres; R.'s Inc. 746*l* and Ho; Pop. 536.) Late Fell. of Corpus Coll. Cam 1823. [18]

HILL, Dennis, *Gressenhall Rectory, East Dereham, Norfolk.*—Ch. Coll. Cam. B.A. 1805; Deac. 1806 and Pr. 1807 by Bp. of Nor. R. of Gressenhall, Dio. Nor. 1807. (Patron, King's Coll. Cam; Tithe, 760*l* 3*s* 3*d*; Glebe, 50 acres; R.'s Inc. 780*l* and Ho; Pop. 991.) [19]

HILL, Edward, *Little Langford Rectory, Heytesbury.*—St. Edm. Hall, Ox. B.A. 1839, M.A. 1842; Deac. 1841 and Pr. 1842 by Bp of Ox. R. of Little Langford, Dio. Salis. 1863. (Patron, Earl of Pembroke; Tithe, 145*l*; Glebe, 9 acres; R.'s Inc. 150*l* and Ho; Pop. 80, Groveley 40.) Formerly C. of Britwell Salome 1841, Charlton in Donhead 1847–63. [20]

HILL, Edward, *Sheering Rectory, Harlow, Essex.*—Ch. Ch. Ox. B.A. 1831, M.A. 1833. R. of Sheering, Dio. Roch. 1849. (Patron, Ch. Ch. Ox; Tithe, 509*l*; Glebe, 16 acres; R.'s Inc. 536*l* and Ho; Pop 499.) [21]

HILL, Edward, *Ashurst Rectory, Steyning, Sussex.*—Magd. Coll. Ox. M.A. 1857. Deac. 1860 and Pr. 1862 by Bp of Wor. R. of Ashurst, Dio. Chich. 1865. (Patron, Magd. Coll. Ox; Glebe, 8 acres; R.'s Inc. 406*l* and Ho; Pop. 372.) [22]

HILL, Edward, *Great Woolston Rectory, Fenny Stratford, Bucks.*—Wad. Coll. Ox. 3rd cl. Lit. Hum. and B.A. 1846, M.A. 1851; Deac. 1847 and Pr. 1848 by Bp of Ox. R. of Great and Little Woolston, Dio. Ox. 1853. (Patron, Ld Chan; Tithe, 120*l*; Glebe, 1 acre; R.'s Inc. 280*l* and Ho; Pop. 296.) Formerly C. of Little Woolston 1850–54. [23]

HILL, Edward James, *Panfield Rectory, near Braintree, Essex.*—St. John's Coll. Cam. B.A. 1847, M.A. 1850; Deac. 1848 and Pr. 1849 by Bp of Roch. R. of

Panfield, Dio. Roch. 1852. (Patron, the present R; Tithe, 500*l*; Glebe, 7 acres; R.'s Inc. 500*l* and Ho; Pop. 308.) Rural Dean; Surrogate. [1]

HILL, Francis Thomas, *Terling Vicarage, Witham, Essex.*—Deac. 1847 and Pr. 1848 by Bp of Wor. V. of Terling, Dio. Roch. 1860. (Patron, Lord Rayleigh; Tithe, comm. 279*l*; Glebe, 11 acres; V.'s Inc. 310*l* and Ho; Pop. 902.) Formerly C. of Loxley, Warw. and Clifton; P. C. of Escot, Devon. Author, *Lectures on the Titles and Offices of the Holy Spirit*; *Lectures on the Evil Spirit*; occasional Sermons. [2]

HILL, George, *Sacombe Rectory, Ware, Herts.*—Dub. A.B. 1841, A.M. 1846; Deac. 1846, Pr. 1847. R. of Sacombe, Dio. Roch. 1852. (Patron, Abel Smith, Esq; Tithe, 337*l* 17*s* 6*d*; Glebe, 8 acres; R.'s Inc. 331*l* and Ho; Pop. 314.) [3]

HILL, George, *St. Winnow, Lostwithiel, Cornwall.*—St. Edmd. Hall, Ox. B.A. 1835, M.A. 1838; Deac. 1839 by Bp of Ex. Pr. 1840 by Bp of Lich. V. of St. Winnow with St. Nighton's C. Dio. Ex. 1864. (Patrons, D. and C. of Ex; Tithe, 300*l*; Glebe, 20 acres; V.'s Inc. 320*l* and Ho; Pop. 1115.) Formerly C. of Torquay 1846–64. [4]

HILL, George Benjamin, *Collingtree Rectory, near Northampton.*—Pemb. Coll. Ox. and St. Bees. R. of Collingtree, Dio. Pet. 1855. (Patron, Rev. G. B. Hill; R.'s Inc. 400*l* and Ho; Pop. 237.) [5]

HILL, George Frederick, *Acle, Norfolk.*—Univ. Coll. Dur; Deac. 1841, Pr. 1842. P. C. of Repps with Bastwick P. C. Norfolk, Dio. Nor. 1850. (Patrons, Governors of King Edward the Sixth's Grammar Sch. Norwich; Tithe—App. 18*l* 4*s* 6*d*, Imp. 400*l* and 33 acres of Glebe; P. C.'s Inc. 156*l*; Pop. 293.) [6]

HILL, Henry Thomas, *Felton Vicarage, Bromyard, Herefordshire.*—Corpus Coll. Cam. B.A. 1837, M.A. 1840; Deac. 1838 and Pr. 1839 by Bp of Herf. R. of Felton, Dio. Herf. 1851. (Patron, Thomas Hill, Esq; Tithe—Imp. 25*l* 18*s* 9*d*, V. 195*l*; Glebe, 9½ acres, and a farm of 37 acres; V.'s Inc. 255*l* and Ho; Pop. 149.) R. of Preston-Wynne, Dio. Herf. 1858. (Patron, Bp of Herf; V.'s Inc. 88*l*; Pop. 182.) Lect. of Bromyard; Rural Dean of Frome 1855. Formerly P. C. of Lye, Worcestershire, 1839–43; C. of Wolverley 1843–51. Author, Assize and other Sermons; *Thoughts on Churches and Churchyards* (a Tract), 3 eds. Bell and Daldy, 1856, 6*d*; *Sermon for the S.P.C.K. and S.P.G.* (Preached in Herf. Cathl), 1857, 3*d*; *Church Restoration: What is it? Whence is it?* Rivingtons, 1864. [7]

HILL, Herbert, *The King's School, Warwick.*—New Coll. Ox. B.A. 1832, M.A. 1837; Deac. 1837 and Pr. 1838 by Bp of Ox. Head Mast. of King's Sch. Warwick. Author, *Short Sermons on some Leading Principles of Christian Life*, Masters, 1854, 6*s*. [8]

HILL, Holden Donald, *The Parsonage, Kenilworth.*—Emman. Coll. Cam. B.A. 1858, M.A. 1861; Deac. 1858 and Pr. 1859 by Bp of Carl. P. C. of St. John's, Kenilworth, Dio. Wor. 1864. (Patrons, Trustees; P. C.'s Inc. 70*l* and Ho; Pop. 1100.) Formerly C. of St. John's, Keswick, 1858. [9]

HILL, Hopkins, *Ocle-Pitchard Vicarage, near Hereford.*—St. John's Coll. Cam. B.A. 1834; Deac. 1836 and Pr. 1837 by Bp of Llan. V. of Ocle-Pitchard, Dio. Herf. 1845. (Patron, Thomas Hill, Esq; Tithe, 190*l* 16*s*; Glebe, 6 acres; V.'s Inc. 206*l* and Ho; Pop. 299.) Formerly C. of Llangattock juxta Usk, and Mow Rock, Worc. [10]

HILL, Isaac, *Helperthorpe Vicarage, Duggleby, Yorks.*—St. John's Coll. Cam. B.A. 1847; Deac. 1847 and Pr. 1848 by Bp of Nor. V. of Helperthorpe with Luttons Ambo C. Dio. York, 1863. (Patrons, D. and C. of York; V.'s Inc. 250*l* and Ho; Pop. Helperthorpe 146, Luttons Ambo 432.) Formerly R. of Newbourne, Suffolk, 1855–63. [11]

HILL, James, 10, *Bedford-street, Bedford-square, London, W.C.*—Caius Coll. Cam. B.A. 1859; Deac. 1859 and Pr. 1860 by Bp of Lon. C. of St. George's, Bloomsbury, 1859. [12]

HILL, James, *Royal Hospital, Greenwich.*—Dub. A.B. 1834, A.M. 1841, B.D. 1853; Deac. 1836, Pr 1837. Head Mast. and Asst. Chap. in the Greenwich Hospital Schools. Formerly Local Inspector under the Church Education Society; Clerical Superintendent of the National Society's Training Institutions, Westminster, 1843. Author, *Educational Reports.* [13]

HILL, James, *Normanby Rectory, Pickering, Yorks.*—New Coll. Ox. B.A. 1836, M.A. 1840; Deac. 1838, Pr. 1839. R. of Normanby, Dio. York, 1848. (Patron, Rev. J. R. Hill; Tithe, 591*l*; Glebe, 10 acres; R.'s Inc. 601*l* and Ho; Pop. 234.) [14]

HILL, Joel Hawkins, *Emmanuel Church, Camberwell, Surrey, S.*—Literate; Deac. 1863 by Bp of St. D. Pr. 1864 by Bp of Win. C. of Emmanuel, Camberwell. Formerly C. of Kilvey, Glamorganshire. [15]

HILL, John, *Castle Morton, Upton-on-Severn, Worcestershire.*—C. of Castle Morton. [16]

HILL, John, *Ridgway Cottage, Sutton, Hereford.*—R. of Henllan-Amgoed with Eglwys-vair-Acherrig P. C. Dio. St. D. 1836. (Patrons, Landed Proprietors; Henllan-Amgoed, Tithe, 90*l*; Eglwys-vair-Acherrig, Tithe—Imp. 35*l*, P. C. 70*l*; R.'s Inc. 160*l*; Pop. 445.) [17]

HILL, John, *The Citadel, Hawkstone, Shrewsbury.*—Brasen. Coll. Ox. B.A. 1825, M.A. 1828; Deac. 1825, Pr. 1826. C. of Weston-under-Red Castle 1825; R. of Great Bolas, Salop, Dio. Lich. 1831. (Patron, Viscount Hill; Tithe, 318*l*; Glebe, 49 acres; R.'s Inc. 386*l*; Pop. 278.) [18]

HILL, John Edward, *Welshpool, Montgomeryshire.*—Ch. Ch. Ox. B.A. 1845, M.A. 1850; Deac. 1848 and Pr. 1849 by Bp of Ex. V. of Welsh Pool with Christ Church P. C. Dio. St. A. 1865. (Patron, Bp of St. Asaph; V.'s Inc. 275*l* and Ho; Pop. 4794.) Formerly C. of Ashburton 1848–50, Welsh Pool 1850–65. [19]

HILL, John George Henry, *Dieppe.*—Emman. Coll. Cam. B.A. 1850, M.A. 1856; Deac. 1849 and Pr. 1850 by Bp of Chich. Brother of St. Katherine's Hospital, Regent's Park, Lond. 1856; British Consular Chap. at Dieppe. Author, *Die Waldenser*; *Jesus and Jesuit.* [20]

HILL, John Harwood, *Cranoe Rectory, Market Harborough, Leicestershire.*—St. Peter's Coll. Cam. B.A. 1834; Deac. 1834 by Bp of Carl. Pr. 1835 by Bp of Pet. R. of Cranoe, Dio. Pet. 1837. (Patron, Earl of Cardigan; Glebe, 142 acres; R.'s Inc. 312*l* and Ho; Pop. 107.) V. of Welham, near Market Harborough, Dio. Pet. 1841. (Patron, Ld Chan; Tithe—Imp. 30*l*, V. 105*l*; Glebe, 44 acres; V.'s Inc. 240*l*; Pop. 65.) Surrogate 1852. Formerly C. of Glaston 1834, Corby 1835. Author, *A Funeral Sermon* (on the Death of Robert, 6th Earl of Cardigan), 1837; *The Chronicles of the Christian Ages*, 2 vols. Uppingham, 1842; *History of Langton and a Portion of the Gartree Hundred of Leicestershire*, illustrated with Etchings by the Author, imp. 4to. 1867. [21]

HILL, John Henry.—British Chap. at Athens. [22]

HILL, John Oakley, *Bladington, near Chipping Norton.*—Ch. Ch. Ox. B.A. 1825, M.A. 1827; Deac. 1826 by Bp of Herf. Pr. 1827 by Bp of Ox. V. of Bladington, Dio. G. and B. 1843. (Patrons, D. and C. of Ch. Ch. Ox; Glebe, 4 acres; V.'s Inc. 125*l*; Pop. 396.) Chap. to the Stow-on-the-Wold Union 1852. [23]

HILL, John Wilbraham, *Waverton Rectory, Chester.*—Brasen. Coll. Ox. B.A. 1829, M.A. 1834; Deac. 1829 and Pr. 1831 by Bp of Lich. P. C. of Waverton, Dio. Ches. 1844. (Patrons, Eccles. Commis; Tithe—App. 441*l* 10*s*; Glebe, 20 acres; P. C.'s Inc. 110*l* and Ho; Pop. 736.) Formerly C. of Stanton-upon-Hine Heath and of Lee Brockhurst, Salop, 1829, Broughton, Flintshire, 1832. Author, *On the Disturbed State of the Country, and Apprehensions of the Pestilence spreading over Europe* (a Sermon), Shrewsbury, 1831, 6*d*; *Assize Sermon*, 1833, 1*s*; *Funeral Sermon on the Death of William Sheen*, 1838, 1*s*; Editor of *Psalms and Hymns for the Use of Churches*, 4th ed. 1853, 1*s*; and various articles in Church of England Magazines. [24]

HILL, Joseph, *Monnington-on-Wye, Herefordshire.*—Wor. Coll. Ox. B.A. 1857; Deac. 1857 and Pr. 1858 by Bp of Lin. R. of Monnington-on-Wye, Dio. Herf. 1864. (Patron, Sir V. Cornewall, Bart; Tithe, 228*l*; Glebe, 33 acres and Ho; Pop. 90.) Formerly C. of Edwinstowe, Ollerton, Old Weston, Kimbolton. [1]

HILL, Melsup, *Shelsley Rectory, near Worcester.*—Jesus Coll. Cam. Sen. Opt. 3rd cl. Lit. Hum. and B.A. 1840; Deac. 1841 and Pr. 1842 by Bp of Dur. R. of Shelsley-Beauchamp, Dio. Wor. 1857. (Patron, Earl of Dudley; Tithe, 482*l* 17*s*; Glebe, 12 acres; R.'s Inc. 500*l* and Ho; Pop. 556.) Formerly P. C. of St. John's, Kidderminster, 1845–57. [2]

HILL, Nicholas Frank, *Burmington, Shipston-on-Stour.*—C. of Burmington. [3]

HILL, Pascoe Grenfell, 34, *Montague-place, Russell-square.*—Dub. A.B. 1834; Deac. 1835 and Pr. 1836 by Bp of Ex. R. of St. Edmund's the King with St. Nicholas Acons R. City and Dio. Lon. 1863. (Patrons, Crown and Abp of Cant; R.'s Inc. 306*l* and Ho; Pop. 501.) Chap. to R.N. Formerly Chap. to the Westminster Hospital, Broad Sanctuary; Morning Reader at Westminster Abbey. Author, *Fifty Days on Board a Slave Vessel*, 3*s* 6*d*; *Visit to Cairo*, S.P.C.K; *Journey through Palestine*; *Coasts of South Africa.* [4]

HILL, Reginald Hay, *Luddenham, Kent.*—Trin. Hall, Cam. LL.B. 1864; Deac. 1865, Pr. 1866. C. of Luddenham, near Faversham. Formerly C. of Trinity, Maidstone, 1865–66. [5]

HILL, Reginald Pyndar, *Bromsberrow Rectory, near Ledbury.*—Emman. Coll. Cam. B.A. 1843, M.A. 1846. R. of Bromsberrow, Dio. G. and B. 1856. (Patron, Earl Beauchamp; Tithe, 362*l*; Glebe, 55 acres; R.'s Inc. 444*l* and Ho; Pop. 305.) [6]

HILL, Richard, *Timsbury Rectory, near Bath.*—Ball. Coll. Ox. B.A. 1838, M.A. 1841; Deac. 1839, Pr. 1840. R. of Timsbury, Dio. B. and W. 1841. (Patron, Ball. Coll. Ox; Tithe, 300*l*; Glebe, 64¾ acres; R.'s Inc. 480*l* and Ho; Pop. 1551.) Late Blundell Fell. Ball. Coll. Ox. [7]

HILL, Richard, *Royton, Oldham.*—Corpus Coll. Cam. B.A. 1839; Deac. 1839 and Pr. 1840 by Bp of Lich. P. C. of Royton, Dio. Man. 1845. (Patron, R. of Prestwich; Tithe—App. 50*l*; Glebe, 50 acres; P. C.'s Inc. 150*l*; Pop. 7493.) Surrogate. [8]

HILL, Richard Humphry, *Oxford.*—Magd. Coll Ox. 2nd cl. Lit. Hum. and B.A. 1846, M.A. 1849, B.C.L. 1852, D.C.L. 1854; Deac. 1849 by Bp of Ox. Pr. 1856 by Bp of Ban. Head Mast. of Magd. Coll. Sch. Ox; Precentor and Hon. Canon of Bangor 1854. Formerly Head Mast. of Beaumaris Gr. Sch. Anglesey, 1849–64. [9]

HILL, Richard Humphry, *Britford, Salisbury.*—Magd. Coll. Ox. D.C.L. 1846. V. of Britford, Dio. Salis. 1849. (Patrons, D. and C. of Salis; V.'s Inc. 300*l*; Pop. 826.) [10]

HILL, Rowland, *Mansel Lacy House, near Hereford.*—Wor Coll. Ox. B.A. 1840; Deac. 1842 and Pr. 1843 by Bp of Herf. V. of Mansel Lacy, Dio. Herf. 1853. (Patron, Sir R. Price, Bart; Tithe—Imp. 269*l* 3*s* 8*d*, V. 91*l* 15*s* 9*d*; Glebe, 3½ acres; V.'s Inc. 162*l*; Pop. 331.) P. C. of Wormsley, Dio. Herf. 1854. (Patron, Sir. W. B. Broughton, Bart; Tithe—Imp. 19*s* 9*d*; Glebe, 4 acres; P. C.'s Inc. 60*l*; Pop. 121.) [11]

HILL, Rowley, 19, *Connaught-square, W.* and *National Club, Whitehall, London, S.W.*—Trin. Coll. Cam. B.A. 1859, M.A. 1863; Deac. 1860 and Pr. 1861 by Abp of Cant. P. C. of St. Luke's, Marylebone (new district), Dio. Lon. 1864. (Patron, R. of St. Mary's, Marylebone; P. C.'s Inc. 400*l*; Pop. 10,000.) Formerly C. of Ch. Ch. Dover and St. Mary's, Marylebone, Lond. Author, *Sundry Lessons on the Collects and Gospels*, Nisbet; etc. [12]

HILL, Samuel Paris, *Bulmer, New Malton, Yorks.*—Univ. Coll. Dur. B.A. 1854; Deac. 1854 and Pr. 1855 by Bp of Dur. C. of Wales, near Rotherham. Formerly C. of Bulmer and Whenby. [13]

HILL, The Venerable Thomas, *Hasland Hall, Chesterfield.*—Trin. Coll. Cam. B.A. 1810. M.A. 1813, B.D. 1822; Deac. 1811 and Pr. 1812 by Bp of Lin. Archd. of Derby 1847. (Value, 200*l*.) Can. Res. with the Prebendal Stalls of Offley and Flixton annexed, in Lich. Cathl. 1851. (Value, 500*l* and Res.) P. C. of Hasland, Dio. Lich. 1851. (Patron, V. of Chesterfield; P. C.'s Inc. 50*l*; Pop. 1107.) [14]

HILL, Thomas Barton.—Wad. Coll. Ox. B.A. 1851, Deac. 1851 by Bp of Ox. Pr. 1854 by Bp of Ches. C. of St. George's-in the-East, Lond. Formerly 2nd Mast. of Godolphin Gr. Sch. 1857. [15]

HILL, Thomas Henry Noel, *Berrington, Shrewsbury.*—St. John's Coll. Cam. B.A. 1830; Deac. 1831, Pr. 1832. R. of Berrington and Sutton R. Dio. Lich. 1846. (Patron, Lord Berwick; Tithe—Imp. 73*l* 13*s*, R. 520*l*; Glebe, 31¼ acres; R.'s Inc. 556*l* and Ho; Pop. Berrington 772, Sutton 75.) [16]

HILL, Thomas Leonard, *Walcot, Bath.*—St. John's Coll. Cam. 2nd Jun. Opt. and B.A. 1830, M.A. 1833; Deac. 1834, Pr. 1835. Min. of Portland Chapel, Walcot. Late Lect. of Kingsbridge, Devon, and Chap. to the Kingsbridge Union. [17]

HILL, Thomas Smythe, *The Infirmary, Salisbury.*—Magd. Coll. Ox. B.C.L. 1849, M.A. 1865; Deac. 1847, Pr. 1849. Chap. of the Infirmary, Salisbury, 1853. Formerly C. of Coggeshall, Essex, 1847, Holy Trinity, Dorchester. [18]

HILL, William, *Peterborough.*—V. of Peterborough, Dio. Pet. 1865. (Patron, Bp of Pet; V.'s Inc. 300*l* and Ho; Pop. 3170.) Hon. Can. of Pet. 1865. [19]

HILL, William Alfred, *Maidstone.*—Wor. Coll. Ox. M.A. P. C. of St. Peter's, Maidstone, Dio. Cant. 1857. (Patron, the present P. C; P. C.'s Inc. 200*l*; Pop. 3610.) [20]

HILL, William Henry, *St. Andrew's Lodge, Birmingham.*—Trin. Coll. Cam. M.A. 1840, *ad eund.* Ox. 1843; Deac. 1837 and Pr. 1838 by Bp of G. and B. P. C. of St. Andrew's, Bordesley, Dio. Wor. 1850. (Patrons, Bp of Wor. and five Trustees alt; P. C.'s Inc. 320*l*; Pop. 8000.) Surrogate. Formerly P. C. of Ironbridge, Salop. Author, *Twenty Reasons for not being a Romanist*, and various Sermons and Tracts. [21]

HILLIARD, John Ashby Stafford, *Little Wittenham, Abingdon.*—St. John's Coll. Ox. B.A. 1852; Deac. 1854 and Pr. 1855 by Bp of Pet. R of Little Wittenham, Dio. Ox. 1861. (Patron, W. E. Hilliard, Esq; Tithe, 370*l* 18*s* 3*d*; R.'s Inc. 404*l* and Ho; Pop. 134.) Formerly C. of Preston, Rutland, 1854, South Stoke, Oxon, 1857–61. [22]

HILLIARD, John Crosier, *Cowley Rectory, Uxbridge.*—St. John's Coll. Ox. B.A. 1843, M.A. 1846; Deac. 1844 and Pr. 1845 by Bp of B. and W. R. of Cowley, Dio. Lon. 1851. (Patron, W. E. Hilliard, Esq; Tithe, 46*l*; Glebe, 40 acres; R.'s Inc. 135*l* and Ho; Pop. 311.) [23]

HILLIARD, Joseph Stephen, *Christ Church Parsonage, Ealing, Middlesex, W.*—St. John's Coll. Ox. B A. 1848, M.A. 1852; Deac. 1850 and Pr. 1851. P. C. of Ch. Ch. Ealing, Dio. Lon. 1859. (Patron, Bp of Lon; P. C.'s Inc. 350*l* and Ho; Pop. 5000.) Formerly C. of Boughton Malherbe, Kent. [24]

HILLIER, Edward John, *Cardington Vicarage, near Bedford.*—Trin. Coll. Cam. 4th Wrang. 1st Tyrwhitt's Heb. Scho. B.A. 1847, M.A. 1850; Deac. 1850 and Pr. 1852 by Bp of Ely. V. of Cardington, Dio. Ely, 1856. (Patron, Trin. Coll. Cam; Tithe—Imp. 1351*l* 10*s* and 5 acres of Glebe, V. 250*l* 10*s* and 22 acres of Glebe; V.'s Inc. 255*l* and Ho; Pop. 1419.) Formerly 2nd Mast. and Math. Tut. of King Edw. the Sixth's Sch. Bury St. Edmunds, 1851–56; Fell. of Trin. Coll. Cam; Examiner for the Math. Trip. 1856. [25]

HILLIS, William, 322, *Upper Parliament-street, Liverpool.*—St. Aidan's; Deac. 1863 and Pr. 1864 by Bp of Ches. C. of St. Clement's, Toxteth Park, Liverpool, 1866. Formerly C. of Trinity, Birkenhead, 1863–65, Hexham, Northumberland, 1865–66. [26]

HILLMAN, Charles, 1, *Argyll-street, Regent-street, London, W.*—Clare Coll. Cam. B.A. 1844, M.A. 1847; Deac. 1846 and Pr. 1847 by Bp of Nor. Formerly C. of the Chapel of Ease, Islington, Lond. [27]

HILLS, George William, 6, *Wellington-street, Islington, N.*—St. Bees; Deac. 1858, Pr. 1859. C. of St. Mary's, Islington, Lond. 1864. Formerly C. of Hopton by Lowestoft, 1858, St. Paul's, Clapham, 1860, Tooting, Graveney, 1860, Mortlake 1863. [1]

HILLS, Thomas, *Clown Rectory, Chesterfield.*—V. of Elmton, Dio. Lich. 1863. (Patron, Duke of Portland; Glebe, 6 acres; V.'s Inc. 120*l*; Pop. 430.) C. of Clown 1865. Formerly C. of Whittington and Brampton, Derbyshire, Knoyle, Wilts. [2]

HILLS, Thomas Charles, *Alma-villas, Uttoxeter-road, Derby.*—St. Bees; Deac. 1862 and Pr. 1863 by Bp of Lich. Sec. for North of England and Scotland to the Patagonian or South American Missionary Society. Formerly C. of St. Werburgh's, Derby, 1862–64. [3]

HILLS, William Jeffreys, *Long Lane, Derby.*—Trin. Coll. Ox. 1848, Jesus Coll. Ox. 1849, 2nd cl. Lit. Hum. and B.A. 1852, M.A. 1853; Deac. 1853 and Pr. 1854 by Bp of G. and B. P. C. of Long Lane, Dio. Lich. 1862. (Patron, V. of Sutton-on-the-Hill.) Formerly C. of Westbury-Leigh, near Westbury, Wilts. [4]

HILLYARD, E. A., *Norwich.*—R. of St. Lawrence's, City and Dio. Nor. 1861. (Patron, Ld. Chan; R.'s Inc. 82*l*; Pop. 877.) Formerly Chap. of the Norwich Union 1861–64. [5]

HILLYARD, Temple, *Southam Rectory, Rugby,* and *The Residentiary House, Abbey-square, Chester.*—Brasen. Coll. Ox. B.A. 1829, M.A. 1832; Deac. 1834 and Pr. 1836 by Bp of Lich. R. of Southam, Dio. Wor. 1841. (Patron, the Crown; Glebe, 338 acres; R.'s Inc. 600*l* and Ho; Pop. 1674.) Can. Res. of Ches. Cathl. 1848. (Value, 500*l* and Res.) Formerly C. of Marston upon-Dove 1834–38; V. of Wormleighton, Warwickshire, 1838–41. [6]

HILLYER, Charles, *Somerleyton, Lowestoft, Suffolk.*—Ch. Miss. Coll; Deac. 1850 by Bp of Lon. Pr. 1851 by Bp of Rupert's Land. R. of Ashby, Suffolk, Dio. Nor. 1859. (Patron, Charles Lucas, Esq; Tithe, 204*l*; Glebe, 23a. 3r. 29p; R.'s Inc. 236*l* 10*s*; Pop. 70.) Formerly Missionary to Rupert's Land; Exam. Chap. to Bp of Rupert's Land. [7]

HILLYER, George William, *Coldharbour Parsonage, Dorking.*—St. Bees; Deac. 1844 and Pr. 1846 by Bp of Nor. P. C. of Ch. Ch. Coldharbour, Dio. Win. 1853. (Patron, Trustees; P. C.'s Inc. 150*l* and Ho; Pop. 531.) [8]

HILTON, Alfred G., *Hampnett Rectory, near Northleach.*—Ch. Coll. Cam. B.A. 1853, M.A. 1856; Deac. 1853 and Pr. 1854 by Bp of G. and B. C. (sole charge) of Hampnett with Stowell, Glouc. 1866. Formerly C. of St. Mark's, Lower Easton, 1853, Kempsford, Glouc. 1854–66. [9]

HILTON, Arthur Denne, *St. John's Parsonage, Hillingdon, Uxbridge.*—Wad. Coll. Ox. B.A. 1846, M.A. 1849; Deac. 1847 and Pr. 1848 by Bp of Lon. P. C. of St. John's, Hillingdon, Dio. Lon. 1851. (Patron, Bp of Lon; P. C.'s Inc. 110*l* and Ho; Pop. 1299.) Formerly C. of Uxbridge 1847–49, Banbury 1849–51. Author, *The Pastor Visiting from House to House,* 1851, 2*s*; *Aid to Parochial Visiting, a Manual for keeping a Record concerning each Parishioner,* 3rd ed. 1860, Mozley, cloth 1*s*, roan 1*s* 6*d*. [10]

HILTON, Clarence Jones, *Badlesmere Rectory, Feversham, Kent.*—Jesus Coll. Cam. B.A. 1836, M.A. 1839; Deac. 1839, Pr. 1840. R. of Badlesmere with Leaveland, Dio. Cant. 1851. (Patron, Lord Sondes; Tithe, 400*l*; Glebe, 13 acres; R.'s Inc. 413*l* and Ho; Pop. Badlesmere 133, Leaveland 94.) [11]

HILTON, Henry, *Milstead Rectory, Sittingbourne, Kent.*—Wor. Coll. Ox. B.A. 1833, M.A. 1836. R. of Milstead, Dio. Cant. 1843. (Patron, the present R; Tithe, 275*l* 10*s* 5*d*; R.'s Inc. 285*l* and Ho; Pop. 245.) [12]

HILTON, Henry Denne, *Orlingbury, near Wellingborough, Northants.*—St. John's Coll. Ox. B.A. 1845, M.A. 1847; Deac. and Pr. 1845. R. of Orlingbury, Dio. Pet. 1854. (Patron, the present R; Tithe, 3*l* 5*s*; Glebe, 280 acres; R.'s Inc. 400*l* and Ho; Pop. 307.) Formerly Chap. to Bp of Moray and Ross, and Incumb. of Holy Trinity, Elgin. [13]

HILTON, Joseph, *Endellion, Wadebridge, Cornwall.*—C. of Endellion. [14]

HIME, Maurice W., *Jamaica.*—Late C. of St. Mary's, Cardiff. [15]

HINCHLIFFE, Edward, *Mucklestone Rectory, near Market Drayton.*—Ch. Coll. Ox. B.A. 1822, M.A. 1826; Deac. 1823, Pr. 1825. R. of Mucklestone, Dio. Lich. 1850. (Patrons, Trustees of Lord Crewe; Tithe, 1036*l*; Glebe, 18 acres; R.'s Inc. 1054*l* and Ho; Pop. 771.) [16]

HINCHLIFFE, E. H., *Gotham, Notts.*—C. of Gotham and Ratcliffe-on-Soar. [17]

HINCKESMAN, Robert, *Ogbourne St. George, Marlborough, Wilts.*—Queens' Coll. Cam. B.A. 1855, M.A. 1858. C. in sole charge of Ogbourne St. George, Wilts. • [18]

HINCKLEY, John, *Sheriff Hales, Newport, Salop.*—St. Mary Hall, Ox. B.A. 1818, M.A. 1820; Deac. 1819 by Bp of Lich. Pr. 1820 by Bp of Ches. P. C. of King's Bromley, Staffs, Dio. Lich. 1829. (Patron, Can. of Alrewas and Weeford in Lich. Cathl; Tithe—Ecclesiastical Commissioners, 322*l* 17*s* 6*d*, Imp. 7*l*, P. C. 189*l* 14*s*; Glebe, 11 acres; P. C.'s Inc. 224*l*; Pop. 638.) V. of Sheriff Hales with Woodcote C. Dio. Lich. 1832. (Patron, Duke of Sutherland; Sheriff Hales. Tithe—Imp. 800*l* 7*s* 6*d*, V. 361*l*; Glebe, 13 acres; Woodcote, Tithe, 325*l* 12*s*; V.'s Inc. 700*l*; Pop. Sheriff Hales 16, Woodcote 150.) [19]

HIND, Charles, *Vernon House, Bolton-le-Moors,*—Dub. A.B. 1850, A.M. 1860; Deac. 1850 and Pr. 1851 by Bp of Win. P. C. of St. Paul's, Bolton-le-Moors, Dio. Man. 1866. (Patrons, Five Trustees; P. C.'s Inc. 150*l*; Pop. 6120.) Formerly C. of Rotherhithe 1850, Stapenhill, Derbyshire, 1856, Bolton-le-Moors 1863. [20]

HIND, J. Smithard, *Cramlington, Northumberland.*—P. C. of Cramlington, Dio. Dur. 1860. (Patron, Sir M. W. Ridley; P. C.'s Inc. 100*l*; Pop. 2430.) [21]

HIND, Robert.—Dur. Licen. Theol. 1851. Chap. of H.M.S. "Cambridge." [22]

HIND, William Marsden, *Pinner, Middlesex.*—Dub. A.B. 1839, A.M. 1842; Deac. 1839 and Pr. 1841 by Bp of Down and Connor. P. C. of Pinner, Dio. Lon. 1861. (Patron, V. of Harrow; Glebe, 26½ acres; P. C.'s Inc. 88*l* and Ho; Pop. 2100.) Formerly C. of Derriagby 1839–44, Pulverbach 1845–48, Stapenhill 1849–55, Lock Chapel, Lond. 1855–58, Harrow 1858–61. [23]

HINDE, Benjamin, *Featherston, Yorkshire.*—Ch. Ch. Ox. B.A. 1857; Deac. 1858 by Abp of York. C. of Featherston. Formerly C. of Cantley. [24]

HINDE, John Fitz-Richard, *Dalby Parva, Melton Mowbray.*—St. John's Coll. Cam. B.A. 1844; Deac. 1845, Pr. 1846. V. of Dalby Parva, Dio. Pet. 1861. (Patron, E. B. Hartopp, Esq; Tithe, 222*l*; Glebe, 57 acres; V.'s Inc. 308*l* and Ho; Pop. 183.) [25]

HINDE, Thomas, *Featherston Vicarage, Pontefract.*—Ch. Ch. Ox. 2nd cl. Lit. Hum. 1808, B.A. 1809, M.A. 1812; Deac. 1812 by Bp of Lin. Pr. 1814 by Bp of Ox. V. of Featherston, Dio. York, 1824. (Patron, Ch. Ch. Ox; Tithe—App. 849*l* 1*s*, V. 199*l* 6*s*; V.'s Inc. 256*l* and Ho; Pop. 2406.) [26]

HINDE, Thomas Bryer, *Bradfield, near Reading.*—Trin. Coll. Cam. B.A. 1863, M.A. 1867; Deac. 1864 and Pr. 1865 by Bp of Rip. C. of Bradfield. Formerly C. of Kildwick, Leeds. [27]

HINDE, William Henry Fitz-Simon, *Flamstead, near Dunstable.*—Univ. Coll. Ox. B.A. 1847, M.A. 1850; Deac. 1848, Pr. 1849. P. C. of Flamstead, Dio. Roch. 1858. (Patron, Univ. Coll. Ox; P. C.'s Inc. 130*l*; Pop. 1919.) Formerly C. of Kingsey, Bucks. [28]

HINDLE, Joseph, *Higham, Rochester.*—St. John's Coll. Cam. B.A. 1818, M.A. 1821, B.D. 1828; Deac. 1821, Pr. 1822. V. of Higham, Dio. Roch. 1829. (Patron, St. John's Coll. Cam; Tithe—Imp. 750*l*, V. 539*l* 9*s*; Glebe, ½ acre; V.'s Inc. 550*l*; Pop. 1064.) Late Fell. of St. John's Coll. Cam. [29]

HINDLEY, Hugh Johnson, *St. George's Parsonage, Everton, Liverpool.*—P. C. of St. George's,

Everton, Dio. Ches. 1855. (Patrons, Trustees; P. C.'s Inc. 350*l* and Ho; Pop. 8550.) [1]

HINDLEY, Joseph, *Cockermouth.*—C. of Cockermouth. [2]

HINDS, John Thomas, *Pulham Rectory, Sherborne, Dorset.*—Trin. Coll. Cam. B.A. 1825, M.A. 1832; Deac. 1828, Pr. 1829. R. of Pulham, Dio. Salis. 1832. (Patron, Rev. T. F. M. Halsey; Tithe, 418*l* 15*s*; Glebe, 54½ acres; R.'s Inc. 499*l* and Ho; Pop. 302.) [3]

HINDS, The Right Rev. Samuel, 40, *Clarendon-road, Notting-hill, London, W.*—Queen's Coll. Ox. 2nd cl. Lit. Hum. and B.A. 1815, Latin Essay and M.A. 1818, B.D. and D.D. 1831; Deac. 1818 and Pr. 1819 by Bp of Lon. Formerly Missionary to the Negroes of Barbados; Prin. of Codrington Coll. Barbados; Vice-Prin. of St. Alban Hall, Ox. 1827; V. of Yardley, Herts, 1834; a Rural Dean of the Dio. of Lin; Preb. of Castleknock in St. Patrick's Cathl. Dublin; Incumb. of the united Parishes of Castleknock, Clonsilla, and Mulhuddert, Dublin; Exam. Chap. to the Abp of Dublin; First Chap. to the Lords-Lieutenant of Ireland (the Earls of Bessborough and Clarendon); Dean of Carlisle 1848; Bp of Norwich 1849; resigned the see 1857. Author, *Introduction to Logic*, from Dr. Whately's *Elements of Logic*, 1827; *The History of the Rise and Progress of Christianity* (being the opening Chapter of the Article *Ecclesiastical History* in the *Encyclopædia Metropolitana*), 2 vols. 3 eds. 1828–46; *The Catechist's Manual and Family Lecturer*, 1829; *The Three Temples of the One True God contrasted*, 1830; *An Inquiry into the Proofs, Nature and Extent of Inspiration, and into the Authority of Scripture*, 1831; *Sonnets and other Short Poems*, 1834; *A Visitation Sermon* (preached at Baldock, 1837), 1837; *The Latest Official Documents relating to New Zealand*, 1838; Dr. Hampden's Consecration *Sermon*, 1840; *Scripture and the Authorised Version*, 2 eds. 1845-53; Episcopal Charges, etc. [4]

HINE, George Henry, 1, *Gloucester-street, Pimlico, London, S.W.*—Sid. Coll. Cam. B.A. 1823, M.A. 1828; Deac. 1824, Pr. 1828. Chap. to the Westminster House of Correction 1834. [5]

HINE, Veasey Germain, *Abbots Kerswell, Newton Abbot.*—Trin. Coll. Cam. B.A. 1842; Deac. 1845 by Bp of Ex. Pr. 1855 by Bp of Wor. V. of Abbots Kerswell, Dio. Ex. 1865. (Patron, Ld Chan; Tithe, 204*l*; Glebe, 60 acres; V.'s Inc. 304*l* and Ho; Pop. 437.) Formerly C. of Brixham, Rugby and Christow. [6]

HINES, Roger, *East Hatley, Gamlingay, Cambs.*—Univ. Coll. Dur. 2nd cl. Math. et Phy. and B.A. 1848, M.A. 1851; Deac. 1851 and Pr. 1852 by Bp of Lin C. of East Hatley 1862. Formerly C. of Bawtry and Austerfield 1851–55 and 1857–60, North Searle 1856, Great Grimsby 1860-61; 2nd Mast. St. Mary's Coll. Windermere, 1855. [7]

HINGESTON, Francis Charles, *Ringmore Rectory, Ivybridge, Devon.*—Ex. Coll. Ox. Double Hon. 4th cl. Lit. Hum. and Math. 1855, B.A. 1855, M.A. 1858; Deac. 1856 and Pr. 1859 by Bp of Ox. R. of Ringmore with Okenbury Chap. Dio. Ex. 1860. (Patron, the present R; Tithe, Ringmore, 229*l*, Okenbury, 6*l*; Glebe, 101 acres; R.'s Inc. 400*l* and Ho; Pop. 280.) Dom. Chap. to the Baroness Le Despencer; Diocesan Inspector of Schools, Woodleigh Deanery. Formerly C. of Holywell, Oxford, 1856–58; P. C. of Hampton Gay, Oxon, 1858–60. Author, *Specimens of Ancient Cornish Crosses, Fonts, &c.*, Cleaver, 1850; *The Poems of Francis Hingeston, edited by his Son*, Longmans; *The Chronicle of England by John Capgrave*, 1858; *The Illustrious Henrys by John Capgrave*, 1859; *Royal and Historical Letters during the Reign of Henry II.* 1860, these edited for the Lords of H.M. Treasury under the direction of the Master of the Rolls; also a translation of *The Illustrious Henrys of Capgrave*, Longmans, 1859; etc. [8]

HINGSTON, A. N., *Churchstow, Kingsbridge, Devon.*—V. of Churchstow with Kingsbridge, Dio. Ex. 1866. (Patron, Ld Chan; V.'s Inc. 200*l* and Ho; Pop. 2000.) [9]

HINGSTON, George W. D., *Farnborough, Kent.*—Dub. A.B. 1862; Philosophical Societies Prize, Divin. Compos. Prize, 1864; Deac. 1865 and Pr. 1866 by Abp of Cant. C. of Farnborough, near Bromley, 1867. Formerly C. (sole charge) of Cudham 1865–66. [10]

HINTON, George Stephen, *Clutton, near Bristol.*—Literate; Deac. 1864. C. of Clutton 1867. Formerly C. of St. Columb Major, Cornwall, 1864, Carnmenellis, Redruth, 1864. [11]

HINTON, Zebulon Wright, *Feckenham, Bromsgrove, Worcestershire.*—Dub. A.B. 1842; Deac. 1842 and Pr. 1843 by Bp of Meath. V. of Feckenham, Dio. Wor. 1855. (Patroness, Mrs. R. Hutchinson; Tithe, —Imp. 1039*l* 13*s* 4*d*, V. 277*l* 10*s*; Glebe, 10½ acres; V.'s Inc. 386*l* and Ho; Pop. 2709.) [12]

HINXMAN, Charles, *Barford St. Martin, Salisbury.*—Ball. Coll. Ox; Deac. 1846 and Pr. 1847 by Bp of Salis. R. of Barford St. Martin, Wilts, Dio. Salis. 1860. (Patron, All Souls Coll. Ox; Tithe, 560*l*; Glebe, 89 acres; R.'s Inc. 625*l* and Ho; Pop. 519.) Chap. to the Countess Dowager of Dunmore. Formerly P. C. of St. Andrew's, Dunmore, 1850–61. [13]

HINXMAN, John Newton, *Great Durnford Vicarage, Salisbury.*—Trin. Coll. Ox. B.A. 1841, M.A. 1844; Deac. 1843, Pr. 1844. V. of Durnford, Dio. Salis. 1849. (Patron, Bp of Salis; Tithe—App. 494*l* 10*s*, V. 105*l*; Glebe, 30 acres; V.'s Inc. 149*l* and Ho; Pop. 553.) [14]

HIPPISLEY, Robert William, *Quar Wood, near Stow-on-the-Wold, Glouc.*—Ex. Coll. Ox. B.A. 1841, M.A. 1844; Deac. 1842 and Pr. 1843 by Bp of G. and B. R. of Stow-on-the-Wold, Dio. G. and B. 1843. (Patron, the present R; R.'s Inc. 560*l* and Ho; Pop. 2250.) Formerly C. of Stowe St. Edwards 1842. [15]

HIRON, Samuel Franklin, *The Schoolhouse, Chipping Campden, Glouc.*—Dub. A.B. 1858, B.C.L. and D.C.L. 1863, D.C.L. *comitatis causâ*, Ox. 1864; Deac. 1859 by Bp of Wor. Pr. 1860 by Bp of Lon. Head Mast. of Chipping Campden, Gr. Sch. 1862; C. of Aston-sub-Edge, Glouc. Formerly Prin. of Jun. Department of Birmingham and Edgbaston Proprietary Sch. 1858–62; Asst. C. of St. Philip's, Birmingham, 1859–61. [16]

HIRSCH, David, 40, *Price-street, Birkenhead.*—Univ. of Berlin; Deac. 1846 and Pr. 1847 by Bp of Ches. Min. of the German Church, Liverpool. (Patrons, Proprietors.) [17]

HIRST, Thomas, *Holmesfield Parsonage, Chesterfield.*—Pemb. Coll. Cam. Sen. Opt. B.A. 1832; Deac. 1834 and Pr. 1335 by Bp of Lich. P. C. of Holmesfield Dio. Lich 1850. (Patron, Charles Cawton, Esq; Glebe, 80 acres; P. C.'s Inc. 97*l* and Ho; Pop. 527.) Formerly C. of Beighton 1834–36, Tickhill 1836–37, Childerditch 1837-41, Wirksworth 1841–44, Bakewell with Mastership of Gr. Sch. and Chap. of Parochial Union 1844–50. [18]

HIRST, Thomas, *The Precincts, Canterbury.*—Clare Coll. Cam. B.A. 1850, M.A. 1855; Deac. 1850 and Pr. 1851 by Bp of Rip. Min. Can. of Cant. Cathl. 1852. (Value, 227*l* and Ho.) R. of St. Martin's with St. Paul's, City and Dio. Cant. 1859. (Patrons, Abp and D. and C. of Cant. alt; Tithe—St. Martin's, 210*l*; Glebe, 1 acre; St. Paul's, Tithe—App. 77*l*, Imp. 441*l*, V. 19*l*; R.'s Inc. 320*l*; Pop. St. Martin's 199, St. Paul's 1653.) [19]

HIRST, W., *Cumberworth, Yorkshire.*—P. C. of Cumberworth, Dio. Rip. 1866. (Patron, W. B. Beaumont, Esq; P. C.'s Inc. 148*l*; Pop. 813.) [20]

HITCHCOCK, John, *Milverton, Warwickshire.*—C. of Milverton. [21]

HITCHCOCK, William Henry, *Brooking Parsonage, Totnes.*—Univ. Coll. Ox. B.A. 1855, M.A. 1858; Deac. 1855 and Pr. 1858 by Bp of G. and B. C. of Dartington (sole charge) 1864. Formerly C. of Flymbridge, Gloucestershire, 1855, Bremhill, Wilts, 1860. [22]

HITCHCOCK, William Maunder, *Whitburn Rectory, Sunderland, Durham.*—Wad. Coll. Ox. B.A. 1858; Deac. 1858 by Abp of Cant. Pr. 1859 by Bp of G. and B. R. of Whitburn, Dio. Dur. 1866. (Patron, Bp of Dur; Tithe, 860*l*; Glebe, 320*l*; R.'s Inc. 1180*l* and Ho; Pop. 1400.) Dom. Chap. to Bp of Dur. Formerly C. of St. James's, Cheltenham, 1858-60; P. C. of Bussage, Glouc. 1860–62, Shildon, Dur. 1862. [23]

HITCHES, J. H., *Willesden, London, W.*—C. of Willesden. [1]

HITCHINGS, H. J.—Chap. R.N. [2]

HITCHINS, Alfred.—St. Bees, 1852; Deac. 1852, Pr. 1853. Formerly C. of Swinton, near Manchester. [3]

HOARE, Arthur Malortie, *Fawley, Southampton.*—St. John's Coll. Cam. 1st cl. Cl. Trip. Hulsean Prize 1846, Bachelor's Essay 1846, B.A. 1844, M.A. 1847; Deac. 1848 and Pr. 1849 by Bp of Ely. R. of Fawley, Dio. Win. 1863. (Patron, Bp of Win; Tithe, 950*l*; Glebe, 17 acres; R.'s Inc. 990*l* and Ho; Pop. 1195.) Rural Dean 1864. Formerly Fell. and Cl. Lect. of St. John's Coll. Cam; R. of Calbourne, Isle of Wight, 1853–63. [4]

HOARE, Edward, *Tunbridge Wells.*—Trin. Coll. Cam. 5th Wrang. and B.A. 1834; Deac. and Pr. 1836. P. C. of Trinity, Tunbridge Wells, Dio Cant. 1853. (Patron, V. of Tunbridge; P. C.'s Inc. 700*l* and Ho; Pop. 5146.) [5]

HOARE, Edward Hatch, *Barkby Vicarage, near Leicester.*—Dub. A.B. 1824, and Trin. Coll. Cam. M.A. 1826. V. of Barkby, Dio. Pet. 1828. (Patron, W. A. Pochin, Esq; Tithe—App. 2*l*, V. 12*s* 8*d*; V.'s Inc. 250*l* and Ho; Pop. 791.) [6]

HOARE, Edward H., *Dunton, Winslow, Bucks.*—C. of Dunton. [7]

HOARE, Edward Thomas, *St. Helen's Green, Isle of Wight.*—Asst. C. of St. Helen's, Ryde. Formerly C. of Crewkerne, Somerset, 1858; C. in sole charge of Sevington St. Michael, with Dinnington, Somerset, 1859. [8]

HOARE, E. V., *Stibbard, Guist, Norfolk.*—C. of Guist. [9]

HOARE, Francis, *Newcastle-under-Lyme.*—Deac. 1857, Pr. 1858. C. in sole charge of Newcastle 1864. Formerly C. of Wigton 1857, Hanley 1859, Shelton 1861. [10]

HOARE, George Tooker, *Godstone Vicarage, Redhill, Surrey.*—St. John's Coll. Cam. B.A. 1843, M.A. 1847; Deac. 1844 and Pr. 1845 by Bp of Salis. V. of Godstone, Dio. Win. 1865. (Patron, the present V; Tithe, 540*l*; Glebe, 10 acres; V.'s Inc. 560*l* and Ho; Pop. 1058.) Formerly P. C. of Tandridge, Surrey, 1853–65. [11]

HOARE, James O'Bryen, *Earl's Colne, Halstead, Essex.*—C. of Earl's Colne. [12]

HOARE, James Raper, *Ladock, Truro.*—Wor. Coll. Ox. 4th cl. Lit. Hum. and B.A. 1833; Deac. 1835, Pr. 1836. C. of Ladock, Cornwall, 1864. Formerly C. of Weldon, Northants, 1835, Eynsford, Kent, 1839, Stanley St. Leonards, Glouc. 1854. [13]

HOARE, James Samuel, *Murston Rectory, Sittingbourn, Kent.*—St. John's Coll. Cam. 6th Wrang. and B.A. 1846, M.A. 1849; Deac. 1849, Pr. 1850. R. of Murston, Dio. Cant. 1866. (Patron, St. John's Coll. Cam; Tithe, comm. 620*l*; Glebe, 40 acres; R.'s Inc. 700*l* and Ho; Pop. 572.) Late Fell. of St. John's Coll. Cam; C. of Godstone, Surrey. Author, *Village Sermons*, Nisbet and Co. [14]

HOARE, Richard, *Woodside, near Leeds.*—St. Bees; Deac. 1857 and Pr. 1858 by Bp of Carl. P. C. of Woodside, Dio. Rip. 1865. (Patrons, Crown and Bp of Rip. alt; P. C.'s Inc. 150*l* and Ho; Pop. 2718.) Formerly C. of Beckermet, Cumberland, 1857; P. C. of Sarn, North Wales, 1860–65. [15]

HOARE, Walter Marsham, *Great Marlow.*—Ex. Coll. Ox. B.A. 1865, M.A. 1866; Deac. 1864 and Pr. 1865 by Bp of Ox. Asst. C. of Great Marlow 1864. [16]

HOARE, William Henry, *Oakfield, Crawley, Sussex.*—St. John's Coll. Cam. Fell. of, 1833; 2nd Chan's Medallist and B.A. 1831, M.A. 1834; Deac. and Pr. by Bp of Win. Sec. to Bp of Newcastle, New South Wales. Formerly C. of All Saints', Southampton, 1841. Author *The Harmony of the Apocalypse with other Prophecies of Holy Scripture*, 1848; *Outlines of Ecclesiastical History before the Reformation*, 1852, 2 eds; *Three Letters to Sir George Grey on the Secular Education Bill of W. J. Fox, Esq., M.P. for Oldham*, 1*s*, 1850, 2nd ed. 1852; *The Veracity of the Book of Genesis*, 1*s*, Longmans, 1860; *Letter to Bishop Colenso on the Pentateuch Critically Examined*, Rivingtons, 1863, 4 eds; *Age and Authorship of the Pentateuch*, Rivingtons, 1863, 2 eds. [17]

HOARE, William Worth, *St. Paul's Parsonage, Stalybridge.*—Deac. and Pr. 1835. P. C. of St. Paul's, Staley, Dio. Ches. 1839. (Patrons, Trustees; P. C.'s Inc. 200*l* and Ho; Pop. 3919.) [18]

HOBART, The Hon. William Arthur, *Conisholme Rectory, Louth, Lincolnshire.*—Theol. Coll. Lichfield; Deac. 1861 and Pr. 1862 by Bp of Roch. R. of Conisholme, Dio. Lin. 1863. (Patron, Earl de Grey and Ripon; Tithe, 180*l* 2*s* 6*d*; Glebe, 74 acres; R.'s Inc. 295*l* and Ho; Pop. 167.) Formerly C. of Theydon-Garnon, Essex, 1861–63. [19]

HOBBINS, Frederic Charles Toole, *Butley Priory, Wickham Market.*—King's Coll. Lond. Theol. Assoc. 1855; Deac. 1855 and Pr. 1856 by Bp of Nor. P. C. of Butley with Capel St. Andrew, Dio. Nor. 1865. (Patron, Lord Rendlesham; P. C.'s Inc. 140*l*; Pop. Butley 375, Capel 231.) Formerly C of Butley, St. Bartholomew's, Bethnal Green, and St. Peter's, Stepney, Lond; Chap. of Infirmary, Derby. [20]

HOBBINS, Frederick John, 11, *East India-road, Limehouse, E.*—King's Coll. Lond. Theol. Assoc; Deac. 1864 and Pr. 1865 by Bp of Lon. C. and afternoon Lect. of St. Anne's, Limehouse, 1867. Formerly C. of Ch. Ch. Spitalfields 1864–67. [21]

HOBBS, Septimus, *West Compton Rectory, Dorchester.*—Ch. Miss. Coll. Islington; Deac. 1841 and Pr. 1842 by Bp of Lon. R. of Compton Abbas West, Dio. Salis. 1866. (Patron, R. Williams, Esq; Tithe, 156*l*; Glebe, 2 acres; R.'s Inc. 160*l* and Ho; Pop. 117.) Formerly Ch. Missionary in India and Ceylon 1842–62. [22]

HOBDAY, William, *Turvey, Bedford.*—St. Bees; Deac. 1864 and Pr. 1865 by Bp of Ches. C. at Turvey 1867. Formerly C. of Mottram-in-Longendale, Cheshire, 1864–67. [22]

HOBHOUSE, Reginald, *St. Ive Rectory, Liskeard.*—Ball. Coll. Ox. B.A. 1839, M.A. 1842; Deac. 1841 and Pr. 1842 by Bp of Herf. R. of St. Ive, Dio. Ex. 1844. (Patron, the Crown; Tithe, 437*l* 10*s*; Glebe, 80 acres; R.'s Inc. 497*l* and Ho; Pop. 2593.) Formerly C. of Leonard's, Bridgnorth, 1841; R. of Riseholme and P. C. of South Carlton, Lincolnshire, 1843. Author, *Ministerial Watchfulness* (a Visitation Sermon), Masters, 1848; *The Cornish Bishopric* (a Letter to the Earl of St. Germans), Whittaker, 1860, 6*d*. [23]

HOBKIRK, J. H. C., *Christian Malford, Chippenham.*—C. of Christian Malford, Wilts. [24]

HOBLYN, Edward, *Mylor Vicarage, Falmouth.*—Univ. Coll. Ox. B.A. 1804; Deac. 1808 by Bp of Win. Pr. 1809 by Bp of Roch. V. of Mylor with Mabe, Dio. Ex. 1823. (Patron, Bp of Ex; Mylor, Tithe—Imp. 453*l*, V. 215*l*; Mabe, Tithe—Imp. 41*l* 14*s* 1*d*, V. 170*l*; Glebe, 14 acres; V.'s Inc. 385*l* and Ho; Pop. Mylor 1600, Mabe 600.) Chap. of St. Peter's Dist. Flushing. (Patron, the V. of Mylor; Pop. 1006.) Author, *Sermons*, 1811; *On the Prophetic* 1260 *Days*, 1821; *The House of Prayer* (a Sermon), 1844; *The Millennium—What is it?* 1863. [25]

HOBSON, George Harrison, *Parkfield, Birkenhead.*—Dub. A.B. 1863; Deac. 1864 and Pr. 1865 by Bp of Ches. C. of St. Paul's, Birkenhead, 1865. Formerly C. of Vauxhall, Liverpool, 1864. [26]

HOBSON, Leonard, *Woodsetts, near Worksop.*—St. John's Coll. Cam. 12th Sen. Opt. and B.A. 1830; Deac. 1830 and Pr 1831 by Abp of York. P. C. of Woodsetts, Dio. York, 1847. (Patron, Abp of York; Tithe, 200*l*; Glebe, 7 acres; P. C.'s Inc. 220*l* and Ho; Pop. 164.) Formerly C. of Ardwick-le-Street 1830, Dartfield 1843–44. [27]

HOBSON, R., *Claughton, Birkenhead.*—C. of Ch. Ch. Claughton. [28]

HOBSON, Samuel, *Marsham, Norfolk.*—St. Cath. Coll. Cam. LL.B. 1831. V. of Tuttington, Norfolk, Dio. Nor. 1853. (Patron, Bp of Nor; Tithe—App. 200*l*, V. 105*l*; Glebe, 24 acres; V.'s Inc. 157*l*; Pop. 202.) Author, *What mean ye by this Service?* (The Question Discussed in the Trial of George Herbert, Richard Hooker, Charles Simeon, Reginald Heber, and Thomas Scott, on the

Charge of Heresy), 2 eds. 3s 6d; *Letters to a Waverer*, 7s; *A Letter to the Poor-Law Commissioners, with Remarks on the Case of Rex v. Jodrell*, 1s; *Be Sure Your Sin will Find You Out* (a Sermon preached to a Village Congregation on the Sunday after the Execution of Charles Daines, the Hempnall Murderer), 2d; *A Plea for the Aged and Infirm Poor, with a Few Hints to Employers Generally, and to the Guardians of the Poor in Particular, as to the Means of Improving the Condition and Promoting the Respectability and Independence of the Labouring Classes*, 6d; *Certain Misstatements and Errors Exposed* (a Conversation between a Village Schoolmaster and an Anabaptist), 3d; *The Wages of Incendiarism*, 1s; *The Vale of Probation*, 2s 6d; *The First Adam* (a Course of Sermons preached to a Village Congregation), 3s 6d; *The Nature and Design of the New Poor-Law Explained in an Address to the Labouring Classes*, 2 eds. 4d; *The Young Man's Guide in the Choice of a Benefit Society*, 1s; *The Root of all Evil* (a Sermon preached to a Village Congregation on the Sunday before the Execution of J. B. Rush, the Stanfield Murderer), 2 eds. 2d; *How should Protestants meet the Aggressions of Rome? and the Trial of the Cardinal*, 6s; *The Claims of the Church of England, and the Insufficiency of Voluntaryism*, 6s; *Church-Rate Abolition and its Consequences, A Dream*, 6d; *The Confession and Absolution sanctioned by the Anglican and Roman Churches respectively*, 1866, 1s 6d; and numerous other Sermons and Tracts. [1]

HOBSON, S. A., *Isleworth, Middlesex, W.*—C. of St. John's, Isleworth. [2]

HOBSON, Thomas Verah, *Woodfield Cottage, Swinton, near Rotherham.*—Deac. 1831 and Pr. 1833 by Abp of York. P. C. of Melton-on-the-Hill, Dio. York. 1860. (Patron, A. F. W. Montagu, Esq; Tithe—Imp. 250l, V. 75l; Glebe, 46 acres; P. C.'s Inc. 150l; Pop. 169.) [3]

HOBSON, William, *Siseland Rectory, near Norwich.*—St. Cath. Coll. Cam. B.D. 1830; Deac. 1816, Pr. 1817. R. of Siseland, Dio. Nor. 1819. (Patron, the present R; Tithe, 132l 15s; Glebe, 17 acres; R.'s Inc. 174l and Ho; Pop. 76.) P. C. of Thurton, Norfolk, Dio. Nor. 1828. (Patron, Sir T. B. Proctor-Beauchamp, Bart; Tithe—Imp. 290l; Glebe, 7 acres; P. C.'s Inc. 94l; Pop. 246.) [4]

HOBSON, W. F., *Hounslow, W.*—Chap. to the Forces. [5]

HOBSON, William Leonard, *Rose Hill, Cantley, Doncaster.*—St. Bees; Deac. 1866 by Abp of York. C. of Cantley 1866. [6]

HOBSON, William Thomas, *Ellesmere House, Clifton Park-row, Clifton.*—Dub. A.B. 1858, A.M. 1864; Deac. 1859 by Bp of Cork, Pr. 1860 by Bp of Meath. Assoc. Sec. of Colonial and Continental Ch. Soc. Formerly C. of Monkstown, co. Dublin, 1857–63, St. Paul's, Prince's Park, Liverpool, 1863–67. [7]

HOBSON, William Topham, *Beckingham, Gainsborough.*—Corpus Coll. Cam. B.A. 1835, M.A. 1842; Deac. 1835 and Pr. 1836 by Bp of Ches. V. of Beckingham, Dio. Lin. 1854. (Patron, Preb. of Southwell; Tithe, 103l; Glebe, 74 acres; V.'s Inc. 220l and Ho; Pop. 450.) Formerly C. of Rochdale 1835–39; R. of Strelly, Notts, 1842–52. [8]

HOBSON, William Willes, *Loddon, near Norwich.*—St. John's Coll. Cam. B.A. 1837; Deac. 1837, Pr. 1840. P. C. of Hales with Heckingham, Norfolk, Dio. Nor. 1844. (Patron, Sir W. B. Smyth, Bart; Hales, Tithe, Imp. 246l; Heckingham, Tithe, Imp. 134l 3s 2d; P. C.'s Inc. 65l; Pop. Hales 315, Heckingham 317.) [9]

HOCKEN, H., *Wolverton, Bucks.*—C. of St. Mary's, Wolverton. Formerly C. of Fenny Stratford. [10]

HOCKEN, William, *St. Endellion, Wadebridge Cornwall.*—St. John's Coll. Cam. B.A. 1831; Deac. 1831 and Pr. 1833 by Bp of Ex. R. of St. Endellion, Dio. Ex. 1833. (Patron, Ld Chan; Tithe—Prebs. of St. Endellion, 399l 19s, and 40 acres of Glebe, R. 232l 10s; Glebe, 18 acres; R.'s Inc. 282l and Ho; Pop. 1192.) [11]

HOCKIN, Frederick, *Phillack Rectory (Cornwall), Hayle.*—St. John's Coll. Cam. B A. 1849, M.A. 1866; Deac. 1849, Pr. 1850. R. of Phillack with Gwithian R. Dio. Ex. 1853. Patron, the present R; Phillack, Tithe, 387l 0s 6d; Glebe, 21½ acres; Gwithian, Tithe, 235l; Glebe, 5 perches; R.'s Inc. 630l and Ho; Pop. Phillack 5381, Gwithian, 774.) Author, *Assurance* (a Sermon), Church Press Co. 1865. [12]

HOCKIN, William, *The Chaplaincy, Exeter.*—Ex. Coll. Ox. B.A. 1820, M.A. 1862; Deac. 1821 and Pr. 1822 by Bp of Ex. Chap. of the Devon and Exeter Hospital, Exeter, 1841. (Patrons, Trustees; Chap.'s Inc. 210l and Ho.) [13]

HOCKING, John Hocking, *Gwalior, Bengal.*—Ex. Coll. Ox. B.A. 1858; Deac. 1858 and Pr. 1859 by Bp of Ex. Formerly C. of St. Mary's, Truro, and of Penzance. [14]

HOCKLEY, Thomas, *Arundel, Sussex.* [15]

HODD, Albert Harry, *Wigan.*—Univ. Coll. Dur. Scho. and Fell; Deac. 1858 and Pr. 1859 by Bp of Lich. C. of Wigan. Formerly C. of Chesterton, Staffs, 1858, St. Leonard's, Bilston, 1862. [16]

HODGE, Henry Vere, *Middleton, Tamworth.*—Ex. Coll. Ox. B.A. 1826, M.A. 1828; Deac. 1827, Pr. 1828. P. C. of Middleton, Dio. Wor. 1836. (Patron, Lord Middleton; P. C.'s Inc. 100l; Pop. 484.) [17]

HODGE, William H. O'Bryen, 16, *Westbourne Park-road, London, W.*—Magd. Hall, Ox. B.A. 1856, M.A. 1858; Deac. 1857 and Pr. 1858 by Bp of Wor. Min. of St. Peter's Temporary Church, Paddington, 1866. Formerly C. of Bp Ryder's Ch. Birmingham, 1857–61; Asst. Chap. Lock Chapel, London, 1861–65. [18]

HODGE, William Henry, *Wombwell, Barnsley.*—St. Aidan's; Deac. 1866 by Abp of York. C. of Wombwell 1866. [19]

HODGENS, Thomas, *Westerleigh, Chipping Sodbury.*—Dub. A.B. 1848; Deac. 1849 and Pr. 1850 by Bp of B. and W. C. of Pucklechurch and Westerleigh, Glouc. Formerly C. of Birmingham. [20]

HODGES, Abraham, *Carlisle.*—P. C. of St. Stephen's, Carlisle, Dio. Carl. 1865. (Patron, Bp of Carl; P. C.'s Inc. 100l; Pop. 2778.) [21]

HODGES, Frederic Thomas Amelius Parry, *Lyme Regis, Dorset.*—New Coll. Ox. B.C.L. 1829, D.C.L. 1838. V. of Lyme Regis, Dio. Salis. 1833. (Patron, Bp of Salis; Tithe—App. 53l 15s; Glebe, 11 acres; V.'s Inc. 218l and Ho; Pop. 2537.) V. of North Clifton, Notts, Dio. Lin. 1832. (Patron, Bp of Lin; Tithe—App. 15l 6s 6d, V. 9l 15s 4d; V.'s Inc. 150l and Ho; Pop. 1110.) Preb. of Salis. and Lin; Fell. of Winchester Coll; Surrogate. [22]

HODGES, G. B.—C. of Ch. Ch. Clapham, Surrey. [23]

HODGES, George Samuel, *Wingates, Bolton-le-Moors.*—Jesus Coll. Cam. 2nd cl. Cl. Trip. B.A. 1851; Deac. 1851 and Pr. 1852 by Bp of Win. P. C. of Wingates, Dio. Man. 1861. (Patron, V. of Dean; Glebe, 6 acres; P. C.'s Inc. 100l and Ho; Pop. 1857.) Formerly C. of Fladbury, Worc. Author, *Ruth and other Poems*, Simpkin, Marshall and Co., 1865. [24]

HODGES, Henry, *Alphamstone Rectory, Bures, Essex.*—Univ. Coll. Ox. B.A. 1830; Deac. 1834 and Pr. 1835 by Bp of Chich. R. of Alphamstone, Dio. Roch. 1838. (Patron, Ld Chan; Tithe, 448l 10s; Glebe, 24 acres; R.'s Inc. 486l and Ho; Pop. 317.) [25]

HODGES, James, *Shippon, Abingdon, Berks.*—Trin. Coll. Cam. B.A. 1849, M.A. 1852; Deac. 1849 and Pr. 1850 by Bp of Roch. P. C. of Shippon, Dio. Ox. 1865. (Patron, Bp of Ox; Tithe, 50l; Glebe, 1 acre; P. C.'s Inc. 100l and Ho; Pop. 250.) Formerly P. C. of St. Mary's Middleton, Leeds, 1853–58, Lane End, Bucks, 1858–65. [26]

HODGES, John Julius, *Onibury, Ludlow.*—Queens' Coll. Cam B.A. 1828, M.A. 1831; Deac. 1828 and Pr. 1829 by Bp of Herf. R. of Onibury, Dio. Herf. 1841. (Patron, Earl of Craven; Tithe, 345l; Glebe, 90 acres; R.'s Inc. 430l; Pop. 375.) [27]

HODGES, Joseph Henry, *Offenham, Evesham.*—Ex. Coll. Ox. 2nd cl. Lit. Hum. 1853, and B.A. 1854; Deac. 1854 by Bp of Lon. Pr. 1855 by Bp of B. and W. Travelling Sec. of S.P.G. 1860. Formerly C. of Longbridge Deverell. [28]

HODGES, Thomas, *Charmouth, Dorset.* [29]

HODGES, Thomas, *Saltersford House, Holmes Chapel, Middlewich, Cheshire.*—Ball. Coll. Ox. B.A 1814, M.A. 1817; Deac. 1814 and Pr. 1815 by Bp of Ches. [1]

HODGES, Thomas, *Appleby, Westmoreland.*—St. John's Coll. Cam. B.A. 1865; Deac. 1865, Pr. 1866. C. of St. Lawrence's, Appleby, 1865. [2]

HODGES, William, *Elsecar Parsonage, Barnsley.*—Deac. 1849 and Pr. 1850 by Bp of Lin. P. C. of Elsecar, Dio. York, 1860. (Patron, Earl Fitzwilliam; Tithe, 100*l*; Glebe, 1 acre; P. C.'s Inc. 135*l* and Ho; Pop. 1912.) Formerly C. of St. Mary's, Nottingham, 1849–51, Wentworth, Yorks, 1851–60. [3]

HODGETTS, Joseph Hope, *Hambledon, Hants.*—Emman. Coll. Cam. B.A; Deac. 1863, Pr. 1865. C. of Hambledon. [4]

HODGINS, Edward Pringle, *St. Stephen's Parsonage, 65, Oxford-street, Liverpool.*—Dub. A.B. 1839, A.M. 1842, B.D. 1852, D.D. 1854; Deac. 1839 by Bp of Down and Connor, Pr. 1840 by Bp of Limerick. P. C. of St. Stephen's, Edge Hill, Liverpool, Dio. Ches. 1863. (Patrons, R. of West Derby and P. C.'s of St. Mary's and St. Jude's, Edge Hill; P. C.'s Inc. 252*l* and Ho; Pop. 8003.) Formerly C. of Luckinabacky 1839, Carrigrohan 1842; P. C. of East Ferry 1856, all three in Dio. of Cork, Cloyne and Ross. [5]

HODGKIN, Joseph, *Treales, Kirkham, Preston.*—St. Bees; Deac. 1853 by Abp of York, Pr. 1854 by Bp of Madras. P. C. of Treales, Dio. Man. 1858. (Patron, V. of Kirkham; P. C.'s Inc. 100*l*; Pop. 632.) Formerly C. of Treales 1854–58. [6]

HODGKINSON, George Christopher, *The Lodge, Louth, Lincolnshire.*—Trin. Coll. Cam. 1833, 14th Wrang. 2nd cl. Cl. Trip. B.A. 1837, M.A. 1841; Deac. 1842, Pr 1843. Head Mast. of King Edward's Sch. Louth. Late Prin. of Dioc. Training Coll. York; Sec. of the National Soc. and Prin. of the Royal Agricultural Coll. Cirencester. Author, *Ordination Sermon* (preached in Wor. Cathl), 1843; *Sermon at Bury*, 1844; *Tract on the Rubric*, 1844; *The Doctrine of the Church*, Rivingtons, 1854; *The Civil Service of India*, 1864. [7]

HODGKINSON, George Langton, *Gainsborough.*—Pemb. Coll. Ox. B.A. 1860, M.A. 1863; Deac. 1861 and Pr. 1862 by Bp of Lin. P. C. of Trinity, Gainsborough, 1867. (Patron, Bp of Lin; P. C.'s Inc. 100*l* and Ho; Pop. 2436.) Chap. to Bp of Lin. Formerly C. of Gainsborough 1861–62, East Retford 1863–67. [8]

HODGKINSON, John, *Strensall Vicarage, York.*—St. John's Coll. Cam. B.A. 1830, M.A. 1833; Deac. 1831, Pr. 1832. V. of Strensall, Dio. York, 1843. (Patron, Abp of York; Tithe, 90*l*; Glebe, 91 acres; V.'s Inc. 300*l* and Ho; Pop. 506.) Formerly C. of Gayton and Stowe 1831, Knottingley 1833, Bolton Percy 1836. [9]

HODGKINSON, Robert John, *Uppingham, Rutland.*—St. Peter's Coll. Cam. B.A. 1849, M.A. 1852; Deac. 1850, Pr. 1851. Mast. of the Lower Sch. Uppingham, 1855. [10]

HODGSON, Beilby Porteus, *Hartburn Vicarage, Morpeth, Northumberland.*—Trin. Coll. Cam. B A. 1832; Deac. 1833 by Bp of Carl. Pr. 1835 by Bp of Lin. V. of Hartburn, Dio. Dur. 1856. (Patron, Bp of Dur; V.'s Inc. 800*l* and Ho; Pop. 746.) Formerly V. of Hillingdon, near Uxbridge, Middlesex, 1840–56; also Clerk in Orders of St. George's, Hanover-square, Lond. 1843–56. [11]

HODGSON, Charles, *Barton-le-Street Rectory, New Malton, Yorks.*—Magd. Coll. Cam. B.A. 1824, M.A. 1826; Deac. 1823 by Bp of Lin. Pr. 1824 by Abp of York. R. of Barton-le-Street with Butterwick C. Dio. York, 1833. (Patron, H. C. M. Ingram, Esq; Tithe, 400*l* 16*s*; R.'s Inc. 450*l* and Ho; Pop. 454.) Formerly C. of Falkingham 1825–33. [12]

HODGSON, Christopher, *Playford Parsonage, Ipswich.*—St. Bees; Deac. 1855 and Pr. 1856 by Bp of Nor. P. C. of Playford, Dio. Nor. 1858. (Patron, Marquis of Bristol; P. C.'s Inc. 79*l* and Ho; Pop. 275.) P. C. of Culpho, Suffolk, Dio. Nor. 1860. (Patron, B. Gurdon, Esq; P. C.'s Inc. 55*l*; Pop. 56.) Formerly C. of Burgh, Woodbridge. [13]

HODGSON, C. A., *Bisham, Great Marlow.*—C. of Bisham. [14]

HODGSON, Diston Stanley, *Grammar Schoolhouse, Bolton-le-Moors.*—Corpus Coll. Cam. 21st Sen. Opt. and B.A. 1841, M.A. 1845; Deac. 1841 and Pr. 1842 by Bp of Ches. Head Mast. of the Bolton-le-Moors Gr. Sch. 1845; Dom. Chap. at Smithill's Hall, near Bolton. [15]

HODGSON, Edward Franks, *Holton-le-Beckering Rectory, Wragby, Lincolnshire.*—R. of Holton with Beckering R. Dio. Lin. 1844. (Patron, C. Turnor, Esq; Tithe, 267*l*; Glebe, 24 acres; R.'s Inc. 310*l* and Ho; Pop. 179.) Rural Dean. [16]

HODGSON, George Courtenay, *Barton Vicarage (Westmoreland), near Penrith.*—St Bees 1847; Deac. 1848 and Pr. 1849 by Bp of Ches. V. of Barton, Dio. Carl. 1855. (Patron, Earl of Lonsdale; Tithe—App. 79*l* 1*s*, Imp. 236*l* 11*s* 9*d*, V. 18*l* 8*s* 4*d*; Glebe, 75½ acres; V.'s Inc. 200*l* and Ho; Pop. 941.) Rural Dean; Chap. of the West Ward Union, Westmoreland, 1855. [17]

HODGSON, Henry Wade, *Vicarage, King's Langley, Herts.*—Univ. Coll. Dur. B.A. 1840, M.A. 1843; Fell. and Chap. of Univ. Coll. 1841; Deac. 1842 and Pr. 1843 by Bp of Dur. V. of King's Langley, Dio. Roch. 1855. (Patron, Abp of Cant; Tithe, 220*l*; Glebe, 15 acres; V.'s Inc. 460*l* and Ho; Pop. 980.) Formerly P. C. of Irton and Drigg, Cumberland, 1845. [18]

HODGSON, Henry William, *Ashwell Vicarage, Baldock, Herts.*—Ball. Coll. Ox; Deac. 1843, Pr. 1844. V. of Ashwell, Dio. Roch. 1851. (Patron, Bp of Roch; Tithe—App. 750*l*, V. 669*l*; V.'s Inc. 680*l* and Ho; Pop. 1507.) [19]

HODGSON, James, *Bloxham Vicarage, Banbury.*—Trin. Coll. Cam. B.A. 1848, M.A. 1851; Deac. 1848 and Pr. 1849 by Bp of G. and B. V. of Bloxham, Dio. Ox. 1852. (Patron, Eton Coll; Glebe, 171 acres; V.'s Inc. 290*l* and Ho; Pop. 1366.) Formerly C. of St. John Baptist's, Bristol, 1848–50; P. C. of St. Mark's, New Swindon, 1850–52. [20]

HODGSON, John, *Wolverley Vicarage, near Kidderminster.*—Wad. Coll. Ox. B.A. 1851, M.A. 1856; Deac. 1851 and Pr. 1852 by Bp of Ex. C. of Wolverley 1864; Chap. of 1st Worcestershire Rifles. Formerly C. of Kinver, Staffs, 1854–58, Calstock, Cornwall, 1858–61, Bedworth, Warwickshire, 1861–64. [21]

HODGSON, John, 3, *Broad Sanctuary, Westminster, S.W.*—Sec. to the Clergy Mutual Assurance Soc. [22]

HODGSON, John, *Hoxne Vicarage, near Scole, Suffolk.*—Jesus Coll. Cam. M.A. 1832; Deac. 1829, Pr. 1830. V. of Hoxne with Denham V. Dio. Nor. 1843. (Patron, Sir E. Kerrison; V.'s Inc. 450*l* and Ho; Pop. Hoxne 1218, Denham 282.) [23]

HODGSON, John Dryden, *Great Bedwyn Vicarage, near Hungerford, Wilts.*—St. Peter's Coll. Cam. Sen. Opt. 2nd cl. Cl. Trip. and B.A. 1844, M.A. 1847; Deac. 1846 and Pr. 1847 by Bp of Roch. V. of Great Bedwyn, Dio. Salis. 1855. (Patron, Marquis of Ailesbury; V.'s Inc. 260*l*; Pop. 1067.) Rural Dean; Dom. Chap. to Marquis of Ailesbury. [24]

HODGSON, John Fisher, *Horsham Vicarage, Sussex.*—Ch. Ch. Ox. B.A. 1835, M.A. 1837; Deac. 1835 and Pr. 1836. V. of Horsham, Dio. Chich. 1840. (Patron, Abp of Cant; Tithe—Imp. 1004*l* 14*s*, V. 756*l* 12*s*; Glebe, 3 acres; V.'s Inc. 740*l* and Ho; Pop. 6165.) Preb. of Chichester 1860; Rural Dean and Surrogate 1840. [25]

HODGSON, John George, *Croydon Vicarage, S.*—Trin. Coll. Cam. B.A. 1835, M.A. 1838; Deac. 1835, Pr. 1836. V. of Croydon, Dio. Cant. 1846. (Patron, Abp of Cant; Tithe—App. 5*l* 18*s* 1*d*, Imp. 1128*l* 14*s* 9*d*, V. 526*l* 16*s*; Glebe, 27 acres; V.'s Inc. 790*l* and Ho; Pop. 9824.) Rural Dean. [26]

HODGSON, John James, *Holbeach, Lincolnshire.*—Magd. Coll. Cam. B.A. 1858, M.A. 1861; Deac. 1858 and Pr. 1859 by Bp of Ely. C. of Holbeach 1862.

Formerly C. of Trinity, Ely, 1858–60, St. Lawrence's, York, 1860–62. [1]

HODGSON, John Willoughby, 18, *Buckingham-place, Brighton.*—Dioc. Coll. Chich; Deac. 1849 and Pr. 1850 by Bp of Chich. Late Lect. of Portslade, Sussex, 1852–58. [2]

HODGSON, Joseph Stordy, *Aikton Rectory, Wigton, Cumberland.*—Trin. Coll. Cam. Wrang. and B.A. 1839; Deac. 1834, Pr. 1835. R. of Aikton, Dio. Carl. 1858. (Patron, Earl of Lonsdale; Tithe—Imp. 5*l* 12*s* 1*d*, R. 488*l*; R.'s Inc. 550*l* and Ho; Pop. 806.) Hon. Can. of Carl; Rural Dean; Surrogate. Formerly R. of Brinklow, near Coventry, 1840–58. Author, *Considerations on Phrenology*, 1839; *Duty of Private Judgment* (a Visitation Sermon at Coventry in 1844). [3]

HODGSON, Octavius Arthur, *The Vicarage, Alton, Hants.*—Magd. Coll. Ox. B.A. 1840, M.A. 1846; Deac. 1841 and Pr. 1842 by Bp of Salis. V. of Alton with Thedden C. Dio. Win. 1862. (Patrons, D. and C. of Win; V.'s Inc. 580*l* and Ho; Pop. 3769.) Surrogate. Formerly Min. Can. of Win. Cathl. 1845–62; Chap. of St. Mary's Coll. Winchester, 1852–62. [4]

HODGSON, Rice Joseph, 6, *Blandford-square, London, N.W.*—Lin. Coll. Ox. B.A. 1847; Deac. 1847, Pr. 1848. Formerly C. of Hanover Chapel, Regent-street. [5]

HODGSON, Richard, *Pilton Rectory, Oundle, Northants.*—Queen's Coll. Ox. B.A. 1831, M.A. 1855; Deac. 1851 and Pr. 1852 by Bp of Lich. R. of Pilton, Dio. Pet. 1858. (Patron, Lord Lilford; Tithe, 160*l*; Glebe, 10 acres; R.'s Inc. 170*l* and Ho; Pop. 144.) Formerly C. of Warton and Freckleton, Lancashire. [6]

HODGSON, Samuel Edward, *Aylesford, Maidstone.*—C. of Aylesford. [7]

HODGSON, Thomas Douglas, *East Woodhay Rectory (Hampshire), near Newbury.*—Trin. Coll. Cam. B.A. 1819, M.A. 1822; Deac. and Pr. 1820. R. of East Woodhay with Ashmansworth C. Dio. Win. 1825. (Patron, Bp of Win; East Woodhay, Tithe, 1005*l* 12*s* 6*d*; Glebe, 51 acres; Ashmansworth, Tithe, 371*l* 3*s* 4*d*; Glebe, 27 acres; R.'s Inc. 1480*l* and Ho; Pop. Woodhay 712, Ashmansworth 201.) [8]

HODGSON, Thomas Edward, *Scarthwaite Caton, Lancaster.*—Trin. Coll. Cam. B.A. 1850, M.A. 1853; Deac. 1850 and Pr. 1851 by Bp of Lich. Formerly C. of Holbrooke, Derbyshire, 1850–54, Romsey Abbey, Hants, 1854–55, St. Mark's, Brighton, 1856–59, St. James's, Dover, 1860–64. [9]

HODGSON, Walter Cotton, *Swepston, near Ashby-de-la-Zouch.*—Trin. Coll. Cam. B.A. 1850, M.A. 1854; Deac. 1851 and Pr. 1852 by Bp of Rip. R. of Swepston with Snareston, Dio. Pet. 1865. (Patron, the present R; Tithe, 765*l*; Glebe, 106 acres; R.'s Inc. 995*l* and Ho; Pop. 921.) Formerly C. of Bradford 1851–54, St. Matthew's, Stoke Newington, 1855, Hingham, Norfolk, 1856–61; V. of Watton, Norfolk, 1861–65. [10]

HODGSON, William, *Cheltenham.*—Queen's Coll. Ox. B.A. 1826, M.A. 1829; Deac. 1828 and Pr. 1829 by Bp of Win. Formerly P. C. of St. Peter's, Cheltenham, 1845–66. [11]

HODGSON, William, *Streatham School, London, S.*—St. Cath. Coll. Cam. Schô. Sen. Opt. Math. Prizeman 1843–44, Latin Declamation Prizeman 1843, B.A. 1846, M.A. 1851; Deac. 1849 and Pr. 1850 by Bp of Salis. Mast. of Streatham Sch. Formerly 2nd Mast. of Marlborough Gr. Sch; C. of Ogbourne St. Andrew, Marlborough. [12]

HODGSON, William, *Trysull, Wolverhampton.*—St. Peter's Coll. Cam. B.A. 1861, M.A. 1866; Deac. 1862 and Pr. 1863 by Bp of Lon. C. of Trysull 1866. Formerly C. of St. Philip's, Stepney, 1862. [13]

HODGSON, William, *Christ Church Parsonage, Colne, Lancashire.*—Literate; Deac. 1835 by Bp of York, Pr. 1838 by Bp of Ches. P. C. of Ch. Ch. Colne, Dio. Man. 1838. (Patrons, Hulme's Trustees; Glebe, ½ acre; P. C.'s Inc. 185*l* and Ho; Pop. 2817.) Formerly C. of Haworth, near Bradford, 1835–37, Ch. Ch. Colne, 1837–38. [14]

HODSON, Charles William, *St. James's Parsonage, Hampstead-road, London, N.W.*—Trin. Coll. Cam. B.A. 1848; Deac. 1848 and Pr. 1849 by Bp of Rip. Min. of St. James's Chapel, Hampstead-road, Dio. Lon. 1863. Formerly C. of High Harrogate 1848–51, Sevington St. Michael 1851–58; P. C. of Lopen, Somerset, 1852–59; Sen. C. of Kensington 1859–62. [15]

HODSON, George, *Henwick Hill, near Worcester.*—Magd. Hall, Ox. Hon. 4th cl. Lit. Hum. 1832, B.A. 1833, M.A. 1837; Deac. 1832 and Pr. 1833 by Bp of Wor. R. of St. Andrew's, City and Dio. Wor. 1845. (Patrons, D. and C. of Wor; Glebe, 10 acres; R.'s Inc. 106*l*; Pop. 1768.) [16]

HODSON, George Hewitt, *Cookham-Deane, Maidenhead, Berks.*—Trin. Coll. Cam. Bell's Univ. Scho. 1837, 1st cl. Cl. Trip. and B A. 1840, M.A. 1843; Deac. and Pr. 1843 by Bp of G. and B. P. C. of Cookham-Deane, Dio. Ox. 1845. (Patron, V. of Cookham; Tithe, 89*l*; P. C.'s Inc. 109*l*; Pop. 743.) Rural Dean; Sen. Fell. and Coll. Preacher of Trin. Coll. Cam. Editor, *Twelve Years of a Soldier's Life in India by Major Hodson*, 1859. [17]

HODSON, Grenville Heber Frodsham Elton, *North Petherton, near Bridgwater.*—Emman. Coll. Cam. B.A. 1850. P. C. of Michaelchurch, Dio. B. and W. 1856. (Patron, Sir P. Acland, Bart; Tithe, 22*l*; Glebe, 22 acres; P. C.'s Inc. 61*l*; Pop. 21.) C. of North Newton 1857. Formerly C. of Chew Magna, near Bristol, 1851–53. [18]

HODSON, James Stephen, 62, *Great King-street, Edinburgh.*—Mert. Coll. Ox. 1st cl. Lit. Hum. and B.A. 1837, M.A. 1840, D.D. 1855; Deac. 1839 and Pr. 1841 by Bp of Win. Rector of the Academy, Edinburgh, 1854; Chap. to the Bp of Edinburgh 1867. Formerly P. C. of Great Longstone, Derbyshire, 1846–55. [19]

HODSON, John Johnston, *Yelvertoft (Northants), near Rugby.*—St. Mary Hall, Ox. B.A. 1820, M.A. 1823; Deac. and Pr. 1821. R. of Yelvertoft, Dio. Pet. 1828. (Patron, Earl of Craven; R.'s Inc. 512*l* and Ho; Pop. 691.) [20]

HOGAN, Alexander Ferrier, *Llanvihangel Crucorney, near Abergavenny.*—Dub. A.B. 1859; Deac. 1859 and Pr. 1860 by Bp of Llan. C. of Llanvihangel Crucorney. Formerly C. of Aberdare. [21]

HOGAN, Arthur Riky, *Watlington Vicarage, Oxon.*—Dub. A.B. 1855, A.M. 1858, *com. causâ* Ox. M.A. 1860; Deac. 1856 by Bp of B. and W. Pr. 1857 by Bp of G. and B. V. of Watlington, Dio. Ox. 1865. (Patron, T. Shaen Carter, Esq; Tithe, 100*l*; Glebe, 63 acres; V.'s Inc. 265*l* and Ho; Pop. 1933.) Formerly C. of Corsham, Wilts, 1856–58; Dom. Chap. to the Earl of Normanton 1859; C. of Piddletown, Dorset, 1860–62. Author, various papers in *Natural History Review*, of which Mr. Hogan was formerly one of the Editors and proprietors. [22]

HOGARTH, David, *Portland, Weymouth, Dorset.*—Univ. of Edin. M.A. 1830; Deac. and Pr. 1833. R. of Portland, Dio. Salis. 1838. (Patron, Bp of Win; Tithe, 120*l*; Glebe, 20 acres; R.'s Inc. 207*l*; Pop. 8468.) [23]

HOGARTH, George, *The Vicarage, Barton-upon-Humber, Lincolnshire.*—St. Cath. Coll. Cam. B.A. 1852, M.A. 1855; Deac. 1853 and Pr. 1854 by Abp of York. V. of Barton-upon-Humber, Dio. Lin. 1858. (Patron, G. C. Uppleby, Esq; Tithe, 230*l*; Glebe, 5 acres; V.'s Inc. 250*l* and Ho; Pop. 3797.) Surrogate. Formerly C. of Scarborough 1853, Rowley St. Peter 1855, Hornsea 1855, Holy Trinity, Westminster, 1857. [24]

HOGARTH, Henry, *Hatfield, Doncaster.*—Magd. Hall, Ox. B.A. 1831, M.A. 1834; Deac. 1832 by Bp of Lich. Pr. 1834 by Abp of York. P. C. of Hatfield, Dio. York, 1848. (Patron, Hon. H. A. Coventry; Tithe—Imp. 2161*l* 19*s*; Glebe, 47 acres; P. C.'s Inc. 150*l*; Pop. 2564.) [25]

HOGG, Christopher Haynes, *High Ercall, near Wellington, Salop.*—Corpus Coll. Cam. B.A. 1850, M.A. 1856; Deac. 1849 and Pr. 1850 by Bp of Ches. Head Mast. of High Ercall Gr. Sch. 1856. Formerly Mast. of Nantwich Gr. Sch. 1842, Mast. of Audlem Gr.

Sch. 1849; C. of Burleydam 1849, Clunbury, Salop, 1852. [1]

HOGG, Edward, *Fornham St. Martin Rectory, Bury St. Edmunds.*—St. Peter's Coll. Cam. B.A. 1806, R. of Fornham St. Martin, Dio. Ely, 1814. (Patron, Lord J. Manners; R.'s Inc. 305*l* and Ho; Pop. 350.) [2]

HOGG, John Roughton, *Torquay.*—Ch. Coll. Cam. B.A. 1835, M.A. 1839; Deac. 1835 and Pr. 1836 by Bp of Ex. P. C. of St. Mark's, Torwood, near Torquay, Dio. Ex. 1855. (Patron, Sir L. Palk, Bart. M.P; P. C.'s Inc. from pew rents; Pop. 2419.) Formerly P. C. of Lower Brixham, Devon. [3]

HOGGAN, C. A., *Talaton Rectory, Ottery, Devon.*—R. of Talaton, Dio. Ex. 1860. (Patron, Rev. L. P. Welland; Tithe, 333*l*; Glebe, 60 acres; R.'s Inc. 460*l* and Ho; Pop. 367.) [4]

HOHLER, Frederic Williams, *Winstone Rectory, Cirencester.*—Deac. 1835 and Pr. 1836 by Bp of G. and B. R. of Colesbourne, Dio. G. and B. 1837. (Patron, John Henry Elwes, Esq; Tithe—Imp. 242*l* 14*s*, R. 127*l* 3*s*; Glebe, 31 acres; R.'s Inc. 158*l*; Pop. 261.) R. of Winstone, Dio. G. and B. 1839. (Tithe, 206*l*; Glebe, 80 acres; R.'s Inc. 290*l* and Ho; Pop. 230.) [5]

HOITT, Henry Thomas, *Lydbrook Parsonage, Ross.*—Pemb. Coll. Ox. B.A. 1859, M.A. 1862; Deac. 1860 and Pr. 1862 by Bp of G. and B. P. C. of Lydbrook, Dio. G. and B. 1866. (Patron, the Crown; P. C.'s Inc. 130*l* and Ho; Pop. 2000.) Formerly C. of Bream 1860–66. [6]

HOLBECH, Charles William, *Farnborough, Banbury.*—Ball. Coll. Ox. 3rd cl. Lit. Hum. B.A. 1838, M.A. 1841; Deac. 1840 by Bp of Wor. Pr. 1841 by Bp of Roch. V. of Farnborough, Dio. Wor. 1842. (Patron, the present V; Tithe, 385*l*; V.'s Inc. 385*l* and Ho; Pop. 402.) Formerly C. of Chelsfield, Kent, 1840–42. [7]

HOLBERTON, Robert, *Norbiton Parsonage, Kingston-on-Thames.*—Ex. Coll. Ox. B.A. 1821, M.A. 1826; Deac. 1823, Pr. 1824. P. C. of Norbiton, Dio. Win. 1850. (Patron, V. of Kingston-on-Thames; P. C.'s Inc. 277*l* and Ho; Pop. 5041.) Chap. of the Kingston Union 1850; Surrogate. Formerly R. of St. John's, Antigua, 1827–50; Rural Dean of Antigua 1828–42; Archd. of Antigua 1843–50. [8]

HOLBROOKE, Frederick George, *Portslade Vicarage, Shoreham, Sussex.*—Ex. Coll. Ox. M.A. 1851; Deac. and Pr. 1857 by Bp of Herf. V. of Portslade, Dio. Chich. 1858. (Patroness, the Countess Delawarr; V.'s Inc. 171*l* and Ho; Pop. 1103.) R. of Hangleton, Dio. Chich. 1863. (Patroness, the Countess Delawarr; R.'s Inc. 240*l*; Pop. 51.) [9]

HOLBROW, Thomas, *Coleford, Gloucestershire.*—Pemb. Coll. Cam. B.A 1853; Deac. 1854 and Pr. 1855 by Bp of G. and B. P. C. of Coleford, Dio. G. and B. 1866. (Patron, Bp of G. and B; P. C.'s Inc. 150*l* and Ho; Pop. 2800.) Formerly C. of Standish and Hardwicke 1854–64, Almondsbury 1864–66. [10]

HOLCOMBE, George Francis, *Arnold Vicarage, near Nottingham.*—St. John's Coll. Cam. B.A. 1811, M.A. 1814. V. of Arnold, Dio. Lin. 1812. (Patron, Duke of Devonshire; Tithe, 223*l* 15*s*; V.'s Inc. 310*l* and Ho; Pop. 4642.) R. of Brinckley, Newmarket, Cambs, Dio. Ely, 1817. (Patron, St. John's Coll. Cam; R.'s Inc. 251*l* and Ho; Pop. 317. Late Fell. of St. John's Coll. Cam. [11]

HOLDEN, Atkenson Alexander, *Hawton Rectory, Newark, Notts.*—Ch. Ch. Ox. B.A. 1830, M.A. 1832; Deac. 1831, Pr. 1833. R. of Hawton, Dio. Lich. 1866. (Patron, C. N. Newdegate, Esq; Tithe, 750*l*; Glebe, 62 acres; R.'s Inc. 862*l* and Ho; Pop. 246.) Formerly V. of Spondon, near Derby. [12]

HOLDEN, Harrington William, *Middleton, Beverley, Yorks.*—Queen's Coll. Birmingham, Warnford Scho; Deac. 1860 and Pr. 1861 by Bp of Wor. C. of Middleton in-the-Wolds 1866. Formerly C. of All Saints', Birmingham, 1860–61, Catton, York, 1862–63, Ebberston with Allerston 1864–65. [13]

HOLDEN, Henry, *Grammar Schoolhouse, Durham.*—Ball. Coll. Ox. 1st cl. Lit. Hum. and B.A. 1837, M.A. 1841; Deac. 1839 and Pr. 1840 by Bp of Lon. Head Mast. of the Cathl. Sch. Dur. 1853; Hon. Can. of Dur. 1867. Formerly Head Mast. of the Uppingham Gr. Sch. 1845–53. [14]

HOLDEN, Hubert Ashton, *Ipswich.*—Trin. Coll. Cam. B.A. 1845, M.A. 1848, LL.D. 1863; Deac. 1848 by Bp of Ely, Pr. 1858 by Bp of Nor. Head Mast. of Queen Elizabeth's Sch. Ipswich, 1858. Formerly Fell. and Tut. of Trin. Coll. Cam. 1847–54; Asst. Tut. 1848–53; Vice-Prin. of Cheltenham Coll. 1853–58. Editor, *Aristophanis Comœdiæ Undecim*, 1848, 15*s*, 4th ed. 1867, 21*s*; *Foliorum Silvula*, 1852, 7*s*, 2nd ed. in two parts, Part I. 6*s*, Part II. 7*s* 6*d*; 4th ed. in three parts, Part I. 7*s* 6*d*, Part II. 5*s*, Part III. 8*s*; *Folia Silvulæ*, being translations of selections from the preceding. Vol. I. 1865, 10*s* 6*d*; *Foliorum Centuriæ*, 1852, 7*s*. 2nd ed. 1858, 3rd ed. 1864. Editor of the following works for the Syndics of the Univ. Press, Cam: *Minucii Felicis Octavius*, 1853, 9*s* 6*d*; *Cæsar Morgan on the Trinity of Plato*, 1853, 4*s*; *Cicero De Officiis*, 1854, 9*s* 6*d*. [15]

HOLDEN, Philip Melancthon, *Upminster Rectory, Romford, Essex.*—King's Coll. Lond. Theol. Assoc; Deac. and Pr. 1854. R. of Upminster, Dio. Roch. 1862. (Patrons, Trustees of the late J. R. Holden, Esq; Tithe, 1052*l*; Glebe, 23 acres; R.'s Inc. 1098*l* 4*s* 3*d* and Ho; Pop. 1342.) Formerly C. of Hammersmith 1854. [16]

HOLDEN, William Thomas, 3, *Mylne-street, Clerkenwell, London, E.C.*—Dub. A.B. 1862; Deac. 1862 and Pr. 1863 by Bp of Lon. C. of St. James's, Clerkenwell, 1862. [17]

HOLDER, Caddell, *St. Juliot, Camelford, Cornwall.*—Trin. Coll. Ox. B.A. 1827, M.A. 1832; Deac. 1827 and Pr. 1828 by Bp of G. and B. R. of St. Juliot, Dio. Ex. 1863. (Patron, the Rev. R. Rawle; R.'s Inc. 125*l* and Ho; Pop. 226.) Formerly C. of Rangeworthy 1827, Alveston 1828; V. of Avenbury, Herf. 1856. Author, *Family Prayers*, 1830; *Sermons*, 1846. [18]

HOLDER, Cornelius Benjamin, *Manchester.*—Literate; Deac. 1855 and Pr. 1856 by Bp of Man. R. of All Souls, Ancoats, Manchester, Dio. Man. 1862. (Patrons, D. and C. of Man; R.'s Inc. 300*l*; Pop. 11,263.) Formerly C. of St. John's, Chadderton, Oldham. [19]

HOLDERNESS, James, *Holloway-street, Exeter.*—St. Cath. Coll. Cam. B.A. 1859; Deac. 1851 by Bp of Victoria, Pr. 1860 by Bp of Roch. Chap. of the Devon and Exeter Female Penitentiary 1867. Formerly Missionary to Seamen at Hong Kong 1849–55; C. of Saffron Walden 1859. [20]

HOLDERNESS, William, *Buckfast Abbey, Buckfastleigh, Devon.*—St. Bees; Deac. 1845 and Pr. 1846 by Bp of Ches. C. of Law Tranchard 1867. Formerly C. of Cockerham, near Lancaster, 1845; Chap. of Thames Ch. Mission 1846–53; Chap. of Portland Prison, 1853–57; Chap. of the Prison, Dartmoor, 1857–65; C of Sourton 1865–67. [21]

HOLDICH, Charles Walter, *Leicester.*—Sid. Coll. Cam. B.A. 1864; Deac. 1866 and Pr. 1867 by Bp of Pet. C. of St. Margaret's, Leicester, 1866. [22]

HOLDICH, John Henry, *Bulwick Rectory, Wansford.*—Clare Coll. Cam. B.A. 1834, M.A. 1837; Deac. 1834 and Pr. 1835 by Bp of Pet. R. of Bulwick, Dio. Pet. 1862. (Patron, Thomas Tryon, Esq; Tithe, 34*l*; Glebe, 304 acres; R.'s Inc. 484*l* and Ho; Pop. 462.) Formerly C. of Draughton 1834–45; R. of Shankton 1845–48; C. of Deene 1848–62. [23]

HOLDICH, Thomas Peach, 22, *Norland-square, Notting-hill, London, W.*—Ball. Coll. Ox. B.A. 1826, M.A. 1829; Deac. 1827 and Pr. 1829 by Bp of Pet. P. C. of St. James's, Norland-square, Dio. Lon. 1854. (Patron, Bp of Lon; P. C.'s Inc. 500*l*; Pop. 7800.) Formerly R. of Dingley, Northants. [24]

HOLDING, John, *Ashampstead Parsonage, Reading.*—St. John's Coll. Ox. B.A. 1821, M.A. 1824; Deac. 1822 and Pr. 1823 by Bp of Lin. P. C. of Ashampstead, Dio. Ox. 1847. (Patrons, Rev. W. Sykes and Simeon's Trustees; Tithe—Imp. 212*l* 1*s* 6*d*, P. C. 70*l*; Glebe, 23 acres; P. C.'s Inc. 100*l* and Ho; Pop. 385.) [25]

HOLDITCH, Hamnet, *Caius College, Cambridge.*—Caius Coll. Cam. B.A. 1822, M.A. 1825; Deac. 1823 by Bp of G. and B. President and Sen. Fell. of Caius Coll. Cam. Author, Mathematical Papers in Transactions and Journals. [1]

HOLDSWORTH, George Alexander, *Sevenhampton Parsonage, Cheltenham.*—St. John's Coll. Cam. B.A. 1850, M.A. 1854; Deac. 1852 and Pr. 1853 by Bp of Ely. P. C. of Sevenhampton, Dio. G. and B. 1862. (Patrons, Walter Laurence Laurence, Esq. and Goodwin Craven, Esq. alt; P. C.'s Inc. 60*l* and Ho; Pop. 543.) Formerly C. of St. James's, Upper Edmonton, Middlesex, and Bicester, Oxon. [2]

HOLDSWORTH, John, *Lotherdale Parsonage, Crosshills, Leeds.*—St. John's Coll. Cam. B.A. 1838; Deac. 1839, Pr. 1847. P. C. of Lotherdale, Dio. Rip. 1847. (Patron, V. of Carleton; P. C.'s Inc. 100*l* and Ho; Pop. 819.) Formerly 2nd Mast. of the Skipton Gr. Sch. 1840–47. Author, *Introductory Address to the Members of the Literary Institution, Skipton,* 1840; *A Sermon,* in Aid of the National Society, Skipton, 1840; *Basket of Flowers,* 1847. [3]

HOLE, Charles, *Shanklin, Isle of Wight.*—Trin. Coll. Cam. Wrang. and B.A. 1846; Deac. 1846 and Pr. 1847 by Bp of Ox. C. of Shanklin. Formerly C. of St. Mary's, Reading, 1846–52. Author, *A Brief Biographical Dictionary,* Macmillan, 1865, 4*s* 6*d*, 2nd ed. 1866; *Genealogical Stemmas of the Kings of England and France,* Macmillan, 1866, 1*s*. [4]

HOLE, Charles Henry, *Worcester College, Oxford.*—Scho. of Wor. Coll. Ox. [5]

HOLE, Francis, *Broad Hempston Vicarage, Totnes, Devon.*—Magd. Hall, Ox. B.A. 1847, M.A. 1851; Deac. 1849 and Pr. 1850 by Bp of Pet. V. of Broad Hempston, Dio. Ex. 1856. (Patron, the Crown; V.'s Inc. 325*l* and Ho; Pop. 661.) [6]

HOLE, Francis Robert, *South Huish, near Kingsbridge, Devon.*—Ch. Coll. Cam. B.A. 1861; Deac. 1862 and Pr. 1863 by Bp of Ches. C. of South Huish. [7]

HOLE, Frederick Francis, *Spreyton Vicarage, Okehampton, Devon.*—Trin. Coll. Cam. B.A. 1837, M.A. 1841; Deac. 1838 and Pr. 1840 by Bp of Ex. V. of Spreyton, Dio. Ex. 1862. (Patron, Rev. W. B. Doveton; Tithe, comm. 118*l*; Glebe, 89 acres; V.'s Inc. 200*l* and Ho; Pop. 358.) Formerly C. of Northover and Weston Bampfylde, and Lect. at Ilchester, Somerset. [8]

HOLE, Henry Tubal, 5, *Sydney-place, Bath.*—Deac. 1859 and Pr. 1860 by Abp of Cant. C. of St. John's, Weston, Bath, 1865. Formerly C. of Capel-le-Ferne, Dover, 1859, Worplesdon, Guildford, 1860. [9]

HOLE, John Eldon, *Washford Pyne, Morchard Bishop, Devon.*—Corpus Coll. Cam. B.A. 1854; Deac. 1854 and Pr. 1855 by Bp of B. and W. R. of Washford Pyne, Dio. Ex. 1858. (Patron, C. C. Tucker, Esq; Tithe, 90*l*; Glebe, 105*l*; R.'s Inc. 200*l* and Ho; Pop. 182.) Formerly C. of Ashbrittle, Somerset, 1854; R. of Stoke Pero, Somerset, 1855–57. [10]

HOLE, Matthew Harvey, *Harbury Vicarage, Leamington.*—St. John's Coll. Cam. 1st cl. Cl. Trip. B.A. 1847, M.A. 1850; Deac. 1850 and Pr. 1851 by Bp of Lon. V. of Harbury, Dio. Wor. 1865. (Patron, John Hudson, Esq; Glebe, 190 acres; V's Inc. 300*l* and Ho; Pop. 1296.) Formerly Head Mast. of Alford Gr. Sch. 1854; C. of Willoughby, Lincolnshire, 1856. [11]

HOLE, Nathaniel John Brassey, *Broadwood Kelly Rectory, Winkleigh, Devon.*—Pemb. Coll. Cam. B.C.L. 1831; Deac. 1832 by Bp of Ex. Pr. 1837 by Bp of Ely. R. of Broadwood-Kelly, Dio. Ex. 1837. (Patron, the present R; Tithe, 218*l*; Glebe, 73 acres; R.'s Inc. 260*l* and Ho; Pop. 342.) [12]

HOLE, Robert, *North Tawton Rectory, Okehampton, Devon.*—Univ. Coll. Ox. B.A. 1846; Deac. 1848 and Pr. 1849 by Bp of Ex. R. of North Tawton, Dio. Ex. 1850. (Patron, the present R; Tithe, 797*l* 15*s* 10*d*; Glebe, 189*l*; R.'s Inc. 986*l* and Ho; Pop. 1849.) Patron of Chumleigh, North Devon. [13]

HOLE, Samuel Reynolds, *Caunton Manor, Newark, Notts.*—Brasen. Coll. Ox. B.A. 1844; Deac. and Pr. 1844. V. of Caunton, Dio. Lin. 1850. (Patron, Bp of Rip; Glebe, 123 acres; V.'s Inc. 195*l*; Pop. 396.) Author, Contributor to First Series of *Sermons for the Christian Seasons.* [14]

HOLE, William Brassey, *St. Luke's Vicarage, Maidenhead.*—Ex. Coll. Ox. B.A. 1840, M.A. 1845; Deac. 1840 by Bp of Win. Pr. 1841 by Bp of Ely. V. of Luke's, Maidenhead, Dio. Ox. 1866. (Patron, Bp of Ox; Tithe, 50*l*; V.'s Inc. 70*l* and Ho; Pop. 2400.) Formerly R. of Woolfardysworthy, Devon, 1841–66. [15]

HOLESGROVE, William, *Woodbridge.*—St. Cath. Coll. Cam. B.A. 1852, M.A. 1857; Deac. 1852 and Pr. 1853 by Bp of G. and B. Chap. of the Seckford Hospital, Woodbridge, 1861. Formerly C. of St. George, Gloucestershire, and Felixstowe, Suffolk. Editor, *The Prayer Book, a Companion in Sorrow and Sickness,* 2*s*. [16]

HOLFORD, John Henry, 8, *Well-walk, Hampstead, N.W.*—Wad. Coll. Ox. B.A. 1854, M.A. 1860; Deac. 1855 and Pr. 1856 by Bp of Chich. C. of Ch. Ch. Hampstead, 1860. Formerly C. of Broadwaters, Sussex, 1855–60. [17]

HOLIWELL, Walter Currer, *Trentham, Stoke-on-Trent.*—C. of Trentham. [18]

HOLLAND, Charles, *Petworth Rectory, Sussex.*—Univ. Coll. Ox. B.A. 1839, M.A. 1842; Deac. 1840 and Pr. 1841 by Bp of Lon. R. of Petworth, Dio. Chich. 1859. (Patron, Lord Leconfield; Tithe, 856*l*; Glebe, 146 acres; R.'s Inc. 1076*l* and Ho; Pop. 3368.) Formerly P. C. of Shipley, near Horsham, Sussex, 1851–59. Author, *The Scripture Expositor, or District Visitor's Scripture Assistant,* 8 vols. 1*l* 1*s*. [19]

HOLLAND, Charles, *Eastville Parsonage, Boston.*—St. Cath. Coll. Cam. B.A. 1843; Deac. 1843, Pr. 1844. P. C. of Eastville, Dio. Lin. 1855. (Patrons, the Bp of Lin. and Trustees; P. C.'s Inc. 80*l* and Ho; Pop. 246.) P. C. of Midville, near Boston, Dio. Lin. 1855. (Patrons, Trustees; P. C.'s Inc. 80*l*; Pop. 152.) Formerly C. of Tydd St. Mary, Linc. [20]

HOLLAND, Charles Dudding, *North Mundham Vicarage, Chichester.*—Caius Coll. Cam. B.A. 1838. V. of North Mundham with Hunston V. Dio. Chich. 1856. (Patron, J. B. Fletcher, Esq; North Mundham, Tithe—Imp. 256*l*, V. 257*l*; Hunston, Tithe, 375*l*; V.'s Inc. 645*l* and Ho; Pop. North Mundham 426, Hunston 176.) [21]

HOLLAND, Edward, *Camerton Rectory, Bath.*—Magd. Hall, Ox. 2nd cl. Lit. Hum. and B.A. 1840, M.A. 1844; Deac. 1841 by Bp of B. and W. Pr. 1842 by Bp of Salis. R. of Camerton, Dio. B. and W. 1851. (Patron, John Jarrett, Esq; Tithe, 417*l* 7*s* 9*d*; Glebe, 53 acres; R.'s Inc. 493*l* and Ho; Pop. 1368.) [22]

HOLLAND, Erskine William, 33, *Upper Brunswick-place, Brighton.*—Wor. Coll. Ox. B.A. 1829, M.A. 1835; Deac. 1831 by Bp of Roch. Pr. 1831 by Bp of Chich. R. of Dunsfold, Godalming, Surrey, Dio. Win. 1838. (Patron, Ld Chan; Tithe, 540*l*; Glebe, 38 acres; R.'s Inc. 595*l* and Ho; Pop. 716.) Author, *Spiritual Husbandry, or Ministerial Seed-time and Harvest* (a Visitation Sermon at Guildford), 1860, 6*d*; *Albert the Good, In Memoriam,* Brighton. [23]

HOLLAND, Francis James.—Trin. Coll. Cam. B.A. 1850, M.A. 1853; Deac. and Pr. 1851. Min. of Quebec Chapel, Marylebone, Dio. Lon. 1861 (Patrons, Exors. of late Rev. J. H. Gurney.) Formerly V. of St. Dunstan's, Canterbury, 1853–61. [24]

HOLLAND, Frederick Whitmore, 6, *Portsea-place, Connaught-square, London, W.*—Trin. Coll. Cam. B.A. 1860, M.A. 1864; Deac. 1862, Pr. 1863. Asst. Min. of Quebec Chapel, Marylebone, 1865. Formerly C. of St. Andrew's, Manchester. [25]

HOLLAND, George Thomas, *South Cockerington, Louth, Lincolnshire.*—Ch. Coll. Cam. B.A. 1827. V. of South Cockerington, Dio Lin. 1846. (Patron, Bp of Lin; Tithe—App. 23*l*, V. 19*l* 2*s*; V.'s Inc. 165*l*; Pop. 300.) [26]

HOLLAND, John Murray, *New College, Oxford.*—New Coll. Ox. B.A. 1841, M.A. 1845; Deac. 1842, Pr. 1843. Fell. of New Coll. Ox. [27]

HOLLAND, Philip Esme Stewart, *Stonehouse, Gloucestershire.*—Wor. Coll. Ox. B.A. 1865; Deac.

1866 and Pr. 1867 by Bp of G. and B. C. of Stonehouse 1866. [1]

HOLLAND, Richard George, *Bromley Common, Kent, S.E.*—Kenyon Coll. Ohio, U.S.A., B.A. 1857, M.A. 1860; Deac. 1859 and Pr. 1860 by Abp of Cant. C. of Trinity, Bromley, 1866. Formerly C. of Sittingbourne, Kent, 1859–62, Faversham, Kent, 1862–66. [2]

HOLLAND, Stewart, 39, *Crown-street, Bury St. Edmunds.*—Dub. A.B. 1860; Deac. 1862 and Pr. 1863 by Bp of Lin. C. of St. James's, Bury St. Edmunds, 1865. Formerly C. of Sutton St. Nicholas, Lincolnshire, 1862–64, Washington, Sussex, 1864–65. [3]

HOLLAND, Thomas Agar, *Poynings Rectory, Hurst Pierpoint, Sussex.*—Wor. Coll. Ox. B.A. 1825, M.A. 1829; Deac. 1826 by Bp of Lin. Pr. 1827 by Bp of Chich. R. of Poynings, Dio. Chich. 1846. (Patron, Ld Chan; Tithe, 273*l*; Glebe, 90 acres; R.'s Inc. 380*l* and Ho; Pop. 261.) Formerly R. of Greatham, Hants, 1838–46; V. of Oving, Sussex, 1827–38. Author, *The Visible Church, its necessary Existence and Progressive Constructure* (a Visitation Sermon), 1831; *A Memento of the Protestant Reformation* (a Tercentenary Sermon), *with Notes and Appendix*, 1835, 2 eds; *Harvest Time* (a Sermon), 1836, 4 eds; *The Queen's Accession, or the English Church and Monarchy* (a Sermon), *with Notes and Appendix*, 1837; *Clergy and Laity, their mutual and equal interest in the Church* (a Visitation Sermon), 1841; *A Time of War, or War justifiable on Christian principles, with Reflections concerning the present War* (a Fast-day Sermon), 1855; *The Sabbath made for Man under both Dispensations* (a Sermon with Notes), 1861; *Sacerdotalism and Mariolatry* (a Letter on Dr. Manning's Church-Dedication Sermons in London and Brighton), *with a Letter on the Church Union Calendar*, 1864; *Poynings* (an article in the Sussex Archæological Collections), 1863; *Dryburgh Abbey and other Poems*, 1845, 2nd ed. [4]

HOLLAND, William, *Cold Norton Rectory, Maldon, Essex.*—Ch. Ch. Ox. Stud. of, B.A. 1819, M.A. 1821; Deac. 1820 and Pr. 1821 by Bp of Ox. R. of Cold Norton, Dio. Roch. 1824. (Patrons, the Governors of the Charterhouse; Tithe, 397*l*; Glebe, 42 acres; R.'s Inc. 435*l* and Ho; Pop. 207.) Rural Dean; Chap. to the late Duke of Somerset. [5]

HOLLAND, William, *Huntingfield Rectory, Halesworth, Suffolk.*—Lin. Coll. Ox. B.A. 1840; Deac. 1840 and Pr. 1841 by Bp of Lin. R. of Huntingfield with Cookley R. Dio. Nor. 1848. (Patron, Lord Huntingfield; Huntingfield, Tithe, 538*l* 9*s*; Glebe, 144½ acres with a manor; Cookley, Tithe, 405*l* 0*s* 9*d*; Glebe, 3½ acres; R.'s Inc. 1155*l* and Ho; Pop. Huntingfield 369, Cookley 252.) [6]

HOLLAND, W., *Evesham, Worcestershire.*—C. of Evesham. [7]

HOLLEY, Edward, *Hackford, next Reepham, Norfolk.*—Caius Coll. Cam. B.A. 1829; Deac. 1830 and Pr. 1831 by Bp of Nor. R. of Burgh St. Peter, near Aylsham, Dio. Nor. 1831. (Patron, J. H. Holley, Esq; Tithe, 260*l*; Glebe, 12 acres; R.'s Inc. 278*l*; Pop. 227.) R. of Hackford with Whitwell, *alias* Reepham All Saints V. Dio. Nor. 1836. (Patron, J. H. Holley, Esq; Hackford, Tithe, 213*l*; Glebe, 24 acres; Whitwell, Tithe—App 326*l*, V. 221*l* 18*s*; R.'s Inc. 533*l*; Pop. Hackford 761, Whitwell 487.) [8]

HOLLEY, Henry Hunt, *Marsham Hall, Norwich.*—Trin. Hall, Cam. B.A. 1859; Deac. 1862 and Pr. 1853 by Bp of Ely. R. of Brampton, Dio. Nor. 1867. (Patron, Rev. H. P. Marsham; Tithe, 154*l*; Glebe, 20 acres; R.'s Inc. 184*l* and Ho; Pop. 195.) Formerly C. of Thetford in Stretham, Isle of Ely, 1862–63, Burgh next Aylsham 1864–67. [9]

HOLLEY, John, *Barton St. Andrew Rectory, Stoke-Ferry, Norfolk.*—St. Peter's Coll. Cam. B.A. 1836; Deac. and Pr. 1836. R. of Barton St. Andrew, Dio. Nor. 1856. (Patron, Ld Chan; Land in lieu of Tithe, 324 acres; R.'s Inc. 270*l* and Ho; Pop. 484.) C. of Barton St. Mary and All Saints. Formerly Chap. of the D. of Calton, Staffs, 1851–56. [10]

HOLLIER, Thomas Henry, *Priston Rectory, Bath.*—St. John's Coll. Cam. B.A. 1855; Deac. 1855 and Pr. 1856 by Abp of York. R. of Priston, Dio. B. and W. 1863. (Patron, W. V. Jenkins, Esq; Tithe, 411*l*; Glebe, 47 acres; R.'s Inc. 502*l* and Ho; Pop. 292.) Formerly C. of Seaton Ross 1855–56, Matherne 1857–63. [11]

HOLLINGS, Richard, *St. John's Parsonage, Newport, Isle of Wight.*—St. John's Coll. Ox. B A. 1830; Deac. 1832, Pr. 1834. Min. of St. John's, Newport, Dio. Win. 1846; Surrogate. Author, *Little Children's Prayers Answered*, 18th ed. 2*d*; *Handbill on Confirmation.* [12]

HOLLINGWORTH, Henry, *Cuckfield, Sussex.*—King's Coll. Cam. 1st cl. Cl. Trip. B.A. 1864, M.A. 1867; Deac. 1865 by Bp of Lin. C. of Cuckfield 1866; Fell. of King's Coll. Cam. [13]

HOLLINGWORTH, John Graham, *Standish, Wigan.*—Ex. Coll. Ox. B.A. 1852; Deac. 1853 and Pr. 1854 by Bp of Rip. P. C. of Coppull, near Chorley, Dio. Man. 1855. (Patron, R. of Standish; P. C.'s Inc. 166*l* and Ho; Pop. 1230.) Formerly C. of Stanley, Wakefield. Author, *A Catechism on the Nature and Offices of the Church*, Rivingtons, 1857. [14]

HOLLINGWORTH, Joseph, *Skelmersdale, Ormskirk, Lancashire.*—St. Cath. Hall, Cam. B.A. 1843, M.A. 1848; Deac. 1843 and Pr. 1844 by Bp of Ches. P. C. of Skelmersdale, Dio. Ches. 1850. (Patron, V. of Ormskirk; Tithe, Imp. 220*l*; P. C.'s Inc. 160*l* and Ho; Pop. 1028.) [15]

HOLLINGWORTH, Ollive, *Parsonage House, Turnham-green, W.*—Sid. Coll. Cam. B.A. 1835, M.A. 1858; Deac. 1836 and Pr. 1837 by Bp of Win. P. C. of Ch. Ch. Chiswick, Dio. Lon. 1858. (Patron, Bp of Lon; P. C.'s Inc. 300*l* and Ho; Pop. 2623.) Formerly V. of Stalisfield, Kent, 1840–58. [16]

HOLLINS, James, *St. Clement's Parsonage, Bristol.*—Literate; Deac. 1847 and Pr. 1848 by Bp of Lich. P. C. of St. Clement's, Bristol, Dio. G. and B. 1855. (Patrons, Trustees; P. C.'s Inc. 200*l* and Ho; Pop. 5301.) Author, *Holy Bible, the Foundation Rock of the Church of England*, 3*s*; *Salvation is of the Jews*; *Pastoral Recollections, &c.* 1857, 5*s*. [17]

HOLLIS, George Parry, *Dodington Rectory, Bridgwater.*—St. Alban Hall, Ox. B.A. 1824. R. of Dodington, Dio. B. and W. 1831. (Patron, Duke of Buckingham; Tithe, 90*l*; Glebe, 18½ acres; R.'s Inc. 120*l* and Ho; Pop. 98.) [18]

HOLLIS, Robert, *Whaplode Drove, Croyland, Lincolnshire.*—St. Bees; Deac. 1849 and Pr. 1850 by Bp of Ches. P. C. of Whaplode Drove, Dio. Lin. 1866. (Patrons, Feoffees; P. C.'s Inc. 400*l* and Ho; Pop. 844.) Formerly C. of Spalding. [19]

HOLLOND, Edmund, *Benhall Lodge, Saxmundham.* [20]

HOLLOWAY, Edward John, *Wantage.*—Caius Coll. Cam. 3rd cl. Cl. Trip. B.A. 1857, M.A. 1866; Deac. 1861 by Bp of Ex. Pr. 1863 by Bp of Ox. C. of Wantage 1863. Formerly C. of Carnmenellis, Cornwall, 1861–63. [21]

HOLLOWAY, George, *Prescot, Lancashire.*—Dub. A.B. 1852, A.M. 1866; Deac. 1854 by Bp of Llan. Pr. 1855 by Bp of Meath. C. of Prescot 1863. Formerly C. of Hillsborough 1854–57, Downpatrick 1858–62. [22]

HOLLOWAY, John Frederick Evans, *Gordon House*, 110, *Lansdowne-place, Brighton.*—Trin. Coll. Cam. B.A. 1848, M.A. 1853; Deac. 1856 and Pr. 1857 by Bp of Chich. [23]

HOLLWAY, Thomas, *Spilsby, Lincolnshire.*—St John's Coll. Cam. B.A. 1823, M.A. 1826; Deac. 1824 by Bp of Salis. Pr. 1825 by Bp of G. and B. Preb. of Lin. 1843. Author, *The Doctrine of the Presence of Christ in the Holy Eucharist as maintained by the Church of England* 1854. [24]

HOLLYWOOD, John, *Dodworth-road, Barnsley.*—Dub. A.B. 1865; Deac. 1865 and Pr. 1866 by Bp of Rip. C. of St. George's, Barnsley, 1865. [25]

HOLMAN, William Henry.—Lin. Coll. Ox. B.A. 1848, M.A. 1854; Deac. 1848 and Pr. 1849 by Bp of Ex. Chap. of H.M.S. "Formidable." Formerly Chap. to the community on Pitcairn's Island, South Pacific. [26]

HOLME, Arthur Phidias, *Fishers Quay, Great Yarmouth*.—Trin. Coll. Cam. B.A. 1857, M.A. 1862; Deac. 1859 and Pr. 1860 by Bp of Nor. Min. of St. Andrew's, Great Yarmouth. Formerly Asst. C. of Great Yarmouth. [1]

HOLME, Christopher, *Greywell, Odiham, Hants*.—Dur. B.A. 1851, M.A. 1855; Deac. 1855 by Bp of Lon. Pr. 1856 by Bp of Win. C. of Greywell 1866. Formerly Asst. Mast. in Kensington Gr. Sch. and Cl. Mast. in St. Peter's Sch. Eaton-square. Author, *Notes on St. Mark's Gospel*, Longmans, 1863, 2s 6d. [2]

HOLME, Edward, *Odiham, Hants*.—St. Bees; Deac. 1854 and Pr. 1855 by Bp of Rip. C. of Odiham 1855. Formerly Chap. to House of Correction, Northallerton. [3]

HOLME, George Ward, *Warkworth, Northumberland*.—Univ. Coll. Dur; Deac. 1856 and Pr. 1857 by Bp of Dur. C. of Warkworth 1862. Formerly C. of Trinity, South Shields, 1856–59, Gateshead 1859–62 [4]

HOLME, James, *East Cowton, Northallerton, Yorks*.—Caius Coll. Cam. Sen. Opt. and B.A. 1825; Deac. 1825 and Pr. 1826 by Bp of Dur. Formerly P. C. of Low Harrogate 1827; V. of Kirkleatham, Yorks, 1839. Author, *Mount Grace Abbey* (a Poem), 5s; *Correspondence and Brief Memorial Sketches of Mrs. Pregrave*, 3s 6d; *Leisure Musings and Devotional Meditations in Humble Strains of Poetry*, 2s 6d; *Psalms and Hymns, Original and Select, for Public Worship*, 1s; *A Sermon* (preached after the Death of the Hon. Lady Turner), 2d; *Mercy for the Fatherless*, 1d; *Hymns and Sacred Poetry by the Brothers Thomas and James Holme*, 1s. [5]

HOLME, John, *Lower Peover, Knutsford, Cheshire*.—Deac. and Pr. 1829. P. C. of Lower Peover, Dio. Ches. 1838. (Patron, Lord De Tabley; Tithe—App. 32*l* 18s; P. C.'s Inc. 100*l*; Pop. 109.) Formerly Chap. of Tabley Chapel, Budworth, 1831–65. [6]

HOLME, Meyrick, *Marston-Meysey (Wilts), near Fairford*.—Brasen. Coll. Ox. B.A. 1836, M.A. 1837; Deac. 1839 and Pr. 1840 by Bp of G. and B. P. C. of Marston-Meysey, Dio. G. and B. 1840. (Patron, R. of Hampton-Meysey; P. C.'s Inc. 80*l* and Ho; Pop. 215.) [7]

HOLME, Robert, *Greenwich, S.E.*—Corpus Coll. Cam. B.A. 1851, M.A. 1854; Deac. 1852, Pr. 1853. Prin. and Chap. of Greenwich Hosp. Sch; Fell. of Corpus Coll Cam. [8]

HOLME, Thomas, *East Cowton, Northallerton, Yorks*.—V. of East Cowton, Dio. Rip. 1842. (Patron, St. John the Baptist's Hospital Kirkby-Ravensworth; Tithe, 213*l* 6s 8d; Glebe, ½ acre; V.'s Inc. 213*l*; Pop. 472.) [9]

HOLME, Thomas, *Mardale, Penrith*.—Queen's Coll. Ox. B.A. 1835, M.A. 1838; Deac. 1836, Pr. 1837. P. C. of Mardale, Dio. Carl. 1858. (Patron, V. of Shap; P. C.'s Inc. 120*l*; Pop. 500.) Formerly R. of Puttenham, Herts, 1849–58. [10]

HOLME, Thomas Redmayne, *St. James's Vicarage, Whitehaven*.—Emman. Coll. Cam. B.A. 1848, M.A. 1857; Deac. 1852 and Pr. 1853 by Bp of Ches. V. of St. James's, Whitehaven, Dio. Carl. 1867. (Patron, Earl of Lonsdale; Tithe, 7*l*; V.'s Inc. 150*l* and Ho; Pop. 5500.) Formerly C. of Hyde, Cheshire, 1852–53; Chap. R.N. 1853–65; C. of Willerby 1865–67. [11]

HOLMES, Alleyne James, *Soham, Cambs*.—Oriel Coll. Ox. B.A. 1851, M.A. 1856; Deac. 1853 and Pr. 1854 by Bp of Wor. C. of Soham with Barway 1858. Formerly C. of St. John's, Coventry, 1853–55, St. Thomas's, Coventry, 1855–58. [12]

HOLMES, Arthur, 5, *Camden-place, Cambridge*.—St. John's Coll. Cam. migrated to Clare, 1864, Bell Scho. 1856, Craven Scho. 1856, Porson Prizes 1856, 1857, '58, Browne Medal for Greek Ode 1857, '58, Chan.'s Medal for English Poem 1858, 2nd in 1st cl. Cl. Trip. and B.A. 1859, M.A. 1862; Deac. 1860 and Pr. 1861 by Bp of Ely. Fell. of St. John's Coll. 1860–62; Fell. and Lect. of Clare Coll. 1864; Lect. of St. John's Coll. 1860; Lect. of Emman. Coll. 1865; Deputy Public Orator of Cambridge 1867. Formerly C. of All Saints', Cambridge, 1860–61. Author, *The Midias of Demosthenes with English Notes*, Johnson, Cambridge, 5s; *A Sermon preached in the Chapel of Clare College*, 1866; *The Nemean Odes of Pindar* (a prelection before the Council of the Senate), 1867. General Editor of the *Catena Classicorum*, 1867. Contributor to the *Sabrinae Corolla*, the *Arundines Cami*, *Folia Silvulae*, etc. [13]

HOLMES, B. J., *Ossett, Wakefield*.—C. of Ossett with Gawthorpe. [14]

HOLMES, Charles Allison, *Oakhouse, Greetham, Oakham*.—St. Cath. Coll. Cam. B.A. 1847; Deac. 1847 and Pr. 1848 by Bp of Pet. Formerly C. of Market Overton, Rutland. [15]

HOLMES, Charles Richard, *Haley Hill, Halifax*.—Magd. Coll. Cam. Sch. of, B.A. 1849, M.A. 1852; Deac. 1849 and Pr. 1850 by Bp of Rip. P. C. of Haley Hill, Dio. Rip. 1855. (Patron, E. Akroyd, Esq; P. C.'s Inc. 257*l* and Ho; Pop. 5235.) Formerly C. of Coley, Halifax, 1849–53, Horncastle 1853–54. Author, *The Necessity for Free Churches and the Sin of Pew Rents*, 1859; *The Offertory*, 1860; *All Saints and All Souls*; *The Church and the Million*; etc. [16]

HOLMES, Charles Rivington, *Bromley, Poplar, London, E.*—Clare Coll. Cam. 3rd cl. Cl. Trip. B.A. 1856, M.A. 1862; Deac. 1857 and Pr. 1858 by Bp of Lon. P. C. of St. Michael and All Angels', Bromley, Dio. Lon. 1864. (Patrons, the Crown and Bp of Lon. alt; P. C.'s Inc. 300*l* and Ho; Pop. 24,000.) Formerly C. of St. John's, Limehouse, 1857; Vice-Prin. of Dioc. Training Coll. Culham, Oxon, 1863. [17]

HOLMES, Edward, *Wakerley, Stamford*.—Corpus Coll. Cam. B.A. 1844; Deac. 1845, Pr. 1846. R. of Wakerley, Dio. Pet. 1853. (Patron, Marquis of Exeter; Glebe, 3 acres; R.'s Inc. 100*l* and Ho; Pop. 223.) Chap to the Stamford Gaol 1851. Formerly C. of St. Michael's, Stamford. [18]

HOLMES, Edward Adolphus, *St. Margaret's Rectory, South Elmham, near Harleston, Norfolk*.—Emman. Coll. Cam. Sen. Opt. and B.A. 1832, M.A. 1835; Deac. 1833 by Bp of Nor. Pr. 1833 by Abp of York. R. of St. Margaret with St. Peter, South Elmham, Dio. Nor. 1833. (Patron, Sir Shafto Adair, Bart; St. Margaret, Tithe—Imp. 1*l* 8s, R. 139*l* 1s; Glebe, 63 acres; St. Peter, Tithe, 145*l*; Glebe, 25 acres; R.'s Inc. 348*l* and Ho; Pop. St. Margaret 152, St. Peter 88.) Rural Dean. [19]

HOLMES, Edward Molloy, *Churchill, Chipping Norton*.—Dub. A.B. 1851; Deac. 1853 and Pr. 1854 by Bp. of Win. C. of Churchill with Cornwell, Oxon, 1857, Formerly C. of Brown Candover with Chilton Candover, Hants, 1853–57. [20]

HOLMES, Edward William.—Trin. Coll. Cam. Jun. Opt. and B.A. 1857; Deac. 1858 and Pr. 1859 by Bp of Rip. Formerly C. of Trinity, Wakefield. [21]

HOLMES, Francis Greame, *Denham, Wickham Market, Suffolk*.—St. John's Coll. Cam. B.A. 1851, M.A. 1854; Deac. 1853 and Pr. 1854 by Bp of Dur. C. of Denham. [22]

HOLMES, George Gorham, *Holme Vicarage, York*.—St. John's Coll. Cam. Sen. Opt. 2nd cl. Cl. Trip. and B.A. 1846, M.A. 1849, B.D. 1856; Deac. 1849 by Bp of Ely, Pr. 1850 by Bp of Pet. V. of Holme-on-Spalding-Moor, Dio. York, 1865. (Patron, St. John's Coll. Cam; V.'s Inc. 650*l* and Ho; Pop. 1913.) Late Fell. of St. John's Coll. Cam; C. of King's Stanley, Glouc. [23]

HOLMES, Henry, *Durleigh, Bridgwater*.—Chap. of Den. of Durleigh, Dio. B. and W. 1866. (Patron, Rev. G. R. Harding; Chap.'s Inc. 25*l*; Pop. 158.) [24]

HOLMES, Henry Cautley, *Garthorpe Vicarage, Melton Mowbray*.—St. Cath. Coll. Cam. B.A. 1837, M.A. 1840; Deac. 1838, Pr. 1839. V. of Garthorpe, Dio. Pet. 1864. (Patron, Earl of Dysart; V.'s Inc. 150*l* and Ho; Pop. 113.) [25]

HOLMES, Isaac, *Kirkdale Industrial Schools, Liverpool*.—Dub. A.B. 1849; Deac. 1849 and Pr. 1850 by Bp of Ches. Chap. of the Kirkdale Industrial Schools, Liverpool, 1855. (Salary, 250*l*.) Formerly Head Mast. to the Liverpool Corporation North Schools 1842; Chap.

to the Liverpool Workhouse 1851–55. Author, *Thieves, Beggars and Prostitutes* (a Pamphlet), 1853; *Liverpool in the Dark* (a Lecture), 1854. [1]

HOLMES, James, *The Hollins, Sowerby Bridge, Normanton.*—Deac. 1866 and Pr. 1866 by Bp of Rip. C. of Sowerby Bridge 1865. [2]

HOLMES, James Ivory, *Baring-crescent, Exeter.*—Trin. Coll. Cam. 2nd Sen. Opt, and B.A. 1805, M.A. 1808; Deac. 1808 by Abp of York, Pr. 1809 by Bp of Nor. Formerly Hon. Chap. to the Female Penitentiary, Exeter, 1821; Sec. to the Devon and Exeter Ch. Miss. Soc. 1822. Author, *The Fulfilment of the Revelation of St. John Displayed*, 1815 and 1819; *Justification by Faith* (a Sermon), 1822; *The Inspiration of the Mosaic Account of Creation*, 1856; etc. [3]

HOLMES, James Roberts, *Brookland, New Romney, Kent.*—Pemb. Coll. Cam. B.A. 1848, M.A. 1851; Deac. 1849 and Pr. 1850 by Bp of Lich. V. of Brookland, Dio. Cant. 1858. (Patrons, D. and C. of Cant; V.'s Inc. 130*l*; Pop. 459.) C. of Brenzett. [4]

HOLMES, James Waldby, *New Mill Parsonage, Huddersfield.*—Clare Coll. Cam. B.A. 1839, M.A. 1842; Deac. 1839 and Pr. 1840 by Abp of York. P. C. of New Mill, Dio. Rip. 1843. (Patron, V. of Kirkburton; P. C.'s Inc. 150*l* and Ho; Pop. 2803.) [5]

HOLMES, John Garraway, *Reading.*—Univ. Coll. Ox. B.A. 1862; Deac. 1863 by Bp of Pet. C. of Ch. Ch. Reading. Formerly C. of Lutterworth 1862. [6]

HOLMES, Joseph, *Swineshead Vicarage, Spalding, Lincolnshire.*—Trin. Coll. Cam. B.A. 1844, M.A. 1847; Deac. 1847 and Pr. 1848 by Bp of Lich. V. of Swineshead, Dio. Lin. 1848. (Patron, Trin. Coll. Cam; Glebe, 62 acres; V.'s Inc. 240*l* and Ho; Pop. 1903.) [7]

HOLMES, Melville, *Trinity Church Rectory, Chesterfield.*—St. John's Coll. Cam. B.A. 1845; Deac. 1845 by Bp of Salis. and Pr. 1846 by Bp of Lich. R. of Trinity, Chesterfield, Dio. Lich. 1867. (Patrons, Trustees; R.'s Inc. 300*l* and Ho; Pop. 4800.) Formerly C. of Haselbury Bryan, Dorset, 1845; P. C. of Tansley, Derbyshire, 1846–47. [8]

HOLMES, Peter, *Wellington Villa, Mannamhead, Plymouth.*—Magd. Hall, Ox. B.A. 1840, M.A. 1844, D.D. 1859; Deac. 1840 and Pr. 1841 by Bp of Ex. C. of Egg-Buckland, Devon; Fell. of the Royal Soc. of Antiquaries; Dom. Chap. to the Countess of Rothes. Formerly Head Mast. of the Plymouth Gr. Sch. Author, *Observations on the Standard of Doctrine in the Church of England*, 1848; *Translation of Bishop Bull's Defensio Fidei Nicaenae*, 2 vols. for the Anglo-Catholic Library, Oxford, 1851–52; *Translation of Bishop Bull's Judicium Ecclesiae Cathol.* ib. 1855; *Treatise on Diocesan Synods*, 1852. [9]

HOLMES, Richard, *Eldersfield Vicarage, near Tewkesbury.*—St. Peter's Coll. Cam. B.A. 1845; Deac. 1846, Pr. 1847. V. of Eldersfield, Dio. Wor. 1851. (Patron, the present V; Tithe—Imp. 715*l* 5*s*, V. 290*l*; Glebe, 4 acres; V.'s Inc. 298*l* and Ho; Pop. 782.) [10]

HOLMES, Richard B., *Christ Church Parsonage, Gloucester.*—P. C. of Ch. Ch. Gloucester, Dio. G. and B. 1830. (Patrons, Trustees; P. C.'s Inc. 150*l* and Ho.) [11]

HOLMES, Samuel, *Dorking, Surrey.*—P. C. of St. Paul's, Dorking, Dio. Win. 1866. (Patrons, Trustees; P. C.'s Inc. 250*l* and Ho; Pop. 1355.) Can. of Rip. 1863. (Value, 500*l*.) Formerly V. of Huddersfield 1855–66. [12]

HOLMES, Samuel, *Bishop Wearmouth, Durham.*—C. of Bishop Wearmouth. [13]

HOLMES, Thomas, *Wilberfoss, York.*—P. C. of Wilberfoss, Dio. York, 1822. (Patrons, Lord Leconfield and others; P. C.'s Inc. 67*l* and Ho; Pop. 632.) [14]

HOLMES, Thomas Pattison, *Wisbech, Cambs.*—St. John's Coll. Cam. B.A. 1815. P. C. of Gaybirn, near Wisbech, Dio. Ely, 1817. (Patron, V. of Wisbech; P. C.'s Inc. 80*l*.) P. C. of Wisbech Chapel of Ease, Dio. Ely, 1831. (Patrons, Trustees; P. C.'s Inc. 350*l*.) [15]

HOLMES, Thomas White, *Congham Rectory, Castle Rising, Norfolk.*—Corpus Coll. Cam. B.A. 1812; Deac. 1813, Pr. 1814. R. of Congham, Dio. Nor. 1861. (Patron, John Roper, Esq; Pop. 315.) Formerly P. C. of Hardley, Norfolk, 1845–61. [16]

HOLROYD, James John, *White Hall, near Colchester.*—Ch. Coll. Cam. B.A. 1830, M.A. 1835; Deac. and Pr. 1830 by Bp of Lon. R. of Abberton, Essex, Dio. Roch. 1830. (Patron, Ld Chan; Tithe, 314*l*; Glebe, 50 acres; R.'s Inc. 360*l* and Ho; Pop. 269.) Author, *Translation of some of Lessing's Works*, 1838. [17]

HOLROYD, John, *Bardsey Vicarage, Wetherby, Yorks.*—Trin. Coll. Cam. B.A. 1819, St. Cath. Hall, Cam. M.A. 1822; Deac. 1822, Pr. 1829. V. of Bardsey, Dio. Rip. 1849. (Patron, G. L. Fox, Esq; Tithe—App. 38*l* 16*s*, Imp. 25*l*, V. 136*l*; Glebe, 130 acres; V.'s Inc. 304*l* and Ho; Pop. 390.) [18]

HOLT, Eardley Chauncy, *Tottenham, N.* and 4, *Eccleston-street, Chester-square, London, S.W.*—Brasen. Coll. Ox. B.A. 1839, M.A. 1842; Deac. 1841 and Pr. 1842 by Bp of Win. Formerly C. of Barcheston. [19]

HOLT, Edward Kaye, *Sancton, Brough, Yorks.*—St. John's Coll. Cam. B.A. 1854; Deac. 1858 and Pr. 1859 by Abp of York. V. of Sancton, Dio. York, 1865. (Patron, Hon. Charles Langdale; Glebe, 3½ acres; V.'s Inc. 300*l*; Pop. 476.) Formerly C. and Mast. of the Church Sch. Market Weighton, 1858–60; C. of Wheldrake 1860–65; Reviser of the *Key to Morrison's Arithmetic.* [20]

HOLT, John Mussendine, *Keelby, Ulceby, Lincolnshire.*—St. John's Coll. Cam. Wrang. and B.A. 1846, M.A. 1849; Deac. 1847 and Pr. 1848 by Bp of Pet. V. of Keelby, Dio. Lin. 1855. (Patron, Earl of Yarborough; Glebe, 61 acres; V.'s Inc. 90*l*; Pop. 842.) [21]

HOLT, Robert, *Adstock Rectory, Buckingham.*—St. John's Coll. Cam. late Scho. of, Cl. and Math. Hons. B.A. 1846, M.A. 1850; Deac. 1846 and Pr. 1847 by Bp of Ox. C. in sole charge of Adstock 1861. Formerly C. of Soulbury, Bucks, 1846, Wardington, Oxon, 1848, Mursley, Bucks, 1852. [22]

HOLT, Robert Fowler, 18, *Russell-street, Reading.*—Brasen Coll. Ox. B.A. 1813, M.A. 1815; Deac. 1815, Pr. 1821. Chap. to the Union, Slough, Bucks, 1836. [23]

HOLT, William Henry, *Elmhurst, Congleton, Cheshire.*—St. John's Coll. Cam. B.A. 1822; Deac. 1828 and Pr. 1831 by Bp of Lich. V. of Biddulph, Staffs, Dio. Lich. 1831. (Patron, J. Bateman, Esq; Tithe—Imp. 181*l* 8*s*, V. 90*l* 10*s*; Glebe, 34 acres; V.'s Inc. 104*l*; Pop. 3130.) [24]

HOLTHOUSE, Charles Scrafton, *Helidon Vicarage, Daventry, Northants.*—St. John's Coll. Ox. B.A. 1839, M.A. 1842; Deac. 1842 and Pr. 1843 by Bp of Lin. V. of Helidon, Dio. Pet. 1845. (Patron, the present V; Glebe, 60 acres; V.'s Inc. 190*l* and Ho; Pop. 449.) Formerly V. of Catesby, Northants, 1849. [25]

HOMAN, John, *Sapcote Rectory, Hinckley, Leicestershire.*—Dub. A.B. 1831, M.A. 1834; Deac. 1836 by Abp of Dub. Pr. 1846 by Bp of Ches. R. of Sapcote, Dio. Pet. 1856. (Patron, Thomas Frewen, Esq; Tithe—Imp. 1*l* 1*s*, R. 1*l* 10*s*; Glebe, 276 acres; R.'s Inc. 600*l* and Ho; Pop. 668.) Dom. Chap. to Lord Castlemaine 1840. Formerly Chap. of the Don. of Dolphinholme, Lanc. 1846–53; P. C. of Ellel, Lanc. 1853–56. [26]

HOMBERSLEY, William, *Normacot, Longton, Staffs.*—Ch. Ch. Ox. B.A. 1840, M.A. 1843; Deac. 1844, Pr. 1845. P. C. of Normacot, Dio. Lich. 1858. (Patron, Duke of Sutherland; P. C.'s Inc. 122*l* and Ho; Pop. 1697.) [27]

HOME, James Campbell, *Rawcliffe Parsonage, Garstang, Lancashire.*—Clare Hall, Cam. B.A. 1840, M.A. 1843; Deac. 1840, Pr. 1841. P. C. of Out-Rawcliffe, Dio. Man. 1847. (Patron, V. of St. Michael's-on-Wyre; Tithe—Imp. 5*l* 6*s* 8*d*; P. C.'s Inc. 110*l* and Ho; Pop. 771.) [28]

HOME, John, *Bradley, Bromsgrove, Worcestershire.*—Corpus Coll. Cam. LL.B. 1850; Deac. and Pr. 1850. R. of Bradley, Dio. Wor. 1864. (Patron, Bp of Wor; R.'s Inc. 300*l*; Pop. 310.) Formerly Chap. of Don. of Dormstone 1851–64. [29]

HOMER, Henry, *Barlestone, Leicester.*—Jesus Coll. Cam. B.A. 1843; Deac. 1843 by Bp of Herf. Pr. 1844 by Bp of Lich. C. of Barlestone. [1]

HOMER, Thomas, *Frieston, Boston, Lincolnshire.*—Trin. Coll. Cam. B D. 1825, D.D. 1834. V. of Frieston with Butterwick V. Dio. Lin. (Patron, L. Hitchen, Esq; V.'s Inc. 895*l*; Pop. Frieston 1059, Butterwick 605.) [2]

HOMFRAY, Kenyon, *Penyclawdd Parsonage, Monmouth.*—Magd. Hall, Ox. B.A. and M.A. 1837; Deac. 1836 by Bp of Ex. Pr. 1837 by Bp of Llan. P. C. of Llangoven with Pen-y-Clawdd P. C. Dio. Llan. 1852. (Patrons, D. and C. of Llandaff; P. C.'s Inc. 100*l* and Ho; Pop. Llangoven 137, Pen-y-Clawdd 53.) Formerly C. of St. Pierre 1836, Llanvihangel Ystern Llewern 1840; Chap. to Usk Gaol 1843–52. [3]

HOMFRAY, Samuel Francis Wingfield Clark, *Bintree, Guist, Norfolk.*—St. Cath. Coll. Cam. B.A. 1844, M.A. 1847; Deac. 1844 and Pr. 1845 by Bp of Ex. R. of Bintree with Themelthorpe, Dio. Nor. 1863. (Patron, Lord Hastings; Bintree, Tithe, 415*l* 12*s* 4*d*; Glebe, 13 acres; Themelthorpe, Tithe, 131*l*; Glebe, 19 acres; R.'s Inc. 525*l* 8*s* 10*d* and Ho; Pop. Bintree 406, Themelthorpe 68.) Chap. to Lord Hastings. Formerly C. of Falmouth 1844–46; V. of Barney, Norfolk, 1846–68; V. of Norton Pudding, Norfolk, 1846–63. Author, *Baptismal Regeneration*, 1846, 1*s*; *Lukewarmness the National Sin* (a Sermon), 1854, 6*d*. [4]

HOMFRAY, Watkin, *West Retford Rectory, East Retford, Notts.*—Ex. Coll. Ox. B.A. 1845, M.A. 1849; Deac. 1852 and Pr. 1854 by Bp of Lich. R. of West Retford, Dio. Lin. 1866. (Patron, John Hood, Esq; R.'s Inc. 600*l* and Ho; Pop. 637.) Formerly R. of Acton Beauchamp, Worcestershire, 1855–66. [5]

HONE, Evelyn Joseph, *Wentworth, Rotherham.*—Wad. Coll Ox. Scho. and Hody Exhib. 3rd cl. Lit. Hum. B.A. 1860, M.A. 1863; Deac. 1860 and Pr. 1861 by Abp of York. P. C. of Wentworth, Dio. York, 1865. (Patron, Earl Fitzwilliam; Glebe, 55 acres; P. C.'s Inc. 120*l* and Ho; Pop. 1270.) Formerly C. of Doncaster 1860, St. Giles'-in-the-Fields, Lond. 1865. [6]

HONE, Joseph Frederic, *Tirley Vicarage, Tewkesbury.*—Univ. Coll. Ox. 3rd cl. Lit. Hum. and B.A. 1825, M.A. 1828; Deac. 1825, Pr. 1826. V. of Tirley, Dio. G. and B. 1827. (Patron, Ld Chan; Glebe, 200 acres; V.'s Inc. 417*l* and Ho; Pop. 539.) Author, *A Visitation Sermon*, 1835, 1*s*; *Comments on the Epistles as appointed to be Read at the Communion Table on the Sundays and Holidays throughout the Year*, 1842, 6*s*. [7]

HONE, The Ven. Richard Brindley, *Hales-Owen Rectory (Worcestershire), near Birmingham.*—Brasen. Coll. Ox. B.A. 1827, M.A. 1831; Deac. 1828 by Bp of Glouc. Pr. 1829 by Bp of Win. V. of Hales-Owen, Dio. Wor. 1836. (Patron, Lord Lyttelton; Glebe, 4 acres; R.'s Inc. 849*l* and Ho; Pop. 6643.) Hon. Can. of Wor. Cathl. 1845; Archd. of Wor. 1849. (Value, 200*l*.) Author, *Lives of Eminent Christians*, 4 vols. S.P.C.K. 4*s* 6*d* each vol; *The Future Life of Blessedness*, 1863; Thirteen *Charges* (delivered to the Clergy of the Archd. of Wor); several single Sermons; Thirty-one *New Years' Addresses*. [8]

HONEY, Charles Robertson, *Copthill House, Bedford.*—Magd. Hall, Ox. 2nd cl. Maths. B.A. 1866; Deac. 1866 by Bp of Ely. C. of Oakley, Beds, 1866. Formerly 2nd Mast. of Sutton Coldfield Sch. 1857–62. [9]

HONNYWILL, John Blake, *Sompting Vicarage, Shoreham, Sussex.*—St John's Coll. Cam. B.A. 1846; Deac. 1848 and Pr. 1849 by Bp of Wor. V. of Sompting, Dio. Chich. 1863. (Patrons, H. P. Crofts, Esq; Tithe, 290*l*; V.'s Inc. 200*l* and Ho; Pop. 628.) Formerly P. C. of St. George's, Altrincham, 1856–59. [10]

HONY, The Ven. William Edward, *Baverstock Rectory, Salisbury, Wilts.*—Ex. Coll. Ox. B.A. 1810, M.A. 1813, B.D. 1824. R. of Baverstock, Dio. Salis. 1827. (Patron, Ex. Coll. Ox; Tithe, 262*l*; Glebe, 57 acres; R.'s Inc. 322*l* and Ho; Pop. 168.) Preb. of Salis. 1841; Archd. of Salis. 1846; Can. Res. of Salis. 1857. Late Fell. of Ex. Coll. Ox. [11]

HONYMAN, William Macdonald.—Wor. Coll. Ox. B.A. 1845, M.A. 1847; Deac. 1846, Pr. 1847. Formerly C. of Stoke-upon-Tern. [12]

HONYWOOD, Philip James, *Colne-Wake Rectory, Halstead, Essex.*—Trin. Coll. Ox. B.A. 1831; Deac. and Pr. 1834 by Bp of Lon. R. of Colne-Wake, Dio. Roch. 1866. (Patron, Earl of Verulam; R.'s Inc. 550*l* and Ho; Pop. 535.) Formerly R. of Markshall, Essex. [13]

HOOD, Elisha William, *Ilston Rectory, Swansea.*—Wad. Coll. Ox. B.A. 1823, M.A. 1827; Deac. 1826 and Pr. 1833 by Bp of Lon. R. of Ilston, Dio. St. D. 1865. (Patron, Thomas Penrice, Esq; R.'s Inc. 300*l* and Ho; Pop. 295.) Formerly V. of Nazeing, Essex, 1834–64. [14]

HOOK, Walter, *Vicar's Close, Chichester.*—Ch. Ch. Ox. 2nd cl. Law and Mod. Hist. B.A. 1860, M.A. 1863; Deac. 1863 by Bp of Salis. Pr. 1864 by Bp of Chich. P. C. of St. Bartholomew's, Chichester, Dio. Chich. 1866. (Patron, Bp of Chich; P. C.'s Inc. 55*l*; Pop. 300.) Succentor of Chich. Cathl. [15]

HOOK, The Very Rev. Walter Farquhar, *The Deanery, Chichester.*—Born, 13th March, 1798; Ch. Ch. Ox. B.A. 1820, M.A. 1824, D.D. 1837; Deac. 1821 by Bp of Herf. Pr. 1822 by Bp of Ox. Dean of Chich. 1859. (Patron, the Crown; Dean's Inc. 1000*l* and Ho.) Chap. in Ordinary to the Queen 1837; F.R.S. 1863. Formerly V. of Trinity, Coventry, 1828–37, of Leeds 1837–59; Preb. of Caistor in Lin. Cathl. 1831; Select Preacher, Univ. of Ox. 1833 and 1858; appointed a Royal Commissioner on Division of Parishes 1855, on Cathedrals 1857, on Middle-class Education 1865. Author, *The Peculiar Character of the Church of England, independently of its Connection with the State* (a Sermon), 4to. 1822; *An Attempt to demonstrate the Catholicism of the Church of England, and other Branches of the Episcopal Church* (a Sermon at the Consecration of the Rt. Rev. M. H. Luscombe), 4to. 1825; *The S P.C.K. recommended to the Support of Churchmen* (a Sermon), 1830; *The Last Days of our Lord's Ministry* (a Course of Lectures for Passion-week), 1832; *Hear the Church* (a Sermon, preached at the Chapel-Royal), 1832, 28 eds; *Questions and Answers on Confirmation*, 1834; *The Sin and Danger of Lukewarmness* (a Sermon), 1834; *The Church and the Establishment* (Two Sermons), 1834; *Private Prayers*, 1836; *The Catholic Clergy of Ireland, their Cause defended* (a Sermon), 1836; *Five Sermons* (preached before the University of Oxford), 1837; *The Gospel and the Gospel only, the Basis of Education* (a Sermon), 1839, 2 eds; *A Call to Union on the Principles of the English Reformation* (a Visitation Sermon, with Notes and Appendix), 1839, 4 eds; *The Novelties of Romanism, or Popery refuted by Tradition* (a Sermon), 1840, 2 eds; *Sermons on Various Subjects*, 1 vol. 1841; *A Letter to the Bishop of Ripon on the State of Parties in the Church of England*, 1841; *Prayers for Young Christians*, 1841, 2 eds; *A Book of Family Prayer*, 1841, 4 eds; *Sermons*, 1 vol. 1842; *Peril of Idolatry* (a Sermon), 1842; *Reasons for contributing towards the Support of an English Bishop at Jerusalem, in a Letter to a Friend*, 1842, *A Church Dictionary*, 1842, 9 eds; *Mutual Forbearance recommended in Things Indifferent* (a Sermon at the Consecration of a Church), 1843, 2 eds; *Take heed what ye hear* (a Sermon, with a Preface, on some of the existing Controversies in the Church), 1844; *Ecclesiastical Biography* 8 vols. 1845–52; *The Church of England Vindicated against Romanism and Ultra-Protestantism* (a collection of Sermons), 1845; *Parochial Sub-division* (a Sermon), Leeds, 1845; *Pastoral Advice to Young People preparing for Confirmation*, 1846; *Helps to Self-examination*, Leeds, 1846; *On the Means of rendering more Efficient the Education of the People* (a Letter to the Bishop of St. David's), 1846, 10 eds; *Sermons, suggested by the Miracles of our Lord and Saviour Jesus Christ*, 2 vols. 1847–48; *The Golden Censers of the Sanctuary* (Sermons at the Consecration of St. James's, Morpeth), 1847; *The Three Reformations—Lutheran, Roman, Anglican* (with a Postscript), 1847, 3 eds; *The Mother of our Lord and Mariolatry* (a Sermon), 1847; *The Invocation of Saints, a Romish Sin: the Communion of Saints,* *an Article of the Creed* (a Sermon), 1847; *I magnify mine Office* (a Sermon), Leeds, 1847; *The Eucharist, a Sacrament and a Sacrifice* (a Sermon), 1847; *Auricular Confession* (a Sermon, with Preface, Appendix and copious Notes), 1848; *A Pastoral Address to a Young Communicant*, Leeds, 1848; *Our Holy and Beautiful House, the Church of England* (a Sermon), 1848; *Marriage with a Deceased Wife's Sister* (in answer to the Letters of W. Procter), 1849; *The Nonentity of Romish Saints*, and *The Inanity of Romish Ordinances* (two Sermons), 1849, 3 eds; *Gorham v. The Bishop of Exeter* (a Letter to Sir Walter Farquhar, Bart. on the Present Crisis in the Church), 1850; *Naaman the Syrian* (a Sermon), Sheffield, 1851; *The Duty of English Churchmen, and the Progress of the Church in Leeds*, 1851; *On Institutions for Adult Education* (a Pamphlet), 1852; *Discourses bearing on the Controversies of the Day*, 1853; *Our Lord's Agony* (No. 3 of *Tracts for Englishmen*); *Lives of the Archbishops of Canterbury, from the Mission of Augustine to the Death of Howley*, 5 vols. 1860–64. Editor of *The Cross of Christ, or Meditations on the Death and Passion*, 1844; *The Crucified Jesus* (a Commentary), 1846; Synge's *Direction for spending of One Day Well*, 1846; *Short Meditations for Every Day in the Year*, Leeds, 1846; Synge's *Rules for the Conduct of Human Life*, 1846; *The Christian taught by the Church's Services*, 1847; Dean Comber's *Friendly and Seasonable Advice to the Roman Catholics*, 1847; Spinckes's *The Sick Man Visited*, 1847; Abridgment of Bishop Hamilton's *Family Prayers*, 1848; Sorocold's *Prayers for a Week*, 1848; *Treatise on the Eighty-fourth Psalm*, 1848; *The Common Prayer Book the Best Companion*, 1849; Reading's *History of Our Lord and Saviour Jesus Christ*, 1849; *Companion to the Altar*, 1849; *Church School Hymn-book*, 1850; *Eat and Eat Not* (a Tract), S.P.C.K. [1]

HOOKE, A., *Shotteswell Vicarage, Banbury.*—Wor. Coll. Ox. M.A. 1859; Deac. 1859 and Pr. 1860 by Bp of Pet. V. of Shotteswell, Dio. Wor. 1864. (Patroness, the Baroness North; Glebe, 93 acres; V.'s Inc. 220*l* and Ho; Pop. 320.) Formerly C. of Chipping Warden 1859–63; P. C. of Wroxton, 1863–64. [2]

HOOKE, David, 16, *Crimbles-street, Leeds.*—St. John's Coll. Cam; Deac. 1863 and Pr. 1864 by Bp of Rip. C. of St. John's, Leeds, 1866. Formerly C. of Burley, near Leeds, 1863–66. [3]

HOOKER, William, *Stodmarsh, Canterbury.*—Pemb. Coll. Ox. B.A. 1832; Deac. 1834 and Pr. 1835 by Bp of Lich. Chap. of the Don. of Stodmarsh, Dio. Cant. 1849. (Patron, Archd. of Cant; Tithe, 95*l* 12*s* 3*d*; Glebe, 27 acres; P. C.'s Inc. 132*l*; Pop. 145.) [4]

HOOKEY, George Stephen, *Ogbourne St. Andrew Vicarage, Wilts.*—Wad. Coll. Ox. B.A. 1843, M.A. 1847; Deac. 1843 by Bp of Win. Pr. 1844 by Bp of Dur. V. of Ogbourne St. Andrew, Dio. Salis. 1858. (Patrons, D. and C. of Windsor; V.'s Inc. 200*l* and Ho; Pop. 518.) Formerly P. C. of St. James's, Plymouth, 1847–58. [5]

HOOKINS, Philip, *Great Barford Parsonage, Banbury.*—Trin. Hall, Cam. B.A. 1830. P. C. of Great Barford, Dio. Ox. 1852. (Patron, John Hall, Esq; P. C.'s Inc. 70*l* and Ho; Pop. 332.) C. of Milton, near Adderbury, Oxon. Formerly P. C. of Milcome, Oxon, 1854–60. [6]

HOOLE, Charles Holland, *Christ Church, Oxford.*—Sen. Stud. and Tut. of Ch. Ch. Ox. [7]

HOOLE, John, *The Paragon, Blackheath, S.E.*—Wad. Coll. Ox. 2nd cl. Lit. Hum. and B.A. 1826, M.A. 1830; Deac. 1827 and Pr. 1830 by Bp of Lon. Formerly C. of Poplar 1827–33. [8]

HOOLE, William Spooner, *St. James's Parsonage, Briercliffe, Burnley, Lancashire.*—Brasen. Coll. Ox. B.A. 1845, M.A. 1847; Deac. 1847 by Bp of Rip. Pr. 1848 by Abp of York. P. C. of Briercliffe, Dio. Man. 1851. (Patrons, Hulme's Trustees; Tithe—Imp. 30*l*, App. 10*l*; P. C.'s Inc. 250*l* and Ho; Pop. 2024.) Formerly C. of St. James's, Sheffield, 1847, Weaverham, Cheshire, 1849. [9]

HOOLEY, Samuel Cutler, *Tottington, Thetford, Norfolk.*—Deac. 1841 and Pr. 1844 by Bp of Ex. V. of Tottington, Dio. Nor. 1858. (Patrons, Trustees of Chigwell Free Schools; Tithe—Imp. 447*l*. V. 62*l*; V.'s Inc. 83*l*; Pop. 308.) P. C. of Sturston, Norfolk, Dio. Nor. 1861. (Patron, Lord Walsingham; P. C.'s Inc. 28*l*; Pop. 75; no church.) Formerly C. of Belchamp St. Paul's, Essex. Author, *Sermons*, 3*s*; *The Sabbath was made for Man*, 1*d*; *A Few Words on the Lord's Day*, 1*d*. [10]

HOOPER, Francis Bodfield, *Upton Warren Rectory, Bromsgrove, Worcestershire.*—Ch. Coll. Cam. B.A. 1834; Deac. 1834, Pr. 1835. R. of Upton Warren, Dio. Wor. 1836. (Patron, Earl of Shrewsbury; Tithe, 650*l*; Glebe, 80¾ acres; R.'s Inc 800*l* and Ho; Pop. 338.) Author, *Revelation Expounded*, 2 vols. pp. 1116, 14*s*; *Summary of the Revelation Expounded*, 6*d*; *Daniel's Prophecies Collated and Expounded*, 6*d*; *Reply to Dr. Wild and the Edinburgh Review on Essays and Reviews*, 6*d*; *A Guide to the Apocalypse*, 3*s* 6*d*; *Palmoni, an Essay on the Mystical System of the Ancients*, 12*s*; *The Old and New Dispensations contrasted with Reference to Points at present controverted*, 1*s*; all published by Rivingtons. [11]

HOOPER, Haines Edward, *Chedworth, near Northleach.*—Jesus Coll. Ox. B.A. 1857, M.A. 1860; Deac. 1858 and Pr. 1860 by Bp of G. and B. C. of Chedworth 1858. [12]

HOOPER, Henry, *Shaw, near Melksham, Wilts.*—Wad. Coll. Ox. B.A. 1854; Deac. 1866 and Pr. 1867 by Bp of Salis. C. of Shaw 1866. [13]

HOOPER, John, *Meopham Vicarage, Gravesend, Kent.*—St. John's Coll. Cam Somerset Scho. B.A. 1823, M.A. 1824; Deac. 1823, Pr. 1824. V. of Meopham, Dio. Roch. 1854. (Patron, Abp of Cant; Tithe—App. 800*l*, V. 400*l* 10*s*; Glebe, 7 acres, V.'s Inc. 530*l* and Ho; Pop. 1140.) [14]

HOOPER, John Wilmore, *Hexham.*—Dur; Deac. 1865 and Pr. 1867 by Bp of Dur. C. of Hexham 1866. Formerly C. of Gateshead. [15]

HOOPER, Richard, *Upton Vicarage, Wallingford.*—Trin. Coll. Cam. B.A. 1844, M.A. 1854; Deac. 1845 by Bp of Ex. Pr. 1846 by Bp of Ely. V. of Upton and Aston Upthorpe, Berks, Dio. Ox. 1862. (Patron, Bp of Ox; Tithe, 138*l*; Glebe, 2 acres; V.'s Inc. 138*l* and Ho; Pop. 475.) Formerly C. of Trinity, Exeter, 1845, St. Stephen's, Westminster, 1849. Editor, *Chapman's Homer*, 5 vols. 1857–58; *Iliad*, 2nd ed. 2 vols. 1865; *Chilcot on Evil Thoughts*, 1851, 2nd ed. 1853. Author, *Life of Dryden*, Aldine Poets, 1865; *A Plea for Seasons and Places of Spiritual Retirement*, Oxford, 1860; Sermons, Reviews, etc. [16]

HOOPER, Richard Hope, *Nash Rectory, Stony Stratford.*—Lin. Coll. Ox. B.A. 1845, M.A. 1848; Deac. 1845 by Bp of Ex; Pr. 1846 by Bp of Ox. R. of Thornton with Nash, Dio. Ox. 1861. (Patron, Hon. R. Cavendish; Tithe, 200*l*; V.'s Inc. 200*l*; Pop. 573.) Dioc. Inspector of Schs. for Deanery of Buckingham. Formerly C. of Coleshill, Berks, 1854–61. [17]

HOOPER, Samuel Hobbs, *The Vicarage, Drax, Selby, Yorks.*—St. Aidan's; Deac. 1851 and Pr. 1852 by Bp of Rip. V. of Drax, Dio. York, 1855. (Patroness, Lady Wheler; V.'s Inc. 135*l* and Ho; Pop. 1231.) Formerly C. of Trinity, Ripon, 1851–54. Author, *My Dissenting Brother and how shall I treat him?* Selby, 1864, 6*d*. [18]

HOOPER, William Nixon, *Winchester.*—Corpus Coll. Cam. B.A. 1824, M.A. 1827. P. C. of Littleton, Hants, Dio. Win. 1832. (Patrons, D. and C. of Win; Tithe—App. 103*l* and 10¾ acres of Glebe; P. C.'s Inc. 77*l*; Pop. 109.) Min. Can. and Precentor of Win. Cathl. 1839. (Value, 150*l*.) Chap. to Bp Morley's Coll. Win. 1839. [19]

HOOPPELL, Robert Eli, *South Shields.*—St. John's Coll. Cam. Wrang. 1855, 1st cl. Moral Sci. Trip. 1856, B.A. 1855, M.A. 1858; Deac. 1857 and Pr. 1859 by Bp of Ban. Head Mast. of the Marine Sch. of South Shields, 1861. (Salary, 350*l*.) Fell. of the Royal Astronomical Soc. 1865. Formerly 2nd and Math Mast. of Beaumaris Gr. Sch. 1855–61; Chap. at Menai Bridge,

Anglesey, 1859–61. Author, *British Dealings with China* (a Sermon), 1859; *The Crimes and Tendencies to Crime of the Present Day* (a Sermon), 1865; *Reason and Religion, or the Leading Doctrines of Christianity*, Mackintosh, 1867, 5s; *Tabular Forms for facilitating the Calculation of certain Nautical Problems*. 1866. [1]

HOOSON, William, *Bulwell, Notts.*—St. Mary Hall, Ox. M.A. 1864; Deac. 1861 and Pr. 1862 by Bp of Lin. C. of Bulwell 1867. Formerly C. of Long Bennington 1862, Welby 1864, Newark 1865. [2]

HOPE, Charles Augustus, *Barwick-in-Elmet Rectory, Milford Junction, Yorks.*—Ex. Coll. Ox. B.A. 1849, M.A. 1852. R. of Barwick-in Elmet, Dio. Rip. 1852. (Patron, Duchy of Lancaster; R.'s Inc. 800*l* and Ho; Pop. 1198.) [3]

HOPE, Charles Stead, *Hornby, Lancaster.*—Sid. Coll. Cam. Sen. Opt. B.A. 1864, M.A. 1867; Deac. 1867 by Bp of Man. C. of Hornby 1867. [4]

HOPE, James, *Halifax.*—Deac 1850, Pr. 1851. P. C. of Trinity, Halifax, Dio. Rip. 1862. (Patron, V. of Halifax; P. C.'s Inc. 300*l* and Ho; Pop. 4500.) Surrogate. [5]

HOPE, John, *Caldicot, Monmouth.*—New Coll Ox. B.A. 1858, M.A. 1860; Deac. 1860 by Bp of Roch. C. of Caldicot; Chap. to Dow. Duchess of Beaufort. [6]

HOPE, John, *Stapleton Rectory, Carlisle.*—Deac. 1820, Pr. 1821. R. of Stapleton, Dio. Carl. 1834. (Patron, Earl of Carlisle; Tithe, 17*l* 12*s* 2*d*; Glebe, 90 acres; R.'s Inc. 100*l* and Ho; Pop. 984.) [7]

HOPE, Richard Mellor, *Newborough Parsonage, Sudbury, Derby.*—Trin. Hall, Cam. LL.B; Deac. 1831, Pr. 1832. P. C. of Newborough, Dio. Lich. 1860. (Patron, V. of Hanbury; P. C.'s Inc. 107*l* and Ho; Pop. 788.) Formerly V. of St. Michael's, Derby, 1847–56. [8]

HOPE, Sackett, 5, *Museum-villas, Oxford.*—Queen's Coll. Ox. B.A. 1862, M.A. 1865; Deac. 1863 and Pr. 1864 by Bp of Ox. C. of St. John Baptist's, Oxford, 1863. [9]

HOPE, Thomas, 7, *Forefield-place, Lyncombe Hill, Bath*—Univ. Coll. Ox. B.A. 1825, M.A. 1828; Deac. 1826 by Bp of B. and W. Pr. 1828 by Bp of Bristol. [10]

HOPE, William, *St Peter's Parsonage, Derby.*—St. Cath. Hall, Cam. B.A. 1846, M.A. 1849; Deac. 1846 and Pr. 1847 by Bp of Pet. V. of St. Peter's with Normanton C. Derby, Dio. Lich. 1847. (Patrons, Rev. Charles Wright and Rev. Henry Wright; St. Peter's, Tithe—Imp. 111*l* 2*s* 7*d*, V. 111*l* 13*s* 4*d*; Normanton, Tithe—Imp. 49*l* 16*s*, V. 13*l* 14*s*; Glebe, 12½ acres; V.'s Inc. 348*l* and Ho; Pop. St. Peter's 13021, Normanton 437.) Surrogate; Dom. Chap. to Earl Ferrers 1847. [11]

HOPKINS, Benjamin, *Barbon, Kirkby Lonsdale, Westmoreland.*—St. John's Coll. Cam. B.A. 1826. P. C. of Barbon, Dio. Ches. 1842. (Patron, V. of Kirkby Lonsdale; Tithe—App. 1*l* 7*s* 5½*d*, Imp. 147*l*; P. C.'s Inc. 85*l*; Pop. 364.) [12]

HOPKINS, Charles, *Polebrook, Oundle, Northants.*—St. Cath. Coll. Cam. 3rd cl. Cl. Trip. and B.A. 1857; Deac. 1858 and Pr. 1859 by Bp of Pet. R. of Polebrook, Dio. Pet. 1863. (Patron, Bp of Pet; Tithe, 155*l*; Glebe, 30 acres; R.'s Inc. 350*l* and Ho; Pop. 488.) Dom. Chap. of Bp of Pet. Formerly C. of Aylestone, near Leicester. [13]

HOPKINS, Evan Henry.—C. of St. Mark's, Victoria Docks, West Ham, Essex. [14]

HOPKINS, Favill John, *Conington, St. Ives, Hunts.*—Sid. Coll. Cam. B.A. 1845, M.A. 1848; Deac. 1845 and Pr. 1846 by Bp of Ely. V. of Caxton, Dio. Ely, 1852. (Patrons, D. and C. of Windsor; Glebe, 8 acres; V.'s Inc. 115*l* and Ho; Pop. 450.) C of Knapwell 1866. Formerly C. of Woolley, Hunts, 1845, Partney, Lincolnshire, 1847, Tempsford, Beds, 1850. [15]

HOPKINS, Frank Laurence, *Trinity Hall, Cambridge.*—Trin. Hall, Cam. 11th Wrang. 1859; Deac. 1862 and Pr. 1865. Fell. and Tut. of Trinity Hall; V. of St. Edward's, Cambridge, Dio. Ely, 1866. (Patron. Trin. Hall, Cam; Pop. 605.) [16]

HOPKINS, Henry Gordon, 2, *York-villas, Cheltenham.*—Corpus Coll. Ox. 3rd cl. Law and Mod. Hist. B.A. 1862, M.A. 1864; Deac. 1863 by Bp of Lich. Pr. 1864 by Bp of Dur. C. of Ch. Ch. Cheltenham 1866. Formerly C. of Sedgefield Asst. Mast. at Repton Sch. [17]

HOPKINS, John, *Ebbw Vale, Newport, Monmouthshire.*—Divinity Sch. Abergavenny; Deac. 1859 and Pr. 1860 by Bp of Llan. C. of Ebbw Vale 1862. Formerly C. of Beaufort 1859–62. [18]

HOPKINS, John, *Corseinon, Swansea.*—Lampeter; Deac. 1863 by Bp of St. D. Pr. 1864 by Bp of Herf. C. of Corseinon 1864. Formerly C. of Clydach 1863–64. Author, *Social Prayer* (a Sermon); *The Relation between Christianity and Natural Theology* (a Prize Essay). [19]

HOPKINS, John.—C. of St. Michael's, South Hackney, Lond. [20]

HOPKINS, Robert Smythe, *Hilderstone, Stone, Staffs.*—Dub. Scho. of, First Hons. in Sci. and Cl. Ethical Moderator, Downe's Prizeman, Berkeley Gold Medallist, B.A. 1841; Deac. 1858 and Pr. 1859 by Bp of G. and B. P. C. of Hilderstone, Dio. Lich. 1863. (Patron, John Bourne, Esq; P. C.'s Inc. 120*l* and Ho; Pop. 448.) Formerly C. of Lydbrook, Forest of Dean, Glouc. 1858–63. [21]

HOPKINS, T. H. T., *Magdalen College, Oxford.*—Magd. Coll. Ox. B.A. 1856, M.A. 1858. Fell. and Tut. of Magd. Coll. Ox. [22]

HOPKINS, William Bonner, *The Vicarage, Littleport, Cambs.*—Caius Coll, and St. Cath. Hall, Cam. 2nd Smith's Prize, 2nd Wrang. and B.A. 1844, M.A. 1847, B.D. 1854; Deac. 1846 and Pr. 1848 by Bp of Ely. V. of Littleport, Dio. Ely, 1866. (Patron, Bp of Ely; Tithe, 1940*l*, less 100*l* a year for new district; Glebe, 35 acres; V.'s Inc. 1907*l* and Ho; Pop. 3728.) Hon. Can. of Ely 1865. Late Fell. and Math. Lect. of Caius Coll. Cam; Fell. and Tut. of St. Cath. Hall, Cam; Dom. Chap. to late Bp of Ely; V. of St. Peter's, Wisbech, 1854–66. Author, *Some Points of Christian Doctrine considered with Reference to certain Theories put forth by the Right Hon. Sir J. Stephen, &c.*, 1849, 3*s* 6*d*; *Geometrical Optics*, with an Atlas of large plates, 1853, 10*s*; *Apostolic Missions* (Five Sermons preached before the Univ. in 1852), 1853, 5*s*; *Inaugural Address* to the Isle of Ely Church Schoolmasters' Association, 1855, 4*d*; *Seven Sermons on the Words spoken by Christ our Lord upon the Cross*, Bell and Daldy, 1866, 2*s* 6*d*; *Notes of Lectures on Confirmation*, 1866, 3*d*. [23]

HOPKINS, William Henry, *Werneth, Stockport.*—Dub. A.B. 1847; Deac. 1848, Pr. 1849. P. C. of St. Paul's, Werneth, Dio. Ches. 1856. (Patron, G. Andrew, Esq; P. C.'s Inc. 150*l* and Ho; Pop. 3464. [24]

HOPKINS, William Robert, *Drypool, Hull.*—Dub. A.B. 1848; Deac. 1855 and Pr. 1857 by Bp of Lin. C. of Drypool 1866. Formerly C. of Lenton, Notts, 1855–59, Binbrooke, Lincolnshire, 1859–64, Kirkby, Misperton, Yorks. 1864–66. [25]

HOPKINS, William Toovey, *Nuffield Rectory, Henley-on-Thames.*—Pemb. Coll. Ox. B.A. 1816, M.A. 1832. R. of Nuffield, Dio. Ox. 1828. (Patronesses, Miss F. Burdett and Lady Langham; Tithe, 446*l*; Glebe, 62 acres; R.'s Inc. 521*l* and Ho; Pop. 259.) Rural Dean [26]

HOPKINSON, Francis, *The Dell, Malvern Wells.*—Magd. Coll. Cam. LL.B. 1847, LL.D. 1856; Deac. 1844 and Pr. 1845 by Bp of Lin. P. C. of St. Peter's, Malvern Wells, Dio. Wor. 1859. (Patron, the present P. C; P. C.'s Inc. 180*l*; Pop. 558.) [27]

HOPKINSON, William, *Great Gidding, Stilton, Hunts.*—V. of Great Gidding, Dio. Ely. 1865. (Patron, Hon. G. W. Fitzwilliam; V.'s Inc. 120*l* and Ho; Pop. 543.) Formerly C. of St. Mary's, Wisbech. [28]

HOPPER, Augustus Macdonald, *Starston Rectory, Harleston, Norfolk.*—Trin. Coll. Cam. Sen. Opt. 1st cl. Cl. Trip. and B.A. 1839, M.A. 1842; Deac. 1842 and Pr. 1844 by Bp of Ely. R. of Starston, Dio. Nor. 1845. (Patron, the present R; Tithe, 663*l*; Glebe, 28 acres; R.'s Inc. 715*l* and Ho; Pop. 481.) Hon. Can. of

Nor. 1854; Rural Dean 1865; Dioc. Inspector of Schs; Proctor in Convocation for Dio. Nor. Late Fell of St. John's Coll. Cam. 1841. [1]

HOPPER, Ralph Lambton, *St. George's Vicarage, Bristol.*—St. John's Coll. Cam. B.A. 1825, M.A. 1828. V. of St. George's, Brandon-hill, City and Dio. Bristol, 1844. (Patrons, D. and C. of Bristol; V.'s Inc. 294*l*; Pop. 5284.) [2]

HOPTON, John, *Canon-Frome Court, Ledbury, Herefordshire.*—Brasen. Coll. Ox. B.A. 1804, M.A. 1807; Deac. 1805, Pr. 1806. V. of Canon-Frome, Dio. Herf. 1808. (Patron, the present V; Tithe, 181*l* 7*s*; Glebe, 7 acres; V.'s Inc. 250*l*; Pop. 115.) Preb. of Bartonsham in Herf. Cathl. 1832. (Value, 36*l*.) R. of Munsley, Dio. Herf. 1865. (Patron, the present R; R.'s Inc. 250*l*; Pop. 234.) [3]

HOPTON, Michael, *Staunton Long Vicarage, Much Wenlock, Salop.*—Trin. Coll. Cam. B.A. 1861, M.A. 1867; Deac. 1862 and Pr. 1863 by Bp of Herf. V. of Staunton Long, Dio. Herf. 1866. (Patrons, D. and C. of Herf; Tithe, 132*l*; Glebe, 99½ acres; V.'s Inc. 210*l* and Ho; Pop. 234.) Formerly C. of Cradley 1862, Hentland 1865. [4]

HOPTON, William Parsons, *Bishops-Frome Vicarage, Bromyard, Herefordshire.*—Trin. Coll. Ox. 2nd cl. Lit. Hum. and B.A. 1823, M.A. 1826; Deac. 1825, Pr. 1826. V. of Bishops-Frome, Dio. Herf. 1826. (Patron, Rev. J. Hopton; Tithe—App. 17*l*, Imp. 8*l* 6*s* 6*d*, V. 496*l*; Glebe, 120 acres; V.'s Inc. 672*l* and Ho; Pop. 1014.) Lect. at Bromyard 1828; Preb. of Herf. 1858. [5]

HOPWOOD, Frank George, *Winwick Rectory, Warrington.*—Ch. Ch. Ox. B.A. 1833, M.A. 1840; Deac. 1833 and Pr. 1834 by Bp of Ches. R. of Winwick, Dio. Ches. 1855. (Patron, Earl of Derby; Pop. 704.) Formerly P. C. of Knowsley, Lancashire, 1840–55. [6]

HOPWOOD, William.—C. of St. Philip's, Salford, Manchester. [7]

HORAN, J., *Coombe Keynes, Wareham, Dorset.*—C. of Coombe Keynes and Wool. [8]

HORDERN, Houstowne J., *Kingsdown, Sittingbourne, Kent.*—R. of Kingsdown, Dio. Cant. 1856. (Patron, Lord Kingsdown; R.'s Inc. 245*l*; Pop. 96.) [9]

HORDERN, James, *Doddington Vicarage, Sittingbourne, Kent.*—V. of Doddington, Dio. Cant. (Patron, Archd. of Cant; V.'s Inc. 300*l* and Ho; Pop. 476.) [10]

HORDERN, Joseph, *Burton Agnes Vicarage, near Hull.*—Brasen. Coll. Ox. B.A. 1816, M.A. 1820; Deac. 1817 and Pr. 1819 by Bp of Ches. V. of Burton Agnes with Harpham C. Dio. York, 1855. (Patron, Hon. and Rev. Augustus Duncombe; Tithe—App. 887*l* 14*s* 3*d*; V. 736*l* 10*s*; Glebe, 192 acres; V.'s Inc. 945*l* and Ho; Pop. Burton Agnes 723, Harpham 274.) Rural Dean. Formerly V. of Rostherne and Rural Dean of East Frodsham, Cheshire, 1821. Author, *Plain Directions for Reading to the Sick*, 4th ed. Rivingtons, 1830; *Sermons*, 1830; *Armour of Light* (four Sermons preached in Advent), 1851. [11]

HORDERN, Joseph Calverley.—St. Aidan's; Deac. 1855 and Pr. 1856 by Abp of York. Chap. of H.M.S. "Dauntless." Author, *Sermons preached to Seafaring Men*, 1860. [12]

HORE, Alexander Hugh, *Dover.*—Trin. Coll. Ox. 3rd cl. Lit. Hum. and B.A. 1852. Chap. to the Forces. [13]

HORE, Edmund Creek, *Manchester.*—St. Bees; Deac. 1854. R. of Levenshulme, Dio. Man. 1860. (Patrons, Trustees; Pop. 2538.) Formerly C. of St. Philip's, Bradford-road, Manchester. [14]

HORE, William Strong, *Penrose Villas, Barnstaple, Devon.*—Queens' Coll. Cam. Jun. Opt. and B.A. 1830, M.A. 1839; Deac. 1831 by Bp of B. and W. Pr. 1832 by Bp of Ex. V. of Shebbear with Sheepwash, Dio. Ex. 1855. (Patron, Ld Chan; Tithe—Imp. 398*l* 11*s* 8*d*, V. 334*l*; V.'s Inc. 334*l* and Ho; Pop. 1636.) Formerly R. of St. Clement's, Oxford, 1850–55. [15]

HORLEY, Edward, *Eaton-Socon, St. Neots, Beds.*—Emman. Coll. Cam. 29th Wrang. and B.A. 1848. M.A. 1851; Deac. 1848, Pr. 1849. V. of Eaton-Socon, Dio. Ely, 1861. (Patron, J. G. Atkinson, Esq; Tithe, 270*l*; Glebe, 20 acres; V.'s Inc. 350*l* and Ho; Pop. 2766.) Formerly P. C. of St. Chadd's, Stafford, 1855–60.) [16]

HORLEY, Engelbert, *Deane near Bolton, Lancashire.*—Queen's Coll. Ox. B.A. 1858 M.A. 1860; Deac. 1859 by Bp of Lich. Pr. 1861 by Bp of Man. C. of Deane 1861. Formerly C. of St. Chadd's, Stafford, 1859, Brill with Boarstall, Bucks, 1860. [17]

HORLOCK, Holled Darrell Cave Smith, *Box House, Chippenham.*—Magd. Hall, Ox. B.A. 1830, M.A. 1834, B.D. 1842, D.D. 1843; Deac. 1830 and Pr. 1831 by Bp of Salis. V. of Box, Dio. G. and B. 1831. (Patron, the present V; Tithe—App. 10*l*, Imp. 498*l* 8*s* 10*d*, V. 408*l* 6*s* 2*d*; V.'s Inc. 490*l*; Pop. 2051.) Author, *An Explanation of the Lord's Prayer*, 5*s*; *An Exposition of the Parables*, 6*s*; *Sabbath Recollections*, 2*s* 6*d*; *The Saviour's Welcome to Little Children*, 6*d*; *An Address on the Evils arising from Revels*, 6*d*; *The Parochial Magazine*, 6*d*. [18]

HORN, George Thomas, *St. Thomas's Rectory, Haverfordwest.*—Pemb. Coll. Ox. B.A. 1855, M.A. 1857; Deac. 1856 and Pr. 1857 by Bp of Llan. R. of St. Thomas's, Haverfordwest, Dio. St. D. 1866. (Patron, Ld Chan; R.'s Inc. 260*l* and Ho; Pop 1600.) Formerly C. of Dixon, near Monmouth, 1856–58; P. C. of Marton, Salop, 1858–61; C. of Nash and Llanwern, Monmouthshire, 1861–63; P. C. of Beachley, Gloucestershire, 1863–66. [19]

HORN, Thomas, *St. Thomas's Rectory, Haverfordwest.*—St. Edm. Hall, Ox. B.A. 1826, M.A. 1827; Deac. 1826 and Pr. 1827 by Bp of Pet. Formerly R. of St. Thomas's, Haverfordwest, 1851–66. Author, *Sermons on Various Subjects*, 1832; *Exhortation to the Belief and Practice of Religion*, 1838; *History and Antiquities of Mursley, with Biographical Notices of Sir John Fortescue, of Salden House, in the time of Elizabeth and James I.* published in the *Records of Buckinghamshire*, 1854–56; *The Churchman in Humble Life* (a true account), in *The Penny Post.* [20]

HORNBY, Charles E., *Much Dewchurch, Hereford.*—Ch. Ch. Ox. B.A. 1857, M.A. 1862; Deac. 1864 and Pr. 1865 by Bp of Salis. C. of Much Dewchurch 1865. Formerly C. of Mere, Wilts, 1864–65. [21]

HORNBY, Edward James Geoffrey, *Bury Rectory, Lancashire.*—Mert. Coll. Ox. 2nd cl. Lit. Hum. and B.A. 1839, M.A. 1844; Deac. 1839, Pr. 1840. R. of Bury, Dio. Man. 1850. (Patron, Earl of Derby; Tithe—App. 49*l* 5*s*, R. 448*l* 5*s*; R.'s Inc. 2240*l* and Ho; Pop. 16,959.) Hon. Can. of Man. 1850; Surrogate; Rural Dean. [22]

HORNBY, George, *Brasenose College, Oxford.*—Brasen. Coll. Ox. B.A. 1812, M.A. 1814, B.D. 1826. Fell. of Brasen. Coll. Ox. [23]

HORNBY, James John, *Winchester.*—Brasen. Coll. Ox. B.A. 1849, M.A. 1852; Deac. 1854. 2nd Mast. of the College, Winchester; Fell. of Brasen. Coll. Ox Formerly Prin. of Bp Cosin's Hall, Durham. [24]

HORNBY, Robert, *Bayston Hill, Shrewsbury.*—Downing Coll. Cam. B.A. 1830, M.A. 1834; Deac. and Pr. 1830. P. C. of Bayston Hill, Dio. Lich. 1833. (Patron, P. C. of St. Julian's, Shrewsbury; Glebe, 46 acres; P. C.'s Inc. 100*l*; Pop. 605.) [25]

HORNBY, Robert William Bilton, *Clifton Garth, York.*—Dur. B.A. 1842, M.A. 1845, B.D. 1852, D.D. 1856; Deac. 1844 by Bp of Nor. Pr. 1845 by Bp of Rip. [26]

HORNBY, Thomas, *Walton-on-the-Hill, Liverpool.*—Ch. Ch. Ox. B.A. 1824, M.A. 1828. V. of Walton-on-the-Hill, Dio. Ches. 1848. (Patron, J. S. Leigh, Esq; Tithe—R. 2082*l* 8*s* 10*d*, V. 109*l* 12*s* 2*d*; V.'s Inc. 110*l*; Pop. 6246.) [27]

HORNBY, William, *St. Michael's-on-Wyre Vicarage, Garstang, Lancashire.*—Ch. Ch. Ox. B.A. 1833, M.A. 1836; Deac. and Pr. 1834. V. of St. Michael's-on-Wyre, Dio. Man. 1847. (Patron, the present V; Tithe—Imp. 1067*l* 11*s* 9*d*, V. 480*l*; Glebe, 25 acres; V.'s Inc. 480*l* and Ho; Pop. 565.) Hon. Can. of Man. 1850; Rural Dean. [28]

HORNE, Edward Larkin, *Whissendine Vicarage, Oakham.*—Clare Coll. Cam. B.A. 1858; Deac. 1858 and Pr. 1859 by Bp of Roch. V. of Whissendine, Dio. Pet. 1864. (Patron, B. W. Horne, Esq; V.'s Inc. 160*l* and Ho; Pop. 693.) Formerly C. of Great Dunmow, Essex, 1858. [1]

HORNE, Edward Lewis, *Great Marlow, Bucks.*—Ex. Coll. Ox. B.A. 1860, M.A. 1864; Deac. 1862 and Pr. 1864 by Bp of Ox. C. of Great Marlow 1862. [2]

HORNE, F. E., *Drinkstone Rectory, Bury St. Edmunds.*—R. of Drinkstone, Dio. Ely, 1865. (Patron, Rev. W. Horne; Tithe, 546*l* 10*s*; Glebe, 85 acres; R.'s Inc. 700*l* and Ho; Pop. 496.) [3]

HORNE, John, *Early Parsonage, Reading.*—Ball. Coll. Ox. 4th cl. Lit. Hum. B.A. 1845, M.A. 1848; Deac. 1847 and Pr. 1848 by Bp of Ox. P. C. of St. Peter's, Early, Dio. Ox. 1856. (Patron, V. of Sonning; Glebe, 2 acres; P. C.'s Inc. 175*l* and Ho; Pop. 774.) Chap. to the Earl of Caithness 1848. Formerly C. of Rotherfield Greys 1847, Sonning, Berks, 1848–56. [4]

HORNE, William, *Christ Church Parsonage, Roxeth, Harrow, Middlesex.*—Caius Coll. Cam. Jun. Opt. B.A. 1859, M.A. 1863; Deac. 1860 and Pr. 1861 by Bp of Lon. P. C. of Roxeth, Dio. Lon. 1866. (Patrons, Trustees; P. C.'s Inc. 190*l* and Ho; Pop. 890.) [5]

HORNER, Francis D'Altry, *Wath, Ripon.*—Dub. A.B. 1860, A.M. 1864; Deac. 1861 and Pr. 1862 by Bp of Ches. C. in sole charge of Wath 1866. Formerly C. of St. Bartholomew's, Liverpool, 1861–63, Normanton 1863–66. [6]

HORNER, John Stewart Hippisley, *Mells Rectory, Frome, Somerset.*—Ex. Coll. Ox. B.A. 1834, M.A. 1835; Deac. and Pr. 1835 by Bp of B. and W. R. of Mells with Leigh-upon-Mendip C. Dio. B. and W. 1835. (Patron, the present R; Mells, Tithe, 603*l*; Glebe, 16 acres; Leigh, Tithe, 200*l*; Glebe, 66 acres; R.'s Inc. 914*l* and Ho; Pop. 782.) Preb. of Wells 1842. [7]

HORNER, Joseph, *Everton Vicarage, Biggleswade, Beds.*—Clare Coll. Cam. B.A. 1838, M.A. 1841. V. of Everton with Tetworth V. Dio. Ely, 1840. (Patron, Clare Coll. Cam; Tithe—Imp. 205*l*, V. 70*l*; V.'s Inc. 204*l* and Ho; Pop. Everton 248, Tetworth 261.) Late Fell. of Clare Coll. Cam. [8]

HORNIBROOK, Samuel, *Maidstone.*—Dub. A.B. 1847; Deac. 1847, Pr. 1848. Chap. of the Kent County Lunatic Asylum; Asst. C. of Trinity, Maidstone. [9]

HORROX, James, *Dinnington Rectory, Rotherham.*—Trin. Coll. Cam. B.A. 1826; Deac. 1826, Pr. 1828. R. of Dinnington, Dio. York, 1840. (Patron, Ld Chan; R.'s Inc. 135*l* and Ho; Pop. 272.) [10]

HORROX, James Holt, 66, *Mosley-street, Blackburn.*—Brasen. Coll. Ox. Hulmeian and Reed Exhib. 3rd cl. Lit. Hum. B.A. 1857; Deac. 1862 and Pr. 1863 by Bp of St. D. C. of Ch. Ch. Blackburn, 1867. Formerly C. of Lamphey, Pembroke, 1862–63, Raglan and Llandenny, Monmouthshire, 1863–67. [11]

HORSBURGH, William, *Willington, Durham.*—Dub. A.B. 1860; Deac. 1862 by Bp of Ossory, Pr. 1864 by Bp of Dur. C. of Willington 1863. Formerly C. of Gorey 1862, St. Andrew's Buckland 1863. Author, *Two Sermons, Almsgiving and the Offertory*, 1863. [12]

HORSFALL, James, *Drighlington, Leeds.*—Deac. 1831 and Pr. 1833 by Abp of York. P. C. of Drighlington, Dio. Rip. 1844. (Patron, Bp of Rip; P. C.'s Inc. 84*l*; Pop. 4274.) Head Mast. of Drighlington Gr. Sch. (Patron, St. Peter's Coll. Cam.) [13]

HORSFALL, Richard, *Dacre Parsonage, Ripley, Yorks.*—Queens' Coll. Cam. B.A. 1825; Deac. 1826, Pr. 1827. P. C. of Dacre, Dio. Rip. 1852. (Patrons, D. and C. of Rip; Glebe, 5 acres; P. C.'s Inc. 105*l* and Ho; Pop. 721.) Formerly C. of Normanby, near Pickering, 1833. Author, *Scriptural Sermons*, 1863, 2*s* 6*d*; *Gospel Sermons*, 3*s*; *Evangelical Sermons*, 1867, 3*s* 6*d*. [14]

HORSFALL, Thomas, *Ripon.*—Chap. of the Gaol, Ripon. [15]

HORSFORD, Thomas Fahie, 3, *Leamington-road Villas, Westbourne Park, London, W.*—Wad. Coll. Ox. B.A. 1819, M.A. 1821; Deac. 1821 by Bp of Ches. Pr. 1821 by Bp of Lon. [16]

HORSLEY, Edward Lamont, *Great Barford Vicarage, Beds.*—Jesus Coll. Cam. B.A. 1846; Deac. 1848, Pr. 1850. C. of Roxton with Great Barford. [17]

HORSLEY, Henry, *Northleach Vicarage, Glouc.*—St. John's Coll. Cam. B.A. 1836, M.A. 1854. V. of Northleach, Dio. G. and B. 1855. (Patron, Bp of G. and B; V.'s Inc. 280*l* and Ho; Pop. 1404.) Surrogate. [18]

HORSMAN, Samuel James O'Hara, *Beanlands, Kildwick, Yorks.*—Dub. A.B. 1857; Deac. 1858 by Bp of Pet. Pr. 1860 by Bp of Lon. Patron of R. of Rattlesden, Suffolk. [19]

HORT, Charles Josiah, *Cork.*—Dub. A.B. 1840; Deac. 1842 by Bp of Wor. Pr. 1845 by Abp of Dub. Chap. to the Forces, Cork. [20]

HORT, Fenton John Anthony, *St. Ippolyt's Vicarage, Hitchen, Herts.*—Trin. Coll. Cam. 1st cl. Cl. Trip. and B.A. 1850, M.A. 1853; Deac. 1854 by Bp of Ox. Pr. 1856 by Bp of Ely. V. of St. Ippolyt's with Great Wymondley, Dio. Roch. 1857. (Patron, Trin. Coll. Cam; V.'s Inc. 330*l* and Ho; Pop. 1266.) [21]

HORTON, Edward, *Powick, Worcester.*—Wor. Coll. Ox. B.A. 1835, M.A. 1838; Deac. 1838 by Bp of Wor. Pr. 1839 by Bp of Ox. Chap. to the Worcester Co. and City Lunatic Asylum 1852. Late Fell. of Wor. Coll. Ox. [22]

HORTON, George Lewis Wilmot, *Garboldisham Rectory, East Harling, Norfolk.*—Trin. Coll. Cam. B.A. 1847, M.A. 1850; Deac. 1849, Pr. 1850. R. of Garboldisham, Dio. Nor. 1850. (Patroness, Hon. Mrs. Montgomerie; Tithe, 605*l*; Glebe, 50 acres; R.'s Inc. 660*l* and Ho; Pop. 701.) [23]

HORTON, George William, *Wellow, Bath.*—Trin. Coll. Cam. B.A. 1853; Deac. and Pr. 1854. V. of Wellow, Dio. B. and W. 1859. (Patron, Rev. J. A. Wallace; Tithe—App. 10*l* 7*s* 2*d*, Imp. 258*l* 11*s* 6*d*, V. 353*l* 12*s*; Glebe, 61 acres; V.'s Inc. 427*l* and Ho; Pop. 1087.) [24]

HORTON, H.—C. of Bishop Ryder's Church, Birmingham. [25]

HORTON, John, *Frome Selwood, Somerset.*—C. of Trinity, Frome. [26]

HORTON, W. G., *Wilmcote, near Stratford-on-Avon.*—P. C. of Wilmcote, Dio. Wor. 1863. (Patron, Bp of Wor; Pop. 424.) [27]

HORWOOD, Edward Russell, *Maldon Vicarage, Essex.*—Brasen. Coll. Ox. 3rd cl. Lit. Hum. B.A. and M.A. 1843; Deac. 1844 and Pr. 1845 by Bp of Lin. V. of All Saints', Maldon, Dio. Roch. 1850. (Patron, the present V; Tithe, 239*l* 10*s*; Glebe, 40 acres; V.'s Inc. 365*l* and Ho; Pop. 3507.) J. P. for county of Essex and borough of Maldon; Surrogate. Formerly C. of Tring 1844, Trinity, Gray's-inn-road, and Asst. Chap. of Royal Free Hosp. Lond. 1845–47; C. of Ch. Ch. Marylebone, 1847–60. Author, *Church Extension* (a Sermon), 1847. [28]

HORWOOD, Thomas George, *Kirkdale, Liverpool.*—St. Mary Hall, Ox. B.A. 1863; Deac. 1863 and Pr. 1864 by Bp of Man. C. of St. Mary's, Kirkdale. Formerly C. of St. James's, Accrington, 1863. [29]

HORWOOD, Webb Davis, *Aberystwith.*—Deac. 1847, Pr. 1848. P. C. of Aberystwith, Dio. St. D. 1867. (Patron, Bp of St. D; P. C.'s Inc. 300*l* and Ho; Pop. 5561.) Formerly P. C. of Pontypool 1852–67. Author, *Remarks on a Few of the Principal Features of the Middle Ages*, 1843. [30]

HOSE, Frederick, *Dunstable Rectory, Beds.*—Queens' Coll. Cam. B.A. 1830, M.A. 1833; Deac. and Pr. 1830. R. of Dunstable, Dio. Ely, 1845. (Patron, Ld Chan; Tithe, 115*l*; R.'s Inc. 180*l* and Ho; Pop. 4470.) Rural Dean; Surrogate. [31]

HOSE, George Frederick, *Trinity Clergy House, Great Portland-street, London, W.*—St. John's Coll. Cam. B.A. 1861, M.A. 1867; Deac. 1861 and Pr. 1862 by Bp of Ely. C. of Trinity, Marylebone, 1865. Formerly C. of Roxton with Great Barford, Beds, 1861–65. [32]

HOSE, Henry Judge, *Dulwich College, S.*—Asst. Mast. in Dulwich Coll. Sch. [1]

HOSE, John Christian, *Antwerp House, Primrose-hill-road, London, N.W.*—King's Coll. Lond. B.A. 1854; Deac. 1857 and Pr. 1859 by Bp of Lon. C. of St. Saviour's, South Hampstead, 1857. [2]

HOSE, Thomas Charles, *Little Wymondley, Stevenage, Herts.*—Literate; Deac. 1858 and Pr. 1859 by Bp of Pet. P. C. of Little Wymondley, Dio. Roch. 1862. (Patron, U. Heathcote, Esq; Glebe, 4 acres; P. C.'s Inc. 45*l* and Ho; Pop. 318.) Formerly C. of Sapcote, Leic. 1858–60, Harpenden, Herts. 1860–62. [3]

HOSEGOOD, J., *Long Sutton, Lincolnshire.*—C. of St. Nicholas', Long Sutton. [4]

HOSEGOOD, Samuel, *Thelbridge Rectory, Morchard Bishop, Devon.*—R. of Thelbridge, Dio. Ex. 1860. (Patron, the present R; R.'s Inc. 300*l*; Pop. 259.) Formerly R. of Wayford, Somerset, 1853–57. [5]

HOSKEN, Charles Henry, *Cubert Vicarage, Grampound, Cornwall.*—Queens' Coll. Cam. B.A. 1841; Deac. 1841, Pr. 1842. V. of Cubert, Dio. Ex. 1850. (Patron, the present V; Tithe—Imp. 322*l*, V. 178*l*; V.'s Inc. 200*l* and Ho; Pop. 420.) [6]

HOSKEN, Cuthbert Edgecumbe, *Luxulyan, Bodmin, Cornwall.*—Ex. Coll. Ox. B.A. 1841; Deac. 1842 and Pr. 1843 by Bp of Ex. V. of Luxulyan, Dio. Ex. 1853. (Patron, Sir Colman Rashleigh, Bart; Tithe, 231*l* 5*s*; Glebe, 13½ acres; V.'s Inc. 233*l* and Ho; Pop. 1329.) Formerly C. of St. Blazey 1842; V. of St. Blazey 1844. [7]

HOSKEN, Thomas Butterfill, *Llandevailog-Vach, Brecon.*—Wor. Coll. Ox. B.A. 1853; Deac. 1855 by Bp of G. and B. Pr. 1856 by Bp of Llan. R. of Llandevailog-Vach, Dio. St. D. 1862. (Patron, Ld Chan; Tithe, 328*l*; Glebe, 26 acres; R.'s Inc. 380*l* and Ho; Pop. 222.) Formerly C. of Bisley, Glouc. 1855–57, Stapleton, Bristol, 1857–59, Llangasty, Brecon, 1859–62. [8]

HOSKIN, Peter Charles Mellish, *Malvern.*—Jesus Coll. Cam. Sen. Opt. and B.A. 1839, M.A. 1843; Deac. 1839 by Bp of Lin. Pr. 1840 by Abp of York. C. of Trinity, Great Malvern, 1862. Formerly C. of Moor Monkton, Yorks, 1839; Asst. C. of Regent-square Chapel, St. Pancras, Lond. 1842. [9]

HOSKING, Henry, *Hope-upon-Dinmore, Herefordshire.*—Magd. Hall, Ox. B.A. 1851; Deac. 1852 and Pr. 1854 by Bp of Ex. C. of Hope-upon-Dinmore. Formerly C. of St. Martin's, St. Mary's, and St. Agnes', Scilly Isles, 1851–57, Phillack 1857, Carnmenellis 1860. [10]

HOSKING, Henry John, *Bunny Vicarage, Nottingham.*—Brasen. Coll. Ox. B.A. 1857, M.A. 1860; Deac. 1858 and Pr. 1859 by Bp of Ches. R. of Thorpe-in-Glebis, Notts, Dio. Lin. 1859. (Patron, the present R; Tithe, 119*l*; R.'s Inc. 150*l*; Pop. 36; no church.) V. of Bunny with Bradmore, Notts, Dio. Lin. 1864. (Patron, Rev. J. R. W. Boyer; V.'s Inc. 500*l* and Ho; Pop. Bunny 273, Bradmore 296.) Formerly C. of Rock Ferry, Cheshire, 1858–60. [11]

HOSKINS, Arthur, *Cheltenham.*—P. C. of St. Peter's, Cheltenham, Dio. G. and B. 1867. (Patrons, Trustees; P. C.'s Inc. 150*l*; Pop. 3855.) Formerly C. of St. Peter-le-Bailey, Oxford. [12]

HOSKINS, Edgar, *All Saints', Margaret-street, London, W.*—Ex. Coll. Ox. B.A. 1853, M.A. 1857; Deac. 1857 by Bp of Ox. Pr. 1858 by Bp of Salis. C. of All Saints', Marylebone, Lond. Formerly C. of Wilton, Wilts, 1857, St. Martin's, Salisbury, 1858. [13]

HOSKINS, George Richard, *Higham, near Cockermouth.*—Pemb. Coll. Ox. B.A. 1854, M.A. 1857; Deac. 1854 and Pr. 1855 by Bp of Lich. P. C. of Setmurthy, Dio. Carl. 1866. (Patrons, the Inhabitants; Glebe, 27*l*; P. C.'s Inc. 46*l*; Pop. 166.) Even. Lect. at All Saints', Cockermouth, 1866; Surrogate. Formerly C. of Wednesbury 1854–55, Cockermouth, 1856–59; P. C. of St. Bridget's, Beckermet, 1859–66. [14]

HOSKINS, Henry, *North Perrott Rectory, Crewkerne, Somerset.*—Oriel Coll. Ox. 2nd cl. Lit. Hum. B.A. 1812, M.A. 1815; Deac. 1813 by Bp of B. and W. Pr. 1814 by Bp of Glouc. R. of North Perrott, Dio. B. and W. 1814. (Patron, Henry William Hoskins, Esq; Tithe, 300*l*; Glebe, 44¾ acres; R.'s Inc. 380*l* and Ho; Pop. 401.) Preb. of Shalford in Wells Cathl. Formerly R. of Frome St. Quintin, Dorset, 1827–65. [15]

HOSKINS, Henry Charles Thomas, *Clipsham Rectory, Oakham, Rutland.*—Ball. Coll. Ox. B.A. 1848; Deac. 1848 and Pr. 1849 by Bp of B. and W. R. of Clipsham, Dio. Pet. 1858. (Patron, J. M. Paget, Esq; R.'s Inc. 250*l* and Ho; Pop. 213.) Formerly C. of St. Mark's, North Audley-street, Lond. [16]

HOSKINS, William Edward, *Chiddingstone Rectory, Edenbridge, Kent.*—Brasen. Coll. Ox. B.A. 1819, M.A. 1821; Deac. 1824 by Bp of Lin. Pr. 1824 by Bp of Lon. R. of Chiddingstone, Dio. Cant. 1852. (Patron, Abp of Cant; Tithe, 868*l*; Glebe, 11 acres; R.'s Inc. 879*l* and Ho; Pop. 1156.) Formerly C. of Acton, Middlesex, 1823–31, Tachbrook-Bishops, Warwickshire, 1831–33, Rickmansworth, Herts, 1833–35, Croydon, Surrey, 1835–36; R. of St. Alphage with St. Mary Northgate, Canterbury, 1836–45; V. of St. John's, Thanet, 1845–52; Rural Dean of Westbere 1845–52. Author, occasional sermons. [17]

HOSKYNS, C., *Wootton Wawen, Henley-in-Arden, Warwickshire.*—C. of Wootton Wawen. [18]

HOSKYNS, Henry James, *Blaby Rectory, near Leicester.*—Univ. Coll. Ox. B.A. 1830, M.A. 1833; Deac. 1834 by Bp of Salis. Pr. 1838 by Bp of Ox. R. of Blaby with Countesthorpe C. Dio. Pet. 1844. (Patron, Ld Chan; Glebe, 400 acres; R.'s Inc. 600*l* and Ho; Pop. Blaby 1028, Countesthorpe 993.) Formerly C. of Appleton, Berks, 1834–45. [19]

HOSKYNS, John Leigh, *Aston-Tyrrold Rectory, Wallingford, Berks.*—Magd. Coll. Ox. 2nd cl. Lit. Hum. and B.A. 1839, M.A. 1843; Deac. 1840 by Bp of Ox. Pr. 1842 by Bp of Herf. R. of Aston-Tyrrold, Dio. Ox. 1845. (Patron, Magd. Coll. Ox; Tithe, 278*l*; Glebe, 36 acres; R.'s Inc. 338*l* and Ho; Pop. 395.) Rural Dean. Formerly C. of Dunchurch 1840–41, Lugwardine, Herefordshire, 1841–45. [20]

HOSMER, Arthur Henry, *Guernsey.*—Oriel Coll. Ox. B.A. 1846, M.A. 1848. Formerly C. of Combe Florey, Somerset; Min. of All Saints' Chapel, Guernsey, 1857–65. [21]

HOSTE, George Charles, *Boyton Rectory, near Woodbridge, Suffolk.*—Caius Coll. Cam. 19th Sen. Opt. and B.A. 1835, M.A. 1838; Deac. 1836 by Bp of Win. Pr. 1838 by Bp of Nor. R. of Boyton, Dio. Nor. 1865. (Patrons, Trustees of Mrs. Warner's Charity; Tithe, 388*l*; Glebe, 28*l*; R.'s Inc. 408*l* and Ho; Pop. 254.) Formerly C. of Stokesby and Runham 1836, Reepham 1847, Fakenham 1849, all in Norfolk, Bucklesham, Suffolk, 1851; R. of Heigham, next Norwich, 1856–65. Author, *Singleness of Heart, or a Few Years in the Life of Richard Beck, a Domestic Servant*, Jarrolds, Lond. 1854. [22]

HOSTE, James Richard Philip, *Cropredy Vicarage, Banbury.*—Clare Coll. Cam. B.A. 1847; Deac. 1848 and Pr. 1849 by Bp of Rip. V. of Cropredy, Dio. Ox. 1860. (Patron, Bp of Ox; Tithe—App. 120*l* 15*s*, V. 99*l* 13*s*; Glebe, 71 acres; V.'s Inc. 300*l* and Ho; Pop. 1057.) Formerly R. of Stanhoe, Norfolk, 1853–60. [23]

HOTCHKIN, Robert Charles Herbert, *Thimbleby Rectory, Horncastle, Lincolnshire.*—Emman. Coll. Cam. B.A. 1824. R. of Thimbleby, Dio. Lin. 1831. (Patrons, Trustees; R.'s Inc. 451*l* and Ho; Pop. 374.) [24]

HOTHAM, Edwin, *Crowcombe Rectory, Taunton.*—New Coll. Ox. B.A. 1830, M.A. 1833; Deac. 1831 and Pr. 1834 by Bp of Roch. R. of Crowcombe, Dio. B. and W. 1853. (Patron, R. Harvey, Esq; Tithe, 351*l* 10*s*; Glebe, 63 acres; R.'s Inc. 412*l* and Ho; Pop. 573.) [25]

HOTHAM, Frederick Harry, *Rushbury Rectory, Church Stretton, Salop.*—Ch. Ch. Ox. B.A. 1846, M.A. 1850, and Theol. Coll. Wells; Deac. 1849, Pr. 1850. R. of Rushbury, Dio. Herf. 1851. (Patron, Bp of Wor; Tithe, 386*l*; Glebe, 70 acres; R.'s Inc. 450*l* and Ho; Pop. 576.) [26]

HOTHAM, Henry, *Woodnesborough Vicarage, Sandwich, Kent.*—Jesus Coll. Cam. B.A. 1844. V. of Woodnesborough, Dio. Cant. 1847. (Patrons, D. and C.

of Roch; Tithe—App. 1163*l* 18*s* 5*d*, Imp. 211*l* 10*s* 7*d*, V. 436*l* 4*s* 9*d*; V.'s Inc. 460*l* and Ho; Pop. 889.) [1]

HOTHAM, Henry John, *Trinity College, Cambridge.*—Trin. Coll. Cam. B.A. 1844, M.A. 1847. Fell. of Trin. Coll. Cam. Formerly P. C. of St. Michael's, Cambridge, 1853–57. [2]

HOTHAM, John Hallett, *Sutton-at-Hone, Dartford, Kent.*—Magd. Coll. Ox. B.A. 1834, M.A. 1839; Deac. 1835, Pr. 1836. V. of Sutton-at-Hone, Dio. Cant. 1836. (Patrons, D. and C. of Roch; Tithe—App. 892*l* 13*s*, V. 473*l* 4*s* 2*d*; Glebe, 21 acres; V.'s Inc. 520*l* and Ho; Pop. 842.) [3]

HOTHAM, William Francis, *Buckland Rectory, Reigate, Surrey.*—Ch. Ch. Ox. B.A. 1841, M.A. 1843; Deac. 1841, Pr. 1842. R. of Buckland, Dio. Win. 1853. (Patron, All Souls Coll. Ox; Tithe, 290*l*; R.'s Inc. 342*l* and Ho; Pop. 369.) Late Fell. of All Souls Coll. Ox. [4]

HOUBLON, Thomas Archer, *Peasemore Rectory, Newbury, Berks.*—Oriel Coll. Ox. B.A. 1830, M.A. 1834; Deac. 1831 and Pr. 1832 by Bp of Salis. R. of Peasemore, Dio. Ox. 1837. (Patron, C. Eyre, Esq; Tithe, 689*l* 18*s* 1*d*; Glebe, 76 acres; R.'s Inc. 800*l* and Ho; Pop. 832.) [5]

HOUCHEN, Bircham, *Swaffham, Norfolk.*—Sid. Coll. Cam. B.A. 1843, M.A. 1846; Deac. 1844, Pr. 1845. Chap. to the Swaffham House of Correction; Chap. to the Swaffham Union. [6]

HOUCHEN, Edward, *Farnham, near Knaresborough.*—Caius Coll. Cam. B.A. 1854; Deac. 1856 and Pr. 1857 by Bp of Nor. C. of Farnham. Formerly C. of Sherburn and Fenton. [7]

HOUGH, George, *Crosland Parsonage, near Huddersfield.*—Deac. 1824 and Pr. 1825 by Abp of York. P. C. of Crosland, Dio. Rip. 1829. (Patron, V. of Almondbury; P. C.'s Inc. 150*l* and Ho; Pop. 2259.) [8]

HOUGH, George D'Urban John, *House of Detention, Clerkenwell, E.C.*—Pemb. Coll. Ox. B.A. 1858; Deac. 1858 and Pr. 1859 by Bp of Wor. Chap. of House of Detention, Clerkenwell, Dio. Lon. 1867. (Patrons, Magistrates of Middlesex; Chap's Inc. 250*l*.) Formerly C. of Dodderhill, Worc. 1858–60; C. in sole charge of Wilsford, Salisbury, 1861–66. [9]

HOUGH, Thomas George Pattinson, *Ham Parsonage, Kingston-on-Thames.*—Caius Coll. Cam. B.A. 1842, M.A. 1845; Deac. 1842 and Pr. 1843 by Bp of Nor. P. C. of Ham, Dio. Win. 1848. (Patron, V of Kingston; P. C.'s Inc. 105*l* and Ho; Pop. 1265.) [10]

HOUGH, William, *Fern Hill, Fleetwood, Lancashire.*—P. C. of Hambleton, Dio. Man. 1836. (Patron, V. of Kirkham; Tithe—App. 214*l* 12*s* 8*d*, Imp. 1*l* 13*s* 4*d*; Glebe, 60 acres; P. C.'s Inc. 140*l*; Pop. 366.) [11]

HOUGHTON, C., *Misterton, Lutterworth.*—C. of Misterton. [12]

HOUGHTON, Charles Adams, *New-street, Salisbury.*—Ex. Coll. Ox. Scho. of, English Essay 1862, B.A. 1860, M.A. 1863; Deac. 1863. C. of Coombe Bissett, Hornington and West Harnham, 1864. Author, *Consider Your Ways* (a Sermon), 1864, 2*d*. [13]

HOUGHTON, Edward James, *The Vicarage, Boston Spa, near Tadcaster.*—Ch. Ch. Ox. B.A. 1860, M.A. 1863; Deac. 1860 and Pr. 1861 by Bp of Win. V. of Boston Spa, Dio. York, 1866. (Patron, D. and C. of Ch. Ch. Ox; V.'s Inc. 200*l* and Ho; Pop. 1200.) Formerly C. of Twyford, Hants; Sen. C. of Alvechurch, Worc. 1863–66; C. and Lect. of St. Philip's, Birmingham, 1866. [14]

HOUGHTON, John, *Matching Vicarage, Harlow, Essex.*—Corpus Coll. Cam. B.A. 1828, M.A. 1832; Deac. 1828 and Pr. 1829 by Bp of Lon. V. of Matching, Dio. Roch. 1837. (Patrons, Trustees of Felstead Sch. on the nomination of the Bp of Roch; Tithe—App. 440*l* and 56 acres of Glebe, V. 246*l* 10*s*; Glebe, 10 acres; V.'s Inc. 256*l* and Ho; Pop. 665.) [15]

HOUGHTON, Robert Walpole, *Halstead, Essex.*—Dub. A.B. 1828; Deac. 1831 by Bp of Kildare, Pr. 1834 by Bp of Lich. Chap. to the Halstead Union, 1847. Author, *A Sermon on Justification* (for the benefit of the Church Pastoral Aid Society), 1842; *Advent, or the Words of Scripture on the Glorious Advent of the Lord Jesus Christ, together with the Restoration of Judah and Israel*, 1848; *Catechetical Exercises, or Introductory Questions on the Study of Holy Scripture*, 1852; Six vols. of Sermons—I. *On the Word of God*; II. *On the Holy Trinity*; III. *On the Perfection of Christ's Work*; IV. *On the Validity of the Apostolic Church of England*; V. *On the Lord's Supper*; VI. *On the Holy Spirit in the Church*, 1867. [16]

HOUGHTON, William, *Preston Rectory, Wellington, Salop.*—Brasen. Coll. Ox; Hulme's Exhib. B.A. 1850, M.A. 1853; Deac. 1852 and Pr. 1853 by Bp of Herf. R. of Preston-upon-the-Wild-Moors, Dio. Lich. 1860. (Patron, St. John C. Charlton, Esq; Tithe, 120*l*; Glebe, 19 acres; R.'s Inc. 160*l* and Ho; Pop. 228.) Author, Natural History articles in Dr. Smith's *Dictionary of the Bible*, and various papers in scientific and literary journals: *An Essay on the Canticles, with a Translation of the Poem and Short Explanatory Footnotes*, Trübner, 1865. [17]

HOUGHTON, William, *Manaccan Vicarage, Helston, Cornwall.*—V. of Manaccan, Dio. Ex. 1865. (Patron, Bp of Ex; V.'s Inc. 200*l* and Ho; Pop. 505.) [18]

HOULBROOK, William, *Wyke Parsonage, Normanton.*—Trin. Coll. Cam. B.A. 1832, M.A. 1835; Deac. 1833 and Pr. 1834 by Abp of York. P. C. of Wyke, Dio. Rip. 1844. (Patrons, the Crown and Bp of Rip alt; P. C.'s Inc. 155*l* and Ho; Pop. 3016.) Formerly C. of St. Mary's, Hull, 1833, Bradford 1838. [19]

HOULDEY, William Ephraim, *Hylton-road, Sunderland.*—King's Coll. Lond. Theol. Assoc. 1866; Deac. 1866 by Bp of Dur. C. of Deptford, Durham, 1866. [20]

HOULDITCH, Edward, *Cathedral House, Gloucester.*—St. John's Coll. Cam. B.A. 1823; Deac. 1824 by Bp of Ches. Pr. 1825 by Bp of Ex. R. of Matson, near Gloucester, Dio. G. and B. 1833. (Patrons, D. and C. of Glouc; Tithe, 1*l*; R.'s Inc. from lands, 209*l*; Pop. 32.) [21]

HOULDITCH, Henry Lovelace, *Holcombe Burnell Vicarage, Exeter.*—Ch. Coll. Cam. B.A. 1832; Deac. 1832, Pr. 1833. V. of Holcombe Burnell, Dio. Ex. 1835. (Patron, Bp of Ex; Tithe, 145*l*; Glebe, 100 acres; V.'s Inc. 209*l* and Ho; Pop. 242.) Formerly C of Challacombe, Devon. [22]

HOULISTON, Alexander Furnice, 21, *Lower Calthorpe-street, Mecklenburgh-square, London, W.C.*—King's Coll. Lond. Theol. Assoc; Deac. 1865 and Pr. 1866 by Bp of Lon. C. of St. Peter's, Regent-square, Lond. 1865. [23]

HOUSE, Thomas Hammond, *Winterbourne-Anderstone, Blandford, Dorset.*—Wor. Coll. Ox. B.A. 1841, M.A. 1842; Deac. 1842, Pr. 1843. R. of Winterbourne-Anderstone, Dio. Salis. 1847. (Patron, St. B. Tregonwell; R.'s Inc. 150*l*; Pop. 62.) R. of Winterbourne-Zelstone, Dio. Salis. 1855. (Patron, J. J. Farquharson, Esq; R.'s Inc. 260*l* and Ho; Pop. 199.) [24]

HOUSEMAN, John, *Holywell Vicarage, near Northampton.*—Ex. Coll. Ox. B.A. 1856, M.A. 1859; Deac. 1857 and Pr. 1858 by Bp of St. D. C. in sole charge of Holywell 1866. Formerly C. of Clyro, Radnor, 1857–59, Stony Stratford 1859–61 and 1863–66, Itchenstoke, Hants, 1861–63. [25]

HOUSEMAN, Thomas, *Harthill, Worksop.*—St. John's Coll. Cam. B.A. 1859, M.A. 1862; Deac. 1858 and Pr. 1859 by Abp of York. C. of Harthill 1859. Formerly C. of Aston, Rotherham, 1859. [26]

HOUSMAN, George Vernon, *Quebec.*—St. John's Coll. Cam. B.A. 1844; Deac. 1844 and Pr. 1845 by Bp of Roch. Chap. to the Bp of Quebec. Formerly C. of St. Paul's, Kensington, Lond. [27]

HOUSMAN, Harry, *Richmond, Surrey, S.W.*—C. of St. Matthias', Richmond. [28]

HOUSMAN, Joseph Brettell, *Scalby, Scarborough.*—Wor. Coll. Ox. B.A. 1866; Deac. 1866 by Abp of York. C. of Scalby, Yorks, 1866. [29]

HOUSON, Henry, *Brant-Broughton (Lincolnshire), near Newark.*—St. John's Coll. Cam. B.A. 1811,

M.A. 1814; Deac. 1811, Pr. 1812. R. of Brant-Broughton, Dio. Lin. 1820. (Patron, Sir R. Sutton, Bart; Tithe, 691*l* 1*s*; Glebe, 4 acres; R.'s Inc. 780*l* and Ho; Pop. 755.) R. of Great Coates, Lincolnshire, Dio. Lin. 1820. (Patron, Sir R. Sutton, Bart; Tithe, 645*l* 5*s*; Glebe, 76½ acres; R.'s Inc. 765*l* and Ho; Pop. 206.) [1]

HOW, Augustus George, *Bromley St. Leonards, Middlesex.*—Deac. and Pr. 1840 by Bp of Chich. V. of Bromley St. Leonards, Dio. Lon. 1849. (Patron, J. Walter, Esq. M.P; Tithe—Imp. 196*l* 5*s*; V.'s Inc. 200*l* and Ho; Pop. 23,849.) [2]

HOW, William Walsham, *Whittington Rectory, Oswestry, Salop.*—Wad. Coll. Ox. 3rd cl. Lit. Hum. B.A. 1845, M.A. 1847, *ad eund.* Dur. 1848; Deac. 1846 and Pr. 1847 by Bp of Wor. R. of Whittington, Dio. St. A. 1851. (Patron, Capt. Lloyd; Tithe, 955*l*; Glebe, 58 acres; R.'s Inc. 1000*l* and Ho; Pop. 1500.) Hon. Can. of St. A. 1860; Rural Dean of Oswestry 1853; Dioc. Inspector of Schs. 1852. Formerly C. of St. George's, Kidderminster, 1846, Holy Cross, Shrewsbury, 1848. Author, *Psalms and Hymns*; *Plain Words*, 1st series, 2*s*; *Plain Words*, 2nd series, 2*s*; *Practical Sermons*, 2*s*; *Lent Sermons on Psalm LI.* 1*s*; *Evening Psalter, Pointed for Chanting*, 1*s*; *Canticles, pointed, with appropriate Chants*, 1*s*; *Prayers for Schools*, 3*d*; *Three All Saints Summers*, 2*s* 6*d*; *Freedom for Colonial Churches*, 6*d*; all published by Morgan, London. [3]

HOWARD, Francis George, *Merton House, Grantchester, Cambridge.*—Triu. Coll. Cam. 26th Wrang. B.A. 1866; Deac. 1866 by Bp of Ely. C. of Grantchester 1866. [4]

HOWARD, Garton, *Fenny-Bentley, Ashbourne, Derbyshire.*—Corpus Coll. Cam. B.A. 1839; Deac. 1839 and Pr. 1840 by Bp of Wor. R. of Fenny-Bentley, Dio. Lich. 1842. (Patron, Bp of Lich; Tithe, 62*l* 10*s*; R.'s Inc. 132*l*; Pop. 305.) [5]

HOWARD, George Broadley, *Baltonsborough Parsonage, Glastonbury.*—St. John's Coll. Cam. 3rd cl. Cl. Trip. B.A. 1852; Deac. 1853 and Pr. 1854 by Bp of Lon. C. of Baltonsborough, Somerset, 1866. Formerly C. of St. Barnabas', Kensington, 1853–55; Asst. Chap. in India 1856–64. Author, *The Christians of St. Thomas and their Liturgies* (a translation from Syriac MSS. obtained in Travancore), Parkers, 1864. [6]

HOWARD, Henry Charles, *Fordcombe Parsonage, Tunbridge Wells.*—Deac. 1862 and Pr. 1863 by Bp of Lon. C. in sole charge of Fordcombe 1865. Formerly C. of St. Matthew's, Canonbury, 1862–63, and Trinity, Islington, Lond. 1863–65. Author, *Christ in the Storm*; *Care, Prayer, and Peace*; *Sacrifice of Isaac*; and other Sermons published by Judd and Glass, and Seeleys. [7]

HOWARD, The Very Rev. and Hon. Henry Edward John, *Donington Rectory, near Wolverhampton.*—Ch. Ch. Ox. 2nd cl. Lit. Hum. B.A. 1817, M.A. 1819, B.D. 1834, D.D. 1838; Deac. and Pr. 1820 by Abp of York. Succentor of York Cathl. with the Prebendal Stall of Holme annexed, 1822. (Value, 246*l*.) Dean of Lich. 1833 with R. of Tatenhill, Staffs, annexed. (Value, 1524*l* and Res.) R. of Donington, Dio. Lich. 1834. (Patron, Duke of Sutherland; Tithe, 250*l*; Glebe, 257 acres; R.'s Inc. 715*l* and Ho; Pop. 456.) Author, *Translations from Claudian*, Murray, 1823; *The Pentateuch, translated from the LXX, with Notes*, Macmillans, 1835, 8*s* 6*d*, 1857, 10*s* 6*d*; *Scriptural History, Old and New Testament, in Familiar Lessons*, Burns, 1851. [8]

HOWARD, Henry H. Nimmo, *Raunds, Thrapstone, Northants.*—C. of Raunds. [9]

HOWARD, Henry St. John, *Parsonage, Pitlochrie, Perthshire.*—Downing Coll. Cam. 1st cl. Civil Law, S.C.L. 1849, B.C.L. 1853; Deac. 1849 and Pr. 1850 by Bp of Wor. Incumb. of Pitlochrie and Blair Athole, Dio. St. Andrew, Dunkeld and Dunblane, 1866. (Patrons, Trustees; Glebe, 3½ acres; Incumb.'s Inc. 140*l* and Ho; Congregation 84.) Formerly C. of Whitwash 1849, and Ashow, Warwickshire, 1850; C. of St. Andrew's, Aberdeen, 1852; Incumb. of Laurencekirk, Dio. Brechin, 1853; C. of Little Sodbury, Gloucestershire, 1864. [10]

HOWARD, John, *Goodshaw Parsonage, Rawtenstall, Manchester.*—St. Bees, 1846; Deac. 1846 by Bp of Ches. Pr. 1848 by Bp of Man. P. C. of Goodshaw, Dio. Man. 1854. (Patrons, Hulme's Trustees; P. C.'s Inc. 176*l* and Ho; Pop. 4808.) [11]

HOWARD, John, *Kirkonchan Vicarage, Douglas, Isle of Man.*—St. Bees. V. of Kirkonchan, Dio. S. and M. 1847. (Patron, the Crown; V.'s Inc. 150*l* and Ho; Pop. 14,195.) [12]

HOWARD, John Flory, *Yattendon Rectory, Newbury, Berks.*—Trin. Coll. Ox. B.A. 1822, M.A. 1824, B.C.L. 1829; Deac. 1823 and Pr. 1824 by Bp of Salis. R. of Frilsham, Berks, Dio. Ox. 1828. (Patron, Robert Floyd, Esq; Tithe, 197*l* 7*s* 6*d*; Glebe, 29 acres; R.'s Inc. 219*l*; Pop. 183.) R. of Yattendon, Dio. Ox. 1829. (Patron, the present R; Tithe—Imp. 5*l* 12*s*, R. 413*l*; Glebe, 56 acres; R.'s Inc. 460*l* and Ho; Pop. 263.) [13]

HOWARD, Robert, *Rawden Parsonage, Leeds.*—P. C. of Rawden, Dio. Rip. 1865. (Patroness, Mrs. Emmett; P. C.'s Inc. 120*l* and Ho; Pop. 2576.) [14]

HOWARD, Thomas, *Ballaugh Rectory, Ramsey, Isle of Man.*—Deac. 1807 and Pr. 1809 by Bp of S. and M. R. of Ballaugh, Dio. S. and M. 1836. (Patron, the Crown; Tithe, 300*l*; Glebe, 27 acres; R.'s Inc. 350*l* and Ho; Pop. 1228.) Author, *Plain and Practical Sermons*, 2 vols. Nisbet, 1827, 1850, 5*s* each. [15]

HOWARD, Thomas, *Grammar School, Newchurch-in-Rossendale, Lancashire.*—Dur. and Dub. A.B; Deac. 1860, Pr. 1862. Formerly C. of Edenfield, Bury, 1860–62. [16]

HOWARD, Thomas Henry, *Warmley Parsonage, near Bristol.*—Queens' Coll. Cam. B.A. 1837, M.A. 1840; Deac. 1837 and Pr. 1838 by Abp of York. P. C. of Warmley, Dio. G. and B. 1860. (Patron, Bp of G. and B; Glebe, 6 acres; P. C.'s Inc. 90*l* and Ho; Pop. 2016.) Formerly P. C. of Wadsley, near Sheffield, 1846–58. [17]

HOWARD, Thomas Henry, 75, *Kingsdown-parade, Bristol.*—Queens' Coll. Cam. B.A. 1866; Deac. 1866 by Bp of G. and B. C. of St. James's, Bristol, 1866. [18]

HOWARD, The Hon. William, *Whiston Rectory, Rotherham.*—Ch. Ch. Ox. 3rd cl. Lit. Hum. 3rd cl. Math. et Phy. and B.A. 1837, M.A. 1840; Deac. 1838 and Pr. 1839 by Bp of Win. R. of Whiston, Dio. York, 1841. (Patron, Earl of Effingham; Tithe—Imp. 22*l* 16*s*, R. 420*l*; Glebe, 150 acres; R.'s Inc. 720*l* and Ho; Pop. 1185.) Preb. of Driffield in York Cathl. 1862; Dom. Chap. to Earl of Effingham; Proctor for Chapter of York in Convocation. [19]

HOWARD, William, *Clifton Rectory, Nottingham.*—New Coll. Ox. B.C.L. 1830. R. of Clifton, Dio. Lin. 1866. (Patron, Sir J. Clifton, Bart; R.'s Inc. 500*l* and Ho; Pop. 382.) Chap. of the County Gaol. Formerly R. of St. Peter's, Nottingham, 1854–66. [20]

HOWARD, William, *Great Witchingham Rectory, near Norwich.*—New Coll. Ox. LL.B. 1830; Deac. 1827 by Bp of Herf. Pr. 1828 by Bp of Win. R. of Little Witchingham, *alias* Witchingham St. Faith, consolidated with Great Witchingham St. Mary V. Dio. Nor. 1836. (Patron, New Coll. Ox; Little Witchingham, Tithe, Imp. 238*l* 14*s* 3*d*; Glebe, 7 acres; Great Witchingham, Tithe—App. 5*l*, Imp. 488*l* 12*s*, V. 261*l* 8*s*; Glebe, 34½ acres; R.'s Inc. 540*l* and Ho; Pop. Little Witchingham 33, Great Witchingham 642.) [21]

HOWARD, William Henry, *St. Thomas's Vicarage, Exeter.*—St. John's Coll. Cam. B.A. 1833, M.A. 1836; Deac. 1835 and Pr. 1836 by Bp of B. and W. V. of St. Thomas's, Exeter, Dio. Ex. 1845. (Patron, J. H. Buller, Esq; V.'s Inc. 226*l* and Ho; Pop. 4533.) P. C. of Oldridge, Devon, Dio. Ex. 1847. (Patron, the V. of St. Thomas's, Exeter; P. C.'s Inc. 64*l*.) [22]

HOWARD, W. H., *St. Petersburg.*—Asst. Chap. at St. Petersburg. Formerly C. of Westerham, Kent. [23]

HOWARD, William Wilberforce, *Privy Council Office, Whitehall, London, S.W.*—Sid. Coll. Cam. 16th Wrang. and B.A. 1846, M.A. 1849; Deac. 1851 and Pr. 1852 by Bp of Ely. Fell. and Math. Lect. of Sid. Coll. 1846; H.M. Inspector of Schs. 1855. [24]

HOWARTH, Henry, 15, *Grosvenor-street, London, W.*—St. John's Coll. Cam. Sen. Opt. and B.A. 1823, M.A. 1826, B.D. 1833; Deac. 1823 by Bp of Ely, Pr. 1824 by Bp of Lich. R. of St. George's, Hanover-square, Dio. Lon. 1845. (Patron, Bp of Lon; R.'s Inc. 1000*l* and Ho; Pop. 22,016.) Rural Dean; Chap. in Ordinary to the Queen 1855. Late Fell. of St. John's Coll. Cam; Hulsean Lect. 1835. [1]

HOWARTH, Thomas, *Broombank House, Sheffield.*—St. John's Coll. Cam. B.A. 1845, M.A. 1850; Deac. 1849 and Pr. 1850 by Abp of York. Formerly C. of St. George's, Sheffield. [2]

HOWE, John, *Knowle, near Birmingham.*—Trin. Coll. Cam. B.A. 1847, M.A. 1850; Deac. 1848, Pr. 1849. P. C. of Knowle, Dio. Wor. 1855. (Patron, George Unett, Esq; Tithe—Imp. 612*l*; P. C.'s Inc. 140*l* and Ho; Pop. 1200.) Surrogate. [3]

HOWE, Richard Boutein, *Berkeley Cottages, Stoke, Devonport.*—Pemb. Coll. Cam. B.A. 1839; Deac. 1841 and Pr. 1842 by Abp of York. Chap. of H.M. Dockyard, Devonport. Formerly Mast. of Barnsley Gr. Sch. 1839–45; Chap. of the Dockyard and Hospital, Malta; Chap. of H.M.S. "Hibernia." [4]

HOWELL, Alfred William, *Aylesbury.*—Wor. Coll. Ox. B.A. 1849, M.A. 1852; Deac. 1849 and Pr. 1850 by Bp of Lich. Head Mast. of the Endowed Schs. and Chap. of the Union, Aylesbury. Formerly Cl. Mast. of Christ's Hospital, Lond. [5]

HOWELL, David, *St. John's Vicarage, Cardiff.*—Deac. 1855 and Pr. 1856 by Bp of Llan. V. of St. John's, Cardiff, Dio. Llan. 1864. (Patrons, D. and C. of Glouc; Tithe, 48*l* 3*s* 3*d*; V.'s Inc. 320*l* and Ho; Pop 8666.) Surrogate. Formerly C. of Neath, 1855–57; Asst. Sec. to the Church Pastoral Aid Soc. 1857–61; V. of Pwllheli 1861–64. [6]

HOWELL, George, *Llangattock Rectory, Crickhowell, Brecon.*—Lampeter 1836; Deac. 1836 and Pr. 1837 by Bp of St. D. R. of Llangattock with Llangenny, Dio. St. D. 1851. (Patron, Duke of Beaufort; Tithe—Llangattock, 525*l* 12*s*, Llangenny, 320*l*; Glebe—Llangattock, 21½ acres, Llangenny, 8½ acres; R.'s Inc. 905*l* and Ho; Pop. Llangattock 5758, Llangenny 470.) Rural Dean. Author, Sermons and Articles in the Welsh monthly magazine *The Haul*, published in Llandovery. [7]

HOWELL, Henry, *Curdridge Parsonage, Botley, Southampton.*—Deac. 1837 by Abp of Cant. Pr. 1838 by Abp of York. P. C. of Curdridge, Dio. Win. 1841. (Patron, R. of Bishops Waltham; Glebe, 7½ acres; P. C.'s Inc. 108*l*; Pop. 534.) Surrogate. [8]

HOWELL, Hinds, *Drayton, near Norwich.*—Mert. Coll. Ox. B.A. 1833, M.A. 1860; Deac. 1833 and Pr. 1834 by Bp of Ex. R. of Drayton with Hellesdon R. Dio. Nor. 1855. (Patron, Bp of Nor; Drayton, Tithe, 258*l*; Glebe, 25 acres; Hellesdon, Tithe, 442*l*; Glebe, 29 acres; R.'s Inc. 762*l*; Pop. Drayton 451, Hellesdon 496.) Hon. Can. of Nor. 1856; Rural Dean of Taverham. Formerly R. of Bridestow with Sourton, Devon, 1846–55. [9]

HOWELL, Howell, *Kilvey, Swansea.*—Deac. 1859 and Pr. 1860 by Abp of Cant. C. of Kilvey, Llansamlet, 1865. Formerly C. of Snargate and Snave, Kent, 1859–61; Chap. to the Kent County Prisons 1861–62; Sen C. of Trinity, Maidstone, 1862–64. [10]

HOWELL, Hugh, *Llanfyrnach Rectory (Pembrokeshire), near Llanboidy, Carmarthenshire.*—Lampeter, 1st cl. 1830; Deac. 1830 and Pr. 1831 by Bp of St. D. R. of Llanfyrnach, Dio. St D. 1844. (Patron, Ld Chan; Tithe—Imp. 6*l*, R. 247*l*; Glebe, 25 acres; R.'s Inc. 267*l* and Ho; Pop. 934.) R. of Penrieth, Pembrokeshire, Dio. St. D. 1844. (Patron, Ld Chan; Tithe—Imp. 30*l*, R. 70*l*; R.'s Inc. 101*l*; Pop. 370.) [11]

HOWELL, John, *Llangattock, Crickhowell, Brecon.*—St. Bees; Deac. 1855 and Pr. 1857 by Bp of Rip. C. of Llangattock with Llangenny 1859. Formerly C. of St. Bartholomew's, Meltham, Huddersfield, 1855–59. [12]

HOWELL, Oswald John, *Littlehampton, Sussex.*—Deac. 1836, Pr. 1837. Formerly V. of Thurmaston, Leicestershire, 1845–54. [13]

HOWELL, William, *Llanedy, Llanelly, Carmarthenshire.*—Lampeter; Deac. 1865, Pr. 1866. C. in sole charge of Llanedy 1865. [14]

HOWELL, William Charles, *High Cross, Tottenham, N.*—Brasen Coll. Ox. 1st cl. Math. et Phy. B.A. 1840, M.A. 1842; Deac. 1842 and Pr. 1843 by Bp of Lon. P. C. of Trinity, Tottenham, Dio. Lon. 1865. (Patron, V. of Tottenham; P. C.'s Inc. 300*l*; Pop. 5061.) Formerly C. of St. George's-in-the-East, Lond; Chap. at Havre. [15]

HOWELLS, Edward, *The College, Hereford.*—Ch. Ch. Ox. B.A. 1810, M.A. 1826; Deac. 1810 by Bp of Salis. Pr. 1811 by Bp of Herf. Min. Can. and Custos of Herf. Cathl. 1853; V. of Preston-on-Wyre with Blakemere V. Herefordshire, Dio. Herf. 1821. (Patrons, D. and C. of Herf; Glebe, 6 acres; V.'s Inc. 250*l*; Pop. Preston 277, Blakemere 175.) [16]

HOWELLS, John, *Cyfartha, Merthyr-Tydvil.*—P. C. of Cyfartha, Dio. Llan. (Patrons, the Crown and Bp of Llan. alt; P. C.'s Inc. 130*l*; Pop. 7888.) [17]

HOWES, Charles, *The Close, Norwich.*—Trin. Hall and Clare Coll. Cam; Sen. Opt. B.A. 1835, M.A. 1838; Deac. 1837, Pr. 1838. Late Fell. of Dulwich Coll. Surrey. [18]

HOWES, George Plumptre, *Wilton, near Salisbury.*—Pemb. Coll. Cam. Scho. and Prizeman of, 3rd cl. Cl. Trip. B.A. 1865, M.A. 1868; Deac. 1866 and Pr. 1867 by Bp of Salis. C. of Wilton 1866. Formerly Asst. Mast. of Rossall Sch. [19]

HOWES, Henry, *Spixworth Rectory, near Norwich.*—Caius Coll. Cam. B.A. 1836, M.A. 1839; Deac. 1838 and Pr. 1839 by Bp of Nor. R. of Spixworth, Dio. Nor. 1855. (Patron, John Longe, Esq; Tithe, 360*l*; Glebe, 7½ acres; R.'s Inc. 360*l* and Ho; Pop. 44.) Formerly R. of Barton-St.-Andrew, Norfolk, 1841–55. [20]

HOWES, John George, *St. Peter's College, Cambridge.*—St. Peter's Coll. Cam. 7th Wrang. and B.A. 1843, M.A. 1846; Deac. 1844 and Pr. 1846 by Bp of Ely. P. C. of St. Mary's-the-Less, Cambridge, Dio. Ely, 1846. (Patron, St. Peter's Coll. Cam; Tithe—App. 4*l* 9*s* 6*d*; P. C.'s Inc. 135*l*; Pop. 800.) Parke Fell. of St. Peter's Coll. Cam; Rural Dean. [21]

HOWES, Thomas George Francis, *Belton Rectory (Suffolk), near Yarmouth.*—Oriel Coll. Ox. B.A. 1830, M.A. 1840; Deac. 1830 and Pr. 1831 by Bp of Nor. R. of Belton, Dio. Nor. 1837. (Patron, Bp of Nor; Tithe, 444*l*; Glebe, 19 acres; R.'s Inc. 464*l* and Ho; Pop. 516.) Rural Dean. [22]

HOWES, William Atkinson, *Northampton.*—St. Bees; Deac. 1863 and Pr. 1864 by Bp of Lich. Formerly C. of St. Paul's, Stafford, 1863–65, St. Edmund's, Northampton, 1865–67. [23]

HOWLETT, Frederick, *Flimwell Parsonage, Ticehurst, Sussex.*—Wor. Coll. Ox. B.A. 1844, M.A. 1851; Deac. 1847, Pr. 1848. P. C. of Flimwell, Dio. Chich. 1856. (Patron, Bp of Chich; P. C.'s Inc. 115*l* and Ho; Pop. 811.) Formerly P. C. of Winster, Westmoreland, 1851–56. [24]

HOWLETT, John Henry, 9, *Young-street, Kensington, London, W.*—Pemb. Coll. Cam. B.A. 1804, M.A. 1807. Reader at the Chapel Royal, Whitehall; R. of Foston, Dio. Pet. 1834. (Patron, Sir Charles Lamb, Bart; Tithe, 200*l*; R.'s Inc. 245*l* and Ho; Pop. 27.) [25]

HOWLETT, John Henry, *Meppershall Rectory, Biggleswade.*—St. John's Coll. Cam. Bell's Univ. Scho. 1830, 2nd cl. Cl. Trip. Wrang. and B.A. 1833, M.A. 1836, B.D. 1844; Deac. 1837, Pr. 1838. R. of Meppershall, Dio. Ely, 1845. (Patron, St. John's Coll. Cam; Tithe, 535*l*; Glebe, 83 acres; R.'s Inc. 580*l* and Ho; Pop. 541.) Formerly Fell. of St. John's Coll. Cam. 1834; Chap. of Horningsea, Cambs, 1838. [26]

HOWLETT, Robert, *Hopton-by-Lowestoft.*—Pemb. Coll. Ox. B.A. 1821; Deac. 1821 by Bp of Lon. Pr. 1822 by Bp of Nor. P. C. of Hopton-by-Lowestoft, Dio. Nor. 1861. (Patrons, D. and C. of Nor; P. C.'s Inc. 150*l*; Pop. 297.) Formerly P. C. of Longham with Wendling, Norfolk, 1841-61. [27]

HOWLETT, Thomas Lea, *St. Paul's Parsonage,* 17, *Barkham-terrace, Southwark, S.*—Queens' Coll. Cam.

B.D; Deac. 1849 and Pr. 1850 by Bp of Wor. P. C. of St. Paul's, Westminster Bridge-road, Dio. Win. 1857. (Patrons, Trustees; P. C.'s Inc. 360*l* and Ho; Pop. 7699.) Formerly Sec. to the London Society for Promoting Christianity amongst the Jews 1854-57. Author, *The Only Sacrifice for Sin*, 1867. [1]

HOWMAN, Edward James, *Bedworth Rectory, Nuneaton.*—Univ. Coll. Ox. B.A. 1851, M.A. 1854; Deac. 1854 by Bp of Ex. Pr. 1854 by Bp of G. and B. R. of Bedworth, Dio. Wor. 1864. (Patron, Earl of Aylesford; Tithe, 270*l*; Glebe, 200 acres; R.'s Inc. 565*l*; Pop. 5656.) Formerly V. of Exhall, Coventry, 1856-64. [2]

HOWMAN, Edward John, *Bexwell Rectory, Downham Market, Norfolk.*—Corpus Coll. Cam. B.A. 1819, M.A. 1830; Deac. 1820 and Pr. 1821 by Bp of Nor. R. of Bexwell, Dio. Nor. 1831. (Patron, Bp of Nor; Tithe, 345*l*; Glebe, 46 acres; R.'s Inc. 435*l* and Ho; Pop. 94.) P. C. of West Dereham, Dio. Nor. 1842. (Patron, Rev. Leonard Jenyns; Stipend, 33*l*; Augmentation Land, 25 acres; P. C.'s Inc. 95*l*; Pop. 679.) Author, *Thoughts on the Rating Question*, 1842, 1*s*; *Collective Lessons on the Catechism for National Schools*, 1843, 4*d*. [3]

HOWMAN, George Ernest, *Barnsley Rectory, Cirencester.*—Ball. Coll. Ox. B.A. 1818, M.A. 1821. R. of Barnsley, Dio. G. and B. 1841. (Patron, Sir J. Musgrave, Bart; Tithe, 323*l* 3*s*; Glebe, 10½ acres; R.'s Inc. 353*l* and Ho; Pop. 327.) Mast. of St. Nicholas' Hospital, Salisbury; Hon. Can. of Bristol, 1845. [4]

HOWORTH, William, *Whitton Rectory, Ipswich.*—Caius Coll. Cam. B.A. 1827, M.A. 1830; Deac. 1829 and Pr. 1830 by Bp of Nor. R. of Whitton with Thurleston R. Dio. Nor. 1835. (Patron, Bp of Nor; Tithe—Imp. 175*l* 0*s* 6*d*, R. 273*l*; Glebe, 39½ acres; R.'s Inc. 285*l*; Pop. 565.) Hon. Can. of Nor. 1863; Rural Dean. Author, *Sermons, Doctrinal and Practical*, 1839, 4*s* 6*d*; etc. [5]

HOWSE, Frederick, *Beauchamp House, East Reach, Taunton.*—St. John's Coll. Cam. Scho. Hare's Exhib. Sen. Opt. B.A. 1846, M.A. 1849; Deac. 1846 and Pr. 1847 by Bp of B. and W. Chap. of the Taunton and Somerset County Hospital 1853. (Patrons, the Governors; Stipend, 52*l* 10*s*.) Chap. of the Somerset County Gaol, Taunton, 1858. (Patrons, the County Magistrates; Stipend, 250*l*.) Formerly C. of Trinity, Taunton, 1846-56. [6]

HOWSE, Walter, *King's College, London, W.C.*—Ch. Coll. Cam. Wrang. B.A. 1850, M.A. 1853; Deac. 1852 and Pr. 1853 by Bp of Lon. P. C. of St. Mary's, Ilford, Dio. Lon. 1866. (Patron, Marquis of Salisbury; Pop. 10.) Math. Lect. in King's Coll. Lond. Formerly C. of St. Pancras, Lond. [7]

HOWSON, Francis, *Shelford, Nottingham.*—Lin. Coll. Ox. Scho. of, B.A; Deac. 1856 and Pr. 1858 by Bp of Ches. C. in sole charge of Shelford 1863. Formerly C. of Bickerstaffe, Lancashire, and Barton Mills, Suffolk. [8]

HOWSON, The Very Rev. John Saul, *The Deanery, Chester.*—Trin. Coll. Cam. 1st cl. Cl. Trip. and Wrang. 1837, Members' Prizeman 1837, '38, Norrisian Prizeman 1840, B.A. 1837, M.A. 1841, D.D. 1861; Deac. 1845 and Pr. 1846 by Bp of Ches. Dean of Chester 1867 (Value 1150*l* and Ho.) V. of St. Peter's, Wisbech, Dio. Ely, 1866. (Patron, Bp of Ely; Tithe, 1311*l*; Glebe, 51 acres; V.'s Inc. 1235*l* and Ho; Pop. 9276.) Exam. Chap. to the Bp of Ely 1865. Formerly Prin. of Liverpool Coll. 1849-67. Hulsean Lect. at Cambridge 1862. Author, *Norrisian Prize Essay*, 1840; *Good and Bad Habits* (three Sermons), Rivingtons, 1846; *Sunday Evening* (Short Sermons for Family Reading), Longmans, 1849; *History of the Mediterranean* (a Lecture), Murray, 1850; *The Way to do Good and the Way to do Harm* (a Sermon), Longmans, 1855; Sermons, *Hagar and Arabia*, 1864, and *Moses succeeded by Joshua*, 1863; Joint Author with the Rev. J. Conybeare of *The Life and Epistles of St. Paul*, 2 vols. 4to. Longmans, 1852, 8vo. ed. 1856, People's ed. 1862; *Sermons to Schoolboys*, Longmans, 1858; *An Essay on Deaconesses*, 1862; *Hulsean Lectures on the Character of St. Paul*, 1864. Contributor to *Quarterly Review* and other periodicals. [9]

HOWSTON, Frederic, *Ham House, Charlton Kings, Cheltenham.*—Queen's Coll. Ox. Lady Elizabeth Hastings' Exhib. of, B.A. 1853, M.A. 1856; Deac. 1854 and Pr. 1855 by Abp of York. Formerly C. of Dowdeswell, near Cheltenham, and Kirby Moorside, Yorks. Fell. of the Historical and Genealogical Soc. of Great Britain. [10]

HOYLAND, John, *Felkirk Vicarage, near Barnsley.*—Wor. Coll. Ox. B.A. 1853, M.A. 1856; Deac. 1855 by Abp of York, Pr. 1856 by Bp of Carl. V. of Felkirk, Dio. York, 1860. (Patron, Abp of York; V.'s Inc. 140*l* and Ho; Pop. 1125.) Formerly C. of Burton Agnes 1855, Ecclesfield, near Sheffield, 1858. [11]

HOYLE, James, *Burton-Dassett Vicarage, Rugby.*—St. John's Coll. Cam. B.A. 1827; Deac. 1827 and Pr. 1828 by Bp of Lin. V. of Burton-Dassett, Dio. Wor. 1861. (Patrons, Lord Willoughby de Broke and R. W. Blencowe, Esq; V.'s Inc. 180*l* and Ho; Pop. 655.) Formerly V. of Strubby, Linc. 1832-61. [12]

HOYLE, J., *Paddock, Huddersfield.*—Deac. 1865 by Bp of Rip. C. of All Saints', Paddock, 1865. [13]

HOYSTED, C. W., *Bishopworth, near Bristol.*—C. of St. Peter's, Bishopworth. [14]

HOYSTED, J. D., *Clack, near Chippenham.*—P. C. of Clack, Dio. Salis. 1866. (Patron, G. Goldney, Esq.) [15]

HUBBACK, Mark G., *Eckington, Chesterfield.*—Dur. B.A. 1858, M.A. 1866; Deac. 1861, and Pr. 1863 by Bp of Lich. C. of Eckington 1864. Formerly C. of Baslow, Chesterfield, 1861-63. [16]

HUBBARD, Arthur, 9, *Cleveland-row, St. James's, London, S.W.*—Ch. Coll. Cam. B.A. 1820; Deac. 1822, Pr. 1833. Lect. of Watford, Herts. [17]

HUBBARD, Henry, *Cheriton Rectory, Alresford, Hants.*—St. Cath. Coll. Cam. B.A. 1818, M.A. 1821; Deac. 1818 and Pr. 1819 by Bp of Lin. R. of Hinton Ampner, Hants, Dio. Win. 1822. (Patron, Bp of Win; Tithe, 469*l*; Glebe, 100 acres; R.'s Inc. 529*l* and Ho; Pop. 362.) R. of Cheriton with Kilmiston C. Titchborne C. and Beaworth C. Dio. Win. 1825. (Patron, Bp of Win; Cheriton, Tithe, 496*l* 10*s*; Glebe, 150 acres; Kilmiston, Tithe, 350*l* 7*s*; Titchborne, Tithe, 494*l* 10*s*; Beaworth, Tithe, 159*l*; R.'s Inc. 1662*l* and Ho; Pop. Cheriton 621, Kilmiston 193, Titchborne 308, Beaworth 127.) Chap. of St. Cross Hospital, Winchester. [18]

HUBBARD, T., *Newbury, Berks.*—P. C. of St. John's, Newbury, Dio. Ox. 1860. (Patron, Bp of Ox; P. C.'s Inc. 150*l*; Pop. 2008.) [19]

HUBBERSTY, Robert Curteis, *Cartmel, Newton-in-Cartmel, Lancashire.*—St. Peter's Coll. Cam. B.A. 1838, M.A. 1842; Deac. 1845, Pr. 1846. P. C. of Cartmel, Dio. Carl. 1854. (Patron, Duke of Devonshire; P. C.'s Inc. 180*l*; Pop. 950.) Surrogate. Formerly V. of Helpstone 1852. [20]

HUBERT, Henry Samuel Musgrave, *Baldon-Marsh Rectory, near Oxford.*—Ch. Coll. Cam. B.A. 1836, M.A. 1840; Deac. 1837 and Pr. 1838 by Bp of Lon. R. of Baldon-Marsh, Dio. Ox. 1858. (Patron, Sir J. Willoughby, Bart; Tithe, 107*l*; R.'s Inc. 120*l*; and Ho; Pop. 342.) Author, *Emblematical Sermons*, 1850, 5*s*; *England's Towers, or the Church of England, under God, the National Bulwark against Popery*, 1851, 5*s*; *Homiletical Sermons*, 1854, 4*s*; *The Church-rate Knot Untied*, 1855, 6*d*; *Jerville* (a Tale), 1856, 5*s*; *Readings for the Thoughtful*, 1856, 1*s* 6*d*. [21]

HUDDLESTONE, George James, *Tunworth Rectory, Basingstoke, Hants.*—Mert. Coll. Ox. B.A. 1824, M.A. 1827; Deac. and Pr. 1825 by Bp of Salis. R. of Tunworth, Dio. Win. 1844. (Patron, F. J. E. Jervoise, Esq; Tithe, 181*l*; R.'s Inc. 200*l* and Ho; Pop. 118.) [22]

HUDSON, Albert, *Swinton Parsonage, near Manchester.*—Trin. Coll. Cam. 2nd cl. Cl. Trip. B.A. 1864, M.A. 1867; Deac. 1865 and Pr. 1866 by Bp of Man. C. of Swinton 1865. [23]

HUDSON, Anthony Thomas, *Wiveton Rectory, Clay-next-the-Sea, Norfolk.*—Jesus Coll. Cam. B.A. 1843; Deac. 1844 by Bp of Pet. Pr. 1845 by Bp of Nor. R. of Wiveton, Dio. Nor. 1846. (Patron, B. B.

Cabbell, Esq; Tithe, 221*l*; Glebe, 36 acres; R.'s Inc. 256*l* and Ho; Pop. 232.) [1]

HUDSON, Charles Walter, *Trowell Rectory, near Nottingham.*—St. Cath. Coll. Cam. LL.B. 1835; R. of Trowell, Dio. Lin. 1858. (Patron, Lord Middleton; R.'s Inc. 500*l* and Ho; Pop. 343.) Formerly R. of Saundby, Notts, 1838–58; V. of North Wheatley, East Retford, Notts, 1838–58. [2]

HUDSON, Edward, 3, *Albert-street, Grosvenor-place, London, S.W.*—Formerly C. of St. John's, Clapham. [3]

HUDSON, Edward Taylor, *St. Paul's School, London, E.C.*—Trin. Coll. Cam. 2nd cl. Cl. Trip. and Jun. Opt. 1848, B.A. 1849, M.A. 1852; Deac. 1851 and Pr. 1852 by Bp of Lon. Chap. (3rd Mast.) of St. Paul's Sch; C. of St. Botolph's Without, Aldersgate, 1865. Formerly C. of St. James's, Norland, Kensington, 1851–53; Asst. Mast. of the Kensington Gr. Sch. 1849–54; Chap. of Bridewell Hospital and Min. of the Precinct 1861–64. [4]

HUDSON, Frank.—Corpus Coll. Cam. B.A. 1851; Deac. 1852 by Bp of Wor. Pr. 1853 by Bp of Chich. Formerly C. of Cocking, Chichester. [5]

HUDSON, F. W., *Great Wilbraham, Cambridge.*—V. of Great Wilbraham, Dio. Ely, 1863. (Patron, Heir of late James Hicks, Esq; V.'s Inc. 250*l*; Pop. 596.) Formerly C. of Stevenage, Herts. [6]

HUDSON, George Townshend, *Harthill, Sheffield.*—Trin. Coll. Ox. B.A. 1827, M.A. 1831; Deac. 1827 and Pr. 1829 by Bp of Chich. R. of Harthill, Dio. York, 1848. (Patron, Duke of Leeds; Tithe, 715*l*; R.'s Inc. 725*l* and Ho; Pop. 673.) Formerly C. of Pagham, Sussex, 1827, Bintree with Themelthorpe, Norwich, 1834, West Harptree, Somerset, 1837, Stiffkey with Morston, Norfolk, 1842; Resident Dom. Chap. to H.M. Adelaide, Queen Dowager, 1842–49. [7]

HUDSON, Joseph, *Chillingham Vicarage, Alnwick.*—St. Peter's Coll. Cam. Sen. Opt. and B.A. 1816, M.A. 1819; Deac. 1816 by Bp of Ches. Pr. 1817 by Bp of Carl. V. of Chillingham, Dio. Dur. 1866. (Patron, Bp of Dur; V.'s Inc. 384*l* and Ho; Pop. 328.) Formerly Fell. of St. Peter's Coll. Cam; Chap. to the Forces in Canada, 1826–36; P. C. of Hexham 1845–66. [8]

HUDSON, Joseph, *Catwick Rectory, Skirlaugh, Hull.*—St. Peter's Coll. Cam. B.A. 1857, M.A. 1860; Deac. 1857 and Pr. 1859 by Bp of Dur. R. of Catwick, Dio. York, 1862. (Patron, Ld Chan; Tithe, 90*l*; Glebe, 63 acres; R.'s Inc. 202*l* and Ho; Pop. 270.) Formerly C. of Alston, Cumb. 1857–59, Riston, near Hull, 1859–62. [9]

HUDSON, Joseph, *Dodworth, Barnsley, Yorks.*—Univ. Coll. Dur. Licen. Theol. 1845; Deac. 1845 and Pr. 1846 by Bp of Dur. P. C. of Dodworth, Dio. Rip. 1847. Patron, V. of Silkstone; P. C.'s Inc. 125*l* and Ho; Pop. 2117.) Formerly C. of Alston, Cumberland, 1845–47. Author, *The History and Principles of the Book of Common Prayer Practically Explained*, Nisbet, 1857, 2*s*. *John Senior, or I've brought Myself to this*, S.P.C.K. No. 1346. [10]

HUDSON, Thomas Percy, *Trinity College, Cambridge.*—Fell. and Tut. of Trin. Coll. Cam. Author, *Treatise on Plane Trigonometry*; and *Treatise on Arithmetic*. [11]

HUDSON, William, *Blackburn.*—Trin. Coll. Cam. 1st cl. Cl. Trip. 1859, 2nd cl. Theol. Trip. 1860, B.A. 1859, M.A. 1863; Deac. 1861 and Pr. 1863 by Bp of Man. C. of St. Peter's, Blackburn, 1861. [12]

HUET, Henry Frederick.—St. Edm. Hall, Ox. B.A. 1851, M.A. 1853; Deac. 1851 by Bp of G. and B. Pr. 1852 by Bp of Llan. Formerly C. of Milborne Port, Somerset. [13]

HUFF, Edmund, *Little Cawthorpe, Louth, Lincolnshire.*—Queens' Coll. Cam. 2nd Tyrwhitt Heb. Scho. Univ. Prizeman, B.A. 1836. R. of Little Cawthorpe, Dio. Lin. 1853. (Patronage, Sequestrated; Tithe, 71*l*; Glebe, 13 acres; R.'s Inc. 84*l*; Pop. 223.) Author, *First Principles of the Laws of England.* [14]

HUGHES, Albert, *Middle Rasen, Market Rasen, Lincolnshire.*—St. John's Coll. Ox. B.A. 1858, M.A. 1861; Deac. 1859 and Pr. 1860 by Bp of Lin. C. in sole charge of Middle Rasen 1864. [15]

HUGHES, Alfred Thomas, *Aberavon Vicarage, Taibach, Glamorganshire.*—Divinity Sch. Abergavenny; Deac. 1852 by Bp of St. D. Pr. 1854 by Bp of Llan. V. of Aberavon with Baglan, Dio. Llan. 1864. (Patron, Griffith Llewellyn, Esq; Aberavon, Tithe, 50*l* 2*s*; Glebe, 1 acre; Baglan, Tithe, 140*l*; V.'s Inc. 203*l* and Ho; Pop. Aberavon 2916, Baglan 715.) Formerly C. of Mynyddyslwyn; P. C. of Upper Machen 1855. [16]

HUGHES, Annesley Paul, *Teynham Vicarage, Sittingbourne, Kent.*—Dub. A.B. 1832, A.M. 1835; Deac. and Pr. 1835. V. of Teynham, Dio. Cant. 1860. (Patron, Archd. of Cant; V.'s Inc. 250*l* and Ho; Pop. 919.) Formerly P. C. of Upper Gornal, near Dudley, 1848–57; P. C. of All Saints', Gordon-square, Lond. 1857–60. [17]

HUGHES, Arthur Horsley, *Darlington.*—Dub. A.B. 1852, A.M. 1860; Deac. 1853 and Pr. 1854 by Bp of Ches. P. C. of Trinity, Darlington, Dio. Dur. 1865. (Patron, Archd. of Dur; P. C.'s Inc. 300*l* and Ho; Pop. 4993.) Formerly C. of St. Mark's, Liverpool, 1853–54, Birch, Essex, 1855–60, St. Nicholas', Durham, 1860–65. [18]

HUGHES, Augustus, 4, *Museum-villas, Oxford.*—Ch. Ch. Ox. B.A. 1865, M.A. 1867; Deac. 1865 and Pr. 1866 by Bp of Ox. C. of St. Giles', Oxford, 1865. [19]

HUGHES, Charles, *Tockholes, Preston.*—Dub. A.B. 1855; Deac. 1856, Pr. 1857. P. C. of Tockholes, Dio. Man. 1861. (Patron, V. of Blackburn; P. C.'s Inc. 150*l* and Ho; Pop. 2542.) [20]

HUGHES, Charles Joseph, *Perivale Rectory, Ealing,* and *Castlebar Court, Ealing, Middlesex, W.*—St. John's Coll. Cam. Wrang. B.A. 1852, M.A. 1855, LL.D. 1863; Deac. 1855 and Pr. 1856 by Bp of Lon. R. of Perivale, Dio. Lon. 1861. (Patroness, Lady Croft; Tithe, 270*l*; Glebe, 3 acres; R.'s Inc. 300*l* and Ho; Pop. 48.) Formerly C. of St. Mark's, Hamilton-terrace, Lond. 1855–57. Author, *Mathematical Formulæ*, 1854, 2*s*. [21]

HUGHES, Daniel, *Church Gates, Ruthin.*—Jesus Coll. Ox. B.A. 1855, M.A. 1858; Deac. 1863 and Pr. 1864 by Bp of St. A. 2nd Mast. of Ruthin Gr. Sch. Dio. St. A. 1860. [22]

HUGHES, David, *Newbold-on-Avon, Warwickshire.*—C. of Newbold with Long Lawford. [23]

HUGHES, Edward, *Meliden Parsonage, St. Asaph, Flintshire.*—Queens' Coll. Cam. B.A. 1842; Deac. 1842 and Pr. 1843 by Bp of St. A. P. C. of Melidden, Dio. St. A. 1844. (Patron, Bp of St. A; Tithe—App. 350*l*, Imp. 18*l*; P. C.'s Inc. 183*l* and Ho; Pop. 590.) [24]

HUGHES, Evan Owen, *Llanddeiniolen Rectory, near Carnarvon.*—Jesus Coll. Ox. B.A. 1827, M.A. 1830. R. of Llanddeiniolen, Dio. Ban. 1853. (Patron, Ld Chan; R.'s Inc. 350*l* and Ho; Pop. 2401.) [25]

HUGHES, Henry, *Haddenham, Isle of Ely.*—St. Mary Hall, Ox. Careswell Exhib. B.A. 1844, M.A. 1848; Deac. 1844 and Pr. 1845 by Bp of Lich. P. C. of Haddenham, Dio. Ely, 1847. (Patron, Archd. of Ely; Tithe—App. 1850*l* and 80 acres of Glebe, P. C. 285*l* and 1 acre of Glebe; P. C.'s Inc. 285*l*; Pop. 1976.) Formerly C. of Holy Trinity, Burton-on-Trent, 1844–47. Author, *A Funeral Sermon*, 1849; *A Funeral Sermon*, 1865. [26]

HUGHES, Henry Erskine Mackenzie, *Frome, Somerset.*—St. Alb. Hall, Ox; B.A. and M.A. 1865; Deac. 1866 by Bp of B. and W. C. of St. John Baptist's, Frome, 1866. [27]

HUGHES, Henry Hunter, *Layham Rectory, Hadleigh, Suffolk.*—St. John's Coll. Cam. 3rd Wrang. and B.A. 1817, M.A. 1820, B.D. 1827; Deac. 1821 and Pr. 1822 by Bp of Ely. R. of Layham, Dio. Ely, 1836. (Patron, St. John's Coll. Cam; Tithe, 800*l*; Glebe, 71 acres; R.'s Inc. 898*l* and Ho; Pop. 534.) Formerly Fell. and Tut. of St. John's Coll. Cam. [28]

HUGHES, H. W. P., *Hulland, Ashborne, Derbyshire.*—P. C. of Hulland, Dio. Lich. 1866. (Patrons

Rev. C. Evans and J. C. B. Borough, Esq. alt; P. C.'s Inc. 73*l*; Pop. 639.) [1]

HUGHES, Hugh, 18, *Chadwell-street, Myddelton-square, London, E.C.*—St. Peter's Coll. Cam. D.D. 1847; Deac. 1823 by Bp of Ches. Pr. 1824 by Abp of York. R. of St. John's, Clerkenwell, Dio. Lon. 1839. (Patron, Ld Chan; R.'s Inc. 340*l* and Ho.) Author, *Discourses on the Female Characters of Holy Writ*, 3 vols. Hamilton, 1845 '46 '47; *Remarkable Scenes of the Bible*, Blackwood; various single Sermons. [2]

HUGHES, Hugh Pritchard, *Shuttleworth, Bury.*—St. Bees; Deac. 1843 and Pr. 1844 by Bp of Ches. P. C. of Shuttleworth, Dio. Man. 1845. (Patrons, the Crown and Bp alt; Glebe, 1 acre; P. C.'s Inc. 162*l* 10*s*; Pop. 3013.) C. of St. John's in the Wilderness, Shuttleworth. Formerly C. of St. George's, Hyde, 1843, Dolphinholme, near Lancaster, 1844. [3]

HUGHES, Hugh Robert, *Madyn Dysw, Amlwch, Anglesey.*—New Inn Hall, Ox. B.A. 1848, M.A. 1852; Deac. 1851 and Pr. 1852 by Bp of Ban. P. C. of Penrhos Lligwy, Amlwch, Dio. Ban. 1852. (Patron, Lord Boston; Tithe, 95*l*; P. C.'s Inc. 95*l*; Pop. 530.) P. C. of Llanwenllwyfo, Dio. Ban. 1865. (Patron, Bp of Ban; Tithe, 174*l*; P. C.'s Inc. 174*l*; Pop. 535.) Chap. to the High Sheriff of Anglesey 1866. Formerly C. of Llanengrad and Llanallgo 1851–52, Llanwenllwyfo 1852–66. [4]

HUGHES, Jacob, *Llanrian, Trevyne, Haverfordwest, Pembrokeshire.*—Lampeter; Deac. 1835 by Bp of St. D. Pr. 1836 by Bp of Llan. V. of Llanrian, Dio. St. D. 1844. (Patron, Bp of St. D; Tithe—App. 220*l* 18*s*, V. 109*l* 8*s*; V.'s Inc. 136*l*; Pop. 1017.) P. C. of Llanreithan, Pembrokeshire, Dio. St. D. 1844. (Patrons, V.-Choral of St. David's; Tithe—App. 102*l*; P. C.'s Inc. 83*l*; Pop. 188.) [5]

HUGHES, James, *Temple Chambers, Falcon-court, Fleet-street, London, E.C.*—Assoc. Sec. of Ch. Pastoral Aid Soc. [6]

HUGHES, James, *Berrow, Ledbury, Worcestershire.*—P. C. of Berrow, Dio. Wor. 1858. (Patrons, D. and C. of Wor; P. C.'s Inc. 100*l*; Pop. 458.) [7]

HUGHES, James, *Crumlin, Newport, Monmouthshire.*—Deac. and Pr. 1842 by Bp of Llan. R. of Llanhilleth, Monmouthshire, Dio. Llan. 1843. (Patron, Earl of Abergavenny; Tithe—Imp. 22*l*, R. 75; R.'s Inc. 110*l*; Pop. 1020.) Sunday Even. Lect. at Crumlin. [8]

HUGHES, James, *Bodedeyrn, Bangor.*—Jesus Coll. Ox. B.D. 1843. Fell. of Jesus Coll. Ox; P. C. of Bodedeyrn, Dio. Ban. (Patron, Jesus Coll. Ox; P. C.'s Inc. 120*l* and Ho; Pop. 1084.) [9]

HUGHES, James, *Llanbedr Rectory, Conway.*—Jesus Coll. Ox. B.A. 1844, M.A. 1846; Deac. 1844 and Pr. 1845 by Bp of Ban. R. of Llanbedr-y-cenin with Caerhun V. Dio. Ban. 1864. (Patron, Bp of Ban; Tithe, comm. 350*l*; Glebe, 8 acres; R.'s Inc. 375*l* and Ho; Pop. Llanbedr 489, Caerhun 1315.) Formerly C. of Llanenghenedl 1844–47, Dwygyfylchi 1847–49, Pentraeth 1849–64. [10]

HUGHES, James Roydon, *Newnton Longville Rectory, Bletchley, Bucks.*—New Coll. Ox. B.A. 1831, M.A. 1837; Deac. 1837, Pr. 1838. R. of Newnton Longville, Dio. Ox. 1843. (Patron, New Coll. Ox; Tithe, 453*l* 13*s*; Glebe, 16 acres; R.'s Inc. 460*l* and Ho; Pop. 547.) Preb. of Chich. 1841. (Value, 10*l* 15*s* 4*d*.) Formerly Fell. of New Coll. Ox; Exam. Chap. to Bp of Chich. 1841–43; Select Preacher of Univ. of Ox. 1845–56. [11]

HUGHES, Jenkin, *Alconbury Vicarage, near Huntingdon.*—Jesus Coll. Ox. 3rd cl. Lit. Hum. B.A. 1828, M.A. 1831; Deac. 1828 and Pr. 1829 by Bp of Llan. V. of Alconbury, Dio. Ely, 1838. (Patrons, D. and C. of Westminster; Tithe—App. 64*l* 6*s* 8*d*, V. 6*l* 6*s* 8*d*; Glebe, 191 acres; V.'s Inc. 300*l* and Ho; Pop. 1470.) Formerly Mast. of Abergavenny Gr. Sch. 1828–32; C. of St. John's, Westminster, 1832–38. [12]

HUGHES, John, *Titchfield, Fareham, Hants.*—Lampeter, B.A. 1866; Deac. 1864 and Pr. 1865 by Bp of St. D. C. of Titchfield with Crofton 1866. Formerly C. of Laugharne, Carmarthenshire, 1864–66. [13]

HUGHES, John, *Tregaron Vicarage, Lampeter, Cardiganshire.*—V. of Tregaron, Dio. St. D. 1839. (Patron, Bp of St. D; V.'s Inc. 160*l* and Ho; Pop. 1740.) [14]

HUGHES, John, *Penally, Tenby, Pembrokeshire.*—V. of Penally, Dio. St. D. 1819. (Patron, Bp of St. D; Tithe—Imp. 180*l* 1*s* 10*d*, V. 90*l* 0*s* 11*d*; V.'s Inc. 78*l*; Pop. 545.) [15]

HUGHES, John, *Ceidio, Nefyn, Carnarvonshire.*—Brasen. Coll. Ox. B.A. 1846; Deac. 1847 and Pr. 1848 by Bp of Ban. P. C. of Ceidio, Dio. Ban. 1855. (Patron, Thomas Love P. Jones Parry, Esq; Tithe—Imp. 90*l*; P. C.'s Inc. 85*l*; Pop. 153.) C. of Llandudwen, near Nefyn. [16]

HUGHES, John, *Cwmdu Rectory, Crickhowell.*—Lampeter; Deac. 1836 and Pr. 1837 by Bp of St. D. R. of Llanvihangel Cwmdu, Brecon, Dio. St. D. 1849. (Patron, Duke of Beaufort; Tithe, 442*l*; Glebe, 52 acres; R.'s Inc. 522*l* and Ho; Pop. 1052.) Formerly C. of Morvil, Pembrokeshire, 1836, Llanelly, Brecon, 1838. [17]

HUGHES, John, *Congleton Parsonage, Cheshire.*—Dub. A.B. 1838; Deac. 1838 and Pr. 1839 by Bp of Ches. P. C. of Congleton, Dio. Ches. 1842. (Patrons, the Mayor and Corporation; Tithe—App. 252*l* 10*s*; Glebe, 26 acres; P. C.'s Inc. 150*l* and Ho; Pop. 3734.) Surrogate. [18]

HUGHES, John, *Penbryn, Newcastle-Emlyn, Cardiganshire.*—Literate; Deac. 1821, Pr. 1822. V. of Penbryn with Bettws C. and Brongwyn C. Dio. St. D. 1838. (Patron, Bp of St. D; Penbryn, Tithe—App. 25*l*, Imp. 355*l*, V. 320*l*; Bettws, Tithe—Imp. 82*l* 10*s*; V. 77*l* 10*s*; Brongwyn, Tithe—Imp. 70*l* 6*s*; V. 68*l* 14*s*; V.'s Inc. 466*l*; Pop. Penbryn 1575, Bettws 419, Brongwyn 339.) [19]

HUGHES, John, *Longcot Parsonage, Shrivenham, Berks.*—Oriel Coll. Ox. B.A. 1846, M.A. 1849; Deac. 1847 and Pr. 1848 by Bp of Dur. P. C. of Longcot, Dio. Ox. 1853. (Patron, Ld Chan; Tithe, 270*l*; Glebe, ½ acre; P. C.'s Inc. 300*l* and Ho; Pop. 692.) [20]

HUGHES, John, *Gwernafield Parsonage, Mold, Flintshire.*—Literate; Deac. 1852 by Bp of Llan. Pr. 1854 by Bp of G. and B. P. C. of Gwernafield, Dio St. A. 1858. (Patron, V. of Mold; Glebe, 60 acres; P. C.'s Inc. 250*l* and Ho; Pop. 1243.) Formerly C. of Llansannan, Denbighshire; P. C. of Llangorwen, Aberystwith. Author, *Welsh Reformers*, Nisbet, 1867, 6*s*. [21]

HUGHES, John Bickley, *Tiverton, Devon.*—Magd. Coll. Ox. B.A. 1838, M.A. 1841; Deac. 1841, Pr. 1842. Head Mast. of Blundell's Sch. Tiverton; Surrogate; Local Sec. to the Ex. Dioc. Architectural Soc; Sec. to the Tiverton Local Board of Education. Formerly Asst. Mast. of Marlborough Coll. C. of St. Thomas's, Tiverton, 1847–66. [22]

HUGHES, John Edward, *Runcorn, Cheshire.*—St. Cath. Coll. Cam. Scho. of, 1862, B.A. 1864; Deac. 1865 and Pr. 1866 by Bp of Ches. C. of Weston, near Runcorn, 1865. [23]

HUGHES, John Thomas, *Montgomery.*—Queen's Coll. Birmingham, Warnford Scho; Deac. 1865 by Bp of Herf. Pr. 1866 by Bp of Wor. C. of Montgomery, and Chap. to the County Gaol 1867. Formerly C. of Norbury, Salop, 1865. [24]

HUGHES, John Young, *Greenwich, S.E.*—St. Cath. Coll. Cam. B.A. 1841, M.A. 1853; Deac. 1841, Pr. 1842. Min. of Ch. Ch. Greenwich, Dio. Lon. 1849. (Patron, V. of Greenwich; Min.'s Inc. 180*l*.) [25]

HUGHES, Joseph, *Whitby.*—Queens' Coll. Cam. Sen. Opt. and B.A. 1842, M.A. 1856; Deac. 1842 by Bp of St. A. Pr. 1844 by Abp of York. P. C. of Aislaby, Whitby, Dio. York, 1857. (Patron, A. Stephenson, Esq; P. C.'s Inc. 110*l*; Pop. 330.) Surrogate. Author, *The Royal Nuptials* (a Coll. Prize Poem); *Elegy on David Pennant, Esq*; and sundry Sermons and Welsh publications. [26]

HUGHES, Joseph, *Llanwddyn, Oswestry.*—Lampeter, Sen. Scho. and Prizeman, B.D. 1863; Deac. 1856 and Pr. 1857 by Bp of St. D. P. C. of Llanwddyn, Dio. St. A. 1859. (Patron, Earl of Powis; P. C.'s Inc. 261*l* and Ho; Pop. 529.) Formerly C. of Lampeter 1856–58, Trinity, Felinfoch, Llanelly, 1858–59. [27]

HUGHES, Joseph, *Tickenhall, Derby.*—C. of Tickenhall. [1]

HUGHES, Joshua, *Llandingat Vicarage, Llandovery, Carmarthenshire.*—Queens' Coll. Cam. B.A. 1842. V. of Llandingat with Llanvair-ar-y-bryn, Dio. St. D. 1846. (Patron, Bp of St. D; Llandingat, Tithe—App. 520*l*, V. 130*l*; Glebe, 23 acres with a house; Llanvair-ar-y-bryn, Tithe—App. 444*l* 16*s*, Imp. 4*l*, V. 111*l* 4*s*; V.'s Inc. 323*l* and Ho; Pop. Llandingat 2229, Llanvair-ar-y-bryn 1559.) Surrogate; Rural Dean. [2]

HUGHES, Morgan, *Bettws Parsonage, Llanelly.*—Lampeter, Sen. Scho. 1857; Deac. 1859 and Pr. 1861 by Bp of Llan. P. C. of Bettws, Dio. St. D. 1865. (Patron, Bp of St. D; Tithe, 10*l*; P. C.'s Inc. 98*l* and Ho; Pop. 1547.) Formerly C. of Cyfartha 1859, Cardiff 1862; P. C. of Llanulid, near Swansea, 1864. [3]

HUGHES, Morris, *Pentraeth, Anglesey.*—Deac. 1811 and Pr. 1812 by Bp of Ban. P. C. of Pentraeth with Llanbedr-Goch C. Dio. Ban. 1854. (Patron, Bp of Ban; Pentraeth, Tithe—App. 290*l* 11*s* 3*d* and 1½ acres of Glebe; Llanbedr-Goch, Tithe—App. 118*l* 10*s* 9*d*; P. C.'s Inc. 365*l*; Pop. Pentraeth 962, Llanbedr-Goch 356.) [4]

HUGHES, Nathaniel Thomas, *Kegworth, Leicestershire.*—Jesus Coll. Ox. B.A. 1857; Deac. 1861 by Bp of Pet. Pr. 1862 by Bp of Lin. Sen. C. of Kegworth 1864. Formerly Asst. Cl. Mast. at the Oakham Gr. Sch; C. of Lynby with Papplewick, Notts. 1862–64. [5]

HUGHES, Reginald, *Glyn Vicarage, Llangollen, Denbighshire.*—Jesus Coll. Ox. Hon. 4th cl. Math. et Phy. B.A. 1851, M.A. 1853; Deac. 1852 and Pr. 1853 by Bp of Ban. P. C. of Llansantffraid Glyn-Ceiriog, Llangollen, Dio. St. A. 1860. (Patron, Lord Arthur Edwin Hill Trevor, M.P; Tithe, 150*l*; Glebe, 7 acres; P. C.'s Inc. 200*l* and Ho; Pop. 738.) Formerly Asst. Cl. and Math. Mast. of the Cowbridge Sch. Glamorgan, 1851–52, 2nd Mast. of Ruthin Sch. 1852–60; C. of Llanbedr 1854–60. [6]

HUGHES, Richard, *Holland-terrace, Edge-hill, Liverpool.*—Corpus Coll. Cam. Scho. Prizeman and Jun. Opt. B.A. 1848, M.A. 1858; Deac. 1849 and Pr. 1850 by Bp of Wor. P. C. of St. Catherine's, Edge-hill, Dio. Ches. 1863. (Patrons, Trustees; P. C.'s Inc. 250*l*; Pop. 5600.) Formerly C. of Portman Chapel, Marylebone, Lond. 1851–55, Ch. Ch. Brighton, 1856–58, St. Michael's, Aberystwith, 1858–60. Author, *Memoir of Ven. Archdeacon Hughes.* [7]

HUGHES, Richard, *Llanvihangel-yn-Howyn, Valley, Holyhead.*—St. Bees; Deac. 1858 and Pr. 1859 by Bp of Ches. C. of Llanvihangel-yn-Howyn 1867. Formerly C. of Great Budworth, Cheshire, Llantrisant 1862, and Bodedern, Anglesey, 1863. [8]

HUGHES, Richard Owen, *Llanrhaiadr-in-Kinmerch, Denbigh.*—Lampeter 1848–49; Deac. 1850 and Pr. 1852 by Bp of St. D. P. C. of St. James's, Llanrhaiadr-in-Kinmerch, Dio. St. A. 1859. (Patron, Bp of St. A; P. C.'s Inc. 150*l*; Pop. 479.) Formerly C. of Blaenporth 1850–53, Ruthin and Llanrhyd 1853–57, Llanfair Dyffyn Clwyd 1857–59. [9]

HUGHES, Robert Edward, *Shennington Rectory (Glouc.) near Banbury.*—New Inn Hall, Ox. B.A. 1835, M.A. 1838; Deac. 1836 and Pr. 1838 by Bp of Wor. R. of Shennington, Dio. Wor. 1846. (Patron, Earl of Jersey; Glebe, 200 acres; R.'s Inc. 348*l* and Ho; Pop. 415.) R. of Alkerton, Dio. Ox. 1846. (Patron, the present R; Glebe, 91 acres; R.'s Inc. 170*l*; Pop. 194.) Formerly C. of St. Mary's, Bungay, Suffolk. [10]

HUGHES, Robert Henry Matthews, *Llansantffraid-yn-Mechan Vicarage (Montgomeryshire), near Oswestry.*—Jesus Coll. Ox. B.A. 1836, M.A. 1838; Deac. 1837 by Bp of Roch. Pr. 1838 by Bp of St. A. V. of Llansantffraid-yn-Mechan, Dio. St. A. 1846. (Patron, Bp of St. A; Tithe—App. 573*l* 16*s*, Imp. 24 15*s* V. 216*l* 10*s*; V.'s Inc. 230*l* and Ho; Pop. 973.) [11]

HUGHES, Robert Vaughan, *The Wyelands, near Chepstow.* [12]

HUGHES, Thomas, *Higher Sutton, near Macclesfield.*—Dub; Deac. 1846 and Pr. 1848 by Bp of Ches. P. C. of St. James's, Sutton, Dio. Ches. 1847. (Patrons, Five Trustees; P. C.'s Inc. 143*l*; Pop. 1448.) Formerly C. of Old Church, Macclesfield, 1846. Author, *Sermon on the Death of Mrs. Henrey,* 1853. [13]

HUGHES, Thomas, *Clocaenog Rectory, near Ruthin, Denbighshire.*—Jesus Coll. Ox. B.A. 1825, M.A. 1828; Deac. 1826 and Pr. 1827 by Bp of Ban. R. of Clocaenog, Dio. St. A. 1846. (Patron, Bp of Llan; Tithe, 342*l*; Glebe, 3½ acres; R.'s Inc. 342*l* and Ho; Pop. 439.) Formerly C. of Llanbedr 1826–34, Ruthin 1834–40; Lect. of St. Peter's, Ruthin, 1830–40; C. of Llandyrnog 1840–46. Author, *Communion Tracts* (for his Parishioners). Editor, *Poems in English and Latin by the Rev. D. Hughes, with Additions by the Editor,* 1865. [14]

HUGHES, Thomas, *Llandrillo-yn-Rhôs, Conway, Denbighshire.*—Lampeter; Deac. and Pr. 1842 by Bp of St. D. V. of Llandrillo-yn-Rhôs, Dio. St. A. 1855. (Patron, Bp of St. A; Tithe—Imp. 4*l*, App. 640*l*, V. 310*l*; Glebe, 2½ acres; V.'s Inc. 400*l* and Ho; Pop. 747.) Formerly C. of Lampeter 1842–43, Llanarmon 1843–44; P. C. of Colwin, Denbighshire, 1844–55. [15]

HUGHES, Thomas Alexander, *Aylmer, Birmingham.* Dub. A.B. 1857, A.M. 1867; Deac. 1857 and Pr. 1858 by Bp of Lich. Assoc. Sec. for Irish Church Missions, Birmingham. Formerly C. of Burton-on-Trent 1857–59, Davenham, Cheshire, 1860–65. [16]

HUGHES, Thomas Collingwood, *South Tawton, Exeter.*—Downing Coll. Cam. B.A. 1829; Deac. 1829 and Pr. 1830 by Bp of Nor. V. of South Tawton, Dio. Ex. 1860. (Patrons, D. and C. of Windsor; V.'s Inc. 141*l* and Ho; Pop. 1541.) Formerly C. of Wheatacre and Thorpe, and Burlingham, Norfolk, and Bradfield and Mistrey, Essex; P. C. of Cerne Abbas, Dorset, 1845 [17]

HUGHES, T. H. Cecil, *Powick, Worcester.*—Brasen. Coll. Ox. B.A. 1865; Deac. 1866 and Pr. 1867 by Bp of Wor. C. of Powick 1866. [18]

HUGHES, Thomas Jones, *The Vicarage, Llanasa, Holywell.*—Trin. Coll. Cam. Scho. of, Wrang. B.A. 1844, M.A. 1847; Deac. and Pr. 1846 by Bp of Ban. V. of Llanasa, Dio. St. A. 1860. (Patron, Bp of St. A; Tithe, 299*l*; Glebe, 12 acres; V.'s Inc. 299*l* and Ho; Pop. 2679.) Formerly C. of Llanfaes and Penmon 1846, Northop 1850. Author, *Essay on the Laws and Principles of English and Welsh Syntax.* [19]

HUGHES, Thomas Sneyd, *Horncastle, Lincolnshire.*—St. Bees 1836; Deac. 1837, Pr. 1838. P. C. of Mareham-on-the-Hill with High Toynton P. C. Dio. Lin. 1867. (Patron, Bp of Man; P. C.'s Inc. 160*l*; Pop. 425.) [20]

HUGHES, William, *Caerwys Rectory, Holywell.*—Lampeter, B.D. 1853; Deac. 1833 and Pr. 1834 by Bp of St. D. R. of Caerwys, Dio. St. A. 1859. (Patron, Bp of Llan; Tithe, 425*l*; Glebe, 5 acres; R.'s Inc. 425*l* and Ho; Pop. 853.) Formerly P. C. of St. David's, Liverpool, 1845–54. Author, *Treatise on Infant Baptism;* several Addresses to the Liverpool Cambrian Society. [21]

HUGHES, William, *Llanwnws, near Aberystwith.*—P. C. of Llanwnws, Dio. St. D. (Patron, T. P. B. Chichester; P. C.'s Inc. 106*l*; Pop. 1295.) [22]

HUGHES, William, *Ciliau Aeron, Carmarthen.*—St. John's Coll. Cam. B.A. 1833, M.A. 1836; Deac. 1833 and Pr. 1834 by Bp of St. D. P. C. of Llanddewi Aberarth, Dio. St D. 1847. (Patron, Bp of St. D; P. C.'s Inc. 370*l*; Pop. 1468.) Formerly R. of Cilian Aeron 1836–62. [23]

HUGHES, William, *Bettws Rectory, Corwen, Merionethshire.*—St. Bees; Deac. 1843 and Pr. 1844 by Bp of Ches. R. of Bettws-Gwerfil-Goch, Dio. St. A. 1851. (Patron, Bp of St. A; Tithe, 142*l* 2*s* 6*d*; Glebe, 13 acres; R.'s Inc. 162*l* and Ho; Pop. 258.) Formerly C. of Cockerham, Lancashire, 1843–45; Llanvaelog and Ceirchiog, Anglesey, 1845–46, Ruabon, Denbighshire, 1846–48, Castle Caerinion, Montgomeryshire, 1848–51. [24]

HUGHES, William, *Llanllynvi Rectory, near Carnarvon.*—Jesus Coll. Ox. B.A. 1849, M.A. 1851; Deac. 1850 and Pr. 1851 by Bp of Ban. R. of Llanllynvi, Dio. Ban. 1863. (Patron, Bp of Ban; Tithe, 262*l* 10*s*; Glebe, 1½ acres; R.'s Inc. 268*l* 10*s*; Pop. 2362.) P. C. of Beddgelert, Dio. Ban. 1854. (Patron, John Priestley, Esq; Glebe, 1½ acres; P. C.'s Inc. 93*l* and Ho;

Pop. 1375.) Formerly C. of Llangwyfan, Anglesey, 1850. [1]

HUGHES, William, *Ebbw Vale, Tredegar, Monmouthshire.*—C. of Ebbw Vale. [2]

HUGHES, William, *Wennington, near Romford, Essex.*—St. John's Coll. Cam. B.A. 1835, M.A. 1838; Deac. 1835 and Pr. 1836 by Bp. of Herf. R. of Wennington, Dio. Roch. 1865. (Patron, Ld Chan; Tithe, comm. 421*l* 5*s*; Glebe, 4 acres; R.'s Inc. 430*l*; Pop. 130.) Formerly C. of Aston Botterell, Salop, 1835-49, Taynton 1850-64, and Tibberton, Gloucestershire, 1864-65, all three sole charges. [3]

HUGHES, William Henry, *Kislingbury Rectory, Weedon, Northants.*—Lin. Coll. Ox. B.A. 1831, M.A. 1834; Deac. 1832, Pr. 1833. R. of Kislingbury, Dio. Pet. 1849. (Patron, the present R; R.'s Inc. 559*l* and Ho; Pop. 723.) [4]

HUGHES, William Holled, *Horley Vicarage, Surrey.*—Lin. Coll. Ox. B A. 1821; Deac. 1821, Pr. 1828. V. of Horley, Dio. Win. 1853. (Patrons, Govs. of Christ's Hospital; Tithe, 430*l*; Glebe, 2 acres; V.'s Inc. 450*l* and Ho; Pop. 1587.) Formerly C. of Horley for 30 years; previously C. of Crediton. [5]

HUGHES, William Lloyd, *Granville House, Hull.*—Queen's Coll. Birmingham; Deac. 1862 and Pr. 1863 by Abp of York. Chap. of the Sculcoates Union, Hull, 1863. Formerly C. of St. Paul's, Hull, 1862-67. [6]

HUGHES, William O'Farrel, *Upwood, near Huntingdon.*—Emman. Coll. Cam. Sen. Opt. 1861, 2nd cl. Theol. Hons. B.A. 1861, M.A. 1865; Deac. 1862 by Bp of Ely, Pr. 1863 by Bp of Win. P. C. of Upwood with Great Raveley P. C. Dio. Ely, 1865. (Patron, R. H. Hussey, Esq; P. C.'s Inc. 78*l*; Pop. 706.) Formerly C. of Burwell, Cambs, 1862-65 [7]

HUGO, Thomas, 57, *Bishopsgate-street Within, London, E.*—Wor. Coll. Ox. B.A. 1842, M.A. 1850; Deac. 1842 and Pr. 1843 by Abp of Cant. P. C. of All Saints', Bishopsgate-street, City and Dio. Lon. 1858. (Patron, Bp of Lon; P. C.'s Inc. 300*l*.) Formerly C. of St. Botolph's, Bishop-gate. Author, *A Form of Self-examination, with Confession, &c., from Bishop Andrewes*; *Christian Children, their Duties and Privileges*; *Catalogue of Works illustrated by T. and J. Bewick, Wood Engravers*; *The Voice of the Dead* (a Sermon on the Death of the Duke of Wellington); *The Education of a Soul for Heaven* (a Sermon); *A Memoir of Gundulf, Bishop of Rochester*, 1077-1108; *A Course of Sermons on the Lord's Prayer, with Illustrations from the Fathers*; *Why are yo not a Communicant?* (a Sermon) etc. [8]

HULBERT, Bertram Brooke, *Marton Vicarage, near Rugby.*—St. Peter's Coll. Cam. B.A. 1849, M.A. 1853; Deac 1851 and Pr. 1852 by Bp of Wor. V. of Marton, Warwickshire, Dio. Wor. 1854. (Patron, the present V; Glebe, 112 acres; V.'s Inc. 140*l*; Pop. 410.) [9]

HULBERT, Charles Augustus, *Almondbury Vicarage, Huddersfield.*—Sid. Coll. Cam. Crosse Theol. Scho. 1834, Tyrwhitt Heb. Scho. 1835, B.A. 1834, M.A. 1837; Deac. 1834 and Pr. 1835 by Bp of Lon. V. of Almondbury, Dio. Rip. 1867. (Patron, Sir J. W. Ramsden, Bart; Glebe, 22*l*; V.'s Inc. 600*l* and Ho; Pop. 2730.) Hon. Can. of Rip. 1866. Formerly C. of St. Mary's, Islington, Lond. 1834-39; P. C. of Slaithwaite, Huddersfield, 1839-67. Author, *Celestial Musings, a Poetical Sketch of the Heavens*, 1826, 1*s*; *Poetical Recreations*, 1828, 5*s*; *On the Genius of Milton* (a College Prize Declamation), 1834, 1*s*; *Letter to C. Woodward, Esq. on the Islington Literary and Scientific Institution*, 1837, 1*s*; *Children, Instruments of Power to the Church* (a Sermon), 1839, 6*d*; *Theotokos, or the Mother of Our Lord* (a Sermon on the Song of the Blessed Virgin, with a Discussion of the Question "Is Mary to be called the Mother of God?"), 1842, 2*s* 6*d*; *Sabbath Recreations*, 1844, 6*d*; *The Church of Our Fathers, a Poem with Music*, 1844; *The Gospel Revealed to Job, or Patriarchal Faith and Practice, illustrated in Thirty Lectures on the Book of Job*, Longmans, 1853, 12*s*; *The Sword of the Spirit* (a Sermon preached at the Visitation of the Bp of Ripon), 1853, 3*d*; *Annals of the Church in Slaithwaite*, 1864. [10]

HULBERT, Charles Augustus, jun., *Slaithwaite, Huddersfield.*—Caius Coll. Cam. Jun. Opt. B.A. 1861, M.A. 1865; Deac. 1861 by Bp of Rip. Pr. 1862 by Bp of Lon. P. C. of Slaithwaite with Lingards, Dio. Rip. 1867. (Patron, V. of Huddersfield; P. C.'s Inc. 200*l*; Pop. 3716.) Formerly C. of Trinity, Tunbridge Wells, 1861, Bowdon, Cheshire, 1865. [11]

HULBERT, Charles Butler, *Atherton-quay Cottage, Warrington.*—Dub. A.B. 1852; Deac. 1855 by Bp of Ex. Pr. 1856 by Bp of B. and W. C. in sole charge of Bank Quay, Warrington, 1866. Formerly C. of All Hallows, Exeter, 1855, St. Paul's, Shadwell, Lond. 1858, Great Grimsby 1861. [12]

HULBERT, James Lacy, *Ixworth, Suffolk.*—Caius Coll. Cam. Jun. Opt. B.A. 1863; Deac. and Pr. 1863. P. C. of Ixworth, Dio. Ely, 1867. (Patron, Rev. R. Cartwright; P. C.'s Inc. 101*l* and Ho; Pop. 1080.) Formerly C. of St. Mary's, Bury St. Edmunds; Afternoon Lect. of St. Anne's, Limehouse, Lond. 1863-65. [13]

HULBERT, Reginald Mottershead, *Almondbury, Huddersfield.*—Caius Coll. Cam. B.A. 1866; Deac. 1866 by Bp of Rip. C. of Almondbury 1867. Formerly Asst. C. of Slaithwaite 1866. [14]

HULEATT, Hugh, *Woolwich.*—Sen. Chap. to the Forces, Woolwich. [15]

HULL, Charles William, *Royal Grammar School, Guildford.*—Queen's Coll. Ox. 2nd Cl. Lit. Hum. B.A. 1864; Deac. 1866 by Bp of Win. 2nd Mast. of Guildford Royal Gr. Sch. 1867. [16]

HULL, Edward, *St. Mary's School for the Blind, Liverpool.*—Chap. of St. Mary's Sch. for the Blind. [17]

HULL, Francis James, *Netherbury, Beaminster, Dorset.*—Univ. Coll. Dur. B.A. 1852, Licen. Theol. 1853, M.A. 1855; Deac. 1853. Formerly C. of Netherbury, 1853-54. [18]

HULL, John, *Eaglescliffe Rectory, Yarm, Yorks.*—Brasen. Coll. Ox. B.A. 1823, M.A. 1826; Deac. 1826, Pr. 1827. R. of Eaglescliffe, Dio. Dur. 1864. (Patron, Bp of Man; Tithe, 664*l*; R.'s Inc. 1049*l* and Ho; Pop. 698.) Hon. Can. of Man; Rural Dean; Examining Chap. to the Bp of Man. Formerly V. of Poulton-le-Fylde 1835-64. Author, *Manual for a Sunday School Teacher*, S.P.C.K; *Observations on a Petition for the Revision of the Liturgy*, 1840. [19]

HULL, John Dawson, *Wickhambrook Vicarage, Newmarket.*—Dub. A.B. 1823; Deac. 1824, Pr. 1825. V. of Wickhambrook, Dio. Ely, 1859. (Patron, Ld Chan; Tithe—Imp. 52*l* 15*s*; V. 350*l*; Glebe, 5 acres; V.'s Inc. 360*l* and Ho; Pop. 1452.) Surrogate. Formerly C. of Bengworth, Evesham. Author, *The Church of God*; *Lays of Many Years*, 1854; *The Rural Parsonage*, 1857; *The Cluster Crushed*, 1867. [20]

HULL, John Winstanley, *North Muskham, Newark, Notts.*—Brasen. Coll. Ox. B.A. 1847; Deac. 1848 and Pr. 1850 by Bp of Man. V. of North Muskham, Dio. Lin. 1853. (Patron, Bp of Rip; V.'s Inc. 300*l* and Ho; Pop. 820.) Formerly P. C. of Grimsargh. Translator, *Gieseler's Ecclesiastical History*, Vols. III. IV. and V. for *Clark's Foreign Theological Library*, 1853-54. [21]

HULL, Richard, *Upper Stondon Rectory, Biggleswade, Beds.*—St. John's Coll. Cam. B.A. 1840; Deac. 1842 and Pr. 1843 by Bp of Ely. R. of Upper Stondon, Dio. Ely, 1844. (Patron, the present R; Glebe, 85 acres; R.'s Inc. 125*l* and Ho; Pop. 66.) [22]

HULLAH, Thomas, *Calstock Rectory, Tavistock, Cornwall.*—Brasen. Coll. Ox. B.A. 1845, M.A. 1847; Deac. 1846 and Pr. 1847 by Bp of Win. R. of Calstock, Dio. Ex. 1865. (Patron, Prince of Wales; Tithe, 440*l*; Glebe, 67 acres; R.'s Inc. 510*l* and Ho; Pop. 7090.) Formerly C. of Plympton St. Mary, Devon, 1846-49, Holne, Devon, 1849-57; P. C. of Tideford, Cornwall, 1857-65. [23]

HULME, George.—Ball. Coll. Ox. B.A. 1836, M.A. 1839; Deac. 1837, Pr. 1838. Dom. Chap. to H.M. the King of Hanover. [24]

HULME, Samuel Joseph, 1, *Park-villas, Oxford.*—Wad. Coll. Ox. 2nd cl. Lit. Hum. and B.A. 1845,

M.A. 1848; Deac. 1848 by Bp of Ox. Pr. 1855 by Bp of Wor. R. of St. Martin's Carfax, Oxford, Dio. Ox. 1863. (Patron, Ld Chan; R.'s Inc. 62*l*; Pop. 377.) Formerly Cl. Moderator in Univ. Ox. 1858; Fell. of Wad. Coll. Ox. 1847; Tut. 1850; Vice-Mast. of Leamington Coll. 1852–58. [1]

HULME, Thomas, *Brightside Parsonage, Sheffield.*—St. Bees; Deac. 1848 and Pr. 1849 by Bp of Lich. P. C. of Brightside with Grimesthorpe, Dio. York, 1850. (Patrons, the Crown and Abp of York alt; Glebe, ½ acre; P. C.'s Inc. 300*l* and Ho; Pop. 10,101.) [2]

HULME, William, *Brampton Abbots Rectory, Ross, Herefordshire.*—Ball. Coll. Ox. B.A. 1839, M.A. 1841; Deac. 1840 and Pr. 1841 by Bp of Ox. R. of Brampton Abbots, Dio. Herf. 1855. (Patron, Bp of Herf; Tithe, 323*l*; Glebe, 6 acres; R.'s Inc. 335*l* and Ho; Pop. 257.) [3]

HULTON, Arthur Emilius, *Stockdalewath, near Carlisle.*—Trin. Coll. Cam. 21st Wrang. and B.A. 1834, M.A. 1837; Deac. 1848, Pr. 1849. P. C. of High Head, or Ive Gill, near Carlisle, Dio. Carl. 1853. (Patron, V. of Dalston; Glebe, 14 acres; P. C.'s Inc. 94*l*; Pop. 126.) [4]

HULTON, Campbell Basset Arthur Grey, *Emberton Rectory, Newport Pagnel, Bucks.*—Brasen. Coll. Ox. 2nd cl. Lit. Hum. Denyer's Theol. Prize Essay 1837, B.A. 1836, M.A. 1837; Deac. 1839 and Pr. 1840 by Bp of Ches. R. of Emberton, Dio. Ox. 1860. (Patron, Rev. C. G. Hulton; R.'s Inc. 560*l* and Ho; Pop. 624.) Formerly C. of St. Mary's, 1839–40, and St. Michael's, Manchester, 1842–44; R. of St. Paul's, Manchester, 1845. Author, *A Catechetical Help to the Study of Bishop Butler's Analogy*, Rivingtons, 3rd ed. 3*s* 6*d*. [5]

HULTON, Henry Edward, *Sonning, Reading.*—Trin. Coll. Ox. B.A. 1862, M.A. 1864; Deac. 1863 and Pr. 1865 by Bp of Ox. C. of Sonning 1863. [6]

HULTON, William, *Weston, Southampton.*—C. of Weston. [7]

HULTON, William Preston, *Weston, Southampton.*—P. C. of Weston, Dio. Win. 1865. (Patron, the present P. C; P. C.'s Inc. 40*l*; Pop. 260.) [8]

HUMBERT, Lewis Macnaughtan, *St. Cross Hospital, Winchester.*—St. John's Coll. Ox. B.A. 1842, M.A. 1845; Deac. 1843 and Pr. 1844 by Bp of Win. Mast. of St. Cross Hospital 1855. (Patron, Bp of Win; Value 250*l* and Res.) Hon. Sec. of the Win. Branch of the S.P.G; Hon. Sec. of the Diocesan Ch. Building Soc; Organising Sec. of Additional Curates' Soc. Author, *The Teacher's Strength* (a Sermon to Sunday School Teachers); *History of St. Cross Hospital*, 4th ed. Tanner, Winchester; several Occasional Sermons. [9]

HUMBLE, Charles Prince, *Helston, Cornwall.*—St. John's Coll. Cam. B.A. 1846; Deac. 1847 by Bp of Pet. Pr. 1848 by Bp of Ex. [10]

HUMBLE, Henry, *St. Ninian's, Perth.*—Univ. Coll. Dur. B.A. 1837, M.A. 1842; Deac. 1843, Pr. 1844. Dom. Chap. to Lord Forbes 1844; Can. and Precentor of St. Ninian's, Perth. Formerly C. of Newburn, Northumberland, 1842. [11]

HUMBLE, J. R., *Master's Lodge, Spalding, Lincolnshire.*—Dur. and St. Aidan's; Deac. 1863 and Pr. 1864 by Bp of Dur. C. of Spalding 1867. Formerly C. of Deptford, Durham, 1863–65, Monkwearmouth 1865–67 [12]

HUMBLE, Michael Maughan, *Sutton Rectory, Chesterfield.*—Emman. Coll. Cam. B.A. 1833; Deac. 1835, Pr. 1836. R. of Sutton with Duckmanton V. Dio. Lich. 1839. (Patron, R. Arkwright, Esq; Tithe, 300*l*; Glebe, 58½ acres; R.'s Inc. 365*l* and Ho; Pop. 507.) [13]

HUME, Abraham, 24, *Clarence-street, Everton, Liverpool.*—Dub. A.B. 1843, LL.B. and LL.D. 1851, D.C.L. *ad eund.* Cam. 1856, *ad eund.* Ox. 1857, Hon. LL.D. of Glasgow Univ. 1843; Deac. 1843 and Pr. 1844 by Bp of Ches. P. C. of Vauxhall, Liverpool, Dio. Ches. 1847. (Patrons, the Crown and Bp of Ches. alt; P. C.'s Inc. 200*l*; Pop. 8512.) Fell. of the Soc. of Antiquaries. Author, *The Learned Societies and Printing Clubs of the United Kingdom*, 1847, 8*s* 6*d*; *Description of the Antiquities found at Hoylake, in Cheshire* (with map and plates), 1847, 2*s*; *Sir Hugh of Lincoln, or an Examination of an Ancient Tradition respecting the Jews*, 1849, 2*s*; *Missions at Home, or a Clergyman's Account of a Portion of the Town of Liverpool* (with map and coloured statistical table), 1850, 1*s*; *Suggestions for the Advancement of Literature and Learning in Liverpool*, 1851; 1*s*; *Liverpool, Ecclesiastical and Social*, 1858, 1*s* 6*d*; etc. [14]

HUME, Abraham, *Hadleigh, Suffolk.*—King's Coll. Cam. B.A. 1842, M.A. 1845; Deac. 1846, Pr. 1847. P. C. of Kersey, Suffolk, Dio. Ely, 1848. (Patron, King's Coll. Cam; Tithe, Imp. 420*l*; P. C.'s Inc. 135*l*; Pop. 604.) Sen. Fell. of King's Coll. Cam. [15]

HUME, Charles, 33, *Islip-street, Kentish-town-road, London, N.W.*—King's Coll. Lond. Theol. Assoc. 1st cl. 1860; Deac. 1861 and Pr. 1862 by Bp of Lon. C. of Trinity, Haverstock-hill, 1863. Formerly C. of Willesden 1861–63. [16]

HUME, Charles, 31, *Mecklenburgh-square, London, W.C.*—R. of St. Michael's, Wood-street, with St. Mary Staining R. City and Dio. Lon. 1849. (Patrons, the Ld Chan. and Parishioners alt; Tithe, comm. 100*l*; R.'s Inc. 260*l*; Pop. St. Michael's 214, St. Mary Staining 161.) [17]

HUME, Charles John, *Meonstoke, Bishops Waltham, Hants.*—Wad. Coll. Ox. 2nd cl. Lit. Hum. B.A. 1821, M.A. 1825; Deac. 1822, Pr. 1824. R. of Meonstoke with Parochial Chap. of Soberton, Dio. Win. 1832. (Patron, Bp of Win; Meonstoke, Tithe, 280*l*; Glebe, 27¾ acres; Soberton, Tithe, 1007*l* 18*s* 11*d*; Glebe, 13 acres; R.'s Inc. 1079*l* and Ho; Pop. Meonstoke 429, Soberton 582.) Formerly Fell. of Wad. Coll. Ox; C. of Ashbury, Berks, Elvetham, Hants, and Farnham, Surrey. [18]

HUME, George, *Melksham Vicarage, Wilts.*—King's Coll. Cam. B.A. 1823, M.A. 1828; Deac. 1823 and Pr. 1824 by Bp of Salis. V. of Melksham with Seend C. and Earl-Stoke C. Dio. Salis. 1825. (Patrons, D. and C. of Salis; Tithe, comm. 1200*l*; Glebe, 50*l*; V.'s Inc. 1250*l* and Ho; Pop. Melksham 3655, Seend 1086, Earl-Stoke 378.) Surrogate. Formerly Fell. of King's Coll. Cam. [19]

HUME, William Wheler, *St. Leonards-on-Sea, Sussex.*—P. C. of St. Mary Magdalen's, St. Leonards, Dio. Chich. 1852. (Patron, Bp of Chich; P. C.'s Inc. 650*l*; Pop. 7106.) [20]

HUME-ROTHERY, William, 3, *Richmond-terrace, Middleton, near Manchester.*—St. Bees; Deac. 1848 and Pr. 1849 by Bp of Man. Formerly C. of Mossley, Ashton-under-Lyne, 1848–51; Incumb. of the Episcopal Chapel, Selkirk, Scotland, 1851–57; C. in sole charge of Holm Cultram, Cumberland, 1857–61; C. of Hexham, Northumberland, 1862–64. Author, *Wheat and Tares*, 1865. [21]

HUMFREY, Robert Pargiter, *Thorpe Mandeville (Northants), near Banbury.*—Lin. Coll. Ox. B.A. 1836, M.A. 1837; Deac. 1837, Pr. 1838. R. of Thorpe Mandeville, Dio. Pet. 1841. (Patron, the present R; Glebe, 174 acres; R.'s Inc. 350*l* and Ho; Pop. 164) [22]

HUMFREY, Thomas Craven, *Trawden Parsonage, near Colne, Lancashire.*—St. Bees; Deac. 1844 and Pr. 1845 by Bp of Ches. P. C. of Trawden, Dio. Man. 1845. (Patrons, Crown and Bp of Man. alt; P. C.'s Inc. 150*l* and Ho; Pop. 1516.) Formerly Min. of Portwood, Cheshire, 1844–45. [23]

HUMFREY, William Cave, *Laughton Rectory, Welford, Leicestershire.*—St. Peter's Coll. Cam. B.A. 1826; Deac. 1827, Pr. 1828. R. of Laughton, Dio. Pet. (Patron, the present R; Tithe, 108*l* 1*s* 9*d*; Glebe, 25 acres; R.'s Inc. 247*l* and Ho; Pop. 152.) Rural Dean. [24]

HUMPHREY, William Barnard, *Warminster, Wilts.*—Magd. Hall, Ox. Exhib. of Lin. and Lusby Scho. of Magd. Hall, B.A. 1865; Deac. 1865, Pr. 1866. Asst. C. of Warminster 1865. [25]

HUMPHREY, William Topley, *East Stockwith, Gainsborough.*—Deac. 1836 and Pr. 1837 by Bp of Lon. P. C. of East Stockwith, Dio. Lin. 1862. (Patron,

Bp of Lin; P. C.'s Inc. 80*l* and Ho; Pop. 350.) Formerly Prin. of Cotyam Coll. Travancore, 1838–40; Ch. Miss. at Myaveram 1841–42; Chap. in Arracan 1843–46; Chap. of Chittagong 1847, Moulmein 1847–52; C. of Brigg 1853–54; Chap. of Singapore 1853–58, Akyab 1858, Barrackpore 1858–60, St. John's, Calcutta, 1860–61; C. of Northwood, Stoke-on-Trent, 1861–62; has a Medal for Services with the Troops in the Pegu War of 1852. [1]

HUMPHREYS, Henry Sockett, *Duchess-road, Edgbaston, Birmingham.*—King's Coll. Lond. Assoc. 1849; Deac. 1849 and Pr. 1850 by Bp of Pet. Chap. to the Birmingham General Hospital, 1856. Formerly C. of Ch. Ch. Birmingham, 1850–56. [2]

HUMPHREYS, Robert, *Capel Curig (Carnarvonshire), Llanrwst.*—Queens' Coll. Cam. B.A. 1843; Deac. 1843, Pr. 1844. P. C. of Capel Curig Chapelry, Llandegai, Dio. Ban. 1848. (Patron, Bp of Ban; P. C.'s Inc. 180*l*.) [3]

HUMPHREYS, Thomas, *Wentnor Rectory, Bishop's Castle, Salop.*—Jesus Coll. Ox. B.A. 1828, M.A. 1831; Deac. 1830 and Pr. 1831 by Bp of Lich. R. of Wentnor, Dio. Herf. 1861. (Patron, Ch. Ch. Ox; Tithe, 210*l* 5*s*; Glebe, 70 acres; R.'s Inc. 272*l* 5*s* and Ho; Pop. 646.) Formerly C. of Dawley 1830–33, Wentnor 1834–60, Norbury, 1839–62, all in Salop. [4]

HUMPHRY, William Gilson, 6, *St. Martin's-place, Trafalgar-square, London, W.C.*—Trin. Coll. Cam. B.A. 1837, M.A. 1840, B.D. 1850; Deac. 1842 and Pr. 1843 by Bp of Ely. V. of St. Martin's-in-the Fields, Dio. Lon. 1855. (Patron, Bp of Lon; V.'s Inc. 950*l* and Ho; Pop. 16,382.) Preb. of St. Paul's 1852; Hulsean Lect. 1849 and 1850; Exam. Chap. to the late Bp. of Lon. 1847–56. Formerly Fell. of Trin. Coll. Cam. Author, *A Commentary on the Book of the Acts of the Apostles*, 1847, 2nd ed. 1854; *The Doctrine of a Future State* (the Hulsean Lecture for 1849), 1850; *The Early Progress of the Gospel* (the Hulsean Lecture for 1850), 1851; *An Historical and Explanatory Treatise on the Book of Common Prayer*, 1853, 2nd ed. 1856; *The Miracles* (the Boyle Lecture for 1857), 1858; *The Character of St. Paul* (the Boyle Lecture for 1858), 1859. Editor of *Theophilus of Antioch*, Pitt Press, 1852; *Theophylact on St. Matthew*, ib. 1854. One of the Authors of *A Revised Version of St. John's Gospel, and the Epistles to the Romans and Corinthians*, 1857–58. [5]

HUNGATE, F. W., *Clay Cross, Chesterfield.*—C. of Clay Cross. [6]

HUNNYBUN, James, *Nayland, Suffolk.*—Caius Coll. Cam. M.A. 1855; Deac. and Pr. 1856 by Bp of Ban. P. C. of Nayland, Dio. Ely, 1867. (Patron, Sir Charles Rowley; P. C.'s Inc. 140*l* and Ho; Pop. 1061.) Formerly C. of Hadleigh, Suffolk. [7]

HUNNYBUN, William Martin, *Withiell-Florey, Dulverton, Somerset.*—Caius Coll. Cam. B.A. 1860, M.A. 1864; Deac. 1862 and Pr. 1863 by Bp of St. D. P. C. of Withiell-Florey, Dio. B. and W. 1866. (Patron, Sir T. B. Lethbridge; P. C.'s Inc. 59*l*; Pop. 164.) Formerly C. of Steynton, Pembrokeshire. [8]

HUNT, Augustus Archer, *Tipton St. John's Parsonage, Ottery St. Mary, Devon.*—Ex. Coll. Ox. B.A. 1841, M.A. 1844; Deac. 1843 and Pr. 1844 by Bp of Ex. P. C. of Tipton St. John's, Dio. Ex. 1845. (Patron, V. of Ottery St. Mary; Glebe, 6 acres; P. C.'s Inc. 80*l* and Ho; Pop. 470.) [9]

HUNT, Edward George, *Plympton St. Mary, Devon.*—Ex. Coll. Ox. 2nd cl. Lit. Hum. B.A. 1846, M.A. 1849; Deac. 1849 and Pr. 1850 by Bp of Ex. P. C. of Plympton St. Mary, Dio. Ex. 1865. (Patrons, D. and C. of Windsor; P. C.'s Inc. 152*l*; Pop. 3060.) Formerly C. of Kingston, Devon, 1849, Upper Brixham with Churston 1852, Ottery St. Mary 1855, Plympton St. Mary 1863. [10]

HUNT, Frederick, *Oulton, Aylesham, Norfolk.*—New Inn Hall, Ox. B.A. 1853; Deac. 1855, Pr. 1856. V. of Oulton, Dio. Nor. 1863. (Patron, Rev. S. Cooke; V.'s Inc. 153*l*; Pop. 357.) Formerly C. of Oulton. [11]

HUNT, Henry Warwick, 27, *Soho-square, London, W.*—Trin. Coll. Cam. M.A; Deac. 1859, Pr. 1860. C. of St. Anne's, Soho. Formerly C. of St. John's, Westminster. [12]

HUNT, James, *Northmoor Green, Bridgwater.*—Emman. Coll. Cam. 1852; Deac. 1854 by Bp of B. and W. Pr. 1861 by Bp of Ossory. P. C. of Northmoor Green, Dio. B. and W. 1864. (Patron, V. of North Petherton; P. C.'s Inc. 110*l*; Pop. 760.) Formerly 3rd Mast. of Ipswich Coll; Head Mast. of Wrexham Coll; Incumb. of the Episcopal Mission, Wick, N. B. Author, various Sermons and Poems. [13]

HUNT, John William, 7, *Coburg-terrace, Hull.*—St. Aidan's; Deac. 1859 and Pr. 1860 by Bp of Lich. P. C. of St. James's, Hull, Dio. York, 1862. (Patron, V. of Trinity, Hull; P. C.'s Inc. 200*l*.) [14]

HUNT, Joseph, *Fifehead Magdalen Vicarage, Blandford, Dorset.*—Queen's Coll. Ox. B.A. 1836, M.A. 1840. V. of Fifehead Magdalen, Dio. Salis. 1848. (Patron, Bp of G. and B; Tithe, 251*l*; Glebe, 24½ acres; V.'s Inc. 301*l* and Ho; Pop. 200.) Formerly Fell. of Queen's Coll. Ox. [15]

HUNT, Oliver, *Stratford-on-Avon.*—Emman. Coll. Cam. B.A. 1863, M.A. 1867; Deac. 1865 and Pr. 1866 by Bp of Wor. Formerly C. of Bickenhill, Warwickshire, 1865–67. [16]

HUNT, Richard William Treen, *Byton (Herefordshire), near Presteigne.*—St. John's Coll. Cam. B.A. 1849; Deac. 1851, Pr. 1852. R. of Byton, Dio. Herf. 1854. (Patron, Ld Chan; Tithe, comm. 135*l*; Glebe, 1 acre; R.'s Inc. 141*l*; Pop. 214.) [17]

HUNT, Robert Shapland, *Mark Beech Parsonage, Eden Bridge, Kent.*—Ex. Coll. Ox. B.A. 1841, M.A. 1844; Deac. 1841, Pr. 1842. P. C. of Mark Beech, Dio. Cant. 1852. (Patroness, Hon. Mrs. Talbot; Glebe, 10½ acres; P. C.'s Inc. 69*l* and Ho; Pop. 289.) [18]

HUNT, Thomas Henry, *Badsey Parsonage, Evesham, Worcestershire.*—Ch. Ch. Ox. B.A. 1849, M.A. 1852; Deac. 1851, Pr. 1852. P. C. of Badsey, Dio. Wor. 1852. (Patron, Ch. Ch. Ox; Glebe, 153 acres; P. C.'s Inc. 240*l* and Ho; Pop. 546.) P. C. of Wickhamford, Worcestershire, Dio. Wor. 1852. (Patron, Ch. Ch. Ox; Tithe—App. 234*l*, P. C. 40*l*; Glebe, 12 acres; P. C.'s Inc. 50*l*; Pop. 124.) [19]

HUNT, William, *Weston-super-Mare.*—P. C. of Trinity, Weston-super-Mare, Dio. B. and W. 1861. (Patrons, Trustees; Pop. 2500.) [20]

HUNT, William, *Congresbury Vicarage, Bristol.*—Trin. Coll. Ox. B.A. 1864; Deac. 1865 and Pr. 1866 by Bp of B. and W. V. of Congresbury with Wick St. Lawrence C. Dio. B. and W. 1867. (Patron, Rev. W. Hunt; V.'s Inc. 820*l* and Ho; Pop. Congresbury 1190, Wick 270.) Formerly C. of Trinity, Weston-super-Mare, 1865–67. [21]

HUNT, William, *Bancroft's Hospital, Mile-end, London, E.*—Corpus Coll. Cam. 17th Wrang. and B.A. 1846, M.A. 1849; Deac. and Pr. 1846. Mast. and Chap. of Bancroft's Hosp. 1855. (Patron, the Drapers' Company.) Sunday Even. Lect. of St. Michael's, Cornhill. Formerly Prof. and Tut. in Queen's Coll. Birmingham. [22]

HUNT, William Cornish, *Odell Rectory, Bedford.*—Ch. Ch. Ox. B.A. 1858; Deac. 1860 by Bp of Salis. Pr. 1860 by Bp of Lich. R. of Odell, Dio. Ely, 1863. (Patron, Crewe Alston, Esq; Tithe, 20*l*; Glebe 384 acres, woods 33 acres; R.'s Inc. 460*l* and Ho; Pop. 494.) Formerly C. of West Felton, Salop, 1860–62, Uffington, Linc. (sole charge) 1862–64. [23]

HUNT, William Thorley Gignac, *Prestwood Parsonage, Great Missenden.*—Ch. Ch. Ox. B.A. 1859, M.A. 1863; Deac. 1861 and Pr. 1862 by Bp of Ox. P. C. of Prestwood, Dio. Ox. 1866. (Patron, Rev. T. Evetts; P. C.'s Inc. 120*l* and Ho; Pop. 947.) Formerly C. of St. John's, Lacey-green, Bucks, 1861, Dinton, Bucks, 1863. [24]

HUNT, Wray Richard, 30, *Bedford-street North, Liverpool.*—Dub A.B. 1837, A.M. 1861; Deac. 1839 and Pr. 1840 by Bp of Down and Connor. P. C. of St. Columba's, Liverpool, Dio. Ches. 1857. (Patrons, Bp of Ches. and Archd. and R. of Liverpool; P. C.'s Inc. 260*l*.) [25]

HUNTER, Alexander, *Tanworth Vicarage, Hockley Heath, Warwickshire.*—Trin. Coll. Cam. B.A. 1830, M.A. 1835; Deac. 1836 and Pr. 1837 by Bp of Wor. V. of Tanworth, Dio. Wor. 1854. (Patron, Earl Amherst; Tithe—Imp. 1223*l* 5*s* 8*d*, V. 507*l*; Glebe, 40 acres; V.'s Inc. 576*l* and Ho; Pop. 804.) [1]

HUNTER, David, *Stanway, Colchester.*—P. C. of All Saints', Stanway, Dio. Roch. 1864. (Patron, Bp of Roch; Pop. 513.) Formerly R. of Howell, Lincolnshire, 1859–64. [2]

HUNTER, George Rivers, *Okeford Fitzpaine Rectory, Blandford, Dorset.*—Wad. Coll. Ox. B.A. 1819. R. of Okeford Fitzpaine, Dio. Salis. 1816. (Patron, Lord Rivers; Tithe, 505*l*; Glebe, 74 acres; R.'s Inc. 608*l* and Ho; Pop. 685.) [3]

HUNTER, Henry, *Warboys, Huntingdon.*—C. of Warboys 1849. [4]

HUNTER, Joseph, *Kirkby Fleetham, Bedale, Yorks.*—Ch. Coll. Cam. B.A. 1857, M.A. 1860; Deac. 1866 and Pr. 1867 by Bp of Rip. C. of Kirkby Fleetham 1866. [5]

HUNTINGFORD, Edward, *Eagle House, Hammersmith, Middlesex, W.*—New Coll. Ox. B.C.L. 1845, D.C.L. 1848; Deac. 1843 by Bp of Ox. Pr. 1844 by Bp of G. and B. Head Mast. of Eagle House Sch. Hammersmith. Formerly Fell. of New Coll. Ox. Author, *Thoughts on some Portions of the Revelation*, 1862; *An Inquiry by the Light of Scripture into the Doctrine of the Lord's Presence in the Holy Communion*, 1855, 1*s*; *The Schoolboy's Way to Eternal Life*, 1857, 3*s* 6*d*; *A Practical Interpretation of the Apocalypse*, 1858, 7*s* 6*d*. [6]

HUNTINGFORD, George William, *Littlemore Parsonage, near Oxford.*—New Coll. Ox. B.A. 1837, M.A. 1840; Deac. 1838, Pr. 1839. P. C. of Littlemore, Dio. Ox. 1851. (Patrons, Oriel Coll. Ox. and C. Crawley, Esq; Glebe, 6 acres; P. C.'s Inc. 180*l* and Ho; Pop. 700.) Formerly Fell. of New Coll. Ox. 1835–49; Asst. Mast. in Winchester Coll. 1838–47. [7]

HUNTINGFORD, Henry, *Hampton Bishop Rectory, Herefordshire.*—New Coll. Ox. LL.B. 1814; Deac. 1811 and Pr. 1812 by Bp of Herf. R. of Hampton Bishop, Dio. Herf. 1822. (Patron, Bp of Herf; Tithe—App. 172*l*, R. 413*l* 15*s*; Glebe, 5 acres; R.'s Inc. 480*l* and Ho; Pop. 1047.) Can. of Herf. Cathl. 1838. Rural Dean. [8]

HUNTINGTON, George, *Tenby Rectory, South Wales.*—St. Bees 1846–47, M.A. by Abp of Cant. 1855; Deac. 1848 and Pr. 1849 by Bp of Man. R. of Tenby, Dio. St. D. 1867. (Patron, the Crown; Glebe, 62*l* 10*s*; R.'s Inc. 384*l* and Ho; Pop. 3197.) Dom. Chap. to the Earl of Crawford and Balcarres; Surrogate. Formerly C. of Wigan; Clerk in Orders, Manchester Cathl. 1855–67; R. of St. Stephen's, Salford, 1863–66. Author, *Sermons for Holy Seasons of the Church*, 1st series, 1856, 6*s*, 2nd series, 1862, 6*s*; *The Church's Work in our Large Towns*, 1863, 4*s*; *Amusements and the Need of supplying Healthy Recreation for the People*, 6d and 1*s*; *How Fathers and Mothers may make or mar the Happiness of their Children and their Homes*, 1*d*; *The Preaching of the Gospel to the Poor*, 2*d*; *The Unity of the Church*, 1*d*; *The Autobiography of John Brown, the Cordwainer*, 1867, 3*s* 6*d*; various Tracts for S.P.C.K. Editor, *Plain Words for Plain People*; *Church of the People*; etc. [9]

HUNTINGTON, Henry John.—Ch. Coll. Cam. B.A. 1846; Deac. 1847, Pr. 1848. British Chap. at Leghorn and Kissingen. [10]

HUNTINGTON, William, *St. John's Rectory, Manchester.*—Trin. Coll. Cam. 10th Sen. Opt. and B.A. 1820, M.A. 1826; Deac. 1822, Pr. 1826. R. of St. John's, Manchester, Dio. Man. 1831. (Patrons, the D. and C. of Man; R.'s Inc. 400*l*; Pop. 12,469.) Dom. Chap. to the Earl of Zetland. Author, *An Address to the Inhabitants of St. John's District*, 1823, 3*d*; *A Sermon on the Death of the Rev. Dr. Morton*, 1844, 1*s*; *An Address to the Operatives of Manchester*, 1850, 6*d*; *A Sermon against the Infallibility claimed by the Church of Rome*, 1*s*. [11]

HUNTLEY, James Webster, *Thursby Vicarage, Carlisle.*—St. John's Coll. Cam. B.A. 1822, M.A. 1825; Deac. 1823, Pr. 1824. V. of Thursby, Dio. Carl. 1830. (Patrons, D. and C. of Carl; Tithe—App. 150*l*, V. 209*l*; Glebe, 23 acres; V.'s Inc. 240*l* and Ho; Pop. 568.) V. of Kirkland, near Penrith, Dio. Carl. 1836. (Patrons, D. and C. of Carl; Tithe—App. 500*l*, V. 100*l*; V.'s Inc. 225*l*; Pop. 481.) [12]

HUNTLEY, John Thomas, *Binbrooke, Market Rasen, Lincolnshire.*—Trin. Coll. Cam. B.A. 1813, M.A. 1817; Deac. 1815, Pr. 1816. R. of Binbrooke St. Mary with Binbrooke St. Gabriel V. Dio. Lin. 1845. (Patron, Ld Chan; R.'s Inc. 310*l*; Pop. 1334.) Author, *Visitation Sermon*, 1826. [13]

HUNTLY, Benjamin Corke, *Dulwich College, S.*—St. John's Coll. Cam. Wrang. B.A. 1865; Deac. 1866 by Bp Anderson for Bp of Lon. C. of Trinity, Sydenham, 1866; Asst. Mast. Dulwich Coll. 1866. [14]

HUNTSMAN, Edmund John, *Walsall Wood, Staffs.*—Jesus Coll. Cam. Sen. Opt. B.A. 1852, M.A. 1855; Deac. 1853 by Bp of Nor. Pr. 1854 by Bp of Meath. P. C. of Walsall Wood, Staffs, Dio. Lich. 1859. (Patron, V. of Walsall; P. C.'s Inc. 101*l* 14*s* and Ho; Pop. 1701.) Formerly C. of Wangford, Suffolk, 1853–57, St. Peter's, Birmingham, 1857–59. [15]

HURLE, Robert Gleadowe, *Mitcheldean, Gloucester.*—St. John's Coll. Cam. B.A. 1865; Deac. 1865, Pr. 1866. C. of Mitcheldean 1865. [16]

HURLOCK, Joseph, 5, *Hanover-crescent, Brighton.*—Wad. Coll. Ox. 2nd cl. Lit. Hum. and B.A. 1821, M.A. 1824; Deac. and Pr. 1823 by Bp of Chich. Formerly P. C. of Ixworth, Suffolk; Chap. to the Sussex Co. Hospital, Brighton, 1843–67. [17]

HURNALL, J., *Egginton, Leighton Buzzard.*—Emman. Coll. Cam. B.A. 1825, M.A. 1832; Deac. 1828 by Bp of Kildare, Pr. 1832 by Bp of Win. P. C. of Egginton, Dio. Ely, 1860. (Patrons, Parishioners; P. C.'s Inc. 105*l*; Pop. 439.) Formerly C. of South Stonham, Hants, 1832, Godshill, Isle of Wight, 1836, Kelmarsh, Northants, 1841, Stocking Pelham, Herts, 1846. [18]

HURST, Blythe, *Dipton Collierley, Gateshead, Durham.*—Literate; Deac. 1842, Pr. 1843. P. C. of Collierley, Dio. Dur. 1854. (Patron, Bp of Dur; P. C.'s Inc. 300*l*; Pop. 3223.) Author, *Christianity no Priestcraft* (a Pamphlet against Socialism), 1840. [19]

HURST, Francis Thomas, *Ridgewell Vicarage, Halstead.*—St. Cath. Coll. Cam. Scho. 19th Wrang. B.A. 1857, M.A. 1860; Deac. 1859 and Pr. 1860 by Bp of Rip. V. of Ridgewell, Dio. Roch. 1862. (Patron, St. Cath. Coll. Cam; Tithe, 136*l*; Glebe, 125 acres; V.'s Inc. 420*l* and Ho; Pop. 795.) Formerly Fell. of St. Cath. Coll. Cam; C. of Trinity, Richmond, Yorks. [20]

HURST, John, *Thakeham Rectory, Petworth, Sussex.*—R. of Thakeham, Dio. Chich. 1818. (Patron, Duke of Norfolk; Tithe, 710*l*; Glebe, 27 acres; R.'s Inc. 737*l* and Ho; Pop. 559.) [21]

HURST, Samuel Sheppard, *Great Yarmouth.*

HURST, William, *St Martin's Vicarage, near Chirk, Salop.*—Clare Coll. Cam. B.A. 1834, M.A. 1847; Deac. 1836 and Pr. 1838 by Bp of Lin. V. of St. Martin's, Dio. St. A. 1842. (Patron, Lord A. E. Hill Trevor; Tithe—Imp. 862*l*, V. 261*l*; Glebe, 60 acres; V.'s Inc. 374*l* and Ho; Pop. 2351.) [22]

HURT, John Francis, *Bilborough Rectory, near Nottingham.*—Trin. Coll. Cam. B.A. 1851; Deac. 1852 by Bp of Lin. Pr. 1853 by Bp of Pet. R. of Strelley with Bilborough, Dio. Lin. 1853. (Patron, J. T. Edge, Esq; Glebe, 165 acres; R.'s Inc. 390*l* and Ho; Pop. Strelley 253, Bilborough 232.) Formerly C. of Barrow-on-Humber and New Holland 1852. [23]

HURT, Robert, *Carlby Rectory, Stamford, Lincolnshire.*—Jesus Coll. Cam. B.A. 1853; Deac. 1837 by Abp of York, Pr. 1838 by Bp of Nor. R. of Carlby, Dio. Lin. (Patrons, Marquis of Exeter and Sir E. Smith, Bart; Glebe, 250 acres; R.'s Inc. 260*l* and Ho; Pop. 183.) [24]

HURT, William Thomas, *Sutton-upon-Lound, Retford, Notts.* Trin. Coll. Cam. B.A. 1832, M.A. 1836; Deac. 1834 and Pr. 1835 by Abp of York. V. of Sutton-upon-Lound with Scrooby V. Dio. Lin. 1842. (Patron,

Duke of Portland; Sutton-upon-Lound, Tithe—Imp. 5*l*, V. 2*l*; Glebe, 106 acres; Scrooby, Tithe—Imp. 95*l*, V. 31*l* 10*s*; Glebe, 33 acres; V.'s Inc. 248*l*; Pop. Sutton-upon-Lound 916, Scrooby 256.) [1]

HUSBAND, Edward, *Atherstone, Warwickshire.*—St. Aidan's; Deac. 1866 by Bp of Wor. C. of St. Mary's, Atherstone, 1866. Author, *Women Preachers*, 2*d*; *Prisoners of Hope*, 3*d*; *The Manner of the Real Presence in the Holy Eucharist*, 3*d*; *Truths of the Catholic Religion*, Masters, 1867, 6*d*; "*Lead kindly Light*" and "*We March to Victory*," set to music, Novello, 1866. [2]

HUSBAND, George Radclyffe, *Brandesburton, Beverley, Yorks.*—King's Coll. Lond; Deac. 1851 and Pr. 1852 by Abp of York. C. of Brandsburton 1867. Formerly C. of Hutton Bushell, near York, and Saltwood, Kent. [3]

HUSBAND, John, *Selattyn Rectory, Oswestry, Salop.*—Magd. Coll. Cam. Jun. Opt. and B.A. 1821, M.A. 1825; Deac. 1821 and Pr. 1822 by Bp of Ely R. of Selattyn, Dio. St. A. 1853. (Patroness, Mrs. Lloyd; Tithe, 815*l*; Glebe, 85 acres; R.'s Inc. 871*l* and Ho; Pop. 675.) Formerly Fell. of Magd. Coll. Cam. Author, *Parochial Sermons on Popery*, 1829. [4]

HUSBAND, John Edward Colville, *Heavitree, near Exeter.*—Literate; Deac. 1853 by Bp of Ex. Pr. 1854 by Bp of Wor. Formerly C. of Whitchurch-Canonicorum, Dorset, and Selattyn, Salop. [5]

HUSSEY, Arthur Law, *Peterley House, Great Missenden, Bucks.*—Ch. Ch. Ox. B.A. 1853, M.A. 1856; Deac. 1855 and Pr. 1856 by Bp of Ox. Formerly Fell. of St. Peter's Coll. Radley. [6]

HUSSEY, Charles John, *Belvedere, Erith, S.E.*—Ch. Coll. Cam. B.A. 1856, M.A. 1864; Deac. 1859 and Pr. 1860 by Abp of Cant. C. of All Saints', Belvedere, 1867. Formerly C. of Brenchley, Kent, 1859; Miss. C. of Ch. Ch. Blackfriars-road, Southwark, 1865. [7]

HUSSEY, Eyre W., *Lyneham, Chippenham.*—Ch. Ch. Ox. B.A. 1862, M.A. 1865; Deac. 1863 and Pr. 1864 by Bp of G. and B. P. C. of Lyneham, Dio. Salis. 1866. (Patron, G. Walker Heneage, Esq; P. C.'s Inc. 147*l* and Ho; Pop. 1034.) Formerly C. of Pucklechurch, Bristol. [8]

HUSSEY, Henry Llewellyn, *Withecombe Raleigh, Exmouth, Devon.*—St. John's Coll. Cam. B.A. 1846, M.A. 1849; Deac. 1846 and Pr. 1847 by Bp of Ex. P. C. of Withecombe Raleigh, Dio. Ex. 1853. (Patrons, Trustees of Lord Rolle; Tithe—Imp. 200*l*; P. C. 210*l*; Glebe, 4 acres; P. C.'s Inc. 214*l* and Ho; Pop. 2145.) Dom. Chap. to Lady Rolle. [9]

HUSSEY, James M'Connel, 2, *Claremont-place, Brixton-road, London, S.*—Ex. Coll. Ox. B.A. 1843; Deac. 1844, Pr. 1845. P. C. of Ch. Ch. Brixton, Dio. Win. 1855. (Patron, the present P. C; P. C.'s Inc. 700*l*; Pop. 3776.) Afternoon Preacher at the Foundling Hospital, Lond. [10]

HUSSEY, William Law, *Ringstead Rectory, Lynn, Norfolk.*—Ch. Ch. Ox. 1831, 4th cl. Lit. Hum. B.A. 1835, M.A. 1837; Deac. 1836 and Pr. 1837 by Bp of Ox. R. of Great Ringstead, Dio. Nor. 1862. (Patron, H. Styleman le Strange, Esq; Tithe, 600*l*; Glebe, 150 acres; R.'s Inc. 800*l* and Ho; Pop. 650.) Hon. Can. of Manchester 1856. Formerly C. of Witham, Essex, 1845–48; Asst. Min. of Curzon Chapel, Lond. 1850–52; V. of Kirkham, Lancashire, 1852–62. [11]

HUSTLER, George, *Stillingfleet, Escrick, Yorks.*—Univ. Coll. Ox. B.A. 1848; Deac. 1849, Pr. 1850. V. of Stillingfleet, Dio. York, 1859. (Patrons, D. and C. of York; V.'s Inc. 412*l* and Ho; Pop. 810.) Formerly P. C. of Acaster Selby, Yorks, 1850–59. [12]

HUSTWICK, Edward Thorold, *Sheffield.*—Jesus Coll. Cam. B.A. 1859, M.A. 1864; Deac. 1860 and Pr. 1861 by Bp of Ely. Asst. Chap. and C. of Sheffield 1864. Formerly C. of Ramsey, Hunts, 1860. [13]

HUSTWICK, Robert, *Morcott Rectory, Uppingham, Rutland.*—Queens' Coll. Cam. B.A. 1825, M.A. 1828; Deac. 1826, Pr. 1827. R. of Morcott, Dio. Pet. 1834. (Patroness, Mrs. Mary Thorold; Tithe—App. 52*l* and 4 acres of Glebe, R. 388*l*; Glebe, 21 acres; R.'s Inc. 410*l* and Ho; Pop. 494.) [14]

HUTCHESON, William, *Chewstoke, Bristol.*—St. Mary Hall, Ox. B.A. 1818, M.A. 1820; Deac. 1820 by Bp of Glouc. Pr. 1821 by Bp of Bristol. R. of Ubley, Somerset, Dio. B. and W. 1827. (Patron, Ld Chan; Tithe, 200*l*; Glebe, 70 acres; R.'s Inc. 240*l*; Pop. 307.) [15]

HUTCHINGS, Robert Sperke, *Alderbury, Salisbury.*—Ch. Ch. Ox. double 2nd cl. Fell. Exhib. of, B.A. 1843, M.A. 1847; Deac. 1845 and Pr. 1846 by Bp of Ex. V. of Alderbury with Pitton C. and Farley C. Dio. Salis. 1865. (Patron, Bp of Salis; Tithe, Alderbury, 75*l*, Farley 103*l*; Glebe, 50*l*; V.'s Inc. 477*l* and Ho; Pop. 1334.) Rural Dean. Formerly C. of Kingsteignton, Devon, 1845–47; P. C. of Monkton Wyld, Dorset, 1850–65. [16]

HUTCHINS, Charles George, *Trinity Church, Guildford.*—Magd. Hall, Ox. B.A. 1860, M.A. 1863; Deac. 1860 by Bp of Ches. Pr. 1861 by Bp of Herf. C. of Trinity and St. Mary's, Guildford, 1863. Formerly C. of St. Mary's, Bridgnorth, 1860–62, Bromfield, Salop, 1862–63. Author, *Our Nightly Rest and its Lessons* (a Sermon), 1864, 6*d*. [17]

HUTCHINS, George William, *Horton, Northampton.*—Magd. Hall, Ox. B.A. 1839, M.A. 1842; Deac. 1840 and Pr. 1841 by Bp of Rip. P. C. of Horton with Piddington P. C. Dio. Pet. 1864. (Patron, Rev. Sir Henry John Cumming, Bart; P. C.'s Inc. 100*l* and Ho; Pop. 1178.) Formerly C. of Horbury, Yorks, 1840–43, Chew Magna and Dundry 1843–50, West Charlton 1850–53, Doddington 1853–61, and Minehead, Somerset, 1863–64. [18]

HUTCHINS, Henry, *Maxstoke Vicarage, Coleshill, Warwickshire.*—Trin. Hall, Cam. B.A. 1839; Deac. 1841 by Bp of Lich. Pr. 1842 by Bp of Herf. V. of Maxstoke, Dio. Wor. 1848. (Patron, Lord Leigh; Tithe—Imp. 214*l* 4*s* 4*d*; Glebe, 4½ acres; V.'s Inc. 100*l* and Ho; Pop. 322.) Formerly C. of Bobbington and Colwich, Staffs. Author, *A Sermon on the Fast-day*, 1847; *Address to Parents on bringing up their Children*, 1848, 4*d*; *Psalms and Hymns for Public Worship very carefully selected*, 1855, 8*d*. [19]

HUTCHINS, James, *Telscombe, Rodmell, Sussex.*—St. John's Coll. Ox. B.A. 1818, Ch. Ch. M.A. 1822; Deac. 1818 and Pr. 1819 by Bp of Ox. R. of Telscombe, *alias* Telescombe, Dio. Chich. 1825. (Patron, the present R; Tithe—Imp. 40*l*, R. 236*l*; Glebe, 6 acres and pasturage for 20 sheep; R.'s Inc. 244*l*; Pop. 156.) V. of Piddinghoe, Newhaven, Sussex, Dio. Chich. 1825. (Patron, the present V; Tithe—Imp. 452*l* 15*s* 9*d*, V. 170*l*; Glebe, 4 acres; V.'s Inc. 175*l*; Pop. 243.) [20]

HUTCHINS, Richard Masters, *Spillman's Court, Rodborough, near Stroud.*—Trin. Coll. Cam. B.A. 1842, M.A. 1845; Deac. 1841 and Pr. 1842 by Bp of G. and B. [21]

HUTCHINS, W. H. H., *All Saints' Rectory, Saltfleetby, Louth, Lincolnshire.*—R. of All Saints', Saltfleetby, Dio. Lin. 1867. (Patron, Magd. Coll. Ox; Tithe, 311*l*; Glebe, 28 acres; R.'s Inc. 353*l* and Ho; Pop. 195.) [22]

HUTCHINSON, Benjamin, *St. Michael's Vicarage, St. Albans, Herts.*—V. of St. Michael's, St. Albans, Dio. Roch. 1850. (Patron, Earl of Verulam; V.'s Inc. 305*l* and Ho; Pop. 1291.) [23]

HUTCHINSON, Charles Edward, *Amport Vicarage, Andover, Hants.*—Trin. Coll. Ox. B.A. 1813, M.A. 1816; Deac. 1814, Pr. 1815. V. of Amport, Dio. Win. 1864. (Patrons, D. and C. of Chich; V.'s Inc. 920*l* and Ho; Pop. 706.) Can. Res. *of Chich. with Prebendal Stall of Ippthorne annexed, 1828. (Value of Canonry, 800*l* and Res; Preb. Stall of Ippthorne, 12*l*.) [24]

HUTCHINSON, Charles Henry, *Westdean Vicarage, Chichester.*—Ex. Coll. Ox. B.A. 1845, M.A. 1847; Deac. 1847 and Pr. 1848 by Bp of Chich. V. of Westdean, Dio. Chich. 1849. (Patrons, D. and C. of Chich; Tithe, 200*l*; Glebe, 40*l*; V.'s Inc. 270*l* and Ho; Pop. 680.) [25]

HUTCHINSON, Charles Pierrepont, *Forton, Gosport, Hants.*—Trin. Coll. Cam. 2nd cl. Cl. Trip. Sen. Opt. B.A. 1854, M.A. 1857; Deac. 1856 and Pr. 1857 by Bp of Rip. P. C. of St. John's, Forton, Dio. Win. 1866. (Patron, R. of Alverstoke; P. C.'s Inc. 300*l*; Pop. 6425.) Formerly C. of St. James's, Bradford, Yorks, 1856, Alverstoke, Hants, 1858, Chilham, Kent, 1859. Folkestone 1864. [1]

HUTCHINSON, Charles Ring, *Pitstone (Bucks), near Tring, Herts.*—Brasen. Coll. Ox. 2nd cl. Lit. Hum. and B.A. 1849; Deac. 1851 and Pr. 1852 by Bp of Lon. P. C. of Pitstone, or Pightlesthorne, Dio. Ox. 1855. (Patron, Earl Brownlow; Glebe, 36 acres; P. C.'s Inc. 175*l* and Ho; Pop. 463.) Formerly C. of Sunbury, Middlesex. [2]

HUTCHINSON, Christopher Blick, *Rugby.*—St. John's Coll. Cam. Fell. of, 1853, 1st cl. Cl. Trip. B.A. 1851, M.A. 1854; Deac. 1853 by Bp of Man. Pr. 1854 by Bp of Ely. Mast. in Rugby Sch. 1858. Formerly Composition Mast. in King Edward's Sch. Birmingham, 1855. [3]

HUTCHINSON, Cyril George, *Batsford Rectory, Moreton-in-the Marsh, Glouc.*—Ch. Ch. Ox. B.A. 1822, M.A. 1824; Deac. 1826, Pr. 1828. R. of Batsford, Dio. G. and B. 1841. (Patrons, Ch. Ch. Ox; Tithe, 253*l*; Glebe, 96½ acres; R.'s Inc. 370*l* and Ho; Pop. 130.) Rural Dean of Campden 1849; Hon. Can. of Glouc. 1852. Author, *Prayers, chiefly selected from the Liturgy*; *Two Plain Sermons on Baptism and Confirmation*, 1837; *Plain Sermons on Church Ministry and Sacraments*, 1841; *Thoughts on Church Matters*, 1845; *Visitation Sermons*, 1846. [4]

HUTCHINSON, Edmund, *Greatham, Stockton-on-Tees.*—Dur. Licen. in Theol. 1860, B.A. 1862, M.A. 1867; Deac. 1861 and Pr. 1863 by Bp of Dur. C. of Greatham 1864. Formerly C. of Shildon 1861, Easington 1862. [5]

HUTCHINSON, Francis Edmund, *Tisbury Vicarage, Salisbury.*—Univ. Coll. Ox. Bedford Scho. Exhib. 4th cl. Lit. Hum. and B.A. 1852; Deac. 1854 and Pr. 1855 by Bp of Ox. V. of Tisbury, Dio. Salis. 1858. (Patron, Lord Arundell; Tithe—App. 947*l* 12*s* and 12 acres of Glebe, Imp. 50*l* 5*s*, V. 440*l*; Glebe, 3 acres; V.'s Inc. 450*l* and Ho; Pop. 2303.) Formerly C. of Barford St. Michael and Milcombe, Oxon, 1854–57, Alverstoke, Hants, 1857–58. [6]

HUTCHINSON, George Henry Hely, *Westport Vicarage, Malmesbury, Wilts.*—Caius Coll. Cam. B.A. 1821, M.A. 1825; Deac. and Pr. 1829. V. of Westport St. Mary with Brokenborough C. and Charlton C. Dio. G. and B. 1837. (Patron, Ld Chan; Tithe, comm. 525*l*; Glebe, 39 acres; V.'s Inc. 580*l* and Ho; Pop. Westport 1615, Brokenborough 275, Charlton 621.) [7]

HUTCHINSON, H., *Mansfield, Notts.*—C. of St. John's, Mansfield. [8]

HUTCHINSON, Henry John, *Brompton, Scarborough.*—Literate; Deac. and Pr. 1847 by Bp of Rip. V. of Brompton with Snainton P. C. Dio. York, 1861. (Patron, Sir G. Cayley, Bart; V.'s Inc. 103*l*; Pop. 1484.) Formerly C. of Hurst, Ashton-under-Lyne [9]

HUTCHINSON, James, *Great Berkhampstead Rectory, Herts.*—St. John's Coll. Ox. B.A. 1825, M.A. 1829; Deac. 1828, Pr. 1829. R. of Great Berkhampstead, Dio. Roch. 1851. (Patron, Duke of Cornwall; Tithe, 434*l* 16*s* 8*d*; Glebe, 2 acres; R.'s Inc. 437*l* and Ho; Pop. 3585.) Rural Dean; Chap. to the Duke of Cambridge. Formerly British Chap. at Rome 1836–49. [10]

HUTCHINSON, John Robinson, *Hurrock Wood, Penrith.*—Magd. Coll. Cam. Scho. of, 1829, Wrang. and B.A. 1834, St. John's Coll. Cam. Fell. of 1834, M.A. 1837, B.D. 1845; Deac. 1836 by Bp of Roch. Pr. 1839 by Bp of Ely. Sen. Fell. of St. John's Coll. Cam. 1848. [11]

HUTCHINSON, Stephen, *Soulby, Brough, Westmoreland.*—Literate; Deac. 1824 and Pr. 1825 by Bp of Carl. P. C. of Soulby, Dio. Carl. 1834. (Patron, Sir G. Musgrave; Tithe—App. 17*l* 13*s* 4*d*, Imp. 54*l* 3*s* 4*d*; Glebe, 150 acres; P. C.'s Inc. 96*l*; Pop. 453.) Chap. to the East Ward Union, Kirkby Stephen, 1849. [12]

HUTCHINSON, Thomas, *Ditchling Vicarage, Hurstpierpoint, Sussex.*—Clare Coll. Cam. B.A. 1831, M.A. 1835; Deac. 1831 and Pr. 1832 by Bp of Lin. V. of Ditchling, Dio. Chich. 1855. (Patron, Richard Hunter, Esq; Tithe—App. 370*l* 5*s*, Imp. 102*l*, V. 210*l* 5*s*; Glebe, 48 acres; V.'s Inc. 305*l* and Ho; Pop. 1068.) Editor, *Holy Thoughts and Musings in a Foreign Land*, 2nd ed. Masters, 1866. [13]

HUTCHINSON, Thomas, *Grantsfield, Leominster, Herefordshire.*—St. John's Coll. Cam. B.A. 1838, M.A. 1841; Deac. 1839 and Pr. 1840 by Bp of Herf. P. C. of Kimbolton with Middleton-on-the-Hill, Dio. Herf. 1841. (Patron, Bp of Herf; P. C.'s Inc. 150*l*; Pop. 989.) Formerly C. of Hentland 1839–41 [14]

HUTCHINSON, Thomas Neville, *Hillmorton-road, Rugby.*—St. John's Coll. Cam. B.A. 1854, M.A. 1859; Deac. 1854 and Pr. 1855 by Bp of Ches. Natural Philosophy Mast. in Rugby Sch. 1865. Formerly Vice-Prin. of the Dioc. Training Coll. Chester, 1854; 2nd Mast. of King Edward Sch. Birmingham, 1860. [15]

HUTCHINSON, William, *Howden, Yorks.*—P. C. of Laxton, near Howden, Dio. York, 1850. (Patron, V. of Howden; Tithe—Imp. 229*l* 12*s*; P. C.'s Inc. 50*l*; Pop. 790.) V. of Howden, Dio. York, 1862. (Patron, Ld Chan; V.'s Inc. 178*l* and Ho; Pop. 3953.) Mast. of the Gr. Sch. Howden. [16]

HUTCHINSON, William, *Checkley Rectory, Cheadle, Staffs.*—Brasen. Coll. Ox. B.A. 1822, M.A. 1824; Deac. 1824 and Pr. 1825 by Bp of Salis. R. of Checkley with Hollington C. Dio. Lich. 1839. (Patron, Edward Philips, Esq; Tithe, 575*l* 5*s*; Glebe, 146 acres; R.'s Inc. 924*l* 10*s* and Ho; Pop. 1257.) [17]

HUTCHINSON, William, *Newton Heath Rectory, Manchester.*—Emman. Coll. Cam. B.D. 1835; Deac. 1824 and Pr. 1826 by Bp of Lin. R. of Newton Heath, Dio. Man. 1824. (Patrons, D. and C. of Man; Tithe—App. 159*l* 3*s* 8*d*; Glebe, 30 acres; R.'s Inc. 295*l* and Ho; Pop. 11,241.) [18]

HUTCHINSON, William Henry, *Leckhampton, Cheltenham.*—Pemb. Coll. Cam. B.A. 1859, M.A. 1864; Deac. 1860 and Pr. 1862 by Bp of G. and B. P. C. of St. Philip and St. James's, Leckhampton, Dio. G. and B. 1864. (Patrons, Trustees.) Formerly C. of Leckhampton 1860–63, St. Mark's, Gloucester, 1863–64. [19]

HUTCHINSON, William Hilton, *Welney Rectory, Wisbech.*—St. Bees 1845; Deac. 1846 and Pr. 1847 by Bp of Ches. R. of Welney, Dio. Nor. 1862. (Patron, C. Watson Townley, Esq; Tithe, 1258*l*; Glebe, 13 acres; R.'s Inc. 1280*l* and Ho; Pop. 1200.) Formerly C. of Weverham, Cheshire, 1846–48; R. of Welney, Lincolnshire, 1848–62. [20]

HUTCHINSON, William P. H., *Blurton Parsonage, Stoke upon-Trent.*—All Souls' Coll. Ox. B.A. 1833, M.A. 1848; Deac 1833 and Pr. 1834 by Bp of Lich. P. C. of Blurton, Dio. Lich. 1865. (Patron, Duke of Sutherland; P. C.'s Inc. 400*l* and Ho; Pop. 2730.) Formerly C. of Dunchurch 1833–36, Trinity, Rotherhithe, 1836–50; P. C. of Hanford, Staffs, 1850–65. [21]

HUTCHISON, Robert Pender, *Christ Church, Old Kent-road, London, S.E.*—Corpus Coll. Cam. B.A. 1843; Deac. 1843, Pr. 1844. P. C. of Ch. Ch. Camberwell, Dio. Win. 1850. (Patrons, Trustees of Hyndman's Bounty; P. C.'s Inc. about 370*l*; Pop. 8176.) Author, *Sermons to Children*; *Life and Death to the Christian* (a Sermon); *The Bible the Defender of the Church against Sectarian Error as to the Kingdom of Heaven, Baptismal Regeneration and Sponsorship.* [22]

HUTT, Charles John, 6, *Carlton-terrace, Cranegrove, Holloway-road, London, N.*—Caius Coll. Cam. B.A. 1850. 2nd Mast. of Islington Prop. Gr. Sch; Reader at St. James's, Holloway, Lond. [23]

HUTT, Richard Goode, 9, *Bloomfield-terrace, Gateshead.*—Deac. 1857 and Pr. 1858 by Bp of Grahamstown. C. of St. Cuthbert's, Bensham, Gateshead, 1866. Formerly S.P.G. Miss. at the Bolotwa, South Africa, 1857–62; Prin. of the Kafir Training Institution,

Grahamstown, 1862–63; Acting Colonial Chap. St. George's Cathl. Grahamstown, 1863–66. [1]

HUTT, William Wayman, *Hockwold Rectory, Brandon, Norfolk.*—Caius Coll. Cam. B.A. 1845, M.A. 1848; Deac. 1846, Pr. 1847. Sen. Fell. of Caius Coll. Cam; R. of Hockwold with Wilton V. Dio. Nor. 1860. (Patron, Caius Coll. Cam; Tithe—App. 180*l* 12*s*; R. 635*l*, V. 91*l*; Glebe, 92 acres; R.'s Inc. 1060*l* and Ho; Pop. 803.) [2]

HUTTON, Augustus Henry Dell, *Bridge-road, Stockton-on-Tees.*—Trin. Coll. Cam. 2nd cl. Cl. Trip. and B.A. 1856, M.A. 1859; Deac. 1857 and Pr. 1859 by Bp of Lin. C. of Trinity, Stockton-on-Tees, 1865. Formerly C. of Market Rasen, Linc. 1857–59, Trinity, Stockton-on-Tees, 1860–61, Benacre, Suffolk, 1861–65. [3]

HUTTON, Edmund Forster Drummond, *Aylmerton Rectory, Norwich.*—Corpus Coll. Ox. S.C.L. 1856, B.A. 1856, M.A. 1860; Deac. 1856, Pr. 1857. R. of Aylmerton with Runton R. Cromer, Dio. Nor. 1861. (Patron, John Ketton, Esq; Tithe, 420*l*; Glebe, 62 acres; R.'s Inc. 490*l* and Ho; Pop. Aylmerton 250, Runton 510.) Formerly C. of Ch. Ch. Worthing 1856–58, Runton 1859–60; R. of Trimingham 1860–61. [4]

HUTTON, Francis P. B. N., *Gold's Hill, West Bromwich.*—St. John's Coll. Cam. B.A. 1849, M.A. 1852; Deac. 1849 and Pr. 1850 by Bp of Lich. Chap. to Messrs. Bagnall's Iron Works. Formerly C. of St. James's, Wednesbury, 1849–52, Trinity, Ely, 1852–53. [5]

HUTTON, George Thomas, *Gate Burton Rectory, Gainsborough, Lincolnshire.*—Trin. Coll. Cam. B.A. 1832; Deac. 1838 by Abp of York, Pr. 1839 by Bp of Lin. R. of Gate Burton, Dio. Lin. 1842. (Patron, W. Hutton, Esq; Tithe, 120*l*; Glebe, 18 acres; R.'s Inc. 160*l* and Ho; Pop. 115.) P. C. of Knaith, Lincolnshire, Dio. Lin. 1842. (Patron, W. Hutton, Esq; Tithe —Imp. 260*l*; P. C.'s Inc. 40*l*; Pop. 105.) Formerly C. of Trowell, Notts, 1838, Hawton, Notts, 1840. [6]

HUTTON, Henry, *Filleigh Rectory, South Molton, Devon.*—Ball. Coll. Ox. B.A. 1820, M.A. 1823; Deac. 1820 and Pr. 1821 by Bp of Lon. R. of Filleigh with East Buckland, Dio. Ex. 1833. (Patron, Earl Fortescue; Filleigh, Tithe, 97*l*; Glebe, 88½ acres; East Buckland, Tithe, 140*l*; Glebe, 28 acres; R.'s Inc. 363*l* and Ho; Pop. Filleigh 311, East Buckland 151.) [7]

HUTTON, Henry Frederick, *Spridlington Rectory, Market Rasen, Lincolnshire.*—Trin. Coll. Ox. B.A. 1832, M.A. 1855; Deac. 1834 and Pr. 1835 by Bp of Lin. R. of Spridlington, Dio. Lin. 1841. (Patron, the present R; Glebe, 430 acres; R.'s Inc. 488*l* and Ho; Pop. 454.) Rural Dean. [8]

HUTTON, Henry Wollaston, *Vicar's Court, Lincoln.*—Trin. Coll. Ox. B.A. 1857, M.A. 1860; Deac. 1859 and Pr. 1860 by Bp of Lin. R. of St. Mary Magdalene's, Lincoln, Dio. Lin. 1862. (Patrons, D. and C. of Lincoln; R.'s Inc. 120*l*; Pop. 625.) Min. Can. of Lin. Cathl. Formerly C. of Southwell, Notts, 1860–62. [9]

HUTTON, Robert Rosseter, *Barnet, N.*—Trin. Coll. Ox. 3rd cl. Lit. Hum. and B.A. 1848, M.A. 1850; Deac. 1849 and Pr. 1850 by Bp of Lon. R. of Chipping Barnet, Dio. Roch 1866. (Patron, the Crown; Tithe, 390*l*; Glebe, 89 acres; R.'s Inc. 550*l*; Pop. 2900.) Formerly C. of St. Barnabas', Kensington, 1849–50, Chipping Barnet 1851–55; Chap. of Colney Hatch Asylum 1855–60; P. C. of Ch. Ch. Warminster, Wilts, 1860–66. Author, *England's Strength in Time of War* (a Sermon), 1854; *I commend you to God, and to the Word of His Grace* (a Sermon), 1855. [10]

HUTTON, Rufus, *St. Nicholas' Vicarage, near Teignmouth, Devon.*—Ex. Coll. Ox. B.A. 1829; Deac. 1831 by Bp of B. and W. Pr. 1832 by Bp of Ex. V. of St. Nicholas', Dio. Ex. 1834. (Patron, Lord Clifford; Tithe, 41*l*; Glebe, 22 acres; V.'s Inc. 130*l* and Ho; Pop. 1148.) [11]

HUTTON, Thomas, *Stilton Rectory, Hunts.*—Dub. A.B. 1843, A.M. 1849; Deac. 1844 and Pr. 1845 by Bp of Lich. R. of Stilton, Dio. Ely, 1859. (Patron, Bp of Pet; Glebe, 265 acres; R.'s Inc. 500*l* and Ho; Pop. 724.) Formerly Chap. to the Northampton County Gaol 1850–59. [12]

HUTTON, Thomas Palmer, *Yockleton Rectory, Shrewsbury.*—Magd. Coll. Ox. 3rd cl. Lit. Hum. M.A. 1832; Deac. 1828 and Pr. 1829 by Abp of Cant. R. of Yockleton, Salop, Dio. Herf. 1866. (Patron, W. E. S. Owen, Esq; R.'s Inc. 550*l* and Ho; Pop. 492.) Formerly V. of Sompting, Sussex, 1855–62, Hemel Hempsted 1862–66. [13]

HUTTON, Vernon Wollaston, 92, *Upper Kennington-lane, London, S.*—Trin. Coll. Cam. 2nd cl. Theol. Hons. B.A. 1864; Deac. 1855 and Pr. 1866 by Bp of Win. C. of St. Mary's the Less, Lambeth, 1865. [14]

HUTTON, William, *Higher Ardwick, Manchester.*—Dub. A.B. 1850, Licen. Theol. of Univ. Dur. 1850; Deac. 1850 and Pr. 1852 by Bp of Lich. R. of St. Philip's, Bradford-road, Manchester, Dio Man. 1857. (Patrons, Trustees; R.'s Inc. 300*l*; Pop. 10,540.) Formerly C. of West Bromwich, and Tamworth, Staffs. [15]

HUTTON, William, *Beetham, Milnthorpe, Westmoreland.*—Queen's Coll. Ox. B.A. 1829, M.A. 1832; Deac. and Pr. 1830. V. of Beetham, Dio. Carl. 1844. (Patron, Chan. of the Duchy of Lancaster; Tithe, 83*l*; V.'s Inc. 160*l* and Ho; Pop. 1021.) [16]

HUTTON, Wyndham Madden, *St. Paul's Parsonage, Tipton, Staffs.*—St. Edm. Hall, Ox. and St. Bees; Deac. 1856 and Pr. 1857 by Bp of Man; P. C. of St. Paul's, Tipton, Dio. Lich. 1861. (Patron, P. C. of Tipton; P. C.'s Inc. 310*l* and Ho; Pop. 10,028.) Formerly C. of Kirkham and Plungar; V. of Plungar 1860–61. Author, *Poems*, Pickering, 1851. [17]

HUXLEY, Thomas Scott, *Watling-street, Canterbury.*—Ex. Coll. Ox. B.A. 1845; Deac. 1845 by Abp of Cant. Pr. 1846 by Bp of Lon. R. of St. Andrew with St. Mary Bredman, Canterbury, Dio. Cant. 1865. (Patrons, Abp and D. and C. of Cant; Tithe, 75*l*; R.'s Inc. 200*l* and Ho; Pop. St. Andrew 523, St. Mary Bredman 360.) C. of All Saints', Canterbury. [18]

HUXTABLE, Anthony, *Sutton Waldron, Blandford, Dorset.*—Trin. Coll. Cam. B.A. 1833, M.A. 1838; Deac. 1833 by Bp of B. and W. Pr. 1834 by Bp of Bristol. R. of Sutton Waldron, Dio. Salis. 1834. (Patron, H. C. Sturt, Esq; Tithe, 162*l*; Glebe, 32 acres; R.'s Inc. 204*l*; Pop. 248.) Preb. of Salis. and Rural Dean of Shaftesbury. Proctor in Convocation for two years for Dio. of Salis; Archd. of Dorset 1862, but resigned on account of ill-health same year. [19]

HUXTABLE, Edgar, *Weston-Zoyland, Bridgwater.*—St. John's Coll. Cam. Sen. Opt. 1st cl. Cl. Trip. 1844, B.A. 1845, M.A. 1848; Deac. 1846, Pr. 1847. Preb. of Wells 1853. V. of Weston-Zoyland, Dio. B. and W. 1861. (Patron, Bp of B. and W; Tithe, 200*l*; V.'s Inc. 350*l* and Ho; Pop. 876.) Formerly Vice-Prin. of Wells Theol. Coll. 1848; Sub-Dean of Wells 1849. Author, *The Ministry of St. John the Baptist, and the Baptism and Temptation of the Lord Jesus Christ*, 1848, 4*s* 6*d*; *What Means the Use of Sponsors in the Baptism of Infants?* (a Sermon preached in Wells Cathl.) 1851, 1*s*; *Sermons, chiefly Expository* (preached in Wells Cathl.) 1854, 4*s* 6*d*. [20]

HUXTABLE, Henry Constantine, *St. Mary's Parsonage, Port Louis, Mauritius.*—King's Coll. Lond. Worsley Scho. Theol. Assoc. 1849; M.A. by Abp of Cant. 1866; Deac. 1849 by Bp of Lon. Pr. 1851 by Bp of Madras. Dioc. Sec. of S.P.G. in Dio. of Mauritius, and Incumb. of St. Mary's Port Louis, 1867. Formerly Mis. of S.P.G. at Christianagram in Tinnevelly, S. India, 1850; Prin. of the Missionary Institution of Sawyerpooram, Madras, 1852; C. in sole charge of Hendford, near Yeovil, 1858–60, R. of Bettiscombe, Somerset, 1859–67. [21]

HUYSHE, Francis John, *Chippenham.*—Brasen. Coll. Ox. 2nd cl. Lit. Hum. B.A. 1864; Deac. 1866 by Bp of G. and B. C. of Chippenham 1866. [22]

HUYSHE, John, *Clyst-Hydon Rectory, Cullompton, Devon.*—Brasen. Coll. Ox. 1st cl. Math. et Phy. and B.A. 1822, M.A. 1824; Deac. 1828 and Pr. 1829 by Bp of B. and W. R. of Clyst-Hydon, Dio. Ex. 1831. (Patroness, Mrs. Huyshe; Tithe, 370*l*; Glebe, 88 acres;

R.'s Inc. 520*l* and Ho; Pop. 329.) Formerly C. of Rockbeare 1828–31. Author, *A Treatise on Logic*, Oxford, 1822; *A Sermon preached in Chapel Royal, H.M. Dockyard, Devonport, on laying the Memorial Stone of the Devonport, Stonehouse, and Cornwall Hospital*, Plymouth, 1862. [1]

HYATT, John Carter, *Queensbury, near Halifax.*—Magd. Hall, Ox. B.A. 1852; Deac. 1854 and Pr. 1855 by Bp of Nor. P. C. of Queensbury, Dio. Rip. 1859. (Patrons, Crown and Bp of Rip. alt; P. C.'s Inc. 300*l* and Ho; Pop. 5850.) Formerly C. of Fincham, Norfolk, 1854–56, St. James's, Halifax, 1856–58. [2]

HYDE, Charles Frederick, *The Parsonage, Dilton Marsh, Westbury, Wilts.*—Corpus Coll. Cam. B.A. 1854, M.A. 1861; Deac. 1854 and Pr. 1855 by Bp of Salis. P. C. of Dilton Marsh, Dio. Salis. 1862. (Patron, Bp of Salis; Glebe, 7 acres; P. C.'s Inc. 300*l* and Ho; Pop. 1561.) [3]

HYDE, Charles Richard, *Liverpool.*—St. John's Coll. Cam. LL.B. 1853; Deac. 1852 and Pr. 1853 by Bp of Carl. P. C. of St. Matthew's, Liverpool, Dio. Ches. 1867. (Patron, R. of Liverpool; P. C.'s Inc. 300*l*; Pop. 18,000.) Surrogate. Formerly C. of Wetheral, Carlisle, Calne, Wilts, North Meols, Lancashire, and St. Peter's Liverpool. [4]

HYDE, Henry Woodd Cook, 14, *Queen's-row, Grove-lane, Camberwell, London, S.*—Emman. Coll. Cam. LL.B. 1816; Deac. 1817, Pr. 1819. Chap. to the Camberwell Union; Wednesday Even. Lect. of St. Antholin's, Watling-street, City of Lond. 1836. [5]

HYDE, William, *Donyatt Rectory, Ilminster, Somerset.*—Emman. Coll. Cam. B.A. 1822, M.A. 1825; Deac. 1823, Pr. 1824. R. of Donyatt, Dio. B. and W. 1847. (Patron, R. T. Combe, Esq; Tithe, 131*l*; Glebe, 31½ acres; R.'s Inc. 206*l* and Ho; Pop. 494.) [6]

HYDE, William Henry,—King's Coll. Lond. B.A. 1854; Deac. and Pr. 1855 by Bp of Pet. C. of West Hackney, Middlesex. Formerly C. of St. Margaret's, Leicester, St. James's, Wednesbury, and St. Mary's, Haggerston, Lond. [7]

HYMAN, Orlando Haydon Bridgeman, *Wadham College, Oxford.*—Wad. Coll. Ox. 1st cl. Lit. Hum. and B.A. 1834, M.A. 1840. Fell. of Wad. Coll. Ox. [8]

HYMERS, John, *Brandsburton Rectory, Beverley, Yorks.*—St. John's Coll. Cam. 2nd Wrang. and B.A. 1826, M.A. 1829, B.D. 1836, D.D. 1841; Deac. 1833 by Bp of Lin. Pr. 1834 by Bp of Carl. R. of Brandsburton, Dio. York, 1852. (Patron, St. John's Coll. Cam; Tithe, 1083*l* 11*s* 6*d*; Glebe, 144 acres; R.'s Inc. 1200*l* and Ho; Pop. 811.) Fell. of the Royal Society, and of the Royal Geological Society. Formerly Lady Margaret Preacher in the Univ. and Fell. and Tut. of St. John's Coll. Cam. Author, *The Elements of the Theory of Astronomy*, 2nd ed. Cam. 1840, 14*s*; *Treatise on the Theory of Algebraical Equations*, 2nd ed. 1848, 9*s* 6*d*; *Treatise on Analytical Geometry of Three Dimensions*, 3rd ed. 1848, 10*s* 6*d*; *Treatise on Differential Equations, and the Calculus of Finite Differences*, 1839, 10*s*; *Treatise on Trigonometry, Plane and Spherical*, 3rd ed. 1841, 8*s* 6*d*; *Treatise on the Integral Calculus*, 3rd ed. 1844, 10*s* 6*d*; *Treatise on Conic Sections*, 3rd ed. 1845, 7*s* 6*d*; *Bishop Fisher's Funeral Sermons on Lady Margaret and her Son Henry VII. with Notes and an Appendix*, Cam. 1840. [9]

HYNE, Charles Wright Noble, *Bibury, Fairford, Glouc.*—Clare Coll. Cam. B.A. 1853, M.A. 1856; Deac. 1855 and Pr. 1856 by Bp of Ely. C. of Bibury with Winson 1863. Formerly C. of Barton, Cambs; C. and Even. Lect. of St. Nicholas', Newcastle-on-Tyne; C. of Lower Beeding, Sussex. [10]

HYSON, John Bezaleel, *Crewkerne, Somerset.*—Church Miss. Coll; Deac. 1860 and Pr. 1861 by Bp of Lich. C. of Crewkerne 1862; Chap. of Dorset County Lunatic Asylum. Formerly C. of St. Mark's, Wolverhampton. [11]

IAGO, William, *Edgehill Fore-street, Bodmin, Cornwall.*—St. John's Coll. Cam. B.A. 1859; Deac. 1859 and Pr. 1861 by Bp of B. and W. Chap. of the Cornwall County Lunatic Asylum at Bodmin. (Patrons, Committee of Visiting Magistrates; Chap.'s Inc. 200*l*; Pop. 450.) Formerly C. of Bridgwater 1859, Surbiton 1861. [12]

IAGOE, Joshua R., *Montrose.*—Incumb. of English Episcopal Chapel, Montrose. [13]

IBBETSON, Joseph, *Ayton, Northallerton, Yorks.*—St. John's Coll. Cam. B.A. 1823, M.A. 1843; Deac. 1824 by Bp of Dur. Pr. 1825 by Abp of York. P. C. of Nunthorpe in Cleveland, Dio. York, 1825. (Patrons, Isaac Wilson and W. R. I. Hopkins, Esqrs; Glebe, 18 acres; P. C.'s Inc. 50*l*; Pop. 160.) P. C. of Newton in Cleveland, Dio. York, 1825. (Patron, the Trustee of the late T. K. Staveley, Esq; Glebe, 40 acres; P. C.'s Inc. 48*l*; Pop. 122.) P. C. of Ayton in Cleveland, Dio. York, 1827. (Patron, G. Marwood; Tithe—Imp. 610*l*; Glebe, 28 acres; P. C.'s Inc. 90*l* and Ho; Pop. 1528.) Formerly C. of Darlington 1824–25. [14]

IBBOTSON, Anthony, *Leeds.*—Deac. and Pr. 1823 by Abp of York. Formerly P. C. of Rawden, Yorks, 1823–58. [15]

IBOTSON, William Haywood, *Edwinstowe Vicarage, Ollerton, Notts.*—Magd. Coll. Cam. B.A. 1837, M.A. 1840. V. of Edwinstowe with Carburton C. and Ollerton C. Dio. Lin. 1854. (Patrons, D. and C. of Lin; Tithe—App. 1570*l*, V. 869*l* 1*s*; Glebe, 16 acres; V.'s Inc. 890*l* and Ho; Pop. Edwinstowe 1444, Carburton 177, Ollerton 932.) [16]

ICK, William Richard, *Peasmarsh Vicarage, Staplehurst, Kent.*—Sid. Coll. Cam. 24th Wrang. and B.A. 1841, M.A. 1845, B.D. 1852; Deac. 1843 and Pr. 1844 by Bp of Ely. V. of Peasmarsh, Dio. Chich. 1858. (Patron, Sid. Coll. Cam; Tithe, 432*l* 9*s*; Glebe, 4 acres; V.'s Inc. 440*l* and Ho; Pop. 906.) Formerly Fell. and Dean of Sid. Coll. Cam; C. of Middleton-on-the Wolds, Brandesburton, and Sigglesthorne, all in Yorks, and St. George's, Douglas, Isle of Man. [17]

IGGLESDEN, Marten, *St. Lawrence Rectory, Newland, near Maldon, Essex.*—King's Coll. Lond. Theol. Assoc; Deac. 1861 and Pr. 1862 by Bp of Roch. C. in sole charge of St. Lawrence 1863. Formerly C. of Bradwell-juxta-Mare, Maldon. [18]

IGGULDEN, William Henry, *East Hyde Parsonage, Luton, Beds.*—Emman. Coll. Cam. Jun. Opt. B.A. 1850, M.A. 1854; Deac. 1851 and Pr. 1852 by Bp of Lin. V. of East Hyde, Dio. Ely, 1859. (Patron, L. Ames, Esq; V.'s Inc. 188*l* and Ho; Pop. 420.) Formerly C. of Louth 1851–53, Luton, East Hyde, 1853–59. [19]

ILBERT, Peregrine Arthur, *Thurlestone Rectory, Kingsbridge, Devon.*—Trin. Coll. Ox. B.A. 1832, M.A. 1835; Deac. 1833, Pr. 1834. R. of Thurlestone, Dio. Ex. 1839. (Patroness, Mrs. Ann Ilbert; Tithe, 329*l* 10*s*; Glebe, 36 acres; R.'s Inc. 408*l* and Ho; Pop. 437.) [20]

ILDERTON, Thomas, *Felton Vicarage, Alnwick, Northumberland.*—St. Peter's Coll. Cam. B.A. 1834, M.A. 1837; Deac. 1834, Pr. 1835. V. of Felton with Long Framlington P. C. Dio. Dur. 1850. (Patron, Ld Chan; Tithe—Imp. 1026*l* 6*s* 3*d*, V. 160*l* 13*s*; Glebe, 100 acres; V.'s Inc. 275*l* and Ho; Pop. Felton 1591, Long Framlington 667.) [21]

ILES, John Hodgson, *Wolverhampton.*—Lin. Coll. Ox. 2nd cl. Lit. Hum. and B.A. 1849, M.A. 1852; Deac. 1852 by Bp of G. and B. Pr. 1853 by Bp of Wor. R. of St. Peter's, Wolverhampton, Dio. Lich. 1860. (Patron, Bp of Lich; R.'s Inc. 750*l* and Ho; Pop. 11,000.) Surrogate. Formerly Fell. of Lin. Coll. Ox. 1855–61; Asst. Mast. of King Edw. VI. Gr. Sch. Bromsgrove, 1852–58; Sen. C. of St. Peter's, Wolverhampton, 1858–60. [22]

ILIFF, Frederick, *Chessington Parsonage, Kingston-on-Thames.*—Trin. Coll. Cam. B.A. 1850, M.A. 1853; Deac. 1857 by Bp of Derry, Pr. 1858 by Abp of York. C. of Malden with Chessington, 1866. Formerly C. of Trinity, North Shields, 1860, Hermitage Mission, Wapping, 1864. Author, *Songs of the Sea Ports*, 1861; *Songs of* *the Heavenly Home*, 1861; *One Hundred Evening Hymns*, 1862. [1]

ILIFF, Frederick, *Gateforth, Selby, Yorks.*—Trin. Coll. Cam. B.A. 1823, M.A. 1826, D.D. 1838; Deac. 1823, Pr. 1824. P. C. of Gateforth, Dio. York, 1862. (Patron, H. Osbaldiston, Esq; P. C.'s Inc. 105*l*; Pop. 174.) Editor of the *Biblia Ecclesiæ Polyglotta*, 4to. Bagster and Son; *Hexapla Psalter*, ib. [2]

ILIFF, George, *The Hall School, Bishopwearmouth.*—Deac. 1855 by Bp of Man. Pr. 1857 by Bp of Dur. Head Mast. of Hall Sch. Sunderland. Author, *An English Education, what it means and how it may be carried out*, 3rd ed. 1861, London, Bell and Daldy, 6*d*. [3]

ILLINGWORTH, Edward Arthur, 3, *Mecklenburgh-street, Mecklenburgh-square, London, W.C.*—Trin. Coll. Cam. B.A. 1830, M.A. 1833; Deac. 1831 and Pr. 1832 by Bp of Lon. Chap. to the Middlesex Ho. of Correction 1839. [4]

IMAGE, John, *Brighton.*—Chap. of the Union, Brighton. [5]

IMAGE, W. T., *Wickham Market, Suffolk.*—V. of Wickham Market, Dio. Nor. 1866. (Patron, Ld Chan; V.'s Inc. 208*l* and Ho; Pop. 1571.) [6]

IMRIE, John, *Rectory, Saxmundham, Suffolk.*—Ch. Coll. Cam. Jun. Opt. B.A. 1860, M.A. 1863; Deac. 1861 and Pr. 1862 by Bp of Man. R. of Saxmundham, Dio. Nor. (Patron, W. Long, Esq; Tithe, 300*l*; Glebe, 39a. 1r. 5p; R.'s Inc. 371*l* and Ho; Pop. 1200.) Formerly C. of St. Anne's, Lancaster, 1861, Southwold 1863, Saxmundham 1864. [7]

INCE, Edward Cumming, *Meltham Mills Parsonage, Huddersfield.*—Jesus Coll. Cam. B.A. 1847; Deac. 1848, Pr. 1849. P. C. of Meltham Mills, Dio. Rip. 1853. (Patrons, W. L. and Charles Brook, Esqrs; Tithe—Imp. 5*l*, App. 41*l*; P. C.'s Inc. 150*l* and Ho; Pop. 1196.) Author, *An Address from a Minister to his Flock on the Day of Humiliation*, Huddersfield, 1854; *Sunday Feasts*, 1854. [8]

INCE, William, *Exeter College, Oxford.*—Lin. Coll. Ox. 1842, 1st cl. Lit. Hum. and B.A. 1846. M.A. 1849; Deac. 1849, Pr. 1852. Sub-Rector and Tut. of Ex. Coll. Ox. [9]

INCHBALD, William, *The College, Cheltenham.*—St. Cath. Coll. Cam. B.A. 1842; Deac. 1848, Pr. 1850. Asst. Mast. in Cheltenham Coll. Formerly 2nd Mast. of Qu. Elizabeth's Gr. Sch. Crediton, Devon, 1853–58. [10]

INCLEDON, Charles Porter, *Howard Hill, Sheffield.*—Wor. Coll. Ox. B.A. 1847; Deac. 1849, Pr. 1850. Formerly Asst. Min. of St. Mary's, Greenwich. [11]

INCLEDON, George William Rooke.—Corpus Coll. Cam. B.A. 1854; Deac. 1855, Pr. 1856. Chap. of H.M.S. "Aurora." Formerly C. of Mylor and Mabe, Cornwall. [12]

INGE, Francis George, *Aberford, South Milford, Yorkshire.*—Ch. Ch. Ox. 3rd Lit. Hum. Slade Exhib. B.A. 1864, M.A. 1866; Deac. 1865 and Pr. 1866 by Abp of York. C. of Aberford. [13]

INGE, George, *Thorpe Constantine, Tamworth.*—Ch. Ch. Ox. B.A. 1821, All Souls Coll. Ox. M.A. 1826; Deac. 1823, Pr. 1824. R. of Thorpe Constantine, Dio. Lich. 1824. (Patron, W. Inge, Esq; R.'s Inc. 90*l* and Ho; Pop. 54.) Fell. of All Souls Coll. Ox. [14]

INGE, John Edward Alexander, *Athelington Rectory, Wickham Market, Suffolk.*—Trin. Hall, Cam. B.A. 1854; Deac. and Pr. 1854 by Bp of Wor. R. of Athelington, Dio. Nor. 1863. (Patron, Ld Chan; Glebe, 16a. 2r. 6p; R.'s Inc. 155*l* and Ho; Pop. 115.) [15]

INGE, John Robert, *Seamer Vicarage, Scarborough.*—Trin. Coll. Cam. B.A. 1827, M.A. 1830; Deac. 1828, Pr. 1829. V. of Seamer with Cayton C. Dio. York, 1847. (Patron, Lord Londesborough; Seamer, Tithe—App. 175*l*, Imp. 603*l* 18*s*, V. 32*l* 18*s*; Cayton, Tithe—Imp. 488*l* 9*s* 6*d*, V. 23*l* 8*s*; V.'s Inc. 426*l* and Ho; Pop. Seamer 1305, Cayton 534.) Dom. Chap. to Lord Londesborough. [16]

INGE, William, *Crayke, near York.*—Wor. Coll. Ox. 1st cl. Lit. Hum. 1853, M.A. 1853. C. of Crayke 1857. [17]

INGHAM, Thomas Barker, *Rainhill, Prescot, Lancashire.*—Queens' Coll. Cam. B A. 1828, M.A. 1831. P. C. of Rainhill, Dio. Ches. 1842. (Patron, Rev. J. Brierley; Tithe—App. 108*l*, Imp. 165*l*; P. C.'s Inc. 180*l*; Pop. 2608.) [18]

INGLE, John, *Exeter.*—Trin. Coll. Cam. 1844, B.A. 1846, M.A. 1852; Deac. 1846 by Bp of Lin. Pr. 1848 by Bp of Ex. C. of St. Olave's, Exeter. Formerly Head Mast. of the Cathl. Sch. Ely, 1852. Author, *Church and Meeting House*, 1*s*; *Puseyites no Friends of Popery*, 1*s*; *Queen's Letters and State Services*, 1*s*; *Ritual Beauty no Mark of Romanism*, 1*s*; *The Synod no Treason*; *The Two Synods*; *What is the Use of our Cathedrals?* (Letter to Lord Stanley on True Principles of Cathedral Reform), 1855, 1*s*; *Tract on Good Friday*; etc. [19]

INGLEBY, Charles, *Woodbank, Cheadle, Staffs.*—Ex. Coll. Ox. M.A. 1844; Deac. 1846, Pr. 1847. Formerly C of Cauldon, Staffs. [20]

INGLES, D., *Cookham Dean, near Maidenhead.*—C. of Cookham Dean. Formerly C. of Stoke-upon-Trent. [21]

INGRAM, Arthur Henry Winnington, *Harvington Rectory, near Evesham, Worcestershire.*—Ch. Ch. Ox. 3rd cl. Lit. Hum. and B.A. 1841, M.A. 1847; Deac. 1841 and Pr. 1842 by Bp of Herf. R. of Harvington, Dio. Wor. 1845. (Patrons, D. and C. of Wor; Land in lieu of Tithe, 218 acres; R.'s Inc. 347*l* and Ho; Pop. 452.) Dioc. Inspector of Schs. 1849; Rural Dean of Pershore 1853; Hon. Can. of Wor. Cathl. 1854. Late Fell. of Ch. Ch. Ox. [22]

INGRAM, Arthur John, 7, *Whitehall, London, S.W.*—Queens' Coll. Cam. B.A. 1864; Deac. 1864 and Pr. 1865 by Bp of Lon. C. of St. Mary-le-Strand, Westminster, 1864; Asst. Sec. of the Addit. Curates' Soc. [23]

INGRAM, Delaval Shafto, *Tunbridge, Kent.*—St. John's Coll. Cam. B.A. 1862, M.A. 1865, 1st cl. Cl. Trip. 1862; Deac. 1865 and Pr. 1866 by Abp of Cant. Asst. Cl. Mast. of Tunbridge Sch. and C. of the Sch. Chapel. [24]

INGRAM, Edward Winnington, *Stanford-on-Teme Rectory, Stourport, Worcestershire.*—Trin. Coll. Cam. B.A. 1837, M.A. 1841; Deac. 1839, Pr. 1840. R. of Stanford-on-Teme, Dio. Herf. 1845. (Patron, Sir T. E. Winnington, Bart; Tithe, 243*l* 10*s*; Glebe, 68¼ acres; R.'s Inc. 323*l* and Ho; Pop. 201.) [25]

INGRAM, Henry Manning, 3, *Little Dean's-yard, Westminster, S.W.*—Trin. Coll. Cam. 38th Wrang. 3rd cl. Cl. Trip. and B.A. 1847, M.A. 1850; Deac. 1850 and Pr. 1851 by Bp of Nor. 2nd Mast. of Westminster Sch. Formerly Chap. of Trin. Coll. Cam. 1852; Asst. C. of St. Michael's, Highgate, 1858. [26]

INGRAM, Hugh, *Steyning, Sussex.*—Ch. Ch. Ox. B.A. 1850, M.A. 1853; Deac. 1853 by Bp of Ox. Pr. 1855 by Bp of G. and B. Stud. of Ch. Ch. Formerly Asst. C. of Bussage, Glouc. 1854–55; P. C. of Offenham, Worc. 1864. [27]

INGRAM, Robert, *Chatburn, Clitheroe, Lancashire.*—Jesus Coll. Cam. B.A. 1830, M.A. 1833; Deac. 1830 and Pr. 1831 by Bp of Lin. P. C. of Chatburn, Dio. Man. 1838. (Patrons, Hulme's Trustees; P. C.'s Inc. 166*l*; Pop. 605.) [28]

INGRAM, Rowland, *Great Ellingham, Attleburgh, Norfolk.*—Trin. Coll. Cam. B.A. 1827, M.A. 1830; Deac. 1827, Pr. 1828. Chap. to the Earl of Carnwath 1840; R. of Great Ellingham with Little Ellingham V. Dio. Nor. 1860. (Patron, Rev. Rowland Ingram; Great Ellingham, Tithe—App. 53*l* 13*s*; Imp. 524*l* 6*s* 10*d*, R. 311*l* 3*s* 2*d*, Little Ellingham, Tithe, 430*l*, R.'s Inc. 750*l* and Ho; Pop. 1099.) [29]

INGRAM, William Clavell, *The Vicarage, Kirk Michael, Isle of Man.*—Jesus Coll. Cam. Jun. Opt. B.A. 1857, M.A. 1864; Deac. 1859 and Pr. 1860 by Bp of Chich. V. of Kirk Michael, Dio. S. and M. 1864. (Patron, the Crown; Glebe, 30 acres; V.'s Inc. 180*l* and Ho; Pop. 1416.) Surrogate; Chap. to Bp of S. and M. 1864. Formerly Math. Tut. Lancing Coll. 1858; Head Mast. of St. Paul's Sch. Cosham, 1860; Chap. to the Forces 1863. [30]

INMAN, Edward, *Bremhill, Chippenham.*—Oriel Coll. Ox. B.A. 1857, M.A. 1861; Deac. 1858 and Pr. 1859 by Bp of Salis. C. of Bremhill. Formerly C. of Pewsey, Wilts, 1858–60, Batheaston 1860–63. [1]

INMAN, Henry, *North Scarle, Newark.*—Deac. 1850, Pr. 1851 by Bp of Man. R. of North Scarle, Lincolnshire, 1859. (Patron, Ld Chan; Tithe, 260*l*; Glebe, 33*a* 1*r* 17*p*; R.'s Inc. 320*l* and Ho; Pop. 600.) Formerly P. C. of Newburgh, Lancashire, 1859. Author, *Meditations on Holy Scripture.* [2]

INMAN, James Williams, *Chudleigh, Devon.*—St. John's Coll. Cam. Bell's Univ. Scho. 1830, 18th Wrang. 3rd in 2nd cl. Cl. Trip. and B.A. 1833, M.A. 1836; Deac. 1835 by Bp of Pet. Pr. 1836 by Bp of Ely. C. of St. Paul's, Knighton, 1863; Mast. of Pynsent's Gr. Sch. Chudleigh. Formerly C. of Broughton, Kettering, 1835; Fell. of St. John's Coll. Cam. 1835–37; Mast. of Grantham Gr. Sch. 1837–58; Dom. Chap. to the Earl of Hardwicke, 1850. Author, *Orcoma, or The Reclaimed,* a Drama, 1852; *Carm. Anglic. Versiones* 1864. Editor, and Reviser of *Inman's Nautical Tables,* Rivingtons, 1*l* 1*s*, 1867. [3]

INMAN, Simon, *Low Wray, Windermere.*—Ch. Coll. Cam. Jun. Opt. B.A. 1862, M.A. 1865; Deac. 1862 and Pr. 1863 by Bp of Carl. P. C. of Low Wray, Dio. Carl. 1865. (Patron, J. Dawson, Esq; Pop. 110.) Formerly C. of Brough, Westmoreland, 1862–65. [4]

INMAN, Thomas, *South Leverton, Notts.*—C. of South Leverton. [5]

INNES, James, *Convict Prison, Dartmoor, Devon.*—Ch. Miss. Coll. Islington; Deac. 1836 and Pr. 1838 by Bp of Lon. Chap. of the Convict Prison, Dartmoor, 1867. Formerly Chap. of the Refuge, Fulham, 1856. [6]

INNES, John Brodie, *Downe, Bromley, Kent.*—Trin. Coll. Ox. B.A. 1839, M.A. 1842; Deac. 1839, Pr. 1840. P. C. of Downe, Dio. Cant. 1846. (Patron, Abp of Cant; P. C.'s Inc. 111*l*; Pop. 496.) [7]

INNES, John Clarke.—Stud. in Arts, Queen's Coll. Belfast, 1839–42, Stud. in Theol. Univ. of Edin. 1842–43, and New Coll. Edin. 1843–44, St. Aidan's Licen. in Theol. 1849, M.A. and Ph. D. Leipsic, 1845; Deac. 1849 and Pr. 1850 by Bp of Win. C. of Trinity, Lambeth. Author, *Lectures on Passion Week*; *The Bright Light in the Clouds*; *The Family in Heaven.* [8]

INNES, Stephen Mountcashell, *Southampton.*—St. Aidan's; Deac. 1855 and Pr. 1857 by Bp of Ches. V. of St. Michael's, Southampton, Dio. Win. 1864. (Patron, Ld Chan; V.'s Inc. 150*l* and Ho; Pop. 1992.) Dom. Chap. to the Earl of Mountcashell. Formerly C. of Billinge, Lancashire; Min. of Zion Chapel, Southampton, 1858-64. [9]

INSKIP, Robert Mills.—Chap. and Naval Instructor of H.M.S. "Britannia." [10]

INSLEY, William P., *Flixborough, Lincolnshire.*—C. of Flixborough. [11]

IRBY, George Powel, *St. James's, Clapton, London, N.E.*—Merton Coll. Ox. B.A. 1860, M.A. 1863; Deac. 1861 and Pr. 1863 by Bp of Pet. C. of St. James's, Clapton, 1866. Formerly C. of Weedon 1861–65, Winwick near Rugby, 1865–66. [12]

IRBY, The Hon. Llewellyn Charles Robert, *Whiston, near Northampton.*—Brasen. Coll. Ox. B.A. 1844, M.A. 1845; Deac. 1846 and Pr. 1848 by Bp of Ox. R. of Whiston, Dio. Pet. 1851. (Patron, Lord Boston; Tithe, 250*l* 10*s*; Glebe, 5 acres; R.'s Inc. 286*l* and Ho; Pop. 69.) [13]

IRBY, Thomas William, *Rushmere Rectory, Lowestoft.*—R. of Rushmere, Dio. Nor. 1842. (Patrons, Lord Boston and F. W. Irby, Esq; R.'s Inc. 220*l* and Ho; Pop. 121.) [14]

IRELAND, George Lewis De Courcy.—Dub. A.B. 1850; Deac. 1852 and Pr. 1853 by Bp of Ches. C. of St. Paul's, Covent Garden, Lond. Formerly C. of St. John's, Liverpool, and Dursley, Gloucestershire. [15]

IRELAND, George William Rossiter, *Sampford Peverell, Tiverton, Devon.*—R. of Sampford Peverell, Dio. Ex. 1857. (Patrons, Trustees of Mrs. Ireland; Tithe—App. 18*l*, R. 390*l*; R.'s Inc 400*l* and Ho; Pop. 720.) [16]

AA

IRELAND, Thomas, *Oldham.*—Dub. A.B. 1844, A.M. 1852; Deac. 1844 and Pr. 1845 by Bp of Ches. P. C. of Wernith, Oldham, Dio. Man. 1847. (Patrons, the Crown and Bp of Man. alt; P. C.'s Inc. 300*l* and Ho; Pop. 6700.) Chap. to Henshaw's Blue Coat Sch. Oldham. [17]

IRELAND, William Milton, *Holybourne, Alton, Hants.*—V. of Holybourne, Dio. Win. 1862. (Patrons, D. and C. of Win; V.'s Inc. 111*l*; Pop. 643.) [18]

IRELAND, William Stanley De Courcy, *Chalford, Stroud, Gloucestershire.*—P. C. of Chalford, Dio. G. and B. 1864. (Patron, Archd of Glouc; P. C.'s Inc. 150*l* and Ho; Pop. 2008.) Formerly C. of Dursley, Glouc. [19]

IREMONGER, Frederick Assheton, *Bullington Parsonage, Micheldever, Hants.*—Pemb. Coll. Ox. B.A. 1839, M.A. 1842; Deac. 1839 and Pr. 1840 by Bp of Win. P. C. of Bullington with Tufton, Dio. Win. 1857. (Patron, W. Iremonger, Esq; P. C.'s Inc. 260*l* and Ho; Pop. Bullington 171, Tufton 142.) Formerly C. of Ludgershall, Wilts. [20]

IREMONGER, Thomas Lascelles, *Goodworth-Clatford Vicarage, Andover, Hants.*—Ball. Coll. Ox. B.A. 1836; Deac. 1838, Pr. 1839. V. of Goodworth-Clatford, Dio. Win. 1839. (Patron, W. Iremonger, Esq; Tithe—Imp. 24*l* 8*s*, V. 165*l*; Glebe, 70 acres; V.'s Inc. 245*l* and Ho; Pop. 427.) V. of Wherwell, Dio. Win. 1844. (Patron, W. Iremonger, Esq; Tithe—Imp. 595*l*, V. 205*l*; Glebe, 5 acres; V.'s Inc. 220*l*; Pop. 626.) [21]

IRONS, William Josiah, 12, *Michael's-grove, Brompton, London, S.W.*—Queen's Coll. Ox. 1829, M.A. 1835, B.D. and D.D. 1854; Deac. 1835, Pr. 1836. P. C. of Brompton, Dio. Lon. 1842. (Patron, Bp of Lon; P. C.'s Inc. 639*l*; Pop. 9650.) Preb. of St. Paul's 1860. Formerly C. of St. Mary's, Newington, 1835–37; P. C. of St. Peter's, Walworth, 1837–38; V. of Barkway with Reed, Herts, 1838–42. Author, *The Whole Doctrine of Final Causes,* 1836; *The Perpetuity of the Church* (a Sermon), 1837; *The Received Faith* (a Farewell Sermon), 1838; *The Difficulties of the Church* (a Visitation Sermon), 1839; *The Church of England Defended against the "Church of England Quarterly Reviewer,"* 1839; *The Church Discipline Bill* (a Letter to the Bishop of Exeter), 1843; *A Remonstrance addressed to the Quarterly Reviewer respecting his recent Article on the Rubrics,* 2 eds. 1843; *Our Blessed Lord regarded in his Earthly Relationships* (Four Sermons), 1844; *A Manual for Christians preparatory to Confirmation,* 3 eds. 1846; *A Manual for Unbaptized Children, preparatory to Baptism,* 1846; *A Manual for Unbaptized Adults, preparatory to their Baptism,* 1846; *The Theory of (Mr. Newman's) Development Examined,* 1846; *Should the State oblige us to Educate?* (A Letter to Lord John Russell), 1846; *On the Holy Catholic Church* (Parochial Lectures, 1st Series), 1847; *On the Apostolical Succession* (2nd Series), 1847; *Ecclesiastical Jurisdiction* (3rd Series), 1847; *An Answer to the Rt. Rev. Dr. Wiseman's Letter, entitled Conversion,* 1847; *Dies Iræ* (translated), 4to. 1848; *An Epitome of the Bampton Lectures of the Rev. Dr. Hampden,* 1848; *Fifty-two Propositions, a Letter to the Rev. Dr. Hampden, submitting to him certain Assertions, Assumptions and Implications in his Bampton Lectures, reduced to the Form of Propositions,* 1848; *The Judgments on Baptismal Regeneration,* 1850; *The Present Crisis in the Church of England,* 1850; *Sequel to the Present Crisis, in Reply to the Revs. W. Maskell and T. W. Allies,* 1850; *The Christian Servant's Book,* 6 eds. 1851; *Metrical Psalter* (from the Latin and Original), 1857; *The Preaching of Christ* (a Series of Sermons for the People), 1st Series, 1858, 2nd Series, 1859; *A Letter on Subscription in the Church of England in Answer to Dean Stanley,* 1863; *Two Sermons at St. Paul's Cathedral on the Canon of Scripture*; *Prayers for Lent*; *The Interpretation of Scripture* (a Sermon); *The Bible and its Interpreters,* 1866; *Prayers for Little Children*; *Prayers for Lent, Apologia Ecclesiæ Anglicanæ* (addressed to Dr. Newman); *Hymns, Jesus Christ the*

Son of God: 1, *The Sacred Life*; 2, *The Sacred Word*; 3, *The Sacred Work*, Hayes, Lyall-place, Eaton-square, 1867. [1]

IRVIN, Joseph, *Brotherton Vicarage, South Milford Junction, Yorks.*—Deac. 1825 and Pr. 1826 by Abp of York. V. of Brotherton, Dio. York, 1856. (Patrons, D. and C. of York; Tithe—App. 263*l*, V. 95*l*; V.'s Inc. 300*l* and Ho; Pop. 1425.) Formerly V. of Brompton with Snainton, Yorks, 1829–56; P. C. of Hackness with Harwood Dale, Yorks, 1842–56. [2]

IRVIN, Thomas, *Ormsby Vicarage, Middlesborough-on-Tees.*—Deac. 1818, Pr. 1819. V. of Ormsby with Eston P. C. Dio. York, 1837. (Patron, Abp of York; Tithe—App. 219*l* 15*s*, V. 186*l* 13*s* 9*d*; V.'s Inc. 224*l* and Ho; Pop. Ormsby 3464, Eston 2835.) [3]

IRVINE, Alexander Campbell, *Walsall, Staffs.*—Ball. Coll. Ox. B.A. 1848, M.A. 1850; Deac. 1849 and Pr. 1850 by Bp of Ox. Min. of St. Paul's, Walsall, Dio. Lich. 1858. (Patrons, Govs. of Queen Mary's Gr. Sch. Walsall; Min.'s Inc. 50*l*.) Head Mast. of Queen Mary's Sch. Walsall. (Salary, 300*l* and Ho.) Formerly P. C. of Longfleet, Dorset, 1850–58. [4]

IRVINE, Gorges Mervyn D'Arcy, 2, *East-hill-terrace, Wandsworth, Surrey, S.W.*—Dub. 2nd cl. Lit. Hum. and A.B. 1848, A.M. 1859, *ad eund.* Ox. M.A. 1860; Deac. 1848 and Pr. 1849 by Bp of Ex. Chap. of Wandsworth and Clapham Unions 1860. (Salary, 200*l*.) Dom. Chap. to the Duke of Leinster. Formerly C. of Lamerton, Devon, 1848–50, Sancreed, Cornwall, 1851, St. Saviour's, Bath, 1851–57, Rock, Worcestershire (sole charge), 1857–60. Author, various Sermons and Tracts. [5]

IRVINE, James, *Leigh Vicarage, near Manchester.*—V. of Leigh with West Leigh C. Dio. Man. 1839. (Patron, Lord Lilford; Tithe—App. 30*l*; Imp. 401*l* 8*s* 4*d*, V. 9*s* 6*d*; V.'s Inc. 270*l* and Ho; Pop. 6912.) [6]

IRVINE, John William, *Chelmsford.*—Ch. Ch. Ox. B.A. 1859, M.A. 1864; Deac. 1864 and Pr. 1865 by Bp of Roch. C. of Chelmsford 1865. Formerly Asst. Mast. at Charterhouse 1859–64; C. of Nalstead, Essex, 1864. [7]

IRVINE, Walter, 15, *St. Mary's-terrace, Newcastle-on-Tyne.*—Dub. A.B. 1840; Deac. 1840, Pr. 1841. P. C. of All Saints', Newcastle-on-Tyne, Dio. Dur. 1852. (Patron, V. of Newcastle-on-Tyne; P. C.'s Inc. 300*l*; Pop. 15,510.) [8]

IRVINE, William Henry, *Foxearth, Sudbury.*—Trin. Coll. Cam. B.A. 1855, M.A. 1858; Deac. 1856 and Pr. 1857 by Bp of B. and W. C. of Foxearth, Essex, 1858. Formerly C. of Bradford, Somerset, 1856–58. [9]

IRVING, James, *Talkin Parsonage, Milton, Carlisle.*—Dub. A.B. 1841; Deac. 1842 by Bp of Llan. Pr. 1843 by Bp of Wor. C. of Hayton, Cumberland, 1848. Formerly C. of Timolin 1842–44, Kellistown 1844–45, Walsall 1845–46, Burton Latimer 1846–47, Broseley 1847–48. [10]

IRVING, John, *Millom Vicarage, Ulverstone.*—Queen's Coll. Ox. B.A. 1826, B.L. 1854, M.A. 1856; Deac. 1855 and Pr. 1856 by Bp of Pet. V. of Millom, Dio. Carl. 1865. (Patron, Chan. of Duchy of Lancaster; Tithe, 128*l*; Glebe, 60*l*; V.'s Inc. 198*l* and Ho; Pop. 3000.) Rural Dean; Surrogate. Formerly C. of Grendon, Northants, 1855–56, Wetheral, Carlisle, 1857; P. C. of Stainmore 1857–65. [11]

IRVING, John William, *Broughton Rectory, Newport Pagnell, Bucks.*—Trin. Coll. Cam. B.A. 1841, M.A. 1844; Deac. 1841 and Pr. 1842 by Bp of Rip. R. of Broughton, Dio. Ox. 1854. (Patron, W. B. Tyringham, Esq; Glebe, 11 acres; R.'s Inc. 97*l* and Ho; Pop. 155.) Formerly P. C. of Trinity, Batley Carr, Dewsbury. [12]

IRVING, R., *Liverpool.*—C. of St. Saviour's, Liverpool. [13]

IRVING, Robert Gill, *Elland, Halifax.*—St. Bees; Deac. 1863 and Pr. 1864 by Bp of Rip. C. of Elland, Yorks, 1863. [14]

IRWIN, John, *St. Mary's Parsonage, Berwick-upon-Tweed.*—Dub. A.B. 1852, A.M. 1856; Deac. 1852 by Bp of Dur. Pr. 1854 by Bp of Carl. P. C. of St. Mary's, Berwick-upon-Tweed, Dio. Dur. 1858. (Patrons, D. and C. of Dur; P. C.'s Inc. 260*l* and Ho; Pop. 2062.) Chap. of Berwick Gaol. Formerly Sen. C. of St. Nicholas', Newcastle-upon-Tyne, 1852–58; Chap. of Newcastle Prisons 1856–58; Even. Lect. of St. Nicholas, Newcastle, 1856–58; Hon. Chap. of Victoria Blind Asylum, Juvenile Reformatory. [15]

IRWIN, Thomas Nesbitt, *Charlinch Rectory, Bridgwater.*—Dub. A.B. 1838; Deac. 1838 by Abp of Dub. Pr. 1839 by Bp of Killaloe. R. of Charlynch, Dio. B. and W. 1858. (Patron, G. Goldney, Esq; R.'s Inc. 430*l*; Pop. 241.) Formerly P. C. of Ellesmere Port, Cheshire, 1844–58; C. of Tarah, Dio. Meath, 1839–40; P. C. of Gartree, Connor, 1840–44. [16]

IRWINE, Arthur Parke, *Bingley, Yorks.*—Dub. A.B. 1838, A.M. 1843; Deac. 1840 and Pr. 1841 by Abp of Cant. V. of Bingley, Dio. Rip. 1862. (Patron, Bp of Rip; Tithe—Imp. 410*l*, V. 300*l*; Glebe, 3 acres; V.'s Inc. 596*l* and Ho; Pop. 9045.) Surrogate. Formerly Sec. to the Ch. Pastoral Aid Soc. [17]

ISAAC, Charles Powys, *Boningale, Shifnall, Salop.*—Ball. Coll. Ox. B.A. 1852, M.A. 1856; Deac. 1854 and Pr. 1855 by Bp of Herf. P. C. of Boningale, Dio. Lich. 1856. (Patron, C. T. Whitmore, Esq; P. C.'s Inc. 250*l*; Pop. 187.) [18]

ISAAC, David Lloyd, *Llangathen, Llandilo-Vawr, Carmarthenshire.*—Lampeter 1854; Deac. 1855, Pr. 1856. C. of Llangathen. Author, *The Silurians; or, Contributions to the History of Gwent and Morgannwg.* [19]

ISAAC, Edward Whitmore, *Buckley Parsonage, Mold.*—Oriel Coll. Ox. B.A. 1859; Deac. 1860 by Bp of Lon. Pr. 1861 by Bp of Wor. C. of Buckley, Hawarden, 1867. Formerly C. of Kidderminster, 1860, Hanley Castle 1865, Kidderminster (again) 1866. [20]

ISAAC, William Deacon.—Literate; Deac. 1844 by Bp of G. and B. Pr. 1845 by Bp of Llan. Formerly P. C. of Hartshill, Staffs, 1856–61. [21]

ISAAC, William Lister, *Pirton Rectory, Worcester.*—Trin. Coll. Cam. M.A. 1835; Deac. 1831, Pr. 1832. R. of Pirton with Croome D'Abitot, Dio. Wor. 1833. (Patron, Earl of Coventry; Pirton, Tithe, 94*l* 12*s*; Glebe, 140 acres; Croome D'Abitot, Tithe, 194*l* 17*s*; Glebe, 26 acres; R.'s Inc. 530*l* and Ho; Pop. Pirton 212, Croome D'Abitot 212.) Rural Dean; Dioc. Inspector of Schs. [22]

ISAACS, Albert Augustus.—Corpus Coll. Cam. B.A. 1850, M.A. 1854; Deac. 1850 and Pr. 1851 by Bp of Pet. P. C. of Ch. Ch. Leicester, Dio. Pet. (Patrons, Trustees; P. C.'s Inc. 300*l* and Ho; Pop. 7000.) Formerly C. of Peterborough 1850. Author, *The Dead Sea*, 5*s*; *A Pictorial Tour in the Holy Land*, 2*s* 6*d*; Sermons, *Wars and Fightings, The Watchman*, and *The Pastor*; *The Cottage Tracts*; *The Voyage of St. Paul*; *The Path of the Just.* [23]

ISAACSON, James, *Newmarket, Suffolk.*—New Inn Hall, Ox. B.A. 1840, M.A. 1842; Deac. and Pr. 1841 by Bp of Lich. R. of St. Mary's, Newmarket, Dio. Ely, 1856. (Patron, Duke of Rutland; Tithe, 73*l*; Glebe, 38½ acres; R.'s Inc. 300*l* and Ho; Pop. 2002.) [24]

ISAACSON, John Frederick, *Freshwater Rectory, Yarmouth, Isle of Wight.*—St. John's Coll. Cam. 3rd Sen. Opt. 1st cl. Cl. Trip. and B.A. 1825; Deac. 1825 and Pr. 1826 by Bp of Ely. R. of Freshwater, Dio. Win. 1839. (Patron, St. John's Coll. Cam; Tithe, 801*l* 10*s*; Glebe, 6 acres; R.'s Inc. 816*l* and Ho; Pop. 1678.) Formerly Fell. and Tut. of St. John's Coll. Cam; Tut. of King's Coll. Cam. [25]

ISARD, James Chapman, *Woodbury Park, Tunbridge Wells.*—St. John's Coll. Cam. B.A. 1850, M.A. 1854; Deac. 1851 and Pr. 1852 by Bp of Man. Formerly C. of Ch. Ch. Salford, and Abbey, Bath; P. C. of Brothertoft, Lincolnshire. [26]

ISHAM, Arthur, *Weston Turville Rectory, Wendover, Bucks.*—All Souls Coll. Ox. 4th cl. Lit. Hum. and B.A. 1832, M.A. 1835; Deac. 1833 and Pr. 1834 by Bp of Ox. R. of Weston Turville, Dio. Ox. 1837. (Patrons, All Souls Coll. Ox; Tithe, 98*l* 11*s* 7½*d*; Glebe, 290 acres; R.'s Inc. 545*l* and Ho; Pop. 724.) Rural Dean

1838. Formerly Fell. of All Souls Coll. Ox. Author, *Sermons on the Death of the Rev. Spencer Thornton, Vicar of Wendover*, 1850, 1s; *Jacob and Israel, or Discriminative Use of their Titles, &c.* 1854, 1s 6d; *Suggestions, Scriptural and Historical, for the Abatement of Dissension and Schism among the People of England and Wales*, 1857, 10s 6d. [1]

ISHAM, Robert, *Lamport Rectory, Northampton.*—Brasen. Coll. Ox. B.A. 1828, M.A. 1829; Deac. 1829 and Pr. 1830 by Bp of Pet. R. of Lamport with Faxton C. Dio. Pet. 1845. (Patron, Sir C. Isham, Bart; Tithe, 717l 15s; Glebe, 60 acres; Faxton, Tithe, 236l; Glebe, 40 acres; R.'s Inc. 1047l and Ho; Pop. 370.) [2]

ISHERWOOD, Richard, *Hoby, near Leicester.*—St. John's Coll. Cam. Scho. of; Deac. 1866 by Abp of York, Pr. 1867 by Bp of Pet. C. of Hoby and Rotherby 1867. Formerly Asst. Math. Mast. at Rossall Sch. near Fleetwood. [3]

IVATT, Alfred William, *Coveney Rectory, Ely.*—Sid. Coll. Cam. B.A. 1845, M.A. 1848. R. of Coveney with Manea C. Dio. Ely, 1852. (Patron, Lord Rokeby; Coveney, Tithe, 231l 12s 3d; Glebe, 80 acres; Manea, Tithe, 356l; R.'s Inc. 820l and Ho; Pop. Coveney 550, Manea 1206.) [4]

IVE, Simon, *Yarde House, Taunton.*—Caius Coll. Cam. B.A. 1858, M.A. 1863; Deac. 1862 and Pr. 1863 by Bp of Ely. C. of St. James's, Taunton, 1864. Formerly C. of Ickleton, Cambridge, 1862–64. [5]

IVES, Cornelius, *Bradden House, near Towcester, Northants.*—Ex. Coll. Ox. B.A. 1815, M.A. 1817; Deac. and Pr. 1816. R. of Bradden, Dio. Pet. 1818. (Patron, the present R; Glebe, 192 acres; R.'s Inc. 235l and Ho; Pop. 140.) Author, *A Compendious History of the Church of God*, 1820, 2s 6d; *Sermons Originally composed for a Country Congregation*, 1832, 6s; *Memoir of Bishop Van Mildert*, prefixed to his Works, 1838. [6]

IVES, Robert J., *Wigginton, near Banbury.*—St. Mark's Coll. Chelsea; Deac. 1863 by Bp of Tasmania. C. of Wigginton 1863. [7]

IVES, William, *Haltwhistle Vicarage, Northumberland.*—Ball. Coll. Ox. B.A. 1822, M.A. 1829; Deac. 1824 by Bp of Ely, Pr. 1825 by Bp of Llan. V. of Haltwhistle, Dio. Dur. 1829. (Patron, Bp of Man; Tithe—Imp. 576l 15s 2d, V. 735l 3s; Glebe, 360 acres; Pop. 5200.) [8]

IZARD, Percy P., *Hythe, near Southampton.*—C. of Hythe. [9]

IZARD, William Chantler, *Slindon Rectory, Arundel, Sussex.*—Ch. Coll. Cam. B.A. 1845, M.A. 1848; Deac. 1845 and Pr. 1846 by Bp of Lin. R. of Slindon, Dio. Chich. 1865. (Patron, W. T. Tilley, Esq; Tithe, 364l 13s 4d; Glebe, 42 acres; R.'s Inc. 372l and Ho; Pop. 618.) Formerly C. of Low Toynton and Greetham, Linc. 1845, St. Dunstan's, Stepney, 1848. Head Mast. of Stepney Gr. Sch. 1850. [10]

IZOD, Thomas, *Honiton, Devon.*—Literate; Deac. 1853. Mast. of Gr. Sch. Honiton. Formerly Vice-Prin. of Culham Training Coll. near Abingdon, Berks, 1853–57. [11]

IZON, William York Seymour, *Yardley Gobion, Stony Stratford.*—Brasen. Coll. Ox. B.A. 1853; Deac. 1856 and Pr. 1857 by Bp of Roch. C. of Potterspury, Northants, 1858. Formerly C. of Kimpton, Herts, 1856. [12]

JACKMAN, William, *Falkenham Vicarage, near Ipswich.*—Trin. Hall, Cam. 1st cl. Law Trip. B.C.L. 1824; Deac. 1828, Pr. 1833. V. of Falkenham, Dio. Nor. 1842. (Patron, Ld Chan; Tithe—Imp. 75l, V. 346l; Glebe, 23½ acres; V.'s Inc. 374l and Ho; Pop. 270.) Hon. Can. of Nor. Cathl. 1854; Rural Dean; Dioc. Inspector of Schs. [13]

JACKSON, Augustus, *Perry-street, Gravesend.*—St. John's Coll. Cam. 6th Jun. Opt. Coll. Prizeman, B.A. 1859, M.A. 1862; Deac. 1860 and Pr. 1861 by Bp of Lon. C. in sole charge of All Saints' Mission, Perry-street, near Gravesend, 1867. Formerly C. of Stoke Newington 1860, and St. Saviour's, Hoxton, 1863. [14]

JACKSON, Blomfield, *Stoke Newington, and King's College, London.*—Ex. Coll. Ox. 4th cl. Lit. Hum. B.A. 1862, M.A. 1865; Deac. 1862 and Pr. 1863 by Bp of Lon. Sen. C. of Stoke Newington 1862; Cl. Mast. in King's Coll. Lond. 1865. [15]

JACKSON, Charles, *Bentley Parsonage, Farnham, Hants.*—St. John's Coll. Ox. B.A. 1835. P. C. of Bentley, Dio. Win. (Patron, Archd. of Surrey; Tithe—App. 808l 0s 11d; P. C.'s Inc. 115l and Ho; Pop. 721.) Sec. of the British and Foreign Bible Soc. [16]

JACKSON, Charles Bird, *Northwood, Stoke-upon-Trent.*—Brasen. Coll. Ox. B.A. 1843, M.A. 1846; Deac. 1845 by Bp of Lin. Pr. 1847 by Bp of Rip. P. C. of Northwood, Dio. Lich. 1848. (Patrons, the Crown and Bp of Lich. alt; P. C.'s Inc. 175l and Ho; Pop. 6099.) [17]

JACKSON, Curtis, *Newstead, Notts.*—St. John's Coll. Cam. B.A. 1839, M.A. 1844; Deac. 1839 and Pr. 1840 by Bp of Lin. Formerly V. of Hucknall Torkard, Notts, 1847–62. [18]

JACKSON, Edmund Frederick, 1, *Church-place, Warrington, Lancashire.*—St. Aidan's; Deac. 1865, Pr. 1866. C. of Warrington 1867. Formerly C. of Sturry, near Canterbury, 1865. [19]

JACKSON, Edward, *Leeds.*—Trin. Hall, Cam. LL.B. 1829. P. C. of St. James's, Leeds, Dio. Rip. 1846. (Patron, V. of Leeds; P. C.'s. Inc. 150l.) Surrogate; Chap. of the Leeds Workhouse. [20]

JACKSON, Edward Downes, *Marple, Stockport.*—P. C. of Marple, Dio. Ches. 1866. (Patron, R. of Stockport; P. C.'s Inc. 150l and Ho; Pop. 3338.) Formerly C. of Penistone, Sheffield. [21]

JACKSON, Edward Dudley, *Heaton Norris Rectory, Stockport.*—Trin. Hall, Cam. 1st cl. Law Trip. and LL.B. 1827; Deac. 1827, Pr. 1828. R. of Heaton Norris, Dio. Man. 1843. (Patrons, D. and C. of Man; R.'s Inc. 280l and Ho; Pop. 7490.) Author, *The Crucifixion and other Poems*, 1833; *The Devotional Year, or Companion to the Liturgy of the Church of England*, 1835; *Scripture History*, 1837; *English Grammar, History, and Geography, for the Use of Grammar Schools*; *Grammar School Atlas*, 1838; *Lays of Palestine*, 1850. [22]

JACKSON, Francis George.—Trin. Coll. Ox. B.A. 1836, M.A. 1839; Deac. 1837 and Pr. 1838 by Bp of Lin. Chap. to the Dow. Countess of Ellesmere. Formerly C. of Billesley, Warwickshire. [23]

JACKSON, Francis William, *Bolton Percy, Tadcaster.*—Dub. A.B. 1864, A.M. 1867; Deac. 1865 by Bp of Rip. Pr. 1866 by Abp of York. C. of Bolton Percy 1865. Formerly C. of Emley, near Wakefield, 1865. [24]

JACKSON, Frederic, *Parson-Drove, Wisbech, Cambs.*—St. John's Coll. Cam. B.A. 1840; Deac. 1842, Pr. 1843. P. C. of Parson-Drove, Dio. Ely, 1844. (Patrons, Trustees; P. C.'s Inc. 284l and Ho; Pop. 876.) Author, *Practical Sermons*, Hatchards, 1st Series, 1850, 2nd Series, 1853, 5s. [25]

JACKSON, Frederick, *West Lynn Rectory, Norfolk.*—Trin. Coll. Cam. 3rd cl. Cl. Trip. B.A. 1857, M.A. 1861; Deac. 1858 and Pr. 1859 by Bp of Ely. R. of West Lynn, Dio. Nor. 1863. (Patron, Rev. C. H. Townshend; Tithe, 400l; Glebe, 28 acres; R.'s Inc. 450l and Ho; Pop. 469.) Formerly C. of Wisbech St. Mary 1858–61. [26]

JACKSON, Frederick, *Carlton, Snaith, Yorks.*—C. of Carlton. [27]

JACKSON, Frederick Christian, *Ruan Rectory, Helston, Cornwall.*—St. John's Coll. Cam. B.A. 1848; Deac. and Pr. 1849 by Bp of Ex. R. of the united R.'s of Grade and Ruan Minor, Dio. Ex. 1853. (Patron, the present R; Grade, Tithe, 295l; Glebe, 5½ acres; Ruan Minor, Tithe, 101l 5s; Glebe, 5 acres; R.'s Inc. 396l and Ho; Pop. Grade 327, Ruan Minor 260.) Rural Dean. [28]

JACKSON, George, *Royal Naval Hospital Haslar.*—Caius Coll. Cam. 25th Wrang. B.A. 1838, M.A. 1843; Deac. 1842, Pr. 1843 by Bp of Nor. Chap. to Royal Naval Hospital, Haslar, 1866. Formerly Chap.

of the Dockyard, Bermuda, 1857–66; C. of Burstall, Suffolk. [1]

JACKSON, George, *North Reston Vicarage, Louth, Lincolnshire.*—Queens' Coll. Cam. B.A. 1823, M.A. 1826; Deac. 1824, Pr. 1825. V. of North Reston, Dio. Lin. 1827. (Patron, the present V; Tithe, 216*l* 9*s* 2*d*; Glebe, ¼ acre; V.'s Inc. 220*l* and Ho; Pop. 44.) R. of South Reston, Dio. Lin. 1849. (Patron, Duchy of Lancaster; Tithe, 6*l* 5*s* 6*d*; Glebe, 132 acres; R.'s Inc. 140*l*; Pop. 235.) [2]

JACKSON, George, *Manchester.*—C. of St. Andrew's, Manchester. [3]

JACKSON, George Ernest Mann, *Marcham, near Abingdon, Berks.*—Trin. Coll. Cam. B.A. 1865; Deac. 1866 by Bp of Ox. C. of Marcham 1866. [4]

JACKSON, Gilbert Charles, *Tockenham, Wilts.*—R. of Tockenham, Dio. Salis. 1865. (Patron, Ld Chan; R.'s Inc. 283*l* and Ho; Pop. 157.) Formerly V. of Glossop, Derbyshire, 1857; C. of Godney, Somerset. [5]

JACKSON, Gildart, *Parsonage, Leith.*—St. John's Coll. Cam. 16th Sen. Opt. 1860, B.A. 1860, M.A. 1863; Deac. 1861 and Pr. 1862 by Bp of Dur. Incumb. of St. James's, Leith, 1865. (Patron, the Vestry of St. James's; P. C.'s Inc. 230*l* and Ho.) Chap. to the Forces, Leith Fort. Formerly C. of Berwick 1861-65. [6]

JACKSON, H., *Kettering, Northants.*—Pemb. Coll. Ox. 2nd cl. Lit. Hum; Deac. 1865 and Pr. 1866 by Bp of Pet. C. of Kettering. [7]

JACKSON, Henry James, *Monk Frystone, Milford Junction, Yorks.*—P. C. of Monk Frystone, Dio. York, 1854. (Patron, Abp of York; P. C.'s Inc. 114*l*; Pop. 1093.) [8]

JACKSON, H. M.—Chap. of H.M.S. "Black Prince." [9]

JACKSON, James, 5, *Charterhouse-square, London, E.C.*—Brasen. Coll. Ox. B.A. 1825, M.A. 1827; Deac. 1826, Pr. 1827. V. of St. Sepulchre's, Dio. Lon. 1850. (Patron, St. John's Coll. Ox; V.'s Inc. 677*l*; Pop. 12,084.) Rural Dean. [10]

JACKSON, John, *Little Blakenham Rectory, Ipswich.*—Pemb. Coll. Cam. B.A. 1836, M.A. 1839; Deac. 1837 and Pr. 1838 by Bp of Nor. R. of Nettlestead, Suffolk, Dio. Nor. 1838. (Patron, the present R; Tithe, 196*l*; Glebe, 4 acres; R.'s Inc. 210*l*; Pop. 105.) R. of Little Blakenham, Dio. Nor. 1847. (Patron, the present R; Tithe, 244*l*; Glebe, 33 acres; R.'s Inc. 294*l* and Ho; Pop. 146.) [11]

JACKSON, John, *Butterwick, Boston, Lincolnshire.*—St. Cath. Hall, Cam. Jun. Opt. and B.A. 1833, M.A. 1836; Deac. 1833 and Pr. 1834 by Bp of Lin. Mast. of the Gr. Sch. Butterwick. Formerly C. of Benington, Lincolnshire, 1833-54. Author, *Sermon for the Fast-day on Cholera*, 1849. [12]

JACKSON, John, *Ledbury.*—R. of Ledbury, Dio. Herf. 1860. (Patron, Bp of Herf; Tithe—App. 552*l*, Imp. 61*l*, R. 460*l*; Glebe, 1 rood; R.'s Inc. 656*l* and Ho; Pop. 5598.) Surrogate; Chap. of St. Catherine's Hospital, Ledbury. [13]

JACKSON, John, *Great Bowden, Market Harborough, Leicestershire.*—Queen's Coll. Ox. B.A. 1849, M.A. 1852; Deac. 1849, Pr. 1852. C. of Great Bowden. [14]

JACKSON, J., *Wenden Vicarage, Saffron Walden.*—Ch. Coll. Cam. B.A. 1847, M.A. 1850; Deac. 1848 and Pr. 1849 by Bp of Nor. R. and V. of Wendens-Ambo, Dio. Roch. 1861. (Patron, Marquis of Bristol; Tithe, 125 acres; R. and V.'s Inc. 220*l* and Ho; Pop. 419.) [15]

JACKSON, John Charles, *Sutton-place, Lower Clapton, Hackney, London, N.E.*—St. John's Coll. Ox. B.A. 1850, M.A. 1855; Deac. 1854 and Pr. 1855 by Bp of Lon. Head Mast of Hackney Ch. of Eng. Sch. 1854. [16]

JACKSON, John Edward, *Leigh Delamere Rectory, Chippenham.*—Brasen. Coll. Ox. 2nd cl. Lit. Hum. and B.A. 1827, M.A. 1830; Deac. 1834, Pr. 1836. R. of Leigh Delamere with Sevington C. Dio. G. and B. 1845. (Patron, Sir John Neeld, Bart; R.'s Inc. 280*l* and Ho; Pop. 113.) V. of Norton, Wilts, Dio. G. and B. 1846. (Patron, Sir John Neeld, Esq. M.P; Tithe—Imp. 77*l* 14*s*, V. 100*l*; V.'s Inc. 100*l*; Pop. 112.) Rural Dean; Hon. Can. of Bristol Cathl. 1855; Fell. of the Soc. of Antiquaries. Author, *History of the Parish of Grittleton, Wilts*, 4to. 1843; *Guide to Farleigh, Hungerford, Somerset*, 2*s*; *The Nation's Guide to Scripture* (Visitation Sermon), 1846; *Sermon* (at Festival of Sons of the Clergy in Bristol Cathl.), *with Appendix, Account of the Charity, &c.* Bristol, 1846; *History of the Ruined Church of St. Mary Magdalene, Doncaster*, 4to. Bell and Daldy, 1853, 10*s* 6*d*; *Moderation, the Standard Rule of the Church of England* (Visitation Sermon), 1854; *A Sermon* (for the Additional Curates Soc.), 1854; *A Sermon* (preached at the Consecration of St. Paul's, Chippenham, and Langley Burrell), 1855; *History and Description of St. George's Church, Doncaster* (destroyed by fire, 1853), with 15 plates and 45 woodcuts, 4to. Nichols and Sons, 42*s*. 1855; *Wiltshire Topographical Collection of John Aubrey* (greatly enlarged, with 45 plates and many hundred coats of arms), 1862; Bull, Devizes, and Longmans, London; Articles in *Wilts Archæological Magazine*, viz., *Opening Address*; *Leland's Journey through Wilts in* 1540–42, *with Notes*; *Anglo-Saxon Cemetery at Harnham, near Salisbury*; *Maud Heath's Causey*; *Kingston House, Bradford, Wilts*; *Murder of Henry Long, Esq*; *Wiltshire Seals*; *History of Chippenham, of Kington St. Michael, and of Longleat*; *Charles Lord Stourton and the Hartgills, &c.* [17]

JACKSON, J. Russell, *Moulton, Spalding.*—M.A. 1859; Deac. 1857 and Pr. 1858 by Bp of Ely. V. of Moulton, Dio. Lin. 1866. (Patroness, Mrs. M. Johnson; V.'s Inc. 450*l* and Ho; Pop. 2000.) Formerly R. of All Saints and St. Julian's, Norwich, 1860. [18]

JACKSON, John Stuart, *The Rectory, Coton, Cambs.*—Caius Coll. Cam. 5th Wrang. and B.A. 1851, M.A. 1857; Deac. 1851 and Pr. 1852 by Bp of Ely. C. of Coton 1867. Formerly Fell. of Caius Coll. Cam. Missionary of the S.P.G. at Delhi 1854–57; P. C. of St. Peter's, Adelaide, South Australia, 1861–64. Author, *Solutions of Senate House Problems*, Macmillan, 1851; *Missions to the Heathen*, No. 34, The Delhi Miss. Soc. for Prom. Christ. Know. 1858. [19]

JACKSON, Jonathan, *Southport, Lancashire.*—St. Cath. Hall, Cam. B A. 1829, M.A. 1846; Deac. 1831, Pr. 1832. P. C. of Trinity, Southport, Dio. Ches. 1837. (Patrons, Trustees; P. C.'s Inc. 550*l* and Ho.) [20]

JACKSON, Joseph, *Rectory, Staple Fitzpaine, Taunton.*—Dub. A.B. 1860; Deac. 1862 and Pr. 1863 by Bp of Lich. C. of Bickenhall, near Taunton, 1866. Formerly C. of St. George's, Wolverhampton, 1862–65, St. James's, Taunton, 1865–66. [21]

JACKSON, Joseph Marshall, *Bow-Brickhill Rectory, Fenny Stratford, Bucks.*—Lin. Coll. Ox. B.A. 1831. R. of Bow-Brickhill, Dio. Ox. 1840. (Patron, Queens' Coll. Cam; R.'s Inc. 430*l* and Ho; Pop. 546.) [22]

JACKSON, J. R., *St. Mary Church, Devon.*—C. of St. Mary Church. [23]

JACKSON, Laurence, *Barby Rectory, Rugby.*—Corpus Coll. Cam. B.A. 1857, M.A. 1862; Deac. 1857 and Pr. 1858 by Bp of Lin. R. of Barby Dio. Pet. 1867. (Patron, J. Jackson, Esq; Tithe, 273*l* 11*s* 3*d*; Glebe, 506 acres; R.'s Inc. 1200*l* and Ho; Pop. 645.) Formerly C. of Laneham 1857, Wold Newton and Butterwick 1860, Old Radford 1860, Hilmorton 1862, Grandborough 1864, Braceborough 1865–67. [24]

JACKSON, Luke, *Hucknall Torkard, Nottingham.*—St. John's Coll. Cam. B.A. 1811, M.A. 1814; Deac. 1811, Pr. 1812. [25]

JACKSON, Nathan, *Over Vicarage, Winsford, Cheshire.*—Brasen. Coll. Ox. B.A. 1851, M.A. 1854; Deac. 1853, Pr. 1854. V. of Over, Dio. Ches. 1863. (Patron, Bp of Ches; Tithe, 18*l* 11*s* 10*d*; V.'s Inc. 150*l* and Ho; Pop. 1191.) Formerly C. of Delamere, Chester, 1853–54, and again 1859. [26]

JACKSON, Richard Henry, *Llanellian Rectory, Abergele, Denbighshire.*—Jesus Coll. Ox. B.A. 1834, M.A. 1838; Deac. 1838 and Pr. 1839 by Bp of St. A. R. of Llanellian, Dio. St. A. 1859. (Patron, Bp. of St. A; R's

Inc. 250*l* and Ho; Pop. 548.) Author, *Welsh Highland Agriculture* (a Prize Essay at the Rhuddlan Royal Eisteddfod), 1850; *Comparison of the Working Classes of England, Ireland, Scotland, and Wales* (Prize Essay at the Tremadoc Royal Eisteddfod), 1851. [1]

JACKSON, Robert, *Wonastow Vicarage, near Monmouth.*—V. of Wonastow, Dio. Llan. (Patron, Sir W. Pilkington, Bart; Tithe, 105*l* 14*s*; V.'s Inc. 124*l* and Ho; Pop. 150.) [2]

JACKSON, Robert David, *Kilburn, Oswaldkirk, York.*—Deac. 1850 and Pr. 1854 by Abp of York. C. of Kilburn 1864. Formerly C. of Stillington 1854-64. [3]

JACKSON, Robert Hall, *Salford Priors, near Evesham.*—Ex. Coll. Ox. B.A. 1859, M.A. 1866; Deac. 1860 and Pr. 1861 by Bp of G. and B. C. of Salford Priors 1862. Formerly C. of Swindon, Wilts, 1860. [4]

JACKSON, Samuel, *Magdalene College, Cambridge.*—Magd. Coll. Cam. B.A. 1854, M.A. 1857; Deac. 1857 and Pr. 1858 by Bp of Ely. Dean, Prælector and Fell. of Magd. Coll. Cam. [5]

JACKSON, Thomas, *Hatton Parsonage, Warwick.*—Wor. Coll. Ox. B.A; Deac. 1834 and Pr. 1835 by Bp of Wor. P. C. of Hatton, Dio. Wor. 1857. (Patrons, Trustees; P. C.'s Inc. 250*l* and Ho; Pop. 1259.) Formerly P. C. of Ovingham and Mickley, Northumberland, 1838; V. of Collierley, Durham, 1842. [6]

JACKSON, Thomas, *Stoke Newington Rectory, London, N.*—St. Mary Hall, Ox. 3rd cl. Lit. Hum. and B.A. 1834, M.A. 1837; Deac. 1835 and Pr. 1836 by Bp of Lon. R. of Stoke Newington, Dio. Lon. 1852. (Patron, Bp of Lon; Tithe, 100*l*; R.'s Inc. 1043*l* and Ho; Pop. 4117.) Preb. of Weldland in St. Paul's Cathl. 1850 (Value, 2*l*). Author, *Questions on Adams's Roman Antiquities*; *A Manual of Logic*; *Examination Questions and Papers adapted to the Use of Theological Students*; *The Duty of bearing each other's Burthens* (a Sermon preached before the Lord Mayor, &c.); *A Pastoral Letter to the Inhabitants of St. Peter's, Stepney*; *Stepney Tracts* (5 Numbers); *Addresses delivered at the Opening of Commercial Schools*; *The Introductory Lecture on Method, at the Opening of Queen's College, Harley-street*; *Discourse to the Students of the Battersea Normal College*, 1847; *Sermon on the Death of the Duke of Wellington*; *The Shaking of the Nations* (a Sermon); *What is Education* (a Sermon)? *Sermons preached chiefly on Public Occasions*, 1863; *Our Dumb Companions, being Conversations of a Father with his Children on Horses, Dogs, Donkeys, and Cats*, 1865; *Lecture on the History of Stoke Newington*. Formerly Editor of *The English Journal of Education*. [7]

JACKSON, Thomas, *Ogley Hay, near Walsall, Staffs.*—P. C. of Ogley Hay, Dio. Lich. 1856. (Patron, Bp of Lich; P. C.'s Inc. 170*l*; Pop. 2490.) Formerly C. of St. James's, Longton, Staffs. [8]

JACKSON, Thomas Molineux, *Osbournby Vicarage, Folkingham, Lincolnshire.*—Brasen. Coll. Ox. B.A. 1844, M.A. 1847; Deac. 1848 and Pr. 1849 by Bp of Ches. V. of Osbournby, Dio. Lin. 1864. (Patrons, Halme's Trustees; V.'s Inc. 250*l* and Ho; Pop. 613.) Formerly C. of Over, Cheshire, 1848; P. C. of Little Marsden, Lancashire, 1852–64. [9]

JACKSON, Thomas Norfolk, *Filey, Yorks.*—Ch. Coll. Cam. Scho. of, 1828, B.A. 1830, M.A. 1833; Deac. 1831, Pr. 1832. P. C. of Filey, Dio. York, 1831. (Patrons, Rev. R. Brooke 2 turns, and Admiral Mitford 1 turn; Tithe—Imp. 30*l* 9*s* 0½*d*; P. C.'s Inc. 95*l* and Ho; Pop. 2244.) [10]

JACKSON, William, *Lowther Rectory, Penrith.*—Queen's Coll. Ox. 2nd cl. Lit. Hum. 1811, B.A. 1812, M.A. 1814, B.D. 1827, D.D. 1832; Deac. 1815 and Pr. 1816 by Bp of Ches. Provost of Queen's Coll. Ox; R. of Lowther, Dio. Carl. 1828. (Patron, Earl of Lonsdale; Tithe, 92*l* 4*s* 10*d*; Glebe, 251 Westmoreland acres; R.'s Inc. 315*l* and Ho; Pop. 427.) Rural Dean. Dom. Chap. to the Earl of Lonsdale. Formerly Fell. Tut. and Bursar of Queen's Coll. Ox; Whitehall Preacher 1827; Chancellor of the Dio. of Carl. 1846–55; R. of Cliburn, Westmoreland, 1841–58; Archd. and Can. of Carl. 1856–62. [11]

JACKSON, William, *Heathfield Vicarage, Hurstmonceaux, Sussex.*—Queen's Coll. Ox. Hon. 4th cl. Math. et Phy. and B.A. 1842, M.A. 1854; Deac. 1842, Pr. 1843. V. of Heathfield, Dio. Chich. 1858. (Patron, Bp of Chich; Tithe—App. 400*l* and 18 acres of Glebe; V. 462*l* 5*s*; Glebe, 17 acres; V.'s Inc. 592*l* and Ho; Pop. 1892.) Organising Sec. to the S.P.G. for the Archdeaconry of Lewes. Formerly P. C. of St. John's, Hurstmonceaux, 1854–58. Author, *The Sufficiency of Holy Scripture* (Mrs. Denyer's Prize Essay), 1846, 2*s*; *The Church's Doctrine of Predestination the Consolation of the Elect* (Mrs. Denyer's Prize Essay), 1847, 1*s*; *Sermons preached in Village Churches*, 1853, 7*s* 6*d*, 2nd ed. 1854, 5*s*. Editor of *Stories and Catechisings on the Collects*, 3 vols. 1853–54, 12*s* 6*d*; *Stories and Lessons on the Catechism*, 3 vols. 1854–56. [12]

JACKSON, William, 6, *King-square, London, E.C.*—Deac. 1866 by Bp Anderson for Bp of Lon. C. of St. Thomas's, Charterhouse, 1866. [13]

JACKSON, W., *Ashton-in-Makerfield, Wigan.*—C. of Trinity, Ashton-in-Makerfield. [14]

JACKSON, W., *Waterfall, Leek, Staffs.*—C. of Waterfall and Cauldon. [15]

JACKSON, William Edward, *Lilbourne Vicarage, near Rugby.*—Deac. 1853 and Pr. 1855 by Bp of Wor. V. of Lilbourne, Dio. Pet. 1858. (Patron, Ld Chan; V.'s Inc. 150*l* and Ho; Pop. 292.) [16]

JACKSON, William Henry, *Chesterton, Newcastle-under-Lyne.*—Brasen. Coll. Ox. B.A. 1847. P. C. of Chesterton, Dio. Lich. 1850. (Patrons, the Crown and Bp of Lich. alt; P. C.'s Inc. 150*l*; Pop. 4067.) [17]

JACKSON, William Hippisley, *Hambleton, Rutland.*—C. of Hambleton with Braunston. [18]

JACKSON, William Nelson, *Kingsey Vicarage, near Thame, Oxon.*—V. of Kingsey, Dio. Ox. 1833. (Patrons, D. and C. of Roch; Tithe—App. 131*l* 15*s*, V. 362*l*; V.'s Inc. 365*l* and Ho; Pop. 237.) [19]

JACKSON, William Vincent, *Trinity Parsonage, Nottingham.*—Ex. Coll. Ox. Magd. Hall, Meke Scho. of, 3rd cl. Law and Mod. Hist. B.A. 1862, M.A. 1865; Deac. 1863 and Pr. 1864 by Bp of Lin. C. of Trinity, Nottingham, 1863. [20]

JACOB, Edwin, *King's College, Fredericton, New Brunswick.*—Corpus Coll. Ox. B.A. 1814, M.A. 1818, B.D. and D.D. 1829; Deac. and Pr. 1818 by Bp of Glouc. Prin. of King's Coll. Fredericton, 1829. Formerly C. of St. Michael's, Gloucester, 1818–20, Clifton 1820–27; R. of St. Pancras, Chichester, 1827–29. Author, *The Authority, Nature, and Duties of the Christian Ministry* (an ordination Sermon), 1818; *The Principles and Objects of King's College, New Brunswick* (Sermon before the Univ. first assembled on Advent Sunday, 1829); *Oration at the first Encænia of the College*, 1830, and others in several subsequent years; *Twelve Sermons, intended for the Propagation of the Gospel*, 1835, gratuitously circulated; *The Experience, Prospects, and Purposes of King's College, Fredericton*, 1851, reprinted at length in the Journals of the House of Assembly; *Presidential Discourse before the Fredericton Athenæum*, 1853; etc. [21]

JACOB, George Andrew, *Christ's Hospital, Newgate-street, London, E.C.*—Wor. Coll. Ox. 1st cl. Lit. Hum. and B.A. 1829, M.A. 1832, B.D. and D.D. 1852; Deac. 1831 by Bp of Ox. Pr. 1832 by Bp of Wor. Head Mast. of Christ's Hospital, Lond. Formerly Head Mast. of King Edward VI. Gr. Sch. Bromsgrove, 1832; Prin. of Sheffield Coll. Sch. 1843. Author, *Bromsgrove Latin Grammar*, 4th ed. 1858; *Bromsgrove Greek Grammar*, 3rd ed. 1861; *Elementary Latin Grammar*, new ed. 1867; *Elementary Greek Grammar*, new ed. 1863; *Letter to Sir Robert Peel on National Education*, 1839; *Sermon before the University of Oxford* 1841; *Tirocinium Gallicum*, 1849; *Four Sermons before the University of Oxford* 1858. [21]

JACOB, James John, *Horningsham, near Warminster, Wilts.*—Emman. Coll. Cam. B.A. 1845, M.A. 1848; Deac. 1846 and Pr. 1847 by Bp of Salis. P. C. of Horningsham, Dio. Salis. 1858. (Patron, Bp of Salis; P. C.'s Inc. 300*l* and Ho; Pop. 1065.) Formerly C. of Fisherton, near Salisbury. [22]

JACOB, John Alexander.—Dub. A.B. 1848; Deac. 1848 and Pr. 1850 by Abp of Dub. C. of St. Stephen's Paddington, Lond. [1]

JACOB, Levi Rees, *Llanllugan, Shrewsbury.*—St. Bees 1850; Deac. 1851, Pr. 1852. P. C. of Llanllugan, Montgomeryshire, 1863. (Patron, Lord of the Manor; P. C.'s Inc. 60*l*; Pop. 304.) Formerly C. of Llangadvan. [2]

JACOB, The Ven. Philip, *Crawley Rectory, Winchester.*—Corpus Coll. Ox. B.A. 1825, M.A. 1828; Deac. 1827 and Pr. 1828 by Bp of Llan. Archd. of Win. 1860. (Archd.'s Inc. 200*l*.) R. of Crawley with Hunton C. Dio. Win. 1831. (Patron, Bp of Win; Tithe, Crawley, 660*l*, Hunton, 190*l*; Glebe, 8 acres; R.'s Inc. 850*l* and Ho; Pop. 502.) Can. Res. of Win. Cathl. 1834. (Value, 850*l* and Res.) Exam. Chap. to the Bp of Win; Sec. to the Win. Dioc. Board of Education. Formerly C. of Newport, Monmouthshire, 1827. Author, Charges and Sermons. [3]

JACOB, Stephen Hall.—Chap. of H.M.S. "Seringapatam." [4]

JACOB, William Borman, *Calne, Wilts.*—Emman. Coll. Cam. Sen. Opt. 3rd cl. Cl. Trip. and B.A. 1833, M.A. 1836; Deac. 1836, Pr. 1837. [5]

JACOBS, the Very Rev. Henry, *Christ Church, Canterbury, New Zealand.*—Queen's Coll. Ox. 1st cl. Lit. Hum. and B.A. 1845, M.A. 1848. Dean of Christ Church, New Zealand. Formerly Michel Fell. of Queen's Coll. Ox. [6]

JACOBSON, William Bowstead Richards, *Sion College, London Wall, E.C.*—Ch. Ch. Ox. 3rd cl. Lit. Hum. B.A. 1864, M.A. 1866; Deac. 1864 and Pr. 1865 by Bp of Lon. C. of St. Mary's, Charterhouse, Lond. 1864. [7]

JACOX, Francis, *Prestwood, near Charlwood, Crawley, Sussex.*—St. John's Coll. Cam. B.A. 1847; Deac. 1847, Pr. 1848. Formerly C. of Wellingborough, Northants, 1847–48. [8]

JACSON, Edward, *Thruxton Rectory, near Hereford.*—Trin. Coll. Cam. B.A. 1849; Deac. 1849 and Pr. 1850 by Bp of Ches. R. of Thruxton with Kingston V. Dio. Herf. 1858. (Patron, Bp of Herf; Thruxton, Tithe, 102*l*; Glebe, 16 acres; Kingston, Tithe—App. 575*l* 14*s*, V. 436*l* 5*s*; R.'s Inc. 800*l* and Ho; Pop. Thruxton 65, Kingston 460.) Rural Dean. Formerly R. of Easthope, Salop, 1852–58. Author, *Harvest Thanksgiving Lecture*, 1857. [9]

JAMES, Alfred, *The Rock Rectory, Bewdley, Worcestershire*—Univ. Coll. Dur. 1st cl. Lit. Hum. and B.A. 1854, M.A. 1857, Fell. of the Univ. 1855; Deac. 1855 by Bp of Man. Pr. 1857 by Bp of Dur. R. of Rock with Heightington C. Dio. Herf. 1862. (Patron, J. H. James, Esq; Tithe, 1110*l*; Glebe, 30 acres; R.'s Inc. 1160*l* and Ho; Pop. 910.) Formerly Chap. Lect. and Bursar of Univ. Coll. Dur; C. of St. Mary-le-bow, Durham; P. C. of Wragby, near Wakefield. [10]

JAMES, Benjamin Fuller, 1, *Little Dean's-yard, Westminster, S.W.*—Ex. Coll. Ox. 2nd cl. Lit. Hum. and B.A. 1846, M.A. 1848. Asst. Mast. in Westminster Sch. [11]

JAMES, Charles Caldecott, *Eton, Bucks.*—King's Coll. Cam. 3rd cl. Cl. Trip. 10th Jun. Opt. and B.A. 1853, M.A. 1856; Deac. 1853 and Pr. 1854 by Bp of Lin. Asst. Mast. at Eton Coll. 1855. Formerly Fell. of King's Coll. Cam. [12]

JAMES, David, *Pant-teg Rectory, Pont-y-Pool, Monmouthshire.*—M.A. by Abp of Cant. 1849, Heidelberg Ph. D. 1853; Deac. 1826 and Pr. 1827 by Bp of St. D. R. of Pant-teg, Dio. Llan. 1856. (Patron, C. H. Leigh, Esq; Tithe, comm. 343*l* 9*s*; Glebe, 24 acres; R.'s Inc. 370*l* and Ho; Pop. 2828.) Formerly C. of Granston, Pembrokeshire, 1826, Jordanston 1827, Almondbury, Yorks, 1829–36; P. C. of St. Mary's, Kirkdale, Liverpool, 1836–53; Warden to the Welsh Educational Institution at Llandovery 1853–54; P. C. of Marsden, Yorks, 1854–56. Author, *A Sermon proving the Scriptural and Apostolic Origin of the Rite of Confirmation as it is at this Time observed in the Church of England*, 1835, 2nd ed. as a Tract, 1850; *The Patriarchal Religion of Britain, or a Complete Manual of Ancient British Druidism*, 1836; *The Conduct of the Romish Church with Regard to the Bible* (a Sermon), 1838; *The Doctrine of the Trinity* (a Lecture), 1839; *Three Letters on the Irish System of Education, as Introduced into the Corporation Schools of Liverpool*; *The Pope's Supremacy Disproved, and the Apostolic Origin and National Independence of the British Church demonstrated*, 1854; *Peter without a Primacy, and the Pope a Usurper* (a Sermon), 1851; *A Lecture on Purgatory*, 1851; *The Siege of Derry* (a Lecture), 1851. [13]

JAMES, David, *Llandderfel Rectory, Corwen, Merionethshire.*—Deac. 1866, Pr. 1867. C. of Llandderfel 1866. [14]

JAMES, David Lloyd, *Pont-Robert Vicarage, near Welshpool.*—St. Bees; Deac. 1851 and Pr. 1852 by Bp of St. A. V. of Pont-Robert, Dio. St. A. 1853. (Patron, Bp of St. A; Tithe, 200*l*; Glebe, 4 acres; V.'s Inc. 205*l* and Ho; Pop. 612.) Formerly C. of Castle Caereinion 1851–52. Author, several controversial treatises and letters on *The Spirit of the Church* and *The Church of the Welsh* in the *Herald Cymraeg*, Carnarvon, 1867. [15]

JAMES, David Owen, *Mathry Vicarage, Haverfordwest.*—Jesus Coll. Ox. B.A. 1849, M.A. 1854; Deac. 1850 and Pr. 1851 by Bp of Llan. V. of Mathry, Dio. St. D. 1865. (Patron, Bp of St. D; Tithe, 190*l*; Glebe, 89 acres; V.'s Inc. 350*l* and Ho; Pop. 976.) Formerly C. of Aberavon with Baglan 1850, Margam 1851–58; R. of Llanychllwyddog with Llanllawer 1858–65. [16]

JAMES, Edward, *Peakirk Rectory, Market Deeping.*—R. of Peakirk, Dio. Pet. 1865. (Patrons, D. and C. of Pet; R.'s Inc. 335*l* and Ho; Pop. 250.) [17]

JAMES, Edward Boucher, *The Vicarage, Carisbrooke, Isle of Wight, and Oxford and Cambridge Club, Pall-mall, London, S.W.*—Queen's Coll. Ox. 2nd cl. Lit. Hum. and B.A. 1842, M.A. 1846; Deac. 1848 and Pr. 1853 by Bp of Ox. V. of Carisbrooke with Northwood C. Isle of Wight, Dio. Win. 1858. (Patron, Queen's Coll. Ox; Carisbrooke, Tithe—Imp. 1106*l*, V. 452*l*; Glebe, 3 acres; Northwood, Tithe, 710*l*; Glebe, 50 acres; V.'s Inc. 1280 and Ho; Pop. Carisbrooke 4238, Northwood 1943.) Formerly Fell. Tut. Dean and Bursar of Queen's Coll. Ox. 1845 to 1858; Sen. Proctor 1856–57. Contributor to Dr. Smith's *Dictionary of Greek and Roman Geography*, 1854. [18]

JAMES, Edward Knight, *Penmaen Rectory, Swansea.*—Lampeter; Deac. and Pr. 1838. R. of Penmaen, Dio. St. D. (Patron, the Prince of Wales; Tithe, 101*l* 14*s* 6*d*; Glebe, 58 acres; R.'s Inc. 210*l* and Ho; Pop. 123.) [19]

JAMES, Edward Stanley, *Letcombe Regis Vicarage, Wantage, Berks.*—Mert. Coll. Ox. B.A. 1846, M.A. 1850; Deac. 1846 and Pr. 1847 by Bp of Win. V. of Letcombe Regis, Dio. Ox. 1852. (Patrons, D. and C. of Win; Tithe—App. 651*l* 10*s*, V. 85*l* 18*s* 3*d*; Glebe, 29½ acres; V.'s Inc. 202*l* and Ho; Pop. 431.) [20]

JAMES, Enoch Rhys, *Prestatyn, near Rhyl.*—Lampeter; Deac. 1856 and Pr. 1857 by Bp of St. A. P. C. of Prestatyn, Dio. St. A. 1861. (Patrons, Crown and Bp alt; Tithe, 233*l*; Glebe, 10 acres; P. C.'s Inc. 233*l* and Ho; Pop. 700.) Formerly C. of Rhuddlan 1856–57, Ysceifiog 1858–60. [21]

JAMES, Francis Joseph, *Stockton-on-Tees Vicarage, Durham.*—V. of Stockton-on-Tees, Dio. Dur. 1847. (Patron, Bp of Dur; Tithe—Imp. 187*l* 2*s* 8*d*, V. 165*l*; V.'s Inc. 256*l* and Ho; Pop. 9494.) [22]

JAMES, George, *Gloucester.*—Dub. A.B. 1862; Deac. 1863 and Pr. 1864 by Bp of G. and B. Min. Can. and Librarian of Glouc. Cathl. and Chap. to the Gloucester Infirmary 1864. Formerly C. of St. Mary-de-Lode, Gloucester. [23]

JAMES, George Burder, *Hatford, near Faringdon, Berks.*—King's Coll. Lond. Theol. Assoc; Deac. 1862 and Pr. 1863 by Bp of Roch. R. of Hatford, Dio. Ox. 1864. (Patron, Rev. S. Paynter; Tithe, 259*l*; Glebe, 53 acres; R.'s Inc. 379*l* and Ho; Pop. 122.) Formerly C. of Therfield, near Royston, Herts. [24]

JAMES, Henry, *Cransley Vicarage, Wellingborough.*—Deac. 1857 and Pr. 1858 by Bp of Lich. V. of Cransley, Dio. Pet. 1864. (Patron, W. S. Rose, Esq; Modus, 18*l*; Glebe, 39 acres; V.'s Inc. 99*l* and Ho; Pop. 350.) Formerly C. of Lapley, Staffs, 1857–59, All Saints', Northampton, 1859–62, Cransley, Northants, 1862–64. [1]

JAMES, Henry Daniel, *Calcutta.*—Magd. Hall, Ox. B.A. 1844, M.A. 1847. Asst. Chap. to H.M.'s East India Government on the Bengal Establishment. [2]

JAMES, Henry Pigott, *Madras.*—St. Bees 1850. Chap. to H.M.'s East India Government on the Madras Establishment. [3]

JAMES, Herbert.—King's Coll. Cam. B.A. 1846, M.A. 1849; Deac. 1848 and Pr. 1849 by Bp of Nor. Fell. of King's Coll. Cam. Formerly P. C. of Goodnestone, Kent, 1855–65. [4]

JAMES, Horatio, *High Harrogate, Knaresborough, Yorks.*—Corpus Coll. Cam. B.A. 1832, M.A. 1835; Deac. and Pr. 1832. P. C. of High Harrogate, Dio. Rip. 1858. (Patron, Bp of Rip; P. C.'s Inc. 260*l* and Ho; Pop. 4327.) Surrogate; Hon. Can. of Rip. 1864. Formerly V. of Sheepshed, Leicestershire, 1848–58. Author, *Sermons on the Levitical Types*, 1847, 4*s* 6*d*; *Lectures on the 17th and 18th Chapters of Revelation*, 1850, 4*s*. [5]

JAMES, James, *Llanbadarn-Trevegloys, Lampeter, Cardiganshire.*—V. of Llanbadarn-Treveglwys, Dio. St. D. 1838. (Patron, Bp of St. D; Tithe—Imp. 175*l*, V. 70*l*; V.'s Inc. 85*l*; Pop. 948.) V. of Kilkennin, near Lampeter, Dio. St. D. (Patron, Bp of St. D; V.'s Inc. 65*l*; Pop. 603.) [6]

JAMES, James Caddy, *St. John's, Worcester.*—St. John's Coll. Cam. Sen. Opt. and B.A. 1843, M.A. 1846; Deac. and Pr. 1844 by Bp of Herf. Sen. C. of St. John-in-Bedwardine, Worcester, 1851. [7]

JAMES, James William, *Puncheston Rectory, Fishguard, Pembrokeshire.*—Jesus Coll. Ox. B.A. 1811, M.A. 1814, R. of Puncheston, Dio. St. D. 1825. (Patron, the present R; Tithe, 107*l* 10*s*; Glebe, 45 acres; R.'s Inc. 147*l* and Ho; Pop. 231.) R. of Llanychaer, near Fishguard, Dio. St. D. 1825. (Patron, the present R; Tithe, 75*l*; R.'s Inc. 79*l*; Pop. 194.) [8]

JAMES, John, *Long Sutton Vicarage, Langport, Somerset.*—Dub. A.B. 1848, A.M. 1851; Deac. 1848 and Pr. 1854 by Bp of B. and W. V. of Long Sutton, Dio. B. and W. 1859. (Patrons, D. and C. of Wells; Tithe—Imp. 400*l*, V. 332*l*; Glebe, 17 acres; V.'s Inc. 250*l* and Ho; Pop. 958.) Formerly Head Mast. of the Rectory Sch. Bath, 1839–59. [9]

JAMES, John, *Avington Rectory, Hungerford, Berks.*—Queen's Coll. Ox. 2nd cl. Lit. Hum. and B.A. 1828, M.A. 1831; Deac. 1830 by Bp of Lich. Pr. 1831 by Bp of Lon. R. of Avington, Dio. Ox. 1853. (Patron, Sir Robert Burdett, Bart; Tithe, 299*l* 10*s*; Glebe, 6 acres; R.'s Inc. 280*l* and Ho; Pop. 104.) Surrogate 1855. Formerly R. of Rawmarsh, Yorks, 1831–43; V. of Pinhoe, Devon, 1844; P. C. of Tor Mohun and Cockington, Devon, 1844–48; P. C. of Headington Quarry, Oxon, 1851–53. Author, *Wesleyan Methodism, its Relation to the Church of Christ in England*, Rivingtons, 1835, 4*d*; *A Manual of Christian Doctrine*, Burns, 1840, 6*d*; *A Voice from Rome*, Burns, 1842, 1*s*; *An Act of Humiliation for Prevailing National and Parochial Sins*, 1843; *A Harmonised Summary of the Four Gospels*, Parker, Oxford, 1854, 4*d*; *The Rubric as to Ornaments of the Church and of the Ministers thereof, its Authorised Interpretation*, Parker, 1866, 6*d*. Editor, *Voices of the Sea*, Mackintosh, 3*s*. [10]

JAMES, John, *Prebendal House, Peterborough.*—St. John's Coll. Ox. B.A. 1803, M.A. 1807, B.D. and D.D. 1834; Deac. 1806 by Bp of Ox. Pr. 1807 by Bp of Nor. Can. Res. of Pet. Cathl. 1829. (Value, 500*l* and Res.) P. C. of Glinton, Dio. Pet. 1850. (Patrons, D. and C. of Pet; P. C.'s Inc. 300*l*; Pop. 421.) Formerly V. of St. John the Baptist's, Peterborough. Author, *A Comment upon the Collects appointed to be used in the Church of England on Sundays and Holidays throughout the Year*, 1826, 16th ed. 3*s* 6*d*; *Christian Watchfulness in the Prospect of Sickness, Mourning, and Death*, 1840, 8th ed. 6*s*; *Sunday Lessons with Commentary*, 1840; *The Christian Temple* (a Visitation Sermon), 1844; *Practical Commentary on the Ordination Services*, 1846, 7*s* 6*d*; *Evangelical Life as seen in the Example of our Lord Jesus Christ*, 2nd ed. 7*s* 6*d*; *A Devotional Comment on the Morning and Evening Services in the Book of Common Prayer*, 2 vols. 2nd ed. 10*s* 6*d*; *The Mother's Help towards instructing her Children in the Excellences of the Catechism and the Occasional Services*; *The Happy Communicant, or the Soldier Armed, a True Story*, 3*d*; all published by Rivingtons. [11]

JAMES, John, 9, *Seymour-street, Liverpool.*—Lampeter, B.D. 1857; Deac. 1849 and Pr. 1851 by Bp of St. D. P. C. of St. David's (Welsh Ch.) Liverpool, Dio. Ches. 1857. (Patron, R. Gladstone, Esq; P. C.'s Inc. 203*l*; Pop. 7442.) [12]

JAMES, John, *Southtown, Gorleston, Great Yarmouth.*—Min. of St. Mary's Chapel, Southtown, Dio. Nor. 1864. (Patron, V. of Gorleston.) [13]

JAMES, J. B., *Gamlingay Vicarage (Cambs), near Biggleswade.*—V. of Gamlingay, Dio. Ely, 1847. (Patron, Bp of Ely; V.'s Inc. 315*l* and Ho; Pop. 2004.) R. of Gamlingay, Dio. Ely, 1849. (Patron, Mert. Coll. Ox; R.'s Inc. 300*l*.) [14]

JAMES, John Burleigh, *Knowbury, Ludlow, Salop.*—St. John's Coll. Cam. B.A. 1834, M.A. 1850; Deac. 1836, Pr. 1837. P. C. of St. Paul's, Knowbury, Dio. Herf. 1841. (Patron, Bp of Wor; P. C.'s Inc. 90*l*; Pop. 655.) Author, *My Duty*, Rivingtons; *Thoughts on the Fathers*, ib; *A Sermon*, ib. [15]

JAMES, J. F., *Hackford, Reepham, Norfolk.*—C. of Hackford with Whitwell 1866. Formerly C. of St. Margaret's, Lynn Regis. [16]

JAMES, Joseph Hobart, *St. Stephen's, Canterbury.*—Corpus Coll. Cam. B.A. 1835; Deac. 1836 and Pr. 1837 by Abp of Cant. R. of All Saints', and St. Mildred with St. Mary-de-Castro R. City and Dio. Cant. 1839. (Patron, Ld Chan; R.'s Inc. 130*l*; Pop. All Saints' 457, St. Mary-de-Castro 2281.) [17]

JAMES, Josiah, *Abbey-Dore, near Hereford.*—St. John's Coll. Cam. B.A. 1829, M.A. 1832; Deac. 1829, Pr. 1830. R. of Abbey-Dore, Dio. Herf. 1839. (Patrons, Co-heirs of the late Duchess of Norfolk; Tithe, 680*l*; Glebe, 9 acres; R.'s Inc. 688*l*; Pop. 551.) [18]

JAMES, Moorhouse, *Bedford, Leigh, near Manchester.*—Jesus Coll. Cam. B.A. 1835, M.A. 1844. P. C. of Bedford, Leigh, Dio. Man. 1843. (Patron, V. of Leigh; Tithe—App. 9*s* 6*d*, Imp. 73*l* 11*s* 10*d*; P. C.'s Inc. 150*l*; Pop. 6558.) [19]

JAMES, Octavius, *Clarghyll Hall, Alston, Cumberland.*—St. John's Coll. Cam. B.A. 1841, M.A. 1848; Deac. 1841, Pr. 1842. R. of Kirkhaugh, Northumberland, Dio. Dur. 1846. (Patron, R. W. Saunder, Esq; Tithe, 80*l* 4*s*; Glebe, 2 acres; R.'s Inc. 100*l*; Pop. 223.) [20]

JAMES, Richard Lee, *Watford Vicarage, Herts.*—Clare Coll. Cam. LL.B. 1852; Deac. 1853, Pr. 1854. V. of Watford, Dio. Roch. 1855. (Patron, Earl of Essex; Tithe—Imp. 1424*l* 19*s* 5*d*, V. 669*l* 8*s* 11*d*; V.'s Inc. 670*l* and Ho; Pop. 5889.) Chap. of the D. of Oxhey, near Watford, Dio. Roch. 1856. (Patron, T. H. S. Estcourt, Esq; Chap.'s Inc. 55*l*.) [21]

JAMES, Robert, *Ubbeston, Yoxford, Suffolk.*—Ch. Miss. Coll. Islington; Deac. 1845 by Bp of Lon. Pr. 1846 by Bp of Roch. V. of Ubbeston, Dio. Nor. 1855. (Patron, Rev. E. Holland; Tithe, 315*l*; Glebe, 6¾ acres; V.'s Inc. 324*l*; Pop. 206.) [22]

JAMES, Robert William, *Southleigh Rectory, Colyton, Devon.*—Pemb. Coll. Ox. B.A. 1832. R. of Southleigh, Dio. Ex. 1847. (Patron, C. Gordon, Esq; Tithe, 226*l*; Glebe, 30 acres; R.'s Inc. 266*l* and Ho; Pop. 331.) Rural Dean. [23]

JAMES, Samuel Benjamin, *Winkfield, Windsor.*—Dub. A.B. 1851, A.M. 1864, Ox. M.A. *com. causâ*, 1865; Deac. 1855 and Pr. 1856 by Abp of York. C. of Winkfield, Berks. Formerly C. of Cottingham with Skidby, Yorks, 1855, St. Nicholas', Worcester, 1856–57. Author, *Duty and Doctrine*, 2nd ed. 1866; *The Church and Society*, 1867, etc. [24]

JAMES, Thomas, *Pembroke.*—C. of St. Dogmael's, Pembroke. [1]

JAMES, Thomas, *Netherthong Parsonage, Huddersfield.*—Deac. 1840, Pr. 1841. P. C. of Netherthong, Dio. Rip. 1846. (Patron, V. of Almondbury; P. C.'s Inc. 150*l* and Ho; Pop. 1640.) [2]

JAMES, Thomas, *Guildford, Surrey.*—Chap. of the Union, Guildford. [3]

JAMES, Thomas, *Rhos-Llanerchrugog, Wrexham.*—C. of Rhos-Llanerchrugog. [4]

JAMES, Walter Hill, *Woodford, Torquay.*—Ball. Coll. Ox. B.A. 1850, M.A. 1856; Deac. 1853 and Pr. 1854 by Bp of Ex. C. of St. Matthias' Chapel, Torwood, 1865. Formerly C. of St. Kenwyn and St. Kea, Cornwall, 1853–55, Heavitree, Devon, 1857–58, St. Mary Major, Exeter, 1858–60; V. of Croft, Lincolnshire, 1860–65. [5]

JAMES, William Browne, *Fen Ditton Rectory, near Cambridge.*—Jesus Coll. Cam. B.A. 1825, M.A. 1828. R. of Fen Ditton, Dio. Ely, 1844. (Patron, Bp of Ely; R.'s Inc. 440*l* and Ho; Pop. 581.) [6]

JAMES, William Edward, 6, *Nelson-place, Bath.*—Dub. A.B. 1854, A.M. 1859; Deac. and Pr. 1855. C. of Trinity, Bath. [7]

JAMES, William Evan, *Abergwili Vicarage, Carmarthen.*—Jesus Coll. Ox. Hon. 4th cl. Lit. Hum. B.A. 1852, M.A. 1855; Deac. 1854 and Pr. 1856 by Bp of St. D. V. of Abergwili, Dio. St. D. 1861. (Patron, Bp of St. D; Glebe, 4 acres; V.'s Inc. 175*l* and Ho; Pop. 2197.) Welsh Exam. Chap. to Bp. of St. D. Formerly C. of St. Peter's, Carmarthen; Vice-Prin. of the Carmarthen Training Coll. 1853. [8]

JAMES, William Richard, *Newton-upon-Trent Vicarage, Newark.*—Caius Coll. Cam. B.A. 1855; Deac. 1856 and Pr. 1857 by Bp of Lon. V. of Newton-upon-Trent, Dio. Lin. 1863. (Patrons, Lord and Lady Thomas Hay; Tithe, 224*l*; V.'s Inc. 226*l* and Ho; Pop. 325.) Formerly C. of Trinity, Sloane-street, Lond. 1856–59, Hailsham, Sussex, 1860–63. [9]

JAMESON, Francis James, *Coton Rectory, near Cambridge.*—Late Fell. and Tut. of St. Cath. Coll. Cam. Fell. of Caius Coll. 6th Wrang. and B.A. 1850, Norrisian Theol. Prizeman 1852, M.A. 1853, Select Preacher 1862; Deac. 1852 and Pr. 1853 by Bp of Ely. R. of Coton, Dio. Ely, 1862. (Patron, St. Cath. Coll. Cam; Glebe, 143 acres; R.'s Inc. 224*l* and Ho; Pop. 311.) Formerly C. of St. Sepulchre's, Cambridge, 1852–62. Author, *Solutions of Senate-House Riders,* 1851; *Analogy between the Doctrines and Miracles* (Norrisian Prize Essay), 1852; *Brotherly Counsels to Students,* 1859; *Life's Work* (Sermons preached before the University of Cambridge) 1863; all published by Macmillan and Co. [10]

JAMESON, George Browne.—Wad. Coll. Ox. B.A. 1864; Deac. 1865 and Pr. 1866 by Bp of Ox. Formerly C. of St. Cross, Oxford. [11]

JAMESON, Joseph, *Ripon.*—Deac. 1816 and Pr. 1817 by Abp of York. Precentor and Min. Can. of Rip. Cathl. 1821. (Value, 300*l*.) P. C. of Cleasby, Yorks, Dio. Rip. 1826. (Patrons, D. and C. of Rip; Tithe—Imp. 57*l* 15*s*; Glebe, 120 acres; P. C.'s Inc. 200*l* and Ho; Pop. 189.) [12]

JAMESON, J., *Warwick.*—V. of St. Nicholas', Warwick, Dio. Wor. 1859. (Patron, Earl of Warwick; V.'s Inc. 218*l* and Ho; Pop. 2499.) [13]

JAMIESON, J. Awdry, *Tiverton, Devon.*—C. of St. Paul's, Tiverton. [14]

JAMIESON, William, *Amsterdam.*—British Chap. at Amsterdam and Utrecht. [15]

JANNINGS, George, *The Parsonage, Thorne, Yorks.*—Dub. A.B. 1850, Theol. Licen. and Prizeman of Dur; Deac. 1852 and Pr. 1853 by Bp of Dur. P. C. of Thorne, Dio. York, 1856. (Patron, the Hon. H. A. Coventry; Tithe—Imp. 1640*l*; Glebe, 40 acres; P. C.'s Inc. 160*l* and Ho; Pop. 3381.) Surrogate. Formerly C. of St. John's, Upper Holloway, Lond. Author, *Address to the Schoolmasters' Association of Doncaster,* Bell and Daldy, 4*d*. [16]

JANVRIN, Francis William, *Great Toller Vicarage, near Dorchester.*—Univ. Coll. Ox. B.A. 1857, M.A. 1859; Deac. 1860 and Pr. 1861 by Bp of B. and W. V. of Great Toller, Dio. Salis. 1864. (Patron, Frederick Janvrin, Esq; Tithe, comm. 92*l*; Glebe, 76 acres, let for 90*l*; V.'s Inc. 200*l* and Ho; Pop. 500.) Formerly C. of Portishead, Somerset, 1860–62, Wool, Dorset, 1863–64. [17]

JANVRIN, James Henry, *Brighton.*—Oriel Coll. Ox. B.A. 1840, M.A. 1843; Deac. 1841 and Pr. 1842 by Bp of Win. [18]

JAQUES, Kinton, *Leyland, Preston.*—Brasen. Coll. Ox. B.A. 1860, M.A. 1863; Deac. 1861 and Pr. 1862 by Bp of Man. C. of Leyland 1861. [19]

JAQUET, J. H.—C. of St. Peter's, Croydon, Surrey. [20]

JARBO, Peter John, *Calcutta.*—Deac. 1852 and Pr. 1853 by Bp of Madras. Chap. of the East India Government in Bengal 1859. Formerly Chap. of the Sailors' Home, North Shields; Morn. Preacher at Gillingham, Kent; previously Missionary of the S.P.G. in India, Author, *Sermons,* in Tamil and English. [21]

JARRATT, John, *North Cave, near Brough, Yorks.*—St. John's Coll. Cam. 1st Jun. Opt. and B.A. 1822, M.A. 1825; Deac. and Pr. 1822 by Bp of B. and W. V. of North Cave with Cliffe, Dio. York, 1830. (Patrons, H. Burton, Esq. and Sarah Burton, Hotham Hall; North Cave, Tithe—App. 1*l*, Imp. 158*l* 2*s* 6*d*, V. 56*l* 13*s*; Glebe, 55 acres; Cliffe, Tithe, 186*l* 15*s*; Glebe, 1 rood; V.'s Inc. 275*l* and Ho; Pop. 1281.) Can. and Preb. of Bole in York Cathl. 1858. [22]

JARRATT, Robert, *Bourton-on-the-Hill Rectory, Moreton-in-the-Marsh, Glouc.*—St. John's Coll. Cam. B.A. 1822, M.A. 1825; Deac and Pr. 1823. R. of Bourton-on-the-Hill with Moreton-in-the-Marsh, Dio. G. and B. 1855. (Patron, Lord Redesdale; Glebe, 700 acres; R.'s Inc. 700*l* and Ho; Pop. 1926.) Chap. to the Duke of St. Albans 1825. [23]

JARRETT, Thomas, *Trunch Rectory, North Walsham, Norfolk.*—St. Cath. Coll. Cam. 34th Wrang. 7th in 1st cl. Cl. Trip. and B.A. 1827, M.A. 1831; Deac. 1829 and Pr. 1830 by Bp of Lin. R. of Trunch, Dio. Nor. 1832. (Patron, St. Cath. Coll. Cam; Tithe, 412*l*; Glebe, 23 acres; R.'s Inc. 435*l* and Ho; Pop. 464.) Professor of Arabic 1831; Regius Professor of Hebrew in Cam. Univ. with Canonry of Ely Cathl. annexed, 1854. (Value, 600*l* and Res.) Formerly Fell. of St. Cath. Coll. Cam. 1828–32. Author, *A Grammatical Index to the Hebrew Text of the Book of Genesis, including a Hebrew Grammar,* 1830, 6*s*; *Essay on Algebraic Development, containing a New Notation for Series,* 1831, 5*s* 6*d*; *A New Hebrew Lexicon, Part I. Hebrew and English, the Words being arranged under their permanent Letters; Part II. English and Hebrew, with an Introduction containing a Hebrew Grammar and Analysis of the Book of Genesis, and an Appendix containing a Chaldee Grammar and Dictionary of the Chaldee Words in the Old Testament,* 1848, 20*s*; *A New Way of Marking the Sounds of English Words,* Quaritch, Lond. 1858, 1*s*; *The Holy Gospel and the Acts of the Apostles; so printed as to show the Sound of each Word without Change of Spelling,* ib. 1859, 7*s* 6*d*; *P. Virgilii Maronis Opera edidit et Syllabarum Quantitates novo eo que facili modo notavit,* Deighton, Bell and Co., 1866. [24]

JARRETT, Wilfrid Lawson, *Offchurch Vicarage, Leamington.*—St. John's Coll. Cam. B.A. 1824, M.A. 1827; Deac. 1827, Pr. 1828. V. of Offchurch, Dio. Wor. 1851. (Patrons, Lord and Lady Guernsey; Tithe—Imp. 400*l*, V. 300*l*; Glebe, 7 acres; V.'s Inc. 400*l* and Ho; Pop. 304.) [25]

JARVIS, Edwin George, *Hackthorn, near Lincoln.*—Trin. Coll. Cam. M.B. 1840; Deac. 1843 and Pr. 1844 by Bp of Lin. V. of Hackthorn with Cold Hanworth R. annexed, Dio. Lin. 1844. (Patron, W. Cracroft-Amcotts, Esq; Tithe, 113*l* 3*s* 6*d*; Glebe, 170 acres; V.'s Inc. 280*l*; Pop. Hackthorn 234, Cold Hanworth 91.) [26]

JARVIS, Frederic, *All Saints' Parsonage, Spicer-street, Spitalfields, London, N.E.*—St. Bees; Deac. 1857 and Pr. 1858 by Abp of York. P. C. of All Saints', Spicer-street, Mile End New Town, Dio. Lon. 1866.

(Patron, Bp of Lon; P. C.'s Inc. 300*l* and Ho; Pop. 12,000.) Formerly C. of Thorganby, Yorks, 1857, Nuneaton, Warwickshire, 1859, Spitalfields, Lond. 1863. [1]

JARVIS, Henry, *Clare House, Maze Hill, St. Leonards-on-Sea.*—Ch. Coll. Cam. B.A. 1843, M.A. 1847; Deac. 1844, Pr. 1845. Formerly C. of Trinity, Hanisfield, Macclesfield, 1844, Witney, Oxon, 1845; Sec. to the Lond. Soc. for Promoting Christianity among the Jews, 1846; C. of Park Chapel, Chelsea, 1855. [2]

JAY, William James, *Elvedon Rectory, near Thetford.*—St. Cath. Hall, Cam. Scho. of, B.A. 1847, M.A. 1850; Deac. 1847 and Pr. 1848 by Bp of Roch. R. of Elvedon, Dio. Ely, 1865. (Patron, H.H. Prince Duleep Singh; R.'s Inc. net, 300*l* and Ho; Pop. 193.) Formerly C. of Goldhanger, near Maldon, 1847-49; Asst. Chap. on Bengal Establishment 1850–60; Chap. of East India Hospital, Poplar, 1860–66. [3]

JEAFFRESON, Charles Babington, *Christ Church Rectory, Heaton Norris, Stockport.*—Pemb. Coll. Cam. B.A. 1841, M.A. 1844; Deac. 1842, and Pr. 1844 by Bp of Ches. R. of Ch. Ch. Heaton Norris, Dio. Man. 1846. (Patron, Bp of Man; Tithe—App. 206*l* 10*s*; R.'s Inc. 300*l* and Ho; Pop. 7490.) Surrogate. Formerly C. of Wilmslow, Cheshire, 1842–46. Author, *Sermons*, 1859, 5*s*; *Sermons*, 1866, 5*s*. [4]

JEAFFRESON, Christopher, *Edmonton, Middlesex.*—Pemb. Coll. Cam. Sen. Opt. B.A. 1816, M.A. 1828; Deac. 1816, Pr. 1817. Chap. of the Edmonton Union 1842. [5]

JEAKES, James, *Harrow-on-the-Hill, N.W.*—St. Peter's Coll. Cam. Wrang. and Sen. in Nat. Sci. Trip. 1853, B.A. 1852, M.A. 1855; Deac. 1853 and Pr. 1854 by Bp of Ely. Fell. of St. Peter's Coll. Cam. 1855; Hon. Fell. of King's Coll. Lond; C. of Harrow 1855. [6]

JEBB, John, *Peters'ow Rectory, near Ross, Herefordshire.*—Dub. A.B. 1826, A.M. 1829, D.D. 1862; Deac. 1828, Pr. 1829. R. of Peterstow, Dio. Herf. 1843. (Patron, James Barrett, Esq; Tithe, 395*l*; Glebe, 25 acres; R.'s Inc. 421*l* and Ho; Pop. 276.) Preb. of Preston Wynne in Herf. Cathl. 1858; Prælector of Hereford 1863. Formerly R. of Dunurlin, Ireland, 1831–32; Preb. of Donoughmore, in Limerick Cathl. 1832–43. Author, *The Divine Economy of the Church*, 1840; *The Choral Service of the United Church of England and Ireland*, 1843; *A Literal Translation of the Book of Psalms with Dissertations, &c.* 2 vols. 1846; *Three Lectures on the Cathedral Service*, 1841; *A Dialogue on the Choral Service*, 1842; *The Choral Responses and Litanies of the United Churches of England and Ireland*, 2 vols. folio. Vol. I. 1847, Vol. II. Cocks and Co. 1857; *Six Letters on the Present State of the Church*, 1851; *A Plea for what is left of the Cathedrals*, 1852; *Hints on Reading the Liturgy*, 1853; Sermons—*On Emigration*, 1838; *On Psalm* cxxxii. 7, 8, 9 (published among the Sermons preached at the Consecration of Leeds Parish Church), 1841; *Truth and Unity* (preached at Hereford), 1843; *Wisdom Justified of all her Children*, 1844; *The Ministerial Office*, and *The Sealing of the Holy Spirit* (both inserted in *Practical Sermons*), 1845; *The Principle of Ritualism Defended*, Rivingtons, 1856; *The Ritual, Law, and Custom of the Church Universal*, Rivingtons, 1866. [7]

JECKELL, Joseph John, *Norwich.*—St. John's Coll. Cam. Jun. Opt. B.A. 1851; Deac. 1853 and Pr. 1854 by Bp of Nor. Assoc. Sec. of the Jews' Society, Norwich. Formerly C. of All Saints', South Elmham, 1853, East and West Rudham 1855, St. Helen's and St. Clement's, Ipswich, 1856, Abbey Church, Bath, 1860. [8]

JEFF, William, *Farnworth, Warrington.*—Deac. 1817 and Pr. 1818 by Bp of Ches. P. C. of Farnworth, Dio. Ches. 1832. (Patron, V. of Prescot; P. C.'s Inc. 300*l* and Ho; Pop. 6447.) [9]

JEFFCOATT, Tom, *Hitchin, Herts.*—Trin. Coll. Cam. B.A. 1856, M.A. 1859; Deac. 1855, Pr. 1856. C. of St. Ippolyt's, Great Wymondley. Formerly C. of Rostherne, Cheshire, 1860. [10]

JEFFCOCK, John Thomas, *The Vicarage, Wolstanton, Stoke-on-Trent.*—Oriel Coll. Ox. 2nd cl. Lit. Hum. B.A. 1857, M.A. 1859; Deac. 1859 and Pr. 1860 by Bp of Nor. V. of Wolstanton, Dio. Lich. 1867. (Patron, Ralph Sneyd, Esq; Tithe, 350*l*; Glebe, 36 acres; V.'s Inc. 400*l* and Ho; Pop. 2800.) Formerly C. of Swaffham, Norfolk, 1859-61; P. C. of St. Saviour's, Hoxton, Lond. 1861–67. Author, *Memoir of his Brother Mr. Parkin Jeffcock*, Bemrose and Lothian, 1867, 3*s* 6*d*. [11]

JEFFERIES, Edward, *Grasmere, Westmoreland.*—Dub. A.B. 1847, A.M. 1865; Deac. 1848 and Pr. 1849 by Bp of Ches. R. of Grasmere, Dio. Carl. 1862. (Patron, General Le Fleming; R.'s Inc. 109*l* and Ho; Pop. 604.) Formerly C. of Grasmere 1840–62. [12]

JEFFERSON, Joseph, *North Stainley, Ripon.*—St. John's Coll. Cam. 2nd Jun. Opt. 3rd cl. Cl. Trip. and B.A. 1845; Deac. 1848 and Pr. 1849 by Bp of Rip. P.C. of North Stainley, Dio. Rip. 1851. (Patron, D. and C. of Rip; P. C.'s Inc. 300*l* and Ho; Pop. 514.) [13]

JEFFERSON, Joseph Dunnington, *Thicket Priory, York.*—St. John's Coll. Cam. Wrang. and B.A. 1830, M.A. 1833; Deac. 1831 and Pr. 1832 by Abp of York. P. C. of Thorganby, near York, Dio. York, 1832. (Patron, the present P. C; Glebe, 1 acre; P. C.'s Inc. 50*l*; Pop. 407.) Preb. of Osbaldwick in York Cathl. 1852. Author, *Sermon* (on the Liturgy), 1840; *Sermon* (on Family Worship), 1841; *Sermon* (on the Death of two Infants), 1847; *Sermon* (at the Consecration of St. Mary's, Ellerton), 1848; various other Sermons. [14]

JEFFERSON, Lancelot, *Brough, Westmoreland.*—Queen's Coll. Ox. B.A. 1806, M.A. 1810; Deac. 1808 and 1809 by Bp of Win. V. of Brough, Dio. Carl. 1828. (Patron, Queen's Coll. Ox; Tithe—Imp. 107*l* 0*s* 4¾*d*, V. 66*l* 0*s* 6*d*; Glebe, 40 acres; V.'s Inc. 305*l* and Ho; Pop. 1056.) Hon. Can. of Carl; Surrogate; Rural Dean of Kirkby-Stephen 1857. [15]

JEFFERY, Frederick, *Sway Parsonage, Lymington, Hants.*—St. John's Coll. Cam. 10th Jun. Opt. and B.A. 1837, M.A. 1840; Deac. 1837, Pr. 1838. P. C. of Sway, Dio. Win. 1843. (Patron, Bp of Win; Glebe, 2 acres; P. C.'s Inc. 116*l*; Pop. 694.) Dom. Chap. to Viscount Molesworth. [16]

JEFFREYS, David, *Taliaris, Llandilo, Carmarthenshire.*—Lampeter; Deac. 1825, Pr. 1826. P. C. of Taliaris, Dio. St. D. 1866. (Patron, William Peel, Esq; Glebe, 8 acres; P. C.'s Inc. 111*l* and Ho; Pop. 100.) Formerly C. of Llanganten 1825–35, St. Bride's Major 1838–42, North Llantwit 1843-50; R. of Newborough, Anglesey, 1851–66. [17]

JEFFREYS, Henry Anthony, *Hawkhurst Parsonage, Staplehurst, Kent.*—Ch. Ch. Ox. B.A. 1832, M.A. 1834. P. C. of Hawkhurst, Dio. Cant. 1839. (Patron, Ch. Ch. Ox; Tithe—App. 959*l* 11*s* 5½*d*; P. C.'s Inc. 250*l* and Ho; Pop. 2537.) Stud. of Ch. Ch. Ox. [18]

JEKYLL, Joseph, *Hawkridge, Dulverton, Somerset.*—St. John's Coll. Cam. B.A. 1831; Deac. 1833, Pr. 1834. R. of Hawkridge with Withypoole, C. Dio. B. and W. 1847. (Patron, Rev. G. Jekyll; Hawkridge, Tithe, 84*l* 5*s*; Glebe, 316 acres; Withypoole, Tithe, 161*l*, Glebe, 30 acres; R.'s Inc. 406*l* and Ho; Pop. Hawkridge 110, Withypoole 307.) [19]

JELF, George Edward, *Aylesbury.*—Ch. Ch. Ox. B.A. 1856, M.A. 1859; Deac. 1858 and Pr. 1859 by Bp of Ox. C. of St. Mary's, Aylesbury, 1866. Formerly C. of St. Michael's, Highgate, 1858–60, St. James's, Clapton, 1860–66. [20]

JELF, Richard William, *King's College, London, W.C.* and *Christ Church, Oxford.*—Ch. Ch. Ox. 2nd cl. Lit. Hum. and B.A. 1820, Oriel Coll. M.A. 1823, Ch. Ch. B.D. 1821, D.D. 1839; Deac. 1823 and Pr. 1824 by Bp of Ox. Canon of Ch. Ch. Oxford (Value, 700*l* and Res); Prin. of King's Coll. Lond. 1844; Sub-Almoner to the Queen. Formerly Fell. and Tut. of Oriel Coll. Ox; Public Examiner 1825; Preceptor to H.R.H. Prince George of Cumberland (King of Hanover), 1826-39; Bampton Lecturer 1844. Author, *Sermons, Doctrinal and Practical*, 1835; *Via Media, or the Church of England our Providential Path between Romanism and Dissent* (a Sermon), 1842; *An Inquiry into the Means of Grace, their mutual Connection and combined Use, with special Reference to the Church of England*

(Eight Sermons), 1844; *A Sermon preached at the Festival of the Sons of Clergy* (printed in the Report), 1845; *The Efficacy of Christian Repentance*; *The Maintenance of the Christian Ministry of Divine Appointment* (Two Sermons inserted in *Practical Sermons*), Vol. I. 1845; *Concio ad Clerum Provinciæ Cantuariensis* (John xiv. 27), 1847; *Grounds for laying before the Council of King's College, London, certain Statements contained in the Theological Essays, by the Rev. F. D. Maurice*, 1853. [1]

JELF, William Edward, *Caerdeon, Dolgelly, North Wales.*—Ch. Ch. Ox. 1829, 1st cl. Lit. Hum. and B.A. 1833, M.A. 1836, B.D. 1844; Deac. 1834, Pr. 1835. Formerly Tut. of Ch. Ch. Ox. 1836–49; Censor 1841–49; Public Examiner 1841–55; Jun. Proctor 1843; Bampton Lect. 1857; Whitehall Preacher 1846–48. Author, *Greek Grammar*, 2 vols. 1842, 2nd ed. 1851; *Sermons*, preached at Whitehall; *Every One Salted with Fire* (preached before the University), 1846; *Appendix to Eton Greek Grammar*, for the use of Eton School, 1849; *Aristotle's Ethics, with English Notes*, 1855; *Bampton Lectures—Christianity Comprehensive and Definite*, 1857, 3rd ed. 1859. [2]

JELLICOE, George Streynsham, *St. Peter's Parsonage, Chorley, Lancashire.*—All Souls Coll. Ox. B.A. 1850, M.A. 1853; Deac. 1853 and Pr. 1854 by Bp of Win. P. C. of St. Peter's, Chorley, Dio. Man. 1860. (Patron, R. of Chorley; P. C.'s Inc. 150*l* and Ho; Pop. 2207.) Formerly C. of Caterham, and of Weybridge, Surrey, Pear Tree Green, Southampton. Author, *Songs of the Church, a Supplemental Hymnal*, Novello, 1867. [3]

JELLICORSE, William, *Clunbury Parsonage, Ludlow, Salop.*—Magd. Coll. Cam. B.A. 1854. P. C. of Clunbury, Dio. Herf. 1856. (Patron, Earl of Powis; Tithe—Imp. 472*l* 12*s* 6*d*; P. C.'s Inc. 120*l* and Ho; Pop. 1029.) [4]

JELLIE, Harry R., *Alberbury, near Shrewsbury.*—C. of Alberbury. [5]

JELLY, John Bonafous, *Macclesfield.*—Dub. A.B. 1848; Deac. 1851 by Abp of Dub. Pr. 1852 by Bp of Killaloe. C. of Macclesfield 1861. Formerly C. of Clonbullogue, Dublin, 1858, and St. Michael's, Manchester, 1860. [6]

JEMISON, William Henry, *Coneysthorpe, Malton, Yorks.*—Dub. A.B. LL.B. 1856; Deac. 1861 and Pr. 1862 by Bp of Carl. C. of Barton-le-Street, Yorks, 1864. Formerly Barrington Lect. on Political Economy, Dublin, 1857–60; C. of St. Nicholas', Whitehaven, 1861–64. [7]

JENKIN, Charles, *Herringswell Rectory, Mildenhall, Suffolk.*—St. Peter's Coll. Cam. B.A. 1814, M.A. 1818, B.D. and D.D. 1828; Deac. 1814 and Pr. 1818 by Bp of Nor. R. of Herringswell, Dio. Ely, 1853. (Patron, Rev. J. T. H. Tooke; Glebe, 363 acres; R.'s Inc. 279*l* and Ho; Pop. 203.) [8]

JENKIN, Evan Alfred, *Tregynnon, Montgomeryshire.*—Caius Coll. Cam. B.A. 1854, M.A. 1857; Deac. 1854 by Bp of Man. Pr. 1858 by Bp of Llan. P. C. of Tregynnon, Dio. St. A. 1868. (Patron, Lord Sudeley; Tithe, 90*l*; P. C.'s Inc. 180*l*; Pop. 703.) Formerly C. of Devizes. [9]

JENKIN, George, *Norton Parsonage, Worcester.*—Dub. A.B. 1846, A.M. 1849; Deac. and Pr. 1847 by Bp of Ches. P. C. of Norton-juxta-Kempsey, Dio. Wor. 1864. (Patrons, D. and C. of Wor; P. C.'s Inc. 100*l* and Ho; Pop. 661.) Formerly C. of Churchill, Worcester. [10]

JENKIN, John Fothergill, *Rochdale.*—St. John's Coll. Cam. B.A. 1860, M.A. 1863; Deac. 1862 and Pr. 1863 by Bp of Ches. C. of Rochdale 1865. Formerly C. of Cheadle, Hulme, near Stockport, 1862–63, Mossley, near Manchester, 1863–65. [11]

JENKINS, Alfred Augustus, *Barnack (Northants), near Stamford.*—King's Coll. Lond. Theol. Assoc; Deac. 1857 and Pr. 1858 by Bp of Pet. C. of Barnack 1859. Formerly C. of Raunds, Northants. [12]

JENKINS, Charles Edward, 14, *Rue des Champs Elysées, Brussels.*—Magd. Coll. Cam. Jun. Opt. 4th in 2nd cl. Cl. Trip. and B.A. 1850, M.A. 1853; Deac. 1850 and Pr. 1851 by Bp of Ely. Chap. of the British Chapel Royal at Brussels 1856. Formerly Fell. of Magd. Coll. Cam. [13]

JENKINS, David, *St. Goran, St. Austell, Cornwall.*—Ex. Coll. Ox. B.A. 1818. V. of St. Goran, Dio. Ex. 1824. (Patron, Bp of Ex; Tithe—App. 543*l*, V. 326*l*; V.'s Inc. 339*l* and Ho; Pop. 1054.) [14]

JENKINS, David, *Rhes-y-Cae, Holywell, Flintshire.*—Lampeter, Scho. and Prizeman; Deac. 1851 and Pr. 1852 by Bp of Llan. P. C. of Rhes-y-Cae, Dio. St. A. 1854. (Patron, Bp of St. A; Glebe, 4 acres; P. C.'s Inc. 234*l* and Ho; Pop. 627.) [15]

JENKINS, David, *Millbank Cottage, Carmarthen.*—Lampeter, B.D. 1863; Deac. 1857 and Pr. 1858 by Bp of St. D. P. C. of Llanllwch, Dio. St. D. 1861. (Patron, Bp of St. D; P. C.'s Inc. 160*l*; Pop. 896.) P. C. of Llangain, Dio. St D. 1865. (Patron, F. Bledworth, Esq; P. C.'s Inc. 100*l*; Pop. 393.) Surrogate; Hon. Chap. to the Independent Order of Oddfellows of Carmarthen. Formerly C. of St. John's, Llanelly, 1857, and Merthyr and St. David's, Carmarthen, 1858. [16]

JENKINS, Edward, *Billinghay Vicarage, Sleaford, Lincolnshire.*—Deac. 1830, Pr. 1831. V. of Billinghay with Walcott, Dio. Lin. 1832. (Patron, the Hon. G. W. Fitzwilliam; Glebe, 252 acres; V.'s Inc. 550*l* and Ho; Pop. Billinghay 1642, Walcott 605.) [17]

JENKINS, Edward, *St. Mellon's Vicarage, near Cardiff.*—Literate; Deac. 1838 and Pr. 1839 by Bp of Llan. V. of St. Mellon's with Llanederne V. Dio. Llan. 1846. (Patron, Bp of Llan; St. Mellon's, Tithe—App. 302*l* 15*s*, V. 111*l* 12*s* 2*d*; Glebe, 39 acres; Llanederne, Tithe—App. 155*l*, Imp. 40*l*, V. 60*l*; Glebe, 10 acres; V.'s Inc. 253*l* and Ho; Pop. St. Mellon's 688, Llanederne 289.) [18]

JENKINS, Edward, *Aberthin House, near Cowbridge.*—Jesus Coll. Ox. Scho. of, B.A. 1864, M.A. 1866; Deac. 1866 by Bp of Llan. C. of Cowbridge and Welsh St. Donatts 1866. [19]

JENKINS, Evan, *Llangyniew Rectory, near Welshpool.*—M.A. 1855 by Abp of Cant; Deac. 1822 and Pr. 1823 by Bp of Llan. R. of Llangyniew, Dio. St. A. 1862. (Patron, Ld Chan; Tithe, 394*l*; Glebe, 20 acres; R.'s Inc. 480*l* and Ho; Pop. 306.) Can. of Llan. Formerly R. of Dowlais, Glamorgan, 1827–62. Author, *Chartism Unmasked*, 1840, more than 21,000 copies sold; numerous Sermons in Welsh and English. [20]

JENKINS, Evan, *The Rectory, Flint.*—Jesus Coll. Ox. B.A. 1855; Deac. 1856 and Pr. 1857 by Bp of St. A. R. of Flint, Dio. St. A. 1865. (Patron, Bp of St. A; Tithe, 311*l*; R.'s Inc. 311*l* and Ho; Pop. 3068.) Formerly C. of Nerthop 1856–65. [21]

JENKINS, Evan, *Loughor Rectory, Llanelly.*—R. of Loughor, Dio. St. D. 1865. (Patron, Ld Chan; R.'s Inc. 200*l* and Ho; Pop. 1238.) [22]

JENKINS, George, *Manaton Rectory, Moretonhampstead, Exeter.*—Lin. Coll. Ox. B.A. 1844, M.A. 1847, Theol. Coll. Chichester; Deac. 1844 by Bp of Win. Pr. 1847 by Bp of Chich. R. of Manaton, Dio. Ex. 1852. (Patron, Rev. W. Carwithen; Tithe—App. 34*l* 8*s*, R. 230*l*; Glebe, 40 acres; R.'s Inc. 280*l* and Ho; Pop. 415.) [23]

JENKINS, Henry, *Stanway Rectory, Colchester.*—Magd. Coll. Ox. 1803, B.A. 1806, M.A. 1809, B.D. 1827; Deac. 1809, Pr. 1811. R. of Stanway, Dio. Roch. 1830. (Patron, Magd. Coll. Ox; Tithe, 776*l*; Glebe, 78¾ acres; R.'s Inc. 883*l* and Ho; Pop. 531.) Formerly Fell. of Magd. Coll. Ox. Author, *A Lecture on Colchester Castle*, 1852, 2*s* 6*d*; *Appendix to same*, 1853, 1*s* 6*d*; *On Roman Roads from Colchester*, in *Journal of the British Archæological Association*, 1863. [24]

JENKINS, Hinton Best, *Tamworth.*—C. of Tamworth. [25]

JENKINS, Isaac Domere, *St. Fagan's Rectory, Aberdare.*—Ch. Coll. Cam. 1st cl. Civil Law Trip. LL.B. 1854; Deac. 1851, Pr. 1852. P. C. of St. Fagan's, Aberdare, Dio. Llan. 1855. (Patron, Bp of Llan; P. C.'s Inc. 150*l* and Ho; Pop. 1740.) Formerly C. of Aberdare, 1851–55. [26]

JENKINS, James, *Blakesley Vicarage, Towcester, Northants.*—St. Aidan's; Deac. 1860 and Pr. 1861 by Bp of Ches. V. of Blakesley, Dio. Pet. 1863. (Patron, J. W. Wight, Esq; V.'s Inc. 300*l* and Ho; Pop. 777.) [1]

JENKINS, Jenkin, *Little Waltham, Chelmsford.*—Lin. Coll. Ox. B.A. 1843, M.A. 1845; Deac. 1843 and Pr. 1844 by Bp of Ex. Min. of Black Chapel, Great Waltham, 1866. Formerly C. of Brampford Speke, Exeter, 1843–46, Little Leighs, Essex, 1846, Great Leighs 1847–66. [2]

JENKINS, John Card, *Brussels.*—Magd. Coll. Cam. B.A. 1859; Deac. 1859 and Pr. 1860 by Bp of Lon. Asst. Chap. of the Chapel Royal, Brussels, 1860. [3]

JENKINS, John Clarke, *Braunston, near Rugby.*—Lin. Coll. Ox. B.A. 1818, M.A. 1821; Deac. 1822, Pr. 1823. V. of Ashby St. Leonard's, Northants, Dio. Pet. 1840. (Patroness, Lady Senhouse; Tithe, 20*l*; Glebe, 66 acres; V.'s Inc. 140*l* and Ho; Pop. 300*l*.) [4]

JENKINS, John Gower, *Edinburgh.*—Univ. Coll. Dur. Licen. Theol. 1853; Deac. 1853 and Pr. 1854 by Bp of Dur. Formerly C. of Kirkby-in-Malhamdale, Yorks, 1854–58; P. C. of St. Osyth, Essex, 1858–61. [5]

JENKINS, John David, *Oxford.*—Fell. of Jesus Coll. Formerly C. of St. Paul's, Oxford. [6]

JENKINS, John Horner, *Hazlewood, Belper, Derbyshire.*—Trin. Coll. Cam. Sen. Opt. and B.A. 1834; Deac. 1836, Pr. 1847. P. C. of Hazlewood, Dio. Lich. 1846. (Patron, Bp of Lich; P. C.'s Inc. 160*l*; Pop. 2286.) [7]

JENKINS, John Rees, *Roath, Cardiff.*—Queens' Coll. Cam. 1st Math. Scho. and Prizeman of, 1862, B.A. 1864; Deac. 1865 and Pr. 1867 by Bp of Llan. C. of Roath 1865. [8]

JENKINS, Maurice Edward, 65, *James-street, Blackburn.*—Ch. Coll. Cam. B.A. 1864; Deac. 1866 by Bp of Man. C. of Trinity, Blackburn, 1866. [9]

JENKINS, Owen, *Longworth Rectory, Faringdon, Berks.*—Jesus Coll. Ox. B.A. 1822, M.A. 1824, B.D. 1833; Deac. 1823, Pr. 1824. R. of Longworth, Dio. Ox. 1841. (Patron, Jesus Coll. Ox; Tithe—Imp. 117*l* 17*s* 6*d*, R. 800*l* 13*s* 9*d*; R.'s Inc. 870*l* and Ho; Pop. 1131.) Formerly Fell. of Jesus Coll. Ox. [10]

JENKINS, R. J.—Chap. of H.M.S. "Colossus." [11]

JENKINS, Rhys Thomas, *Mydrim Vicarage, St. Clear, Carmarthenshire.*—Lampeter, Prizeman 1843; Deac. 1842 and Pr. 1843 by Bp of St. D. V. of Mydrim with Llanvihangel Abercowin C. Dio. St. D. 1847. (Patron, Bp of St. D; V.'s Inc. 90*l* and Ho; Pop. Mydrim 992, Llanvihangel Abercowin 893.) P. C. of Llanginning, Carmarthenshire, Dio. St. D. 1854. (Patron, C. G. Philipps, Esq; Tithe—Imp. 200*l*; Glebe, 183 acres; P. C.'s Inc. 100*l*; Pop. 378.) Formerly C. of Newchurch, Carmarthenshire. [12]

JENKINS, Richard, *Trefdraeth, Anglesey.*—Dub. A.B. 1852; Deac. 1854 by Bp of St. D. Pr. 1855 by Bp of Ely. C. of Trefdraeth and Llangwyfan; Chap. to the Earl of Lisburne. Formerly P. C. of Gwnnws, Cardiganshire, 1856–61; C. of St. Michael's, Aberystwith. [13]

JENKINS, Robert Charles, *Lyminge Rectory, Hythe.*—Trin. Coll. Cam. B.A. 1841, M.A. 1844; Deac. 1841 and Pr. 1842 by Bp of Lon. R. and V. of Lyminge with the Chapelry of Paddlesworth, Dio. Cant. 1854. (Patron, the present R; Tithe—Lyminge, 769*l* 5*s*, Paddlesworth, 90*l*; Glebe, 72*l*; R.'s Inc. 922*l* 5*s* and Ho; Pop. Lyminge 938, Paddlesworth 57.) Formerly C. of Willesden 1841–43; P. C. of Ch. Ch. Turnham Green, 1843–54. Author, *On the Rite of the Presanctified*, 1840; *A Plea for Christian Peace and Unity*, 1842; *The Judgment of Cardinal Cajetan on the Immaculate Conception, with Introduction*, 1858; *The Life and Times of Cardinal Julian of the House of Cesarini*, 1861; *The Rest of the Churches* (a Sermon), 1862; *Some Account of the Church or Minster of St. Mary and St. Eadburg in Lyminge from its Foundation in 633 till its Surrender by Archbishop Cranmer in 1546*, 1858; various papers in the Transactions of the Kent Archæological Soc; Pamphlets, Sermons, etc. [14]

JENKINS, Thomas, *Great Trefgarn Rectory, Haverfordwest, Pembrokeshire.*—Lampeter; Deac. 1824 and Pr. 1825 by Bp of St. D. R. of Great Trefgarn, Dio. St. D. 1826. (Patron, David Evans, Esq; Tithe, 37*l*; R.'s Inc. 60*l* and Ho; Pop. 86.) P. C. of Spittal, Pembrokeshire, Dio. St. D. 1839. (Patrons, Precentor of St. D. Cathl. and Chancellor of St. Paul's Cathl. Lond; Tithe, App. 152*l*; Glebe, 32 acres; P. C.'s Inc. 80*l*; Pop. 392.) [15]

JENKINS, Thomas, *Caerphilly, Cardiff.*—P. C. of St. Martin's, Caerphilly, Dio. Llan. 1865. (Patrons, D. and C. of Llan; P. C.'s Inc. 120*l*; Pop. 1198.) [16]

JENKINS, Thomas, *Church-street, Beaumaris.*—Dub. A.B. 1858; Deac. 1860 and Pr. 1861 by Bp of Ban. Chap. to the Anglesey Gaol 1866. Formerly C. of Clynnog, Llandudno, and Carnarvon. [17]

JENKINS, William, *Llangammarch, Builth, Brecknockshire.*—Deac. 1813, Pr. 1814. V. of Llangammarch with Llanwrtyd C. and Llanddewi-Abergwessin C. Dio. St. D. 1838. (Patron, Bp of St. D; Llangammarch, Tithe—App. 238*l* 13*s* 4*d*, V. 119*l* 6*s* 8*d*; Llanwrtyd, Tithe—App. 127*l* 7*s* 1*d*, V. 60*l* 14*s* 0½*d*; Llanddewi-Abergwessin, Tithe—App. 58*l*, V. 29*l*; V.'s Inc. 209*l*; Pop. Llangammarch 1078, Llanwrtyd 607, Llanddewi-Abergwessin 111.) [18]

JENKINS, William, *Michaelston-y-Vedw, Newport, Monmouthshire.*—Deac. 1842, Pr. 1843. R. of Michaelston-y-Vedw, Dio. Llan. 1851. (Patron, Colonel C. K. K. Tynte; Tithe, 495*l* 8*s* 8*d*; Glebe, 17 acres; R.'s Inc. 530*l* and Ho; Pop. 512.) [19]

JENKINS, William Henry, *The Mission House, Anchor-street, Shoreditch, N.E.*—Theol. Assoc. King's Coll. Lond. 1852; Deac. 1852 and Pr. 1853 by Bp of Lon. P. C. of Trinity, Shoreditch, Dio. Lon. 1867. (Patrons, the Crown and Bp of Lon. alt; P. C.'s Inc. 200*l*; Pop. 6000.) Formerly C. of St. Margaret's, Westminster, 1852–64; Sen. C. of Greenwich 1865–66; C. of Ch. Ch. East Greenwich 1866–67. [20]

JENKINS, William James, *Fillingham Rectory, near Lincoln.*—Ball. Coll. Ox. B.A. 1841, M.A. 1846; Deac. 1843 and Pr. 1845 by Bp of Ox. R. of Fillingham, Dio. Lin. 1852. (Patron, Ball. Coll. Ox; Glebe, 467 acres; R.'s Inc. 846*l* and Ho; Pop. 316.) Dom. Chap. to the Earl of Cardigan. Formerly Fell. of Ball. Ox; C. of Ramsgate 1848–52. Author, *Synchronistical Annals of the Kings and Prophets of Israel and Judah*, 4to. 1842, 5*s*; *Prose Hymns for Children*, Masters; etc. [21]

JENKINS, William Marsden, *Llanllwchaiarn Newtown, Montgomeryshire.*—Jesus Coll. Ox. B.A. 1864; Deac. 1865 and Pr. 1866 by Bp. of St. A. C. of Llanllwchaiarn. [22]

JENKINSON, George, *Lowick Parsonage, Berwick-on-Tweed.*—St. Bees; Deac. 1822 by Bp of Lin. Pr. 1823 by Bp of Ox. P. C. of Lowick, Dio. Dur. 1829. (Patrons, D. and C. of Dur; Tithe—App. 184*l* 1*s* 2*d*, Imp. 155*l* 17*s* 2*d*; Glebe, 147 acres; P. C.'s Inc. 354*l* and Ho; Pop. 1946.) [23]

JENKINSON, John Simon, *The Vicarage, Church-road, Battersea, London, S.W.*—Magd. Hall, Ox. B.A. 1827; Deac. 1829 and Pr. 1830 by Bp of B. and W. V. of Battersea with Ch. Ch. C. Dio. Win. 1847. (Patron, Earl Spencer; Tithe—Imp. 45*l*, V. 980*l* 5*s* 9*d*; V.'s Inc. 995*l* and Ho; Pop. 7908.) Formerly R. of Sudbourn with Orford, 1831–34; P. C. of St. Mary-in-the-Castle, Hastings, 1834–47. Author, *A Collection of Psalms and Hymns*, 1833; *On Confirmation*, 1837; *Marriage with a Deceased's Wife's Sister not forbidden by the Word of God*, 1849. [24]

JENKINSON, J. H., *Reading.*—C. of St. Mary's, Reading. [25]

JENKINSON, Thomas Barge, *Parkstone, Poole, Dorset.*—Pemb. Coll. Ox. B.A. 1852; Deac. 1853 and Pr. 1856 by Bp of Ches. Formerly C. of Mottram-in Longendale 1853–56, Rowstone, Lincolnshire, 1857–58, Christchurch, Hants, 1863–64. [26]

JENKS, David, *Little Gaddesden, Hemel-Hempstead, Herts.*—St. John's Coll. Cam. B.A. 1807, M.A. 1811; Deac. 1808, Pr. 1809. R. of Little Gaddesden, Dio. Roch. 1829. (Patron, Earl Brownlow; Tithe, 270*l*;

Glebe, 16 acres; R.'s Inc. 340*l* and Ho; Pop. 386.) Rural Dean. Formerly R. of Aldbury, Herts, 1818-62. [1]

JENKYN, James, *Cawood, Selby, Yorks.*—Sid. Coll. Cam. B.A. 1814, M.A. 1818; Deac. 1815, Pr. 1819. P. C. of Cawood, Dio. York, 1853. (Patron, Abp of York; P. C.'s Inc. 300*l* and Ho; Pop. 1290.) [2]

JENKYN, William Osborn, *Sittingbourne, Kent.*—Ch. Coll. Cam. Scho. of, and 25th Sen. Opt. B.A. 1845, M.A. 1849; Deac. 1845 and Pr. 1846 by Bp of Ely. C. of Sittingbourne and Iwade 1865. Formerly P. C. of Charlton, Salisbury, and Chap. to Earl Nelson 1850-60; Asst. Chap. at St. Petersburg 1860-63. [3]

JENKYNS, Charles, *Tucking-Mill, Camborne, Cornwall.*—Clare Hall, Cam. B.A. 1833; Deac. 1833, Pr. 1834. P. C. of Tucking-Mill, Dio. Ex. 1853. (Patrons, the Crown and Bp of Ex. alt; P. C.'s Inc. 200*l*; Pop. 3769.) [4]

JENKYNS, Henry, *The College, Durham.*—Corpus Coll. Ox. 1813, Double 1st cl. 1816, B.A. 1817, Fell of Oriel Coll. 1818, M.A. 1819, B.D. and D.D. 1841; Deac. 1820 and Pr. 1821 by Bp of Ox. Can. Res. of Dur. Cathl. 1839. (Value, 1000*l* and Res.) Formerly Prof. of Greek in Univ. of Dur. 1833, and of Divinity 1841. Editor of *Cranmer's Remains*, 4 vols. Ox. Univ. Press, 1833, 48*s*. [5]

JENNER, Alfred Herbert, *Wenvoe Rectory, Cardiff.*—Trin. Hall Cam. S.C.L. 1849, LL.B. 1852; Deac. 1851 and Pr. 1852 by Bp of Llan. R. of Wenvoe, Dio. Llan. 1853. (Patron, R. F. Jenner, Esq; Tithe, 364*l* 12*s*; Glebe, 22 acres; R.'s Inc. 386*l* and Ho; Pop. 504.) [6]

JENNER, Charles Herbert, *St. Mary's, Stafford.*—Trin. Hall, Cam. B.A. 1830, M.A. 1834; Deac. 1832 and Pr. 1834 by Bp of Nor. R. of Merthyr-Dovan, Dio. Llan. 1834. (Patron, R. F. L. Jenner, Esq; Glebe, 16 acres; R.'s Inc. 138*l*; Pop. 143.) C. of St. Mary's, Stafford, 1861. Formerly C. of Heydon, Stratford St. Mary, Peldon, Bishop's Cleeve, Frampton, Old Sodbury, Alberbury, Aldridge, Warbleton, Bromsgrove, Ellastone; R. of Wenvoe. [7]

JENNER, Stephen, *The Vicarage, Camberwell, London, S.*—St. John's Coll. Cam. Sen. Opt. B.A. 1834, M.A. 1839; Deac. 1835 and Pr. 1836 by Bp of Lon. Even. Preacher at St. John's, Westminster. Author, *The Queen's Supremacy Vindicated*, 1851, 1*s*; *An Answer to Archdeacon Wilberforce on the Doctrine of the Holy Eucharist*, 1854, 3*s* 6*d*; *Truth's Conflicts and Truth's Triumphs*, 1854, 10*s* 6*d*. [8]

JENNINGS, George Pryme, *Anston, Rotherham, Yorks.*—Dub. A.B. 1847; Deac. 1847, Pr. 1848. C. of Anston. Author, *Parochial Addresses*; etc. [9]

JENNINGS, Henry, *Watton, Great Driffield, Yorks.*—Univ. Coll. Ox. B.A. 1819, M.A. 1821. V. of Watton, Dio. York, 1839. (Patron, Richard Bethell, Esq; Tithe—Imp. 666*l*, V. 21*l*; V.'s Inc. 110*l*; Pop. 343.) [10]

JENNINGS, James Knight, *Wellington House, Weston-super-Mare.*—Queens' Coll. Cam. Cl. and Math. Prizemen 1835 and 1836, Jun. Opt. and B.A. 1838, M.A. 1842; Deac. 1838, Pr. 1840. Prin. of Wellington Sch. Weston-super-Mare, 1861. Chap. of Don. of Catcott, Dio. B. and W. 1867. (Patron, A. Henniker, Esq; Chap.'s Inc. 60*l*; Pop. 600.) Formerly Librarian of Queens' Coll. Cam; C. of Church Brampton 1838; Asst. Min. of Milverton Chapel, Leamington, 1842; C. of Burton Latimer and Carbrooke 1844, Highgate 1845, Lavenham and Brent Eleigh 1846; Chap. of the Infant Orphan Asylum, Wanstead, 1849; Asst. Min. of Trinity Chapel, Conduit-street, Lond. 1850, Belgrave Chapel, 1855, Somers Town Chapel, St. Pancras, 1857, &c. Editor, *Poems and Glossary of Dialect of West of England*, 2nd ed. enlarged and improved, J. R. Smith, London, 1865. [11]

JENNINGS, John, *St. John's Rectory, Westminster, London, S.W.*—R. of St. John's, Westminster, Dio. Lon. 1832. (Patron, the Crown; R.'s Inc. 355*l* and Ho; Pop. 10,461.) Can. Res. of Westminster Abbey 1837. (Value, 1200*l* and Res.) Rural Dean; Dom. Chap. to the Marquis of Downshire. [12]

JENNINGS, Thomas Fryer, *Weston-super-Mare.*—Wad. Coll. Ox. B.A. 1816, M.A. 1819. C. of Emmanuel Ch. Weston-super-Mare 1864. [13]

JENOUR, Alfred, *Blackpool, Lancashire.*—Deac. 1822, Pr. 1823. P. C. of Blackpool, Dio. Man. 1834. (Patrons, Five Trustees; Glebe, 55 acres; P. C.'s Inc. 340*l* and Ho; Pop. 1957.) Formerly C. of Mountsorrel; R. of Pilton; P. C. of Regent-square Chapel, Lond; R. of Kittisford 1851. Author, *Isaiah, translated from the Hebrew, with Commentary*, 2 vols. Seeley's, 1832, 24*s*; *Pastor's Wedding Gift*, 1831, 6*d*; *Treatise on Languages*, 1832, 3*s* 6*d*; *Job, translated from the Hebrew, with Critical Notes*, 1841, 3*s* 6*d*; *The Droppings of the Thundercloud* (Sermon), 1847; *The First Shock of the Great Earthquake*, 1848; *Fenelon's Dialogues on Eloquence, from the French, with an Introductory Essay*, 1849, 2*s* 6*d*; *Rationale Apocalypticum, or Systematic Exposition of the Revelation of St. John*, 2 vols. Hatchard, 1852, 28*s*. [14]

JENOUR, Henry, *Portland, Weymouth, Dorset.*—Deac. 1816 and Pr. 1817 by Bp of Nor. P. C. of St. John's, Portland, Dio. Salis. 1840. (Patrons, Hyndman's Trustees; P. C.'s Inc. 60*l*; Pop. 8468.) [15]

JENOUR, H. C., *Burton-Joyce, Nottingham.*—V. of Burton-Joyce with Bulcote C. Dio. Lin. 1863. (Patron, Earl of Chesterfield; V.'s Inc. 150*l*; Pop. 834.) [16]

JENYNS, Charles Fitzgerald Gambier, *Melbourn, Royston, Cambs.*—Emman. Coll. Cam. B.A. 1850, M.A. 1853; Deac. 1851, Pr. 1852. V. of Melbourn, Dio. Ely, 1853. (Patrons, D. and C. of Ely; Tithe—App. 860*l*, V. 220*l*; Glebe, 37 acres; V.'s Inc. 300*l* and Ho; Pop. 1637.) Surrogate. [17]

JENYNS, Leonard, *Darlington-place, Bath.*—St. John's Coll. Cam. B.A. 1822, M.A. 1825; Deac. 1823, Pr. 1824. Formerly V. of Swaffham Bulbeck, Cambs. Author, *A Manual of British Vertebrate Animals*, Longmans; *Observations in Natural History*, Van Voorst; *Observations in Meteorology*, Ib; *Memoir of Professor Henslow*, Ib. [18]

JEPHSON, John Hilton, *Long Crendon, Thame, Oxon.*—Magd. Hall Ox. B.A. 1851; Deac. 1852 and Pr. 1853 by Bp of Rip. C. of Chearsley, Aylesbury, 1861. Formerly C. of Stanley, Wakefield, 1852-53, Chievely, Berks, 1853-56, Curridge, Berks, 1856-60. [19]

JEPHSON, William, *Hinton-Waldrist Rectory, Faringdon, Berks.*—Corpus Coll. Cam. B.A. 1841, M.A. 1844; Deac. and Pr. 1843 by Bp. of Lon. R. of Hinton-Waldrist, Dio. Ox. 1853. (Patron, J. L. Symonds, Esq; Glebe, 400 acres; R.'s Inc. 400*l* and Ho; Pop. 329.) Dioc. Inspector of Schs. Formerly C. of St. John's, Westminster, 1844-53. [20]

JEPSON, George, 36, *Great Ormond-street, London, W.C.*—St. John's Coll. Cam. B.A. 1837, M.A. 1847; Deac. 1837 and Pr. 1838 by Bp of Lin. Chap. to the New Prison, Clerkenwell, Lond. 1843. [21]

JERDEIN, Charles, *Stoke Goldington, Newport Pagnell.*—Dub. A.B. 1857, A.M. 1860; Deac. 1861 and Pr. 1862 by Bp of Ox. R. of Gayhurst with Stoke Goldington R. Bucks, Dio. Ox. 1865. (Patron, Lord Carington; Gayhurst, Tithe, 48*l*; Stoke Goldington, Tithe, 120*l*; Glebe, 232 acres; R.'s Inc. 580*l*; Pop. Gayhurst 129, Stoke Goldington 963.) Formerly C. of Banbury 1861, Gayhurst and Stoke Goldington 1863. [22]

JEREMIE, Frederick John, *Hibaldstow Vicarage, Kirton in Lindsey, Lincolnshire.*—Trin. Coll. Cam. 12th Sen. Opt. and B.A. 1835, M.A. 1838; Deac. 1836 and Pr. 1837 by Bp of Win. V. of Hilbaldstow, Dio. Lin. 1851. (Patrons, Bp of Lin. and M.D. Dalison, Esq. alt; Tithe, comm. for 242 acres; V.'s Inc. 424*l* and Ho; Pop. 775.) Chap. to the Duke of St. Albans. Formerly Min. of Trinity Episcopal Chapel, Guernsey, 1836-45; C. of St. Michael's-in-the-Vale, Guernsey, 1845-51. Author, the Articles *Guernsey, Sir John Jeremie, Customary Law of Normandy, Legion of Honour, War of the Succession, Simondi, Wace*, and numerous other Articles in the Supplement to the *Penny Cyclopædia*; *A Visitation Sermon* (preached before the Bp of Lin.), 1852; *Cottage Gardens* in *Macmillan's Magazine*, 1863. [23]

JEREMIE, The Very Rev. James Amiraux, *The Deanery, Lincoln.*—Trin. Coll. Cam. Norrisian Prizeman 1823, and again in 1825, B.A. 1824, Hulsean Prizeman 1824, Members' Prizeman 1826, M.A. 1827, B.D. 1850, D.D. by Royal Mandate 1850, Hon. D.C.L. of Ox. 1862; Deac. and Pr. 1830 by Bp of Lin. Sen. Fell. of Trin. Coll. Cam; Dean of Lincoln 1864; Regius Professor of Divinity in the Univ. of Cam. 1850; R. of Somersham with Colne C. and Pidley C. Huntingdonshire, Dio. Ely, 1850 (annexed to the Regius Professorship). (Somersham, Tithe, 537*l* 10*s*; Glebe, 20 acres; Colne, Tithe, 540*l* 2*s*; Glebe, ¼ acre; Pidley, Tithe, 478*l*; R.'s Inc. 1575*l* and Ho; Pop. Somersham 1621, Colne, 385, Pidley 569.) Formerly Christian Advocate in the Univ. of Cam. 1833–34; Exam. Chap. to (Dr. Kaye) late Bp of Lincoln; Dean, and Professor of Classical Literature in the East India Coll. Haileybury 1833–50; Sub-Dean and Can. of Lincoln, 1848–64. Author, *The Office and Mission of St. John the Baptist* (Norrisian Medal), 1823; *The Doctrines of Our Saviour, as derived from the four Gospels, are in perfect Harmony with the Doctrines of St. Paul as derived from the Epistles* (Hulsean Prize), 1824; *No Valid Argument can be drawn from the Incredulity of the Heathen Philosophers against the Truth of the Christian Religion* (Norrisian Medal), 1825; *The Last Discourses of Our Saviour considered in Reference to the Divine Origin of Christianity* (Christian Advocate's Treatise), 1833; The Articles on *The History of the Christian Church in the Second and Third Centuries*; *Roman History, from Constantine to the Death of Julian, &c. in the Encyclopædia Metropolitana*; *Commemoration Sermons* (preached in the Chapel of Trinity College, Cambridge), 1834; *Commemoration Sermon*, 1842, 2 eds; *The Third Centenary of Trinity College, Cambridge*, 1846, 2 eds; *Commemoration Sermon*, 1849; *Parental Affection, Christian Benevolence, St. John, &c.* (preached in the Chapel of E. I Coll. Haileybury); *Sermon on the Day of General Thanksgiving* (preached in Lincoln Cathedral); *Sermons* (preached before the Univ. of Cam.); *On the Death of the Rev. J. J. Blunt, B.D.* (Margaret Professor of Divinity), 2 eds; *The Fallacy of Appearances; On the Days appointed for General Humiliation and Prayer*, 1854 and 1855, 2 eds; *Concio ad Clerum Provinciæ Cantuariensis in Æde Paulina V. die Novembri, MDCCCLII. habita, jussu Reverendissimi* (At the Festival of the Sons of the Clergy in St. Paul's Cathedral), 1856; *On the Death of the Prince Consort; On the Reopening of Great St. Mary's Church*; etc. [1]

JERMYN, The Ven. Hugh Willoughby, *Nettlecombe Rectory, near Taunton.*—Trin. Hall, Cam. B.A. 1841, M.A. 1847; Deac. 1842, Pr. 1843. R. of Nettlecombe, Dio. B. and W. 1858. (Patron, Sir W. C. Trevelyan, Bart; Tithe, 480*l*; Glebe, 60 acres; R.'s Inc. 600*l* and Ho; Pop. 327.) Formerly Archd. of St. Christopher's, West Indies. [2]

JERRAM, James, *Fleet Rectory (Lincolnshire), near Wisbech.*—Wad. Coll. Ox. 3rd cl. Lit. Hum. and B.A. 1826, M.A. 1830; Deac 1827, Pr. 1828. R. of Fleet, Dio. Lin. 1853. (Patron, Rev. R. Dods; Tithe, 1236*l*; Glebe, 87 acres; R.'s Inc. 1388*l* and Ho; Pop. 1312.) Author, *Memoirs of Rev. Charles Jerram, late Rector of Witney*, 1855. [3]

JERRAM, Samuel John, *Chobham, Bagshot, Surrey.*—Wor. Coll. Ox. B.A. 1838, M.A. 1843. V. of Chobham, Dio. Win. 1854. (Patron, J. Thornton, Esq; Tithe—App. 4*s* 6*d*, Imp. 507*l* 13*s* 11*d*, V. 22*l* 10*s* 2½*d*; V.'s Inc. 168*l*; Pop. 2040.) [4]

JERRARD, Frederick William Hill, *Long Stratton St. Mary, Norfolk.*—Caius Coll. Cam. 8th Wrang. and B.A. 1833, M.A. 1836; Deac. 1839, Pr. 1840. R. of Long Stratton St. Mary, Dio. Nor. 1842. (Patron, Caius Coll. Cam; Tithe, 424*l*; Glebe, 40 acres; R.'s Inc. 490*l* and Ho; Pop. 743.) Formerly Sen. Fell of Caius Coll. Cam. [5]

JERVIS-EDWARDS, Thomas, *Manor House, Chester.* [6]

JERVOIS, Sampson Thomas Henry.—Brasen. Coll. Ox. B.A. 1846, M.A. 1852; Deac. 1847, Pr. 1849. P. C. of Downham, Dio. Man. 1853. (Patrons, Hulme's Trustees; Glebe, 2 acres; P. C.'s Inc. 130*l* and Ho; Pop. 433.) Chap. to the late Marquis of Thomond 1848–51. [7]

JESSON, Cornelius, *Enville Rectory (Staffs), near Stourbridge.*—Emman. Coll. Cam. B.A. 1824, M.A. 1827; Deac. 1826 and Pr. 1827 by Bp of Lich. R. of St. Bride's, Netherwent, Monmouthshire, Dio. Llan. 1829. (Patron, T. Perry, Esq; Tithe, 140*l*; Glebe, 41¾ acres; R.'s Inc. 192*l*; Pop. 171.) R. of Enville, Dio. Lich. 1837. (Patron, the present R; Tithe, 912*l* 12*s* 6*d*; Glebe, 70 acres; R.'s Inc. 1154*l* and Ho; Pop. 850.) [8]

JESSON, Frederick, *Grantham, Lincolnshire.*—P. C. of St. John's, Spittlegate, Grantham, Dio. Lin. 1842. (Patron, V. of Grantham; P. C.'s Inc. 300*l* and Ho; Pop. 3803.) Chap. of the Union, Spittlegate, and Chap. of Grantham Gaol; Hon. Chap. to Lincolnshire Rifle Volunteers. [9]

JESSOPP, Augustus, *The School House, Norwich.*—St. John's Coll. Cam. B.A. 1848, M.A. 1852; Deac. 1848 and Pr. 1850 by Bp of Ely. Head Mast. of King Edward VI. Sch. Norwich. Formerly Mast. of Helston Gr. Sch. 1855. Author, *The Middle-class Examinations, What will they do for us?* Bell and Daldy, 1860; *Norwich School Sermons*, 1864; *Tales by Emile Souvestre, with Life of the Author*, Nutt, 1861; *A Manual of Greek Accidence*, Macmillan, 1865. [10]

JESSOPP, John, *Cheshunt, Herts.*—St. John's Coll. Cam. B.A. 1837, M.A. 1841; Deac. 1839 and Pr. 1840 by Abp of York. Chap. of Surrey Co. Gaol 1855. Formerly British Consular Chap. at Ostend 1840; Chap. to the King of the Belgians 1842; Chap. H. E. I. C. S. 1844; Morning Preacher, Asylum for Female Orphans, Lambeth, 1846; Even. Lect. St. Mary's, Newington, 1847; P. C. of Trinity, Newington, 1848. Author, *Woman, in Eight Chapters*, 1851, 3*s* 6*d*. [11]

JESTON, Henry Playsted, *Cholesbury, Tring.*—Wor. Coll. Ox. B.A. 1821, M.A. 1824; Deac. 1821 by Bp of Lich. Pr. 1822 by Bp of Ches. P. C. of Cholesbury, Dio. Ox. 1830. (Patrons, Trustees; Tithe, 33*l* 2*s* 6*d*; Glebe, 8 acres; P. C.'s Inc. 71*l* 10*s* and Ho; Pop. 103.) J. P. for Bucks and Herts. Accompanied Bp Coleridge to the West Indies 1824; Dom. Chap. to Sir Ralph Woodford, Trinidad, 1825; P. C. of Wigginton 1841–47; British Chap. at Kissengen 1855–61. [12]

JEUDWINE, William, *Chicheley Vicarage, Newport Pagnell.*—V. of Chicheley, Bucks, Dio. Ox. 1860. (Patron, C. M. Chester, Esq; V.'s Inc. 120*l* and Ho; Pop. 265.) [13]

JEX-BLAKE, Charles Thomas, *Lyng, Norwich.*—Jesus Coll. Cam. Sen. Opt. and B.A. 1842, M.A. 1845; Deac. 1843 and Pr. 1844 by Bp of Nor. R. of Lyng, Dio. Nor. 1867. (Patron, Rev. H. Lombe; Tithe, comm. 528*l*; Glebe, 58 acres; R.'s Inc. 600*l* and Ho; Pop. 590.) Formerly P. C. of St. Martin's-at-Oak, Norwich, 1854–62; V. of Gayton, Norfolk, 1862–67. [14]

JEX-BLAKE, Thomas William, *Rugby.*—Univ. Coll. Ox. B.A. 1855, M.A. 1857; Deac. 1856 by Bp of Ox. Pr. 1857 by Bp of Win. Asst. Mast. at Rugby Sch. 1858. Formerly Fell. of Queen's Coll. Ox. 1855–58. Author, *Long Vacation in Continental Picture Galleries*, 1858, 3*s* 6*d*. [15]

JEX-BLAKE, William Francis, *Great Dunham, Swaffham, Norfolk.*—Caius Coll. Cam. B.A. 1854. R. of Great Dunham, Dio. Nor. 1862. (Patron, R. B. Humfrey, Esq; Tithe—App. 9*l*, R. 562*l*; Glebe, 44 acres; R.'s Inc. 611*l* and Ho; Pop. 493.) Formerly C. of Great Snoring, Norfolk. [16]

JICKLING, Francis, *Beeston Rectory, Scottow, Norwich.*—Emman. Coll. Cam. B.A. 1860; Deac. 1860 and Pr. 1861 by Bp of B. and W. R. of Beeston St. Lawrence with Ashmanhaugh P. C. Dio. Nor. 1863. (Patron, Sir J. H. Preston, Bart; Tithe, 145*l*; Glebe, 140*l*; R.'s Inc. 310*l* and Ho; Pop. 195.) Formerly C. of Bathford 1860–63. [17]

JOBERNS, Charles Henry, 12, *St. Ann's-terrace, Derby.*—St. John's Coll. Ox B.A. 1863, M.A. 1865; Deac. 1863 and Pr. 1864 by Bp of Lich. C. of All Saints', Derby, 1863. [18]

JODRELL, Charles Philip Paul, *Wramplingham, Wymondham, Norfolk.*—Brasen. Coll. Ox. B.A. 1845, M.A. 1846; Deac. 1845 and Pr. 1846 by Bp of Ely. R. of Wramplingham, Dio. Nor. 1861. (Patron, Rev. H. P. Marsham; Tithe, 260*l*; Glebe, 34 acres; R.'s Inc. 305*l* and Ho; Pop. 194.) Formerly C. of Wood Dalling, Norfolk; R. of Bayfield, Norfolk, 1855–61. [1]

JODRELL, Sir Edward Repps, Bart., *Salt Park, Norfolk.*—Queen's Coll. Ox. B.A. 1848, M.A. 1851; Deac. 1850 and Pr. 1851 by Bp of Lon. Formerly R. of Saxlingham, Norfolk, 1855–61. [2]

JODRELL, Henry, *Gisleham, near Wangford, Suffolk.*—Ex. Coll. Ox. B.A. 1839, M.A. 1842; Deac. 1840, Pr. 1841. R. of Gisleham, Dio. Nor. 1844. (Patron, Ld Chan; Tithe, 410*l*; Glebe, 7 acres; R.'s Inc. 410*l* and Ho; Pop. 267.) Chap. to the Duke of Leeds. [3]

JOHN, Ebenezer, *Abercarn, Newport, Monmouthshire.*—Divinity Sch. Abergavenny; Deac. 1859 and Pr. 1860 by Bp of Llan. C. of Abercarn and Crumlin 1862. Formerly C. of Nantyglo 1859–61, Aberystruth 1861–62. [4]

JOHNES, Thomas William, *All Saints' Vicarage, Leicester.*—Univ. Coll. Dur. Licen. Theol. 1837, M.A. 1847; Deac. 1837 and Pr. 1838 by Bp of Ches. V. of All Saints' with St. Leonard's V. (no Church), Dio. Pet. 1851. (Patron, Ld Chan; Tithe, All Saints' 1*l* 10*s*, St. Leonard's 3*l*; V.'s Inc. 145*l* and Ho; Pop. All Saints' 5945, St. Leonard's 441.) Surrogate. Author, *A Farewell Sermon*, 1841. [5]

JOHNS, Bennett George, *The Blind School, St. George's Fields, London, S.E.*—Deac. 1846, Pr. 1848. Chap. of the Blind Sch. 1851. (Chan.'s Inc. 300*l* and Ho.) Author, *History of the Jews between Old and New Testaments*, 1*s* 6*d*; *History of Spain*, 2*s* 6*d*; *Dictation Lessons*; *Collects and Catechisings*; *Book of Poetry*; *Sermons to the Blind*, 3*s* 6*d*; *Blind People, their Work and Ways*, Murray, 7*s* 6*d*; *History of England*; various Educational Works. Contributor to the *Quarterly* and *Edinburgh Review*, *Frazer's Magazine*, and other periodicals. [6]

JOHNS, Charles Alexander, *Winton House, Winchester.*—Dub. A.B. 1841; Deac. 1841, Pr. 1842. Formerly C. of Yarnscombe 1841–42; Chap. to the National Society's Training Schools 1842–44; Head Mast. of Helston Gr. Sch. and C. of Portleven 1844–49; C. of Beenham 1849–56. Fell. of the Linnæan Soc. Author, *Botanical Rambles*; *Forest Trees of Britain*, 2 vols; *Week at the Lizard*; *Birds' Nests*; *Rambles in British Isles*; *Flowers of the Field*, 2 vols. S.P.C.K; *Gardening for Children*; *Ammemon*; *The Governess*; etc. [7]

JOHNS, John White, *Crowan Vicarage, Camborne, Cornwall.*—St. John's Coll. Cam. B.A. 1831, M.A. 1842; Deac. 1831, Pr. 1832. V. of Crowan, Dio. Ex. 1842. (Patron, Rev. Hender Molesworth St. Aubyn; Tithe—Imp. 494*l* 15*s*, V. 470*l*; Glebe, 45 acres; V.'s Inc. 460*l* and Ho; Pop. 4131.) [8]

JOHNS, Thomas, 7, *Windsor-terrace, Neath, Glamorganshire.*—Lampeter, Creaton Prize 1864; Deac. 1864 and Pr. 1865 by Bp of St. D. C. of Cadoxton-juxta-Neath 1867. Formerly C. of St. Peter's, Carmarthen, 1864, and Chap. of Carmarthen Union Workhouse 1868. [9]

JOHNS, Thomas, *Chard, Somerset.*—C. of Chard. [10]

JOHNS, William, *Junior Carlton Club, London, S.W.*—Dom. Chap. to the Earl of Courtown. [11]

JOHNS, William Stabback, *Yspytty-Ystrad-Meuric, Cardiganshire.*—C. of Yspytty-Ystrad-Meuric. [12]

JOHNSON, Ambrose James, *Oxwick, Fakenham, Norfolk.*—C. of Oxwick and Helhoughton. [13]

JOHNSON, Andrew, *Southwark Grammar School, S.E.*—Trin. Coll. Cam. B.A. 1853; Deac. 1853 and Pr. 1854 by Bp of Lon. Head Mast. of the Southwark Gr. Sch. Formerly C. of St. Clement's, Eastcheap, and St. Martin's Orgar, City of Lond. Author, *Bacon's Novum Organum newly translated, with Notes*, Bell and Daldy, 1859, 6*s*. [14]

JOHNSON, Arthur, 36, *Canonbury-square, Islington, London, N.*—Ch. Ch. Ox. B.A. 1826; Deac. 1831 by Bp of B. and W. Pr. 1832 by Bp of Ex. Lect. of St. Vedast, Foster-lane, London. [15]

JOHNSON, Bertie Entwisle, *Childs Ercall, Market Drayton, Salop.*—St. Peter's Coll. Cam. B.A. 1817, M.A. 1821; Deac. 1818 and Pr. 1819 by Bp of Ches. P. C. of Childs Ercall, Dio. Lich. 1844. (Patron, Richard Corbet, Esq; Tithe, Imp. 730*l*; P. C.'s Inc. 65*l* and Ho; Pop. 470.) R. of Hinstock, Salop, Dio. Lich. 1850. (Patron, Richard Corbet, Esq; Tithe, 527*l* 17*s* 6*d*; Glebe, 14½ acres; R.'s Inc. 556*l* and Ho; Pop. 791.) Formerly C. of High Legh; P. C. of Over Peover; R. of Lymm, Cheshire. [16]

JOHNSON, Charles Augustus, *Enborne Rectory, Newbury, Berks.*—Brasen. Coll. Ox. B.A. 1841; Deac. 1848 and Pr. 1850 by Bp of Ox. R. of Enborne, Dio. Ox. 1850. (Patron, Earl of Craven; Tithe, 450*l*; Glebe, 80 acres; R.'s Inc. 520*l* and Ho; Pop. 412.) R. of Hampstead-Marshal, Berks, Dio. Ox. 1850. (Patron, Earl of Craven; Tithe, 290*l*; Glebe, 17¾ acres; R.'s Inc. 311*l*; Pop. 299.) [17]

JOHNSON, Edmund, 24, *Upper Park-street, Clifton.*—Dub. A.B. 1840, A.M. 1843; Deac. 1842 and Pr. 1843 by Bp of Lon. C. of Trinity, Clifton, 1866. Formerly Prin. of the Coll. Benares, 1843–45; Prin. of Ch. M. Coll. Cottayam, 1850–54; in charge of Pallam Miss. District, in Travancore, 1854–58; C. of Melcombe Regis, Dorset, 1862. [18]

JOHNSON, Edward Frederick, *Hinton Blewett Rectory, Bristol.*—St. John's Coll. Cam. Scho. of; Deac. 1856 and Pr. 1857 by Bp of St. D. R. of Hinton Blewett, Dio. B. and W. 1867. (Patroness, Mrs. Johnson; Tithe, 170*l*; Glebe, 80 acres; R.'s Inc. 320*l* and Ho; Pop. 302.) Surrogate. Formerly C. of Builth 1856; P. C. of Llanebwedd, Radnorshire, 1857; C. of Hinton Blewett 1863. [19]

JOHNSON, Edward Henry.—Preb. of Hova Ecclesia in Chich. Cathl. 1841. Formerly V. of Poling, Sussex, 1841–59. [20]

JOHNSON, Edward Ralph, *Northenden Rectory, Manchester.*—R. of Northenden, Dio. Ches. 1866. (Patrons, D. and C. of Ches; Tithe, 417*l*; Glebe, 42 acres; R.'s Inc. 546*l* and Ho; Pop. 1430.) [21]

JOHNSON, Francis Charles, *White Lackington Vicarage, Ilminster.*—V. of White Lackington, Dio. B. and W. 1825. (Patron, Bp of B. and W; Tithe—App. 295*l* 13*s* and 37¾ acres of Glebe; V. 224*l* 12*s*; Glebe, 3 roods; V.'s Inc. 227*l* and Ho; Pop. 260.) [22]

JOHNSON, Frederick, *Hemington Parsonage, Oundle, Northants.*—St. Cath. Hall, Cam. B.A. 1829, M.A. 1833; Deac. and Pr. 1830. R. of the Consolidated Benefices of Luddington 1850, with Hemington 1833, Dio. Pet. (Patron, Duke of Buccleuch; Glebe, 318 acres; R.'s Inc. 500*l* and Ho; Pop. Luddington 128, Hemington 152.) [23]

JOHNSON, Frederick Alfred, *Stratford St. Andrew, Saxmundham.*—R. of Stratford St. Andrew, Dio. Nor. 1859. (Patron, Ld Chan; R.'s Inc. 154*l*; Pop. 181.) [24]

JOHNSON, Frederick Pigot, *Floore, Weedon, Northants.*—Ch. Ch. Ox. B.A. 1848, M.A. 1850; Deac. 1849, Pr. 1850. V. of Floore, Dio. Pet. 1865. (Patron, Ch. Ch. Ox; V.'s Inc. 500*l*; Pop. 1138.) Formerly C. of Whittington, Salop; P. C. of Market Harborough 1856–65. [25]

JOHNSON, George Alexander, *Lidget Green, Bradford, Yorks.*—Dub. A.B. 1857; Deac. 1857 and Pr. 1858 by Bp of Kilmore. C. of Great Horton, Bradford, 1866. Formerly C. of Kilbryan, Roscommon, Belturbet, Cavan, and Otley, Yorks. [26]

JOHNSON, The Very Rev. George Henry Sacheverell, *The Deanery, Wells.*—Queen's Coll. Ox. Ireland Scho. 1827, Double 1st cl. 1828, B.A. 1829, Math. Scho. 1831, M.A. 1833; Deac. and Pr. 1834 by Bp of Ox. Dean of Wells 1854. (Value, 1000*l* and Res.) V. of Wells, Dio. B. and W. 1855. (Patrons, D. and C. of Wells; V.'s Inc. 600*l* and Ho; Pop. 4525.) Formerly Public Examiner of the Univ. of Ox. 1834 and 1839;

Savilian Prof. of Astronomy 1839–42; Prof. of Moral Philosophy 1842–45; Whitehall Preacher 1852. Author, *Treatise on Optics*, 1835; *Sermons* (preached in Wells Cathl.), 1 vol. 1857. [1]

JOHNSON, Henry Frank, *High Wych, Sawbridgeworth, Herts.*—Trin. Coll. Cam. S.C.L. 1857, B.C.L. 1861; Deac. 1856 by Bp of Win. Pr. 1860 by Bp of Roch. P. C. of High Wych, Dio. Roch. 1862. (Patron, V. of Sawbridgeworth; P. C.'s Inc. 120*l*; Pop. 900.) Formerly C. of Richmond, Surrey, 1858. [2]

JOHNSON, Henry Isaac, *Grahamstown, South Africa.*—Ch. Coll. Cam. B.A. 1853, M.A. 1857; Deac. 1853 and Pr. 1854 by Bp of Chich. Formerly Asst. Mast. at Brighton Coll. [3]

JOHNSON, James Thomas, *Britwell Salome Rectory, near Wallingford, Berks.*—St. John's Coll. Ox. 3rd cl. Lit. Hum. and B.A. 1835, M.A. 1839; Deac. 1836 and Pr. 1837 by Bp of Lin. R. of Britwell Salome, Dio. Ox. 1851. (Patron, Marquis of Lansdowne; Tithe, 240*l*; Glebe, 18½ acres; R.'s Inc. 260*l* and Ho; Pop. 217.) [4]

JOHNSON, Job, *Denby, Huddersfield.*—Dub; Deac. 1849, Pr. 1850. P. C. of Denby, Dio. Rip. 1851. (Patron, V. of Penistone; Glebe, 22 acres; P. C.'s Inc. 150*l*; Pop. 2262.) [5]

JOHNSON, John, 7, *Grosvenor-road, Highbury New Park, London, N.*—St. Cath. Hall, Cam. M.A. 1836; Deac. and Pr. 1835 by Bp of Lich. Dist. Sec. of the Ch. Miss. Soc. Formerly P. C. of Horton, Staffs. Author, *Sermons*, 2 vols. 12*s*. [6]

JOHNSON, John, *Causeway Cottage, Carr's Hill, Gateshead, Durham.*—Dur. Licen. in Theol. 1855; Deac. 1855 and Pr. 1856 by Bp of Man. C. of Gateshead Fell 1863. Formerly C. of Pittington 1855–63. [7]

JOHNSON, John, *Kirkby, Prescot, Lancashire.*—Queens' Coll. Cam. B.A. 1861; Deac. 1862 and Pr. 1863 by Bp of Ches. C. of Kirkby, Walton-on-the-Hill, 1863. [8]

JOHNSON, John, *Heskin Hall, near Chorley.*—St. Bees; Deac. 1853 and Pr. 1854 by Bp of Man. P. C. of Wrightington, Dio. Man. 1857. (Patron, R. of Eccleston; Tithe—App. 599*l* 4*s*; P. C.'s Inc. 100*l*.) Formerly C. of Bacup 1853–57. [9]

JOHNSON, John Barham, *Welborne, East Dereham, Norfolk.*—Corpus Coll. Cam. B.A. 1841, M.A. 1845; Deac. 1842 by Bp of B. and W. Pr. 1844 by Bp of Nor. R. of Welborne, Dio. Nor. 1844. (Patron, the present R; Tithe, 240*l*; Glebe, 41 acres; R.'s Inc. 290*l* and Ho; Pop. 200.) Formerly C. of Nailsea 1842–43. [10]

JOHNSON, John Edward, *Palm Villa, Russell-terrace, Leamington.*—St. John's Coll. Cam. LL.B. 1832; Deac. 1829 and Pr. 1830 by Bp of Lin. Formerly C. of Harpenden, Herts, and Chaddesley Corbett, Worc. [11]

JOHNSON, John Edward, *Sheffield.*—Sid. Coll. Cam. B.A. 1859; Deac. 1859 and Pr. 1860 by Bp of Win. P. C. of St. Jude's, Moorfields, Sheffield, Dio. York, 1864. (Patrons, Crown and Abp of York; P. C.'s Inc. 300*l*; Pop. 6254.) [12]

JOHNSON, John Fairbairn, *Abb Kettleby Vicarage, Melton Mowbray.*—Univ. Coll. Dur. B.A. 1847, M.A. 1855; Deac. 1847 and Pr. 1848 by Bp of Dur. V. of Abb Kettleby with Holwell V. Dio. Pet. 1850. (Patron, Rev. T. Bingham; Abb Kettleby, Tithe, 3*s* 4*d*; Holwell, Tithe—Imp. 50*l* 11*s* 1*d*, V. 120*l*; Glebe, 92 acres; V.'s Inc. 297*l* and Ho; Pop. 371.) [13]

JOHNSON, J. H., *Tilshead Vicarage, Devizes, Wilts.*—V. of Tilshead, Dio. Salis. 1837. (Patron, Ld Chan; V.'s Inc. 200*l* and Ho; Pop. 500.) C. of Rollestone, Wilts. [14]

JOHNSON, John Lovick, *Cockley Clay, near Swaffham, Norfolk.*—St. Edm. Hall, Ox. B.A. 1845, M.A. 1848. Formerly C. of Cockley Clay. [15]

JOHNSON, John Munnings, *Scoulton Rectory, Thetford, Norfolk.*—Queens' Coll. Cam. B.A. 1828; Deac. 1829, Pr. 1830. R. of Scoulton, Dio. Nor. 1847. (Patron, J. Weyland, Esq; Tithe, 450*l*; Glebe, 53 acres; R.'s Inc. 500*l* and Ho; Pop. 329.) Chap. to Lord Berners 1850. [16]

JOHNSON, John Richard, *Candlesby, Spilsby, Lincolnshire.*—Trin. Coll. Cam. B.A. 1848, M.A. 1853; Deac. 1849 and Pr. 1851 by Bp of Lon. V. of Orby, Dio. Lin. 1864. (Patron, Bp of Lin; Tithe, 113*l* 14*s* 8*d*; Glebe, 85*l*; V.'s Inc. 221*l*; Pop. 357.) Formerly Asst. C. of St. Bartholomew's, Bethnal Green, 1849–51; C. of Moorby, Lincolnshire, 1852–64, Haltham 1852–60, Wood Enderby 1860–64. [17]

JOHNSON, Joseph Holden, *Sherburn, Milford Junction, Yorks.*—St. Cath. Hall, Cam. B.A. 1851; Deac. 1851 and Pr. 1852 by Bp of Man. C. of Sherburn and Micklefield. Formerly C. of Ellenbrook 1851–54, Harpurhey 1854–57, Royton 1857–62, all three in Lancashire. [18]

JOHNSON, Joseph William, *Moulton, Spalding, Lincolnshire.*—Trin. Coll. Cam. 7th Sen. Opt. B.A. 1859, M.A. 1862; Deac. 1860 and Pr. 1861 by Bp of Win. Head Mast. of the Upper Sch. Moulton, 1861; Dioc. Inspector of Schs. for Rural Deanery of South Holland 1862. Formerly Vice-Prin. and Gov. Lect. in Math. of the Winchester Dioc. Training Sch. for Masters 1859–61. [19]

JOHNSON, Paul, *Overstrand, Northrepps, Norfolk.*—St. John's Coll. Cam. B.A. 1811, M.A. 1814; Deac. 1813 and Pr. 1814 by Bp of Nor. R. of Sidestrand, Norfolk, Dio. Nor. 1834. (Patrons, Chan. of the Duchy of Lancaster and Proprietors of Manor Farm alt; Tithe, 106*l* 4*s*; Glebe, 2½ acres; R.'s Inc. 108*l*; Pop. 145.) R. of Overstrand, Dio. Nor. 1841. (Patron, J. H. Gurney, Esq; Tithe, 80*l*; Glebe, 1½ acres; R.'s Inc. 84*l* and Ho; Pop. 251.) [20]

JOHNSON, Peter, *Wembworthy Rectory, Chulmleigh, Devon.*—Ex. Coll. Ox. B.A. and M.A. 1812, B.D. 1823. R. of Wembworthy, Dio. Ex. 1830. (Patron, the present R; Tithe, 170*l*; Glebe, 40 acres; R.'s Inc. 210*l* and Ho; Pop. 345.) Preb. of Ex. 1842. [21]

JOHNSON, Philip, *Netteswell Rectory, Harlow, Essex.*—Ch. Coll. Cam. B.A. 1822, M.A. 1825; Deac. 1823, Pr. 1824. R. of Netteswell, Dio. Roch. 1835. (Patron, C. Phelips, Esq; Tithe, 230*l*; Glebe, 5 acres; R.'s Inc. 234*l* and Ho; Pop. 335.) [22]

JOHNSON, Robert, *Chislet Vicarage, near Canterbury.*—St. John's Coll. Cam. B.A. 1854, M.A. 1857; Deac. 1855 and Pr. 1856 by Bp of Lin. V. of Chislet, Dio. Cant. 1858. (Patron, Abp of Cant; Tithe—App. 1121*l* 3*s*, Imp. 154*l*, V. 241*l* 12*s*; V.'s Inc. 255*l* and Ho; Pop. 1072.) Formerly C. of King's Stanley, Glouc. 1856–58. [23]

JOHNSON, Robert Henry, *Claybrook Vicarage, Lutterworth, Leicestershire.*—Brasen. Coll. Ox. B.A. 1802, M.A. 1805; Deac. 1805 and Pr. 1806 by Bp of Herf. V. of Claybrook with Wibtoft C. and Little Wigston C. Dio. Pet. 1816. (Patron, the Crown; Tithe—Imp. 151*l* 2*s* 6*d*, V. 284*l* 18*s* 10*d*; V.'s Inc. 510*l* and Ho; Pop. 1274.) R. of Lutterworth, Dio. Pet. 1816. (Patron, the Crown; R.'s Inc. 654*l* and Ho; Pop. 2289.) [24]

JOHNSON, Robert William, *Packwood Parsonage, Hockley Heath, near Birmingham.*—Magd. Coll. Cam. B.A. 1837, M.A. 1840; Deac. 1837 and Pr. 1838 by Bp of Win. P. C. of Packwood, Henley-in-Arden, Dio. Wor. 1839. (Patron, Philip Wykeham Martin, Esq. Leamington; Tithe—Imp. 318*l* 10*s*; Glebe, 5 acres; P. C.'s Inc. 150*l* and Ho; Pop. 292.) [25]

JOHNSON, Rothwell Underwood Moore John, *Allington, Grantham.*—Magd. Coll. Cam. B.A. 1843; Deac. 1845 and Pr. 1846 by Bp of Nor. C. of Muston, Leicestershire, 1861, and West Allington, Lincolnshire, 1865. Formerly C. of Mundesley, Norfolk, 1845, Hilgay 1847, Wisbeach, Cambs, 1852, Newbold Pacey, Warwickshire, 1855, Uffington, Lincolnshire, 1859. [26]

JOHNSON, Samuel, *Atherton, near Manchester.*—Lin. Coll. Ox. B.A. 1820, M.A. 1823; Deac. 1820 and Pr. 1821 by Abp of York. P. C. of Atherton, Dio. Man. 1836. (Patron, Lord Lilford; Tithe—Imp. 118*l* 4*s* 8*d*; Glebe, 10½ acres; P. C.'s Inc. 147*l*; Pop. 5641.) Formerly C. of Radcliffe, near Manchester, 1822–36. [27]

JOHNSON, Stenning, *North Pallant, Chichester.*—Mert. Coll. Ox. B.A. 1841; Deac. 1841 and Pr. 1842 by Bp of Ex. V. of Ramboldswyke, Chichester, Dio. Chich. 1865. (Patrons, D. and C. of Chich; Tithe, comm. 210*l*; Glebe, 14 acres; V.'s Inc. 246*l*; Pop. 582.) Min. Can. of Chich. 1865; Rural Dean; Chap. to Chichester Infirmary. Formerly R. of West Itchenor, Chichester, 1847–65. [1]

JOHNSON, Thomas, 4, *Stanley-terrace, Preston.*—St. Bees; Deac. 1857, Pr. 1858. P. C. of St. Mark's, Preston, Dio. Man. 1865. (Patrons, V. of Preston and Trustees of Ch. Ch. alt; P. C.'s Inc. 300*l*; Pop. 5730.) Formerly C. of St. Peter's, Oldham, Pontefract, and Preston. [2]

JOHNSON, Thomas, *Hinton Ampner, New Alresford, Hants.*—C. of Hinton Ampner and Kilmeston; Dom. Chap. to Lord Rodney. [3]

JOHNSON, William, *Repton, Burton-on-Trent.*—Emman. Coll. Cam. 1st cl. Cl. Trip. B.A. 1853, M.A. 1856; Deac. 1855 and Pr. 1856 by Bp of Lich. Asst. Mast. of Repton Sch. 1855. [4]

JOHNSON, William, *Llanbadrig, near Bangor.*—Dub. A.B. 1846, A.M. 1862; Deac. 1847 by Bp of Ban. Pr. 1848 by Abp of York. V. of Llanbadrig, Dio. Ban. 1852. (Patron, Ld Chan; Tithe—Imp. 380*l* 1*s* 6*d*, V. 180*l* 1*s* 6*d*; Glebe, ½ acre; V.'s Inc. 198*l*; Pop. 1187.) Exam. Chap. to Bp of Ban. Formerly 2nd Mast. of Ruthin Gr. Sch. 1846; C. of Cyffylliog, Denbighshire, 1848. [5]

JOHNSON, William, 6, *Egerton-terrace, Polygon, Ardwick, Manchester.*—Dur. Licen. in Theol. 1865, B.A. 1866; Deac. 1866 by Bp of Man. C. of St. Peter's, Oldham-road, Manchester, 1866. [6]

JOHNSON, William Cooper, *Diptford Parsonage, Ivybridge, Devon.*—Mert. Coll. Ox. B.A. 1833; Deac. and Pr. 1834. R. of Diptford, Dio. Ex. 1837. (Patron, the present R; Tithe, 559*l* 5*s*; Glebe, 2 acres; R.'s Inc. 560*l* and Ho; Pop. 747.) [7]

JOHNSON, William Cowper, *Yaxham Rectory, East Dereham, Norfolk.*—Corpus Coll. Cam. 33rd Wrang. and B.A. 1837, M.A. 1841; Deac. 1837 and Pr. 1839 by Bp of Lin. R. of Yaxham, Dio. Nor. 1843. (Patron, the present R; Tithe, 515*l*; Glebe, 46 acres; R.'s Inc. 585*l* and Ho; Pop. 479.) Rural Dean. [8]

JOHNSON, William Henry, *Witham-on-the-Hill Vicarage, Bourne, Lincolnshire.*—V. of Witham-on-the-Hill, Dio. Lin. 1835. (Patron, General Johnson; V.'s Inc. 107*l* and Ho; Pop. 548.) [9]

JOHNSON, Woodthorpe, *Grainsby Rectory, Grimsby, Lincolnshire.*—St. John's Coll. Cam. B.A. 1837, M.A. 1839; Deac. 1837 and Pr. 1838 by Bp of Lin. R. of Grainsby, Dio. Lin. 1844. (Patrons, Trustees of T. Sands, Esq; Tithe, 269*l*; Glebe, 57 acres; R.'s Inc. 350*l* and Ho; Pop. 124.) V. of Waith, Great Grimsby, Dio. Lin. 1859. (Patrons, W. Haigh, Esq. and Mrs. Haigh; V.'s Inc. 86*l*; Pop. 43.) Formerly C. of Healing 1837, Ravendale 1838, Messingham 1840, Wold Newton 1843–53. [10]

JOHNSTON, Charles Henry, *Coalpit Heath, Bristol.*—St. Edm. Hall, Ox. B.A. 1842, M.A. 1846; Deac. 1843 and Pr. 1844 by Bp of G. and B. P. C. of Coalpit Heath, Dio. G. and B. 1848. (Patron, Bp of G. and B; P. C.'s Inc. 150*l* and Ho; Pop. 1610.) Formerly P. C. of St. Michael's, Two Mile Hill, Bristol. Author, *A Visitation Sermon*, Masters, 1856, 1*s*. [11]

JOHNSTON, Charles William Joseph, *Sproxton Vicarage, Melton Mowbray.*—Emman. Coll. Cam. Sen. Opt. and B.A. 1835, M.A. 1838; Deac. 1835 and Pr. 1836 by Bp of Lin. V. of Sproxton with Saltby V. Dio. Pet. 1847. (Patron, Duke of Rutland; Sproxton, Tithe, 9*s*; Glebe, 71 acres; Saltby, Glebe, 79 acres; V.'s Inc. 274*l* and Ho; Pop. Sproxton 455, Saltby 292.) [12]

JOHNSTON, George, *Barnstaple, Devon.*—King's Coll. Aberdeen, Huttonian Scho. 1815, 1st Huttonian Prizeman 1819, M.A. 1819; Ch. Coll. Cam. B.D. 1839; Deac. 1838 and Pr. 1839 by Bp of Ex. Head Mast. of the Gr. Sch. and Chap. of the Workhouse and Gaol, Barnstaple. [13]

JOHNSTON, George, *Broughton, near Huntingdon.*—Sid. Coll. Cam. Jun. Opt. 3rd cl. Cl. Trip. and B.A. 1829, M.A. 1832; Deac. 1829, Pr. 1832. R. of Broughton, Dio. Ely, 1837. (Patron, the present R; Glebe, 370 acres; R.'s Inc. 400*l* and Ho; Pop. 376.) [14]

JOHNSTON, George Liddell, *Vienna.*—Univ. Coll. Dur. Licen. Theol. 1849; Deac. 1849 by Bp of Dur. Pr. 1850 by Bp of Ex. Chap. to the British Embassy, Vienna, 1856. [15]

JOHNSTON, George Thomson, *Longton Rectory, Staffs.*—Trin. Coll. Cam. C. of Longton 1866. Formerly C. of Long Preston, Yorks. [16]

JOHNSTON, Henry Cromwell, *Langham, Oakham, Rutland.*—Caius Coll. Cam. Sen. Opt. B.A. 1858; M.A. 1862; Deac. 1858 and Pr. 1859 by Bp of Chich. C. of Langham 1865. Formerly C. of Westham, Sussex, 1859–62, Norbiton, Surrey, 1862–65. [17]

JOHNSTON, Henry Graydon, *Brompton Ralph, Wiveliscombe, Somerset.*—Dub. A.B. 1846; Deac. 1847 by Abp of Dub. Pr. 1848 by Abp of Armagh. C. of Brompton Ralph 1865. Formerly C. of Sheringham 1857, High Wycombe 1858, Accrington 1859, Shirley 1861, Silverstone 1863. [18]

JOHNSTON, Hugh William, *The Rectory, North Cray, Kent.*—Trin. Coll. Cam. Cl. Trip. B.A. 1859, M.A. 1862; Deac. 1861 and Pr. 1862 by Bp of Wor. R. of North Cray, Dio. Cant. 1864. (Patron, R. E. Vansittart, Esq; Tithe, 363*l*; Glebe, 90*l*; R.'s Inc. 453*l* and Ho; Pop. 560.) Formerly C. of Chaddesley Corbett, Worc. 1861, Salehurst, Sussex, 1863. [19]

JOHNSTON, James Aitken, 48, *Upper Stamford-street, London, S.*—Literate; Deac. 1834 and Pr. 1836 by Bp of Jamaica. P. C. of St. John's, Waterloo-road, Lond. Dio. Win. 1848. (Patron, Abp of Cant; P. C.'s Inc. 500*l*; Pop. 10,262.) Surrogate. [20]

JOHNSTON, John Talbot, *Beccles, Suffolk.*—Deac. 1839, Pr. 1840. R. of Beccles, Dio. Nor. 1855. (Patron, Rev. E. Holland; Tithe, 350*l*; R.'s Inc. 386*l*; Pop 4266.) Surrogate. Author, *The Existence and Office of Memory in the Future State* (a Sermon). [21]

JOHNSTON, William, *Brislington, near Bristol.*—Dub. A.B. 1848, A.M. 1864; Deac. 1849 by Bp of Tuam, Pr. 1850 by Abp of Armagh. Chap. at Brislington House Asylum 1860. Formerly C. of Maguiresbridge 1849–53, St. James's, Bristol, 1853–56, Thornhaugh with Wansford 1856–59. [22]

JOHNSTON, William Boys, *Cranley, Guildford.*—Ch. Ch. Ox. B.A. 1857, M.A. 1860; Deac. 1858 and Pr. 1859 by Bp of Carl. C. of Cranley 1866. Formerly C. of Levens 1858, Moulsham 1861, Swaffham 1863. [23]

JOHNSTON, William Downes, *Milton Rectory, next Gravesend, Kent.*—St. John's Coll. Ox. B.A. 1826, M.A. 1829; Deac. 1827 by Bp of Lon. Pr. 1829 by Bp of Bristol. R. of Milton-next-Gravesend, Dio. Roch. 1860. (Patrons, Ld Chan. two turns, and Bp of Roch. one turn; Tithe, comm. 325*l* 11*s*; R.'s Inc. 350*l* (net, 270*l*) and Ho; Pop. 1624.) Formerly C. of Yetminster 1827–30, Tunbridge Wells 1831–35, Laddesdown 1835–40; R. of Ifield 1838–60; C. of Milton 1840–60. Author, *The Blessings of Baptism*, S.P.C.K. 1842; *An Order for Family Prayer, on the Plan of a Liturgy*, 1844, 6*d*; *A Short Family Liturgy*, 1851, 6*d*. [24]

JOHNSTONE, Bolton Waller, *Farndon Parsonage, near Chester.*—Dub. A.B. 1844, A.M. 1854; Deac. 1846 by Abp of York, Pr. 1847 by Bp of Dur. P. C. of Farndon, Dio. Ches. 1854. (Patron, Marquis of Westminster; Tithe—Imp. 400*l*; P. C. 2*l*; Glebe, 40 acres; P. C.'s Inc. 100*l* and Ho; Pop. 992.) Author, *Sermons*, 1854. [25]

JOHNSTONE, Charles, *Sutton Hall, Thirsk, Yorks.*—Trin. Coll. Cam. B.A. 1823, M.A. 1824; Deac. 1825 and Pr. 1826 by Abp of York. V. of Feliskirk, Yorks, Dio. York, 1827. (Patron, Abp of York; Tithe—App. 430*l*; Glebe, 150 acres; V.'s Inc. 700*l*; Pop. 878.) Can. Res. of York with the Preb. Stall of Wetwang annexed 1845. (Value, 1200*l* and Res.) [26]

JOHNSTONE, Charles, *Hackness Parsonage, Scarborough.*—Univ. Coll. Dur. B.A. 1852; Deac. 1852,

Pr. 1853. P. C. of Hackness with Harwood-Dale P. C. Dio. York, 1856. (Patron, Sir J. V. B. Johnstone, Bart; Hackness, Tithe—Imp. 22*l*; Glebe, 4 acres; Harwood-Dale, Tithe, 220*l*; Glebe, 10 acres; P. C.'s Inc. 280*l* and Ho; Pop. Hackness 444, Harwood-Dale 214.) Formerly C. of Hackness. [1]

JOHNSTONE, Frederick Richard, *St. Mark's Parsonage, Broadwater, Tunbridge Wells.*—Ex. Coll. Ox. 3rd cl. Lit. Hum. B.A. 1853, M.A. 1856; Deac. 1855 and Pr. 1856 by Bp of Wor. P. C. of St. Mark's, Broadwater, Dio. Chich. 1866. (Patron, Earl of Abergavenny; P. C.'s Inc. 180*l* and Ho; Pop. 700.) Formerly C. of Hagley, Worc. 1855–57, Marston, Yorks, 1857–64. [2]

JOHNSTONE, George Henry, *Sutton St. Nicholas, Hereford.*—Trin. Coll. Cam. B.A. 1840. R. of Sutton St. Nicholas, Dio. Herf. 1847. (Patron, J. Johnston, Esq; R.'s Inc. 220*l* and Ho; Pop. 251.) [3]

JOHNSTONE, John, *Haxey Vicarage, Bawtry.*—St. John's Coll. Cam. B A. 1837, M.A. 1859; Deac. 1837 and Pr. 1838 by Bp of Lon. V. of Haxey and Westwood R. Dio. Lin. 1861. (Patron, Abp of York; Glebe, 108 acres; V.'s Inc. 960*l* and Ho; Pop. 2157.) Formerly C. of Hampton; P. C. of All Saints', Rotherhithe; R. of Bramshurst, Hants; R. and V. of Overton; R. of Tadley. Author, *The Way of Life in Sermons preached before the Queen*, London, Hatchards. [4]

JOHNSTONE, John.—C. of St. John's, Walworth, Surrey. [5]

JOHNSTONE, Thomas Bryan, *Clutton Rectory, near Bristol.*—Trin. Coll. Cam. B.A. 1811, M.A. 1815; Deac. 1812 and Pr. 1813 by Bp of Win. R. of Clutton, Dio. B. and W. 1815. (Patron, Earl of Warwick; Tithe, 308*l*; Glebe, 56 acres; R.'s Inc. 396*l* and Ho; Pop. 1149.) Chap. to the Clutton Union 1838. [6]

JOHNSTONE, William Henry, *Bromsgrove House, Croydon, Surrey.*—St. John's Coll Cam. 13th Wrang. and B.A. 1842, M.A. 1845; Deac. 1844 and Pr 1845 by Abp of Cant. Formerly Asst. Prof. of Math. and Cl. in Military Coll. Addiscombe, 1842–61, and Chap. 1844–61. Author, *Israel after the Flesh, or the Judaism of the Bible separated from its Spiritual Religion*, 1850, 10*s* 6*d*; *Sunday and the Sabbath*, 1853, 1*s* 6*d*; *Israel in the World, or the Mission of the Hebrews to the Great Military Monarchies*, 1854, 3*s* 6*d*; *The Image of the Invisible, or the Life of Christ viewed in Relation to St. Peter's Promise that we are to be Partakers of the Divine Nature*, 1856, 1*s* 6*d*; *Forgiveness and Absolution, a Timely Tract*, and various Sermons. [7]

JOLLEY, George Martin Guise, *Wanstead, Essex.*—King's Coll. Lond. and Clare Hall, Cam. B.A. 1851, M.A. 1854; Deac. and Pr. 1851. C. of Wanstead. Formerly Chap. of the South Metropolitan Industrial Schs; C. of St. George the Martyr's, Southwark. [8]

JOLLEY, William Rowe, *Corse Vicarage, Gloucester.*—St. Peter's Coll. Cam. B.A. 1852, M.A. 1858; Deac. 1850 and Pr. 1851 by Bp of Wor. V. of Corse, Dio. G. and B. 1867. (Patron, Ld Chan; Tithe, 202*l*; Glebe, 181 acres; V.'s Inc. 443*l* and Ho; Pop. 525.) Formerly Chap. of H.M.S. "Illustrious;" Tut. to H.R.H. Prince Arthur; C. of Aston, near Birmingham, 1850–52, St. Bride's, Liverpool, 1852–54. [9]

JOLLIFFE, Thomas Robert, *Babington, Frome, Somerset.*—Trin. Coll. Cam. B.A. 1804, M.A. 1807. R. of Babington, Dio. B. and W. 1810. (Patron, J. T. Jolliffe, Esq; Tithe, 123*l*; Glebe, 6 acres; R.'s Inc. 175*l*; Pop. 129.) [10]

JOLLYE, Albert Palmer, *Seaham Harbour, Durham.*—Dur. Licen. in Theol. 1864; Deac. 1864 by Bp of Dur. C. of St. John's, Seaham Harbour, 1864. [11]

JOLLYE, Hunting, *Wingfield Parsonage, Harleston, Norfolk.*—Jesus Coll. Cam. Sen. Opt. and B.A. 1821, M.A. 1824; Deac. and Pr. 1824. P. C. of Wingfield, Dio. Nor. 1853. (Patron, Bp of Nor; Tithe, 298*l*; P. C.'s Inc. 360*l* and Ho; Pop. 593.) [12]

JONA, Henry, 5, *Addington-road, Bow, E.*—King's Coll. Lond. Assoc; Deac. 1861 and Pr. 1862 by Bp of Lon. Lect. in Divinity at King's Coll. Lond. 1864; C. of Bow, *pro tem.* Formerly C. of Bow 1861–64. [13]

JONAS, Edwin Waldron, 12, *St. Michael's-terrace, Plymouth.*—Dub. A.B. 1856, A.M. 1867; Deac. 1857 and Pr. 1858 by Bp of Ex. Chap of the Devonport Borough Gaol; Cl. Mast. of Devonport and Stoke Gr. Sch. Formerly C. of St. Mellion 1857–60. [14]

JONAS, John George, *Exmouth House, Stoke, Devonport.*—St. John's Coll. Cam. 1st Sen. Opt. Prizeman and Exhib. B.A. 1850, M.A. 1853; Deac. 1853 and Pr. 1855 by Bp. of Ex. Mast. of the Devonport and Stoke Gr. Sch. Formerly C. of St. John's Chapel, Devonport, 1853–55. [15]

JONES, Albert, *Holmer Vicarage, near Hereford.*—St. John's Coll. Ox. 2nd cl. Math. et Phy. and B.A. 1822, M.A. 1824; Deac. 1823 and Pr. 1823 by Bp of Herf. Min. Can. of Herf. Cathl. 1822. (Value, 150*l*.) V. of Holmer with Huntington P. C. Dio. Herf. 1850. (Patrons, D. and C. of Herf; Holmer, Tithe, Eccles. Commis. 8*l* 15*s*, App. 267*l* 11*s* and 35 acres of Glebe, Imp. 20*l*, V. 222*l* 10*s*; Glebe, 12 acres; Huntington, Tithe—App. 85*l* 15*s*, V. 57*l*; V.'s Inc. 399*l* 10*s* and Ho; Pop. Holmer 1083, Huntington 154.) Formerly Chap. of Price's Hospital, Hereford, 1837–65. [16]

JONES, Alfred, *Aske's Hospital, Haberdashers'-walk, Hoxton, London, N.*—King's Coll. Lond; Deac. 1849 and Pr. 1850 by Bp of Lon. Chap. of Aske's Hospital 1854, Head Mast. 1864. (Mast.'s Inc. 200*l* and Ho.) Formerly C. of St. John's and St. Matthew's, Westminster, 1849; Sec. of Sunday Rest Association 1860–67. Author, *A Letter to the City Mission*, 1845; *A Few Words on the State of Westminster*, 1846; *The Proper Names of the Old Testament Scriptures Expounded and Illustrated*, 4to, Bagster, 1856, 24*s*; *Sunday Rest Question*, 1863, 1*s*. [17]

JONES, Ambrose, *Stannington Vicarage, Cramlington, Northumberland.*—St. John's Coll. Cam. B.A. 1848, M.A. 1851; Deac. 1850 and Pr. 1851 by Bp of Ches. V. of Stannington, Dio. Dur. 1867. (Patron, Bp of Ches; Tithe, 342*l*; Glebe, 19 acres; V.'s Inc. 379*l* and Ho; Pop. 1058.) Formerly P. C. of Elworth, Cheshire, 1850–67. [18]

JONES, Basil Morgan, *Llanwenarth Rectory, Abergavenny.*—Jesus Coll. Ox. Hon. 4th in Maths. and B.A. 1863, M.A. 1866; Deac. 1866 and Pr. 1867 by Bp of Llan. C. of Llanwenarth, Monmouthshire, 1866. [19]

JONES, Bulkeley Owen, *The Cloisters, Ruthin, Denbighshire.*—Brasen. Coll. Ox. B.A. 1846, M.A. 1851; Deac. 1847 and Pr. 1848 by Bp of Ban. Warden of Ruthin with Llanrhyd R. Dio. St. A. 1851. (Patrons, D. and C. of Westminster; Tithe, 462*l* 1*s*; Warden's Inc. 463*l* and Ho; Pop. Ruthin 1299, Llanrhyd 965.) [20]

JONES, B. Wilkes, *Sibson, near Atherstone, Leicestershire.*—C. of Sibson. [21]

JONES, Charles, *Cwm Bach, Aberdare.*—Literate; Deac. 1860 and Pr. 1866 by Bp of Llan. C. of Aberdare 1865. Formerly C. of Abersychan, Monmouthshire, 1860–65. [22]

JONES, Charles, *Cardigan.*—Lampeter; Deac. 1860 and Pr. 1861 by Bp of St. D. C. of St. Mary's, Cardigan, 1860. [23]

JONES, Charles, *Matlock Rectory, Derbyshire.*—Theol. Coll. Birmingham; Deac. 1863 and Pr. 1864 by Bp of Ches. C. of Matlock 1867. Formerly C. of Congleton 1863–65, Chesterfield 1866–67. [24]

JONES, Charles Alfred, 1, *Dean's-yard, Westminster, S.W.*—St. John's Coll. Cam. 15th Wrang. B.A. 1857, M.A. 1860; Deac. 1858 and Pr. 1859 by Bp of Ely. Sen. Math. Mast. in Westminster Sch. Formerly C. of St. Clement's, Cambridge, 1858–60; Chap. of St. John's Coll. Cam. 1861–62. Author, *History of the Jesus Lane Sunday School*, 1864; Joint-Editor, *Algebraical Exercises Progressively Arranged*, Macmillans, 1867. [25]

JONES, Charles Parry, *Prospect House, St. David's.*—Lampeter; Deac. 1856 by Bp of Herf. Pr. 1857 by Bp of St. D. Min. Can. of St. David's. (Patrons, D. and C. of St. D; M. C.'s Inc. 150*l*.) Formerly C. of Aberystwith 1856–58, Letterstone 1858–59. [26]

JONES, Charles Powell, *Forcester Vicarage, Stonehouse, Gloucestershire.*—Deac. 1828, Pr. 1829. V. of Forcester with Chapel, Dio. G. and B. 1837. (Patron,

Rev. H. W. Bloxsome; Tithe—Imp. 100*l*, V. 260*l*; Glebe, 5½ acres; V.'s Inc. 273*l* and Ho; Pop. 262.) [1]

JONES, Charles William, *Pakenham Vicarage, Bury St. Edmunds.*—Caius Coll. Cam. B.A. 1848, M.A. 1851; Deac. 1848 and Pr. 1849. V. of Pakenham, Dio. Ely, 1861. (Patron, the present V; Tithe, 265*l* 2*s*; Glebe, 68 acres; V.'s Inc. 323*l* and Ho; Pop. 1130.) Formerly C. of Pakenham 1848. Author, *Reading Books for Adult and other Schools*, Longmans. [2]

JONES, Charles William Frederick, *Bangor, N. Wales.*—Jesus Coll. Ox. B.A. 1857, M.A. 1858; Deac. 1858 by Bp of St. A. Pr. 1859 by Bp of Ban. Min. Can. in Bangor Cathl. 1863. (M. C.'s Inc. 150*l*.) Formerly C. of Penmorva with Dolbenmaen, Carnarvonshire, 1858–61, Yalding, Kent, 1861–62, West Farleigh, Kent, 1862–63. [3]

JONES, Christopher Jay, *Westbury-on-Severn, Gloucester.*—Brasen. Coll. Ox. B.A. 1852, M.A. 1855; Deac. 1852, Pr. 1853. V. of Westbury-on-Severn, Dio. G. and B. 1858. (Patrons, Custos and Coll. of Vicars-Choral in Herf. Cathl; Tithe—App. 628*l* and 42 acres of Glebe, V. 291*l* 4*s*; V.'s Inc. 299*l* and Ho; Pop. 2501.) Rural Dean 1865. Formerly C. of Sutton St. Nicholas, Herefordshire. [4]

JONES, Daniel, *Llawhaden Vicarage, Narberth, Pembrokeshire.*—Deac. 1816 and Pr. 1817 by Bp of St. D. V. of Llawhaden with Bletherston C. Dio. St. D. 1836. (Patron, Bp of St. D; Llawhaden, Tithe—App. 210*l* and 170 acres of Glebe, V. 105*l*; Glebe, 47 acres; Bletherston, Tithe—App. 116*l* 13*s* 4*d*, V. 58*l* 6*s* 8*d*; R.'s Inc. 220*l* and Ho; Pop. Llawhaden 647, Bletherston 255.) [5]

JONES, Daniel, *Ystradowen, Cowbridge, Glamorgunshire.*—P. C. of Ystradowen, Dio. Llan. 1866. (Patron, Bp of Llan; P. C.'s Inc. 52*l*; Pop. 248.) [6]

JONES, Daniel Lewis, *Gwyddelwern, Corwen, Merionethshire.*—V. of Gwyddelwern, Dio. St. A. 1829. (Patron, Bp of St. A; Tithe—App. 560*l*, V. 140*l*; Glebe, 5 acres; V.'s Inc. 170*l*; Pop. 1541.) [7]

JONES, D., *Trawsvynydd, Carnarvon.*—R. of Trawsvynydd, Dio. Ban. 1862. (Patron, Bp of Ban; R.'s Inc. 200*l* and Ho; Pop. 1517.) [8]

JONES, David, *Upper Bangor, Carnarvonshire.*—Dub. A.B. 1862, A.M. 1865; Deac. 1862, Pr. 1863. C. of St. James's, Upper Bangor, 1866. Formerly C. of Holywell 1862–65, Bagillt 1865–66. [9]

JONES, David, *Kilgwrwg, Usk, Monmouthshire.*—C. of Kilgwrwg. [10]

JONES, David, *Brynford Parsonage, Holywell, Flintshire.*—Lampeter; Deac. 1851, Pr. 1852. P. C. of Brynford, Dio. St. A. 1853. (Patron, Bp of St. A; Tithe, 69*l*; Glebe, 4 acres; P. C.'s Inc. 159*l*; Pop. 910.) [11]

JONES, David, *Stanley St. Leonards, Stroud, Glouc.*—Deac. 1821, Pr. 1822; P. C. of Stanley St. Leonards, Dio. G. and B. 1839. (Patrons, Trustees of late Mrs. Cumberland; Glebe, 110 acres; P. C.'s Inc. 200*l*; Pop. 864.) [12]

JONES, David, *Abergorlech, Lampeter, Cardiganshire.*—P. C. of Abergorlech, Dio. St. D. 1832. (Patron, V. of Llanybyther; P. C.'s Inc. 60*l*.) [13]

JONES, David, *Bishopston, Swansea.*—Deac. 1825, Pr. 1826. R. of Bishopston, Dio. St. D. 1831. (Patron, Bp of Llan; Tithe, 236*l* 0*s* 8*d*; R.'s Inc. 250*l* and Ho; Pop. 418.) V. of Pennard, Glamorganshire, Dio. St. D. 1849. (Patron, Thomas Penrice, Esq; Tithe—Imp. 142*l*, V. 78*l*; V.'s Inc. 79*l*; Pop. 321.) [14]

JONES, David, *Llanarmon Dyffryn Ceiriog, Llangollen, Denbighshire.*—Jesus Coll. Ox. B.A. 1839, M.A. 1842; Deac. 1839, Pr. 1840. R. of Llanarmon, Dio. St. A. 1848. (Patron, Bp of St. A; R.'s Inc. 250*l* and Ho; Pop. 315.) [15]

JONES, David, *Llandewi-Velfrey Vicarage, Narberth, Pembrokeshire.*—Deac. 1811 by Bp of Llan. Pr. 1812 by Bp of St. D. V. of Llandewi-Velfrey, Dio. St. D. 1830. (Patron, Ld Chan; Tithe—Imp. 200*l*, V. 200*l*; Glebe, 46 acres; V.'s Inc. 260*l* and Ho; Pop. 790.) R. of Crinow, Pembrokeshire, Dio. St. D. 1830. (Patron, Ld Chan; Tithe, 50*l*; Glebe, 1 acre; R.'s Inc. 87*l*; Pop. 70.) Formerly V. of Castlemartin, Pembrokeshire, 1814–38. [16]

JONES, David, *Brechva, near Carmarthen.*—R. of Brechva, Dio. St. D. 1856. (Patrons, Families of Tragib and Aberathy alt; Tithe, 21*l* 16*s* 10*d*; R.'s Inc. 80*l*; Pop. 122.) [17]

JONES, David, 16, *Park-row, Greenwich, S.E.*—Queens' Coll. Cam. B.D. 1830; Deac. 1808 and Pr. 1809 by Bp of St. D. Chap. to the Greenwich Union 1839; Surrogate 1824; Dom. Chap. to Lord Saye and Sele. Formerly Chap. to Marine Society 1816–60; Chap. to the "Dreadnought" Hospital Ship 1820–54. Author, *Lectures on the Lord's Prayer* (for the use of Boys on board the Marine Soc. Ships), Greenwich, 1858. [18]

JONES, David, *Hope Rectory, Ludlow.*—Ch. Ch. Coll. Brecon; Deac. 1814, Pr. 1815. R. of Hope Bagget, Dio. Herf. 1840. (Patron, Duke of Cleveland; Tithe, 78*l* 16*s*; Glebe, 26 acres; R.'s Inc. 120*l* and Ho; Pop. 82.) [19]

JONES, David, *Llanguick, Neath, Glamorganshire.*—P. C. of Llanguick, Dio. St. D. 1860. (Patron, F. E. Lloyd, Esq; P. C.'s Inc. 120*l*; Pop. 6338.) [20]

JONES, David, *Llandinam, Llanidloes, Montgomeryshire.*—Lampeter; Deac. 1834 and Pr. 1835 by Bp of St. D. V. of Llandinam, Dio. Ban. 1839. (Patron, Bp of Ban; Tithe—App. 730*l*, V. 190*l*; V.'s Inc. 500*l*; Pop. 1574.) P. C. of Banhaglog, near Llanidloes, Dio. Ban. (Patron, Bp of Ban.) Formerly C. of Llanidloes 1834–38, Llandinam 1839. [21]

JONES, David, *Mountain Ash, Aberdare.*—Jesus Coll. Ox. Hon. 4th cl. in Math. 1858, B.A. 1858, M.A. 1861; Deac. 1858, Pr. 1859. P. C. of St. Margaret's, Mountain Ash, Dio. Llan. 1863. (Patron, Bp of Llan; P. C.'s Inc. 300*l* and Ho; Pop. 7,500.) Formerly C. of Aberdare 1858–63. [22]

JONES, David, *Llantysilio, Llangollen.*—St. Bees; Deac. 1853 and Pr. 1854 by Bp of St. A. P. C. of Llantysilio, Dio. St. A. 1862. (Patron, Sir W. W. Wynn, Bart; Tithe, Imp. 412*l*; Glebe, 46 acres; P. C.'s Inc. 125*l* and Ho; Pop. 1120.) Formerly C. of Llanfair-caereinion 1853, Llangyniew 1856, Castle Caereinion 1858, Corwen 1860. [23]

JONES, David, *Llangollen.*—Lampeter; Deac. 1864 and Pr. 1865 by Bp of St. A. C. of Llangollen 1864. [24]

JONES, David, *Clydach, Swansea.*—Lampeter; Deac. 1864 by Bp of St. D. Asst. C. of Clydach, 1864. [25]

JONES, David, *Slaidburn, near Clitheroe.*—St. Bees; Deac. and Pr. 1828. R. of Slaidburn with Dalehead C. Dio. Rip. 1861. (Patron, Leonard Wilkinson, Esq; Tithe, 513*l*; Glebe, 10 acres; R.'s Inc. 568*l* and Ho; Pop. 1481.) Formerly C. of Slaidburn 1828, Woodbridge, Suffolk, 1838, Wymondham, Norfolk, 1839–52; Sunday Even. Lect. at the Parish Ch. and Chap. to Wymondham Bridewell 1839–62. [26]

JONES, David, *Aberdare.*—C. of St. Fagan's, Aberdare. [27]

JONES, David, *Bodedeyrn, Bangor.*—C. of Bodedeyrn. [28]

JONES, David, *Golborne, Warrington.*—C. of Golborne. [29]

JONES, David Joseph, *Llanarth Vicarage, Carmarthen.*—Lampeter 1845–47; Deac. 1847, Pr. 1848. V. of the United V.'s of Llanarth and Llanina, Dio. St. D. 1853. (Patron, Bp of St. D; Llanarth, Tithe—App. 303*l* 8*s* 4*d*, Imp. 4*l* 17*s* 6*d*, V. 151*l* 14*s* 2*d*; Llanina, Tithe—App. 46*l* 13*s* 4*d*, V. 45*l* 16*s* 8*d*; V.'s Inc. 210*l* and Ho; Pop. Llanarth 2216, Llanina 498.) [30]

JONES, D. J., *Rhymney, Newport, Monmouthshire.*—C. of Rhymney. [31]

JONES, David Lewes, *Mothvey Vicarage, Llandovery, Carmarthenshire.*—Lampeter; Deac. 1828, Pr. 1829. V. of Mothvey, St. Dio. D. 1850. (Patron, Bp of St. D; Tithe—App. 280*l*, V. 140*l*; Glebe, 7 acres; V.'s Inc. 157*l* and Ho; Pop. 1118) C. of Talley 1867. [32]

JONES, David Secretan, *Lee, Kent.*—Univ. Coll. Ox. 3rd cl. Lit. Hum. B.A. 1857; Deac. 1858 by Bp of G. and B. C. of Lee 1864. Formerly C. of Swindon, Wilts. [33]

JONES, David Thomas, *Wark, near Hexham.*—C. of Wark. [1]

JONES, Denis Edward, *Stamford, Lincolnshire.*—Lin. Coll. Ox. B.A. 1830; Deac. 1830, Pr. 1831. R. of St. John's with St. Clement's, Stamford, Dio. Lin. 1833. (Patrons, Marquis of Exeter two turns, and R. Newcomb, Esq. one turn; Tithe, 12*s*; Glebe, 47 acres; R.'s Inc. 209*l* and Ho; Pop. 1199.) Chap. to the Stamford and Rutland Infirmary. [2]

JONES, Ebenezer, *Nerquis Mold, Flintshire.*—Lampeter; Deac. 1852 and Pr. 1853 by Bp of Llan. P. C. of Nerquis, Dio. St. A. 1856. (Patron, V. of Mold; Tithe, 43*l*; P. C.'s Inc. 120*l*; Pop. 842.) Formerly C. of Llansantffraid, Merionethshire. [3]

JONES, Ebenezer, *Llanefydd Vicarage, Rhyl.*—Dub. A.B. 1853; Deac. 1854 and Pr. 1855 by Bp of Llan. V. of Llanefydd, Dio. St. A. 1865. (Patron, Bp of St. A; Tithe—App. 464*l*, V. 260*l*; Glebe, 3 acres; V.'s Inc. 280*l* and Ho; Pop. 1136.) Formerly C. of Aberdare 1853–57, Llanelly 1857–61, Llanefydd 1861–65. [4]

JONES, Edward, *Bistre Parsonage, Mold, Flintshire.*—P. C. of Bistre, Dio. St. A. 1842. (Patron, V. of Mold; P. C.'s Inc. 180*l* and Ho; Pop. 2347.) [5]

JONES, Edward, *West Peckham Vicarage, Maidstone.*—Corpus Coll. Cam. 10th Sen. Opt. and B.A. 1828, M.A. 1831; Deac. 1834 by Bp of Win. Pr. 1835 by Abp of Cant. V. of West Peckham, Dio. Cant. 1839. (Patrons, D. and C. of Roch; Tithe—App. 282*l* 1*s* 7*d*; V. 309*l* 5*s* 2*d*; Glebe, 17 acres; V.'s Inc. 274*l* and Ho; Pop. 446.) [6]

JONES, Edward, *Gwaenysgor, Rhyl.*—Jesus Coll. Ox. B.A. 1825; Deac. 1826, Pr. 1827. R. of Gwaenysgor, Dio. St. A. 1850. (Patron, Bp of St. A; Tithe—Imp. 1*l*, R. 175*l*; Glebe, 12 acres; R.'s Inc. 200*l* and Ho; Pop. 322.) [7]

JONES, Edward, *Nantglyn, near Denbigh.*—Jesus Coll. Ox. B.A. 1850, M.A. 1853; Deac. 1849 and Pr. 1850 by Bp of St. A. V. of Nantglyn, Dio. St. A. 1863. (Patron, Bp of St. A; Tithe, 180*l*; Glebe, 1½ acres; V.'s Inc. 180*l* and Ho; Pop. 320.) Formerly C. of Flint 1849-50; P. C. of Llanarmon and Llanrhaiadr 1852–60. Editor, *Y Cenadwr Eglwysig* (the Church Missionary); a serial published by the Church Missionary Society. [8]

JONES, Edward Evans, *Gorsedd Parsonage, Holywell, Flintshire.*—St. Bees; Deac. 1849 and Pr. 1850 by Bp of St. A. P. C. of St. Paul's, Gorsedd, Dio St. A. 1853. (Patron, Bp of St. A; Glebe, 2 acres; P. C.'s Inc. 220*l* and Ho; Pop. 639.) [9]

JONES, Edward Henry, *Tooting, Surrey, S.*—King's Coll. Lond. Assoc. 1866; Deac. 1866 by Bp of Win. C. of Tooting. [10]

JONES, Edward Lloyd, *Llangerniew Vicarage, Conway.*—Jesus Coll. Ox. B.A. 1825; Deac. and Pr. 1825. V. of Llangerniew, Dio. St. A. 1843. (Patron, Bp of St. A; Tithe, 271*l* 6*s* 10*d*; Glebe, 20¼ acres; V.'s Inc. 310*l* and Ho; Pop. 1245.) [11]

JONES, Edward Newton, *Penkhull, Stoke-upon-Trent.*—Jesus Coll. Ox. B.A. 1844; Deac. 1844 and Pr. 1845 by Bp of Herf. P. C. of Penkhull, Dio. Lich. 1860. (Patron, T. W. Minton; P. C.'s Inc. 180*l*; Pop. 2110.) Formerly P. C. of Bagillt, Flintshire, 1850 55; P. C. of Lynesach with Softly, Durham, 1855–60. Author, Sermons, *The Power and Mercy of God as exemplified in His Dealings with Men*; *The Preaching of the Cross*; *The Late War with Russia*; *The Love of Money the Root of all Evil, or the Sin of Gambling*; "*Be Still and know that I am God*" (on the occasion of the wreck of the "Royal Charter"), 1859; *The Apostles Preaching Christ*, 4*d*; *Gossip, its Character and Results*, 4*d*. [12]

JONES, Edward Rhys, *Limehouse Rectory, London, E.*—Brasen. Coll. Ox. 1st cl. Lit. Hum and B.A. 1839, M.A. 1843; Deac. 1841, Pr. 1842. R. of Limehouse, Dio. Lon. 1850. (Patron, Brasen. Coll. Ox; Glebe, 437 acres; R.'s Inc. 700*l* and Ho; Pop. 15,609.) Rural Dean. Formerly Michel Fell. of Queen's Coll. Ox. 1842; Fell. of Brasen. Coll. Ox. 1843. [13]

JONES, Evan, *Llanvihangel ar-arth, Carmarthen.*—Lampeter, B.D. 1860; Deac. 1853 and Pr. 1854 by Bp of Llan. V. of Llanvihangel-ar-arth. Dio. St. D. 1860. (Patrons, W. P. Lewes, Esq. alt. with W. O. Brigstocke and T. Elliott, Esqs; Tithe, 78*l*; Glebe, 50*l*; V.'s Inc. 160*l* and Ho; Pop. 1780.) Formerly C. of Radyr 1853, Llandyssilio Gogo 1856, Llandyssul 1858. [14]

JONES, Evan, *Lampeter, Cardiganshire.*—Lampeter, B.D. 1854; Deac. and Pr. 1833. P. C. of St. Alban's, Llanddewi-Aberath, Dio. St. D. 1853. (Patrons, Proprietors of Ty-Glyn Estate; P. C.'s Inc. 60*l*.) Formerly Sen. Cl. Tut. in the Free Gr. Sch. Winwick, Lancashire, Author, *A Statistical Account of the Population of St. Bartholomew's District, Liverpool, in* 1844. [15]

JONES, Evan, *Cadoxton-juxta-Neath, Glamorganshire.*—C. of Cadoxton. [16]

JONES, Evan, *Pentrebach, Merthyr Tydvil.*—King's Coll. Lond; Deac. 1866 by Bp of Llan. C. of St. John's, Pontyrhun, Pentrebach, 1866. Author, *Poems and Essays* in Welsh contributed to Welsh periodicals. [17]

JONES E., *Cardiff.*—C. of St. Mary's, Cardiff. [18]

JONES, E., *Taibach, Glamorganshire.*—C. of Margam with Taibach. [19]

JONES, Francis, *Morton-Pinckney Parsonage, Banbury.*—Oriel Coll. Ox. B.A. 1831, M.A. 1837; Deac. 1836 by Bp of Ely, Pr. 1837 by Bp of G. and B. P. C. of Morton-Pinckney, Dio. Pet. 1837. (Patron, Oriel Coll. Ox; Tithe—Imp. 163*l* 3*s*; Glebe, 125 acres; P. C.'s Inc. 250*l* and Ho; Pop. 570.) Formerly Head Mast. of Uffculme Gr. Sch. Devon. Author, *Village Church Sermons*, 1841. [20]

JONES, Francis Innes, *Darley Abbey Parsonage, near Derby.*—St. Bees; Deac. 1851, Pr. 1852. P. C. of Darley Abbey, Dio. Lich. 1854. (Patrons, T. W. Evans, Esq. M.P. and Samuel Evans, Esq; Glebe, 2 acres; P. C.'s Inc. 300*l* and Ho; Pop. 967.) Formerly C. of Elland, Yorks, 1851-53, St. Michael's, Stockwell, Lond. 1853-54. [21]

JONES, Frederick Edward Lloyd, *Newgate, London, E.C.*—Corpus Coll. Cam. Bacon Scho. B.A. 1854, M.A. 1857; Deac. 1855 and Pr. 1856 by Bp of Nor. Ordinary of Newgate. Formerly C. of Great Cressingham and Bodney, Norfolk; Sen. C. of Greenwich. [22]

JONES, Frederick Foster, *Kemerton, Tewkesbury.*—Pemb. Coll. Cam. B.A 1859; Deac. 1860 and Pr. 1861 by Bp of Roch. C. of Kemerton 1865. Formerly C. of Little Bardfield 1860, Kilmersdon 1862. [23]

JONES, Frederick Havard, *Grantham.*—Emman. Coll. Cam. 27th Wrang. and B.A. 1855, M.A. 1858; Deac. 1856 and Pr. 1857 by Bp of Lin. 2nd Mast. of the Gr. Sch. Grantham, 1858. Formerly C. of South Collingham and Langford-cum-Holme, Notts, 1856–58. [24]

JONES, George, *Wrecclesham, Farnham, Surrey.*—C. of Wrecclesham. [25]

JONES, George, *Tintern Magna, Chepstow, Monmouthshire.*—Deac. 1849 by Bp of Herf. Pr. 1850 by Bp of Llan. P. C. of Chapel Hill, near Chepstow, Dio. Llan. 1851. (Patron, Duke of Beaufort; P. C.'s Inc. 75*l*; Pop. 497.) Chap. to the Chepstow Union 1852. [26]

JONES, George Alfred, *Mossley Parsonage, Ashton-under-Lyne.*—P. C. of Mossley, Dio. Man. 1864. (Patron, R. of Ashton; P. C.'s Inc. 300*l* and Ho; Pop. 9000.) Formerly C. of Ashton-under-Lyne. [27]

JONES, George John Avery, *Lowesby Vicarage, Billesdon, near Leicester.*—St. Peter's Coll. Cam. B.A. 1848; Deac. 1848 and Pr. 1849 by Bp of Pet. V. of Lowesby, Dio. Pet. 1849. (Patron, Sir F. T. Fowke, Bart; Tithe, 6*l* 13*s* 4*d*; Glebe, 56 acres; V.'s Inc. 120*l*; Pop. 259.) [28]

JONES, George Woven, *Longgrove Parsonage, Ross, Herefordshire.*—M.D; Deac. 1844, Pr. 1845. P. C. of Longgrove, Dio. Herf. 1857. (Patroness, Mrs. Marriott; Glebe, 2 acres; P. C.'s Inc. 104*l* and Ho; Pop. 742.) Formerly C. of Trinity Chapel, Bordesley, Birmingham, 1844, Newent 1848, and Alvington, Gloucestershire, 1852. [29]

JONES, George W., *Lye, near Stourbridge.*—C. of Lye. [30]

JONES, Griffith Arthur, *Llanegryn, Machynlleth, Merionethshire.*—Jesus Coll. Ox. B.A. 1851, M.A.

1853; Deac. 1851 and Pr. 1852 by Bp of Ban. P. C. of Llanegryn, Dio. Ban. 1857. (Patrons, Peter Titley, Esq. and others; Tithe, Imp. 327*l*; P. C.'s Inc. 87*l*; Pop. 652.) Formerly C. of Gwalchmai, near Holyhead. Author, in conjunction with the Rev. C. W. Heaton and the Rev. Lewis Gilbertson, *Y Psallwyr neu Psalmau Dafydd, wedi eu nodi au haddasu i'r Tônau Cyntefig* (the Psalter, pointed, in Welsh, for Chanting to the Tones of the Church), Oxford, 1854, 2*s* 6*d*; *Y Caniadau a Chredo S. Athanasius wedi eu nodi a'u haddasu i'r Tônau Cyntefig* (the Canticles, in the same form), 1854, 6*d*; *Ffurf igynnal Gwylnos*, 2*d*; *Bedydd Esgob*, 3*d*. [1]

JONES, Harry, 2, *Duchess-street, Portland-place, London, W.*—St. John's Coll. Cam. B.A. 1846, M.A. 1849; Deac. 1848, Pr. 1849. P. C. of St. Luke's, Berwick-street, St. James's, Westminster, Dio. Lon. 1858. (Patron, R. of St. James's; P. C.'s Inc. 300*l*; Pop. 9219.) Formerly C. of Baddow, Essex, 1848–49, Drinkstone, Suffolk, 1850–52, St. Mark's, North Audley-street, Lond. 1852–57, St. Mary's, Marylebone, 1858. Author, *Church of England and Common Sense*, Macmillans, 3*s* 6*d*; *Holiday Papers*, Hardwicke, 6*s*; *Priest and Parish*, 6*s*; and *Life in the World* (Sermons), Rivingtons, 5*s*. [2]

JONES, Harry Longueville.—Magd. Coll. Cam. Fell. of, Wrang. and B.A. 1828, M.A. 1831; Deac. 1829 and Pr. 1832 by Bp of Ely. Formerly one of H.M. Inspectors of Schs. Editor of the *Archæologia Cambrensis*. [3]

JONES, Henry, *Thornes Parsonage, Wakefield.*—Bp Cosin's Hall, Dur. Licen. in Theol. 1854; Deac. 1854 by Bp of Dur. Pr. 1855 by Bp of Man. for Bp of Dur. P. C. of Thornes, Dio. Rip. 1859. (Patron, V. of Wakefield; Glebe, 6 acres; P. C.'s Inc. 200*l* and Ho; Pop. 1798.) Hon. Chap. of 3rd Battalion West York Rifle Volunteers. Formerly C. of Trinity, Hartlepool, and of Wakefield. [4]

JONES, Henry, *Boxford, near Colchester.*—Ex. Coll. Ox. 2nd cl. Lit. Hum. and B.A. 1819, M.A. 1826; Deac. 1824 and Pr. 1825 by Bp of Glouc. P. C. of Shelley, Suffolk, Dio. Nor. 1852. (Patroness, Mrs. J. M. Cripps; P. C.'s Inc. 75*l*; Pop. 142.) Mast. of the Gr. Sch. Boxford, 1850. Formerly Prin. of Codrington Coll. Barbados, 1835–46. [5]

JONES, Henry, *Great Ilford, London, E.*—Lampeter; Sen. Scho. of; Deac. 1860 and Pr. 1861 by Bp of Llan. C. of Great Ilford 1866. Formerly C. of Wakes Colne 1863–66. [6]

JONES, Henry, *Osmotherley, Northallerton, Yorks.*—Dub. A.B. 1844, A.M. 1848; Deac. 1844 and Pr. 1845 by Bp of Rip. V. of Osmotherley, Dio. York. 1852. (Patron, Ld Chan; Tithe—App. 18*s*, Imp. 209*l* 11*s*; V.'s Inc. 113*l*; Pop. 1320.) Author, *Letter to Earl Grey on the Irish Church, with some Remarks on Sacrilege*, 1846; *Lecture on the Primitive Christianity of Britain and its Independence of Rome*, 1848; *Letter to Lord John Russell, pointing out the True Way of opposing Rome and strengthening the Church of England* (occasioned by his Durham Letter), 1850; *Six Lectures on the Church as distinguished from Rome and Ultra-Protestantism*, 1851; etc. [7]

JONES, Henry, 63, *Hope-street, Liverpool.*—St. John's Coll. Cam. B.A. 1863, M.A. 1866; Deac. 1863 and Pr. 1864 by Bp of Ches. Miss. C. of St. Paul's, Liverpool, 1866. Formerly C. of St. Aidan's, Kirkdale, 1863–64, Garston 1864–66. [8]

JONES, Henry Berkeley, *Whalley Range, Manchester.*—C. of Whalley Range. [9]

JONES, Henry Charles Pryce, *Clergy Orphan School, St. Thomas's Hill, Canterbury.*—Wor. Coll. Ox. B.A. 1855, M.A. 1862; Deac. 1857 and Pr. 1858 by Abp of Cant. Asst. Mast. of the Clergy Orphan Sch. Canterbury. Formerly C. of Hern Hill, near Faversham, 1860–65. [10]

JONES, Henry David, 39, *Cumberland-street, London, S.W.*—St. John's Coll. Cam. B.A; Deac. 1865 and Pr. 1866 by Abp of York. Asst. C. of St. Gabriel's, Pimlico. Formerly C. of St. James's, Hull. [11]

JONES, Henry Denson, 119, *Highfield, Sheffield.*—Pemb. Coll. Cam. B.A. 1841; Deac. 1841, Pr. 1842. P. C. of Heeley, Dio. York, 1846. (Patrons, the Crown and Abp of York alt; P. C.'s Inc. 180*l*; Pop. 5563.) Author, *God's Providence, the Queen's Inheritance* (a Sermon), 1842, 1*s*. [12]

JONES, Henry William, *Hunslet, Leeds.*—St. Aidan's 1857. C. of St. Mary's, Hunslet. [13]

JONES, Henry Wynne, *Penmynydd, Bangor.*—Jesus Coll. Ox. B.A. 1837, M.A. 1844; Deac. 1839, Pr. 1840. P. C. of Penmynydd Dio. Ban. 1850. (Patron, Preb. of Penmynydd in Ban. Cathl; Tithe—App. 434*l* 4*s* 3*d*; Glebe, 6 acres; P. C.'s Inc. 98*l* and Ho; Pop. 446.) Rural Dean. [14]

JONES, Herbert, *Blaenpenal, Tregaron, Cardiganshire.*—Lampeter; Deac. 1850 and Pr. 1851 by Bp of Llan. P. C. of Blaenpenal, Dio. St. D. 1853. (Patron, P. C. of Llanddewi Brefi; Tithe—Imp. 101*l*; P. C.'s Inc. 123*l*; Pop. 522.) Formerly C. of Mynyddyslwyn, Monmouthshire, 1851, Oakwood, Glamorganshire, 1852. [15]

JONES, Herbert Walsingham, *Sculthorpe Rectory, Fakenham, Norfolk.*—Trin. Coll. Cam. B.A. 1849, M.A. 1852; Deac. 1850 and Pr. 1851 by Bp of Nor. R. of Sculthorpe, Dio. Nor. 1359. (Patron, Sir Willoughby Jones, Bart; R.'s Inc. 600*l* and Ho; Pop. 680.) Formerly Asst. C. of Runton, Norfolk. [16]

JONES, Hubert Francis, *Vicarage, St. Thomas the Martyr's, Oxford.*—Queen's Coll. Ox. B.A. 1857, M.A. 1860; Deac. 1857 and Pr. 1858 by Bp of B. and W. C. of St. Thomas the Martyr's, Oxford, 1860. Formerly C. of Cheddar, Somerset, 1857–60. [17]

JONES, Hugh, *Holywell Vicarage, Flintshire.*—Jesus Coll. Ox. B.A. 1836, M.A. 1839; Deac. 1839, Pr. 1840. V. of Holywell, Dio. St. A. 1844. (Patron, Jesus Coll. Ox; Tithe—Imp. 958*l* 19*s* 3*d*, V. 271*l* 5*s*; Glebe, 40 acres; V.'s Inc. 365*l* and Ho; Pop. 6536.) Can. of St. Asaph Cathl. 1860. (Value, 350*l*.) Rural Dean. Formerly Fell. of Jesus Coll. Ox. 1839. Author, *The Christian's Example* (Eight Sermons preached in Lent, 1848), 3*s*; *The Evil of Consenting to Popery* (a Sermon), 1849, 3*d*; *Our Warfare and our Weapons* (a Visitation Sermon), 1855; *A Collection of* 400 *Psalms and Hymns for Public Worship*, Holywell, 1*s* 2*d*. [18]

JONES, The Ven. Hugh Chambres, 13, *Portland-place, London, W.*, and *Brynsteddfod, Conway.*—Ch. Ch. Ox. B.A. 1805, M.A. 1807; Deac. 1806 and Pr. 1807 by Bp of Ox. Treasurer of St. Paul's Cathl. Lond. 1816. Late Archd. of Essex 1823–61. Formerly V. of West Ham, Essex, 1807–45; R. of Aldham, Essex, 1823–40, Dom. Chap. and Sec. to William, 3rd Duke of Portland, 1807–9; Exam. Chap. to Dr. W. Howley, Bp of Lon. 1813–28. [19]

JONES, Hugh Hughes, *Llanidan Vicarage, Anglesey.*—King's Coll. Lond. and Emman. Coll. Cam. B.A. 1846; Deac. 1847 and Pr. 1848 by Bp of Wor. V. of Llanidan with Llanedwen C. Llanddaniel C. and Llanfairycwymwd C. Dio. Ban. 1850. (Patron, Lord Boston; Llanidan, Tithe—Imp. 370*l*, V. 185*l*; Llanedwen, Tithe—Imp. 130*l*, V. 65*l*; Llanddaniel, Tithe—Imp. 160*l*, V. 80*l*; Llanfairycwymwd, Tithe—Imp. 26*l*, V. 13*l*; V.'s Inc. 343*l* and Ho; Pop. Llanidan 1323, Llanedwen 273, Llanddaniel 443, Llanfairycwymwd 37.) Author, *The Spiritual Portraiture of the True Believers* (a Sermon). [20]

JONES, Hugh William, *Nantyglo, Monmouthshire.*—St. Bees; Deac. 1865 by Bp of Llan. C. of Nantyglo 1865. [21]

JONES, James, *Rhydymwyn, Mold.*—King's Coll. Lond. Theol. Assoc. 1855; Deac. 1856 and Pr. 1857 by Bp of St. A. P. C. of Rhydymwyn, Dio. St. A. 1865. (Patron, Bp of St. A; Tithe, 236*l* 9*s*; Glebe, 1¾ acres; P. C.'s Inc. 278*l*; Pop. 700.) Formerly C. of Llanuwchllyn 1856, Llansantffraid Glyndyfrdwg 1858, Holywell 1860, Ysceifiog 1861, Rhydymwyn 1863. [22]

JONES, James, *Fir Grove, Ruthin, Denbighshire.*—Jesus Coll. Ox. 3rd cl. Lit. Hum. and B.A. 1831, M.A. 1835; Deac. 1832 and Pr. 1833 by Bp of Ban. R. of Llanfwrog, near Ruthin, Dio. St. A. 1851. (Patron, Bp of St. D; Tithe, 456*l*; Glebe, 8½ acres; R.'s Inc. 486*l*; Pop. 1425.) Surrogate. [23]

JONES, James, *Swansea.*—C. of Swansea. [24]

JONES, James, *Hirnant, Llanfyllin, Montgomeryshire.*—C. of Hirnant. [1]

JONES, James, *Llangoed, Anglesey.*—C. of Llangoed. [2]

JONES, James Evans, *Bagillt Parsonage, Holywell, Flintshire.*—Univ. Coll. Dur. Licen. Theol. 1848; Deac. 1848 and Pr. 1850 by Bp of Dur. P. C. of Bagillt, Dio. St. A. 1856. (Patron, V. of Holywell; Glebe, 2 acres; P. C.'s Inc. 190*l* and Ho; Pop. 2935.) Formerly P. C. of Lynesach, Durham, 1848–56. [3]

JONES, James Foster, *Coelbren, Ystradgynlais, near Swansea.*—Queen's Coll. Birmingham; Deac. 1858 and Pr. 1859 by Bp of Ban. P. C. of Capel-Coelbren, Dio. St. D. 1862. (Patron, R. of Ystradgynlais; P. C.'s Inc. 100*l*.) Formerly C. of Ystradgynlais. [4]

JONES, Jenkin, *Gwersyllt Parsonage, Wrexham.*—Lampeter; Deac. 1847, Pr. 1848. P. C. of Gwersyllt, Dio. St. A. 1858. (Patron, V. of Gresford; Tithe, 81*l* 17*s* 6*d*; Glebe, 7 acres; P. C.'s Inc. 150*l* and Ho; Pop. 1593) Formerly P. C. of Gwernafield, Mold, 1850–58. [5]

JONES, Joel, *Llanllwchairn, Cardigan.*—C. of Llanllwchairn. [6]

JONES, The Ven. John, *Waterloo, near Liverpool.*—St. John's Coll. Cam. B.A. 1815, M.A. 1819; Deac. 1815 by Bp of Lin. Pr. 1815 by Bp of Ches. P. C. of Ch. Ch. Waterloo, Dio. Ches. 1850. (Patrons, Trustees; Pop. 2046.) Archd. of Liverpool 1855. (Value, 200*l*) Author, *Sermons*, 10*s* 6*d*; *Lectures on the Acts of the Apostles*, 2 vols. 1841, 10*s* 6*d*; *Lectures on the Types*, 2 vols. 10*s* 6*d*; *The Wedding Gift*, 4 eds. 3*s* 6*d*. [7]

JONES, John, *Dowlais Rectory, Glamorganshire.*—Lond. Univ. B.A. 1858; Deac. 1860 and Pr. 1861 by Bp of Llan. R. of Dowlais, Dio. Llan. 1862. (Patron, Marquis of Bute; R.'s Inc. 150*l* and Ho; Pop. 15,590.) Formerly C. of Dowlais 1860–62. [8]

JONES, John, *Llandysilio-Gogo, near New Quay, Cardiganshire.*—Literate; Deac. 1853 and Pr. 1854 by Bp of St. D. V. of Llandysilio-Gogo, Dio. St. D. 1858. (Patron, Bp of St. D; Tithe—App. 313*l* 9*s*, without House or Glebe; V.'s Inc. 230*l*; Pop. 800.) Formerly C. of Llandysul. Author, *A Critical Commentary on the Pentateuch and New Testament*, 4 vols. Llanidloes, 1845, 54*s*; *A Critical Exposition of the Old and New Testaments for the Use of Sunday Schools*, 5 vols. Machynlleth and Aberystwith, 1864, 56*s*; *A Christian Day-book, or 365 Tracts on every Point of Theology*, Machynlleth, 2nd ed. 1864, 1*s* 6*d*; *A Historical Exposition on the New Testament*, Llanidloes, 1841, 2*s* 6*d*; *The Teacher's Companion, or Instructions how to read the Bible properly*, 3rd ed. ib. 1845, 4*d*; *A Reward for a Child, or a Catechism founded on the Holy Scripture*, 7th ed; *A Treatise on the Millennium, or an Answer to the Question, Will the End of the World take place in 1867?* Aberystwith, 6*d*; numerous Sermons, Pamphlets, Tracts, and Welsh Translations. [9]

JONES, John, *Blaenavon, Pontypool, Monmouthshire.*—Literate; Deac. 1839 by Bp of Llan. Pr. 1840 by Bp of Roch. P. C. of Blaenavon with Capel Newydd P. C. Dio. Llan. 1842. (Patron, Thomas Hill, Esq; P. C.'s Inc. 300*l* and Ho; Pop. 5876.) [10]

JONES, John, *Llandderfel, Corwen, Merionethshire.*—Deac. 1837 and Pr. 1838 by Bp of St. D. R. of Llandderfel, Dio. St. A. 1840. (Patron, Bp of Llan; Tithe, 322*l*; Glebe, 14 acres; R.'s Inc. 360*l* and Ho; Pop. 839.) [11]

JONES, John, *Cilypebyll Rectory, Swansea.*—Lampeter, Scho. of, and 1st cl. in Classics, B.D. 1861; Deac. 1852 and Pr. 1854 by Bp of Llan. R. of Cilypebyll, Dio. Llan. 1860. (Patron, Bp of Llan; Tithe, 115*l*; Glebe, 13 acres; R.'s Inc. 135*l* and Ho; Pop. 1346.) Formerly C. of Tredegar, and Chap. to the Bedwellty Union 1852; C. of Margam and Taibach 1858. [12]

JONES, John, *Llansadwrn Vicarage, Llangadock, Carmarthenshire.*—Deac. 1819 and Pr. 1821 by Bp of St. D. V. of Llansadwrn with Llanwrda, Dio. St. D. 1834. (Patroness, Lady Lucy Foley; Tithe—Imp. 263*l* 14*s* 9*d* and 5 acres of Glebe, V. 87*l* 18*s* 3*d*; Glebe, 3 acres; Llanwrda, Tithe—Imp. 157*l* 10*s*, V. 52*l* 10*s*; V.'s Inc. 200*l* and Ho; Pop. Llansadwrn 1099, Llanwrda 611.) [13]

JONES, John, *Nevern Vicarage, Newport, Haverfordwest.*—Lampeter; Deac. 1845 and Pr. 1846 by Bp of Llan. V. of Nevern with Kilgwyn C. Dio. St. D. 1852. (Patron, Ld Chan; Tithe—Imp. 585*l* 7*s* 6*d*, V. 193*l* 2*s* 6*d*; V.'s Inc. 205*l* and Ho; Pop. 1436.) [14]

JONES, John, *Llangwm Vicarage, Corwen, Merionethshire.*—Literate; Deac. 1813 by Bp of St. A. Pr. 1814 by Bp of Ban. V. of Llangwm, Dio. St. A. 1830. (Patron, Bp of St. A; Tithe—Sinecure R. 250*l* and 22¾ acres of Glebe, V. 152*l*; Glebe, 12 acres; V.'s Inc. 192*l* and Ho; Pop. 986.) [15]

JONES, John, *Llanvihangel-Geneu-r-Glyn, Aberystwith.*—Literate; Deac. 1820 and Pr. 1821 by Bp of St. D. V. of Llanvihangel-Geneu-r-Glyn, Dio. St. D. 1844. (Patron, Bp of St. D; Tithe—Imp. 1035*l*, Parish Clerk 10*l*, V. 285*l*; Glebe, 110 acres; V.'s Inc. 300*l* and Ho; Pop. 3433) [16]

JONES, John, *Llanaber, Barmouth, Merionethshire.*—R. of Llanaber with Barmouth C. Dio. Ban. 1843. (Patron, Prince of Wales; R.'s Inc. 225*l*; Pop. 1600.) [17]

JONES, John, *Bryllys Parsonage, Hay, Breconshire.*—Lampeter; Deac. 1832, Pr. 1833. R. of Llanelieu, Breconshire, Dio. St. D. 1849. (Patron, Earl of Ashburnham; Tithe, 89*l* 15*s* 8*d*; R.'s Inc. 90*l*; Pop. 93.) V. of Bryllys, Dio. St. D. 1852. (Patron, W. D. Wilkins, Esq; Tithe—App. 118*l*; V. 172*l* 7*s* 9*d*; V.'s Inc. 172*l* and Ho; Pop. 305.) Surrogate. [18]

JONES, John, *Llanarmon-yn-Iâl Vicarage (Denbighshire), near Mold.*—New Inn Hall, Ox. B.A. 1835, M.A. 1838; Deac. 1835 by Bp of Ban. Pr. 1836 by Bp of St. A. V. of Llanarmon-yn-Iâl, Dio. St. A. 1851. (Patron, Bp of St. A; Tithe—Sinecure R 455*l*, Imp. 7*l* 10*s*, V. 242*l* 9*s* 11*d*; Glebe, 84 acres; V.'s Inc. 340*l* and Ho; Pop. 1119.) [19]

JONES, John, *Llanarmon Mynydd Mawr, Llanrhaiadr, Oswestry.*—Literate; Deac. 1858 and Pr. 1863 by Bp of St. D. P. C. of Llanarmon Mynydd Mawr, Dio. St. A. 1863. (Patron, V. of Llanrhaiadr; Glebe, 31 acres; P. C.'s Inc. 213*l*; Pop. 200.) Formerly C. of Ystradgynlais 1858, St. Dogmell's 1861. [20]

JONES, John, *Reepham Vicarage, Lincoln.*—Dub. A.B. 1848, A.M. 1852; Deac. 1848 and Pr. 1849 by Bp of Ban. V. of Reepham, Dio. Lin. 1855. (Patron, the Mercers' Company; Tithe, 361*l*; Glebe, 15½ acres; V.'s Inc. 380*l* and Ho; Pop. 436.) Author, *A Family and School Liturgy*, 1842. [21]

JONES, John, *Yspytty-ystwith, Aberystwith.*—C. of Yspytty-ystwith. [22]

JONES, John, *Milton, Stoke-upon-Trent.*—C. of Milton. [23]

JONES, John, *Honley Parsonage, Huddersfield.*—P. C. of Honley with Brockholes P. C. Dio. Rip. 1863. (Patron, V. of Almondbury; P. C.'s Inc. 180*l* and Ho; Pop. 4626.) [24]

JONES, John, *Castle-street, Brecon.*—Literate; Deac. 1865 by Bp of Win. for Bp of St. D. C. of St. John's, Brecon, 1865. [25]

JONES, John, *Abergwessin Parsonage, Builth, Brecon.*—Lampeter, Eldon Welsh Scho. 1859, Sen. Scho. 1860; Deac. 1861 and Pr. 1862 by Bp of St. D. P. C. of Llanvihangel-Abergwessin with Llanddewi-Abergwessin P. C. Dio. St. D. 1865. (Patron, Bp of St. D; Tithe, Llanvihangel—Imp. 120*l*, P. C. 60*l*; Llanddewi—Imp. 58*l*, P. C. 29*l*; Glebe, 14 acres; P. C.'s Inc. 189*l* and Ho; Pop. Llanvihangel 355, Llanddewi 111.) Formerly C. of Llanedi, Carmarthenshire, 1861–65. [26]

JONES, John, *Rhosllanerchrugog, Ruabon.*—St. Bees; Deac. 1855, Pr. 1856. P. C. of Rhosllanerchrugog, Dio. St. A. 1864. (Patrons, Crown and Bp of St. A. alt; P. C.'s Inc. 284*l*; Pop. 6620.) [27]

JONES, John, *Gwersyllt, Wrexham.*—Jesus Coll. Ox. Scho. of, 1862; B.A. 1866; Deac. by Bp of St. A. 1867. C. of Gwersyllt 1867. [28]

JONES, John, *Stella, Ryton, Durham.*—C. of St. Cuthbert's, Stella. [29]

JONES, John, *Llanvillo Rectory, Brecon.*—R. of Llanvillo with Llandevailog-Tre'r-Graig C. Dio. St. D.

1865. (Patron, T. Watkins, Esq; Tithe, 327*l*; Glebe, 53 acres; R.'s Inc. 350*l* and Ho; Pop. Llanville 263, Llandevailog-Tre'r-Graig 38.) [1]

JONES, J., *Rowsley Parsonage, Bakewell.*—St. John's Coll. Cam. Sen. Opt. 1836; Deac. 1838 and Pr. 1839 by Bp of Salis. P. C. of Rowsley, Dio. Lich. 1856. (Patron, Duke of Rutland; P. C.'s Inc. 50*l* and Ho; Pop. 320.) [2]

JONES, J., *Llanarthney, Carmarthen.*—C. of Llanarthney. [3]

JONES, J., *Caerwent, Chepstow.*—C. of Caerwent and Llanvair Discoed. [4]

JONES, J., *Llannon, Swansea.*—C. of Llannon and Llanddarog. [5]

JONES, John Balmer, *Radley College, Abingdon.*—Trin. Coll. Cam. B.A. 1861, M.A. 1865; Deac. 1863 by Bp of Tasmania for Bp of Ox. Pr. 1865 by Bp of Ex. Math. Mast. at St. Peter's Coll. Radley 1866. Formerly C. of St. Ives, Cornwall, 1863–66. [6]

JONES, John Bowen, *Bedwellty, Newport, Monmouthshire.*—St. Bees; Deac. 1865 by Bp of Llan. C. of Bedwellty. [7]

JONES, John Bulkeley Goodman, *Llangristiolus, Bangor.*—Jesus Coll. Ox. B.A. 1840, M.A. 1842; Deac. 1841 and Pr. 1843 by Bp of Ban. R. of Llangristiolus with Cerrigceinwen C. Dio. Ban. 1863. (Patron, Bp of Ban; Tithe, 461*l*; Glebe, 7 acres; R.'s Inc. 500*l* and Ho; Pop. 1346.) Formerly C. of Clocaenog 1841; P. C. of Bodedeyrn, Anglesey, 1843. [8]

JONES, John Cartwright, *Shelton Rectory, Newark, Notts.*—Ch. Ch. Ox. B.A. 1854, M.A. 1856; Deac. 1854 and Pr. 1855 by Bp of Lich. R. of Shelton, Dio. Lin. 1863. (Patron, G. Maltby, Esq; R.'s Inc. 330*l* and Ho; Pop. 127.) Formerly C. of Breaston, Derbyshire; P. C. of Thrumpton, Notts, 1857–63. [9]

JONES, John David, *Llanvihangel-y-Croyddin, near Aberystwith.*—Lampeter; Deac. 1855 and Pr. 1856 by Bp of Llan. V. of Llanvihangel-y-Croyddin, Dio. St. D. 1859. (Patron, Bp of St. D; Tithe, 181*l*; Glebe, 15 acres; V.'s Inc. 196*l*; Pop. 1695.) Formerly C. of Glyntaff; P. C. of Llangorwen, Aberystwith. [10]

JONES, John David, *Colwyn, Conway.*—Lampeter; Deac. and Pr. 1857 by Bp of Ban. P. C. of St. Catherine's, Colwyn, Dio. St. A. 1866. (Patron, V. of Llandrillo-yn-Rhos; Tithe, 37*l*; P. C.'s Inc. 170*l*; Pop. 570.) Formerly C. of Rhyl. [11]

JONES, John Davies, *Llangristiolus, Bangor.*—Lampeter; Deac. 1866 by Bp of St. D. for Bp of Ban. C. of Llangristiolus with Cerrigceinwen 1866. [12]

JONES, John Edward, *Llanthewy Parsonage, Caerleon.*—Jesus Coll. Ox. B.A. 1854, M.A. 1857; Deac. 1856 and Pr. 1857 by Bp of Lich. P. C. of Llanthewy Vach, Dio. Llan. 1858. (Patron, Bp of Llan; Tithe—App. 90*l*; Glebe, 98 acres; P. C.'s Inc. 119*l* and Ho; Pop. 185.) C. in sole charge of Llandegveth 1864. Formerly C. of Alfreton, Derbyshire, 1856–57. [13]

JONES, J. E., *Taibach, Glamorganshire.*—C. of Taibach with Margam. [14]

JONES, John Edwyn, 25, *Cantelowes-road, Camden-square, London, N.W.*—Jesus Coll. Ox. B.A. 1863; Deac. 1864 and Pr. 1865 by Abp of York. C. of St. Thomas's, Camden-town, 1867. Formerly Sen. C. of St. Jude's, Moorfields, Sheffield, 1864–66. [15]

JONES, John Fowell, *Saul Vicarage, Stonehouse, Glouc.*—Ball. Coll. Ox. B.A. 1813, M.A. 1817; Deac. 1814 by Bp of B. and W. Pr. 1815 by Bp of Glouc. V. of Saul, Dio. G. and B. 1825. (Patron, V. of Standish; Tithe—App. 115*l*, P. C. 42*l*; Glebe, 6 acres; V.'s Inc. 120*l* and Ho; Pop. 359.) R. of Gwernesney, Monmouthshire, Dio. Llan. 1830. (Patron, Duke of Beaufort; Tithe, 90*l* 7*s*; Glebe, 27 acres; R.'s Inc. 130*l* and Ho; Pop. 57.) P. C. of Moreton-Valence, Glouc. Dio. G. and B. 1830. (Patron, Bp of G. and B; Tithe—App. 365*l* and 40 acres; P. C.'s Inc. 85*l*; Pop. 157.) Formerly C. of Broadwell 1818–29, Sevenoaks, Kent, 1829–30. [16]

JONES, John G., *Somerby, Brigg, Lincolnshire.*—R. of Somerby, Dio. Lin. 1861. (Patron, Ld Chan; R.'s Inc. 200*l*; Pop. 120.) [17]

JONES, John Herbert, *Waterloo, Liverpool.*—Jesus Coll. Cam. 18th Wrang. and B.A. 1844, M.A. 1847, Deac. 1845 and Pr. 1846 by Abp of Cant. P. C. of St. John's, Waterloo, Dio. Ches. 1865. (Patrons, Five Trustees; P. C.'s Inc. from pew-rents.) Formerly Fell. of Jesus Coll. Cam; P. C. of St. Augustine's, Everton, Liverpool, 1847–65. Author, *Norrisian Prize Essay*. 1846, 2*s* 6*d*. [18]

JONES, John Lloyd, *Kingsland, Leominster.*—C. of Kingsland. [19]

JONES, John Morgan, *Caerhun, Conway.*—St. Bees; Deac. 1865 and Pr. 1867 by Bp of Ban. C. of Caerhun 1865. [20]

JONES, John Owen, *Llangwyvan Rectory, Denbigh.*—Dub. A.B. 1836; Deac. 1837, Pr. 1838. R. of Llangwyvan, Dio. St. A. 1857. (Patron, Bp of Llan; R.'s Inc. 225*l* and Ho; Pop. 246.) Formerly C. of Llandyrnog. [21]

JONES, John Powell, *Llantrisant Vicarage, Pontypridd.*—Lampeter, B.D. 1855; Deac. 1846 by Bp of Dur. for Bp of St. D. Pr. 1847 by Bp of St. D. V. of Llantrisant, Dio. Llan. 1865. (Patrons, D. and C. of Glouc; Tithe, 609*l* 7*s*; Glebe, 16 acres; V.'s Inc. 660*l* and Ho; Pop. 5492.) Formerly Asst. Tut. at Lampeter; C. and subsequently R. of Longhor, Carmarthenshire. [22]

JONES, John Price, *Newcastle-Emlyn, Carmarthenshire.*—Lampeter 1833–35; Deac. 1836 by Bp of Glouc. Pr. 1838 by Bp of St. D. P. C. of Newcastle-Emlyn, Dio. St. D. 1843. (Patron, Bp of St. D; P. C.'s Inc. 158*l*; Pop. 2426.) Formerly C. of Newcastle-Emlyn 1837–43. [23]

JONES, John Rees, *Burghill Vicarage, near Hereford.*—Deac. 1842, Pr. 1844. V. of Burghill, Dio. Herf. 1850. (Patron, B. Biddulph, Esq; Tithe—Imp. 481*l* 12*s* 11*d*, V. 2*l* 18*s* 6*d*; V.'s Inc. 102*l* and Ho; Pop. 934.) [24]

JONES, J. R., 54, *Upper Brunswick-place, Hove, Brighton.* [25]

JONES, John Samuel, *Clare street, Liverpool.*—Deac. 1858 by Bp of Meath, Pr. 1859 by Bp of Down and Connor. P. C. of Ch. Ch. Liverpool, Dio. Ches. 1862. (Patrons, Trustees; P. C.'s Inc. 300*l*; Pop. 7725.) Formerly C. of Skerry and Rathcavan, Dio. Connor, 1858, Drummaul, Dio. Connor, and Armaghbreague, Dio. Armagh, 1861, St. Stephen's, Spitalfields, Lond. 1861–62. Author, *Letter to the Attorney-General on the Pew-Rent Clauses of the Church Building Bill*, 1864. [26]

JONES, John Samuel, *Llanuwchllyn Parsonage, Corwen.*—Queens' Coll. Cam. B.A. 1862; Deac. 1863 and Pr. 1864 by Bp of St. A. P. C. of Llanuwchllyn, Dio. St. A. 1865. (Patron, Sir W. W. Wynn, Bart; Tithe, 49*l*; P. C.'s Inc. 200*l*; Pop. 1129.) Formerly C. of Rhuabon 1863–65. [27]

JONES, John Skinner, *Penmon Parsonage, Beaumaris, Anglesey.*—Jesus Coll. Ox. Scho. of, 3rd cl. Lit. Hum. and B.A. 1852, M.A. 1855; Deac. 1853 and Pr. 1854 by Bp of Ban. P. C. of Llanfaes and Penmon, Anglesey, Dio. Ban. 1862. (Patron, Sir R. B. Williams Bulkeley, Bart, M.P., Baron Hill, Beaumaris; Llanfaes, Tithe—Imp. 140*l*; Glebe, 12 acres; Penmon, Tithe, 80*l*; Glebe, 4 acres; P. C.'s Inc. 163*l* and Ho; Pop. Llanfaes 249, Penmon 226.) Dioc. Inspector of Schs. Formerly C. of Llandegfan, Anglesey, 1854–62. [28]

JONES, The Ven. John Wynne, *Heneglwys Rectory, Llangefni, Anglesey.*—Jesus Coll. Ox. B.A. 1827, M.A. 1830; Deac. 1827, Pr. 1828. R. of Heneglwys with Trêvwalchmai C. Dio. Ban. 1844. (Patron, Bp of Ban; Heneglwys, Tithe, 250*l* 5*s*; Glebe, 19 acres; Trêvwalchmai, Tithe, 205*l*; R.'s Inc. 590*l*; Pop. Heneglwys 510, Trêvwalchmai 768.) Archd. of Ban. 1863; Can. Res. of Ban. Cathl. 1863 (Value, 350*l*). [29]

JONES, Jonathan, *Guilsborough, Northants.*—Head Mast. of the Guilsborough Gr. Sch. [30]

JONES, Joseph, *Burleigh-on-the-Hill, Oakham, Rutland.*—V. of Burleigh-on-the-Hill, Dio. Pet. 1819. (Patron, G. Finch, Esq; V.'s Inc. 375*l*; Pop. 237.) [31]

JONES, Joseph Peter, *Ivington, Leominster, Herefordshire.*—P. C. of Ivington, Dio. Herf. (Patron, V. of Leominster; P. C.'s Inc. 150*l*; Pop. 750.) P. C. of

Ford, Dio. Herf. (Patron, J. H. Arkwright, Esq; P. C.'s Inc. 53*l*; Pop. 29.) [1]

JONES, Joshua, *King William's College, Isle of Man.*—Lin. Coll. Ox. Johnson Math. Scho. 1853, Sen. Math. Scho. 1854, B.A. 1852, M.A. 1856, D.C.L. 1866; Deac. 1854 and Pr. 1855 by Bp of Ches. Prin. and Dean of the Chapel, King William's Coll. Isle of Man, 1865. Formerly C. of Dodleston, Cheshire, 1854–55, Trinity, Manchester, 1856–57; Vice-Prin. of the York Training Coll. 1859–61; Head Mast. of the Liverpool Institute 1862–65. Author, *Classical Studies, their True Position and Value in Education*, Longmans, 2*s*. [2]

JONES, Kenneth Linton, *North Cave, Brough, Yorks.*—Ch. Coll. Cam. B.A. 1866; Deac. 1866 by Abp of York. C. of North Cave with South Cliffe 1866. [3]

JONES, Latimer Maurice, *The Vicarage, Carmarthen.*—Lampeter, Sen. Scho. B.D. 1864; Deac. 1857 and Pr. 1858 by Bp of G. and B. V. of Carmarthen, Dio. St. D. 1863. (Patron, Bp of St. D; Tithe, 7*l*; V.'s Inc. 300*l* and Ho; Pop. 4570.) Formerly C. of Stratton St. Margaret, Wilts, 1857–60, Swansea 1860–61, Carmarthen 1861–63. Author, *The Welsh People and the Welsh Tongue*, Carmarthen, 1862. [4]

JONES, Lewis, *Llanbeulan, Holyhead.*—R. of Llanbeulan with Ceirchiog C. Llanvaelog C. and Llechylched C. Dio. Ban. (Patron, Bp of Ban; R.'s Inc. 900*l* and Ho; Pop. 1887.) Min. Can. of Ban. 1866. [5]

JONES, Lewis David, *Union-street, Carmarthen.* [6]

JONES, Lewis Price, *Abersefin, near Brecon.*—Literate; Deac. 1821 and Pr. 1822 by Bp of St. D. R. of Llanbadarnfawr, Radnorshire, Dio. St. D. 1832. (Patron, Bp of St. D; Tithe, 256*l*; Glebe, 37 acres; R.'s Inc. 297*l*; Pop. 475.) [7]

JONES, Lewis Usk, *Penrhos, near Raglan.*—Lampeter; Deac. 1863 by Bp of Llan. C. of Penrhos 1863. [8]

JONES, L.—C. of St. John's, Leeds. [9]

JONES, Llewellyn, *Bromsgrove.*—Trin. Coll. Cam. B.A. 1862, M.A. 1866; Deac. 1864 and Pr. 1865 by Bp of Wor. C. of Bromsgrove 1864. [10]

JONES, Llewelyn Wynne, *Connah's Quay, Northop, Flintshire.*—Dub. A.B. 1844, A.M. 1852; Deac. 1845, Pr. 1846. P. C. of Connah's Quay, Dio. St. A. 1860. (Patron, V. of Northop; P. C.'s Inc. 301*l*; Pop. 1422.) Formerly Sen. C. of Oswestry. Author, *The New Reformation in Ireland*, 1852, 1*s* 6*d*. [11]

JONES, Morgan, *St. Margaret's, near Hereford.*—Jesus Coll. Ox. B.A. 1828. P. C. of St. Margaret's with St. Michaelchurch-Eskley P. C. Dio. Herf. 1828. (Patron, Earl of Oxford; St. Margaret's, Tithe—App. 4*l* 18*s* 10*d*, Imp. 106*l* 1*s* 4*d*, P. C. 64*l*; Michaelchurch-Eskley, Tithe—Imp. 146*l* 14*s*; P. C. 36*l* 6*s* 8*d*; P. C.'s Inc. 167*l*; Pop. St. Margaret's 343, St. Michaelchurch-Eskley 448.) [12]

JONES Morgan, *Ystabyfera, Swansea.*—Lampeter; Deac. 1863 and Pr. 1865 by Bp of St. D. C. of Llanguicke and Ystabyfera 1866. Formerly C. of Ystradffyn 1863, Llanelly 1865. [13]

JONES, Morris, *Dafen, Llanelly, Carmarthenshire.*—C. of Dafen. [14]

JONES, Morris, *Llanfairpwllgwngyll, Anglesey.*—C. of Llanfairpwllgwngyll with Llandysilio. [15]

JONES, Mortimer Lloyd, *St. John's Parsonage, Walthamstow.*—Corpus Coll. Cam. Heb. Coll. Prize, 2nd cl. Theol. Trip. and B.A. 1856, M.A. 1861; Deac. 1856 and Pr. 1857 by Bp of Lon. P. C. of St. John's, Walthamstow, Dio. Lon. 1862. (Patron, V. of Walthamstow; Pop. 1300.) Formerly C. of St. Luke's, Chelsea, 1856–60, St. Mary's, Walthamstow, 1860–62. [16]

JONES, Neville, *St. George's, Bolton, Lancashire.*—St. Cath. Coll. Cam. B.A. 1832; Deac. 1832 and Pr. 1833 by Bp of Lin. P. C. of St. George's, Bolton, Dio. Man. 1847. (Patron, V. of Bolton-le-Moors; P. C.'s Inc. 300*l*; Pop. 14,288.) Surrogate. [17]

JONES, Owen, *St. Ishmael's, Ferryside, Carmarthen.*—Jesus Coll. Ox. B.A. 1853, M.A. 1856; Deac. 1852 and Pr. 1853 by Bp of St. D. V. of St. Ishmael's, Dio. St. D. 1855. (Patron, Ld Chan; Tithe, 186*l* 8*s* 6*d*; Glebe, 60 acres; V.'s Inc. 220*l* and Ho; Pop. 1211.) P. C. of Ferryside, Dio. St. D. 1855. (Patron, the V. of St. Ishmael's; P. C.'s Inc. 45*l*.) [18]

JONES, Owen, *Pentrevoelas, Llanrwst, North Wales.*—St. Bees; Deac. 1851 and Pr. 1852 by Bp of Man. P. C. of Pentrevoelas, Dio. St. A. 1857. (Patron, C. W. Wynne Finch, Esq; P. C.'s Inc. 242*l* and Ho; Pop. 534.) Formerly C. of St. James's, Accrington, 1851–53, Ysceifiog, Flintshire, 1853–55; P. C. of Capel Garmon, Llanrwst, 1855–57. Author, *Christmas Carols* (Welsh) *with Music*, Hughes, Wrexham. [19]

JONES, Owen, *Towyn Vicarage, Machynlleth, Merionethshire.*—Lampeter; Deac. 1830 and Pr. 1831 by Bp of St. D. V. of Towyn, Dio. Ban. 1841. (Patron, Bp of Ban; Tithe—App. 793*l* 10*s*, Imp. 6*l* 10*s*, V. 180*l*; V.'s Inc. 239*l* and Ho; Pop. 1673.) [20]

JONES, Owen Williams, *Thomas-street, Holyhead, Anglesey.*—Dub. A.B. 1856; Deac. 1856 and Pr. 1857 by Bp of Ban. C. of Holyhead 1859. Formerly C. of Llanvihangel-yn-Howyn 1856–59. [21]

JONES, Owen Wynne, *Llanfaethlu, Holyhead.*—Literate; Deac. 1860 by Bp of Ban. C. of Llanfaethlu and Llanfurog 1863. Formerly C. of Llangristiolus 1860. One of the Editors of the *Brython* Quarterly Journal. [22]

JONES, Peter, *Hindley, near Wigan.*—Dub. A.B. 1848; Deac. 1850 and Pr. 1851 by Bp of Ches. P. C. of St. Peter's, Hindley, Dio. Ches. 1866. (Patrons, Trustees; Pop. 3600.) Formerly C. of All Saints' Hindley, 1853 63. [23]

JONES, Pryce Wilson, *Llangennech, Llanelly.*—C. of Llangennech, Carmarthenshire. [24]

JONES, Rees, *Penmaen, Blackwood, Newport, Monmouthshire.*—Lampeter; Deac. 1845, Pr. 1846. P. C. of Penmaen, Dio. Llan. 1846. (Patrons, the Crown and Bp of Llan. alt; P. C.'s Inc. 150*l*; Pop. 2686.) [25]

JONES, Rees, *Eglwysilan Vicarage, Pontypridd.*—Lampeter; Deac. 1853, Pr. 1854. V. of Eglwysilan, Dio. Llan. 1860. (Patrons, D. and C. of Llan; Tithe, 140*l*; V.'s Inc. 180*l* and Ho; Pop. 4000.) [26]

JONES, Rhys, *Abberley, Stourport.*—C. of Abberley, Worcestershire. [27]

JONES, Richard, *Bettws-y-Coed, Llanrwst, Carnarvonshire.*—Lampeter; Deac. 1843 and Pr. 1844 by Bp of Ban. P. C. of Dolwyddelan, Carnarvonshire, Dio. Ban. 1847. (Patron, Lord Willoughby D'Eresby; Tithe—Imp. 102*l*, App. 8*l*; P. C.'s Inc. 110*l*; Pop. 811.) [28]

JONES, Richard, *Gisburn, Skipton, Yorks.*—Deac. 1821 and Pr. 1822 by Abp of York. V. of Gisburn, Dio. Rip. 1822. (Patron, Ld Chan; Tithe, 282*l*; Glebe, 125*l*; V.'s Inc. 407*l* and Ho; Pop. 1755.) Rural Dean. [29]

JONES, Richard, *Llanvihangel-y-Traethan, Tan-y-bwlch, Merionethshire.*—P. C. of Llanvihangel-y-Traethan with Llandecwyn P. C. Dio. Ban. 1861. (Patron, Bp of Ban; P. C.'s Inc. 250*l*; Pop. 957.) [30]

JONES, Richard, *Treveglwys Vicarage, Caersws, Montgomeryshire.*—Lampeter; Deac. 1843, Pr. 1844. V. of Treveglwys, Dio. Ban. 1860. (Patron, Rev. J. W. Griffith; Tithe, 186*l*; Glebe, 10 acres; V.'s Inc. 196*l* and Ho; Pop. 1398.) Formerly C. of Capel Cûrig and Dolwyddelan 1843–47; P. C. of Dolwyddelan and Bettws-y-Coed 1847–60. [31]

JONES, Richard Bowen, *Killymaenllwyd (Carmarthenshire), near Narberth.*—Jesus Coll. Ox. B.A. 1835; Deac. 1835, Pr. 1836. R. of Killymaenllwyd, Dio. St. D. 1841. (Patron, Ld Chan; Tithe, 278*l* 10*s*; R.'s Inc. 280*l*; Pop. 640.) [32]

JONES, Richard Devereux, *Pond's Bridge, Ramsey, Huntingdon.*—Dub. A.B. 1862, A.M. 1866; Deac. 1863 and Pr. 1864 by Bp of Ches. P. C. of Pond's Bridge, Dio. Ely, 1867. (Patron, Bp of Ely; Tithe, comm. 70*l*; P. C.'s Inc. 150*l*; Pop. 780.) Formerly 2nd Mast. Liverpool Coll. Middle Sch. 1861–67. [33]

JONES, Richard Parry, *Gaerwen, Anglesey.*—Trin. Coll. Cam. Sen. Opt. and B.A. 1841, M.A. 1844; Deac. 1841, Pr. 1842. R. of Llanvihangel-Ysceiviog with Llanfinnan P. C. Anglesey, Dio. Ban. 1847. (Patron

Dean of Ban; R.'s Inc. 360*l* and Ho; Pop. Llanvihangel-Ysceiviog 1213, Llanfinnan 112.) Editor of the *Cymro*, a Welsh Periodical. [1]

JONES, Richardson, *Blodwell Cottage, Oswestry.*—King's Coll. Lond. Assoc. 1863; Deac. 1863 and Pr. 1864 by Bp of St. A. C. of Llanyblodwel 1863. [2]

JONES, Robert, *Branxton Vicarage, Coldstream (Northumberland).*—St. Bees; Deac. 1829, Pr. 1830. V. of Branxton, Dio. Dur. 1834. (Patrons, D. and C. of Dur; Tithe—Imp. 221*l* 12*s*, V. 108*l*; Glebe, 384 acres; V.'s Inc. 233*l* and Ho; Pop. 255.) Author, *A Sermon* (preached before the Society of the Sons of the Clergy of Northumberland), 1841; *The Plague Spots in the Church of England* (a Tract); *The Battle of Flodden*, Blackwoods; Sermons in *Church of England Magazine*. [3]

JONES, Robert, *All Saints' Parsonage, Rotherhithe, London, S.E.*—Jesus Coll. Ox. B.A. 1837; Deac. 1837, Pr. 1838. P. C. of All Saints', Rotherhithe, Dio. Win. 1841. (Patron, R. of Rotherhithe; P. C.'s Inc. 300*l* and Ho; Pop. 6212.) Chap. to the Rotherhithe Union 1855; Metropolitan Sec. to the Cambrian Institute. Editor of *Roscoe's Wanderings in Wales*; *Y Caniedydd*. [4]

JONES, Robert, *Cromford, Derbyshire.*—Pemb. Coll. Ox. 3rd cl. Lit. Hum. and B.A. 1829, M.A. 1834; Deac. 1834, Pr. 1835. P. C. of Cromford, Dio. Lich. 1839. (Patron, Frederick Arkwright, Esq; Glebe, 26 acres; P. C.'s Inc. 190*l* and Ho; Pop. 1140.) [5]

JONES, Robert, *Llangynog, Llanfyllen, Montgomeryshire.*—R. of Llangynog, Dio. St. A. 1850. (Patron, Bp of St. A; R.'s Inc. 130*l* and Ho; Pop. 601.) [6]

JONES, R., *Llandewi-Rytherch, Abergavenny.*—C. of Llandewi-Rytherch. [7]

JONES, Robert Griffith, *Rhuddlan, Rhyl.*—St. Bees; Deac. 1854 by Bp of Ches. Pr. 1855 by Bp of St. A. C. of Rhuddlan 1859. Formerly C. of Llanarmon in Yale 1854–59, Bettws yn Rhôs 1859, Caerwys 1859. Author, *St. Asaph Clerical Directory and Church Almanack*; and other small Pamphlets and Manuals. [8]

JONES, Robert Harries, *The Vicarage, Llanidloes, Montgomeryshire.*—Univ. Göttingen, M.A. and Ph.D; Deac. 1847 by Bp of Ches. Pr. 1848 by Bp of Man; V. of Llanidloes, Dio. Ban. 1867. (Patron, Bp of Ban; Glebe, 1½ acres; V.'s Inc. 247*l* and Ho; Pop. 3983.) Formerly C. of Hollinwood 1847–49; Sen. C. of Oldham 1850; C. of Bolton 1852–57, Walmsley 1858–59, Bury 1860, Penmon and Llanfaes 1861, Llanfairfechan 1861–67. Author, *The Japhetic Races* (an Inaugural Address at Göttingen); *The Affinity of European Languages* (a Lecture at Bolton); *Landmarks in the Reign of Henry VIII* (a Lecture); *The Inquisition* (a Lecture); Translations from the Russian of Marlinska, Poushkin, and Lermontoff, for *Bolton Chronicle*. Editor, *Y Cymro* 1851 to 1853; etc. [9]

JONES, Robert Pugh, *Caius College, Cambridge.*—Scho. of Caius Coll. [10]

JONES, Samuel, *Flemingstone, Cowbridge, Glamorganshire.*—R. of Flemingstone, Dio. Llan. 1859. (Patron, Earl of Dunraven; R.'s Inc. 200*l*; Pop. 68.) [11]

JONES, Samuel Flood, *The Cloisters, Westminster Abbey, London, S.W.*—Pemb. Coll. Ox. B.A. 1851, M.A. 1854; Deac. 1852 and Pr. 1853 by Bp of Lon. Min. of St. Matthew's, Spring-gardens, Dio. Lon. 1854. (Patron, V. of St. Martin-in-the-fields; Min.'s Inc. 200*l*.) Lect. at Bow, Middlesex, 1858; Min. Can. of Westminster 1859. Author, *The Throne of Grace* (a Course of Sermons on Prayer), 1854, 2*s* 6*d*; *Progress and Prosperity* (New Year's Sermon), 1859; *Hymns of Prayer and Praise especially suited for the Sick-room*, Dalton and Lucy, Lond. 6*d*; *The Westminster Abbey Special Evening Service and Festival Book*, Novello, 1867, 1*s* 6*d*. [12]

JONES, Samuel Rowland, *Hindley, Wigan.*—C. of Hindley. [13]

JONES, Theophilus, *Brixton, Earl's Plympton, Devon.*—Brasen. Coll. Ox. Hon. 4th cl. and B.A. 1845, M.A. 1848; Deac. 1848 and Pr. 1849 by Bp of Ex. P. C. of Brixton, Dio. Ex. 1866. (Patrons, D. and C. of Windsor; P. C.'s Inc. 103*l*; Pop. 691.) Formerly C. of Stowford. Author, *Accession Service*, 6*d*; *Royal Supremacy*, 6*d*; *Society for the Propagation of the Gospel, and Queen's Letter*, 6*d*. [14]

JONES, Thomas, *Tanlan, Pencarreg, Carmarthenshire.*—Deac. 1824, Pr. 1825. V. of Pencarreg, Dio. St. D. 1835. (Patron, Pryse Pryse, Esq; Tithe—Imp. 220*l*, V. 110*l*; V.'s Inc. 160*l*; Pop. 1208.) [15]

JONES, Thomas, *Llanbeder, near Crickhowell.*—Abergavenny Div. Sch; Deac. 1849 by Bp of Herf. Pr. 1850 by Bp of Llan. R. of Llanbeder with Patrishow C. Dio. St. D. 1860. (Patron, Duke of Beaufort; Tithe, Llanbeder, 217*l*, Patrishow, 58*l*; Glebe, 36 acres; R.'s Inc. 320*l*; Pop. Llanbeder 280, Patrishow 73.) Formerly C. of Kilvey, near Swansea, 1853–60. [16]

JONES, Thomas, *Merthyr-Cynog, near Brecon.*—V. of Merthyr-Cynog, Dio. St. D. 1846. (Patron, J. L. V. Watkins, Esq; Tithe—Imp. 410*l*; V.'s Inc. 100*l*; Pop. 917.) [17]

JONES, Thomas, *Sporle, Swaffham, Norfolk.*—V. of Sporle with Great and Little Palgrave R.'s, Dio. Nor. 1845. (Patron, Eton Coll; Sporle and Great Palgrave, Tithe—Imp. 929*l* 4*s* 6*d*, and 106½ acres of Glebe; Little Palgrave, Tithe, 120*l*; V.'s Inc. 303*l*; Pop. 806.) [18]

JONES, Thomas, *Llanengan Rectory, Pwllheli, Carnarvonshire.*—St. Cath. Coll. Cam. Scho. and 1st Hebrew Prizeman, B.A. 1833; Deac. 1833 and Pr. 1834 by Bp of Wor. R. of Llanengan, Dio. Ban. 1860. (Patron, Bp of Llan; Tithe, 413*l*; Glebe, 10 acres; R.'s Inc. 433*l* and Ho; Pop. 1021.) Surrogate 1849; Rural Dean of Lleyn 1867; Dioc. Inspector of Schs. in Deanery of Lleyn. Formerly C. of St. Clement's, Worcester, 1833–35, Llangelynin 1835–49; V. of Pwllheli 1849–60. Author, *Welsh Church Tune and Chant Book*, 4 eds. 1859–66, 5th ed. enlarged 1866, Macintosh, 2*s* 6*d*. [19]

JONES, Thomas, *Henley-in-Arden, Warwickshire.*—St. John's Coll. Cam. B.A. 1833, M.A. 1837; Deac. 1833 and Pr. 1834 by Bp of Wor. P. C. of Henley-in-Arden, Dio. Wor. 1842. (Patrons, the Inhabitants; Glebe, 21 acres; P. C.'s Inc. 160*l*; Pop. 1069.) Surrogate. Formerly P. C. of Bearley, Warwickshire, 1846–65. [20]

JONES, Thomas, *Llandysul, near Carmarthen*—Lampeter; Deac. 1862 and Pr. 1863 by Bp of St. D. C. of Llandysul 1865. Formerly C. of Llanelly 1862; P. C. of Glyncollwn, Brecon, 1863. [21]

JONES, Thomas, *St. Bride's Major, Bridgend, Glamorganshire.*—Literate; Deac. 1849 and Pr. 1850 by Bp of Herf. V. of St. Bride's Major with Wick, P. C. Dio. Llan. 1864. (Patron, Capt. Warlow; Tithe, 293*l* 12*s* 6*d*; Glebe, 1½ acres; V.'s Inc. 297*l* and Ho; Pop. 1249.) Formerly C. of Llangeinor 1849–55; V. of Colwinstowe 1855–64. [22]

JONES, T., *Bryneglwys, Eglwys, Denbighshire.*—C. of Bryneglwys. [23]

JONES, T., *Llantrisant, Pontypridd.*—C. of Llantrisant. [24]

JONES, T. D., *Llangristiolus, Anglesey.*—C. of Llangristiolus. [25]

JONES, Thomas Evan, *Egglestone, Barnard Castle, Durham.*—Univ. Coll. Dur. Licen. Theol. 1849; Deac. 1849 and Pr. 1850 by Bp of Dur. P. C. of Egglestone, Dio. Dur. 1857. (Patron, R. of Middleton-in-Teesdale; Glebe, 56 acres; P. C.'s Inc. 110*l*; Pop. 788.) Formerly Sen. C. of Barnard Castle, Durham. [26]

JONES, Thomas Evans, *Selattyn Rectory, Oswestry.*—Dub. A.B. 1860, A.M. 1866; Deac. 1861 and Pr. 1862 by Bp of St. A. C. of Selattyn 1864. Formerly C. of Brymbo 1861–64. [27]

JONES, T. F., *Kilmersdon, Bath.*—C. of Kilmersdon. [28]

JONES, Thomas Henry, *Greetham Vicarage, Rutland.*—Pemb. Coll. Cam. B.A. 1845 M.A. 1849; Deac. 1845 and Pr. 1846 by Bp of Ox. V. of Greetham, Dio. Pet. 1857. (Patron, G. Finch, Esq; V.'s Inc. 200*l* and Ho; Pop. 706.) Surrogate. Formerly P. C. of St. Peter's, Croydon, Surrey, 1854–57; Morn. Preacher of Abp Tenison's Chapel; P. C. of St. Luke's, St. James's, Westminster. [29]

JONES, Thomas Hughes, *Pendoylan Vicarage, Cardiff.*—Lampeter; Welsh Scho. B.D. 1842; Deac. 1842 and Pr. 1843 by Bp of Herf. V. of Pendoylan, Dio. Llan. 1847. (Patrons, D. and C. of Llan; Tithe, 107*l* 7*s* 5*d*; Glebe, 57 acres, let for 104*l* 10*s*; V.'s Inc. 211*l* 17*s* 5*d* and Ho; Pop. 380.) P. C. of Talygarn (sinecure) Dio. Llan. 1866. (P. C.'s Inc. 63*l* 10*s*.) Formerly C. of Beaufort and Maesteg. Author, *Mormonism Unmasked* (a Sermon), Llandovery, 1853, 4*d*. [1]

JONES, Thomas James, *Atlow Rectory, Ashbourn.*—Corpus Coll. Cam. Scho. of, B.A. 1856; Deac. 1856 and Pr. 1857 by Bp of Lich. R. of Atlow, Dio. Lich. 1867. (Patron, H. C. Okeover, Esq; Tithe, 110*l*; Glebe, 50*l*; R.'s Inc. 160*l* and Ho; Pop. 124.) Formerly C. of Elvaston 1857–58, Bromshall 1859; Head Mast. of Tideswell Gr. Sch. 1859–63; Chap. of Don. of Okeover 1863–67. Author, *Mathematical and Commercial Tables*, 4*d*; *To the Redbreast* (Music), Novello, 2*s*; *The Scotch Emigrant* (ditto), ib. 2*s* 6*d*. [2]

JONES, Thomas Jeffrey, *Minera Parsonage, Wrexham.*—P. C. of Minera, Dio. St. A. 1863. (Patron, V. of Wrexham; P. C.'s Inc. 120*l* and Ho; Pop. 1714.) [3]

JONES, Thomas Roberts, *Trinity Parsonage, Huddersfield.*—Edinburgh Univ. M.A. by Abp of Cant; Deac. 1843, Pr. 1844. P. C. of Trinity, Huddersfield, Dio. Rip. 1857. (Patron, B. H. Davies, Esq; P. C.'s Inc. 300*l* and Ho; Pop. 3316.) Formerly C. of St. Mary's, Kelbrook, Thornton-in-Craven 1843, and P. C. of same, 1844–51; P. C. of Ch. Ch. Battersea, 1851; V. of Hoos, Sussex, 1852–57. Author, *Exposition of the Thirty-nine Articles by the Reformers*, 1847, 2nd ed. 1867. [4]

JONES, Thomas Samuel, *Worcester.*—St. John's Coll. Cam. Jun. Opt. and B.A. 1839; Deac. 1839, Pr. 1840. Chap. of St. Oswald's Hospital, Worcester. [5]

JONES, Thomas William, *Llanybri, Llanstephan, near Carmarthen.*—Lampeter; Deac. 1846 and Pr. 1847 by Bp of Llan. P. C. of Llanybri, Dio. St. D. 1861. (Patroness, Miss Lloyd; Glebe, 60 acres; P. C.'s Inc. 150*l* and Ho; Pop. 410.) P. C. of Llandilo Abercowin, Dio. St. D. 1866. (Patron, J. W. M. G. Hughes, Esq; Tithe, 64*l*; P. C.'s Inc. 76*l*; Pop. 77.) Formerly C. of St. Mary's-on-the-Hill 1846, Maesteg, Glamorganshire, 1847–50, St. Paul's, Liverpool, 1850–55; P. C. of Llanavan 1855–61. [6]

JONES, Timothy, *St. Margaret's Vicarage, Leicester.*—Magd. Hall, Ox. B.A. 1842, M.A. 1843. V. of St. Margaret's with Knighton C. Dio. Pet. 1852. (Patron, the Preb. of Leicester St. Margaret in Lin. Cathl; Tithe—App. 36*l* 8*s* 9*d*, V. 13*l* 15*s*; V.'s Inc. 390*l* and Ho; Pop. 13,909.) Rural Dean. [7]

JONES, Walter, *Llansilin Vicarage, Oswestry.*—Jesus Coll. Ox. 2nd cl. Lit. Hum. and B.A. 1819, M.A. 1822; Deac. 1820, Pr. 1821. V. of Llansilin, Dio. St. A. 1827. (Patron, Bp of St. A; Tithe, 262*l* 0*s* 10*d*; Glebe, 3 acres; V.'s Inc. 300*l*; Pop. 1913) [8]

JONES, Walter Powell, *Llyswen, near Hereford.*—Lampeter; Deac. 1851 and Pr. 1852 by Bp of St. D. R. of Llyswen, Dio. St. D. 1855. (Patron, Sir J. Bailey, Bart; Tithe, 105*l*; Glebe, 37 acres; R.'s Inc. 180*l* and Ho; Pop. 226.) Formerly C. of St. David's, Merthyr-Tydvil. [9]

JONES, William, *Llanellen Vicarage, Abergavenny, Monmouthshire.*—Literate; Deac. 1826 and Pr. 1827 by Bp of Llan. V. of Llanellen, Dio. Llan. 1850. (Patron, C. J. K. Tynte, Esq; Tithe—Imp. 32*l* 17*s* 8½*d*, V. 132*l* 3*s* 8*d*; Glebe, 15 acres; V.'s Inc. 155*l* and Ho; Pop. 373.) Formerly V. of Llangathen, Dio. St. D. 1847–49. [10]

JONES, William, *Burton-on-Trent.*—Trin. Coll. Cam. B.A. 1857, M.A. 1860; Deac. 1857 and Pr. 1858 by Bp of Lich. P. C. of Burton-on-Trent, Dio. Lich. 1860. (Patron, Marquis of Anglesey; P. C.'s Inc. 200*l*; Pop. 4463.) Surrogate. Formerly C. of Trinity, Burton-on-Trent. [11]

JONES, William, *Baschurch, Shrewsbury.*—Ch. Ch. Ox. B.A. 1826, M.A. 1829; Deac. 1827, Pr. 1829. V. of Baschurch, Dio. Lich. 1837. (Patron, Ld Chan; Tithe—Imp. 2000*l*, V. 346*l*; Glebe, 46 acres; V.'s Inc. 392*l* and Ho; Pop. 1277.) [12]

JONES, William, *Llanbadarn-Vawr, Radnorshire.*—C. of Llanbadarn-Vawr. [13]

JONES, William, *Llandwrog Rectory, Carnarvon.*—M.A. by Abp of Cant; Deac. 1818 and Pr. 1820 by Bp of St. D. R. of Llandwrog, Dio. Ban. 1862. (Patron, Bp of Llan; Tithe, 491*l*; Glebe, 22*l*; R.'s Inc. 520*l* and Ho; Pop. 711.) Preb. of Llandaff 1851. Formerly C. of Vaynor 1818–35; V. of Llanvihangel Gwenr Glyn 1835–44; P. C. of Bedwellty 1844–46; P. C. of Tredegar 1846–59; V. of Llanover 1859–62. [14]

JONES, William, 14, *College-green, Bristol.*—Emman. Coll. Cam. Wrang. B.A. 1859, M.A. 1863; Deac. 1860 and Pr. 1862 by Bp of Lich. C. of St. Augustine's, Bristol, 1866. Formerly C. of Shareshill, Staffs, 1860–62, Wellington, Somerset, 1862–65. [15]

JONES, William, *The Rectory, Llanenddwyn, Barmouth, Merionethshire.*—Glasgow Univ. and Lampeter; Deac. 1835 by Bp of Roch. Pr. 1836 by Bp of St. D. R. of Llanenddwyn with Llanddwywe C. Dio. Ban. 1862. (Patron, Bp of Ban; Tithe, comm. 350*l*; Glebe, 4 acres; R.'s Inc. 350*l* and Ho; Pop. Llanenddwyn 891, Llanddwywe 368.) Formerly V. of Nevyn 1842–62; previously C. of Llandovery 1835–37, Llanbeulan 1837–42. Author, *A Portrait of the True Philosopher* (a Lecture), 1831; *The Character of the Welsh as a Nation in the present Age* (a Prize Essay in Welsh and English), Carnarvon, 1840, 7*s*; *A Prize Essay on the Cause of Adversity and Prosperity* (in Welsh), 1842; *A Prize Essay on the Present State of France, and the Causes which have operated in producing it* (in Welsh), Holywell, 1848; *The Patriotism of the present Age* (an Oration delivered at the Aberffraw Royal Eisteddfod), 1849; *An Essay on the Province of Judgment and Imagination in Prose and Poetical Compositions*; *The Resurrection* (a Poem), Ruthin, 1853, 1*s* 6*d*; "*Wherewithal shall a Young Man cleanse his Way*" (a Sermon), Carnarvon, 1862. [16]

JONES, William, *Market Deeping, Lincolnshire.*—St. Bees; Deac. 1863 and Pr. 1864 by Bp of St. A. C. of Market Deeping 1865. Formerly C. of Llanllwchaiarn, Montgomeryshire, 1863–65. [17]

JONES, William, *Brymbo, Wrexham.*—St. Bees; Deac. 1854 by Bp of Ches. for Bp of Lich. Pr. 1854 by Bp of Lich. P. C. of Brymbo, Dio. St. A. 1856. (Patron, V. of Wrexham; Tithe, 147*l*; Glebe, 2 acres; P. C.'s Inc. 300*l* and Ho; Pop. 5475.) [18]

JONES, William, *Billingsley, Bridgnorth, Salop.*—R. of Billingsley, Dio. Herf. 1855. (Patron, Duke of Cleveland; Tithe, 188*l*; Glebe, 12 acres; R.'s Inc. 209*l*; Pop. 144.) [19]

JONES, William, *Frisby Vicarage, Melton Mowbray.*—St. John's Coll. Cam. Sen. Opt. and B.A. 1836; Deac. 1837, Pr. 1838. V. of Frisby-on-the-Wreak, Dio. Pet. 1841. (Patron, Ld Chan; V.'s Inc. 200*l* and Ho; Pop. 424.) P. C. of Kirby Bellars, Dio. Pet. 1865. (Patron, Sir R. Burdett, Bart; P. C.'s Inc. 84*l*; Pop. 243.) [20]

JONES, William, *Carngiwch, Pwllheli, Carnarvonshire.*—C. of Carngiwch. [21]

JONES, William, *Llantrisant, Glamorganshire.*—C. of Llantrisant. [22]

JONES, William, *Morton House, Oswestry.*—St. Bees; Deac. 1846 by Bp of Ches. Pr. 1848 by Bp of Man. C. of Morton, Salop. [23]

JONES, William, *Dowlais, Glamorganshire.*—St. Bees; Deac. 1863 by Bp of Ely for Bp of Llan. C. of Dowlais 1863. [24]

JONES, The Ven. William Basil, *Bishopthorpe Vicarage, York.*—Trin. Coll. Ox. Scho. of; Ireland Univ. Scho. 1842; 2nd cl. Lit. Hum. and B.A. 1844, M.A. 1847. V. of Bishopthorpe with Middlethorpe Dio. York, 1865. (Patron, Abp of York; Tithe, 18*l*; Glebe, 60 acres; V.'s Inc. 300*l* and Ho; Pop. 559.) Archd. of York, *alias* the West Riding, 1867 (Value, 180*l*). Preb. of Grindall in York Minster, 1863; Exam. Chap. to the Abp of York. Formerly Michel Fellow of Queen's; Fell. and Tut. of Univ. Coll. Ox; Mast. of the Schs. 1848; Cl. Mod. 1856, 1860; Sen.

Proctor 1861; Select Preacher 1860, 1866. P. C. of Haxby, Dio. York, 1863; Cursal Preb. in St. David's Cathl. 1859. Author, *Vestiges of the Gael in Gwynedd*, 1851; *Christ College, Brecon, its History and Capabilities, considered with Reference to a Measure now before Parliament*, 1853; *The History and Antiquities of St. David's* (jointly with E. A. Freeman, Esq.), 1856; *The Responsibility of Man to the Law of God* (Assize and Univ. Sermon), 1859; *Religion and Morality* (Univ. Sermon), 1861; *Notes on the Œdipus Tyrannus of Sophocles, adapted to the Text of Dindorf*, 1862; *The Clergyman's Office* (a Sermon), 1864; *The New Testament, illustrated, with a Plain Explanatory Commentary for Private Reading* (jointly with Archd. Churton), 1865; *Judgment, Mercy and Faith* (Univ. Sermon), 1866; *A Charge*, 1867; several Papers in Literary and Antiquarian Journals. [1]

JONES, William Brookbank Borrowdale, *Hollins Grove, Lower Darwen, Lancashire.*—St. Bees; Deac. 1862 and Pr. 1863 by Bp of Man. C. of Trinity, Over Darwen, 1864. Formerly C. of St. Matthew's, Manchester, 1862–64. [2]

JONES, William Evan, *Garth-Beibio Rectory, Welshpool.*—St. Bees; Deac. 1845 and Pr. 1846 by Abp of Cant. R. of Garth-Beibio, Dio. St. A. 1850. (Patron, Bp of St. A; Tithe, 227*l*; Glebe, 9½ acres; R.'s Inc. 240*l* and Ho; Pop. 326.) [3]

JONES, William Henry, *Mottram-in-Longdendale Vicarage, near Manchester.*—Brasen. Coll. Ox. Queen's Coll. Ox. Exhib. B.A 1843, M.A. 1845; Deac. 1844 and Pr. 1845 by Bp of Ches. V. of Mottram-in-Longendale, Dio. Ches. 1853. (Patron, Bp of Ches; Tithe, 38*l* 17*s* 6*d*; Glebe, 4 acres; V.'s Inc. 180*l* and Ho; Pop. 4298.) Inventor and Patentee (see Official Catalogue of the Great Exhibition of 1851, Cl. xxix. No. 95.) Author, *Form of Prayer, to be used in Sunday Schools*; *The Temple of Pleasure and the Lord's Day*, 2nd ed; *A Letter to Viscount Palmerston on the Necessity for the Revision of the Marquis of Blandford's "New Parishes Act,"* 1857, 6*d*; *A Letter to the Earl of Shaftesbury on Church Rates*, 2nd ed. 1859, 6*d*; *Suggestions for a Church Rate Relief Bill* (addressed by permission to Sir George Grey, Bart.), 1862; *The Muffled Peal* (a record of the Cotton Famine), 1863; all published by Hatchards. [4]

JONES, William Henry, *Bradford-on-Avon Vicarage, Wilts.*—Magd. Hall, Ox. Boden Sanscrit Scho. 1837, B.A. 1840, M.A. 1843; Deac. 1841 and Pr. 1842 by Bp of Lon. V. of Bradford with Westwood R. Dio. Salis. 1851. (Patrons, D. and C. of Bristol; Bradford, Tithe, 391*l* 3*s* 6*d*; Westwood, Tithe, 190*l*; Glebe, 21 acres; V.'s Inc. 602*l* and Ho; Pop. Bradford 3261, Westwood 469.) Surrogate; Rural Dean; Chap. to Lord Westbury. Author, *Our Work and our Teaching, as Ministers of Christ* (a Visitation Sermon), 1851; *Literary Institutions, their Use and Usefulness* (a Lecture delivered at the Opening of the Bradford Literary Institution), 1852; *History of the Parish of Bradford-on-Avon*, and many other papers in the *Wiltshire Archæological Magazine*; *Domesday for Wiltshire* (transcribed and edited, with Introduction and Illustrative Notes), 1865. [5]

JONES, William Lloyd, *Washfield Rectory, Tiverton.*—Emman. Coll. Cam. B.A. 1855; Deac. 1855 and Pr. 1857 by Bp of S. and M. R. of Washfield, Dio. Ex. 1865. (Patron, J. F. Worth, Esq; Tithe, 407*l*; Glebe, 35 acres; R.'s Inc. 450*l* and Ho; Pop. 471.) Formerly C. of St. Thomas's, Douglas, Isle of Man, 1855, Hagley, Worc. 1860, Woolborough, Devon, 1862, St. Mary Major, Exeter, 1864, South Molton 1865. [6]

JONES, William Price, *Clee Vicarage, Great Grimsby, Lincolnshire.*—Ch. Ch. Ox. B.A. 1844, M.A. 1852; Deac. 1844 and Pr. 1845 by Bp of Lich. V. of Clee with Cleethorpes, Dio. Lin. 1850. (Patron, Bp of Lin; Tithe, App. 265*l*; Glebe, 45 acres; V.'s Inc. 300*l* and Ho; Pop. 1555.) Surrogate. [7]

JONES, William Richard, *Llandinam, Montgomeryshire.*—Jesus Coll. Ox. B.A. 1862; Deac. 1863 by Bp of Ban. C. of Banhadlog in Llandinam 1863. [8]

JONES, William Taylor, *Sydenham College, Sydenham, S.E.*—Queens' Coll. Cam. B.A. 1849, M.A. 1853; Deac. 1849 by Bp of Lich. Pr. 1850 by Bp of Roch. Prin. of Sydenham Coll. and Exam. of Coll. of Preceptors. Formerly Chap. of Romford Union 1849–56; Morning Preacher, St. Edward's, Romford, 1857. [9]

JONES, William Taylor, *Forest Hill, Sydenham, S.E.*—C. of Forest Hill. [10]

JONES, William Thomas, *Tilford, Farnham, Surrey.*—Pemb. Coll. Ox. B.A. 1856, M.A. 1858; Deac. 1857 and Pr. 1858 by Bp of Win. P. C. of Tilford, Dio. Win. 1865. (Patron, Archd. of Surrey; P. C.'s Inc. 250*l* and Ho; Pop. 450.) Formerly C. of Farnham 1857–65. [11]

JONES, William West, *St. John's College, Oxford.*—St. John's Coll. Ox. Fell. of, 1860; Deac. 1861 and Pr. 1862 by Bp of Ox. P. C. of Summertown, Dio. Ox. 1864. (Patron, St. John's Coll. Ox; P. C.'s Inc. 120*l*; Pop. 1088.) Formerly C. of St. Matthew's, City-road, Lond. 1861–64. [12]

JOPLIN, Frederic, *Harswell Rectory, York.*—Queen's Coll. Cam. B.A. 1846, M.A. 1849; Deac. 1847, Pr. 1848. R. of Harswell, Dio. York, 1860. (Patron, Sir C. Slingsby, Bart; R.'s Inc. 200*l* and Ho; Pop. 89.) Formerly C. of Ramsey, Hunts. [13]

JORDAN, Gibbes, *Oakhurst, East-Wood-Hay, near Newbury.*—Queen's Coll. Ox. B.A. 1852; Deac. 1853, Pr. 1854. C. of East-Wood-Hay with Ashmanworth. [14]

JORDAN, John, *Church Enstone Vicarage, Oxon.*—Clare Coll. Cam. Coll. Priseman, B.A. 1826; Deac. 1827 by Bp of Glouc. Pr. 1830 by Bp of Ox. V. of Church Enstone, Dio. Ox. 1840. (Patron, Viscount Dillon; Tithe—App. 1244*l* 14*s* 11*d* and 53 acres of Glebe, V. 300*l*; Glebe, 25 acres; V.'s Inc. 350*l* and Ho; Pop. 1198.) Formerly C. of Little Dean 1827, Handborough 1830, Somerton 1836. Author, *A Curate's Views of Church Reform, Temporal, Spiritual, and Educational*, 1837; other Pamphlets on the same subject; *A Reply to certain Allegations of the Rev. G. Faussett, D.D*; *An Appeal to the Bishop of Oxford*; *The Crisis Come*; *Review of Tradition, as taught by the Writers of the Tracts for the Times*, 1840; *The Holy Baptist*, a Scriptural Poem in five Cantos, 1843; *Memoir of the Hailstorm that occurred in the County of Oxford*, 1843, read before the Ashmolean Society; *Scriptural Views of the Sabbath of God*, 1848; *A Parochial History of Enstone*, 1857. [15]

JOSCELYNE, Henry, *Fewcott, Bicester.*—New Inn Hall, Ox. B.A. 1862; Deac. 1857 and Pr. 1861 by Bp of Ox. Asst. C. of Ardley, Bicester, 1866. Formerly C. of Holywell, Oxford, 1857–61; Chap. of the City Gaol Oxford, 1861–66. [16]

JOSE, Stephen Prust, *Clifton.*—Pemb. Coll. Ox. B.A. 1853, M.A. 1857; Deac. 1856 and Pr. 1857 by Bp of Win. Min. of Dowry Chapel, Clifton, 1865. Formerly C. of Heckfield and Rotherwick, Hants, 1856–59, Emmanuel, Weston-super-Mare, 1859–63. [17]

JOSEPH, Alexander, *Chatham.*—Brasen. Coll. Ox. B.A. 1845, M.A. 1848; Deac. and Pr. 1848 by Abp of York. P. C. of St. John's, Chatham, Dio. Roch. 1861. (Patron, R. of Chatham; P. C.'s Inc. 300*l* and Ho; Pop. 5168.) Rural Dean. Formerly C. of Nafferton, Yorks, 1848, Romford 1851, Curzon Chapel, Lond. 1856, St. John's, Paddington, 1858. [18]

JOSLING, William James, *Christ's College, Cambridge.*—Ch. Coll. Cam. 12th in 1st cl. Cl. Trip. 1862, 1st cl. Theol. Trip. 1863, Carus Prize for Undergraduates 1859, and for Bachelors 1863, B.A. 1862, M.A. 1865; Deac. 1863 and Pr. 1864 by Bp of Ely. Fell. and Asst. Tut. of Ch. Coll. Formerly C. of St. Andrew's the Great, Cambridge, 1863–65. [19]

JOURDAIN, Francis, *The Parsonage, Derwent, Sheffield.*—Pemb. Coll. Ox. B.A. 1856, M.A. 1859; Deac. 1858 and Pr. 1859 by Bp of Man. P. C. of Derwent, Dio. Lich. 1862. (Patron, the Duke of Devonshire; Glebe, 111 acres; P. C.'s Inc. 85*l* and Ho; Pop. 165.) Formerly C. of St. Peter's, Manchester, 1858, St. Philip's, Hulme, 1860. [20]

JOWETT, Benjamin, *Balliol College, Oxford.*—Ball. Coll. Ox. Hertford Univ. Scho. 1837, 1st. cl. Lit. Hum. and B.A. 1839, M.A. 1842; Deac. 1842 and Pr.

1845 by Bp of Ox. Fell. and Tut. of Ball. Coll. Ox. 1838; Member of the Commission appointed to arrange the Examinations for Admission to the East Indian Civil Service 1854; Regius Prof. of Greek in the Univ. of Ox. 1855; Exam. in Lit. Hum. 1849, 1850, 1858. Author, *St. Paul's Epistles to the Thessalonians, Galatians and Romans*; *Critical Notes and Dissertations*, 1855, 2nd ed. 1859; *On the Interpretation of Scripture* (an Essay in *Essays and Reviews*), 1860. [1]

JOWETT, Edward, *Carlton-Miniott, Thirsk, Yorks.*—Caius Coll. Cam. B.A. 1835; Deac. 1835, Pr. 1836. P. C. of Carlton-Miniott, Dio. York, 1843. (Patron, Abp of York; Tithe—App. 263*l*, P. C. 73*l*; Queen Anne's Bounty Land, 20 acres; P. C.'s Inc. 105*l*; Pop. 314.) Author, *The Wisdom of God in the Works of Creation* (a Lecture), 6*d*. [2]

JOWETT, James Forbes, *Kingston Bagpuze Rectory, Abingdon, Berks.*—St. John's Coll. Ox. B.A. 1819, M.A. 1822, B.D. 1825; Deac. 1819 and Pr. 1820 by Bp of Ox. R. of Kingston Bagpuze, Dio. Ox. 1828. (Patron, St. John's Coll. Ox; Tithe, 385*l*; Glebe, 28 acres; R.'s Inc. 420*l* and Ho; Pop. 283.) [3]

JOWITT, John Henry.—Dur. Licen. Theol. 1854, B.A. 1855; Deac. 1855 and Pr. 1856 by Bp of Ox. Travelling Sec. of the Additional Curates' Soc. [ ]

JOWITT, W.—Head Mast. of the City Middle Class Sch. Lond. [4]

JOY, Henry, *Cheltenham.*—Dub. and Wor. Coll. Ox. M.A. 1863; Deac. and Pr. 1860 by Bp of St. A. C. of Cheltenham 1862. Formerly C. of Bronington, Salop, 1860–62. [5]

JOY, John Holmes, *Lullingstone, Dartford, Kent.*—C. of Lullingstone. [6]

JOY, Samuel, *Hill Top, Ambleside.*—Wor. Coll. Ox. B.A. 1856, M.A. 1859; Deac. 1857, Pr. 1858. Formerly C. and Lect. of Leeds 1857–59, P. C. of Bramley, Yorks, 1859–66. [7]

JOY, William, *Shudy Camps, Linton, Cambs.*—Scho. of Trin. Coll. Cam. 1838, Sen. Opt. 2nd cl. Cl. Trip. and B.A. 1839, M.A. 1842; Deac. and Pr. 1842 by Bp of G. and B. V. of Shudy Camps, Dio. Ely, 1863. (Patron, Trin. Coll. Cam; V.'s Inc. 150*l* and Ho; Pop. 351.) Formerly C. of Heapham with Springthorpe, Gainsborough. [8]

JOYCE, Charles, *Denham, near Uxbridge.*—C. of Denham. [9]

JOYCE, Francis Hayward, *Harrow-on-the-Hill, Middlesex.*—Ch. Ch. Ox. 2nd cl. Lit. Hum. and B.A. 1851, M.A. 1854; Deac. 1858 by Bp of Ox. V. of Harrow-on-the-Hill, Dio. Lon. 1862. (Patron, Lord Northwick; V.'s Inc. 756*l* and Ho; Pop. 2620.) Rural Dean. Stud. of Ch. Ch. Ox. [10]

JOYCE, Henry Morrogh, *Nichol Forest, Longtown, Cumberland.*—Bp. Hat. Hall, Dur. Licen. in Theol. 1855; Deac. 1855 and Pr. 1856 by Bp of Nor. P. C. of Nichol Forest, Dio. Carl. 1862. (Patron, R. of Kirk-Andrews-upon-Esk; P. C.'s Inc. 150*l* and Ho; Pop. 1216.) Formerly C. of Lopham, Norfolk, 1855–58, Kelloe, Durham, 1858–62. [11]

JOYCE, James Gerald, *Strathfieldsaye Rectory, Winchfield, Hants.*—Magd. Hall, Ox. 2nd cl. Lit. Hum. and B.A. 1846; Deac. 1846 by Bp of Wor. Pr. 1847 by Bp of Ox. R. of Strathfieldsaye, Dio. Win. 1855. (Patron, Duke of Wellington; Tithe, 962*l*; Glebe, 12½ acres; R.'s Inc. 978*l* and Ho; Pop. 827.) Formerly C. of St. Michael's, Coventry, 1846–47, Wing, 1847–50; V. of Burford with Fullbrook 1850–55. [12]

JOYCE, James Wayland, *Burford Rectory (Salop), near Tenbury.*—Ch. Ch. Ox. B.A. 1832, M.A. 1835; Deac. and Pr. 1838. R. of Burford, 3rd portion, Dio. Herf. 1842. (Patron, Lord Northwick; Tithe, 409*l* 2*s* 9*d*; Glebe, 49 acres; R.'s Inc. 471*l* and Ho; Pop. 326.) Proctor in Conv. for Dio. Herf. Author, *England's Sacred Synods, a Constitutional History of the Convocations of the Clergy, &c.* Rivingtons, 1855; *The Duty of the Civil Power to Promote the Faith of the National Church* (Assize Sermon), 1857; *The National Church* (an Answer to an Essay on the National Church in *Essays and Reviews*), 1861; *Appeals in Matters Spiritual*, 1862; *Concio ad Clerum* (Latin Sermon preached at the opening of Convocation), Rivingtons, 1866. [13]

JOYCE, William Henry, *Dorking, Surrey.*—Univ. Coll. Ox. B.A. 1840, M.A. 1865; Deac. 1842, Pr. 1843. V. of Dorking, Dio. Win. 1850. (Patron, G. Cubitt, Esq. M.P; Tithe—Imp. 154*l* 8*s* 6*d*, V. 541*l* 2*s* 6½*d*; Glebe, 5 acres; V.'s Inc. 550*l*; Pop. 3308.) Surrogate [14]

JOYNES James Leigh, *Eton College, Bucks.*—King's Coll. Cam. B.A. 1848, M.A. 1850. Asst. Mast. in Eton Coll. [15]

JOYNES, John, 12, *Hutchinson-place, Gravesend.*—Emman. Coll. Cam. B.A. 1848, M.A. 1852; Deac. 1849, Pr. 1850. P. C. of St. James's, Gravesend, Dio. Roch. 1851. (Patron, R. of Gravesend; Pop. 3215.) [16]

JOYNES, Richard, *Great Holland Rectory, Colchester.*—Corpus Coll. Ox. B.A. 1839, M.A. 1842, B.D. 1851; Deac. 1842 and Pr. 1843 by Bp of Ox. R. of Great Holland, Dio. Roch. 1861. (Patron, Corpus Coll. Ox; Tithe, 750*l*; Glebe, 70 acres; R.'s Inc. 835*l* and Ho; Pop. 467.) Hon. Can. of Roch. 1866; Rural Dean 1866; Hon. Organizing Sec. to S.P.G. for the Archd. of Colchester; Surrogate. Formerly P. C. of Trinity, Milton-next-Gravesend, 1845–61; Lect. of St. George's, Gravesend, 1846; Fell. of Corpus Coll. Ox. 1847. [17]

JOYNES, Robert, *Gravesend.*—St. John's Coll. Cam. B.A. 1843, M.A. 1846; Deac. and Pr. 1844. R. of Gravesend, Dio. Roch. 1846. (Patron, Ld Chan; Tithe, 284*l* 10*s* 6*d*; Glebe, 22½ acres; R.'s Inc. 361*l*; Pop. 4670.) Surrogate. [18]

JOYNES, William, *South Hill, Gravesend.*—Trin. Coll. Cam. B.A. 1852, M.A. 1855; Deac. 1853, Pr. 1855. V. of Chalk, Dio. Roch. 1856. (Patron, Ld Chan; Tithe—Imp. 481*l* 10*s* 10*d*; Glebe, 30 acres; V. 198*l* 10*s*; V.'s Inc. 200*l*; Pop. 382.) Sinecure R. of Merston, Dio. Roch. 1864. (Patron, Ld Chan; R.'s Inc. 89*l*.) Formerly C. of St. George's, Gravesend. [19]

JUBB, Henry, *Dunham-on-Trent, near Newark, Notts.*—Jesus Coll. Cam. LL.B. 1855; Deac. 1854 and Pr. 1856 by Bp of Ex. V. of Dunham with Ragnall and Durlton, Dio. Lin. 1856. (Patron, Bp of Man; V.'s Inc. 268*l*; Pop. 694.) Formerly Asst. C. of Bridewest and Stourton, near Exeter. [20]

JUDD, Richard, *Hills-road, Cambridge.*—Corpus Coll. Cam. C. of St. Paul's, Cambridge. [21]

JUDGE, John, *Leighton Parsonage, near Welshpool.*—St. Bees, 1st cl. 1846–48; Deac. 1848 and Pr. 1849 by Bp of Ches. P. C. of Trelystan with Leighton, Dio. Herf. 1853. (Patron, John Naylor, Esq. Leighton Hall; Tithe—App. 292*l* 10*s*; P. C.'s Inc. 150*l* and Ho; Pop. 573.) Formerly C. of Liscard, near Liverpool, 1848–51, Bollington, near Macclesfield, 1851–53. [22]

JUDKIN, Thomas James, 49, *Euston-square, London, N. W.*—Caius Coll. Cam. B.A. 1815, M.A. 1818; Deac. 1816, Pr. 1817. P. C. of Somers Chapel, Somerstown, Dio. Lon. 1828. (Patron, V. of St. Pancras; P. C.'s Inc. 400*l*.) Author, *Twelve Signs of the Times*; *Popish Aggression* (Sermons); *Church and Home Psalmody, and Bygone Moods* (Sonnets). [23]

JUDSON, Robert Kershaw, *Mallinson's, Ashton-under-Lyne.*—St. John's Coll. Cam. B.A. 1866; Deac. 1866 by Bp of Man. C. of St. James's, Hurst Brook, Ashton-under-Lyne, 1866. [24]

JUKES, George Morse.—Dom. Chap. to Lord Kinnaird. Formerly British Chap. at Havre. [25]

JUKES, Joseph Hordern, *Withington, near Hereford.*—Wad. Coll. Ox. B.A. 1857, M.A. 1863; Deac. 1858 and Pr. 1861 by Bp of Herf. C. of Church Withington 1866. Formerly C. in sole charge of Preston-Wynne 1858–66. [26]

JUKES, Robert Boswell, *Ostend.*—Corpus Coll. Cam. B.A. 1838; Deac. 1839, Pr. 1840. British Consular Chap. at Ostend. [27]

JUKES, William Malone, *Ennerdale, Whitehaven, Cumberland.*—St. Bees; Deac. 1843 and Pr. 1844 by Bp of Ches. P. C. of Ennerdale, Dio. Ches. 1848. (Patron, Henry Curwen, Esq; Tithe—Imp. 68*l*; P. C's Inc. 76*l*; Pop. 499.) [28]

JULIAN, John, 50, *Mandale-road South, Stockton-on-Tees.*—St. Aidan's; Deac. 1866 and Pr. 1867 by Abp of York. C. of Thornaby, Yorks, 1866. Author, *The English Bible and its Translators*, 1864, 6d. [1]

JULIUS, Archibald Æneas, *Southery Rectory, Downham, Norfolk.*—St. John's Coll. Cam. B.A. 1842, M.A. 1848; Deac. 1842 and Pr. 1844 by Bp of Lin. R. of Southery, Dio. Nor. 1855. (Patron, Rev. Edmund Hall; Tithe, 650*l* 10*s* 6*d*; Glebe, 104 acres; R.'s Inc. 804*l* and Ho; Pop. 1164.) [2]

JULIUS, Henry Richard, *Wrecclesham, Parsonage, Farnham, Surrey.*—St. John's Coll. Cam. B.A. 1839, M.A. 1842; Deac. 1839, Pr. 1840. P. C. of Wrecclesham, Dio. Win. 1846. (Patron, Bp of Win; P. C.'s Inc. 350*l* and Ho; Pop. 1271.) Formerly C. of St. Andrew's, Farnham, 1839–46. [3]

JUMP, Edward, *Underbarrow, Milnthorpe.*—Literate; Deac. 1867 by Bp of Carl. C. of Crook, Kendal, 1867. [4]

KAHN, Joseph, *Rudwell, Herts.*—C. of Radwell. [5]

KANE, James Percy, *Cowley, Oxford.*—Trin. Coll. Ox. B.A. 1856, M.A. 1858; Deac. 1856 and Pr. 1858 by Bp of Ox. C. of Cowley 1857. [6]

KANE, Richard Nathaniel, *Mortlake, Surrey, S.W.*—Oriel Coll. Ox. B.A. 1859, M.A. 1862; Deac. 1860 by Bp of Llan. C. of Mortlake with East Sheen 1864. Formerly C. of St. Wooles, Newport, Monmouth and Trevethian, Pontypool. [7]

KANT, W.—C. of St. Paul's, Birmingham. [8]

KARNEY, Charles Lumsdaine, *Sutton Scotney, Micheldever Station.*—Trin. Coll. Cam. B.A. 1863; Deac. 1864 and Pr. 1865 by Bp of Win. C. of Wonston, Hants, 1866. Formerly C. of Lingfield, Surrey, 1864. [9]

KARR, J. S., *Berkeley Vicarage, Glouc.*—V. of Berkeley, Dio. G. and B. 1839. (Patron, Lord Fitzhardinge; Pop. 4039.) Dom. Chap. to the Duke of Roxburghe. [10]

KARSLAKE, John Wollaston, *Culmstock Vicarage, Wellington, Somerset.*—Magd. Coll. Cam. Jun. Opt. B.A. 1835; Deac. 1836, Pr. 1837. V. of Culmstock, Dio. Ex. 1841. (Patrons, D. and C. of Ex; Tithe, comm. 355*l*; Glebe, 4 acres; V.'s Inc. 360*l* and Ho; Pop. 1102.) [11]

KARSLAKE, William Heberden, *Meshaw Rectory, South Molton, Devon.*—Oriel Coll. Ox. B.A. 1830. R. of Meshaw, Dio. Ex. 1832. (Patron, Rev. W. Karslake; Tithe, 113*l*; Glebe, 83¾ acres; R.'s Inc. 203*l* and Ho; Pop. 250.) R. of Creacombe, near South Molton, Dio. Ex. 1832. (Patron, Rev. W. Karslake; Tithe, 44*l* 11*s* 6*d*; Glebe, 100 acres; R.'s Inc. 194*l*; Pop. 63.) Rural Dean. [12]

KARSLAKE, William Henry, *Westcott, Dorking.*—Mert. Coll. Ox. Fell. and Tut. of, 1st cl. Lit. Hum. M.A. 1848; Deac. 1855 and Pr. 1862 by Bp of Ox. P. C. of Westcott, Dio. Win. 1866. (Patron, A. K. Barclay, Esq; P. C.'s Inc. 155*l* and Ho; Pop. 1060.) Formerly P. C. of St. Andrew's, Hove, Sussex, 1862. Author, *An Exposition of the Lord's Prayer, Devotional, Doctrinal, and Practical*, 7*s* 6*d*; *Aids to the Study of Logic*, 2 vols. 5*s*; *The Past, the Present, and the Future, a Manual for those who are about to be Confirmed*, 1*s* 6*d*. [13]

KATTERNS, W., *Ashted, near Birmingham.*—C. of St. James's, Ashted. [14]

KAY, Edward Birt, *Hedon, Hull.*—Lin. Coll. Ox. B.A. 1854; Deac. 1857 and Pr. 1858 by Abp of York. P. C. of Marfleet, Dio. York, 1864. (Patron, Herbert Robinson; P. C.'s Inc. 54*l*; Pop. 175.) Formerly C. of Oversilton 1857–59, Hedon and Preston 1859–62. [15]

KAY, John Lowder, *Sydenham, S.E.*—Magd. Hall, Ox. B.A. 1844, M.A. 1846. C. of St. Bartholomew's, Sydenham. Formerly C. of St. Peter's, Everton, Liverpool, and Trinity, Dorchester. [16]

KAY, William, *Great Leighs Rectory, Chelmsford.*—Lin. Coll. Ox. 1st cl. Lit. Hum. 2nd cl. Math. et Phy. and B.A. 1839, M.A. 1842, B.D. and D.D. 1855; Deac. and Pr. 1844. R. of Great Leighs, Dio. Roch. 1866. (Patrons, Lin. Coll; R.'s Inc. 878*l*; Pop. 909.) Formerly Fell. of Lin. Coll. Ox. 1840; Prin. of Bishop's Coll. Calcutta, 1849–65. Author, *The Promises of Christianity*, Parker, 1856; *The Psalms, translated from the Hebrew, with Notes*, Lepage, Calcutta, 1863; *Crisis Hupfeldiana*, Parker, 1865. [17]

KAY, William Leonard, *Newcastle-on-Tyne.*—St. Bees; Deac. 1853 and Pr. 1854 by Bp of Rip. P. C. of Ch. Ch. Newcastle, Dio. Dur. 1861. (Patron, Bp of Dur; P. C.'s Inc. 300*l* and Ho; Pop. 10,000.) Surrogate. Formerly C. of Otley, Yorks, and All Saints, Newcastle. [18]

KAYE, John, *Harvington, Evesham.*—C. of Harvington. [19]

KAYE, The Ven. William Frederick John, *Lincoln.*—Ball. Coll. Ox. 2nd cl. Math. et Phy. and B.A. 1844, M.A. 1847; Deac. and Pr. 1846. Archd. of Lincoln 1863; Can. of Lincoln 1863; R. of Riseholme, Linc. Dio. Lin. 1846. (Patrons, Ball. Coll. Ox; R.'s Inc. 150*l*; Pop. 93.) P. C. of South Carlton, Linc. Dio. Lin. 1847. (Patron, Bp of Lin; Tithe, Eccles. Commis. 480*l*; P. C.'s Inc. 200*l*; Pop. 181.) Chap. to the Bp of Lin. Formerly Official to Archdeacon H. K. Bonney. Author, *A Sermon preached at the Visitation of the Bishop of Lincoln* 1849; *A Visitation Sermon*, 1850; *A Sermon on the Privileges of the Lord's Day*; *Charges to Clergy and Churchwardens of the Archdeaconry of Lincoln*, 1863–66. [20]

KAYSS, John Bainbridge, *School Frigate "Conway," Rock Ferry, Birkenhead.*—Dub. A.B. 1859; Deac. 1860 and Pr. 1861 by Bp of Carl; Chap. of the Sch. Frigate "Conway," Rock Ferry. Formerly C. of Urswick, near Ulverstone, and Bromfield, Aspatria, Cumberland. [21]

KEANE, John Espy, *St. Jude's Parsonage, Old Bethnal-green-road, London, N.E.*—P. C. of St. Jude's, Bethnal-green, Dio. Lon. 1844. (Patron, Bp of Lon; P. C.'s Inc. 300*l* and Ho; Pop. 14,039.) Chap. to the Bethnal-green Union. [22]

KEANE, William, *Whitby Parsonage, Yorks.*—Emman. Coll. Cam. B.A. 1840, M.A. 1843; Deac. 1841 and Pr 1843 by Bp of Ely. R. of Whitby with St. Michael's C. and St. John's C. Dio. York, 1853. (Patron, Abp of York; Tithe, App. 2820*l*; R.'s Inc. 654*l* and Ho; Pop. 12,830.) Surrogate; Dom. Chap. to the Marquis of Conyngham; Fell. of Royal Astronomical Soc. Formerly Can. of St. Paul's Cathl. Calcutta, and Assoc. Sec. to the Ch. Miss. Soc. Author, *Hinduism and Romanism*; *Public Instruction of Indian Government*; *The Irish Mission to the Heathen English*; *Sermons on St. Paul's Cathedral (Calcutta) Mission*; *Funeral Sermon on the Rev. Dr. Scoresby*; *The Knightsbridge Decision no Compromise.* [23]

KEARNEY, John Batchelor, *The Precincts, Canterbury.*—St. John's Coll. Cam. 20th Wrang. and B.A. 1850, M.A. 1853; Deac. 1852 and Pr. 1853 by Bp of Dur. Author, *On Elementary Mechanics*, 1847; *On the Theory of Parallels*; *On the Theory of Quadratic Factors*; *The National Anthem, Harmonised in the Modern Style*, 1851; *Church Songs for Christmas*, 1856. [24]

KEATCH, Frederic, *The Quinton, Birmingham.* Queens' Coll. Cam. B.A. 1863, M.A. 1867; Deac. 1864 and Pr. 1865 by Bp of Worc. C. of The Quinton 1864. [25]

KEATE, John Charles, *Hartley-Wespall Rectory, Hartfordbridge, Hants.*—Ball. Coll. Ox. B.A. 1844, M.A. 1847; Deac. 1845 and Pr. 1846 by Bp of Ox. R. of Hartley-Wespall, Dio. Win. 1849. (Patrons, D. and C. of Windsor; Tithe, 389*l*; Glebe, 30 acres; R.'s Inc. 419*l* and Ho; Pop. 343.) [26]

KEATING, William, M.A., 29, *Carlton-hill East, London.* [27]

KEBBEL, Carsten Dirs, *The Parsonage, Hatherden, Andover.*—Univ. Coll. Ox; P. C. of Smannell with Hatherden, Dio. Win. 1857. (Patrons, Winchester Coll; P. C.'s Inc. 100*l* and Ho; Pop. 650.) Author, *Sermons on the Harmony of the Sacrament*, etc., Bell and Daldy; *A Guide to True Conversion*; *The Way of Christian Holiness, and Neglect of Public Worship*, S.P.C K. [1]

KEBLE, Thomas, *Bisley Vicarage, Stroud, Glouc.*—Corpus Coll. Ox. 2nd cl. Lit. Hum. 2nd cl. Math. et Phy. and B.A. 1811, M.A. 1815, B.D. 1824. V. of Bisley, Dio. G and B. 1827. (Patron, Ld Chan; Tithe—Imp. 1204*l*, V. 750*l*; Glebe, 17 acres; V.'s Inc. 767*l* and Ho; Pop. 1497.) Formerly Fell. of Corpus Coll. Ox. [2]

KEBLE, Thomas, *Flaxley. Newnham, Glouc.*—Magd. Coll. Ox. B.A. 1846, M.A. 1849; Deac. 1849 and Pr. 1850 by Bp of Ex. C. of Flaxley. Formerly C. of Bussage, Glouc. [3]

KEDDLE, Robert Antram, *Hutchlands, Netherbury, Dorset.*—Jesus Coll. Cam. B.A. 1856; Deac. 1858 and Pr. 1859 by Bp of B. and W. R. of Hook, Dio. Salis. 1862. (Patrons, Duke of Cleveland and Earl of Sandwich, alt; Tithe, 49*l* 13*s* 4*d*; Glebe, 42 acres; R.'s Inc. 100*l*; Pop. 247.) [4]

KEDDLE, Samuel Sherrin, *Combe St. Nicholas, Somerset.*—C. of Combe St. Nicholas. [5]

KEELING, Charles Neville, *Chorley, Lancashire.*—St. John's Coll. Cam. B.A. 1864; Deac. 1866 by Bp of Ches. C. of St. Philip's, Chorley, 1866. [6]

KEELING, Francis, *Adstone, Northants.*—Deac. 1837 and Pr. 1838 by Abp of York. P. C. of Adstone, Dio. Pet. 1865. (Patrons, Sons of the Clergy Corporation; P. C.'s Inc. 130*l*; Pop. 165.) Formerly C. of Hook, Yorks. [7]

KEELING, James, 41, *Blandford-square, London, N.W.*—P. C. of St. Paul's, Lisson-grove, Dio. Lon. 1854. (Patrons, Trustees; P C.'s Inc. 210*l*; Pop. 8850.) [8]

KEELING, J., *Idle, near Leeds.*—C. of Idle. [9]

KEELING, William, *Barrow Rectory, Bury St. Edmunds.*—St. John's Coll. Cam. B.A. 1826, M.A. 1829, B.D. 1836; Deac. and Pr. 1829. R. of Barrow, Dio. Ely, 1845. (Patron, St. John's Coll. Cam; Tithe, 828*l*; Glebe, 77 acres; R.'s Inc. 880*l* and Ho; Pop. 1030.) Formerly Fell. of St. John's Coll. Cam. Author, *Liturgiæ Britannicæ*, 1842, 2nd ed. 1851. [10]

KEELING, William Graham, *Edmonton, N.*—St. John's Coll. Ox. B.A. 1857, M.A. 1864; Deac. 1858 and Pr. 1859 by Bp of Lin. C. of Edmonton 1864. Formerly C. of Blyton, Lin. 1858–64. [11]

KEELING, William Hulton, *Northampton.*—Head Mast. of Northampton Gr. Sch. 1867. Formerly Asst. Mast. at Rossall Sch. Fleetwood. [12]

KEELING, William Robert, *Blackley Rectory, near Manchester.*—St. John's Coll. Cam. B.A. 1832; Deac. 1835 and Pr. 1836 by Bp of Ches. R. of Blackley, Dio. Man. 1838. (Patrons, D. and C. of Man; Tithe—App. 203*l* 11*s* 3*d*; R.'s Inc. 200*l* and Ho; Pop. 3112.) Formerly C. of St. Mary's, Manchester, 1835–38. [13]

KEENE, Benjamin Ruck, *Erwarton Rectory, Ipswich.*—Trin. Coll. Cam. B.A. 1849; Deac. 1850 and Pr. 1851 by Bp of Chich. R. of Erwarton with Woolverstone R Dio. Nor. 1858. (Patron, J. Berners, Esq; Erwarton, Tithe, 305*l*; Glebe, 48 acres; Woolverstone, Tithe, 239*l*; Glebe, 30 acres; R.'s Inc. 613*l* and Ho; Pop. Erwarton 243, Woolverstone 239.) Formerly C. of Forest Row, Sussex, 1850–57. V. of Bentley 1851–58 [14]

KEENE, Charles Edmund Ruck, *Swyncombe House, Henley-on-Thames.*—All Souls Coll. Ox. B.A. 1815, M.A. 1819. Preb. of Wells. [15]

KEENE, Henry Ruck, *Bentley Vicarage, near Ipswich.*—Univ. Coll. Dur. B.A. 1853, M.A. 1856; Deac. 1854 by Bp of Dur. Pr. 1855 by Bp of Man. V. of Bentley, Dio. Nor. 1858. (Patron, Rev. C. E. R. Keene; Tithe, 218; V.'s Inc. 200*l* and Ho; Pop. 453.) Formerly C. of St. Oswald's, Durham. [16]

KEENE, Thomas Pacey.—Ch. Coll. Cam. LL.B. 1856. Deac. 1857 by Bp of Pet. Pr. 1858 by Bp of Man. Sen. Chap. of the Calcutta Dioc. Addit. Clergy Soc. and Surrogate, India, 1859. Formerly C. of St. Mark's, Peterborough, 1857–58, St. Margaret's Chapel, Bath, 1867. [17]

KEER, William Brown, *Bombay.*—St. Bees; Deac. 1858 and Pr. 1859 by Bp of Ches. Harbour Chap. Bombay. Formerly C. of Liverpool 1858–60, Wilsden, Bradford, 1860, St. Paul's, Dock-street, Whitechapel, Lond. 1861. Author, *The Good Confession and the Fight of Faith*; *Numbering our Days or Thoughts for the New Year.* [18]

KEIGHTLEY, George Wilson, *Dunsby Rectory, Bourn, Lincolnshire.*—Pemb. Coll. Ox. B.A. 1848, M.A. 1851; Deac. 1850 and Pr. 1852 by Bp of Lon. R. of Dunsby, Dio. Lin. 1853. (Patrons, Govs. of Charterhouse, Lond; Tithe, 180*l*; Glebe, 7 acres; R.'s Inc. 189*l* and Ho; Pop. 195.) Formerly C. of Enfield, Lond. 1850. [19]

KEIGWIN, James Philip, *Isle of Cumbrae, Greenock, Scotland.*—Wad. Coll. Ox. B.A. 1832, M.A. 1838; Deac. 1835 and Pr. 1836 by Bp of Ex. Incumb. of St. Andrew's, Cumbrae; Can. of the Coll. Ch. Cumbrae. [20]

KEITCH, Robert S., 6, *Charlotte-terrace, Rouel-road, Bermondsey, Surrey.*—St. Aidan's; Deac. 1866 by Bp of Win. C. of Bermondsey. [21]

KEITH, William Alexander, *Burham, Rochester.*—St. Mary Hall, Ox. B.A. 1852, M.A. 1854; Deac. 1855 and Pr. 1856 by Bp of Lich. C. of Burham 1858. Formerly C. of Ch. Ch. Derby, 1855–56, Repton 1856–57, All Saints', Maidstone, 1857. [22]

KELK, Arthur Hastings, *St. Stephen's Vicarage, Burmantofts, Leeds.*—Caius Coll. Cam. Jun. Opt. B.A. 1859; Deac. 1859 and Pr. 1860 by Bp of Lin. V. of St. Stephen's, Burmantofts, Leeds, Dio. Rip. 1865. (Patrons, Five Trustees; V.'s Inc. 300*l* and Ho; Pop. 9000.) Formerly C. of Sutton-Bonington, Notts, 1859; Theol. Tut. of Protestant Coll. Malta, 1861; C. of St. George's, Leeds, 1861. [23]

KELK, Theophilus Henry Hastings, *Newbolt, Ashby-de-la-Zouch.*—Jesus Coll. Cam. B.A. 1828; Deac. 1831 and Pr. 1833 by Bp of Lin. Formerly C. of Worthington, Ashby-de-la-Zouch, 1831–40; Mast. of Osgathorpe Gr. Sch. 1834–53. [24]

KELLY, Frederic Festus, *Stockport, Cheshire.*—Trin. Hall, Cam. LL.B. 1860, LL.M. 1863; Deac. 1861 and Pr. 1862 by Bp of Ely. C. of Stockport 1864. [25]

KELLY, George Fitzroy, *St. John's Parsonage, Pembroke Dock, South Wales.*—Dub. Scho. 1818, Twice Cl. Prizeman, B.A. 1820, M.A. 1828; Deac. 1827 by Abp of Dub. Pr. 1828 by Bp of Ferns. P. C. of St. John's, Pembroke Dock, Dio. St. D. 1844. (Patron, the Crown; P. C.'s Inc. 371*l* and Ho; Pop. 10,190.) Acting Chap. to the Troops at Pembroke; Surrogate 1845. Formerly C. of St. Mary's, Dublin, 1830–40; P. C. of Baxtergate Chapel, Whitby, Yorks. Author, *Masonic Sermons*; *Practical Sermons*; *Butler's Analogy in Question and Answer*, Watson, Dublin. [26]

KELLY, Henry Plimley, *Parsonage House,* 112, *New North-road, London, N.*—Caius Coll. Cam. B.A. 1855, M.A. 1858; Deac. 1855 by Bp of Colombo, Pr. 1856 by Bp of Lon. P. C. of Ch. Ch. Hoxton, Dio. Lon. 1860 (Patron, P. C. of St. John's, Hoxton; P. C.'s Inc. 370*l* and Ho; Pop. 7610.) [27]

KELLY, James, *Princes-park, Liverpool.*—Dub. A.B. 1831, Downe's Prizeman for Divinity Composition, and Reading of the Liturgy, A.M. 1840; Deac. 1832 by Bp of Ossory, Pr. 1833 by Bp of Killaloe. P. C. of St. George's, Liverpool, Dio. Ches. 1863. (Patron, W. Titherington, Esq; P. C.'s Inc. 250*l*; Pop. 4002.) Formerly P. C. of Sandgate, Kent, 1839; R. of Stillorgan, Dublin; R. and V. of Killishee 1845; Min. of St. Peter's Chapel, Westminster, 1848. Author, *The Eternal Purpose of God*, 4*s*; *The Apocalypse interpreted in the Light of the Day of the Lord*, 2 vols. 12*s*; *Apocalyptic Interpretation*, 1*s*; *National Education in Ireland*, 1*s*; *Union or Alliance: Which is it?* 3*d*; *Scripture Truth extracted from Tractarian Superstition and Rationalising Subtlety*, 6*d*; *Inspiration: a Dialogue*, 1*s*; etc. [28]

KELLY, James Davenport, *Christ Church Parsonage, near Ashton-under-Lyne.*—Wad. Coll. Ox. Scho. Hody Hebrew Exhib. Kennicott Hebrew Scho. 2nd cl. Lit. Hum. B.A. 1851, M.A. 1854; Deac. 1852 by Bp of Ox. Pr. 1853 by Bp of Man. P. C. of Ch. Ch. Ashton-under-Lyne, Dio. Man. 1865. (Patrons, Crown and Bp alt; P. C.'s Inc. 390*l* and Ho; Pop. 1093.) Formerly C. of St. John's, Blackburn, 1853; Vice-Prin. of Elizabeth Coll. Guernsey, 1855; R. of St. James's, Manchester, 1860. [1]

KELLY, John Alexander, *Dixon road, Monmouth.*—Dub. A.B. 1862; Deac. 1862 and Pr. 1864 by Bp of G. and B. C. of St. Thomas's, Monmouth, 1867. Formerly C. of St. Paul's, Dean Forest, 1862–66. [2]

KELLY, Joshua, *Bath.*—Assoc. Sec. to Ch. Pastoral Aid Soc. [3]

KELLY, Walter, *Preston Vicarage, Brighton.*—Caius Coll. Cam. Wrang. and B.A. 1827, M.A. 1830; Deac. 1827, Pr. 1829. V. of Preston with Hove, Dio. Chich. 1834. (Patron, Bp of Chich; Preston, Tithe, App. 13*l*, V. 304*l* 5*s*; Glebe, 4 acres; Hove, Tithe, App. 220*l*, V. 93*l* 10*s*; Glebe, 1 acre; V.'s Inc. 612*l* and Ho; Pop. Preston 1044, Hove 9624.) [4]

KELLY, William, *Shipley Parsonage, near Leeds.*—Dub. A.B. 1841; Deac. 1842 and Pr. 1843 by Bp of Rip. P. C. of Shipley, Dio. Rip. 1845. (Patrons, Simeon's Trustees; Tithe, App. 20*l*, Imp. 30*l* 0*s* 6*d*; P. C.'s Inc. 346*l* and Ho; Pop. 7095.) Formerly C. of Clayton, Yorks, 1842. [5]

KELSALL, Henry S., *Smallthorne, Stoke-upon-Trent.*—King's Coll. Lond. Theol. Assoc. 1850; Deac. 1850 and Pr. 1851 by Bp of Herf. P. C. of Smallthorne, Dio. Lich. 1859. (Patron, R. of Norton-on-the-Moors; P. C.'s Inc. 160*l* and Ho; Pop. 1727.) [6]

KELSON, Henry, *Folkington Rectory, Willingdon, Sussex.*—Sid. Coll. Cam. B.A. 1816, M.A. 1819; Deac. 1817 by Bp of Ex. Pr. 1818 by Abp of Cant. R. of Folkington, Dio. Chich. 1842. (Patron, Earl De la Warr; Tithe, 270*l*; Glebe, 10 acres; R.'s Inc. 235*l* and Ho; Pop. 150.) V. of Lullington, Seaford, Sussex, Dio. Chich. 1840. (Patron, Bp of Chich; Tithe—App. 210*l*; V.'s Inc. 38*l*; Pop. 13.) [7]

KEMBLE, Charles, *Vellore, Bath.*—Wad. Coll. Ox. B.A. 1841, M.A. 1844; Deac. 1842 and Pr. 1843 by Bp of Win. R. of Bath, Dio. B. and W. 1859. (Patrons, Simeon's Trustees; R.'s Inc. 450*l* net and Ho; Pop. 2347.) Preb. of Wells, 1866; Surrogate. Formerly C. of St. Michael's, Stockwell, Surrey, 1842–44; P. C. of same, 1844–59; Sunday Even. Lect. at Ch. Ch. Spitalfields, 1848–51. Author, *Church Psalmody*, 3 eds; *The Venite, pointed for Chanting*, 2 eds. 3*d*; *Manual for Communicants*, 1846, 4*d* and 1*d*; *England's Wants*, 1851, 1*s*; *Seventeen Sermons*, Seeleys, 1851, 5*s*; *Selection of Psalms and Hymns*, 1853, various eds. from 2*d* to 12*s*, Shaw & Co; *Occasional Sermons*, 1857, 7*s* 6*d*; various single Sermons; etc. [8]

KEMBLE, Nicholas Freeze Younge, *Hesket Parsonage, Carlisle.*—Univ. Coll. Dur. B.A. and Licen. Theol. 1847, M.A. 1851; Deac. 1848 and Pr. 1849 by Bp of Pet. P. C. of Hesket and P. C. of Armathwaite, Dio. Carl. 1865. (Patron, of Hesket D. and C. of Carlisle, of Armathwaite Earl of Lonsdale; Tithe, of Hesket 18*l* 5*s*, of Armathwaite 16*s* 8*d*; Glebe, of Hesket 60 acres, of Armathwaite 47 acres; P. C.'s Inc. of Hesket 175*l* and Ho, of Armathwaite 95*l* 16*s* 8*d*; Pop of Hesket and Armathwaite combined 2050.) Organizing Sec. of S.P.G. for the Dio. of Carl. 1864. Formerly C. of Harston, Leic. 1848–49; Rothbury, Northum. 1849–52; P. C. of Sebergham, Carl. 1852–65. [9]

KEMBLE, William, *West Hanningfield Rectory, Chelmsford.*—Lin. Coll. Ox. B.A. 1833, M.A. 1836; Deac. 1833 and Pr. 1834 by Bp of Ox. R. of West Hanningfield with R. of South Hanningfield, Dio. Roch. 1842. (Patrons, the Trustees of the present R; South Hanningfield, Tithe, 360*l*; Glebe, 20 acres; Pop. 235; West Hanningfield, Tithe, 788*l*; Glebe, 24 acres; R.'s Inc. 930*l* and Ho; Pop. 527.) Rural Dean of Danbury. Formerly C. of Bucknell, Oxon, 1833, Swindon, Wilts, 1834, Hapton, Bucks, 1838. [10]

KEMM, William Henry, *Haydon, Sherborne, Dorset.*—C. of Haydon. [11]

KEMP, Augustus, *Corfe Mullen, Wimborne, Dorset.*—Caius Coll. Cam. B.A. 1839, M.A. 1843; Deac. 1840 and Pr. 1841 by Bp of Nor. [12]

KEMP, Edward Curtis, 51, *King-street, Great Yarmouth.*—St. John's Coll. Cam. B.A. 1817, M.A. 1820, 12th Wrang. P. C. of St. George's, Great Yarmouth, Dio. Nor. 1865. (Patrons, Trustees; P. C.'s Inc. 200*l*.) Formerly Chap. at Berlin to H.R.H. the Duke of Cambridge; C. of Lyndhurst 1825, East Dereham 1828; R. of Whissonsett and Horningtoft 1829. Author, *The Refutation of Nonconformity on its own Professed Principle, in Reply to Conder, Binney, Pye Smith, &c.*, Whittaker, Lond. 1830, 5*s*; *Scripture and Calvinism, an Answer to Mr. Scott's Reply to Tomline*, Bell and Daldy, 1843, 8*s*; *Isaaci Watts ii. Carm. Fascis qui inscribitur "Divine Songs," Latinè redditorum*, 2*s* 6*d*, Bell and Daldy. [13]

KEMP, George, *President's House, Sion College, London, E.C.*—Corpus Coll. Cam. B.A. 1840, M.A. 1843; Deac. 1841 and Pr. 1842 by Bp of Lon. R. of St. Alphage's, London-wall, Dio. Lon. 1856. (Patron, Bp of Lon; R.'s Inc. 319*l*; Pop. 699.) Formerly Chap. of the Royal Orthopœdic Hospital, Lond. 1847–56; C. of St. George's, Hanover-square, St. Dionis', Fenchurch-street, St. Giles's, Cripplegate, Lond. [14]

KEMP, Henry, *Kyre Wyard, Tenbury.*—Dub. A.B. 1849, A.M. 1852; Deac. 1849 and Pr. 1850 by Bp of Herf. R. of Kyre Wyard, Dio. Her. 1865. (Patron, Wm. Lacon Childe, Esq; Tithe, 170*l*; Glebe, 42 acres; R.'s Inc. 220*l* and Ho; Pop 152.) Formerly Asst. C. of Cleobury Mortimer; Head Mast. of Cleobury Mortimer Sch. Author, *Elementary Religious Catechism*, 8th ed. 3*d*, Macintosh. [15]

KEMP, Henry William, 33, *George-street, Hull.*—Corpus Coll. Cam. 29th Wrang. B.A. 1843; Deac. 1843, Pr. 1844. P. C. of St. John's, Hull, Dio. York, 1847. (Patron, V. of Holy Trinity, Hull; P. C.'s Inc. 220*l*.) Author, *Sermons*, 1 vol. Seeleys, 1854, 10*s* 6*d*; several single Sermons. [16]

KEMP, John, *Birstal, near Leeds.*—St. John's Coll. Ox. B.A. 1849, M.A. 1853; Deac. 1850 and Pr. 1851 by Bp of Rip. C. of Birstal. [17]

KEMP, Robert, *Wissett Vicarage, Halesworth, Suffolk.*—Deac. 1832 by Bp of Nor. Pr. 1833 by Bp of Win. P. C. of Walpole, Suffolk, Dio. Nor. 1840. (Patron, Ch. Patronage Soc; Tithe—Imp. 31*l* 7*s* 10*d*; P. C.'s Inc. 90*l*; Pop. 540.) V. of Wissett, Dio. Nor. 1842. (Patron, Sir John Hartopp, Bart; Tithe—Imp. 452*l* 10*s* 2*d*, V. 90*l*; V.'s Inc. 105*l* and Ho; Pop. 427.) Author, *Short Sermons*, 5*s*; *Funeral Sermon* (on the death of the Rev. E. Griffin), Ipswich, 1833, 1*s*. [18]

KEMP, Thomas Cooke, *East Meon Vicarage, Petersfield, Hants.*—Caius Coll. Cam. B.A. 1811. V. of East Meon with Froxfield C. and Steep C. Dio. Win. 1826. (Patron, Bp of Win; East Meon, Glebe, 13 acres; Tithe, App. 1128*l*, V. 680*l*; Froxfield, Tithe—App. 770*l*, V. 230*l*; Steep, Tithe—Imp. 300*l*, V. 230*l*; V.'s Inc. 1140*l* and Ho; Pop. East Meon 1486, Froxfield 637, Steep 903.) [19]

KEMP, Thomas Cooke, *Filey, Yorks.*—St. Aidan's 1859; Deac. 1859 and Pr. 1860 by Bp of Pet. C. of Filey. Formerly C. of Kegworth, near Derby, 1859–60. Author, *Sermon on Relinquishing the Curacy of Kegworth*, 1860, 6*d*. [20]

KEMP, Sir William Robert, Bart., *Gissing Hall, Diss, Norfolk.*—Corpus Coll. Cam. M.A. 1813; Deac. 1811, Pr. 1812. R. of Gissing, Dio. Nor. 1816. (Patron, the present R; Tithe, 497*l*; Glebe, 38 acres; R.'s Inc. 554*l*; Pop. 481.) [21]

KEMPE, Alfred Arrow, *Wexham Rectory, Slough, Bucks.*—Magd. Coll. Cam. B.A. 1838; Deac. 1838, Pr. 1839. R. of Wexham, near Slough, Bucks, Dio. Ox. 1846. (Patron, Ld Chan; Tithe, 7*l* 17*s* 6*d*; Glebe, 20 acres; R.'s Inc. 375*l* and Ho; Pop. 196.) Formerly C. of St. Peter's, Walworth, Lond. [22]

KEMPE, Edward Marshall, *Linkinhorne Vicarage, Callington, Cornwall.*—Ex. Coll. Ox. B.A. 1827; Deac. 1828, Pr. 1829. V. of Linkinhorne, Dio. Ex. 1833. (Patron, W. Hickens, Esq; Tithe—Imp. 390*l*, V. 292*l*; Glebe, 75 acres; V.'s Inc. 382*l* and Ho; Pop. 2551.) [23]

KEMPE, George Henry, *Bicton Parsonage, Exeter.*—Ex. Coll. Ox. 3rd cl. Lit. Hum. 2nd cl.

Math. et Phy. B.A. 1831, M.A. 1835; Deac. 1832, Pr. 1833. R. of Bicton, Dio. Ex. 1845. (Patrons, Heirs of Lord Rolle; Tithe, 170*l* 16*s* 11*d*; Glebe, 50 acres; R.'s Inc. 260*l*; Pop. 150.) Dom. Chap. to Lady Rolle. [1]

KEMPE, James Cory, *Merton Rectory, Beaford, Devon.*—St. John's Coll. Cam. B.A. 1836; Deac. 1837 by Bp of Lin. Pr. 1838 by Bp of B. and W. R. of Huish, Devon, Dio. Ex. 1844. (Patron, Lord Clinton; Tithe, 117*l*; Glebe, 56 acres; R.'s Inc. 170*l* and Ho; Pop. 171.) R. of Merton, Dio. Ex. 1845. (Patron, Lord Clinton; Tithe, 365*l*; Glebe, 65 acres; R.'s Inc. 455*l* and Ho; Pop. 820.) [2]

KEMPE, John Edward, *St. James's Rectory, 197, Piccadilly, London, W.*—Clare Coll. Cam. 1st cl. Cl. Trip. Sen. Opt. B.A. 1833, M.A. 1837; Deac. 1833 and Pr. 1834 by Bp of Ex. R. of St. James's, Westminster, Dio. Lon. 1853. (Patron, Bp of Lon; Glebe Houses, 720*l*; R.'s Inc. 1150*l* and Ho; Pop. 26,107.) Preb. of St. Paul's 1861. Hon. Chap. to Her Majesty, 1864; Proctor in Convocation for Middlesex 1866; Rural Dean of St. James's. Formerly C. of Tavistock and of Barnet; P. C. of St. John's, St. Pancras, and St. Barnabas', Kensington, Lond. Author, *Lectures on Job*, 2*s* 6*d*; *Lectures on Elijah*; single Sermons, etc. [3]

KEMPE, Reginald, *Niton, Isle of Wight.*—Formerly R. of Hawkwell, Essex, 1858. [4]

KEMPLAY, R. W., *Stillingfleet, Yorkshire.*—C. of Stillingfleet. [5]

KEMPSON, Edwin, *Castle Bromwich, Birmingham.*—Trin. Coll. Cam. Scho. Wrang. B.A. 1823, M.A. 1826; Deac. 1824, Pr. 1825. P. C. of Castle Bromwich 1833. (Patron, Earl of Bradford; Tithe, 400*l*; P. C.'s Inc. 450*l*; Pop. 613.) [6]

KEMPSON, Edwin Alfred, *Claverdon Vicarage, Warwick.*—St. John's Coll. Cam. Jun. Opt. 3rd cl. Cl. Trip. B.A. 1852, M.A. 1855; Deac. 1853 and Pr. 1854 by Bp of Win. V. of Claverdon with Norton-Lindsey C. Dio. Wor. 1862. (Patron, Archd. of Wor; Tithe, 229*l* 10*s*; Glebe, 60 acres; V.'s Inc. 420*l* and Ho; Pop. Claverdon 755, Norton-Lindsey 157.) Formerly C. of Send with Ripley, Surrey, 1853–56, Hales Owen, Worcestershire, 1856 62. [7]

KEMPSON, Frederick, *Rochdale.*—St. Bees; Deac. 1861 and Pr. 1862 by Bp of Rip. C. of Rochdale, 1864. Formerly C. of Batley, Yorks, 1861. [8]

KEMPSON, George A. E., *Bedworth, Warwickshire.*—Emman. Coll. Cam. B.A. 1861, M.A. 1867; Deac. 1863 by Bp of Nor. Pr. 1866 by Bp of Ely. C. of Bedworth 1866. Formerly C. of St. Nicholas', Great Yarmouth, 1863–64, Mere, Wilts, 1865–66, Hopton, Suffolk, 1866. [9]

KEMPTHORNE, John, *Wedmore Vicarage, near Weston-super-Mare.*—St. John's Coll. Cam. Sen. Opt. 2nd cl. Cl. Trip. and B.A. 1825, M.A. 1845; Deac. 1827 by Bp of Lich. Pr. 1827 by Bp of B. and W. V. of Wedmore, Dio. B. and W. 1827. (Patron, Bp of B. and W; Tithe—App. 343*l* 2*s* 6*d*, Imp. 180*l*, V. 210*l*; Glebe, 71 acres; V.'s Inc. 365*l* and Ho; Pop. 2283.) [10]

KEMPTHORNE, John, *St. Paul's School, St. Paul's-churchyard, London, E.C*—Trin. Coll. Cam. B.A. 1857; Deac. 1858 by Bp of Ely. Sub-Mast. of St. Paul's Sch. 1858; C. of Herne-hill, Camberwell. [11]

KEMPTHORNE, The Ven. Richard, *Elton Rectory, Oundle, Hunts.*—St. John's Coll. Cam. 27th Wrang. B.A. 1827, M.A. 1834; Deac. 1828 by Bp of Lich. Pr. 1828 by Bp of Ches. R. of Elton, Dio. Ely, 1860. (Patron, Univ. Coll. Ox; Glebe, 490 acres; R.'s Inc. 750*l* and Ho; Pop. 947.) Rural Dean of Yaxley, Hunts, 1865. Formerly Archd. of St. Helena and Colonial Chap. 1839–60; C. of Tarvin, Cheshire, 1828–31. Author, *Monitor's Key to Church Catechism*, 2nd ed. Suter, Cheapside, Lond; *Monitor's Key, &c.*, 3rd ed. [12]

KENAH, S., *Sheffield.*—C. of St. Luke's, Sheffield. [13]

KENDALL, Edward Kaye, 20, *Arundel Gardens, W.*—St. John's Coll. Cam. 17th Wrang. 1856, B.A. 1856, M.A. 1859; Deac. 1857 and Pr. 1858 by Bp of Toronto. P. C. of St. Mark's, Notting-hill, Dio. Lon. 1863. (Patron, Miss E. F. Kaye, for 40 years, then the Bishop; P. C.'s Inc. uncertain; Pop. 3500.) Formerly C. of St. John's, Notting-hill, 1860–63. [14]

KENDALL, Francis John Hext, *Lanlivery Vicarage, Bodmin, Cornwall.*—Ex. Coll. Ox. B.A. 1828, M.A. 1829; Deac. 1829 and Pr. 1830 by Bp of Ex. V. of Lanlivery, Dio. Ex. 1844. (Patron, Nicholas Kendall, Esq; Tithe—Imp. 372*l* 10*s*, V. 304*l* 10*s*; Glebe, 20 acres; V.'s Inc. 319*l* and Ho; Pop. 1657.) V. of Talland, Cornwall, Dio. Ex. 1862. (Patron, N. Kendall, Esq; V.'s Inc. 110*l*; Pop. 800.) [15]

KENDALL, Henry, *Startforth Vicarage, Barnard Castle, Yorks.*—Literate; Deac. 1813 and Pr. 1814 by Abp of York. V. of Startforth, Dio. Rip. 1826. (Patron, Earl of Lonsdale; Tithe—Imp. 66*l* 16*s* 2*d*, V. 112*l* 5*s* 3*d*; Glebe, 26 acres; V.'s Inc. 150*l* and Ho; Pop. 802.) [16]

KENDALL, Herbert Peter, *Hampton Lucy, Warwick.*—St. John's Coll. Cam. Scho. of, 1858–63, B.A. 1859, M.A. 1863; Deac. 1860 and Pr. 1861 by Bp of Rip. Head Mast. of the Gr. Sch. Hampton Lucy, 1864. (Patron, H. S. Lucy, Esq.) Formerly Asst. C. of Batley 1860–62, Head Mast. of the Free Gr. Sch. Batley, Yorks, 1860–64; C. of Ch. Ch. Liversedge, 1862–64. [17]

KENDALL, James, *Lanteglos Vicarage, Fowey, Cornwall.*—St. John's Coll. Cam. B.A. 1834; Deac. 1834, Pr. 1835 by Bp of Ex. V. of Lanteglos, Dio. Ex. 1842. (Patron, the executors of the late T. Robins; Tithe—Imp. 315*l*, V. 225*l*; Glebe, 8 acres; V.'s Inc. 245*l* and Ho; Pop. 1271.) Formerly C. of Perranzabuloe 1834–37, St. Stephen's and St. Dennis's 1837, Lanliglos 1837–42. [18]

KENDALL, John, *Church-Hulme, Middlewich, Cheshire.*—St. Bees; Deac. 1832 and Pr. 1833 by Bp of Ches. P. C. of Church-Hulme, Dio. Ches. 1849. (Patron, V. of Sandbach; P. C.'s Inc. 150*l*; Pop. 1023.) Formerly C. of Buttermere, Cumb. 1832–38, St. George's, Chorley, 1838–46, Church-Hulme 1846–49. [19]

KENDALL, John Hutton Fisher, *Holbeck Parsonage, Leeds.*—St. Bees; Deac. 1839 and Pr. 1840 by Bp of Rip. P. C. of Holbeck, Dio. Rip. 1855. (Patron, V. of Leeds; Tithe, App. 28*l* 19*s* 9*d*; P. C.'s Inc. 319*l* and Ho; Pop. 9248.) [20]

KENDALL, Robert, *Bethnal Green, London, E.*—C. of St. Bartholomew's, Bethnal Green. [21]

KENDALL, Walter, *East Lulworth, Wareham, Dorset.*—V. of East Lulworth, Dio. Salis. 1859. (Patron, J. Weld, Esq; V.'s Inc. 109*l*; Pop. 453.) [22]

KENDALL, Walter William, *Birch Parsonage, Middleton, Manchester.*—Brasen. Coll. Ox. B.A. 1848, M.A. 1851; Deac. 1849 and Pr. 1850 by Bp of Dur. P. C. of Birch, Dio. Man. 1857. (Patron, R. of Middleton; P. C.'s Inc. 149*l* and Ho; Pop. 3773.) Formerly C. of Heworth, Gateshead, 1849–53, Middleton 1853 57. [23]

KENDALL, W., *St. Thomas's Parsonage, Castle Town, Stafford.*—St. Cath. Coll. Cam. B A. 1849. V. of St. Thomas's, Castle Town, Staffs, Dio. Lich. 1866. (Patron, James Tyrer, Esq; V.'s Inc. 300*l* and Ho; Pop. 1300.) Formerly C. of St. James's, Manchester, 1849–52, and of St. Jude's, Manchester, 1852–54. [24]

KENNARD, Robert Bruce, *Marnhull Rectory, Dorset.*—St. John's Coll. Ox. 3rd cl. Lit. Hum. B.A. 1848, M.A. 1851; Deac. 1849 and Pr. 1850 by Bp of Nor. R. of Marnhull, Dio. Salis. 1858. (Patron, R. W. Kennard, Esq. M.P; Tithe, 1024*l*; Glebe, 26 acres; R.'s Inc. 1076*l* and Ho; Pop. 1444.) Formerly C. of Wymondham, Norfolk. Author, *The Evidences of Religion, Natural and Revealed*, Rivingtons, 1852, 2*s* 6*d*; *A Plea for the Maintenance of our National Christianity*, Bell and Daldy, 1855, 2*s*; *A Protest addressed to the Bishop of Salisbury on the Appearance of the Episcopal Manifesto*, Hardwicke, 1861, 2nd ed. 1*s*; *Essays and Reviews, their Origin, History, General Character*, &c. Hardwicke, 1863, 6*s*; *A Letter to the Bishop of St. David's on the Theory of the Supernatural*, Hardwicke, 1864; *The Unity of the Material and Spiritual Worlds* (a Sermon preached before the University of Oxford), Rivingtons, 1866, 1*s*. [25]

KENNAWAY, Charles Edward, *Chipping Campden Vicarage, Glouc.*—St. John's Coll. Cam. 15th

Wrang. B.A. 1822, M.A. 1825; Deac. 1828 and Pr. 1829 by Bp of B. and W. V. of Campden, Dio. G. and B. 1832. (Patron, Earl of Gainsborough; Tithe, 335*l*; Glebe, 400 acres; V.'s Inc. 735*l* and Ho; Pop. 1975.) Hon. Can. of Glouc; Surrogate. Formerly Foundation Fell. of St. John's Coll. Cam. P. C. of Ch. Ch. Cheltenham, 1840–43, Trinity, Brighton, 1843–47. Author, *Manual of Baptism*, Rivingtons, 4*s* 6*d*; *Sermons at Cheltenham*, Hatchards, 12*s*; *Sermons at Brighton*, 2 vols. Rivingtons, each 6*s* 6*d*; *Sermons to the Young*, 5*s* 6*d*; *Sermons on the Lord's Prayer*, 4*s* 6*d*; *Poems*, Rivingtons, 5*s* 6*d*; *Consolatio*, 12th ed. 5*s* 6*d*; *Family Prayers*, 5th ed. Nisbet, 1*s* 6*d*; *Life of the Duke of Wellington* (a Lecture), 1*s* 6*d*; *Thoughts on the War*, 1*s*; *The War and the Newspapers* (a Lecture); *The Irish Famine* (two Sermons); various single Sermons and Tracts; *Tone of Prophecy and Miracle*, Parker, Oxford, 1867. [1]

KENNAWAY, William Bampfylde.—St. John's Coll. Ox. B.A. 1853, M.A. 1857; Deac. 1854, Pr. 1855. Formerly C. of Buckingham. [2]

KENNEDY, Benjamin Hall, *Shrewsbury.*—St. John's Coll. Cam. 1823, Sen. Opt. 1st in 1st cl. Cl. Trip. and B.A. 1827, M.A. 1830, D.D. 1836; Deac. 1829 by Bp of Ely, Pr. 1830 by Bp of Lin. R. of West Felton, Dio. Lich. 1865. (Patrons, Trustees of late Rev. W. Burbury; R.'s Inc. 1023*l*; Pop. 1067.) Preb. of Lich. 1843; Head Mast. of Shrewsbury Sch. 1836. Formerly Fell. of St. John's Coll. Cam. 1828–36. Author, *Latin Grammar*; *Greek Grammar*; *Child's Latin Primer*; *Tirocinium Latinum*; *Palæstra Latina*; *Latin Vocabulary*; *Palæstra Stili Latini*, all published by Longmans; *Sermon* (preached at Bath, on the Tercentenary Festival of the Grammar Sch.), 1853. [3]

KENNEDY, B. S., *Kennington, Surrey.*—P. C. of St. James's Chapel, Kennington. [4]

KENNEDY, J. D., *Guernsey.*—R. of St. Sampson's, Guernsey, Dio. Win. 1859. (Patron, the Gov; R.'s Inc. 120*l* and Ho; Pop. 2455.) [5]

KENNEDY, J. M.—P. C. of Rowlstone with Llancillo, Dio. Herf. (Patron, Mr. King; P. C.'s Inc. 200*l*; Pop. 219.) Formerly C. of Spitalfields, Lond. [6]

KENNEDY, Lewis Drummond, *Theddlethorpe, St. Helen's, Alford, Lincolnshire.*—Ch. Coll. Cam. B.A. 1840, M.A. 1843; Deac. 1841 and Pr. 1842 by Bp of Lin. R. of Theddlethorpe with Mablethorpe St. Peter R. Dio. Lin. 1861. (Patron, Lord Willoughby de Eresby; Theddlethorpe, Tithe, 449*l* 9*s* 2*d*, and Glebe, 26 acres; Mablethorpe, Tithe, 67*l*, Modus, 36*l*, and Glebe, 10 acres; R.'s Inc. 600*l* and Ho; Pop. Theddlethorpe 426, Mablethorpe 82.) [7]

KENNEDY, William James, *Privy Council Office, Downing-street, London, S.W.*—St. John's Coll. Cam. B.A. 1837, M.A. 1844. One of H.M.'s Inspectors of Schs. Author, *A Clergyman's Apology for favouring the Removal of Jewish Disabilities*, 1847, Parker. [8]

KENNEY, Arthur, *Bourton Rectory, near Rugby.*—R. of Bourton-on-Dunsmore, Dio. Wor. 1839 (Patron, B. Shuckburgh, Esq; Tithe, 14*l* 8*s* 3*d*; R.'s Inc. 350*l* and Ho; Pop. 382.) Rural Dean. [9]

KENNEY, Frederick, *Ashton Vicarage, Warrington.*—Ch. Ch. Ox. B.A. 1837, M.A. 1845; Deac. 1841, Pr. 1842. V. of St. Thomas's, Ashton-in-Makerfield, Dio. Ches. 1858. (Patron, R. of Ashton-in Makerfield; Tithe, 126*l* 12*s*; Glebe, 23 acres; V.'s Inc. 280*l* and Ho; Pop. 6863.) Formerly C. of Middleton, near Manchester. [10]

KENNICOTT, Benjamin Centum, *All Saints' Parsonage, Monkwearmouth, Durham.*—Oriel Coll. Ox. B.A. 1842; Deac. 1842 and Pr. 1843 by Bp of Dur. P. C. of All Saints', Monkwearmouth, Dio. Dur. 1844. (Patrons, the Crown and Bp of Dur. alt; Glebe, ½ acre; P. C.'s Inc. 163*l* and Ho; Pop. 3492.) [11]

KENNICOTT, Richard Dutton, *Stockton-upon-Tees.*—Univ. Coll. Ox. B.A. 1818. P. C. of Trinity, Stockton-upon-Tees, Dio. Dur. 1845. (Patron, Bp of Dur; P. C.'s Inc. 300*l*; Pop. 4267.) [12]

KENNION, Alfred, *Eastington, Stonehouse, Glouc.*—Trin. Coll. Cam. B.A. 1851, M.A. 1854; Deac. 1852 and Pr. 1853 by Bp of Ely. C. of Eastington 1855. Author, *Ecce Homo Unmasked*, Seeleys, 6*d*. [13]

KENNION, Robert Winter, *Acle Rectory, Norwich.*—St. John's Coll. Cam. B.A. 1837, M.A. 1840; Deac. 1854 and Pr. 1855 by Bp of Win. R. of Acle, Dio. Nor. 1858. (Patron, Lord Calthorpe; Tithe, 693*l* 11*s*; Glebe, 11 acres; R.'s Inc. 693*l* 11*s* and Ho; Pop. 926.) Formerly C. of Alton, Hants. Author, *Unity and Order, the Handmaids of Truth*, 1866, Mackintosh, 2*s* 6*d*. [14]

KENNY, Henry Torrens, *Banningham Rectory, North Walsham, Norfolk.*—Dub. A.B. 1845; Deac. 1850, Pr. 1853. R. of Banningham, Dio. Nor. 1857. (Patrons, J. S. Dawber, Esq. and Rev. W. Leeper; Tithe, 375*l*; Glebe, 17¾ acres; R.'s Inc. 406*l* and Ho; Pop. 302.) [15]

KENNY, Lewis Stanhope, *Kirkby-Knowle Rectory, Thirsk, Yorks.*—Trin. Coll. Ox. B.A. 1850, M.A. 1852; Deac. 1851 and Pr. 1852 by Bp of Rip. R. of Kirkby-Knowle with Bagby C. Dio. York, 1857. (Patroness, Lady Frankland Russell; Tithe, 180*l* 18*s* 9*d*; Glebe, 57 acres; Bagby, Tithe, 205*l* 17*s*; Glebe, 3 acres; R.'s Inc. 404*l* 6*s* and Ho; Pop. 504.) Formerly C. of Catterick 1851, Lancaster 1853. [16]

KENRICK, Jarvis, *Caterham, Croydon, Surrey.*—Trin. Coll. Cam. Jun. Opt. and B.A. 1827; Deac. 1829, Pr. 1830. R. of Caterham, Dio. Win. 1857. (Patron, the present R; Tithe, 401*l*; Glebe, 5 acres; R.'s Inc. 406*l*; Pop. 815.) Formerly C. of Denington, Cheshire. [17]

KENSIT, George Robert, *Betchworth Vicarage, Reigate, Surrey.*—Wad. Coll. Ox. B.A. 1826, M.A. 1830; Deac. 1828 and Pr. 1829 by Bp of B. and W. V. of Betchworth, Dio. Win. 1835. (Patrons, D. and C. of Windsor; Tithe—Imp. 293*l* 5*s* 4*d*, V. 200*l*; V.'s Inc. 220*l* and Ho; Pop. 628.) [18]

KENT, Alfred, *Coln St. Aldwyn Vicarage, near Fairford, Glouc.*—Ch. Coll. Cam. B.A. 1845, M.A. 1860; Deac. 1846 and Pr. 1847 by Bp of Wor. V. of Coln St. Aldwyn, Dio. G. and B. 1853. (Patrons, D. and C. of Glouc; Glebe, 75 acres; V.'s Inc. 135*l* and Ho; Pop. 516.) [19]

KENT, Charles, *Ludlow.*—Queens' Coll. Cam. B.C.L. 1834; Deac. 1833 and Pr. 1834 by Bp of Nor. V. of Ludford, Herf. Dio. Herf. 1838. (Patron, E. L. Charlton, Esq; Tithe—Imp. 103*l* 4*s* 10*d*, V. 183*l* 0*s* 1*d*; V.'s Inc. 200*l*; Pop. 319.) P. C. of Elton, Herf. Dio. Herf, 1844. (Patron, Rev. H. Cowdell; Tithe—Imp. 441*l* 3*s* 4*d*. P. C. 56*l* 6*s* 9*d*; P. C.'s Inc. 150*l*; Pop. 108.) [20]

KENT, Frederic William, *Cold Norton, Maldon, Essex.*—St. John's Coll. Cam. B.A. 1860, M.A. 1866. Deac. 1864 and 1865 by Bp of Roch. C. of Cold Norton 1866. Formerly C. of St. Peter and St. Michael's, St. Albans. [21]

KENT, George Davies, *Stratford-Tony Rectory, near Salisbury.*—Corpus Coll. Ox. 2nd cl. Lit. Hum. and B.A. 1824, M.A. 1827, B.D. 1835. R. of Stratford-Tony, *alias* Stratford St. Anthony, Dio. Salis. 1848. (Patron, Corpus Coll. Ox; Tithe, 257*l*; Glebe, 48 acres; R.'s Inc. 409*l* and Ho; Pop. 161.) Formerly Fell. of Corpus Coll. Ox. [22]

KENT, Roger, *Burley Dam, Nantwich, Cheshire.*—Brasen. Coll. Ox. B.A. 1837, M.A. 1840; Deac. 1837 and Pr. 1838 by Bp of Ches. Dom. Chap. to Viscount Combermere; P. C. of Burley Dam, Dio. Ches. 1853. (Patron, Viscount Combermere; P. C.'s Inc. 100*l*.) [23]

KENTISH, Thomas Blackburn, *Monyash Parsonage, Buxton, Derbyshire.*—P. C. of Monyash or Monish, Dio. Lich. 1859. (Patron, V. of Bakewell; P. C.'s Inc. 100*l* and Ho; Pop. 460.) Formerly P. C. of Earl Sterndale, Derbyshire, 1856–59. [24]

KENWORTHY, Edwin, *Orton, Penrith.*—C. of Orton. [25]

KENWORTHY, James Wright, 61, *Oakley-square, London, N.W.*—St. Bees; Deac. 1857 and Pr. 1858 by Abp of York. C. of Camden Town, Lond. 1866. Formerly C. of Wetwang, Yorks, 1858, St. Stephen's, Westminster. Author, *Reminiscences of a Visit to Rome*, 1866, Masters; *Sermons and Lectures*. [26]

KENWORTHY, Joseph, *Ackworth Rectory, Pontefract.*—Caius Coll. Cam. B.A. 1838; Deac. and Pr. 1839 by Bp of Salis. R. of Ackworth, Dio. York, 1844. (Patron, Chan. of the Duchy of Lancaster; Tithe, 162*l*; Glebe, 152 acres; R.'s Inc. 480*l* and Ho; Pop. 1813.) [1]

KENYON, Charles Orlando, *Great Ness, Shrewsbury.*—Ch. Ch. Ox. B.A. 1839, M.A. 1841; Deac. 1839 by Bp of St. A. Pr. 1841 by Bp of Lich. V. of Great Ness, Dio. Lich. 1850. (Patron, Ld Chan; Tithe—App. 54*l* 6*s*, Imp. 163*l*, V. 338*l*; Glebe, 11 acres; V.'s Inc. 337*l* and Ho; Pop. 578.) Author, *Harvest Thanksgivings*, 1856. [2]

KENYON, John, *Brenckburne, Morpeth.*—Dur. 4th cl. Lit. Hum. B.A. 1854, M.A. 1858. Licen. Theol. 1855; Deac. 1856 and Pr. 1857 by Bp of Dur. P. C. of Brenckburne, Dio. Dur. 1865. (Patron, C. H. Cadogan, Esq. and co.-trustees; P. C.'s Inc. 6*l* 13*s* 4*d* and Ho; Pop. 200.) [3]

KEOGH, George Patrick, *Stratford, Essex.*—P. C. of St. Paul's, Stratford, Dio. Lon. 1864. (Patrons, Trustees; P. C.'s Inc. 300*l*; Pop. 6200.) [4]

KEPPEL, The Hon. Edward Southwell, *Quidenham, Attleborough, Norfolk.*—Caius Coll. Cam. M.A. 1820; Deac. 1823 and Pr. 1824 by Bp of Nor. R. of Quidenham with Snetterton R. Dio. Nor. 1824. (Patron, Earl of Albemarle; Tithe, Quidenham, 215*l*; Glebe, 60½ acres; Tithe, Snetterton, 440*l*; Glebe, 66¾ acres; R.'s Inc. 776*l* and Ho; Pop. Quidenham 111, Snetterton 237.) Deputy Clerk of the Closet to Her Majesty 1841; Rural Dean of Rockland 1842; Hon. Can. of Nor. Cathl. 1844. [5]

KEPPEL, William Arnold Walpole, *Haynford, Norwich.*—Trin. Coll. Cam. B.A. 1826; Deac. 1828, Pr. 1829. R. of Haynford, Dio. Nor. 1857. (Patron, Rev. H. P. Marsham; Tithe, 425*l*; Glebe, 35 acres; R.'s Inc. 464*l*; Pop. 643.) [6]

KER, William, *Tipton Parsonage, Staffs.*—Dub A.B. 1826, A.M. 1835; Deac. 1826, Pr. 1827. P. C. of Tipton *alias* Tibbington, Dio. Lich. 1847. (Patron, J. S. Hellier, Esq; Tithe, App. 287*l* 9*s* 7*d*; P. C.'s Inc. 420*l*; Pop. 12,199.) [7]

KER, W. Palgrave, *Mucheiney, Somerset.*—C. of Muchelney and Drayton. [8]

KERMODE, William, *The Parsonage, Ramsey, Isle of Man.*—King Wm. Coll. Isle of Man and Dub; Deac. 1839 and Pr. 1840 by Bp of S. and M. P. C. of St. Paul's, Ramsey, Dio. S. and M. 1843. (Patron, Bp of S. and M; P. C.'s Inc. 160*l* and Ho; Pop. 3000.) Surrogate 1847; Hon. Chap. 3rd Isle of Man Volunteer Rifle Corps 1861. Formerly C. of St. James's, Kirk Patrick, 1839, Lezayre, Isle of Man, 1840. [9]

KERR, Charles, *Winslow, Bucks.*—Trin. Coll. Cam. B.A. 1820, M.A. 1821; Deac. 1823 and Pr. 1824 by Abp of York. [10]

KERR, George Putland, *Parsonage, Upper Hopton, Normanton.*—Queens' Coll. Cam. B.A. 1848; Deac. 1848 and Pr. 1849 by Bp of Rip. P. C. of Hopton, Dio. Rip. 1861. (Patron, V. of Mirfield; P. C.'s Inc. 137*l*; Pop. 1211.) Formerly C. of Mirfield 1848–61. [11]

KERR, The Right Hon. Lord Henry Francis Charles.—St. John's Coll. Cam. M.A. 1821; Deac. 1820, Pr. 1821. Formerly R. of Dittisham, Devon, 1827–52. [12]

KERR, St. George, *The Parsonage, Langrick, near Boston.*—Dub. A.B. 1851, A.M. 1854; Deac. 1857 and Pr. 1858 by Bp of Wor. P. C. of Llangriville, Dio. Lin. 1862. (Patrons, Trustees; P. C.'s Inc. 91*l* and Ho; Pop. 312.) P. C. of Thornton-le-Fen, Dio. Lin. 1862. (Patrons, Trustees; P. C.'s Inc. 84*l*; Pop. 193.) Called to the Bar and Member of the Oxford Circuit 1851; formerly C. of St. Swithin's, Worcester, and of Crowle with Upton Snodsbury. [13]

KERR, William Frederick, *Marston Sicca Rectory, near Stratford-on-Avon.*—St. John's Coll. Cam. B.A. 1836; Deac. 1836 and Pr. 1837 by Bp of Pet. R. of Marston Sicca, Dio. G. and B. 1839. (Patron, Fisher Tomes, Esq; R.'s Inc. 430*l* and Ho; Pop. 380.) Formerly C. of Farndon, Northants, Geddington 1836–37, Bastow, Derbyshire, 1838–39. [14]

KERR, William Mignot, *Nevendon, Wickford, Essex.*—St. John's Coll. Cam. B.A. 1841. R. of Nevendon, Dio. Roch. 1850. (Patron, Rev. V. Edwards; Tithe, 266*l*; Glebe, 7 acres; R.'s Inc. 281*l*; Pop. 205.) [15]

KERRICH, Richard Edward, 13, *Free School-lane, Cambridge.*—Ch. Coll. Cam. 7th Sen. Opt. and B.A. 1823, M.A. 1826; Deac. 1830, Pr. 1831. [16]

KERRY, C., *Topcliffe, Yorkshire.*—C. of Topcliffe. [17]

KERRY, William, *Portland-square, Bristol.*—St. John's Coll. Cam. B.A. 1842, M.A. 1845; Deac. 1842 and Pr. 1843 by Bp of Lon. P. C. of St. Jude's, Bristol, Dio. G. and B. 1864. (Patrons, Crown and Bp of G. and B. alt; P. C.'s Inc. 200*l* and Ho; Pop. 4039.) Formerly C. of St. Andrew's, Holborn, 1843–44, P. C. of St. Thomas's, Bethnal Green, Lond. 1844–64. [18]

KERSHAW, Edmund Dickie, *Trinity College, Cambridge.*—Trin. Coll. Cam. B.A. 1851, M.A. 1854 *ad eund.* Ox. 1859; Deac. 1854 and Pr. 1855 by Bp of Wor. Dom. Chap. to A. B. Cochrane, Esq., M.P. Formerly C. of Hampton-Lucy, near Warwick. [19]

KERSHAW, George Senior Wilkinson, *Boughton Ollerton, Notts.*—Queens' Coll. Cam. Scho. and Prizeman, 1849, Queen's Coll. Ox. 2nd cl. Lit. Hum. and B.A. 1854; Deac. 1855 and Pr. 1856 by Bp of Herf. V. of Egmanton, Dio. Lin. 1857. (Patron, Duke of Newcastle; V.'s Inc. 160*l* and Ho; Pop. 386.) P. C. of Boughton, Dio. Lin. 1866. (Patron, Chapter of Southwell; Tithe, 250*l*; P. C.'s Inc. 250*l* and Ho; Pop. 400.) Formerly C. of Bromyard, Herf. 1855–57.). [20]

KERSHAW, George William, *Thwaite St. George Rectory, Stonham, Suffolk.*—Wor. Coll. Ox. B.A. 1830, M.A. 1833. R. of Thwaite St. George, Dio. Nor. 1841. (Patron, John Sheppard, Esq; Tithe, 240*l*; Glebe, 21 acres; R.'s Inc. 270*l* and Ho; Pop. 147.) Rural Dean. Author, *Sermons*, 1846. [21]

KERSHAW, Henry, *Greenhow Hill, Ripon.*—Deac. 1851, Pr. 1852. P. C. of Greenhow Hill, Dio. York, 1858. (Patrons, D. and C. of Rip; P. C.'s Inc. 60*l*; Pop. 748.) Formerly C. of Leeds. [22]

KERSHAW, James Clegg, *Walton-le-Dale, near Preston.*—Emman. Coll. Cam. Sen. Opt. and B.A. 1854, M.A. 1857; Deac. 1855 and Pr. 1856 by Bp of Man. P. C. of Walton-le-Dale, Dio. Man. 1857. (Patron, V. of Blackburn; Tithe—Imp. 387*l* 3*s* 3*d*; P. C.'s Inc. 300*l* and Ho; Pop. 3257.) Formerly C. of Blackburn. [23]

KERSHAW, John Atherton, *Lathom Parsonage, Ormskirk, Lancashire.*—Trin. Coll. Cam. B.A. 1843, M.A. 1846; Deac. 1844 and Pr. 1845 by Bp of Ches. P. C. of St. James's, Lathom, Dio. Ches. 1856. (Patron, V. of Ormskirk; Glebe, 4 acres; P. C.'s Inc. 90*l* and Ho; Pop. 914.) [24]

KERSHAW, John Albert, *Easingwold, Yorkshire.*—St. Cath. Coll. Cam. B.A. 1861; Deac. 1863 and Pr. 1864 by Bp of Dur. C. of Easingwold 1865. [25]

KERSHAW, Thomas Atherton, *Milton Rectory, Northampton.*—Brasen. Coll. Ox. B.A. 1840, M.A. 1842; Deac. 1840, Pr. 1841. R. of Milton, Dio. Pet. 1844. (Patron, T. Kershaw, Esq; R.'s Inc. 340*l* and Ho; Pop. 668.) [26]

KERSLEY, Thomas Henry, *Middleton Vicarage, King's Lynn, Norfolk.*—Dub A.B. 1850; Deac. 1852 and Pr. 1853 by Bp of Ches. V. of Middleton, Dio. Nor. 1856. (Patron, the present V; Tithe—App. 99*l* 18*s*, Imp. 432*l* 2*s* 5*d*, V. 313*l* 9*s* 9*d*; Glebe, 12 acres; V.'s Inc. 396*l* and Ho; Pop. 894.) Can. and Sub-Dean of the Collegiate Ch. of Middleham, Yorks, 1855. Formerly 2nd Mast. of Maidstone Gr. Sch; Asst. Cl. and Math. Tut. and Lib. of King William's Coll. Isle of Man; C. of Devizes, Wilts. [27]

KESTON, C.—C. of St. Jude's, Whitechapel, Lond. [28]

KETCHLEY, Walter Guy, *Ripley Parsonage, near Derby.*—Literate; Deac. 1859 and Pr. 1860 by Abp of York. P. C. of Ripley, Dio. Lich. 1862. (Patrons, Francis Wright, Esq. and Trustees; Glebe, 58 acres; P. C.'s Inc. 300*l* and Ho; Pop. 5199.) Formerly C. of

Lythe, Yorks, 1859–60; Chap. of D. of Bempton, Yorks, 1860–62; P. C. of Speeton, Yorks, 1860–62. [1]

KETLEY, Joseph.—Queens' Coll. Cam. B.A. 1840, M.A. 1843; Deac. 1840 and Pr. 1841 by Bp of Win. Author, *The Atonement* (a Sermon); *National and Individual Examination* (a Sermon); *Ministerial Responsibility* (a Sermon). Editor of *The Liturgies and other Documents of Edward VI.* for the Parker Society. [2]

KETTLE, Henry Francis, 4, *Queen's-terrace, Victoria-park, E.*—King's Coll. Lond; Deac. 1864 and Pr. 1865 by Bp of Lond. Chap. to City of Lond. Hospital, for Diseases of the Chest. Formerly C. of St. Simon's, Bethnal Green, Lond. [3]

KETTLE, Robert, *Woking Vicarage, Surrey.*—Trin. Coll. Cam. B.A. 1858, M.A. 1861; Deac. 1858 and Pr. 1859 by Bp of Win. C. of Woking 1862. Formerly C. of St. Matthew's, Brixton, 1858, Binstead, Alton, Hants, 1860. [4]

KETTLE, William Arundel, *Bath.*—St. Bees, 1850. Formerly C. of Weston-Bampfylde, Somerset. [5]

KETTLEWELL, Samuel, *St. Mark's Parsonage, Woodhouse, Leeds.*—Univ. Coll. Dur. M.A. 1860; Deac. 1848 and Pr. 1849 by Bp of Rip. P. C. of St. Mark's, Woodhouse, Dio. Rip. 1851. (Patrons, Trustees of St. Peter's, Leeds; P. C.'s Inc. 370*l* 16*s* and Ho; Pop. 6072.) Author, *Catechism on Gospel History*, Rivingtons, 2*s* 6*d*. [6]

KETTON, John, *Grammar School, Hutton, Preston.*—Queens' Coll. Cam. B.A. 1839, M.A. 1843; Deac. 1839 and Pr. 1840 by Bp of Ches. Head Mast. of the Free Gr. Sch. Hutton, 1851. Formerly C. of St. Peter's, Preston, 1839–41; P. C. of St. John's, Houghton, Stanwix, Carlisle, 1841–48; C. of Holy Trinity, Preston, 1848–50, Bury 1850, Preston 1850–51. [7]

KEWLEY, Francis, *Jesus College, Oxford.*—Fell. and Tut. of Jesus Coll. Ox. [8]

KEWLEY, George Robinson, *St. John's Parsonage, Kidderminster.*—Univ. Coll. Dur. Fell of, B.A. 1845, M.A. 1849; Deac. 1845 by Bp of Nor. Pr. 1846 by Bp of Wor. P. C. of St. John's, Kidderminster, Dio. Wor. 1857. (Patron, V. of Kidderminster; P. C.'s Inc. 200*l* and Ho.) Formerly C. of Kidderminster. [9]

KEWLEY, Joseph William, *Thorpe Rectory, Ashbourne, Derbyshire.*—St. Edm. Hall, Ox. B.A. 1851; Deac. 1850 and Pr. 1852 by Bp of S. and M. R. of Thorpe, Dio. Lich. 1860. (Patron, Bp of Lich; Tithe, comm. 90*l*; Glebe, rent 59*l*; R.'s Inc. 149*l* and Ho; Pop. 204.) Formerly C. of Foxdale, Isle of Man, 1850–54; Examiner in King William's Coll. Isle of Man, 1850–54; Dioc. Inspector of Schs. 1853–54; P. C. of Cauldon and of Waterfall and C. of Calton, Dio. Lich. 1854–60. [10]

KEWLEY, Thomas Bigby, *Woodfield, Hatfield, Herts.*—Magd. Coll. Cam. B.A. 1844, M.A. 1847; Deac. 1844 and Pr. 1845 by Bp of Lon. Travelling Sec. for the Additional Curates' Soc. Formerly C. of Bishop's Hatfield. [11]

KEY, Henry Cooper, *Stretton-Sugwas, Herefordshire.*—Ch. Ch. Ox. B.A. 1841, M.A. 1844; Deac. 1842, Pr. 1844. R. of Stretton-Sugwas, Dio. Herf. 1846. (Patron, B. E. Bailey, Esq; Tithe, 192*l* 7*s*; Glebe, 29¼ acres; R.'s Inc. 222*l* and Ho; Pop. 209.) Rural Dean of Weston 1852.) [12]

KEYMER, Nathaniel, *Christ's Hospital, Hertford.*—Pemb. Coll. Cam. Sen. Opt. and B.A. 1836, M.A. 1839; Deac. 1837, Pr. 1839. Head Mast. of Christ's Hospital, Hertford, 1837; Chap. to the General Infirmary, Hertford. [13]

KEYS, William.—Dub. A.B. 1851, A.M. 1854, Oxon. (*ad eund.*) 1855; Deac. and Pr. 1851 by Bp of Lin. P. C. of St. Thomas's, Scarborough, Dio. York, 1856. (Patron, Earl Bathurst; P. C.'s Inc. 125*l*; Pop. 2821.) Surrogate. Formerly C. of Mansfield, Notts. Author, *National Humiliation* (a Sermon). [14]

KIDD, James, 112, *Bloomsbury, Birmingham.*—King's Coll. Lond. Assoc. 1862; Deac. 1862 and Pr. 1863 by Bp of Wor. Sen. C. of Halesowen 1864. Formerly C. of St. Matthew's, Duddeston, Birmingham, 1862. [15]

KIDD, Philip Chabert, *Skipton Vicarage, Yorks.*—Ch. Ch. Ox. B.A. 1841, M.A. 1845; Deac. and Pr. 1841. V. of Skipton, Dio. Rip. 1843. (Patron, Ch. Ch. Ox; Tithe—Imp. 169*l* 1*s*, V. 109*l*; Glebe, 240 acres; V.'s Inc. 307*l* and Ho; Pop. 4790.) Surrogate of York 1845, and Ripon 1849. [16]

KIDD, Richard Bentley Porson, *Heigham Potter Vicarage, near Norwich.*—Emman. Coll. Cam. B.A. 1833, M.A. 1836; Deac. and Pr. 1833. V. of Heigham Potter, Dio. Nor. 1843. (Patron, Bp of Nor; V.'s Inc. 200*l* and Ho; Pop. 439.) Late R. of St. Swithin's, Norwich; formerly V. of Bedingham, Norfolk; previously Chap. to the City Gaol, Norwich, and to the Norfolk and Norwich Magdalen. Author, *Testimonies and Authorities in Confirmation of the XXXIX. Articles*, Cam. 10*s* 6*d*; *Lectures on the Errors of Romanism*; *Psalms and Hymns adapted to the Collects, &c*; *Encouragements in Critical Times* (a Visitation Sermon), 1846; various other Sermons. [17]

KIDD, Thomas William, *Byley, Middlewich, Cheshire.*—Dur. B.A. 1858, Licen. Theol. 1859, M.A. 1861; Deac. 1859 and Pr. 1860 by Bp of Ches. P. C. of Byley with Lees, Dio. Ches. 1865. (Patron, V. of Middlewich; P. C.'s Inc. 110*l* and Ho; Pop. 519.) Formerly C. of Alton 1859. [18]

KIDD, William John, *Didsbury Rectory, near Manchester.*—St. Bees; Deac. 1834 and Pr. 1835 by Bp of Ches. R. of Didsbury, Dio. Man. 1841. (Patrons, representatives of the late J. Darwell, Esq; Tithe—App. 149*l*, Imp. 17*s* 3*d*; Glebe, 5 acres; R.'s Inc. 232*l* and Ho; Pop. 808.) Formerly C. of St. Ann's, Manchester, 1834–36; P. C. of St. Matthew's, Manchester, 1836–41. Author, *Reflections on Unitarianism*; *Christian Unity, with special References to Wesleyan Methodism*; *The Doctrine of the Church of England, compared with the Church of Rome, on Intercession and Creature-Worship*; *The Gordian Knot of Infidelity, or the Impossibility of the Bible being False*; *The Bible a Message from God, or the Internal Evidence for the Truth of the Bible*; *The Sunday Question viewed in the Light of Holy Scripture*; *Bible-Class Notes on the Epistle to the Hebrews*; *Hymns for Sunday Schools, compiled and arranged for every Sunday and Great Festival throughout the Year*; Lectures. [19]

KILBY, Thomas, *St. John's Parsonage, Wakefield.*—Queen's Coll. Ox. 1816; Deac. 1818 by Bp of Ches. Pr. 1821 by Abp of York. P. C. of St. John's, Wakefield, Dio. Rip. 1825. (Patron, V. of Wakefield; P. C.'s Inc. 190*l* and Ho; Pop. 4262.) Surrogate. Author, *Wakefield and its adjacent Scenery, by an Amateur*, 1843, 21*s*; *Sermons* 1846, 6*s* 6*d*; *Sermons on Papal Aggression, Death of the Duke of Wellington, Day of General Humiliation*; *Wakefield, embracing its Ancient and Picturesque Combinations* (14 plates and letter-press), fol. 1853, 42*s*; *Sermons*, 1866, 7*s* 6*d*. [20]

KILLICK, John Henry, *Oakamoor Parsonage, Cheadle, Staffordshire.*—St. John's Coll. Cam. B.A. 1858, M.A. 1863; Deac. 1859 and Pr. 1860 by Bp of Lin. P. C. of Oakamoor, Dio. Lich. 1865. (Patron, R. of Cheadle; P. C.'s Inc. 72*l*; Pop. 600.) Formerly C. of East Leake with West Leake 1859–65. [21]

KILLICK, Richard Henry, *St. Clement Danes, Strand, London, W.C.*—Queens' Coll. Cam. B.A. 1841, M.A. 1844; Deac. 1841 and Pr. 1842 by Bp of Pet. R. of St. Clement Danes, Westminster, Dio. Lon. 1859. (Patron, Marquis of Exeter; R.'s Inc. 360*l*; Pop. 15,592.) Formerly C. of Saddington, Leicester, 1841, Barley, Herts, 1842; V. of Stratton, Cornwall, 1845, Erchfont, Wilts, 1850. Author, *The Speech of the Dead* (a Sermon), 1851, 1*s*; *Earthly Service Exchanged for Heavenly* (a Sermon), 1853, 6*d*. [22]

KILLIN, Richard, *Clynnog Vicarage, Carnarvon.*—Lampeter Scho. and 1st cl; Deac. 1848 by Bp of Win. Pr. 1849 by Bp of Llan. V. of Clynnog, Dio. Ban. 1864. (Patron, Bp of Ban; Tithe, comm. 290*l*; V.'s Inc. 300*l* and Ho; Pop. 1671.) Formerly C. of Dowlais 1848–50, Ysceifiog, 1850–51; P. C. of St. David's, Ffestiniog, 1851–65. [23]

KILLOCH, William Bryan, *Edmondthorpe, Oakham.*—St. Peter's Coll. Cam. B.A. 1830; Deac. 1831, Pr. 1832. R. of Edmondthorpe, Dio. Pet. 1846. (Patron,

Ld Chan; Tithe, 486*l*; Glebe, 200*l*; R.'s Inc. 1120*l* and Ho; Pop. 230.) [1]

KILNER, James Maze, *Chester.*—St. Bees; Deac. 1852 and Pr. 1853 by Bp of Lich. Chap. of Chester Castle. (Salary, 300*l*.) [2]

KILVERT, Robert, *Langley-Burrell Rectory, Chippenham.*—Oriel Coll. Ox. B.A. 1826, M.A. 1829; Deac. 1827, Pr. 1828. R. of Langley-Burrell, Dio. G. and B. 1855. (Patron, Rev. R. M. Ashe; Tithe, 235*l*; Glebe, 113 acres; R.'s Inc. 400*l* and Ho; Pop. 367.) Formerly R. of Hardenhuish, Wilts, 1838–55. [3]

KILVERT, Robert Francis, *Clyro, near Hays, Radnorshire.*—Wad. Coll. Ox. B.A. 1862, M.A. 1866; Deac. 1863 and Pr. 1864 by Bp of G. and B. C. of Clyro with Bettws Clyro 1865. Formerly C. of Langley-Burrell, Wilts, 1863–64. [4]

KINCHANT, John Robert Nathaniel, *Nantiago, Llanvair, Waterdine, near Knighton, Radnorshire.*—Queens' Coll. Cam. B.A. 1828; Deac. 1828 and Pr. 1329 by Bp of Herf. P. C. of Llanvair Waterdine, Dio. Herf. 1833. (Patron, Earl of Powis; Tithe—Imp. 375*l*; P. C.'s Inc. 80*l*; Pop. 611.) P. C. of Bettws, Salop, Dio. Herf. 1833. (Patron, Earl of Powis; P. C.'s Inc. 38*l*; Pop. 520.) Surrogate. [5]

KINDER, John, *Auckland, New Zealand.*—Trin. Coll. Cam. B.A. 1842, M.A. 1845; Deac. 1846, Pr. 1848. Formerly Mast. of Uttoxeter Gr. Sch. 1846–55. [6]

KINDER, Ralph, *Lumb-in-Rossendale, Newchurch, Manchester.*—Deac. 1843, Pr. 1844. P. C. of Lumb, Dio. Man. 1846. (Patrons, the Crown and Bp of Man. alt; P. C.'s Inc. 160*l*; Pop. 2647.) [7]

KINDERSLEY, Richard Cockburn, *Brampford Speke, Exeter.*—Trin. Coll. Cam. B.A. 1853, M.A. 1856; Deac. 1855 and Pr. 1856 by Bp of Ox. V. of Brampford with Cowley R. Dio. Ex. 1857. (Patron, Ld Chan; Tithe, 196*l* 7*s* 8*d*; Glebe, 40 acres; V.'s Inc. 240*l* and Ho; Pop. 496.) Formerly C. of Holy Trinity, Windsor, 1855–57. [8]

KING, Alexander, *Sherrington Rectory, Newport Pagnel, Bucks.*—Oriel Coll. Ox. B.A. 1846, M.A. 1849; Deac. 1847 by Bp of Wor. Pr. 1848 by Bp of Ely. R. of Sherrington, Dio. Ox. 1849. (Patron, Bp of Ox; Tithe, 402*l*; Glebe, 16 acres; R.'s Inc. 435*l* and Ho; Pop. 839.) Formerly C. of Broadwas, near Worcester. [9]

KING, Bryan, *Avebury Vicarage, Calne.*—Brasen. Coll. Ox. 3rd cl. Lit. Hum. and B.A. 1834, M.A. 1837; Deac. 1836 and Pr. 1837 by Bp of Ox. V. of Avebury, Dio. Salis. 1863. (Patron, Ld Chan; Tithe, 90*l* 2*s* and 20*l* Pension; Glebe, 100 acres; V.'s Inc. 316*l* and Ho; Pop. 725.) Formerly Fell. of Brasen. Coll. Ox; P. C. of St. John's, Bethnal Green, Lond. 1837–41; R. of St. George's-in-the-East 1842–62. Author, *The Recovery of the Lost Sheep of the Church of England by Home Missions in her Large and Destitute Parishes, a Sermon,* 1856; *A Warning against the Sin of Sacrilege, a Sermon,* 2nd ed. 1859; *Sacrilege and its Encouragement, in a Letter,* 4th ed. 1860; *Sacrilege and its Encouragement, in a Second Letter,* 1860; all published by Masters. [10]

KING, Charles, *Stratford-sub-Castle, Salisbury.*—Magd. Coll. Ox. 4th cl. Lit. Hum. and B.A. 1831, M.A. 1834; Deac. 1834, Pr. 1835. Pr.-Vic. of Salis. Cathl. 1835; Procurator of the Vicars 1846; P. C. of Stratford-sub-Castle, Dio. Salis. 1852. (Patrons, D. and C. of Salis; Tithe, App. 578*l* 17*s*; P. C.'s Inc. 100*l*; Pop. 332.) [11]

KING, Charles, *Longburton Vicarage, Sherborne, Dorset.*—Emman. Coll. Cam. B.A. 1809; Deac. 1819, Pr. 1820. V. of Longburton with Holnest Chapelry, Dio. Salis. 1867. (Patron, C. Cosens, Esq; V.'s Inc. 275*l* and Ho; Pop. Longburton 336, Holnest 147.) Formerly C. of Road, Somerset. [12]

KING, Charles William, *Durham.*—Trin. Coll. Ox. Open Scholarship 1850, 2nd cl. Lit. Hum B.A. 1853, M.A. 1855; Deac. 1854 by Bp of Ox. Pr. 1855 by Bp of Rip. H.M. Inspector of Schs. for Durham and Northumberland. Formerly C. of Woodhorn, Northumberland, 1855–59; R. of St. Mary-le-Bow, Durham, 1859–67; Prin. of Female Training Coll. Durham, 1859–64. [13]

KING, Edward, *Corney House, Penrith.*—Jesus Coll. Cam. B.A. 1853; Deac. 1854 and Pr. 1855 by Bp of Carl. C. of Penrith. [14]

KING, Edward, *Cuddesdon Vicarage, Wheatley, Oxon.*—Oriel Coll. Ox. V. of Cuddesdon, Dio. Ox. 1863. (Patron, Bp of Ox; V.'s Inc. 260*l* and Ho; Pop. 560.) Prin. of Cuddesdon. Theol. Coll. Formerly C. of Wheatley; Chap. and Asst. Lect. at Cuddesdon Coll. [15]

KING, Frank Bowes, *Burstwick Vicarage, Hull.*—Clare Coll. Cam. B.A. 1846, M.A. 1849; Deac. 1846 and Pr. 1848 by Abp of York. V. of Burstwick, Dio. York, 1852. (Patron, Sir Clifford Constable, Bart; Tithe, 31*l*, Glebe, 110 acres; V.'s Inc. 236*l* and Ho; Pop. 726.) Author, *A Short Plain Sermon on Holy Baptism,* Hull, 1850, 6*d*; *A Hymn Book,* 1856. [16]

KING, Frederick Meade, *Shipbourne, near Tunbridge.*—Pemb. Coll. Ox. B.A. 1858, M.A. 1862; Deac. 1858 and Pr. 1859 by Bp of B. and W. C. of Shipbourne. Formerly C. of Lyng, Somerset, 1858. [17]

KING, George, *Worsted Vicarage, Norfolk.*—Corpus Coll. Cam. B.A. 1827, M.A. 1830; Deac. 1829, Pr. 1830. V. of Worsted, Dio. Nor. 1844. (Patrons, D. and C. of Nor; Tithe—App. 618*l* 9*s* and 50 acres of Glebe; V. 270*l* 9*s* 6*d*; Glebe, 4 acres; V.'s Inc. 281*l* and Ho; Pop. 751.) C. of Westwick, Norfolk; Rural Dean. Formerly Fell. of Corpus Coll. Cam. 1829. [18]

KING, James, *Gateshead, Durham.*—C. of Trinity, Gateshead. [19]

KING, James Carleton, *Bury Vicarage, Petworth, Sussex.*—St. Mary Hall, Ox. B.A. 1851; Deac. 1853 and Pr. 1854 by Bp of Ox. V. of Bury, Dio. Chich. 1856. (Patrons, D. and C. of Glouc; Tithe, comm. 364*l*; Glebe, 11 acres; V.'s Inc. 370*l* and Ho; Pop. 500.) [20]

KING, Sir James Walker, Bart., 8, *St. Peter's-square, Hammersmith, W.*—Dub. A.B. 1817, A.M. 1832; Deac. 1818 by Bp of Kilmore, Pr. 1821 by Bp of Dromore. Formerly Dom. Chap. to Earl of Enniskillen 1818; Chap. to Marquis of Anglesey 1830–33; V. of Rathmore, Kildare. [21]

KING, John Freeman, *Maldon, Essex.*—C. of Maldon. [22]

KING, John Myers, *Cutcombe Vicarage, Dunster, Somerset.*—Ball. Coll. Ox. 2nd cl. Lit. Hum. and B.A. 1823; Deac. 1827, Pr. 1828. V. of Cutcombe wth Luxborough C. Dio. B. and W. 1832. (Patron, Ld Chan; Cutcombe Tithe—Imp. 114*l* 14*s* 6*d*, V. 292*l* 1*s*; Glebe, 1½ acres; Luxborough, Tithe—Imp. 141*l*, V. 115*l*; V.'s Inc. 408*l* and Ho; Pop. Cutcombe 793, Luxborough 521.) Author, *Ecclesia Cura, or a Parson's Cares,* 1*s*; *The Parson's Home,* 2*s* 6*d*; *A Sermon* (preached at the opening of King's Brompton new Church, 1854), 6*d*; *Georgics of Virgil in English Verse*; *Æneid of Virgil in English Verse,* 7*s* 6*d*; *Lays of Palestine,* 7*s* 6*d*; *Legends of the West,* 1851. [23]

KING, John Richard, *Oxford.*—Ball. Coll. Ox. Scho. 1st. cl. Lit. Hum. and B.A. 1857, M.A. 1860, at Mert. Coll. Denyer Theol. Prize Essay 1863; Deac. 1861 and Pr. 1862 by Bp of Ox. V. of St. Peter's-in-the-East, Oxford, Dio. Ox. 1867. (Patron, Mert. Coll. Ox; V.'s Inc. 150*l*; Pop. 1174.) Formerly Fell. and Tut. of Mert. Coll. Ox. 1859–66; C. of All Saints', Oxford, 1862–65. Author, *The Grant of Repentance in the Case of Postbaptismal Sin* (Denyer Essay), 1863, 1*s* 6*d*. [24]

KING, John William, *Bassingham Rectory, Lincolnshire.*—Corpus Coll. Ox. 2nd cl. Lit. Hum. and B.A. 1814, M.A. 1818, B.D. 1827. V. of Ashby-de-la-Launde, Sleaford, Dio. Lin. 1822. (Patron, the present V; V.'s Inc. 300*l*; Pop. 176.) R. of Bassingham, Dio. Lin. 1832. (Patron, Corpus Coll. Ox; Tithe, 630*l*; R.'s Inc. 645*l* and Ho; Pop. 928.) Formerly Fell. of Corpus Coll. Ox. [25]

KING, Joseph, *Farnham, Wickham Market, Suffolk.*—Queens' Coll. Cam. B.A. 1841, M.A. 1844; Deac. 1841, Pr. 1842. P. C. of Farnham, Dio. Nor. 1845. (Patron, William Long, Esq; Tithe—Imp. 240*l*; Glebe, 6 acres; P. C.'s Inc. 112*l* and Ho; Pop. 184.) [26]

KING, Richard, *Prestwich, Manchester.*—Ch. Coll. Cam. B.A. 1844; Deac. 1843 and Pr. 1844 by Bp of Lon. Chap. to the Co. Lunatic Asylum, Prestwich. Author, *Angels' Work*, 2s; *Singers of the Sanctuary*, 2s 6d. [1]

KING, Richard, *Pevensey, Eastbourne, Sussex.*—C. of Pevensey. [2]

KING, Richard Henry, *Little Glemham Rectory, Wickham Market, Suffolk.*—Mert. Coll. Ox. B.A. 1847, M.A. 1851; Deac. 1848, Pr. 1849. R. of Little Glemham with Great Glemham P. C. Dio. Nor. 1849. (Patron, Earl of Guilford; Little Glemham, Tithe, 305*l*; Glebe, 7 acres; Great Glemham, Tithe—Imp. 352*l* 14*s* 8*d* and 2¾ acres of Glebe, P. C. 95*l*; Glebe, 28 acres; R.'s Inc. 400*l* and Ho; Pop. Little Glemham 325, Great Glemham 354.) [3]

KING, R. A., *Bradford, Yorks.*—C. of Bradford. [4]

KING, Robert Collins, *Northampton.*—Ch. Coll. Cam. Sen. Opt. and B.A. 1851, M.A. 1854; Deac. 1851 and Pr. 1852 by Bp of Man. P. C. of St. Katharine's, Northampton, Dio. Pet. 1863. (Patrons, Hyndman's Trustees; Pop. 2638.) Formerly Sen. C. of St. Martin's, Birmingham. [5]

KING, Samuel, *Cantley Vicarage, Doncaster.*—Corpus Coll. Cam. B.A. 1847, M.A. 1850; Deac. 1847 and Pr. 1848 by Abp of York. V. of Cantley, Dio. York, 1854. (Patron, J. W. Childers, Esq; Tithe—2*l* 15*s* 3*d*, V. 1*l*; V.'s Inc. 240*l* and Ho; Pop. 663.) [6]

KING, Samuel William, *Saxlingham-Nethergate Rectory, near Norwich.*—St. Cath. Coll. Cam. B.A. 1844, M.A. 1847; Deac. 1846 by Bp of Ches. Pr. 1848 by Bp of Man. R. of Saxlingham-Nethergate with Saxlingham-Thorpe R. Dio. Nor. 1851. (Patron, J. Steward, Esq; Tithe, 805*l*; Glebe, 27 acres; R.'s Inc. 835*l* and Ho; Pop. Saxlingham-Nethergate 586, Saxlingham-Thorpe 141.) F.G.S. F.S.A. and F.R.G.S. Author, *Italian Valleys of the Alps*, Murray. [7]

KING, Thomas, *Lyttelton House, Malvern Link, Worcestershire.*—Ball. Coll. Ox. B.A. 1832, M.A. 1835; Deac. 1833 and Pr. 1834 by Bp of Herf. P. C. of Little Malvern, Dio. Wor. 1863. (Patron, Earl Somers; P. C.'s Inc. 44*l*; Pop. 104.) Formerly C. of Trinity, St. Pancras, Lond; R. of Pencombe, Herf. 1856–62. Author, *A Letter to the Inhabitants of Holy Trinity District, St. Pancras, on the Occasion of opening a Unitarian Chapel therein.* [8]

KING, Thomas, *Ordsall Rectory, East Retford, Notts.*—R. of Ordsall, Dio. Lin. 1841. (Patron, Lord Wharncliffe; Tithe, 480*l*; Glebe, 27 acres; R.'s Inc. 515*l* and Ho; Pop. 1911.) [9]

KING, Walker, *Lower Hardres, Canterbury.*—Emman. Coll. Cam. S.C.L. 1856; Deac. 1857 and Pr. 1858 by Bp of B. and W. C. of Lower Hardres 1865. Formerly C. of Cutcombe and Luxborough 1857–65; Dioc. Inspector of Schs. for Deanery of Dunster 1858–65. [10]

KING, Walker, *Leigh Rectory, Rochford, Essex.*—Oriel Coll. Ox. B.A. 1850, M.A. 1853; Deac. 1850, Pr. 1851. R. of Leigh, Dio. Roch. 1859. (Patron, Bp of Roch; Tithe, 500*l*; Glebe, 4 acres; R.'s Inc. 510*l* and Ho; Pop. 1473.) Formerly C. of Stone, near Dartford, Kent, 1850-59. [11]

KING, Watson, *Plaxtole, Sevenoaks, Kent.*—St. John's Coll. Cam. Sen. Opt. and B.A. 1838, M.A. 1839; Deac. 1838 and Pr. 1839 by Bp of Rip. R. of Plaxtole, Dio. Cant. 1864. (Patron, Abp of Cant; Tithe, 397*l*; Glebe, 2 acres; R.'s Inc. 480*l*; Pop. 1144.) Formerly Chap. to the Co. Gaol, Maidstone, 1851. [12]

KING, William Clark, *Norham Vicarage, near Berwick on-Tweed.*—Corpus Coll. Cam. B.A. 1822, M.A. 1843: Deac. 1824 by Bp of Lin. Pr. 1825 by Bp of Nor. V. of Norham, Dio. Dur. 1855. (Patrons, D. and C. of Dur; Tithe—App. 2328*l* 17*s* 11*d*, V. 194*l* 15*s* 3*d*; V.'s Inc. 597*l* and Ho; Pop. 2930.) Rural Dean. [13]

KING, William Thomas Pearse Meade, *Norton Rectory, Atherstone, Leicestershire.*—Trin. Coll. Cam. B.A. 1846, M.A. 1849; Deac. 1847 and Pr. 1848 by Bp of B. and W. R. of Norton-juxta-Twycross, Dio. Pet. 1850. (Patron, Ld Chan; R.'s Inc. 390*l* and Ho; Pop. 451.) [14]

KING, William Wilson, *Fleet Marston, Aylesbury.*—Dub. A.B. 1849, A.M. 1857; Deac. and Pr. 1849 by Bp of Lich. R. of Fleet Marston, Dio. Ox. 1862. (Patron, the present R; R.'s Inc. 250*l*; Pop. 23.) Formerly C. of Ch. Ch. Stone, Staffs; V. of Milwich, Staffs, 1849. [15]

KINGDON, Alfred Cory, *Tollerton, Nottingham.*—Caius Coll. Cam. Jun. Opt. and B.A. 1851; Deac. 1851, Pr. 1852. C. of Tollerton. Formerly C. of Trinity, Nottingham, Walcot, near Bath, and St. John's, Derby. [16]

KINGDON, Charles Frederick, 31, *Maida Hill West, London, W.*—Dur. Licen. in Theol. 1847; Deac. 1847 and Pr. 1848 by Bp of Ches. Formerly C. of St. Stephen's, Liverpool, 1847. [17]

KINGDON, George Thomas, *Ivy Bridge, Devon.*—Trin. Coll. Cam. 1st Jun. Opt. 2nd cl. Cl. Trip. and B.A. 1838, M.A. 1842; Deac. 1841, Pr. 1842. P. C. of Ivy Bridge, Dio. Ex. 1862. (Patrons, Lady Rogers and W. Cotton, Esq. alt; P. C.'s Inc. 100*l*; Pop. 1348.) Surrogate. Formerly R. of Pyworthy, Devon, 1853 62. [18]

KINGDON, Godfrey, *Spondon, near Derby.*—V. of Spondon, Dio. Lich. 1866. (Patron, W. D. Lowe, Esq; Glebe, 88 acres; V.'s Inc. 280*l* and Ho; Pop. 1523.) [19]

KINGDON, Hollingworth Tully, *Salisbury.*—Trin. Coll. Cam. B.A. 1858; Deac. 1859 by Bp of Ox. Pr. 1860 by Bp of Salis. Vice-Prin. of Salisbury Dioc. Theol. Coll. 1864. Formerly C. of Sturminster-Marshall, Dorset, 1859, Devizes 1863. [20]

KINGDON, James Durant, *Sutton-Valence, Staplehurst, Kent.*—Trin. Coll. Cam. Sen. Opt. 2nd cl. Cl. Trip. and B.A. 1854, M.A. 1857; Deac. 1857 and Pr. 1858 by Bp of Wor. Head Mast. of Sutton-Valence Gr. Sch. Formerly Asst. Mast. in Gr. Sch. Bromsgrove, 1854. Mast. in King's Coll. Sch. Lond. [21]

KINGDON, John, *Michaelstow, Camelford, Cornwall.*—Pemb. Coll. Ox. B.A. 1831; Deac. 1832, Pr. 1833. R. of Michaelstow, Dio. Ex. 1849. (Patron, the Prince of Wales, in right of the Duchy of Cornwall; Tithe, 235*l*; R.'s Inc. 300*l* and Ho; Pop. 219.) Formerly V. of North Petherwin, Devon, 1833–49. [22]

KINGDON, Samuel Nicholson, *Bridgerule Vicarage (Devon and Cornwall), near Holsworthy.*—Trin. Coll. Cam. Jun. Opt. 2nd cl. Cl. Trip. and B.A. 1828, M.A. 1832, Sid. Coll. B.D. 1839; Deac. 1828 and Pr. 1829 by Bp of Ex. V. of Bridgerule, Dio. Ex. 1844. (Patron, the present V; Tithe—Imp. 132*l* 18*s*, V. 154*l* 5*s*; Glebe, 50 acres, other Land Endowments, 130 acres; V.'s Inc. 300*l* and Ho; Pop. 410.) Formerly Fell. of Sid. Coll. Cam. Author, *The History and Sacred Obligation of the Sabbath*, Seeleys, 1856; *Schism and its Results* (a Tract), Seeleys; *Address on St. John* iii. 3, Macintosh, 1865; etc. [23]

KINGLAKE, F. C., *West Monkton, Taunton.*—C. of West Monkton. [24]

KINGLAKE, William Chapman, *Monkton Rectory, Taunton.*—Trin. Coll. Cam. Chan.'s Gold Medal for English Poem 1830, again 1832; B.A. 1834, M.A. 1841; Deac. 1835 and Pr. 1836 by Bp of B. and W. R. of Monkton, Dio. B. and W. 1838. (Patron, the present R; Tithe, 640*l*; Glebe, 55¾ acres; R.'s Inc. 1000*l* and Ho; Pop. 1153.) [25]

KINGSBURY, Thomas Luck, 10, *Warrior-square, Hastings.*—Trin. Coll. Cam. B.A. 1848, M.A. 1851; Deac. 1848 by Bp of Roch. Pr. 1849 by Bp of Salis. Chap. to Marquis of Ailesbury. Formerly Asst. Chap. on H.E.I.C.'s Establishment at Bombay 1851–53; P. C. of Savernake, Wilts, 1854–61; Chap. of Trin. Coll. Cam. [26]

KINGSFORD, Brenchley, *Shadwell Rectory, London, E.*—Ex. Coll. Ox. 3rd cl. Lit. Hum. and B.A. 1843, M.A. 1849; Deac. 1846 and Pr. 1847 by Abp of Cant. R. of St. Paul's, Shadwell, Dio. Lon. 1862. (Patron, Bp of Lon; Pop. 8499.) Formerly C. of West Farleigh, Maidstone, 1846–51, Bishop's Bourne, near Canterbury, 1852–59; P. C. of Hythe, Kent, 1859–62. [27]

KINGSFORD, Frederick William, *The Terrace, Upper Clapton, N.E.*—Clare Coll. Cam. B.A.

1855, M.A. 1861; Deac. 1855 and Pr. 1856 by Bp of Nor. P. C. of St. Thomas's, Stamford Hill, Dio. Lon. 1861. (Patron, R. of Hackney; P. C.'s Inc. 210*l*; Pop. 4400.) Formerly C. of East Dereham, Norfolk, 1855–57, St. Martin's-in-the-Fields, Lond. 1858; Chap. at Allahabad, H.E.I.C.S. 1858–61. [1]

KINGSFORD, Philip, *Hanley Grange, Upton-on Severn.*—Jesus Coll. Cam. B.A. 1854, M.A. 1857; Deac. 1855 and Pr. 1856 by Bp of Wor. Chap. to Sir Edmund Lechmere 1865. Formerly Prof. of Mathematics at Royal Military Coll. Sandhurst, 1854; C. of Malvern Wells 1855, Newland 1860, Malvern Link 1862. [2]

KINGSFORD, Sampson, *Atherstone.*—St. John's Coll. Cam. Fell. 1851, Sen. Opt. 1st cl. Cl. Trip. B.A. 1848, M.A. 1851; Deac. 1851 and Pr. 1853 by Bp of Ely. Head Mast. of Gr. Sch. Atherstone. Formerly 2nd Mast. of Rossall Sch. 1849–55; Head Mast of Chard Gr. Sch. and P. C. of Chillington, Somerset, 1855–57; Head Mast. of Ludlow Gr. Sch. 1857–65. [3]

KINGSFORD, Sampson, *Faversham, Kent.*—Trin. Coll. Cam. B.A. 1814; Deac. 1816, Pr. 1817. Head Mast. of Faversham Gr. Sch. 1847. [4]

KINGSFORD, Septimus, *Ospringe, Kent.*—Trin. Coll. Cam. 2nd Sen. Opt. B.A. 1862, M.A. 1865; Deac. 1863 and Pr. 1864 by Abp of Cant. C. of Ospringe 1863. [5]

KINGSLEY, Charles, *Eversley Rectory, Winchfield, Hants.*—Magd. Coll. Cam. Scho. and Prizeman, Sen. Opt. 1st cl. Cl. Trip. and B.A. 1842; Deac. 1842 and Pr. 1843 by Bp of Win. R. of Eversley, Dio. Win. 1844. (Patron, Rev. Sir W. H. Cope, Bart; Tithe, 585*l*; Glebe, 60 acres; R.'s Inc. 500*l* and Ho; Pop. 829.) Prof. of Modern History in Univ. of Cam; Chap. in Ordinary to Her Majesty; Chap. to the Prince of Wales; Dom. Chap. to Viscount Sydney. Author, *The Roman and the Teuton* (a series of Lectures before the University of Cambridge), 12*s*; *Two Years Ago*, 3rd ed. 6*s*; *Westward Ho!* 4th ed. 6*s*; *Alton Locke, Tailor and Poet*, 4*s* 6*d*; *Hypatia, or New Foes with an Old Face*, 4th ed. 6*s*; *Yeast*, 5*s*; *Miscellanies*, 2nd ed. 2 vols. 12*s*; *The Saint's Tragedy*, 3rd ed. 5*s*; *Andromeda, and other Poems*, 3rd ed. 5*s*; *The Water Babies, a Fairy Tale for a Land Baby*, 6*s*; *Glaucus, or the Wonders of the Shore*, 5*s*; *The Heroes, or Greek Fairy Tales for My Children*, 3*s* 6*d*; *Village Sermons*, 6th ed. 2*s* 6*d*; *The Gospel of the Pentateuch*, 2nd ed. 4*s* 6*d*; *Good News of God*, 3rd ed. 6*s*; *Sermons for the Times*, 3rd ed. 3*s* 6*d*; *Town and Country Sermons*, 6*s*; *Sermons on National Subjects*, 1st series, 2nd ed. 5*s*; 2nd series, 2nd ed. 5*s*; *Alexandria and her Schools* (being Four Lectures delivered at the Philosophical Institution, Edinburgh), 5*s*; *The Limits of Exact Science as applied to History* (an Inaugural Lecture delivered before the University of Cambridge), 2*s*; *Phaethon, or Loose Thoughts for Loose Thinkers*, 3rd ed. 2*s*; *What then does Dr. Newman mean?* (a pamphlet), 1864, 1*s*; *The Ancien Régime*, 1867; *The Water of Life* (Sermons), 1867; all published by Macmillans, Lond. and Cam. [6]

KINGSLEY, John, *Dunham Massey, Altrincham, Cheshire.*—Dub. A.B. 1834, A.M. 1847; Deac. 1835 and Pr. 1836 by Bp of Ches. P. C. of Dunham Massey, Dio. Ches. 1855. (Patron, Earl of Stamford; P. C.'s Inc. 480*l*; Pop. 4569.) Surrogate. Formerly C. of Bowden 1835–54. [7]

KINGSLEY, William Towler, *South Kilvington Rectory, Thirsk, Yorks*—Sid. Coll. Cam. Wrang. and B.A. 1838, M.A. 1841, B.D. 1848; Deac. and Pr. 1842 by Bp of Ely. R. of South Kilvington, Dio. York, 1859. (Patron, Sid. Coll. Cam; R.'s Inc. 550*l* and Ho; Pop. 360.) Formerly Fell. and Tut. of Sid. Coll. Cam. [8]

KINGSMILL, C.—C. of St. Matthew's, Pell-street, St. George's-in-the-East, Lond. [9]

KINGSMILL, Henry, *Buxted Rectory, Uckfield, Sussex.*—Trin. Coll. Ox. B.A. 1835. R. of Buxted, Dio. Chich. 1846. (Patron, Abp of Cant; Tithe, 1030*l*; Glebe, 50 acres; R.'s Inc. 1105*l* and Ho; Pop. 1248.) [10]

KINGSMILL, William Major, *Bredicot Rectory, Worcester.*—Jesus Coll. Cam. B.A. 1847, M.A. 1854; Deac. 1848 and Pr. 1849 by Bp of Lon. R. of Bredicot with Tibberton V. Dio. Wor. 1865. (Patrons, D. and C. of Wor; R.'s Inc. 290*l* and Ho; Pop. Bredicot 53, Tibberton 309.) Formerly Asst. C. of St. Mary's, Tothill Fields, Westminster, 1848–51, Broad Clyst, near Exeter, 1852–65. [11]

KINGSTON, Clement Usill, *Sutton St. Edmund, near Wisbeach.*—Clare Coll. Cam. B.A. 1838; Deac. 1848, Pr. 1850. C. of Sutton St. Edmund 1849 and Guyhirne 1848. Formerly 2nd Mast. of Ashbourne Gr. Sch. [12]

KINGSTON, John.—Dur. Licen. in Theol. 1855; Deac. 1855 and Pr. 1857 by Bp of Man. C. of St. Peter's, River-lane, Islington, Lond. Formerly R. of Cattistock, Dorset, 1859–63; Dom. Chap. to the King of Hanover 1862–63; Prov. Grand Chap. to the Freemasons of Dorset 1861–62. Author, "*With Well Doing ye May Put to Silence the Ignorance of Foolish Men*" (a Sermon before the Dorset Freemasons), 1862; etc. [13]

KINLESIDE, R. V. C., *North Luffenham, Rutland.*—C. of North Luffenham. [14]

KINNEAR, George, *Upton, Torquay.*—Dur. B.A. 1850, M.A. 1857; Deac. 1850 and Pr. 1851 by Bp of Rip. C. of Upton. [15]

KINNEAR, Henry Gott, *Old Malton, Yorks.*—Ch. Ch. Ox. B.A. 1851, M.A. 1854; Deac. 1852 and Pr. 1854 by Bp of Roch. Formerly Clerk in Orders, and Precentor of Trinity, Hull. [16]

KINSMAN, Andrew Guyse, *Gildersome Parsonage, Leeds.*—Clare Hall, Cam. B.A. 1814, M.A. 1817; Deac. 1814, Pr. 1815. P. C. of Gildersome, Dio. Rip. (Patron, V. of Batley; Glebe, 6 acres; P. C.'s Inc. 120*l* and Ho; Pop. 2701.) [17]

KINSMAN, Richard Byrn, *Tintagel Vicarage, near Camelford, Cornwall.*—Trin. Coll. Cam. B.A. 1834, M.A. 1847; Deac. 1834, Pr. 1835. V. of Tintagel, Dio. Ex. 1851. (Patrons, D. and C. of Windsor; Tithe—App. 239*l* 13*s*, Imp. 4*l* 13*s* 9*d*, V. 268*l*; Glebe, 95 acres; V.'s Inc. 390*l* and Ho; Pop. 900.) Editor of *Sermons* by Rev. George Kemp, 1842, Smith and Elder; *Sermons* by Rev. W. Hichens, Rivingtons, 10*s*. [18]

KIRBY, Henry Thomas Murdoch, *Mayfield Vicarage, Hurst Green, Sussex.*—St. John's Coll. Cam. Jun. Opt. and B.A. 1844, M.A. 1847; Deac. 1844, Pr. 1845. V. of Mayfield, Dio. Chich. 1845. (Patron, the present V; Tithe—Imp. 1223*l* 4*s* 9*d*, V. 710*l*; Glebe, 52 acres; V.'s Inc. 1050*l* and Ho; Pop. 1799.) [19]

KIRBY, Henry William, *Bewholme, Hull.*—St. John's Coll. Cam. 1850, 3rd Sen. Opt. and B.A. 1853, M.A. 1857; Deac. 1853 and Pr. 1854 by Bp of Lin. P. C. of Nunkeeling, near Sigglesthorne, Dio. York, 1857. (Patron, T. C. Dixon, Esq; P. C.'s Inc. 90*l* and Ho; Pop. 271.) Formerly C. of Sneenton 1853. [20]

KIRBY, Reginald Rivers, *Hadlow Down, Uckfield.*—St. John's Coll. Cam. B.A. 1852, M.A. 1867; Deac. 1852 and Pr. 1853 by Bp of G. and B. P. C. of Hadlow Down, Dio. Chich. 1855. (Patron, Rev. H. T. M. Kirby; Glebe, 7 acres; P. C.'s Inc. 126*l* and Ho; Pop. 981.) Formerly C. of St. Mark's, Lower Easton, Bristol. Editor of *The Hadlow Down Magazine*. [21]

KIRBY, Richard Heighway, *Haverthwaite Parsonage, near Ulverston.*—St. John's Coll. Cam. 1838, 12th Wrang. and B.A. 1840, M.A. 1843; Deac. 1842 and Pr. 1843 by Bp of Lon. P. C. of Haverthwaite, Dio. Carl. 1853. (Patrons, P. C. of Colton and Bp of Carl. alt; P. C.'s Inc. 132*l* and Ho; Pop. 1099.) Formerly P. C. of Taddington, Derbyshire, 1848–53. [22]

KIRBY, William Walter, 19, *Woburn square, W.C.* and 8, *Serjeants'-inn, Fleet-street, London, E.C.*—Queens' Coll. Cam. B.A. 1850, M.A. 1856; Deac. 1850 and Pr. 1851 by Abp of Cant. R. of St. Dunstan's-in-the East, City and Dio. Lon. 1862. (Patron, Abp of Cant; Tithe, 333*l* 6*s* 8*d*; R.'s Inc. 350*l*; Pop. 971.) Sec. of South American Miss. Soc. Formerly V. of Appledore with Ebony, Kent, 1856–62. Editor, *South American Missionary Magazine*, Bi-monthly, 2*d*. [23]

KIRK, William Boyton, *Shankhill, Lurgan, Ireland.*—Dub. and St. Aidan's; Deac. 1860. Formerly C. of Burslem 1860. [24]

KIRKBY, Edward Ernest Ward, *Trinity College, Cambridge.*—Trin. Coll. Cam. Scho. 5th in 2nd cl. Cl. Trip. B.A. 1862; Deac. 1863 and Pr. 1864 by Bp of Ely. Chap. of Trin. Coll. Cam; C. of Trumpington, Cambs, 1863. [1]

KIRKBY, William, *Wandsworth-common, Surrey, S.W.*—Jesus Coll. Cam. B.A. 1850, M.A. 1853; Deac. 1851 and Pr. 1852 by Bp of Lin. Chap. of the R. V. Patriotic Asylum, Wandsworth-common, 1858. [2]

KIRKHAM, John William, *Llanbrynmair Rectory, North Wales.*—Jesus Coll. Ox. B.A. 1842, M.A. 1845; Deac. 1842 and Pr. 1843 by Bp. of St. A. R. of Llanbrynmair, Dio. Ban. 1851. (Patron, Bp of St. A; Tithe, 315*l*; Glebe, 4 acres; R.'s Inc. 330*l* and Ho; Pop. 1998.) Surrogate; Rural Dean of Cyfeilio 1863; Dom. Chap. to the Marquis of Ailsa 1847. Author, some Welsh Catechisms and Devotional Books. [3]

KIRKMAN, Joshua, *Thurlow-road, Hampstead, London, N.W.*—Queens' Coll. Cam. B.A. 1851, M.A. 1855; Deac. 1852 and Pr. 1853 by Bp of Pet. Incumb. of St. John's Chapel, Downshire-hill, Hampstead, Dio. Lon. 1861; Chap. to the Soldiers' Daughters' Home, Hampstead. Formerly Incumb. of St. Paul's Episcopal Chapel, Aberdeen; V. of Field Dalling, Norfolk, 1855–59; C. of St. Giles-in-the-Fields, Lond. 1859–61. [4]

KIRKMAN, Thomas Penyngton, *Croft Rectory, Warrington.*—Dub. A.B. 1834, A.M. 1848. R. of Croft with Southworth R. Dio. Ches. (Patron, Earl of Derby; R.'s Inc. 200*l* and Ho; Pop. 1100.) F.R.S. [5]

KIRKNESS, William John, *Forrabury Rectory, Boscastle, Cornwall.*—Queens' Coll. Cam. B.A. 1831, M.A. 1837; Deac. 1832 and Pr. 1833 by Bp of Ex. R. of Forrabury, Dio. Ex. 1843. (Patrons, last turn, W. Kirkness, Esq. present turn, J. R. Avery, Esq; Tithe, 62*l* 10*s*; Glebe, 9 acres; R.'s Inc. 83*l* and Ho; Pop. 366.) R. of Minster, Cornwall, Dio. Ex. 1843. (Patrons, last turn, W. Kirkness, Esq. present turn J. R. Avery, Esq; Tithe, 261*l* 10*s*; Glebe, 40 acres; R.'s Inc. 331*l*; Pop. 505.) [6]

KIRKPATRICK, Francis, *West Hoathly Vicarage, East Grinstead, Sussex.*—Dub. A.B. 1825; Deac. 1827, Pr. 1828. V. of West Hoathly, Dio. Chich. 1850. (Patron, Ld Chan; Tithe—Imp. 337*l* 19*s* 3*d*, V. 225*l* 8*s* 2*d*; Glebe, 9 acres; V.'s Inc. 210*l* and Ho; Pop. 1120.) [7]

KIRKPATRICK, James.—St. Peter's Coll. Cam. B.A. 1830, M.A. 1833; Deac. 1831, Pr. 1832. Formerly C. of Southery, Downham, Norfolk. [8]

KIRTON Charles.—Dub. A.B. 1852; Deac. 1852 and Pr. 1853 by Bp of Cork. P. C. of St. Andrew's, Bethnal Green, Dio. Lon. 1864. (Patron, Bp of Lon; P. C.'s Inc. 250*l*; Pop. 9913.) [9]

KIRWAN, Edward Dominick Geoffrey Martin, *Wootton-Wawen Vicarage, Henley-in-Arden, Warwickshire.*—King's Coll. Cam. B.A. 1837, M.A. 1841; Deac. 1838 and Pr. 1839 by Bp of Lin. V. of Wootton-Wawen, Dio. Wor. 1854. (Patron, King's Coll. Cam; Tithe—Imp. 4000*l*, V. 143*l* 17*s* 6*d*; Glebe, 70 acres; V.'s Inc. 298*l* and Ho; Pop. 676.) [10]

KIRWAN, John Henry, *St. Anne's, Buck Mills, Bideford, Devon.*—King's Coll. Cam. B.A. 1840, M.A. 1843; Deac. 1842 by Bp of Lin. Pr. 1843 by Bp of B. and W. P. C. of Buck Mills, Dio. Ex. 1863. (Patroness, Mrs. Elwes; Glebe, 18 acres; P. C.'s Inc. 69*l* 10*s* and Ho; Pop. 249.) Fell. of King's Coll. Cam. Formerly C. of St. Feock, Cornwall. [11]

KIRWAN, Richard, *Gittisham Rectory, Honiton, Devon.*—Emman. Coll. Cam. B.A. 1853, M.A. 1856; Deac. 1855 and Pr. 1856 by Bp of Roch. R. of Gittisham, Dio. Ex. 1860. (Patron, Richard Marker, Esq; Tithe, 322*l*; Glebe, 47 acres; R.'s Inc. 418*l* and Ho; Pop. 355.) Rural Dean. Formerly C. of Little Bardfield, Essex, 1855–57, Gosfield, Essex, 1857–60. [12]

KIRWOOD, George Henry, *Hereford.*—St. Bees; M.A. by Abp of Cant; Deac. 1846 and Pr. 1847 by Bp of Lich. V. of St. Martin's, City and Dio. Herf. 1857. (Patrons, D. and C. of Windsor; V.'s Inc. 290*l* and Ho; Pop. 1450.) Formerly P. C. of Ivington, Herefordshire. [13]

KIRWOOD, Robert, *Chester-le-street, Durham.*—St. Bees; Deac. 1853, Pr. 1854. R. of Chester-le-street, Dio. Dur. 1865. (Patrons, H. Joliffe, Esq. and Trustees alt; Tithe, 446*l*; R.'s Inc. 460*l*; Pop. 4124.) Formerly C. of St. Andrew's, Newcastle-on-Tyne. [14]

KISSACK, Edward William, *Kirk Andreas, Isle of Man.*—Dub. A.B. 1861; Deac. 1862 and Pr. 1863 by Bp of S. and M. C. of Kirk Andreas 1862. [15]

KITCAT, David, *Lasborough, Wotton-under-Edge, Glouc.*—Trin. Coll. Ox. B.A. 1850, M.A. 1852; Deac. 1854 and Pr. 1855 by Bp of Salis. R. of Lasborough, Dio. G. and B. 1859. (Patron, R. S. Holford, Esq; R.'s Inc. 150*l*.) Formerly C. of Wilton, Wilts. [16]

KITCAT, John, *Swallowfield, Reading.*—Oriel Coll. Ox. B.A. 1841, M.A. 1851; Deac. 1844 and Pr. 1845 by Bp of Chich. P. C. of Swallowfield, Dio. Ox. 1855. (Patrons, D. and C. of Herf; Tithe—Imp. 75*l* 3*s* 4*d*, P. C. 80*l*; Glebe, 18 poles; P. C.'s Inc. 160*l*; Pop. 1265.) [17]

KITCHIN, Francis, *St. Peter's, York.*—Jesus Coll. Cam. B.A. 1864; Deac. 1866 by Abp of York. C. of St. Helen's, York, 1866; Asst. Mast. at St. Peter's Sch. York. [18]

KITCHIN, George William, *Christ Church, Oxford.*—Ch. Ch. Ox. Double 1st cl. and B.A. 1850, M.A. 1853; Deac. 1852 and Pr. 1859 by Bp of Ox. Jun. Proctor; Select Preacher before the Univ. of Ox; Tut. to H.R.H. the Crown Prince of Denmark; Hon. Fell. of King's Coll. Lond; Literary Superintendent of the Clarendon Press, Oxford, 1865; Chap. to the Bp of Ches. 1865; Whitehall Preacher 1866 and 1867. Author, *Bacon's Novum Organum*, 2 vols. with English Notes and Translation, Univ. Press, Oxford, 1855; *Bacon's Advancement of Learning*, with Notes, Bell and Daldy, 1860; *Prayers for the Use of Twyford School*, 2nd ed. 1860; *A Lecture on Lectures*, 1859; *Sermons preached before the University of Oxford.* Editor, *Spenser's Faery Queene*, Book I., Clarendon Press Series, 1867; *Catalogue of MSS. in the Library of Christ Church, Oxford*, Macmillan, 1867. [19]

KITCHIN, Joseph, *Wasdale Head, Holm Rook, Cumberland.*—Deac. and Pr. 1820. P. C. of Wasdale Head, Dio. Carl. 1820. (Patron, P. C. of St. Bees; P. C.'s Inc. 80*l*; Pop. 49.) [20]

KITCHING, Robert, *Westow, Kirkham, Yorks.*—St. Cath. Coll. Cam. B.A. 1851, M.A. 1856; Deac. 1851 and Pr. 1852 by Abp of York. V. of Westow, Dio. York, 1860. (Patron, Abp of York; Tithe, 113*l*; V.'s Inc. 320*l*; Pop. 635.) Formerly C. of Ellerburne 1851–53, Pickering 1853–58; V. of Buckthorpe 1858–60. [21]

KITCHING, Walton, 14, *Devonshire-place, Portland-place, London, W.*—St. John's Coll. Cam. B.A. 1852, M.A. 1855; Deac. 1853, Pr. 1854. [22]

KITCHING, William Vistirin, *Great Finborough, Stowmarket.*—St. John's Coll. Cam. B.A. 1845, M.A. 1853; Deac. 1847 and Pr. 1848 by Bp of Pet. V. of Great Finborough, Dio. Nor. 1860. (Patron, Bp of Nor.; Tithe, 146*l* 2*s* 9*d*; Glebe, 7½ acres; V.'s Inc. 172*l* 2*s* 9*d*; Pop. 419.) Formerly C. of Gretworth 1847, Brackley, 1848, Carlston Rode 1852. [23]

KITCHINGMAN, John, *Shelton, Newcastle-under-Lyne.*—Theol. Coll. Lichfield; Deac. 1860 and Pr. 1861 by Bp of Lich. C. of Shelton 1866. Formerly C. of St. Peter's, Stoke-upon-Trent, 1860–66. [24]

KITCHINGMAN, Philip, *Bonby, Barton-on-Humber.*—Pemb. Coll. Ox. B.A. 1830, M.A. 1834; Deac. 1832, Pr. 1833. V. of Bonby, Dio. Lin. 1867. (Patron, Earl of Yarborough; Tithe, 290*l*; V.'s Inc. 300*l* and Ho; Pop. 471.) Formerly C. of Bonby. [25]

KITSON, Edward.—Ball. Coll. Ox. 2nd cl. Lit. Hum. and B.A. 1822, M.A. 1827; Deac. 1826 by Abp of Cashel, Pr. 1827 by Bp of Ox. Formerly Fell. of Ball. Coll. Ox. Retired Chap. Royal Navy. [26]

KITSON, Edward B. Blake, *Denford, Thrapstone, Northants.*—Ch. Coll. Cam. Bell. Univ. Scho. 1861, 1st Sen. Opt. in Math. Trip. 13th in 2nd cl. Cl. Trip. 1864, B.A. 1864, M.A. 1867; Deac. 1866 by Abp of York for Bp of Pet. Pr. 1867 by Bp of Pet. C. of Denford with Ringstead 1866. [27]

KITSON, Francis John, *Hemyock Rectory (Devon), near Wellington.*—St. John's Coll. Ox. B.A.

1838, M.A. and B.D. 1848; Deac. 1834, Pr. 1835. R. of Hemyock with Culm Davy Chapelry, Dio. Ex. 1854. (Patron, F. L. Popham, Esq; Tithe, 700*l*; Glebe, 104 acres; R.'s Inc. 604*l* and Ho; Pop. 1004.) [1]

KITSON, James Buller, *Morval Vicarage, East Looe, Cornwall.*—Ex. Coll. Ox. B.A. 1834; Deac. 1834, Pr. 1835. V. of Morval, Dio. Ex. 1858. (Patron, Ld Chan; Tithe—Imp. 260*l* 7*s*, V. 213*l* 18*s*; Glebe, 121½ acres; V.'s Inc. 333*l* and Ho; Pop. 765.) Chap. to Bp of Ex. 1842. Formerly V. of Pelynt, Cornwall, 1841–58. [2]

KITSON, John Francis, *Antony Vicarage (Cornwall), near Devonport.*—Ex. Coll. Ox. B.A. 1841, M.A 1845. V. of Antony, Dio. Ox. 1845 (Patron, W. H. P. Carew, Esq; Tithe—Imp. 287*l* 3*s* 2*d*, V. 308*l* 13*s* 6*d*; Glebe, 6 acres; V.'s Inc. 320*l* and Ho; Pop. 3887.) [3]

KITSON, Thomas, *Shiphay House, Torquay.*—Ball. Coll. Ox. 2nd cl. Lit. Hum. 1819, Fell. of Ex. Coll. 1819, B.A. 1823, M.A. 1824; Deac. 1821 by Bp of Bristol, Pr. 1821 by Bp of Ex. C. of Haccombe, Devon. Formerly C. of Combeinteignhead and Chap. to the Newton-Abbot Union. Previously Fell. of Ex. Coll. Ox. [4]

KITTERMASTER, Frederic Wilson, *Edgton, Aston-on-Clun, Salop.*—Pemb. Coll. Ox. Hon. 4th cl. Math. et Phy. and B.A. 1847, M.A. 1849; Deac. 1848 and Pr. 1849 by Bp of Ches. P. C. of Edgton 1865. (Patron, Humphrey Sandford, Esq; Glebe, 4 acres; P. C.'s Inc. 120*l*; Pop. 191.) Hon. Chap. to the Shropshire Artillery Volunteers 1860. Formerly C. of Bangor 1848, St. James's, Ratcliff, Lond. 1851, St. Paul's, Lisson-grove, Lond. 1853, St. Chad's, Shrewsbury, 1856. Author, *Rhyddlan Castle* (a Prize Poem); *A Poem on the Consecration of Sandford and Shippon Churches, Berks,* 1855, 2nd ed; *Sermon on the Death of the Duke of Wellington*; *Blessed are they that Mourn* (a Funeral Sermon on the Death of the Rev. H. S. Polehampton, Chaplain at Lucknow during the Siege); *A Sermon occasioned by the decease of Robert Burton, Esq. of Longner Hall, Salop*; *A Sermon on the Death of W. R. Stokes, Esq. of Shrewsbury*; *The Sword of the Lord and of Gideon* (a Sermon preached before the Shropshire Artillery); *Fight the Good Fight of Faith* (a Tract for Volunteers); *The Moslem and the Hindoo* (a Poem on the Sepoy Revolt), 3*s* 6*d*; *Poetry and Religious Feeling* (a Lecture); *The River Avon* (a Lecture); *Warwickshire Arms and Lineages,* 5*s*. [5]

KITTO, John Fenwick, *St. Matthias' Parsonage, Poplar, London, E.*—St. Alban Hall, Ox. 2nd cl. Math. B.A. 1860; Deac. 1862 and Pr. 1863 by Bp of Lon. P. C. of St. Matthias', Poplar, Dio. Lon. 1867. (Patron, Bp of Lon; P. C.'s Inc. 320*l* and Ho; Pop. 5000.) Formerly C. of St. Pancras, Lond. 1862–66. [6]

KITTO, J. W., *Whitnash, Leamington.*—C. of Whitnash. [7]

KITTOE, Edward Hooper, *Old Chester-road, Erdington, Birmingham.*—Ex. Coll. Ox. B.A. 1844; Deac. 1846 and Pr. 1847 by Bp of Nor. P. C. of St. Michael's Boldmere, Dio. Wor. 1857. (Patron, R. of Sutton-Coldfield; Glebe, 55 acres; P. C.'s Inc. 150*l* and Ho; Pop. 648.) Formerly C. of Chadwell Essex. [8]

KLAMBOROWSKI, Adolphus, *Hinckley, Leicestershire.*—Lond. Univ. B.A. 1863; Deac. 1865 and Pr. 1866 by Bp of Pet. C. of Hinckley 1865. [9]

KLANERT, Charles, *Iping Rectory, Midhurst, Sussex.*—St. Peter's Coll. Cam. Sen. Opt. and B.A. 1831, M.A. 1834; Deac. 1831 and Pr. 1832 by Bp of Chich. R. of Iping with Chithurst, Dio. Chich. 1851. (Patron, Lord Leconfield; Tithe, 315*l*; Glebe, 28 acres; R.'s Inc. 404*l* and Ho; Pop. Iping 404, Chithurst 215.) Formerly C. of Petworth 1831–51. [10]

KNAGGS, William, *Buslingthorpe, Leeds.*—St. Bees; Deac. 1864. C. of St. Michael's, Buslingthorpe 1864. [11]

KNAPP, Charles Tyrrell, *Wells, Norfolk.*—Ex. Coll. Ox. and St. Aidan's; Deac. 1861 and Pr. 1862 by Bp of Lich. C. of Wells 1864. Formerly C. of Wellington, Salop, 1860–62, Herley and Hornton, Oxon, 1862–64. [12]

KNAPP, Henry, *Swaton Vicarage, Folkingham, Lincolnshire.*—St. John's Coll. Ox. B.A. 1833, M.A. 1836. V. of Swaton with Spanby R. Dio. Lin. 1840. (Patroness, Mrs. Knapp; Spanby, Tithe—Imp. 164*l*, V. 81*l*; V.'s Inc. 525*l* and Ho; Pop. Swaton 297, Spanby 75.) Rural Dean. [13]

KNAPP, H. J.—Chap. to Sailors, Constantinople. [14]

KNAPP, John George Francis Henry, *St. John's Parsonage, Portsea, Hants.*—King's Coll. Lond. Theol. Assoc. 1850; Deac. 1850 and Pr. 1851 by Bp of Lich. P. C. of St. John's, Portsea, Dio. Win. 1853. (Patrons, Trustees; P. C.'s Inc. 300*l* and Ho; Pop. 6696.) Surrogate 1854; Chap. to the 5th Hants Rifle Volunteer Corps. Author, *The Christian Sabbath*; *Sins of the Tongue*; *The Church in the Circus*; *Precious Stones from a Strange Quarry,* etc. [15]

KNAPP, John Harvey.—St. John's Coll. Cam. B.A. 1848, M.A. 1852; Deac. 1849, Pr. 1850. Chap. and Naval Instructor of H.M.S. "Britannia." [16]

KNAPP, Joseph Greenway, *Church Honeybourne, Broadway, Worcestershire.*—C. of Church Honeybourne. [17]

KNAPP, Thomas Lloyd, *Hacconby, near Bourn, Lincolnshire.*—St. John's Coll. Ox. B.A. 1864, M.A. 1867; Deac. 1865 and Pr. 1866 by Bp of Lin. C. of Morton with Hacconby 1865. [18]

KNAPTON, Augustus James, *Boldre, Lymington, Hants.*—Ex. Coll. Ox. B.A. 1826, M.A. 1829; Deac. 1828 and Pr. 1829 by Bp of Salis. Formerly C. of Ebbesborne-Wake; P. C. of Anstey, Wilts. [19]

KNAPTON, Henry Pearce, *Ilex House, Weston-super-Mare.*—Queens' Coll. Cam. 1858, Wrang. 3rd cl. Cl. Trip. 3rd cl. Theol. Trip; Deac. 1859 and Pr. 1860 by Bp of Lon. Formerly C. of St. Michael's, Strand, Lond. 1859; Head Mast. of Weston-super-Mare Coll. [20]

KNATCHBULL, Henry Edward, *Campsey-Ash Rectory, Market Wickham, Suffolk.*—Wad. Coll. Ox. B.A. 1830; Deac. and Pr. 1832. R. of Campsey-Ash, Dio. Nor. 1867. (Patron, Lord Rendlesham; Tithe, 432*l*; Glebe, 9¾ acres; R.'s Inc. 451*l* and Ho; Pop. 379.) Formerly V. of North Elmham, Norfolk, 1833–67. [21]

KNATCHBULL, Wadham, *Cholderton Lodge, Marlborough, Wilts.*—Ch. Ch. Ox. B.A. 1816, M.A. 1823; Deac. 1816 and Pr. 1819 by Bp of Salis. Preb. of Combe the 2nd in Wells Cathl. 1822. (Value, 3*l* 15*s* 6*d*.) Formerly R. of Sutton Mandeville, Wilts, 1831–39. [22]

KNATCHBULL, Wyndham, *Westbere Rectory, Canterbury.*—Ch. Ch. Ox. B.A. 1808, All Souls Coll. M.A. 1812, B.D. 1826, D.D. 1823. R. of Westbere, Dio. Cant. 1811. (Patron, Ld Chan; Tithe—App. 90*l*, R. 275*l*; Glebe, 2 acres; R.'s Inc. 277*l* and Ho; Pop. 220.) R. of Aldington with Smeeth P. C. Hythe, Kent, Dio. Cant. 1823. (Patron, Abp of Cant; Aldington, Tithe, 982*l* 12*s* 4*d*; Smeeth, Tithe, 469*l* 4*s*; R.'s Inc. 1451*l* and Ho; Pop. Aldington 686, Smeeth 486.) Rural Dean. [23]

KNATCHBULL-HUGESSEN, *Cheriton Rectory, Sandgate, Kent.*—Ball. Coll. Ox. B.A. 1852; Deac. 1864 and Pr. 1865 by Abp of Cant. R. of Cheriton, Dio. Cant. 1866. (Patron, Rev. T. Brockman; R.'s Inc. 570*l* and Ho; Pop. 623.) Formerly C. of Boxley, Kent, 1864–67. [24]

KNEVETT, John, *Needham, Harleston, Norfolk.*—P. C. of Needham, Dio. Nor. 1834. (Patrons, Exors. of the late A. Adair, Esq; Tithe—Imp. 310*l* 5*s*, P. C. 25*l* 17*s*; P. C.'s Inc. 75*l*; Pop. 395.) [25]

KNIGHT, Charles, *Honfleur.*—Caius Coll. Cam. B.A. 1859; Deac. 1860 by Abp of York. British Chap. at Honfleur. [26]

KNIGHT, Charles Bridges, *Chawton Rectory, Alton, Hants.*—Trin. Coll. Cam. B.A. 1825, M.A. 1828; Deac. 1827 by Bp of Win. Pr. 1828 by Abp of Cant. R. of Chawton, Dio. Win. 1837. (Patron, Edward Knight, Esq; Tithe, 500*l*; Glebe, 65 acres; R.'s Inc. 560*l* and Ho; Pop. 464.) Rural Dean of Alton 1851. [27]

KNIGHT, Charles Rumsey, *Tythegston Court, Bridgend, Glamorganshire.*—Wad. Coll. Ox. B.A. 1839, M.A. 1841; Deac. 1840, Pr. 1841. Chap. of the Don. of Ewenny, Dio. Llan. 1863. (Patroness, Miss E. Turbervill; Chap.'s Inc. 70*l*; Pop. 270.) Rural Dean. [28]

KNIGHT, David Thomas, *Earls Barton Vicarage, Northampton.*—Lin. Coll. Ox. B.A. 1832, M.A. 1834; Deac. 1832 and Pr. 1833 by Bp of Pet. V. of Earls Barton, Dio. Pet. 1842. (Patron, Edward Thornton, Esq; Glebe, 285 acres; V.'s Inc. 266*l* 15*s* and Ho; Pop. 1557.) [1]

KNIGHT, Delaval, *Ford (near Coldstream), Northumberland.*—Univ. Coll. Dur. B.A. 1850; Deac. 1851 and Pr. 1852 by Bp of Dur. C. of Ford. Formerly C. of Longbridge, Deveril, Wilts. [2]

KNIGHT, Edmund Hinds, *Laceby Rectory, Great Grimsby.*—R. of Laceby, Dio. Lin. 1862. (Patron, R. Haynes, Esq; Tithe, 535*l*; Glebe, 18 acres; R.'s Inc. 590*l* and Ho; Pop. 1021.) [3]

KNIGHT, Edward Bridges, *Holme Parsonage, Peterborough.*—Ex. Coll. Ox. B.A. 1852; Deac. 1852 by Bp of G. and B. Pr. 1855 by Bp of Chich. P. C. of Holme, Dio. Ely, 1865. (Patron, William Wells, Esq; Tithe, 195*l*; Glebe, 3 acres; P. C.'s Inc. 300*l* and Ho; Pop. 640.) Formerly C. of Fordcomb, Kent, and St. Peter's, Penshurst. [4]

KNIGHT, Edward Doddridge, *Nottage Court, Bridgend, Glamorganshire.*—Ex. Coll Ox. B.A. 1829; Deac. 1832 and Pr. 1833 by Bp of Llan. R. of Newton Nottage, Dio. Llan. 1858. (Patrons, Rev. E. D. Knight 2 turns, Sir J. B. Guest 1 turn; Tithe, 400*l* 14*s*; Glebe, 12*l*; R.'s Inc. 412*l* 14*s*; Pop. 1082.) Rural Dean. Formerly P. C. of Tredegar 1838–46; R. of Llandough, Glamorganshire, 1846–58. [5]

KNIGHT, George, *Hungerton Vicarage, Leicester.*—St. Edm. Hall, Ox. 3rd cl. Lit. Hum. and B.A. 1835, M.A. 1838; Deac. 1836 and Pr. 1837 by Bp of Lin. V. of Hungerton united with Twyford V. with Thorpe Satchville C. Dio. Pet. 1843. (Patron, Rev. E. Q. Ashby; Hungerton, Glebe, 60 acres; Tithe—Twyford with Thorpe Satchville, Imp. 240*l*, V. 90*l*; Glebe, 52 acres; V.'s Inc. 320*l* and Ho; Pop. Hungerton 302, Twyford 372, Thorpe Satchville 171.) C. of Keyham; Rural Dean. [6]

KNIGHT, Henry Charles, *Yr Allt Goch, Beaumaris.*—Queens' Coll. Cam. M.A. "tanquam nobilis;" Deac. 1838, Pr. 1839. [7]

KNIGHT, Henry J., *Flyford Favel Rectory, Worcester.*—R. of Abberton, Dio. Wor. 1862. (Patron, W. Laslett, Esq; Tithe, 173*l* 10*s*; Glebe, 2½ acres; R.'s Inc. 193*l*; Pop. 62.) R. of Flyford Favel, Dio. Wor. 1862. (Patron, W. Laslett, Esq; Glebe, 100 acres; R.'s Inc. 107*l* and Ho; Pop. 173.) [8]

KNIGHT, James, *Greenwich, S.E.*—St. Cath. Coll. Cam. B.A. 1846, M.A. 1855; Deac. 1847 and Pr. 1848 by Bp of Carl. C. of Greenwich 1866. Formerly C. of Ch. Ch. Carlisle, 1847–49, St. Paul's, Sheffield, 1851–55, Headingley, Leeds, 1855–57, Pulborough, Sussex, 1857–66. [9]

KNIGHT, James William, *Grammar School-house, Lichfield.*—Head Mast. of the Gr. Sch. Lichfield. [10]

KNIGHT, John, *Heytesbury, Wilts.*—Queens' Coll. Cam. B.A. 1832, M.A. 1835; Deac. 1832 and Pr. 1833 by Bp of Lich. Mast. of Hungerford Hospital, Heytesbury, 1836. (Patrons, Chan. of the Ch. Salisbury, and D. and C. of Salis.) P. C. of Heytesbury with Knook, Dio. Salis. 1836. (Patron, Bp of Salis; P. C.'s Inc. 360*l*; Pop. Heytesbury 1103, Knook 208.) Preb. of Tytherington in Heytesbury Coll. Ch. 1836; Surrogate. [11]

KNIGHT, John George, *Wrotham, Sevenoaks, Kent.*—Caius Coll. Cam. Jun. Opt. B.A. 1863, M.A. 1866; Deac. 1865 and Pr. 1866 by Abp of Cant. C. of Wrotham 1867. Formerly C. of Birling, near Maidstone, 1865–67. [12]

KNIGHT, John Walker, *Washington, Hurstpierpoint, Sussex.*—Magd. Coll. Ox. 2nd cl. Lit. Hum. and B.A. 1849, M.A. 1852; Deac. 1852 by Bp of Ox. Pr. 1853 by Bp of Pet. Fell. of Magd. Coll. Ox. V. of Washington, Dio. Chich. 1865. (Patron, Magd. Coll. Ox; Tithe—Imp. 398*l* 5*s* 6*d*, V. 201*l* 14*s* 6*d*; Glebe, 14 acres; V.'s Inc. 235*l* and Ho; Pop. 908.) Formerly C. of Brafield-on-the-Green, Northants, 1852–62. [13]

KNIGHT, J., *Tytherington, Warminster, Wilts.*—P. C. of Tytherington, Dio. Salis. 1836. (Patron, Bp of Salis; Pop. 111.) [14]

KNIGHT, Richard, *North Marston Parsonage, Winslow, Bucks.*—St. Peter's Coll. Cam. B.A. 1835, M.A. 1847. P. C. of North Marston, Dio. Ox. 1847. (Patrons, D. and C. of Windsor; Tithe, App. 519*l* 12*s*; P. C.'s Inc. 150*l* and Ho; Pop. 644.) [15]

KNIGHT, Robert Hervey, *Weston-Favell, near Northampton.*—St. John's Coll. Ox. B.A. 1816, M.A. 1819; Deac. 1817, Pr. 1819. R. of Weston-Favell, Dio. Pet. 1842. (Patron, the present R; Land in lieu of Tithe, 104 acres; R.'s Inc. 240*l* and Ho; Pop. 470.) [16]

KNIGHT, Robert Joseph, *Harrow Weald, Middlesex.*—Trin. Coll. Cam. 12th Wrang. and B.A. 1846, M.A. 1849; Deac. 1851, Pr. 1852. P. C. of Harrow Weald, Dio. Lon. 1861. (Patron, V. of Harrow; P. C.'s Inc. 150*l* and Ho; Pop. 1119.) Formerly C. of Harrow. [17]

KNIGHT, Thomas, *Ford Rectory (Coldstream), Northumberland.*—St. Peter's Coll. Cam. B.A. 1817; Deac. 1818, Pr. 1819. R. of Ford, Dio. Dur. 1819. (Patron, Marquis of Waterford; Tithe—Imp. 1052*l*, R. 1380*l*; Glebe, 7 acres; R.'s Inc. 1380*l* and Ho; Pop. 2072.) [18]

KNIGHT, Thomas, *St. Mary's Hall, Southsea, Hants.*—St. John's Coll. Cam. B.A. 1843; Deac. 1844 and Pr. 1845 by Bp of Lich. Min. of St. Mary's, Portsmouth, Dio. Win. 1847. [19]

KNIGHT, V. C., *Pucklechurch, Bristol.*—C. of Pucklechurch. [20]

KNIGHT, William, *Oughtibridge Parsonage, near Sheffield.*—Deac. 1848 and Pr. 1849 by Bp of Rip. P. C. of Oughtibridge 1852. Formerly C. of Honley, near Huddersfield, 1848–52. [21]

KNIGHT, William, *Steventon Rectory, Overton, Hants.*—Ex. Coll. Ox. B.A. 1822, M.A. 1824; Deac. 1822 and Pr. 1823 by Bp of Win. R. of Steventon, Dio. Win. 1823. (Patron, Rev. Gilbert Alder; Tithe, 500*l*; Glebe, 56 acres; R.'s Inc. 600*l* and Ho; Pop. 167.) Chap. to the Earl of Winchilsea and Nottingham 1827. [22]

KNIGHT William *St. Michael's, Bristol.*—Ball. Coll. Ox. B.A. 1813, M.A. 1816; Deac. 1813 by Bp of Ex. Pr. 1814 by Bp of Herf. R. of St. Michael's, City and Dio. Bristol, 1816. (Patrons, J. S. Harford, Esq. and Trustees; R.'s Inc. 250*l*; Pop. 4922.) Hon. Can. of Bristol 1864. Author, *Lectures on Prophecy.* [23]

KNIGHT, William, *High Ham Rectory, Langport, Somerset.*—Wor. Coll. Ox. 3rd cl. Lit. Hum. and B.A. 1839, M.A. 1842. R. of High Ham, Dio. B. and W. 1862. (Patrons, Wor. Coll. Ox; Tithe—App. 21*l*, R. 455*l*; Glebe, 55 acres; R.'s Inc. 509*l* and Ho; Pop. 1283.) Chap. to Bp of Lon. Formerly Fell. of Wor. Coll. Ox; Sec. of the Ch. Missionary Soc. Author, *Church Missionary Atlas*, Seeleys, 4th ed. 1865; several pamphlets on India and Missions. [24]

KNIGHTLEY, Henry Charles, *Combrook, Kineton, Warwickshire.*—Jesus Coll. Cam. B.A. 1836; Deac. 1838 and Pr. 1839 by Bp of Nor. P. C. of Combrook. Formerly C. of Wilby, Norfolk, 1838–39. [25]

KNIGHTLY, Valentine, *Preston Capes Rectory, Daventry, Northants.*—Ch. Ch. Ox. B.A. 1834, M.A. 1837; Deac. 1835 by Bp of Pet. Pr. 1836 by Bp of Ely. R. of Preston Capes, Dio. Pet. 1836. (Patron, Sir C. Knightly, Bart; Tithe 200*l*; Glebe, 156 acres; R.'s Inc. 412*l* and Ho; Pop. 320.) R. of Charwelton, Northants, Dio. Pet. 1837. (Patron, Sir C. Knightly, Bart; Tithe, 550*l*; Glebe, 90 acres; R.'s Inc. 640*l*; Pop. 214.) [26]

KNIPE, Elliott A., *Bingley, Yorks.*—C. of Bingley. [27]

KNIPE, James J. R. Leigh, *Chesterford, Essex.*—Dub. A.B. 1858, A.M. 1861; Deac. 1861 by Bp of Wor. Pr. 1864 by Bp of Roch. C. of Chesterford 1863. Formerly C. of Atherstone, Warwickshire, 1861–63. [28]

KNIPE, Randolph, *Water-Newton Rectory (Hunts), near Wansford.*—Clare Coll. Cam. B.A. 1838. R. of Water-Newton, Dio. Ely, 1846. (Patron, E. S.

Knipe, Esq; Tithe, 237*l*; Glebe, 25 acres; R.'s Inc. 298*l* and Ho; Pop. 149.) [1]

KNIPE, Thomas Wenham, *Woodsford Rectory, Dorchester.*—Corpus Coll. Cam. B.A. 1845; Deac. 1845 by Bp of Pet. Pr. 1847 by Bp of Salis. R. of Woodsford, Dio. Salis 1849. (Patron, H. C. Sturt, Esq; Tithe, 250*l*; Glebe, 6 acres; R.'s Inc. 153*l* and Ho; Pop. 193.) P. C. of Tincleton, Dorset, Dio. Salis. 1849. (Patron, H. C. Sturt, Esq; Tithe—App. 87*l* 10*s*, P. C. 120*l*; Glebe, 5 acres; P. C.'s Inc. 130*l*; Pop. 154.) [2]

KNOCKER, Walter G., *Margate.*—C. of St. John's, Margate. [3]

KNOLLYS, Erskine William, *Clapton, N.E.*—Brasen. Coll. Ox. B.A. 1865; Deac. 1866 by Bp of Lon. C. of St. James's, Clapton, 1866. [4]

KNOLLYS William Frederick Erskine, 1, *Marlborough-terrace, Victoria-road Kensington, W.*—Mert. Coll. Ox. Hon. 4th cl. B.A. 1837, M.A. 1840; Deac. 1832 and Pr. 1840 by Bp of Roch. Hon. Chap. to Bp of Lon. and Dom. Chap. to Lord Walsingham. Formerly R. of Quedgeley, near Gloucester, 1842–61; P. C. of Barking-side and Aldborough Hatch, near Ilford, Essex, 1861–63. [5]

KNOTT, John Clark, *Stanford-le Hope Rectory, Romford, Essex.*—Ch. Coll. Cam. B.A. 1843, M.A. 1859; Deac. 1843 and Pr. 1844 by Abp of York. R. of Stanford-le-Hope, Dio. Roch. 1848. (Patron, the present R; Tithe—Imp. 82*l* 3*s*, R. 840*l*; Glebe, 28 acres; R.'s Inc. 904*l* and Ho; Pop. 504.) [6]

KNOTT, John William, *East Ham Vicarage, Essex.*—Magd. Hall, Ox. 2nd cl. Lit. Hum. and B.A. 1844, Brasen. Coll. M.A. 1846. Fell. of Brasen. Coll. Ox. V. of East Ham, Dio. Lon. 1866. (Patron, Brasen. Coll. Ox; V.'s Inc. 1000*l* and Ho; Pop. 1909.) Formerly V. of St. Saviour's, Leeds, 1851–59. [7]

KNOTT, Robert Rowe, 135, *High Holborn, London, W.C.*—St. John's Coll. Cam. B.A. 1819, M.A. 1824. Chap. of the West London Union. Formerly Chap. of the Don. of Tarrant-Crawford, Dorset, 1849. [8]

KNOWLES, Charles, *Winteringham Rectory, near Brigg, Lincolnshire.*—Emman. Coll. Cam. B.A. 1854, M.A. 1857; Deac. 1854 and Pr. 1855 by Bp of Lich. Dixie Fell. of Emman. Coll. R. of Winteringham, Dio. Lin. 1866. (Patron, Emman. Coll. Cam; Tithe, 192*l*; Glebe, 290 acres; R.'s Inc. 843*l* and Ho; Pop. 850.) Formerly C. of St. Luke's, Leek, and Chesterton, Cambridge. [9]

KNOWLES, Edward Hadarezer, *The Abbey Hill, Kenilworth.*—Queen's Coll. Ox. 2nd cl. Lit. Hum. and B.A. 1842, M.A. 1843; Deac. 1849 by Bp of Ox. Pr. 1851 by Bp of Ches. Formerly Michel Fell. of Queen's Coll. Ox; Math. and 2nd Cl. Mast. of St. Bees Sch. 1843. Author, *Notes on the Epistle to the Hebrews*, Rivingtons, 1867, 6*s* 6*d*. [10]

KNOWLES, George Ramsden, *Lincoln.*—Dur. B.A. 1862, Licen. in Theol. 1863; Deac. 1863, Pr. 1865. P. C. of North Carlton, Dio. Lin. 1867. (Patron, Lessee of Preb; P. C.'s Inc. 35*l*; Pop. 163.) Formerly C. of St. Thomas's, Toxteth Park, Liverpool, 1863, St. Martin's, Lincoln, 1864. [11]

KNOWLES, John Dickenson, *Glossop Vicarage, Derbyshire.*—St. Peter's Coll. Cam. B.A. 1851, M.A. 1854; Deac. 1852 and Pr. 1853 by Bp of Ches. V. of Glossop, Dio. Lich. 1865. (Patron, Lord Foley; Tithe, 352*l*; V.'s Inc. 377*l* and Ho; Pop. 3982.) Formerly C. of Halifax; P. C. of Rawdon, Yorks, 1858–65. Author, *Gold and Pearls* and *Effie's Dream Garden*. [12]

KNOWLES, John Lambert, *Bushey, Watford, Herts.*—Pemb. Coll. Ox. B.A. 1846, M.A. 1849; Deac. 1846 and Pr. 1847 by Bp of Lich. P. C. of St. Peter's Chapel of Ease, Bushey Heath, Dio. Roch. 1846. (Patron, R. of Bushey; P. C.'s Inc. 120*l*; Pop. 2000.) Formerly C. of St. Chad's, Lichfield, St. John's, Stratford, Essex, and St. Peter's, Brighton. Author, *False Teaching Prevalent at Our Lord's Second Advent* (a Sermon), 1854. [13]

KNOWLES, Robert James, 8, *Tavistock-terrace, Upper Westbourne Park, London, W.*—St. Cath. Coll. Cam. B.A. 1856, M.A. 1859; Deac. 1856 and Pr. 1857 by Bp of Lon. C. of St. Luke's, Paddington, Lond. [14]

KNOWLING, George, *Vicarage, Wellington, Somerset.*—Pemb. Coll. Ox. B.A. 1849, M.A. 1852; Deac. 1849 and Pr. 1850 by Bp of Ex. V. of Wellington with West Buckland and Trinity Chapel, Dio. B. and W. 1865. (Patroness, Mrs. Pulman; Tithe, 984*l*; Glebe, 4*l*; V.'s Inc. 1108*l* and Ho; Pop. 6907.) Surrogate. Formerly C. of St. Paul's, Devonport, 1849, East Stonehouse 1851; Min. of St. Paul's, East Stonehouse, 1852. [15]

KNOX, Andrew, *The Abbey, Birkenhead.*—Dub. A.B. 1820; Deac. and Pr. 1821. P. C. of Birkenhead, Dio. Ches. (Patrons, Trustees; P. C.'s Inc. 153*l*; Pop. 12,730.) Surrogate. [16]

KNOX, George, *Waddon, Croydon, Surrey.*—Sid. Coll. Cam. Scho. of, B.A. 1837, M.A. 1855; Deac. 1837 by Bp of St. D. Pr. 1838 by Bp of G. and B. Sec. to the Ch. Miss. Soc. for the Metropolitan District, 1864. Formerly Chap. to the Hon. E.I.C. on the Madras Establishment; C. of St. John's, Ousebridge, York; Sen. C. of All Souls', Marylebone, Lond; Sec. to Ch. Miss. Soc. for South-east District 1858. [17]

KNOX, The Very Rev. Henry Barry, *Hadleigh, Suffolk.*—Dub. A.B. 1828, A.M. 1832; Deac. and Pr. 1833. R. of Hadleigh, Dio. Ely, 1841. (Patron, Abp of Cant; Tithe, 1325*l*; R.'s Inc. 1345*l* and Ho; Pop. 3606.) Co-Dean of Bocking 1841. [18]

KNOX, Joseph, *Cliftonville, Brighton.*—Dub. A.M. 1828; Deac. and Pr. 1830. Retired Chap. H. E. I. C. S. Madras Establishment. [19]

KNOX, Robert Augustus, *Shobrooke, Crediton, Devon.*—Dub. A.B. and A.M. 1840; Deac. 1841 and Pr. 1842 by Bp of Ex. R. of Shobrooke, Dio. Ex. 1865. (Patron, Bp of Ex; Pop. 630.) Formerly C. of Sherford 1841, Stokenham 1844, and Shobrooke 1847. [20]

KNOX, Thomas, *Runwell Rectory, Wickford, Essex.*—St. John's Coll. Ox. B.A. 1842, M.A. 1844; Deac. 1842 and Pr. 1843 by Bp of Ox. R. of Runwell, Dio. Roch. 1843. (Patron, the present R; Tithe, 556*l*; Glebe, 23 acres; R.'s Inc. 584*l* and Ho.) R. of Ramsden Crays, Essex, Dio. Roch. 1843. (Patron, the present R; Tithe, 310*l*; Glebe, 90 acres; R.'s Inc. 400*l*; Pop. 262.) Formerly Fell. of St. John's Coll. Ox. [21]

KNYVETT, Charles William, *West Heslerton Rectory, Malton, Yorks.*—Ch. Ch. Ox. B.A. 1818, M.A. 1821; Deac. 1819, Pr. 1820. R. of West Heslerton with East Heslerton, Dio. York, 1847. (Patron, the Crown; R.'s Inc. 465*l* and Ho; Pop. 603.) [22]

KOE, Robert Louis, *Privy Council Office, Whitehall, London, S.W.*—Ch. Coll. Cam. B.A. 1843, M.A. 1846; Deac. 1844, Pr. 1845. One of H M. Inspectors of Schs. [23]

KUPER, Charles Augustus Frederick, *Trelleck Vicarage, Chepstow.*—Mert. Coll. Ox. B.A. 1829, M.A. 1832; Deac. 1830, Pr. 1833. V. of Trelleck with Penalt, Dio. Llan. 1842. (Patron, Prince of Wales; Trelleck, Tithe, 310*l*; Glebe, 12 acres; Penalt, Tithe, 156*l*; Glebe, 28 acres; V.'s Inc. 480*l* and Ho; Pop. Trelleck 991, Penalt 458.) Formerly Chap. to the Garrison, Corfu, 1834–42. [24]

KYNASTON, Herbert, *St. Paul's School, St. Paul's-churchyard, London, E.C.*—Ch. Ch. Ox. Coll. Prize for Latin Hexameters, 1st cl. Lit. Hum. and B.A. 1831, M.A. 1833, B.D. and D.D. 1849; Deac. and Pr. 1834 by Bp of Ox. Head Mast. of St. Paul's Sch. 1838; R. of St. Nicholas-Cole-Abbey with St. Nicholas-Olave R. City and Dio. Lon. 1850. (Patrons, Ld Chan. and D. and C. of St. Paul's alt; Tithe, comm. 130*l*; R.'s Inc. 270*l*; Pop. St. Nicholas-Cole-Abbey 230, St. Nicholas-Olave 355.) Preb. of Holborn in St. Paul's Cathl; Select Preacher of the Univ. of Ox. 1842. Author, *Miscellaneous Poems*, Fellowes, 1840. [25]

KYNASTON, John, *Billingborough Vicarage, near Folkingham.*—Ch. Ch. Ox. B.A. 1826, M.A. 1829; Deac. 1826 and Pr. 1827 by Bp of Lich. V. of Billingborough, Dio. Lin. 1855. (Patron, Earl Fortescue; Glebe, 140 acres; V.'s Inc. 340*l* and Ho; Pop. 1149.) [26]

KYTE, Joseph Wiggins, *Dunham-hill, Frodsham, Cheshire.*—St. Aidan's; Deac. 1865 and Pr. 1867 by Bp of Ches. C. of Thornton-in-the-Moors, Cheshire, 1865. [27]

LA BARTE, William White, *Lavington, Petworth.*—Dub. A.B. 1847, A.M. 1851, *ad eund.* Ox. 1853; Deac. 1847 and Pr. 1848 by Bp of Ches. C. of Lavington with Graffham, Petworth 1866. Formerly Lect. on Theology, St. Aidan's, and C. of Trinity, Birkenhead; C. of Mullabrack, Armagh, St. Thomas's, Ryde, Alverstoke, Hants, Enfield, Middlesex, Chislehurst, Kent, Leaden, Essex, and St. John's, Newbury, Berks; Chap. and Director of St. Margaret's Sisterhood, East Grinstead. [1]

LABATT, E.—Dom. Chap. to the Earl of Enniskillen. [2]

LABORDE, Horatio William, *Island of St. Vincent, West Indies.*—Caius Coll. Cam. B.A. 1845; Deac. 1845, Pr. 1846. British Chap. at St. Vincent. [3]

LACE, John William, *Pill, Bristol.*—Univ. Coll. Ox. B.A. 1855, M.A. 1856; Deac. 1855 by Bp of B. and W. Pr. 1856 by Bp of G. and B. P. C. of Ch. Ch. Pill, Dio. B. and W. 1867. (Patron, V. of Easton-in-Gordano; P. C.'s Inc. 180*l*; Pop. 1800.) Formerly C. of St. Paul's, Cheltenham, 1855, St. Cuthbert's, Wells, 1861. [4]

LACEY, Edward, *Milton, Gravesend.*—St. Bees 1852; Deac. 1854 by Bp of Dur. Pr. 1855 by Bp of Man. Formerly C. of St. Luke's, Berwick-street, Oxford-street, Lond. [5]

LACON, Frederick, *Headless-Cross, Redditch.*—Wor. Coll. Ox. B.A. 1846; Deac. 1846 and Pr. 1847 by Bp of Wor. P. C. of Headless-Cross, Dio. Wor. 1850. (Patrons, R. of Ipsley, V. of Tardebigge and V. of Feckenham alt; P. C.'s Inc. 175*l*; Pop. 1748.) [6]

LACY, Charles, 25, *Finsbury-square, London, E.C.*—Ch. Ch. Ox. 1st cl. Math. et. Phy. B.A. 1816, M.A. 1824, *ad eund.* Cam. 1833; Deac. 1818 and Pr. 1819 by Bp of Ox. R. of Allhallows, London-wall, City and Dio. Lon. 1839. (Patron, Ld Chan; R.'s Inc. 1700*l* and Ho; Pop. 1999.) Formerly P. C. of Tring, Herts, 1819–39, Wigginton, Herts, 1819–39; R. of Altherpe, Linc. 1837–39. [7]

LADBROOKE, John Arthur, *Falmouth.*—Dur. A.B. 1860; Deac. 1860 and Pr. 1861 by Bp of Nor. Chap. to Seamen's Mission, Falmouth, 1863. Formerly C. of Moulton, Norfolk, 1860–63. [8]

LADDS, Thomas, *Leighton-Bromswold, Kimbolton, Hunts.*—Caius Coll. Cam. 24th Wrang. and B.A. 1829, M.A. 1832; Deac. 1830, Pr. 1831. V. of Leighton-Bromswold, Dio. Ely, 1849. (Patron, Bp of Ely; Tithe—Eccles. Commis. and Lessees, 185*l* 3*s* 9*d*, V. 140*l* 9*s* 10*d*; Glebe, 82 acres; V.'s Inc. 195*l*; Pop. 450.) [9]

LAFONT, Ogle Russell, *Hinxworth Rectory, Baldock, Herts.*—St. John's Coll. Ox. B.A. 1849, M.A. 1852; Deac. 1850 and Pr. 1851 by Bp of Roch. R. of Hinxworth, Dio. Roch. 1852. (Patrons, Trustees of Rev. J. Lafont; R.'s Inc. 320*l* and Ho; Pop. 320.) [10]

LAGDEN, Richard Dowse, *Castleton, Sherborne, Dorset.*—Clare Coll. Cam. B.A. 1824; Deac. and Pr. 1837. R. of Stock Gayland, Dio. Salis. 1861. (Patron, Rev. H. F. Yeatman; Tithe, 185*l* 2*s* 9*d*; Glebe, 42¾ acres; R.'s Inc. 221*l*; Pop. 50.) Chap. of Sherborne Union 1856. Formerly P. C. of North Wootton, Dorset, Dio. Salis. 1834. [11]

LAIDMAN, Samuel Lancaster, *Highfield, Pemberton, Wigan.*—Dur. Theol. Licen. 1859; Deac. 1859 and Pr. 1861 by Bp of Rip. C. of Pemberton 1867. Formerly C. of St. Mark's, Longwood, 1859–62, Trinity, Bickerstaffe, 1862–65, Meole Brace, Salop, 1865, and Stretton, Cheshire, 1867. [12]

LAING, Henry, *Brighton.*—Trin. Hall, Cam. LL.B. 1810, LL.D. 1816; Deac. 1811, Pr. 1812. [13]

LAING, J. Fenwick, *Walsall.*—Lich. Theol. Coll; Deac. 1866 by Bp of Win. for Bp of Lich. Pr. 1867 by Bp of Lich. C. of Caldmore District, Walsall, 1866. Formerly Solicitor and Notary Public. [14]

LAING, Malcolm Strickland, *Calcutta.*—St. Bees; Deac. 1853, Pr. 1854. Chap. to the East India Government, Calcutta. Formerly C. of Chettle, Dorset. [15]

LAING, William, *Colchester, Essex.*—St. John's Coll. Cam. Jun. Opt. 2nd cl. Cl. Trip. and B.A. 1835, M.A. 1844; Deac. 1839 and Pr. 1840 by Bp of Ex. R. of St. Martin's, Colchester, Dio. Roch. 1858. (Patronage, *in dispute*; R.'s Inc. 150*l*; Pop. 994.) [16]

LAING, William, *Langley Parsonage, Oldbury, Birmingham.*—Ch. Coll. Cam; Deac. 1844 and Pr. 1845 by Bp of Wor. P. C. of Langley, Dio. Wor. 1846. (Patrons, the Crown and Bp of Wor. alt; P. C.'s Inc. 300*l* and Ho; Pop. 5825.) Author, *An Appeal to Christians on the subject of Horse-racing* (a Pamphlet), 1836, 1*s*. [17]

LAKE, William Charles, *Huntspill Rectory, Bridgwater, Somerset.*—Ball. Coll. Ox. Vinerian Scho. 1st cl. Lit. Hum. and B.A. 1838, Latin Essayist 1840; Deac. 1842, Pr. 1844. R. of Huntspill, Dio. B. and W. 1858. (Patron, Ball. Coll. Ox; Tithe, 691*l* 16*s* 4*d*; Glebe, 49 acres; R.'s Inc. 792*l* and Ho; Pop. 1017.) Preacher at the Chapel Royal, Whitehall; Preb. of Wells. Formerly Tut. of Ball. Coll. Ox. 1842; Public Examiner 1853; Fell. of Ex. Coll. Ox. [18]

LAKES, John, *Guernsey.*—Clare Coll. Cam. B.A. 1823; Deac. 1825 and Pr. 1826 by Bp of Ex. P. C. of St. James's, Guernsey, Dio. Win. 1848. (Patrons, the Congregation; P. C.'s Inc. 300*l*.) [19]

LAKIN, John Marsh, *Gilmorton Rectory, Lutterworth, Leicestershire.*—Wor. Coll. Ox. B.A. 1839, M.A. 1843; Deac. 1840, Pr. 1841. R. of Gilmorton, Dio Pet. 1851. (Patron, the present R; R.'s Inc. 650*l* and Ho; Pop. 853.) Rural Dean. [20]

LAKIN, Storer Marshall, *The Close, Salisbury.*—Sid. Coll. Cam. Sen. Opt. and B.A. 1859, M.A. 1862; Deac. 1851 and Pr. 1852 by Bp of Lon. Min. Can. of Salis. Cathl. 1856. [21]

LALLEMAND, Frederick Aime, 2, *Devonshire-street, Ardwick, Manchester.*—Caius Coll. Cam. B.A. 1858, M.A. 1862; Deac. 1859 and Pr. 1860 by Bp of Ches. C. in sole charge of District of St. Matthew, Hyde-road, Manchester. Formerly C. of St. John's, Buglawton, 1859–64, St. John's, Leicester, 1865. [22]

LAMB, Benjamin, *Boston.*—Emman. Coll. Cam. Sen. Opt. B.A. 1864, M.A. 1867; Deac. 1865 by Bp of Ely for Bp of Lin. Pr. 1866 by Bp of Lin. C. of Boston 1865. [23]

LAMB, Charles Edward, *Sheffield.*—Corpus Coll. Cam. B.A. 1853; Deac. 1853 and Pr. 1854 by Bp of Lin. P. C. of St. Mary's, Sheffield, Dio. York, 1866. (Patron, V. of Sheffield; P. C.'s Inc. 300*l*; Pop. 16,294.) Formerly Mayor's Chap. Boston, Lincolnshire. [24]

LAMB, Edward, *Welbeck Abbey, Worksop, Notts.*—Corpus Coll. Cam. B.A. 1850; Deac. 1851, Pr. 1852. Dom. Chap. to the Duke of Portland. [25]

LAMB, Francis William, *Shrivenham, Berks.*—Pemb. Coll. Cam. B.A. 1855 M.A. 1859; Deac. 1856 and Pr. 1857 by Bp of Wor. C. of Shrivenham 1866. Formerly C. of St. John's, Coventry, 1856–59, Aldridge, Staffs, 1863–66. [26]

LAMB, George Fleming, *Amberley, near Stroud.*—Oriel Coll. Ox. B.A. 1864; Deac. 1865 and Pr. 1866 by Bp of Wor. C. of Amberley 1867. Formerly C. of St. John's, Ladywood, Birmingham, 1865–67. [27]

LAMB, James, *Cumrew, Carlisle.*—C. of Cumrew and Renwick. [28]

LAMB, James Henry, *Manorbier, Tenby.*—Ch. Coll. Cam. B.A. 1855, M.A. 1858; Deac. 1856 and Pr. 1857 by Bp of Ely. V. of Manorbier, Dio. St. D. 1864. (Patron, Ch. Coll. Cam; Tithe, 30*l*; Glebe, 55 acres; V.'s Inc. 200*l* and Ho; Pop. 750.) Formerly Fell. of Ch. Coll. Cam; C. of Hapton, Norfolk. [29]

LAMB, John, *Caius College, Cambridge.*—Caius Coll. Cam. B.A. 1848, M.A. 1851; Deac. 1850 and Pr. 1851 by Bp of Ely. Sen. Fell. of Caius Coll; Hulsean Lect. 1860. Author, Hulsean Lectures, *The Seven Words spoken against the Lord Jesus*, [30]

LAMB, Matthias Mawson, *Swinbrook Parsonage, Burford, Oxon.*—Corpus Coll. Cam. B.A. 1845, M.A. 1848; Deac. 1846 and Pr. 1847 by Bp of G. and B. P. C. of Swinbrook, Dio. Ox. 1867. (Patron, Lord Redesdale; P. C.'s Inc. 100*l* and Ho; Pop. 190.) R. of Widford, Glouc. Dio. Ox. 1867. (Patron, Lord Redesdale; R.'s Inc. 86*l*; Pop. 43.) Formerly C. of Sapperton, Glouc. 1850–65, Moreton-in-the-Marsh 1865–67. [31]

LAMB, Robert, 3, *Shakspeare-street, Ardwick, Manchester.*—St. John's Coll. Ox. 2nd cl. Lit. Hum. and B.A. 1835, M.A. 1840; Deac. 1837 and Pr 1838 by Bp of Ches. R. of St. Paul's, Manchester, Dio. Man. 1849. (Patrons, D. and C. of Man; Endow. 60*l*; R.'s Inc. 300*l*; Pop. 6609.) Surrogate. Formerly C. of Kirkham, Lancashire, 1837–40; Prin. of the Western Gr. Sch. Brompton, Lond. 1840–44; P. C. of St. Mary's, Preston, 1844–49. Author, *Sermons on Passing Seasons and Events,* 7*s*; *Selections from Articles contributed to Fraser's Magazine,* 2 vols. 14*s*; and numerous single Sermons, Tracts and Articles in Reviews and Magazines. [1]

LAMB, Thomas Davis, *West Hackney Rectory, London, N.*—St. Mary Hall, Ox; S.C.L. 1839; Deac. 1839 and Pr. 1842 by Bp of Chich. R. of West Hackney, Dio. Lon. 1846. (Patron, W. A. Tyssen Amhurst, Esq; Tithe, 257*l*; Glebe, 1 acre; R.'s Inc. 776*l* and Ho; Pop. 8060.) Dom. Chap. to the Earl of Mexborough 1855; Preacher at St. George's, Albemarle-street, Lond. Formerly C. of Playden, Essex; R. of Windlesham and Bagshot, Surrey. Author, *Analysis of Pearson on the Creed*; *Sermons on the Eucharist*; various Pamphlets and single Sermons. [2]

LAMB, William Dunn, *Cobridge, Stoke-upon-Trent.*—St. Bees 1839; Deac. and Pr. 1840 by Bp of Rip. P. C. of Ch. Ch. Cobridge, Dio. Lich. 1846. (Patron, R. of Burslem; P. C.'s Inc. 85*l* and Ho; Pop. 8378.) [3]

LAMBARDE, C. J., *Moggerhanger, St. Neots, Beds.*—Emman. Coll. Cam. B.A. 1856; Deac. 1858 and Pr. 1859. P. C. of Moggerhanger, Dio. Ely. (Patron, E. F. Dawkins, Esq; P. C.'s Inc. 100*l*; Pop. 503.) [4]

LAMBART, W. H., *Leamington.*—Min. of Trinity Chapel, Leamington. [5]

LAMBE, George, *St. Austell, Cornwall.*—St. John's Coll. Cam. B.A. 1848, M.A. 1855; Deac. 1851 and Pr. 1852 by Bp of Ex. P. C. of Charlestown, St. Austell, Dio. Ex. 1861. (Patrons, the Crown and Bp of Ex. alt; P. C.'s Inc. 160*l*; Pop. 3367.) Formerly C. of Tor Mohun and Cockington. [6]

LAMBERT, Alfred, *Monk Bretton Parsonage, Barnsley, Yorks.*—Pemb. Coll. Cam. B.A. 1840: Deac. 1840 and Pr. 1841 by Bp of Rip. P. C. of Monk Bretton, Dio. York, 1842. (Patron, V. of Royston; P. C.'s Inc. 143*l* and Ho; Pop. 2489.) [7]

LAMBERT, Anthony Lewis, *Chilbolton Rectory, Stockbridge, Hants.*—Trin. Coll. Ox. B.A. 1825, M.A. 1828; Deac. 1826, Pr. 1827. R. of Chilbolton, Dio. Win 1848. (Patron, Bp of Win; Tithe, 620*l*; Glebe, 10 acres; R.'s Inc. 630*l* and Ho; Pop. 398.) Rural Dean of Chilbolton 1850. [8]

LAMBERT, Brooke, *St. Mark's Parsonage, Whitechapel, E.*—Brasen. Coll. Ox. B.A. 1858, M.A. 1861, B.C.L. 1863; Deac. 1858, Pr. 1859. P. C. of St. Mark's, Whitechapel, Dio. Lon. 1865. (Patron, Bp of Lon; P. C.'s Inc. 300*l* and Ho; Pop. 11,383.) Formerly C. of Ch. Ch. Preston, 1858–60, St. John's, Worcester, 1860–63, Hillingdon 1863–64, St. Mark's, Whitechapel, 1864–65. [9]

LAMBERT, F. F., *Kidderminster.*—C. of St. George's, Kidderminster. [10]

LAMBERT, George, *Osbaldwick, near York.*—St. John's Coll. Cam. B.A. 1847, M.A. 1851; Deac. 1847, Pr. 1848. Formerly C. of Dunnington, and Fulford, Yorks. [11]

LAMBERT, G. H., *Leafield, Witney.*—C. of Leafield, Oxon. [12]

LAMBERT, H., *Graveney Vicarage, Faversham, Kent.*—V. of Goodnestone with Graveney V. Dio. Cant. 1864. (Patrons, Abp of Cant. and J. H. Lade, Esq; V.'s Inc. 500*l* and Ho; Pop. Goodneston 78, Graveney 234.) [13]

LAMBERT, Johnson, *Bowes (Barnard Castle), Yorks.*—Deac. 1820, Pr. 1821. P. C. of Bowes, Dio. Rip. 1828. (Patron, T. Harrison, Esq; Tithe—Imp. 173*l*; Glebe, 28 acres; P. C.'s Inc. 74*l*; Pop. 849.) [14]

LAMBERT, John Jeffery, *Great Coates Rectory, Ulceby, Lincolnshire.*—C. of Great Coates 1864. [15]

LAMBERT, Richard Joseph Farran, *Burrington, Wrington, Somerset.*—St. John's Coll. Ox. B.A. 1864. C. of Burrington. Formerly Asst. C. of Attworth and South Roxall, Freshford, Bath. [16]

LAMBERT, Richard Umfraville, *Wells, Somerset.*—Trin. Coll. Cam. 2nd cl. Cl. Trip. and B.A. 1852, M.A. 1855; Deac. 1853 and Pr. 1854 by Bp of Ox. C. of St. Cuthbert's, Wells. Formerly C. of Devizes, and Holt, Wilts. [17]

LAMBERT, Richard William, *Swell Vicarage, Langport, Somerset.*—Pemb. Coll. Ox. B.A. 1823, M.A. 1826. V. of Fivehead with Swell V. Dio. B. and W. 1840. (Patrons, D. and C. of Bristol; Fivehead, Tithe—App. 251*l* 16*s*, V. 166*l* 9*s* 4*d*; Swell, Tithe, 176*l*; Glebe, 28 acres; V.'s Inc. 357*l* and Ho; Pop. Fivehead 489, Swell 110.) [18]

LAMBERT, William, *Pennington Parsonage, Lymington, Hants.*—Ex. Coll. Ox. B.A. 1836, M.A. 1841; Deac. 1837 and Pr. 1838 by Bp of Nor. P. C. of Pennington, Dio. Win. 1849. (Patron, V. of Milford; P. C.'s Inc. 100*l* and Ho; Pop. 753.) [19]

LAMBERT, William Henry, *Stoke-Edith Rectory, Ledbury, Herefordshire.*—Mert. Coll. Ox. B.A. 1857, M.A. 1859; Deac. 1857 and Pr. 1858 by Bp of Herf. R. of Stoke-Edith with West-Hide P. C. Dio. Herf. 1858. (Patroness, Lady Emily Foley; R.'s Inc. 490*l* and Ho; Pop. Stoke-Edith 332, West-Hide 174.) [20]

LAMBERT, W. H., *Silsoe, Beds.*—C. of Silsoe. [21]

LAMBRICK, Samuel Stratford, *Cholmondeley, Cheshire.*—Formerly C. of Claverley, Salop. [22]

LAMERT, Matthew, *Bedford.*—St. Edm. Hall, Ox. B.A. 1865; Deac. 1865 by Bp of B. and W. Pr. 1866 by Bp of Ely. Asst. Cl. Mast. in Bedford Gr. Sch. [23]

LA MOTHE, Claude Hoskins, *Clyton Villa, Fallowfield, Manchester.*—St. John's Coll. Cam. B.A. 1864, M.A. 1867; Deac. 1864 and Pr. 1867 by Bp of Man. C. of Withington, Manchester. [24]

LA MOTTE, George Crespigny, *Denton Rectory, Canterbury.*—Ball. Coll. Ox. 4th cl. Lit. Hum. B.A. 1834, M.A. 1838; Deac. 1837 by Bp of Rip. Pr. 1838 by Abp of Cant. R. of Denton, Dio. Cant. 1846. (Patron, the present R; Tithe, 211*l*; Glebe, 6 acres; R.'s Inc. 218*l* and Ho; Pop. 183.) P. C. of Swingfield, Dio. Cant. 1862. (Patron, the present P. C; P. C.'s Inc. 60*l*; Pop. 418.) Dom. Chap. to the Earl of Tenterden. Formerly P. C. of Swingfield 1849–59. [25]

LA MOTTE, George Grimshaw, 6, *Montpellier-crescent, Brighton.*—Emman. Coll. Cam. B.A. 1837, M.A. 1841; Deac. 1838, Pr. 1839. Formerly P. C. of Coxley, Wells, Somerset, 1856–63. [26]

LAMPEN, John, *St. John's Rectory, Antony, near Devonport.*—Ex. Coll. Ox. B.A. 1825, M.A. 1830; Deac. 1827 and Pr. 1828 by Bp of Ex. R. of St. John's, Cornwall, Dio. Ex. 1863. (Patron, W. H. Pole Carew, Esq; R.'s Inc. 200*l* and Ho; Pop. 213.) Surrogate. Formerly P. C. of St. John Baptist's, Devonport, 1831. [27]

LAMPEN, Stephen Pering, *The Vicarage, New Wortley, Leeds.*—Rostock, Germany, M.A. and Ph. D. 1867; Ch. Miss. Coll. Islington; Deac. 1851 and Pr. 1852 by Bp of Rip. V. of New Wortley, Dio. Rip. 1865. (Patrons, Crown and Bp of Rip. alt; V.'s Inc. 320*l* and Ho; Pop. 12,000.) Formerly C. of Slaithwaite 1851–56, Huddersfield 1856–57; P. C. of Scammonden 1857–65. Author, *A Word to the Doubter,* 1858, 2*s* per 100. [28]

LAMPET, W. E. L., *East Pennard, Shepton Mallet, Somerset.*—C. of East Pennard with West Bradley. [29]

LANCASTER, George, *Grindleton Parsonage, Clitheroe.*—St. Bees; Deac. 1842 and Pr. 1843 by Bp of Ches. P. C. of Grindleton, Dio. Rip. 1855. (Patron, V. of Mitton; Tithe—Imp. 212*l*; P. C.'s Inc. 95*l* and Ho; Pop. 920.) Formerly C. of Slaidburn, Yorks. [30]

LANCASTER, Richard Thomas, *Brighton.*—Ex. Coll. Ox. 2nd cl. Lit. Hum. and B.A. 1819, M.A. 1821; Deac. and Pr. 1826. Author, *Six Forms of Prayer to the Book of Family Prayer,* 1844. [31]

LANCE, John Edwin, *Buckland St. Mary, Chard, Somerset.*—Deac. 1817, Pr. 1819. R. of Buckland

St. Mary, Dio. B. and W. 1832. (Patrons, Trustees of the late Lieut.-General Popham; Tithe, 350*l*; Glebe, 37½ acres; R.'s Inc. 388*l*; Pop. 715.) Preb. of Wells 1841; Rural Dean. [1]

LANCE, William Henry, *Thurlbear, Taunton, Somerset.*—King's Coll. Lond. Theol. Assoc. 1858; Deac. 1858 by Bp of B. and W. C. of Thurlbear with Stoke St. Mary 1859. Formerly C. of Bishops Lydiard, Somerset, 1858–59. [2]

LANCHESTER, Charles Preston, *Blofield, Norwich.*—Clare Coll. Cam. B.A. 1857, M.A. 1863; Deac. 1858 by Bp of Nor. Asst. C. of Blofield. Formerly Head Mast. of the Lower Sch. Rossall. [3]

LANDER, John, *Donnington Rectory, Ledbury, Herefordshire.*—Pemb. Coll. Ox. B.A. 1839, M.A. 1842; Deac. 1843 and Pr. 1844 by Bp of G. and B. R. of Donnington, Dio. Herf. 1845. (Patron, Rev. R. Webb; Tithe, 200*l*; Glebe, 27½ acres; R.'s Inc. 240*l* and Ho; Pop. 105.) [4]

LANDER, Thomas, *Hertingfordbury, Herts.*—Corpus Coll. Cam. B.A. 1855, M.A. 1864; Deac. 1856 and Pr. 1857 by Abp of Cant. Chap. of Hertford Workhouse. Formerly C. of Westerham, Kent. [5]

LANDON, Charles Whittington, *Ashford Rectory, Barnstaple, Devon.*—King's Coll. Lond. Theol. Assoc. 1854; Deac. 1854 and Pr. 1855 by Bp of B. and W. R. of Ashford, Dio. Ex. 1861. (Patron, Ld Chan; Tithe, 85*l*; Glebe, 8 acres; R.'s Inc. 110*l*; Pop. 157.) [6]

LANDON, George, *Richard's Castle Rectory, Ludlow, Salop.*—Wor. Coll. Ox. B.C.L; Deac. 1828 and Pr. 1829 by Bp of Ex. R. of Richard's Castle, Dio. Herf. 1837. (Patron, Bp of Wor; R.'s Inc. 800*l* and Ho; Pop. 710) [7]

LANDON, James Timothy Bainbridge, *Ledsham Vicarage, South Milford, Yorks.*—Magd. Coll. Ox. 1st cl. Lit. Hum. and B.A. 1840, M.A. 1842; Deac. 1842, Pr. 1843. V. of Ledsham, Dio. York, 1855. (Patron, Rev. C. Wheler; Tithe—App. 301*l* 10*s*, Imp. 3*l*, V. 366*l* 0*s* 6*d*; Glebe, 52 acres; V.'s Inc. 400*l* and Ho; Pop. 1146.) Formerly Fell. of Magd. Coll. and Public Exam. in Lit. Hum. Oxford. [8]

LANDON, John W. R., *Braunton Vicarage, Barnstaple, Devon.*—Wor. Coll. Ox. M.A. 1823; Deac. 1824, Pr. 1825. V. of Braunton, Dio. Ex. 1826. (Patron, Bp of Ex; Tithe, 536*l*; Glebe, 38 acres; V.'s Inc. 570*l* and Ho; Pop. 2168.) V. of Bishopston, Wilts, Dio. G. and B. 1826. (Patron, Bp of G. and B; V.'s Inc. 240*l* and Ho; Pop. 716.) [9]

LANDON, Whittington Henry, *Slebech, Haverfordwest.*—P. C. of Slebech with Mynwere P. C. and Newton P. C. Dio. St. D. 1851. (Patron, Baron de Rutzen; P. C.'s Inc. 320*l*; Pop. 435.) [10]

LANDOR, Charles Wilson, *Lindridge Vicarage, Tenbury, Worcestershire.*—Wor. Coll. Ox. B.A. 1835, M.A. 1837; Deac. 1835 by Bp of Lich. Pr. 1836 by Bp of Wor. V. of Lindridge, Dio. Herf. 1847. (Patrons, D. and C. of Wor; Tithe—App. 479*l*, V. 565*l*; Glebe, 103 acres; V.'s Inc. 565 and Ho; Pop. 687.) Formerly Rural Dean and R of Over Whitacre, Wichenford. [11]

LANDOR, Robert Eyres, *Birlingham Rectory, Pershore, Worcestershire.*—Wor. Coll. Ox. B.A. 1801, M.A. 1804; Deac. 1804, Pr. 1805. R. of Birlingham, Dio. Wor. 1829. (Patron, the present R; Tithe—App. 14*l* 19*s* 6*d*; Glebe, 84 acres; R.'s Inc. 240*l* and Ho; Pop. 353.) Formerly Chap. in Ordinary to the Prince Regent. Author, *Four Tragedies*; *The Impious Feast*; *The Fawn of Sertorius*; *The Fountain of Arethusa.* [12]

LANE, Alfred William, *Greenford, Southall, Middlesex.*—Caius Coll. Cam. Wrang. B.A. 1836, M.A. 1842; Deac. 1845, Pr. 1846. C. of Greenford. [13]

LANE, Ambrose, *Pendleton, Manchester.*—Dub. A.B. 1823; Deac. 1824, Pr. 1825. P. C. of Pendleton, Eccles, Dio. Man. 1834. (Patron, V. of Eccles; P. C.'s Inc. 200*l*.) [14]

LANE, Charles, *Wrotham, Sevenoaks, Kent.*—Queen's Coll. Ox. 3rd cl. Lit. Hum. and B.A. 1814, M.A. 1817; Deac. 1816, Pr. 1817. R. of Wrotham, Dio. Cant. 1845. (Patron, Abp of Cant; Glebe, 20 acres; R.'s Inc. 1025*l* and Ho; Pop. 1119.) Rural Dean of Shoreham 1845. [15]

LANE, Charlton, *Hampstead, N.W.*—Jesus Coll. Cam. B.A. 1819, M.A. 1823; Deac. 1820, Pr. 1821. P. C. of Hampstead, Dio. Lon. 1864. (Patron, Sir T. Maryon Wilson; P. C.'s Inc. 760*l* and Ho; Pop. 3271.) Prof. of Rhetoric in Gresham Coll. Lond. Formerly P. C. of St. Mark's, Kennington, 1832–64. [16]

LANE, Charlton George, *Little Gaddesden, Great Berkhamsted.*—Ch. Ch. Ox. B.A. 1860, M.A. 1867; Deac. 1862 and Pr. 1864 by Bp of Wor. C. of Little Gaddesden 1866; Chap. and Librarian to Earl Brownlow. Formerly C. of Great Witley, Worcester. [17]

LANE, Edmund, 2, *Henrietta-street, Bath.*—Magd. Hall, Ox. 3rd cl. Lit. Hum. and B.A. 1839, M.A. and D.C.L. 1851; Deac. 1840 and Pr. 1841 by Bp of Rip. C. of Bathampton; Dom. Chap. to the Earl of Airlie; Asst. Mast. of Somersetshire Coll. Bath. Formerly Cl. Mast. of the Civil and Military Dept. Proprietary Coll. Bath, R. of St. Mary's, Manchester, 1844–58. [18]

LANE, Edward Aldous, *St. Paul's Parsonage, Hull.*—St. John's Coll. Cam. 25th Wrang. B.A 1858, M.A. 1860; Deac. 1860 and Pr. 1861 by Bp of G. and B. P. C. of St. Paul's, Hull, Dio. York, 1866. (Patrons, Crown and Abp of York alt; P. C.'s Inc. 410*l* and Ho; Pop. 15,000.) Surrogate. Formerly C. of Strood 1860–62; V. of Marske-in-Cleveland 1862–66. [19]

LANE, Ernald, *All Souls College, Oxford.*—All Souls Coll. Ox. Fell. of B.A. 1860, M.A. 1862; Deac. 1862 and Pr. 1863 by Bp of Ox. Fell. of All Souls Coll. [20]

LANE, Francis Charles de Lona, *Whissonsett Rectory, Swaffham, Norfolk.*—M.A. 1863 by Abp of Cant; Deac. 1857 and Pr. 1858 by Abp of Cant. Dom. Chap. to the Duke of Leeds; R. of Whissonsett with Horningtoft, Dio. Nor. 1865. (Patron, Capt. Douglas Lane; Tithe, 660*l*; Glebe, 93 acres; R.'s Inc. 750*l* and Ho; Pop. 940.) Formerly C. of Wrotham, Kent, 1857–65. [21]

LANE, G. P., *Loughborough.*—C. of Loughborough. [22]

LANE, John Reynolds, *Aynhoe, Banbury.*—Trin. Coll. Ox. M.A. 1862; Deac. 1861 and Pr. 1862 by Bp of Ox. C. of Aynhoe 1863. Formerly C. of Great Haseley, Tetsworth, 1861–62. [23]

LANE, Joseph, *Attleburgh, Norfolk.* [24]

LANE, Richard, *Brixton Lodge, Plympton, Devon.*—Queen's Coll. Ox. B.A. 1835; Deac. 1837, Pr. 1839. P. C. of Wembury, Devon, Dio. Ex. 1848. (Patrons, D. and C. of Windsor; Tithe—App. 380*l*; P. C.'s Inc. 85*l*; Pop. 561.) [25]

LANE, Samuel, *Frome Vauchurch, Dorchester.*—Ex. Coll. Ox. B.A. 1825, M.A. 1828; Deac. 1825, Pr. 1826. R. of Frome Vauchurch with Batcombe R. Dio. Salis. 1828. (Patrons, Duke of Cleveland and Dowager Countess of Sandwich; Frome Vauchurch, Tithe, 170*l*; Glebe, 45 acres; Batcombe, Tithe, 122*l*; Glebe, 34 acres; R.'s Inc. 432*l* and Ho; Pop. Frome Vauchurch 171, Batcombe 184.) Formerly C. of Chilfrome, Dorset; Rural Dean 1836. [26]

LANE, Thomas Leveson, *Wasperton Vicarage, near Warwick.*—St. John's Coll. Cam. B.A. 1823, M.A. 1830; Deac. 1827 by Bp of Herf. Pr. 1828 by Bp of Lich. V. of Wasperton, Dio. Wor. 1834. (Patron, R. of Hampton-Lucy; Tithe—App. 290*l*, V. 108*l*; Glebe, 44¼ acres; V.'s Inc. 232*l* and Ho; Pop. 269.) V. of Baswich, or Berkswich, Staffs. Dio. Lich. 1836. (Patrons, J. N. Lane, Esq. and Rev. C. Inge; Tithe—App. 295*l*, Imp. 15*l*, V. 164*l*; V.'s Inc. 237*l* and Ho; Pop. 938.) Rural Dean. [27]

LANE, William Meredith, *The Vicarage, Normanton.*—Trin. Coll. Cam. 22nd Wrang. B.A. 1861, M.A. 1864; Deac. 1863 and Pr. 1864 by Bp of G. and B. V. of Normanton, Dio. York, 1866. (Patron, Trin. Coll. Ox; Tithe, 139*l* 6*s*; Glebe, 76 acres; V.'s Inc. 250*l* and Ho; Pop. 3973.) Formerly Vice-Prin. of the Royal Agricultural Coll. Cirencester 1863–65; C. of Cirencester 1863–65, West Ham, Essex, 1865–66. [28]

LANFEAR, Walter Francis, *St. John's Parsonage, Southall Green, Middlesex.*—Queens' Coll. Cam. B.A. 1845; Deac. and Pr. 1846. P. C. of St. John's,

Southall Green, Dio. Lon. 1850. (Patrons, Five Trustees; P. C.'s Inc. 200*l* and Ho; Pop. 474.) Chap. of St. Marylebone Schools, Southall. [1]

LANFEAR, William Francis, *Christ Church Parsonage, Weston-super-Mare.*—Queens' Coll. Cam. B.A. 1838; Deac. and Pr. 1838 by Bp of B. and W. P. C. of Ch. Ch. Weston-super-Mare, Dio. B. and W. 1855. (Patrons, Trustees; P. C.'s Inc. 207*l* and Ho; Pop. 1597.) Formerly Chap. to the English Congregation at Wiesbaden, Germany, 1842–47. [2]

LANG, Dashwood, *West Leigh Vicarage, Bideford, Devon.*—St. Alban Hall, Ox. B.A. 1829; Deac. 1830 and Pr. 1831 by Bp of Ex. V. of West Leigh, Dio. Ex. (Patrons, D. and C. of Ex; Tithe—App. 198*l* 10*s*. V. 169*l* 12*s*; Glebe, 45 acres; V.'s Inc. 239*l* and Ho; Pop. 491.) Rural Dean of Barnstaple 1838. [3]

LANG, Ernest Augustus, *Manchester.*—St. John's Coll. Ox. B.A. 1849. R. of St. Mary's, Manchester, Dio. Man. 1857. (Patrons, D. and C. of Man; R.'s Inc. 200*l*; Pop. 3507.) Formerly C. of St. James's, Birch, Manchester. [4]

LANG, James Henry, *Old Charlton, Kent.*—Magd. Coll. Cam. 16th Sen. Opt. and B.A. 1843, M.A. 1849; Deac. 1843 and Pr. 1844 by Bp of Roch. Additional Chap. H.M.S. "Fisgard" 1866; Chap. to Woolwich Division of Royal Marine Light Infantry. Formerly C. of Charlton; Chap. and Naval Instructor of H.M.SS. "Grampus," "Arrogant," "Juno," "Dido," "Liffey," and "Wellesley." [5]

LANG, James Thomason, *Wisbeck.*—Caius Coll. Cam. 12th Wrang. and B.A. 1866, 1st. cl. Theo. Trip. 1867; Deac. 1867 by Bp of Ely. C. of Wisbech St. Peter's 1867. [6]

LANG, Owen Charles Seymour, *Bradfield Combust Rectory, Bury St. Edmunds.*—Trin. Coll. Cam. B.A. 1856, M.A. 1859; Deac. 1856 and Pr. 1857 by Bp of Win. R. of Bradfield Combust, Dio. Ely, 1865. (Patron, the present R; Tithe, 224*l*; R.'s Inc. 231*l* and Ho; Pop. 173.) Formerly R. of Pwllcrochon, near Pembroke, 1857–65. [7]

LANG, Robert, *Petworth, Sussex.*—Trin. Coll. Cam. B.A. 1862, M.A. 1866; Deac. 1863 and Pr. 1864 by Bp of Carl. C. of Petworth 1865. Formerly C. of Kendal 1863–65. [8]

LANG, William Francis Dashwood.—Wad. Coll. Ox. B.A. 1866; Deac. 1866 by Bp Anderson for Bp of Lon. C. of St. George's, Campden Hill, Kensington, 1866. [9]

LANGDALE, Edward, *East Hoathley Rectory, Hurst Green, Sussex.*—Jesus Coll. Cam. B.A. 1824; Deac. 1825 and Pr. 1826 by Bp of Chich. R. of East Hoathley, Dio. Chich. 1828. (Patron, Earl of Abergavenny; R.'s Inc. 270*l* and Ho; Pop. 615.) [10]

LANGDALE, George Augustus, *Compton, Petersfield.*—St. John's Coll. Cam. B.A. 1840, M.A. 1843; Deac. 1840 and Pr. 1841 by Bp of Lin. V. of Compton with Up. Marden, Dio. Chich. 1854. (Patron, the present V; Tithe, Compton, 131*l*, Up. Marden, 348*l*; Glebe, 38 acres; V.'s Inc. 517*l* and Ho; Pop. Compton 266, Up. Marden 297.) [11]

LANGDALE William John, 2, *Ormond-terrace, Regent's-park, London, N.W.* [12]

LANGDON, Alfred, *Sedgfield, Durham.*—C. of Sedgfield. [13]

LANGDON, Charles, *Queen-Camel Vicarage, Ilchester, Somerset.*—Queens' Coll. Cam. B.A. 1829. V. of Queen-Camel, Dio. B. and W. 1832. (Patron, P. St. John Mildmay, Esq; Tithe—Imp. 864*l* and 72¾ acres of Glebe, V. 190*l*; Glebe, 41½ acres; V.'s Inc. 242*l* and Ho; Pop. 734.) [14]

LANGDON, George Leopold, *Paul's Cray Rectory, Kent.*—R. of Paul's Cray, Dio. Cant. 1858. (Patron, Viscount Sidney; R.'s Inc. 500*l* and Ho; Pop. 532.) Dom. Chap. to Viscount Sidney; Patron of Glanville Wootton R. Dorset. Formerly C. of Paul's Cray. [15]

LANGDON, John, *Grammar Schoolhouse, Yeovil.*—St. John's Coll. Cam. B.A. 1833, M.A. 1856. V. of Mudford, Yeovil, Dio. B. and W. 1853. (Patrons, D. and C. of Wells; Tithe—App. 25*l*, Imp. 330*l* 1*s* 6*d* and 40¾ acres of Glebe, V. 230*l* 12*s* 6*d*; Glebe, ¾ acre; V.'s Inc. 232*l*; Pop. 421.) Head Mast. of Yeovil Gr. Sch; Chap. of the Yeovil Union; Surrogate. [16]

LANGDON, Thomas William Spicer, *Lopen, Ilminster.*—Pemb. Coll. Ox. B.A. 1845; Deac. 1845 by Bp of Ches. Pr. 1846 by Bp of Man. P. C. of Lopen, Dio. B. and W. 1859. (Patron, Earl Poulett; Tithe, Imp. 200*l*; P. C.'s Inc. 77*l*; Pop. 419.) Formerly C. of South Perrott with Mosterton, Dorset. [17]

LANGFORD, Edward Henry, *Marksbury, Bristol.*—Sid. Coll. Cam. B.A. 1834; Deac. 1835, Pr. 1836. R. of Marksbury, Dio. B. and W. 1843. (Patron, F. L. Popham, Esq; Tithe, 247*l* 10*s*; Glebe, 17 acres; R.'s Inc. 265*l* and Ho; Pop. 307.) P. C. of Brislington, Bristol, Dio. B. and W. 1843. (Patron, F. L. Popham, Esq; Tithe, 170*l*; P. C.'s Inc. 200*l*; Pop. 1489.) [18]

LANGFORD, John Frere, *Cranfield, near Newport Pagnell.*—Ball. Coll. Ox. B.A. 1864; Deac. 1865 by Bp of Ox. Pr. 1866 by Bp of Ely. C. of Cranfield 1866. Formerly C. of Newport Pagnell 1865–66. [19]

LANGFORD, John Thomas.—C. of Trinity, Brompton, Lond. [20]

LANGHORNE, Frederick, *Preston, Lancashire.*—P. C. of Trinity, Preston, Dio. Man. 1852. (Patrons, V. of Preston and Trustees alt; P. C.'s Inc. 150*l*; Pop. 4287.) [21]

LANGHORNE, John, *Tunbridge, Kent.*—Ch. Coll. Cam. Scho. 1st cl. Cl. Trip. B.A. 1859, M.A. 1862; Deac. 1862 and Pr. 1864 by Abp of Cant. C. of Hildenborough 1862, and Asst. Cl. Mast. in Tunbridge Sch. Formerly 2nd Mast. of Wakefield Gr. Sch. [22]

LANGHORNE, William Henry, 4, *Lyall-place, Eaton-square, London, S.W.*—Queens' Coll. Cam. B.A. 1854, M.A. 1858; Deac. 1854 by Bp of Dur. Pr. 1855 by Bp of Man. C. of St. Paul's, Knightsbridge, 1862. Formerly C. of Alnwick 1854–57, All Saints, Knightsbridge, 1858–61. Author, *The Consecration of Churches and Cemeteries* (a Sermon). [23]

LANGHORNE, William Henry, *Shorewell Villa, De Beauvoir-road, London, N.*—King's Coll. Lond. Assoc. 1865; Deac. 1865, Pr. 1866. C. of St. Peter's, De Beauvoir-square, 1865. [24]

LANGLEY, Daniel Baxter, *The Rectory, Yardley-Hastings, Northampton.*—St. John's Coll. Cam. 1st cl. in Law, S.C.L. 1828, LL.D. 1841; Deac. 1828 and Pr. 1829 by Bp of Pet. R. of Yardley-Hastings with Denton R. Dio. Pet. 1856. (Patron, Marquis of Northampton; Glebe, Yardley-Hastings, 300 acres; Denton, 144 acres; R.'s Inc. 600*l* and Ho; Pop. Yardley-Hastings 1152, Denton 578.) J.P. for Bucks; as Rector, Lord of the Manor of a portion of Yardley-Hastings. Formerly C. of Pilton, Northants, 1828–34; V. of Olney, Bucks, 1834–56. Author, *Olney Lectures*; *Naaman the Syrian*; *Christian Laconics*; *Morning and Evening Prayers for Private Use*; various Tracts, Sermons, etc. [25]

LANGLEY, John, *Southampton.*—Magd. Hall, Ox. B.A. 1823, M.A. 1827; Deac. 1823, Pr. 1824. Min. of St. Peter's, Southampton, Dio. Win. 1846. (Patron, R. of All Saints; Min.'s Inc. 200*l*; Pop. 1550.) [26]

LANGLEY, John, *Wallingford Rectory, Berks.*—R. of Wallingford St. Leonard's with Sotwell C. Dio. Ox. 1829. (Patron, Bp of Ox; St. Leonard's, Tithe—App. 43*l*, R. 44*l* 3*s*; Sotwell, Tithe—Imp. 153*l* 9*s* 7*d*, R. 120*l* 1*s*; R.'s Inc. 175*l* and Ho; Pop. St. Leonard's 1030, Sotwell 149.) R. of St. Mary's, Wallingford, Dio. Ox. 1829. (Patron, Bp of Ox; R.'s Inc. 150*l*; Pop. 1198.) Surrogate. [27]

LANGLEY, John Piercy, *Olney Vicarage, Bucks.*—St. John's Coll. Cam. 2nd cl. Cl. Trip. Jun. Opt. B.A. 1852, M.A. 1855; Deac. 1852 and Pr. 1853 by Bp of Ox. V. of Olney, Dio. Ox. 1856. (Patron, Earl of Dartmouth; Glebe, 9 acres; V.'s Inc. 160*l* and Ho; Pop. 2357.) Formerly C. of Olney 1852–56. [28]

LANGLEY, Thomas, *Ganerew House, Ross, Herefordshire.*—St. John's Coll. Cam. B.A. 1832; Deac. 1833 and Pr. 1834 by Bp of Roch. R. of Ganerew, Dio.

Herf. 1853. (Patroness, Mrs. Marriott; Tithe—App. 7*l* 10*s*, R. 100*l*; Glebe, 14 acres; R.'s Inc. 120*l*; Pop. 116.) Author, miscellaneous Sermons and Tracts. [1]

LANGLEY, William, *Wymondham, Oakham.*—Dur. B.A. 1856, M.A. 1861; Deac. 1857 and Pr. 1859 by Bp of Man. C. of Wymondham, Leicestershire, 1863. Formerly C. of St. Luke's, Heywood, Lancashire, 1857–60, Linton, Herefordshire, 1860–63. [2]

LANGMEAD, George Winne, *Royal Military Asylum, Chelsea, S.W.*—Ex. Coll. Ox. B.A. 1834, M.A. 1847; Deac. 1835 and Pr. 1836 by Bp of Ex. Chap. to the Forces; Chap. to the Royal Military Asylum, Chelsea, 1860. Formerly C. of Sampford Spiney, Devon, 1835, St. Saviour's, Dartmouth, 1837; Chap. to the Plymouth Garrison 1841; Chap. to the Camp at Chobham 1853. [3]

LANGSHAW, Thomas Wall, *West Grinstead, near Horsham, Sussex.*—St. John's Coll. Cam. B.A. 1829; Deac. 1830, Pr. 1831. R. of West Grinstead, Dio. Chich. 1849. (Patron, Lord Leconfield; Tithe, 1128*l* 8*s* 6*d*; Glebe, 100 acres; R.'s Inc. 1270*l* and Ho; Pop. 1403.) [4]

LANGSTAFF, George William, *Whatton, Notts.*—Magd. Hall, Ox. B.A. 1859; Deac. 1852 by Bp of S. and M. Pr. 1859 by Abp of York. V. of Whatton, Dio. Lin. 1864. (Patron, T. D. Hall, Esq; V.'s Inc. 205*l* and Ho; Pop. 763.) Formerly C. of Filey, Yorks. [5]

LANGSTON, Earle Augustus, 38, *Langham-street, Portland-place, London, W.*—Brasen. Coll. Ox. B.A. 1865; Deac. 1866 and Pr. 1867 by Bp of Lon. C. of St. Luke's, Berwick-street, Soho, 1866. [6]

LANGSTON, Stephen Hurt, *Southborough Parsonage, Tunbridge Wells.*—Wad. Coll. Ox. 2nd cl. Cl. and B.A. 1814, M.A. 1820; Deac. 1815 by Bp of G. and B. Pr. 1816 by Bp of Nor. P. C. of Southborough, Dio. Cant. 1847. (Patrons, five Trustees; P. C.'s Inc. 150*l* and Ho; Pop. 2038.) [7]

LANGTON Arthur, *Plumstead, Aylsham, Norfolk.* Wad. Coll. Ox. B.A. 1823, M.A. 1837; Deac. 1823, Pr. 1824. R. of Matlaske, Norfolk, Dio. Nor. 1837. (Patron, Duchy of Lancaster; Tithe, 132*l* 15*s*; Glebe, 50 acres; R.'s Inc. 183*l*; Pop. 163.) R. of Plumstead, Norfolk, Dio. Nor. 1837. (Patron, Duchy of Lancaster; Tithe, 187*l* 12*s*; Glebe, 11 acres; R.'s Inc. 192*l*; Pop. 342.) [8]

LANGTON, Augustus Wenman, *Fransham Rectory, East Dereham, Norfolk.*—Caius Coll. Cam. B.A. 1827, M.A. 1831; Deac. 1829, Pr. 1830. R. of Little Fransham, Dio. Nor. 1840. (Patron, the present R; Tithe, 314*l*; Glebe, 37 acres; R.'s Inc. 358*l* and Ho; Pop. 256.) V. of Kempston, Norfolk, Dio. Nor. 1842. (Patron, Earl of Leicester; Tithe—Imp. 170*l*, V. 106*l* 5*s*; Glebe, 30 acres; V.'s Inc. 151*l*; Pop. 48.) [9]

LANGTON, Thomas Hamilton, *Kirmond, Market Rasen, Lincolnshire.*—Magd. Coll. Cam. B.A. 1830; Deac. 1831, Pr. 1833. V. of Kirmond, Dio. Lin. 1833. (Patron, C. Turnor, Esq; Tithe—Imp. 140*l*, V. 120*l*; V.'s Inc. 146*l*; Pop. 73.) Formerly C. of Langton by Spilsby. [10]

LANGWORTHY, John, *Backwell, Bristol.*—Magd. Hall, Ox. B.A. 1842, M.A. 1846; Deac. 1842, Pr. 1843. V. of Backwell, Dio. B. and W. 1843. (Patroness, Mrs. Uniacke; Tithe—Sinecure R. 167*l* 7*s* 1½*d*, Imp. 19*l* 16*s* 6*d*, V. 167*l* 7*s* 1½*d*; V.'s Inc. 175*l*; Pop. 926.) [11]

LANGWORTHY, W. H.—C. of St. Saviour's, Chelsea. [12]

LANPHIER, Joseph, *Nottingham.*—Dub. A.B. 1852; Deac. 1852, Pr. 1853. C. of St. Paul's, Nottingham. Formerly C. of Kilcoe and Missionary to Roman Catholics on Cape Clear, co. Cork, Ireland, 1852–57; C. of Kirklington 1857. [13]

LANPHIER, William Henry, *Long Compton, Shipston-on-Stour.*—Cuddesdon 1856; Deac 1856 and Pr. 1858 by Bp of Ox. V. of Long Compton, Dio. Wor. 1861. (Patron, Eton Coll; Tithe, 20*l*; Glebe, 125 acres; V.'s Inc. 190*l* and Ho; Pop. 703.) Formerly Asst. C. of Clewer. [14]

LARGE, William John Agg, *Balham Hill, Streatham, Surrey, S.*—Caius Coll. Cam. C. of Balham Hill. Formerly C. of Marston-Sicca, Glouc. [15]

LARKEN, Edmund Roberts, *Burton-by-Lincoln, Lincolnshire.*—Trin. Coll. Ox. B.A. 1833, M.A. 1836; Deac. 1833, Pr. 1834. R. of Burton-by-Lincoln, Dio. Lin. 1843. (Patron, Lord Monson; Tithe, 510*l*; Glebe, 12 acres; R.'s Inc. 543*l* and Ho; Pop. 171.) Dom. Chap. to Lord Monson 1842. [16]

LARKEN, William Pechin, *Ufford, Woodbridge, Suffolk.*—Jesus Coll. Cam. B.A. 1826, M.A. 1830; Deac. 1826, Pr. 1827. R. of Ufford, Dio. Nor. 1836. (Patron, F. C. Brooke, Esq; Tithe, 331*l*; Glebe, 35 acres; R.'s Inc. 376*l* and Ho; Pop. 656.) Rural Dean. [17]

LARKING, Lambert Blackwell, *Ryarsh Vicarage, Maidstone.*—Brasen. Coll. Ox. 2nd cl. Lit. Hum. and B.A. 1820, M.A. 1823; Deac. 1820 and Pr. 1821 by Bp of Lon. V. of Ryarsh, Dio. Cant. 1830. (Patron, Hon. J. W. Stratford; Tithe—Imp. 253*l* 17*s*, V. 399*l* 1*s* 9*d*; Glebe, 12 acres; V.'s Inc. 400*l* and Ho; Pop. 447.) V. of Burham, near Aylesford, Dio. Roch. 1837. (Patron, C. Milner, Esq; Tithe—Imp. 385*l* 5*s* 4*d*, V. 183*l* 17*s* 10*d*; Glebe, 35 acres; V.'s Inc. 220*l*; Pop. 775.) Chap. to Viscountess Falmouth. Editor of *The Hospitallers in England.* [18]

LARPENT, George Porter de Hochepied, *Thorpe Morieux, Bildeston, Suffolk.*—Emman. Coll. Cam. B.A. 1859, M.A. 1862; Deac. 1862 by Bp of Ely, Pr. 1863 by Bp of Win. C. of Thorpe Morieux 1862. [19]

LASCELLES, Edwin, *Newton St. Loe, Bristol.*—Pemb. Coll. Ox. B.A. 1860; Deac. 1861 and Pr. 1862 by Bp of G. and B. C. of Newton St. Loe 1863. Formerly C. of Dumbleton 1861. [20]

LASCELLES, The Hon. James Walter, *Goldsborough Rectory, Knaresborough.*—Ex. Coll. Ox. B.A. 1852; Deac. 1855 by Bp of G. and B. Pr. 1857 by Bp of Rip. R. of Goldsborough, Dio. Rip. 1857. (Patron, Earl of Harewood; Tithe, 291*l*; R.'s Inc. 500*l* and Ho; Pop. 451.) Formerly C. of Cirencester. [21]

LASCELLES, Rowley, *Elson Parsonage, near Gosport.*—Ex. Coll. Ox. B.A. 1862; Deac. 1862 and Pr. 1863 by Bp of St. D. P. C. of St. Thomas's, Elson, Dio. Win. 1865. (Patron, R. of Alverstoke; P. C.'s Inc. 150*l* and Ho; Pop. 1530.) Formerly C. of St. Mary's, Brecknock. [22]

LATHAM, Frederick, *Helpringham Vicarage, Sleaford, Lincolnshire.*—Clare Hall, Cam. B.C.L. 1837; Deac. 1837 and Pr. 1838 by Bp of Lin. V. of Helpringham, Dio. Lin. 1855. (Patron, the present V; Glebe, 85 acres; V.'s Inc. 180*l* and Ho; Pop. 912.) [23]

LATHAM, Henry, *Trinity Hall, Cambridge.*—Trin. Coll. Cam. B.A. 1845, Trin. Hall, Cam. M.A. 1848; Deac. 1848 and Pr. 1850 by Bp of Ely. Vice-Mast. Fell. and Tut. of Trin. Hall, Cam. Author, *Geometrical Problems on the Properties of the Conic Sections,* 1848, 3*s* 6*d*. [24]

LATHAM, John, *Little Eaton Parsonage, Derby.*—Queens' Coll. Cam. B.D. 1847; Deac. 1825, Pr. 1826. P. C. of Little Eaton, Dio. Lich. 1848. (Patron, V. of St. Alkmund's, Derby; P. C.'s Inc. 300*l* and Ho; Pop. 775.) Can. Res. of Lich. 1864; Chap. of the Female Training Coll. Derby. Author, *The Idolatry of the Church of Rome* (a Sermon); *A Visitation Sermon.* [25]

LATHAM, John Larking, *Lydden Vicarage, Dover.*—Wor. Coll. Ox. B.A. 1850, M.A. 1853; Deac. 1852 and Pr. 1853 by Abp of Cant. V. of Lydden, Dio. Cant. 1865. (Patron, Abp of Cant; Tithe, 130*l*; Glebe, 1½ acres; V.'s Inc. 130*l* and Ho; Pop. 198.) Formerly C. of Alkham, near Dover, 1852, East Malling, Maidstone, 1857. [26]

LATHAM, Lawrence, *Quenington Rectory, Fairford, Glouc.*—Pemb. Coll. Ox. B.A. 1821; Deac. 1822, Pr. 1823. P. C. of Ampney St. Mary, Glouc. Dio. G. and B. 1833. (Patron, M. H. Beach, Esq; P. C.'s Inc. 72*l*; Pop. 125.) R. of Quenington, Dio. G. and B. 1834. (Patron, M. H. Beach, Esq; R.'s Inc. 180*l* and Ho; Pop. 426.) [27]

LATHAM, Mortimer Thomas, *Tattershall, Boston.*—Brasen. Coll. Ox. B.A. 1840; Deac. 1840 and Pr. 1841 by Bp of Lon. P. C. of Tattershall, Dio. Lin.

1846. (Patron, Earl Fortescue; P. C.'s Inc. 110*l*; Pop. 848.) Surrogate. Formerly C. of Billingborough and Swaton 1841, Sleaford and Quarrington 1841–46. [1]

LATHAM, Richard, *Catworth-Magna Rectory, Kimbolton, Hunts.*—Brasen. Coll. Ox. B.A. 1825, M.A. 1827. R. of Catworth-Magna, Dio. Ely, 1835. (Patron, Brasen. Coll. Ox; R.'s Inc. 347*l* and Ho; Pop. 640.) Formerly Fell. of Brasen. Coll. Ox. [2]

LATHAM, Samuel, *Lichfield.*—Emman. Coll. Cam. B.A. 1857, M.A. 1861; Deac. 1860 and Pr. 1861 by Bp of Chich. Formerly Asst. Mast. at Brighton Coll. 1857–64. [3]

LATIMER, Edward William Forty, *Waddesdon Rectory, Aylesbury, Bucks.*—Lin. Coll. Ox. B.A. 1827, M.A. 1828. R. of the 2nd portion of Waddesdon, Dio. Ox. 1829. (Patron, Duke of Marlborough; R.'s Inc. 178*l* and Ho.) R. of the 1st portion of Waddesdon 1830. (Patron, Duke of Marlborough; R.'s Inc. 220*l* and Ho; Pop. 1786.) [4]

LA TOUCHE, James, *Stokesay, Ludlow, Salop.*—Dub. A.B. 1848; Deac. 1851 by Bp of Tuam, Pr. 1851 by Bp of Cork. V. of Stokesay, Dio. Herf. 1856. (Patron, R. Marston, Esq; Tithe—Imp. 242*l* 1*s*, V. 351*l* 2*s*; Glebe, 5½ acres; V.'s Inc. 363*l*; Pop. 552.) [5]

LATREILLE, George Birkett.—King's Coll. Lond; Deac. 1862, Pr. 1863. C. of St. Mark's, Tollington-park, Islington, Lond. Formerly C. of St. George the Martyr's, Southwark. [6]

LA TROBE, John Antes.—St. Edm. Hall, Ox. B.A. 1826, M.A. 1829; Deac. 1826, Pr. 1827. Hon. Can. of Carl. Formerly P. C. of St. Thomas's, Kendal, 1840–65. Author, *The Music of the Church*; *The Instructions of Chenaniah*, 1838; *The Solace of Song*; *Scripture Illustrations*, 1838; *More Plain Words to Plain People*, 1842; *Sacred Lays and Lyrics*, 1850; *Songs for the Times*, 1852; Visitation and other single Sermons. [7]

LATTEN, William, *Brightlingsea Vicarage, Colchester.*—St. John's Coll. Cam. B.A. 1824, M.A. 1827; Deac. 1824 and Pr. 1825 by Bp of Lon. V. of Brightlingsea, Dio. Roch. 1836. (Patron, Bp of Pet; V.'s Inc. 212*l* and Ho; Pop. 2585.) [8]

LATTER, Arthur S., *North Mimms, Hatfield, Herts.*—Queen's Coll. Ox. 3rd cl. Lit. Hum. B.A. 1850, M.A. 1852; Deac. 1850 and Pr. 1852 by Bp of Ox. V. of North Mimms, Dio. Roch. 1864. (Patron, R. W. Gaussen, Esq; V.'s Inc. 300*l* and Ho; Pop. 1095.) Formerly C. of Wiggington 1850–52, Henley-on-Thames 1852–54, Chinnor 1854–55, All Saints', Fulham, 1855–64. [9]

LAUGHARNE, Thomas, *Mundesfield House, Bromyard, Herefordshire.*—St. Cath. Coll. Cam. B.A. 1839, M.A. 1847; Deac. 1840 and Pr. 1841 by Bp of Lich. R. of Bridenbury, Dio. Herf. 1859. (Patron, E. Higginson, Esq; Tithe, 53*l* 9*s*; Glebe, 15 acres; R.'s Inc. 63*l*; Pop. 32.) Formerly C. of Wellow. [10]

LAUGHARNE, Thomas Robert John, *Burton-in-Wirral, near Chester.*—Jesus Coll. Ox. Hon. 4th cl. Lit. Hum. B.A. 1843, M.A. 1845; Deac. 1843 and Pr. 1844 by Bp of G. and B. P. C. of Burton, Dio. Ches. 1866. (Patron, W. Congreve, Esq; P. C.'s Inc. 75*l*; Pop. 425.) Dom. Chap. to the Earl of Pomfret. Formerly C. of Acton Turville, and St. John's, Gloucester; Whitnash, Warwickshire; Mast. of Gr. Sch. Buckingham; C. of Calverton, Bucks, 1858–66. [11]

LAUGHLIN, John William, 1, *Furnival's-inn, London, E.C.*—Dub. A.B. 1839, A.M. 1865; Deac. 1844 by Bp of Ossory, Pr. 1845 by Bp of Derry. P. C. of St. Peter's, Saffron-hill, Dio. Lon. 1856. (Patron, R. of St. Andrew's, Holborn; P. C.'s Inc. 260*l*; Pop. 7149.) Author, *The Infidel Tendency of Romanism* (a Lecture), 6*d*; *The Preliminaries of Repentance* (a Sermon), 4*d*. [12]

LAURENCE, Frederick John Ross, *Tiptree Heath Rectory, Kelvedon, Essex.*—Ex. Coll. Ox. S.C.L. 1844, M.A. 1861; Deac. 1843 and Pr. 1844 by Bp of Lon. R. of Tiptree Heath, Dio. Roch. 1866. (Patron, Bp of Roch; Glebe, 13 acres; R.'s Inc. 305*l* and Ho; Pop. 853.) Formerly C. of Witham and Chap. of the Witham Union 1843–45; C. in sole charge of Little Warley 1845–66; Chap. at E.I.C. Military Depôt, Warley, Brentwood, 1845–62. [13]

LAURENCE, George, *Thurgarton, Norwich.*—Emman. Coll. Cam. B.A. 1856, M.A. 1859; Deac. 1857 by Bp of Wor. Pr. 1858 by Bp of Ex. C. of Thurgarton 1865. Formerly C. of Loxbear, near Tiverton, 1857–59, Ticknall, Derby, 1860–61, St. John's, Lowestoft, 1861–63, Rockland, Norwich, 1863–65. [14]

LAURENCE, John Alfred, *Bergh Apton, Norwich.*—Emman. Coll. Cam. Jun. Opt. B.A. 1859; Deac. 1860 and Pr. 1861 by Bp of Nor. C. of Bergh Apton 1860. [15]

LAURENCE, Percival, *East Claydon, Winslow, Bucks.*—Trin. Coll. Cam. B.A. 1852, M.A. 1855; Deac. 1853 and Pr. 1854 by Bp of Wor. Sinecure R. of Buckland, Sittingbourne, Dio. Cant. (Patron, Sir J. T. Tyrell, Bart; R.'s Inc. 167*l*; Pop. 18.) C. of East Claydon. Formerly C. of St. Peter's, Woking, and of Ickham with Well, Kent. [16]

LAURENCE, Richard, *Chigwell, Essex.*—Dub. A.B. 1846, A.M. 1849; Deac. 1847 by Bp of Wor. Pr. 1848 by Bp of Ches. P. C. of Chigwell Row, Dio. Roch. 1860. (Patrons, the Crown and Bp of Roch. alt; P. C.'s Inc. 200*l*; Pop. 665.) Formerly C. of Tunbridge. [17]

LAURENCE, Robert French, *Chalgrove, Tetsworth, Oxon.*—Ch. Ch. Ox. B.A. 1828, M.A. 1831; Deac. 1830 by Bp of Bristol, Pr. 1831 by Bp of Ox. V. of Chalgrove with Berwick-Salome R. Dio. Ox. 1832. (Patrons, Ch. Ch. Ox; Chalgrove, Tithe, 152*l* 7*s* 6*d*; Glebe, 3½ acres; Berwick-Salome, Tithe, 200*l*; Glebe, 7½ acres; V.'s Inc. 375*l* and Ho; Pop. Chalgrove 549, Berwick-Salome 151.) Formerly C. of Kirtlington, Oxon, 1830–31; P. C. of Great and Little Hampton, Worcestershire, 1831–32. Author, *Remarks on the Hampden Controversy*, 1836; *An Examination of the Theories of Absolution and Confession, lately propounded in the University of Oxford*, 1847; *An Inquiry into the Circumstances attendant upon the Condemnation of Dr. Hampden in* 1836, 1848; *A Letter to a Friend on certain Suggestions recently made by Archdeacon Hare, as to the Measures to be adopted for the Removal of Doubts on the Doctrine of Regeneration*, 1850; *A Letter to the Rev. Dr. M'Neile, on certain Topics touched upon in his Correspondence with Archdeacon Wilberforce*, 1850; *The Order for the Visitation of the Sick, with a Series of Supplemental Services founded thereon, and generally expressed in the Language of the Church*, etc. 1851; *The Churchman's Assistant at Holy Communion, being so much of the Order of Administration as is engaged with the actual Celebration of that Sacrament, with Additions and Directions for the Use of Communicants*, 1860; *Provision for the Future* (a Sermon before a Benefit Club), 1865; *The Canticles arranged for Antiphonal Chanting according to the Anglican Use*, 1866. [18]

LAURENT, Felix, *Saleby, Alford, Lincolnshire.*—St. Alban Hall, Ox. B.A. 1818, M.A. 1821; Deac. 1818, Pr. 1819. V. of Saleby, Dio. Lin. 1847. (Patrons, Trustees of the Alford Gr. Sch; V.'s Inc. 241*l* and Ho; Pop. 244.) [19]

LAURIE, Anthony.—C. of Wandsworth, Surrey. [20]

LAURIE, Richard, *Bow, Crediton, Devon.*—Queens' Coll. Cam. B.A. 1835; Deac. and Pr. 1836 by Bp of Ex. C. of Bow, Devon. Formerly C. of Crawys Morchard. [21]

LAURIE, Titus Edward, *Calder Bridge, near Whitehaven.*—St. Bees; Deac. 1866 by Bp of Carl. C. of Calder Bridge, Cumberland. [22]

LAW, Arthur, *Chipping Camden, Gloucestershire.*—C. of Chipping Camden. [23]

LAW, Edward, *St. Petersburg.*—Ch. Ch. Ox. B.A. 1812, M.A. 1815, B.D. and D.D. 1844. Chap. to the British Embassy at St. Petersburg. [24]

LAW, Francis, *Samlesbury Parsonage, Preston.*—Queens' Coll. Cam. B.A. 1826; Deac. 1827 by Bp of Killaloe, Pr. 1828 by Bp of Cloyne. P. C. of Samlesbury, Dio. Man. 1832. (Patron, V. of Blackburn; Tithe—Imp. 136*l* 14*s*; P. C.'s Inc. 150*l* and Ho; Pop. 1215.) Author, *Tracts on Romish Controversy*. [25]

LAW, Frederick Henry, *Lullington Vicarage, Burton-on-Trent.*—Corpus Coll. Cam. B.A. 1849, M.A. 1854; Deac. 1849 and Pr. 1850 by Bp of Dur. V. of Lullington, Dio. Lich. 1859. (Patron, C. R. Colvile, Esq; M.P; Tithe—Imp. 730*l*; Glebe, 60 acres; V.'s Inc. 140*l* and Ho; Pop. 235.) P. C. of Coton-in-the-Elms, Dio. Lich. 1865. (Patroness, Lady Wilmot Horton; Tithe—Imp. 267*l* 7*s* 6*d*; P. C.'s Inc. 80*l* and Ho; Pop. 353.) Formerly P. C. of Berrow, Worc. 1854–59. [1]

LAW, George Henry, *Locking, Weston-super-Mare.*—St. John's Coll. Cam. M.A. 1847; Deac. 1845 and Pr. 1846 by Bp of B. and W. V. of Locking, Dio. B. and W. 1857. (Patrons, Merchant-Adventurers, Bristol; Tithe—Imp. 44*l*, V. 170*l*; Glebe, 25½ acres; V.'s Inc. 200*l*; Pop. 152.) Formerly C. of Leighland, Somerset, 1845–46; Principal Surrogate, Lichfield, 1847–57. [2]

LAW, The Very Rev. Henry, *The Deanery, Gloucester.*—St. John's Coll. Cam. B.A. 1820, M.A. 1823; Deac. and Pr. 1821 by Bp of Ches. Dean of Gloucester 1862. (Value, 1224*l* with Res.) Formerly Fell. of St. John's Coll. Cam; Archd. of Wells with the Prebendal Stalls of Huish and Brent in Wells Cathl. annexed, 1826; Can. Res. of Wells Cathl. 1828; R. of Weston-super-Mare 1840. Author, *Christ is All*, 3 vols; various Charges. [3]

LAW, Henry, *Clayton Vicarage, near Doncaster.*—Deac. 1860 and Pr. 1861 by Abp of York. V. of Frickley with Clayton, Dio. York, 1862. (Patron, William Aldam, Esq; Glebe, 50 acres; V.'s Inc. 140*l* and Ho; Pop. 312.) Formerly C. of Fenwick, Yorks, 1860–62. [4]

LAW, James Edmund, *Little Shelford Rectory, Cambridge.*—St. John's Coll. Cam. B.A. 1850, M.A. 1853; Deac. 1851 and Pr. 1852 by Bp of Ely. R. of Little Shelford, Dio. Ely, 1852. (Patron, Jas. Edmund Law, Esq; R.'s Inc. 390*l* and Ho; Pop. 474.) Formerly C. of All Saints', Sawtry, Hunts, 1851–52. [5]

LAW, James Thomas, *Banwell, Somerset.*—Ch. Coll. Cam. 2nd Sen. Opt. and B.A. 1812, M.A. 1815; Deac. 1814 and Pr. 1815 by Bp of Ches. Chan. of the Dio. of Lich. 1821. Formerly Fell. of Ch. Coll. Cam; Special Commissary of the Dio. of B. and W. 1840; Hon. Warden of Queen's Coll. Birmingham, 1846. Author, *Ecclesiastical Statutes at large*, 5 vols; *Church Building Acts; Forms of Ecclesiastical Law; Catechetical Exposition of the Apostles' Creed*; various Charges and Pamphlets. [6]

LAW, John, *Elvetham Rectory, Hartford Bridge, Hants.*—Queens' Coll. Cam. B.A. 1824; Deac. 1825, Pr. 1826. R. of Elvetham, Dio. Win. 1841. (Patron, Lord Calthorpe; Tithe, 303*l* 3*s* 10*d*; Glebe, 13 acres; R.'s Inc. 321*l* and Ho; Pop. 475.) [7]

LAW, Joseph, *South Hylton, Sunderland.*—Trin. Coll. Cam. Jun. Opt. and B.A. 1817; Deac. 1817, Pr. 1820. P. C. of Ford, or South Hylton, Dio. Dur. 1843. (Patron, Bp of Dur; P. C.'s Inc. 300*l* and Ho; Pop. 2036.) Formerly C. of Whittingham, Northumberland, 1817–35, Sunderland, 1835–43. Author, *The Scripture Doctrine of the Divine Unity and of the Person of Christ Asserted and Defended, with an Appendix on Phil.* ii. 6–11, 1827; *Consistent Interpretations of Prophecies relating to the House of Judah, the Church of Christ, the Romish Papacy and its Church*, etc. Mackintosh, 1865, 14*s*. [8]

LAW, Patrick Comerford, *North Repps Rectory, Norwich.*—Dub. A.B. 1818; Deac. and Pr. 1828 by Bp of Killaloe. R. of North Repps, Dio. Nor. 1830. (Patron, Duchy of Lancaster; Tithe, 581*l* 10*s*; Glebe, 9 acres; R.'s Inc. 590*l* and Ho; Pop. 625.) Rural Dean of Repps 1842; Chap. to the Marquis of Cholmondeley. [9]

LAW, Robert A., *Hertford.*—C. of All Saints', Hertford. [10]

LAW, Robert Vanbrugh, *Christian-Malford, Chippenham, Wilts.*—St. Peter's Coll. Cam. 1st Sen. Opt. and B.A. 1822, M.A. 1825; Deac. 1823, Pr. 1824. R. of Christian-Malford, Dio G. and B. 1835. (Patron, Bp of G. and B; Tithe, 700*l*; Glebe, 116 acres; R.'s Inc. 900*l* and Ho; Pop. 898.) Rural Dean; Treasurer of Wells Cathl. 1829. (Value, 130*l*.) [11]

LAW, T., *Stockton-on-Tees.*—C. of St. Thomas's, Stockton-on-Tees. [12]

LAW, William, *Marston-Trussell Rectory, Welford, Northants.*—Queens' Coll. Cam. B.A. 1834. R. of Marston-Trussell, Dio. Pet. 1845. (Patron, the present R; R.'s Inc. 435*l* and Ho; Pop. 219.) [13]

LAW, William, *Pelton, Fence Houses, Durham.*—Deac. 1866 by Bp of Dur. C. of Pelton 1866. [14]

LAWFORD, Charles, *Winterborne Stoke Vicarage, near Salisbury.*—Trin. Coll. Cam. B.A. 1841, M.A. 1844; Deac. 1843 and Pr. 1844 by Abp of Cant. V. of Winterborne-Stoke, Dio. Salis. 1847. (Patron, Lord Ashburton; Tithe—App. 95*l*, Imp. 131*l* 9*s*, V. 220*l*; Glebe, 2 acres; V.'s Inc. 240*l* and Ho; Pop. 383.) V. of Berwick St. James, Wilts, Dio. Salis. 1847. (Patron, Lord Ashburton; Tithe—Imp. 132*l* 11*s* 6*d*, V. 30*l*; Glebe, 15 acres; V.'s Inc. 69*l*; Pop. 252.) Hon. Sec. to Salisbury Dioc. Ch. Building Association. [15]

LAWLESS, George.—Chap. to the Forces, Sheerness. [16]

LAWLEY, The Hon. Stephen Willoughby, *Escrick Rectory, York.*—Ball. Coll. Ox. 2nd cl. Lit. Hum. and B.A. 1845, M.A. 1852; Deac. 1846, Pr. 1848. R. of Escrick, Dio. York, 1848. (Patron, Lord Wenlock; Tithe, 406*l*; Glebe, 90 acres; R.'s Inc. 505*l* and Ho; Pop. 855.) Formerly Sub-Dean of York 1852. [17]

LAWRANCE, Robert, *Bleadon, Weston-super-Mare.*—St. John's Coll. Cam. Scho. of, B.A. 1851, M.A. 1854; Deac. 1852 and Pr. 1853 by Bp of Nor. C. of Bleadon 1867. Formerly C. of Burnham Deepdale 1852–55, Mattishall, Norfolk, 1855–61; Asst. Mast. in Epsom Coll. 1864–66. [18]

LAWRANCE, Robert, *Bleadon Rectory, Weston-super-Mare, Somerset.*—St. Edm. Hall, Ox. B.A. 1821, M.A. 1824; Deac. 1821, Pr. 1822. R. of Bleadon, Dio. B. and W. 1850. (Patron, Bp of Win; Tithe, 623*l* 8*s* 10*d*; Glebe, 19 acres; R.'s Inc. 555*l* and Ho; Pop. 623.) [19]

LAWRANCE, Walter John, *Aylesford, Maidstone.*—Trin. Coll. Cam. 2nd cl. Cl. Trip. B.A. 1862, M.A. 1865; Deac. 1863, Pr. 1864. C. of Aylesford 1864. Formerly C. of St. Paul's, Chatham 1863. [20]

LAWRENCE, Arthur, *St. Ewe Rectory, St. Austell, Cornwall.*—St. Mary Hall, Ox. B.A. 1856; Deac. 1856, Pr. 1858. R. of St. Ewe, Dio. Ex. 1864. (Patrons, Sir Charles Sawle, Bart. and Major Carlyon; Tithe, 653*l*; Glebe, 100 acres; R.'s Inc. 730*l* and Ho; Pop. 1434.) Formerly C. of Parkham, Bideford. [21]

LAWRENCE, Charles, *Rectory, Lee, S.E.*—King's Coll. Lond. Theol. Assoc. 1st cl; Deac. 1854, Pr. 1855. R. of Lee, Dio. Roch. 1864. (Patron, Ld Chan; Tithe, 410*l*; Glebe, 19 acres; R.'s Inc. 550*l* and Ho; Pop. 2729.) Formerly C. of St. Martin's, Birmingham, 1854; St. Marylebone, Lond. 1855; Tut. to H.R.H. the Duke of Edinburgh 1856; British Chap. at Geneva 1856; R. of Tolleshunt Knights 1857; Chap. to Dr. Villiers, Bp of Carlisle and Durham 1857. [22]

LAWRENCE, George Guerard, *Springdale, Huddersfield.*—St. Edm. Hall, Ox. B.A. 1846, M.A. 1848; Deac. 1856 and Pr. 1857 by Abp of York. P. C. of St. Paul's, Huddersfield, Dio. Rip. 1862. (Patron, V. of Huddersfield; P. C.'s Inc. 300*l* and Ho; Pop. 5219.) Formerly P. C. of Shirley, Hants. Author, *Three Months in America in* 1863, 1864, 6*d*; *Tour in the Southern States of America in* 1866, Simpkin, Marshall and Co., 1866; *Lectures on Ritualism*, 1867, 1*s*; *Lectures on the Established Church*, Mackintosh, 1867, 2*d*. each. [23]

LAWRENCE, Hezekiah.—British Chap. at Dantzic. [24]

LAWRENCE, James, *Alexandra-terrace, Prince's-road, Liverpool.*—Brasen. Coll. Ox. Hon. 4th cl. Math. B.A. 1849, M.A. 1852; Deac. 1850, Pr. 1851. Chap. of the S.P.G. to Emigrants sailing from Liverpool 1867. Formerly C. of St. George's, Everton, Liverpool, 1851–55; P. C. of Ellel, near Lancaster, 1856–64, St. Michael's, Liverpool, 1864–65. [25]

LAWRENCE, John Algernon, *Crewkerne, Somerset.*—Jesus Coll. Cam. LL.B. 1863; Deac. 1864,

Pr. 1865. Sen. C. of Crewkerne 1866. Formerly C. of Waddesdon, Bucks, and St. Mary's, Southampton. [1]

LAWRENCE, Neville George Murray, *Forebridge Parsonage, Stafford.*—Queen's Coll. Ox. B.A. 1849, M.A. 1852; Deac. 1851 and Pr. 1852 by Bp of Ches. P. C. of Forebridge, Dio. Lich. 1853. (Patron, P. C. of Castlechurch; P. C.'s Inc. 150*l* and Ho; Pop. 2531.) [2]

LAWRENCE, Richard Gwynne, *Edgmond, Newport, Salop.*—Wells Theol. Coll. 1858–59, St. John's Coll. Cam. B.A. 1858; Deac. 1859 and Pr. 1860 by Bp of B. and W. C. of Edgmond 1865. Formerly C. of West Chinnock with Chiselborough 1859–61, Westbury-on-Trym 1861–63, Welshpool 1864–65. [3]

LAWRENCE, Thomas, *Hanwell, London, W.*—Chap. of the Kensington Cemetery, Hanwell. [4]

LAWRENCE, T. E., *Northop, Flintshire.*—C. of Northop. [5]

LAWRENCE, William Barton, 7, *Clifton Vale, Clifton.*—Chap. of the Bristol House of Correction. [6]

LAWRENCE, William Robert, *Ewyas Harold Vicarage, Hereford.*—Dur. B.A. 1847, Licen. Theol. 1848, M.A. 1850; Deac. 1848 and Pr. 1849 by Bp of Ches. V. of Ewyas Harold, Dio. Herf. 1866. (Patron, Bp of G. and B; Tithe, 85*l* 5*s*; Glebe, 50 acres; V.'s Inc. 146*l* and Ho; Pop. 450.) Formerly C. of St. Martin's, Liverpool, 1848; P. C. of St. Michael's, Two Mile-hill, near Bristol, 1852; P. C. of Chipping Sodbury 1861. [7]

LAWSON, Basil Ranaldson, *Wythburn, Keswick, Cumberland.*—St. Bees; Deac. 1834 and Pr. 1836 by Bp of Ches. P. C. of Wythburn, Dio. Carl. 1851. (Patron, V. of Crosthwaite; P. C.'s Inc. 84*l*.) [8]

LAWSON, Frederick Pike, *Northampton.*—Trin. Coll. Cam. Sen. Opt. B.A. 1856, M.A. 1859; Deac. 1857 and Pr. 1858 by Bp of Pet. C. in sole charge of St. Peter's, Northampton, 1857. [9]

LAWSON, George Nicholas Gray, *Littleton Drew Rectory, near Chippenham, Wilts.*—St. John's Coll. Cam. B.A. 1838, M.A. 1843; Deac. 1838 and Pr. 1839 by Bp of Ox. R. of Littleton Drew, Dio. G. and B. 1849. (Patron, Bp of G. and B; Tithe, 120*l*; Glebe, 68 acres; R.'s Inc. 210*l*; Pop. 233.) Formerly C. of Uffington, Berks, 1838, West Grinstead 1842; P. C. of Dilton's Marsh, Westbury, Wilts, 1844. Author, *Plain and Practical Sermons*, Masters, 1847, 10*s* 6*d*; *The Woman of Samaria—The Church in Mystery* (a Visitation Sermon), 1850; *A Sermon* (preached before the Chippenham Branch of the Wilts Friendly Soc.), 1853; *Catechism of the Fall and Restoration of Man*, Masters, 1859. [10]

LAWSON, George Robert, *Pitminster Vicarage, Taunton, Somerset.*—Trin. Coll. Cam. B.A. 1828, M.A. 1835; Deac. 1829, Pr. 1830. V. of Pitminster, Dio. B. and W. 1837. (Patron, the present V; Tithe—Imp. 300*l*, V. 535*l*; Glebe, 2 acres; V.'s Inc. 540*l* and Ho; Pop. 1572.) [11]

LAWSON, James, *Buckminster Vicarage, Colsterworth, Leicestershire.*—St. Alban Hall, Ox. 3rd cl. Lit. Hum. B.A. 1828, M.A. 1831; Deac. and Pr. 1830 by Bp of Ches. V. of Buckminster with Sewsterne, Dio. Pet. 1834. (Patron, Earl of Dysart; Buckminster, Tithe—Imp. 371*l*, V. 3*l* 19*s*; Glebe, 80 acres; Sewsterne, Tithe—Imp. 300*l*, V. 4*l*; V.'s Inc. 166*l* 10*s* and Ho; Pop. 655.) Author, *A Defence of Poesy, and other Poems*, 1842; *The Ocean Tribute*; *Thoughts in Verse and Prose*, 1844. [12]

LAWSON, John, *Seaton-Carew, West Hartlepool.*—St. Alban Hall, Ox. 2nd cl. Lit. Hum. and B.A. 1829; M.A. 1833; Deac. 1831, Pr. 1832. P. C. of Seaton-Carew, Dio. Dur. 1835. (Patron, the present P. C; Glebe, 16 acres; P. C.'s Inc. 150*l*; Pop. 884.) [13]

LAWSON, John Archibald, *St. Mary's, Southampton.*—Deac. 1858 and Pr. 1859 by Bp of Lich. C. of St. Mary's, Southampton, 1863; Surrogate. Formerly C. of Tamworth, St. Stephen's, Islington, Lond. and All Saints', Southampton, 1862. [14]

LAWSON, John Sharpe, 4, *Peel-terrace, Regent road, Salford.*—Caius Coll. Cam. B.A. 1865, LL.B. 1867; Deac. 1865 and Pr. 1866 by Bp of Man. C. of St. Bartholomew's, Salford. Author, *Christ the Way, the Truth and the Life* (a Sermon in words of one syllable). [15]

LAWSON, Robert, *Upton-upon-Severn, Worcestershire.*—Ch. Ch. Ox. 4th cl. Lit. Hum. and B.A. 1844, M.A. 1847; Deac. 1846 and Pr. 1848 by Bp of Ox. R. of Upton-upon-Severn, Dio. Wor. 1864. (Patron, Bp of Wor; R.'s Inc. 100*l* and Ho; Pop. 2676.) Stud. of Ch. Ch. Ox. Formerly P. C. of Offenham, Worcestershire, 1848–64. [16]

LAWSON, William De Lancey, *Fishponds, Bristol.*—Magd. Coll. Cam. Wrang. and B.A. 1834, M.A. 1837; Deac. 1835 by Bp of Roch. and Pr. 1835 by Bp of Carl. for Bp of Ely. Formerly Fell. of Magd. Coll. Cam; C. of Oakham 1836, Kentish-town 1840; P. C. of St. Andrew's, Bethnal Green, 1841, P. C. of St. John's, Uxbridge Moor, 1845. Author, *Arithmetic Explained*, 2nd ed. 1*s*, and *Questions and Examples*, 1865, 1*s* 6*d*. [17]

LAWSON, William Lipsett, *Lynton Parsonage, Barnstaple.*—Dub. A.B 1850, A.M. 1854; Deac. 1851, Pr. 1855. P. C. of Lynton with Countesbury P. C. Dio. Ex. 1866. (Patron, Archd. of Barnstaple; P. C.'s Inc. 150*l* and Ho; Pop. 1219.) Formerly C. of Trinity, Hulme, Manchester. [18]

LAWSON, William Morrell.—St. John's Coll. Cam. 1825, 3rd Sen. Opt. and B.A. 1826, M.A. 1831; Deac. 1827, Pr. 1828. Author, *The Study of Mathematics and Natural Philosophy* (an Introductory Lecture delivered to the Students of Queen's Coll. Birmingham); *The Irish Famine* (three Sermons). [19]

LAWTON, Mark Anthony, *Kilnwick-Percy Vicarage, Pocklington, Yorks.*—Jesus Coll. Cam. B.A. 1839, Deac. 1839 and Pr. 1840 by Abp of York. V. of Kilnwick-Percy, Dio. York, 1847. (Patron, Abp of York; Tithe, App. 160*l*, V. 119*l*; Glebe, 22 acres; V.'s Inc. 134*l* and Ho; Pop. 132.) Formerly V. of Salton. [20]

LAXTON, William, *Holt, Trowbridge, Wilts.*—Trin. Coll. Ox. 2nd cl. Lit. Hum. and B.A. 1832, M.A 1835. V. of Atworth with South Wraxhall, Wilts, Dio. Salis. 1848. (Patrons, D. and C. of Bristol; Tithe—App. 397*l* and 16½ acres of Glebe; V. 255*l* 2*s* 6*d*; Glebe, 1½ acres; V.'s Inc. 256*l*; Pop. 949.) [21]

LAY, Henry Reeve, *Holgate, near Much Wenlock, Salop.*—Trin. Coll. Cam. B.A. 1858; Deac. 1860, Pr. 1861. R. of Holgate, Dio. Herf. 1861. (Patron, Bp of Herf; R.'s Inc. 275*l*; Pop. 196.) [22]

LAYARD, Charles Clement, *Wembley, Sudbury, Middlesex.*—St. John's Coll. Cam. 1837, and St. Bees, 1842–43; Deac. 1843, Pr. 1844. P. C. of St. John's, Wembley, Dio. Lon. 1858. (Patronesses, Misses Copland; P. C.'s Inc. 130*l*; Pop. 896.) Formerly Chap. to the Hon. Trinity House Almshouses, Mile-end, Lond. 1849–58; V. of Mayfield, Staffs. Author, *Sabbath Trumpets*; *British and Foreign Bible Society Jubilee Hymns*; *Statement of Circumstances connected with the Refusal of the Bishop of Exeter to license the Rev. C. C. Layard to the P. C. of Escott, Devon.* [23]

LAYARD, John Thomas, *Swafield Rectory, North Walsham, Norfolk.*—Ch. Coll. Cam. Jun. Opt. 3rd cl. Cl. Trip. and B.A. 1845; Deac. 1845, Pr. 1846. R. of Swafield, Dio. Nor. 1850. (Patron, Chan. of the Duchy of Lancaster; Tithe, 220*l*; R.'s Inc. 240*l* and Ho; Pop. 172.) [24]

LAYCOCK, Samuel Field, *Cross-lane, Salford.*—St. John's Coll. Cam. B.A. 1866; Deac. 1866 by Bp of Man. C. of Ch. Ch. Salford, 1866. [25]

LAYCOCK, William, *Southowram Parsonage, Halifax.*—St. Cath. Coll. Cam. B.A. 1849; Deac. 1848 and Pr. 1850 by Bp of Rip. P. C. of St. Anne's-in-the-Grove, or Chapel-le-Breers, Halifax, Dio. Rip. 1853. (Patron, V. of Halifax; Glebe, 12½ acres; P. C.'s Inc. 300*l* and Ho; Pop. 6068.) Formerly C. of Gawber, near Barnsley, 1848–50, St. Peter's, Burnley, 1851–53. [26]

LAYNG, Edward, *Milwich Vicarage, near Stone, Staffs.*—St. John's Coll. Cam. B.A. 1845, M.A. 1848; Deac. 1846 and Pr. 1847 by Bp of Wor. V. of Milwich, Dio. Lich. 1856. (Patron, L. G. Dive, Esq; Tithe, comm. 140*l*; Glebe, 1½ acres; V.'s Inc. 143*l* and Ho; Pop. 567.)

Formerly C. of Beedon 1846, Standish 1848, Badby 1850, Down Hatherley 1853. [1]

LAYNG, Henry, *Foulden, Brandon, Norfolk.*—Sid. Coll. Cam. B.A. 1852, M.A. 1859; Deac. 1853 and Pr. 1854 by Abp of York. C. of Oxburgh and Foulden 1857. Formerly C. of Ferry Fryston, Yorks, 1853–57. [2]

LAYNG, Thomas Francis, *Marden, near Hereford.*—Sid. Coll. Cam. B.A. 1830, M.A. 1833, B.D. and D.D. 1845; Deac. 1831, Pr. 1832. V. of Marden, Dio. Herf. 1850. (Patrons, D. and C. of Herf; Tithe—App. 410*l* 4*s* and 30 acres of Glebe; Tithe—Imp. 16*l*, V. 310*l*; Glebe, 2½ acres; V.'s Inc. 296*l* and Ho; Pop. 929.) C. of Wisteston, Hereford. Formerly Head Mast. of Hereford Sch. Author, *A Farewell Sermon*, 1833; *The Plague Stayed* (a Sermon in *Church of England Magazine*), 1847. [3]

LAYNG, William, *Creeton Rectory, Stamford, Lincolnshire.*—Sid. Coll. Cam. Sen. Opt. and B.A. 1841, M.A. 1844; Deac. 1842 and Pr. 1843 by Bp of Pet. R. of Creeton with Counthorpe, Dio. Lin. 1850. (Patron, Ld Chan; Tithe, comm. 138*l*; Glebe, 32 acres; R.'s Inc. 181*l* and Ho; Pop. 180.) Formerly 2nd Mast. Oundle Gr. Sch. 1841–42; C. of Harrowden, Northants, 1842–43, Strubby and Maplethorpe, Linc. 1843–45, Overstone, Northants, 1845–50, Swayfield, Linc. 1850–56. Author, Sermons in *Church of England Magazine*; Poetry in various Magazines; *A Christmas Carol*, with music by Mrs. Farebrother, Ollivier, 1864. [4]

LAYTON, H. G., *Gloucester.*—Chap. of the County Prison, Gloucester. [5]

LAYTON, Thomas Charles Lichfield, *Marston Bigot, near Frome, Somerset.*—Pemb. Coll. Ox. B.A. 1846; Deac. 1846, Pr. 1847. C. of Marston Bigot. Formerly R. of St. Aldate's, Oxford, 1856; Asst. C. of St. Andrew's, Plymouth; Fell. of Pemb. Coll. Ox. 1854. [6]

LAZENBY, Matthew, *Alnham Vicarage, Alnwick.*—Dur. Licen. in Theol; Deac. 1855, Pr. 1856. V. of Alnham, Dio. Dur. 1866. (Patron, Duke of Northumberland; Tithe, 154*l* 7*s* 11*d*; Glebe, 8 acres; V.'s Inc. 207*l* and Ho; Pop. 295.) Formerly C. of Gateshead 1855, South Hetton, Easington, 1857, Eglingham 1862. [7]

LAZONBY, Henry Paul, *Thistleton, Rutland.*—Jesus Coll. Cam. B.A. 1834; Deac. 1840 and Pr. 1841 by Bp of Pet. C. of Thistleton. Formerly C. of Somerby. [8]

LEA, Abel Humphrys, *Loxley Vicarage, Warwick.*—Wor. Coll. Ox. B.A. 1851, M.A. 1853; Deac. 1852 and Pr. 1853 by Bp of Wor. C. of Loxley. Formerly Sub-V. of Stratford-on-Avon 1854–57. [9]

LEA, Frederic Simcox, *Trinity Parsonage, Tredegar-square, Mile-end-road, London, E.*—Wad. Coll. Ox. 1st cl. Lit. Hum. 3rd cl. Math. et Phy. and B.A. 1851, M.A. 1854; Deac. 1851 and Pr. 1852 by Bp of Win. P. C. of Trinity, Stepney, Dio. Lon. 1855. (Patron, Bp of Lon; P. C.'s Inc. 250*l*; Pop. 10,478.) Formerly Clifton Fell. of Brasen. Coll. Ox. 1853–56; C. of Alverstoke 1851–53, Middleton Cheney 1853–55. [10]

LEA, George, *Edgbaston, Birmingham.*—Wad. Coll. Ox. 2nd cl. Lit. Hum. and B.A. 1826, M.A. 1829; Deac. 1827, Pr. 1828. P. C. of St. George's, Edgbaston, Dio. Wor. 1864. (Patron, Lord Calthorpe; P. C.'s Inc. 350*l*; Pop. 3178.) Formerly P. C. of Ch. Ch. Birmingham, 1840. [11]

LEA, Job, *Bickerton, near Malpas, Cheshire.*—St. Bees; Deac. 1843 and Pr. 1845 by Bp of Ches. P. C. of Shocklach, Dio. Ches. 1864. (Patrons, Trustees of Sir R. Puleston; P. C.'s Inc. 117*l*; Pop. 414.) Formerly C. of Wallasey 1843–45, St. Chad's, Malpas, 1857–60, Worthenbury 1861–64. [12]

LEA, Josiah Turner, *Far-Forest Parsonage, Bewdley, Worcestershire.*—Univ. Coll. Ox. B.A. 1844; Deac. and Pr. 1846 by Bp of Herf. P. C. of Far-Forest, Dio. Herf. 1853. (Patrons, Rectors of Ribbesford and Rock alt; Tithe, 5*l*; Glebe, 2 acres; P. C.'s. Inc. 129*l* and Ho; Pop. 655.) [13]

LEA, William, *St. Peter's Vicarage, Droitwich, Worcestershire.*—Brasen. Coll. Ox. 2nd cl. Lit. Hum. 1841, B.A. 1842; Deac. 1843, Pr. 1845. V. of St. Peter's, Droitwich, Dio. Wor. 1849. (Patron, Earl Somers; Tithe, 170*l* 3*s*; V.'s Inc. 170*l* and Ho; Pop. 854.) Hon. Can. of Wor. 1858. [14]

LEACH, Francis George, *St. Petrox Rectory, Pembroke.*—Pemb. Coll. Ox. B.A. 1819, M.A. 1822; Deac. 1820 and Pr. 1821 by Bp of Ox. R. of Stackpool Elidur, Dio. St. D. 1831. (Patron, Earl of Cawdor; Tithe, 207*l*; Pop. 273.) R. of St. Petrox, Dio. St. D. 1839. (Patron, Earl of Cawdor; Tithe, 46*l*; Glebe, 45 acres; R.'s Inc. 120*l* and Ho; Pop. 78.) Chap. to the Union, Pembroke, 1853. Formerly Philip's Fell. of Pemb. Coll. Ox. 1819–21; Chap. to the Earl of Cawdor 1821. [15]

LEACH, Henry, *All Saints' Parsonage, Bradford, Yorks.*—Emman. Coll. Cam. B.A. 1852, M.A. 1856; Deac. 1853 and Pr. 1854 by Bp of Nor. P. C. of All Saints', Horton, Bradford, Dio. Rip. 1864. (Patron, F. S. Powell, Esq., M.P; Pop. 7000.) Formerly Cl. Mast. in Ipswich Gr. Sch. 1853–58; C. of St. Thomas's, Portman-square, Lond. 1858–63. [16]

LEACH, John, *Warrington.*—P. C. of Trinity, Warrington, Dio. Ches. 1863. (Patron, Rt. Rev. H. Powys; P. C.'s Inc. 180*l*.) [17]

LEACH, John, *Lakenham, Norwich.*—Caius Coll. Cam. Sen. Opt. B.A. 1861, M.A. 1864; Deac. 1862, Pr. 1863. C. of St. Mark's, Lakenham, 1862. [18]

LEACH, John Henry, *Gillingham Vicarage, Chatham.*—Brasen. Coll. Ox. Fell. of, 2nd cl. Lit. Hum. and B.A. 1851, M.A. 1854; Deac. 1856 and Pr. 1858 by Bp of Ox. V. of Gillingham with Lidsing C. Dio. Roch. 1867. (Patron, Brasen. Coll. Ox; Tithe, 622*l*; Glebe, 15 acres; V.'s Inc. 680*l* and Ho; Pop. Gillingham 9412, Lidsing 30.) Formerly Head Cl. Mast. of Grosvenor Coll. Bath, Asst. Mast. of Highgate Gr. Sch. [19]

LEACH, Octavius, *Hubberstone Rectory, Milford, Pembrokeshire.*—Jesus Coll. Ox. B.A. 1824, M.A. 1827; Deac. 1826, Pr. 1827. R. of Hubberstone, Dio. St. D. 1844. (Patron, Ld Chan; Tithe, 180*l*; Glebe, 9 acres; R.'s Inc. 186*l* and Ho; Pop. 1270.) [20]

LEACH, Richard Ebenezer, *Holmfirth Parsonage, Huddersfield.*—Literate; Deac. 1822 by Bp of Ches. Pr. 1824 by Abp of York. P. C. of Holmfirth, Dio. Rip. 1832. (Patron, V. of Kirkburton; P. C.'s Inc. 190*l* and Ho; Pop. 5447.) [21]

LEACH, Robert Burton, *Sutton Montis, Ilchester.*—Brasen. Coll. Ox. B.A. 1860, M.A. 1862; Deac. 1863 and Pr. 1864 by Bp of Ox. R. of Sutton Montis, Dio. B. and W. 1864. (Patroness, Mrs. Burton Leach; Tithe, 147*l*; Glebe, 37 acres; R.'s Inc. 300*l* and Ho; Pop. 150.) Formerly Hulme Exhib. of Brasen. Coll. 1859–62; Fell. of Radley Coll. 1862–64. [22]

LEACH, Thomas, *Thornton Vicarage, Lancaster.*—Trin. Coll. Cam. Sen. Opt. and B.A. 1846; Deac. 1847, Pr. 1848. V. of Thornton-in-Lonsdale, Dio. Rip. 1848. (Patrons, D. and C. of Wor; Tithe—App. 410*l* and 180½ acres of Glebe, V. 100*l*; Glebe, 3½ acres; V.'s Inc. 120*l* and Ho; Pop. 534.) [23]

LEACHMAN, Edmund, 124, *New North-road, London, N.*—St. John's Coll. Cam. B.A. 1847, M.A. 1851; Deac. 1848 by Bp of Nor. Pr. 1849 by Bp of Man. C. of Ch. Ch. Hoxton 1863; Chap. of St. Luke's Hospital, Lond. 1854. [24]

LEACHMAN, Francis Joseph, 20, *Compton-terrace, Islington, London, N.* and *Park-place, Margate.*—Trin. Coll. Cam. B.A. 1854, M.A. 1857, Assoc. of King's Coll. Lond; Deac. 1859 and Pr. 1860 by Abp of Cant. Formerly C. of Fordwich, Kent, 1859–61, Exford, Somerset, 1861–62, Howe, near Norwich, 1863–66. [25]

LEACROFT, Charles Holcombe, *Dethwick, Chesterfield.*—Trin. Coll. Cam. B.A. 1847, M.A. 1851; Deac. 1847, Pr. 1848. P. C. of Dethwick, Dio. Lich. 1860. (Patron, Thomas Hallowes, Esq; P. C.'s Inc. 110*l*; Pop. 935.) P. C. of Brackenfield, Derbyshire, Dio. Lich. 1857. (Patron, R. of Morton; P. C.'s Inc. 80*l*; Pop. 317.) [26]

LEAH, Thomas, *St. Keyne's Rectory, Liskeard.*—Queens' Coll. Cam. B.A. 1830; Deac. 1831 by Bp of G. and B. Pr. 1832 by Bp of Ex. R. of St. Keyne, Dio. Ex. 1833. (Patron, Admiral Cory; Tithe, 140*l*; Glebe, 25 acres; R.'s Inc. 165*l* and Ho; Pop. 181.) [27]

LEAHY, Daniel.—Maynooth Coll; Deac. and Pr. by (Roman Catholic) Bp of Limerick. Formerly C. of Ellastone 1858, Field Dalling, Norfolk; Asst. C. of St. Peter's, Saffron hill, Lond. Previously a Priest of the Church of Rome. [1]

LEAK, John Custance, *Holt, Norfolk.*—Trin. Hall, Cam. S.C.L. 1828, LL.B. 1833; Deac. 1829 and Pr. 1830 by Bp of Nor. R. of Barningham Parva, Norfolk, Dio. Nor. 1831. (Patrons, G. D. Grave, Esq. and others; Tithe, 260*l*; R.'s Inc. 260*l*; Pop. 273.) Formerly C. of Hempstead by Holt. [2]

LEAKEY, Henry Palmer, *Bradninch, Devon.*—P. C. of Bradninch, Dio. Ex. 1864. (Patrons, D. and C. of Windsor; P. C.'s Inc. 185*l*; Pop. 1796.) [3]

LEAKEY, John Arundell, *Topsham, Exeter.*—Queen's Coll. Ox. B.A. 1844; Deac. 1846 and Pr. 1848 by Bp of Salis. P. C. of Topsham, Dio. Ex. 1857. (Patrons, D. and C. of Ex; P. C.'s Inc. 300*l*; Pop. 2995.) Formerly C. of St. Michael's, Chester-square, Lond. [4]

LEAKEY, Peter N., *Droxford, Hants.*—C. of Droxford. [5]

LEAR, Francis, *Bishopstone Rectory, Salisbury.*—Ch. Ch. Ox. B.A. 1846, M.A. 1849; Deac. 1847 and Pr. 1848 by Bp of Salis. R. and V. of Bishopstone, Dio. Salis. 1850. (Patron, Earl of Pembroke; Tithe, 960*l*; Glebe, 32 acres; R.'s Inc. 995*l* and Ho; Pop 685.) Rural Dean of Chalke 1851–62; Preb. of Bishopstone in Salis. Cathl. 1856; Dom. Chap. to the late Bp of Salis. 1852–54; Exam. Chap. to present Bp 1854; Chan. of Salis. Cathl. 1861–64; Canon Residentiary of Salis. 1862; Precentor of Salis. 1864. Author, occasional Sermons. [6]

LEARY, Thomas Humphrys Lindsay, *Grammar School House, Derby.*—Brasen. Coll. Ox. Div. Exhib. 1849, B.A. 1853; Deac. 1858 by Bp of Lich. Head Mast. of the Derby Gr. Sch. 1859. Editor of *Homer's Iliad*, and of *Herodotus*, in *Weale's Classical Series*, 1857–59. [7]

LEATHERDALE, George, *Golden Valley, Alfreton, Derbyshire.*—Deac. 1856 by Abp of Cant. Pr. 1857 by Bp of Mauritius. C. of Ironville, Alfreton, Derbyshire. Formerly P. C. of St. John's, Moka, Mauritius, 1857; C. of St. Mary's, Hemel Hempstead, 1862. [8]

LEATHERDALE, John.—St. John's Coll. Cam. B.A. 1827. Formerly R. of Little Plumstead 1854–63. [9]

LEATHES, Carteret Henry, *Limpenhoe Vicarage, Norwich.*—St. John's Coll. Cam. Sen. Opt. and B.A. 1855; Deac. 1855 and Pr. 1856 by Bp of Nor. R. of Southwood with Limpenhoe V. Dio. Nor. 1856. (Patron, Rev. T. H. C. Day; Tithe, Southwood, 145*l*; Glebe, 6½ acres; Limpenhoe, Tithe—Imp. 48*l*, V. 130*l*; Glebe, 3½ acres; R.'s Inc. 296*l* and Ho; Pop. Southwood 39, Limpenhoe 227.) Formerly C. of Gunthorpe, Norfolk, 1855–56. [10]

LEATHES, Frederic, *Reedham Rectory, Acle, Norfolk.*—Emman. Coll. Cam. B.A. 1815; Deac. 1817 and Pr. 1818 by Bp of Nor. R. of Reedham with Freethorpe, Dio. Nor. 1844. (Patron, J. F. Leathes, Esq; Tithe, 615*l*; Glebe, 116 acres; Net Value, 607*l* and Ho; Pop. Reedham 836, Freethorpe 425) R. of Wickhampton, Dio. Nor. 1836. (Patron, J. F. Leathes, Esq; Tithe, 195*l*; Glebe, 16 acres; R.'s Inc. 220*l*; Pop. 119.) [11]

LEATHES, Stanley, 4, *Golden-square, London, W.*—Jesus Coll. Cam. Tyrwhitt Scho. B.A. 1852, M.A. 1855; Deac. 1856 and Pr. 1857 by Bp of Salis. Preacher and Asst. Min. of St. James's, Westminster; Prof. of Heb. in King's Coll. Lond. Formerly C. of St. Martin's, Salisbury, 1856, St. Luke's, Soho, Lond. 1858, St. James's, Westminster, and Clerk in orders, 1860. Author, *The Birthday of Christ, &c*; *Three Sermons before the University of Cambridge*, Bell and Daldy, 1866, 2*s*; *Human Wisdom and Divine Power* (a Sermon), Bell and Daldy, 1866. [12]

LEAVER, Henry Cozens, *Pen Selwood Rectory, Bourton, Bath.*—Pemb. Coll. Ox. B.A. 1846, M.A. 1849; Deac. 1848 and Pr. 1849 by Bp of Lich. R. of Pen Selwood, Dio. B. and W. 1852. (Patrons, Earl of Egremont's Trustees, and Sir H. H. Hoare, Bart; Tithe, 156*l* 12*s* 8*d*; Glebe, 47 acres; R.'s Inc. 217*l* and Ho; Pop. 442.) Formerly V. of Shepton-Montague, Somerset, 1850–52. [13]

LEAVER, Tay, *Epping, Essex.*—Caius Coll. Cam. B.A. 1853, M.A. 1856; Deac. 1855 and Pr. 1856 by Bp of Ox. C. of Epping 1866. Formerly C. of High Wycombe and Amersham, Bucks, 1855–58, St. Thomas's, Stamford Hill, and Upper Clapton 1858–61, St. Michael's, Highgate, 1861–66. [14]

LEAVER, Thomas Charles Hyde, *St. John's College, Oxford.*—St. John's Coll. Ox. B.A. 1836, M.A. 1840; Deac. 1837, Pr. 1838. Fell. of St. John's Coll. Ox. Formerly R. of Rockhampton 1848–59. [15]

LEAVY, P. A.—C. of St. Andrew's, Bethnal Green, Lond. [16]

LEAY, William, *Downside Parsonage, Bath.*—St. Edm. Hall, Ox. B.A. 1843, M.A. 1846; Deac. 1843 by Bp of Ches. Pr. 1844 by Bp of Ox. P. C. of Ch. Ch. Downside, Dio. B. and W. 1852. (Patron, V. of Norton-Midsomer; P. C.'s Inc. 92*l* and Ho; Pop. 697.) Author, *A Pastor's Pocket-book and New Year's Gift for* 1855; *Supplemental Psalmody*; *A Selection of Hymns, chiefly original*, 1859; *Ecclesiastical Architecture*, 1859. [17]

LE BAS, Henry Vincent, *Bedfont Vicarage, near Hounslow, Middlesex.*—Univ. Coll. Ox. B.A. 1850, M.A. 1853; Deac. 1852 and Pr. 1854 by Bp of Ox. V. of Bedfont, Dio. Lon. 1859. (Patron, Bp of Lon; Tithe—App. 619*l*, Imp. 210*l*, V. 327*l* 1*s* 2*d*; Glebe, 16 acres; V.'s Inc. 345*l* and Ho; Pop. 1150.) Formerly C. of Trinity, Windsor, 1852, St. James's, Paddington, 1855, St. Mark's, North Audley-street, 1856. [18]

LE BRETON, The Very Rev. William Corbet, *St. Saviour's Rectory, Jersey.*—Pemb. Coll. Ox. 3rd cl. Lit. Hum. and B.A. 1835, M.A. 1837; Deac. 1839 and Pr. 1840 by Bp of Ox. Dean of Jersey 1850; R. of St. Saviour's, Jersey, Dio. Win. 1850. (Patron, the Governor; Tithe—uncertain, chiefly derived from apples; Glebe, 27 verges, or 12 statute acres; Dean and R.'s Inc. 600*l* and Ho; Pop. 3723.) Formerly Fell. of Ex. Coll. Ox. [19]

LECHMERE, Anthony Berwick, *Hanley-Castle Vicarage, Upton-on-Severn, Worcestershire.*—Ch. Ch. Ox. B.A. 1824, M.A. 1826; Deac. and Pr. 1826. V. of Welland, Worc. Dio. Wor. 1828. (Patron, Ld Chan; Tithe, 388*l*; V.'s Inc. 389*l* and Ho; Pop. 802.) V. of Hanley-Castle, Dio. Wor. 1839. (Patron, Sir A. Lechmere, Bart; V.'s Inc. 680*l* and Ho; Pop. 1175.) Hon. Can. of Wor. Cathl; Rural Dean. [20]

LE COCQ, Bonamy, *Bridgwater, Somerset.*—Literate; Deac. 1827 by Bp of B. and W. Pr. 1828 by Bp of Win. C. of St. John's the Baptist, Bridgwater. [21]

LEDGER, Edmund, *The Rectory, Duxford, Cambridgeshire.*—Corpus Coll. Ox. 4th Wrang. B.A. 1863, M.A. 1866; Deac. 1865 and Pr. 1866 by Bp of Ely. R. of Duxford St. Peter, Dio. Ely, 1866. (Patron, Corpus Coll. Ox.; Tithe, 500*l*; Glebe 12¾ acres; R.'s Inc. 516*l* and Ho; Pop. 841.) [22]

LEDSAM, Daniel, *Sand Hill, Birmingham.*—St. John's Coll. Cam. B.A. 1835, M.A. 1839; Deac. 1836, Pr. 1840. P. C. of St. Mark's, Birmingham, Dio. Wor. 1841. (Patrons, Trustees; P. C.'s Inc. 160*l*; Pop. 10,899.) [23]

LEE, Alfred Theophilus, *Bella Hill, Carrickfergus, Ireland.*—Ch. Coll. Cam. Prizeman and B.A. 1853, M.A. 1856; Deac. 1853 by Bp of Rip. Pr. 1853 by Bp of Dur. Dom. Chap. to Marquis of Donegal 1857. Formerly R. of Ahoghill 1858; Sen. C. and Lect. of Tetbury, Glouc. 1853–57. Author, *Slavery of Sin*, 1853, 6*d*.; *Address to Candidates for Confirmation*, 1855, 1*s*; *Address to the Churchmen of England on the Increase in the Episcopate proposed by the Cathedral Commission*, 1855, 6*d*. [24]

LEE, Augustus Charles, *Oxford and Cambridge Club, London.*—Trin. Coll. Cam. B.A. 1859; Deac. 1860 and Pr. 1861 by Bp of B. and W. Formerly C. of Chewton-Mendip, Somerset, 1860–62; Barming, Kent, 1862–65. [25]

LEE, Charles, *Kentish-town, London, N.W.*—P. C. of Trinity, Kentish-town, Dio. Lon. 1860. (Patrons, D. and C. of St. Paul's; P. C.'s Inc. 300*l*; Pop. 16,821.) [1]

LEE, Charles, *Yaxley Vicarage, Stilton, Hunts.*—Mert. Coll. Ox; Deac. 1824 and Pr. 1825 by Bp of Lin. V. of Yaxley, Dio. Ely, 1836. (Patron, Ld Chan; Tithe, Imp. 328*l* 15*s*; Glebe, 92 acres; V.'s Inc. 185*l* and Ho; Pop. 1411.) [2]

LEE, Charles, *Hope, Shelton, Staffordshire.*—C. of Hope. [3]

LEE, C. E., *Presteign, Radnorshire.*—C. of Presteign. [4]

LEE, Edmund, *St. Peters', Preston, Lancashire.*—Dub. A.B. 1862, A.M. 1864; Deac. 1862 by Abp of Dub. Pr. 1864 by Bp of Limerick. C. of St. Peter's, Preston, 1866. Formerly C. of Radford, near Nottingham, 1865–66. [5]

LEE, Edward Henry, *Cliffe Rectory, Rochester.*—New Inn Hall, Ox. B.A. 1841; Deac. 1842 and Pr. 1843 by Abp of Cant. C. of Cliffe-at-Hoo (sole charge) 1850. Diocesan Inspector of Schools. Formerly C. of Hadleigh, Suffolk, 1842, Saltwood, Kent, 1846. [6]

LEE, Frederick George, 23, *Coleshill-street, Eaton-square, London, S.W.*—St. Edm. Hall, Ox. S.C.L. 1854; Deac. 1854 and Pr. 1856 by Bp of Ox. Formerly Dom. Chap. to the Duke of Leeds 1858–60; C. of Sunningwell and Kennington, Berks, 1854–56; Incumb. of St. John's Episcopal Ch. Aberdeen, 1860-64. Author, *Lays of the Church*, Masters, 1851; *A Form for the Admission of a Chorister*, 1854; *Poems*, 2nd ed. 3*s* 6*d*; *The Martyr of Vienne and Lyons* (a Prize Poem), 1854; *Our Village and its Story*, 1855; *Petrovilla and other Poems*, 1858, 3*s*. [7]

LEE, Godfrey Bollas, *Winchester College.*—New Coll. Ox. B.A. 1839; Deac. 1845 and Pr. 1846 by Bp of Ox. Warden of Winchester Coll. 1861. [8]

LEE, Harry, *North Bradley Vicarage, Trowbridge, Wilts.*—New Coll. Ox. B.A. 1815, M.A. 1819, B.D. 1827. Preb. of Putson-Major in Herf. Cathl. 1827; (Value, 30*l*.) Fell. of the Coll. of St. Mary, Winchester, 1828; V. of North Bradley, Dio. Salis. 1832. (Patron, Win. Coll; Tithe—Imp. 460*l*, V. 640*l*; Glebe, 4 acres; V.'s Inc. 650*l* and Ho; Pop. 1788.) [9]

LEE, Henry, *Jackfield, Broseley, Salop.*—Dur. B.A. 1852, M.A. 1855; Deac. 1852 by Bp of Wor. Pr. 1853 by Bp of Ox. R. of Jackfield, Dio. Herf. 1863. (Patrons, F. B. Harries, Esq. and R. of Broseley alt; P. C.'s Inc. 150*l*; Pop. 1500.) Formerly C. of Enmore, Somerset, and Ashbury, Berks. [10]

LEE, Henry Thomas, *South Raynham Vicarage, Brandon, Norfolk.*—Trin. Coll. Cam. B.A. 1833, M.A. 1844; Deac. 1844 by Bp of G. and B. Pr. 1844 by Bp of Llan. V. of Helhoughton with South Raynham V. Dio. Nor. 1846. (Patron, Marquis Townshend; Helhoughton, Tithe—Imp. 299*l* 14*s*, V. 184*l* 12*s* 6*d*; Glebe, 26 acres; South Raynham, Tithe—Imp. 185*l*, V. 106*l* 8*s* 6*d*; Glebe, 28 acres; V.'s Inc. 390*l* and Ho; Pop. Helhoughton 346, South Raynham 129.) Rural Dean. [11]

LEE, John, *Tilstock Parsonage, Whitchurch, Salop.*—Pemb. Coll. Ox. B.A. 1855; Deac. 1855 by Bp of Man. Pr. 1856 by Bp of Dur. P. C. of Tilstock, Dio. Lich. 1857. (Patron, R. of Whitchurch; Glebe, 110 acres; P. C.'s Inc. 130*l* and Ho; Pop. 593.) Formerly C. of St. Hilda's, South Shields. [12]

LEE, John Irwin, *Leeds.*—C. of St. Andrew's, Leeds. [13]

LEE, John Morley, *Botley, Southampton.*—St. John's Coll. Cam. 8th Sen. Opt. and B.A. 1848, M.A. 1851; Deac. 1850 and Pr. 1851 by Bp of Ely. R. of Botley, Dio. Win. 1855. (Patron, H. Lee, Esq; Tithe, 391*l* 17*s* 8*d*; Glebe, 12 acres; R.'s Inc. 400*l*; Pop. 860.) Rural Dean of Droxford. [14]

LEE, John Robinson, *Magdalen College, Cambridge.*—Magd. Coll. Cam. B.A. 1857; Deac. 1859, Pr. 1860. Fell. of Magd. Coll. Cam. Formerly C. of Bardsea, Ulverstone, 1860. Author, *History of Market Drayton*; *Translation of Antigone.* [15]

LEE, John Walter, *Hartlebury, Worcestershire.*—Emman. Coll. Cam. 4th Jun. Opt. and B.A. 1851, M.A. 1856; Deac. 1852 by Bp of Rip. Pr. 1864 by Bp of Wor. Head Mast. of Queen Elizabeth's Gr. Sch. Hartlebury. Formerly 2nd Mast. of the Chelmsford Gr. Sch. [16]

LEE, John William, *Alphington, near Exeter.*—Dub. A.B. 1828, A.M. 1831; Deac. 1828, Pr. 1829. C. of Alphington. Formerly C. of Tedburn, Exeter, and St. Paul's, Honiton, Devon. [17]

LEE, Lancelot J., *New College, Oxford.*—Fell. of New Coll. Ox. [18]

LEE, Matthew Henry, *Morland, Penrith.*—Brasen. Coll. Ox. B.A. 1854, M.A. 1857; Deac. 1856 and Pr. 1857 by Bp of Man. C. of Morland. Formerly C. of Longsight, Manchester. [19]

LEE, Melville Lauriston, *Bridport Rectory, Dorset.*—Magd. Coll. Cam. B.A. 1843; Deac. 1844 and Pr. 1845 by Bp of Ex. R. of Bridport, Dio. Salis. 1851. (Patron, Earl of Ilchester; Tithe, 13*l*; Glebe, 16 acres; R.'s Inc. 270*l* and Ho; Pop. 4645.) Surrogate. [20]

LEE, Philip Henry, *Stoke Bruerne Rectory, Towcester, Northants.*—Brasen. Coll. Ox. B.A. 1827, M.A. 1830; Deac. 1828 by Bp of Ox. Pr. 1829 by Bp of Ches. R. of Stoke Bruerne, Dio. Pet. 1836. (Patron, Brasen. Coll. Ox; Tithe, 559*l* 6*s* 6*d*; Glebe, 66 acres; R.'s Inc. 650*l* and Ho; Pop. 824.) Rural Dean of Brockley, N.E. Division, 1840; Chap. to Lord Stanley 1845. Formerly Fell. of Brasen. Coll. Ox. 1827–36. [21]

LEE, Philip Henry, *Farnham, Dorset.*—Wor. Coll. Ox. B.A. 1851, M.A. 1854; Deac. 1852 and Pr. 1853 by Bp of Man. R. of Farnham, Dio. Salis. 1866. (Patron, Ld Chan; R.'s Inc. 149*l* and Ho; Pop. 121.) Formerly C. of Penwortham, Lanc. 1852–54, Mathon, Worc. 1855, Middleton Cheney, Northants, 1855–58 (sole charge); V. of Pattishall 1st Div. 1859. [22]

LEE, Richard, *St. Dunstan's Rectory, Stepney, London, E.*—Lin. Coll. Ox. B.A. 1829, M.A. 1840; Deac. 1828 and Pr. 1829 by Bp of Lin. R. of Stepney, Dio. Lon. 1847. (Patron, Brasen. Coll. Ox; R.'s Inc. 900*l* and Ho; Pop. 27,607.) Dom. Chap. to the Earl of Mexborough. Formerly V. of Aslackby, Linc. 1829–38; R. of Darley, Derbyshire, 1838–47. Author, *Sermons*, 1831, 4*s*; *Sermons, Occasional and Practical*, 1841, 7*s*. [23]

LEE, Robert, *Scarborough, Yorks.*—Pemb. Coll. Cam. B.A. 1854; Deac. 1855 and Pr. 1857 by Bp of Rip. Formerly Sen. C. of Scarborough, and C. of Rothwell. [24]

LEE, Roger, 24, *Wellington Esplanade, Lowestoft.*—Trin. Coll. Cam. B.A. 1852, M.A. 1856; Deac. 1856 and Pr. 1857 by Bp of Nor. C. of Gunton, Suffolk, 1860. Formerly C. of Chedgrave, Norfolk, 1856; Chap. to the House of Industry, Oulton, Suffolk, 1858; Dom. Chap. to the late and the present Earl of Gosford, 1858–65. [25]

LEE, Sackville Usher Bolton, *Exeter.*—Oriel Coll. Ox. 3rd cl. Lit. Hum. and B.A. 1828, M.A. 1835; Deac. 1830, Pr. 1838. Preb. of Ex. Cathl. 1858, and Canon Res. 1865. Formerly R. of Allhallows-on-the-Walls, Exeter, 1846–61, and of Allhallows in Goldsmith-street, Exeter, 1861–66. [26]

LEE, Stanlake, *Broughton Rectory, Stockbridge.*—Queen's Coll. Ox. B.A. 1840; Deac. 1840 and Pr. 1841 by Bp of Ox. R. of Broughton with Bossington R. Dio. Win. 1842. (Patron, T. Baring, Esq. M.P; Broughton, Tithe, 770*l*; Glebe, 34 acres; Bossington, Tithe, 140*l*; R.'s Inc. 969*l* and Ho; Pop. Broughton 1001, Bossington 45.) [27]

LEE, Thomas, *Ossett Parsonage, Dewsbury, Yorks.*—St. Cath. Coll. Cam. B.A. 1853. P. C. of Ossett-cum-Gawthorpe, Dio. Rip. 1858. (Patron, V. of Dewsbury; Tithe, Ossett, Imp. 201*l* 8*s* 9*d*; Glebe, 1½ acres; Gawthorpe, Imp. 88*l* 10*s* 9*d*; V.'s Inc. 160*l* and Ho; Pop. 4932.) Formerly C. of St. Giles's, Lond. [28]

LEE, Thomas Booth, *Woolverstone, Suffolk.*—C. of Woolverstone. Formerly C. of Kirk Christ, Lezayre, and St. Olave's, Ramsey, Isle of Man. [29]

LEE, Thomas Faulkner, *Grammar Schoolhouse, Lancaster.*—Queens' Coll. Cam. B.A. 1848, M.A. 1851; Deac. 1848 and Pr. 1849 by Bp of Roch. P. C. of Ch.

Ch. Lancaster, Dio. Man. 1857. (Patroness, Mrs. Murray.) Head Mast. of the Royal Gr. Sch. Lancaster, 1850. Formerly 2nd Mast. of the St. Albans Gr. Sch. 1848–50. Author, *Short Account of the Abbey of St. Albans*; Papers on Archæological Subjects; Sermons. [1]

LEE, Thomas Jones, *Luton, Beds.*—Wor. Coll. Ox. 3rd cl. Lit. Hum. B.A. 1849, M.A. 1850; Deac. 1849 and Pr. 1850 by Bp of B. and W. V. of Ch. Ch. Luton, Dio. Ely, 1863. (Patron, William Goodwin, Esq; Tithe, 105*l*; V.'s Inc. 250*l*; Pop. 6658.) Formerly C. of Bridgwater 1849–52, Banwell 1852–59, Buckley, Flintshire, 1857–61. Author, *The Book of Common Prayer, a Form of Sound Words*, 1862, 6*d*; *Louise Gulliford, or Recollections of the Cholera, a Tale*; *The Baptists in Error. a Dialogue*; *Resignation, a Sermon on the Sudden Death of the Rev. T. G. James.* [2]

LEE, Thomas William, *Hartford House, Winchfield, Hants.*—Trin. Coll. Cam. Bracketed 1st in 2nd cl. Cl. Trip. 21st Sen. Opt. and B.A. 1857, M.A. 1860; Deac. 1860 and Pr. 1861 by Bp of Salis. Formerly Asst. Mast. in Marlborough Coll. 1859–63. [3]

LEE, Walter, *Billericay, Essex.*—Head Mast. of the Gr. Sch. Billericay. [4]

LEE, William Blackstone, *Wootton, Woodstock, Oxon.*—New Coll. Ox. B.A. 1816, M.A. 1820; Deac. 1817, Pr. 1818. R. of Wootton, Dio. Ox. 1836. (Patron, New Coll. Ox; Tithe, 259*l* 10*s* 6*d*; Glebe, 564 acres; R.'s Inc. 845*l* and Ho; Pop. 1238.) [5]

LEE, William Gurden, *Shelton Rectory, Kimbolton, Beds.*—Lin. Coll. Ox; Deac. 1853 and Pr. 1854 by Bp of Pet. R. of Shelton, Dio. Ely, 1866. (Patron, Lord St. John; Glebe, 45 acres; R.'s Inc. 232*l*; Pop. 150.) Formerly C. of Stanwick 1853–54, Shapwith with Ashcott 1854–66. [6]

LEE, W. Hill, *Leicester.*—C. of Ch. Ch. Leicester. Formerly C. of St. Mark's, Old-street, Lond. and St. Mary's, Liverpool, 1864. [7]

LEE, William Molland, *Christ Church Parsonage, Sandown, Isle of Wight.*—St. John's Coll. Cam. B.A. 1835, M.A. 1842; Deac. 1835 by Bp of Carl. Pr. 1836 by Bp of Ex. P. C. of Ch. Ch. Sandown, Dio. Win. 1862. (Patrons, Trustees; Glebe, 18 acres; Inc. variable—about 200*l* and Ho; Pop. 1760.) Surrogate. Formerly C. of King's Kerswell 1835, St. Columb Major 1838; R. of Adverdiscott, *alias* Alscott, 1838. [8]

LEECH, William, *Flitcham Parsonage, Castle Rising, Norfolk.*—Queen's Coll. Ox. B.A. 1829, M.A. 1833; Deac. 1830 and Pr. 1831 by Bp of Nor. V. of Shernborne, Lynn, Norfolk, Dio. Nor. 1833. (Patron, Bp of Nor; Glebe, 65 acres; V.'s Inc. 120*l*; Pop. 144.) P. C. of Flitcham, Dio. Nor. 1843. (Patron, Earl of Leicester; Tithe—Imp. 700*l*; P. C.'s Inc. 80*l* and Ho; Pop. 533.) [9]

LEECH, William Henry, *Egremont, Cumberland.*—Brasen. Coll. Ox; Deac. 1818 by Bp of Carl. Pr. 1826 by Bp of Ches. R. of Egremont, Dio. Ches. 1835. (Patron, General Wyndham; Tithe—Imp. 2*l*, R. 207*l* 4*s* 3*d*; Glebe, 32 acres; R.'s Inc. 260*l* and Ho; Pop. 3481.) [10]

LEECH, William Poole, *Flitcham Parsonage, Castle Rising, Norfolk.*—Dub. A.B. 1856; Deac. 1857 and Pr. 1858 by Bp of Nor. Asst. C. of Flitcham. [11]

LEEFE, John Ewbank, *Cresswell Parsonage, Morpeth.*—Trin. Coll. Cam. 24th Wrang. 4th in 3rd cl. Cl. Trip. and B.A. 1835, M.A. 1839; Deac. 1838 and Pr. 1840 by Bp of Ox. P. C. of Cresswell, Dio. Dur. 1849. (Patron, A. J. C. Baker, Esq; Tithe—App. 91*l* 14*s* 8*d*; Glebe, 1 acre; Endow. 100*l*; P. C.'s Inc. 102*l* 10*s* and Ho; Pop. 508.) [12]

LEEKE, William, *Holbrooke, Derby.*—Queens' Coll. Cam. B.A. 1828, M.A. 1832; Deac. 1829 and Pr. 1830 by Bp of Chich. P. C. of Holbrooke, Dio. Lich. 1840. (Patron, Thomas William Evans, Esq; Tithe—App. 6*l* 5*s* 10*d*; Imp. 55*l* 10*s* 6*d*; P. C.'s Inc. 157*l* 10*s*; Pop. 1003.) Formerly C. of Westham, Sussex, 1829, Brailsford, Derbyshire, 1831. Rural Dean of Duffield 1849. Author, *A Few Suggestions for increasing the Incomes of many of the smaller Livings, and for the almost total Abolition of Pluralities, more especially addressed to the Members of both Houses of Parliament*, 1838; *Memorial to the Archbishop of Canterbury, from seventy-two of the Clergy of Derbyshire, on the Abolition of Pluralities*, 1839; Papers on *The Observance of the Lord's Day*; *History of Lord Seton's Regiment* (the 52nd Light Infantry) *at the Battle of Waterloo, &c. &c.* [13]

LEEMAN, Alfred, *Aldenham Grammar School, Watford, Herts.*—Scho. of St. John's Coll. Cam. 2nd cl. Cl. Trip. Sen. Opt. B.A. 1839, M.A. 1842; Deac. 1841. Head. Mast. of Aldenham Gr. Sch. 1843. [14]

LEEPER, William, *All Saints' Vicarage, Kings Lynn.*—Dub. A.B. 1846, A.M. 1862; Deac. 1846 by Bp of Lich. Pr. 1848 by Bp of Nor. V. of All Saints', Lynn-Regis, Dio. Nor. 1855. (Patron, Bp of Nor; Tithe, 190*l*; V.'s Inc. 300*l* and Ho; Pop. 4534.) Chap. of the Lynn Union. Formerly C. of St. John's, Derby, 1846, St. Margaret's, Lynn, 1848; P. C. of Stoke Ferry 1855. [15]

LEES, John, 2, *Duerdin-villas, Tollington-park, Upper Holloway, London, N.*—Corpus Coll. Cam. B.A. 1841, M.A. 1853; Deac. 1841 and Pr. 1842 by Bp of Lich. P. C. of St. Mark's, Tollington-park, Dio. Lon. 1854. (Patron, P. C. of St. John's, Upper Holloway; P. C.'s Inc. 450*l*; Pop. 6873.) [16]

LEES, John Lowder Laycock, *West Wratting Vicarage, near Cambridge.*—St. Bees 1850; Deac. 1852 and Pr. 1853 by Bp of Lich. V. of West Wratting, Dio. Ely, 1866. (Patrons, D. and C. of Ely; Glebe, 134 acres; V.'s Inc. 250*l* and Ho; Pop. 770.) P. C. of West Wickham, Dio. Ely. (Patron, Lord Hardwicke; P. C.'s Inc. 80*l*; Pop. 500.) Formerly C. of the "Working Man's Wooden Church," Luton, and Tankersley, Yorks; P. C. of St. Michael's, Islington, 1862. [17]

LEES, Thomas, *Wreay Parsonage, Carlisle.*—Emman. Coll. Cam. 18th Sen. Opt. and B.A. 1852, M.A. 1855; Deac. 1854 and Pr. 1855 by Bp of Carl. P. C. of Wreay, Dio. Carl. 1865. (Patrons, D. and C. of Carl; Tithe, 30*l* 11*s* 7*d*; Glebe, 76 acres; P. C.'s Inc. 92*l* and Ho; Pop. 166.) Formerly C. of Kirkby-Thore, Westmoreland 1854–55, Greystoke 1855–65. [18]

LEES, William, *Sidlow Bridge, Horley, Surrey.*—P. C. of Sidlow Bridge, Dio. Win. 1862. (Patrons, R. Clutton and C. Sherrard, Esqs. alt; P. C.'s Inc. 75*l* and Ho; Pop. 550.) [19]

LEES, William, *Norley, near Frodsham, Cheshire.*—St. John's Coll. Cam. B.A. 1831, M.A. 1834; Deac. 1831 and Pr. 1832 by Bp of Ches. P. C. of Norley, Dio. Ches. 1862. (Patron, S. Woodhouse, Esq; P. C.'s Inc. 64*l*; Pop. 728.) Formerly C. of St. Peter's, Oldham, 1836. [20]

LEESON, Frederick Charles, *New St. George's, Staleybridge, Ashton-under-Lyne.*—St. Cath. Coll. Cam. B.A. 1851. P. C. of New St. George's, Staleybridge, Dio. Man. 1850. (Patron, R. of Ashton-under-Lyne; P. C.'s Inc. 135*l*; Pop. 4047.) [21]

LEESON, John Edmund, *Old St. George's Parsonage, Staleybridge, Ashton-under-Lyne.*—St. Bees 1842. P. C. of Old St. George's, Staleybridge, Dio. Man. 1850. (Patron, Earl of Stamford; P. C.'s Inc. 135*l* and Ho.) [22]

LEESON, William, *Thurstonland, Huddersfield.*—Dub. A.B. 1863; Deac. 1866 by Bp of Rip. C. of Thurstonland 1866. [23]

LEETE, Thomas Troughton, *Poling Vicarage, Arundel, Sussex.*—Caius Coll. Cam. B.A. 1836, M.A. 1845; Deac. 1836 and Pr. 1837 by Bp of Lin. V. of Poling, Dio. Chich. 1859. (Patron, Bp of Chich; Tithe, comm. 220*l*, Glebe, 2¾ acres; V.'s Inc. 236*l* and Ho; Pop. 206.) Formerly C. of William, Herts, 1836, Bishops Stortford 1840, St. John's, Reading, 1844, Poling 1847-59. Author, *Nature of a Christian Fast*, 1844; *The One Mediator*, 1844, 1*s*; *Christian Armour*, 1858. [24]

LEE-WARNER, George Brydges, *The Vicarage, Dane John, Canterbury.*—Brasen. Coll. Ox. B.A. 1834, M.A. 1837; Deac. 1844, Pr. 1847. V. of St. Mary Bredin, City and Dio. Cant. 1851. (Patron, H. Lee-Warner, Esq; Tithe, 30*l*; Glebe, 21*l*; Augmentation by Queen Anne's Bounty 69*l* 10*s* 4*d*; V.'s Inc. 120*l* 10*s* 4*d*; Pop. 1700.) [25]

LEE-WARNER, Henry James, *Thorpland, Fakenham, Norfolk.*—St. John's Coll. Cam. B.A. 1825, M.A. 1828. Hon. Can. of Nor. Cathl; Rural Dean. Formerly Chap. of the D. of Great Walsingham 1835. [1]

LEE-WARNER, James, *University College, Oxford.*—Trin. Coll. Ox. 2nd cl. Lit. Hum. 1859; Chan. Prize for Lat. Essay; Deac. 1866 by Bp of Lon. Fell. and Lect. Univ. Coll. 1866. Formerly Asst. Mast. in Westminster Sch. 1862–66. [2]

LEE-WARNER, John, *Great Walsingham, Norfolk.*—Chap. of Don. of Great Walsingham, Dio. Nor. 1855. (Patron, H. J. Lee-Warner, Esq; Chap.'s Inc. 168*l*; Pop. 512.) [3]

LEE-WARNER, Septimus Henry, *Walsingham Parsonage, Norfolk.*—St. John's Coll. Cam. B.A. 1842, M.A. 1849; Deac. 1843, Pr. 1844. V. of Houghton-in-the-Dale, Dio. Nor. 1853. (Patron, Rev. P. H. Lee-Warner; Tithe, 135*l*; Glebe, 29 acres; V.'s Inc. 156*l* and Ho; Pop. 191.) P. C. of Little Walsingham, Dio. Nor. 1859. (Patron, H. J. Lee-Warner, Esq; Glebe, 2 acres; P. C.'s Inc. 168*l*; Pop. 1069.) [4]

LEE-WARNER, T. H., *Elmore, near Gloucester.*—P. C. of Elmore, Dio. G. and B. 1865. (Patron, Sir J. W. Guise; P. C.'s Inc. 73*l*; Pop. 374.) Formerly C. of East Woodhay, Hants. [5]

LE FEUVRE, Philip Alfred, *Oak-walk, St. Peter's, Jersey.*—Wad. Coll. Ox. B.A. 1848, M.A. 1851; Deac. 1850 and Pr. 1856 by Bp of Win. Chap. of Rozel Manor Chapel, Jersey, Dio. Win. (Patron, P. R. Lempriere, Esq.) Formerly C. of St. Matthew's, 1850, St. Luke's, 1856. [6]

LE FEUVRE, Philip Horton, *Wisbech St. Mary, Cambridge.*—C. of Wisbech St. Mary. [7]

LEFROY, Anthony Cottrell, *Church Crookham Parsonage, Farnham, Surrey.*—Ch. Ch. Ox. B.A. 1834, M.A. 1839; Deac. 1837 and Pr. 1838 by Bp of Lon. P. C. of Crookham with Ewshott P. C. Hants, Dio. Win. 1841. (Patron, V. of Crondall; P. C.'s Inc. 78*l* and Ho; Pop. 1283.) [8]

LEFROY, William, 4, *St. James'-road, Liverpool.*—Dub. A.B. 1863, A.M. 1867; Deac. 1864 and Pr. 1865 by Bp of Cork. P. C. of St. Andrew's, Liverpool, Dio. Ches. 1866. (Patron, Robertson Gladstone, Esq; P. C.'s Inc. 400*l*; Pop. 4000.) Formerly C. of Ch. Ch. Cork, 1864–66. [9]

LEGARD, Francis Digby, *Whitwell, York.*—Univ. Coll. Ox. B.A. 1851; Deac. 1855 and Pr. 1856 by Bp of Lin. P. C. of Whitwell, Dio. York, 1858. (Patron, Sir E. A. H. Lechmere, Bart; P. C.'s Inc. 110*l*.) Formerly C. of Flixborough and Burton-upon-Stather, Linc. [10]

LE GEYT, Charles James, *St. Matthias' Parsonage, Stoke Newington, London, N.*—Ex. Coll. Ox. B.A. 1853, M.A. 1855; Deac. 1853 and Pr. 1854 by Bp of Ox. P. C. of St. Matthias', Stoke Newington, Dio. Lon. 1858. (Patrons, the Crown and Bp. of Lon. alt; P. C.'s Inc. 260*l* and Ho; Pop. 9000.) Formerly Chap. of Magd. Coll. Ox. 1853–58; C. of Clifton-Hampden and Hursley. Author, *The Warning of Esau* (a Sermon), 1860, Masters; *Digging again the Wells* (a Sermon), 1867, G. J. Palmer; *Catholic Ritual of the Church in England* (a Lecture), 1866, Masters. [11]

LEGG, William, *West Farleigh, Maidstone.*—Magd. Coll. Ox. B.A. 1859, M.A. 1862; Deac. 1859 and Pr. 1860 by Bp of Ely. C. of West Farleigh 1863. Formerly C. of Orton Longueville, Hunts, and Tutor to Lord Douglas Gordon, son of the Marquis of Huntly. [12]

LEGGATT, G. B., *Westborough, Lincolnshire.*—C. of Westborough. Formerly C. of Radbourne, Derbyshire. [13]

LEGGE, Alfred, *Barnack, Northamptonshire.*—St. Peter's Coll. Cam. B.A. 1862. Deac. 1864 and Pr. 1865 by Bp of Wor. C. of Barnack 1866. Formerly C. of Redditch 1864. [14]

LEGGE, Hon. Augustus.—C. of St. Mary's, Bryanston-square, and Assist. Min. of Brunswick Chapel, Marylebone, Lond. [15]

LEGGE, Augustus George, *Elmham Vicarage, Thetford, Norfolk.*—Ch. Ch. Ox. B.A. 1857; Deac. 1858 and Pr. 1859 by Bp of Nor. V. of North Elmham, Dio. Nor. 1867. (Patron, Lord Sondes; Tithe, comm. 463*l* 2*s* 6*d*; Glebe, 8 acres; Pop. 1252.) Formerly C. of Doning with Dilham, Norwich, 1858; Campsea Ashe, Suffolk, 1860. [16]

LEGGE, Eugene E. P., *Litton Cheney, Dorchester.*—Wad. Coll. Ox. B.A. 1865; Deac. 1866. Formerly C. of Bampton with Petton 1866–67. [17]

LEGGE, The Hon. Henry, *Blackheath, Kent.*—Ch. Ch. Ox. B.A. 1824, All Souls Coll. B.C.L. 1835, D.C.L. 1840; Deac. 1826, Pr. 1827. V. of Lewisham, Kent, Dio. Lon. 1831. (Patron, Earl of Dartmouth; Tithe—Imp. 420*l* 3*s* 9*d*, V. 1006*l* 19*s* 6*d*; Glebe, 72 acres; V.'s Inc. 1113*l* and Ho; Pop. 10,386.) Formerly Fell. of All Souls Coll. Ox. 1825. [18]

LEGGE, Henry, *East Lavant Rectory, Chichester.*—Ch. Ch. Ox. B.A. 1824. R. of East Lavant, Dio. Chich. 1838. (Patron, Lord Willoughby De Broke; Tithe, 493*l* 12*s*; R.'s Inc. 510*l* and Ho; Pop. 421.) [19]

LEGGE, Henry James, *Brimscombe Parsonage, Stroud, Glouc.*—St. Alban Hall, Ox. B.A. 1823, M.A. 1835; Deac. 1823 and Pr. 1824 by Bp of Salis. P. C. of Brimscombe, Dio. G. and B. 1841. (Patron, David Ricardo, Esq; Tithe, 276*l*; Glebe, 17 acres; P. C.'s Inc. 334*l* and Ho; Pop. 1430.) [20]

LEGGE, William, *Ashtead Rectory, Epsom, Surrey.*—Ch. Ch. Ox. B.A. 1824; Deac. 1825 by Bp of Ox. Pr. 1826 by Bp of Herf. R. of Ashtead, Dio. Win. 1826. (Patrons, Heirs of the late Hon. Col. Howard; Tithe, 553*l* 12*s* 6*d*; Glebe, 12 acres; R.'s Inc. 497*l* and Ho; Pop. 729.) [21]

LEGGETT, Robert, *Claydon, Ipswich.*—Caius Coll. Cam. B.A. 1839. C. of Claydon and Coddenham; Chap. of the Bosmere and Claydon Union. [22]

LEGH, H. Edmund, 1, *Montpelier-place, Brighton.*—B.A. 1863, M.A. 1867; Deac. 1864 and Pr. 1865 by Abp of Cant. Asst. C. of Ch. Ch. Brighton, 1867. Formerly C. of Ch. Ch. Tunbridge Wells, 1864–65, Trinity, Tunbridge Wells, 1865–66. [23]

LEGH, John Robert, *Astley, Salop.*—St. John's Coll. Cam. B.A. 1855, M.A. 1859; Deac. 1856 and Pr. 1857 by Bp of Wor. P. C. of Astley, Dio. Lich. 1861. (Patrons, Trustees of Shrewsbury Sch; Glebe, 3 acres; P. C.'s Inc. 96*l* and Ho; Pop. 240.) Chap. to Shrewsbury Incorporation of the Poor 1864. Formerly C. of St. George's, Birmingham, 1856, Blandford 1857; V. of Tarrant Monkton, Dorset, 1858. [24]

LE GRICE, Frederick, *Great Gransden (Hunts), near Caxton.*—Clare Hall, Cam. 10th Wrang. and B.A. 1820, M.A. 1823; Deac. 1821, Pr. 1824. V. of Great Gransden, Dio. Ely, 1832. (Patron, Clare Hall, Cam; Tithe—Imp. 484*l* 5*s* 6*d*, V. 102*l* 10*s*; Glebe, 93 acres; V.'s Inc. 200*l*; Pop. 641.) Formerly Fell. of Clare Hall, Cam. [25]

LE HARDY, Clement, *St. Peter's Rectory, Jersey.*—Pemb. Coll. Ox. B.A. 1830, M.A. 1833; Deac. 1831, Pr. 1832. R. of St. Peter's, Jersey, Dio. Win. 1848. (Patron, The Governor; Tithe, 40*l*; Glebe, 6 acres; R.'s Inc. 135*l* and Ho; Pop. 2671.) [26]

LEICESTER, Morton Amos, *Langridge, Somerset.*—Cam. B.A. 1849, M.A. 1853; Deac. 1853, Pr. 1855. C. of Langridge. Formerly C. of Marston Bigott, Leigh, Staffs. [27]

LEICESTER, Robert, *Much Woolton, near Liverpool.*—Clare Coll. Cam. B.A. 1822, M.A. 1825; Deac. 1822, Pr. 1823. P. C. of Woolton, Dio. Ches. 1826. (Patron, V. of Childwall; Glebe, 2 acres; P. C.'s Inc. 220*l* and Ho; Pop. 3538.) [28]

LEICESTER, William Henry, *Marthall, Knutsford.*—Ch. Coll. Cam. B.A. 1845, M.A. 1846; Deac. 1846 and Pr. 1847 by Bp of Lich. P. C. of Marthall, Dio. Ches. 1864. (Patron, Lord Egerton; P. C.'s Inc. 165*l*; Pop. 525.) Formerly C. of Eversholt, Beds, and Freehay, Staffs. [29]

LEIGH, Arthur H. Austen, *Bray Vicarage, Maidenhead.*—St. John's Coll. Ox. B.A. 1858, M.A. 1859, 2nd cl. Lit. Hum. 1st cl. in Law and Mod. Hist; Deac. 1864, Pr. 1865. C. of Bray, 1867. Formerly C. of Ch. Ch. Marylebone, 1865–66. [30]

LEIGH, Augustus Austen, *King's College, Cambridge.*—King's Coll. Cam. Fell. of; Deac. 1865 by

Bp of Lin. Formerly Asst. C. of Henley-on-Thames 1865-67. [1]

LEIGH, Charles Brian, *Goldhanger Rectory, Maldon, Essex.*—Ch. Coll. Cam. B.A. 1837; Deac. 1839 and Pr. 1840 by Bp of Lon. R. of Goldhanger with Little Totham R. Dio. Roch. 1846. (Patron, the present R; Goldhanger, Tithe, 589*l*; Glebe, 28 acres; Little Totham, Tithe, 368*l*; Glebe, 7 acres; R.'s Inc. 995*l* and Ho; Pop. Goldhanger 545, Little Totham 346.) [2]

LEIGH, Daniel, *Aberdare.*—Deac. 1861 and Pr. 1862 by Bp of Llan. C. of St. Elvan's, Aberdare, 1867. Formerly C. of Merthyr Tydvil. [3]

LEIGH, Edmund, *Tredegar, Monmouthshire.*—Literate; Deac. 1843 and Pr. 1844 by Bp of Llan. P. C of Tredegar, Dio. Llan. 1866. (Patron, P. C. of Bedwellty; P. C.'s Inc. 300*l*; Pop. 7630.) Formerly P. C. of Bedwellty 1846. [4]

LEIGH, Francis, *Caverswall Vicarage, Cheadle, Staffs.*—Magd. Hall, Ox. Hon. 4th cl. Lit. Hum. and B.A. 1842; Deac. 1844 and Pr. 1845 by Bp of Lich. C. of Caverswall and Werrington. [5]

LEIGH, Francis Joseph, *Nympsfield Rectory, Stonehouse, Glouc.*—Ox. and Dub. 2nd cl. Math. B.A. 1842, M.A. 1845; Deac. 1843 by Bp of Lin. Pr. 1844 by Bp of G. and B. R. of Nympsfield, Dio. G. and B. 1861. (Patron, Ld Chan; Tithe, 258*l*; Glebe, 27 acres; R.'s Inc. 300*l* and Ho; Pop. 373.) Formerly C. of Ch. Ch. Newark, 1843, Newington Bagpath with Owlpen 1844-52; Min. of St. Paul's, Jersey, 1852-61. [6]

LEIGH, James Edward Austen, *Bray Vicarage, Maidenhead, Berks.*—Ex. Coll. Ox. 2nd cl. Lit. Hum. and B.A. 1820, M.A. 1826; Deac. 1822, Pr. 1823. V. of Bray, Dio. Ox. 1852. (Patron, Bp of Ox; Tithe—App. 2300*l*, V. in lieu of Tithe, 402 acres; Glebe, 5 acres; V.'s Inc. 500*l* and Ho; Pop. 2547.) [7]

LEIGH, the Hon. James Wentworth, *Stoneleigh Vicarage, Kenilworth.*—Trin. Coll. Cam. Hon. M.A. 1860; Deac. 1862 and Pr. 1863 by Bp of Wor. V. of Stoneleigh, Dio. Wor. 1864. (Patron, Lord Leigh; V.'s Inc. 460*l* and Ho; Pop. 683.) Formerly C. of Bromsgrove 1863. Author, *Sacred Music in the Temple of God* (Sermon preached in the Cathedral at the Worcester Musical Festival 1866). [8]

LEIGH, Richard, 134, *Marine Parade, Brighton.*—Brasen. Coll. Ox. B.A. 1830; M.A. 1835; Deac. 1832 and Pr. 1833 by Bp of Salis. Formerly R. of Halsall 1843. [9]

LEIGH, Robert, *Hyde, Manchester.*—Queens' Coll. Cam. B.A. 1831, M.A. 1844; Deac. 1833 and Pr. 1834 by Bp of Lich. P. C. of St. Thomas's, Hyde, Dio. Man. 1858. (Patrons, Crown and Bp of Man. alt; P. C.'s Inc. 150*l*; Pop. 8267.) Formerly P. C. of Milford, Derbyshire, 1846-56. [10]

LEIGH, Thomas Gerrard, *Walton on-the-Hill Rectory, Liverpool.*—Brasen. Coll. Ox. B.A. 1825, M.A. 1827; Deac. 1825, Pr. 1826. R. of Walton-on-the-Hill, Dio. Ches. 1847. (Patron, J. S. Leigh, Esq; Tithe, 2082*l* 8*s* 10*d*, V. 109*l* 12*s* 2*d*; R.'s Inc. 2100*l* and Ho; Pop. 6246.) [11]

LEIGHTON, David Hillcoat, *Worlingham Rectory, Beccles, Suffolk.*—Trin. Coll. Cam. B.A. 1830, M.A. 1834. R. of Worlingham, Dio. Nor. (Patron, Ld Chan; Tithe, 303*l*; Glebe, 47½ acres; R's Inc. 360*l* and Ho; Pop. 199.) [12]

LEIGHTON, Francis, *Cardeston Rectory, Shrewsbury.*—Trin. Coll. Cam. B.A. 1827, M.A. 1830; Deac. 1826, Pr. 1827. R. of Cardeston, Dio. Herf. 1828. (Patron, Sir Baldwin Leighton, Bart; Tithe—Imp. 121*l* 1*s* 6*d*, R. 267*l*; Glebe, 30 acres; R.'s Inc. 340*l*; Pop. 294.) [13]

LEIGHTON, Francis Knyvett, *All Souls College, Oxford.*—Magd. Coll. Ox. Prizeman Latin Verse 1826, 2nd cl. Lit. Hum. and B.A. 1828, All Souls Coll. M.A. 1831; Deac. 1831 by Bp of Bristol, Pr. 1832 by Bp of Ox. R. of East Lockinge, Dio. Ox. 1858 (*annexed* to the Wardenship of All Souls Coll; Pop. 318); Warden of All Souls Coll. Ox. 1858; Rural Dean of Oxford 1858; Proctor in Convocation for the Dio. of Ox. 1857. Formerly R. of Harpeden, and Rural Dean of Henley, 1841-58; Vice-Chan. of Ox. 1866-67. [14]

LEIGHTON, James, *Bispham Vicarage, Fleetwood, Lancashire.*—Ch. Miss. Coll. Islington; Deac. 1854 by Bp of Ches. Pr. 1856, at Agra, by Bp of Madras. V. of Bispham, Dio. Man. 1861. (Patron, Rev. Charles Hesketh; Glebe, 3 acres; V.'s Inc. 220*l* and Ho; Pop. 457.) Formerly Missionary of Ch. Miss. Soc. at Agra 1854-58, at Amristar 1858-60. Author, *The Soldiers' Manual, chiefly for Hospitals,* Tract Society, Agra. [15]

LEIGHTON, John, 5, *Queen's Parade, Cheltenham*—St. John's Coll. Cam. Scho. B.A. 1848, M.A. 1855; Deac. 1848 by Bp of G. and B. Pr. 1849 by Bp of Ex. Boarding-House Mast. and Mast. in the Civil and Military Department of the Cheltenham Coll. 1862. Formerly 2nd Mast. of Chudleigh Gr. Sch. 1848-58, and Asst. C. of Hennock for the District of Chudleigh Knighton, 1848-58; Math. Mast. of the Somersetshire Coll. Bath, 1858-62. [16]

LEIR, Charles Edward, *March, Cambs.*—Oriel Coll. Ox. B.A. 1864; Deac. 1865 and Pr. 1866 by Bp of Ely. C. of March 1865. [17]

LEIR, William Marriott, *Ditcheat Rectory, Castle Carey, Somerset.*—Wad. Coll. Ox. B.A. 1828, M.A. 1836; Deac. and Pr. by Bp of B. and W. R. of Ditcheat, Dio. B. and W. 1861. (Patron, Rev. William Leir; Tithe—App. 1*l* 2*s* 4*d*, R. 773*l* 17*s* 8*d*; Glebe, 103 acres; R.'s Inc. 883*l* and Ho; Pop. 1218.) Formerly R. of West Bagborough 1855-61. [18]

LE MAISTRE, George John, *St. Aubyn's School, Jersey.*—Dub. A.B. 1851, A.M. 1854; Deac. 1852 and Pr. 1854 by Bp of Win. Head Mast. of St. Aubyn's Sch; Chap. of St. Aubyn's 1856. [19]

LE MAISTRE, James, LL.D., *Adlingfleet, Yorks.* [20]

LE MAISTRE, W., *St. Heliers, Jersey.*—C. of St. Heliers. [21]

LE MAISTRE, W. B., *The Great Trench, Hildenborough, Kent.* [22]

LEMAN, Thomas Orgill, *Brampton Rectory, Wangford, Suffolk.*—Wor. Coll. Ox. B.A. 1826, M.A. 1848; Deac. 1827, Pr. 1828. R. of Brampton, Dio. Nor. 1837. (Patron, Rev. G. O. Leman; Tithe, 433*l* 5*s* 6*d*; Glebe, 11¾ acres; R.'s Inc. 451*l* and Ho; Pop. 310.) Rural Dean. [23]

LEMANN, Francis Gregory, *Langford Vicarage, Lechlade, Berks.*—King's Coll. Cam. B.A. 1827, M.A. 1831; Deac. 1828 and Pr. 1829 by Bp of Ely. V. of Langford, Dio. Ox. 1855. (Patron, the present V; Tithe, 133*l*; Glebe, 106 acres; V.'s Inc. 330*l* and Ho; Pop. 701.) [24]

LE MARCHANT, Joshua, *Woolverton, Newbury.*—C. of Woolverton. [24]

LE MARCHANT, Robert, *Little Risington, Burford, Oxon.*—Dub. A.B. 1840, M.B. 1841, A.M. 1845, M.D. 1845; Deac. 1849 and Pr. 1850 by Bp of Chich. R. of Little Risington, Glouc. Dio. G. and B. 1862. (Patron, Ld Chan; Tithe, comm. 8*l*; Glebe, 174 acres; R.'s Inc. 400*l* and Ho; Pop. 250.) Formerly Sen. C. of Harberton, Totnes, 1857-59, Dawlish, Devon, 1859-62. [25]

LE MARCHANT, William Hirzel, *Stonehouse, Glouc.*—Dub. A.B. 1836 *ad eund.* Ex. Coll. Ox. 1839, M.A. 1839, D.D. 1864. V. of Haresfield, Glouc. Dio. G. and B. 1853. (Patron, D. J. Niblett, Esq; V.'s Inc. 263*l* and Ho; Pop. 612.) [26]

LE MESURIER, George Frederick, *Tormarton, Chipping Sodbury.*—Ex. Coll. Ox. B.A. 1855, M.A. 1858; Wells, 1856-57; Deac. 1857 and Pr. 1858 by Bp of Ox. C. of Tormarton with West Littleton and Acton Turville 1863. Formerly C. of Welford, Berks. [27]

LE MESURIER, Henry, *Grammar Schoolhouse, Bedford.*—New Coll. Ox. B.A. 1828, M.A. 1831. 2nd Mast. of Bedford Gr. Sch. [28]

LE MESURIER, John, *Bembridge, Ryde, Isle of Wight.*—Ch. Ch. Ox 3rd cl. Lit. Hum. 1st cl. Math. et Phy. and B.A. 1841, M.A. 1844; Deac. 1843 and Pr. 1844 by Bp of Lon. P. C. of Bembridge, Dio. Win. 1851. (Patron, V. of Brading; P. C.'s Inc. 100*l*; Pop. 783) [29]

LEMON, Charles, *Gerrans, Cornwall.*—C. of Gerrans. [30]

LEMON, John, 9, *Rodney-place, Clifton.*—King's Coll. Lond. Theol. Assoc; Deac. 1862 and Pr. 1863 by Bp of Win. C. of Ch. Ch. Clifton, 1867. Formerly C. of St. Jude's, Southwark, 1862–66. [1]

LE MOTTEE, William, *Helion-Bumpstead Vicarage (Essex), near Haverhill, Cambs.*—Trin. Coll. Cam. 13th Wrang. and B A. 1835, M.A. 1838; Deac. 1837, Pr. 1838. V. of Helion-Bumpstead, Dio. Roch. 1857. (Patron, Trin. Coll. Cam; Tithe—Imp. 711*l* 9*s* 9*d*, V. 274*l* 16*s*; Glebe, 3 acres; V.'s Inc. 284*l* and Ho; Pop. 887.) Formerly Chap. to the Garrison, Guernsey, 1849–57. [2]

LEMPRIERE, Daniel Mathew, *St. Heliers, Jersey.*—Pemb. Coll. Ox. B.A. 1846; Deac. 1847 by Bp of Ox. Pr. 1848 by Bp of Win. Chap. to the Jersey Hospital and Prison 1854. [3]

LEMPRIERE, Everard, *Meethe Rectory, Hatherleigh, Devon.*—R. of Meethe, Dio. Ex. 1824. (Patron, Rev. F. D. Lempriere; Tithe, 223*l* 10*s*; Glebe, 25 acres; R.'s Inc. 258*l* and Ho; Pop. 289.) [4]

LEMPRIERE, Francis Drouet, *Newton St. Petrock Rectory, Highampton, Devon.*—Trin. Coll. Cam. B.A. 1817, M.A. 1823; Deac. 1818 by Bp of Ex. Pr. 1820 by Bp of Lon. R. of Newton St. Petrock, Dio. Ex. 1824. (Patron, the present R; Tithe, 141*l* 10*s*; Glebe, 80 acres; R.'s Inc. 204*l* and Ho; Pop. 231.) Author, *Lessons on the Prophecies, &c.* 1829, 4*s* 6*d*; *The Catechism of the Church* (a Sermon), 1840, 1*s* 6*d*; *Lectures on the Collects*, Rivingtons, 1845, 12*s*; *A Catechism on the Unity of the Church*, Masters, 1861, 8*d*. [5]

LE NEVEU, Thomas, *Jersey.*—Dub. and St. Mary Hall, Ox. B.A. 1853; Deac. 1852 by Bp of Lich. Pr. 1853 by Bp of Win. R. of St. John's, Jersey, Dio. Win. 1863. (Patron, the Governor; R.'s Inc. 120*l* and Ho; Pop. 1815.) Formerly C. of St. Heliers. [6]

LENNARD, John Barrett, *Fauls Parsonage, Prees, Salop.*—Magd. Coll. Cam. B.A. 1864, M.A. 1867; Deac. 1864 and Pr. 1865 by Bp of Lon. P. C. of Fauls, Dio. Lich. 1866. (Patron, V. of Prees; Tithe, 50*l*; Glebe, 6 acres; P. C.'s Inc. 58*l* and Ho; Pop. 504.) Formerly C. of St. Jude's, Chelsea, 1864–66. [7]

LENNY, Christian, *Stubbings, Maidenhead, Berks.*—St. John's Coll. Cam. B.D. 1842, D.D. 1848; Deac. 1827, Pr. 1828. C. of St. James's, Stubbings. Author, *Shakespeare for Schools*, 2nd ed. 1865, 2*s* 6*d*. [8]

LENNY, Henry Stokes Noel, *Sandhurst, Wokingham.*—Trin. Coll. Cam. B.A. 1857; Deac. 1859 and Pr. 1860 by Abp of Cant. C. of Sandhurst 1866. Formerly C. of St. Peter's, Isle of Thanet, 1859–60, Burford, Oxford, 1861–66. [9]

LEONARD, Francis Burford, *Brook House, Newport, Monmouthshire.*—Wad. Coll. Ox. B.A. 1827, M.A. 1831; Deac. 1830, Pr. 1831. R. of Kemeys Inferior, Dio. Llan. 1846. (Patron, Rev. W. C. Risley; Tithe—Imp. 24*l*, R. 148*l*; R.'s Inc. 194*l*; Pop. 122.) P. C. of Llandevand, Monmouthshire, Dio. Llan. 1853. (Patron, Bp of Llan; Tithe—App. 30*l* 5*s* 9*d*; P. C.'s Inc. 48*l*.) [10]

LEONINI, P.—C. of St. James's the Less, Westminster, 1864. [11]

LEPARD, Samuel Campbell, *Canterbury.*—Wor. Coll. Ox B.A. 1857, M.A. 1860; Deac. 1857 and Pr. 1858 by Abp of Cant. Chap. of East Kent County Prisons, Canterbury, 1861; C. of St. Paul's and St. Martin's, Canterbury, 1862. Formerly C. of Ashford, Kent, 1857–61. [12]

LE PELLEY, John L., *Brompton, Chatham.*—Caius Coll. Cam. B.A. 1862, M.A. 1865; Deac. 1863, Pr. 1864. C. of Brompton 1864. [13]

LERMIT, Gerald Thomson, *Dedham Grammar School, near Colchester.*—St. John's Coll. Cam. Jun. Opt. and B.A. 1849, M.A. 1852; Deac. 1849, Pr. 1850. Head Mast. of the Dedham Gr. Sch. 1853. [14]

LESH, Edward, *Langtoft, Great Driffield, Yorks.*—St. Bees; Deac. 1853 and Pr. 1854 by Abp of York. C. of Langtoft 1864. Formerly C. of East Acklam and of Myton-upon-Swale. [15]

LESLIE, R. G., *Anstey, Buntingford, Herts.*—C. of Anstey. [16]

LESLIE, Robert T.—Chap. of the West Derby Workhouse, Everton, Liverpool. [17]

LESTER, Edward, *Victoria Villa, Derby-road, Bootle, Liverpool.*—Ch. Coll. Cam; Deac. 1856 by Bp of Ex. Pr. 1858 by Bp of Nor. Min. of the Episcopal Chapel, North Shore, Kirkdale, Liverpool, 1859, Asst. Chap. of Walton Cemetery, Liverpool. Formerly C. of St. Petrock, Exeter, 1856, Thorndon, Suffolk, 1857–59. [18]

LESTER, John William, *Lower Norwood, Surrey.*—Ch. Coll. Cam. B A. 1849, Ph.D. and D.D. of Giessen Univ. 1860; Deac. 1849 by Bp of Ches. Pr. 1850 by Abp of York. P. C. of St. Luke's, Norwood, Dio. Win. 1858. (Patron, Abp of Cant; P. C.'s Inc. 200*l*; Pop. 7098.) Chap. of the Lambeth Industrial Schs; Dom. Chap. to Lord Oranmore and Browne. Formerly P. C. of Ashton-Hayes, Cheshire, 1853–57. Author, *Criticism*, 3 eds. 1847, '48, '53, 10*s* 6*d* and 5*s* each; *Orations*, 1851, 4*s*; *Do You Love God? The Waters near the Stones*; *I Hearkened and Heard*; *Yet there is Room*; *Who shall Roll us away the Stone? Scarcely Saved*; *Man's True Dwelling-place*; *Faint, yet Pursuing*; *Will a Man rob God? The Lame take the Prey*; *Watchman, What of the Night? The Mountain Burned with Fire* (Tracts), 1*d* each; *A Letter to the Archbishops and Bishops on the Order for Morning Prayer*, 1854, 6*d*; *Suggestions for Increasing the Efficiency of the Church of England*, 1856; various Sermons and Tracts. [19]

LESTER, Lester, *Monkton Wyld, Charmouth, Dorset.*—Downing Coll. Cam. 1st cl. Law Trip. S.C.L. 1855; Deac. 1858 and Pr. 1863 by Bp of Salis. P. C. of Monkton Wyld, Dio. Salis. 1865. (Patroness, Mrs. E. Hodson; P. C.'s Inc. 146*l* and Ho; Pop. 362.) Formerly C. of Swanage, Dorset, 1858–65. Author, *Sermon for Shipwrecked Mariners' Society*, 1861; *A Few Words upon the Observance of Good Friday*, 1863; *The Sacrifice of Praise* (Sermon before Choral Association), 1867. [20]

LESTER, Thomas, *Elm Tree House, Hull.*—St. Bees, Librarian, 1st cl. Prizeman; Deac. 1850 and Pr. 1851 by Bp of Ches. P. C. of St. Luke's, Hull, Dio. York, 1859. (Patron, V. of Hull; P. C.'s Inc. 280*l*; Pop. 7360.) Formerly Sen. C. of Ch. Ch. Salford, 1852–57. [21]

LESTER, Thomas Major, *St. Mary's, Kirkdale, Liverpool.*—Ch. Coll. Cam. B.A. 1852, M.A. 1866; Deac. 1852 and Pr. 1853 by Bp of Ches. P. C. of St. Mary's, Kirkdale, Dio. Ches. 1855. (Patrons, Trustees; P. C.'s Inc. 300*l*; Pop. 14,730.) Surrogate. Author, *Essays*, 4*s*; Tracts, *Tribulation*; *A Word to Children*; *A Promise for the Year*; *A Word to the Tried*. [22]

L'ESTRANGE, Alfred Guy Kingham.—Ex. Coll. Ox. B.A. 1856; Deac. 1859 by Abp of Cant. C. of All Saints', Knightsbridge, Lond. Formerly C. of Trinity, Maidstone, 1859. [23]

LE SUEUR, Abraham, *Grouville Rectory, St. Heliers, Jersey.*—Magd. Hall, Ox. 1841; Deac. 1842, Pr. 1843. R. of Grouville with St. Pierre de la Rocque C. Jersey, Dio. Win. 1851. (Patron, the Crown; Glebe, 3 acres; R.'s Inc. 118*l* and Ho; Pop. 2622.) Formerly C. of St. Heliers, and of St. Peter's Port, Guernsey. [24]

LE SUEUR, Joshua, *Victoria College, Jersey.*—St. John's Coll. Cam. B.A. 1852, M.A. 1855; Deac. 1854 by Bp of Win. Math. Mast. Victoria Coll. 1852. [25]

LETCHWORTH, Arnold, *Saltburn-by-the-Sea, Yorks.*—Ex. Coll. Ox. B.A. 1863, M.A 1866; Deac. 1864 and Pr. 1865 by Abp of Cant. C. of Saltburn 1867. Formerly C. of Ch. Ch. Folkestone 1864–66. [26]

LETCHWORTH, Henry Howard, *Witham, Essex.*—Oriel Coll. Ox. B.A. 1859, M.A. 1861; Deac. 1859 and Pr. 1860 by Bp of G. and B. C. of Witham 1867. Formerly C. of Stapleton, near Bristol, 1859–61, St. Saviour's, Paddington, Lond. 1862–64, and St. John's, Notting-hill, 1864–67. [27]

LETHBRIDGE, Elford Copland, *West Thurrock, near Romford, Essex.*—Magd. Hall, Ox. B.A. 1855, M.A. 1857; Deac. 1855 and Pr. 1856 by Bp of Ex. V. of West Thurrock with Purfleet C. Dio. Roch. 1863. (Patron, W. H. Whitbread, Esq; Tithe, 312*l*; Glebe, 3 acres; V.'s Inc. 320*l* and Ho; Pop. 1039.) Formerly C. of Buckland Monachorum 1855—58, West Thurrock, 1858–63. [28]

LETTS, John Davis, *Tottenham, Middlesex, N.*—Trin. Coll. Cam. B.A. 1848, M.A. 1853. P. C. of St.

Ann's, Hanger-lane, Tottenham, Dio. Lon. 1861. (Patron, F. Newsam, Esq.) Dom. Chap. to Earl Ferrers 1855. [1]

LEVERETT, John, *Balsall Heath, Birmingham.* —Emman. Coll. Cam. B.A. 1858, M.A. 1861; Deac. 1860 and Pr. 1861 by Bp of Wor. C. of Balsall Heath 1860. [2]

LEVESON, Charles A., *High-street, Putney, S.W.*—Dur. B.A. 1858; Deac. 1858 by Bp of Lich. Pr. 1860 by Bp of Ches. [3]

LEVESON, Wilfred, *Liverpool.*—Trin. Coll. Cam. B.A. 1851; Deac. 1851 and Pr. 1852 by Bp of Lich. P. C. of St. Barnabas', Liverpool, Dio. Ches. 1857. (Patrons, Trustees; P. C.'s Inc. 300*l*.) Surrogate. Formerly C. of St. Andrew's, Liverpool. [4]

LEVETT, John, *Swinton, Rotherham, Yorks.*—St. Cath. Hall, Cam. B.A. 1844, M.A. 1847; Deac. 1844 and Pr. 1845 by Bp of Pet. P. C. of Swinton, Dio. York, 1851. (Patron, Earl Fitzwilliam; P. C.'s Inc. 360*l* and Ho; Pop. 2317.) Formerly C. of Kettering 1844, Langham 1847, Wentworth 1848. [5]

LEVIEN, John, *Enmore Rectory, Bridgwater.*—Wad. Coll. Ox. B.A. and M.A. 1842; Deac. 1843 and Pr. 1844 by Bp of Lon. R. of Enmore, Dio. B. and W. 1860. (Patron, the present R; Tithe, comm. 220*l*; Glebe, 22 acres; R.'s Inc. 285*l* and Ho; Pop. 314.) Formerly C. of Trinity, Marylebone, Lond. 1843–48, Holt and Little Witley, Worcester, 1848–58. [6]

LEVY, Thomas Bayley, *Knight's Enham Rectory, near Andover.*—Ex. and Queen's Coll. Ox. 2nd Fell. of Queen's Coll. 3rd cl. Lit. Hum. and B.A. 1834, M.A. 1838; Deac. 1835 and Pr. 1836 by Bp of Ox. R. of Knight's Enham, Hants, Dio. Win. 1856. (Patron, Queen's Coll. Ox; Tithe, 218*l*; Glebe, 29 acres; R.'s Inc. 250*l* and Ho; Pop. 159.) Formerly C. of Sparsholt, Berks, 1836, Kirkby Thore, Westmoreland, 1838; Chap. of Queen's Coll. Ox. 1843; R. of South Weston, Oxon, 1855. [7]

LEWELLIN, Charles Lloyd, *Coychurch, Bridgend, Glamorganshire.*—Lampeter 1855; Deac. 1855 and Pr. 1856 by Bp of St. D. R. of Coychurch with Peterstone-super-Montem C. Dio. Llan. 1861. (Patron, Earl of Dunraven; Coychurch, Tithe, 255*l*; Glebe, 36 acres; Peterstone, Tithe, 75*l*; R.'s Inc. 498*l* and Ho; Pop. Coychurch 1215, Peterstone 216.) [8]

LEWELLIN, The Very Rev. Llewelyn, *Lampeter, Cardiganshire.*—Jesus Coll. Ox. 1st cl. Lit. Hum. and B.A. 1822, M.A. 1824, B.C.L. 1827, D.C.L. 1830; Deac. 1822 and Pr. 1823 by Bp of Ox. Prin. of Lampeter 1827; V. of Lampeter, Dio. St. D. 1833. (Patron, Bp of St. D; Tithe—App. 176*l*; Glebe, 80 acres; V.'s Inc. 250*l*; Pop. 1542.) Sin. R. of Llangeler, Dio. St. D. 1843. (Patron, Bp of St. D; R.'s Inc. 244*l*.) Dean of St. D. 1840. (Value, 226*l*.) Chap. to the present and late Bp of St. D. Formerly Mast. of the Schools, Oxford, 1825–26. [9]

LEWELLIN, Richard T., *Finchampstead, near Wokingham, Berks.*—C. of Finchampstead. [10]

LEWES, David Laugharne, *Bodenham, Leominster.* [11]

LEWES, John Meredith, *Mattersey, Bawtry, Notts.*—Trin. Coll. Cam. 3rd cl. Cl. Trip. Jun. Opt. B.A. 1843, M.A. 1865; Deac. 1844 and Pr. 1845 by Bp of Herf. V. of Mattersey, Dio. Lin. 1862. (Patron, Bp of Ches; Glebe, 130 acres; V.'s Inc. 260*l* and Ho; Pop. 436.) Formerly Chap. to H.M.'s Forces 1854–56; R. of Hascomb, Surrey, 1859–62. [12]

LEWES, Thomas, *Great Barrington (Glouc.), near Burford.*—Brasen. Coll. Ox. B.A. 1815, M.A. 1817. V. of Great Barrington, Dio. G. and B. 1820. (Patron, Lord Dynevor; Tithe—Imp. 222*l* 10*s*, V. 199*l* 15*s* 1*d*; Glebe, 41¾ acres; V.'s Inc. 258*l*; Pop. 496.) V. of Taynton, Dio. Ox. 1819. (Patron, Lord Dynevor; V.'s Inc. 56*l* and Ho; Pop. 341.) [13]

LEWIN Richard, *Yateley Parsonage, Winchfield, Hants.*—P. C. of Yateley, Dio. Win. 1831. (Patron, the Master of St. Cross Hosp; Tithe, Imp. 572*l* 15*s* 11*d*; P. C.'s Inc. 75*l* and Ho; Pop. 1332.) Surrogate. [14]

LEWINTON, A. L., *Reading.*—Head Mast. of St. Michael's Gr. Sch. Reading. [15]

LEWIS, A. A., *Berkeley, Gloucestershire.*—C. of Berkeley. [16]

LEWIS, C. W.—C. of St. George's-in-the-East, Lond. [17]

LEWIS, Daniel, *Llanelly, Abergavenny.*—Lampeter; Deac. 1864 by Bp of St. D. C. of Llanelly 1864. [18]

LEWIS, Daniel, *Runcorn, Cheshire.*—Queen's Coll. Birmingham; Deac. 1866 by Bp of Ches. C. of Runcorn 1866. [19]

LEWIS, David, *Trefnant Rectory, Rhyl.*—Jesus Coll. Ox. B.A. 1849, M.A. 1852; Deac. 1850 and Pr. 1851 by Bp of Ban. R. of Trefnant, Dio. St. A. 1855. (Patrons, the Crown and Bp of St. A. alt; Tithe, 377*l*; Glebe, 8 acres; P. C.'s Inc. 377*l* and Ho; Pop. 639.) [20]

LEWIS, David, *Llangeinor, Bridgend, Glamorganshire.*—Lampeter; Deac. 1830 and Pr. 1831 by Bp of St. D. C. of Llangeinor 1856. [21]

LEWIS, David, *Briton Ferry, Glamorganshire.*—P. C. of Briton Ferry, Dio. Llan. 1863. (Patron, Earl of Jersey; Tithe, 145*l*; Glebe, 252 acres; P. C.'s Inc. uncertain; Pop. 3781.) [22]

LEWIS, David, *Llangevni, Anglesey.*—St. Aidan's; Deac. 1855 and Pr. 1856 by Bp of Ches. C. of Llangevni. [23]

LEWIS, David, *Llandugwydd Parsonage, Llechryd, Carmarthen.*—Emman. Coll. Cam. B.A. 1862; Deac. 1863 and Pr. 1864 by Bp of St. D. P. C. of Llandugwydd, Dio. St. D. 1865. (Patron, Bp of St. D; Glebe, 4 acres; P. C.'s Inc. 140*l* and Ho; Pop. 1050.) Formerly C. of Aberystwith 1863–65. [24]

LEWIS, David, *Brook Cottage, Llanbister, Radnorshire.*—Lampeter; Deac. 1854 by Bp of St. D. Pr. 1855 by Bp of B. and W. P. C. of Llanano with Llanbadarn Vynydd, Dio. St. D. 1856. (Patron, Rev. H. R. Pechell; P. C.'s Inc. 135*l*; Pop. Llanano 358, Llanbadarn Vynydd 609.) [25]

LEWIS, David Phillips, *Guildsfield Vicarage, Welshpool.*—St. John's Coll. Cam. B.A. 1842, M.A. 1845; Deac. 1843 by Bp of G. and B. Pr. 1844 by Bp of Herf. V. of Guildsfield, Dio. St. A. 1863. (Patron, Bp of St. A; Tithe, comm. 351*l*; Glebe, 15 acres; V.'s Inc. 370*l* and Ho; Pop. 2150.) Formerly C. of Sudeley 1843, Oswestry 1845, Welshpool 1847; P. C. of Buttington 1850. [26]

LEWIS, Edward, *Steventon, Micheldever Station, Hants.*—C. of Steventon. [27]

LEWIS, Edward, *Port-Eynon Rectory, Swansea.*—St. Cath. Coll. Cam. B.A. 1850; Deac. 1850 and Pr. 1851 by Bp of Wor. R. of Port-Eynon, Dio. St. D. 1856. (Patron, Ld Chan; Tithe, 121*l*; Glebe, 30 acres; R.'s Inc. 151*l* and Ho; Pop. 297.) [28]

LEWIS, Edward Freke, *Portskewett Rectory, Chepstow, Monmouthshire.*—Univ. Coll. Ox. B.A. 1823, M.A. 1824; Deac. 1823 by Bp of Llan. Pr. 1824 by Bp of Bristol. R. of Portskewett, with St. Pierre, Dio. Llan. 1839. (Patron, Charles Lewis, Esq; Portskewett, Tithe, 236*l*; Glebe, 46 acres; St. Pierre, Tithe, 119*l* 13*s*; Glebe, 1 acre; R.'s Inc. 450*l* and Ho; Pop. Portskewett 175, St. Pierre 92.) P. C. of Mounton, Dio. St. D. (Patron, C. Morgan, Esq; P. C.'s Inc. 87*l*; Pop. 90.) [29]

LEWIS, Evan, *Llanfair Talhairn Rectory, Abergele.*—Lampeter, Sen. Scho. B.D. 1855; Deac. 1843, Pr. 1844. R. of Llanfair Talhaiarn, Dio. St. A. 1866. (Patron, Bp of St. A; Tithe, 410*l*; Glebe, 10 acres; R.'s Inc. 433*l* and Ho; Pop. 1309.) Formerly Asst. Tut. at Lampeter; Head Mast of Cardigan Gr. Sch. Cardigan; C. of Whittington, and of Morton Chapel, Salop; P. C. of St. Catherine Colwyn, Conway, 1855–66. [30]

LEWIS, Evan, *Dolgelly, Merionethshire.*—Jesus Coll. Ox. B.A. 1841, M.A. 1863; Deac. 1842 by Bp of Ban. R. of Dolgelly, Dio. Ban. 1866. (Patron, Ld Chan; Tithe, 500*l*; Glebe, 6 acres; R.'s Inc. 505*l*; Pop. 3271.) Formerly P. C. of Llanvihangel-Ysceiving, Anglesey, 1845; C. of Llanllechid 1847–58; V. of Aberdare 1859–66. Author, *Treatise on the Apostolic Succession*, 1851, 4*s* 6*d*; *A Defence of the Doctrine and Polity of the Church*, 1852, 1*s*; *Exposure of the Wesleyan Succession*, 1858, 1*s*; a Club Sermon, and some articles in periodicals. [31]

LEWIS, Forster, *Wotton Fitzpaine, Charmouth, Dorset.*—St. John's Coll. Ox. Hon. 4th Law and Mod. Hist. B.A. 1855, M.A. 1858; Deac. 1857 and Pr. 1858 by Bp of B. and W. R. of Wotton Fitzpaine, Dio. Salis. 1864. (Patron, present R; Tithe, comm. 250*l*; R.'s Inc. 250*l* and Ho; Pop. 307.) Formerly C. of Congresbury with Wick St. Lawrence 1857–59, Grittleton 1862–63, Wotton Fitzpaine 1863–64. [1]

LEWIS, Francis, *St. Pierre, Chepstow, Monmouthshire.*—Univ. Coll. Ox. B.A. 1802, M.A. 1805, B.D. 1826; Deac. 1805 by Bp of Llan. Pr. 1806 by Bp of Glouc. V. of Holme Lacy, Herf. with Bolstone C. Dio. Herf. 1826. (Patron, Sir E. F. S. Stanhope, Bart; Tithe, 603*l*; V.'s Inc. 640*l* and Ho; Pop. Holme Lacy, 307, Bolstone 61.) R. of Llanvair Kilgidin, Monmouthshire, Dio. Llan. 1831. (Patron, Lord Tredegar; Tithe, 276*l* 2*s*; Glebe, 84 acres; R.'s Inc. 423*l* and Ho; Pop. 296.) [2]

LEWIS, George Bridges, *Northaw Parsonage, Barnet, N.*—Oriel Coll. Ox. B.A. 1846, M.A. 1853. P. C. of Northaw, Dio. Roch. 1857. (Patron, J. A. Trenchard, Esq; P. C.'s Inc. 120*l* and Ho; Pop. 551.) Formerly C. of Malden and Chessington, Surrey. [3]

LEWIS, George Tucker, *Exminster, near Exeter.*—Queen's Coll. Ox. 3rd cl. Lit. Hum. B.A. 1838; Deac. 1839, Pr. 1840 by Bp of Ex. Chap. to Devon County Lunatic Asylum 1845. [4]

LEWIS, Gerrard, *Margate.*—St. Cath. Hall. Cam. 1st cl. Ordinary Deg. and B.A. 1854; Deac. 1854, Pr. 1855. C. of Trinity, Margate. Formerly C. of St. John's, Margate, and St. Mary's, Leamington. [5]

LEWIS, Sir Gilbert Frankland, Bart., *Moccas, Herefordshire.*—Magd. Coll. Cam. B.A. 1830, M.A. 1833; Deac. 1831, and Pr. 1833 by Bp of Herf. Can. of Worcester 1856; Rural Dean. Formerly R. of Gladestry 1832; Preb. of Herf. 1845; R. of Monnington-on-Wye 1832–64. [6]

LEWIS, Henry, *Vicarage, Stowmarket.*—Pemb. Coll. Ox. M.A. 1848; Deac. 1846, Pr. 1847, V. of Stowmarket with Stowupland V. Dio. Nor. 1861. (Patrons, Reps. of late Rev. A. G. H. Hollingsworth; Tithe, 333*l* 11*s* 8*d*; Glebe, 5 acres; V.'s Inc. 384*l* and Ho; Pop Stowmarket 3563, Stowupland 193.) [7]

LEWIS, Henry, *Briton Ferry, Glamorganshire.*—Queen's Coll. Birmingham; Deac. 1861 by Bp of Llan. C. of Briton Ferry 1866. Formerly C. of Rhymney 1861, and Gellygaer. [8]

LEWIS, James, *Llanilar, Aberystwith.*—V. of Llanilar, Dio. St. D. 1861. (Patron, Bp of St. D; V.'s Inc. 95*l* and Ho; Pop. 947.) [9]

LEWIS, John, *Buttington Parsonage, Welshpool.*—St. John's Coll. Cam. B.A. 1852; Deac. 1852 and Pr. 1853 by Bp of Lich. P. C. of Buttington, Dio. St. A. 1863. (Patron, V. of Welshpool; P. C.'s Inc. 180*l* and Ho; Pop. 935.) Formerly C. of Albrighton 1852; Chap. to Salop Infirmary 1853–63; C. of St. Alkmond's, Shrewsbury, 1856. [10]

LEWIS, John, *Llanbeblig, Carnarvon.*—C. of Llanbeblig 1864. [11]

LEWIS, John, *Welland House, Spalding, Lincolnshire.*—Lampeter B.D. 1867; Sid. Coll. Cam; Deac. 1832 by Bp of Bristol, Pr. 1833 by Bp of Llan. Chap. to the Spalding Gaol 1844. Formerly C. of Penarth and Lavernock, near Cardiff. [12]

LEWIS, John, *Bonvilstone, Cardiff.*—Lampeter, 1834–38; Deac. 1838 and Pr. 1839 by Bp of St. D. P. C. of Bonvilstone, Dio. Llan. 1865. (Patron, Richard Bassett, Esq; Tithe, 44*l*; Glebe, 52 acres; P. C.'s Inc. 99*l*; Pop. 291.) Formerly C. of Gartheli and Bettws Leiki 1838, Llanwyddelan, Montgomery, 1840, Machynlleth 1848, Llanbedr and Caerhûn, Carnarvon, 1858, Llandefeilog 1864. [13]

LEWIS, J. Clarke, *Alverdiscott, Barnstaple, Devon.*—C. of Alverdiscott. [14]

LEWIS, John Rees, *Cascob Rectory, Presteign, Radnorshire.*—Lampeter; Deac. 1831 and Pr. 1832 by Bp of St. D. R. of Cascob, Dio. St. D. 1835. (Patron, Bp of St. D; Tithe, 143*l*; Glebe, 14 acres; R.'s Inc. 163*l* and Ho; Pop. 153.) [15]

LEWIS, John Tomkins.—Dub. A.B. 1859, A.M. 1865; Deac. 1859 and Pr. 1860 by Bp of G. and B. C. of St. James's, Paddington, Lond. 1864. [16]

LEWIS, John William, *Kingston-on-Thames.*—Caius Coll. Cam. 2nd cl. Cl. Trip. B.A. 1864; Deac. 1865 and Pr. 1866 by Bp of G. and B. C. of All Saints', Kingston-on-Thames, 1867. Formerly C. of St. Philip and St. Jacob's, Bristol, 1865–67. [17]

LEWIS, Joseph Pollard, *Milford Haven.*—Lampeter, B.A. 1865; Deac. 1865 and Pr. 1866 by Bp of St. D. C. of Steynton with Johnston, Pembrokeshire, 1865. [18]

LEWIS, Lewis, *Llanthony-Abbey, Abergavenny.*—P. C. of Llanthony-Abbey, Dio. Llan. 1855. (Patron, John Morgan, Esq; P. C.'s Inc. 55*l*.) P. C. of Cwmyoy, Dio. Llan. 1855. (Patron, John Morgan, Esq; P. C.'s Inc. 68*l*; Pop. 649.) [19]

LEWIS, Lewis, *The Rectory, Denbigh.*—Jesus Coll. Ox. B.A. 1841, M.A. 1844; Deac. 1841 by Bp of Ban. Pr. 1842 by Bp of St. A. R. of Denbigh, Dio. St. A. 1855. (Patron, Bp of St. A; Tithe, 400*l*; R.'s Inc. 400*l*; Pop. 4593.) Formerly Fell. of Jesus Coll. Ox. [20]

LEWIS, Lewis, *Llanycil, Bala, Merionethshire.*—C. of Llanycil 1864. [21]

LEWIS, Lewis Charles, *Peterston-super-Ely, near Cardiff.*—Queen's Coll. Ox; Deac. and Pr. 1842 by Bp of Llan. R. of Peterston-super-Ely, Dio. Llan. 1856. (Patron, Sir T. D. Aubrey and Colonel Wood; Tithe, 269*l*; Glebe, 20 acres; R.'s Inc. 279*l*; Pop. 285.) [22]

LEWIS, Lewis Owen, *Asby, Appleby, Westmoreland.*—St. Bees; Deac. 1867 by Bp of Carl. C. of St. Peter's, Asby, 1867. [23]

LEWIS, Lewis Thomas, *Llanbedr-Dyffryn Clwyd, Ruthin.*—Lampeter, Scho. B.D. 1854; Deac. 1846 and Pr. 1847 by Bp of Llan. C. of Llanbedr-Dyffryn Clwyd 1860. Formerly C. of Aberystruth 1846–49, Selattyn, Salop, 1849–51, Llansantffraidylyn-Ceiriog 1851–60. [24]

LEWIS, Lewis Woodward, *Leysdown Vicarage, Kent.*—Lin. Coll. Ox. M.A; Deac. 1855 and Pr. 1857 by Abp of Cant. V. of Leysdown with Harty P. C. Dio. Cant. 1862. (Patrons, Abp of Cant. 3 turns and Family of Major Munn 1 turn; Tithe, comm. 265*l*; Glebe, 5 acres; V.'s Inc. 340*l* and Ho; Pop. Leysdown 215, Harty 159.) Formerly C. of Mersham 1855–58, Luddenham 1858–60; C. of Faversham and Chap. to the Union 1860–62. [25]

LEWIS, Michael, *Cotgrave, Nottingham.*—C. of Cotgrave. [26]

LEWIS, Philip, *Bursledon, Southampton.*—Univ. Coll. Ox. B.A. 1835, M.A. 1836; Deac. 1836, Pr. 1837. P. C. of Bursledon, Dio. Win. 1850. (Patron, Win. Coll; Tithe—App. 74*l*, P. C. 37*l*; P. C.'s Inc. 116*l* and Ho; Pop. 659.) [27]

LEWIS, Richard, *Hooe, Plymstock, Devon.*—P. C. of Hooe, Dio. Ex. 1861. (Patroness, Lady Rogers; P. C.'s Inc. 79*l*; Pop. 1082.) [28]

LEWIS, Richard, *Lampeter Velfry Rectory, Narberth, Pembrokeshire.*—Late Scho. of Wor. Coll. Ox. Hon. 4th cl. Lit. Hum. 1842, B.A. 1843, M.A. 1846; Deac. 1844, Pr. 1846. R. of Lampeter Velfry, Dio. St. D. 1851. (Patron, Ld Chan; Tithe, 475*l*; Glebe, 27 acres; R.'s Inc. 532*l* and Ho; Pop. 951.) Preb. of St. D; Rural Dean; Organising Sec. of the S.P.G. [29]

LEWIS, Richard, 56, *Warwick-street, Rugby.*—Jesus Coll. Ox. B.A. 1860, M.A. 1863; Deac. 1865 and Pr. 1866 by Bp of Wor. Formerly C. of Brownsover, Warwickshire, 1865–67. [30]

LEWIS, Robert George, *Charlton-road, Blackheath, S.E.*—Wad. Coll. Ox. B.A. 1828, M.A. 1831. P. C. of St. John's, Blackheath, Dio. Lon. 1853. (Patron, Wm. Angerstein, Esq; P. C.'s Inc. 250*l*.) [31]

LEWIS, Thomas, *Manafon Rectory, Berriew, Montgomeryshire.*—Jesus Coll. Ox. B.A. 1829; Deac. 1830, Pr. 1831. R. of Manafon, Dio. St. A. 1851. (Patron, Bp of St. A; Tithe, 460*l*; Glebe, 9 acres; R.'s Inc. 469*l* and Ho; Pop. 701.) [32]

LEWIS, Thomas, B.A., *Rye, Sussex.*—Chap. of the Union, and C. of Rye. [33]

LEWIS, Thomas, *Llanavan Vawr Vicarage, Builth, Breconshire.*—Lampeter; Deac. 1847 and Pr. 1848 by Bp of Llan. V. of Llanavan Vawr with Llanfihangel Bryn Pabuan C. and Llanavanfechan, Dio. St. D. 1868. (Patron, Bp of St. D; Tithe, 275*l* 6*s* 8*d*; Glebe, 20 acres; V.'s Inc. 275*l* 6*s* 8*d* and Ho; Pop. 1440.) Surrogate. [1]

LEWIS, Thomas Henry, 6, *Richard's-terrace, Canton, Cardiff.*—Deac. 1864 by Bp of Llan. C. of Canton 1865. Formerly C. of Llanvabon 1864. [2]

LEWIS, Titus, *Llanelly, Breconshire.*—Asst. C. of Llanelly 1864. [3]

LEWIS, Walter Sunderland, *Trinity Parsonage, Ripon.*—Trin. Coll. Cam. 17th Wrang. B.A. 1843, M.A. 1846; Deac. 1843, Pr. 1844. P. C. of Trinity, Ripon, Dio. Rip. 1848. (Patrons, Simeon's Trustees; P. C.'s Inc. 350*l* and Ho; Pop. 2848.) Chap. of the Ho. of Correction, Ripon. Formerly Math. Mast. of Bishop's Coll. Bristol, 1843; C. of St. Werburgh's, Bristol, 1844; Chap. of Trin. Coll. Cam. 1846. Author, *Preaching to the Unconverted*, 1856, 6*d*; *Landmarks of Faith*, 1858, 2*s* 6*d*; *The Threshold of Revelation, an Investigation into the True Province and Character of the First Chapters of Genesis*, Rivingtons, 6*s*. [4]

LEWIS, William, *Sedgley Vicarage, Dudley.*—St. John's Coll. Cam. B.A. 1824, M.A. 1847; Deac. 1824, Pr. 1825. V. of Sedgley, Dio. Lich. 1837. (Patron, Earl of Dudley; Tithe—Imp. 148*l* 3*s*, V. 444*l*; Glebe, 7 acres; V.'s Inc. 594*l* and Ho; Pop. 10,270.) Rural Dean. [5]

LEWIS, William, *Nantyglo, Tredegar, Monmouthshire.*—Deac. 1862 and Pr. 1863 by Bp of Llan. C. of Nantyglo. [6]

LEWIS, William, *Pont Dolanog Parsonage, Llanfyllin, Montgomeryshire.*—Lampeter; Deac. 1847, Pr. 1848. P. C. of Pont Dolanog, Dio. St. A. (Patron, Bp of St. A; P. C.'s Inc. 160*l*; Pop. 450.) Formerly C. of Bagillt 1853–54. [7]

LEWIS, William John, *Llandonna, Beaumaris, Anglesey.*—Jesus Coll. Ox. B.A 1815, M.A. 1818. P. C. of Llandonna, Dio. Ban. 1822. (Patron, Lord Boston; P. C.'s Inc. 75*l*; Pop. 567.) [8]

LEWTHWAITE, George, *Adel, Leeds.* [9]

LEWTHWAITE, Joseph, *Warmsworth, Doncaster.*—Ch. Coll. Cam. B.A. 1859, M.A. 1862; Deac. 1860 and Pr. 1861 by Bp of Lin. C. of Warmsworth. Formerly C. of Barrow-on-Humber. [10]

LEWTHWAITE, Thomas, *Lockwood, Huddersfield.*—Lond. Coll. of Divinity; Deac. 1866 by Bp of Rip. C. of Lockwood 1866. [11]

LEWTY, Thomas Cooper, *The Vicarage, Rowston, Sleaford, Lincolnshire.*—St. John's Coll. Cam. Sen. Opt. B.A. 1858, M.A. 1861; Deac. 1859 and Pr. 1860 by Bp of Lin. V. of Rowston *alias* Rowlston, Dio. Lin. 1862. (Patron, B. H. Thorold, Esq; Glebe, 10 acres; V.'s Inc. 180*l* and Ho; Pop. 224.) Formerly C. of Coddington, Notts, 1859, P. C. of same 1861. [12]

LEY, Augustin, *Buxton, Derbyshire.*—Ch. Ch. Ox. B.A. 1865; Deac. 1867 by Bp of Wor. C. of Buxton 1867. [13]

LEY, Jacob, *Staverton Vicarage, Daventry, Northants.*—Ch. Ch. Ox. B.A. 1826, M.A. 1829, B.D. 1840; Deac. 1827, Pr. 1828. V. of Staverton, Dio. Pet. 1858. (Patron, Ch. Ch. Ox; Glebe, 362 acres; V.'s Inc. 672*l* and Ho; Pop. 486.) Formerly V. of St. Mary Magdalene's, Oxford, 1845–58. [14]

LEY, John, *Waldron, Hurst Green, Sussex.*—Ex. Coll. Ox. B.A. 1826, M.A. 1829, B.D. 1841; Deac. 1829, Pr. 1831. R. of Waldron, Dio. Chich. 1850. (Patron, Ex. Coll. Ox; Tithe, 616*l*; Glebe, 38 acres; R.'s Inc. 646*l* and Ho; Pop. 1132.) [15]

LEY, Richard, *Cumnor, Abingdon, Berks.*—Brasen. Coll. Ox. B.A. 1844, M.A. 1847; Deac. 1851 and Pr. 1852 by Bp of Ox. C. of Cumnor. [16]

LEY, William Clement, *King's Caple, Ross, Herefordshire.*—Magd. Coll. Ox. C. of King's Caple. [17]

LEY, William Henry, *Sellack, Ross, Herefordshire.*—Trin. Coll. Ox. 1st cl. Lit. Hum. and B.A. 1835; Deac. 1838, Pr. 1839. V. of Sellack with King's Caple C. Dio. Herf. 1841. (Patrons, D. and C. of Herf; Sellack, Tithe—App. 300*l*, V. 132*l*; Glebe, 97¾ acres; King's Caple, Tithe—App. 380*l*, V. 172*l* 10*s*; Glebe, 2 acres; V.'s Inc. 420*l*; Pop. Sellack 345, King's Caple 320.) Formerly Fell. of Trin. Coll. Ox. 1836–39; Head Mast. of the Herf. Cathl. Sch. 1839–41. [18]

LIAS, John James, *Lambourne, Hungerford, Berks.*—Emman. Coll. Cam. B.A. 1861, M.A. 1867; Deac. 1858 and Pr. 1860 by Bp of Salis. P. C. of Eastbury, Dio. Ox. 1867. (Patron, Bp of Ox; P. C.'s Inc. 120*l*; Pop. 300.) Formerly C. of Shaftesbury 1858, Folkestone 1865. [19]

LIBERTY, Nathaniel, 6, *Elm-place, Brompton, London, S.W.*—King's Coll. Lond. Theol. Assoc. 1850; Deac. 1850 and Pr. 1851 by Bp of Rip. C. of St. Mary's, West Brompton. [20]

LICHFIELD, The Right Rev. the Lord Bp of, *Eccleshall Castle, Staffs.*—(See Appendix.) (Episcopal Jurisdiction—the Cos. of Derby and Stafford, and a portion of the Co. of Salop; Inc. of See, 4500*l*; Pop. 1,121,404; Acres, 1,740,607; Deaneries, 49; Benefices, 625; Curates, 254; Church sittings, 305,938. [21]

LICHTENSTEIN, Isidore, *Ingham, North Walsham, Norfolk.*—Queens' Coll. Cam. B.A. 1853; Deac. 1853 and Pr. 1854 by Bp of Nor. C. of Ingham. Formerly C. of Worlingworth with Southolt. [22]

LICKORISH, Richard, *Wolston, Coventry.*—Sid. Coll. Cam. B.A. 1819; Deac. 1820, Pr. 1821. P. C. of Ryton-upon-Dunsmore, Coventry, Dio. Wor. 1822. (Patron, Preb. of Lich; P. C.'s Inc. 126*l*; Pop. 557.) [23]

LIDDELL, The Very Rev. Henry George, *The Deanery, Christ Church, Oxford.*—Ch. Ch. Ox. Double 1st cl. Lit. Hum. B.A. 1833, M.A. 1835; Deac. 1836, Pr. 1838. Dean of Ch. Ch. Ox. 1855. (Value, 2800*l*.) Hon. Chap. in Ordinary to the Queen. Formerly Dom. Chap. to his late R.H. Prince Albert, 1845; Select Preacher, Ox. 1842 and 1847; Mast. of the Schools, Public Examiner, Proctor, 1846; Head Mast. of Westminster Sch. 1846–55. Author, *Greek-English Lexicon* in conjunction with the Rev. Dr. Scott, Mast. Ball. Coll. Ox. 1st ed. 1843, 2nd, 1846, 3rd, 1849, 4th, 1855, 5th, 1861; *History of Rome*, 1st ed. 1855, last ed. 1866. [24]

LIDDELL, The Hon. Robert, 36, *Wilton-crescent, London, S.W.*—Ch. Ch. Ox. B.A. 1829, All Souls Coll. M.A. 1834, *ad eund.* Dur. 1835; Deac. 1833 by Bp of Ox. Pr. 1834 by Bp of Roch. P. C. of St. Paul's, Knightsbridge, Dio. Lon. 1851. (Patron, Bp of Lon; P. C.'s Inc. 1000*l* and Ho; Pop. 13,844.) Formerly Fell. of All Souls Coll. Ox. 1834–36; V. of Barking, Essex, 1836–51. [25]

LIDDELL, William Wren, *South Cerney, Cirencester.*—Ch. Ch. Ox. B.A. 1845, M.A. 1847; Deac. 1847 and Pr. 1848 by Bp of Dur. V. of South Cerney with Cerney Wick C. Dio. G. and B. 1862. (Patron, Bp of G. and B; V.'s Inc. 242*l*; Pop. 1006.) Formerly C. of Easington. [26]

LIDDON, H. J., *Cat's Hill, Bromsgrove.*—P. C. of Cat's Hill, Dio. Wor. 1864. (Patron, V. of Bromsgrove; P. C.'s Inc. 120*l*; Pop. 2393.) [27]

LIDDON, Henry Parry, *Salisbury.*—Ch. Ch. Ox. 2nd cl. Lit. Hum. and B.A. 1850, Johnson Theol. Scho. 1851, M.A. 1853; Deac. 1852 and Pr. 1853 by Bp of Ox. Preb. of Salis. 1864; Chap. to Bp of Salis. Formerly Stud. of Ch. Ch. Ox; Vice-Prin. of Cuddesdon 1854–59. Author, *Lenten Sermons*, 1858; *The Divinity of Our Lord and Saviour Jesus Christ*, Bampton Lectures for 1866, Rivingtons, 1867, 14*s*. [28]

LIGHT, Henry William Maure, *Wroughton Vicarage, Swindon, Wilts.*—Univ. Coll. Ox. B.A. 1831; Deac. 1833 by Bp of Salis. Pr. 1834 by Bp of G. and B. V. of Wroughton, Dio. G. and B. 1840. (Patron, Bp of Win; Tithe, 240*l*; Glebe, 46 acres; the Sin. R. of Wroughton; Tithe, 21*l* 14*s* 8*d*; Glebe, 46 acres; V.'s Inc. 330*l* and Ho; Pop. 1721.) Formerly V. of Bramshaw, New Forest. [29]

LIGHT, John, *Notting-hill, Kensington, W.*—Dub. A.B. 1845, A.M. 1853; Deac. 1845, Pr. 1846. P. C. of All Saints', Notting-hill, Dio. Lon. (Patron, Rev. Dr. Walker; Pop. 4000.) Formerly Sen. C. of Ashton-under-Lyne. Author, *The Mission of Charity*; *The Rest of the Righteous.* [1]

LIGHT, William Edward, *St. James's Rectory, Dover.*—St. John's, Coll. Cam. 3rd cl. Cl. Trip. Wrang. and B A. 1842, M.A. 1845; Deac. 1842 by Bp of Lon. Pr. 1844 by Bp of Roch. R. of St. James's, Dover, Dio. Cant. 1857. (Patron, Abp of Cant; Tithe, 45*l*; R.'s Inc. 400*l* and Ho; Pop. 4000.) Formerly Assoc. Sec. of Ch. Miss. Soc. 1852–55. Author, *Twenty-four Sermons chiefly on Personal Religion*, Nisbet, 1865, 5*s*; etc. [2]

LIGHTBOURN, Joseph Fraser, *Bermuda.*—Jesus Coll. Ox. B.A. 1825; Deac. 1827, Pr. 1828. R. of Pembroke and Devon, Bermuda. [3]

LIGHTFOOT, John Nicholas, *Cofton, Exeter.*—Ex. Coll. Ox. B.A. 1847, M.A. 1851; Deac. 1848, Pr. 1849. P. C. of Cofton, Dio. Ex. 1860. (Patron, Earl of Devon; P. C.'s Inc. 100*l*; Pop. 450.) Formerly C. of Cofton. [4]

LIGHTFOOT, John Prideaux, *Exeter College, Oxford.*—Ex. Coll. Ox. 1st cl. Lit. Hum. and B.A. 1824, D.D. 1854; Deac 1830, Pr. 1832. Hon. Can. of Pet. Cathl. 1853; R. of Ex. Coll. Ox. 1854; V. of Kidlington (*annexed* to the Rectorship of Ex. Coll. Ox.), Dio. Ox. 1854. (Tithe, 21*l* 17*s* 9*d*; Glebe, 209 acres; V.'s Inc. 310*l* and Ho; Pop. 1507.) [5]

LIGHTFOOT, Joseph Barber, *Trinity College, Cambridge.*—Trin. Coll. Cam. Sen. Classic and Sen. Chan.'s Medallist 1851, Norrisian Prizeman 1853, Wrang. and B.A. 1851, M.A. 1854; Deac. 1854 and Pr. 1858 by Bp of Man. Hulsean Prof. of Div. and Fell. and late Tut. of Trin. Coll. Cam; Hon. Chap. in Ordinary to the Queen; Exam. Chap. to the Bp of Lond. Author, *St. Paul's Epistle to the Galatians*, Macmillans, 2nd ed. 1866; Sermons, etc. [6]

LIGHTFOOT, Nicholas Francis, *Islip Rectory, Thrapston, Northants.*—Ex. Coll. Ox. B.A. 1833, M.A. 1836; Deac. 1834, Pr. 1836. R. of Islip, Dio. Pet. 1855. (Patroness, Mrs. Wm. Stopford; R.'s Inc. 400*l* and Ho; Pop. 627.) Formerly V. of Cadbury, Devon, 1846–55. [7]

LIGHTFOOT, Reginald Prideaux, *Vicarage, Towcester.*—Ball. Coll. Ox. B.A. 1859, M.A. 1861; Deac. 1859 by Bp of Man. Pr. 1860 by Bp of Pet. V. of Towcester, Dio. Pet. 1867. (Patron, Bp of Lich; Tithe, 50*l*; V.'s Inc. 300*l* and Ho; Pop. 2715.) Dom. Chap. to Bp of Pet; Dioc. Inspector of Schs. Formerly C. of Preston Deanery 1859, Kidlington, Oxon, 1861; V. of Preston Deanery, Northants, 1863–67. [8]

LIGHTFOOT, William Barber, *Basingstoke, Hants.*—Trin. Coll. Cam. Wrang. 2nd cl. Cl. Trip. and B.A. 1845, M.A 1848; Deac. 1846, Pr. 1848. Head Mast. of the Queen's Gr. Sch. Basingstoke. [9]

LIGHTON, Sir Christopher Robert, Bart., *Ellastone (Staffs), Ashbourne.*—St. John's Coll. Cam. B.A. 1843, M.A. 1846; Deac. 1845 and Pr. 1846 by Bp of Wor. V. of Ellastone, Dio. Lich. 1848 (Patron, W. Davenport Bromley, Esq; Tithe, 193*l*; Glebe, 7 acres; V.'s Inc. 210*l* and Ho; Pop. 1230.) Formerly C. of St. Luke's, Birmingham, 1845, Ch. Ch. Epsom, 1848. Author, *Does Rome teach Salvation by Christ alone? If not, is her Teaching Christian?* (a Pamphlet) Ashbourne. [10]

LILLEY, Edmund, *Tenterden, Kent.*—Wor. Coll. Ox. B.A. 1829, M.A. 1833, B.D. 1851; Deac. 1830 by Bp of Wor. Pr. 1831 by Bp of Glouc. P. C. of Smallhythe, Dio. Cant. 1865. (Patrons, the Householders; P. C.'s Inc. 131*l*; Pop. 250.) Chap. of Tenterden Union. Formerly Min. of Peckham Chapel, Surrey, 1833; Chap. of Taddyport, and Even. Lect. of Great Torrington, Devon. [11]

LILLIE, William, *Didsbury, Manchester.*—King's Coll. Lond. Theol. Assoc; Deac. 1857 and Pr. 1858 by Bp of Wor. C. of Didsbury. Formerly C. of St. Peter's, Saffron-hill, Lond. 1859. [12]

LILLINGSTON, Edward, *Cheltenham.*—Emman. Coll. Cam. B.A. 1835, M.A. 1856; Deac. 1835 by Bp of Roch. Pr. 1837 by Bp of Nor. P. C. of Trinity, Cheltenham, Dio. G. and B. 1864. (Patron, R. of Cheltenham.) Formerly C. of St. Margaret's, Ipswich, 1837, Hampton-in-Arden 1838–41; P. C. of All Saints', Derby, 1841–48, St. George's, Edgbaston, 1849–64. Author, *Sermons*, 1849. [13]

LILLINGTON, Frederick, *Hasfield, near Gloucester.*—Brasen. Coll. Ox. Scho. M.A; Stud. of Wells; Deac. 1861 and Pr. 1862 by Bp of B. and W. Formerly C. of Trull, Somerset. [14]

LILLISTONE, J. S., *Jesus College, Cambridge.*—Fell. of Jesus Coll. [15]

LILLY, Peter, *Colluton, Paignton, Devon.*—St. John's Coll. Cam. Wrang. 3rd cl. Cl. Trip. and B.A. 1849, M.A. 1852; Deac. 1853, Pr. 1854. P. C. of Collaton, Dio. Ex. 1864. (Patron, Rev. J. R. Hogg; P. C.'s Inc. 150*l*; Pop. 345.) Formerly C. of Kegworth, Derbyshire. [16]

LIMPUS, Henry Francis, *The Minor Canonries, Llandaff.*—Magd. Hall, Ox. B.A. 1860; Deac. 1861 and Pr. 1862 by Bp of Ely. Min. Can. of Llan. 1867; C. of Llandaff 1867. Formerly C. of St. Neots, Hunts, 1861–65, Colwall, Herefordshire, 1865–67. [17]

LIMRICK, John, *The Rectory, Bolas Magna, Wellington, Salop.*—Dub. A.B. 1835; Deac. 1838 and Pr. 1839 by Bp of Kildare. C. in sole charge of Bolas Magna 1865. Formerly C. of Gaeshill, King's Co. Ireland, 1838–41, Trinity, Leicester, 1841–42, St. Chad's, Shrewsbury, 1842–44, Crewe (sole charge) 1844–46, Brailes (sole charge) 1847–56, Coleshill, Warw. 1857–62, Bayston Hill 1863–65. Author, *Lectures Expository and Practical for every Sunday in the Year as set forth in the Book of Common Prayer, for the Use of Sunday-school Teachers*, 1863, 5*s*. [18]

LINCOLN, The Right Rev. John JACKSON, Lord Bp of Lincoln, *London, S.W.*, and *Riseholme, near Lincoln.*—Pemb. Coll. Ox. 1st cl. Lit. Hum. and B.A. 1833, Ellerton Theol. Prize Essayist 1834, M.A. 1836, B.D. and D.D. 1853; Deac. 1835 and Pr. 1836 by Bp of Ox. Consecrated Bp of Lin. 1853. (Episcopal Jurisdiction, the counties of Lincoln and Notts; Inc. of See, 5000*l*; Pop. 706,026; Acres, 2,302,814; Deaneries, 33; Benefices, 810; Curates, 181; Church Sittings, 238,831.) His Lordship is Visitor of King's Coll. Cam. and of Brasen. Lin. and Ball. Colls. Ox. and also of Eton Coll. His Lordship was formerly Select Preacher to the Univ. of Ox. 1845, 1850, 1862, and 1866, Boyle Lect. 1853; R. of St. James's, Westminster, 1846–53. Author, *The Leading Points of the Christian Character* (six Sermons), 1844; *Sanctifying Grace, and the Grace of the Ministry* 1847; *The Day of Prayer and the Day of Thanksgiving* (two Sermons preached on those days), 1849; *The Sinfulness of Little Sins*, 1849; *Rome and her Claims* (a Sermon), 1850; *The Spirit of the World, and the Spirit which is of God*, 1850; *Repentance, its Necessity, Nature and Aids* (a course of Lent Sermons), 1851; *An Address to the Newly Confirmed, preparatory to the Holy Communion*, 1852; *Sunday a Day of Rest or a Day of Work* (a few Words to Working Men), 1853; *War, its Evils and Duties* (a Sermon), 1854; *The Witness of the Spirit* (Sermons preached before the Univ. of Ox.), 1854; *God's Word and Man's Heart* (Sermons preached before the Univ. of Ox.) [19]

LINDLEY, William, *Thirsk Parsonage, Yorks.*—P. C. of Thirsk, Dio. York, 1843. (Patron, Abp of York; Tithe—App. 2072*l* 9*s* 2*d*; P. C.'s Inc. 150*l* and Ho; Pop. 2956.) P. C. of Sandhutton, Thirsk, Dio. York, 1843. (Patron, Abp of York; Tithe—App. 243*l* 10*s*, P. C. 62*l* 10*s*; P. C.'s Inc. 115*l*; Pop. 297.) [20]

LINDON, Thomas Angell, *St. Peter's Parsonage, Halliwell, Bolton, Lancashire.*—St. Edm. Hall, Ox. B.A. 1851, M.A. 1854; Deac. 1851 and Pr. 1852 by Bp of Salis. P. C. of St. Peter's, Halliwell, Dio. Man. 1854. (Patrons, Trustees; Endow. 33*l*, Fees, Pew-rents, 167*l*; P. C.'s Inc. 200*l* and Ho; Pop. 3241.) [21]

LINDSAY, Henry, *Kettering Rectory, Kettering.*—Trin. Coll. Cam. B.A. 1846 M.A. 1853; Deac. 1847 and Pr. 1848 by Bp of Pet. R. of Kettering, Dio. Pet. 1863. (Patron, G. L. Watson, Esq; Glebe, 400 acres; R.'s Inc. 1090*l* and Ho; Pop. 5845.) Chap. of Kettering Union 1863; Surrogate. Formerly C. of Sibbertoft, Northants, 1847–50; P. C. of St. Mary's, Ide Hill, 1850–63; Organising Sec. to the S.P.G. for the Archd. of Maidstone 1857–63; Chap. to the Sevenoaks Union 1850–57. [1]

LINDSAY, John, *Stanford-on-Avon Vicarage, near Rugby.*—Dub. A.B. *ad eund.* Sid. Coll. Cam. 1811, M.A. 1812. V. of Stanford-on-Avon, Dio. Pet. 1818. (Patroness, Baroness Braye; V.'s Inc. 85*l* and Ho; Pop. 42.) V. of Swinford, Leic. Dio. Pet. 1818. (Patroness, Baroness Braye; V.'s Inc. 216*l*; Pop. 402.) [2]

LINDSAY, Thomas, *St. Oswald's Grove, Manchester.*—St. Aidan's; Deac. 1857 and Pr. 1858 by Bp of Ches. C. of St. George's, Manchester, 1866. Formerly C. of Ch. Ch. Chester, 1857–60, Brampton, near Chesterfield, 1860, St. Barnabas', Manchester, 1860–61, St. Mary's, Whitechapel, Lond. 1861–62, St. James's, Heywood, Manchester, 1862–63, Rathmolyon, Meath, 1863–66. [3]

LINDSAY, William John Coussmaker, *Llanvaches Rectory, Caerleon, Monmouthshire.*—Dub. A.B. 1855; Deac. 1855 and Pr. 1856 by Bp of Roch. R. of Llanvaches, Dio. Llan. 1857. (Patron, Lord Tredegar; Tithe, 200*l*; Glebe, 9 acres; R.'s Inc. 212*l* and Ho; Pop. 235.) Chap. to the Earl of Crawford and Balcarres. Formerly C. of Danbury, Essex, 1855–57. [4]

LINDSELL, Edward, *Broom Hall, Biggleswade, Beds.*—Jesus Coll. Cam. B.A. 1827, M.A. 1830; Deac. 1825, Pr. 1826. [5]

LINGHAM, George, *Bengeo, Hertford.*—C. of Bengeo. Formerly C. of St. Botolph's, Aldgate, Lond. [6]

LINGHAM, John Fentiman, *St. Mary's Rectory, Church-street, Lambeth, London, S.*—Trin. Coll. Cam. B.A. 1843, M.A. 1854. R. of Lambeth, Dio. Win. 1854. (Patron, Abp of Cant; Tithe, 1090*l* 19*s* 3*d*; R.'s Inc. 1560*l* and Ho; Pop. 26,080.) Rural Dean; Dom. Chap. to Lord Londesborough. [7]

LINGHAM, Thomas Lawford, *Hertingfordbury, Herts.*—Univ. and King's Coll. Lond. B.A. 1853; Deac. 1854 and Pr. 1855 by Abp of Cant. C. of Hertingfordbury. Formerly Asst. C. of Ash-next-Sandwich. [8]

LINGLEY, Thomas.—C. of Ch. Ch. Highbury, Islington, Lond. [9]

LINGWOOD, Thomas John, *Maidenhead, Berks.*—Ch. Coll. Cam. Jun. Opt. and B.A. 1838; Deac. and Pr. 1840 by Bp of Herf. P. C. of St. Mary's, Maidenhead, Dio. Ox. 1865. (Patron, E. F. Maitland, Esq; P. C.'s Inc. 190*l* and Ho; Pop. 3303.) Formerly C. of Long Newnton. [10]

LINKLATER, Robert, *Frome Selwood, Somerset.*—C. of Frome Selwood. [11]

LINSKILL, John Anthony Pearson, *Beaudesert Rectory, Henley-in-Arden, Warwickshire.*—Dur. English Essay and B.A. 1837. R. of Beaudesert, Dio. Wor. 1857. (Patron, Ld Chan; Tithe, 170*l* 15*s*; Glebe, 140 acres; R.'s Inc. 330*l* and Ho; Pop. 172.) Formerly Dom. Chap. to Lord Dinorben; R. of Bicknor, Kent, 1852–57; Chap. to the Military Prisons, Fort Clarence, Chatham, and Military Prison, Weedon. [12]

LINTHWAITE, Henry, *Whitton, Cheshire.*—Jesus Coll. Cam. Jun. Opt. and B.A. 1844; Deac. 1847, Pr. 1848. Head Mast. of the Gr. Sch. Whitton. Formerly C. of the Mediety of West Walton-Lewis, Norfolk. [13]

LINTON, Charles Robert, *Bath.*—Corpus Coll. Cam. B.A. 1866; Deac. 1867 by Bp Hobhouse for Bp of B. and W. C. of St. Saviour's, Bath, 1867. [14]

LINTON, Henry, *Birkenhead.*—P. C. of St. Paul's, Birkenhead, Dio. Ches. 1866. [15]

LINTON, Henry, *St. Peter-le-Bailey, Oxford.*—Magd. Coll. Ox. B.A. 1824, M.A. 1827; Deac. 1826 by Bp of Ox. Pr. 1827 by Bp of Lin. R. of St. Peter-le-Bailey, Oxford, Dio. Ox. 1856. (Patrons, Trustees; Glebe, 8 acres; R.'s Inc. 258*l*; Pop. 1153.) Author, *A Paraphrase and Notes of the Epistles of St. Paul,* Mackintosh, 1857, 7*s* 6*d*. [16]

LINTON, Hewett, *Tadmarton, near Banbury.*—St. Aidan's; Deac. 1861 and Pr. 1862 by Bp of Win. C. of Tadmarton 1863. Formerly C. of St. Paul's, Bermondsey. [17]

LINTON, Hewett, *Nassington Vicarage, Wansford, Northants.*—St. John's Coll. Cam. B.A. 1818, M.A. 1821; Deac. 1820 and Pr. 1821 by Bp of Pet. V. of Nassington with Yarwell C. Dio. Pet. 1829. (Patron, Bp of Pet; Nassington, Glebe, 110 acres; Yarwell, Glebe, 1 acre; V.'s Inc. 190*l* and Ho; Pop. Nassington 718, Yarwell 402.) [18]

LINTON, James, *Hemingford House, St. Ives, Hunts.*—Magd. Coll. Ox. B.A. 1822, M.A. 1823; Deac. 1823, Pr. 1824. Formerly Fell. of Magd. Coll. Ox. 1823–28. [19]

LINTON, Robert Mayer, *Boroughbridge, Yorks.*—Dub. A.B. 1867; Deac. 1866 and Pr. 1867 by Bp of Rip. C. of Copgrove 1866. [20]

LINTOTT, J., *Newcastle-on-Tyne.*—Chap. of the Infirmary, and Lect. at St. John's, Newcastle-on-Tyne. [21]

LINTOTT, J. Cooper, 24, *Neale-street, Camberwell, S.*—King's Coll. Lond. Theol. Assoc. 1866; Deac. 1866 by Bp of Win. C. of St. George's, Camberwell, 1866. [22]

LIPSCOMB, Charles Henry, *Temple Ewell Rectory, Dover.*—Queen's Coll. Ox; Deac. 1846 by Bp of Ely, Pr. 1846 by Bp of Carl. R. and V. of Temple Ewell, Dio. Cant. 1862. (Patron, B. J. Angell, Esq; Tithe, 127*l* 10*s*; Glebe, 56 acres; R.'s Inc. 172*l* 10*s*; Pop. 420.) Chap. to the Dover Union; Surrogate. Formerly C. of Barking, Essex, 1847–52; Sen. C. of Daventry 1852–62. [23]

LIPSCOMB, Francis, *Welbury, Northallerton, Yorks.*—Univ. Coll. Ox. B.A. 1821, M.A. 1824; Deac. 1821, Pr. 1822. R. of Welbury, Dio. York, 1832. (Patron, Ld Chan; Tithe, 334*l*; Glebe, 63 acres; R.'s Inc. 365*l* and Ho; Pop. 258.) Rural Dean. [24]

LIPSCOMB, Frederick, *Frogmore Parsonage, St. Albans.*—Queen's Coll. Ox. B.A. 1847, M.A. 1850; Deac. 1848 and Pr. 1849 by Bp of Roch. P. C. of Frogmore, Dio. Roch. 1859. (Patron, Rev. M. R. Southwell; Glebe, 4 acres; P. C.'s Inc. 160*l* and Ho; Pop. 975.) Formerly C. of Abbot's Langley, Herts, 1847–52; Hampstead, Middlesex, 1852–55; P. C. of Nether Wasdale, Cumberland, 1856–58. [25]

LIPSCOMB, Harry Curteis, *Staindrop Vicarage, Darlington, Durham.*—Dur. B.A. 1843, M.A. 1844; Deac. 1844, Pr. 1845. V. of Staindrop with Cockfield R. Dio. Dur. 1846. (Patron, Duke of Cleveland; Tithe, Staindrop—Imp. 301*l* 13*s* 7*d*; Cockfield, Tithe, 214*l* 1*s* 10*d*; Glebe, 32 acres; V.'s Inc. 545*l* and Ho; Pop. Staindrop 1848, Cockfield 956.) Dom. Chap. to the Duke of Cleveland. Author, *History of Staindrop Church,* fol. Whittaker and Co. 1852, 15*s*. [26]

LIPSCOMB, Henry Alchorne, 9, *The Grove, Gravesend.*—Ex. Coll. Ox. B.A. 1862, M.A. 1864; Deac. 1863 and Pr. 1864 by Bp of Roch. Chap. of St. Andrew's Waterside Church Mission, Gravesend. [27]

LIPTROTT, James, *Coombe, Shoreham, Sussex.*—Wor. Coll. Ox. B.A. 1832; Deac. 1833, Pr. 1834. C. of Coombe. [28]

LISTER, Henry, *Hawridge Rectory, Berkhampstead.*—St. Cath. Coll. Cam. B.A. 1844; Deac. 1844 by Bp of Rip. Pr. 1845 by Bp of Lin. R. of Hawridge, Dio. Ox. 1865. (Patrons, Trustees of Rev. H. Du Cane; Pop. 276.) Surrogate. Formerly P. C. of Boxmoor, Herts, 1845–65. [29]

LISTER, John, *Croughton Rectory, Brackley, Northants.*—St. Cath. Coll. Cam. Sen. Opt. and B.A. 1831; Deac. 1830 by Bp of Roch. Pr. 1831 by Abp of York. R of Croughton, Dio. Pet. 1849. (Patron, the present R; R.'s Inc. 630*l*. and Ho; Pop. 580.) Formerly P. C. of Stanley 1833–34; V. of Thorpe, Surrey, 1844–49. [30]

LISTER, Thomas Llewellyn, *Lime Tree Cottage, Newport, Monmouthshire.*—Jesus Coll. Ox. B.A. 1861, M.A. 1865; Deac. 1862 and Pr. 1863 by Bp of Llan. C. of St. Mark's and St. Woolos, Newport. [31]

LITCHFIELD, Francis, *Farthinghoe Rectory, Brackley, Northants.*—Mert. Coll. Ox. B.A. 1815; M.A.

1818; Deac. and Pr. 1817 by Bp of Pet. R. of Farthinghoe, Dio. Pet. 1836. (Patron, Alfred Rush, Esq; Tithe, 455*l* 17*s* 4*d*; R.'s Inc. 460*l* and Ho; Pop. 392.) R. of Great Linford, Dio. Ox. 1836. (Patron, Rev. W. Uthwat; Tithe, 406*l* 3*s* 9*d*; R.'s Inc. 417*l* and Ho; Pop. 557.) [1]

LITCHFIELD, Isaac Smith, *Buckland-Ripers Rectory, Dorchester.*—Trin. Coll. Ox. B.A. 1823, M.A. 1830; Deac. 1824, Pr. 1826. R. of Buckland-Ripers, Dio. Salis. 1841. (Patron, Q. H. Stroud, Esq; Tithe, 200*l*; Glebe, 9 acres; R.'s Inc. 214*l* and Ho; Pop. 113.) [2]

LITLE, George Alexander Magrath, *Lewes.* —Ch. Coll. Cam. Sen. Opt. and B.A. 1842, M.A. 1845; Deac. 1842 by Bp of Lon. Pr. 1843 by Abp of Cant. Chap. of the Royal Naval Prison, Lewes, 1862. Formerly Sen. C. of Dursley 1854; Chap. of the Dursley Union 1855. [3]

LITLER, Joseph Bellot, *Brassington Vicarage, Wirksworth.*—Brasen. Coll. Ox. M.A. 1856; Deac. 1857 and Pr. 1858 by Bp of Herf. V. of Brassington, Dio. Lich. 1865. (Patron, Tidd Pratt, Esq; Tithe, 10*l*; Glebe, 35*l* 8*s*; V.'s Inc. 97*l* and Ho; Pop. 721.) Formerly C. of Stanton-upon-Arrow 1857, Lockington 1859, Kilnwick-by-Watton 1863. [4]

LITTLE, George Savile Lumley, *The Parsonage, Buildwas, Iron Bridge, Salop.*—Trin. Coll. Cam. B.A. 1859; Deac. 1860 and Pr. 1861 by Bp of Rip. P. C. of Buildwas, Dio. Lich. 1862. (Patron, Walter Moseley, Esq; P. C.'s Inc. 68*l*; Pop. 282.) Formerly C. of Liversedge, near Leeds, 1861, Beaminster, Dorset, 1862. [5]

LITTLE, Joseph Russell, *Park House, Tunbridge.*—St. John's Coll. Cam. Jun. Opt. and 2nd cl. Cl. Trip. B.A. 1855, M.A. 1858; Deac. 1857 and Pr. 1858 by Abp of Cant. Asst. Mast. in Tunbridge Sch. 1857. Formerly C. of Hildenborough 1857–59. [6]

LITTLE, Thomas, *Princes Risborough, Bucks.*—Dub. A.B. 1855, A.M. 1858; Deac. 1856 and Pr. 1857 by Bp of Lon. P. C. of Princes Risborough, Dio. Ox. 1864. (Patron, Bp of Ox; Glebe, 80 acres; P. C.'s Inc. 180*l* and Ho; Pop. 1440.) [7]

LITTLE, Thomas Palling, *Oxenhall Parsonage, Newent, Glouc.*—Trin. Coll. Ox. B.A. 1841, M.A. 1843; Deac. 1841, Pr. 1842. P. C. of Pauntley, Dio G. and B. 1848. (Patron, Bp of G. and B; Tithe—Imp. 450*l*; Glebe, 14 acres; P. C.'s Inc. 80*l*; Pop. 233.) P. C. of Oxenhall, Glouc. Dio. G. and B. 1848. (Patron, Bp of G. and B; Tithe—Imp. 440*l*; Glebe, 17 acres; P. C.'s Inc. 80*l*; Pop. 272.) [8]

LITTLE, William John Knox, *Sherborne, Dorset.*—Trin. Coll. Cam. 3rd cl. Cl. Trip. 1862; Deac. 1863 and Pr. 1864 by Bp of Man. Asst. Mast. Sherborne Gr. Sch. Formerly Asst. Mast. Royal Gr. Sch. Lancaster, 1862; C. of Ch. Ch. Lancaster, 1863. [9]

LITTLEDALE, Richard Frederick, 10, *Beresford-terrace, London, W.*—Dub. Univ. Scho. 1852, 1st cl. Cl. and Gold Medal, 1854, 1st cl. Div. Biblical Greek Prize, and Berkeley Greek Gold Medal, 1856, A.B. 1855, A.M. 1858, LL.D. 1862, D.C.L. *com. causâ* Ox. 1862; Deac. 1856 by Bp of Nor. Pr. 1857 by Bp of Lon. Formerly C. of St. Matthew's in Thorpe Hamlet, 1856–57, St. Mary's the Virgin, Soho, Lond. 1857–61. Author, *Application of Colour to the Decoration of Churches,* Masters, 1857; *Philosophy of Revivals,* Bell and Daldy, 1860; *Religious Communities of Women in the Early Church,* Masters, 1862; *Offices of the Holy Eastern Church,* Williams and Norgate, 1863; *The Mixed Chalice,* a Letter to the Bishop of Exeter, Palmer, 1863; *Carols for Christmas and other Seasons,* Masters, 1863; *Unity and the Rescript, a Reply to Bishop Ullathorne,* Palmer, 1864; *Catholic Ritual in Church of England,* 12 eds. 1865; *The North Side of the Altar,* 5 eds. 1864; *The Elevation of the Host,* 2 eds. 1865; *Incense, a Liturgical Essay,* 3 eds. 1866. Joint Editor of *The Priest's Prayer-Book,* 1864; *The People's Hymnal,* Masters, 1867; etc. [10]

LITTLEHALES, Walter Gough, *Chieveley, Newbury, Berks.*—New Coll. Ox. B.A. 1859, M.A. 1861; Deac. 1860 and Pr. 1863 by Bp of Ox. C. of Chieveley with Oare 1860. [11]

LITTLEHALES, William, *Compton Bishop, Axbridge, Somerset.*—Ex. Coll. Ox. B.A. 1830, M.A. 1846; Deac 1831, Pr. 1832. V. of Compton Bishop, Dio. B. and W. 1848. (Patron, Preb. of Copton Bishop, in Wells Cathl; Tithe—App. 71*l* 2*s* 9*d* and 80 acres of Glebe, V. 203*l* 17*s* 3*d*; Glebe, 5 acres; V.'s Inc. 200*l* and Ho; Pop. 663.) [12]

LITTLEJOHN, William Douglas, *Sydenham Vicarage, Oxon.*—Corpus Coll. Cam. B.A. 1837; Deac. 1837 and Pr. 1838 by Bp of Chich. V. of Sydenham, Dio. Ox. 1844. (Patrons, Trustees; V.'s Inc. 130*l* and Ho; Pop 397.) [13]

LITTLER, Joseph, *East Crompton, Oldham, Lancashire.*—St. Bees; Deac. 1841 and Pr. 1842 by Bp of Ches. P. C. of East Crompton, Dio. Man. 1845. (Patrons, the Crown and Bp of Man. alt; P. C.'s Inc. 170*l*; Pop. 3414.) Formerly C. of Halliwell 1841–44, St. Andrew's, Liverpool, 1844. Author, occasional Sermons. [14]

LITTLEWOOD, Alfred Samuel, *Turnworth, Blandford.*—Trin. Coll. Ox. B.A. 1851, M.A. 1854; Deac. 1853 and Pr. 1854 by Bp of Salis. R. of Turnworth, Dio. Salis. 1862. (Patron, Bp of Salis; V.'s Inc. 160*l*; Pop. 150.) Formerly C. of Heytesbury, Wilts, 1853–59, Tretire 1859. [15]

LITTLEWOOD, James Lawrence, *Bebington, near Birkenhead.*—Trin. Coll. Ox. B.A. 1861, M.A. 1864; Deac. 1863 and Pr. 1864 by Bp of Ches. C. of Bebington 1863. [16]

LITTLEWOOD, John Henry, *Patrick Brompton, near Bedale, Yorks.*—St. Bees; Deac. 1860 and Pr. 1861 by Bp of Ches. C. of Hornby, near Catterick, 1866. Formerly C. of Trinity Runcorn, Cheshire, 1860–62; Asst. Chap. of the West Riding Prison, Wakefield, 1862–65; C. in sole charge of East Acklam, York, 1865, Patrick Brompton 1865–66. [17]

LITTLEWOOD, Samuel, *Edington, Westbury, Wilts.*—St. John's Coll. Cam. B.D. 1833; Deac. 1819 and Pr. 1820 by Bp of Salis. P. C. of Edington, Dio. Salis. 1826. (Patron, S. W. Taylor, Esq; Tithe—Imp. 1300*l*; P. C.'s Inc. 160*l*; Pop. 994.) Author, *A Letter to the Rev. Dr. Whately in Vindication of the Universal and Perpetual Obligation of the Moral Law as contained in the Mosaic Code, occasioned by his Essay on its Abolition,* Rivingtons, 1830; *A Specimen of a Humble Trial to develope some leading Principles and Feelings, and trace some Associations of the Mind and Spirit of St Paul,* Rivingtons, 1836; *A Letter to the Rev. William Maskell, M.A., occasioned by the Publication of his Sermon preached at the Triennial Visitation of the Bishop of Exeter,* 1848. [18]

LITTLEWOOD, William Edensor, *Hipperholme Grammar School, Halifax.*—Pemb. Coll. Cam. Wrang. Chan.'s English Medallist 1851, B.A. 1854, M.A. 1860; Deac. 1857 and Pr. 1858 by Bp of Rip. Head Mast. of Hipperholme Gr. Sch. 1861. (Patrons, Trustees; Inc. 227*l* Ho. Garden and Field.) Formerly C. of St. John's, Wakefield, 1857–61. Author, *Garland from the Parables,* 1857; *Essentials of English History,* Longmans, 3rd ed. 1867, 3*s*. [19]

LITTON, Edward Arthur, *Naunton Rectory, Andoversford, Cheltenham.*—Ball. Coll. Ox. Double 1st cl. 1835, B.A. 1836, M.A. 1840; Deac. 1840, Pr. 1841. R. of Naunton, Dio. G. and B. 1860. (Patron, Bp of G. and B; Tithe, 130*l*; Glebe, 53 acres, with an allotment of 444¾ acres; R.'s Inc. 600*l* and Ho; Pop. 535.) Exam. Chap. to the Bp of Dur. Formerly R. of St. Clement's, City and Dio. Ox. 1858; Bampton Lect. for 1856; Fell. of Oriel Coll. and Vice-Prin. of St. Edm. Hall, Ox. Author, *Sermon on John* iii. 5, 1850; *University Reform; The Church of Christ in its Idea, &c.* 1851; *Intellectual Religionism Portrayed; The Gospel not a Ceremonial Law* (University Sermons), 1853–54; *The Connection of the Old and New Testaments* (the Bampton Lectures), 1856; *Guide to the Study of the Holy Scriptures,* Seeleys, 1861, 3*s* 6*d*. [20]

LIVEING, Henry Thomas, *Tansor Rectory, Oundle, Northants.*—Pemb. Coll. Cam. 1827, Prizeman 1826 '27, '28, B.A. 1829, M.A. 1832; Deac. 1831 and Pr. 1832 by Bp of Lon. R. of Tansor, Dio. Pet. 1859. (Patrons, D. and C. of Lin; Glebe, 235 acres; R.'s Inc. variable; Pop. 248.) Rural Dean. Formerly C. of Wix, Essex, 1831, Hadleigh, Suffolk, 1838, Polstead, Suffolk, 1835; P. C. of Uxbridge-Moor 1843; V. of Bedfont, Middlesex, 1844–58. [1]

LIVESEY, John, *Upperthorpe, Sheffield.*—St. John's Coll. Cam. B.A. 1827, M.A. 1830; Deac. 1827 by Bp of Lon. Pr. 1828 by Bp of Ely. P. C. of St. Philip's, Sheffield, Dio. York, 1831. (Patron, V. of Sheffield; P. C.'s Inc. 157*l*; Pop. 18,461.) Military Chap. at Sheffield 1836. Author, various Sermons and Pamphlets. [2]

LIVESEY, Thomas Alexander, *High School, Stony Knolls, Broughton, Manchester.*—Univ. Coll. Dur. Heb. Prizeman 1858, Licen. in Theol. 1859; Deac. 1859, Pr. 1860. Formerly C. of St. George's, Barnsley, Yorks, of Worthen, Salop, and St. Luke's, Halliwell, Lancashire. Author, *English Grammar Simplified*, Barnsley, 1*s*; *Grace and Peace* (Sermon on leaving Worthen), Bolton. [3]

LIVINGSTON, Thomas Gott, 6, *Victoria-place, Carlisle.*—Magd. Hall, Ox B.A. 1852, M.A. 1854; Deac. 1853, and Pr. 1854 by Bp of Ox. Min. Can. of Carl. Cathl. 1855 (Value 150*l*.) Formerly Precentor of Carl. Cathl. 1855–68. [4]

LIVINGSTONE, R. G., *Oxford.*—C. of St. Mary the Virgin's, Oxford. [5]

LIVINGSTONE, Richard John, *Trinity Parsonage, Northwich, Cheshire.*—Trin. Coll. Cam. 1st in Middle Bachelor's Moral Sciences Trip. 1852, B.A. 1851, M.A. 1854; Deac. 1854 and Pr. 1855 by Bp of Ches. P. C. of Trinity, Northwich, Dio. Ches. 1861. (Patron, Bp of Ches; P. C.'s Inc. 150*l*; Pop. 1202.) Formerly Organising Sec. to S.P.C.K. and C. of Padgate, Lancashire. [6]

LIVIUS, Henry George, *Keinton-Mandeville Rectory, Somerton, Somerset.*—St. Edm. Hall. Ox. B.A. 1845, M.A. 1848; Deac. 1845, Pr. 1846. R. of Keinton-Mandeville, Dio. B. and W. 1851. (Patrons, Trustees; Tithe, 105*l*; Glebe, 72 acres; R.'s Inc. 170*l* and Ho; Pop. 538.) [7]

LIVIUS, Henry Samuel, *Berkeley square, Bristol.*—Trin. Coll. Cam. B.A. 1819, M.A. 1822; Deac. 1819 by Bp of Lin. Pr. 1826 by Bp of Nor. Chap. to the Bristol Orphan Asylum. [8]

LIVIUS, William Grinfield, *Stratford-on-Avon.*—St. Edm. Hall, Ox. B.A. 1860; Deac. 1861 and Pr. 1862 by Bp of Salis. Pr. Chap. of Trinity, Stratford, 1866. Formerly C. of St. Peter's, Marlborough, 1861–63, Mickleham 1863–65, Shinfield 1865–66. [9]

LLANDAFF, The Right Rev. Alfred OLLIVANT, Lord Bishop of Llandaff, *Athenæum Club, London, S.W.* and *Bishop's Court, Llandaff.*—Trin. Coll. Cam. Craven Scho. 1820, Senior Chancellor's Medallist, 6th Wrang. and B.A. 1821, Senior Member's Prizeman 1822–23, Tyrwhitt's Heb. Scho. 1822, M.A. 1824, B.D. and D.D. 1836. Consecrated Bishop of Llandaff 1849. (Episcopal Jurisdiction—the Counties of Monmouth and Glamorgan excepting the Deanery of Gower in the latter; Inc. of See, 4200*l*; Pop. 421,336; Acres, 797,864; Deaneries, 6; Benefices, 226; Churches, 286; Curates, 89; Church Sittings, 64,268.) His Lordship is Treasurer of Llandaff Cathl; was formerly Fell. of Trin. Coll. Cam; Vice-Prin. of St. Dav. Coll. Lampeter, 1827–43; Regius Prof. of Div. at Cambridge, 1843–60. Author, *A Sermon* (preached at the Consecration of the Chapel of St. Dav. Coll. Lampeter), 1827; *The Necessity of a Decent Celebration of Public Worship* (a Sermon), 1828; *An Analysis of the Text of the History of Joseph*, 1828; *A National School Sermon*, 1829; *Sermons* (preached in St. Dav. Coll. Lamp.) 1831; *The Principles that should influence a Christian Student* (a Sermon), 1841; *The Introductory Lecture to the Course delivered before the University of Cambridge in Lent Term*, 1844; *A Charge at his Primary Visitation*, 1851; *A Charge*, 1854; *A Few Remarks upon the Missionary Bishops' Bill and the Church Protestant Defence Society* 1854; *Some Remarks on the Condition of the Fabric of Llandaff Cathedral* 1856; *Charges at Visitations*, 1857, '60, '63 and '66; etc. [10]

LLEWELLIN, J., *Wiveliscombe, Somerset.*—C. of Wiveliscombe. [11]

LLEWELLIN, John Cleeves, *Trevethin, Pontypool.*—Lampeter; Deac. 1851, Pr. 1853. V. of Trevethin, Dio. Llan. 1863. (Patrons, D. and C. of Llan; Tithe—App. 56*l* 10*s* 10*d*, Imp. 53*l* 11*s* 9*d*; V.'s Inc. 500*l* and Ho; Pop. 7930.) Formerly C. of St. Thomas's, Haverfordwest, and Narberth and Robeston-Wathan, Pembrokeshire, P. C. of Michaelstone-super-Avon. [12]

LLEWELLYN, A. J. C.—Queen's Coll. Ox. B.A. 1858. Formerly C. of Easton Royal and Wilcot, Wilts. [13]

LLEWELLYN, David, *Easton, Pewsey, Wilts.*—Deac. 1818, Pr. 1819. Chap. of the D. of Easton Royal, Dio. Salis. 1839. (Patron, Marquis of Ailesbury; Chap's Inc. 120*l*; Pop. 463.) Chap. of the Pewsey Union. [14]

LLEWELLYN, David, *Puddington Rectory, Crediton, Devon.*—Deac. 1826, Pr. 1827. R. of Puddington, Dio. Ex. 1835. (Patron, Wm. Blaydon Gamlen, Esq; Tithe, 131*l*; Glebe, 68 acres; R.'s Inc. 177*l* and Ho; Pop. 210.) [15]

LLEWELLYN, William, *Llanfrynach, Cowbridge, Glamorganshire.*—V. of Llanfrynach with Penllyne C. Dio. Llan. 1850. (Patron, Earl of Dunraven; V.'s Inc. 135*l*; Pop. 286.) P. C. of Llangeinor, Dio. Llan. 1829. (Patron, C. R. M. Talbot, Esq; P. C.'s Inc. 71*l*; Pop. 363.) [16]

LLEWELYN, David Nicholas, *Penarth, Glamorganshire.*—Corpus Coll. Cam. B.A. 1865; Deac. 1866 by Bp of Llan. C. of Penarth and Lavernock 1866. [17]

LLEWELYN, Richard Pendrill, *Llangynwyd Vicarage, Bridgend, Glamorganshire.*—Deac. 1836 and Pr. 1837 by Bp of Llan. V. of Llangynwyd with Baidan C. and Maestig C. Dio. Llan. 1841. (Patron, J. D. Llewelyn, Esq; Tithe—Imp. 147*l*, V. 170*l*; Glebe, 2 acres; V.'s Inc. 170*l* and Ho; Pop. 7002.) [18]

LLOYD, Albany Rossendale, *Hengoed Parsonage, Oswestry, Salop.*—Trin. Coll. Cam. B.A. 1840, M.A. 1862; Deac. 1840 and Pr. 1841 by Bp of Ches. P. C. of Hengoed, Dio. St. A. 1854. (Patron, the present P. C; Glebe, 4 acres; P. C.'s Inc. 71*l* and Ho; Pop. 700.) Formerly C. of Padiham, St. John's, Liverpool, and Selattyn. Author, *History of England in Verse, from King Egbert to Queen Victoria*, 1846, 2*s* 6*d*; *The Birth of the Storms* (a Poem), 6*d*; *The Island Spectres* (an Allegory), 1855, 2*s* 6*d*; *The Missionary Hymn-book*, 1856, 1*s*; *Astronomical Recreation Cards with Rules*, 1862, 5*s*; and several Hymns and Tracts. [19]

LLOYD, Benjamin Marner, 140, *Craven-street, Liverpool.*—St. Bees; Deac. 1866 and Pr. 1867 by Bp of Ches. C. of St. Stephen's, West Derby, 1866. [20]

LLOYD, Charles, *Bettws-Bledwrs Rectory, Lampeter, Cardiganshire.*—Jesus Coll. Ox. B.A. 1829, M.A. 1835; Deac. 1831 and Pr. 1832 by Bp of Nor. R. of Bettws-Bledwrs, Dio. St. D. 1836. (Patron, Bp of St. D; Tithe—Imp. 4*l*, R. 122*l*; Glebe, 10 acres; R.'s Inc. 150*l* and Ho; Pop. 222.) Formerly R. of Cellan, Cardiganshire, 1838. [21]

LLOYD, Charles, *Chalfont St. Giles' Rectory, Slough, Bucks.*—R. of Chalfont St. Giles, Dio. Ox. 1859. (Patron, Bp of Ox; R.'s Inc. 615*l* and Ho; Pop. 1217.) Rural Dean; Chap. to the Bp of Ox. [22]

LLOYD, Charles Albert, *Rand, Wragby, Lincolnshire.*—Caius Coll. Cam. B.A. 1852. R. of Rand, Dio. Lin. 1854. (Patrons, W. Wyld and J. Hall, Esqrs; Tithe, 439*l*; R.'s Inc. 450*l*; Pop. 165.) [23]

LLOYD, Charles Williams, *Aldham Rectory, Ipswich.*—Magd. Coll. Cam. 1830, Prize Essayist and B.A. 1832, M.A. 1835; Deac. 1833 and Pr. 1834 by Bp of Lon. R. of Aldham, Dio. Ely, 1848. (Patron, Sir Thomas Barrett Lennard; Tithe, 315*l* 18*s* 6*d*; Glebe, 45 acres; R.'s Inc. 370*l* and Ho; Pop. 207.) Formerly

Asst. Min. of St. Peter's, Marylebone, Lond. 1833–38; V. of Gosfield, Essex. 1838–48. [1]

LLOYD, David, *Bodewryd, Almwch, Anglesey.*—Dub. A.B. 1847; Deac. 1847 and Pr. 1848 by Bp of Ban. P. C. of Bodewyrd, Dio. Ban. 1847. (Patron, Lord Stanley of Alderley; P. C.'s Inc. 174*l*; Pop. 26.) [2]

LLOYD, David, *Trefonen Rectory, Oswestry, Salop*—Lampeter; Deac. 1847 by Bp of St. D. Pr. 1848 by Bp of Herf. P. C. of Trefonen, Dio. St. A. 1850. (Patron, Earl Powys; Glebe, 9 acres; P. C.'s Inc. 210*l* and Ho; Pop. 1284.) [3]

LLOYD, Erasmus, R. W., *Legbourne, Louth, Lincolnshire.*—C. of Legbourne. [4]

LLOYD, Francis Brown, 9, *Norland-square, Notting-hill, London, W.*—M.D; Deac. 1859, Pr. 1861. Formerly C. of Trinity, Coventry, 1859, Gosforth 1862, Hotham 1863, Adbaston 1864, West Wratting 1865, Stetchworth 1866. [5]

LLOYD, Francis Llewelyn, *Aldworth, Reading, Berks.*—St. John's Coll. Cam. B.A. 1840, M.A. 1843, B.D. 1850; Deac. 1841 and Pr. 1842 by Bp of Ely. V. of Aldworth, Dio. Ox. 1859. (Patron, St. John's, Coll. Cam; Tithe—Imp. 409*l* 10*s* and 27 acres of Glebe, V. 102*l* 10*s*; Glebe 16 acres; V.'s Inc. 450*l*; Pop. 275.) Formerly C. of Wilnecote, Staffs; Sen. Fell. of St. John's Coll. Cam. [6]

LLOYD, George, *Darlington.*—Deac. 1861 and Pr. 1862 by Bp of Rip. C. of St. Paul's, Darlington, 1866. Formerly C. of Thurstonland 1861–66. Formerly Editor of *Irish Sunday School Teachers' Magazine.* [7]

LLOYD, George, *Gresley Parsonage, Ashby-de-la-Zouch.*—Deac. 1840, Pr. 1841. P. C. of Church Gresley, Dio. Lich. 1860. (Patron, Rev. Dr. Lloyd; Tithe—Imp. 250*l*; P. C.'s Inc. 125*l* and Ho; Pop. 2317.) Formerly P. C. of Willesley 1841; C. of Gresley. [8]

LLOYD, George Newton, *Shrawardine Rectory, Shrewsbury.*—Dur. B.A. 1855, M.A. 1859; Deac. 1855 and Pr. 1856 by Bp of Ely. C. of Shrawardine 1858. Formerly C. of Doddington 1855–57, Tenbury 1858. [9]

LLOYD, Henry Robert, *St. Mark's Parsonage, Kennington, London, S.*—Trin. Coll. Cam. B.A. 1831, M.A. 1837; Deac. 1833 and Pr. 1834 by Bp of St. D. P. C. of Kennington, Dio. Win. 1864. (Patron, Abp of Cant; P. C.'s Inc. 600*l* and Ho; Pop. 26,345) Chap. to the Abp of Cant. Formerly V. of Owersby, Linc. 1850–64. [10]

LLOYD, Henry William, *Cholsey, Wallingford, Berks.*—Magd. Coll. Cam. B.A. 1831, M.A. 1835; Deac. 1831, Pr. 1832. V. of Cholsey with Moulsford, Dio. Ox. 1837. (Patron, Ld Chan; Tithe—Imp. 675*l*; V. 220*l* 9*s* 10*d*; V.'s Inc. 450*l* and Ho; Pop. 1127.) Author, *Scripture Questioner*; *Parochial Visiting Cards*; *Happy Jack*; *What is True Religion? An Address to Candidates after Confirmation*; *A Letter to the Rev. T. Carter* (in reply to his work, *Rome Catholic and Rome Papal.*) [11]

LLOYD, Jacob, *Crosswood, Aberystwith.*—Lampeter; Deac. 1856 and Pr. 1857 by Bp of Llan. C. of Llanwnws and Llanavan-y-Trawscoed 1864; Dom. Chap. to the Earl of Lisburne. Formerly Chap. to Lewis's Charity, Gellygaer, 1856; C. of Narberth Pembroke, 1856. [12]

LLOYD, John, *Cerrig-y-Druidion Rectory, near Corwen.*—Deac. 1811, Pr. 1812. R. of Cerrig-y-Druidion, Dio. St. A. 1841. (Patron, Bp of St. A; Tithe, 352*l*; Glebe, 82 acres; R.'s Inc. 500*l* and Ho; Pop. 1243.) [13]

LLOYD, John, *Llandilo-Graban, Builth, Radnorshire.*—St. John's Coll. Cam. B.A. 1848; Deac. and Pr. 1849 by Bp of Nor. P. C. of Llandilo-Graban, Dio. St. D. 1853. (Patron, Bp of St. D; Tithe—App. 250*l*; Glebe, 10 acres; P. C.'s Inc. 75*l*; Pop. 263.) P. C. of Llanstephan, near Hay, Dio. St. D. 1854. (Patron, Bp of St. D; Tithe, App. 180*l* and 2 acres of Glebe; P. C.'s Inc. 69*l*; Pop. 231.) [14]

LLOYD, John, *Montgomery.*—Emman. Coll. Cam. Wrang. and B.A. 1832, M.A. 1835; Deac. 1836, Pr. 1837. R. of Llanmerewig, Dio. St. A. (Patron, Bp of St. A; Tithe, 132*l*; Glebe, 8 acres; R.'s Inc. 137*l*; Pop. 148.) [15]

LLOYD, John, *Llanvapley, Abergavenny.*—R. of Llanvapley, Dio. Llan. 1861. (Patron, Earl of Abergavenny; R.'s Inc. 231*l* and Ho; Pop. 156.) [16]

LLOYD, Julius, 6, *Lyall-place, Eaton-square, London, S.W.*—Trin. Coll. Cam. Scho. of, 1851, Wrang. 1852, 1st cl. Moral Sci. Trip. 1853, B.A. 1852, M.A. 1855; Deac. 1855 and Pr. 1856 by Bp of Roch. C. of St. Peter's, Pimlico, 1866. Formerly C. of Brentwood 1855, St. Peter's, Wolverhampton, 1858, Trysull, Staffs, 1862. Author, *Life of Sir Philip Sidney*, Longmans, 1862; *Sermons*, Wolverhampton, 1862; *Cambridge Sermons*, Bell and Daldy, 1866. [17]

LLOYD, Martin John, *Depden Rectory, Bury St. Edmunds.*—St. John's Coll. Cam. B.A. 1829, M.A. 1834. R. of Depden, Dio. Ely, 1836. (Patron, Ld Chan; Tithe, 462*l* 10*s*; Glebe, 24 acres; R.'s Inc. 492*l* and Ho; Pop. 265.) [18]

LLOYD, Maurice, *The Rectory, Montgomery.*—Emman. Coll. Cam. B.A. 1824, M.A. 1827; Deac. 1825, Pr. 1826. R. of Montgomery, Dio. Herf. 1831. (Patron, Ld Chan; Tithe, 480*l*; Glebe, 30 perches; R.'s Inc. 486*l*; Pop. 1276.) Rural Dean. [19]

LLOYD, Morris, *Llanelltyd, Dolgelly, Merionethshire.*—St. Bees; Deac. 1860 and Pr. 1861 by Bp of Ban. P. C. of Llanelltyd, Dio. Ban. 1866. (Patrons, Misses Lloyd and Mrs. Ffoulkes; P. C.'s Inc. 62*l*; Pop. 465.) Formerly C. of Llanvihangel-y-traethan 1860–61, Llanbeulan 1861–66. [20]

LLOYD, Newton Rossendale, *Milnsbridge, near Huddersfield.*—Deac. 1846, Pr. 1847. P. C. of Milnsbridge, Dio. Rip. 1864. (Patron, V. of Almondbury, P. C.'s Inc. 150*l* and Ho; Pop. 2903.) Formerly P. C. of Mold Green, Huddersfield. Author, *Mustard Seed* (a Lecture). [21]

LLOYD, Rhys Jones, *Troedyraur Rectory, near Newcastle-Emlyn.*—Ex. Coll. Ox. B.A. 1850; Deac. 1851 and Pr. 1852 by Bp of St. D. R. of Troedyraur, Dio. St. D. 1852. (Patron, Ld Chan; Tithe, 307*l*; Glebe, 12 acres; R.'s Inc. 319*l* and Ho; Pop. 974.) Rural Dean. Formerly C. of Lampeter 1851. [22]

LLOYD, Robert, *Blo-Norton Hall, East Harling.*—Jesus Coll. Cam. Sen. Opt. B.A. 1842, M.A. 1845; Deac. 1843 and Pr. 1844 by Bp of Lich. R. of Blo-Norton, Dio. Nor. 1863. (Patron, C. B. Goldson, Esq; Tithe, 336*l*; Glebe, 20 acres; R.'s Inc. 370*l*; Pop. 370) [23]

LLOYD, R., *Boston Spa, Tadcaster, Yorks.*—C. of Boston Spa. [24]

LLOYD, Samuel Webb, M.A.—Asst. Min. of Grosvenor Chapel, South Audley-street, Lond. [25]

LLOYD, Thomas, *Christleton Rectory, near Chester.*—R. of Christleton, Dio. Ches. 1843. (Patron, Rev. E T. Evans; Tithe, 638*l* 7*s* 10*d*; R.'s Inc. 910*l* and Ho; Pop. 1006.) [26]

LLOYD, Thomas, *Gilfachwen, Llandyssul, Carmarthen.*—Jesus Coll. Ox. B.A. 1824, M.A. 1825; Deac. 1826 and Pr. 1827 by Bp of St. D. R. of Llanfair Orllwyn, Cardiganshire, Dio. St. D. 1831. (Patron, Bp of St. D; Tithe, 120*l*; Glebe, 25 acres; R.'s Inc. 150*l*; Pop. 427.) [27]

LLOYD, Thomas, *Hanley Castle, near Upton-on-Severn.*—Ch. Ch. Ox. 2nd cl. Lit. Hum. B.A. 1834, M.A. 1837; Deac. 1838, Pr. 1839. Head Mast. of Hanley Castle Gr. Sch. 1845. [28]

LLOYD, Thomas B., *Whitehall, Shrewsbury.*—St. John's Coll. Cam. B.A. 1846, M.A. 1849; Deac. 1848 and Pr. 1849 by Bp of Lich. P. C. of St. Mary's, Shrewsbury, Dio. Lich. 1854. (Patrons, Trustees of Shrewsbury Sch. Livings; Tithe, Imp. 991*l*; P. C.'s Inc. 366*l*; Pop. 3966.) Formerly Asst. C. of Lilleshall 1848–51; V. of Meole Brace, Salop, 1851–54. [29]

LLOYD, Thomas Richard, *Llanfynydd, Wrexham, Flintshire.*—Jesus Coll. Ox. B.A. 1843; Deac. 1843 and Pr. 1844 by Bp of St. A. P. C. of Llanfynydd, Dio. St. A. 1843. (Patron, V. of Hope; Tithe, 148*l*; P. C.'s Inc. 150*l*; Pop. 1133.) Author, *Welsh Carols*; *Essay on Druidism*; *Songs of the Land we Live in.* [30]

LLOYD, Thomas Richard, *Strata Florida, Tregaron, Cardiganshire.*—Queen's Coll. Ox; Deac. 1847 and Pr. 1848 by Bp of St. D. P. C. of Strata Florida, Dio.

St. D. 1861. (Patron, Colonel Powell; P. C.'s Inc. 80*l*; Pop. 868.) Formerly P. C. of Eglwys Newydd, Cardiganshire, 1851-61. [1]

LLOYD, William, *Lillingstone-Lovell (Oxon), near Buckingham.*—Brasen. Coll. Ox. B.A. 1822, M.A. 1825; Deac. 1823, Pr. 1824. R. of Lillingstone-Lovell Dio. Ox. 1827. (Patron, Ld Chan; Tithe, 183*l* 13*s*; Glebe, 40 acres; R.'s Inc. 226*l* and Ho; Pop. 185.) Chap. to Viscount Dungannon 1837. [2]

LLOYD, William, *Manerdivy, Newcastle-Emlyn, Pembrokeshire.*—R. of Manerdivy, Dio. St. D. 1846. (Patron, Ld Chan; Tithe—Imp. 70*l*, R. 270*l*; Glebe, 40 acres; R.'s Inc. 320*l*; Pop. 896.) R. of Whitchurch Dio. St. D. 1850. (Patron, Thomas Lloyd, Esq; Tithe, 140*l*; R.'s Inc. 145*l*: Pop. 318.) [3]

LLOYD, William, *Draycot, Shardlow, Derbyshire.*—Jesus Coll. Ox. B.A. 1829, M.A. 1833; Deac. 1831 by Bp of Roch. Pr. 1832 by Abp of York. P. C. of Wilne, near Derby, Dio. Lich. 1857. (Patron, Bp of Lich; P. C.'s Inc. 85*l*; Pop. 1183.) [4]

LLOYD, William Henry, *Christ Church Parsonage, Eastbourne, Sussex.*—Magd. Coll. Ox. 2nd cl. Nat. Sci. B.A. 1856, M.A. 1859; Deac. 1857, and Pr. 1859 by Bp of Ox. P. C. of Ch. Ch. Eastbourne, Dio. Chich. 1864. (Patron, V. of Eastbourne; P. C.'s Inc. 100*l* and Ho; Pop. 1700.) Formerly C. of Claydon, Bucks, 1857-59, St. Clement's, Worcester, 1859-61, Trinity, Eastbourne, 1861-64. [5]

LLOYD, W. Valentine.—Chap. of H.M.S. "Scylla." [6]

LLOYD, Yarburgh Gamaliel.—Trin. Coll. Cam. B.A. 1836, M.A. 1842; Deac. 1836, Pr. 1837. Formerly V. of Dunston, Dio. Lin. 1847. [7]

LOBB, S. B., *Frome, Somerset.*—C. of Ch. Ch. Frome. [8]

LOBLEY, Joseph Albert, *Hamer, Rochdale.*—Trin. Coll. Cam. Fell. of, 8th Wrang. 2nd cl. Cl. Trip. B.A. 1863, M.A. 1866; Deac. 1863 and Pr. 1864 by Bp of Ely. V. of All Saints', Hamer, Dio. Man. 1867. (Patron, Bp of Man; V.'s Inc. 360*l*; Pop. 3300) Formerly C. of Bourne, Cambs, 1863; Conventional District of Hamer 1866. [9]

LOCK, Charles Snow, *Colchester.*—Ball. Coll. Ox. 3rd cl. Lit. Hum. and B.A. 1844, M.A. 1851. P. C. of St. Botolph's, Colchester, Dio. Roch. 1853. (Patron, Ball. Coll. Ox; Tithe, App. 230*l* 7*s*; P. C.'s Inc. 148*l*; Pop. 6228.) [10]

LOCK, William Edwardes, *Oswaldkirk Rectory, York.*—St. John's Coll. Cam. S.C.L. 1854; Deac. 1862 and Pr. 1863 by Bp of Rip. C. of Oswaldkirk 1867. Formerly C. of Danby-wisk with Yafforth. [11]

LOCKE, Edward, *East Somerton, Great Yarmouth.*—St. Bees; Deac. 1855 and Pr. 1856 by Bp of Nor. C. of Winterton and East Somerton 1866. Formerly C. of Tilney St. Lawrence, Lynn, 1855, Runcton with Holme 1857. [12]

LOCKER, Richard, *Aston, Stone, Staffs.*—Dur. Theol. Licen. 1853; Deac. 1853 and Pr. 1854 by Bp of Lich. P. C. of Aston, Dio. Lich. 1858. (Patron, Hon. E. S. Jervis; P. C.'s Inc. 150*l*.) Chap. to the Stone Union 1858. Formerly C. of Barlaston, Staffs, 1853-58. [13]

LOCKETT, William, *Little Dean, Newnham, Gloucestershire.*—Queens' Coll. Cam. 1851, Jun. Opt. 3rd cl. Cl. Trip. and B.A. 1854; Deac. 1854, Pr. 1855. P. C. of Little Dean, Dio. G. and B. 1865. (Patrons, Mayor and Corporation of Gloucester; P. C.'s Inc. 90*l*; Pop. 887.) Formerly C. of Moseley. [14]

LOCKEY, Francis, *Swainswick, Bath.*—Magd. Coll. Cam. LL.B. 1826; Deac. 1822, Pr. 1823. Author, *The Dangers threatening the Religious and Civil Liberties of the British Nation by the Admission of Roman Catholics to Political Power, &c.* 1819. [15]

LOCKHART, Samuel John Ingram, *St. Mary-Bourne, Andover, Hants.*—Lin. Coll. Ox. B.A. 1826, M.A. 1831; Deac. 1827, Pr. 1828. V. of Hurstbourne Priors with St. Mary-Bourne, Dio. Win. 1843. (Patron, Bp of Win; Hurstbourne Priors, Tithe—Imp. 358*l* 5*s* 5*d*, V. 199*l* 14*s* 7*d*; St. Mary-Bourne, Tithe—Imp. 1347*l* 19*s* 6*d*, V. 110*l*; V.'s Inc. 310*l* and Ho; Pop. Hurstbourne Priors 437, St. Mary-Bourne 1188.) Formerly Dom. Chap. and Sec. to the Bp of Quebec. [16]

LOCKWOOD, Edward Isaac, *Belstead Rectory, Ipswich.*—Jesus Coll. Cam. Coll. Prizeman, B.A. 1820, M.A. 1823; Deac. 1822 and Pr. 1823 by Bp of Ches. R. of Belstead, Dio. Nor. 1846. (Patron, the present R; Tithe, 307*l* 15*s*; Glebe, 54 acres; R.'s Inc. 388*l* and Ho; Pop. 292.) [17]

LOCKWOOD, George Palmer, *Rectory-house, Tryon's-place, Tudor-road, Hackney, London, N.E.*—Trin. Coll. Cam. B.A. 1852, M.A. 1852. R. of South Hackney, Dio. Lon. 1850. (Patron, W. G. T. Tyssen Amherst, Esq; Tithe, 209*l* 4*s*; R.'s Inc. 475*l* and Ho; Pop. 15,548.) [18]

LOCKWOOD, John William, *Kingham Rectory, Chipping Norton, Oxon.*—Ch. Ch. Ox. B.A. 1821, M.A. 1823; Deac. and Pr. 1826. R. of Kingham, Dio. Ox. 1836. (Patron, the present R; Tithe, 678*l* 3*s* 3*d*; Glebe, 75 acres; R.'s Inc. 886*l* and Ho; Pop. 678.) Formerly R. of Chelsea 1836. [19]

LOCKWOOD, John William Knollys, *Pocklington, Yorks.*—Trin. Coll. Cam. B.A. 1830; Deac. 1832 by Bp of Lin. Pr. 1833 by Abp of York. R. of Everingham, Dio. York, 1842. (Patroness, Mrs. Martin; Tithe, 80*l*; Glebe, 13 acres; R.'s Inc. 250*l* and Ho; Pop. 321.) [20]

LOCKYER, Edmund Leopold, *Westcot Barton Rectory, Woodstock.*—Emman. Coll. Cam. B.A. 1846, M.A. 1850; Deac. 1846 and Pr. 1847 by Bp of Win. R. of Westcot-Barton, Dio. Ox. 1852. (Patron, Rev. J. Y. Seagrave; Glebe, 208 acres, R.'s Inc. 220*l* and Ho; Pop. 270.) [21]

LOCOCK, Alfred Henry, *Lemsford, Welwyn, Herts.*—Trin. Coll. Cam. Wrang. and B.A. 1852, 1st cl. Nat. Sci. Trip. 1853, M.A. 1855; Deac. 1854, Pr. 1855. P. C. of Lemsford, Dio. Roch. 1859. (Patroness, Countess Cowper; P. C.'s Inc. 200*l* and Ho; Pop. 490.) Formerly C. of Chedgrave and Langley, Norfolk, and Southborough, Kent, 1857. [22]

LOCOCK, William, *East Haddon Vicarage, near Northampton.*—Caius Coll. Cam. Sen. Opt. and B.A. 1851; Deac. 1852 and Pr. 1853 by Bp of Lon. V. of East Haddon, Dio. Pet. 1854. (Patrons, Rev. W. Smyth and Mrs. Sawbridge; Tithe, 10*l*; Glebe, 94 acres; V.'s Inc. 200*l* and Ho; Pop. 727.) Author, *Theory and Practice of Perspective, together with the Application of the same to Drawing from Nature.* [23]

LODGE, Aneurin Lloyd, *Wavertree, near Liverpool.*—Jesus Coll. Ox. B.A. 1845; Deac. 1845 by Bp of Rip. Pr. 1846 by Bp of St. A. P. C. of Wavertree, Dio. Ches. 1859. (Patron, V. of Childwall; P. C.'s Inc. 135*l*; Pop. 3065.) Formerly C. of Rhuddlan, Flintshire. [24]

LODGE, Barton, *Colchester.*—Corpus Coll. Cam. B.A. 1829, M.A. 1831; Deac. 1831 and Pr. 1832 by Bp. of Lon. R. of St. Mary Magdalene's, Colchester, Dio. Roch. 1852. (Patron, Ld Chan; Glebe, 136 acres; R.'s Inc. 374*l* and Ho; Pop. 1127.) Mast. of the Hospital of King James, Colchester. Formerly Chap. at Buenos Ayres 1842-47; Vice-Chap. at Lisbon 1856-57. [25]

LODGE, Samuel, *Horncastle, Lincolnshire.*—Lin. Coll. Ox. B.A. 1850, M.A. 1854; Deac. 1851 and Pr. 1854 by Bp of Lin. R. of Scrivelsby with Dalderby R. Dio. Lin. 1867. (Patron, Hon. Champion Dymoke; Tithe, 700*l*; Glebe, 52 acres; R.'s Inc. 820*l*; Pop. Scrivelsby 153, Dalderby 33.) Head Mast. of Horncastle Gr. Sch. 1854; Chap. of 9th Lincolnshire Volunteers. Author, *Scriptural Reasons for Volunteer Movement* (a Sermon), Parkers. [26]

LODGE, Thomas, *Skerton Parsonage, near Lancaster.*—Trin. Coll. Cam. B.A. 1848, M.A. 1851; Deac. 1848 and Pr. 1849 by Bp of Rip. P. C. of Skerton, Dio. Man. 1855. (Patrons, Trustees; Tithe—Imp. 74*l*; P. C.'s Inc. 120*l* and Ho; Pop. 1556.) [27]

LOFT, James Edmund Wallis, *Healing Rectory, Ulceby, Lincolnshire.*—Corpus Coll. Cam. B.A. 1854, M.A. 1858; Deac. 1855 and Pr. 1857 by Bp of Lin. R. of Healing, Dio. Lin. 1859. (Patrons, A. A. Wallis, Esq. and Rev. J. P. Parkinson, D.C.L; Tithe, 360*l*;

Glebe, 21 acres; R.'s Inc. 290*l* and Ho; Pop. 96.) Formerly C. of Healing 1855–59. [1]

LOFT, John, *Wyham Rectory, Louth, Lincolnshire.*—Caius Coll. Cam. B.A. 1813, M.A. 1816; Deac. 1816 and Pr. 1817 by Bp of Lin. R. of Wyham with Cadeby C. Dio. Lin. 1818. (Patron, Magd. Coll. Ox; Tithe, 315*l*; Glebe, 6 acres; R.'s Inc. 390*l* and Ho; Pop. 135.) V. of Nun Ormsby, Dio. Lin. 1818. (Patronesses, Misses E. and S. Ansell; V.'s Inc. 87*l*; Pop. 155.) Rural Dean of Southesk. [2]

LOFTIE, Arthur Gershom, *Longtown, Cumberland.*—Dub. A.B. 1866; Deac. 1867 by Bp of Carl. C. of Arthuret. [3]

LOFTIE, William John, *Corsham, near Chippenham.*—C. of Corsham. [4]

LOFTY, Fitzroy Fuller, *Monk Sherborne, near Basingstoke.*—St. John's Coll. Cam. B.A. 1850, M.A. 1854; Deac. 1853 and Pr. 1854 by Bp of Ely. C. of Monk Sherborne 1865. Formerly C. of Kingclere 1859, Stretham-cum-Thetford, Isle of Ely, 1853–55, Rotherfield-Greys, Oxon, 1855–58, Thursley, Surrey, 1861–62, Hartpury, Gloucester, 1862–65. [5]

LOGAN, Crawford, *Everton, Liverpool.*—Ch. Coll. Cam. B.A. 1855, M.A. 1858; Deac. 1858 and Pr. 1859 by Bp of Ches. C. of St. George's, Everton. Formerly C. of St. Philip's, Liverpool, 1858. [6]

LOHR, Charles William, *Bedingham Vicarage (Norfolk), near Bungay.*—Corpus Coll. Cam. B.A. 1839; Deac. 1842 and Pr. 1843 by Bp of Nor. V. of Bedingham, Dio. Nor. 1846. (Patron, C. W. Uuthank, Esq. Lay Imp. on nomination of Bp of Nor; Tithe, 142*l* 10*s*; Glebe, 9 acres; V.'s Inc. 190*l* and Ho; Pop. 288.) Formerly C. of Rackheath, near Norwich, 1842–46. Author, *Church Establishments Expedient and Beneficial,* 1847. [7]

LOMAS, Holland, *Walton Breck, Liverpool.*—St. Mary Hall, Ox. B.A. 1848, M.A. 1860; Deac. 1848 and Pr. 1849 by Bp of Man. P. C. of Walton-Breck, Dio. Ches. 1855. (Patron, John Stock, Esq; P. C.'s Inc. 300*l*.) Formerly P. C. of St. Luke's, Leeds, 1851–54. Author, *Idleness and Industry contrasted* (a Series of Six Lectures). [8]

LOMAX, Charles Henry, *Droylesden, Manchester.*—C. of Droylesden and of Holy Cross, Clayton, Manchester. [9]

LOMAX, John, *Lathom, Ormskirk.*—Chap. of Don. of Lathom, Dio. Ches. 1865. (Patron, Lord Skelmersdale; Chap.'s Inc. 100*l* and Ho.) Almoner of Lathom; Dom. Chap. to Lord Skelmersdale. [10]

LOMBE, Edward, *Swanton Morley Rectory, East Dereham.*—Corpus Coll. Cam. B.A. 1846; Deac. 1849 by Bp of Pet. Pr. 1851 by Bp of Ely. R. of Swanton Morley, with Worthing R. Dio. Nor. 1863. (Patron, Rev. H. Lombe; R.'s Inc. 1065*l* and Ho; Pop. Swanton Morley 769, Worthing 170.) [11]

LOMBE, Edward, jun., *Eriswell Rectory, Mildenhall, Suffolk.*—R. of Eriswell, Dio. Ely, 1853. (Patron, T. B. Evans, Esq; R.'s Inc. 550*l* and Ho; Pop. 473.) [12]

LOMBE, Henry, *Bylaugh Hall, East Dereham, Norfolk.* [13]

LONDON, The Right Hon. and Right Rev. Archibald Campbell TAIT, Lord Bp of London, *London House, St. James's-square, S.W.* and *The Palace, Fulham, Middlesex, S.W.*—Ball. Coll. Ox. Scho. 1830, 1st cl. Lit. Hum. and B.A. 1833, Fell. of Ball. 1834, M.A. 1836, D.C.L. 1848, D.D. (*per literas Regius*) 1856; Deac. 1836 and Pr. 1838 by Bp of Ox. Consecrated Bp of Lon. 1856. (Inc. of See, 10,000*l*; Episcopal Jurisdiction, the Counties of London and Middlesex, and certain Parishes in Essex, Herts, Kent, and Surrey; Pop. 2,570,079; Acres, 246,157; Deaneries, 2; Benefices, 324; Curates, 258; Church Sittings, 396,841.) His Lordship is one of Her Majesty's Most Hon. Privy Council; Dean of Her Majesty's Chapels Royal; Provincial Dean of Canterbury; a Lord of Trade and Plantations; Official Trustee of the British Museum; Official Governor of King's College, London; Visitor of Harrow Sch. (in conjunction with the Abp of Cant.); Visitor of Highgate Sch; a Governor of the Charterhouse; Fell. of the Royal Soc. His Lordship was formerly Fell. and Tut. of Ball. Coll. Ox. 1834; Public Examiner in Lit. Hum. Ox. 1841; Head Mast. of Rugby Sch. 1842–49; Select Preacher in the Univ. of Oxford 1844–45; Dean of Carlisle 1849–56; one of the Royal Commissioners to Report on the Univ. of Oxford 1850. Author, *Five Sermons* (preached in Oxford), 1843; *Suggestions offered to the Theological Student,* 1846; *Four Sermons* (connected with Confirmation), 1847; *Lessons for School Life,* 1850; *Episcopal Charge at Primary Visitation,* 1858; *The Dangers and Safeguards of Modern Theology, containing "Suggestions offered to the Theological Student under present Difficulties"* (a revised edition), *and other Discourses,* Murray, 1861; *A Charge,* 1862; *The Word of God and the Ground of Faith,* Parts 1 and 2; various Pamphlets and Tracts. [14]

LONDON, George, *St. George's Parsonage, Altrincham.*—St. Aidan's; Deac. 1853 and Pr. 1854 by Bp of Ches. P. C. of Altrincham, Dio. Ches. 1859. (Patron, V. of Bowdon; P. C.'s Inc. 360*l* and Ho; Pop. 2800.) Formerly C. of St. Clement's, Liverpool; P. C. of Burneside, Kendal, 1854–59; Rural Dean of Kendal. [15]

LONG, Charles Edward.—St. John's Coll. Ox. B.A. 1855, M.A. 1858; Deac. 1856 and Pr. 1858 by Bp of Lin. Formerly C. of East Ravendale, Lincolnshire, 1857. [16]

LONG, The Ven. Charles Maitland, *Settrington Rectory, Malton, Yorks.*—Trin. Coll. Cam. B.A. 1826, M.A. 1830; Deac. 1826 by Bp of Salis. Pr. 1827 by Bp of Lin. R. of Settrington, Dio. York, 1846. (Patron, Earl Brownlow; Glebe, 1100 acres; R.'s Inc. 1200*l* and Ho; Pop. 871.) Archd. of the East Riding of Yorks, 1854. (Value, 200*l*.) Preb. of York 1855. [17]

LONG, David, *Parkside, Cambridge.*—Corpus Coll. Cam. B.A. 1855, Caius Coll. Cam. M.A. 1858; Deac. 1856 and Pr. 1857 by Bp of Lin. Fell. of Caius Coll. Cam. Formerly C. of Grantham 1859. [18]

LONG, Frederick Edward, *Butterton, Newcastle-under Lyne, Staffs.*—King's Coll. Cam. B.A. 1840, M.A. 1844; Deac. 1841 and Pr. 1842 by Bp of Lich. P. C. of Butterton, Dio. Lich. 1856. (Patron, Sir W. and Lady Pilkington; P. C.'s Inc. 90*l*; Pop. 379.) Fell. of King's Coll. Cam. [19]

LONG, Henry Churchman, *Newton Rectory, Long Stratton, Norfolk.*—Ch. Coll. Cam. B.A. 1832; Deac. 1832 and Pr. 1833 by Bp of Nor. R. of Newton Fletman with Swainsthorpe, Dio. Nor. 1835. (Patron, the present R; Tithe, 362*l* 7*s*; Glebe, 23 acres; Swainsthorpe, Tithe, 245*l*; Glebe, 45 acres; R.'s Inc. 760*l* and Ho; Pop. Newton 328, Swainsthorpe 338.) P. C. of Dunston, Norfolk, Dio. Nor. 1841. (Patron, R. K. Long, Esq; P. C.'s Inc. 30*l*; Pop. 83.) [20]

LONG, Henry Frederick, *Ferry Hill Parsonage, Durham.*—Dur. Open Scho. 1847 and 1848, Latin Prose Prize 1848, Van Mildert Scho. 1850, B.A. 1851, M.A. 1854; Deac. 1852 and Pr. 1853 by Bp of Dur. P. C. of Ferry Hill, Dio. Dur. 1864. (Patrons, D. and C. of Dur; Tithe, 276*l* 2*s* 6*d*; Glebe, 58*l* 5*s*; P. C.'s Inc. 334*l* 7*s* 6*d* and Ho; Pop. 1100.) Fell. of the Univ. of Dur. 1851. Formerly Lect. in Univ. of Dur. and Bursar and Censor of Univ. Coll; Examiner 1854, 1856–66; Pro-Proctor 1855–66. [21]

LONG, Robert, *St. Simon's Parsonage, Upper Chelsea, S.W.*—Corpus Coll. Cam. 18th Wrang. and Fell. of Corpus Coll. Cam. Crosse Univ. Scho; Deac. 1856 and Pr. 1857 by Bp of Lon. P. C. of St. Simon's, Upper Chelsea, Dio. Lon. 1864. (Patrons, Trustees; P. C.'s Inc. *uncertain*; Pop. 3959.) Formerly C. of St. George's, Bloomsbury, and Sec. to the Church Miss. Soc. [22]

LONG, R. Denn, *Inworth Rectory, Kelvedon, Essex.*—R. of Inworth, Dio. Roch. 1861. (Patron, T. Poynder, Esq; Tithe, 378*l*; Glebe, 71 acres; R.'s Inc. 446*l* and Ho; Pop. 202.) [23]

LONG, William Duncan, *The Vicarage, Godalming, Surrey.*—Dub. A.B. 1837, A.M. 1840, *ad eund.*

Ox. M.A. 1860, *ad eund.* Cam. 1864; Deac. 1839 and Pr. 1840 by Bp of Ches. V. of Godalming, Dio. Win. 1865. (Patron, Bp of Win; Tithe, 600*l*; Glebe, 2 acres; V.'s Inc. 640*l* and Ho; Pop. 2694.) Surrogate. Formerly C. of Davenham, Cheshire, 1839–41; V. of Dunany, co. Louth, Ireland, 1841–45; Min. of St. Matthew's, Liverpool, 1846; Sunday Aft. Preacher of Trinity, Liverpool; P. C. of St. Bartholomew's, Birmingham, 1847–50; Min. of Trinity Chapel, Woolwich, 1850–51; C. of St. George the Martyr's, Southwark, and Min. of St. John's Chapel, London-road, 1852–55; P. C. of St. Paul's, Bermondsey, 1855–59; Aft. Lect. of St. John's, Horselydown, Southwark, 1859; R. of Bermondsey 1859–65. Author, *Anniversary Sermon of the Trinitarian Bible Society*, 1861. [1]

LONGDEN, Robert Knight, *Brent Eleigh, Suffolk.*—Trin. Hall, Cam. LL.B. 1841; Deac. 1843 and Pr. 1844 by Bp of Nor. R. of Brent Eleigh, Dio. Ely, 1860. (Patroness, Mrs. Brown; Tithe, 463*l*; Glebe, 9 acres; R.'s Inc. 560*l* and Ho; Pop. 228.) Formerly C. of Groton. [2]

LONGDEN, William George, *St. Columba's College, Dublin.*—Queens' Coll. Cam. B.A. 1859, M.A. 1862; Deac. 1860 and Pr. 1861 by Bp of Ely. Fell. of Queens' Coll. 1860; Warden of St. Columba's Coll. 1864. Formerly C. of St. Andrew's, Wells-street, Lond; Fell. and Math. Tut. of St. Peter's Coll. Radley, 1859; C. of Sunningwell, Berks, 1860. [3]

LONGE, Henry Browne, *Monewden Rectory, Market Wickham.*—Downing Coll. Cam. B.A. 1825, M.A. 1828; Deac. 1827 and Pr. 1828 by Bp of Ely. R. of Monewden, Dio. Nor. 1847. (Patron, A. Arcedeckne, Esq; R.'s Inc. 265*l* and Ho; Pop. 223.) [4]

LONGE, Robert, *Coddenham Vicarage, Needham Market, Suffolk.*—Caius Coll. Cam. B.A. 1822; Deac. 1823 and Pr. 1824 by Bp of Nor. V. of Coddenham with Crowfield C. Dio. Nor. 1834. (Patron, the present V; Coddenham, Tithe, 644*l*; Glebe, 28 acres; Crowfield, Tithe—Imp. 260*l* 1*s*, V. 126*l*; V.'s Inc. 1050*l* and Ho; Pop. Coddenham, 903, Crowfield 353.) Rural Dean of Bosmere. [5]

LONGFIELD, Charles, *Hawthorn House, Hanley Castle, near Upton-on-Severn.*—Dur. Licen. in Theol; Deac. 1865 and Pr. 1866 by Bp of Wor. C. of Hanley Castle 1867. Formerly C. of Elmbridge and Wychbold 1865. [6]

LONGHURST, Alfred Augustus, *Fotheringhay, Vicarage, Oundle, Northants.*—Queens' Coll. Cam. B.A. 1850, M.A. 1854; Deac. 1852 and Pr. 1853. V. of Fotheringhay, Dio. Pet. 1859. (Patron, Lord Overstone; Tithe, 1*l* 10*s*; Glebe, 93 acres; V.'s Inc. 200*l* and Ho; Pop. 246.) Formerly C. of Bygrave, Herts. [7]

LONGHURST, John, *Dunton Bassett Vicarage, Lutterworth.*—Queens' Coll. Cam. B.A. 1824, M.A. 1828; Deac. 1823 and Pr. 1824 by Bp of Lin. V. of Dunton Bassett, Dio. Pet. 1845, second time, 1863. (Patron, the present V; Tithe, 11*l* 2*s* 6*d*; Glebe, 32 acres; V.'s Inc. 80*l* and Ho; Pop. 528.) Formerly C. of Knaptoft with Shearsby and Mowsley 1823, Kirkby-Mallory with Earl's Shilton 1824–34; Hinckley Sec. of S.P.C.K. and S.P.G. for 28 years. [8]

LONGHURST, W. H. R., *Savernake, Marlborough, Wilts.*—C. of Savernake. [9]

LONGLAND, Charles Pitman, *Rotherfield-Greys, Henley-on-Thames.*—St. Bees, 1845; Deac. 1846 and Pr. 1847 by Bp of Chich. C. of Trinity, Rotherfield-Greys; Chap. of the Union, Henley-on-Thames. [10]

LONGLANDS, William Arthur, *Eling, near Southampton.*—Jesus Coll. Cam. B.A. 1854; Deac. 1855 and Pr. 1856 by Abp of Cant. C. of Eling 1864. Formerly C. of Crayford 1855–62, Farnborough, Kent, 1862–64. [11]

LONGLEY, John, *Scaleby, Carlisle.*—Corpus Coll. Cam. B.A. 1866; Deac. 1866 by Bp of Carl. C. of Scaleby 1866. [12]

LONGLEY, Thomas, *Hutton, near Preston.* [13]

LONGMIRE, Joseph Leopold, *Sandiacre Rectory, near Nottingham.*—Lin. Coll. Ox. B.A. 1840, M.A. 1844; Deac. 1843 and Pr. 1844 by Bp of G. and B. R. of Sandiacre, Dio. Lich. 1849. (Patron, Bp of Lich; Glebe, 31 acres; R.'s Inc. 120*l*; Pop. 1012.) [14]

LONGMORE, Philip Alexander, *Newbury, Berks.*—Emman. Coll. Cam. B.A. 1847, M.A. 1850; Deac. 1848 and Pr. 1849 by Bp of Roch. P. C. of Hermitage, Dio. Ox. 1852. (Patron, Marquis of Downshire; P. C.'s Inc. 150*l* and Ho; Pop. 434.) Formerly C. of Bygrave, Herts. 1849–52. [15]

LONGSDON, Henry John, *Seacroft Parsonage, near Leeds.*—Trin. Coll. Cam. Sen. Opt. and B.A. 1850, M.A. 1856; Deac. 1850 and Pr. 1851 by Bp of Nor. P. C. of Seacroft, Dio. Rip. 1854. (Patron, V. of Whitkirk; P. C.'s Inc. 135*l* and Ho; Pop. 1306.) Formerly Chap. to the English Residents at Lucerne, Switzerland, and at Messina, Sicily. [16]

LONGUEVILLE, John Gibbons, *Eccleston Rectory, near Chester.*—Wad. Coll. Ox. 1st cl. Lit. Hum. and B.A. 1833, M.A. 1836; Deac. 1834 and Pr. 1836 by Bp of Ches. R. of Eccleston, Dio. Ches. 1854. (Patron, Marquis of Westminster; Tithe, 271*l* 16*s* 8*d*; Glebe, 47 acres; R.'s Inc. 363*l* and Ho; Pop. 849.) [17]

LONSDALE, James Gylby, *King's College, London, W.C.*—Ball. Coll. Ox. 1st. cl. Lit. Hum. 2nd cl. Math. et Phy. and B.A. 1837, M.A. 1840; Deac. 1842 and Pr. 1846 by Bp of Ox. Fell. of Ball. Coll. Ox; Prof. of Cl. Lit. King's Coll. Lond. Chap. to the late Bp of Lin. [18]

LONSDALE, John Gylby, *Lichfield.*—Trin. Coll. Cam. B.A. 1841, M.A. 1845; Deac. 1845 and Pr. 1846 by Bp of Lich. V. of St. Mary's, Lichfield, Dio. Lich. 1865. (Patrons, D. and C. of Lich; V.'s Inc. 480*l* and Ho; Pop. 2683.) Can. of Lich. 1855. (Can.'s Inc. 500*l*.) Formerly Sec. to the Nat. Soc. for the Education of the Poor 1849; Reader at the Temple Ch. Lond. 1851; Chap. to the late Bp of Lich. [19]

LONSDALE, William, *Duke-street, Grosvenor-square, London, W.*—St. John's Coll. Cam. B.A. 1819, M.A. 1838; Deac. 1821 and Pr. 1823 by Bp of Lon. Head Mast. of the Commercial and Coll. Sch. Duke-street, Grosvenor-square; Chap. of the Brentford Union, Middlesex. [20]

LOOSEMORE, Robert Wood, *St. Mark's Parsonage, Low Moor, Bradford, Yorks.*—St. Cath. Hall, Cam. Div. Prizeman, 3rd Jun. Opt. and B.A. 1855, M.A. 1858; Deac. 1855 and Pr. 1856 by Bp of Ex. P. C. of St. Mark's, Low Moor, Dio. Rip. 1857. (Patron, Gathorne Hardy, Esq; P. C.'s Inc. 168*l* and Ho; Pop. 1563.) Formerly C. of Perranzabuloe, Cornwall, 1855–57. [21]

LORAINE, Nevison, *Liverpool.*—Nonconformist Coll; Deac. 1859 and Pr. 1860 by Bp of Lon. Patron and *Locum Tenens* of Trinity, Liverpool, 1860. Formerly C. of St. Giles-in-the-Fields, Lond. 1859. Author, *The Lord's Prayer*, 1860, 3*s*; *The Voice of the Prayer-Book*, Longmans, 1867, 4*s* 6*d*. [22]

LORD, Alfred, *Mithian, Chacewater, Cornwall.*—Literate; M.R.C.S. formerly practising in London; Deac. 1844 and Pr. 1845 by Bp of Ex. P. C. of Mithian, Dio. Ex. 1847. (Patrons, the Crown and Bp alt; P. C.'s Inc. 150*l*; Pop. 2085.) Formerly C. of Tresco and Bryher, Scilly Isles, 1844–47. Author, *Luther, or Rome and the Reformation, a Poem*, 1841, 3*s*; *A Sermon on the Operations of the Holy Spirit*, J. H. Parker, 1852; *A Sermon on the Grace of God and the Danger of receiving it in vain*, 1859. [23]

LORD, Edmund, *Whittlesford, Cambridge.*—Jesus Coll. Cam. B.A. 1855, M.A. 1858; Deac. 1856 and Pr. 1857 by Bp of Nor. V. of Whittlesford, Dio. Ely, 1862. (Patron, Jesus Coll. Cam; Tithe, 11*l* 6*s* 8*d*; Glebe, 76½ acres; V.'s Inc. 200*l*; Pop. 800.) Formerly C. of Reedham 1855, Besthorpe 1857, Ten Mile Bank, Hilgay, 1859. [24]

LORD, F. B., *Farnborough Rectory, Bath.*—R. of Farnborough, Dio. B. and W. 1867. (Patron, the present R; Tithe, 304*l*; Glebe, 77 acres; R.'s Inc. 500*l* and Ho; Pop. 965.) Formerly C. of Chilton Foliatt, Berks. [25]

LORD, John Octavus, *Northiam Rectory, Staplehurst, Kent.*—Literate; Deac. 1851 and Pr. 1852 by Bp of Lon. R. of Northiam, Sussex, Dio. Chich. 1856.

(Patron, Rev. J. O. Lord; Tithe, 737*l* 18*s* 10*d*; Glebe, 30 acres; R.'s Inc. 790*l* and Ho; Pop. 1260.) [1]

LORD, Thomas Ebenezer, *Howden-Panns, Newcastle-on-Tyne.*—Deac. 1850 and Pr. 1851 by Bp of Lich. R. of Howden-Panns, Dio. Dur. 1860. (Patrons, the Crown and Bp of Dur. alt; Tithe, 196*l* 3*s* 8*d*; R.'s Inc. 180*l*; Pop. 3443.) Formerly C. of West Rainton, Durham. [2]

LORING, Edward Henry, *Gillingham Rectory, Beccles.*—Trin. Coll. Cam. B.A. 1845, M.A. 1848; Deac. 1846, Pr. 1847. R. of Gillingham All Saints' with Gillingham St. Mary, Dio. Nor. 1867. (Patron, Lord G. Beresford; Tithe, 462*l* 10*s*; Glebe, 59¾ acres; R.'s Inc. 600*l* and Ho; Pop. 390.) Formerly Asst. C. of Cranley near Guildford, 1846–53; V. of Cobham, Surrey, 1853–67. [3]

LORING, Henry Nele, *Southwick, near Fareham, Hants.*—Ex. Coll. Ox. B.A. 1832, M.A. 1836; Deac. 1835 and Pr. 1836 by Bp of Salis. Min. of Boarhunt and Southwick, Dio. Win. 1860. (Patron, Thomas Thistlethwayte, Esq; Pop. Boarhunt 267, Southwick, 607.) Formerly C. of Alvediston, Wilts, 1835, Romsey, Hants, 1837, Bishopstoke, Hants, 1842, Farley, Wilts, 1859. [4]

LORY, Frederick Aylmer Pendarves, *Seaview, Christchurch, Hants.*—Ex. Coll. Ox. B.A. 1861; Deac. 1863 and Pr. 1864 by Bp of Win. C. of Christchurch 1865. Formerly C. of Sholing 1863. [5]

LORY, H. C.—Chap. of H.M.S. "Terrible." Formerly C. of St. Clement's with St. Paul's, Truro. [6]

LOSH, James, *Long Newton, Darlington.*—Jesus Coll. Cam. B.A. 1841, M.A. 1847; Deac. 1841 and Pr. 1842 by Bp of Ches. R. of Long Newton, Dio. Dur. 1866. (Patron, Bp of Ches; Tithe, 610*l* 6*s* 4*d*; Glebe, 10 acres; R.'s Inc. 637*l* and Ho; Pop. 353.) Formerly Chap. to the Swinton Industrial Schs. near Manchester; P. C. of Odd Rode, Cheshire, 1857–66. [7]

LOSH, James, *Ponsonby Parsonage, near Whitehaven.*—Dur. B.A. 1857, Licen. in Theol. 1857, M.A. 1866; Deac. 1858 and Pr. 1860 by Bp of Wor. P. C. of Ponsonby, Dio. Carl. 1861. (Patron, William Stanley, Esq; Glebe, 50*l*; P. C.'s Inc. 81*l* 10*s* 6*d* and Ho; Pop. 111.) P. C. of Bridget's, Beckermet, Dio. Carl. 1866. (Patron, Thomas Irwin, Esq; Glebe, 29*l* 4*s*; P. C.'s Inc. 57*l* 14*s* and Ho; Pop. 657.) Surrogate 1866; Dioc. Inspector of Schs. 1866. Formerly C. of Corley 1858–60, Keresley and Coundon, Warwickshire, 1860–61. [8]

L'OSTE, Charles Alfred, *St. Mary's Rectory, Colchester.*—Caius Coll. Cam. B.A. 1813; Deac. 1813 and Pr. 1814 by Bp of Salis. R. of St. Mary-at-the-Walls, Colchester, Dio. Roch. 1855. (Patron, Bp of Roch; Tithe—App. 6*l*, R. 101*l*; Glebe, 13 acres; R.'s Inc. 255*l* and Ho; Pop. 1505.) [9]

LOTT, Frederick Edwin, *Bampton, Faringdon, Oxon.*—St. Alban Hall, Ox. B.A. 1841, M.A. 1843; Deac. 1841 by Bp of Ex. Pr. 1842 by Bp of Rip for Bp of Ex. V. of Bampton-Lew, Dio. Ox. 1857. (Patrons, D. and C. of Ex; V.'s Inc. 300*l* and Ho; Pop. 182.) Formerly C. of Luppitt, Devon, of Colyton, Devon, of Minster Lovell, and Islip, Oxon; P. C. of Leafield and of Ascott-under-Wychwood, Oxon, 1849. [10]

LOTT, William Buckland, *Barton Mills Rectory, Mildenhall, Suffolk.*—Ball. Coll. Ox. B.A. 1843, M.A. 1850; Deac. 1848 and Pr. 1849 by Bp of Ex. R. of Barton Mills 1863. (Patron, Ld Chan; Tithe, 423*l*; R.'s Inc. 550*l* and Ho; Pop. 531.) Formerly Asst. C. of Milverton. [11]

LOUGHBOROUGH, Ralph Lindsay, *Pirton, Hitchin, Herts.*—Literate; Deac. 1849, Pr. 1850. V. of Pirton, Dio. Roch. 1851. (Patron, R. Lindsay, Esq; Tithe—Imp. 550*l*; Glebe, 164 acres; V.'s Inc. 248*l* and Ho; Pop. 1023.) Author, *Times of Restoration, a Caution for the Times* (a Sermon with Notes and Illustrations), 2*s*. [12]

LOUGHNAN, Timothy, *Queen's-square, Bath.*—Dub. A.B. 1848, A.M. 1856; Deac. 1848 by Bp of Tuam, Pr. 1850 by Bp of Salis. Min. of St. Mary's Chapel, Queen's-square, Bath, Dio. B. and W. 1852. (Patron, the Proprietor; Min.'s Inc. 400*l*.) Author, *An Answer to certain Statements in the Essay entitled "On the Study of the Evidences of Christianity," in "Essays and Reviews,"* Bell and Daldy, 1861, 1*s*. [13]

LOVATT, H., *Burntwood, near Lichfield.*—C. of Burntwood. [14]

LOVE, George, *Luton, Beds.*—C. of Luton. [15]

LOVEBAND, Anthony William, *Tor Down, Barnstaple.*—Wor. Coll. Ox. B.A. 1843, M.A. 1846; Deac. 1844, Pr. 1845. Formerly C. of Yarnscombe, Landkey and Swimbridge, Devon. [16]

LOVEBAND, William Chorley, *Georgeham Rectory, near Barnstaple.*—King's Coll. Lond. Theol. Assoc. 1861; Deac. 1861 and Pr. 1862 by Bp of Ex. R. of Georgeham, Dio. Ex. 1867. (Patrons, Rev. W. Furadon and H. Deue, Esq., Trustees; Tithe, 507*l*; Glebe, 42 acres; R.'s Inc. 580*l* and Ho; Pop. 873.) Formerly C. of Stoke Climsland 1861–64, Swimbridge and Landkey 1864–66. [17]

LOVEDAY, Thomas, *Williamscote, Oxon.*—Magd. Coll. Ox. B.A. 1810, M.A. 1813, B.D. 1823; Deac. 1813, Pr. 1814. Formerly Fell. of Magd. Coll. Ox. 1818; Select Preacher 1819 and 1823; R. of East Ilsley, Berks, 1831–66. [18]

LOVEDAY, William Taylor, *Arlescote, Banbury.*—Formerly C. of Shotteswell, near Kineton. [19]

LOVEJOY, William, *Haltwhistle, Northumberland.*—Literate; Deac. 1866 and Pr. 1867 by Bp of Carl. C. of Midgeholme, near Brampton, Cumberland, 1866. [20]

LOVEKIN, Alfred Peter.—King's Coll. Lond. Theol. Assoc. and M.A. 1845; Deac. 1845 and Pr. 1849 by Bp of Lon. Gov. Chap. at Point de Galle, Ceylon. Formerly C. of St. John's, Glastonbury. [21]

LOVELOCK, Edward Henry, *Mildenhall Vicarage, Soham.*—St. John's Coll. Cam. B.A. 1849, M.A. 1855; Deac. 1849 and Pr. 1850 by Bp of Win. C. of Mildenhall and Surrogate 1851. Formerly C. of St. James's, Clapham, 1849–51. [22]

LOVELY, George, *Calcutta.*—Dub; Deac. 1849, Pr. 1850. Formerly C. of Ewell. Author, *Nature and Offices of the Holy Ghost; The Jews in their Present Condition and Future Prospects; Friendship with God, and the Saint's Death* (three Tracts). [23]

LOVERIDGE, J.—C. of St. Philip's, Bethnal Green, Lond. [24]

LOVETT, Robert, *Pickwell Rectory (Leicestershire), near Oakham.*—R. of Pickwell, Dio. Pet. 1856. (Patron, Earl of Gainsborough; Tithe, 527*l*; R.'s Inc. 535*l* and Ho; Pop. 169.) Dom. Chap. to the Earl of Roden. [25]

LOVETT, P. C., *Wellington House, Minehead, Somerset.* [26]

LOVETT, R., *Exeter.*—Min. of Bedford Chapel, Exeter, 1864. [27]

LOW, Charles, *Brampton, Cumberland.*—King's Coll. Lond; Deac. 1865 and Pr. 1866 by Bp of Carl. C. of Brampton 1865. [28]

LOW, John Low, *Forest of Teesdale, Barnard Castle, Durham.*—Dur. Licen. Theol. 1844, M.A. 1849; Deac. 1844 and Pr. 1845 by Bp of Dur. C. of Forest with Harwood, Middleton-in-Teesdale. [29]

LOWDER, Charles Fuge.—Ex. Coll. Ox. 2nd cl. Lit. Hum. B.A. 1843, M.A. 1845; Deac. 1843, Pr. 1844. P. C. of St. Peter's, Old Gravel-lane, London, Dio. Lon. 1866. (Patrons, Trustees.) Formerly C. of St. Barnabas', Pimlico. Author, *Penitents' Path* (Tract), 1850, 6*d*. [30]

LOWDER, William Henry, *Whitmore Reans, Wolverhampton.*—St. Edm. Hall, Ox. B.A. 1860, M.A. 1862; Deac. 1860, Pr. 1861. C. in sole charge of St. Andrew's District, Wolverhampton, 1866. Formerly C. of Bisley, Glouc. 1860, Leek, Staffs, 1864. [31]

LOWE, Charles, *Worsley, near Manchester.*—C. of St. Mark's, Worsley. [32]

LOWE, Charles Benjamin, *Tydd St. Mary Rectory, Wisbech.*—Trin. Coll. Cam. Sen. Opt. and B.A. 1835, M.A. 1838; Deac. 1836 and Pr. 1837 by Bp of Lich. R. of Tydd St. Mary, Dio. Lin. 1866. (Patron, Ld Chan; Tithe, 1250*l*; Glebe, 77 acres; R.'s Inc. 1300*l* and Ho; Pop. 977.) Formerly V. of Duddington 1853–60; R. of South Collingham, Notts, 1860–66. [33]

LOWE, Edward Clarke, *St. John's College, Hurstpierpoint, Sussex.*—Lin. Coll. Ox. 3rd cl. Lit. Hum. and B.A. 1846, M.A. 1849, B.D. 1860, D.D. 1860; Deac. 1847 and Pr. 1848 by Bp of Ex. Fell. of St. Nicholas Coll. Shoreham, 1849; Head. Mast. of St. John's Middle Sch. Hurstpierpoint, 1850. Author, *The Lord and Giver of Life* (a Sermon), 1s; *The Image of God* (a Sermon), 6d; *Erasmi Coloquia Selecta*, 3s 6d; *An English Primer of Religious and General Instruction*, 2s 6d; *St. Nicholas College and its Schools, a Letter to Sir John Coleridge*, 2 eds. 1s; *A Plea for Poor Scholars, a Letter to the Rector of Lincoln College*, 1s; *George Herbert's Church Porch, with Notes.* [1]

LOWE, Edward Henry, *Long Melford, Suffolk.*—Sid. Coll. Cam. Found. Scho. of, 8th Jun. Opt. 1867; Deac. 1867 by Bp of Ely. C. of Long Melford 1867. [2]

LOWE, Edward Jackson, *New Buckenham, Attleborough, Norfolk.*—St. Edm. Hall, Ox. B.A. 1852, M.A. 1855; Deac. 1852, Pr. 1853. P. C. of New Buckenham, Dio. Nor. 1866. (Patrons, the Inhabitants; P. C.'s Inc. 110*l* and Ho; Pop. 656.) Formerly C. of St. Bartholomew's District, Islington, Lond. 1856, Herringfleet 1862. [3]

LOWE, F. Pyndar, *Kingsclere, Hants.*—C. of Kingsclere. [4]

LOWE, George, *Upper Ottery Vicarage, Honiton, Devon.*—Mert. Coll. Ox. B.A. 1836; Deac. 1837, Pr. 1838. V. of Upper Ottery, Dio. Ex. 1841. (Patrons, D. and C. of Ex; Tithe—App. 690*l* and 76 acres of Glebe, V. 431*l*; Glebe, 4 acres; V.'s Inc. 437*l* and Ho; Pop. 940.) [5]

LOWE, George William, *Boston, Lincolnshire.*—Dur. B.A. 1855; Deac. 1855 and Pr. 1856 by Abp of York. Chap. of Boston 1864. [6]

LOWE, Henry Edward, *Atherstone, Warwickshire.*—Trin. Coll. Cam. Jun. Opt. B.A. 1837, M.A. 1840; Deac. 1837, Pr. 1839. Formerly Asst. C. of Bewdley, Worcestershire, 1837, Rushall, Staffs, 1840; P. C. of Wollaston, Salop, 1844; Asst. C. of Market Bosworth 1848; Asst. Mast. in Atherstone Gr. Sch. 1858–64. [7]

LOWE, John, *Ardley Rectory, near Bicester, Oxon.*—Lin. Coll. Ox. B.A. 1814, M.A. 1839; Deac. 1813 and Pr. 1814 by Abp of York. R. of Ardley, Dio. Ox. 1815. (Patron, Duke of Marlborough; Tithe, 285*l*; Glebe, 60 acres; R.'s Inc. 340*l* and Ho; Pop. 169.) Formerly P. C. of Swinton, Yorks, 1814–44; Aft. Lect. of Wath-upon-Dearne for 30 years. [8]

LOWE, John, *Abbotts Bromley Vicarage, Lichfield.*—V. of Abbotts Bromley Dio. Lich. 1848. (Patron, Marquis of Anglesey; Tithe—Imp. 389*l*, V. 83*l*; V.'s Inc. 188*l* and Ho; Pop. 1538.) [9]

LOWE, Joseph, *Bolton, Lancashire.*—Trin. Coll. Cam. Sen. Opt. 3rd cl. Cl. Trip. and B.A. 1853, M.A. 1856; Deac. 1853 and Pr. 1855 by Bp of Man. P. C. of Holy Trinity, Bolton, Dio. Man. 1856. (Patron, Bp of Man; P. C.'s Inc. 300*l*; Pop. 11,000.) Formerly C. of Deane, near Bolton. [10]

LOWE, Josiah Beatson, *Erskine-street, Liverpool.*—Dub. A.B. 1839; Deac. 1839 by Bp of Kildare, Pr. 1840 by Abp of Dub. P. C. of St. Jude's, Walton-on-the-Hill, Liverpool, Dio. Ches. 1850. (Patrons, Trustees; P. C.'s Inc. 400*l*.) Author, *Lectures on the Festivals of the Jews*, 1847; *The History of the Cross* (Lectures in Passion Week), 1849; *The Worship of the Virgin*, 1851, 4*d*; *Mormonism*, 1851, 4*d*; *Mormonism Exposed*, 1852, 6*d*; *The Church of Christ not a Roman Catholic Body, in Reply to the Rev. W. H. Anderdon*, 1854; *The Idolatry of the Church of Rome* (a Lecture), 1854; *The Immaculate Conception* (a Lecture), 1855; etc. [11]

LOWE, Julius Conran, *Durham.*—Queen's Coll. Ox. B.A. 1846, M.A. 1854; Deac. 1846 and Pr. 1847. Min. Can. and Sacrist. of Dur. Cathl. 1854; Mast. of the Dur. Elementary Gr. Sch. [12]

LOWE, R. B., B.A., *Newton in Makerfield, Lancashire.*—C. of Newton in Makerfield. [13]

LOWE, Richard Lomas, *Muckton Rectory, Louth, Lincolnshire.*—Dur; Deac. 1858 and Pr. 1859 by Bp of Lich. C. of Muckton with Burwell 1866. Formerly Missionary Pr. in Vancouver Island 1860–65. [14]

LOWE, Richard Thomas, *Lea Rectory, Gainsborough, Lincolnshire.*—Ch. Coll. Cam. Sen. Opt. and B.A. 1825, M.A. 1835; Deac. 1825 and Pr. 1830 by Bp of Lin. R. of Lea, Dio. Lin. 1852. (Patron, Sir Charles Henry John Anderson, Bart; Tithe, 392*l* 8*s* 10*d*; Glebe, 42¼ acres; R.'s Inc. 440*l* and Ho; Pop. 194.) Formerly British Chap. in Madeira 1832–52. Author, *Primitiæ et Novitiæ Faunæ et Floræ Maderæ*, Cambridge, 1831 and 1838, and Van Voorst, 1851; *The Fishes of Madeira*, 4to, and 8vo, 1843; *Memoirs on Zoology and Botany*, in the *Linnæan Society's Transactions*, *Cambridge Philosophical Society's Transactions*, and *London Zoological Society's Transactions*, in the *Zoological Journal*, 1824–34, *Proceedings of the Zoological Society*, 1830–54, *Hooker's Botanical Miscellany*, *Annals of Philosophy*, &c; *A Catechism on Confirmation for Young Persons*, Funchal, 1842; *A Catechism on Confirmation for Adults*, 1842; *Conformity, the Means of Peace and Union*, 1846; *Protest, with Appendix on Missions*, 1848; *Facts and Documents*, 1851; *Hymns for the Christian Seasons*, 1854. [15]

LOWE, Thomas, *Bolton-le-Moors.*—St. John's Coll. Cam. B.A. 1852. P. C. of All Saints', Bolton, Dio. Man. 1863. (Patron, T. Tipping, Esq; P. C.'s Inc. 128*l*; Pop. 3294.) Formerly C. of East Rudham, Norfolk, and Lever Bridge, Bolton. [16]

LOWE, Thomas, *Willingdon, Hurst Green, Sussex.*—Oriel Coll. Ox. B.A. 1836, M.A. 1839; Deac. 1841, Pr. 1852. V. of Willingdon, Dio. Chich. 1850. (Patrons, D. and C. of Chich; Tithe—App. 310*l* 10*s*, V. 155*l* 5*s*; Glebe, 4½ acres; V.'s Inc. 180*l*; Pop. 709.) Rural Dean 1867. Formerly Vice-Prin. of the Chich. Diocesan Coll. and P. C. of St. Bartholomew's, Chichester. Author, *The Kingdom of God* (a Visitation Sermon); *Why are Children Baptised* (a Tract); *The Long Journey* (a Tract); *Burnham Pottery, a Tale*, Macintosh, 3*d*. [17]

LOWE, William, *Bunbury, Tarporley, Cheshire.*—Dub. A.B. 1848, A.M. 1857; Deac. 1850 and Pr. 1851 by Bp of Ches. P. C. of Bunbury with Caveley C. and Peckforton C. Dio. Ches. 1864. (Patrons, Haberdashers' Co; P. C.'s Inc. 120*l* and Ho; Pop. 2820.) Formerly C. of Handley 1850, Bickerton 1850, Malpas 1853, Tilston 1855, Bunbury 1861–64. [18]

LOWE, W.—C. of St. Jude's, Edge Hill, Liverpool. [19]

LOWNDES, Charles, *Hartwell Rectory, Aylesbury.*—Trin. Coll. Cam. B.A. 1831, M.A. 1835; Deac. 1833 and Pr. 1834 by Bp of Lich. R. of Hartwell with Little Hampden C. Dio. Ox. 1855. (Patron, Royal Astronomical Soc. of Lond; Hartwell, Glebe, 93 acres; Little Hampden, Tithe, 65*l*; Glebe, 9 acres; R.'s Inc. 250*l* and Ho; Pop. Hartwell 137, Little Hampden 68.) [20]

LOWNDES, Charles Clayton, *St. Mary's Parsonage, Windermere, Westmoreland.*—Brasen. Coll. Ox. M.A. 1852; Deac. and Pr. 1850 by Bp of Ches. P. C. of Applethwaite, Dio. Carl. 1855. (Patron, Bp of Carl; P. C.'s Inc. 120*l* and Ho; Pop. 1235.) Asst. Tut. of Windermere Coll. Formerly Lect. of St. Cuthbert's, Carlisle, and 2nd Mast. of the Carlisle Gr. Sch. Author, *The Scholar's Hymn-book*, Carlisle, 1853; *Sermon on the Fast-day*, ib. 1854. [21]

LOWNDES, Edward Spencer, *Cleobury Mortimer, Salop.*—Ch. Coll. Cam. 1st cl. Moral Sci. Trip. B.A. 1854, M.A. 1857; Deac. 1854, Pr. 1855. C. in sole charge of Cleobury Mortimer. Formerly C. of Handsworth and Chesterton, Staffs. Author, *Two Sermons on Christian Temperance, with Preface and Notes*, Parkers, 1865. [22]

LOWNDES, Matthew, *Buckfastleigh Vicarage, Ashburton, Devon.*—V. of Buckfastleigh, Dio. Ex. 1861. (Patron, the present V; V.'s Inc. 285*l* and Ho; Pop. 2544.) [23]

LOWNDES, Richard, *Sturminster-Newton Vicarage, Blandford.*—Ch. Ch. Ox. B.A. 1844, M.A. 1847; Deac. 1844 and Pr. 1845 by Bp of Lon. V. of Sturminster-Newton, Dio. Salis. 1862. (Patron, Lord Rivers; Tithe—Imp. 185*l*, V. 775*l*; Glebe, 81 acres; V.'s Inc. 940*l* and Ho; Pop. 1880.) Formerly R. of Poole St. Michael, *alias* Poole Keynes, 1854–62. [24]

LOWNDES, William Charles Selby, *North Crawley, Newport Pagnell, Bucks.*—Ch. Coll. Cam. B.A. 1840; Deac. 1841, Pr. 1842. R. of North Crawley, Dio. Ox. 1856. (Patroness, Miss Duncombe; R.'s Inc. 230*l* and Ho; Pop. 981.) [1]

LOWRY, Charles Blomfield, *Darlington*—St. Bees; Deac. 1858 and Pr. 1860 by Bp of Rip. C. of St. Cuthbert's, Darlington. Formerly C. of Illingworth. [2]

LOWRY, Charles Henry, *The College, Northleach, Cheltenham.*—Queen's Coll. Ox. 4th cl. Lit. Hum. 2nd cl. Math. et Phy. and B.A. 1845, M.A. 1849; Deac. 1847, Pr. 1851. Head Mast. of the Coll. Gr. Sch. Northleach. (Patron, Queen's Coll. Ox.) Formerly Fell. of Queen's Coll. Ox. [3]

LOWRY, John, *Burgh-by-Sands, Carlisle.*—Magd. Coll. Cam; Deac. 1817, Pr. 1818. V. of Burgh-by-Sands, Dio. Carl. 1838. (Patron, Ld Chan; Tithe—Parliamentary Grant, and Eccles. Comm. 59*l* 6*s* 6*d*, V. 23*l*; Glebe, 92 acres; V.'s Inc. 120*l* and Ho; Pop. 986.) [4]

LOWRY, Joseph, *Chichester.*—Chap. of Chichester Union. [5]

LOWRY, Thomas, *Watermillock House, Penrith.*—Literate; Deac. 1825 by Abp of York, Pr. 1826 by Bp of Ches. R. of Watermillock, Dio. Carl. 1826. (Patron, R. of Greystoke; Tithe, 6*l* 13*s* 4*d*; Glebe, 22 acres; R.'s Inc. 140*l* and Ho; Pop. 521.) [6]

LOWTH, Alfred James, *St. James's Villas, Winchester.*—Formerly P.C. of Branksea, Dio. Salis. 1854. [7]

LOWTH, Arthur, *Winchester.*—R. of St. Swithin's, Winchester, Dio. Win. 1865. (Patron, Ld Chan; R.'s Inc. 80*l*; Pop. 170.) [8]

LOWTHER, Beresford, *Vowchurch, Hereford.*—Ex. Coll. Ox. B.A. 1837; Deac. 1837 and Pr. 1838 by Bp of Salis. V. of Vowchurch, Dio. Herf. 1838. (Patron, Preb. of Putson Major in Herf. Cathl; Tithe—App. 154*l* 6*s* 11*d*, V. 233*l*; Glebe, 1 acre; V.'s Inc. 274*l*; Pop. 333.) Dom. Chap. to the Earl of Lonsdale; C. of Turnaston. [9]

LOWTHER, Georges Paulin, *Orcheston St. George Rectory, Devizes, Wilts.*—St. Mary Hall, Ox. B.A. 1815, M.A. 1819; Deac. 1815, Pr. 1816. R. of Orcheston St. George, Dio. Salis. 1830. (Patron, Wad. Coll. Ox; Tithe, 500*l* 9*s* 9*d*; Glebe, 43 acres; R.'s Inc. 600*l* and Ho; Pop. 296.) Rural Dean 1832; Preb. of Salis. 1841; Proctor in Convocation for the Dio. of Salis. from 1835; Dom. Chap. to the Earl of Lonsdale. [10]

LOWTHER, Henry, *Distington, Whitehaven.*—Trin. Coll. Cam. B.A. 1810, M.A. 1813. R. of Bolton, Dio. Carl. 1822. (Patron, Earl of Lonsdale; Tithe, 436*l* 17*s* 4½*d*; R's. Inc. 520*l* and Ho; Pop. 1048.) R. of Distington, Dio. Carl. 1813. (Patron, Earl of Lonsdale; R.'s Inc. 311*l* and Ho; Pop. 785.) [11]

LOWTHER, John Mordaunt, *Whicham Rectory, Ravenglass, Cumberland.*—St. Bees, 1848. R. of Whicham, Dio. Carl. 1865. (Patron, Earl of Lonsdale; Tithe, 166*l*; Glebe, 61 acres; R.'s Inc. 253*l* and Ho; Pop. 327.) Surrogate. Formerly P. C. of Hensingham, Cumberland, 1851–65. [12]

LOWTHER, William St. George Penruddocke, *Sheepstor, Plymouth.*—Dub. and Theol. Coll. Chich; Deac. 1858, Pr. 1860. C. of Sheepstor; Chap. to the Duke of Leinster. Formerly C. of Woodborough 1858. [13]

LOWTHIAN, John, *Brampton, Cumberland.*—St. Bees; Deac. 1844, Pr. 1845. P. C. of Farlam, near Brampton, Dio. Carl. 1848. (Patron, Earl of Carlisle; P. C.'s Inc. 130*l*; Pop. 1311.) Formerly C. of Lamley, Northumberland. [14]

LOXHAM, Richard, *Great Lever Hall, Bolton-le-Moors, Lancashire.*—Dur. B.A. 1843, M.A. 1846; Deac. 1844 by Bp of Ches. Pr. 1848 by Bp of Man. Formerly C. of Rufford, Lancashire, 1848–49, Formby 1845–46. [15]

LOXHAM, Thomas, *Great Lever, Bolton-le-Moors.*—Dur. B.A. 1845, M.A. 1848; Deac. 1843 and Pr. 1846 by Bp of Ches. R. of Great Lever, Dio. Man. 1851. (Patron, Earl of Bradford; Tithe, App. 3*l*; R.'s Inc. 180*l*; Pop. 722.) Formerly C. of Bolton-le-Moors 1845–51. [16]

LOY, James, *Witney, Oxon.*—Dur. Licen. Theol. 1855; Deac. 1855 by Bp of Win. Pr. 1856 by Bp of Lich. C. of Witney. Formerly C. of Darlaston, Staffs, 1855. [17]

LUARD, Arthur Charles, *Wadworth Vicarage, Doncaster.*—Dur. B.A. 1855; Deac. 1855, Pr. 1856. V. of Wadworth, Dio. York, 1861. (Patron, W. Walker, Esq; Glebe, 148 acres; V.'s Inc. 156*l* and Ho; Pop. 656.) Formerly C. of Witton-le-Wear. [18]

LUARD, Bixby Garnham, *Hatfield-Peverell, Chelmsford.*—St. Peter's Coll. Cam. B.A. 1858, M.A. 1865; Deac. 1858 and Pr. 1859 by Bp of Roch. V. of Hatfield-Peverell, Dio. Roch. 1860. (Patron, John Wright, Esq; Glebe, 5 acres; V.'s Inc. 66*l* and Ho; Pop. 1311.) Formerly C. of Saffron Walden 1858. [19]

LUARD, Edward, *Winterslow Rectory, near Salisbury.*—St. John's Coll. Cam. Jun. Opt. and B.A. 1818, M.A. 1825; Deac. 1818 and Pr. 1819 by Bp of Pet. R. of Winterslow, Dio. Salis. 1846. (Patron, St. John's Coll. Ox; Tithe, 887*l*; Glebe, 57 acres; R.'s Inc. 950*l* and Ho; Pop. 904.) Formerly C. of Grafton Regis 1818–19, Little Houghton and Bradfield 1819–20, Morley 1821–28, Scawby, Lincolnshire, 1829–46. [20]

LUARD, Henry Richards, *Trinity College, Cambridge.*—Trin. Coll. Cam. B.A. 1847, M.A. 1850; Deac. and Pr. 1855. P. C. of St. Mary's the Great, Cambridge, Dio. Ely, 1860. (Patron, Trin. Coll. Cam; P. C.'s Inc. 104*l*; Pop. 758.) Fell. of Trin. Coll. Cam; Registrar of the Univ. Author, *Life of Porson*, in the *Cambridge Essays* for 1857; *Lives of Edward the Confessor*, in the Government Series of Mediæval Chronicles, 1858; *Catalogue of the MSS. in the Cambridge University Library—the Theological Portion*; *Remarks on the Cambridge University Commissioners' New Statutes for Trinity College* 1858; *Bartholomæi de Cotton Historia Anglicana*, 1859; *Epistolæ Roberti Grosseteste*, 1861; *Annales Monastici*, vols. 1–4, 1864–67; *Rud's Diary*, 1860; *The Correspondence of Porson* 1867. [21]

LUARD, Octavius, *Aunsby Rectory, Folkingham, Lincolnshire.*—St. John's Coll. Cam. Sen. Opt. and B.A. 1827, M.A. 1830; Deac. 1827 and Pr. 1828 by Bp of Lin. R. of Aunsby, Dio. Lin. 1856. (Patron, J. Archer Houblon, Esq; Tithe—App. 6*l*, R. 245*l*; Glebe, 12 acres; R.'s Inc. 266*l*; Pop. 140.) Formerly C. of Willoughton 1827–36, Blyborough 1827–46, Scotton 1853–56. [22]

LUARD, Thomas Garnham, *Stansted-Mountfitchet Vicarage, Bishops Stortford, Herts.*—Wad. Coll. Ox. B.A. 1843, M.A. 1851; Deac. 1845 by Bp of Lon. Pr. 1846 by Bp of Roch. V. of Stansted-Mountfitchet, Dio. Roch. 1852. (Patron, E. F. Maitland, Esq; Tithe—Imp. 315*l* 15*s*, V. 306*l* 14*s*; Glebe, 2 acres; V.'s Inc. 318*l* and Ho; Pop. 1769.) [23]

LUBBOCK, Henry Hammond, *Gunton Rectory, Norwich.*—Caius Coll. Cam. B.A. 1858; Deac. 1859, and Pr. 1860 by Bp of Ely. R. of Gunton with Hanworth V. Dio. Nor. 1866. (Patron, Lord Suffield; Tithe, 206*l*; Glebe, 75 acres; R.'s Inc. 280*l* and Ho; Pop. Gunton 78, Hanworth 227.) Formerly C. of Stow-cum-Quy, Cambridge, 1859–60, Gunton and Suffield 1860, R. of Bradfield, 1st Mediety, Norfolk, 1864–66. [24]

LUBBOCK, Richard, *Eccles, Attleborough, Norfolk.*—Pemb. Coll. Cam. B.A. 1819, M.A. 1822; Deac. 1821, Pr. 1824. R. of Eccles, Dio. Nor. 1837. (Patron, Sir T. Beevor, Bart; Tithe, 255*l*; Glebe, 27 acres; R.'s Inc. 279*l*; Pop. 194.) Chap. to the Guiltcross Union. Author, *Observations on the Fauna of Norfolk*, 1846. [25]

LUBY, Edmund, *Glasson Parsonage, Lancaster.*—Dub. A.B. 1839; Deac. 1839, Pr. 1840. P. C. of Glasson, Dio. Man. 1850. (Patrons, Trustees; P. C.'s Inc. 100*l* and Ho; Pop. 857.) [26]

LUCAS, Charles, *Filby House, Norwich.*—Trin. Hall, Cam. B.A. 1826; Deac. 1826, Pr. 1827. R. of Filby, Dio. Nor. 1848. (Patron, the present R; Tithe, 588*l* 5*s* 2*d*; Glebe, 20½ acres; R.'s Inc. 606*l*; Pop. 517.) [27]

LUCAS, C. H., *Edith Weston, Rutland.*—R. of Edith Weston, Dio. Pet. 1860. (Patron, B. Lucas, Esq; R.'s Inc. 155*l*; Pop. 387.) [28]

LUCAS, Charles John, *Burgh St. Margaret, Aele, Norfolk.*—Magd. Coll. Cam. B.A. 1835, M.A. 1848; Deac. 1836, Pr. 1837. R. of Burgh St. Margaret with St. Mary R. Dio. Nor. 1862. (Patron, Rev. W. Lucas; Tithe, 446*l* 10*s*; Glebe, 22½ acres; R.'s Inc. 500*l*; Pop. 554.) R. of Billockby, Dio. Nor. 1862. (Patrons, Family of Lucas; Tithe, 147*l* 10*s*; Glebe, 1¾ acres; R.'s Inc. 150*l* 5*s*; Pop. 46.) Formerly R. of Thrigby 1852–62. [1]

LUCAS, Gibson, *Enfield House, Southampton.*—Trin. Coll. Cam. B.A. 1821; Deac. 1822, Pr. 1823. R. of St. Lawrence's with St. John's R. Southampton, Dio. Win. 1854. (Patron, Ld Chan; R.'s Inc. 156*l*; Pop. St. Lawrence 359, St. John 733.) [2]

LUCAS, John Jackson, *Addingham, Leeds.*—St. Aidan's; Deac. 1858 and Pr. 1859 by Bp of Ches. C. of Addingham 1865. Formerly C. of St. Mary Magdalen's, Finch-street, Liverpool, 1858, St. Andrew's, Bradford, 1860, Idle 1862. [3]

LUCAS, John Ponsonby, *Rhossili Rectory, Swansea.*—New Inn Hall, Ox. B.A. 1851; Deac. 1851 by Bp of Ely, Pr. 1853 by Bp of Lich. R. of Rhossili, Dio. St. D. 1855. (Patron, Ld Chan; Tithe, 104*l*; Glebe, 51 acres; R.'s Inc. 150*l* and Ho; Pop. 294.) V. of Llangennith, Dio. St. D. 1855. (Patron, Thomas Penrice, Esq; Tithe—Imp. 155*l* 17*s*, App. 6*l* 10*s*, V. 65*l* 8*s*; V.'s Inc. 72*l* and Ho; Pop. 384.) Formerly C. of Tempsford, Beds, 1851, Whitchurch, Salop, 1853, Fladbury, Worcestershire, 1854. [4]

LUCAS, Richard Gay, *Mulbarton Rectory, Norwich.*—Univ. Coll. Ox. B.A. 1837; Deac. 1838, Pr. 1839. R. of Mulbarton with Kenningham R. Dio. Nor. 1842. (Patron, Rev. J. H. Steward; Mulbarton, Tithe, 531*l* 3*s* 3*d*; Glebe, 73 acres; R.'s Inc. 625*l* and Ho; Pop. 525.) [5]

LUCAS, William.—Prin. of the Hall and East Riding Proprietary Coll. Yorkshire. Formerly Mast. in Elizabeth Coll. and C. of the Vale, Guernsey; Head Mast. of the Gr. Sch. Carmarthen, 1864. [6]

LUCAS, William Henry, *Sopley Vicarage, Ringwood, Hants.*—Mert. Coll. Ox. 2nd cl. Lit. Hum. 1st. cl. Math. et Phy. elected Fell. of Brasenose 1844, B.A. 1843, M.A. 1845; Deac. 1848 by Bp of Ox. Pr. 1849 by Bp of Lon. V. of Sopley, Dio. Win. 1866. (Patron, H. Compton, Esq; Tithe, 330*l*; Glebe, 30 acres; V.'s Inc. 360*l* and Ho; Pop. 908.) Lect. of Rodborough, Glouc. Dio. G. and B. 1851. (Patron, Brasen. Coll. Ox; Lect.'s Inc. 235*l*.) Formerly C. of St. Peter's, Walthamstow, 1848; P. C. of Milford, Surrey, 1852; C. of Lyndhurst 1856. [7]

LUCE, Edmund Jones, *St. Paul's, Truro.*—Dub. A.B. 1848, A.M. 1852; Deac. 1849 and Pr. 1850 by Bp of Ox. P. C. of St. Paul's, Truro, Dio. Ex. 1864. (Pop. 3300.) Chap. of the Truro Union. Formerly Chap. of the Amersham Union; Mast. of Amersham Gr. Sch. [8]

LUCENA, Lorenzo, *Oxford.*—Deac. 1830, Pr. 1831. Formerly Professor of Spanish Literature at the Royal Institution Sch. Liverpool. [9]

LUCEY, Ebenezer Curling, *St. Margaret's at-Cliffe, Dover.*—Lin. Coll. Ox. B.A. 1858, M.A. 1861; Deac. 1858 and Pr. 1859 by Abp of Cant. V. of St. Margaret's-at-Cliffe, Dio. Cant. 1866. (Patron, Abp of Cant; V.'s Inc. 180*l*; Pop. 831.) Formerly C. in sole charge of Dymchurch, Kent, 1858, Biddenden, Staplehurst, 1860–66. [10]

LUCKMAN, Edward, *Bowers Gifford Rectory, Rayleigh, Essex.*—Queens' Coll. Cam. B.A. 1864; Deac. 1864 and Pr. 1865 by Abp of Cant. C. in sole charge of Bowers Gifford 1867. Formerly C. of Badlesmere with Leveland, Kent, 1864–67. [11]

LUCKMAN, William Grant, 9, *Johnstone-street, Bath.*—Queens' Coll. Cam. B.A. 1854, M.A. 1857; Deac. 1854 and Pr. 1855 by Bp of B. and W. Chap. of St. John's Hospital, and C. of St. John's Chapel, Bath, 1863. Formerly Asst. C. of Charlcombe, Bath. [12]

LUCKOCK, Herbert Mortimer, *Newnham, Cambridge.*—Jesus Coll. Cam. 2nd Cl. Trip. 1st cl. Theol. Trip. Crosse Div. Scho. Tyrwhitt Heb. Scho. Carus Prize 1860, Scholefield Prize 1860, Members' Prizeman 1860, 1861 and 1862, B.A. 1858, M.A. 1862; Deac. 1860 by Bp of Ox. Pr. 1862 by Bp of Ely. V. of All Saints', Cambridge, Dio. Ely 1865. (Patron, Jesus Coll. Cam; Glebe, 70*l*; V.'s Inc. 150*l*; Pop. 1400.) Chap. to Lord Carington. Formerly Cl. Lect. and Fell. of Jesus Coll; Div. Lect. at King's Coll; R. of Gayhurst with Stoke Goldington, Bucks, 1863. [13]

LUCKOCK, Reginald Mortimer, *Godolphin School, Hammersmith, W.*—Corpus Coll. Cam. Math. Hons. B.A. 1863, M.A. 1866; Deac. 1864 and Pr. 1865 by Bp of Lon. Formerly C. of St. John's, Hammersmith, 1864–67. [14]

LUCKOCK, Thomas George Mortimer, *Upper Berwick House, Shrewsbury.*—St. John's Coll. Cam. Jun. Opt. and B.A. 1829, M.A. 1832; Deac. 1829, Pr. 1831. P. C. of Little Berwick, Salop, Dio. Lich. 1833. (Patrons, Earl of Tankerville and others; P. C.'s Inc. 56*l*; Pop. 186.) [15]

LUCKOCK, Thomas Gilbert, 10, *Carlton-place, Clifton.*—St. John's Coll. Cam. B.A. 1854; Deac. 1854 by Bp of G. and B. Pr. 1855 by Bp of B. and W. Dom. Chap. to the Earl of Ducie 1857; Min. of Emmanuel Ch. Clifton, Dio. G. and B. 1866. (Patrons, Simeon's Trustees.) Formerly C. of St. Matthias', Weir, Bristol. [16]

LUCY, John, *Hampton-Lucy, Warwickshire.*—Trin. Coll. Cam. B.A. 1814, M.A. 1817; Deac. 1814, Pr. 1815. R. of Hampton-Lucy, Dio. Wor. 1815. (Patron, Geo. Lucy, Esq; Tithe, 1325*l*; Glebe, 10 acres; R.'s Inc. 1435*l* and Ho; Pop. 435.) V. of Charlecote, Warw. Dio. Wor. 1823. (Patron, Geo. Lucy, Esq; Tithe, 217*l* 6*s*; Glebe, 1 acre; V.'s Inc. 229*l*; Pop. 245.) [17]

LUDGATER, Henry, *Roding-Aythorp, Great Dunmow, Essex.*—Trin. Coll. Cam. B.A. 1838, M.A. 1841. R. of Roding-Aythorp, Dio. Roch. 1849. (Patron, the present R; Tithe, 372*l* 9*s* 8*d*; R's Inc. 385*l*; Pop. 269.) [18]

LUDLOW, Arthur Rainey, *Littleton-upon-Severn, Almondsbury, Glouc.*—Oriel Coll. Ox. B.A. 1831, M.A. 1835; Deac. 1833 by Bp of Roch. Pr. 1834 by Bp of Carl. R. of Littleton-upon-Severn, Dio. G. and B. 1855. (Patron, R. C. Lippincott, Esq; Tithe, 1*l* 18*s* 10*d*; R.'s Inc. 55*l*; Pop. 195.) Formerly C. of Paddington 1837–41; Mayor of Bristol's Chap. 1852. Author, *Manual of Prayers*, Bristol, 1847; *Baptism*, Bristol, 1865. [19]

LUDLOW, Edward, *Winterbourne St. Martin, Dorchester.*—St. Edm. Hall, Ox. B.A. 1824, M.A. 1827; Deac. 1825 and Pr. 1826 by Bp of B. and W. V. of Winterbourne St. Martin, Dio. Salis. 1837. (Patron, Bp of Salis; Tithe—Imp. 8*l*, V. 110*l*; V.'s Inc. 120*l* and Ho; Pop. 458.) Surrogate 1857. Formerly C. of Walton, Somerset, 1825–27, Winkfield, Wilts, 1827–31, Norton St. Philip, Somerset, 1831–37. [20]

LUDLOW, John Thomas, *Compton-Greenfield Rectory, Bristol.*—Oriel Coll. Ox. B.A. 1835, M.A. 1840. R. of Compton-Greenfield, Dio. G. and B. 1846. (Patron, R. C. Lippincott, Esq; Tithe, 148*l* 10*s*; Glebe, 50 acres; R.'s Inc. 228*l* and Ho; Pop. 52.) [21]

LUDLOW, Thomas Binfield, *Slapton Rectory, Leighton Buzzard.*—Ch. Ch. Ox. Hon. 4th cl. Lit. Hum. 3rd cl. Math. et Phy. and B.A. 1845, M.A. 1848; Deac. 1845, Pr. 1846. R. of Slapton, Dio. Ox. 1853. (Patrons, D. and C. of Ch. Ch. Ox; Tithe—Tithe Farm, 174 acres; Glebe, 15 acres; R.'s Inc. 310*l* and Ho; Pop. 325.) [22]

LUDLOW, William, *Kirton Vicarage, Boston, Lincolnshire.*—St. Peter's Coll. Cam. B.A. 1829, M.A. 1835; Deac. 1829, Pr. 1830. V. of Kirton, Dio. Lin. 1846. (Patrons, the Mercers' Company, who are Imps. of a Land Allotment of 600 acres, letting for 1000*l* per annum; V.'s Inc. 420*l* and Ho; Pop. 2131.) Preb. of Kerswell in Ex. Cathl. 1847. (Value, 2*l* 13*s* 4*d*.) British Chap. at Wildbad. Formerly R. of St. Botolph's, Aldgate, Lond. [23]

LUFKIN, Henry Everitt, *East Donyland Rectory, Colchester.*—St. John's Coll. Cam. Sen. Opt. B.A. 1855, M.A. 1858; Deac. 1857 and Pr. 1858 by Bp of Ely. R. of East Donyland, Dio. Roch. 1863. (Patron, P. Havens, Esq; R.'s Inc. 209*l*; Pop. 1052.) Formerly C. of Nayland 1857, Carlton and Friston with Snape 1859. [24]

LUGARD, Frederick Grueber, *St. Clement's, Worcester.*—Trin. Coll. Cam. B.A. 1831, M.A. 1856; Deac. 1831, Pr. 1832. R. of St. Clement's, Worcester, Dio. Wor. 1865. (Patrons, D. and C. of Wor; Tithe, 7*l*; R.'s Inc. 170*l* and Ho; Pop. 2500.) Formerly Chap. in Madras 1837–64. [1]

LUGG, John.—Clare Coll. Cam. B.A. 1844. Chap. of H.M.S. "St. Vincent." [2]

LUKE, Francis Vyvyan, *Weeting, Brandon, Norfolk.*—St. Peter's Coll. Cam. B.A. 1818, M.A. 1821; Deac. and Pr. 1818 by Bp of Lon. R. of Frinton, Colchester, Dio. Roch. 1818. (Patron, S. Lushington, Esq; Tithe, 160*l* 10*s*; Glebe, 27 acres; R.'s Inc. 190*l*; Pop. 30.) Formerly C. of Weeting, Norfolk, 1837. Author, *Sermon on the Death of Mrs. Angerstein, of Weeting Hall.* [3]

LUKE, William Henry Colbeck, *Elmswell Rectory, Bury St. Edmunds.*—Oriel Coll Ox. B.A. 1853, M.A. 1857, Wells 1853–54; Deac. 1854 by Bp of Win. Pr. 1856 by Bp of Ely. R. of Elmswell, Dio. Ely, 1863. (Patron, W. Luke, Esq; Tithe, 420*l*; Glebe, 45 acres; R.'s Inc. 500*l* and Ho; Pop. 759.) Formerly C. of Oundle, Northants, East Retford, Notts, and Chislehurst, Kent. [4]

LUKIN, James, *Pwllcrochan, Pembroke.*—Brasen. Coll. Ox. B.A. 1849; Deac. 1851 and Pr. 1852 by Bp of G. and B. R. of Pwllcrochan, Dio. St. D. 1865. (Patrons, Trustees of Mrs. Lukin; Tithe, 175*l*; Glebe, 10 acres; R.'s Inc. 214*l* and Ho; Pop. 264.) Formerly R. of Bradfield-Combust, Suffolk, 1862–65. Author, *Handbook of Natural Philosophy*, Cassell, 1*s*. [5]

LUKIN, W. H., *Friskney, Lincolnshire.*—C. of Friskney [6]

LUKIS, William Collings, *Wath Rectory, near Ripon.*—Trin. Coll. Cam. 3rd Jun. Opt. B.A. 1840, M.A. 1843, *ad eund.* Ox. 1854; Deac. 1841 and Pr. 1842 by Bp of Salis. R. of Wath, Dio. Rip. 1862. (Patron, Marquis of Ailesbury; Tithe, 918*l*; Glebe, 69 acres, 137*l*; R.'s Inc. 1055*l* and Ho; Pop. 718.) F.S.A. and Fell. of the Royal Society of Antiquaries, Copenhagen. Formerly C. of Bradford-on-Avon 1841–46; P. C. of East Grafton, Wilts, 1846–50; V. of Great Bedwyn, Wilts, 1850–55; Dom. Chap. to Marquis of Ailesbury 1850; Rural Dean of Marlborough 1851–61; R. of Collingbourne, Ducis, Wilts, 1855–62. Author, *Specimens of Ancient Church Plate, &c.*, 4to, 1845, 21*s*; *An Account of Church Bells, &c.* 1857, 6*s*; *Danish Cromlechs and Burial Customs compared with those of Brittany, the Channel Islands, &c*; *A Few Words to Rural Deans on Church Bells*, 1858; *A Few Words to Churchwardens on Church Bells*, 1858. [7]

LUMB, Henry, *Lowther, near Penrith.*—Dur. B.A. 1862, M.A. 1866; Deac. 1862 and Pr. 1863 by Bp of Man. C. of Lowther 1864. Formerly C. of Bury, Lancashire, 1862–64. [8]

LUMB, William Eedson, *Halford Parsonage, Craven Arms, Salop.*—Trin. Coll. Cam. B.A. 1830, M.A. 1834; Deac. 1831 and Pr. 1832 by Abp of York. P. C. of Sibdon, Dio. Herf. 1841. (Patron, James Baxter, Esq. Sibdon Castle; P. C.'s Inc. 50*l*; Pop. 69.) P. C. of Halford, Dio. Herf. 1843. (Patroness, Baroness Windsor; Glebe, 4 acres; P. C.'s Inc. 40*l* and Ho; Pop. 141.) Formerly 2nd Mast. of Gr. Sch. Ripon, 1829–37; C. of Winksley, near Ripon, 1831, Sedbergh, Yorks, 1837–40, Winstanstow, Salop, 1841–43. [9]

LUMBY, Joseph Rawson, 33, *Jesus lane, Cambridge.*—Magd Coll. Cam. B.A. 1858; Deac. and Pr. 1858 by Bp of Ely. C. of Girton, Cambs, 1860. Formerly Fell. of Magd. Coll. Cam. [10]

LUMSDAINE, Edwin Sandys, *Upper Hardres Rectory, Canterbury.*—St. John's Coll. Ox. B.A. 1807, M.A. 1808; Deac. 1809 and Pr. 1810 by Bp of Lin. R. of Upper Hardres with Stelling C. Dio. Cant. 1815. (Patrons, the present R. and Heirs of Lady Hardres; Tithe, 700*l*; Glebe, 43 acres; R.'s Inc. 740*l* and Ho; Pop. Upper Hardres 271, Stelling 309.) [11]

LUMSDEN, Henry Thomas, 15, *Lower Berkeley-street, Portman-square, London, W.*—St. John's Coll. Cam. B.A. 1831; Deac. 1832 and Pr. 1833 by Bp of Nor. P. C. of St. Thomas's, Portman-square, Dio. Lon. 1858. (Patron, the Crown; P. C.'s Inc. 250*l*; Pop. 9782.) Formerly P. C. of St. Peter's, Ipswich, 1837–58. [12]

LUND, Thomas, *Brindle Rectory, near Chorley, Lancashire.*—St. John's Coll. Cam. 4th Wrang. B.A. 1828, M.A. 1831, B.D. 1837; Deac. 1830 and Pr. 1831 by Bp of Lin. R. of Brindle, Dio. Man. 1864. (Patron, Duke of Devonshire; Tithe, 500*l*; Glebe, 11 acres with 18 houses; R.'s Inc. 700*l* and Ho; Pop. 1501.) Preb. of Lichfield. Formerly Chap. of Horningsey, near Cambridge, 1831–38; Fell. of St. John's Coll. Cam. 1829–41; R. of Morton, Derbyshire, 1841–64. Author, *Wood's Algebra*, 11th ed. revised and enlarged, 1841, 12*s* 6*d*, 12th ed. 1845, 13th ed. 1848, 14th ed. 1852, 15th ed. 1857, 16th ed. 1861; *Key to Wood's Algebra*, 1860, 7*s* 6*d*; *Companion to Wood's Algebra*, 1845, 7*s* 6*d*, 2nd ed. 1852, 3rd ed. 1860; *A Short and Easy Course of Algebra*, 1850, 2*s* 6*d*; 2nd ed. 1851, 3rd ed. 1856, 4th ed. 1859, 5th ed. 1860, 6th ed. 1863; *Key to Same*, 2*s* 6*d*; *Elements of Geometry and Mensuration*, in three parts, Part I. 1854, 1*s* 6*d*; Part II. 1855, 2*s*; Part. III. 1859, 3*s* 6*d*; *Geometrical Exercises*, 1859, 3*s* 6*d*; *The Necessity of a Studious and Learned Clergy, A Visitation Sermon*, 1845, 1*s*; *The True Theory of Missions according to Holy Scripture*, 1854, 1*s*; *The Reading and Deportment of the Clergy during Divine Service*, 1862, 6*d*; *A Key to Bishop Colenso's Biblical Arithmetic*, 1st and 2nd ed. 1*s*. [13]

LUND, Thomas William May, *Liverpool.*—Sid. Coll. Cam. B.A. 1866, 2nd cl. Cl. Trip; Deac. 1866 by Bp of Ches. C. of St. Philip's, Hardware-street, Liverpool, 1866. [14]

LUND, William, *Dunnington, York.*—Literate; Deac. 1821 and Pr. 1822 by Abp of York. [15]

LUNDIE, William Compton, M.A., *Spital House, Berwick-on-Tweed.* [16]

LUNEY, T. Hodson R., *Churchstow, Kingsbridge, Devon.*—C. of Churchstow and Kingsbridge 1864. [17]

LUNN, John Robert, *Marton Vicarage, Ouseburn, Yorks.*—St. John's Coll. Cam. Fell. of, 1855, B.A. 1853, M.A. 1856, B.D. 1863; Deac. 1855 and Pr. 1856 by Bp of Ely. V. of Marton with Grafton V. Dio. Rip. 1864. (Patron, St. John's Coll. Cam; V.'s Inc. 200*l* and Ho; Pop. 454.) Formerly Sadlerian Lect. at St. John's Coll. Cam. 1857. Author, *Of Motion, an Elementary Treatise*, 1859; *Service for the Holy Eucharist for Chorus and Organ*, Novello, Lond. 1861. [18]

LUPTON, James, *The Cloisters, Westminster Abbey, London, S.W.*—Ch. Ch. Ox. 2nd cl. Math. et Phy. and B A. 1823, M.A. 1825; Deac. 1824 and Pr. 1825 by Bp of Ox. V. of Blackbourton, Oxon, Dio. Ox. 1827. (Patron, Ch. Ch. Ox; V.'s Inc. 250*l* and Ho; Pop. 200.) Min. Can. of St. Paul's Cathl. 1829. (Value, 150*l*.) Min. Can. of the Coll. Ch. of St. Peter's, Westminster, 1829. (Value, 105*l*.) R. of St. Michael's, Queenhithe, with St. Trinity R. City and Dio. Lon. 1832. (Patrons, D. and C. of Cant. and D. and C. of St. Paul's alt; Fire Act Commutation in lieu of Tithe, 160*l*; R.'s Inc. 270*l*; Pop. St. Michael's 548, St. Trinity 553.) Author, *Church-rates, and the Possibility of Augmenting the Value of Church Property, by a Transfer of it from Bishops and Chapters to a Commission*, 1836; *The Public Schools Bill*, 1867; Sermons occasional. [19]

LUPTON, Joseph Hirst, *St. Paul's School, London, E.C.*—St. John's Coll. Cam. Fell. of, Members' Prizeman, B.A. 1858, M.A. 1861; Deac. 1859 and Pr. 1860 by Bp of Lon. Sur-Master of St. Paul's School. Formerly C. of St. Paul's Avenue-road, Hampstead, 1859–64. Author, *Wakefield Worthies*, 1864. Editor of Dean Colet's *Treatise on the Sacraments*, Bell and Daldy, 1867. [20]

LUSCOMBE, Alexander Popham, *Harbertonford, Totnes, Devon.*—St. John's Coll. Cam. B.A. 1842; Deac. 1846 and Pr. 1847 by Bp of Ches. P. C. of Harbertonford, Dio. Ex. 1859. (Patron, V. of Harberton; P. C.'s Inc. 170*l*; Pop. 533.) Formerly C. of Harberton; P. C. of Flockton, Yorks, 1855–58. [21]

LUSCOMBE, Edmund Peard, *Melbecks Parsonage, Reeth, Yorks.*—St. John's Coll. Cam. B.A. 1838;

Deac. 1840 and Pr. 1841 by Bp of Rip. P. C. of Melbecks, in the Parish of Grinton, Dio. Rip. 1841. (Patron, V. of Grinton; P. C.'s Inc. 150*l* and Ho; Pop. 2173.) [1]

LUSCOMBE, F. P. Epworth, *Old Lakenham, Norwich.*—Dub. 1836, Heb. Prizeman; Deac. 1839 and Pr. 1840 by Bp of Ches. P. C. of Arminghall, Dio. Nor. 1861. (Patrons, D. and C. of Nor; P. C.'s Inc. 80*l* from Qu. Anne's Bounty and Stipend from D. and C. of Nor; Pop. 80.) [2]

LUSCOMBE, Richard James, *Moorlinch Vicarage, Ashcott, Bath, Somerset.*—Wor. Coll. Ox. B.A. 1833, M.A. 1835; Deac. 1833, Pr. 1834 by Bp of B. and W. V. of Moorlinch with Stawell C. and Sutton-Mallet C. Dio. B. and W. 1847. (Patron, the present V; Tithe—Imp. 290*l*, V. 330*l*; Glebe, 95 acres; V.'s Inc. 500*l* and Ho; Pop. Moorlinch 334, Stawell 173, Sutton-Mallet 139.) [3]

LUSH, Alfred, *Beaminster, Dorset.*—Corpus Coll. Cam. B.A. 1849, M.A. 1852; Deac. 1849 and Pr. 1850 by Bp of Win. C. of Beaminster 1862. Formerly C. of Odiham and Greywell 1849, Kibworth 1858, Shrivenham 1860. [4]

LUSH, William, *Waterlooville, Portsmouth.*—King's Coll. Lond. Theol. Assoc. 1856; Deac. 1858 and Pr. 1859 by Bp of Pet. P. C. of Waterlooville, Dio. Win. 1862. (Patrons, Bp of Win. and Win. Coll; P. C.'s Inc. 130*l* and Ho; Pop. 243.) Formerly C. of Worthington, Great Dalby, Leicestershire, Creaton, Northants. Author, *The Poor Man's Hymn-book*, 1858, 4*d*; *The Remembrancer Hymn-book*, 1867. [5]

LUSHINGTON, Charles.—Ch. Ch. Ox. B.A. 1828, M.A. 1830; Deac. 1830, Pr. 1831. Formerly V. of Walton-on-Thames 1851–64. [6]

LUSIGNAN, Constantine Adolphus, *Wyresdale Parsonage, Lancaster.*—Dub. A.B. 1854, A.M. and *ad eund.* Ox. 1865; Deac. 1854 and Pr. 1855 by Bp of Ches. P. C. of Wyresdale, Dio. Man. 1863. (Patron, V. of Lancaster: Tithe, 39*l*; Glebe, 11 acres; P. C.'s Inc. 184*l* and Ho; Pop. 524.) Formerly C. of Frodsham, Cheshire, 1854–56, Wyresdale (sole charge), 1856-63. [7]

LUSIGNAN, Michael William, 2, *Little Bush-lane, Thames-street, London, E.C.*—Lect. of Allhallows, Upper Thames-street [8]

LUTENER, T. B., *Shrewsbury.*—P. C. of St. Michael's, Shrewsbury, Dio. Lich. 1854. (Patron, P. C. of St. Mary's; P. C.'s Inc. 198*l*; Pop. 3681.) [9]

LUTENER, William, *Harthill Rectory, Handley, Cheshire.*—St. John's Coll. Cam. B.A. 1847; Deac. 1849, Pr. 1850. R. of Harthill, Dio. Ches. 1850. (Patron, T. T. Drake, Esq; Tithe, 42*l*; Glebe, 18¼ acres; R.'s Inc. 130*l* and Ho; Pop. 122.) [10]

LUTMAN, Adrian Henry, *Yeovil.*—Dub. A.B. 1853, A.M. 1857; Deac. 1853 by Abp of Dub. Pr. 1854 by Bp of Cork. P. C. of Hendford, Yeovil, Dio. B. and W. 1867. (P. C.'s Inc. 165*l*; Pop. 4230.) Formerly C. of Bloxwich 1856, St. John the Baptist's, Peterborough, 1857, Yeovil 1864. [11]

LUTT, Edward Kefford, *Harmston Vicarage, Lincoln.*—Sid. Coll. Cam. Haberdashers' Company's Exhib. Latin Declamation Prizeman, B.A. 1844, M.A. 1847, *ad eund.* Ox. 1853; Deac. 1844 and Pr. 1845 by Bp of Lin. V. of Harmston, Dio. Lin. 1862. (Patron, the present V; Glebe, 18 acres and Ho; Pop. 414.) Formerly C. of Easton, near Winchester, and Bower-Chalke 1859; P. C. of Avediston, Wilts, 1861. Author, *The Maynooth Grant*; *The Papal Aggression.* [12]

LUTTMAN-JOHNSON, Henry William Robinson, *Binderton, Chichester.*—Trin. Coll. Ox. 1st cl. Lit. Hum. and B.A. 1823, M.A. 1826; Deac. 1825 by Bp of Ox. Formerly C. of Sandford, Oxon, 1825. [13]

LUTTRELL, Alexander Fownes, *East Quantoxhead Rectory, Bridgwater, Somerset.*—Ex. Coll. Ox. B.C.L. 1816; Deac. 1816 and Pr. 1817 by Bp of B. and W. R. of East Quantoxhead, Dio. B. and W. 1817. (Patron, John Fownes Luttrell, Esq; Tithe, 265*l*; Glebe, 28 acres; R.'s Inc. 332*l* and Ho; Pop. 339.) [14]

LUTTRELL, Alexander Henry Fownes, *Minehead Vicarage, Somerset.*—Pemb. Coll. Cam. B.A. 1829; Deac. 1831 and Pr. 1832 by Bp of B. and W. V. of Minehead, Dio. B. and W. 1832. (Patron, H. F. Luttrell, Esq; Tithe—Imp. 104*l* 2*s* 3*d*, V. 200*l*; Glebe, 26½ acres; V.'s Inc. 274*l* and Ho; Pop. 1582.) [15]

LUTTRELL, Thomas Fownes, *Dunster Castle, Somerset.*—Deac. 1817, Pr. 1819. P. C. of Dunster, Dio. B. and W. 1821. (Patron, J. F. Luttrell, Esq; Tithe, Imp. 200*l*; P. C.'s Inc. 130*l*; Pop. 1112.) V. of Carhampton, Somerset, Dio. B. and W. 1834. (Patron, J. F. Luttrell, Esq; Tithe—Imp. 505*l*, V. 280*l*; Glebe, 3 acres; V.'s Inc. 290*l*; Pop. 706.) [16]

LUXFORD, George Curteis, *Higham House, Hurst Green, Sussex.*—Trin. Coll. Cam. B.A. 1833, M.A. 1837; Deac. 1836 by Bp of Lin. Pr. 1839 by Bp of Chich. Formerly R. of Middleton, Sussex, 1847. [17]

LUXMOORE, Charles C., *Lamborne, Hungerford.*—C. of Lamborne. [18]

LUXMOORE, John, *Llanymynech Rectory, Oswestry, Salop.*—Pemb. Coll. Cam. B.A. 1825, M.A. 1829; Deac. 1825 by Bp of St. A. Pr. 1826 by Bp of Ex. V. of Berriew, Montgomeryshire, Dio. St. A. 1827. (Patron. Bp of St. A; Tithe—Imp. 805*l*, V. 445*l* 7*s* 6*d*; Glebe, 1 acre; V.'s Inc. 446*l* and Ho; Pop. 2155.) R. of Llanymynech, Dio. St. A. 1829. (Patron, Bp of St. A; Tithe, 380*l*; Glebe, 22 acres; R.'s Inc. 472*l* and Ho; Pop. 951.) Rural Dean. [19]

LUXMOORE, John Reddaway, *Ashford, Bakewell, Derbyshire.*—St. Bees 1855; Deac. 1857 and Pr. 1858 by Bp of Lich. P. C. of Ashford, Dio. Lich. 1861. (Patron, V. of Bakewell; Tithe—App. 16*l* 13*s* 4*d*, Imp. 110*l*; Glebe, 33 acres; P. C.'s Inc. 120*l* and Ho; Pop. 829.) Formerly C. of Ashford. [20]

LUXTON, John, *Bundley Rectory, North Tawton, Devon.*—St. Peter's Coll. Cam. B.A. 1847; Deac. 1848, Pr. 1849. R. of Bundley, or Boundleigh, Dio. Ex. 1855. (Patron, Earl of Egremont; R.'s Inc. 232*l* and Ho; Pop. 279.) P. C. of Brushford, Dio. Ex. 1849. (Patron, G. Luxton, Esq; P. C.'s Inc. 51*l*; Pop. 132.) [21]

LYALL, F. J., *Derby.*—C. of St. Michael's, Derby. [22]

LYALL, William Godden, *Frome Castle Rectory, Bromyard, Herefordshire.*—Ch. Coll. Cam. B.A. 1827, M.A. 1830. R. of Frome Castle, Dio. Herf. 1843. (Patron, F. T. Freeman, Esq; Tithe, 270*l*; Glebe, 55¾ acres; R.'s Inc. 330*l* and Ho; Pop. 160.) [23]

LYALL, William Hearle, 39, *Beaufort-gardens, Brompton, S.W.*—St. Mary Hall, Ox. and Theological Coll. Wells. M.A. 1852; Deac. 1852 and Pr. 1853 by Bp of Lon. R. of St. Dionis Backchurch, City and Dio. Lon. 1853. (Patrons, D. and C. of Cant; Fire Act Commutation in lieu of Tithe, 200*l*; Rents, Bequests, &c., 287*l*; R.'s Inc. 497*l*; Pop. 534.) Formerly Asst. C. of Ch. Ch. St. Pancras, 1852–53. [24]

LYDE, James.—Univ. Coll. Lond. M.R.C.S. and L.A.C. 1841, St. Bees 1853; Deac. 1854 and Pr. 1855 by Bp of Ches. Formerly C. of Waberthwaite. [25]

LYDE, William, *Wigton Vicarage, Cumberland.*—Queens' Coll. Cam. Mathematical Prizeman, 24th Wrang. and B.A. 1851, M.A. 1855; Deac. 1855 by Bp of Ches. Pr. 1856 by Bp of Carl. V. of Wigton, Dio. Carl. 1857. (Patron, Bp of Carl; Tithe—Imp. 10*s*, V. 2*l* 15*s*; V.'s Inc. 300*l* and Ho; Pop. 6023.) Surrogate. Formerly Sen. C. of Wigton 1856-57; Asst. C. of Holy Trinity, Whitehaven, 1855–56; Chaplain of Wigton Workhouse; Math Mast. of King Edward VI. Gr. Sch. Bath, 1851–55. [26]

LYFORD, Stewart, *Slymbridge, Dursley, Gloucestershire.*—Dub. A.B. 1855; Deac. 1857, and Pr. 1858 by Abp of York. C. of Slymbridge 1866. Formerly C. of Hedon and Preston 1857–59, Heytesbury 1859–63, Coleford, Gloucestershire, 1863–66. [27]

LYNDE, T. G., *Haggerstone, London, N.E.*—C. of St. Columba's, Haggerstone. Formerly C. of Eynesbury, Hunts. [28]

LYNE, Charles, 8, *Buldon-terrace, Dawlish, Devon.*—St. John's Coll. Cam. B.A. 1825, M.A. 1842; Deac. 1825, Pr. 1826. Preb. in Ex. Cathl. 1842. Formerly V. of Tywardreath 1851; P. C. of St. Sampson 1854; R. of Roche, Cornwall, 1834–40; R. of Tywardreath,

Cornwall, 1840–48, 1851–62. Author, *Modern Methodism not in Accordance with the Principles and Plans of the Rev. John Wesley, during any Portion of his Life*; *Modern Methodism a Schism* (an exposure of the Wesleyan *Tracts for the Times*); *Modern Methodism, or a Dialogue on the Cry of "No Popery;"* three Tracts, 1842–44; *The Authority, Character, and Responsibility of the Christian Ministry* (a Sermon at the Bp of Exeter's Visitation, published by command), 1845; *National Education* (a Sermon on the Anniversary of the Devon and Exeter National Schools), 1847; *A Sermon preached at the Consecration of the Church of St. Mary-the-Virgin, at Biscovey, Cornwall*, 1849; four *Pastoral Letters*, and Tracts on the Blessed Sacraments; etc. [1]

LYNE, Charles Names Lyne, *Dixton-road, Monmouth.*—Magd. Hall, Ox. B.A. 1858, M.A. 1860; Deac. 1858 by Bp of Ex. Pr. 1860 by Bp of Salis. C. of St. Mary's, Mon. 1867. Formerly C. of St. Sampson, Cornwall, 1859–62, St. Endellion, Cornwall, 1862–63, Newton Abbot, Devon, 1863–65. Author, *Tractarianism considered, &c.* 1866. [2]

LYNE, Charles Philip, *Tower-street, Emsworth, Hants.*—Queen's Coll. Ox. B.A. 1807, M.A. 1826; Deac. 1809. Pr. 1810. V. of East Marden, Sussex, Dio. Chich. 1817. (Patron, Preb. of East Marden; Tithe, 162*l* 13*s* 5*d*; V.'s Inc. 118*l*; Pop. 63.) R. of West Thorney, Sussex, Dio. Chich. 1833. (Patron, Philip Lyne, Esq; R.'s Inc. 320*l*; Pop. 93.) [3]

LYNE, Joseph Leycester.—Trin. Coll. Glenalmond, Perthshire; Deac. 1860 by Bp of B. and W. for Bp of Ex. Formerly C. of Claydon, Suffolk; Ignatius, Superior of the Anglican Order of St. Benedict, the Priory of St. Mary and St. Dunstan, Norwich, established January, 1864. [4]

LYNES, John, *Claremount, Weymouth.*—Ch. Coll. Cam. B.A. 1844, M.A. 1847; Deac. 1847 and Pr. 1849 by Bp of Pet. Formerly V. of Buckland Monachorum, Devon, and Melchbourne, Beds. [5]

LYNES, William, *Mountsorrel, Loughborough, Leicestershire.*—Univ. Coll. Lond. and Queen's Coll. Birmingham; Deac. 1865 and Pr. 1866 by Bp of Wor. C. of Mountsorrel. Formerly C. of Bedworth, Warwickshire. [6]

LYNN, George Goodenough, *Coniscliffe Vicarage, Durham.*—Ch. Coll. Cam. B.A. 1833, M.A. 1835; Deac. 1832, Pr. 1833. V. of Coniscliffe, Dio. Dur. 1858. (Patron, Bp of Dur; Tithe—Imp. 186*l*, V. 124*l*; Glebe, 60 acres; V.'s Inc. 254*l* and Ho; Pop. 434.) Formerly P. C. of Hampton-Wick, Middlesex, 1834–58. Author, *Are the People to be Educated or not?* (a Pamphlet), 1839; *What is Dissent?* 1840; *Sermons*, 1841; *Revealed Religion*, 1845. [7]

LYON, Gilbert, *Calstone, Wilts.*—Jesus Coll. Cam. B.A. 1859; Deac. 1858 and Pr. 1859 by Bp of G. and B. C. of Calstone and Blackland, Wilts. Formerly C. of All Saints', Bristol, 1858, Ashprington, Totnes. [8]

LYON, James, *Wherwell, Hants.*—Jesus Coll. Cam. B.A. 1850, M.A. 1855; Deac. 1851 by Bp of Lich. Pr. 1853 by Bp of Win. Formerly C. of Dogmersfield. [9]

LYON, James Radcliffe, *Pulford Rectory, Cheshire, near Wrexham.*—Brasen. Coll. Ox. B.A. 1808, M.A. 1811; Deac. 1808. P. C. of Ringley, Prestwich, Lanc. Dio. Man. 1817. (Patrons, Rs. of Prestwich, Bury, and Middleton; P. C.'s Inc. 250*l* and Ho.) R. of Pulford, Dio. Ches. 1818. (Patron, Marquis of Westminster; Tithe, 200*l*; Glebe, 7 acres; R.'s Inc. 214 and Ho; Pop. 354.) [10]

LYON, Joseph, *Maghull Parsonage, Liverpool.*—Trin. Coll. Ox. B.A. 1857, M.A. 1863; Deac. 1859 and Pr. 1860 by Bp of Rip. P. C. of Maghull, Dio. Ches. 1865. (Patron, R. of Halsall; P. C.'s Inc. 145*l* and Ho; Pop. 1150.) Formerly C. of Clapham, Yorks, 1859–63, Bangor, 1863–65. [11]

LYON, Ralph John, *Wickwar Rectory, Wotton-under-Edge, Glouc.*—Trin. Coll. Cam. B.A. 1851, M.A. 1854; Deac. 1852 and Pr. 1853 by Bp of Salis. R. of Wickwar, Dio. G. and B. 1864. (Patron, Lord Ducie; Tithe, 430*l*; Glebe, 80 acres; R.'s Inc. 530*l* and Ho; Pop. 950.) Formerly C. of Haydon, Dorset, 1852, Melcombe Regis, Dorset, 1854, Weston-super-Mare, Somerset, 1861, Dalston, Cumberland, 1862. [12]

LYON, Samuel Edmund, *East Stratton, Micheldever, Hants.*—Wad. Coll. Ox. B.A. 1845; Deac. 1845, Pr. 1846. C. of East Stratton 1859. Formerly C. of West Tisted, Hants, 1845–49; P. C. of Farncombe, Surrey, 1849–59. [13]

LYON, Samuel John, *Farndish, Wellingborough.*—Trin. Coll. Cam. B.A. 1844, M.A. 1848; Deac. 1844 and Pr. 1845 by Bp of Ches. R. of Farndish, Beds, Dio. Ely, 1859. (Patron, M. Chester, Esq; Glebe, 130 acres; R.'s Inc. 195*l*; Pop. 67.) Formerly P. C. of Moorfields, Sheffield. [14]

LYON, William Hector, *Castleton, Sherborne, Dorset.*—Trin. Coll. Cam. B.A. 1850, M.A. 1853; Deac. 1850 and Pr. 1851 by Bp of Salis. P. C. of Castleton, Dio. Salis. 1854. (Patron, G. D. W. Digby, Esq; Tithe, P. C. 20*l* and Bounty Land; P. C.'s Inc. 78*l*; Pop. 157.) V. of Oborne, Dorset, Dio. Salis. 1854. (Patron, G. D. W. Digby, Esq; Tithe, 168*l*; Glebe, 7 acres; V.'s Inc. 172*l*; Pop. 140.) [15]

LYONS, John, *Wednesbury, Staffs.*—Dub. A.B. 1829, A.M. 1834; Deac. 1830 and Pr. 1832 by Bp of Cloyne. V. of Wednesbury, Dio. Lich. 1859. (Patron, Ld Chan; Tithe, App. 10*l*, Imp. 220*l*, V. 230*l*; V.'s Inc. 355*l* and Ho; Pop. 16,000.) Formerly V. of Tillingham, Essex, 1852. [16]

LYS, Francis George, *Madras.*—St. John's Coll. Cam. Jun. Opt. 1858, 2nd cl. Theol. Trip. 1859; B.A. 1858, M.A. 1861; Deac. 1859 and Pr. 1861 by Bp of Lin. Asst. Chap. in Madras Presidency (Salary, 660*l*.), 1864. Formerly C. of Warsop, Notts, Holy Trinity, Gainsborough, Chesterton, Staffs, and Menheniot, Cornwall. [17]

LYS, John Thomas, *Exeter College, Oxford.*—Ex. Coll. Ox. 2nd cl. Lit. Hum. 1812, B.A. 1813, M.A. 1816, B.D. 1826. Fell. of Ex. Coll. Ox. [18]

LYSAGHT, William Pulleine, *Hurst, Twyford, Berks.*—Trin. Coll. Cam. B.A. 1859, M.A. 1862; Deac. 1860 and Pr. 1862 by Bp of Ox. C. of Hurst, Berks, 1864. Formerly C. of Langley, Bucks, 1860–64. [19]

LYSONS, Samuel, *Hempstead Court, near Gloucester.*—Ex. Coll. Ox. 3rd cl. Lit. Hum. 1829, B.A. 1831, M.A. 1835; Deac. 1830, Pr. 1831. R. of Rodmarton, Glouc. Dio. G. and B. 1833. (Patron, the present R; Glebe, 525 acres; R.'s Inc. 650*l* and Ho; Pop. 401.) Author, *Conjectures concerning the Identity of the Patriarch Job*, 1832; *The Formularies of Christian Faith* (a Sermon), 1843; *Christian Fables, or the Fables of Æsop Christianised, and adapted with Christian Morals*, 1850; *Christian Fables*, &c. in French, Société des Livres Religieux, Toulouse. [20]

LYTHE, Richard, *Skirlaugh, Hull.*—Deac. 1829, Pr. 1830. V. of Swine with Skirlaugh C. Dio. York, 1839. (Patron, William Wilberforce, Esq; Tithe—Imp. 477*l* 12*s* 8*d*, V. 18*l* 3*s* 4*d*; Glebe, 19 acres; V.'s Inc. 116*l* and Ho; Pop. Swine 1034, Skirlaugh 687.) Chap. to the North Skirlaugh Union 1838. [21]

LYTTELTON, The Hon. William Henry, *Hagley Rectory, Stourbridge, Worcestershire.*—Trin. Coll. Cam. 3rd cl. Cl. Trip. and M.A. 1841; Deac. 1843 by Bp of Pet. Pr. 1844 by Bp of Ox. R. of Hagley, Dio. Wor. 1847. (Patron, Lord Lyttelton; Tithe, 580*l*; Glebe, 53 acres; R.'s Inc. 580*l* and Ho; Pop. 962.) Hon. Can. of Wor. Cathl. 1850; Principal Registrar of Dio. of Wor. 1861. Formerly C. of Kettering 1843; P. C. of Sunningdale, Ox. 1845. Chap. of D. of Frankley; Chap. to Earl Spencer 1846. Author, *Dangers to Truth from Controversy and Agitation, with an Appendix on the Controversy on Baptism* (a Visitation Sermon), 1850; *Some Reasons of Want of Success in the Christian Ministry* (an Ordination Sermon), 1850; *Holy Scripture the Witness to the Revelation of God in all Facts* (a Sermon); *The Testimony of Scripture to the Authority of Conscience and of Reason* (a Tract); *The Original Order of Nature our Model and the Spirit of God our Guide in the Work of Education* (a Sermon); *Church Establishments: their Lawfulness and Advantages, Social and Religious* (a Lecture); *Two Sermons on the Duty and Joy of Frequent Public Worship; Some Reasons why I value Daily Service* (a Tract), 1866; Editor of *Sermons on the Holy Communion* (preached at Hagley). [1]

MABER, Chasty, *Howsham, York.*—St. Bees 1854; Deac. 1856 by Bp of Carl. Pr. 1857 by Abp of York. C. of Scrayingham, York. 1858. Formerly C. of Birdsall and Asst. C. of Wharram-le-Street and Wharram-Percy, Yorks, 1856–58. [2]

MABERLY, Thomas Astley, *Cuckfield Vicarage, Sussex.*—Ch. Ch. Ox. 1st. cl. Math. B.A. 1832, M.A. 1836; Deac. 1836 and Pr. 1837 by Bp of Lon. V. of Cuckfield, Dio. Chich. 1841. (Patron, Bp of Chich; Tithe—Imp. 1304*l* 17*s* 1½*d*, V. 621*l* 4*s* 2½*d*; Glebe, 47 acres; V.'s Inc. 706*l* and Ho; Pop. 2000.) Formerly C. of St. Andrew's, Holborn, Lond. 1836–41. [3]

M'ALLISTER, James Adair, *Plumstead Vicarage, Kent.*—Dub. A.B. 1846, A.M. 1858; Deac. 1848 and Pr. 1849. V. of Plumstead, Dio. Lon. 1864. (Patron, the present V; V.'s Inc. 800*l* and Ho; Pop. 24,502.) Formerly C. of St. Simon's, Liverpool, and St. Paul's, Princes-park. Liverpool. [4]

M'ALLISTER, John, 6, *Park Villas, Plumstead, S.E.*—Dublin; Deac. 1855 by Bp of B. and W. Pr. 1856 by Bp of G. and B. P. C. of St. Nicholas', Plumstead, 1865. (Patron, V. of Plumstead; P. C.'s Inc. 300*l*; Pop. 10,500.) [5]

M'ANALLY, David, *Parsonage, Penge, Surrey, S.E.*—Theol. Assoc. King's Coll. Lond. 1850; Deac. 1850, Pr. 1851. P. C. of Penge, Dio. Win. 1857. (Patrons, Court of Watermen and Lightermen; P. C.'s Inc. 600*l* and Ho; Pop. 6500.) Surrogate 1867. Formerly C. of St. Marylebone, Lond. [6]

MACARTNEY, Sydney Parkyns, *Kenilworth.*—Clare Coll. Cam. B.A. 1866, 10th Sen. Opt; Deac. 1866 by Bp of Wor. C. of St. John's, Kenilworth, 1866. [7]

MACAULAY, Daniel, *Bishop Stortford, Herts.*—Dub. A.B. 1844; Deac. 1846 and Pr. 1847 by Bp of Wor. P. C. of Trinity, Newtown, Bishop Stortford, Dio. Roch. 1867. (Patron, V. of Bishop Stortford; P. C.'s Inc. 300*l*; Pop. 1490.) [8]

MACAULAY, John, *Aldingham Rectory, Ulverstone, Lancashire.*—St. Peter's Coll. Cam. B.A. 1829, M.A. 1832. R. of Aldingham, Dio. Carl. 1849. (Patron, the Crown; Tithe—Imp. 16*l* 12*s*, R. 1060*l*; R.'s Inc. 1100*l* and Ho; Pop. 1011.) Rural Dean; Surrogate; Hon. Can. of Carl. [9]

MACAULAY, John Heyrick, *Highbridge, Somerset.*—Trin. Coll. Cam. 2nd cl. Cl. Trip. 1853; B.A. 1853, M.A. 1864; Deac. 1856 and Pr. 1857 by Bp of Wor. P. C. of Highbridge, Dio. B. and W. 1859. (Patrons, Colonel and Mrs. Luttrell; P. C.'s Inc. 186*l* and Ho; Pop. 756.) Formerly C. of St. John in Bedwardine, Worcester, 1856–58; Stoke-upon-Trent 1858–59. [10]

MACAULAY, Samuel Heyrick, *Hodnet Rectory, Drayton-in-Hales, Salop.*—Jesus Coll. Cam. B.D. 1846; Deac. 1836, Pr. 1838. R. of Hodnet, Dio. Lich. 1828. (Patron, A. C. Heber-Percy, Esq; Tithe, 2390*l*; Glebe, 21½ acres; R.'s Inc. 2380*l* and Ho; Pop. 1714.) [11]

M'CALL, John Henry Grice, *Cemetery Lodge, Carlisle.*—Corpus Coll. Cam. B.A. 1864; Deac. 1866 by Bp of Win. C. of St. James's, Denton Holme, Carlisle, 1866. [12]

M'CALL, William, 9, *Hilldrop-road, Tufnell-park, London, N.*—Dub. 1st Abp King's and 1st Regius Professor's Div. Prem. A.B. 1842, A.M. 1857; Deac. 1844 and Pr. 1845 by Bp of Down and Connor. P. C. of St. George's, Tufnell-park, Islington, Dio. Lon. 1864. (Patrons, Trustees; P. C.'s Inc. 400*l*.) Formerly P. C. of St. Mary's, St. George's-in-the-East, Lond. 1850–64. [13]

M'CALLAN, John Ferguson, *St. Matthew's Parsonage, Nottingham.*—Queen's Coll. Belfast, B.A. 1854, Prize for Essay on the Baconian Philosophy 1855, M.A. 1856; Deac. 1857, Pr. 1858. C. of St. Matthew's, Nottingham, 1860. Formerly C. of St. Mark's, Liverpool, 1857–60. [14]

M'CALMONT, Thomas, *Highfield Uplands, near Southampton,* and *Elm Grove Cottage, Hillbutts, near Wimborne Minster, Dorset.*—Dub. A.B. 1829, ad eund. Wor. Coll. Ox. B.A. 1829; Deac. 1832 and Pr. 1833 by Bp of Lin. [15]

M'CANN, James, *Huddersfield.*—St. Aidan's, Hon. M.A; Deac. 1863 and Pr. 1864 by Bp of Rip. C. of St. Paul's, Huddersfield. Formerly C. of Holmfirth 1863. Author, *Inter relations of Prayer, Providence, and Science*, 1*s*, Simpkin; *Anti-Secularist Lectures, with Appendix*, 5*s*, Simpkin. [16]

M'CAROGHER, John Ommaney, *Nuthurst Rectory, Horsham, Sussex.*—Magd. Coll. Ox. B.A. 1846, M.A. 1849; Deac. 1849 by Bp of Ox. Pr. 1850 by Bp of Chich. R. of Nuthurst, Dio. Chich. 1859. (Patron, Bp of Lon; R.'s Inc. 345*l* and Ho; Pop. 767.) Chap. to Duke of Richmond. Formerly C. of Nuthurst. [17]

M'CARTHY, Charles P.—C. of Meltham Mills, near Huddersfield. Formerly Sec. to Naval and Military Bible Soc. [18]

MACCARTHY, Egerton Francis Mead, 47, *Hagley-road, Edgbaston, near Birmingham.*—Emman. Coll. Cam. Wrang. 1860, B.A. 1860, M.A. 1864; Deac. 1862 and Pr. 1863 by Bp of Nor. Second Mast. at King Edward's Sch. Birmingham, 1866. Formerly Math. Mast. of King Edward's Sch. Norwich, 1860. C. of St. Matthew's, Thorpe Hamlet, Norfolk, 1862; Math. Mast. at Bedford Gr. Sch. 1864. [19]

MACCARTHY, Francis Michael, 66, *Myddelton-square, Clerkenwell, London, E.C.*—St. Peter's Coll. Cam. B.A. 1828, M.A. 1832; Deac. 1829 and Pr. 1830 by Bp of Pet. P. C. of St. Mark's, Clerkenwell, Dio. Lon. 1848. (Patron, Bp of Lon; P. C.'s Inc. 500*l*; Pop. 10,417.) Formerly V. of Lodera, Dorset; Rural Dean of Bridport 1835–48. [20]

MACCARTIE, Joseph, *Raughton-Head, Carlisle.*—Dub. A.M. 1865; Deac. and Pr. 1855 by Bp of Ches. P. C. of Raughton-Head, Dio. Carl. 1865. (Patrons, Trustees; Glebe, 4½ acres; P. C.'s Inc. 97*l* and Ho; Pop. 468.) Formerly R. of St. Jude's, Manchester, 1857–65. Author, Sermons on the *Indian Mutiny, Cotton Famine, Cattle Plague,* and on *Ritualism*, Hatchards. [21]

M'CAUL, Alexander Israel, *Rectory*, 37, *King William-street, London, E.C.*—St. John's Coll. Ox. B.A. 1858, M.A. 1860; Deac. 1859 and Pr. 1860 by Bp of Lon. R. of St. Magnus', City and Dio. Lon. 1863. (Patrons, Abp of Cant. and Bp of Lon. alt; R.'s Inc. 353*l* and Ho; Pop. 867.) Divinity Lect. at King's Coll. Lond. Formerly C. of St. Magnus' 1859–63. [22]

M'CAUL, Joseph Benjamin, 10, *Bedford-row, W.C. and British Museum, W.C*; as Chap. to the Bp of Roch. 5, *Montague-street, Russell-square, London, W.C.*—King's Coll. Lond. Theol. Assoc. 1850, Deac. 1851 and Pr. 1852 by Bp of Lon. Corresponding Chap. to Bp of Roch; one of the Assistant Librarians in the British Museum 1846–49, reappointed 1851; Hon. Can. of Rochester; R. of St. Michael Bassishaw; Lect. of Ch. Ch. Spitalfields; Chap. to the Company of Girdlers, Lond. Formerly Censor, Reader, and Divinity Lect. King's Coll. Lond. 1852–54; C. of St. Magnus' the Martyr 1851–54. Author, *The Abbé Migne and the Bibliothèque Universelle du Clergé* (Four Essays privately printed); *The Ten Commandments, The Christian's Spiritual Instructor and Rule of Daily Life* (Ten Lectures); *The Rev. Thomas Hartwell Horne, B.D., a Sketch; Reminiscences, Personal and Bibliographical, of T. H. Horne, B.D., with a Preface by the Rev. J. B. M'Caul; Bishop Colenso's Criticism criticised, in a Series of Eight Letters, with Notes and a Postscript*; various Sermons, etc. [23]

M'CAUSLAND, H. W., *Cheddon Fitzpaine, Taunton.*—C. of Cheddon-Fitzpaine. [24]

M'CHEANE, James Henry, *Trinity Parsonage, Leeds.*—Lin. Coll. Ox. formerly Fell. of, 3rd cl. Lit. Hum. B.A. 1856, M.A. 1859; Deac. 1858 and Pr. 1859 by Bp of Rip. P. C. of Holy Trinity, Leeds, Dio.

Rip. 1862. (Patrons, V. of Leeds, Recorder and V. of St. John's; P. C.'s Inc. 250*l* and Ho.) 2nd Mast. of Leeds Gr. Sch. Formerly C. of Leeds. Chap. to the 1st West Riding Artillery Volunteers. Author, *A Sermon on the Death of Keble*, 1866. [1]

M'CLEAN, Donald Stewart, *Cannock Chase, Staffordshire.*—Dub. A.B. 1854; Deac. 1856 and Pr. 1857 by Bp of Herf. C. of St. Ann's, Cannock Chase, 1866. Formerly C. of All Saints', Paddington, Lond. and Letton, Herf. [2]

M'CLELLAN, John Brown, *Bottisham Vicarage, near Cambridge.*—Trin. Coll. Cam. Fell. 1859, B.A. Double 1st in Cl. and Math. Hons. and Wrang. Gold Medallist 1858, M.A. 1861; Deac. 1860 and Pr. 1861 by Bp of Ely. V. of Bottisham, Dio. Ely, 1861. (Patron, Trin. Coll. Cam.; Glebe, 240 acres; V.'s Inc. 360*l* and Ho; Pop. 732.) Author, *Everlasting Punishment and the Oxford Declaration of* 1864, Macmillans, 1864, 1*s*. [3]

M'COMAS, Charles Edward Archibald, *Halton, Preston Brook, Cheshire.*—Dub. A.B. LL.B. 1863, Jun. Mod. 1863, Abp King's Prize 1864, Theo. Exhib. Prize 1866; Deac. 1866 and Pr. 1867 by Bp of Ches. C. of Halton 1866. [4]

M'CONECHY, James, 41, *Bryanston-street, Portman-square, London, W.*—Ball. Coll. Ox. B.A. 1858, M.A. 1861; Deac. 1858 and Pr. 1859 by Bp of Ox. Asst. Pr. and C. of St. George's, Hanover-square, Lond. 1866. Formerly C. of St. Paul's Iron Ch. Camden-hill, Kensington, 1860, Sonning, near Reading, 1858. [5]

M'CONKEY, Andrew, *West Derby, Liverpool.*—Dub. A.M. P. C. of St. James's, West Derby, Dio. Ches. 1847. (Patroness, Mrs. Thornton; P. C.'s Inc. 50*l*.) [6]

M'CORMICK, John H.—C. of St. Stephen's, Marylebone, Lond. [7]

M'CORMICK, Joseph, 36, *Manor-road, Lewisham High Road, S.E.*—St. John's Coll. Cam. B.A. 1857, M A. 1860; Deac. 1858, Pr. 1859. P. C. of St. Peter's, Deptford, 1867. (Patron, W. W. Drake, Esq.) Formerly C. of St. Peter's, Regent-square, Lond. 1867; R. of Dunmore East, Waterford; Asst. Min. of St. Stephen's, Marylebone. [8]

M'CORMICK, William Thomas, 9, *Upper Woodbine-street, North Shields.*—King's Coll. Lond. Theol. Assoc; Deac. 1860 by Bp of Lon. Pr. 1861 by Bp of Wor. Chap. to Sailors on the Tyne. Formerly C. of St. Clement's, Birmingham, 1860, Bonchurch, Isle of Wight, 1862, St. George's, Birmingham, 1862. Author, *Dips into Literature*, 1859, 8*d*; *Lifeboats off Tynemouth Bar*, 1864. [9]

M'COWEN, Thomas James Craig, *Walton-on-Thames Vicarage, Surrey.*—Deac. 1860 and Pr. 1861 by Bp of Lich. V. of Walton-on-Thames, Dio. Win. 1864. (Patron, G. Robinson, Esq; V.'s Inc. 260*l* and Ho; Pop. 2244.) Formerly C. of Wheaton Aston, Penkridge, Staffs, Holcombe, Lanc. (sole charge), Westport, St. Mary, Wilts (sole charge). [10]

***M'CUBBIN, John,** *Christ Church Parsonage, Bacup, Manchester.*—St. Bees; Deac. 1847 by Bp of Ches; Pr. 1848 by Bp of Man. P. C. of Ch. Ch. Bacup, Dio. Man. 1854. (Patrons, Trustees; P. C.'s Inc. 300*l*; Pop. 5730.) [11]

MACDONA, Henry Victor.—Dub. A.B. 1860, A.M. 1863; Deac. 1861 and Pr. 1862 by Bp of Man. C. of Blackpool, 1867. Formerly C. of St. Matthias', Salford, 1861–63, Stockport 1863, St. Peter's, Ashton-under-Lyne, 1863–65, St. James's, Notting-hill, 1866. Author, *Sermons*; E. Paul, London. [12]

MACDONA, John Cumming, *Sephton Rectory, Liverpool.*—C. in sole charge of Sephton 1866. Formerly C. of Charlesworth 1859–60, Moseley 1860–63, Sephton, 1863–65. Author, *Sermons*; *Journey through the Dark Valley*; *Day of Salvation*; *Death of the Prince Consort*, *Gospel Wedding*; *Tears of Jesus*; E. Paul, London. [13]

MACDONALD, Jacob, *Blewbury Vicarage, Wallingford, Berks.*—Caius Coll. Cam. LL.B. 1829. V. of Blewbury with Upton C. and Alston-Upthorpe C. Dio. Ox. 1836. (Patron, Bp of Ox; Tithe—App. 1125*l* 2*s* and 217½ acres of Glebe, V. 232*l* 16*s*; Glebe, 1¾ acres; V.'s Inc. 236*l* and Ho; Pop. 639.) Surrogate. [14]

MACDONALD, J. L.—C. of All Saints', Paddington, Lond. Formerly C. of St. Bride's, Liverpool. [15]

M'DONALD, James William, M.A., *Pembroke College, Oxford.* [16]

MACDONALD, Reginald Chambers.—Sid. Coll. Cam. Scho. of, B.A. 1859; Deac. 1859 by Abp of Cant. Itinerating Miss. in North Tinnevelly under Ch. Mis. Soc. 1859. [17]

MACDONALD, Thomas Mosse, *Trinity Parsonage, Nottingham.*—St. Aidan's, M.A. 1859 by Abp of Cant; Deac. 1849 and Pr. 1850 by Abp of Cant. P. C. of Trinity, Nottingham, Dio. Lin. 1851. (Patrons, Trustees; P. C.'s Inc. 520*l*; Pop. 9239.) Preb. of Lin. 1864. Formerly C of Bromley, Kent, 1849. Author, *The Church Catechism and Confirmation*, 1862, 6*d*; *Expository Notes on the Gospel of St. John*; *Questions on the Miracles of our Lord*. [18]

MACDONALD, William Maurice, *Calstone Willington Rectory, Calne, Wilts.*—R. of Calstone Willington, Dio. Salis. 1841. (Patron, Marquis of Lansdowne; Tithe, 82*l*; R.'s Inc. 192*l* and Ho; Pop. 36.) R. of Blackland, near Calne, Dio. Salis. 1844. (Patron, Rev. James Mayo; Tithe, App. 7*l*; R. 131*l*; R.'s Inc. 165*l*; Pop. 54.) Rural Dean; Surrogate. [19]

M'DONNELL, George Alcock.—Dub. A.B; Deac. 1854 and Pr. 1855 by Abp of Dub. C. of St. George's in-the East, Lond. Formerly C. of St. Andrew's, Dublin, All Saints', St. John's Wood, Lond. and St. Peter's, Walworth, Lond. 1857. Author, *Man's Life and Destiny* (Sermons), Bell and Daldy, 2*s* 6*d*. [20]

MACDONOGH, Terence Michael, *Bransgore Parsonage, near Ringwood, Hants.*—Deac. and Pr. 1827 by Bp of Llan. P. C. of Bransgore, Dio. Win. 1841. (Patron, T. Jesson. Esq; Glebe, 6 acres; P. C.'s Inc. 110*l* and Ho; Pop. 650.) Author, *A Memoir of Nicholas Ferrar*, 1829; *Lectures on Prayer, &c.* 1833; *An Abridgment of Manton on the Epistle of James*, 1842. [21]

M'DONOUGH, J. T., *Friezland, Greenfield, near Manchester.*—C. of Friezland. [22]

M'DOUALL, Patrick George, *Kirk-Newton Vicarage, Wooler, Northumberland.*—Ch. Ch. Ox. B.A. 1845, M.A. 1847; Deac. 1846 and Pr. 1847 by Bp of Roch. V. of Kirk-Newton, Dio. Dur. 1856. (Patron, Trustees of the Marquis of Bute; Tithe—Imp. 653*l* 4*s* 6*d*, V. 631*l*; Glebe, 7 acres; V.'s Inc. 681*l* and Ho; Pop. 1503.) [23]

M'DOUALL, William Sutherland, *Owsden Rectory. Newmarket, Suffolk.*—Ch. Ch. Ox. B.A. 1843, M.A. 1845; Deac. 1845, Pr. 1846. R. of Owsden, Dio. Ely, 1854. (Patron, B. J. M. Praed, Esq; Tithe, 26*l* 10*s*; Glebe, 338 acres; R.'s Inc. 380*l* and Ho; Pop. 346.) Dom. Chap. to the Marchioness of Bute 1848. [24]

MACDOUGALL, Henry, *Outwell Rectory, Wisbech.*—Brasen. Coll. Ox. M.A. 1847; Deac. 1845 and Pr. 1846 by Bp of Win. Chap. to the Forces 1847, Half Pay 1861. [25]

MACDOUGALL, James, *Hanney Vicarage, Wantage, Berks.*—Brasen. Coll. Ox. 3rd cl. Lit. Hum. and B.A. 1834, M.A. 1842; Deac. 1835 and Pr. 1836 by Bp of Lich. V. of Hanney with East Hanney C. Dio. Ox. 1849. (Patrons, D. and C. of Salis; Tithe—App. 450*l*, V. 130*l*; Glebe, 60 acres; V.'s Inc. 250*l* and Ho; Pop. 947.) Author, *Sleeping at Church* (a Tract). [26]

M'DOWALL, Robert Scott, *Bournemouth, Ringwood, Hants.*—Lin. Coll. Ox. B.A. 1853; Deac. 1854 and Pr. 1855 by Bp of Lin. C. of Bournemouth 1864. Formerly Asst. Mast. of Newark Gr. Sch. and General Preacher in Dio. of Lin. [27]

MACDOWALL, William, *Rillington, New Malton, Yorks.*—V. of Rillington, Dio. York, 1865. (Patron, Sir G. Strickland, Bart; Glebe, 40 acres; V.'s Inc. 260*l* and Ho; Pop. 884.) [28]

M'DOWELL, G. H. W.—Chap. of H.M.S. "Challenger." [29]

M'DOWELL, John Ramsay, *St. Just Vicarage, Penzance.*—Dub. Univ. Scho. 1846, A.B. 1851, A.M. 1856; Deac. 1852 and Pr. 1853 by Bp of Rip. V. of St. Just in Penwith, Dio. Ex. 1867. (Patron, Ld Chan;

Tithe, comm. 484*l*; Glebe, 12 acres; V.'s Inc. 500*l* and Ho; Pop. 5777.) Formerly C. of St. Mary's, Barnsley, 1852, St. Edmund's, Salisbury, 1855, Fisherton 1858, Bolton Percy 1864; P. C. of Whitwood Mere, Yorks, 1865. [1]

M'EWEN, Archibald, *Dumfries.*—Magd. Coll. Cam. 12th Sen. Opt. B.A. 1840, M.A. 1843; Deac. 1840 by Bp of Salis. Pr. 1841 by Bp of Chich. Incumb. of St. Mary's, Episcopal Church, Dumfries. Formerly C. of Semington, Wilts, 1840–46. [2]

M'FARLANE, James Duncan, *Staveley Rectory, Chesterfield.*—St. Edm. Hall, Ox. B.A 1838, M.A. 1846. R. of Staveley, Dio. Lich. 1847. (Patron, Duke of Devonshire; Tithe—Imp. 605*l* 10*s* 0¾*d*, R 605*l* 10*s* 0¾*d*, Glebe, 92 acres; R.'s Inc. 752*l* and Ho; Pop. 6831.) Rural Dean. [3]

MACFARLANE, Thomas, *Llandilo-Vawr, Carmarthenshire.*—Marischal Coll. Aberdeen, M.A. 1853; Deac. 1864 and Pr. 1865 by Bp of St. D. C. of Llandilo-Vawr 1864. Formerly Sen. Cl. Asst. in Cheltenham Gr. Sch. [4]

MACFARLANE, William Charles, *Dorchester Parsonage, near Oxford.*—Magd. Hall, Ox. B.A. 1852, M A. 1855; Deac. 1853 and Pr. 1854 by Bp of Ox. P. C. of Dorchester, Dio. Ox. 1856. (Patron, Rev. H. W. Burrows; Tithe—App. 96*l*, Imp. 330*l* 17*s* 2*d*, P. C. 12*s*; Glebe, 1½ acres; P. C.'s Inc. 110*l* and Ho: Pop. 1097.) [5]

M'GACHEN, John Drummond, *The Parsonage, St. Bartholomew's, Bethnal Green, London, N.E.*—Pemb. Coll. Ox. B.A. 1848, M.A. 1855; Deac. 1848 and Pr. 1849 by Abp of York. P. C. of St. Bartholomew's, Bethnal Green, Dio. Lon. 1860. (Patron, Bp of Lon; P. C.'s Inc. 300*l* and Ho; Pop. 9922.) [6]

MACGACHEN, Nicolas Howard, *Portsmouth.*—Pemb. Coll. Ox. B.A. 1849. C. of Portsmouth. Formerly C. of Brading, Isle of Wight. Author, *The City of the Desert and Prize Poems,* 1850. [7]

M'GHEE, Robert James, *Holywell Rectory, St. Ives, Hunts.*—Dub. Scho. of, 1807, A.B. 1811, A.M. 1840, *ad eund.* Trin. Coll. Cam. 1854; Deac. 1812 by Bp of Clonfert, Pr. 1812 by Bp of Ferns. R. of Holywell with Needingworth, Dio. Ely, 1846. (Patron, Duke of Manchester; Tithe, 4*l* 9*s*; Glebe, 424 acres; R.'s Inc. 580*l* and Ho; Pop. 826.) Author, Two Pamphlets in Defence of the Bible Society, 1815 and 1818; *Truth and Error Contrasted, and Reflections on Solemn Duties and Responsibilities of the Church of England in Reference to the Church of Rome,* Dublin, 1830; Pamphlets, from 1831 to 1833; *The Last Stand for the Church* (a Letter to the Deans, Archdeacons, and Clergy of Ireland), 1832; *The King and the Church Vindicated and Delivered* (an Address to the House of Lords, with a solemn appeal to the Abp of Canterbury), Dublin, 1833; *A Letter to the Clergy of Ireland, in Reply to a Letter of Archdeacon Stopford, afterwards Bishop of Meath,* 1834; *Episcopal and Clerical Duty considered in Reference to Ireland* (a Letter to the Bishop of Down and Connor, on his Charge against the Irish Home Mission), Dublin, 1835; *Romanism as it Rules in Ireland,* 2 vols. Dublin, 1836; *A Report of all the Speeches, Letters, and Documents on the Detection of Dens and the other Papal Works, during the Years* 1835, '36, '37; Joint Author with the Rev. Dr. O'Sullivan: *Secret Statutes of the Province of Leinster,* reprinted, with Translations, Notes, and Comments, London, 1838; *Notes of the Douay Bible and Rheimish Testament, with a List of Roman Catholic Bishops, Priests, Patrons, and Subscribers through Ireland, with a Preface detailing the History of the Work,* Dublin, 1839; *Speech delivered to the Electors of the University of Dublin, to prove the Establishment of the Papal Laws in Ireland,* Dublin, 1840; *Laws of the Papacy, set up by Roman Catholic Bishops, to subvert the Authority of their Lawful Sovereign in Ireland*-in 1852, 2nd ed. London, 1841; *The Nature and Obligation of Oaths in the Church of Rome,* Dublin, 1844; *Reflections on the Endowment of the College of Maynooth, and on the Doctrine of Expediency,* Dublin, 1844; *Secular without Scriptural Education considered* (two Sermons), 1846; *Scriptural Education based upon Divine Authority and Inspiration of the Scriptures* (a Sermon), 1847; *The Irish Prelates and Clergy vindicated* (a National Education Sermon), 1853; *Sermon* to Young Men's Christian Association, 1851; *No True Allegiance to a Protestant Sovereign permitted by the Church of Rome* (a Reply to Lord Arundel and Surrey), 1848; *Expository Lectures on the Epistle to the Ephesians,* 4th ed. 2 vols. 1849; *Justice for Ireland, or the Rejected Memorial* (an Appeal to the Earl of Clarendon on the Papal Laws in Ireland), 1849; *The Church of Rome, her present Moral Theology, Scriptural Instruction, and Canon Law* (a Report on the Documents of the Papacy deposited in the Universities, certified by the Vice-Chancellor of Cam. in compliance with a requisition from the County of Huntingdon), 1852; *Maynooth, its Sayings and Doings, or the Maynooth Commission Analysed and Tested* (in Letters to the Earl of Harrowby), 1856; Funeral Sermons: *On the Death of J. H. North, Esq. M.P*; *On the Death of the Very Rev. Henry Dawson, Dean of St. Patrick*; *On the Death of the Hon. Judge Foster*; *Ultramontanism Past and Present* (a Letter to Lord Palmerston), 1862; *Is there not a Cause? an Appeal to Archbishops, Bishops, and Clergy,* 1863; *Poor Gentlemen of Liége, a History of the Jesuits in England and Ireland for the last Sixty Years* (translated from Cretineau Joly, with Notes and Comments), 1863; *Appeal to the House of Lords on the Oaths Bill,* 1866; numerous occasional Sermons. [8]

M'GHEE, Robert James Leslie, *Curragh, Kildare.*—Chap. to the Forces. [9]

M'GHIE, John Poulett, *Portsmouth Vicarage.*—Queen's Coll. Ox. B.A. 1827, M.A. 1830. V. of Portsmouth, Dio. Win. 1839. (Patron, St. Mary's Coll. Win; V.'s Inc. 565*l* and Ho; Pop. 10,833.) Rural Dean. [10]

M'GILL, George Henry, *Christchurch Parsonage, Watney-street, St. George's-in-the-East, London, E.*—Brasen. Coll. Ox. B.A. 1841, M.A. 1844; Deac. 1841 and Pr. 1842 by Bp of Ches. P. C. of Ch. Ch. St. George's-in-the-East, Dio. Lon. 1854. (Patron, Brasen. Coll. Ox; P. C.'s Inc. 300*l* and Ho; Pop. 13,145.) [11]

M'GILL, John, *Stoke Ferry, Brandon, Norfolk.*—St. Bees; Deac. 1856 and Pr. 1857 by Bp of Nor. P. C. of Stoke Ferry, Dio. Nor. 1858. (Patron, Ld Chan; Tithe, Imp. 562*l* 17*s* 6*d*; P. C.'s Inc. 120*l*; Pop. 791.) [12]

M'GLYNN, F. F., 35, *Norfolk-road, Brighton.*—C. of St. Margaret's Chapel, Brighton, 1860. Formerly C. of Trinity, Maidstone, 1855–58, Thedden Chapel, Alton, Hants, 1858–60. [13]

M'GOWAN, Alexander John, *Stanley Parsonage, Chester-le-street, Durham.*—Dub. A.B. 1860; Deac. 1863 by Bp of Cork, Pr. 1864 by Bp of Killaloe. C. in charge of Conventional District of Stanley 1865. (C.'s Inc. 140*l* and Ho; Pop. 1600.) Formerly C. of St. John's, Limerick, and Asst. Chap. to the Garrison, Limerick, 1863; C. of Boston Spa, Yorks, 1865. [14]

M'GOWAN, Earle, *Holmside, Chester-le-Street, Durham.*—Dub. A.B. 1854, A.M. 1866; Deac. 1857 by Bp of Rip. Pr. 1858 by Bp of Lich. P. C. of Holmside, Dio. Dur. 1865. (Patron, the Crown; P. C.'s Inc. 300*l*; Pop. 1500.) Formerly C. of Chester-le-Street 1862. [15]

M'GRATH, Henry Walter.—Dub. A.B. 1827, A.M. 1830; Deac. and Pr. 1829. Hon. Can. of Man. 1858. Formerly R. of Kersall, Manchester, 1852–65. [16]

M'GRATH, William Carroll, *All Saints' Parsonage, Paddock, Huddersfield.*—Dub. A.B. 1825, A.M. 1830; Deac. 1829 by Bp of Meath, Pr. 1830 by Bp of Kildare. P. C. of All Saints', Paddock, Dio. Rip. 1843. (Patron, V. of Huddersfield; P. C.'s Inc. 155*l* and Ho; Pop. 3940.) [17]

MACGREGOR, Sir Charles, Bart., *Swallow Rectory, Caistor, Lincolnshire.*—St. Cath. Coll. Cam. B.A. 1842, M.A. 1852; Deac. 1843 by Bp of Ely, Pr. 1844 by Bp of Lich. R. of Swallow, Dio. Lin. 1854. (Patron, Earl of Yarborough; R.'s Inc. 410*l* and Ho; Pop. 239.) Rural Dean 1850. Author, *Remarks on Dr. Hook's Letter in the* "Times," Oct. 5, 1850; *An Attempt to Enquire into the History of the Law concerning Convocations, and the*

Expediency of revising them at the Present Time; *Notes on Genesis*, 1 vol; *India* (a Sermon). [1]

M'GUINNESS, William Nesbitt, 31, *Gibson-square Islington, London, N.*—Dub. Univ. Scho. 1855, A.B. 1858, A.M. 1867; Deac. 1859 and Pr. 1860 by Bp of Man. Lon. Dioc. Home Miss. 1866. Formerly C. of St. Mary's, Preston, 1859; Min. of Verulam Chapel, Lambeth, 1861; Min. of St. Paul's, Accrington, 1864. Author, *Moral Reasons for the Establishment of a State Church in a Christian Country*, Preston, 1860. [2]

MACHELL, James, *Penny-bridge, Ulverston.*—Brasen. Coll. Ox. B.A. 1827, M.A. 1829; Deac. 1827 and Pr. 1829 by Bp of Ches. [3]

MACHELL, Richard Beverley, *Roos Rectory, Hull.*—Magd. Coll. Cam. B.A. 1846; Deac. 1846, Pr. 1848. R. of Roos, Dio. York, 1866. (Patron, Sir Tatton Sykes, Bart; Tithe, 212*l* 6*s*; Glebe, 343 acres; R.'s Inc. 696*l* 19*s* and Ho; Pop. 652.) Formerly C. of Birdsall and Wharram-le-street 1846, Newton Kyme 1848, Bishop Wearmouth 1849; V. of Barrow-on-Humber 1849; Lect. on Sir John Nelthorpe's Foundation 1849. [4]

MACHEN, Edward, *Staunton Rectory, Colford, Glouc.*—Deac. 1842 by Bp of Salis. Pr. 1842 by Bp of G. and B. R. of Staunton, Dio. G. and B. 1857. (Patron, the present R; Tithe, 149*l* 5*s* 2*d*; Glebe, 10 acres; R.'s Inc. 163*l* and Ho; Pop. 202.) Formerly R. of Micheldean, Glouc. 1847–57. [5]

MACHUGH, George Edward, *Pembroke Dock, South Wales.*—Dub. A.B. 1862, A M. 1866; Deac. 1863 and Pr. 1864 by Bp of St. D. C. of St. John's, Pembroke Dock, 1863. [6]

MACHUTCHIN, Mark Wilks, *Talke Parsonage, Stoke-upon-Trent.*—St. Bees 1858; Deac. 1858 and Pr. 1859 by Bp of Lich. P. C. of Talke, Dio. Lich. 1859. (Patron, V. of Andley; Glebe, 22 acres; P. C.'s Inc. 250*l* and Ho; Pop. 2039.) Formerly C. of Audley, Staffs, 1856–59. [7]

M'ILWAINE, James, *Hambleton, Poulton le-Fylde, Lancashire.*—St. Bees; Deac. 1859 and Pr. 1860 by Bp of Ches. C. of Hambleton, 1861. Formerly C. of Byley with Yatehouse 1859–61. [8]

M'ILWAINE, W. R.—Chap. of H.M.S. "Jason." [9]

M'INTIRE, Travers, *Langcliffe Settle, Yorks.*—Dub. A.B. 1848; Deac. 1848, Pr. 1849. P. C. of Langcliffe, Dio. Rip. 1864. (Patron, Rev. G. B. Paley; P. C.'s Inc. 108*l*; Pop. 376.) Chap. of the Settle Union Workhouse 1865. [10]

M'INTOSH, Joseph, *Llanervul, Welshpool, Montgomeryshire.*—Ch. Ch. Ox. B.A. 1841; Deac. 1842, Pr. 1843. R. of Llanervul, Dio. St. A. 1860. (Patron, Bp of St. D; Tithe, 400*l*; Glebe, 22 acres; R.'s Inc. 417*l* and Ho; Pop. 827.) Formerly R. of Llanwyddelan 1847–60; P. C. of Llanllugan 1851–60, both in Montgomeryshire. [11]

MACKARNESS, George Richard, *Ilam Vicarage, Ashbourne, Staffs.*—Mert. Coll. Ox. 3rd cl. Lit. Hum. and B.A. 1845, M.A. 1848; Deac. 1846 by Bp of Salis. Pr. 1848 by Bp of Pet. V. of Ilam, Dio. Lich. 1854. (Patron, J. Watts-Russell, Esq; Tithe, 410*l* 5*s*; Glebe, 1½ acres and Ho; V.'s Inc. 360*l* and Ho; Pop. 243.) Fell. of St. Nicholas' Coll. Lancing 1866. Formerly Fell. of St. Columba's Coll. Ireland, 1846–47; C. of Barnwell, Peterborough, 1848–54. [12]

MACKARNESS, Henry Smith, *Ash Vicarage, near Sandwich, Kent.*—King's Coll. Cam. B.A. 1851, M.A. 1859; Deac. and Pr. 1852. V. of Ash, Dio. Cant. 1857. (Patron, Abp of Cant; Tithe—Imp. 333*l*, V. 290*l*; Glebe, 3 acres; V.'s Inc. 300*l* and Ho; Pop. 1582.) Formerly R. of St. Mary's, Romney, Kent, 1853–57; Fell. of King's Coll. Cam. [13]

MACKARNESS, John Fielder, *The Rectory, Honiton.*—Mert. Coll. Ox. 2nd cl. Lit. Hum. Fell. of Ex. Coll. 1844, B.A. 1844, M A. 1847; Deac. 1844 by Bp of Ox. Pr. 1845 by Bp of Wor. R. of Honiton, Dio. Ex. 1855. (Patron, Earl of Devon; R.'s Inc. 800*l* and Ho; Pop. 3301.) Preb. of Ex. 1858; Dom. Chap. to Lord Lyttelton 1855; P. C. of Monkton, Dio. Ex. 1867. (Patrons, D. and C. of Ex; P. C.'s Inc. 50*l*.) Chap. of Honiton Union 1866; Proctor in Convocation for Dio. Ex. 1865. Formerly V. of Tardebigge, Worcestershire, 1845–55; Hon. Can. of Wor. Cathl. [14]

MACKAY, Sween Macdonald, *Langton-by-Wragby, Lincolnshire.*—Wor. Coll. Ox. B.A. 1847, M.A. 1850; Deac. 1847 and Pr. 1848 by Bp of Lin. V. of Langton, Dio. Lin. 1859. (Patrons, Earl Manvers and C. Turnor, Esq. alt; Tithe, 230*l*; Glebe, 45 acres; V.'s Inc. 350*l* and Ho; Pop. 321.) Formerly C. of Gainsborough 1847–50; V. of Skillington 1850–59. [15]

MACKEE, Thomas John, *Brampton Vicarage, near Huntingdon.*—Dub. A.B. 1814, A.M. 1817; Deac. 1814 by Bp of Cork, Pr. 1815 by Bp of Kildare. V. of Brampton, Dio. Ely, 1844. (Patrons, Bp of Ely and Preb. of Brampton, in Lin Cathl; Tithe—App. 93*l* 10*s*; V.'s Inc. 179*l* and Ho; Pop. 1270.) Formerly Incumb. of Mellifont and Tullyallen, Dio. Armagh, 1831–44. Author, *Morning Musings by an Old Pastor*, 1859, 3*s* 6*d*. [16]

MACKENZIE, Charles, 52, *Leadenhall-street, London, E.C.*—Pemb. Coll. Ox. B.A. 1828, M.A. 1831; Deac. 1830 and Pr. 1831 by Bp of Salis. R. of the united parishes of Allhallows, Lombard-street with St. Benet's, Gracechurch, with St. Leonard's, Eastcheap, Dio. Lon. 1866. (Patrons, D. and C. of Cant; R.'s Inc. 600*l* and Ho; Pop. Allhallows 300, St. Benet 278, St. Leonard 111.) Preb. of St. Paul's 1852. Founder of Metropolitan Evening Classes for Young Men 1848, and Chairman of the Council of City of London Coll. for Young Men 1862. Formerly Head Mast of St. Olave's Gr. Sch. 1832–36; V. of St. Helen's, Bishopsgate 1836–46. R. of St. Benet's, Gracechurch with St. Leonard's, Eastcheap, 1846–66; Prin. of Westbourne Coll. 1855–64. Author, *History of the Church in a Course of Lectures*, 2 eds; *Young Christian's Glossary*; various Sermons and Lectures. [17]

M'KENZIE, Douglas, *Chaffcombe, Ilminster.*—C. of Chaffcombe, Somerset. [18]

MACKENZIE, Duncan Campbell, *Westgate, Chichester.*—Theol. Coll. Chich; Deac. 1852 by Bp of Rip. Pr. 1854 by Bp of Win. Chap. to the Chichester Union. Formerly P. C. of St. Bartholomew's, Chichester, 1854–60. [19]

MACKENZIE, The Ven. Henry, *Collingham, Notts, and Sub-Deanery, Lincoln.*—Pemb. Coll. Ox. Hon. 4th cl. Lit. Hum. and B.A. 1834, M.A. 1838; Deac. 1834 by Bp of Roch. Pr. 1835 by Abp of Cant. Archd. of Nottingham 1866; R. of South Collingham, Dio. Lin. 1866. (Patron, Bp of Pet; Tithe, 5*l*; Glebe, 213 acres; R.'s Inc. 472*l* and Ho; Pop. 863.) Sub-Dean of Lincoln 1864; Chap. to Bp of Lin. 1855. Formerly C. of Wool, Dorset, 1834–35; Asst. Chap. at Rotterdam, 1835; Asst. C. of St. Peter's, Walworth, Lond. 1836–37; Mast. of Bancroft's Hospital 1837–40; P. C. of St. James's, Bermondsey, 1840–43; P. C. of Great Yarmouth 1844–48; V. of St. Martin's-in-the-Fields, Lond. 1848–55; Preb. of Lin. 1858–64; R. of Tydd St. Mary 1855–66; Proctor in Convocation for Clergy of Lincoln 1857. Author, *Historical* (Prize) *Essay on the Life of Offa, King of Mercia*, Smith, Elder and Co. 1840; *A Commentary on the Gospels and Acts*, ib. 1847; *On the Parochial System*, J. W. Parker, 1850; *Ordination Lectures delivered at Riseholme* (3 series), Rivingtons, 1862; *Meditations on Psalm XXXI. or Thoughts for Hours of Retirement*, ib. 1864; occasional Sermons and Pamphlets. [20]

MACKENZIE, Henry, *St. Chad's Parsonage, Whitchurch, Salop.*—Magd. Hall, Ox. B.A. 1853, M.A. 1859; Deac. 1854 and Pr. 1855 by Bp of Ely. P. C. of St. Chad's, Malpas, Dio. Ches. 1859. (Patron, R. of Malpas; Glebe, 12 acres; R.'s Inc. 137*l* 8*s* 4*d* and Ho; Pop. 871.) Formerly C. of Luton, Beds, 1854–56, St. James's, Bristol, 1856–58, Gawsworth, near Macclesfield, 1858–59. [21]

MACKENZIE, Roderick Bain.—Ex. Coll. Ox. B.A. 1858, M.A. 1860; Deac. 1858 and Pr. 1859 by Bp of Lon. Formerly C. of St. Philip's, Bethnal Green, Lond. 1858. [22]

MACKENZIE, William.—Dom. Chap. to the Duke of Sutherland. [23]

MACKENZIE, William Bell, 19, *Canonbury-park North, Islington, London, N.*—Magd. Hall, Ox. 3rd cl. Lit. Hum. and B.A. 1833; Deac. and Pr. 1834. P. C. of St. James's, Holloway, Dio. Lon. 1838. (Patrons, Five Trustees; P. C.'s Inc. 700*l*; Pop. 5563.) Author, *Justified Believer*, R.T.S.; *Saul of Tarsus*, Seeleys; *Married Life*, ib; *Dwellings of the Righteous*, ib; *Redeeming Love*, ib; *Bible Characters*, ib; various other Books and Tracts. [1]

MACKERETH, Miles, *Ottringham, Hull.*—St. Cath. Coll. Cam. B.A. 1831, M.A. 1837; Deac. 1831 by Abp of York, Pr. 1844 by Bp of Nor. P. C. of Ottringham, Dio. York, 1848. (Patron, F. Watts, Esq; P. C.'s Inc. 85*l*; Pop. 644.) C. of Halsham, Yorks. [2]

MACKERITH, Charles, *Middleton Vicarage, Pickering, Yorks.*—V. of Middleton, Dio. York. (Patrons, Rev. A. Caley and T. Smith, Esq; V.'s Inc. 110*l* and Ho; Pop. 1654.) Formerly Chap. of Don. of Old Byland, Yorks, 1829–66. [3]

MACKIE, Charles, *Quarley Rectory, Andover, Hants.*—R. of Quarley, Dio. Win. 1821. (Patron, St. Katherine's Hospital, Regent's-park, Lond; Tithe, 342*l* 17*s* 10*d*; R.'s Inc. 345*l* and Ho; Pop. 182.) [4]

MACKIE, George, *Chilvers Coton Vicarage, Nuneaton.*—Pemb. Coll. Cam. B.A. 1834, D.D. 1847 by Abp Howley; Deac. 1835 and Pr. 1836 by Bp of Ex. V. of Chilvers Coton, Dio. Wor. 1859. (Patron, C. N. Newdegate, Esq. M.P; Glebe, 38 acres; V.'s Inc. 183*l* and Ho; Pop. 2764.) Formerly C. of St. Eval, Cornwall, 1835–36; Exam. Chap. to Bp of Quebec, 1836–58, and Bp's Official and Eccles. Commissary 1843–58. [5]

MACKIE, John, *Bristol.*—Chap. of the Royal Infirmary, Bristol; Surrogate. [6]

M'KIMM, D. J., *Rashcliffe, Huddersfield.*—P. C. of Rashcliffe, Dio. Rip. 1864. (Patron, P. C. of Lockwood; P. C.'s Inc. 150*l* and Ho; Pop. 4140.) [7]

MACKINNON, John, *Bloxholm Rectory, Sleaford, Lincolnshire.*—Pemb. Coll. Cam. B.A. 1814, M.A. 1818; Deac. 1815 and Pr. 1816 by Bp of Lin. R. of Bloxholm and Digby V. Dio. Lin. 1825. (Patron, The Right Hon. R. C. Nesbit-Hamilton; Bloxholm, Tithe, 209*l* 5*s* 2*d*; Glebe, 18½ acres; Digby, Tithe, 240*l*; Glebe, 1 acre; R.'s Inc. 478*l* and Ho; Pop. Bloxholm 115, Digby 330.) Author, *The Peace* (a Thanksgiving Sermon), 1815, 1*s*; *On the Importance of Christian Union*, 1817, 6*d*; *The Public and Private Character of George III* (a Sermon), 1820. [8]

MACKINTOSH, James, *The Cloisters, Bristol.*—St. John's Coll. Cam. Exhib. Sen. Opt. and B.A. 1847; Deac. 1850 and Pr. 1851 by Bp of G. and B. Head Mast. of the Cathl. Gr. Sch. Bristol, 1855. Author, *The Christian's Faith and Jacob's Sin* (two Sermons), Bristol, 1851, 1*s* 6*d*. [9]

MACKLACHLAN, Archibald Neil Campbell, *Newton-Valence Vicarage, Alton, Hants.*—Ex. Coll. Ox. B.A. 1841, M.A. 1844. V. of Newton-Valence, Dio. Win. 1860. (Patron, Rev. T. Snow; V.'s Inc. 512*l* and Ho; Pop. 340.) Formerly Chap. of St. Cross Hospital, Winchester. [10]

MACKNESS, George, *The Beeches, Aldridge, near Walsall.*—Lin. Coll. Ox. Scho. of, B.A. 1856, M.A. 1859; Deac. 1858 by Abp of Cant. Pr. 1858 by Bp of Lich. C. of Aldridge 1866. Formerly Asst. C. of Hinstock, Salop, 1858–60, C. of Stonham Aspal, Suffolk, 1860–63, St. John Baptist's, Woking, Surrey, 1863–66. Author, *Receiving from God, not giving to God, the Central Idea of Holy Communion*, Masters, 1867, 2*d*. [11]

M'KNIGHT, W. H. E.—Dom. Chap. to the Earl of Suffolk and Berkshire. [12]

MACKONOCHIE, Alexander Heriot, *St. Alban's Clergy House, Brooke-street, Holborn, London, E.C.*—Wad. Coll. Ox. B.A. 1848; Deac. 1848, Pr. 1849. P. C. of St. Alban's, Gray's-inn-lane, Dio. Lon. 1862. (Patron, J. G. Hubbard, Esq. M.P; P. C.'s Inc. 150*l*.) Formerly C. of St. George's-in-the-East, Lond. [13]

MACKRETH, Thomas, *Halton Rectory, near Lancaster.*—St. Peter's Coll. Cam. B.D. 1827, D.D. 1859; Deac. 1812, Pr. 1813. R. of Halton, Dio. Man. 1854. (Patron, J. Hastings, Esq; Tithe, 489*l*; R.'s Inc. 500*l* and Ho; Pop. 670.) Hon. Can. of Man. 1854; Surrogate. Formerly Vice-Commissary of the Archdeaconry of Richmond, and Rural Dean. Author, *Churchwarden's Manual*, Rivingtons, 2*s* 6*d*; *Four Charges to Churchwardens*; etc. [14]

MACLACHLAN, Ewan Hugh, *Tudely Vicarage, Tunbridge, Kent.*—Pemb. Coll. Ox. 2nd cl. Lit. Hum. and B.A. 1844, M.A. 1847; Deac. and Pr. 1845 by Bp of Ox. C. of Tudely and Capel. [15]

MACLAGAN, William Dalrymple, *The Vicarage, Enfield, Middlesex.*—St. Peter's Coll. Cam. B.A. 1856, M.A. 1860; Deac. 1856 and Pr. 1857 by Bp of Lon. C. in sole charge of Enfield; Hon. Sec. to the Lond. Dioc. Ch. Building Soc. Formerly C. of St. Saviour's, Paddington, 1856–58, St. Stephen's, Marylebone, 1858–60. [16]

M'LAUGHLIN, Hubert, *Boraston Rectory (Salop), near Tenbury.*—Dub. A.B. 1828, A.M. 1832; Deac. 1829, Pr. 1831. R. of Burford, 1st Portion, Dio. Herf. 1838. (Patron, Lord Northwick; 1st Portion, Tithe, 516*l* 7*s* 1*d*; Glebe, 22 acres; R.'s Inc. 572*l* and Ho; Pop. 445.) Rural Dean 1843; Surrogate; Dom. Chap. to Lord Crofton; Preb. of Herf. Formerly British Chap. at Nice. Author, *Sermon on the Duty of Private Judgment*; *English Scenes, a Cantata*, Words and Music; *Consider the Lilies, an Anthem for Harvest Festivals*; etc. [17]

MACLEAN, A. S., *Lichfield.*—C. of St. Chad's, Lichfield. [18]

MACLEAN, Frederick, *Ripponden, Yorks.*—Chap. of the Coll. Ripponden. [19]

M'LEAN, George Gavin, *Horsham, Sussex.*—Wad. Coll. Ox. M.A. 1861; Deac. and Pr. 1862 by Bp of Chich. C. of Horsham 1862. [20]

MACLEAN, Hippisley, *The Vicarage, Caistor, Lincolnshire.*—Caius Coll. Cam. B.A. 1829; Deac. 1831 and Pr. 1832 by Bp of Lich. V. of Caistor with Holton-le-Moor C. and Clixby C. Dio. Lin. 1844. (Patron, Bp of Lin; Tithe, 180*l*; Glebe, 80 acres; V.'s Inc. 320*l* and Ho; Pop. 2141.) Chap. to the Caistor Union; Rural Dean; Patron of Sudbury Gr. Sch. Formerly C. of St. Michael's and P. C. of Ch. Ch. Coventry. [21]

MACLEAN, Richard, *Great Redisham, Halesworth, Suffolk.*—P. C. of Great Redisham, Dio. Nor. 1858. (Patron, Rev. Alex. B. Campbell; Tithe, Imp. 100*l*; P. C.'s Inc. 64*l*; Pop. 182.) [22]

MACLEAR, George, *The Crescent, Bedford.*—Dub. A.B. 1821, Trin. Coll. Cam. M.A. 1825; Deac. 1822, Pr. 1823. Chap. of Bedford Co. Prison; Chap.'s Inc. 250*l*. Author, *Christian Freedom and Popish Bondage* (a Sermon), 1*s* 8*d*. [23]

MACLEAR, George Frederick, 24, *Elgin Crescent, Notting-hill, W*, and *King's College, London, W.C.*—Trin. Coll. Cam. Carus, Burney, Maitland, Hulsean, and Norrisian Prizeman, 1st cl. Theol. Trip. 2nd cl. Cl. Trip. B.A. 1855, M.A. 1860, B.D. 1867; Deac. 1856 and Pr. 1857 by Bp of Ely. Head Mast. of King's Coll. Sch. Lond. 1866; Reader at the Temple Church 1865. Formerly Asst. Min. at Curzon Chapel, Mayfair, and St. Mark's, Notting-hill, London. Author, *Incentives to Virtue, Natural and Revealed* (Burney Prize Essay), 1855; *The Cross and the Nations* (Hulsean Prize Essay), 1857; *The Christian Statesman and our Indian Empire* (Maitland Prize Essay), 2nd ed. 1859; *Mission of the Middle Ages* (Maitland Prize Essay), 1861; *The Witness of the Eucharist* (Norrisian Prize Essay), 1863; *Class Book of Old Testament History*, 3rd ed. 1866; *Class Book of New Testament History*, 2nd ed. 1867; *Shilling Book of Old Testament History*, 1866; *Shilling Book of New Testament History*, 1867; all published by Macmillans. [24]

MACLEAY, Alexander, *Chellaston, Derby.*—Deac. 1866 by Bp of Ches. C. of Chellaston 1867. Formerly C. of St. James's, Haydock, Lancashire, 1866. [25]

M'LEOD, Charles Middleton, *Harlow, Essex.*—Trin. Coll. Cam. B.A. 1825, M.A. 1828. Min. of St. John the Baptist's, Harlow. [26]

M'LEOD, Nicholas Kenneth, *The Parsonage, Ellon, Aberdeenshire.*—Marischal Coll. Aberdeen, M.A. 1855, Bp Hatfield's Hall, Dur. Licen. in Theol. 1859; Deac. 1859 and Pr. 1860 by Bp of Roch. Incumb. of Ellon. (Inc. 150*l*, Ho. and 2 acres of land.) Formerly C.

of Little Horkesley, Essex, 1859, St. Andrew's, Aberdeen, 1860–62. [1]

MACLURE, Edward C., *Habergham Eaves, Whalley, Lancashire.*—Brasen. Coll. Ox. Hulme's Exhib. B.A. 1856, M.A. 1858; Deac. 1857 and Pr. 1858 by Bp of Wor. P. C. of Habergham Eaves, Dio. Man. 1863. (Patrons, Hulme's Trustees; P. C.'s Inc. 360*l* and Ho; Pop. 11,533.) Formerly Fell. of Brasen. Coll. Ox; Sen. C. of St. Pancras; C. of St. John's, Ladywood. [2]

MACMICHAEL, John Fisher, *Ripon, Yorks.*—Trin. Coll. Cam. Wrang. 2nd cl. Cl. Trip. and B.A. 1837; Deac. 1844, Pr. 1845. Head Mast. of Ripon Gr. Sch; C. of Bishop Monkton. Editor of *Xenophon's Anabasis, with Notes,* 1847; *Greek Testament, with Notes,* 1853. Author, *Our Duty as Members of the House of God* (Ordination Sermon), 1854. [3]

MACNAMARA, Thomas Binstead, *West Cowes, Isle of Wight.*—Magd. Hall, Ox. B.A. 1846, M.A. 1849; Deac. 1847 and Pr. 1849 by Bp of Ox. Formerly P. C. of St. George's, Waterloo, Portsmouth, 1853. [4]

MACNAUGHT, John, 8, *Catharine-place, Bath.*—Wad. Coll. Ox. 1846, 4th cl. Lit. Hum. and B.A. 1847; Deac. 1849 and Pr. 1850 by Bp of Ches. Min. of Laura Chapel, Bath, 1867. Formerly P. C. of St. Chrysostom's Everton, Liverpool, 1853–61. Author, *The Doctrine of Inspiration,* Longmans, 2 eds; etc. [5]

M'NEILE, E. H., *Liverpool.*—P. C. of St. Paul's, Princes-park, Liverpool, Dio. Ches. 1867. (Patrons, Trustees; P. C.'s Inc. 900*l*; Pop. 11,000.) Formerly C. of St. Emmanuel's, Bristol. [6]

M'NEILE, Hugh, *Albury House, Liverpool.*—Dub. A.B. 1815, A.M. 1822, B.D. and D.D. 1841 (*honoris causâ*); Deac. 1820 and Pr. 1821 by Bp of Raphoe. Hon. Can. of Ches. Cathl. 1845; Canon Residentary of Chester 1860. (Inc. 500*l* and Ho.) Formerly R. of Albury 1822–34; P. C. of St. Jude's, Liverpool, 1834–48, St. Paul's Princes-park, Liverpool, 1848–67. Author, *Ordination Sermon,* 1828; *Seventeen Sermons,* 1826, 12*s*; *Lectures on Miracles,* 1833, 3*s*; *Letters to a Friend,* 1834, 3*s*; *Lectures on the Church of England,* 1841, 7*s*; *Lectures on the Prophecies relative to the Jewish Nation,* 4*s* 6*d*; *Sermons on the Second Advent,* 4*s* 6*d*; *The Church and the Churches,* 1846, 12*s*; *Lectures on the Sympathies, Sufferings, and Resurrection of our Lord Jesus Christ,* 1845, 3*s*; all published by Hatchard, London; *The Adoption and other Sermons preached in Chester Cathedral,* Nisbet, 1864, 5*s*; and numerous single Sermons and Lectures. [7]

M'NIVEN, Charles, *Patney Rectory, Devizes, Wilts.*—Trin. Coll. Cam. B.A. 1816, M.A. 1819. R. of Patney, Dio. Salis. 1848. (Patron, Bp of Win; R.'s Inc. 239*l* and Ho; Pop. 154.) [8]

MACPHAIL, E. W. St. Maur, *Forscote, Bath.*—C. of Forscote. Formerly C. of Chewton Mendip. [9]

MACRAY, William Dunn, 7, *Park-crescent, Oxford.*—Magd. Coll. Ox. Hon. 4th cl. Lit. Hum. and B.A. 1848, M.A. 1851; Deac. 1850 and Pr. 1851 by Bp of Ox. Chap. of New Coll. Ox. 1850; Chap. of Magd. Coll. 1856; Assistant in the Bodleian Library 1840. Formerly Chap. of Ch. Ch. 1851–56; Asst. C. of St. Mary Magdalene's, Oxford, 1850–67. Author, *A Manual of British Historians to A.D.* 1600, 1845; *Catalogue of the Library at Bicton House, Devon,* 4to (privately printed), 1850; several Sermons in *Sermons for the Christian Seasons,* 1853; *Catalogus Codd. MSS. Ric. Rawlinson in Bibl. Bodleiana,* Fasc. I. 4to, 1862; *Chronicon Abbatiæ de Evesham, ad Annum* 1418, 8vo, 1863; *Index to the Catalogue of Ashmolean MSS. in Bodleian Library,* 4to, 1867. [10]

MACRORIE, William Kenneth, *The Parsonage, Accrington.*—Brasen. Coll. Ox. Hulmian Exhib. B.A. 1852, M.A. 1855; Deac. 1855 and Pr. 1857 by Bp of Ox. P. C. of Accrington, Dio. Man. 1865. (Patrons, Hulme's Trustees; Glebe, 46 acres; P. C.'s Inc. 370*l* and Ho; Pop. 13,000.) Formerly Fell. of St. Peter's Coll. Radley, 1855–58; C. of Deane, Lancashire, 1858–60; P. C. of Wingates, Bolton-le-Moors, 1860–61; R. of Wapping, Lond. 1861–65. [11]

MACSORLEY, A. K., *Arkengarth-Dale, Richmond, Yorks.*—P. C. of Arkengarth-Dale, Dio. Rip. 1862. (Patron, Sir J. Lowther, Bart; P. C.'s Inc. 123*l*; Pop. 1147.) [12]

M'SORLEY, Hugh, *St. Paul's Parsonage, Tottenham, London, N.*—Dub. Royal Exhib. and Univ. Scho. Prizeman in Cl. Math. Logic and Hebrew Ethical Moderatorship, Jun. A.B. 1850, A.M. 1866; Deac. 1850 by Abp of Dub. Pr. 1852 by Bp of Down and Connor. P. C. of St. Paul's, Tottenham, Dio. Lon. 1861. (Patron, V. of Tottenham; P. C.'s Inc. 240*l* and Ho; Pop. 2265.) Formerly C. of St. George's, Belfast, 1850, Aughrim, Galway, 1852; Chap. R.N. 1853; C. of All Saints', Gordon-square, Lond. 1856, St. Peter's, Hammersmith, 1858. St. Jude's, Chelsea, 1859–60. Author, *Words of our Lord Jesus on the Cross* (Seven Sermons), 3*s*; *Temptation* (Six Sermons), 2*s*; *Thoughts on Popery,* 4*d*; *Tottenham Tracts*—No. 1, *The Lord's Table,* No. 2, *The Lord's Day,* No. 3, *Infant Baptism,* No. 4, *Confession,* No. 5, *The Confessional,* No. 6, *The Elect,* No. 7, *The Priest, Altar, and Vestments,* No. 8, *The Sacrifice of the Mass,* 1*d* each, J. F. Shaw; *The Protestant Vindicator,* Macintosh, 1*s*. [13]

M'SWINEY, John H. Herbert, *Cronstadt.*—Chap. to the Russia Co. Cronstadt. [14]

MACVICAR, J. D., *Worcester.*—Trin. Coll. Cam. B.A. 1862, M.A. 1866; Deac. 1864 and Pr. 1865 by Bp of Win. C. of St. Martin's, Worcester, 1867. Formerly C. of Weybridge, Surrey, 1864–67. [15]

MACY, Vincent Hardwicke, *Oxhill Rectory, Kineton, Warwickshire.*—St. Bees; Deac. 1855 and Pr. 1856 by Bp of G. and B. R. of Oxhill, Dio. Wor. 1864. (Patron, Rev. W. D. Bromley; R.'s Inc. 260*l* and Ho; Pop. 373.) Formerly C. of St. Mary Redcliff, Bristol; Chap. of Codrington Coll. Barbados. [16]

MADAN, George, *The Rectory, Dursley, Gloucestershire.*—Ch. Ch. Ox. 1st cl. Math. et Phy. and B.A. 1829; Deac. 1831 and Pr. 1832. Hon. Can. of Bristol 1853; R. of Dursley, Dio. G. and B. 1865. (Patron, Bp of G. and B; R.'s Inc. 350*l* and Ho; Pop. 2477.) Formerly V. of St. Mary, Redcliff, Bristol, 1852–65. [17]

MADAN, James Russel, *Mission House, Warminster.*—Queen's Coll. Ox. Scho. of, 3rd cl. Lit. Hum. B.A. 1864, M.A. 1867; Prin. of Mission House, Warminster; Asst. C. of Warminster. Formerly Asst. C. of Dursley 1865–67. [18]

MADAN, Nigel, *Polesworth Vicarage, Tamworth.*—Trin. Coll. Cam. B.A. 1862, M.A. 1866; Deac. 1864, Pr. 1865. V. of Polesworth, Dio. Wor. 1866. (Patron, Ld Chan; Tithe, 62*l*, augmentation by Charity, 450*l*; Glebe, 2 acres; V.'s Inc. 512*l* and 2 Hos; Pop. 1800.) Formerly C. of Ashburne, Dio. Lich. 1864–66. [19]

MADAN, Spencer, *Standon Rectory, Eccleshall, Staffs.*—Ch. Ch. Ox. B.A. 1857, M.A. 1858; Deac. 1858 and Pr. 1859 by Bp of Lich. R. of Standon, Dio. Lich. 1862. (Patrons, Trustees of the late Rev. Jos. Salt; Tithe, 480*l*; Glebe, 80 acres; R.'s Inc. 600*l* and Ho; Pop. 347.) Formerly C. of Standon 1858–62. [20]

MADDEN, Wyndham Monson, *Wakefield.*—St. John's Coll. Cam. Sen. Opt. and B.A. 1845; Deac. 1846, Pr. 1847. P. C. of Trinity, Wakefield, Dio. Rip. 1853. (Patrons, Trustees; P. C.'s Inc. 250*l*; Pop. 3719.) [21]

MADDISON, Arthur Roland, *Croft, Boston, Lincolnshire.*—Mert. Coll. Ox. 2nd cl. Law and Modern History, B.A. and S.C.L. 1867; Deac. 1867 by Bp of Lin. C. of Croft 1867. [22]

MADDISON, Charles John, *Douglas, Isle of Man.*—Deac. 1840, Pr. 1841. V. of Stottesdon, Salop, Dio. Herf. 1846. (Patron, Duke of Cleveland; Tithe—Imp. 200*l* 8*s*, V. 484*l* 14*s*; Glebe, 27 acres; V.'s Inc. 680*l* and Ho; Pop. 905.) [23]

MADDISON, George, *The Vicarage, Grantham.*—Jesus Coll. Cam. B.A. 1832, M.A. 1835; Deac. 1832 by Abp of York, Pr. 1833 by Bp of Ely. V. of Grantham, Dio. Lin. 1856. (Patron, Bp of Lin; V.'s Inc. 1250*l* and Ho; Pop. 7108.) Preb. of Lincoln 1864; Rural Dean of Cambridge; Chap. to Bp of Wor. Formerly Fell. of St. Cath. Coll. Cam. 1832–39; V. of All Saints', Cambridge, 1838–56; Surrogate for the Archd. of Ely 1846–56. [24]

MADDOCK, Benjamin, *Edgerton Lodge, Tadcaster, Yorks.*—Corpus Coll. Cam. 2nd Sen. Opt. and B.A. 1810, M.A. 1813; Deac. 1810 and Pr. 1811 by Bp of Lin. V. of Tadcaster, Dio. York, 1830. (Patron, Lord Londesborough; Tithe—App. 6*l*, Imp. 598*l* 18*s* 9½*d*, V. 165*l* 3*s*; Glebe, 5 acres; V.'s Inc. 244*l* and Ho; Pop. 3126.) [1]

MADDOCK, Edward Knight, *St. Margaret's, Twickenham, S.W.*—St. Cath. Coll. Cam. B.A. 1833, M.A. 1836; Deac. 1833 and Pr. 1834 by Bp of Win. Chap of the Royal Naval Female Sch. St. Margaret's, Isleworth; Clerical Sec. of the Indian Female Instruction Society. Formerly P. C. of St. Stephen's, Lindley, Huddersfield, 1837; Chap. H.E.I.C.S. 1842. [2]

MADDOCK, Henry John, *Ryde, Isle of Wight.*—Wor. Coll. Ox. B.A. 1833, M.A. 1836; Deac. 1834, Pr. 1835. Formerly C. of Wootton, Isle of Wight. [3]

MADDOCK, Henry William, *Boundary House, St. John's Wood, London, N.W.*—Brasen. Coll. Ox. Fell. of, 1827, 2nd cl. Lit. Hum. 1827, B.A. St. John's, 1827, M.A. Brasen. 1830; Deac. 1827 and Pr. 1828 by Bp of Ox. P. C. of All Saints', St. John's Wood, Dio. Lon. 1850. (Patron, G. J. Eyre, Esq; P. C.'s Inc. about 400*l*; Pop. 5481.) Formerly V. of Kington, Herefordshire, 1835–50. [4]

MADDOCK, Philip Bainbrigge, *Staverton, Trowbridge.*—Literate; Deac. 1849, Pr. 1850. P. C. of Staverton, Dio. Salis. 1859. (Patron, R. of Trowbridge; P. C.'s Inc. 100*l*; Pop. 580.) Formerly C. of Winkfield, Wilts. [5]

MADDOCK, Samuel, *Ropley Vicarage, Alresford, Hants.*—Brasen. Coll. Ox. B.A. 1812, M.A. 1815; Deac. and Pr. 1811. V. of Bishops Sutton with Ropley Chapelry, Dio. Win. 1818. (Patroness, Mrs. Deacon; Bishops Sutton, Tithe—Imp. 677*l* 7*s*, V. 197*l* 3*s* 6*d*; Glebe, 21 acres; Pop. 537; Ropley, Tithe—Imp. 753*l* 11*s*, V. 250*l*; Glebe, 7 acres and Ho; Pop. 796.) Author, *Sermons for Seamen* (3 eds.); *Farewell Sermons* (8 eds.), 1817. [6]

MADDOCK, William Herbert, 3, *College Grounds, Great Malvern.*—St. John's Coll. Ox. Fell. of, 1858–65, 3rd cl. Lit. Hum. B.A. 1862, M.A. 1865; Deac. 1864 and Pr. 1865 by Bp of Wor. Asst. Mast. in Malvern Coll. [7]

MADDY, Henry William, *Down-Hatherley Vicarage, Gloucester.*—Trin. Coll. Cam. B.A. 1850, M.A. 1853; Deac. 1852 and Pr. 1853 by Bp of Wor. V. of Down-Hatherley, Dio. G. and B. 1856. (Patron, Ld Chan; V.'s Inc. 300*l* and Ho; Pop. 199.) Formerly C. of Nuthurst, Warwickshire, 1852–54, St. Briavell's, Glouc. 1855–56. [8]

MADDY, Joseph, *Penhow Rectory, Caerleon, Monmouthshire.*—Lampeter; Deac. 1852, Pr. 1853. R. of Penhow, Dio. Llan. 1861. (Patron, John Cave, Esq; R.'s Inc. 200*l* and Ho; Pop. 293.) Formerly C. of Magor and Redwick. [9]

MAGEE, George, *Acton-Scott Rectory, near Shrewsbury.*—Dub. A.B. 1827; Deac. 1828, Pr. 1831. R. of Acton-Scott, Dio. Herf. 1856. (Patron, F. W. Pendarvis, Esq; R.'s Inc. 250*l* and Ho; Pop. 207.) [10]

MAGNAY, Claude, *Hemyock (Devon), near Wellington, Somerset.*—Clare Coll. Cam. B.A. 1844; Deac. 1845 and Pr. 1846 by Bp of Win. C. of Hemyock. Formerly C. of Holwell, Dorset. Author, *The Rest, a Tale,* 2*s* 6*d*, 1849; *Reginald Greme,* 1850, 3*s*; *Selwood, and other Poems,* 1853; Ditto, enlarged, 4*s*, Masters, 1855; *Duty, a Poem,* 1855, 6*d*; *Sermons, Practical and Suggestive,* 1855, 6*s*. [11]

MAGRATH, James.—Dub. A. B. 1859; Deac. 1856 and Pr. 1857 by Bp of Lich. Formerly C. of Beteley 1857–60, Codicote, Herts, 1860, Bix, Henley-on-Thames, 1860–64, Hollesley, Suffolk, 1864. [12]

MAGRATH, John Richard, *Queen's College, Oxford.*—Oriel Coll. Ox. Scho. of, 1856, 1st cl. Lit. Hum. 1860, Johnson Theol. Scho. 1861, B.A. 1860, M.A. 1863; Deac. 1863 and Pr. 1864 by Bp of Ox. Fell. Dean and Tut. of Queen's Coll. Ox. Formerly Mast. of the Schs. Ox. 1864–65; Select Preacher 1867. [13]

FF

MAGUINNESS, John Thomas, *St. Stephen's Vicarage, Burmantofts, Leeds.*—St. Aidans 1866; Deac. 1866 by Bp of Rip. C. of St. Stephen's, Burmantofts, 1866. [14]

MAGUIRE, Robert, 39, *Myddelton-square, Clerkenwell, London, E.C.*—Dub. A.B. 1847, A.M. 1855; Deac. 1849 and Pr. 1850 by Bp of Cork. P. C. of Clerkenwell, Dio. Lon. 1857. (Patrons, the Inhabitants; P. C.'s Inc. 350*l*; Pop. 26,667.) Sunday Aft. Lect. at St. Luke's, Old-street, 1856; Early Sund. Morn. Lect. at St. Swithin's, Cannon-street, 1864. Author, *Papal Indulgences,* Seeleys, 1852; *Perversion and Conversion, or Cause and Effect,* 1853; *History of the Early Irish Church,* 1854; *The Seven Churches of Asia,* 1857; *Expository Lectures on Bunyan's Pilgrim's Progress,* 1859; *Annotations of Cassell's Illustrated Bunyan,* 1863; *Self: its Dangers, Doubts, and Duties,* Shaw, 1863; *Mottoes for the Million, or Evenings with my Working Men,* ib. 1867. [15]

MAHON, George, *Vobster Parsonage, Frome, Somerset.*—Magd. Hall, Ox. B.A. 1852, M.A. 1855; Deac. 1853, Pr. 1854. P. C. of Vobster with Leigh-upon-Mendip C. Dio. B. and W. 1860. (Patron, R. of Mells; P. C.'s Inc. 60*l* and Ho; Pop. 716.) Formerly C. of Leigh-upon-Mendip. [16]

MAHON, Sir William Vesey Ross, Bart., *Rawmarsh Rectory, near Rotherham, Yorks.*—Dub. A.M. 1837; Deac. 1836, and Pr. 1837. R. of Rawmarsh, Dio. York, 1844. (Patron, Ld Chan; Tithe, 134*l* 10*s* 1*d*; Glebe, 170 acres; R.'s Inc. 550*l* and Ho; Pop. 4000.) Dom. Chap. to the Marquis of Sligo. [17]

MAIN, Robert, *Radcliffe Observatory, Oxford.*—Queens' Coll. Cam. 6th Wrang. and B.A. 1834, M.A. 1837, Pemb. Coll. Ox. M.A. 1860; Deac. 1836, Pr. 1837. Radcliffe Observer at Oxford 1860. Formerly Fell. of Queens' Coll. Cam. 1836–38; 1st Asst. at the Royal Observatory, Greenwich. Author, *Rudimentary Astronomy* (Weale's Series), 1852; *Sermons,* 1 vol. 1860; *Translation of Brünnow's Astronomy,* Deighton, Bell and Co. 1860; *Spherical Astronomy,* ib. 1863; Several papers in *Memoirs of the Royal Astronomical Society of London.* [18]

MAIN, Thomas John, *Royal Naval College, Portsmouth.*—St. John's Coll. Cam. Sen. Wrang. and B.A. 1838, M.A. 1841; Deac. 1841 and Pr. 1842 by Bp of Ely. Prof. of Mathematics at the Royal Naval Coll. Portsmouth; Chap. of H.M.S. "Excellent," Gunnery Ship Portsmouth, 1857. Formerly Fell. of St. John's Coll. Cam. Author, various works on the Marine Steam Engine, Longmans. [19]

MAINE, John T., *Bighton Wood, Alresford, Hants.*—Trin. Coll. Cam. M.A. [20]

MAINE, Lewin George, *St. Lawrence Vicarage, Reading.*—King's Coll. Lond. Theol. Assoc. 1856, M.A. by Abp of Cant; Deac. 1856, Pr. 1857. V. of St. Lawrence, Reading, Dio. Ox. 1866. (Patron, Bp of Ox; V.'s Inc. 250*l* and Ho; Pop. 3636.) Formerly C. of St. Philip's, Clerkenwell, 1856–59, Stanford-in-the-Vale, Berks, 1859–66. Author, *The Second Advent* (a Sermon), Rivingtons, 1864; *A Berkshire Village,* 1866. [21]

MAINGUY, James, *Hainton, Wragby, Lincolnshire.*—Pemb. Coll. Ox. B.A. 1826, M.A. 1830; Deac. 1827 and Pr. 1828 by Bp of Ches. V. of Hainton, Dio. Lin. 1865. (Patron, E. Heneage, Esq; V.'s Inc. 270*l*; Pop. 302.) Formerly R. of St. Mary de Castro, Guernsey, 1843–60; R. of St. Martin's, Guernsey, 1860–65. [22]

MAINWARING, Charles Henry, *Whitmore Rectory, Newcastle-under-Lyne.*—Oriel Coll. Ox. B.A. 1843; Deac. 1844 and Pr. 1845 by Bp of Lich. R. of Whitmore, Dio. Lich. 1848. (Patron, Captain Mainwaring; Tithe, 275*l*; Glebe, 27 acres; R.'s Inc. 310*l* and Ho; Pop. 345.) [23]

MAINWARING, Edward, *Calverhall Parsonage, Whitchurch, Salop.*—Brasen. Coll. Ox. B.A. 1814; Deac. 1815, Pr. 1816. P. C. of Calverhall, Dio. Lich. 1843. (Patron, T. T. Heywood, Esq; Glebe, 2 acres; P. C.'s Inc. 82*l* and Ho; Pop. 209.) [24]

MAIR, Henry, *Donhead Lodge, Donhead St. Andrew, Salisbury.*—Trin. Coll. Cam. B.A. 1811, M.A. 1814; Deac. 1812, Pr. 1813. [25]

MAIRIS, Henry, E. H., *Long Ashton, Bristol.*—C. of Long Ashton. [1]

MAIS, John, *Tintern, Chepstow, Monmouthshire.*—Queens' Coll. Cam. B.D. 1837; Deac. 1814 and Pr. 1815 by Bp of B. and W. R. of Tintern, Dio. Llan. 1827. (Patron, Rev. H. Vaughan Hughes; Tithe, 64*l* 11*s* 1*d*; R.'s Inc. 150*l*; Pop. 335.) Formerly Chap. of the Infirmary, Bristol. [2]

MAISTER, Arthur, *Kexby, Yorks.*—Ball. Coll. Ox. 2nd cl. Lit. Hum. 1825, B.A. 1826, M.A. 1829; Deac. 1826, Pr. 1827. P. C. of Kexby, Dio. York, 1853. (Patron, Lord Wenlock; Tithe—App. 4*l* 8*s* 10*d*; Glebe, 35 acres; P. C.'s Inc. 123*l* and Ho; Pop. 182.) [3]

MAISTER, Henry, *Skeffling, Hull.*—New Inn Hall, Ox. B A. 1839, M.A. 1850; Deac. 1839 and Pr. 1840 by Abp of York. P. C. of Easington, Dio. York, 1858. (Patron, Abp of York; Glebe, 23 acres; P. C.'s Inc. 66*l* and Ho; Pop. 666.) V. of Kilnsea, Dio. York, 1858. (Patron, Leonard Thompson, Esq; Tithe, 55*l* 9*s* 4*d*; Glebe, 32 acres; V.'s Inc. 122*l* 11*s* 4*d*; Pop. 181.) Formerly P. C. of Thornaby, near Stockton, 1845–50; C. of Routh, Beverley, 1850–57. [4]

MAITLAND, Brownlow, 41, *Montague-square, London, W.*—Trin. Coll. Cam. 7th Wrang. B.A. 1837, M.A. 1840; Deac. 1841 by Bp of Chich. Pr. 1842 by Bp of Lin. Min. of Brunswick Chapel, Marylebone, Dio. Lon. 1849. (Patron, the Crown.) Formerly Sec. and Chap. to Gen. Sir P. Maitland, G.C.B. Governor of the Cape of Good Hope. [5]

MAITLAND, John Whitaker, *Loughton Rectory, Essex.*—Trin. Hall, Cam. B.A. 1854, M.A. 1857; Deac. 1854 and Pr. 1856 by Bp of Roch. R. of Loughton, Dio. Roch. 1856. (Patron, the present R; Tithe, comm. 518*l*; Glebe, 43 acres; R.'s Inc. 580*l* and Ho; Pop. 1527.) Formerly C. of Bishop Stortford 1854–56. [6]

MAITLAND, Thomas Henry, *South Molton Parsonage, Devon.*—Oriel Coll. Ox. 3rd cl. Lit. Hum. and B.A. 1830, M.A. 1832; Deac. 1831 and Pr. 1832. P. C. of South Molton, Dio. Ex. 1833. (Patrons, D. and C. of Windsor; Tithe—App. 910*l* and 240 acres of Glebe; P. C.'s Inc. 248*l* and Ho; Pop. 3830.) [7]

MAJENDIE, Arthur, *Lamborne, Berks.*—C. of Lamborne. [8]

MAJENDIE, Henry William, *Speen Vicarage, Newbury, Berks.*—Trin. Coll. Cam. B.A. 1812, M.A. 1818; Deac. 1814, Pr. 1815. V. of Speen, Dio. Ox. 1819. (Patron, Bp of Ox; Tithe—App. 120*l*, V. 16*l*; Glebe, 7 acres; V.'s Inc. 220*l* and Ho; Pop. 729.) Preb. of Ban. 1818. (Value, 318*l* 5*s* 8*d*.) Preb. of Salis. 1824; Rural Dean 1827. [9]

MAJENDIE, Henry William, *Cropredy, Oxon.*—Ex. Coll. Ox. B.A. 1862, M.A. 1866; Deac. 1866 by Bp of Ox. C. of Cropredy 1866. [10]

MAJENDIE, Stuart, *Barnwell, Oundle, Northants.*—Ch. Ch. Ox. B.A. 1822; Deac. 1822 and Pr. 1823 by Bp of Ban. R. of Barnwell St. Andrew and Barnwell All Saints' R. Dio. Pet. 1860. (Patron, Duke of Buccleuch; R.'s Inc. 308*l*; Pop. 355.) Formerly V. of Longdon, Staffs, 1823–60. [11]

MAJOR, John Richardson, 42, *Bloomsbury-square, London, W.C.*—Trin. Coll. Cam. B.A. 1819, M.A. 1827, D.D. 1838; Deac. 1821 by Bp of Lon. Pr. 1821 by Bp of Nor. Formerly Mast. of Wisbech Gr. Sch. 1826–30; V. of Wartling, Hurst Green, Sussex, 1846–51; Head Mast. of King's Coll. Sch. Lond. 1830–66. Editor of *Stephen's Greek Thesaurus*; *Five Plays of Euripides*; *Gospel of St. Luke*; *Milton's Paradise Lost*; Portions of *Homer, Virgil, Herodotus, and Xenophon*; *Guide to the Reading of the Greek Tragedians*; *Questions on Mitford's History of Greece*; *Latin Grammar, Exercises, and Reader*; *Initia Græca*; *Initia Homerica*, and other School Books. [12]

MAJOR, John Richardson, *The College, Wye, Kent.*—Ex. Coll. Ox. B.A. 1843, M.A. 1847; Deac. 1851 and Pr. 1852 by Bp of Lon. Head Mast. of Wye Coll. 1867. Formerly Mast. of Thetford Gr. Sch; Sec. of the Photographic Soc. of Lond. 1856; Mast. in King's Coll. Sch. Lond. 1846–56; Head Mast. of the Crypt Sch. Gloucester, 1856–67. Author, *Scripture Maps, with Key.* Editor of *The Photographic Journal for* 1856. [13]

MAJOR, Seymour Edward, 34, *St. Paul's-road, Walworth, S.*—C. of St. Paul's, Walworth. [14]

MALAM, William, *Youlgreave Vicarage, Bakewell, Derbyshire.*—Dub. Scho. of, A.B. 1849, Caius Coll. Cam. Scho. of, B.A. 1864; Deac. 1856 by Bp of Rip. Pr. 1857 by Abp of York. V. of Youlgreave, Dio. Lich. 1865. (Patron, Duke of Devonshire; V.'s Inc. 230*l* and Ho; Pop. 2111.) Formerly C. of Trinity, Sheffield, 1856–57, St. Peter's, Hull, 1858–59, Ch. Ch. Bradford, 1860–61, Freckenham, Suffolk, 1861–64; P. C. of Dishforth and Marton-le-Moor, Yorks, 1864–65. [15]

MALAN, Salomon Cesar, *Broadwindsor, Beaminster, Dorset.*—Ball. Coll. Ox. Boden Sanscrit Scho. 1834; Pusey and Ellerton Heb. Scho. 2nd cl. Lit. Hum. and B.A. 1837, M.A. 1843; Deac. 1838 by Bp of Calcutta, Pr. 1843 by Bp of Win; V. of Broadwindsor, Dio. Salis. 1845. (Patron, Bp of Salis; Tithe—App. 530*l*, Imp. 2*l* 10*s*, V. 50*l*; Glebe, 7 acres; V.'s Inc. 650*l* and Ho; Pop. 1516.) Sec. to the Asiatic Soc. of Bengal 1839; Mem. of the Soc. of Northern Antiquaries, Copenhagen, 1840; formerly Sen. Cl. Prof. at Bishop's Coll. Calcutta, 1838; Rural Dean and Dioc. Inspector of Schs. 1846–53. Author, *Persomache Herodotica, a Tabular Analysis of Herodotus,* Oxford, 1835; *An Outline of Bishop's College and of its Missions*, Burns, 1843; *Family Prayers*, 1844; *A Plain Exposition of the Apostles' Creed*, Crewkerne, 1847; *A Systematic Catalogue of the Eggs of British Birds*, Van Voorst, 1848; *List of British Birds*, ib. 1849; *Who is God in China—Shin or Shang-Te? Remarks on the Etymology of Elohim and of Theos, and on the rendering of those Terms into Chinese*, 8vo, Bagster, 1855; *Three Months in the Holy Land* ("Journal of Sacred Literature"); *A Vindication of the Authorised Version*, Bell and Daldy, 1856; *The Threefold Santsze-King, or Triliteral Classic of China, translated into English, with Notes*, Nutt, 1856; *Magdala and Bethany*, Masters, 1857; *The Coasts of Tyre and Sidon*, ib. 1858; *A Letter to the Right Hon. the Earl of Shaftesbury, on the Buddhistic and Pantheistic Tendency of the Chinese and Mongolian Versions of the Bible published by the British and Foreign Bible Society*, Bell and Daldy, 1856; *Aphorisms on Drawing*, Longmans, 1856; *Letters to a Young Missionary*, Masters, 1858; *Prayers and Thanksgivings for the Holy Communion, translated from Armenian, Coptic, and other Eastern Rituals, for the Use of the Clergy*, Masters, 1859; *Meditations and Prayers of S. Ephraem, translated from the Russian*, Masters, 1859; *The Gospel according to St. John, translated from the Eleven oldest Versions, except the Latin, viz., the Syriac, Ethiopic, Armenian, Sahidic, Memphitic, Gothic, Armenian, Georgian, Slavonic, Anglo-Saxon, Arabic, and Persian, with Foot Notes to every Translation, and a Criticism on all the* 1340 *Alterations proposed by "the Five Clergymen" in their Revision of that Gospel*, Masters, 1862; *Preparation for the Holy Communion, translated from Coptic, Armenian, and other Eastern originals, for the Use of the Laity*, Masters, 1863; *Meditations on our Lord's Passion, translated from the Armenian of Matthew Vartabed*, Masters, 1863; *A Manual of Daily Prayers, translated from Armenian and other Eastern originals*, Masters, 1863; *Philosophy, or Truth? Remarks on the first five Lectures by the Dean of Westminster on the Jewish Church, with Plain Words on Questions of the Day, regarding Faith, the Bible, and the Church*, Masters, 1865; *History of the Georgian Church, translated from the Russian of P. Joselian*, Saunders and Otley, 1866; *Sermons by Gabriel, Bishop of Imereth, translated from the Georgian*, Saunders and Otley, 1867; *Repentance, translated from the Syriac of S. Ephraem*, Masters, 1867; *Thoughts for every Day in Lent, translated from Eastern Fathers and Divines*, Masters, 1867; *On Ritualism*, Saunders and Otley, 1867; *An Outline of the Early Jewish Church, from a Christian Point of View*, Saunders and Otley, 1867. [16]

MALCOLM, Archibald, *Dune-Tew, Deddington, Oxon.*—Trin. Coll. Cam. B.A. 1837, M.A. 1842; Deac. 1838 and Pr. 1839 by Bp of Wor. V. of Dune-Tew, Dio. Ox. 1841. (Patron, Sir Henry William Dashwood, Bart;

Glebe, 180 acres; V.'s Inc. 280*l* and Ho; Pop. 407.) [1]

MALDEN, Bingham Sibthorpe, *Pattingham, Wolverhampton.*—Caius Coll. Cam. B.A. 1853; Deac. 1853 by Bp of Chich. Pr. 1855 by Bp of Nor. C. of Pattingham. Formerly C. of St. George the Martyr with St. Mary Magdalen's, Canterbury. [2]

MALDEN, Clifford, *St. Lawrence, Ventnor, Isle of Wight.*—Trin. Coll. Cam. B.A. 1855, M.A. 1859; Deac. 1856 and Pr. 1857 by Bp of Ox. R. of St. Lawrence, Dio. Win. 1865. (Patron, Hon. E. Pelham; R.'s Inc. 110*l* and Ho; Pop. 80.) Formerly C. of Datchet, Windsor; P. C. of Raughton Head, Carlisle, 1860-65. [3]

MALDEN, Myers Dallas, *Farnham, Surrey.*—Emman. Coll. Cam. B.A. 1858; Deac. 1858 and Pr. 1860 by Bp of Roch. Sen. C. of Farnham 1865. Formerly C. of Bengeo, Herts, 1860-62, St. Paul's, Tiverton, 1862-65. [4]

MALE, Arthur Somery, *More Rectory, Bishops Castle, Salop.*—St. Peter's Coll. Cam. B.A. 1847, M.A. 1850; Deac. 1848 and Pr. 1849 by Bp of Herf. R. of More, Dio. Herf. 1860. (Patron, Rev. T. F. More; Tithe, 250*l*; Glebe, 15 acres; R.'s Inc. 270*l* and Ho; Pop. 280.) Formerly C. of Bitterley, near Ludlow, 1849, Bremhill, Wilts, 1850-60. [5]

MALE, Christopher Parr, *Cotes Heath, Stone, Staffs.*—Ch. Coll. Cam. B.A. 1843, M.A. 1847; Deac. 1846 and Pr. 1847 by Bp of Wor. P. C. of Cotes Heath, Dio. Lich. 1863. (Patron, V. of Eccleshall; P. C.'s Inc. 150*l* and Ho; Pop. 471.) Formerly Asst. Mast. in King Edward's Sch. Birmingham. [6]

MALET, James Hudson, *Pembroke.*—V. of Martle Twy, Pembrokeshire, Dio. St. D. 1846. (Patron, Hon. Captain Greville; Tithe—Imp. 100*l* 5*s* 7*d*, V. 80*l* 4*s* 5*d*; Glebe, 4 acres; V.'s Inc. 108*l*; Pop. 703.) Chap. of Her Majesty's Dockyard, Pembroke, 1845. [7]

MALET, William Wyndham, *Ardeley Vicarage, Buntingford, Herts,* and 7, *Whitehall, London, S.W.*—Magd. Hall, Ox; Deac. 1835 and Pr. 1836 by Bp of Nor. V. of Ardeley, Dio. Roch. 1843. (Patrons, D. and C. of St. Paul's Cathl; Tithe—Imp. 556*l*, V. 180*l*; Glebe, 50 acres; V.'s Inc. 285*l* and Ho; Pop. 574.) Hon. Sec. to the Tithe Redemption Trust, 7, Whitehall. Formerly C. of Dowlish Wake, Somerset, 1837, St. Cuthbert's, Wells, 1840, St. John's, Bedminster, 1840-43; previously on the Bombay Establishment of the Hon. E.I.C.'s Civil Service, 1823-34. Author, Pamphlets *On Church Extension by Restoration of Alienated Tithes,* 1840; *Letter to Lord Lyttelton on Behalf of the Tithe Redemption Trust,* 1846; *Letter to Rt. Hon. Justice Coleridge on the Education of the Children of the Poor,* 1847; *Letter to the Rt. Hon. M. T. Baines, M.P, on the New Poor Law, in Behalf of Local Self-Government,* 1848; *Letter to the Archbishop of Canterbury on the Funds of the Church,* 1849; *Sermon on the Militia Service,* 1852; *Letter to the Earl of Aberdeen on Church-rates not Required if Tithes were Restored,* 1853; *Errand to the South, or a Six Months' Visit to the Carolinas and Virginia in 1862 during the Civil War,* Bentley, 1863. [8]

MALIM, George, *Higham-Ferrers, Northants.*—Lin. Coll. Ox. 3rd cl. Lit. Hum. and B.A. 1830, Deac. 1830, Pr. 1831. V. of Higham-Ferrers with Chelveston C. Dio. Pet. 1837. (Patron, Earl Fitzwilliam; Tithe, 180*l*; Land and other sources, 185*l*; V.'s Inc. 365*l* and Ho; Pop. 1606.) Rural Dean; Surrogate. [9]

MALIM, Henry, *Hatcham, Deptford, S.E.*—C. of St. James's, Hatcham, 1864. [10]

MALKIN, William, 9, *Lansdowne-circus, Leamington.*—Magd. Coll. Cam. B.A. 1816; Deac. and Pr. 1816. P. C. of Hunningham, Leamington, Dio. Wor. 1863. (Patron, Ld Chan; P. C.'s Inc. 70*l*; Pop. 253.) Formerly Chap. Hon. E.I.C. Service, 1816-48. Author, *Sermons on the Truth of the Christian Religion,* 1825, 12*s*. [11]

MALLAM, Benjamin, *Poole-Keynes Rectory (Wilts), near Cirencester.*—St. John's Coll. Ox. 4th cl. Lit. Hum. B.A. 1850, M.A. 1853; Deac. 1852 and Pr. 1853 by Bp of G. and B. R. of Poole-Keynes, Dio. G. and B. 1862. (Patron, Chan. of Duchy of Lancaster; Tithe, 5*l* 14*s* 4*d*; Glebe, 213 acres; R.'s Inc. 370*l* and Ho; Pop. 130.) Formerly Sen. C. of St. Peter's, Burnley, Lancashire, 1856-62. [12]

MALLESON, Edward, *Baldersby Parsonage, Thirsk.*—Queen's Coll. Ox. B.A. 1853, M.A. 1856; Deac. 1852, Pr. 1853. P. C. of Baldersby, Dio. York, 1863. (Patroness, Viscountess Downe; P. C.'s Inc. 300*l* and Ho; Pop. 713.) Formerly C. of All Saints', Oxford, and Horspath, near Oxford, Dalton, Yorks; V. of Wold Newton, York, 1860-63. Author, *The Life of Faith* (a Sermon on the Death of the Rev. Dr. Neale), Hayes, 1866, 6*d*. [13]

MALLESON, Frederick Amadeus, *Enfield, Claughton, Birkenhead.*—Dub. A.B. 1858, A.M. 1860; Deac. 1853, Pr. 1855. Formerly C. of West Kirby 1853, St. Anne's, Birkenhead, 1855-56. [14]

MALLINSON, James Gill, *Breedon, Ashby-de-la-Zouch.*—St. Bees 1847; Deac. 1847, Pr. 1848. C. of Breedon. Formerly C. of St. Jude's, Manchester. [15]

MALLINSON, Richard, *Arkholme Parsonage, near Lancaster.*—Literate; Deac. 1817, Pr. 1818. P. C. of Arkholme, Dio. Man. 1829. (Patron, V. of Melling; P. C.'s Inc. 60*l* and Ho; Pop. 331.) [16]

MALLINSON, Whiteley, *Cross Stone, Todmorden, Yorks.*—Magd. Coll. Cam. Wrang. and B.A. 1839; M.A. 1842; Deac. 1840, Pr. 1841. P. C. of Cross Stone, Dio. Rip. 1845. (Patron, V. of Halifax; P. C.'s Inc. 300*l* and Ho; Pop. 8045.) Formerly Fell. of Magd. Coll. Cam. [17]

MALLOCK, Rawlin, *Yeovil, Somerset.*—Magd. Coll. Cam. B.C.L. 1822; Deac. 1823 and Pr. 1824 by Bp of Ex. [18]

MALLOCK, William, *Cheriton-Bishop Rectory, near Exeter.*—Ball. Coll. Ox. B.A. 1831, M.A. 1834, B.D. 1841; Deac. 1832, Pr. 1833. R. of Cheriton-Bishop, Dio. Ex. 1844. (Patron, Bp of Ex; Tithe, 399*l*; Glebe, 50 acres; R.'s Inc. 459*l* and Ho; Pop. 696.) [19]

MALLORY, George, *Old Hall, Moberley, Knutsford, Cheshire.*—Deac. 1829, Pr. 1830. R. of Moberley, Dio. Ches. 1832. (Patroness, Mrs. Mallory; Tithe, 600*l*; Glebe, 94 acres; R.'s Inc. 775*l*; Pop. 1245.) [20]

MALONE, Richard, *St. Paul Vicarage, near Penzance.*—Queens' Coll. Cam. Scho. of, 1st Sen. Opt. B.A. 1846, M.A. 1849; Deac. 1846 by Bp of Chich. Pr. 1849 by Bp of Lon. V. of St. Paul, Cornwall, Dio. Ex. 1866. (Patron, Ld Chan; V.'s Inc. 580*l* and Ho; Pop. 2168.) Formerly C. of Bexhill, Sussex, 1846-47; Tut. to the Earl of Kintore 1847-49; C. of St. Michael's, Pimlico, 1849; P. C. of Ch. Ch. Plymouth, 1849-50, P. C. of St. Matthew's, Westminster, 1851-66. [21]

MALPAS, Henry, *Clifton, Bristol.*—St. Edm. Hall, Ox. B.A. 1840, M.A. 1847; Deac. 1840, Pr. 1841. Chap. to the Clifton Union. Formerly C. of Corse, Gloucester. [22]

MALPAS, Joseph Henry, *Awre Vicarage, Newnham, Glouc.*—Ex. Coll. Ox. B.A. 1813, M.A. 1816; Deac. 1813 by Bp of Lich. Pr. 1813 by Bp of Ches. V. of Awre, Dio. G. and B. 1826. (Patron, the Haberdashers' Company; Tithe—Imp. 400*l*, V. 450*l* 7*s* 2*d*; Glebe, 6½ acres; V.'s Inc. 560*l* and Ho; Pop. 447.) Formerly C. of Measham, Derbyshire, 1813-26. [23]

MALPAS, William, *Portsmouth.*—Pemb. Coll. Ox. B.A. 1845, M.A. 1848; Deac. 1846 and Pr. 1847 by Bp of G. and B. Formerly Chap. to the Mariners' Chapel, Gloucester, 1855-58; C. of Ch. Ch. South Mimms, near Barnet, and St. Mary's, Portsmouth. [24]

MALTBY, Brough, *Farndon, near Newark, Notts.*—St. John's Coll. Cam. Scho. of, 1847, 1st cl. Prizeman, B.A. 1850, M.A. 1853; Deac. 1850 and Pr. 1851 by Bp of Herf. V. of Farndon, Dio. Lin. 1864. (Patron, Bp of Lin; Glebe, 52 acres; V.'s Inc. 300*l* and Ho; Pop. 692.) Formerly C. of Westbury, Salop, 1850, Whatton, Notts, 1851-64; Off. Min. of Sibthorpe 1855-64; Dioc. Inspector of Schs. for the Rural Deaneries of Newark and Bingham, Notts, 1856. [25]

MALTBY, James William, *Morton Rectory, Alfreton, Derbyshire.*—St. John's Coll. Cam. B.A. 1852; Deac. 1852 and Pr. 1854 by Bp of Lin. R. of Morton,

Dio. Lich. 1864. (Patrons, St. John's Coll. Cam. and G. Turbatt, Esq. alt; R.'s Inc. 360*l* and Ho; Pop. 594.) Formerly C. of Gotham and Clifton, Notts. [1]

MALTHUS, Henry, *Effingham Vicarage, Leatherhead, Surrey.*—Trin. Coll. Cam. B.A. 1829, M.A. 1832; Deac. 1829 and Pr. 1834 by Bp of Win. V. of Donnington, Sussex, Dio. Chich. 1837. (Patron, Bp of Ox; Tithe—Imp. 224*l* 3*s* 6*d*, V. 317*l* 3*s* 5*d*; Glebe, 15 acres; V.'s Inc. 367*l* and Ho; Pop. 188.) V. of Effingham, Dio. Win. (Patron, Ld Chan; Tithe—Imp. 413*l* 19*s*, V. 120*l* 10*s*; Glebe, 9 acres; V.'s Inc. 135*l* and Ho; Pop. 612.) [2]

MAN, John Thomas, *Cardiff.*—King's Coll. Lond. Theol. Assoc; Deac. 1849 and Pr. 1850 by Bp of Win. Chap. of the Sailors' Home and C. of St. Mary's, Cardiff, 1861. Formerly C. of Heckfield, Hants, 1849, St. Giles'-in-the-Fields, Lond. 1851, St. John's, Southwark, 1853, Waltham Abbey, Essex, 1856, Little Stukeley, Hunts, 1856, Stonehouse, Devon, 1859. [3]

MANBEY, William, *Doddinghurst Rectory, near Ingatestone, Essex.*—Queen's Coll. Ox. B.A. 1829, M.A. 1832; Deac. 1830, Pr. 1831. R. of Doddinghurst, Dio. Roch. 1849. (Patroness, Mrs. Manbey; Tithe, 630*l* 7*s* 3*d*; Glebe, 18 acres; R.'s Inc. 687*l* and Ho; Pop. 394.) [4]

MANBY, Aaron, *Farnham Lodge, Knaresborough, Yorks.*—St. John's Coll. Cam. Jun. Opt. and B.A. 1847; Deac. and Pr. 1848 by Abp of York. V. of Nidd, near Knaresborough, Dio. Rip. 1854. (Patron, Duchy of Lancaster; Tithe, 35*l*; Glebe, 46 acres; V.'s Inc. 103*l*; Pop. 141.) [5]

MANBY, Charles, *Bisbrooke, near Uppingham, Rutland.*—C. of Bisbrooke. [6]

MANBY, Edward Francis, *Poulton-le-Sands, near Lancaster.*—Ch. Coll. Cam. B.A. 1840; Deac. 1841, Pr. 1842. R. of Poulton-le-Sands, Dio. Man. 1842. (Patron, V. of Lancaster; Glebe, 17 acres; R.'s Inc. 180*l* and Ho; Pop. 2228.) [7]

MANBY, John Ralph George, *Overton, near Lancaster.*—Brasen. Coll. Ox. B.A. 1836, M.A. 1840. P. C. of Overton, Dio. Man. 1838. (Patron V. of Lancaster; Tithe, Imp. 41*l* 14*s*; P. C.'s Inc. 155*l*; Pop. 305.) [8]

MANCHESTER, The Right Rev. James Prince LEE, Lord Bishop of Manchester, *Mauldeth Hall, near Manchester.* — Trin. Coll. Cam. Craven Scho. 1827, B.A. 1828, M.A. 1831, B.D. and D.D. 1848. Consecrated Bp of Man. 1848. (Episcopal Jurisdiction, the Deaneries of Amounderness, Blackburn, Manchester and Leyland; the Deanery of Tunstal (being such parts of the Deaneries of Kendal and Kirkby Lonsdale as are in Lancashire) and the Parish of Leigh; Inc. of See, 4200*l*; Pop. 1.679,326; Acres, 845,904; Deaneries, 15; Benefices, 384; Curates, 203; Church Sittings, 301,536.) His Lordship was formerly Fell. of Trin. Coll. Cam; Asst. Mast. of Rugby Sch. 1830–38; Head Mast. of King Edward VI.'s Sch. Birmingham, 1838–48. Author, *A Charge* (at the Primary Visitation), 1851; *A Sermon for the S.P.G.* (published in the Society's Report), 1853; *A Charge*, 1855; *A Sermon on the Death of the Prince Consort*, 1862. [9]

MANCLARKE, Richard Palgrave, *Woodland, Ulverston, Lancashire.*—Wad. Coll. Ox. B.A. 1849, M.A. 1852; Deac. 1851 and Pr. 1852 by Abp of York. P. C. of Woodland, Dio. Carl. 1861. (Patrons, Landowners; P. C.'s Inc. 68*l*; Pop. 303.) Formerly C. of Cotesbach, Leic. 1853–58; P. C. of Kilnwick, Yorks, 1858–61. [10]

MANCLARKE, William Palgrave, *Norwich.*—Jesus Coll. Cam. B.A. 1817, M.A. 1820; Deac. 1818 and Pr. 1819 by Bp of Nor. Incapacitated by blindness. [11]

MANDALE, Blain, *Ripple Rectory, Deal.*—R. of Ripple, Dio. Cant. 1827. (Patrons, Sir J. G. Sinclair and Rev. A. B. Mesham; R.'s Inc. 200*l* and Ho; Pop. 254.) [12]

MANDALE, Blain, *Bishops Itchington, Leamington.*—Trin. Coll. Cam. B.A. 1847, M.A. 1849; Deac. 1848 by Bp of Ches. Pr. 1849 by Bp of Lich. V. of Bishops Itchington with Chadshunt C. and Gaydon C. Dio. Wor. 1866. (Patron, Bp of Lich; Tithe, 308*l* 9*s*; Glebe, 230 acres; V.'s Inc. 560*l* and Ho; Pop. 927.) Formerly C. of Heanor 1848, Staveley 1851, North Wingfield 1863. [13]

MANDUELL, Matthewman, *Tetford, Horncastle, Lincolnshire.*—Queen's Coll. Ox. B.A. 1830; Deac. 1831 and Pr. 1832 by Bp of Lin. C. of Tetford. [14]

MANGIN, Edward Nangreave, *Woodhorn Vicarage, Morpeth, Northumberland.*—Wad. Coll. Ox. B.A. 1839, M.A. 1839; Deac. 1840 by Bp of Rip. Pr. 1841 by Bp of Dur. V. of Woodhorn with Newbiggen C. Dio. Dur. 1865. (Patron, Bp of Dur; Tithe, 620*l*; Glebe, 70 acres; V.'s Inc. 620*l* and Ho; Pop. Woodhorn 1506, Newbiggen 948.) Formerly V. of Horsley, Glouc. 1849–61; R. of Howick, Northumberland, 1862–65. [15]

MANGIN, Samuel Wareing, 12, *Highbury New Park, London, N.*—Wad. Coll. Ox. B.A. 1843; Deac. 1844 by Bp of G. and B. Pr. 1845 by Bp of B. and W. P. C. of St. Columba's, Haggerston, Dio. Lon. 1863. (Patrons, Trustees; P. C.'s Inc. 200*l*; Pop. 7000.) Formerly P. C. of St. Matthias', Stoke Newington, Lond. 1854–58, Holy Trinity, Headington Quarry, Oxon. 1858–63. [16]

MANGLES, Albert, *Beech Hill, Woking, Surrey.*—Mert. Coll. Ox. 2nd cl. Lit. Hum. and B.A. 1829, M.A. 1832; Deac. 1832, Pr. 1833. P. C. of Horsell, Surrey, Dio. Win. 1840. (Patrons, Three Landowners; Tithe, Imp. 420*l* 19*s* 3*d*; P. C.'s Inc. 83*l*; Pop. 788.) [17]

MANGLES, Arthur Onslow, 25, *Lewes-crescent, Brighton.*—Magd. Coll. Ox. B.A. 1858; Deac. 1858, Pr. 1859. C. of Brighton 1864. Formerly C. of Churchstoke, Salop, 1858, Steeple Aston, Oxon, 1861, Horspath, Oxford, 1862. [18]

MANING, Naasson, *Hooe Vicarage, near Battle, Sussex.*—Dub. A.B 1834; Deac. 1835 by Bp of Kildare, Pr. 1836 by Bp of St. A. V. of Hooe, Dio. Chich. 1857. (Patron, Alfred Jones, Esq; Tithe, 337*l*; Glebe, 3 acres; V.'s Inc. 342*l* and Ho; Pop. 496.) Formerly C. of Monastreven, Ireland, 1835, Whittington, Salop, 1836; P. C. of Trinity, Huddersfield, 1838–57. [19]

MANING, Parsons James, *Farsley Parsonage, Leeds.*—Deac. 1839, Pr. 1840. P. C. of Farsley, Dio. Rip. 1846. (Patron, V. of Calverley; P. C.'s Inc. 150*l* and Ho; Pop. 3117.) [20]

MANING, Thomas Anthony, *Isleham Vicarage, Soham, Cambs.*—Dub. A.B. 1843, A.M. 1855; Deac. 1847 and Pr. 1848 by Bp of Pet. V. of Isleham, Dio. Ely, 1855. (Patron, Bp of Pet; Tithe—App. 620*l*, Imp. 112*l* 10*s*, V. 496*l* 8*s*; V.'s Inc. 500*l* and Ho; Pop. 1925.) Formerly C. of Fiskerton, Linc. [21]

MANING, Thomas Henry, *Clayton, Bradford, Yorks.*—Dub. A.B. 1840; Deac. 1842 by Bp of Rip. Pr. 1843 by Bp of Pet. P. C. of Clayton, Dio. Rip. 1851. (Patron, V. of Bradford; Tithe—App. 20*l*, Imp. 23*l* 9*s* 3½*d*; P. C.'s Inc. 100*l*; Pop. 3228.) [22]

MANISTY, James, *Easington Rectory, Castle Eden, Durham.*—Lin. Coll. Ox. B.A. 1828, M.A. 1831. R. of Easington, Dio. Dur. 1862. (Patron, Bp of Dur; R.'s Inc. 1100*l* and Ho; Pop. 1536.) Rural Dean. Formerly P. C. of Shildon, Durham, 1834–62. [23]

MANLEY, John, *Merstham, Reigate, Surrey.*—Univ. Coll. Ox. B.A. 1813, M.A. 1818; Deac. 1816, Pr. 1817. R. of Merstham, Dio. Win. 1839. (Patron, Abp of Cant; Tithe, 580*l*; Glebe, 25¾ acres; R.'s Inc. 615*l* and Ho; Pop. 846.) Formerly C. of Amersham, Bucks, and East Peckham and Wrotham, Kent; V. of Godmersham and of Westwell, Kent. [24]

MANLEY, John Jackson, *Cottered Rectory, Buntingford, Herts.*—Ex. Coll. Ox. 3rd cl. Lit. Hum. and B.A. 1852, M.A. 1855. Theol. Coll. Wells; Deac. 1853, Pr. 1854. R. of Cottered with Broadfield, R. Dio. Roch. 1861. (Patron, the present R; Glebe, 320 acres; R.'s Inc. 500*l* and Ho; Pop. 489.) Formerly C. of Dawlish 1854–55, Tiverton 1856–57; V. of Buckfastleigh, Devon,

1858–60. Author, *Religious Agitation* (a Sermon), Dawlish. [1]

MANLEY, John Thomas, *Tunbridge, Kent.*—Trin. Coll. Cam. B.A. 1852, M.A. 1855; Deac. 1852 and Pr. 1853 by Bp of Win. V. of Tunbridge, Dio. Cant. 1864. (Patroness, Mrs. Deacon; Tithe, 900*l*; V.'s Inc. 1000*l* and Ho; Pop. 3308.) Formerly C. of Clapham 1852–55; P. C. of Mortlake, Surrey, 1855–64. [2]

MANLEY, Mortimer, *Rainham Vicarage, Romford, Essex.*—Queens' Coll. Cam. B.A. 1845, M.A. 1853; Deac. 1845 and Pr. 1846 by Bp of Nor. C. in sole charge of Rainham 1865. Formerly C. of Baconsthorpe, Norfolk, 1845–54, Mistley, Essex, 1854–63; C. in sole charge of Stoke, Kent, 1863–65. [3]

MANLEY, Nicholas Mortimer, *Morton Rectory, Norwich.*—St. John's Coll. Cam. late Platt. Fell. of St. John's, Tyrwhitt Hebrew Scho. 17th Wrang. and B.A. 1838, M.A. 1841; Deac. 1841 and Pr. 1842 by Bp of Ely. R. of Morton-on-the-Hill, Dio. Nor. 1860. (Patron, T. T. Berney, Esq; Tithe, 180*l*; Glebe, 6 acres; R.'s Inc. 190*l* and Ho; Pop. 147.) Formerly C. of Stibbard, Norfolk, 1843–57; Morton-on-the-Hill 1857–60. [4]

MANLEY, Orlando, *St. Paul's Parsonage, Devonport.*—Trin. Coll. Cam. B.A. 1844; Deac. 1846 and Pr. 1847 by Bp of Ex. P. C. of St. Paul's, Devonport, Dio. Ex. 1865. (Patrons, Crown and Bp alt; P. C.'s Inc. 300*l* and Ho; Pop. 8750.) Formerly C. of St. Keverne, Cornwall, 1846–54, Helston 1854–57; P. C. of St. John's, Truro, 1857–65. [5]

MANLEY, Richard Henry, *Handley, Salisbury.*—Clare Coll. Cam. Fell. of, 1858, Burney Prizeman, Chan.'s Medallist for Legal Studies, 1st cl. Moral Sci. Trip. Wrang. and B.A. 1857, M.A. 1860; Deac. 1858 and Pr. 1859 by Abp of York. C. of Handley with Gussage St. Andrew, Dorset. Formerly C. of North Cave, Yorks, 1858–62, North Luffenham, Rutland, 1862–63, Edith Weston 1863. Author, *The Discipline afforded by External Events and Circumstances, and by Intercourse with others in forming the Moral Character* (Burney Prize Essay). [6]

MANLEY, William Lewis, *Treleigh, Redruth, Cornwall.*—Ch. Coll. Cam. B.A. 1846; Deac. 1846, Pr. 1847. P. C. of Treleigh, Dio. Ex. 1848. (Patrons, the Crown and Bp of Ex. alt; P. C.'s Inc. 150*l*; Pop. 2349.) Chap. to the Redruth Union. [7]

MANN, Charles Noel, *St. Issey Vicarage, Cornwall.*—Clare Hall, Cam. B.A. 1845; Deac. 1849 and Pr. 1851 by Bp of Herf. V. of St. Issey, Dio. Ex. 1865. (Patrons, D. and C. of Ex; Tithe, 223*l*; Glebe, 51½ acres; V.'s Inc. 279*l* and Ho; Pop. 756.) Formerly C. of Much Marcle, Herfs, 1849; R. of Mawgan and St. Martin-in-Meneage, Cornwall, 1855. [8]

MANN, Frederick William, *Forest Rectory, Guernsey.*—St. Peter's Coll. Cam. Scho. of, B.A. 1849, M.A. 1852; Deac. 1850 and Pr. 1852 by Bp of Rip. R. of Forest, Guernsey, Dio. Win. 1867. (Patron, Lieut. Gov. of Guernsey; Tithe, 12*l*; Glebe, 20*l*; R.'s Inc. 99*l* and Ho; Pop. 670.) Formerly C. of Patrick Brompton and Hunton, Bedale, Yorks, 1850–53; Wyham with Cadeby and Nun Ormsby, Lincolnshire, 1853–67. [9]

MANN, Joseph, *Kellington Vicarage (Yorks), near Ferry-bridge.*—Trin. Coll. Cam. B.A. 1830, M.A. 1833; Deac. 1833 by Bp of Carl. Pr. 1838 by Bp of Ely. V. of Kellington, Dio. York, 1840. (Patron, Trin. Coll. Cam; Tithe—Imp. 1067*l* 5*s* and 111 acres of Glebe, V. 331*l* 19*s*; Glebe, 38 acres; V.'s Inc. 359*l* and Ho; Pop. 1352.) Formerly Fell. of Trin. Coll. Cam. [10]

MANN, Robert, *Long Whatton Rectory, Loughborough.*—St. John's Coll. Cam. 10th Sen. Opt. and B.A. 1831; Deac. 1831 and Pr. 1832 by Bp of Nor. R. of Long Whatton, Dio. Pet. 1852. (Patron, Ld Chan; R.'s Inc. 380*l* and Ho; Pop. 779.) Dom. Chap. to Lord St. Leonards. [11]

MANN, William Henry Galfridus, *Lichfield.*—Trin. Coll. Cam. B.A. 1816, M.A. 1819; Deac. 1820 by Bp of Glouc. Pr. 1820 by Bp of Salis. Registrar of Dio. Lich. Formerly V. of Bowdon, Cheshire, 1821–56. [12]

MANNERS, John, 6, *Victoria Park-square, London, N.E.*—Corpus Coll. Cam. B.A. 1833, M.A. 1837; Deac. 1841, Pr. 1842. C. in sole charge of St. James's-the-Less, Bethnal Green, Lond. [13]

MANNERS, Otho Augustus, *Hawnby, Helmsley, Yorks.*—Sid. Coll. Cam. B.A. 1843; Deac. 1844 by Abp of York, Pr. 1845 by Bp of Rip. R. of Hawnby, Dio. York, 1852. (Patron, Robert Tennant, Esq; Tithe, 173*l* 2*s* 2*d*; Glebe, 29 acres; R.'s Inc. 214*l* and Ho; Pop. 746.) Chap. of Don. of Old Byland, Dio. York, 1866. (Patron, Sir G. O. Wombwell, Bart; Tithe, Imp. 38*l*; Chap.'s Inc. 56*l* and Ho; Pop. 157.) [14]

MANNING, Alexander, *Long-street, Devizes.*—St. Cath. Coll. Cam. B.A. 1828; Deac. 1828 by Bp of Nor. Pr. 1830 by Bp of Lin. Chap. to the Devizes Gaol. [15]

MANNING, Charles Robertson, *Diss Rectory, Norfolk.*—Corpus Coll. Cam. B.A. 1847, M.A. 1850; Deac. 1848 and Pr. 1850 by Bp of Nor. R. of Diss, Dio. Nor. 1857. (Patron, the present R; Tithe, 903*l*; Glebe, 11 acres; R.'s Inc. 919*l* and Ho; Pop. 3710.) Surrogate; Magistrate of Norfolk; Hon. Sec. of the Norfolk and Norwich Archæological Soc. Author, *A List of Monumental Brasses remaining in England*, Rivingtons. [16]

MANNING, Frederick James, *Springfield, Chelmsford.*—Lin. Coll. Ox. Scho. of, 2nd cl. Lit. Hum. and B.A. 1842, M.A. 1845, B.D. and D.D. 1860; Deac. 1845 and Pr. 1846 by Bp of Lon. C. of Springfield 1852; Head Mast. of Trinity Sch. Springfield, 1857. Formerly C. of Hampstead 1845, Ch. Ch. Westminster, 1851. Author, *Catechetical Examinations for the Use of Parochial Schools*, Simpkin, Marshall and Co; *Morning and Evening Prayers for Schools*, No. 711, S.P.C.K; *Our Christian Simplicity in Danger* (a Sermon at Hampstead), Parker, 1851; *Called to be Saints* (a Sermon), Masters; *The Son of Consolation* (a Sermon), ib. 1856. [17]

MANNING, George William, *Little Petherick, St. Issey, Cornwall.*—St. Bees; Deac. 1838, Pr. 1840. R. of Little Petherick, Dio. Ex. 1862. (Patrons, Exors. of late Sir W. Molesworth; Tithe, 172*l* 10*s*; Glebe, 75*l*; R.'s Inc. 247*l* 10*s* and Ho; Pop. 236.) Formerly C. of Neston, Cheshire, 1838–40, Whittlesey St. Andrew 1841, North Leigh, Devon, 1841–42, Sutton St. Edmund 1842–43, Cheadle, Staffs, 1844; P. C. of St. Juliot, Cornwall, 1844–62, Lesnewth, Cornwall, 1844 55. [18]

MANNING, William, *Elizabeth College, Guernsey.*—Deac. 1851 by Bp of Ex. Pr. 1854 by Bp of Rip. Mast. of the Lower Sch. Elizabeth Coll. and Chap. of the Hospital of St. Peter's Port, Guernsey; Inspector of the Parochial Schs. of Guernsey. [19]

MANSEL, Henry Longueville, *Christ Church, Oxford.*—St. John's Coll. Ox. 1839, Double 1st cl. and B.A. 1843, M.A. 1847, B.D. 1852, D.D. 1867; Deac. 1844 and Pr. 1845 by Bp of Ox. Regius Professor of Ecclesiastical History and Can. of Ch. Ch. 1866; Hon. Can. of Pet; Chap. to Bp of Pet. Formerly Fell. and Tut. of St. John's Coll. Ox; Reader in Moral and Metaphysical Philosophy, Magd. Coll. 1855; Waynflete Professor of Philosophy 1859. Author, *Logic from the Text of Aldrich, with Notes*, Oxford, 1849, 2nd ed. 1852, 3rd ed. 1856; *Prolegomena Logica, an Inquiry into the Psychological Character of Logical Processes*, 1851; *The Limits of Demonstrative Science Considered*, 1853; *Man's Conception of Eternity, an Examination of Mr. Maurice's Theory*, 1854; *Psychology the Test of Moral and Metaphysical Philosophy* (an Inaugural Lecture), 1855; *The Philosophy of Kant* (a Lecture), 1856; Article *Metaphysics*, in 8th ed. of the *Encyclopædia Britannica*, 1857; *The Limits of Religious Thought* (Bampton Lecture for 1858), Murray, 2nd ed. 1858, 3rd ed. 1859, 4th ed. 1859, 5th ed. 1867; *The Witness of the Church to the Promise of Christ's Coming* (a Sermon preached in Cathedral, Canterbury, 1864, at the Consecration of the Bishops of Peterborough, Tasmania, and the Niger), 1864; *The Philosophy of the Conditioned*, 1866. [20]

MANSEL, James Temple, 3, *Leicester-villas, Clifton.*—Ch. Ch. Ox. Stud. of, B.A. 1825, M.A. 1827; Deac. 1825 by Bp of Ox. Pr. 1826 by Abp of Cashel.

Formerly C. of Bagshot, Surrey, 1827–29; Min. of the English Chapel, St. Servan, France, 1830–33; C. of Monmouth 1834–37, Dunkeswell, Devon, 1838–44; Chap. of the Bristol House of Correction 1850–65. [1]

MANSEL, Owen Luttrell, *Church Knowle Rectory, Wareham, Dorset.*—Trin. Coll. Cam. B.A. 1849, M.A. 1852; Deac. 1850, Pr. 1851. R. of Church Knowle, Dio. Salis. 1852. (Patron, J. C. Mansel, Esq; Tithe—Imp. 13*l*, R. 292*l*; R.'s Inc. 310*l* and Ho; Pop. 511.) [2]

MANSELL, James.—Caius Coll. Cam. Cl. and Math. Scho. B.A. 1858; Deac. 1860 and Pr. 1861 by Bp of Win. Min. Can. of Lin. 1865. Formerly C. of Lambeth and Asst. Chap. to the Union, 1860; C. of Trinity, Lambeth, 1861; Preacher in Danish at the Danish Church, Wellclose-square, Lond. 1863; C. of St. Thomas's, Portman-square, Lond. 1863–65. [3]

MANSELL, William S., *Martin Hussingtree, Worcester.*—King's Coll. Lond. Theol. Assoc; Deac. 1864 by Bp of Lich. Pr. 1867 by Bp of Wor. C. of Martin Hussingtree 1867. Formerly C. of Trinity, Shrewsbury, and St. George's, Lilleshall, Salop. [4]

MANSFIELD, Arthur, *Shirehampton, Bristol.*—Ch. Ch. Ox. B.A. 1850, M.A. 1853; Deac. 1850, Pr. 1852. P. C. of Shirehampton, Dio. G. and B. 1859. (Patron, P. C. of Westbury-on-Trym; Glebe, 7 acres; P. C.'s Inc. 37*l* and Ho; Pop. 731.) Formerly C. of Shirehampton. [5]

MANSFIELD, Edward, *Highnam Parsonage, near Gloucester.*—Ex. Coll. Ox. B.A. 1842; Deac. 1843 and Pr. 1844 by Bp of G. and B. P. C. of Highnam, Dio. G. and B. 1851. (Patron, T. G. Parry, Esq; P. C.'s Inc. 126*l* and Ho; Pop. 357.) [6]

MANSFIELD, George, *St. John's Parsonage, North Brixton, London, S.*—Dub. A.B. 1833; Deac. 1838 and Pr. 1839 by Abp of Cant. P. C. of St. John's, Brixton, Dio. Win. 1864. (Patron, W. H. Stone, Esq; Pop. 4967.) Formerly R. of Allhallows the Great and the Less, Lond. 1856–60; P. C. of St. Peter's, Saffron-hill, Lond. 1851–56; V. of Finchingfield, Essex, 1860–64. Author, *Spiritual Conservatism,* 1840; *Look to your Children,* 1849; *Picture of Grace,* Macintosh, 1866, 1*s*. [7]

MANSFIELD, Joseph, *Blandford St. Mary, Dorset.*—Trin. Coll. Ox. B.A. 1837, M.A. 1839; Deac. 1840, Pr. 1841. R. of Blandford St. Mary, Dio. Salis. 1850. (Patroness, Lady Le Poer Trench; Tithe, 300*l*; Glebe, 42 acres; R.'s Inc. 400*l* and Ho; Pop. 409.) Formerly C. of Rockland St. Mary, Norwich, and Shipton Moyne, Gloucestershire; P. C. of New Swindon, Wilts. [8]

MANT, Frederick Woods, *Woodmancote, Micheldever Station, Hants.*—New Inn Hall, Ox. S.C.L. 1841, 2nd cl. Lit. Hum. and B.A. 1844; Deac. 1841 by Bp of Rip. Pr. 1841 by Abp of Dub. P. C. of Woodmancote with Popham, Dio. Win. 1858. (Patron, Lord Ashburton; Tithe—Woodmancote, 168*l* 10*s*; Glebe, 13 acres; Popham, App. 43*l*; P. C.'s Inc. 210*l*; Pop. Woodmancote 87, Popham 124.) Formerly V. of Stanford, Norfolk, 1851–58, and V. of Tottington, Norfolk, 1851–58. Author, *The Rubi,* 1840; *Reginald Vere,* 1848: *Two Sermons* for the 5th of November; *Sermon on the Holy Communion,* 1852; *On the Morning Service,* 1853; *A Sermon* (for Coggeshall Schools), 1853; *A Visitation Sermon,* 1854; *Saxon Ballads and Lays,* Bell and Daldy, 1857. [9]

MANT, Richard, *Clevedon House, Somerset.* [10]

MANTELL, The Very Rev. Edward Reginald, *Gretford Rectory, Stamford.*—Emman. Coll. Cam. Scho. of, B.A. 1821, M.A. 1825; Deac. 1822 by Bp of Bristol, Pr. 1823 by Bp of Ches. R. of Gretford with Wilsthorpe, Dio. Lin. 1859. (Patron, Ld Chan; Tithe, 194*l*; Glebe, 185 acres; R.'s Inc. 525*l* and Ho; Pop. 270.) Surrogate 1832; Hon. Preb. of Louth in Lin. Cathl. 1845; Dean of Stamford (Peculiar) 1863; Rural Dean of Ness 1864. Formerly C. of Dartford, Kent 1823, Bexley, Kent, 1826, Ticehurst, Sussex, 1828; V. of Louth and Tetney, Linc. 1831–59. [11]

MANUS, John L. S., *Braxted, Dunmow, Essex.*—Dur. M.A. 1853; Deac. 1853 and Pr. 1854 by Bp of Pet. C. in sole charge of Braxted 1867. Formerly C. of Good Easter, Essex, 1862–67. [12]

MANWARING, Charles Woollaston, *Stone, near Rotherham.*—Dub. A.M; Deac. 1861 by Bp of Ely, Pr. 1862 by Abp of York. Dom. Chap. to the Earl of Scarborough. Formerly C. of Stainton with Hellaby. [13]

MAPLETON, David, *Meanwood Vicarage, Leeds.*—St. John's Coll. Ox. B.A. 1845, M.A. 1865; Deac. 1846 and Pr. 1847 by Bp of Lich. V. of Meanwood, Dio. Rip. 1850. (Patronesses, Mrs. and Miss Beckett; V.'s Inc. 150*l* and Ho; Pop. 1321.) [14]

MAPLETON, Harvey Mallory, *Badgworth, Weston-super-Mare.*—St. John's Coll. Ox. B.A. 1848, M.A. 1861; Deac. 1849 and Pr. 1850 by Bp of Wor. R. of Badgworth, Dio. B. and W. 1861. (Patron, Sir Charles Mordaunt, Bart. M.P; Tithe, 486*l*; Glebe, 58 acres; R.'s Inc. 600*l*; Pop. 279.) Formerly C. of Nether Whitacre, Warw. 1849–53, Frankley, Worc. 1854–55, Broughton, Oxon, 1855–57; P. C. of Dunstall, Staffs, 1857–61. [15]

MAPLETON, James Henry, *Tarrington, Ledbury, Herefordshire.*—Wor. Coll. Ox. B.A. 1838; Deac. 1839, Pr. 1840. R. of Aylton, Herefordshire, Dio. Herf. 1844. (Patron, Earl of Oxford; Tithe—App. 40*l* 13*s*, R. 124*l* 11*s* 6*d*; Glebe, 23 acres; R.'s Inc. 157*l*; Pop. 89.) [16]

MARAH, William Hennessey, *Little Compton, Moreton-in-the-Marsh, Glouc.*—King's Coll. Lond. Theol. Assoc. Deac. 1852 and Pr. 1853 by Bp of Ox. P. C. of Little Compton, Dio. G. and B. 1857. (Patron, Ch. Ch. Ox; Tithe—Imp. 227 acres of Glebe; P. C.'s Inc. 65*l*; Pop. 398.) Formerly C. of Churchill and Cornwell, Oxon, 1852–55, Ch. Ch. St. Pancras, Lond. 1855–57. [17]

MAROON, Walter, *Edgefield Rectory, Thetford, Norfolk.*—Wor. Coll. Ox. B.A. and S.C.L. 1846; Deac. 1846 and Pr. 1847 by Bp of Win. R. of Edgefield, Dio. Nor. 1848. (Patron, John Maroon, Esq; Tithe, 574*l*; Glebe, 17 acres; R.'s Inc. 604*l* and Ho; Pop. 682.) [18]

MARCUS, Lewis, *St. Paul's Parsonage, Artillery-place West, London, E.C.*—Queens' Coll. Cam. B.A. 1827, M.A. 1831; Deac. 1827 and Pr. 1828 by Bp of Lin. P. C. of St. Paul's, Finsbury, Dio. Lon. 1846. (Patron, R. of St. Luke's; P. C.'s Inc. 360*l* and Ho; Pop. 5896.) Prof. of Latin in the City of London Coll. for Ladies, Finsbury. Formerly Head Mast. of the Holbeach Gr. Sch. Linc. Author, *Village Psalmody.* [19]

MARDEN, Owen, 22, *Norfolk-square, Brighton.*—Trin Hall, Cam. 1st cl. Law Trip. and LL.B. 1818–19; Deac. 1819 by Bp of Salis. Pr. 1820 by Bp of Glouc. V. of Climping, near Arundel, Sussex, Dio. Chich. 1833. (Patron, Eton Coll; Tithe—Imp. 425*l* 3*s* 3*d*, and 7 acres of Glebe, V. 225*l*; Glebe, 45 acres; V.'s Inc. 303*l* and Ho; Pop. 331.) Formerly R. of Trusthorpe, Linc. 1824–31; R. of Greetham, Linc. 1831–33; Incumb. of Hove Chapel, Brighton, 1838–57. [20]

MARE, William Salmon, *Bramham Vicarage, Tadcaster.*—Magd. Coll. Cam. B.A. 1839, M.A. 1842, Licen. in Theol. Univ. Dur. 1848; Deac. 1843 and Pr. 1844 by Bp of Dur. V. of Bramham, Dio. York, 1862. (Patrons, D. and C. of Ch. Ch. Ox; Tithe, 110*l*; Glebe, 72 acres; V.'s Inc. 300*l* and Ho; Pop. 1381.) Formerly C. of Morpeth 1844–53; P. C. of Owlesbury 1853–62; Dom. Chap. to Earl of Durham. [21]

MARETT, Charles, *St. Clement's Rectory, St. Heliers, Jersey.*—Pemb. Coll. Cam. B.A. 1837, M.A. 1846; Deac. 1839, Pr. 1841. R. of St. Clement's, Jersey, Dio. Win. 1842. (Patron, the Governor of Jersey; R.'s Inc. 150*l* and Ho; Pop. 1448.) [22]

MARGESSON, William, *Mountfield Vicarage, Hurst Green, Sussex.*—R. of Whatlington, near Battle, Sussex Dio. Chich. 1821. (Patron, the present R; Tithe, 228*l* 15*s*; Glebe, 9 acres; R.'s Inc. 239*l*; Pop. 343.) V. of Mountfield, Dio. Chich. 1836. (Patron, Earl de la Warr; Tithe—Imp. 173*l* and 20 acres of Glebe, V. 314*l*; Glebe, 20 acres; V.'s Inc. 334*l* and Ho; Pop. 585.) [23]

MARGETTS, Francis Thomas, *Aldburgh, Hull.*—Clare Coll. Cam. B.A. 1843, M.A. 1846; Deac. 1844, Pr. 1846. V. of Aldburgh with Colden Parva P. C. Dio.

York, 1863. (Patron, Ld Chan; V.'s Inc. 500*l*; Pop. 1095.) Formerly V. of Duxford, Cambs, 1853–63. [1]

MARGOLIOUTH, Moses, *Branches-park, Newmarket, Cambs.*—Deac. and Pr. 1844. Dom. Chap. to Sir Robert Pigot, Bart., Branches Park, Newmarket. Formerly C. of Wyton, Hants; Exam. Chap. to Bp of Kildare. Author, *The Fundamental Principles of Modern Judaism Investigated*, 1843, 10*s*; *Israel's Ordinances Examined*, 1844, 2*s*; *An Exposition of the Fifty-third Chapter of Isaiah*, 1846, 7*s* 6*d*; *The Antiquities of the Jews in Great Britain*, 1846, 7*s* 6*d*; *A Pilgrimage to the Land of My Fathers*, 2 vols. 1851, 1*l* 12*s*; *The History of the Jews in Great Britain*, 3 vols. 1851, 1*l* 12*s*; *Vestiges of Genuine Freemasonry amongst the Ruins of Asia and Africa*, 1852, 1*s*; *Genuine Freemasonry indissolubly connected with Revelation*, 1852, 1*s*; *Holmfirth's Solemn Voice*, 1852, 6*d*; *The Apostle's Triple Benediction* (a Farewell Sermon), 1853, 6*d*; *Genuine Repentance and its Effects, forming an Exposition of the Fourteenth Chapter of Hosea*, 1854, 5*s*; *The Anglo-Hebrews, their Past Wrongs and Present Grievances*, 1856, 3*s* 6*d*; *The Lord's Anointed* (a Coronation Sermon preached in the British Chapel at Moscow on the enthronement of Alexander II.), 1856, 1*s*; *The Quarrel of God's Covenant* (a Fast-Day Sermon), 1857, 6*d*; *The Gospel and its Mission* (a Sermon), 1860, 6*d*; *What is Man?* (a Sermon), 1860; *The End of the Law, being a Preliminary Examination of "Essays and Reviews,"* 1861, 3*s*; *The True Light* (a Farewell Sermon on St. Bartholomew's Day), 1862, 6*d*; *England's Crown of Rejoicing* (a Sermon on the Marriage of the Prince of Wales, 1863, 1*s*; *Sacred Minstrelsy, a Lecture on Biblical and Post-Biblical Hebrew Music*, 1863, 2*s* 6*d*; *The Spirit of Prophecy, an Exposition in Four Sermons of Rev.* i. 7, xxii. 20, 1864, 2*s* 6*d*; *The Haidad, a Harvest Thanksgiving Sermon, with Preface and Appendixes for careful Perusal*, 1864, 1*s*; *Abyssinia, its Past, Present, and probable Future*, 1866, 3*s*. Works ready for the Press: *The Hebrew Old Testament, with Critical, Philological, Historical, Polemical, and Expository English Comments, the principal portion of which are original*, 5 vols. 4to; *The History of the Jews from the Great Dispersion to A.D.* 1860, 12 vols. 8vo; *Essays on the Poetry and Music of the Hebrews, Biblical and Post-Biblical*, 2 vols; *The Light of the Gentiles and the Glory of Israel* (Thirty Sermons), 2 vols; *Miscellaneous Lectures*, 2 vols. [2]

MARILLIER, Jacob Francis, *St. Paul's Parsonage, Bedminster, near Bristol.*—Trin. Coll. Cam. B.A. 1847, M.A. 1850; Deac. 1848 and Pr. 1850 by Bp of G. and B. P. C. of St. Paul's, Bedminster, Dio. G. and B. 1852. (Patron, Bp of G. and B; P. C.'s Inc. 150*l* and Ho; Pop. 4416.) Formerly C. of St. Paul's, Bedminster, 1848–52. [3]

MARKBY, Edward, *Swanland, near Brough, Yorks.*—Corpus Coll. Cam. B.A; Deac. 1864 and Pr. 1865 by Bp of Rip. C. of North Ferriby (sole charge) 1867. Formerly C. of Kirkburton 1864 67. [4]

MARKBY, Thomas, *Trinity Hall, Cambridge.*—Trin. Coll. Cam. B.A. 1846, M.A. 1849; Deac. 1848 and Pr. 1849 by Bp of Lon. Sec. to the Syndicate for conducting Local Examinations. Author, *The Man Christ Jesus*, Rivingtons, 1862, 9*s* 6*d*. [5]

MARKER, George Townsend, *The Vicarage, Uffculme, Devon.*—Ball. Coll. Ox. B.A; Deac. 1818 and Pr. 1819 by Bp of Ex. V. of Uffculme, Dio. Ex. 1833. (Patron, Bp of Ex; V.'s Inc. 600*l* and Ho; Pop. 2020.) Formerly C. of Upper Ottery, Devon, 1818–33. [6]

MARKHAM, Charles Warren, *Goddington, Bicester, Oxon.*—Magd. Coll. Cam. the Reading Prize and B.A. 1857, M.A. 1861; Deac. 1858 by Bp of Pet. Pr. 1859 by Bp of Man. R. of Goddington, Dio. Ox. 1866. (Patron, Corpus Coll. Ox; R.'s Inc. 334*l*; Pop. 85.) Formerly C. of Oundle, Northants, 1858–60; V. of Owston, near Doncaster, 1860–62, P. C. of Tong, Bradford, 1862. [7]

MARKHAM, William Rice, *Morland Vicarage, Penrith.*—Ch. Ch. Ox. B.A. 1824; Deac. 1826, Pr. 1827. V. of Morland, Dio. Carl. 1828. (Patrons, D. and C. of Carl; Tithe—Imp. 10*l*, App. 359*l* 12*s* 1½*d*, V. 32*l*; Glebe, 180 acres; V.'s Inc. 150*l* and Ho; Pop. 1336.) [8]

MARLAND, Henry, *Haugham, Louth, Lincolnshire.*—St. Cath. Coll. Cam. B.A. 1847, M.A. 1850. V. of Haugham, Dio. Lin. 1859. (Patron, H. Chaplin, Esq; V.'s Inc. 250*l*; Pop. 115.) [9]

MARLAND, John, *Ventnor Parsonage, Isle of Wight.*—Dub. A.B. 1848; Deac. 1850, Pr. 1851. P. C. of Ventnor, Dio. Win. 1856. (Patron, John Hambrough, Esq; Pop. 1767.) Surrogate 1859. Formerly C. of West Deeping, Linc. 1854–56. [10]

MARLEN, Henry, *All Saints' Parsonage, Liverpool.*—St. Bees 1844; Deac. 1845 and Pr. 1847 by Bp of Ches. P. C. of All Saints', Liverpool, Dio. Ches. 1847. (Patrons, the Crown and Bp of Ches. alt; P. C.'s Inc. 300*l*; Pop. 10,000.) Author, *The Poetic Reciter, or Beauties of the British Poets*; *The Arithmetician's Assistant*; *The Catechist's Assistant, or Manual of Religious Instruction*; various Books for the use of Schools. [11]

MARRETT, Clement Augustus, *Forteval, Guernsey.*—Pemb. Coll. Ox. 3rd cl. Lit. Hum. and B.A. 1846; Deac. 1847, Pr. 1848. P. C. of Forteval, Dio. Win. 1866. (Patron, The Governor; Tithe, 30*l*; Glebe, 15 vergees; P. C.'s Inc. 110*l* and Ho; Pop 365.) Formerly C. of St. Andrew's, Plymouth, 1847, Tattingstone, Ipswich, 1851, Guilden Morden 1856, St. Peter Port, Guernsey, 1860. [12]

MARRETT, Edward Lawrence, *Lesbury Vicarage, Alnwick, Northumberland.*—St. Mary Hall, Ox. B.A. 1850, M.A. 1855; Deac. 1851 and Pr. 1852 by Bp of Dur. V. of Lesbury, Dio. Dur. 1858. (Patron, Ld Chan; Tithe, 308*l*; Glebe, 3 acres; V.'s Inc. 312*l* and Ho; Pop. 1202.) Formerly C. of Holy Trinity, Stockton-on-Tees, 1851–53, St. Michael's, St. Albans, Herts, 1853–54; R. of Morborne, Hunts, 1854–58. [13]

MARRINER, John, *Clapham Vicarage (Yorks), near Lancaster.*—Trin. Coll. Cam. B.A. 1828; Deac. 1829 and Pr 1830 by Bp of Dur. V. of Clapham, Dio. Rip. 1841. (Patron, Bp of Ches; Tithe—App. 924*l*, Imp. 1*l* 10*s*, V. 42*l*; Glebe, 18 acres; V.'s Inc. 300*l* and Ho; Pop. 1768.) Rural Dean. Formerly P. C. of Austwick Chapel-of-Ease. [14]

MARRINER, John, *Silsden, Leeds.*—Deac. 1860 and Pr. 1861 by Bp of Lich. P. C. of Silsden, Dio. Rip. 1865. (Patron, Sir Richard Tufton, Bart; P. C.'s Inc. 150*l* and Ho; Pop. 2800.) [15]

MARRINER, William, *Calbourne, Isle of Wight.*—Lin. Coll. Ox. Lord Crewe's Exhib. Goldsmith's Exhib. 1852–54, 3rd cl. Lit. Hum. and S.C.L. 1855; Deac. 1855 by Bp of Man. Pr. 1857 by Bp of Dur. C. of Calbourne. Formerly C. of Castle Eden, Durham' Holy Rhood, Southampton, and Weobley, Herf. [16]

MARRIOTT, C. Bertie.—Min. of Berkeley Chapel, May Fair, Lond. [17]

MARRIOTT, Charles Harwick, *Rendham Vicarage, Saxmundham, Suffolk.*—Deac. 1853 and Pr. 1854 by Bp of Chich. V. of Rendham, Dio. Nor. 1855. (Patrons, Trustees; Tithe—Imp. 411*l* 5*s*, V. 98*l* 17*s* 1*d*; Glebe, 15 acres; V.'s Inc. 105*l* and Ho; Pop. 384.) C. of Cransford, Suffolk. [18]

MARRIOTT, Cockburn Peel, *Richmond, Yorks.*—Corpus Coll. Cam. Jun. Opt. 2nd cl. Cl. Trip. and B.A. 1856; Deac. 1857 by Bp of Roch. Mast. of the Richmond Gr. Sch. 1864. Formerly Asst. Mast. of the Gr. Sch. Felstead, and Morn. Lect. at Black Chapel, Great Waltham, Essex; C. of Trinity, Vauxhall, Lond. [19]

MARRIOTT, Edmund Harwick, *Farnhurst Parsonage, Haslemere, Sussex.*—Deac. 1848 and Pr. 1849 by Bp of Chich. P. C. of Farnhurst, Dio. Chich. 1852. (Patron, Earl of Egmont; Tithe—Imp. 229*l* 8*s*; Glebe, 60 acres; P. C.'s Inc. 116*l* and Ho; Pop. 771.) [20]

MARRIOTT, Fitzherbert Adams, *Chaddesley-Corbett Vicarage, Kidderminster.*—Oriel Coll. Ox. B.A. 1833, M.A. 1836; Deac. 1835 and Pr. 1836 by Bp of Pet. V. of Chaddesley-Corbett, Dio. Wor. 1860. (Patron, Ld Chan; Glebe, 209 acres; V.'s Inc. 525*l* and Ho; Pop. 1457.) Chap. to the Earl de Grey and Ripon. Formerly R. of Cotesbach, Leic. 1842–43; Archd. of

Hobart Town, and Chap. to Bp of Tasmania, 1843-54. [1]

MARRIOTT, Harvey, *Grammar School, Leeds.*—Bp Hat. Hall, Dur. B.A. 1851, M.A. 1856; Deac. 1857 and Pr. 1859 by Bp of Wor. Scho. 1849. Fell. of Dur. Univ. 1854; Asst. Mast. in the Leeds Gr. Sch. 1864. Formerly C. of Morton Bagot and Oldberrow, Warw. 1857-58, St. Helen's and St. Alban's, Worcester, 1858-60, St. James's-the-Less, Plymouth, 1861-64. [2]

MARRIOTT, H. F. Smith, *Horsmonden, Staplehurst, Kent.*—R. of Horsmonden, Dio. Cant. 1866. (Patrons, Reps. of late Sir W. M. S. Marriott; R.'s Inc. 596*l* and Ho; Pop. 1385.) Formerly C. of Christian Malford 1864. [3]

MARRIOTT, John, *Hythe, Southampton.*—Oriel Coll. Ox. B.A. 1830, M.A. 1833. P. C. of Hythe St. John, Dio. Win. 1863. (Patron, R. of Fawley; P. C.'s Inc. 170*l*; Pop. 654.) Formerly C. of Buckland 1832-34, Bradfield, Berks, 1834-63. [4]

MARRIOTT, Oswald, *Goxhill Vicarage, Barton-on-Humber, Lincolnshire.*—St. John's Coll. Cam. B.A. 1827; Deac. 1828 and Pr. 1830 by Bp of Lich. and Coventry. V. of Goxhill, Dio. Lin. 1851. (Patron, Ld Chan; Tithe—Imp. 5*s*, V. 1*l* 10*s*; Glebe, 115 acres; V.'s Inc. 210*l* and Ho; Pop. 1100.) [5]

MARRIOTT, Randolph Charles, *Radipole, Weymouth.*—St. John's Coll. Cam. B.A. 1859; Deac. 1859 and Pr. 1860 by Bp of Ex. C. of Radipole 1865. Formerly C. of Loddiswell with Buckland-Tout-Saints, Devon, 1859, Wellington, Somerset, 1862. [6]

MARRIOTT, Richard Walker, *Aldborough, Boroughbridge, Yorks.*—Lin. Coll. Ox. B.A. 1851, M.A. 1854; Deac. 1852, Pr. 1853. V. of Aldborough, Dio. Rip. 1863. (Patrons, D. and C. of York; V.'s Inc. 380*l* and Ho; Pop. 900.) [7]

MARRIOTT, Walter Henry, *Rodford, Westerleigh.*—Dub. Hebrew Prizeman B.A. 1855, M.A. 1858; Deac. 1860 and Pr. 1862 by Bp of G. and B. C. of Westerleigh 1865. Formerly C. of St. Philip and Jacob's, Bristol, 1861, Chipping, Sodbury, Glouc. [8]

MARRIOTT, Wharton Booth, *Eton, Bucks.*—Trin. Coll. Ox. 1842, 2nd cl. Lit. Hum. and B.A. 1846, B.C.L. 1849, M.A. 1856; Deac. 1849 and Pr. 1850 by Bp of Ox. Fell. of Ex. Coll. Ox; Preacher in Dio. Ox. 1863. Formerly Asst. Mast. of Eton Coll. 1850. Author, *What is the Meaning of the Word Priest as used in the Church of England?* 1856, J. Mitchell, 1*s* 6*d*; *Selections from Ovid's Metamorphoses, with English Notes*, Eton, 1862, 4*s* 6*d*; *The Adelphi of Terence, with English Notes and Introduction*, Rivingtons, 1863, 3*s* 6*d*; *Urenica—The Wholesome Words of Holy Scripture concerning Questions still disputed in the Church*, Rivingtons, 1865, 4*s* 6*d*; *Vestiarium Christianum*, Day and Son, 1867, 1*l* 5*s*. [9]

MARRIOTT, William Henry, *Thrussington Vicarage, Leicester.*—Lin. Coll. Ox. B.A. 1855, M.A. 1857; Deac. 1856 and Pr. 1857 by Bp of Lin. V. of Thrussington, Dio. Pet. 1867. (Patroness, Mrs Bishopp; V.'s Inc. 280*l* and Ho; Pop. 574.) Formerly C. of Swaby, Linc. 1856-58, Glooston, Leic. 1859-67. [10]

MARSDEN, Benjamin, *Glascomb Vicarage, (Radnorshire), near Kington.*—Lampeter; Deac. 1827 and Pr. 1828 by Bp of St. D. V. of Glascomb with Colva C. and Rhulen C. annexed, Dio. St. D. 1851. (Patron, Bp of St. D; Glascomb, Tithe—App. 206*l* and 11½ acres, V. 135; Glebe, 1½ acres; Colva, Tithe—App. 95*l*, V. 62*l*; Rhulan, Tithe—App. 49*l* 10*s*, V. 33*l*; V.'s Inc. 230*l* 5*s* and Ho; Pop. Glascomb 463, Colva 185, Rhulan 111.) [11]

MARSDEN, Charles Bateman, 37, *Highfield-road, Birmingham.*—Emman. Coll. Cam. B.A. 1860, M.A. 1864; Deac. 1861 and Pr. 1862 by Bp of Ex. C. of St. Peter's, Birmingham, 1863. Formerly C. of Tiverton 1861. [12]

MARSDEN, Charles John, *Gargrave Vicarage, Yorks.*—Ch. Ch. Ox. B.A. 1838, M.A. 1840. V. of Gargrave, Dio. Rip. 1852. (Patron, the present V; Tithe—Imp. 78*l* 12*s* 6*d*, V. 794*l* 15*s*; V.'s Inc. 822*l* and Ho; Pop. 1403.) [13]

MARSDEN, Charles John Delabene, *Hooton-Roberts Rectory, Rotherham.*—Lin. Coll. Ox. M.A. 1833; Deac. 1834 and Pr. 1835 by Bp of Ches. R. of Hooton-Roberts, Dio. York, 1860. (Patron, Earl Fitzwilliam; Tithe, 255*l*; Glebe, 64 acres; R.'s Inc. 340*l* and Ho; Pop. 241.) Formerly V. of Bolton-upon-Dearne, Yorks, 1849-60. [14]

MARSDEN, Edward, *Aston, Runcorn, Cheshire.*—St. John's Coll. Cam. B.A. 1839, M.A. 1842; Deac. 1839, Pr. 1840. P. C. of Aston, Dio. Ches. 1844. (Patron, Sir Arthur Aston; Tithe—App. 64*l* 17*s* 6*d*; Glebe, 13 acres; P. C.'s Inc. 90*l*; Pop. 616.) [15]

MARSDEN, John Buxton, *Birmingham.*—St. John's Coll. Cam. B.A. 1827, M.A. 1830; Deac. 1827, Pr. 1828. P. C. of St. Peter's, Birmingham, Dio. Wor. 1851. (Patron, R. of St. Philip's, Birmingham; P. C.'s Inc. 300*l*; Pop. 4356.) Surrogate. Author, *Sermons*, 1834, 6*s*; *Discourses for the Festivals of the Church of England*, 1840, 12*s*; *Sermons on the Old Testament*, 1847, 6*s*; *Churchmanship of the New Testament*, 1848, 6*s*; *The History of the Early Puritans*, 1850, 10*s*; *The History of the Later Puritans*, 1852, 10*s*; *A History of Christian Sects and Churches*, Bentley, 1855, eight Monthly Parts, 3*s* 6*d* each. [16]

MARSDEN, John Frank, *St. Stephen's Parsonage, Bradford, Yorks.*—St. John's Coll. Cam. B.A. 1863; Deac. 1863 and Pr. 1865 by Bp of Rip. P. C. of St. Stephen's, Bowling, Dio. Rip. 1866. (Patron, Charles Hardy, Esq; P. C.'s Inc. 196*l* and Ho; Pop. 1500.) Formerly C. of St. Stephen's, Bowling, 1863-66. [17]

MARSDEN, John Howard, *Great Oakley Rectory, Harwich, Essex.*—St. John's Coll. Cam. 1st Bell's Univ. Scho. 1823, Sen. Opt. 1st cl. Cl. Trip. and B.A. 1826, Seatonian Prizeman and M.A. 1829, B.D. 1836; Deac. and Pr. 1827 by Bp of Ely. R. of Great Oakley, Dio. Roch. 1840. (Patron, St. John's Coll. Cam; Tithe, 900*l*; Glebe, 57 acres; R.'s Inc. 957*l* and Ho; Pop. 1038.) Can. of Man. Cathl. 1858. (Value, 600*l*.) Rural Dean; Dom. Chap. to the Bp of Man. Formerly Select Preacher of the Univ. of Cam. 1834, 1837, and 1847; Hulsean Lect. 1843 and 1844; Disney Prof. of Archæology 1851. Author, *Hulsean Lectures*, 2 vols. 1843-44; *Sermon* (preached before the Univ. of Cam.), 1847; *Two Introductory Lectures on the Study of Archæology*, 1851; Articles in Reviews and various Pamphlets. [18]

MARSDEN, Jonathan, *Dafen, Llanelly.*—Lampeter; Deac. 1857 and Pr. 1858 by Bp of St. D. C. of Dafen, 1864. Formerly C. of Llandilofawr, 1861, St. Dogmell's, 1858. [19]

MARSDEN, Jonathan William, *Llanegwad, near Carmarthen.*—Lampeter; Deac. 1857 and Pr. 1858 by Bp of St. D. C. of Llanegwad 1864. Formerly C. of Glascombe, Radnorshire, 1857; Sen. C. of Neath, Glamorganshire, 1858-59; C. in sole charge of Cowbridge 1860; C. of Haigh, near Wigan, 1861-62, St. Peter's, Carmarthen, 1863. [20]

MARSDEN, Samuel Edward, *Evesham.*—Trin. Coll. Cam. M.A. 1858; Deac. 1855 and Pr. 1856 by Bp of Herf. P. C. of Bengeworth, Dio. Wor. 1861. (Patroness, Mrs. J. C. Marsden; P. C.'s Inc. 175*l* and Ho; Pop. 1259.) Dioc. Inspector of Schs. Formerly C. of St. Peter's, Hereford, and Lilleshall, Salop. [21]

MARSDEN, Thomas, *Burstow Rectory (Surrey), near Crawley.*—Corpus Coll. Cam. 13th Sen. Opt. and B.A. 1834; Deac. 1834, Pr. 1836. R. of Burstow, Dio. Win. 1858. (Patrons, Ld Chan; Tithe, 600*l*; Glebe, 43 acres; R.'s Inc. 672*l* and Ho; Pop. 927.) Formerly V. of Child-wickham, Glouc. 1843-57. [22]

MARSDEN, William, *Chester.*—V. of St. John the Baptist's, City and Dio. Ches. 1838. (Patron, Marquis of Westminster; V.'s Inc. 300*l*; Pop. 3259.) [23]

MARSDEN, William.—C. of St. John's, Longsight, Manchester. Formerly C. of St. Saviour's, Chorlton-on-Medlock. [24]

MARSDEN, William Green, *Sherborne, Dorset.*—Queens' Coll. Cam. B.A. 1861; Deac. 1862, Pr. 1863. C. of Sherborne. Formerly C. of Headley, Hants. [25]

MARSH, Charles Earle, *Sall, Reepham, Norfolk.*—Pemb. Coll. Cam. B.A. 1843, M.A. 1846. R. of Sall, Dio. Nor. 1847. (Patron, Pemb. Coll. Cam; Tithe, 568*l* 10*s*; Glebe, 30 acres; R.'s Inc. 628*l*; Pop. 241.) [1]

MARSH, Felix Augustus, 53, *Wrotham-road, Gravesend.*—St. John's Coll. Cam. B.A. 1846, M.A. 1853; Deac. 1846 by Bp of Pet. Pr. 1847 by Bp of Roch. P. C. of Ch. Ch. Milton, Dio. Roch. 1855. (Patron, R. of Milton; P. C.'s Inc. 300*l*; Pop. 5631.) Chap. to H.M.'s Forces. Formerly C. of Gravesend 1846. [2]

MARSH, George Henry, *Great Snoring Rectory, Fakenham, Norfolk.*—St. John's Coll. Cam. Sen. Opt. 2nd in 1st cl. Cl. Trip. and B.A. 1836, M.A. 1839, B D. 1846. R. of Great Snoring with Thursford R. Dio. Nor. 1851. (Patron, St. John's Coll. Cam; Great Snoring, Tithe, 545*l*; Glebe, 16 acres; Thursford, Tithe, 294*l* 15*s*; R.'s Inc. 840*l* and Ho; Pop. Great Snoring 594, Thursford 322.) Formerly Fell. of St. John's Coll. Cam. 1837-40. [3]

MARSH, Henry Augustus, *Tuxford Vicarage, Notts.*—Trin. Coll. Cam. B.A. 1840, M.A. 1843; Deac. 1844, Pr. 1845. V. of Tuxford, Dio. Lin. 1849. (Patron, Trin. Coll. Cam; Land in lieu of Tithe, 136 acres; V.'s Inc. 300*l* and Ho; Pop. 1034.) Surrogate 1850; Rural Dean 1855; Justice of the Peace 1858. Formerly Fell. of Trin. Coll. Cam. [4]

MARSH, John, *Thorncombe, Chard, Devon.*—St. Cath. Coll. Cam. B.A. 1834; Deac. 1836 and Pr. 1837 by Bp of B. and W. C. of Thorncombe, Devon. Formerly C. of Burstock, Dorset. [5]

MARSH, John Kirk, *Brampton Vicarage, Chesterfield.*—Queens' Coll. Cam. B.A. 1830, M.A. 1834; Deac. 1830 and Pr. 1831 by Bp of Ches. V. of Brampton, Dio. Lich. 1867. (Patron, Bp of Lich; Tithe, 90*l*; Glebe, 14 acres; V.'s Inc. 300*l* and Ho; Pop. 1059.) Formerly C. of Knaresborough 1830; P. C. of Brimington, Derby, 1836-52, Chap. of H.M.'s Convict Establishments at Woolwich and Chatham, 1852-67. [6]

MARSH, John William, *Bleasby Vicarage, Southwell, Notts.*—Wad. Coll. Ox. B.A. 1844; Deac. 1845, Pr. 1846. V. of Bleasby with Morton, P. C. Dio. Lin. 1848. (Patron, Southwell Coll. Ch; Morton, Tithe—App. 113*l*, V. 3*l*; V.'s Inc. 188*l* and Ho; Pop. Bleasby 332, Morton 142.) [7]

MARSH, Richard, *Witton, Northwich, Cheshire.*—Sid. Coll. Cam. Sen. Opt. B.A. 1862, M.A. 1865; Deac. 1864 by Bp of Ches. Pr. 1865 by Bp of St. A. C. of Witton, Northwich. Formerly Math. Mast. of King Wm.'s Coll. Isle of Man. 1862; C. of Runcorn and Mast. of Gr. Sch. 1864. [8]

MARSH, Richard William Bishop, *Plaistow, Stratford, Essex.*—St. John's Coll. Cam. Sen. Opt. and B.A. 1839, M.A. 1843; Deac. 1840, Pr. 1841. P. C. of Plaistow, Dio. Lon. 1842. (Patron, V. of West Ham; P. C.'s Inc. 300*l* and Ho; Pop. 11,214.) Chap. to the Plashet Industrial Schs. 1853. Author, *Fast-day Sermons; Every Parish a Family of Christ* (a Sermon). [9]

MARSH, Theodore Henry, *Cawston Rectory, near Norwich.*—Pemb. Coll. Cam. B.A. 1847, M.A. 1851; Deac. 1848 and Pr. 1850 by Bp of Ex. R. of Cawston, Dio. Nor. 1855. (Patron, Pemb. Coll. Cam; Tithe, 1015*l* 18*s* 6*d*; R.'s Inc. 1020*l* and Ho; Pop. 1019.) [10]

MARSH, William, *Wethersfield, Braintree, Essex.*—Caius Coll. Cam. 28th Wrang. and B.A. 1838, Trin. Hall, M.A. 1841; Deac. 1840 and Pr. 1841 by Bp of Ely. V. of Wethersfield, Dio. Roch. 1854. (Patron, Trin. Hall, Cam; Rectorial Tithe—App. 1105*l* and 51 acres of Glebe, V. 376*l*; Glebe, 2 acres; V.'s Inc. 346*l*; Pop. 1727.) Formerly Fell. and Tut. of Trin. Hall, Cam. [11]

MARSH, William Heath, *Lammas, Buxton, Norfolk.*—Corpus Coll. Cam. B.A. 1823; Deac. 1823 and Pr. 1824 by Bp of Nor. R. of Lammas with Hautbois Parva, Dio. Nor. 1833. (Patron, the present R; Tithe, 250*l*; Glebe, 36 acres; R.'s Inc. 304*l* and Ho; Pop. Lammas 291, Hautbois Parva 25.) [12]

MARSHALL, Alfred Ethelwolf, *Rendlesham, Woodbridge, Suffolk.*—St. Bees, 1st cl. Prizeman; Deac. 1854 by Bp of Down and Connor, Pr. 1855 by Bp of Nor. C. of Rendlesham 1858. Formerly Asst. C. of Woodbridge 1854-58. [13]

MARSHALL, Benjamin Arthur, *St. Cuthbert's Parsonage, Carlisle.*—St. Peter's Coll. Cam. B.A. 1835, M.A. 1843; Deac. 1835 and Pr. 1836 by Bp of Ches. P. C. of St. Cuthbert's, City and Dio. Carl. 1853. (Patrons, D. and C. of Carl; Glebe, 36 acres, let at 72*l*; D. and C. 5*l* 6*s* 8*d*, Queen Anne's Bounty, 33*l* 10*s* 10*d*, Cottage, 7*l* 16*s*, Eccles. Commis. 33*l*, Consols, 9*l* 9*s* 6*d*; P. C.'s Inc. 161*l* 11*s* and Ho; Pop. 3138.) Formerly C. of Great Budworth 1835-38, St. Mark's 1839-46, and St. Luke's, Liverpool, 1847-50, Tattenhall, Cheshire, 1850-53. Author, *Byzantium and other Poems*, 1831, 4*s* 6*d*; various articles in Magazines; *The People's Church Hymn Book*, 1857, 4*d*. [14]

MARSHALL, Charles, 9, *South-street, Finsbury, London, E.C.*—Trin. Coll. Cam. B.A. 1833, M.A. 1836, Deac. 1833, Pr. 1834. V. of St. Bride's with Bridewell annexed, City and Dio. Lon. 1846. (Patrons, D. and C. of Westminster; V.'s Inc. 451*l*; Pop. 5656.) Lect. at St. Antholin's, Lond; Preb. of St. Paul's Cathl. 1856; Hon. Sec. of the City of London National Schools. [15]

MARSHALL, Charles, *Harpurhey Rectory, Manchester.*—M.A. 1850; Deac. 1844 and Pr. 1845 by Bp of Ches. R. of Harpurhey with Moston, Dio. Man. 1854. (Patrons, Trustees; R.'s Inc. 300*l* and Ho; Pop. 5126.) [16]

MARSHALL, Edward, *Sandford, Steeple Aston, Oxon.*—Corpus Coll. Ox. 4th cl. Lit. Hum. and B.A. 1838, M.A. 1840; Deac. 1839 and Pr. 1840 by Bp of Ox. Diocesan Inspector of Schools. Formerly Scho. and Fell. of Corpus Coll. Ox; C. of Enstone 1839-40, Somerton 1840-44, St. Mary Magdalene's, Oxford, 1846-60, Hempton 1862-64. Author, *An Account of Sandford, in the Deanery of Woodstock*, Oxford, 1866. [17]

MARSHALL, Edward Douglass, 18, *Marine-parade, Lowestoft.*—St. Cath. Coll. Cam. B.A. 1852, M.A. 1855; Deac. 1852 and Pr. 1854 by Bp of Rip. Chap. of the Oulton House of Industry, Lowestoft, 1859. [18]

MARSHALL, Frederick Anthony Stansfeld, *Minster Precincts, Peterborough.*—Caius Coll. Cam. B.A. 1839, M.A. 1842; Deac. 1840, Pr. 1841. Min. Can. of Pet. Cathl. 1850 and Precentor 1865. (Value, 150*l*.) Formerly Chap. to the Peterborough Union 1850-57. [19]

MARSHALL, Francis Catton, 4, *Park-side, Cambridge.*—Corpus Coll. Cam. 5th Jun. Opt. B.A. 1856, M.A. 1866; Deac. 1863 by Bp of B. and W. Pr. 1867 by Bp of Ely. C. of Trinity, Cambridge, 1867. Formerly Sen. Asst. Mast. in King William's Coll. Isle of Man. 1856-60; Head Mast. of the Gr. Sch. and C. of St. Mary's, Bridgwater, 1863; C. of Grantchester, Cambridge, 1866. [20]

MARSHALL, George, *Pudsey, Leeds.*—Dub. A.B. 1844; Deac. 1844, Pr. 1845. P. C. of St. Paul's, Pudsey, Dio. Rip. 1846. (Patrons, the Crown and Bp of Rip. alt; P. C.'s Inc. 150*l*; Pop. 1976.) [21]

MARSHALL, George, *Pirton Vicarage, Tetsworth, Oxon.*—Ch. Ch. Ox. Craven Scho. 1837, 2nd cl. Lit. Hum. 3rd cl. Math. et Phy. and B.A. 1840, M.A. 1842; Deac. 1843, Pr. 1844. Mast. of the Schs. 1846; Sen. Proctor 1853; Moderator 1855; Censor of Ch. Ch. V. of Pirton, Dio. Ox. 1857. (Patron, Ch. Ch. Ox; V.'s Inc. 238*l* and Ho; Pop. 5.) Rural Dean. [22]

MARSHALL, Henry Bernard, *Blakemere, Hereford.*—Wor. Coll. Ox. B.A. 1860, M.A. 1863; Deac. 1862 and Pr. 1863 by Bp of Her. C. of Preston-on-Wye with Blakemere. [23]

MARSHALL, Henry James, *Bettws Vicarage, Newtown, Montgomeryshire.*—Corpus Coll. Ox. B.A. 1840, M.A. 1844; Deac. 1841 and Pr. 1842 by Bp of B. and W. V. of Bettws, *alias* Bettws Cae dewen, Dio. St. A. 1854. (Patron, Ld Chan; Tithe—Imp. 230*l*, V. 230*l*; Glebe, 4 acres; V.'s Inc. 234*l* and Ho; Pop. 730.) [24]

MARSHALL, Henry James, *Clapton Rectory, near Bristol.*—St. John's Coll. Cam. B.A. 1842, M.A. 1848; Deac. 1847 and Pr. 1848 by Bp of Lich. R. of Clapton-in-Gordano, Dio. B. and W. 1860. (Patron, Walter Bernard, Esq; Tithe, comm. 210*l*; Glebe, 35 acres; R.'s Inc. 250*l* and Ho; Pop. 178.) Formerly C. of Belper, Derbyshire, 1847–49, Dunkerton, Bath, 1850, Sutton-Montis 1850, Dilton's Marsh 1851, Melksham, Wilts, 1852–53; Sec. for the S.W. District of the Lond. Soc. for Promoting Christianity amongst the Jews, 1854–56; Asst. Min. of Margaret Chapel and Lect. of Walcot, Bath, 1856–59; Incumb. of St. Peter's Chapel, Montrose, Scotland, 1859–60. [1]

MARSHALL, James, 2, *Little Dean's-yard, Westminster, London, S.W.*—Ch. Ch. Ox. B.A. 1842, M.A. 1846; Deac. 1843 and Pr. 1844 by Bp of Ox. Asst. Mast. in Westminster Sch. [2]

MARSHALL, James, *Brenckburne, Morpeth.*—Univ. Coll. Dur. B.A. 1865; Deac. 1866 and Pr. 1867 by Bp of Dur. C. of Brenckburne 1866. [3]

MARSHALL, Jenner, *Westcott Barton Manor, Oxon.*—Wor. Coll. Ox. 1835, B.A. 1839, M.A. 1843; Deac. 1841 and Pr. 1842 by Bp of Ox. Formerly C. of Barford St. Michael, Ox. 1841; Asst. C. of Broughton 1847; C. of North Aston, 1848, Barford St. John, Adderbury, 1851. [4]

MARSHALL, John, *Eastbourn, Darlington.*—Dub. A.B. 1835; Deac. 1835 and Pr. 1836 by Bp of Ches. Head Mast. of Queen Elizabeth's Gr. Sch. Darlington 1845. Formerly Head Mast. of the Bentham Gr. Sch. and P. C. of Chapel-le-Dale 1842–45. [5]

MARSHALL, John, *Greetland Parsonage, Halifax.*—Dub. Div. Prizeman, A.M. 1864; Deac. and Pr. 1853 by Bp of Man. P. C. of Greetland, Dio. Rip. 1861. (Patron, V. of Halifax; Inc. uncertain; Pop. 2800.) Formerly C. of St. Philip's, Salford, Pontefract, and Rothbury. [6]

MARSHALL, J. H., *Bury St. Edmunds.*—2nd Mast. of the Gr. Sch. Bury St. Edmunds, and C. of Great Barton, Suffolk. [7]

MARSHALL, John William M., *Marnham, Newark, Notts.*—St. Aidan's; Deac. 1861 and Pr. 1862 by Bp of Ches. C. of Marnham. Formerly C. of St. Aidan's, Kirkdale, Liverpool, 1862, North Leverton 1862. [8]

MARSHALL, Joseph William, *Birchfield, Birmingham.*—Trin. Coll. Cam. B.A. 1858; Deac. 1859 by Bp of Wor. Pr. 1860 by Bp of Lon. P. C. of Birchfield, Dio. Lich. 1864. (Patron, R. of Handsworth; P. C.'s Inc. 330*l*; Pop. 1550.) Formerly C. of Martley, St. Martin's, Birmingham, and Handsworth. [9]

MARSHALL, Peter, *Greenheys, Manchester.*—Dub. A.B. 1850, A.M. 1857; Deac. 1850, Pr. 1851. R. of St. John Baptist's, Hulme, Dio. Man. 1858. (Patron, Bp of Man; R.'s Inc. 300*l*; Pop. 8370.) Formerly C. of St. Nicholas', Great Yarmouth, 1850, Trinity, Hulme, Manchester, 1852. Author, *Confirmation Instructions*, 2*d*; *Sermons on Absolution*, 1867, Whittaker, 3*d*. [10]

MARSHALL, Richard, *Whittonstall Parsonage, by Stocksfield-on-Tyne, Northumberland.*—Deac. 1821 and Pr. 1822 by Bp of Carl. P. C. of Whittonstall, Dio. Dur. 1837. (Patrons, D. and C. of Dur; Tithe, App. 380*l*; Glebe, 8 acres; P. C.'s Inc. 200*l* and Ho; Pop. 219.) Formerly C. of Gilcrux 1821, Allenby 1824, Shotley 1826, Bamburgh 1829. [11]

MARSHALL, Robert Manning, *Hedenham Rectory, Bungay.*—Ex. Coll. Ox. B.A. 1855, M.A. 1857; Deac. 1856 and Pr. 1857 by Bp of Nor. R. of Hedenham, Dio. Nor. 1859. (Patron, J. L. Bedingfeld, Esq; Tithe, 458*l*; Glebe, 29 acres; R.'s Inc. 458*l* and Ho; Pop. 280.) Formerly C. of Creeting St. Mary, Suffolk, 1856–59. [12]

MARSHALL, Stirling Frederick, *Farnham-Royal Rectory, Eton, Bucks.*—Wad. Coll. Ox. B.A. 1838, M.A. 1841. R. of Farnham-Royal, Dio. Ox. 1854. (Patron, Eton Coll; Tithe, 310*l* 10*s* 11*d*; Glebe, 18 acres; R.'s Inc. 543*l* and Ho; Pop. 1044.) Conduct of Eton Coll. [13]

MARSHALL, Thomas Edward, *Gedling, Nottingham.*—Emman. Coll. Cam. 1835, B.A. 1837, M.A. 1841; Deac. 1838 and Pr. 1839 by Bp of Lin. C. of Gedling. Formerly V. of Gringley-on-the-Hill, Linc. 1853–61. [14]

MARSHALL, Thomas Outram, *Batcombe, Dorchester.*—New Coll. Ox. B.A. 1866; Deac. 1866 by Bp of Salis. C. of Batcombe 1866. [15]

MARSHALL, William, *Ilton Vicarage, Ilminster, Somerset.*—Univ. Coll. Ox. B.A. 1852, M.A. 1855. V. of Ilton, Dio. B. and W. 1852. (Patron, Bp of B. and W; Tithe—Imp. 275*l* and 26 acres of Glebe, V. 138*l* and 5 acres of Glebe; V.'s Inc. 198*l* and Ho; Pop. 492.) [16]

MARSHALL, William, *Heaton Norris, Stockport.*—St. Bees; Deac. 1860 and Pr. 1861 by Abp of York. C. of Ch. Ch. Heaton Norris, 1865. Formerly C. of St. Philip's, Sheffield, 1860 61, St. Peter's, Huddersfield, 1863 65. [17]

MARSHALL, William John, *Yatton Lodge, Ross, Herefordshire.*—Queens' Coll. Cam. B.A. 1843; Deac. 1844 and Pr. 1845 by Bp of Pet. Formerly R. of Grendon-Underwood, Oxon, 1855–62; C. of Much Marcle, Hereford, 1862. [18]

MARSHALL, William Knox, *Wragby Vicarage, Lincolnshire.*—Dub. A.B. 1832, A.M. and B.D. 1855; Deac. 1832 and Pr. 1833 by Bp of Lich. R. of Panton with Wragby V. Dio. Lin. 1860. (Patron, C. Turnor, Esq; Tithe, Panton, 421*l*, Wragby 63*l*; Glebe, Panton, 25 acres, Wragby 34 acres; R.'s Inc. Panton, 463*l* and Ho; D.'s Inc. Wragby, 185*l* and Ho; total, 648*l*; Pop. Wragby 619, Panton 136.) Preb. of Pratum Majus in Herf. Cathl. 1856; Official of the Royal Peculiar of Bridgnorth 1856; Surrogate. Formerly C. of Tamworth 1833; R. of St. Mary Magdalene's, Bridgnorth, Salop, 1833–60. [19]

MARSHAM, C. D. Bullock, *Edgcott, Bicester, Oxon.*—R. of Edgcott, Dio. Ox. 1861. (Patron, R. B. Marsham, Esq; R.'s Inc. 210*l*; Pop. 182.) [20]

MARSHAM, Henry Philip, *Rippon Hall, Hevingham, Norwich.*—Trin. Hall, Cam. S.C.L. 1842, B.C.L. 1846; Deac. 1842 and Pr. 1843 by Bp of Nor. R. of Stratton-Strawless, Dio. Nor. 1859. (Patron, the present R; Tithe, 287*l*; Glebe, 30 acres; R.'s Inc. 330*l*; Pop. 202.) Formerly R. of Brampton, Norfolk, 1843–58; C. of Stratton-Strawless 1842–58; Patron of the Rectories of Haynford, Wramplingham, and Brampton, Norfolk. [21]

MARSHAM, Jacob Joseph, *Shorne, Gravesend, Kent.*—Ch. Ch. Ox. B.A. 1826, M.A. 1830; Deac. 1827 and Pr. 1828 by Abp of York. V. of Shorne, Dio. Roch. 1837. (Patrons, D. and C. of Roch; Tithe—App. 618*l* 10*s*, V. 392*l* 10*s*; V.'s Inc. 400*l*; Pop. 963.) Chap. to the Earl of Harewood. [22]

MARSHAM, The Hon. John, *Sutton, near Mansfield, Notts.*—Downing Coll. Cam. B.A. 1865; Deac. 1866 and Pr. 1867 by Bp of Ox. C. of Middleton Stoney, Oxon. 1866. [23]

MARSHAM, Thomas John Gordon, *Saxlingham Rectory, Holt, Norfolk.*—Magd. Coll. Cam. M.A. 1847; Deac. 1845 and Pr. 1847 by Bp of Nor. R. of Saxlingham, Dio. Nor. 1861. (Patron, Rev. Sir E. Repps Jodrell, Bart; Tithe, 474*l* 8*s*; Glebe, 28 acres; R.'s Inc. 474*l* and Ho; Pop. 156.) Formerly C. of Stratton-Strawless 1845. [24]

MARSLAND, George, *Beckingham Rectory (Lincolnshire), near Newark.*—Brasen. Coll. Ox. B.A. 1834, M.A. 1837. R. of Beckingham with Stragglethorpe C. and Fenton C. Dio. Lin. 1837. (Patron, G. Marsland, Esq; R.'s Inc. 700*l* and Ho; Pop. Beckingham 431, Stragglethorpe 90, Fenton 103.) [25]

MARSLAND, William Bourne, *Dorking, Surrey.*—Clare Hall, Cam. Sen. Opt. B.A. 1840; Deac. 1840, Pr. 1841. Formerly Mast. of the Gr. Sch. Totnes. [26]

MARSON, Charles, 4, *Hagley-grove, Edgbaston, Birmingham.*—Ch. Ch. Ox. 4th cl. Lit. Hum. B.A. 1845, M.A. 1847; Deac. 1845 by Abp of Cant. Pr. 1849 by Bp of Ely. P. C. of Ch. Ch. Birmingham, 1864. (Patron, Bp of Wor; P. C.'s Inc. 350*l*; Pop. 6000.) Preb. of Lich. 1864. Formerly C. of Biddenden, Kent, 1845, Kimbolton, Hunts, 1847, St. George the Martyr's, Queen-square, Bloomsbury, Lond. 1851, St. John's, Woking, Surrey, 1854; Assoc. Sec. of Ch. Miss. Soc. Metropolitan District, 1861. Author, *An Exposition of the Lord's Prayer by John Calvin (translated from the Latin)*, Seeleys, 1843; *Readiness for Death and Judgment* (a Sermon), 1846. [27]

MARSTON, Charles Dallas, *Kersal Rectory, Manchester.*—Caius Coll. Cam. Jun. Opt. 3rd cl. Cl. Trip. and B.A. 1848, M.A. 1852; Deac. 1848 and Pr. 1849 by Bp of Nor. R. of Kersal, Dio. Man. 1866. (Patrons, Trustees; R.'s Inc. 855*l* and Ho; Pop. 976.) Formerly P. C. of Ch. Ch. Hougham-in-Dover, Kent, 1850–62; R. of St. Mary's, Bryanston-square, Lond. 1862–66. Author, *Manual of Inspiration of Scripture*; *Fundamental Truths*; *Exposition of the Epistles*; *Advent Sermons*; *The Teaching of the Church of England on the Lord's Supper*; various Tracts. [1]

MARTER, Richard, *Bright-Waltham Rectory, Wantage, Berks.*—Ex. Coll. Ox; Deac. 1816 by Bp of Salis. Pr. 1817 by Bp of Glouc. R. of Bright-Waltham, Dio. Ox. 1841. (Patron, T. R. Harman, Esq; Tithe, 700*l*; Glebe, 86 acres; R.'s Inc. 805*l* and Ho; Pop. 450.) [2]

MARTIN, Charles, *Christ Church, Oxford.*—New Coll. Ox. B.A. 1863, M.A. 1866, Scho. of New Coll. 1859, Stanhope Essay 1862, Stud. and Tut. of Ch. Ch. 1864; Deac. 1865 and Pr. 1866 by Bp of Ox. [3]

MARTIN, Edward Brace, *West Grinstead Rectory, Horsham.*—Ex. Coll. Ox. B.A. 1859, M.A. 1861; Deac. 1860 and Pr. 1862 by Bp of Chich. R. of West Grinstead, Dio. Chich. 1864. (Patron, Earl of Ilchester; Glebe, 20 acres; R.'s Inc. 265*l* and Ho; Pop. 250.) Formerly C. of Alderbury 1860–64. [4]

MARTIN, Edward William.—St. John's Coll. Cam. Sen. Opt. 2nd cl. Cl. Trip. and B.A. 1832, M.A. 1851; Deac. 1832 and Pr. 1834 by Bp of Roch. Formerly C. of Laughton, Linc. [5]

MARTIN, Francis, *Trinity College, Cambridge.*—Trin. Coll. Cam. Univ. Scho. B.A. 1824, M.A. 1827; Deac. 1833 by Bp of Roch. Pr. 1833 by Bp of Lin. Sen. Fell. of Trin. Coll. Cam. [6]

MARTIN, Francis William Wykeham, *Chacombe Vicarage (Northants), near Banbury.*—Ball. Coll. Ox. B.A. 1832; Deac. and Pr. 1843 by Bp of Pet. V. of Chacombe, Dio. Pet. 1843. (Patron, Charles Wykeham Martin, Esq; Tithe—Imp. 199*l* 16*s*, V. 241*l* 10*s*; Glebe, 30 acres; V.'s Inc. 311*l* and Ho; Pop. 468.) [7]

MARTIN, George, *St. Breward Vicarage, Bodmin, Cornwall.*—St. John's Coll. Cam. 27th Sen. Opt. and B.A. 1837, M.A. 1840, B.D. 1847, D.D. 1852; Deac. 1838, Pr. 1839. V. of St. Breward, Cornwall, Dio. Ex. 1851. (Patrons, D. and C. of Ex; Tithe—App. 150*l*, V. 290*l*; Glebe, 70 acres; V.'s Inc. 335*l* and Ho; Pop. 705.) Formerly Asst. C. of Launceston 1858. [8]

MARTIN, Glanville.—Sid. Coll. Cam. B.A. 1833; Deac. 1834 and Pr. 1835 by Bp of Ex. Formerly R. of Otterham, Cornwall, 1850–61. [9]

MARTIN, Henry, *Bristol.*—V. of St. Nicholas' with St. Leonard's, Bristol, Dio. G. and B. 1858. (Patrons, D. and C. of Bristol; V.'s Inc. 300*l*; Pop. 2039.) [10]

MARTIN, Henry, 48, *New Kent-road, London, S.E.*—Deac. 1866 by Bp of Win. C. of St. George-the-Martyr's, Southwark, Surrey. [11]

MARTIN, Henry Arthur, *Laxton Vicarage, Newark, Notts.*—St. Mary Hall, Ox. B.A. 1855, M.A. 1857; Deac. 1856 and Pr. 1857 by Bp of Wor. V. of Laxton with Moorhouse, Dio. Lin. 1858. (Patron, Earl Manvers; Tithe, 225*l* 3*s* 9*d*; Glebe, 4 acres; V.'s Inc. 231*l* and Ho; Pop. 613.) Formerly C. of Hallow, near Worcester. [12]

MARTIN, Henry John, *Parsonage, West Hartlepool.*—Trin. Coll. Cam. Jun. Opt. and 3rd cl. Cl. Trip. B.A. 1852, M.A. 1862; Deac. 1853 and Pr. 1854 by Bp of Ox. P. C. of West Hartlepool, Dio. Dur. 1866. (Patron, Bp of Dur; P. C.'s Inc. 370*l* and Ho; Pop. 11,000.) Formerly C. of Morebath, Devon, 1854–66, Trinity, Exeter, 1856–60, St. Thomas's, Exeter, 1861–62; Assoc. Sec. to Ch. Miss. Soc. for Cam. and adjoining Counties, 1862–66. [13]

MARTIN, Hezekiah, *Thatcham Vicarage, Newbury, Berks.*—Corpus Coll. Cam. Jun. Opt. B.A. 1857; Deac. 1856 and Pr. 1859 by Bp of Chich. V. of Thatcham, Dio. Ox. 1866. (Patron, Rev. H. Martin; Glebe, 40 acres; V.'s Inc. 460*l* and Ho; Pop. 1972.) Formerly C. of East Guildford with Playden, Sussex, 1856–59, St. Paul's, Stepney, Lond. 1860, Elsing, Norf. 1862, St. Peter's, Folkestone, 1864. [14]

MARTIN, John, *Cambridge.*—Sid. Coll. Cam. 9th Sen. Opt. and B.A. 1839, M.A. 1842; Deac. 1839 and Pr. 1842 by Bp of G. and B. P. C. of St. Andrew's the Great, Cambridge, Dio. Ely, 1858. (Patrons, D. and C. of Ely; P. C.'s Inc. 130*l*; Pop. 2578.) Formerly C. of Dawlish, Devon. Author, *Charity under Persecution* (a Sermon on behalf of the Plymouth Sisterhood), Masters, 6*d*; *Christian Burial and Unconsecrated Cemeteries* (a Sermon), ib. 6*d*; *War a Calamity*, Rivingtons, 1854, 6*d*; *Modern Christianity in its Relation to the Divine Government* (a Sermon), 1855, 6*d*. [15]

MARTIN, Richard, *Menheniot Vicarage, Liskeard, Cornwall.*—Oriel Coll. Ox. 1st cl. Lit. Hum. and B.A. 1823, Ex. Coll. M.A. 1826; Deac. 1827 and Pr. 1829 by Bp of Ox. V. of Menheniot, Dio. Ex. 1831. (Patrons, D. and C. of Ex; Tithe, 1134*l*; Glebe, 20 acres; V.'s Inc. 800*l* and Ho; Pop 2423.) Formerly Fell. Tut. and Public Exam. of Ex. Coll. Ox. [16]

MARTIN, Richard, *Challacombe Rectory, Barnstaple, Devon.*—Corpus Coll. Cam. Deac. 1859 and Pr. 1860 by Bp of Ex. M.A. 1860. R. of Challacombe, Dio. Ex. 1861. (Patron, Earl Fortescue; Tithe, 180*l*; Glebe, 60 acres; R.'s Inc. 250*l* and Ho; Pop. 270.) [17]

MARTIN, Robert, *Anstey Pastures, near Leicester.*—Queens' Coll. Cam. Sen. Opt. and B.A. 1832, M.A. 1835; Deac. and Pr. 1833 by Bp of Lin. V. of Ratby with Groby C. Leic. Dio. Pet. 1833. (Patron, Earl of Stamford and Warrington; Tithe—Imp. 214*l*, V. 132*l* 10*s*; Glebe, 50 acres; V.'s Inc. 300*l*; Pop. 1264.) V. of Breedon, Leic. Dio. Pet. 1833. (Patron, Earl of Stamford and Warrington; Glebe, 10 acres; V.'s Inc. 200*l*; Pop. 1245.) Min. of Newtown Linford, Leic. Dio. Pet. 1834. (Patron, Earl of Stamford and Warrington; Min.'s Inc. 100*l*; Pop. 467.) Chap. to the Earl of Stamford and Warrington 1838. [18]

MARTIN, Robert Marshall, *Christ Church Parsonage, Spa Road, Bermondsey, London, S.E.*—St. Edm. Hall, Ox. B.A. 1841; Deac. 1842 and Pr. 1843 by Bp of Rip. P. C. of Ch. Ch. Bermondsey, Dio. Win. 1845. (Patrons, the Crown and Bp of Win. alt; P. C.'s Inc. 300*l* and Ho; Pop. 5672.) Formerly C. of Ossett, near Wakefield, 1842, St. George the Martyr, Southwark, 1843. [19]

MARTIN, William, *Grantchester Vicarage, near Cambridge.*—Corpus Coll. Cam. Sen. Opt. 1st cl. Cl. Trip. and B.A. 1841, M.A. 1844; Deac. 1843 by Bp of Herf. for Bp of Lich. Pr. 1845 by Bp of G. and B. V. of Grantchester, Dio. Ely, 1850. (Patron, Corpus Coll. Cam; Glebe, 100 acres; V.'s Inc. 303*l* 10*s* and Ho; Pop. 696.) Formerly Fell. Asst. Tut. and Cl. Lect. of Corpus Coll. Cam. 1841–51. Author, *A Visitation Sermon*, 1858. [20]

MARTIN, William, *Steeple Morden Vicarage, Royston.*—New Hall Coll. Ox. Fell. of, M.A. 1853; Deac. 1857 by Bp of Lon. Pr. 1862 by Bp of Ex. V. of Steeple Morden, Dio. Ely, 1865. (Patron, New Coll. Ox; Tithe, 371*l*; Glebe, 322*l*; V.'s Inc. 707*l* and Ho; Pop. 913.) Formerly C. of East Buckland, Devon, and Chap. of Devon County Sch. [21]

MARTIN, William Eyoott, *The Precincts, Rochester.*—Pemb. Coll. Ox. B.A. 1849, M.A. 1853; Deac. and Pr. 1850 by Bp of G. and B. Min. Can. Librarian and Sacristan of Roch. Cathl. 1858. Formerly C. of Boughton-Malherbe, Kent. [22]

MARTIN, William George, *Licensed Victuallers' Asylum, Old Kent-road, London, S.E.*—St. John's Coll. Cam. Coll. Prizeman 1846–47, Exhib. 1847. Jun. Opt. and B.A. 1848; Deac. 1848 and Pr. 1849 by Bp of Win. Chap. to the Licensed Victuallers' Asylum 1850. (Patrons, the Trustees and Governors.) [23]

MARTIN, Walter Willasey, *Church-square, Taunton.*—Brasen. Coll. Ox. B.A. 1860, M.A. 1865; Deac. 1863 and Pr. 1864 by Bp of B. and W. Sen. C. of St. Mary's, Taunton, 1865. Formerly C. of Trinity, Bridgwater, 1863. [24]

MARTINDALE, Arthur Frederic, *Hadnall, near Shrewsbury.*—St. Bees; Deac. 1866 and Pr. 1867 by Bp of Ches. for Bp of Lich. C. of Hadnall, 1866. [1]

MARTINDALE, Robert, 10, *Custom-house-terrace, Victoria-docks, London, E.*—St. Bees; Deac. 1835 and Pr. 1837 by Bp of Ches. Formerly C. of Batley, near Dewsbury. [2]

MARTINE, John Melville, *Edburton Rectory, Hurstpierpoint, Sussex.*—Univ. Coll. Edin. B.A. 1841, M.A. 1848, D.D. 1863; Deac. and Pr. 1841. R. of Edburton, Dio. Chich. 1866. (Patron, Abp of Cant; Tithe, 420*l* 15*s*; Glebe, 3 acres; R.'s Inc. 426*l* and Ho; Pop. 300.) Formerly P. C. of Shipley, Sussex; V. of Farningham, Kent. Author, *Lectures on Old Testament History*; *Lectures on the Beatitudes*; *Church of England Hymnal*, 2nd ed., dedicated by express permission to the Abp of Canterbury. [3]

MARTINEAU, Arthur, 61, *Westbourne-terrace, Hyde-park, London, W.*—Trin. Coll. Cam. 3rd in 1st cl Cl. Trip. and B.A. 1829, M.A. 1832; Deac. 1837 by Bp of Lich. Pr. 1838 by Bp of Rip. R. of St. Mildred's, Bread-street, with St. Margaret Moyses R. City and Dio. Lon. 1864. (Patrons, Ld Chan with Mrs. Benson and Mr. Andrew; R.'s Inc. 220*l*; Pop. St. Mildred's, 86, St. Margaret's 137.) Hon. Chap. to Bp of Lon. Formerly Fell. of Trin. Coll. Cam. 1831–36; V. of Whitkirk 1838–63; Rural Dean of Wetherby, and afterwards of Whitkirk 1847–63; V. of Alkham with Capel, Kent, 1863–64. Author, *No Need of a Living Infallible Guide in Matters of Faith* (four Sermons), Leeds, 1850; *Church History in England*, Longmans, 1853, 2nd ed. 1854. [4]

MARTYN, Charles John, 15, *Lansdown-place, Cheltenham,* and *Palgrave Priory, Diss, Norfolk.*—Ch. Ch. Ox. B.A. 1858, M.A. 1861; Deac. 1859 and Pr. 1860 by Bp of Nor. C. of St. Luke's, Cheltenham, 1865. Formerly C. of Palgrave, Suffolk, 1859–64. Author, *Two Sermons*, published by request for private circulation, preached at Palgrave in 1861 and 1864. [5]

MARTYN, Henry, *Grammar School, Norwich.*—Under-Mast. of the Gr. Sch. Norwich. [6]

MARTYN, John, *Ibberton Rectory, Blandford, Dorset.*—St. John's Coll. Cam. B.A. 1839; Deac. 1841 and Pr. 1842 by Bp of Ex. R. of Ibberton, Dio. Salis. 1855. (Patron, Lord Rivers; Tithe, 190*l*; Glebe, 57 acres; R.'s Inc. 270*l* and Ho; Pop. 237.) R. of Bellchalwell, Dorset, Dio. Salis. 1862. (Patron, Lord Rivers; Pop. 158.) Chap. of Don. of Woolland, Dorset, Dio. Salis. (Patron, M. Williams, Esq; Pop. 132.) [7]

MARTYN, John, *Penistone, Sheffield.*—Caius Coll. Cam. Jun. Opt. Math. Trip. B.A. 1867; Deac. 1867 by Abp of York. C. of Midhope, Sheffield, 1867. [8]

MARTYN, Thomas, *Ludgershall Rectory (Bucks), near Thame.*—Queen's Coll. Ox. R. of Ludgershall, Dio. Ox. 1821. (Patron, the present R; Tithe, 75*l*; R.'s Inc. 500*l* and Ho; Pop. 536.) [9]

MARTYN, William Waddon, *Lifton Rectory, Exeter.*—Trin. Coll. Ox. B.A. 1855; Deac. 1856 and Pr. 1857 by Bp of Ex. R. of Lifton, Dio. Ex. 1863. (Patron, H. Bradshaw, Esq; R.'s Inc. 500*l* and Ho; Pop. 1441.) Formerly C. of Kingsteignton, and of Hartland, Devon. [10]

MARVIN, William Harry, *Higham Gobion Rectory, Silsoe, Beds.*—St. John's Coll. Ox. B.A. 1850, M.A. 1854; Deac. 1851, Pr. 1852. R. of Higham Gobion, Dio. Ely, 1857. (Patron, J. H. Marvin, Esq; Tithe, 300*l*; Glebe, 30 acres; R.'s Inc. 360*l* and Ho; Pop. 121.) Formerly C. of Burton, Salop. [11]

MARWOOD, G. Willis, *Allerston, near Pickering, Yorks.*—Pemb. Coll. Cam. B.A. 1861, M.A. 1866; Deac. 1863 and Pr. 1864 by Bp of Man. C. of Ebberston with Allerston 1866. Formerly C. of Ch. Ch. Bolton-le-Moors. [12]

MARYCHURCH, Henry Weldy, *St. Paul's Parsonage, Blackburn.*—St. Edm. Hall, Ox. B.A. 1838, M.A. 1841. P. C. of St. Paul's, Blackburn, Dio. Man. 1850. (Patron, V. of Blackburn; P. C.'s Inc. 300*l* and Ho; Pop. 9718.) [13]

MASHEDER, Thomas, 3, *Eton-road, Haverstock-hill, N.W.*—Sid. Coll. Cam. 3rd Sen. Opt. B.A. 1865; Deac. 1866 and Pr. 1867 by Bp of Lon. C. of All Souls, South Hampstead. [14]

MASHITER, Benjamin, *Woodford Parsonage, Stockport.*—Dub. A.B. 1842; Deac. and Pr. 1842 by Bp of Ches. C. of Woodford, in the parish of Prestbury, Dio. Ches. 1842. (Patron, V. of Prestbury; Tithe—Imp. 224*l*; C.'s Inc. 50*l* and Ho; Pop. 392.) C. of Handforth, Cheshire. [15]

MASKELL, Joseph, *Tower-hill, London, E.C.*—King's Coll. Lond. Assoc. 1852; Deac. 1852 and Pr. 1853 by Bp of Salis. C. of All Hallows, Barking, 1860; Hon. Sec. of the City of Lond. Coll. 1861. Formerly C. of Allington 1852–55; West Lulworth, Dorset, 1855–56; and C. in sole charge of Bermondsey 1859. Author, *Lecture on the History of Bridport*, 1855; *Sermon for the Litton Friendly Society, Bridport*, 1856; *Notes on the Sepulchral Brasses of All Hallows, Barking*, 1861; *Collections towards the History and Antiquities of All Hallows, Barking*, 1864. [16]

MASKERY, Edward James, *Morpeth, Northumberland.*—Dub. A.B. 1848; Deac. 1848 by Bp of Lin. Pr. 1849 by Bp of Win. C. of Morpeth 1854. [17]

MASKERY, John, *Royal Medical Benevolent College, Epsom, Surrey.*—Wad. Coll. Ox. 3rd cl. Lit. Hum. and B.A. 1846, M.A. 1855; Deac. 1848 and Pr. 1849 by Bp of Lich. Asst. Mast. in the Royal Benevolent Medical College. [18]

MASKEW, H. E., M.A., *Shorncliffe.*—Chap. to the Forces. [19]

MASKEW, Thomas Ratsey, *Grammar School House, Dorchester*—Sid. Coll. Cam. B.A. 1842, M.A. 1846; Deac. 1842, Pr. 1843. Head Mast. of Dorchester Gr. Sch. 1846; Chap. to Dorchester Union; Surrogate. Formerly R. of Swyre, Dorset, 1856–61. Author, *Annotations on the Acts of the Apostles*, 2nd ed. 1847, 5*s*. [20]

MASON, Abraham, *Great Broxted Vicarage, Dunmow, Essex.*—Brasen. Coll. Ox. B.A. 1837, M.A. 1840; Deac. 1840 and Pr. 1841 by Abp of York. V. of Broxted, Dio. Roch. 1846. (Patron, Richard Benyon, Esq. M.P; Tithe, 200*l*; V.'s Inc. 200*l* and Ho; Pop. 782.) [21]

MASON, Alfred William, *Moulsham Parsonage, Chelmsford.*—Trin. Coll. Cam. B.A. 1843, M.A. 1847; Deac. 1843, Pr. 1844 by Abp of Cant. P. C. of St. John's, Moulsham, Dio. Roch. 1859. (Patron, R. of Chelmsford; Glebe, 2 acres; P. C.'s Inc. 300*l* and Ho; Pop. 4229.) Rural Dean of Chelmsford 1864. Formerly C. of Bocking 1843, St. Thomas's, Stamford Hill, 1848, Loughton 1854, Chelmsford 1858. [22]

MASON, Charles, *Bilsby Vicarage, Alford, Lincolnshire.*—Wor. Coll. Ox. B.A. 1856; Deac. 1857 and Pr. 1858 by Bp of Lin. V. of Bilsby, Dio. Lin. 1858. (Patron, the V; Tithe—Imp. 225*l*, V. 150*l*; Glebe, 19 acres; V.'s Inc. 180*l* and Ho; Pop. 572.) V. of Farlsthorp, Dio. Lin. 1840. (Patroness, Mrs. J. Kipling; Tithe—Imp. 170*l*, V. 35*l*; Glebe, 47 acres; V.'s Inc. 98*l*; Pop. 135.) Formerly C. of Bilsby and Farlsthorp. [23]

MASON, Edmund Thomas, *Buxton, Derbyshire.*—Ch. Coll. Cam. B.A. 1860; Deac. 1861 by Bp. of Dur. Pr. 1862 by Abp of York. Chap. of Devonshire Hospital, Buxton, 1865. Formerly C. of Coxwold 1861–63, Kirkby in Ashfield 1863. [24]

MASON, George, *Devonport.*—New Inn Hall, Ox. B.A. 1852, Wells Theol. Coll. 1852–53; Deac. 1853 by Bp of Salis. Pr. 1855 by Bp of Ex. C. of St. Stephen's, Devonport. Formerly C. of Alfington. [25]

MASON, George Holditch.—C. of Carisbrooke, Isle of Wight. Formerly C. of St. James's, Norwich. [26]

MASON, Henry Payne, *Beesby, Alford, Lincolnshire.*—Trin. Coll. Cam. B.A. 1831; Deac. 1832 and Pr. 1833 by Bp of Chich. R. of Beesby-le-Marsh, Dio. Lin. 1839. (Patron, Ld Chan; Tithe, 221*l* 17*s* 7*d*; Glebe, 42½ acres; R.'s Inc. 264*l*; Pop. 174.) [27]

MASON, Henry Williams, *Wigginton, Tring, Herts.*—Ch. Ch. Ox. Student of, B.A. 1848, M.A. 1851; Deac. 1849 by Bp of Ox. Pr. 1850 by Bp of Wor. P. C. of Wigginton, Dio. Roch. 1858. (Patron, Ch. Ch. Ox; Glebe, 89 acres; P. C.'s Inc. 184*l*; Pop. 641.) Formerly C. of Barford, near Warwick. [28]

MASON, Jackson, *Pickhill, Thirsk, Yorks.*—Trin. Coll. Cam. 2nd cl. Cl. Trip. B.A. 1856, M.A. 1859; Deac. 1858 and Pr. 1859 by Abp of York. V. of Pickhill with Roxby, Dio. Rip. 1859. (Patron, Trin. Coll. Cam; V.'s Inc. 200*l* and Ho; Pop. 783.) Formerly C. of Cantley, near Doncaster, 1858-59. [1]

MASON, Jacob Montagu, *Silk Willoughby Rectory, Sleaford, Lincolnshire.*—R. of Silk Willoughby, Dio. Lin. 1856. (Patron, Earl Dysart; Tithe, 625*l* 1*s*, Glebe, 11½ acres; R.'s Inc. 652*l* and Ho; Pop. 237.) [2]

MASON, J.—C. of St. John's, Leicester. [3]

MASON, J.—C. of Worsbrough, Yorks. [4]

MASON, John, *Sherburn Vicarage, New Malton, Yorks.*—Deac. 1831 and Pr. 1832 by Abp of York. V. of Sherburn, Dio. York, 1834. (Patron, Sir G. Chomley, Bart; Tithe—Imp. 84*l*, V. 84*l*; Glebe, 4 acres; V.'s Inc. 150*l* and Ho; Pop. 744.) Rural Dean of Buckrose East 1855. Formerly P. C. of Knapton, Yorks, 1842–66. [5]

MASON, John, *Fir Tree, Bishop's Auckland, Durham.*—P. C. of Fir Tree, Dio. Dur. 1862. (Patron, Crown and Bp alt; P. C.'s Inc. 200*l*; Pop. 1782.) [6]

MASON, John Mason, *Whitfield Rectory, Hexham.*—St. John's Coll. Cam. Sen. Opt. and B.A. 1844; Deac. 1844 and Pr. 1845 by Bp of Dur. R. of Whitfield, Dio. Dur. 1860. (Patron, Mrs. Blackett-Ord; Tithe, 260*l*; Glebe, 47 acres; R.'s Inc. 330*l* and Ho; Pop. 400.) [7]

MASON, John Wharton, *Hagg Cottage, Richmond, Yorks.*—Univ. Coll. Dur. B.A. 1844, M.A. 1847; Deac. 1845 and Pr. 1846 by Bp of Rip. P. C. of Marrick, near Richmond, Dio. Rip. 1847. (Patron, F. Morley, Esq; Tithe—Imp. 292*l* 6*s* 1*d*, P. C. 2*s*; Glebe, 40 acres; P. C.'s Inc. 120*l*; Pop. 462.) [8]

MASON, John Williams, *Furthoe (Northants), near Stony Stratford.*—Jesus Coll. Ox. B.A. 1842. R. of Furthoe, Dio. Pet. 1843. (Patron, Jesus Coll. Ox; Tithe, 31*l*; R.'s Inc. 144*l*; Pop. 16.) [9]

MASON, Joseph, *East Tytherley, Stockbridge, Hants.*—Queen's Coll. Ox. B.A. 1840, M.A. 1843; Deac. 1841 by Bp of Roch. Pr. 1842 by Bp of Herf. Chap. of the D. of East Tytherley, Dio. Win. 1851. (Patron, Sir Lionel Goldsmid, Bart; Chap.'s Inc. 40*l*; Pop. 352.) Formerly Chap. to H.M.'s Forces in the Crimea. [10]

MASON, Peter, *Kimbolton.*—Emman. Coll. Cam. Sen. Opt. and B.A. 1853; Deac. 1856 and Pr. 1857 by Bp of Wor. C. of Kimbolton 1865. Formerly C. of Exford 1859–61, Uley 1861–64, Woodbridge 1864–65. [11]

MASON, Peter Hamnett, *St. John's College, Cambridge.*—St. John's Coll. Cam. 11th Wrang. and B.A. 1849, M.A. 1852; Deac. 1852, Pr. 1854. Fell. and Heb. Lect. of St. John's Coll. Cam. 1854. Joint Author of Mason and Bernard's *Hebrew Grammar* מֵי מְנֻחוֹת *Gently Flowing Waters* (with Exercises and Key, and *Commentary on and New Translation of Isaiah* liii.) 2 vols. Cambridge, 1853. Author of *A Plea for accurate Hebrew Study*, Cambridge, 1855. [12]

MASON, Richard Evans, *Earsdon, Newcastle-on-Tyne.*—Dub. A.B. 1852, A.M. 1858; Deac. 1852 by Abp of Dub. Pr. 1853 by Bp of Cork. V. of Earsdon, Dio. Dur. 1857. (Patrons, several Landholders; V.'s Inc. 140*l*; Pop. 8000.) Chap. of Seaton-Delaval, Earsdon, Dio. Dur. 1860. (Patron, Lord Hastings; C.'s Inc. 60*l*; Pop. 2876.) Formerly C. of All Saints', Newcastle, and Shotton, Durham. [13]

MASON, Richard Williams, *Llanfair, Harlech.*—Jesus Coll. Ox. 2nd cl. Lit. Hum. B.A. and M.A. 1839; Deac. 1841 and Pr. 1843 by Bp of Ox. R. of Llanfair, Dio. Ban. 1859. (Patron, Bp of Ban; Tithe, 150*l*; R.'s Inc. 210*l* and Ho; Pop. 426.) Formerly P. C. of Penrhos Llugwy, Anglesey, 1844; Stip. C. to Bp Bethel at Llandyrnog, Denbigh, 1857. [14]

MASON, Robert Boyle Monck, *Normanton-road, Derby.*—Dub. Queen's Scho. and Prof. of Div Prize, 1847, A.B. 1847, A.M. 1854; Deac. 1848 and Pr. 1850 by Bp of Dur. P. C. of Ch. Ch. Derby, Dio. Lich. 1863. (Patrons, Trustees; P. C.'s Inc. 190*l*; Pop. 5000.) Formerly C. of Gateshead, 1848; P. C. of Worton, Wilts, 1851, Ch. Ch. Battersea, 1853. [15]

MASON, Skinner Chart, *Urchfont Vicarage, Devizes, Wilts.*—St. Cath. Hall, Cam. B.A. 1845, M.A. 1855; Deac. 1845, Pr. 1846. V. of Urchfont with Stert C. Dio. Salis. 1860. (Patrons, D. and C. of Windsor; Tithe, 300*l*; Glebe, 2 acres; V.'s Inc. 380*l* and Ho; Pop. 1459.) Formerly C. of Winkfield, Berks, 1846–49, Sherborne 1849–53; R. of Magdalen Laver, Essex, 1853–55; R. of St. Clement Danes, Lond. 1855–60. [16]

MASON, William, *Kirkby Malzeard, Yorkshire.*—Trin. Coll. Cam. 12th Wrang. and B.A. 1826; Deac. and Pr. 1828. C. of Kirkby Malzeard 1866. Formerly V. of Normanton, 1833–66. [17]

MASON, William, *Cobham, Surrey.*—Ch. Coll. Cam. Found. Scho. Sen. Opt. B.A. 1852, M.A. 1855; Deac. 1854 and Pr. 1856 by Bp of Lin. C. of Cobham, Surrey, 1861. Formerly C. of Barford, near Warwick. [18]

MASON, William, *Sacriston Parsonage, Durham.*—Deac. 1859 and Pr. 1860 by Bp of Carl. P. C. of Sacriston, Dio. Dur. 1864. (Patrons, Crown and Bp of Dur. alt; P. C.'s Inc. 300*l* and Ho; Pop. 3000.) Formerly C. (sole charge) of Waberthwaite, Northumberland, 1859–63; Stower Provost and Todbere, Dorset, 1863–64. [19]

MASSEY, Charles, *West Bromwich, Staffs.*—Dub. and St. Bees Theol. Coll; Deac. 1858 and Pr. 1859 by Bp of Lich. P. C. of St. Peter's, West Bromwich, Dio. Lich. 1860. (Patron, Bp of Lich; P. C.'s Inc. 300*l*; Pop. 6330.) Formerly C. of Trinity, Smethwick, 1858. [20]

MASSEY, John Cooke, *The Vicarage, Rugeley.*—Ex. Coll. Ox. B.A. 1865; Deac. 1866 Pr. 1867. C. of Rugeley 1866. [21]

MASSEY, Thomas, *Hatcliffe Rectory, Great Grimsby, Lincolnshire.*—St. John's Coll. Cam. Sen. Opt. and B.A. 1833; Deac. 1833 and Pr. 1834 by Abp of York. R. of Hatcliffe with West Ravendale P. C. Dio. Lin. 1840. (Patron, Chapter of Southwell Coll. Ch; Hatcliffe, Tithe, 314*l* 7*s* 3*d*; Glebe, 4 acres; West Ravendale, Glebe, 27 acres; R.'s Inc. 350*l* and Ho; Pop. Hatcliffe 159, West Ravendale 50.) V. of East Ravendale, Linc. Dio. Lin. 1841. (Patron, Trin. Coll. Cam; Tithe—Imp. 188*l* 4*s*, V. 58*l* 4*s* 6*d*; Glebe, 43½ acres; V.'s Inc. 127*l*; Pop. 94.) [22]

MASSEY, Thomas Hackety, *Faringdon Rectory, near Alton, Hants.*—King's Coll. Lond. Theol. Assoc. 1852. R. of Faringdon, Dio. Win. 1857. (Patron, the present R; Tithe, 592*l*; R.'s Inc. 760*l* and Ho; Pop. 535.) Formerly C. of St. Mark's, Marylebone, Lond. [23]

MASSINGBERD, Francis Charles, *Ormsby Rectory, Alford, Lincolnshire.*—Magd. Coll. Ox. 2nd cl. Lit. Hum. and B.A. 1822, M.A. 1823; Deac. 1824 by Bp of Ox. Pr. 1825 by Bp of Lin. R. of Ormsby South with Ketsby R. Calceby V. and Triby R. Dio. Lin. 1825. (Patrons, Massingberd Trustees; Tithe—Imp. 92*l* 11*s*, R. 888*l*; Glebe, 59 acres; R.'s Inc. 968*l* and Ho; Pop. Ormsby and Ketsby 261, Calceby 66, Triby 79.) Chancellor of Lin. Cathl. 1862. Formerly Preb. of Thorngate in Lin. Cathl. 1847. Author, *Considerations on Church Reform*, Rivingtons, 1832; *English Reformation*, 2 eds. 1847; Pamphlets on Convocation, &c; *Letter to Rev. W. Goode*, 1851; *Letter to Dr. Jeremie*, 1851. [24]

MASSINGHAM, John Deacon, *St. Paul's Parsonage, Warrington.*—Dub. A.B. 1851, A.M. 1854; Deac. 1851 and Pr. 1852 by Bp of Lich. P. C. of St. Paul's, Warrington, Dio. Ches. 1863. (Patron, Lord Lilford; P. C.'s Inc. 210*l* and Ho; Pop. 9266.) Surrogate; Chap. to the Warrington Union; Lect. for the Church Institution of London. Formerly C. of All Saints', Derby, 1851–53; P. C. of St. Paul's, Derby, 1853–63. Author, *Infidel Objections to Holy Scripture weighed in the Balances and found Wanting*, 3d; *The Church of England in Relation to the State and the People*, 3d; *One Hundred Questions for Roman Catholics*; *Little Mary, or a Child's Influence*; *Summary of English History*; *History of the Jesuits*; *Letters to Mr. Smedley in Defence of the Church of England*; *A Public Discussion for Two Nights at Derby with Charles Williams, Baptist Minister, on the Property, Endowments, and System of the Church of England as opposed to Dissent*; *What about*

the Prayer Book? or, The Objector Refuted, and her Church of England Defended, 1d; *Are these Things True? or, The Aggressor Exposed, and the Church of England Defended*, 1d; *Lectures Delivered in the Philosophical Hall, Huddersfield*, 4d; *Williams Unmasked; or, the Misstatements and False Quotations of a Liberation Society Lecturer Exposed*, 2d; *The Scriptural Connection of Church and State*, 4d; *The Assailant Answered; or, the Union of the Church and State of England, both Scriptural and Advantageous to the Nation*; *The Assailant again Answered; or the Fictions, Fallacies, and Misstatements of the Rev. W. Walters Exposed*, 1d; *The Liberation Society; its Objects, Character, and Advocates*; *The Liberation Society, What it Really Wants*, 2d; *The State-Church Controversy*, 4d; *Tithes, not National Property, proved to be the Gifts of Individuals, not of the State*, 2d; also, Occasional Sermons and Articles in *The Church of England Magazine*, *The London Pulpit*, *Church of England Sunday School Quarterly Magazine*, etc. [1]

MASTER, Augustus Chester, *Preston All Saints', Cirencester.*—New Inn Hall, Ox. B.A. 1847; Deac. 1848, Pr. 1849. V. of Preston All Saints', Dio. G. and B. 1861. (Patroness, Miss Master; V.'s Inc. 350*l*; Pop. 217.) Formerly P. C. of Perlethorpe, Notts, 1851–58; R. of Broadwas, Worc. 1858–61. [2]

MASTER, George Francis, *Stratton, Cirencester.*—Univ. Coll. Ox. B.A. 1841, M.A. 1842; Deac. 1841, Pr. 1842. P. C. of Baunton, Glouc. Dio. G. and B. 1843. (Patroness, Miss Master; Tithe, 100*l*; Glebe, 5 acres; P. C.'s Inc. 100*l*; Pop. 122.) R. of Stratton, Dio. G. and B. 1844. (Patroness, Miss Jane Master; Glebe, 375 acres; R.'s Inc. 330*l* and Ho; Pop. 396.) [3]

MASTER, George Streynsham, *West Dean Rectory, Salisbury.*—Brasen. Coll. Ox. B.A. 1845, M.A. 1848; Deac. 1846, Pr. 1847 by Bp of Lich. R. of West Dean with East Grinstead, Dio. Salis. 1865. (Patron, Rev. Henry Glossop; Tithe, 625*l*; Glebe, 90 acres; R.'s Inc. 700*l* and Ho; Pop. 446.) Formerly P. C. of Welsh-Hampton, Salop, 1847–59; V. of Twickenham 1859–65. Author, *A Plea for the Faithful Celebration of the Occasional Services of the Church of England*, Rivingtons, 1858. [4]

MASTER, Gilbert Coventry, *Huyton, near Prescot, Lancashire.*—Ex. Coll. Ox. B.A. 1862; Deac. 1862, Pr. 1863. C. of Huyton 1864. Formerly C. of St. Barnabas', Liverpool, 1862–64. [5]

MASTER, James Streynsham, *Chorley Rectory, Lancashire.*—Ball. Coll. Ox. 2nd cl. Lit. Hum. and B.A. 1820, M.A. 1823; Deac. 1822, Pr. 1824. R. of Chorley, Dio. Man. 1846. (Patrons, the present R; Tithe, 1042*l*; Glebe, 26 perches; R.'s Inc. 1042*l* and Ho; Pop. 3187.) Hon. Can. of Man. Cathl. 1854; Rural Dean of Leyland. [6]

MASTER, Oswald, *Cold Norton, Maldon, Essex.*—Brasen. Coll. Ox. B.A. 1849, M.A. 1852; Deac. 1851, Pr. 1852. C. of Cold Norton. Formerly C. of Huyton 1851. [7]

MASTER, William, *Bucknell Rectory, Bicester, Oxon.*—New Coll. Ox. B.C.L. 1821; Deac. 1819 and Pr. 1821 by Bp of Herf. R. of Bucknell, Dio. Ox. 1833. (Patron, New Coll. Ox; Glebe, 362 acres; R.'s Inc. 400*l* and Ho; Pop. 291.) [8]

MASTERS, James Hoare, *Lower Beeding Vicarage, Horsham, Sussex.*—Emman. Coll. Cam. B.A. 1856, M.A. 1859; Deac. 1856 and Pr. 1857 by Bp of Win. V. of Lower Beeding with St. John's C. Dio. Chich. 1861. (Patron, W. E. Hubbard, Esq; Tithe, 134*l*; Glebe, 20 acres; P. C.'s Inc. 135*l* and Ho; Pop. 1100.) Formerly C. of All Saints', Southampton. [9]

MASTERS, John Smalman, *Shrewsbury House, Shooter's Hill, Kent, S.E.*—Jesus Coll. Ox. B.A. 1825, M.A. 1828; Deac. 1829 and Pr. 1830 by Bp of Roch; P. C. of Ch. Ch. Shooter's Hill, Dio. Roch. 1865. (Patron, J. S. Masters.) Formerly C. of Greenwich. [10]

MASTERS, William Caldwell, *Ivy Cottage, Hitchin, Herts.*—Magd. Coll. Ox. B.A. 1865; Deac. 1866 by Bp of Roch. C. of St. Mary's, Hitchin, 1866. [11]

MATCHETT, Abraham, *Halesworth, Suffolk.*—C. of Halesworth. [12]

MATCHETT, Henry Horace, *Alkborough, Brigg, Lincolnshire.*—Emman. Coll. Cam. B.A. 1851, M.A. 1855; Deac. 1853 and Pr. 1854 by Bp of Wor. C. in sole charge of Alkborough 1866. Formerly C. of Claines, Worcestershire; Chap. R.N. 1854–62. [13]

MATCHETT, Jonathan Chase, *The Close, Norwich.*—St. John's Coll. Cam. B.A. 1821, M.A. 1824; Deac. 1821, Pr. 1822. P. C. of St. Mary-in-the-Marsh, City and Dio. Nor. 1824. (Patrons, D. and C. of Nor; P. C.'s Inc. 105*l*; Pop. 451.) V. of Easton, Norfolk, Dio. Nor. 1834. (Patron, E. R. Fellowes, Esq; Tithe—Imp. 31*l* 10*s*, V. 170*l*; Glebe, 28¾ acres; V.'s Inc. 190*l*; Pop. 233.) Min. Can. and Sacrist. of Nor. Cathl. 1824. (Value 20*l*.) [14]

MATHER, Edward, *Ringley Parsonage, Manchester.*—Brasen. Coll. Ox. B.A. 1858, M.A. 1863; Deac. 1859 and Pr. 1860 by Bp of Lich. C. of Ringley 1861. Formerly C. of Alton, Staffs, 1860–61. [15]

MATHER, Edward Lushington, *Bootle, Liverpool.*—Brasen. Coll. Ox. B.A. 1848, M.A. 1851; Deac. 1849, Pr. 1850. P. C. of Ch. Ch. Bootle, Dio. Ches. 1866. (Patrons, Trustees; P. C.'s Inc. 260*l* and Ho; Pop. 2250.) Formerly C. of Iver, Bucks, and Calne, Wilts. [16]

MATHER, Frederic Vaughan, *Clifton.*—Trin. Coll. Cam. Wrang. and B.A. 1847, M.A. 1855; Deac. 1847, Pr. 1848. P. C. of St. Paul's, Clifton, Dio. G. and B. 1853. (Patrons, Simeon's Trustees; Pop. 1444.) Exam. Chap. to Bp of G. and B. [17]

MATHER, George, *Huntley Hall, Cheadle, Staffs.*—Trin. Coll. Cam. B.A. 1845, M.A. 1848; Deac. 1846, Pr. 1847. P. C. of St. Chad's, Freehay, Dio. Lich. 1847. (Patron, R. of Cheadle; P. C.'s Inc. 164*l*; Pop. 630.) Rural Dean of Cheadle 1857. Formerly P. C. of Oakamoor, Cheadle, 1854–65. [18]

MATHER, Herbert, *Training College, Carmarthen.*—Trin. Coll. Cam. B.A. 1863, M.A. 1867; Deac. 1866 and Pr. 1867 by Bp of St. D. Prin. of National Society's Training Coll. Carmarthen, 1867. Formerly Vice-Prin. of same Coll. 1865–67. [19]

MATHESON, Charles, *St. John's College, Oxford.*—St. John's Coll. Ox. B.A. 1854, M.A. 1857; Deac. 1855, Pr. 1856. Fell. of St. John's Coll. Ox. [20]

MATHEWS, George F., *St. Mary's Vicarage, Bungay.*—Dub. Hebrew Prize, A.B. 1848; Deac. 1848 and Pr. 1849 by Abp of Armagh. P. C. of St. Mary's, Bungay, Dio. Nor. 1865. (Patron, Duke of Norfolk; P. C.'s Inc. 180*l* and Ho; Pop. 1996.) Formerly Sec. to Ch. Miss. Soc; P. C. of Woodville 1854; V. of Ravenstone, Bucks, 1860–65. [21]

MATHEWS, Henry Staverton, *Bentworth Rectory, Alton, Hants.*—Clare Coll. Cam. B.A. 1841, M.A. 1845; Deac. and Pr. 1843 by Bp of Pet. R. of Bentworth, Dio. Win. 1847. (Patron, the present R; Tithe, 937*l* 10*s*; Glebe, 90 acres; R.'s Inc. 1027*l* and Ho; Pop. 647.) [22]

MATHEWS, Murray Alexander, *Weston-super-Mare.*—Mert. Coll. Ox. 3rd cl. Lit. Hum. M.A. 1862; Deac. 1861 and Pr. 1862 by Bp of B. and W. C. of Weston-super-Mare 1863. Formerly C. of St. Mary Magdalen's, Taunton, 1861–63. Author, *The Everlasting Love*, Taunton, 1867, 3*s*. [23]

MATHEWS, Thomas, *Erryd Mansion, Kilycwm, near Llandovery, Carmarthenshire.*—Lampeter; many prizes and Sen. and Heb. Scho. B.D. 1860; Deac. 1852 and Pr. 1853 by Bp of St. D. V. of Kilycwm, Dio. St. D. 1859. (Patron, W. H. H. Campbell-Davys, Esq; V.'s Inc. 200*l*; Pop. 1380.) Surrogate 1861. Formerly C. of Llanllwny, Carmarthenshire, 1852; Stip. C. of Llanrhidian and Penclawdd, Glamorganshire, 1853–59. [24]

MATHEWS, William Arnold, *Laughton Vicarage, Gainsborough.*—Corpus Coll. Ox. B.A. 1861; Deac. 1862 and Pr. 1863 by Bp of Lin. V. of Laughton with Wildsworth C. Dio. Lin. 1865. (Patron, H. C. M. Ingram, Esq; V.'s Inc. 260*l* and Ho; Pop. Laughton 365, Wildsworth 150.) Formerly C. of St. Peter's, Radford, Notts, 1862. [25]

MATHIAS, George, *Royal Hospital, Chelsea, London, S.W.*—St. John's Coll. Cam. B.A. 1838, M.A. 1841; Deac. and Pr. 1839 by Bp of Nor. Chap. to the Royal Hospital, Chelsea, 1845; Chap. in Ordinary to the Queen. [1]

MATHIAS, George H. Duncan, *East Cowes, Isle of Wight.*—King's Coll. Cam. 1st cl. Cl. Trip. B.A. 1856, M.A. 1860; Deac. 1856 and Pr. 1857 by Bp of Lin. Formerly C. of Lamborne Woodlands, Berks; P. C. of East Moulsey, Surrey. [2]

MATHIE, Benjamin, *Hendon Rectory, Sunderland.*—Univ. Coll. Dur. B.A. 1848, M.A. 1852; D.C.L. 1861; Deac. 1849 and Pr. 1850 by Bp of Dur. R. of Hendon, Dio. Dur. 1854. (Patron, Bp of Dur; Tithe, 100*l*; R.'s Inc. 430*l* and Ho; Pop. 11,451.) [3]

MATHISON, William Collings, *Trinity College, Cambridge.*—Trin. Coll. Cam. B.A. 1839, M.A. 1842; Deac. 1843 and Pr. 1844 by Bp of Ely. Sen. Fell. and Tut. of Trin. Coll. Cam. [4]

MATHWIN, John, *Tanfield Vicarage, Gateshead, Durham.*—Univ. Coll. Dur. Licen. Theol. 1852; Deac. 1852 and Pr. 1853 by Bp of Dur. V. of Tanfield, Dio. Dur. 1857. (Patron, Lord Ravensworth; Tithe—App. 7*l*, Imp. 376*l* 2*s*, V. 73*l*; Glebe, 2 acres; V.'s Inc. 220*l* and Ho; Pop. 4593.) Formerly C. of Tanfield. [5]

MATSON, Robert, *Piddington, near Thame, Oxon.*—Deac. 1849 by Bp of Ex. Pr. 1851 by Bp of Lin. C. in sole charge of Piddington 1866. Formerly C. of Bridestowe with Sourton, Devon, 1851, Spanby, Lincolnshire, 1853, Morpeth, Northumberland, 1854–59; held appointments in West Indies 1859; C. of Adstock, Bucks, 1861, Thorverton, Devon, 1862, Sidbury, Devon, 1864, Gilling, York (sole charge), 1864. [6]

MATTHEW, David Sutton, *Wainfleet St. Mary, Boston.*—Emman. Coll. Cam. 18th Wrang. and B.A. 1851, M.A. 1854; Deac. 1852 and Pr. 1853 by Bp of Lon. P. C. of Wainfleet St. Mary's, Linc. Dio. Lin. 1859. (Patron, Bethlehem Hosp; P. C.'s Inc. 201*l* and Ho; Pop. 730.) Formerly C. of All Saints', Islington, 1852, St. Bride's, Fleet-street, Lond. 1854, Alford, Linc. 1857. [7]

MATTHEW, Henry James, *Allahabad, Bengal.*—Trin. Coll. Cam. 2nd cl. Cl. Trip. 1859, Carus Prize, 1858, B.A. 1859, M.A. 1862; Deac. 1861 and Pr. 1862 by Abp of Cant. East India Chap. 1866; Military Chap. Allahabad 1867. [8]

MATTHEW, John, *Chelvey, Bristol.*—Ball. Coll. Ox. B.A. 1821, M.A. 1830; Deac. 1822, Pr. 1823. R. of Chelvey, Dio. B. and W. 1831. (Patron, J. Cooke, Esq; Tithe, 100*l*; Glebe, 19¾ acres; R.'s Inc. 145*l*; Pop. 54.) [9]

MATTHEWS, Andrew, *Gumley, Market Harborough.*—Lin. Coll. Ox. B.A. 1836, M.A. 1839; Deac. 1837, Pr. 1838. R. of Gumley, Dio. Pet. 1853. (Patrons, D. and C. of Lin; Tithe, 18*s* 4*d*; R.'s Inc. 400*l* and Ho; Pop. 214.) [10]

MATTHEWS, Henry, *Magdalen Laver, near Ongar, Essex.*—Queen's Coll. Ox. B.A. 1852, M.A. 1855; Deac. 1853, Pr. 1854. C. of Magdalen Laver 1867. Formerly C. of Gratwich and Kingstone, Staffs. [11]

MATTHEWS, James, *Sherburn Vicarage, Milford Junction, Yorks.*—Wad. Coll. Ox. B.A. 1825, M.A. 1827; Deac. 1826 by Bp of Ox. Pr. 1827 by Bp of Cashel for Bp of Ox. V. of Sherburn, Dio. York, 1831. (Patron, the Preb. of Fenton, in York Cathl; Tithe—App. 137*l* 3*s* 4½*d*, Imp. 13*l* 6*s*, V. 18*l* 11*s* 3*d*; Glebe, 100 acres; V.'s Inc. 135*l* and Ho; Pop. 2918.) V. of Fenton-Kirk, near Tadcaster, Dio. York, 1830. (Patron, the Preb. of Fenton, in York Cathl; Glebe, 70 acres; V.'s Inc. 100*l*; Pop. 711.) [12]

MATTHEWS, James Bolomey, *Rushden Vicarage, Buntingford, Herts.*—Trin. Coll. Cam. Sen. Opt. B.A. 1855, M.A. 1858; Deac. 1855 and Pr. 1856 by Bp of Ely. V. of Rushden, Dio. Roch. 1858. (Patrons, D. and C. of Lin; Tithe—App. 219*l*, V. 123*l* 10*s*; Glebe, 27 acres; V.'s Inc. 155*l* and Ho; Pop. 291.) Formerly C. of Layham, Suffolk. [13]

MATTHEWS, John, *Knowstone, South Molton, Devon.*—V. of Knowstone with Molland V. Dio. Ex. 1853. (Patron, Sir William Throckmorton; Knowstone, Tithe—Lect. 99*l* 13*s* 2*d*, V. 339*l*; Molland, Tithe—Imp. 138*l*, V. 301*l*; V.'s Inc. 666*l*; Pop. Knowstone 511, Molland 598.) [14]

MATTHEWS, Joseph, *Haughley, near Stowmarket, Suffolk.*—C. of Haughley. Formerly C. of Chenies, Bucks. [15]

MATTHEWS, Joseph, *St. David's College, Lampeter, Cardiganshire.*—St. John's Coll. Cam. 20th Wrang. and B.A. 1846, M.A. 1849; Deac. 1850 and Pr. 1851 by Bp of Ex. Prof. of Physical Science, Lampeter; Preb. of St. D. [16]

MATTHEWS, J. T., *Shiffnal, Salop.*—Mast. of Shiffnal Gr. Sch. [17]

MATTHEWS, Richard Browne, *Shalford Vicarage, Guildford.*—Jesus Coll. Cam. B.A. 1847, M.A. 1850. V. of Shalford, Dio. Win. 1856. (Patron, Ld Chan; Tithe—Imp. 109*l* 9*s*, V. 180*l*; V.'s Inc. 330*l* and Ho; Pop. 1293.) [18]

MATTHEWS, Timothy Richard, *North Coates, Great Grimsby.*—Caius Coll. Cam. B.A. 1853; Deac. 1853, Pr. 1854. C. of North Coates 1859. Formerly C. of St. Mary's, Nottingham. Author, *Times for Holy Worship.* [19]

MATTHEWS, William, *Hawes, Bedale, Yorks.*—Queens' Coll. Cam. Coll. Prizeman 1836–37, B.A. 1838; Deac. 1839 by Bp of Rip. Pr. 1841 by Bp of Ches. P. C. of Hawes. Dio. Rip. 1863. (Patron, V. of Aysgarth; Tithe—Imp. 186*l*; Glebe, 76 acres; P. C.'s Inc. 153*l* 17*s* 6*d* and Ho; Pop. 1708.) Formerly P. C. of Cowgill-in-Dent, Dio. Rip. 1841–63. Author, *Letter to Rev. T. L. Green in Reply to his "Transubstantiation as taught by Christ and His Apostles,"* 1830, 2*s* 6*d*; *A Voice from the Grave* (a Sermon in Cowgill Church), 1860, 1*s*; numerous papers in *Notes and Queries*; etc. [20]

MATTHEY, Alphonso.—King's Coll. Lond. Theol. Assoc; Deac. 1856 by Bp of Ox. Pr. 1857 by Bp of Lon. C. of St. John's Chapel, Park-road, St. John's Wood, Lond. Formerly C. of St. Thomas's, Stepney, Lond. Ruswarp, Yorks, and Little Stanmore, Middlesex. Author, *A Musical Version of the Evening Service.* [21]

MATTHIAS, Thomas, *Borth, Llanvihangel-Geneu-r-Glyn, Cardiganshire.*—Lampeter; Scho. and Bates' Prizeman 1862; Deac. 1865 and Pr. 1866 by Bp of St. D. C. of Borth 1865. [22]

MATURIN, Benjamin, *Lymington, Hants.*—Dub. A.B. 1837, A.M. 1865; Deac. 1839 by Bp of Dromore, Pr. 1840 by Bp of Derry. C. of Lymington 1852; Surrogate. Formerly C. of Ringwood, Hants, and Biddenham, Beds. Author, *The Lord's Supper examined and explained, and the Duty of celebrating it recommended and enforced,* Nisbet, 2*s*. [23]

MATURIN, Washington Shirley, *Thurgarton, Hanworth, Norfolk.*—Deac. 1849, Pr. 1850. R. of Thurgarton, Dio. Nor. 1852. (Patron, Bp of Nor; Tithe, 235*l*; Glebe, 10 acres; R.'s Inc. 260*l*; Pop. 273.) [24]

MAUD, Henry Landon, *Assington, near Sudbury, Suffolk.*—Trin. Coll. Cam. B.A. 1850; Deac. 1853, Pr. 1854. V. of Assington, Dio. Ely, 1866. (Patron, John Gurdon, Esq; Tithe, 300*l*; Glebe, 50 acres; V.'s Inc. 400*l* and Ho; Pop. 747.) Formerly C. of Brigstock with Stanion, Northants, and St. Giles'-in-the-Fields, Lond. [25]

MAUD, John Primatt, *The Vicarage, Ancaster, near Grantham.*—Trin. Hall, Cam. LL.B. 1851; Deac. 1860 and Pr. 1861 by Bp of Ches. V. of Ancaster, Dio. Lin. 1862. (Patron, the present V; Glebe, 120 acres; V.'s Inc. 190*l* and Ho; Pop. 682.) Formerly C. of St. Paul's, Tranmere, Cheshire, 1860, Langtoft, Linc. 1861. [26]

MAUDE, C. W., *Great Munden, Ware, Herts.*—R. of Great Munden, Dio. Roch. 1863. (Patron, the Crown; R.'s Inc. 750*l* and Ho; Pop. 457.) [27]

MAUDE, Francis Henry, *Trinity Parsonage, Ipswich.*—St. Bees; Deac. 1845 and Pr. 1846 by Bp of Dur. P. C. of Trinity, Ipswich, Dio. Nor. 1848. (Patrons, Three Trustees; P. C.'s Inc. 200*l* and Ho; Pop. 2326.) [28]

MAUDE, Joseph, *Chirk Vicarage, Denbighshire.*—Queen's Coll. Ox. 1st cl. Math. et Phy. 1826, B.A. 1827, M.A. 1830; Deac. 1828 and Pr. 1829 by Bp of Lin. V. of Chirk, Dio. St. A. 1852. (Patron, Bp of St. A; Tithe—Imp. 62*l* 14*s*, V. 507*l* 6*s*; Glebe, 2¼ acres; V.'s Inc. 570*l* and Ho; Pop. 1630.) Chap. to Bp of St. A. 1840; Hon. Can. of St. A. 1854; Rural Dean. [1]

MAUDE, Ralph, *Mirfield Vicarage, Dewsbury*—Brasen. Coll. Ox. B.A. 1824, M.A. 1827; Deac. 1825, Pr. 1826. V. of Mirfield, Dio. Rip. 1827. (Patron, Joshua Ingham, Esq; V.'s Inc. 255*l* and Ho; Pop. 5452.) [2]

MAUDE, Thomas, *Hasketon Rectory, Woodbridge, Suffolk.*—Jesus Coll. Cam. B.A. 1827; Deac. 1828, Pr. 1830. R. of Hasketon, Dio. Nor. 1845. (Patron, the present R; Tithe—Imp. 187*l* 18*s* 3*d*, R. 396*l* 16*s* 5*d*; Glebe, 37 acres; R.'s Inc. 402*l* and Ho; Pop. 145.) [3]

MAUGHAM, Henry Macdonald, *Sandwich, Kent.*—King's Coll. Lond. 1848, Oriel Coll. Ox. 3rd cl. Math. et Phy. and B.A. 1852, M.A. 1855; Deac. 1853 by Bp of Ox. Pr. 1855 by Bp of Win. C. of St. Peter's, Sandwich, 1867. Formerly C. of Reigate 1855, Chertsey 1858, Kirton 1860, Sturry 1865. [4]

MAUGHAN, George, *East Kirkby Vicarage, Spilsby, Lincolnshire.*—St. Cath. Coll. Cam. B.A. 1854, M.A. 1858; Deac. 1854 and Pr. 1855 by Bp of Lin. V. of East Kirkby, Dio. Lin. 1857. (Patron, J. Banks, Stanhope, Esq. M.P; Glebe, 118 acres; V.'s Inc. 170*l* and Ho; Pop. 432.) Formerly C. of Basford, Notts, 1854–57. [5]

MAUGHAN, John, *Bewcastle Rectory, Brampton, Cumberland.*—Dub. A.B. 1830; Deac. and Pr. 1833 by Bp of Ches. R. of Bewcastle, Dio. Carl. 1836. (Patrons, D. and C. of Carl; Tithe, 60*l*; Glebe, 40 acres; R.'s Inc. 120*l* and Ho; Pop. 1091.) Formerly C. of Melling, near Liverpool, 1833 37. Author, *Memoir on the Roman Station and Runic Cross at Bewcastle,* 1*s*; *Memoir on the old Roman Road, called the Maiden Way, from the Roman Wall into Scotland,* and other Antiquarian Papers. [6]

MAUGHAN, John Archibald Collingwood, *Prudhoe, Northumberland.*—Univ. Coll. Dur. and Cuddesdon Coll; Deac. 1863 and Pr. 1865 by Bp of Dur. P. C. of Mickley, Ovingham, Dio. Dur. 1867. (Patron, W. B. Wrightson, Esq; P. C.'s Inc. 93*l* and Ho; Pop. 2800.) Formerly C. of Horton, Northumberland, 1863–67. [7]

MAUGHAN, Joseph, *Holdforth-street, New Wortley, near Leeds.*—King's Coll. Lond. Theol. Assoc. 1860; Deac. 1860 and Pr. 1861 by Bp of Ex. P. C. of New Wortley (Conventional District), Dio. Rip. 1867. (Patron, Bp of Rip; P C.'s Inc. 150*l*; Pop. 4700.) Formerly C. of St. Blazey, Cornwall, 1860, St. Philip's, 1862; Assoc. Sec. of Colonial and Continental Ch. Soc. Stepney, Lond. 1862; C. and Lect. of Whitechapel 1864. [8]

MAUGHAN, Robert, *Heatherycleugh Parsonage, Darlington.*—Univ. Coll. Dur. Licen. Theol. 1841; Deac. 1841, Pr. 1842. P. C. of Heatherycleugh, Stanhope, Dio. Dur. 1865. (Patron, Bp of Dur; P. C.'s Inc. 400*l* and Ho.) Formerly C. of Stanhope. [9]

MAUGHAN, Simpson Brown, *Widdrington Vicarage, Morpeth, Northumberland.*—Clare Coll. Cam. and St. Bees; Deac. 1834 by Bp of Dur. Pr. 1836 by Bp of Carl. V. of Widdrington, Dio. Dur. 1853. (Patron, Lord Vernon; Tithe, 50*s*; V.'s Inc. 75*l* 3*s* 8*d* and Ho; Pop. 502.) Formerly C. of Ch. Ch. Tynemouth, 1834–35, Hebron, Bothal, 1836–60; Chap. to the Morpeth Union, 1838–63. Author, *The Obligation imposed upon the Church to preach the Gospel to the World* (a Sermon), 1845. [10]

MAUGHAN, William, *Benwell Parsonage, Newcastle-on-Tyne.*—St. Bees; Deac. 1833, Pr. 1834. P. C. of St. James's, Benwell, Dio. Dur. 1843. (Patron, V. of Newcastle-on-Tyne; Glebe, 12 acres; P. C.'s Inc. 186*l* and Ho; Pop. 4323.) [11]

MAUGHAN, William Morland, *Little Witley, Worcester.*—Dur. 1863; Deac. 1866 by Bp of Wor. C. of Holt and Little Witley 1866. [12]

MAUL, Richard Compton, *Rickinghall Rectory, Botesdale, Suffolk.*—Caius Coll. Cam. B.A. 1843, M.A. 1848; Deac. 1845 and Pr. 1846 by Bp of Nor. R. of Rickinghall Superior with Rickinghall Inferior R. Dio. Nor. 1850. (Patron, G. St. Vincent Wilson, Esq; Tithe, 1052*l*; Glebe, 43 acres; R.'s Inc. 1116*l* and Ho; Pop. Rickinghall Superior 742, Rickinghall Inferior 437.) [13]

MAUL, Richard Graham, 14, *Bloomsbury-street, London, W.C.*—St. John's Coll. Cam. B.A. 1842, M.A. 1846; Deac. 1843 and Pr. 1844 by Bp of Ex. P. C. of St. John's, Drury-lane, Dio. Lon. 1855. (Patron, Sir Walter James; P. C.'s Inc. 160*l*; Pop. 2983.) [14]

MAULE, George, *Ampthill Rectory, Beds.*—Univ. Coll. Ox. B.A. 1837; Deac. 1838 and Pr. 1839 by Bp of Lin. R. of Ampthill, Dio. Ely, 1846. (Patron, Ld Chan; Corn rent, 150*l*; Glebe, 47 acres; R.'s Inc. 280*l* and Ho; Pop. 2144.) Surrogate 1854; Chap. to the Ampthill Union 1854. [15]

MAULE, Henry Augustus, *Godmanchester, Hunts.*—St. Peter's Coll. Cam. B.A. 1821, M.A. 1836; Deac. 1822 and Pr. 1823 by Bp of Lin. P. C. of Raveley Parva, Hunts, Dio. Ely, 1828. (Patron, Earl of Sandwich; Tithe, Imp. 45*l*; P. C.'s Inc. 59*l*; Pop. 60.) Chap. to the Hunts County Gaol and House of Correction 1828; Mast. of the Hospital of St. John the Baptist in Huntingdon, 1836. [16]

MAULE, Thomas Carteret, *Cheam Rectory, Ewell, Surrey.*—St. John's Coll. Ox. Fell. of, 3rd cl. Lit. Hum. and B.A. 1839, M.A. 1843, B.D. 1848. R. of Cheam, Dio. Win. 1856. (Patron, St. John's Coll. Ox; Tithe, 683*l*; Glebe, 26 acres; R.'s Inc. 655*l* and Ho; Pop. 1156.) [17]

MAULE, William, *Eynesbury Rectory, St. Neots, Hunts.*—Trin. Coll. Cam. B.A. 1848, M.A. 1853; Deac. 1849 and Pr. 1850 by Bp of Ely. R. of Eynesbury, Dio. Ely, 1851. (Patron, Earl of Sandwich; R.'s Inc. 430*l* and Ho; Pop. 1314.) [18]

MAUNDER, Charles, *Walton Vicarage, Ipswich.*—Queens' Coll. Cam. B.A. 1839, M.A. 1842; Deac. 1839 and Pr. 1840 by Bp of Lon. V. of Walton with Felixstow V. Dio. Nor. 1857. (Patron, the present V; Walton, Tithe—Imp. 376*l* 14*s* 2*d*, V. 213*l* 17*s* 2*d*; Glebe, 3 acres; Felixstow, Tithe—Imp. 303*l* 6*s*, V. 176*l* 15*s* 2*d*; V.'s Inc. 399*l* and Ho; Pop. Walton, 988, Felixstow 673.) Chap. of Landguard Fort. [19]

MAUNSELL, Frederick Webster, *Iwerne-Courtnay, Blandford, Dorset.*—Dub. A.B. 1851, A.M. 1854; Deac. 1852 by Bp of Killaloe and Clonfert, Pr. 1853 by Bp of Meath. R. of Iwerne-Courtnay with Farrington C. Dio. Salis. 1861. (Patron, Lord Rivers; R.'s Inc. 372*l* and Ho; Pop. 620.) Formerly C. of Critchill and Farnham, Dorset. [20]

MAUNSELL, G., *Broomfield, Chelmsford.*—C. of Broomfield. [21]

MAUNSELL, George Edmond, *Thorpe-Malsor, Kettering.*—Ch. Ch. Ox. B.A. 1838; Deac. 1840, Pr. 1841. R. of Thorpe-Malsor, Dio. Pet. 1842. (Patron, T. P. Maunsell, Esq; Tithe, 17*l* 2*s* 3*d*; R.'s Inc. 300*l* and Ho; Pop. 297.) Chap. to the Earl of Westmoreland 1842; Rural Dean 1858. Author, *Miscellaneous Poems,* Smith, Elder and Co. 1861, 5*s*. [22]

MAURICE, John Frederick Denison, 2, *York-terrace, Regent's-park, London, N.W.*—Ex. Coll. Ox. B.A. 1831, M.A. 1835; Deac. 1834, Pr. 1835. P. C. of St. Peter's, Vere-street, Dio. Lon. 1860. (Patron, the Crown; P. C.'s Inc. 450*l*.) Formerly Chap. and Preacher to the Hon. Soc. of Lincoln's-inn, 1846; Prof. of Div. in King's Coll. Lond. Author, *Has the Church or the State the Power to Educate the Nation?* (a course of Lectures), 1839; *The Kingdom of Christ,* 2 vols. 1841; *Christmas-day and other Sermons,* 1843; *The Epistle to the Hebrews,* 1846; *The Religions of the World and their Relations to Christianity,* 1847; *The Lord's Prayer* (nine Sermons preached in Lincoln's-inn Chapel), 1848; *The Prayer-Book considered in Reference to the Romish System* (nineteen Sermons, ditto), 1849; *The Church, a Family* (twelve Sermons, ditto), 1850; *The Old Testament* (nineteen Sermons, ditto), 1851; *The Prophets and Kings of the Old*

Testament, 1853; *Sermons on the Sabbath-day*, 1853; *Theological Essays*, 1853; *Learning and Working* (six Lectures on the Foundation of Colleges for Working Men, 1854); *The Indian Crisis* (five Sermons), 1857, 2s 6d; *Lectures on the Apocalypse, or Book of Revelation of St. John the Divine*, 1861, 10s 6d; *What is Revelation? a Series of Sermons on the Epiphany, to which are added Letters to a Theological Student on the Bampton Lectures of Mr. Mansel*, 10s 6d; *Sequel to the Inquiry, "What is Revelation?" Letters in Reply to Mr. Mansel's Examination of "Strictures on the Bampton Lectures,"* 6s; *The Claims of the Bible and of Science; a Correspondence between a Layman and the Rev. F. D. Maurice, on some Questions arising out of the Controversy respecting the Pentateuch*, 4s 6d; *The Gospel of the Kingdom of Heaven* (a course of Lectures on the Gospel of Luke), 1864, 9s; all published by Macmillan and Co; *Modern Philosophy, a Treatise on Moral and Metaphysical Philosophy from the Fourteenth Century to the French Revolution, with a Glimpse into the Nineteenth Century*, 1862, 10s 6d; *Mediæval Philosophy*, 2nd ed. 5s; *Philosophy of the First Six Centuries*, 2nd ed. 3s 6d; *Ancient Philosophy*, 4th ed. 5s; these Philosophical Manuals published by Griffin, Bohn and Co. [1]

MAURICE, John Pierce, *Mitchelmersh, Romsey, Hants.*—R. of Mitchelmersh, Dio. Win. 1840. (Patron, Bp of Win; R.'s Inc. 550*l*; Pop. 718.) [2]

MAURICE, Lyttelton Henry Powys, *Nutley Parsonage, Reigate.*—Caius Coll. Cam. and Theol. Coll. Lichfield; Deac. 1864 by Bp of Lich. Pr. 1865 by Bp of Ches. P. C. of Nutley Lane, Dio. Win. 1866. (Patron, William Phillipps, Esq; P. C.'s Inc. 100*l* and Ho.) Formerly C. of Wednesbury 1864, King's Hill, Wednesbury, 1864. [3]

MAURICE, Mortimer, *Crantock, New Quay, Cornwall.*—St. Edm. Hall, Ox. B.A. 1851, M.A. 1855; Deac. 1851 and Pr. 1853 by Bp of G. and B. P. C. of Crantock, Dio. Ex. 1860. (Patron, Lord Churston; P. C.'s Inc. 78*l*; Pop. 381.) Formerly C. of Trinity, Clifton, near Bristol. [4]

MAURICE, Peter, *New College, Oxford.*—Jesus Coll. Ox. B.A. 1826, New Coll. Ox. M.A. 1829, B.D. 1837, D.D. 1840; Deac. and Pr. 1827 by Bp of Ban. V. of Yarnton, near Oxford, Dio. Ox. 1858. (Patrons, All Souls Coll. Ox. one turn, and Sir G. Dashwood, three turns; V.'s Inc. 290*l*; Pop. 294.) Formerly Chap. of New Coll. Ox. 1828; Chap. of All Souls Coll. Ox. 1837; C. of Kennington, Berks, 1829–54. Author, *Popery in Oxford* (a Tract), 1832; *Popery of Oxford Confronted, Repudiated, Disavowed* (a Pamphlet), 1837; *Key to the Popery of Oxford*, 1838; *Postscript to the Popery of Oxford*, 1851. Composer of an *Evening Service in E*, "*With Angels and Archangels*," *Choral Harmony*, 1854; *Tunes, in Four Parts, for Congregational Worship*, 1855; *Supplement to the Choral Harmony*, 1858. [5]

MAURICE, Thomas, *Harnhill Rectory, Cirencester.*—Mert. Coll. Ox. 3rd cl. Lit. Hum. and B.A. 1830, M.A. 1833; Deac. 1831 and Pr. 1832 by Bp of Salis. R. of Harnhill, Dio. G. and B. 1840. (Patron, George Bengough, Esq; Tithe, 123*l* 10*s*; Glebe, 23 acres; R.'s Inc. 152*l* and Ho; Pop. 88.) V. of Driffield, Glouc. Dio. G. and B. 1840. (Patron, George Bengough, Esq; Glebe, 180 acres; V.'s Inc. 225*l* and Ho; Pop. 132.) J. P. for Gloucester and Wilts. [6]

MAXFIELD, John, *Norwell Vicarage, Newark, Notts.*—V. of Norwell with Carlton-on-Trent C. Dio. Lin. 1853. (Patron, Bp of Rip; V.'s Inc. 365*l* and Ho; Pop. Norwell 736, Carlton-on-Trent 290.) [7]

MAXWELL, Charles, *Wyddial Rectory, Buntingford, Herts.*—Ball. Coll. Ox. 3rd cl. Lit. Hum. and B.A. 1833; Deac. 1834 and Pr. 1835 by Bp of Bristol. R. of Wyddial, Dio. Lon. 1838. (Patroness, Mrs. Ellis; Tithe, 326*l*; Glebe, 14 acres; R.'s Inc. 340*l* and Ho; Pop. 213.) [8]

MAXWELL, Edward, *High Roding Rectory, Dunmow, Essex.*—Trin. Coll. Cam. B.A. 1839, M.A. 1842; Deac. 1841 and Pr. 1842 by Bp of Rip. R. of High Roding, Dio. Roch. 1857. (Patron, Earl of Roden; Tithe, comm. 487*l*; Glebe, 25*l*; R.'s Inc. 517*l* and Ho; Pop. 469.) Formerly C. of Ch. Ch. Leeds, 1841; Min. of St. John's, Barnsley, 1845; C. of Trinity, Calne, 1853, St. Peter's, Ipswich, 1856. Author, *Evangelical Assent and Consent*, Hunt, 1863, 6*d*. [9]

MAXWELL, George.—St. John's Coll. Cam. B.A. 1824; Deac. 1825, Pr. 1826. Formerly V. of Winterbourne Whitchurch, Dorset, 1849–65. [10]

MAY, Edmund.—Dom. Chap. to the Earl of Radnor. [11]

MAY, Edward John, *Nottingham.*—Wor. Coll. Ox. B.A. 1842, M.A. 1845. Head Mast. of the Coll. Sch. Nottingham; C. of Strelly and Bilbrough, Notts. Formerly Head Mast. of Brewers' Company Sch. Lond. [12]

MAY, Edward William, *Allington, Bridport.*—Ch. Coll. Cam. B.A. 1859, M.A. 1862; Deac. 1859 and Pr. 1863 by Bp of Ex. C. of Allington 1864; Patron of Roborough, Devon. Formerly C. of North Molton, Devon, and St. Peter's, Regent-square, Lond. [13]

MAY, Frederic Schiller, 15, *Craven-terrace, Upper Hyde Park-gardens, London, W.*—Caius Coll. Cam. 3rd cl. Cl. Trip. 1856, 2nd cl. Theol. Trip. 1857, B.A. 1856, M.A. 1860; Deac. 1856 and Pr. 1857 by Bp of Nor. C. of Ch. Ch. Paddington, 1859; Hon. Chap. to Bp of Illinois. Formerly C. of Ashwell-Thorpe 1856–59. Scandinavian Editor for Anglo-Continental Society. Author, *Vindication of Apostolic Succession of Church of Sweden*, 1862; *On Intercommunion of Anglican and Scandinavian Churches*, 1863; *Letter to Rev. J. Vahl on the Anglican Doctrine of the Eucharist*, Copenhagen, 1866. [14]

MAY, Henry Thomas, *South Petherwin, Launceston.*—New Coll. Ox. M.A; Deac. 1839 by Bp of Ox. Pr. 1840 by Bp of Win. V. of South Petherwin with Trewen, Dio. Ex. 1850. (Patron, Univ. of Ox; Tithe, 308*l*; Glebe, 14 acres; V.'s Inc. 340*l* and Ho; Pop. South Petherwin 876, Trewen 178.) Formerly C. of St. Paul's, Southsea, 1839, Kingston, Portsea, 1841; P. C. of Milton, Portsea, 1847. [15]

MAY, James Lewis, *West Putford Rectory, Brandis Corner, North Devon.*—Queens' Coll. Cam. B.A. 1836; Deac. 1836 and Pr. 1837 by Bp of Ex. R. of West Putford, Dio. Ex. 1837. (Patron, the present R; Tithe, 203*l*; Glebe, 90 acres; R.'s Inc. 260*l* and Ho; Pop. 362.) [16]

MAY, John, *Ugborough Vicarage, Ivybridge, Devon.*—Ex. Coll. Ox. B.A. 1825; Deac. and Pr. 1826 by Bp of Nor. V. of Ugborough, Dio. Ex. 1845. (Patron, the Grocers' Company; Tithe, Imp. 436*l* 9*s*; V.'s Inc. 300*l* and Ho; Pop. 1226.) [17]

MAY, John, *Hanwell, Middlesex.*—St. Cath. Hall, Cam. B.A. 1836, M.A. 1839; Deac. 1838 and Pr. 1839. Chap. to the Co. of Middlesex Lunatic Asylum at Hanwell 1844. [18]

MAY, Robert Costall, 12, *Munster-terrace, Fulham, S.W.*—Trin. Coll. Cam. 2nd cl. Cl. Trip. B.A. 1854, M.A. 1857; Deac. 1855 by Bp of Lon. Pr. 1856 by Bp of Win. C. of Fulham 1865. Formerly C. of St. Thomas's, Stepney, 1855, St. Giles'-in-the-Fields 1857. [19]

MAY, Thomas, *Leigh Vicarage, Tunbridge, Kent.*—Ch. Coll. Cam. B.A. 1820, M.A. 1823; Deac. 1821, Pr. 1822. V. of Leigh, Dio. Cant. 1830. (Patron, the present V; Tithe—Imp. 555*l*, V. 510*l* 15*s*; Glebe, 3 acres; V.'s Inc. 447*l* and Ho; Pop. 1047.) [20]

MAY, William, *Landbeach, Cambridge.*—Corpus Coll. Cam. B.A. 1866; Deac. 1866 by Bp of Ely. C. of Landbeach 1866. [21]

MAYALL, Robert, *Blackburn, Lancashire.*—Dur. Licen. in Theol. 1863; Deac. 1863 and Pr. 1864 by Abp of York. C. of Blackburn 1865. Formerly C. of Pontefract 1863–65. [22]

MAYBERRY, Charles, *Hirwain, near Pont-y-prydd.*—Jesus Coll. Ox. B.A. 1825, M.A. 1828. R. of Penderyn, Dio. St. D. 1831. (Patron, William Winter, Esq; Tithe, 306*l*; Glebe, 4½ acres; R.'s Inc. 311*l*; Pop. 1331.) C. of Ystradvelte, Breconshire. [23]

MAYD, William, *Withersfield Rectory, Haverhill, Suffolk.*—Ex. Coll. Ox. B.A. 1821, M.A. 1822; Deac. 1821 by Bp of Win. Pr. 1822 by Bp of Nor. R. of Withersfield, Dio. Ely, 1827. (Patron, the present R;

Tithe, 600*l* 9*s*; Glebe, 44 acres; R.'s Inc. 645*l* and Ho; Pop. 640.) Rural Dean. Author, *Village Sermons*, 1 vol; *Sunday Evening, a Short and Plain Exposition of the Gospel for every Sunday in the Year*, 1863, 3*s* 6*d*. [1]

MAYE, Henry Stanton, *Liverpool College, Liverpool.*—Lond. B.A. 1862; Deac. 1864, Pr. 1865. Head Mast. of the Lower Sch. Liverpool Coll. 1863 Formerly C. of St. Philip's, Liverpool, 1864–65. [2]

MAYER, H., *Wold-Newton, Bridlington, Yorks.*—V. of Wold-Newton, Dio. York, 1863. (Patron, Viscount Downe; V.'s Inc. 113*l*; Pop. 351.) [3]

MAYERS, Henry, *Weston Rectory, near Beccles.*—Trin. Hall, Cam. B.A. 1845; Deac. 1846 and Pr. 1847 by Bp of Ches. R. of Weston, Dio. Nor. 1859. (Patron, Ld Chan; Tithe, comm. 350*l*; Glebe, 2 acres; R.'s Inc. 350*l*; Pop. 261.) Formerly C. of Walkden Moor, Lanc. 1846; Chap. in Scotland 1849–52; C. of Witheringsett, Suffolk, 1856, Topcroft, Norfolk (sole charge), 1857–58. Wootton, Isle of Wight, 1859. [4]

MAYERS, Michael John, *Winchester.*—R. of St. Peter's, Cheesehill, Winchester, Dio. Win. 1865. (Patron, Ld Chan; R.'s Inc. 185*l*; Pop. 992.) Formerly British Chap. at Marseilles; Min. of Castelnau Chapel, Barnes, Surrey. [5]

MAYHEW, Anthony Lawson, *Zenith Houses, St. Margaret's, Rochester.*—Wad. Coll. Ox. B.A. 1863; Deac. 1865 and Pr. 1866 by Bp of Lich. C. of St. Margaret's, Rochester, 1867. Formerly C. of St. Paul's, Derby, 1865–67. [6]

MAYHEW, Caleb B.—C. of Christ Chapel, St. John's Wood, Lond. 1864. Formerly C. of Maryport, Cumberland. [7]

MAYHEW, H. C., *Abington, Northants.*—C. of Abington. [8]

MAYHEW, Samuel Martin, *St. Paul's, Bermondsey, London, S.E.*—King's Coll. Lond. Theol. Assoc. 1854; Deac. 1854 and Pr. 1855 by Bp of Win. P. C. of St. Paul's, Bermondsey, Dio. Win. 1864. (Patrons, Crown and Bp of Win. alt; P. C.'s Inc. 300*l*; Pop. 9770.) Formerly C. of Newdegate, Surrey. [9]

MAYHEW, Thomas Rabett, *Warehorne Rectory, Ashford, Kent.*—Queen's Coll. Ox. B.A. 1839, M.A. 1842; Deac. 1840, Pr. 1841. R. of Warehorne, Dio. Cant. 1866. (Patron, Ld Chan; Tithe, 330*l*; Glebe, 40 acres; R.'s Inc. 420*l* and Ho; Pop. 412.) Formerly V. of Darsham 1851–66; P. C. of Dunwich, Suffolk, 1851–66. [10]

MAYNARD, Forster, *Kirk-Bramwith Rectory, Doncaster.*—Caius Coll. Cam. B.A. 1828, M.A. 1837; Deac. 1828, Pr. 1829. R. of Kirk-Bramwith Dio. York, 1850. (Patron, Chan. of the Duchy of Lancaster; Tithe, 455*l*; Glebe, 53 acres; R.'s Inc. 540*l* and Ho; Pop. 226.) [11]

MAYNARD, John, *Sudborne Rectory, Woodbridge, Suffolk.*—Ex. Coll. Ox. B.A. 1822, M.A. 1824; Deac. 1823, Pr. 1824. R. of Sudborne with Orford C. Dio. Nor. 1842. (Patron, the Crown; Sudborne, Tithe, 502*l* 0*s* 5*d*; Orford, Tithe, 317*l*; R.'s Inc. 846*l* and Ho; Pop. Sudborne 525, Orford 948.) Chap. to the Marquis of Hertford. [12]

MAYNARD, John Martin, *Matlock.*—Pemb. Coll. Ox. 2nd cl. Lit. Hum. and B.A. 1847, M.A. 1849; Deac. 1848 and Pr. 1849 by Abp of York. P. C. of Trinity, Matlock, Dio. Lich. 1859. (Patrons, Trustees; Pop. 1258.) Formerly C. of Ch. Ch. Cheltenham. [13]

MAYNARD, Robert, *Wormleighton Vicarage, Leamington.*—Wad. Coll. Ox. B.A. 1836, M.A. 1838; Deac. 1837, Pr. 1838. V. of Wormleighton, Dio. Wor. 1841. (Patron, Earl Spencer; Tithe 40*l*; Glebe, 40 acres; V.'s Inc. 100*l* and Ho; Pop. 203.) [14]

MAYNARD, Thomas Richard, *Canterbury.*—Queens' Coll. Cam. B.A. 1851, M.A. 1855; Deac. 1851 and Pr. 1853 by Bp of Roch. Chap. to the Forces 1855. Formerly C. of Aylesford, Kent, 1851–53, All Saints', Paddington, 1854–55. [15]

MAYNARD, Walter, *Great Glemham, Wickham Market, Suffolk.*—Ex. Coll. Ox. B.A. 1853, M.A. 1855. C. of Great Glemham. Formerly C. of Horfield, Glouc. [16]

MAYNARD, William, 17, *Percy-street, Liverpool.*—Caius Coll. Cam. B.A. 1828; Deac. and Pr. 1830 by Bp of Lon. Min of the Mariners' Ch. Liverpool, Dio. Ches. 1832. (Patrons, Trustees; Min's Inc. 250*l*.) [17]

MAYNARD, William Suffield Forster, *Mosterton, near Crewkerne.*—Dub. A.B. 1858; Deac. 1860 and Pr. 1861 by Bp of B. and W. C. of South Perrott with Mosterton 1865. Formerly C. of Midsomer-Norton 1860, Hemington with Hardington 1861. [18]

MAYNE, James, *Romansleigh Rectory, South Molton, Devon.*—St. John's Coll. Cam. B.A. 1846; Deac. 1846 and Pr. 1847 by Bp of Ches. R. of Romansleigh, Dio. Ex. 1865. (Patron, Sir T. D. Acland; R.'s Inc. 200*l* and Ho; Pop. 230.) Formerly C. of Melling, Lancaster, of Constantine, Cornwall, of Bridestowe, and Silverton, Devon; Chap. of Killerton Chapel, Devon, for five years. [19]

MAYNE, John Pascoe, *Tidcombe Portion, Tiverton, Devon.*—Deac. 1849, Pr. 1850. C. of Tidcombe Portion. [20]

MAYNE, Jonathan, *Gloucester.*—St. John's Coll. Cam. B.A. 1861; Deac. 1862 and Pr. 1863 by Bp of Ex. C. of St. Catherine's, Gloucester, 1867. Formerly C. of Gwennap, Cornwall, 1862–64, St. Mark's, Gloucester, 1864–67. [21]

MAYNE, William Gibbons, *St. John's Parsonage, Ingrow, near Keighley, Yorks.*—Dub. A.B. 1826, A.M. 1836, M.A. Ox. 1867; Deac 1832 by Bp of Dromore, Pr. 1834 by Bp of Ferns. P. C. of Ingrow with Hamworth, Dio. Rip. 1846. (Patron, Bp of Rip; P. C.'s Inc. 145*l* and Ho; Pop. 4072.) Formerly C. of St. John's, Dublin, 1832, St. John's, Manchester, 1836, St. George's, Wigan, 1841. [22]

MAYO, Charles Erskine, *Colesgrove, Cheshunt, Herts.*—Clare Hall, Cam. B.A. 1833, M.A. 1836; Deac. 1833 and Pr. 1834 by Bp of Ches. Formerly V. of Lenaham, Notts, 1843–56. [23]

MAYO, Charles Theodore, *St. Andrew's Parsonage, Hillingdon, near Uxbridge.*—Ball. Coll. Ox. B.A. 1855, M.A. 1857; Deac. 1857 and Pr. 1858 by Bp of Win. P. C. of St. Andrew's, Hillingdon, Dio. Lon. 1865. (Patron, Bp of Lon; P. C.'s Inc. 240*l* and Ho; Pop. 2500.) Formerly C. of St. John's, Redhill, Surrey. [24]

MAYO, James, *Bircham Newton, Lynn, Norfolk.*—C. of Bircham Newton with Tofts. [25]

MAYO, Job, *Stokenchurch, Oxon.*—Literate; Deac. 1823 and Pr. 1825 by Abp of York. P. C. of Stokenchurch, Dio. Ox. 1849. (Patron, Ld Chan; Tithe, 135*l*; P. C.'s Inc. 140*l*; Pop. 1412.) [26]

MAYO, Robert, *Ovington, Alresford, Hants.*—Ch. Ch. Ox. B.A. 1856. C. of Ovington. [27]

MAYO, Theodore, *Leigh on Mendip, Frome.*—Trin. Coll. Cam. B.A. 1862, M.A. 1865; Deac. 1867. C. of Leigh on Mendip 1867. [28]

MAYO, William, *Folke, Sherborne.*—Magd. Hall, Ox. B.A. 1828, M.A. 1830; Deac. 1828 and Pr. 1829 by Bp of Glouc. R. of Folke, Dorset, Dio. Salis. 1865. (Patrons, D. and C. of Salis; R.'s Inc. 390*l* and Ho; Pop. 332.) P. C. of North Wootton, Dorset, Dio. Salis. 1865. (Patron, G. W. D. Digby, Esq; P. C.'s Inc. 67*l*; Pop. 76.) Formerly C. of Didmarton and Oldbury-on-the-Hill, Glouc. 1828; Steeple Langford, Wilts, 1833; Chap. of St. Nicholas' Hospital, Salisbury, 1841; Chap. of the Wilts County Gaol 1843. [29]

MAYOR, Charles, *Wavendon, Woburn, Beds.*—St. John's Coll. Cam. B.A. 1842, M.A. 1845; Deac. 1845 and Pr. 1846 by Bp of Nor. C. of Wavendon, Bucks, 1848. [30]

MAYOR, John Eyton Bickersteth, *St. John's College, Cambridge.*—St. John's Coll. Cam. B.A. 1848, M.A. 1851; Deac. 1855 and Pr. 1857 by Bp of Ely. Fell. of St. John's Coll. Cam. Author, *Thirteen Satires of Juvenal*, 1853; *Cambridge in the 17th Century*, 1854; *Life of Nicholas Ferrar*, 1855; *Life of Matthew Robinson*, 1856; *Early Statutes of St. John's College, Cambridge*, Part I. 1859, all published by Macmillans. [31]

MAYOR, Joseph, *Cossington Rectory, Loughborough.*—Deac. 1848, Pr. 1850. R. of Cossington, Dio. Pet. 1859. (Patron, the present R; R.'s Inc. 450*l* and

Ho; Pop. 408.) Formerly R. of Scorborough with Leconfield P. C. Yorks, 1852–59. [1]

MAYOR, Joseph Bickersteth, 27, *Kensington-square, London, W.*—St. John's Coll. Cam. B.A. 1851, M.A. 1854. Head Mast. of Kensington Sch. Formerly Fell. and Tut. of St. John's Coll. Cam. [2]

MAYOR, Robert Bickersteth, *Frating Rectory, Colchester.*—St. John's Coll. Cam. 3rd Wrang. and B.A. 1842, M.A. 1845, B.D. 1852; Deac. 1845 and Pr. 1850 by Bp of Wor. R. of Frating with Thorington R. Dio. Roch. 1863. (Patron, St. John's Coll. Cam; Tithe, 820*l*; Glebe, 106 acres; R.'s Inc. 985*l* and Ho; Pop. Frating 235, Thorington 424.) Formerly Nadin Div. Stud. 1844; Fell. of St. John's Coll. Cam. 1845; Math. Mast. Rugby Sch. 1845–63. [3]

MAYOR, William, *Winksley, Ripon.*—Queen's Coll. Birmingham; Deac. 1861 by Bp of Dur. Pr. 1865 by Bp of Rip. P. C. of Winksley with Grantley, Dio. Rip. 1865. (Patrons, D. and C. of Rip; Tithe—App. 16*l*, Imp. 8*l* 7*s* 6*d*; Glebe, 5 acres; P. C.'s Inc. 150*l*; Pop. 350.) Formerly C. of Horton, Morpeth, Northumberland, 1861; St. John's, Kensal Green, Lond. 1862, St. Jude's, Mildmay Park, Islington, 1863, Ch. Chapel, Maida Hill, 1864, Trinity, Ripon, 1864. [4]

MAYOR, William, *Thornley Vicarage, Ferryhill, Durham.*—Bp Hat. Hall, Dur. Barry Univ. Scho. B.A. 1856, M.A. 1860; Deac. 1855 and Pr. 1856 by Bp of Man. V. of Thornley, Dio. Dur. 1862. (Patron, V. of Kelloe; V.'s Inc. 300*l* and Ho; Pop. 3454.) Surrogate; J.P. for Durham. Formerly C. of St. Nicholas', Durham, Easington, and Ch. Ch. North Shields. [5]

MAYOU, Benjamin, *Baddesley Parsonage, Atherstone, Warwickshire.*—Lin. Coll. Ox. King's Coll. Lond. Theol. Assoc. 1849; Deac. 1850 and Pr. 1851 by Bp of Lich. P. C. of Baddesley-Ensor, Dio. Wor. 1867. (Patrons, the Inhabitants; Tithe—Imp. 61*l* 15*s* 9*d*; P. C. 9*l* 14*s* 1*d*; P. C.'s Inc. 67*l* 11*s* 8*d* and Ho; Pop. 872.) Formerly Asst. C. of Wilnecote 1850–59; C. of Wilnecote 1859–61, Polesworth, Tamworth, 1861–64, Tamworth 1865–67. [6]

MAYOW, Mayow Wynell, *St. Mary's, West Brompton, London S.W.*—Ch. Ch. Ox. B.A. 1833, M.A. 1837; Deac. 1833, Pr. 1834. P. C. of St. Mary's, West Brompton, Dio. Lon. 1860. (Patron, P. C. of Brompton; P. C.'s Inc. 300*l*; Pop. 4236.) Formerly V. of Market Lavington, Wilts, 1836–60. Author, *A Letter to the Archdeacon of Wilts*, 1847; *A Letter to the Rev. W. Maskell*, 1850; *A Second Letter to the Rev. W. Maskell*, 1850; *A Few Words to Soldiers and Sailors called to active Service*, Masters, 1854, *Eight Sermons on the Priesthood, Altar, and Sacrifice*, Parkers, 1867. [7]

MAYOW, Philip Wynell, *Easton, Wells, Somerset.*—Trin. Coll. Cam. B.A. 1836, M.A. 1839; Deac. 1837, Pr. 1838. P. C. of Easton, Dio. B. and W. 1845. (Patron, V. of Wells; P. C.'s Inc. 66*l*; Pop. 259.) [8]

MEABY, G. K., *Bradford, Yorks.*—C. of St. Luke's, Bradford. [9]

MEAD, Richard Yawler, *Tredington Rectory, Shipston-on-Stour.*—St. John's Coll. Cam. B.A. 1856, M.A. 1859; Deac. 1856 and Pr. 1857 by Bp of Lich. C. of Tredington 1866. Formerly C. of Wellington, Salop, 1856; P. C. of Berwick-Bassett, Wilts, 1859; C. of St. Saviour's, Bath, and Heytesbury, Wilts. [10]

MEADE, De Courcy, *Weston, near Bath.*—Ex. Coll. Ox. 2nd cl. Lit. Hum. and B.A. 1846; Deac. 1849 and Pr. 1850 by Bp of Llan. C. of Weston 1856. Formerly C. of Ibberton and Woolland, Dorset. [11]

MEADE, Edward, *Winkfield Rectory, Trowbridge, Wilts.*—Wad. Coll. Ox. 2nd cl. Lit. Hum. and B.A. 1829, M.A. 1832; Deac. 1831 and Pr. 1832 by Bp of Wor. R. of Winkfield, Dio. Salis. 1842. (Patrons, Trustees; Tithe, 260*l*; Glebe, 18 acres; R.'s Inc. 300*l* and Ho; Pop. 340.) Formerly P. C. of St. Peter's, Malvern Wells, Author, various Sermons. [12]

MEADE, John, *Newton-Purcell Rectory, near Buckingham.*—St. Peter's Coll. Cam. B.A. 1836; Deac. 1836 and Pr. 1837 by Bp of Lin. R. of Newton-Purcell with Shelswell C. Dio. Ox. 1843. (Patron, J. Harrison, Esq; Newton-Purcell, Tithe, 132*l* 12*s* 4*d*; Glebe, 28 acres; Shelswell, Tithe, 186*l* 2*s* 2*d*; R.'s Inc. 352*l*; Pop. Newton-Purcell 105, Shelswell 44.) [13]

MEADE, J., *Thornbury, Glouc.*—Asst. Mast. of the Gr. Sch. Thornbury. [14]

MEADE, Richard John, *Castle-Cary Vicarage, Somerset.*—Ball. Coll. Ox. 2nd cl. Lit. Hum. and B.A. 1815, M.A. 1818; Deac. 1816 and Pr. 1817. Can. of Coombe the 15th in Wells Cathl. 1863; V. of Castle-Cary, Dio. B. and W. 1845. (Patron, Bp of B. and W; Tithe—Imp. 291*l* 10*s* and 65 acres of Glebe, V. 358*l* 15*s*; Glebe, 10 acres; V.'s Inc. 374*l* and Ho; Pop. 2060.) Formerly C. of Norton St. Philip 1820; R. of Marston Bigot 1821–34; P. C. of Ch. Ch. Frome, 1834–45; Chap. to the late Earl of Cork. Author, *A Sermon* (on quitting the Chaplaincy of the English Church at Boulogne-sur-Mer); *The Papal Intrusion* (a Sermon). Editor of *A Collection of Psalm Tunes, Introits, and Chants of the best Composers.* [15]

MEADE, The Hon. Sidney, *Reading.*—Salis. Theol. Coll; Deac. 1866 by Bp of Ox. C. of St. Mary's, Reading, 1866. [16]

MEADE, Wakefield Suft, *Arkengarth Dale, Richmond, Yorks.*—Clare Coll. Cam. B.A. 1852, M.A. 1855; Deac. 1853 and Pr. 1854 by Bp of Ches. C. of Arkengarth Dale 1866. Formerly C. of Tarporley, Cheshire; Chap. at Albany, Western Australia. [17]

MEADE, William, *Binegar, Shepton-Mallett, Somerset.*—Ball. Coll. Ox. B.A. 1843, M.A. 1847. R. of Binegar, Dio. B. and W. 1851. (Patron, Bp of B. and W; Tithe, 260*l*; Glebe, 44 acres; R.'s Inc. 310*l*; Pop. 302.) [18]

MEADE-RAY, Henry William Gainsborough, *The Elms, Duffield-road, Derby.*—St. Bees; Deac. 1841 and Pr. 1842 by Bp of Ches. [19]

MEADOWS, Thomas, *Duke's Field, Runcorn, Cheshire.*—Dub. A.B. 1862, A.M. 1865; Deac. 1863 and Pr. 1864 by Bp of Ches. C. of Trinity, Runcorn, 1864. Formerly C. of All Souls', Liverpool, 1863. [20]

MEADOWS, William Spencer Harris, *Chigwell Vicarage, Essex.*—Lin. Coll. Ox. B.A. 1826, M.A. 1830; Deac. and Pr. 1827. V. of Chigwell, Dio. Roch. 1855. (Patron, Bp of Roch; Tithe—Eccles. Commis. 900*l* and 56½ acres of Glebe, V. 500*l*; Glebe, 7½ acres; V.'s Inc. 500*l* and Ho; Pop. 1224.) Rural Dean; Dom. Chap. to Earl Waldegrave. [21]

MEAKIN, John Alexander Deverell, *Speenhamland, Newbury, Berks.*—St. John's Coll. Cam. B.A. 1826, M.A. 1829; Deac. 1827 and Pr. 1828 by Bp of Nor. P. C. of Speenhamland, Dio. Ox. 1845. (Patron, V. of Speen; P. C.'s Inc. 175*l* and Ho; Pop. 1767.) [22]

MEALY, Richard Ridgeway Parry, *Perfeddgoed, near Bangor.*—St. John's Coll. Ox. B.A. 1823, M.A. 1827; Deac. 1824, Pr. 1825. [23]

MEARA, William, *Ebenezer-terrace, Plumstead, Kent, S.E.*—Dub. Downes' Prize Essayist 1843, Biblical Greek Prize 1844, 1st cl. Lit. Hum. and A B. 1835; Deac. 1844 by Bp of Ches. Pr. 1845 by Bp of Down and Connor. C. of St. Margaret's, Plumstead, 1866. Formerly Asst. C. of St. Stephen's Bow, Lond. 1860; C. of Wootton Wawen, Warwickshire, 1863; Surrogate for Archd. of Oxford 1865. Author, *An Instruction preparatory to Confirmation*, 1859; *A Pastoral Address on Parental Duty*, 1859; *A Dissertation on the Sacrament of Baptism*, Rivingtons, 1861. [24]

MEARS, Samuel Owen, *Haverfordwest, Pembrokeshire.*—Trin. Coll. Cam. B.A. 1832; Deac. 1833 and Pr. 1834 by Bp of St. D. P. C. of Uzmaston, Pembrokeshire, Dio. St. D. 1840. (Patrons, D. and C. of St. D; Tithe, App. 205*l*; P. C.'s Inc. 102*l*; Pop. 610.) P. C. of St. Martin's, Haverfordwest, Dio. St. D. 1856. (Patron, H. W. Bowen, Esq; Tithe—App. 232*l*; P. C.'s Inc. 86*l*; Pop. 2120.) Chap. to Lady Milford; Dom. Chap. to the Rev. J. H. A. Phillips. Formerly Asst. C. of Rudboxton, Pembrokeshire. [25]

MEARS, William, *York, Swan River, Australia.*—Queen's Coll. Ox. B.A. 1832; Deac. 1832, Pr. 1833. Min. of York, Swan River. [26]

MEASHAM, Richard.—Sid. Coll. Cam. 1st Div. Prizeman, 1st cl. Cl. Trip. and B.A. 1851; Deac. 1851 and Pr. 1852 by Bp of Ex. Chap. of H.M.S. "Indus." Formerly C. of St. Andrew's, Plymouth. [1]

MEDCALF, David, *Charsfield Parsonage, Wickham Market, Suffolk.*—Dub. A.B. 1852, A.M. 1859; Deac. 1853 and Pr. 1855 by Abp of Dub. P. C. of Charsfield, Dio. Nor. 1865. (Patron, Earl Howe; Tithe, Imp. 160*l*; P. C.'s Inc. 110*l* and Ho; Pop. 480.) Formerly C. of St. Nicholas' Within, Dublin, 1853, St. Mary's, Leicester, 1857, Ch. Ch. Derby, 1860, Drypool, Hull, 1864. [2]

MEDCALF, William, *Manston Rectory, Blandford.*—St. John's Coll. Cam. Scho. of, B.A. 1854, M.A. 1857; Deac. 1854 and Pr. 1855 by Abp of York. R. of Manston, Dio. Salis. 1867. (Patron, J. T. Leather, Esq; Glebe, 52 acres; R.'s Inc. 450*l* and Ho; Pop. 152.) Formerly C. of Oarfield 1854–57, Chalcombe 1857–65; P. C. of Appleton-le-Moors 1865–67. [3]

MEDD, Arthur Octavius, *Escrick, York.*—Univ. Coll. Ox. B.A. 1864, Wells Theol. Coll. 1864; Deac. 1864 and Pr. 1865 by Bp of Ox. C. of Escrick 1867. Formerly C. of Banbury 1864–67. [4]

MEDD, Peter Goldsmith, *University College, Oxford.*—King's Coll. Lond. Hon. Fell. of, Theol. Assoc. 1849, Univ. Coll. Ox. 1st cl. Lit. Hum. and B.A. 1852, M.A. 1855; Deac. 1853 and Pr. 1859 by Bp of Ox. Fell. Sen. Tut. and Dean of Univ. Coll. Ox; C. of St. John Baptist's, Oxford. Author, *Christian Meaning of the Psalms and Supernatural Character of Christian Truth*, Parkers, 1862; *The Perfected Work of the Spirit*, ib. 1864; *Fundamental Principle of the Christian Ministry*, ib. 1867; *Office of Intercession for the Church*, ib. 1864; *Household Prayer*, Rivingtons, 1864. Co-Editor with Rev. W. Bright of *Latin Version of the Prayer Book*, Rivingtons, 1865; Essay on *Eucharistic Sacrifice*, in *Church and the World* 1st Series. [5]

MEDLAND, Alfred, 6, *Oxford-terrace, Bath.*—Ch. Miss. Coll. Islington; Deac. 1853 by Bp of Lon. Pr. 1856 by Bp of Madras. C. of St. Mark's, Lyncombe, Bath, 1861. Formerly Miss. of Ch. Miss. Soc. at Meerut, India, 1854–61. [6]

MEDLAND, Joseph Gould, *St. Martin's, Kentish-town, London, N.W.*—P. C. of St. Martin's, St. Pancras, Dio. Lon. 1864. (Patron, J. D. Allcroft, Esq; P. C.'s Inc. 200*l*.) [7]

MEDLAND, Thomas, *Steyning Vicarage, Sussex.*—Corpus Coll. Ox. 1st cl. Lit. Hum. and B.A. 1824, M.A. 1827, B.D. 1836; Deac. 1828 and Pr. 1829 by Bp of Ox. V. of Steyning, Dio. Chich. 1840. (Patron, Duke of Norfolk; Tithe—App. 15*l*, Imp. 293*l* 16*s* 4*d*, V. 410*l*; Glebe, 33½ acres; V.'s Inc. 500*l* and Ho; Pop. 1620.) Formerly C. of St. James's, Dover, 1831. [8]

MEDLAND, William, *Charlwood, Surrey.*—Ch. Coll. Cam. B.A. 1859, M.A. 1863; Deac. 1859 and Pr. 1860 by Abp of York. C. of Charlwood 1865. Formerly C. of St. Paul's, York, 1859; Newchurch, Isle of Wight, 1863. [9]

MEDLEY, George Rowland, 8, *Mersea-road, Colchester.*—Corpus Coll. Cam. B.A. 1838; Deac. 1838 and Pr. 1839 by Bp of Nor. R. of St. Nicholas', Colchester, Dio. Roch. 1846. (Patron, Ball. Coll. Ox; Tithe, 1*l* 10*s*; Glebe, 30 acres; R.'s Inc. 145*l*; Pop. 1036.) Surrogate. [10]

MEDLICOTT, Joseph, *Potterne, Devizes, Wilts.*—Queens' Coll. Cam. B.A. 1827; Deac. 1827, Pr. 1828. V. of Potterne, Dio. Salis. 1837. (Patron, Bp of Salis; Tithe—App. 840*l*, V. 601*l*; Glebe, 22 acres; V.'s Inc. 632*l* and Ho; Pop. 1235.) Formerly C. of All Cannings 1827–31, Potterne 1831–37. [11]

MEDLICOTT, Walter Edward, *Stoke-next-Guildford, Surrey.*—Ch. Ch. Ox. B.A. 1864, M.A. 1867; Deac. 1866 by Bp of Chich. C. of Stoke-next-Guildford 1866. [12]

MEDLYCOTT, Hubert James, *Brington, Northampton.*—Trin. Coll. Cam. B.A. 1864; Deac. 1866 and Pr. 1867 by Bp of Pet. C. of Brington 1866. [13]

MEDWIN, Thomas Rea, *Stratford-on-Avon.*—Wor. Coll. Ox. 2nd cl. Lit. Hum. and B.A. 1831, M.A. 1834; Deac. 1834 and Pr. 1835 by Bp of G. and B. Min. of Holy Cross Chapel, Stratford-on-Avon, Dio. Wor. 1843 (Patrons, Trustees Min.'s Inc. 70*l*.) Head Mast. of the Stratford-on-Avon Gr. Sch. Author, *A Manual of the History of Greek and Roman Literature, translated from the German of Aug. Matthiæ*, Rivingtons, 1841; *Sermons*, 1851, 5*s*; *An Address on the Tercentenary of the Grammar School of Stratford on-Avon*, 1853. [14]

MEE, John, *St. Jude's Parsonage, Southwark, S.*—Ch. Coll. Cam. Scho. of, B.A. 1849, M.A. 1853; Deac. 1849 by Bp of Wor. Pr. 1849 by Bp of Lich. P. C. of St. Jude's, Southwark, Dio. Win. 1864. (Patrons, Trustees; P. C.'s Inc. 410*l* and Ho; Pop. 6968.) Sec. of Ch. Miss. Soc. Formerly C. of All Saints', Derby, 1849–50; P. C. of Riddings, Derby, 1850–54; Assoc. Sec. of Ch. Miss. Soc. for Eastern District 1854–57; Clerical Sec. of British and Foreign Bible Soc. 1857–61; Dean of Grahamstown 1861–64. [15]

MEE, William Chapman, *Hayton, Retford, Notts.*—Ch. Coll. Cam. B.A. 1841, M.A. 1844; Deac. 1842, Pr. 1843. V. of Hayton, Dio. Lin. 1845. (Patron, Abp of York; Tithe—Imp. 178*l* 10*s*, V. 84*l*; Glebe, 35 acres; V.'s Inc. 163*l* and Ho; Pop. 258.) P. C. of West Burton, Notts, Dio. Lin. 1849. (Patron, John Barrow, Esq; Glebe, 18¾ acres; P. C.'s Inc. 56*l*; Pop. 67.) [16]

MEEKINS, Reuben William, 6, *Brent-villas, Hendon, N.W.*—Dub. A.B. 1857, A.M. 1863; Deac. 1857 and Pr. 1858 by Bp of Lon. C. of Hendon 1866. Formerly C. of St. Michael's, Pimlico, Lond. 1857–59, St. Matthew's, Marylebone, 1859–64, St. Thomas's, Camden New Town, 1864. [17]

MEERES, Henry, *Haddenham Vicarage, Thame.*—Clare Hall, Cam. Coll. Prizeman 1839 and 1840, 4th Sen. Opt. and B.A. 1840, M.A. 1843; Deac. 1841, Pr. 1842. V. of Haddenham, Dio. Ox. 1855. (Patrons, D. and C. of Roch; V.'s Inc. 370*l* and Ho; Pop. 1623.) Formerly V. of Rolvenden, Kent, 1854–55. [18]

MEERES, Horace, *Horsmonden, Staplehurst, Kent.*—Ex. Coll. Ox. 4th cl. Lit. Hum. and B.A. 1860, M.A. 1863; Deac. 1863 and Pr. 1864 by Abp of Cant. C. of Horsmonden 1863. [19]

MEFFRE, Joseph C.—Chap. to the French Hospital, Bath-street, Lond. [20]

MEGGISON, Septimus Stanley, *Bolam, Newcastle-on-Tyne.*—Trin. Coll. Cam. B.A. 1814; Deac. 1815, Pr. 1816. V. of Bolam, Dio. Dur. 1817. (Patron, Ld Chan; Tithe—Imp. 246*l* 18*s* 6*d*, V. 72*l* 10*s* 6*d*; Glebe, 130 acres; V.'s Inc. 260*l* and Ho; Pop. 685.) Author, *The Real Roman Catholic Religion* (a Tract), 1829, 2*d*; *Selections from Luther's Table Talk*, 1832, 5*s*; *A Series of Questions on the Church Catechism*, 1839, 1*s*; *A Key to* Ditto, 1839, 8*d*; *Our Baptismal Services*, 1846, 6*d*. [21]

MEGGY, George William, *Corhampton, Southampton.*—Wad. Coll. Ox. B.A. 1862; Deac. 1866 by Bp of Win. C. of Eton and Corhampton, Hants. [22]

MEIGH, Josiah, *Walsall, Staffs.*—C. of St. Peter's, Walsall. [23]

MELHUISH, Charles, *Highbray, Barnstaple, Devon.*—St. John's Coll. Cam. B.A. 1822, M.A. 1826; Deac. 1822 and Pr. 1823 by Bp of Ex. R. of Highbray, Dio. Ex. 1843. (Patron, Sir P. F. P. Acland, Bart; Tithe, 368*l*; Glebe, 89½ acres; R.'s Inc. 458*l*; Pop. 295.) Formerly Mast. of the Gr. Sch. South Molton, Devon, 1822–43. [24]

MELHUISH, George Edward.—Mert. Coll. Ox. B.A. 1858, M.A. 1860; Deac. 1858 and Pr. 1859 by Bp of Salis. Formerly C. of Bradford-on-Avon 1858. [25]

MELHUISH, Thomas Bremridge, *Poughill Rectory, Crediton, Devon.*—Ex. Coll. Ox. B.A. 1834; Deac. 1836, Pr. 1837. R. of Poughill, Dio. Ex. 1861. (Patron, Ld Chan; R.'s Inc. 230*l* and Ho; Pop. 356.) [26]

MELLAND, William, *Harescombe Rectory, near Stroud.*—Deac. 1850 and Pr. 1851 by Bp of Lich. R. of Harescombe with Pitchcombe, Dio. G. and B. 1867. (Patron, the present R; R.'s Inc. 180*l* and Ho; Pop. 316.) Formerly P. C. of Rushton, Staffs, 1853–63. [27]

MELLER, Thomas William, *Woodbridge, Suffolk.*—Trin. Coll. Cam. Scho. of, 10th Wrang. B.A.

1831, M.A. 1834; Deac. 1831 and Pr. 1832 by Bp of Ely. R. of Woodbridge, Dio. Nor. 1844. (Patron, Major Rouse; Tithe, 329l 4s; Glebe, 62l 10s; R.'s Inc. 428l and Ho; Pop. 2095.) Surrogate. Formerly P. C. of Haddenham, Ely, 1832; Prin. of Collegiate Sch. Sheffield, 1836; C. of Glossop 1842; Chap. of the Sekeford Almshouses, Suffolk; Editorial Superintendent of the Bible Society 1848. Author, *Pusey or the Fathers?* 1843. [1]

MELLERSH, William Peachey, *Cheltenham.*—St. John's Coll. Cam. B.A. 1833, M.A. 1836; Deac. 1834 and Pr. 1835 by Abp of Cant. P. C. of Salperton, Dio. G. and B. 1840. (Patron, J. Browne, Esq; P. C.'s Inc. 100l; Pop. 184.) [2]

MELLISH, William John, *Orston Vicarage, near Nottingham.*—Queens' Coll. Cam. B.A. 1852, M.A. 1855; Deac. 1852 and Pr. 1853 by Bp of Salis. V. of Orston with Thoroton C. Dio. Lin. 1855. (Patrons, D. and C. of Lin; Glebe, 95 acres; V.'s Inc. 200l and Ho; Pop. Orston 500, Thoroton 220.) Formerly C. of Halstock, Dorset, 1852–55. [3]

MELLISS, James King, *Eastbourne, Sussex.*—King's Coll. Lond. Assoc. 1860; Deac. 1860 and Pr. 1861 by Bp of Lich. C. of St. Mary's, Eastbourne, 1864. Formerly C. of Crich, Derbyshire, 1860. [4]

MELLO, John Magens, *Brampton, Chesterfield.*—St. John's Coll. Ox. B.A. 1859, M.A. 1863; Deac. 1859, Pr. 1860. R. of St. Thomas's, Brampton, Dio. Lich. 1863. (Patron, Bp of Lich; R.'s Inc. 300l and Ho; Pop. 5259.) F.G.S., and F.A.S.L. Formerly C. of All Saints', Derby, 1859–63. Author, *Holy Scripture and Modern Science*, Bemrose, 1866, 6d. [5]

MELLOR, Thomas Vernon, *Idridgehay, Wirksworth, Derbyshire.*—St. John's Coll. Cam. B.A. 1844, M.A. 1847; Deac. 1845 and Pr. 1847 by Bp of Lich. P. C. of Idridgehay, Dio. Lich. 1855. (Patrons, R. Cresswell and James Milnes, Esqrs. alt; Tithe, 7l; Glebe, 35 acres; P. C.'s Inc. 59l; Pop. 639.) [6]

MELLOR, W. J., *Colwick Rectory, Nottingham.*—R. of Colwick, Dio. Lin. 1860. (Patron, J. Chaworth Musters, Esq; R.'s Inc. 220l and Ho; Pop. 110.) [7]

MELVILL, Henry, *Barnes Rectory, Surrey.*—St. John's Coll. Cam. 2nd Wrang. and B.A. 1821, St. Peter's Coll. Cam. M.A. 1824, B.D. 1836; Deac. 1824 and Pr. 1825 by Bp of Ely. R. of Barnes, Dio. Lon. 1863. (Patrons, D. and C. of St. Paul's; R.'s Inc. 400l and Ho; Pop. 2359.) Chap. in Ordinary to the Queen 1853; Can. Res. of St. Paul's 1856. (Value, 1000l.) Formerly Fell. and Tut. of St. Peter's Coll. Cam; Prin. of the Hon. E.I.C.'s Coll. Haileybury, 1843; Chap. of the Tower of London 1840. Author, *Sermons* (preached before the Univ. of Cam. to which are added *Two Sermons* at Great St. Mary's), Cam. 1836, 2 eds; *Four Sermons* (preached before the Univ. of Cam. to which are added *Two Sermons* at Great St. Mary's), 2 eds. 1837; *Religious Education* (a Sermon), 1838; *Protestantism and Popery*, 1839; *Sermons* (preached at Cam.) 2 eds. 1840; *Sermons*, 2 vols. 1840; *Sermons on Certain of the Less Prominent Facts and References in Sacred History*, 2 vols. 1843–45; *Sermons* (preached on public occasions), 1846; *A Selection of Sermons* (from the Lectures delivered in St. Margaret's, Lothbury, in 1850, '51, '52, '53; *Funeral Sermon for the Rev. W. Howell.* [8]

MELVILLE, David, *Witley Rectory, Stourport, Worcestershire.*—Brasen. Coll. Ox. M.A. 1840; Deac. 1840 by Bp of Ox. Pr. 1844 by Bp of Dur. R. of Great Witley, Dio. Wor. 1857. (Patron, Earl of Dudley; Tithe, 400l; R.'s Inc. 420l and Ho; Pop. 445.) Hon. Can. of Wor; Rural Dean. Formerly Tut. in the Univ. of Dur. 1842–51; Prin. of Bp Hat. Hall, Dur. 1846–51; R. of Shelsley-Beauchamp with Shelsley-Walsh, near Worcester, 1845–57. [9]

MELVILLE, Frederick Abel Leslie, *Welbourn Rectory, Grantham.*—Trin. Coll. Cam. B.A. 1862, M.A. 1865; Deac. 1863 and Pr. 1865 by Abp of Cant. R. of Welbourn, Dio. Lin. 1867. (Patron, Earl de Grey and Ripon; R.'s Inc. 550l and Ho; Pop. 664.) Formerly C. of Goodnestone, Kent, 1863, Livermere, Suffolk, 1866. [10]

MELVILLE, William James, *Warrington.*—St. Peter's Coll. Cam. B.A. 1858; Deac. 1859 and Pr. 1860 by Bp of Ches. P. C. of St. Ann's, Warrington, Dio. Ches. 1864. (Patron, W. Beaumont, Esq; P. C.'s Inc. 303l; Pop. 3000.) Formerly C. of Stanley, Liverpool, 1859–61, Home Mission, Warrington, 1862–64. [11]

MELVILLE, William Rylance, *Matlock Rectory, Derbyshire.*—St. Peter's Coll. Cam. Scho. of, B.A. 1835, M.A. 1838; Deac. 1835 and Pr. 1836 by Abp of York. R. of Matlock, Dio. Lich. 1839. (Patron, Bp of Lich; Tithe, 335l; Glebe, 26 acres; R.'s Inc. 400l and Ho; Pop. 2994.) Surrogate. Formerly V. of Willoughby-on-the-Wolds, Notts, 1836. [12]

MENCE, Richard, *Bockleton Parsonage, Tenbury.*—P. C. of Bockleton, Dio. Herf. 1864. (Patron, Rep. of the late Rev. J. J. Miller; P. C.'s Inc. 130l and Ho; Pop. 346.) [13]

MENDHAM, John, *Clophill Rectory, Ampthill, Beds.*—St. Edm. Hall, Ox. B.A. 1821, M.A. 1825; Deac. 1823, Pr. 1824. R. of Clophill, Dio. Ely, 1841. (Patron, Earl de Grey; R.'s Inc. 446l and Ho; Pop. 1169.) Author, *Translation of the Seventh General Council, the Second of Nice.* [14]

MENET, John, *Hockerill, Bishop Stortford.*—Ex. Coll. Ox. B.A. 1845, M.A 1847; Deac. 1848 and Pr. 1849 by Bp of Man. P. C. of Hockerill, Dio. Roch. 1851. (Patron, Bp of Lon; P. C.'s Inc. 100l; Pop. 1467.) [15]

MENGE, John Peter, *Park-villas, Lower Norwood, S.*—Ch. Miss. Coll; Deac. 1835 by Bp of Lon. Pr. 1860 by Bp of Win. Chap. of Norwood Cemetery 1860. Formerly Mast. of the German Sch. Savoy, and Asst. Min. of the German Ch. Savoy, 1837–40; C. of St. Paul's, Herne Hill, 1859–60. Author, *Voice from the Cemetery*, 6d; *Hebrew Chrestomathy*, E. Menge, Lower Norwood, 1867, in two parts, 3s 6d each. [16]

MENSOR, Meyer, *Bury Lane, near Warrington.*—C. of Bury Lane 1864. [17]

MENZIES, Frederick, *West Shefford Rectory, Hungerford.*—Brasen. Coll. Ox. Pusey and Ellerton Heb. Scho. B.A. 1837, M.A. 1840; Deac. 1839 and Pr. 1840 by Bp of Win. R. of West Shefford, Dio. Ox. 1866. (Patron, Brasen. Coll. Ox; Tithe, 822l; Glebe, 110 acres; R.'s Inc. 1012l and Ho; Pop. 538.) Formerly Vice-Prin. and Fell. of Brasen. Coll. Ox. [18]

MENZIES, William, 4, *Portland-terrace, Winchester.*—Queens' Coll. Cam. B.A. 1835, M.A. 1838; Deac. 1835, Pr. 1836. R. of Winnall, Hants, Dio. Win. 1853. (Patron, Bp of Win; Tithe, 170l; R.'s Inc. 170l; Pop. 120.) Chap. to the Hants Co. Hospital, 1855. [19]

MERCER, Edward, *Eccleshill Parsonage, Leeds.*—Corpus Coll. Cam. B.A. 1847, M.A. 1860; Deac. 1847 and Pr. 1848 by Bp of Rip. P. C. of Eccleshill, Dio. Rip. 1853. (Patron, V. of Bradford; Glebe, 1 acre; P. C.'s Inc. 75l and Ho; Pop. 4482.) [20]

MERCER, Thomas Warren, *Northallerton Vicarage, Yorks.*—Trin. Coll. Ox. B.A. 1820, M.A. 1824; Deac. 1820, Pr. 1821. V. of Northallerton with Deighton C. Dio. York, 1849. (Patrons, D. and C. of Dur; Tithe, Imp. 1292l 10s 7d, V. 522l; Glebe, 220 acres; V.'s Inc. 742l and Ho; Pop. Northallerton 3332, Deighton 141.) Chap. to the Duke of Bedford. Formerly R. of Wheeley, Essex. [21]

MERCER, William, *Leavy-Greave, Sheffield.*—Trin. Coll. Cam. B.A. 1835, M.A. 1840. P. C. of St. George's, Sheffield, Dio. York, 1840. (Patron, V. of Sheffield; P. C.'s Inc. 400l; Pop. 10,538.) Author, *A Visitation Sermon*, 1845; *Addresses*; *The Church Psalter and Hymn-book, containing the Words and the Music together, for the Use of Congregations and Families*, Cramer and Co. [22]

MERCIER, Jerome John, *Hanwell, W.*—St. Mark's Coll. Chelsea; Deac. 1862 and Pr. 1863 by Bp of Lon. Tut. of St. Mark's Coll. Chelsea, 1856; C. of Hanwell 1867. [23]

MERCIER, Lewis Page, *Woolwich.*—Univ. Coll. Ox. 3rd cl. Lit. Hum. and B.A. 1841, M.A. 1855; Deac. 1843, Pr. 1845. Chap. of the Foundling Hospital, Lond. 1857. Formerly 2nd Mast. Glasgow Coll. Sch. 1842; Asst. Min. of St. Andrew's Episcopal Chapel,

Glasgow, and Chap. to the Garrison, 1843; Asst. Cl. Mast. Tunbridge Sch. 1845; 2nd Mast. Edgbaston Sch. 1846; Head Mast. Edgbaston Sch. 1849; Provincial Grand Chap. to the Freemasons, Warw. 1850. Author, *Manual of Greek Prosody*, 1843, 3s 6d; *Sermon* (in aid of repairs of Church), Glasgow, 1843, 1s; *First Greek Selections*, 1851, 4s; *Masonic Sermon* (preached at Coventry); *Masonic Sermon* (preached at Leamington), 1853, 1s. [1]

MEREDITH, Edward, *Ightfield Rectory, Whitchurch, Salop.*—Ch. Ch. Ox. 1st cl. Math. et Phy. 2nd cl. Lit. Hum. and B.A. 1815, M.A. 1818; Deac. 1817 and Pr. 1818 by Bp of Ox. R. of Ightfield, Dio. Lich. 1865. (Patron, Rev. H. H. Price; Tithe, 174*l*; Glebe, 72 acres; R.'s Inc. 350*l* and Ho; Pop. 360.) Formerly P. C. of Longdon-upon-Terne 1845–65. Author, *The Sacrament of the Lord's Supper.* [2]

MEREDITH, James, *The Vicarage, Abergele, Denbighshire.*—Dub. A.B. 1824; Deac. 1824, Pr. 1825. V. of Abergele, Dio. St. A. 1848. (Patron, Bp of St. A; Tithe—App. 1487*l*, V. 490*l*; Glebe, 1 acre; V.'s Inc. 490*l* and Ho; Pop. 3308.) Hon. Can. of St. A. 1860; Rural Dean of Denbigh 1844; Surrogate. [3]

MEREDITH, John, *Uppington, Wellington, Salop.*—Chap. of the D. of Uppington, Dio. Lich. 1840. (Patron, Duke of Cleveland; Chap.'s Inc 70*l*; Pop. 95.) Head Mast. of Donington Sch. in Wroxeter. [4]

MEREDITH, Richard, *Hagbourne Vicarage, Wallingford, Berks.*—St. Edm. Hall, Ox. B.A. 1823, M.A. 1826; Deac. 1823 by Bp of Wor. Pr. 1824 by Bp of Herf. V. of Hagbourne, Dio. Ox. 1825. (Patron, the present V; Tithe—Imp. 1040*l*, V. 200*l*; Glebe, 11 acres; V.'s Inc. 240*l* and Ho; Pop. 795.) [5]

MEREDITH, Thomas, *Newborough, Anglesey.*—Queen's Coll. Birmingham; Deac. 1861 and Pr. 1862 by Bp. of Ban. R. of Newborough, Dio. Ban. 1866. (Patron, Ld Chan; Tithe, 250*l*; R.'s Inc. 253*l*; Pop. 920.) Formerly C. of Amlwch 1861–64, Glanogwen 1864–67. [6]

MEREDITH, William, *Llanfrynach, Brecon.*—C. of Llanfrynach. [7]

MEREDYTH, John, *St. Peter's, Stockport.*—Dub. A.B. 1826, A.M. 1832, *ad eund.* Ox. 1853; Deac. 1833 by Bp of Killaloe, Pr. 1835 by Bp of Lich. C. in sole charge of St. Peter's, Stockport, 1844. Formerly C. of Bowdon 1834, St. Paul's, Leeds, 1841. Author, *Scripture Calendar*, Seeleys, 1844. [8]

MEREDYTH, Thomas Edward, *Burleydam, Cheshire.*—Magd. Coll. Cam. Scho. of, 1846, B.A. 1848, M.A. 1867; Deac. 1848 and Pr. 1849 by Bp of Lich. P. C. of Burleydam, Dio. Ches. 1867. (Patron, Viscount Combermere; Tithe, 10s 6d; Glebe, 48 acres; P. C.'s Inc. 96*l* and Ho.) Chap. R.N. 1852; Dom. Chap. to Viscount Combermere. Formerly C. of Audlem, Staffs, 1848, Wem, Salop, 1849–52; Chap. of H.M.S. Dockyard at the Cape 1857, and at Chatham 1866. [9]

MERES, Harry John, 24, *Dawson-street, Manchester.*—Emman. Coll. Cam. 2nd cl. Cl. Trip. B.A. 1860, M.A. 1865; Deac. 1861 and Pr. 1862 by Bp of Wor. C. of St. Bartholomew's, Salford, 1866. Formerly C. of St. Luke's, Birmingham, 1861–66. [10]

MEREST, John William Drage, *Wem Rectory, Salop.*—Deac. and Pr. 1824. R. of Wem, Dio. Lich. 1846. (Patron, Duke of Cleveland; Tithe, 2100*l*; Glebe, 38¾ acres; R.'s Inc. 2192*l* and Ho; Pop. 3003.) Dom. Chap. to the Duke of Cleveland. [11]

MEREWEATHER, John Davies, *Venice.*—St. Edm. Hall, Ox. B.A. 1842; Deac. 1843, Pr. 1844. British Chap. at Venice. Formerly Government Chap. in N. S. Wales. Author, *The Type and the Antitype, or Circumcision and Baptism*; *Diary on Board an Emigrant Ship*; *Diary of a Working Clergyman in Australia and Tasmania.* [12]

MEREWETHER, Francis, *Woolhope Vicarage, Ledbury, Herefordshire.*—Trin. Hall, Cam. B.C.L. 1832; Deac. and Pr. 1829 by Bp of Herf. V. of Clehonger, Herfs, Dio. Herf. 1833. (Patron, Bp of Herf; Tithe, App. 180*l*, V. 165*l*; Glebe, ½ acre; V.'s Inc. 166*l*; Pop. 451.) V. of Woolhope, Dio. Herf. 1841. (Patrons, D. and C. of Herf; Tithe, App. 503*l* 10s, V. 292*l* 16s; V.'s Inc. 620*l* and Ho; Pop. 803.) [13]

MEREWETHER, Henry Robert, *Tenterden Vicarage, Kent.*—St. Alban Hall, Ox. B.A. 1840; Deac. 1842 and Pr. 1843 by Bp of Herf. V. of Tenterden, Dio. Cant. 1859. (Patrons, D. and C. of Cant; V.'s Inc. 350*l* and Ho; Pop. 2856.) Formerly C. of Latchingdon. [14]

MERIVALE, Charles, *Lawford Rectory, Manningtree, Essex.*—St. John's Coll. Cam. Browne's Medallist 1829, Sen. Opt. 1st cl. Cl. Trip. and B.A. 1830, B.D. 1840, Hon. D. C. L. Ox. 1866; Deac. 1833, Pr. 1834. R. of Lawford, Dio Roch. 1848. (Patron, St. John's Coll. Cam; Tithe, 720*l*; Glebe, 40 acres; R.'s Inc. 760*l* and Ho; Pop. 842.) Chap. to the Speaker of the House of Commons 1863. Formerly Fell. of St. John's Coll. Cam. 1833; Tut. and Select Preacher 1838; Whitehall Preacher 1840; Hulsean Lect. Cam. 1862. Author, *Six Sermons*, 1838; *Whitehall Sermons*, 1842; *History of the Romans*, Vols. I.–VII. Longmans, 1850–62; *The Conversion of the Roman Empire* (Boyle Lectures for 1864), 1864; *The Conversion of the Northern Nations* (Boyle Lectures for 1865), 1865. [15]

MERREFIELD, George Nelmes, *St. Stephen's Rectory, Salford.*—Magd. Hall, Ox; Deac. and Pr. by Bp of Rip. R. of St. Stephen's, Salford, Dio. Man. 1866. (Patrons, D. and C. of Man; R.'s Inc. 260*l* and Ho; Pop. 12,031.) Formerly C. of St. Philip's, Hulme; R. of St. James's, Manchester. [16]

MERRIMAN, George, *Reading.*—Ex. Coll. Ox. B.A. 1859, M.A. 1863; Deac. 1861 and Pr. 1862 by Bp of Ox. Asst. C. of St. Giles', Reading, 1864. Formerly Asst. C. of Banbury 1861–64. [17]

MERRIMAN, Henry Gordon, *Guildford.*—New Coll. Ox. 2nd cl. Lit. Hum. and B.A. 1846, M.A. 1850, B.D. 1861, D.D. 1861; Deac. 1847 and Pr. 1848 by Bp of Ox. Head Mast. of the Royal Gr. Sch. Guildford 1859. Formerly Asst. Mast. of Winchester Coll. 1847; Tut. of New Coll. Ox. 1849; Head Mast. of Bridgnorth Sch. Salop, 1850. [18]

MERRIMAN, Joseph, *Surrey County School, Cranley, Guildford.*—St. John's Coll. Cam. 5th Wrang. B.A. 1860, M.A. 1863; Deac. 1862 and Pr. 1863 by Bp of Ely. Fell. of St. John's Coll. Cam; Head Mast. of Surrey County Sch. [19]

MERRIMAN, William Henry Robert, *Shapwick, Bath.*—Brasen. Coll. Ox. B.A. 1846, M.A. 1850, Deac. 1846 by Bp of Salis. Pr. 1848 by Bp of B. and W. Formerly C. of St. John's, Frome, 1846, Dinder 1848; P.C. of Dilton Marsh, Wilts, 1851–58, Greinton 1859. [20]

MERRY, Charles M., *Wetherby, Tadcaster.*—Deac. 1855 and Pr. 1856 by Abp of Cant. C. of Spofforth 1855; Chap. to the Union Workhouse, Wetherby, 1865. Author, *Lecture on Education*, 1854; *Young Children, a Plea on their Behalf*, 1857; *Pulpit Echoes*, 1859; *Divine Charge to Teachers*, 1859; various single Sermons. [21]

MERRY, Samuel Williamson, *Peterborough.*—Jesus Coll. Cam. 47th Jun. Opt. and B.A. 1849, M.A. 1852; Deac. 1849 by Bp of Ches. Pr. 1850 by Bp of Lich. P. C. of St. Mark's, Peterborough, Dio. Pet. 1860. (Patron, Bp of Pet; P. C.'s Inc. 300*l* and Ho; Pop. 3170.) Formerly P. C. of Astley, Warwickshire, 1853–56; C. of St. James's, Bristol, 1857–60. [22]

MERRY, William Walter, *Oxford.*—Ball. Coll. Ox. Scho. of, B.A. 1857, M.A. 1860; Fell. and Tut. of Lin. Coll; Deac. 1860 and Pr. 1861 by Bp of Ox. P. C. of All Saints', City and Dio. Ox. 1862. (Patron, Lin. Coll. Ox; P. C.'s Inc. 65*l*; Pop. 478.) [23]

MERTENS, Frederick Mounteney Dirs, *New Shoreham, Sussex.*—Queen's Coll. Ox. B.A. 1852, M.A. 1856; Deac. 1853 by Bp of Chich. Fell. of St. Nicholas' Coll; Head Mast. of St. Saviour's Sch. Shoreham. [24]

MESHAM, Arthur Bennett, *Wootton Rectory, Canterbury.*—Corpus Coll. Ox. 2nd cl. Lit. Hum. and B.A. 1822, M.A. 1825, B.D. 1833; Deac. and Pr. 1825. R. of Wootton, Dio. Cant. 1834. (Patron, J. W. H. Brydges, Esq; Tithe, 260*l*; Glebe, 15¼ acres; R.'s Inc. 275*l* and Ho.; Pop. 163.) Rural Dean 1846; Chap. to the Marquis of Downshire. [25]

MESSENGER, James Bryant, *Werrington Parsonage (Devon), near Launceston.*—Clare Coll. Cam. B.A. 1847, M.A. 1850; Deac. 1847, Pr. 1849. Chap. of D. of Werrington, Dio. Ex. 1849. (Patron, A. H. Campbell, Esq; Glebe, 5 acres; Chap.'s Inc. 120*l* and Ho; Pop. 664.) [1]

MESSENGER, John Farnham, *The Wardenry, Farley Hospital, Salisbury.*—St. John's and Lin. Colls. Ox. 3rd cl. Lit. Hum. 3rd cl. Math. and B.A. 1859, M.A. 1862; Deac. 1860, Pr. 1861. Warden of Farley Hospital 1864; Sen. C. of Farley and Pitton 1863. Formerly C. of Plaitford, Wilts, 1860–63. [2]

MESSENGER, William, *Great Marsden, Colne, Lancashire.*—Univ. Coll. Dur. Licen. Theol. 1841; Deac. 1842, Pr. 1843. P. C. of Great Marsden, Dio. Man. 1845. (Patrons, the Crown and Bp of Man. alt; P. C.'s Inc. 180*l* and Ho; Pop. 3057.) [3]

MESSITER, George Malim, *Repton, Derbyshire.*—Wad. Coll. Ox. B.A. 1841, M.A. 1843; Deac. 1847 and Pr. 1850 by Bp of Lichfield. 3rd Mast. in Repton Sch. 1850. [4]

MESSITER, George Terry Moulton, *Payhembury, Ottery St. Mary, Devon.*—Ex. Coll. Ox. B.A. 1860, M.A. 1864; Deac. 1862 and Pr. 1863 by Bp of B. and W. V. of Payhembury, Dio. Ex. 1864. (Patron, Rev. W. Michel; Tithe, comm. 147*l*; Glebe, 81 acres; V.'s Inc. 280*l*. and Ho; Pop. 532.) Formerly C. of Stoke St. Gregory, Taunton, 1862-64. [5]

MESSITER, Richard, *Caundle Marsh Rectory, Sherborne, Dorset.*—Corpus Coll. Ox. B.A. 1820, M.A. 1824; Deac. 1823, Pr. 1824. R. of Caundle Marsh, Dio, Salis. 1828. (Patron, Sir H. A. Hoare, Bart; Tithe, 96*l*; Glebe, 35 acres; R.'s Inc. 170*l*; Pop. 84.) R. of Caundle Purse, Dio. Salis. 1829. (Patron, Sir H. A. Hoare, Bart; Tithe, 162*l*; Glebe, 23 acres; R'.s Inc. 177*l*; Pop. 185.) R. of Bratton St. Maur, Somerset, Dio. B. and W. 1829. (Patrons, Sir R. Lopes and J. Hodges, Esq. alt; R.'s Inc. 161*l*; Pop. 80.) Formerly P. C. of Caundle Stourton, Dorset, 1830–64. [6]

METCALF, William Layton, *West Camel Rectory, Ilchester, Somerset.*—St. John's Coll. Cam. B.A. 1839, M.A. 1842; Deac. 1839, Pr. 1841. R. of West Camel, Dio. B. and W. 1848. (Patron, Bp of B and W; Tithe, 250*l*; Glebe, 80½ acres; R.'s Inc. 316*l* and Ho; Pop. 338.) Formerly C. of Huddersfield 1840–48; Scarborough 1844–48. Author, Articles in Kitto's *Biblical Cyclopædia.* [7]

METCALFE, Benjamin Eamonson, *York.*—Sid. Coll. Cam. Sen. Opt. and B.A. 1841, M.A. 1844; Deac. 1842, Pr. 1843. V. of Huntington, Yorks, Dio. York, 1851. (Patrons, Sub-Chanters and V.-Choral of York Cathl; Tithe—App. 437*l* 9*s*, V. 123*l* 15*s* 6*d*; V.'s Inc. 125*l*; Pop. 671.) V.-Choral of York Cathl. 1852. [8]

METCALFE, Frederick, *Lincoln College, Oxford.*—St. John's Coll. Cam. Jun. Opt. 2nd cl. Cl. Trip. and B.A. 1838, Lin. Coll. Ox. M.A. 1845, B.D. 1855; Deac. 1845, Pr. 1846. P. C. of St. Michael's, Oxford, Dio. Ox. 1849. (Patron, Lin. Coll. Ox; P.C.'s Inc. 100*l*; Pop. 971.) Fell. of Lin. Coll. Ox. Author, *The Oxonian in Norway*, 2 eds. Hurst and Blackett, 1857; *The Oxonian in Thelmarcken*, 2 vols. Hurst and Blackett, 1858; *History of German Literature*, Longmans, 1858. Translator from the German of *Prof. A. Becker's Gallus and Charicles, being Scenes from the Lives of the Ancient Romans and Greeks*, each in 1 vol. 3 eds. Longmans. [9]

METCALFE, Frederick, *Great Chesterford, Essex.*—Corpus Coll. Cam. B.A. 1847, M.A. 1850; Deac. 1848 and Pr. 1849 by Bp of Man. C. of Great Chesterford 1858. Formerly C. of Little Shelford, Cambs, 1850–58. [10]

METCALFE, George, *Christchurch Rectory, Upwell, Cambs.*—Clare Coll. Cam. Scho. and Exhib. B.A. 1855, M.A. 1858; Deac. 1856 and Pr 1857 by Bp of Ely. R. of Christchurch, Upwell, Dio. Nor. 1862. (Patron, C. W. Townley, Esq; Tithe, 1594*l*; Glebe, 5 acres; R.'s Inc. 1594*l*; Pop. 850.) Formerly P. C. of St. Peter's, Norwich, 1859. [11]

METCALFE, George Morehouse, *Hinton Hall, Peterchurch, near Hereford.*—Wor. Coll. Ox. B.A. 1860, M.A. 1863; Deac. 1860 and Pr. 1861 by Bp of Herf. C. in sole charge of Peterchurch 1862. Formerly Asst. C. of St. Margaret's with Michaelchurch, Eskley, 1860. [12]

METCALFE, James, *Devonport.*—P. C. of St. Aubyn's, Devonport, Dio. Ex. 1864. (Patron, R. of Devonport; P. C.'s Inc. 120*l*.) Chap. of the Royal Albert Hospital, Devonport; Chap. of the Plymouth, Devonport, and Stonehouse Cemetery. [13]

METCALFE, John, *Inge House, Hawes, Yorkshire.* [14]

METCALFE, Joseph Powell, *Bilbrough, York.*—Sid. Coll. Cam. 17th Sen. Opt. B.A. 1847, M.A. 1850; Deac. 1847 and Pr. 1848 by Bp of Rip. R. of Bilbrough, Dio. York, 1856. (Patron, T. Fairfax, Esq; Tithe, 270*l*; R.'s Inc. 274*l*; Pop. 214.) Formerly C. of Collingham 1847, Bilbrough 1852. Author, *School Round Book*; *Metrical Anthems*; *Rounds, Catches, and Canons of England* jointly with Dr. Rimbault. [15]

METCALFE, Wallace, *St. Andrew Ilketshall, Bungay, Suffolk.*—St. John's Coll. Camb. B.A. 1833, M.A. 1838; Deac. 1834, Pr. 1835. V. of St. Andrew Ilketshall, Dio. Nor. 1859. (Patron, M. B. Metcalfe, Esq; Tithe 130*l* 7*s*; Glebe, 29 acres; V.'s Inc. 200*l* and Ho; Pop. 315.) Formerly C. of Brockdish, Norfolk. [16]

METCALFE, William, *Everton, Bawtry, Notts.*—Jesus Coll. Cam. 8th Sen. Opt. and B.A. 1837; Deac. 1838, Pr. 1839. V. of Everton, Dio. Lin. 1847. (Patron, the present V; Tithe—Imp. 448*l* 16*s* 9*d*, V. 78*l*; Glebe, 112 acres; V.'s Inc. 230*l* and Ho; Pop. 849.) [17]

METCALFE, William, *Yeadon Parsonage, Leeds.*—Clare Coll. Cam Coll. Prizeman, Sen. Opt. and B.A. 1815; Deac. 1815 by Bp of Lon. Pr. 1816 by Bp of Ches. P. C. of Yeadon St. John's, Dio. Rip. 1844. (Patron, R. of Guiseley; Tithe, App. 111*l*; P.C.'s Inc. 180*l* and Ho; Pop. 4259.) [18]

METCALFE, William Henry, *Exmouth.*—Cam. M.A. 1863; Deac. 1861 and Pr. 1862 by Bp of Herf. C. of Withycombe Rawleigh 1867. Formerly C. of Whimple, near Exeter. [19]

METCALFE, William Richardson, *Buckden, Skipton, Yorks.*—Deac. 1833, Pr. 1834. P. C. of Hubberholme, Dio. Rip. 1847. (Patron, V. of Arncliffe; P. C.'s Inc. 80*l*; Pop. 335.) [20]

METHOLD, John William, *Wighton, Little Walsingham, Norfolk.*—Trin. Coll. Cam. B.A. 1822. V. of Wighton, Dio. Nor. 1835. (Patrons, D. and C. of Nor; Tithe—App. 578*l*, V. 232*l*; Glebe, 22 acres; V.'s Inc. 254*l*; Pop. 612.) R. of Hempstead Holt, Dio. Nor. 1835. (Patrons, D. and C. of Nor; Pop. 280.) [21]

METHUEN, Francis Paul, *All Cannings Rectory, near Devizes.*—Trin Coll. Cam. B.A. 1846, M.A. 1854; Deac. 1854 and Pr. 1856 by Bp of Ely. C. of All Cannings 1861; Chap. to Lord Rolle. Formerly C. of Trinity, Cambridge, 1854–59. [22]

METHUEN, Henry Hoare, *All Cannings, near Devizes.*—Ex. Coll. Ox. B.A. 1840; Deac. 1848 and Pr. 1849 by Abp of Cant. C. of Etchilhampton 1856. Formerly C. of Bridge, Canterbury, 1849–50, Northbourne, Deal, 1851–52, Stanford Dingley, near Reading, 1855. [23]

METHUEN, Thomas Anthony, *All Cannings Rectory, Devizes.*—Deac. 1804, Pr. 1805. R. of All Cannings with Etchilhampton, Dio. Salis. 1809. (Patron, Lord Ashburton; Tithe, 1204*l* 5*s*; Glebe, 36½ acres; R.'s Inc. 1243*l* and Ho; Pop. 1013.) R. of Garsdon with Lea V. Wilts, Dio. G. and B. 1814. (Patron, F. Gale, Esq; Garsdon, Tithe, 165*l*; Glebe, 14 acres; Lea, Tithe—Imp. 35*l*, V. 189*l* 9*s*; Glebe, 43¾ acres; R.'s Inc. 360*l* and Ho; Pop. Garsdon 206, Lea 432.) Author, *Memoir of the Rev. R. P. Beachcroft*, 1830. [24]

METIVIER, Charles.—Pemb. Coll. Ox. B.A. 1859, M.A. 1863; Deac. 1861 and Pr. 1862 by Bp of G. and B. C. of St. George's, Bloomsbury, Lond. Formerly C. of Tewkesbury, and Walton, Cardiff, 1861–63, St Clement's, Bristol, 1863. [25]

MEYER, Horace, *East Tisted Rectory, Alton, Hants.*—St. Cath. Coll. Cam. B.A. 1855, M.A. 1859; Deac. 1855 and Pr. 1856 by Bp of Wor. R. of East Tisted, Dio. Win. 1864. (Patron, J. W. Scott, Esq; R.'s

Inc. 390*l* and Ho; Pop. 220.) Chap. to Lord Rollo. Formerly C. of Ch. Ch. Birmingham, 1855–56; V. of North Mimms, Herts, and Rural Dean of Barnet, 1856–64. [1]

MEYLER, William, *St. Lawrence Rectory, Haverfordwest, Pembrokeshire.*—St. John's Coll. Cam. B.A. 1836. R. of St. Lawrence, Pembrokeshire, Dio. St. D. 1847. (Patron, Ld Chan; Tithe, 81*l* 10*s*; Glebe, 30 acres; R.'s Inc. 101*l* and Ho; Pop. 205.) P C. of St. Edrin's, near Haverfordwest, Dio. St. D. (Patron, Ld Chan; Tithe—App. 70*l*; P.C.'s Inc. 122*l*; Pop. 118.) [2]

MEYNELL, Henry, *Denstone Parsonage, Ashburne, Derbyshire.*—Brasen. Coll. Ox. B.A. 1850, M.A. 1851; Deac. 1851 and Pr. 1852 by Bp of Ox. C. in sole charge of Denstone; Fell. of St. Nicholas' Coll. Lancing. Formerly C. of Kidlington, Oxon. 1851; P. C. of Fauls, Salop, 1857. [3]

MEYRICK, Edward, *Ramsbury, Hungerford, Wilts.*—Magd. Coll. Ox. B.A. 1833, M.A. 1836; Deac. 1838 by Bp of Ox. Formerly Fell. of Magd. Coll. Ox. [4]

MEYRICK, Edwin, *Wyndersham House, Amesbury.*—Queen's Coll. Ox. B.A. 1836, M.A. 1839; Deac. 1838, Pr. 1839. Formerly V. of Chisledon, Wilts, 1847-66. [5]

MEYRICK, Frederick, *Palace Plain, Norwich.*—Trin. Coll. Ox. 2nd cl. Lit. Hum. and B.A. 1847; Deac. 1850, and Pr. 1852 by Bp of Ox; Fell. of Trin. Coll. Ox. 1847, Tut. 1851; Mast. of the Schs. 1855; Select Preacher before the Univ. 1855; Public Examiner in Classics 1856; Whitehall Preacher 1856; Proctor 1857; One of H.M. Inspectors of Schs. 1859; Select Preacher before the Univ. 1865–67. Author, *What is the Working of the Church of Spain?* 1850; *The Practical Working of the Church of Spain*, 1851; *Clerical Tenure of Fellowships*, 1854; *Two Sermons preached before the University of Oxford*, 1854; *Liguori's Theory of Truthfulness*, Mozley, 1854, 1*s* 6*d*; *Liguori's Theory of Theft*, ib. 1854, 1*s* 6*d*; *Liguori's Glories of Mary*, ib. 1854, 1*s* 6*d*; *Liguori's Theology discussed in Nineteen Letters with Archbishop Manning*, ib. 1854, 2*s*; *An Examination of the Rev. R. I. Wilberforce's Charges against the Church of England*, 1855, 2*s*; *Moral and Devotional Theology of the Church of Rome*, 1856, 6*s*; *God's Revelation and Man's Moral Sense* (a Sermon before the Univ. of Ox. 1856); *The Outcast and the Poor of London*, 1858, 7*s*; *University and Whitehall Sermons*, Parkers, 1859, 4*s*; *But isn't Kingsley right after all?* Rivingtons, 1864, 6d; *On Dr. Newman's Rejection of Liguori's Doctrine of Equivocation*, ib. 1864, 1*s*; *Sulle Chiese Suburbicarie, una Lettera ad un Uomo di Stato*, ib. 1864, 6*d*; *Jehovah or Baal?* (a Sermon before the Univ. of Ox.) ib. 1865, 1*s*; *Patriotism* (a Sermon to Volunteers), 1866, Bacon, Norwich, 1*d*; *The Bible, the Church, Conscience* (a Sermon before the Univ. of Ox.), Rivingtons, 1867, 6*d*; *Our Schools of the Prophets* (do.) ib. 1867, 1*s*; *Intercommunion* (do.), ib. 1867, 1*s*. Editor of *Ecclesiæ Anglicanæ Religio, Disciplina, Ritusque Sacri*, Rivingtons, 1853, 2nd ed. 1857, 1*s*; *Della Religione, Disciplina e Riti Sacri della Chiesa Anglicana*, ib. 1854, 2nd ed. 1867, 1*s*; *La Santa Chiesa Cattolica*, ib. 1855, 1*s* 6*d*; *La Supremazia Papale, al Tribunale dell' Antichita*, ib. 1856, 1*s*; *Historia Transubstantiationis Papalis*, ib. 1858, 1*s* 6*d*; *Bevergii Tractatus de Ecclesiæ consensu*, ib. 1861, 6*d*; *Preces Privatæ Lanceloti Andrewes*, ib. 1865, 1*s*; *Papal Supremacy tested by Antiquity*, Parkers, 1855, 2nd ed. 1862, 1*s*. [6]

MEYRICK, Llewellyn, *Magdalen College, Oxford.*—Magd. Coll. Ox. B.A. 1852, M.A. 1855; Deac. 1853, Pr. 1854. Fell. of Magd. Coll. Ox. [7]

MEYRICK, Maurice, *Kennet Cottage, Plaistow, Essex, E.*—P. C. of Trinity, Barking-road, West Ham, Dio. Roch. 1867. (Patron, Bp of Roch; P. C.'s Inc. 200*l*; Pop. 6500.) Formerly C. of Shaftesbury, Dorset, and St. Stephen's, Westminster; Min. of Barking-road District 1860–67. [8]

MEYRICKE, Robert, *Ludlow, Salop.*—Queens' Coll. Cam. B.A. 1824; Deac. 1824, Pr. 1825. Reader of Ludlow 1825. [9]

MICHELL, Eardley Wilmot, *Shirley Vicarage, near Derby.*—Queens' Coll. Cam. B.C.L. 1840; Deac. 1837 and Pr. 1838 by Bp of Win. V. of Shirley, Dio. Lich. 1847. (Patron, Earl Ferrers; Tithe—App. 10*s*, V. 153*l* 17*s* 6*d*; Glebe, 9¾ acres; V.'s Inc. 170*l* and Ho; Pop. 301.) Author, *Plain Consideration of the Christian Sabbath; On Confirmation and the Lord's Supper; On Bible Societies and the Bible; Examination of the First Psalm; Visitation Sermon; Church Missionary Jubilee Sermon.* [10]

MICHELL, Richard, *Magdalen Hall, Oxford.*—Wad. Coll. Ox. 1st cl. Lit. Hum. and B.A. 1824, M.A. 1827; Lin. Coll. B.D. 1836; Deac. 1831 by Bp of Ox. Pr. 1832 by Bp of Roch. R. of South Moreton, near Wallingford, Berks, Dio. Ox. 1856. (Patron, Magd. Hall, Ox; Tithe—Imp. 3*l*. R. 45*l*; Glebe, 97 acres; R.'s Inc. 225*l* and Ho; Pop. 371.) Vice-Prin. and Tut. of Magd. Hall, Ox; Public Orator in the Univ. of Ox. 1848. Formerly Fell. and Tut. of Lin. Coll. Ox; Pub. Examiner in 1829, 1833, 1835, 1839, and 1854; Prælector of Logic 1839–49; Bampton Lect. 1849. Author, *The Nature and Comparative Value of the Christian Evidences considered generally* (Bampton Lectures for 1849), 1849. [11]

MICHELL, William, *Barwick, near Yeovil, Somerset.*—Trin. Hall, Cam. LL.B.; Deac. 1826, Pr. 1827. R. of Barwick, Dio. B. and W. 1827. (Patron, J. Newman, Esq; Tithe—Imp. 132*l*, R. 100*l*; Glebe, 45 acres; R.'s Inc. 180*l*; Pop. 458.) Formerly R. of Cotleigh, Devon, 1827–61. [12]

MICHELL, William, *Chantry, Frome, Somerset.*—New Coll. Ox. B.A. 1852, M.A. 1856; Theol. Coll. Chich; Deac. 1853 and Pr. 1854 by Bp of Chich. P. C. of Chantry, Dio. B. and W. 1864. (Patron, Rev. J. G. C. Fussell; P. C.'s Inc. 90*l*; Pop. 264.) Formerly C. of Brighton 1853–9; All Saints', Guernsey, 1860–64. Author, *The Bible and its Translations*, 1*s*; *Our Title to Sonship, and other Sermons*, 1864, 2nd ed. Masters, 3*s* 6*d*; *The Churches of Asia as Types of Individual Character, and other Sermons*, Masters, 5*s*; *Our Curate's Budget*, Parkers, monthly, 3*d*. [13]

MICHELL, William Philip, *Carhampton, Dunster.*—Emman. Coll. Cam. B.A. 1856; Deac. 1856 and Pr. 1858 by Bp of Ox. C. of Carhampton with Rode Huish 1865. Formerly C. of Drayton Beauchamp, Bucks, 1856–58; Ludgvan, Cornwall, 1858–65. [14]

MICKLEBURGH, James, *Ashill, near Ilminster, Somerset.*—Trin. Coll. Cam. B.A. 1828, M.A. 1831; Deac. 1829 by Bp of G. and B. Pr. 1831 by Abp of Cant. R. of Ashill, Dio. B. and W. 1833. (Patron, Preb. of Ashill in Wells Cathl; Tithe—Imp. 220*l* 10*s* 8*d* and 60¼ acres of Glebe, R. 118*l* 13*s* 4*d*; R.'s Inc. 322*l* 10*s* 8*d* and Ho; Pop. 445.) Author, *The Index to the Maps of the Society for the Diffusion of Useful Knowledge*, 1846; *Prayers for National Schools*, 1851. [15]

MICKLETHWAIT, John Heaton, *Painthorpe House, near Wakefield.*—Trin. Coll. Cam. B.A. 1839, M.A. 1843; Deac. 1840, Pr. 1841. P. C. of Chapelthorpe, near Wakefield, Dio. Rip. 1841. (Patron, V. of Great Sandall; Glebe, 106 acres; P. C.'s Inc. 214*l* 9*s* and Ho; Pop. 2021.) Formerly C. of Denton, near Otley, 1840–41; P. C. of Scissett, near Huddersfield, 1842–43. [16]

MICKLETHWAIT, John Nathaniel, *Taverham Hall, Norwich.*—Magd. Coll. Cam. B.A. 1835, M.A. 1838; Deac. 1835 and Pr. 1836 by Bp of Nor. Travelling Fell. of Magd. Coll. Cam. [17]

MICKLETHWAIT, Richard Greaves, *Ardsley Parsonage, Barnsley, Yorks.*—St. Cath. Coll. Cam. B.A. 1839; Deac. 1839, Pr. 1840. P. C. of Ardsley, Dio. York, 1844. (Patron, V. of Darfield; Tithe—App. 101*l* 10*s*, Imp. 101*l* 10*s* 10*d*; P. C.'s Inc. 120*l* and Ho; Pop. 1712.) [18]

MICKLETHWAIT, Sotherton Nathaniel, *Hickling Vicarage, Stalham, Norfolk.*—Magd. Coll. Cam. B.A. 1846, M.A. 1849; Deac. 1848, Pr. 1849. V. of Hickling, Dio. Nor. 1849. (Patron, N. Micklethwait, Esq; Tithe—Imp. 814*l*, V. 344*l*; V.'s Inc. 414*l*; Pop. 767.) [19]

MICKLETHWAIT, William, *Chapeltown, Sheffield.*—St. Aidan's; Deac. 1855 and Pr. 1856 by Bp of Ches. P. C. of Chapelton, Dio. York 1857. (Patrons, the Crown and Abp of York alt; P. C.'s Inc. 160*l* and Ho; Pop. 4063.) Formerly C. of Birkenhead. [1]

MIDDLEMIST, Robert, *Harrow-on-the Hill, Middlesex.*—Ch. Coll. Cam. B.A. 1843, M.A. 1816. Math. Mast. at Harrow Sch. [2]

MIDDLETON, Alfred, *Kingsbridge, Devon.*—Head Mast. of the Kingsbridge Gr. Sch. [3]

MIDDLETON, Charles Henry, *Thorpe Audlin, Pontefract.*—Ch. Coll. Cam. F.L.S., B.A. 1851; Deac. 1851 and Pr. 1852 by Bp of Lich. Chap. of the Borough Gaol, Leeds; C. of Badsworth 1867. [4]

MIDDLETON, Henry, *Codnor Parsonage, Alfreton, Derbyshire.*—St. Cath. Hall, Cam. B.A. 1833; Deac. 1834 and Pr. 1835 by Abp of York. P. C. of Codnor, Derbyshire, Dio. Lich. 1845. (Patrons, the Crown and Bp of Lich. alt; P. C.'s Inc. 150*l*; Pop. 3829.) [5]

MIDDLETON, Henry Abdy.—Brasen. Coll. Ox. B.A. 1847, M.A. 1850; Deac. 1848, Pr. 1849. Chap. of H.M.S. "Cumberland." [6]

MIDDLETON, John Clement, *Great Greenford Rectory, Hounslow, Middlesex.*—King's Coll. Cam. B.A. 1832, M.A. 1835; Deac. 1833, Pr. 1834. R. of Great Greenford, Dio. Lon. 1850. (Patron, King's Coll. Cam; Tithe, 600*l*; Glebe, 40½ acres; R.'s Inc. 680*l* and Ho; Pop. 600.) Formerly Fell. of King's Coll. Cam. [7]

MIDDLETON, John Douglas, *Tettenhall Regis, Staffordshire.*—Corpus Coll. Ox. B.A. 1855, M.A. 1858; Deac. 1858 and Pr. 1859 by Bp. of Win. P. C. of Ch. Ch. Tettenhall Regis, 1866. (Patron, Lord Wrottesley.) Formerly C. of Carisbrook, Isle of Wight, 1858-60, St. Saviour's, Paddington, Lond. [8]

MIDDLETON, Joseph Empson, *St. Bees, Whitehaven.*—Trin. Coll. Cam. B.A. 1830; Deac. 1830, Pr. 1831. C. of St. Bees and Theol. Tut. of the Coll. Author, *Lectures on Ecclesiastical History* (for the use of St. Bees Coll.), 1850, 12*s*. Editor, *Grotius de Veritate*; ditto, *with English Notes*, Rivingtons, 1855, 6*s*. [9]

MIDDLETON, Sholto, *Bruton, Somerset.*—Head Mast. of the King's Sch. Bruton, 1864. Formerly 2nd Mast. of Blundell's Sch. Tiverton. [10]

MIDDLETON, Thomas, *St. George's, Manchester.*—Magd. Hall, Ox. B.A. 1842, M.A. 1844. R. of St. George's, Manchester, Dio. Man. 1849. (Patron, Bp of Ches; P. C.'s Inc. 270*l*; Pop. 24,212.) [11]

MIDDLETON, William John, *Brompton, Northallerton, Yorks.*—Queens' Coll. Cam. Sen. Opt. and B.A. 1829, M.A. 1835; Deac. 1832 and Pr. 1833 by Abp of York. P. C. of Brompton, Dio. York, 1844. (Patrons, D. and C. of Dur; Tithe—Imp. 301*l*, P. C. 220*l*; Glebe, 1 acre; P. C.'s Inc. 240*l* and Ho; Pop. 1398.) [12]

MIDGLEY, Edward James, *Medomsley, Gateshead.*—Deac. and Pr. 1838. P. C. of Medomsley, Dio. Dur. 1838. (Patron, Bp of Dur; Tithe—Imp. 183*l* 19*s* 1*d*; Glebe, 60 acres; P. C.'s Inc. 250*l* and Ho; Pop. 856.) [13]

MIDGLEY, James, *Ickham, Sandwich.*—St. John's Coll. Cam. 1st cl. Moral Sci. Trip. B.A. 1858, M.A. 1866; Deac. 1859, Pr. 1860. C. in sole charge of Ickham 1861. Formerly C. of St. James's, Bradford, Yorks, 1859–61. [14]

MIDLETON, The Very Rev. Viscount William John, *Peper-Harrow, Godalming, Surrey.*—Ball. Coll. Ox. 1st cl. Lit. Hum. and B.A. 1820, M.A. 1823; Deac. 1822 by Bp of Ban. Pr. 1822 by Bp of Win. Chap. in Ordinary to the Queen 1847. Formerly C. of Ashtead, Surrey, 1822–25; R. of Castle Rising, Norfolk, 1825–39; R. of Bath 1839–54; Can. Res. of Wells and Preb. of Yatton 1855–63; Dean of Exeter 1863–67. [15]

MIDWINTER, Nathaniel, *St. Michael's Rectory, Winchester.*—Magd. Hall, Ox. B.A. 1842, M.A. 1844; Deac. 1842, Pr. 1843. R. of St. Michael's, City and Dio. Win. 1844. (Patron, Bp of Win; Modus, 16*l*; Glebe, 1 acre; R.'s Inc. 130*l* and Ho; Pop. 542.) Formerly Hon. Sec. to the Hampshire Ch. Sch. Soc. Author, *The Sunday School Teacher*, 4th ed; *Inaugural Address Hants Charity School Society*; *Not Forsaken*, a Ballad Tale, Macintosh. [16]

MILBURN, William, *Redcar, Yorks.*—Univ. Coll. Dur. Hebrew Priseman, Sen. Cl. 1836 and 1837, Licen. Theol. 1837; Deac. 1837 and Pr. 1838 by Bp of Dur. P. C. of Redcar, Dio. York, 1854. (Patron, Earl of Zetland; P. C.'s Inc. 43*l*; Pop. 1330.) Formerly C. of Houghton-le-Spring and Wolsingham. [17]

MILDMAY, The Ven. Carew Anthony St. John, *Chelmsford Rectory, Essex.*—Oriel Coll. Ox. B.A. 1822, M.A. 1825. R. of the Sinecure R. of Shorewell, Isle of Wight, Dio. Win. (Patroness, Lady St. John Mildmay; Tithe—Imp. 238*l*, Sinecure R. 468*l* and 3 acres of Glebe, V. 192*l* and 2 acres of Glebe; Sinecure R.'s Inc. 474*l*.) R. of Chelmsford, Dio. Roch. 1826. (Patroness, Lady St. John Mildmay; Tithe, 565*l*; Glebe, 15 acres; R.'s Inc. 590*l* and Ho; Pop. 4178.) Archd. of Essex 1861. (Value, 200*l*.) Formerly V. of Burnham, Essex, 1827–58. [18]

MILES, Charles Popham, *Monk Wearmouth, Durham.*—Caius Coll. Cam. B.A. 1837, M.A. 1850; Deac. 1837 and Pr. 1838 by Bp of Lond. P. C. of St. Peter's, Monk Wearmouth, Dio. Dur. 1867. (Patron, Sir Hedworth Williamson, Bart; P. C.'s Inc. 300*l* and Ho; Pop. 17,000.) Formerly C. of St. Ann's, Limehouse, and Chap. to the Sailors' Home, Lond. 1837, St. Luke's, Chelsea, 1839, Bishop Wearmouth 1841; P. C. of St. Jude's, Glasgow, 1843; Principal of the Protestant College, Malta, 1858. Author, *Lectures on the Book of Daniel*, 2 vols. 10*s*, Nisbet, 1842; *The Voice of the Glorious Reformation*, Dalton, 1843, 8*s*; *Memoir of Frank Mackenzie*, 1857, 6*s*, 4th ed; Pamphlets on the Scottish Episcopal Church; etc. [19]

MILES, Henry, *Llanafanfawr, near Builth.*—Deac. 1865 by Bp of St. D. C. of Llanafanfawr 1865. [20]

MILES, Henry Broadway, *Burleston, near Dorchester.*—Literate; Deac. 1852 and Pr. 1853 by Bp of Rip. R. of Athelhampton with Burleston R. Dio. Salis. 1854. (Patron, G. J. Wood, Esq; R.'s Inc. 226*l*; Pop. 120.) Hon. Sec. of the Church of England Temperance Association, in Dio. of Salis. Formerly C. of Greenhow-hill, Yorks. [21]

MILES, Henry Edmund, *Huntley Rectory, near Gloucester.*—Magd. Coll. Cam. B.A. 1844, M.A. 1864; Deac. 1845, Pr. 1846. R. of Huntley, Dio. G. and B. 1866. (Patron, Rev. H. Miles; Tithe, 250*l*; Glebe, 65 acres; R.'s Inc. 300*l* and Ho; Pop. 530.) Formerly P. C. of Rennington, Northumberland, 1854–59; P. C. of Acklington, Northumberland, 1859. [22]

MILES, Henry Hugh, *Clifton Rectory, Biggleswade, Beds.*—Ex. Coll. Ox. B.A. 1851, M.A. 1854; Deac. 1853 and Pr. 1854 by Bp of Wor. R. of Clifton, Beds, Dio. Ely, 1858. (Patron, Rev. H. H. Miles; Glebe, 6 acres; R.'s Inc. 450*l* and Ho; Pop. 2000.) Formerly C. of Weethley, Warw. [23]

MILES, Lomas, *Coreley Rectory, Tenbury.*—Queen's Coll. Ox. B.A. 1832, M.A. 1835; Deac. 1833, Pr. 1834. R. of Coreley, Salop, Dio. Herf. 1858. (Patron, A. F. Haliburton, Esq; R.'s Inc. 300*l* and Ho; Pop. 381.) Formerly R. of Willoughby-Waterless, Leic. 1847–58. [24]

MILES, Philip Edward, *Owslebury, Winchester.*—Caius Coll. Cam. B.A. 1853; Deac. 1855 and Pr. 1856 by Bp of Lin. P. C. of Owslebury, Dio. Win. 1865. (Patron, Rev. R. Buston; Glebe, 2 acres; P. C.'s Inc. 170*l* and Ho; Pop. 520.) Formerly C. of Barrow-upon-Humber, Linc. Bytham-Parva, Wadenhoe, Northants. [25]

MILES, Robert Henry William, *Bingham, Notts.*—Ch. Ch. Ox. B.A. 1841; Deac. 1843, Pr. 1844. R. of Bingham, Dio. Lin. 1845. (Patron, Earl of Chesterfield; Tithe, 1416*l* 4*s*; Glebe, 33¾ acres; R.'s Inc. 1546*l* and Ho; Pop. 1918.) Preb. of Lincoln 1864. [26]

MILES, Stephen, *Cottesmore, near Oakham, Rutland.*—Ch. Coll. Cam. B.A. 1858; Deac. 1858 and Pr. 1859 by Bp of Pet. C. of Cottesmore with Barrow 1858. [27]

MILES, Thomas, *Stockton Rectory, Heytesbury, Wilts.*—St. Cath. Coll. Cam. B.A. 1817, M.A. 1839. R. of Stockton, Dio. Salis. 1856. (Patron, Bp of Win; R.'s Inc. 440*l* and Ho; Pop. 288.) [28]

MILFORD, Robert Newman, *Bishop Knoyle Rectory, Salisbury.*—Ball. Coll. Ox. B.A. 1851, M.A. 1854; Deac. 1853, Pr. 1854 by Bp of Win. R. of Bishop Knoyle, Dio. Salis. 1865. (Patron, Bp of Win;

R.'s Inc. 850*l* and Ho; Pop. 1038.) Chap. to Bp of Win. Formerly C. of Stockwell Chapel 1853–54; R. of Brightwell, Berks, 1860. Author, *Farnham, and its Borough*, Longmans, 1860, 1*s* 6*d*. [1]

MILLAR, James Ogilvy, *The Vicarage, Tamworth.*—Ch. Coll. Cam. B.A. 1849, M.A. 1852, LL.D. 1864; Deac. 1851 by Bp of B. and W. Pr. 1852 by Bp of Ex. V. of Tamworth, Dio. Lich. 1865. (Patron, C. H. W. A Court Hessington, Esq; V.'s Inc. 300*l* and Ho; Pop. 7000.) Rural Dean; Surrogate. Formerly C. of South Petherton, Somerset, 1851–53, Cirencester 1853–55; Asst. Min. of St. John, Edinburgh, 1855–60; P. C. of Elson, Hants, 1860–65. [2]

MILLARD, Charles Sutton, *Costock Rectory, Loughborough.*—St. John's Coll. Cam. B.A. 1858; Deac. 1858 by Bp of G. and B. Pr. 1859 by Bp of Lin. R. of Costock, Dio. Lin. 1859. (Patron, the present R; Tithe, 49*l* 9*s*; Glebe, 353*l* 15*s*; R.'s Inc. 403*l* 4*s* and Ho; Pop. 440.) Formerly C. of Tormarton, Glouc. 1858–59. [3]

MILLARD, Frederick Maule, *St. Michael's College, Tenbury.*—Magd. Coll. Ox. 3rd cl. Lit. Hum. 1857, B.A. 1858, M.A. 1861; Deac. 1859 and Pr. 1860 by Bp of Ox. Head Mast. of St. Michael's Coll. Tenbury; Fell. of Magd. Coll. Ox. 1867. [4]

MILLARD, Henry Shaw, *Clifton, Bristol.*—St. John's Coll. Cam. B.A. 1855; Deac. and Pr. 1856. Formerly C. of Carleton and Ashby. [5]

MILLARD, James Elwin, *Basingstoke, Hants.*—Magd. Coll. Ox. Fell. of, 3rd cl. Lit. Hum. and B.A. 1845, M.A. 1848, B.D. 1854, D.D. 1859; Deac. 1846 and Pr. 1847 by Bp of Ox. V. of Basingstoke, Dio. Win. 1864. (Patron, Magd. Coll. Ox; Tithe, 497*l* 11*s*; Glebe, 1 acre; V.'s Inc. 532*l*; Pop. 4654.) Formerly C. of Bradfield, Berks, 1846; Head Mast. Magd. Coll. Sch. Oxford, 1846. Author, *The Island Choir, or the Children of the Child Jesus*, 1847; *Historical Notices of the Office of Choristers*, 1848; *The Christian Knight, a Confirmation Address*, 1851, all published by Masters; *The Sin of Blood Guiltiness* (Sermon preached before the Univ. of Ox), Parker, 1862. [6]

MILLARD, Jeffery Watson, *Shimpling Rectory, Scole, Norfolk.*—Wor. Coll. Ox. B.A. 1852, M.A. 1855; Theol. Coll. Wells; Deac. 1853 and Pr. 1854 by Bp of Ox. R. of Shimpling, Dio. Nor. 1854. (Patron, the present R; Tithe, 230*l*; Glebe, 31 acres; R.'s Inc. 297*l* 12*s* and Ho; Pop. 219.) [7]

MILLER, Charles, *Harlow Vicarage, Essex.*—Magd. Coll. Ox. B.A. 1817, M.A. 1819; Deac. 1817, Pr. 1818. V. of Harlow, Dio. Roch. 1831. (Patron, Hon. W. North; Tithe—Imp. 700*l* 10*s* 6*d*, V. 396*l* 5*s* 6*d*; V.'s Inc. 411*l* and Ho; Pop. 1183.) [8]

MILLER, C. H., *Huddersfield.*—C. of Huddersfield. [9]

MILLER, Edward, *The Parsonage, Bognor, Sussex.*—Trin. Coll. Cam. B.A. 1823, M.A. 1826; Deac. 1823 by Bp of Ches. Pr. 1824 by Bp of Bristol. P. C. of Bognor, Dio. Chich. 1838. (Patron, Abp of Cant; P. C.'s Inc. 107*l* and Ho; Pop. 2523.) Formerly C. of Shaftesbury 1823–25, Bognor 1828–31, St. Mary's, Lambeth, 1833–39. Author, *Sermons* (preached at Bognor), 1st Series, 1844, 2nd Series, 1852, 9*s*; *The Battle Axe of God* (a Sermon preached on the Day of the Funeral of the Duke of Wellington), 1852, 1*s*; *War from the North* (a Sermon preached on the Fast-day), 1854, 1*s*; *The Second and Third Seals* (a Sermon preached on the Thanksgiving-day), Rivingtons, 1854, 1*s*; *India and Retribution* (a Sermon), Van Voorst, 1857, 1*s*; *Church Choral Associations* (a Sermon preached in Norwich Cathl), 1861, 6*d*; *England's Irreparable Loss* (a Sermon on the Death of the Prince Consort), 1861, 6*d*. [10]

MILLER, Edward, 5, *Cotham-park, Clifton, Bristol.*—New Coll. Ox. 2nd cl. Lit. Hum. and B.A. 1847, M.A. 1851; Deac. 1848 and Pr. 1850 by Bp of Ox. Formerly Fell. and Tut. of New Coll. Ox. 1851–56. [11]

MILLER, Francis Richard, *Kineton Vicarage, Warwickshire.*—Wor. Coll. Ox. B.A. 1824, M.A. 1827; Deac. 1825, Pr. 1826. V. of Kineton, Dio. Wor. (Patron, Lord Willoughby De Broke; V.'s Inc. 116*l* and Ho; Pop. 1077.) [12]

MILLER, George, *Radway Vicarage, Kineton, Warwickshire.*—Magd. Coll. Ox. 1846, 4th cl. Lit. Hum. and B.A. 1850, M.A. 1852; Deac. 1854 and Pr. 1855 by Bp of Ex. V. of Radway, Dio. Wor. 1858. (Patron, the present V; Tithe—Imp. 144*l* 14*s*, V. 48*l*; V.'s Inc. 111*l* and Ho; Pop. 375.) [13]

MILLER, George, 16, *North-street, Westminster, S.W.*—Trin. Hall Cam. 2nd cl. Cl. Trip. B.A. 1862, M.A. 1866; Deac. 1865 and Pr. 1866 by Bp of Lond. C. of St. John's, Westminster, 1866. [14]

MILLER, George Dempster, *Woodkirk Vicarage, Wakefield.*—Wad. Coll. Ox. B.A. 1836, M.A. 1839; Deac. 1837 by Bp of Roch. Pr. 1838 by Bp of Chich. V. of Woodkirk, *alias* West Ardsley, Dio. Rip. 1846. (Patron, Earl of Cardigan; Glebe, 185 acres; P. C.'s Inc. 320*l* and Ho; Pop. 1650.) Formerly C. of Heathfield, Sussex, 1837–39; P. C. of Morley, near Leeds, 1839–41; V. of Skenfrett, Mon. 1841–46. [15]

MILLER, Henry, *Ashbury, Shrivenham, Berks.*—Magd. Coll. Ox. Fell. of, Hon. 4th cl. Lit. Hum. B.A. 1850, M.A. 1852; Deac. 1854 and Pr. 1855 by Bp of Ex. V. of Ashbury, Dio. Ox. 1860. (Patron, Magd. Coll. Ox; Tithe, 57*l*; Glebe, 60*l*; V.'s Inc. 435*l* and Ho; Pop. 742*l*.) Formerly C. of Littleham with Exmouth, Devon, 1854; V. of Radway, Warwick, 1858. Author, *The Question of Inspiration plainly stated*, Parkers, 1861, 1*s*; *Letter to Parishioners of Ashbury on the Observance of Holy Week*, 1867. [16]

MILLER, James Webber, *Birdham Rectory, Chichester.*—Ex. Coll. Ox. B.A. 1842; Deac. 1843 and Pr. 1844 by Bp of Chich. R. of Birdham, Dio. Chich. 1861. (Patrons, D. and C. of Chich; R.'s Inc. 400*l* and Ho; Pop. 436.) Formerly R. of St. Andrew's, Chichester, 1857–61. [17]

MILLER, John.—St. John's Coll. Cam. Jun. Opt. and 2nd cl. Cl. Trip. B.A. 1841, M.A. 1844; Deac. 1842 and Pr. 1843 by Bp of Win. Formerly P. C. of Ch. Ch. Brockham, Surrey, 1847–49; C. of St. Thomas's, Winchester, 1850–54; P. C. of St. Paul's, Preston, 1854–66. [18]

MILLER, John Cale, *Greenwich.*—Lin. Coll. Ox. B.A. 1835, M.A. 1838; Deac. 1836, Pr. 1837. V. of Greenwich with St. Mary C. Dio. Lon. 1866. (Patron, the Crown; V.'s Inc. 700*l*; Pop. 3000.) Surrogate; Chap. to Lord Calthorpe. Formerly R. of St. Martin's, Birmingham. Author, *Sermons*, 1838. [19]

MILLER, John Robert Charlesworth, *Goddington, Oxon.*—Corpus Coll. Ox. Scho. and Fell. of 1865, B.A. 1859, M.A. 1861; Deac. 1860 by Bp of Ox. Pr. 1861 by Bp of Salis. R. of Goddington, Dio. Ox. 1866. (Patron, Ch. Ch. Coll. Ox; Glebe, 201 acres; R.'s Inc. 361*l* and Ho; Pop. 78.) Formerly C. of Winkfield, Wilts, 1860–62, Bradford-on-Avon, Wilts, 1862–65, Puddletown, Dorset, 1865–66. [20]

MILLER, Joseph Augustus, *Ile-Brewers, near Taunton.*—Deac. 1856 and Pr. 1857 by Bp of Ox. V. of Ile-Brewers, Dio. B. and W. 1862. (Patron, Prince of Wales; V.'s Inc. 225*l* and Ho; Pop. 270.) Formerly C. of Windsor. Author, *Saul, the First King of Israel*; *A Commentary on the Epistles to the Hebrews*; *The Third Commandment*; *The Co-operation of the Laity with the Clergy on Church Parishes.* [21]

MILLER, Michael Hodsoll, 1, *Belsize-square, Hampstead, London, N.W.*—St. John's Coll. Cam. 19th Wrang. and B.A. 1815, M.A. 1818; Deac. 1817 by Bp of Ely, Pr. 1817 by Bp of Lon. Chap. to the Duke of Buccleuch. Formerly Fell. of Clare Coll. Cam; V. of Scarborough 1828–48; P. C. of Hopton, Suffolk, 1848. [22]

MILLER, Stanley, *Dennington, Framlingham, Suffolk.*—Ch. Coll. Cam. Sen. Opt. B.A. 1823; Deac. 1824 and Pr. 1825 by Bp of Ox. V. of Tannington with Brundish C. Suffolk, Dio. Nor. 1837. (Patron, Bp of Nor; V.'s Inc. 270*l* and Ho; Pop. 697.) [23]

MILLER, Thomas, *Haileybury College, Hertford.*—Trin. Coll. Cam. 1st cl. Cl. Trip. B.A. 1862, M.A. 1865; Deac. 1863 by Bp of Rip. Pr. 1864 by Bp of Ely. Fell. of Queens' Coll. Cam. and Mast. at Haileybury Coll. Formerly C. of St. Paul's, Covent Garden, 1866; Asst. Chap. to English Ch. at Rome 1866–67. [24]

MILLER, Thomas.—C. of St. George's, Newcastle-under-Lyme. [1]

MILLER, Thomas Elton, *West Ravendale, Grimsby*—C. of West Ravendale. [2]

MILLER, William Coase, *Wellingborough.*—King's Coll. Lond. Theol. Assoc. 1863; Deac. 1863 by Bp of Pet. C. of Wellingborough 1863. [3]

MILLER, William Sanderson.—C. of Bishop's Itchington, Warw. [4]

MILLETT, Humphrey Davy, *Leicester.*—Clare Coll. Cam. B.A. 1841; Deac. 1842, Pr. 1843. Chap. of the Blaby Union; Mast. in the Coll. Sch. Leicester. [5]

MILLETT, William, *Lyng Rectory, East Dereham, Norfolk.*—R. of Lyng, Dio. Nor. 1863. (Patron, Rev. H. Lombe; R.'s Inc. 400*l* and Ho; Pop. 590.) [6]

MILLIGAN, Henry Mawson, *Cricksea Rectory, Maldon, Essex.*—St. Cath. Hall, Cam. B.A. 1844; Deac. 1845 and Pr. 1846 by Bp of Lich. R. of Cricksea with Alethorne V. Dio. Roch. 1862. (Patron, J. H. Candy, Esq; R.'s Inc. 400*l* and 2 Hos; Pop. 564.) Formerly Head Mast. of the Sutton Valence Gr. Sch. 1848–62. [7]

MILLINGTON, Thomas Street, *Woodhouse Eaves, Loughborough*—Deac. 1848, Pr. 1849. P. C. of Woodhouse Eaves, Leic. Dio. Pet. 1853. (Patrons, Lords of Six Manors adjoining; P. C.'s Inc. 230*l* and Ho; Pop. 1125.) Min. of the Iron Church, Leamington, 1864. Author, *Testimony of the Heathen to the Truths of Holy Writ*, Seeleys, 1864, 21*s*. [8]

MILLNER, Thomas Darnton, *Bulford, Amesbury, Wilts.*—P. C. of Bulford, Dio. Salis. 1853. (Patron, Dr. Southby; P. C.'s Inc. 75*l*; Pop. 383.) C. of Wendron, Cornwall. [9]

MILLNER, William.—Wor. Coll. Ox. B.A. and M.A. 1828. R. of St. Antholin's with St. John Baptist's, City and Dio. Lon. 1858. (Patrons, Crown and D. and C. of St. Paul's alt; R.'s Inc. 222*l*; Pop. 395.) Formerly P. C. of Kentish-town 1848–58. [10]

MILLS, Alfred Wilson, *St. Erth Vicarage, Hayle, Cornwall.*—Lin. Coll. Ox. B.A. 1857, M.A. 1860; Deac. 1858 and Pr. 1859 by Bp of Ox. V. of St. Erth, Dio. Ex. 1864. (Patrons, D. and C. of Exeter; V.'s Inc. 250*l* and Ho; Pop. 2558.) Surrogate. Formerly C. of Steeple Aston, Oxon, 1858, Blockley, Worcester, 1861. Author, *Night Schools*, Houlston and Wright, 1866. [11]

MILLS, Barrington Stopford Thomas, *Lawshall Rectory, Bury St. Edmunds.*—Ch. Ch. Ox. B.A. 1844, M.A. 1847; Deac. 1847, Pr. 1848. R. of Lawshall, Dio. Ely, 1858. (Patron, Trustees of the late Sir Wm. Middleton; Tithe, 700*l*; Glebe, 40 acres; R.'s Inc. 750*l* and Ho; Pop. 903.) Formerly C. of Great Canford and Kinson, near Wimborne, Dorset. [12]

MILLS, Cecil, *Barford Rectory, Warwick.*—Ch. Ch. Ox. B.A. 1862, M.A. 1864; Deac. 1863 and Pr. 1864 by Bp of Win. R. of Barford, Dio. Wor. 1865. (Patron, J. Mills, Esq; R.'s Inc. 1000*l* and Ho; Pop. 750.) Formerly C. of Farnham, Surrey, 1863–65. [13]

MILLS, Frederick, *The Parsonage, Lindfield, Sussex.*—Deac. 1860 and Pr. 1861 by Bp of Carl. P. C. of Lindfield, Dio. Chich. 1862. (Patron, W. Mossom Kearns, Esq; Pop. 1917.) Formerly C. of Bampton, Westmoreland, 1860, Dalston, Carlisle, 1861. [14]

MILLS, Frederick Russell, *Esholt Parsonage, near Leeds.*—Trin. Coll. Cam. B.A. 1840, M.A. 1844; Deac. 1841 and Pr. 1842 by Bp of Herf. P. C. of Esholt with Hawkesworth P. C. Dio. Rip. 1854. (Patron, W. R. C. Stansfield, Esq; Tithe—Imp. 15*s* 4*d*; P. C.'s Inc. 130*l* and Ho; Pop. Esholt 869, Hawkesworth 237.) Dioc. Inspector of Schs. for Rural Deanery of Otley 1867. [15]

MILLS, James Bassnett, *Hemswell Parsonage, Kirton-in-Lindsey, Lincolnshire.*—Queen's Coll. Ox. M.A. 1827; Deac. 1836 by Bp of Glouc. Pr. 1849 by Bp of Herf. P. C. of Hemswell, Dio. Lin. 1853. (Patron, the present P. C.; Tithe—Imp. 900*l*; Glebe, 3 acres; P. C.'s Inc. 50*l* and Ho; Pop. 465.) Chap. of St. Edmund's Chapel, Spital, Linc. (Patrons, D. and C. of Lin.) Dom. Chap. to the Earl of Zetland. Author, *An Apology for the Church of England*, 1830; *The Christian Priesthood*, 1836. [16]

MILLS, James Fuller Humfrys, *Hockerton Rectory, Southwell.*—St. Edm. Hall, Ox. B.A. 1853; Deac. 1853 and Pr. 1854 by Bp of Lin. R. of Hockerton, Dio. Lin. 1856. (Patroness, Mrs. Whetham; Tithe, 230*l*; Glebe, 40 acres; R.'s Inc. 282*l* 10*s* and Ho; Pop. 108.) Formerly C. of St. Peter's, Nottingham, 1854–55. [17]

MILLS, John, *Orton-Waterville (Hunts), near Peterborough.*—Pemb. Coll. Cam. B.A. 1831, M.A. 1834; Deac. 1832, Pr. 1833. R. of Orton-Waterville, Dio. Ely, 1837. (Patron, Pemb. Coll. Cam; R.'s Inc. 375*l*; Pop. 289.) Formerly Fell. of Pemb. Coll. Cam. [18]

MILLS, Malkin, *Thorpe-Arnold Vicarage, Melton-Mowbray.*—Literate; Deac. 1817, Pr. 1818. V. of Thorpe-Arnold with Brentingby C. Dio. Pet. 1852. (Patron, Duke of Rutland; Thorpe-Arnold, Tithe—Imp. 85*l* 0*s* 9*d*, V. 248*l* 12*s*; Brentingby, Tithe, 72*l*; Glebe, 39 acres; V.'s Inc. 400*l* and Ho; Pop. 124.) [19]

MILLS, Robert Twyford, *Halse Vicarage, Taunton.*—Magd. Coll. Ox. 4th cl. Lit. Hum. and B.A. 1842, M.A. 1844; Deac. 1843, Pr. 1844. V. of Halse, Dio. B. and W. 1844. (Patroness, Mrs. Frobi[illegible] —Imp. 327*l* 16*s* 6*d*, V. 135*l*; Glebe, 4 acre[illegible] 200*l* and Ho; Pop. 453.)

MILLS, Samuel, *St. Andrew's, St. He*[illegible] —Dub. A.B. 1857, A.M. 1864; Deac. 1858 b[illegible] of Meath, Pr. 1859 by Bp of Down and Connor. C. of St. Andrew's, St. Heliers, Jersey, 1867. Formerly C. of Newtownland co. Down, Ireland, 1858, St. John's, Lancaster, 1859, Albert Memorial Ch. Man. 1865, St. Luke's, Hallewell, 1866. [21]

MILLS, Thomas, *Yalding, Maidstone.*—P. C. of St. Margaret's, Yalding, Dio. Cant. 1852. (Patron, V. of Yalding; P. C.'s Inc. 150*l*; Pop. 801.) [22]

MILLS, Thomas, *Great Saxham, Suffolk.*—R. of Great Saxham, Dio. Ely, 1829. (Patron, W. Mills, Esq; R.'s Inc. 330*l*; Pop. 270.) [23]

MILLS, Walter, *Berwick St. John, Wilts.*—Deac. 1851 and Pr. 1854 by Bp of Ex. C. of Berwick St. John, 1866. Formerly C. of Buckland-in-the-Moor, Devon. [24]

MILLS, William, *Harpham, near Hull.*—Queens' Coll. Cam. Scho. of, and Grad. in Math. Honors, B.A. 1840, M.A. 1844, *ad eund.* Ox. 1848; Deac. 1845 and Pr. 1846 by Bp of Pet. C. of Burton Agnes 1865. Formerly C. of Witney, Ox. 1847–64. Author, *In Memoriam*, a Poem, 1860; *Sermon on the Death of the Rector of Witney*, 1863. [25]

MILLS, William, *Hindon, Wilts.*—King's Coll. Lond. Assoc. 1849; Deac. 1849 and Pr. 1850 by Bp of Salis. P. C. of Hindon, Dio. Salis. 1867. (Patron, Ld Chan; P. C.'s Inc. 75*l*; Pop. 604.) Formerly C. of East and West Stower, Dorset. [26]

MILLS, William Henry, *Stapleton, Bristol.*—Caius Coll. Cam. B.A. 1865; Deac. 1865 and Pr. 1866 by Bp of G. and B. C. of Stapleton 1865. [27]

MILLS, William Lewis.—Queens' Coll. Cam. B.A. 1830; Deac. 1832 and Pr. 1833 by Bp of Wor. C. of St. John's, Battersea, Surrey. [28]

MILLS, William Woodward, 43, *Canonbury-road, London, N.*—Wad. Coll. Ox. B.A. 1854, M.A. 1857; Deac. 1855 and Pr. 1856 by Bp. of Lon. Third Mast. of the Islington Proprietary Sch. Lond; C. of St. John's, Hoxton. Formerly C. of St. Thomas's, Liberty of the Rolls, Chan. Lane, Lond. 1855–58. [29]

MILLS, William Yarnton, *Miserden Rectory, Cirencester.*—Trin. Coll. Ox. B.A. 1826, M.A. 1827; Deac. 1829 and Pr. 1830 by Bp of Ox. R. of Miserden, Dio. G. and B. 1848. (Patron, the present R; Tithe, 431*l*; Glebe, 86½ acres; R.'s Inc. 523*l* and Ho; Pop. 503.) [30]

MILMAN, The Very Rev. Henry Hart, *The Deanery, St. Paul's, London, E.C.*—Brasen. Coll. Ox. 1st cl. Lit. Hum. and B.A. 1813, M.A. 1816, B.D. and D.D. 1849; Deac. 1816 by Bp of Lon. Pr. 1816 by Bp of Ox. Dean of St. Paul's 1849. (Value, 2000*l* and Res.) Formerly V. of St. Mary's, Reading, 1817–35; Prof. of Poetry, Ox. 1821–31; Bampton Lect. 1827; R. of St.

Margaret's, Westminster, and Can. of Westminster, 1835–49. Author, *Poems*, 3 vols. Murray, 1826; *Bampton Lectures*, Oxford, 1827; *History of the Jews*, 3 vols. Murray, 1829; *History of Christianity from the Birth of Christ to the Abolition of Paganism in the Roman Empire*, 3 vols. ib. 1840; *History of Latin Christianity*, 6 vols. ib; *Life and Works of Horace*, ib. 1842. [1]

MILMAN, John White M'Kinley, *Sykehouse Parsonage, Snaith, Yorks.*—St. John's Coll. Cam. B.A. 1842; Deac. 1842, Pr. 1843. P. C. of Sykehouse, Dio. York, 1851. (Patrons, D. and C. of Dur; Glebe, 21 acres; P. C.'s Inc. 320*l*; Pop. 623.) [2]

MILMAN, William Henry, *Sion College-gardens, London-wall, London, E.C.*—Ch. Ch. Ox. 1843, B.A. 1847, M.A. 1850; Deac. 1849 by Bp of Ox. Pr. 1850 by Bp of Lon. R. of St. Augustine's with St. Faith's R. City and Dio. Lon. 1857. (Patrons, D. and C. of St. Paul's; Fire-Act Commutation, 172*l*; R.'s Inc. 300*l*; Pop. St. Augustine's 110, St. Faith's 761.) Librarian of Sion Coll. 1857; Min. Can. of St. Paul's Cathl. 1859. Formerly C. of Ch. Ch. Hoxton, Lond. [3]

MILNE, Henry, *Letchworth Rectory, Hitchin, Herts.*—Brasen. Coll. Ox. B.A. 1842, M.A. 1845; Deac. 1843 and Pr. 1844. R. of Letchworth, Dio. Roch. 1859. (Patron, Rev. C. Alington; R.'s Inc. 300*l* and Ho; Pop. 85.) Formerly Sen. C. of St. Andrew's, Holborn, Lond. 1845. C. of Bushey, Herts, 1848; V. of Harlington, near Dunstable, 1854–58. [4]

MILNE, Henry, *Home-Hale Rectory, Shipdham, Norfolk.*—Brasen. Coll. Ox. Scho. of, and Hulme's Exhib. B.A. 1837, M.A. 1840; Deac. 1839 and Pr. 1840 by Bp of Win. R. of Holme-Hale, Dio. Nor. 1844. (Patron, the present R; Tithe, 571*l* 14*s* 8*d*; Glebe, 56 acres; R.'s Inc. 685*l* and Ho; Pop. 464.) Formerly C. of Privett, Hants, 1839–44. [5]

MILNE, John Haworth, *Itchingfield Rectory, Horsham, Sussex.*—Brasen. Coll. Ox. B.A. 1850, M.A. 1853; Deac. 1851 and Pr. 1852 by Abp of Cant. R. of Itchingfield, Dio. Chich. 1862. (Patron, Rev. J. H. Milne; Tithe, comm. 408*l*; Glebe, 70 acres; R.'s Inc. 450*l* and Ho; Pop. 377.) Formerly C. of West Farleigh, Kent, 1851–52, Hammersmith 1853; V. of Thatcham, Berks, 1855–62. [6]

MILNE, Nathaniel, *Radcliffe Rectory, Manchester.*—St. John's Coll. Cam. B.A. 1832, M.A. 1835; Deac. 1833 and Pr. 1834 by Bp of Ches. R. of Radcliffe, or Ratcliffe Tower, Dio. Man. 1838. (Patron, Earl of Wilton; Tithe, 160*l*; Glebe, 49½ acres; R.'s Inc. 510*l* and Ho; Pop. 4000.) Surrogate. [7]

MILNER, Charles Frederick, *Archbishop Tenison's Grammar School, St. Martin-in-the-Fields, London, W.C.*—King's Coll. Lond; Deac. 1849 and Pr. 1850 by Bp of Rip. Head Mast. of Abp Tenison's Sch. Lond. Formerly P. C. of Shadwell, Yorks, 1851–57. Author, *Holy Truths* (a Catechism for Schools), Masters, 3*d*; *Pastor's Gift*, ib. 1855, 1*s* 6*d*. [8]

MILNER, Edward William, *Plymouth.*—Pemb. Coll. Cam. B.A. 1836, M.A. 1839; Deac. 1840 by Bp of Dur. Pr. 1841 by Abp of Cant. Chap. to the Forces, Devonport. [9]

MILNER, J.—C. of Frating with Thorington, Essex. [10]

MILNER, James, *Stockton-on-Tees.*—Trin. Coll. Cam. B.A. 1845, M.A. 1848; Deac. 1846 by Bp of Wor. Pr. 1847 by Bp of Dur. R. of Elton, near Stockton-on-Tees, Dio. Dur. 1852. (Patrons, T. Wade and T. J. and J. Hogg, Esqrs; Tithe, 150*l*; Glebe, 75 acres; R.'s Inc. 214*l*; Pop. 108.) [11]

MILNER, James George, *Bellerby, Bedale, Leyburn, Yorks.*—Deac. 1820 and Pr. 1823 by Bp of Ches. P. C. of Hamsterley, Durham, Dio. Dur. 1825. (Patron, Henry Chaytor, Esq; Tithe—Imp. 83*l*; P. C.'s Inc. 75*l* and Ho; Pop. 522.) P. C. of Bellerby, Yorks, Dio. Rip. 1829. (Patron, J. C. Chaytor, Esq; P. C.'s Inc. 80*l*; Pop. 391.) [12]

MILNER, John.—Queen's Coll. Ox. B.A. 1845; Deac. 1845 and Pr. 1846 by Bp of Carl. Chap. and Naval Instructor of H.M.S. "Hector." Author, *The Alcestis of Euripides, with copious English Notes*, Sydney, New South Wales; *A Few Plain Words on Baptismal Regeneration*, Masters; *Hints as to the Right Interpretation of the Apocalypse*, ib; *Letters on the Day-Year Theory*, Greenock. [13]

MILNER, Joseph, *Castor, Peterborough.*—St. Cath. Hall, Cam. Sen. Opt. 2nd cl. Cl. Trip. and B.A. 1847, M.A. 1850; Deac. 1851, Pr. 1852. C. of Upton, near Peterborough; Fell. of St. Cath. Coll. Cam. [14]

MILNER, Richard, *Barnoldswick Parsonage, (Yorks), near Colne.*—St. John's Coll. Cam. B.A. 1822; Deac. 1824 and Pr. 1825 by Bp of Ches. P. C. of Barnoldswick, Dio. Rip. 1840. (Patron, R. Hodson, Esq; Glebe, 9 acres; P. C.'s Inc. 180*l* and Ho; Pop. 3478.) [15]

MILNER, William, 4, *Egerton-grove, Stratford-road, Hulme, Manchester.*—Dub. A.B. 1852, A.M. 1855; Deac. 1852 and Pr. 1853 by Bp of Lich. C. of St. George's, Hulme, Manchester, 1852. Formerly C. of Forsbrook, Staffs, 1852, St. George's, Hulme, 1854, Broughton-in-Airedale 1856, St. George's, Hulme, 1861. [16]

MILNER, William Holme, *The Vicarage, Horncastle, Lincolnshire.*—Deac. 1827 and Pr. 1828 by Bp of Carl. V. of Horncastle, Dio. Lin. 1853. (Patron, Bp of Carl; Tithe, 6*l* 7*s* 6*d*; Glebe, 370 acres; V.'s Inc. 750*l* and Ho; Pop. 4987.) Preb. of Weston Rivall in Lin. Cathl; Rural Dean; Dioc. Inspector of Schs; Surrogate. Formerly C. of Morland, Westmoreland, 1833–45; V. of Penrith 1845–53. [17]

MILNER, William Kirkbank, *Knaresdale Rectory, Northumberland.*—Bp Hat. Hall, Dur. B.A. 1849, Licen. Theol. 1850; Deac. 1850 and Pr. 1851 by Bp of Rip. R. of Knaresdale, Dio. Dur. 1866. (Patron, Lord Chan; Tithe, 117*l*; Glebe, 30 acres; R.'s Inc. 160*l* and Ho; Pop. 500.) Formerly C. of Sharow, Ripon, 1850–52, Hamsterley, Durham, 1852–66. [18]

MILNES, Benjamin.—C. of Ocle Pitchard, near Hereford. [19]

MILNES, Herbert, *Winster, near Matlock, Derbyshire.*—Deac. 1864, Pr. 1865. V. of Winster, Dio. Lich. 1866. (Patrons, Freeholders, &c. of Winster; Glebe, 36 acres; V.'s Inc. 113*l*; Pop. 958.) Formerly C. of Crick, near Derby, 1864–66. [20]

MILNES, Nicholas Bourne, *Collyweston Rectory (Northants), Stamford.*—Trin. Coll. Ox. B.A. 1849, M.A. 1853; Deac. 1849 and Pr. 1850. R. of Collyweston, Dio. Pet. 1854. (Patron, Ld Chan; Tithe, 252*l*; Glebe, 50 acres; R.'s Inc. 380*l* and Ho; Pop. 473.) [21]

MILTON, William, *Broomfield, Sheffield.*—Wor. Coll. Ox. B.A. 1839, M.A. 1842; Deac. 1839 and Pr. 1840 by Bp of Rip. Min. of the District of Broomhall, Sheffield. Formerly P. C. of New Radford, Notts, 1845. Author, *Sermons, Christian Mercifulness, its Nature and Reward*; *Piety and Patriotism*; *Parting Words*, Allens, Nottingham. [22]

MILTON, William, *Newbury, Berks.*—Ex. Coll. Ox. 2nd cl. Lit. Hum. and B.A. 1843, M.A. 1845; Deac. 1846 and Pr. 1847 by Bp of Rip. C. of Newbury 1859. Formerly C. of Little Marlow. Author, *The Sacrificial Vestments, Are they Legal?* Rivingtons, 1866; *On the Morality of the Old Testament*, Rivingtons, 1867. [23]

MILWARD, Henry, *Paulton Parsonage, Bristol.*—Wad. Coll. Ox. B.A. 1840; Deac. 1840 and Pr. 1841 by Bp of B. and W. P. C. of Paulton, Dio. B. and W. 1842. (Patron, V. of Chewton, Mendip; Tithe, 67*l*; Glebe, 54 acres; P. C.'s Inc. 200*l* and Ho; Pop. 1958.) Preb. of East Harptree in Wells Cathl. [24]

MILWARD, Henry Charles, *Nechells, Birmingham.*—Ch. Coll. Cam. late Sch. of, 33rd Wrang. and B.A. 1855, M.A. 1860; Deac. 1855 and Pr. 1856 by Bp of Lich. P. C. of St. Clement's, Nechells, Birmingham, Dio. Wor. 1862. (Patron, P. C. of St. Matthew's, Duddeston; P. C.'s Inc. 320*l* and Ho; Pop. 9000.) Formerly C. of Great Barr 1855–56; Miss. Can. of St. Paul's Cathl. Calcutta, 1856–60; C. of Ch. Ch. Birmingham 1860–62. [25]

MINCHIN, Harry Holdsworth, *Woodford, Daventry.*—Wad. Coll. Ox. B.A. 1855, M.A. 1857; Deac. 1856 and Pr. 1858 by Bp of Ox. V. of Woodford-cum-Membris, Dio. Pet. 1865. (Patron, Ld Chan; Tithe, 70*l*;

Glebe, 138 acres; V.'s Inc. 240*l* and Ho; Pop. 800.) Formerly C. of St. Peter's-in-the-East, Oxford; R. of Wormley, Herts, 1860. [1]

MINCHIN, Henry Charles, *Gloucester.*—Dub. A.M. 1847, *ad eund.* Ox. 1854; Deac. and Pr. 1843. V. of St. Mary-de-Lode with Trinity V. City and Dio. Glouc. 1861. (Patrons, D. and C. of Glouc; V.'s Inc. 300*l*; Pop. 4250.) Formerly P. C. of High Cross, Herts, 1857–61. [2]

MINCHIN, John Champneys, *Walthamstow, Essex.*—New Coll. Ox. B.A. 1824, M.A. 1829; Deac. 1822 and Pr. 1824 by Bp of Herf. R. of St. Mildred's with St. Mary Colechurch R. City and Dio. Lon. 1837. (Patrons, Ld Chan and Mercers' Company alt; Fire Act Commutation, 170*l*; R.'s Inc. 280*l*; Pop. 421.) [3]

MINGAYE, George, *Wilby Rectory, Stradbrooke, Suffolk.*—Caius Coll. Cam. B.A. 1812, M.A. 1819. R. of Wilby, Dio. Nor. 1838. (Patron, the present R; Tithe, 647*l*; Glebe, 51 acres; R.'s Inc. 734*l* and Ho; Pop. 560.) [4]

MINNITT, Robert, *Healey Vicarage, near Rochdale.*—Dub. A.B. 1831; Deac. 1834 by Bp of Dromore, Pr. 1855 by Bp of Ches. V. of Healey, Dio. Man. 1850. (Patrons, the Crown and Bp of Man. alt; V.'s Inc. 250*l* and Ho; Pop. 2758.) Formerly P. C. of Heywood, Lanc. 1835–50. [5]

MINNS, George William Waller, *East Dereham, Norfolk.*—St. Cath. Coll. Cam. LL.B. 1859; Deac. 1860 and Pr. 1862 by Bp of Ox. C. of East Dereham 1866. Formerly C. of Charney, Berks, 1860–62, Burnham Overy, Norfolk, 1863–64. Author, *Mural Paintings at Witton*, 1859; *Acoustic Vases*, 1865 (published by Norfolk Archæol. Soc); *Notes upon Rood Screens*, 1867, Norwich. [6]

MINSHULL, Thomas E., *Castle Bromwich, Birmingham.*—C. of Castle Bromwich. [7]

MINTON, Samuel.—Wor. Coll. Ox. B.A. 1842, M.A. 1844; Deac. 1843 by Bp of Herf. Pr. 1844 by Bp of G. and B. C. of Brighton. Formerly P. C. of Penkhull, Staffs; P. C. of St. Silas', Liverpool, 1851–57; Min. of Percy Chapel, Lond. 1857–63; P. C. of Eaton Chapel, Eaton-square, Lond. 1864. Author, *Complete Exposure of Dr. Cahill* (a Lecture); *The Evangelicals and Edinburgh*; *The Romish Doctrine of Intention*; *Second Challenge to Dr. Cahill*; *Facts and Fictions*; *An Exposure of the Inconsistencies, Fictions, and Fallacies of Dr. Newman's Lectures at Birmingham*; *Romish Tactics and Romish Morals*; *Has the Church of Rome any Pope, &c*; *Dr. Cahill, the Priests and the Madiai*; *Speaking Lies in Hypocrisy*; *Guerilla Warfare*; *The Confessional*; *Ye are Complete in Him* (a Sermon); *Righteousness and Redemption* (a Sermon); *Popular Lectures on Unitarianism*; *The Sabbath Argument*; *Letter to the Bishop of London on Liturgical Revision*, Longmans. [8]

MINTON, Thomas William, *Darlington.*—Deac. 1825, Pr. 1826. Formerly P. C. of Trinity, Darlington, 1847–65. [9]

MIREHOUSE, John Herbert, *Colsterworth Rectory, near Grantham,* and *Hambrook, Gloucestershire.*—Clare Coll. Cam. B.A. 1861, M.A. 1865; Deac. 1862 by Abp of York, and Pr. 1863 by Bp of G. and B. R. of Colsterworth, Dio. Lin. 1864. (Patron, Rev. Henry Mirehouse, Preb. of South Grantham; R.'s Inc. 600*l* and Ho; Pop. 1169.) Formerly C. of Fishponds 1862–64. [10]

MIRRIELEES, William, *Berwick-on-Tweed.*—Queen's Coll. Ox. 2nd cl. Lit. Hum. and B.A. 1850, M.A. 1853; Deac. 1851 and Pr. 1852 by Bp of Salis. Head Mast. of the Berwick Gr. Sch. Formerly C. of Upton Scudamore, Wilts; Second Mast. of the Gr. Sch. and Lect. at Bishop Stortford, and C. of Perry Green, Much Hadham, Herts. [11]

MITCHELL, Charles, *Knutsford, Cheshire.*—Chap. to the Knutsford House of Correction. [12]

MITCHELL, Henry, *Bosham Vicarage, Emsworth, Sussex.*—Lin. Coll. Ox. B.A. 1841, M.A. 1844; Deac. 1842, Pr. 1843. V. of Bosham, Dio. Chich. 1845. (Patrons, D. and C. of Chich; Tithe—App. 1366*l* 11*s*; Glebe, 11 acres; V.'s Inc. 270*l* and Ho; Pop. 1158.) [13]

MITCHELL, Henry, *Longparish, Hants.*—St. John's Coll. Cam. Scho. and Prizeman of, 3rd Sen. Opt. B.A. 1852; Deac. 1853 and Pr. 1854 by Bp of Win. C. of Longparish. Formerly C. of Beaconsfield 1863, Chessington 1864. [14]

MITCHELL, Josiah, *Alberbury, Salop.*—All Souls Coll. Ox. B.A. 1856, M.A. 1859; Deac. 1857, Pr. 1858. V. of Alberbury, Dio. Herf. 1866. (Patron, All Souls' Coll. Ox; Tithe, 280*l*; Glebe, 38*l*; V.'s Inc. 332*l* and Ho; Pop. 1035.) Formerly C. of Ampthill, Beds, 1857–60, St. Simon's, Jersey, 1860–66. [15]

MITCHELL, John Butler.—Corpus Coll. Cam. B.A. 1860, M.A. 1863; Deac. 1859 by Bp of Man. Pr. 1860 by Bp of Pet. Formerly C. of Medbourne with Holt, Leic. 1859–63, and East Stoke with Syerston 1863, Syerston and Elston, Notts, 1864–67. [16]

MITCHELL, J. B., *Tavistock.*—P. C. of St. Paul's, Tavistock, Dio. Ex. 1858. (Patron, Duke of Bedford; P. C.'s Inc. 150*l*; Pop. 1323.) [17]

MITCHELL, John Hollings, *Cullingworth, Bingley, Yorks.*—Ch. Coll. Cam. B.A. 1843, M.A. 1860; Deac. 1843 and Pr. 1844 by Bp of Rip. P. C. of Cullingworth, Dio. Rip. 1847. (Patron, the Crown and Bp of Rip. alt; P. C.'s Inc. 150*l* and Ho; Pop. 1943.) [18]

MITCHELL, J. W., *Leadgate, Gateshead.*—P. C. of Leadgate, Dio. Dur. 1864. (Patrons, Crown and Bp of Dur. alt; P. C.'s Inc. 200*l*; Pop. 3413.) Formerly C. of Lanchester, Durham. [19]

MITCHELL, Muirehead, *University Club, London, S.W.*—Univ. Coll. Ox. B.A. 1832, M.A. 1835. One of H.M. Inspectors of Schs. [20]

MITCHELL, Oliver, 208, *Walworth Road, S.*—Jesus Coll. Cam. Scho. of, B.A. 1855; Deac. 1856, Pr. 1857. P. C. of All Saints', Walworth, Dio. Lon. 1865. (Patron, Bp of Lon; P. C.'s Inc. 200*l*; Pop. 8,000.) Formerly C. of Holy Rhood, Southampton, and St. Peter's, Walworth. [21]

MITCHELL, Robert, *Hanging Heaton, Dewsbury.*—P. C. of St. Paul's, Hanging Heaton, Dio. Rip. 1859. (Patron, V. of Dewsbury; P. C.'s Inc. 150*l* and Ho; Pop. 2219.) [22]

MITCHELL, St. John, *Pentney Parsonage, Swaffham, Norfolk.*—St. Edm. Hall, Ox. B.A. 1839. P. C. of Pentney, Dio. Nor. 1851. (Patron, Rev. R. Hankinson; Tithe—Imp. 7*l* 4*s* 6*d*; P. C.'s Inc. 70*l* and Ho; Pop. 642.) P. C. of West Bilney, Lynn-Regis, Dio. Nor. 1852. (Patron, J. Dalton, Esq; P. C.'s Inc. 70*l*; Pop. 253.) [23]

MITCHELL, St. John, *Kirk Malew, Isle of Man.*—C. of Kirk Malew. [24]

MITCHELL, Thomas, *Kingston-on-Thames.*—Oriel Coll. Ox. B.A. 1840; Deac. 1844, Pr. 1845. C. of Kingston-on-Thames 1859–67. [25]

MITCHELL, Thomas, *Clawson Vicarage, Melton-Mowbray.*—Trin. Coll. Cam. B.A. 1845, M.A. 1848; Deac. and Pr. 1845 by Bp of Lin. V. of Long Clawson, Dio. Pet. 1848. (Patron, T. Mitchell, Esq; Tithe, 5*l*; Glebe, 123 acres; V.'s Inc. 200*l*; Pop. 850.) Author, *The Glory of the Latter House* (a Sermon), Melton-Mowbray, 6*d*; *Palestine Revisited, and other Poems*, Nottingham. [26]

MITCHELL, Walter, *St. Bartholomew's Hospital, London, E.C.*—Queens' Coll. Cam. B.A. 1841, M.A. 1844; Deac. 1841 and Pr. 1842 by Abp of York. Hospitaller of St. Bartholomew's Hospital 1846; V. of St. Bartholomew's the Less, 1861; Reader of Ch. Ch. Newgate-street, 1846. Formerly Lect. on Natural Philosophy at St. Bartholomew's Hosp. Author, *The Properties of Matter*; *Statics*; *Crystallography*; and *Mineralogy* in "*Orr's Circle of the Sciences*," 1855. [27]

MITCHINSON, Henry Clarke, *Christ Church Parsonage, Rotherhithe, London, S.E.*—Clare Hall, Cam. Sen. Opt. 3rd cl. Cl. Trip. and B.A. 1849, M.A. 1853; Deac. 1850 and Pr. 1851 by Bp of Lin. P. C. of Ch. Ch. Rotherhithe, Dio. Win. 1864. (Patrons, Hyndman's Trustees; P. C.'s Inc. 300*l* and Ho; Pop. 4616.) Formerly 2nd Mast. of East Retford Gr. Sch. 1849; Chap. of the East Retford Union 1856; Even. Lect. of St. Saviour's, Clarborough, 1856; C. of Trinity, Marylebone, Lond. 1860–64. [28]

MITCHINSON, John, *King's School, Canterbury.*—Pemb. Coll. Ox. Scho. and Fell. of, 1st cl. Cl. and 1st cl. Nat. Sci. B A. 1855, M.A. 1857, B. and D.C.L. 1864; Deac. 1858 by Bp of Lon. Pr. 1860 by Abp of Cant. Head Mast. of the King's Sch. Canterbury, 1859. Formerly Head Mast.'s Asst. in Merchant Taylors' Sch. and C. of St. Philip's, Clerkenwell, Lond; Cl. Examiner in Durham Univ. 1861 and 1867. [1]

MITCHINSON, Thomas York.—St. John's Coll. Cam. B.A. 1849; Deac. 1850 and Pr. 1851 by Bp of Wor. Formerly C of St. Leonard's, Shoreditch, Lond. [2]

MITTON, A. T., *Huddersfield.*—C. of Huddersfield. Formerly C. of Sheepshed. [3]

MITTON, H. A., *Heaton Parsonage, near Bradford, Yorks.*—Ch. Coll. Cam. B.A. 1859, M.A. 1864; Deac. 1860 and Pr. 1861 by Bp of Rip. P. C. of Heaton, Dio. Rip. 1864. (Patrons, Earl of Rosse, B. Wood, John Hollings, and Joseph Wood, Esqs. Rev. W. Kelly; P. C.'s Inc. 48*l* and Ho; Pop. 2000.) Formerly C. of St. Paul's, Shipley, 1860–64. [4]

MITTON, Joseph, *Baildon Parsonage, Leeds.*—Jesus Coll. Cam. B.A. 1833; Deac. 1833, Pr. 1834. P. C. of Baildon, Dio. Rip. 1848. (Patrons, Trustees; Tithe—Imp. 124*l* 6*s*; P. C.'s Inc. 157*l* and Ho; Pop. 5000.) [5]

MITTON, Welbury, *St. Paul's Parsonage, Manningham, Bradford, Yorks.*—Deac. 1827 and Pr. 1828 by Abp of York. P. C. of St. Paul's, Manningham, Dio. Rip. 1847. (Patron, John Hollings, Esq; Endow. 150*l*; Pew rents, &c. 150*l*; P. C.'s Inc. 270*l* and Ho; Pop. 8000.) Surrogate. Formerly C. of Arncliffe 1828–31, Ripon 1831–34, Aldborough, 1834–37. [6]

MOBERLY, Charles Edward, *Rugby.*—Ball. Coll. Ox. B.A. 1840, M.A. 1843; Deac. 1846 and Pr. 1848 by Bp of Ox. Asst. Mast. of Rugby Sch. 1859. Formerly P. C. of Beeston, near Leeds, 1855–59. Author, *Lectures on Logic.* [7]

MOBERLY, Frederick Showers, *Wells, Somerset.*—Trin. Coll. Cam. B.A. 1853, M.A. 1856; Deac. 1860 by Bp of B. and W. Pr. 1862 by Bp of Ex. Priest-Vicar of Wells Cathl. and Vice Prin. of Wells Theol. Coll. 1866. Formerly Asst. C. of Exmouth 1860–62. [8]

MOBERLY, George, *Brighstone Rectory, Newport, Isle of Wight.*—Ball. Coll. Ox. 1st cl. Lit. Hum. and B.A. 1825; English Essay 1826, M.A. 1828, D.C.L. 1836; Deac. 1826 and Pr. 1828 by Bp of Ox. R. of Brighstone or Brixton, Dio. Win. 1866. (Patron, Bp of Win; Tithe, 515*l*; Glebe, 5 acres, R.'s Inc. 680*l* and Ho; Pop. 630.) Fell. of Win. Coll. Formerly Fell. and Tut. of Ball. Coll. Ox; Public Examiner in the Univ. of Ox. 1830 and 1833; Select Preacher 1833, 1858, and 1863; Head Mast. of Win. Coll. 1835–66. Author, *Practical Sermons,* 1838; *Sermons Preached at Winchester College,* 1844, 2nd series, *with a Preface on Fagging,* 1848; *The Sayings of the Great Forty Days between the Resurrection and Ascension, regarded as the Outlines of the Kingdom of God* (five Sermons), 1844; Second Ed. with *An Examination of Mr. Newman's Theory of Development,* 1846; *The Proposed Degradation and Declaration Considered* (a Letter addressed to the Mast. of Ball.) Ox. 1845; *All Saints, Kings and Priests* (Two Sermons on the Papal Aggression, Winchester), 1850; *The Law of the Love of God* (an Essay), 1854; *Sermons on the Beatitudes,* Ox. 1860; *Five Short Letters to Sir William Heathcote on the Studies and Discipline of Public Schools,* Rivingtons, 1861. [9]

MOBERLY, George Herbert, *Corpus Christi College, Oxford.*—Corpus Coll. Ox. B.A. 1859, M.A. 1861; Deac. 1860, Pr. 1861. Fell. of Corpus Coll. Ox. Formerly C. of St. Peter's-in-the-East, Oxford 1860–63, Assington, Suffolk, 1864–65. [10]

MOBERLY, Henry Edward, *Winchester.*—New Coll. Ox. 3rd cl. Lit. Hum. and B.A. 1845, M.A. 1848; Deac. 1846, Pr. 1847. Fell of New Coll. Ox; Asst. Mast. of Win. Coll. [11]

MOCATTA, William Abraham, *Eccleston, St. Helens, Lancashire.*—Dub. A.B. 1853, A.M. 1856; *ad eund.* Ox. et Cam 1856; Deac. 1854 and Pr. 1855 by Bp of Ches. P. C. of St. Thomas's, Eccleston, Dio. Ches. 1861. (Patrons, Exors. of the late P. Greenall, Esq; P. C.'s Inc. 180*l* and Ho; Pop. 3206.) Formerly C. of Ch. Ch. Southport, 1854–57; V. of Bispham; 1857–61. [12]

MOCKLER, James, *Denby, near Derby.*—Dub. A.B. 1844, A.M. 1852; Deac. 1844 and Pr. 1845 by Bp of Lich. V. of Denby, Dio. Lich, 1845. (Patron, Wm. D. Lowe, Esq; Tithe—Imp. 350*l*; V. 12*l*; Glebe, 37 acres; V.'s Inc. 140*l*; Pop. 1338.) Formerly a Captain in the 59th Foot. [13]

MOE, John Brathwaite, *Barbados.*—King's Coll. Lond. 1st cl. Assoc. 1853; Deac. 1854 and Pr. 1855 by Abp of Cant. Formerly C. of Knockholt 1854–55, Holy Trinity, Maidstone, Kent, 1855–56, Dartford, Kent, 1856–58, Prestbury 1858. [14]

MOERAN, Thomas Warner, 109, *Upper Parliament-street, Liverpool.*—Dub. A.B. 1844; Deac. and Pr. 1845. P. C. of St. Matthew's, Toxteth-park, Dio. Ches. 1854. (Patrons, Trustees; Inc. from Pew-rents; Pop. 8004.) [15]

MOFFAT, Charles, *Minster-yard, Lincoln.*—Hon. Chap. of the Lincoln Lunatic Asylum. [16]

MOFFATT, Christopher William, *Brussels.*—British Chap. at Brussels. [17]

MOGGRIDGE, Matthew Weston, *Long Ditton, Kingston-on-Thames.*—Univ. Coll. Ox. B.A.; Deac. 1864 and Pr. 1865 by Bp of Pet. C. of Long Ditton 1866. Formerly C. of St. John's, Leicester, 1864. [18]

MOGRIDGE, Henry Fullelove, *Old Radnor Vicarage, near Kington, Herefordshire.*—St. John's Coll. Cam. B.A. 1830, M.A. 1835. V. of Old Radnor with Ednol C. and Kinnerton C. Dio. Herf. 1834. (Patrons, D. and C. of Wor; Tithe—App. 1333*l* 10*s* and 3 acres of Glebe; V.'s Inc. 200*l* and Ho; Pop. 1349.) [19]

MOGRIDGE, Henry Twells, *All Saints', Hereford.*—St. Peter's Coll. Cam. B.A. 1865; Deac. 1866 by Bp of G. and B. C. of All Saints', Hereford, 1866. [20]

MOGRIDGE, H. P., *Great Badminton, Chippenham.*—C. of Great Badminton, Gloucestershire. [21]

MOILLIET, J. L., *Abberley Rectory, Stourport, Worcestershire.*—R. of Abberley, Dio. Herf. 1865. (Patroness, Mrs. Moilliet; Tithe, 333*l* 8*s* 6*d*; Glebe, 4 acres; R.'s Inc. 350*l* and Ho; Pop. 692.) [22]

MOLESWORTH, John Edward Nassau, *Rochdale.*—Trin. Coll. Ox. B.A. 1812, M.A. 1817, B.D. and D.D. 1838; Deac. 1813, Pr. 1814. V. of Rochdale, Dio. Man. 1839. (Patron, Bp of Man; Tithe—App. 68*l* 15*s* 6*d*, Imp. 1292*l* 9*s*; Glebe, 200 acres; V.'s Inc. 1730*l* and Ho; Pop. 25,280.) Author, *Sermons on* various subjects; *Answer to Davison on the Origin and Intent of Primitive Sacrifice; The Passover, pointing out Errors, &c; St. Paul's Key to Types of Gen.* xxii; *Sermon* on the Consecration of Bishops Broughton and Mountain; *Sermon* on the Primary Visitation of Abp Howley; *Visitation Sermons,* before the Archd. and Clergy of Cant; *Domestic Chaplain,* 2 vols; *The Penny Sunday Reader,* first 5 vols; *Remarks upon the Cases of Dr. Hampden and the Rev. J. P. Lee, in Reference to proposed Modifications of the Law of Electing Bishops, &c.* [23]

MOLESWORTH, Rennell Francis Wynn, *Bideford, Devon.*—Brasen. Coll. Ox. B.A. 1849, M.A. 1851; Deac. 1850 and Pr. 1851 by Abp of Cant. Evening Lect. at St. Mary's, Bideford. Formerly C. of Preston next Wingham 1850–52, Ramsgate 1852–55, Betshanger 1857–63, Sutton 1864–65, St. Peter's, Canterbury, 1866–67. Author, *Lecture upon Unity,* 1st ed. 1857, 3rd ed. Masters, 1859, 4*d.* [24]

MOLESWORTH, Robert Francis, *Coston Rectory, Melton Mowbray.*—Deac. 1863 and Pr. 1864 by Bp of Chich. R. of Coston, Dio. Pet. 1865. (Patron, Ld Chan; Tithe, 320*l*; Glebe, 36 acres; R.'s Inc. 390*l* and Ho; Pop. 150.) Dom. Chap. to Viscount Molesworth. Formerly C. of St. Anne's, Lewes, 1863, Trinity, West Cowes, 1864–65. [25]

MOLESWORTH, Samuel, *Addlestone, near Weybridge, Surrey.*—C. of Addlestone. [26]

MOLESWORTH, Thomas, *Gosport.*—Corpus Coll. Cam. B.A. 1851; Deac. 1852 and Pr. 1853 by Bp of

Lon. Chap. to the Forces 1855. Formerly C. of Trinity, Tottenham, 1852–54, Hitchin, Herts, 1854–55. [1]

MOLESWORTH, Walter, *Painswick, Gloucestershire.*—Ch. Coll. Cam. B.A. 1854; Deac. 1854 and Pr. 1855 by Bp of Ely. C. of Painswick. Formerly C. of St. Peter-at-Arches, Lincoln. [2]

MOLESWORTH, William Nassau, *Spotland Vicarage, Rochdale.*—Pem. Coll. Cam. Prizeman, Sen. Opt. and B.A. 1839, M.A. 1843; Deac. 1839 by Abp of Cant. Pr. 1840 by Bp of Ches. V. of St. Clement's, Rochdale, Dio. Man. 1844. (Patron, V. of Rochdale; V.'s Inc. 700*l* and Ho; Pop. 7500.) Surrogate. Formerly P. C. of St. Andrew's, Manchester. Author, *The Strong Man disturbed in his Palace* (a Sermon on behalf of the National Society); *A Lecture on the System of Religious Education, established by the Reformers*, 1842; *An Essay on the Religious Importance of Secular Instruction; Plain Lectures on Astronomy; A Lecture on the History of Industrial Progress* (delivered before the Rochdale Equitable Pioneers' Co-operative Society, and published by them); *A History of the Reform Bill of* 1832, Chapman and Hall, 1865, 10*s* 6*d*; *On the Great Importance of an Alliance between England and France* (a Prize Essay), 1860; *On Upper and Middle Class Education* (a Prize Essay), 1866. [3]

MOLESWORTH-ST. AUBYN, St. Aubyn Hender, *Swindon Parsonage, Dudley.*—Ch. Ch. Ox. B.A. 1856, M.A. 1859; Deac. 1858, Pr. 1859. P. C. of Swindon, Dio. Lich. 1867. (Patron, V. of Wombourne; P. C.'s Inc. 100*l* and Ho; Pop. 600.) Formerly C. of Ledsham, Yorks, 1858; Budock, Cornwall, 1860; Swindon, 1862. [4]

MOLINEUX, Thomas, *Lewes, Sussex.*—Trin. Coll. Ox. B.C.L. R. of Waberthwaite, Cumberland, Dio. Carl. 1847. (Patron, Lord Muncaster; Tithe—App. 2*s*, Imp. 2*s* 6*d*, R. 105*l*; R.'s Inc. 135*l* and Ho; Pop. 198.) [5]

MOLONY, Charles Arthur, *Hougham, Dover.*—Lin. Coll. Ox. B.A. 1848, M.A. 1851; Deac. 1849, Pr. 1850. V. of Hougham, Dio. Cant. 1854. (Patron, Abp of Cant; Tithe—App. 557*l* 10*s*; Glebe, 97 acres; V. 190*l* 14*s* 6*d*; Glebe, 4 acres; V.'s Inc. 190*l*; Pop. 1569.) [6]

MOLONY, Charles Walker, *Canterbury.*—C. of St. George-the-Martyr's, Canterbury. Formerly C. of Gatcombe, Isle of Wight. [7]

MOLSON, William, *Hogsthorpe, Alford, Lincolnshire.*—Queens' Coll. Cam. B.A. 1832; Deac. 1832 by Bp of Nor. Pr. 1833 by Bp of Lin. V. of Hogsthorpe, Dio. Lin. 1846. (Patron, Bp of Lin; Glebe, 167 acres; V.'s Inc. 300*l*; Pop. 874.) [8]

MOLYNEUX, Bryan W., *Cold Weston, Ludlow.*—C. of Cold Weston, Salop. [9]

MOLYNEUX, Capel, 44, *Onslow-square, London, S.W.*—Ch. Coll. Cam. B.A. 1826; Deac. 1828 by Bp of Wor. Pr. 1829 by Bp of Herf. P. C. of St. Paul's, Onslow-square, Brompton, Dio. Lon. 1860. (Patron, C. J. Freake, Esq.) Formerly Min. of the Lock Chapel, Harrow-road, Lond. Author, *Israel's Fortune*, 4*s* 6*d*; *The World to Come*, 4*s* 6*d*; *Gethsemane*, 4*s* 6*d*; *Broken Bread*, 5*s*. [10]

MOLYNEUX, George More, *Compton Rectory, Guildford.*—Trin. Coll. Ox. B.A. 1821, M.A. 1822; Deac. 1828 by Bp of Ches. Pr. 1828 by Bp of Lin. R. of Compton, Dio. Win. 1828. (Patron, J. M. Molyneux, Esq; Tithe, 438*l* 15*s*; Glebe, 71½ acres; R.'s Inc. 538*l* and Ho; Pop. 502.) [11]

MOLYNEUX, Henry George, *Steeple-Gidding, Oundle.*—Magd. Coll. Cam. Scho. of, 1852, 3rd cl. Math. and Theol. Trip. and B.A. 1855, M.A. 1858; Deac. 1856 and Pr. 1857 by Bp of Ely. R. of Steeple-Gidding, near Huntingdon, Dio. Ely, 1859. (Patron, J. Heathcote, Esq; Tithe, 175*l*; Glebe 6 acres; R.'s Inc. 190*l*; Pop. 118.) Formerly C. of Great Stukeley and Kings-Ripon, Hunts. [12]

MOLYNEUX, John Charles, *Mount Radford House, Exeter.*—Ch. Coll. Cam. LL.B. 1866; Deac. 1867. Asst C. of St. Olave's, Exeter; Asst. Mast. in Mount Radford Sch. [13]

MOLYNEUX, John William Henry, *Sudbury, Suffolk.*—Trin. Coll. Cam. 27th Wrang. and B.A. 1841; Deac. 1842, Pr. 1843. P. C. of St. Gregory's with St. Peter's P. C. Sudbury, Dio. Ely, 1855. (Patron, Bp of Ely; Tithe—Imp. 298*l* 10*s* 9*d*; Glebe, 9 acres; P. C.'s Inc. 138*l* and Ho; Pop. St. Gregory, 2781, St. Peter's 1880.) Author, *What is a Christian?* (a Sermon) 1858; *The Manifestation of the Sons of God*, 1853; *Symbolism not Formalism*, 1854; *Letter to Bishop of Ely on Appropriation of Seats in Churches*; *The Altar and Lights on Altar* (correspondence with Bishop of Ely), Longmans, 1865; *Private Prayers from Bishop Andrewes' Devotions*, Rivingtons, 1866. [14]

MOLYNEUX, Reginald Edward, *Waltham St. Lawrence, Maidenhead, Berks.*—Ex. Coll. Ox. B.A. 1859, M.A. 1862; Deac. 1860 and Pr. 1861 by Bp of B. and W. C. of Waltham St. Lawrence. Formerly C. of Cheddar, Somerset, 1860–62, Boldre, Hants, 1862–65. [15]

MOLYNEUX, William, *Twineham Rectory, Cuckfield, Sussex.*—Ch. Ch. Ox. B.A. 1848, M.A. 1851; Deac. 1849 and Pr. 1850 by Bp of Herf. R. of Twineham, Dio Chich. 1859. (Patron, Sir C. Goring; Tithe, comm. 400*l*; Glebe, 4 acres; R.'s Inc. 420*l* and Ho; Pop. 339.) Formerly C. of St. Paul's, Covent-garden, Lond. [16]

MONCKTON, Inglis George, *Coven Parsonage, near Wolverhampton.*—Wad. Coll. Ox. B.A. 1856, M.A. 1858; Deac. 1856 by Bp of Ox. Pr. 1857 by Bp of Lich. P. C. of Coven, Dio. Lich. 1857. (Patron, V. of Brewood; Tithe, 50*l*; P. C.'s Inc. 146*l* and Ho; Pop. 746.) Formerly C. of Woodstock 1856–57. [17]

MONCREIFF, George Robertson, *Privy Council-office, Downing-street, London, S.W.*—Ball. Coll. Ox. 2nd cl. Lit. Hum. 1st cl. Math. et Phy, and B.A. 1838, M.A. 1843; Deac. 1840, Pr. 1841. One of H.M. Inspectors of Schs. 1850. Formerly R. of Tattenhall, Cheshire, 1842 55. Author, *Confirmation Records*, 1848, 2nd ed. 1853, 2*s* 6*d*; *Not Priests but Servants* (a Visitation Sermon), 1849; *The Soldier's Rest* (a Funeral Sermon), 1849; *Confirmation Lectures*, 1850, 2nd ed. 1854, 4*d*; *Confirmation Dialogues*, 1850, 1*d*; *Memoir of Thomas Birth, D.D.* Hatchards, 1851, 14*s*. [18]

MONCRIEFF, William Scott, *Tiverton.*—Trin. Coll. Cam. B.A. 1848, M.A. 1851; Deac. 1848, Pr. 1849. P. C. of St. Paul's, Tiverton, Dio. Ex. 1864. (Patrons, Trustees; P. C.'s Inc. 550*l* and Ho; Pop. 2622.) Formerly C. of Norham, Durham, and Upper Chelsea; P. C. of St. Simon's, Chelsea, Lond. [19]

MONEY, Charles F. S., *St. John's Parsonage, Upper Lewisham-road, Deptford, London, S.E.*—Corpus Coll. Cam. B.A. 1845, M.A. 1850; Deac. 1845, Pr. 1846. P. C. of St. John's, Deptford, Dio. Lon. 1855. (Patron, J. S. S. Lucas, Esq; P. C.'s Inc. 120*l* and Ho; Pop. 7626.) Formerly in the Colonial-office; late Assoc. Sec. of the Ch. Miss. Soc. Author, *Paraphrase on the Lord's Prayer*; *Formation of God's Image in the Soul*, 6*d*; *Retirement and Prayer*, 3*d*; *Revolution in China, and its bearing upon Missionary Efforts*; etc. [20]

MONEY, Frederick, *Offham, Maidstone.*—Caius Coll. Cam. B.A. 1821; Deac. 1818 and Pr. 1821 by Bp of Nor. R. of Offham, Dio. Cant. 1832. (Patron, Ld Chan; Tithe, 324*l* 13*s* 4*d*; Glebe, 8 acres; R.'s Inc. 368*l*; Pop. 411.) [21]

MONK, Herbert, *Newton-in-Makerfield, Lancashire.*—C. of St. Peter's, Newton-in-Makerfield. [22]

MONK, Joseph, 14, *Surrey-terrace, Upper Lewisham-road, S.E.*—St. Cath. Coll. Cam. Scho. of, B.A. 1859, M.A. 1867; Deac. 1859 and Pr. 1860 by Abp of York. Asst. Min. of Ch. Ch. Deptford, and Chap. of the London Dioc. Home Mission 1866. Formerly C. of Trinity and Chap. of the Charterhouse Hull, 1859–61; C. of St. Clement's, Cambridge, and temporary sole charge of Little Shelford, 1862; C. of Balsham, Cambs, 1863–65; Sen. C. of All Saints', Islington, Lond. 1865–66. [23]

MONK, William, *Wymington Rectory, Higham Ferrers, Beds.*—St. John's Coll. Cam. B.A. 1855, 2nd in 1st cl. Moral Sci. Trip. 1856, Univ. Moral Phil. Prizeman 1856, M.A. 1858, *ad eund.* M.A. Ox. 1858; Deac. 1855 and Pr. 1856 by Bp of Ely. R. of Wymington, Dio. Ely, 1864. (Patron, the present R; Glebe, 166 acres; R.'s Inc. 230*l* and Ho; Pop. 349.) Formerly C. of St. Andrew's-the-Less, Cambridge, 1855–58; Wimpole, Rampton, and Arrington, Cambs, 1859–61; Bassingbourne, Cambs, 1861-62; Wixoe, Suffolk, 1862–64. Fell. of the Royal Astronomical Soc. and Soc. of Antiquaries, of London, 1855; Hon. Corresponding Assoc. of the Genealogical and Historical Soc. for Counties of Bedford and Northampton, 1864, and of the Anthropological Soc. 1864; Prin. Founder and first Hon. Sec. of the Cambridge Church Missionary and Gospel Propagation Union 1856–57; Founder, Prin. Organizer, and first Hon. Sec. of the University's Mission to Central Africa 1858–59; Hon. Sec. to the Cambridge branches of the London City Mission, of the Turkish Missions Aid Soc. and of the English Church Missions to Roman Catholics, 1856–57; Hon. Sec. to the Ruridecanal Chapter of the Deanery of Clare, Suffolk, 1863–64, and of the Deanery of Clapham, Beds, 1864; Hon. Sec. to the Soc. of Antiquaries for the co. of Northants 1864; Hon. Sec. to the Additional Curates' Soc. 1864, and the Curates' Augmentation Fund 1866, each for the Deanery of Clapham; Hon. Sec. to the Central African Mission for co. of Bedford 1867; Member of the Archæological and Architectural Socs. for co. of Bucks 1865, for co. of Bedford 1865, and for Archdeaconry of Northampton 1865. Editor of *Dr. Livingstone's Cambridge Lectures, with a Preface by Prof. Sedgwick, and a Map granted by the Royal Geographical Society, &c.*, 1st ed. 1858, 2nd ed. 1860, Deighton, Bell, and Co. 6*s* 6*d*. Author, *The Advancement of the Church of Christ by the Monarchs of the Earth* (a Sermon in the presence of the Prince of Wales), Deighton, Bell, and Co. 1861, 6*d*; *Livingstone and Central Africa Mission Correspondence* (read at the Meeting of the British Association at Cambridge), 1862; *On the Importance of preserving Ecclesiastical Monuments, illustrated by some Remarks on the Parish Church of Wymington*, (a Paper read before the Bedfordshire Archæological and Architectural Soc. at Bedford), 1866; etc. [1]

MONKHOUSE, George, *Garrigill Parsonage, Alston, Penrith.*—St. Bees; Deac. 1849, Pr. 1850. C. in sole charge of Garrigill 1851. [2]

MONKHOUSE, Henry Clarke, *Fiskerton, Lincoln.*—Trin. Coll. Cam. B.A. 1853, M.A. 1859; Deac. 1856 by Bp of Lon. Pr. 1858 by Bp of Lin. C. of Fiskerton 1863. Formerly C. of St. Luke's, Berwick-street, Lond. 1856–57, Haydor, Linc. 1858–61, Horsington, Linc. 1861–63. [3]

MONKHOUSE, John, *Church Oakley, Basingstoke, Hants.*—Queen's Coll. Ox. B.A. 1856, M.A. 1859; Deac. 1858 and Pr. 1859 by Bp of Ox. R. of Church Oakley, Dio. Win. 1862. (Patron, Queen's Coll. Ox; Tithe, 380*l*; Glebe, 26 acres; R.'s Inc. 320*l* and Ho; Pop. 287.) [4]

MONKHOUSE, Philip Edmund, *Queen's School, Basingstoke.*—Mert. Coll. Ox. B.A. 1864, M.A. 1865; Deac. 1865 by Bp of Salis. 2nd Mast. of Queen's Sch. Basingstoke, 1867. Formerly C. of Compton Basset, Wilts, 1865; Mast. of the Tower Sch. Rossall, Fleetwood, 1866. [5]

MONNINGTON, George, *Bitteswell Vicarage, Lutterworth, Leicestershire.*—Wor. Coll. Ox. B.A. 1825; Deac. 1825, Pr. 1827. V. of Bitteswell, Dio. Pet. 1844. (Patrons, Haberdashers' Company and Christ's Hospital; Glebe, and Land in Lieu of Tithe, 327 acres; V.'s Inc. 437*l* and Ho; Pop. 438.) [6]

MONRO, Horace George, *Highmore, Henley-on-Thames.*—Trin. Coll. Cam. B.A. 1854, M.A. 1857; Deac. 1855 and Pr. 1856 by Bp of Win. P. C. of Highmore, Dio. Ox. 1860. (Patron, R. of Rotherfield-Greys; P. C.'s Inc. 94*l* 5*s* and Ho; Pop. 333.) Formerly C. of Trinity, Winchester. [7]

MONRO, Hugh, 11, *Chester-place, Regent's-park, London, W.*—Ex. Coll. Cam. B.A. 1851; Deac. 1852 and Pr. 1853 by Bp of Lon. Formerly C. of Ch. Ch. St. Pancras, and Abp Tenison's Chapel, St. James's, Lond. [8]

MONRO, Percy, *Colden Common Parsonage, near Winchester.*—Ex. Coll. Ox. B.A. 1849, M.A. 1859; Deac. 1849 by Bp of Lon. Pr. 1851 by Bp of Win. P. C. of Colden Common, Dio. Win. 1851. (Patrons, V. of Twyford, and P. C. of Owslebury, alt; Glebe, 4 acres; P. C.'s Inc. 148*l* and Ho; Pop. 652.) [9]

MONRO, Robert, *Canon Frome, Ledbury, Herefordshire.*—St. John's Coll. Cam. Scho. of, 2nd cl. Cl. Trip. and Jun. Opt. B.A. 1852; Deac. 1855 by Bp of Cashel, Pr. 1858 by Bp of Kilmore. C. of Canon Frome 1866. Formerly C. of Kilmeaden, Waterford, 1855, Hazelmere, Bucks, 1859, Cusop, Herf. 1861, Marwood, Devon, 1864. [10]

MONRO, Robert Douglas, 4, *Gloucester-terrace, Blackheath, S.E.*—Wad. Coll. Ox. B.A. 1862, M.A. 1866; Deac. 1863 and Pr. 1864 by Abp of Cant. C. of Greenwich 1866. Formerly C. of Bexley 1863. [11]

MONSARRAT, Henry, *St. Thomas's Parsonage, Kendal.*—Dub. A.B. 1855, A.M. 1860; Deac. 1856 by Abp of Dub. Pr. 1856 by Bp of Ches. P. C. of St. Thomas's, Kendal, Dio. Carl. 1865. (Patrons, Trustees; P. C.'s Inc. 210*l* and Ho; Pop. 2090.) Formerly Asst. Chap. to Dublin Female Penitentiary 1856; Asst. Chap. to Carysfort, Dio. Dub. 1857; Sen. C. of Cheltenham 1861. [12]

MONSELL, John Samuel Bewley, *Egham Vicarage, Surrey.*—Dub. Downes' Prizeman, Heb. Premiums, A.B. 1832, LL.D. 1856; Deac. 1834 by Bp of Limerick, Pr. 1835 by Bp of Ferns. V. of Egham, Dio. Win. 1853. (Patroness, Miss Gostling; Tithe—Imp. 1088*l*, V. 162*l*; Glebe, 50 acres; V.'s Inc. 350*l* and Ho; Pop. 3817.) Rural Dean of Stoke. Formerly Chan. of the Dio. of Connor; R. of Ramoan, Antrim, Ireland, and Exam. Chap. to the Bp of Down and Connor. Author, *Parish Musings*, 10th thousand, Rivingtons; *Spiritual Songs*, 6th thousand, Longmans; *His Presence, not His Memory*, 5th ed. ib; *Beatitudes*, 3rd ed. ib; *Hymns of Love and Praise*, Bell and Daldy; *The Passing Bell and other Poems*, ib; *Our New Vicar*, ib; *Prayers and Litanies*, Masters; *No Sect on Earth*, 8th thousand, Masters; etc. [13]

MONSON, The Hon. Evelyn John, *Croft Vicarage, Boston, Lincolnshire.*—Mert. Coll. Ox. B.A. 1863, M.A. 1865; Deac. 1864 and Pr. 1865 by Bp of Ex. V. of Croft, Dio. Lin. 1865. (Patron, Lord Monson; V.'s Inc. 480*l* and Ho; Pop. 784.) Chap. to Lord Monson. Formerly C. of St. Mary's Church, Devon, 1864–65. [14]

MONSON, Thomas John, *Kirby-underdale, Yorks.*—Univ. Coll. Dur. B.A. 1848, M.A. 1851; Deac. 1848, Pr. 1849. R. of Kirby-underdale, Dio. York, 1859. (Patron, Ld Chan; R.'s Inc. 900*l* and Ho; Pop. 333.) Formerly V. of Kirkby-Fleetham, Yorks, 1854–59. [15]

MONTAGU, Edgar, *Kettlestone Rectory, Fakenham, Norfolk.*—Caius Coll. Cam. 2nd cl. Cl. Trip. Sen. Opt. B.A. 1842, M.A. 1845; Deac. 1843 and Pr. 1845 by Bp of Nor. R. of Kettlestone, Dio. Nor. 1864. (Patron, the present R; Tithe, 300*l*; Glebe, 43 acres; aug. under Lord Westbury's Act, 175*l*; R.'s Inc. 540*l* and Ho; Pop. 200.) [16]

MONTAGU, George, *Epwell, Banbury.*—Wor. Coll. Ox. C. of Epwell 1857. [17]

MONTAGU, James, *Hawkwell, near Rochford, Essex.*—R. of Hawkwell, Dio. Roch. 1865. (Patron, R. Bristow, Esq; R.'s Inc. 460*l* and Ho; Pop. 334.) [18]

MONTAGUE, John, *King's School, Warwick.*—Sid. Coll. Cam. B.A. 1847, M.A. 1857; Deac. 1849 and Pr. 1853 by Bp of Wor. 2nd. and Math. Mast. of the King's Sch. Warwick, 1857. Formerly Head Mast. of the Vicar's Sch. Leamington-Priors, and C. of Leamington-Priors 1847-53. [19]

MONTEFIORE, Thomas Law, *Charmouth, Dorset.*—Trin. Coll. Cam. B.A. 1848, M.A. 1851; Deac. 1849 and Pr. 1850 by Bp of G. and B. R. of Catherston-Leweston, Dio. Salis. 1858. (Patroness, Mrs Hildyard; Tithe, 50*l*, Bounty, 17*l* 18*s* 8*d*; Glebe, 9 acres; R.'s Inc. 81*l*; Pop. 32.) Formerly C. of Westbury-on-Severn 1849–56, Wotton-Fitzpaine, Dorset, 1856-58. Author, *Cathechesis Evangelica, being Questions and Answers on the Textus Receptus, Part I. St. Matthew*, 1862, 6*s* 6*d*. [20]

MONTFORD, Edward Edwards, *Farnah Hall, near Derby.*—Corpus Coll. Cam. 5th Sen. Opt. and B.A. 1852, M.A. 1855; Deac. 1853 and Pr. 1854 by Bp of Pet. Formerly C. of Northborough, Northants, 1853–56, Deeping St. James, Linc. 1856–58. [1]

MONTGOMERY, James Francis, 7, *Walker-street, Edinburgh.*—Univ. Coll. Dur. Theol. Prizeman 1856, B.A. 1858, M.A. 1861; Deac. 1856 and Pr. 1857 by Bp of Salis. Incumb. of St. Paul's Episcopal Ch. Edinburgh, 1864. Formerly C. of Puddletown, Dorset, 1856, St. Paul's, Edinburgh, 1858. Author, *Words from the Cross* (Lent Lectures), Grant, Edinburgh, 1864, 2s. [2]

MONTGOMERY, Robert, *Holcott Rectory, near Northampton.*—St. Peter's Coll. Cam. B.A. 1823, M.A. 1826; Deac. 1824, Pr. 1825. R. of Holcott, Dio. Pet. 1825. (Patron, the present R; R.'s Inc. 350*l* and Ho; Pop. 517.) [3]

MONTRIOU, Edwin Carvick, *Parsonage, Over Darwen, Lancashire.*—Pemb. Coll. Cam. B.A. 1838, M.A. 1851; Deac. 1839, Pr. 1840. P. C. of Trinity, Over Darwen, Dio. Man. 1846. (Patron, V. of Blackburn; P. C.'s Inc. 300*l* and Ho; Pop. 14,000.) Surrogate. [4]

MONYPENNY, James Isaac, *Hadlow Vicarage, Tunbridge.*—Wad. Coll. Ox. B.A. 1820, M.A. 1825; Deac. 1822, Pr. 1823. V. of Hadlow, Dio. Cant. 1841. (Patron, the present V; Tithe—Imp. 1076*l* 4*s* 1*d*, V. 427*l*; Glebe, 4 acres; V.'s Inc. 1100*l* and Ho; Pop. 2568.) [5]

MONYPENNY, P. Howard, *The Priory, Pittenweem, Scotland.*—Dub. A.B.; Deac. 1861 and Pr. 1862 by Bp of Ches. Incumb. of St. John's Episcopal Ch. Pittenweem, Dio. St. Andrew's, 1866. (Patrons, Trustees; Incumbent's Inc. 150*l* and Ho.) Formerly C. of St. Thomas's, Wigan, 1860–62; Coleshill, Warwickshire, 1863–66. [6]

MOODY, Clement, *The Vicarage, Newcastle-upon-Tyne.*—Magd. Hall, Ox. B.A. 1844, M.A. 1845. V. of St. Nicholas', Newcastle-upon-Tyne, Dio. Dur. 1853. (Patron, Bp of Dur; Tithe—App. and Eccles. Commiss. 1268*l* 6*s* 8*d*, Imp. 238*l*, V. 241*l* 5*s* 1*d*; V.'s Inc. 490*l* and Ho; Pop. 7487.) Mast. of St. Mary Magdalen Hospital, Newcastle-upon-Tyne. Editor of *New Eton Latin* and *Greek Grammar.* Author, *The New Testament explained in Words of Holy Scripture*; *Cathedral Reform*; Sermons; etc. [7]

MOODY, George, *Gilston Rectory, Herts, near Harlow.*—St. John's Coll. Cam. B.A. 1830, M.A. 1833; Deac. 1832 and Pr. 1833 by Bp of Ches. R. of Gilston, Dio. Roch. 1841. (Patron, Bp of Roch; Tithe, 290*l* 6*s*; Glebe, 17 acres; R.'s Inc. 310*l* and Ho; Pop. 270.) [8]

MOODY, Henry Riddell, *Chartham Rectory, near Canterbury.*—Oriel Coll. Ox. Double 1st cl. B.A. 1815, M.A. 1817; Deac. and Pr. 1817 by Bp of Lon. R. of Chartham, Dio. Cant. 1822. (Patron, Abp of Cant; Tithe, 800*l*; Glebe, 32 acres; R.'s Inc. 825*l* and Ho; Pop. 1094.) Hon. Can. of Cant. 1866. Formerly C. of South Weald, Essex, 1817–22. Author, *Hints to Young Clergymen*, Rivingtons; *Occasional Sermons*; etc. [9]

MOODY, James Leith, *Walmer, Kent.*—St. Mary Hall, Ox. B.A. 1840, M.A. 1862; Deac. 1840 and Pr. 1841 by Bp of Lin. Chap. to the Forces. [10]

MOON, Charles, 36, *Canonbury-road, Islington, N.*—King's Coll. Lond. Theol. Assoc. 1866; Deac. 1866 by Bp Anderson for Bp of Lon. C. of St. Bartholomew's, Islington, 1866. [11]

MOON, Edward Graham, *Fetcham Rectory, Leatherhead, Surrey.*—Magd. Coll. Ox. B.A. 1847, M.A. 1850; Deac. 1849 and Pr. 1851 by Bp of Ox. R. of Fetcham, Dio. Win. 1859. (Patron, T. Sidney, Esq; Tithe, 298*l* 11*s*; Glebe, 90 acres; R.'s Inc. 363*l* and Ho; Pop. 399.) Formerly C. of St. John's, Worcester, 1849–51, Bredon, Worc. 1851–52, Fetcham 1853–59. [12]

MOON, George, 85, *Nicholas-street, Mile-end-road, London, N.E.*—Lond. B.A. 1857; Deac. 1858 and Pr. 1859 by Bp of Rip. C. and Lect. of St. Mary's, Whitechapel, Lond. 1864. Formerly C. of Woodside, near Leeds, 1856, Macclesfield, 1860, St. Matthew's, Bethnal Green, 1861. [13]

HH

MOONEY, T. Plunket, 1, *Dinton-villas, Tooting, S.*—Dub. A.B. 1859; Deac. 1859 and Pr. 1860 by Bp of Down and Connor. Min. of Singlegate District and Afternoon Lect. of Mitcham, Dio. Win. 1867; Deputation Sec. of the London Association in Aid of Moravian Missions, 32, Sackville-street, W. Formerly C. of Coleraine 1859, St. Peter's, Ipswich, 1861, St. Michael's, Stockwell, Surrey, 1864. [14]

MOONEY, W. J., *Rosedale, Pickering, Yorks.*—P.C. of Rosedale, Dio. York, 1864. (P. C.'s Inc. 100*l*; Pop. 446.) Formerly C. of St. Mary's, Widnes, Warrington. [15]

MOOR, Allen Page.—Trin. Coll. Cam. B.A. 1846, M.A. 1849; Deac. 1848 by Bp of Lon. Pr. 1849 by Abp of Cant. Fell. of St. Augustine's Missionary Coll. 1847; Sub-Warden of the same 1849. [16]

MOOR, C. T., *Shrewsbury.*—C. of St. Alkmond's, Shrewsbury. [17]

MOOR, D., *North Weald, Epping, Essex.*—C. of North Weald. [18]

MOOR, Edward James, *Great Bealings, Woodbridge, Suffolk.*—Trin. Coll. Cam. B.A. 1821; Deac. 1822, Pr. 1823. R. of Great Bealings, Dio. Nor. 1844. (Patron, Lord Henniker; Tithe—Imp. 8*l* 10*s*, R. 300*l*; Glebe, 20 acres; R.'s Inc. 347*l* and Ho; Pop. 338.) Hon. Can. of Nor; Rural Dean. Formerly C. of Bucklesham and Newbourn, and Wetheringsett and Brockford; P. C. of Brightwell with Kesgrave. Author, *Twelve Plain Sermons*, 3rd ed. 2*s*; *Eleven Village Sermons*, 2*s*; *Letters for the Poor*, 2nd ed. 1*s* 6*d*; *Cottage Letters*, 2nd ed. 1*s*. 6*d*; *The Wreck and the Rock*, 2*s*; *The Harvest*, 1*s* 6*d*; *David, his Character*, &c. 2*s*; *The Prodigal Son*, 1*s* 6*d*; *Tracts on Common Things*, all published by W. Hunt and Co. [19]

MOOR, John Frewen, *Sion-place, Bath.*—Brasen. Coll. Ox. B.A. 1821, M.A. 1824; Deac. 1822 and Pr. 1823 by Bp of Ely. Author, *Two Assize Sermons*, (preached at Lewes), 1839. [20]

MOOR, John Frewen, jun., *Ampfield Parsonage, Romsey, Hants.*—Oriel Coll. Ox. B.A. 1846, M.A. 1848; Deac. 1846 by Bp of Win. Pr. 1848 by Abp of York. P. C. of Ampfield, Dio. Win. 1853. (Patron, Sir William Heathcote, Bart. M.P; Tithe, 37*l* 15*s* 11*d*; Glebe, $2\frac{1}{4}$ acres; P. C.'s Inc. 109*l* and Ho; Pop. 464.) Formerly C. of Hawley, Hants, 1846–48, Barton Agnes, Yorks, 1848–53. Author, *Morning and Evening Devotions for the Aged, chiefly from the Devotions of Bishop Cousin and of Bishop Wilson*, Oxford, 1850; *A Warning to Young Men* (a Sermon), 1862. [21]

MOOR, Richard Watson, *Stoke St. Gregory, Taunton*—P. C. of Stoke St. Gregory, Dio. B. and W. 1830. (Patrons, D. and C. of Wells; P. C.'s Inc. 120*l*; Pop. 1139.) [22]

MOORE, Albert, *Westbury, Wilts.*—Magd. Coll. Cam. B.A. 1861, M.A. 1866; Deac. 1864 and Pr. 1865 by Bp of Salis. C. of Westbury 1864. [23]

MOORE, Alfred Edgar, *Horkstow Vicarage, Barton-on-Humber, Lincolnshire.*—Jesus Coll. Cam. Scho. and Prizeman of, 5th Sen. Opt. B.A. 1866; Deac. 1866 and Pr. 1867 by Bp of Lin. V. of Horkstow, Dio. Lin. 1867. (Patron, Earl of Yarborough; Tithe—Imp. 255*l* 0*s* 1*d*, V. 255*l* 0*s* 1*d*; Glebe, 1 rood 25 perches; V.'s Inc. 256*l* and Ho; Pop. 245.) Formerly C. of New Sleaford, Lincolnshire, 1866. [24]

MOORE, Augustus William George, *Burnsall Rectory, Skipton, Yorks.*—St. John's Coll. Cam. B.A. 1864, M.A. 1867; Deac. 1864 and Pr. 1866 by Bp of Ches. C. of Burnsall 1866. Formerly C. of Tarporley, Cheshire, 1864–66. [25]

MOORE, Bernard, *Bayfield, Holt, Norfolk.*—Jesus Coll. Cam. B.A. 1824; Deac. 1824 by Bp of G. and B. Pr. 1826 by Bp of Chich. R. of Bayfield, Dio. Nor. 1826. (Patron, Major E. Jodrell; R.'s Inc. 150*l*; no Church; Pop. 30.) Formerly C. of Buxton, Derbyshire, 1831–38; R. of Staveley 1838–47; R. of Sutton, Norfolk, 1847–62. [26]

MOORE, Calvert Fitzgerald, *Cloford, Frome, Somerset.*—St. John's Coll. Cam. B.A. 1811, M.A. 1816; Deac. 1812, and Pr. 1813. Chap. in Ordinary to the

Queen 1825. Formerly R. of Hinton Martell 1825; R. of Belleau, Lincolnshire, 1835. [1]

MOORE, Carter William Daking, *The Grove, Blackheath, Kent,* and *Easton, near Stamford.*—St John's Coll. Cam. B.A. 1841, M.A. 1847; Deac. 1842, Pr. 1843. Dom. Chap. to Viscount Valentia. [2]

MOORE, Cecil Gurden, *Lindsey Parsonage, near Ipswich.*—Jesus Coll. Cam. B.A. 1858, M.A. 1861; Deac. 1860 and Pr. 1861 by Bp of Chich. P. C. of Lindsey, Dio. Ely, 1865. (Patron, King's Coll. Cam; P. C.'s Inc. 110*l*; Pop. 316.) Formerly C. of Maresfield, Sussex, 1860–65. [3]

MOORE, Charles.—Chap. to the Forces, Newbridge. [4]

MOORE, Charles, *Wyberton Rectory, Boston.*—R. of Wyberton, Dio. Lin. 1859. (Patron, Rev. T. R. Mayhew; R.'s Inc. 600*l* and Ho; Pop. 608.) Dom. Chap. to the Earl of Northesk. [5]

MOORE, Charles Avery, *Sutterton Vicarage, near Spalding.*—Trin. Hall, Cam. B.C.L. 1840; Deac. 1840, Pr. 1841. V. of Sutterton, Dio. Lin. 1859. (Patron, the Crown; Glebe, 495 acres; V.'s Inc. 1032*l* and Ho; Pop. 898.) [6]

MOORE, Corbett Metcalfe, *Beechamwell, Swaffham, Norfolk.*—Trin. Coll. Cam. B.A. 1851, Deac. 1852 and Pr. 1853 by Bp of Herf. R. of Beechamwell St. Mary with Beechamwell St. John R. Dio. Nor. 1855. (Patron, John Fielden, Esq; Tithe, 176*l* 5*s*; Glebe, 91 acres; R.'s Inc. 284*l* and Ho; Pop. 356.) C. of Shingham, Norfolk. Formerly C. of St. Andrew's, Ancoats, Manchester. [7]

MOORE, C. M.—C. of St. John's, Westminster. [8]

MOORE, Daniel, *Trinity Parsonage, Paddington, London, W.*—St. Cath. Coll. Cam. Norrisian Prizeman 1837 and 1839, Hulsean Prizeman 1840, Select Preacher 1844, 1851, 1861, Hulsean Lect. 1864, B.A. 1840, M.A. 1844; Deac. 1840 and Pr. 1841 by Bp of Lon. P. C. of Trinity, Paddington, Dio. Lon. 1866. (Patron, Bp of Lon; P. C.'s Inc. 1000*l* and Ho; Pop 13,497.) Tuesday Morn. Lect. at St. Margaret's, Lothbury, 1856. (Value, 370*l*.) Hon. Chap. in Ordinary to the Queen. Formerly P. C. of Camden Ch. Camberwell, 1844–66. Author, *Daily Devotion, or Prayers framed on the successive Chapters of the New Testament,* 7*s* 6*d*; *Christian Consolation,* 5*s*; *Romanism as set forth in its own acknowledged Formularies,* 5*s*; *Sermons preached before the University of Cambridge,* 3*s*; *The Christian System vindicated against the more Popular Forms of Modern Infidelity* (three Hulsean and Norrisian Prize Essays), 4*s*; *Discourses on the Lord's Prayer,* 5*s*; *Family Duties,* 2*s* 6*d*; *Thoughts on Preaching,* 7*s* 6*d*; *The Spiritual Mind,* 6*d*; *The Divine Authority of the Pentateuch,* 7*s* 6*d*; *The Age and the Gospel* (Hulsean Lectures for 1864), 5*s*; also several Tracts published by the S.P.C.K. [9]

MOORE, Edward, *Whitchurch Rectory, near Reading.*—R. of Whitchurch, Dio. Ox. 1840. (Patron, Bp of Ox; Tithe, 100*l*; Glebe, 290 acres; R.'s Inc. 500*l* and Ho; Pop. 857.) Dom. Chap. to Lord Brougham. [10]

MOORE, Edward, *Boughton-Malherbe Rectory, Maidstone.*—Brasen. Coll. Ox. B.A. 1841, M.A. 1843; Deac. 1842, Pr. 1843. R. of Boughton-Malherbe, Dio. Cant. 1843. (Patrons, Heirs of Earl Cornwallis; Tithe, 306*l*; Glebe, 6 acres; R.'s Inc. 320*l* and Ho; Pop. 408.) [11]

MOORE, Edward, *Gatcombe Rectory, Newport, Isle of Wight.*—Pemb. Coll. Ox. 1st cl. Lit. Hum. and 1st cl. Math. B.A. 1857, M.A. 1860; Fell. and Tut. of Queen's Coll; Deac. 1859 and Pr. 1861 by Bp of Ox. R. of Gatcombe, Dio. Win. 1864. (Patron, Univ. of Ox; Tithe, 560*l*; Glebe, 38 acres; R.'s Inc. 624*l* and Ho; Pop. 280.) Prin. of St. Edmund Hall, and Lect. of Queen's Coll. Ox. [12]

MOORE, Edward, *Frittenden Rectory, Staplehurst, Kent.*—R. of Frittenden, Dio. Cant. 1848. (Patron, the present R; Tithe, 412*l*; Glebe, 13½ acres; R.'s Inc. 439*l* and Ho; Pop. 898.) [13]

MOORE, Edward, *Spalding, Lincolnshire.*—St John's Coll. Cam. B.A. 1835, M.A. 1838; Deac. and Pr. 1835 by Bp of Lin. P. C. of Spalding, Dio. Lin. 1866. (Patrons, Trustees; P. C.'s Inc. 1200*l* and Ho; Pop. 8723.) F.A.S; Chairman of the Quarter Sessions at Spalding. Formerly V. of Weston St. Mary, Lincolnshire, 1835–66. [14]

MOORE, The Hon. Edward George, *The Cloisters, Windsor Castle,* and *West Ilsley Rectory, East Ilsley, Berks.*—St. John's Coll. Cam. M.A. 1819. Can. Res. of St. George's Chapel, Windsor, 1834. (Value, 800*l* and Res.) R. of West Ilsley, Dio. Ox. 1840. (Patrons, D. and C. of Windsor; R.'s Inc. 550*l* and Ho; Pop. 432.) [15]

MOORE, Francis Joseph, *Ashby, Brigg, Lincolnshire.*—Trin. Coll. Cam. B.A. 1849; Deac. 1850, Pr. 1851. C. of Messingham with Bottesford, Lincolnshire, 1863. Formerly C. of St. John's, Fulham, 1855–60, Abp Tenison's Chapel, Lond. 1860–61. [16]

MOORE, Francis Wellington, *Duffield Vicarage, near Derby.*—St. Bees 1845; Deac. 1845 by Bp of Ches. Pr. 1846 by Bp of Wor. V. of Duffield, Dio. Lich. 1858. (Patron, Rowland Smith, Esq; Tithe—App. 5*l*, Imp. 1623*l* 16*s* 5*d* and 120 acres of Glebe, V. 66*l* 16*s* 3*d* and 12 acres of Glebe; V.'s Inc. 173*l* and Ho; Pop. 1642.) Surrogate 1859 Formerly C. of Weston-upon-Trent. Author, *A Sermon on the Death of Parkin Jeffcock, Esq. in the Oaks Colliery,* Bemrose, 1867. [17]

MOORE, Frederick James, *Foxdale, Isle of Man.*—Dub. A.B. 1861; Deac. 1863 and Pr. 1864 by Bp of Ches. P. C. of Foxdale, Dio. S. and M. 1865. (Patron, Bp of S. and M; P. C.'s Inc. 100*l*.) Formerly C. of St. Paul's, Chester, 1863–65. [18]

MOORE, George, *Southholme, Gainsborough.*—Ex. Coll. Ox. Exhib. of, B.A. 1865; Deac. 1866 and Pr. 1867 by Bp of Lin. C. of Trinity, Gainsborough, 1867. Formerly C. of Partney, Spilsby, 1866. [19]

MOORE, George Bridges, *Tunstall Rectory, Sittingbourne, Kent.*—Ch. Ch. Ox. B.A. 1831, M.A. 1836; Deac. 1833 and Pr. 1834 by Abp of Cant. R. of Tunstall, Dio. Cant. 1837. (Patron, Abp of Cant; Tithe, 510*l* 10*s*; Glebe, 9 acres; R.'s Inc. 530*l* and Ho; Pop. 207.) [20]

MOORE, George Henry, *Heyhouses Parsonage, near Whalley, Lancashire.*—St. Bees, and Queens' Coll. Cam; Deac. 1844 and Pr. 1845 by Bp of Ches. P. C. of Heyhouses, Dio. Man. 1846. (Patron, Le Gendre Starkie, Esq; Tithe—Imp. 4*l* 13*s* 9*d*; Glebe, ½ acre; P. C.'s Inc. 123*l* and Ho; Pop. 1616.) [21]

MOORE, Henry, 45, *Bridge-street, Derby.*—Dub. A.B. 1844; Deac. 1846 and Pr. 1847 by Bp of Lich. Chap. to the Derby Co. Gaol 1855. Author, *Private Prayers for Morning and Evening, with Prayers upon entering and leaving Church, and Graces before and after Meat, and numerous Mental Prayers,* 1*s*. [22]

MOORE, Henry, 3, *St. James's-place, Exeter.*—Wor. Coll. Ox. Fell. of, B.A. 1853, M.A. 1856; Deac. 1854 by Bp of Ox. Pr. 1856 by Bp of Nor. C. of St. James's, Exeter, 1863. Formerly C. of Walpole St. Peter, Norfolk, 1855, Louth, Linc. 1859. [23]

MOORE, The Ven. Henry, *Lichfield.*—Clare Coll. Cam. B.A. 1819, M.A. 1822; Deac. and Pr. 1819 by Bp of Lich. Can. and Precentor of Lich. 1865. (Value, 500*l*.) Archd. of Stafford 1855. (Value, 200*l*.) Formerly V. of Eccleshall, Staffs, 1822–56; V. of Penn St. Bartholomew, Staffs, 1836–56; V. of St. Mary's, Lichfield, 1856–65. [24]

MOORE, Henry Dawson, *Misterton Parsonage, Gainsborough.*—St. John's Coll. Cam. B.A. 1852; Deac. 1852 and Pr. 1853 by Abp of York. P. C. of Misterton, Notts, Dio. Lin. 1856. (Patrons, D. and C. of York; Tithe—App. 1260*l*; Glebe, 17 acres; P. C.'s Inc. 110*l*; Pop. 1089.) Formerly C. of Blaydon, near Newcastle-on-Tyne. [25]

MOORE, Henry Dodwell, 12, *Barking-road, Poplar, E.*—Pemb. Coll. Ox. 2nd cl. Math. B.A. 1862, M.A. 1865; Deac. 1863 and Pr. 1864 by Bp of Lon. C. of St. Michael's, Bromley, Middlesex, 1865. Formerly C. of Barkingside and Aldborough Hatch, Essex, 1863–65. [26]

MOORE, Henry Headley, *Over Darwen, Lancashire.*—Wor. Coll. Ox. 2nd cl. Law and Modern History,

B.A. 1864; Deac. 1864 and Pr. 1865 by Bp of Man. C. of St. John's, Over Darwen, 1864. [1]

MOORE, James, *Oldfield-road, Salford, Manchester.*—Magd. Coll. Cam. Sen. Opt. Coll. Prizeman, B.A. 1836; Deac. 1839 and Pr. 1840 by Abp of Cant. R. of St. Bartholomew's, Salford, Dio. Man. 1842. (Patrons, Trustees; R.'s Inc. 265*l* and Ho; Pop. 10,893.) Surrogate 1852. Author, *Teetotalism and the Bible* (a Sermon), 2*d*. [2]

MOORE, James, 47, *Princes-street, Rotherhithe, London, S.E.*—Wor. Coll. Ox. B.A. 1859, M.A. 1862; Deac. 1859 and Pr. 1860. C. of Rotherhithe 1862. Formerly C. of Hoby with Rotherby, near Leicester, 1859–62. [3]

MOORE, James Henry, *Cloford, Frome, Somerset.*—Univ. Coll. Dur. B.A. 1848, M.A. 1851; Deac. 1848 and Pr. 1850 by Bp of Rip. V. of Cloford, Dio. B. and W. 1865. (Patron, Rev. J. S. H. Horner; V.'s Inc. 74*l*; Pop. 218*l*.) Formerly P. C. of St. Edmund's, Mells, Somerset, 1857–63; P. C. of Eighton Banks, Durham, 1863–65. [4]

MOORE, John, *Thetford, Norfolk.*—St. John's Coll. Cam. Coll. Prizeman, B.A. 1834, M.A. 1837; Deac. 1835, Pr. 1836. R. of Kilverstone, Dio. Nor. 1853. (Patron, Ld Chan; Tithe—Imp. 20*l*, R. 140*l*; R.'s Inc. 150*l*; Pop. 39.) [5]

MOORE, John James Stevenson, *Swansea.*—Dub. A.B. 1855; Deac. 1855 and Pr. 1856 by Bp of Ches. Chap. of Missions to Seamen, Swansea. Formerly C. of Ch. Ch. Chester. [6]

MOORE, John Leach Mitchell, *Tamworth.*—Ch. Coll. Cam. B.A. 1865; Deac. 1866 and Pr. 1867 by Bp of Lich. C. of Hopwas 1866. [7]

MOORE, John Walter, *Hordley Rectory, Ellesmere, Salop.*—Ex. Coll. Ox. B.A. 1836, M.A. 1838; Deac. 1836 by Bp of Salis. Pr. 1838 by Bp of Ches. R. of Hordley, Dio. Lich. 1839. (Patron, J. R. Kenyon, Esq. Q.C; Tithe, App. 16*l*, Imp. 70*l*, R. 272*l*; Glebe, 52 acres; R.'s Inc. 400*l* and Ho; Pop. 291.) Formerly C. of Arborfield, Berks, 1836, Alderley, Cheshire, 1837, St. Mary's, Reading, 1839. Author, various Sermons and Pamphlets. [8]

MOORE, Joseph, *Buckland Vicarage, Farringdon, Berks.*—Lin. Coll. Ox. 2nd cl. Lit. Hum. and B.A. 1836, M.A. 1838; Deac. 1838 and Pr. 1839 by Bp of Ox. V. of Buckland, Dio. Ox. 1842. (Patron, Bp of Ox; Tithe, App. 873*l*, V. 270*l*; Glebe, 58 acres; V.'s Inc. 375*l* and Ho; Pop. 912.) P. C. of Littleworth, Faringdon, Berks, Dio. Ox. 1838. (Patron, Bp of Ox; P. C.'s Inc. 82*l*; Pop. 337.) Dom. Chap. to the Earl of Morley. [9]

MOORE, The Ven. Joseph Christian, *Kirk Andreas Rectory, Isle of Man.*—St. Edm. Hall, Ox. B.A. 1827, M.A. 1844; Deac. 1828 and Pr. 1829 by Bp of Lich. R. of Kirk Andreas, Dio. S. and M. 1844. (Patron, the Crown; R.'s Inc. 800*l* and Ho; Pop. 1955.) Archd. of the Isle of Man, 1844. (Value, 700*l*.) Formerly P. C. of Measham, Derbyshire. [10]

MOORE, Josiah Samuel, *Crofton Rectory, Wakefield.*—Trin. Coll. Cam. B.A. 1846; Deac. 1846, Pr. 1847. R. of Crofton, Dio. York, 1858. (Patron, Duchy of Lancaster; R.'s Inc. 350*l* and Ho; Pop. 402.) Formerly R. of Stoke-Edith, Herefordshire, 1850–58. [11]

MOORE, Lethbridge, C. E., *Sheringham, Cromer, Norfolk.*—Caius Coll. Cam. B.A. 1856, M.A. 1859; Deac. 1857 and Pr. 1858 by Bp of Lon. V. of Sheringham, Dio. Nor. 1862. (Patron, Bp of Nor; V.'s Inc. 90*l*; Pop. 1289.) Chap. of D. of Weyborn, included in parish of Sheringham. (Patron, Earl of Oxford; Value, 50*l*.) Formerly C. of Ch. Ch. Hampstead, Lond. 1857–60. [12]

MOORE, Peter Halhed, *Pill, Bristol.*—Brasen. Coll. Ox. B.A. 1852, M.A. 1855; Deac. 1854 and Pr. 1856 by Bp of Salis. P. C. of Ch. Ch. Pill, Dio. B. and W. 1863. (Patron, Rev. T. H. Mirehouse; P. C.'s Inc. 116*l* and Ho; Pop. 1800.) Formerly C. of South Broom, Devizes, 1854–56, St. George's, Somerset, 1857–58; P. C. of Lovington, Somerset, 1858–63. [13]

MOORE, Philip Hughes, 2, *Lower Trafalgar-terrace, Swansea.*—St. John's Coll. Cam. B.A. 1863; Deac. 1864. C. of Swansea 1864. [14]

MOORE, Richard, *Lund Vicarage, Preston.*—Brasen. Coll. Ox. B.A. 1814, M.A. 1817; Deac. 1815 and Pr. 1817 by Bp of Ches. V. of Lund, Dio. Man. 1820. (Patrons, D. and C. of Ch. Ch. Ox; Tithe—Imp. 690*l*, V. 165*l* 5*s* 8*d*; Glebe, 92 acres; V.'s Inc. 364*l* and Ho; Pop. 733.) Surrogate. Formerly C. of Kirkham 1815, Whittington 1817. [15]

MOORE, Richard Ravencroft, *Warrington.*—Dub. A.B. 1854; Deac. 1854. C. of St. Paul's, Warrington. Formerly C. of St. Chrysostom's, Everton, Liverpool. [16]

MOORE, Robert Stephen, *Albert-road, Tamworth.*—St. John's Coll. Cam. B.A. 1851, M.A. 1861; Deac. 1852 and Pr. 1853 by Bp of Dur. Sen. C. of Tamworth 1866. Formerly C. of Elsdon 1852, Godalming 1857, Wellington, Somerset, 1859; P. C. of Hulland, Derbyshire, 1861. [17]

MOORE, Thomas, *West Harptree Vicarage, near Bristol.*—V. of West Harptree, Dio. B. and W. 1842. (Patron, Prince of Wales; Tithe—Imp. 159*l* 17*s* 6*d*, V. 221*l* 12*s* 6*d*; Glebe, 51¼ acres; V.'s Inc. 302*l* and Ho; Pop. 539.) [18]

MOORE, Thomas Barrington Geary, *Broxbourne Vicarage, Hoddesdon, Herts.*—Pemb. Coll. Ox. B.A. 1826, M.A. 1832; Deac. 1827 and Pr. 1828 by Bp of Ox. V. of Broxbourne, Dio. Roch. 1853. (Patron, Bp of Roch; Tithe—App. 211*l* 18*s*, V. 147*l* 8*s*; V.'s Inc. 350*l* and Ho; Pop. 949.) [19]

MOORE, William, *Brimpsfield Rectory, Painswick, Glouc.*—Pemb. Coll. Ox. 2nd cl. Lit. Hum. and B.A. 1814, M.A. 1818; Deac. 1819, Pr. 1820. R. of Brimpsfield with Cranham, Dio. G. and B. 1829. (Patron, W. Goodrich, Esq; Brimpsfield, Tithe, 295*l*; Glebe, 32 acres; Cranham, Tithe, 162*l*; Glebe, ¼ acre; R.'s Inc. 506*l* and Ho; Pop. Brimpsfield 392, Cranham 424.) [20]

MOORE, William Burton, *Evington Vicarage, Leicester.*—St. Bees, Librarian 1845; Deac. 1845, Pr. 1846. V. of Evington, Dio. Pet. 1846. (Patron, Bp of Pet; Tithe—Imp. 63*l* 1*s* 2*d*, V. 15*l* 17*s*; V.'s Inc. 109*l* and Ho; Pop. 275.) Formerly C. of Longwood, Huddersfield, 1845. [21]

MOORE, William Clarke, *Ilfracombe, Devon.*—St. John's Coll. Ox. B.A. 1849, M.A. 1851; Deac. 1850 and Pr. 1851 by Bp of Lon. P. C. of SS. Philip and James's, Ilfracombe, Dio. Ex. 1857. (Patron, W. H. Stone, Esq; P. C.'s Inc. uncertain; Ho; Pop. 1291.) Formerly C. and Sunday Even. Lect. of St. Mary's, Newington, Lond. Author, *Words of Counsel and of Doctrine* (Sermons), Ilfracombe, 1858, 3*s*; Occasional Sermons. [22]

MOORE, William Thomas, 2, *Surrey terrace, Lakenham, Norwich.*—Emman. Coll. Cam. B.A. 1860, M.A. 1864; Deac. 1862 and Pr. 1864 by Bp of Nor. P. C. of St. John de Sepulchre, Norwich, Dio. Nor. 1865. (Patrons, D. and C. of Nor; P. C.'s Inc. 140*l*; Pop. 2219.) Formerly C. of Heigham, Norwich, 1862–65. [23]

MOORHOUSE, James, 8, *Southampton-street, Fitzroy-square, London, W.*—St. John's Coll. Cam. Sen. Opt. and B.A. 1853; Deac. 1853 and Pr. 1854. P. C. of Paddington, Lond. Dio. Lon. 1867. (Patron, Bp of Lon; P. C.'s Inc. 1200*l*; Pop. 5817.) Formerly C. of Sheffield 1855–61; P. C. of St. John's, Charlotte-street, Fitzroy-square, Lond. 1861–67. [24]

MOORHOUSE, Matthew B., *Tintwistle, near Manchester.*—Queen's Coll. Ox. B.A. 1862, M.A. 1864; Deac. 1863 and Pr. 1864 by Bp of Ches. C. of Tintwistle, Cheshire, 1863. [25]

MOORSOM, Joseph Robertson, *Southoe Rectory, Hunts.*—Univ. Coll. Ox. 2nd cl. Lit. Hum. and B.A. 1843, M.A. 1846; Deac. and Pr. 1845. R. of Southoe, with Hail Weston V. annexed, Dio. Ely, 1848. (Patron, Richard Moorsom, Esq; R.'s Inc. 300*l* and Ho; Pop. Southoe 281, Hail Weston 440.) [26]

MOORSOM, Robert Maude, *Sadberge, Darlington.*—Trin. Coll. Cam. B.A. 1854, M.A. 1858; Deac. 1857 and Pr. 1859 by Bp of Man. P. C. of Sadberge, Dio.

Dur. 1861. (Patron, Bp of Man; P. C.'s Inc. 325*l*; Pop. 414.) Formerly C. of Poulton-le-Fylde 1857–59, Barnham Broom 1861. [1]

MOOYAART, Richard James, *St. John's Parsonage, Ladywood, Birmingham.*—Trin. Coll. Cam. 3rd cl. Cl. Trip. B.A. 1855, M.A. 1858; Deac. 1856 and Pr. 1857 by Bp of Win. P. C. of St. John's, Ladywood, Dio. Wor. 1865. (Patron, R. of St. Martin's, Birmingham; P. C.'s Inc. 400*l* and Ho; Pop. 12,000.) Formerly C. of St. Matthew's, Brixton, 1856–58, St. Andrew's, Plymouth, 1859–61, Upper Chelsea, Lond. 1861–64. [2]

MORAN, Francis John Clay, 18, *Gloucester-place, Park-road, Peckham, S.E.*—King's Coll. Lond. Theol. Assoc. 1862; Deac. 1862 and Pr. 1863 by Bp of Win. P. C. of St. Philip's, Old Kent-road, Camberwell, Dio. Win. 1865. (Patron, Bp of Win; P. C.'s Inc. 200*l*; Pop 6000.) Formerly C. of St. Mary Magdalene's, Old Kent-road, Southwark. [3]

MORAN, John Fleming, *Slaithwaite, Huddersfield.*—Dub. A.B. 1865; Deac. 1866. C. of Slaithwaite 1866. [4]

MORAN, John Henry.—Magd. Hall, Ox. B.A. 1830; Deac. 1830 and Pr. 1831 by Bp of Ches. P. C. of St. Thomas's, Liberty of the Rolls, Chancery-lane, Lond. Dio. Lon. 1866. (Patrons, Hyndman's Trustees; P. C.'s Inc. 200*l*.) Formerly Chap. to H.M. Prison for Female Convicts, Brixton, 1853–66. Author, *The Doctrine and Order of the Church of England proved to be in Harmony with the Teaching of the Apostles*, 1st ed. 1844, 2nd ed. 1849, 6*d*; *Faith turned to Sight* (a Funeral Sermon), 1855, 2*d*. [5]

MORAN, Lawrence Fitzmaurice, *Macclesfield.*—Dub. A.B. 1848; Deac. 1849 and Pr. 1850 by Bp of Man. C. of Crompton-road District, Macclesfield. [6]

MORANT, Henry John, *Newnham Rectory, Winchfield, Hants.*—Trin. Coll. Cam. B.A. 1840, M.A. 1845; Deac. 1845 and Pr. 1846 by Bp of Llan. C. in sole charge of Newnham 1866. Formerly C. of Coltishall, Norfolk, 1850; P. C. of King's Walden, Herts, 1854–58; Plaitford, Hants, 1861. [7]

MORCOM, William Genn, *Louth, Lincolnshire.*—Ex. Coll. Ox. B.A. 1863, M.A. 1865; Deac. 1864 and Pr. 1865 by Bp of Lin. V. of Little Grimsby, near Louth, Dio. Lin. 1866. (Patrons, Reps. of late Lord Frederick Beauclerk; Glebe, 64 acres; V.'s Inc. 112*l*; Pop. 55.) C. of Louth 1864. [8]

MORDACQUE, Louis Henry, *Haslingden, Lancashire.*—Brasen. Coll. Ox. Scho. of, Hulme's Exhib. 3rd cl. Lit. Hum. B.A. 1846, M.A. 1847; Deac. 1848 and Pr. 1849 by Bp of Man. P. C. of Haslingden, Dio. Man. 1849. (Patrons, Hulme's Trustees; P. C.'s Inc. 300*l* and Ho; Pop. 9034.) [9]

MORE, Robert Henry Gayer, *Burton, Much-Wenlock, Salop.*—Ch. Coll. Cam. B.A. 1825, M.A. 1836; Deac. 1826 and Pr. 1829 by Bp of Herf. P. C. of Burton, Dio. Herf. 1833. (Patron, V. of Much-Wenlock; P. C.'s Inc. 56*l*.) Chap. of Don. of Shipton, Dio. Herf. (Patron, T. Mytton, Esq.) [10]

MORE, Thomas Frederick.—Pemb. Coll. Cam. B.A. 1815; Deac. 1816, Pr. 1817. R. of Shelve, near Shrewsbury, Dio. Herf. (Patron, R. B. More, Esq; Tithe, 43*l*; Glebe, 17¾ acres; R.'s Inc. 85*l*; Pop. 78.) Formerly R. of More, Salop, 1833–65. [11]

MOREHEAD, George Jeffrey, *Easington Rectory, Redcar, Yorks.*—Univ. Coll. Dur. Licen. Theol. 1837; Deac. 1837 and Pr. 1838 by Abp of York. R. of Easington with Liverton C. Dio. York, 1840. (Patron, Ld Chan; Tithe, 614*l*; Glebe, 111 acres; R.'s Inc. 714*l* and Ho; Pop. Easington 566, Liverton 186.) [12]

MORGAN, Aaron Augustus, *Bristol Lodge, Brighton.*—St. John's Coll. Cam. Sen. Opt. and B.A. 1844, Tyrwhitt's and Univ. Heb. Scho. 1847, M.A. 1847; Deac. 1845 and Pr. 1846 by Bp of Nor. P. C. of St. John's, Brighton, Dio. Chich. 1862. (Patron, V. of Brighton; P. C.'s Inc. 90*l*.) Formerly R. of Bradley, Linc. 1846–55; Chap. to the Army Work Corps in the Crimea. Author, *Ecclesiastes Metrically Paraphrased, being a Retranslation of the original Hebrew*, Bosworth, 1856, 4to, 21*s*; *The Mind of Shakspere, as exhibited in his Works*, Chapman and Hall, 1860, 6*s* 6*d*. [13]

MORGAN, Charles Augustus, *Machen Rectory, Newport, Monmouthshire.*—Ch. Ch. Ox. B.A. 1825, M.A. 1833; Deac. 1825 and Pr. 1826 by Bp of Llan. R. of Machen, Dio. Llan. 1831. (Patron, Lord Tredegar; Tithe—Imp. 14*l*, R. 469*l* 6*s* 9*d*; Glebe, 1½ acres; R.'s Inc. 471*l* and Ho; Pop. 2700.) Chan. of Llan. Cathl. 1851; Chap. in Ordinary to the Queen 1829; Rural Dean. Author, *An Assize Sermon*, Monmouth. [14]

MORGAN, Charles James, *Leamington.*—Lin. Coll. Ox. B.A. 1844, M.A. 1846; Deac. 1846 and Pr. 1847 by Bp of Llan. Formerly C. of Matherne, Monmouth, 1846–51. [15]

MORGAN, David, *Aberystruth Rectory, Blaina, near Tredegar, Monmouthshire.*—Lampeter, Heb. Scho. B.D. 1853; Deac. 1842 and Pr. 1843 by Bp of G. and B. R. of Aberystruth with Abertilery C. Monmouthshire, Dio. Llan. 1858. (Patron, Earl of Abergavenny; Tithe—Imp. 5*l* 10*s*; R.'s Inc. 315*l*; Pop. 10,000.) Surrogate. [16]

MORGAN, David, *Aberyskir, Brecknock.*—R. of Aberyskir, Dio. St. D. 1859. (Patron, Rev. W. L. Jones; R.'s Inc. 140*l*; Pop. 125.) [17]

MORGAN, David, *Cross-town, Cowbridge, Glamorganshire.*—Literate; Deac. 1828, Pr. 1829. V. of Llancarvon, near Cowbridge, Dio. Llan. 1837. (Patron, Ld Chan; Tithe—App. 325*l* 10*s* 2*d*, V. 245*l*; Glebe, 15 acres; V.'s Inc. 320*l*; Pop. 668.) Author, *The Difference between the Church of England and the Societies of Dissenters*, Cardiff, 1841, 1*s*. [18]

MORGAN, David, *Penarth, Cardiff.*—C. of Penarth; Min. Can. of Llan. (Value, 150*l*.) [19]

MORGAN, David, *St. Tyfaelog, Pontlottyn, near Rhymney, Glamorganshire.*—Magd. Hall, Ox. Lusby Scho. B.A. 1866; Deac. 1866 by Bp of Win. for Bp of Llan. C. of St. Tyfaelog, Gelligaer, 1866. [20]

MORGAN, David, *Festiniog, near Carnarvon.*—Dioc. Theol. Institute, Abergavenny; Deac. 1861 by Bp of Llan. C. of St. David's, Festiniog, 1866. Formerly C. of Pentrebach 1861–66. [21]

MORGAN, D., *Chorlton on-Medlock, Manchester.*—C. of St. Luke's, Chorlton-on-Medlock. [22]

MORGAN, David Evan, *Moylgrove (Pembrokeshire), near Cardigan.*—Literate; Deac. 1822 and Pr. 1823 by Bp of St. D. V. of Bayvil with Moylgrove P. C. Dio. St. D. 1846. (Patron, Ld Chan; Bayvil, Tithe—Imp. 111*l* and 12 acres of Glebe, V. 15*l*; Moylgrove, Tithe—Imp. 155*l*, V. 60*l* 3*s* 6*d*; Glebe, 2 acres; V.'s Inc. 260*l*; Pop. Bayvil 118, Moylgrove 429.) [23]

MORGAN, Edmond John, *Fakenham-Magna Rectory, Ixworth, Suffolk.*—Wad. Coll. Ox. B.A. 1842, M.A. 1846; Deac. 1844 and Pr. 1845 by Bp of Lon. R. of Fakenham-Magna, Dio. Ely, 1856. (Patron, Duke of Grafton; Tithe, 271*l* 15*s* 9*d*; Glebe, 32 acres; R.'s Inc. 283*l* and Ho; Pop. 196.) Formerly C. of Trinity, St. Giles'-in-Fields, Lond. 1844–49; P. C. of St. Matthias', Malvern Link, 1849–52. [24]

MORGAN, Edward, *Syston, near Leicester.*—V. of Syston, Dio. Pet. 1814. (Patron, Univ. of Ox; Tithe—Imp. 2*l* 5*s*; V.'s Inc. 125*l*; Pop. 1656.) V. of Ratcliffe-on-the-Wreak, Dio. Pet. 1818. (Patron, Ld Chan; V.'s Inc. 191*l* and Ho; Pop. 126.) [25]

MORGAN, Edward Olmius, *Middleton Parsonage, Chirbury, Salop.*—Trin. Coll. Cam. Sen. Opt. 3rd cl. Cl. Trip. B.A. 1840, M.A. 1845; Deac. 1840 and Pr. 1841 by Abp of York. P. C. of Scropton, Derbyshire, Dio. Lich. 1865. (Patron, John Broadhurst, Esq; Tithe, 12*l*; Glebe, 16 acres; P. C.'s Inc. 80*l*; Pop. 520.) C. of Middleton. Formerly 2nd Mast. of Stockwell Gr. Sch. 1844–50. [26]

MORGAN, Evan, *Llandyssil Vicarage, near Carmarthen.*—Deac. 1831 and Pr. 1832 by Bp of St. D. V. of Llandyssil with Capel Dewi C. Dio. St. D. 1849. (Patron, Bp of St. D; Llandyssil, Tithe—Sinecure R. 794*l*; V.'s Inc. 220*l* and Ho; Pop. 2788.) [27]

MORGAN, Evan, *Ystrad-ralsarn, Carmarthen.*—Lampeter; Deac. 1851 and Pr. 1852 by Bp of St. D. V. of Llanvihangel Ystrad, Dio. St. D. 1867. (Patron,

Bp of St. D; Tithe, 125*l*; Glebe, 25*l*; V.'s Inc. 180*l*; Pop. 1162.) Formerly C. of Borth and Rhydmeirionyd 1851; P. C. of Llanychaiarn 1854; R. of Ciliau Aeron 1862–67. [1]

MORGAN, Francis Henry, *Guisborough, Yorks.*—Wor. Coll. Ox. B.A. 1846; Deac. 1847, Pr. 1848. P. C. of Guisborough, Dio. York, 1862. (Patron, Abp of York; P. C.'s Inc. 176*l*; Pop. 4615.) Surrogate. Formerly C. of Windsor. [2]

MORGAN, Frederick Payler, *Willey Rectory, Lutterworth.*—St. John's Coll. Ox. 1827; Deac. 1827 by Bp of Lin. R. of Willey, Dio. Wor. 1843. (Patron, the present R; Glebe, 175 acres; R.'s Inc. 256*l* and Ho; Pop. 120.) [3]

MORGAN, George, *Poole, Dorset.*—Dub. A.B. 1840; Deac. 1841 and Pr. 1842 by Bp of Pet. P. C. of St. Paul's, Poole, Dio. Salis. 1854. (Patrons, Trustees; P. C.'s Inc. 200*l*.) Surrogate. [4]

MORGAN, George Frederic, *Teversall, Mansfield, Notts.*—Ch. Ch. Ox. B.A. 1841, M.A. 1844; Deac. 1844 and Pr. 1845 by Bp of Nor. C. of Teversall. [5]

MORGAN, Henry, *Nunhead-road, Peckham-rye, S.E.*—St. John's Coll. Cam LL.B. 1822. Chap. of Nunhead Cemetery. Formerly P. C. of Withington, Salop. [6]

MORGAN, Henry, *Street Aston, Lutterworth.*—St. Aidan's; St. John's Coll. Cam. B.D. 1866; Deac. 1855 and Pr. 1856 by Bp of Herf. C. of Monk's Kirby 1865. Formerly C. of Upton Bishop 1855–58, Weston Begard 1863. [7]

MORGAN, Henry, *Henvenw, Lampeter, Cardiganshire.*—P. C. of Henvenw, Dio. St. D. 1854. (Patron, Bp of St. D; Tithe, App. 190*l* 10*s*; P. C.'s Inc. 129*l*; Pop. 1067.) P. C. of Aberayon, Dio. St. D. 1854. (Patrons, the Inhabitants; P. C.'s Inc. 65*l*.) [8]

MORGAN, H., *St. Athan Rectory, Cowbridge, Glamorganshire.*—R. of St. Athan, Dio. Llan. 1854. (Patron, Rev. W. Rayer; R.'s Inc. 370*l* and Ho; Pop. 357.) [9]

MORGAN, Henry Arthur, *Jesus College, Cambridge.*—Jesus Coll. Cam. 26th Wrang. B.A. 1853, M.A. 1856; Deac. 1859 by Bp of Wor. Pr. 1860 by Bp of Ely. Sadlerian Lect. of Jesus Coll. 1853; Ley Fell. 1858; Math. Lect. 1858; Foundation Fell. 1860; Tut. 1863. Formerly Dean of Jesus Coll. Author, *A Collection of Problems and Examples in Mathematics, selected from the Jesus College Examination Papers, with Answers*, Macmillans, 1858; *The Northern Circuit, or Brief Notes of Sweden, Finland, and Russia*, ib. 1862. [10]

MORGAN, Henry Charles, *Goodrich Vicarage, Ross, Herefordshire.*—Brasen. Coll. Ox. B.A. 1813, M.A 1816; Deac. 1815, Pr. 1816. V. of Goodrich, Dio. Herf. 1830. (Patron, Bp of Herf; Tithe—App. 155*l*, V. 370*l*; Glebe, 33 acres; V.'s Inc. 436*l* and Ho; Pop. 796.) [11]

MORGAN, Hugh, *Rhyl, Flints.*—Jesus Coll. Ox. B.A. 1847, M.A. 1849; Deac. 1849, Pr. 1850. P. C. of Rhyl, Dio. St. A. 1855. (Patron, V. of Rhuddlan; Glebe, 4 acres; P. C.'s Inc. 155*l* and Ho; Pop. 2965.) Surrogate. [12]

MORGAN, H. T., *Newbury, Berks.*—C. of St. John's, Newbury. [13]

MORGAN, James, *Bronllys Castle, Hay, Brecknockshire.*—Trin. Coll. Ox. B.A. 1823, M.A. 1824; Deac. 1826, Pr. 1827. V. of Talgarth, Brecknock, Dio. St. D. 1832. (Patrons, D. and C. of Windsor; Tithe—App. 540*l* and 22 acres of Glebe, V. 225*l*; Glebe, 22 acres; V.'s Inc. 310*l*; Pop. 1330.) V. of Llangorse, Brecknockshire, Dio. St. D. 1836. (Patrons, D. and C. of Windsor; Tithe—App. 168*l* 15*s* 6*d*, V. 131*l* 4*s* 6*d*; Glebe, 14 acres; V.'s Inc. 160*l* and Ho; Pop. 414.) [14]

MORGAN, James, *Sutton Valence, Staplehurst, Kent.*—St. Peter's Coll. Cam. Scho. of, Sen. Opt. B.A. 1867; Deac. 1867 by Abp of Cant. C. of Sutton Valence with East Sutton, and 2nd Mast. in Sutton Valence Gr. Sch. 1867. [15]

MORGAN, James Blacker, *Hamilton-terrace, Milford, Pembrokeshire.*—Dub. Vice-Chan.'s Prize 1846, B.A. 1846; Deac. 1853 by Abp of Dub. Pr. 1854 by Bp of Meath. Assoc. Chap. of Missions to Seamen, Milford Haven. Formerly C. of St. Peter's, Walsall. [16]

MORGAN, James Morrison, *Dalton-in-Furness Vicarage, Ulverston.*—V. of Dalton-in-Furness, Dio. Ches. 1849. (Patron, Duchy of Lancaster; Tithe—Imp. 405*l*; V.'s Inc. 155*l* and Ho; Pop. 6456.) Dom. Chap. to the Earl of Cork and Orrery. Surrogate. [17]

MORGAN, John, *Llandudno Rectory, near Conway.*—Jesus Coll. Ox. B.A. 1843; Deac. 1843 and Pr. 1844 by Bp of St. A. R. of Llandudno, Dio. Ban. 1857. (Patron, Archd. of Merioneth; Tithe, 227*l* 14*s*; Glebe, 32*l*; R.'s Inc. 324*l* and Ho; Pop. 2316.) Surrogate. Formerly C. of Pentrevoelas, Clocaenog, and Llanrhaiadr. [18]

MORGAN, John, *Kiffig Parsonage, Narberth, Carmarthenshire.*—Lampeter; Deac. and Pr. 1844 by Bp of St. D. P. C. of Kiffig, Dio. St. D. 1845. (Patron, V. of Langharne; Tithe—Imp. 185*l*, P. C. 40*l*; Glebe, 20 acres; P. C.'s Inc. 91*l* and Ho; Pop. 468.) P. C. of Marros, Carmarthenshire, Dio. St. D. 1845. (Patron, V. of Langharne; Tithe—Imp. 72*l* 10*s*, P. C. 16*l*; Glebe, 104 acres; P. C.'s Inc. 75*l*; Pop. 130.) [19]

MORGAN, John, *Glanogwen, Bangor.*—Univ. Coll. Dur. Exhib. Licen. Theol. 1850; Deac. 1850 and Pr. 1851 by Bp of St. A. P. C. of Glanogwen, Dio. Ban. 1864. (Patron, Lord Penrhyn; P. C.'s Inc. 250*l* and Ho; Pop. 5264.) Formerly R. of Yspytty Ifan, Denbighshire, 1854-64. [20]

MORGAN, John, *Abernant Vicarage, near Carmarthen.*—V. of Abernant with Convil V. Dio. St. D. 1856. (Patron, Duke of Leeds; Abernant, Tithe—Imp. 270*l*, V. 73*l* 10*s*; Glebe, 100 acres; Convil, Tithe—Imp. 400*l*, V. 142*l* 10*s*; Glebe, 50 acres; V.'s Inc. 345*l* and Ho; Pop. Abernant 793, Convil 1703.) [21]

MORGAN, John, *Nantyglo, Tredegar, Monmouthshire.*—Jesus Coll. Ox. Hon. 4th cl. Lit. Hum. and B A. 1845, M.A. 1847; Deac. 1847 by Bp of Ox. Pr. 1847 by Bp of St. D. P. C. of Nantyglo, Dio. Llan. 1857. (Patrons, Crown and Bp of Llan. alt; P. C.'s Inc. 180*l* and Ho; Pop. 4450.) [22]

MORGAN, John, *Pontnewynydd, Pontypool, Monmouthshire.*—Literate; Deac. 1850 and Pr. 1851 by Bp of Llan. P. C. of Pontnewynydd, Dio. Llan. 1852. (Patron, P. C. of Trevethin; P. C.'s Inc. 146*l* and Ho; Pop. 2753.) [23]

MORGAN, John David, *Llanspythid, Brecon.*—Lampeter; Deac. 1839, Pr. 1840. P. C. of Llaniltid or St. Illtyd, Brecon, Dio. St. D. 1841. (Patron, V. of Devynock; P. C.'s Inc. 94*l*; Pop. 273.) V. of Llanspythid, Dio. St. D. 1853. (Patron, Marquis Camden; Tithe—Imp. 240*l*, V. 120*l*; Glebe, 7 acres; V.'s Inc. 120*l* and Ho; Pop. 289.) [24]

MORGAN, John Parry, *Llanidloes Vicarage, Montgomeryshire.*—Lampeter; Deac. 1832, Pr. 1833 V. of Llanidloes, Dio. Ban. 1851. (Patron, Bp of Ban; Tithe—App. 396*l*, Imp. 318*l*, V. 130*l*; V.'s Inc. 180*l* and Ho; Pop. 3987.) Surrogate. [25]

MORGAN, John Parry, *Mold, Flintshire.*—Lampeter, Scho. Prizeman and Sub.-Librarian of, B.A. 1865; Deac. 1865 and Pr. 1866 by Bp of St. A. C. of Mold 1867. Formerly C. of Holywell 1865. [26]

MORGAN, John Williams, *Beaufort, Newport, Monmouthshire.*—Cowbridge Gr. Sch; Deac. 1838 and Pr. 1839 by Bp of Llan. P. C. of Beaufort, Dio. Llan. 1851 (Patrons, the Crown and Bp of Llan. alt; P. C.'s Inc. 130*l* and Ho; Pop. 5880.) [27]

MORGAN, Joseph, *Pyecombe Rectory, Brighton.*—R. of Pyecombe, Dio. Chich. 1843. (Patron, Ld Chan; Tithe—App. 7*l* 10*s*, Imp. 6*s*, R. 313*l* 13*s*; Glebe, 29 acres; R.'s Inc. 333*l* and Ho; Pop. 283.) [28]

MORGAN, Joseph, *St. Andrew Rectory, near Cardiff.*—R. of St. Andrew, Dio. Llan. 1849. (Patron, Ld Chan; Tithe, 367*l*; R.'s Inc. 375*l* and Ho; Pop. 570.) [29]

MORGAN, Lewis, *Llangadock-Vawr, Carmarthenshire.*—Lampeter 1845, B.D. 1855; Deac. 1845 by Bp of Nor. Pr. 1846 by Bp of St. D. V. of Llangadock-Vawr with Llanthoysaint V. Dio. St. D. 1861. (Patron, Bp of St. D; V.'s Inc. 270*l* and Ho; Pop. 1650.) Formerly V. of Llandebie, Carmarthenshire. [30]

MORGAN, Lewis, *West Bradenham Vicarage, Thetford, Norfolk.*—Dub. A.B. 1842, A.M. 1846; Deac. 1846 and Pr. 1847 by Bp of Dur. V. of West Bradenham, Dio. Nor. 1860. (Patron, Bp of Nor; Tithe, 169*l* 9*s*; Glebe, 60 acres; V.'s Inc. 325*l* and Ho; Pop. 381.) Formerly Chap. to the Univ. of Dur. Author, *Athens and Modern Greece*; *Glimpses of the Middle Ages*; *History of the Catacombs at Rome.* [1]

MORGAN, Llewellyn, *Pentyrch, Cardiff.*—C. of Pentyrch. [2]

MORGAN, Morgan, *Roath, near Cardiff.*—Deac. 1851 and Pr. 1852 by Bp of Llan. V. of Rumney, Dio. Llan. 1862. (Patrons, D. and C. of Bristol; Tithe, 45*l*; Glebe, 40 acres; V.'s Inc. 122*l*; Pop. 356.) Formerly C. of Melincryddan, Neath, 1851; P. C. of Pentyrhun 1852, Bonvilstone 1853. [3]

MORGAN, Morgan, *Conway, Carnarvonshire.*—Trin. Coll. Ox. B.A. 1837, M.A. 1845. V. of Conway, Dio. Ban. 1838. (Patron, Sir David Erskine, Bart; Tithe—Imp. 68*l*, V. 68*l*; V.'s Inc. 125*l*; Pop. 1855.) [4]

MORGAN, Morgan Rice, *Llansamlet Vicarage, Swansea.*—Lampeter, Welsh and Heb. Scho; Deac. 1837 and Pr. 1838 by Bp of St. D. V. of Llansamlet with Kilvey C. Dio. St. D. 1842. (Patron, Bp of St. D; Tithe—Imp. 200*l*, P. C. 46*l* 13*s* 6*d*; Glebe, 2 acres; V.'s Inc. 310*l* and Ho; Pop. 5103.) P. C. of St. John's-juxta-Swansea, Dio. St. D. 1842. (Patrons, Messrs Vivian and Sons; Tithe, Imp. 36*l*; P. C.'s Inc. 98*l*; Pop. 2738.) Chap. to the Union, Swansea; Surrogate. Author, many articles in the Welsh periodicals. [5]

MORGAN, M., *Bognor, Sussex.*—Chap. of St. Michael's Sch. Bognor. [6]

MORGAN, Philip Howel, *Llanhamllêch Rectory, near Brecon.*—Jesus Coll. Ox. B.A. 1839, M.A. 1841; Deac. 1840 and Pr. 1841 by Bp of Ox. R. of Llanhamllêch, Dio. St. D. 1864. (Patron, Sir Joseph Russell Bailey, Bart., M.P; Tithe, 255*l*; Glebe, 45*l*; R.'s Inc. 300*l* and Ho; Pop. 314.) P. C. of Bettws-Penpont, near Brecon, Dio. St. D. 1842. (Patrons, the Landholders; P. C.'s Inc. 125*l*; Pop. 119.) P. C. of Battle, Brecon, Dio. St. D. 1859. (Patron, Col. Ll. V. Watkins; P. C.'s Inc. 73*l*; Pop. 118.) [7]

MORGAN, Rees Herbert, *Bedwellty, Newport, Monmouthshire.*—Literate; Deac. 1847 and Pr. 1848 by Bp of Llan. P. C. of Bedwellty, Dio. Llan. 1860. (Patron, Bp of Llan; P. C.'s Inc. 180*l* and Ho; Pop. 3127.) Formerly P. C. of Llanguick, Glamorganshire, 1853–60. [8]

MORGAN, Richard Turnill, 35, *Crimbles-street, Leeds.*—Brasen. Coll. Ox. B.A. 1865; Deac. 1865 and Pr. 1866 by Bp of Rip. C. of St. Thomas's, Leeds, 1865. [9]

MORGAN, Samuel Christopher, *The Parsonage, Aldershot.*—Wad. Coll. Ox. B.A. 1859, M.A. 1862; Deac. 1860 and Pr. 1861 by Bp of Llan. P. C. of Aldershot, Dio. Win. 1863. (Patrons, Lay Impropriators; Tithe, Imp. 365*l*; P. C.'s Inc. 180*l* and Ho; Pop. 7700.) Formerly C. of Chepstow 1860, Newland, Glouc. 1862. [10]

MORGAN, Samuel Francis, *Chepstow.*—Jesus Coll. Ox. B.A. 1813, M.A. 1816; Deac. 1815 and Pr. 1816 by Bp of Ox. V. of Chepstow, Dio. Llan. 1856. (Patron, D. H. D. Burr, Esq; Tithe, Imp. 138*l* 14*s* 8*d*, V. 124*l* 2*s*; Glebe, 66 acres; V.'s Inc. 250*l* and Ho; Pop. 3455.) Formerly R. of All Saints', Birmingham, 1835–56. [11]

MORGAN, Theophilus, *Glanhonddu House, Llanfihangel-Crucorney, near Abergavenny.*—V. of Walterstone, Herfs, near Abergavenny, Dio. Herf. 1830. (Patron, E. Higginson, Esq; Tithe, App. 65*l* 15*s* 6*d*, V. 80*l* 12*s* 6*d*; V.'s Inc. 150*l*; Pop. 173.) R. of Oldcastle, near Abergavenny, Dio. Llan. 1830. (Patron, E. Higginson, Esq; Tithe—Imp. 5*l*, R. 48*l*; R.'s Inc. 75*l*; Pop. 60.) [12]

MORGAN, Thomas, *Llangennech, Llanelly, Carmarthenshire.*—P. C. of Llangennech, Dio. St. D. 1839. (Patron, E. Rose Tunno, Esq; Tithe, Imp. 93*l* 16*s*; P. C.'s Inc. 90*l*; Pop. 923.) [13]

MORGAN, Thomas, *Brilley Vicarage, near Hereford.*—Jesus Coll. Cam. Scho. of, B.A. 1849, M.A. 1852; Deac. 1852 and Pr. 1853 by Bp of Wor. V. of Brilley with Michaelchurch R. Dio. Herf. 1860. (Patron, Bp of Wor; Tithe, Brilley 165*l*, Michaelchurch 165*l* 11*s*; Glebe, 4 acres; V.'s Inc. 350*l* and Ho; Pop. Brilley 517, Michaelchurch 138.) Formerly C. of Great Witley, Worc. 1852–57, Hampton, Evesham, 1857–60. [14]

MORGAN, Thomas, *Llantillio-Pertholey Vicarage, near Abergavenny.*—Jesus Coll. Ox. B.A. 1824, M.A. 1827; Deac. 1825 by Bp of G. and B. Pr. 1826 by Bp of Llan. V. of Llantillio-Pertholey, Dio. Llan. 1858. (Patrons, D. and C. of Llan; Tithe, 264*l*; Glebe, 60 acres; V.'s Inc. 300*l* and Ho; Pop. 984.) Formerly C. of Llantillio-Pertholey 1831–58. [15]

MORGAN, Thomas, *Llanfor Rectory, near Bala, Merionethshire.*—Lampeter, Greek Prizeman and Hebrew Prizeman; Deac. 1851 and Pr. 1852 by Bp of Ban. R. of Llanfor, Dio. St. A. 1858. (Patron, Bp of St. A; Tithe, 298*l*; Glebe, 3½ acres; R.'s Inc. 310*l* and Ho; Pop. 762.) Surrogate; Rural Dean. Formerly C. of Llanycil, Merionethshire. [16]

MORGAN, Thomas George, *Wheelock Parsonage, Sandbach, Cheshire.*—P. C. of Wheelock, Dio. Ches. 1843. (Patron, V. of Sandbach; Tithe, App. 49*l* 14*s* 3*d*, Imp. 75*l*; P. C.'s Inc. 155*l* and Ho; Pop. 1869.) [17]

MORGAN, William, *Llandegai, Bangor, Carnarvonshire.*—Queens' Coll. Cam. B.A. 1842, M.A. 1846; Deac. 1842 and Pr. 1843 by Bp of Ban. P. C. of Llandegai, Dio. Ban. 1845. (Patron, Bp of Ban; Tithe, App. 340*l*; P. C.'s Inc. 300*l*; Pop. 3050.) Author, Sermons in the *Haul.* [18]

MORGAN, William, *Cadoxton-juxta-Barry, Cardiff.*—R. of Cadoxton, Dio. Llan. 1859. (Patrons, R. F. Jenner, Esq. and others; R.'s Inc. 100*l*; Pop. 279.) [19]

MORGAN, William, *The Moat, Kerry, Montgomeryshire.*—Emman. Coll. Cam. B.D. 1825; Deac. 1812 and Pr. 1818 by Bp of Llan. V. of Kerry with Dolfor C. Dio. St. A. 1846. (Patron, Bp of St. D; Kerry, Tithe—App. 810*l*, V. 550*l*; Glebe, 99 acres; V.'s Inc. 600*l* and Ho; Pop. 1520.) [20]

MORGAN, William, *Ystradyfodwg, Pontypridd, Glamorganshire.*—P. C. of Ystradyfodwg, Dio. Llan. 1858. (Patron, V. of Llantrisant; P. C.'s Inc. 120*l*; Pop. 3857.) [21]

MORGAN, William Augustus, *Egloskerry, Launceston.*—Wad. Coll. Ox. S.C.L; Deac. 1801, Pr. 1802. P. C. of Tresmere, near Launceston, Dio. Ex. 1821. (Patron, Ld Chan; Tithe—Imp. 130*l*; P. C.'s Inc. 110*l*; Pop. 148.) [22]

MORGAN, William Leigh, *Cardiff.*—Deac. 1832, Pr. 1833. V. of St. Mary's, Cardiff, Dio. Llan. 1844. (Patron, Marquis of Bute; Tithe—App. 26*l*, V. 61*l* 12*s*; V.'s Inc. 350*l*; Pop. 24,288.) V. of Roath, Glamorganshire, Dio. Llan. 1844. (Patron, Marquis of Bute; Tithe—App. 160*l*, Imp. 72*l* 10*s*, V. 75*l*; V.'s Inc. 120*l*; Pop. 3044.) Preb. of Llan. 1855; Rural Dean; Dom. Chap. to the Marchioness of Bute. [23]

MORGAN, William Lewis, *St. John's, Ovenden, Halifax.*—Dub. A.B. 1848, A.M. 1852; Deac. 1848 by Bp of Ely, Pr. 1849 by Bp of Rip. P. C. of Bradshaw, Dio. Rip. 1853. (Patron, V. of Halifax; P. C.'s Inc. 150*l*; Pop. 2171.) [24]

MORGAN, William Richard, *Tunbridge, Kent.*—C. of Tunbridge 1864. [25]

MORICE, Charles, *River Vicarage, Dover.*—St. John's Coll. Cam. B.D. V. of River with Guston P. C. Dio. Cant. 1867. (Patron, Abp of Cant; Tithe, 168*l*; Glebe, 3 acres; V.'s Inc. 170*l* and Ho; Pop. River 445, Guston 436.) Formerly Chap. to the Forces; C. of Charing, Kent, 1858. [26]

MORICE, Richard William, *Hoddesdon Parsonage, Herts.*—Trin. Coll. Cam. B.A. 1831, M.A. 1836; Deac. 1831, Pr. 1832. P. C. of Hoddesdon, Dio. Roch. 1843. (Patron, Bp of Lon; Glebe, 2 acres; P. C.'s Inc. 220*l* and Ho; Pop. 2203.) Dioc. Inspector of Schs. 1852. Author, *Sermons*, 1838. [27]

MORICE, Thomas Richards, *Jesus College, Oxford.*—Jesus Coll. Ox. 3rd cl. Lit. Hum. and B.A. 1851,

M.A. 1853; Deac. 1852 and Pr. 1854 by Bp of Ox. Fell. of Jesus Coll. Ox. 1852. Formerly Asst. C. of St. Paul's, Oxford, 1853–54. [1]

MORISON, George, 3, *Salutary Mount, Heavitree, Exeter.*—Trin. Coll. Cam. B.A. 1834, M.A. 1840; Deac. and Pr. 1836 by Bp of Barbados. Formerly Chap. to the Hon. East India Company on the Bombay Establishment 1840–57. [2]

MORLAND, Benjamin, *Shabbington Vicarage, (Bucks), near Thame, Oxon.*—V. of Shabbington, Dio. Ox. (Patroness, Mrs. M. Wroughton; Tithe, 395*l*; Glebe, 97 acres; V.'s Inc. 565*l* and Ho; Pop. 371.) [3]

MORLEY, David Benjamin, *Walpole St. Peter, Highway, Wisbech.*—King's Coll. Lond. Theol. Assoc; Deac. 1860 and Pr. 1862 by Bp of Nor. C. of Walpole St. Peter 1863. Formerly C. of Marham, Norfolk, 1860–63. [4]

MORLEY, George Bentley, *St. Catherine's College, Cambridge.*—St. John's Coll. Cam. Porson Prizeman 1851, Sen. Opt. 1st in 2nd cl. Cl. Trip. and B.A. 1852, M.A. 1855; Deac. 1854 and Pr. 1855 by Bp of Ely. Fell. of St. Cath. Coll. Cam. 1854; 2nd Mast. in St. Andrew's Coll. Bradfield, Berks. [5]

MORLEY, Thomas Aldersey, *St. George's, Pendleton, Manchester.*—Dub. A.B. 1851, A.M. 1860; Deac. 1851 and Pr. 1852 by Bp of Man. P. C. of Charlestown-in-Pendleton, Dio. Man. 1863. (Patron, Bp of Man; P. C.'s Inc. 300*l*; Pop. 6900.) Formerly C. of St. Paul's, Bury, 1851–54, Ellenbrook, Worsley, 1854–63. [6]

MORLEY, William, *Mavis Enderby, Spilsby, Lincolnshire.*—R. of Mavis Enderby, Dio. Lin. 1834. (Patron, the present R; R.'s Inc. 370*l*; Pop. 169.) C. of Raithby. [7]

MORPHEW, John Cross, *Crimplesham, Stoke Ferry, Norfolk.*—St. Peter's Coll. Cam. B.A. 1833. P. C. of Crimplesham, Dio. Nor. 1850. (Patron, Bp of Nor; Tithe—App. 503*l* 15*s* 8*d* and 58½ acres of Glebe, P. C.'s Inc. 70*l*; Pop. 328.) P. C. of Ryston with Roxham P. C. Downham Market, Dio. Nor. 1859. (Patrons, D. and C. of Nor; P. C.'s Inc. 61*l*; Pop. 87.) [8]

MORPHY, Richard, *Norton, near Stockton-on-Tees.*—C. of Norton. [9]

MORRALL, Cyrus, *Plâs-Yolyn, Ruabon.*—Brasen. Coll. Ox. B.A. 1825, M.A. 1828; Deac. 1828 and Pr. 1829 by Bp of St. A. Formerly P. C. of St. Michael's, Liverpool, 1835–56; V. of North Leigh, Oxon. 1856–61. [10]

MORRALL, John, *Whitchurch, Salop.*—Brasen. Coll. Ox. 2nd cl. Lit. Hum. and B.A. 1817, M.A. 1820; Deac. 1819 and Pr. 1820 by Bp of Ox. Fell. of Brasen. Coll. Ox. 1819. [11]

MORRELL, George Kidd, *Moulsford, Wallingford, Berks.*—St. John's Coll. Ox. 3rd cl, Lit. Hum. and B.C.L. 1838, D.C.L. 1842; Deac. 1836 and Pr. 1837 by Bp of Ox. P. C. of Moulsford, Dio. Ox. 1846. (Patron, H. B. Morrell, Esq; Tithe, 23*l* 13*s*; Glebe, 3 acres; P.C.'s Inc. 60*l*; Pop. 180.) Surrogate. Formerly Fell. of St. John's Coll. Ox. [12]

MORRELL, Robert Price, *Woodham-Mortimer Rectory, Maldon, Essex.*—Ball. Coll. Ox. 3rd cl. Lit. Hum. and B A. 1826, M.A. 1829; Deac. 1829, Pr. 1830. R. of Woodham-Mortimer, Dio. Roch. 1835. (Patron, G. Round, Esq; Tithe, 360*l*; Glebe, 42½ acres; R.'s Inc. 400*l* and Ho; Pop. 324.) Formerly Fell. of Magd. Coll. Ox. 1828–35. [13]

MORRELL, The Right Rev. Thomas Baker, D.D., *Edinburgh.*—Ball. Coll. Ox. B.A. 1836, M.A. 1839; Deac. 1839 and Pr. 1840 by Bp of Ches. Consecrated Coadjutor Bp of Edinburgh 1863. Formerly R. of Henley-on-Thames 1852–63. [14]

MORRES, Arthur Philip, *Alderbury, Wilts.*—Wad. Coll. Ox. B.A. 1859; Deac. 1859 and Pr. 1860 by Bp of B. and W. Chap. of the Aldebury Union. Formerly C. of Bishop's Lydeard 1859. [15]

MORRES, H. R., *Finedon, Higham Ferrers, Northants.*—C. of Finedon. [16]

MORRES, Robert Elliot, *Chedington Rectory, Crewkerne.*—Wad. Coll. Ox. B.A. 1848, M.A. 1851, Theol. Coll. Wells, 1849; Deac. 1850 by Bp of B. and W. Pr. 1851 by Bp of Salis. R. of Chedington, Dio. Salis. 1867. (Patron, W. T. Cox, Esq; Tithe, 128*l*; Glebe, 40 acres; R.'s Inc. 194*l* and Ho; Pop. 163.) Formerly C. of Sharpwick with Ashcott 1850, Thurloxton, Somerset, 1856; R. of Chedington 1864; P. C. of Bicknoller, Somerset, 1864–67. [17]

MORRES, Thomas, *Chapel Green, Wokingham, Berks.*—Brasen. Coll. Ox. B.A. 1817, M.A. 1820; Deac. 1819 and Pr. 1820 by Bp of Salis. P. C. of Wokingham, Dio. Ox. 1820. (Patron, Bp of Ox; Tithe—App. 1710*l* 1*s* 4*d*; Glebe, 30 acres; P. C.'s Inc. 275*l*; Pop. 2445.) Surrogate. [18]

MORRICE, William David, *The Vicarage, Longbridge-Deverill, Warminster, Wilts.*—St. John's Coll. Cam. 2nd Sen. Opt. and B.A. 1839, M.A. 1842; Deac. 1840 and Pr. 1841 by Bp of Rip. V. of Longbridge-Deverill with Monkton-Deverill C. and Crockerton C. Dio. Salis. 1852. (Patron, Marquis of Bath; Longbridge-Deverill, Tithe—Imp. 415*l*, V. 158*l*; Glebe, 8 acres; Monkton-Deverill, Tithe—Imp. 133*l* and 51 acres of Glebe, V. 60*l*; Glebe, ½ acre; Crockerton, Tithe, 139*l*; V.'s Inc. 531*l* and Ho; Pop. Longbridge-Deverill and Crockerton 1197, Monkton-Deverill 205.) Preb. of Salis; Rural Dean. Formerly C. of Leeds 1840–42, Clovelly, North Devon, 1842–47, St. Andrew's Chapel, Plymouth, 1847–49, Westbury, Wilts, 1850–51, Oldland, Glouc. 1852. [19]

MORRIS, Adolphus Philipse, *East Harnham, Salisbury.*—Wor. Coll. Ox. B.A. 1846; Deac. 1847. Pr. 1848. P. C. of East Harnham, Dio. Salis. 1861. (Patron, V. of Britford, Wilts; P. C.'s Inc. 70*l*; Pop. 461.) [20]

MORRIS, Alfred George.—C. of Stapleton and Fishponds, near Bristol. [21]

MORRIS, Ambrose, *Rotherhithe, S.E.*—Deac. 1866 by Bp of Man. C. of St. Mary's, Rotherhithe, 1866. Formerly C. of St. Paul's, Pendleton, Manchester, 1865. [22]

MORRIS, David, 24, *Everton-villas, Liverpool.*—Lond. B.A. 1864; Deac. 1865 by Bp of St. A. for Bp of Ches. Pr. 1866 by Bp of Ches. C. of St. Mary's, Kirkdale, 1865; Mast. in Liverpool Coll. [23]

MORRIS, David Winter, *Pembroke.*—C. of St. Mary's, Pembroke. [24]

MORRIS, Ebenezer, *Llanelly Vicarage, Carmarthenshire.*—Deac. 1813 and Pr. 1814 by Bp of St. D. P. C. of Llannon, near Llanelly, Dio. St. D. 1815. (Patron, R. G. Thomas, Esq; Tithe—Imp. 775*l*; Glebe, 3 acres; P. C.'s Inc. 96*l*; Pop. 1656.) P. C. of Llandarog, near Carmarthen, Dio. St. D. 1818. (Patron, Bp of St. D; Tithe, Eccles. Commis. 819*l* and 4 acres of Glebe; P. C.'s Inc. 100*l*; Pop. 970.) V. of Llanelly with St. John's C. and Trinity C. Dio. St. D. 1820. (Patron, R. G. Thomas, Esq; Tithe—Imp. 2090*l* and 40 acres of Glebe; V.'s Inc. 96*l* and Ho; Pop. 12,270.) Rural Dean of Kidwelly; Surrogate 1830; Dom. Chap. to the Earl of Lisburne. Author, *Seasons and Jesuits on the Church.* [25]

MORRIS, Eli, *Sutton Cheney, Hinckley, Leicestershire.*—St. Peter's Coll. Cam. B.A. 1850; Deac. 1850, Pr. 1851. C. of Sutton Cheney. Formerly C. of Wolverhampton Coll. Ch. [26]

MORRIS, Francis Orpen, *Nunburnholme Rectory, Hayton, Yorks.*—Wor. Coll. Ox. 2nd cl. Lit. Hum. and B.A. 1833; Deac. 1834 and Pr. 1835 by Abp of York. R. of Nunburnholme, Dio. York, 1854. (Patron, Abp of York; Tithe—Imp. 14*l*; Glebe, 120 acres; R.'s Inc. 260*l* and Ho; Pop. 281.) Formerly P. C. of Hanging Heaton, Yorks; C. of Taxall, Cheshire, Ch. Ch. Doncaster, Ordsall, Notts, Crambe and Huttons Ambo, Yorks; V. of Nafferton, Yorks; Chap. to the late Duke of Cleveland. Author, *A History of British Birds*, 6 vols. 5*l*; *A Natural History of the Nests and Eggs of British Birds*, 3 vols. 3*l* 3*s*; *A Natural History of British Butterflies*, 20*s*; *A Natural History of British Moths*, 4 vols. 6*l*; *A Bible Natural History*, 10*s* 6*d*; *A Book of Natural History*, 10*s* 6*d*; *A Guide to an Arrangement of British Birds*, 1*s* 6*d*; *An Essay on Scientific Nomenclature*, 6*d*; *The Country Seats of the Noblemen and Gentlemen of Great Britain and Ireland*, in Parts, 2*s* 6*d* each; *An Essay on* *the Eternal Duration of the Earth*, 1s; *National Adult Education*, 6d; *An Essay on Baptismal Regeneration*, 2s; *A Family Prayer for Morning and Evening*, 1d; *A Morning and Evening Prayer for a Child*, 3s per 100; *A Prayer to be used before Reading the Holy Scriptures*, 3s per 100; *Memento of Confirmation*, 5s per 100; *The Sponsor's Memorial*, 3s 6d per 100; *The Communicant's Memorial*, 3s 6d per 100; *The Ministerial Credential*, 4s per 100; *None but Christ*, 3d; *Farewell Address to the Inhabitants of Ordsall*, 1d; *Extracts from the Works of the Rev. John Wesley*, 1s; *Possibilities in a Parish*, 3d; *A Plan for the Safe Delivery of every Letter under the New System*, 3d; *A Plan for the Detection of Thefts by Letter-Carriers*, 3d; *The Present System of Hiring Farm Servants in the East Riding of Yorkshire, with Suggestions for its Improvement*, 3d; *An Account of the Siege of Killowen*, 3d; *An Account of the Battle of the Monongahela River*, 3d; *A Farewell Address to the Inhabitants of Crambe and Huttons Ambo*, 1d; *Comfort for the Contrite*, Texts of Holy Scripture, 3d; *The Precepts of the Bible*, 3d; *The Maxims of the Bible*, 6d; *A Practical Solution of the Church-rate Difficulty*, 6d; *A Letter on Supremacy*, 6d; *The Gamekeeper's Museum*, 1s; *A Catechism of the Catechism*, 6d; *Plain Sermons for Plain People*, 1s each; *The Churchman's Belief*, 1s per 24; *The Yorkshire Hymn Book*, 8d; *Records of Animal Sagacity*, 5s; *Anecdotes in Natural History*, 5s; Various articles in the *Magazine of Natural History*, *Zoologist*, *Naturalist*, *Entomologist*; etc. [1]

MORRIS, George, *King's Kerswell, Newton Abbott, Devon.*—P. C. of King's Kerswell, Dio. Ex. 1859. (Patron, V. of St. Mary Church; P. C.'s Inc. 120*l* and Ho; Pop. 903.) [2]

MORRIS, George, *St. Allen Rectory, Truro.*—Ball. Coll. Ox. B.A. 1812, M.A. 1814; Deac. 1815, Pr. 1816. R. of St. Allen, Dio. Ex. 1842. (Patron, Bp of Ex; Tithe—Imp. 271*l* 5*s*, R. 147*l* 1*s* 7*d*; Glebe, 118 acres; R.'s Inc. 217*l* and Ho; Pop. 687.) [3]

MORRIS, George, 144, *Queen's-road, Dalston, London, N.E.*—St. John's Coll. Cam. B.A. 1855, M.A. 1859; Deac. 1855 and Pr. 1856 by Bp of Lin. P. C. of St. Stephen's, Haggerston, Dio. Lon. 1865. (Patrons, Crown and Bp of Lon; P. C.'s Inc. 200*l*; Pop. 7,500.) Formerly C. of Dunham, Notts, 1855, West Hackney 1858, St. Mary's, Haggerston, 1861. [4]

MORRIS, George Sculthorpe, *Bretforton Vicarage, Evesham.*—St. John's Coll. Cam. Sen. Opt. and B.A. 1835; Deac. 1836, Pr. 1837. V. of Bretforton, Dio. Wor. 1845. (Patron, Admiral Morris; Tithe, 19*s* 3*d*; Glebe, 90 acres; V.'s Inc. 246*l* and Ho; Pop. 565.) [5]

MORRIS, Henry, *Reading.*—Trin. Hall, Cam. B.A. 1853, M.A. 1856; Deac. 1854 and Pr. 1855 by Bp of Lon. P. C. of Trinity, Reading, Dio. Ox. 1866. (Patron, Rev. George Hulme; P. C.'s Inc. 250*l*.) Formerly C. of All Souls', Marylebone, Lond. 1854, St. Thomas's, Ryde, 1855, Lewknor, Oxon, 1861. [6]

MORRIS, Henry, *Tenby, S. Wales.* [7]

MORRIS, Henry Budd, *Colney Hatch, London, N.*—Caius Coll. Cam. B.A. 1862, M.A. 1865; Deac. 1864 and Pr. 1865 by Bp of Rip. Chap. R.N. Formerly C. of St. Andrew's, Leeds, 1864–66. [8]

MORRIS, James, *Little Dawley, Wellington, Salop.*—St. Cath. Hall, Cam. B.A. 1842; Deac. 1842, Pr. 1843. P. C. of Little Dawley, Dio. Lich. 1845. (Patrons, the Crown and Bp of Lich. alt; P. C.'s Inc. 150*l* and Ho; Pop. 2327.) [9]

MORRIS, James, *Llanallgo Rectory, Anglesey.*—Deac. 1855 and Pr. 1856 by Bp of Llan. R. of Llaneugrad with Llanallgo, Dio. Ban. 1863. (Patron, Bp of Llan; Tithe, 216*l*; Glebe, 1½ acres; R.'s Inc. 230*l* and Ho; Pop. Llaneugrad 276, Llanallgo 480.) Formerly C. of Bedwellty, Neath, and Michaelstone-super-Avon. Author, *St. Bartholomew's Day, or the Two Thousand*, reprinted from the *Haul*; *Gwyl-y-Cynhauaf, a Selection of Tunes and Hymns for Harvest-Home Services*, 1867. [10]

MORRIS, John, *Narberth, Pembrokeshire.*—C. of Narberth. [11]

MORRIS, John, *Askham Bryan, York.*—P. C. of Askham Bryan, Dio. York, 1866. (Patron, W. Morris, Esq; P. C.'s Inc. 200*l* and Ho; Pop. 362.) [12]

MORRIS, John Alfred, *Woodland Cottage, near Pontypridd, Glamorganshire.*—St. Bees; Deac. 1864 by Bp of Llan. C. of Llanwonno with St. David's, Rhondda, 1864. [13]

MORRIS, Joseph Lewis, *Fillongley Vicarage, Coventry.*—Wor. Coll. Ox. Hon. 4th cl. Math. et Phy. 1846, B.A. 1847, M.A. 1849; Deac. and Pr. 1848 by Bp of Win. V. of Fillongley, Dio. Wor. 1856. (Patron, Ld Chan; Tithe, 330*l* 12*s*; Glebe, 4½ acres; V.'s Inc. 358*l* and Ho; Pop. 1105.) Formerly C. of Highclere, Hants. [14]

MORRIS, Joseph William, *Ystrad-Meurig, Aberystwith.*—Mast. of Ystrad-Meurig Gr. Sch. Formerly P. C. of Yspytty-Ystwith, Cardiganshire, 1846–59. [15]

MORRIS, Laurence Stuart, *Thornton Rectory, Skipton, Yorks.*—Ch. Coll. Cam. B.A. 1832, M.A. 1835; Deac. 1833 by Bp of Roch. Pr. 1834 by Abp of York. R. of Thornton, Dio. Rip. 1834. (Patron, the present R; Land in lieu of Tithe, 158 acres; Glebe, 80 acres; R.'s Inc. 308*l* and Ho; Pop. 2112.) Rural Dean of Skipton 1859; Hon. Can. of Rip. 1864. [16]

MORRIS, Robert, *Fryern-Barnet, Middlesex.*—Ch. Ch. Ox. 1st cl. Math et Phy. 1829, B.A. 1830, M.A. 1833; Deac. 1831 and Pr. 1832 by Bp of Lon. R. of Fryern-Barnet, Dio. Lon. 1850. (Patrons, D. and C. of St. Paul's; Tithe, 270*l*; Glebe, 8 acres; R.'s Inc. 290*l*; Pop. 3314.) Rural Dean of Enfield 1858. Formerly C. of Trinity, St. Giles', Lond. 1831, and P. C. of same, 1838. [17]

MORRIS, Robert John, *Whitstable Parsonage, near Canterbury.*—Jesus Coll. Cam. B.A. 1837. V. of Seasalter, near Canterbury, Dio. Cant. 1848. (Patrons, D. and C. of Cant; Tithe—App. 225*l* and 38 acres of Glebe, V. 160*l*; Glebe, 1 rood; V.'s Inc. 161*l*; Pop. 1378.) P. C. of Whitstable, Dio. Cant. 1848. (Patron, Abp of Cant; Tithe—Imp. 935*l*; P. C.'s Inc. 155*l* and Ho; Pop. 3675.) [18]

MORRIS, Robert Leslie, *Verum House, Sandown, Isle of Wight.*—Pemb. Coll. Ox. Scho. of, B.A. 1861, M.A. 1863; Deac. 1863 and Pr. 1864 by Bp of Salis. C. of Ch. Ch. Sandown 1865. Formerly C. of St. James's, Poole, Dorset, 1863. [19]

MORRIS, Theodore Joseph, *Vicarage, Hampton-in-Arden, Birmingham.*—Lin. Coll. Ox. B.A. 1859, M.A. 1863; Deac. 1861 and Pr. 1862 by Bp of Wor. V. of Hampton-in-Arden with Nuthurst, C. Dio. Wor. 1866. (Patron, W. C. Alston, Esq; Tithe, 647*l*; Glebe, 62 acres; V.'s Inc. 705*l* and Ho; Pop. Hampton-in-Arden 796, Nuthurst 117.) Formerly C. of Hampton-in-Arden 1859. [20]

MORRIS, Thomas, *Eastham, Worcester.*—C. of Eastham. [21]

MORRIS, Thomas Edward, *Carleton Vicarage, Skipton, Yorks.*—Ch. Ch. Ox. 2nd cl. Lit. Hum. and B.A. 1835, M.A. 1838; Deac. 1837 and Pr. 1838 by Bp of Ox. V. of Carleton, Dio. Rip. 1854 (Patrons, D. and C. of Ch. Ch. Ox; Tithe, 300*l*; Glebe, 114 acres; V.'s Inc. 414*l* and Ho; Pop. 890.) Rural Dean. Formerly Tut. of Ch. Ch. Ox. 1838–45. Author, *A Sermon preached before the University* 1843. [22]

MORRIS, Thomas Whitaker, *Ashton-under-Lyne.*—St. Bees; Deac. 1845 and Pr. 1847 by Bp of Ches. Surrogate 1851. Formerly P. C. of St. Peter's, Ashton-under-Lyne, 1848–65. [23]

MORRISH, William John, *Ledbury Union House, Herefordshire.*—Magd. Hall, Ox. B.A. 1833, M.A. 1834. Chap. to the Ledbury Union. [24]

MORRISON, William, *Midsomer-Norton, Bath.*—Ch. Ch. Ox. B.A. 1856, M.A. 1858; Deac. 1856, Pr. 1857. V. of Midsomer-Norton, Dio. B. and W. 1867. (Patron, Ch. Ch. Ox; Tithe, 340*l*; Glebe, 1 acre; V.'s Inc. 350*l* and Ho; Pop. 2064.) Formerly Chap. of Ch. Ch. Oxford. [25]

MORRISON, William Robert, *St. James's Parsonage, Halifax.*—Dub. A.B. 1846, A.M. 1856; Deac. 1852, Pr. 1853 by Abp of York. P. C. of St. James's,

Halifax, Dio. Rip. 1859. (Patron, V. of Halifax; P. C.'s Inc. 350*l* and Ho; Pop. 14,388.) Surrogate. Formerly C. of Brighouse, Yorks. Author, *The Plenary Inspiration of Scripture proved both by External and Internal Evidence* (a Sermon), 3*d*; *The Yoke of Bondage* (a Sermon), 3*d*; *Addresses to Young Men*, 5 Parts, 2*d* each; *New Years' Addresses*; etc. [1]

MORROW, Thomas Knox Magee, *Birkenhead.*—P. C. of St. James's, Birkenhead, 1863. (Patrons, Trustees.) [2]

MORSE, Anthony South, *Lakenham, near Norwich.*—Corpus Coll. Cam. B.A. 1856; Deac. 1856 and Pr. 1857 by Bp of Nor. C. of Caister, and of St. Mark's, Lakenham. [3]

MORSE, Charles, *St. Michael's Rectory, Norwich.*—Queens' Coll. Cam. B.C.L. 1835; Deac. 1837 and Pr. 1838 by Abp of York. R. of St. Michael's-at-Plea, Norwich, Dio. Nor. 1839. (Patrons, Sir T. B. Leonard and J. Morse, Esq; R.'s Inc. 60*l*; Pop. 379.) P. C. of St. Mary Coslany, Norwich, Dio. Nor. 1839. (Patron, Marquis Townshend; P. C.'s Inc. 70*l*; Pop. 1498.) Formerly Member of the Royal Coll. of Surgeons. [4]

MORSE, Francis, *Vicarage, Nottingham.*—St. John's Coll. Cam. 14th Sen. Opt. 1st cl. Cl. Trip. B.A. 1842, M.A. 1845; Deac. 1843 and Pr. 1844 by Bp of Nor. V. of St. Mary's, Nottingham, Dio. Lin. 1864. (Patron, Earl Manvers; V.'s Inc. 800*l* and Ho; Pop. 6000.) Preb. of Lin; Rural Dean; Surrogate. Formerly C. of North Cove, Suffolk, and Tamworth; P. C. of St. John's, Ladywood, Birmingham, 1854–64; Select Preacher to Univ. of Cam. 1857–59; Hulsean Lect. 1863. Author, *Working for God* (Sermons before the University of Cambridge), 5*s*; Various Tracts for S.P.C.K. [5]

MORSE, Herbert George, *Trinity College, Cambridge.*—Trin. Coll. Cam. B.A. 1861, M.A. 1864; Deac. 1863 and Pr. 1864 by Bp of Ely. Formerly C. of St. Clement's, Cambridge, 1863. [6]

MORSE, Thomas, D. C., *Stretford Rectory, Manchester.*—King's Coll. Lond. 1st cl. 1851; Deac. 1851 and Pr. 1852 by Bp of Salis. R. of Stretford, Dio. Man. 1864. (Patrons, D. and C. of Man; R.'s Inc. 370*l* and Ho; Pop. 3882.) Formerly R. of West Grimstead, Wilts, and Dioc. Inspector of Schs. 1855–64. [7]

MORSHEAD, Henry John, *Kelly Rectory, Tavistock, Devon.*—Ex. Coll. Ox. B.A. 1829, M.A. 1832; Deac. 1831 and Pr. 1832 by Bp of Ex. R. of Kelly, Dio. Ex. 1837. (Patron, A. Kelly, Esq; Tithe, 250*l*; Glebe, 73 acres; R.'s Inc. 370*l*; Pop. 217.) V. of St. Cleather, Cornwall, Dio. Ex. 1837. (Patron, J. Carpenter Garnier, Esq; Tithe, 90*l*; Glebe, 73 acres; V.'s Inc. 165*l*; Pop. 229.) [8]

MORSHED, John Anderson, *Salcombe-Regis Vicarage, Sidmouth, Devon.*—Ex. Coll. Ox. B.A. 1831, M.A. 1845. V. of Salcombe-Regis, Dio. Ex. 1854. (Patrons, D. and C. of Ex; Tithe—App. 170*l* 5*s*, V. 151*l* 5*s*; Glebe, 9 acres; V.'s Inc. 186*l* and Ho; Pop. 434.) [9]

MORSON, J. C. F., *Llandow, Cowbridge, Glamorganshire.*—C. of Llandow and Monknash. [10]

MORTIMER, Christian, *Middle, Salop.*—Clare Coll. Cam. B.A. 1858, M.A. 1861; Deac. 1859 and Pr. 1860 by Bp of Herf. C. of Middle 1864. [11]

MORTIMER, George Ferris Whidborne, 72, *Eccleston-square, London, S.W.*—Queen's Coll. Ox. 1st cl. Lit. Hum. and B.A. 1826, M.A. 1829, B.D. and D.D. 1841. Preb. of St. Paul's. Formerly Head Mast. of the City of Lond. Sch. [12]

MORTIMER, Thomas Gwynne, *Castle Bigh, Haverfordwest.*—Jesus Coll. Ox. B.A. 1853, M.A. 1855; Deac. 1854 and Pr. 1855 by Bp of Ox. R. of Castle Bigh, Pembrokeshire, Dio. St. D. 1866. (Patron, Ld Chan; Pop. 227.) Formerly C. of Abingdon, Berks. [13]

MORTIMER, William Basset.—Pemb. Coll. Ox. B.A. 1862; Deac. 1862, Pr. 1863. Formerly C. of Alfreton with Somercotes, Derbyshire, 1862. [14]

MORTLOCK, Charles, *The Vicarage, Pennington, near Ulverston.*—Caius Coll. Cam. B.A. 1841, M.A. 1846; Deac. 1841 by Abp of Cant. Pr. 1842 by Bp of Pet. V. of Pennington, Dio. Carl. 1851. (Patron, Duchy of Lancaster; Glebe, 65 acres; V.'s Inc. 216*l* and Ho; Pop. 879.) Formerly C. of Newton Heath, near Manchester, 1841–42, St. Martin's 1842–43; Miss. of S.P.G. 1843; R. of Turk's Island, Bahamas, 1844–48; V. of All Saints and V. of St. Leonard's, Leicester, 1848–51. [15]

MORTLOCK, Edmund, *Moulton Rectory (Suffolk), near Newmarket.*—Ch. Coll. Cam. 14th Wrang. and B.A. 1808, M.A. 1811, B.D. 1840; Deac. 1810, Pr. 1811. R. and V. of Moulton, Dio. Ely, 1845. (Patron, Ch. Coll. Cam; Tithe—App. 2*l* 10*s*, R. 615*l*; Glebe, 170 acres; R. and V.'s Inc. 730*l* and Ho; Pop. 518.) Formerly Fell. of Ch. Coll. Cam. Author, *Four Sermons on the Trinity* (preached before the Univ. of Cam.) *with copious Notes*, Rivingtons, 6*s* 6*d*; *Explanation and Defence of the Athanasian Creed*, ib. 2*s*; *Baptism from the Bible* (a Visitation Sermon), ib. 1*s*. [16]

MORTLOCK, E., *Lewisham, Kent, S.E.*—Min. of Southend Chapel, Lewisham, Dio. Lon. 1863. [17]

MORTLOCK, Edward Thomas, *Rudston Vicarage, Bridlington, Yorks.*—Caius Coll. Cam. B.A. 1849, M.A. 1852; Deac. 1849 and Pr. 1850 by Bp of Pet. V. of Rudston, Dio. York, 1856. (Patron, Abp of York; V.'s Inc. 260*l* and Ho; Pop. 605.) Formerly V. of North-Frodingham, Yorks, 1854–56. [18]

MORTON, A. H. Aylmer, *United University Club, Pall-mall East, London, S.W.*—King's Coll. Cam. Fell. of; Deac. 1861 and Pr. 1863 by Bp of Ox. Chap. to the Earl of Fife. Formerly C. of All Saints', Knightsbridge, and of Curzon Chapel, May Fair, Lond. [19]

MORTON, David, *Harleston Rectory, near Northampton.*—Trin. Coll. Cam. Wrang. and B.A. 1822, M.A. 1831; Deac. 1823 by Bp of Bristol, Pr. 1826 by Bp of Ely. R. of Harleston, Dio. Pet. 1831. (Patron, Earl Spencer; Land in lieu of Tithe, 313 acres; Glebe, 10 acres; R.'s Inc. 580*l* and Ho; Pop. 652.) Chap. R.N. [20]

MORTON, Edward Howard, *Tatterford Rectory, Rougham, Norfolk.*—Trin. Coll. Cam. B.A. 1852, M.A. 1863; Deac. 1852 by Bp of Chich. Pr. 1853 by Bp of Wor. R. of Tatterford with Tatterset, Dio. Nor. 1857. (Patron, J. S. Scott Chad, Esq; Tithe, 685*l*; Glebe, 50 acres; R.'s Inc. 750*l* and Ho; Pop. 275.) Formerly C. of Midhurst 1852, Pillerton, Warwickshire, 1853, St. Martin's, Worcester, 1854–57. Author, *A Visitation Sermon*, Rivingtons, 1867, 6*d*. [21]

MORTON, Francis Clarke, *Wadsley Parsonage Sheffield.*—Dub. A.B. 1849, A.M. 1852; Deac. 1849 and Pr. 1850 by Bp of Wor. P. C. of Wadsley, Dio. York, 1858. (Patroness, Miss Harrison; P. C.'s Inc. 239*l* and Ho; Pop. 5264.) Formerly C. of St. Stephen's, Birmingham, and St. James's, Sheffield. [22]

MORTON, George Gustavus, *Acton, London, W.*—Dub. A.B. 1853, A.M. 1862; Deac. 1854 by Bp of Cork, Pr. 1855 by Bp of Ossory. Formerly C. of Borris, Carlow, 1854–59, Ch. Ch. St. George's-in-the-East, Lond. 1860–62, Acton 1863–66. [23]

MORTON, Hector, *Prittlewell, Chelmsford.*—C. of Prittlewell. [24]

MORTON, Henry, *Thorpe, near Newark, Notts.*—Dub. A.B. 1846; Deac. 1847 by Bp of Tuam, Pr. 1847 by Bp of Killaloe. R. of Thorpe, Dio. Lin. 1866. (Patron, Ld Chan; Tithe, 225*l*; Glebe, 40 acres; R.'s Inc. 305*l* and Ho; Pop. 107.) Formerly C. of Wark, Northumberland, 1848–51, South Shields 1851–56; R. of Knaresdale, Northumberland, 1856–66. [25]

MORTON, James Henry, *Chittlehamholt, South Molton, Devon.*—Dub. A.B. 1850, A.M. 1853; Deac. 1856 and Pr. 1857 by Bp of Ex. C. of St. John's, Chittlehamholt. [26]

MORTON, John, *Cleeve Prior Vicarage, Evesham.*—Wor. Coll. Ox. B.A. 1837, M.A. 1843; Deac. 1837 and Pr. 1838 by Bp of Wor. V. of Cleeve Prior, Dio. Wor. 1857. (Patrons, D. and C. of Wor; Glebe, 111 acres; V.'s Inc. 230*l* and Ho; Pop. 340.) Formerly C. of Wolstone, near Coventry. [27]

MORTON, John Francis, *Dalston, Carlisle.*—Dub. A.B. 1865; Deac. 1866 by Bp of Cork for Bp of Carl. Pr. 1867 by Bp of Carl. C. of Dalston 1866. [28]

MORTON, Joshua.—C. of St. Stephen's, Spitalfields, Lond. [1]

MORTON, Richard, *Rothwell Vicarage, near Kettering.*—St. Cath. Coll. Cam. Scho. of, B.A. 1840, M.A. 1853; Deac. 1840 and Pr. 1841 by Bp of Ches. V. of Rothwell with Orton, Dio. Pet. 1855. (Patroness, Miss Hall; V.'s Inc. 160*l* and Ho; Pop. Rothwell 2285, Orton 69.) R. of Glendon, Dio. Pet. 1857. (Patrons, Trustees of late John Boothe, Esq; R.'s Inc. 85*l*; Pop. 83.) Surrogate. Formerly C. of Barrowford, Lanc. 1840–42, St. Cuthbert's, York, 1842, Geddington, Northants, 1842–45; Mast. of Gr. Sch. Kettering, 1845–55, and Chap. of Union Workhouse 1847–55. [2]

MORTON, Thomas, *Fairford, Glouc.*—C. of Fairford. [3]

MORTON, T. Fitzhardinge, *Handsworth, near Birmingham.*—C. of St. Michael's, Handsworth. [4]

MORTON, William, 57, *York-road, Hove, Brighton.*—Trin. Coll. Ox. B.A. 1857, M.A. 1860; Deac. 1859 and Pr 1860 by Bp of Wor. C. of St. Patrick and St. James's, Hove, 1867. Formerly Sub-Vicar of Stratford-on-Avon 1859–66. [5]

MORTON, W., *Lynesack, Bishop Auckland, Durham.*—P. C. of Lynesack with Softley, Dio. Dur. 1861. (Patron, Bp of Dur; P. C.'s Inc. 300*l*; Pop. 1120.) [6]

MOSELEY, Henry, *Olveston Vicarage, Bristol.*—St. John's Coll. Cam. 7th Wrang. and B.A. 1826, M.A. 1829; Deac. 1827 and Pr. 1828 by Bp of B. and W. V. of Olveston, Dio. G. and B. 1854. (Patrons, D. and C. of Bristol; Tithe—App. 120*l*, Imp. 178*l* 10*s*, V. 708*l*; Glebe, 37 acres; V.'s Inc. 865*l* and Ho; Pop. 1699.) Can. Res. of Bristol Cathl. (Value, 700*l* and Res.) Chap. in Ordinary to the Queen 1855; Fell. of the Royal Soc; Corresponding Member of the Institute of France. Formerly Prof. of Natural Philosophy and Astronomy in King's Coll. Lond. [7]

MOSELEY, Herbert Henry, *Holt, Trowbridge, Wilts.*—St. John's Coll. Cam. B.A. 1853; Deac. 1853, Pr. 1854. P. C. of Holt, Dio. Salis. 1865. (Patrons, D. and C. of Bristol; Tithe, comm. 150*l*; P. C.'s Inc. 150*l*; Pop. 825.) Formerly C. of St. Augustine's Bristol. [8]

MOSES, William Stainton, *Maughold, Isle of Man.*—Ex. Coll. Ox. B.A. 1863, M.A. 1865; Deac. 1863 and Pr. 1865 by Bp of S. and M. C. of Maughold 1863. [9]

MOSLEY, Peploe Paget, *Rolleston Rectory, Burton-on-Trent.*—Jesus Coll. Cam. B.A. 1816, M.A. 1818; Deac. 1817, Pr. 1818. R. of Rolleston, Dio. Lich. 1834. (Patron, Sir Oswald Mosley, Bart; Tithe—Imp. 2*l* 6*s* 7*d*, R. 387*l* 10*s*; Glebe, 79½ acres; R.'s Inc. 680*l* and Ho; Pop. 608.) [10]

MOSLEY, Richard, *Rotherham Vicarage, Yorks.*—Trin. Coll. Cam. B.A. 1830, M.A. 1833. V. of Rotherham, Dio. York, 1842. (Patron, Earl of Effingham; Tithe—Imp. 211*l* 3*s* 6*d*, V. 11*l* 10*s* 9*d*; V.'s Inc. 190*l* and Ho; Pop. 15,035.) [11]

MOSLEY, Rowland, *Egginton Rectory, Burton-on-Trent.*—Ex. Coll. Ox. B.A. 1852; Deac. 1853, Pr. 1854. R. of Egginton, Dio. Lich. 1857. (Patrons, Sir H. Every, Bart., S. C. Pole, and J. Leigh, Esqrs.; Tithe, 315*l*; Glebe, 53 acres; R.'s Inc. 470*l* and Ho; Pop. 355.) Formerly C. of Anslow, Burton-on-Trent, 1854–57. [12]

MOSS, John James, *East Lydford Rectory, Somerton.*—R. of East Lydford, Dio. B. and W. 1864. (Patron, Rev. P. S. Newell; R.'s Inc. 180*l* and Ho; Pop. 178.) [13]

MOSS, Richard, *Christ Church Parsonage, Blackburn.*—Dub. A.B. 1851, A.M. 1854, B.D. and D.D. 1866; Deac. 1851 and Pr. 1852 by Bp of S. and M. P. C. of Ch. Ch. Blackburn, Dio. Man. 1860. (Patrons, V. of Blackburn and others alt; P. C.'s Inc. 300*l* and Ho; Pop. 6642.) Formerly C. of St. Mary's, Blackburn. [14]

MOSSE, Henry Moore, *Heage Parsonage, Belper.*—Dub. Cl. and Heb. Prizeman of, A.B. 1846; Deac. 1848 and Pr. 1849 by Bp of Ches. P. C. of Heage, Dio. Lich. 1855. (Patron, V. of Duffield; Glebe, 3 acres; P. C.'s Inc. 180*l* and Ho; Pop. 2286.) Formerly C. of Ch. Ch. Liverpool, 1848, Brailsford, Derbyshire, 1852. [15]

MOSSE, Samuel Tenison, *Great Smeaton Rectory, North Allerton, Yorks.*—Dub. A.B. 1833, A.M. 1840; Deac. 1834 by Bp of Roch. Pr. 1835 by Bp of Lin. R. of Great Smeaton with Appleton-upon-Wisk P. C. Dioc. Rip. and York, 1866. (Patron, Robert Barry, Esq; Tithe, 500*l*; Glebe, 33 acres; Appleton, Tithe, 187*l*; Glebe, 6½ acres; R.'s Inc. 720*l* and Ho; Pop. Great Smeaton 461, Appleton 466.) Formerly C. of Tisbury, Wilts; V. of Buckland, Kent, 1856–66. Author, *A Key to Ordination for Divinity Students*, 1837; *Archæologic and Graphic Illustrations of Ashbourne Church, Derbyshire*, fol. E. G. Moon, 1843, 63*s*; etc. [16]

MOSSMAN, Thomas Wimberley, *Torrington Rectory, near Wragby.*—St. Edm. Hall, Ox. B.A. 1849; Deac. 1849 and Pr. 1850 by Bp of Lin. R. of East and West Torrington V. Dio. Lin. 1859. (Patron, C. Turnor, Esq; Tithe, 310*l*; Glebe, 43 acres; R.'s Inc. 360*l* and Ho; Pop. 285.) Formerly C. of Donington-on-Bain 1849; V. of Randby, Linc. 1854–59. Author, *Sermons*, 5*s*; *A Glossary of the Principal Words used in a Figurative, Typical, or Mystical Sense in the Holy Scriptures, with their Signification, gathered from the Sacred Writers themselves, or from the Works of the Ancient Fathers*, Masters, 1*s* 8*d*; *Followers of the Lamb* (a Sermon), ib. 1867. [17]

MOSSOP, Charles, *Etton (Northants), near Market Deeping.*—St. John's Coll. Cam. B.A. 1816, M.A. 1819; Deac. 1816 and Pr. 1817 by Bp of Lin. R. of Etton, Dio. Pet. 1853. (Patron, Earl Fitzwilliam; Glebe, 200 acres; R.'s Inc. 380*l*; Pop. 160.) [18]

MOSSOP, Isaac, *Wood-Plumpton Parsonage, Preston.*—St. Bees 1824; Deac. 1826 and Pr. 1827 by Bp of Ches. P. C. of Wood-Plumpton, Dio. Man. 1836. (Patron, V. of St. Michael-on-Wyre; Glebe, 86 acres; P. C.'s Inc. 175*l* and Ho; Pop. 1462.) [19]

MOSSOP, John, *Covenham St. Bartholomew, Louth, Lincolnshire.*—St. John's Coll. Cam. B.A. 1827; Deac. 1828, Pr. 1829. R. of Covenham St. Bartholomew, Dio. Lin. 1829. (Patrons, Heirs of S. Harrold, Esq. and Rev. C. D. Holland; Corn-rents in lieu of Tithe, 145*l*; Glebe, 62 acres; R.'s Inc. 240*l*; Pop. 298.) Author, *British Land Birds* (in Verse and Prose). [20]

MOSTYN, George Thornton.—Dub. A.B. 1830. Min. of St. John's, Kilburn Park, Willesden, Dio. Lon. 1862. Formerly P. C. of St. Thomas's, Eccleston, Lanc. 1845–57. Author, *The Ministry of the Angels*. [21]

MOSTYN, Hon. H. Wynne, *Buckworth Rectory, Huntingdon.*—R. of Buckworth, Dio. Ely, 1863. (Patron, R. E. D. Shafto, Esq; R.'s Inc. 380*l* and Ho; Pop. 201.) Formerly C. of Badsworth, Yorks. [22]

MOTHERSOLE, William Frederick.—Trin. Coll. Cam. Jun. Opt. B.A. 1855, M.A. 1858; Deac. 1856 by Bp of Man. C. of St. Marylebone, Lond. Formerly C. of St. Philip's, Bradford-road, Manchester. [23]

MOTT, Henry Samuel, *Much Hadham, Ware, Herts.*—St. John's Coll. Cam. B.A. 1841, M.A. 1844; Deac. 1843 and Pr. 1844 by Bp of Lon. Formerly C. of Furneux Pelham with Brent, Herts, 1843–59, Ickworth and Horringer, Suffolk, 1860–63. [24]

MOTTRAM, Charles John Macqueen, *Kidderminster.*—Magd. Hall, Ox. B.A. 1841; Deac. 1841, Pr. 1842. P. C. of St. George's, Kidderminster, Dio. Wor. 1852. (Patron, V. of Kidderminster; P. C.'s Inc. 300*l*.) [25]

MOTTRAM, C. P., *Smethwick, Birmingham.*—C. of St. Matthew's, Smethwick. [26]

MOTTRAM, Joshua, 6, *Halliford-street, Islington, London, N.*—Min. of Miss. Ch. Rosemary-street, Islington, 1865. [27]

MOULD, James George, *Bath.*—Corpus Coll. Cam. 2nd Smith's Prizeman, 2nd Wrang. and B.A. 1838, M.A. 1841, B.D. 1849; Deac. 1840, Pr. 1848. Fell. and Tut. of Corpus Coll. Cam. [28]

MOULD, John, *The Vicarage, Oakham, Rutland.*—St. John's Coll. Cam. Wrang. and B.A. 1838, M.A. 1841; Deac. 1839, Pr. 1841. V. of Oakham with Egleton C. Langham C. and Brooke C. Dio. Pet. 1865. (Patron, George Finch, Esq; Tithe, 650*l*; V.'s Inc. 950*l* and Ho;

Pop. Oakham 2959, Egleton 181, Langham 636, Brooke 112.) Surrogate. Formerly V. of Tamworth 1854–65. [1]

MOULD, Joseph, 6, *Bernard-street, Russell-square, London, W.C.*—Clare Coll. Cam. Sen. Scho. of, Cl. Prizeman, B.A. 1845, M.A. 1851; Deac. 1845 and Pr. 1846 by Bp of Lich. Min. of Woburn Chapel, St. Pancras, Lond. 1862; Chap. of the Holborn Union. Formerly Preacher at Quebec Chapel, Marylebone, 1848–49; Preacher to Magdalen Hospital 1851–55. [2]

MOULE, Frederick John, *Fordington, Dorchester.*—Corpus Coll. Cam. B.A. 1855, M.A. 1858; Deac. 1857 and Pr. 1859 by Bp of Salis. C. of Fordington 1857. Formerly Chap. to the Dorset County Lunatic Asylum 1860–66. [3]

MOULE, George Evans, *Ningpo, China.*—Corpus Coll. Cam. Sen. Opt. 3rd cl. Cl. Trip. and B.A. 1850; Deac. 1851 and Pr. 1852 by Bp of Salis. British Chap. at Ningpo. Formerly Chap. of the Dorset Co. Hospital, 1855–57. [4]

MOULE, Henry, *Fordington Vicarage, Dorchester.*—St. John's Coll. Cam. B.A. 1821, M.A. 1828; Deac. 1824 and Pr. 1825 by Bp of Salis. V. of Fordington, Dio. Salis. 1829. (Patron, the Preb. of Fordington in Salis. Cathl; Tithe—App. 691*l*, V. 224*l*; V.'s Inc. 325*l* and Ho; Pop. 2199.) Surrogate. Author, *Two Conversations on the Service for the Public Baptism of Infants,* 1844, 2 eds. 2*d*; *Scraps of Sacred Verse,* 1846, 5*s*; *Barrack Sermons,* 1845, 1847, 2*s* 6*d*; *Scriptural Church Teaching,* 1848, 2*s* 6*d*; *Two Conversations on Confirmation,* 1849, 2*d*; *Three Sermons on the Profession contained in the Words, "A Member of Christ the Child of God, and an Inheritor of the Kingdom of Heaven,"* 4*d*; *Five Lectures on Revelation* iv. v. vi. *and* vii. 1853, 2*s*; *Eight Letters to Prince Albert on the Dwellings and Conditions of the Working Classes and Poor of Fordington,* 1854, 1*s*; *Three Letters on Self-Supporting Boarding Schools for Children of the Working Classes,* 1856; *National Health and Wealth,* 1859, 1*s*; *Hope against Hope* (a Narrative), 1*s*; *Rules for Reading Scripture in Letters addressed to Bishop Colenso,* 1*s*; *Sixty Original Hymns,* published by Nisbet, and by Macintosh. [5]

MOULLIN, Daniel Alfred, 44, *Trinity-square, Southwark, London, S.E.*—Dub. A.B. 1842; Deac. 1843, Pr. 1844. P. C. of Trinity, Southwark, 1848. (Patron, Bp of Lon.) [6]

MOULLIN, George Alaric, *West Woodhay Rectory, Newbury, Berks.*—Dub. A.B. 1846; Deac. 1848 and Pr. 1849 by Bp of Lin. R. of West Woodhay, Dio. Ox. 1855. (Patron, Rev. J. Sloper; Tithe, 241*l* 3*s* 3*d*; Glebe, 12 acres; R.'s Inc. 260*l* and Ho; Pop. 130.) [7]

MOULTRIE, Gerard, *Barrow Gurney, Bristol.*—Ex. Coll. Ox. 3rd cl. Lit. Hum. B.A. 1851, M.A. 1856; Deac. 1852 by Bp of Lich. Pr. 1858 by Bp of Dur. Chap. of the D. of Barrow Gurney, Dio. B. and W. 1864. (Patron, J. H. Blagrave, Esq; Chap.'s Inc. 66*l* and Ho; Pop. 321.) Formerly Mast. of Shrewsbury Sch. 1852–55; Chap. to the Dowager Marchioness of Londonderry 1855–64. [8]

MOULTRIE, John, *Rugby Rectory, Warwickshire.*—Trin. Coll. Cam. Bell's Univ. Scho. 1828, Trin. Coll. Scho. 1822, B.A. 1823, M.A. 1826; Deac. 1825 by Bp of Lin. Pr. 1825 by Bp of Ely. R. of Rugby, Dio. Wor. 1825. (Patron, Earl of Craven; Glebe, 179 acres; R.'s Inc. 714*l* and Ho; Pop. 4899.) Hon. Can. of Wor; Rural Dean. Author, *My Brother's Grave and other Poems,* 1837; *Dream of Life; Lays of the English Church, &c.* 1843; *Memoir and Poetical Remains of W. S. Walker,* 1852; *Sermons* (preached at Rugby), 1852; *Altars, Hearths, and Graves,* 1854. [9]

MOUNT, Charles Bridges, *Netherbury, Beaminster, Dorset.*—New Coll. Ox. B.A. 1849, M.A. 1852. Fell. of New Coll. Ox; C. of Netherbury. [10]

MOUNT, Francis John, *Horsham, Sussex.*—Oriel Coll. Ox. B.A. 1854, M.A. 1858; Deac. 1855 and Pr. 1857 by Bp of Chich. C. of Horsham 1855. [11]

MOUNTAIN, Jacob Henry Brooke, *Blunham Rectory, St. Neots, Beds.*—Trin. Coll. Cam. Sen. Opt. B.A. 1810, M.A. 1814, B.D. 1836, D.D. 1842; Deac. 1811, Pr. 1812. R. of Blunham, Dio. Ely, 1831. (Patroness, Countess Cowper; Glebe, 450 acres; R.'s Inc. 810*l* and Ho; Pop. 647.) Preb. of Lin. 1819; Rural Dean of Shefford; Surrogate; Commissary for Archdeaconry of Bedford. Author, *Twelve Advent Sermons,* Rivingtons, 1834; *Twenty-one Sermons for the Times,* ib. 1835; *Summary of Lactantius,* ib. 1839; *The Church on Earth the appointed Way to the Heavenly Church,* 1845; *The Acts of the Apostles considered,* 1851; numerous single Sermons. [12]

MOUNTAIN, Jacob Jehoshaphat Salter, *Jersey.*—King's Coll. Univ. of Windsor, Nova Scotia, B.A. 1845, M.A. 1855, B.C.L. and D.C.L. 1858; Deac. 1847 and Pr. 1849 by Bp of Quebec. Formerly Travelling Missionary in the Canadian Backwoods 1847–49; Incumb. of Coteau du Lac, Canada, 1849–57; C. of Milston, Wilts, 1858. [13]

MOUNTFIELD, David, *Newport Rectory, Salop.*—St. John's Coll. Cam. B.A. 1850, M.A. 1853; Deac. 1850 and Pr. 1851 by Bp of Lich. R. of Newport, Dio. Lich. 1864. (Patron, Ld Chan; Tithe, 180*l*; R.'s Inc. 275*l*; Pop. 3051.) Chap. of the Newport Union; Surrogate. Formerly C. of Burton-on-Trent 1850, St. Chad's, Shrewsbury, 1853; P. C. of Oxon, Salop, 1854. Author, *Letters on the Revision of the Prayer Book,* 1860; *The Powers of Convocation,* 1861; *Two Hundred Years Ago,* 1862. [14]

MOUSLEY, William, *Ashby Hall, near Welford, Rugby.*—Queens' Coll. Cam. Sen. Opt. and B.A. 1822, M.A. 1825; Deac. 1823 and Pr. 1824 by Bp of Pet. V. of Cold-Ashby, Dio. Pet. 1829. (Patron, the present V; Glebe, 119 acres; V.'s Inc. 230*l* and Ho; Pop. 446.) Formerly C. of Cold-Ashby 1823–29. Author, *Plain Sermons on some of the Leading Truths of the Gospel,* 1829, 5*s*; *Moral Strength, or the Nature and Conquest of Evil Habits considered,* 1843, 4*s*; *Contemplations on the Redeemer's Grace and Glory,* 1863, 2*s*. [15]

MOWATT, James, *Sidney College, Cambridge.*—Sid. Coll. Cam. B.A. 1858, M.A. 1861; Deac. 1859 and Pr. 1860 by Bp of Ely. Fell. and Cl. Lect. of Sid. Coll. Cam. Formerly Head Mast. of Qu. Elizabeth's Sch. Ipswich. [16]

MOXON, Charles St. Denys, *Hempton Parsonage, Fakenham, Norfolk.*—Emman. Coll. Cam. 1st cl. Law Trip. B.C.L. 1850; Deac. 1850 and Pr. 1851 by Bp of Nor. P. C. of Hempton, Dio. Nor. 1856. (Patron, the Crown; P. C.'s Inc. 95*l* and Ho; Pop. 459.) R. of Pudding Norton, Dio. Nor. 1864. (Patron, A. W. Biddulph, Esq; Pop. 17.) Formerly C. of Fakenham. Author, *Introduction to Mineralogy,* 3*s* 6*d*; *The Characteristic Fossils of British Strata,* 12*s*. Editor of *Ray's Wisdom of God in Creation; Ray's Miscellaneous Discourses; Werner's External Character of Minerals* (Wernerian Club). [17]

MOYLE, Vyvyan Henry, *North Ormesby, Middlesborough, Yorks.*—Pemb. Coll. Ox; Deac. 1859, Pr. 1862. C. in sole charge of Ormesby 1863. Formerly C. of Coatham, Redcar, 1859. [18]

MOYSEY, Frederick Luttrell.—Ch. Ch. Ox. B.A. 1838, M.A. 1861; Deac. 1836 by Bp of Ox. Pr. 1848 by Bp of B. and W. Formerly Asst. C. of Trinity, Bath, 1838; Asst. Min. of Margaret's Chap. Bath, 1839; V. of Combe St. Nicholas, Somerset, 1840–61, V. of Shilmouth, Devon, 1861–65. [19]

MOZLEY, Arthur, *Emmanuel Hospital, Westminster, S.W.*—Oriel Coll. Ox. B.A. 1840, M.A. 1844; Deac. 1843 by Bp of Wor. Pr. 1844 by Bp of Lich. Mast. of Emmanuel Hospital, Westminster, 1859. Formerly Asst. Mast. King Edward's Sch. Birmingham; C. of Eckington 1841–49, Hingham 1849–55, St. Gabriel's, Pimlico, 1855–59. [20]

MOZLEY, James Bowling, *Old Shoreham Vicarage, Sussex.*—Oriel Coll. Ox. 3rd cl. Lit. Hum. and B.A. 1834. M.A. 1838, B.D. 1846; Deac. 1838 and Pr. 1844 by Bp of Ox. V. of Old Shoreham, Dio. Chich. 1856. (Patron, Magd. Coll. Ox; Tithe—Imp. 310*l* 9*s*, V. 155*l* 4*s* 1*d*; V.'s Inc. 430*l* and Ho; Pop. 282.) Author, *Treatise on the Augustinian Doctrine of Predestination,* Murray, 1855; *The Primitive Doctrine of Baptismal Regeneration,* ib. 1856; *Review of the Baptismal Controversy,* Rivingtons, 1862; *Bampton Lectures on*

Miracles, Rivingtons, 1865; *Subscription to the Articles, a Letter to Professor Stanley*, Parkers, 1863; *Observations on the Colonial Church Question*, Rivingtons, 1867. [1]

MUCKLESTON, Edward, *Haseley Rectory, Warwick.*—Wor. Coll. Ox. M.A; Deac. and Pr. by Bp of Lich. R. of Haseley, Dio. Wor. 1865. (Patron, William Lyon, Esq; Tithe, 200*l*; Glebe, 100*l*; R.'s Inc. 300*l* and Ho; Pop. 209.) [2]

MUCKLESTON, John, *Lichfield.*—Ch. Ch. Ox. 2nd cl. Lit. Hum; Deac. 1823 and Pr. 1824 by Bp of Lich. P. C. of Wichnor, Dio. Lich. 1832. (Patron, T. J. Levett, Esq; Glebe, 50 acres; P. C.'s Inc. 67*l*; Pop. 152.) [3]

MUCKLESTON, Rowland, *Dinedor, Hereford.*—Wor. Coll. Ox. Open Foundation Scho. 1831, 1st cl. Lit. Hum. and B.A. 1833, M.A. 1836. Fell. of Wor. Coll. 1836; Deac. and Pr. 1837 by Bp of Ox. R. of Dinedor, Dio. Herf. 1855. (Patron, Wor. Coll. Ox; Tithe—App. 64*l* 4*s*, Imp. 28*l*, R. 276*l* 11*s*; R.'s Inc. 389*l*; Pop. 270.) Formerly Tut. and Vice-Provost of Wor. Coll. Ox; Mast. of the Sch. 1838; Public Examiner in Cl. 1847; Moderator 1854; twice Public Examiner for the Univ. Latin Scholarships. [4]

MUDGE, William, *Pertenhall Rectory (Beds), near Kimbolton.*—Queens' Coll. Cam. B.A. 1823; Deac. 1823, Pr. 1824. R. of Pertenhall, Dio. Ely, 1842. (Patron, John Beedham, Esq; Tithe, 30*l* 7*s* 6*d*; Glebe, 280 acres; R.'s Inc. 315*l* and Ho; Pop. 404.) Author, *Thirty Sermons*, 2 eds. 7*s* 6*d*; *Sixteen Discourses on the Tabernacle of Moses*, 2 eds. 5*s*; *A Country Clergyman's Advice to his Flock*, 2*s* 6*d*; *Goodness and Mercy*, R.T.S; *Suggestions on Scripture Interpretation*, 9*d*; *Popery a Trap and a Snare to Unwary Protestants* (a Tract), Brit. Ref. Soc; *An Essay on Missions*, Nisbet, 1*s* 6*d*. [5]

MUDRY, John, 7, *Clifton road, St. John's Wood, London, N.W.*—Deac. 1811, Pr. 1812. Min. of the French Episcopal Ch. Bloomsbury, Dio. Lon. 1845. (Patrons, Trustees; Min's Inc. 100*l* and Ho.) [6]

MULCASTER, John Scott, *Great Salkeld Rectory, Penrith.*—Dub. A.B. 1834, A.M. 1837; Deac. 1834 and Pr. 1835 by Bp of Carl. R. of Great Salkeld, Dio. Carl. 1855. (Patron, Bp of Carl; Tithe—App. 315*l*; R.'s Inc. 346*l* and Ho; Pop. 502.) Formerly Asst. C. of Greystoke, Cumberland, 1836–55. [7]

MULCASTER, Richard, *Ulverston.*—Dur. B.A. 1853, M.A. 1867; Deac. 1854 and Pr. 1855 by Bp of Carl. C. of Ulverston 1866. Formerly C. of Grinsdale, Cumberland. [8]

MULES, Charles Marwood Speke, *Curry-Rivell Vicarage, Taunton.*—King's Coll. Lond; Deac. 1862 and Pr. 1863 by Bp of S. and M. V. of Curry-Rivell with Weston C. Dio. B. and W. 1864. (Patron, William Speke, Esq; V.'s Inc. 310*l* and Ho; Pop. 1287.) Formerly C. of Kirk Michael, Isle of Man. [9]

MULES, C. O., *Whorlton, Durham.*—C. of Whorlton. [10]

MULES, Francis, *Bittadon, Barnstaple, Devon.*—R. of Bittadon, Dio. Ex. 1842. (Patron, William A. Yoe, Esq; Tithe, 72*l*; Glebe, 23 acres; R.'s Inc. 102*l*; Pop. 65.) [11]

MULES, F. H., *Romford, Essex.*—C. of Romford. [12]

MULES, James, *Mayland, near Maldon, Essex.*—Trin. Hall, Cam. Coll. Prizeman 1814, 1st cl. Law Trip. and LL.B. 1816; Deac. 1816 by Bp of B. and W. Pr. 1818 by Bp of Ex. C. of Mayland. Formerly C. of West Wratting, Cambs. [13]

MULES, John Hawkes, *Moulton Rectory, Long Stratton, Norfolk.*—Trin. Coll. Cam. B.A. 1839; Deac. 1838, Pr. 1839. R. of Great Moulton, Dio. Nor. 1865. (Patron, W. L. Chute, Esq; Tithe, 460*l*; Glebe, 23 acres; R.'s Inc. 500*l* and Ho; Pop. 460.) Formerly V. of Payhembury, Devon. [14]

MULES, Philip, *Belvoir Castle, Grantham.*—Brasen. Coll. Ox. B.A. 1836, Ex. Coll. M.A. 1839, B.D. 1851; Deac. 1838 and Pr. 1839 by Bp of Ox. Dom. Chap. to the Duke of Rutland. Formerly Fell. of Ex. Coll. Ox; Exam. Chap. to the Bp of Gibraltar 1842–47 [15]

MULLENEUX, William, *Landfield House, Waterloo, near Liverpool.*—Emman. Coll. Cam. B.A. 1843, M.A. 1849; Deac. 1843, Pr. 1844. [16]

MULLENS, George Oakman, *Chedzoy Rectory, Bridgwater, Somerset.*—Jesus Coll. Cam. B.A. 1852, M.A. 1855; Deac. 1853 and Pr. 1854 by Bp of Lin. R. of Chedzoy, Dio. B. and W. 1855. (Patron, the present R; Tithe—App. 2*l*, R. 385*l* 5*s*; Glebe, 29 acres; R.'s Inc. 405*l* and Ho; Pop. 442.) [17]

MULLENS, Richard Herbert, *Acton Turville, Chippenham.*—Jesus Coll. Cam. B.A. 1858, M.A. 1861; Deac. 1859 and Pr. 1860 by Bp of Ely. C. of Acton Turville 1865. Formerly C. of Monk's Eleigh, Suffolk, 1859–62, Huish, Devon, 1863–64. [18]

MULLER, J. S., *Norwich.*—Min. Can. of Nor. 1865. Formerly C. of Great Chart, Kent, 1864. [19]

MULLER, Theodor, *Selworthy, Minehead, Somerset.*—Univ. of Basle, Switzerland; Deac. and Pr. 1840. R. of Selworthy, Dio. B. and W. 1864. (Patron, Sir T. Dyke Acland, Bart; Tithe, 270*l*; Glebe, 59 acres; R.'s Inc. 300*l* and Ho; Pop. 434.) Formerly Miss. of the Ch. Miss. Soc. in Egypt and Palestine 1825–36; Chap. to the Niger Expedition 1841–43, V. of Morebath, Devon, 1852–64. [20]

MULLINS, George Henry, *Uppingham, Rutland.*—Brasen. Coll. Ox. Hon. 4th cl. Lit. Hum. et Math. B.A. 1859, M.A. 1862; Deac. 1862 and Pr. 1863 by Bp of Ox. Asst. Mast. in Uppingham Sch. Formerly C. of St. Philip and St. James's, Oxford, 1862–64. [21]

MUNBY, George Frederick Woodhouse, *Church Missionary College, Islington, London, N.*—Trin. Coll. Cam. B.A. 1856, M.A. 1859, *ad eund.* Ox. 1860; Deac. 1856 and Pr. 1857 by Bp of Lon. Tut. at the Ch. Miss. Coll. Islington, 1856. [22]

MUNBY, John Pigott, *Hovingham, New Malton, Yorks.*—Lin. Coll. Ox. B.A. 1833. P. C. of Hovingham, Dio. York, 1842. (Patron, Earl of Carlisle; Tithe, Imp. 65*l* 8*s*; P. C.'s Inc. 105*l*; Pop. 1208.) [23]

MUNBY, Joseph Edwin, *Leeds.*—Trin. Coll. Cam. B.A. 1862, M.A. 1865; Deac. 1863 and Pr. 1865 by Bp of Rip. C. of Leeds 1866. Formerly C. of Masham, Yorks, 1863–66. [24]

MUNDY, Thomas Browning, *Wolverhampton.*—Dur. B.A. 1852, M.A. 1855; Deac. 1855 and Pr. 1856 by Bp of Lich. C. of St. Peter's, Wolverhampton. [25]

MUNFORD, George, *East Winch, Lynn-Regis, Norfolk.*—Magd. Hall, Ox. 1818; Deac. 1820 and Pr. 1823 by Bp of Nor. V. of East Winch, Dio. Nor. 1849. (Patron, G. Edwards, Esq; Tithe—Imp. 3*l* 10*s*, V. 184*l*; Glebe, 22 acres; V.'s Inc. 212*l* and Ho; Pop. 434.) Author, *An Analysis of the Domesday Book of the County of Norfolk*, J. R. Smith, 1858; etc. [26]

MUNGEAM, William Martin, 6, *Anchor-terrace, Bridge-street, Southwark, London, S.E.*—St. John's Coll. Cam. B.A. 1837; Deac. 1837 and Pr. 1838 by Abp of Cant. P. C. of St. Peter's, Southwark, Dio. Win. 1848. (Patrons, Hyndman's Trustees; P. C.'s Inc. 235*l*; Pop. 5044.) One of the five Readers of Ch. Ch. Newgate-street, Lond. 1842. (Value, 8*l*.) Formerly Chap. of the Queen's Prison, Southwark, 1844–48. [27]

MUNN, George Shaw, *Madresfield Rectory, near Worcester.*—Trin. Coll. Ox. B.A 1842, M.A. 1845; Deac. 1843, Pr. 1844. R. of Madresfield, Dio. Wor. 1857. (Patron, Earl Beauchamp; R.'s Inc. 250*l* and Ho; Pop. 271.) [28]

MUNN, Henry, *Liddington, Swindon, Wilts.*—Emman. Coll. Cam. Wrang. and B.A. 1850, M.A. 1853; Deac. 1850, Pr. 1851. R. of Liddington, Dio. G. and B. 1862. (Patron, Duke of Marlborough; R.'s Inc. 350*l* and Ho; Pop. 440.) Formerly C. of Edmonton. [29]

MUNN, John Read, *Ashburnham Vicarage, Battle, Sussex.*—Wor. Coll. Ox. B.A. 1830; Deac. 1830 and Pr. 1831 by Bp of Chich. V. of Ashburnham with Penhurst R. Dio. Chich. 1840. (Patron, Earl of Ashburnham; Ashburnham, Tithe, 265*l*; Glebe, 6 acres; Penhurst, Tithe, 156*l*; Glebe, 60 acres; V.'s Inc. 465*l* and Ho; Pop. Ashburnham 844, Penhurst 105.) [30]

MUNRO, H. A. J.—Sen. Fell. of Trin. Coll. Cam. [31]

MURDOCH, Edward Sloane, 78, *Maudland Bank, Preston.*—Dub. A.B. 1858; Deac. 1858 by Bp of Killaloe, Pr. 1858 by Bp of Kilmore. C. of Emmanuel District, Preston, 1866. Formerly C. of St. Peter's, Preston, 1863. [1]

MURIEL, Edward Morley, *Ruckinge Rectory, Ashford, Kent.*—Caius Coll. Cam. B.A. 1843, M.A. 1846; Deac. and Pr. 1847. R. of Ruckinge, Dio. Cant. 1861. (Patron, Abp of Cant; R.'s Inc. 300*l* and Ho; Pop. 429.) Formerly C. of Sandhurst and Newenden, Kent. [2]

MURIEL, William C., *Debden Rectory, Saffron Walden.*—St. Peter's Coll. Cam. B.A. 1862; Deac. 1862 and Pr. 1863 by Bp of Lich. R. of Debden, Dio. Roch. 1867. (Patron, Sir Francis Vincent; Tithe, 960*l*; Glebe, 54 acres; R.'s Inc. 1082*l* and Ho; Pop. 942.) Formerly C. of Sheen, near Ashbourne, 1862–64; Chap. of High Legh, Cheshire, 1864–67. [3]

MURPHY, Joseph Patrick, *West Cliffe, Preston.*—Dub. A.B. 1851, LL.B. 1854; Deac. 1851, Pr. 1852. Chap. of the Preston House of Correction 1857. (Salary, 300*l*.) Formerly C. of St. George's, Sutton, Macclesfield, 1851, Trinity, Preston, 1854, Preston 1855. [4]

MURRAY, David Rodney, *Brampton Bryan (Herefordshire), near Shrewsbury.*—Ch. Ch. Ox. B.A. 1814. R. of Brampton Bryan, Dio. Herf. 1826. (Patron, Earl of Oxford; Tithe—Imp. 159*l*, R. 345*l*; Glebe, 16 acres; R.'s Inc. 375*l*; Pop. 430.) R. of Cusop, Herefordshire, near Hay, Brecknockshire, Dio. Herf. (Patron, Earl of Oxford; Tithe, 210*l*; R.'s Inc. 220*l*; Pop. 218.) V. of Beedon, near Newbury, Berks, Dio. Ox. 1828. (Patron, Sir J. Reade, Bart; Tithe—Imp. 30*l*, V. 146*l* 2*s*; Glebe, 28½ acres; V.'s Inc. 176*l*; Pop. 317.) [5]

MURRAY, Edward Albert, 24, *Upper Gloucester-place, Dorset-square, London, N.W.*—Trin. Coll. Cam. B.A. 1863; Deac. 1864 and Pr. 1865 by Bp of Lon. Formerly C. of St. Paul's, Lisson-grove, 1864, St. John's, Stratford, Essex, 1865; Acting British Consular Chap. at Oporto 1866–67. [6]

MURRAY, Francis Henry, *Chislehurst, Bromley, Kent, S.E.*—Ch. Ch. Ox. 3rd cl. Lit. Hum. and B.A. 1841, M.A. 1845; Deac. 1843 by Bp of Ox. Pr. 1844 by Bp of Wor. R. of Chislehurst, Dio. Cant. 1846. (Patron, Bp of Wor; Tithe, comm. 575*l*; Glebe, 14 acres; R.'s Inc. 600*l* and Ho; Pop. 1311.) Author, *Devotions for the Seasons of the Christian Year*, Masters, 3*s* 6*d* per 100; *Catena of Authorities upon the Altar and the Eucharistic Sacrifice*, ib. 1*s* 6*d*; *Prayers for Parochial Schools*, ib. 6*d*; *Form of Self-Examination*, ib. 3*d*. [7]

MURRAY, Frederick William, *Stone Rectory, Dartford, Kent.*—Ch. Ch. Ox. B.A. 1851, M.A. 1855; Deac. 1854 and Pr. 1855 by Bp of Roch. R. of Stone, Dio. Roch. 1859. (Patron, Bp of Roch; Tithe, 932*l*; Glebe, 6 acres; R.'s Inc. 938*l* and Ho; Pop. 824.) Formerly R. of Leigh, Essex, 1856–59. [8]

MURRAY, George, *Dedham Vicarage, Colchester.*—V. of Dedham, Dio. Roch. 1854. (Patron, Duchy of Lancaster; V.'s Inc. 200*l* and Ho; Pop. 1734.) [9]

MURRAY, George William, *Bromsgrove Vicarage, Worcestershire.*—Mert. Coll. Ox. B.A. 1830, M.A. 1834; Deac. 1830, Pr. 1831. V. of Bromsgrove, Dio. Wor. 1861. (Patrons, D. and C. of Wor; Tithe, App. 1227*l* and 75 acres of Glebe, V. 1101*l*; Glebe, 2 acres; V.'s Inc. 1105*l* and Ho; Pop. 7553.) Chap. of the Bromsgrove Union. Formerly R. of Handsworth, Staffs, 1848–61; Rural Dean; Proctor for the Dio. of Lich. [10]

MURRAY, George William, *Shrivenham Vicarage, Berks.*—Queen's Coll. Ox. B.A. 1850, M.A. 1853; Deac. 1851 and Pr. 1852 by Bp of Win. V. of Shrivenham with Watchfield C. Dio. Ox. 1859. (Patron, Ld Chan; V.'s Inc. 600*l* and Ho; Pop. Shrivenham 1135, Watchfield 431.) Surrogate; Chap. to the Earl of Cork and Orrery. Formerly R. of Welton-le-Wold, Lincolnshire. [11]

MURRAY, Henry, *Colney Hatch, Herts.*—Chap. of the Co. Lunatic Asylum, Colney Hatch. [12]

MURRAY, James, *North Walsham, Norfolk.*—Dub. A.B. 1847, A.M. 1862; Deac. 1847 and Pr. 1848 by Bp of Ches. V. of North Walsham and R. of Antingham St. Margaret, Dio. Nor. 1854. (Patron, Bp of Nor; Tithe, 420*l*; Glebe, 2 acres; V.'s Inc. 455*l* and Ho; Pop. 2865.) Surrogate. Formerly C. of Tintwistle, Manchester, 1847; C. in sole charge of St. Stephen's, Norwich, 1849–51; P. C. of St. Giles's, Norwich, 1850–54. [13]

MURRAY, Jeffreys Wilkins, *St. John's, Truro, Cornwall.*—Oriel Coll. Ox. B.A. 1844, M.A. 1848; Deac. 1845 by Bp of Herf. Pr. 1846 by Bp of Lich. P. C. of St. John's, Kenwyn, Dio. Ex. 1865. (Patron, V. of St. Kenwyn; P. C.'s Inc. 164*l*; Pop. 2600.) Formerly C. of Ashton-Eyre, Salop, 1845; P. C. of Llandilo-Graban 1847; C. of St. Mary's, Reading, 1848, St. Mary's, Truro, 1854, Gwithian, Cornwall, 1857, St. Kea 1857. Author, *Baptism, Confirmation, Holy Communion*, 1858, 4*d*; *A Comparative Scale of Creation according to Mosaic Records and Geological Facts*, 1861, 1*s* 6*d*; *Gerennius*, 1*s*; *The Doctrine of the Incarnation as affecting the Natural History of Man* (a Sermon preached before the University of Oxford), 1863, 1*s*. [14]

MURRAY, John, *Wickhambrook, Newmarket.*—Sid. Coll. Cam. B.A. 1833; Deac. 1855 and Pr. 1856 by Bp of Ely. C. of Wickhambrook, Suffolk. [15]

MURRAY, John, *Hartington, Ashbourne, Derbyshire.*—Dub. A.B. 1850; Deac. 1851 and Pr. 1852 by Bp of Lich. P. C. of Biggin, Dio. Lich. 1865. (Patron, Duke of Devonshire; Glebe, 1 acre; P. C.'s Inc. 130*l* and Ho; Pop. 399.) Formerly P. C. of Marazion, Cornwall, 1857–64. [16]

MURRAY, John, *Reading.*—Caius Coll. Cam. B.A. 1850; Deac. 1850 and Pr. 1851 by Bp of Ex. C. of St. Giles's, Reading, 1863. Formerly C. of Stoke Climsland, Cornwall, 1850, Broughton, Oxon, 1853, Banbury, 1854; V. of Wroxton and Balscott 1854–63; Dioc. Inspector of Schs. 1853. [17]

MURRAY, John Hale, *Bridgwater, Somerset.*—Wor. Coll. Ox. B.A. 1832. C. of Trinity, Bridgwater. Formerly Min. of St. Mary Magdalene's Chapel, Holloway, Bath. [18]

MURRAY, William, *St. John's Parsonage, Sheffield.*—Dub. A.B. 1849; Deac. 1849 and Pr. 1850 by Bp of Lich. C. of St. John's, Sheffield, 1865. Formerly C. of Fenton, Staffs, 1849, Malborough and South Huish, Devon, 1852, Sherford, Devon, 1865. [19]

MURTON, William, *Sutton, Peterborough.*—St. John's Coll. Cam. Jun. Opt. and B A. 1844, M.A. 1847; Deac. 1845, Pr. 1846. P. C. of Sutton, Dio. Pet. 1851. (Patron, Bp of Pet; Tithe, App. 194*l* 9*s* 5*d*; Glebe, 22 acres; P. C.'s Inc. 210*l*; Pop. 112.) [20]

MUSCROFT, James Wilson, *Barnsley, Yorks.*—Ch. Coll. Cam. B.A. 1861, M.A. 1865; Theol. Coll. Lichfield 1862; Deac. 1863 by Bp of Win. Pr. 1864 by Bp of Lich. C. of Worsborough Dale, Yorks, 1867. Formerly C. of Colwick and Even. Lect. at Rugeley, Staffs, 1863–66; C. of St. George's, Barnsley, 1866–67. [21]

MUSGRAVE, The Ven. Charles, *Halifax Vicarage, Yorks.*—Trin. Coll. Cam. 10th Wrang. B.A. 1814, M.A. 1817, B.D. 1830, D.D. 1837; Deac. 1817 by Bp of Ely, Pr. 1817 by Bp of Nor. V. of Halifax, Dio. Rip. 1827. (Patron, the Crown; V.'s Inc. 1804*l* and Ho; Pop. 46,965.) Preb. of Givendale in York Cathl. 1833. (Value, 45*l* 1*s*.) Archd. of Craven 1836. (Value, 200*l*.) Formerly Fell. of Trin. Coll. Cam; V. of Whitkirk, Leeds, 1821. Author, several Sermons and Charges. [22]

MUSGRAVE, George, *Shillington Manor, Beds,* and *Borden Hall, Kent,* and *Sussex-gardens, Hyde Park, London, W.*—Brasen. Coll. Ox. 2nd cl. Lit. Hum. B.A. 1819, M.A. 1822; Deac. 1822 and Pr. 1823 by Bp of Lon. Impropriator of R. of Borden, Kent, 550*l*. Formerly C. of St. Michael and St. Mary Steyning, Lond. 1822–23, All Souls', Langham-place, 1824, Marylebone 1826–29; R. of Bexwell, Norfolk, 1835–38; V. of Borden, Kent, 1838–54. Author, *Translations from Tasso and Petrarch*, 1822; *The Book of Psalms, in Blank Verse, from the Hebrew Psalter*, Rivingtons, 1833; *Plain and Simple Instruction for the Rural Poor*, ib. 1843; *Difficulties Explained for Cottage Readers*, ib. 1844; *The Crow-*

keeper; *or, Thoughts in the Fields*, Rivingtons, 1847; *The Parson, Pen, and Pencil*, *A Tour in France*, Bentley, 1848; *Rambles in Normandy*, Bogue, 1855; *Hymns for Agricultural Congregations*, Rivingtons, 1856; *A Pilgrimage into Dauphiné*, Hurst and Blackett, 1857; *Byroads and Battle-fields in Picardy*, Bell and Daldy, 1861; *Cautions to Tourists on Impositions and Indecencies, by Viator Verax*, Ridgway, 1863; *Ten Days in a French Parsonage*, S. Low, Son, and Marston, 1864; *The Odyssey of Homer* (translated from the Original Greek), *in English Blank Verse*, 2 vols. Bell and Daldy, 1865; *Nooks and Corners in Old France*, Hurst and Blackett, 1867; *Vice-Presidential Lectures at Institutes—On the Races of Mankind*; *on France*; *on the Relation of Music to Design*; *on the Customs and Manners of the Ancient Egyptians*; *Sermons*; etc. 1852–60. [1]

MUSGRAVE, Vernon, *Hascombe Rectory, Godalming, Surrey.*—Trin. Coll. Cam. Jun. Opt. and B.A. 1853, M.A. 1856, Theol. Coll. Wells; Deac. 1854 and Pr. 1855 by Bp of Chich. R. of Hascombe, Dio. Win. 1862. (Patron, E. Tompson, Esq; R.'s Inc. 180*l* and Ho; Pop. 396.) Formerly V. of Mattersey, Notts, 1855–62. [2]

MUSGRAVE, Sir William Augustus, Bart., *Chinnor Rectory, Tetsworth, Oxon.*—Ch. Ch. Ox. B.A. 1812, M.A. 1815; Deac. 1814 and Pr. 1815 by Bp of Glouc. R. of Chinnor, Dio. Ox. 1816. (Patron, the present R; Tithe, App. 51*l* 15*s*, Imp. 1*l* 2*s*, R. 509*l*; Glebe, 11 acres; R.'s Inc. 520*l* and Ho; Pop. 1296.) R. of Emmington, Oxon, Dio. Ox. 1827. (Patron, P. T. Wykeman, Esq; Tithe, 160*l*; Glebe, 2 acres; R.'s Inc. 162*l* and Ho; Pop. 88.) [3]

MUSGRAVE, William Peete, *Etton Rectory, Beverley, Yorks.*—Trin. Coll. Cam. 1st Sen. Opt. and B.A. 1835, M.A. 1838; Deac. 1837 by Bp of Ely, Pr. 1838 by Bp of Herf. Can. Res. and Preb. Episcopi of Herf. Cathl. 1844. (Value, 587*l* 19*s* 10*d* and Res.) R. of Etton, Dio. York, 1854. (Patron, Abp of York; Corn-rent, 636*l*; Glebe, 40 acres; R.'s Inc. 700*l* and Ho; Pop. 502.) Formerly C. of Trumpington, Cambs, 1837–40; I of Eaton Bishop, Herefordshire, 1841–54. [4]

MUSKETT, H. J., *Clippesby House, Norwich.*—St. Peter's Coll. Cam. B.A. 1843, M.A. 1846; Deac. 1843 and Pr. 1845 by Bp of Nor. R. of Clippesby, Dio. Nor. 1860. (Patron, the present R; Tithe, comm. 246*l* 11*s*; Glebe, 3 acres; R.'s Inc. 250*l*; Pop. 97.) [5]

MUSSELWHITE, Thomas Ralph, *West Mersea, Colchester.*—Magd. Hall, Ox. B.A. 1850; Deac. 1850, Pr. 1851. V. of West Mersea, Dio. Roch. 1863. (Patron, T. May, Esq; V.'s Inc. 231*l*; Pop. 944.) Surrogate. Formerly C. of Trentham, Staffs, and Aston-in-Edgmond, Salop; R. of St. Andrew's, Aston, Salop. [6]

MUSSON, Francis, *Haley Hill, Halifax.*—St. Bees 1851; Deac. 1853 and Pr. 1854 by Bp of Rip. C. of Haley Hill. Formerly C. of Elland, and Chap. to the Halifax Union. [7]

MUSSON, Spencer C., *Stapleford, near Cambridge.*—C. of Stapleford. [8]

MYDDELTON, Thomas, *East Ferry, Scotton, Lincolnshire.*—Sid. Coll. Cam. B.A. 1840; Deac. 1841 and Pr. 1842 by Bp of Lin. C. of Scotton. Formerly C. of Wildsworth, Linc. [9]

MYDDELTON-EVANS, John, *Pitsford, Northants.*—Ex. Coll. Ox. B.A. 1859, M.A. 1862; Wells Theol. Coll; Deac. 1860 and Pr. 1861 by Bp of B. and W. C. of Pitsford 1866. Formerly C. of Ilminster, Somerset, and Sibbertoft, Northants. [10]

MYERS, Alfred, *All Saints Parsonage, Stonebridge, Kingsland, London, N.E.*—Deac. 1844 and Pr. 1845 by Bp of Lon. P. C. of All Saints', Shoreditch, Dio. Lon. 1856. (Patron, Bp of Lon; P. C.'s Inc. 500*l* and Ho; Pop. 5930.) Formerly P. C. of Ch. Ch. Barnet, 1844–53. [11]

MYERS, Alfred Joseph, *Deptford, Kent, S.E.*—C. of St. John's, Deptford. [12]

MYERS, Charles John, *Flintham Vicarage, Newark, Notts*, and *Dunningwell, Millom, Broughton-in-Furness, Cumberland.*—Trin. Coll. Cam. 5th Wrang. B.A. 1823, M.A. 1826; Deac. and Pr. 1829. V. of Flintham, Dio. Lin. 1829. (Patron, Trin. Coll. Cam; V.'s Inc. 365*l* and Ho; Pop. 524.) R. of the 1st Mediety of Ruskington, Linc. Dio. Lin. 1832. (Patron, the present R; R.'s Inc. 400*l*; Pop. 1089.) Formerly Fell. of Trin. Coll. Cam. 1825–29. Author, *Elementary Treatise on the Differential Calculus*, 1827, 2*s* 6*d*. [13]

MYERS, Thomas, *Trinity Rectory, Minster-yard, York.*—Trin. Coll. Cam. Hulsean Prizeman 1829. 1st Sen. Opt. and B.A. 1830, Norrisian Prizeman 1832 and 1834, M.A. 1833; Deac. 1832, Pr. 1833. R. of Trinity Goodramgate with St. John Delpike R. and St. Maurice V. City and Dio. York, 1857. (Patron, Abp of York; R.'s Inc. 250*l* and Ho; Pop. Trinity Goodramgate 431, St. John Delpike 2573, St. Maurice 428.) Preacher at York Castle. Formerly V. of Sheriff-Hutton, New York, 1848–57. Author, *The Hulsean Prize for* 1829, 2*s* 6*d*; *The Norrisian Essays for* 1832–34, 5*s*; *Advent Sermons* (preached before the Univ. of Cam.) 1843, 5*s*; Translator of *Ezekiel and Daniel, with Calvin's Comments*, 1849–52, 4 vols. 25*s*, Pitcairn, Edinburgh. [14]

MYERS, Thomas, *Auckland St. Andrew, Durham.*—Trin. Coll. Cam. B.A. 1858; Deac. 1858 by Bp of G. and B. C. of Auckland St. Andrew. [15]

MYLIUS, Frederick Henry, *Elmdon Rectory, Birmingham.*—St. Cath. Coll. Cam. LL.B. 1859; Deac. 1857 and Pr. 1859 by Bp of Wor. R. of Elmdon, Dio. Wor. 1863. (Patron, G. F. I. Lillingstone, Esq; Tithe, 200*l*; Rent from Glebe, 40*l*; R.'s Inc. 240*l* and Ho; Pop. 206.) Formerly an Officer in the Army 1845–54; C. of Ch. Ch. Birmingham, 1857–58; St. George's, Edgbaston, 1858–64. [16]

MYNORS, Edmund Baskerville, *Ashley Rectory, Tetbury, Wilts.*—St. Mary Hall, Ox. B.A. 1845, M.A. 1848; Deac. 1848 and Pr. 1849 by Bp of Herf. R. of Ashley, Dio. G. and B. 1863. (Patron, Duchy of Lancaster; R.'s Inc. 220*l* and Ho; Pop. 90.) Formerly C. of East and West Cranmore, Somerset. [17]

MYNORS, Thomas Hassall, *St. Patrick's Parsonage, Hockley Heath, Warwickshire.*—Wad. Coll. Ox. B.A. 1842; Deac. 1842, Pr. 1843. P. C. of St. Patrick's, Dio. Wor. 1847. (Patron, V. of Tanworth; Glebe, 40 acres; P. C.'s Inc. 150*l* and Ho; Pop. 1142.) [18]

MYNORS, Walter Baskerville, *Llanwarne Rectory, Ross, Herefordshire.*—Oriel Coll. Ox. B.A. 1850. R. of Llanwarne, Dio. Herf. 1855. (Patron, the present R; Tithe—App. 17*l* 6*s*, Imp. 106*l* 5*s*, R. 339*l* 4*s*; R.'s Inc. 359*l* and Ho; Pop. 383.) [19]

MYTTON, D. F. G., *Llandyssil, Montgomeryshire.* [20]

NADIN, Joseph, *The Parsonage, Crewe.*—St. Aidan's; Deac. 1850 and Pr. 1851 by Bp of Ches. P. C. of Crewe, Dio. Ches. 1858. (Patrons, Trustees; P. C.'s Inc. 300*l* and Ho; Pop. 12,000.) Surrogate. Formerly Min. of St. Mary's, Leamington, and Sec. to the Soc. for Irish Ch. Missions. Author, *Lectures on the Romish Controversy*. [21]

NAGLE, William, 1, *Blackheath-villas, Blackheath, Kent, S.E.*—Caius Coll. Cam. 1st Sen. Opt. B.A. 1839, M.A. 1842; Deac. 1840 by Bp of Lin. Pr. 1841 by Bp of Ox. P. C. of Bransgore, Dio. Win. 1867. (Patrons, Trustees; Glebe, 5 acres; P. C.'s Inc. 115*l* and Ho; Pop. 700.) Formerly C. of St. Leonard's, Wallingford, 1840–42; Chap. on the Madras Establishment 1842–61. [22]

NAIRNE, Spencer, *Hunsdon Rectory, Ware, Herts.*—Emman. Coll. Cam. Sen. Opt. B.A. 1856, M.A. 1859; Deac. 1856 and Pr. 1858 by Bp of Salis. R. of Hunsdon, Dio. Roch. 1861. (Patron, C. Phelips, Esq; Tithe, 280*l*; Glebe, 70*l*; R.'s Inc. 350*l* and Ho; Pop. 500.) Formerly C. of Trinity, Weymouth. [23]

NAISH, Thomas, *Sible Hedingham, Halstead, Essex.*—Lin. Coll. Ox. B.A. 1844; Deac. 1851 and Pr. 1852 by Bp of Chich. C. of Sible Hedingham 1865. Formerly C. of Surbiton. [24]

NALSON, Joshua, *Halling Vicarage, Rochester.*—Queens' Coll. Cam. B.A. 1834; Deac. 1838 by Bp of Win. Pr. 1844 by Bp of Ox. V. of Halling, Dio. Roch.

1852. (Patrons, D. and C. of Roch; Tithe—App. 243*l* 5*s* 7*d*, V. 152*l* 1*s* 4*d*; Glebe, 32 acres; V.'s Inc. 214*l* and Ho; Pop. 760.) [1]

NANKIVELL, John Robert, *Crediton, Devon.*—Ex. Coll. Ox; B.A. 1849, M.A. 1852; Deac. 1850 and Pr. 1851 by Bp of Ex. Chap. of Crediton 1867. Formerly C. of Thorverton 1850, Hulsh 1854; Chap. to Torbay and Dartmouth Mission to Seamen 1860. Author, *A Manual of Hymns and Prayers for Seamen* 1864, Granford, Brixham. [2]

NANNEY, Lewis M., *Caenby Rectory, Market Rasen, Lincolnshire.*—R. of Caenby, Dio. Lin. 1863. (Patron, Sir C. M. L. Monck, Bart; Tithe, 150*l*; Glebe, 61 acres; R.'s Inc. 350*l* and Ho; Pop. 125.) [3]

NANNEY, T. Middleton, *Saxby Vicarage, Market Rasen, Lincolnshire.*—V. of Saxby with Frisby R. Dio. Lin. 1863. (Patron, Earl of Scarborough; Tithe, Imp. 19*l* 10*s*; Glebe, 24 acres; V.'s Inc. 99*l* and Ho; Pop. Saxby 112, Frisby 108.) [4]

NANTES, Daniel, *Powderham Rectory, near Exeter.*—Trin. Coll. Cam. Sen. Opt. and B.A. 1817, M.A. 1820; Deac. 1818, Pr. 1819. R. of Powderham, Dio. Ex. 1825. (Patron, Earl of Devon; Tithe, 270*l*; Glebe, 93 acres; R.'s Inc. 515*l* and Ho; Pop. 238.) [5]

NANTES, William Hamilton, *East Stonehouse Parsonage, Plymouth*—Trin. Coll. Cam. B.A. 1834, M.A. 1844; Deac. 1834 and Pr. 1835 by Bp of Ex. P. C. of East Stonehouse, Dio. Ex. 1847. (Patron, V. of St. Andrew's, Plymouth; Tithe, 5*l*; Glebe, 17*l*; P. C.'s Inc. 250*l* and Ho; Pop. 15,000.) Formerly Asst. C. of Powderham, Devon, 1834–35; C. of Shipton George, Dorset, 1836–37, West and Middle Chinnock, Somerset, 1837–41, Bishops Caundle, Dorset, 1841–44; P. C. of St. Paul's, Jersey, 1844–47. [6]

NAPIER, Alexander, *Holkham Vicarage, Wells, Norfolk.*—Trin. Coll. Cam. B.A. 1838, M.A. 1847. V. of Holkham, Dio. Nor. 1847. (Patron, Earl of Leicester; Tithe—Imp. 400*l*, V. 200*l*; Glebe, 1 acre; V.'s Inc. 201*l* and Ho; Pop. 603.) R. of Egmere with Waterden R. near Walsingham, Dio. Nor. 1847. (Patron, Earl of Leicester; Egmere, Tithe, 24*l*; Waterden, Tithe, 194*l* 10*s*; Glebe, 18 acres; R.'s Inc. 211*l* and Ho; Pop. Egmere 56, Waterden 44.) [7]

NAPIER, Charles Walter Albin, *Wiston Rectory, Steyning, Sussex.*—Ch. Ch. Ox. B.A. 1839; Deac. 1841 by Bp of B. and W. Pr. 1842 by Bp of G. and B. R. of Wiston, Dio. Chich. 1850. (Patron, C. Goring, Esq; Tithe—Imp. 64*l*, R. 436*l*; Glebe, 3½ acres; R.'s Inc. 442*l* and Ho; Pop. 311.) [8]

NAPIER, The Hon. Henry Alfred, *Swyncombe Rectory, Henley-on-Thames.*—Ch. Ch. Ox. B.A. 1820, M.A. 1822; Deac. and Pr. 1821 by Bp of Ox. R. of Swyncombe, Dio. Ox. 1826. (Patron, Ld Chan; Tithe, 415*l*; R.'s Inc. 415*l* and Ho; Pop. 446.) Author, *Historical Notices of the Parishes of Swyncombe and Ewelme, Oxfordshire*, Oxford, 1858. [9]

NAPIER, John Warren, *Stretton Parsonage, Penkridge, Staffs.*—Trin. Coll. Cam. B.A. 1855; Deac. 1856 by Bp of B. and W. P. C. of Stretton, Dio. Lich. 1857. (Patron, Lord Hatherton; P. C.'s Inc. 73*l* and Ho; Pop. 273.) Formerly Asst. C. of Holy Trinity, Taunton. [10]

NAPLETON, John Charles, *All Saints Parsonage, Lower Marsh, Lambeth, London, S.*—Wor. Coll. Ox. B.A. 1833; Deac. 1833 and Pr. 1834 by Bp of Ox. P. C. of All Saints', Lambeth, Dio. Win. 1858. (Patron, P. C. of St. John's, Lambeth; P. C.'s Inc. 250*l*; Pop. 5452.) Formerly P. C. of Hatfield, near Leominster, 1844–58; Grendon-Bishop, Herf. 1849–58. Author, *Daily Service in the Cottage*, 3*d*; *Present Condition of the Working Classes*, 1855, 6*d*; *Infant Education* (a Sermon, Leominster), 6*d*; *The Acknowledgment of St. Paul by the Corinthians*, 1859. [11]

NAPPER, Campion, *Farlington, Easingwold, Yorks.*—St. Alban Hall, Ox. P. C. of Farlington with Marton P. C. Dio. York. (Patron, Abp of York; Farlington, Tithe—App. 209*l*, P. C. 94*l* 5*s*; Glebe, 7 acres; P. C.'s Inc. 146*l*; Pop. Farlington 174, Marton, 168.) [12]

NARES, Owen Alexander, *Letterston Rectory, Haverfordwest.*—Lampeter; Scho. and Prizeman; Deac. 1856 by Bp of Llan. Pr. 1857 by Bp of St. D. R. of Letterston with Llanfair-nant-y-Gof, 1865. (Patron, the Ld Chan; Tithe, Letterston 153*l*, Llanfair 143*l*; Glebe, Letterston 80 acres, Llanfair 22 acres; R.'s Inc. 460*l* and Ho; Pop. 720.) Formerly Min. Can of St. D.'s Cathl. 1856–59; V. of Warren with St. Twinels, Pembrokeshire, 1859–65. [13]

NARES, Robert, *Driffield, Yorks.*—St. John's Coll. Cam. B.A. 1854. Chap. of the Union and C. of Driffield. Formerly C. and Lect. of Great Torrington, and Chap. of the Torrington Union, Devon. [14]

NASH, Frederick Gifford, *Berden Parsonage, Bishop Stortford, Essex.*—Pemb. Coll. Cam. B.A. 1842, M.A. 1845; Deac. 1844, Pr. 1845. P. C. of Berden, Dio. Roch. 1851. (Patrons, Govs. of Christ's Hospital, Lond; Tithe—Imp. 360*l*, P. C. 150*l*; Glebe, 3 acres; P. C.'s Inc. 165*l* and Ho; Pop. 414.) [15]

NASH, George, *St. Michael's Parsonage, Louth, Lincolnshire.*—Dub. A.B. 1836, A.M. 1852; Deac. 1850 and Pr. 1851 by Bp of Rip. P. C. of St. Michael's, Louth, Dio. Lin. 1863. (Patron, R. of Louth; P. C.'s Inc. 200*l* and Ho; Pop. 2500.) Formerly C. of Bramley, Leeds, 1850, Weston, Notts, 1855. Author, *The Christian Priesthood a Reality*, 1861, Bell and Daldy. [16]

NASH, George Edward, *High Halstow, Rochester.*—V. of Allhallows-Hoo, near Rochester, Dio. Roch. 1836. (Patrons, D. and C. of Roch; Tithe, App. 660*l*, V. 276*l*; V.'s Inc. 276*l*; Pop. 236.) C. of High Halstow. [17]

NASH, George Lloyd, *Tolpuddle Vicarage, Dorchester.*—Ch. Ch. Ox. B.A. 1849, M.A. 1852; Deac. 1851, Pr. 1852. V. of Tolpuddle, Dio. Salis. 1852. (Patron, Ch. Ch. Ox; Tithe—App. 400*l* and 10 acres of Glebe; V.'s Inc. 250*l* and Ho; Pop. 461.) Rural Dean. [18]

NASH, Henry, 41, *Great Ormond street, Queen-square, W.C.*—Trin. Coll. Cam. B.A. 1865; Deac. 1866 by Bp of Lon. C. of St. George-the-Martyr, Bloomsbury, Lond. 1866. [19]

NASH, James, *Clifton, Bristol.*—Trin. Coll. Ox. B.A. 1830, M.A. 1833; Deac. 1831, Pr. 1832. P. C. of St. Peter's, Clifton-wood, Dio. G. and B. 1855. (Patrons, Simeon's Trustees; P. C.'s Inc. 90*l*; Pop. 2519.) [20]

NASH, James Palmer, *Old Alresford, Hants.*—Ch. Ch. Coll. Ox. B.A. 1865; Deac. 1866 by Bp of Win. Pr. 1867. C. of Old Alresford 1866. [21]

NASH, Nigel Fowler, *Newnham, Gloucestershire.*—Pemb. Coll. Ox. B.A. 1865; Deac. 1866 and Pr. 1867 by Bp of G. and B. C. of Newnham 1867. Formerly C. of Leckhampton 1866–67. [22]

NASH, Robert Seymour, *Old Sodbury Vicarage, Chippenham.*—Trin. Coll. Cam. Sen. Opt. B.A. 1844, M.A. 1847; Deac. 1845, Pr. 1846. V. of Old Sodbury, Dio. G. and B. 1856. (Patrons, D. and C. of Wor; V.'s Inc. 500*l* and Ho; Pop. 809.) Surrogate. Formerly C. of Stone, Wor. [23]

NASH, Thomas Augustus, *Oxford.*—Wor. Coll. Ox. B.A. 1859; Deac. 1860 and Pr. 1861 by Bp of Ox. C. of St. Aldate's, Oxford, 1860. [24]

NASH, William, *Belleau Rectory, Alford, Lincolnshire.*—Caius Coll. Cam. B.A. 1854; Deac. and Pr. 1855. R. of Belleau with Aby, Dio. Lin. 1861. (Patron, Lord Willoughby de Eresby; Tithe, 180*l*; Glebe, 170 acres; R.'s Inc. 380*l* and Ho; Pop. Belleau 214, Aby 407.) Formerly C. of Kilmahon 1855, St. Luke's, Berwick-street, 1858, and St. George's, Hanover-square, Lond. 1861. [25]

NASH, Zachary, *Christchurch, Hants.*—St. Cath. Coll. Cam. B.A. 1840, M.A. 1844; Deac. 1843 and Pr. 1844 by Bp of Lin. Sen. C. of Christchurch 1857; Surrogate. [26]

NATERS, Charles John, *Horspath, Oxford.*—Univ. Coll. Dur. Licen. Theol. 1859; Deac. 1859 by Bp of Lich. Pr. 1860 by Bp of Rip. Asst. C. of Horspath 1863. Formerly C. of Burley, Yorks, 1859, High Ercall, Salop, 1859–60, North Pickenham, Linc. 1860, Baldersley, near Thirsk, 1861, Horbury, near Wakefield, 1863. [27]

NATHAN, Henry, *Fishguard, Pembrokeshire.*—Lampeter; Deac. 1833 by Bp of Win. Pr. 1839 by Bp of St. D. R. of Jordanstone, Pembrokeshire, Dio. St. D. 1848. (Patrons, Sir James John Hamilton Bart., and Lady Hamilton; Tithe, 87*l*; Glebe, 6 acres; R's Inc. 105*l*; Pop. 139.) Formerly C. of Penmaen, Glamorganshire, 1834–39. Author, *A Sermon*, 1853. [1]

NAYLOR, Christopher, *Gloucester.*—2nd Mast. of St. Mary de Crypt Gr. Sch. Gloucester. [2]

NEALE, Edward P., *Horsey-next-the-Sea, Yarmouth, Norfolk.*—Trin. Coll. Cam. B.A. 1825, M.A. 1831; Deac. 1825, Pr. 1826. P. of Horsey-next-the Sea, Dio. Nor. 1857. (Patron, R. Rising, Esq. of Horsey; Tithe—Imp. 70*l* 1*s* 6*d*, V. 83*l* 1*s* 8*d*; Glebe, ½ acre; V.'s Inc. 160*l* and Ho; Pop. 206.) Formerly C. of Chelmondiston, Suffolk. Author, *Seven Lectures on the History of Gideon*, 1843, 2*s* 6*d*. [3]

NEALE, Erskine, *Exning Vicarage, Newmarket.*—Emman. Coll. Cam. B.A. 1828, M.A. 1832; Deac. 1829, Pr. 1830. V. of Exning with Lanwade C. Dio. Ely, 1854. (Patrons, D. and C. of Cant; Glebe, 240 acres; V.'s Inc. 450*l* and Ho; Pop. Exning 1348, Lanwade 36.) Dom. Chap. to the Earl of Huntingdon, Formerly V. of Allingfleet, Yorks, and R. of Kirton, Suffolk. Author, *The Closing Scene*; *Life of the Duke of Kent*; *The Bishop's Daughter*; *The Life Book of a Labourer*; *The Old Minor Canon*; *The Earthly Resting Places of the Just*; *The Dangers and Duties of a Christian*; *Reasons for Supporting the S.P.G.* [4]

NEALE, Frederick, *Wootton Vicarage, near Bedford.*—St. Alban Hall, Ox. B.A. 1850, M.A. 1853. V. of Wootton, Dio. Ely, 1852. (Patroness, Miss Esther Maria Neale; Tithe, 8*l*; V.'s Inc. 400*l* and Ho; Pop. 1349.) Translator of M. Verri's *Political Economy*, Paris, 1823. [5]

NEALE, Richard.—C. of St. Giles's, Cripplegate, Lond. [6]

NEALE, R. L.—Chaplain of H.M.S. "Highflyer.' [7]

NEAME, Walter, *Banbury.*—Clare Coll. Cam. B.A. 1861; Deac. 1862 and Pr. 1863 by Bp of Ely. C. of Banbury 1864. Formerly C. of Hadleigh, Suffolk, 1862. [8]

NEAME, W. J. R., *Child Okeford, Dorset.*—C. of Child Okeford. Formerly C. of Marston Magna. [9]

NEARY, Denis Creighton, *South Ossett Parsonage, Wakefield.*—Dub. A.B. 1856, A.M. 1859; Deac. 1847 and Pr. 1848 by Bp of Rip. P. C. of South Osset, Dio. Rip. 1850. (Patron, the Crown and Bp of Rip. alt; P. C.'s Inc. 170*l* and Ho; Pop. 4000.) Formerly C. of Ossett-cum-Gawthorpe. Author, *Sermons and Lectures.* [10]

NEATE, Richard Henry, *St. Paul's Vicarage, Walden, Herts.*—Trin. Coll. Cam. B.A. 1840, M.A. 1843; Deac. 1841 and Pr. 1842 by Bp of Lon. V. of St. Paul's, Walden, Dio. Roch. 1857. (Patrons, D. and C. of St. Paul's Cathl. Lond; Tithe—Imp. 603*l*, V. 34*l* 3*s* 2*d*; Glebe, 7 acres; V.'s Inc. 171*l* and Ho; Pop. 1123.) Formerly C. of Chiswick, Middlesex, 1843–57. [11]

NEAVE, Henry Lyttelton, *Epping Vicarage, Essex.*—Ch. Ch. Ox. B.A. 1820, M.A. 1823; Deac. 1822 by Bp of Ban. Pr. 1822 by Bp of Lon. V. of Epping, Dio. Roch. 1824. (Patron, H. J. Conyers, Esq; Tithe—Imp. 400*l*, V. 820*l*; Glebe, 11 acres; V.'s Inc. 842*l* and Ho; Pop. 2105.) [12]

NEBLETT, Augustus, *Womersley, Pontefract.*—St. Bees; Deac. 1858 and Pr. 1859 by Bp of Ches. C. of Womersley 1863. Formerly C. of Weaverham 1858, Dringhouses 1860, Oxcombe 1862. [13]

NEEDHAM, John James, *Lee, S.E.*—Bp Hatfield's Hall, Dur. B.A. and Licen. in Theol. 1855, M.A. 1858; Deac. 1855 and Pr. 1856 by Bp of Lich. Sen. C. of Lee, Kent, 1865. Formerly Sen. C. of St. Paul's, Warrington, 1863. Author, *The Christian Volunteer*; *Jesus and the Daughters of Jerusalem*; Sermons, various. [14]

NEELY, Andrew Craig, *Ashton Rectory, Towcester, Northants.*—Dub. A.B. 1839, A.M. 1858; Deac. 1843 by Bp of Kilmore, Pr. 1845 by Bp of Down and Connor. R. of Ashton, Dio. Pet. 1853. (Patron, Ld Chan; Glebe, 232 acres; R.'s Inc. 400*l* and Ho; Pop. 374.) [15]

NEIL, Charles, 7, *Weymouth-terrace, N.E.*—Trin. Hall, Cam. B.A. 1862, M.A. 1866; Deac. 1865 and Pr. 1866 by Bp of Salis. P. C. of St. Paul's, Bethnal Green, Dio. Lon. 1866. (Patron, Bp of Lon; P. C.'s Inc. 200*l*; Pop. 6000.) Formerly C. of Bradford Abbas, Dorset, 1865–66. [16]

NELSON, Daniel, *Kirk-Bride Rectory, Ramsey, Isle of Man.*—Deac. 1831 and Pr. 1833 by Bp of S. and M. R. of Kirk-Bride, Dio. S. and M. 1847. (Patron, the Crown; Glebe, 2¾ acres; R.'s Inc. 300*l* and Ho; Pop. 919.) [17]

NELSON, Edward Hamilton, 61, *Avenue-road, Regent's-park, London, N.W.*—Dub. A.B. 1840, A.M. 1852; Deac. 1842 and Pr. 1843 by Bp of Dur. P. C. of St. Stephen's-the-Martyr, St. Mary-le-bone, Dio. Lon. 1849. (Patron, Bp of Lon; P. C.'s Inc. 750*l*; Pop. 9621.) Formerly C. of Hunstanworth, Durham, 1842–49. Author, *Sermon on Romanism*, Hexham, 1849. [18]

NELSON, Hector, *Training School, Lincoln.*—St. John's Coll. Ox. M.A. 3rd cl. Lit. Hum. 2nd cl. Math; Deac. 1843, Pr 1844. Preb. of Lin. 1865; Principal of Training School, Lincoln. [19]

NELSON, James, *Luddenden Parsonage, via Manchester.*—Magd. Coll. Cam. Jun. Opt. B.A. 1836, M.A. 1839; Deac. 1836 by Abp of York, Pr. 1837 by Bp of Rip. P. C. of Luddenden, Dio. Rip. 1838. (Patron, V. of Halifax; P. C.'s Inc. 300*l* and Ho; Pop. 5080.) Formerly C. of Morley 1836, Coley 1837. [20]

NELSON, John Gudgeon, *Aldborough Rectory, Norwich.*—King's Coll. Lond. Theol. Assoc. 1848; Deac. 1849 and Pr. 1850 by Bp of Nor. R. of Aldborough, Dio. Nor. 1860. (Patron, Lord Suffield. Tithe, 200*l*; Glebe, 26 acres; R.'s Inc. 240*l* and Ho; Pop. 305.) Formerly C. of Ashby, Oby, and Thirne, 1849, Suffield and Gunton 1854. [21]

NELSON, The Hon. John Horatio, *Scottow Vicarage, near Norwich.*—Trin. Coll. Cam. M.A. 1846; Deac. 1847, Pr. 1848. R. of Belaugh with Scottow V. Dio. Nor. 1857. (Patron, Bp of Nor; Tithe, Belaugh, 226*l*, Scottow—App. 500*l* and 27 acres of Glebe, V. 230*l* and 17 acres of Glebe; R. and V.'s Inc. 500*l* and Ho; Pop. Belaugh 154, Scottow 454.) Formerly R. of Trimley St. Mary, Suffolk, 1853–57. [22]

NELSON, Thomas Sherlock, *St. Peter-at-Arches Rectory, Lincoln.*—Clare Hall, Cam. B.A. 1845, M.A. 1848; Deac. 1846, Pr. 1847. R. of the united Parishes of St. Peter-at-Arches with St. Benedict's, City and Dio. Lin. 1851. (Patron, Bp of Lin; St. Peter-at-Arches, Tithe, 9*l* 4*s*; Glebe, 5 acres; R.'s Inc. 225*l* and Ho; Pop. St. Peter-at-Arches 562, St. Benedict 653.) Rural Dean; Surrogate. [23]

NEMBHARD, Henry, *Instow, Bideford.*—R. of Instow, Dio. Ex. 1866. (Patron, A. S. Willett, Esq; R.'s Inc. 150*l*; Pop. 614.) [24]

NEPEAN, Evan, 21, *Bolton-street, Piccadilly, London, W.*—Trin. Coll. Cam. B.A. 1823, M.A. 1826; Deac. 1823, Pr. 1824. Min. of Grosvenor Chapel, South Audley-street, Dio. Lon. 1830. (Patron, R. of St. George's, Hanover-square; Min.'s Inc. 700*l*.) Chap. in Ordinary to the Queen 1848; Can. of Westminster 1860. Formerly R. of Heydon, Norfolk, 1831–61. [25]

NEPEAN, Evan Yorke, *Bucknall Rectory, Horncastle, Lincolnshire.*—Queen's Coll. Ox. B.A. 1848, M.A. 1851; Deac. 1849 and Pr. 1850 by Bp of Salis. R. of Bucknall, Dio. Lin. 1859. (Patron, Lord Monson; R.'s Inc. 250*l* and Ho; Pop. 406.) Formerly C. of Midgham, and Even. Lect. of Thatcham, Berks. [26]

NESFIELD, Charles, *Headon, Tuxford, Notts.*—Jesus Coll. Cam. B.A. 1827, M.A. 1831; Deac. 1827 and Pr. 1828 by Bp of Lon. V. of Headon with Upton, Dio. Lin. 1864. (Patron, G. H. Vernon, Esq; V.'s Inc. 220*l*; Pop. 282.) Formerly V. of Stratton, Wilts, 1833–64. [27]

NESFIELD, J. C., *Highgate, London, N.*—C. of St. Michael's, Highgate. [28]

NESS, Edward, *Elkstone Rectory, Cirencester.*—St. Mary Hall, Ox. B.A. 1826, M.A. 1832. R. of Elkstone, Dio. G. and B. 1846. (Patron, Hon. R. K. Craven; Tithe, 356*l* 5*s*; Glebe, $77\frac{3}{4}$ acres; R.'s Inc. 435*l* and Ho; Pop. 320.) Dom. Chap. to Earl Craven. [1]

NESS, John Derby, *Morthoe, Ilfracombe, Devon.*—Lin. Coll. Ox. B.A. 1825; Deac. 1826 and Pr. 1827 by Bp of Ex. V. of Morthoe, Dio. Ex. 1830. (Patrons, D. and C. of Ex; V.'s Inc. 128*l*; Pop. 347.) [2]

NETHERCLIFT, Thomas Martin, *Northallerton, Yorks.*—Ch. Coll. Cam. B.A. 1856; Deac. 1858 and Pr. 1859 by Bp of Roch. Chap. to the North Riding House of Correction, Northallerton, 1865. Formerly C. of St. Mary's, Greenhithe, 1858, Longton on the Swale, Yorks, 1860, Hornby Catterick, York, 1862, Northallerton, Yorks, 1864. [3]

NETHERWOOD, John, *Appleby, Westmoreland.*—Corpus Coll. Cam. B.A. 1828, M.A. 1829; Deac. 1829, Pr. 1830. [4]

NETTLESHIP, Arthur, *Minsterworth Vicarage, Gloucester.*—Trin. Coll. Ox. B.A. 1849, M.A. 1852; Theol. Coll. Wells; Deac. 1851 and Pr. 1852 by Bp of Win. V. of Minsterworth, Dio. G. and B. 1854. (Patron, Bp of G. and B; Tithe, Imp. 600*l*; Glebe, 6 acres; V. 16*l*; Glebe, 27 acres; V.'s Inc. 121*l* and Ho; Pop. 463.) [5]

NEUCATRE, Henry Sidney, *South Kyme Parsonage, Sleaford, Lincolnshire.*—St John's Coll. Cam. B.A. 1824, M.A. 1828; Deac. 1824 and Pr. 1825 by Bp of Nor. P. C. of South Kyme, Dio. Lin. 1837. (Patron, Hon. C. H. Cust; Tithe—Imp. 789*l*; Glebe, $1\frac{1}{2}$ acres; P. C.'s Inc. 106*l* and Ho; Pop. 1004.) [6]

NEUMANN, John Stubbs, *Hockliffe Rectory, Leighton Buzzard, Beds.*—St. Peter's Coll. Cam. B.A. 1837, M.A. 1841; Deac. 1838 and Pr. 1839 by Bp of Ches. R. of Hockliffe, Dio. Ely, 1842. (Patron, the present R; Tithe—Imp. 333 acres, R. 306*l*; Glebe, 24 acres; R.'s Inc. 462*l* and Ho; Pop. 416) [7]

NEVILE, Charles, *Fledborough Rectory, Newark, Notts.*—Trin. Coll. Ox. 3rd cl. Lit. Hum. 2nd cl. Math. and Phys. B.A. 1839, M.A. 1842; Deac. 1839 and Pr. 1841 by Bp of Lin. R. of Fledborough, Dio. Lin. 1853. (Patron, Earl Manvers; Tithe, rent charge, 315*l*; Glebe, 6 acres; R.'s Inc. 327*l* and Ho; Pop. 115.) Rural Dean. Formerly C. of Thorney 1839–45, Wickenby 1845–53. [8]

NEVILE, Henry, *Wickenby Rectory, Wragby, Lincolnshire.*—R. of Wickenby, Dio. Lin. 1863. (Patron, the present R; R.'s Inc. 330*l* and Ho; Pop. 288.) [9]

NEVILL, Gerard, *Tilton Vicarage, Leicester.*—St. Cath. Coll. Cam. B.A. 1839, M.A. 1843; Deac. 1840, Pr. 1841. V. of Tilton, Dio. Pet. 1843. (Patrons, E. A. Holden, Esq. Rev. H. T. Adnutt, and H. Nevile, Esq. in rotation; Tithe, 380*l*; Glebe, 5 acres; R.'s Inc. 42*l* and Ho; Pop. 432.) [10]

NEVILL, Henry Ralph, *Great Yarmouth, Norfolk.*—Univ. Coll. Ox. 2nd cl. Lit. Hum. 1844, M.A. 1850; Deac. 1848, Pr. 1849. P. C. of St. Nicholas', Great Yarmouth, Dio. Nor. 1858. (Patrons D. and C. of Nor; Tithe—App. 60*l*; P. C.'s Inc. 365*l*; Pop. 30,338.) Hon. Can. of Nor. 1860. Formerly P. C. of St. Mark's, Lakenham, near Norwich, 1850–58. [11]

NEVILL, S. T., *Shelton, Staffordshire.*—C. of Scarisbrook. R. of Shelton, Dio. Lich. 1865. (Patron, Rev. J. H. Murray; R.'s Inc. 620*l*; Pop. 8617.) [12]

NEVILLE, Hastings Mackelcan, 20, *Monument-lane, Edgbaston, Birmingham.*—Clare Coll. Cam. B.A. 1862; Deac. 1863 by Bp of Ex. Pr. 1865 by Bp of Wor. C. of St. John's, Ladywood, Birmingham, 1865. Formerly C. of St. Peter's and St. Paul's, Barnstaple, 1863. [13]

NEVILLE, The Hon. Latimer, *Heydon Rectory, Royston, Essex.*—Magd. Coll. Cam. 3rd in 2nd cl. Cl. Trip. M.A. 1849; Deac. 1850, Pr. 1851. R. of Heydon with Little Chishall, Dio. Roch. 1851. (Patron, Lord Braybrooke; Heydon, Tithe, 430*l* 8*s* 8*d*; Glebe, $94\frac{3}{4}$ acres; R.'s Inc. 700*l* and Ho; Pop. Heydon 270, Little Chishall 110.) Mast. of Magd. Coll. Cam. 1853. Formerly Fell. of Magd. Coll. Cam. [14]

NEVILLE, Nigel, *Montgomery.*—St. John's Coll. Cam. B.A. 1857, M.A. 1860; Deac. 1859 and Pr. 1860 by Bp of Ely. C. of Montgomery 1864. Formerly C. of Withersfield, Suffolk, 1859–60, Sopworth and Badminster, Glouc. 1860–64. [15]

NEVILLE, Seymour, *Wraysbury Vicarage (Bucks), near Staines.*—Magd. Coll. Cam. Jun. Opt. and B.A. 1845; Deac. 1846, Pr. 1848. V. of Wyrardisbury *alias* Wraysbury, Dio. Ox. 1856. (Patrons, D. and C. of Windsor; Glebe, 18 acres; V.'s Inc. 215*l*; Pop. 720.) Formerly C. of Stanton St. Gabriel, Dorset, 1846, St. John's, Windsor, 1847; Min. Can. of St. George's Chapel, Windsor, 1848; Fell. of Magd. Coll. Cam. 1845–48. [16]

NEVILLE, William Frederick, *Butleigh Vicarage, Glastonbury, Somerset.*—Magd. Coll. Cam. Scho. of, Sen. Opt. B.A. 1840, M.A. 1843; Deac. 1841 by Bp of B. and W. Pr. 1842 by Bp of G. and B. V. of Butleigh with Baltonsborough C. Dio. B. and W. 1845. (Patron, R. Neville Grenville, Esq; Butleigh, Tithe—Imp. 227*l*, V. 268*l*; Glebe, 49 acres; Baltonsborough, Tithe—App. 8*l* 10*s* 2*d*, Imp. 52*l*, V. 175*l*; Glebe, 5 acres; V.'s Inc. 538*l* and Ho; Pop. Butleigh 1038, Baltonsborough 763.) Preb. of Barton St. David in Wells Cathl. 1851; Rural Dean of Glastonbury 1851. Formerly C. of Butleigh 1841–45. [17]

NEVILLE-ROLFE, Edward Fawcett, *Cannes, France.*—Trin. Coll. Cam. B.A. 1842, M.A. 1846; Deac. 1844 and Pr. 1845 by Bp of Ches. English Chap. at Cannes. Formerly C. of Amwell, Herts. [18]

NEVIN, Thomas, *Battyeford, Mirfield, Dewsbury.*—St. John's Coll. Cam. 18th Sen. Opt. and B.A. 1834, M.A. 1837; Deac. 1836 by Abp of York, Pr. 1837 by Bp of Dur. P. C. of Ch. Ch. Battyeford, Dio. York. (Patron, V. of Mirfield; P. C.'s Inc. 180*l*; Pop. 3115) Organising Sec. to the S.P.G. for the Dio. of Rip. [19]

NEVINS, William, *Miningsby Rectory, Lincolnshire.*—Deac. 1838 and Pr. 1840 by Bp of Herf. R. of Miningsby, Linc. Dio. Lin. 1843. (Patron, Duchy of Lancaster; R.'s Inc. 274*l* and Ho; Pop. 143.) Author, *The Clergy's Privilege and Duty of Daily Intercession* (a Sermon preached at the Visitation of the Bp of Lin.) Masters, 1846; *The Scriptural Doctrine of the Holy Communion*, ib. 1855; *Prayer for the Priesthood* (a Sermon), ib. 1857. [20]

NEVINSON, Charles, *Browne's Hospital, Stamford.*—Wad. Coll. Ox. 1st cl. Lit. Hum. and B.A. 1838, M.A. 1840; Deac. 1840 and Pr. 1841 by Bp of Ox. Warden of Browne's Hospital 1845. Editor, *The Later Writings of Bishop Hooper*, Parker Soc. [21]

NEW, John, *Duncton Rectory, Petworth, Sussex.*—St. John's Coll. Ox. B.A. 1851; Deac. 1849 and Pr. 1850 by Bp of Chich. R. of Duncton, Dio. Chich. 1859. (Patron, Lord Leconfield; Tithe, 420*l*; Glebe, 7 acres; R.'s Inc. 520*l*; Pop. 258.) C. of Burton with Coates 1853. Formerly C. of Duncton 1849–59. [22]

NEWALL, Frederick James, *Bourton (Dorset), near Wincanton, Somerset.*—Trin. Coll. Cam. B.A. 1831, M.A. 1834; Deac. 1832 by Bp of Chich. Pr. 1832 by Bp of Ex. P. C. of Bourton, Gillingham, Dio. Salis. 1834. (Patrons, Trustees; Glebe, 5 acres; P. C.'s Inc. 100*l*; Pop. 931.) [23]

NEWALL, Samuel, *Clifton-road, Rugby.*—Queens' Coll. Cam. B.A. 1830, M.A. 1833; Deac. 1830 and Pr. 1831 by Bp of Ches. V. of Clifton-upon-Dunsmore with Brownsover C. near Rugby, Dio. Wor. 1853. (Patron, Earl of Bradford; Tithe, Imp. 121*l*, V. 75*l*; Glebe, 15 acres; V.'s Inc. 150*l*; Pop. 732.) Surrogate 1857. Formerly P. C. of Ch. Ch. Tunstall, 1843–53. [24]

NEWBALD, Samuel Wilberforce, *Pontefract.*—Wad. Coll. Ox. 3rd cl. Lit. Hum. and B.A. 1842, M.A. 1845; Deac. 1842, Pr. 1843. Head Mast. of the King's Sch. Pontefract; C. of Pontefract. [25]

NEWBOLD, Arthur George, *Thornton Vicarage, Horncastle, Lincolnshire.*—Magd. Hall, Ox. B.A. 1839. V. of Thornton, Dio. Lin. 1851. (Patrons, D. and C. of Lich; Tithe—App. 145*l* 5*s*, V. 174*l* 3*s* 10*d*; Glebe, $2\frac{3}{4}$ acres; V.'s Inc. 179*l* and Ho; Pop. 114.) [26]

NEWBOLD, Charles Hutchinson, *Hindley Parsonage, Wigan.*—St. Aidan's; Deac. 1853 and Pr. 1854 by Bp of Ches. P. C. of Hindley, Dio. Ches. 1863.

(Patron, R. of Wigan; P. C.'s Inc. 300*l* and Ho; Pop. 5906.) Formerly C. of Wigan. [1]

NEWBOLT, George Digby, *Knotting Rectory, near Bedford.*—Brasen. Coll. Ox. B.A. 1852; Deac. 1853 and Pr. 1854 by Bp of Roch. R. of Knotting with Souldrop, Dio. Ely, 1856. (Patron, Duke of Bedford; R.'s Inc. 300*l* and Ho; Pop. Knotting 185, Souldrop 276.) Formerly C. of Hitchin, Herts. [2]

NEWBOLT, William Henry, *Paulerspury, Towcester, Northants.*—New Coll. Ox. B.A. 1829, M.A. 1833; Deac. 1829 by Bp of Herf. Pr. 1830 by Bp of Salis. R. of Paulerspury, Dio. Pet. 1842. (Patron, New Coll. Ox; Tithe, 863*l* 19*s* 9*d*; Glebe, 62 acres; R.'s Inc. 925*l*; Pop. 1238.) Formerly Fell. of New Coll. Ox. [3]

NEWBY, Alfred, *Gransden-Parva Rectory, Caxton, Cambs.*—St. John's Coll. Cam. B.A. 1832, M.A. 1835; Deac. 1832 and Pr. 1834 by Bp of Lin. R. of Gransden-Parva, Dio. Ely, 1856. (Patron, Bp of Ely; Glebe, 425 acres; R.'s Inc. 325*l* and Ho; Pop. 298.) [4]

NEWBY, Alfred Ryle, *Benwick, Ramsey, Cambs.*—St. Bees; Deac. 1860 and Pr. 1861 by Bp of Lich. C. of Benwick 1862. Formerly C. of Ripley, 1860. [5]

NEWBY, George, *Borrowdale Parsonage, Crosthwaite, Keswick.*—St. Bees; Deac. 1824, Pr. 1825. P. C. of Borrowdale, Dio. Carl. 1838. (Patron, V. of Crosthwaite; Glebe, 2 acres; P. C.'s Inc. 80*l*; Pop. 422.) Author, *Pleasures of Melancholy* (a Poem), Keswick, 1842; *Henllyware, or the Druid's Temple near Keswick* (a Poem), Longmans, 1854. [6]

NEWBY, Henry, *Mears Ashby Vicarage, Northampton.*—Wor. Coll. Ox. B.A. 1844, M.A. 1847; Deac. 1845 and Pr. 1846 by Bp of Pet. V. of Mears Ashby, Dio. Pet. 1857. (Patrons, Trustees; Glebe, 154 acres; V.'s Inc. 200*l* and Ho; Pop. 525.) Formerly C. of Wootton, Northants, Kidlington and Water-Eaton, near Oxford. [7]

NEWBY, John, *Owthorne, Patrington, Yorks.*—C. of Owthorne. [8]

NEWBY, Richard John, *Whetstone, near Leicester.*—Ch. Coll. Cam. B.A. 1850, M.A. 1853; Deac. 1850 and Pr. 1851 by Bp of Nor. V. of Whetstone, Dio. Pet. 1859. (Patron, Charles Brook, Esq; Tithe—Imp. 30*l*, V. 175*l*; Glebe, 58 acres; V.'s Inc. 300*l*; Pop. 1057.) Formerly C. of Burnham-Westgate, Norfolk, 1851–52, Crosby Ravensworth, Westmoreland, 1853–57. [9]

NEWCOME, Edward William, *Leavesden Vicarage, Watford, Herts.*—Ball. Coll. Ox. B.A. 1844, M.A. 1861; Deac. 1847, Pr. 1858 by Bp of Roch. P. C. of Leavesden, Dio. Roch. 1855. (Patron, V. of Watford; Tithe, 116*l*; Glebe, 6 acres; P. C.'s Inc. 116*l* and Ho; Pop. 770.) Formerly C. of Ashwell, Herts, 1847–49. [10]

NEWCOME, Henry Justinian, *Shenley Rectory, Barnet, Herts.*—Trin. Coll. Ox. B.A. 1837; Deac. 1838 by Bp of G. and B. Pr. 1841 by Bp of Lin. R. of Shenley, Dio. Roch. 1849. (Patron, the present R; Tithe, 1064*l* 13*s*; Glebe, 24 acres; R.'s Inc. 1116*l* and Ho; Pop. 902.) [11]

NEWCOME, William Cyrill, *Boothby Pagnel Rectory, Grantham.*—Trin. Coll. Cam. B.A. 1837, M.A. 1843; Deac. 1842 and Pr. 1843 by Bp of Lin. R. of Boothby Pagnel, Dio. Lin. 1846. (Patron, T. Fardell, Esq; Tithe, 337*l* 14*s*; Glebe, 121 acres; R.'s Inc. 477*l* and Ho; Pop. 112.) [12]

NEWDIGATE, Alfred, *Kirk Hallam, near Derby.*—Ch. Ch. Ox. 3rd cl. Maths. and B.A. 1851, M.A. 1854; Deac. 1853 and Pr. 1855 by Bp of Ox. V. of Kirk Hallam with Mapperley, Dio. Lich. 1856. (Patron, Lieut.-Col. Newdigate; Tithe, 250*l*; Glebe, 58*l*; V.'s Inc. 309*l*; Pop. 535.) Formerly Asst. C. of Aylesbury 1853–56. [13]

NEWDIGATE, Charles John, *West Hallam, Derby.*—Ch. Ch. Ox. B.A. 1845, M.A. 1851; Deac. 1847 and Pr. 1848 by Bp of Lich. R. of West Hallam, Dio. Lich. 1848. (Patron, F. Newdigate, Esq; Tithe, 256*l* 10*s*; Glebe, 46 acres; R.'s Inc. 290*l*; Pop. 559.) [14]

NEWELL, Christian Frederick, *The Rectory, Chiselborough, near Ilminster, Somerset.*—Clare Coll. Cam. Wrang. and B.A. 1840, M.A. 1843; Deac. 1843, Pr. 1844. R. of Chiselborough with West Chinnock R. Dio. B. and W. 1866. (Patron, Earl of Ilchester; Tithe, 400*l*; Glebe, 52 acres; R.'s Inc. 506*l* and Ho; Pop. 972.) Formerly P. C. of Broadstairs, Kent, 1850–66. Author, *The Crisis and its Duties* (a Tract), 1854; *Parting Words*, 1866. [15]

NEWENHAM, Bagenal Burdett, *Bilton Vicarage, near York.*—King's Coll. Lond. Theol. Assoc. 1849; Deac. 1849 and Pr. 1850 by Bp of Ex. V. of Bilton, Dio. York, 1866. (Patron, Abp of York; V.'s Inc. 300*l*; Pop. 936.) Formerly P. C. of Gateforth, Yorks, 1859–62. [16]

NEWENHAM, Edward H.—C. of Holywell, St. Ives, Hunts. [17]

NEWENHAM, William Thomas, *Knotty Ash Parsonage, Liverpool.*—Dub. A.B. 1850, A.M. 1865; Deac. 1851 and Pr. 1852 by Bp of Ches. P. C. of St. John's, Knotty Ash, Dio. Ches. 1853. P. C.'s Inc. 200*l* and Ho; Pop. 1500.) Formerly C. of St. Augustin's, Liverpool, 1850. Author, *Antiquated Spots round Cheltenham*, 1849, 2*s*; *Volunteer of the Cross*, 1860, 2*d*; *Brotherly Love*, 1860, 2*d*. [18]

NEWHAM, John, *Calais.*—Emman. Coll. Cam. B.A. 1850, M.A. 1855; Deac. 1851 and Pr. 1852 by Abp of York. Minister of Castelnau Proprietary Chapel, Barnes, Surrey, 1866; Consular Chap. at Calais. Formerly P. C. of Mount Sorrel, North End, Leic. 1855–61. [19]

NEWHAM, William Leighton, *Barrow-on-Soar Vicarage, Loughborough.*—St. John's Coll. Cam. Double 1st cl. and B.A. 1847, M.A. 1850; Deac. 1848 and Pr. 1849 by Bp of Ely. V. of Barrow-on-Soar, Dio. Pet. 1854. (Patron, St. John's Coll. Cam; Glebe, 199 acres; V.'s Inc. 450*l* and Ho; Pop. 1800.) Fell. of St. John's Coll. Cam. 1847; Patron of the P. C.'s of Quorndon, Mount Sorrel, and Woodhouse. [20]

NEWINGTON, Frank, *Wool, near Wareham.*—St. John's Coll. Ox. B.A. 1845; Deac. 1845 and Pr. 1846 by Bp of Win. V. of Combe-Keynes, Dorset, Dio. Salis. 1860. (Patron, Edward Weld, Esq; Tithe, 98*l*; Glebe, 25 acres; V.'s Inc. 125*l* and Ho; Pop. 163.) P. C. of Wool, Dio. Salis. 1860. (Patron, Bp of Salis; Tithe, 60*l*; P. C.'s Inc. 72*l*; Pop. 590.) Formerly C. of Breamore, Hants, 1846, Broad Chalke, Wilts, 1856. [21]

NEWINGTON, Philip, *Wilmington, Kent.*—Wor. Coll. Ox. B.A. 1842, M.A. 1854; Deac. 1844 and Pr. 1845 by Bp of Lin. C. of Wilmington 1867. Formerly C. of Addlethorpe, Lin. 1844, Oxted, Surrey, 1848, Boughton Malherbe, Kent, 1860. [22]

NEWLAND, Henry, *Scissett Parsonage, Huddersfield.*—Dub. A.B. 1847, A.M. 1852; Deac. 1849 and Pr. 1850 by Bp of Man. P. C. of St. Augustine's, Scissett, Dio. Rip. 1854. (Patron, W. B. Beaumont, Esq. M.P; P. C.'s Inc. 150*l* and Ho; Pop. 4634.) [23]

NEWLING, William, *Liskeard, Cornwall.*—St. John's Coll. Cam. B.A. 1845; Deac. 1845, Pr. 1846. P. C. of Herodsfoot, Cornwall, Dio. Ex. 1851. (Patron, R. of Duloe; Tithe, 69*l* 10*s*; Glebe, 2 acres; P. C.'s Inc. 70*l* and Ho; Pop. 453.) [24]

NEWLOVE, Richard, *Thorner Vicarage, Leeds.*—Clare Coll. Cam. B.A. 1835, M.A. 1838; Deac. 1835 and Pr. 1836 by Abp of York. V. of Thorner, Dio. Rip. 1839. (Patron, Ld Chan; Tithe, 60*l*; Glebe, 84 acres; V.'s Inc. 150*l* and Ho; Pop. 1047.) Rural Dean; Chap. to the Earl of Harewood. [25]

NEWMAN, Charles Durnford, *Sutton Coldfield, Warwickshire.*—Wad. Coll. Ox. 2nd cl. Lit. Hum. 3rd cl. Math. and B.A. 1843, M.A. 1854; Deac. 1857 by Bp of B. and W. Pr. 1858 by Bp of Ex. C. of Sutton Coldfield 1866. Formerly Head Mast. of St. John's Academy, Newfoundland, 1845; Head Mast. of the Truro Gr. Sch. 1853–66; C. of Kenwyn, Cornwall, 1857; St. Erme, Cornwall, 1864. [26]

NEWMAN, Edward, *Ecclesall Parsonage, Sheffield.*—Ch. Miss. Coll. Islington; Deac. 1843 and Pr. 1844 by Bp of Lon. P. C. of Ecclesall, Dio. York, 1856. (Patron, V. of Sheffield; Glebe, 40 acres; P. C.'s Inc. 417*l* and Ho; Pop. 2876.) Formerly Miss. in Jamaica and in Southern India. Author, *A Brief Sketch of the Life and Character of the Rev. Henry Farish*, 1857;

A Sermon on the Death of H. M. Greaves, Esq. 1859. [1]

NEWMAN, Francis B., *Burton Latimer, Wellingborough.*—St. Cath. Coll. Cam. M.A. C. of Burton Latimer. (Patron, Rev. Francis B. Newman; Inc. 1100*l*; Pop. 1150.) [2]

NEWMAN, Frederick, *Henstridge (Somerset), near Blandford, Dorset.*—Trin. Coll. Cam. B.A. 1852; Deac. 1852 and Pr. 1853 by Bp of G. and B. C. of Henstridge. [3]

NEWMAN, Frederick Samuel, *Thorp Arch Vicarage, Tadcaster.*—Queen's Coll. Ox. 3rd cl. Lit. Hum. Hon. 4th cl. Math. 1858, B.A. 1858, M.A. 1861; Deac. 1859 and Pr. 1860 by Abp of York. C. in sole charge of Thorp Arch. 1864. Formerly C. of Clifford, Yorks, 1859-61, Hawton, Newark, 1861-62, Barwick in Elmet 1862-64. [4]

NEWMAN, Frederick William, *Halifax.*—St. Peter's Coll. Cam. B.A. 1851, M.A. 1854; Deac. 1854 and Pr. 1855 by Bp of Rip. C. of Trinity, Halifax. Formerly C. of Illingworth, Yorks, and St. Paul's, King Cross, Halifax. [5]

NEWMAN, Henry, *Stanley Lodge, West Hallam, Derby.*—Ball. Coll. Ox. B.A. 1861, M.A. 1864; Deac 1864 and Pr. 1865. P. C. of Stanley, Lich. 1867. (Patron, Sir Henry Wilmot, Bart; Glebe, 12 acres; P. C.'s Inc. 75*l* and Ho; Pop. 534.) Formerly C. of Chellaston. [6]

NEWMAN, Henry Brown, *Little Bromley Rectory, Manningtree, Essex.*—Wad. Coll. Ox. B.A. 1819, M.A. 1825; Deac. 1821, Pr. 1822. R. of Little Bromley, Dio. Roch. 1838. (Patron, Wad. Coll. Ox; Tithe, 560*l*; Glebe, 11 acres; R.'s Inc. 530*l* and Ho; Pop. 371.) Formerly Fell. of Wad. Coll. Ox. [7]

NEWMAN, James, *Maindee, near Newport, Monmouthshire.*—Dub. A.B. 1850; Deac. 1850 and Pr. 1851 by Bp of Herf. P. C. of Maindee, Dio. Llan. 1866. (Patrons, Provost and Fellows of Eton Coll; Pop. 2200.) Formerly C. of Bromyard, Herf. 1850-54; Min. of Brockhampton Chapel, Bromyard, 1852-54; C. of St. Mary's, Brecon, 1854-59, St. John's, Maindee, 1860-66. [8]

NEWMAN, John, *Worsborough Parsonage, Barnsley, Yorks.*—P. C. of Worsborough, Dio. York, 1862. (Patron, R. of Darfield; P. C.'s Inc. 150*l* and Ho; Pop. 5381.) [9]

NEWMAN, Thomas Harding, D.D., *Magdalen College, Oxford.*—Fell. of Magd. Coll. Ox. [10]

NEWMAN, Thomas Henry, *Cheriton Bishop, near Exeter.*—St. John's Coll. Cam. 16th Sen. Opt. B.A. 1853, M.A. 1856; Deac. 1853 and Pr. 1855 by Bp of Ex. C. of Cheriton Bishop. Formerly C. of St. Paul's, Honiton, 1853, Shutford, near Bunbury, 1855, Hittisleigh 1857. [11]

NEWMAN, William Alexander, *The Hill, Upton-on-Severn, Worc.*—Trin. Coll. Ox. B.A. 1862, M.A. 1866; Deac. 1863 by Bp of Roch. Pr. 1865 by Abp of Cant. C. of Upton-on-Severn 1866. Formerly C. of St. Martin's, Canterbury, 1864-65. [12]

NEWMAN, William James, *Hockworthy Vicarage (Devon), near Wellington, Somerset.*—Wad. Coll. Ox. B.A. 1842, M.A. 1846; Deac. 1844 and Pr. 1845 by Bp of Ex. V. of Hockworthy, Dio. Ex. 1860. (Patron, the present V; V.'s Inc. 280*l* and Ho; Pop. 373.) Rural Dean. Formerly C. of Street, Devon, 1844-47, Uffculme, Devon, 1847-52, Hockworthy 1852-60. [13]

NEWMAN, William Symons, *Coryton Rectory, Lew Down, Devon.*—Wad. Coll. Ox. 3rd cl. Lit. Hum. and B.A. 1840, M.A. 1842; Deac. 1841 and Pr. 1842 by Bp of Ox. R. of Coryton, Dio. Ex. 1853. (Patron, T. H. Newman, Esq; Tithe, 160*l*; Glebe, 70 acres; R.'s Inc. 220*l* and Ho; Pop. 238.) Rural Dean. [14]

NEWMARCH, Charles Francis, *Leverton Rectory, Boston.*—St. Alban Hall, Ox. 2nd cl. Lit. Hum. and B.A. 1833, M.A. 1835; Deac. and Pr. 1835 by Bp of G. and B. R. of Leverton, Dio. Lin. 1853. (Patrons, Ld Chan. and A. Booth, Esq. alt; Glebe, 420 acres; R.'s Inc. 930*l* and Ho; Pop. 770.) [15]

NEWMARCH, Charles Henry, *Belton Vicarage, Uppingham, Rutland.*—Corpus Coll. Cam. B.A. 1855; Deac. 1854 and Pr. 1855 by Bp of G. and B. R. of Wardley with Belton V. Rutland, Dio. Pet. 1856. (Patron, Ld Chan; Tithe, Wardley, 157*l* 9*s*; Glebe, 25 acres; Belton, Glebe, 60 acres; R. and V.'s Inc. 327*l* and Ho; Pop. Wardley 68, Belton 461.) Rural Dean 1857; Local Sec. to Church Building Soc. Joint Author (with Prof. Buckman) of *Illustrations of the Remains of Roman Art*, 4to. 2 eds. Bell, 1850 and 1851, 21*s*. Author, under assumed names, of several Books and Pamphlets, published by Longmans, Masters, and Hamilton, Adams, and Co. [16]

NEWMARCH, Henry, *Hessle Vicarage, Hull.*—St. Mary Hall, Ox. B.A. 1827; Deac. 1828, Pr. 1829 R. of Boultham, Linc. Dio. Lin. 1829. (Patron, R. Ellison, Esq; Tithe, 6*s* 4*d*; Glebe, 20 acres; R.'s Inc. 124*l*; Pop. 95.) V. of Hessle, Dio. York, 1837. (Patron, Ld Chan; Tithe, 80*l*; Glebe, 180 acres; V.'s Inc. 396*l* and Ho; Pop. 1625.) Chap. to Earl of Stratford 1837. Author, Sermons, *Confirmation a Consecration of ourselves unto the Lord*; *Faithfulness and Order essential to the Edification of the Church*; *Life a Vapour* (preached during the prevalence of the Cholera); *God the Warrior's Covering* (preached on the Death of the Duke of Wellington); *Prayer for the Queen the Duty of the People*; *Glory to God and Good Will to Man inseparable in the True Christian*; *A New Pulpit, but no New Doctrine* (preached on the reopening of Hessle Ch.); *The Armour of Light the best Defence in War* (Fast-day Sermon); Tracts, *Perilous Times made less Perilous by Religion and Loyalty*; *Baptismal Grace always given, but not always Efficacious*; *The Protestant and the Romanist not "True Yokefellows;" The Glad Worshipper the most Profitable in the House of God.* [17]

NEWNHAM, George William, *Combe-Down, Bath.*—Corpus Coll. Ox. 2nd cl. Lit. Hum. 3rd cl. Math. et Phy. and B.A. 1827, M.A. 1830; Deac. 1831 and Pr. 1832 by Bp of B. and W. P. C. of Combe-Down, Dio. B. and W. 1842. (Patron, V. of South Stoke; P. C.'s Inc. 45*l* and Ho; Pop. 960.) Formerly P. C. of Coleford, Kilmersdon, 1832-40, Monkton-Combe, near Bath, 1845-63. [18]

NEWPORT, Henry, *Grammar Schoolhouse, Exeter.*—Pemb. Coll. Cam. 1st of 2nd cl. Cl. Trip. Sir W. Brown's Univ. Medallist for Greek and Latin Odes 1849, B.A. 1845, M.A. 1849; Deac. 1850 and Pr. 1851 by Bp of Ox. Head Mast. of Exeter Gr. Sch. 1852. (Stipend, 40*l* and Ho.) Chap. of St. John's Hospital Chapel, Exeter, 1852. Author, *Two Prize Poems* (Greek and Latin), Cam. Univ. Press. [19]

NEWPORT, John, *Stroud, Glouc.*—Wor. Coll. Ox. B.A. 1808; Deac. 1808, Pr. 1809. [20]

NEWTON, Alfred, *Brighton College.*—St. John's Coll. Cam. 11th Wrang. 1847, B.A. 1846, M.A. 1852, Theol. Coll. Wells; Deac. 1847 and Pr. 1851 by Bp of Chich. Vice-Principal of Brighton Coll. [21]

NEWTON, Charles, *Timberland, Sleaford, Lincolnshire.*—St. Bees; Deac. 1859 and Pr. 1860 by Bp of Lich. C. of Timberland 1866. Formerly C. of Hope, Hanley, Staffs, 1859-61; C. (sole charge) of Reddal Hill, Staffs, 1861-66. [22]

NEWTON, Francis John, *North Scarle, Collingham, near Newark.*—Univ. Coll. Dur. B.A. 1846, M.A. 1847; Deac. 1848, Pr. 1849. [23]

NEWTON, Henry, *Ashburne, Derbyshire.*—C. of Ashburne 1864. Formerly C. of Helmsley, Yorks, 1861-63. [24]

NEWTON, Hibbert.—Dub. A.B. 1829; Deac. 1845 by Bp of Gibraltar, Pr. 1847 by Bp of Win. C. of St. George's, Southwark. Formerly C. of St. Cuthbert's, York, 1853. Author, *Religious Liberty*, 1853, 1*s*; *The Resurrection of Israel* (a Poem), 1855, 3*s* 6*d*. [25]

NEWTON, Horace, *Park-terrace, Nottingham.*—St. John's Coll. Ox. Scho. of, Math. Honors, B.A. 1864, M.A. 1867; Deac. 1865 and Pr. 1866 by Bp of Lin. C. of St. Mary's, Nottingham. [26]

NEWTON, John Farmer, *Kirkby-in-Cleveland, Stokesley, Yorks.*—Jesus Coll. Cam. B.A. 1816; Deac. 1817, Pr. 1818. V. of Kirkby-in-Cleveland, Dio. York,

1841. (Patron, the sinecure R; Tithe—App. 630*l*, V. 155*l*; V.'s Inc. 158*l*; Pop. 804.) [1]

NEWTON, John Horsley, *Cambo, Newcastle-on-Tyne.*—Trin. Coll. Cam. B.A. 1834; Deac. 1835 and Pr. 1836 by Abp of York. P. C. of Cambo, Dio. Dur. 1855. (Patron, V. of Hartburn; Tithe, 48*l* 19*s*; P. C.'s Inc. 122*l* 19*s*; Pop. 780.) Formerly C. of St. Denis and Naburn, York; C. (sole charge) of Kirkharle, Northumberland, 1839–55. [2]

NEWTON, Joseph Knight, *Sutton Scotney, Micheldever Station.*—St. Aidan's; Deac. 1863, Pr. 1864. C. of Wonston with Hunton, Hants, 1867. Formerly C. of Micheldever 1863; P. C. of Burrowa, New South Wales, 1866. [3]

NEWTON, J. T., *Shelley Rectory, Romford, Essex.*—R. of Shelley, Dio. Roch. 1861. (Patron, J. Tomlinson, Esq; R.'s Inc. 250*l* and Ho; Pop. 178.) [4]

NEWTON, William, *Ousebridge, York.*—C. of St. John's, Ousebridge. [5]

NEWTON, W. A.—C. of All Saints', Kensington-park, Middlesex. Formerly C. of St. Stephen's, Paddington. [6]

NEWTON, William Fretwell, *Littleport, Ely, Cambridge.*—Caius Coll. Cam. B.A. 1856, M.A. 1860; Deac. 1856 and Pr. 1857 by Bp of Ches. C. of Littleport. Formerly C. of St. Bride's, Liverpool, 1856–57; Sen. C. of St. Mary's, Bury St. Edmunds, 1857–62; Chap. to the Suffolk General Hospital 1861–62; C. of Ch. Ch. Birmingham, 1862–63, Histon 1863. [7]

NIBLETT, Edward Henry, *Redmarley Rectory (Worcestershire), near Newent.*—Ex. Coll. Ox. B.A. 1834; Deac. 1834, Pr. 1835. R. of Redmarley-d'Abitot, Dio. Wor. 1853. (Patron, D. T. Niblett, Esq; Tithe, 900*l*; Glebe. 56 acres; R.'s Inc. 900*l* and Ho; Pop. 1265.) [8]

NICHOL, John Scrymeour, *Hetton Rectory, Fence Houses, Durham.*—St. Bees; Deac. 1825 by Bp of Carl. Pr. 1826 by Bp of Ches. R. of Hetton-le-Hole, Dio. Dur. 1847. (Patron, Bp of Dur; R.'s Inc. 377*l* 18*s* 2*d*; Pop. 7300.) Formerly C. of Kirkandrews on Esk 1825–28, Worth 1828–32, Helton 1832–47. [9]

NICHOLAS, E. P., *East Lavington, Wilts.*—C. of East Lavington. [10]

NICHOLAS, George Davenport, *Clewer, Windsor.*—Pemb. Coll. Ox. B.A. 1859, M.A. 1862; Deac. 1860 and Pr. 1861 by Bp of Ox. C. of Clewer 1865. Formerly Asst. C. of Trinity, Windsor, 1860; Vice-Prin. of the Theol. Coll. St. John's, Newfoundland. Author, *Will a Man rob God? or, Tithes the Rule of Almsgiving,* Rivingtons, 6*d*. [11]

NICHOLAS, Tressilian George, *West Molesey Parsonage, Kingston-on-Thames, S.W.*—Wad. Coll. Ox. Hon. Double 4th cl. 1842, B.A. 1843, M.A. 1846; Deac. 1845 and Pr. 1846 by Bp of Ox. P. C. of West Molesey, Dio. Win. 1863. (Patroness, Mrs. Croker; Glebe, 24 acres; P. C.'s Inc. 100*l* and Ho; Pop. 459.) Formerly C. of St. Lawrence's, Reading, 1845–46; P. C. of West Molesey 1846–59; V. of Lower Halstow, Kent, 1859–63. Author, *Poems,* 1851; *Sermon before the Lord Mayor and Sheriffs of London,* 1858. [12]

NICHOLETTS, William, *Chipstable Rectory, Taunton.*—Pemb. Coll. Ox. B.A. 1853. R. of Chipstable, Dio. B. and W. 1858. (Patron, Charles H. Dare, Esq; Tithe, 270*l*; R.'s Inc. 350*l* and Ho; Pop. 361.) Formerly C. of Monksilver, Somerset. [13]

NICHOLL, Charles Iltid, *Hinton St. Mary, Blandford, Dorset.*—P. C. of Hinton, Dio. Salis. 1863. (Patron, V. of Iwerne-Minster; P. C.'s Inc. 350*l*.) Formerly C. of Hinton. [14]

NICHOLL, D., *Bodenham, near Leominster.*—C. of Bodenham. [15]

NICHOLL, E. P., *Laycock Vicarage, Chippenham.*—V. of Laycock, Dio. G. and B. 1864. (Patron, H. F. Talbot, Esq; V.'s Inc. 250*l* and Ho; Pop 1100.) [16]

NICHOLL, John Richard, *Streatham Rectory, Surrey.*—Ex. Coll. Ox. B.A. 1831, M.A. 1833; Deac. 1832, Pr. 1833. R. of Streatham, Dio. Win. 1843. (Patron, Duke of Bedford; Tithe, 1200*l* 10*s*; Glebe, 1½ acres; R.'s Inc. 1300*l* and Ho; Pop. 1728.) Rural Dean; Chap. to the Bp of St. D. [17]

NICHOLL, Robert, *Farnley, near Leeds.*—C. of Farnley. Formerly C. of St. Matthew's, Sheffield. [18]

NICHOLLS, G., *Redruth, Cornwall.*—C. of Redruth. [19]

NICHOLLS, Henry, *Hawkhurst Lodge, Burdocks, Horsham.*—Wad. Coll. Ox. B.A. 1859, M.A. 1862; Deac. 1859 and Pr. 1860 by Bp of Win. Formerly C. of Shirley, Southampton, 1859–61; V. of Madehurst 1861–66. [20]

NICHOLS, William Luke, *Keynsham House, near Bath.*—Queen's Coll. Ox. B.A. 1825, M.A. 1828; Deac. 1827, Pr. 1828. Formerly Min. of Trinity, Bath, 1839–46; V. of Buckland-Monachorum, Devon, 1846–51. Author, *Reliquiæ Romanæ, a Roman Villa Described,* 4to, Bath, 1833; *Inaugural Address* at the first Meeting of the Plymouth Branch of the Diocesan Architectural Soc. Exeter, 1848. Editor *of Kilvert's Remains,* Bath, 1867, 12*s*, Simpkin and Marshall. [21]

NICHOLS, William Powley, *Challacombe, Devon.*—C. of Challacombe. [22]

NICHOLSON, Aldwell, *Southampton.*—C. of St. Peter's, Southampton. Formerly C. of All Souls', Marylebone, Lond. [23]

NICHOLSON, George Joseph, *Chipstead, Sevenoaks, Kent.*—St. Aidan's; Deac. 1857 and Pr. 1858 by Bp of Ches. C. of Chevening, Kent, 1864. Formerly C. of Prestbury, Cheshire, 1858–62, Thornton-in-the-Moors 1862–64. [24]

NICHOLSON, Henry, *Dodderhill Vicarage, Droitwich.*—Emman. Coll. Cam. B.A. 1833, M.A. 1843; Deac. 1833 and Pr. 1834 by Abp of York. V. of Dodderhill with Elmbridge C. Dio. Wor. 1864. (Patrons, Trustees of Mrs. Nicholson; Dodderhill, Tithe—App. 3*l*, Imp. 540*l* 1*s*, V. 204*l* 1*s* 6*d*; Elmbridge, Tithe, 342*l* 4*s* 6*d*; V.'s Inc. 560*l* and Ho; Pop. Dodderhill 1750, Elmbridge 391.) Formerly V. of Wiston by Welland, Northants. [25]

NICHOLSON, Henry Donaldson.—Trin. Coll. Cam. B.A. 1852, M.A. 1855; Deac. 1853 and Pr. 1854 by Bp of Roch. Formerly C. of St. Alban's and of Barking, Essex. [26]

NICHOLSON, Henry Isaac, *Great Paxton, Buckden, Hunts.*—Jesus Coll. Cam. B.A. 1828; Deac. 1830, Pr. 1832. V. of Great Paxton with Little Paxton C. and Toseland C. Dio. Ely, 1840. (Patrons, D. and C. of Lin; Great Paxton, Glebe, 95 acres; Little Paxton, Tithe, App. 10*l*, V. 4*l* 16*s*; Glebe, 55 acres; V.'s Inc. 300*l* and Ho; Pop. Great Paxton 411, Little Paxton 247, Toseland 217.) [27]

NICHOLSON, Horatio Langrishe, 2, *Woodsome-villas, Forest Hill, S.E.*—Dub. Scho. of, B.A. 1855, M.A. 1859, *ad eund.* Ox. M.A. 1860; Scho. and Exhib. Medallist and 1st Prize in Oratory, 1st cl. and Medallist in Cl; Deac. 1856 by Bp of Killaloe, Pr. 1857 by Abp of Dub. P. C. of St. Saviour's, Brockley Hill, Forest Hill, 1866. (Patron, the present P. C; P. C.'s Inc. 660*l*; Pop. 2800.) Formerly C. of Aughrim 1856, Kingstown 1857; Lect. of Holy Trinity, Newington, 1859; C. of St. Matthew's, Paddington, 1860; P. C. of St. James's, Kennington, 1862, Chapel of Ease, Bathwick, 1864. Author, several *Sermons.* Editor of the *Appendix Hymnal,* Novello, 1866, 1*s* and upwards. [28]

NICHOLSON, John, *Elsdon, near Newcastle-on-Tyne.*—St. Bees; Deac. 1855 and Pr. 1856 by Abp of York. P. C. of Byrness, Dio. Dur. 1860. (Patron, R. of Elsdon; P. C.'s Inc. 75*l*.) [29]

NICHOLSON, J. H., *Welford, Berks.*—C. of Welford. [30]

NICHOLSON, John Young, *Aller Rectory, Langport, Somerset.*—Emman. Coll. Cam. B.A. 1844, M.A. 1847, B.D. 1854; Deac. 1845 and Pr. 1846 by Bp of Ely. R. of Aller, Dio. B. and W. 1858. (Patron, Emman. Coll. Cam; Tithe, 500*l*; Glebe, 66 acres; R.'s Inc. 600*l* and Ho; Pop. 518.) Formerly Fell. and Asst. Tut. of Emman. Coll. Cam; C. of St. Paul's, Cambridge. [31]

NICHOLSON, Jonah Peter, *Muker, near Richmond, Yorks.*—St. Bees; Deac. 1848 and Pr. 1849 by Bp of Carl. C. in sole charge of Muker 1866. Formerly C. of Dacre, near Penrith, 1848, Longton, near Preston, 1850, Wisbeach St. Mary, 1861, Milton, near Southsea, 1863. [32]

NICHOLSON, Mark Anthony, *Hanslope Vicarage, Stony Stratford, Bucks.*—Univ. Coll. Dur. Licen. Theol. and M.A. 1837; Deac. 1837 and Pr. 1838 by Bp. of Ches. V. of Hanslope with Castlethorpe C. Dio. Ox. 1851. (Patron, Bp of Ox; Tithe—App. 1400*l*, V. 70*l*; Glebe, 20 acres; V.'s Inc. 152*l*; Pop. Hanslope 1792, Castlethorpe 338.) [1]

NICHOLSON, Octavius, 54, *Oxford-street, Liverpool.*—St. Aidan's; Deac. 1860 and Pr. 1862 by Bp of Lich. C. of St. Augustine's, Everton, 1864. Formerly C. of Broughton, Stafford, 1860–63, Doddington, Cheshire, 1864. [2]

NICHOLSON, Patrick Charles, *St. Philip's Rectory, Salford, Manchester.*—Trin. Coll. Cam. B.D. 1848. R. of St. Philip's, Salford, Dio. Man. 1849. (Patrons, D. and C. of Man; R.'s Inc. 250*l*; Pop. 11,415.) Dom. Chap. to the Earl of Carlisle. [3]

NICHOLSON, Richard, *Beechingstoke Rectory, Devizes.*—Oriel Coll. Ox. B.A. 1850, M.A. 1852; Deac. 1851 and Pr. 1852 by Bp of G. and B. R. of Beechingstoke, Dio Salis. 1858. (Patron, G. H. Walker Heneage, Esq; Tithe, 293*l*; Glebe, 32 acres; R.'s Inc. 361*l* and Ho; Pop. 180.) Formerly C. of Stapleton 1851, Cherington 1853; P. C. of St. Mark's, Easton, Bristol, 1855. [4]

NICHOLSON, Richard, *Cumberland-place, Burnley.*—St. Bees; Deac. 1846 and Pr. 1847 by Bp of Ches. P. C. of St. Paul's, Lane Bridge, Burnley, Dio. Man. 1851. (Patrons, the Crown and Bp of Man. alt; P. C.'s Inc. 150*l*; Pop. 4420.) [5]

NICHOLSON, William, *The Parsonage, Onecote, Leek, Staffs.*—St. John's Coll. Cam. B.A. 1853, M.A. 1859; Deac. 1855 and Pr. 1857 by Bp of Man. P. C. of Onecote with Bradnop P. C. Dio. Lich. 1866. (Patron, V. of Leek; Glebe, 95 acres; P. C.'s Inc. 115*l* and Ho; Pop. 916.) Formerly C. of Trinity, Over Darwen, 1855, Leek 1859, Horncastle 1861. [6]

NICHOLSON, William, *King's-Nympton Rectory, South Molton, Devon.*—R. of King's-Nympton, Dio. Ex. 1853. (Patron, the present R; Tithe, 462*l* 18*s* 10*d*; R.'s Inc. 475*l* and Ho; Pop. 697.) [7]

NICHOLSON, William, *Wickham, Newbury, Berks.*—Trin. Coll. Ox. 2nd cl. Lit. Hum. and B.A. 1829, M.A. 1831; Deac. 1832, Pr. 1833. R. of Welford with Wickham C. Dio. Ox. 1836. (Patron, the present R; Tithe, 1400*l*; Glebe, 200*l*; R.'s Inc. 1600*l* and Ho; Pop. 1030.) [8]

NICHOLSON, W. Trevor, *Llanvihangel-vach-Cilvargen, Llandilo-Vawr, Carmarthenshire.*—Dub. A B. 1855; Deac. and Pr. 1855. R. of Llanvihangel-vach-Cilvargen, Dio. St. D. 1838. (Patron, Earl Cawdor; R.'s Inc. 113*l*; Pop. 58.) Formerly C. of Send with Ripley, Surrey, 1863, Cardiff. Author, *Gospel Thoughts, or Christ in the Prayer Book*, 1859, 5*s*. [9]

NICKLIN, John, *Green Gown, Blackburn.*—St. Bees; Deac. 1850 by Bp of Lich. Pr. 1851 by Bp of Man. C. of the Pleckgate Conventional District, Blackburn, 1865. [10]

NICKOLL, F. W.—Chap. of H.M.S. "Ocean." [11]

NICOL, Walter, *Denton Rectory, Manchester.*—Univ. Glasgow, M.A. 1848; Deac. 1848 and Pr. 1849 by Bp of Lich. R. of Denton, Dio. Man. 1853. (Patron, Earl of Wilton; Glebe, 17 acres; R.'s Inc. 197*l* and Ho; Pop. 3127.) [12]

NICOLAS, Percy, *Benares, India.*—Ch. Coll. Cam. 2nd cl. Cl. Trip. B.A. 1858, M.A. 1861; Deac. 1859 and Pr. 1860 by Bp of Roch. Chap. to H. M.'s Forces, Benares, 1866. Formerly C. of Great Oakley, Essex, 1859, Tottenham, Middlesex, 1862. P. C. of Plympton St. Maurice, Devon, 1864. [13]

NICOLAY, Charles Grenfell, *Bahia.*—Librarian of King's Coll. Lond. British Chap. at Bahia. Editor of *Manual of Geographical Science*, 10*s* 6*d*; *Atlas of Physical and Historical Geography*, 5*s*. [14]

NICOLL, Charles, *King's Somborne Vicarage, Stockbridge, Hants.*—Ex. Coll. Ox. B.A. 1826; Deac. 1828 and Pr. 1829 by Bp of Nor. V. of King's Somborne with Little Somborne C. Dio. Win. 1850. (Patroness, Lady Mill; Tithe—Imp. 357*l* 16*s* 6*d*, V. 761*l* 19*s* 8*d*; Glebe, 6 acres; V.'s Inc. 786*l* and Ho; Pop. King's Somborne 1241, Little Somborne 87.) [15]

NICOLL, C. A. S., *East Grimstead, near Salisbury.*—C. of East Grimstead. [16]

NICOLLS, Jasper Hume, *Lennoxville College, Canada East.*—Oriel Coll. Ox. B.A. 1840, M.A. 1843, D.D. 1850. Prin. of Lennoxville Coll. Canada. [17]

NICOLS, Bartholomew, *Mill Hill, Hendon, Middlesex.*—St. Peter's Coll. Cam. B.A. 1821, M.A. 1824; Deac. 1821 and Pr. 1822 by Bp of Win. P. C. of St. Paul's, Mill Hill, Dio. Lon. 1841. (Patron, V. of Hendon; P. C.'s Inc. 125*l*; Pop. 1188.) [18]

NICOLSON, Alexander Dunbar.—St. Peter's Coll. Cam. 8th Sen. Opt. and B.A. 1850, M.A. 1855; Deac. 1850, Pr. 1851. Chap. at Nowshera, Bengal. Formerly C. of Ripley, and of Hampsthwaite, Yorks. [19]

NIGHTINGALE, George, *Sherborne, Dorset.*—St. Cath. Coll. Cam. B.A. 1835, M.A. 1838; Deac. 1836 and Pr. 1837 by Bp of Ches. R. of Holcombe, Dio. Man. 1849. (Patron, R. of Bury; R.'s Inc. 180*l* and Ho; Pop. 2511.) [20]

NIHILL, Henry Daniel, *St. Michael's Church, Mark-street, Finsbury, E.C.*—Jesus Coll. Ox. 3rd cl. Lit. Hum. 3rd cl. Nat. Sci. and B.A. 1857; Deac. 1857 and Pr. 1858 by Bp of St. A. C. of St. Michael's, Shoreditch, 1866. Formerly C. of Whittington, Salop, 1857, St. Alban's District, Cheetwood, Manchester, 1862. [21]

NIND, Philip Henry, *Woodcote, Henley-on-Thames,* and *United University Club, Suffolk-street, Pall-mall, London, W.*—Ch. Ch. Ox. B.A. 1829, M.A. 1831; Deac. 1829 by Bp of Ox. and Pr. 1830 by Bp of G. and B. V. of South Stoke with Woodcote, Dio. Ox. 1844. (Patrons, D. and C. of Ch. Ch. Ox; Tithe, comm. 128*l* 15*s*; Glebe, 70 acres; V.'s Inc. 150*l* and Ho; Pop. 800.) Surrogate. [22]

NINIS, George Wyatt, *Stockport, Cheshire.*—St. Bees; Deac. 1853 and Pr. 1854 by Bp of Rip. Min. of Stockport Moor Chapel. Formerly C. of Queenshead, near Halifax; C. of Hyson Green. [23]

NISBET, John Marjoribanks, *Ramsgate Vicarage, Kent.*—Ball. Coll. Ox. B.A. 1846, M.A. 1849; Deac. 1848 and Pr. 1849 by Bp of Lich. V. of Ramsgate, Dio. Cant. 1861. (Patron, Abp of Cant; V.'s Inc. 480*l* and Ho; Pop. 9243.) Rural Dean. Formerly R. of Deal 1856–61. [24]

NISBET, Matthew Alexander, *Campden, Chipping Campden, Gloucestershire.*—Jesus Coll. Cam. Scho. of, Sen. Opt. in Math. Trip. B.A. 1860, M.A. 1863; Deac. 1861 and Pr. 1862 by Bp of G. and B. Sen. C. of Campden 1867. Formerly C. of Longborough, Gloucestershire. [25]

NISBETT, James Meade, M.A.—Dom. Chap. to Lord Dunalley. [26]

NIVEN, Henry, *Bishampton Vicarage, Pershore, Worcestershire.*—St. John's Coll. Cam. Wrang. and B.A. 1837, M.A. 1840; Deac. 1839 and Pr. 1841 by Bp of Salis. V. of Bishampton, Dio. Wor. 1850. (Patron, Bp of Wor; Tithe, 17*s* 4*d*; Glebe, 100 acres; V.'s Inc. 140*l* and Ho; Pop. 469.) [27]

NIVEN, James, *Adstock Rectory, Buckingham.*—R. of Adstock, Dio. Ox. 1867. (Patron, the present R; R.'s Inc. 450*l* and Ho; Pop. 385.) Formerly V. of Swanbourne, Bucks, 1852–67. [28]

NIVEN, William, 5, *Walton-place, London, S.W.*—Sid. Coll. Cam. B.D. 1849; Deac. 1834 and Pr. 1835 by Bp of Win. P. C. of St. Saviour's, Upper Chelsea, Dio. Lon. 1840. (Patron, R. of Upper Chelsea; P. C.'s Inc. 450*l*; Pop. 8837.) Formerly C. of Surlingham, Norfolk, 1834–36; Chap. of St. George's Hospital, Lond. 1836–39. Author, *Thoughts on the Kingdom of God*, 2*s*. 6*d*; *The Victory over Death, an Exposition of* 1 *Cor. xv.* 2*s* 6*d*; etc. [29]

NIX, Charles Devas, *St. John's Parsonage, Hatfield-Broad-Oak, Harlow, Essex.*—Trin. Coll. Cam. B.A. 1854, M.A. 1857; Deac. 1854 and Pr. 1855 by Bp of Chich. P. C. of St. John's, Hatfield-Broad-Oak, Dio. Roch. 1860. (Patron, V. of Hatfield; P. C.'s Inc. 75*l* and Ho; Pop. 410.) Formerly C. of Worth, Sussex. [30]

NIXON, Edward, *Kelsall, Chester.*—Corpus Coll. Cam. Sen. Opt. 1860; Deac. 1861 and Pr. 1862 by Bp of Ches. C. of Delamere, Cheshire, 1861. [1]

NIXON, The Right Rev. Francis Russell. —St. John's Coll. Ox. Fell. of, 3rd cl. Lit. Hum. B.A. 1827, M.A. 1841, D.D. 1842; Deac. 1827 and Pr. 1828 by Bp of Ox. Formerly C. of Leyton, Essex, and Sevenoaks, Kent; P. C. of Plaistow, Essex; Chap. at Naples; P. C. of Sandgate, Kent; V. of Ash-next-Sandwich, Kent; consecrated first Bp of Tasmania, 24 Aug. 1842, resigned 17th Dec. 1868. Author, *Visitation Sermon*, 1840; *Lectures on the Church Catechism*, Rivingtons, 1843, 18*s*; *Charges*, 1846, '51, '55. [2]

NIXON, William, *Sutton, Woodbridge, Suffolk.*—Wor. Coll. Ox. B.A. 1852. V. of Sutton, Dio. Nor. 1855. (Patrons, Trustees of late J. Nixon, Esq; Tithe, App. 431*l*; Glebe, 33 acres; V.'s Inc. 440*l*; Pop. 618.) [3]

NIXSON, Joseph Mayer, *Rampton, Cambridge.* C. of Rampton. [4]

NOAD, George Frederick, *Wye College, Ashford, Kent.*—Wor. Coll. Ox. S.C.L. 2nd cl. Lit. Hum. and B.A. 1836, B.C.L. 1838, D.C.L. 1846; Deac. 1837 and Pr. 1839 by Bp of B and W. Head Mast. of Wye College. Formerly Head Mast. of Holybourne Gr. Sch. 1850. [5]

NOBBS, G. H.—Chap. of Norfolk Island. [6]

NOBLE, H. B., *Bradford, Wilts.*—C. of Bradford with Westwood. [7]

NOBLE, John, *Nether-Broughton Rectory, Melton-Mowbray.*—Sid. Coll. Cam. B.A. 1826; Deac. 1827, Pr. 1828. R. of Nether-Broughton, Dio. Pet. 1847. (Patrons, Hon. P. P. Bouverie and Rev. W. H. Sawyer alt; Tithe—Imp. 1*l* 10*s*, R. 9*s*; Glebe, 266 acres; R.'s Inc. 440*l* and Ho; Pop. 519.) Rural Dean. [8]

NOBLE, John Padmore, *Lodsworth, near Petworth, Sussex.*—Ch. Coll. Cam. B.A. 1858, M.A. 1861; Deac. 1860 and Pr. 1861 by Bp of Ely. C. of Lodsworth. Formerly C. of Ampthill, Beds, 1860. [9]

NOBLE, R., *Grimstone, Loughboro', Leicestershire.* —P. C. of Grimstone, Dio. Pet. 1866. (Patron, V. of Rothley; P. C.'s Inc. 43*l*; Pop. 190.) [10]

NOBLE, Samuel Henry Brierly, *Frowlesworth, near Lutterworth, Leicestershire.*—Emman. Coll. Cam. B.A. 1863; Deac. 1864 and Pr. 1865 by Bp of Wor. R. of Frowlesworth, Dio. Pet. 1865. (Patrons, Trustees; Tithe, 400*l*; Glebe, 60 acres; R.'s Inc. 530*l* and Ho; Pop. 296.) Formerly C. of Dunchurch, 1864-65. [11]

NOBLE, William, *Pitchcott Rectory, Aylesbury, Bucks.*—R. of Pitchcott, Dio. Ox. 1847. (Patrons, Heirs of the late Captain Saunders; R.'s Inc. 333*l* and Ho; Pop. 45.) [12]

NOCKELLS, William, *Ifield, Gravesend, Kent.*—St. John's Coll. Cam. B.A. 1847, M.A. 1850; Deac. 1854 and Pr. 1856 by Bp of Roch. R. of Ifield, Dio. Roch. 1860. (Patron, Rev. W. H. Edmeades; Glebe, 8½ acres; R.'s Inc. 120*l* and Ho; Pop. 88.) Formerly C. of Stanstead-Abbots, Herts. [13]

NODDER, Joseph, *Ashover Rectory, Chesterfield.* —Wad. Coll. Ox. B.A. 1811, M.A. 1814; Deac. 1812, Pr. 1813. R. of Ashover, Dio. Lich. 1835. (Patron, the present R; Tithe, 540*l*; Glebe, 165 acres; R.'s Inc. 760*l* and Ho; Pop. 2351.) Rural Dean 1837. [14]

NOEL, Augustus William, *Stanhoe Rectory, King's Lynn, Norfolk.*—Trin. Coll. Cam. Hon. M.A. 1840; Deac. 1840 and Pr. 1841 by Bp of G. and B. R. of Stanhoe with Barwick V. Dio. Nor. 1860. (Patron, Admiral G. H. Seymour, C.B; Tithe, Stenhoe, comm. 480*l*, Barwick, 10*l*; Glebe, 30 acres; R.'s Inc. 510*l* and Ho; Pop. Stanhoe 468, Barwick 26.) Formerly C. of Cropredy, Oxon, 1851–61. [15]

NOEL, David, *Llanfabon, Pontypridd, Glamorganshire.*— Lampeter; Deac. 1848, Pr. 1849. V. of Llanfabon, Dio. Llan. 1860. (Patrons, D. and C. of Llan; V.'s Inc. 120*l* and Ho; Pop. 2500.) Formerly C. of St. Mary's, Cardiff, 1850, Gelligaer 1854. [16]

NOEL, The Hon. Leland, *Exton Vicarage, Oakham.*—Trin. Coll. Cam. B.A. 1822, M.A. 1823; Deac. 1823, Pr. 1824. V. of Exton, Dio. Pet. 1832. (Patron, Earl of Gainsborough; Glebe, 16 acres; V.'s Inc. 372*l* and Ho; Pop. 835.) Hon. Can. of Pet. Cathl. 1850. [17]

NOEL-FEARON, Henry, 3, *Danes Inn, Strand, W.C.*—St. John's Coll. Cam. B.A. 1837, M.A. 1840. F.R.S; Deac. 1837 and Pr. 1838 by Bp of Ches. C. of St. James's Garlick Hythe, Thames-street, 1866; Thursday Morning Lect. St. Peter's, Cornhill, 1852. Formerly C. of Colne, Lancashire, Trinity, Clapham, and St. Clement Danes, Strand; P. C. of Verulam Chapel, Lambeth; Prof. of British Hist. and Archeol. in the R. Soc. of Literature, Lond. Author, *Universal Mythology*, Parker, 1838; *Cradle of the Twin Giants*, 2 vols. Bentley, 1849; *Echoes of the Universe*, 7th ed. Bentley, 1862; *History of the Hampden Controversy*, Smith and Elder, 1848; *Shores and Islands of the Mediterranean*, 3 vols. Bentley, 1851; *Sin, its Causes and Consequences*, Allen, 1860; *Scenes in the Life of Christ*, Smith and Elder, 1853; *Christian Politics*, Hope, 1854; *Preachers and Preaching*, Bohn, 1858. Translations—*Meditations Poetiques*, *Lamartine*, Parker, 1838; *Calmet's Phantom World*, 2 vols. Bentley, 1850; *Wieland's Republic of Fools*, 2 vols. Allen, 1860. Formerly Editor of the *Churchman*, *British Churchman*, *Church of England Quarterly Review*, and *Literary Gazette*. [18]

NOLAN, Thomas, 34, *Brunswick-square, London, W.C.*—Dub. A.B. 1831, A.M. 1833, *ad eund.* Cam. 1851, Scho. 1827, B.D. 1857; Deac. 1833 by Bp of Killaloe, Pr. 1834 by Bp of Raphoe. P. C. of St. Peter's, Regent-square, Dio. Lon. 1857. (Patrons, D. and C. of St. Paul's; P. C.'s Inc. 400*l* from pew rents; Pop. 10,666.) Formerly C. of St. Peter's, Stockport, 1837; P. C. of St. Barnabas', Liverpool, 1841; Min. of St. John's Chapel, Bedford-row, Lond. 1849; V. of Acton, Cheshire, 1854. Author, *Vicarious Sacrifice*, 1860. [19]

NOOTT, Edward Henry Lane, *Dudley.*—Corpus Coll. Cam. B.A. 1839. P. C. of St. John's, Dudley, Dio. Wor. 1845. (Patron, V. of Dudley; P. C.'s Inc. 260*l* and Ho; Pop. 6370.) [20]

NOOTT, John Frederick, *Frostenden Hermitage, near Wangford, Suffolk.*—Queens' Coll. Cam. B.A. 1844; Deac. 1844 and Pr. 1845 by Bp of Nor. R. of Blyford, near Wangford, Dio. Nor. 1860. (Patrons, Exors. of Rev. J. Day; R.'s Inc. 60*l*; Pop. 193.) Chap. of the Blything Union, Suffolk, 1865. (Salary 50*l*.) P. C. of Dunwich, Dio. Nor. 1867. (Patron, F. Barne, Esq; P.C.'s Inc. 53*l*; Pop. 227.) Formerly C. of Westhall 1844–57, Wangford and Reydon 1857–60. [21]

NORCLIFFE, Charles Best, *York* and *Langton Hall, Malton.*—Univ. Coll. Dur. B.A. 1855, M.A. 1858; Deac. 1856 and Pr. 1857 by Abp of York. Fell. of Dur. Author, *Best's Farming Book*, 1857; *Agricultural Statistics*, 1858; *Christian Diligence* (a Sermon), 1860; *The Priory and Peculiar of Snaith*, 1861; *Some Account of the Parish of Holy Trinity, York*, 1862; Editor of *The York Diocesan Calendar*, 1863; etc. [22]

NORGATE, Edward, *Rollesby Rectory, Norfolk.* —Corpus Coll. Cam. Deac. 1867, Pr. 1868. C. of Rollesby 1867. Formerly C. of Newmarket. [23]

NORGATE, Louis Augustus, *Foxley, near Elmham, Norfolk.*—Corpus Coll. Cam. B.A. 1834; Deac. 1836 by Bp of Lin. Pr. 1836 by Bp of Ely. P. C. of Bylaugh, Norfolk, Dio. Nor. 1836. (Patron, Rev. H. Lombe; Tithe, Imp. 208*l*; P. C.'s Inc. 80*l*; Pop. 82.) R. of Foxley, Dio. Nor. 1840. (Patron, Rev. H. Lombe; Tithe, 390*l*; Glebe, 20 acres; R.'s Inc. 410*l* and Ho; Pop. 278.) Rural Dean of Sparham 1858. [24]

NORGATE, Thomas Starling, *Sparham Rectory, near Norwich.*—Caius Coll. Cam. B.A. 1832; Deac. and Pr. 1832 by Bp of Nor. R. of Sparham, Dio. Nor. 1840. (Patron, Rev. Henry Lombe; Tithe, rent charge, 481*l* 18*s*; Glebe, 91 acres; R.'s Inc. 564*l* and Ho; Pop. 354.) Formerly P. C. of Brioingham 1832; C. of Cley next the Sea 1835–39, Banningham and Swanton Abbots, all in Norfolk. Author, *Homer's Iliad, reproduced in Dramatic Blank Verse*, 1864; *Homer's Odyssey, reproduced in Dramatic Blank Verse*, 1863, 12*s*; *The Battle of the Frogs and the Mice, an Homeric Fable, reproduced in Dramatic Blank Verse*, 1863, 1*s*; published in London and Edinburgh by Williams and Norgate. [25]

NORMAN, Alfred Merle, *Newbottle, Fence Houses, Durham.*—Ch. Ch. Ox. B.A. 1852, M.A. 1858; Deac. 1856 and Pr. 1857 by Bp of Pet. R. of Burnmoor, Dio. Dur. 1866. (Patrons, Crown and Bp of Dur. alt; R's. Inc. 200*l*; Pop. 1700.) Formerly C. of Kibworth 1856–58, Sedgefield 1858–64, Houghton-le-Spring 1864–66. [1]

NORMAN, Charles, *Boxtead Vicarage, Nayland, Essex.*—V. of Boxtead, Dio. Roch. 1841. (Patron, Bp of Roch; Tithe—Imp. 582*l* 15*s* and 61 acres of Glebe, V. 224*l* 15*s*; Glebe, 3 acres; V.'s Inc. 229*l* and Ho; Pop. 935.) [2]

NORMAN, Charles Frederick, *Portishead Rectory, Bristol.*—R. of Portishead, Dio. B. and W. 1854. (Patron, the present R; Tithe, 625*l*; R.'s Inc. 729*l* and Ho; Pop. 1201.) [3]

NORMAN, Charles Manners Richard, *Northwold Rectory (Norfolk), near Brandon.*—St. John's Coll. Cam. Hon. M.A. 1820; Deac. 1824 by Bp of Lon. Pr. 1824 by Bp of Ely. R. of Northwold, Dio. Nor. 1833. (Patron, Bp of Nor; Tithe, 896*l*; Glebe, 57 acres; R.'s Inc. 946*l* and Ho; Pop. 1375.) [4]

NORMAN, Denham Rowe, *Middleton Vicarage, Wirksworth, Derbyshire.*—King's Coll. Lond. 1st cl. Theol. Assoc. 1855; Deac. 1855 and Pr. 1856 by Bp of Lich. P. C. of Middleton-by-Wirksworth, Dio. Lich. 1858. (Patron, V. of Wirksworth; Tithe, 8*l* 12*s*; P. C.'s Inc. 140*l* and Ho; Pop. 1226.) Formerly C. of Wirksworth and Ashton, near Warrington. [5]

NORMAN, Frederic John, *Bottesford Rectory (Leicestershire), near Nottingham.*—Caius Coll. Cam. B.A. 1838; Deac. 1838 by Bp of Win. Pr. 1839 by Bp of Pet. R. of Bottesford, Dio. Pet. 1846. (Patron, Duke of Rutland; R.'s Inc. 1000*l* and Ho; Pop. 1415.) Rural Dean. [6]

NORMAN, George, *Marston Parsonage, Stafford.*—St. Peter's Coll. Cam. B.A. 1822, M.A. 1826, *ad eund.* Ox. 1861; Deac. 1822 by Bp of Nor. Pr. 1824 by Bp of Lich. P. C. of Marston, Dio. Lich. 1836. (Patron, R. of St. Mary's, Stafford; Tithe, 100*l*; Glebe, 12 acres; P. C.'s Inc. 150*l* and Ho; Pop. 206.) P. C. of St. John's, Whitgreave, Dio. Lich. 1836. (Patron, R. of St. Mary's, Stafford; P. C.'s Inc. 40*l*.) Formerly Head Mast. of King Edward's Gr. Sch. Stafford. [7]

NORMAN, James Charles, *Chantry Cottage, Berkeley, Glouc.*—Magd. Coll. Ox. B.A. 1853, M.A. 1856; Deac. 1853 and Pr. 1856 by Bp of Dur. Chap. to Lord Fitzhardinge. Formerly C. of Morpeth 1854–58; R. of Warehorne, Kent, 1858–63. Author, *School Prayers*; occasional Sermons. [8]

NORMAN, John, *Coates Parsonage, Whittlesey, Cambs.*—Queens' Coll. Cam. B.A. 1842, M.A. 1847. P. C. of Coates, Dio. Ely, 1861. (Patrons, Ld Chan. and Mr. Childers, alt; P. C.'s Inc. 70*l* and Ho; Pop. 1394.) Formerly C. of St. Andrew's, Whittlesey. [9]

NORMAN, John Burton, *Whitchurch Rectory, Edgware, N.W.*—Queen's Coll. Ox. B.A. 1852, M.A. 1865; Deac. 1853 and Pr. 1854 by Bp of Carlisle. P. C. of Grinsdale, Dio. Carl. 1855. (Patron, Joseph Dacre, Esq; P. C.'s Inc. 130*l*; Pop. 105.) C. (sole charge) of Little Stanmore, or Whitchurch, Middlesex 1865. [10]

NORMAN, Manners Octavius, *Harby Rectory, Melton Mowbray.*—Corpus Coll. Cam. B.A. 1844; Deac. 1844 and Pr. 1845 by Bp of Pet. R. of Harby, Dio. Pet. 1853. (Patron, Duke of Rutland; Glebe, 459¾ acres; R.'s Inc. 560*l* and Ho; Pop. 655.) Rural Dean. [11]

NORMAN, Richard Whitmore, *St. Peter's College, Radley, near Abingdon.*—Ex. Coll. Ox. B.A. 1851, M.A. 1854; Deac. 1852 and Pr. 1853 by Bp of Ox. Warden of St. Peter's Coll. Radley, 1861. Formerly Fell. of St. Peter's Coll. Radley, and C. of St. Thomas's, Oxford, 1852–57; Head Mast. of St. Michael's Coll. Tenbury, 1857. Author, *Manual of Prayers for the Use of Schools*, 1856, 2nd ed. 1862; *Occasional Sermons*, 1860; *Sermons preached in Radley College Chapel*, 1864. [12]

NORMAN, William, *Wanstead, Essex.*—Chap. to the Infant Orphan Asylum, Wanstead. [13]

NORRIS, Charles, *Melton-Constable, Holt, Norfolk.*—Caius Coll. Cam. B.A. 1854; Deac. 1854 and Pr. 1855 by Bp of Nor. R. of Melton-Constable with Burgh Parva R. Dio. Nor. 1855. (Patron, Lord Hastings; Tithe, 242*l*; Glebe, 33 acres; R.'s Inc. 282*l*; Pop. 118.) V. of Briston, near Dereham, Norfolk, Dio. Nor. 1855. (Patron, Lord Hastings; Tithe—Imp. 449*l* 8*s* 1*d*, V. 234*l* 8*s* 1*d*; V.'s Inc. 320*l*; Pop. 931.) [14]

NORRIS, Charles Edward, *Pendleton, Manchester.*—Emman. Coll. Cam. B.A. 1857, M.A. 1860; Deac. 1862 and Pr. 1863 by Bp of Roch. Sen. C. in charge of St. Thomas's, Pendleton, 1867; Organizing Sec. to the National Soc. for the Dio. of Man. 1867. Formerly 2nd Mast. of the Stockport Gr. Sch; C. of Clavering-with-Langley, Essex, 1862–65; 2nd C. of St. Thomas's, Pendleton, 1862–65. [15]

NORRIS, George Montgomery, *Wissett, near Wangford, Suffolk.*—Emman. Coll. Cam. B.A. 1852, M.A. 1857; Deac. 1855 and Pr. 1856 by Bp of Ches. C. of Frostenden, near Wangford, 1865. Formerly C. of St. Philip's, Liverpool, 1855; Burgh, near Aylsham, 1859; Kessingland, near Wangford, 1861. [16]

NORRIS, George P., *Rosecraddock, Liskeard, Cornwall.*—R. of East Anstey, near Dulverton, Devon, Dio. Ex. (Patron, T. S. Jessop, Esq; Tithe, 168*l*; R.'s Inc. 175*l* and Ho; Pop. 227.) [17]

NORRIS, James, *Corpus Christi College, Oxford.*—Corpus Coll. Ox. 2nd cl. Lit. Hum. and B.A. 1818, M.A. 1822, B.D. 1829, D.D. 1843. President of Corpus Coll. Ox. 1843. [18]

NORRIS, John Elye, *Ashby-by-Partney, Spilsby, Lincolnshire.*—Jesus Coll. Cam. B.A. 1838; Deac. 1841 and Pr. 1842 by Bp of Lin. R. of Ashby, Dio. Lin. 1842. (Patron, Rev. Luke Fowler; R.'s Inc. 240*l* and Ho; Pop. 240.) [19]

NORRIS, John Pilkington, *The Abbey House, Bristol.*—Trin. Coll. Cam. 1st cl. Cl. Trip. and B.A. 1846, M.A. 1849; Deac. 1849 and Pr. 1850 by Bp of Ely. P.C. of Hatchford, Dio. Win. 1865. (Patron, Hon. Capt. Egerton, R.N; P.C.'s Inc. 95*l*; Pop. 300.) Can. of Bristol 1865. Formerly one of H.M.'s Inspectors of Schools 1849–64; C. (sole charge) of Lewknor, Oxon. 1864–65; Fell. of Trin. Coll. Cam. Author, *Translation of Demosthenes de Corona* 1849; *Education Reports*, 1849–64; *On the Inspiration of the New Testament Writers*, Macmillans, 1864; *Ordination Sermons*, Rivingtons, 1866. [20]

NORRIS, Thomas, *Tugby Vicarage, Leicester.*—Dub. A.B. 1850, Dur. Licen. Theol. 1851; Deac. 1851 and Pr. 1852 by Bp of Pet. V. of Tugby with East-Norton C. Dio. Pet. 1862. (Patron, Lord Berners; V.'s Inc. 300*l* and Ho; Pop. Tugby 360, East-Norton 139.) Formerly C. of Alexton. [21]

NORRIS, William, *Warblington Rectory, Havant, Hants.*—Trin. Coll. Ox. B.A. 1816, M.A. 1819; Deac. 1818 by Bp of Herf. Pr. 1819 by Bp of Salis. R. of Warblington, Dio. Win. 1827. (Patron, the present R; Tithe, 486*l*; Glebe, 44 acres; R.'s Inc. 574*l* and Ho; Pop. 452.) Rural Dean of S.E. Droxford 1846. Author, *Sermons on the History of our Blessed Saviour*, Rivingtons, 1830; *The Annals of Adelaide*, on the list of the S.P.C.K. and S.P.G. 1852. [22]

NORRIS, William Arthur, *Oaksey Rectory, Cirencester.*—Trin. Coll. Cam. B.A. 1854, M.A. 1857; Deac. 1854, Pr. 1855. R. of Oaksey, Dio. G. and B. 1860. (Patron, Capt. Mullins; R.'s Inc. 460*l* and Ho; Pop. 450.) Formerly C. of Langley, Worc. 1854–56, Alresford 1856–57, Feliskirk, Yorks, 1857–60. [23]

NORRIS, William Foxley, *Buckingham.*—Trin. Coll. Ox. B.A. 1848, M.A. 1850; Deac. 1848, Pr. 1849. V. of Buckingham, Dio. Ox. 1862. (Patron, Bp of Ox; V.'s Inc. 500*l* and Ho; Pop. 3247.) Surrogate. Formerly C. of Trinity, Cirencester. [24]

NORRIS, William Sheard, *Trinity, South Shields.*—Bp Hat. Hall, Dur. Scho. of, Licen. in Theol. 1863, B.A. 1864, Div. Prize and Fell. of Univ. 1865; Deac. 1863 and Pr. 1864 by Bp of Ches. C. of South Shields 1866. Formerly C. of St. Silas's, Liverpool, 1863. [25]

NORTH, Isaac William, *The Grove, Blackheath, Kent.*—Trin. Coll. Cam. B.A. 1833, M.A. 1836; Deac.

1834, Pr. 1835. Min. of Trinity, Greenwich, Dio. Lon. 1851. (Patron, V. of Greenwich.) Author, *Sermons on the Liturgy*, 1844, 5s; *Visitation Sermon*, 1850; *A Week in the Isles of Scilly*, 1850; *Sermons preached in Trinity Church, Greenwich*, 1854, 2s 6d. [1]

NORTH, Jacob Hugo, *Brighton.*—Trin. Coll. Cam. B.A. 1834, M.A. 1837. P. C. of St. George's Chapel, Brighton, Dio. Chich. 1851. (Patron, L. Peel, Esq; P. C.'s Inc. 250*l*.) [2]

NORTH, James, 1, *Bedford-street North, Liverpool.*—Brasen. Coll. Ox. B.A. 1825, M.A. 1826; Deac. 1828 and Pr. 1829 by Bp of Ches. P. C. of St. Catherine's, Liverpool, Dio. Ches. 1833. (Patrons, Trustees; P. C.'s Inc. 250*l*; Pop. 9679.) [3]

NORTH, Joseph, *Banwell, Weston-super-Mare.*—Deac. and Pr. by Bp of Kilmore. C. of Banwell 1866. Formerly C. of St. Clement's and Temple, Bristol. [4]

NORTH, The Venerable William, *Llangoedmore, Cardigan.*—Jesus Coll. Ox. Scho. of, B.A. 1829, M.A. 1832; Deac. 1831 and Pr. 1832 by Bp of Ox. Archd. of Cardigan with Preb. of Llandyfriog 1860. (Value, 200*l*.) R. of Llangoedmore, Cardiganshire, Dio. St. D. 1845. (Patron, St. D. Coll. Lampeter; Tithe, 440*l*; R.'s Inc. 440*l*; Pop. 902.) Prof. of Latin at Lampeter. Formerly C. of St. John's, Brecon, 1833–40. Author, *A Charge*, 1862–65; various occasional Sermons. [5]

NORTHCOTE, George B., *Feniton Rectory, Honiton, Devon.*—R. of Feniton, Dio. Ex. 1860. (Patrons, G. B. Northcote, Esq. 2 turns, and B. Woolley, Esq. 1 turn; R.'s Inc. 400*l* and Ho; Pop. 361.) [6]

NORTHCOTE, Henry Mowbray, *Monk Okehampton Rectory, Hatherleigh, Devon.*—New Coll. Ox. B.A. 1849; Deac. 1850 and Pr. 1851 by Bp of Ox. R. of Monk Okehampton, Dio. Ex. 1853. (Patron, Sir S. Northcote, Bart; Tithe, 126*l*; Glebe, 40 acres; R.'s Inc. 175*l* and Ho; Pop. 272.) [7]

NORTHCOTE, Stafford Charles, *Upton-Pyne Rectory, near Exeter.*—Ball. Coll. Ox. B.A. 1819, M.A. 1821; Deac. 1820, Pr. 1821. R. of Upton-Pyne, Dio. Ex. 1821. (Patron, Sir S. H. Northcote; Tithe, 400*l*; Glebe, 90 acres; R.'s Inc. 580*l* and Ho; Pop. 455.) [8]

NORTHEY, A. E.—C. of St. Martin's-in-the-Fields, Lond. Formerly C. of All Saints', Huntingdon. [9]

NORTHEY, Edward William, *Hawkhurst, Staplehurst, Kent.*—Corpus Coll. Ox. B.A. 1855, M.A. 1857; Deac. 1856 and Pr. 1857 by Bp of Lich. C. of Hawkhurst. Formerly P. C. of Atlow, Derbyshire, 1864. [10]

NORTON, Hector, *Longfield, Dartford, Kent.*—Magd. Coll. Cam. B.A 1850; Deac. 1850, Pr. 1851. R. of Longfield, Dio. Roch. 1864. (Patron, Bp of Roch; R.'s Inc. 193*l*; Pop. 188.) Formerly C. of Ecclesfield, near Sheffield, and St. Mary's, Southampton. [11]

NORTON, Josiah, *High Beech Parsonage, Loughton, N.E.*—St. John's Coll. Cam Sen. Opt. and B.A. 1851, M.A. 1854; Deac. 1851 and Pr. 1852 by Bp of Win. P. C. of St. Paul's, High Beach, 1865. (Patron, Bp of Roch; P. C.'s Inc. 200*l* and Ho; Pop. 530.) Formerly C. of St. Mary's, Southampton; P. C. of South Baddesley 1856. [12]

NORTON, John, *Worplesdon, Guildford, Surrey.*—C. of Worplesdon 1867. Formerly C. of Spilsby 1856–57, Horne, Surrey, 1858–67. [13]

NORVAL, William, *Fulham, London, S.W.*—Dub. A.B. 1829, M.A. 1831; Deac. and Pr. 1840. Chap. of the Union Workhouse, Fulham. Formerly R. of Ickleford, Herts, 1851–59. [14]

NORWICH, The Hon. and Right Rev. John Thomas PELHAM, Lord Bishop of Norwich, *The Palace, Norwich.*—Ch. Ch. Ox. B.A. 1832, D.D. (per Literas Regias) 1857; Deac. 1834, Pr. 1835. Consecrated Bishop of Norwich 1857. (Episcopal Jurisdiction—the County of Norfolk, and part of the County of Suffolk; Income of See, 4500*l* and Res; Population, 667,704; Acres, 1,994,525; Deaneries, 41; Benefices, 910; Curates, 253; Church Sittings, 294,777.) His Lordship was formerly R. of Bergh Apton, Norfolk, 1837–52; P. C. of Ch. Ch. Hampstead, 1852–55; R. of St. Marylebone, Lond. 1855–57. Author, *A Charge at the Primary Visitation*, 1858. [15]

NORWOOD, Curteis H., *Sibertswold, Dover.*—Brasen. Coll. Ox. B.A. 1862, M.A. 1864; Deac. 1864 by Abp of Cant. C. of Sibertswold 1864. [16]

NORWOOD, George, *Mersham Rectory, Ashford, Kent.*—Oriel Coll. Ox. B.A. 1801, M.A. 1825; Deac. 1803 and Pr. 1804 by Abp of Cant. R. of Mersham, Dio. Cant. 1840. (Patron, Abp of Cant; Tithe, 630*l* 10*s* 6*d*; Glebe, 40 acres; R.'s Inc. 710*l* and Ho; Pop. 752.) [17]

NORWOOD, Samuel, *Royal Grammar School, Whalley, Blackburn.*—Lond. Univ. Deac. 1865 and Pr. 1867 by Bp of Man. Head Mast. of Gr. Sch. Whalley; C. of St. James's, Clitheroe, Lanc. 1865. [18]

NORWOOD, Thomas Wilkinson, *The Rectory, Chelsea.*—St. John's and Queens' Coll. Cam. B.A. 1851; Deac. 1851 and Pr. 1852 by Bp of Ches. C. in charge of the Onslow District of Chelsea 1867. Formerly C. of St. Paul's, Cheltenham, and Chap. of the Union; C. of Bollington and North Rode, Cheshire. [19]

NOSWORTHY, J. T., *Bierley, Bradford, Yorks.*—C. of Bierley. [20]

NOSWORTHY, Stephen, *Buckland-Filleigh, Highampton, Devon.*—Sid. Coll. Cam. B.A. 1813; Deac. 1813 and Pr. 1814 by Bp of Ex. R. of Buckland-Filleigh, Dio. Ex. 1842. (Patron, Bp of Ex; Tithe, 210*l*; Glebe, 87 acres; R.'s Inc. 260*l*; Pop. 258.) [21]

NOSWORTHY, William, 30, *East Southernhay, Exeter.*—St. John's Coll. Cam. B.A. 1850, M.A. 1864; Deac. 1850 and Pr. 1851 by Bp of Ex. Bodleian Lect. in Trin. Ch. Exeter, 1866. Formerly C. of Wembworthy, North Devon, 1863. [22]

NOTLY, Charles, *Eye, Suffolk.*—St. John's Coll. Cam. B.D. 1838; Deac. 1837 by Bp of Chich. Pr. 1838 by Bp of Nor. P. C. of Redlingfield, near Eye, Suffolk, Dio. Nor. 1842. (Patron, William Adair, Esq; Tithe, Imp. 251*l*; P. C.'s Inc. 71*l*; Pop. 203.) Head Mast. of the Eye Gr. Sch. 1836; Chap. to the Hartismere Union 1838. [23]

NOTT, Percy Wemyss Phillips, *Kew, Surrey, S.W.*—Trin. Coll. Cam. B.A. 1861, M.A. 1864; Deac. 1861 and Pr. 1862 by Bp of Ely. V. of Kew with Petersham, Dio. Win. 1867. (Patron, the Crown; V.'s Inc. 520*l*; Pop. Kew 1099, Petersham 637.) Formerly C. of Hitcham, Suffolk, 1861–63, Kew 1863–67. [24]

NOTTIDGE, Septimus, *Askingdon, Rockford, Essex.*—Jesus Coll. Cam. B.A. 1834. R. of Ashingdon, Dio. Roch. 1846. (Patron, the present R; Tithe, 285*l*; Glebe, 20 acres; R.'s Inc. 305*l*; Pop. 99.) C. of South Fambridge, near Rochford. [25]

NOTTLEY, W. G. C., *Ratlinghope, Shrewsbury.* P. C. of Ratlinghope, Dio. Herf. 1866. (Patrons, C. B. and W. Hawkins, Esqs; P. C.'s Inc. 65*l*; Pop. 285.) Formerly C. of Lane End, High Wycombe. [26]

NOURSE, Anis Henry, *St. Mary's, Priory, Cogs, Witney.*—Deac. 1853 and Pr. 1854 by Bp of Llan. P. C. of Cogs, Dio. Ox. 1862. (Patron, Eton Coll; P. C.'s Inc. 120*l* and Ho; Pop. 714.) Formerly C. of Llangattock-Llingoed, Monmouth, 1853–56, Standlake, Oxon, 1856–62. [27]

NOURSE, William, *Clapham Rectory, Worthing, Sussex.*—St. Alban Hall, Ox. B.A. 1802, M.A. 1808. R. of Clapham, Dio. Chich. 1821. (Patroness, Lady Brooke-Pechell; Tithe—Imp. 157*l* 6*s* 3*d*, V. 157*l* 6*s* 3*d*; V.'s Inc. 175*l* and Ho; Pop. 249.) [28]

NOURSE, W. G.—C. of Stanton-upon-Hine-Heath, Shrewsbury. Formerly C. of Bentley, Farnham, Hants. [29]

NOWELL, Thomas Whitaker, *Poplar Rectory, London, E.*—Brasen. Coll. Ox. B.A. 1846. R. of Poplar, Dio. Lon. 1860. (Patron, Brasen. Coll. Ox; R.'s Inc. 600*l* and Ho; Pop. 34,950.) Formerly Fell. of Brasen. Coll. Ox; R. of Wapping, Lond. 1853–60. [30]

NOWERS, James Henry, *The Vicarage, Weston St. Mary, near Spalding.*—Deac. 1845 by Bp of Guiana, Pr. 1850 by Bp of Lich. V. of Weston St. Mary, Dio. Lin. 1866. (Patron, Ld Chan; Tithe, 163*l*; other sources 131*l*; Glebe, 1$\frac{3}{4}$ acres; V.'s Inc. 294*l* and Ho; Pop. 760.) Formerly Chap. of Convict Department, Wakefield Prison; C. of Sutton-on-the-Hill; Asst. Chap. of Portland Prison. [1]

NOYES, Frederick Robert Halsey Herbert, *Tarporley, Cheshire.*—Univ. Coll. Dur. Fell.'s Prize 1861, Math. Prize 1861, B.A. 1861; Deac. 1862 and Pr. 1863 by Bp of Chich. C. of Tarporley 1866. Formerly C. of Waldron 1862. [2]

NOYES, John Henry, *Ketton Vicarage (Rutland), near Stamford.*—Trin. Coll. Cam. B.A. 1849, M.A. 1852; Deac. 1849, Pr. 1850. V. of Ketton with Tixover, Dio. Pet. (Patron, Dean of Roch; Glebe, 27 acres; V.'s Inc. 150*l* and Ho; Pop. Ketton 1053, Tixover 129.) Rural Dean. [3]

NUGEE, George, *Wymering Vicarage, near Portsmouth.*—Trin. Coll. Cam. 2nd cl. Cl. Trip. Eng. and Latin Oration Prize, Jun. Opt. and B.A. 1842, M.A. 1846; Deac. 1845 and Pr. 1846 by Bp of Lon. R. of Widley with Wymering V. Dio. Win. 1858. (Patron, F. G. Nugee, Esq; Tithe, Widley, 255*l*, Wymering, Imp. 536*l*, V. 434*l*; R. and V.'s Inc. 700*l* and Ho; Pop. Widley 725, Wymering 1071.) Founder and Hon. Clerical Sec. to the London Diocesan Penitentiary, and First Warden of St. Mary Magdalene, Highgate. Author, *The Necessity for Christian Education to elevate the Native Character in India* (the Maitland Prize), 1846; *Instructions on Confirmation*; *The Holy Women of the Gospel* (Lent Lectures, 1st Series), Masters; *The Words from the Cross as applied to our Deathbeds* (Lent Lectures, 2nd Series), ib; *Conversion* (a Sermon); *The Lame Man Healed at the Temple Gate* (Sermon on Church-Dispensaries); *Spirit of Romanism* (a Sermon); *The Penitential*; *A Letter to the Bishop of London on the Subject of a London Church Mission*; etc. [4]

NUNN, Abraham Augustus, *Parr Parsonage, St. Helens, Lancashire.*—Dub. A.B. 1841; Deac. 1842, Pr. 1843. P. C. of Parr, Dio. Ches. 1848. (Patron, P. C. of St. Helens; P. C.'s Inc. 163*l* and Ho; Pop. 4712.) [5]

NUNN, F., *Lancing, Sussex.*—Asst. Mast. of SS. Mary and Nicholas' Sch. Lancing. [6]

NUNN, Joseph, 194, *Oxford-road, Manchester.*—St. John's Coll. Cam. 2nd cl. Cl. Trip. and Jun. Opt. M.A; Deac. 1857, Pr. 1858. R. of St. Thomas's, Ardwick, Dio. Man. 1867. (Patrons, D. and C. of Man; R.'s Inc. 300*l*; Pop. 10,147.) Formerly C. of Ch. Ch. Everton, St. Mary's, Marylebone, Lond. St. Paul's, Kersall Moor, and St. Thomas's, Ardwick, Manchester. [7]

NUNN, Preston, *Church Stretton, Salop.*—Deac. 1815 and Pr. 1815 by Abp of York. C. of Church Stretton 1822. Formerly C. of Stanton Long. [8]

NUNN, S., *Heaton Norris, Manchester.*—C. of Ch. Ch. Heaton Norris. [9]

NUNN, Thomas, *Stansted Rectory, Sevenoaks, Kent.*—Sid. Coll. Cam. B.A. 1825, M.A. 1828; Deac. and Pr. 1826. R. of Stansted, Dio. Cant. 1854. (Patron, Abp of Cant; Tithe, 429*l*; Glebe, 58 acres; R.'s Inc. 480*l* and Ho; Pop. 403.) Author, *A Sermon on the Death of the Rev. W. B. Harrison, Vicar of Goudhurst, Kent*, 1849, 6*d*; *A Letter to the Rev. F. D. Eyre, M.A.* 1852, 3*d*. [10]

NUNN, Thomas Partridge, *West Pennard Parsonage, Wells.*—St. Mary Hall, Ox. B.A. 1844, M.A. 1846. P. C. of West Pennard, Dio. B. and W. 1850. (Patron, Bp of B. and W; Tithe—App. 309*l* 19*s* 8*d* and 1 acre of Glebe; P. C.'s Inc. 100*l* and Ho; Pop. 836.) [11]

NUNN, William Eastgate Middleton, *Stansted Rectory, Sevenoaks, Kent.*—Dub. A B. 1866; Deac. 1866 by Bp of Roch. C. of Ash, near Sevenoaks. [12]

NUNNS, Robert Augustine Luke, *Appledram, Chichester.*—Ch. Coll. Cam. B.A. 1858; Deac. 1858 and Pr. 1859 by Bp of Lin. P. C. of Appledram, Dio. Chich. 1865. (Patrons, D. and C. of Chich; P. C.'s Inc. 64*l*; Pop. 120.) R. of St. Olave's, Chichester. Formerly C. of Orston and Thoroton, Notts, 1858–60; Funtington, Chich. 1860–65. [13]

NUNNS, Thomas Jackson, 9, *Eliot-place, Blackheath.*—St. John's Coll. Cam. Scho. and Exhib. of, Members' Univ. Prize for Latin Essay, 1st cl. Cl. Trip. B.A. 1857, M.A. 1861; Deac. 1859 and Pr. 1860 by Bp of Rip. Formerly Asst. Mast. at St. Andrew's Coll. Bradfield, 1857–58, at Leeds Gr. Sch. 1859-60; Head Mast. of Helston Gr. Sch. 1861. [14]

NURSEY, C. R. W., *Woolwich.*—C. of St. Thomas's, Woolwich. [15]

NURSEY, Perry, *Crostwick, Norwich.*—Sid. Coll. Cam. B.A. 1822; Deac. 1822 and Pr. 1823 by Bp of Nor. R. of Crostwick, Dio. Nor. 1863. (Patron, Bp of Nor; R.'s Inc. 200*l*; Pop. 144.) Formerly C. of Burlingham. [16]

NUSSEY, Edward Richard, *Longney Vicarage, Gloucester.*—Oriel Coll. Ox. B.A. 1851; Deac. 1851 and Pr. 1852 by Bp of Pet. V. of Longney, Dio. G. and B. 1865. (Patron, Ld. Chan; V.'s Inc. 125*l* and Ho; Pop. 500.) Formerly C. of Oundle 1852; Whiston, Yorks, 1853–57; Easton with Barnham, Suffolk, 1858–59; Ware, Herts, 1860–64. [17]

NUSSEY, Joshua, *Oundle Vicarage, Northants.*—St. Cath. Hall. Cam. B.A. 1822, M.A. 1825; Deac. 1823, Pr. 1824. V. of Oundle, Dio. Pet. 1845. (Patron, Ld Chan; Tithe, Imp. 600*l*; Glebe, 263 acres; V.'s Inc. 600*l* and Ho; Pop. 3217.) Surrogate; Dom. Chap. to Lord Blayney. Formerly C. of St. Margaret's and St. John's, Westminster; R. of Poughill, Devon, 1837–45. Author, *Sermon on the Prevailing Epidemic of* 1837, 1837; *Rights and Duties of Incumbents in Reference to Churchyards* (a Letter to a Churchwarden), 1849. [18]

NUTT, Charles Henry, *East Harptree Vicarage, Bristol.*—Magd. Coll. Ox. 3rd cl. Lit. Hum. and B A. 1851, M.A. 1853; Deac. 1852 by Bp of Ox. Pr. 1855 by Bp of B. and W. V. of East Harptree, Dio. B. and W. 1864. (Patron, Bp of B. and W; Tithe—App. 72*l* and 72 acres of Glebe, V. 126*l*; Glebe, 4$\frac{1}{2}$ acres; V.'s Inc. 132*l* and Ho; Pop. 657.) [19]

NUTT, George, *Shaw, Melksham, Wilts.*—Wor. Coll. Ox. B.A. 1838. P. C. of Shaw and Whittey P. C. Dio. Salis. 1851. (Patron, V. of Melksham; P. C.'s Inc. 105*l*; Pop. 596.) [20]

NUTT, J. W., *All Souls' College, Oxford.*—Corpus Coll. Ox. B.A. 1856, M.A. 1858, 1st cl. Cl. 1855, Hebrew Scho. 1856–57, Sanskrit, 1857; Deac. 1859 by Bp of Ox. Fell. of All Souls' Coll. Ox. Formerly Asst. Inspector of Schs. 1860–67; Under-Librarian of the Bodleian 1867. [21]

NUTT, Robert, *Carisbrooke, Isle of Wight.*—Wor. Coll. Ox. B.A. 1849, M.A. 1850; Deac. 1854 and Pr. 1856 by Bp of Pet. Asst. C. of Carisbrooke 1867. Formerly C. of Newport, Isle of Wight. [22]

NUTT, William Young, *Cold-Overton Rectory, (Leicestershire), near Oakham.*—Deac. 1812, Pr. 1814. R. of Cold-Overton, Dio. Pet. 1852. (Patron, T. Frewen, Esq; Tithe, 276*l*; Glebe, 45 acres; R.'s Inc. 334*l* and Ho; Pop. 106.) [23]

NUTTALL, William.—Queens' Coll. Cam. B.A. 1843; Deac. 1843 by Bp of Herf. Pr. 1844 by Bp of Lich. Formerly Chap. of the English Church at the Hague; R. of Oxcombe, Lincolnshire, 1856–63. [24]

NUTTER, William Henry, *Newport, Isle of Wight.*—Ch. Coll. Cam. B.A. 1861, M.A. 1865; Deac. 1867 by Bp of Win. C. of St. Thomas's, Newport, Isle of Wight, 1867. [25]

NUTTING, George Horatio, *Chasleton Moreton-in-Marsh, Oxon.*—R. of Chasleton, Dio. Ox. 1863. (Patron, the present R; R.'s Inc. 550*l*; Pop. 218.) Formerly R. of Sherfield-on-Loddon, Hants, 1859–63. [26]

OAK, Charles Anthony, *St. Leonards-on-Sea, Sussex.*—St. John's Coll. Cam. Sen. Opt. and B.A. 1840, M.A. 1843; Deac. 1841 and Pr.

1842 by Bp of Carl. Formerly C. of St. John's-in-the Vale, Keswick, 1841, St. Cuthbert's, Carlisle, and Min. of Upperby Church, near Carlisle, 1844.) [1]

OAKDEN, Joseph, *Congleton, Cheshire.*—Dur. Licen. Theol. 1850; Deac. 1850 and Pr. 1851 by Bp of Rip. P. C. of St. Stephen's, Congleton, Dio. Ches. 1852. (Patrons, the Crown and Bp of Ches. alt; P. C.'s Inc. 150*l*; Pop. 3411.) [2]

OAKELEY, Arthur, *Lydham, near Bishop's-Castle, Salop.*—New Inn Hall, Ox. B.A. 1840, M.A. 1841, Deac. 1841 and Pr. 1843 by Bp of Herf. R. of Lydham, Dio. Herf. 1842. (Patron, Sir C. W. A. Oakeley, Bart; Tithe—Imp. 53*l* 6*s* 8*d*, R. 246*l* 10*s* 6*d*; R.'s Inc. 415*l*; Pop. 205.) [3]

OAKELEY, James, *Llanishen Parsonage, Chepstow.*—Jesus Coll. Ox. B.A. 1852; Deac. 1853 and Pr. 1857 by Bp of Ox. P. C. of Llanishen with Trelleck Grange, Dio. Llan. 1861. (Patron, Duke of Beaufort; Glebe, 176 acres; P. C.'s Inc. 188*l* 12*s* and Ho; Pop. 457.) [4]

OAKES, Hervey Aston Adamson, *Nowton Rectory, Bury St. Edmunds.*—Jesus Coll. Cam. B.A. 1827; Deac. 1827, Pr. 1828. R. of Nowton, Dio. Ely, 1844. (Patron, Marquis of Bristol; Tithe, 345*l*; Glebe, 10 acres; R.'s Inc. 345*l*; Pop. 186.) [5]

OAKES, Orbell Plampin, *Hawkedon Rectory, Bury St. Edmunds.*—Emman. Coll. Cam. B.A. 1847. R. of Hawkedon, Dio. Ely, 1850. (Patron, H. J. Oakes, Esq; Tithe, 371*l*; Glebe, 41½ acres; R.'s Inc. 413*l* and Ho; Pop. 321.) [6]

OAKES, William Frederick, *Tibberton Parsonage, Newport, Salop.*—P. C. of Tibberton, Dio. Lich. 1861. (Patron, R. of Edgmond; P. C.'s Inc. 100*l* and Ho; Pop. 538.) Formerly C. of Stainland, Yorks. [7]

OAKLEY, Edwin, *Heacham, Lynn, Norfolk.*—Bp Hat. Hall, Dur. B.A. 1858; Deac. 1859 and Pr. 1860 by Bp of Nor. C. of Heacham 1862. Formerly C. of Lopham 1859–61, Burnham Deepdale 1861–62. [8]

OAKLEY, George Robert, *Lowesby, Leicester.*—Dub. A.B. 1827, A.M. 1837; Deac. 1830 and Pr. 1831 by Bp of Lin. C. of Lowesby. [9]

OAKLEY, John.—C. and Clerk in Orders of St. James's, Westminster; Sec. to the Lond. Dioc. Board of Education. [10]

OAKLEY, William Henry, *Wyfordby Rectory, Melton Mowbray.*—Dub. A.B. 1828; Deac. 1833 and Pr. 1834 by Bp of Lin. R. of Wyfordby, Dio. Pet. 1846. (Patron, Sir W. Edm. Cradock Hartopp, Bart; Tithe—App. 72*l*, R. 72*l*; Glebe, 64½ acres; R.'s Inc. 214*l* and Ho; Pop. 144.) C. of Freeby, Leicestershire; Surrogate. [11]

OATES, Alfred, *High-street, Maryport, Cumberland.*—Moravian Coll. Niesky, Prussia; Deac. 1866 by Bp of Dur. Pr. 1866 by Bp of Carl. C. of Maryport 1866. [12]

OATES, John, *Guernsey.*—Lin. Coll. Ox. 2nd cl. Lit. Hum. and B.A. 1846, M.A. 1851; Deac. 1848 by Abp of York, Pr. 1849 by Bp of Wor. Vice-Prin. of Elizabeth Coll. Guernsey. Formerly C. of Scarborough, and St. Mark's, St. John's Wood, Lond. Author, *Letter on the Intrusion of a Romish Episcopate in England, to the Bishop of Worcester*, 1850; *A Reply to Letters of Mr. Backhouse, and a Lover of Truth, on Confirmation*, Scarborough, 1854; *The Spirit of Adoption* (a Sermon before the University of Oxford), Rivingtons, 1867. [13]

OATES, John William, *Newnham, Winchfield.*—Ch. Ch. Ox. Exhib. B.A. 1859, M.A. 1862; Deac. 1859 by Bp of Wor. Pr. 1862 by Bp of Man. C. in sole charge of Newnham and Mapledérwell, Hants, 1863. Formerly C. of Bedworth 1859–61, Blackburn 1862–63. [14]

OATES, Richard, *Edge Hill, Liverpool.*—St. Bees 1852; Deac. 1852 and Pr. 1853 by Bp of Ches. Formerly C. of Workington 1852, Ch. Ch. Everton, Liverpool, 1855, St. Paul's, Liverpool, 1864. [15]

O'BRIEN, Edward, *Thornton-Curtis, Lincolnshire.*—Dub. and St. Bees; Deac. 1848 and Pr. 1850 by Bp of Man. V. of Thornton-Curtis, Dio. Lin. 1851. (Patron, C. Wynn, Esq; Glebe, 114 acres; V.'s Inc. 350*l*; Pop. 483.) [16]

O'BRIEN, James, 61, *Upper Brunswick-place, Brighton.*—Magd. Hall, Ox. 1837, D.D. 1863; Deac. 1841 by Bp of Ches. Pr. 1842 by Bp of Llan. Min. of St. Patrick's, Hove, Brighton, Dio. Chich. 1859. (Built by Dr. O'Brien at his own cost.) [17]

O'BRIEN, John, *Henfield Vicarage, Hurstpierpoint, Sussex.*—Dub. and Queen's Coll. Ox. B.A. 1843, M.A. 1846; Deac. 1844, Pr. 1845. V. of Henfield, Dio. Chich. 1851. (Patron, Bp of Chich; Tithe, comm. 412*l* 9*s* 9*d*; Glebe, ¾ acre; V.'s Inc. 472*l* 9*s* 9*d* and Ho; Pop. 1662.) Formerly C. of St. Helens, Lancashire, 1844, Ashton-under-Lyne 1846, Warnham, Sussex, 1848. [18]

O'BRIEN, Philip Stephen, 171, *Grove-street, Faulkner-square, Liverpool.*—Dub. A.B. 1864, LL.B. 1864; Deac. 1865 by Bp of Rip. Pr. 1866 by Bp of Ches. C. of St. Bride's, Liverpool, 1866. Formerly C. of St. Thomas's, Bradford, Yorks, 1865. [19]

O'BRIEN, Richard, *Hesketh Rectory, near Preston.*—Dub. A.B. 1854, A.M. 1857; Deac. 1860 and Pr. 1861 by Abp of Dub. R. of Hesketh with Becconsall P. C. Dio. Man. 1864. (Patron, Sir T. G. Hesketh, Bart. M.P; R.'s Inc. 300*l*; Pop. 804.) Formerly C. of St. Jude's, Dublin, 1860–61, Wendy, Cambs, 1861–63, Coppenhall, Cheshire, 1863–64. Author, *The Odes of Horace translated into English Verse with the Original Measures preserved throughout*, Lond. 1860, 2*s* 6*d*. [20]

O'CALLAGHAN, Robert.—Dom. Chap. to Viscount Lismore. [21]

O'CARROLL, J., *Congresbury, Bristol.*—C. of Congresbury, Somerset. [22]

O'CONNOR, Dionysius Prittie, *Biscathorpe Rectory, Louth, Lincolnshire.*—Dub. A.B. 1839, A.M. 1843; Deac. 1839 by Bp of Ches. Pr. 1840 by Bp of Wor. R. of Gayton-le-Wold with Biscathorpe R. Dio. Lin. 1857. (Patron, Ld Chan; Tithe, 250*l* 1*s*; Glebe, 200 acres; R.'s Inc. 450*l* and Ho; Pop. Gayton-le-Wold 118, Biscathorpe 90.) C. of Calcethorpe. Formerly C. of Anderby with Cumberworth, Lincolnshire, 1841–48; V. of Fotherby, near Louth, 1847–57. [23]

O'CONNOR, William Anderson, 21, *Grafton-street, Manchester.*—Dub. A.B.; Deac. 1853, Pr. 1854. R. of St. Simon's with St. Jude's, City and Dio. Man. 1858. (Patron, Bp of Man; R.'s Inc. 212*l*; Pop. 4515.) Formerly C. of St. Nicholas', Liverpool, 1853, St. Thomas's, Liverpool, 1854, St. Michael's and St. Olave's, Chester, 1855. Author, *Essay on Miracles*, Parkers, 1862; Lectures and Tracts in Defence of the Church; etc. [24]

ODDIE, George Augustus, *Aston Rectory, Stevenage, Herts.*—Univ. Coll. Ox. B.A. 1842; Deac. 1844 and Pr. 1845 by Bp of Salis. R. of Aston, Dio. Roch. 1848. (Patron, the present R; Tithe, 460*l*; Glebe, 42½ acres; R.'s Inc. 505*l* and Ho; Pop. 639.) [25]

ODELL, M. C., *Shorncliffe.*—Dub. A.B. 1849. Chap. to the Forces. Formerly Sec. to Bp of Victoria, and Tut. at St. Paul's Coll. Hong Kong, 1849–57; Incumb. of St. Thomas's, Mauritius, 1853–63. [26]

O'DONEL, Constantine, *Allendale, Carlisle.*—P. C. of St. Peter's, Allendale, Dio. Dur. 1851. (Patron, P. C. of Allendale; P. C.'s Inc. 130*l*.) Min. of Allenheads Chapel, Allendale, Dio. Dur. 1851. (Patron, W. B. Beaumont, Esq; Min.'s Inc. 50*l*.) [27]

O'DONNELL, Henry, *Whittington, Worcester.*—Dub. A.B. 1850, A.M. 1853; Deac. 1852, Pr. 1853. V. of Upton Snodbury, Dio. Wor. 1864. (Patron, the present R; Tithe, 120*l*; Glebe, 1¼ acres; V.'s Inc. 125*l*; Pop. 358.) Formerly C. of Lymington, Hants. Author, *The Water-Brooks*, 1*s*; *Hecuba, in English Verse*, 1*s*. [28]

O'DONOGHUE, Francis Talbot, *Walsden Vicarage, Todmorden, Lancashire.*—Dub. A.B. 1841; Deac. 1841 and Pr. 1842 by Bp of Ches. V. of Walsden, Dio. Man. 1865. (Patrons, Crown and Bp of Man. alt; V.'s Inc. 300*l* and Ho; Pop. 3934.) Dom. Chap. to the Marquis of Westmeath. Formerly P. C. of Over Peover 1842–52, Godolphin 1852–55, Wellington, Staffs, 1855–60; V. of Tickenham, Somerset, 1860–65. Author, *St. Knighton's Keive, a Cornish Tale*, Smith, Elder and Co. 1864; *Donnington Hall, a Novel*, Saunders, Otley and Co. 1865. [29]

O'DONOGHUE, Frederic Freeman, *Biddulph, Congleton.*—Dub. A.B; Deac. 1836, Pr. 1838. C. of Biddulph, Staffs, 1862. Formerly C. of Newall and of Chellaston, Derbyshire. [1]

O'FLAHERTY, Theobald Richard, *Capel Parsonage, Dorking.*—St. John's Coll. Cam. B.A. 1843; Deac. 1843 and Pr. 1844 by Bp of Win. P. C. of Capel, Dio. Win. 1848; Glebe, 1 acre; P. C.'s Inc. 100*l* and Ho; Pop. 743.) Chap. to Dorking Union 1851. Formerly C. of Odiham 1843, Tadley 1846. [2]

OGDEN, William, *St. Peter's Parsonage, Ashton-under-Lyne.*—St. John's Coll. Cam. B.A. 1853, M.A. 1857; Deac. 1853 and Pr. 1854 by Bp of Pet. P. C. of St. Peter's, Ashton-under-Lyne, Dio. Man. 1865. (Patron, R. of Ashton; P. C.'s Inc. 300*l* and Ho; Pop. 11,694.) Surrogate. Formerly C. of Ashton-under-Lyne. [3]

OGILVIE, Charles Atmore, *Christ Church, Oxford,* and *The Rectory, Ross, Herefordshire.*—Ball. Coll. Ox. 1st cl. Lit. Hum. and B.A. 1815, Chancellor's Prizeman for English Essay 1817, M.A. 1818, B.D. and D.D. 1842; Deac. 1817 and Pr. 1818 by Bp of Ox. R. and V. of Ross, Dio. Herf. 1839. (Patron, Bp of Herf; Tithe, App. 118*l*, R. and V. 790*l*; Glebe, 98½ acres; R. and V.'s Inc. 1100*l* and Ho; Pop. 4346.) Regius Prof. of Pastoral Theology in the Univ. of Ox. with Canonry of Ch. Ch. annexed, 1842. (Patron, the Crown; Value, 800*l* and Res.) Fell. of Ball. Coll. 1816; Dom. and Exam. Chap. to the late Dr. Howley, Abp of Cant; Bampton Lect. 1836; Select Preacher 1844. Author, *The Divine Glory manifested in the Conduct and Discourses of Our Lord* (Bampton Lectures for 1836); *Considerations on Subscription to the Thirty-nine Articles*, 1845; *Sermons* (preached before the Univ. of Ox.) 1847; *Sermon* (at a Visitation of the Bp of Ex); *Sermon* (at a Visitation of the Bp of Herf); *On Subscription to the Thirty-nine Articles as by Law required of Candidates for Holy Orders and of the Clergy*, Parkers, 1863. [4]

OGLE, Edward Chaloner, *Kirkley, Newcastle-on-Tyne.*—Mert. Coll. Ox. B.A. 1820, M.A. 1821; Deac. and Pr. 1823 by Bp of Salis. Preb. of Salis 1828. [5]

OGLE, James Ambrose, *Sedgeford Vicarage, Lynn, Norfolk.*—Brasen. Coll. Ox. 4th cl. Math. et Phy. and B.A. 1846, M.A. 1849; Deac. 1848, Pr. 1849. V. of Sedgeford, Dio. Nor. 1858. (Patrons, D. and C. of Nor; Tithe, 330*l*; Glebe, 4 acres; V.'s Inc. 332*l* and Ho; Pop. 742.) Rural Dean. [6]

OGLE, Octavius, 20, *Park-crescent, Oxford.*—Wad. Coll. Ox. Scho. of, 2nd cl. Lit. Hum. 2nd cl. Math. B.A. 1850, M.A. 1853, Vinerian Univ. Scho. 1849; Deac. 1852 and Pr. 1854 by Bp of Ox. Chap. to the Warneford Asylum 1854. Formerly Public Exam. in the Cl. Moderation Schs. Ox. 1854–55; Mast. of the Schs. 1863; Fell. 1850, Sen. Tut. and Sub-Rector, Lin. Coll. Ox; C. of St. Giles's, Oxford, 1859. Author, *Letter to Vice-Chancellor on Responsions Examination*, Hammans, Oxford, 1863; *Copybook of Sir Amias Poulet's Letters* (edited for the Roxburghe Club), Nichols and Sons, 1866. [7]

OGLE, William, *Corpus Christi College, Oxford.*—Corpus Coll. Ox. 2nd cl. Lit. Hum. and B.A. 1849, M.A. 1852. Fell. of Corpus Coll. Ox. [8]

OGLE, William Reynolds, *Bishops Teignton Vicarage, Teignmouth, Devon.*—Trin. Coll. Ox. B.A. 1839, M.A. 1841; Deac. 1840 and Pr. 1841 by Bp of Lich. V. of Bishops Teignton, Dio. Ex. 1856. (Patron, the present V; Tithe—Imp. 499*l* 9*s* 10*d*, V. 217*l* 0*s* 8*d*; Glebe, 8 acres; V.'s Inc. 330*l* and Ho; Pop. 750.) Formerly C. of Watton, Herts, 1848. Author, *The Bible in the Collects adapted for Schools and Families*, Macintosh. [9]

O'GRADY, Thomas, *Hognaston, Ashbourne, Derbyshire.*—St. Bees; Deac. 1854, Pr. 1855. P. C. of Hognaston, Dio. Lich. 1855. (Patron, Bp of Lich; Tithe, —App. 195*l* 8*s* and 26½ acres of Glebe, P. C. 7*l* 15*s*; P. C.'s Inc. 55*l*; Pop. 295.) [10]

OHLSON, G., *Hull.*—C. of Trinity, Hull, 1867. Formerly Asst. Chap. at St. Pierre, Calais. [11]

OKE, William S. Amways, *Winterbourne Clenstone, near Blandford, Dorset.*—Wad. Coll. Ox. B.A. 1839; Deac. 1840, Pr. 1841. C. of Winterbourne Clenstone. Formerly C. of Ch. Ch. Nailsea, Somerset. [12]

OKES, Richard, *King's College, Cambridge.*—King's Coll. Cam. Browne's Medallist 1819–20, B.A. 1822, M.A. 1826, D.D. 1848; Deac. 1822, Pr. 1827. Provost of King's Coll. Cam. 1850. Formerly Mast. of Eton Coll. 1838–50. [13]

OLDACRES, Edward William, *Lichfield.*—Clare Coll. Cam. B.A. 1821, M.A. 1825; Deac. 1822, Pr. 1823. [14]

OLDACRES, Samuel Lealand, *Woodborough, Southwell, Notts.*—Emman. Coll. Cam. B.A. 1831; Deac 1832 and Pr. 1833 by Abp of York. P. C. of Woodborough, Dio. Lin. 1840. (Patron, Chap. of Southwell Coll. Ch; Glebe, 55 acres; P. C.'s Inc. 110*l*; Pop. 893.) Mast. of the Woodborough Free Sch. 1837. [15]

OLDERSHAW, Henry, *Lichfield.*—Brasen. Coll. Ox. Hulme's Exhib. B.A. 1826, M.A. 1827; Deac. 1827 and Pr. 1828 by Bp of Lich. Formerly C. of Weston-upon-Trent, Staffs, 1827; Chan.'s V. in Lich. Cathl. 1836; P. C. of Wall, Lichfield, 1843–59. [16]

OLDFIELD, Charles, *Stamford.*—Trin. Coll. Cam. B.A. 1857, M.A. 1861; Deac. 1857, Pr. 1858. R. of St. Michael's, Stamford, Dio. Lin. 1867. (Patron, Marquis of Exeter; R.'s Inc. 180*l*; Pop. 1305.) Formerly C. of Halesowen 1857. [17]

OLDFIELD, Christopher Holroyd, *The Quinton, near Birmingham.*—Ch. Coll. Cam. B.A. 1849; Deac. 1849 and Pr. 1851 by Bp of Pet. R. of The Quinton, Dio. Wor. 1857. (Patron, R. of Halesowen; Tithe, 120*l*; Glebe, 6 acres; R.'s Inc. 220*l* and Ho; Pop. 2495.) Formerly C. of Wellingborough, and St. Mary's, Brighton. [18]

OLDFIELD, Edward, *Llysfaen, Conway, Carnarvonshire.*—St. John's Coll. Cam. B.A. 1817, M.A. 1820; Deac. 1818, Pr. 1819. R. of Llysfaen, Dio. St. A. 1835. (Patron, Bp of St. A; Tithe—App. 56*l* 4*s* 8¼*d*, Imp. 1*l* 10*s*, R. 232*l* 16*s* 2*d*; R.'s Inc. 260*l* and Ho; Pop. 908.) [19]

OLDFIELD, Edward Colnett, *Minchinhampton Rectory, Gloucestershire.*—Trin. Coll. Cam. B.A. 1852, M.A. 1855; Deac. 1852, Pr. 1853. R. of Minchinhampton, Dio. G. and B. 1865. (Patron, H. D. Ricardo, Esq; R.'s Inc. 500*l* and Ho; Pop. 1703.) Formerly C. of Horsley. [20]

OLDFIELD, George Biscoe, *East Woodhay, Newbury.*—Ex. Coll. Ox. B.A. 1862, M.A. 1866; Deac. 1864 and Pr. 1865 by Bp of Lon. C. of Woolton Hill, Newbury, 1865. Formerly C. of Putney, Surrey. [21]

OLDHAM, James, *Doverdale Rectory, Droitwich, Worcestershire.*—Trin. Coll. Ox. S.C.L. 1853, B.A. 1855, M.A. 1857; Deac. 1855 and Pr. 1856 by Bp of St. D. R. of Doverdale, Dio. Wor. 1857. (Patroness, Mrs. Curtler; Tithe, 200*l*; Glebe, 40 acres; R.'s Inc. 240*l* and Ho; Pop. 43.) Formerly C. of Hay, South Wales. [22]

OLDHAM, John Lane, *Audley End, Saffron-Walden, Essex*—Magd. Coll. Cam. B.A. 1854, M.A. 1858; Deac. 1854 and Pr. 1856 by Bp of Roch. Dom. Chap. to Lord Braybrooke; Fell. of the Geological Soc. of Lond. Formerly C. of Littlebury, Essex. [23]

OLDHAM, John Roberts, *Ottershaw Parsonage, Weybridge, Surrey.*—P. C. of Ottershaw, Dio. Win. 1865. (Patron, Sir E. Colebrooke, Bart; P. C.'s Inc. 150*l* and Ho; Pop. 594.) [24]

OLDHAM, Joseph, *Clay Cross Parsonage, Derbyshire.*—St. John's Coll. Cam. B.D. 1855; Deac. 1845, Pr. 1846. P. C. of Clay Cross, Dio. Lich. 1851. (Patron, R. of North Wingfield; Glebe, 2½ acres; P. C.'s Inc. 115*l* and Ho; Pop. 4922.) [25]

OLDHAM, Ralph, *Myton-on-Swale, Boroughbridge, Yorks.*—Dub. A.B. 1836; Deac. and Pr. 1840 by Bp of Tuam. V. of Myton-on-Swale, Dio. York, 1862. (Patron, Abp of York; V.'s Inc. 180*l* and Ho; Pop. 155.) [26]

OLDHAM, Richard Samuel, *Glasgow.*—Wad. Coll. Ox. Kennicott Hebrew Scho. 1847, B.A. 1846, M.A. 1849; Deac. 1846 and Pr. 1847 by Bp of Lon. Incumb. of St. Mary's, Glasgow, 1851. Formerly C. of St. John's, St. Pancras, and of St. Barnabas', Kensington,

Lond; Dom. Chap. to the late Earl of Elgin. Author, *Mirror of Prophecy*, Rivingtons; various single Sermons. [1]

OLDKNOW, Joseph, *Trinity Parsonage, Bordesley, Birmingham.*—Ch. Coll. Cam. B.A. 1831, M.A. 1835; D.D. Trin. Coll. Hartford, U.S.A. 1857; Deac. 1832 and Pr. 1833 by Bp of Lin. P. C. of Trinity, Bordesley, Dio. Wor. 1841. (Patron, V. of Aston; P. C.'s Inc. 300*l* and Ho; Pop. 12,000.) Author, *Vindication of the Church and Clergy of England*, 1834; *The Catholic Church*, 1839; *The Sect everywhere spoken against*, 1842; *The Duty of promoting Christian Unity*, 1844; *Sacerdotal Remission and Retaining of Sins*, 1845; *Grounds for abiding in the Church of England*, 1845; *Zeal without Knowledge as exhibited in the Church of England*, 1847; *A Letter to the Rev. J. C. Miller on the Comparative Relations of the Church of Englnd to the Church of Rome and the Protestant Bodies*, 1848; *Admission into a State of Salvation by Holy Baptism*, 1850; *The Evil of forsaking the Church of England for the Communion of Rome*, 1850; *The Church and its Civil Power and our Duty to ourselves in Days of Excitement*, 1851; *Revival in the Church of England and the House of God sanctified by His Presence*, 1853; *The Mother of our Lord and the Reverence due to her*, 1855; *The Validity of the Holy Orders in the Church of England*, 1857; *A Month in Portugal*, 1855; *Apostolical Succession*, 1864; *Anti-Ritual Proceedings* (a Letter to to the Clergy of Birmingham), 1866; *The Evangelical System contrasted with that of the Church of England*, 1867; *Puritan Objections to the Book of Common Prayer*, 1867. [2]

OLDRID, John Henry, *Alford, Lincolnshire.*—Magd. Hall, Ox. B.A. 1834, M.A. 1851; Deac. and Pr. 1834 by Bp of Lin. V. of Alford with Rigsby, C. Dio. Lin. 1863. (Patron, Bp of Lin; V.'s Inc. 150*l*; Pop. Alford 2658, Rigsby 102.) Formerly P. C. of Garscott, Bucks, 1834; Lect. of Boston 1844. [3]

OLDRINI, Thomas John, *Beeston Vicarage, near Nottingham.*—Queen's Coll. Ox. B.A. 1850, M.A. 1853; Deac. 1851, Pr. 1852. V. of Beeston, Dio. Lin. 1854. (Patron, Duke of Devonshire; Glebe, 110 acres; V.'s Inc. 300*l* and Ho; Pop. 3195.) Author, *Sermon on the Fast-day*, 1855. [4]

OLDROYD, William Robert, *Whitburn, Sunderland.*—St. Bees; Deac. 1865 and Pr. 1867 by Bp of Dur. C. of Whitburn 1866. [5]

O'LEARY, John, *The Borough Gaol, Manchester.*—Chap. to the Borough Gaol, Manchester. [6]

OLIVE, John, *Ayot St. Lawrence Rectory, Welwyn, Herts.*—Wor. Coll. Ox. B.A. 1826, M.A. 1829; Deac. 1827, Pr. 1830. R. of Ayot St. Lawrence, Dio. Roch. 1830. (Patron, G. H. Ames, Esq; Tithe, 176*l*; Glebe, 10 acres; R.'s Inc. 180*l* and Ho; Pop. 122.) [7]

OLIVER, Charles Norwood.—Queens' Coll. Cam. B.A. 1858, M.A. 1862; Deac. 1859, Pr. 1860. C. of St. Augustine's, Haggerston. Formerly C. of St. Stephen's, Willington, 1859. [8]

OLIVER, George William.—Ch. Coll. Cam. B.A. 1858, M.A. 1863; Deac. 1859 by Bp of Ox. Pr. 1861 by Bp of Ely. Formerly C. of Wardington, Oxon, 1859, St. Peter's, Bedford, 1861, St. Barnabas', Kensington, 1863, St. Neots, Hunts, 1865. [9]

OLIVER, John, *London Diocesan Penitentiary, Highgate, London, N.*—Queens' Coll. Cam. B.A. 1844, M.A. 1847. V. of Warmington, Oundle, Northants, Dio. Pet. 1844. (Patron, Earl of Westmoreland; Tithe, 25*l*; V.'s Inc. 127*l*; Pop. 724.) Warden of the London Dioc. Penitentiary. Formerly Chap. to King's Coll. Hospital, Lond. [10]

OLIVER, John Paul.—Chap. R.N. Formerly Chap. to H.M.S. "Cumberland," 1857. [11]

OLIVER, Robert Bennett, *Whitwell, Isle of Wight.*—Trin. Coll. Cam. B.A. 1859, M.A. 1862; Deac. 1860 and Pr. 1861 by Bp of Lin. P. C. of Whitwell, Dio. Win. 1866. (Patron, the present P. C; P. C.'s Inc. 93*l*; Pop. 570.) Formerly C. of Bawtry and of Whitwell. [12]

OLIVER, Samuel, *Calverton Vicarage, Nottingham.*—Deac. 1825 and Pr. 1826 by Abp of York. V. of Calverton, Dio. Lin. 1826. (Patron, Bp of Man; Glebe, 210 acres; V.'s Inc. 160*l* and Ho; Pop. 1372.) Author, *Emma Whiteford*, 2*s*; *Plain Questions for Dissenters* (a Card), 1*d*; *A Plain Argument for the Church* (a Card), 1*d*; *War, and its Probable Consequences*, 6*d*; *Village Lectures on some controverted Articles of Catholic Faith*; etc. [13]

OLIVER, William, *Filleigh, South Molton, Devon.*—C. of Filleigh. [14]

OLIVER, William, *Hadnall, Shrewsbury.*—St. Peter's Coll. Cam. B.A. 1834, M.A. 1839; Deac. 1835, Pr. 1836. P. C. of Hadnall, Dio. Lich. 1840. (Patron, R. of Middle; P. C.'s Inc. 173*l*; Pop. 456.) [15]

OLIVER, William, *Fulford, Stone, Staffs.*—P. C. of Fulford, Dio. Lich. 1824. (Patron, T. Allen, Esq; Tithe, Imp. 89*l* 7*s* 6*d*; P. C.'s Inc. 129*l*.) P. C. of Barlaston, near Stone, Dio. Lich. 1834. (Patron, Duke of Sutherland; Tithe, Imp. 136*l* 6*s* 1*d*, P. C. 80*l*; P. C.'s Inc. 150*l*; Pop. 637.) [16]

OLIVER, William Hutchinson, *Stapleford Rectory, Hertford.*—Trin. Coll. Cam. B.A. 1841, M.A. 1844; Deac. 1841 and Pr. 1843 by Bp of Ely. R. of Stapleford, Dio. Roch. 1862. (Patron, Abel Smith, Esq; R.'s Inc. 300*l* and Ho; Pop. 226.) Formerly C. of Tonwell and Waterford, Herts. [17]

OLIVER, William Macjanlay, *Bovinger Rectory, Ongar, Essex.*—St. Peter's Coll. Cam. 17th Wrang. and B.A. 1831, M.A. 1834. R. of Bovinger, or Bobbingworth, Dio. Roch. 1838. (Patron, C. Cure, Esq; Tithe, 446*l* 5*s*; Glebe, 35 acres; R.'s Inc. 484*l* and Ho; Pop. 334.) [18]

OLIVIER, Alfred, *Derby.*—Min. of St. James's District, St. Peter's, Derby, Dio. Lich. 1865. [19]

OLIVIER, Dacres, *Wilton Rectory, Salisbury.*—Ch. Ch. Ox. B.A. 1853, M.A. 1855; Deac. 1854 and Pr. 1855 by Bp of Nor. R. of Wilton with Netherhampton P. C. Dio. Salis. 1867. (Patron, Earl of Pembroke; Tithe, 323*l*; Glebe, 29 acres; R.'s Inc. 490*l* and Ho; Pop. Wilton 1930, Netherhampton 182.) Dom. Chap. to the Earl of Pembroke 1865. Formerly C. of Yarmouth, Norfolk, 1854–59; Chap. to Bp of Moray and Ross 1859-60; C. of Wilton 1860–67. [20]

OLIVIER, Henry Arnold, *Crowhurst Rectory, Battle, Sussex.*—Ball. Coll. Ox. B.A. 1849, M.A. 1854; Deac. 1849 by Bp of Herf. Pr. 1851 by Bp of Salis. R. of Crowhurst, Dio. Chich. 1861. (Patron, T. Papillon, Esq; R.'s Inc. 180*l* and Ho; Pop. 430.) C. of Ham, Wilts. Formerly Asst. C. of St. Stephen's, Brighton, and of All Saints', Colchester. [21]

OLLIVANT, Edward, *Llandewi Rytherch, Abergavenny.*—Trin. Coll. Cam. B.A. 1839, M.A. 1842; Deac. 1841, Pr. 1842. P. C. of Llandewi-Rytherch, Dio. Llan. 1865. (Patron, Bp of Llan; P. C.'s Inc. 250*l* and Ho; Pop. 339.) Exam. Chap. to the Bp of Llan. 1850. Formerly Mast. of Wye Gr. Sch. and C. of Wye, Kent. [22]

OLVER, Henry Haine, *Port View, Saltash, Cornwall.*—Corpus Coll. Cam. Sen. Opt. and B.A. 1849; Deac. 1850 by Bp of B. and W. Pr. 1852 by Bp of Wor. Formerly 2nd Mast. of Kingsbridge Gr. Sch. Devon, 1852. [23]

O'MELIA, Frederick, *Walpole St. Andrew, Lynn, Norfolk.*—Dub. A.B. 1857; Deac. 1858 and Pr. 1860 by Bp of Meath. C. of Walpole St. Andrew 1867. Formerly C. of All Saints', Portsea, 1863–67. [24]

OMMANNEY, Edward Aislabie, *Chew Magna Vicarage, Bristol.*—Ex. Coll. Ox. 3rd cl. Lit. Hum. and B.A. 1827, M.A. 1831; Deac. 1829, Pr. 1830. V. of Chew Magna, Dio. B. and W. 1841. (Patrons, Bp of B. and W. and others in turn; Tithe—Imp. 98*l* 2*s* 9*d*, V. 416*l* 15*s*; Glebe, 120 acres; V.'s Inc. 750*l* and Ho; Pop. 1855.) Preb. of Wells 1848; Rural Dean of Chew 1850. [25]

OMMANNEY, George Druce Wynne, *Whitchurch, Bristol.*—Trin. Coll. Cam. Sen. Opt. 2nd cl. Cl. Trip. and B.A. 1842, M.A. 1846; Deac. 1843 and Pr. 1844 by Bp of Lin. C. of Whitchurch 1862. [26]

O'NEIL, Simeon Wilberforce, *Wantage, Berks.*—C. of Wantage. Formerly C. of Clewer. [27]

O'NEILL, Arthur Alexander, *Crewe, Cheshire.*—King's Coll. Lond. Theol. Assoc. 1858; Deac. 1858 and Pr. 1859 by Bp of Lin. C. of Crewe 1866. Formerly C. of Carrington, Lincolnshire, 1858, Horwich, Lancashire, 1860, St. George's, Chorley, 1861. [1]

O'NEILL, Henry, *Queeniborough, Leicester.*—V. of Queeniborough, Dio. Pet. 1866. (Patron, Thomas Frewen, Esq; Glebe, 9 acres; V.'s Inc. 106*l*; Pop. 511.) [2]

O'NEILL, James, *Luton Vicarage, Beds.*—Deac. 1845, Pr. 1846. V. of Luton, Dio. Ely, 1862. (Patron, the present V; V.'s Inc. 900*l* and Ho; Pop. 9102. [3]

O'NEILL, John Mortlock, *Bradford, Taunton*—Caius Coll. Cam. B.A. 1850; Deac. 1855 and Pr. 1858 by Bp of Ex. C. of West Buckland, Somerset, 1866. Formerly C. of St. Ives, Cornwall, 1855; Tedburn St. Mary, 1858; Silverton 1860; Burlescombe 1861. [4]

O'NEILL, Owen Lucas, *Newton St. Petrock, Exeter.*—Queens' Coll. Cam. B.A. 1844; Deac. 1844, Pr. 1845. P. C. of Abbot's Bickington, Devon, Dio. Ex. 1855. (Patrons, Trustees of Lord Rolle; Tithe—Imp. 16*l* 16*s*, P. C. 45*l*; P. C.'s Inc. 87*l*; Pop. 71.) C. of Cornworthy, Devon. Formerly C. of Skilgate, Somerset, 1860. [5]

ONION, Thomas Clarke, *Lancaster.*—St. Cath. Hall, Cam. B.A. 1845, M.A. 1853; Deac. 1844, Pr. 1845. Chap. to the Lancaster Co. Asylum; Chap. to the Dowager Duchess of Leeds. Formerly Chap. to the Birmingham Borough Lunatic Asylum. [6]

ONLEY-PRATTENTON, George Deakin, *Alfrick, near Worcester.*—St. John's Coll. Ox. B.A. 1850, M.A. 1865; Deac. 1852 and Pr. 1853 by Bp of Lich. C. of Alfrick and Lulsley. [7]

ONSLOW, Alexander William, *Trinity College, Cambridge.*—Scho. of Trin. Coll. Cam. [8]

ONSLOW, Arthur Cyril, *Newington Rectory, Newington-butts, London, S.*—Ch. Ch. Ox. B.A. 1809, M.A. 1811; Deac. 1810, Pr. 1811. R. of St. Mary's with St. Matthew's C. Newington, Dio. Lon. 1812. (Patron, Bp of Lon; Tithe, 120*l*; R.'s Inc. 900*l* and Ho; Pop. 13,282.) [9]

ONSLOW, Charles, *Wimborne Minster, Dorset.*—Trin. Coll. Cam. B.A. 1831, M.A. 1838; Deac. 1838 and Pr. 1839 by Bp of B. and W. Priest of the Royal Peculiar of Wimborne Minster, Dio. Salis. 1849. (Patrons, the 12 Govs. of Queen Elizabeth's Gr. Sch; Tithe, Imp. 2416*l* on 11,966 acres; Annual Stipend, 250*l*; Pop. 4807.) Rural Dean 1853; Surrogate 1852; Preb. of Salis. 1863; Chap. of the Wimborne and Cranborne Union. [10]

ONSLOW, Middleton, *East Peckham Vicarage, Tunbridge, Kent.*—Queens' Coll. Cam. B.A. 1828, M.A. 1832; Deac. 1829, Pr. 1830. V. of East Peckham, Dio. Cant. 1853. (Patrons, D and C. of Cant; Tithe—App. 907*l* 12*s* 6*d*, V. 454*l* 13*s* 5*d*; Glebe, 8 acres; V.'s Inc. 840*l* and Ho; Pop. 423.) Rural Dean of North Malling 1854. [11]

ONSLOW, Phipps, *Upper Sapey, Worcester.*—Ex. Coll. Ox. B.A. 1846; Deac. 1847 and Pr. 1848 by Bp of Wor. R. of Upper Sapey, Dio. Herf. 1859. (Patron, Sir T. E. Winnington, Bart. M.P; Tithe, 298*l*; Glebe, 40 acres; R.'s Inc. 335*l* and Ho; Pop. 260.) Formerly C. of Longdon 1847, March 1850. Author, *What is the Church?* (a Lecture), 1862, 6*d*. [12]

ONSLOW, Thomas George, *Catmore Rectory, Wantage, Berks.*—Deac. 1850 and Pr. 1851 by Bp of Lon. R. of Catmore, Dio. Ox. 1853. (Patron, C. Eyre, Esq; Tithe, 186*l* 8*s*; R.'s Inc. 190*l* and Ho; Pop. 121.) [13]

ONSLOW, William Lake, *Sandringham, Lynn, Norfolk.*—Emman. Coll. Cam. B.A. 1842, M.A. 1845; Deac. 1843 and Pr. 1844 by Bp of Nor. R. of Sandringham with Babingley R. Dio. Nor. 1866. (Patron, J. Motteaux, Esq; Glebe, 32 acres; R.'s Inc. 195*l* and Ho; Pop. Sandringham 56, Babingley 67.) Formerly Chap. of H.M.S. "Racoon." [14]

OPENSHAW, Thomas, *Kentisbury Rectory, Barnstaple, Devon.*—St. John's Coll. Cam. B.A. 1851; Deac. 1851 and Pr. 1853 by Bp of Man. R. of Kentisbury, Dio. Ex. 1864. (Patron, the present R; Tithe, 270*l*; Glebe, 74 acres; R.'s Inc. 440*l* and Ho; Pop. 385.) Formerly P. C. of Brakenfield, Derbyshire, 1853–58; P. C. of Friarmere, Rochdale, 1858–64. [15]

OPENSHAW, Thomas Williams, *Bristol.*—Brasen. Coll. Ox. Somerset Scho. Hulmeian Exhib. B.A. 1860, M.A. 1863; Deac. 1862, Pr. 1863. 2nd Mast. of Bristol Gr. Sch. Formerly C. of Octagon Chapel, Bath 1862. [16]

ORAM, Henry Austin, *Leeds.*—St. John's Coll. Cam. B.A. 1839; Deac. 1846 and Pr. 1848 by Bp of Ches. C. of All Saints', Leeds. Formerly Head Mast. of the Modern Free Sch. Macclesfield; Chap. to the Union Workhouse, Macclesfield. Author, *Examples in Arithmetic*; *Examples in Algebra*; *Latin Derivation.* [17]

ORANGE, Thomas, *St. Lawrence Rectory, St. Heliers, Jersey.*—Literate; Deac. 1824 and Pr. 1825 by Bp of Win. R. of St. Lawrence, Jersey, Dio. Win. 1842. (Patron, the Gov; Tithe, 60*l*; Glebe, 20 acres; R.'s Inc. 150*l* and Ho.) Formerly C. of St. Owen, Jersey, 1824–26, Serk 1826–29, St. Heliers 1829–41, St. Saviour's, Jersey, 1841–42. [18]

ORDE, Leonard Shafto, *Edinburgh.*—Queens' Coll. Cam. B.A. 1830, M.A. 1842. Min. of St. Paul's, Edinburgh, 1859; Dom. Chap. to the Duke of Northumberland. Formerly P. C. of Alnwick, Northumberland, 1854–59. [19]

O'REGAN, Thomas, *Donington-Wood Parsonage, Newport, Salop.*—Dub. A.B. 1845; Deac. 1845 and Pr. 1846 by Bp of Lich. P. C. of Donington-Wood, Dio. Lich. 1850. (Patron, Duke of Sutherland; Tithe, 200*l*; Glebe, 257 acres; P. C.'s Inc. 665*l* and Ho; Pop. 1351.) [20]

O'REILLY, Charles James, *Riversdale, Melton Mowbray.*—Dub. Primate's Heb. Prize, A.B. 1862; Deac. 1862 and Pr. 1863 by Bp of Lich. C. of Melton Mowbray. [21]

O'REILLY, C. T., *Burton on-Trent.*—C. of Trinity, Burton-on-Trent. [22]

O'REILLY, James, *King's College, London, W.C.*—Formerly C. of St. Peter's, Walworth, Lond. [23]

ORFORD, James, *Fonnereau-road, Ipswich.*—Caius Coll. Cam. B.A. 1817, M.A. 1820; Deac. 1817, Pr. 1818. Chap. of the Tattingstone Union, Ipswich, 1831. [24]

ORGER, Edward Redman, *St. Augustine's College, Canterbury.*—Pemb. Coll. Ox. 2nd cl. Lit. Hum. and B A. 1849, M.A. 1852; Deac. 1851, Pr. 1852. Fell. of St. Augustine's Coll. 1855; Sub-Warden 1866. [25]

ORGER, John Goldsmith, *Cranford Rectory, Kettering, Northants.*—Wad. Coll. Ox. 2nd cl. Lit. Hum. and B.A. 1844; Deac. 1846 and Pr. 1847 by Bp of Salis. R. of Cranford St. Andrew with Cranford St. John R. Dio. Pet. 1856. (Patron, Sir G. Robinson; Cranford St. Andrew, Tithe, 10*l* 8*s* 4*d*; Glebe, 140 acres; Cranford St. John, Glebe, 205 acres; R.'s Inc. 356*l* and Ho; Pop. Cranford St. Andrew 228, Cranford St. John 325.) [26]

ORGILL, V. T. T., *Brentwood, Essex.*—St. Alb. Hall, Ox. B.A. 1862; Deac. 1863 and Pr. 1865 by Bp of Lich. C. of Brentwood 1866. Formerly C of Kidsgrove, Staffs, 1863, Dalton-in Furness, Lancashire, 1865. [27]

ORLEBAR, Augustus, *Willington Vicarage, Bedford.*—Wad. Coll. Ox. 4th cl. Lit. Hum. M.A. 1850; Deac. 1847, Pr. 1848. V. of Willington, Dio. Ely, 1858. (Patron, Duke of Bedford; Tithe, comm. 235*l*; Glebe, 17 acres; V.'s Inc. 290*l* and Ho; Pop. 290.) Organizing Sec. to the Additional Curates' Soc. for Dio. Ely 1863. Formerly C. of All Saints', Lewes, 1847–49, Hagley, Worc. 1850–52; R. of Farndish, Beds, 1852–58. [28]

ORLEBAR, John Charles, *Whipsnade Rectory, near Dunstable, Beds.*—St. Bees; Deac. 1839 and Pr. 1840 by Bp of Ches. R. of Whipsnade, Dio. Ely, 1858. (Patron, Ld Chan; Tithe, 185*l* 14*s* 6*d*; Glebe, 20 acres; R.'s Inc. 230*l* and Ho; Pop. 180.) Formerly C. of Downham, Lanc. 1839, Hockcliffe with Chalgrave, Beds, 1841; P. C. of Heath and Reach 1842, with P. C. of Billington, Beds, 1843–58. [29]

O'RORKE, Henry Thomas, *Brighton.*—Dub. A.B. 1854, A.M. 1859; Deac. 1857 and Pr. 1858 by Bp of Lich. Asst. Min. of St. Mary's, Brighton. Formerly C. of Burton-on-Trent 1857–59, Basildon, Berks, All Saints', Maidstone, 1859–60, Beddington, Surrey, 1860. [1]

ORMANDY, Thomas, *Whitbeck, Bootle, Whitehaven.*—St. Bees; Deac. 1820 and Pr. 1821 by Bp of Ches. P. C. of Whitbeck, Dio. Carl. 1850. (Patron, Earl of Lonsdale; Tithe—Imp. 89*l* 17*s* 4*d*; Glebe, 7 acres; P. C.'s Inc. 120*l* and Ho; Pop. 213.) [2]

ORME, Frederick, *Lyndon Rectory, Uppingham.*—Jesus Coll. Cam. B.A. 1835, M.A. 1861; Deac. 1836 and Pr. 1837 by Bp of Lin. R. of Lyndon, Dio. Pet. 1864. (Patron, E. N. Conant, Esq; Tithe, 190*l*; R.'s Inc. 190*l* and Ho; Pop. 126.) Formerly R. of Edith Weston 1856–60. [3]

ORME, James Bond, *Angmering Rectory, Arundel.*—Brasen. Coll. Ox. M.A. 1862; Deac. 1863 and Pr. 1864 by Bp of Chich. R. of East Angmering with West Angmering V. Dio. Chich. 1866. (Patroness, Lady Brooke Pechell; Tithe, 305*l*; Glebe, 38 acres; R.'s Inc. 360*l* and Ho; Pop. 1050.) Formerly C. of Hurstpierpoint 1863–65, Sutton, Sussex, 1865–66. [4]

ORMEROD, Arthur Stanley, *Halvergate, Acle, Norfolk.*—Ex. Coll. Ox. 3rd cl. Lit. Hum. B.A. 1843, M.A. 1846; Deac. 1844, Pr. 1845. V. of Halvergate, Dio. Nor. 1853. (Patron, Bp of Nor; Tithe—Imp. 330*l*, V. 236*l*; Glebe, 44 acres; V.'s Inc. 340*l* and Ho; Pop. 541.) Surrogate. [5]

ORMEROD, Oliver, *Presteign Rectory, Radnorshire.*—Brasen. Coll. Ox. B.A. 1829, M.A. 1832. R. of Presteign with Discoed C. Dio. Herf. 1841. (Patron, Earl of Oxford; Presteign, Tithe—Imp. 83*l* 2*s* 10*d*, R. 1300*l*; R.'s Inc. 1400*l* and Ho; Pop. Presteign 2272, Discoed 111.) [6]

ORMEROD, The Ven. Thomas Johnson, *Redenhall Rectory, Harleston, Norfolk.*—Brasen. Coll. Ox. 1st cl. Lit. Hum. 1829, B.A. 1830, M.A. 1833; Deac. 1834 and Pr. 1835 by Bp of Ox. Archd. of Suffolk 1846. (Value, 180*l*.) R. of Redenhall with Harleston C. Dio. Nor. 1847. (Patron, Bp of Nor; Tithe, 1000*l*; Glebe, 28 acres; R.'s Inc. 1100*l* and Ho; Pop. Redenhall 434, Harleston 1302.) Formerly Exam. Chap. to Bp of Nor; Fell. of Brasen. Coll. Ox. 1831; Select Preacher Univ. of Ox. 1845. Author, Articles on the German Reformation, in the *Encyclopædia Metropolitana*; Archidiaconal Charges; etc. [7]

ORMISTON, James, 55, *Cloudesley-terrace, Islington, N.*—King's Coll. Lond; Deac. 1863 and Pr. 1864 by Bp of Carl. C. of the Conventional District of St. David, Islington, 1866. (C.'s Inc. 200*l*; Pop. 8000.) Formerly C. in sole charge of Wythop. Cumberland, 1863–66; Chap. of Cockermouth Railway, 1863–65. Author, *The Faithful Friend, or a Balm for every Wound*, 1860, 1*s*; *Protest against the Ritualists' Confessional*, 1867, 6*d*. [8]

ORMOND, John, *Great Kimble, Tring, Bucks.*—Pemb. Coll. Ox. Fell of, B.A. 1850, M.A. 1853; Deac. 1852, Pr. 1853. V. of Great Kimble, Dio. Ox. 1857. (Patron, G. H. C. Hampden, Esq; Tithe, comm. 150*l*; Glebe, 40 acres; V.'s Inc. 200*l* and Ho; Pop. 408.) Formerly C. of Shalfleet, Isle of Wight, 1852, Great Hampden, Bucks, 1854–57. [9]

ORMSBY, George Albert, *Eglingham Vicarage, Alnwick.*—Dub. A.B. 1865; Deac. 1866 by Bp of Dur. C. of Eglingham 1866. [10]

ORMSBY, William Arthur, *Smallburgh Rectory, Norwich.*—Univ. Coll. Ox. 1831, Hon. 4th cl. Lit. Hum. and B.A. 1834, M.A. 1837; Deac. 1837, Pr. 1838. R. of Smallburgh, Dio. Nor. 1853. (Patron, Bp of Nor; Tithe, 430*l*; Glebe, 28 acres; R.'s Inc. 472*l* and Ho; Pop. 559.) Hon. Sec. to the Norwich Dioc. Board of Education. [11]

ORNSBY, George, *Fishlake Vicarage, Doncaster.*—Dur. Licen. in Theol. 1841; Deac. 1841 and Pr. 1842 by Bp of Dur. V. of Fishlake, Dio. York, 1850. (Patrons, D. and C. of Dur; Glebe, 226 acres; V.'s Inc. 400*l* and Ho; Pop. 645.) Formerly C. of Newburn, Northumberland, 1841–43, Sedgefield, Durham, 1843–44, Whickham, Durham, 1845–50. Author, *Sketches of Durham*, 1846. [12]

ORPEN, Edward Chatterton, *Dean Prior Vicarage, near Ashburton, Devon.*—Trin. Hall, Cam. B.A. 1854, M.A. 1857; Deac. 1854 and Pr. 1855 by Bp of Ches. V. of Dean Prior, Dio. Ex. 1866. (Patron, Lord Churston; Tithe, 228*l*; Glebe, 92 acres; V.'s Inc. 330*l* and Ho; Pop. 380.) Formerly C. of Marton, Cheshire, 1854–56, Newtown, Hants, 1856–57; Stibbard, Norfolk, 1858–60; C. in sole charge of Ashton Keynes, Wilts, 1860–66. [13]

ORR, Alexander, *Salehurst Vicarage, Hurst Green, Sussex.*—Oriel Coll. Ox. B.A. 1836; Deac. 1837 and Pr. 1838 by Bp of Down and Connor. V. of Salehurst, Dio. Chich. 1860. (Patron, Charles Hardy, Esq; Tithe, 615*l*; V.'s Inc. 620*l* and Ho; Pop. 2012.) Formerly R. of Lambeg, Dio. Down and Connor, 1847. [14]

ORR, R., *Milton, Gravesend.*—C. of Christchurch, Milton. [15]

ORR, William Holmes, *Bishop's Sutton, Bristol.*—St. Bees; Deac. 1859 and Pr. 1860 by Bp of Lich. C. in sole charge of Bishop's Sutton 1866. Formerly C. of Sneyd, Lancashire, and Bilston, Staffs; Chap. to Labourers on Bristol and North Somerset Railway. Author, *Teachers and Teaching*, Macintosh, 1864. [16]

ORTON, Frederic.—C. of Bermondsey, Lond. [17]

ORTON, John Swaffield, *Beeston Rectory, Swaffham, Norfolk.*—King's Coll. Lond. Theol. Assoc; Deac. 1860 and Pr. 1861 by Bp of Win. R. of Beeston-next-Mileham, Dio. Nor. 1865. (Patron, Rev. C. B. Barnwell; Tithe, 550*l*; Glebe, 30 acres; R.'s Inc. 600*l* and Ho; Pop. 615.) Formerly C. of Shalfleet 1860, and Yarmouth, Isle of Wight, 1863. [18]

ORTON, Owen, *Trinity College, Glenalmond, Perthshire.*—Corpus Coll. Ox. 2nd cl. Lit. Hum. B.A. 1861, M.A. 1864; Deac. 1862 and Pr. 1864 by Bp of G. and B. Theol. Tut. in Trinity Coll. Glenalmond, 1865. Formerly C. of Tortworth 1862, Cromhall 1864. [19]

OSBORN, Edward, *Maldon, Essex.*—St. Peter's Coll. Cam. B.A. 1823, M.A. 1826; Deac. 1826 and Pr. 1828 by Bp of Lon. Formerly V. of Asheldam, Essex, 1850–59. [20]

OSBORN, Montagu Francis Finch, *Kibworth-Beauchamp Rectory, Market Harborough, Leicestershire.*—Ball. Coll. Ox. B.A. 1845, M.A. 1848; Deac. and Pr. 1850 by Bp of Ox. R. of Kibworth-Beauchamp, Dio. Pet. 1851. (Patron, Mert. Coll. Ox; R.'s Inc. 835*l* and Ho; Pop. 1334.) Rural Dean 1865. Formerly Fell. of Mert. Coll. Ox. Author, *A Few Words on the Representation of the University of Oxford*, 1853; *Letter on the Representation of the University of Oxford*, 1860; *A Church Hymn Book*, 4th ed. 1865. [21]

OSBORN, William Cook. *South Hill House, Bath.*—St. John's Coll. Cam. B.A. 1839, M.A. 1842; Deac. 1839, Pr. 1840. Chap. of the Gaol, Bath, 1843. (Salary, 200*l*.) Formerly C. of Melksham 1842. Author, *The Prevention of Crime*; *The Plea of Not Guilty*; *The Prisoners' Character Book and Educational Register*; *The Imprisonment of Children*; *The Cry of Ten Thousand Children*; *The Preservation of Youth from Crime*; *The Non-Imprisonment of Children*; etc. [22]

OSBORNE, George, *Stainby Rectory, Colsterworth, Grantham.*—St. John's Coll. Cam. B.A. 1824, M.A. 1828; Deac. 1824 and Pr. 1825 by Bp of Lin. R. of Stainby with Gunby R. Dio. Lin. 1825. (Patron, Rev. B. S. Kennedy; Stainby, Glebe, 256 acres; Gunby, Glebe, 165 acres; R.'s Inc. 475*l* and Ho; Pop. Stainby 179, Gunby 175.) Rural Dean. [23]

OSBORNE, George Yarnold, *Fleetwood, Lancashire.*—Sid. Coll. Cam. Scho. of, B.A. and M.A. 1839; Deac. 1840 and Pr. 1842 by Bp of Ches. P. C. of Fleetwood, Dio. Man. 1850. (Patron, the Rev. Sir P. H. Fleetwood, Bart; P. C.'s Inc. 170*l*; Pop. 4258.) Author, *History of Prestbury*, Macclesfield, 1840; *Bible Stories*, Fleetwood, 1854. [24]

OSBORNE, John Francis, 29, *St. Giles's-plain, Norwich.*—Deac. 1839 and Pr. 1840 by Bp of Lon. R. of Eccles-next-the-Sea, Dio. Nor. 1857. (Patron, Chas. Lombe, Esq; R.'s Inc. 80*l*; Pop. 28.) Chap. to the Norfolk and Norwich Hospital; C. of St. Simon and St. Jude's, Norwich, 1861. Formerly Even. Lect. of St.

Stephen's, Norwich. Author, *The Bible and its Uses*, 1855, 1*s*; *Sermon on Mary Magdalene; A Fast-day Sermon*; etc. [1]

OSBORNE, Peter Mann, *Heavitree, near Exeter.*—Ex. Coll. Ox. B.A. 1800, M.A. 1803; Deac. 1801, Pr. 1802. [2]

OSBORNE, Philip, *Garthorpe Vicarage, Melton Mowbray.* — St. Cath. Coll. Cam. B.C.L. 1828; Deac. 1829 and Pr. 1830 by Bp of Lin. C. of Garthorpe. [3]

OSBORNE, Lord Sidney Godolphin, *Durweston Rectory, Blandford, Dorset.*—Brasen. Coll. Ox. B.A. 1830; Deac. 1831 and Pr. 1832 by Bp of Lin. R. of Durweston with Bryanston R. Dio. Salis. 1841. (Patron, Lord Portman; Tithe, Durweston, 263*l*; Glebe, 111 acres; Bryanston, Tithe, 177*l*; R.'s Inc. 500*l* and Ho; Pop. Durweston 364, Bryanston 206.) Author, *Hints to the Charitable for the Amelioration of the Condition of the Poor*; *Gleanings in Ireland*; Pamphlets on Poor Law; *The Lady Eva*, Boone; *Immortal Sewerage*, Parker; *Scutari*, Dickenson. [4]

OSBORNE, William Alexander, *Rossall School, Fleetwood, Lancashire.*—Trin. Coll. Cam. Craven Scho. 1st Cl. and Sen. Chancellor's Medallist 1836–37, B.A. 1838; Deac. 1838 and Pr. 1839 by Abp of Cant. Head Mast. of Rossall Gr. Sch. 1849. Formerly Head Mast. of Macclesfield Gr. Sch. Editor, *Horace* (1st vol. of Greek and Latin Classics), Longmans, 1848, 1*s* 6*d*. [5]

OSMAN, Joseph Wheeler, 54, *Lansdowne-square, Cardiff.*—Deac. 1858 and Pr. 1859 by Bp of Lich. C. of St. Mary's, Cardiff, 1866. Formerly C. of St. George's, Wolverhampton, 1860–62; Chap. of South Staffordshire General Hospital 1862; Sen. C. of Bishop Wearmouth 1864. [6]

OSTREHAN, Joseph Duncan, *Creech St. Michael, Taunton.*—Wor. Coll. Ox. B.A. 1852; Deac. 1853 and Pr. 1854 by Bp of Lon. V. of Creech St. Michael, Dio. B. and W. 1851. (Patrons, C. Creswell, Esq. and Mrs. Creswell; V.'s Inc. 500*l* and Ho; Pop. 1121.) Formerly Asst. Chap. to the H.E.I.C. on the Madras Establishment. [7]

OSWALD, Henry Murray.—Ch. Ch. Ox. B.A. 1855, M.A. 1860; Deac. 1856 and Pr. 1857 by Bp of Lin. Formerly C. of Alnwick, Northumberland, and Witham, Essex. [8]

OSWELL, Henry Lloyd, *Shrewsbury.*—Ch. Ch. Ox. B.A. 1835, M.A. 1838; Deac. 1837 and Pr. 1838 by Bp of Lon. P. C. of St. George's, Shrewsbury, Dio. Lich. 1866. (Patron, V. of St. Chad's, Shrewsbury; P. C.'s Inc. 150*l*; Pop. 2581.) Chap. of Millington's Hospital. Formerly C. of Trinity, Coleham, Shrewsbury. [9]

OTTER, George, *Hucknall Torkard, Nottingham.*—Jesus Coll. Cam. M.A. V. of Hucknall Torkard, Dio. Lin. 1862. (Patron, Duke of Portland; V.'s Inc. 140*l*; Pop. 2836.) Formerly C. of Whaplode Drove, Lincolnshire, 1850–62. [10]

OTTER, Robert William, *Aisthorpe, near Lincoln.*—Pemb. Coll. Cam. B A. 1837. R. of Aisthorpe with West Thorpe, *alias* Thorpe-in-the-Fallows, V. Dio. Lin. 1850. (Patron, the present R; Aisthorpe, Tithe, 287*l* 8*s* 7*d*; West Thorpe, Tithe, 72*l*; R.'s Inc. 365*l*; Pop. Aisthorpe 150, West Thorpe 54.) Formerly C. of Broxholme and North Carlton, 1838–47, Scampton 1848–50. [11]

OTTER, The Ven. William Bruere, *Cowfold Vicarage, Horsham, Sussex.*—St. Peter's Coll. Cam. B.A. 1828, M.A. 1838; Deac. 1829, Pr. 1830. V. of Cowfold, Dio. Chich. 1839. (Patron, Bp of Lon; Tithe, 587*l*; Glebe, 33 acres; R.'s Inc. 610*l* and Ho; Pop. 946.) Preb. of Chich. 1850; Archd. of Lewes 1855. [12]

OTTLEY, Charles M'Mahon, *Fenny Stratford, Bucks.*—C. of Fenny Stratford. [13]

OTTLEY, Francis John, *Eton College, Windsor.*—Oriel Coll. Ox. 1st cl. Math. et Phy. and B.A. 1848, Sen. Math. Scho. 1849, M.A. 1851; Deac. 1852 and Pr. 1853 by Bp of Ox. Asst. Math. Mast. Eton Coll; C. of Boveny, Bucks. [14]

OTTLEY, George L., *Ridley House, Herne, Kent.* [15]

OTTLEY, John Bridges, *Thorpe Acre Parsonage, Loughborough.*—Oriel Coll. Ox. 1st cl. Lit. Hum. 1818, B.A. 1819, M.A. 1823; Deac. 1824 by Bp of Ox. Pr. 1824 by Bp of Chich. P. C. of Thorpe Acre, Dio. Pet. 1845. (Patron, Bp of Pet; Glebe, 1½ acres; P. C.'s Inc. 150*l* and Ho; Pop. 195.) Formerly Fell. of Oriel Coll. Ox. [16]

OUGH, Charles, 26, *Spencer-road, Hornsey-road, Holloway, N.*—King's Coll. Lond. Assoc. 1862; Deac. 1863 and Pr. 1864 by Bp of G. and B. C. of St. Barnabas', Holloway, Islington, 1867. Formerly C. of Hanham, Bristol, 1863. [17]

OULD, Fielding, *Tattenhall Rectory, Chester.*—R. of Tattenhall, Dio. Ches. 1855. (Patron, Bp of Ches; R.'s Inc. 300*l* and Ho; Pop. 1262.) Surrogate. [18]

OULD, Fielding Frederick, 8, *Peckitt-street, York.*—St. Aidan's; Deac. 1861 and Pr. 1863 by Bp of Dur. Assoc. Sec. Ch. Pastoral Aid Soc. 1867. Formerly C. of Monk-Hesleden, Durham, 1861, Berwick-on-Tweed 1864, Davenham, Cheshire, 1865–66. [19]

OUSELEY, Sir Frederick Arthur Gore, Bart., *St. Michael's College, Tenbury, Worcestershire.*—Ch. Ch. Ox. B.A. 1846, M.A. 1849, Mus. Bach. 1850, Mus. Doc. 1854; Deac. 1849 by Bp of Lon. Pr. 1855 by Bp of Herf. P. C. of St. Michael's, Tenbury, Dio. Herf. 1856. (Patron, the present P. C; P. C.'s Inc. 70*l*.) Prof. of Music in the Univ. of Ox. 1855. (Value, 130*l*.) Precentor of Herf. Cathl. Composer, *Sweet Echo* (a Glee), Oxford, 1845; *Services and Anthems*, Novello, 1853; *Collection of Services*, ib. 1853; *St. Polycarp* (an Oratorio), ib. 1855. [20]

OUSELEY, Gideon J. R., 6, *St. Stephen-square, Norwich.*—Deac. 1859 and Pr. 1860 by Bp of Down and Connor. [21]

OUTRAM, George Sanford, *Norwich.*—Ch. Coll. Cam. Sen. Opt. and B.A. 1852; Deac. 1853 by Abp of York, Pr. 1854 by Bp of Madras for Abp of York. R. of All Saints' and St. Julian's, City and Dio. Nor. 1864. (Patron, Rev. C. F. Soulthorpe; R.'s Inc. 260*l*; Pop. All Saints' 667, St. Julian's 1361.) Formerly C. of Hapton, Norfolk; P. C. of Beeley, Derbyshire, 1856–64. [22]

OUVRY, Peter Thomas, *Wing (Bucks), near Leighton-Buzzard.*—Trin. Coll. Cam. Sen. Opt. and B.A. 1834, M.A. 1837; Deac. 1836 by Bp of Lin. for Bp of Pet. Pr. 1837 by Bp of Glouc. for Bp of Pet. V. of Wing Dio. Ox. 1850. (Patron, Lord Overstone; Tithe—App. 45*l* 19*s* 10½*d*, V. 61*l* 19*s*; Glebe, 220 acres; V.'s Inc. 461*l* 19*s* and Ho; Pop. 1504.) R. of Grove, Bucks, Dio. Ox. 1860. (Patron, Lord Overstone; R.'s Inc. 75*l*; Pop. 19.) Formerly C. of Mears Ashby, near Northampton, 1836–37, St. John's, Paddington, 1838–47; P. C. of Linslade, Bucks, 1848–50. [23]

OUVRY-NORTH, John North, *East Acton, Middlesex, W.*—Trin. Coll. Cam. B.A. 1849, M.A. 1852; Deac. and Pr. 1848 by Bp of Ox. Formerly V. of Mentmore, Bucks, 1848–60. [24]

OVENS, Thomas, *Halstead, Essex.*—Dub. A.B. 1843; Deac. 1844, Pr. 1845. V. of Halstead, Dio. Roch. 1864. (Patron, Bp of Roch; Tithe, 472*l*; Glebe, 5 acres; V.'s Inc. 485*l* and Ho; Pop. 3368.) Formerly Min. of St. Paul's Chapel, Writtle, Essex, 1846–64. [25]

OVER, Edward, 39, *North End, Croydon, Surrey.*—St. Cath. Hall, Cam. B.A 1839, M.A. 1843; Deac. 1842 and Pr. 1843 by Bp of Lon. [26]

OVERTON, Charles, *Cottingham Vicarage, near Hull.*—Deac. 1829 by Abp of York, Pr. 1830 by Bp of Ches. V. of Cottingham, Dio. York, 1841. (Patron, Bp of Ches; Cottingham, Tithe, App. 968*l* 14*s* 10*d* and 441½ acres of Glebe; V.'s Inc. 235*l* 13*s* 8*d* and Ho; Pop. 3131.) Author, *Ecclesia Anglicana* (Poem), Rivingtons, 1853, 5*s*; *Tracts on Confirmation*, &c. Seeleys, 1843; *Cottage Lectures on Pilgrim's Progress*, ib. 1847, 1st and 2nd series, 3*s* 6*d* each; *The Expository Preacher, or St. Matthew's Gospel practically Expounded*, 2 vols. Nisbet, 1850, 15*s*; *Life of Joseph*, 1866, 4*s* 6*d*. [27]

OVERTON, Isle Grant, *Rothwell Rectory, Caistor, Lincolnshire.*—Corpus Coll. Ox. 2nd cl. Lit. Hum. and B.A. 1831, M.A. 1834, B.D. 1841; Deac. 1834 by Bp of Ox. Pr. 1835 by Bp of Lin. R. of Rothwell, Dio. Lin. 1844.

(Patron, Lord Yarborough; R.'s Inc. 520*l* and Ho; Pop. 245.) Formerly Fell. of Corpus Coll. Ox; C. of Cuxwold, Linc. 1834. [1]

OVERTON, John, *Sessay Rectory, Thirsk, Yorks.*—Trin. Coll. Cam. English Declamation Prize 1817, B.A. 1820, M.A. 1823, Seatonian Prize Poem 1824; Deac. 1819 by Bp of Ex. Pr. 1820 by Abp of York. R. of Sessay, Dio. York, 1836. (Patron, Viscount Downe; Tithe, 619*l*; Glebe, 66¾ acres; R.'s Inc. 740*l* and Ho; Pop. 456.) [2]

OVERTON, John, *Rougham Vicarage, Norfolk.*—Magd. Hall, Ox. B.A. 1835, M.A. 1838; Deac. 1835, Pr. 1836. V. of Rougham, Dio. Nor. 1846. (Patron, Ld Chan; Tithe, 355*l*; Glebe, 1 acre; V.'s Inc. 231*l*; Pop. 409.) [3]

OVERTON, John Henry, *Legbourn Parsonage, Louth, Lincolnshire.*—Lin. Coll. Ox. Scho. of, B.A. 1858, M.A. 1860; Deac. 1858 and Pr. 1859 by Bp of G. and B. P. C. of Legbourn, Dio. Lin. 1860. (Patron, J. L. Fytche, Esq; P. C.'s Inc. 260*l* and Ho; Pop. 512.) Formerly C. of Quedgeley, Glouc. 1858. Author, *Two Assize Sermons at Lincoln*, Louth, 1865, 6*d*. [4]

OVERTON, S. C., *Stretton, near Warrington.*—C. of Stretton. Formerly C. of Hackness, Yorks. [5]

OVERTON, Thomas, *Black Notley Rectory, Braintree, Essex.*—St. John's Coll. Cam. 5th Wrang. and B.A. 1828, M.A. 1831, B.D. 1838; Deac. 1836 by Bp of Lin. Pr. 1837 by Bp of Ely. R. of Black Notley, Dio. Roch. 1858. (Patron, St. John's Coll. Cam; Tithe, 497*l*; Glebe, 26 acres; R.'s Inc. 584*l* and Ho; Pop. 489.) Formerly Fell. of St. John's Coll. Cam. [6]

OWEN, Charles Gustavus, *Pinxton Rectory, Alfreton, Derbyshire.*—R. of Pinxton, Dio. Lich. 1864. (Patron, D. Ewes Coke, Esq; R.'s Inc. 300*l* and Ho; Pop. 1367.) [7]

OWEN, Charles Henry, *Alderwasley, Wirksworth, Derbyshire.*—Chap. of Don. of Alderwasley, Dio. Lich. 1865. (Patron, A. F. Hurt, Esq; Chap.'s Inc. 120*l* and Ho; Pop. 372.) Formerly C. of Wirksworth. [8]

OWEN, David, *Bettws, Bridgend, Glamorganshire.*—St. Bees; Deac. 1858 and Pr. 1861 by Bp of Llan. C. of Bettws 1858. [9]

OWEN, David, *Eglwysfach Vicarage, Conway, Denbighshire.*—Deac. 1817, Pr. 1819. V. of Eglwysfach, Dio. St. A. 1826. (Patron, Bp of St. A; Tithe—Imp. 717*l*, Parish Clerk, 16*l*, V. 252*l*; Glebe, 1½ acres; V.'s Inc. 260*l* and Ho; Pop. 1530.) Author, *A Vocabulary of English Words of One Syllable, with a Welsh Translation, for the Use of Village Schools in the Principality*, Llanrwst, 1850, 8*d*. [10]

OWEN, David, *Llanvawr, Corwen, Merionethshire.*—C. of Llanvawr. [11]

OWEN, David, *Gyffylliog, Ruthin.*—St. Bees; Deac. 1864 and Pr. 1865 by Bp of St. A. C. of Gyffylliog 1864. [12]

OWEN, Donald Millman, *Balliol College, Oxford.*—Ball. Coll. Ox. 2nd cl. Lit. Hum. and B.A. 1852, M.A. 1855; Deac. 1853, Pr. 1854. Fell. of Ball. Coll. Ox. [13]

OWEN, Edmund John, *Tretire Rectory, near Ross.*—Brasen. Coll. Ox. Somerset Scho. B.A. 1855; Deac. 1856. C. of Tretire 1860. Formerly C. of Hope-under-Dinmore and Tenbury. [14]

OWEN, Edward, *St. Peter's Parsonage, Oldham.*—Clare Coll. Cam. B.A. 1852; Deac. 1853 and Pr. 1854 by Bp of Ban. P. C. of St. Peter's, Oldham, Dio. Man. 1861. (Patron, R. of Prestwich; P. C.'s Inc. 300*l* and Ho; Pop. 7100.) [15]

OWEN, Edward, *Sedlescombe Rectory, Battle, Sussex.*—Sid. Coll. Cam. B.A. 1844, M.A. 1847; Deac. 1843 and Pr. 1844 by Bp of Lin. R. of Sedlescombe, Dio. Chich. 1861. (Patron, Ld Chan; Tithe, 333*l* 6*s* 5*d*; Glebe, 60*l*; R.'s Inc. 438*l* and Ho; Pop. 703.) Formerly R. of Halton, Bucks, 1846–57; Incumb. of Laura Chapel, Bath, 1857–61. [16]

OWEN, Edward Henry, *Forres, Scotland.*—Jesus Coll. Cam. B.A. 1854; Deac. 1855 and Pr. 1856 by Bp of Man. Incumb. of St. John's, Forres, Dio. Moray and Ross, 1859. Formerly C. of Penwortham, Lancashire, and Rippingale, Lincolnshire. [17]

OWEN, Edward John, *Llanvair-Dyfryn-Clwyd Rectory, Ruthin, Denbighshire.*—Downing Coll. Cam. B.A. 1827, M.A. 1856. V. of Llanvair-Dyfryn-Clwyd, Dio. Ban. 1848. (Patron, Bp of Ban; Tithe—App. 581*l* 6*s* 8*d*, V. 290*l* 13*s* 4*d*; V.'s Inc. 301*l* and Ho; Pop. 1263.) [18]

OWEN, Edward Vaughan, *Llwydiarth Parsonage, Welshpool.*—St. Aidan's; Deac. 1858 and Pr. 1859 by Bp of Pet. P. C. of Llwydiarth, Dio. St. A. 1867. (Patron, Sir W. W. Wynne, Bart; P. C.'s Inc. 230*l*; Pop. 322.) Formerly C. of Corwen and of Llwydiarth. [19]

OWEN, George Welsh, *Calverleigh, Tiverton, Devon.*—New Inn Hall, Ox. B.A. 1832, M.A. 1836; Deac. 1834, Pr. 1835. R. of Calverleigh, Dio. Ex. 1841. (Patron, G. W. Owen, Esq; Tithe, 85*l* 13*s*; Glebe, 72 acres; R.'s Inc. 186*l*; Pop. 86.) [20]

OWEN, Henry, *Trusthorpe, near Alford.*—Dub. A.B. 1844; Deac. 1845 and Pr. 1846 by Bp of Rip. R. of Trusthorpe, Dio. Lin. 1859. (Patron, the present R; Glebe, 445*l*; R.'s Inc. 450*l* and Ho; Pop. 295.) V. of Sutton-in-the-Marsh, Dio. Lin. 1859. (Patron, Bp of Lin; V.'s Inc. 80*l*; Pop. 368.) Formerly C. of Otley, Yorks, 1845, St. Martin's, Birmingham, 1851; Assoc. Sec. to Irish Church Missions 1854. [21]

OWEN, Henry, *Llangefni Rectory, Anglesey.*—Jesus Coll. Cam. B.A. 1822, M.A. 1853; Deac. 1822 and Pr. 1823 by Bp of Ban. R. of Llangefni with Tregeian, Dio. Ban. 1850. (Patron, Bp of Ban; Tithe, 515*l*; Glebe, 1 acre; R.'s Inc. 525*l* and Ho; Pop. 1856.) Rural Dean; Proctor in Convocation for Dio. Ban. Author, *Three Sermons on Regeneration* (in Welsh). [22]

OWEN, Henry, *Heveningham Rectory, Yoxford, Suffolk.*—Magd. Coll. Cam. B.A. 1828, M.A. 1831; Deac. 1828 and Pr. 1829 by Bp of Nor. R. of Heveningham, Dio. Nor. 1838. (Patron, Ld Chan; Tithe, 480*l*; Glebe, 40 acres; R.'s Inc. 594*l* and Ho; Pop. 354.) Rural Dean; Chap. to Earl Stradbroke. Formerly R. of Wilby, Suffolk, 1830–38. [23]

OWEN, Hugh, *Llanerchymedd, Anglesey.*—Jesus Coll. Ox. B.A. 1844; Deac. 1846 and Pr. 1847 by Bp of Ban. P. C. of Llanerchymedd with Rhodogeidio C. and Gwredog C. Dio. Ban. 1853. (Patron, Bp of Ban; Glebe, 17 acres; P. C.'s Inc. 120*l* and Ho; Pop. 1277.) Formerly C. of Llanerchymedd 1850–53, Trefdraeth, Anglesey, 1846–50. [24]

OWEN, Hugh, *Bradfield Rectory, North Walsham, Norwich.*—R. of Bradfield, 1st Mediety, Dio. Nor. 1866. (Patron, Lord Suffield; R.'s Inc. 180*l* and Ho; Pop. 226.) Formerly C. of Llanstadwell, Pembrokeshire, and East Leake, Notts. [25]

OWEN, Hugh Davies, *Trefdraeth Rectory (Anglesey), near Bangor.*—Jesus Coll. Ox. 2nd cl. Lit. Hum. 1816, B.A. 1817, M.A. 1819, B.D. and D.D. 1834; Deac. 1819 and Pr. 1820 by Bp of Ban. R. of Trefdraeth with Llangwyvan C. Dio. Ban. 1849. (Patron, Bp of Ban; Trefdraeth, Tithe, 380*l* 10*s*; Llangwyvan, Tithe, 242*l*; Glebe, 9¾ acres; R.'s Inc. 622*l* and Ho; Pop. Trefdraeth 921, Llangwyvan 200.) Rural Dean. [26]

OWEN, Hugh Davies, jun., *Llangadwaladr, Bangor.*—Jesus Coll. Ox. B.A. 1852, M.A. 1855; Deac. 1854 by Bp of Ban. Pr. 1855 by Bp of Ches. C. of Llangadwaladr. [27]

OWEN, Hugh Thomas, *Trevor Traian, Ruabon.*—Jesus Coll. Ox. B.A. 1863, M.A. 1866; Deac. 1863 and Pr. 1864 by Bp of St. A. P. C. of Trevor Traian, Dio. St. A. 1865. (Patroness, Mrs. Ironmonger; P. C.'s Inc. 98*l*; Pop. 1700.) Formerly C. of Hirnant 1863. [28]

OWEN, James, *Myrtle Hill, Llechryd, Newcastle-Emlyn, Cardiganshire.*—Lampeter; Deac. 1829, Pr. 1830. P. C. of Llechryd, Dio. St. D. 1833. (Patron, T. E. Lloyd, Esq; Tithe, Imp. 36*l* 6*s*; P. C.'s Inc. 109*l*; Pop. 454.) [29]

OWEN, James Hughes, *Barkingside, Essex.*—C. of Barkingside. Formerly C. of Aylesbury; Math. Mast. in Aylesbury Gr. Sch. [30]

OWEN, James Richard, *Llanverres Rectory, Ruthin, Denbighshire.*—Jesus Coll. Ox. B.A. 1834, M.A. 1838. R. of Llanverres, Dio. St. A. 1854. (Patron, Bp of St. A; Tithe, 308*l*; R.'s Inc. 328*l* and Ho; Pop. 754.) [1]

OWEN, John, *Chaplain's House, City Prison, Holloway, London, N.*—Lampeter, B.D 1858; Deac. 1844 and Pr. 1845 by Bp of St. D. Chap. of the City Prison, Holloway, Lond. Formerly C. of St. Clement Danes, Strand, Lond. [2]

OWEN, John, *Llaniestyn Rectory, Pwllheli, Carnarvonshire.*—Jesus Coll. Ox B.A. 1812, M.A. 1815; Deac. 1812 and Pr. 1813 by Bp of Ban. R. of Llaniestyn with Llandegwining C. and Penllêch C. Dio. Ban. 1852. (Patron, Bp of Ban; Llaniestyn, Tithe—Imp. 6*l*. R. 375*l*; Glebe, 18 acres; Llandegwining, Tithe, 140*l*; Penllêch, Tithe, 190*l*; R.'s Inc. 742*l* and Ho; Pop. Llaniestyn 1012, Llandegwining 142, Penllêch 261.) Rural Dean of Lelyn; Hon. Can. of Ban, 1862. [3]

OWEN, John, *Llaneilian Rectory, Amlwch, Anglesey.*—Jesus Coll. Ox. B.A. 1816, M.A. 1818; Deac. and Pr. 1816. R. of Llaneilian with Coedanna C. and Rhosbeirio C. Dio. Ban. 1837. (Patron Bp of Ban; Llaneilian, Tithe, 227*l*; Glebe, 18 acres; Coedanna, Tithe, 140*l*; Rhosbeirio, Tithe, 58*l* 15*s*; R.'s Inc. 500*l* and Ho; Pop. Llaneilian 1282, Coedanna 275, Rhosbeirio 26.) [4]

OWEN, John, *Erryrys, Mold.*—Jesus Coll. Ox. B.A. 1851; Deac. 1852 and Pr. 1853 by Bp of St. A. R. of Erryrys, Dio. St. A. 1862. (Patrons, Crown and Bp of St. A. alt; Glebe, 24 acres; R.'s Inc. 300*l*; Pop. 900.) Formerly C. of Eglwys Rhos for nine years. [5]

OWEN, John, *Bower Chalke, near Salisbury.*—Lampeter; Deac. 1859 and Pr. 1860 by Bp of Salis. C. of Bower Chalke. [6]

OWEN, John, *Hooton, Eastham, Chester.*—Trin. Coll. Cam. B.A. 1850, M.A. 1853; Deac. 1851 and Pr. 1852 by Bp of Ches. P. C. of Hooton, Dio. Ches. 1862. (Patron, R. C. Naylor, Esq; P. C.'s Inc. 150*l*; Pop. 1100.) Formerly C. of All Saints', Paddington, Lond. [7]

OWEN. John, *Ipswich.*—Queens' Coll. Cam. B.A. 1833; Deac. 1833, Pr. 1834. P. C. of St. Margaret's with St. John's C. Ipswich, Dio. Nor. 1854. (Patrons, Simeon's Trustees; Tithe, Imp. 61*l* 4*s*; Glebe, 44 acres; P. C.'s Inc. 300*l* and Ho; Pop. 8108.) Surrogate. [8]

OWEN, John Maurice Dorset, *Hindringham Vicarage, Thetford, Norfolk.*—Brasen. Coll. Ox. 2nd cl. Lit. Hum. and B.A. 1850, M.A. 1853; Deac. 1852 and Pr. 1853 by Bp of Nor. V. of Hindringham, Dio. Nor. 1860. (Patrons, D. and C. of Nor; Tithe, 322*l*; V.'s Inc. 328*l* and Ho; Pop. 781.) Formerly C. of Martham, Norfolk. [9]

OWEN, John Smith, *Mount Pleasant, Norwich.*—Dub. A.B. 1862, LL.B. 1863; Deac. 1863 and Pr. 1864 by Bp of Nor. C. of St. Stephen's, Norwich, 1863. [10]

OWEN, Joseph Buttersworth, 40, *Cadogan-place, Chelsea, London, S.W.*—St. John's Coll. Cam. M.A. 1832; Deac. 1833 and Pr. 1834. P. C. of St. Jude's, Chelsea, Dio. Lon. 1859. (Patron, R. of Up. Chelsea; P. C.'s Inc. 300*l*; Pop. 4561.) Formerly Lect. of St. Andrew's Holborn, and St. Swithin's, Cannon-street Lond. Author, *Lectures—Home*; *Health*; *Young England*; *English Charities*; *Mendicity*; *Popular Insurance*; *Portraiture of a Life*; *Polemical Lectures on Infallibility*; *Trial of the Seven Bishops*; *Rabbinism the Type of Romanism*; *The Power of the Keys*; *Church of England Antagonistic to Popery and Semi Popery*; *Popery in Connection with English History*; *Social Blessings of the Reformation*; vols. of Sermons on the Sabbath; Confirmation; Assize Sermons, and on the Principal Public Events of the last Twenty Years; *Biography of the Pottery Schoolmaster*; *The Village Voluntary*; *The Staffordshire Primer*; numerous Reward-books for Schools. [11]

OWEN, Lewis Edward, *Chilton Foliat, Wilts.*—Ex. Coll. Ox. B.A. 1866; Deac. 1867 by Bp of Salis. C. of Chilton Foliat 1867. [12]

OWEN, Lewis Welsh, *Colchester.*—Ball. Coll. Ox. 2nd cl. Lit. Hum. and B.A. 1834, M.A. 1838; Deac. 1837 and Pr. 1838 by Bp of Ox. R. of Holy Trinity, Colchester, Dio. Roch. 1839. (Patron, Ball. Coll. Ox; Tithe, 23*l* 12*s* 6*d*; Glebe, 50 acres; R.'s Inc. 180*l*; Pop. 875.) V. of Mark's-Tey, Colchester, Dio. Roch. 1839. (Patron, Ball. Coll. Ox; Tithe, 235*l*; Glebe, 32 acres; V.'s Inc. 310*l* and Ho; Pop. 396.) Rural Dean; Surrogate; Sec. for the Colchester Dist. of the S.P.G. and S.P.C.K; Chap. to Bp of Roch. 1867. Formerly Fell. of Ball. Coll. Ox. [13]

OWEN, Loftus, *Writtle, Chelmsford.*—Min. of St. Paul's Chapel, Writtle, Dio. Roch. 1865. (Patron, V. of Writtle; Min.'s Inc. 100*l*.) [14]

OWEN, Octavius Freire, 23, *Carlton-hill East, St. John's-wood, London, N.W.*—Ch. Ch. Ox. 1835, B.A. 1839, M.A. 1843; Deac. 1841, Pr. 1842. Dom. Chap. to the Duke of Portland; Provincial Grand Masonic Chap. of the Province of Surrey 1854. Formerly P. C. of Stratton Audley 1842–46; V. of St. Mary's Leicester, 1846–48; R. of Burstow, Surrey, 1848–55; V. of Child's Wickham, Glouc. 1855–58. Author, *Schools of Ancient Philosophy*, R.T.S; *Translation of the Organon of Aristotle*, Bohn; *Refutation of Spinoza by Leibnitz*, Constable. Editor, *Gay's Fables*, Routledge. Contributor to *Sharpe's Magazine*, *Eliza Cook's Journal*, *The Critic*, *The Atlas*, *The Morning Chronicle*. Formerly Editor of *The Freemasons' Magazine*. [15]

OWEN, Owen, *Gidley, Oakhampton, Devon*—R. of Gidley, Dio. Ex. 1863. (Patron, Rev. T. Whipham; R.'s Inc. 75*l*; Pop. 184.) [16]

OWEN, Owen, *Kelbrook, Colne.*—P. C. of Kelbrook, Thornton in-Craven, Dio. Rip. 1866. (Patron, R. of Thornton-in-Craven; P. C.'s Inc. 120*l*.) Formerly C. of Morley, Leeds. [17]

OWEN, Philip, *Cerrig-y-Druidion, Denbighshire.*—C. of Cerrig-y-Druidion. [18]

OWEN, Richard, *Llanfair, Ruthin.*—Deac. 1858 and Pr. 1859 by Bp of St. A. C. of Llanfair 1866. Formerly C. of Llangyniew 1858, Llansantffraid 1860, Llandrillo 1862. [19]

OWEN, Richard, *Well street, Ruthin.*—Deac. 1862 and Pr. 1863 by Bp of St. A. C. of Ruthin with Llanrhyd 1867. Formerly C. of Ruthin 1862–63, Elerch, Llanbadarnfawr, 1864–67. [20]

OWEN, Richard Evan, *Llanerch, Churchstoke, Salop.*—Brasen. Coll. Ox. B.A. 1810, M.A. 1813; Deac. 1812, Pr. 1813. P. C. of Hyssington, Montgomeryshire, Dio. Herf. 1822. (Patron, the present P. C; Tithe—Imp. 170*l*, P. C. 11*l*; P. C.'s Inc. 128*l*; Pop. 341.) R. of Snead, Montgomeryshire, Dio. Herf. 1849. (Patron, the present R; Tithe, 80*l*; R.'s Inc. 90*l*; Pop. 59.) [21]

OWEN, Richard Trevor, *Ruabon, Denbighshire.*—Jesus Coll. Ox. Scho. of, 3rd cl. Math. B.A. 1859, M.A. 1862; Deac. 1860 and Pr. 1861 by Bp of St. A. C. of Ruabon 1865. Formerly C. of Llangollen 1860; Asst. Mast. at Llandovery Coll. Institution 1863; C. of Northop 1863. [22]

OWEN, Robert Deaville, *Boroughbridge, Yorks.*—Trin. Coll. Cam. B.A. 1845, M.A. 1851; Deac. 1847 and Pr. 1848 by Bp of Rip. P. C. of Boroughbridge, Dio. Rip. 1854. (Patron, V. of Aldborough; P. C.'s Inc. 300*l* and Ho; Pop. 909.) [23]

OWEN, Thomas Cæsar, *Llanbedrog Rectory, Pwllheli, Carnarvonshire.*—Jesus Coll. Ox. B.A. 1827; Deac. and Pr. 1828 by Bp of Ban. R. of Llanbedrog with Llangian C. and Llanfihangel-Bachellaeth C. Dio. Ban. 1852. (Patron, Bp of Ban; Tithe, 649*l*; Glebe, 8 acres; R.'s Inc. 665*l* and Ho; Pop. Llanbedrog 469, Llangian 1088, Llanfihangel-Bachellaeth 312.) Formerly C. of Llanfihangel-y-Pennant with Criccieth, Carnarvonshire, 1828; Dwygyfylchi C. and Llangelynin C. and P. C. 1836–52. [24]

OWEN, Walter Charles Edward, *St. John's Parsonage, Huddersfield.*—Dub. A B. 1859, A.M. 1861; Deac. 1860 and Pr. 1861 by Bp of Rip. P. C. of St. John's, Huddersfield, Dio. Rip. 1865. (Patron, Sir J. W. Ramsden; P. C.'s Inc. 200*l* and Ho; Pop. 4466.) Formerly C. of Huddersfield. [25]

OWEN, William, *Damerham Vicarage, Salisbury.*—Magd. Hall, Ox. B.A. 1853; Deac. 1854 and Pr. 1855 by Abp of Cant. V. of Damerham, Dio. Salis.

1862. (Patron, Earl of Chichester; V.'s Inc. 330*l* and Ho; Pop. 697.) Formerly P. C. of St. Stephen's, Tunbridge, 1856–62. [1]

OWEN, William Hicks, *Rhyllon, St. Asaph.*—Magd. Coll. Cam. B.A 1823, M.A. 1833; Deac. 1824 and Pr. 1825 by Bp of St. A. Sen. V. of St. Asaph. Dio. St. A. 1827. (Patron, Bp of St. A; V.'s Inc. 250*l*.) V. of Tremeirchion, Dio. St. A. 1829. (Patron, Bp of St. A; V.'s Inc. 340*l* and Ho; Pop. 707.) Rural Dean; Surrogate. [2]

OWENS, Frederick James, *Oswaldtwistle, Accrington.*—Dub. A.B. 1859, A.M. 1865; Deac. 1863 and Pr. 1864 by Bp of Man. C. of Oswaldtwistle, 1863. [3]

OWGAN, Joseph Bullen, 28, *Hamilton-square, Birkenhead.*—Dub. A.B. 1847, A M. 1862; Deac. 1860 and Pr. 1861 by Bp of Ches. C. of St. James's, Walton-on-the-Hill, Liverpool, 1863. Formerly C. of St. Thomas's, Park-lane, Liverpool, 1860. Author, various Translations of the Classics, Kelly, Dublin. [4]

OWSTON, Francis, *Manor House, Pirbright, Guildford, Surrey.*—St. Cath. Coll. Cam. Skirne Scho. B.A. 1848, M.A. 1855; Deac. 1849, Pr. 1850. P. C. of Pirbright, Dio. Win. 1851. (Patron, Henry Halsey, Esq; Tithe, App. 380*l*; P. C.'s Inc. 110*l* and Ho; Pop. 599.) Chap. of the London Necropolis, Woking. Formerly 2nd Mast. of Bishop's Coll. Bristol, 1848; C. of Trinity, Over Darwen, 1849. [5]

OWSTON, Thomas, *Sutterby, Spilsby, Lincolnshire.*—Queens' Coll. Cam. B.A. 1831, M.A. 1834. R. of Sutterby, Dio. Lin. 1848. (Patron, Ld Chan; Tithe, 118*l* 18*s*; Glebe, 17 acres; R.'s Inc. 135*l*; Pop. 40.) [6]

OXENDEN, Ashton, *Pluckley Rectory, Ashford, Kent.*—Univ. Coll. Ox. B A. 1831; Deac. 1833 and Pr. 1834 by Abp of Cant. R. of Pluckley with Pevington R. Dio. Cant. 1848. (Patron, Abp of Cant; Tithe, 706*l*; Glebe, 34 acres; R.'s Inc. 684*l* and Ho; Pop. 777.) Hon. Can. of Cant. 1864. Author, *Cottage Library*, 6 vols; *Cottage Sermons*, 2 vols; *Barham Tracts*; etc. [7]

OXENDEN, Charles, *Barham Rectory, Canterbury.*—Ch. Coll. Cam. B.A. 1820; Deac. 1823, Pr. 1824. R. of Barham 1846. (Patron, Abp of Cant; R.'s Inc. 800*l* and Ho; Pop. 1090.) Rural Dean. Author, *Lent Sermons on the Penitential Psalms*, 1837; *Statistical Tables of the Principal Provincial Hospitals* on a large Map; sundry Articles on Hospital Management in *Farr's Medical Almanacs.* [8]

OXENDEN, Montagu, *Eastwell, Ashford, Kent.*—Ex. Coll. Ox. B.A. 1821, M.A. 1824; Deac. 1823 by Abp of York, Pr. 1824 by Bp of Lin. R. of Luddenham, Kent, Dio. Cant. 1827. (Patron, Ld Chan; Tithe, App. 386*l*; Glebe, 2 acres; R.'s Inc. 400*l*; Pop. 264.) R. of Eastwell, Dio. Cant. 1837. (Patron, Earl of Winchilsea; Tithe, 196*l* 14*s*; Glebe, 20½ acres; R.'s Inc. 222*l* and Ho; Pop. 126.) [9]

OXENHAM, F. N., *Torwood, Torquay.*—Ex. Coll. Ox. B.A. 1862, M.A. 1865; Deac. 1864 by Bp of Ox. Pr. 1865 by Bp of Ex C. of St Mark's, Torwood. [10]

OXFORD, The Right Reverend Samuel WILBERFORCE, Lord Bishop of Oxford, 26, *Pall-mall, London*, and *Cuddesdon Palace, near Wheatley, Oxfordshire.*—Oriel Coll. Ox. 2nd cl. Lit. Hum. 1st cl. Phy et Math. and B.A. 1826, M.A. 1829, B.D. and D.D. 1845; Deac. 1828 and Pr. 1830 by Bp of Ox. Consecrated Bp of Ox. 1845. (Episcopal Jurisdiction, the counties of Oxford, Berks and Bucks; Inc. of See, 5000*l*; Pop. 515,083; Acres, 1,385,779; Rural Deaneries, 31; Benefices, 609; Curates, 249; Church Sittings, 217,415.) His Lordship is Lord High Almoner to Her Most Gracious Majesty; Chancellor of the Most Noble Order of the Garter; Co-Visitor of Wor. Coll. Ox. His Lordship was formerly Archd. of Surrey; Dean of Westminster; Select Preacher 1837–44. Author, *The Life of William Wilberforce, by his Sons* (Isaac and Samuel), 5 vols. 1838; *Six Sermons* (preached before the Univ. of Ox. in 1837, '38, '39), 1839; *A History of the Protestant Episcopal Church in America*, 1840; *A Selection of Psalms and Hymns for Public Worship*, Newport, Isle of Wight, 1840; *An Archidiaconal Charge*, 1840; *A Second Charge*, 1841; *Four Sermons* (preached before the Queen in 1841 and 1842), published by Command, 3 eds. 1842–48; Three *Archidiaconal Charges*, in 1842, '43, '44; *Agathos, and other Sunday Stories*, 8th ed. 1843; *The Rocky Island, and other Parables*, 20th ed. 1849; *Sermons*, 5th ed. 1844; *Scripture Reading Lessons*, 1845; *Eucharistica—Devotions and Prayers on the Most Holy Eucharist, from Old English Divines*; *A Charge and Sermon at the Bishop's General Ordination*, 1846; *Pride, a Hindrance to True Knowledge* (a Sermon), 2nd ed. 1847; *A Charge to the Clergy at his Second Visitation*, 1851; *Miscellaneous Sermons*, 1 vol. 1854; *Rome, her New Dogma and our Duties*, 1855; *The Principles of the English Reformation* (a Sermon), 1855; *Addresses to the Candidates for Ordination on the Questions in the Ordination Service*, 1860; "*Cast in Meal*," *or the Poison rendered Harmless* (a Sermon), 1861; *The Revelation of God the Probation of Man* (two Sermons), 1861; *Sermons preached before the University of Oxford* (2nd Series, 1847–62), 1863. [11]

OXLEE, John, *Oversilton, near Northallerton.*—Deac. 1835 by Bp of Roch. Pr. 1836 by Abp of York. R. of Cowsby, Dio. York, 1863. (Patron, Thomas W. Lloyd, Esq; Tithe, 127*l* 12*s*; Glebe, 18 acres; R.'s Inc. 149*l* 17*s* 10*d* and Ho; Pop. 96.) P. C. of Oversilton, Dio. York, 1848. (Patron, Trin. Coll. Cam; Tithe—App. 314*l*; Glebe, 15 acres; P. C.'s Inc. 98*l*; Pop. 255.) [12]

OXLEE, John Arthur Osiris, 16, *Grosvenor-street, Chester.*—Queen's Coll. Birmingham; Deac. 1866 by Bp of Ches. C. of St. Mary's-on-the-Hill with Upton, Chester, 1866 [13]

OXLEY, John Swaby, *Long Bennington Vicarage, Grantham.*—Queens' Coll. Cam. B.A. 1841; Deac. 1842 and Pr. 1843 by Bp of Rip. V. of Long Bennington with Foston C. Dio. Lin. 1860. (Patron, Duchy of Lancaster; V.'s Inc. 500*l* and Ho; Pop. 1545.) Formerly V. of Clent, Worcestershire, 1855–60. [14]

OZANNE, Richard James, *St. Andrew's Rectory, Guernsey.*—Pemb. Coll. Ox. 3rd cl. Lit. Hum. and B.A. 1846, M.A. 1848; Deac. 1847 and Pr. 1848 by Bp of Lich. R. of St. Andrew's, Guernsey, Dio. Win. 1858. (Patron, the Gov; R.'s Inc. 150*l* and Ho; Pop. 1049.) Formerly V. of Alfreton, Derbyshire; P. C. of St. Matthew's, Guernsey, 1854–58. [15]

PACE, Henry Horatio, *Bombay.*—St. Bees; Deac. 1853 and Pr. 1854 by Bp of Ches. Chap. to the East India Government, Bombay. Formerly C. of St. Paul's, Preston. [16]

PACKE, Christopher, *Ruislip Vicarage, Uxbridge, Middlesex.*—Wor. Coll. Ox. B.A. 1814, M.A. 1825; Deac. 1814 and Pr. 1815 by Abp of Cant. Min. Can. of St. Paul's 1817. (Value, 150*l*.) Pr. in Ordinary to the Queen 1821. (Value, 58*l*.) Min. Can. of Windsor. (Value, 73*l* 11*s* 6*d* and Ho.) V. of Ruislip, Dio. Lon. 1834. (Patrons, D. and Cans. of Windsor; Tithe—App. 599*l* and 252 acres of Glebe, V. 462*l*; V.'s Inc. 465*l* and Ho; Pop. 1100.) [17]

PACKE, Henry Vere, *Shangton Rectory, Market Harborough, Leicestershire.*—Brasen. Coll. Ox. Hon. 4th cl. B.A. 1848; Deac. 1849, Pr. 1850. R. of Shangton, Dio. Pet. 1858. (Patron, Sir C. Isham, Bart; Tithe, 316*l* 6*s* 4*d*; Glebe, 29 acres; R.'s Inc. 320*l* and Ho; Pop. 82.) Formerly C. of Barnham Broom-cum-Kimberley, Norfolk. [18]

PACKE, William James, *Kidderminster.*—Ch. Ch. Ox. 2nd cl. in Nat. Sci. B.A. 1855, M.A. 1863; Deac. 1857 and Pr. 1858 by Bp of Roch. C. of Kidderminster 1865. Formerly C. of Heydon with Little Chishall 1858–65. [19]

PACKER, Arthur, *St. Paul's Parsonage, Halliwell, Bolton-le-Moors.*—Deac. 1852, Pr. 1853. P. C. of St. Paul's, Halliwell, Dio. Man. 1855. (Patron, J. H.

Ainsworth, Esq; P. C.'s Inc. 170*l* and Ho; Pop. 2712.) [1]

PACKER, Charles, *Longwood, near Huddersfield.*—St. John's Coll. Cam. B.A. 1848, M.A. 1862; Deac. 1848 and Pr. 1849 by Bp of Rip. P. C. of Longwood, Dio. Rip. 1851. (Patron, V. of Huddersfield; Glebe, 17 acres; P. C.'s Inc. 165*l* and Ho; Pop. 3400.) Formerly C. of Huddersfield 1848–51. Author, *Marriage with a Deceased Wife's Sister, Arguments against it drawn from Holy Scripture*, 1858, 1*d*. [2]

PACKER, John Graham, *Thurmaston Vicarage, Leicester.*—Trin. Coll. Cam. 1st Jun. Opt. B.A. 1836, M.A. 1840; Deac. 1836 by Abp of York, Pr. 1838 by Bp of Lon. V. of Thurmaston, Dio. Pet. 1866. (Patron, W. Pochin, Esq; V.'s Inc. 120*l* and Ho; Pop. 893.) Formerly C. of Kirksmeaton, Yorks, 1836, St. Matthew's, Bethnal Green, 1838; P. C. of St. Peter's, Bethnal Green, 1841–66. Author, *Twelve Sermons*, 1840; *Sermons on the Lord's Prayer*, 1849; *Theopoles*, 1853; *Lectures on Death*, 1856. [3]

PACKER, Richard Waldegrave, *Woodton Rectory, Bungay, Norfolk.*—St. Cath. Coll. Cam. B.A 1823, M.A. 1832; Deac. 1829 and Pr. 1830 by Bp of Chich. R. of Woodton, Dio. Nor. 1832. (Patron, King's Coll. Cam; Tithe, 621*l*; Glebe, 24 acres; R.'s Inc. 696*l* and Ho; Pop. 531.) [4]

PACKER, Richard Waldegrave, jun., *Witcham Vicarage, near Ely.*—V. of Witcham, Dio. Ely, 1846. (Patrons, D. and C. of Ely; V.'s Inc. 150*l* and Ho; Pop. 495.) [5]

PACKMAN, Cyrus Hugh Larken, 10, *Tennyson-street, Prince's-road, Liverpool.*—Clare Coll. Cam. Scho. of, and Johnson Exhib. B.A. 1860, M.A. 1866; Deac. 1865 and Pr. 1866 by Bp of Ches. C. of Grassendale, Liverpool, 1865; Asst. Mast. Upper Sch. Liverpool Coll. Formerly 2nd Mast. in Bath Gr. Sch. 1863–65. [6]

PACKMAN, Robert Collier, *Langdon Hills Rectory, Horndon-on-the-Hill, Essex.*—St. Peter's Coll. Cam. B.A. 1820. Priest in Ordinary to the Queen 1825. (Value, 58*l*.) Librarian and 9th Min. Can. of St. Paul's, 1829. (Value, 150*l*.) R. of Langdon Hills, Dio. Roch. 1825. (Patrons, D. and C. of St. Paul's; R.'s Inc. 442*l* and Ho; Pop. 289.) [7]

PACKWOOD, James, *Sutton Coldfield, Warwickshire.*—Deac. 1821 and Pr. 1822 by Abp of York. C. of Sutton Coldfield. [8]

PADDON, Thomas Henry, *High Wycombe, Bucks*—Trin. Coll. Ox. B.A. 1830, M.A. 1852; Deac. and Pr. 1831 by Bp of B. and W. V. of High Wycombe, Dio. Ox. 1844. (Patron, Lord Carington; V.'s Inc. 384*l* and Ho; Pop. 7804.) Formerly C. of Wellesbourne, Warwickshire, 1833–34, Alverstoke, Hants, 1835–37. Author, *World Gained and Soul Lost* (Tract), 3*d*; *Outlines of Sermons preached at High Wycombe*. [9]

PADLEY, Augustus Frederick, *Bailgate, Lincoln.*—Ch. Coll. Cam. B.A. 1845, M.A. 1848; Deac. 1845 and Pr. 1846 by Bp of Lin. V. of St. Peter-at-Gowts, Lincoln, Dio. Lin. 1860. (Patron, Bp of Lin; V.'s Inc. 110*l*; Pop. 2055.) Chap. of the Lincoln Union 1845. Formerly P. C. of Greetwell, Lincoln, 1851. Author, *Solutions to Trigonometrical Problems*, 1841. [10]

PADLEY, Charles John Allen Newton, *Bulwell, Notts.*—Ex. Coll. Ox. B.A. 1841; Deac. 1842, Pr. 1843. C. of Bulwell. [11]

PADLEY, James Sandby, *Ireleth, Dalton-in-Furness, Lancashire.*—P. C. of Ireleth, Dio. Carl. 1865. (Patron, V. of Dalton; P. C.'s Inc. 100*l* and Ho.) Formerly C. of Dalton. [12]

PAGAN, Samuel, *Lever Bridge, Bolton le-Moors.*—St. John's Coll. Cam. 29th Wrang. and B.A. 1840; Deac. 1841 and Pr. 1842 by Bp of Dur. P. C. of Lever Bridge, Dio. Man. 1845. (Patrons, the Crown and Bp of Man. alt; P. C.'s Inc. 170*l*; Pop. 2844.) [13]

PAGE, Alexander Shaw, *Selsley Parsonage, Stonehouse, Gloucestershire.*—St. John's Coll. Cam. Hulsean Exhib. Jun. Opt. and B.A. 1852; Deac. 1852 and Pr. 1853 by Abp of Cant. P. C. of Selsley, Dio. G. and B. 1864. (Patron, S. S. Marling, Esq; P. C.'s Inc. 108*l* and Ho; Pop. 650.) Formerly C. of Bexley, Kent,

1852–54, St. James's, Preston, 1854–56, St. Paul's, Preston, 1856–57; P. C. of St. Anne's, Lancaster, 1857–64. [14]

PAGE, Cyril William, 7, *James-street, Buckingham-gate, London, S.W.*—Ch. Ch. Ox. Stud. of, B.A. 1827, M.A. 1829. P. C. of Ch. Ch. Westminster, Dio. Lon. 1843. (Patron, R. of St. Margaret's, Westminster; P. C.'s Inc. 200*l*; Pop. 6874.) Author, *A Letter to the Bishop of London upon certain Circumstances connected with the National Society*, 1846. [15]

PAGE, James Augustus, *Tintwistle Parsonage, Mottram, Cheshire.*—Dub. A.B. 1845, A.M. 1865; Deac. 1845 and Pr. 1846 by Bp of Ches. P. C. of Tintwistle, Dio. Ches. 1846. (Patrons, Trustees; P. C.'s Inc. 130*l* and Ho; Pop. 3586.) District Sec. of Brit. and For. Bible Soc. Formerly C. of Lymm, Cheshire, 1845–46. Author, *Protestant Ballads*. [16]

PAGE, R., *Rochester.*—C. of St. Nicholas', Rochester. [17]

PAGE, Robert Lay, *The Clergy House, Coatham, Redcar, Yorks.*—St. John's Coll. Cam. B.A. 1861, M.A. 1864; Deac. 1862 and Pr. 1863 by Bp of Rip. P. C. of Coatham, Dio. York, 1866. (Patroness, Mrs. Newcomen; P. C.'s Inc. 150*l*; Pop. 727.) Formerly C. of St. Peter's, Leeds, 1862–66. [18]

PAGE, Thomas, *Pembroke College, Oxford.*—Fell. of Pemb. Coll. [19]

PAGE, Vernon, *St. Tudy Rectory, Bodmin, Cornwall.*—Ch. Ch. Ox. B.A. 1840, M.A. 1842; Deac. 1841 and Pr. 1842 by Bp of Ox. R. of St. Tudy, Dio. Ex. 1858. (Patron, Ch. Ch. Ox; Tithe, 577*l* 7*s* 3*d*; Glebe, 25 acres; R.'s Inc. 623*l* and Ho; Pop. 570.) [20]

PAGET, Edward, *Christ Church, Oxford.*—Stud. of Ch. Ch. [21]

PAGET, Edward Heneage, *Stuston Rectory, Scole, Suffolk.*—St. John's Coll. Ox. B.A. 1852, M.A. 1855; Deac. 1856 and Pr. 1857 by Bp of Nor. R. of Stuston, Dio. Nor. 1860. (Patron, Sir E. Kerrison, Bart; Tithe, 209*l* 13*s*; R.'s Inc. 220*l* and Ho; Pop 232.) Formerly C. of East Tuddenham. [22]

PAGET, Edward James, *Steppingley Rectory, Ampthill.*—Ch. Ch. Ox. B A. 1828, M.A. 1832; Deac. 1835 and Pr. 1836 by Bp of Ox. R. of Steppingley, Dio. Ely, 1864. (Patron, Ld Chan; Tithe, 234*l*; Glebe, 28 acres; R.'s Inc. 280*l* and Ho; Pop. 365.) Formerly R. of Swithland, Leic. 1841–58. [23]

PAGET, Francis Edward, *Elford Rectory, Lichfield.*—Ch. Ch. Ox. B.A. 1832, M.A. 1835. R. of Elford, Dio. Lich. 1835. (Patrons, Heirs of the late Hon. F. G. Howard; Tithe, 19*l* 7*s* 4*d*; Glebe, 240½ acres; R.'s Inc. 400*l* and Ho; Pop. 461.) Rural Dean of Tamworth and Tutbury. Formerly Chap. to the Bp of B. and W. Author, *Tales of the Village*, 3 vols. 1842; *St. Antholin's, or Old Churches and New*, 3 eds. 1842; *The Idolatry of Covetousness* (a Sermon), 1842; *The Warden of Berkingholt, or Rich and Poor*, 1843; *The Churchman's Calendar for 1844, as set forth in the Book of Common Prayer*, 1843; *Luke Sharp, or Knowledge without Religion* (a Tale of Modern Education), 1845; *The Christian's Day*, 1845; *Prayers on Behalf of the Church and her Children in Times of Trouble*, 1845; *Sermons on the Duties of Daily Life*, 2 eds. 1847; *The Living and the Dead* (a Course of Practical Sermons on the Burial Service), 1845; *Sermons for Saints' Days*, 1848. [24]

PAGET, Thomas Bradley, *Welton, Brough, Yorks.*—Trin. Coll. Cam. B.A. 1834, M.A 1839; Deac. 1836, Pr. 1837. V. of Welton with Melton, Dio. York, 1845. (Patroness, Miss Sophia Broadley; Tithe, 52*l*; Glebe, 342 acres; V.'s Inc. 600*l*; Pop. 863.) Preb. of York; Rural Dean; Chap. to the Abp of York. [25]

PAGLAR, Charles, *Copdock, near Ipswich.*—St. John's Coll. Cam. B.D. 1844; Deac. 1843 and Pr. 1844 by Bp of Nor. C. of Copdock 1858; Chap. of the East Suffolk Hospital. Formerly Chap. of the Ipswich Union 1849–58. [26]

PAGLAR, Edward Brandon, *Tibshelf, Alfreton, Derbyshire.*—Queens' Coll. Cam. B.A. 1858; Deac. 1858 by Bp of Pet. C. of Tibshelf. Formerly C. of Grendon 1858. [27]

PAIGE, Lewis, *Trinity Parsonage, Hartlepool, Durham.*—Deac. 1833, Pr. 1834. P. C. of Trinity, Hartlepool, Dio. Dur. 1852. (Patron, V. of Hart; P. C.'s Inc. 300*l* and Ho; Pop. 5638.) [1]

PAIGE, William Michael Tucker, *Ilsington Vicarage, Newton Abbot, Devon.*—Trin. Coll. Cam. B.A. 1829; Deac. 1830 and Pr. 1831 by Bp of Ex. C. of Ilsington 1835. [2]

PAIN, Andrew R., *Bury, Huntingdon.*—P. C. of Bury, Dio. Ely, 1848. (Patron, Duke of Manchester; P. C.'s Inc. 167*l*; Pop. 362.) [3]

PAIN, Arthur Wellesley, *Holbrook, Ipswich.*—St. Cath. Coll. Cam. B.A. 1865; Deac. 1866 and Pr. 1867 by Bp of Nor. Formerly C. of Holbrook 1866–67. [4]

PAIN, Edmund, *Stoke Hammond, Bletchley Station, Bucks.*—C. of Stoke Hammond [5]

PAIN, John Lloyd, *Aughton, Ormskirk, Lancashire.*—Brasen. Coll. Ox. 3rd cl. Lit. Hum. and B.A. 1854, M.A. 1857; Deac. 1856 and Pr. 1857 by Bp of Ches. C. of Aughton. Formerly C. of St. Luke's, Liverpool. [6]

PAIN, Thomas Holland, *Stone Vicarage, Kidderminster, Worcestershire.*—Brasen. Coll. Ox. B.A. 1853, M.A. 1856; Deac. 1856 and Pr. 1857 by Bp of Ches. C. of Stone 1859. Formerly C. of St. Thomas's, Liverpool, 1856–59. [7]

PAIN, Thomas Lloyd, 50, *Falkner-street, Liverpool.*—Brasen. Coll. Ox. 2nd cl. Lit. Hum. and B.A. 1821, M.A. 1824; Deac. 1826, Pr. 1827. P. C. of St. Thomas's, Liverpool, Dio. Ches. 1834. (Patrons, Simeon's Trustees; P. C.'s Inc. 289*l*; Pop. 4984.) [8]

PAINE, Edwin, *Dalston House, Dalston, Cumberland.*—Sen. Asst. C. of Dalston. Formerly C. of St. James's, Whitehaven. [9]

PAINE, Jesse, *Ash, Whitchurch, Salop.*—St. John's Coll. Cam. B.A. 1857; Deac. 1857 and Pr. 1859 by Bp of Lich. C. of Ash 1859. [10]

PAITSON, John, *Nether Wasdale Parsonage, St. Bees, Cumberland.*—Dur. B.A. 1854; Deac. 1854 by Bp of Dur. Pr. 1855 by Bp of Man. P. C. of Nether Wasdale, Dio. Ches. 1857. (Patron, P. C. of St. Bees; P. C.'s Inc. 63*l* and Ho; Pop. 192.) Formerly C. of Bamborough, Northumberland. [11]

PALAIRET, Richard.—Wor. Coll. Ox. B.A. 1828, M.A. 1846; Deac. 1832, Pr. 1834. Preb. of Wells 1855. Formerly V. of Norton St. Philip, Bath, 1837–66. [12]

PALEY, Francis Henry, *Penn Vicarage, Wolverhampton.*—Ch. Coll. Cam. B.A. 1848, M.A. 1851. V. of Penn, Dio. Lich. 1856. (Patron, Bp of Lich; Tithe—App. 682*l* 10*s*, Imp. 37*l* 10*s*, V. 165*l*; Glebe, 52¾ acres; V.'s Inc. 315*l* and Ho; Pop. 913.) [13]

PALEY, George Barber, *Freckenham, near Soham, Suffolk.*—St. Peter's Coll. Cam. 25th Wrang. and B.A. 1822, M.A. 1825, B.D. 1833; Deac. 1825 and Pr. 1826 by Bp of Ely. R. and V. of Freckenham, Dio. Ely, 1835. (Patron, St. Peter's Coll. Cam; R. and V.'s Inc. 620*l* and Ho; Pop. 477.) Rural Dean. Author, *Form of Prayer, with Paraphrase on the Litany*, 1839; *Tract for the Foundry*, 1846, 3*d*; *Saul of Tarsus* (a Dramatic Sketch), 3*s* 6*d*. [14]

PALEY, John, *Great Longstone, Buxton, Derbyshire.*—St. Peter's Coll. Cam. B.A. 1838; Deac. 1840 and Pr. 1841 by Bp of G. and B. P. C. of Great Longstone, Dio. Lich. 1867. (Patron, V. of Bakewell; P. C.'s Inc. 200*l* and Ho; Pop. 868.) Formerly P. C. of Hook, Yorks, 1843–59, Codsall, Staffs, 1859–67. [15]

PALEY, Thomas, *Ufford Rectory, Stamford.*—St. John's Coll. Cam. B.A. 1833, M.A. 1836, B.D. 1843; Deac. 1833 by Abp of York, Pr. 1834 by Abp of Cant. R. of Ufford with Bainton, Dio. Pet. 1847. (Patron, St. John's Coll. Cam; Tithe, 513*l* 5*s*; Glebe, 40 acres; R.'s Inc. 560*l* and Ho; Pop. Ufford 307, Bainton 217.) Formerly Fell. of St. John's Coll. Cam. Author, *The Church the Great Power of God, seen in the Faith and Patience of the Saints* (a Sermon), 1848; *A Word for the Bible Society*, 1851; *The Church Catechism construed Scripturally.* [16]

PALIN, Charles William, *Knaptoft, Lutterworth.*—St. Cath. Coll. Cam. B.A. 1846, M.A. 1849; Deac. 1846 and Pr. 1847 by Bp of Ely. C. of Knaptoft. Formerly P. C. of Nether Dean 1847. [17]

PALIN, Edward, *Linton, Ross, Herefordshire.*—St. John's Coll. Ox. 1st cl. Lit. Hum. and B.A. 1848, M.A. 1850, B.D. 1856; Deac. 1853 and Pr 1855 by Bp of Ox. V. of Linton, Dio. Herf. 1865. (Patron, St. John's Coll. Ox; Tithe, 555*l*; Glebe, 69 acres; V.'s Inc. 650*l* and Ho; Pop. 915.) Formerly P. C. of Summertown, Oxford, 1856–60; Public Examiner Lit. Hum. 1861 62; Fell. and Rector of St. John's Coll. Oxford. [18]

PALIN, William, *Stifford Rectory, Romford, Essex.*—Trin. Coll. Cam. B.A. 1833, M.A. 1839; Deac. 1833 and Pr. 1834 by Bp of Lon. R. of Stifford, Dio. Roch. 1834. (Patron, R. B. Wingfield, Esq; Tithe, 450*l*; Glebe, 26 acres; R.'s Inc. 495*l* and Ho; Pop. 326.) Author, *Bellingham*, 3*s* 6*d*; *Village Lectures on the Litany*, 3*s* 6*d*; *History of the Church of England*, 1688–1717, 8*s* 6*d*; *Sermon on the Weekly Offertory*, 1*s*; *Suggestions for the Foundation of a Clergy Colleges* (privately circulated), 1849; also numerous Contributions to the leading Church Periodicals; Editor of *The Churchman's Magazine.* [19]

PALK, Henry, *Shillingford Rectory, Exeter.*—St. Mary Hall, Ox. B.C.L. 1844; Deac. 1844 by Bp of Roch. Pr. 1845 by Bp of Wor. R. of Dunchideock with Shillingford R. Dio. Ex. 1846. (Patron, Sir L. Palk, Bart; Dunchideock, Tithe, 142*l*; Shillingford, Tithe, 90*l*; Glebe, 75 acres; R.'s Inc. 260*l* and Ho; Pop. Dunchideock 155, Shillingford 64.) R. of Bridfort, Dio. Ex. 1846. (Patron, Sir L. Palk, Bart; R.'s Inc. 305*l* and Ho; Pop. 576.) Rural Dean. [20]

PALK, Wilmot Henry, *Ashcombe Rectory, near Dawlish, Devon.*—Trin. Coll. Cam. B.A. 1819; Deac. 1819 by Bp of Lon. Pr. 1820 by Bp of Lin. R. of Ashcombe, Dio. Ex. 1820. (Patron, Ld Chan; Tithe, 247*l*; Glebe, 31 acres; R.'s Inc. 297*l* and Ho; Pop. 242.) V. of Chudleigh, Dio. Ex. 1848. (Patrons, Trustees for the Inhabitants; Tithe, 550*l*; Glebe, 1 acre; V.'s Inc. 555*l* and Ho; Pop. 2108.) [21]

PALLETT, Thomas Carter, *Hockerill, Bishop Stortford.*—Lin. Coll. Ox. 2nd cl. Cl. Trip. B.A. 1860, M.A. 1862; Deac. 1860, Pr. 1861. C of Great Hallingbury, Essex, 1860. [22]

PALMER, Charles, *Lighthorne Rectory, Kineton, Warwickshire.*—Ch. Ch. Ox. B.A. 1805, M.A. 1808. R. of Lighthorne, Dio. Wor. (Patron, Lord Willoughby De Broke; Tithe, 347*l*; R.'s Inc. 357*l* and Ho; Pop. 391.) P. C. of Chesterton, near Kineton, Dio. Wor. 1848. (Patron, Lord Willoughby de Broke; Tithe, Imp. 658*l* 5*s* 1*d*; P. C.'s Inc. 85*l*; Pop. 217.) [23]

PALMER, Charles Edward, *Great Torrington, Devon.*—St. Peter's Coll. Cam. 1820, B.A. 1823, M.A. 1826; Deac. 1823, Pr. 1824. Formerly Asst. C. of Wear-Gifford, Devon, 1824–57. [24]

PALMER, Charles Edwin, *Evenwood, Darlington.*—Deac. 1861 and Pr. 1863 by Bp of Dur. P. C. of Evenwood, Dio. Dur. 1864. (Patrons, Crown and Bp of Dur. alt; P. C.'s Inc. 300*l* and Ho; Pop. 1949.) Formerly C. of Trinity, Hartlepool, 1861–63. [25]

PALMER, Charles Samuel, *Eardisley Vicarage, Hereford.*—Ex. Coll. Ox. B.A. 1854, M.A. 1855; Deac. 1854 and Pr. 1855 by Bp of Ox. V. of Eardisley, Dio. Herf. 1866. (Patron, W. Perry Herrick, Esq; Tithe, comm. 255*l*; V.'s Inc. 255*l* and Ho; Pop. 831.) Formerly C. of Sunningdale, Berks, 1854–55; P. C. of Owston and R. of Withcote, Leicestershire, 1855–66. [26]

PALMER, Edmund Richard Hopper Griffith, *South Somercotes Rectory, Louth.*—Queen's Coll. Ox. B.A. 1818; Deac. 1819 and Pr. 1820 by Bp of Lin. R. of South Somercotes, Dio. Lin. 1864. (Patron, Duchy of Lancaster; Tithe, 569*l* 12*s* 9*d*; Glebe, 29¾ acres; R.'s Inc. 626*l* and Ho; Pop. 406.) Formerly R. of Greetham 1848–49; V. of North Somercotes 1849–64. [27]

PALMER, Edwin, *Balliol College, Oxford.*—Ball. Coll. Ox. B.A. 1845, M.A. 1850; Deac. 1854 by Bp of Ox. Fell. of Ball. Coll. 1845. [28]

PALMER, Ellis.—Min. of the Brill Mission Chapel, St. Pancras, Lond. Formerly C. of Bloxwich; C. of the Floating Chapel, Worcester. [1]

PALMER, Feilding, *Eastcliff, Chepstow.*—Trin. Coll. Cam. Wrang. and B.A. 1839, M.A. 1842; Deac. 1841 and Pr. 1842 by Bp of G. and B. Formerly Scho. and Chap. of Trin. Coll. Cam; C. of St. John's, Cheltenham, 1841–45; V. of Felmersham, Beds, 1846–67. [2]

PALMER, Francis.—Mert. Coll. Ox. B.A. 1850. Min. of St. George's, Albemarle-street, Lond. 1866. Formerly C. of St. Mary's, Dover, and Kidderminster. [3]

PALMER, George, *Brampton, Faringdon, Oxon.*—C. of Brampton. [4]

PALMER, George Horsley, *Mixbury Rectory (Oxon) near Brackley.*—Ex. Coll. Ox. B.A. 1847. M.A. 1859; Deac. 1850 and Pr. 1851 by Bp of Ox. R. of Mixbury, Dio. Ox. 1852. (Patron, Bp of Ox; Tithe, 105*l*; Glebe, 64 acres; R.'s Inc. 200*l* and Ho; Pop. 381.) [5]

PALMER, George Thomas, *Linwood, Market Rasen, Lincolnshire.*—R. of Linwood, Dio. Lin. 1861. (Patron, Sir G. Aston, Bart; Tithe, 395*l*; Glebe, 90 acres; R.'s Inc. 494*l*; Pop. 261.) [6]

PALMER, George Thomas, 53, *Lowndes-square, London, S.W.*—Brasen. Coll. Ox. B.A. 1824, M.A. 1827; Deac. 1835 and Pr. 1837 by Bp of Chich. [7]

PALMER, G. W., *Claydon, Banbury.*—P. C. of Claydon, Dio. Ox. 1864. (Patron, Bp of Ox; P. C.'s Inc. 125*l*; Pop 317.) [8]

PALMER, Henry, *Little Laver, Ongar, Essex.*—Ch. Ch. Ox. B.A. 1822, M.A. 1826; Deac. and Pr. 1823. R. of Little Laver, Dio. Roch. 1824. (Patron, R. Palmer, Esq; Tithe, 260*l*; Glebe, 90 acres; R.'s Inc. 325*l* and Ho; Pop. 111.) [9]

PALMER, Henry, *Sullington Rectory, Steyning, Sussex.*—Trin. Coll. Cam. B.A. 1858, M.A. 1860; Deac. 1858 by Bp of Ely, Pr. 1859 by Bp of Chich. R. of Sullington, Dio. Chich. 1859. (Patroness, Mrs. Palmer; Tithe, comm. 435*l*; R.'s Inc. 450*l* and Ho; Pop. 241.) Formerly C. of All Saints' and St. John's, Huntingdon. 1858–59. [10]

PALMER, Henry Carew, *Bowden Hill, Laycock, Wilts.*—Sid. Coll. Cam. B.A. 1856, M.A. 1859; Deac. 1857 and Pr. 1858 by Bp of Salis. Fell. of Sid. Coll; P. C. of Bowden Hill, Dio. G. and B. 1863. (Patrons, Trustees; Pop. 400.) Formerly C. of Wootton-Bassett. [11]

PALMER, Henry James, *Stoneyton House, Aberdeen.*—Magd. Hall, Ox. B.A. 1860, M.A. 1867; Deac. 1863 and Pr. 1864 by Bp of Ches. Incumb. of St. Mary's, Aberdeen, 1866. Formerly C. of Wallasey 1863–66; 2nd Mast. of Tower Sch. Liscard, Cheshire, 1859–66. Author, *Plain Words to Protestants*, Palmer, 2*d*; *Office for Confirmation Classes*, 2*d*. [12]

PALMER, Henry Vaughan, *Lawrence Cottage, York.*—Deac. 1860, Pr. 1861. C. of St. Margaret's, York. [13]

PALMER, James Howard, *St. Andrew's College, Bradfield, Reading.*—Ex. Coll. Ox. B.A. 1862, M.A. 1866; Deac. 1864 and Pr. 1865 by Bp of Ox. Asst. Mast. in St. Andrew's Coll. 1862. [14]

PALMER, James Nelson, *Breamore Rectory, near Salisbury.*—St. John's Coll. Ox. B.A. 1856, M.A. 1857; Deac. 1857 and Pr. 1858 by Bp of Wor. R. of Breamore, Dio. Win. 1865. (Patron, the present R; Tithe, 877*l* 6*s* 8*d*; R.'s Inc. 890*l* and Ho; Pop. 565.) Formerly C. of Shipston-on-Stour 1857–59, Breamore 1861–64. [15]

PALMER, Jordan, *Streatham, Surrey, S.*—Lin. Coll. Ox. B.A. 1851, M.A. 1854; Deac. 1852 by Bp of Ex. Pr. 1853 by Bp of B. and W. Chap. of the Royal Asylum of St. Ann's Society; Organizing Sec. to the Bp of Win.'s Surrey Fund. Formerly C. of St. Stephen's, Camden-town, and of Streatham. [16]

PALMER, Lewis Henry, *East Carlton Rectory, Northants.*—Ch. Ch. Ox. B.A. 1840, M.A. 1844; Deac. 1841, Pr. 1842. R. of East Carlton, Dio. Pet. (Patron, Sir John Henry Palmer, Bart; Tithe, 322*l* 10*s* 9*d*; R.'s Inc. 336*l* and Ho; Pop. 70.) [17]

PALMER, Philip Hall, *Woolsthorpe Rectory, Grantham.*—Jesus Coll. Cam. B.A. 1824, M.A. 1828; Deac. 1826, Pr. 1827. R. of Woolsthorpe, Dio. Lin. 1844. (Patron, Duke of Rutland; Tithe, 80*l*; Glebe, 100 acres; R.'s Inc. 210*l* and Ho; Pop. 615.) [18]

PALMER, Richard, *Purley Rectory, Reading.*—Ch. Ch. Ox. B.A. 1817, M.A. 1820; Deac. 1822 and Pr. 1823 by Bp of Ox. R. of Purley, Dio. Ox. 1844. (Patron, Ld Chan; Tithe, 300*l*; Glebe, 48 acres; R.'s Inc. 359*l* and Ho; Pop. 193.) [19]

PALMER, Rodney Drake, *Broadway, Ilminster, Somerset.*—King's Coll. Fredericton, B.A. 1844; Deac. 1847 and Pr. 1850 by Bp of Fredericton. P. C. of Broadway, Dio. B. and W. 1857. (Patron, Rev. Dr. W. Palmer; Tithe—Imp. 277*l*, P. C. 62*l*; Glebe, 43 acres; P. C.'s Inc. 200*l*; Pop. 431.) Lect at Chard, Somerset. [20]

PALMER, Septimus, *High Bickington Rectory, Barnstaple, Devon.*—St. Peter's Coll. Cam. B.A. 1824, M.A. 1827; Deac. 1825 and Pr. 1826 by Bp of Ex. R. of High Bickington, Dio. Ex. 1850. (Patron, the present R; Tithe, 448*l* 17*s* 6*d*; Glebe, 160 acres; R.'s Inc. 450*l* and Ho; Pop. 738.) [21]

PALMER, Thomas, *Trimley St. Martin Rectory, near Ipswich.*—R. of Trimley St. Martin, Dio. Nor. 1860. (Patron, the present R; Tithe, 500*l*; Glebe, 22 acres; R.'s Inc. 534*l* and Ho; Pop. 582.) [22]

PALMER, Walter Vaughan, *Belchalwell, Blandford.*—C. of Belchalwell 1866. Formerly Missionary at Capetown; C of Lyford, Berks, and Campton Abbas, Dorset. [23]

PALMER, William, *Whitchurch-Canonicorum, Bridport, Dorset.*—Magd. Hall, Ox. B.A. 1831, M.A. 1833. V. of Whitchurch-Canonicorum with Chideock C. Marshwood C. Stanton St. Gabriel C. and Monkton-Wyld P. C. Dio. Salis. 1846. (Patron, Bp of Salis; Whitchurch-Canonicorum, Tithe—App. 410*l*, V. 514*l*; Chideock, Tithe—App. 300*l*, V. 230*l*; Marshwood, Tithe—App. 230*l*, V. 280*l*; Stanton St. Gabriel, Tithe—App. 105*l*, V. 70*l*; V.'s Inc. 1094*l* and Ho; Pop. Whitchurch-Canonicorum 1283, Chideock 794, Marshwood 473, Stanton St. Gabriel 75.) Surrogate. Formerly Fell. of Wor. Coll Ox. Author, *Origines Liturgicæ, or Antiquities of the English Ritual*, 2 vols. Ox. 1839, 4 eds; *The Apostolical Jurisdiction and Succession of the Episcopacy in the British Churches, vindicated against the Objections of Dr. Wiseman in the Dublin Review*, 1840; *A Treatise on the Church of Christ* (designed chiefly for the use of Students in Theology), 2 vols. 1842, 3 eds; *A Compendious Ecclesiastical History, from the Earliest Period to the Present Time*, 1842, 2 eds; *An Examination of the Rev. R. W. Sibthorp's Reasons for his Secession from the Church*, 1842; *Letters to N. Wiseman, D.D. on the Errors of Romanism, in Respect to the Worship of Saints, Satisfaction, Purgatory, Indulgences, and the Worship of Images and Relics* (with a Supplement), 1842, 3 eds; *A Narrative of Events connected with the Publication of* "The Tracts for the Times," *with Reflections on existing Tendencies to Romanism, and on the present Duties and Prospects of Members of the Church*, 1843, 2 eds; *The Doctrine of Development and Conscience, considered in Relation to the Evidences of Christianity and of the Catholic System*, 1846; *The Victory of Faith* (a Sermon on behalf of the Church Societies), 1850; *A Statement of Circumstances connected with the Proposal of Resolutions at a Special General Meeting of the Bristol Church Union*, 1850. [24]

PALMES, William Lindsay, *Hornsea Vicarage, Hull.*—Trin. Coll. Cam. Sen. Opt. and B.A. 1836, M.A. 1839; Deac. 1844 and Pr. 1845 by Bp of Win. V. of Hornsea with Long Riston R. Dio. York, 1848. (Patron, Ld Chan; Hornsea, Tithe—Imp. 9*l* 15*s*, V. 15*l*; Glebe, 70 acres; Riston, Tithe, 114*l*; Glebe, 172 acres; V.'s Inc. 474*l* and Ho; Pop. Hornsea 1063, Long Riston 401.) Rural Dean of North Holderness. [25]

PALMOUR, John, *West-place, Lancaster.*—Jesus Coll. Ox. B.A. 1855; Deac. 1857 and Pr. 1858 by Bp of Man. C. of St. Mary's, Lancaster. [26]

PALMOUR John Dawkins, *Cresselly, Pembroke.*—Lampeter 1827; Deac. 1828 and Pr. 1829 by Bp of St. D. P. C. of Reynoldston, Pembrokeshire, Dio. St. D. 1831. (Patron, Sir R. Phillips, Bart; Tithe, 33*l*; Glebe, 30 acres; R.'s Inc. 70*l*; Pop. 106.) V. of Jeffreyston, Dio. St. D. 1854. (Patrons, D. and C. of St. D; Tithe, App. 206*l* 3*s* 7*d*; Glebe, 55 acres; V.'s Inc. 140*l*; Pop. 634.) [1]

PANCKRIDGE, William.—C. of St. Matthew's, City-road and Head Mast. of the Middle Class Sch. St. Thomas's, Charterhouse, Lond. [2]

PANNELL, John, *Ludgershall, Wilts.*—St. Mary Hall, Ox. B.A. 1809, M.A. 1811. R. of Ludgershall, Dio. Salis. 1824. (Patron, J. Smith, Esq; Tithe, 427*l*; R.'s Inc. 442*l*; Pop. 536.) [3]

PANTER, Frederick Downes, *Rushford Lodge, Thetford, Norfolk.*—Trin. Coll. Ox. B.A. 1832; Deac. 1835, Pr. 1836. Chap. of the D. of Rushford, Dio. Nor. 1848. (Pop. 170.) R of Brettenham, Dio. Nor. 1848. (Patron, Sir Robert J. Buxton, Bart; Tithe, 200*l*; Glebe, 18 acres; R.'s Inc. 210*l*; Pop. 72.) Dioc. Inspector of Schs. for the Deaneries of Rockland and Thetford; District Sec. for the Deaneries of Rockland and Thetford for the S.P.G. [4]

PANTIN, John Wicliff, *Westcote Rectory, Chipping Norton.*—Pemb. Coll. Ox. Scho. of, B.A. 1850, M.A. 1854; Deac. 1850 and Pr. 1852 by Bp of G. and B. R. of Westcote, Dio. G. and B. 1866. (Patron, the present R; Tithe, 200*l*; Glebe, 100*l*; R.'s Inc. 300*l* and Ho; Pop. 245.) Formerly C. of Llangasty, Brecon, 1856–59, St. Matthias', Stoke Newington, 1859–64, St. Barnabas', Pimlico 1864–66. [5]

PANTING, Lawrence, *Chebsey Vicarage, Eccleshall, Staffs.*—St. John's Coll. Cam. B.A. 1832, M A. 1835. V. of Chebsey, Dio. Lich. 1838. (Patrons, D. and C. of Lich; Tithe—App. 463*l*; V. 70*l*; Glebe, 94 acres and ten cottages; V.'s Inc. 285*l* and Ho; Pop. 514.) [6]

PAPILLON, John, *Lexden Rectory, Colchester.*—Univ. Coll. Ox. B.A. 1828, M.A. 1858; Deac. 1830, Pr. 1831. R. of Lexden, Dio. Roch. 1841. (Patron, Philip Oxenden Papillon, Esq; Tithe, 660*l*; Glebe, 29 acres; R.'s Inc. 700*l* and Ho; Pop. 1263.) Formerly C. of East Langdon, near Dover, 1830–35; R. of Bonnington, Kent, 1831–41; R. of Knowlton, Kent, 1836–41; C. of Chillenden, Kent, 1840–41. [7]

PARAMORE, D. R., *East Norton, Leicester.*—Fell. of St. John's Coll. Ox; C. of East Norton. [8]

PARAMORE, John Huxtable, *Dunterton, near Tavistock, Devon.*—Corpus Coll. Cam. B.A. 1845. R. of Dunterton, Dio. Ex. 1866. (Patron, Rev. N. T. Royse; Pop. 181.) Formerly V. of Islington, Norfolk, 1855–66. [9]

PARDOE, Arthur, *Stanton Lacy House, Ludlow.*—Jesus Coll. Cam. B.A. 1843. Formerly R. of Hook 1859; V. of Sidmouth, Devon, 1856–58. [10]

PARDOE, George, *Alkham Vicarage, near Dover.*—St. John's Coll. Ox. B.A. 1845, M A. 1850. V. of Alkham with Capel-le Ferne, Dio. Cant. 1864. (Patron, Abp of Cant; Alkham, Tithe—App. 500*l* 9*s* 8*d*, and 9 acres of Glebe, V. 215*l* 0*s* 4*d*; Glebe, 3 acres; Capel-le-Ferne, Tithe—App. 175*l*, Imp. 41*l* 10*s* 6*d*, V. 100*l*; V.'s Inc. 318*l* and Ho; Pop. Alkham 520, Capel le-Ferne 193.) Formerly C. of Wolverley. [11]

PARDOE, John, *Leyton, Essex.*—St. John's Coll. Cam. B.A. 1836, M.A. 1840; Deac. 1837, Pr. 1838. V. of Leyton, Dio. Lon. 1848 (Patron, John Pardoe, Esq; Tithe—Imp. 370*l*, V. 394*l*; Glebe, ¾ acre; V.'s Inc. 430*l* and Ho; Pop. 2398.) [12]

PARDOE, John, *Hitchin, Herts.*—Trin. Coll. Cam. B.A. 1861; Deac. 1864 and Pr. 1865 by Bp of Roch. C. of St. Ippolyt's and Great Wymondley 1866. Formerly C. of Hitchin 1864-66. [13]

PARE, Frederick Harry, *Adelaide crescent, Brighton.*—Ch. Ch. Ox. B.A. 1821, M.A. 1824; Deac. and Pr. 1823 by Bp of Win. [14]

PAREZ, Claude Hubert, *Carlisle.*—One of H.M.'s Inspectors of Schs. Formerly Fell. of Pemb. Coll. Cam. [15]

PARHAM, Frank, *Netherbury, Bridport, Dorset.*—Ch. Ch. Ox; Deac. 1862 by Bp of Killaloe, Pr. 1863 by Bp of Ches. C. of Netherbury 1866. Formerly Tut. in St. Columba's Coll. Dublin; C. of Milltown, Dublin. [16]

PARIS, Samuel Stanley, *Forthampton House, near Tewkesbury, Glouc.*—Deac. 1820, Pr. 1821. P. C. of Chaseley, Worc. Dio. Wor. 1847. (Patron, V. of Longdon; P. C.'s Inc. 154*l*; Pop. 307.) [17]

PARISH, William Douglas, *Selmeston, Lewes.*—Trin. Coll. Ox. S.C.L; Deac. 1859, Pr. 1861. V. of Selmeston with Alciston V. Dio. Chich. 1863. (Patrons, D. and C. of Chich; Glebe, 5 acres; V.'s Inc. 330*l* and Ho; Pop. 417.) Formerly C. of Firle and Beddingham. [18]

PARISH, William Samuel, *Cherry Hinton Vicarage, near Cambridge.*—St. Peter's Coll. Cam. 26th Wrang. and B.A. 1838, M.A. 1841; Deac. 1839 and Pr. 1840 by Bp of Ely. V. of Cherry Hinton, Dio. Ely, 1851. (Patron, St. Peter's Coll. Cam; V.'s Inc. 164*l* and Ho; Pop. 734.) Chap. of the Cambridge Lunatic Asylum. Formerly Fell. of St. Peter's Coll. Cam. [19]

PARK, James Allan, *Methwold Vicarage, Brandon, Norfolk.*—Oriel Coll. Ox. B.A. 1851, Dur. Licen. Theol. 1852; Deac. 1852, Pr. 1853. V. of Methwold, Dio. Nor. 1853. (Patron, Ld Chan; Tithe—App. 32*l* 5*s*, and 7½ acres of Glebe, Imp. 1102*l* 10*s* 2*d*, and 133 acres of Glebe, V. 340*l*; V.'s Inc. 340*l* and Ho; Pop. 1509.) [20]

PARK, James Allan, *Elwick Hall Rectory, Castle Eden, Durham.*—R. of Elwick Hall, Dio. Dur, 1828. (Patron, Bp of Man; R.'s Inc. 542*l*; Pop. 206.) Hon. Can. of Dur. [21]

PARK, John, *Walney Parsonage, Ulverston.*—P. C. of Walney, Dio. Ches. 1846. (Patron, V. of Dalton-in-Furness; P. C.'s Inc. 85*l* and Ho.) [22]

PARK, John, *Rampside Parsonage, Ulverston.*—Emman. Coll. Cam. B.A. 1853; Deac. 1853, Pr. 1854. P. C. of Rampside, Dio. Carl. 1859. (Patron, V. of Dalton-in-Furness; P. C.'s Inc. 100*l* and Ho; Pop. 75.) Formerly C. of Petham, Kent, 1853–55, St. John's, Lancaster, 1855–58, Glentworth, Lincolnshire, 1858–59. [23]

PARKE, Edward, *Blackley, Manchester.*—R. of St. Andrew's, Blackley, Dio. Man. 1816. (Patron, Bp of Man; Pop 1000.) Formerly C. of Blackley. [24]

PARKER, Arthur Townley, *Royle Hall, Burnley, Lancashire.*—Trin. Coll. Cam. B.A. 1852, M.A. 1855; Deac. 1853, and Pr. 1855 by Bp of Man. R. of Burnley Dio. Man. 1855. (Patron, R. Townley Parker, Esq; Glebe, 226 acres; R.'s Inc. 2200*l* and Ho; Pop. 9000.) Hon. Can. of Man. 1866; Rural Dean of Whalley 1866; Surrogate. Formerly C. of Deane, Lancashire, 1853-55. [25]

PARKER, Arthur William, *Southampton.*—Lin. Coll. Ox. 2nd cl. Lit. Hum. B.A. 1863, M.A. 1867; Deac. 1864 and Pr. 1865 by Bp of Lon. C. of St. Mary's, Southampton, 1866. Formerly C. of Trinity, St. Giles'-in-the-Fields, Lond. 1864–66. [26]

PARKER, Charles, *Bodiam Vicarage, Hurst Green, Sussex.*—Caius Coll. Cam. B.A. 1835, M.A. 1839; Deac. 1836 and Pr. 1837 by Bp of Lon. V. of Bodiam, Dio. Chich. 1851. (Patron, T. Cubitt, Esq; Tithe, 321*l*; Glebe, 10 acres; V.'s Inc. 341*l* and Ho; Pop. 303.) [27]

PARKER, Charles, *Ford, Shrewsbury.*—P. C. of Ford, or Foord, Dio. Herf. 1863. (Patron, J. Naylor, Esq; P. C.'s Inc. 91*l*; Pop. 351.) [28]

PARKER, Charles Frederick, *Ringshall, Stowmarket, Suffolk.*—Pemb. Coll. Ox. B.A. 1806, M.A. 1809; Deac. 1810, Pr. 1811. R. of Ringshall, Dio. Nor. 1819. (Patron, Pemb. Coll. Ox; Tithe, 462*l* 12*s* 5*d*; Glebe, 88 acres; R.'s Inc. 655*l* and Ho; Pop. 359.) Formerly Fell. of Pemb. Coll. Ox. [29]

PARKER, Charles Hubert, *Great Comberton, Pershore, Worcestershire.*—Lin. Coll. Ox. B.A. 1822, M.A. 1825; Deac. 1823, Pr. 1824. R. of Great Comberton, Dio. Wor. 1826. (Patron, the present R; Glebe, 19 acres; R.'s Inc. 336*l* and Ho; Pop. 247.) [30]

PARKER, Charles William, *Bulphan Rectory, Romford, Essex.*—Wad. Coll. Ox. B.A. 1856, M.A. 1859; Deac. 1858, Pr. 1859. R. of Bulphan, Dio. Roch. 1862. (Patron, J. S. Hands, Esq; Tithe, 410*l*; Glebe, 15 acres;

R.'s Inc. 436*l* and Ho; Pop. 268.) Formerly C. of Overton cum Tyfield 1859. [1]

PARKER, Edward, *Oxendon Rectory, Northampton.*—Oriel Coll. Ox. 3rd cl. Lit. Hum. and B.A. 1830, M.A. 1832; Deac. 1833 and Pr. 1834 by Abp of Cant. R. of Oxendon Magna, Dio. Pet. 1843. (Patron, the present R; R.'s Inc. 420*l* and Ho; Pop. 236.) Rural Dean. [2]

PARKER, Edward B., *Oxendon Rectory, Northampton.*—Pemb. Coll. Ox. M.A. 1863; Deac. 1862, Pr. 1863. Formerly C. of Frodingham, of Kirton-in-Lindsey, and of Owston, Lincolnshire. [3]

PARKER, Edwin James, *Waltham St. Lawrence, Reading.*—Pemb. Coll. Ox. B.A. 1814, M.A. 1817, B.D. 1847; Deac. 1819 and Pr. 1820 by Bp of Ox. V. of Waltham St. Lawrence, Dio. Ox. 1834. (Patron, Lord Braybrooke; Tithe—Imp. 310*l*, V. 40*l*; Glebe, 118 acres; V.'s Inc. 220*l*; Pop. 848.) [4]

PARKER, Franke, *Luffingcott, Launceston.*—Trin. Coll. Cam. B.A. 1827, M.A. 1831; Deac. 1829 and Pr. 1831 by Bp of Ex. R. of Luffingcott, Dio. Ex. 1838. (Patron, Henry Bradshaw, Esq; Tithe, 68*l* 5*s*; Glebe, 40*l*; R.'s Inc. 108*l* 5*s*; Pop. 71.) Surrogate. Formerly C. of Sampford Peverell, Devon, 1829–31, Starcross, Devon, 1831–32. Author, *The Church*, Folio, with large chart of Authors chronologically arranged, J. H. Parker, London, 1851, 3*l* 3*s*; *Chronology*, 8vo, with extended table in folio, J. H. Parker, 1858, 21*s*; *Replies to the First and Second Parts of Bishop Colenso on the Pentateuch*, Clifford, Exeter, 1863, 9*s* 6*d*; *Replies to Third and Fourth Parts of same*, ib. 1864, 7*s* 6*d*; *A Light upon Thucydides, with Remarks on Dr. Pusey's "Daniel the Prophet," and Dr. Temple's Essay "On the Education of the World,"* Williams and Norgate, 1865, 7*s* 6*d*; *The Athenian Year*, ib. 1866, 1*s*. [5]

PARKER, Frederick William, *Moughtrey, Newton, Montgomeryshire.*—Pemb. Coll. Ox. 3rd cl. Lit. Hum. and B.A. 1846, M.A. 1849; Deac. and Pr. 1848 by Bp of St. A. P. C. of Moughtrey or Mochtre, Dio. St. A. 1863. (Patron, Bp of St. A; Tithe, 155*l*; Brecon Coll. 31*l*; Pop. 526.) Formerly C. of Welshpool 1848–63. [6]

PARKER, George, *Sacriston, Durham.*—St. Bees; Deac. 1867 by Bp of Dur. C. of Sacriston 1867. [7]

PARKER, Henry, *Ilderton Rectory, near Alnwick, Northumberland.*—Wor. Coll. Ox. B.A. 1824, M.A. 1830; Deac. 1826 and Pr. 1827 by Bp of Dur. R. of Ilderton, Dio. Dur. 1840. (Patron, Duke of Northumberland; Tithe—Imp. 195*l*, V. 120*l*; Glebe, 50 acres; R.'s Inc. 150*l* and Ho; Pop. 571.) Formerly C. of Chillingham and Chatton. [8]

PARKER, Henry, *St. Mary-in-the-Marsh Rectory, Romney, Kent.*—Corpus Coll. Cam. B.A. 1842, M.A. 1845; Deac. 1842 and Pr. 1843 by Abp of Cant. R. of St. Mary-in-the-Marsh, Dio. Cant. 1857. (Patron, Abp of Cant; Tithe, 300*l*; Glebe, 3½ acres; R.'s Inc. 315*l* and Ho; Pop. 175.) Formerly C. of Whitedale and Seasalter, Kent. [9]

PARKER, Henry John, M.A.—Gresham Prof. of Divinity, Lond. [10]

PARKER, James, *Norton, near Malton, Yorks.*—St. Cath. Coll. Cam. B.A. 1834, M.A. 1837; Deac. 1834 and Pr. 1835 by Bp of Lich. Formerly P. C. of St. Mary's, Preston, 1838–42; V. of Ellerburne, Yorks, 1842–57; P. C. of Taddington, Derbyshire, 1857–65. [11]

PARKER, James Benjamin, *Hitchin, Herts.*—St. Mary Hall, Ox. M.A. 1867; Deac. 1865 and Pr. 1866 by Bp of Roch. C. of St. Saviour's, Hitchin, 1865. [12]

PARKER, James Dunne, *Bowes House, Barnard Castle.*—Dub. A.B. 1854, LL.B. 1857, LL.D. 1864, Jun. and Sen. Scho. and Prizeman in Lit. Sc. and Laws, Queen's Coll. Belfast and Galway, Theol. Scho. St. Aidan's; D.C.L. Dur. 1865; Deac. 1859 by Bp of Ches. Pr. 1860 by Bp of Dur. P. C. of Bowes, Dio. Rip. 1867. (Patron, P. H. Stanton, Esq; Tithe, Imp. 212*l* 12*s* 6*d*; Glebe, 28 acres; P. C.'s Inc. 90*l*; Pop. 849.) Formerly C. of All Saints', Newcastle-on-Tyne, 1859; C. in sole charge of Cockfield, Durham, 1863. [13]

PARKER, John, *Wysall Vicarage, Nottingham.*—Dur. Gisborne Scho. B.A. 1853, M.A. 1856; Deac. 1856 and Pr. 1857 by Bp of Lich. V. of Wysall with Willoughby-in-the-Wolds, Notts, Dio. Lin. 1867. (Patrons, Sir James Campbell and others; Glebe, 200 acres; V.'s Inc. 400*l* and Ho; Pop. Wysall 274, Willoughby 573.) Formerly C. of Long Eaton, Derby, 1855, Aston-on-Trent, 1860. [14]

PARKER, John, *Sinnington, Pickering, Yorks.*—Deac. 1826, Pr. 1827. P. C. of Sinnington, Dio. York, 1852. (Patron, J. Proud, Esq; Tithe, 15*l* 11*s* 4*d*; Glebe, 51 acres; P. C.'s Inc. 93*l* and Ho; Pop. 607.) [15]

PARKER, John Allen, *Heywoods, Birch, near Bury, Lancashire.*—St. Bees; Deac. 1865 and Pr. 1866 by Bp of Man. C. of Ashworth, near Rochdale. [16]

PARKER, John Webster, *St. Alban's Vicarage, Rochdale.*—Brasen. Coll. Ox. B.A. 1847, M.A. 1849; Deac. 1848 and Pr. 1849 by Bp of Pet. V. of St. Alban's Rochdale, Dio. Man, 1856. (Patron, V. of Rochdale; V.'s Inc. 300*l* and Ho; Pop. 5391.) [17]

PARKER, Matthew, *Perry Barr, Birmingham.*—Queen's Coll. Cork, and St. Bees; Deac. 1864 by Bp of Ches. Pr. 1865 by Bp of St. A. C. of Perry Barr 1866. Formerly C. of St. John's, Liverpool, 1864–65. [18]

PARKER, Richard, *Claxby, near Spilsby, Lincolnshire.*—Corpus Coll. Cam. B.A. 1837, M.A. 1840; Deac. 1837 and Pr. 1839 by Bp of Lin. R. of Well with Claxby V. and Dexthorpe annexed, Dio. Lin. 1852. (Patrons, Rt. Hon. R. A. C. Nisbet-Hamilton and Lady Mary C. Nesbit-Hamilton; Tithe, comm. 409*l* 10*s* 6*d*; Glebe, 22 acres; R.'s Inc. 450*l* and Ho; Pop. Well 99, Claxby 103, Dexthorpe 35.) Formerly C. of Gunby 1837–52, Bratoft 1839–44, Orby 1844–52. [19]

PARKER, Richard, *Wykeham Rectory, Fareham, Hants.*—Queen's Coll. Ox. Hon. 4th in Mod. Hist. B.A. 1858, M.A. 1861; Deac. 1858 and Pr. 1860 by Bp of Ely. R. of Wykeham, or Wickham, Dio. Win. 1863. (Patron, W. Rashleigh, Esq; Tithe, comm. 577*l* 11*s* 2*d*; Glebe, 53 acres; R.'s Inc. 700*l* and Ho; Pop. 1019.) Formerly C. of Turvey, Beds, Elton, Hunts, Moulsoe, Bucks, Great Tew, Oxon. [20]

PARKER, William, *Saham Tony Rectory, Watton, Norfolk.*—New Coll. Ox. B.A. 1811, M.A. 1815; Deac. 1812, Pr. 1813. R. of Saham Tony, Dio. Nor. 1833. (Patron, New Coll. Ox; Tithe, 1122*l*; R.'s Inc. 1200*l* and Ho; Pop. 1286.) Hon. Can. of Nor. 1852. Formerly Fell. of New Coll. Ox. [21]

PARKER, William, *Little Comberton Rectory, Pershore, Worcestershire.*—Trin. Coll. Ox. B.A. 1815, M.A. 1818; Deac. 1817 and Pr. 1818 by Bp of Wor. R. of Little Comberton, Dio. Wor. 1826. (Patron, the present R; Glebe, 150 acres; R.'s Inc. 265*l*; Pop. 257.) Formerly C. of Elmley Castle, Worc. [22]

PARKER, William Henry, *Castle Donington, Derby.*—St. Bees; Deac. 1858 and Pr. 1859 by Bp of Pet. C. of Castle Donington 1858. [23]

PARKER, William Henry, *Hanley, Staffs.*—C. of Hanley; Dom. Chap. to the Marquis Townshend. [24]

PARKER, William Russell, *Willingale-Spain, Ongar, Essex.*—Corpus Coll. Cam. Sen. Opt. and B.A. 1836, M.A. 1839; Deac. 1836 by Bp of Lon. Pr. 1837 by Abp of Cant. R. of Willingale-Spain, Dio. Roch. 1858. (Patron, the Crown, on nomination of the Bp of Roch; Tithe, 322*l* 12*s* 6*d*; Glebe, 14½ acres; R.'s Inc. 350*l* and Ho; Pop. 220.) [25]

PARKES, Francis B., *Southwick Rectory, Shoreham, Sussex.*—Ch. Ch. Ox. B.A. 1835, M.A. 1837; Deac. and Pr. 1836 by Bp of Lich. R. of Southwick, Dio. Chich. 1858. (Patron, Ld Chan; Tithe—Imp. 106*l* 16*s* 2*d*, R. 179*l* 17*s*; R.'s Inc. 210*l* and Ho; Pop. 1358.) Formerly P. C. of Broughton, Salop, 1840–58. [26]

PARKES, Samuel Hadden, *The Mount, St. Leonards-on-Sea.*—Jesus Coll. Cam. B.A. 1854, M.A. 1862; Deac. 1855, Pr. 1856. P. C. of St. Leonards-on-Sea, Dio. Chich, 1865. (Patron, Rev. R. T. Marsh; P. C.'s Inc. 650*l*; Pop. 1693.) Formerly C. of St. George's, Wolverhampton, 1855–57, St. George's, Bloomsbury, Lond. 1857–65. Author, *Flower Shows of Window Plants for the Working Classes* (a paper read before the

British Association for the Promotion of Social Science); *Window Gardens for the People*; *Clean and Tidy Rooms*; and *How to grow a Plant and win a Prize*. [1]

PARKES, William Joseph, *Hilgay Rectory, near Downham Market.*—Trin. Coll. Cam. 22nd Sen. Opt. and B.A. 1836, M.A. 1839; Deac. 1839 by Bp of Lin. Pr. 1840 by Bp of Roch. R. of Hilgay with St. Mark's C. Dio. Nor. 1844. (Patron, the present R; Tithe, 1600*l*; Glebe, 85 acres; R.'s Inc. 1730*l* and Ho; Pop. 1624.) [2]

PARKHOUSE, William Heathman, *Exeter.*—Magd. Hall, Ox. B.A. 1862, M.A. 1865; Deac. 1862 and Pr. 1864 by Bp of Ex. R. of Allhallows, Goldsmith-street, Exeter, Dio. Ex. 1867. (Patrons, D. and C. of Ex; R.'s Inc. 90*l*; Pop. 371.) Formerly C. of St. Lawrence, Exeter, 1862-67. [3]

PARKIN, Charles, *Lenham Vicarage, Maidstone.*—Brasen. Coll. Ox. B.A. 1822, M.A. 1824; Deac. 1823 and Pr. 1825 by Abp of York. V. of Lenham, Dio. Cant. 1827. (Patron, A. Akers, Esq; Tithe—Imp. 1205*l*, V. 650*l*; Glebe, 8 acres; V.'s Inc. 670*l* and Ho; Pop. 2016.) [4]

PARKIN, Dynely Deane, *Weaverham, Northwich, Cheshire.*—St. Bees; Deac. 1865 and Pr. 1866 by Bp of Rip. C. of Weaverham 1867. Formerly C. of Wensley, Yorks, 1865–67. [5]

PARKIN, James, *Oakford, Bampton, Devon.*—Pemb. Coll. Ox. B.A. 1810, M.A. 1813; Deac. 1812 by Bp of Ox. Pr. 1813 by Bp of Salis. R. of Oakford, Dio. Ex. 1813. (Patron, the present R; Tithe, 425*l*; Glebe, 90 acres; R.'s Inc. 505*l*; Pop. 629.) [6]

PARKIN, John, *Halton Parsonage, Hastings.*—Queens' Coll. Cam. Scho. of, 16th Wrang. and B.A. 1829, M.A. 1832; Deac. 1832 and Pr. 1833 by Bp of Lich. P. C. of St. Clement's, Halton, Dio. Chich. 1838. (Patron, Bp of Chich; P. C.'s Inc. 153*l* and Ho; Pop. 997.) Dom. Chap. to Earl Waldegrave; Surrogate. Formerly C. of Wellington, Salop. [7]

PARKIN, Lewis, *The Rectory. Ingatestone. Essex.*—St. John's Coll. Ox. 2nd cl. Math. et Phy. and S.C.L. 1844, B.A. 1856, M.A. 1857; Deac. 1845 by Bp of Dur. Pr. 1846 by Bp of Lich. R. of Ingatestone with Buttsbury P. C. Dio. Roch. 1860. (Patron, Lord Petre; Ingatestone, Tithe, 561*l*; Glebe, 1 acre; Buttsbury, Tithe, 330*l*; Glebe, 1 acre; R.'s Inc. 560*l* and Ho; Pop. Ingatestone 882, Buttsbury 531.) Rural Dean. Formerly C. of St. Mary and St. Nicholas, South Kelsey, 1848. [8]

PARKIN, William, 62, *Redcliffe-road, West Brompton, London, S.W.*—Formerly P. C. of West Hatch, Somerset, 1857–67. [9]

PARKINSON, Arthur Mackeson, *Morley Parsonage, Leeds.*—Jesus Coll. Cam. B.A. 1830; Deac. 1835, Pr. 1836. P. C. of Morley with Churwell, Dio. Rip. 1857. (Patron, V. of Bately; Tithe—App. 109*l*, Imp. 375*l* 8*s*; Glebe, 1 acre; P. C.'s Inc. 150*l* and Ho; Pop. 8404.) Formerly C. of Cawthorne, near Barnsley, 1837–57. [10]

PARKINSON, John Allen, *Maldon, Essex*—Corpus Coll. Cam. B.A. 1844, M.A. 1850; Deac. 1845 and Pr. 1846 by Bp of Nor. R. of Hazeleigh, near Maldon, Dio. Roch. 1852. (Patrons, H. S. Blake and B. Kerr, Esqs; Tithe, 292*l* 10*s*; Glebe, 15 acres; R.'s Inc. 310*l*; Pop. 106.) Author, *The Martyrdom of King Charles I.* (a Sermon), 1850; Contributions to Reviews, Periodicals, &c. [11]

PARKINSON, John Posthumus, *Ravendale, Grimsby.*—Magd. Coll. Ox. 2nd cl. Lit. Hum. B.A. 1831, M.A. 1834, D.C.L. 1845; Deac. 1832 and Pr. 1833 by Bp of Lin. Rural Dean and J.P. for the Parts of Lindsey in the co. of Lin. Formerly Fell. of Magd. Coll. Ox. and Proctor, 1841–42; P. C. of Marsh Chapel 1835–46. Author, *Analysis of Butler's Analogy*. Editor of *Bishop Andrewes' Sermons*, 5 vols. in Anglo-Catholic Library; *Giles Witherne, or the Reward of Disobedience, a Tale for the Young*, 6 eds. 1*s*. [12]

PARKINSON, Richard, *Lawbrooks, Shere, Guildford.* [13]

PARKINSON, Richard, *Steeple Ashton, Wilts.*—C. of Steeple Ashton. [14]

PARKINSON, Stephen, *St. John's College, Cambridge.*—St. John's Coll. Cam. Sen. Wrang. 2nd Smith's Prizeman, B.A. 1845, M.A. 1848, B.D. 1855. Pres. Tut. and Fell. of St. John's Coll. Author, *An Elementary Treatise on Mechanics*, Macmillans, 3rd ed. 1863, 9*s* 6*d*; *A Treatise on Optics*, ib. 2nd ed. 1866, 10*s* 6*d*. [15]

PARKINSON, Thomas, *Austwick Parsonage, near Lancaster.*—Queen's Coll. Birmingham; Deac. 1864 and Pr. 1865 by Bp of Rip. C. of Clapham with Austwick, Yorks, 1867. Formerly C. of Bardsey 1864–67. [16]

PARKINSON, William, *Langenhoe Rectory, Colchester, Essex.*—St. John's Coll. Cam. 1st cl. Cl. Trip. Sen. Opt. and B.A. 1838, M.A. 1841; Deac. 1840 by Bp of Ely, Pr. 1841 by Bp of Lin. R. of Langenhoe, Dio. Roch. 1843. (Patroness, Countess Waldegrave; Tithe, 480*l*; Glebe, 30 acres; R.'s Inc. 510*l* and Ho; Pop. 169.) Formerly C. of Caunton, Notts, 1841–43. Author, *Poems*, 1856. [17]

PARKS, William, *Openshaw, Manchester.*—Dub. A.B. 1832; Deac. 1840 and Pr. 1841 by Bp of Ches. R. of Openshaw, Dio. Man. 1843. (Patrons, Trustees; R's. Inc. 300*l*; Pop. 4123.) Formerly P. C. of Rainow, Macclesfield, 1840–43. Author, *Tracts and Addresses from* 1850–60, 3*s* 6*d*; *Five Sermons on the Five Points*, 3rd ed. 1863, 2*s*; *Baptism, its Use and Abuse*, 1862, 1*s*; and many Tracts. [18]

PARKYN, Jonathan Clouter.—St. John's Coll. Cam. B.A. 1859; Deac. 1859 by Bp of Ex. Pr. 1860 by Bp of G. and B. Chap. R.N. Formerly C. of Woolborough 1859. [19]

PARLBY, John Hall, *Manadon, Plymouth.*—Univ. Coll. Ox B.A. 1827, M.A. 1830; Deac. 1828, Pr. 1829. A Magistrate for Devon. [20]

PARMENTER, Thomas Arthur, *The Rectory, Little Steeping, Spilsby.*—St. John's Coll. Cam. B.A. 1853; Deac. 1856 and Pr. 1857 by Bp of Lin. C. in sole charge of Little Steeping. Formerly C. of Bunny, Notts, 1856; Rempstone, Notts, 1864. [21]

PARMINTER, George Henry, *Wynard House, Magdalen-hill, Exeter.*—Trin. Coll. Cam. B.A. 1842; Deac. 1843 and Pr. 1844 by Bp of Ex. R. of St. John's with St. George's R. Exeter. Dio. Ex. 1852. (Patrons, Ld Chan. and D. and C. of Ex. alt; R.'s Inc. 160*l*; Pop. St. John 653, St. George 596.) Author, *Materials for a Grammar of the Modern English Language*, 1856, 3*s* 6*d*. [22]

PARMINTER, Henry.—St. John's Coll. Cam. B.A. 1849; Deac. 1850, Pr. 1851. Chap. of H.M.S. "Duke of Wellington." [23]

PARMINTER, William George, *Stuttgardt.*—Deac. 1835, Pr. 1838. Chap. at Stuttgardt. Formerly Prin. of the Kingsbridge Coll. Sch. 1858; Chap. at Abbeville 1836–37; Chap. at Dieppe 1838–48. [24]

PARMITER, John, *Clare Hall-road, Halifax.*—Ch. Coll. Cam. B.A. 1859; Deac. 1860 and Pr. 1861 by Bp of Herf. C. of Halifax 1863. Formerly C. of Eastnor, Herefordshire, 1860–62. [25]

PARNELL, Charles, 44, *Great Mersey-street, Liverpool.*—St. John's Coll. Cam. B.A. 1851; Deac. 1852, Pr. 1853. C. of St. James's Mission Chapel, Liverpool. Formerly C. of St. Stephen's, Devonport, 1852–59. [26]

PARNELL, Frank, *Hurstpierpoint.*—Ch. Ch. Ox. Jun. Stud. of, 3rd cl. Lit. Hum. B.A. 1860, M.A. 1863; Deac. 1861 and Pr. 1862 by Bp of Chich. C. of Hurstpierpoint 1861. [27]

PARNELL, The Hon. George Damer, *Long Cross, Chertsey, Surrey.*—Downing Coll. Cam. B.A. 1839, M.A. 1843. P. C. of Longcross, Dio. Win. 1861. (Patron, W. Tringham, Esq; Pop. 133.) Formerly P. C. of St. Thomas's, Elson, 1857; C. of Ash, Kent. [28]

PARNELL, Richard, *The Parsonage, North Bow, London. E.*—Dub. A.B. 1844; Deac. 1845 and Pr. 1846 by Bp of Lich. P. C. of St. Stephen's, Old Ford, Dio. Lon. 1857. (Patrons, five Trustees; P. C.'s Inc. 300*l* and Ho; Pop. 7158.) Formerly C. of Bow, Middlesex; Chap. of Mile-end Workhouse. Author, *The*

Man of Sorrows (a Gospel History, in Rhyme, for Children), 1845; *The Accommodating Spirit of Popery* (a Lecture), 1852. [1]

PAROISSIEN, Charles, *Hardingham Rectory, Attleborough, Norfolk.*—Clare Coll. Cam. Wrang. and B.A. 1817, M.A. 1820. R. of Hardingham, Dio. Nor. 1839. (Patron, Clare Coll. Cam; Tithe, 770*l* 8*s* 7*d*; R.'s Inc. 771*l* and Ho; Pop. 527.) Formerly Fell. of Clare Coll. Cam. [2]

PARR, Edward George Codrington, 11, *High-street, Doncaster.*—Brasen. Coll. Ox. B.A. 1865; Deac. 1866 and Pr. 1867 by Abp of York. C. of St. James's, Doncaster, 1866. [3]

PARR, Henry, *Campsall, Doncaster.*—Magd. Coll. Ox. and St. Bees; Deac. 1845 and Pr. 1847 by Bp of Ches. C. of Campsall. Formerly Sen. C. of Tunbridge 1859; V. and Patron of St. Mary Magdalene's, Taunton, 1849–58; Surrogate 1849–58. Author, *Church of England Psalmody* (a Collection of Psalms, Tunes, Chants, &c.); *The Canticles Pointed for Chanting*; Contributor to Burke's *Landed Gentry, Visitation of Seats, Historic Lands*, &c; Nicholls's *Topographer*, and other Genealogical and Antiquarian Publications. [4]

PARR, John, *Parkstone Parsonage, Poole, Dorset.*—Ex. Coll. Ox. M.A. 1855; Deac. 1855 and Pr. 1857 by Bp of Pet. P. C. of Parkstone, Dio. Salis. 1858. (Patron, the present P. C; P. C.'s Inc. 130*l* and Ho; Pop. 900.) Formerly C. of Badby and Newnham, Northants. [5]

PARR, John Owen, *Preston Vicarage, Lancashire.*—Brasen. Coll. Ox. B.A. 1818, M.A. 1830. V. of Preston, Dio. Man. 1840. (Patrons, Hulme's Trustees; Tithe, 9*l*; V.'s Inc. 665*l* and Ho; Pop. 6513.) Hon. Can. of Man. 1853; Rural Dean. [6]

PARR, John Owen, jun., *Hinstock Rectory, Market Drayton, Salop.*—Deac. 1848, Pr. 1849. C. in sole charge of Hinstock. [7]

PARR, Robert Henning, *Scarborough.*—Trin. Coll. Cam. B.A. 1849, M.A. 1854; Deac. 1854 and Pr. 1855 by Abp of York. P. C. of St. Martin's, Scarborough, Dio. York, 1863. (Patrons, Trustees.) Formerly Precentor and C. of Hull. [8]

PARR, Thomas Gnosall, *The Close, Lichfield.*—St. John's Coll. Cam. B.A. 1822, M.A. 1825; Deac. 1822, Pr. 1823. P. C. of St. Michael's, Lichfield, Dio. Lich. 1831. (Patron, V. of St. Mary's, Lichfield; P. C.'s Inc. 140*l*; Pop. 2004.) Dean's Vicar of Lich. Cathl. 1829. (Value, 68*l*.) [9]

PARRIER, H. T., *Devizes, Wilts.*—Chap. of the Union Workhouse, Devizes. [10]

PARRINGTON, Matthew, *The Training College, Chichester.*—Ch. Coll. Cam. B.A. 1830, M.A. 1834. R. of Fishbourne, Chichester, Dio. Chich. 1856. (Patron, Ld Chan; Tithe—App. 10*l* 14*s*, R. 176*l* 16*s*; Glebe, 13½ acres; R.'s Inc. 189*l*; Pop. 341.) Preb. of Chich; Prin. of the Training Coll. Chichester. [11]

PARROTT, Richard, *Great Amwell Vicarage, Ware, Herts.*—Wad. Coll. Ox. B.A. 1852, M.A. 1858; Deac. 1854 and Pr. 1855 by Bp of St. D. V. of Great Amwell, Dio. Roch. 1864. (Patroness, Mrs. Richard Parrott; Tithe—Imp. 518*l* 11*s* 6*d*, V. 239*l*; Glebe, 65 acres; V.'s Inc. 372*l* and Ho; Pop. 650.) Surrogate. Formerly Min. of Fitzroy Chapel, Lond. 1859; C. of Ware, Herts, and St. Leonards-on Sea; Dom. Chap. to the Earl of Lisburne. Author, occasional Sermons. [12]

PARRY, David, *Devynock Vicarage, Brecknockshire.*—V. of Devynock with Ystradveilte P. C. Dio. St. D. 1862. (Patron, Bp of St. D; V.'s Inc. 400*l* and Ho; Pop. Devynock 881, Ystradveilte 668.) Rural Dean. [13]

PARRY, David, *Darowen Rectory, Machynlleth, Montgomeryshire.*—Jesus Coll. Ox. B.A. 1850; Deac. 1851 and Pr. 1852 by Bp of St. A. R. of Darowen, Dio. Ban. 1856. (Patron, Bp of Ban; Tithe, 241*l*; Glebe, 23 acres; R.'s Inc. 250*l* and Ho; Pop. 1168.) Formerly P. C. of Nerquis, Flintshire, 1853–55. [14]

PARRY, Edward, *Acton Rectory, Middlesex, W.*—Ball. Coll. Ox. 1st cl. Lit. Hum. and B.A. 1852, M.A. 1855; Deac. 1854 by Bp of Dur. Pr. 1855 by Bp of Man. R. of Acton, Dio. Lon. 1859. (Patron, Bp of Lon; Tithe, 1037*l* 1*s* 10*d*; R.'s Inc. 1060*l* and Ho; Pop. 3300.) Chap. to the Bp of Lon; Rural Dean. Formerly Tut. of the Univ. and Chap. of Univ. Coll. Dur. Author, *Memoir of Rear-Admiral Sir W. Edward Parry*, 1856. [15]

PARRY, Edward Humffreys, *Surfleet, Spalding, Lincolnshire.*—Pemb. Coll. Cam. B.A. 1841; Deac. 1843 and Pr. 1845 by Bp of Barbados. P. C. of Surfleet, Dio. Lin. 1851. (Patron, Rev. J. Conant; P. C.'s Inc. 132*l*; Pop. 953.) Formerly Mast. of the Codrington Gr. Sch. and Chap. on the Society's Trust Estates, Barbados. [16]

PARRY, Edward St. John, *The College, Leamington.*—Ball. Coll. Ox. B.A. 1848, M.A. 1851. Prin. of Leamington Coll. Formerly Warden of Queen's Coll. Birmingham; Prof. of Cl. at Trin. Coll. Toronto, Canada. [17]

PARRY, Erasmus, *Criccieth Rectory, Pwllheli, Carnarvonshire.*—Lampeter; Deac. 1844, Pr. 1845. R. of Criccieth with Trevlys C. and Ynyscynhaiarn C. Dio Ban. 1863. (Patron, Bp of Ban; Criccieth, Tithe, 130*l*; Glebe, 1¾ acres; Trevlys, Tithe, 34*l*; Ynyscynhaiarn, Tithe, 160*l*; R.'s Inc. 330*l* and Ho; Pop. Criccieth 769, Trevlys 91, Ynyscynhaiarn 3138.) Formerly C. of Llanenghenedl, and Caerhun, Carnarvonshire. [18]

PARRY, Frederick William, *Bickerton, Malpas, Cheshire.*—Emman. Coll. Cam. S.C.L. 1849, LL.B. 1852; Deac. 1850 and Pr. 1851 by Bp of Ches. P. C. of Bickerton, Dio. Ches. 1857. (Patron, R. of Malpas; Glebe, 1 acre; P. C.'s Inc. 124*l* and Ho; Pop. 1348.) Formerly Asst. C. of St. Thomas's, Newcastle-on-Tyne, and Wendover, Bucks. [19]

PARRY, Henry, *Oswestry.*—Univ. Coll Lond. B.A; Deac. 1864 by Bp of St. A. C. of Trinity, Oswestry, 1864. [20]

PARRY, Henry, *Bylchau, near Denbigh.*—New Inn Hall, Ox. B.A. 1842; Deac. 1842 and Pr. 1843 by Bp of St. A. R. of Bylchau, Dio. St. A. 1854. (Patrons, the Crown and Bp of St. A. alt; R.'s Inc 378*l* and Ho; Pop. 537.) Formerly C. of Llanasa, Flintshire, and Chap. to the Holywell Union. [21]

PARRY, Howard Lewis, *Clearwell Vicarage, Coleford, Glouc.*—St. Peter's Coll. Cam. 5th Sen. Opt. and B.A. 1845, M.A. 1865; Deac. 1845 by Abp of Cant. Pr. 1846 by Bp of Lon. V. of Clearwell, Dio. G. and B. 1857. (Patroness, Dowager Countess of Dunraven; Tithe, 36*l*; Glebe, 6 acres; V.'s Inc. 200*l* and Ho: Pop. 1244.) Dom. Chap. to the Dowager Countess of Dunraven. Formerly C. of Sandhurst, Kent, 1845–48, Newent, Glouc. 1848–56. [22]

PARRY, James Abraham Peters, *Beaufort, Monmouthshire.*—St. Bees; Deac. 1862 by Bp of Llan. C. of Beaufort. [23]

PARRY, John, *Radir, Glamorganshire.*—Literate; Deac. 1843 and Pr. 1844 by Bp of St D. C. of Radir. Formerly C. of Amlwch. [24]

PARRY, John, *Wolverhampton.*—V. of St. Luke's, Wolverhampton, Dio. Lich. 1861. (Patrons, Trustees; V.'s Inc. 150*l*; Pop. 4500.) [25]

PARRY, John Peers, *Stony Stretton, Yockleton, Salop.*—St. John's Coll. Cam. B.A. 1839, M.A. 1842; Deac. 1841 and Pr. 1842 by Bp of Dur. Formerly C. of Eaton, Salop. [26]

PARRY, Morris, *Criccieth, Portmadoc, Carnarvonshire.*—Lampeter; Deac. 1842 and Pr. 1843 by Bp of St. D. R. of Llanvihangel-y-Pennant, Dio. Ban. 1863. (Patron, Bp of Ban; R.'s Inc. 127*l*; Pop. 735.) Formerly C. of Rhostie, Cardiganshire, 1842–43, Llanvihangel-y-Pennant 1843. [27]

PARRY, Thomas, *Walthamstow Vicarage, Essex.*—Wad. Coll. Ox. B.A. 1828, M.A. 1838; Deac. 1829 by Bp of Herf. Pr. 1830 by Bp of Wor. V. of Walthamstow, Dio. Lon. 1851. (Patron, Edward Warner, Esq; Tithe—Imp. 552*l* 6*s* 3*d*, V. 601*l*; V.'s Inc. 614*l* and Ho; Pop. 3122.) [28]

PARRY, Thomas William, *Hereford.*—St. Mary Hall, Ox. B.A. 1854, M.A. 1857; Deac. 1856 and Pr. 1857 by Bp of Ely. R. of St. Nicholas', Hereford, Dio.

Herf. 1859. (Patron, Ld Chan; Tithe, 150*l*; Glebe, 20 acres; R.'s Inc. 200*l*; Pop. 1533.) Formerly C of Luton, Beds. [1]

PARRY, William, *Romsey, Hants.*—Magd. Coll. Ox. B.A. 1854, M.A. 1857; Deac. 1855 by Bp of Ches. Pr. 1856 by Bp of Carl. V. of Timsbury, Dio. Win. 1863. (Patrons, J. Fleming and T. Chamberlayne, Esqs; Tithe—Imp. 283*l*, V. 24*l*; V.'s Inc. 76*l* 8*s* 10*d*; Pop. 226.) Member of Royal Asiatic Soc. 1855. Formerly Chap. of Tirhoot. Bengal, 1859–61. [2]

PARRY, William Henry, *Brecknock.*—Ch. Coll. Cam. Scho. of, Ridout Prizeman and Master's Prizeman, B.A. 1856, M.A. 1859; Deac. 1862 and Pr. 1863 by Bp of St. D. Asst. C. of St. John's and St. Mary's, Brecknock; 2nd Mast. of Christ's Coll. Brecknock. [3]

PARRY, William Warner.—Wor. Coll. Ox. B.A. 1857, M.A. 1859; Deac. 1859 and Pr. 1860 by Bp of Ches. Chap. and Naval Instructor of H.M.S. "Malacca." Formerly C. of St. Mary's, Hulme, Manchester, 1859. [4]

PARSON, John Campbell, *Much Hadham, Ware, Herts.*—Trin. Coll. Ox. B.A. 1865; Deac. 1866 by Bp of Roch. C. of Much Hadham. [5]

PARSON, William Henry, *Lynchmere, Shotter Mill, Liphook, Sussex.*—Magd. Hall, Ox. B.A. 1826 M.A. 1830; Deac. 1827 and Pr. 1828 by Bp of Win; P. C. of Lynchmere, Dio. Chich. 1849. (Patron, the present P. C; Tithe, Imp. 51*l* 6*s* 8*d*; P. C.'s Inc. 60*l*; Pop. 283.) [6]

PARSONS, Andrew Evered, *Haydon Vicarage, Sherborne, Dorset.*—Wor. Coll. Ox. B.A. 1841, M.A. 1850; Deac. 1849 by Bp of Pet. Pr. 1850 by Bp of Ox. V. of Haydon, Dio. Salis. 1856. (Patron, G. D. W. Digby, Esq; Tithe, 126*l*; Glebe, 20 acres; V.'s Inc. 155*l* and Ho; Pop. 131.) R. of Goathill, Somersetshire, Dio. B. and W. 1864. (Patron, G. D. W. Digby, Esq; R.'s Inc. 98*l*; Pop. 57.) Formerly C. of St. Mary-the-More, Wallingford. [7]

PARSONS, Augustus James, *St. Anne's Rectory, Lewes, Sussex.*—Trin. Coll. Cam. B.A. 1859; Deac. 1859 and Pr. 1860 by Bp of Chich. R. of St. Anne's, Lewes, Dio. Chich. 1862. (Patron, Ld Chan; Tithe—Imp. 193*l* 10*s* R. 130*l*; Glebe, 3 acres; R.'s Inc. 156*l* and Ho; Pop. 980.) [8]

PARSONS, Charles, *Penarth Rectory, Cardiff.*—Jesus Coll. Ox. 3rd cl. Lit. Hum. B.A. 1852, M.A. 1855; Deac. 1855 and Pr. 1856 by Bp of Llan. R. of Penarth with Lavernock R. Dio. Llan. 1863. (Patroness, Baroness Windsor; Tithe, 187*l* 10*s*; Glebe, 7 acres; R.'s Inc. 200*l* and Ho; Pop. 1500.) Formerly C. of St. Mary's, Cardiff, 1855–59, Roath 1859–63. [9]

PARSONS, F., *Heaton Reddish, Manchester.*—Dub. A.B. 1847, A.M. 1851; Deac. 1848, Pr. 1849. R. of Heaton Reddish, Dio. Man. 1865. (Patrons, Trustees; R.'s Inc. 200*l*; Pop. 6000.) Formerly C. of Oldham. [10]

PARSONS, Francis Crane, *Goathurst, Bridgwater, Somerset.*—Wor. Coll. Ox. B.A. 1830, M.A. 1833; Deac. 1830, Pr. 1832. R. of Goathurst, Dio. B. and W. 1845. (Patron, Col. C. C. K. Kynte; Tithe, 235*l*; Glebe, 62 acres; R.'s Inc. 412*l* and Ho; Pop. 304.) [11]

PARSONS Frederic James, *Selborne Vicarage, Alton, Hants.*—Magd. Coll. Ox. 1st cl. Lit. Hum and B.A. 1820, M.A. 1823, B.D. 1834; Deac. and Pr. 1834. V. of Selborne, Dio. Win. 1842. (Patron, Magd. Coll. Ox; Tithe—Imp. 578*l* 5*s* 6*d*, V. 274*l* 7*s* 4*d*; Glebe, 17 acres; V.'s Inc. 288*l* and Ho; Pop. 1110.) [12]

PARSONS, Henry, *St. Leonard's, Bridgnorth, Salop.*—Trin. Coll. Ox. B.A. 1861; Deac. 1861 and Pr. 1862 by Bp of Ox. C. of St. Leonard's and Afternoon Lect. at Badger 1864. Formerly C. of Welford and Wickham, Berks, 1861–63. [13]

PARSONS, Henry, *Sandhurst Rectory, Wokingham. Berks.*—Ball. Coll. Ox. Scho. of, 1816, B.A. 1820, M.A. 1823; Deac. 1820 and Pr. 1822 by Bp of Pet. R. of Sandhurst, Dio. Ox. 1850. (Patron, Bp of Ox; Tithe—App. 150*l* and 34 acres of Glebe; P. C.'s Inc. 208*l* and Ho; Pop. 1271.) Formerly P. C. of Upton St. Leonard's, Glouc. 1833–46. [14]

PARSONS, John Tournay, *Much Dewchurch Vicarage, Ross, Herefordshire.*—Ball. Coll. Ox. B.A. 1848; Deac. 1849 by Bp of Salis. Pr. 1850 by Bp of Herf. V. of Much Dewchurch, Dio. Herf. 1850. (Patron, Bp of G and B; Tithe—App. 300*l*, V. 440*l*; Glebe, 4 acres; V.'s Inc. 440*l* and Ho; Pop. 608.) [15]

PARSONS, Lawrence John, *Shorncliffe.*—St. John's Coll. Cam. B.A. 1849, M.A. 1853; Deac. 1850 and Pr. 1851 by Bp of Lin. Chap. to the Forces, Shorncliffe. Formerly Asst. Chap. to the Forces, Shorncliffe. [16]

PARTINGTON, Charles Edward, *Stoke-Mandeville Vicarage, Aylesbury, Bucks.*—Wor. Coll. Ox. B.A. 1853, M.A. 1855; Deac. 1853 and Pr. 1854 by Bp of Ches. V. of Stoke-Mandeville with Buckland, Dio Ox. 1858. (Patrons, D. and C. of Lin; V.'s Inc. 133*l* and Ho; Pop. Stoke-Mandeville 364, Buckland 372.) Formerly C. of Frodsham 1852–55, Stand, Manchester, 1855–58. [17]

PARTINGTON, Henry, *Wath, Rotherham, Yorks.*—Ch. Ch. Ox. B.A. 1830, M.A. 1832; Deac. 1831 and Pr. 1832 by Bp of Ox. V. of Wath-upon-Dearne with P. C. of Adwick-upon-Dearne, Dio. York, 1833. (Patrons, D. and C. of Ch. Ch. Oxford; Tithe, App. 2074*l* 12*s* and 29 acres of Glebe, V. 250*l*; Glebe, 30 acres; V.'s Inc. 390*l*; Pop. Wath, 1690, Adwick 226.) Lect. of Wath 1847. (Patrons, Trustees of the late Mrs. Ellis; Value, 52*l* 10*s*.) [18]

PARTRIDGE, Joseph Sutcliffe, *Stratford-le-Bow, London, E.*—C. of Bow. [19]

PARTRIDGE, Walter John, *Caston Rectory, Attleborough, Norfolk.*—Corpus Coll. Cam. B.A. 1837, M.A. 1840; Deac. 1838 and Pr. 1839 by Bp of Nor. R. of Caston, Dio. Nor. 1850. (Patron, the present R; Tithe, 517*l*; Glebe, 50 acres; R.'s Inc. 585*l* and Ho; Pop. 510.) [20]

PARTRIDGE, William Edwards, *Horsendon House (Bucks), near Tring.*—Brasen. Coll. Ox. B.A. 1832; Deac. 1833, Pr. 1834. V. of Ilmer, Bucks, Dio. Ox. 1833. (Patron, the present R; Tithe—Imp. 72*l*, V. 104*l* 4*s*; Glebe, 1¾ acres; V.'s Inc. 116*l*; Pop. 79.) R. of Horsendon, Dio. Ox. 1844. (Patron, the present R; Tithe, 148*l* 13*s*; Glebe, 20 acres; R.'s Inc. 184*l*; Pop. 45.) [21]

PASCOE, Richard Corbett, *The Close, Exeter.*—Magd. Hall, Ox. 3rd cl. Lit. Hum. and B.A. 1851, M.A. 1854; Deac. 1855 by Bp of Ox. Pr. 1856 by Bp of B. and W. Fell. of Ex. Coll. Ox. 1856; Prin. of Theol. Coll. Exeter, 1861. Formerly C. of Harberton 1856–58; Vice Prin. of Lichfield Theol. Coll. 1858–61; Vice-Prin. Theol. Coll. Exeter, 1861; R. of St. Stephen's, Exeter, 1862–63. [22]

PASCOE, Thomas, *St. Hilary Vicarage, Marazion, Cornwall.*—Jesus Coll. Cam. B.A. 1810; Deac. 1811 and Pr. 1812 by Bp of Ex. V. of St. Hilary, Dio. Ex. 1814. (Patrons, Duke of Leeds and others; Tithe, Imp. 393*l* 11*s*, V. 248*l* 3*s*; Glebe, 36 acres; V.'s Inc. 380*l* and Ho; Pop. 1914.) [23]

PASKE, Edward, *Creeting St. Peter Rectory, Needham Market, Suffolk.*—Clare Hall, Cam. B.A. 1813, M.A. 1816; Deac. 1815 and Pr. 1817 by Bp of Nor. R. of Creeting St. Peter, Dio. Nor. 1818. (Patron, the present R; Tithe, 401*l* 10*s*; Glebe, 7 acres; R.'s Inc. 410*l* and Ho; Pop. 248.) V. of Battisford, Suffolk, Dio. Nor. 1821. (Patron, the present V; Tithe, 400*l* 5*s*; Glebe, 1 acre; V.'s Inc. 402*l*; Pop. 504.) [24]

PASKE, George Alexander, *Needham Market, Suffolk.*—Clare Coll. Cam. B.A. 1824, M.A. 1828; Deac. 1825 and Pr. 1826 by Bp of Nor. P. C. of Needham-Market, Dio. Nor. 1828. (Patron, R. of Barking; Glebe, 23 acres; P. C.'s Inc. 85*l*; Pop. 1377.) P. C. of Willisham, Suffolk, Dio. Nor. 1837. (Patron, Rev. E. B. Sparke; Tithe—Imp. 246*l* 15*s*, and 4½ acres of Glebe; Glebe, 24 acres; P. C.'s Inc. 61*l*; Pop. 186.) [25]

PASSAND, Henry John, *Shipton-on-Cherwell Rectory, Woodstock, Oxon.*—St. Alban Hall, Ox. B.A. 1824, M.A. 1827. R. of Shipton-on-Cherwell, Dio. Ox. 1831. (Patron, W. Turner, Esq; R's Inc. 321*l* and Ho; Pop. 131.) [26]

PASSY, Frederic Charles George, *Wilshamstead Vicarage, Beds.*—Emman. Coll. Cam. B.A. 1832; Deac. 1834 and Pr. 1835 by Bp of Lin. V. of Wilshamstead, *alias* Wilstead, Dio. Ely, 1843. (Patron, Heirs of Lord Carteret; Glebe, 269 acres; V.'s Inc. 400*l* and Ho; Pop. 1032.) [1]

PATCH, Henry, *Bridgnorth, Salop.*—St. John's Coll. Cam. B.A. 1854, M.A. 1857; Deac. 1856 and Pr. 1857 by Bp of Nor. C. of Bridgnorth. Formerly C. of Southwold, Suffolk. [2]

PATCH, Hubert Mornington, *Hungerford, Berks.*—Clare Coll. Cam. B.A. 1862, M.A. 1866; Deac. 1864 and Pr. 1865 by Bp of Ex. C. of St. Lawrence's Hungerford, 1867. Formerly C. of Lower Brixham 1864, St. Luke's, Torquay, 1866. [3]

PATCH, James Terry, *Homburg.*—British Chap. at Homburg. [4]

PATCH, Joseph, *Blawith, Ulverston.*—Queens' Coll. Cam. Jun. Opt. and B.A. 1841, M.A. 1844; Deac. 1841 and Pr. 1842 by Abp of York. P. C. of Blawith, Dio Carl. 1847. (Patron, Duke of Buccleuch; Tithe, Imp. 6*l* 6*s*: P. C.'s Inc. 66*l*; Pop. 193.) [5]

PATCHELL, William Gibson, *Holbeach, Lincolnshire.*—Dub. A.B. 1846; Deac. 1847 and Pr. 1848 by Bp of Lin. V. of Holbeach, Dio. Lin. 1867. (Patron, Bp of Lin; Glebe, 8 acres; V.'s Inc. 993*l* and Ho; Pop. 4956.) Formerly C. of St. Mary's, Nottingham; P. C. of Drove End, Lincolnshire, 1855–67. [6]

PATCHETT, William, *Haworth Grammar School, Yorks.*—St. John's Coll. Cam. B.A. 1852, M.A. 1855; Deac. 1853 and Pr. 1854 by Abp of York. Head Mast. of Haworth Gr. Sch. Formerly C. of Harringworth, Northants, and Lythe, Yorks. [7]

PATCHETT, William Henry, *Sawley, Ripon.*—St. Cath. Hall, Cam Jun. Opt. and B.A. 1845; Deac. 1847 and Pr. 1848 by Abp of York. P. C. of Sawley, Dio. Rip. 1858. (Patrons, D. and C. of Rip; Glebe, 6 acres; P. C.'s Inc. 110*l* and Ho; Pop. 446.) Formerly C. of Dishforth and Skipworth; P. C. of Winksley, Yorks, 1856–65. [8]

PATER, J. Saunders, *Histon, Cambridge.*—C. of Histon. [9]

PATERSON, David James, *Chelford Parsonage, Congleton, Cheshire.*—Trin. Coll. Cam. B.A. 1845; Deac. 1849 and Pr. 1850 by Bp of Herf. P. C. of Chelford, Dio. Ches. 1853. (Patron, J. Dixon, Esq., Astle Hall; Glebe, 40 acres; P. C.'s Inc. 114*l* and Ho.) Author, *The Lord's Day* (a Tract), 1853, 3*d.* [10]

PATERSON, George Mapletoft, *Brome Rectory, Scole, Suffolk.*—Lin. Coll. Ox. B.A. 1845, M.A. 1846; Deac. 1845 and Pr. 1846 by Bp of Ox. R. of Brome with Oakley, Dio. Nor. 1847. (Patron, Sir Edward Kerrison, Bart; Brome, Tithe, 231*l*; Glebe, 26 acres; Oakley, Tithe, 351*l*; Glebe, 25 acres; R.'s Inc. 658*l* and Ho; Pop. Brome 291, Oakley 332.) Dom. Chap. to Lord Grey. [11]

PATEY, George Phelps, *Grammar School, Plympton, Devon.*—Head Mast. of Plympton Gr. Sch. Formerly C. of Bickleigh and Shepstor, Plympton. [12]

PATEY, Macnamara, *Canford, Wimborne, Dorset.*—St. Cath Coll. Cam. B.A. 1849; Deac. 1850 by Bp of Man Pr. 1851 by Bp of Salis. Chap. of the Union, Poole, Dorset. Formerly Lieut. in the Royal Marines. [13]

PATEY, Thomas Maurice, *Hampreston Rectory, Wimborne, Dorset.*—St. Cath. Hall, Cam. Sen. Opt. and B.A. 1844; Deac. 1844, Pr. 1846. R. of Hampreston, Dio. Salis. 1857. (Patrons, Rev. H. T. Glyn and others; Tithe—Imp. 53*l* 10*s*, R. 302*l* 5*s* 10*d*; Glebe, 8 acres; R.'s Inc. 315*l* and Ho; Pop. 1341.) [14]

PATON, Alexander, *Tuddenham Vicarage, Ipswich.*—Queens' Coll. Cam. B.A. 1835, M.A. 1839. V. of Tuddenham St. Martin, Dio. Nor. 1846. (Patroness, Mrs. Lillingstone; Tithe—Imp. 220*l* 12*s*, V. 110*l* 6*s*; Glebe, 3 acres; V.'s Inc. 114*l* and Ho; Pop. 394.) [15]

PATON, George, *Ramsey, Isle of Man.*—C. of St. Paul's, Ramsey. [16]

PATTEN, F. A. Murray, *Gosport, Hants.*—Dub. A.B. 1833; Deac. 1833 by Bp of Meath, Pr. 1864 by Bp of Limerick. Formerly C. of St. Matthew's, Gosport. [17]

PATTENDEN, George Edwin, *Grammar Schoolhouse, Boston.*—St. Peter's Coll. Cam. B.A. 1846, M.A. 1850. P. C. of the Chapel of Ease, Boston, Dio. Lin. 1856. (Patrons, Trustees; P. C.'s Inc. 100*l*.) Head Mast. of the Boston Gr. Sch. 1850. [18]

PATTENSON, John Cooke Tylden, *Sutton St. Ann's Rectory, Loughborough.*—Dur. B.A. 1844, M.A. 1849; Deac. 1846, Pr. 1847. R. of Sutton-Bonnington St. Ann's, Dio. Lin. 1855. (Patron, Ld Chan; Glebe, 5 acres; R.'s Inc. 300*l* and Ho; Pop. 881.) P. C. of Kingston on-Soar, Nottingham, Dio. Lin. 1855. (Patron, Lord Belper; Glebe, 10 acres; P. C.'s Inc. 100*l*; Pop. 197.) Formerly C. of Keston, Kent, 1850–55. [19]

PATTENSON, Robert Cane, *Melmerby Rectory, Penrith, Cumberland.*—St. Mary Hall, Ox. B.C.L. 1842; Deac. 1842, Pr. 1843. R. of Melmerby, Dio. Carl. 1844. (Patron, Rev. John Hall; Tithe, 118*l*; Glebe, 76 acres; R.'s Inc. 200*l* and Ho; Pop. 307.) Formerly C. of St. Stephen's, Bristol, 1842–44. [20]

PATTERSON, James William, *The Hollies, Stanley, near Wakefield.*—Deac. 1866. C. of Stanley 1866. [21]

PATTERSON, William St. George, *The Close, Lichfield.*—Dub. A.B. 1840, A.M. 1843; Deac. 1841 and Pr. 1842 by Bp of Chich. Div. Lect. Sub-Chanter and Succentor of Lich. Cathl. 1846. [22]

PATTESON, John, *Thorpe Rectory, Norwich.*—Corpus Coll. Cam. 25th Wrang. and B.A. 1836; Deac. 1837 and Pr. 1839 by Bp of Salis. R. of Thorpe, Dio. Nor. 1867. (Patron, William Birkbeck, Esq; R.'s Inc. 657*l* and Ho; Pop. 1456.) Formerly P. C. of St. Jude's, Chelsea, 1844–56; R. of Ch. Ch. Spitalfields, Lond. 1856–67. [23]

PATTESON, Thomas, *Hambledon Vicarage, Horndean, Hants.*—Ex. Coll. Ox. B.A. 1830, M.A. 1832. V. of Hambledon, Dio. Win. 1841. (Patron, Bp of Win; Tithe, App. 979*l* 16*s*, V. 749*l* 15*s* 6*d*; V.'s Inc. 765*l* and Ho; Pop. 1810.) Surrogate. [24]

PATTESON, William Frederick, *St. Helen's-square, Norwich.*—Trin. Coll. Cam. B.A. 1824, M.A. 1860; Deac. 1823, Pr. 1824. P. C. of St. Helen's, Norwich, Dio. Nor. 1825. (Patrons, Trustees; P. C.'s Inc. 206*l* and Ho; Pop. 507.) Hon. Can. of Nor; Rural Dean. [25]

PATTINSON, William, *Kirkbampton Rectory, Carlisle.*—St. Peter's Coll. Cam. Sen. Opt. and B.A. 1839, M.A. 1850; Deac. 1842 and Pr. 1843. R. of Kirkbampton, Dio Carl. 1845. (Patrons, Earl of Lonsdale and Sir W. Briscoe, alt; Tithe—Eccles. Commis. 58*l* 6*s* 6*d*, R. 94*l* 4*s*; Glebe, 8 acres; R.'s Inc. 115*l* and Ho; Pop. 119.) [26]

PATTINSON, William John, *Laxton (Northants), near Uppingham.*—St. Cath. Coll. Cam. LL.B. 1852; Deac. 1851, Pr. 1852. V. of Laxton, Dio. Pet. 1853. (Patron, Lord Carbery; V.'s Inc. 360*l*; Pop. 119.) [27]

PATTISON, Edward, *Bradfield St. George, Bury St. Edmunds.*—Queens' Coll. Cam. B.A. 1825; Deac. 1826 by Bp of B. and W. Pr. 1827 by Bp of Nor. R. of Gedding, Suffolk, Dio. Ely, 1831. (Patron, William Sorsby, Esq. Doncaster; Tithe, 150*l*; Glebe, 5½ acres; R.'s Inc. 158*l* 16*s*; Pop. 147.) C. of Rushbrooke, Suffolk, 1836. Formerly C. of Little Eversden, Cambs. 1826; Letheringham, Suffolk, 1827–31. [28]

PATTISON, George, *Carnforth, Lancaster.*—Queens' Coll. Cam. B.A. 1865; Deac. 1866 and Pr. 1867 by Bp of Man. C. of Carnforth with Priest-Hutton District 1866. Formerly C. of St. John's, Blackburn, 1866. [29]

PATTISON, James Balfour, *Sulby, Isle of Man.*—P. C. of St. Stephen's, Sulby, Dio. S. and M. 1866. (Patron, Bp of S. and M; P. C.'s Inc. 60*l*.) Formerly C. of St. Philip's, Hulme, Manchester. [30]

PATTISON, Mark, *Lincoln College, Oxford.*—Oriel Coll. Ox. B.A. 1837; Lin. Coll. M.A. 1840, B.D. 1851; Deac. 1840, Pr. 1841. Fell. of Lin. Coll. 1840, and R. of same 1861. [31]

PATTRICK, Beaufoy, *Monewden, Market Wickham, Suffolk.* C. of Monewden. [1]

PAUL, Charles Kegan, *Sturminster-Marshall Vicarage, Wimborne, Dorset.*—Ex. Coll. Ox. B.A. 1849. V. of Sturminster-Marshall. Dio. Salis. 1862. (Patron, Eton Coll; V.'s Inc. 303*l* and Ho; Pop. 850.) Formerly Conduct of Eton Coll; C. of Eton, Bucks. [2]

PAUL, Dolben, *Stevenage, Herts.*—Ch. Ch. Ox. B.A. 1854; Deac. 1856 and Pr. 1857 by Bp of Lin. C. of Stevenage. Formerly C. of Barrowby, Lincolnshire, 1857–58, Sibbertoft, Northants, 1858–63. [3]

PAUL, Frederick Bateman, *St. Blasey Vicarage, St. Austell, Cornwall.*—Dur. Theol. Licen. 1859; Deac. 1859 and Pr. 1860 by Bp of Ex. V. of St. Blasey, Dio. Ex. 1868. (Patron, T. T. S. Carlyon, Esq; V.'s Inc. 120*l* and Ho; Pop. 2700.) Formerly Assist. C. of Ottery St. Mary, 1859. [4]

PAUL, George Woodfield, *Finedon, Higham Ferrers.*—Magd. Coll. Ox. B A. 1843, M.A. 1845; Deac. 1844 by Bp of Ox. Pr. 1845 by Bp of Pet. V. of Finedon, Dio. Pet. 1848. (Patron, the present V; V.'s Inc. 1010*l* and Ho; Pop. 1880.) Formerly Fell. of Magd. Coll. Ox. resigned 1848. [5]

PAUL, John, 2, *Lansdowne-place, Worcester.*—Magd. Hall, Ox. B.A. 1841; Deac. 1841 and Pr. 1842 by Bp of Ches. C. of Warndon, Worc. 1867. Formerly P. C. of Twigworth, Gloucestershire; Min. of St. Peter's Chapel, Pimlico, Lond. Author, *Six Sermons on Christian Union*, 1852, 4*s* 6*d*. [6]

PAUL, Robert Bateman, *St Mary's Rectory, Stamford.*—Ex. Coll. Ox. 2nd cl. Lit. Hum. 1819, Fell. of Ex. 1818, B.A. 1821, M.A. 1822, Pub. Exam. in Lit. Hum. 1826; Deac. and Pr. 1822 by Bp of Ox. R. of St. Mary's Stamford, Dio. Lin. 1864. (Patron, Marquis of Exeter; R.'s Inc. 88*l* and Ho; Pop. 359.) Preb. of Lin. 1867. Formerly P. C. of Kentish-town, Lond; for some years Archd. of Nelson, New Zealand. Author, *Grecian Antiquities*; *History of Germany*. [7]

PAULET, Lord Charles, *Wellesbourne Vicarage, Warwickshire.*—Clare Hall, Cam. M.A. 1825; Deac. 1828 by Bp of Lin. Pr. 1830 by Bp of Wor. V. of Wellesbourne, Dio. Wor. 1830. (Patron, Ld Chan; Tithe—Imp, 312*l* 11*s* 6*d*, V. 367*l*; Glebe, 69 acres; V.'s Inc. 470*l* and Ho; Pop. 1542.) Preb. of Salis. 1833. [8]

PAULET, Charles Newton, *Kirk-Hammerton, York.*—Magd. Hall, Ox. M.A; Deac. 1853 and Pr. 1854 by Bp of Herf. P. C. of Kirk-Hammerton Dio. Rip. 1855. (Patron, the present P. C; Tithe 19*l* 11*s*; Glebe, 44 acres; P. C.'s Inc. 123*l* 16*s* and Ho; Pop. 400.) Formerly C. of Churchstoke, Montgomery, 1853. [9]

PAULETT, John David, 11, *Warrington-place, Staleybridge.*—Deac. 1860 and Pr. 1861 by Abp of York. C. of St. Paul's, Stayley, 1864. Formerly C. of Chaceltown, near Sheffield, 1860, Kimberworth 1861, Tankersley 1863. [10]

PAULI, Christian Abraham Manasseh, *Redmire, Bedale, Yorks.*—Dub. A.B. 1855; Deac. 1855 and Pr. 1856 by Bp of Rip. P. C. of Bolton with Redmire P. C. Dio. Rip. 1856. (Patron, R. of Wensley; Bolton, Glebe, 24 acres; Redmire, Tithe—App. 184*l* 10*s*; Glebe, 24 acres; P. C.'s Inc. 167*l* 12*s*; Pop. Bolton 250, Redmire 420.) [11]

PAULI, John, *Hednesford, Cannock, Stafford.*—Lich. Theol. Coll; Deac. 1861 and Pr. 1862 by Bp of Lich. C. in sole charge of Hednesford 1864. Formerly C. of St. John's, Longton, 1861–64. [12]

PAULL, Henry Andrew, *East Wickham, Plumstead, Kent, S.E.*—P. C. of East Wickham, Dio. Lon. 1854. (Patron, Rev. W. Acworth; P. C.'s Inc. 172*l*; Pop. 836.) [13]

PAULL, William, *Handley, near Chester.*—St. John's Coll. Cam. Sen. Opt. 3rd cl. Cl. Trip. and B.A. 1827, M.A. 1830; Deac. 1827 and Pr. 1831 by Bp of Lin. R. of Handley, Dio. Ches. 1850 (Patrons, D. and C. of Ches; Tithe, 255*l* 19*s* 1*d*; Glebe, 10½ acres; R.'s Inc. 278*l* and Ho; Pop. 364.) Formerly Chap. of Chester Infirmary 1840–50. [14]

PAULSON, George Robert, *Addington Rectory, Maidstone.*—Ball. Coll. Ox. M.A. 1828; Deac. and Pr. 1823. R. of Addington, Dio. Cant. 1834. (Patron, Hon. John Wingfield Stratford; Tithe, 223*l* 4*s*; Glebe, 26 acres; R.'s Inc. 226*l* and Ho; Pop. 262.) [15]

PAVER, Richard, *Brayton Vicarage, Selby, Yorks.*—Deac. 1816 and Pr. 1817 by Abp of York. V. of Brayton, Dio. York, 1819. (Patron, Lord Londesborough; Tithe, App. 137*l* 10*s*, Imp. 217*l* 16*s*, V. 57*l* 16*s*; V.'s Inc. 288*l* and Ho; Pop. 1381.) P. C. of Barlow, Brayton, 1819. (Patron, G. H. Thompson, Esq; P. C.'s Inc. 30*l*; Pop. 239.) [16]

PAVEY, Alfred, *Aslackton Lodge, near Nottingham.*—Queen's Coll. Ox. B.A. 1854, M.A. 1857; Deac. 1854 and Pr. 1856 by Bp of Man. P. C. of Scarrington with Aslackton, Dio Lin. 1867. (Patrons, D. and C. of Lin; Glebe, 36 acres; P. C.'s Inc. 200*l* and Ho; Pop. 641.) Formerly C. of Trinity, Bolton, and St. James, Heywood, near Manchester, and Bingham, Notts, 1859. [17]

PAXTON, William Archibald, *Otterden Rectory, Feversham, Kent.*—Trin. Coll. Ox. B.A. and M.A. 1844; Deac. 1843, Pr. 1845. R. of Otterden, Dio. Cant. 1850. (Patron, the present R; Tithe, 242*l* 10*s*; Glebe, 191 acres; R.'s Inc. 400*l* and Ho; Pop. 194.) [18]

PAYNE, Alfred, *Enville Hall, Stourbridge.*—Trin. Coll. Ox. B.A. 1856, M.A. 1859; Deac. 1859 by Bp of Win. Pr. 1861 by Bp of Pet. C. of Enville 1866; Dom. Chap. to the Earl of Stamford and Warrington. Formerly C. of Yately, Hants, and Markfield, Leicestershire. [19]

PAYNE, David Bruce, *The Beach, Lower Walmer.*—Dur. B.A. 1848, M.A. 1851, B.D. 1862, D.D. 1864; Deac. 1850 and Pr. 1851 by Abp of Cant. C. of Walmer 1850, and Chap. to St Bartholomew's Hospital, Sandwich, 1863. [20]

PAYNE, Edward, *Swalcliffe Vicarage, Banbury, Oxon.*—New Coll. Ox. B.A. 1829, M.A. 1832; Deac. 1832 by Bp of Ox. Pr. 1833 by Bp of Win. V. of Swalcliffe with Shutford C. and Epwell C. Dio. Ox. 1837. (Patron, New Coll. Ox; V.'s Inc. 320*l* and Ho; Pop. Swalcliffe 379, Shutford 386, Epwell 358.) Rural Dean of Deidington 1847. Formerly C. of Old Alresford, Hants, 1832–33, Pagham, Sussex, 1834, St. Michael's, Winchester, 1835–36. [21]

PAYNE, James, *Church Green, Witney.*—Queen's Coll. Ox. B.A. 1862; Deac. 1866 and Pr. 1867 by Bp of Ox. C. of Ducklington with Hurdwick 1866. Formerly Cl. Prof. at the International Coll. Boulogne-sur-Mer [22]

PAYNE, John Burnell, 15, *Long Wall-street, Oxford.*—Univ. Coll. Lond. B.A. 1858; Downing Coll. Cam. 2nd cl. Cl. Trip. 1st cl. Moral Sci. Trip; Deac. 1865 by Bp of Ox. Formerly Asst Mast. at Wellington Coll. Wokingham, 1864–67. [23]

PAYNE, John Hervey, *Colney Rectory, Norwich.*—Caius Coll Cam. B.A. 1839; Deac. 1840 and Pr. 1841 by Bp of Nor. V. of Earlham St. Mary with Bowthorpe, Norfolk, Dio. Nor. 1849. (Patron, Bacon T. Frank, Esq; Earlham St. Mary, Tithe—Imp. 159*l*, V. 120*l*; Bowthorpe, Tithe—Imp. 110*l*; V.'s Inc. 155*l*; Pop. Earlham 131, Bowthorpe 88.) R. of Colney, Dio. Nor. 1866. (Patron, J. Scott, Esq; Tithe, 229*l*; R.'s Inc. 240*l* and Ho; Pop. 84.) [24]

PAYNE, John Vaughan, *Gloucester.*—New Inn Hall, Ox. B.A. 1849, M.A. 1852; Deac. 1851 by Bp of Ex. Pr. 1866 by Bp of G. and B. C. of Ch. Ch. Gloucester, 1863. [25]

PAYNE, Randolph, 7, *Norfolk-terrace, Brighton.*—Magd. Hall, Ox. B.A. 1846; Deac. 1847 and Pr. 1849 by Bp of Salis C. of St. Paul's, Brighton. Formerly C. of Wiston, Sussex [26]

PAYNE, Richard, *Downton Vicarage, Salisbury.*—New Coll. Ox. B.C.L. 1835; Deac. 1835, Pr. 1836. V. of Downton with Nunton, Dio. Salis. 1841. (Patron, Win Coll; Tithe—Imp. 1612*l* and 126½ acres of Glebe, V. 929*l* 5*s*; Glebe, 5¾ acres; V.'s Inc. 930*l* and Ho; Pop. 2375.) Rural Dean of Wilton; Preb. of Salis. 1861. [27]

PAYNE, S. W.—Chap. of H.M.S. "Caraçoa." [28]

PAYNE, William, *Reading.*—Trin. Coll. Cam. B.A. 1851, M.A. 1854; Deac. 1851 and Pr. 1852 by Bp of Ely. P. C. of St. John's, Reading, Dio. Ox. 1857.

(Patron, Rev. F. Trench.) Formerly C. of St. Andrew's the Great, Cambridge, 1851–54. [1]

PAYNTER, Francis, *Stoke Rectory, Guildford.*—R. of Stoke-next-Guildford, Dio. Win. 1862. (Patron, the Rev. S. Paynter; Tithe, 693*l*; R.'s Inc. 700*l* and Ho; Pop. 3797.) [2]

PAYNTER, Samuel, *Stoke Hill, Guildford.*—Trin. Coll. Cam. B.A. 1823, M.A. 1827. Formerly R of Stoke-next-Guildford, Surrey, 1831–58. [3]

PAYNTER, W. Cambourne, *Redbourne, Herts.*—C. of Redbourne. [4]

PEACE, Peter, *Devizes.*—Wor. Coll. Ox. B.A. 1833, M.A. 1836, B.D. 1844; Deac. 1835 and Pr. 1836 by Bp of Bristol. Formerly C. of St. Nicholas', Bristol, 1835–46, Enmore Green, Dorset, 1847–61. Author, *An Address for the Labouring Poor*, and *A Plea for Small Farms.* [5]

PEACE, William, *Yatesbury, Wilts.*—C. of Yatesbury. [6]

PEACH, Charles, *Turnditch, Derby.*—Ch. Coll. Cam. Sen. Opt. and 3rd cl. Cl. Trip. 1847; Deac. 1848 and Pr. 1849 by Bp of Pet. P C. of Turnditch, Dio. Lich. 1865. (Patron, V. of Duffield; P. C.'s Inc. 70*l* and Ho; Pop. 324) [7]

PEACH, Henry John, *Tutbury Vicarage, Burton-on Trent.*—Emman. Coll. Cam. Sen. Opt. 3rd cl. Cl. Trip. and B.A. 1840, M.A 1843; Deac. 1841 and Pr. 1842 by Bp of Pet. V. of Tutbury, Dio. Lich. 1844. (Patron, Sir O. Mosley, Bart; Tithe, 156*l*; Glebe, 110 acres; V.'s Inc. 290*l* and Ho; Pop. 1982.) Formerly C. of Walton-on-the-Wolds, Leicestershire, 1841–43. [8]

PEACHE, Alfred, *Mangotsfield, Bristol.*—Wad. Coll. Ox. B.A. 1842, M.A. 1845; Deac. 1842, Pr. 1843. P. C. of Mangotsfield with Downsend C. Dio. G. and B. 1859. (Patron the present P. C; P. C.'s Inc. 280*l*; Pop. 4222.) Formerly C. of Heckfield-cum-Mattingley, Hants. [9]

PEACOCK, Edward, *Road Hill Parsonage, near Bath.*—Trin. Coll. Cam. Sen. Opt. and B.A. 1843, M A. 1846; Deac. 1844 and Pr. 1846 by Bp of Salis. P. C. of Road Hill, Wilts, Dio. Salis. 1858. (Patron, V. of North Bradley, Wilts; P. C.'s Inc. 149*l* and Ho; Pop. 407.) Dioc. Inspector of Schs. Formerly C, of Gussage All Saints', Donhead St. Mary, Wilts, Berwick St. John, Maddington, Wilts. [10]

PEACOCK, John, *Wellingore Vicarage, Grantham.*—Lin. Coll. Ox. B.A. 1842. V. of Wellingore, Dio. Lin. 1845. (Patrons, D. and C. of Lin; V.'s Inc. 210*l* and Ho; Pop. 943.) [11]

PEACOCK, Wilkinson Affleck, *Ulceby Rectory, Alford, Lincolnshire.*—Corpus Coll. Cam. B.A. 1837; Deac. 1838, Pr. 1839. R. of Ulceby with Fordington, Dio. Lin. 1848. (Patron, the present R; R.'s Inc. 740*l*; Pop. 212.) [12]

PEACOCKE, William James, *Upton, Southwell, Notts.*—Dub. A.B. 1848; Deac. 1849 and Pr. 1850 by Bp of Lin. V. of Upton, Dio, Lin. 1859. (Patron, Chapter of Southwell; Glebe, 41 acres; V.'s Inc. 290*l* and Ho; Pop. 587.) Formerly C. of Lenton, Notts, Hoby, Leic. and Ch. Ch. Newark, Notts. [13]

PEAKE, George, *Aston Vicarage, Birmingham.*—Mert. Coll. Ox. B.A. 1813, M.A. 1822. V. of Aston, Dio. Wor. 1852. (Patrons, Trustees; Tithe—App. 400*l*, Imp. 622*l* 5*s* 9*d*, V. 1800*l*; V.'s Inc. 1800*l* and Ho; Pop. 30,634.) Surrogate. [14]

PEAKE, Henry, *Monk-street, Abergavenny, Monmouthshire.*—Jesus Coll Ox. 2nd cl. Lit. Hum. and B.A. 1833; Deac. 1834, Pr. 1835. Head Mast. of Gr. Sch. Abergavenny, 1834. Formerly C. of Llangattock-juxta-Usk. [15]

PEAKE, James Room, *Whitchurch, Salop.*—Head Mast. of the Gr. Sch. Whitchurch. [16]

PEAKE, John Dawson, *Laleham (Middlesex), Chertsey.*—St. John's Coll. Cam. Sen. Opt. and B.A. 1852; Deac. 1853 and Pr. 1854 by Bp of Pet. V. of Laleham, Dio. Lon. 1859. (Patron, Ld Chan; Tithe, 96*l*; Glebe, 16 acres; V.'s Inc. 120*l*; Pop. 613.) Formerly C. of Kirkby-la-Thorpe with Asgarby, Linc. [17]

PEAKE, John R., *Ellesmere Vicarage, Salop.*—V. of Ellesmere, Dio. Lich. 1864. (Patron, Earl Brownlow; Tithe—Imp. 2591*l* 10*s*, V. 430*l*; V.'s Inc. 530*l* and Ho; Pop. 6071.) [18]

PEAKE, Thomas Cross, *Hallaton Rectory, Leicestershire.*—Sid. Coll. Cam, 30th Wrang. and B.A. 1839, M.A. 1842; Deac. 1841 and Pr. 1842 by Bp of Ely. R. of Hallaton with Blaston St. Michael C. Dio. Pet. 1843. (Patrons, Rev. G. O. Fenwicke, and C. Bewicke, Esq; Hallaton, Glebe, 460 acres; Blaston St. Michael, Tithe, 76*l*; Glebe, 6 acres; R.'s Inc. 700*l* and Ho; Pop. Hallaton 696, Blaston St. Michael 68.) Formerly Fell. of Sid. Coll. Cam. [19]

PEARCE, Robert John, *Rossall, Fleetwood, Lancashire.*—Caius Coll. Cam. 3rd Wrang. B.A. 1864, M.A. 1867; Deac, 1865, Pr. 1866. Fell. of Caius Coll. Cam; Sen. Math. Mast. at Rossall Sch. 1867. Formerly C. of St. Mary's, Windermere, 1866-67 [20]

PEARCE, Thomas, *Morden Vicarage, Blandford, Dorset.*—Lin. Coll. Ox. B.A. 1843, M A. 1848; Deac. 1845 and Pr. 1846 by Bp of Lich. V. of Morden, Dio Salis. 1853. (Patroness, Miss Drax; Tithe—Imp. 309*l*, V. 160*l*; Glebe, 90 acres; V.'s Inc. 280*l* and Ho; Pop. 939.) Deputy Grand Master of Freemasons for Dorset. Formerly C. of Golden Hill, Staffs, of Highcliff, Hants, and of Waterperry, Oxon. [21]

PEARMAN, Augustus John, *Rainham Vicarage, Sittingbourne, Kent.*—Pemb. Coll. Ox B.A. 1853, M.A. 1856; Deac. 1854 by Bp of Ely, Pr. 1856 by Abp of Cant. V. of Rainham, Dio. Cant. 1866. (Patron, Abp of Cant; Tithe, 520*l*; Glebe, 3 acres; V.'s Inc. 550*l* and Ho; Pop. 1422.) Formerly V. of Bethersden, Kent, 1857–66. [22]

PEARMAN, J. A., *Hanley, Staffs.*—C. of Hanley. [23]

PEARMAN, Morgan Thomas, *Staplehurst, Kent.*—Pemb. Coll. Ox. B.A. 1857, M.A. 1859; Deac. 1858 and Pr. 1859 by Abp of Cant. C. of Staplehurst 1862. Formerly C. of Cranbrooke 1858-62. [24]

PEARS, Edmund Ward, *St. Peter's Rectory, Dorchester.*—Magd. Coll. Ox. B.A 1833, M.A. 1836. R. of St. Peter's Dorchester, Dio. Salis. 1864. (Patron, Ld Chan; R.'s Inc. 164*l* and Ho; Pop 1213.) Formerly C. of Stoke Goldington. [25]

PEARS, Stewart Adolphus, *Repton, Burton-on-Trent, Staffs.*—Corpus Coll. Ox. 2nd cl. Lit. Hum. and B.A. 1836, Ellerton Theol. Prize and M.A. 1839, Denyer Theol. Prize 1841, B.D. 1846; Deac. 1839, Pr. 1843. Head Mast. of Repton School 1854; Rural Dean. Author, *Correspondence of Sir Philip Sidney*; *Sermons* (preached at Harrow). [26]

PEARSE, Arthur Henry.—Corpus Coll. Ox. 2nd cl. Math. et Phy. and B.A. 1852, M.A 1855; Deac. 1855 and Pr. 1856 by Bp of Ox. Formerly C. of Easthampstead; Chap. of the Easthampstead Union Workhouse. [27]

PEARSE, Beauchamp K. W., *Ascot Heath, near Staines.*—P. C. of Ascot Heath, Dio. Ox. 1866. (Patron, Bp of Ox; P. C.'s Inc. 100*l*; Pop. 800.) [28]

PEARSE, George, *Martham Vicarage, Yarmouth, Norfolk.*—Caius Coll. Cam. B.A. 1820, M.A. 1831; Deac. 1821 and Pr 1822 by Bp of Nor. V. of Martham, Dio. Nor. 1834. (Patrons, D. and C. of Nor; Tithe—App. 628*l* 18*s* 2*d*, and 46 acres of Glebe, V. 363*l* 17*s* 9*d*; Glebe, 9 acres; V.'s Inc. 383*l* and Ho; Pop. 1092.) [29]

PEARSE, George Wingate, *Walton Rectory, Fenny-Stratford, Bucks.*—Corpus Coll. Ox. 3rd cl. Lit. Hum. and B.A. 1845, M.A. 1848; Deac. 1848 and Pr. 1849 by Bp of Ox. R. of Walton, Dio. Ox. 1851 (Patrons, Rev. V. Ellis and the Ld Chan; Tithe, 208*l* 5*s* 6*d*; Glebe, 47 acres; R.'s Inc. 304*l* and Ho; Pop. 95.) Formerly Fell. of Corpus Coll. Ox. [30]

PEARSE, Henry, *St. John's Rectory, Bedford.*—Corpus Coll Cam. Wrang. and B.A. 1829, M.A. 1832; Deac. 1829, Pr. 1830. R. of St. John's, Bedford, Dio. Ely, 1835. (Patron, the Corporation; Glebe, 11 acres; R.'s Inc. 171*l* and Ho; Pop. 465.) Rural Dean. [31]

PEARSE, Henry Thornton, *Litchfield Rectory, Hants.*—Ch. Ch. Ox. B.A. 1859, M.A. 1864; Deac. 1860 by Bp of Roch. R. of Litchfield, Dio. Win. 1865. (Patron, W. H. Kingsmill, Esq; Glebe, 1 acre; Tithe, 400*l*; R.'s Inc. 389*l* and Ho; Pop. 107.) Formerly C. of Ovington-cum-Tilbury 1860. [1]

PEARSE, John Gilberd, *Exeter.*—Cam. B.A. 1849; Deac. 1850, Pr. 1851. R. of Allhallows-on-the-Walls, Exeter, 1861. (Patrons, D. and C. of Ex; R.'s Inc. 100*l*; Pop. 1002.) Formerly C. of St. David's, Exeter, and Kenn, Devon. [2]

PEARSE, John Thomas, *Birkenhead.*—Trin. Coll. Cam. Bell's Univ Scho. 1849, Coll. Scho. 1851, 1st cl. Cl. Trip. and B.A. 1852, M.A. 1855; Deac. 1854 and Pr. 1857 by Bp of Salis. Head Mast. of the Proprietary S h. Birkenhead. Formerly Asst. Mast. of King's Sch. Sherborne, 1852–60. [3]

PEARSE, Robert Wilson, *Gaywood Rectory, Lynn, Norfolk.*—Brasen. Coll. Ox. B.A. 1849, M.A. 1852, and Wells; Deac 1851, Pr. 1852. R. of Gaywood, Dio. Nor. 1854. (Patron, R. Bagge, Esq; Tithe, 630*l*; Glebe, 18½ acres; R.'s Inc. 660*l* and Ho; Pop. 1368.) [4]

PEARSE, Samuel Winter, *Cadleigh, Ivybridge, Devon.*—Ex. Coll. Ox. B.A. 1803; Deac. 1806 and Pr. 1808 by Bp of Ex. P. C. of Shaugh with Sampford-Spiney, Devon, Dio. Ex. 1807. (Patrons, D. and C. of Windsor; Shaugh, Tithe—App. 295*l*; Sampford-Spiney, Tithe—App. 172*l* 10*s*; P. C.'s Inc. 150*l*; Pop. Shaugh 570, Sampford-Spiney 565.) [5]

PEARSE, Thomas, *Westoning Vicarage, Woburn, Beds.*—St. John's Coll. Cam. B.A. 1819, M.A. 1822; Deac. 1820 and Pr. 1821 by Bp of Lin. V. of Westoning, Dio. Ely, 1823. (Patron, Rev. J. W. C. Campion; Tithe - App. 355*l*, V. 260*l*; Glebe, 20 acres; V.'s Inc. 296*l* and Ho; Pop. 784.) [6]

PEARSE, Thomas, *Fittleton Rectory, Amesbury, Wilts.*—Magd. Coll. Ox. 3rd cl. Cl. B.A. 1839, B.D. 1850; Deac. 1840 and Pr. 1842 by Bp of Ox. R. of Fittleton, Dio. Salis. 1855. (Patron, Magd. Coll. Ox; Tithe—Imp. 64*l* 16*s*, R. 461*l* 7*s* 8*d*; Glebe, 32 acres; R.'s Inc. 525*l* and Ho; Pop. 393.) Dom. Chap. to Baroness North. Formerly C. of Wardington, Oxon, 1842–45, Sible Hedingham, Essex, 1847–51. [7]

PEARSE, Vincent, *Hanwell Rectory, Banbury.*—Lin. and Ex. Colls. Ox. 3rd cl. Cl. 1856, B.A. 1857, M.A. 1859; Deac. 1860 by Bp of Pet. Pr. 1861 by Bp of Wor. R. of Hanwell, Dio. Ox. 1861. (Patron, Earl De La Warr; Glebe, 27 acres; R.'s Inc. 320*l* and Ho; Pop. 305.) Formerly C. of Hartwell, Northants, and Barcheston, Warwickshire. [8]

PEARSON, Alleyne Ward, *Madras, India.*—Pemb. Coll. Cam. 1st cl. Moral Sci. Trip. Moral Philosophy Prizeman, and B.A. 1855; Deac. 1855 by Bp of Ox. Chap. at Arcot, Madras. Formerly Asst. C. of Sunningdale, Berks. [9]

PEARSON, Arthur, *Springfield Rectory, Chelmsford.*—Trin. Coll. Cam. B.A. 1827, M.A. 1830; Deac and Pr. 1827. R. of Springfield with Trinity C. Dio. Roch. 1827. (Patron, the present R; Tithe, 866*l*; Glebe, 55¾ acres; R.'s Inc. 1000*l* and Ho; Pop. 2566.) Surrogate. [10]

PEARSON, Arthur Cyril, *Wookey, near Wells, Somerset.*—Ball. Coll. Ox. B.A; Deac. 1862 and Pr. 1863 by Bp of Man. C of Wookey. Formerly C. of Longsight, Manchester, 1862–63, Cranbrook 1864. [11]

PEARSON, Charles Buchanan, *Knebworth Rectory, Stevenage Herts.*—Oriel Coll. Ox. 2nd cl. Lit. Hum. and B.A. 1828, M.A. 1831; Deac. 1830, Pr 1831. R. of Knebworth, Dio. Roch. 1838. (Patron, Sir E. Bulwer Lytton, Bart; Tithe, 538*l*; Glebe, 70 acres; R.'s Inc. 590*l* and Ho; Pop. 250.) Preb. of Fordington in Salis. Cathl. 1832. Author, *Plain Sermons to a Country Congregation*, 1838; *Thoughts on the Management Clauses*, 1848; *Church Expansion*, 1853. [12]

PEARSON, Charles Richardson Jervis, *The Vicarage, Bishop Stortford, Herts.*—King's Coll. Lond. 1st cl. Assoc. 1860; Deac. 1860 and Pr. 1861 by Bp of Lon. C. of Bishop Stortford 1867. Formerly C. of Bromley St. Leonard, Middlesex, 1861–62, Emman. Ch. Forest Gate, 1863–67. [13]

PEARSON, Christopher Ridley, *Tunbridge Wells.*—Queens' Coll. Cam. B.A. 1849, M.A. 1852; Deac. 1849 by Abp of Cant. Pr. 1850 by Bp of Win. P. C. of St. James's, Tunbridge Wells, Dio. Cant. 1862. (Patron, P. C. of Trinity; P. C.'s Inc. from pew-rents; Pop. 3500.) Formerly C. of Walmer 1849–50, Tunbridge Wells 1850–53; P. C. of Mark, Somerset, 1853–60; V. of Standon, Herts, 1860–62. [14]

PEARSON, Edward, 8, *Blossom-street, York.*—Wor. Coll. Ox. B.A. 1852, M.A. 1855; Deac. 1852 by Bp of Nor. Pr. 1853 by Bp of Ely. C. of All Saints', York, 1866. Formerly C. of St. Nicholas', Great Yarmouth, 1852, Barrow, Suffolk, 1854, St. Martin's, Liverpool, 1855, Alverstoke with Anglesey, Hants, 1856, St. Paul's, Birmingham, 1857, Ch. Ch. Westminster, 1858, St. Peter's with Normanton, Derby, 1859. [15]

PEARSON, Frederick, *Sutton, near Potton, St. Neots.*—Trin. Hall, Cam. B.A. 1855, M.A. 1858; Deac. 1856 and Pr. 1857 by Bp of Ely. C. of Sutton, Beds, 1856. [16]

PEARSON, Frederick Thorpe, *St. George's, Whitwick, Ashby de-la-Zouch.*—Queen's Coll. Ox. B.A. 1844, M.A. 1847. P. C. of St. George's, Whitwick, Dio. Pet. (Patron, V. of Whitwick; P. C.'s Inc. 140*l* and Ho; Pop. 2000.) Formerly Min. of St. Peter's Chapel, Pimlico, Lond. 1852–58, Dawlish 1858–60, Loughborough, 1860. [17]

PEARSON, George, *Combe Vicarage, near Hungerford.*—New Inn Hall, Ox. B.A. 1851, M.A. 1855; Deac. 1852 and Pr. 1854 by Bp of Ox. V. of Combe, Dio. Win. 1856. (Patrons, D. and C. of Windsor; Tithe—App. 249*l* 1*s* 1*d*, V. 120*l* 18*s* 5*d*; V.'s Inc. 140*l* and Ho; Pop. 225.) Author, *Questions and Answers on Aldrich's Logic*, 2 eds. 1850. [18]

PEARSON, George Charles, *Hopebourne House, near Canterbury*, and *Oxford and Cambridge Club, Pall-mall, London, S.W.*—Ch. Ch. Ox. 2nd cl. Lit. Hum. and B.A. 1836, M.A. 1838; Deac. 1839 and Pr. 1840 by Abp of Cant. C. of Challock, Canterbury. Formerly P. C. of St. Gregory the Great, Canterbury, 1852. [19]

PEARSON, George Frederick, *Chichester.*—Wor. Coll. Ox. B.A. 1847, M.A. 1858; Deac. 1848 and Pr. 1849 by Bp of Win. Min. Can. of Chich. 1862. Formerly Vicar-Choral of York Minster 1857; P. C. of Pollington-cum-Balne, Yorks, 1852. [20]

PEARSON, Henry, *Henley Vicarage, Ipswich.*—St. Cath. Hall, Cam. Wrang. and B.A. 1841, M.A. 1844; Deac. 1841, Pr. 1843. V. of Henley, Dio. Nor. 1850. (Patrons, D. and C. of Nor; Tithe—App. 240*l* and 49½ acres of Glebe, V. 116*l*; Glebe, 16 acres; V.'s Inc. 148*l* and Ho; Pop. 293.) Formerly C. of Atlow, Derbyshire. [21]

PEARSON, Henry, *Derby.*—C. of All Saints', Derby. [22]

PEARSON, Henry Daniel, *Richmond, Surrey.*—Wor. Coll. Ox. B.A. 1844, M.A. 1848; Deac. 1845 by Abp of Cant Pr. 1847 by Bp of Win. C. of Richmond. Formerly C. of Croydon, Hambledon, Sydenham, and Curzon Chapel, Surbiton. Author, *Poems by an Undergraduate*; *Tales of Christian Joy and Sorrow*; etc. [23]

PEARSON, Henry Hollingworth, *Norton Vicarage, near Sheffield.*—Lin. Coll. Ox. B.A. 1830, M.A. 1833; Deac. 1836, Pr. 1837. V. of Norton, Dio. Lich. 1844. (Patron, Henry Wilson, Esq; Tithe—Imp. 14*l* 8*s*, V. 22*l*; Glebe, 136 acres; V.'s Inc. 286*l* and Ho; Pop. 2500.) [24]

PEARSON, Henry Richard Storr, *Lythe Vicarage, Whitby, Yorks.*—Dur. B.A. 1851, M.A. 1854, Licen. Theol; Deac. 1851 and Pr. 1852 by Abp of York. V. of Lythe-cum-Ugthorpe, Dio. York, 1858. (Patron, Abp of York; Tithe—Imp. 421*l* and 556 acres of Land; Glebe, 2 acres; V.'s Inc. 300*l* and Ho; Pop. 2108.) Formerly C. of Hotham, Yorks, 1853–57. [25]

PEARSON, Henry Spencer, *Yeaveley Parsonage, Ashbourne, Derbyshire.*—Dub. A.B. 1846; Deac. 1846, Pr. 1847. P. C. of Yeaveley, Dio. Lich. 1851. (Patron, V. of Shirley; Tithe—App. 45*l*; Glebe, 2½ acres; P. C.'s Inc. 90*l* and Ho; Pop. 295.) [26]

PEARSON, Hugh, *Sonning Vicarage, Reading.* —Ball. Coll. Ox. B.A. 1839, M.A 1841; Deac. and Pr. 1841. V. of Sonning, Dio. Ox. 1841. (Patron, Bp of Ox; Tithe—Imp. 1052*l* 5*s*, V. 514*l*; Glebe, 3 acres; V.'s Inc. 514*l* and Ho; Pop. 1825.) Rural Dean of Henley-on-Thames 1864. [1]

PEARSON, Hugh, *Mickleover, near Derby.*—Caius Coll. Cam. B A. 1865; Deac. 1866 and Pr. 1867 by Bp of Lich. C. in sole charge of Mickleover. Formerly Asst. C. of All Saints', Derby, 1866–67. [2]

PEARSON, James, *St. John's Parsonage, Workington, Cumberland.*—Trin. Coll. Cam. Scho. of, 15th Wrang. Fell. of the Cam. Phil. Soc. B.A. 1848, M.A. 1852; Deac. 1851 and Pr. 1852 by Bp of Ches. P. C. of St. John's, Workington, Dio. Carl. 1862. (Patron, R. of Workington; Glebe, ½ acre; P. C.'s Inc. 160*l* and Ho; Pop. 3400.) Formerly C. of Scarisbrook 1851; Prof. of Math. Sandhurst, 1857; P. C. of Altcar 1856; R. of St. Edmund's and Math. Mast. of the Cathl. Sch. Norwich, 1852. Author, *A Treatise on the Calculus of Finite Differences*; Sermons; etc. [3]

PEARSON, James Hugh, *Heydour, Sleaford.*—Magd. Hall, Ox. B.A. 1863, M.A. 1866; Deac. 1864 and Pr. 1866 by Bp of Lin. C. of Heydour 1864. [4]

PEARSON, John, *Suckley Rectory, near Worcester.*—R. of Suckley with Alfrick C. and Lulsley C. Dio. Wor. 1838. (Patron, the Crown; Suckley, Tithe—Imp. 41*l* 8*s* 6*d*, R. 340*l*; Glebe, 3 acres; Alfrick, Tithe, 240*l*; Glebe, 2½ acres; Lulsley, Tithe, Imp. 9*l* 16*s*, R. 152*l*; Glebe, 3½ acres; R.'s Inc. 749*l* and Ho; Pop. Suckley 584, Alfrick 474, Lulsley 149.) Rural Dean; Hon. Can. of Worcester. [5]

PEARSON, John, *Herongate, Brentwood.*—Trin. Coll. Cam. B.A. 1827, M.A. 1830; Deac. 1829 and Pr. 1830 by Bp of Chich. R. of East Horndon, Dio. Roch. 1831. (Patron, the present R; Tithe, 344*l*; Glebe, 36 acres; R.'s Inc. 350*l*; Pop. 475.) R. of Little Warley, Essex, Dio. Roch. 1837. (Patron, the present R; Tithe, 287*l* 10*s*; Glebe, 32 acres; R.'s Inc. 322*l* and Ho; Pop. 485.) Rural Dean of Billericay 1845. [6]

PEARSON, John Batteridge, *Emmanuel College, Cambridge.*—St. John's Coll. Cam. B.A. 1855, M.A. 1858; Deac. 1856 and Pr. 1857 by Bp of Ely. C. of St. Andrew's, Cambridge, 1867; Fell. of Emman. Coll. Cam. [7]

PEARSON, John Garencieres, *The Vicarage, Darlington.*—Univ. Coll. Dur. Licen. Theol. 1840; Deac. 1840 and Pr. 1841 by Bp of Dur. P. C. of St. Cuthbert's, Darlington, Dio. Dur. 1860. (Patron, Duke of Cleveland; P. C.'s Inc. 230*l*; Pop. 6196.) Formerly C. of St. Ann's, Newcastle, 1840, Wingate Grange 1841, Tyne mouth 1842, Little Staughton, Beds, 1843; P. C. of St. Paul's, Newcastle, 1846; Chap. to the Legation and British Residents, Lima, 1849; C. of St. Cuthbert's, Darlington 1856. [8]

PEARSON, Josiah Brown, *St. John's College Cambridge.*—St. John's Coll. Cam. Fell. of, 1st cl. Moral Sci. Trip. Burney Prize 1864, B.A. 1864, M.A. 1867; Deac. 1865 and Pr. 1866 by Bp of Ely. Formerly C. of St. Michael's, Cambridge, 1865–67. Author, *The Divine Personality*; *The Burney Prize Essay for* 1864, 1*s* 6*d*, Bell and Daldy. [9]

PEARSON, Robert Keath, *Edstone Vicarage, Kirkby-Moorside, Yorks.*—Deac. 1828, Pr. 1829. V. of Great Edstone, Dio. York, 1843. (Patron, G. W. Dowker. Esq; Tithe, 31*l* 10*s*; Glebe, 105 acres; V.'s Inc. 180*l* and Ho; Pop. 152.) [10]

PEARSON, Samuel, *Brown Edge, Burslem, Staffs.*—St. Bees 1841; Deac. 1843 and Pr. 1844 by Bp of Nor. P. C. of Brown Edge, Dio. Lich. 1853. (Patron, Bp of Lich; P. C.'s Inc. 150*l*; Pop. 670.) [11]

PEARSON, Thomas, *East Lavington, Wilts.* —V. of East Lavington, Dio. Salis. 1860. (Patron, Ch. Ch. Ox; V.'s Inc. 300*l* and Ho; Pop. 1583.) [12]

PEARSON, Thomas Layton, *St. Cross Parsonage, Knutsford.*—Lond. Univ. B.A. 1864; Deac. 1865 and Pr. 1866 by Bp of Ches. C. of St. Cross, Knutsford, 1865. [13]

PEARSON, Thomas Rhodes Walton, 8, *Providence-row, Queen's-square, Leeds.*—St. Cath. Coll. Cam. previously of Ch. Coll. B.A. 1859; Deac. 1864 by Bp of Rip. C. of St. Peter's, Leeds, 1866. Chaplain of the Leeds Infirmary 1866; Sunday Even. Lect. of St. Simon's, Leeds, 1867; Sec. of the Yorkshire Ch. of England Scripture Readers' Soc. 1867; Memb. of the Leeds Ch. Institute, and Phil. and Lit. Soc. Formerly C. of St. Matthew's, Leeds, 1864. [14]

PEARSON, William, *New Hutton, Kendal, Westmoreland.*—P. C. of New Hutton, Dio. Carl. 1862. (Patron, V. of Kendal; Glebe, 85 acres; P. C.'s Inc. 87*l*; Pop. 316.) [15]

PEARSON, William, *North Rode, Congleton, Cheshire.*—Univ. Coll. Ox. 3rd cl. Lit. Hum. B.A. 1832, M.A. 1833; Deac 1834 and Pr. 1835 by Bp of Lich. P. C. of North Rhode, Dio. Ches. 1863. (Patron, Rev. J. Daintry; Tithe, 150*l*; Glebe, 3 acres; P. C.'s Inc. 155*l* and Ho; Pop. 288.) Formerly C. of Norton, Derbyshire, 1834, Prestbury, Cheshire, 1844. [16]

PEARSON, William Henley.—Ch. Ch. Ox. 2nd cl. Lit. Hum. and B.A. 1835, M.A. 1838; Deac. 1836 and Pr. 1837. Preb. of Swallowcliffe in Heytesbury Coll. Ch. 1838; Dom. Chap. to Viscount St. Vincent. Formerly R. of St. Nicholas', Guildford, 1837. Author, *Visitation Sermon* (at Guildford), 1852. [17]

PEART, Thomas W., *Rose Cottage, Douglas, Isle of Man.*—St. Aidan's, Deac. 1864. C. of St. George's, Douglas. Formerly C. of Hindley, Wigan. [18]

PEART, William Fiddian, *Breck Triangle, Halifax.*—St. Cath. Coll. Cam. 1st Sen. Opt. B.A. 1845, M.A 1851; Deac. 1845 and Pr. 1846 by Bp of Wor. C. of Sowerby 1861. Formerly C. of Rowley Regis 1845, St. James's, Bath, 1855, Shepton Mallett 1860. [19]

PEASE, George, *Darrington Vicarage, near Pontefract.*—St. John's Coll. Cam. B.A. 1819, M.A. 1823; Deac. 1822 and Pr. 1823 by Abp of York. V. of Darrington, Dio. York, 1831. (Patron, Abp of York; Tithe, 262*l*; Glebe, 210 acres; V.'s Inc. 512*l* and Ho; Pop. 744.) Formerly C. of Seighford, Staffs, 1823–25; Tachbrook, Warwickshire, 1825–31. [20]

PEASE, George Clifford, *Routh Rectory, Beverley.*—Magd. Coll. Cam. B.A. 1845, M.A. 1849; Deac. 1845 and Pr. 1847 by Bp of Pet. R. of Routh, Dio. York, 1865. (Patron, Lord Londesborough; Tithe, 516*l*; Glebe, 3 acres; R.'s Inc. 525*l* and Ho; Pop. 180.) Formerly V. of Paul with Thorngumbald, Yorks, 1856. [21]

PEAT, Abraham, *Thorley Vicarage, Yarmouth, Isle of Wight.*—V. of Thorley, Dio. Win. 1864. (Patron, C. R. Colvile, Esq; V.'s Inc. 100*l* and Ho; Pop. 143.) [22]

PEAT, John, *Vicarage, East Grinstead, Sussex.*—St. Peter's Coll. Cam. Coll. Prizeman 1831 and 1832, Sen. Opt. and B.A. 1833, M.A. 1836. M.A. *ad eund.* Ox; Deac. 1835 by Bp of Lin. Pr. 1836 by Abp of Cant. V. of East Grinstead, Dio. Chich. 1863. (Patroness, the Dowager Countess Amherst; Tithe—Imp. 1300*l*, V. 500*l*; Glebe, 3 acres; V.'s Inc. 500*l* and Ho; Pop. 2855.) Surrogate. Formerly C. of Sevenoaks 1850–54; P. C. of Weald Chapel, Sevenoaks, 1854–60; R. of Hangleton, near Brighton, 1860–64. Author, *Discourses on the Afflictive Dispensations of Providence*, 1840, 2*s*; *Poems*, 1840, 1*s*; *Songs of the Moral Sympathies*, 1840, 1*s*; *A Translation of the Sapphic Odes of Horace*, 1845, 3*s* 6*d*; *Thoughts on a Plurality of Worlds, a Poem*, 1856, 1*s*; *The Fair Evanthe, a Poem*, 1858, 3*s* 6*d*; etc. [23]

PECHELL, Horace Robert, *Bix Rectory, Henley-on-Thames, Oxon.*—Ch. Ch. Ox. B.A. 1813, M.A. 1814; Deac. 1817 and Pr. 1818 by Bp of Ox. R. of Bix, Dio. Ox. 1822. (Patron, Earl of Macclesfield; Tithe, 625*l* 2*s* 6*d*; Glebe, 45 acres; R.'s Inc. 659*l* and Ho; Pop. 342.) Chan. and Can. of Llanbister in the Collegiate Ch. of Brecon, 1829. (Value, 60*l*.) Formerly Fell. of All Souls' Coll. Ox. [24]

PECK, Edward Ansley, *Houghton Rectory, Hunts.*—Trin. Coll. Cam. B.A. 1838, M.A. 1841; Deac. 1840 and Pr. 1841 by Bp of Ely. R. of Houghton, Dio. Ely, 1846. (Patron, Duke of Manchester; R.'s Inc. 300*l* and Ho; Pop. 484.) [25]

PECKOVER, Edmund George, *Christ's Hospital*, and 13, *King Edward-street, London, E.C.*—St. John's Coll. Cam. Scho. of, Cl. Hon. 1st in 3rd cl. Cl. Trip. B.A. 1859, M.A. 1862; Deac. 1863 and Pr. 1864 by Bp of Lon. Cl. Mast. in Ch. Hospital, Lond. Formerly C. of Ch. Ch. Lee, 1863-65. [1]

PECKSTON, Thomas, 11, *Newmarket-terrace, Cambridge-heath, London, N.E.*—Trin. Coll. Cam. B.A. 1841, M.A. 1845; Deac. 1845 and Pr. 1846 by Bp of Lin. Chap. of the Bethnal-green Workhouse 1865; Hon. Clerical Sec. of Queen Adelaide's Dispensary for the Sick Poor of Bethnal Green 1849. Formerly Asst. Min. of St, Peter's, Bethual Green; Math. Mast. of the Coll. Gr. Sch. Southwell, Notts, 1845–46; Head Mast. of Beverley Gr. Sch. Berks, 1842–45. [2]

PEDDER, Edward, *Lancaster.*—Brasen. Coll. Ox. B.A. 1842, M.A. 1845; Deac. 1843 and Pr. 1844 by Bp of Ches. P. C. of St. John's, Lancaster, Dio. Man, 1862. (Patron, V. of Lancaster; Glebe, 50 acres; P. C.'s Inc, 203*l* and Ho; Pop. 1885.) Formerly C. of Lancaster. [3]

PEDDER, John, *Meldon Rectory, Newcastle-on-Tyne.*—Dur. 1st cl Math. et Phy; Bp Maltby's Math. Prize 1843 and 1845, B A. 1845, M A. 1848; Deac. 1847 and Pr. 1848 by Bp of Dur. R. of Meldon, Dio. Dur. 1859. (Patrons, D and C. of Dur; Tithe, 230*l*; R.'s Inc. 288*l* and Ho; Pop. 144.) Formerly Prin. of Bp Hat. Hall, Durham, and Fell. and Tutor of Dur. Univ. [4]

PEDDER, William Newland, *Clevedon, Somerset.*—Wor. Coll. Ox. B.A. 1818, M.A. 1821; Deac. 1819, Pr. 1820. V. of Clevedon, Dio. B. and W. 1830. Patron, Bp of Wor, Tithe—App. 120*l*, V. 500*l*; Glebe, 10 acres; V.'s Inc. 515*l* and Ho; Pop. 2995.) [5]

PEDDER, Wilson, *St. Helen Vicarage, Church-town, Gorstang, Lancashire.*—Brasen. Coll. Ox. B.A. 1840, M.A. 1842; Deac. 1841 by Bp. of B. and W. Pr. 1842 by Bp of Ely. V. of Church-town, Dio. Man. 1859 (Patrons, R. Pedder and T. Pedder, Esqs; V.'s Inc. 400*l* and Ho; Pop. 4251.) Surrogate, Formerly V. of Compton-Dando 1847; P. C. of Horrington; Even. Lect. of St. Cuthbert's, Wells; Vice-Prin. of Wells for 5 years. Author, *The Work of the Church*, 6*d*; *The Position of our Church as to Rome*, 3*d*. [6]

PEEL, Charles Steers, *Rousham Rectory, Port-town, Oxford.*—Wor. Coll. Ox. B.A. 1843, M.A. 1847; Deac. 1845 and Pr. 1846 by Bp of Lich. R. of Rousham, Dio. Ox. 1859. (Patron, C. C. Dormer, Esq; R.'s Inc. 260*l* and Ho; Pop. 131.) Formerly R. of Syresham, Northants, 1850-59. [7]

PEEL, Edmund, *Baldon-Toot, Oxford.*—Brasen. Coll. Ox. M.A; Deac. 1848 and Pr. 1849 by Bp of B. and W. V. of Baldon-Toot, Dio. Ox. 1861. (Patron, Bp of Ox; V.'s Inc. 20*l* and Ho; Pop. 240.) [8]

PEEL, Francis William, *Burghwallis Rectory, Doncaster.*—Wor. Coll. Ox. B.A, 1845, M A. 1847; Deac. 1850 and Pr. 1851 by Bp of Ox. R. of Burghwallis, Dio. York, 1856. (Patron, William Peel, Esq; R.'s Inc. 275*l* and Ho; Pop. 197.) Formerly C. of White Waltham, and Shottesbrook, Berks, 1850–56. [9]

PEEL, Frederick, *Cowleigh, West Malvern, Worc.*—C. of Cowleigh. [10]

PEEL, Herbert A., *Handsworth, Birmingham.*—R. of Handsworth, Dio. Lich. 1860. (Patron, Rev. Dr. Peel; Tithe, 1300*l*; Glebe, 85 acres; R.'s Inc. 1502*l* and Ho; Pop. 3524.) [11]

PEEL, The Very Rev. John, *The Deanery, Worcester*—Ch. Ch. Ox. B.A. 1822, M.A. 1826, B.D. and D.D. 1845; Deac. 1825, Pr. 1826. V. of Stone, Worc. Dio. Wor. 1828. (Patron, Ld Chan; Tithe, 718*l* 16*s*; Glebe, 94 acres; V.'s Inc. 865*l* and Ho; Pop. 475.) Dean of Worcester 1845. (Value, 1150*l* and Ho.) [12]

PEEL, Robert, *Hampton, Middlesex, S.W.*—Univ. Coll. Ox. B.A. 1814, M.A. 1817. C. of Hampton, Middlesex. Formerly Head Mast. of the Hampton Gr. Sch. [13]

PEERS, John Witherington, *Tetsworth, Oxon.*—St. Cath. Coll. Cam. B.A. 1832, M.A. 1836; Deac. 1832 and Pr. 1833 by Bp of Chich. V. of Tetsworth, Dio. Ox. 1841. (Patrons, Trustees; Tithe—App. 215*l* 8*s*, V. 115*l*; Glebe, 1½ acres; V.'s Inc. 135*l* and Ho; Pop. 481.) [14]

PEERS, William Henry, *Westerham, Edenbridge, Kent.*—St. Cath. Coll. Cam. Jun. Opt. B.A. 1864, M.A. 1867; Deac. 1864 and Pr. 1865 by Bp of G. and B. C. of Westerham 1867. Formerly C. of Trinity, Tewkesbury, and St. John's, Tredington, 1864–67. [15]

PEETE, William Willox.—Wad. Coll. Ox. B.A. 1819, M.A. 1824; Deac. 1822 by Abp of Cant. Pr. 1823 by Bp of Lon. [16]

PEGLAR, John James, *Stow Vicarage, Salop.*—Emman. Coll. Cam. B.A. 1856, M.A. 1860; Deac. 1859 and Pr. 1860 by Bp of Herf. C. of Stow 1867. Formerly C. of Aymestrey, Herf. 1859-66. [17]

PEILE, Arthur Lewis Babington, *Ventnor, Isle of Wight.*—Jesus Coll. Cam. B.A. 1852; Deac. 1853 and Pr. 1854 by Bp of Roch. P. C. of Holy Trinity, Ventnor, Dio. Win. 1862. (Patronesses, Misses Percy and Mrs. Thompson; P. C.'s Inc. 100*l*; Pop. 1500.) Surrogate. Formerly C. of Bishop's Hatfield, Herts, and Wimbledon, 1859. [18]

PEILE, Thomas Williamson, 37, *St. John's Wood Park, London, N.W.*—Trin. Coll. Cam. 1st cl. Math. and Cl. Davies' Univ. Scho. Chan.'s Medallist, B.A. 1828, M.A. 1831, D.D. 1843; Deac. and Pr. 1830 by Bp of Ches. P. C. of St. Paul's, Avenue-road, Dio. Lon. 1860. (Patron, P. C. of Hampstead; P. C.'s Inc. 600*l* from pew-rents; Pop. 2500.) Formerly Head Mast. of Repton Sch. 1841–54; V. of Luton, Beds, 1857–60. Author, *Annotations on the Epistles*, 4 vols. 2nd ed. 1853, 42*s*; *Miracle of Healing Power*, 1862, 5*s*; *Sermons, Doctrinal and Didactic, bearing on the Religious Topics of the Day*, 6*s*. [19]

PEILL, John Newton, *Newton Tony Rectory, Marlborough, Wilts.*—Queens' Coll. Cam. 7th Wrang. and B.A. 1831, M.A. 1834, B.D. 1841; Deac. 1833, Pr. 1834. R. of Newton Tony, Dio. Salis. 1853. (Patron, Queens' Coll. Cam; Tithe, 441*l*; Glebe, 43 acres; R.'s Inc. 600*l* and Ho; Pop. 351.) Fell. of the Royal Astronomical Soc. Formerly Fell. Tut. and Bursar of Queens' Coll. Cam. [20]

PELL, Beauchamp Henry St. John, *Ickenham Rectory, Uxbridge, Middlesex.*—Trin. Coll. Cam. B.A. 1847, M.A. 1851; Deac. 1848 and Pr. 1849 by Bp of Lin. R. of Ickenham, Dio. Lon. 1859. (Patron, T. T. Clarke, Esq; Tithe, 40*l* 2*s* 7*d*; Glebe, 13 acres; R.'s Inc. 380*l* and Ho; Pop. 351.) Formerly C. of Iden, Sussex, and Ashwell, Herts. [21]

PELLEW, George Israel, *East Tuddenham, Norwich.*—C. of East Tuddenham. Formerly P. C. of St. Mark's, Lakenham, 1858, C. of St. Nicholas', Great Yarmouth. [22]

PELLY, R. P., *Raymond Percy, Wanstead, Essex.*—Trin. Coll. Cam. B.A. 1863, M.A. 1867; Deac. 1864 by Bp of Win. Pr. 1865 by Bp of Lon. C. of Wanstead 1865. Formerly C. of Mitcham, Surrey, 1864–65. [23]

PEMBER, Frederick, *Folkingham, Lincolnshire.*—Ch. Ch. Ox. B.A. 1859; Deac. 1860 and Pr. 1861 by Bp of Ox. C. of Folkingham 1867. Formerly C. of Amersham. [24]

PEMBERTON, Arthur Gore, *Kensal-green Parsonage, Harrow-road, London, W.*—Dub. Hons. 1832; Deac. 1833 and Pr. 1834 by Bp of Lin. P. C. of St. John's, Kensal-green, Dio. Lon. 1844. (Patron, Bp of Lon; Glebe, 2 acres; P. C.'s Inc. 253*l* and Ho; Pop. 5794.) Chap. of the Kensal-green Cemetery, Middlesex. Author, *Exhortation to Parents, Children, and Teachers, with Prayers for Use of Sunday and Daily Schools*; *Introduction to Acts of the Apostles*. Editor of *Sermons by Modern Divines, with Introductory Essay*; *Essay on Ritualism*. [25]

PEMBERTON, Charles Leigh, *Curry-Mallett Rectory, Taunton.*—Trin. Coll. Cam, B.A. 1850, M.A. 1853; Deac. 1851, Pr. 1852. R. of Curry Mallett with Curland C. Dio. B. and W, 1853. (Patron, the Duchy of Cornwall; Curry-Mallett, Tithe, 430*l*; Glebe, 45 acres; Curland, Tithe, 85*l*; Glebe, 10 acres; R.'s Inc. 570*l* and Ho; Pop. Curry-Mallett 549, Curland 247.) [26]

PEMBERTON, Edward.—Jesus Coll. Ox. B.A. 1851, M.A. 1854; Deac. 1853 and Pr. 1854 by Bp of Ely. Chap. of H.M.S. "Bristol." Formerly C. of St. Gregory and St. Peter's, Sudbury. [1]

PEMBERTON, Stanley, *Little Hallingbury Rectory, Bishop Stortford.*—Ch. Ch. Ox. B.A. 1833; Deac. 1835, Pr. 1837. R. of Little Hallingbury, Dio. Roch. 1849. (Patron, Charterhouse, Lond; Tithe, 474*l*; Glebe, 28 acres; R.'s Inc. 520*l* and Ho; Pop. 514.) [2]

PENDERED, William Leeman, *Haydon Bridge, Carlisle.*—St. John's Coll. Cam. Sen. Opt. 2nd cl. Cl. Trip. and B.A. 1846, M.A. 1849; Deac. 1852 and Pr. 1853 by Bp of Roch. C. of St. Paul's, Alnwick; Head Mast. of Gr. Sch. Haydon Bridge 1865. Formerly C. of Wootton-Rivers 1858; 2nd Mast. of Brentwood Sch. Essex; Asst. Mast. of Tunbridge Sch. 1846. [3]

PENFOLD, William, *Ruardean (Glouc.), near Ross, Herefordshire.*—Lin. Coll. Ox. B.A. 1823, M.A. 1826. V. of Ruardean, Dio. G. and B. 1851. (Patron, Bp of G. and B; Tithe, 100*l*; V.'s Inc. 100*l*; Pop. 897.) Chap. to the Duke of Beaufort. [4]

PENGELLEY, Edward, *Glinton (Northants), near Market Deeping, Lincolnshire.*—Corpus Coll. Cam. Math. and Cl. Hons. and B.A. 1848, M.A. 1851; Deac. 1848 and Pr. 1849 by Bp of Pet. C. of Glinton 1850. Author, Sermons in "*The Pulpit*;" Contributions to *The Gentleman's Magazine*. [5]

PENGELLEY, William Henry, *Great Gonerby Rectory, Grantham.*—Corpus Coll. Cam. Scho. of, B.A. 1851, M.A. 1860; Deac. 1851 and Pr. 1852 by Bp of Pet. R. of Great Gonerby, Dio. Lin. 1866. (Patron, V. of Grantham; R.'s Inc. 300*l* and Ho; Pop. 1145.) Formerly C. of Ch. Ch. St. George's-in-the-East, Lond. 1856, Grantham 1858, Bourne 1859, Grantham 1862. [6]

PENGELLY, John Wotton, *St. Michael's Parsonage, Blackburn.*—St. Bees; Deac. 1844, Pr. 1845. P. C. of St. Michael's, Blackburn, Dio. Man. 1846. (Patron, V. of Blackburn; P. C.'s Inc. 300*l* and Ho; Pop. 6317.) Formerly C. of Haslingdon 1864. [7]

PENISTAN, Joseph.—St. John's Coll. Cam. B.A. 1845, M.A. 1848; Deac. 1846, Pr. 1847. Formerly Head Mast. of Guisborough Gr. Sch. 1846–50; Mast. of the Liverpool Literary Institution; C. of Fordham, Cambs. [8]

PENLEAZE, John, *Torrington Rectory, Highampton, Devon.*—Magd. Coll. Ox. B.A. 1830; Deac. 1832 and Pr. 1833 by Bp of Nor. R. of Black Torrington, Dio. Ex. 1834. (Patron, Lord Poltimore; Tithe, 450*l*; Glebe, 191 acres; R.'s Inc. 600*l* and Ho; Pop. 1020.) Formerly C. of All Saints', Hereford. [9]

PENLEY, Francis Thorpe.—Corpus Coll. Cam. B.A. 1856; Deac. 1856 and Pr. 1857 by Bp of G. and B. Formerly C. of Oddington, and St. Luke's, Gloucester. [10]

PENLEY, Lionel Banks, *Trimpley, Kidderminster.*—Corpus Coll. Cam. B.A. 1858; Deac. 1858 by Bp of Wor. P. C. of Trinity, Trimpley, 1866. Formerly C. of Stretton-on-Dunsmore. [11]

PENNEFATHER, William.—Dub. A.B. 1841; Deac. 1841 and Pr. 1842 by Bp of Ches. P. C. of St. Jude's, Mildmay Park, Islington, Dio. Lon. 1864. (Patron, P. C. of St. Paul's, Islington; P. C.'s Inc. 400*l* and Ho; Pop. 6620.) Formerly P. C. of Ch. Ch. Barnet, South Mimms, 1852–64. [12]

PENNEL, R. Lewin, *Hurstpierpoint, Sussex.*—Fell. of St. Nicholas' Coll. Lancing, and Asst. Mast. of St. John's Sch. Hurstpierpoint. [13]

PENNETHORNE, Gregory Walton, *The Close, Chichester.*—Jesus Coll. Cam. Scho. and 1st Math. Prizeman of, Sen. Opt. B.A. 1860, M.A. 1863; Deac. 1860 by Bp of Lin. Pr. 1861 by Bp of Chich. R. of St. Andrew's, Chichester, Dio. Chich. 1861. (Patrons, D. and C. of Chich; R.'s Inc. 75*l*; Pop. 613.) Vice-Prin. of the Theol. Coll. Chichester. Formerly C. of Beeston 1861. [14]

PENNEY, John William Watkin, *Stewartville House, Glasgow.*—Univ. Coll. Dur. Scho. of, B.A. 1859, M.A. 1862, B.C.L. 1864, D.C.L. 1866; Deac.

LL

1860 and Pr. 1861 by Bp of Carl. Incumb. of St. John's, Glasgow, 1865. (Patrons, Bp and Churchwardens; Incumb.'s Inc. 200*l*.) Formerly C. of Drigg, Cumb. 1860–62; Incumb. of Kilmarnock 1862–65. [15]

PENNINGTON, Arthur Robert, *Utterby Rectory, near Louth, Lincolnshire.*—Trin. Coll. Cam. 8th Jun. Opt. B.A. 1838, M.A. 1841; Deac. 1838 and Pr. 1839 by Bp of Win. R. of Utterby, Dio. Lin. 1854. (Patron, Rev. T. E. Norris; Glebe, 20 acres; R.'s Inc. 190*l* and Ho; Pop. 324.) Author, *A Farewell Sermon at Ryde*, 1855; *Carisbrook Castle, a Poem*, 1*s*; *Henri Arnaud, or the Glorious Return of the Waldenses of Piedmont to their Native Villages in* 1689–90, *a Poem*, 1864, 4*s* 6*d*. [16]

PENNINGTON, Gervase Rainey, *Stockingford Parsonage, Nuneaton.*—St. John's Coll. Cam. B.A. 1858, M.A. 1861; Deac. 1859 and Pr. 1860 by Bp of B. and W. P. C. of Stockingford, Dio. Worc. 1864. (Patron, V. of Nuneaton; Tithe, 100*l*; Glebe, 11½ acres; P. C.'s Inc. 120*l* and Ho; Pop. 1610.) Formerly C. of Widcombe, Bath, 1859–64. [17]

PENNINGTON, Lewis Theodore, *Mickleover, near Derby.*—St. Bees 1851; Deac. 1853 and Pr. 1854 by Bp of G. and B. Formerly Asst. Min. of St. John's, Moulsham, 1859; C. of Workington, Cumberland. Author, *An Address to the Working Classes*. [18]

PENNY, Benjamin, *Leamington.*—Brasen. Coll. Ox. B.C.L. and D.C.L. 1834; Deac. 1837, Pr. 1838. [19]

PENNY, Charles, *Grammar Schoolhouse, Crewkerne, Somerset.*—Pemb. Coll. Ox. 2nd cl. Lit. Hum. and B.A. 1831, M.A. 1833, B.D. and D.D. 1850; Deac. 1832 by Bp of B. and W. Pr. 1834 by Bp of Salis. Head Mast. of Crewkerne Gr. Sch. 1838; R. of Chaffcombe, Somerset, Dio. B. and W. 1848. (Patron, Earl Poulett; Tithe, 160*l*; Glebe, 28 acres; R.'s Inc. 195*l*; Pop. 246.) Dom. Chap. to Earl Poulett and Lord Raglan; Surrogate 1848. Formerly C. of Bicknoller 1832–34, Sutton-Courtney 1834–36, Dorchester 1836–37, West Ilsly, Berks, 1837–38. Author, *To follow Christ the Way of Safety* (Sermon preached before the Univ. of Ox.), privately printed, 1851. [20]

PENNY, Charles, *West Coker Rectory, near Yeovil, Somerset.*—Wor. Coll. Ox. B.A. 1840, M.A. 1842; Deac. 1840 and Pr. 1841 by Bp of B. and W. R. of West Coker, Dio. B. and W. 1846. (Patron, Rev. Charles Penny; Tithe, 430*l* 11*s*; Glebe, 18 acres; R.'s Inc. 500*l* and Ho; Pop. 1012.) [21]

PENNY, Charles William, *Wellington College, Wokingham, Berks.*—Corpus Coll. Ox. 1st cl. Math. 1860. B.A. 1861, M.A. 1863; Deac. 1862 and Pr. 1866 by Bp of Ox. Tut. and Asst. Mast. at Wellington College, 1861. [22]

PENNY, Edmund Henry, *Great Stambridge Rectory, Rochford, Essex.*—Brasen. Coll. Ox. B.A. 1818, M.A. 1821. R. of Great Stambridge, Dio. Roch. 1839. (Patron, Charterhouse, Lond; Tithe, 706*l*; Glebe, 20 acres; R.'s Inc. 736*l* and Ho; Pop. 363.) Formerly Reader and Asst. Mast. of the Charterhouse. [23]

PENNY, Edward, *Great Mongeham Rectory, Deal, Kent.*—St. John's Coll. Ox. 3rd cl. Lit. Hum. and B.A. 1831, M.A. 1835; Deac. 1832 and Pr. 1833 by Abp of Cant. R. of Great Mongeham, Dio. Cant. 1849. (Patron, Abp of Cant; Tithe, 499*l* 15*s*; Glebe, 1½ acres, with a Ho. and Buildings; R.'s Inc. 504*l* and Ho; Pop. 349.) One of the six preachers in Cant. Cathl. 1843; Hon. Can. of Canterbury, and Rural Dean of Sandwich, 1866. Author, *The Holiness of the Christian Priesthood* (Isaiah lii. 11; a Sermon preached in Cant. Cathl. at the Visitation of Abp of Cant. 1844); *The Sacrifice of Christ* (1 Cor. v. 7; a Sermon preached in Cant. Cathl. 1857); *The Least in the Kingdom of God* (Luke vii. 28; a Sermon preached in Cant. Cathl. 1861). [24]

PENNY, Edward Gorton, *Rangeworthy, Chipping Sodbury, Glouc.*—Ch. Coll. Cam. B.A. 1847, M.A. 1852; Deac. 1847, Pr. 1848. P. C. of Rangeworthy, Dio. G. and B. 1855. (Patron, V. of Thornbury; P. C.'s Inc. 150*l* and Ho; Pop. 250.) Formerly C. of Fulbeck, Linc. [25]

PENNY, Edward Lewton, *The Hospital, Bedworth, Warwickshire.*—Pemb. Coll. Ox. B.A. 1859,

M.A. 1861; Deac. 1859 and Pr. 1860 by Abp of York. C. of Bedworth 1864. Formerly C. of St. Jude's, Moorfields, Sheffield, 1859, Holy Trinity and Chap. of Charterhouse, Hull, 1862. [1]

PENNY, George Harry, *Abbotsbury Vicarage, Dorchester.*—St. Bees; Deac. 1849 and Pr. 1850 by Abp of York. V. of Abbotsbury, Dio. Salis. 1857. (Patron, Lord Ilchester; V.'s Inc. 150*l* and Ho; Pop. 1089.) Formerly C. of Abbotsbury, Rotherham 1849, Cauldon 1851, Heytesbury 1853. [2]

PENNY, James, *Blandford, Dorset.*—St. John's Coll. Cam. Wrang. and B.A. 1842, M.A. 1845. R. of Steepleton-Iwerne, Dorset, Dio. Salis. 1850. (Patron, Lord Rivers; Tithe, 95*l*; R.'s Inc. 95*l*; Pop. 59.) Head Mast. of the Milton-Abbas Sch. in Blandford 1848. [3]

PENNY, John, *Cuxwold Rectory, Caistor, Lincolnshire.*—Emman. Coll. Cam. B.A. 1816, M.A. 1827; Deac. 1816 by Bp of Ches. Pr. 1819 by Bp of Lin. R. of Cuxwold, Dio. Lin. 1858. (Patron, H. Thorold, Esq; Tithe, 314*l* 19*s* 8*d*; Glebe, 1½ acres; R.'s Inc. 317*l*; Pop. 83.) Formerly Chap. to Millbank Prison 1837–58. [4]

PENRHYN, Oswald Henry Leycester, *Bickerstaffe, Ormskirk.*—Ball. Coll. Ox. B.A 1849, M.A. 1852; Deac. 1852 and Pr. 1853 by Bp of G. and B. P. C. of Bickerstaffe, Dio. Ches. 1858. (Patron, Earl of Derby; P. C.'s Inc. 230*l* and Ho; Pop. 1800.) Formerly Asst. C. of Upton St. Leonard's 1852–56, Winwick, Lanc. 1856–58. [5]

PENRICE, Charles Berners, *Plumstead Parva, Norwich.*—Trin. Coll. Cam. Sen. Opt. B.A. 1850, M.A. 1853; Deac. 1851 and Pr. 1852 by Bp of Nor. R. of Little Plumstead, Dio. Nor. 1863. (Patron, John Penrice, Esq; Tithe, 468*l*; Glebe, 54 acres; R.'s Inc. 555*l* and Ho; Pop. 319.) Formerly C. of Witton and Brundall 1851; R. of Bracon Ash 1854; C. of Skeyton 1856; Travelling Sec. to Addit. Curates Soc. 1858–62. [6]

PENROSE, Charles Thomas, *North Hykeham, Lincoln.*—Trin. Coll. Cam. Bell's Scho. and 2nd in 1st cl. Cl. Trip. B.A. 1839, M.A. 1842; Deac. 1842 and Pr. 1856 by Bp of Lin. P. C. of North Hykeham, Dio. Lin. 1858. (Patron, Bp of Lin; P. C.'s Inc. 210*l* and Ho; Pop. 462.) Formerly Head Mast. of King Edward's Sch. Sherborne, 1845–50. Author, *Eight Village Sermons,* 1858, 2*s* 6*d*; *Private Orations of Demosthenes,* 5*s*. [7]

PENROSE, John, *Exmouth, Devon.*—Ball. Coll. Ox. 3rd cl. Lit. Hum. and B.A. 1836, Lin. Coll. M.A. 1839. Formerly Fell. of Lin. Coll. Ox. [8]

PENRUDDOCK, Isaac, *Lyminster, near Arundel.*—C. of Lyminster. Formerly C. of East Thorpe. [9]

PENRUDDOCKE, John Hungerford, *South Newton Vicarage, near Salisbury.*—Clare Hall, Cam. B.A. 1851, M.A. 1854; Deac. 1853 and Pr. 1854 by Bp of Wor. V. of South Newton, Dio. Salis. 1860. (Patron, Earl of Pembroke; Tithe, comm. 250*l*; V.'s Inc. 260*l* and Ho; Pop. 717.) Chap. of the Wilton Union. Formerly P. C. of Berwick-Bassett, Wilts, 1854–58; C. of Lapworth, Warwick, 1853–54, South Newton 1858. [10]

PENRUDDOCKE, Thomas, *Fyfield Manor House, Pewsey, Wilts.*—Clare Coll. Cam. B.A. 1857; Deac. 1859 and Pr. 1860 by Bp of St. Asaph. Formerly C. of Bettws-cum-Dolforwyn 1859–61, Collingbourne Ducis, Wilts, 1862–63, Tangley-cum-Faccombe, 1863–67. [11]

PENTREATH, Frederick Richard, *Market Rasen, Lincolnshire.*—Wor. Coll. Ox. 1st cl. Mods. 2nd cl. Lit. Hum. B.A. 1857, M.A. 1859; Deac. 1858 by Bp of Lin. Head Mast. of the De Aston Sch. Market Rasen. Formerly Head Master's Asst. at the Charterhouse, Lond. [12]

PEPPER, Thomas Staples, *Little Missenden Vicarage, Amersham, Bucks.*—St. Aidan's 1851; Deac. 1851 and Pr. 1852 by Bp of Ches. C. of Little Missenden 1855. [13]

PEPPIN, Stephen Francis Bedford, *Cathedral-green, Wells.*—St. Edm. Hall, Ox. B.A. 1854, M.A. 1856; Deac. 1855 and Pr. 1856 by Bp of B. and W. Min. Can. of Wells 1852; P. C. of Herrington, Dio. B. and W. 1865. (Patron, V. of Wells; P. C.'s Inc. 300*l*; Pop. 868.) Formerly C. of Kilmersdon, Somerset, and St. Thomas', East Wells. [14]

PEPPIN, Sydenham Henry, *Branscombe Vicarage, Sidmouth, Devon.*—Wad. Coll. Ox. B.A. 1811; Deac. 1811 and Pr. 1812 by Bp of Ex. V. of Branscombe, Dio. Ex. 1837. (Patrons, D. and C. of Ex; Tithe—App. 268*l*, V. 225*l*; Glebe, 8 acres; V.'s Inc. 250*l* and Ho; Pop. 936.) [15]

PEPYS, Herbert George, *Hallow Vicarage, near Worcester.*—Trin. Coll. Cam. Sen. Opt. B.A. 1852, M.A. 1855; Theol. Coll. Wells; Deac. 1853 by Bp of Ely, Pr. 1854 by Bp of Wor. V. of Grimley with Hallow, Dio. Wor. 1854. (Patron, Bp of Wor; Grimley, Tithe—App. 280*l*, V. 170*l*; Hallow, Tithe—App. 382*l* 2*s* 6*d*, V. 330*l*; Glebe, 26 acres; V.'s Inc. 625*l* and Ho; Pop. Grimley 776, Hallow 1507.) Formerly C. of Kidderminster 1853–54. [16]

PERCEVAL, Arthur, *Woolfardisworthy, Bideford.*—P. C. of Woolfardisworthy, Dio. Ex. 1865. (Patroness, Mrs. L. E. Hawkes; P. C.'s Inc. 65*l*; Pop. 776.) [17]

PERCEVAL, Henry, *Elmley-Lovett Rectory, Droitwich.*—Brasen. Coll. Ox. B.A. 1820, M.A. 1823; Deac. 1822, Pr. 1823. R. of Elmley-Lovett, Dio. Wor. 1837. (Patron, Ch. Coll. Cam; Tithe, 545*l*; Glebe, 30 acres; R.'s Inc. 605*l* and Ho; Pop. 353.) [18]

PERCIVAL, George, *Lane End, near Stoke-on-Trent.*—C. of Lane End. [19]

PERCIVAL, James Stanley, *Quinton Rectory, Northampton.*—Emman. Coll. Cam. B.A. 1855, M.A. 1858; Deac. 1856 and Pr. 1857 by Bp of Win. C. in charge of Quinton, Northants, 1866. Formerly C. of Effingham, Surrey, 1856–58, Bramdean, Hants, 1858–61; P. C. of Freefolk and C. of Laverstoke, Hants, 1861–66. [20]

PERCIVAL, John, M.A., *Clifton, Bristol.*—Head. Mast. of the Coll. Clifton. [21]

PERCIVAL, Thomas.—C. of Hetton-le-Hole, Durham. [22]

PERCY, Barnard Elliott, *Headborne-Worthy, Winchester.*—Lin. Coll. Ox. B.A. 1995; Deac. 1833 and Pr. 1834 by Bp of Lich. Formerly Min. of Cockerham, Lancashire. [23]

PERCY, Henry, *Residentiary Houses, Carlisle Cathedral.*—St. John's Coll. Cam. B.A. 1837, M.A. 1842. Can. Res. of Carl. Cathl. 1847. (Value, 1000*l* and Res.) R. of Graystoke, Penrith, Dio. Carl. 1853. (Patron, H. W. Askew, Esq; Tithe—App. 6*l* 13*s* 4*d*, Imp. 15*l* 1*s*, R. 418*l* 5*s* 1½*d*; R.'s Inc. 500*l*; Pop. 1307.) [24]

PERCY, Philip Henry, *Garford-street, Poplar, E.*—King's Coll. Lond; Deac. 1854 and Pr. 1855 by Abp of Cant. Miss. C. of Poplar, Lond. Formerly C. of West Hackney, East Retford, St. Leonard's, Deal, and Eastchurch, Kent. [25]

PERCY, William John.—St. John's Coll. Cam. B.A. 1839, M.A. 1842; Deac. 1839 and Pr. 1840 by Bp of B. and W. Patron of Silton, Dorset, and formerly R. 1851–59. Formerly Provincial Grand Chap. to the Freemasons for Dorset. Author, *Masonic Sermons,* 1844, 3*s*. [26]

PERCY, William John Edward, *Blandford, Dorset.*—St. John's Coll. Cam. B.A. 1864; Deac. 1866 by Bp of Salis. C. of Blandford 1866. [27]

PERFECT, Arthur P., *Brighton.*—C. and Lect. of St. Peter's, Brighton. [28]

PERFECT, Henry Theodore, *Chelwood Cottage, near Bristol.*—King's Coll. Lond. Theol. Assoc. 1st cl; Deac. 1854 and Pr. 1855 by Bp of B. and W. V. of Stanton Drew with Pensford C. Dio. B. and W. 1866. (Patron, Archd. of Bath; Tithe, 242*l*; Inc. 236*l*; Pop. Stanton Drew 523, Pensford 312.) Formerly Asst. C. of Ilminster, Somerset, 1854, Weare 1857. [29]

PERKINS, Benjamin Roberts, *Wotton-under-Edge Vicarage, Glouc.*—Lin. Coll. Ox. 2nd cl. Lit. Hum. B.A. 1824, Ch. Ch. Ox. B.C.L. 1831; Deac. 1824 by Bp of Lin. Pr. 1825 by Bp of Ox. Mast. of the Domus Scholarum and V. of Wootton-under-Edge, Dio. G. and B. 1828. (Patron, Ch. Ch. Ox; Tithe—App. 969*l* 12*s* 6*d*;

V.'s Por. 43*l* 6*s* 8*d* and Ho; Glebe, 20 acres; Pop. 3673.) Formerly Chap. of Ch. Ch. Ox. 1825–31. [1]

PERKINS, Charles Mathew, *Badminton Vicarage, Chippenham.*—Lin. Coll. Ox. B.A. 1859, M.A. 1862; Deac. 1860, Pr. 1861. C. of Badminton and Sopworth 1862. Formerly C. of Wootton-under-Edge 1860–62. [2]

PERKINS, George, *Grammar School, Manchester.*—Brasen. Coll. Ox. B.A. 1846, M.A. 1849; Deac. 1848 and Pr. 1850 by Bp of Man. Second Mast. of Manchester Gr. Sch. 1862. Formerly Mast. of Lower Sch. 1847, 2nd Mast.'s Asst. 1855, High Mast.'s Asst. 1857; C. of St. John's, Broughton, 1848. [3]

PERKINS, James Edward, 10, *Richmond-place, Bradford, Yorks.*—St. Aidan's; Deac. 1860, Pr. 1861. C. of St. Andrew's, Lister-hill, Bradford, 1862. Formerly C. of Holmfirth 1860–62. [4]

PERKINS, Thomas Norwood, *Oldham, Colchester.*—St. John's Coll. Cam. B.A. 1866; Deac. 1867 by Bp of Roch. C. of Oldham. [5]

PERKINS, William, *Twyford, near Buckingham.*—Lin. Coll. Ox. B.A. 1818, M.A. 1820; Deac. 1819 by Bp of Salis. Pr. 1820 by Bp of Ches. C. of Twyford. Formerly C. of Geddington, Oxon, 1820. [6]

PERKINS, William Henry, *The Parsonage, Child's Hill, Hendon, N.W.*—Deac. 1841 and Pr. 1842 by Bp of Calcutta. P. C. of Child's Hill, Dio. Lon. 1860. (Patrons, Trustees; Pop. 906.) Formerly C. of Ch. Ch. Hampstead; Missionary to the S.P.G. in India 1834–49. Author, Tracts in Hindustani. [7]

PEROWNE, Edward Henry, *Corpus Christi College, Cambridge.*—Corpus Coll. Cam. Porson Prizeman 1848, Members' Prizeman 1849–52, 14th Jun. Opt. Sen. Classic and B.A. 1850, M.A. 1853, B.D. 1860, *ad eund.* M.A. Ox. 1857; Deac. 1850 and Pr. 1851 by Bp of Nor. Fell. and Tut. of Corpus Coll; Preacher of H.M. Chapel Royal, Whitehall, 1864–66; Hulsean Lect. 1866. Formerly C. of St. John's, Maddermarket, Norwich, 1850–51. Author, *The Christian's Daily Life, a Life of Faith,* 1860; *Corporate Responsibility,* 1862; *Counsel to Undergraduates on entering the University,* 1863; *Ordination Sermon,* Whitehall Chapel, 1865; *Hulsean Lectures, The Godhead of Jesus,* 1866, Deighton, Bell, and Co. [8]

PEROWNE, John, *Norwich.*—R. of Carlton with Ashby R. Norfolk, Dio. Nor. 1863. (Patron, Sir W. B. Proctor, Bart. and Sir Charles Rich. Bart; Carlton Tithe, 170*l*; Glebe, 5 acres; Ashby, Tithe, 172*l*; Glebe, 28 acres; R.'s Inc. 350*l* and Ho; Pop. Carlton 79, Ashby 257.) Formerly R. of St. John's, Maddermarket, Norwich 1835. [9]

PEROWNE, John James Stewart, *St. David's College, Lampeter.*—Corpus Coll. Cam. Bell's Univ. Scho. 1842, Crosse Scho. and B.A. 1845, Members' Prizes (Latin Essay) 1844 '46 '47, Tyrrwhitt's Hebrew Scho. 1848, Examiner for Cl. Trip. 1851–52, Select Preacher 1858–61, M.A. 1848; Deac. 1847, Pr. 1848. Fell. of Corpus Coll. Cam; Vice-Prin. of St. David's Coll; Preb. of St. David's and Asst. Reader at Lincoln's Inn; Exam. Chap. to the Bp of Nor. Formerly Lect. in Divinity, King's Coll. Lond; Asst. Tut. of Corpus Coll. Cam. Author, *The Labour and Strength of the Christian Ministry* (a Sermon). Editor of *Rogers on the XXXIX. Articles*; *Al Adjrumiieh* (an Elementary Arabic Grammar); *The Book of Psalms, a New Translation, with Notes, Critical, and Exegetical,* 2 vols. Bell and Daldy; Articles on the Pentateuch, Zechariah, &c. in Dr. Smith's *Dictionary of the Bible*; *The Feast of Harvest* (a Sermon). [10]

PEROWNE, Thomas Thomason, *Stalbridge Rectory, Blandford, Dorset.*—Corpus Coll. Cam. Wrang. 1847, Tyrrwhitt's Heb. Scho. 1850, Norrisian Prizeman 1854, B.A. 1847, M.A. 1850, B.D. 1858; Deac. and Pr. 1848 by Bp of Ely. R. of Stalbridge, Dio. Salis. 1867. (Patron, Corpus Coll. Cam; Tithe, 1200*l*; Glebe, 53 acres; R.'s Inc. 1300*l* and Ho; Pop. 1920.) Formerly C. of St. Michael's, Cambridge, 1848–53. Fell. and Heb. and Div. Lect. of Corpus Coll. and Exam. Chap. to the Bp of Nor; C. in sole charge of The Holy Sepulchre, Cambridge, 1862. Author, *Essential Coherence of the Old and New Testaments,* 1858, 6*s*; *Memoir of the Rev. T. G. Ragland,* 1861, 6*s* 6*d*; occasional Sermons, and Articles in Smith's *Dictionary of the Bible.* [11]

PERRAM, George Jubb.—Caius Coll. Cam. 1840; Clare Coll. Cam. Wrang. and B.A. 1843, M.A. 1847; Deac. 1843, Pr. 1844, C. of St. Peter's, Walworth, Surrey. Formerly British Chap. at Düsseldorf; C. of Clymping, Sussex. [12]

PERRIN, Frederick Eugene, *Waddington (Yorks), Clitheroe, Lancashire.*—Dub. A.B. 1845. A.M. 1848; Deac. 1848 and Pr. 1850 by Bp of Man. C. in sole charge of Whitewell-in-Bowland 1852; Chap. of Waddington Hospital, 1855. [13]

PERRIN, George, *Wellington, Somerset.*—Dub. 3rd Sen. Mod. in Ethics and Logics, A.B. 1854; Deac. 1854 by Bp of Meath, Pr. 1855 by Bp of Ches. C. of Runnington, Somerset, 1860. Formerly C. of Howth, near Dublin, 1854, St. Jude's, Liverpool, 1856, Wickham-Skeith, Suffolk, 1858. [14]

PERRING, Alfred Reginald, *Embleton Parsonage, Cockermouth.*—St. Bees 1855; Deac. 1856 and Pr. 1857 by Bp of Carl. P. C. of Embleton, Dio. Carl. 1861. (Patron, Earl of Lonsdale; Tithe—Imp. 196*l*; P. C.'s Inc. 190*l* and Ho; Pop. 363.) P. C. of Lorton, Dio. Carl. 1864. (Patron, Earl of Lonsdale; P. C.'s Inc. 100*l*; Pop. 581.) C. of Mosser, Cockermouth. Formerly C. of Bury and Rusland, Lanc. [15]

PERRING, Charles, 19, *Devonshire-place, Marylebone, London, W.*—Pem. Coll. Cam. B.A. 1825, M.A. 1828. [16]

PERRING, Charles Augustus, *Upper Vicarage, Pattishall, Towcester.*—St. Bees; Deac. 1853, Pr. 1854. V. of Holy Cross, Pattishall, Northants, Dio. Pet. 1867. (Patron, Ld Chan; Tithe, 35*l*; Glebe, 110*l*; V.'s Inc. 145*l* and Ho; Pop. 800.) Surrogate. Formerly P. C. of St. John's, Keswick, 1854–55, St. Paul's, Leeds, of St. James's, Whitehaven. [17]

PERROTT, O. G. D., *Marlborough, Wilts.*—C. of St. Mary's, Marlborough. [18]

PERRY, Alfred John, *Bury St. Edmunds.*—Dub. A.B. 1853; Deac. 1853 and Pr. 1854 by Bp of Lon. Chap. of the Suffolk General Hospital (Salary, 60*l*) and Chap. of the Bury Incorporation (Salary, 40*l*). Formerly C. of Plaistow, Essex, 1853, Stanningfield, Suffolk, 1856, Lackford, Suffolk, 1860. Author, *The Christian's Choice,* 1856; *The Old Year and the New,* 1864; *A Few Words on the Real Presence,* Macintosh, 1866. [19]

PERRY, Edward, *Llangattock-Vivon-Avel, near Monmouth.*—Wor. Coll. Ox. B.A. 1826. V. of Llangattock-Vivon-Avel with Llanvanair P. C. and St. Maugham P. C. Dio. Llan. 1844. (Patron, J. E. W. Rolles, Esq; Llangattock-Vivon-Avel, Tithe, Imp. 176*l* 3*s* 4*d*, V. 209*l* 7*s* 7*d*; St. Maugham, Tithe, Imp. 50*l* 8*s* 4½*d*, V. 108*l*; V.'s Inc. 348*l*; Pop. Llangattock-Vivon-Avel 497, St. Maugham 191.) [20]

PERRY, Edwin Creswell, *Seighford, Stafford.*—Caius Coll. Cam. B.A. 1855, M.A. 1858; Deac. 1855 and Pr. 1856 by Bp of Lich. V. of Seighford, Dio. Lich. 1861. (Patron, Francis Eld, Esq; Tithe—Imp. 342*l* 6*s*, V. 64*l* 17*s* 2*d*; Glebe, 54 acres; V.'s Inc. 212*l* and Ho; Pop. 808.) Author, *The Confessional, its Unscriptural Character and Injurious Tendencies,* 1859, 1*s*. [21]

PERRY, Frederick.—P. C. of St. Saviour's, Fitzroy-square, St. Pancras, Dio. Lon. 1861. (Patron, Bp of Lon; P. C.'s Inc. 300*l* and Ho; Pop. 7000.) [22]

PERRY, George Booth, 2, *Marsham-street, Maidstone.*—Trin. Coll. Cam. B.A. 1860; Deac. 1861 by Abp of York, Pr. 1863 by Bp of Dur. C. of Trinity, Maidstone, 1867. Formerly C. of Trinity, Stockton-on-Tees, 1861, Winteringham, Lincolnshire, 1864, St. Swithin's, Lincoln, 1865, St. John's, Withyham, Sussex, 1865 67. [23]

PERRY, George Gresley, *Waddington Rectory, near Lincoln.*—Corpus Coll. Ox. Fell of, 2nd cl. Lit. Hum. and B.A. 1840, M.A. 1843; Deac. 1844 and Pr. 1845 by Bp of Ox. R. of Waddington, Dio. Lin. 1852. (Patron, Lin. Coll. Ox; R.'s Inc. 865*l* and Ho; Pop. 905.) Rural Dean; Preb. of Lin; Fell. of Lin. Coll. 1842, Tut. 1847–52, Master of the Schs. 1847–48.

Author, *History of the Church of England*, 3 vols. 1861-64; and divers smaller works. [1]

PERRY, G. H. A., *St. Mary Cray, Kent.*—Deac. 1854, Pr. 1855. C. of Orpington with St. Mary Cray. [2]

PERRY, John, *Perranzabuloe, Truro.*—Ball. Coll. Ox. 3rd cl. Lit. Hum. 1825, B.A. 1826, M.A. 1830; Deac. 1827 and Pr. 1829 by Bp of B. and W. V. of Perranzabuloe, Dio. Ex. 1846. (Patrons, D. and C. of Ex; Tithe, comm. 415*l*; Glebe, 2 acres; V.'s Inc. 430*l*; Pop. 2649.) [3]

PERRY, Samuel Edgar, 4, *Brunswick place, Cambridge.*—Trin. Coll. Cam. B.A. 1864; Deac. 1865 and Pr. 1866 by Bp of Ely. C. of St. Andrew's-the-Less, Cambridge, 1865. [4]

PERRY, Samuel Gideon Frederick, *Tottington Parsonage, Bury.*—Trin. Coll. Cam. B.A. 1841, M.A. 1844. P. C. of Tottington, Dio. Man. 1849. (Patron, R. of Bury; Tithe, App. 82*l* 5*s*; P. C.'s Inc. 150*l* and Ho; Pop. 5119.) [5]

PERRY, Thomas Walter, 20, *Clifton-terrace, Brighton.*—Literate; Deac. 1845 and Pr. 1846 by Bp of Chich. C. of St. Michael's, Brighton. Formerly C. of St. Mary's, Addington, Bucks. Author, *Lawful Church Ornaments* (being an Historical Examination of the Judgment of the Rt. Hon. Stephen Lushington, D.C.L. in the case of Westerton *v.* Liddell, &c. and of "Aids for determining some disputed Points in the Ceremonial of the Church of England," by the Rev. W. Goode, with *An Appendix* on the Judgment of the Rt. Hon. Sir John Dodson, D.C.L. in the Appeal, Liddell *v.* Westerton), Masters, and J. H. Parker, 1857. [6]

PERRY, William.—C. of St. Peter's, Bethnal Green, Lond. [7]

PERRY, William Parker, *Stadhampton Parsonage, near Wallingford.*—Wad. Coll. Ox. B.A. 1827, M.A. 1845; Deac. 1828, Pr. 1830. P. C. of Chislehampton with Stadhampton, Dio. Ox. 1840. (Patron, Rev. J. Witherington Peers; P. C.'s Inc. 167*l* and Ho; Pop. Chislehampton 133, Stadhampton 329.) [8]

PERRYN, Gerard Alexander, *Trafford Hall, Chester.*—Brasen. Coll. Ox. B.A. 1846, M.A. 1849; Deac. 1850 and Pr. 1851 by Bp of Ches. P. C. of Guilden Sutton, near Chester, Dio. Ches. 1851. (Patron, Sir J. T. Stanley, Bart; Tithe—Imp. 227*l* 5*s*; P. C.'s Inc. 49*l*; Pop. 223.) [9]

PERTWEE, Arthur, 5, *Canning-place, Leicester.*—Pemb. Coll. Ox. B.A. 1860, M.A. 1863; Deac. 1861 and Pr. 1863 by Bp of Dur. C. of St. Margaret's, Leicester, 1865. Formerly C. of Brancepeth, Durham, 1861–64. [10]

PETCH, George, *Oddington Rectory, Oxford.*—Lin. Coll. Ox. 2nd cl. Lit. Hum. and B.A. 1847, M.A. 1850; Deac. 1850, Pr. 1851. R. of Oddington, Dio. Ox. 1857. (Patron, Trin. Coll. Ox; Modus, 2*l*; R.'s Inc. 325*l* and Ho; Pop. 169.) Formerly Fell. and Tut. of Trin. Coll. Ox. 1847. [11]

PETER, Lewis Morgan, *Treviles, Grampound, Cornwall.*—Ex. Coll. Ox. B.A. 1840, M.A. 1843; Deac. 1840 and Pr. 1841 by Bp of Ex. Formerly P. C. of Cornelly, Cornwall, 1847. [12]

PETER, Robert Godolphin, *Cavendish, Suffolk.*—Jesus Coll. Cam. 1st cl. Cl. Trip. B.A. 1842, M.A. 1845; Deac. 1845 and Pr. 1846 by Bp of Ely. R. of Cavendish, Dio. Ely, 1860. (Patron, Jesus Coll. Cam; Tithe, 730*l*; Glebe, 72 acres; R.'s Inc. 800*l* and Ho; Pop. 1300.) Formerly Fell. and Tut. of Jesus Coll. Author, *Manual of Prayer for Students*, 1859, 1*s* 6*d*. [13]

PETERBOROUGH, The Right Rev. Francis JEUNE, *The Palace, Peterborough.*—Pemb. Coll. Ox. 1st cl. Lit. Hum. and B.A. 1827, M.A. 1830, D.C.L. 1834, D.D; Deac. 1832 and Pr. 1833 by Bp of Ox. Consecrated Bp of Pet. 1864. (Episcopal Jurisdiction, Counties of Leicester, Northampton and Rutland; Inc. of See, 4500*l*; Pop. 486,977; Acres, 1,240,327; Deaneries, 18; Benefices, 550; Curates, 184; Church Sittings, 196,222.) His Lordship was formerly Tut. of Pemb. Coll. Ox. 1830–34; Mast. of Pemb. Coll. with Canonry in Glouc. Catbl. 1843; Head Mast. of King Edward's Sch. Birmingham, 1834–38; Dean of Jersey and R. of St. Heliers, 1838–44; Public Examiner at Ox. 1834; Select Preacher 1845; one of Her Majesty's Commissioners of Inquiry for the Univ. of Ox. 1850; a Member of the Hebdomadal Council at Oxford, 1854 and 1863; Vice-Chan. of the Univ. 1859; Dean of Lincoln 1864. Author, *Sermons* (preached before the Univ. of Ox); *A Sermon* (preached at the Tercentenary Anniversary of King Edward's Sch. Birmingham); *Sermon* (preached at the Consecration of Dr. Jackson, Bp of Lin.) 1853. [14]

PETERS, Charles Powell, *Pitchford Rectory, Shrewsbury.*—Queen's Coll. Ox. B.A. 1831, M.A. 1837; Deac. 1833, Pr. 1834. R. of Pitchford, Dio. Lich. 1867. (Patrons, Heirs of Earl of Liverpool; R.'s Inc. 240*l* and Ho; Pop. 180.) Formerly Preb. of Lich 1852; C. of Pitchford. [15]

PETERS, Henry, *The Rectory, Sunderland.*—R. of Sunderland with St. John's P. C. Dio. Dur. 1848. (Patron, Bp of Dur; R.'s Inc. 420*l* and Ho; Pop. 17,107.) Hon. Can. of Dur. 1855; Surrogate. [16]

PETERS, Michael Nowell, *Penzance.*—St. Peter's Coll. Cam. B.A. 1823, M.A. 1846; Deac. 1823, Pr. 1824. V. of Madron with Morvah, Dio. Ex. 1838. (Patron, the present V; Madron, Tithe—Imp. 431*l* 10*s*, V. 660*l*; Glebe, ¼ acre; Morvah Tithe—Imp. 68*l*, V. 69*l*; Glebe, ½ acre; Penzance, Tithe—Imp. 19*l*, V. 152*l* 10*s*; Glebe, 4 acres; V.'s Inc. 890*l*; Pop. Madron 2330, Morvah 380.) [17]

PETERS, Thomas, *Eastington Rectory, Stonehouse, Glouc.*—St. Alban Hall, Ox. B.A. 1834; Deac. 1836, Pr. 1837. R. of Eastington, Dio. G. and B. 1837. (Patron, the present R; Tithe, 525*l*; Glebe, 60 acres; R.'s Inc. 615*l* and Ho; Pop. 1647.) [18]

PETERS, Thomas, *Wellington, Somerset.*—Ch. Coll. Cam. B.A. 1857; Deac. 1859 by Bp of Wor. Pr. 1860 by Bp of Lon. C. of Wellington. [19]

PETERSON, William, *Sissinghurst, Cranbrook, Kent.*—P. C. of Sissinghurst, Dio. Cant. 1853. (Patron, Rev. J. Boys and others; P. C.'s Inc. 130*l*.) [20]

PETHERICK, George William, *Wilton-terrace, Salford.*—Dub. A.B. 1862; Deac. 1863 and Pr. 1864 by Bp of Man. Sen. C. of Ch. Ch. Salford, 1867. Formerly C. of St. Bartholomew's, Salford, 1863, St. Saviour's District, Manchester, 1865. [21]

PETO, James, *Preston Vicarage, Faversham, Kent.*—Trin. Hall, Cam. LL.B. 1814; Deac. 1814 and Pr. 1815 by Bp of Ely. V. of Preston-by-Faversham, Dio. Cant. 1837. (Patron, Abp of Cant; Tithe—App. 416*l* 12*s* 3*d*, V. 415*l*; V.'s Inc. 322*l* and Ho; Pop. 1535.) [22]

PETRIE, J., *Bury, Lancashire.*—C. of St. John's, Bury. [23]

PETTAT, Charles Richard, *Ashe Rectory, Andover-road, Hants.*—Univ. Coll. Ox. B.A. 1834; Deac. 1838, Pr. 1839. R. of Ashe, Dio. Win. 1845. (Patron, William Beach, Esq; Tithe, 450*l*; Glebe, 26 acres; R.'s Inc. 476*l* and Ho; Pop. 145.) R. of Deane, Hants, Dio. Win. 1845. (Patron, William Beach, Esq; Tithe, 325*l*; Glebe, 56 acres; R.'s Inc. 397*l*; Pop. 135.) Rural Dean. [24]

PETTITT, George, 31, *Bath-row, Birmingham.*—Ch. Miss. Coll. Islington; Deac. 1831 and Pr. 1832 by Bp of Lon. P. C. of St. Jude's, Birmingham, Dio. Wor. 1856. (Patrons, Crown and Bp of Wor. alt; P. C.'s Inc. 300*l*; Pop. 4810.) Formerly Chap. to the General Hospital, Birmingham, 1855–56; Miss. to the Ch. Miss. Soc. in South India and Ceylon 1833–55. Author, *A History of the Church Missionary Society's Mission in Tinnevelly, South India*, 1850, 7*s*; *Sermons on the Creed, in the Tamil Language*, Palamcottah, South India. [25]

PETTITT, John, *Wortley, Leeds.*—St. John's Coll. Cam. B.A. 1855, M.A. 1858; Deac. 1855 and Pr. 1856 by Bp of Ches. P. C. of Wortley, Dio. Rip. 1859. (Patrons, Trustees; P. C.'s Inc. 160*l*; Pop. 4724.) Formerly C. of Wybunbury, Cheshire. [26]

PETTITT, William, *St. Mary's Parsonage, Carlisle.*—Trin. Coll. Cam. B.A. 1860, M.A. 1863; Deac.

1861 and Pr. 1862 by Bp of Wor. Sen. C. of St. Mary's, Carlisle, 1866. Formerly C. of St. Martin's, Birmingham, 1861, West Ham, Essex, 1863. [1]

PEYTON, Algernon, *Doddington Rectory, March, Cambs.*—R. of Doddington with March C. and Benwick C. Dio. Ely, 1811. (Patron, Sir Henry Peyton; Doddington, Tithe, 3697*l* 13*s* 10*d*; Glebe, 53½ acres; March, Tithe, 5280*l* 10*s* 6*d*; Glebe, 5 acres; R.'s Inc. 10,090*l* and Ho; Pop. 8722.) Rural Dean. [2]

PHABAYN, John Finden Smith, *Charlton Horethorne, Sherborne, Somerset.*—Queen's Coll. Ox. B.A. 1832, M.A. 1834; Deac. 1833, Pr. 1834. V. of Charlton Horethorne, Dio. B. and W. 1844. (Patron, G. D. W. Digby, Esq; Tithe—Imp. 395*l*, V. 325*l*; Glebe, 40 acres; V.'s Inc. 385*l* and Ho; Pop. 506.) Formerly C. of Castle Cary, Somerset, 1836. [3]

PHAYRE, Richard, *West Raynham Rectory, Brandon, Norfolk.*—Dub. A.B. 1830; Deac. 1831 and Pr. 1832 by Bp of Lich. R. of the consolidated R.'s of East and West Raynham, Dio. Nor. 1841. (Patron, Marquis Townshend; East Raynham, Tithe, 359*l* 10*s*; West Raynham, Tithe, 390*l* 5*s*; Glebe, 153½ acres; R.'s Inc. 935*l* and Ho; Pop. East Raynham 139, West Raynham 369.) [4]

PHEAR, John, *Earl Stonham, Suffolk.*—Pemb. Coll. Cam. 13th Wrang. and B.A. 1815; Deac. 1817 and Pr. 1818 by Bp of Ex. R. of Earl Stonham, Dio. Nor. 1823. (Patron, Pemb. Coll. Cam; Tithe, 659*l*; Glebe, 31¾ acres; R.'s Inc. 698*l* and Ho; Pop. 752.) Formerly Fell. and Tut. of Pemb. Coll. Cam. [5]

PHEAR, Samuel George, *Emmanuel College, Cambridge.*—Emman. Coll. Cam. 4th Wrang. and B.A. 1852, B.D. 1861; Deac. 1853, Pr. 1854. Fell. and Tut. of Emman. Coll. Cam; Chap. to the Bp of Ely. [6]

PHELP, P. H., *Derby.*—Chap. to the Derbyshire Infirmary, Derby. Formerly C. of St. Mark's, Albert-road, St. Pancras, Lond. [7]

PHELPS, Arthur Whitmarsh, *The Vicarage, Compton Chamberlayne, Salisbury.*—Wor. Coll. Ox. B.A. 1858, M.A. 1861; Deac. 1858 and Pr. 1859 by Bp of Salis. V. of Compton Chamberlayne, Dio. Salis. 1863. (Patron, C. Penruddocke, Esq; Tithe, 20*l*; Glebe, 2 acres; V.'s Inc. 87*l* and Ho; Pop. 348.) Formerly C. of Berwick St. Leonard 1858–62; R. of Pertwood, Wilts, 1859–63. [8]

PHELPS, Charles Martin, *Milnsbridge, Huddersfield,*—King's Coll. Lond; Deac. 1865 by Bp of Rip. C. of Milnsbridge 1865. [9]

PHELPS, Edward Spencer, *Portsmouth.*—Wad. Coll. Ox. B.A. 1835; Deac. 1835, Pr. 1836. Chap. of H.M. Dockyard, Portsmouth, 1836. [10]

PHELPS, Hubert Hunter, *Old Hutton Parsonage, Kendal.*—Corpus Coll. Cam. B.A. 1853, M.A. 1857; Deac. 1854 and Pr. 1856 by Bp of Ox. P. C. of Old Hutton and Holmscales, Dio. Carl. 1864. (Patron, Archd. Cooper; P. C.'s Inc. 107*l* and Ho; Pop. 406.) Formerly C. of Trinity, Reading, and St. Pancras, Chichester. [11]

PHELPS, John, *Vicarage, Hatherleigh, N. Devon.*—Queen's Coll. Ox. B.A. 1824, M.A. 1830; Deac. and Pr. 1829 by Bp of Salis. V. of Hatherleigh, Dio. Ex. 1862. (Patrons, Trustees of J. Ireland, Esq; Tithe—Imp. 335*l* 15*s*, V. 224*l* 10*s*; Glebe, 51 acres; V.'s Inc. 202*l* and Ho; Pop. 1645.) Formerly P. C. of Burcombe 1829; R. of Little Langford and C. of Stapleford, Wilts, 1845. [12]

PHELPS, John, *Carew Vicarage, near Pembroke.*—Jesus Coll. Ox. B.A. 1829, M.A. 1831. V. of Carew, Dio. St. D. 1844. (Patron, Bp of St. D; Tithe, App. 481*l* and 33 acres of Glebe, V. 90*l*; Glebe, 2 acres; V.'s Inc. 195*l* and Ho; Pop. 993.) [13]

PHELPS, John, *Houghton, Carlisle.*—All Souls' Coll. Ox. M.A. 1859; Deac. 1860 by Abp of Cant. Pr. 1861 by Bp of Carl. P. C. of Houghton, Dio. Carl. 1864. (Patrons, Trustees; P. C.'s Inc. 83*l* and Ho; Pop. 883.) Formerly C. of Ch. Ch. Ramsgate, 1860–61, Houghton 1861–64. [14]

PHELPS, Peter, *Ambleston, Haverfordwest.*—Lampeter, Heb. Prizeman and Sen. Heb. Scho. 1850; Deac. 1851 and Pr. 1853 by Bp of St. D. V. of Ambleston, Dio. St. D. 1866. (Patron, Ld Chan; Tithe, 142*l* 12*s*; Glebe, 73 acres; V.'s Inc. 200*l* and Ho; Pop. 524.) Formerly C. of Letterston 1851–56, Angle 1856–58; V. of Llanstadwell 1858–66. [15]

PHELPS, P. A., *Wraxall, Bristol.*—C. of Wraxall, Somerset. [16]

PHELPS, Philip Edmund, 17, *Ruby place, Bathwick-hill, Bath.*—Deac. 1862, Pr. 1864. Min. of the Octagon Chapel, Bath, Dio. B. and W. 1867. Formerly C. of Mansergh, Westmoreland, 1862–64, St. Jude's, Whitechapel, Lond. 1864–65; C. and Min. of St. Paul's, Bethnal Green, 1865–66; C. of St. James's, Norland, Notting-hill. Lond. 1866–67. [17]

PHELPS, Robert, *Sidney-Sussex College, Cambridge.*—Trin. Coll. Cam. 5th Wrang. and B.A. 1833, M.A. 1836, B.D. 1843, D.D. per Lit. Reg. 1843; Deac. 1840 by Bp of Herf. Pr. 1840 by Bp of Lich. Mast. of Sid. Coll. Cam. 1843; R. of Willingham, Dio. Ely, 1848. (Patron, Bp of Ely; Tithe, App. 670*l*, R. 699*l* 8*s* 6½*d*; Glebe, 80 acres; R.'s Inc. 899*l* and Ho; Pop. 1630.) Formerly Fell. and Taylor Lect. of Sid. Coll. Cam. Author, *A Treatise on Optics.* [18]

PHELPS, Thomas, *Froxfield, Petersfield, Hants.*—Magd. Hall, Ox. B.A. 1860, M.A. 1864; Deac. 1861, Pr. 1862. C. of Froxfield. Formerly C. of Bransgore, Hants, 1861. [19]

PHELPS, Thomas Prankard, *Ridley Rectory, Wrotham, Kent.*—Wor. Coll. Ox. B.A. 1838. R. of Ridley, Dio. Roch. 1855. (Patron, W. Lambart, Esq; Tithe, 180*l*; Glebe, 30 acres; R.'s Inc. 230*l* 10*s* and Ho; Pop. 101.) Hon. Can. of Roch. [20]

PHELPS, William Whitmarsh, *Rawul Pindee, East Indies.*—Queen's Coll. Ox. B.A. 1849, M.A. 1852; Deac. 1850, Pr. 1851; Asst. Chap. at Rawul Pindee. Formerly Chap. at Peshawur 1854. [21]

PHILIPPS, George, *Rodwell, Weymouth.*—Jesus Coll. Ox. B.A. 1849, M.A. 1851; Deac. 1850 by Bp of G. and B. Pr. 1851 by Bp of Ex. Sen. C. of Trinity, Weymouth, 1864. Formerly C. of Malmesbury Abbey, Wilts, 1850–52; Sen. C. of St. George's, Ramsgate, 1852–59; Precentor of Sherborne Abbey 1859–64. Author, *Canticles pointed for Chanting*, 1855, 2nd ed. 1861; *The Seasons of the Church and the Preacher's Duty*, 1859; *Secular Education*, 1864; *Church Music and the Choral Service*, 1865. [22]

PHILIPPS, Henry, *Pittville Lawn, Cheltenham.*—Queen's Coll. Ox. M.A; Deac. 1842 and Pr. 1843 by Bp of Salis. [23]

PHILIPPS, James, *Wiston Vicarage, Haverfordwest.*—Jesus Coll. Ox. B.A. 1833; Deac. 1834, Pr. 1835. V. of Wiston, Dio. St. D. 1839. (Patron, Earl Cawdor, Glebe, ¾ acre; V.'s Inc. 170*l* and Ho; Pop. 718.) [24]

PHILIPPS, James Erasmus, *Warminster Vicarage, Wilts.*—Ch. Ch. Ox. 3rd cl. Lit. Hum. 1846, B.A. 1847, M.A; Deac. 1848 and Pr. 1850 by Bp of Salis. V. of Warminster, Dio. Salis. 1859. (Patron, Bp of Salis; Tithe—App. 29*l* 15*s*, V. 40*l*; V.'s Inc. 415*l* and Ho; Pop. 3829.) Surrogate. Formerly C. of Wilton, Alderbury, Wilts. Author, *Seven Common Faults*, 1*s*; *Your Duty and Mine*, 1*s*; *Things Rarely Met With*, 1*s*; *Woman's Work in Foreign Missions*, 2*d*; *The Selection and Training of Missionaries*, 1*d*; all published by Rivingtons. [25]

PHILIPPS, Sir James Evans, Bart., *Osmington Vicarage, Weymouth*—Queen's Coll. Ox. 2nd cl. Lit. Hum. and B.A. 1817, M.A. 1820; Deac. 1817 by Bp of Glouc. Pr. 1818 by Bp of Salis. V. of Osmington, Dio. Salis. 1832. (Patron, Bp of Salis; Tithe, 252*l*; Glebe, 6 acres; V.'s Inc. 259*l* and Ho; Pop. 448.) Rural Dean. Author, *Sermons.* [26]

PHILIPPS, James Henry Alexander, late GWYTHER, *Picton Castle Haverfordwest.*—Trin. Coll. Cam. B.A. 1837, M.A. 1840; Deac. 1838 and Pr. 1839 by Bp of Wor. V. of St. Mary's, Haverfordwest, Dio. St. D. 1859. (Patron, the present V; V.'s Inc. 130*l*; Pop. 1525.) Rural Dean. Formerly V. of Madeley, Salop, 1841–59. [27]

PHILIPPS, James Joseph, *St. Florence, Tenby.*—Lampeter, Scho. 1864–65, B.A. 1866; Deac.

1866 by Bp of St. D. C. of St. Florence, Pembrokeshire, 1866. [1]

PHILIPS, E., *Rostherne, Cheshire.*—C. of Rostherne. [2]

PHILIPS, Gilbert Henderson, *The Mount, York.*—Brasen. Coll. Ox. B.A. 1845, M.A. 1848; Deac. 1846 and Pr. 1847 by Bp of Ches. V. of Brodsworth, Dio. York, 1867. (Patron, Abp of York; Tithe, 60*l*; Glebe, 413*l*; V.'s Inc. 473*l* and Ho; Pop. 412.) Chap. to Abp of York 1864. Formerly C. of Mobberley, Cheshire, 1846–48. P. C. of Dringhouses, York, 1848–67. [3]

PHILIPS, R., *Salisbury.*—Chap. of the Dioc. Training Sch. Salisbury. [4]

PHILIPSON, William, *Bradley, Great Grimsby.*—St. John's Coll. Cam. Jun. Opt. and B.A. 1853; Deac. 1854 and Pr. 1855 by Bp of Wor. R. of Bradley, Dio. Lin. 1853. (Patron, Sir J. Nelthorpe, Bart; Tithe, 217*l*; Glebe, 6¾ acres; R.'s Inc. 227*l*; Pop. 108.) [5]

PHILLIMORE, George, *Radnage Rectory (Bucks), Stokenchurch.*—Ch. Ch. Ox. B.A. 1829. M.A. 1832; Deac. 1831 by Bp of Ox. Pr. 1832 by Bp of Lin. R. of Radnage, Dio. Ox. 1851. (Patron, Ld Chan; Tithe, 304*l* 9*s* 10*d*; Glebe, 6½ acres; R.'s Inc. 311*l* and Ho; Pop. 478.) [6]

PHILLIMORE, Greville, *Down Ampney, near Cricklade.*—Ch. Ch. Ox. B.A. 1842, M.A. 1844; Deac. and Pr. 1843 by Bp of Ox. V. of Down Ampney, Dio. G. and B. 1851. (Patron, Ch. Ch. Ox; Tithe—App. 320*l*, V. 300*l*; Glebe, 19 acres; V.'s Inc. 320*l*; Pop. 429.) Surrogate. [7]

PHILLIPPS, Alfred, *Long Preston, near Leeds.*—King's Coll. Lond. Assoc. 1863; Deac. 1864 and Pr. 1866 by Bp of Rip. C. of Long Preston 1864. [8]

PHILLIPPS, Charles Lisle Marsh, *Sheepshed Vicarage, Loughborough, Leicestershire.*—Magd. Coll. Cam. Jun. Opt. and B.A. 1835, M.A. 1838; Deac. 1844 and Pr. 1845 by Bp of Pet. V. of Sheepshed, Dio. Pet. 1856. (Patron, A. L. M. P. de Lisle, Esq; Tithe, 58*l*; V.'s Inc. 362*l* and Ho; Pop. 3339.) Formerly V. of Queeniborough, Leicester, 1846–56. [9]

PHILLIPPS, Thomas, *Dewsall Vicarage, near Hereford.*—Jesus Coll. Cam. B.A. 1825, M.A. 1836; Deac. 1825 by Bp of Glouc. Pr. 1826 by Bp of B. and W. V. of Dewsall with Callow, Dio. Herf. 1838. (Patron, Rev. W. B. Mynors; Tithe, comm. 200*l*; Glebe, 2 acres; V.'s Inc. 225*l*; Pop. Dewsall 36, Callow 137.) Formerly C. of Harston, Gloucestershire, 1825, Berrow, Somerset, 1826. [10]

PHILLIPPS, William, *Buckland Rectory, Broadway, Glouc.*—Deac. 1828, Pr. 1829. R. of Buckland, Dio. G. and B. 1848. (Patron, Sir T. Phillipps, Bart; Glebe, 227 acres; R.'s Inc. 260*l* and Ho; Pop. 355.) [11]

PHILLIPS, Abel, *Uckfield, Sussex.*—C. of Uckfield. [12]

PHILLIPS, Alfred, *The Vicarage, Bushbury, Staffs.*—Jesus Coll. Cam. Wrang. and B.A. 1824, M.A. 1837, B.D. and D.D. 1841; Deac. and Pr. 1832 by Bp of Chich. V. of Bushbury, Dio. Lich. 1864. (Patrons, A. Hordern, Esq. and others; V.'s Inc. 159*l* and Ho; Pop. 2051.) [13]

PHILLIPS, Arthur, *Curland, Taunton.*—C. of Curland. [14]

PHILLIPS, Charles, 12, *Stanhope-street, Gloucester-gate, Regent's-park, London, N.W.*—Trin. Coll. Cam. B.A. 1840; Deac. 1841, Pr. 1842. P. C. of St. Matthew's, St. Pancras, Dio. Lon. 1849. (Patron, V. of St. Pancras; P. C.'s Inc. 250*l*; Pop. 7768.) [15]

PHILLIPS, Edward, *Surbiton, Kingston-on-Thames, S.W.*—St. Peter's Coll. Cam. B.A. 1829, M.A. 1832. P. C. of St. Mark's, Surbiton, Dio. Win. 1845. (Patrons, Sir E. Antrobus and others; P. C.'s Inc. 150*l*; Pop. 3291.) [16]

PHILLIPS, Evan, *Aberannell, Builth.*—Ch. Miss. Coll. Islington; Deac. 1861 and Pr. 1866 by Bp of St. D. C. of the Church of the Lamb of God, Abergwessin, 1866. Formerly C. of Llandilo-Fawr 1861–63, Margam 1863-65, Brynmawr 1865–66. [17]

PHILLIPS, Evan Owen, *Aberystwith, Cardigan.*—Corpus Coll. Cam. Prizeman, 1846–7–8–9, 18th Wrang. and B.A. 1849; Deac. 1849 and Pr. 1850 by Abp of York. V. of Llanbadarn-Fawr, Dio. St. D. 1861. (Patron, Bp of St. D; V.'s Inc. 170*l* and Ho; Pop. 6244.) P. C. of Aberystwith, Dio. St. D. 1861. (Patron, Bp of St. D; Pop. 5561.) Surrogate; Rural Dean; Fell. of Corpus Coll. Cam. 1864. Formerly Warden of the Welsh Coll. Llandovery, 1854. [18]

PHILLIPS, Frederick Parr, *Stoke d'Abernon, Cobham, Surrey.*—Ch. Ch. Ox. B.A. 1840, M.A. 1844. R. of Stoke d'Abernon, Dio. Win. 1862. (Patron, the present R; R.'s Inc. 480*l* and Ho; Pop. 368.) [19]

PHILLIPS, George, *Queens' College, Cambridge.*—Queens' Coll. Cam. 8th Wrang. and B.A. 1829, M.A. 1832, B.D. 1839, D.D. 1858; Deac. 1831 and Pr. 1832 by Bp of Ely. Vice-Chan. and Pres. of Queens' Coll. Cam. 1857. Formerly Fell. and Tut. of Queens' Coll. Cam. 1831–46; R. of Sandon, Essex, 1846–57. Author, *The Elements of Syriac Grammar*, 1st ed. 1837, 2nd ed. 1845; *The Psalms in Hebrew, with a Critical, Exegetical, and Philological Commentary*, 2 vols. 1846. [20]

PHILLIPS, George, *Penmorva Rectory, Dôlbenmaen, Carnarvonshire.*—Queen's Coll. Ox. B.A. 1830; Deac. 1831, Pr. 1832. R. of Penmorva with Dôlbenmaen C. Dio. Ban. 1853. (Patron, Bp of Ban; Tithe, 290*l*; Glebe, 12 acres; R.'s Inc. 320*l* and Ho; Pop. Penmorva 1104, Dôlbenmaen 387.) [21]

PHILLIPS, George, *Upper Edmonton, Middlesex, N.*—Queens' Coll. Cam. B.A. 1842, M.A. 1845; Deac. 1842 and Pr. 1843 by Bp of Lon. P. C. of St. James's, Edmonton, Dio. Lon. 1850. (Patron, V. of Edmonton; P. C.'s Inc. 280*l*; Pop. 2945.) [22]

PHILLIPS, George, *Grammar Schoolhouse, Chard, Somerset.*—Queens' Coll. Cam. Scho. of, Sen. Opt. B.A. 1855, M.A. 1858; Deac. 1855 and Pr. 1856 by Bp of Roch. Head Mast. of the Gr. Sch. Chard; P. C. of Chillington, Dio. B. and W. 1861. (Patron, Earl Powlett; P. C.'s Inc. 67*l*; Pop. 313.) Chap. to the Chard Union. Formerly C. of West and South Hanningfield 1855–57; Asst. Mast. in Walthamstow Gr. Sch. 1858–61. [23]

PHILLIPS, G. N., *Eling, Southampton.*—V. of Eling, Dio. Win. 1863. (Patrons, Trustees of Rev. W. J. G. Phillips; V.'s Inc. 700*l*; Pop. 2442.) Surrogate. [24]

PHILLIPS, George William, *Chipping Ongar, Essex.*—C. of Chipping Ongar. Formerly C. of Writtle, Essex. [25]

PHILLIPS, Henry Frederick, *Rochester.*—Univ. Coll. Ox. B.A. 1855; Deac. 1855 and Pr. 1856 by Bp of Roch. P. C. of St. Peter's, Rochester, Dio. Roch. 1860. (Patrons, D. and C. of Roch; Pop. 4361.) Formerly C. of St. Margaret's, Rochester. [26]

PHILLIPS, Henry George, *Great Welnetham Rectory, Bury St. Edmunds.*—Emman. Coll. Cam; Deac. and Pr. 1815. R. of Great Welnetham, Dio. Ely, 1816. (Patron, F. Wing, Esq; Tithe, 390*l*; Glebe, 50 acres; R.'s Inc. 400*l* and Ho; Pop. 504.) V. of Mildenhall; Dio. Ely, 1818. (Patron, Sir H. E. Bunbury; Tithe, 30*l*, Glebe, 327 acres; V.'s Inc. 460*l*; Pop. 4046.) [27]

PHILLIPS, Hugh Moreton, *Stirchley Rectory, Dawley, Salop.*—Wor. Coll. Ox. B.A. 1818, M.A. 1822; Deac. 1819, Pr. 1820. R. of Stirchley, Dio. Lich. 1827. (Patrons, Revell Phillips, Esq. and others; Tithe, 190*l*; Glebe, 45½ acres; R.'s Inc. 260*l* and Ho; Pop. 310.) [28]

PHILLIPS, James, *Abington House School, Northampton.*—Dub. A.B. 1860, A.M. 1868; Deac. 1860 and Pr. 1861 by Bp of Pet. C. of Weston Favell 1866. Formerly C. of St. Sepulchre's, Northampton, 1860. [29]

PHILLIPS, John Bartholomew, *New Church Rectory, Rossendale, Manchester.*—All Souls' Coll. Ox. 3rd cl. Lit. Hum. and B.A. 1836, M.A. 1840; Deac. 1838, Pr. 1839. R. of New Church, in Rossendale, Dio. Man. 1850. (Patron, V. of Whalley; Glebe, 200 acres; R.'s Inc. 500*l* and Ho; Pop. 6481.) Formerly P. C. of St. Andrew's, Manchester, 1844–45; C. of Liverpool 1845–50. Author, *Prayers for the Dead*, and other Sermons. [30]

PHILLIPS, John Croxon, *Tyn-y-Rhôs, Chirk.*—Ch. Coll. Cam. B.A. 1825, M.A. 1826; Deac. 1826, Pr. 1827. [31]

PHILLIPS, John Rodney B., *Fazeley, Tamworth.*—C. of Fazeley. [1]

PHILLIPS, Owen, *Lawrenny, near Pembroke.*—R. of Lawrenny, Dio. St. D. 1852. (Patrons, Heirs of H. Barlow, Esq; Tithe, 168*l* 10*s*; Glebe, 20 acres; R.'s Inc. 198*l*; Pop. 339.) Formerly C. of Martletwy, Pembrokeshire. [2]

PHILLIPS, Robert, *Christ Church, Leeds.*—St. Bees; Deac. 1864 and Pr. 1866 by Bp of Rip. C. of Ch. Ch. Leeds, 1866. Formerly C. of New Wortley 1864. [3]

PHILLIPS, Samuel Church, *Gloucester House, Tetbury.*—St. Aidan's; Deac. 1862 and Pr. 1864 by Bp of G. and B. C. of Tetbury 1866. Formerly C. of Stapleton 1862, Lydney 1863, Lea 1864. [4]

PHILLIPS, Samuel John, *Rossall School, Fleetwood, Lancashire.*—Pemb. Coll. Cam. B.A. 1845, M.A. 1848; Deac. 1848 and Pr. 1849 by Bp of Lon. Vice-Mast. of Rossall Sch. Formerly 2nd Mast. of same 1855. [5]

PHILLIPS, Sidney, *South End House, Croydon.*—Brasen. Coll. Ox. B.A. 1863, M.A. 1866; Deac. 1864, Pr. 1866. Formerly Asst. C. of Newland, Worcestershire, 1864–67. [6]

PHILLIPS, Spencer William, *Ickleford, near Hitchin, Herts.*—Univ. Coll. Ox. B.A. 1856, M.A. 1859; Deac. 1857 and Pr. 1858 by Bp of Roch. C. in sole charge of Ickleford 1866. Formerly C. of Ifield, Kent, 1857-60, Romford, 1860–63, Aylesford 1863–66. [7]

PHILLIPS, Thomas Lloyd, *Beckenham, Kent, S.E.*—Univ. Coll. Lond. B.A. 1856, Jesus Coll. Ox. B.A. 1866; Deac. 1858 and Pr. 1859 by Abp of Cant. C. of Beckenham 1858. Formerly Sec. to the Editorial Department of the Brit. and For. Bible Soc. [8]

PHILLIPS, Thompson, *Holme Eden Parsonage, Carlisle.*—St. John's Coll. Cam. B.A. 1856, M.A. 1860; Deac. 1856 by Bp of Roch. Pr. 1857 by Bp of Wor. P. C. of Holme Eden, Dio. Carl. 1861. (Patroness, Mrs. Peter Dixon; P. C.'s Inc. 120*l* and Ho; Pop. 1180.) Rural Dean. Formerly C. of St. Peter's, Coventry, 1856–58, All Saints', Paddington, Lond. 1858–61. [9]

PHILLIPS, William Davies, *Crunwere Rectory, Narberth, Pembrokeshire.*—Jesus Coll. Ox. B.A. 1828; Deac. 1830 by Bp of Chich. Pr. 1832 by Bp of St. D. R. of Crunwere, Dio. St. D. 1839. (Patron, Ld Chan; Tithe, 105*l*; Glebe, 62 acres; R.'s Inc. 148*l* and Ho; Pop. 261.) V. of Amroath, Pembrokeshire, Dio. St. D. 1850. (Patron, C. P. Callen, Esq; Tithe—Imp. 103*l* 18*s*, V. 62*l*; Glebe, 28 acres; V.'s Inc. 180*l*; Pop. 889.) Rural Dean. [10]

PHILLIPS, William Parr, *Woodford Rectory, Essex, N.E.*—Trin. Coll. Ox. B.A. 1831; Deac. 1831 and Pr. 1832 by Bp of Win. R. of Woodford, Dio. Lon. 1832. (Patron, Lord Cowley; Tithe, 670*l*; Glebe, 15 acres; R.'s Inc. 700*l* and Ho; Pop. 2613.) [11]

PHILLOTT, Edward, *Stanton Drew, Pensford, Somerset.*—C. of Stanton Drew with Pensford. [12]

PHILLOTT, Henry Wright, *Staunton-on-Wye Rectory, near Hereford.*—Ch. Ch. Ox. 2nd cl. Lit. Hum. 3rd cl. Math. et Phy. and B.A. 1838, M.A. 1840; Deac. 1839 and Pr. 1840 by Bp of Ox. R. of Staunton-on-Wye, Dio. Herf. 1850. (Patron, Ch. Ch. Ox; Land in lieu of Tithe, 324 acres; R.'s Inc. 400*l* and Ho; Pop. 675.) Rural Dean 1854. Author, *Education the Business of Life* (a Charterhouse Founder's Day Sermon), 1851; *The Days of the Flood* (a Sermon), 1852; *Watchfulness the Duty of the Clergy* (a Visitation Sermon), 1854. [13]

PHILLPOTTS, Arthur Archbold, *Harton, South Shields.*—Dur. B.A. 1853, M.A. 1858; Deac. 1855 and Pr. 1857 by Bp of Dur. P. C. of Harton, Dio. Dur. 1864. (Patrons, D. and C. of Dur; P. C.'s Inc. 300*l* and Ho.) Formerly C. of Boldon 1855, Brancepeth 1857, Sedgefield 1859, Newbottle 1864. [14]

PHILLPOTTS, Henry John, *Lamerton Vicarage, Tavistock.*—Ch. Ch. Ox. B.A. 1855; Deac. 1855, Pr. 1856. V. of Lamerton, Dio. Ex. 1860. (Patron, J. H. Tremayne; Tithe—Imp. 310*l* 16*s* 11*d*, V. 397*l*; V.'s Inc. 400*l* and Ho; Pop. 1517.) Chap. to the Bp of Ex. Formerly C. of St. Gluvias. [15]

PHILLPOTTS, Thomas, *St. Feock, Truro.*—King's Coll. Cam. B.A. 1829, M.A. 1833; Deac. 1830 by Bp of Lin. Pr. 1832 by Bp of G. and B. V. of St. Feock, Dio. Ex. 1844. (Patron, Bp of Ex; Tithe—Imp. 232*l* 18*s* 9*d*, V. 204*l*; Glebe, 3 acres; V.'s Inc. 204*l* and Ho; Pop. 2411.) Chap. to the Bp of Ex. Formerly Fell. of King's Coll. Cam. [16]

PHILLPOTTS, The Ven. William John, *St. Gluvias, Penryn, Cornwall.*—Oriel Coll. Ox. B.A. 1830, M.A. 1832. Preb. of Ex. 1840; Archd. of Cornwall 1845. (Value, 330*l*.) V. of St. Gluvias with Budock V. Dio. Ex. 1845. (Patron, Bp of Ex; St. Gluvias, Tithe—Imp. 237*l* 11*s*, V. 269*l* 0*s* 6*d*; Glebe, 15 acres; Budock, Tithe—Imp. 380*l*, V. 420*l*; V.'s Inc. 519*l*; Pop. St. Gluvias 4760, Budock 1369.) [17]

PHILP, William Pellowe, *Jarrow-on-Tyne.*—Deac. 1846 by Bp of Ex. Pr. 1847 by Bp of Dur. R. of Jarrow, Dio. Dur. (Patrons, Lady James and T. D. Brown, Esq. alt; Tithe, 85*l*; Glebe, 50 acres; P. C.'s Inc. 230*l* and Ho; Pop. 7418.) Formerly C. of St. John's, Gateshead Fell. [18]

PHILPOT, Benjamin, *Lydney, Gloucestershire.*—Ch. Coll. Cam. Fell. of, 9th Sen. Opt. M.A. 1812; Deac. 1815, Pr. 1817. V. of Lydney, with Aylburton, Dio. G. and B. 1859. (Patrons, D. and C. of Herf; Tithe, comm. 670*l*; V.'s Inc. 700*l* and Ho; Pop. Lydney 2285, Aylburton 604.) Formerly R. of Cressingham, Norfolk; Archd. of Sodor and Man, and R. of Kirk Andrews. Author, *Nine Lectures on the Second Advent*, 4*s* 6*d*; *Lectures on Ruth*, Nisbet, 3*s* 6*d*; etc. [19]

PHILPOT, George, *Gorton, Manchester.*—Caius Coll. Cam. B.A. 1849, M.A. 1854; Deac. 1849 and Pr. 1850 by Bp of Roch. R. of Gorton, Dio. Man. 1864. (Patrons, D. and C. of Man; R.'s Inc. 300*l* and Ho; Pop. 7017. (Formerly C. of St. Thomas's, Ardwick, near Manchester. [20]

PHILPOT, William Benjamin, 20, *South-terrace, Littlehampton.*—Trin. Coll. Cam; Wor. Coll. Ox. Fell. of, 2nd cl. Lit. Hum. and B.A. 1848, M.A. 1851; Deac. 1848 and Pr. 1849 by Bp of Ox; Private Tutor. Author, *Heavenly and Earthly Service*, S.P.C.K. [21]

PHILPOTT, Henry Charles, *Earl's Croome, Worcester.*—St. John's Coll. Ox. B.A. 1817, M.A. 1820; Deac. and Pr. 1818. R. of Earl's Croome, Dio. Wor. 1855. (Patron, Rev. Charles Dunne; Tithe, 226*l* 16*s*; Glebe, 4 acres; R.'s Inc. 234*l* and Ho; Pop. 189.) [22]

PHILPOTT, John, *Hinxhill Rectory, Ashford, Kent.*—St. John's Coll. Cam. B.A. 1833, M.A. 1836; Deac. 1834 by Abp of Cant. Pr. 1835 by Bp of Lon. R. of Hinxhill, Dio. Cant. 1837. (Patrons, Dean and C. of Cant and Sir C. Honeywood alt; Tithe, 200*l*; Glebe, 12 acres; R.'s Inc. 225*l* and Ho; Pop. 128.) R. of Brook, Dio. Cant. 1852. (Patrons, D. and C. of Cant. and Sir C. Honeywood alt; Tithe, 148*l* 14*s*; Glebe, 20 acres; R.'s Inc. 200*l*; Pop. 120.) Chap. of East Ashford Union. [23]

PHILPOTT, Richard Stamper, *Chewton Mendip Vicarage, Wells.*—St. Cath. Hall, Cam. B.A. 1850; Deac. 1850 and Pr. 1852 by Bp of Win. V. of Chewton Mendip with Emborough C. Farington-Gurney C. and Stone Easton C. Dio. B. and W. 1858. (Patron, R. P. Philpott, Esq; Chewton-Mendip, Tithe—Imp. 352*l* 10*s*, V. 235*l* 4*s*; Glebe, 31 acres; Emborough, Tithe—Imp. 141*l* 1*s* and 1 acre of Glebe, V. 74*l* 8*s* 6*d*; Glebe, 2 acres; Farington-Gurney, Tithe—Imp. 25*l*, V. 88*l*; V.'s Inc. 450*l* and Ho; Pop. Chewton-Mendip 976, Emborough 178, Farington-Gurney 482, Stone Easton 431.) Dom. Chap. to the Duke of Hamilton and Brandon 1851. Formerly C. of Ch. Ch. Epsom, Surrey. [24]

PHILPOTT, T. H., *Rock, near Bewdley, Worcestershire.*—C. of Rock. [25]

PHINN, Charles Perceval, *Long Critchill Rectory, Salisbury.*—Ball. Coll. Ox. 1st cl. Lit. Hum. and B.A. 1850; Deac. 1852 by Bp of Salis. Pr. 1853 by Bp of G. and B. R. of Moor Critchill with Long Critchill R. Dio. Salis. 1864. (Patron, Henry Gerard Sturt, Esq; Tithe, 357*l*; Glebe, 114 acres; R.'s Inc. 445*l* and Ho;

Pop. Moor Critchill 342, Long Critchill 145.) Formerly C. of St. Mary's, Melcombe Regis, 1852–53, St. James's, Bristol, 1853–56; P. C. of Coxley, Somerset, 1856–57; R. of All Saints', Chichester, 1861-62, R. of St. Pancras, Chichester, 1857–64. [1]

PHIPPS, The Hon. Augustus Frederick, *Euston Rectory, near Thetford.*—Trin. Coll. Cam. M.A. 1831; Deac. and Pr. 1834 by Bp of Lin. R. of Euston with Fakenham-Parva R. and Barnham R. Dio. Ely, 1850. (Patron, Duke of Grafton; Euston, Tithe, 274*l* 10*s* 3*d*; Glebe, 2 acres; Barnham, Tithe, 435*l* 2*s* 3*d*; R.'s Inc. 709*l* and Ho; Pop. Euston 225, Barnham 475.) Chap. in Ordinary to the Queen 1847; Rural Dean 1862. Formerly R. of Halesworth, Suffolk, 1834–39; R. of Boxford, Suffolk, 1839–50. [2]

PHIPPS, Edward James, *Stansfield Rectory, Clare, Suffolk.*—Ex. Coll. Ox. B.A. 1827; Deac. 1829 and Pr. 1838 by Bp of B. and W. R. of Stansfield, Dio. Ely, 1853. (Patron, Ld Chan; Tithe, 500*l*; Glebe, 86 acres; R.'s Inc. 623*l* and Ho; Pop. 549.) Formerly R. of Devizes, Wilts, 1833–53. Author, *Catechism on the Holy Scriptures*, for Church Schools, Masters, 1850, 3rd ed. 1867, 1*s*; *The Real Question as to Altar Lights*; *Christ's Body Present by Consecration, and Offered in the Sacrament of the Altar*, Longmans, 1865. [3]

PHIPPS, George William, *Husband's Bosworth Rectory, near Rugby.*—St. Peter's Coll. Cam. B.A. 1843, M.A. 1847; Deac. 1844 by Bp of Lin. Pr. 1848 by Bp of Pet. R. of Husband's Bosworth, Dio. Pet. 1856. (Patron, John W. Lamb, Esq; R.'s Inc. 1012*l* and Ho; Pop. 934.) Formerly C. of Husband's Bosworth. [4]

PHIPPS, Pownoll William, 2, *Holland-road, Brighton.*—Pemb. Coll. Ox. M.A. 1861; Deac. 1859 and Pr. 1860 by Bp of Lon. C. of St. John the Baptist's, Hove, near Brighton, 1864. Formerly C. of Shepperton, Middlesex, 1859-61, Iver, Bucks, 1861–63. [5]

PICOOPE, George John, *Yarwell, Wansford, Northants.*—Brasen. Coll. Ox. B.A. 1842, M.A. 1845; Deac. 1845 and Pr. 1847 by Bp of Ches. C. of Yarwell 1864. Formerly C. of Brindle 1849–64. [6]

PICKARD, Henry Adair, *Gledhow Lodge, Leeds.*—Ch. Ch. Ox. 2nd cl. Lit. Hum. and B.A. 1855, M.A. 1858; Deac. 1856 and Pr. 1858 by Bp of Ox. Stud. of Ch. Ch. Ox; one of H.M. Inspectors of Schs. Formerly C. of Sandford, and Abingdon, Berks; Tut. of Ch. Ch. Ox. [7]

PICKERING, George, *Ulverston.*—Deac. 1822 by Bp of Ox. Pr. 1824 by Abp of York. P. C. of Trinity, Ulverston, Dio. Carl. 1839. (Patron, Rev. A. Peache; P. C.'s Inc. 150*l*; Pop. 2116.) Chap. of the Ulverston Union 1847. [8]

PICKERING, Henry Valentine, *Brandeston Vicarage, Wickham Market, Suffolk.*—Pemb. Coll. Cam. B.A. 1844; Deac. 1844 and Pr. 1845 by Bp of Nor. V. of Brandeston, Dio. Nor. 1862. (Patron, C. Austin, Esq; Tithe, 120*l*; Glebe, 15 acres; V.'s Inc. 154*l* and Ho; Pop. 469.) Formerly P. C. of Ashfield with Thorpe. [9]

PICKERING, James Henry, *Shipton Parsonage, York.*—Ch. Ch. Ox. B.A. 1838; Deac. 1840 and Pr. 1841 by Abp of Cant. V. of Overton with Shipton P. C. Dio. York, 1849. (Patron, Hon. P. Dawnay; Endow. 30*l*; V.'s Inc. 336*l* and Ho; Pop. 763.) [10]

PICKFORD, Edward Matthew, *Tilston Rectory, Farndon, Cheshire.*—Brasen. Coll. Ox. B.A. 1838, M.A. 1841; Deac. 1840, Pr. 1841. R. of Tilston, Dio. Ches. 1850. (Patrons, Marquis of Cholmondeley and T. T. Drake, Esq. alt; Glebe, 38 acres; R.'s Inc. 350*l* and Ho; Pop. 817.) [11]

PICKFORD, Francis, *Hagworthingham Rectory, Spilsby, Lincolnshire.*—Queens' Coll. Cam. B.A. 1824, M.A. 1825; Deac. 1825, Pr. 1826. R. of Hagworthingham, Dio. Lin. 1839. (Patron, Bp of Lin; Tithe, 311*l*; Glebe, 54 acres; R.'s Inc. 395*l* and Ho; Pop. 666.) Rural Dean. [12]

PICKFORD, James John, *Great Gaddesden, Herts.*—C. of Great Gaddesden. [13]

PICKLES, Joseph Samuel, 156, *Queen's-road, Everton, Liverpool.*—St. John's Coll. Cam. B.A. 1859, M.A. 1862; Deac. 1859 and Pr. 1860 by Bp of Ches. Miss. C. of St. Saviour's, Everton, 1866. Formerly C. of St. Saviour's, Liverpool, 1859–66. [14]

PICKSLAY, Frederick Richard, *Longnor, near Buxton.*—St. Bees; Deac. 1853 and Pr. 1854 by Bp of Lich. C. of Longnor. [15]

PICTHALL, Charles Grayson, *Chillesford, Orford, Suffolk.*—Ch. Coll. Cam. B.A. 1846. R. of Chillesford, Dio. Nor. 1857. (Patron, Rev. W. E. Pooley; Tithe, 293*l* 6*s* 1*d*; Glebe, 32 acres; R.'s Inc. 364*l*; Pop. 214.) [16]

PICTHALL, Wallis Marmaduke, *Cold Ash, Thatcham, near Newbury, Berks.*—Ch. Coll. Cam. B.A. 1853; Deac. 1853 by Bp of Ely, Pr. 1854 by Bp of Nor. P. C. of Cold Ash, Dio. Ox. 1865. (Patron, V. of Thatcham; P. C.'s Inc. 100*l*; Pop. 750.) Formerly C. of Sudbourne, Suffolk, 1853–63. [17]

PICTON, John Owen, *Desford Rectory, Leicester.*—Deac. 1847, Pr. 1848. R. of Desford, Dio. Pet. 1861. (Patron, Ld Chan; Tithe—Imp. 83*l* 16*s* 3*d*, R. 6*l* 0*s* 9*d*; R.'s Inc. 195*l* and Ho; Pop. 981.) Formerly C. of Rowde, Wilts, and St. George's, Leicester. [18]

PIDCOCK, Benjamin, *St. Luke's Parsonage, Leek, Staffs.*—Corpus Coll. Cam. Jun. Opt. and B.A. 1843; Deac. 1843, Pr. 1844. P. C. of St. Luke's, Leek, Dio. Lich. 1845. (Patrons, Crown and Bp of Lich. alt; P. C.'s Inc. 300*l* and Ho; Pop. 5081.) [19]

PIDCOCK, William, *Addlestone Parsonage, near Weybridge Station, Surrey.*—Queens' Coll. Cam. B.A. 1835, M.A. 1836; Deac. 1835 and Pr. 1837 by Bp of Win. P. C. of St. Paul's, Addlestone, Dio. Win. 1845. (Patron, Bp of Win; P. C.'s Inc. 278*l* and Ho; Pop. 2337.) Chap. of Chertsey Union 1858. Formerly C. of Chertsey and Chap. of the Chertsey Union, 1837–45. [20]

PIDCOCK, William Hugh, *Little Torrington, Devon.*—Corpus Coll. Cam. B.A. 1861; Deac. 1863 and Pr. 1864 by Bp of Win. C. of Little Torrington 1867. Formerly C. of Trinity, Winchester, 1863–65, St. John's, Winchester, 1865–67. [21]

PIDSLEY, F., *Bordesley, Birmingham*—C. of Trinity, Bordesley. [22]

PIERCY, John, *Rushock Rectory, Droitwich.*—St. Cath. Hall, Cam. S.C.L. 1829, LL.B. 1831; Deac. 1829, Pr. 1831. R. of Rushock, Dio. Wor. 1845. (Patron, Ld Chan; Tithe, 298*l* 2*s* 7½*d*; Glebe, 21 acres; R.'s Inc. 329*l* and Ho; Pop. 159.) [23]

PIERCY, John Morpott William, *Slawston Vicarage, Market Harborough, Leicestershire.*—Clare Coll. Cam. B.A. 1839, M.A. 1845; Deac. 1840, Pr. 1841. V. of Slawston, Dio. Pet. 1847. (Patron, Earl of Cardigan; Corn Rent, 56*l*; Glebe, 52 acres; V.'s Inc. 173*l* and Ho; Pop. 246.) R. of Glooston, Leicestershire, Dio. Pet. 1848. (Patron, Earl of Cardigan; Glebe, 185 acres; R.'s Inc. 255*l* and Ho; Pop. 157*l*.) Formerly C. of Pickwell, Leicestershire, 1840–43, Wymeswold 1843–46. [24]

PIERITZ, George Wildon, *Hardwicke Rectory, Royston, Cambs.*—Caius Coll. Cam. Tyrwhitt Heb. Scho. B.A. 1846, M.A. 1852; Deac. 1846 by Abp of York, Pr. 1846 by Bp of Rip. R. of Hardwicke, Dio. Ely, 1864. (Patron, Bp of Ely; Tithe, comm. 256*l*; Glebe, 44 acres; R.'s Inc. 310*l* and Ho; Pop. 250.) [25]

PIERPOINT, Richard Deare, *Hill Lodge, Woodbridge-road, Ipswich.*—St. John's Coll. Cam. Jun. Opt. and 3rd cl. Cl. Trip. B.A. 1861, M.A. 1864; Deac. 1861 and Pr. 1862 by Bp of Nor. C. of St. Clement's and St. Helen's, Ipswich. Formerly C. of Acle, Norfolk. 1861. [26]

PIERPOINT, Richard William, *Southbourne Parsonage, Eastbourne, Sussex.*—St. John's Coll. Cam. Sen. Opt. 1836, M.A. 1840; Deac. 1837, Pr. 1838; P. C. of Trinity, Eastbourne, Dio. Chich. 1847. (Patron, V. of Eastbourne; P. C.'s Inc. 250*l* and Ho; Pop. 3796.) [27]

PIERSON, George James, *Norton Vicarage, Baldock, Herts.*—Jesus Coll. Cam. Sen. Opt. and B.A. 1839, M.A. 1842; Deac. 1840 and Pr. 1841 by Bp of G. and B. V. of Norton, Dio. Roch. 1842. (Patrons, Rev. J. B. Watson and G. D. Wade, Esq; Glebe, 58½ acres; V.'s Inc. 90*l* and Ho; Pop. 352.) Formerly Chap. of the D. of Little Wymondley, Herts, 1843. [1]

PIERSON, William Frederick, *The Parsonage, Settle, Yorks.*—Emman. Coll. Cam. B.A. 1845, M.A. 1848; Deac. 1845 and Pr. 1846 by Bp of Ches. P. C. of Settle, Dio. Rip. 1848. (Patrons, Trustees; Glebe, ½ acre; P. C.'s Inc. 120*l* and Ho; Pop. 1586.) Surrogate 1859. Formerly C. of Blackburn. [2]

PIETERS, John William, *St. John's College, Cambridge.*—St. John's Coll. Cam. 9th Wrang. and B.A. 1847, M.A. 1850, B.D. 1857; Deac. 1849 and Pr. 1851 by Bp of Ely. Fell. of St. John's Coll. Cam. 1848. Formerly C. of Wotton, Surrey, 1849–50. [3]

PIGGOTT, Francis Allen, *Worthing, Sussex.*—Trin. Coll. Cam. B.A. 1843, M.A. 1846; Deac. 1843, Pr. 1844. Prin. of Worthing Coll. 1860. Formerly C. of Chapel of Ease, Worthing, 1843, Trinity with St. Mary's, Guildford, 1847; C. of Broadwater, and Chap. of Steyning Union, Sussex, 1854. [4]

PIGGOTT, Samuel Rotton, *Bredgar Vicarage, Sittingbourne, Kent.*—St. Edm. Hall, Ox. 1830, B.A. 1833; Deac. 1834 and Pr. 1835 by Bp of Lin. V. of Bredgar, Dio. Cant. 1849. (Patron, Sir E. Dering, Bart; Tithe—Imp. 375*l*, V. 204*l*; Glebe, 1½ acres; V.'s Inc. 204*l* and Ho; Pop. 547.) Editor, *Noah and his Days* (a Poem, with Preface, a Dissertation on Prophecy and Notes), 2*s* 6*d*. [5]

PIGGOTT, Thomas, *Burton New Road, Lincoln.*—King's Coll. Lond. Theol. Assoc; Deac. 1866 by Bp of Lin. C. of St. Martin's, Lincoln, 1867. Formerly C. of Willoughby, Spilsby, 1866–67. [6]

PIGOT, Edward, *Whittington Rectory, Kirk Lonsdale, Lancashire.*—Brasen. Coll. Ox. B.A. 1841, M.A. 1844; Deac. 1841 and Pr. 1842. R. of Whittington, Dio. Man. 1857. (Patron, E. Hornby, Esq; Tithe, 326*l* 10*s*; R.'s Inc. 420*l* and Ho; Pop. 421.) Formerly V. of St. Thomas's, Ashton-in-Makerfield, Lanc. 1848–57; Surrogate 1847. [7]

PIGOT, Henry Septimus, *Horwich Parsonage, Bolton-le-Moors, Lancashire.*—Brasen. Coll. Ox. B.A. 1848, M.A. 1851; Deac. 1849 and Pr. 1850 by Bp of Nor. P. C. of Horwich, Dio. Man. 1853. (Patron, V. of Deane; P. C.'s Inc. 334*l* and Ho; Pop. 3471.) Formerly C. of Lopham, Norfolk. [8]

PIGOT, Hugh, *The Vicarage, Wisbech St. Mary, Cambs.*—Brasen. Coll. Ox. B.A. 1842, M.A. 1845; Deac. 1843 and Pr. 1844 by Abp of Cant. V. of Wisbech St. Mary, Dio. Ely, 1863. (Patron, Bp of Ely; Tithe, 879*l*; Glebe, 33*l* 16*s*; V.'s Inc. 912*l* 16*s* and Ho; Pop. 1887.) Formerly C. of Hadleigh, Suffolk, 1843–63. Author, *Death in the Lord* (a Sermon), 1855; *The Blessed Life* (a Course of Lectures, on the Beatitudes), 2nd ed. 1855, 4*s*; "*He Descended into Hell*" (a Sermon), 1857; *History of Hadleigh*, Lowestoft, 1859, 4to. 18*s*, 8vo. 12*s*; *The Sorrow and the Joy of Parting* (a Farewell Sermon), 1863; *The Education of the Poor* (a Sermon), 1865; *A Guide to the Town of Hadleigh*, 1866; *The Choral Movement* (a Sermon), 1867; *Suffolk Superstitions*, Bradbury and Evans, 1867; Articles in the *Churchman's Magazine*, and *Gentleman's Magazine*. [9]

PIGOT, John David, *Cuxham Rectory, Tetsworth, Oxon.*—Mert. Coll. Ox. B.A. 1837; Deac. 1838 and Pr. 1839 by Bp of Lin. R. of Cuxham, Dio. Ox. 1853. (Patron, Mert. Coll. Ox; Tithe, 192*l*; Glebe, 24 acres; R.'s Inc. 215*l* and Ho; Pop. 177.) [10]

PIGOT, John Tayleur, *Fremington Vicarage, Barnstaple, Devon.*—Brasen. Coll. Ox. B.A. 1844, M.A. 1847; Deac. 1844 and Pr. 1845 by Bp of Ches. V. of Fremington, Dio. Ex. 1855. (Patron, the present V; Tithe, 289*l*; V.'s Inc. 375*l* and Ho; Pop. 1245.) Rural Dean of Barnstaple 1857. Formerly Min. Can. of Roch. Cathl. 1847–55, and Even. Lect. at Frindsbury, near Rochester, 1853–55. Author, *Our Present Help* (Sermon on Fast-Day, 1854); *Two Sermons for the present Crisis* 1854. [11]

PIGOT, Octavius Frederick, *Bradshaw, near Wigan.*—Dur. Licen. Theol. 1852; Deac. 1853 and Pr. 1854 by Bp of Ches. C. of Haigh, near Wigan, 1858. Formerly C. of Ashton-in-Makerfield, 1853, Chorlton-cum-Hardy, near Manchester, 1856. [12]

PIGOTT, Arthur James, *Uffington Parsonage, Shrewsbury.*—Mert. Coll. Ox. 2nd cl. Lit. Hum. and B.A. 1838; Deac. 1839 by Bp of Chich. Pr. 1840 by Bp of Lich. P. C. of Uffington, Dio. Lich. 1856. (Patron, A. W. Corbet, Esq; Glebe, 6 acres; P. C.'s Inc. 57*l* and Ho; Pop. 180.) P. C. of Battlefield, Dio. Lich. (Patron, A. W. Corbet, Esq; P. C.'s Inc. 233*l*; Pop. 81.) Author, *Important Truths for Important Times* (six Letters to his Parishioners), 1851. [13]

PIGOTT, C. F. C., *Edgmond Rectory, Newport, Salop.*—R. of Edgmond, Dio. Lich. 1865. (Patron, the present R; Tithe, 2397*l* 19*s* 6*d*; R.'s Inc. 2440*l* and Ho; Pop. 952.) Formerly R. of Llanwenarth with Govillon, Monmouthshire, 1861–65. [14]

PIGOTT, George Granado Graham Foster, *Abington Pigotts Rectory, Royston, Cambs.*—St. Peter's Coll. Cam. LL.B. 1830; Deac. and Pr. 1831 by Bp of Lin. R. of Abington Pigotts or Abington-in-the-Clay, Dio. Ely, 1850. (Patron, the present R; Tithe, 362*l*; Glebe, 28 acres; R.'s Inc. 390*l* and Ho; Pop. 228.) [15]

PIGOTT, G. O. Smyth, *Kingston Seymour, Somerset.*—R. of Kingston Seymour, Dio. B. and W. 1854. (Patroness, Mrs. Pigott; R.'s Inc. 305*l*; Pop. 336.) [16]

PIGOTT, George William, *Upton Magna Rectory, Shrewsbury.*—Ex. Coll. Ox. Hon. 4th cl. Lit. Hum. and B.A. 1848; Deac. 1848 and Pr. 1849 by Bp of Lich. R. of Upton Magna with Withington, Dio. Lich. 1854. (Patron, A. W. Corbet, Esq; Tithe, 733*l*; Glebe, 45 acres; R.'s Inc. 778*l* and Ho; Pop. 452.) [17]

PIGOTT, Randolphe Henry, *Grendon Rectory, Bicester.*—St. John's Coll. Cam. B.A. 1860; Deac. 1861 and Pr. 1862 by Bp of Ox. R. of Grendon-Underwood, Dio. Ox. 1862. (Patrons, Trustees of G. W. Pigott, Esq, Tithe, 80*l*; Glebe, 250 acres; R.'s Inc. 360*l* and Ho; Pop. 450.) Formerly C. of Chipping Norton 1861. Author, *Margery the Martyr*, 1863, and other religious tales. [18]

PIGOTT, Richard Paynton, *Ellisfield Rectory, Basingstoke, Hants.*—Trin. Coll. Ox; Deac. 1836 and Pr. 1837 by Bp of Win. R. of Ellisfield, Dio. Win. 1837. (Patroness, Mrs. Brocas; Tithe, 402*l*; Glebe, 20 acres; R.'s Inc. 420*l* and Ho; Pop. 255.) [19]

PIGOTT, Shreeve Botry, *Great Bradley, near Newmarket.*—St. Peter's Coll. Cam. B.A. 1835; Deac. 1835, Pr. 1836. R. of Great Bradley, Suffolk, Dio. Ely, 1864. (Patrons, Trustees of William Phillips, Esq; Tithe, 640*l*; Glebe, 50 acres; R's Inc. 700*l*; Pop. 460.) Formerly C. of Hardingstone, Northants, 1835, Bramley, Hants, 1837–42; R. of Crawley, Sussex, 1842; V. of Great Wilbraham, Cambs, 1848. [20]

PIGOTT, Wellesley Pole, *Fovant Rectory, Salisbury.*—New Inn Hall, Ox. B.A. 1835, M.A. 1836; Deac. 1835 and Pr. 1836 by Bp of Salis. R. of Fovant, Dio. Salis. 1836. (Patron, Earl of Pembroke; Tithe, 540*l*; Glebe, 45 acres; R.'s Inc. 563*l* and Ho; Pop. 600.) R. of Fugglestone St. Peter with Bemerton, Wilts, Dio Salis. 1836. (Patron, Earl of Pembroke; Fugglestone, Tithe, 550*l*; Glebe, 6 acres; R.'s Inc. 550*l*; Pop. 609.) [21]

PIGOTT, William, *Whaddon Vicarage, Stony-Stratford, Bucks.*—New Coll. Ox. B.C.L. 1835; Deac. 1836 by Bp of Ox. Pr. 1837 by Bp of Lin. V. of Whaddon, Dio. Ox. 1850. (Patron, New Coll. Ox; Glebe, 242 acres; V.'s Inc. 300*l* and Ho; Pop. 493.) [22]

PIGOTT, W. G. F., *Abington-in-the-Clay, Cambs.*—C. of Abington. [23]

PIGOU, Francis.—Dub. A.B. 1853; Deac. 1855 by Bp of Ox. P. C. of St. Philip's, Regent-street, Lond. (Patron, R. of St. James's, Westminster.) Lect. of St. Paul's, Kensington. Formerly C. of Stoke-Talmage, Oxon. [24]

PIGOU, Henry, *Little Bredy, Dorchester.*—Pemb. Coll. Cam. B.A. 1853, M.A. 1859; Deac. 1856 and Pr. 1857 by Bp of Ches. C. of Long Bredy with Little Bredy 1866. Formerly C. of Halton, Cheshire, Greywell, Hants, and Bourne End, Herts. [25]

PIGOU, Henry Clarence, *Wyke Regis Rectory, Weymouth, Dorset.*—Univ. Coll. Ox. Scho. of, B.A. 1844, M.A. 1848; Deac. 1845, Pr. 1846. R. of Wyke Regis, Dio. Salis. 1855. (Patron, Bp of Win; Tithe, 550*l*; Glebe, 26¾ acres; R.'s Inc. 676*l* and Ho; Pop. 1006.) [1]

PIKE, Sidney, 32, *Mostyn-road, Brixton, S.*—Caius Coll. Cam. Sen. Opt. in Math. Trip. B.A. 1864; Deac. 1864 and Pr. 1865 by Bp of Win. C. of Ch. Ch. North Brixton, Surrey, 1864. [2]

PIKE, William Bennett, *Downing College, Cambridge.*—Trin. Coll. Cam. Wrang, 2nd cl. Cl. Trip. and B.A. 1853, Downing Coll. M.A. 1856; Deac. 1855 and Pr. 1856 by Bp of Ely. Fell. Tut. and Chap. of Downing Coll. Cam. 1855. [3]

PILDITCH, John, *Westbury, Wilts.*—Queen's Coll. Cam. Clarke's Scho. and Librarian, S.C.L. 1865; Deac. 1856 by Bp of Wor; Pr. 1857 by Bp of St. D. for Bp of Ex. C. of Westbury 1866. Formerly P. C. of Falfield Thornbury, Gloucestershire, 1864–66. [4]

PILKINGTON, Charles, *Stockton Rectory, Southam, Warwickshire.*—New Coll. Ox. B C.L. 1827; Deac. 1825 and Pr. 1826 by Bp of Herf. Preb. of Wyndham in Chich. Cathl. 1834. (Value, 11*l*.) R. of Stockton, Dio. Wor. 1835. (Patron, New Coll. Ox; Glebe, 218½ acres; R.'s Inc. 286*l* and Ho; Pop. 548.) Rural Dean of Dassett Magna, in the Dio. of Wor. 1838; Can. Res. of Chich. Cathl. 1850. (Value, 400*l* and Res.) Chancellor of the Cathl. Ch. of Chich. 1854. [5]

PILKINGTON, Charles Henry, *Fair Oak, Bishopstoke, Hants.*—New Coll. Ox. 3rd cl. Lit. Hum. 2nd cl. Math. B.A. 1858, M.A. 1861; Deac. 1860 and Pr. 1861 by Bp of Win. Fell. of New Coll. Ox; C. of Bishopstoke 1860. [6]

PILKINGTON, J. G. — Clerical Sec. of the Bishop of London's Fund. Formerly Min. of St. Matthew's Mission Church, St. Mary's, Newington, Surrey. [7]

PILKINGTON, Nicholas Gee, *Feltham, Hounslow, W.* — Dur. B.A. 1849, M.A. 1851; Deac. 1850, Pr. 1851. Chap. to the County of Middlesex Industrial Sch. Feltham, 1861. (Patrons, Visiting Justices; Chap.'s Inc. 300*l* and Ho.) Formerly Sen. C. of Horsham 1852; Chap. to Newcastle Borough Gaol, and Even. Lect. of St. Andrew's 1853; Chap. to County Bridewell, Walsingham, 1857–61. [8]

PILKINGTON, Richard, 1, *Ham-terrace, West Ham, Essex.*—Queens' Coll. Cam. B.A. 1850, M.A. 1853; Deac. 1850 and Pr. 1851 by Bp of Ches. [9]

PILKINGTON, William, *Campbell-road, Thornton-heath, London, S.*—St. Bees; Deac. 1862 and Pr. 1863 by Bp of Ches. C. of Ch. Ch. Croydon, 1867. Formerly C. of St. Jude's, Liverpool, 1863. [10]

PILLING, John Rushworth, *Longham, Thetford, Norfolk.*—Magd. Hall, Ox. B.A. 1849; Deac. 1850 and Pr. 1851 by Bp of Ches. P. C. of Longham with Wendling R. Dio. Nor. 1864. (Patron, Ld Chan; Longham, Tithe, Imp. 285*l*; Glebe, 64 acres; Wendling, Tithe, 30*l* 4*s* 6*d*; Glebe, 60 acres; P. C.'s Inc. 155*l* and Ho; Pop. Longham 320, Wendling 371.) Formerly C. of Cheadle 1850–57, Upwell, Cambs, 1857–61, Wells, Norfolk, 1861–63; V. of Binham, Norfolk, 1863–64. [11]

PILLING, William, *Arnesby, Leicester.*—St. John's Coll. Cam. B.A. 1852, M.A. 1857; Deac. 1852, Pr. 1853. V. of Arnesby, Dio. Pet. 1865. (Patron, the present V; V.'s Inc. 190*l*; Pop. 573.) Formerly C. of Whalley 1852–54; P. C. of Grimsargh, Preston, 1854–65. [12]

PILSON, Robert, *Birts-Morton Rectory, Tewkesbury.*—Dub. A.M; Deac. and Pr. by Bp. of Down and Connor. R. of Birts-Morton, Dio. Wor. 1858. (Patron, C. Pilson, Esq; Tithe, 330*l*; Glebe, 28 acres; R.'s Inc. 400*l* and Ho; Pop. 318.) Author, *Tradition, Infallibility, and Private Judgment*; *Mode of Baptism, an Address to Baptists*; *Light in the Evening, or Memorials of H. W*; *The Lord our Righteousness.* [13]

PINCHES, Thomas, *Braddyl-place, Ulverston.*—St. John's Coll. Cam. B.A. 1862; Deac. 1864, Pr. 1866. C. of Trinity, Ulverston, 1864. [14]

PINCK, Robert, *Riggs House, Hawes, Yorks.*—St. Bees; Deac. 1851 and Pr. 1852 by Bp of Rip. P. C. of Hardrow and Lunds P. C. Yorks. Dio. Rip. 1854. (Patrons, Lord Wharncliffe and V. of Aysgarth alt; P. C.'s Inc. 190*l*; Pop. 552.) [15]

PINCKNEY, Robert, *The Rectory, Chilfrome, Dorset.*—R. of Chilfrome, Dio. Salis. 1862. (Patron, J. Pinckney, Esq; R.'s Inc. 200*l* and Ho; Pop. 120.) [16]

PINCKNEY, William Philip, *Trinity Parsonage, Rotherfield-Greys, Henley-on-Thames.*—Trin. Coll. Cam. B.A. 1832, M.A. 1836. P. C. of Trinity, Rotherfield-Greys, Dio. Ox. 1848. (Patron, Bp of Ox. next turn; P. C.'s Inc. 125*l* and Ho; Pop. 1235.) [17]

PINCOTT, Edward London, *Dupplin Castle, Perthshire.*—Caius Coll. Cam. B.A. 1861, M.A. 1866; Deac. 1862 and Pr. 1863 by Bp of Lin. Dom. Chap. to the Earl of Kinnoul. Formerly C. of Southwell, Notts, 1862. [18]

PINCOTT, William Henry, *Bexley Heath, Kent, S.E.*—St. Aidan's; Deac. 1859 and Pr. 1860 by Abp of Cant. P. C. of Ch. Ch. Bexley Heath, Dio. Cant. 1866. (Patron, Viscount Sydney; Tithe, 160*l*; P. C.'s Inc. 270*l*; Pop. 3500.) Formerly C. of Dartford 1859. [19]

PINDER, George, *Hartford Vicarage, Huntingdon.*—St Bees; Deac. 1844 and Pr. 1845 by Bp of Ches. V. of Hartford, Dio. Ely, 1860. (Patron, the present V; Glebe, 64 acres; V.'s Inc. 185*l* and Ho; Pop. 341.) Formerly R. of Woolley, Hunts, 1857–60. [20]

PINDER, Humphrey Senhouse, *Bratton-Fleming, Barnstaple.*—Caius Coll. Cam. Fell. of, Wrang. and B.A. 1827, M.A. 1830; Deac. 1828, Pr. 1829. R. of Bratton-Fleming, Dio. Ex. 1838. (Patron, Caius Coll. Cam; Tithe, 485*l*; Glebe, 257 acres; R.'s Inc. 650*l* and Ho; Pop. 686.) [21]

PINDER, John Hothersall, *Wells, Somerset.*—Caius Coll. Cam. B.A. 1816, M.A. 1823; Deac. and Pr. 1818. Precentor 1840, and Can. Res. and Preb. of Litton in Wells Cathl. 1852. (Value, 400*l* and Res.) Author, *Sermons on the Common Prayer*; *Sermons on the Holy Days of the Church*; *Meditations and Prayers on the Ordination Services.* [22]

PINDER, North, *Greys Rectory, Henley-on-Thames.*—Trin. Coll. Ox. 1st cl. Lit. Hum. 1850, B.A. 1853, M.A. 1855; Deac. 1855, Pr. 1856. R. of Rotherfield-Greys, Dio. Ox. 1861. (Patron, Trin. Coll. Ox; R.'s Inc. 714*l* and Ho; Pop. 365.) Formerly Fell. and Tut. of Trin. Coll. [23]

PINHORN, Charles Avery, *Gillingham, Dorset.*—Dub. A.B. 1862; Salisbury Theol. Coll; Deac. 1864 and Pr. 1865 by Bp of Salis. Asst. C. of Gillingham 1864. [24]

PINHORN, George, *Brimfield Rectory, near Ludlow.*—St. Edm. Hall, Ox. 3rd cl. Lit. Hum. and B.A. 1830, M.A. 1833; Deac. 1830, Pr. 1832. R. of Brimfield, Dio. Herf. 1832. (Patron, Bp. of Herf; Tithe—App. 155*l*, Imp. 3*s* 4*d*, R. 125*l*; Glebe, 5 acres; R. N.'s Inc. 156*l*; Pop. 665.) P. C. of Ashford Bowdler, Salop, Dio. Herf. 1835. (Patron, C. Walker, Esq; Tithe, Imp. 108*l* 16*s*; P. C.'s Inc. 70*l*; Pop. 106.) Formerly C. of Rock, Worcestershire, 1830. Author, *A Consecration Sermon*, 1834; *Providence of God over the British Church, &c.* 1837; *Letter to the Bishop of London, asserting the Hypothetical Interpretation of the Baptismal Service*, 1842; *A Short and Easy Way for ascertaining the Doctrine of the Church of England*, 1848; *The Noiseless Power of Truth*, 1848; *The Russian Antichrist*, 1854; *The Bible and the Church*, 1864; *Ritualism, or "Graves which appear not,"* 1866. [25]

PINHORNE, George Stanley, *Beckermet, Whitehaven, Cumberland.*—St. John's Coll. Cam. B.A. 1849; Deac. 1850 and Pr. 1851 by Bp of Lich. P. C. of St. John's, Beckermet, Dio. Carl. 1859. (Patron, Jonas L. Burns, Esq; P. C.'s Inc. 112*l* and Ho; Pop. 492.) Formerly C. of Eskdale, Cumberland. [26]

PINKERTON, John Saltwell, *St. John's College, Oxford.*—St. John's Coll. Ox. 3rd cl. Lit. Hum. 1833, B.A. 1834, M.A. 1837, B.D. 1843. Sinecure R. of Leckford, Dio. Win. 1855. (Patron, St. John's Coll. Ox; Tithe, Sinecure R. 532*l* and 30 acres of Glebe;

Sinecure R.'s Inc. 562*l*.) Chap. of St. John's Coll. Ox. [1]

PINNEY, John Charles, *Coleshill, Warwickshire.*—Caius Coll. Cam. B.A. 1860. M.A. 1864; Deac. 1861 by Bp of G. and B. Pr. 1862 by Abp of Cant. C. of Coleshill 1866. Formerly C. of Beckenham 1861–62; Min. of St. Paul's Chapel, Beckenham, 1864–66. [2]

PINNEY, William, *Stainburn, Otley, Yorks.*—Ch. Coll. Cam. B.A. 1850; Deac. 1851 and Pr. 1852 by Bp of Herf. P. C. of Stainburn, Dio. Rip. 1856. (Patron, V. of Kirkby-Overblow; P. C.'s Inc. 75*l*; Pop. 243.) Formerly C. of Potterne, Wilts. [3]

PINNIGER, Richard Broome, *Whichford Rectory, Long Compton, Warwickshire.*—Pemb. Coll. Ox. B.A. 1825, M.A. 1827; Deac. 1828, Pr. 1829. R. of Whichford with Stourton, Dio. Wor. 1839. (Patron, Ch. Ch. Ox; Glebe, 490 acres; R.'s Inc. 814*l* and Ho; Pop. 746.) [4]

PINNOCK, George, *East Dean, Eastbourne, Sussex.*—Deac. 1827 and Pr. 1829 by Bp. of Jamaica in Jamaica. V. of East Dean with Friston V. Dio. Chich. 1846. (Patrons, Bp and D. and C. of Chich; East Dean, Tithe, 265*l*; Glebe, 35 acres; V.'s Inc. 300*l* and Ho; Pop. East Dean 367, Friston 78.) Formerly C. in Jamaica; C. of Stogursey, Somerset, 1832, Madron, Cornwall, 1836. [5]

PINNOCK, William Henry, *Somersham Rectory, St. Ives, Hunts.*—Corpus Coll. Cam. 1st cl. Law Trip. S.C.L. 1843, B.C.L. 1849, D.C.L. and LL.D. 1854 *ad eund.* Ox. 1859; Deac. 1843 and Pr. 1844 by Bp of Ely. C. of Somersham. Author, *The Laws and Usages of the Church and the Clergy*, 5 vols. 5*s*. each; *The Ornaments and Goods of the Church, with the Laws and Usages*, 5*s*; *The Ecclesiastical Vestments, with the Laws and Usages*, 5*s*; *The Laws and Usages affecting Curates, Lecturers, and Chaplains*, 5*s*; *The Laws and Usages affecting the Conduct, Order, and Ritual of Public Worship*, vol. E, 5*s*, vol. F, 6*s* 6*d*; *Analysis of Scripture History*, 3*s* 6*d*; *Analysis of New Testament History and Criticism*, 4*s*; *Analysis of History of the Reformation and the Early English Church*, 4*s* 6*d*; *Annotations, Critical and Exegetical, on the Greek Text of St. Paul's Epistle to the Romans*, 4*s*; *Pinnock's Catechisms of the Arts and Sciences*, 9*d* each; *History of England*, 6*s*; *History of Greece*; *History of Rome*; *Latin Grammar on Ollendorff's Method*, 4*s*; *Analytical Latin Vocabulary*, 1*s* 6*d*; *Use of the Globes*, 4*s*; *English Grammar, on a New Principle*, 1*s* 6*d*; *Scripture Facts*, 2*s*; *Iconology*, 7*s* 6*d*; *Ancient History*, 1*s* 6*d*; *Modern History*, 1*s* 6*d*; *Astronomy made Easy*, 1*s* 6*d*; *Geography made Easy*, 1*s* 6*d*; *Nature Displayed*, 3*s*; *Elements of Latin Familiarised*, 1*s* 6*d*; *Picture of the British Empire*, 5*s* 6*d*; *Analysis of Ecclesiastical History*, 3*s* 6*d*; *Rubrics for Communicants, a Guide to the Holy Communion*, 1*s* 6*d*; *Church Choirs and Church Music*, 6*d*; *The Law of the Rubric and Transition Period of the Church of England*, 1866, 3*s*. [6]

PINWILL, Edmund, *Colnbrook, Bucks.*—C. of Colnbrook. [7]

PINWILL, William James, *Horley Vicarage, Banbury, Oxon.*—Trin. Coll. Cam. B.A. and M.A. 1824. V. of Horley with Hornton V. Dio. Ox. 1853. (Patron, Ld Chan; V.'s Inc. 395*l* and Ho; Pop. Horley 337, Hornton 514.) Chap. to Lord Kingsale. [8]

PIRIE, Henry George, *The Parsonage, Dunoon, Scotland.*—Aberdeen and Edinburgh; Deac. 1846 and Pr. 1847 by Bp of Glasgow. Incumb. of Trinity, Dunoon, Dio. Argyll 1848. (Patron, Bp of Argyll and others; Glebe, 2 acres; Incumb.'s Inc. 120*l* and Ho.) [9]

PITCAIRN, James Pelham, *Eccles, Manchester.*—Jesus Coll. Cam. Scho. of, 2nd Prizeman, Sen. Opt. and B.A. 1846, M.A. 1851; Deac. 1846 and Pr. 1847 by Bp of Ches. V. of Eccles, Dio. Man. 1862. (Patron, Ld Chan; V.'s Inc. 900*l* and Ho; Pop. 13,079.) Dom. Chap. to the Duke of Roxburghe 1854. Formerly R. of St. John's, Longsight, 1850–62. [10]

PITCHER, Amos William, *Horton-in-Ribblesdale, Settle, Yorks.*—Stud. of the Univ. Bonn, and King's Coll. Lond; Deac. 1858, Pr. 1859. P. C. of Horton-in-Ribblesdale, Dio. Rip. 1866. (Patron, Bp of Rip; P. C.'s Inc. 104*l* and Ho; Pop. 417.) Formerly C. of Low Harrowgate 1858–60, Trinity, Salford; Asst. Min. Park Chapel, Chelsea, 1862-64; Chap. of the City of London Hospital for Diseases of the Chest 1864–66. Author, *Le Jugement futur*, Paris, 1857; *Das zukünftige Gericht*, Bonn, 1857–58. [11]

PITCHFORD, John Watkins, *Laburnum Villa, Tattenhall, Chester.*—Dub. A.B. 1862, A.M. 1865; Deac. 1866 by Bp of Ches. C. of Tattenhall 1866. [12]

PITMAN, Edward Rogers, *Rugeley, Staffs.*—Ch. Coll. Cam. Scho. of, 1st cl. Cl. Trip. and B.A. 1843, M.A. 1846; Deac. 1844 and Pr. 1846 by Bp of Salis. P. C. of Pipe-Ridware, Dio. Lich. 1853. (Patron, Bp of Lich; Tithe, 45*l*; Glebe, 3 acres; P.C.'s Inc. 75*l*; Pop. 93.) Head Mast. of Rugeley Gr. Sch. Author, *Iphigenia in Tauris, with English Notes*, 1856. [13]

PITMAN, Henry Rogers, *Basford, near Nottingham.*—Clare Coll. Cam. 1837, 2nd Sen. Opt. and B.A. 1841; Deac. 1843 and Pr. 1844 by Bp of Dur. V. of Basford, Dio. Lin. 1848. (Patron, Ld Chan; Glebe, 150 acres; V.'s Inc. 260*l*; Pop. 6518.) Chap. to the Basford Union 1855. [14]

PITMAN, Maurice William, 8, *Dacre Park, Lee, S.E.*—Queen's Coll. Ox. B.A. 1848; Deac. 1849, Pr. 1850. Formerly C. of Trinity, St. Giles-in-the-Fields, Lond. 1849–51, Louth, Lincolnshire, 1851, Cliffe Regis, Northants, 1851–53, Stonton Wyville, Leicestershire, 1853–54, Greenwich 1854–66. Author, *The Good and Faithful Servant* (a Funeral Sermon), 1866. [15]

PITMAN, Thomas, *Eastbourne.*—Wad. Coll. Ox. B.A. 1825, M.A. 1827; Deac. 1826, Pr. 1827. V. of Eastbourne, Dio. Chich. 1828. (Patron, Treasurer of Chich. Cathl; Tithe, comm. 556*l*; Glebe, 4 acres; V.'s Inc. 556*l* and Ho; Pop. 2000.) Surrogate; Preb. of Chich. 1841. [16]

PITMAN, William Daniel, *Chippenham.*—Ex. Coll. Ox. Scho. of, 1862, B.A. 1866; Deac. 1867 by Bp of G. and B. C. of Chippenham 1867. [17]

PITMAN, William Parr, *Aveton-Gifford, Ivybridge, Devon.*—Ex. Coll. Ox. B.A. 1834, M.A. 1838; Deac. 1835, Pr. 1836. R. of Aveton-Gifford, Dio. Ex. 1847. (Patron, the present R; Tithe, 667*l*; Glebe, 97 acres; R.'s Inc. 817*l*; Pop. 839.) [18]

PITT, Charles, *Malmesbury, Wilts.*—Ch. Ch. Ox. B.A. 1822, M.A. 1825. V. of Malmesbury with Rodbourne C. and Corston C. Dio. G. and B. 1829. (Patron, Ld Chan; Tithe—Imp. 186*l* 8*s* 6*d*, V. 430*l* 3*s*; Glebe, 2 acres; V.'s Inc. 433*l*; Pop. Malmesbury 1928, Rodbourne 162, Corston 315.) Surrogate. Formerly R. of Ashton-Keynes 1834–66. [19]

PITT, Charles Whitworth, *Stapleford Abbotts Rectory, Romford, Essex.*—Brasen. Coll. Ox. B.A. 1824, M.A. 1829; Deac. 1825 and Pr. 1826 by Bp of Lon. R. of Stapleford Abbotts, Dio. Roch. 1841. (Patron, Ld Chan; Tithe, 530*l*; Glebe, 20 acres; R.'s Inc. 560*l*; Pop. 502.) [20]

PITT, Joseph, *Rendcomb Rectory, Cirencester.*—Oriel Coll. Ox. B.A. 1838, M.A. 1840; Deac. and Pr. 1844. R. of Rendcomb, Dio. G. and B. 1844. (Patron, the present R; Tithe, 440*l*; Glebe, 24 acres; R.'s Inc. 460*l* and Ho; Pop. 246.) [21]

PITTAR, Arthur Charles, *Ashton Hayes Parsonage, Chester.*—Dub. A.B. 1850; Deac. 1850, Pr. 1851. P. C. of Ashton Hayes, Dio. Ches. 1863. (Patron, W. Atkinson, Esq; P. C.'s Inc. 160*l*; Pop. 626.) Formerly P. C. of Riddings with Somercotes, Derbyshire, 1854–63. [22]

PITTS, Thomas, *St. George's Parsonage, Halifax.*—Queens' Coll. Cam. B.A. 1838; Deac. 1838 by Bp of Roch. Pr. 1839 by Bp of Rip. P. C. of St. George's, Sowerby, Dio. Rip. 1841. (Patron, V. of Halifax; P. C.'s Inc. 150*l* and Ho; Pop. 2707.) Formerly C. of Otley, 1838–41 [23]

PITTS, Thomas, *Emmanuel College, Cambridge.*—Emman. Coll. Cam. 16th Wrang. and Fell. of, 1865; Deac. 1866 by Bp of Ely. [24]

PIX, George Banastre, *Acaster-Selby, Tadcaster, Yorks.*—Lin. Coll. Ox. B.A. 1846, M.A. 1850; Deac. 1849 and Pr. 1851 by Bp of Wor. P. C. of Acaster-

Selby, Dio. York, 1859. (Patron, Sir W. M. Milner, Bart; P. C.'s Inc. 50*l*; Pop. 154.) Formerly Vice-Prin. of York Training Coll; Head Mast. of Gr. Sch. Trinidad, West Indies, 1853–56. [1]

PIX, Henry, *Wimborne-Minster, Dorset.*—Emman. Coll. Cam. Wrang. and B.A. 1843, M.A. 1846; Deac. 1845 and Pr. 1846 by Bp of Herf. 2nd Mast. of Wimborne Gr. Sch. 1856. Formerly Sen. Math. Mast. in Marlborough Coll. 1847–55. Author, *Arithmetic and Algebra,* 1844; *Examples in Arithmetic* 1851, 1857, 1861, and 1864. [2]

PIXELL, Charles Henry Vincent, *Skirwith Parsonage, Penrith.*—Trin. Coll. Cam. B.A. 1862, M.A. 1867; Deac. 1863 and Pr. 1864 by Bp of Wor. P. C. of Skirwith, Dio. Carl. 1866. (Patron, C. Parker, Esq; Glebe, 2 acres; P. C.'s Inc. 110*l* and Ho; Pop. 315.) Formerly C. of St. Peter's and St. Michael's, Coventry. [3]

PIXELL, Henry, *South Bank, Leamington.*—Clare Coll. Cam. B.A. 1823, M.A. 1826; Deac. 1823, Pr. 1824. [4]

PIZEY, Charles Thomas, *Camberwell, Surrey, S.*—St. Cath. Coll. Cam. B.A. 1851. Head Mast. of the Collegiate Sch. Camberwell. Formerly C. of St. George's, Everton, and Holy Trinity, Liverpool. [5]

PIZEY, John Frederick, *Beaujaiet, or Bozeat Vicarage, Wellingborough, Northants.*—Dub. A.B. 1846; Deac. 1847 and Pr. 1848 by Bp of Chich. V. of Beaujaiet with Strixton R. Dio. Pet. 1853. (Patron, Earl Spencer; Beaujaiet, Tithe, 30*l*; Glebe, 123 acres; Strixton, Tithe—App. 6*l* 19*s* 8*d*, Imp. 85*l* 10*s*, R. 93*l* 1*s* 8*d*; V.'s Inc. 230*l* and Ho; Pop. Beaujaiet 955, Strixton 61.) [6]

PLACE, Joseph, *Great Casterton Rectory, near Stamford.*—St. John's Coll. Cam. M.A. R. of Great Casterton with Pickworth R. Dio. Pet. 1861. (Patron, Marquis of Exeter; R.'s Inc. 500*l* and Ho; Pop. Casterton 323, Pickworth 151.) [7]

PLAFORD, G.—Chap. to the Labourers on the New Railways in the North of London. [8]

PLANT, Samuel, *Weston-upon-Trent, Stafford.*—Brasen. Coll. Ox. B.A. 1844, M.A. 1847; Deac. 1845 and Pr. 1846 by Bp of Lich. V. of Weston-upon-Trent, Dio. Lich. 1849. (Patrons, Rev. C. Inge and J. Newton Lane, Esq. alt; Tithe—Imp. 95*l* and 12½ acres of Glebe, V. 25*l*; Glebe, 1½ acre; V.'s Inc. 105*l* and Ho; Pop. 503.) Formerly C. of Hanley, Staffs, 1843–49. Author, *Parochial Sermons,* 1857, 5*s*. [9]

PLATER, Charles Eaton, *Aldington, Hythe, Kent.*—Ch. Coll. Cam. Sen. Opt. 3rd cl. Cl. Trip. and B.A. 1847, M.A. 1850; Deac. 1847 by Bp of Lon. Pr. 1848 by Abp of Cant. C. of Aldington 1847. [10]

PLATER, Herbert, *Newark, Notts.*—Mert. Coll. Ox. Postmaster, 2nd cl. Lit. Hum. and B.A. 1849, M.A. 1852. Head Mast. of Newark Gr. Sch. [11]

PLATT, Arthur Mountjoy, *Balscott, Banbury,*—Jesus Coll. Cam. LL.B. 1866; Deac. 1866 and Pr. 1867 by Bp of Ox. C. of Wroxton with Balscott 1866. [12]

PLATT, George, *Sedbergh Vicarage, near Kendal.*—Trin. Coll. Cam. Sen. Opt. 2nd in 1st cl. Cl. Trip. and B.A. 1828, M.A. 1831; Deac. 1829 by Bp of Nor. Pr. 1831 by Bp of Lich. V. of Sedbergh, Dio. Rip. 1841. (Patron, Trin. Coll. Cam.; Tithe—Imp. 129*l*, V. 16*l*; Glebe, 140 acres; V.'s Inc. 400*l* and Ho; Pop. 2070.) Surrogate. [13]

PLATT, George Moreton, *Whitkirk, near Leeds.*—Trin. Coll. Cam. Bell's Scho. 1854, 8th Jun. Opt. 10th Classic, B.A, 1857, M.A. 1860; Deac. 1860 and Pr. 1862 by Bp of Rip. V. of Whitkirk, Dio. Rip. 1863. (Patron, Trin. Coll. Cam; Tithe, 54*l*; Glebe, 155*l*; V.'s Inc. 230*l* and Ho; Pop. 1726.) Formerly Asst. C. of Masham 1860–62; P. C. of Cautley and Dowbiggin 1862–63. [14]

PLATT, Herbert Edwyn, *Sherborne, Dorset.*—Trin. Coll. Cam. Sen. Opt. B.A; Deac. 1864 and Pr. 1865 by Bp of Salis. C. of Sherborne. [15]

PLATT, Thomas Duodecimus, *Portsea, Hants.*—Trin. Coll. Cam. B.A. 1852; Deac. 1852, Pr. 1853. P. C. of Trinity, Portsea, Dio. Win. 1854. (Patron, V. of St. Mary's, Portsea; P. C.'s Inc. 220*l*; Pop. 10,315.) Surrogate. [16]

PLATTEN, John Clethero, *North Barsham, Fakenham, Norfolk.*—Caius Coll. Cam. B.A. 1833, M.A. 1836; Deac. 1833, Pr. 1835. R. of North Barsham, Dio. Nor. 1843. (Patron, Earl of Oxford; Tithe, 334*l* 7*s*; Glebe, 20 acres; R.'s Inc. 350*l* and Ho; Pop. 57.) [17]

PLATTEN, T. E., *Steeple Morden, Royston, Cambs.*—C. of Steeple Morden. [18]

PLATTEN, Thomas Parlett, *Chellesworth Rectory, Bildeston, Suffolk.*—Emman. Coll. Cam. Prizeman 1833, Sen. Opt. and B.A. 1834, M.A. 1837; Deac. 1835 by Bp of Lin. Pr. 1836 by Bp of Ely. R. of Chellesworth, Dio. Ely, 1852. (Patron, Ld Chan; Tithe, comm. 273*l* 7*s*; Glebe, 30 acres; R.'s Inc. 300*l* and Ho; Pop. 273.) [19]

PLENDERLEATH, William Charles, *Cherhill Rectory, Calne.*—Wad. Coll. Ox. B.A. 1852, M.A. 1855; Deac. 1855 by Bp of G. and B. Pr. 1856 by Bp of Llan. R. of Cherhill, Dio. Salis. 1860. (Patron, Bp of Salis; Tithe, comm. 199*l*; R.'s Inc. 200*l* and Ho; Pop. 364.) Formerly C. of Frodsham, Cheshire, and Bedminster, Somerset; Fell. of the Philological Soc. Author, *The Parish Priest's Visiting List, with Remarks on Parochial Visitation,* 1858. [20]

PLOW, Antony John, *Todmorden, Lancashire.*—Queens' Coll. Cam. B.A. 1855; Deac. 1856 and Pr. 1857 by Bp of Lon. V. of Todmorden, Dio. Man. 1863. (Patron, V. of Rochdale; Glebe, 120*l*; V.'s Inc. 200*l* and Ho; Pop. 5200.) Formerly C. of Staines 1856, Rochdale 1863. [21]

PLOW, Henry Anthony, *Bradley Rectory, Andover-road, Hants.*—Queens' Coll. Cam. B.D. 1847; Deac. 1845, Pr. 1846. R. of Bradley, Dio. Win. 1852. (Patron, C. E. Rumbold, Esq; Tithe, 185*l*; Glebe, 21 acres; R.'s Inc. 235*l* and Ho; Pop. 106.) Formerly P. C. of Wield, near Alresford, 1852. [22]

PLOWS, William, *Barnham Parsonage, Thetford.*—Pemb. Coll. Ox. B.A. 1851, M.A. 1854; Deac. 1852 and Pr. 1853 by Bp of Lon. C. of Euston with Barnham and Little Fakenham 1866. Formerly C. of St. Bartholomew's, Bethnal Green, Lond. 1853, St. Peter's, Sible Hedingham, 1857–61, Trinity, Westminster, 1861–63, Kentford, Newmarket, 1863–66. Author, *Hymns for the Great Festivals set to Original Tunes,* Novello, 1864, 2*s* 6*d*. [23]

PLUCKNETT, Charles, *Holton, Wincanton, Somerset.*—St. John's Coll. Cam. B.A. 1816, M.A. 1820; Deac. 1816, Pr. 1817. R. of Holton, Dio. B. and W. 1833. (Patron, the present R; Tithe, 110*l*; Glebe, 38¾ acres; R.'s Inc. 164*l*; Pop. 208.) C. of Bratton St. Maur, Wincanton. [24]

PLUCKNETT, William, *Horsted-Keynes, East Grinstead, Sussex.*—St. John's Coll. Cam. B.A. 1820, M.A. 1823; Deac. 1821, Pr. 1822. R. of Horsted-Keynes, Dio. Chich. 1840. (Patron, Thomas R. Davis, Esq; Tithe, comm. 505*l*; Glebe, 70 acres; R.'s Inc. 550*l* and Ho; Pop. 644.) [25]

PLUME, William Henry, *Framingham-Pigot Rectory, near Norwich.*—Queens' Coll. Cam. B.A. 1839; Deac. 1840 by Bp of Win. Pr. 1845 by Bp of Nor. R. of Framingham-Pigot, Dio. Nor. 1845. (Patron, Bp of Nor; Tithe, 221*l* 6*s* 8*d*; Glebe, 25 acres; R.'s Inc. 260*l* and Ho; Pop. 312.) [26]

PLUMER, Charles John, *Elstree Rectory, Edgeware, Herts.*—Ball. Coll. Ox. 2nd cl. Lit. Hum. and B.A. 1821, M.A. 1824; Fell. of Oriel 1821; Deac. 1824 and Pr. 1827 by Bp of Ox. R. of Elstree, Dio. Roch. 1849. (Patron, Ld Chan; Glebe, 200 acres; R.'s Inc. 300*l* and Ho; Pop. 402.) Formerly Fell. of Oriel Coll. Ox. [27]

PLUMMER, John Taylor, *Hartley Maudit Rectory, Alton, Hants.*—Brasen. Coll. Ox. B.A. 1846, M.A. 1849; Deac. 1846, Pr. 1847. R. of Hartley Maudit, Dio. Win. 1847. (Patroness, Mrs. A. H. Douglas; Glebe, 11 acres; R.'s Inc. 255*l* and Ho; Pop. 92) Formerly C. of Tring, Herts, 1846. Author, *The Dignity of Little Children* (a Sermon), Rivingtons, 2nd ed. 6*d*; *The Resur-*

rection of the Just and their Condition in a Future State, Rivingtons, 1866, 5s. [1]

PLUMMER, Matthew, *Heworth Parsonage, Gateshead, Durham.*—Jesus Coll. Cam. B.A. 1831, M.A. 1834; Deac. 1831, Pr. 1832. P. C. of Heworth, Dio. Dur. 1834. (Patrons, Lady James and Thomas Drewett Brown, Esq; Tithe—App. 202*l* 16*s* 4*d*, Imp. 37*l* 1*s* 8*d*; P. C.'s Inc. 266*l* and Ho; Pop. 3100.) Formerly C. of Heworth 1831–34. Author, *The Clergyman's Assistant*, 1846, 3*s* 6*d*; *Observations. on the Book of Common Prayer*, 1847, 4*s* 6*d*. [2]

PLUMMER, William Henry, *Fleet, Winchfield, Hants.*—Trin. Coll. Cam. B.A. 1851; Deac. 1852, Pr. 1857. P. C. of Fleet, Dio. Win. 1860. (Patron, J. W. M. Lefroy, Esq; P. C.'s Inc. 75*l* and Ho.) Formerly C. of Griston, Norfolk. [3]

PLUMPTRE, Charles Pemberton, *Claypole Rectory, Newark, Notts.*—Sid. Coll. Cam. B.A. 1862; Deac. 1863 and Pr. 1864 by Bp of Ox. R. of Claypole, Dio. Lin. 1865. (Patron, C. J. Plumptre, Esq; Glebe, 470 acres; R.'s Inc. 737*l* and Ho; Pop. 774.) Formerly C. of Claydon, Winslow, Bucks, 1863. [4]

PLUMPTRE, Edward Hayes, *King's College, W.C.* and 4, *Gloucester-road, London, N.W.*—Univ. Coll. Ox. Scho. of, Double 1st cl. B.A. 1844, M.A. 1847; Deac. 1846 and Pr. 1847 by Bp of Ox. Prof. of Exegesis of New Testament and Chap. of King's Coll. Lond; Dean of Queen's Coll. 168, Harley-street; Preb. of St. Paul's, 1863; Exam. Chap. to Bp of G. and B; Boyle Lect. 1866–67. Formerly Fell. of Brasen. Coll. Ox. 1844–47; Asst. Preacher at Lincoln's Inn 1851–58; Select Preacher, Oxford, 1851–53; Prof. of Pastoral Theology, King's Coll. Lond. 1853–63. Author, *The Calling of a Medical Student* (Four Sermons), 1849, 1*s* 6*d*; *The Study of Theology and the Ministry of Souls* (Three Sermons), 1853; *King's College Sermons*, 1860; *Dangers Past and Present*, 1862; *Lazarus, and other Poems*, 1865, 5*s*; articles in Smith's *Dictionary of the Bible*; *Master and Scholar, and other Poems*, 1866; *Theology and Life*, 1865; *Sophocles, a New Translation with Biographical Essay*, 1865, 2nd ed. 1867; *Christ and Christendom, Boyle Lectures for* 1866; all published by Strahan. [5]

PLUMPTRE, Frederick Charles, *University College, Oxford.*—Univ. Coll. Ox. 2nd cl. Lit. Hum. and B.A. 1817, M.A. 1820, B.D. 1836, D.D. 1837; Deac. 1819 by Bp of Dur. Pr. 1825 by Bp of Ox. Mast. of Univ. Coll. Ox. 1836; Vice-Chan. of the Univ. of Ox. 1848. Formerly Fell. and Tut. of Univ. Coll. Ox. [6]

PLUMPTRE, Henry Western, *Eastwood, Nottingham.*—Univ. Coll. Ox. B.A. 1859, M.A. 1862; Deac. 1860, Pr. 1861. R. of Eastwood, Dio. Lin. 1863. (Patron, C. J. Plumptre, Esq; Glebe, 165 acres; R.'s Inc. 300*l* and Ho; Pop. 1860.) Formerly C. of Goodnestone, Kent, 1860–63. [7]

PLUMPTRE, B. B., *North Coates, Lincolnshire.*—R. of North Coates, Dio. Lin. 1818. (Patron, Duchy of Lancaster; R.'s Inc. 382*l*; Pop. 290.) [8]

PLUMPTRE, Robert William, *Corfe-Mullen, Wimborne, Dorset.*—Univ. Coll. Ox. Coll. Prizeman for Latin Verse, 4th cl. Lit. Hum. and B.A. 1848, M.A. 1850; Deac. 1849 and Pr. 1850 by Bp of Lich. P. C. of Corfe-Mullen, Dio. Salis. 1858. (Patron, Eton Coll; Tithe, 386*l*; Glebe 3 acres; P. C.'s Inc. 413*l* and Ho: Pop. 725.) Formerly C. of Wombourn with Trysull, Staffs, 1849–52, Pluckley, Kent, 1852, Min. of St. Thomas's, Ferryside, Carmarthenshire, 1852–54; C. of Boxley, Kent, 1855–58. Author, *A Militia Sermon*, Army Scripture Readers' Soc. 1855. [9]

PLUMPTRE, William Alfred, *Woodstock.*—Univ. Coll. Ox. B.A. 1852, M.A. 1858; Deac. 1853 and Pr. 1854 by Bp of Lich. Chap. to the Duke of Marlborough 1867. Formerly Miss. in Madras 1858–62. [10]

PLUMSTEAD, Jonathan, *Eston, Guisborough, Yorks.*—C. of Eston. Formerly C. of Willington, Durham. [11]

POCHIN, Edward Norman, *Sileby Vicarage, Mount Sorrel, Leicestershire.*—Trin. Coll. Cam. B.A. 1851, M.A. 1854; Deac. 1851 and Pr. 1852 by Bp of Pet. V. of Sileby, Dio. Pet. 1856. (Patron, W. Pochin, Esq; V.'s Inc. 152*l* and Ho; Pop. 1572.) [12]

POCHIN, William Henry, *Ramsgill Parsonage, Ripon, Yorks.*—St. Bees; Deac. 1843 and Pr. 1844 by Bp of Ches. P. C. of Ramsgill, Dio. Rip. 1852. (Patron, V. of Masham; P. C.'s Inc. 133*l* and Ho; Pop. 523.) [13]

POCKLINGTON, Duncan, *Tythby, near Nottingham.*—C. of Tythby. [14]

POCKLINGTON, Joseph Nelsey, *St. Michael's Rectory, Hulme, Manchester.*—St. Cath. Hall, Cam; Deac. 1848 and Pr. 1850 by Bp of Man. R. of St. Michael's, Hulme, Dio. Man. 1864. (Patrons, Hugh Birley, Esq. and others; Pop. 8900.) Formerly C. of St. Matthew's, Manchester, 1848, Trinity, Salford, 1854; R. of Trinity 1859; C. of St. Michael's, Hulme, 1861. [15]

POCKLINGTON, Roger, *Walesby Vicarage, Ollerton, Notts.*—Ex. Coll. Ox. B.A. 1825, M.A. 1829; Deac. 1829 and Pr. 1830 by Abp of York. V. of Walesby, Dio. Lin. 1833. (Patron, Earl of Scarborough; Tithe, 12*l*; Glebe, 157 acres; V.'s Inc. 158*l* and Ho; Pop. 327.) R. of Skegness, Spilsby, Linc. Dio. Lin. 1834. (Patron, Earl of Scarborough; Tithe, 180*l*; Glebe, 16 acres; R.'s Inc. 200*l*; Pop. 322.) [16]

POCOCK, Charles, *Rouslench Rectory, Evesham.*—Ch. Ch. Ox. B.A. 1826, M.A. 1830; Deac. 1827 and Pr. 1828 by Bp of Chich. R. of Rouslench, Dio. Wor. 1838. (Patron, Sir Charles Rous-Boughton, Bart; Glebe, 290 acres; R.'s Inc. 407*l* and Ho; Pop. 306.) [17]

POCOCK, Francis, *Monkton Combe, Bath.*—St. Aidan's; Deac. 1855 by Abp of Cant. Pr. 1856 by Bp of Sierra Leone. P. C. of Monkton Combe, near Bath, Dio. B. and W. 1863. (Patron, V. of South Stoke; Tithe, 15*l*; P. C.'s Inc. 50*l*; Pop. 331.) Formerly Chap. to Bp of Sierra Leone 1855–58; C. of Little Faringdon 1858. [18]

POCOCK, Frederick Pearce, *Alfred House School, Bow, Middlesex, E.*—St. Peter's Coll. Cam. B.A. 1841, M.A. 1844; Deac. 1842 and Pr. 1843 by Bp of Lon. Chap to the City of Lond. Union 1844; Prin. of Alfred House Sch. 1859; C. of St. Paul's, Great Portland-street, Marylebone, 1865. Editor of *Bishop Burnet's Pastoral Care*, 1839; *Dr. Bisse's Beauty of Holiness on the Common Prayer, with a Rationale on Cathedral Worship*, 1841; *Bowdler's Theological Essays*, S.P.C.K. 1843; *Simpson's Euclid*, Allman, 1853. [19]

POCOCK, George, 209, *Albany-street, Regent's-park, London, N.W.*—Trin. Hall, Cam. LL.B. 1826; Deac. 1826 by Bp of Lin. Pr. 1827 by Bp of Lon. P. C. of St. Paul's, Great Portland-street, Marylebone, Dio. Lon. 1843. (Patron, the Crown; P. C.'s Inc. from Pew-rents.) Wednesday Even. Lect. at St. Lawrence's, Jewry, Dio. Lon. 1857. (Patrons, the Parishioners of St. Mary Magdalen's, Milk-street.) [20]

POCOCK, George Hume Innes, *Pentrich Vicarage, Belper, Derbyshire.*—St. Bees; Deac. 1853 and Pr. 1854 by Bp of Nor. V. of Pentrich, Dio. Lich. 1855. (Patron, Duke of Devonshire; Tithe, 80*l*; Glebe, 27 acres; V.'s Inc. 150*l*; Pop. 336.) Formerly C. of Mundesley, Norfolk, 1853–55. [21]

POCOCK, John Carne, *Angle Vicarage, near Pembroke.*—Cuddesdon; Deac. 1856 and Pr. 1857 by Bp of Ox. V. of Angle, Dio. St. D. 1859. (Patron, Bp of St. D; V.'s Inc. 84*l* and Ho; Pop. 512.) [22]

PODMORE, John Buckley, *West Hackney, London, N.E.*—Jesus Coll. Cam. B.A. 1853; Deac. 1853, Pr. 1855. P. C. of St. Michael's, West Hackney, Dio. Lon. 1863. Formerly C. of St. James's, Ashted. [23]

PODMORE, Richard Hillman, *Rockbeare Vicarage, near Exeter.*—Trin. Coll. Cam. B.A. 1843, M.A. 1847; Deac. 1846 and Pr. 1847 by Bp of Ex. V. of Rockbeare, Dio. Ex. 1864. (Patron, Bp of Ex; Tithe, 150*l*; Glebe, 21 acres; V.'s Inc. 148*l* and Ho; Pop. 540.) Formerly C. of St. Columb-Major. [24]

PODMORE, Thompson, *Elstree Hill, Herts.*—St. John's Coll. Ox. 1st cl. Lit. Hum. and B.A. 1846, M.A. 1850; Deac. 1847, Pr. 1848. Formerly Fell. of St. John's Coll. Ox. [25]

PODMORE, William Henry, *Queen's Park, Chester.*—Dub. A.B. 1859; Deac. 1859 and Pr. 1860 by Bp of Ox. Formerly Organizing Sec. to the National

Soc. for the Dio. of Manchester; Asst. C. of St. Mary's, Hulme, 1863. [1]

POINGDESTRE, George, *St. Anastasius Grammar School, Jersey.*—Pemb. Coll. Ox. B.A. 1844, M.A. 1854; Deac. 1844 and Pr. 1846 by Bp of Win. P. C. of St. Matthew's, Jersey, Dio. Win. 1848. (Patrons, the R.'s of St. Helier's, St. Lawrence's, and St. Peter's, Jersey; P. C.'s Inc. 50*l*; Pop. 2255.) Prin. of St. Anastasius' Gr. Sch. 1854. [2]

POLAND, Frederick William, *The Vicarage, Paignton, South Devon.*—Emman. Coll. Cam. Jun. Opt. B.A. 1849, M.A. 1853; Deac. 1849 and Pr. 1850 by Bp of Ex. V. of Paignton with Marldon C. Dio. Ex. 1861. (Patrons, J. G. J. Templer, 2 turns, Sir Stafford Northcote, 1 turn; Tithe, Paignton, 430*l*, Marldon 235*l*; Glebe, 7 acres; R.'s Inc. 665*l* and Ho; Pop. Paignton 3076, Marldon 554.) Author, *Notes on Confirmation*, Parker, 1857, 6*d*; *Earnest Exhortations on Practical Subjects*, Masters, 1861, 3*s* 6*d*. [3]

POLE, Edward, *Templeton Rectory, Tiverton, Devon.*—Ex. Coll. Ox. B.A. 1828, M.A. 1831; Deac. 1828 and Pr. 1829 by Bp of Ex. R. of Templeton, Dio. Ex. 1833. (Patron, Sir W. T. Pole, Bart; Tithe, 160*l*; Glebe, 86 acres; R.'s Inc. 224*l* and Ho; Pop. 217.) [4]

POLE, Reginald, *Yeovilton Rectory, Ilchester, Somerset.*—Ex. Coll. Ox. B.A. 1822; Deac. 1823, Pr. 1824. R. of Yeovilton, Dio. B. and W. 1839. (Patron, Bp of B. and W; Tithe—Imp. 4*l*, V. 410*l*; Glebe, 65 acres; R.'s Inc. 528*l* and Ho; Pop. 342.) [5]

POLE, Richard, *Wolverton Rectory, near Newbury.*—Ball. Coll. Ox. 3rd cl. Lit. Hum. and B.A. 1824, M.A. 1826; Deac. 1825, Pr. 1826. R. of Wolverton, Dio. Win. 1844. (Patron, Duke of Wellington; Tithe, 290*l*; Glebe, 80 acres; R.'s Inc. 340*l* and Ho; Pop. 146.) R. of Ewhurst, Hants, Dio. Win. 1847. (Patron, Duke of Wellington; Tithe, 100*l*; R.'s Inc. 105*l*; Pop. 12.) Rural Dean. [6]

POLE, Van Notten Watson Buller, *Upper Swell Rectory, Stow-on-the-Wold, Glouc.*—Ball. Coll. Ox. B.A. 1825; Deac. 1826 and Pr. 1827 by Bp of G. and B. R. of Upper Swell, Dio. G. and B. 1828. (Patron, Charles Van Notten Pole, Esq; Tithe, 30*l*; Glebe, 5 acres; R.'s Inc. 87*l* and Ho; Pop. 65.) R. of Condicote, Glouc. Dio. G. and B. 1840. (Patrons, Rev. W. Bishop and others; Tithe, 6*l* 13*s*; Glebe, 212 acres; R.'s Inc. 263*l*; Pop. 182.) [7]

POLE, William Chandos, *Radborne Rectory, Derby.*—Ch. Ch. Ox. B.A. 1856, M.A. 1862; Deac. 1857 and Pr. 1858 by Bp of Lich. R. of Radborne, Dio. Lich. 1866. (Patron, E. S. C. Pole, Esq; Tithe, 225*l*; Glebe, 130 acres; R.'s Inc. 400*l* and Ho; Pop. 225.) Formerly C. of Ashbourne 1857 59, R. of Trusley, Derbyshire, 1859–66. [8]

POLEHAMPTON, Edward Thomas William, *Hartfield Vicarage, Tunbridge Wells.*—Pemb. Coll. Ox. B.A. 1847, M.A. 1850; Deac. 1849 and Pr. 1851 by Bp of Ox. R. and V. of Hartfield, Dio. Chich. 1859. (Patron, Earl Delawarr: Tithe, 900*l*; Glebe, 1½ acres; R. and V.'s Inc. 902*l* and Ho; Pop. 1451.) Chap. to Earl Powlett. Formerly P. C. of Great Bricet 1855. Co-Editor with the Rev. T. S. Polehampton, of *Memoir, Letters, and Diary of the late Rev. S. Polehampton, Chaplain at Lucknow*, 1858. [9]

POLEHAMPTON, John, *Ightham Rectory, Sevenoaks, Kent.*—Pemb. Coll. Ox. B.A. 1848, M.A. 1851; Deac. 1849 and Pr. 1851 by Bp of Lin. R. of Ightham, Dio. Cant. 1866. (Patron, Thomas Coleman, Esq; R.'s Inc. 540*l* and Ho; Pop. 1152.) Formerly C. of Sneinton, Notts; Tut. of St. Columba's, Dublin, 1851–53; C. of Leigh, Tunbridge, of Sevenoaks, and St. Mary's, Dover. [10]

POLEHAMPTON, Thomas Stedman, *Ellel Parsonage, Lancaster.*—Pemb. Coll. Ox. 1846, 2nd cl. Math. et Phy. and B.A. 1850, M.A. 1852; Deac. 1850 by Bp of Ox. Pr. 1851 by Bp of Salis. P. C. of Ellel, Dio. Man. 1864. (Patron, V. of Cockerham; Tithe—Imp. 184*l* 5*s*; P. C.'s Inc. 150*l* and Ho; Pop. 1277.) Formerly C. of Chaffcombe, Somerset, 1851–53, Beltshanger, Kent, 1853–57, Ross, Herefordshire, 1857-59, Hartfield, Sussex, 1860–61, St. Ann's, Highgate Rise, Lond. 1861–63, Torwood, Devon, 1863–64. Author, *Three Assize Sermons* (at Maidstone), 1855. Co-Editor with the Rev. E. T. W. Polehampton, of *Memoir, Letters, and Diary of the late Rev. Henry S. Polehampton, Chaplain at Lucknow*, 1858; *Steps in the Christian's Life on Earth*, Masters, 1864, 1*s* 6*d*. [11]

POLEY, William Weller, *Brandon House, Brandon, Suffolk.*—Queens' Coll. Cam. B.A. 1837, M.A. 1840; Deac. 1839 and Pr. 1840 by Bp of Nor. R. of Santon, Norfolk, Dio. Nor. 1857. (Patroness, Duchess Dow. of Cleveland; R.'s Inc. 80*l*; Pop. 35.) P. C. of Santon Downham, Suffolk, Dio. Ely, 1857. (Patroness, Duchess Dow. of Cleveland; P. C.'s Inc. 50*l*; Pop. 80.) Formerly C. of Attleborough, Norfolk, 1843–52. [12]

POLHILL, Frederick C., *Sundridge, Kent.* [13]

POLHILL, Henry Western Onslow, *Ashurst Rectory, Tunbridge Wells.*—Univ. Coll. Ox. B.A. 1837, M.A. 1843; Deac. 1838 and Pr. 1839 by Abp of Cant. R. of Ashurst, Dio. Cant. 1861. (Patroness, Countess Delawarr; Tithe, 185*l*; Glebe, 30 acres; R.'s Inc. 207*l* and Ho; Pop. 247.) Formerly R. of Illington, Norfolk, 1851–61. [14]

POLLARD, Edward, *Evedon Rectory, Sleaford, Lincolnshire.*—St. Edm. Hall, Ox. B.A. 1827; Deac. 1827 and Pr. 1828 by Bp of Lin. R. of Evedon, Dio. Lin. 1837. (Patron, Hon. M. E. G. Finch Hatton; Tithe—App. 26*l* 2*s* 6*d*, Imp. 6*l*, R. 300*l*; Glebe, 56 acres; R.'s Inc. 370*l* and Ho; Pop. 62.) V. of Ewerby, Linc. Dio. Lin. 1837. (Patron, Ld Chan; Tithe—Imp. 13*l* 0*s* 3½*d*, V. 48*l* 8*s*; Glebe, 5 acres; V.'s Inc. 68*l*; Pop. 473.) [15]

POLLARD, George Cox, *South Walsham Rectory, Blofield, Norfolk.*—Queens' Coll. Cam. 17th Wrang. and B.A. 1847, M.A. 1850; Deac. 1851 and Pr. 1855 by Bp of Ely. R. of South Walsham, St. Lawrence, Dio. Nor. 1858. (Patron, Queens' Coll. Cam; Tithe, 516*l*; Glebe, 59½ acres; R.'s Inc. 633*l* 18*s* and Ho; Pop. 220.) Formerly Fell. of Queens' Coll. Cam. 1849–58. [16]

POLLARD, Henry Smith, *Everdon Rectory, Daventry.*—Lin. Coll. Ox. B.A. 1833, M.A. 1837. R. of Everdon, Dio. Pet. 1863. (Patron, Eton Coll; Tithe, 251*l*; Glebe, 166 acres; R.'s Inc. 510*l* and Ho; Pop. 740.) Formerly V. of Edlington, Lincolnshire, 1852–57; V. of Coombe-Bissett and P. C. of Homington, Salisbury, 1857–63. [17]

POLLEXFEN, John Hutton, *Colchester.*—Queens' Coll. Cam. B.A. 1843, M.A. 1847; Deac. 1844 by Bp of Rip. Pr. 1846 by Bp of Win. R. of St. Runwald's, Colchester, Dio. Roch. 1851. (Patron, C. G. Round, Esq; R.'s Inc. 140*l*; Pop. 320.) [18]

POLLOCK, James S., *Bordesley, near Birmingham.*—C. of Trinity, Bordesley. Formerly C. of St. John's, Hammersmith. [19]

POLLOCK, Thomas Benson, *St. Alban's, Birmingham.*—Dub. A.M. C. of St. Alban's, Birmingham. Formerly C. of St. Thomas's, Stamford Hill, Middlesex. [20]

POLLOCK, William, *Bowdon Vicarage, Altrincham, Cheshire.*—V. of Bowdon, Dio. Ches. 1856. (Patron, Bp of Ches; Tithe, App. 1891*l* 19*s*, V. 401*l* 10*s*; V.'s Inc. 470*l* and Ho; Pop. 4026.) Surrogate; Rural Dean. [21]

POLLOCK, William James, *The Vicarage, Keswick.*—Dub. A.B. Wad. Coll. Ox. 1st cl. Lit. Hum. A.M; Deac. 1854 and Pr. 1855 by Bp of Ches. C. of Crosthwaite 1863. Formerly C. of Bootle 1854, St. Matthew's, Salford, 1856, Cheltenham 1857; Incumb. of St. Peter's Chapel, Montrose, 1860–62. [22]

POLWHELE, Edward, *St. Stephen's Vicarage, Saltash, Cornwall.*—Trin. Coll. Cam. B.A. 1837; Deac. 1838 and Pr. 1839 by Bp of Ex. V. of St. Stephen's-by-Saltash, Dio. Ex. 1858. (Patrons, D. and C. of Windsor; Tithe, 30*l*; Glebe, 7 acres; V.'s Inc. 176*l* and Ho; Pop. 1387.) Formerly P. C. of St. Stephen's-by-Launceston 1845–53. [23]

POMERY, John, *St. Erme Rectory, Truro.*—Ex. Coll. Ox. B.A. 1804; Deac. 1804 and Pr. 1806 by Bp of Ex. R. of St. Erme, Dio. Ex. 1831. (Patrons,

Trustees; Tithe, 514*l*; Glebe, 80 acres; R.'s Inc. 594*l* and Ho; Pop. 554.) [1]

PONSFORD, William, *Drewsteignton, Chagford, Devon.*—Trin. Coll. Ox. M.A. 1823; Deac. 1820, Pr. 1821. R. of Drewsteignton, Dio. Ex. 1846. (Patron, the present R; Tithe, 614*l*; R.'s Net Inc. 776*l* and Ho; Pop. 1067.) [2]

PONSONBY, Frederick John, *Hampton Court Palace, Middlesex.*—Mert. Coll. Ox. M.A. 1862; Deac. 1862 and Pr. 1863 by Bp of Ox. Chap. at Hampton Court Palace, Dio. Lon. 1867. (Patron, the Queen; Chap.'s Inc. 105*l* and Res; Inhabitants 400.) Formerly C. of St. Giles's, Reading, 1862-67. [3]

PONSONBY, The Hon. Walter William Brabazon, *Canford, Wimborne, Dorset.*—Trin. Coll. Cam. B.A. 1840, M.A. 1843; Deac. and Pr. 1845. V. of Canford Magna with Chapelry of Kinson annexed, Dio. Salis. 1846. (Patron, Sir Ivor B. Guest, Bart; Tithe—Imp. 881*l* 0*s* 10*d*; Glebe, 150 acres; V.'s Inc. 353*l* and Ho; Pop. 2145.) [4]

PONTIFEX, A., *Cheverell Parva, East Lavington, Wilts.*—C. of Little Cheverell. [5]

POOKE, William Henry, *Keevil, Trowbridge, Wilts.*—Wor. Coll. Ox. B.A. 1835, M.A. 1837. V. of Keevil, Dio. Salis. 1839. (Patrons, D. and C. of Win; Tithe, 101*l*; V.'s Inc. 260*l*; Pop. 669.) [6]

POOLE, Alexander, *Trinity Parsonage, Chesterfield.*—St. Edm. Hall, Ox. B.A. 1822. P. C. of Trinity, Chesterfield, Dio. Lich. 1838. (Patrons, Trustees; P. C.'s Inc. 130*l* and Ho; Pop. 3814.) Chap. to the Chesterfield Union. [7]

POOLE, Alexander, 21, *Berkeley-square, Bristol.*—St. John's Coll. Cam. 5th Jun. Opt. B.A. 1855, M.A. 1859; Deac. 1855, Pr. 1856. Precentor, Sacristan, and Min. Can. of Bristol Cathl. 1861. (Value, 175*l*.) C. of St. Peter's, Clifton, 1862. Formerly C. of Walton, Derbyshire, 1855, Ch. Ch. Salford, 1857, St. Mark's, Brighton, 1858; P. C. of Bussage, Stroud, 1861. [8]

POOLE, Alfred, *Purbrooke, Cosham, Hants.*—St. Edm. Hall, Ox. 3rd cl. Lit. Hum. and B.A. 1848, M.A. 1852; Deac. 1848 and Pr. 1850 by Abp of York. P. C. of Purbrook, Dio. Win. 1861. (Patron, R. of Farlington; P. C.'s Inc. 50*l*; Pop. 350.) Formerly Asst. Mast. of the Gr. Sch. Harlow; C. of St. Barnabas', Pimlico, Lond. [9]

POOLE, Edward, *Llanvihangel-rhyd-Ithan, Radnorshire.*—Trin. Hall, Cam. Scho. of, B.A. 1827, M.A. 1841; Deac. 1829 by Bp of Roch. Pr. 1830 by Bp of Lon. P. C. of Llandewi-Ystrad-Ennan with Llanvihangel-rhyd-Ithan P. C. Dio. St. D. 1856. (Patron, Chan. of the Coll. Church of Christ, Brecon, as Prebendal R. of Llanbister; Tithe, 48*l*; Glebe, 69*l*; P. C.'s Inc. 150*l*; Pop. 1047.) Dom. Chap. to Lord Kensington. [10]

POOLE, Edward, *Alvaston, Derby.*—St. Bees; Deac. 1834 and Pr. 1835 by Abp of York. V. of Boulton, Derby, Dio. Lich. 1838. (Patrons, Proprietors of Estates; Glebe, 80 acres; V.'s Inc. 130*l*; Pop. 224.) V. of Alvaston, Dio. Lich. 1846. (Patrons, the Parishioners; Glebe, 76 acres; V.'s Inc. 170*l*; Pop. 558.) [11]

POOLE, Edward, *Liverpool.*—Chap. to the Infirmary, Liverpool. [12]

POOLE, Frederick John, *Bishop Monkton Vicarage, Ripon.*—Wor. Coll. Ox. B.A. 1853, M.A. 1860; Deac. 1854 and Pr. 1855 by Bp of Rip. V. of Bishop Monkton, Dio. Rip. 1865. (Patrons, D. and C. of Rip; V.'s Inc. 300*l* and Ho; Pop. 530.) Formerly C. of St. John's, Leeds, of Trinity, Westminster, and of Ryton, Durham. [13]

POOLE, George, *Burntwood Parsonage, near Lichfield.*—Queens' Coll. Cam. B.A. 1846; Deac. 1846, Pr. 1847. P. C. of Burntwood, Dio. Lich. 1852. (Patron, V. of St. Mary's, Lichfield; Glebe, 6 acres; P. C.'s Inc. 90*l* and Ho; Pop. 1634.) Formerly P. C. of Hammerwich, Staffs, 1852-58. [14]

POOLE, George Alfred.—Deac. 1854 and Pr. 1855 by Bp of Rip. C. of St. Paul's, Ball's Pond, Islington, Lond. Formerly C. of St. Margaret's, Ipswich, and Melcombe Regis, Dorset. [15]

POOLE, George Ayliffe, *Welford Vicarage, Northants.*—Emman. Coll. Cam. B.A. 1831, M.A. 1838; Deac. 1832, Pr. 1833. V. of Welford, Dio. Pet. 1843. (Patron, Bp of Pet; Tithe—App. 181*l* 15*s*, V. 163*l* 5*s*; Glebe, 80 acres; V.'s Inc. 230*l* and Ho; Pop. 1099.) Author, *Sermons on the Apostles' Creed*, 1837; *On the Admission of Lay Members to the Synods of the Church in Scotland*, 1838; *Testimony of St. Cyprian against Rome*, 1838; *The Life and Times of St. Cyprian*, 1840; *The Present State of Parties in the Church of England*, 1842; *Twelve Practical Sermons on the Holy Communion*, 1843; *A History of England*, 2 vols. 1845; *A History of Ecclesiastical Architecture in England*, 1848; *Sir Raoul de Broc and his Son Tristram, a Tale of the Twelfth Century*, 1849; several Sermons, Tracts, Papers, and occasional Pamphlets. [16]

POOLE, John, 10, *South Crescent, Bedford-square, London, W.C.* [17]

POOLE, John Copeland, *Claycoton Rectory, Rugby.*—St. Peter's Coll. Cam. B.A. 1847, M.A. 1851; Deac. 1847, Pr. 1849. R. of Claycoton, Dio. Pet. 1852. (Patron, Rev. J. T. H. Smith; Tithe, 295*l*; Glebe, 75 acres; R.'s Inc. 395*l*; Pop. 112.) [18]

POOLE, Richard, *St. Albans.*—C. of St. Michael's, St. Albans, 1867. Formerly C. of Welford with Wickham, Berks. [19]

POOLE, Robert, *Ripon.*—St. Cath. Hall, Cam. B.A. 1823, M.A. 1826; Deac. 1823 and Pr. 1824 by Abp of York. Min. Can. and V. of Ripon Cathl. 1824. (Value, 300*l*.) Rural Dean. Formerly P. C. of Bishop Thornton, Ripon, 1836; V. of Bishop Monkton, Ripon, 1836. [20]

POOLE, Robert, *St. Decuman's Vicarage, near Taunton.*—Ex. Coll. Ox. B.A. 1829; Deac. 1830, Pr. 1831. V. of St. Decuman's, Dio. B. and W. (Patron, the Preb. of St. Decuman's in Wells Cathl; Tithe—App. 540*l*, V. 230*l* 10*s*; V.'s Inc. 237*l*; Pop. 3196.) [21]

POOLE, Robert Blake, *Broad Somerford, Chippenham.*—Brasen. Coll. Ox. B.A. 1860, M.A. 1864; Deac. 1862 and Pr. 1863 by Bp of B. and W. C. of Dauntsey, Wilts, 1866. Formerly C. of Ilchester 1862, Banwell 1864. [22]

POOLE, Robert Burton, *Clifton College, Bristol.*—Univ. Coll. Ox. B.A. 1862, M.A. 1867; Deac. 1864 and Pr. 1865 by Bp of G. and B. C. of St. Paul's, Clifton, 1866; Asst. Mast. in Clifton Coll. 1863. Formerly C. of St. George, Gloucestershire, 1864–66. [23]

POOLE, Robert Henry, *Rainton Rectory, Durham.*—Wor. Coll. Ox. B.A. 1849, M.A. 1851; Deac. 1849 and Pr. 1850 by Bp of Lich. R. of Rainton, Dio. Dur. 1859. (Patron, Bp of Dur; R.'s Inc. 310*l* and Ho; Pop. 4096.) Surrogate. Formerly P. C. of St. Thomas's, Leeds, 1854–59, Beeston, Leeds, 1859. [24]

POOLE, Samuel Gower, *Bow-road, London, E.*—St. Bees 1841; Deac. 1840 and Pr. 1841 by Bp of Ches. Chap. to the Tower Hamlets Cemetery 1851, and of the Industrial Sch. Forest Lane, West Ham, Essex. Formerly Even. Lect. of Ch. Ch. Spitalfields, 1854. [25]

POOLE, Thomas, *Letwell, Worksop.*—St. John's Coll. Cam. B.A. 1829, M.A. 1832; Deac. 1832 by Bp of Lich. Pr. 1832 by Bp of Lin. P. C. of Firbeck with Letwell P. C. Dio. York, 1838. (Patron, Abp of York; Firbeck, Tithe, App. 200*l*; Letwell, Tithe, App. 210*l*; Glebe, 14 acres; P. C.'s Inc. 265*l*; Pop. Firbeck 195, Letwell 139.) [26]

POOLE, William, *Hentland, Ross, Herefordshire.*—Oriel Coll. Ox. 4th cl. Lit. Hum. and B.A. 1841, M.A. 1845; Deac. 1844, Pr. 1845. P. C. of Hentland with Hoarwithy, Dio. Herf. 1854. (Patron, Rev. Canon Morgan; P. C.'s Inc. 210*l*; Pop. 647.) Rural Dean 1856; Preb. of Herf. 1857. Formerly P. C. of Little Dewchurch 1854. [27]

POOLE, William James, *Aberffraw Rectory, (Anglesey), near Bangor.*—Jesus Coll. Ox. B.A. 1835; Deac. 1836 by Bp of Ox. Pr. 1837 by Bp of Ban. R. of Aberffraw, Dio. Ban. 1850. (Patron, Prince of Wales; Tithe, 846*l*; Glebe, 9 acres; R.'s Inc. 900*l* and Ho; Pop. 1288.) [28]

POOLEY, George Frederick, *Cransford Rectory, Woodbridge, Suffolk.*—Ch. Coll. Cam. LL.B. 1848. R. of Cransford, Dio. Nor. 1846. (Patron, G. W. Pooley, Esq; Tithe, 343*l* 4*s*; Glebe, 44 acres; R.'s Inc. 409*l* and Ho; Pop. 284.) P. C. of Bruisyard, Suffolk, Dio. Nor. 1846. (Patron, Earl of Stradbroke; Tithe—Imp. 92*l*; P. C.'s Inc. 60*l*; Pop. 222.) [1]

POOLEY, James, *Standlake Rectory, Witney.*—Ch. Coll. Cam. B.A. 1851; Deac. 1851 and Pr. 1852 by Bp of Lin. C. in sole charge of Standlake 1863. Formerly C. of Limber, Linc. 1851–56; Sen. C. of Hambleden, Bucks, 1856–62. [2]

POOLEY, John George, *Stonham Aspal Rectory, Stonham, Suffolk.*—Corpus Coll. Cam. B.A. 1859; Deac. 1859 and Pr. 1860 by Bp of G. and B. R. of Stonham Aspal, Dio. Nor. 1864. (Patron, Sir W. Middleton; R.'s Inc. 700*l* and Ho; Pop. 694.) Formerly C. of St. Peter's, Bristol, 1859. [3]

POOLEY, John Henry, *Scotter Rectory, Kirton-in-Lindsey, Lincolnshire.*—St. John's Coll. Cam. 1st cl. Cl. Trip. 2nd Sen. Opt. Norrisian Prizeman 1828, B.A. 1825, M.A. 1828, B.D. 1837; Deac. 1827, Pr. 1828. R. of Scotter, Dio. Lin. 1833. (Patron, Bp. of Pet; Glebe, 744 acres; R.'s Inc. 1000*l* and Ho; Pop. 1167.) Rural Dean of Corringham 1839; Preb. of Asgarby in Lin. Cathl. 1845. Formerly Fell. of St. John's Coll. Cam. and Select Preacher before the Univ. of Cam; C. of St. James's, Westminster, 1832–33. Author, *Norrisian Prize Essay on our Saviour's Parables*, 1829; *Bishop Marsh's Sermon on National Education, with Preface and Introduction*, 1839; *The Case of the Rev. W. T. Humphrey, Missionary of the Church Missionary Society, considered*, 1843. [4]

POORE, Charles Harwood, *Collingbourne-Kingston Vicarage, Ludgershall, Wilts.*—Queens' Coll. Cam. B.A. 1833. V. of Collingbourne-Kingston, Dio. Salis. 1839. (Patrons, D. and C. of Win; V.'s Inc. 275*l* and Ho; Pop. 903.) Formerly Min. Can. of Win. Cathl. [5]

POPE, Alexander, *Frogmore, Kingsbridge, Devon.*—Queens' Coll. Cam. B.A. 1840; Deac. 1841 and Pr. 1842 by Bp of Ex. C. of Sherford, Devon, 1857. [6]

POPE, Benjamin, *Nether-Stowey Vicarage, Bridgwater, Somerset.*—Ch. Ch. Ox. B.A. 1801, M.A. 1803; Deac. 1804, Pr. 1805. V. of Nether-Stowey, Dio. B. and W. 1824. (Patrons, D. and C. of Windsor; Tithe, 300*l*; Glebe, 47 acres; V.'s Inc. 480*l* and Ho; Pop. 876.) V. of Ogborne St. George, Wilts, Dio. Salis. 1826. (Patrons, D. and C. of Windsor; Tithe—App. 698*l*, V. 250*l*; V.'s Inc. 270*l* and Ho; Pop. 534.) Hon. Can. of St. George's, Windsor. Formerly Min. Can. 1817. [7]

POPE, Edwin, *Paddock Wood, Staplehurst, Kent.*—Univ. Coll. Ox. B.A. 1851, M.A. 1854; Deac. 1853 and Pr. 1854 by Abp of Cant. P. C. of Paddock Wood 1859. (Patron, G. C. Courthoupe, Esq; Endow. 217*l*; P. C.'s Inc. 225*l*; Pop. 898.) [8]

POPE, George, *Rempstone Rectory, Loughborough.*—Sid. Coll. Cam. 20th Wrang. 2nd cl. Nat. Sci. Trip. and B.A. 1853, M.A. 1856; Deac. 1855 and Pr. 1856 by Bp of Ely. Fell. of Sid. Coll. Cam; Mast. of St. John's Sch. Hurstpierpoint. R. of Rempstone, Dio. Lin. 1867. (Patron, Sid. Coll. Cam; R.'s Inc. 478*l*; Pop. 337.) Formerly Math. Mast. of the Gr. Sch. Norwich; Prof. of Maths. at the Royal Military Coll. Sandhurst; C. of Blickling. Author, *A Class-book of Elementary Chemistry*, Stanford, 1864. [9]

POPE, Septimus, *Christon, Weston-super-Mare, Somerset.*—Queen's Coll. Ox. B.A. 1836, M.A. 1838; Deac. 1836, Pr. 1837. R. of Christon, Dio. B. and W. 1842. (Patron, C. R. Wainwright, Esq; Tithe, 92*l*; Glebe, 13 acres; R.'s Inc. 120*l* and Ho; Pop. 81.) [10]

POPE, Thomas, *Christchurch Vicarage, Newport, Monmouthshire.*—Univ. Coll. Ox. B.A. 1821. V. of Christchurch, Dio. Llan. 1839. (Patron, Eton Coll; Tithe—Imp. 150*l*, V. 265*l*; Glebe, 90 acres; V.'s Inc. 385*l* and Ho; Pop. 3004.) V. of Nash, near Newport, Dio. Llan. 1840. (Patron, Eton Coll; Tithe—Imp. 30*l*, V. 26*l*; Glebe, 1½ acres; V.'s Inc. 95*l*; Pop. 284.) Rural Dean of the Western Div. of Netherwent. [11]

POPE, William, *Cossington Rectory, Bridgwater.*—Univ. Coll. Ox. 3rd cl. Lit. Hum. B.A. 1863, M.A. 1866; Deac. 1864 and Pr. 1865 by Bp of Man. R. of Cossington, Dio. B. and W. 1866. (Patron, E. G. Broderip, Esq; Tithe, 222*l*; Glebe, 55 acres; R.'s Inc. 260*l* and Ho; Pop. 250.) Formerly C. of St. Luke's, Cheetham, 1864–66. [12]

POPE, William Alexander, *St. Albans, Herts.*—Trin. Coll. Cam. B.A. 1863, M.A. 1867; Deac. 1864, Pr. 1866 by Bp of Roch. C. of St. Stephen's, St. Albans, 1864. [13]

POPE, William Langley, *Dartmouth, Devon.*—Pemb. Coll. Ox. B.A. 1845, M.A. 1852, D.D. 1863; Deac. 1846 and Pr. 1847 by Bp of Nor. Formerly C. of St. Nicholas', Great Yarmouth, 1846–48. Author, *Christian Union and Progress* (a Tract); *Jesus and the Doctors* (a Sermon), 1856, Whittaker and Co; *Poetical Legends of the Channel Islands*, 1857, Saunders, Otley and Co. [14]

POPE, William Law, *Tunbridge Wells, Kent.*—Wor. Coll. Ox. B.A. 1818, M.A. 1820; Deac. 1820 and Pr. 1821 by Bp of Ox. Min. of the Chapel-of-Ease, Tunbridge Wells, Dio. Cant. 1825. (Patrons, Trustees; Min.'s Inc. 275*l*.) Sen. Fell. of Wor. Coll. Ox. [15]

POPHAM, John, *Stepney, London, E.*—C. of Stepney. [16]

POPHAM, John Leyborne, *Chilton Folliatt Rectory, Hungerford, Wilts.*—Wad. Coll. Ox. B.A. 1832, M.A. 1838; Deac. 1834 by Abp of Cant. Pr. 1835 by Bp of Lin. R. of Chilton Folliatt, Dio. Salis. 1835. (Patron, F. L. Popham, Esq; Tithe, 720*l*; Glebe, 30 acres; R.'s Inc. 750*l* and Ho; Pop. 691.) Preb. of Salis. 1849; Rural Dean of Marlborough 1839; Chap. to the Bp of Salis. 1854. [17]

POPHAM, William, *Christchurch Parsonage, Bradford-on-Avon, Wilts.*—Oriel Coll. Ox. B.A. 1837, M.A. 1844; Deac. 1845 and Pr. 1846 by Bp of Salis. P. C. of Christchurch, Bradford-on-Avon, Dio. Salis. 1848. (Patron, V. of Bradford; P. C.'s Inc. 150*l* and Ho; Pop. 2028.) [18]

PORT, George Richard, *Sedgeberrow, Evesham, Worcestershire.*—Brasen. Coll. Ox. B.A. 1824; Deac. 1825, Pr. 1826. R. of Grafton-Flyford, Worc. Dio. Wor. 1855. (Patron, Earl of Coventry; Glebe, 270 acres; R.'s Inc. 220*l* and Ho; Pop. 225.) Dom. Chap. to the Earl of Ellenborough. [19]

PORTAL, George Raymond, *Albury Rectory, Guildford.*—Ch. Ch. Ox. B.A. 1849, M.A. 1852; Deac. 1850 and Pr. 1851 by Bp of Salis. R. of Albury, Dio. Win. 1858. (Patron, Earl Percy; Tithe, 500*l*; Glebe, 78 acres; R.'s Inc. 580*l* and Ho; Pop. 1200.) Dom. Chap. to the Earl of Carnarvon. Author, *Consideration upon the Presence of Non-Communicants at the Holy Communion*, J. H. Parker; *Sermons on some of the Prevalent Objections to Ritual Observances*, 2 eds; *Personal Faith the only Source of Peace*; *Christian Worship*; *Sermon on Reopening St. Michael's, Cornhill.* [20]

PORTER, Albert John, *Norwich.*—St. John's Coll. Cam. S.C.L. 1857, LL.B. 1862; Deac. 1858 and Pr. 1861 by Bp of Nor. Chap. of the Norwich Union 1865. Formerly C. of Heigham 1858, Geldestone 1861. [21]

PORTER, Charles, *Raunds Vicarage, Thrapstone, Northants.*—Caius Coll. Cam. 3rd Wrang. and B.A. 1819, M.A. 1822, B.D. 1831; Deac. 1821 and Pr. 1822 by Bp of Ely. V. of Raunds, Dio Pet. 1855. (Patron, Ld Chan; Glebe, 205 acres; V.'s Inc. 300*l* and Ho; Pop. 2337.) Formerly Fell. and Tut. of Caius Coll. Cam. [22]

PORTER, Charles Fleetwood, *Dropmore, Maidenhead.*—Caius Coll. Cam. 3rd cl. Cl. Trip. B.A. 1853, M.A. 1856; Deac. 1854 and Pr. 1855 by Bp of Ox. P. C. of Dropmore 1867. (Patron, Hon. G. M. Fortescue; Pop. 350.) Formerly C. of Raunds, Bisham, and Slapton, Berks. [23]

PORTER, Erisey John, *Metfield Parsonage, near Harleston, Norfolk.*—Corpus Coll. Cam. 5th Jun. Opt. and B.A. 1844; Deac. 1847 and Pr. 1848 by Bp of Lin. P. C. of Metfield, Dio. Nor. 1866. (Patrons, the Parishioners; Glebe, 47 acres; P. C.'s Inc. 80*l* and Ho; Pop. 700.) C. of Witheredale 1866. Formerly C. of

Charles, near Plymouth, 1856, Bigbury, Devon, 1857; R. of Middleton Scriven, Salop, 1861. [1]

PORTER, Frederick, *Yedingham, Malton, Yorks.*—St. Bees; Deac. 1846 and Pr. 1847 by Bp of Pet. V. of Yedingham, Dio. York, 1855. (Patron, Earl Fitzwilliam; V.'s Inc. 205*l* and Ho; Pop. 78.) P. C. of Knapton, Dio. York, 1866. (Patron, J. Tindall, Esq; P. C.'s Inc. 48*l*; Pop. 271.) Formerly C. of Warmington, Northants, 1846, Swayfield, Lincolnshire, 1849; V. of Great Gidding 1853. [2]

PORTER, George, *Anstey, Buntingford, Herts.*—Ch. Coll. Cam. B.A. 1865; Deac. 1866 by Bp of Roch. C. of Anstey, and Asst. Cl. Mast. of the Gram. Sch. Bishop Stortford. [3]

PORTER, George, *Littleton Rectory, near Chertsey.*—Ex. Coll. Ox. M.A. 1850; Deac. 1849, Pr. 1850. R. of Littleton, Dio. Lon. 1867. (Patron, T. Wood, Esq; Tithe, 312*l*; R.'s Inc. 326*l* and Ho; Pop. 111.) Formerly R. of Rackenford, Devon, 1861–67. [4]

PORTER, George Henry, *Marlesford Rectory, Wickham Market, Suffolk.*—Caius Coll. Cam. 31st Sen. Opt. and B.A. 1832, M.A. 1835; Deac. 1832 and Pr. 1833 by Bp of Nor. R. of Marlesford, Dio. Nor. 1833. (Patron, A. Archdeckne, Esq; Tithe, 362*l*; Glebe, 30 acres; R.'s Inc. 410*l* and Ho; Pop. 412.) [5]

PORTER, Jackson, *Oddingley Rectory, Droitwich, Worcestershire.*—Corpus Coll. Cam. 8th Sen. Opt. and B.A. 1819, M.A. 1820; Deac. 1820 and Pr. 1821 by Bp of Chich. R. of Oddingley, Dio. Wor. 1852. (Patron, J. H. Galton, Esq; Tithe, 181*l*; Glebe, 13 acres; R.'s Inc. 203*l* and Ho; Pop. 202.) Author, *A Catechism*; various single Sermons. [6]

PORTER, Jacob, *Thetford, Norfolk.*—C. of St. Mary's, Thetford. [7]

PORTER, James, *St. Peter's College, Cambridge.*—St. Peter's Coll. Cam. B.A. 1851, M.A. 1854; Deac. 1853 and Pr. 1856 by Bp of Wor. Fell. of St. Peter's Coll. Cam. 1851. [8]

PORTER, John Leech, *St. John's Parsonage, Studley, Trowbridge.*—Dub. 1st cl. with Medal in Ethics and Logic, 1st cl. Math. Univ. Prize in Div. Heb. Mod. Hist. and in Rhet. and Eng. Lit. and A.B. 1857; Deac. 1857 by Bp of Rip. Pr. 1859 by Bp of Salis. P. C. of St. John's, Studley, Dio. Salis. 1860. (Patron, R. of Trowbridge; Glebe, 4 acres; P. C.'s Inc. 200*l* and Ho; Pop. 335.) Formerly C. of St. Paul's, Shipley, Yorks, 1857, Trowbridge, Wilts, 1859. [9]

PORTER, Lewis, *Moss House, Breightmet, Bolton-le-Moors, Lancashire.*—St. Bees; Deac. 1845 and Pr. 1846 by Bp of Ches. P. C. of Tonge, Dio. Man. 1848. (Patrons, the Crown and Bp of Man. alt; Tithe, App. 5*l* 3*s*; P. C.'s Inc. 160*l*; Pop. 2884.) [10]

PORTER, Reginald, *The Rectory, Kenn, near Exeter.*—Ex. Coll. Ox. B.A. 1855, M.A. 1858; Deac. 1856 and Pr. 1857 by Bp of Ox. R. of Kenn, Dio. Ex. 1858. (Patron, J. H. Ley, Esq; Tithe, 819*l*; Glebe, 50 acres; R.'s Inc. 850*l* and Ho; Pop. 1064.) Formerly C. of Wantage, Berks, 1856–57. [11]

PORTER, Richard Ibbetson, *South Stoke, Wallingford.*—Corpus Coll. Cam. B.A. 1858, M.A. 1862; Deac. 1860 and Pr. 1861 by Bp of Ox. C. of South Stoke 1862. Formerly C. of Stewkley, Bucks, 1860–62. [12]

PORTER, W., *East Hendred, Berks.*—C. of East Hendred. [13]

PORTER, William Carmichael, *Downton, Salisbury.*—Trin. Coll. Cam. 2nd cl. Cl. Trip. B.A. 1860, M.A. 1863; Deac. 1860 by Bp of Ox. Pr. 1862 by Bp of Pet. C. of Downton 1864. Formerly C. of Speen, 1860–61, Addington, Thrapston, 1862–63. [14]

PORTEUS, Beilby, *Edenhall Vicarage, Penrith.*—Ch. Coll. Cam. Coll. Prizeman for Latin Hexameters, and B.A. 1833; Deac. 1836 and Pr. 1837 by Abp of Cant. V. of Edenhall with Longwathby, Dio. Carl. 1840. (Patrons, D. and C. of Carl; Edenhall, Tithe, App. 247*l* 18*s* 2*d*, V. 72*l*; Glebe, 33 acres; Longwathby, Tithe, App. 143*l* 16*s* 2*d*, V. 23*l* 10*s* 8½*d*; Glebe, 22 acres; V.'s Inc. 180*l* and Ho; Pop. Edenhall 335, Longwathby 296.) [15]

PORTEUS, G. B., *Burley, Leeds.*—Literate; Deac. 1867 by Bp of Rip. C. of Burley. [16]

PORTMAN, Fitzhardinge Berkeley, *Staple Fitzpaine, Taunton.*—Ch. Ch. Ox. B.A. 1832, M.A. 1836; Deac. 1835 and Pr. 1836 by Bp of Ox. R. of Staple Fitzpaine with Bickenhall R. and Orchard Portman R. Dio. B. and W. 1840. (Patron, Lord Portman; Staple Fitzpaine, Tithe, 382*l* 10*s*; Glebe, 50 acres; Bickenhall, Tithe, 201*l* 1*s*; Glebe, 12 acres; Orchard Portman, Tithe, 120*l*; Glebe, 28 acres; R.'s Inc. 793*l*; Pop. Staple Fitzpaine 264, Bickenhall 269, Orchard Portman 66.) Rural Dean. Formerly Fell. of All Souls' Coll. Ox. [17]

PORTMAN, Henry Fitzhardinge Berkeley, *Pylle Rectory, Shepton Mallet, Somerset.*—Magd. Coll. Ox. B.A. 1863; Deac. 1864 and Pr. 1865 by Bp of Win. R. of Pylle, Dio. B. and W. 1866. (Patron, Lord Portman; Tithe, 178*l* 4*s* 3*d*; Glebe, 22a. 2r. 25p; R.'s Inc. 218*l* and Ho; Pop. 207.) Formerly C. of Farnham, Surrey, 1864; Chap. to the Sheriff of Somerset 1866. [18]

PORTMAN, The Hon. Walter Berkeley, B.A., *Corton-Denham Rectory, Somerset.*—R. of Corton-Denham, Dio. B. and W. 1861. (Patron, Lord Portman; Tithe, 380*l*; Glebe, 32 acres; R.'s Inc. 420*l* and Ho; Pop. 413.) [19]

POSTANCE, Henry, *The Parsonage, 48, Upper Parliament-street, Liverpool.*—St. Aidan's; Deac. 1856 and Pr. 1857 by Bp of Ches. P. C. of Trinity, Toxteth-park, Dio. Ches. 1858. (Patrons, Trustees; P. C.'s Inc. 250*l*; Pop. 7584.) Formerly C. of St. James's, Toxteth-park, 1856–57. [20]

POSTANCE, Richard, *St. Domingo Vale, Chester.*—Deac. 1859, Pr. 1860. P. C. of St. Titus, Liverpool, 1865. (Patrons, Trustees; P. C.'s Inc. 300*l*; Pop. 10,500.) [21]

POSTLE, John, *Burgh next Aylsham, Norfolk.*—Corpus Coll. Cam. Sen. Opt. and B.A. 1842; Deac. 1842, Pr. 1843. R. and C. of Felmingham, Norfolk, Dio. Nor. 1852. (Patrons, John Postle, Esq. and others; Tithe—App. 351*l* 15*s* 6*d* and 1½ acres of Glebe, V. 148*l* 17*s* 6*d* and 13 acres of Glebe, R. 167*l* 3*s* 6*d*; R.'s Inc. 188*l*; Pop. 434.) Formerly C. of Burgh next Aylsham. [22]

POSTLETHWAITE, Colin, *Misson Vicarage, Bawtry, Notts.*—Dub. A.B. 1832, A.M. 1838; Deac. 1835, Pr. 1836. V. of Misson, Dio. Lin. 1861. (Patron, Ld Chan; Tithe—Imp. 420*l*, V. 100*l*; V.'s Inc. 360*l* and Ho; Pop. 803.) Formerly V. of Elkesley 1849–61. [23]

POSTLETHWAITE, John, *Quatford, near Tasley, Bridgnorth, Salop.*—Queen's Coll. Ox. B.A. 1836, M.A. 1858; Deac. 1837 and Pr. 1838 by Bp of Ches. R. of Tasley, Dio. Herf. 1848. (Patron, E. F. Acton, Esq; Tithe, 212*l*; Glebe, 8½ acres; R.'s Inc. 225*l*; Pop. 78.) [24]

POSTLETHWAITE, John, *Coatham, Redcar, and Wreaksend, Broughton-in-Furness.*—Trin. Coll. Cam. B.A. 1851, M.A. 1854; Deac. 1851 and Pr. 1852 by Abp of York. Pastor of The Homes of the Good Samaritan, Coatham. Formerly C. of Dunnington, York, 1851–52; P. C. of Coatham 1853–65. [25]

POSTLETHWAITE, Thomas George, *The Parsonage, Hatfield Heath, Harlow, Essex.*—St. Peter's Coll. Cam. Fell of, 22nd Wrang. B A. 1843, M.A. 1846; Deac. 1843 and Pr. 1844 by Bp of Win. P. C. of Hatfield Heath, Dio. Roch. 1862. (Patron, V. of Hatfield Broad Oak; P. C.'s Inc. 110*l* and Ho; Pop. 614.) Formerly C. of Petersfield, Hants, 1843–47, Stonehouse, Devon, 1847–51; P. C. of Ch. Ch. Plymouth, 1851–61. [26]

POSTLETHWAITE, Thomas Marshall, *Witherslack, Kirkby-Lonsdale, Westmoreland.*—Queen's Coll. Ox. B.A. 1833; Deac. 1833 and Pr. 1837 by Bp of Ches. P. C. of Witherslack, Dio. Carl. 1846. (Patrons, Trustees of Barwick's Charity; P. C.'s Inc. 197*l* and Ho; Pop. 565.) Formerly P. C. of the Isle of Walney. [27]

POTCHETT, Charles, *Ryhall, near Stamford.*—Clare Coll. Cam. B.A. 1845, M.A. 1851; Deac. 1845 and Pr. 1846 by Bp of Lin. V. of Ryhall with Essendine C. Dio. Pet. 1849. (Patron, Marquis of Exeter; Tithe—Essendine, Imp. 247*l* 0*s* 1*d*, V. 97*l* 10*s*; V.'s Inc. 265*l*; Pop. Ryhall 847, Essendine 193.) [28]

POTCHETT, George Thomas, *Denton Rectory, Grantham, Lincolnshire*.—St. John's Coll. Cam. B.A. 1838; Deac. 1839 and Pr. 1840 by Bp of Lin. R. of Denton, Dio. Lin. 1840. (Patron, Bp of Lin; Tithe, 788*l* 8*s* 9*d*; Glebe, 59 acres; R.'s Inc. 895*l* and Ho; Pop. 637.) [1]

POTE, Edward, *King's College, Cambridge*.—King's Coll. Cam. B.A. 1814, M.A. 1817. Sen. Fell. of King's Coll. Cam. [2]

POTT, Alfred, *East Hendred, Wantage, Berks*.—Magd. Coll. Ox. Fell. of, 2nd cl. Lit. Hum. Univ. Theol. Scho. B.A. 1844, M.A. 1847, B.D. 1854; Deac. 1845 and Pr. 1846 by Bp of Ox. R. of East Hendred, Dio. Ox. 1858. (Patron, Bp of Ox; Tithe, 640*l*; Glebe, 50 acres; R.'s Inc. 720*l* and Ho; Pop. 900.) Rural Dean of Abingdon; Surrogate; Ex. Chap. to Bp of Ox. Formerly V. of Cuddesdon 1852, and Prin. of Theol. Coll. [3]

POTT, Francis, *Northill Rectory, Biggleswade*.—Brasen. Coll. Ox. B.A. 1854, M.A. 1857; Deac. 1856 by Bp of B. and W. Pr. 1857 by Bp of G. and B. R. of Northill, Dio. Ely, 1866. (Patrons, Grocers' Company, Lond; Glebe, 318 acres; R.'s Inc. 535*l* and Ho; Pop. 1364.) Formerly C. of Ticehurst 1861, Ardingley 1858, Bishopsworth, Bristol, 1856. Author, *Te Deum considered Musically and Poetically*, Metzler, 6*d*. [4]

POTTER, Alfred, *Keyworth Rectory, near Nottingham*.—St. John's Coll. Cam. B.A. 1851; Deac. 1850 and Pr. 1851 by Bp of Lin. R. of Keyworth, Dio. Lin. 1860. (Patron, the present R; R.'s Inc. 480*l* and Ho; Pop. 830.) Formerly C. of Ropsley, Linc. 1859–60, Skirbeck, Linc. Author, *Present Depression in Trade, a Divine Judgment*, 1861, 2*d*; *Almsgiving, a Duty and Privilege*, 1862, 6*d*. [5]

POTTER, Charles Augustus, *Shoreham, Sevenoaks, Kent*.—Mert. Coll. Ox. B.A. 1865; Deac. 1866 by Abp of Cant. Asst. C. of Shoreham. [6]

POTTER, James, *Ellington Vicarage, Kimbolton, Hunts*.—St. Peter's Coll. Cam. B.A. 1850; Deac. 1850 and Pr. 1851 by Abp of York. V. of Ellington, Dio. Ely, 1852. (Patron, St. Peter's Coll. Cam; V.'s Inc. 170*l* and Ho; Pop. 413.) [7]

POTTER, Joseph, *Lingwood, near Norwich*.—Dub. A.B. 1828, A.M. 1831; Deac. 1831, Pr. 1832. R. of Fishley, Norfolk, Dio. Nor. 1837. (Patroness, Miss Edwards; Tithe—App. 3*l*, R. 162*l*; Glebe, 5 acres; R.'s Inc. 179*l*; Pop. 19.) P. C. of Lingwood, Dio. Nor. 1847. (Patron, H. N. Burroughes, Esq; Tithe—Imp. 256*l* 15*s* 6*d*; P. C.'s Inc. 60*l* and Ho; Pop. 509.) [8]

POTTER, Lewis Francis, *Thorpe-Achurch, Oundle, Northants*.—Dub. Heb. and Catechetical Prize A.B. 1851, A.M. 1856; Deac. 1853 and Pr. 1854 by Bp of Pet. R. of Thorpe-Achurch with Lilford V. Dio. Pet. 1860. (Patron, Lord Lilford; R.'s Inc. 430*l* and Ho; Pop. Thorpe-Achurch 209, Lilford 179.) Formerly C. of St. Mary's, Lambeth, 1854–57; Asst. Chap. in Leicester County Gaol, 1853–54, Thorpe-Achurch and Lilford-cum-Wigsthorpe 1857–60. [9]

POTTER, Robert, *Bulkington Vicarage, Nuneaton, Warwickshire*.—St. Peter's Coll. Cam. Sen. Opt. and B.A. 1840, M.A. 1843; Deac. 1840 and Pr. 1841 by Bp of Herf. V. of Bulkington, Dio. Wor. 1856. (Patron, Ld Chan; Tithe, 187*l*; V.'s Inc. 253*l* and Ho; Pop. 1858.) Formerly C. of Broadwell, Glouc. [10]

POTTER, Thomas Johnson, *Christ's Hospital, Newgate-street, London, E.C.*—Trin. Coll. Cam. B.A. 1850, M.A. 1853; Deac. 1853 and Pr. 1854 by Abp of York. Asst. Math. Mast. in Christ's Hospital, Sch. [11]

POTTER, William, *Witnesham Rectory, Ipswich*.—St. Peter's Coll. Cam. Wrang. and B.A. 1828, M.A. 1831; Deac. 1829, Pr. 1830. R. of Witnesham, Dio. Nor. 1836. (Patron, St. Peter's Coll. Cam; Tithe, 630*l*; Glebe, 47 acres; R.'s Inc. 690*l* and Ho; Pop. 634.) Rural Dean 1842; Hon. Can. of Nor. 1852; Sec. to the Archd. Branch of the National Soc; Diocesan Inspector of Schs. Formerly Fell. of St. Peter's Coll. [12]

POTTICARY, George Brown Francis, *Girton Rectory, Cambridge*.—Magd. Coll. Ox. B.A. 1823, M.A. 1824; Deac. 1824, Pr. 1825. R. of Girton, Dio. Ely, 1850. (Patron, Bp of Ely; Tithe, 446*l*; Glebe, 20 acres; R.'s Inc. 452*l* and Ho; Pop. 469.) [13]

POTTS, Henry John, *Llangarrin, Ross, Herefordshire*.—Trin. Coll. Cam. B.A. 1846. V. of Llangarrin with St. Weonard's, Dio. Herf. 1855. (Patrons, D. and C. of Herf; Llangarrin, Tithe—App. 709*l* 12*s* and 2¾ acres of Glebe, V. 290*l*; Glebe, 4 acres; St. Weonard's, Tithe—App. 458*l* 17*s* and 18 acres of Glebe, V. 210*l* 3*s*; V.'s Inc. 506*l*; Pop. Llangarrin 473, St. Weonard's 690.) [14]

POTTS, Joseph, *Beccles*.—Emman. Coll. Cam. 32nd Sen. Opt; Deac. 1865 and Pr. 1867 by Bp of Nor. C. of Geldeston, Norfolk, 1865. [15]

POULDEN, James Bedford, *Fylton Rectory, near Bristol*.—St. John's Coll. Cam. B.A. 1822; Deac. 1823 by Bp of Herf. Pr. 1824 by Bp of Salis. R. of Fylton or Filton, Dio. G. and B. 1832. (Patron, R. Poulden, Esq; Tithe, 145*l* 6*s* 8*d*; Glebe, 60 acres; R.'s Inc. 240*l* and Ho; Pop. 340.) [16]

POULTER, James, *High Wycombe, Bucks*.—Dub. A.B. 1847, A.M. 1850; Deac. 1847 and Pr. 1849 by Bp of Ox. Mast. of the Royal Free Gr. Sch. High Wycombe, 1842. (Patrons, Trustees; Stipend, 150*l* and Ho.) [17]

POULTON, William, 13, *Talbot-terrace, Westbourne-park, W.*—Deac. 1851 and Pr. 1852 by Bp of Nor. C. of Stoke Newington 1862. Formerly C. of Aylsham, Norfolk, 1851; St. Martin-in-the-Fields, Westminster, 1855. [18]

POULTON, William H., *Queen's College, Birmingham*.—St. John's Coll. Cam. B.A. 1856, M.A. 1859; Deac. 1857 and Pr. 1858 by Bp of Wor. Prof. of Math. Sub-Warden and Chap. of the Hospital, Queen's Coll. Birmingham [19]

POUND, William, *Appledurcombe, Isle of Wight*.—St. John's Coll. Cam. 6th Wrang. and B.A. 1833, M.A. 1836; Deac. 1835 and Pr. 1836 by Bp of Ely. Prin. of Appledurcombe Sch. Formerly Fell. of St. John's Coll. Cam; Head Mast. of Old Malton Gr. Sch. Author, *The Christ in His own Words and Works, a Solution of all Gospel Difficulties*, Rivingtons. [20]

POVAH, Alfred, *St. Olave's Rectory, Hart-street, Mark-lane, London, E.C.*—Wad. Coll. Ox. 2nd cl. Lit. Hum. B.A. 1847, M.A. 1849; Deac. 1847 and Pr. 1848 by Bp of Lon. R. of St. Olave's, City and Dio. Lon. 1860. (Patrons, Five Trustees; R.'s Inc. 1891*l* and Ho; Pop. 757.) Formerly C. of St. James's, Westminster, 1847–60; Lect. and C. of St. Andrew Undershaft, Lond. 1853–60; Head Mast. of St. Saviour's Gr. Sch. Southwark, 1850–58; Under Mast. of Dulwich Coll. Upper Sch. 1858–60. [21]

POVAH, John Vigden, 16, *Tavistock-square, London, W.C.*—Trin. Coll. Camb. Jun. Opt. and B.A. 1829, M.A. 1831; Deac. 1829, Pr. 1830. 11th Min. Can. of St. Paul's 1833. (Value, 150*l*.) Pr. in Ordinary to the Queen 1833. (Value, 58*l*.) R. of St. Anne's and St. Agnes' with St. John Zachary's R. City and Dio. Lon. 1849. (Patrons, Bp of Lon. and D. and C. of St. Paul's alt.; Fire-Act Commut. 140*l*; R.'s Inc. 365*l*; Pop. St. Anne and St. Agnes 362, St. John Zachary 192.) Div. Lect. in St. Paul's Cathl. 1845. (Value, 185*l*.) [22]

POVAH, Richard Worgan, *St. John's College, Oxford*.—St. John's Coll. Ox. 1st cl. Lit. Hum. 2nd cl. Math. et Phy. and B.A. 1817, M.A. 1820. Fell. of St. John's Coll. Ox. [23]

POWELL, Charles Meares, 31, *Great Portland-street, Langham-place, W.*—Dub. Div. Prizeman, A.B. 1862; Deac. 1862 and Pr. 1864 by Bp of Win. Sen. C. of All Souls', Langham-place, St. Marylebone, 1866. Formerly C. of St. Paul's, Bermondsey, 1863. [24]

POWELL, Edward, *Sowerby, Halifax, Yorks*.—C. of St. George's, Sowerby. [25]

POWELL, Edward Arnett, *Caldecote Rectory, Caxton, Cambs*.—Ch. Coll. Camb. 37th Wrang. B.A. 1830, M.A. 1833; Deac. 1833 and Pr. 1833. R. of Toft with Caldecote, Dio. Ely, 1843. (Patron, Ch. Coll. Cam; Toft, Tithe, 300*l*; Glebe, 26 acres; Caldecote, Tithe, 136*l*; Glebe, ½ acre; R.'s Inc. 474*l*; Pop. Toft 359, Caldecote 93.) [26]

POWELL, Edward Henry, 5, *Albert-buildings, Weston-super-Mare.*—St. John's Coll. Ox. B A. 1848, M.A. 1851; Deac. 1849 and Pr. 1850 by Bp of Ex. C. of Locking, Somerset, 1857. Formerly C. of Lynton, Countesbury and Oare, 1849–51, Wellington, Somerset, 1851–54; R. of Ludchurch and C. of Yerbeston, Pembroke, 1854–56. [1]

POWELL, Edward Parry, *The Gill, Ulverstone, Lancashire,* and *Coedmawr, Carnarvon.*—Jesus Coll. Ox. S.C.L. 1854; Deac. 1856 by Bp of Carl. Formerly C. of Holy Trinity, Ulverstone; Asst. Chap. to the Ulverstone Workhouse. [2]

POWELL, George, *Clapton, Middlesex, N.E.*—Trin. Coll. Cam. B.A. 1841, M.A. 1844; Deac. 1841, Pr. 1842. Min. of St. James's, Clapton, Dio. Lon. 1853. (Patron, R. of Hackney; Min.'s Inc. 350*l*; Pop. 3500.) [3]

POWELL, George Francis Sydenham, *Sutton-Veny, Warminster, Wilts.*—Wad. Coll. Ox. B.A. 1841; Deac. 1843, Pr. 1844. R. of Sutton-Veny, Dio. Salis. 1854. (Patron, G. W. Heneage, Esq; Glebe, 850 acres; R.'s Inc. 1000*l* and Ho; Pop. 794.) Formerly C. of Baverstock and Compton, Bishops Cannings; P. C. of Burcombe; Registrar to the Archdeaconry of Wells. [4]

POWELL, Henry, *Bolton Vicarage, Bolton-le-Moors.*—Literate; Deac. 1836 and Pr. 1837 by Bp of Lon. V. of Bolton-le-Moors, Dio. Man. 1857. (Patron, Bp. of Man; Tithe—Imp. 20*l*, App. 178*l* 4*s* 11*d*; Glebe, 80 acres; V.'s Inc. 350*l* and Ho; Pop. 8000.) [5]

POWELL, Henry, *Mortlake, Surrey.*—Clare Coll. Cam. B.A. 1861, M.A. 1865; Deac. 1862 by Bp of Win. Pr. 1864 by Bp of Lon. C. of Mortlake 1866. Formerly C. of Chertsey 1862, St. Luke's, King's Cross, Lond. 1863, Willesden 1864. [6]

POWELL, Henry William, *Pantycelyn, near Carmarthen.*—Literate; Deac. 1821, Pr. 1822 by Bp of St. D. P. C. of Llanpympsaint with Llanllawddog P. C. Dio. St. D. 1857. (Patron, V. of Abergwili; Llanpympsaint, Tithe—App. 180*l*; Llanllawddog, Tithe—App. 200*l*; P. C.'s Inc. 150*l*; Pop. Llanpympsaint 519, Llanllawddog 725.) Formerly C. of Llanpympsaint and Llanllawddog 1822–33, Cappel-y-ffyn, 1821–22. [7]

POWELL, John, *Warminster, Wilts.*—Dub. A.B. 1850; Deac. 1852 and Pr. 1853 by Bp of Rip. P. C. of Hill-Deverill, Dio. Salis. 1858. (Patron, Preb. of Hill-Deverill; P. C.'s Inc. 75*l*; Pop. 149.) Formerly C. of Brixton-Deverill. [8]

POWELL, John Robert, *Peter's Marland Parsonage, near Great Torrington, North Devon.*—Jesus Coll. Cam. B.C.L. 1851, B.A. 1852, M.A. 1854; Deac. 1853 and Pr. 1854 by Bp of Salis. P. C. of Peter's Marland, Dio. Ex. 1863. (Patron, J. C. Moore Stevens, Esq; Tithe, 63*l*; Glebe, 10 acres; P. C.'s Inc. 75*l* and Ho; Pop. 320.) Formerly C. of Monkton Farleigh, near Bath, 1853–63. [9]

POWELL, John Welstead Sharp, *Abinger Rectory, Dorking.*—St. Edm. Hall, Ox. B.A. 1830, M.A. 1833. R. of Abinger, Dio. Win. 1850. (Patron, W. J. Evelyn, Esq; Tithe, 600*l*; Glebe, 85 acres; R.'s Inc. 660*l* and Ho; Pop. 489.) Rural Dean of the South East District of Stoke; Surrogate. [10]

POWELL, Joseph, *Normanton-on-Soar, Loughborough.*—Dub. A.B. 1831; Deac. and Pr. 1831 by Abp of York. R. of Normanton-on-Soar, Dio. Lin. 1831. (Patrons, John R. Buckley, Esq. with others; Land in lieu of Tithe and ancient Glebe, 456 acres; R.'s Inc. 456*l* and Ho; Pop. 300.) [11]

POWELL, Joseph O., *Whaddon Vicarage, Royston.*—V. of Whaddon, Dio. Ely, 1863. (Patrons, D. and C. of Windsor; Tithe—App. 355*l* and 102 acres of Glebe, V. 100*l*; Glebe, 1 acre; V.'s Inc. 194*l* and Ho; Pop. 319.) [12]

POWELL, Richard, *Fleet, Lincolnshire.*—Dub. A.B. 1831, A.M. 1859; Deac. 1851 and Pr. 1852 by Bp of Ches. C. of Fleet. Formerly C. of Tenterden, Saxby, and Trinity, Dover. [13]

POWELL, Richmond, *South Stoke Rectory, Arundel, Sussex.*—Trin. Coll. Cam. B.A. 1831, M.A. 1834; Deac. 1832 and Pr. 1833 by Bp of Chich. R. of South Stoke, Dio. Chich. 1856. (Patron, Duke of Norfolk; Tithe, 223*l*; Glebe, 15 acres; R.'s Inc. 245*l* and Ho; Pop. 111.) Formerly V. of Bury, Sussex, 1841–56. [14]

POWELL, Robert Powell, *Bellingham Rectory, Hexham.*—Wor. Coll. Ox. B.A. 1840, M.A. 1842; Deac. 1841 and Pr. 1842 by Bp of Ches. R. of Bellingham, Dio. Dur. 1860. (Patrons, Lords Commis. of the Admiralty; Tithe, 203*l*; Glebe, 7 acres and 40 acres of waste land; R.'s Inc. 220*l* and Ho; Pop. 1700.) Surrogate. Formerly Chap. R.N. 1846–58; Chap. of H.M.S. "Albion" during the Crimean war, and was wounded in the attack on Sebastopol, Oct. 17, 1854. [15]

POWELL, Samuel, *Stretford, Leominster, Herefordshire.*—Pemb. Coll. Ox. B.A. 1812, M.A. 1815; Deac. and Pr. 1815. R. of Stretford, Dio. Herf. 1836. (Patron, Arthur Henry Wall, Esq; Tithe, 94*l*; Glebe, 15 acres; R.'s Inc. 125*l*; Pop. 45.) [16]

POWELL, Samuel Hooper, *Sharrow Lodge, Ripon.*—Trin. Coll. Cam. B.A. 1829, M.A. 1830; Deac. 1830, Pr. 1831. [17]

POWELL, Thomas, *Dorstone Vicarage, Hay, Herefordshire.*—V. of Dorstone, Dio. Herf. 1843. (Patron, the present V; V.'s Inc. 446*l* and Ho; Pop. 547.) Dom. Chap. to Lord Gray. [18]

POWELL, T., *Turnastone, Hereford.*—R. of Turnastone, Dio. Herf. (Patroness, Mrs. Robinson; R.'s Inc. 73*l*; Pop. 54.) [19]

POWELL, Thomas Baden, *Newick Rectory, Uckfield Sussex.*—Oriel Coll. Ox. 1st cl. Lit. Hum. 1807, B.A. 1808, M.A. 1811; Deac. 1811 and Pr. 1812 by Abp of Cant. R. of Newick, Dio. Chich. 1818. (Patron, the present R; Tithe, 377*l*; Glebe, 28 acres; R.'s Inc. 404*l* and Ho; Pop. 991.) Hon. Preb. of Sidlesham in Chich. Cathl. 1849. Formerly Fell. of Oriel Coll. Ox. 1808–12; C. of Farningham, Kent, 1811. [20]

POWELL, Thomas Crump, *Munslow Rectory, Church-Stretton, Salop.*—Brasen. Coll. Ox. B.A. 1838; Deac. 1839, Pr. 1840. R. of Munslow, Dio. Herf. 1846. (Patron, the present R; Tithe—App. 6*l*, Imp. 10*l* 10*s*, R. 514*l* 10*s*; Glebe, 125 acres; R.'s Inc. 740*l* and Ho; Pop. 700.) [21]

POWELL, Thomas Edward, *Bisham Vicarage, Maidenhead, Berks.*—Oriel Coll. Ox. B.A. 1845, M.A. 1848; Deac. 1846, Pr. 1848. V. of Bisham, Dio. Ox. 1848. (Patron, G. Vansittart, Esq; Tithe—Imp. 87*l* 12*s* 6*d*, V. 115*l*; V.'s Inc. 179*l* and Ho; Pop. 528.) [22]

POWELL, Thomas Prosser, *Buenos Ayres.*—St. John's Coll. Ox. B.A. 1863; Deac. 1863; Pr. 1864. Asst. Chap. to the English Estancieros in the Campo, Buenos Ayres. Formerly C. of Turnaston and Vowchurch, Herf. 1863–64. [23]

POWELL, Thomas Wade.—St. John's Coll. Cam. 21st Wrang. and B.A. 1853, M.A. 1856; Deac. 1853 and Pr. 1854 by Bp of Rip. Formerly C. of Keighley. Author, *The Scriptural Doctrine of the Influence of the Holy Ghost as illustrated by the Analogy of Nature* (Burney Prize), 1856. [24]

POWELL, William, *Llanvrechva, Monmouthshire.*—Deac. 1821, Pr. 1822. P. C. of Llanvrechva with Cumbrane C. Monmouthshire, Dio. Llan. 1827. (Patrons, D. and C. of Llan; Tithe—App. 348*l* 3*s* 1*d*; Glebe, 6 acres; P. C.'s Inc. 120*l*; Pop. 2554.) P. C. of Llanhenog, Dio. Llan. 1838. (Patrons, D. and C. of Llan; Tithe, App. 150*l*; P. C.'s Inc. 60*l*; Pop. 228.) [25]

POWELL, William, *Christ Church Parsonage, Folkestone.*—Deac. 1847, Pr. 1848. P. C. of Ch. Ch. Folkestone, Dio. Cant. 1850. (Patron, Earl of Radnor; Pop. 3000.) [26]

POWELL, William, *Trefelan Rectory, Talsarn, Carmarthen.*—St. D.; Deac. 1863 and Pr. 1864 by Bp of St. D. R. of Trefelan, Dio. St. D. 1867. (Patron, Bp of St. D; Tithe, comm. 110*l*; Glebe, 3 acres; R.'s Inc. 145*l* and Ho; Pop. 345.) Formerly C. of Llanbadarn Vawr. [27]

POWELL, William Frederick, *Cirencester Parsonage, Glouc.*—St. Peter's Coll. Cam. B.A. 1827 M.A. 1830; Deac. and Pr. 1827 by Bp of Herf. V. of Cirencester with Water Moor C. Dio. G. and B. 1839.

(Patron, Bp of G. and B; Tithe—App. 5*l*, Imp. 99*l*, V. 240*l*; V.'s Inc. 470*l* and Ho; Pop. 6336.) Hon. Can. of Glouc. Cathl. 1854. Formerly C. of Great Malvern, Worc. 1830-33; P. C. of Stroud, Glouc. 1833–39. [1]

POWER, Alexander Bath, *Blackheath, Kent, S.E.*—St. Cath. Coll. Cam. Sen. Opt. and B.A. 1833, M.A. 1837; Deac. 1836 and Pr. 1837 by Bp of Carl. Mast. in the Blackheath Proprietary Sch; Chap. to the Earl of Bessborough. Formerly Prin. of the Norwich Diocesan Normal Schs. 1840. Author, *Lectures and Addresses on Educational and Scientific Subjects.* [2]

POWER, Francis Armstrong, 56, *York-terrace, Everton, Liverpool.*—Dub. A.B. 1837, A.M. 1841; Deac. 1837 and Pr. 1838 by Bp of Ches. P. C. of Bevington, Liverpool, Dio. Ches. 1846. (Patron, the Crown and Bp of Ches. alt; V.'s Inc. 300*l*; Pop. 14,375.) [3]

POWER, Henry, *Farington Parsonage, near Preston, Lancashire.*—St. John's Coll. Cam. B.A. 1831; Deac. 1838, Pr. 1839 by Bp of Ches. P. C. of Farington, near Preston, Dio. Man. 1840. (Patron, P. C. of Penwortham; Tithe—Imp. 152*l* 19*s* 6*d*; Endow. 25*l*; P. C.'s Inc. 130*l* and Ho; Pop. 2492.) Formerly C. of Bacup 1838–39. Author, *Reflections on Important Christian Doctrines,* Macintosh, 1858, 1*s* 6*d.* [4]

POWER, Henry Bolton, *Bramley Parsonage, Guildford, Surrey.*—Oriel Coll. Ox. B.A. 1842, M.A. 1846; Deac. 1843, Pr. 1844. P. C. of Bramley, Dio. Win. 1847. (Patron, Ld Chan; Tithe—Imp. 126*l* 9*s* 11*d*, P. C. 160*l*; Glebe, 1 acre; P. C.'s Inc. 160*l* and Ho; Pop. 1129.) [5]

POWER, John, *Parsonage, Tyler's Green, Amersham, Bucks.*—St. Edmund Hall, Ox. B.A. 1847, M.A. 1853; Deac. 1847, Pr. 1848. P. C. of Tyler's Green, Dio. Ox. 1862. (Patron, Earl Howe; Glebe, 5 acres; P. C.'s Inc. 120*l* and Ho; Pop. 800.) Formerly C. of Buttershaw, Bradford, 1847; P. C. of Shelf, Halifax, 1848. [6]

POWER, John, *Pembroke College, Cambridge.*—Pemb. Coll. Cam. 8th Wrang. and B.A. 1841, M.A. 1844; Deac. 1843, Pr. 1844. Fell. and Tut. of Pemb. Coll. Cam. 1852. [7]

POWER, Joseph, *Clare College, Cambridge.*—Clare Coll. Cam. 10th Wrang. and B.A. 1821, M.A. 1824; Deac. 1822 by Bp of Nor. Pr. 1822 by Bp of Lin. R. of Birdbrook, Dio. Roch. 1866. (Patron, Clare Coll. Cam; Tithe, comm. 600*l*; Glebe, 99 acres; R.'s Inc. 750*l* and Ho; Pop. 600.) Member of the Cambridge Philosophical and Antiquarian Societies, and Foundation Member of the Society of Northern Antiquarians of Copenhagen. Formerly Fell. of Clare Hall 1824-67; Fell. and Tut. of Trin. Hall 1829–44; Univ. Lib. 1845; V. of Littlington, Cambs. 1856. Author, Papers on Scientific Subjects in the *Philosophical Transactions* of London and of Cambridge, as well as others in the Cambridge and Dublin Mathematical Journals. [8]

POWER, Thomas Barratt, *The Vicarage, Upton Bishop, Ross.*—Emman. Coll. Cam. 11th Wrang. and B.A. 1845, M.A. 1848; Deac. 1847 and Pr. 1848 by Bp of Ely. V. of Upton Bishop, Dio. Herf. 1857. (Patrons, D. and C. of Herf; Tithe, 225*l*; Glebe, 202 acres; V.'s Inc. 550*l* and Ho; Pop. 716.) Preb. of Moreton Parva in Herf. Cathl. 1856. Formerly Fell. and Asst. Tut. of Emman. Coll; Head Mast. of the Herf. Cathl. Sch. 1851–57. [9]

POWLES, Edmund Sheppard.—King's Coll. Lond. Theol. Assoc. 1855; Deac. 1855 by Bp of Lon. Chap. of H.M.S. "Octavia." Formerly C. of St. Barnabas', Homerton, Middlesex, 1858. [10]

POWLES, Henry Charles, *Rodmarton Rectory, Cirencester.*—Oriel Coll. Ox. Ireland Exhib. B.A. 1848, M.A. 1851; Deac. and Pr. 1849 by Bp of Roch. C. of Rodmarton 1859. Formerly C. of Whitchurch, Herefordshire. [11]

POWLES, Richard Cowley, *Eliot-place, Blackheath, Kent, S.E.*—Ex. Coll. Ox. 1st cl. Lit. Hum. 1842, B.A. 1845, M.A. 1846; Deac. 1843 by Bp of Ox. Pr. 1851 by Bp of Lon. Formerly Fell. Tut. and Pub. Exam. in Lit. Hum. of Ex. Coll. Ox. [12]

POWLETT, The Hon. Thomas Orde, *Wensley Rectory, Bedale, Yorks.*—Trin. Coll. Cam. B.A. 1844, M.A. 1847; Deac. 1845 and Pr. 1846 by Bp of Rip. R. of Wensley, Dio. Rip. 1850. (Patron, Lord Bolton; Tithe, 1074*l* 10*s*; Glebe, 80 acres; R's Inc. 1202*l* and Ho; Pop. 1638.) [13]

POWLEY, Matthew, *Gibraltar.*—Queen's Coll. Ox. 4th cl. Lit. Hum. and B.A. 1849, M.A. 1853; Deac. 1850, Pr. 1851. Canon and Chap. of Gibraltar. Formerly C. of Wallasey, Cheshire, 1850–59; Chap. of Malaga 1859. [14]

POWLEY, Robert, *Eskdale, Ravenglass, Cumberland.*—Deac. 1812, Pr. 1813. P. C. of Eskdale, Dio. Carl. 1814. (Patron, W Stanley, Esq; P. C.'s Inc. 66*l* and Ho; Pop. 346.) Formerly C. of Grasmere 1812–14. [15]

POWNALL, Alfred, *Norwich.*—St. Cath. Coll. Cam. Crosse's Theol. Scho. 1853, Tyrwhitt's Heb. Scho. 1855, B.A. 1853, M.A. 1856; Deac. 1856 and Pr. 1857 by Bp of Ely. V. of Trowse with Lakenham, Dio. Nor. 1860. (Patrons, D. and C. of Nor; Tithe, Trowse—App. 92*l* 5*s* 8*d*, V. 178*l* 4*s* 6*d*; Glebe, 11 acres; Lakenham, Tithe—App. 44*l* 14*s*, V. 183*l* 7*s*; V.'s Inc. 360*l*; Pop. Trowse 1402, Lakenham 2079.) Formerly Chap. of St. Cath. Coll. Cam. 1856–60; C. of Conington, Hunts, 1857–60. Author, *Shakspere weighed in an Even Balance,* 1864, 3*s* 6*d*, Saunders, Otley, and Co. [16]

POWNALL, Assheton, *South Kilworth Rectory, near Rugby.*—Brasen. Coll. Ox. B.A. 1845, M.A. 1848; Deac. 1845 and Pr. 1846 by Bp of Lich. R. of South Kilworth, Dio. Pet. 1847. (Patron, Ld Chan; Glebe, 256 acres; R.'s Inc. 463*l* and Ho; Pop. 421.) Organizing Sec. of S.P.G. in the Archdeaconry of Leic; Rural Dean 1867. Formerly C. of Edgmond, Salop, 1845–47. [17]

POWNALL, Charles Colyear Beaty, *Milton Ernest Vicarage, near Bedford.*—Clare Hall, Cam. Sen. Opt. and B.A. 1829, M.A. 1832; Deac. 1831 and Pr. 1832 by Bp of Lin. V. of Milton Ernest, Dio. Ely, 1835. Patron, Christopher Turnor, Esq; Glebe, 246 acres; V.'s Inc. 267*l* and Ho; Pop. 485.) Chap. to the Earl of Portmore 1831; Rural Dean of Clapham 1840; Hon. Sec. to the Bedfordshire Board of Education 1844. [18]

POWNALL, George Purves, *St. John's Parsonage, Murray-street, Hoxton, London, N.*—Trin. Coll. Cam. B.A. 1845; Deac. 1846 by Bp of Nor. Pr. 1847 by Bp of Pet. P. C. of St. John's, Hoxton, Dio. Lon. 1864. (Patron, Archd. of Lond; P. C.'s Inc. from fees and pew-rents 800*l* and Ho; Pop. 20,000.) Formerly C. of Dursley, Glouc. 1846, St. Anne's, Soho, St. Giles', Cripplegate, 1848–52; Colon. Chap. of West Australia, 1852; Dean of Perth 1858. [19]

POWYS, The Hon. and Rev. Edward Victor Robert, 33, *Great Cumberland-place, London, W.*—Trin. Coll. Cam. LL.B. 1863; Deac. 1865 and Pr. 1866 by Bp of Rip. Formerly C. of Danby-Wiske with Yafforth, Yorks, 1865–67. [20]

POWYS, Francis Arthur, *St. John's College, Oxford.*—St. John's Coll. Ox. B.A. 1854, M.A. 1857; Deac. 1855 by Bp of Ox. V. of St. Giles', City and Dio. Ox. 1864. (Patron, St. John's Coll. Ox; V.'s Inc. 160*l*; Pop. 1701.) Fell. of St. John's Coll. Ox. Formerly C. of Sonning, Berks. [21]

POWYS, Richard Thomas, *Hullavington Vicarage, near Chippenham.*—Univ. Coll. Ox. B.A. 1820, M.A. 1823; Deac. 1821 and Pr. 1822 by Bp of Ox. V. of Hullavington, Dio. G. and B. 1864. (Patron, Eton Coll; Tithe, 175*l*; Glebe, 84 acres; V.'s Inc. 278*l* and Ho; Pop. 700.) Formerly C. of Whitchurch 1821–22, Caversham 1823–27, Rotherfield-Peppard 1840–49, Purley, Berks, 1854–64; Chap. to the Goring Heath Almshouses, Reading, 1828–64. [22]

POWYS, Thomas Arthur, *Medmenham, Great Marlow.*—St. John's Coll. Ox. B.A. 1826, M.A. 1829; Deac. 1826, Pr. 1827. R. of Sawtry St. Andrew, Hunts, Dio. Ely, 1831. (Patron, Lord Valentia; R.'s Inc. 170*l*; Pop. 386.) Author, *The Reconstruction of the Liturgy,* 1843, 2*s.* [23]

POWYS, William Percy, *Reading.*—Univ. Coll. Ox. B.A. 1862, M.A. 1864; Deac. 1862 and

Pr. 1864 by Bp of Ox. C. of St. Mary's, Reading, 1862. [1]

POYNDER, Clement, *Stroud, Glouc.*—Caius Coll. Cam. B.A. 1859, M.A. 1861; Deac. 1860 and Pr. 1861 by Bp of Man. C. of Stroud 1863. Formerly C. of St. Peter's, Halliwell, Lanc. 1860, Stanley St. Leonard's, Glouc. 1862. [2]

POYNDER, Frederick, 2, *Rutland-place, Charterhouse-square, London, E.C.*—Wad. Coll. Ox. B.A. 1838, M.A. 1840; Deac. 1840 and Pr. 1841 by Bp of Lon. 2nd Mast. of the Charterhouse Sch. 1858. Formerly Chap. to the Bridewell Hospital, Lond. 1849–58; Asst. Mast. in Charterhouse Sch. 1838–49. [3]

POYNDER, Leopold, *Blyborough, Kirton Lindsey.*—Trin. Coll. Cam. Sen. Opt. 1841, Norrisian Prize 1842, B.A. 1841, M.A. 1844; Deac. 1843, Pr. 1844 by Bp of Pet. Formerly C. of Sibbertoft and Weddingworth; Chap. at Calcutta. [4]

POYNTON, Francis John, *Kelston Rectory, Bristol.*—Ex. Coll. Ox. 1846, Symes Scho. 1848, B.A. 1850, Rector's Theol. Essay 1851, M.A. 1853; Deac. 1850 and Pr. 1851 by Bp of Ox. R. of Kelston, Dio. B. and W. 1858. (Patron, Sir J. Neeld, Bart; Tithe, 252*l*; Glebe, 50 acres; R.'s Inc. 332*l* and Ho; Pop. 212.) Formerly C. of Barmington, Warwickshire, 1853–53. [5]

POYNTZ, Newdigate.—C. of St. Mark's, Kennington, Surrey. [6]

POYSER, Thomas John, *Elmdon, Saffron Walden.*—C. of Elmdon, Essex. [7]

PRANCE, Clement Howard, *Hales Owen, Birmingham.*—Trin. Coll. Cam. B.A. 1864; Deac. 1865 and Pr. 1866 by Bp of Wor. Asst. C. of Hales Owen 1865. [8]

PRANCE, Lewis Newcomen, *Haileybury, Herts.*—Trin. Coll. Cam. B.A. 1863, M.A. 1866; Deac. 1864 and Pr. 1865 by Bp of Roch. C. of Little Amwell. Formerly C. of Halley with Woollens Brook. [9]

PRAT, Richard, *Todber, Blandford.*—Mert. Coll. Ox. Postmaster of, 1839, 2nd cl. Lit. Hum. 1841, B.A. 1842; Deac. 1843 and Pr. 1844 by Bp of Chich. C. of Stour Provost and Todber, Dorset, 1860. Formerly C. of Harting, Sussex, 1843–46, Salterton, Devon, 1846–49, Newtown, Hants, 1850–56; Consular Chap. at Christiania 1856–58. [10]

PRATT, Charles, *St. Margaret's, Ware, Herts.*—Magd. Coll. Cam. B.A. 1815, M.A. 1826; Chap. of the Donative Peculiar of Stanstead St. Margaret's, Dio. Roch. 1858. (Patron, the present Chap; Chap's Inc. 6*l*; Pop. 93.) [11]

PRATT, Charles, jun., *Packington Vicarage, Ashby-de-la-Zouch.*—Trin. Coll. Cam. B.A. 1843. V. of Packington, Dio. Pet. 1853. (Patroness, Lady Edith A. Hastings; Tithe—Imp. 15*l* 10*s*, V. 50*l* 10*s*; V.'s Inc. 330*l* and Ho; Pop. 643.) [12]

PRATT, Charles O'Neill, *St. Paul's Parsonage, Burslem, Staffs.*—Dub. A.B. 1836, A.M. 1842; Deac. 1836 by Bp of Down and Connor, Pr. 1837 by Bp of Kildare. P. C. of St. Paul's, Burslem, Dio. Lich. 1864. (Patron, R. of Burslem; P. C.'s Inc. 150*l* and Ho; Pop. 7801.) Surrogate. Formerly C. of Ch. Ch. Macclesfield. Author, *Twenty Sermons, on various Subjects,* 1847; *Metrical Translation of the "Ars Poetica,"* Macclesfield, 1850. [13]

PRATT, Charles Palliner Tidd, *The Parsonage, Bracknell, Beds.*—Jesus Coll. Cam. B.A. 1860; Deac. 1860 and Pr. 1861 by Bp of Ely. P. C. of Bracknell, Dio. Ox. 1865. (Patron, Bp of Ox; Tithe, 12*l*; P. C.'s Inc. 60*l* and Ho; Pop. 807.) Formerly C. of Barrow, Suffolk, 1860, Longworth and Charney (sole charge) 1862–65. [14]

PRATT, Charles Tiplady, *Cawthorne Parsonage, Barnsley.*—Queen's Coll. Ox. B.A. 1860, M.A. 1863; Deac. 1861 and Pr. 1862 by Bp of Lich. C. in sole charge of Cawthorne 1866. Formerly C. of Kidsgrove, Staffs, 1861, Drigg, Cumberland, 1863, Berkeley, Gloucestershire, 1864, Hoyland Swaine Mission 1865. [15]

PRATT, George Henry, *Lincoln.*—Wad. Coll. Ox. B.A. 1855, M.A. 1858; Deac. 1857 and Pr. 1858 by Bp of Lin. P. C. of St. Swithin's, Lincoln, Dio. Lin. 1866. (Patron, Bp of Lin; Tithe, 11*l* 14*s* 6*d*; Glebe, 25 acres; P. C.'s Inc. 300*l* and Ho; Pop. 6100.) Formerly C. of Louth 1857–66; Chap. to Lord Hawke 1864. [16]

PRATT, Henry, *Shepton-Mallett Rectory, Somerset.*—Trin. Coll. Cam. B.A. 1838; Deac. 1842 and Pr. 1843 by Bp of Pet. R. of Shepton-Mallett, Dio. B. and W. 1847. (Patrons, the Prince of Wales and T. Wickham, Esq. alt; Tithe, 787*l* 10*s*; R.'s Inc. 790*l* and Ho; Pop. 5347.) Can. of Pet. 1851. (Value, 500*l* and Res.) [17]

PRATT, James Weston, 16, *South-street, Finsbury-square, London, E.C.*—Trin. Coll. Cam. 1st cl. Cl. Trip. B.A. 1863, M.A. 1866; Deac. 1866 and Pr. 1867 by Bp of Lon. C. of St. Stephen's, Coleman-street, City of Lond. 1866. [18]

PRATT, The Ven. John Henry, *Calcutta.*—Caius Coll. Cam. 3rd Wrang. and B.A. 1833, M.A. 1836. Chap. to the Hon. E.I.C. 1838; Archd. of Calcutta 1850; Fell. of Caius Coll. Cam. Author, *Mathematical Principles of Mechanical Philosophy; Scripture and Science not at Variance.* [19]

PRATT, Joseph, *Paston Rectory, Peterborough.*—Queens' Coll. Cam. B.A. 1807, M.A. 1811; Deac. 1808 and Pr. 1809 by Bp of B. and W. R. of Paston, Dio. Pet. 1811. (Patron, Bp of Pet; Tithe—App. 140*l*, R. 160*l*; Glebe, 243 acres; R.'s Inc. 631*l* and Ho; Pop. 1071.) [20]

PRATT, Josiah, 13, *Finsbury-circus, London, E.C.*—Trin. Coll. Cam. B.A. 1825, M.A. 1828; Deac. 1826 and Pr. 1827 by Bp of Lon. V. of St. Stephen's, Coleman-street, City and Dio. Lon. 1844. (Patrons, the Parishioners; V.'s Inc. 570*l*; Pop. 3324.) [21]

PRATT, Julian, *Harrietsham, Maidstone.*—Trin. Coll. Ox. B.A. 1845, M.A. 1847; Deac. 1846, Pr. 1847. C. of Harrietsham. [22]

PRATT, Philip Cornish.—Pemb. Coll. Cam. B.A. 1851; Deac. 1852 and Pr. 1853 by Bp of Wor. Chap. of H.M.S. "Leander." [23]

PRATT, Philip Edgar, *Minsterley Parsonage, Shrewsbury.*—Ex. Coll. Ox. Scho. of, 3rd cl. Lit. Hum. B.A. 1859, M.A. 1863; Deac. 1859 and Pr. 1860 by Bp of Pet. P. C. of Minsterley, Dio. Herf. 1865. (Patron, Marquis of Bath; P. C.'s Inc. 87*l* and Ho; Pop. 890.) Formerly C. of St. Margaret's, Leicester, 1859–61, Ross, Herefordshire, 1861–65. [24]

PRATT, Robert, *Sandbach, Cheshire.*—St. John's Coll. Cam. 4th Sen. Opt. 1862; Deac. 1862 by Bp of Ches. C. of Sandbach 1862 and Math. Mast. in Sandbach Gr. Sch. [25]

PRATT, Samuel, *Darrington, Pontefract.*—C. of Darrington. [26]

PRATT, Thomas Arthur Cooper, *Madras, India.*—St. Peter's Coll. Cam. B.A. 1852, M.A. 1855; Deac. 1853 and Pr. 1855. Chap. in Madras 1856. Formerly C. of Wymondham, Norfolk, 1854–56. [27]

PRATT, William, *Harpley Rectory, Rougham, Norfolk.*—Trin. Coll. Cam. B.A. 1826; Deac. 1827, Pr. 1828. R. of Harpley, Dio. Nor. 1832. (Patron, Anthony Hamond, Esq; Tithe, 460*l*; Glebe, 90 acres; R.'s Inc. 595*l* and Ho; Pop. 479.) R. of Great Bircham, Dio. Nor. 1832. (Patron, Anthony Hamond, Esq; Tithe, 575*l*; Glebe, 72 acres; R.'s Inc. 647*l* and Ho; Pop. 489.) [28]

PRATTEN, William Sidney, *Hale Vicarage, Beckermet, Whitehaven, Cumberland.*—St. Bees; Deac. 1857 and Pr. 1858 by Bp of Lich. V. of Hale, Dio. Carl. 1861. (Patron, Earl of Lonsdale; V.'s Inc. 82*l*; Pop. 382.) Formerly C. of St. Paul's, Forebridge, Staffs, 1857–61. [29]

PRENTICE, Henry, *Holdford Rectory, Bridgwater.*—Trin. Coll. Ox. B.A. 1850, M.A. 1853; Deac. 1851 and Pr. 1852 by Bp of Win. R. of Holdford, Dio. B. and W. 1866. (Patron, Eton Coll; R.'s Inc. 380*l* and Ho; Pop. 170.) Formerly C. of Preston-Candover, Hants, and Burnham, Bucks. [30]

PRENTIS, A., *Monmouth.*—C. of Monmouth. [31]

PRESCOT, Charles Kenrick, *Stockport Rectory, Cheshire.*—Brasen. Coll. Ox. B.A. 1808, M.A. 1810. R. of Stockport, Dio. Ches. 1324. (Patron, S. Symonds,

Esq; Tithe, 1470*l* 0*s* 3*d*; R.'s Inc. 2200*l* and Ho; Pop. 15.244.) Rural Dean of Warrington. [1]

PRESCOT, Kenrick, *Ponteland, Newcastle-on-Tyne.*—Brasen. Coll. Ox. 1st cl. Lit. Hum. and B.A. 1852, M.A. 1855; Fell. of Mert. Coll. 1853; Deac. 1859, Pr. 1861. V. of Ponteland, Dio. Dur. 1864. (Patron, Mert. Coll. Ox; V.'s Inc. 560*l* and Ho; Pop 1089.) Formerly C. of Stockport 1861–64. [2]

PRESCOT, Oldfeld Kelsall, *North Wraxall, Chippenham.*—Brasen. Coll. Ox. B.A. 1852; Deac. 1853 by Bp of Lon. Pr. 1854 by Bp of Lin. C. of North Wraxall 1861. Formerly C. of Southwell, Notts, 1853–56; P. C. of St. John's, Dukinfield, Cheshire, 1856–60. [3]

PRESCOTT, George Edward, *Digswell Rectory, Welwyn, Herts.*—Trin. Coll. Cam. B.A. 1827, M.A. 1830; Deac. 1832 and Pr. 1833 by Bp of Lin. R. of Digswell, Dio. Roch. 1839. (Patron, the present R; Tithe, 350*l*; Glebe, 42 acres; R.'s Inc. 400*l* and Ho; Pop. 243.) [4]

PRESCOTT, George Frederick, 13, *Oxford-square, London, W.*—Trin. Coll. Cam. B.A. 1850, M.A. 1853; Deac. and Pr. 1853. P. C. of St. Michael's, Paddington, Dio. Lon. 1864. (Patron, W. Gibbs, Esq; P. C.'s Inc. 300*l*; Pop. 3851.) Formerly C. of St. John's, Paddington, and Little Marsden, Lancashire. [5]

PRESCOTT, Isaac Philip, *Priors Marston Vicarage, Daventry.*—Oriel Coll. Ox. B.A. 1837, M.A. 1840; Deac. 1839, Pr. 1840. V. of Priors-Marston, Dio. Wor. 1862. (Patron, Earl Spencer, V.'s Inc. 250*l* and Ho; Pop. 698.) Formerly C. of Romsey, Hants, 1840; Min. of St. Mary's, Portsmouth, 1841–46; C. of the Willingales and Shellow, Essex, 1848, Chelmsford 1856; R. of Willingale-Doe and Shellow 1861; Min. at Barley, Herts, 1861. [6]

PRESCOTT, John Eustace, *Scroope-terrace, Cambridge.*—Corpus Coll. Cam. 12th Wrang. and B.A. 1855, M.A. 1858, B.D. 1867; Deac. 1858 and Pr. 1859 by Bp of Pet. Formerly Fell. of Corpus Coll. Cam; C. of Whissendine 1858–60, All Saints', Hawkhurst, 1860–65. Author, *Every Day Scripture Difficulties*, Pt. I; *Readings on St. Matthew and St. Mark*, 1863, 9*s*, Pt. II; *St. Luke and St. John*, 1866, 9*s*, Longmans; Contributions to various Periodicals. [7]

PRESCOTT, Peter, *City of London Union, Bow-road, E.* St. Mary Hall, Ox. B.A. 1850, M.A. 1853; Deac. 1852, Pr. 1853. Chap. of the City of London Union, Bow-road. (Stipend, 300*l*.) Formerly C. of Camden Church, Camberwell, and Great Ilford, Essex. [8]

PRESCOTT, Thomas, *Caddington Vicarage, Luton.*—V. of Caddington, Dio. Ely, 1862. (Patrons, D. and C. of St. Paul's; Tithe, App. 1036*l*; V.'s Inc. 319*l* and Ho; Pop. 1851.) [9]

PREST, The Ven. Edward, *Gateshead Rectory, Gateshead.*—St. John's Coll. Cam. Jun. Opt. 2nd cl. Cl. Trip. B.A. 1847, M.A. 1850; Deac. 1847 and Pr. 1848 by Bp of Ox. R. of Gateshead, Dio. Dur. 1861. (Patron, Bp of Dur; Tithe, 400*l*; Glebe, 16½ acres; R.'s Inc. 1000*l* and Ho; Pop. 22,000.) Mast. of King James's Hospital, Gateshead, 1861 (included in Rectory); Archd. and Can. of Dur. 1863. (Patron, Bp. of Dur; Canonry 1000*l*, Archdeaconry, 212*l*.) Formerly Chap. to Sherburn Hospital 1851–57; Mast. of Sherburn Hospital 1857–61; Hon. Can. Dur. 1860. Author, several Charges, Addresses, and Sermons. [10]

PRESTON, Alfred Matthew, *Winslow Vicarage, Bucks.*—Trin. Coll. Cam. B.A. 1844; Deac. 1845, Pr. 1847. V. of Winslow, Dio. Ox. 1863. (Patron, Ld Chan; Glebe, 133 acres; V.'s Inc. 220*l* and Ho; Pop. 1890.) Formerly C. of Cheshunt. [11]

PRESTON, Charles Moyes, *Warcop Hall, Warcop, Penrith.*—Queen's Coll. Ox. B.A. 1848; Deac. 1848 and Pr. 1849 by Bp of Dur. V. of Warcop, Dio. Carl. 1855. (Patron, Rev. W. S. Preston; V.'s Inc. 216*l*; Pop. 806.) [12]

PRESTON, George Henry, *Rio Janeiro.*—St. Bees; Deac. 1846 and Pr. 1847 by Bp of Ches. British Chap. at Rio Janeiro. Formerly C. of Minster in Sheppey, Kent, and Donhead St. Andrew, Salisbury. Author, *The Student's Theological Manual, comprising the History of the Canon, Theological Evidences, Biblical Antiquities, Old and New Testament History, Church History, Doctrine and Prophecy*, 1850, 7*s*. 6*d*. [13]

PRESTON, Henry Edmund, *Tasburgh Rectory, Long Stratton, Norfolk.*—Queen's Coll. Cam; Deac. 1835, Pr. 1836. R. of Tasburgh, Dio. Nor. 1837. (Patrons, Trustees of J. Jermy, Esq; Tithe, 287*l*; Glebe, 2½ acres; R.'s Inc. 287*l* and Ho; Pop. 446.) Rural Dean of Depwade; Sunday Even. Lect. at Wymondham. [14]

PRESTON, John D'Arcy Warcop, *Sandgate Parsonage, Kent.*—Wor. Coll. Ox. B.A. 1845, M.A. 1847; Deac. 1847 by Bp of Nor. Pr. 1849 by Abp of York. P. C. of Sandgate, Dio. Cant. 1859. (Patron, Hon. Sir J. D. Bligh; P. C.'s Inc. 280*l* and Ho; Pop. 1965.) Formerly Asst. Chap. to the Forces in the Crimea and at Malta. [15]

PRESTON, John William, *Parkstone, near Poole.*—Dur. B.A. 1851; Deac. 1851 and Pr. 1852 by Bp of Dur. Formerly C. of Bower Chalk and Alvediston. [16]

PRESTON, Lawrence, *Longton, Preston.*—Queens' Coll. Cam. B.A. 1849, M.A. 1853; Deac. 1849, Pr. 1850. P. C. of Longton, Dio. Man. 1852. (Patron, L. Rawstorne, Esq; Tithe—Imp. 328*l*, App. 8*l*; P. C.'s Inc. 260*l*; Pop. 1637.) [17]

PRESTON, Theodore, *Trinity College, Cambridge.*—Trin. Coll. Cam. B.A. 1841, M.A. 1844. Fell. of Trin. Coll. Cam. 1842; Lord Almoner's Reader of Arabic 1854. Author, *A New Translation, with Prolegomena, Annotations, &c. on the Book of Ecclesiastes*, Cambridge, and J. Parker, London; *A Metrical Translation, with copious Notes, of the Makamat Al Hariri*; *Phraseological Notes on the Hebrew Text of the Book of Genesis*; *A Catalogue of the Arabic MSS. presented by Burkhardt to the University Library at Cambridge.* [18]

PRESTON, Thomas, *Swaffham Prior Vicarage, near Cambridge.*—Ex. Coll. Ox. B.A. 1839, M.A. 1843; Deac. 1840 and Pr. 1841 by Bp of Nor. V. of Swaffham Prior with St. Cyriac and St. Mary, Dio. Ely, 1856. (Patrons, Bp of Ely and D. and C. of Ely alt; V.'s Inc. 600*l* and Ho; Pop. 1329.) Formerly C. of the Sequestrated R. of Long Melford, Suffolk. [19]

PRESTON, Thomas Arthur, *The College, Marlborough, Wilts.*—Emman. Coll. Cam. B.A. 1856, M.A. 1859; Deac. 1858 and Pr. 1859 by Bp of Salis. Asst. Mast. of Marlborough Coll. 1858. [20]

PRESTON, William, *Bulmer Rectory, York.*—Queen's Coll. Ox. B.A. 1807, M.A. 1812; Deac. 1806 and Pr. 1806 by Abp of York. R. of Bulmer, Dio. York, 1806. Patron, Earl Fitzwilliam; Tithe, 32*l*; Glebe, 210 acres; R.'s Inc. 395*l* and Ho; Pop. 1077.) V. of Whenby, Yorks, Dio. York, 1806. (Patron, W. Garforth, Esq., Wiganthorpe, York; Tithe, 105*l*; Glebe, 12 acres; V.'s Inc. 130*l*; Pop. 109.) Preb. of Bilton in York Cathl. 1812. Formerly V. of Sculcoates, Hull, 1815–66. [21]

PRESTON, William, *St. James's, Bath.*—St. Aidan's; Deac. 1865 by Bp of Rip. Pr. 1866 by Abp of York. C. of St. James's, Bath, 1866. Formerly C. of Attercliffe, Sheffield, 1865. [22]

PRETYMAN, Frederick, *Great Carlton Vicarage, Louth, Lincolnshire.*—Magd. Coll. Ox. B.A. 1841, M.A. 1844, B.D. 1850. V. of Great Carlton, Dio. Lin. 1850. (Patrons, D. and C. of Lin; V.'s Inc. 598*l* and Ho; Pop. 338.) Rural Dean. Formerly Fell of Magd. Coll. Ox. [23]

PRETYMAN, Henry George Middleton, *Lowick Rectory, Thrapstone, Northants.*—Oriel Coll. Ox. B.A. 1839, M.A. 1843. R. of Lowick, Dio. Pet. 1856. (Patroness, Mrs W. Stopford; R.'s Inc. 353*l* and Ho; Pop. 427.) [24]

PREVOST, The Ven. Sir George, Bart., *Stinchcombe, Dursley.*—Oriel Coll. Ox. 2nd cl. Lit. Hum. 1st cl. Math. et Phy. and B.A. 1825, M.A. 1827; Deac. 1828 and Pr. 1829 by Bp of Glouc. P. C. of Stinchcombe, Dio. G. and B. 1834. (Patron, Bp of G. and B; Tithe, Imp. 240*l*; P. C.'s Inc. 715*l* and Ho; Pop. 346.) Archd. of Gloucester (Value, 200*l*.) 1865; Hon. Can. of Glouc.

1859. Formerly Rural Dean of Dursley 1852 66. Author, *A Manual of Daily Prayers*, 1846. [1]

PRICE, Arthur Henry, *Lugwardine Vicarage, Hereford.*—Wad. Coll. Ox. 4th cl. Lit. Hum. and B.A. 1833, M.A. 1838; Deac. 1834, Pr. 1835. V. of Lugwardine, Dio. Herf. 1862. (Patrons, D. and C. of Herf; Pop. 748.) Formerly C. of King's Capel. [2]

PRICE, Aubrey Charles, *Loat's-road, Clapham-park, S.*—New Coll. Ox. Hon. 4th cl. Lit. Hum. and B.A. 1853; Deac. 1853 by Bp of Ox. Pr. 1854 by Bp of Lon. P. C. of St. James's, Clapham, Dio. Win. 1865. (Patrons, Trustees; P. C.'s Inc. 620*l*; Pop. 5250.) Formerly Fell. of New Coll. Ox; C. of St. George's, Bloomsbury, Lond. 1854–56; R. of Rusholme, Manchester, and Chap. to Bp of Dur. 1856–60; Min. of Lock Chapel, and Chap. of Lock Hospital, Lond. 1860–65. [3]

PRICE, Bartholomew, 11, *St. Giles'-street, Oxford.*—Pemb. Coll. Ox. Exhib. 1837, 1st cl. Math. et Phy. 3rd cl. Lit. Hum. and B.A. 1840, M.A. 1843; Deac. 1841 and Pr. 1848 by Bp of Ox. Fell. of Pemb. Coll. Ox. 1844, Tutor 1846, Public Examiner 1847 and 1853, Moderator 1852, Sedleian Prof. of Natural Philosophy 1853. Fell. of the Royal Soc. Author, *A Treatise on Differential Calculus*, 1848; *A Treatise on Infinitesimal Calculus*, Vol. I. *Differential Calculus*, Oxford Univ. Press, 1852; Vol. II. *Integral Calculus and Calculus of Variations*, 1854; Vol. III. *Statics and Dynamics of a Particle*, 1856; Vol. IV. *Dynamics of Material Systems*, 1862. [4]

PRICE, Charles Parker, *Uxbridge Parsonage, Middlesex.*—Pemb. Coll. Ox. 2nd cl. Lit. Hum. and B.A. 1824, M.A. 1827; Deac. 1826, Pr. 1827. P. C. and Lect. of Uxbridge, Dio. Lon. 1827. (Patrons, Trustees of the late G. Townsend; P. C.'s Inc. 82*l*; Lect.'s Inc. 100*l* and Ho; Pop. 3235.) Chap. to the Uxbridge Union 1836. Author, *A Funeral Sermon on the Death of George IV*; *Sermons*, 1 vol. 1831; occasional Sermons; *The Neglect of the Sacrament of the Lord's Supper* (a Tract). [5]

PRICE, David, *Castle-street, Brecon.*—Lampeter, Scho. of, B.D. 1854; Deac. 1844 by Bp of Nor. Pr. 1844 by Bp of St. D. Chap. to the Brecon County Gaol and House of Correction, Dio. St. D. 1847. (Salary, 100*l*.) Formerly C. of Aberayron, Cardiganshire, 1844–45. [6]

PRICE, David, *Little Marcle Rectory, Ledbury, Herefordshire.*—R. of Little Marcle, Dio. Herf. 1865. (Patron, Bp of Herf; Tithe, 230*l*; Glebe, 30 acres; R.'s Inc. 275*l* and Ho; Pop. 168.) [7]

PRICE, David Bankes, *Llangelynin Rectory, Conway.*—Lampeter, B.D. 1854; Deac. 1847 and Pr. 1848 by Bp of Ban. R. of Llangelynin, Dio. Ban. 1866. (Patron, Bp of Ban; Tithe, 250*l*; Glebe, 2 acres; R.'s Inc. 253*l* and Ho; Pop. 204.) Formerly C. of Holyhead, and of Llandyssilio, Anglesey. [8]

PRICE, Edmund, *Farnborough Rectory, Wantage, Berks.*—Univ. Coll. Ox. B.A. 1858, M.A. 1862; Deac. 1859 and Pr. 1860 by Bp of G. and B. R. of Farnborough, Dio. Ox. 1862. (Patron, Ralph C. Price, Esq; Tithe, 291*l*; Glebe, 22 acres; R.'s Inc. 320*l* and Ho; Pop. 232.) Formerly C. of St. Peter's, Bishopsworth, Bristol, 1859. [9]

PRICE, Edward, *Richmond, Surrey, S.W.*—Chap. to the Richmond Union. [10]

PRICE, Ellis, *Temple Balsall, Knowle, Birmingham.*—King's Coll. Lond. Theol. Assoc. 1864; Deac. 1865 and Pr. 1866 by Bp of Wor. C. of Temple Balsall. [11]

PRICE, Evan, *Dunston Parsonage, Penkridge, Staffs.*—Deac. 1822 and Pr. 1823 by Bp of Llan. P. C. of Dunston, Dio. Lich. 1824. (Patron, Lord Hatherton; Tithe—Imp. 253*l*; Glebe, 1½ acres; P. C.'s Inc. 98*l* and Ho; Pop. 275.) P. C. of Coppenhall in the Par. of Penkridge, Dio. Lich. 1850. (Patron, Lord Hatherton; Tithe, Imp. 142*l*, P. C.'s Inc. 90*l*; Pop. 88.) [12]

PRICE, E., *Trétower, Crickhowell, Brecon.*—P. C. of Trétower, Dio. St. D. 1860. (Patron, M. Morgan, Esq; Tithe, 2*l* 10*s*; Glebe, 26 acres; P. C.'s Inc. 71*l*; Pop. 296.) [13]

PRICE, George Frederick, *Brunswick-road, Norwich.*—New Coll. Ox. Fell. of; Deac. and Pr. by Bp of Ox. R. of St. John's, Maddermarket, Norwich, Dio. Nor. 1863. (Patron, New Coll. Ox; R.'s Inc. 110*l*; Pop. 537.) Dom. Chap. to the Marquis of Abercorn. [14]

PRICE, Henry Hugh, *Ash Parsonage, Whitchurch, Salop.*—Wor. Coll. Ox. B.A. 1850, M.A. 1852; Deac. 1850 and Pr. 1851 by Bp of Lich. P. C. of Ash, Dio. Lich. 1852. (Patron, R. of Whitchurch; Glebe, 29 acres; P. C.'s Inc. 100*l* and Ho; Pop. 545.) [15]

PRICE, Henry Tilley, 1, *Bath-villa, Cheltenham.*—Jesus Coll. Ox. B.A 1840, M.A. 1846; Deac. 1846 and Pr. 1847 by Bp of G. and B. Cl. Mast. in Cheltenham Coll. [16]

PRICE, Howel, *Llanfrynach Rectory, Brecon.*—Lampeter; Deac. 1850 and Pr. 1852 by Bp of Llan. R. of Llanfrynach, Dio. St. D. 1855. (Patrons, Exors. of the late J. P. De Winton, Esq; Tithe, 300*l* 10*s*; Glebe, 2 acres; R's Inc. 303*l* 10*s* and Ho; Pop. 304.) Formerly C. of Aberpergwm, and R. of Kilybebyll, Dio. Llan. [17]

PRICE, Hugh Lewis, *Penmachno, near Llanrwst, Carnarvonshire.*—P. C. of Penmachno, Dio. Ban. 1860. (Patron, Lord Ranelagh; P. C.'s Inc. 200*l* and Ho; Pop. 1425.) [18]

PRICE, Isaac, *Amersham, Bucks.*—Dub. A.B. 1861; Deac. 1864 by Bp of Lon. Pr. 1865 by Bp of Ox. C. of Chesham Bois, Bucks, 1865. Formerly C. of Trent Park Church, near Barnet, 1864. [19]

PRICE, James, *Nantddû, Merthyr-Tydvil.*—St. John's Coll. Cam. B.A. 1846, M.A. 1850; Deac. 1846 by Bp of St. D. Pr. 1847 by Bp of Herf. P. C. of Nantddû, Dio. St. D. 1847. (Patron, R. of Cantreff; P. C.'s Inc. 60*l*; Pop. 95.) [20]

PRICE, James Mansel, *Cuddington Vicarage, Aylesbury.*—All Souls' Coll. Ox. B.A. 1849, M.A. 1852; Deac. 1852 and Pr. 1853 by Bp of Ox. V. of Cuddington, Dio. Ox. 1855. (Patrons, D. and C. of Roch; Tithe, 180*l*; Glebe, 14 acres; V.'s Inc. 200*l* and Ho; Pop. 594.) [21]

PRICE, John, *Llanvihangel-Tor-y-Mynydd Rectory, Chepstow, Monmouthshire.*—Literate; Deac. 1827 and Pr. 1828 by Bp of Llan. R. of Llanvihangel-Tor-y-Mynydd, Dio. Llan. 1847. (Patron, Archd. of Llan; Tithe, 121*l* 0*s* 6*d*; Glebe, 11½ acres; R.'s Inc. 137*l* and Ho; Pop. 195.) P. C. of Kilwrwg, Monmouthshire, Dio. Llan. 1847. (Patron, Archd. of Llan; P. C.'s Inc. 50*l*; Pop. 121.) Chap. to the Chepstow Union. [22]

PRICE, John, *Blethvaugh, Knighton, Radnorshire.*—R. of Blethvaugh or Bleddfa, Dio. St. D. 1835. (Patron, Bp of St. D; Tithe, 200*l*; Glebe, 8 acres; R.'s Inc. 210*l*; Pop. 250.) Chap to the Chepstow Union. [23]

PRICE, John, *Bangor.*—Jesus Coll. Ox. 3rd cl. Lit. Hum. B.A. 1851, M.A. 1863; Deac. 1851 and Pr. 1852 by Bp of Ban. V. of Bangor, Dio. Ban. 1863. (Patron, Bp. of Ban; Tithe, 800*l*; V.'s Inc. 430*l* (there are two V.'s) and Ho; Pop. 10,662.) Formerly P. C. of Glanogwen 1857–63. Author, *Lay Agency as an Auxiliary to the Christian Ministry in Wales.* [24]

PRICE, John, *Stratton-on-the-Foss, Bath.*—R. of Stratton-on-the-Foss, Somerset, Dio. B. and W. 1865. (Patron, Prince of Wales; R.'s Inc. 130*l* and Ho; Pop. 385.) [25]

PRICE, John Bankes, *Coedkernew Vicarage, Castletown, near Cardiff.*—Lampeter, Sen. Scho. of and Bate's Prizeman; Deac. 1850 by Bp of St. D. Pr. 1851 by Bp of Llan. V. of Coedkernew and St. Bride's Wentloog, Dio. Llan. 1860. (Patron, Bp of Llan; Tithe, 62*l*; Glebe, 47 acres; V.'s Inc. 170*l* and Ho; Pop. 404.) Formerly V. of Pyle and Kenfig 1855–60. [26]

PRICE, Joseph Edward, *Hapton Vicarage, Long Stratton, Norfolk.*—Ch. Coll. Cam. B.A. 1860; Deac. 1861 and Pr. 1862 by Bp of Ches. P. C. of Hapton, Dio. Nor. 1863. (Patron, Ch. Coll. Cam; P. C.'s Inc. 100*l* with Ho; Pop. 200.) Formerly C. of St. John's and St. Silas', Liverpool, 1861, St. Margaret's, Dunham Massey, 1862. [27]

PRICE, Lewis, *The Vicarage, Trecastle, Brecon.*—Lampeter; Deac. 1857 and Pr. 1858 by Bp of Llan. V. of Llywell, Dio. St. D. 1862. (Patron, Bp of St. D; Tithe, 209*l*; Glebe, ½ acre; V.'s Inc. 210*l*; Pop. 1603.) Formerly C. of Gellyfaelog, Dowlais, 1857–60, St. John's,

Pontyrhun, Merthyr Tydvil, 1860–62, Llanulid, Trecastle, 1862–64. [1]

PRICE, Lewis, *Pentlow, near Sudbury, Essex.*—C. of Pentlow. [2]

PRICE, Owen Bowen, *Bangor.*—C. of Bangor. [3]

PRICE, Peter, *Erbistock, Ruabon, Flintshire.*—Jesus Coll. Ox. B.A. 1817, M.A. 1819; Deac. and Pr. 1818. R. of Erbistock, Dio. St. A. 1852. (Patron, Bp of St. A; Tithe, 247*l*; Glebe, 30 acres; R.'s Inc. 326*l* and Ho; Pop. 337.) [4]

PRICE, Philip Edward, *Derby.*—Jesus Coll. Ox. B.A. 1862, M.A. 1864; Deac. 1863 by Bp of Lich. 2nd Cl. Mast. of Derby Gr. Sch. [5]

PRICE, Rees, *Brecon.*—Lampeter, B.D. 1853; Deac. 1845 by Bp of Nor. Pr. 1846 by Bp of St. D. V. of St. David's, or Llanfaes, Brecon, Dio. St. D. 1846. (Patrons, Bp and D. and C. of St. D; Tithe—App. 260*l*, V. 77*l*; V.'s Inc. 150*l*; Pop. 1418.) Surrogate. Formerly Mast. of the Coll. Sch. Brecon, 1846–55. [6]

PRICE, Richard.—Oriel Coll. Ox. B.A. 1802, M.A. 1805; Deac. 1809, Pr. 1810. Chap. of H.M.S. "Royal Adelaide." [7]

PRICE, Richard, *York terrace, Whitby.*—Min. of St. Ninian's Chapel, Whitby, Dio. York, 1868. Formerly C. of St. Thomas's, Preston, Wombridge, Salop, and Trinity, Hulme. [8]

PRICE, Richard Edwardes, *Berriew, near Shrewsbury.*—Jesus Coll. Ox. B.A. 1858, M.A. 1860; Deac. 1859. Pr. 1860. C. of Berriew 1859. [9]

PRICE, Robert Cholmeley, *Okeford Fitzpaine, Blandford.*—Ch. Ch. Ox. B.A. 1839, M.A. 1842; Deac. 1842 and Pr. 1843 by Bp of Ox. C. of Okeford Fitzpaine, Dorset. Formerly C. of Deane, Hants. [10]

PRICE, Robert Morgan, *Filkins Parsonage, Lechlade.*—Queens' Coll. Cam. 1833; Deac. 1833 and Pr. 1834 by Bp. of Lin. P. C. of Filkins, Dio. Ox. 1864. (Patron, Bp of Ox; P. C.'s Inc. 63*l* and Ho; Pop. 616.) Formerly Chap. on Bengal Establishment 1841–59. [11]

PRICE, Thomas, *Rûg Chapel, Corwen.*—Jesus Coll. Ox. B.A. 1853, M.A. 1857; Deac. 1854, Pr. 1855. Chap. of Rûg Chapel 1862. (Patrons, Trustees of the Rûg Estate; Glebe, 3 acres; Chap.'s Inc. 84*l*.) Formerly C. of Aber-Avon-with-Baglan 1854, Llanuwchllyn 1859, Llandrillo 1860. [12]

PRICE, Thomas, *The Parsonage, Selly Oak, Birmingham.*—Magd. Hall, Ox. 2nd cl. Lit. Hum. and B.A. 1847, M.A. 1850; Deac. 1848 and Pr. 1849 by Bp of Wor. P. C. of Selly Oak, Dio. Wor. 1862. (Patrons, Trustees; P. C.'s Inc. 200*l*; Pop. 1483.) Formerly Lusby Scho. Magd. Hall, Oxford, 1844; Asst. Mast. in King Edward's Sch. Birmingham, 1847. [13]

PRICE, Thomas Charles, 8, *Charlotte-street, Berkeley-square, Bristol.*—Mert. Coll. Ox. 1836, 2nd cl. Lit. Hum. and B.A. 1838, M A. 1842; Deac. 1841 and Pr. 1842 by Bp of Pet. V. of St. Augustine's-the-Less, Bristol, Dio. G. and B. 1852. (Patrons, D. and C. of Bristol; Glebe, 22 acres; V.'s Inc. 300*l*; Pop. 5192.) Dom. Chap. to Lord Howden. Author, *Faith in the Son of God*, 1845, 4*d*; *Work while it is Day*, 1851, 4*d*; *The Plenary Inspiration of Holy Scriptures*, 1852, 3*d*; *Christ, the only Sacrificing Priest under the Gospel*, 1858, 1*s*. [14]

PRICE, Thomas Oldmeadow, *Park-lane, Norwich.*—St. John's Coll. Cam. B.A. 1862; Deac. 1865 and Pr. 1866 by Bp of Ches. C. of Heigham, Norwich, 1867. [15]

PRICE, William, *Llangwm Vicarage, Usk.*—V. of Llangwm, Dio. Llan. 1858. (Patron, Bp of Llan; V.'s Inc. 83*l* and Ho; Pop. 385.) [16]

PRICE, William. *Llanarth Vicarage, Raglan, Monmouthshire.*—Lampeter; Deac. and Pr. 1831. V. of Llanarth with Bettwys Newydd P. C. Dio. Llan. 1838. (Patrons, D. and C of Llan; Llanarth, Tithe—App. 249*l* 9*s* 0½*d*, V. 213*l* 7*s* 6*d*; Bettwys Newydd, Tithe—App. 80*l* 1*s* 2*d*, V. 51*l* 1*s*; V.'s Inc. 265*l* and Ho; Pop. Llanarth 679, Bettwys 129.) Rural Dean 1846; Preb. of Llan. 1854. [17]

PRICE, William, *Douglas Parsonage, near Ormskirk.*—Deac. 1839 and Pr. 1840 by Bp of Ches. P. C. of Douglas, Dio. Man. 1860. (Patron, R. of Eccleston; P. C.'s Inc. 150*l* and Ho.) [18]

PRICE, William, *Christ Church, Oxford.*—Ch. Ch. Ox. B.A. 1853, M.A. 1856; Deac. 1353 and Pr. 1855 by Bp of Ox. Head Mast. of Ch. Ch. Cathl. Sch; C. of Albury, Oxon. [19]

PRICE, William Henry, *Somerton Rectory, Deddington, Oxon.*—R. of Somerton, Dio. Ox. 1861. (Patron, the present R; R.'s Inc. 325*l* and Ho; Pop. 335.) [20]

PRICHARD, Constantine Estlin, *South Luffenham, Stamford.*—Ball. Coll. Ox. 1st cl. Lit. Hum. and B.A. 1841, M.A. 1844; Deac. 1846 and Pr. 1847 by Bp of Ox. R. of South Luffenham, Dio. Pet. 1854. (Patron, Ball. Coll. Ox; Tithe, 463*l*; Glebe, 45 acres; R.'s Inc. 549*l* and Ho; Pop. 437.) Formerly Fell. of Ball. Coll. Ox. 1843; Vice-Prin. of Wells Coll. 1847; Preb. of Wells 1852; Asst. C. of Wells 1852. Author, *Sermons on the Lord's Prayer*, Rivingtons, 1856, 3*s* 6*d*; *Commentary on the Romans*, Longmans, 1862, 2*s*; *Commentary on Ephesians, Philippians, and Colossians*, Rivingtons, 1865; *Thoughts on Free Inquiry*, Longmans, 1864, 6*s*. [21]

PRICHARD, Howell, *Knockin, Salop.*—C. of Knockin. [22]

PRICHARD, John, *Capel Garmon, Llanrwst, Denbighshire.*—St. Bees; Deac. 1856, Pr. 1857. P. C. of Capel Garmon, Dio. St. A. 1857. (Patron, Bp of St. A; P. C.'s Inc. 120*l*; Pop. 800.) Formerly C. of Llanycil, Bala, 1856. [23]

PRICHARD, Rees, *Garth Hall, Bridgend, Glamorganshire.*—Literate; Deac. 1848 by Bp of Llan. Pr. 1849 by Bp of Herf. V. of Llandyfodwg, Glamorganshire, Dio. Llan. 1851. (Patroness, Miss E. Turberville; Tithe, 70*l* 15*s*; Glebe, 16 acres; V.'s Inc. 127*l*; Pop. 254.) C. of St. John the Baptist's Chapel, Llantrissint. [24]

PRICHARD, Richard, *Newbold Rectory, Shipston-on-Stour.*—Jesus Coll. Ox. 3rd cl. Lit. Hum. and B.A. 1832, M.A. 1834, B.D. 1842; Deac. 1834 by Bp of Ox. Pr. 1836 by Bp of Llan. R. of Newbold-on-Stour, Dio. Wor. 1844. (Patron, Jesus Coll. Ox; Tithe, 510*l*; Glebe, 12 acres; R.'s Inc. 528*l* and Ho; Pop. 498.) Rural Dean 1857. Formerly Fell. of Jesus Coll. Ox. [25]

PRICHARD, Richard Posthumus, *Wilburton, near Ely.*—Jesus Coll. Ox. 4th cl. Lit. Hum. B.A. 1850, M.A. 1855; Deac. 1851 and Pr. 1853 by Bp of Lon. P. C. of Wilburton, Isle of Ely, Dio. Ely, 1862. (Patron, Archd. of Ely; Tithe—App. 570*l* and 170 acres of Glebe; P. C.'s Inc. 181*l*; Pop. 560.) Formerly C. of Wilburton. [26]

PRICHARD, Richard Williams, *Yardley Hastings, Northampton.*—St. John's Coll. Cam. 25th Wrang. B.A. 1858, M.A. 1861; Deac. 1858 and Pr. 1859 by Bp of Pet. C. of Yardley Hastings 1858. [27]

PRICHARD, Robert A., *The Rectory, Thelveton, Scole, Norfolk.*—Magd. Hall, Ox; Deac. 1840 and Pr. 1842 by Bp of G. and B. R. of Thelveton, Norfolk, Dio. Nor. 1864. (Patron, Ld Chan; Tithe, 249*l*; Glebe, 7½ acres; R.'s Inc. 260*l* and Ho; Pop. 154.) [28]

PRICKARD, Thomas Charles, *The Rectory, New Radnor.*—Jesus Coll. Ox; Deac. 1856 and Pr. 1857 by Bp of Roch. R. of New Radnor, Dio. Herf. 1866. (Patron, Ld Chan; Tithe, 297*l*; R.'s Inc. 305*l* and Ho; Pop. 490.) Formerly C. of Wivenhoe, Essex, 1856–58, Stanton, Suffolk, 1859–64, Wilby 1864–65. [29]

PRICKARD, W. E., *The Parsonage, Rhayader, Radnor.*—P. C. of Rhayader, Dio. St. D. 1863. (Patron, V. of Nantmel; P. C.'s Inc. 75*l* and Ho; Pop. 846.) [30]

PRICKETT, Richard, *Loxley Vicarage, Warwick.*—St. Peter's Coll. Cam. Sen. Opt. and B.A. 1816; Deac. 1819, Pr. 1821. V. of Loxley, Dio. Wor. 1850. (Patron, Ld Chan; V.'s Inc. 200*l* and Ho; Pop. 308.) [31]

PRIDDEN, William, *West Stow Rectory, Bury St. Edmunds.*—Pemb. Coll. Ox. B.A. 1832, M.A. 1835; Deac. 1832, Pr. 1833. R. of West Stow with Wordwell, Dio. Ely, 1846. (Patron, R. B. De Beauvoir, Esq; Tithe, 191*l* 15*s*; Glebe, 32 acres; Wordwell, Tithe, App. 2*l*, R. 174*l* 15*s* 9*d*; R.'s Inc. 400*l* and Ho; Pop. West Stow 238, Wordwell 65.) Rural Dean. Author, *The Early Christians*, 1836. [32]

PRIDEAUX, Gostwyck, *Hastingleigh Rectory, Ashford, Kent.*—Sid. Coll. Cam. B.A. 1820; Deac. 1820 and Pr. 1821 by Abp of Cant. R. of Hastingleigh, Dio. Cant. 1833. (Patron, Abp of Cant; Tithe, 233*l*; Glebe, 21 acres; R.'s Inc. 255*l* and Ho; Pop. 198.) V. of Elmsted, near Ashford, Dio. Cant. 1833. (Patron, Abp of Cant; Tithe—App. 300*l*, V. 219*l* 14*s* 6*d*; Glebe, 1 acre; V.'s Inc. 241*l*; Pop. 492.) [1]

PRIDEAUX, Walter Alfred, *Liskeard, Cornwall.*—St. Aidan's; Deac. 1864, Pr. 1865. C. of Liskeard 1866. Formerly C. of Bermondsey, Lond. 1864, Havant, Hants, 1865. [2]

PRIDEAUX, William Henry, *Lenoxville, Canada East.*—Lin. Coll. Ox. Scho. of, 2nd cl. Lit. Hum. B.A. 1852, M.A. 1855; Deac. 1857 and Pr. 1858 by Bp of Wor. Sen. Cl. Mast. Coll. Sch. Lenoxville 1867. Formerly Tut. of Codrington Coll. Barbadoes; Head Mast. of Qu. Eliz. Sch. Worcester; 2nd Mast. of Blundell's Sch. Tiverton, Devon. [3]

PRIDHAM, John, *Rochford, Essex.*—C. of Rochford. [4]

PRIDMORE, Edward Morris, *St. Breage Vicarage, Helston, Cornwall.*—Clare Coll. Cam. B.A. 1839, M.A. 1842; Deac. 1840 and Pr. 1841 by Bp of Ex. V. of Breage with Germoe V. Dio. Ex. 1852. (Patron, the Crown; Tithe, Breage—Imp. 628*l* 10*s*, V. 510*l*; Germoe—Imp. 99*l*, V. 105*l*; V.'s Inc. 910*l* and Ho; Pop. Breage 3289, Fermoe 1015.) Formerly P. C. of Cury and Gunwalloe 1852–64. [5]

PRIEST, William John.—St. Alb. Hall, Ox; Deac. 1859 and Pr. 1860 by Bp of Lich. Formerly C. of Heanor, near Derby, 1859–65. [6]

PRINCE, Samuel, *The Study, Bonsall, near Matlock, Derbyshire.*—Jesus Coll. Cam. B.A. 1846, M.A. 1852; Deac. 1847. [7]

PRINCE, William, *The Parsonage, Newark-on-Trent.*—P. C. of Ch. Ch. Newark, Dio. Lin. 1860. (Patrons, Trustees; P. C.'s Inc. 148*l* and Ho; Pop. 3679.) Formerly P. C. of Pishill-cum-Assendon, Dio. Ox 1854–60. Author, *Doctrines of the Gospel, in Question and Answer.* [8]

PRING, Ellis Roberts, *Talyllyn, Machynlleth, Merionethshire.*—Magd. Coll. Ox. B.A. 1838; Deac. 1839, Pr. 1840. P. C. of Talyllyn with Llanfihangel-y-Pennant P. C. Dio. Ban. 1843. (Patron, Bp of Ban; Talyllyn, Tithe—App. 250*l*; P. C.'s Inc. 74*l*; Pop. 1284; Llanfihangel-y-Pennant, Tithe—App. 190*l*; P. C.'s Inc. 33*l*; Pop. 368.) [9]

PRING, Joseph Charles, *Headington, Oxford.*—Jesus Coll. Ox. B.A. 1824, New Coll. M.A. 1826. V. of Headington, Dio. Ox. (Patron, Rev. T. H. Whorwood, D.D; V.'s Inc. 140*l*; Pop. 1504.) Chap. of New Coll. Ox; Chap. of the Headington Union. [10]

PRINGLE, A. D., *Norwich.*—P. C. of St. James's with Pockthorpe P. C. Norwich, Dio. Nor. 1865. (Patrons, D. and C. of Nor; P. C.'s Inc. 200*l* and Ho; Pop. St. James's 1353, Pockthorpe 2055.) [11]

PRIOR, Alfred Staff, *Whitchurch, Salop.*—St. John's Coll. Cam. B.D. 1866; Deac. 1862 by Abp of York, Pr. 1862 by Bp of Lich. C. of Whitchurch 1862; Chap. of the Whitchurch Union 1865. [12]

PRIOR, George Sayle, *St. Breock Rectory, Wadebridge.*—Queen's Coll. Ox. B.A. R. of St. Breock, Dio. Ex. 1861. (Patron, the present R; Tithe, 966*l* 3*s* 11*d*; Glebe, 94 acres; R.'s Inc. 1150*l* and Ho; Pop. 1866.) Formerly British Chap. at Lisbon 1840. [13]

PRIOR, John, *Sidney Proprietary College, Bath.*—Dur. 1st cl. Cl. B.A. 1846, M.A. 1850; Deac. 1849, Pr. 1850. Cl. Mast. of Sidney Proprietary Coll. 1859. Formerly Head Mast. of Audlem Sch. Nantwich, Cheshire, 1852–57. [14]

PRIOR, John, *Kirklington Rectory, Ripon.*—Dub. A.B. 1825, A.M. 1828; Deac. and Pr. 1827 by Abp of Dub. R. of Kirklington, Dio. Rip. 1853. (Patron, Hon. C. B. Wandesford; Tithe, 866*l*; Glebe, 104 acres; R.'s Inc. 958*l* and Ho; Pop. 471.) Author, Tracts. [15]

PRIOR, John, *Yarcombe, near Chard.*—C. of Yarcombe. [16]

PRIOR, John Laurence, *Lynby Rectory, Nottingham.*—Ex. Coll. Ox. B.A. 1842, M.A. 1844; Deac. 1844 and Pr. 1845 by Bp of Llan. R. of Lynby, Dio. Lin. 1853. (Patron, A. F. W. Montague, Esq; Tithe, 280*l*; Glebe, 21 acres; R.'s Inc. 310*l* and Ho; Pop. 257.) P. C. of Papplewick, near Nottingham, Dio. Lin. 1853. (Patron, F. Wilson, Esq; P. C.'s Inc. 90*l*; Pop. 270.) Formerly C. of Monmouth; V. of Maldon, Essex. [17]

PRIOR, Stephen James, *Newent, Glouc.*—Emman. Coll. Cam; Deac. 1867 by Bp of G. and B. Asst. C. of Newent 1867. [18]

PRITCHARD, Albert R., *Maidstone.*—Lin. Coll. Ox. B.A. 1864, M.A. 1867; Deac. 1866 by Abp of Cant. C. of St. Peter's, Maidstone, 1866. [19]

PRITCHARD, Charles, *Freshwater, Isle of Wight.*—St. John's Coll. Cam. 4th Wrang. and B.A. 1830, Fell. 1832, M.A. 1833; Deac. 1833 and Pr. 1834 by Bp of Ely. Hulsean Lect. in the Univ. of Cam. 1867; Pres. of the Royal Astronomical Society; F.R.S., etc. Formerly Head Mast. of the Clapham Gr. Sch. Author, *The Theory of Statical Couples, and on the Figure of the Earth considered as Heterogeneous*; *Communications to the Royal Astronomical Society*, and *Dictionary of the Bible*; *Vindiciæ Mosaicæ in Reply to Bishop Colenso*; *Two Sermons* (preached by request before the British Association at Nottingham, 1866, and at Dundee, 1867); *Presidential Address* (delivered before the Royal Astronomical Society), 1867; *Essay on the Bible and Science* (before the Church Conference at Wolverhampton), 1867; etc. [20]

PRITCHARD, Charles William, *Silvington, Cleobury Mortimer, Salop.*—Clare Coll. Cam. B.A. 1853; Deac. 1853 and Pr. 1854 by Bp of Lich. R. of Silvington, Dio. Herf. (Patron, Rev. G. Edmonds; R.'s Inc. 100*l*; Pop. 47.) C. of Loughton. Formerly C. of Trinity, Hull. [21]

PRITCHARD, Richard, *Whitchurch, Stratford-on-Avon.*—Magd. Hall, Ox. B.A. 1828; Deac. 1833 by Bp of Lich. Pr. 1834 by Bp of Wor. R. of Whitchurch, Dio. Wor. 1838. (Patron, J. R. West, Esq; Tithe, 286*l* 10*s* 7*d*; Glebe, 77 acres; R.'s Inc. 350*l*; Pop. 234.) Formerly C. of Farewell and Armitage, Staffs, 1833; Mast. of the Royal Free Gr. Sch. and Asst. Min. of Stratford-on-Avon, 1833; C. of Whitchurch 1837–38. [22]

PRITCHARD, William Gee, *Brignall Vicarage, near Darlington.*—St. John's Coll. Cam. Sen. Opt. and B.A. 1835, M.A. 1839; Deac. 1835 by Abp of Cant. Pr. 1838 by Bp of Lin. V. of Brignall, Dio. Rip. 1858. (Patron, Ld Chan; Tithe, 271*l*; Glebe, 62 acres; V.'s Inc. 351*l* and Ho; Pop. 170.) Rural Dean. Formerly P. C. of Ch. Ch. District, Mount Sorrel, Leic. 1844–58. [23]

PRITCHETT, William Henry, *Old Charlton, Kent, S.E.*—Corpus Coll. Cam. Wrang. and B.A. 1846, M.A. 1849; Deac. 1846, Pr. 1848. Fell. of Corpus Coll. Cam; R. of St. Paul's, Charlton, Dio. Lon. 1864. (Patron, Sir T. M. Wilson, Bart; R.'s Inc. 264*l*; Pop. 4000.) Dom. Chap. to the Earl of Stair. [24]

PRITT, Francis Drinkall, *Lancaster.*—Trin. Coll. Cam. Jun. Opt. B.A. 1864, M.A. 1867; Deac. 1864 and Pr. 1865 by Bp of Man. C. of St. John's Lancaster, 1867. Formerly C. of St. Anne's, Lancaster, 1864–67. [25]

PROBERT, Charles, *Bacton Rectory, Hereford.*—Lampeter; Deac. 1831, Pr. 1832. R. of Bacton, Dio. Herf. 1835. (Patron, F. Hamp, Esq; Tithe, 122*l* 9*s*; Glebe, ½ acre; R.'s Inc. 122*l* and Ho; Pop. 154.) V. of Clodock, Dio. Herf. 1836. (Patron, W. Wilkins, Esq; Tithe—Imp. 504*l* 16*s* 6*d*, V. 222*l* 13*s* 9½*d*; V.'s Inc. 224*l* and Ho.) C. of Long Town and Llanfaino, Herefordshire. [26]

PROBERT, Edward.—Dom. Chap. to the Duke of Northumberland. [27]

PROBY, William Henry Baptist, 8, *Shrubland-road, Dalston, London, N.E.*—Trin. Coll. Cam. Tyrwhitt's Heb. Scho. 1855, 1st cl. Theol. Trip. 1856, Carus Greek Test. Prizeman, 1856, B.A. 1855, M.A. 1858; Deac. 1856 by Bp of Win. Pr. 1857 by Bp of Ely. C. of St. Augustine's, Haggerston, 1867. Formerly C. of East

Hatley and Tadlow, Cambs, 1856–61; Incumb. of St. Ternan's, Stonehaven, Dio. Brechin, 1862–65. [1]

PROCTER, Aislabie, *Alwinton Vicarage, Morpeth.*—Pemb. Coll. Cam. B.A. 1828; Deac. 1829 by Bp of Lin. Pr. 1830 by Bp of Bristol. V. of Alwinton with Hallystone P. C. Dio. Dur. 1833. (Patron, Duke of Northumberland; Alwinton, Tithe—Imp. 230*l*; Glebe, 2 acres; Hallystone, Tithe—Imp. 63*l* 6*s* 8*d*; V.'s Inc. 120*l* and Ho; Pop. Alwinton 809, Hallystone 426.) [2]

PROCTER, C., *Windsor.*—C. of Trinity, Windsor. [3]

PROCTER, Charles Tickell, *Salisbury.*—King's Coll. Cam. B.A. 1854, M.A. 1857; Deac. 1858 by Bp of Salis. C. of St. Edmund's, Salisbury, 1858; Fell. of King's Coll. Cam. [4]

PROCTER, Francis, *Witton Vicarage, North Walsham.*—St. Cath. Coll. Cam. 30th Wrang. 2nd cl. Cl. Trip. B.A. 1835, M.A. 1839; Deac. 1836 by Bp of Lin. Pr. 1838 by Bp of Ely. V. of Witton, Dio. Nor. 1847. (Patron, Bp of Nor; Tithe—App. 2*l* 2*s*, V. 120*l* 13*s* 4*d*; Glebe, 5 acres; V.'s Inc. 135*l* and Ho; Pop. 269.) Formerly Fell. and Asst. Tut. of St. Cath.'s Coll. Cam. 1841; C. of Streatley, Beds, 1836, Romsey, Hants, 1840. Author, *A History of the Book of Common Prayer, with a Rationale of its Offices,* Macmillans, 1855, 10*s* 6*d*, 6 eds; *An Elementary History of the Book of Common Prayer,* 1862, 2*s* 6*d*; *Plain Rules about Registration,* 4*s per* 100. [5]

PROCTER, George Allen, 5, *Washington-terrace, Southampton.*—Dub. A.B. 1852, A.M. 1858; Deac. 1856 and Pr. 1857 by Bp of Lich. P. C. of St. James's, Southampton, Dio. Win. 1863. (Patron, Bp of Win; Tithe, 240*l*; P. C.'s Inc. 240*l*; Pop. 6883.) Surrogate. [6]

PROCTER, George William, *Bradstone Rectory, Tavistock.*—Queens' Coll. Cam. B.A. 1844, M.A. 1850; Deac. 1841 by Bp of Ely, Pr. 1846 by Bp of Win. R. of Bradstone, Dio. Ex. 1862. (Patron, Bp of Ex; Tithe, 220*l*; Glebe, 50 acres; R.'s Inc. 285*l* and Ho; Pop. 121.) Formerly P. C. of St. Stephen's, Devonport, 1846–62. [7]

PROCTER, Gilbert, *Egton, Ulverston.*—Ch. Coll. Cam. B.A. 1852, M.A. 1855; Deac. 1853 and Pr. 1854 by Bp of Ches. P. C. of Egton with Newland, Dio. Ches. 1855. (Patron, J. P. Machell, Esq; P. C.'s Inc. 180*l* and Ho; Pop. 1230.) Dioc. Inspector of Schs. Formerly Sen. C. of Ulverston. [8]

PROCTER, John Mathias, *Vicarage, Aldborough Hatch, Ilford, Essex.*—Trin. Coll. Ox. 2nd cl. Lit. Hum. B.A. 1858, M.A. 1861; Deac. 1859 and Pr. 1860 by Bp of Ox. P. C. of Barkingside, Dio. Lon. 1864. (Patron, V. of Ilford; Tithe, 45*l*; Glebe, 20 acres; P. C.'s Inc. 180*l*; Pop. 1557.) V. of Aldborough Hatch, Dio. Lon. 1864. (Patron, the Crown; Tithe, 20*l*; Glebe, 15 acres; V.'s Inc. 90*l* and Ho; Pop. 490.) Formerly C. of North Rode 1859; Fell. of Jesus Coll. Ox. [9]

PROCTER, Lovell James, *Bolton Percy, Tadcaster, Yorks.*—Dur. Licen. in Theol. 1855, B.A. 1858, M.A. 1865; Deac. 1855 and Pr. 1856 by Abp of York. C. of Bolton Percy 1865. Formerly C. of Naburn, Yorks, 1855–57, St. Lawrence's, York, 1859–60; Assoc. of the Central African Mission 1860–63; C. of Beeford, Yorks, 1864. [10]

PROCTER, Nathaniel, *Plymouth.*—Chap. of Royal Naval Hospital, Plymouth. Formerly Chap. of H.M. Dockyard, Pembroke. [11]

PROCTER, Richard, *Kenninghall Vicarage, East Harling, Norfolk.*—St. John's Coll. Cam. B.A. 1824, M.A. 1828; Deac. 1823, Pr. 1825. V. of Kenninghall, Dio. Nor. 1846. (Patron, Bp. of Nor; Tithe, comm. 325*l*; Glebe, 11 acres; V.'s Inc. 335*l* and Ho; Pop. 1405.) [12]

PROCTER, Thomas, *Tweedmouth, Berwick-on-Tweed.*—Dur. B.A. 1849, M.A. 1858; Deac. 1850 and Pr. 1851 by Bp of Dur. V. of Tweedmouth, Dio. Dur. 1864. (Patrons, D. and C. of Dur; V.'s Inc. 300*l*; Pop. 5600.) Surrogate; J. P. for Northumberland. Formerly C. of Berwick-on-Tweed 1860–62, Tweedmouth 1862–64. [13]

PROCTER, William, *Doddington Glebe, Alnwick.*—St. Cath. Hall, Cam. Sen. Opt. and B.A. 1813, M.A. 1816 *ad eund.* Dur. 1854; Deac. 1816 by Bp of Dur. Pr. 1819 by Bp of Ely. Lecturer of Berwick-upon-Tweed, Dio. Dur. 1824. (Patron, Mercers' Company, London.) P. C. of Doddington, Dio. Dur. 1834. (Patron, Duke of Northumberland; Glebe, ½ acre; P. C.'s Inc. 274*l* and Ho; Pop. 795.) Hon. Can. of Dur. 1854. Formerly Fell. of St. Cath. Hall, Cam. Author, Five Discourses—*On the Personal Office of Christ, and of the Holy Ghost; On the Doctrine of the Trinity; On Faith; On Regeneration,* 1824; *The Epiphany* (a Sermon), *with a Chronological Appendix,* 1850, 1*s*; various Pamphlets. [14]

PROCTER, William, *Doddington, Alnwick.*—Ch. Coll. Cam. 2nd cl. Cl. Trip. B.A. 1863; Deac. 1865 and Pr. 1867 by Bp of Dur. C. of Doddington 1865. [15]

PROCTOR, Thomas Beauchamp, *Langley, Norwich.*—Ch. Coll. Cam. B.A. 1812, M.A. 1816; Deac. 1814 by Bp of Nor. Pr. 1815 by Bp of Bristol. Formerly R. of Carleton with Ashby R. Norwich, 1838–63. [16]

PRODGERS, Edwin, *Ayot St. Peter Rectory, Welwyn, Herts.*—Trin. Coll. Ox. B.A. 1807, M.A. 1810, B.D. 1827; Deac. 1808, Pr. 1809. R. of Ayot St. Peter, Dio. Roch. 1842. (Patron, the present R; Tithe, 245*l* 12*s* 6*d*; Glebe, 49 acres; R.'s Inc. 307*l* and Ho; Pop. 234.) [17]

PROPERT, William Peregrine, *St. David's, Haverfordwest.*—Trin. Hall, Cam. Jun. Opt. and B.A. 1856; Deac. 1856, Pr. 1857. Min. Can. of St. David's. [18]

PROSSER, Henry, *Dulas, near Hereford.*—P. C. of Garway, Herefordshire, Dio. Herf. 1821. (Patron, Sir J. Bailey; Tithe—Imp. 230*l*; P. C.'s Inc. 82*l*; Pop. 585.) P. C. of Welsh-Newton, Herefordshire, Dio. Herf. 1821. (Patron, Sir J. Bailey; Tithe—Imp. 40*l*; P. C.'s Inc. 48*l*; Pop. 226.) P. C. of Dulas, Dio. Herf. 1827. (Patron, James Hopton, Esq; Tithe—Imp. 25*l*, P. C. 42*l*; P. C.'s Inc. 80*l*; Pop. 76.) [19]

PROSSER, James, *Thame Vicarage, Oxon.*—St. Cath. Coll. Cam. B.A. 1832, M.A. 1835; Deac. 1832 and Pr. 1833 by Bp of Lin. V. of Thame, Dio. Ox. 1841. (Patrons, Trustees; Tithe, 30*l*; Glebe, 119 acres; V.'s Inc. 175*l* and Ho; Pop. 3245.) Author, *A Key to the Hebrew Scriptures without Points,* 3 eds. 1838, '48, '54, 6*s*; *Examples of the Philosophical Accuracy of the Hebrew Text, when literally translated without Points; The Book of Genesis without Points,* 2*s*; *Parkhurst's Hebrew and Chaldee Grammar without Points,* 3*s*; *An Index of Hebrew Roots,* 6*d*. [20]

PROSSER, John, *Church-Minshull, Middlewich, Cheshire.*—St. Edm. Hall, Ox. B.A. 1842; Deac. 1842, Pr. 1843. P. C. of Church-Minshull, Dio. Ches. 1853. (Patron, H. Brooke, Esq; Tithe—Imp. 120*l*, P. C. 59*l*; Glebe, 30 acres; P. C.'s Inc. 108*l* and Ho; Pop. 392.) [21]

PROSSER, Joseph Camplin, *Devauden, Chepstow.*—Deac. 1828, Pr. 1829. R. of Itton, Monmouthshire, Dio. Llan. 1832. (Patron, W. Curre, Esq; Tithe, 128*l* 18*s* 6*d*; Glebe, 75 acres; R.'s Inc. 232*l* 1*s* 6*d*; Pop. 192.) V. of Newchurch, Monmouthshire, Dio. Llan. 1829. (Patron, Duke of Beaufort; Tithe—Imp. 189*l*, V. 65*l*; Glebe, 56 acres; V.'s Inc. 167*l* and Ho; Pop. 729.) [22]

PROSSER, Samuel, *Margate.*—St. John's Coll. Ox. B.A. 1822, M.A. 1824. P. C. of Trinity, Margate, Dio. Cant. 1846. (Patrons, Trustees; P. C.'s Inc. 280*l*; Pop. 4818.) [23]

PROSSER, William, *Ashby-Folville Vicarage, Melton-Mowbray.*—St. Bees; Deac. 1845, Pr. 1846. V. of Ashby-Folville, Dio. Pet. 1853. (Tithe—Imp. 99*l* 16*s*, V. 85*l* 12*s*; V.'s Inc. 235*l* and Ho; Pop. 450.) [24]

PROTHER, Edward Ramsay, *Chettle, Blandford, Dorset.*—R. of Chettle, Blandford, Dio. Salis. 1866. (Patron, H. Chambers, Esq; Tithe—Imp. 11*l*, R. 187*l*; R.'s Inc. 195*l* and Ho; Pop. 177.) Formerly R. of Farnham, Dorset, 1846–66. [25]

PROTHERO, George, *Whippingham Rectory, East Cowes, Isle of Wight.*—Brasen. Coll. Ox. B.A. 1842; Deac. 1842, Pr. 1843. R. of Whippingham, Dio. Win.

1857. (Patron, Ld Chan; Tithe—Imp. 102*l*, R. 781*l* 16*s*; R.'s Inc. 800*l* and Ho; Pop. 647.) Chap. at Osborne House 1857. Formerly C. of Whippingham 1853–57. [1]

PROTHERO, Thomas, *Malpas Court, Malpas, Monmouthshire.*—Brasen. Coll. Ox. 2nd cl. Lit. Hum. and B.A. 1834, M.A. 1837; Deac. 1835, Pr. 1836. Chap. in Ordinary to the Queen 1853; Patron of the P. C. of Malpas. Formerly Chap. to his late R.H. Prince Albert 1848. Author, *The Irish Famine* (a Fast-Day Sermon), by Royal Command. [2]

PROTHEROE, James Havard, 5, *Brighton-terrace, Cardiff.*—Corpus Coll. Cam. Mawson Scho. 1st Math. Prizeman, 3rd Sen. Opt. and B.A. 1864, M.A. 1867; Deac. 1865 and Pr. 1866 by Bp of Llan. C. of St. John's, Cardiff, 1865. [3]

PROUT, Thomas Jones, *Christ Church, Oxford.*—Ch. Ch. Ox. B.A. 1846, M.A. 1849, Stud. of Ch. Ch. Ox; P. C. of Binsey, Dio. Ox. 1857. (Patron, Ch. Ch. Ox; P. C.'s Inc. 95*l*; Pop. 67.) Fell. of the Geological Soc. [4]

PROUT, William Smart, *Lakenheath, Mildenhall, Suffolk.*—Wor. Coll. Ox. 4th cl. Lit. Hum. and B.A. 1847; Deac. 1848 and Pr. 1850 by Bp of Ches. V. of Lakenheath, Dio. Ely, 1853. (Patrons, D. and C. of Ely; Tithe—App. 170*l*, V. 130*l*; Glebe, 51 acres; V.'s Inc. 158*l*; Pop. 1797.) [5]

PROWDE, George, *Busearp, Whitby.*—St. John's Coll. Cam. Scho. of 11th Sen. Opt. 1859, M.A. 1862; Deac. 1859 and Pr. 1860 by Abp of York. P. C. of Faceby-in-Cleveland, Dio. York, 1866. (Patron, John S. Sutton, Esq; P. C.'s Inc. 85*l*; Pop. 164.) Mast. of Whitby Gr. Sch. 1861. Formerly C. of Aislaby 1859. [6]

PROWDE, John, *Cleckheaton, Normanton.*—St. John's Coll. Cam. B.A. 1863, M.A. 1867; Deac. 1865 and Pr. 1866 by Bp of Rip. C. of Cleckheaton 1865. [7]

PROWDE, Ralph, *Ingleby Greenhow, Northallerton.*—Dur. Hons. in Cl. and Gen. Lit. Ellerton Scho. B.A. 1855; Deac. 1857 and Pr. 1858 by Bp of Man. P. C. of Ingleby Greenhow, Dio. York, 1859. (Patrons, Lord and Lady De L'Isle and Dudley; Tithe, Imp. 565*l* 5*s*; P. C.'s Inc. 130*l* and Ho; Pop. 400.) Tut. to the Family of Lord and Lady De L'Isle and Dudley. Formerly C. of Stretford, Manchester, 1857–58, Marton, near Middlesbrough-on-Tees, 1859. Author, *Christian Prayer* (Sermon). [8]

PROWER, John Mervin, *Purton, Swindon, Wilts.*—Wad. Coll. Ox. B.A. 1806, M.A. 1835; Deac. 1824 and Pr. 1827 by Bp of Salis. V. of Purton, Dio. G. and B. 1827. (Patron, Earl of Shaftesbury; Tithe—Imp. 667*l*, V. 548*l* 17*s* 7*d*; Glebe, 53 acres; V.'s Inc. 698*l* and Ho; Pop. 2087.) Hon. Can. of Bristol. [9]

PRUEN, Hudson Boyce, *Didbrook Vicarage, Winchcomb, Gloucestershire.*—Pemb. Coll. Ox. B.A. 1846, M.A. 1850; Deac. 1848 and Pr. 1849 by Bp of Pet. C. in sole charge of Didbrook and Hayles 1851. Formerly C. of Harrowden, Northants, 1848, Churchill, Worcestershire, 1850. [10]

PRYCE, Hugh Lewis, *The Rectory, Penmachno, near Llanrwst, Carnarvonshire.*—Queens' Coll. Cam. Scho. of and Sandy's Exhib. B.A. 1853; Deac. 1853 and Pr. 1864 by Bp of Ban. R. of Penmachno, Dio. Ban. 1860. (Patron, Lord Penrhyn; Tithe, 153*l*; Glebe, 16*l*; R.'s Inc. 180*l* and Ho; Pop. 1400.) Formerly C. of Llandwrog 1853, Llanaber 1854, Dolgelly 1847. [11]

PRYCE, Shadrach.—Queens' Coll. Cam. Scho. Librarian and Clark's Scho. 8th Sen. Opt. B.A. 1858, M.A. 1867; Deac. 1859 and Pr. 1860 by Bp of Ban. H.M. Inspector of Schs. for Central Wales. Formerly Mast. of the Gr. Sch. and C. of Dolgelly 1859–64; R. of Yspytty, Denbighshire, 1864–67. Author, a Welsh Translation of Dean Goodwin's *Guide to the Parish Church.* [12]

PRYKE, William Emanuel, *St. John's College, Cambridge.*—St. John's Coll. Cam. 2nd cl. in Theol. Trip. 14th Wrang. B.A. 1867; Deac. 1867 by Bp of Ely. C. of Stapleford, Cambridge, 1867. [13]

PRYNNE, George Rundle, *Plymouth.*—St. Cath. Coll. Cam. B.A. 1839, M.A. 1861; Deac. 1841 and Pr. 1842 by Bp of Ex. P. C. of St. Peter's, Plymouth, Dio. Ex. 1848. (Patrons, Trustees; P. C.'s Inc. 400*l*; Pop. 10,325.) Author, *Parochial Sermons*, 1846, 10*s* 6*d*; *Plain Parochial Sermons*, 1856, 10*s* 6*d*; *Christ the only Foundation* (Two Sermons), 1849, 1*s*; *Confession, Penance, and Absolution, as authoritatively taught in the Church of England*, 1852, 6*d*; *A Few Plain Words about what every one must believe and do in order to be Saved*; *Plain Instructions in Confirmation*; *Ascension Day*; *The Eucharistic Manual*, 1864, 1*s*; *We have an Altar*, 2*d*; *The Christian Sacrifice*, 1866, 1*d*; *A Letter to Archdeacon Downall on the Subject of a Charge delivered by him*, Masters, 1867, 1*s*. [14]

PRYOR, John Eade, *Bennington Rectory, Stevenage.*—Magd. Coll. Ox. B.A. 1858, M.A. 1861; Deac. 1859 and Pr. 1860 by Bp of Roch. R. of Bennington, Dio. Roch. 1860. (Patron, the present R; Tithe, 635*l*; Glebe, 90 acres; R.'s Inc. 735*l* and Ho; Pop. 637.) Formerly C. of Shenley, Herts, 1859–60. [15]

PRYSE, James, *Llandwrog, Carnarvonshire.*—Lampeter; Deac. 1851, Pr. 1852. P. C. of St. Thomas's, Llandwrog, Dio. Ban. 1856. (Patron, the R. of Llandwrog; Pop. 2114.) Formerly C. of Llandwrog. [16]

PUCKLE, Benjamin Hale, *Graffham Rectory, St. Neots, Hunts.*—St. Peter's Coll. Cam. B.A. 1843; Deac. 1845 and Pr. 1846 by Abp of Cant. R. of Graffham, Dio. Ely, 1853. (Patron, Duke of Manchester; Glebe, 332 acres; R.'s Inc. 420*l* and Ho. Minus 140*l* in repayment of money borrowed for drainage and building; Pop. 320.) Formerly C. of Little Brickhill, Bucks, 1845–46, Mistley, Essex, 1846–49, Graffham, Hunts, 1849–53. [17]

PUCKLE, Edwin, *Blisworth, near Northampton.*—Magd. Hall, Ox. B.A. 1859; Deac. 1859 and Pr. 1860 by Bp of Pet. C. of Blisworth 1859. [18]

PUCKLE, John, *St. Mary's Parsonage, Dover.*—Brasen. Coll. Ox. 2nd cl. Math. et. Phy. and B.A. 1836, M.A. 1839; Deac. 1836 and Pr. 1832 by Bp of Lon. P. C. of St. Mary the Virgin's, Dover, Dio. Cant. 1842. (Patrons, the Parishioners; P. C.'s Inc. arising from Pew-rents, etc. with Ho; Pop. 8424.) Rural Dean of Dover and Surrogate 1846. Author, *Prayer, the Essential Part of Public Worship*, 1842, 6*d*; *Parochial Sermons*, vol. i. 1847, 9*s*, vol. ii. 1852, vol. iii. 1855, vol. iv. 1861; *Ecclesiastical Sketches of St. Augustine's, Canterbury*, 1849, 3*s* 6*d*; *Insensibility to Blessings and Over-sensitiveness under Trials*, during the Cholera of 1849, 6*d*; *Our Lord's Plea for Unity*, 1852, 6*d*; *Church and Fortress of Dover Castle illustrated from Author's Drawings*, Parkers, 1864, 7*s* 6*d*; etc. [19]

PUDSEY, Charles Douglas, *Goole, Yorks.*—St. Bees; Deac. 1866 by Abp of York. C. of Goole 1866. [20]

PUGH, David, *Abererch, near Pwllheli, Carnarvonshire.*—St. Cath. Coll. Cam. B.A. 1833; Deac. 1833 and Pr. 1834 by Bp of Ban. V. of Abererch with Chap. of Penrhos annexed, Dio. Ban. 1841. (Patron, Bp of Ban; Tithe—App. 490*l*, V. 83*l* 10*s*; Glebe, 10 acres; V.'s Inc. 160*l*; Pop. Abererch 1652, Penrhos 100.) Formerly C. of Dolgellau 1833–41. [21]

PUGH, David, *Llandysilio, Pembrokeshire.*—Lampeter, B.A. 1866; Deac. 1866 by Bp of St. D. C. of Llandysilio and Egremont 1866. [22]

PUGH, Enoch, *Llanfair Caereinion Vicarage, Welshpool.*—Lampeter, Burton Scho. and 1st cl. and Lat. Prizeman 1834, B.D. 1854; Deac. 1834, Pr. 1835. V. of Llanfair Caereinion, Dio. St. A. 1856. (Patron, Bp of St. A; Tithe—Imp. 565*l* 15*s*, V. 314*l* 5*s*; Glebe, 14 acres; Bounty and Allotment Lands, 98 acres; V.'s Inc. 415*l* and Ho; Pop. 2439.) Surrogate 1857. Formerly V. of Abergwili, Carmarthen, 1846–56. Author, *The Duty of Thankfulness* (an Assize Sermon), 1866. [23]

PUGH, Giles, *Shapwick, Bath.*—Magd. Hall, Ox. B.A. 1827; Deac. 1827 and Pr. 1829 by Bp of Bristol. V. of Shapwick with Ashcott P. C. Dio. B. and W. 1864. (Patron, Sir G. G. Montgomery, Bart; Tithe, 265*l*; V.'s Inc. 424*l*; Pop. Shapwick 407, Ashcott 817.) Formerly C. of Hinton Martel, Dorset, 1827, Chalbury 1829, South Newton, Wilts, 1834, St. Thomas's, Salisbury,

1841–44; Chap. to British Embassy at Naples 1845–61. Author, *Spiritualism*, 1857; *Crime at Home and Abroad*, 1858. [1]

PUGH, James, *Llanfoist Rectory, Abergavenny, Monmouthshire.*—Emman. Coll. Cam. S.C.L. 1850, LL.B. 1852; Deac. 1850 and Pr. 1851 by Bp of Wor. R. of Llanfoist, Dio. Llan. 1863. (Patron, Earl of Abergavenny; R.'s Inc. 174*l* and Ho; Pop. 456.) Formerly C. of Bidford and Salford, Warw. 1850–51, Sutterton, Lincoln, 1851–60, St. Andrew's, Cardiff, 1861–63. [2]

PUGH, James Baldwyn, *Vicarage, Hemel Hempstead.*—St. John's Coll. Cam. 37th Wrang. and B.A. 1838, M.A. 1841; Deac. 1838 by Bp of G. and B. Pr. 1840 by Bp of Lich. V. of Hemel Hempstead, Dio. Roch. 1866. (Patron, Bp of Pet; Tithe, 501*l*; V.'s Inc. 660*l* and Ho; Pop. 3785.) Chap. of the Hemel Hempstead Union; Surrogate. Formerly C. of Littleover, Derbyshire, 1838, Stanton-by-Dale 1841; Head Mast. of Gr. Sch. and Min. of St. Paul's, Walsall, 1845; R. of Yockleton, Salop, 1858–66. [3]

PUGH, John, *Llansannan Vicarage, near Abergele, N. Wales.*—Lampeter; Deac. 1847 by Bp of Llan. Pr. 1848 by Bp of St. D. V. of Llansannan, Dio. St. A. 1861. (Patron, Bp of St. D; Glebe, 4 acres; V.'s Inc. 416*l* and Ho; Pop. 1256.) Formerly C. of Llangorse; P. C. of Llanywern, near Brecon. [4]

PUGH, John, *Ambleston, Haverfordwest.*—V. of Ambleston, near Haverfordwest, Dio. St. D. 1824. (Patron, Prince of Wales; Tithe—Imp. 170*l*, V. 141*l* 12*s*; V.'s Inc. 185*l*; Pop. 524.) Formerly R. of Castle Bigh, Haverfordwest, 1816–66. [5]

PUGH, John, *Llanbadarn Vicarage, Aberystwith.*—Lampeter, Scho. of; Deac. 1856 by Bp of Herf. Pr. 1857 by Bp of St. D. V. of Llanbadarn-Vawr, Dio. St. D. 1861. (Patron, Bp of St. D; Tithe, 20*l*; Glebe, 3 acres; V.'s Inc. 300*l* and Ho; Pop. 4923.) Formerly C. of Llanbadarn-Vawr 1856–61. [6]

PUGH, Matthew, *Rishworth, Halifax.*—St. Cath. Coll. Cam. Sen. Opt. and B.A. 1845, M.A. 1848; Deac. 1845 and Pr. 1846 by Bp of Ches. Head Mast. of Rishworth Gr. Sch. Formerly Head Mast. of the Churchhill Sch. Brighton; Head Mast. of Congleton Gr. Sch. Cheshire. [7]

PUGH, Thomas.—C. of St. Sepulchre's and Reader of Ch. Ch. Newgate-street, Lond. [8]

PUGHE, Evan, *Llantrisant Rectory, Bangor.*—Jesus Coll. Ox. B.A. 1828; Deac. 1829 and Pr. 1830 by Bp of Herf. R. of Llantrisant with Llechgynfarny and Llanllibio annexed, Anglesey, Dio. Ban. 1863. (Patron, Bp of Ban; Tithe, comm. 813*l*; Glebe, 19 acres; R.'s Inc. 915*l* and Ho; Pop. 850.) Surrogate 1837; Hon. Sec. to the North Wales Training Coll. 1853; Rural Dean 1866. Formerly C. of Chirbury, Salop, 1829, Beaumaris 1832; V. of Llanidloes and Rural Dean of Arustley, 1837–50; Sen. V. of Bangor and V. Choral of the Cathl. 1850–63. Author, *A Sermon*, 1832; *Teach me, O Lord* (an Anthem), Novello; *Sermons preached at Bangor*, Parkers, 1866; *The Religious Statistics of the Principality*, 1867. [9]

PUGHE, G. R. G., *Mellor Parsonage, Blackburn.*—P. C. of Mellor, Dio. Man. 1864. (Patron, V. of Blackburn; P. C.'s Inc. 150*l* and Ho; Pop. 1718.) Formerly C. of Trinity, Over Darwen. [10]

PUGHE, John, *Newenden, Staplehurst, Kent.*—R. of Newenden, Dio. Cant. 1855. (Patron, Abp of Cant. Tithe, 240*l* 5*s*; Glebe, 2 acres; R.'s Inc. 244*l*; Pop. 137.) [11]

PULESTON, Theophilus Henry Gresley, *Worthenbury Rectory, Wrexham.*—Brasen. Coll. Ox. B.A. 1845; Deac. 1847 and Pr. 1848 by Bp of Wor. R. of Worthenbury, Dio. St. A. 1848. (Patron, Sir R. Puleston; Tithe, 400*l*; R.'s Inc. 400*l* and Ho; Pop. 543.) [12]

PULLEIN, John, *Kirkthorpe Vicarage, Wakefield.*—Clare Hall, Cam. B.A. 1836, M.A. 1839; Deac. 1836 and Pr. 1838 by Abp of York. V. of Warmfield, Wakefield, Dio. York, 1838. (Patrons, Trustees; Tithe—Imp. 250*l*, V. 125*l*; Glebe, 14½ acres; V.'s Inc. 178*l* and Ho; Pop. 1645.) [13]

PULLEINE, John James, *Marlborough College, Wilts.*—Trin. Coll. Cam. B.A. 1865; Deac. 1866 by Bp of Salis. Asst. Mast. of Marlborough Coll. 1865. [14]

PULLEINE, Robert, *Kirkby-Wiske Rectory, Thirsk.*—Emman. Coll. Cam. B.A. 1829, M.A. 1832; Deac. and Pr. 1830 by Bp of Ches. R. of Kirkby-Wiske, Dio. Rip. 1845. (Patron, Duke of Northumberland; Tithe, 643*l*; Glebe, 60 acres; R.'s Inc. 703*l* and Ho; Pop. 866.) [15]

PULLEN, Henry William, *The Close, Salisbury.*—Clare Coll. Cam. B.A. 1859, M.A. 1862; Deac. 1859 and Pr. 1860 by Bp of Ox. Min. Can. of Salis. 1863. Formerly Asst. Mast. in St. Andrew's Coll. Bradfield, 1859; Min. Can. of York 1862. [16]

PULLEN, Joseph, *Cambridge.*—Corpus Coll. Cam. 6th Wrang. and B.A. 1830, M.A. 1833, B.D. 1841. P. C. of St. Benedict's, Cambridge, Dio. Ely, 1847. (Patron, Corpus Coll. Cam; P. C.'s Inc. 155*l*; Pop. 996.) Prof. of Astronomy in Gresham Coll. Lond. Formerly Fell. and Tut. of Corpus Coll. Cam. [17]

PULLER, Charles, *Standon, Ware, Herts.*—Trin. Coll. Cam. 15th Wrang. and Fell. of, B.A. 1857, M.A. 1860; Deac. 1860 by Bp of Ely, Pr. 1861 by Bp of Roch. V. of Standon, Herts, Dio. Roch. 1862. (Patron, the present V; Tithe, 512*l*; Glebe, 15 acres; V.'s Inc. 550*l*; Pop. 1426.) [18]

PULLER, Frederick William.—C. of St. Paul's, Walworth, Lond. [19]

PULLEY, Harry, *The Parsonage, Marton, Chirbury, Salop.*—Ox. B.A. 1852; Deac. 1852, Pr. 1853. P. C. of Marton, Dio. Herf. 1862. (Patron, V. of Chirbury; Glebe, 4 acres; P. C.'s Inc. 43*l* and Ho; Pop. 328.) [20]

PULLIBLANK, Joseph, *St. John's College, Cambridge.*—St. John's Coll. Cam. 1st cl. Theol. Trip. Wrang. and B.A. 1866; Deac. 1867 by Bp of Ely. C. of St. Luke's, New Chesterton, Cambridge, 1867. [21]

PULLIN, John Henry, *Ryton-on-Dunsmore, Coventry.*—St. Bees; Deac. 1852 and Pr. 1853 by Bp of Lich. C. of Ryton-on-Dunsmore. Formerly C. of Monyash, Derbyshire. [22]

PULLING, Charles James, *New Workhouse, Manchester.*—Magd. Hall, Ox. B.A. 1848; Deac. 1849 by Bp of Wor. Pr. 1850 by Bp of Herf. Chap. to the New Workhouse, Crumpsall, Manchester, 1858. Formerly Chap. to the Hereford Union. [23]

PULLING, Edwin William Relhan, *Littlemore, near Oxford.*—Queens' Coll. Cam. B.A. 1839, M.A. 1842, *ad eund.* M.A. Ox. 1846; Deac. 1839 and Pr. 1840 by Abp of Cant. Chap of the County Lunatic Asylum, Littlemore, 1846. (Salary, 180*l* and Ho.) Formerly C. of Dymchurch, Kent, 1839–43, Boxford, Suffolk, 1844–45, Mistley, Essex, 1845–46. [24]

PULLING, Frederick William, *Pinhoe Vicarage, Devon.*—Corpus Coll. Cam. B.A. 1845; Deac. 1847, Pr. 1848. V. of Pinhoe, Dio. Ex. 1863. (Patron, Bp of Ex; Tithe—App. 235*l* 1*s*, V. 265*l* 1*s*; V.'s Inc. 270*l* and Ho; Pop. 508.) Formerly Asst. C. of Modbury; C. of Revelstoke, Devon, 1847–49, Tywardreath, Cornwall, 1850–51. [25]

PULLING, James, *Corpus Christi College Lodge, Cambridge.*—Corpus Coll. Cam. 11th Wrang. and B.A. 1837, M.A. 1840, B.D. 1848, D.D. 1855, Hon. D.C.L. Ox. 1853; Deac. 1840 by Bp of Lich. Pr. 1842, by Bp of Herf. Mast. of Corpus Coll. Cam. 1850; V. of Belchamp St. Paul's, near Clare, Suffolk, Dio. Roch. 1863. (Patrons, D. and C. of St. Paul's; Tithe—App. 303*l*, V. 207*l*; Glebe, 78 acres; V.'s Inc. 320*l* and Ho; Pop. 832.) Formerly Fell. of Corpus Coll. 1838–50; C. of Grantchester 1842–44. [26]

PULLING, William, *Eastnor Rectory, Ledbury, Herefordshire.*—Oriel Coll. Ox. 2nd cl. Lit. Hum. and B.A. 1836, M.A. 1840; Deac. 1838, Pr. 1839. R. of Eastnor, Dio. Herf. 1849. (Patron, Earl Somers; Tithe—Imp. 100*l*, R. 360*l*; Glebe, 61 acres; R.'s Inc. 480*l* and Ho; Pop. 478.) R. of Pixley, Herf. Dio. Herf. 1850. (Patron, Earl Somers; Tithe, 122*l*; Glebe, 50 acres; R.'s Inc. 174*l*; Pop. 110.) Dom. Chap. to Earl Somers. Formerly Fell. and Tut. of Brasen. Coll. Ox. [27]

PULTENEY, Richard Thomas, *Ashley Rectory, Market Harborough.*—Trin. Coll. Ox. B.A. 1833; Deac. 1835 and Pr. 1836 by Bp of Lin. R. of Ashley, Dio. Pet. 1853. (Patron, the present R; Glebe, 246 acres; R.'s Inc. 450*l* and Ho; Pop. 348.) [1]

PURCELL, Francis, *Shrewsbury.*—C. of St Giles's, Shrewsbury. [2]

PURCELL, Goodwin, *Charlesworth, Glossop, Derbyshire.*—Dub; Deac. 1842 and Pr. 1843 by Bp of Ches: P. C. of Charlesworth, Dio. Lich. 1845. (Patrons, the Crown and Bp of Lich. alt; Tithe, 3*l* 10*s*; Glebe, ¾ acre; P. C.'s Inc. 200*l* and Ho; Pop. 2564.) [3]

PURCELL, Handfield Noel, *The Vicarage, Fowey, Cornwall.*—Ex. Coll. Ox. B.A. 1865; Deac. 1866 and Pr. 1867 by Bp of Wor. V. of Fowey, Dio. Ex. 1867. (Patron, Rev. E. J. Treffry; V.'s Inc. 200*l* and Ho; Pop. 1429.) Formerly C. of St. Kenelm, Romsley, Worcestershire. [4]

PURCELL, Usher Williamson, *Wigginton Parsonage, Tamworth.*—Dub. A.B. 1839, M.D. Glasgow 1840; Deac. 1850 and Pr. 1851 by Bp of Pet. P. C. of Wigginton, Dio. Lich. 1865. (Patron, V. of Tamworth; Glebe, 2 acres; P. C.'s Inc. 110*l* and Ho; Pop. 420.) Formerly C. of Sheepy, Leicestershire. [5]

PURCELL, William, *Clifton, Bristol.*—Dub. A.B. 1823, A.M. 1841; Deac. 1827 by Abp of Dub. Pr. 1827 by Bp of Kildare. [6]

PURCELL, William Henry D'Olier, *South Sydenham Rectory, Tavistock, Devon.*—Dub. A.B. 1856; Deac. 1856 and Pr. 1857 by Bp of Ex. R. of South Sydenham, Dio. Ex. 1862. (Patron, J. Carpenter-Garnier, Esq; Tithe, 160*l*; Glebe, 100 acres; R.'s Inc. 300*l* and Ho; Pop. 608.) Formerly C. of Lower Brixham, Devon, and Pershore, Worc. [7]

PURCHAS, John, 7, *Montpelier-villas, Brighton.*—Ch. Coll. Cam. B.A. 1844, M.A. 1847; Deac. 1851-52. Min. of St. James's Chapel, Brighton, 1866. (Patron, V. of Brighton; Min.'s Inc. 180*l*.) Formerly C. of Orwell, Cambs, and St. Paul's, Brighton. Author, *Christ in His Ordinances* (a Farewell Sermon), 1853, 6*d*; *The Book of Feasts, Homilies for the Saints' Days*, 1853, 6*s*; *The Priest's Dream, an Allegory*, 1856, 1*s* 6*d*; *Directorium Anglicanum*, 4to, 17*s* 6*d*; *A Translation of the Cantels of the Sarum Missal, with Directions for the Use of Incense, at the Solemn Celebration of the Holy Communion* (privately printed); *A Portfolio of Photographs of the Ecclesiastical Vestments*, 1858, 25*s*. [8]

PURCHAS, William Henry, *Gloucester.*—Dur. Licen. in Theol. 1857; Deac. 1857 and Pr. 1859 by Bp of Lich. C. of Tredworth St. James's, Gloucester, 1867. Formerly C. of Ticknall, Derbyshire, 1857–59, Lydney, Gloucestershire, 1865–67. [9]

PURCHES, George Christian, *Calne, Wilts.*—Corpus Coll. Cam. B.A. 1845; Deac. 1845, Pr. 1846. C. of Calne; Retired Chap. R.N. [10]

PURDUE, George, *West Challow, Wantage, Berks.*—Mert. Coll. Ox. Jackson Scho. 1843, S.C.L. 1846; Deac. 1848 and Pr. 1851 by Bp of Ox. P. C. of East and West Challow, Dio. Ox. 1853. (Patron, C. C. Ferard, Esq; Tithe, App. 486*l*; Glebe, 31 acres; P. C.'s Inc. 148*l* and Ho; Pop. 583.) Formerly C. of Wantage 1848–54. [11]

PURDY, T. Augustus, 3, *Manor-street, Poplar, London, E.*—Deac. 1851, Pr. 1852. Chap. of the Hackney Union, Homerton, 1860; C. of All Saints', Bishopsgate, 1864. Formerly C. at Melrose and Galashiels 1851; Incumb. of St. Peter's, Galashiels, Scotland, 1852–59; Sen. C. of Homerton, Lond. 1859–60. Author, *The Crucifixion and Last Sayings of our Blessed Lord*, Hackney, 1860. [12]

PURNELL, Thomas, *Staverton Vicarage, near Cheltenham.*—New Inn Hall, Ox. B.A. 1838; Deac. 1838 and Pr. 1840 by Bp of G. and B. V. of Staverton with Boddington C. Dio. G. and B. 1841. (Patron, the present V; Glebe, 300 acres; V.'s Inc. 470*l* and Ho; Pop. Staverton 315, Boddington 400.) Formerly C. of Cam, Glouc. 1838–42. [13]

PURRIER, H. T., *Alton Priors, Marlborough, Wilts.*—C. of Alton Priors. Formerly C. of South Broom, Devizes. [14]

PURSELL, John Reeves, *Angersholme, Fleetwood.*—St. John's Coll. Ox. B.A. 1855, M.A. 1862; Deac. 1856 by Bp of Win. Pr. 1858 by Bp of Chich. Mast. of the Preparatory School, Rossall. Formerly 2nd Mast. of the Gr. Sch. and C. of St. Ann's, Lewes. [15]

PURTON, H. B., *Exhall, near Alcester, Warwickshire.*—C. of Exhall. [16]

PURTON, John, *Oldbury Rectory, Bridgnorth, Salop.*—Trin. Coll. Ox. B.A. 1829, M.A. 1830; Deac. 1830 and Pr. 1831 by Bp of Herf. R. of Oldbury, Dio. Herf. 1834. (Patron, Ld Chan; Tithe, 210*l*; Glebe, 19 acres; R.'s Inc. 265*l* and Ho; Pop. 207.) Rural Dean of Stottesdon 1840. [17]

PURTON, John Smyth, *Chetton Rectory, Bridgnorth*—St. Cath. Coll. Cam. 8th in 1st cl. Cl. Trip. 15th Jun. Opt. B.A. 1847, M.A. 1850, B D. 1857; Deac. 1848 and Pr. 1849 by Bp of Ely. R. of consolidated R.'s of Chetton, Glazeley and Deuxhill with Chap. of Loughton annexed, Salop, Dio. Herf. 1861. (Patron, T. W. Wylde-Browne, Esq; Chetton, Tithe, 567*l* 10*s* 9*d*; Glebe, 11 acres; Glazeley, Tithe, 86*l*; Glebe, 4 acres; Deuxhill, Tithe, 74*l* 17*s*; Glebe, 17½ acres; Loughton, Tithe, 85*l*; R.'s Inc. 870*l* and Ho; Pop. Chetton 490, Glazeley 67, Deuxhill 43, Loughton 100.) Exam. Chap. to Bp of Wor. 1860. Formerly Fell. and Tut. of St. Cath. Coll. 1847–61. Author, *Cicero pro Milone*, Cam. Univ. Press, 1853, 2nd ed. 1864; *An Examination before Matriculation considered in its Bearings on the Neglected Studies of the University of Cambridge* (a Pamphlet); *Corporate Life, a Sermon*, preached before the Univ. of Cambridge, 1857. [18]

PURTON, Walter Onions, *Lancing, Shoreham.*—St. Cath. Coll. Cam. B.A. 1859; Deac. 1859 and Pr. 1860 by Bp of Chich. R. of Coombe, Dio. Chich. 1866. (Patron, Lord Leconfield; Tithe, 212*l*; Glebe, 16 acres; R.'s Inc. 228*l*; Pop. 70.) Formerly C. of Petworth 1859–65, Blackpool 1865–66. Author, *Trust in Trial, or Lessons of Peace in the School of Affliction*, 4*s* 6*d*; *Songs in Suffering, Lyrics and Hymns of Modern Poets for the Use of the Afflicted and Distressed*, 3*s* 6*d*; *Hymn Book for the Sick*, 1*s*; Harvest Tracts and New Year Addresses; Editor of *Home Visitor*, 1*d*, Monthly; all published by W. Hunt and Co. [19]

PURTON, William, *Stottesdon Vicarage, Cleobury Mortimer, Salop.*—Trin. Coll. Ox. 3rd cl. Math. B.A. 1855, M.A. 1857; Deac. 1856 and Pr. 1857 by Bp of Herf. C. in sole charge of Stottesdon 1863. Formerly C. of St. Leonard's, Bridgnorth, 1856–63. [20]

PURVIS, Fortescue Richard, *Redlynch Parsonage, near Downton, Salisbury.*—Jesus Coll. Cam. 2nd cl. Civil Law Trip. 1850–51, S.C.L. 1851, B.C.L. 1854; Deac. 1854 and Pr. 1855 by Bp of Ches. P. C. of Redlynch, Dio. Salis. 1866. (Patron, V. of Downton; Glebe, 2 acres; P. C.'s Inc. 113*l* and Ho; Pop. 1170.) Formerly C. of Hollinfare, Warrington, 1854, Midford, Hants, 1857, Ibsley, Hants, 1858, Wickford, Essex, 1860, Calstone, Wellington and Blackland, Wilts, 1863. [21]

PURVIS, Richard Fortescue, *Whitsbury, Breamore, Hants.*—Jesus Coll. Cam. 1st cl. Law Trip. 1821–22, LL.B. 1825; Deac. 1820, Pr. 1821. V. of Whitsbury, Dio. Win. 1824. (Patron, Vice-Admiral Purvis; Tithe, 291*l* 0*s* 4*d*; Glebe, 12 acres; V.'s Inc. 297*l* and Ho; Pop. 204.) Dom. Chap. to the Earl of Limerick 1846. [22]

PURVIS, William Pye, *Croscombe Rectory, Wells, Somerset.*—St. Cath. Coll. Cam. B.A. 1830, M.A. 1832; Deac. 1831 by Bp of Pet. Pr. 1834 by Bp of Lin. R. of Croscombe, Dio. B. and W. 1838. (Patroness, Miss Eliz. Wylie; Tithe, 205*l*; Glebe, 17½ acres; R.'s Inc. 235*l* and Ho; Pop. 729.) Chap. to the Shepton-Mallet Union 1846. [23]

PUSEY, Edward Bouverie, *Christ Church, Oxford.*—Ch. Ch. Ox. 1st cl. Lit. Hum. and B.A. 1822, Oriel Coll. Ox. Latin Essay 1824, M.A. 1825, B.D. 1832; Ch. Ch. Ox. D.D. 1836. Regius Prof. of Hebrew in the Univ. of Ox. with Canonry of Christchurch annexed, 1828. (Value of Canonry, 700*l* and Res.) Member of the Hebdomadal Council 1854. Formerly Fell. of Oriel Coll. Ox. Author, *An Historical Inquiry into the probable Causes of* *the Rational Character lately predominant in the Theology of Germany*, 2 Parts, 1828–30; *A Sermon* (preached at the Consecration of Grove Chapel, Oxford), 1832; *Remarks on the Prospective and Past Benefits of Cathedral Institutions in the Promotion of Religious Knowledge, occasioned by Lord Henley's Plan for their Abolition*, 1833; *An Earnest Remonstrance to the Author of the Pope's Pastoral Letter to certain Members of the University of Oxford, with a Postscript*, 1836; *Churches in London, with an Appendix containing Answers to Objections raised by the* "Record," *and others, to the Plan of the Metropolis Churches' Fund*, 1837; *Patience and Confidence the Strength of the Church* (a Sermon preached on the 5th of November, before the Univ. of Oxford), 1837; *Appendices* (to the foregoing), 1838; *The Church the Converter of the Heathen* (two Sermons on behalf of the S.P.G.), 1838; *The Confessions of St. Augustine* (Revised from a former Translation by Dr. Pusey), Oxford "Library of the Fathers," 1838; *The Day of Judgment* (a Sermon), 1839; *A Letter to Richard* (Bagot) *Lord Bishop of Oxford, on the Tendency to Romanism, imputed to Doctrines held of old, as now, in the English Church*, 4 eds. 1839; *Scriptural Views of Holy Baptism* (being an enlargement of No. LXVII. of *Tracts for the Times*), 1840; *The Preaching of the Gospel in Preparation for Our Lord's Coming* (a Sermon), 1841; *The Articles treated of in Tract XC. reconsidered, and their Interpretation Vindicated*, 1841; *Christ the Source and Rule of Christian Love* (a Sermon preached at Bristol in Aid of a new Church), with a Preface on *The Relations of our Exertions to our Needs*, 1841; *A Letter to His Grace the Archbishop of Canterbury* (Howley) *on some Circumstances connected with the Present Crisis in the English Church*, 2 eds. 1842; *The Holy Eucharist, a Comfort to the Penitent* (a Sermon), 1843; *God in Love; Whoso receiveth one such Little Child in My name, receiveth Me* (two Sermons), 1844; *The Blasphemy against the Holy Ghost* (a Sermon), 1845; *The Entire Absolution of the Penitent* (two Sermons), 1846; *Chastisements neglected Forerunners of greater* (a Fast-day Sermon), 1847; *Sermons during the Seasons from Advent to Whitsuntide* (Parochial Sermons), 2 vols. Oxford, 1848–53; *Marriage with a Deceased Wife's Sister prohibited by Holy Scripture, as understood by the Church for* 1500 *Years* (Evidence given before the Commission appointed to inquire into the State and Operation of the Law of Marriage), 1849; *The Danger of Riches, Seek God first, and ye shall have all* (two Sermons), 1850; *God withdraws in Lovingkindness also* (a Sermon printed in "Sermons preached at St. Barnabas', Pimlico"), 1850; *The Church of England leaves her Children free to open their Griefs* (a Letter to the Rev. W. U. Richards), 1853; *Postscript to the Letter to the Rev. W. U. Richards in Vindication of the Freedom which the Church of England leaves her Children to whom to open their Griefs*, 1850; *Address at a Meeting of the London Union on Church Matters* (reprinted from the "Guardian"), *with a Postscript*, 1850; *The Royal Supremacy not an Arbitrary Authority, but Limited by the Laws of the Church, of which Kings are Members*, Part I. *Ancient Precedents*, 1859; *A Lecture* (delivered previously to laying the Foundation Stone of All Saints' Church, Marylebone), 1851; *A Letter to the Bishop of London* (Blomfield) *in Explanation of some Statements contained in a Letter by the Rev. W. Dodsworth, to Dr. Pusey, on the Position which he has taken in the Present Crisis*, 1851; *The Rule of Faith, as maintained by the Fathers and the Church of England* (a Sermon preached before the Univ. of Ox.), 1851; *Justification* (a Sermon), 1853; *The Presence of Christ in the Holy Eucharist* (a Sermon preached before the Univ. of Ox.), 1853; *Summary of Objections against the proposed Theological Statute*, 1854; *Collegiate and Professorial Teaching and Discipline, in Answer to Professor Vaughan's Strictures, chiefly as to the Charges against the Colleges of France and Germany*, 1854; *Do all to the Lord Jesus* (a Sermon), 5 eds. 1855; *The Doctrine of the Real Presence, as contained in the Fathers, from the Death of St. John the Evangelist to the Fourth General Council, vindicated in Notes on a Sermon*, "*The Presence of Christ in the Holy Eucharist*," *preached* A.D. 1853, *before the University of Oxford*, 1855; *The Councils of the Church from the Council of Jerusalem*, A.D. 51, *to the Council of Constantinople*, A.D. 381, *chiefly as to their Constitution, but also as to their Objects and History*, 1857; *The Real Presence of the Body and Blood of Our Lord Jesus Christ the Doctrine of the English Church, with a Vindication of the Reception of the Wicked, and of the Adoration of Our Lord Jesus Christ truly present*, 1857; *Repentance, from the Love of God Life-long* (a Sermon), 1857; *God's Prohibition of the Marriage with a Deceased Wife's Sister, Lev. xviii. 6, not to be set aside by an Inference from a Restriction of Polygamy among the Jews, Lev. xviii.* 18, 1860; *Grounds of Objection, to Details at least, of the Statute as now proposed for Middle Class Examinations*, 1861; *Vindication of* "*Grounds of Objection*" *against a leading Article in the* "*Guardian,*" 1861; *A Letter on the* "*Essays and Reviews*" (reprinted from the "Guardian"), 1861; *The Thought of the Love of Jesus for us the Remedy for Sins of the Body* (a Sermon on 1. Cor. vi. 15), 1861; *Pusey and others v. Jowett—The Argument and Decision as to the Jurisdiction of the Chancellor's Court at Oxford*, 1863; *The Spirit Comforting* (a Sermon on Matt. v. 4), 1863; *Everlasting Punishment* (a Sermon), 1864. Editor (in conjunction with the Rev. J. H. Newman, the Rev. J. Keble, and the Rev. C. Marriott), of *Bibliotheca Patrum Ecclesiæ Catholicæ*, 1838–45; Avrillon, *A Guide for Keeping Lent Holy*, 1846; *A Course of Sermons preached at St. Saviour's, Leeds*, 1845; Nonet, *The Life of Jesus Christ* (adapted for Members of the Church in England), 1846; Scupoli, *The Spiritual Combat with the Path of Paradise*, 1846; *Select Works of St. Ephraim*, 1847. [1]

PUSEY, William Bouverie, *Langley Rectory, Maidstone.*—Oriel Coll. Ox. B.A. 1831, M.A. 1834; Deac. 1832 and Pr. 1833. R. of Langley, Dio. Cant. 1842. (Patron, Philip Pusey, Esq; Tithe, 485*l* 14*s* 6*d*; R.'s Inc. 495*l* and Ho; Pop. 386.) [2]

PUTSEY, William, *Kirk-Leasington, Yarm, Yorks.*—Literate; Deac. 1834 and Pr. 1835 by Abp of York. P.C. of Kirk-Leasington, Dio. York, 1838. (Patron, Abp of York; Glebe, 38 acres; P.C.'s Inc. 300*l* and Ho; Pop. 543.) P.C. of Hilton-on-Cleveland, Dio. York, 1847. (Patron, John Hay, Esq; Tithe, 12*l* 12*s*; Glebe, 34 acres; P.C.'s Inc. 55*l*; Pop. 127.) [3]

PUTTOCK, Edward, *Flaxley, near Gloucester.*—King's Coll. Lond. Theol. Stud. 1851; Deac. 1851 and Pr. 1855 by Bp of Ex. C. of Flaxley. Formerly C. of St. Sidwell's, Exeter, 1851; Chap. to the St. John D'el Rey Mining Company, Morro Velho, Brazils, 1856–62; C. of Rockbear, near Exeter, 1863. [4]

PUXLEY, Herbert Boyne Lavallin, *The Parsonage, Cockermouth.*—Brasen. Coll. Ox. B.A. 1858, M.A. 1860; Deac. 1859 and Pr. 1860 by Bp of Carl. P.C. of Cockermouth, Dio. Carl. 1865. (Patron, Earl of Lonsdale; P.C.'s Inc. 100*l* and Ho; Pop. 2285.) Formerly Dom. Chap. to the Earl of Bantry 1860; C. of Cockermouth 1859–65. [5]

PYBUS, George Harrison, *Hudswell, Catterick, Yorks.*—St. Bees 1850; Deac. 1851 and Pr. 1852. P.C. of Hudswell, Dio. Rip. 1856. (Patron, V. of Catterick; P.C.'s Inc. 90*l*.) Chap. of the Union, Richmond, Yorks. [6]

PYCOCK, Joseph, *Newbourne, Woodbridge, Suffolk.*—St. Bees Div. Test. 1834; Deac. 1835 and Pr. 1836. R. of Newbourne, Dio. Nor. 1863. (Patron, Sir Charles Rowley, Bart; Tithe, 220*l*; Glebe, 4 acres; R.'s Inc. 224*l* and Ho; Pop. 168.) Formerly P.C. of Morley with Churwell, near Leeds, 1841–57; V. of Helperthorpe 1857. [7]

PYCROFT, James, 27, *Gloucester-gardens, Hyde-park, W.*—Trin. Coll. Ox. B.A. 1836; Deac. 1840 and Pr. 1841. Formerly P.C. of St. Mary Magdalene's, Barnstaple, 1845–56. Author, *Guide to University Honours*, 2nd ed. 1837; *On School Education*, 1841; *A Course of English Reading, or How and What to Read on Divinity and General Literature*, 4th ed. 1868; *The Collegian's Guide, or Recollections of College Days*, 1843; *Latin and Greek Grammar Practice*, an improvement of

Kerchever Arnold's System, 3rd ed. 1844; *Virgil, with Marginal References and Notes, Illustrated by 6000 Parallel Passages from the Iliad, Odyssey, Hesiod and Theocritus, besides Livy and other Authors*, 1845; *Beaufoy's Prize Lectures on Classical Studies*, 1847; *Literature Compatible with a Busy Life* (a Lecture to the Barnstaple Early Closing Association), 1852; *The Health of Towns Act* (a Letter to his Parishioners), 1853; *Classical versus Useful Knowledge Education*, 1858; *Twenty Years in the Church*, 3 eds. 1859; *Elberton Rectory, being Part Second of "Twenty Years in the Church,"* 2 eds. 1860, '62; *Ways and Words of Men of Letters*, 1861; *Agony Point, or the Groans of Gentility*, 2 vols. 1861; 2nd ed. 1862; *The Cricket Field, or the History and the Science of the Game of Cricket*, 4th ed. 1862; *Dragon's Teeth* (a Novel), 2 vols. 1863. [1]

PYDDOKE, Edward, *France Lynch, Bisley, Glouc.*—Trin. Coll. Cam. B.A. 1832, M.A. 1842; Deac. 1843 and Pr. 1846 by Bp of G. and B. C. of Bisley. Formerly Army Chap. in the East. [2]

PYE, Francis Woolcock, *Blisland Rectory, Bodmin, Cornwall.*—Queens' Coll. Cam. B.A. 1831; Deac. 1831 and Pr. 1832 by Bp of Ex. R. of Blisland, Dio. Ex. 1834. (Patron, the present R; Tithe, 543*l*; Glebe, 40 acres; R.'s Inc. 632*l* and Ho; Pop. 553.) [3]

PYE, Henry John, *Clifton Rectory, Tamworth, Staffs.*—Trin. Coll. Cam. B.A. 1848, M.A. 1852, *ad eund.* Ox. 1853; Deac. 1850 and Pr. 1851 by Bp of Ox. R. of Clifton-Campville with Chilcote, Dio. Lich. 1851. (Patron, H. J. Pye, Esq; Tithe, 717*l*; Glebe, 103 acres; R.'s Inc. 865*l* and Ho; Pop. Clifton-Campville 513, Chilcote 129.) C. of Nemans Heath 1863; Preb. of Lich. Formerly C. of Cuddesdon 1850–51. Author, *Short Ecclesiastical History*, Masters, 1854; *Ought the Sick to be Anointed?* Parkers; *Reasons why all ought to stay in during the Celebration*, Hayes. [4]

PYE, William, *Sapperton Rectory, Cirencester.*—Ch. Ch. Ox. B.A. 1827, M.A. 1830; Deac. 1828 by Bp of Ox. Pr. 1829 by Bp of Wor. R. of Sapperton with Frampton C. Dio. G. and B. 1833. (Patron, Earl Bathurst; Sapperton, Tithe, 67*l* 1*s* 6*d*; R.'s Inc. 600*l* and Ho; Pop. 600.) [5]

PYE, William Pye, *Countess Weir, Topsham, Devon.*—Trin. Coll. Ox. B.A. 1844, M.A. 1847; Deac. 1846 and Pr. 1847 by Bp of Ex. P. C. of Countess-Weir, Dio. Ex. 1856. (Patron, P. C. of Topsham; P. C.'s Inc. 110*l*; Pop. 506.) Formerly C. of Lawhitton, Cornwall. [6]

PYKE, John, *Parracombe Rectory, Barnstaple.*—Ex. Coll. Ox. B.A. 1821, M.A. 1824; Deac. 1822, Pr. 1823. R. of Parracombe, Dio. Ex. 1826. (Patrons the present R; Tithe, 252*l* 10*s*; Glebe, 64 acres; R.'s Inc. 290*l* and Ho; Pop. 410.) Formerly C. of Martinhoe 1822–40. [7]

PYKE, Thomas Massingberd, *Onehouse, Stowmarket.*—Corpus Coll. Cam. B.A. 1841; Deac. 1841, Pr. 1842. R. of Onehouse, Dio. Nor. 1846. (Patron, R. J. Pettiward, Esq; Tithe, 246*l* 10*s*; R.'s Inc. 250*l* and Ho; Pop. 212.) [8]

PYM, William Mills Parry, *Easthope Rectory, Much Wenlock, Salop.*—Caius Coll. Cam. B.A. 1860; Deac. 1862 and Pr. 1863 by Bp of Lich. R. of Easthope, Dio. Herf. 1867. (Patron, M. G. Benson, Esq; Glebe, 36 acres; R.'s Inc. 100*l* and Ho; Pop. 110.) Formerly C. of Little Drayton and Barleydam. [9]

PYNE, Alfred, *Roydon Vicarage, Harlow, Essex.*—St. Peter's Coll. Cam. B.A. 1840. V. of Roydon, Dio. Roch. 1843. (Patron, Earl of Mornington; Tithe—Imp. 637*l* 5*s*, V. 151*l* 0*s* 2*d*; V.'s Inc. 175*l* and Ho; Pop. 910.) Fell. of St. Peter's Coll. Cam. [10]

PYNE, Augustus, *Horning Vicarage, Norwich.*—Caius Coll. Cam. B.A. 1834. V. of Horning, Dio. Nor. 1855. (Patron, Bp of Nor; Tithe—App. 175*l* and 116 acres of Glebe, V. 160*l* 10*s*; Glebe, 7 acres; V.'s Inc. 175*l* and Ho; Pop. 441.) [11]

PYNE, Edward Manners Dillman, *Westacre, Swaffham, Norfolk.*—Emman. Coll. Cam. Coll. Exhib. Jun. Opt. and B.A. 1846; Deac. 1847 and Pr. 1849 by Bp of Nor. Chap. of the D. of Westacre, Dio. Nor. 1853. (Patron, A. Hamond, Esq; Chap.'s Inc. 30*l*; Pop. 415.) R. of Bawsey, Norfolk, Dio. Nor. 1853. (Patron, A. Hamond, Esq; Tithe, 90*l*; R.'s Inc. 100*l*; Pop. 32.) [12]

PYNE, Thomas, *Hook Parsonage, Kingston-on-Thames, S.W.*—St. John's Coll. Cam. B.A. 1824, M.A. 1832; Deac. 1825, Pr. 1826. P. C. of Hook, Dio. Win. 1842. (Patron, Bp of Win; P. C.'s Inc. 80*l* and Ho; Pop. 420.) [13]

PYNE, William, *Oxted Rectory, Godstone, Surrey.*—Pemb. Coll. Ox. B.A. 1822, M.A. 1823; Deac. and Pr. 1823. R. of Oxted, Dio. Win. 1828. (Patron, C. L. H. Masters, Esq; Tithe, 798*l*; Glebe, 36 acres; R.'s Inc. 824*l* and Ho; Pop. 1074.) [14]

PYNE, William, *West Charlton House, Somerton, Somerset.*—Pemb. Coll. Ox. B.A. 1822, M.A. 1825; Deac. 1823, Pr. 1824. R. of Sock or Stock-Dennis, Somerset, Dio. B. and W. 1852. (Patron, J. E. Wyndham, Esq; Tithe, 231*l* 18*s* 6*d*; R.'s Inc. 232*l*; Pop. 26.) [15]

PYNSENT, Ferdinand Alfred, *Bawdeswell, East Dereham, Norfolk.*—Deac. 1847, Pr. 1848. R. of Bawdeswell, Dio. Nor. 1851. (Patron, C. Lombe, Esq; Tithe, 330*l* 14*s* 4*d*; Glebe, 1 acre; R.'s Inc. 332*l*; Pop. 515.) [16]

PYPER, Richard, *Bratton, Westbury, Wilts.*—Downing Coll. Cam. B.A. 1856, M.A. 1863; Deac. 1856 and Pr. 1857 by Bp of Salis. P. C. of Bratton, Dio. Salis. 1858. (Patron, V. of Westbury; Glebe, 3½ acres; P. C.'s Inc. 300*l*; Pop. 741.) Formerly C. of Langton-Matravers, Dorset, 1856–57. [17]

PYPER, Thomas, *Stamford, Lincolnshire.*—St. Cath. Coll. Cam. B.A. 1844; Deac. 1845, Pr. 1847. R. of St. Michael's with St. Andrew's V. and St. Stephen's R. Stamford, Dio. Lin. 1857. (Patron, Marquis of Exeter; Tithe, 4*l* 5*s*; Glebe, 53 acres; P. C.'s Inc. 150*l*; Pop. 1305.) Formerly Asst. C. of All Souls', Brighton. [18]

QUALTROUGH, John, *Kirk-Arbory Vicarage, Castletown, Isle of Man.*—King William's Coll. Isle of Man; Deac. 1837 by Bp of Ches. Pr. 1839 by Bp of S. and M. V. of Kirk-Arbory, Dio. S. and M. 1859. (Patron, the Crown; V.'s Inc. 120*l* and Ho; Pop. 1512.) Formerly C. of Lezayre; P. C. of Sulby 1840–47, of St. Jude's, Isle of Man, 1847–59. [19]

QUANT, William Cheadle, 67, *Ashbourn-road, Derby.*—St. Cath. Hall, Cam. B.A. 1840; Deac. 1841, Pr. 1842. Chap. to the Derby Union 1853. [20]

QUARMBY, George Jonathan, *St. George's Parsonage, Portsea, Hants.*—Lin. Coll. Ox. B.A. 1829; Deac. 1829 and Pr. 1830 by Bp of Lin. P. C. of St. George's, Portsea, Dio. Win. 1854. (Patron, V. of Portsea; P.C.'s Inc. 75*l* and Ho.) [21]

QUARMBY, James Richard, *Goldhanger, Maldon, Essex.*—Lin. Coll. Ox. B.A. 1834; Deac. 1839, Pr. 1840. C. of Goldhanger and Little Totham, Essex, 1849. [22]

QUARRINGTON, Edwin Fowler, *Wellesbourne, Warwick.*—St. Cath. Coll. Cam. Sen. Opt. B.A. 1863; Deac. and Pr. 1863 by Bp of Wor. C. of Wellesbourne 1867. Formerly C. of Stoke, near Coventry, 1863. [23]

QUARRINGTON, Frederick, *The Forest, Walthamstow, Essex.*—Pemb. Coll. Ox. B.A. 1820, M.A. 1825; Deac. 1822, Pr. 1823. P. C. of St. Peter's, Walthamstow, Dio. Lon. 1851. (Patron, V. of Walthamstow; P. C.'s Inc. 150*l* and Ho; Pop. 784.) [24]

QUARTERMAN, John K., 9, *Bowater-crescent, Woolwich.*—Caius Coll. Cam. B.A; Deac. 1866 and Pr. 1867 by Bp of Lon. C. of St. Thomas's, Woolwich, 1867. Formerly C. of St. John's, Stratford, Essex, 1866. [25]

QUAYLE, Thomas, *Arrington, Royston.*—Trin. Coll. Cam. B.A. 1830, M.A. 1833; Deac. 1831, Pr. 1832. V. of Arrington. Dio. Ely, 1860. (Patron, Trin. Coll. Cam.; R.'s Inc. 69*l*; Pop. 302.) Formerly British Chap. at Berne. [26]

QUEKETT, William, *Warrington Rectory, Lancashire.*—St. John's Coll. Cam. B.A. 1826, M.A. 1831; Deac. 1825, Pr. 1836. R. of Warrington, Dio. Ches. 1854. (Patron, Lord Lilford; Tithe—Imp. 432*l* 10*s*, R. 1282*l* 6*s* 6*d*; R.'s Inc. 1290*l* and Ho; Pop. 14,442.) [1]

QUENNELL, William, *Brentwood, Essex.*—Wor. Coll. Ox. 2nd cl. Lit. Hum. and B.A. 1861, M.A. 1864; Deac. 1862 and Pr. 1863 by Bp of Roch. 2nd Mast. of the Gr. Sch. Brentwood. [2]

QUESNEL, Charles Michael, *Gaydon, Southam, Warwickshire.*—Pemb. Coll. Ox. B.A. 1849, M.A. 1852; Deac. 1849, Pr. 1851. C. of Gaydon and Chadshunt, Warw. Formerly C. of Fillongley 1854. [3]

QUICKE, Charles Penrose, *Ashbrittle Rectory, Wellington, Somerset.*—Trin. Coll. Ox. B.A. 1854; Deac. 1857, Pr. 1859. R. of Ashbrittle, Dio. B. and W. 1859. (Patron, J. Quicke, Esq; Tithe, 420*l*; Glebe, 79½ acres; R.'s Inc. 530*l* and Ho; Pop. 500.) Formerly C. of Barwell, Leicestershire, 1857–59. [4]

QUICKE, Edward Henry, *Newton St. Cyres, Exeter.*—Wad. Coll. Ox. B.A. 1844; Deac. 1845, Pr. 1846. V. of Newton St. Cyres, Dio. Ex. 1847. (Patron, J. Quicke, Esq; Tithe—Imp. 351*l* 11*s* 2*d*, V. 360*l*; V.'s Inc. 430*l* and Ho; Pop. 1083.) Rural Dean 1847. [5]

QUICKE, George Andrew, *Radclive, Buckingham.*—New Coll. Ox. B.C.L 1845; Deac. 1845, Pr. 1847. Fell. of New Coll. Ox. R. of Radclive with Chackmore, Dio. Ox. 1864. (Patron, New Coll. Ox; R.'s Inc. 434*l* and Ho; Pop. 356.) Formerly C. of Buttermere, Wilts, 1845-46; Asst. C. of Kintbury, Berks, 1846–48; C. of East Hendred, Berks, 1849–51; R. of Ashbrittle, Somerset, 1855–59. [6]

QUILTER, George, *Canwick Vicarage, Lincoln.*—St. Peter's Coll. Cam. B.A. 1815, M.A. 1818; Deac. 1816 and Pr. 1817 by Bp of Ely. V. of Canwick, Dio. Lin. 1818. (Patron, Mercers' Company; V.'s Inc. 231*l* and Ho; Pop. 228.) [7]

QUIN, Thomas St. John, *Bordeaux.*—British Chap. at Bordeaux. [8]

QUIRK, Charles Thomas, *Golborne Rectory, Warrington, Lancashire.*—St. John's Coll. Cam. Moral Philosophy Prizeman, Wrang. and B.A. 1833, M.A. 1836; Deac. 1834, Pr. 1836. R. of Golborne, Dio. Ches. 1854. (Patron, Earl of Derby; Tithe, App. 158*l*; R.'s Inc. 150*l* and Ho; Pop. 2776.) Surrogate. [9]

QUIRK, George, *Over Kellet Vicarage, Lancaster.*—Wor. Coll. Ox. B.A. 1846, M.A. 1863; Deac. 1846 and Pr. 1847 by Bp of Pet. V. of Over Kellet, Dio. Man. 1862. (Patron, Septimus Booker, Esq; Tithe, 42*l*; Glebe, 190*l*; V.'s Inc. 240*l* and Ho; Pop. 425.) Formerly C. of Bringhurst with Great Easton 1847–60; V. of Luton, Beds, 1860–62. Author, *Farewell Sermon at Luton*, 1862, 1*s*. [10]

QUIRK, James Richard, *Blandford Rectory, Dorset.*—St. Edm. Hall, Ox. B.A. 1841, M.A. 1845; Deac. 1842 and Pr. 1843 by Bp of Lich. R. and V. of Blandford Forum, Dio. Salis. 1863. (Patrons, D. and C. of Winchester; Tithe, App. 157*l* 10*s* and 12 acres of Glebe, V. 112*l* 10*s*; R. and V.'s Inc. 325*l* and Ho; Pop. 4500.) Surrogate. Formerly C. of Clifton Campville, Nuneaton, Willoughby; P. C. of Attleborough, Warwickshire, 1851–63. [11]

RABBETTS, Cicero, *Wanstrow Rectory, Frome, Somerset.*—Wor. Coll. Ox. B.A. 1821. R. of Wanstrow, Dio. B. and W. 1825. (Patroness, Mrs. C. S. Clarke; Tithe, 330*l*; Glebe, 57½ acres; R.'s Inc. 410*l* and Ho; Pop. 454.) [12]

RABBETTS, Francis Deacle, *Cologne.*—St. John's Coll. Cam. B.A. 1853, M.A. 1860; Deac. 1853 and Pr. 1856 by Bp of Man. English Chap. at Cologne. Formerly C. of Habergham-Eaves, Burnley, 1853–56, Hendon, Middlesex, 1856-61; Acting Civil Chap. Gibraltar, 1862; C. of South Witham, Grantham, 1863. Author, *Original Sacred Music*, 1862. [13]

RABY, John, *Greystoke, Penrith.*—Clare Coll. Cam. B.A. 1856; Deac. 1857, Pr. 1858. C. of Greystoke, Cumberland. [14]

RABY, John, *Wetherby in Spofforth, Yorks.*—P. C. of Wetherby-in-Spofforth, Dio. Rip. 1853. (Patron, R. of Spofforth; Tithe, App. 246*l* 7*s* 8*d*; P. C.'s Inc. 130*l*; Pop. 1682.) [15]

RABY, Walter, *Minting, Horncastle, Lincolnshire.*—C. of Minting. [16]

RACKHAM, Hanworth Edward, *Witchford Vicarage, Ely.*—Trin. Hall, Cam. Scho. of, B.A. 1839, M.A. 1849; Deac. 1843 and Pr. 1844 by Bp of Nor. V. of Witchford, Dio. Ely, 1844. (Patrons, D. and C. of Ely; Tithe—App. 421*l* 13*s* 9*d* and 21 acres of Glebe, V. 140*l*; Glebe, 22 acres; V.'s Inc. 240*l* and Ho; Pop. 559.) [17]

RACKHAM, Matthew John, *Pitt-street, Norwich.*—St. Bees 1836; Deac. 1837, Pr. 1838. R. of St. Augustine's, Norwich, Dio. Nor. 1848. (Patrons, D. and C. of Nor; R.'s Inc. 160*l*; Pop. 1890.) C. of Riddlesworth, Norfolk. Formerly C. of South Walsham St. Lawrence 1837, Oulton 1843. [18]

RACKHAM, Robert Alfred, *Whatfield, Ipswich.*—Jesus Coll. Cam. 20th Wrang. and B.A. 1837, M.A. 1840; Deac. 1840, Pr. 1841. R. of Whatfield, Dio. Ely, 1852. (Patron, Jesus Coll. Cam; Tithe, 484*l*; Glebe, 78 acres; R.'s Inc. 500*l* and Ho; Pop. 340.) Formerly Fell. of Jesus Coll. Cam. [19]

RACKHAM, Robert Reeve, *Barney Vicarage, Fakenham, Norfolk.*—Corpus Coll. Cam. Sen. Opt. and B.A. 1847; Deac. 1848 and Pr. 1849 by Bp of Nor. V. of Barney, Dio. Nor. 1863. (Patron, Lord Hastings; Tithe—Imp. 168*l*, V. 104*l*; Glebe, 38 acres; V.'s Inc. 165*l* and Ho; Pop. 283.) Surrogate. Formerly C. of Hunworth and Bale, Norfolk. [20]

RADCLIFFE, Alston William, *North Newnton, Pewsey, Wilts.*—Brasen. Coll. Ox. B.A. 1832, M.A. 1837. V. of North Newnton, Dio. G. and B. 1843. (Patron, the Prebend of Newnton in Salis. Cathl; Tithe—App. 407*l*, V. 76*l*; V.'s Inc. 80*l*; Pop. 376.) [21]

RADCLIFFE, Frederick Adolphus, *Milston Rectory, Amesbury, Wilts.*—R. of Milston with Brigmerston, Dio. Salis. 1863. (Patron, C. E. Rendell, Esq; Tithe, 174*l*; Glebe, 201 acres; R.'s Inc. 331*l* and Ho; Pop. 130.) [22]

RADCLIFFE, Henry Eliot Delme, *South Tidworth Rectory, Marlborough.*—Queen's Coll. Ox. 2nd cl. Lit. Hum. 1855, B.A. 1855, M.A. 1858; Deac. 1856 by Bp of Ox. Pr. 1858 by Bp of Ely. Michel Fell. of Queen's Coll. Ox; R. of South Tidworth, Dio. Win. 1862. (Patron, F. Sloane Stanley, Esq; R.'s Inc. 379*l* and Ho; Pop. 206.) Formerly C. of Riseley and Melchbourne, Beds, 1857–58, Oakley and Bromham, Beds, 1859. [23]

RADCLIFFE, John Randle, *Hillmorton, near Rugby.*—Magd. Hall, Ox. S.C.L. 1851; Deac. 1852 and Pr. 1853 by Bp of Wor. C. of Hillmorton 1865. Formerly C. of Hallow 1852, Eyke 1854, Stoke 1859, Crick 1861. [24]

RADCLIFFE, John William, 38, *East Southernhay, Exeter.*—Lin. Coll. Ox. 3rd cl. Lit. Hum. M.A. 1840; Deac. 1846 and Pr. 1848 by Bp of Ex. Formerly C. of St. Sidwell's, Exeter, 1846–48, Wambrook, Dorset, 1852–56. [25]

RADCLIFFE, Walter, *Warleigh, near Plymouth.* [26]

RADCLIFFE, William Coxe, *Fonthill Gifford, Wilts.*—R. of Fonthill Gifford, Dio. Salis. 1839. (Patron, Lord of the Manor; R.'s Inc. 351*l*; Pop. 430.) [27]

RADCLIFFE, W. H., *Leeds.*—C. of Leeds. [28]

RADFORD, Henry Freer, *Broughton-Astley Rectory, Lutterworth.*—Trin. Coll. Cam. B.A. 1847; Deac. 1848, Pr. 1849. R. of Broughton-Astley, Dio. Pet. 1854. (Patron, H. Radford, Esq; Tithe—App. 80*l*, R. 557*l* 12*s* 4*d*; R.'s Inc. 64*l* and Ho; Pop. 785.) [29]

RADFORD, William Tucker Arundel, *Downe St. Mary, Bow, North Devon.*—Ex. Coll. Ox. 2nd cl. Math. B.A. 1840; Deac. 1842 and Pr. 1843 by Bp of Ex. R. of Downe St. Mary, Dio. Ex. 1843. (Patron, the present R; Tithe, 265*l*; Glebe, 60*l*; R.'s Inc. 355*l* and

Ho; Pop. 426.) Formerly C. of Downe St. Mary 1842–43. [1]

RAE, Eben, *Peel-street, Princes-park, Liverpool.*—Glasgow Univ. and St. Aidan's; Deac. 1862 and Pr. 1863 by Bp of Man. P. C. of St. Cleopas', Toxteth-park, Liverpool, Dio. Ches. 1866. (Patrons, Trustees; P. C.'s Inc. 460*l* and Ho; Pop. 9000.) Formerly C. of All Saints', Goodshaw, 1862, St. Chrysostom's, Everton, Liverpool, 1864. [2]

RAGG, Thomas, *Lawley, near Wellington, Salop.*—Deac. 1858 and Pr. 1859 by Bp of Roch. P. C. of Lawley, Dio. Lich. 1865. (Patron, Bp of Lich; Glebe, 1½ acres; P. C.'s Inc. 100*l* and Ho; Pop. 1647.) Formerly C. of Southfleet, Kent, 1858, Malin's Lee, Salop, 1860. Author, *The Deity, a Poem,* 1834, 4*s*; *The Martyr of Verulam,* 1835, 2*s* 6*d*; *Lyrics from the Pentateuch,* 1837, 5*s*; *Heber, Lays from the Prophets, &c.* 1841, 5*s*; *Scenes and Sketches from Life and Nature,* 1847, 5*s*; *Creation's Testimony to its God,* 1855, 5*s*; *Man's Dreams and God's Realities,* 1857, 2*s* 6*d*; and about 30 smaller works. [3]

RAIKES, Charles Hall, *Chittoe, Chippenham.*—Oriel Coll. Ox. B.A. 1861, M.A. 1864; Deac. 1863 and Pr. 1864 by Bp of Win. P. C. of Chittoe, Dio. Salis 1867. (Patron, J. W. Gooch Spicer, Esq; Glebe, 12 acres; P. C.'s Inc. 150*l* and Ho; Pop. 382.) Formerly C. of Abbotts Ann, Hants, 1863. [4]

RAIKES, Francis, *Carleton-Forehoe, Wymondham, Norfolk.*—Ex. Coll. Ox. 2nd cl. Math. et Phy. B.A 1844, M.A. 1847; Deac. 1846, Pr. 1848. R. of Carleton-Forehoe, Dio. Nor. 1848. (Patron, Lord Wodehouse; Glebe, 93 acres; R.'s Inc. 180*l*; Pop. 127.) R. of Crownthorpe, Norfolk, Dio. Nor. 1848. (Patron, Lord Wodehouse; Tithe, 145*l*; Glebe, 16 acres; R.'s Inc. 170*l*; Pop. 97.) [5]

RAIKES, Frederick Thornton, *Milnthorpe Parsonage, Westmoreland.*—Literate; Deac. 1859, Pr. 1860. P. C. of Milnthorpe, Dio. Carl. 1860. (Patron, V. of Heversham; Glebe, 7 acres; P. C.'s Inc. 247*l* and Ho; Pop. 1073.) Formerly C. of St. George's, Kendal, Westmoreland, 1859–60; previously Lieut. in H.M. 62nd Regt. [6]

RAIKES, Henry Puget, *Cheselborne, Dorset.*—Literate; Deac. 1860 and Pr. 1862 by Bp of Carl. C. of Cheselborne 1863. Formerly C. of Barton 1860. [7]

RAINE, James, *York.*—Dur. B.A. 1851, M.A. 1853. V. of St. Lawrence's, York, Dio. York, 1867. (Patrons, D. and C. of York; Tithe, 45*l*; V.'s Inc. 130*l*; Pop. 2456.) Preb. of York 1866; Fell. of Dur. Univ. [8]

RAINE, John, *Blyth Vicarage, Worksop, Notts.*—Trin. Coll. Cam. Sen. Opt. B.A. 1828, M.A. 1831, *ad eund.* Univ. Coll. Dur. 1839; Deac. 1831 and Pr. 1834 by Bp of Lin. V. of Blyth with Austerfield C. and Bawtry C. Dio. Lin. 1834. (Patron, Trin. Coll. Cam; Tithe—Imp. 2708*l* 9*s*, App. 1953*l* 12*s* 3*d*, V. 720*l* 11*s* 10*d*; V.'s Inc. 751*l* and Ho; Pop. 2086.) Formerly Fell. of Trin. Coll. Cam. [9]

RAINES, Charles Alfred, *Queen-square, Newcastle-on-Tyne.*—St. John's Coll. Cam. Scho. of, B.A. 1840, M.A. 1843; Deac. 1840 and Pr. 1841 by Bp of Dur. P. C. of St. Peter's, Newcastle, Dio. Dur. 1844. (Patron, V. of Newcastle; P. C.'s Inc. 130*l*; Pop. 4559.) Formerly C. of Jarrow 1841–43. [10]

RAINES, Francis Robert, *Milnrow Vicarage, Rochdale, Lancashire.*—Queens' Coll. Cam. M.A. 1845; Deac. 1828 and Pr. 1829 by Bp of Ches. V. of Milnrow, Dio. Man. 1832. (Patron, V. of Rochdale; V.'s Inc. 350*l* and Ho.) Hon. Can. of Man. 1849; Rural Dean of Rochdale 1846; Fell. of Soc. of Antiquaries. Editor of Bishop Gastrell's *Notitia Cestriensis,* 4 vols. 4to, 1845–50; *The Stanley Papers*; *Nicholas Assheton's Journal*; *Memoirs of James, seventh Earl of Derby,* 3 vols; *History of the Lancashire Chantries,* 2 vols. 4to; various Tracts, etc. [11]

RAINES, W., *Clare Hall, Cambridge.*—Fell. of Clare Hall, Cam. [12]

RAINIER, George, *Ninfield, Battle, Sussex.*—Brasen. Coll. Ox. B.A. 1835; Deac. 1837, Pr. 1838. V. of Ninfield, Dio. Chich. 1854. (Patrons, D. and C. of Cant; Tithe, 426*l*; Glebe, 1½ acres; V.'s Inc. 450*l*; Pop. 587.) [13]

RAINSFORD, M.—Min. of Belgrave Chapel, Pimlico, Lond. 1866. [14]

RALPH, Henry F., *Little Horwood, Winslow, Bucks.*—V. of Little Horwood, Dio. Ox. 1866. (Patron, Rev. J. Bartlett; Tithe, 34*l*; V.'s Inc. 110*l* and Ho; Pop. 449.) [15]

RALPH, Solomon Kelly Ferrier, *Walton-on-the-Hill, Liverpool.*—Brasen. Coll. Ox. B.A. 1856. C. of St. Aidan's, Walton-on-the-Hill. Formerly C. of Ch. Ch. Preston, and Holy Island, Durham. [16]

RAM, Abel John, *The Vicarage, West Ham, London, E.*—Oriel Coll. Ox. B.A. 1827, M.A. 1830; Deac. 1827 and Pr. 1829 by Bp of Lich. V. of West Ham, Dio. Roch. 1845. (Patron, the Crown; Tithe, 1100*l*; Glebe, 50*l*; V.'s Inc. 1273*l* and Ho; Pop. 6500.) Rural Dean of Barking. Formerly V. of Towcester and P. C. of Beverley Minster. Author, *Visitation Sermons in Peterborough and York.* [17]

RAM, Edward, 32, *Victoria-street, Norwich.*—King's Coll. Lond; Deac. 1866 and Pr. 1867 by Bp of Nor. C. of All Saints' with St. Julian's, Norwich, 1866. [18]

RAM, George Stopford, *Heston, Hounslow, W.*—Wad. Coll. Ox. B.A. 1861, M.A. 1864; Deac. 1861 and Pr. 1862 by Bp of Lon. Formerly C. of Heston, Middlesex, 1862–63; P. C. of St. John's, Stratford, Essex, 1864–66. [19]

RAM, Stopford James, *Pavenham, Beds.*—St. John's Coll. Cam. B.A. 1849, M.A. 1852; Deac. 1849 by Abp of Armagh, Pr. 1851 by Bp of Pet. P. C. of Pavenham, Dio. Ely, 1860. (Patron, Joseph Tucker, Esq; P. C.'s Inc. 206*l* and Ho; Pop. 520.) Formerly C. of Tynan, Armagh, 1849, Kingstown 1850, Burbage, Leicestershire, 1851; P. C. of Warslow, Staffs, 1851, Ch. Ch. Stratford, Essex, 1854; Assoc. Sec. for Irish Ch. Missions 1857. [20]

RAMADGE, Frederick, 24, *Gloucester-street, Pimlico, London, S.W.*—Fell. of Caius Coll. Cam. [21]

RAMSAY, Allan, *Cheltenham.*—C. of St. John's, Cheltenham. Formerly C. of St. Stephen's, Hull. [22]

RAMSAY, The Very Rev. Edward Bannerman, 23, *Ainslie-place, Edinburgh.*—St. John's Coll. Cam. B.A. 1815, M.A. 1831, Edin. LL.D. 1860; Deac. 1816 and Pr. 1818 by Bp of B. and W. Incumb. of St. John's, Edinburgh, 1830; Dean of the Dio. of Edinb. 1839. Formerly C. of Rodden, Somerset, 1816–24. Author, *Memoir of Sir J. E. Smith,* 1827; *Memoir of Dr. Chalmers,* 1850; *Advent Sermons,* 2 eds. 1851; *Christian Doctrine of the Eucharist,* 2 eds; *Reminiscences of Scottish Life and Character,* 14 eds. 1857; *Diversities of Christian Character,* 1858; *Diversities of Faults in Christian Characters*; *Manual of Catechising,* 10 eds. [23]

RAMSBOTHAM, Thomas, *The Rectory, Heywood, Lancashire.*—Ch. Coll. Cam. B.A. 1843, M.A. 1846; Deac. and Pr. 1843 by Bp of Rip. R. of Heywood, Dio. Man. 1865. (Patron, R. of Bury; R.'s Inc. 400*l* and Ho; Pop. 9231.) Formerly P. C. of Walmersley, Bury, 1854–65. [24]

RAMSDEN, Charles Henry, *Chilham Vicarage, Canterbury.*—Trin. Coll. Cam. B.A. 1841, M.A. 1843; Deac. 1842, Pr. 1843. V. of Chilham with Molash P. C. Dio. Cant. 1862. (Patron, C. S. Hardy, Esq; Glebe, 23 acres; V.'s Inc. 800*l* and Ho; Pop. Chilham 1319, Molash 328.) Formerly C. of Shirland 1846–62. [25]

RAMSDEN, Frederick John, *Uffington Rectory, Stamford.*—Ch. Ch. Ox. B.A. 1859; Deac. 1860 by Bp of Lon. R. of Uffington, Dio. Lin. 1861. (Patron, Earl of Lindsey; Tithe—App. 9*l*, R. 3*l*; R.'s Inc. 837*l* and Ho; Pop. 510.) Formerly C. of Stratford-on-Avon 1860. [26]

RAMSDEN, Thomas Lagden, *North End, East Ham, London, E.*—St. John's Coll. Ox. B.A. 1826, M.A. 1828; Deac. 1828 and Pr. 1829 by Bp of Lon. P. C. of Forest Gate, Dio. Roch. 1852. (Patrons, V. of East and West Ham alt; P. C.'s Inc. 215*l*; Pop. 3792.) Chap. to Little Ilford House of Correction 1839. Formerly C. of St. Clement's, Eastcheap 1828, Mitcham 1830, Balsham 1837, Little Ilford 1839, East Ham 1847. [1]

RAMSDEN, William, *Sudbrooke Rectory, Lincoln.*—Ch. Coll. Cam. B.A. 1825; Deac. 1825 and Pr. 1826 by Bp of Lon. R. of Sudbrooke, Dio. Lin. 1855. (Patron, Bp of Lin; Tithe, 57*l*; R.'s Inc. 160*l* and Ho; Pop. 75.) Formerly R. of Buslingthorpe 1844–55. [2]

RAMSDEN, William Russell.—Dub. A.B. 1853, A.M. 1858; Deac. 1856 and Pr. 1857 by Bp of Ches. Formerly C. of Frodsham, Cheshire, and Boldon, Durham. [3]

RAMSKILL, Edwin James, *Knaresborough.*—St. Cath. Coll. Cam. 20th Sen. Opt. B.A. 1852, M.A. 1855; Deac. 1853 and Pr. 1854 by Bp of Rip. P. C. of Trinity, Knaresborough, Dio. Rip. 1866. (Patron, V. of Knaresborough; P. C.'s Inc. 300*l*; Pop. 2250.) Formerly C. of Knaresborough 1853–66. [4]

RAMUS, Charles Meade, *Playden Rectory, Rye, Sussex.*—Trin. Coll. Cam. B.A. 1847, M.A. 1850; Deac. 1848 and Pr. 1849 by Bp of Win. R. of Playden with East Guildford, Dio. Chich. 1865. (Patron, Rev. Charles Shrubb; Tithe, comm. 450*l*; R.'s Inc. 500*l* and Ho; Pop. 457.) Formerly C. of Boldre 1848; P. C. of South Baddesley, Hants, 1851. Author, *Address to Royal Commissioners for Clerical Subscription in Favour of Abolition of Oath against Simony*, Parkers, 1864. [5]

RANDALL, Edward, *Randalstown, Castle Douglas, Scotland.*—Oriel Coll. Ox. B.A. 1853, M.A. 1858; Deac. 1855 and Pr. 1856 by Bp of Roch. Incumb. of St. Ninian's, Castle Douglas. Formerly C. of Great Chesterford, Essex, Graffham, Sussex; Chap. to Sir H. E. L. Dryden, Bart. Canons Ashby, Northants. Author, *The Word of God*; *God in Three Persons*; *Inauguration Ode on the Opening of the New Town Hall, Castle Douglas*, 1863. [6]

RANDALL, Francis, *Hemingborough, Yorks.*—C. of Hemingborough. [7]

RANDALL, Henry Goldney, *Redcliffe Vicarage, Bristol.*—Queen's Coll. Ox. 2nd cl. Lit. Hum. 2nd cl. Math. and B.A. 1831, M.A. 1834; Deac. 1834 and Pr. 1836 by Bp of Ox. V. of St. Mary Redcliffe, Bristol Dio. G. and B. 1865. (Patron, Bp of G. and B; V.'s Inc. 300*l* and Ho; Pop. 7455.) Rural Dean 1866. Formerly Michel Fell. of Queen's Coll. Ox; P. C. of St Peter's, Bishopworth, Bristol, 1853–65. [8]

RANDALL, The Ven. James, *Binfield, Berks.*—Trin. Coll. Ox. 1809, 1st cl. Lit. Hum. 1812, B.A. 1813, M.A. 1816; Deac. 1828, Pr. 1829. Chap. to the Bp of Ox. 1846; Archd. of Berks 1855; Can. of Bristol 1867. Formerly R. of Binfield, Berks, 1831–59; Fell. of Trin. Coll. Ox. 1818–21. Author, *Sermons*, 1843; *Ordination Sermon*, 1848; *Letter on Court of Appeal in Causes Ecclesiastical*, 1850; *Archidiaconal Charges*. [9]

RANDALL, James Leslie, *Newbury Rectory, Berks.*—New Coll. Ox. B.A. 1851, M.A. 1855; Deac. 1852 and Pr. 1853 by Bp of Ox. R. of Newbury, Dio. Ox. 1857. (Patron, Bp of Ox; Tithe, 363*l*; Glebe, 13 acres; R.'s Inc. 380*l* and Ho; Pop. 4727.) Formerly C. of Warfield, Berks; Fell. of New Coll. Ox. [10]

RANDALL, John Montagu, *Langham-Bishops, Holt, Norfolk.*—King's Coll. Lond. Theol. Assoc. 1838; Deac. 1843 and Pr. 1844 by Bp of Nor. V. of Langham-Bishops, Dio. Nor. 1850. (Patron, Bp of Nor; Glebe, 100 acres; V.'s Inc. 190*l* and Ho; Pop. 350.) Formerly C. of Lowestoft 1843–50. Author, *Titles of our Lord*, R.T.S. 1859. [11]

RANDALL, Richard William, *Woollavington Rectory, Petworth, Sussex.*—Ch. Ch. Ox. 4th cl. Lit. Hum. B.A. 1846, M.A. 1849; Deac. 1847 and Pr. 1848 by Bp of Ox. R. of Woollavington with Graffham R. Dio. Chich. 1851. (Patron, the Bp of Ox. in his own right; Woollavington, Tithe—Imp. 43*l* 14*s*, R. 212*l*; Glebe, 17 acres; Graffham, Tithe, 185*l*; Glebe, 37 acres; R.'s Inc. 417*l* and Ho; Pop. Woollavington 316, Graffham 416.) [12]

RANDALL, William, *Hayes Rectory, Uxbridge, Middlesex.*—R. of Hayes, Dio. Lon. 1860. (Patron, the present R; R.'s Inc. 700*l* and Ho; Pop. 2650.) Formerly C. of Hayes. [13]

RANDOLPH, Charles, *Kimpton Lodge, Andover.*—Clare Coll. Cam. B.A. 1816, M.A. 1825; Deac. 1818, Pr. 1819. R. of Kimpton, Dio. Win. 1832. (Patrons, Exors. of the late G. S. Foyle, Esq; Tithe, 473*l*; Glebe, 50½ acres; R.'s Inc. 510*l* and Ho; Pop 305.) [14]

RANDOLPH, Cyril, *Staple, Sandwich, Kent.*—Ch. Ch. Ox. B.A. 1846, M.A. 1847; Deac. 1849, Pr. 1850. R. of Staple, Dio. Cant. 1863. (Patron, Abp of Cant; Tithe, 600*l*; Glebe, 1½ acres; R.'s Inc. 600*l* and Ho; Pop. 520.) Formerly P. C. of Riverhead 1850–63. [15]

RANDOLPH, Edmund, *Kimpton, Andover.*—Jesus Coll. Cam. B.A. 1844, Tyrwhitt's Hebrew Scho. 1st cl. Cl. Trip. 1846, M.A. 1847; Deac. 1845, Pr. 1846. C. of Kimpton. Formerly C. of Little Hadham; V. of St. Clement's, Cambridge. [16]

RANDOLPH, Edward, John, *Dunnington Rectory, near York.*—Ch. Ch. Ox. B.A. 1836, M.A. 1838; Deac. 1837 and Pr. 1838 by Bp of Ox. R. of Dunnington, Dio. York, 1845. (Patron, Earl Brownlow; Tithe, 320*l*; Glebe, 102 acres; R.'s Inc. 380*l* and Ho; Pop. 850.) Preb. of York 1848; Hon. Sec. to the York Diocesan Board of Education. [17]

RANDOLPH, Francis, *Little Hadham, Bishop Stortford, Herts.*—St. John's Coll. Cam. Sen. Opt. and B.A. 1840, M.A. 1843; Deac. 1841, Pr. 1842. C. of Little Hadham 1858. Formerly C. of Dolton, Devon. [18]

RANDOLPH, Henry Jones, *Marcham Vicarage, Abingdon, Berks.*—St. Edm. Hall, Ox. B.A. 1800, M.A. 1804; Deac. 1802, Pr. 1803. V. of Marcham, Dio. Ox. 1819. (Patron, Ch. Ch. Ox; V.'s Inc. 455*l* and Ho; Pop. 1111.) [19]

RANDOLPH, Herbert, *Tolbury House, Bruton, Somerset.*—Chap. to the Marquis of Downshire 1850. Formerly V. of Abbotsley, Hants, 1839–49. Editor of Sir R. Wilson's *Journal of The French Invasion of Russia in 1812*, 1860. [20]

RANDOLPH, John, *Sanderstead Rectory, Croydon, Surrey, S.*—Brasen. Coll. Ox. B.A. 1843, M.A. 1847; Deac. 1845 and Pr. 1846 by Bp of Chich. R. of Sanderstead, Dio. Win. 1866. (Patron, A. D. Wigsell, Esq; Tithe, 456*l*; Glebe, 18 acres, R.'s Inc. 500*l* and Ho; Pop. 206.) Formerly Chap. of Don. of Tattenhoe, Bucks. [21]

RANDOLPH, John Honywood, *Sanderstead Rectory, Croydon, Surrey, S.*—Ch. Ch. Ox. 2nd cl. Lit. Hum. and B.A. 1812, M.A. 1815; Deac. 1814, Pr. 1815. Preb. of Ealdland in St. Paul's 1822. (Value, 2*l* 10*s*.) Proctor in Convocation for the Clergy of the Archd. of Surrey. Formerly Preacher to the Hon. Soc. of Gray's Inn; Chap. to the British Factory of St. Petersburg; R. of Mistley-cum-Bradfield; V. of Northolt; R. of Burton Coggles; R. of Tobbins; R. of Wainfleet; R. of Saunderstead, Surrey, 1845–66. [22]

RANDOLPH, Leveson Cyril, *East Garston Vicarage, Hungerford, Berks.*—Ch. Ch. Ox. B.A. 1843, M.A. 1848; Deac. 1849 and Pr. 1850 by Bp of Ox. V. of East Garston, Dio. Ox. 1853. (Patron, Ch. Ch. Ox; Tithe—App. 646*l* 1*s* and 134½ acres of Glebe, V. 272*l* 6*s*; Glebe, ½ acre; V.'s Inc. 275*l* and Ho; Pop. 589.) Dom. Chap. to the Duke of Sutherland. [23]

RANDOLPH, Thomas, *72, Harley-street, Cavendish-square, London, W.* and *Much Hadham Rectory, Ware, Herts.*—Ch. Ch. Ox. 2nd cl. Lit. Hum. and B.A. 1809, M.A. 1812; Deac. and Pr. 1812. R. of Much Hadham with Little Hadham and Perry Green C. Dio. Roch. 1812. (Patron, Bp of Lon; Much Hadham, Tithe, 1200*l*; Glebe, 165½ acres; Little Hadham, Tithe, App. 99*l* 10*s*, R. 800*l* 10*s*; Glebe, 126 acres; R.'s Inc. 2147*l* and Ho; Pop. Much Hadham 1172, Little Hadham 864.) Preb. of Cantlers in St. Paul's 1812. (Value, 1500*l*.) Chap. in Ordinary to the Queen 1825. [24]

RANKEN, Charles, *Richmond, Surrey, S.W.*—Ch. Ch. Ox. B.A. 1817, M.A. 1820; Deac. 1820 and Pr. 1821 by Bp of Ox. Chap. of Almshouses, Richmond. Formerly C. and Lect. of Brislington, near Bristol. [25]

RANKEN, Charles Edward, *Sandford Parsonage, Oxford.*—Wad. Coll. Ox. B.A. 1850, M.A. 1852;

Deac. 1852 and Pr. 1853 by Bp of Lich. P. C. of Sandford-on-Thames, Dio. Ox. 1867. (Patroness, Mrs. Hussey; P. C.'s Inc. 95*l* and Ho; Pop. 376.) Formerly C. of St. Modwen's, Burton-on-Trent, 1852–54, Tooting 1854–56; Assoc. Sec. Church of Eng. Educ. Soc. 1856–59; C. of Trinity, Cheltenham, 1859–64, St. John's, Richmond, Surrey, 1864–67. [1]

RANKEN, William Henry, *West Houghton Parsonage, Bolton-le-Moors.*—Corpus Coll. Ox. 2nd cl. Lit. Hum. and 1st cl. Math. B.A. 1854, M.A. 1857; Deac. 1856 and Pr. 1858 by Bp of Ox. Fell. of Corpus Coll. Ox; P. C. of West Houghton, Dio. Man. 1867. (Patron, V. of Deane; Tithe, 65*l* 18*s* 7*d*; Glebe, 14 acres; P. C.'s Inc. 225*l* and Ho; Pop. 3679.) Formerly C. of East Retford 1860–61; P. C. of Sandford-on-Thames 1862–66; V. of Radley, Berks, 1865–67. Author, *Simple Sermons*, Rivingtons, 1867, 5*s*. [2]

RANKING, George, *Dorset House, Tunbridge Wells.*—Ch. Coll. Cam. B.C.L. 1829; Deac. 1826 and Pr. 1827 by Bp of Nor. Formerly V. of Wimbish, Essex, 1860–65. [3]

RANSFORD, Robert Bolton, 8, *Brixton Rise, Surrey, S.*—Clare Coll. Cam. Jun. Opt. Math. Trip. B.A. 1863, M.A. 1866; Deac. 1863 and Pr. 1864 by Bp of Win. C. of St. Matthew's, Brixton, 1863. [4]

RANSOME, John Henry, *Lindale Parsonage, Grange-in-Cartmel, Lancashire.*—Trin. Coll. Cam. B.A. 1857, M.A. 1865; Deac. 1857 and Pr. 1858 by Bp of Man. P. C. of Lindale, Dio. Carl. 1859. (Patron, Bp of Carl; P. C.'s Inc. 71*l* and Ho.) Formerly C. of Warton with Freckleton 1858. [5]

RANSOME, V. F., *Chetnole, Sherborne, Dorset.* C. of Chetnole. [6]

RASHDALL, John, *Dawlish Vicarage, Devon.*—Corpus Coll. Cam. B.A. 1832, M.A. 1835; Deac. 1833, Pr. 1834. V. of Dawlish with St. Mark's C. Dio. Ex. 1864. (Patrons, D. and C. of Ex; Tithe—App. 360*l*, V. 440*l* 3*s*; Glebe, 3 acres; V.'s Inc. 490*l* and Ho; Pop. 3662.) Formerly V. of Great Malvern 1850–56; Min. of Eaton Chapel, Eaton-square, Lond. 1856–64. [7]

RASHDALL, Robert, *Bury St. Edmunds.*—Corpus Coll. Cam. B.A. 1835, M.A. 1841; Deac. 1835 and Pr. 1836 by Bp of G. and B. P. C. of St. John's, Bury St. Edmunds, Dio. Ely, 1841. (Patron, Bp of Ely; P. C.'s Inc. 113*l* and Ho; Pop. 3492.) Treasurer of the Suffolk Soc. for the Relief of Clergymen's Widows and Orphans. [8]

RASHLEIGH, George, *Horton-Kirby, Dartford, Kent.*—Oriel Coll. Ox. B.A. 1806, M.A. 1809; Deac. 1807, Pr. 1808. V. of Horton-Kirby, Dio. Cant. 1818. (Patron, the present V; Tithe—Imp. 970*l* 18*s* 2*d*, V. 266*l*; Glebe, 34 acres; V.'s Inc. 290*l* and Ho; Pop. 867.) R. of Lower Hardres, Kent, Dio. Cant. 1827. (Patron, St. John's Coll. Ox; Tithe, 413*l*; Glebe, 13½ acres; R.'s Inc. 438*l* and Ho; Pop. 233.) [9]

RASHLEIGH, George Cumming, *Hamble-le-Rice, Southampton.*—New Coll. Ox. B.A. 1813, M.A. 1817; Deac. and Pr. 1815. Chap. of Don. of Hamble-le-Rice, Dio. Win. 1850. (Patron, Win. Coll; Tithe, Imp. 136*l*; Chap.'s Inc. 184*l*; Pop. 409.) Fell. of Win. Coll. Formerly Fell. and Sen. Proctor of New Coll. Ox. 1826; P. C. of Hound 1850. [10]

RASHLEIGH, Henry Burville, *Horton-Kirby, Dartford, Kent.*—Ex. Coll. Ox. B.A. 1842; Deac. 1844, Pr. 1845. C. of Horton-Kirby. [11]

RASHLEIGH, Stanhope, *St. Wenn Vicarage, Bodmin, Cornwall.*—Magd. Hall. Ox. B.A. 1852; Deac. 1852, Pr. 1853. V. of St. Wenn, Dio. Ex. 1853. (Patron, William Rashleigh, Esq; Tithe—Imp. 181*l*, V. 161*l*; Glebe, 128 acres; V.'s Inc. 265*l* and Ho; Pop. 580.) Formerly C. of Harberton, Devon, 1852–53. [12]

RATCLIFF, W. H.—C. of St. Mary Magdalen's, Paddington, Lond. Formerly C. of St. Peter's, Leeds. [13]

RATCLIFFE, Thomas, 74, *Belgrave-road, London, S.W.*—St. John's Coll. Cam. Scho. of, Wrang. B.A. 1833, M.A. 1837, B.D. 1863; Deac. 1834 and Pr. 1835 by Bp of Lin. Dom. Chap. to Lord Churchill. Formerly Lect. and Sen. C. of Trinity, Newington, 1859–63, Min. of Berkeley Chapel, Mayfair, Lond. 1863–65. [14]

NN 2

RATE, John, *Lapley Vicarage, Penkridge, Staffs.*—St. Cath. Coll. Cam. B.A. 1840, M.A. 1843; Deac. 1840 and Pr. 1841 by Bp of Ex. V. of Lapley with Wheaton Aston C. Dio. Lich. 1848. (Patron, Major Swinfen; Tithe—Imp. 470*l*, V. 200*l*; Glebe, 22½ acres; V.'s Inc. 270 and Ho; Pop. 828.) Formerly C. of Mawgan and St. Martin, Cornwall, 1840–44; Asst. Min. of Belgrave Chapel, Lond. 1844–48. [15]

RATHBONE, David, *Ashworth Hall, near Rochdale.*—R. of Ashworth, Dio. Man. 1832. (Patron, Lord Egerton; R.'s Inc. 139*l*; Pop. 233.) Surrogate. [16]

RATHBONE, Hardwicke John Reeves, *Bringhurst, Rockingham, West Retford, Notts.*—Clare Coll. Cam. B.A. 1846; Deac. 1846 and Pr. 1847 by Bp of Lon. C. of Bringhurst, Leicestershire. Formerly C. of St. Botolph's, Bishopsgate, Lond. 1846, St. Martin's, Birmingham, 1848, Hasland, Chesterfield, 1851, St. Matthew's, Walsall, 1862, West Retford, Notts, 1863. [17]

RATHNA, George Adam, *St. Aidan's College, Birkenhead.* [18]

RATLIFFE, Thomas, *Godshill Vicarage, Isle of Wight.*—St. John's Coll. Cam. B.A. 1847, M.A. 1850; Deac. 1848, Pr. 1849. V. of Godshill, Dio. Win. 1867. (Patron, Queen's Coll. Ox; Pop. 1156.) Mast. of Godshill, Gr. Sch. Formerly C. of Godshill. [19]

RAVEN, Berney Wodehouse, 63, *Southwark-bridge-road, Southwark, London, S.E.*—St. John's Coll. Cam. B.A. 1858; Deac. 1860 by Bp of Win. C. of St. Peter's, Southwark, 1860. [20]

RAVEN, E., *Codsall, Wolverhampton.*—C. of Codsall. [21]

RAVEN, Eustace H., *Sedbergh, Yorks.*—C. of Sedbergh. [22]

RAVEN, James, *Swindon, Dudley.*—Dur. B.A. 1856, Licen. in Theol. 1857, M.A. 1859; Deac. 1857 by Abp of Cant. Pr. 1858 by Bp of Lich. P. C. of Swindon, Dio. Lich. 1867. (Patron, V. of Wombourn; P. C.'s Inc. 100*l* and Ho; Pop. 600.) Formerly C. of St. Mary's, Kingswinford, 1857–59, Alford 1859–62, Pendleton 1862–67. [23]

RAVEN, J., *Cowley, Cheltenham.*—C. of Cowley. [24]

RAVEN, John, *Mundford, Brandford, Norfolk.*—Emman. Coll. Cam. B.A. 1823; Deac. 1822, Pr. 1823. R. of Langford with Igburgh, Norfolk, Dio. Nor. 1839. (Patron, Lord Ashburton; Tithe, 248*l*; Glebe, 33¾ acres; R.'s Inc. 262*l* and Ho; Pop. Langford 62, Igburgh 192.) R. of Mundford, Dio. Nor. 1839. (Patron, Tidd Pratt, Esq; Tithe, 135*l*; Glebe, 20 acres; R.'s Inc. 140*l*; Pop. 376.) [25]

RAVEN, John James, 17, *South Quay, Great Yarmouth.*—Emman. Coll. Cam. Sen. Opt. B.A. 1857, M.A. 1860, B.D. 1867; Deac. 1857 and Pr. 1859 by Abp of Cant. Head Mast. of Great Yarmouth Gr. Sch. 1866; Min. of St. Mary's, Southtown, 1867. Formerly Asst. C. of Sevenoaks 1857–59; C. of Ellingham, near Bungay, 1862–66; 2nd Mast. of Sevenoaks Gr. Sch. 1857–59; Head Mast. of Bungay Gr. Sch. 1859–66. Contributor to the *Ecclesiastical and Architectural Topography of England*, J. H. Parker. [26]

RAVEN, Nicholas John, *Thornham, Lynn, Norfolk.*—Queens' Coll. Cam. B.A. 1838, M.A. 1841; Deac. 1838, Pr. 1840. V. of the Consolidated Livings of Thornham with Holme-next-the-Sea, Dio. Nor. 1846. (Patrons, Bp of Nor. and L'Estrange Ewen, Esq. alt; Thornham, Tithe—App. 480*l* and 4¾ acres of Glebe, V. 250*l*; Glebe, 14½ acres; Holme-next-the-Sea, Tithe—Imp. 283*l*, V. 170*l*; Glebe, 26 acres; V.'s Inc. 500*l*; Pop. Thornham 728, Holme-next-the-Sea 305.) [27]

RAVEN, Thomas Milville, *Crakehall Parsonage, Bedale, Yorks.*—Deac. 1850 and Pr. 1852 by Bp of Herf. P. C. of Crakehall, Dio. Rip. 1867. (Patron, R. of Bedale; P. C.'s Inc. 100*l* and Ho; Pop. 817.) Chap. to the Earl of Buchan. Formerly C. in sole charge of Scruton, Bedale. [28]

RAVEN, Vincent, *Great Fransham Rectory, Dereham, Norfolk.*—Magd. Coll. Cam. Scho. of, 1834, 10th Wrang. and B.A. 1837, M.A. 1840; Deac. 1838 and

Pr. 1839 by Bp of Ely. R. of Great Fransham, Dio. Nor. 1853. (Patron, Magd. Coll. Cam; Tithe, 534*l*; Glebe, 62½ acres; R.'s Inc. 630*l* and Ho; Pop. 295.) Hon. Fell. of King's Coll. Lond. Formerly Fell. of Magd. Coll. Cam. 1837, Dean 1844, Tut. 1846, President 1850. [1]

RAVEN, Wodehouse Berney Atkyns, *Christchurch Parsonage, Streatham-hill, Surrey, S.*—Trin. Coll. Cam. B.A. 1829, Tyrrwhitt's Heb. Scho. 1829, M.A. 1832; Deac. 1829 by Bp of Ely, Pr. 1831 by Bp of Nor. P. C. of Ch. Ch. Streatham, Dio. Win. 1841. (Patron, R. of Streatham; P. C.'s Inc. 600*l* and Ho; Pop. 2004.) Chap. to the Earl of Cadogan 1838. [2]

RAVENHILL, Henry Everett, *The Vicarage, Buckland Newton, Dorchester.*—Univ. Coll. Ox. 2nd cl. in Law and History, B.A. 1855, M.A. 1858; Deac. 1856 and Pr. 1857 by Bp of B. and W. V. of Buckland Newton with Plush C. Dio. Salis. 1860. (Patrons, D. and C. of Wells; Tithe, 560*l*; Glebe, 19 acres; V.'s Inc. 585*l* and Ho; Pop. 972.) Formerly C. of St. Cuthbert's, Wells, 1856–60. [3]

RAVENHILL, Thomas Holmes, *Arlingham Vicarage, Stonehouse, Glouc.*—Wor. Coll. Ox. B.A. 1843, M.A. 1845; Deac. 1843 and Pr. 1844 by Bp of Salis. V. of Arlingham, Dio. G. and B. 1848. (Patron, John Sayer, Esq; Glebe, 136 acres; V.'s Inc. 250*l* and Ho; Pop. 594.) [4]

RAVENSHAW, Thomas Fitz - Arthur Torin, *Pewsey Rectory, Marlborough.*—Oriel Coll. Ox. B.A. 1851, M.A. 1854; Deac. 1853 and Pr. 1855 by Bp of Ex. R. of Pewsey, Dio. Salis. 1857. (Patron, Earl of Radnor; Tithe, 1011*l*; Glebe, 125 acres; R.'s Inc. 1250*l* and Ho; Pop. 2200.) Formerly C. of Ilfracombe 1854–56, Author, *A New List of the Flowering Plants and Ferns growing wild in the County of Devon*, Bosworth, 1860, 4*s* 6*d*; Co-Editor, *The Festival Psalter, being the Proper Psalms for the Four Great Feasts, adapted to Gregorian Tones*, Masters, 1864, 1*s*. [5]

RAW, Joseph Carter, *Ainderby-Steeple, Northallerton, Yorks.*—Queens' Coll. Cam. B.A. 1841; Deac. 1841, Pr. 1842. V. of Ainderby, Dio. Rip. 1849. (Patron, Ld Chan; Tithe—Imp. 511*l* 9*s*; Glebe, 68 acres; V.'s Inc. 200*l*; Pop. 848.) [6]

RAWDON, James Hamer, *Astbury, Congleton.*—Brasen. Coll. Ox. 2nd cl. Lit. Hum. Hon. 4th cl. Math. B.A. 1858, M.A. 1861; Deac. 1863 by Bp of Man. Pr. 1866 by Bp of Ches. C. of Astbury 1865. Formerly Fell. of St. Peter's Coll. Radley, 1861–62; C. of Halton, Lancashire, 1863–64. [7]

RAWES, John, *Alveston, near Bristol.*—Corpus Coll. Cam. Mawson Scho. 1st Prizeman, B.A. 1826; Deac. 1826, Pr. 1827. P. C. of Alveston, Dio. G. and B. 1846. (Patrons, D. and C. of Bristol; Tithe—App. 160*l*, P. C. 332*l* 10*s*; P. C.'s Inc. 420*l*; Pop. 841.) [8]

RAWES, William Francis, 7, *Palace Garden Terrace, Kensington, W.*—Caius Coll. Cam. B.A. 1837, M.A. 1841; Deac. 1841 and Pr. 1842 by Bp of Herf. Formerly P. C. of St. John's Wembley, Middlesex, 1853–57. [9]

RAWLINGS, James, *St. Pinnock, near Liskeard.*—Queens' Coll. Cam. Scho. of, B.A. 1826, M.A. 1829; Deac. 1826 and Pr. 1827 by Bp of Ex. R. of St. Pinnock, Dio. Ex. 1835. (Patrons, Trustees; Tithe, 285*l*; Glebe, 50*l*; R.'s Inc. 335*l* and Ho; Pop. 513.) [10]

RAWLINGS, William, *Lansallos, West Looe, Cornwall.*—St. Edm. Hall, Ox. 2nd cl. Lit. Hum. and B.A. 1812; Deac. 1813, Pr. 1814. R. of Lansallos, Dio. Ex. 1822. (Patron, Francis Howell, Esq; Tithe, 500*l*; Glebe, 10 acres; R.'s Inc. 518*l* and Ho; Pop. 659.) Author, *Short Sermons*, 1835. [11]

RAWLINS, Charles, *Chaddesden, Derbyshire.*—Trin. Coll. Cam. B.A. 1835; Deac. 1835 by Bp of Nor. Pr. 1836 by Bp of Lin. P. C. of Chaddesden, Dio. Lich. 1851. (Patron, Sir R. Wilmot, Bart; Glebe, 24 acres; P. C.'s Inc. 100*l*; Pop. 465.) [12]

RAWLINS, Christopher, *Allerthorpe Vicarage, Pocklington, Yorks.*—Oriel Coll. Ox. B.A. 1832; Deac. 1833, Pr. 1834. V. of Thornton with Allerthorpe C. Dio. York, 1836. (Patron, Abp of York: Thornton, Tithe—App. 281*l* 5*s*, V. 92*l*; Allerthorpe, Tithe—App. 185*l* 7*s* 4*d*, V. 60*l* 3*s* 8*d*; Glebe, 3 acres; V.'s Inc. 217*l* and Ho; Pop. Thornton 851, Allerthorpe 205.) [13]

RAWLINS, Francis John, *Windsor.*—St. Peter's Coll. Cam. B.A. 1849, M.A. 1854; Deac. 1850 and Pr. 1853 by Bp of Pet. Formerly R. of Fiddington, Somerset, 1855–59. Author, *England's Welcome to the Princess Alexandra* (a Poem), 1863; *Notes on Virginia Water*, 1866, 6*d*. [14]

RAWLINS, James, *Mansfield, Notts.*—St. John's Coll. Ox. B.A. 1812, M.A. 1825; Deac. 1815 by Abp of York, Pr. 1821 by Bp of Ches. C. of Upper Langwith, Derbyshire. [15]

RAWLINS, John Arthur, *Stinchcombe, Dursley, Gloucestershire.*—New Coll. Ox. B.A. 1863, M.A. 1867; Deac. 1865, Pr. 1866. C. of Stinchcombe 1865. [16]

RAWLINS, Richard Randall, *Kneeton Parsonage, Bingham, Notts.*—St. John's Coll. Ox. B.A. 1804; Deac. 1811 and Pr. 1812 by Abp of York. P. C. of Kneeton, Dio. Lin. 1836. (Patroness, Countess of Carnarvon; Tithe, Imp. 3*l* 15*s*; P. C.'s Inc. 57*l* and Ho; Pop. 116.) [17]

RAWLINS, Thomas Samuel Fraser, *Denchworth Vicarage, Wantage, Berks.*—Wor. Coll. Ox. 1848, 2nd cl. Lit. Hum. and B.A. 1852, M.A. 1854; Deac. 1853 by Bp of Ox. Pr. 1854 by Bp of Lich. V. of Denchworth, Dio. Ox. 1858. (Patron, Wor. Coll. Ox; Tithe, 82*l* 10*s*; V.'s Inc. 155*l* and Ho; Pop. 257.) Formerly C. of Clifton Campville, Staffs, 1854–58; Fell. of Wor. Coll. Ox. 1853–62. [18]

RAWLINSON, George, *Oxford.*—Ex. Coll. Ox. 1st cl. Lit. Hum. 1838, Denyer Theol. Prize 1842 and 1843, B.A. 1838, M.A. 1841; Deac. 1841 and Pr. 1842 by Bp of Ex. Camden Prof. of Ancient History, Oxford, 1861. Formerly C. of Merton, Oxon, 1846–47; Cl. Moderator, Ox. 1850, Cl. Examiner 1854 and 1856; Bampton Lect. 1859. Author, *Translation of Herodotus, with Copious Notes*, 4 vols. Murray, 1858–60, 2nd ed. 1862; *The Historical Evidences of the Truth of the Scripture Records, being the Bampton Lectures for* 1859, Murray, 1859, 2nd ed. 1860; *The Contrasts of Christianity with Heathen and Jewish Systems, in Eight Sermons preached before the University of Oxford*, Longmans, 1861; *The Five Great Monarchies of the Ancient Eastern World*, 4 vols. Murray, 1862–67. [19]

RAWLINSON, Henry, *Symondsbury Rectory, Bridport, Dorset.*—St. John's Coll. Ox; Deac. 1837 and Pr. 1838 by Bp of Salis. R. of Symondsbury, Dio. Salis. 1863. (Patroness, Mrs. Bower; Tithe, 770*l*; Glebe, 132 acres; R.'s Inc. 1100*l* and Ho; Pop. 1352.) Formerly C. of Symondsbury, Dorset. [20]

RAWNSLEY, Robert Drummond Burrell, *Halton Holgate Rectory, near Spilsby.*—Magd. Coll. Ox. B.A. 1840, M.A. 1843; Deac. 1841, Pr. 1842. R. of Halton Holgate, Dio. Lin. 1861. (Patron, Lord Willoughby d'Eresby; R.'s Inc. 300*l*; Pop. 531.) Formerly Fell. of Magd. Coll. Ox; V. of Shiplake 1849. Author, *Village Sermons*, 1848; *Sermons, chiefly Catechetical, intended for Parochial Lending Libraries*, 1851, 6*s*; *Village Sermons*, 2nd Series, 1853, 5*s* 6*d*; *Sermons preached in Country Churches*, 1858. [21]

RAWSON, Arthur, *Bromley-common, Kent, S.E.*—Trin. Coll. Cam. M.A; Deac. 1841, Pr. 1842. P. C. of Trinity, Bromley, Dio. Cant. 1843. (Patron, Bp of Wor; P. C.'s Inc. 128*l* and Ho; Pop. 1163.) Formerly C. of Bromsgrove, Worcestershire, 1842. [22]

RAWSON, William, *Seaforth Parsonage, Liverpool.*—Magd. Coll. Cam. B.A. 1815, M.A. 1818; Deac. 1815 at B. and W. Pr. 1815 at Ches. P. C. of Seaforth, Dio. Ches. 1815. (Patron, R. of Sefton; Glebe, 1½ acre; P. C's Inc. 178*l* and Ho; Pop. 2235.) Formerly C. of Wellington, Somerset, 1815. [23]

RAWSON, William, *Aylesbury.*—St. John's Coll. Cam. B.A. 1843, M.A. 1847; Deac. 1842, Pr. 1843. Chap. of the County Gaol, Aylesbury. Formerly C. of Aylesbury. [24]

RAWSTORNE, Robert Atherton, *Balderstone, near Blackburn.*—Brasen. Coll. Ox. B.A. 1846, M.A. 1849; Deac. 1848 and Pr. 1849 by Bp of Man. P. C. of Balderstone, Dio. Man. 1859. (Patron, V. of

Blackburn; P. C.'s Inc. 160*l* and Ho; Pop. 582.) Formerly P. C. of Penwortham, Lanc. 1852–58. [1]

RAWSTORNE, William Edward, *Penwortham, Preston.*—Ch. Ch. Ox. 1st cl. Lit. Hum. B.A. 1842, M.A. 1843; Deac. 1844 by Bp of Ox. Pr. 1845 by Bp of Pet. P. C. of Penwortham, Dio. Man. 1858. (Patron, Lawrence Rawstorne, Esq; Tithe, 35*l*; Glebe, 60*l*; P. C.'s Inc. 180*l*; Pop. 1560.) Formerly R. of Galby, Leic. 1845–50; V. of Ormskirk, Lanc. 1850–53. [2]

RAY, George, *Stathern Rectory, Melton-Mowbray, Leicestershire.*—St. Peter's Coll. Cam. 25th Wrang. and B.A. 1832; Deac. 1833, Pr. 1834. R. of Stathern, Dio. Pet. 1844. (Patron, St. Peter's Coll. Cam; Glebe, 342 acres; R.'s Inc. 620*l* and Ho; Pop. 524.) Formerly Fell. of St. Peter's Coll. Cam. [3]

RAY, Henry, *Hunston, Stowmarket, Suffolk.*—Emman. Coll. Cam. B.A. 1837. P. C. of Hunston, Dio. Ely, 1839. (Patron, J. H. Heigham, Esq; Tithe, Imp. 228*l* 15*s*; P. C.'s Inc. 75*l*; Pop. 172.) [4]

RAY, Henry, *Badwell-Ash, Ixworth, Suffolk.*—Emman. Coll. Cam. B.A. 1837; Deac. 1837 and Pr. 1839 by Bp of Nor. P. C. of Badwell-Ash, Dio. Ely, 1846. (Patroness, Miss Clough; Tithe—App. 6*s* 8*d*, Imp. 357*l* 1*s* 4*d*; P. C.'s Inc. 72*l*; Pop. 527.) Lect. of Ashfield 1846. (Value, 76*l*.) [5]

RAY, Joseph, *Ashton-upon-Mersey, near Manchester.*—R. of Ashton, Dio. Ches. 1866. (Patron, Rev. C. B. Sowerby; Tithe, 699*l*; Glebe, 27 acres; R.'s Inc. 800*l* and Ho; Pop. 1476.) Chap. to Lord Leigh. Formerly C. of St. Philip's, Birmingham. [6]

RAY, Philip William, *Greensted Rectory, Ongar, Essex.*—Clare Hall, Cam. B.A. 1829, M.A. 1832; Deac. 1829, Pr. 1830. R. of Greensted, Dio. Roch. 1837. (Patron, Bp of Lon. in Trust; Tithe, 200*l*; Glebe, 29 acres; R.'s Inc. 270*l* and Ho; Pop. 125.) [7]

RAYMOND, John Mayne St. Clere, *Belchamp Hall, Sudbury.*—Dur. B.A. 1837, M.A. 1840; Deac. 1838 and Pr. 1839 by Bp of Dur. Formerly V. of Dinnington, Northumberland, 1847–58; C. of Borley, Suffolk, 1859. [8]

RAYMOND, Oliver, *Middleton Rectory (Essex), near Sudbury.*—Trin. Hall, Cam. LL.B. 1816; Deac. 1817, Pr. 1818. R. of Middleton, Dio. Roch. 1820. (Patron, the present R; Tithe, 400*l*; Glebe, 40 acres; R.'s Inc. 520*l* and Ho; Pop. 138.) V. of Bulmer with Belchamp-Water, Essex, Dio. Roch. 1826. (Patron, S. M. Raymond, Esq; Bulmer, Tithe—Imp. 662*l*, V. 330*l*; Glebe, 3 acres; Belchamp-Water, Tithe—App. 8*s*, Imp. 655*l* 7*s*, V. 194*l* 8*s* 8*d*; Glebe, 2 acres; V.'s Inc. 588*l*; Pop. Bulmer 758, Belchamp-Water 708.) Rural Dean of Belchamp. [9]

RAYMOND, Oliver Edward, *Bulmer near Sudbury, Suffolk.*—Clare Coll. Cam. B.A. 1849, M.A. 1852; Deac. 1850, Pr. 1851. C. of Bulmer 1859. Formerly C. of Monks-Eleigh, Suffolk. [10]

RAYMOND, Samuel.—Hon. Can. of Gloucester 1850. [11]

RAYMOND, William Francis, *Stockton Rectory, Tenbury, Worcestershire.*—St. Peter's Coll. Cam. B.A. 1830, M.A. 1833; Deac. 1830 and Pr. 1831 by Bp of Bristol. R. of Stockton, Dio. Herf. 1834. (Patron, the present R; Tithe, 220*l*; Glebe, 21 acres; R.'s Inc. 250*l* and Ho; Pop. 129.) V. of Wilsford, Wilts, Dio. Salis. 1835. (Patron, Mast. of St. Nicholas Hospital, Salisbury; Tithe—App. 52*l*, Imp. 217*l*, V. 125*l*; Glebe, 2 acres; V.'s Inc. 250*l* and Ho; Pop. 521.) Rural Dean of Burford, Dio. Herf. 1839; Dioc. Inspector of Schs. 1849; Preb. of Herf. 1857. [12]

RAYNBIRD, Robert, *Wentworth Rectory, near Ely.*—Ch. Coll. Cam. B.A. 1843, M.A. 1846; Deac. 1844 by Bp of Ely, Pr. 1845 by Bp of Herf. R. of Wentworth, Dio. Ely, 1859. (Patrons, D. and C. of Ely; Tithe, 450*l*; Glebe, 19 acres; R.'s Inc. 487*l* and Ho; Pop. 180.) Formerly C. of Stretham, near Ely, 1844–59. [13]

RAYNES, William, *Clare College, Cambridge.*—Clare Coll. Cam. Browne's Medallist 1850, Jun. Opt. in Maths. and 1st cl. Cl. Trip. 1852, B.A. 1852, M.A. 1855; Deac. 1854 and Pr. 1856 by Bp of Ely. Fell. and Tut. of Clare Coll. Cam. Formerly C. of Witham, Essex, 1855–63. [14]

RAYNOR, George, *Kelvedon Hatch, near Brentwood, Essex.*—Clare Hall, Cam. B A. 1849; Deac. 1849, Pr. 1850. C. of Kelvedon Hatch. Formerly C. of Totternhoe, Beds. [15]

RAYSON, William, *Elmfield, Worcester.*—Magd. Hall, Ox. B.A. 1856, M.A. 1858; Deac. 1855 and Pr. 1856 by Bp of Pet. Min. Can. and Sacristan of Wor. Cathl. 1862. (Value, 165*l*.) Formerly C. of St. Margaret's, Leicester, 1855–56, Kemerton 1856–60, Aldridge 1861–62. [16]

READ, Alexander, *Hyde, Manchester.*—Dub. A.B. 1842; Deac. 1843 by Bp of Tuam, Pr. 1844 by Bp of Down and Connor. P. C. of Hyde, Dio. Ches. 1849. (Patron, R. of Stockport; P. C.'s Inc. 300*l*; Pop. 8287.) Surrogate. Formerly C. of Runcorn, Cheshire, 1844–46; P. C. of St. Thomas's, Hyde, 1846–49. [17]

READ, A. P.—C. of Trinity, Gray's-inn-road, Lond. [18]

READ, George, 14, *South Hunter-street, Liverpool.*—Dub. A.B. 1862, A.M. 1865; Deac. 1864 and Pr. 1865 by Bp of Ches. C. of St. Mark's, Liverpool, 1864. [19]

READ, George, *St. Paul's Parsonage, Liverpool.*—P. C. of St. Paul's, Liverpool, 1850. (Patron, G. Ramsden, Esq; P. C.'s Inc. 200*l* and Ho.) [20]

READ, George Preston, *Clapton, London, N.E.*—C. of St. James's, Clapton. [21]

READ, Henry Newport, *St. James's, Exeter.*—Emman. Coll. Cam. Exhib. of B.A. 1849; Deac. 1849 and Pr. 1850 by Bp of Nor. Formerly C. of Earlham with Bowthorpe, near Norwich, 1849–51; 2nd Mast. of Oundle Gr. Sch. Northants, 1851–52; 2nd Mast of Gr. Sch. and Asst. Chap. of St. John's Chapel, Exeter, 1852–59. [22]

READ, Josiah, *South Hylton, Sunderland.*—Dub. A.B. LL.B. C. of South Hylton. [23]

READ, Stephen Gooch, *Alderwasley Parsonage, Wirksworth, Derbyshire.*—Corpus Coll. Cam. B.A. 1855, M.A. 1858; Deac. 1856 and Pr. 1857 by Bp of Roch. R. of Barton Bendish St. Mary with All Saints' R. Stoke Ferry, Norfolk, Dio. Nor. 1865. (Patron, Sir Hanson Berney, Bart; Tithe, comm. for 330 acres; R.'s Inc. 316*l* and Ho; Pop. 495.) Chap. of D. of Alderwasley, Dio. Lich. 1864. (Patron, A. F. Hurt, Esq; Chap.'s Inc. 120*l* and Ho; Pop. 372.) Formerly C. of Hitchin, Herts, 1856–64. [24]

READ, Thomas Frederick Rudston, *Withyham Rectory, Tunbridge Wells.*—Univ. Coll. Ox. B.A. 1830, M.A. 1834; Deac. and Pr. 1835. R. of Withyham, Dio. Chich. 1865. (Patron, Earl Delawarr; Tithe, 600*l*; R.'s Inc. 600*l* and Ho; Pop. 1570.) Formerly R. of Winteringham, Lin. [25]

READ, William, *Worthing, Sussex.*—St. John's Coll. Cam. B.A. 1844, M.A. 1847; Deac. 1845 and Pr. 1846 by Bp of Ches. Chap. of the Chapel of Ease, Worthing, Dio. Chich. 1852. (Patron, R. of Worthing; Chap.'s Inc. 150*l*.) Fell. of the Royal Astronomical Soc. and Royal Microscopical Soc. [26]

READE, Compton, *Magdalen College, Oxford.*—Magd. Coll. Ox. B.A. 1857, M.A. 1859; Deac. 1857 and Pr. 1858 by Bp of Ox. V. of Cassington, Dio. Ox. 1867. (Patron, Ch. Ch. Ox; Glebe, 128 acres; V.'s Inc. 450*l*.) Chap. of Magd. Coll. 1858 and Ch. Ch. Ox. 1862. Formerly C. of Burford 1858, and of Summertown, Oxon, 1861. [27]

READE, Frederick, *Hove, near Brighton.*—St. John's Coll. Cam. B.A. 1830, M.A. 1833; Deac. 1831, Pr. 1832. C. of St. John the Baptist's, Hove, Dio. Chich. 1854. (Patron, V. of Preston.) [28]

READE, George E. P., *Garden Lane, Chester.*—Dub. A.B. 1864; Deac. 1865 and Pr. 1866 by Bp of Ches. C. of St. Mary's-on-the-Hill, Chester, 1866. Formerly C. of St. Peter's, Chester, 1865. [29]

READE, John Chorley, *The Elms, West Derby, near Liverpool.*—St. John's Coll. Cam. B.A. 1852, M.A. 1855; Deac. 1852 and Pr. 1853 by Bp of Ches. Formerly Asst. C. of Ch. Ch. Tintwistle, Cheshire, 1852–

53; Asst. C. of St. Mary-the-Virgin's, West Derby, 1853–61. [1]

READE, Joseph Bancroft, *Bishopsbourne Rectory, Canterbury.*—Caius Coll. Cam. Sen. Opt. and B A. 1825, M.A. 1828; Deac. 1825 and Pr. 1826 by Bp of Lin. F.R.S. R. of Bishopsbourne, Dio. Cant. 1863. (Patron, Abp of Cant; R.'s Inc. 600*l* and Ho; Pop. 416.) Formerly V. of Stone, Bucks, 1839–59; R. of Ellesborough, Bucks, 1859–63. Author, various Papers in the Proceedings of Philosophical Socs. [2]

READE, Richard, *Barkstone Rectory, Grantham.*—Caius Coll. Cam. B.A. 1826. R. of Barkstone, Dio. Lin. 1850. (Patron, the Preb. of North Grantham, in Salis. Cathl; Tithe, 610*l*; Glebe, 18½ acres; R.'s Inc. 633*l* and Ho; Pop. 540.) [3]

READE, William, *Ollerton, Notts.*—St. Cath. Coll. Cam. B.A. 1844, M.A. 1847; Deac. 1844 and Pr. 1847 by Bp of Lin. C. (sole charge) of Ollerton 1859. Formerly C. of Great Catworth, Hants, 1852–58. [4]

READY, Henry, *Hickling, Stalham, Norfolk.*—St. John's Coll. Cam. B.A. 1836; Deac. 1836, Pr. 1837. R. of Waxham with Palling V. Norfolk, Dio. Nor. 1841. (Patron, H. J. Conyers, Esq; Tithe—App. 90*l*, Imp. 162*l* 14*s*, R. 343*l*; Glebe, 20½ acres; R.'s Inc. 464*l* and Ho; Pop. Waxham 75, Palling 442.) [5]

REAVELY, Francis Fenwick, *Kinnersley Rectory, Letton, Herefordshire.*—Trin. Coll. Cam. S.C.L. 1854; Deac. 1854 by Bp of Lin. Pr. 1858 by Bp of Nor. R. of Kinnersley, Dio. Herf. 1858. (Patron, Thomas Reavely, Esq; Glebe, 15 acres; R.'s Inc. 420*l* and Ho; Pop. 280.) [6]

REAY, Thomas Osmotherley, *Hampton Lucy, Warwick.*—Ex. Coll. Ox. B.A. 1857; Deac. 1858; Pr. 1859. C. of Hampton Lucy, 1860. Formerly C. of All Saints', Wellington, Salop, 1858. [7]

REDFERN, Robert Scarr, *Acton Vicarage, Nantwich, Cheshire.*—Queen's Coll. Ox. B.A. 1844, M.A. 1848; Deac. 1845, Pr. 1846. V. of Acton, Dio. Ches. 1857. (Patron, J. Tollemache, Esq; Glebe, 8 acres; V.'s Inc. 627*l* and Ho; Pop. 3125.) Formerly C. of St. Pancras, Lond. [8]

REDFERN, William Thomas, *St. James's Parsonage, Taunton.*—Magd. Hall, Ox. B.A. 1845, M.A. 1846; Deac. 1842, Pr. 1844. P. C. of St. James's, Taunton, Dio. B. and W. 1845. (Patroness, Mrs. S. Cottle; P. C.'s Inc. 260*l* and Ho; Pop. 5136.) Surrogate. [9]

REDFORD, Francis, *St. Paul's Parsonage, Holme-Cultram, Wigton, Cumberland.*—Deac. 1843, Pr. 1844. P. C. of Holme-Low, or Holme St. Paul's, Dio. Carl. 1850. (Patron, P. C. of Holme-Cultram; Glebe, 3 acres; P. C.'s Inc. 120*l* and Ho; Pop. 1521.) Surrogate. [10]

REDHEAD, John Roberts, *Thurnby Vicarage, Leicester.*—St. Edm. Hall, Ox. B.A. 1828; Deac. 1828 by Bp of Roch. Pr. 1830 by Bp of Ches. V. of Thurnby with Stoughton, Dio. Pet. 1832. (Patron, Hon. H. L. Powys Keck, Esq; Thurnby, Tithe—Imp. 67*l* 10*s*, V. 45*l*; Glebe, 2 acres; Stoughton, Tithe—Imp. 220*l*, V. 110*l*; Bushby, Tithe—Imp. 9*l*, V. 50*l*; Glebe, 2 acres; V.'s Inc. 263*l* and Ho; Pop. 375.) [11]

REDHEAD, Theodore John, *Emery Down, Lyndhurst, Hants.*—St. Edm. Hall, Ox. B.A. 1851; M.A. 1856; Deac. 1853 and Pr. 1854 by Bp of Pet. P. C. of Emery Down, Dio. Win. 1864. (Patron, Admiral Boultbee; P. C.'s Inc. 67*l*; Pop. 450.) Chap. of the New Forest Union 1862. Formerly C. of St. Margaret's, Leicester, and of Eling, Hants. [12]

REDHEAD, Thomas Fisher, *Rock-Ferry, Higher Bebington, Birkenhead.*—Dub. Moderator in Science and A.B. 1834; Deac. 1834 and Pr. 1835 by Bp of Ches. P. C. of Higher Bebington, Dio. Ches. 1842. (Patrons, Trustees; Tithe—App. 140*l*; Glebe, ½ acre; P. C.'s Inc. 160*l* and Ho; Pop. 2800.) Author, *Holy Actions and Holy Thoughts the Youth's best Safeguard; Holy Rules of Living essential to Living a Holy Life;* etc. [13]

REDIFER, Alfred, *Finstock Parsonage, near Charlbury, Oxon.*—St. Mary Hall, Ox. B.A. 1852, M.A. 1855; Deac. 1853 and Pr. 1854 by Bp of Pet. P. C. of Finstock with Fawler, Dio. Ox. 1863. (Patron, St. John's Coll. Ox; Tithe, 75*l*; P. C.'s Inc. 75*l* and Ho; Pop. 676.) Formerly C. of Daventry 1853, Hurstpierpoint 1859, Quainton, Bucks (sole charge), 1860. [14]

REDKNAP, William Henry, *Ryde, Isle of Wight.*—Deac. 1850 and Pr. 1852 by Bp of Chich. P. C. of St. James's, Ryde, Dio. Win. 1865. Formerly C. of Portsea; P. C. of Milton, Hants, 1859. Author, *Advent Lectures.* [15]

REDPATH, George D.—C. of Putney, Surrey. [16]

REECE, James, *Braithwell Rectory, Rotherham.*—Deac. 1823 and Pr. 1824 by Abp of York. V. of Braithwell, Dio. York, 1851. (Patron, Ld Chan; Tithe—Imp. 370*l*, R. 269*l*, V. 87*l*; Glebe, 8 acres; V.'s Inc. 305*l* and Ho; Pop. 757.) [17]

REECE, R. M.—C. of Barton-upon-Humber, Lincolnshire. [18]

REECE, William, *Chicklade, near Hindon, Wilts.*—Queens' Coll. Cam. B.A. 1849; Deac. 1852 and Pr. 1853 by Bp of Lin. R. of Pertwood, Dio. Salis. 1863. (Patroness, Mrs. Seymour; Tithe, 80*l*; R.'s Inc. 86*l* 10*s*; Pop. 30.) Formerly C. of Owmby, Lincoln, 1852–54, Chicklade 1854–63. [19]

REED, Christopher, *Chirton House, Tynemouth.*—Ex. Coll. Ox. B.A. 1820, M.A. 1828; Deac. 1828 and Pr. 1829 by Bp of Dur. V. of Tynemouth, Dio. Dur. 1830. (Patron, Duke of Northumberland; Tithe—Imp. 1157*l* 9*s* 8*d*, Churchwardens of Tynemouth, in trust for the Vicar and Poor, 69*l* 11*s* 3*d*; V.'s Inc. 300*l*; Pop. 13,152.) [20]

REED, Edward, 26, *Royal-crescent, Notting-hill, London, W.*—St. John's Coll. Cam. B.A. 1816, M.A. 1819; Deac. 1817 and Pr. 1818 by Bp of Lin. Formerly C. of St. Vedast's, Foster-lane, and Lect. of St. Magnus-the-Martyr's, Lond. [21]

REED, George Varenne, *Hayes Rectory, Bromley, Kent, S.E.*—Jesus Coll. Cam. B.A. 1837, M.A 1840; Deac. 1837, Pr. 1838. R. of Hayes, Dio. Cant. 1854. (Patron, Abp of Cant; Tithe, 230*l*; Glebe, 18 acres; R.'s Inc. 260*l* and Ho; Pop. 598.) Sec. to S.P.G. for the Deanery of West Dartford. Formerly C. of Hayes 1837–39, Tingewick, Bucks, 1839–54. [22]

REED, John, *Newburn Vicarage, Blaydon-on-Tyne.*—Trin. Coll. Cam. B.A. 1825; Deac. 1826 and Pr. 1827 by Bp of Dur. V. of Newburn with Holy Trinity C. and St. Saviour's C. Dio. Dur. 1832. (Patron, Bp of Dur; Tithe—App. 1491*l* 7*s* 10*d*, V. 132*l* 5*s* 10*d*; V.'s Inc. 300*l* and Ho; Pop. 4619.) Lect. of St. Nicholas', Newcastle-on-Tyne, 1832. Formerly C. of Byton, 1826–32. [23]

REED, William, *Training College, Carmarthen.*—Queen's Coll. Ox. B.A. 1833, M.A. 1848; Deac. 1833 by Bp of Lon. Pr. 1834 by Bp of Jamaica. Prin. of the Training Coll. Carmarthen, 1848. Formerly Military Chap. at Fort Augusta, Jamaica, 1834–37; Chap. to the Bp of Jamaica and Deputy Registrar of the Dio. of Jamaica 1836–41; Prin. of the York and Ripon Diocesan Training Schs. 1841–48. [24]

REES, Charles Davies, *Llanwrthwl Rhayader, Brecknockshire.*—Jesus Coll. Ox. B.A. 1837; Deac. 1837 and Pr. 1838 by Bp of St. D. V. of Llanwrthwl, Dio. St. D. 1845. (Patron, Bp of St. D; Tithe—App. 185*l* 6*s* 8*d*, V. 92*l* 13*s*. 4*d*; V.'s Inc. 105*l*; Pop. 556.) [25]

REES, D.—C. of Llanrhaiadr, Glamorganshire. [26]

REES, David Morgan, *Aberporth, Cardigan.*—Deac. 1853, Pr. 1854. R. of Aberporth, Dio. St. D. 1862. (Patron, Bp of St. D; R.'s Inc. 150*l*; Pop. 454.) [27]

REES, Enoch, *Clydach, Swansea.*—Lampeter, Schs. 1836; Deac. 1837 and Pr. 1838 by Bp of St. D. P. C. of Clydach, Dio. St. D. 1847. (Patrons, the Crown and Bp of St. D. alt; P. C.'s Inc. 150*l*; Pop. 2942.) Formerly C. of Llangendeirne 1837, Llanon 1840, Corseinon, near Swansea, 1844. [28]

REES, George, *Llanrhidian, Swansea.*—V. of Llanrhidian with Penclawdd C. Dio. St. D. 1850. (Patrons, Trustees of G. Morgan, Esq; V.'s Inc. 100*l*; Pop. 1993.) [29]

REES, Henry Thomas, *Snaith, Yorks.*—St. Bees 1849. V. of Snaith, Dio. York, 1862. (Patron, G. J. Yarburgh, Esq; V.'s Inc. 500*l* and Ho; Pop. 1582.) Formerly V. of Teynham, Kent, 1856–62. [1]

REES, John, *Bangor, Aberystwith.*—Lampeter; Deac. 1848 and Pr. 1849 by Bp of St. D. P. C. of Bangor, Dio. St. D. 1854. (Patron, V. of Llanbadarnfawr; P. C.'s Inc. 119*l*; Pop. 1919.) Formerly C. of Llangan, Carmarthenshire, 1848–54. [2]

REES, John.—C. of Llanelly, Carmarthenshire. [3]

REES, M.—C. of Beaufort, near Tredegar, Mon. [4]

REES, Samuel George, *Wasing Rectory, near Reading.*—Jesus Coll. Ox. B.A. 1848, M.A. 1853; Deac. 1848 and Pr. 1851 by Bp of Lin. R. of Wasing, Dio. Ox. 1857. (Patron, W. Mount, Esq; Tithe, 94*l*; Glebe, 26 acres; R.'s Inc. 120*l* and Ho; Pop. 76.) [5]

REES, Thomas, *Llanishen Vicarage, Cardiff.*—Deac. 1849, Pr. 1850 by Bp of Llan. P. C. of Llanishen, Dio. Llan. 1862. (Patrons, Baroness Windsor, and C. K. K. Tynte, Esq. alt; Glebe, 3 acres; P. C.'s Inc. 60*l* and Ho; Pop. 300.) P. C. of Lisvane, Dio. Llan. 1862. (Patrons, Baroness Windsor, and C. K. K. Tynte, Esq. alt; P. C.'s Inc. 70*l*; Pop. 500.) Formerly C. of Llanvrechva 1849–54. [6]

REES, T. M., *St. Mellon's, Cardiff.*—C. of St. Mellon's. [7]

REES, William, 6, *Bridge-street, Cardigan.*—Lampeter, Bates' Prizeman 1861, Phillips' Scho. 1862; Sen. Scho. 1863; Deac. 1863 and Pr. 1864 by Bp of St. D. C. of St. Mary's, Cardigan, 1863. [8]

REES, William, *Llanboidy, St. Clears, Carmarthenshire.*—Deac. 1848 by Bp of Llan, Pr. 1850 by Bp of St. D. V. of Llanboidy, Dio. St. D. 1865. (Patron, Bp. of St. D; Tithe, 139*l* 10*s* 10*d*; V.'s Inc. 196*l* 10*s*; Pop. 1800.) Formerly P. C. of Bettws 1851. [9]

REES, William Davies, *Glyn Traian, near Llangollen, Denbighshire.*—Lampeter; Deac. 1841, Pr. 1843. P. C. of Glyn Traian *alias* Pontfadog, Dio. St. A. 1848. (Patron, Bp of St. A.; P. C.'s Inc. 126*l*; Pop. 1499.) [10]

REEVE, Abraham Charles, *Higham, near Colchester.*—Trin. Coll. Cam. B.A. 1832; Deac. 1833, Pr. 1834. P. C. of Higham, Dio. Nor. 1835. (Patrons, Trustees; Tithe, 220*l*; Glebe, 50 acres; P. C.'s Inc. 240*l* and Ho; Pop. 229.) [11]

REEVE, Edward James, *Stondon-Massey Rectory, Brentwood, Essex.*—St. Peter's Coll. Cam. B.A. 1844, M.A. 1847. R. of Stondon-Massey, Dio. Roch. 1849. (Patron, E. Reeve, Esq; Tithe, 336*l*; R.'s Inc. 468*l* and Ho; Pop. 273.) [12]

REEVE, Henry, *Gaol, Leeds.*—Ch. Miss. Coll; Deac. 1852 by Bp of Lon. Pr. 1853 by Bp of Victoria. Chap. of the Leeds Borough Gaol 1867. Formerly Miss. at Shanghae 1857–58; C. of Petworth, St. Agnes, 1859–61, Great Malvern 1861–65; Miss. to British Columbia 1865–67. [13]

REEVE, James Farr, *Thornham Rectory, Eye, Suffolk.*—Wad. Coll. Ox. B.A. 1840; Deac. 1841 and Pr. 1843 by Bp of Nor. R. of Thornham-Magna with Thornham-Parva, Dio. Nor. 1850. (Patron, Lord Henniker; Thornham-Magna, Tithe, 375*l*; Thornham-Parva, Tithe, 136*l*; R.'s Inc. 555*l* and Ho; Pop. Thornham-Magna 282, Thornham-Parva 124.) [14]

REEVE, John William, 112, *Harley-street, London, W.*—Trin. Coll. Cam. B.A. 1833, M.A. 1842; Deac. 1863, Pr. 1864. Min. of Portman Chapel, St. Marylebone, Lond. 1847. [15]

REEVES, Jonathan.—C. of Upper Beeding, Sussex. [16]

REIBEY, James H., *Denbury, Newton Abbott, Devon.*—R. of Denbury, Dio. Ex. 1859. (Patron, the present R; R.'s Inc. 180*l*; Pop. 419.) [17]

REICHEL, Oswald Joseph, *Oxhey Rise, near Watford.*—Queen's Coll. Ox. 2nd cl. Lit. Hum. B.A. 1863 M.A. 1866, B.C.L. 1867; Deac. and Pr. 1865. Vice-Prin. of Cuddesdon Theol. Coll. 1865. Formerly C. of North Hinksey, Berks, 1865. Author, *The Duties of the Church in Respect of Christian Missions* (Ellerton Prize Essay), 1866, Longmans, 1*s*; *Socrates and the Socratic Schools*, from the German of Dr. S. Zeller, Longmans, 1867. [18]

REID, Charles Burton, *Twickenham, Middlesex, S.W.*—St. John's Coll. Cam. Jun. Opt. and B.A. 1835, M.A. 1838; Deac. 1837 and Pr. 1838 by Bp of Lon. Chap. to H.M. Troops, Hounslow Barracks, and at Kneller Hall Military Sch. of Music. [19]

REID, Moses, *Minshull-Vernon, Middlewich, Cheshire.*—Deac. 1843, Pr. 1844. P. C. of Minshull-Vernon, Dio. Ches. 1845. (Patron, Bp of Ches; Tithe, Imp. 262*l* 2*s* 6*d*; P. C.'s Inc. 110*l*; Pop. 619.) [20]

RELTON, Edward William, *Ealing Vicarage, Middlesex, W.*—Pemb. Coll. Cam. Sen. Opt. 2nd cl. Cl. Trip. and B.A. 1839, M.A. 1842; Deac. 1840, Pr. 1841. V. of Ealing, Dio. Lon. 1853. (Patron, Bp of Lon; Tithe—App. 1000*l* and 67¾ acres of Glebe, V. 600*l*; Glebe, 5 acres; V.'s Inc. 750*l* and Ho; Pop. 1639.) Formerly C. of Sheffield and Vice-Prin. of Sheffield Coll. Sch. 1840–42; C. of St. Peter's, Stepney, 1843; P. C. of St. Bartholomew's, Bethnal Green, 1844–53; Rural Dean of Ealing 1859–63. Author, *Plain Lectures on Romanism*, 1850, 4*d*; *The Nature and Condition of Spirits*, Rivingtons, 1855, 1*s*; *Church Rates—What a Vestry can do and what it cannot do*, ib. 1856, 6*d*; *Scepticism and Faith, and the Reward of Faith, Fellowship with God*, Bell and Daldy, 1868, 6*d*; *Hints and Prayers for Sunday School Teachers, with Prayers for Sunday School Children*, Macintosh, 1863, 3*d*; Sundry Sermons on Church Education, Missionary Co-operation, Harvest, Marriage of the Prince of Wales, printed by request. [21]

REMFRY, William Henry, *Rayleigh, Essex.*—St. Aidan's; Deac. 1866 by Bp of Roch. C. of Rayleigh 1866. [22]

REMINGTON, F. H., *Wollaston, Shrewsbury.*—P. C. of Wollaston, Dio. Herf. 1864. (Patron, V. of Alberbury; P. C.'s Inc. 95*l*; Pop. 367.) [23]

REMINGTON, Reginald, *Crow Trees, Melling, Lancashire.*—Pemb. Coll. Ox. B.A. 1855, M.A. 1858, Theol. Coll. Cuddesdon; Deac. 1856 by Bp of Ox. Pr. 1857 by Bp of Roch. Formerly C. of Foxearth 1856, Middleton 1859, Downham (sole charge) 1860, Trinity, Southport, 1864; P. C. of Gilsland with Upper Denton, 1865–67. [24]

REMINGTON, Thomas Machell, *Arkholme Parsonage, Lancaster.*—Trin. Coll. Cam. B.A. 1859, M.A. 1863; Deac. 1860 and Pr. 1861 by Bp of Man. P. C. of Arkholme, Dio. Man. 1866. (Patron, V. of Melling; P. C.'s Inc. 80*l* and Ho; Pop. 331.) Formerly C. of Caton, Lanc. 1860–65; Harthill, near Sheffield, 1865–66. [25]

RENAUD, George, *Silsoe Parsonage, Beds.*—Corpus Coll. Ox. 2nd cl. Lit. Hum. and B.A. 1834, M.A. 1837; Deac. 1838, Pr. 1839. P. C. of Silsoe, Dio. Ely, 1864. (Patroness, Countess Cowper; P. C.'s Inc. 150*l* and Ho; Pop. 713.) [26]

RENAUD, William, *Salisbury.*—Ex. Coll. Ox. 3rd cl. Lit. Hum. and B.A. 1840, M.A. 1844; Deac. 1841, Pr. 1843. Preb. of Salis. Cathl; P. C. of St. Thomas's, Salisbury, Dio. Salis. 1863. (Patrons, D. and C. of Salis; P. C.'s Inc. 140*l*; Pop. 2215.) Lect. of St. Thomas's; Chap. to the Salisbury Union. Formerly C. of St. Thomas's, Salisbury. [27]

RENDALL, Frederick, *Harrow-on-the-Hill, Middlesex, N.W.*—Trin. Coll. Cam. B.A. 1845; Deac. and Pr. 1848. Mast. in Harrow Sch. Formerly Fell. of Trin. Coll. Cam. 1846–48. [28]

RENDALL, Henry, *Great Rollright Rectory, Chipping Norton, Oxon.*—Trin. Coll. Ox. 2nd cl. Lit. Hum. and B.A. 1840; Brasen. Coll. Ox. M.A. 1843; Deac. 1841 and Pr. 1842 by Bp of Ox. R. of Great Rollright, Dio. Ox. 1855. (Patron, Brasen. Coll. Ox; R.'s Inc. 250*l* and Ho; Pop. 410.) Formerly P. C. of Trinity, Stepney, Lond. 1847–55. [29]

RENDELL, Arthur Medland, *Elgin House, Highgate, N.*—Trin. Coll. Cam. 23rd Wrang; Deac. 1866 and Pr. 1867 by Bp of Lon. Assist. Mast. of Sir R. Cholmley's Sch. Highgate. Formerly C. of St. James's, Muswell-hill, 1866. [30]

RENDELL, Edward, *Bampton Vicarage, Tiverton, Devon.*—St. John's Coll. Cam. B.A. 1834; Deac. 1835, Pr. 1836. V. of Bampton, Dio. Ex. 1841. (Patron, Joseph Chichester Nagle, Esq; Tithe—Imp. 720*l*, V. 130*l*; Glebe, 2 acres; V.'s Inc. 130*l* and Ho; Pop. 1971.) Formerly C. of Cove Chapel, Tiverton, 1835–37, Seaton with Beer Chapel 1837–38, Rettendon, Essex, 1838–41. [1]

RENNISON, Thomas, *Queen's College, Oxford.*—Queen's Coll. Ox. 3rd cl. Lit. Hum. 2nd cl. Math. et Phy. and B.A. 1851, M.A. 1854. Fell. and Tut. of Queen's Coll. Ox. [2]

RENOUARD, George Cecil, *Swanscombe Rectory, Dartford, Kent.*—Sid. Coll. Cam. B.A. 1802, M.A. 1805, B.D. 1811. R. of Swanscombe, Dio. Roch. 1818. (Patron, Sid. Coll. Cam; Tithe, 650*l*; Glebe, 40 acres; R.'s Inc. 695*l* and Ho; Pop. 1473.) [3]

RENWICK, Thomas, *Shorwell, Newport, Isle of Wight.*—Ch. Ch. Ox. B.A. 1843; Deac. 1843 and Pr. 1844 by Bp of Ex. R. of Mottistone with Shorwell V. Isle of Wight, Dio. Win. 1854. (Patron, Brasen. Coll. Ox; Mottistone, Tithe—App. 14*l*, R. 200*l*; Glebe, 42½ acres; Shorwell, Tithe—App. 468*l* and 3 acres of Glebe, Imp. 288*l*, V. 192*l*; Glebe, 62 acres; R.'s Inc. 474*l* and Ho; Pop. Mottistone 160, Shorwell 612.) [4]

REVEL, Samuel, *Wingerworth, Chesterfield.*—St. John's Coll. Cam. B A. 1826, M.A. 1829; Deac. 1826 and Pr. 1827 by Bp of Lich. R. of Wingerworth, Dio. Lich. 1828. (Patron, Bp of Lich. Tithe, 248*l* 10*s* and 34*l* 10*s*; Glebe, 14½ acres; Pop. 433.) [5]

REW, Charles, *Cranham Rectory, Romford, Essex.*—St. John's Coll. Ox. B.A. 1834, M.A. 1838, B.D. 1843; Deac. 1837 and Pr. 1838 by Bp of Ox. R. of Cranham, Dio. Roch. 1860. (Patron, St. John's Coll. Ox; Tithe, 560*l*; Glebe, 38 acres; R.'s Inc. 650*l* and Ho; Pop. 385.) Formerly Fell. of St. John's Coll. Ox; C. of All Saints', Marylebone, 1838–46; V. of St. Giles', Oxford, 1846–53. [6]

REW, John James, *Bath.*—St. John's Coll. Cam. B.D. 1864; Deac. 1849, Pr. 1850. Chaplain to House of Industry, Bath. Formerly P. C. of St. Paul's Chapel, Bath. [7]

REY, Francois A., *St. Heliers, Jersey.*—C. of St. Heliers. [8]

REYNARDSON, George Birch, *Eastling Rectory, Feversham, Kent.*—Trin. Coll. Cam. B.A. 1835, M.A. 1838; Deac. 1836, Pr. 1837. R. of Eastling, Dio. Cant. 1842. (Patron, Earl of Winchilsea; Tithe, 489*l*; Glebe, 36 acres; R.'s Inc. 545*l* and Ho; Pop. 399.) [9]

REYNARDSON, John Birch, *Careby Rectory, Stamford, Lincolnshire.*—Corpus Coll. Cam. B.A. 1840, M.A. 1843; Deac. 1841, Pr. 1842. R. of Careby with Holywell and Aunby C. Dio. Lin. 1844. (Patron, Charles T. S. B. Reynardson, Esq; Tithe, 285*l*; Glebe, 79 acres; R.'s Inc. 400*l* and Ho; Pop. Careby 107, Holywell 91, Aunby 58.) [10]

REYNELL, George Carew, *Hydrabad, Bombay.*—Trin. Hall, Cam. B.A. 1859; Deac. 1859 and Pr. 1860 by Bp of Lon. Chap. at Hydrabad. Formerly C. of St. Mary's, Kensington, Lond. 1859. [11]

REYNER, George Fearns, *St. John's College, Cambridge.*—St. John's Coll. Cam. 4th Wrang. and B.A. 1839, M.A. 1842, B.D. 1849. Sen. Fell. of St. John's Coll. Cam. [12]

REYNOLDS, Edward, *Appledore, North Devon.*—P. C. of Appledore, Dio. Ex. 1842. (Patron, V. of Northam; P. C.'s Inc. 150*l*; Pop. 2210.) [13]

REYNOLDS, Edward Morris, *St. Peter's College, Radley, Berks.*—Emman. Coll. Cam. B.A. 1855; Deac. 1855 by Bp of Man. Fell. of St. Peter's Coll. Formerly C. of Trinity, Stockton-on-Tees. [14]

REYNOLDS, George Worthington, *Hoddlesden, near Over Darwen, Lancashire.*—Caius Coll. Cam. B.A. 1855; Deac. 1857 and Pr. 1858 by Bp of Man. P. C. of Hoddlesden, Dio. Man. 1863. (Patrons, V. of Blackburn and W. B. Ranken, Esq. alt; P. C.'s Inc. 150*l*; Pop. 2250.) [15]

REYNOLDS, Henry, *Rotherfield-Peppard Rectory, Henley-on-Thames.*—Jesus Coll. Ox. 2nd cl. Lit. Hum. 1st cl. Math. et Phy. and B.A. 1827, M.A. 1829, B.D. 1841. R. of Rotherfield-Peppard, Dio. Ox. 1848. (Patron, Jesus Coll. Ox; Tithe, 540*l* 10*s*; Glebe, 57 acres; R.'s Inc. 620*l* and Ho; Pop. 386.) Formerly Fell. of Jesus Coll. Ox. [16]

REYNOLDS, Henry, *Elmstead, Colchester.*—Queens' Coll. Cam. B.A. 1841, M.A. 1846; Deac. 1865 by Bp of Roch, Pr. 1866 by Bp of Wor. Formerly C. of Thorington, Essex, 1865, Shipston-on-Stour, Worc. 1866. Author, *Baptism by Christ the only Means of Entrance into the Church of Christ*, 1867, 1*s* 6*d*. [17]

REYNOLDS, Henry Revell, *Markham-Clinton Vicarage, near Tuxford, Notts.*—Trin. Coll. Cam. B.A. 1850, M.A. 1853; Deac. 1851, Pr. 1852. V. of Markham-Clinton with Bevercotes, Dio. Lin. 1863. (Patron, Duke of Newcastle; V.'s Inc. 254*l* and Ho; Pop. 240.) Formerly C. of Westerham, Kent, 1851–56, St. Andrew's, Croydon, Surrey, 1857–63. [18]

REYNOLDS, James Jones, *South Hykeham, Lincoln.*—St. John's Coll. Ox. B.A. 1841; Deac. 1842 by Bp of Salis. Pr. 1843 by Bp of Herf. R. of South Hykeham, Dio. Lin. 1867. (Patron, Ld Chan; Corn Rents, 164*l*; Glebe, 80 acres; R.'s Inc. 275*l*; Pop. 176.) Formerly C. of Abbotshaw, Devon, 1842–49, Hartland, 1849–51, St. John's, Bristol, 1851–52; R. of Shaftesbury 1852–67. Author, *Ancient History of Shaftesbury*, 1862, 2nd ed. 1867. [19]

REYNOLDS, Joseph William, *St. Stephen's Parsonage, Commercial-street, London, N.E.*—King's Coll. Lond. Theol. Assoc. 1849, M.A. 1854; Deac. and Pr. 1849. P. C. of St. Stephen's, Spitalfields, Dio. Lon. 1859. (Patrons, Trustees; P. C.'s Inc. 400*l* and Ho; Pop. 7000.) Formerly Lect. at Ch. Ch. Spitalfields, and Prin. of the Jewish Operative Converts' Institution 1853–59. Author, *The Miracles of Our Lord.* [20]

REYNOLDS, Patrick, *St. Stephen's Parsonage, Birmingham.*—Dub. Scho. 1839, 1st Prizeman, A.B. 1841, 1st cl. Div. 1842, LL.B. 1855; Deac. 1842 and Pr. 1844 by Bp of Ches. P. C. of St. Stephen's, Birmingham, Dio. Wor. 1854. (Patrons, the Crown and Bp of Wor. alt; P. C.'s Inc. 300*l* and Ho; Pop. 16,333.) Formerly C. of Blackley 1842–44; P. C. of Waterhead 1844–54. [21]

REYNOLDS, Robert Vincent, *Buttershaw Parsonage, Bradford, Yorks.*—Deac. 1833 and Pr. 1835 by Bp of Calcutta. P. C. of St. Paul's, Buttershaw, Dio. Rip. 1859. (Patron, C. S. Hardy, Esq; P. C.'s Inc. 300*l* and Ho; Pop. 2247.) Formerly Chap. to the Wakefield Convict Prison. Author, *Rule of Faith*; *Outcasts of England*; *Eight Lectures on the Lord's Prayer*; *Appeal on Behalf of the Heathen*; *Was Ramohun Roy a Christian? Reformatories and Prisons.* [22]

REYNOLDS, Robert Vincent, jun., *Crook, Darlington.*—Deac. 1866 by Bp of Dur. C. of Crook 1866. [23]

REYNOLDS, Samuel Harvey, *Brasenose College, Oxford.*—Brasen. Coll. Ox. B.A. 1857, M.A. 1860; Deac. 1860 by Bp of Ox. Fell. of Brasen. Coll. Ox. [24]

RHOADES, Edward James, *Rugby.*—Pemb. Coll. Ox. B.A. 1857, M.A. 1859; Deac. 1859 by Bp of Wor. Pr. 1860 by Bp of Lon. Asst. C. of Rugby 1859. [25]

RHODES, Francis William, *Bishop Stortford, Herts.*—Trin. Coll. Cam. B.A. 1831, M.A. 1834; Deac. 1831 and Pr. 1832 by Bp of Nor. V. of Bishop Stortford, Dio. Roch. 1849. (Patron, the Precentor of St. Paul's Cathl; Tithe, 356*l*; V.'s Inc. 386*l*; Pop. 2380.) Formerly C. of Oby, Norfolk, 1831–32, Stocking Pelham, Herts, 1832–33; P. C. of Brentwood 1834–43; C. of Madehurst, Sussex, 1844–46. [26]

RHODES, Henry Jackson, *Abingdon Lodge, Tunbridge Wells.*—Corpus Coll. Ox. B.A. 1844, M.A. 1847; Deac. 1846 and Pr. 1847 by Bp of Ox. Formerly C. of St. Anne's, Brookfield, Highgate-rise, Lond. Author, *Handbook to Convocation*, 1852, 2*s* 6*d*. [27]

RHODES, James Armitage, *Carlton, near Pontefract.*—Queens' Coll. Cam. Jun. Opt. and B.A. 1806, M.A. 1809; Deac. and Pr. 1812 by Abp of York. [28]

RHODES, J. W., *Royston.*—Head Mast. of Royston Gr. Sch. [29]

RIADORE, Geldart John Evans, *Cavendish Club, London, W.*—Emman. Coll. Cam. B.A. 1849, M.A. 1860; Deac. 1850 and Pr. 1851 by Bp of Wor. R. of All Saints', Chichester, 1865. (Patron, Abp of Cant; Tithe, 7*l*; Glebe, 2½ acres; R.'s Inc. 26*l*; Pop. 260.) R. of St. Martin's, Chichester, Dio Chich. 1865. (Patrons, D. and C. of Chich; R.'s Inc. 52*l*; Pop. 277.) Formerly C. of Coventry, Dorking; Warden of the House of Charity, Rose-street, Soho, Lond. Dom. Chap. to the Duke of Buccleuch. Author, *Essays*, Rivingtons, 5*s*; *Manual of Theological Instruction for Adults*, ib. 1859. [1]

RIADORE, James Evans, *Tintern House, Charlotte-road, Edgbaston, Birmingham*, and *Cavendish Club, London, W.*—St. Peter's Coll. Cam. Jun. Opt. and B.A. 1852; Deac. 1853 by Bp of Lich. Pr. 1855 by Bp of Ox. C. of St. Luke's, Edgbaston. Formerly C. of St. Alkmund's, Derby, 1853, Sutton Courtney, Berks, Canon Ashby (sole charge), Northants, 1860, Higher Broughton, Manchester, St. Andrew's, Pimlico, and Ch. Ch. Turnham Green. [2]

RIBBANS, E. F. T.—Formerly Head Mast. of the Gr. Sch. and Chap. to the Union, Leek, Staffs. [3]

RICE, The Hon. Aubrey Spring, *Netherbury Vicarage, Bridport.*—Trin. Coll. Cam. M.A. 1846; Deac. 1846 and Pr. 1847 by Bp of Nor. V. of Netherbury and Ash C. Dio. Salis. 1852. (Patron, Bp of Salis; Tithe, 400*l*; Glebe, 3 acres; V.'s Inc. 400*l* and Ho; Pop. 1453.) Rural Dean. Formerly C. of Great Yarmouth 1846, Somerleyton 1848, Saham-Toney 1849. [4]

RICE, Charles Hobbes, *Cheam Rectory, Ewell, Surrey.*—St. John's Coll. Ox. Hon. 4th cl. Lit. Hum. and 3rd cl. Math. 1855, B.A. 1855, M.A. 1859, B.D. 1864; Deac. 1856 by Bp of Ox. Pr. 1862 by Abp of Armagh. Fell. of St. John's Coll. Ox. R. of Cheam, Dio. Win. 1867. (Patron, St. John's Coll. Cam; Tithe, 633*l*; Glebe, 26 acres; R.'s Inc. 655*l* and Ho; Pop. 1156.) Formerly Tut. of St. Columba's Coll. 1856–62; V.-Choral of Armagh Cathl. 1862. Author, *Sermons at St. Columba's*, J. H. and J. Parker, 1863, 3*s* 6*d*, and single Sermons. [5]

RICE, Francis William, *Fairford Vicarage, Glouc.*—Ch. Ch. Ox. B.A. 1826, M.A. 1847; Deac. and Pr. 1828 by Bp of Glouc. V. of Fairford, Dio. G. and B. 1828. (Patrons, D. and C. of Glouc; Tithe, 395*l*; Glebe, 30 acres; V.'s Inc. 485*l* and Ho; Pop. 1654.) Rural Dean. [6]

RICE, Henry, *Great Risington Rectory, Moreton-in-the-Marsh, Glouc.*—Ch. Ch. Ox. B.A. 1836; Deac. 1838 and Pr. 1839 by Bp of Wor. R. of Great Risington, Dio. G. and B. 1856. (Patron, Lord Dynevor; R.'s Inc. 650*l* and Ho; Pop. 499.) Formerly V. of Biddenham, Beds, 1850–56. [7]

RICE, John George, 56, *Vyse-street, Birmingham.*—Dub. Scho. of, 1858, A.B. 1860, A.M. 1864; Deac. 1861 and Pr. 1862 by Bp of Rip. P. C. of St. Michael's, Birmingham, Dio. Wor. 1866. (Patrons, Directors of Ch. of Eng. Cemetery; P. C.'s Inc. 120*l*.) Formerly C. of St. George's, Barnsley, 1861, St. George's, Birmingham, 1865–66. [8]

RICE, John Moreland, *Bramber, Steyning, Sussex.*—Magd. Coll. Ox. B.A. 1848, M.A. 1849, B.D. 1856; Deac. 1848 and Pr. 1849 by Bp of Win. R. of Bramber with Botolph V. Dio. Chich. 1864. (Patron, Magd. Coll. Ox; R.'s Inc. 160*l*; Pop. Bramber 119, Botolph 54.) Formerly Fell. of Magd. Coll. Ox. 1848–54; Chap. to Royal East Kent Mounted Rifles, and P. C. of Wye, Kent, 1854–58. [9]

RICE, Richard, *Eaton Hastings, Lechlade, Berks.*—Mert. Coll. Ox. B.A. 1814, M.A. 1818; Deac. 1815, Pr. 1816. R. of Eaton Hastings, Dio. Ox. 1836. (Patron, the present R; Tithe, 378*l* 5*s*; R.'s Inc. 378*l*; Pop. 185.) [10]

RICE, Richard, *Little Barrington Vicarage, Burford, Oxon.*—Queen's Coll. Ox. Scho. of, 1841, 3rd cl. Lit. Hum. 1845, B.A. 1846, M.A. 1851; Deac. 1848, Pr. 1849. V. of Little Barrington, Dio. G. and B. 1856. (Patron, Ld Chan; V.'s Inc. 100*l* and Ho; Pop. 151.) 2nd Mast. of the Northleach Gr. Sch. 1849. Formerly C. of Menheniot, Cornwall, 1848, Hampnett with Stowell 1849. [11]

RICE, Richard John Howard, *Sutton-Courtney Vicarage, Abingdon, Berks.*—Ex. Coll. Ox. B.A. 1850, M.A. 1853. V. of Sutton-Courtney with Appleford C. Dio. Ox. 1856. (Patrons, D. and C. of Windsor; Tithe—App. 1112*l* 8*s* 11*d*, and 44 acres of Glebe; V.'s Inc. 180*l* and Ho; Pop. 1581.) [12]

RICE, Robert, *St. Columba's College, Dublin.*—Ch. Ch. Ox. B.A. 1860, M.A. 1863; Deac. 1862 by Bp of Ches. Pr. 1863 by Bp of Win. Sub-Warden of St. Columba's 1867. Formerly C. of Donnybrook 1862–64. [13]

RICH, Edward John George Henry, *New College, Oxford.*—New Coll. Ox. B.A. 1841, M.A. 1845. Fell. of New Coll. Ox. [14]

RICH, John, *Chippenham*—Ch. Ch. Ox. B.A. 1848, M.A. 1851; Deac. 1851 by Bp of Ox. Pr. 1856 by Bp of Chich. V. of Chippenham with Tytherton R. Dio. G. and B. 1861. (Patrons, D. and C. of Ch. Ch. Ox; V.'s Inc. 300*l* and Ho; Pop. 4819.) [15]

RICHARDS, Asa, *Llanvabon, Pontypridd.*—Lampeter; Deac. 1866 by Bp of Llan. C. of Llanvabon 1866. [16]

RICHARDS, Charles William, *Ettingshall Parsonage, Wolverhampton.*—Dub. Catechetical Prem. 1835, A.B. 1838, A.M. 1855; Deac. 1838 and Pr. 1839 by Bp of Ches. P. C. of Ettingshall, Dio. Lich. 1852. (Patron Bp of Lich; P. C.'s Inc. 205*l*; Pop. 4728) [17]

RICHARDS, Edward, *Pont Dolanog, Welshpool.*—Jesus Coll. Ox. B.A. 1861, M.A. 1866; Deac. 1862 and Pr. 1863 by Bp of St. A. P. C. of Dolanog, Dio. St. A. 1866. (Patron, Bp of St. A; Tithe, 155*l*; Glebe, 2 acres; P. C.'s Inc. 160*l* and Ho; Pop. 390.) Formerly C. of Bettws-yn-Rhos 1862–66. [18]

RICHARDS, Edward Tew, *Farlington Rectory, Havant, Hants.*—Corpus Coll. Ox. B.A. 1819, M.A. 1822; Deac. 1822 by Bp of Herf. Pr. 1822 by Bp of Ox. R. of Farlington 1826. (Patron, the present R; Tithe, 616*l*; Glebe, 2 acres; R.'s Inc. 620*l* and Ho; Pop. 596.) [19]

RICHARDS, Enoch Valentine, *Hickleton Parsonage, Doncaster.*—B.A. 1856, M.A. 1863; Deac. 1856 and Pr. 1858 by Bp of St. A. P. C. of Hickleton, Dio. York, 1865. (Patron, Viscount Halifax; P. C.'s Inc. 150*l* and Ho; Pop. 127.) Formerly Asst. British Chap. at Nice; C. of Carnarvon 1860–63. [20]

RICHARDS, Frederic Jonathan, *Boxley Vicarage, Maidstone.*—Univ. Coll. Dur. B.A. 1849, M.A. 1853; Deac. 1849 and Pr. 1850 by Bp of Herf. V. of Boxley, Dio. Cant. 1853. (Patrons, D. and C. of Roch; Tithe—App. 684*l* 9*s*, V. 794*l*; Glebe, 5 acres; V.'s Inc. 834*l* and Ho; Pop. 1470.) [21]

RICHARDS, George, *Chitterne, near Heytesbury, Wilts.*—All Souls' Coll. Ox. B.A. 1830, M.A. 1840; Deac. 1830 and Pr. 1832 by Bp of Salis. V. of All Saints' with St. Mary's V. Chitterne, Dio. Salis. 1862. (Patrons, Bp and D. and C. of Salis. alt; Tithe, 115*l*; Glebe, 260*l*; V.'s Inc. 375*l* and Ho; Pop. 710.) Formerly C. of Wokingham 1830–31, Atworth 1831–36; Chap. to Royal Navy 1836–47; R. of Thorneyburn, Northumberland 1852–62. [22]

RICHARDS, George, *Streatham House, Hastings.*—Dom. Chap. to the Earl of Cork and Orrery. [23]

RICHARDS, George, *Tyldesley Parsonage, near Manchester.*—Trin. Coll. Cam. B.A. 1835, M.A. 1839; Deac. 1836 and Pr. 1838 by Bp of Ches. P. C. of Tyldesley with Shackerley, Dio. Man. 1851. (Patron, Lord Lilford; P. C.'s Inc. 180*l* and Ho; Pop. 6029.) Formerly C. of Warrington, and Clerical Prin. of the Chester Diocesan Female Training Sch. and Clergy Daughters' Sch. [24]

RICHARDS, Henry, *Llanystyndwy Rectory, Pwllheli, Carnarvonshire.*—Jesus Coll. Ox. B.A. 1824; Deac. 1824, Pr. 1825. R. of Llanystyndwy, Dio. Ban. 1855. (Patron, Bp of Ban; Tithe, 485*l*; Glebe, 4 acres; R.'s Inc. 485*l* and Ho; Pop. 1126.) Rural Dean. Formerly C. of Llanengan. [25]

RICHARDS, Henry Ebenezer, *Claygate Parsonage, Esher, Surrey.*—St. John's Coll. Cam. B.D. 1855,

D.D. 1860; Deac. 1847 and Pr. 1848 by Bp of Wor. P. C. of Claygate, Dio. Win. 1855. (Patrons, Trustees; P. C.'s Inc. 125*l* and Ho; Pop. 535.) Dom. Chap. to the Earl of Kintore. [1]

RICHARDS, Henry Manning, *Andover, Hants.*—Ch. Ch. Ox. 4th cl. Lit. Hum. and B.A. 1840, M.A. 1843; Deac. 1841 and Pr. 1842 by Bp of Ox. C. of Andover 1858. Formerly C. of Cornwell, Oxon, 1841–44, Andover 1844–55, Sulham, Berks, 1855–58. [2]

RICHARDS, Henry William Parry, *Isleworth Vicarage, Middlesex, W.*—Ch. Ch. Ox. B.A. 1849; Deac. 1850 and Pr. 1851 by Bp of Win. V. of Isleworth, Dio. Lon. 1855. (Patrons, D. and C. of Windsor; Tithe—Imp. 275*l* 7*s* 10*d* and $65\frac{1}{4}$ acres of Glebe, V. 700*l* 10*s*; Glebe, $\frac{1}{2}$ acre; V.'s Inc. 702*l* and Ho; Pop. 4127.) [3]

RICHARDS, Hugh, *Aberdare.*—C. of St. Fagan's, Aberdare. [4]

RICHARDS, James, *Hunwick, Bishop Auckland, Durham.*—Univ. Coll. Dur. B.A. 1845, Licen. Theol. 1846, M.A. 1848; Deac. 1846, Pr. 1847. P. C. of Hunwick, Dio. Dur. 1850. (Patron, P. C. of Auckland; P. C.'s Inc. 296*l* and Ho; Pop. 1487.) [5]

RICHARDS, James, 58, *Brunswick-terrace, Pendleton.*—Sid. Coll. Cam. B.A. 1863; Deac. 1864 and Pr. 1865 by Bp of Ches. C. of St. George's, Pendleton, 1867. Formerly C. of Cheadle, Cheshire, 1864–67. [6]

RICHARDS, James Preston, *Silloth, Carlisle.*—St. Bees; Deac. 1865, Pr. 1866. C. of St. Paul's, Silloth, 1865. [7]

RICHARDS, John, *Guildford.*—Queens' Coll. Cam. B.A. 1817, M.A. 1820; Deac. 1818 by Bp of B. and W. Pr. 1820 by Bp of Win. Surrogate. Formerly C. of Stoke-next-Guildford 1820–31; Chap. of Surrey House of Correction, Guildford, 1822–51; Chap. of the Union Workhouse, Guildford, 1838–66. [8]

RICHARDS, John, *Grammar School, Bradford, Yorks.*—St. John's Coll. Cam. 1st cl. Cl. Trip. B.A. 1835, M.A. 1846; Deac. 1847 by Bp of Wor. Head Mast. of Bradford Gr. Sch. [9]

RICHARDS, John, *Amlwch Parsonage, Anglesey.*—Deac. 1847 and Pr. 1848 by Bp of Ban. P. C. of Amlwch with Llanwenllwyfo, Dio. Ban. 1859. (Patron, Bp of Ban; P. C.'s Inc. 210*l* and Ho; Pop. 5215.) Surrogate. Formerly C. of Holyhead. [10]

RICHARDS, John Brinley, *Llanbister, Penybont, Radnorshire.*—Lampeter, B.D. 1860; Deac. 1849 by Bp of Herf. Pr. 1850 by Bp of St. D. V. of Llanbister, Dio. St. D. 1863. (Patron, Bp of St. D; Tithe, 160*l*; V.'s Inc. 196*l* and Ho; Pop. 1084.) [11]

RICHARDS, John William, *Hellifield, Leeds.*—Corpus Coll. Ox. Fell. and Tut. of, 2nd cl. Lit. Hum. B.A. 1831, M.A. 1834; Deac. 1834 and Pr. 1835 by Bp of Ox. Formerly Head Mast. of Manchester High Sch. 1837–42; P. C. of East Harnham, Salisbury, 1835–59; Sen. C. of Hursley, Hants, 1859–66; C. of Long Preston, Yorks, 1866–67. [12]

RICHARDS, Joseph.—Trin. Coll. Cam. B.A. 1858, M.A. 1863; Deac. 1859 by Bp of Ches. Pr. 1860 by Bp of Lich. Formerly C. of Shawbury, Salop, 1859–63, St. Mary's, Hulme, Manchester, 1863–67. [13]

RICHARDS, Richard, *Taunton.*—St. Aidan's; Deac. 1860 by Abp of Cant. C. of St. James's, Taunton. [14]

RICHARDS, Richard, *Horwich, near Bolton-le-Moors.*—C. of Horwich. [15]

RICHARDS, Robert Edward, *Monart, Torquay.*—Trin. Coll. Cam. Sen. Opt. 2nd cl. Cl. Trip. B.A. 1854, M.A. 1857; Deac. 1856 and Pr. 1857 by Bp of Salis. C. of Tor Mohun with Cockington 1861. Formerly C. of Corfe Castle, Dorset, 1856–61. [16]

RICHARDS, Theodore Edward Maurice, *Hastings, Sussex.*—Jesus Coll. Cam. Rustat Scho. B.A. 1858, M.A. 1861; Deac. 1859 and Pr. 1860 by Bp of Chich. C. of Trinity, Hastings, 1859. [17]

RICHARDS, Thomas, *Hardwick, Wellingborough.*—R. of Hardwick, Northants, Dio. Pet. 1866. (Patrons, Heirs of the late Rev. E. Hughes; R.'s Inc. 300*l*; Pop. 83.) Formerly C. of Misterton, Lutterworth; V. of Naseby, Northants, 1861–66. [18]

RICHARDS, Thomas Hardy, *Llangian, Pwllheli, Carnarvonshire.*—St. Bees; Deac. 1852, Pr. 1853. C. of Llangian. Formerly C. of Llantrisaint and Ceidio, Anglesey. [19]

RICHARDS, Thomas Miller, *Alcombe, Minehead, Somerset.*—Deac. 1834, Pr. 1835. [20]

RICHARDS, Thomas Wallis, *The Vicarage, Leighton Buzzard.*—Sid. Coll. Cam. 1st Sen. Opt. and B.A. 1840, M.A. 1844; Deac. 1840 and Pr. 1841. V. of Leighton Buzzard, Dio. Ely, 1849. (Patron, Preb. of Leighton Buzzard in Lin. Cathl; Tithe, 300*l*; V.'s Inc. 330*l* and Ho; Pop. 4882.) Surrogate. Formerly C. of Holbeach and Mast. of Holbeach Gr. Sch. Author, *Sermons*, 5*s*; *A Sermon before the Court of Foresters*, 6*d*; *On the Service of the Church*, 6*d*; *On the Consecration of a New Cemetery*, 1*s*; *Confirmation*, 2*d*; *Infant Baptism*, 2*d*. [21]

RICHARDS, Thomas William, 4, *Victoria-place South, Clifton.*—Queen's Coll. Birmingham; Deac. 1864 and Pr. 1865 by Bp of Wor. C. of Temple, Bristol, 1866. Formerly C. of Rushock, near Droitwich, 1864–66. [22]

RICHARDS, William, *Penrhyn-Deudraeth, Carnarvon.*—Lampeter; Deac. and Pr. 1857 by Bp of Ban. P. C. of Penrhyn-Deudraeth, Dio. Ban. 1863. (Patrons, Trustees; P. C.'s Inc. 180*l* and Ho; Pop. 1815.) Formerly C. of Penmorfa and Dolbenmaen 1857–58, Llannor, Pwllheli, 1858–63. [23]

RICHARDS, William, *Dawley, Wellington, Salop.*—Queen's Coll. Ox. B.A. 1844, M.A. 1847; Deac. 1845, Pr. 1846. V. of Dawley-Magna, Dio. Lich. 1849. (Patrons, R. Phillips, Esq. and others; Tithe—Imp. 180*l*, V. 6*l*; Glebe, 1 acre; V.'s Inc. 150*l* and Ho; Pop. 3969.) [24]

RICHARDS, William Henry, *Grays Thurrock, Romford, Essex.*—Jesus Coll. Cam. B.A. 1855; Deac. 1856 by Bp of Rip. V. of Grays Thurrock, Dio. Roch. 1862. (Patron, the present V; V.'s Inc. 250*l* and Ho; Pop. 2209.) Formerly C. of Bishop Thornton, Yorks. [25]

RICHARDS, William Steward, *Terwick Rectory, Petersfield.*—Jesus Coll. Ox. B.A. 1831, M.A. 1834; Deac. 1831 by Bp of Roch. Pr. 1832 by Bp of Ox. R. of Terwick, Dio. Chich. 1842. (Patron, T. A. Richards, Esq; Tithe, 173*l*; Glebe, $12\frac{1}{4}$ acres; R.'s Inc. 193*l* and Ho; Pop. 106.) [26]

RICHARDS, William Upton, 137, *Albany-street, Regent's-park, London, N.W.*—Ex. Coll. Ox. B.A. 1833, M.A. 1839; Deac. 1836 and Pr. 1837 by Bp of Lon. P. C. of All Saints', Margaret-street, Dio. Lon. 1849. (Patron, Bp of Lon; P. C.'s Inc. 150*l*; Pop. 2981.) [27]

RICHARDSON, Arthur Hill, *Fishguard, Pembrokeshire.*—Lampeter; Deac. 1828 and Pr. 1829 by Bp of St. D. P. C. of Maner Owen, Pembrokeshire, Dio. St. D. 1830. (Patrons, Vicars-Choral of St. D.'s Cathl; Tithe—App. 80*l*; P. C.'s Inc. 86*l*; Pop. 186.) V. of Llanwnda, Pembrokeshire, Dio. St. D. 1841. (Patrons, D. and C. of St. D; Tithe—App. 220*l*, V. 209*l* 11*s* 7*d*; V.'s Inc. 228*l*; Pop. 1138.) V. of St. Dogwells, Pembrokeshire, Dio. St. D. 1866. (Patrons, Bp and D. and C. of St. D; V.'s Inc. 71*l* and Ho; Pop. 436.) P. C. of Little Newcastle, Pembrokeshire, Dio. St. D. 1866. (Patron, Thomas Morse, Esq; P. C.'s Inc. 54*l*; Pop. 354.) [28]

RICHARDSON, Benjamin, *Glaisdale, Yarm, Yorks.*—St. John's Coll. Cam. B.A. 1830; Deac. 1831, Pr. 1833. P. C. of Glaisdale, Dio. York, 1844. (Patron, Abp of York; Glebe, 3 acres; P. C.'s Inc. 126*l* and Ho; Pop. 1074.) [29]

RICHARDSON, Edmund Augustine, 6, *Montpelier-terrace, Woodhouse Cliff, Leeds.*—Queen's Coll. Ox. Hon. 4th cl. Lit. Hum. B.A. 1858, M.A. 1861; Deac. 1859 and Pr. 1861 by Bp of Rip. 2nd Mast. of Leeds Gr. Sch; Lect. of Trinity, Leeds, 1862. Formerly C. of Roundhay 1859. [30]

RICHARDSON, Francis, *Denshaw Vicarage, Delph, near Manchester.*—Caius Coll. Cam. B.A. 1852, M.A. 1855; Deac. 1852 and Pr. 1853 by Bp of Ches-

V. of Denshaw, Dio. Man. 1863. (Patron, Henry Gartside, Esq; V.'s Inc. 150*l*; Pop. 800.) Formerly C. of Great Budworth 1852–53, St. Thomas's Chapel, Edinburgh, 1854–58; St. Paul's, Kersal, Manchester, 1859–62; St. Peter's, Ashton-under-Lyne, 1862–63. [1]

RICHARDSON, Frederick, *Bollington Parsonage, Macclesfield.*—Caius Coll. Cam. B.A. 1852, M.A. 1855. P. C. of Bollington, Dio. Ches. 1856. (Patron, V. of Prestbury; P. C.'s Inc. 175*l* and Ho; Pop. 5439.) [2]

RICHARDSON, Frederic Henry, *Uppingham.*—St. John's Coll. Ox. B.A. 1865; Deac. 1865 and Pr. 1866 by Bp of Pet. C. of Uppingham 1865. [3]

RICHARDSON, George, *College-street, Winchester.*—St. John's Coll. Cam. 3rd Wrang. B.A. 1860, M.A. 1863; Deac. 1865 and Pr. 1866 by Bp of Ely. Asst. Mast. at Win. Coll; Fell. of St. John's Coll. Cam. [4]

RICHARDSON, Henry Kemp, *Leire Rectory, Lutterworth.*—Trin. Coll. Cam. B.A. 1830, M.A. 1834; Deac. 1832, Pr. 1833. R. of Leire, Dio. Pet. 1834. (Patroness, Countess Cowper; Tithe, 20*l*; Glebe, 130 acres; R.'s Inc. 330*l* and Ho; Pop. 433.) Rural Dean. [5]

RICHARDSON, Herbert Henley, *St. Andrew's Cottage, Isle of Cumbrae, Greenock.*—St. Mary Hall, Ox. B.A. 1858, M.A. 1861; Deac. 1859 and Pr. 1860 by Abp of Cant. Dom. Chap. to the Countess Dowager of Glasgow 1859; Chap. and Jun. Tut. at the Coll. of the Holy Spirit, Cumbrae, 1863. Editor, *The Calendar and Clergy List of the Scottish Episcopal Church*, Rivingtons, 1867, 2*s*; *The Cumbrae College Calendar* (annually), Grant and Son, Edinburgh, 6*d*. [6]

RICHARDSON, John, *Warwick.*—Queen's Coll. Ox. 2nd cl. Lit. Hum. and B.A. 1829, M.A. 1832; Deac. 1833, Pr. 1835. Chap. to the County Gaol, Warwick. [7]

RICHARDSON, John, *St. Mary's Parsonage, Bury St. Edmunds.*—Dub. A.B. 1842, A.M. 1854; Deac. 1842, Pr. 1843. P. C. of St. Mary's, Bury St. Edmunds, Dio. Ely, 1857. (Patrons, Trustees; P. C.'s Inc. 160*l*; Pop. 6604.) Formerly R. of St. Ann's, Manchester, 1852–57. Author, *Real Exhibitors Exhibited*, 1851, 2*s*; *Emblems from and for the Factory*—1. *The Turn-out*, 2. *The Proposal*, 3. *The Deliberation*, 2*d* each; *Gospel Unities*, 2*s*. [8]

RICHARDSON, John, *St. George's Vicarage, Wolverhampton.*—Dub. A.B. 1857, A.M. 1863; Deac. 1857 by Bp of Win. Pr. 1859 by Bp of Lich. V. of St. George's, Wolverhampton, Dio. Lich. 1860. (Patron, Bp of Lich; V.'s Inc. 300*l* and Ho; Pop. 6759.) Surrogate. Formerly C. of St. Mark's, Wolverhampton, 1857, St. George's, Birmingham, 1859. [9]

RICHARDSON, John, *Manor House, Cranborne, Salisbury.*—Deac. 1865 and Pr. 1866 by Bp of Salis. C. of Cranborne 1865. Formerly Asst. Mast. and Sec. to the National Society's Training Coll. Battersea, 1852–61. [10]

RICHARDSON, J., *Sandy Rectory, St. Neots, Beds.*—R. of Sandy, Dio. Ely, 1858. (Patron, F. Pym, Esq; R.'s Inc. 800*l* and Ho; Pop. 2118.) [11]

RICHARDSON, Joseph George, *Worth Matravers, Wareham, Dorset.*—V. of Worth Matravers, Dio. Salis. 1865. (Patron, R. of Swanage; V.'s Inc. 150*l* and Ho; Pop. 350.) [12]

RICHARDSON, Piercy John, 31, *Tredegar-square, Bow, E.*—King's Coll. Lond. Theol. Assoc. 1866; Deac. 1866. C. of St. Luke's Mission, Trinity, Stepney. [13]

RICHARDSON, Richard, *Capenhurst, near Chester.*—Brasen. Coll. Ox. B.A. 1834, M.A. 1845; Deac. 1845, Pr. 1846. P. C. of Capenhurst, Dio. Ches. 1859. (Patron, the present P. C.; Tithe, 150*l*; P. C.'s Inc. 150*l*; Pop. 224.) [14]

RICHARDSON, Thomas, *York.*—Deac. 1819 and Pr. 1820 by Abp of York. R. of St. Martin's Micklegate, City and Dio. York, 1857. (Patrons, Trustees of H. Willoughby, Esq. and others; R.'s Inc. 250*l*; Pop. 727.) 2nd Mast. of the Gr. Sch. and Chap. of the Lunatic Asylum, York. Formerly V. of Bugthorpe, near York, 1843–57. [15]

RICHARDSON, Thomas, 17, *Princes-square, London, E.*—St. Bees; Deac. 1854 and Pr. 1855 by Bp of Win. P. C. of St. Matthew's, Pell-street, Dio. Lon. 1859. (Patron, Bp of Lon; P. C.'s Inc. 300*l*; Pop. 3245.) Lect. at St. George's-in-the-East. Formerly C. of St. Andrew's, Lambeth, 1854, St. George's, Southwark, 1856, St. Olave's, Jewry, 1858. [16]

RICHARDSON, Thomas, *Grove House, St. David's.*—Jesus Coll. Ox. Fell. of; Deac. 1849 by Bp of Ox. Pr. 1850 by Bp of St. D. Min. Can. of St. David's Cathl. (Value, 140*l*.) [17]

RICHARDSON, Thomas Pierson, *Great Barford, St. Neots.*—Trin. Coll. Cam. B.A. 1841, M.A. 1844; Deac. and Pr. 1845. V. of Great Barford with Roxton V. Dio. Ely, 1847. (Patron, Trin. Coll. Cam; V.'s Inc. 298*l* and Ho; Pop. Great Barford 907, Roxton, 688.) Formerly Fell. of Trin. Coll. Cam. Author, *The Mind of Christ in Us* (a Sermon), Bristol, 1867. [18]

RICHARDSON, Thomas Williamson, *Sephton, near Liverpool.*—St. Bees; Deac. 1862 and Pr. 1863 by Bp of Ches. C. of Sephton 1865. Formerly C. of St. Mary's, Kirkdale, Liverpool, 1862, St. Stephen's, Liverpool, 1863. [19]

RICHARDSON, William, *Treasurer's House, St. David's.*—P. C. of St. David's, Dio. St. D. 1820. (Patron, Bp of St. D; Tithe—App. 1048*l* 18*s* 5½*d*; P. C.'s Inc. 125*l*; Pop. 2199.) Can. Res. and Treasurer with the Prebendal Stall of Llandisilio Gogoff annexed 1854. (Value 350*l*.) Rural Dean of Pebidiawke. [20]

RICHARDSON, William, *Miles - Platting, Manchester.*—R. of Miles-Platting, Dio. Man. 1855. (Patron, Sir B. Heywood, Bart; R.'s Inc. 300*l*; Pop. 5153.) [21]

RICHARDSON, William, *The Vicarage, Corwen, Merionethshire.*—Jesus Coll. Ox. Scho. of 4th cl. Lit. Hum. B.A. 1853; Deac. 1853 by Bp. of Ox. Pr. 1854 by Bp. of St. A. V. of Corwen, Dio. St. A. 1866. (Patron, Bp of St. A; Tithe, 489*l* 7*s*; Glebe, 27 acres; V.'s Inc. 510*l* and Ho; Pop. 1935.) Formerly C. of Bala 1854; Chap. of Rhug Chapel 1854; P. C. of St. Mary's, Llywdiarth, 1859. [22]

RICHARDSON, William Esdaile, *Quainton, Winslow, Bucks.*—Trin. Coll. Cam. B.A. 1850; Deac. 1850, Pr. 1851. C. of Quainton 1864. Formerly P. C. of Limslade, Bucks, 1853–64. [23]

RICHARDSON, William James, *Archbishop Tenison's Chapel, Regent-street, London, W.*—Corpus Coll. Cam. B.A. 1851; Deac. 1850, Pr. 1851. Min. of Abp Tenison's Chapel, St. James's, Westminster, 1863. Formerly Preacher of same. [24]

RICHEY, James, *Loxbear Rectory, Tiverton, Devon.*—R. of Loxbear, Dio. Ex. 1854. (Patron, Sir Thomas Dyke Acland, Bart; Tithe, 115*l*; Glebe, 20½ acres; R.'s Inc. 195*l* and Ho; Pop. 126.) Dom. Chap. to the Earl of Charlemont. [25]

RICHINGS, Alfred Cornelius, *Boxmore, near Berkhampstead, Herts.*—Ch. Coll. Cam. M.A. 1843. P. C. of Boxmoor, Dio. Roch. 1865. (Patron, V. of Hemel Hempstead; P. C.'s Inc. 200*l*; Pop. 3813.) Formerly V. of Beaminster, Dorset, 1852–57; R. of Hawridge, Bucks, 1857–65. [26]

RICHINGS, Benjamin, *Mancetter Vicarage, Atherstone, Warwickshire.*—Lin. Coll. Ox. B.A. 1808, M.A. 1811; Deac. 1811, Pr. 1812. V. of Mancetter, Dio. Wor. 1816. (Patron, the present V; V.'s Inc. 230*l* and Ho; Pop. 402.) Author, *The Martyrdom of Robert Glover*, 4*s*; *A Protestant Catechism* (for the use of Schools), 6*d*; *Flowers of Sacred Poetry*, 1*s* 6*d*; forty Tracts, etc. [27]

RICHINGS, Frederic Hartshill, *Atherstone Parsonage, Warwickshire.*—Queens' Coll. Cam. B.A. 1840; Deac. 1840, Pr. 1841. P. C. of Atherstone, Dio. Wor. 1841. (Patron, V. of Mancetter; P. C.'s Inc. 150*l* and Ho; Pop. 3877.) [28]

RICHMOND, Henry James, *Sherburn, Durham.*—Univ. Coll. Dur. Open Scho. 1846, Van Mildert Scho. 1849, B.A. 1849, Fell. of Univ. 1850, M.A. 1852;

Deac. 1851 and Pr. 1852 by Bp of Dur. C. of Pittington, Durham, 1865. Formerly C. of Houghton-le-Spring, Durham, 1851, Haydon Bridge, Northumberland, 1854; Head Mast. of Sch. at Bognor, Sussex, 1854–65; C. of Middleton, Sussex, 1863. [1]

RICHMOND, Henry Sylvester, *Wyck Risington, Rectory, Stow-on-the-Wold, Glouc.*—Queens' Coll. Cam. B.A. 1831, M.A. 1834; Deac. 1831 and Pr. 1833 by Bp of Lin. R. of Wyck Risington, Dio. G. and B. 1853. (Patron, Ld Chan; Tithe, 84*l*; Glebe, 80 acres; R.'s Inc. 250*l* and Ho; Pop. 206.) Author, *The Hope of Christian Parents for their Baptized Children*, 1841, 1*s*; *Αισχυλου Προμηθευς Δεσμωτης* (The Prometheus Bound of Æschylus, the Text newly revised, with Notes, Critical and Explanatory), Pickering, 1846, 6*s*; *The Baptism which Saves*, 1851, 9*d*. [2]

RICHMOND, Thomas Knyvett, 1, *St. George's-place, Hyde Park Corner, London, S.W.*—Ex. Coll. Ox. M.A. 1858; Deac. 1858 and Pr. 1859 by Bp of Nor. Chap. of St. George's Hospital. Formerly C. of St. Nicholas' and Lect. at St. George's, Great Yarmouth. [3]

RICHMOND, William, *Moortown, Leeds.*—Dub. A.B. 1856, A.M. 1859; Deac. 1857 and Pr. 1858 by Bp of Rip. Formerly C. of All Saints', Leeds, 1857–59, Barwick-in-Elmet 1859. [4]

RICHMOND, William Alexander, *Limpley Stoke, Bath.*—Lin. Coll. Ox. B.A. 1857, M.A. 1859; Deac. 1857 and Pr. 1858 by Bp of Ely. Formerly C. of Gazeley with Kentford, Suffolk, 1857–62. [5]

RICHSON, Charles, *The Cathedral, Manchester.*—St. Cath. Coll. Cam. B.A. 1842, M.A. 1845; Deac. 1841 and Pr. 1842 by Bp of Ches. Can. Res. of Man. Cathl. 1854. (Value, 600*l*.) R. of St. Andrew's, Ancoats, Dio. Man. 1854. (Patrons, D. and C. of Man; R.'s Inc. 115*l*; Pop. 16,070.) Formerly Clerk in Orders of Man. Cathl. 1844–54. Author, *The Observance of the Sanitary Laws, Divinely appointed, in the Old Testament Scriptures, sufficient to ward off Preventable Diseases from Christians as well as Israelites* (a Sermon preached in Man. Cathl. with Notes, by John Sutherland, M.D.) Manchester, 1854, 6*d*; *A Lecture on the Position Mechanics' Institutions ought to occupy amongst the Agencies for promoting National Education* (delivered at the Manchester Mechanics' Institution), 1*s*; *A Series of Seven Confirmation Tracts*, 8*d*; *Speculum Parochialium and Clergyman's Memorandum Book* (in 5 Parts, with Appendixes), 3*s*; *Education in Manchester, considered with Reference to the State of Church Day-Schools in that Parish*, 1*s*; *A Letter to the Right Hon. Sir George Grey, M.P. on the Urgent Necessity of additional Legislative Provision for Pauper Education, and especially for Out-Door Pauper Children*, 1*s* 6*d*; *The Scheme of Secular Education proposed by the National Public Schools Association compared with the Manchester and Salford Boroughs Education Bill*, 2*s* 6*d*; *Educational Facts and Statistics of Manchester and Salford*, 6*d*; *The Fallacies involved in certain Parliamentary Returns of Day-Schools and Day-Scholars in England and Wales*, in 1818, 1833, *and* 1851 (published in *The Transactions of the Manchester Statistical Society*); *Elementary Free-Hand Drawing Copies* (in 5 Parts, on the Recommended List of the Department of Practical Art), 4to, single Parts, 6*d*. each, the Series, 2*s* 6*d*; *Diagrams and Instructions for Free-Hand Exercises in Geometrical Forms*, 4to, 1*s* 3*d*; *Lessons on the Delineations of Form*; *The Outline, or First Writing-Book, a Guide to the Correct Formation of the Elements of Letters*, 3 eds. 3*s* 6*d* per dozen; *Gallery Models for the Collective Teaching of Elementary Writing* (on the Committee of Council's List), 4 Books, 1*s* 6*d* each; *Desk Models, or Copy Slips*, 1*s*; *Preparatory Exercises for Current Hand Writing to give Freedom of Movement to the Fingers*, 4½*d*; *Progressive Lessons in Elementary Writing, suggesting Improvements in the Methods of Teaching Writing, &c.* (a Manual for Teachers and Pupil Teachers), (on Committee of Council's List), 3*s* 6*d*; *The School Builder's Guide, and School Furniture Pattern Book*, 3*s*. [6]

RICHTER, Henry William, *Lincoln.*—Deac. 1821 and Pr. 1822 by Abp of York. R. of St. Paul's, Lincoln, Dio. Lin. 1844. (Patron, Archd. of Lin; R.'s Inc. 70*l*; Pop. 789.) Chap. to the Lincoln Co. Gaol. [7]

RICKARDS, Heley Hutchinson Keating, *Dynas Powis, Cardiff.*—Mert. Coll. Ox. B.A. 1835; Deac. 1836 by Bp of Ex. Pr. 1837 by Bp of Llan. R. of Michaelstone-le-Pit, Dio. Llan. 1839. (Patron, Lieut.-Col. G. G. Rous; Tithe, 70*l*; Glebe, 18 acres; R.'s Inc. 100*l*; Pop. 73.) R. of Leckwith with Llandough R. and Cogan R. Dio. Llan. 1863. (Patron, Marquis of Bute; R.'s Inc. 200*l* and Ho; Pop. 650.) [8]

RICKARDS, James, *Sidney-Sussex College, Cambridge.*—Trin. Coll. Cam. B.A. 1834, Sid. Coll. M.A. 1844, B.D. 1851. Fell. of Sid. Coll. Cam. [9]

RICKARDS, John Witherstone, *Ringwood, Hants.*—Caius Coll. Cam. B.A. 1866; Deac. 1867 by Bp of Win. C. of Ringwood. [10]

RICKARDS, Robert Francis Bute, *Constantine Vicarage, Falmouth.*—Ball. Coll. Ox. 1st cl. Math. 4th cl. Lit. Hum. B.A. 1832, M.A. 1840. V. of Constantine, Dio. Ex. 1856. (Patrons, D. and C. of Ex; Tithe—App. 481*l*, V. 486*l* 12*s* 2½*d*; Glebe, 10 acres; V.'s Inc. 516*l* and Ho; Pop. 2014.) Author, *Short Prayers and Plain Questions to assist Young Persons in preparing for the Holy Communion*; *Words by Way of Remembrance* (a vol. of Sermons.) [11]

RICKARDS, Thomas Ascough, *Cosby, near Lutterworth.*—Oriel Coll. Ox. 1st cl. Math. 3rd cl. Lit. Hum. B.A. 1814; Deac. 1814, Pr. 1815. V. of Cosby, Dio. Pet. 1816. (Patron, J. Pares, Esq; Tithe, 15*l*; Glebe, 104 acres; V.'s Inc. 138*l*; Pop. 974.) [12]

RICKETTS, Martin Henry, *Bromyard.*—Ex. Coll. Ox. Hon. 4th cl. Lit. Hum. and B.A. 1847, M.A. 1850; Deac. 1848 and Pr. 1849 by Bp of Wor. P. C. of Hatfield, Dio. Herf. 1862. (Patron, Ld Chan; P. C.'s Inc. 90*l*; Pop. 180.) P. C. of Grendon Bishop, Dio. Herf. 1862. (Patron, V. of Bromyard; P. C.'s Inc. 85*l*; Pop. 199.) Formerly C. of Cleobury-Mortimer. [13]

RICKETTS, St. Vincent Fitzhardinge Lennox, *Hartpury, Gloucester.*—St. John's Coll. Ox. B.A. 1865; Deac. 1866 and Pr. 1867 by Bp of G. and B. C. of Hartpury 1866. [14]

RIDDELL, James, *Balliol College, Oxford.*—Ball. Coll. Ox. 1st cl. Lit. Hum. 3rd cl. Math. et Phy. and B.A. 1845, M.A. 1850; Deac. 1852, Pr. 1856. Fell. and Tut. of Ball. Coll. Ox. 1845; Public Examiner in Lit. Hum. 1858. [15]

RIDDELL, John Charles Buchanan, *Harrietsham Rectory, Maidstone.*—Ch. Ch. Ox. 1833, 4th cl. Lit. Hum. B.A. 1837, M.A. 1841; Deac. 1838, Pr. 1840. R. of Harrietsham, Dio. Cant. 1842. (Patron, All Souls' Coll. Ox; Tithe—Imp. 40*l*, R. 580*l*; Glebe, 62 acres; R.'s Inc. 680*l* and Ho; Pop. 624.) Hon. Can. of Cant. 1864. Formerly Fell. of All Souls' Coll. Ox. 1837. [16]

RIDDING, Charles Henry, *Andover, Hants.*—New Coll. Ox. B.C.L. R. of Rollstone, Wilts, Dio. Salis. 1824. (Patron, Ld Chan; R.'s Inc. 150*l*; Pop. 52.) V. of Andover with Foxcote C. Dio. Win. 1835. (Patron, Win. Coll; V.'s Inc. 400*l*; Pop. Andover 4583, Foxcote 50.) Fell. of Win. Coll. Formerly Fell. of New Coll. Ox; 2nd Mast. of Win. Coll. [17]

RIDDING, Charles Henry, jun., *Slymbridge Rectory, Stonehouse, Gloucestershire.*—Trin. Coll. Ox. 1844, Demy of Magd. Coll. 1847, B.A. 1848, M.A. 1850; Deac. 1849 and Pr. 1850 by Bp of Ox. R. of Slymbridge, Dio. G. and B. 1865. (Patron, Magd. Coll. Ox; Glebe, 344 acres; R.'s Inc. 650*l* and Ho; Pop. 789.) Formerly C. of Theale, Berks, 1849–52, Faccombe with Tangley, Hants, 1852–57; Fell. of Magd. Coll. Ox. 1856–66, and Vice-Pres. 1864–65. [18]

RIDDING, George, *Winchester.*—Ball. Coll. Ox. 1st cl. Lit. Hum. Craven Scho. and B.A. 1851; Ex. Coll. Ox. Latin Essay and M.A. 1853. Fell. of Ex. Coll. Ox; Head Mast. of Winchester Coll. [19]

RIDDING, William, *Meriden, Coventry.*—New Coll. Ox. B.C.L. and M.A. 1856; Deac. 1854 and Pr. 1856 by Bp. of Ox. V. of Meriden, Dio. Wor. 1860. (Patron, Earl of Aylesford; V.'s Inc. 300*l*; Pop. 968.) Formerly Fell. of New Coll. Ox; C. of Paddingham 1858-60. [20]

RIDDLE, John Brimble, *Bedminster, Bristol.*—Wad. Coll. Ox. 3rd cl. Lit. Hum. B.A. 1837, M.A. 1844; Deac. 1844 and Pr. 1845 by Bp of G. and B, V. of St. Thomas's, Bristol, Dio. G. and B. 1852. (Patron, Bp of G. and B; V.'s Inc. 115l; Pop. 1267.) Chap. to Bristol General Cemetery, Bedminster, 1862. (Stipend, 80l.) Formerly C. of St. James's, Bristol, 1844; P. C. of St. Michael's, Two Mile Hill, 1848. Translator, *Gräfenhan's Introduction to Writing Hebrew,* Talboys, Oxford, 1836. [1]

RIDGEWAY, Charles John, *Christ Church Parsonage, Tunbridge Wells.*—Trin. Coll. Cam. B.A. 1863; Deac. and Pr. by Abp of Cant. C. of Ch. Ch. Tunbridge Wells. [2]

RIDGEWAY, Joseph, *Christ Church Parsonage, Tunbridge Wells.*—Dub. A.B. 1822, A.M. 1825; Deac. 1825 and Pr. 1826 by Bp of Meath. P. C. of Ch. Ch. Tunbridge Wells, Dio. Cant. 1857. (Patron, Rev. T. W. Franklyn; P. C.'s Inc. 525l and Ho; Pop. 2452.) Editorial Sec. of Ch. Miss. Soc. Formerly C. of Slane, co. Meath, Armagh, co. Cavan, Delgany, co. Wicklow; R. of High Roding, Essex, 1830-49; P. C. of Penge, Surrey, 1849-58. Author, *Faith once delivered to the Saints; Bible its own Witness; Gospel in Type,* Seeleys; etc. [3]

RIDGEWAY, William Henry, *Sternfield, Saxmundham, Suffolk.*—Magd. Hall, Ox. B.A. 1859, M.A. 1862: Deac. and Pr. by Abp of Cant. R. of Sternfield, Dio. Nor. 1865. (Patron, William Long, Esq; R.'s Inc. 350l and Ho; Pop. 208.) Formerly C. of Ch. Ch. Tunbridge Wells, and Congresbury, Somerset. [4]

RIDGWAY, James, *Diocesan Training College, Culham, Oxon.*—Lin. Coll. Ox. B.A. 1851, M.A. 1854; Deac. 1851 and Pr. 1853 by Bp of Ox. Prin. of Training Coll. Culham. (Salary, 400l.) Author, *On Oxford Local Examinations,* 1858; *Outlines of English History,* 1860; *Westminster Abbey, its Historical Associations,* 1860. [5]

RIDLEY, Charles George, *Grammar School, Spilsby, Lincolnshire.*—Deac. 1858 and Pr. 1866 by Bp of Lin. Head Mast. of the Gr. Sch. Spilsby 1858; Chap. of the Union Workhouse 1863. Formerly C. of Spilsby 1858-65. [6]

RIDLEY, Henry Richard, *Durham.*—Univ. Coll. Ox. B.A. 1828, M.A. 1859; Deac. 1840 and Pr. 1841 by Bp of Dur. P. C. of St. Cuthbert's, Durham, Dio. Dur. 1858. (Patrons, D. and C. of Dur; P. C.'s Inc. 300l; Pop. 3486.) Surrogate. [7]

RIDLEY, Henry Thomas, 81, *Cambridge-street, Pimlico, London, S.W.*—Deac. and Pr. 1853 by Bp of Ex. Sen. C. of St. Gabriel's, Warwick-square, Pimlico, 1861. Formerly C. of St. Columb Major, Cornwall, and St. James's, Devonport. [8]

RIDLEY, James William, Trin. Hall, Cam. 1st in 1st cl. Civil Law Trip. and S.C.L. 1853; Deac. 1853 and Pr. 1854 by Bp of Lich. Chap of H.M.S. "Impregnable." [9]

RIDLEY, Joseph, *Wigan.*—St. Bees; Deac. 1863 and Pr. 1864 by Bp of Ches. C. of St. Catherine's. Wigan, 1863. [10]

RIDLEY, Nicholas James, *Hollington House, East Woodhay, Newbury.*—Ch. Ch. Ox. 2nd cl. Lit. Hum. 1842, B.A. 1843, M.A. 1845; Deac. 1844, Pr. 1845. P. C. of Woolton Hill, East Woodhay, Dio. Win. 1850. (Patron, R. of East Woodhay; P. C.'s Inc. 100l; Pop. 831.) Sec. to Ch. of England Book Hawking Union, 3, Waterloo-place, Lond. [11]

RIDLEY, Oliver Matthew, *Cobham, Gravesend.*—Ch. Ch. Ox. B.A. 1846, M.A. 1866; Deac. 1855 by Abp of Cant. Pr. 1855 by Bp of Nor. V. of Cobham, Kent, Dio. Roch. 1860. (Patron, Earl of Darnley; V.'s Inc. 400l; Pop. 864.) Formerly R. of West Harling, Norfolk, 1855-60. [12]

RIDLEY, Thomas, *Preston Candover, Micheldever Station, Hants.*—St. Cath. Hall, Cam. B.A. 1839; Deac. 1843 and Pr. 1844 by Bp of Win. P C. of Wield, Dio. Win. 1860. (Patron, Earl of Portsmouth; P. C.'s Inc. 80l; Pop. 304.) Formerly Asst. C. of St. James's, Bermondsey, Lond. 1843-44; C. of Bullington with Tufton, Hants, 1844-58. [13]

RIDLEY, Thomas, *St Mary's Parsonage, near Halifax.*—Magd. Hall, Ox. B.A. 1833, M.A. 1838; Deac. 1833, Pr. 1834. P. C. of St. Mary's, Sowerby, Dio. Rip. 1848. (Patrons, the Crown and Bp of Rip. alt; P. C.'s Inc. 150l and Ho; Pop. 1902.) [14]

RIDLEY, William Henry, *Hambleden Rectory, Henley-on-Thames.*—Ch. Ch. Ox. 1st cl. Lit. Hum. 3rd cl. Math. and B.A. 1838, M.A. 1840; Deac. 1839, Pr. 1840. R. of Hambleden, Dio. Ox. 1840. (Patron, the present R; Tithe, 1200l; Glebe, 40 acres; R.'s Inc. 1260l and Ho; Pop. 1350.) Rural Dean of Marlow 1859. Author, *A Plain Tract on Confirmation,* 4d; *Master and his Servants,* 2s; *Holy Communion,* 7d; *How to Give Thanks,* 1d; *The Falling Leaves,* 1d; *Sermons in Plain Language,* 2s; *Every-Day Companion,* 3s. [15]

RIDOUT, George, *Newland Vicarage, Coleford, Glouc.*—Ball. Coll. Ox. 2nd cl. Lit. Hum. and B.A. 1809, LL.B. 1810; Deac. and Pr. 1812 by Bp of Glouc. V. of Newland with Redbrook C. Dio. G. and B. 1832. (Patron, Bp of G. and B; Tithe—App. 1090l, Imp. 10l, V. 525l; Glebe, 25 acres; V.'s Inc. 565l and Ho; Pop. 1085.) Lect. of Newland 1813. (Value, 69l.) [16]

RIDOUT, George, *Sandhurst Rectory, Staplehurst.*—Emman. Coll. Cam. B.A. 1842, M.A. 1845; Deac. 1843 and Pr. 1844 by Bp of Lon. R. of Sandhurst, Kent, Dio. Cant. 1857. (Patron, Abp of Cant; Tithe, 487l; Glebe, 11 acres; R.'s Inc. 750l and Ho; Pop. 1232.) Formerly C. of St. George's, Bloomsbury, Lond. 1843-49; P. C. of Ash, Kent, 1849-57. [17]

RIDOUT, John Dowell, *Bourn Vicarage, near Royston, Cambs.*—Ch. Coll. Cam. 1st. Sen. Opt. 1st in 3rd cl. Cl. Trip. and B.A. 1841, M.A. 1844; Deac. and Pr. 1842 by Bp of Ely. V. of Bourn, Dio. Ely, 1853. (Patron, Ch. Coll. Cam; Tithe, comm. 200l; V.'s Inc. 235l and Ho; Pop. 883.) Formerly Fell. of Ch. Coll. Cam; C. of St. Andrew's the Great, Cambridge, 1843-53. [18]

RIDSDALE, Charles Joseph, *Norwell, Newark, Notts.*—Caius Coll. Cam. Cl. Hons. and B.A. 1863; Deac. 1864 by Abp of Cant. C. of Norwell with Carlton. Formerly C. of Whitstable and Seasalter, Kent, 1864. [19]

RIDSDALE, George John, *South Creake Vicarage, Fakenham, Norfolk.*—Magd. Coll. Cam. B.A. 1851, M.A. 1854; Deac. 1853, Pr. 1855. V. of South Creake, Dio. Nor. 1858. (Patron, Marquis of Townshend; Tithe—Imp. 675l, V. 440l; Glebe, ½ acre; V.'s Inc. 442l and Ho; Pop. 1058.) Private Chap. to the Duke of Devonshire. Formerly C. of Tillington, Sussex. [20]

RIDSDALE, J. W., *Bramhope, Otley, Yorks.*—P. C. of Bramhope, Dio. Rip. (Patrons, Trustees; P. C.'s Inc. 50l; Pop. 312.) P. C. of Poole, Dio. Rip. 1834. (Patron, V. of Otley; P. C.'s Inc. 70l; Pop. 337.) [21]

RIDSDALE, Robert, *Tillington Rectory, Petworth, Sussex.*—Clare Coll. Cam. Fell. of, 1816-26, Sen. Opt. B.A. 1815, M.A. 1818; Deac. 1815 and Pr. 1816 by Bp of Lin. R. of Tillington, Dio. Chich. 1834. (Patron, Lord Leconfield; Tithe, 740l; Glebe, 25 acres; R.'s Inc. 780l and Ho; Pop. 908.) R. of Knockin, Salop, Dio. St. A. 1826. (Patron, Earl of Bradford; Tithe, 328l 2s; Glebe, 1r. 32p; R.'s Inc. 328l; Pop. 289.) Preb. of Chich. 1835. Formerly C. of Hertingfordbury, Herts, 1815-18, St. Andrew's, Hertford, 1819-26; V. of Kirdford 1826-31; R. of North Chapel 1831-34. [22]

RIDSDALE, Thomas Marshall, *Pyrford Vicarage, Woking, Surrey.*—Jesus Coll. Cam. B.A. 1852, M.A. 1855; Deac. 1853 and Pr. 1854 by Bp of Lon. R. of Wisley with Pyrford V. Dio. Win. 1867. (Patron, Earl of Onslow; Wisley, Tithe, 120l 10s; Glebe, 57 acres; Pyrford, Tithe, Imp. 199l 18s 1d; Glebe, 12 acres; R.'s Inc. 268l and Ho; Pop. Wisley 166, Pyrford 381.) Formerly C. of Trinity, St. Giles's-in-the-Fields, Lond. 1853-57; Chap. of Serampore, India, 1857-64; C. of St. Katherine Cree, City, Lond. 1865-66, Wisley with Pyrford 1866-67. [23]

RIDSDEL, Thomas, *Oldbury, Birmingham.*—Queen's Coll. Birmingham, Deac. 1866 by Bp of Wor. C. of Oldbury. [24]

RIDYARD, Robert Tomlinson, 1, *Lord Duncan-street, Cross-lane, Salford.*—St. Bees; Deac. 1861 and Pr. 1862 by Bp of Pet. C. of St. John's, Manchester, 1867. Formerly C. of Sheepshead, Loughborough, 1861–62, Ch. Ch. Salford, 1862–65, St. Matthias', Salford, 1866. [1]

RIGAUD, John, *Magdalen College, Oxford.*—Magd. Coll. Ox. 3rd cl. Lit. Hum. and B.A. 1844, M.A. 1846, B.D. 1854; Deac. 1847 and Pr. 1851 by Bp of Ox. Fell. of Magd. Coll. Ox. C. of St. Mary Magdalen's, Oxford. [2]

RIGBY, George Henry, *Pembury, Tunbridge.*—Trin. Coll. Cam. B.A. 1861, M.A. 1864; Deac. 1861 and Pr. 1862 by Abp of Cant. C. of Pembury 1861. [3]

RIGBY, Joseph, *Hutton Vicarage, Driffield, Yorks.*—Univ. Coll. Ox. B.A. 1811; Deac. 1815 by Bp of Lin. Pr. 1816 by Abp of York. V. of Hutton-Cranswick, Dio. York, 1819. (Patron, Lord Hotham; Tithe—Imp. 182*l* 13*s*, V. 14*l* 16*s*; Glebe, 50 acres; V.'s Inc. 140*l* and Ho; Pop. 1415.) P. C. of Beswick, Yorks, Dio. York, 1819. (Patron, Lord Hotham; Tithe—Imp. 285*l*, P. C. 75*l*; Glebe, 17 acres; P. C.'s Inc. 112*l*; Pop. 252.) Author, *The Spirit of the Age*, 1834; *An Inquiry into the Descent of Christ into Hell*, 1845. [4]

RIGBY, Thomas, *Ramford Holme, Parr, St. Helens.*—Corpus Coll. Cam. B.A. 1864; Deac. 1865 and Pr. 1866 by Bp of Ches. C. of Parr 1865. [5]

RIGBY, Thomas Newton, *Victoria-road, Aston Park, Birmingham.*—Dub. A.B. 1862, A.M. 1866; Deac. 1864 and Pr. 1865 by Bp of Wor. C. of St. Mary's, Birmingham. [6]

RIGBY, Thomas Procter, *Aughton, near Halton, Lancaster.*—St. John's Coll. Cam. 27th Wrang. 3rd cl. Cl. Trip. B.A. 1849, M.A. 1852; Deac. 1849 and Pr. 1850 by Bp of Ches. P. C. of Aughton, Dio. Man. 1856. (Patron, R. of Halton; P. C.'s Inc. 126*l* and Ho; Pop. 130.) Formerly Head Mast. of the Gr. Sch. Horton-in-Ribblesdale, Yorks. [7]

RIGDEN William, *Cann St. Rumbold, near Shaftesbury, Dorset.*—Magd. Hall, Ox. B.A. 1832; Deac. 1833, Pr. 1834. R. of Cann St. Rumbold, Dio. Salis. 1857. (Patron, Earl of Shaftesbury; Tithe, 250*l*; R.'s Inc. 260*l* and Ho; Pop. 547.) Formerly C. of South Newton, near Salisbury. [8]

RIGDEN, W. G., *Kendal.*—C. of Kendal. [9]

RIGG, Arthur, *Chester.*—Ch. Coll. Cam. B.A. 1835, M.A. 1840. Prin. of the Chester Dioc. Training Coll. [10]

RIGG, George, *Saxon-street, Lincoln.*—St. Peter's Coll. Cam. B.A. 1828; Deac. 1829 by Bp of Pet. Pr. 1830 by Bp of Lin. P. C. of St. Peter's with St. Margaret's, Lincoln, Dio. Lin. 1841. (Patrons, Precentor of Lin. Cathl. and Bp of Lin. alt; Tithe, App. 556*l* 10*s*; P. C.'s Inc. 159*l*; Pop. St. Peter's 1028, St. Margaret's 452.) V. of Cherry Willingham, Dio. Lin. 1848. (Patrons, Messrs. Cock, Gordon, and Ellis; Tithe, 100*l*; V.'s Inc. 145*l*; Pop. 173.) [11]

RIGG, John, *Shrewsbury.*—St. John's Coll. Cam. 11th Wrang. 3rd cl. Cl. Trip. and B.A. 1846; Deac. 1853, Pr. 1855. Second Mast. of Shrewsbury Sch. 1861. Formerly Fell. and Asst. Tut. of St. John's Coll. Cam. [12]

RIGG, John, *New Mills (Derbyshire), near Stockport.*—New Inn Hall Ox. M.A. 1843; Deac. 1842, Pr. 1843. P. C. of New Mills, Dio. Lich. 1848. (Patron, V. of Glossop; P. C.'s Inc. 300*l* and Ho; Pop. 4822.) [13]

RIGG, Richard, *Norwich.*—Caius Coll. Cam. 15th Wrang. and B.A. 1831, M.A. 1834. R. of St. Clement's, Norwich, Dio. Nor. 1842. (Patron, Caius Coll. Cam; Tithe, 49*l* 13*s* 6*d*; R.'s Inc. 97*l*; Pop. 770.) [14]

RIGG, Thomas, *Flookburgh Parsonage, Grange-in-Cartmel, Lancashire.*—Dub. A.B; Deac. 1860 and Pr. 1861 by Bp of Ches. P. C. of Flookburgh, Dio. Carl. 1868. (Patron, Duke of Devonshire; P. C.'s Inc. 124*l* 14*s*. and Ho; Pop. 1160.) Formerly C. of Newton Moor, Cheshire, 1860–62; P. C. of Peak Forest, Derbyshire, 1863. [15]

RIGG, William, *Kingston-on-Thames.*—Pemb. Coll. Cam. Scho. 1842, B.A. 1844, M.A. 1847; Deac. 1845 and Pr. 1847 by Bp of Pet. Head Mast. to Queen Elizabeth's Gr. Sch. Kingston-on-Thames, 1848; Chap. to House of Correction; Aft. Lect. at New Malden, Surrey, 1858. Formerly Mast. of Oundle Gr. Sch. Northants, 1844–48; C. of Lutton, near Oundle, 1845–48. [16]

RIGGE, William Postlethwaite, *Lee, Hexham, Northumberland.*—Dub. A.B. 1848; Deac. 1848, Pr. 1849. R. of Lee, Dio. York, 1863. (Patron, W. B. Beaumont, Esq; R.'s Inc. 350*l*; Pop. 2254.) Formerly C. of Eglingham, and of Lee, Northumberland; P. C. of Peak-Forest, Derbyshire, 1859–63. [17]

RIKY, John Benjamin, *Bagborough Rectory, near Taunton.*—St. John's Coll. Cam. B.A. 1851, M.A. 1854; Deac. 1852 and Pr. 1853 by Bp of Wor. R. of Bagborough, Dio. B. and W. 1857. (Patron, the present R; Tithe, 323*l*; Glebe, 72 acres; R.'s Inc. 560*l* and Ho; Pop. 495.) Formerly C. of Abbotts-Morton, Worc. 1852–56. [18]

RILEY, John, *Vernham, Hungerford.*—Queens' Coll. Cam. B.A. 1864; Deac. 1865 and Pr. 1866 by Bp of Win. C. of Vernham 1865. [19]

RILEY, Richard, *Hennock Vicarage, Exeter.*—St. Bees; Deac. 1851 by Bp of Ches. Pr. 1852 by Bp of Win. V. of Hennock with Knighton C. Dio. Ex. 1862. (Patron, the present V; Tithe, 230*l*; Glebe, 20 acres; V.'s Inc. 250*l* and Ho; Pop. 1004.) Formerly C. of St. Peter's, Southwark, Mangotsfield, and St. Peter's, Cheltenham. Author, *Thunderstorms* (a Sermon). [20]

RIMELL, Edgcombe, *Marystow Vicarage, Lew Down, Devon.*—St. John's Coll. Cam. B.A. 1831; Deac. 1831 by Bp of G. and B. Pr. 1834 by Bp of Ex. V. of Marystow with Thrushelton C. Dio. Ex. 1840. (Patron, J. Tremayne, Esq; Marystow, Tithe—App. 13*s* 10*d*, Imp. 86*l* 19*s*, V. 161*l* 7*s*; Glebe, 110 acres; Thrushelton, Tithe—Imp. 130*l*, V. 109*l*; V.'s Inc. 350*l* and Ho; Pop. Marystow 448, Thrushelton 484.) Rural Dean of Tavistock 1856. Author, *Loss of the Kent*, 1825; *Harvest Sermon*, 1840; *Funeral Sermon*, 1851. [21]

RIMINGTON, William, *The Vicarage, Norton Subcorse, near Loddon, Norfolk.*—Trin. Coll. Cam. B.A. 1859; Deac. 1860 and Pr. 1861 by Bp of B. and W. V. of Norton Subcorse, Dio. Nor. 1867. (Patron, Sir H. Hickman Bacon, Bart; Tithe, 161*l* 10*s*; Glebe, 16 acres; V.'s Inc. 189*l* 10*s* and Ho; Pop. 379.) Formerly C. of White Lackington with Sevington St. Mary, Somerset, 1860–62; P. C. of Bolsterstone, Yorks, 1862–67. [22]

RIMMER, John, *Woodhouse, Whitehaven.*—Glasgow Univ. M.A. and M.D. St. Bees; Deac. 1843 and Pr. 1844 by Bp of Ches. P. C. of Ch. Ch. Whitehaven, Dio. Carl. 1847. (Patron, Earl of Lonsdale; P. C.'s Inc. 220*l*; Pop. 4131.) [23]

RING, Bartholomew.—Dub. A.B. 1853; Deac. 1854 by Bp of Killaloe, Pr. 1855 by Abp of Dub. Chap. of H.M.S. "Lion." [24]

RIPLEY, Frederick N., *Herongate, Brentwood, Essex.*—C. of East Horndon, Essex. [25]

RIPLEY, Frederick William, *Highfield House, Lymm, Cheshire.*—Formerly C. of Lymm. [26]

RIPLEY, Horace Charles, *West Horsley, Ripley, Surrey.*—Univ. Coll. Dur. B.A. 1853, M.A. 1857; Deac. 1857, Pr. 1866. C. of West Horsley 1866. Formerly C. of Chester-le-Street 1857, Brancepeth, Durham, 1864; Youlgreave, Derbyshire, 1865. [27]

RIPLEY, William Nottidge, *Earlham, near Norwich.*—Caius Coll. Cam. Wrang. and B.A. 1848, M.A. 1851; Deac. 1849, Pr. 1850. P. C. of St. Giles's, Norwich, Dio. Nor. 1859. (Patrons, D. and C. of Nor; P. C.'s Inc. 80*l*; Pop. 1586.) Formerly C. of Lowestoft, Suffolk. [28]

RIPON, The Right Rev. Robert BICKERSTETH, Lord Bp of Ripon, *The Palace, Ripon, Yorks,* and 1, *Whitehall-gardens, London, S.W.*—Queens' Coll. Cam. B.A. 1841, M.A. 1846, D.D. 1856; Deac. 1841, Pr. 1842. Consecrated Bp of Rip. 1857. (Episcopal Jurisdiction—the Western and Northern parts of the County of York; Inc. of See, 4500*l*; Pop. 1,167,288; Deaneries, 7; Benefices, 439; Curates,

196; Church sittings, 229,726.) His Lordship was formerly R. of St. Giles's-in-the-Fields, Lond. 1851–56; Can. Res. and Treasurer of Salis. Cathl. 1854–56. Author, *Bible Landmarks*, Hatchards; *Means of Grace*, ib; *Sermons*, 1 vol. Nisbet, 1866; various Sermons; Charges to the Clergy delivered in 1858, 1861, and 1864; Lectures in Exeter Hall to the Young Men's Christian Association. [1]

RISK, Andrew Charles, *Crewe, Cheshire.*—C. of Ch. Ch. Crewe. [2]

RISK, John Erskine, *St. Andrew's Chapelry, Plymouth.*—Dub. Heb. Cl. and Logic Prizes and Honors, A.B. 1847, A.M. 1860, *ad eund.* Magd. Hall, Ox. M.A. 1864; Deac. 1853 by Bp of Meath, Pr. 1854 by Bp of Killaloe. P. C. of St. Andrew's Chapel, Plymouth, Dio. Ex. 1867. (Patron, V. of St. Andrew's; P. C.'s Inc. 114*l* and Ho.) Formerly C. of St. Andrew's, 1856–67. Author, *King David the Warrior, with Remarks on the Light in which the New Testament regards War* (a Lecture, 1855); *The Church's Inviolable Deposit* (a Sermon), 1858; *The Church's Prayer for the Magistracy* (a Sermon), 1861; *The Magistrate God's Minister* (a Sermon), Plymouth, 1867; etc. [3]

RISLEY, John Holford, *Akeley Rectory, near Buckingham.*—New Coll. Ox. S.C.L. 1833, B.C.L. 1835, M.A. 1865; Deac. 1837, Pr. 1838. R. of Akeley with Stockholte, Dio. Ox. 1841. (Patron, New Coll. Ox. Tithe, 11*d*; Glebe, 34 acres; R.'s Inc. 184*l* and Ho; Pop. 366.) Chap. to the late Duke of Buckingham. [4]

RISLEY, Robert Wells, *Surbiton, Surrey, S.W.*—Ex. Coll. Ox. M.A. 1861; Deac. 1862 by Abp of Cant. Pr. 1863 by Bp of Win. C. of St. Mark's, Surbiton, 1864. Formerly C. of Egham 1862. [5]

RISLEY, William Cotton, 17, *Upper Southwick-street, Hyde Park, W.*—Ex. Coll. Ox. B.A. 1856, M.A. 1857; Deac. 1858 and Pr. 1860 by Bp of Ox. C. of St. Michael's, Paddington, Lond. Formerly C. of Hambleden, Bucks, Fulbrook, and Kidmore End, Oxon, and St. John's, Paddington. [6]

RITSON, John, *Brinklow Rectory, near Coventry.*—Jesus Coll. Cam. B.A. 1845, M.A. 1850; Deac. 1845 and Pr. 1846 by Bp of Ches. R. of Brinklow, Dio. Wor. 1858. (Patron, Ld Chan; Tithe, 9*l*; Glebe, 120 acres; R.'s Inc. 228*l* and Ho; Pop. 736.) Rural Dean of Rugby; Dioc. Inspector of Schs. Formerly P. C. of Allonby and Organizing Sec. for S.P.G. Dio. Carl. 1850–58. [7]

RIVERS, Henry Frederick, *Luton, Chatham.*—Trin. Coll. Cam. Sen. Opt. B.A. 1857; Deac. 1857 and Pr. 1858 by Bp of Roch. Chap. of Medway Union, Chatham, 1860; C. of St. Mary's, Chatham. Formerly C. of St. Paul's, Chatham, 1857. [8]

RIVETT, Alfred W. L., *Bunwell, Attleborough, Norfolk.*—C. in sole charge of Bunwell 1867. Formerly C. of St. Nicholas', Great Yarmouth. [9]

RIVINGTON, Luke, *Clergy House, All Saints', Margaret-street, London, W.*—Magd. Coll. Ox. Demy and Exhib. of, M.A; Deac. 1861 by Bp of Ox. Pr. 1863 by Bp of Tasmania. C. of All Saints', Margaret-street, 1867. Formerly C. of St. Giles', Oxford, 1861, and again 1864, St. Clement's, Oxford, 1863. Author, *The Inward Part, or Thing signified in the Lord's Supper*, Mowbray, Oxford, 1866, 6*d*. [10]

ROACH, William Harris, *Whiteshill Parsonage, Stroud, Glouc.*—Pemb. Coll. Cam. Sen. Opt. and B.A. 1838; Deac. 1842, Pr. 1843. P. C. of Whiteshill, Dio. G. and B. 1846. (Patron, Bp of G. and B; Glebe, 2 acres; P. C.'s Inc. 54*l* and Ho; Pop. 1516.) [11]

ROBARTS, Charles N., *St. John's, Newbury.*—Ch. Coll. Cam. Jun. Opt. B.A. 1858, M.A. 1861; Deac. 1858 and Pr. 1859 by Bp of Roch. C. of St. John's, Newbury, 1860. Formerly C. of Halstead, Essex, 1858–60. [12]

ROBBINS, George, *Courteenhall Rectory, near Northampton.*—Magd. Coll. Ox. B.A. 1831, M.A. 1834; Deac. 1832 and Pr. 1833 by Bp of Salis. R. of Courteenhall, Dio. Pet. 1851. (Patron, Ld Chan; Tithe, 300*l*; Glebe, 58 acres; R.'s Inc. 396*l* and Ho; Pop. 162.) Rural Dean of Northampton 1851. Formerly British Chap. in Tuscany 1836–50. [13]

ROBBINS, John.—Ch. Ch. Ox. M.A. P. C. of St. Peter's, Bayswater, Dio. Lon. 1862. (Patron, R. Martin, Esq; Pop. 6660.) [14]

ROBBINS, William, *Shropham Vicarage, Larlingford, Norfolk.*—Wor. Coll. Ox. B.A. 1836, M.A. 1845; Deac. 1837 by Bp of Ely, Pr. 1838 by Bp of Nor. V. of Shropham, Dio. Nor. 1850. (Patrons, Mayor and Corporation of Norwich; Tithe, 106*l* 12*s*; Glebe, 45½ acres; V.'s Inc. 300*l* and Ho; Pop. 510.) [15]

ROBERSON, Sidney Philip, *Rowton, High Ercall, Wellington, Salop.*—Wor. Coll. Ox. B.A. 1836; Deac. 1839 by Bp of Ely, Pr. 1841 by Bp of Lich. P. C. of Rowton, Dio. Lich. 1850. (Patron, Duke of Cleveland; P. C.'s Inc. 88*l*; Pop. 780.) Formerly C. of Waters-Upton 1849. [16]

ROBERSON, William Henry Moncrieff, *Tytherington Vicarage, Thornbury, Glouc.*—Lin. Coll. Ox. B.A. 1825, M.A. 1826; Deac. and Pr. 1826. V. of Tytherington, Dio. G. and B. 1830. (Patron, G. M. Taswell, Esq; Tithe—Imp. 450*l*, V. 309*l*; Glebe, 61 acres; V.'s Inc. 406*l* and Ho; Pop. 447.) [17]

ROBERTON, James Matthew, 16, *Devonshire-square, London, N.E.*—Magd. Hall, Ox. B.A. 1851, M.A. 1853; Deac. 1850 and Pr. 1851 by Bp of Win. P. C. of St. Botolph's, without Aldgate, City and Dio. Lon. 1860. (Patron, Bp of Lon; P. C.'s Inc. 300*l*; Pop. 9421.) Lect. at St. Olave's, Jewry. Formerly Sen. C. of All Souls', St. Marylebone, Lond. [18]

ROBERTS, Aaron, 16, *Spilman-street, Carmarthen.*—Jesus Coll. Ox. B.A. 1857, M.A. 1860; Deac. 1858 and Pr. 1860 by Bp of St. D. P. C. of Newchurch, Carmarthen, Dio. St. D. 1861. (Patron, John Davies, Esq; P. C.'s Inc. 100*l*; Pop. 782.) Chap. of County Prison, Carmarthen. (Chap.'s Inc. 100*l*.) Formerly C. of St. Peter's, Carmarthen, 1858–61. [19]

ROBERTS, Albert James, *Tidebrook Parsonage, Mayfield, Sussex.*—St. John's Coll. Ox. B A. 1848, M.A. 1861; Deac. 1850, Pr. 1851. P. C. of Tidebrook, Dio. Chich. 1858. (Patrons, V. of Wadhurst and V. of Mayfield alt; P. C.'s Inc. 53*l* and Ho; Pop. 710.) Formerly C. of Penkridge, Staffs, 1850, St. Stephen's, Islington, Lond. 1853. [20]

ROBERTS, Arthur, *Woodrising Rectory, Shipdham, Norfolk.*—Oriel Coll. Ox. 2nd cl. Lit. Hum. B.A. 1823, M.A. 1829; Deac. 1824 by Bp of Glouc. Pr. 1824 by Bp of Win. R. of Woodrising, Dio. Nor. 1831. (Patron, John Weyland, Esq; Tithe, 250*l*; Glebe, 17 acres; R.'s Inc. 260*l* and Ho; Pop. 97.) Formerly C. of Painswick, Glouc. 1824, St. Lawrence, Isle of Wight, 1824, and Bisley, Glouc. 1825. Author, *Life, Letters, and Opinions of William Roberts, Esq.* Seeleys, 1850; *Plain Sermons for every Sunday, &c. in the Year*, Nisbet, 1st Series, 2 vols. 1851, 10*s*; 2nd Series, 2 vols. 1853, 10*s*; 3rd Series, 2 vols. 1853, 10*s*; *Village Sermons*, 6 vols. Jarrolds; *Sermons on the History of Scripture*, 2 vols. ib; *Analysis of Martin Bucer's Revision of the Prayer Book*, Nisbet, 1*s* 6*d*; *Doctrine of Peter Martyr on Baptism* (Tract); *Sermons on the Pope's Supremacy*; *Mendip Annals, or Labours of Hannah and Martha More*, Nisbet, 5*s*; *Correspondence of Hannah More and Z. Macaulay*, ib. 5*s*; *Sermons on the Parables*, ib. 5*s*; *Plain Sermons on Gospel Miracles*, ib. 1867, 5*s*; etc. [21]

ROBERTS, Arthur, *Barkham, Wokingham, Berks.*—Magd. Coll. Ox. B.A. 1840; Deac. 1840 and Pr. 1841 by Bp of Lon. R. of Barkham, Dio. Ox. 1863. (Patron, John Walter, Esq. M.P; Tithe, 370*l*; Glebe, 16 acres; R.'s Inc. 390*l* and Ho; Pop. 280.) Formerly C. of Halstead, Essex, 1840–43. [22]

ROBERTS, Astley, *Rickmansworth, Herts.*—Trin. Coll. Cam. B.A. 1848, M.A. 1853; Deac. 1848 and Pr. 1850 by Bp of Chich. C. of Rickmansworth 1852. Formerly C. of Northiam, Sussex, 1848. [23]

ROBERTS, Charles Manley, *Monmouth.*—St. John's Coll. Cam. Scho. of, 26th Wrang. B.A. 1857, M.A. 1860; Deac. 1860 and Pr. 1861 by Bp of Herf. Head Mast. of the Gr. Sch. Monmouth; Chap. to the Monmouth Union Workhouse. Formerly 2nd Mast. of Ch. Coll. Brecon. [1]

ROBERTS, Claude William, *The Parsonage, Harrogate Wells, Yorks.*—Caius Coll. Cam. B.A. 1859; Deac. 1860 by Bp of Nor. C. in sole charge of St. Mary's, Harrogate Wells, 1864; Chap. of the Harrogate Bath Hospital 1864. Formerly C. of Scoulton, Norfolk, and Hemingford Abbots, Hunts. Author, *A Few Words on the Weekly Offertory*, 1865. [2]

ROBERTS, Cresswell, 215, *St. Philip's-road, Sheffield.*—Dub. A.B. C. of St. Philip's, Sheffield, 1866. Formerly C. of Cubley, Derbyshire. [3]

ROBERTS, David, *Llanwenllwyvo, Almwch, Anglesey.*—P. C. of Llanwenllwyvo, Dio. Ban. (Patron, P. C. of Almwch; Tithe, App. 172*l* 19*s* and 20 poles of Glebe; P. C.'s Inc. 75*l*; Pop. 546.) [4]

ROBERTS, David, *Llandyrnog Rectory, Denbigh.*—Jesus Coll. Ox. 3rd cl. Lit. Hum. B.A. 1837, M.A. 1839; Deac. 1838 and Pr. 1839 by Bp of Ox. R. of Llandyrnog, Dio. St. A. 1859. (Patron, Bp of St. D; Tithe, comm. 666*l*; Glebe, 24 acres; R.'s Inc. 700*l* and Ho; Pop. 653.) Formerly C. of St. Martin's, Salop, 1839–42; P. C. of Rhos-y-Medre, Denbighshire, 1842–43; P. C. of Llangedwin 1843–52; R. of Caerwys, Flintshire, 1852–59. [5]

ROBERTS, David, *Bryngolen House, Bridgend, Glamorganshire.*—Deac. 1861 and Pr. 1863 by Bp of Llan. C. of Coity with Nolton, Bridgend, 1865. Formerly Welsh C. of Maesteg. [6]

ROBERTS, David, *Mostyn Parsonage, Holywell.*—St. Bees; Deac. 1851 and Pr. 1852 by Bp of St. A. P. C. of Mostyn, Dio. St. A. 1852. (Patron, Bp of St. A; Glebe, 4 acres; P. C.'s Inc. 300*l* and Ho; Pop. 1640.) Formerly C. of Ysceifiog 1851-52. [7]

ROBERTS, David, *Llanelidan Rectory, Ruthin, Denbighshire.*—R. of Llanelidan, Dio. St. A. 1857. (Patron, Bp of St. A; Tithe—Imp. 300*l*, R. 300*l*; Glebe, ½ acre; R.'s Inc. 300*l* and Ho; Pop. 848.) [8]

ROBERTS, Edward, *Bunbury Rectory, Tarporley, Cheshire.*—St. Mary Hall, Ox. M.A. 1863. Preacher of Bunbury with Calveley and Peckforton, Dio. Ches. 1864. (Patron, Haberdashers' Co; Glebe, 28 acres; Preacher's Inc. 120*l* and Ho; Pop. 2820.) [9]

ROBERTS, Edward, *Nelson House, Devonport.*—St. John's Coll. Cam. 3rd cl. Cl. Trip. Wrang. B.A. 1854, M.A. 1857; Deac. 1856 and Pr. 1857 by Bp of Ex. C. of St. Aubyn's Chapel, Devonport, 1864. Formerly C. of Trinity, Plymouth. [10]

ROBERTS, Edward, *Harborne Vicarage, Birmingham.*—Dub. A.B. 1846; Deac. 1846, Pr. 1847. V. of Harborne, Dio. Lich. 1858. (Patrons, D. and C. of Lich; Tithe—App. 262*l* 7*s* 6*d*, and 25¾ acres of Glebe, V. 514*l* 7*s* 6*d*; Glebe, 25 acres; V.'s Inc. 600*l* and Ho; Pop. 1347.) Formerly C. of Harborne 1851–58. [11]

ROBERTS, Edward, *Llangwstenyn, Conway, Carnarvonshire.*—Jesus Coll. Ox. M.A. 1838; Deac. 1837, Pr. 1838. P. C. of Llangwstenyn, Dio. St. A. 1846. (Patron, Bp of St. A; Tithe, App. 281*l* and 7 acres of Glebe; P. C.'s Inc. 150*l*; Pop. 674.) [12]

ROBERTS, Ellis, *Llanvihangel Rectory, Corwen.*—Literate; Deac. 1862 and Pr. 1863 by Bp of St. A. R. of Llanvihangel Glyn-Myvyr, Dio. St. A. 1866. (Patron, Bp of St. A; Tithe, 200*l*; Glebe, 10 acres; R.'s Inc. 200*l* and Ho; Pop. 464.) Formerly C. of Rhos-y-Medre 1862–66. [13]

ROBERTS, Frederick, *Melbury Bubb, Sherborne, Dorset.*—R. of Melbury Bubb, Dio. Salis. 1860. (Patron, Earl of Ilchester; R.'s Inc. 240*l* and Ho; Pop. 136.) [14]

ROBERTS, Gabriel Lloyd, *Ryton Rectory, near Shiffnal.*—St. John's Coll. Cam. B.A. 1843, M.A. 1847; Deac. 1846 and Pr. 1847 by Bp of Ban. R. of Ryton, Dio. Lich. 1863. (Patron, Gabriel Roberts, Esq; Tithe, 445*l*; Glebe, 57½ acres; R.'s Inc. 550*l* and Ho; Pop. 214.) Formerly C. of Llanrhydd 1846–51, St. Asaph 1859–60. [15]

ROBERTS, George, *Thornaby, near Stockton-on-Tees.*—St. Bees; Deac. 1850 and Pr. 1851 by Bp of Rip. P. C. of Thornaby, Dio. York, 1856. (Patron, Abp of York; P. C.'s Inc. 300*l* and Ho; Pop. 3126.) Surrogate. Formerly C. of St. James's, Halifax, 1851–56. [16]

ROBERTS, George, *Norton Disney (Lincolnshire), Newark.*—Magd. Hall, Ox. B.A. 1840; Deac. 1840, Pr. 1842. V. of Norton Disney, Dio. Lin. 1852. (Patron, Viscount St. Vincent; Tithe, 115*l* 13*s*; Glebe, 53 acres; V.'s Inc. 172*l*; Pop. 196.) [17]

ROBERTS, Griffith, *Rhiw Rectory, Pwllheli, Carnarvonshire.*—Dub. A.B. 1822, *ad eund.* Jesus Coll. Ox. M.A. 1825; Deac. 1822, Pr. 1823. P. C. of Bryncroes, Carnarvonshire, Dio. Ban. 1836. (Patron, C. W. G. Wynne, Esq; Tithe—Imp. 181*l* 10*s* 6*d*; P. C.'s Inc. 105*l*; Pop. 889.) R. of Rhiw with Llandudwen C. Dio. Ban. 1837. (Patron, Bp of Ban; Rhiw, Tithe, 100*l*; Glebe, 6 acres; Llandudwen, Tithe, 30*l*; R.'s Inc. 139*l* and Ho; Pop. Rhiw 370, Llandudwen 94.) [18]

ROBERTS, Henry, *Othery Vicarage, Bridgwater.*—St. Edm. Hall, Ox. B.A. 1829; Deac. 1829 and Pr. 1830 by Bp of B. and W. V. of Othery, Dio. B. and W. 1864. (Patron, Bp of B. and W; Tithe, comm. 147*l*; Glebe, 18 acres; V.'s Inc. 180*l* and Ho; Pop. 714.) Formerly C. of Curry Rivell, Somerset, 1829–57; V. of same 1857–64. [19]

ROBERTS, Henry, *Mold, Flintshire.*—C. of Mold. [20]

ROBERTS, H., *Ashton, Chudleigh, Devon.*—R. of Ashton, Dio. Ex. 1861. (Patron, Rev. George Ware; R.'s Inc. 250*l*; Pop. 347.) [21]

ROBERTS, Henry Seymour, *Thornbury, Glouc.*—Queens' Coll. Cam. 1st cl. Civil Law Trip. S.C.L. 1851, LL.B. 1854–55, LL.D. 1860; Deac. 1862 by Abp of York, Pr. 1863 by Bp of G. and B. Head Mast. of the Gr. Sch. Thornbury, and Lect. of Thornbury 1864; Chap. of the Union. Formerly 2nd Mast. of Bristol Gr. Sch. 1855, and C. of St. Andrew's Montpelier, Bristol, 1862; previously Sen. Cl. Mast. at Wimbledon Military Coll. [22]

ROBERTS, Horace, 14, *Bury-place, Bloomsbury-square, London, W.C.*—Magd. Coll. Cam. B.A. 1837, M.A. 1841; Deac. 1838 and Pr. 1839 by Bp of Lon. Surrogate. Formerly Asst. Min. of Bedford Chapel, Bloomsbury. [23]

ROBERTS, Hugh, *Aberdaron, Pwllheli, Carnarvonshire.*—Dub. A.B. 1844; Deac. 1844, Pr. 1845. V. of Aberdaron with Llanfaelrhys P. C. Dio. Ban. 1852. (Patron, Bp of Ban; Aberdaron, Tithe—Imp. 252*l*, Sinecure R. 194*l*, V. 73*l*; Glebe, ½ acre; Llanfaelrhys, Tithe—Imp. 63*l*, Sinecure R. 47*l*, V. 18*l*; V.'s Inc. 125*l*; Pop. Aberdaron 1266, Llanfaelrhys 208.) [24]

ROBERTS, James, *St. David's, Haverfordwest.*—Min. Can. of St. David's. [25]

ROBERTS, James Barry, *Bronington Parsonage, Whitchurch, Salop.*—Dub. A.B. 1860, A.M. 1863; Deac. 1860 and Pr. 1861 by Bp of Ches. P. C. of Bronington, Dio. St. A. 1864. (Patron, Sir J. Hanmer, Bart. M.P; P. C.'s Inc. 110*l*; Pop. 675.) Formerly C. of Malpas, Lower Mediety, 1860–62; Threapwood (sole charge) 1862–64. [26]

ROBERTS, James Clarke, *Wrexham, Flintshire.*—Magd. Hall, Ox. B.A. 1848, M.A. 1853; Deac. 1857 by Bp of B. and W. Pr. 1858 by Bp of St. A. Chap. of the Union and Lect. of Wrexham. Formerly Asst. C. of Long Sutton and East Lambrook, Somerset. [27]

ROBERTS, James Corrall, *Wolston, Coventry.*—Trin. Coll. Ox. B.A. 1818, M.A. 1833. R. of Wolston, Dio. Wor. 1819. (Patron, W. Wilcox, Esq; Tithe—Imp. 540*l* 12*s* 6*d*, R. 79*l* 11*s* 5*d* and 106½ acres of Land in lieu of Tithe; R.'s Inc. 500*l*; Pop. 1263.) [28]

ROBERTS, John, *Llansadwrn, near Bangor (Anglesey).*—R. of Llansadwrn, Dio. Ban. 1845. (Patron, Bp of Ban; Tithe, 400*l*; R.'s Inc. 400*l*; Pop. 419.) [29]

ROBERTS, John, *Llaniestyn, Gwindy, Anglesey.*—C. of Llaniestyn. [30]

ROBERTS, John, *Chelford, near Congleton.*—C. of Chelford. [31]

ROBERTS, John Batthorp, *Shilbottle Vicarage, near Alnwick, Northumberland.*—Benet Coll. Cam. B.A. 1816, M.A. 1819; Deac. 1817 by Bp of Nor. Pr. 1833 by

Abp of Cant. V. of Shilbottle, Dio. Dur. 1849. (Patron, Ld Chan; Tithe, 209*l* 4*s* 7*d*; Glebe, 18 acres; V.'s Inc. 236*l* and Ho; Pop 1050.) [1]

ROBERTS, John Harris, *Denbigh.*—Clare Coll. Cam. B.A. 1843, M.A. 1846. Head Mast. of Denbigh Gr. Sch. Formerly C. of Thornham Magna and Parva, Suffolk. [2]

ROBERTS, John Lindfield, *Thicket, Maidenhead, Berks.*—Wor. Coll. Ox. B.A. 1839, M.A. 1840; Deac. 1844 and Pr. 1845 by Bp of Lin. Chap. to Cookham Union and to Ascot Hospital. Formerly C. of South Weston, Oxon, and Maidenhead, Berks. [3]

ROBERTS, John Llewellyn, *Spratton Vicarage, Northampton.*—Queen's Coll. Ox. 4th cl. Lit. Hum. 3rd cl. Math. et Phy. and B.A. 1847, M.A. 1850; Deac. 1848 and Pr. 1849 by Bp of Ely. V. of Spratton, Dio. Pet. 1862. (Patron, R. J. Bartlett, Esq; V.'s Inc. 400*l* and Ho; Pop. 1086.) Formerly Michel Fell. of Queen's Coll. Ox; P. C. of St. John's Chatham, 1858–62. Author, *Nature and Efficacy of Prayer* (a Sermon before the University of Oxford), Rivingtons, 1865. [4]

ROBERTS, John Mortlock, *Wellington, Somerset.*—C. of Wellington. [5]

ROBERTS, J. Pepys, *Blyton, Gainsborough.*—C. of Blyton, Lincolnshire. Formerly C. of Haverhill, Suffolk. [6]

ROBERTS, John Phillips, *Chichester.*—New Coll. Ox. B.A. 1821, M.A. 1826; Deac. 1822 and Pr 1823 by Bp of Ox. Min. Can. of Chich. 1831. (Value, 75*l* and Ho.) R. of Eastergate, Dio. Chich. 1849. (Patrons, D. and C. of Chich; Tithe, 370*l*; R.'s Inc. 375*l*; Pop. 162.) [7]

ROBERTS, Joseph Charles, *Witherley Rectory (Leicestershire), near Atherstone.*—R. of Witherley, Dio. Pet. 1846. (Patron, the present R; Tithe, 460*l*; R.'s Inc. 522*l* and Ho; Pop. 528.) [8]

ROBERTS, Lewis.—St. Bees; Deac. 1839, Pr. 1840. P. C. of Whitewell, Dio. Man. 1843. (Patrons, Hulme's Trustees; P. C.'s Inc. 133*l*; Pop. 553.) [9]

ROBERTS, Nicholas H., *Shotley, Ipswich.*—C. of Shotley. [10]

ROBERTS, Reginald Jolliffe, 33, *Patshull-road, Kentish-town, N.W.*—Ch. Coll. Cam. 9th Sen. Opt. B.A. 1862, M.A. 1867; Deac. 1862, Pr. 1863. C. of St. Mark's, Regent's-park, 1865. Formerly C. of St. Mary's, Somers-town, Lond. 1862. [11]

ROBERTS, Richard, *Llanwnog Vicarage, Newtown, Montgomeryshire.*—St. Bees; Deac. 1855 and Pr. 1856 by Bp of Llan. V. of Llanwnog, Dio. Ban. 1864. (Patron, Bp of Ban; Tithe, comm. 220*l*; Glebe, 8 acres; V.'s Inc. 248*l* and Ho; Pop. 1631.) Chap. of Caersws Union Workhouse; Surrogate. Formerly C. of Dowlais 1855, Llanidloes 1858, Carnarvon 1860, Llanidloes (second time) 1863. [12]

ROBERTS, Richard Earnshaw, *Richmond, Yorks.*—St. Edm. Hall, Ox. B.A. 1832, M.A. 1835; Deac. 1833 and Pr. 1834 by Abp of York. R. of Richmond, Dio. Rip. 1861. (Patron, Bp of Rip; R.'s Inc. 574*l* and Ho; Pop. 4290.) Surrogate; Rural Dean; Formerly C. of St. James's, Sheffield, 1833–38; P. C. of St. George's, Barnsley, 1838–61. [13]

ROBERTS, Robert, *Haverhill, Suffolk.*—St. John's Coll. Cam. B.A. 1809, M.A. 1812; Deac. 1811 and Pr. 1813 by Bp of Ely. V. of Haverhill, Dio. Ely, 1815. (Patron, Sir G. H. W. Beaumont, Bart; Tithe—Imp. 656*l* 14*s* 6*d*, V. 220*l*; V.'s Inc. 234*l*; Pop. 2434.) V. of Blyton, Lincolnshire, Dio. Lin. 1824. (Patron, Earl of Scarborough; V.'s Inc. 450*l* and Ho; Pop. 746.) [14]

ROBERTS, Robert, *Aldwinckle Rectory, Thrapstone, Northants.*—Corpus Coll. Cam. B.A. 1830. R. of All Saints', Aldwinckle, Dio. Pet. 1838. (Patron, Lord Lilford; R.'s Inc. 315*l* and Ho; Pop. 222.) R. of Waddenhoe, Dio. Pet. 1831. (Patron, G. Capron, Esq; R.'s Inc. 200*l*; Pop. 270.) [15]

ROBERTS, Robert, *Milton-Abbas Vicarage, Blandford, Dorset.*—V. of Milton-Abbas, Dio. Salis. 1842. (Patroness, Mrs. E. Dawson Damer; V.'s Inc. 132*l* and Ho; Pop. 1014.) [16]

ROBERTS, Robert Jones, *Ysceifiog Rectory, Holywell, Flintshire.*—New Inn Hall, Ox. B.A. 1834, M.A. 1836; Deac. 1837 and Pr. 1838 by Bp of St. A. R. of Ysceifiog, Dio. St. A. 1855. (Patron, Bp of St. A; Tithe, 722*l*; Glebe, 8 acres; R.'s Inc. 730*l* and Ho; Pop. 1179.) Formerly C. of Dyserth 1837–43; R. of Denbigh 1843–55. [17]

ROBERTS, Robert Lloyd Anwyl, *Llangynhafal Rectory, Ruthin, Denbighshire.*—R. of Llangynhafal, Dio. St. A. 1857. (Patron, Bp of Llan; R.'s Inc. 405*l* and Ho; Pop. 507.) [18]

ROBERTS, T., *Martin Hussingtree, Worcester.*—C. of Martin Hussingtree. [19]

ROBERTS, Walter Cramer, *Edwardston Vicarage, Boxford, Suffolk.*—Dub. A.B. 1824, A.M. 1831; Deac. 1825, Pr. 1826. V. of Edwardston, Dio. Ely, 1848. (Patron, Charles Dawson, Esq; Tithe—App. 373*l*, V. 260*l*; Glebe, 11 acres; V.'s Inc. 272*l* and Ho; Pop. 462.) [20]

ROBERTS, Watkins Charles, *Radford, Nottingham.*—C. of Radford. [21]

ROBERTS, William, *Fron Goch, Bala, Merionethshire.*—Lampeter; Deac. 1849 by Bp of Wor. for Bp of St. D. Pr. 1850 by Bp of St. D. P. C. of Fron Goch, Dio. St. A. 1859. (Patron, Bp of St. A; P. C.'s Inc. 120*l*; Pop. 650.) Formerly C. of Holywell. [22]

ROBERTS, William, *Northall, Dunstable.*—Emman. Coll. Cam. B.A. 1856; Deac. 1856 and Pr. 1857 by Bp of Roch. C. of Eddlesborough, Bucks, 1865. Formerly C. of Trinity, Milton-next-Gravesend, 1856–61, Woodchurch, Kent, 1861–65. [23]

ROBERTS, William, 2, *Grove-road, Colney Hatch, N.*—Dub. A.B. 1864; Deac. 1856 and Pr. 1857 by Bp of Lon. Chap. of Great Northern Cemetery, Colney Hatch, Dio. Roch. 1861; C. of Friern-Barnet 1861. Formerly C. of Bridge, Kent, 1856, Clandown, Somerset, 1857. [24]

ROBERTS, William Anwyl, *Llandudno, Conway.*—Jesus Coll. Ox. B.A. 1848; Deac. 1849 and Pr. 1850 by Bp of St. A. C. of Llandudno 1856. Formerly C. of Bangor; Mast. of the Gr. Sch. and C. of Dolgellan. [25]

ROBERTS, William Page, *Eye Vicarage, Suffolk.*—St. John's Coll. Cam. B.A. 1861, M.A. 1865; Deac. 1861 and Pr. 1862 by Bp of Ches. V. of Eye, Dio. Nor. 1864. (Patron, Sir E. C. Kerrison, Bart. M.P; Tithe, 451*l* 5*s*; Glebe, 13 acres; V.'s Inc. 480*l* and Ho; Pop. 2430.) Formerly C. of St. Thomas's, Stockport, 1861–64. [26]

ROBERTS, William Pender, *Eggesford Rectory, Wembworthy, Devon.*—St. John's Coll. Cam. B.A. 1845, M.A. 1850; Deac. 1846 and Pr. 1847 by Bp of Ex. C. of Eggesford. [27]

ROBERTSON, Charles Hope, *Crocken Hill, Dartford, Kent.*—Trin. Coll. Cam. Dr. Hooper's Declamation Silver Cup and College Greek Test. Prize. Sen. Opt. and B.A. 1854, M.A. 1860; Deac. 1855 and Pr. 1857 by Bp of Rip. P. C. of Crocken Hill, Dio. Cant. 1866. (Patron, Abp of Cant; P. C.'s Inc. 200*l* and Ho; Pop. 670.) Formerly C. of St. John's, Bradford, 1855–57; P. C. of Muckross, Killarney, 1859–63; V. of St. Margaret's-at-Cliff, Dover, 1863–66. Author, *Gathered Lights Illustrating the Lord's Prayer, selected from Theological Writers*, Rivingtons, 1858, 4*s* 6*d*; etc. [28]

ROBERTSON, David, *Lye Parsonage, Stourbridge, Worcestershire.*—Trin. Coll. Cam. Sen. Opt. B.A. 1861, M.A. 1864; Deac. 1862 and Pr. 1863 by Bp of Wor. P. C. of Ch. Ch. Lye, Dio. Wor. 1866. (Patron, Bp of Wor; Glebe, 20 acres; P. C.'s Inc. 300*l* and Ho; Pop. 6772.) Formerly C. of Halesowen 1862, St. Michael's, Chester-square, Lond. 1865. [29]

ROBERTSON, Divie, *Terry's Cross, Henfield, Hurstpierpoint.*—Wells Theol. Coll. and Ch. Ch. Ox. B.A. 1845; Deac. 1846 and Pr. 1848. [30]

ROBERTSON, G., *Morpeth, Northumberland.*—C. of Morpeth. [31]

ROBERTSON, James, 1, *Apsley-place, Redland, Bristol.*—Pemb. Coll. Ox. 2nd cl. Lit. Hum. 1st cl. Math. et Phy. and B.A. 1831, M.A. 1834; Deac. 1833 and Pr.

1834 by Bp of Ox. R. of Ch. Ch. with St. Ewen's, Bristol, Dio. G. and B. 1859. (Patron, the present R; R.'s Inc. 400*l*; Pop. 1149.) Formerly Head Mast. of St. Paul's Sch. Southsea, 1843–46; Prin. of Bishop's Coll. Bristol, 1846–59. [1]

ROBERTSON, James, *Jesus College, Cambridge.*—Fell. of Jesus Coll. Cam. [2]

ROBERTSON, James, *Burton Leonard, Knaresborough, Yorks.*—Ch. Coll. Cam. B.A. 1829, M.A. 1835; Deac. 1835 and Pr. 1836 by Abp of York. V. of Burton Leonard, Dio. Rip. 1842. (Patrons, D. and C. of York; Tithe, 105*l*; Glebe, 56½ acres; V.'s Inc. 180*l*; Pop. 511.) [3]

ROBERTSON, James, *Rugby.*—Jesus Coll. Cam. Fell. of, M.A. 1862; Deac. 1860 and Pr. 1861 by Bp of Ely. Asst. Mast. in Rugby Sch. [4]

ROBERTSON, James Craigie, *The Precincts, Canterbury.*—Trin. Coll. Cam. B.A. 1834, M.A. 1838; Deac. 1836 by Bp of G. and B. Pr. 1841 by Abp of Cant. Can. of Canterbury 1859. (Patron, the Crown; Value, 1000*l* and Ho.) Prof. of Ecclesiastical History, King's Coll. Lond. 1864. Formerly V. of Bekesbourne, near Canterbury, 1846–59. Author, *How shall we Conform to the Liturgy?* 1843, 2nd ed. 1844; *Bearings of the Gorham Case*, Rivingtons, 1850; *History of the Christian Church*, Vol. I. Murray, 1854, 4th ed. 1866, Vol. II. 1856, 2nd ed. 1862, Vol. III. 1866; *Sketches of Church History during the First Six Centuries*, S.P.C.K. 1855; *Becket, a Biography*, Murray, 1859. Editor, *Heylyn's History of the Reformation*, 2 vols. Eccles. Hist. Soc. 1849; *Bargrave's Alexander VII. and his Cardinals*, Camden Soc. 1866. [5]

ROBERTSON, P., *Berwick-on-Tweed.*—C. of Berwick. [6]

ROBERTSON, Samuel, *Swinstead Vicarage, Bourne, Lincolnshire.*—Ch. Coll. Cam. B.A. 1852, M.A. 1855; Deac. 1854 and Pr. 1855 by Bp of Ches. V. of Swinstead, Dio. Lin. 1862. (Patron, Lord Willoughby D'Eresby; Glebe, 103 acres; V.'s Inc. 115*l* and Ho; Pop. 396.) Formerly C. of Ulverston, Lancashire, and Tilney St. Lawrence, Norfolk. [7]

ROBERTSON, William A. Scott, *Whitehall, Sittingbourne, Kent.*—Ch. Coll. Cam. Scho. 1856, Sen. Opt. and B.A. 1859, M.A. 1862; Deac. 1859 and Pr. 1860 by Bp of B. and W. R. of Elmley, Kent, Dio. Cant. 1866. (Patroness, Miss Robertson; Tithe, 350*l*; R.'s Inc. 350*l*; Pop. 140.) Dom. Chap. to the Earl of Tankerville. Formerly R. of Sutton Montis, Somerset, 1860–64. Author, *The Church's Charge, The Nation's Prayer for the Prince of Wales on his Twenty-first Birthday* (a Village Sermon), Hertford; *A Succession of Righteous Rulers a Manifestation of God's Mercy* (a Sermon), Lond. [8]

ROBERTSON, William Henry, *Durham.*—Ch. Ch. Ox. B.A. 1863, M.A. 1866; Deac. 1863, Pr. 1864. Min. Can. of Dur. 1866. (Value, 300*l*.) Formerly C. of Thorpe Mandeville, Northants, 1863–65, Houghton-le-Spring, Durham, 1865–66. [9]

ROBESON, Hemming, *Forthampton, Tewkesbury.*—Ball. Coll. Ox. 2nd cl. Lit. Hum. Chan.'s Prize for Latin Essay 1856, B.A. 1855, M.A. 1856; Deac. 1857 and Pr. 1858 by Bp of Ox. P. C. of Forthampton, Dio. G. and B. 1863. (Patron, Joseph Yorke, Esq; P. C.'s Inc. 170*l*; Pop. 442.) Formerly C. of Bray, near Maidenhead, 1857–62. [10]

ROBIN, Philip Raulin, *Woodchurch, Birkenhead.*—Brasen. Coll. Ox. B.A. 1837, M.A. 1840; Deac. 1839 and Pr. 1840 by Bp of Ches. R. of Woodchurch, Dio. Ches. 1861. (Patron, the present R; R.'s Inc. 1100*l* and Ho; Pop. 977.) Formerly C. of Woodchurch. [11]

ROBINS, Arthur, *Burnham, Bucks.*—Magd. Hall, Ox. M.A; Deac. 1866 and Pr. 1867 by Bp of Ox. C. in sole charge of Burnham. Formerly C. of St. Clement's, Oxford. [12]

ROBINS, G. A., *Bishopstone Rectory, Hereford.*—R. of Bishopstone, Dio. Herf. 1863. (Patron, Rev. G. H. Davenport; R.'s Inc. 200*l* and Ho; Pop. 288.) [13]

ROBINSON, Alfred, *Humbleton, near Hull.*—Corpus Coll. Cam. B.A. 1846; Deac. 1848 and Pr. 1849 by Bp of Salis. V. of Humbleton with Elsternwick, Dio. York, 1863. (Patron, Ld Chan; V.'s Inc. 280*l* and Ho; Pop. Humbleton 464, Elsternwick 130.) [14]

ROBINSON, Arthur Dalgarno, 6, *Lancaster-terrace, Lancaster-road, Kensington-park, London, W.*—P. C. of St. Andrew's, Silchester-road, Kensington, 1860. (Patron, Bp of Lon.) [15]

ROBINSON, Arthur Edward, *South Marston, Swindon, Wilts.*—New Coll. Ox. B.A. 1857, M.A. 1860; Deac. 1860 by Bp of Ox. Pr. 1861 by Bp of G. and B. Fell. of New Coll. Ox; C. of South Marston 1864. Formerly C. of Highworth, Wilts, 1860. [16]

ROBINSON, Bernard, *Lane Bridge, Whalley, Lancashire.*—C. of Lane Bridge. [17]

ROBINSON, Charles, *Bishop Burton, Beverley, Yorks.*—Queen's Coll. Ox. B.A. 1850, M.A. 1853; Deac. 1851, Pr. 1852. V. of Bishop Burton, Dio. York, 1853. (Patrons, D. and C. of York; Tithe, 13*l* 6*s* 8*d*; Glebe, 50 acres; V.'s Inc. 124*l* and Ho; Pop. 499.) [18]

ROBINSON, Charles Daniel Palmer, *St. Martin's, Guernsey.*—Literate; Deac. 1838 and Pr. 1840 by Bp of Win. R. of St. Martin's, Guernsey, Dio. Win. 1865. (Patron, Gov. of Guernsey; Tithe, 32*l*; Glebe, 8 acres; R.'s Inc. 160*l* and Ho; Pop. 2200.) Formerly P. C. of Alderney 1851–65. [19]

ROBINSON, Charles Edward Ricketts, *Milton next Gravesend.*—Trin. Coll. Cam. B.A. 1851, M.A. 1855; Deac. 1852 and Pr. 1853 by Bp of Win. P. C. of Trinity, Milton next Gravesend, Dio. Roch. 1861. (Patrons, Bp of Roch. and Crown alt; P. C.'s Inc. 340*l*; Pop. 3642.) Hon. Can. of Roch; Rural Dean of Gravesend. Formerly Chap. to Price's Patent Candle Co. 1852; C. of St. Thomas's, Ryde, 1855, Therfield, Herts, 1859. [20]

ROBINSON, Charles James, *Privy Council Office, Downing-street, London, S.W.*—Queen's Coll. Ox. B.A. 1854, M.A. 1856: Deac. 1855 and Pr. 1856 by Bp of Lon. One of H. M. Inspectors of Schs. 1859. Formerly C. of West Ham, 1855, Bishop's Hatfield, Herts, 1856. [21]

ROBINSON, Charles John, *Norton Canon Vicarage, Weobley, Herefordshire.*—Univ. Coll. Dur. Latin Verse Prize 1853, 1st cl. Cl. 1855, Van Mildert Scho. 1855, Fell. of the Univ. 1857–62; B.A. 1855, M.A. 1859; Deac. and Pr. 1857 by Bp of Dur. V. of Norton Canon, Dio. Herf. 1865. (Patrons, D. and C. of Herf; Tithe, 120*l*; Glebe, 29 acres; V.'s Inc. 170*l* and Ho; Pop. 330.) Dom. Chap. to the Earl of Caithness 1861. Formerly Chap. of the Univ. Coll. Dur. 1857–58; C. of Windsor 1858–59, Sevenoaks, Kent, 1859–62; C. in sole charge of Healaugh, Yorks, 1862–63; C. of Great Berkhampstead 1863; P. C. of Harewood, Hereford, 1864–65. Author, *Records of the Family of Cary*, Nichols, Westminster, 1864–65. [22]

ROBINSON, Charles Kirkby, *St. Catherine's Lodge, Cambridge.*—St. Cath. Coll. Cam. Maitland Univ. Prize Essay 1852, 22nd Wrang. B.A. 1849, M.A. 1853, D.D. 1867; Deac. 1849 and Pr. 1850 by Bp of Lin. Master of St. Catherine's Coll. and *ex officio* Can. of Norwich 1861. Formerly C. of Carlton-in-Lindrick, Notts, 1850; Fell. and Asst. Tut. of St. Cath. Coll. 1850–59; P. C. of St. Andrew's the Less, Cambridge, 1859–62. Author, *Missions urged on the State*, 1852, 3*s*; *Old Willie*, R.T.S.; etc. [23]

ROBINSON, Christopher, *Trinity Parsonage, Blackburn.*—Dub. Vice-Chan.'s Prize for Latin and for English Essay, A.B. 1848, LL.D. 1856; Deac. 1848 and Pr. 1849 by Bp of Man. P. C. of Trinity, Blackburn, Dio. Man. 1850. (Patron, V. of Blackburn; P. C.'s Inc. 300*l* and Ho; Pop. 4660.) Surrogate. Formerly C. of Audenshaw 1848. Author, *Ireland* (a Prize Essay), 1847; *The Church and the People*, 1850, 2*s* 6*d*; *Three Lectures on Papal Idolatry*, 1851; *A Sermon on the Funeral of the Duke of Wellington*, 1852; *A Sermon preached at the Midnight Service, New Year's Eve*, 1853 and 1866; *Our Crimean Disasters and National Perplexities a Divine Retribution* (a Sermon), 1853; *Premonitions of the Impending Doom of the Papacy*, 1856, 3*s* 6*d*; *God's Four Sore Judgments against Britain* (Fast-day Sermon),

1857; *The Divine Oracles of Joel, Habakkuk, and Zephaniah*, Rivingtons, 1865, 10*s* 6*d*; *The Immediate Future, The Downfall of the Papal and Mahomedan Powers* (a Sermon), 1867. [1]

ROBINSON, Christopher Gerard, *Middlesborough-on-Tees.*—Dub. A.B. 1864; Deac. 1866 by Abp of York. Asst. C. of St. John's, Middlesborough, 1866. [2]

ROBINSON, David, 4, *Rutland-gate, Hyde-park, London, W.* [3]

ROBINSON, Disney, *Henbury, near Bristol.*—St. John's Coll. Cam. B.A. 1828, M.A. 1831; Deac. 1828 and Pr. 1830 by Abp of York. P. C. of Woolley, Yorks, Dio. York, 1833. (Patron, G. Wentworth, Esq; P. C.'s Inc. 230*l*; Pop. 531.) Author, *The Law and Gospel* (a Course of Sermons on the Ten Commandments); *The Christian's Privilege, or Words of Comfort for his Hours of Sadness*; *The Shield of Truth* (a Parochial Minister's Address to his Flock on the Papal Aggression); etc. [4]

ROBINSON, Edward, *St. Mary's-villas, Battle.*—Trin. Coll. Cam. and Cuddesdon; Deac. 1863 and Pr. 1865 by Bp of Roch. C. of Battle 1866. Formerly C. of Aylesford, Maidstone, and Felstead, Chelmsford. [5]

ROBINSON, Edward, *Deytheur, Oswestry.*—Dub. A.B. 1858, A.M. 1861; Deac. 1858 and Pr. 1859 by Bp of St. A. Mast. of Deytheur Gr. Sch. [6]

ROBINSON, Eustace, *Worcester.*—C. of St. Peter's, Worcester. [7]

ROBINSON, Francis, *Stonesfield Rectory, Woodstock, Oxon.*—Corpus Coll. Ox. B.A. 1823, M.A. 1826; Deac. 1824 and Pr. 1829 by Bp of Ox. R. of Staughton Parva, Beds, Dio. Ely, 1831. (Patron, Corpus Coll. Ox; Glebe, 266 acres; R.'s Inc. 276*l*; Pop. 572.) R. of Stonesfield, Dio. Ox. 1834. (Patron, Duke of Marlborough; Glebe, 140 acres; R.'s Inc. 150*l* and Ho; Pop. 650.) Surrogate. [8]

ROBINSON, George, 22, *Portland-place, Hull.*—Dub; Deac. 1862 and Pr. 1863 by Bp of Carl. C. of St. Stephen's, Hull, 1865. Formerly C. of Ch. Ch. Whitehaven, 1862–63, St. Mary's, Hull, 1864–65, St. Peter's, Hull, 1865. [9]

ROBINSON, George, *Keynsham Vicarage, Bristol.*—Dub. A.M; Deac. 1844, Pr. 1845. V. of Keynsham, Dio. B. and W. 1854. (Patron, Rev. Alfred Peache; Tithe, App. 116*l* 7*s*, Imp. 135*l*, V. 170*l*; Glebe, 8 acres; V.'s Inc. 300*l*; Pop. 2190.) [10]

ROBINSON, George, *Pudsey, near Leeds.*—C. of Pudsey. [11]

ROBINSON, George Alington, *Irby-on-Humber Rectory, Great Grimsby, Lincolnshire.*—Ch. Coll. Cam. B.A. 1830. R. of Thorganby, Caistor, Linc. Dio. Lin. 1841. (Patron, Earl of Yarborough; Tithe, 85*l*; R.'s Inc. 90*l*; Pop. 140.) R. of Irby-on-Humber, Dio. Lin. 1842. (Patrons, Earl of Yarborough and W. Haigh Esq. alt; Tithe, 246*l*; Glebe, 48 acres; R.'s Inc. 306*l* and Ho; Pop. 235.) [12]

ROBINSON, George Croke, *West Bromwich, Staffs.*—Ch. Ch. Ox. Stud of, 2nd cl. Sci. Nat. B.A. 1861, M.A. 1864; Deac. 1863, Pr. 1864. C. of West Bromwich. Formerly C. of St. Peter's, Leeds. [13]

ROBINSON, Sir George Stamp, Bart., *Cranford, Kettering, Northants.*—New Coll. Ox. B.A. 1819, M.A. 1824. Hon. Can. of Pet. 1853. Formerly R. of Cranford 1822–53. [14]

ROBINSON, George Walter, *Barmby Marsh, Howden, Yorks.*—St. John's Coll. Cam; Deac. 1845 and Pr. 1846 by Bp of Rip. P. C. (1864) and Blanchard's Lect. (1863) of Barmby-on-the-Marsh, Dio. York. (Patron, of P. C. Ld-Chan; P. C.'s Inc. 97*l* 13*s* 4*d*; Pop. 436; Patrons of Lectureship, Inhabitants of Barmby; Lect.'s Inc. 95*l* 7*s*.) Formerly C. of Elland, Halifax, 1845–57, after which held ten other Curacies, the last of them being Billing Parva, Northants, 1861–63. Author, *Village Sermons*, 1866, 5*s*. [15]

ROBINSON, Gilbert William, *Walmley Parsonage, Sutton Coldfield.*—St. Peter's Coll. Cam. 1837, B.A. 1869, M.A. 1844; Deac. and Pr. 1839 by Bp of Wor. P. C. of Walmley, Dio. Wor. 1845. (Patroness, Miss Riland; P. C.'s Inc. 100*l* and Ho; Pop. 621.) Author, *Aids to Self-Examination*, 1841, 1*s* 6*d*; etc. [16]

ROBINSON, Henry, *Nenthead Parsonage, Penrith.*—P. C. of Nenthead, Dio. Dur. 1862. (Patron, V. of Alston Moor; P. C.'s Inc. 140*l* and Ho; Pop. 2039.) [17]

ROBINSON, Henry, *Escomb, Bishop Auckland, Durham.*—St. Alban Hall, Ox. B.A. 1842, M.A. 1854; Deac. 1842 and Pr. 1843 by Bp of Ox. Formerly C. of Didcot, Berks, 1842; Mast. in Christ's Hospital, Lond. 1849; R. of Kilkhampton, Cornwall, 1857; C. of Kirkharle, Northumberland, 1862, Chillingham 1864, Escomb, Durham, 1866. [18]

ROBINSON, Henry, *St. Leonards-on-Sea, Sussex.*—Dub. Two Divinity Prizes, and Primate's Heb. Prize, A.B. 1844, A.M. 1852, *ad eund.* Ox. 1864; Deac. 1845, Pr. 1846. Min. of St. Paul's, St. Leonards-on-Sea. Formerly Chap. to the Forces; served in the Crimea and in China. Author, various Sermons; etc. [19]

ROBINSON, Henry, *Haselbeech Rectory, near Northampton.*—Trin. Hall, Cam. B.A. 1835, M.A. 1838; Deac. 1835, Pr. 1836. R. of Haselbeech, Dio. Pet. 1840. (Patron, T. Apreece, Esq; Tithe, 335*l* 18*s* 10*d*; Glebe, 28 acres; R.'s Inc. 350*l* and Ho; Pop. 180.) [20]

ROBINSON, Henry, 115, *Embden-street, Hulme, Manchester.*—St. John's Coll. Cam. 26th Sen. Opt. B.A. 1864; Deac. 1864 by Bp of Man. C. of St. Paul's, Hulme, Manchester. [21]

ROBINSON, H. H., *Burnley, Lancashire.*—C. of Burnley. [22]

ROBINSON, Henry Mowld, *Lancing College, Shoreham, Sussex.*—Pemb. Coll. Ox. B.A. 1862, M.A. 1864; Deac. and Pr. 1863 by Bp of Salis. Asst. Mast. and Fell. of St. Mary's and St. Nicholas' Coll. Lancing. Formerly C. of Cheverel Parva, Wilts, 1863–65. [23]

ROBINSON, Henry Vyvyan, *St. Giles's-in-the-Wood, Great Torrington, Devon.*—P. C. of St. Giles's, Dio. Ex. 1856. (Patrons, Heirs of Lord Rolle; P. C.'s Inc. 95*l* and Ho; Pop. 962.) Rural Dean. [24]

ROBINSON, Hugh George, *Bolton Abbey, Skipton, Yorks.*—Clare Coll. Cam. B.A. 1842, M.A. 1854; Deac. and Pr. 1847. Min. of Bolton Abbey, Dio. Rip. 1864. (Patron, Duke of Devonshire; Min.'s Inc. 120*l* and Ho; Pop. 112.) Preb. of York 1858. Formerly Prin. of York and Ripon Dioc. Training Coll. 1854–64. [25]

ROBINSON, James.—Chap. of H.M.S. "Flora." [26]

ROBINSON, John, *Bowness Rectory, Carlisle.*—R. of Bowness, Dio. Carl. 1855. (Patron, Earl of Lonsdale; R.'s Inc. 400*l*; Pop. 1321.) Surrogate. [27]

ROBINSON, John, *Hollinwood Parsonage, Manchester.*—St. Bees; Deac. 1856 and Pr. 1857 by Bp of Ches. P. C. of Hollinwood, Dio. Man. 1861. (Patron, R. of Prestwich; P. C.'s Inc. 300*l* and Ho; Pop. 6298.) Formerly C. of Oldham 1860, St. Paul's, Warrington, 1857–59. [28]

ROBINSON, John, *Newbiggin Rectory, Temple-Sowerby, Westmoreland.*—Deac. 1813 and Pr. 1814 by Abp of York. R. of Newbiggin, Dio. Carl. 1818. (Patron, W. Crackenthorpe, Esq; Tithe, 72*l*; R.'s Inc. 115*l* and Ho; Pop. 107.) [29]

ROBINSON, John, *Widmerpool Rectory, near Nottingham.*—Trin. Coll. Ox. B.A. 1813; Deac. 1814 by Bp of Salis. Pr. 1816 by Abp of York. R. of Widmerpool, Dio. Lin. 1830. (Patron, F. Robinson, Esq; Land in lieu of Tithe, 450 acres; R.'s Inc. 300*l* and Ho; Pop. 151.) [30]

ROBINSON, John, *Settle, Yorks.*—Oriel Coll. Ox. B.A. 1847, M.A. 1858; Deac. 1848 and Pr. 1851 by Bp of Rip. Formerly Chap. to the Settle Union 1857–66. Editor of *The Parochial Hymn Book*, Parkers, 1860. [31]

ROBINSON, John, *Clifton, near York.*—Corpus Coll. Cam. B.A. 1820, M.A. 1826; Deac. 1821 by Abp of York, Pr. 1823 by Bp of Ox. Formerly V. of St. Lawrence's, York, 1843–67. [32]

ROBINSON, John, *Bradfield, Reading.*—Chap. of the Bradfield Union. [33]

ROBINSON, John, *Broughton-in-Furness, Lancashire.*—St. Cath. Coll. Cam. B.A. 1832, M.A. 1835;

Deac. 1832, Pr. 1833. P. C. of Broughton-in-Furness, Dio. Carl. 1844. (Patron, J. D. Sawrey, Esq; P. C.'s Inc. 108*l* and Ho; Pop. 1183.) [1]

ROBINSON, John, *Swinton, near Manchester.*—St. Bees; Deac. 1846 by Bp of Ches. Pr. 1848 by Bp of Man. Chap. to the Industrial Training Schs. Swinton, 1857. Formerly C. of Newton Heath, Lancashire. [2]

ROBINSON, John Ellill, *Chieveley Vicarage, Newbury, Berks.*—Ch. Ch. Ox. B.A. 1829, M.A. 1832; Deac. 1832, Pr. 1833. V. of Chieveley with Oare C. and Chapelries of Winterbourne and Leckhampstead and Curridge C. Dio. Ox. 1837. (Patrons, Joseph Dand, Esq. and Miss Wasey, alt; Tithe—Imp. 653*l* 10*s*, V. 1168*l* 17*s*; Glebe, 220 acres; V.'s Inc. 1460*l* and Ho; Pop. 1923.) [3]

ROBINSON, J. H., *Burton-on-Trent.*—C. of Burton-on-Trent. [4]

ROBINSON, John James, *Mowcop Parsonage, Stoke-on-Trent.*—Dub. A.B. 1835; Deac. 1843, Pr. 1844. P. C. of Mowcop, Dio. Lich. 1845. (Patron, Bp of Lich; P. C.'s Inc. 126*l* and Ho; Pop. 2135.) [5]

ROBINSON, John Lovell, *Weston Colville, Linton, Cambs.*—Dub. Univ. Scho. A.B. 1845, A.M. 1849; Deac. 1845 by Bp of Tuam, Pr. 1846 by Abp of Dub. R. of Weston Colville, Dio. Ely, 1865. (Patron, Col. John Scriven; Glebe, 375 acres; R.'s Inc. 360*l* and Ho; Pop. 537.) Formerly Treasurer of Cloyne Cathl. [6]

ROBINSON, John William, *North Petherton Vicarage, Bridgwater.*—Dub. A.B. 1855, A.M. 1864; Deac. 1855 by Bp of Ex. Pr. 1857 by Bp of B. and W. V. of North Petherton, Dio. B. and W. 1857. (Patron, the present V; Tithe, comm. 900*l*; V.'s Inc. 900*l* and Ho; Pop. 3151.) Formerly C. of East Teignmouth, Devon, 1855. [7]

ROBINSON, Leighton, *East Guildford, Rye, Sussex.*—C. of East Guildford with Playden. [8]

ROBINSON, Ottywell.—Trin. Coll. Cam. B.A. 1841, M.A. 1845. Chap. at St. Thomas's Hospital, Lond. Formerly C. of St. Mary Magdalene's, Bermondsey, Lond. [9]

ROBINSON, Philip Vyvyan, *Landewednack Rectory, Helstone, Cornwall.*—R. of Landewednack, Dio. Ex. 1844. (Patron, the present R; R.'s Inc. 280*l* and Ho; Pop. 429.) R. of Ruan Major, Cornwall, Dio. Ex. 1844. (Patron, P. V. Robinson, Esq; R.'s Inc. 200*l*; Pop. 141.) [10]

ROBINSON, Richard Barton, *Lytham, Preston.*—Queen's Coll. Ox. B.A. 1826, M.A. 1829; Deac. 1827 and Pr. 1828 by Bp of Ches. P. C. of Lytham, Dio. Man. 1834. (Patron, T. Talbot Clifton, Esq; P. C.'s Inc. 131*l*; Pop. 1615.) Surrogate. [11]

ROBINSON, Richard Hayes, 3, *Woodfield-terrace, Upper Norwood, S.*—King's Coll. Lond; Deac. 1866 by Bp of Dur. for Bp of Carl. C. of St. Paul's, Penge, 1867. [12]

ROBINSON, Robert, *Cumwhitton, Carlisle.*—Queen's Coll. Ox. B.A. 1835; Deac. 1837 and Pr. 1838 by Bp of Dur. P. C. of Cumwhitton, Dio. Carl. 1844. (Patrons, D. and C. of Carl; P. C.'s Inc. 98*l* and Ho; Pop. 574.) Formerly C. of St. Ann's, Newcastle-on-Tyne, 1837, Beaumont and Kirkandrews-on-Eden 1840. [13]

ROBINSON, Robert, *Mallerstang, Kirkby-Stephen, Westmoreland.*—Dub. A.B. 1825; Deac. 1824, Pr. 1825. P. C. of Mallerstang, Dio. Carl. 1844. (Patron, Sir R. Tufton, Bart; P. C.'s Inc. 64*l*; Pop. 232.) [14]

ROBINSON, R., *Chipping, Preston.*—V. of Chipping, Dio. Man. 1864. (Patron, Bp of Man; V.'s Inc. 120*l*; Pop. 1483.) [15]

ROBINSON, Thomas, *Ravenglass, Cumberland.*—St. Bees; Deac. 1838, Pr. 1839. P. C. of Muncaster, Cumberland, Dio. Carl. 1844. (Patron, Lord Muncaster; Tithe, Imp. 167*l* 6*s* 1*d*; P. C.'s Inc. 103*l*; Pop. 580.) [16]

ROBINSON, Thomas, 56, *Great Mersey-street, Liverpool.*—St. Bees; Dub. Theol. Prizeman, A.B. 1859, A.M. 1867; Deac. 1846 and Pr. 1847 by Bp of Ches. P. C. of St. Bartholomew's, Liverpool, Dio. Ches. 1859. (Patrons, Five Trustees; P. C.'s Inc. 350*l*; Pop. 8772.) Formerly C. of St. John's, Dukinfield, 1846–47; Sen. C. of Ashton-under-Lyne 1848–49. Author, *Sunset at Noon,* 1856; *A Voice from the Grave,* 1859. [17]

ROBINSON, The Ven. Thomas, *Master's House, Temple, London, E.C.* and *Precincts, Rochester.*—Trin. Coll. Cam. Bell's Scho. 13th Wrang. and 2nd Medallist, B.A. 1813, M.A. 1816, D.D. 1844; Deac. 1815 by Bp of Ely, Pr. 1816 by Bp of Lin. Mast. of the Temple 1845; Can. of Roch. 1854. Formerly Chap. to the Abp of York; Chap. to Bp of Calcutta; Archd. of Madras; R. of Therfield, Herts, 1853–60. Author, *The Old Testament translated into Persian,* 4 vols; *Six Discourses on the Evidences,* Calcutta, 1819; *Sermons* (preached at Madras), Madras, 1836; *The Last Days of Bishop Heber,* Madras and Lond. 1827; *Three Charges delivered at Madras*; *The Character of St. Paul* (Sermons before the Univ. of Cam.), 1840; *The Twin Fallacies of Rome* (five Sermons at the Temple), 1851; various single Sermons; *Lectures on the Study of the Oriental Languages.* [18]

ROBINSON, Thomas Bond Bird, *Fremington, Barnstaple, Devon.*—C. of Fremington. [19]

ROBINSON, Thomas H. Grantham, *St. James's, Walthamstow, Essex.*—King's Coll. Lond; Deac. 1862 and Pr. 1863 by Bp of Lon. P. C. of St. James's, Walthamstow, Dio. Lon. 1865. (Patron, V. of Walthamstow.) Sec. to Prayer Book and Homily Soc. [20]

ROBINSON, William, *Shakespeare-street, Manchester.*—St. Bees; Deac. 1858 and Pr. 1859 by Bp of Lich. P. C. of St. Clement's, Manchester, Dio. Man. 1866. (Patrons, Trustees; P. C.'s Inc. 150*l*.) Formerly C. in sole charge of Wentworth, Yorks, 1862–63; C. of Ch. Ch. Salford, 1864. [21]

ROBINSON, William, *Stickford, Spilsby, Lincolnshire.*—Literate; Deac. 1819 and Pr. 1820 by Bp of Carl. V. of Stickford, Dio. Lin. 1856. (Patron, Bp of Lin; Glebe, 74 acres; V.'s Inc. 200*l*; Pop. 357.) Formerly P. C. of Wood Enderby, Lincolnshire, 1830–56. [22]

ROBINSON, W. C., *New College, Oxford.*—Fell. of New Coll. Ox. [23]

ROBINSON, William Kay, *The Rookery, Wymondham, Oakham.*—St. John's Coll. Cam. 8th Jun. Opt. B.A. 1853; Deac. 1855, Pr. 1856. Head Mast. of Wymondham Gr. Sch. Leic. Formerly C. of Stonesby, Leic. 1855–57. [24]

ROBINSON, William Scott, *Dyrham Rectory, (Glouc.), near Chippenham.*—Ex. Coll. Ox. B.A. 1826, M.A. 1829. R. of Dyrham, Dio. G. and B. 1828. (Patron, G. W. Blathwayt, Esq; Tithe, 545*l*; R.'s Inc. 555*l* and Ho; Pop. 457.) R. of Fairleigh-Hungerford, Beckington, Somerset, Dio. B. and W. 1832. (Patron, J. T. Holton, Esq; Tithe, 119*l* 10*s*; Glebe, 47½ acres; R.'s Inc. 201*l* and Ho; Pop. 127.) [25]

ROBINSON, William Woolhouse, *Cambridge-villa, Cotham-grove, Kingsdown, Bristol.*—St. John's Coll. Cam. B.A. 1826, M.A. 1829; Deac. 1826 by Bp of B. and W. Pr. 1828 by Bp of Lon. Chap. to the Earl of Plymouth. Formerly C. of Stogursey 1826, Rochford 1826, Yeovil 1837; P. C. of Ch. Ch. Chelsea, 1845; C. of Great Warley, Essex, 1865–67. Author, *Farewell Sermons*; *A Word in Season*; *The Last Great Exhibition*; Series of *Yeovil Handbills*; *A Clergyman's Reasons for Teetotalism*; *Sermon for Trinitarian Bible Society*; *Temperance Comparisons.* [26]

ROBSON, Edward Henry, *St. John's Parsonage, Pendlebury, Lancashire.*—Wor. Coll. Ox. B.A. 1849, M.A. 1851; Deac. 1850 and Pr. 1851 by Bp of Ox. P. C. of St. John's, Pendlebury, Dio. Man. 1856. (Patrons, Bp of Man. V. of Eccles, Oliver Heywood, Esq. Alfred Barton, Esq. and Thomas Cooke, Esq. as Trustees; Tithe, Imp. 13*l* 1*s*; P. C.'s Inc. 220*l* and Ho; Pop. 2610.) Formerly C. of Upton with Chalvey, Slough, Bucks, 1850–52, Prestwich, near Manchester, 1852–56. [27]

ROBSON, George, *Walton-on-the-Wolds, Leicestershire.*—St. Bees; Deac. 1850 and Pr. 1851 by Abp of York. C. of Walton-on-the-Wolds 1867. Formerly C. of Great Ayton, Yorks, 1850–64, Thrussington, Leic. 1864–67. [28]

ROBSON, James, *Ponteland, Newcastle-upon-Tyne.*—C. of Ponteland. [29]

ROBSON, James Stuart.—Dur. B.A. 1841; Deac. 1842, Pr. 1843. Chap. of H.M.S. "Asia." [1]

ROBSON, John Evans, *Hartwith Parsonage, near Ripley, Yorks.*—Deac. 1825 by Bp of Bristol, Pr. 1825 by Abp of York. P. C. of Hartwith, Dio. Rip. 1825. (Patrons, Rev. D. R. Roundell and Samuel Swire, Esq. alt; P. C.'s Inc. 127*l* and Ho; Pop. 1227.) [2]

ROBSON, John Henry, 8, *Wellington-place, Guildford.*—Downing Coll. Cam. B.A. 1865; Deac. 1866 by Bp of Lon. Pr. 1867 by Bp of Win. Chap. to the Surrey County Hospital, Guildford. Formerly C. of Finchley, Middlesex, 1866. [3]

ROBSON, Thomas.—Magd. Hall, Ox. B.A. 1850; Deac. 1850 and Pr. 1851 by Bp of Dur. Formerly V. of Kirkleatham, Yorks, 1854–67. [4]

ROBSON, Thomas William, *Richmond, Yorks.*—Univ. Coll. Ox. B.A. 1830, M.A. 1842; Deac. 1831, Pr. 1833. R. of Marske, near Richmond, Dio. Rip. 1855. (Patron, J. T. D. Hutton, Esq; R.'s Inc. 390*l*; Pop. 263.) Formerly P. C. of Hudswell, Catterick, Yorks, 1833–55. [5]

ROBSON, William Henry Fairfax, *St. Giles's Vicarage, Northampton.*—King's Coll. Lond. Theol. Assoc. 1861; Deac. 1861 by Bp of Lon. Pr. 1863 by Bp of Pet. V. of St. Giles's, Northampton, Dio. Pet. 1864. (Patrons, Simeon's Trustees; V.'s Inc. 250*l* and Ho; Pop. 3690.) Formerly C. of St. Paul's, Whitechapel, Lond. 1861–62, St. Giles's, Northampton, 1862–64. Author, *Farewell Sermon at St. Paul's, Whitechapel,* 1862; *Plain Sermons,* published Monthly by W. Macintosh. [6]

ROCHE, Henry George, *Raynham Vicarage, Romford, Essex.*—St. John's Coll. Cam. LL.B. 1843. V. of Raynham, Dio. Roch. 1847. (Patron, J. G. C. Crosse, Esq; Tithe—Imp. 259*l* 5*s*, V. 430*l*; Glebe, 4 acres; V.'s Inc. 438*l* and Ho; Pop. 924.) Chap. to the Earl of Limerick. [7]

ROCHE, William, *Colney-heath, St. Albans, Herts.*—Trin. Coll. Ox. B.A. 1830, M.A. 1833; Deac. 1831, Pr. 1832. P. C. of Colney-heath, Dio. Roch. 1850. (Patrons, Trustees; P. C.'s Inc. 70*l* and Ho; Pop. 854.) [8]

ROCHESTER, The Right Rev. Thomas Leigh CLAUGHTON, Ld Bishop of Rochester, *Danbury Palace, Chelmsford, Essex.*—Trin. Coll. Ox. B.A. 1831, M.A. 1834; Deac. 1834, Pr. 1836. Consecrated Bp of Rochester 1867. (Episcopal Jurisdiction—the City and Deanery of Rochester, the Co. of Hertford and the Co. of Essex, excepting ten Parishes in the latter; Inc. of See, 5000*l*; Pop. 608,914; Acres, 1,535,450; Deaneries, 36; Benefices, 591; Curates, 240; Church Sittings, 203,643.) His Lordship was formerly V. of Kidderminster 1841-67; Prof. of Poetry at Oxford 1852; Hon. Can. of Wor. 1845. [9]

ROCKE, Thomas James, *Exmouth Vicarage, Devon.*—Downing Coll. Cam. B.A. 1829, M.A. 1845; Deac. 1829, Pr. 1830. V. of Littleham with Exmouth, Dio. Ex. 1843. (Patrons, D. and C. of Ex; Tithe—App. 371*l* 19*s* 10*d*, V. 112*l* 16*s*; V.'s Inc. 160*l* and Ho; Pop. 3904.) [10]

ROCKE, Thomas Owen, *Clungunford Rectory, Shrewsbury.*—Trin. Coll. Cam. B.A. 1845; Deac. 1845, Pr. 1846. R. of Clungunford, Dio. Herf. 1849. (Patron, John Rocke, Esq; Tithe, 538*l*; R.'s Inc. 538*l* and Ho; Pop. 647.) [11]

ROCKETT, Hugh Joseph, *Wythop, Cumberland.*—Wad. Coll. Ox; Deac. 1867 by Bp of Carl. C. of Wythop 1867. [12]

RODD, Charles, *North Hill Parsonage, Launceston.*—Ex. Coll. Ox. B.A. 1829; Deac. 1831 by Bp of B. and W. Pr. 1832 by Bp of Ex. R. of North Hill, Dio. Ex. 1832. (Patron, Francis Rodd, Esq; Tithe, 538*l* 9*s*; Glebe, 62 acres; R.'s Inc. 580*l* and Ho; Pop. 1263.) Formerly C. of St. Just in Roseland 1831–32. [13]

RODD, Frederick Arthur, *Hayfield, Stockport.*—St. Aidan's; Deac. 1857 and Pr. 1858 by Bp of Ches. P. C. of Hayfield, Derbyshire, Dio. Lich. 1863. (Patrons, Freeholders; P. C.'s Inc. 180*l*; Pop. 3360.) Formerly C. of Hurdsfield, Cheshire, 1857–59, Holbrook, Suffolk, 1859–60, High Wycombe 1860, St. John's, Miles Platting. Manchester, 1860–61, St. George's, Bolton, 1861–62. [14]

RODD, Henry Tremayne, *Gwinear Vicarage, Hayle, Cornwall.*—Ex. Coll. Ox. B.A. 1833; Deac. 1834 by Bp of Win. Pr. 1836 by Bp of Ex. V. of Gwinear, Dio. Ex. 1851. (Patron, Bp of Ex; Tithe, 287*l*; Glebe, 34 acres; V.'s Inc. 317*l* and Ho; Pop. 2880.) [15]

RODGERS, Charles Eboral, *Harworth, Tickhill, Notts.*—Trin. Coll. Cam. B.A. 1830, M.A. 1833; Deac. 1831, Pr. 1832. V. of Harworth, Dio. Lin. 1841. (Patron, the present V; Tithe—App. 209*l* 8*s*, Imp. 303*l* 18*s*, V. 108*l* 16*s*; Glebe, 38 acres; V.'s Inc. 686*l* and Ho; Pop. 925.) [16]

RODGERS, Edward, *St. Luke's Parsonage, Nottingham.*—St. Aidan's; Deac. 1851 by Bp of Nor. Pr. 1852 by Bp of Ely. P. C. of St. Luke's, Nottingham, Dio. Lin. 1865. (Patrons, Trustees; P. C.'s Inc. 300*l* and Ho; Pop. 8500.) Formerly C. of New Radford, Notts; Chap. of Borough Gaol, Nottingham; Chap. to Messrs. Copestake, Moore and Co. [17]

RODGERS, Harvey Henry, *Lyne Parsonage, Chertsey, Surrey.*—Trin. Hall, Cam. Jun. Opt. and B.A. 1844; Deac. 1845, Pr. 1846. P. C. of Botleys and Lyne, Dio. Win. 1855. (Patron, Bp of Win; P. C.'s Inc. 110*l* and Ho; Pop. 494.) Formerly C. of St. Saviour's, Upper Chelsea. [18]

RODGERS, John, 17, *Mecklenburgh-square, London, W.C.*—Deac. and Pr. 1848 by Abp of York. P. C. of St. Thomas's, Charterhouse, Lond. Dio. Lon. 1863. (Patron, Bp of Lon; P. C.'s Inc. 400*l*; Pop. 6840.) Formerly P. C. of Worneth, near Chester, 1849–55; Min. of St. Barnabas', Holloway, Lond. 1855–63. Author, *Whose Children ought to be Baptized?* 6*d*; *Death Conquered* (a Sermon), 2*d*. [19]

RODGERS, John Douglass, 8, *Everett-street, Russell-square, London, W.C.*—Clare Hall, Cam. B.A. 1849; Deac. 1849 and Pr. 1850 by Bp of Man. C. of Ch. Ch. Woburn-square, Bloomsbury, 1865. [20]

RODNEY, The Hon. Henry, *Berrington House, Leominster.*—Trin. Coll. Cam. M.A. 1813; Deac. 1815 and Pr. 1816 by Bp of Herf. V. of Eye, Dio. Herf. 1817. (Patron, Ld Chan; Tithe—App. 40*l*, Imp. 215*l*, V. 318*l* 2*s* 2*d*; V.'s Inc. 325*l* and Ho; Pop. 733.) Preb. of Herf. 1826. (Value, 38*l*.) V. of Llanfihangel-Crucorney, Monmouthshire, Dio. Llan. 1828. (Patron, the Prince of Wales; Tithe—Imp. 93*l*, V. 255*l*; V.'s Inc. 260*l* and Ho; Pop. 479.) V. of Llangattock Llingoed, Monmouthshire, Dio. Llan. 1828. (Patron, Bp of Llan; Tithe, 173*l*; V.'s Inc. 175*l* and Ho; Pop. 206.) [21]

RODWELL, Christopher Brown, *Freshford, near Bath.*—Ch. Coll. Cam. B.A. 1835; Deac. 1846 and Pr. 1847 by Bp of Roch. R. of Freshford with Woodwick, Dio. B. and W. 1856. (Patron, the present R; Tithe, 174*l* 15*s*; Glebe, 32 acres; R.'s Inc. 360*l* and Ho; Pop. 584.) Formerly V. of Great and Little Toller, Dorset. [22]

RODWELL, John Medows, *Douglas House, Highbury New Park, London, N.*—Caius Coll. Cam. Scho. of, B.A. 1830, M.A. 1833; Deac. 1831 by Bp of Nor. Pr. 1832 by Bp of Lon. R. of St. Ethelburga's, Bishopsgate, Dio. Lon. 1843. (Patron, Bp of Lon; R.'s Inc. 1060*l*; Pop. 606.) Formerly Sec. to the Additional Curates Fund 1843–58. Translator of the Koran and of the Book of Job, and of various Ethiopic Liturgies. [23]

RODWELL, Robert Mandeville, *High Laver Rectory, Ongar, Essex.*—Ex. Coll. Ox. 3rd cl. Lit. Hum. B.A. 1844, M.A. 1846; Deac. 1845 by Bp of Lon. Pr. 1846 by Bp of Roch. R. of High Laver, Dio. Roch. 1864. (Patron, P. J. Budworth, Esq; Tithe, 520*l*; Glebe, 60 acres; R.'s Inc. 620*l* and Ho; Pop. 471.) Formerly R. of Newcastle, Dio. Limerick, 1848–64. [24]

ROE, Charles, *Little Welnetham, Bury St. Edmunds.*—Trin. Coll. Ox. B.A. 1832, M.A. 1835. R. of Little Welnetham, Dio. Ely, 1849. (Patron, Marquis of Bristol; Tithe, 163*l* 15*s* 9*d*; Glebe, 25 acres; R.'s Inc. 188*l*; Pop. 194.) [25]

ROE, Henry, *Kineton, Warwick.*—Deac. 1865 and Pr. 1866 by Bp of Wor. Asst. C. of Combrook with Compton Verney 1865; Head Mast. of the Middle Sch. Kineton. Formerly Government Lect. on Mathematics at the Metropolitan Training Institution, Highbury. [1]

ROE, Henry Farwell, *Lesnewth, Boscastle, Cornwall.*—Lin. Coll. Ox. B.A. 1850, M.A. 1853; Deac. 1851 and Pr. 1852 by Bp of Ex. R. of Lesnewth, Dio. Ex. 1854. (Patron, Lord Churston; Tithe, 200*l*; Glebe, 45 acres; R.'s Inc. 260*l* and Ho; Pop. 96.) Author, *Two Humiliation Sermons*, Parker, 1854. [2]

ROE, James, 18*a*, *Arbour-square, London, E.*—Dub. A.B. C. of St. Thomas's, Stepney. [3]

ROE, Robert Bradley, *Melbury Osmund Rectory, near Dorchester.*—Corpus Coll. Cam. Spencer's Scho. B.A. 1848, M.A. 1851; Deac. 1849 and Pr. 1850 by Bp of Salis. R. of Melbury Osmund with Melbury Sampford R. Dio. Salis. 1855. (Patron, Earl of Ilchester; Melbury Osmund, Tithe, 177*l*; Glebe, 86 acres; Melbury Sampford, Tithe, 57*l*; R.'s Inc. 398*l* and Ho; Pop. Melbury Osmund 329, Melbury Sampford 60.) Formerly V. of Shepton-Montague, Somerset, 1852–55. [4]

ROE, William Fletcher, *Hammoom, Blandford, Dorset.*—Dub. Scho. of, 1st Cl. Gold Medallist, Hons. in Div. Cl. and Heb. A.B. 1817, St. Mary Hall, Ox. B.A. and M.A. 1853; Deac. 1819 and Pr. 1820 by Bp of Derry. R. of Hammoom, Dio. Salis. 1863. (Patron, Giles Meech, Esq; Tithe, 180*l*; Glebe, 23½ acres; R.'s Inc. 269*l* and Ho; Pop. 80.) Formerly 2nd Mast. of Foyle Coll. Londonderry, 1817–34; Incumb. of Chapel of Ease, Londonderry, 1820–35; Railway Chap. and various Curacies in England and Ireland. [5]

ROFFE, Alfred Augustus, *St. Ives, Hunts.*—St. Augustine's Miss. Coll. Canterbury; Deac. 1865 by Bp of Ox. Pr. 1867 by Bp of Ely. C. of St. Ives 1867. Formerly C. of Thatcham, Berks, 1865–66. [6]

ROGERS, Aaron, *Clifton.*—Jesus Coll. Ox. B.A. 1825, M.A. 1828; Deac. 1827 and Pr. 1828 by Bp of Llan. R. of St. Peter's, Bristol, Dio. G. and B. 1867. (Patrons, Trustees; R.'s Inc. 250*l* and Ho; Pop. 836.) Formerly C. of Llanaben, Monmouthshire, 1827–28; Chap. R.N. 1832; C. of Henbury, Gloucestershire, 1841; P. C. of St. Paul's, Bristol, 1849–67. [7]

ROGERS, Alexander John, *Great Dunmow, Essex.*—Queens' Coll. Cam. B.A. 1839, M.A. 1842; Deac. 1839 and Pr. 1840 by Bp of Win. V. of Lindsell, Dio. Roch. 1864. (Patron, S. Alger, Esq; V.'s Inc. 204*l* and Ho; Pop. 385.) Sen. Chap. (Retired List) Madras Establishment 1842–62. [8]

ROGERS, Alleyne, *Langlands, Stourbridge.*—Dub. A.B. 1837; Deac. 1837 and Pr. 1838 by Abp of Dub. Formerly P. C. of Brockmoor, Staffs; P. C. of St. Peter's, Leighton, Cheshire; V. of Avenbury, Herefordshire. [9]

ROGERS, Charles Mott, *St. Helen's, Ryde.*—Caius Coll. Cam. B.A. 1862; Deac. 1863 and Pr. 1864 by Bp of Salis. C. of St. Helen's, Ryde, 1867. Formerly C. of Castleton and Oborne, Dorset, 1863. [10]

ROGERS, Edward, *Blackford, Ivy Bridge, Devon.*—Ch. Ch. Ox. Stud. of, B.A. 1841, M.A. 1843; Deac. 1843 by Bp of Ox. Pr. 1844 by Bp of Salis. Formerly C. of Penselwood, Somerset, Freshwater, Isle of Wight, Lydford, Devon. Author, *Some Account of the Life and Opinions of a Fifth Monarchy Man*, Longmans, 1867. [11]

ROGERS, E. Ellis, *Beaumaris.*—Mast. in the Gr. Sch. Beaumaris. [12]

ROGERS, Edward Henry, *Thames-Ditton, Kingston-on-Thames, S.W.*—King's Coll. Cam. B.A. 1851, Tyrrwhitt's Heb. Scho. 1853, M.A. 1854. P. C. of Thames-Ditton, Dio. Win. 1860. (Patron, King's Coll. Cam; P. C.'s Inc. 300*l* and Ho; Pop. 1950.) Formerly Fell. of King's Coll. Cam. [13]

ROGERS, Edward J.—Chap. to the Forces, Aldershot. [14]

ROGERS, Foster, *Winchester.*—Asst. Chap. to the House of Correction, Winchester. [15]

ROGERS, George, *Gedney Vicarage (Lincolnshire), near Wisbech.*—St. John's Coll. Cam. B.A. 1835, M.A. 1838; Deac. and Pr. 1839 by Bp of Lin. V. of Gedney, Dio. Lin. 1857. (Patron, the Crown; Tithe—App. 1148*l* 10*s* and 105½ acres of Glebe, Imp. 551*l* 15*s*, V. 1000*l*; Glebe, 19½ acres; V.'s Inc. 1040*l* and Ho; Pop. 1215.) Formerly R. of Braceborough, Lincolnshire, 1844–57. [16]

ROGERS, George Albert, *Oaklands, Hilldrop-road, Tufnell-park, London, N.*—Trin. Coll. Cam. B.A. 1839, M.A. 1842; Deac. and Pr. 1839 by Bp of B. and W. P. C. of St. Luke's, Holloway, Dio. Lon. 1858. (Patrons, Trustees; P. C.'s Inc. 500*l*; Pop. 3500.) Formerly P. C. of Penkridge, Staffs, 1845–47; V. of Leominster, Herf. 1847–51; P. C. of St. Peter's, Regent's-square, Lond. 1851–58. Author, *Jacob's Well*, R.T.S. 1*s* 6*d*; *Bethany*, 5*s*; *The Sure Anchor*, Seeleys, 2*s* 6*d*; *Clapham Sermons*, Hatchards, 6*s*; *The Valour of Faith*, 2*s* 6*d*; etc. [17]

ROGERS, Henry, *Melverley, Oswestry.*—Jesus Coll. Ox. B.A. 1829; Deac. 1830 by Bp of Lich. Pr. 1838 by Bp of St. A. R. of Melverley, Dio. St. A. 1847. (Patron, Bp of St. A; Tithe, 177*l* 11*s*; Glebe, 6 acres; R.'s Inc. 196*l* 11*s* and Ho; Pop. 114.) Formerly C. of Ruyton of the 11 Towns 1830–32. [18]

ROGERS, Herbert Goodenough, *West Kington Rectory, Chippenham.*—Trin. Coll. Ox. B.A. 1866; Deac. 1867 by Bp of G. and B. C. of West Kington 1867. [19]

ROGERS, James Beadon, *Cornworthy, Totnes, Devon.*—Magd. Hall, Ox. B.A. 1847; Deac. 1848, Pr. 1849. V. of Cornworthy, Dio. Ex. 1854. (Patron, George Norsworthy, Esq; Tithe—Imp. 301*l* 2*s*; Glebe, 35 acres; V.'s Inc. 235*l* and Ho; Pop. 479.) [20]

ROGERS, James Charles Warrington, *Motcombe, Wincanton, Dorset.*—Ex. Coll. Ox. B.A. 1848. C. of Motcombe. [21]

ROGERS, James Edwin Thorold, *Oxford.*—Magd. Hall, Ox. B.A. 1846, M.A. 1849. Professor of Political Economy, Oxford, 1862. Formerly C. of Headington, Oxford. Author, *An Introductory Lecture to the Logic of Aristotle*, Oxford, 1859; *Education in Oxford, its Method, its Aid, and its Rewards*, 1861; etc. [22]

ROGERS, James Strangward, 22, *Northampton-park, Canonbury, N.*—C. of St. Jude's, Mildmay-park, Islington; Sec. of the South-West London Protestant Institute. [23]

ROGERS, John, *Habberley Rectory, Shrewsbury.*—Brasen. Coll. Ox. B.A. 1856, M.A. 1859; Deac. 1858 and Pr. 1859 by Bp of Dur. R. of Habberley, Dio. Herf. 1862. (Patron, F. T. Sparrow, Esq; Tithe, 126*l*; Glebe, 22 acres; R.'s Inc. 160*l* and Ho; Pop. 112.) Formerly C. of St. Andrew's, Auckland, Durham, 1858–62. [24]

ROGERS, John, *Foxton, Market Harborough, Leicestershire.*—Dub. A.B. 1825; Deac. 1828 by Bp of Killaloe, Pr. 1829 by Bp of Lin. V. of Foxton, Dio. Pet. 1834. (Patron, Ld Chan; R.'s Inc. 136*l*; Pop. 388.) [25]

ROGERS, John, *Stanage-park, Brampton Brian, Herefordshire.*—St. John's Coll. Cam. B.A. 1840. R. of Stowe, Salop, Dio. Herf. 1865. (Patron, Ld Chan; Glebe, 1½ acres; R.'s Inc. 200*l* and Ho; Pop. 161.) Formerly V. of Amyestrey, Herefordshire, 1850–65. [26]

ROGERS, John, *Llanlleonvel, Builth.*—P. C. of Llanlleonvel, Brecknockshire, Dio. St. D. 1866. (Patron, Bp of St. D; P. C.'s Inc. 60*l*; Pop. 250.) [27]

ROGERS, John Gurney, *Worcester.*—Jesus Coll. Cam. B.A. 1839; Deac. 1840, Pr. 1841. [28]

ROGERS, John Henry, 18, *Portland-square, Bristol.*—Wad. Coll. Ox. B.A. 1865; Deac. 1866 by Bp of G. and B. C. of St. Paul's, Bristol, 1866. [29]

ROGERS, John Thomas, *Barwick-in-Elmet, Milford Junction, Yorks.*—Ch. Coll. Cam. B.A. 1859, M.A. 1863; Deac. 1860 by Bp of Carl. Pr. 1861 by Bp of Rip. C. of Barwick-in-Elmet 1866. Formerly C. of Bramley, Leeds, 1860. [30]

ROGERS, Percy, 52, *Durnford-street, Stonehouse, Devon.*—Clare Coll. Cam. Scho. Prizeman and Exhib. Sen. Opt. and B.A. 1849, M.A. 1861; Deac. 1850 and Pr. 1851 by Bp of Ex. Chap. and Naval Instructor, R.N.

1852; Chap. of H.M.S. "Implacable," Training Ship, Devonport. [1]

ROGERS, Reginald Basset, *Preston, near Uppingham.*—C. of Preston. [2]

ROGERS, Reginald Welford, *The Vicarage, Cookham, Berks.*—Trin. Coll. Cam. Scho. of, 3rd cl. Math. and Cl. Trip. B.A. 1858, M.A. 1861; Deac. 1861 by Bp of Lon. Pr. 1862 by Abp of Cant. V. of Cookham, Dio. Ox. 1864. (Patron, John Rogers, Esq; Tithe, 430*l*; V.'s Inc. 430*l* and Ho; Pop. 1050.) Formerly C. of St. Martin's with St. Paul's, Canterbury, 1863. [3]

ROGERS, Robert, *Fawkham Rectory, Dartford, Kent.*—Dub. Scho. of, 1849, A.B. 1852, Abp King's Div. Prizeman 1853, A.M. 1861; Deac. 1855 by Bp of Meath, Pr. 1856 by Bp of Kilmore. C. in sole charge of Fawkham 1861. Formerly C. of Cloon, Kilmore, 1855, Withington, Manchester, 1856, St. Nicholas', Cork, 1858, Lockwood, Ripon, 1860. [4]

ROGERS, Robert Green, *Yarlington Rectory, Wincanton, Somerset.*—Oriel Coll. Ox. B.A. 1821, M.A. 1824; Deac. 1823, Pr. 1824. R. of Yarlington, Dio. B. and W. 1826. (Patron, the present R; Tithe, 244*l*; Glebe, 38 acres; R.'s Inc. 354*l* and Ho; Pop. 246.) [5]

ROGERS, Robert Roe, *Madeley, Salop.*—St. Aidan's, 1856–57, Hon. and Div. Scho. of; Deac. 1858 and Pr. 1859 by Bp of Herf. Formerly C. of Madeley, Salop, 1858–62, St. Mary's, Haverfordwest, and Chap. of Picton Castle 1863–65. Author, *Farewell Sermon on leaving Madeley*, 1862, 6*d*. [6]

ROGERS, Saltren, *Gwennap Vicarage, Redruth, Cornwall.*—Ex. Coll. Ox. B.A. 1846, M.A. 1848; Deac. 1847, Pr. 1848. V. of Gwennap, Dio. Ex. 1856. (Patrons, D. and C. of Ex; Tithe, 429*l* 7*s* 6*d*; Glebe, 70*l*; V.'s Inc. 540*l* and Ho; Pop. 4124.) Formerly P. C. of Cury with Gunwalloe, Cornwall, 1849–56. [7]

ROGERS, Samuel, *Clayworth, Bawtry, Notts.*—Corpus Coll. Cam; Deac. 1824 and Pr. 1825 by Abp of York. C. of Clayworth. Formerly C. of St. James's, Nottingham, Bulwell, Notts, and Sutton-on-Trent. [8]

ROGERS, Thomas, *Durham.*—New Coll. Ox. Choral Scho. of, B.A. 1862, M.A. 1864; Deac. 1863 and Pr. 1864 by Bp of Ox. Min. Can. of Dur. 1864. (Value, 300*l*.) Chap. of Durham Union 1866. Formerly C. of St. Helen's, Sandford, Abingdon, 1863, Asst. Mast. of St. Andrew's Coll. Bradfield, Berks. [9]

ROGERS, Thomas, *Boncath, Blaenffos, Cardigan.*—Lampeter; Deac. 1850 and Pr. 1852 by Bp of St. D. R. of Llanfihangel Pembedw, Dio. St. D. 1863. (Patron, Ld Chan; Tithe, 100*l*; R.'s Inc. 100*l*; Pop. 287.) P. C. of Capel Colman, Dio. St. D. 1866. (Patron, Mark Anthony Saurin, Esq; P. C.'s Inc. 90*l*; Pop. 157.) Formerly C. of Llanguick 1850–53, Llangunllo 1854–63. [10]

ROGERS, Thomas Percival, *Batheaston Vicarage, Bath.*—Ch. Ch. Ox. 2nd cl. Lit. Hum. and B.A. 1844; Deac. 1845, Pr. 1849. V. of Batheaston with Catherine C. Dio. B. and W. 1851. (Patron, Ch. Ch. Ox; Batheaston, Tithe, 300*l*; Catherine, Tithe, 50*l*; V.'s Inc. 360*l* and Ho; Pop. Batheaston 1698, Catherine 84.) [11]

ROGERS, Thomas Whitwell, *Helsington Parsonage, Milnthorpe, Westmoreland.*—St. John's Coll. Cam. B.A. 1851, M.A. 1857; Deac. 1854 by Bp of Ches. Pr. 1855 by Bp of Lich. P. C. of Helsington, Dio. Carl. 1860. (Patron, V. of Kendal; Glebe, 66 acres; P. C.'s Inc. 121*l* and Ho; Pop. 302.) [12]

ROGERS, William, 3, *Devonshire-square, London, N.E.*—Ball. Coll. Ox. B.A. 1842, M.A. 1844; Deac. 1842, Pr. 1843. R. of St. Botolph's, Bishopsgate, City and Dio. Lon. 1863. (Patron, Bp of Lon; R's Inc. 1700*l* and Ho; Pop. 7069.) Preb. of St. Paul's 1862; Chap. in Ordinary to the Queen. Formerly P. C. of St. Thomas's, Charterhouse, Lond. 1841–63. Author, *A Letter to Lord John Russell on the Educational Prospects of St. Thomas's, Charterhouse.* [13]

ROGERS, William, *Mawnan, Falmouth.*—Ex. Coll. Ox. B.A. 1840, M.A. 1845; Deac. 1841 and Pr. 1842 by Bp of Ex. R. of Mawnan, Dio. Ex. 1842. (Patron, J. J. Rogers, Esq; Tithe, comm. 314*l* 10*s*; Glebe, 38 acres; R.'s Inc. 323*l* and Ho; Pop. 569.) Rural Dean. Formerly C. of Cury and Gunwalloe 1841–42. [14]

ROGERS, William Henry, *Wilmslow, Manchester.*—Dub. A.B. 1857, A.M. 1859, *ad eund.* Ox. 1861; Deac. 1860 and Pr. 1861 by Bp of Man. C. of Wilmslow, Cheshire. Formerly C. of Withington, near Manchester, 1860. [15]

ROGERS, William Rogers Coxwell, *Dowdeswell Rectory, Cheltenham.*—Ex. Coll. Ox. B.A. 1833, M.A. 1836. R. of Dowdeswell, Dio. G. and B. 1854. (Patron, R. C. Rogers, Esq; Tithe, 386*l* 1*s* 3*d*; Glebe, 23 acres; R.'s Inc. 450*l* and Ho; Pop. 350.) [16]

ROGERSON, George Bayldon, *Manningham, Bradford, Yorks.*—St. John's Coll. Cam. Tyrrwhitt's Heb. Scho. 1851, 17th Wrang, and B.A. 1848, M.A. 1851; Deac. and Pr. 1848. Usher of King Charles II.'s Gr. Sch. Bradford, 1851. [17]

ROKEBY, Henry Ralph, *The Manor House, Arthingworth, Northants.*—Downing Coll. Cam. B.A. 1830; Deac. and Pr. 1830. R. of Arthingworth, Dio. Pet. 1830. (Patron, the present R; Tithe, 1*l* 2*s* 6*d*; Glebe, 40 acres; R.'s Inc. 360*l*; Pop. 275.) Surrogate 1839. [18]

ROLFE, Charles, *The Rectory, Shadoxhurst, Ashford, Kent.*—Lin. Coll. Ox. B.A. 1824; Deac. 1825, Pr. 1826. R. of Shadoxhurst, Dio. Cant. 1838. (Patron, Ld Chan; Tithe, 126*l* 10*s*; Glebe, 50 acres; R.'s Inc. 136*l* 10*s* and Ho; Pop. 194.) R. of Orlestone, Kent, Dio. Cant. 1845. (Patron, T. Oliver, Esq; Tithe, 157*l* 18*s* 2*d*; Glebe, 48 acres; R.'s Inc. 193*l*; Pop. 390.) Formerly C. of Chesterfield 1825, St. James's, Nottingham, 1826, Ockbrook, 1827, Harwich 1828, South Normanton 1828. [19]

ROLFE, Charles, *The Vicarage, North Lydbury, Salop.*—King's Coll. Lond. Theol. Assoc. 1856; Deac. 1856 and Pr. 1857 by Bp of Lon. V. of North Lydbury with Norbury, Dio. Herf. 1864. (Patrons, Trustees of the late Rev. John Bright; Tithe, 658*l*; Glebe, 45 acres; V.'s Inc. 700*l* and Ho; Pop. Lydbury 102[illegible] Norbury 412.) Formerly C. of Wimbledon 1856, Shere 1859. [20]

ROLFE, Edmund Nelson, *Morningthorpe Rectory, Long Stratton, Norfolk.*—Caius Coll. Cam. B.A. 1833, M.A. 1841. R. of Morningthorpe, Dio. Nor. 1850. (Patron, Ld Chan; Tithe, 300*l*; Glebe, 7 acres; R.'s Inc. 328*l* and Ho; Pop. 140.) [21]

ROLFE, George Crabb, *Hailey Parsonage, Witney.*—P. C. of Hailey with Crawley P. C. Dio. Ox. 1839. (Patron, Bp of Ox; P. C.'s Inc. 360*l* and Ho; Pop. 1569.) Chap. to the Witney Union. [22]

ROLLES, Robert John, *Cheltenham.*—New Coll. Ox. B.A. 1830, M.A. 1833; Deac. 1831 by Bp of Herf. Pr. 1832 by Bp of Wor. Formerly Fell. of New Coll. Ox. [23]

ROLLESTON, George, *Maltby, Rotherham, Yorks.*—Mert. Coll. Ox. B.A. 1814, M.A. 1817; Deac. 1814 and Pr. 1815 by Abp of York. V. of Maltby, Dio. York, 1816. (Patron, Earl of Scarborough; Tithe—App. 82*l*, Imp. 1*l* 3*s*, V. 81*l* 4*s* 1*d*; Glebe, 4 acres; V.'s Inc. 174*l*; Pop. 858.) V. of Stainton, Yorks, Dio. York, 1816. (Patron, Earl of Scarborough; Tithe—Imp. 54*l* 10*s*; V. 101*l* 10*s*; Glebe, 30 acres; V.'s Inc. 220*l*; Pop. 267.) [24]

ROLLESTON, George, *Stainton-by-Langworth Vicarage, Wragby, Lincolnshire.*—Mert. Coll. Ox. B.A. 1814, M.A. 1820. V. of Stainton-by-Langworth, Dio. Lin. 1823. (Patron, Earl of Scarborough; V.'s Inc. 185*l* and Ho; Pop. 213.) [25]

ROLLESTON, Robert, *Godmanchester Vicarage, Huntingdon.*—Univ. Coll. Ox. B.A. 1842; Deac. 1843, Pr. 1844. V. of Godmanchester, Dio. Ely, 1867. (Patrons, D. and C. of Westminster; Glebe, 190 acres; V.'s Inc. 420*l* and Ho; Pop. 2438.) Formerly P. C. of Seathwaite, Lancashire, 1855–57. [26]

ROLLESTON, Septimus, *Bedford.*—Deac. 1851, Pr. 1852. R. of St. Peter's, Bedford, Dio. Ely, 1866. (Patron, Ld Chan; R.'s Inc. 250*l* and Ho; Pop. 2882.) Formerly V. of Somerby, Leic. 1855–66. [27]

ROLLESTON, William Lancelot, *Scraptoft Vicarage, Leicester.*—St. John's Coll. Cam. B.A. 1840;

Deac. and Pr. 1840. V. of Great Dalby, Dio. Pet. 1842. (Patron, Sir R. Burdett, Bart; Tithe—Imp. 49*l* 7*s* 6*d*, V. 235*l*; Glebe, 1 acre; V.'s Inc. 243*l* and Ho; Pop. 484.) V. of Scraptoft, Dio. Pet. 1849. (Patron, E. B. Hartopp, Esq. M.P; V.'s Inc. 200*l* and Ho; Pop. 108.) [1]

ROLPH, Thomas, *Chisledon Vicarage, Swindon, Wilts.*—St. John's Coll. Cam. B.A. 1829; Deac. 1829, Pr. 1831. V. of Chisledon, Dio. Salis. 1866. (Patron, H. Calley, Esq; V.'s Inc. 200*l* and Ho; Pop. 1206.) Dom. Chap. to Earl Bathurst. Formerly C. of North Cerney and Chap. to the Cirencester Union. [2]

ROLT, Henry George, *Limpsfield, Godstone, Surrey.*—Ball. Coll. Ox. M.A. 1851; Deac. 1852 by Bp of Ox. Formerly C. of Streatfeld Mortimer, Reading, 1852. [3]

ROMANIS, William, *Wigston-Magna, Leicester.*—Emman. Coll. Cam. Sen. Opt. 1st cl. Cl. Trip. and B.A. 1846, M.A. 1849; Deac. 1847 and Pr. 1848 by Bp of G. and B. V. of Wigston-Magna, Dio. Pet. 1863. Patrons, Haberdashers' Co. and Christ's Hospital, alt; Glebe, 115 acres; V.'s Inc. 300*l* and Ho; Pop. 2321.) Formerly Sen. C. of St. Mary's, Reading; C. of Axminster; Cl. Mast. and Lect. at Cheltenham Coll. Author, *Sermons preached at St. Mary's, Reading*, Macmillans, 1862, 6*s*; Second Series, 1864. [4]

ROOKE, Frederick John, *Rampisham Rectory, Dorchester.*—Oriel Coll. Ox. B.A. 1838, M.A. 1841; Deac. 18[illegible]1 by Bp of Lich. Pr. 1843 by Bp of Salis. R. of Rampisham with Wraxall R. Dio. Salis. 1845. (Patron, St. John's Coll. Cam; Rampisham, Tithe, 198*l*; Glebe, 125 acres; Wraxall, Tithe, 165*l*; Glebe, 33 acres; R.'s Inc. 596*l* and Ho; Pop. Rampisham 356, Wraxall 83.) Preb. of Salis. 1859. [5]

ROOKE, George, *Embleton Vicarage, Chathill, Northumberland.*—Mert. Coll. Ox. B.A. 1817, M.A. 1822; Deac. 1822, Pr. 1823. V. of Embleton, Dio. Dur. 1830. (Patron, Mert. Coll. Ox; Tithe, App. 560*l*; Glebe, 200 acres; V.'s Inc. 815*l* and Ho; Pop. 1809.) Hon. Can. of Dur. 185[illegible]. Formerly Fell. of Mert. Coll. Ox. [6]

ROOKE, Thomas, *St. Alban's House, Windsor.*—Dub. A.B. 1848, A.M. 1851, *ad eund.* Ox. 1861; Deac. 1848 and Pr. 1849 by Abp of Armagh. Clerical Sec. of Ch. of Eng. Temperance Reformation Soc. 1865; Chap. to Earl of Donoughmore. Formerly C. of Carnteel, Tyrone, 1848–50, Monkstown, Dublin, 1850–59, Windsor 1859–65. Author, *Biblical Catechist*, Dublin, 1846; *Sermons—On Psalm XC.* 1, 2, Dublin, 1859; *Farewell at Monkstown*, ib. 1859; *On Indian Famine*, Windsor, 1861; *On Death of H.R.H. the Prince Consort*, ib. 1861; *To Windsor Volunteers*, ib. 1863; *On Behalf of the Church of England Temperance Reformation Society*, Partridge, Lond. 1866; another, ib. 1867; *Lay Assistance in Parochial Work*, Windsor; *Formation of Parochial Temperance Societies*, Partridge, Lond. [7]

ROOKE, William Thomas, *Patterdale Rectory, near Penrith.*—St. Bees; Deac. 1852, Pr. 1853. R. of Patterdale, Dio. Carl. 1861. (Patron, Earl of Lonsdale; Tithe, 22*l*; Glebe, 18 acres; R.'s Inc. 135*l* and Ho; Pop. 693.) Formerly C. of Wigton and Chap. of the Wigton Union 1852; C. of Patterdale 1857. [8]

ROOKE, Willoughby John Edward.—Brasen. Coll. Ox. B.A. 1833, M.A. 1836; Deac. 1836, Pr. 1837. Chap. to H.R.H. the Duke of Cambridge. [9]

ROOKER, James Yates, *Lower Gornal, Dudley.*—St. Cath. Coll. Cam; Deac. 1845, Pr. 1846. P. C. of Lower Gornal, Dio. Lich. 1848. (Patron, Earl of Dudley; Glebe, 9 acres; P. C.'s Inc. 200*l* and Ho; Pop. 5915.) Formerly C. of Hathersage, Derbyshire, 1845–48. [10]

ROOKER, John, 10, *Barnsbury square, Islington, London, N.*—Ch. Coll. Cam. B.A. 1853, M.A. 1856; Deac. 1853, Pr. 1854. Director of the Ch. Missionary Children's Home, Highbury-park, Lond; P. C. of Trinity, Cloudesley-square, Islington, Dio. Lon. 1867. (Patrons, Trustees; P. C.'s Inc. 600*l*; Pop. 6504.) Formerly C. of the Lye, Stourbridge, St. Mary's, Cheltenham, and St. George's, Leeds; P. C. of Trinity, Runcorn, 1859–64. [11]

ROOKER, William Yates, *St. Mark's, Dalston, London, N.E.*—P. C. of St. Mark's, Dalston. Formerly Min. of Fitzroy Chapel, St. Pancras, Lond. 1854–63. [12]

ROOKES, Charles, *Exeter.*—Jesus Coll. Cam. LL.B. 1824; Deac. 1826, Pr. 1827. [13]

ROOKIN, Henry, *Upton Grey, Odiham, Hants.*—Queen's Coll. Ox. B.A. 1822, M.A. 1826; Deac. 1823, Pr. 1824. C. of Upton Grey. [14]

ROOM, John, *Eastwood, Keighley, Yorks.*—St. John's Coll. Cam. B.A. 1852; Deac. 1852, Pr. 1853. P. C. of Eastwood, Dio. Rip. 1853. (Patrons, the Crown and Bp of Rip. alt; P. C.'s Inc. 150*l*; Pop. 3442.) Author, *Random Rhymes*, 1855, 1*s*. [15]

ROOPER, Plumer Pott, *Abbotts-Ripton Rectory, Huntingdon.*—Brasen. Coll. Ox. B.A. 1850; Deac. 1851, Pr. 1852. R. of Abbotts-Ripton, Dio. Ely, 1853. (Patron, the present R; Tithe, 560*l* 11*s* 6*d*; R.'s Inc. 620*l* and Ho; Pop. 381.) Formerly C. of Chettle, Dorset, 1851–53. [16]

ROOSE, Joseph, *Over, Winsford, Cheshire.*—C. of St. John's, Over. [17]

ROPER, Arthur Wellington, *Leverington, Wisbech, Cambs.*—Emman. Coll. Cam. B.A. 1838; Deac. 1839, Pr. 1840. C. of Leverington. [18]

ROPER, Charles Rodwell, *Mount Radford House, Exeter.*—St. John's Coll. Ox. B.A. 1821, M.A. 1832; Deac. 1826, Pr. 1827. R. of St. Olave's, Exeter, Dio. Ex. 1840. (Patron, Ld Chan; R.'s Inc. 93*l*; Pop. 945.) Prin. of the Mount Radford Sch. Exeter, 1829. [19]

ROPER, John Riddall, *St. Boniface Villa, Ventnor, Isle of Wight.*—Corpus Coll. Cam. B.A. 1822, M.A. 1825; Deac. 1822 and Pr. 1823 by Bp of Lin. Formerly C. of Whaddon, Bucks, 1822–24, St. John's, Hackney, 1824–27, Gravesend 1827–31; P. C. of St. Margaret's, Brighton, 1832–37. [20]

ROPER, Thomas, *Sudbury, Derby.*—Univ. Coll. Dur. Fell. of, B.A. 1853, M.A. 1856; Deac. 1853 and Pr. 1854 by Bp of Lich. C. of Sudbury 1864. Formerly C. of North Harborne, Staffs, and Bridport, Dorset. [21]

ROPER, Thomas Henry, *Puddlehinton Rectory, Dorchester.*—St. John's Coll. Ox. B.A. 1841, M.A. 1844; Deac. 1842, Pr. 1843. R. of Puddlehinton, Dio. Salis, 1863. (Patron, Eton Coll; R.'s Inc. 300*l* and Ho; Pop. 414.) Formerly Conduct of Eton Coll. [22]

ROSE, Alfred, *Emmanuel College, Cambridge.*—Emman. Coll. Cam. 13th Wrang. Math. Trip. 1863, B.A. 1863, M.A. 1866; Deac. 1864 and Pr. 1865 by Bp of Ely. Fell. and Asst. Tut. of Emman. Coll. Formerly C. of St. George's, Ramsgate, 1865–66. [23]

ROSE, Charles, *St. Michael-le-Belfrey's Parsonage, York.*—St. Cath. Hall, Cam. B.A. 1829, M.A. 1861; Deac. 1829 by Bp of Roch. Pr. 1830 by Abp of York. P. C. of St. Michael-le-Belfrey, York, Dio. York, 1852. (Patrons, D. and C. of York; P. C.'s Inc. 300*l* and Ho; Pop. 2460.) Formerly C. of North Ferriby 1829–42, St. Cuthbert's, York, 1842–52. [24]

ROSE, Edward Joseph, *Weybridge Rectory, Chertsey, Surrey.*—Trin. Coll. Cam. B.A. 1841, M.A. 1844; Deac. 1841, Pr. 1842. R. of Weybridge, Dio. Win. 1855. (Patron, Ld Chan; Tithe, 219*l* 16*s* 4*d*; Glebe, 7 acres; R.'s Inc. 326*l* and Ho; Pop. 1603.) [25]

ROSE, Francis, *Baulking, Uffington, Faringdon, Berks.*—Univ. Coll. Dur. M.A. 1815, D.D. 1846; Deac. 1815 and Pr. 1816 by Bp of Nor. P. C. of Baulking with Woolstone P. C. Dio. Ox. 1856. (Patron, C. Eyre, Esq; Tithe—App. 165*l*, Imp. 155*l*; P. C.'s Inc. 100*l*; Pop. Baulking 181, Woolstone 256.) Author, *A Call to the Communion*; *An Epitome of the Church of England's History*. [26]

ROSE, Frederic, *The Mission Chapel House, Clare Market, W.C.*—Queens' Coll. Cam. B.A. 1863; Deac. 1863 and Pr. 1865 by Bp of Lin. Miss. C. of Clare Market Mission, St. Clement Danes, 1866. Formerly C. of St. Mary's, Nottingham, 1863–64, St. Luke's, Nottingham, 1864–65. [27]

ROSE, George, *Earls-Heaton Parsonage, Dewsbury, Yorks.*—Trin. Coll. Cam. B.A. 1828; Deac. and Pr. 1829. P. C. of Earls-Heaton, Dio. Rip. 1840. (Patron, V. of Dewsbury; Glebe, 4 acres; P. C.'s Inc. 164*l* and Ho; Pop. 4019.) Author, *Family Prayers, suggested by each Chapter in the Gospels*, 1832; *Pastoral Tracts on the Cholera*, 1833; *On which Side are You? A Happy New Year*, 1845; *Friendly Observations addressed to* *the Sculptors and Artists of Great Britain, on some of their Works in the Great Exhibition*, 2 eds. 1851; *Services for the Church of God*, 1852; *Letter to H. Mayhew, Esq. and his Audience of Working Men, on the Connection between the Sabbath, the Lord's Day, and the Eternal Rest in Heaven*, 1853. [1]

ROSE, the Rev. Henry John, *Houghton-Conquest Rectory, Ampthill, Beds.*—St. John's Coll. Cam. 14th Wrang. and B.A. 1821, M.A. 1824, B.D. 1831; Deac. 1825, Pr. 1826. R. of Houghton-Conquest with Houghton-Gildable R. Dio. Ely, 1837. (Patron, St. John's Coll. Cam; Tithe, 829*l* 15*s*; Glebe, 70 acres; R.'s Inc. 840*l* and Ho; Pop. 784.) Rural Dean. Archd. of Bedford 1866. Formerly Fell. of St. John's Coll. Cam. 1824; Hulsean Lect. 1833. Author, *An Answer to the Case of the Dissenters*, 1834; *Translation of Neander's Ecclesiastical History of Three First Centuries*, Vol. I. 1831, 2nd ed. 1841, 10*s* 6*d*; Vol. II. 1842, 12*s*; *The Law of Moses viewed in Connection with the Character and the History of the Jews, &c.* (Hulsean Lectures), 1834, 8*s*; *The Meet Attire of the Spouse of Christ, &c.* (two Sermons preached in Leicestershire), 1851, 1*s* 6*d*; *Ecclesiastical History from* 1700–1858, in the 8vo reprint of the *Encyclopædia Metropolitana*, 1858. Editor of the *Encyclopædia Metropolitana* from 1839; *Bunsen, The Critical School, &c. in Replies to* "Essays and Reviews, 1862." [2]

ROSE, Hugh Francis, *St. Cross Rectory, near Harleston, Suffolk.*—Corpus Coll. Cam. B.A. 1843, M.A. 1847; Deac. 1845 and Pr. 1847 by Bp of Nor. R. of Homersfield with St. Cross, South Elmham R. Dio. Nor. 1855. (Patron, Sir Robert Shafto Adair, Bart; Homersfield, Tithe, 140*l*; Glebe, 8½ acres; St. Cross, South Elmham, Tithe—App. 23*l* 6*s* 8*d*, R. 191*l* 13*s* 4*d*; Glebe, 30 acres; R.'s Inc. 332*l* and Ho; Pop. Homersfield 120, St. Cross, South Elmham, 238.) Formerly C. of Homersfield 1845–55. [3]

ROSE, Hyla Holden, *Erdington, Birmingham.*—Clare Coll. Cam. B.A. 1833, M.A. 1836; Deac. 1835 and Pr. 1836 by Bp of Lin. P. C. of Erdington, Dio. Wor. 1850. (Patron, V. of Aston; P. C.'s Inc. arising from Pew-rents 200*l*; Pop. 3906.) [4]

ROSENBURGH, C. B.—Sinecure R. of Orgarswick, Kent, Dio. Cant. 1829. (Patrons, D. and C. of Cant; R.'s Inc. 39*l*; Pop. 10.) [5]

ROSENTHAL, Samuel, *St. Kea Vicarage, Truro.*—Ch. Coll. Cam. B.A. 1857; Deac. 1859 and Pr. 1860 by Bp of Pet. C. (sole charge) of St. Kea, 1865. Formerly C. of Uppingham 1859–65. [6]

ROSENTHALL, William Lewis, *Holy Trinity Vicarage, Willenhall, Wolverhampton.*—Deac. 1849 and Pr. 1850 by Bp of Lich. V. of Holy Trinity, Willenhall, Dio. Lich. 1853. (Patrons, the Crown and Bp of Lich. alt; V.'s Inc. 200*l* and Ho; Pop. 1936.) [7]

ROSS, Alexander Johnston.—C. of St. Andrew's, Holborn, Lond. [8]

ROSS, Charles Sydenham, *Glastonbury, Somerset.*—Magd. Hall, Ox. B.A. 1839, M.A. 1841; Deac. 1839, Pr. 1840. P. C. of St. John's, Glastonbury, Dio. B. and W. 1865. (Patron, Bp of B. and W; P. C.'s Inc. 150*l*.) Formerly C. of Nettlecombe. [9]

ROSS, Charles Wellard, *Greetham Rectory, Horncastle, Lincolnshire.*—Pemb. Coll. Cam. B.A. 1848, M.A. 1851; Deac. 1848 and Pr. 1849 by Bp of Wor. R. of Greetham, Dio. Lin. 1863. (Patron, Bp of Lin; Tithe, 152*l*; Glebe, 49 acres; R.'s Inc. 232*l* and Ho; Pop. 152.) [10]

ROSS, David, *Rectory, Langton, Northallerton.*—Dur. Licen. of Theol. and Univ. Prizeman 1850; Deac. 1850 and Pr. 1851 by Bp of Man. C. in sole charge of Langton-on-Swale 1866. Formerly Sen. C. of South Hackney 1859–62; C. of Emmanuel, Camberwell, 1855–59; C. in sole charge of Rawmarsh 1862–66. Author, *Doctrine of the Trinity*; *Necessity of the Sabbath*, several Sermons in *The Pulpit*, 1858. [11]

ROSS, George, *Tywardreath Vicarage, St. Austell, Cornwall.*—V. of Tywardreath with Tregaminion C. Dio. Ex. 1863. (Patron, W. Rashleigh, Esq; V.'s Inc. 135*l* and Ho; Pop. 2576.) P. C. of St. Sampson's or Golant, Dio. Ex. 1863. (Patron, W. Rashleigh, Esq; P. C.'s Inc. 53*l*; Pop. 311.) [12]

ROSS, George Gould, *Leatherhead.*—St. Mary Hall, Ox. B.C.L. and M.A. 1856; Deac. 1857 and Pr. 1858 by Bp of Ox. Railway Chaplain at Leatherhead 1864. Formerly C. (sole charge) of Pitchcott and Oving, Bucks, 1858–63. [13]

ROSS, George W., *Biarritz, France.*—Lin. Coll. Ox. B.A. 1828, M.A. 1850; Deac. 1829 and Pr. 1830 by Bp of B. and W. British Chap. at Biarritz. Formerly P. C. of Shepscombe, near Stroud, Glouc. 1854–58. [14]

ROSS, John, *St. Mary's Parsonage, Haggerston, London, N.E.*—Deac. 1848 and Pr. 1849 by Bp of Chich. P. C. of St. Mary's, Haggerston, Dio. Lon. 1859. (Patron, Archd. of Lond; P. C.'s Inc. 450*l* and Ho; Pop. 6136.) [15]

ROSS, John Alexander, *Westwell Vicarage, Ashford, Kent.*—Trin. Coll. Cam. B.A. 1820, M.A. 1823; Deac. and Pr. 1821 by Bp of Lin. V. of Westwell, Dio. Cant. 1839. (Patron, Abp of Cant; Tithe—App. 606, and 39¾ acres of Glebe, V. 317*l* 15*s*, Glebe 7 acres; V.'s Inc. 354*l* and Ho; Pop. 999.) Chap. of the West Ashford Union. [16]

ROSS, John Lockhart, *St. George's Rectory, Cannon-street-road, London, E.*—Oriel Coll. Ox. B.A. 1833, M.A. 1836; Deac. 1834 and Pr. 1835 by Bp of Ches. R. of St. George's-in-the-East, with Calvert-street Chapel and Wellclose-square Chapel, Dio. Lon. 1863. (Patron, Brasen. Coll. Ox; R.'s Inc. 400*l* and Ho; Pop. 26,986.) Formerly Vice-Prin. of Chichester Theol. Coll. 1840–51; V. of Avebury, Wilts, 1852–63. Author, *Lectures on the History of Moses*, 1837; *Reciprocal Obligations of the Church and the Civil Power*, 1848; *Letters on Diocesan Theological Colleges*, 1849; *Letters on Secession to Rome*, Masters, 1849; *Scoto-Ecclesiastica, or Miscellaneous Pieces in Connection with the Scottish Episcopal Church*, ib. 1849; *Traces of Primitive Truth, a Manual for Missions in India and the Colonies*, 1858; *Druidical Temples at Avebury, Wilts*, 1859. Editor of *The Planter's Guide, by the late Sir Henry Stewart, Bart. with the Author's last Improvements, and a Memoir*, 1848, 21*s*. [17]

ROSS, William, *Alderney.*—Dub. A.B. 1848; Deac. 1848, Pr. 1850. P. C. of Alderney 1865. Formerly Mast. in Ch. Coll. Sch. Brecon, 1848; C. of St. David's, Brecon. Author, *Elementary Etymological Manual of the English Language*, Longmans, 1844, 6*d*; *The Teacher's Manual of Method*, Part. I. 1848, 3*s*; *Papers on Teaching and on kindred Subjects*, 1859, Longmans, 5*s*. [18]

ROSSER, Charles Adeane, *Little Drayton, Market Drayton.*—Oriel Coll. Ox. B.A. 1864; Deac. 1865 and Pr. 1866 by Bp of Lich. C. of Little Drayton, 1865. [19]

ROSS-LEWIN, George, *Ross Hill, co. Clare, and Thorneyburn Rectory, Bellingham, Northumberland.*—St. Cath. Coll. Cam. Scho. of, 6th Sen. Opt. Math. and Cl. Prizeman, B.A. 1831, M.A. 1842; Deac. 1832, Pr. 1833. J.P. for co. Clare. R. of Thorneyburn, Dio. Dur. 1866. (Patrons, Lords Commissioners of the Admiralty; Tithe, 196*l*; Glebe, 22 acres; R.'s Inc. 229*l* and Ho; Pop. 340.) Formerly C. of Sutcombe, Devon; Chap. R.N. on board H.M.S. "Britannia," flagship of Admiral Sir Pulteney Malcolm, K.C.B. Mr. Ross-Lewin has served afloat several years, and has British and Turkish Medals. Author, *Sketches of an Experimental Cruise*; *The Supper at Bethany* (a Sermon), 1865; Articles in *Literary Gazette, United Service Journal*; etc. [20]

ROTHERHAM, William, *Bury St. Edmunds.*—Math. Mast. of the Gr. Sch. Bury St. Edmunds. [21]

ROUCH, Frederick, *The Precincts, Canterbury.*—St. John's Coll. Ox. B.A. 1820, M.A. 1824. Min. Can. of Cant. 1827. (Value, 220*l* and Ho.) V. of Littlebourne, Kent, Dio. Cant. 1859. (Patrons, D. and C. of Cant; V.'s Inc. 200*l* and Ho; Pop. 757.) Formerly Min. Can. of Bristol 1825–27; R. of St. George's and St. Mary's, Canterbury, 1829–40; V. of Lower Halstow 1840–59. [22]

ROUGHTON, Francis H., *Keystone, Thrapston, Hunts.*—C. of Keystone. [23]

ROUGHTON, Wentworth Charles, *Harrowden Vicarage, Wellingborough, Northants.*—Emman. Coll. Cam. Jun. Opt. B.A. 1836, M.A. 1839; Deac. and Pr. 1838. V. of Harrowden, Dio. Pet. 1843. (Patron, Earl Fitzwilliam; Tithe, 230*l*; Glebe, 204 acres; V.'s Inc. 550*l* and Ho; Pop. 804.) Rural Dean; Organising Sec. for the S.P.G. for the Archd. of Northampton. [1]

ROUND, Thomas Bennett, *Greywell, Odiham, Hants.*—St. John's Coll. Ox. B.A. 1821, M.A. 1824; Deac. 1821 and Pr. 1822 by Bp of Ox. R. of Rotherwick, Hants, Dio. Win. 1841. (Patron, Bp of Win; Tithe—App. 385*l*, P. C. 11*l* 15*s* 6*d*; R.'s Inc. 55*l*; Pop. 386.) Formerly P. C. of Weston-Patrick, Hants, 1841. [2]

ROUNDELL, Danson Richardson, *Gledstone, near Skipton, Yorks.*—Ch. Ch. Ox. B.A. 1806, M.A. 1809; Deac. 1811 and Pr. 1812 by Abp of York. Formerly Dom. Chap. to Viscount Downe. Patron of Merton R. Yorks. [3]

ROUNTHWAITE, John Frederic, *Neston, Cheshire.*—St. John's Coll. Cam. B.A. 1863, M.A. 1866; Deac. 1864, Pr. 1865. C. of Neston 1867. Formerly C. of Padiham, Lanc. 1864, Duddon in Tarvin, Ches. 1866. [4]

ROUPELL, Francis Pooley, *Walton-on-the Hill Rectory, Epsom, Surrey.*—Trin. Coll. Cam. B.A. 1828, M.A. 1829; Deac. and Pr. 1828. R. of Walton-on-the-Hill, Dio. Win. 1847. (Patron, Sir B. H. Carew; Tithe, 340*l*; Glebe, 46 acres; R.'s Inc. 380*l* and Ho; Pop. 475.) [5]

ROUSE, Rolla Charles Meadows, *The Parsonage, Southwold, Suffolk.*—Trin. Coll. Cam. 10th Wrang. and B.A. 1856, M.A. 1859; Deac. 1856 and Pr. 1857 by Bp of Roch. P. C. of Southwold, Dio. Nor. 1867. (Patron, Rev. E. Hollond; Tithe, 68*l*; Glebe, 5*l*; Queen Anne's Bounty 24*l*; P. C.'s Inc. 150*l* and Ho; Pop. 2159.) Formerly C. of Kendal and Chap. to the Kendal Gaol; P. C. of Ch. Ch. Carlisle; C. of Waltham Holy Cross; P. C. of Oatlands; Chap. of the Convalescent Asylum, Walton-on-Thames. [6]

ROUSE, William Archibald, *Darfield Vicarage, York.*—Trin. Coll. Cam. late Scho. of, 24th Wrang. B.A. 1861, M.A. 1864; Deac. and Pr. by Bp of Wor. Formerly Math. Mast. in Leamington Coll; C. of Wath-upon-Dearne. [7]

ROUSE, Wanford.—C. of Selside, near Kendal. [8]

ROUTH, John Oswald, *Gayle, Hawes, Yorks.*—Ch. Coll. Cam. B.A. 1837, M.A. 1840. Formerly Fell. of Ch. Coll. Cam. [9]

ROUTH, John William, *Tilehurst, Reading.*—Magd. Coll. Ox. B.A. 1839, M.A. 1841; Deac. 1840 and Pr. 1841 by Bp of Ox. R. and V. of Tilehurst, Dio. Ox. 1855. (Patron, Magd. Coll. Ox; Tithe, 980*l*; Glebe, 150 acres; R. and V.'s Inc. 1100*l*; Pop. 1400.) [10]

ROUTLEDGE, Charles Francis, *Halifax.*—King's Coll. Cam. 1st cl. Cl. Trip. B.A. 1862; Deac. 1862 and Pr. 1863 by Bp of Lin. One of H.M. Inspectors of Schs. 1864. Formerly C. of Richmond, Surrey, 1863–64; Fell. of King's Coll. Cam. [11]

ROUTLEDGE, William, *Cotleigh Rectory, Honiton, Devon.*—Dub. A.B. 1828, A.M. 1831, B.D. and D.D. 1852; Deac. 1828 and Pr. 1829 by Bp of B. and W. R. of Cotleigh, Dio. Ex. 1861. (Patroness, Lady Ashburton; Tithe, 210*l*; Glebe, 27 acres; R.'s Inc. 280*l* and Ho; Pop. 188.) Formerly Head Mast. of Bishops Hull Sch. Somerset; C. of Ilminster, Isle Abbots, Cricket Malherbie and Cudworth. Author, *English Edition of the Eton Greek Grammar*, 1854. [12]

ROW, Charles Adolphus, 55, *Gloucester-crescent, Regent's-park, London, N.W.*—Pemb. Coll. Ox. 2nd cl. Lit. Hum. B.A. 1838, M.A. 1841; Deac. 1840, Pr. 1841. Formerly Head Mast. of the Royal Free Gr. Sch. Mansfield, 1848–61. Author, *Letter to Lord John Russell, on the Constitutional Defects of the University and Colleges of Oxford, and Suggestions for a Royal Commission of Inquiry into the Universities*; *Letter to Sir R. Inglis, in Answer to his Speech in the House of Commons on the Oxford University Commission*; *The Nature and Extent of Divine Inspiration as stated by the Writers and deduced from the Facts of the New Testament*, Longmans, 1864, 12*s*. [13]

ROWAN, Robert Strettell, *Wardleworth Vicarage, Rochdale.*—Dub. A.B. 1846, A.M. 1853; Deac. and Pr. 1847. V. of St. James's, Wardleworth, Rochdale, Dio. Man. 1863. (Patron, V. of Rochdale; P. C.'s Inc. 300*l* and Ho; Pop. 7130.) Formerly C. of Rochdale. [14]

ROWBOTTOM, Thomas, *The Cottage, Kegworth, near Derby.*—Deac. 1828 and Pr. 1829 by Abp of York. P. C. of North and South Anston, Dio. York, 1835. (Patron, Abp of York; Tithe, App. 450*l*; P. C.'s Inc. 337*l*; Pop. 1067.) Formerly C. of Kinver, Staffs, and Newton Regis, Warw. [15]

ROWBOTTOM, Frederick, *Episcopal Training College, Edinburgh.*—Dub; Deac. 1858 by Bp of Carl. Prin. of the Episcopal Training Coll. Edinburgh, 1858. Formerly Mast. of the Miss. Coll. Battersea, Lond. 1852–58. [16]

ROWDEN, Edward, *Highworth Vicarage, Wilts.*—New Coll. Ox. B.A. 1802, M.A. 1806; Deac. 1803 by Bp of Ox. Pr. 1804 by Bp of Glouc. V. of Highworth with South Marston C. and Broad Blunsdon C. Dio. G. and B. 1804. (Patron, Bp of G. and B; Tithe—Imp. 1150*l* and about 1500 acres of Glebe, V. 430*l*; Glebe, 100 acres; V.'s Inc. 550*l* and Ho; Pop. 2823.) Surrogate. Formerly Fell. of New Coll. Ox. Author, *A Visitation Sermon*, 1848. [17]

ROWDEN, Francis Marmaduke, *Stanton-Fitzwarren, Highworth, Wilts.*—Wad. Coll Ox. B.A. 1837, M.A. 1840; Deac. 1838, Pr. 1840. R. of Stanton-Fitzwarren, Dio. G. and B. 1851. (Patron, J. A. Trenchard, Esq; R.'s Inc. 250*l*; Pop. 200.) [18]

ROWDEN, Frederick, *Shalfleet, Isle of Wight.*—New Coll. Ox. Fell. of, B.A. 1860, M.A. 1864; Deac. 1864 by Bp of Ches. Pr. 1864 by Bp of Lich. C. of Shalfleet 1866. Formerly C. of St. James's, Wolverhampton, 1864–66. [19]

ROWDEN, Robert, *Winwick Vicarage, Oundle.*—Wad. Coll. Ox. B.A. 1855, M.A. 1860; Deac. 1857 by Bp of Lon. Pr. 1858 by Bp of Wor. V. of Winwick, Dio. Ely, 1863. (Patron, Duke of Buccleuch; Glebe, 84 acres; V.'s Inc. 105*l* and Ho; Pop. 380.) Formerly C. of Danchurch and of Alnwick. [20]

ROWE, Alfred William, *Felstead School, Essex.*—Trin. Coll. Cam. B.A. 1859, M.A. 1862; Deac. 1864 and Pr. 1865 by Bp of Roch. Asst. Mast. of Felstead Sch. [21]

ROWE, George, *Training College, York.*—St. John's Coll. Cam. B.A. 1851, M.A. 1854; Deac. 1851, Pr. 1852. Prin. of the York and Ripon Training Sch. for Masters 1858. Formerly Vice-Prin. and Gov. Lect. in Geography; Chap. to Female Training Sch. York. Author, *The Colonial Empire of Great Britain*, in Four Parts, with Maps, 1864–65, 2*s* each Part, S.P.C.K. [22]

ROWE, James John, *Morchard Bishop Rectory, Devon.*—St. Mary Hall, Ox. B.A. 1826, M.A. 1830; Deac. 1827 and Pr. 1828 by Bp of Chich. R. of Morchard Bishop, Dio. Ex. 1867. (Patron, R. Bartholomew, Esq; Tithe, 550*l*; Glebe, 61 acres; R.'s Inc. 700*l* and Ho; Pop. 1500.) Formerly R. of St. Mary-Arches, Exeter, 1841–67; Rural Dean 1848–50. [23]

ROWE, John, *King Edward's School, Birmingham.*—Trin. Coll. Cam. 3rd cl. Cl. Trip. B.A. 1853, M.A. 1856; Deac. 1854 and Pr. 1855 by Bp of Ex. Asst. Mast. in King Edward VI. Sch. Birmingham. Formerly C. of Street, Devon, and Swavesey, Hunts; 2nd Mast. of Gr. Sch. Walsall. [24]

ROWE, John Ferrier, *Bishops Sutton, Alresford, Hants.*—St. Bees 1861; Deac. 1862 and Pr. 1863 by Bp of Win. C. of Bishops Sutton 1864. Formerly C. of Ropley 1862–64. [25]

ROWE, John George, *Berwick-upon-Tweed.*—Literate; M.A. 1865; Deac. 1855 and Pr. 1856 by Bp of Rip. V. of Berwick-upon-Tweed, Dio. Dur. 1866. (Patrons, D. and C. of Dur; Glebe, 50 acres; V.'s Inc. 472*l* and Ho; Pop. 8000.) Formerly C. of Pateley Bridge 1855–58; P. C. of West Hartlepool 1859–66. [26]

ROWE, Theophilus Barton, *Uppingham.*—St. John's Coll. Cam. Chan.'s Medallist, 3rd in 1st cl. Cl. Trip. 31st Wrang. B.A. 1856, M.A. 1859; Deac. 1859 by Bp of B. and W. Asst. Mast. of the Gr. Sch. Uppingham. Formerly C. of Bathampton, Somerset, 1859–61; Fell. of St. John's Coll. Cam. 1858–61. [1]

ROWLAND, Adam.—C. of Pentrebach, Merthyr Tydvil. [2]

ROWLAND, Charles B., *Martley, Worcester.*—St. John's Coll. Ox. B.A. 1859, M.A. 1859; Deac. 1859 by Bp of Wor. Pr. 1860 by Bp of Lon. C. of Martley; Chap. to the Martley Union. [3]

ROWLAND, David, *St. Dogmael's, Cardigan.*—Lampeter; Deac. 1853 and Pr. 1854 by Bp of St. D. C. of St. Dogmael's, Pembrokeshire. [4]

ROWLAND, Evan, *Bryngwran, Holyhead, Anglesey.*—Literate; Deac. 1860 and Pr. 1865 by Bp of Llan. C. of Bryngwran 1866. Formerly C. of Merthyr Tydvil 1860–66. [5]

ROWLAND, Lewis Thomas, *Tredegar, Monmouthshire.*—Lampeter, Llan. Scho; Deac. 1859 and Pr. 1861 by Bp of Llan. C. of St. George's, Tredegar, 1863. Formerly C. of St. David's, Merthyr Tydvil, 1859–62. [6]

ROWLAND, Thomas, *St. Thomas's, Penybont, Oswestry.*—Llandovery Collegiate Institution; Deac. 1852 and Pr. 1853 by Bp of St. A. R. of Pennant or Penybont, Dio. St. A. 1856. (Patron, Bp of St. A; Tithe—App. 329*l*; Glebe, 30 acres; R.'s Inc. 405*l* and Ho; Pop. 712.) Formerly C. of Rhosygwalian, and Llansantffraid, Llanrwst. Author, *Grammar* (in English) *of the Welsh Language*, 1st ed. 1853, 2nd ed. 1857, Hughes and Butler, Lond; 3rd ed. 1865, Saunderson, Bala. [7]

ROWLAND, William Morgan, *Bishops Castle Vicarage, Salop.*—St. John's Coll. Cam. Sen. Opt. B.A. 1837, M.A. 1843; Deac. 1838, Pr. 1839. V. of Bishops Castle, Dio. Herf. 1842. (Patron, Earl of Powis; Tithe—Imp. 328*l* 17*s* 6*d*, V. 466*l* 15*s*; Glebe, 12 acres; V.'s Inc. 490*l* and Ho; Pop. 2083.) Surrogate; Rural Dean. [8]

ROWLANDS, D., *Gwynfa Parsonage, Llangadock, Carmarthenshire.*—Lampeter, Sen. Scho. of, 1st cl. and Heb. Prizeman; Deac. 1853 and Pr. 1854 by Bp of St. D. P. C. of Gwynfa, Dio. St. D. 1862. (Patron, V. of Llangadock-Vawr; Glebe, 200 acres; P. C.'s Inc. 120*l*; Pop. 1354.) C. of Llangadock with Llandensant 1862. Formerly C. of St. Dogmael's, Pemb. 1853, Pembrey, Carm. 1858. [9]

ROWLANDS, Evan, *Merthyr Tydvil.*—C. of Merthyr Tydvil. [10]

ROWLANDS, Isaac, *Festiniog, Tanybwlch, Carnarvon.*—King's Coll. Lond; Deac. 1864 and Pr. 1865 by Bp of Bangor. C. of Festiniog 1864. [11]

ROWLANDS, James, *Meylltyrne Rectory, Pwllheli, Carnarvonshire.*—R. of Meylltyrne with Bottwnog, C. Dio. Ban. 1860. (Patron, Bp of Ban; R.'s Inc. 180*l* and Ho; Pop. 403.) [12]

ROWLANDS, John, *Bwlch-y-Cibau, Oswestry.*—Corpus Coll. Cam. Scho. of, Cl. Prizeman 1858 and 1860, Div. Prizeman 1859, B.A. 1861, M.A. 1865; Deac. 1861 and Pr. 1862 by Bp of St. B; P. C. of Bwlch-y-Cibau, Dio. St. A. 1863. (Patron, Bp of St. A; P. C.'s Inc. 200*l*; Pop. 500.) Formerly C. of Gresford 1861. [13]

ROWLANDS, John, *Grimston Rectory, Lynn, Norfolk.*—Queens' Coll. Cam. 10th Wrang. and B.A. 1832, M.A. 1835, B.D. 1844; Deac. 1835, Pr. 1836 by Bp of Roch. R. of Grimston, Dio. Nor. 1858. (Patron, Queens' Coll. Cam; Glebe, 620 acres; R.'s Inc. 660*l* and Ho; Pop. 1300.) Formerly Fell. of Queens' Coll. Cam; C. of Haslingfield 1835–39; Great St. Mary's, Cambs, 1844–49; P. C. of Nerquis, Mold, Flints, 1849–53. [14]

ROWLANDS, John Bowen.—C. of St. Margaret's, Rochester. [15]

ROWLANDS, William, *Fishguard Vicarage, Pembrokeshire.*—Lampeter; Deac. 1847 by Bp of St. D. Pr. 1848 by Bp of Llan. V. of Fishguard, Dio. St. D. 1854. (Patron, Ld Chan; Tithe—Imp. 231*l* 6*s* 8*d*, V. 70*l* 13*s* 4*d*; Glebe, 9 acres; V.'s Inc. 185*l* and Ho; Pop. 2084.) Formerly C. of Vaynor, 1847, St. Tydvil, Merthyr, 1848–54. Author, *Twyllwormoniaeth* (a Tract against the Mormons), 1852. [16]

ROWLANDS, William Bowen, *Grammar School, Haverfordwest, Pembrokeshire.*—Jesus Coll. Ox. Scho. of 2nd cl. Lit. Hum. B.A. 1859, M.A. 1865; Deac. 1864 by Bp of St. D. Head Mast. of the Gr. Sch. Haverfordwest, 1864; C. of Narberth, Pembrokeshire, 1864. [17]

ROWLANDSON, M. E., *Bridgwater.*—C. of Bridgwater. [18]

ROWLANDSON, William Henry, 57, *Corpus-buildings, Cambridge.*—Corpus Coll. Cam. 1st cl. Theol. Hon. and Heb. Prize 1866, Greek Test. Prize and Crosse Scho. 1866, 1st Tyrrwhitt Scho. 1867; Deac. 1867 by Bp of Ely. Reader and Catechist, and Div. and Heb. Lect. to Corpus Coll. Cam. 1867. [19]

ROWLATT, John Charles, *The Close, Exeter.*—Emman. Coll. Cam. B.A. 1849; Deac. 1849 and Pr. 1850 by Bp of Ex. Priest-Vicar of Ex. Cathl. 1852; Surrogate; Hon. Sec. and Treasurer to the S.P.C.K. and S.P.G. and Hon. Treasurer to the Exeter Dioc. Church-Building Association. Formerly C. of St. James's, Exeter, 1849–52; R. of St. Paul's, Exeter, 1854–66. [20]

ROWLATT, John Henry, *Upper Holloway, London, N.*—St. John's Coll. Cam. B.A. 1826, M.A. 1829; Deac. 1840 and Pr. 1841 by Bp of Lon. Formerly Librarian to the Hon. Soc. of Middle Temple 1837. [21]

ROWLEY, Adam Clarke, 14, *St. James's-square, Bristol.*—Wad. Coll. Ox. B.A. 1842, M.A. 1846; Deac. 1842 and Pr. 1843 by Bp of G. and B. P. C. of St. Matthias', Weir, Bristol, Dio. G. and B. 1846. (Patrons, the Crown and Bp of G. and B. alt; P. C.'s Inc. 175*l* and Ho; Pop. 4011.) Author, *A Letter of Remonstrance to the Directors of the Great Western Railway on the Subject of Sunday Excursion Trains*, 1852; *Collections from our Ancient Records, and especially Rymer's Fœdera, to show the Limits of the Papal Power in England, and also to prove that no Papal Bull, Brief, Letter, &c. had any Currency in these Realms since Licentiâ Regis*, 1852; *Judgment of the Privy Council in the Case of "Essays and Reviews,"* Hamilton, Adams and Co. 1864; *Joel, A Translation in Metrical Parallelisms according to the Hebrew Method of Punctuation, with Notes and References*, ib. 1867. [22]

ROWLEY, Henry, 5, *Park-place, St. James'-street, London, S.W.*—Deac. 1860 and Pr. 1864 by Bp of Ox. Univ. Miss. to Central Africa. Author, *The Story of the Universities Mission to Central Africa*, Saunders and Otley, 1868. [23]

ROWLEY, Joseph Moss, *Woodbridge, Ipswich.*—Corpus Coll. Cam. B.A. 1843; Deac. 1844, Pr. 1845 by Bp of Ches. P. C. of St. John's, Woodbridge, Dio. Nor. 1846. (Patron, Church Patronage Soc; Tithe, 38*l*; Glebe, 3 acres; P. C.'s Inc. 203*l* and Ho; Pop. 2418.) Formerly C. of Macclesfield 1844–46. [24]

ROWLEY, Julius Henry, *Walesby Rectory, Market Rasen.*—Magd. Coll. Cam. B.A. 1860, M.A. 1864; Deac. 1860 by Bp of Ches. Pr. 1863 by Bp of Chich. R. of Walesby, Dio. Lin. 1865. (Patron, Wm. Angerstein, Esq; R.'s Inc. 440*l*; Pop. 350.) [25]

ROWLEY, Thomas, *Willey Rectory, Broseley, Salop.*—Ch. Ch. Ox. B.A. 1819, M.A. 1822, B.D. and D.D. 1839; Deac. 1821 and Pr. 1822 by Bp of Herf. R. of Willey with Barrow P. C. Dio. Herf. 1854. (Patron, Lord Forester; Willey, Tithe, 252*l* 10*s*; Glebe, 27 acres; Barrow, Tithe—Imp. 283*l* 2*s*; Glebe, 6 acres; R.'s Inc. 345*l* and Ho; Pop. Willey 149, Barrow 365.) Rural Dean. [26]

ROWLEY, Walter Theodoret, *Sarn Parsonage, Newtown, N. Wales.*—King's Coll. Lond. Assoc. 1861; Deac. 1861 and Pr. 1862 by Bp of Lon. C. in charge of Sarn 1866. Formerly C. of Plumstead 1861; St. Mary's, Leamington, 1864–66. [27]

ROWLEY, William Walter, *Combe Lodge, Weston-super-Mare.*—Queen's Coll. Ox. 3rd cl. Lit. Hum. and B.A. 1835, M.A. 1839; Deac. 1836 and Pr. 1837 by Bp of B. and W. P. C. of Emmanuel, Weston-super-Mare, Dio. B. and W. 1847. (Patrons, Trustees; P. C.'s Inc. 250*l*; Pop. 2434.) Formerly R. of Lympsham, Somerset, 1837–44. [28]

ROWNTREE, Mark, *Great Ayton, Northallerton, Yorks.*—St. Bees; Deac. 1864 and Pr. 1865 by Abp of York. C. of Great Ayton in Cleveland, Newton, and Nunthorpe. [1]

ROWSELL, Evan Edward, *Hambledon Rectory, Godalming, Surrey.*—St. John's Coll. Cam. B.A. 1827, M.A. 1830; Deac. 1827 and Pr. 1828 by Bp of Lon. R. of Hambledon, Dio. Win. 1859. (Patron, Earl of Radnor; R.'s Inc. 235*l* and Ho; Pop. 557.) Formerly Fell. of St. John's Coll. Cam; C. of Brinkley, Cambs. [2]

ROWSELL, Herbert.—C. of Trinity, Paddington, London. [3]

ROWSELL, Thomas James, 20, *Finsbury-square, London, E.C.*—St. John's Coll. Cam. B.A. 1838, M.A. 1843; Deac. 1839, Pr. 1840. R. of St. Christopher-le-Stocks with St. Margaret's, Lothbury, R. and St. Bartholomew's, Exchange, R. City and Dio. Lon. 1860. (Patrons, Ld Chan. and Bp of Lon. alt; R.'s Inc. 1300*l* and Ho; Pop. 423.) Dom. Chap. to Duke of Sutherland and Hon. Chap. to the Queen. Formerly P. C. of St. Peter's, Stepney, Lond. 1844–60. [4]

ROWSELL, Thomas Norman.—C. of St. Mark's, Reigate, Surrey. [5]

ROWSELL, Walter Frederick, 35, *Holgate Crescent, York.*—St. John's Coll. Cam. 1st cl. Cl. Hon. B.A. 1860, M.A; Deac. 1863 and Pr. 1864 by Bp of Chich. P. C. of Copmanthorpe, Dio. York, 1867. (Patron, V. of Bishophill, York; P. C.'s Inc. 250*l* and Ho; Pop. 400.) Formerly C. of Preston with Hove, Sussex, 1863–67. [6]

ROWSON, Robert Wilson, *Aylesby, Grimsby.*—Dub. A.B. 1850; Dur. Theol. Licen. 1852; Deac. 1853 and Pr. 1854 by Bp of Lin. P. C. of Aylesby, Dio. Lin. 1864. (Patron, T. Tyrwhitt Drake, Esq; P. C.'s Inc. 73*l*; Pop. 130.) C. of Riby 1853. Formerly 2nd Mast. of Humberstone Gr. Sch. near Grimsby, 1852–60. [7]

ROXBURGH, Alfred Henry, *Southsea.*—Deac. 1850 and Pr. 1852 by Bp of Ex. C. of St. Paul's, Southsea. Formerly C. of Ufton; Chap. of D. of Smallhythe, Kent, 1861. [8]

ROXBY, Edmund Lally, *Corlsend, Wooburn, Bucks.*—Emman. Coll. Cam. B.A. 1866; Deac. 1867. C. of Wooburn 1867. [9]

ROXBY, Henry Meux, *Wellingborough, Northants.*—St. John's Coll. Cam. B.A. 1855, M.A. 1858; Deac. 1856 and Pr. 1857 by Bp of Pet. C. of Wellingborough. [10]

ROXBY, Wilfrid, *Thornford, Sherborne, Dorset.*—Emman. Coll. Cam. B.A. 1860; Deac. 1862 and Pr. 1863 by Bp of Lich. C. of Thornford. Formerly C. of Berrington, Salop, 1862–66. [11]

ROY, Edmund, *Westwood, Kenilworth, Warwickshire.*—Pemb. Coll. Ox. B.A. 1825, M.A. 1828; Deac. 1828 and Pr. 1829 by Bp of Wor. V. of Westwood, Dio. Wor. 1846. (Patron, V. of Stoneleigh; P. C.'s Inc. 150*l*; Pop 620.) [12]

ROY, Richard Clarke.—C. of Skirbeck, near Boston, Lincolnshire. [13]

ROY, Robert Evelyn, *Skirbeck Rectory, Boston, Lincolnshire.*—Corpus Coll. Cam. B.A. 1843, M.A. 1847; Deac. 1843, Pr. 1845. R. of Skirbeck with Trinity C. Dio. Lin. 1853. (Patroness, Mrs. A. C. Roy; Land in lieu of Tithe, 308 acres; R.'s Inc. 676*l* and Ho; Pop. 2837.) [14]

ROYCE, David, *Lower Swell Vicarage, Stow-on-the-Wold, Glouc.*—Ch. Ch. Ox. 3rd cl. Lit. Hum. and B.A. 1840, M.A. 1844; Deac. 1841 and Pr. 1842 by Bp of Win. V. of Lower Swell, Dio. G. and B. 1850. (Patron, Ch. Ch. Ox; Glebe, 103 acres; V.'s Inc. 170*l* and Ho; Pop. 450.) [15]

ROYDS, Charles Leopold, *Aldenham Vicarage, Watford, Herts.*—Wad. Coll. Ox. B.A. 1839; Deac. 1839, Pr. 1840. V. of Aldenham, Dio. Roch. 1850. (Patrons, Trustees of P. Thelluson, Esq; Tithe—Imp. 778*l* 2*s*, V. 110*l*; Glebe, 14 acres; V.'s Inc. 460*l* and Ho; Pop. 1769.) [16]

ROYDS, Charles Smith, *Haughton Rectory, Stafford.*—Ch. Coll. Cam. B.A. 1822, M.A. 1825; Deac. 1823 and Pr. 1824 by Bp of B. and W. R. of Haughton, Dio. Lich. 1831. (Patron, the present R; Tithe, 300*l*; R.'s Inc. 403*l* and Ho; Pop. 516.) P. C. of St. Matthew's, Derrington, Dio. Lich. 1866. (Patron, Rev. C. S. Royds; P. C.'s Inc. 30*l*.) Preb. of Bishop's Hull in Lich. Cathl. 1857; Dom. Chap. to the Marquis of Abercorn. [17]

ROYDS, Charles Twemlow, *Heysham Rectory, Lancaster.*—Ch. Coll. Cam. B.A. 1861, M.A. 1864; Deac. 1862 and Pr. 1863 by Abp of York. R. of Heysham, Dio. Man. 1865. (Patron, Rev. Charles Smith Royds; Tithe, 470*l*; Glebe, 90 acres; R.'s Inc. 587*l* and Ho; Pop. 567.) Formerly C. of Sprotborough, near Doncaster, 1862, and Heysham. [18]

ROYDS, Edward, *Brereton Rectory, Congleton, Cheshire.*—Brasen. Coll. Ox. B.A. 1820, M.A. 1823; Deac. 1844, Pr. 1845. R. of Brereton, Dio. Ches. 1845. (Patron, Rev. Edward Royds; Tithe, 810*l*; Glebe, 20 acres; R.'s Inc. 810*l* and Ho; Pop. 592.) [19]

ROYDS, Francis Coulman, *Coddington, near Chester.*—Brasen. Coll. Ox. B.A. 1847, M.A. 1850; Deac. 1850, Pr. 1851. R. of Coddington, Dio. Ches. 1855. (Patrons, D. and C. of Ches; Tithe—App. 67*l* 10*s*, Imp. 60*l* 5*s*, R. 247*l* 1*s*; Glebe, 6 acres; R.'s Inc. 261*l* and Ho; Pop. 325.) [20]

ROYDS, Nathaniel, *Rectory, Little Barford, St. Neots, Beds.*—Trin. Coll. Cam. B.A. 1859, M.A. 1862; Deac. 1861 and Pr. 1862 by Bp of Pet. R. of Little Barford, Dio. Ely, 1864. (Patron, W. Alington, Esq; Tithe, 259*l*; Glebe, 45 acres; R.'s Inc. 260*l* and Ho; Pop. 120.) Formerly C. of Woodford, Northants, 1861; P. C. of Moggerhanger, Beds, 1863-64. [21]

ROYLE, James Patrick, *Little Bittering, Swaffham, Norfolk.*—Trin. Coll. Cam. B.A. 1834; Deac. 1839, Pr. 1842. R. of Little Bittering, Dio. Nor. 1858. (Patrons, Exors. of the late James Dover, Esq; Tithe, 70*l*; Glebe, 45 acres; R.'s Inc. 114*l*; Pop. 30.) Formerly C. of Wereham and Wretton, Norfolk. [22]

ROYLE, Jermyn Patrick, *Wellow Parsonage, Newark, Notts.*—St. John's Coll. Cam. B.A. 1839; Deac. 1840 and Pr. 1842 by Bp of Nor. P. C. of Wellow, Dio. Lin. 1859. (Patron, Earl of Scarborough; Tithe—App. 190*l*, P. C. 42*l*; Glebe, 24 acres; P. C.'s Inc. 75*l* and Ho; Pop. 468.) Dom. Chap. at Rufford Abbey. Formerly C. of Ollerton, Notts. [23]

ROYLE, J. P.—C. of Hoo, East Dereham, Norfolk. [24]

ROYLE, William George, *East Rusham, near Rougham, Norfolk.*—Queens' Coll. Cam. B.A. 1843; Deac. 1844 and Pr. 1845 by Bp of Nor. C. of Little Massingham, Norfolk, 1866. Formerly C. of Guestling 1854, Pett 1853, Mountfield with Whatlington 1857, Woodmancote 1862, Barlavington 1864, Albury, near Guildford 1860, Andover 1863, Belbroughton 1865. [25]

ROYSTON, Peter, *Stoke by Nayland, Colchester.*—St. Cath. Coll. Cam; Deac. 1859 and Pr. 1861 by Bp of Chich. C. of Stoke by Nayland 1866. Formerly C. of Pulborough 1859–66. [26]

ROYSTON, Peter Sorenson, *Madras.*—Trin. Coll. Cam. 2nd cl. Cl. Trip. Jun. Opt. and B.A. 1853; Deac. 1853, Pr. 1854. Clerical Sec. of the Madras Ch. Miss. Committee 1855. Formerly Res. Tut. of the Ch. Miss. Coll. Islington, Lond. 1853–55. [27]

RUDALL, Alfred, *Penzance.*—Wad. Coll. Ox. B.A. 1865; Deac. 1865 by Bp of Rip. Pr. 1866 by Bp of Ex. P. C. of St. Paul's, Penzance, Dio. Ex. 1866. (Patroness, Mrs. Henry Batten; P. C.'s Inc. 120*l*; Pop. 1500.) Formerly C. of Ch. Ch. Bradford, Yorks, 1865–66. [28]

RUDD, Eric John Sutherland, *Malvern College, Worcestershire.*—St. John's Coll. Cam. 26th Wrang. B.A. 1863, M.A. 1866; Deac. 1864 and Pr. 1865 by Bp of Wor. Asst. Mast. in Malvern Coll. 1865. Formerly 2nd Mast. of Sheffield Collegiate Sch. [29]

RUDD, John, *Stranton, West Hartlepool, Durham.*—V. of Stranton, Dio. Dur. 1858. (Patron, Sir M. W. Ridley; Tithe—Imp. 103*l* 6*s*, V. 220*l*; V.'s Inc. 321*l*; Pop. 3923.) [30]

RUDD, John England, *Covenham, St. Mary, near Louth, Lincolnshire.*—Trin. Coll. Cam. B.A. 1843

Deac. 1845 by Bp of Pet. Pr. 1847 by Bp of Wor. R. of Covenham St. Mary, Dio. Lin. 1848. (Patron, Ld Chan; Tithe, 122*l*; Glebe, 21 acres; R.'s Inc. 152*l* and Ho; Pop. 196.) Formerly C. of St. Mark's, Birmingham, 1845–48, Little Grimsby 1855–66. [1]

RUDD, John Henry Augustus, *Bedford.*—Pemb. Coll. Cam. B.A. 1832: Deac. 1832 by Bp of Lin. Pr. 1833 by Abp of York. P. C. of Elstow, Beds, Dio. Ely, 1852. (Patron, W. H. Whitbread, Esq; Glebe, 22 acres; P. C.'s Inc. 84*l*; Pop. 618.) Formerly Chap. on E.I.C.'s Bengal Establishment 1834–31. [2]

RUDD, Philip, *Billingham Rectory, Stockton-on Tees.*—Univ. Coll. Dur. B.A. 1846, M.A. 1849; Deac. 1848, Pr. 1849. V. of Billingham, Dio. Dur. 1853. (Patrons, D. and C. of Dur; Tithe—App. 332*l*, V. 133*l* 11*s*; Glebe, 112 acres; V.'s Inc. 380*l* and Ho; Pop. 579.) Formerly Fell. and Chap. of Univ. Coll. Dur. 1847, Bursar and Cl. Lect. 1851, Censor 1852. [3]

RUDD, Richard, *Sigglesthorne, Hull.*—Queen's Coll. Ox. B.A. 1848, M.A. 1851; Deac. 1849 and Pr. 1850 by Bp of Dur. C. of Sigglesthorne 1867. Formerly C. of Ch. Ch. Tynemouth.' [4]

RUDDACH, James Stewart, *Castle House, Shooter's Hill, S.E.*—Pemb. Coll. Cam. B.A. 1852; Deac. 1854, Pr. 1856. Min. of Trinity, Woolwich, Dio. Roch. 1860. (Patron, R. of Woolwich; Min.'s Inc. 300*l*.) Formerly C. of King's Langley, Herts, Blandford Forum, Dorset, and St. Mary's, St. Leonards-on-Sea. [5]

RUDDLE, Charles Snelling, *Durrington, near Amesbury, Wilts.*—King's Coll. Lond. Theol. Assoc. 1858; Deac. 1858 and Pr. 1859 by Bp of Win. P. C. of Durrington, Dio. Salis. 1863. (Patrons, D. and C. of Win; P. C.'s Inc. 125*l*; Pop. 449.) Formerly C. of Frensham, Surrey, 1858–63. [6]

RUDGE, Edward, *St. George's-road, Southwark, London, S.*—St. Cath. Coll. Cam. B.C.L. 1843; Deac. 1843 and Pr. 1844 by Bp of Lon. Chap. and Superintendent of King Edward's Sch. St. George's-in-the-Fields; Chap. to the Sadlers' Company. Formerly C. of St. Peter's, Stepney, 1843, St. Luke's, Chelsea, 1844–50, St. Matthew's, Westminster, 1857–59; Chap. of North Surrey District Schs. Norwood, 1850–56. Author, *Psalms and Hymns for Use in the Service of the Church*, 1852, 10*d*. [7]

RUDGE, Frederick.—C. of Barkway, near Royston, Herts. [8]

RUDGE, Frederick, *Tenbury, Worcestershire.*—Pemb. Coll. Ox; Deac. 1814 by Bp of Herf. Pr. 1815 by Bp of B. and W. V. of Eardisland, Herefordshire, Dio. Herf. 1816. (Patron, Bp of Herf; Tithe—App. 586*l* 6*s*. 6*d*, V. 339*l* 11*s*; Glebe, 2½ acres; V.'s Inc. 350*l*; Pop. 894.) [9]

RUDGE, William John, *Stoven Parsonage, Wangford, Suffolk.*—Corpus Coll. Cam. B.A. 1861, M.A. 1865; Deac. 1862, Pr. 1864. P. C. of Stoven, Dio. Nor. 1866. (Patron, Rev. G. O. Leman; Glebe, 4 acres; P. C.'s Inc. 120*l* and Ho; Pop. 170.) Formerly C. of Monks Eleigh, 1862–65, Castle Ashley 1866–67. [10]

RUDIFORD, J., *Keynsham, Bath.*—Chap. of the Union, Keynsham. [11]

RUFFORD, William, *Lower Sapey Rectory, (Worcestershire), near Bromyard.*—Magd. Hall, Ox. B.A. 1844; Deac. 1845 and Pr. 1846 by Bp of Wor. R. of Lower Sapey, *alias* Sapey Pritchard, Dio. Herf. 1846. (Patron, P. Rufford, Esq; Tithe, 226*l* 10*s*; Glebe, 67 acres; R.'s Inc. 284*l* and Ho; Pop. 218.) [12]

RUGELEY, John William Stephenson, *St. Ives, Hunts.*—St. John's Coll. Cam. 8th Sen. Opt. and B.A. 1841, M.A. 1844; Deac. 1841 and Pr. 1848 by Bp of Ely. C. of the Chapelries of Oldhurst and Woodhurst, near St. Ives, 1841; Fell. of the Cambridge Philosophical Soc. [13]

RUGG, Lewis, *Ecchinswell (Hants), near Newbury, Berks.*—V. of Ecchinswell with Sidmonton V. Dio. Win. 1852. (Patron, V. of Kingsclere; Ecchinswell, Tithe—Imp. 624*l* 18*s*, V. 60*l*; Sidmonton, Tithe—Imp. 273*l* 8*s* 4*d*, V. 50*l* 6*s* 8*d*; V.'s Inc. 118*l*; Pop. Ecchinswell 452, Sidmonton 149.) Chap. of the Kingsclere Union. [14]

RULE, John, *Poulton, Cricklade.*—Corpus Coll. Cam. B.A. 1861; Deac. 1863 and Pr. 1864 by Bp of Salis. P. C. of Poulton, Dio. G. and B. 1867. (Patron, Bp of G. and B; Glebe 5 acres; P. C.'s Inc. 42*l*; Pop. 500.) Formerly C. of Warminster 1863–65, Fowey 1865–67. [15]

RULE, Martin Luther, *Buckland, Denham, Somerset.*—Pemb. Coll. Cam. B.A. 1858; Deac. 1859 by Bp of Roch. C. of Buckland. Formerly C. of Stanford-le-Hope 1859. [16]

RUMANN, William, *Sutton St. Ann, Loughborough.*—Univ. Coll. Dur. and Univ. of Leipsic; Deac. 1858 and Pr. 1859 by Bp of Lin. C. of Sutton St. Ann and Kingston-upon-Soar, Notts. [17]

RUMBALL, Charles, *Littlehampton, Sussex.*—Magd. Hall, Ox. B.A; Deac. 1859 by Bp of G. and B. Pr. 1860 by Bp of Ex. V. of Littlehampton, Dio. Chich. 1864. (Patron, Bp of Chich; Tithe, 93*l*; V.'s Inc. 150*l*; Pop. 2350.) Formerly C. of Kingswood, near Bristol, 1860, Falmouth 1861–62, St. James's, Hove, Brighton, 1862–63, St. John's, Kentish-town, Lond. 1864. [18]

RUMBOLL, Abraham Henry, *Thorpe-le-Soken, Colchester.*—Corpus Coll. Cam. B.A. 1857, M.A. 1860; Deac. 1857 and Pr. 1858 by Bp of Ely. V. of Thorpe-le-Soken, Dio. Roch. 1862; V.'s Inc. 250*l*; Pop. 1159.) Formerly C. of Trinity, Cambridge, 1857. [19]

RUMPF, John, *Bluntisham Rectory, St. Ives, Hunts.*—Trin. Coll. Ox. B.A. 1835, M.A. 1841; Deac. 1836 by Bp of Lin. Pr. 1837 by Bp of Nor. R. of Bluntisham, Dio. Ely, 1859. (Patron, Bp of Pet; Tithe, 1070*l*; Glebe, 61 acres; R.'s Inc. 1190*l* and Ho; Pop. 1351.) Formerly C. of Pakefield and Kirkley, Suffolk, 1837–56; R. of Pakefield 1856–59. [20]

RUMSEY, James, *Llandough, Cowbridge.*—Pemb. Coll. Ox. M.A.; Deac. 1853 and Pr. 1862 by Bp of Ox. R. of Llandough with St. Mary's Church, Dio. Llan. 1864. (Patron, C. R. M. Talbot, Esq; R.'s Inc. 325*l*; Pop. 238.) Formerly C. of St. Giles's, Ox. 1862. [21]

RUMSEY, James Richard, *Templecrone, Cliftonville, Brighton.*—St. John's Coll. Cam. Sen. Opt. and B.A. 1848; Deac. 1852, Pr. 1854. Formerly C. of Carlton 1852. Author, *The Babe of Bethlehem*, 1854, Hatchards, 6*d*; *The God of Battles*, ib. 4*d*. [22]

RUMSEY, John Williams, *Rolvenden Vicarage, Staplehurst, Kent.*—Literate; Deac. 1850 and Pr. 1852 by Bp of Roch. V. of Rolvenden, Dio. Cant. 1855. (Patrons, D. and C. of Roch; Tithe, 45*l*; Glebe, 18 acres; V.'s Inc. 200*l* and Ho; Pop. 1483.) Precentor of the Cant. Diocesan Choral Union 1866. Formerly C. of Orsett 1850, Grays 1855. Author, *Canticles for the Christian Seasons*, 3*d*. [23]

RUMSEY, Lacy Henry, *Guildford.*—New Inn Hall, Ox. B.A. 1850, M.A. 1858; Deac. 1853 and Pr. 1854 by Bp of Jamaica. 2nd Mast. of the Guildford Gr. Sch. Formerly Vice-Prin. of Bishop's Coll. Jamaica, and Incumb. of St. John's and St. Mark's, in the Parish of St. Andrew's, Jamaica; Tut. of Trin. Coll. Glenalmond, Scotland; Incumb. of Ipswich, Australia. [24]

RUNDELL, William John.—C. of St. George's, Southwark. Formerly C. of St. James's, Pentonville, Lond. [25]

RUNDLE, Samuel, *Landrake, Cornwall.*—Trin. Coll. Ox. B.A. 1833, M.A. 1836; Deac. 1834 and Pr. 1836 by Bp of Ex. C. of Landrake 1856. Formerly C. of Buckleigh, Devon; Min. of St. Aubyn's Chapel, Devonport. [26]

RUSBRIDGER, John, *Chichester.*—Wad. Coll. Ox. B.A. 1839, M.A. 1841; Deac. 1840, Pr. 1841 by Bp of Chich. Formerly Dom. Chap. to the late Duke of Richmond 1843; C. of Eartham 1850. [27]

RUSBY, Thomas, *Doddington, March, Cambs.*—Magd. Coll. Cam. 5th Sen. Opt. and B.A. 1855, M.A. 1858; Deac. 1855 and Pr. 1856 by Bp of Ely. C. of Doddington, 1864. Formerly C. of St. Ives, Hunts, 1855–64. Author, *The Distinction between Regeneration and Conversion*, 1862, 6*d*; *The Holy Catholic and Apostolic Church*, 2*d*. [28]

RUSBY, W. H. L., *The Hurst, Glossop, Derbyshire.*—Dur; Deac. 1860 and Pr. 1861 by Bp of Lin. Formerly C. of Halton, Lin. 1860–62; V. of Fawley, Berks, 1862–65. [1]

RUSH, Henry John, *Rustington Vicarage, Littlehampton, Sussex.*—Wor. Coll. Ox. 4th cl. Lit. Hum. and B.A. 1843, M.A. 1846; Deac. 1843 and Pr. 1844 by Bp of Chich. V. of Rustington, Dio. Chich. 1858. (Patron, Bp of Chich; Tithe—Imp. 390*l*, V. 127*l*; Glebe, 21 acres; V.'s Inc. 160*l* and Ho; Pop. 300.) Formerly C. of Etchingham, Sussex. [2]

RUSHTON, James, *Long Stowe Rectory, near Caxton, Cambs.*—St. John's Coll. Cam. B.A. 1843, M.A. 1852; Deac. 1843, Pr. 1844. R. of Long Stowe, Dio. Ely, 1852. (Patron, the present R; Glebe, 406 acres; R.'s Inc. 350*l* and Ho; Pop. 264.) [3]

RUSHTON, John, *Blackburn Vicarage, Lancashire.*—Deac. 1822, Pr. 1823, D.D. 1844. V. of Blackburn, Dio. Man. 1854. (Patron, Bp of Man; Glebe, 20 acres; V.'s Inc. 918*l* and Ho; Pop. 12,000.) Hon. Can. of Man. Cathl. 1849; Rural Dean 1854. Formerly C. of Langho 1823; P. C. of Newchurch in Pendle 1825; Surrogate 1846; Archd. of Man. 1843–54; R. of Prestwich 1847–54. [4]

RUSHTON, John Richard, *Hook-Norton Rectory, Chipping-Norton, Oxon.*—Clare Coll. Cam. B.D. 1834; Deac. 1822 and Pr. 1823 by Bp of Ches. P. C. of Hook-Norton, Dio. Ox. 1840. (Patron, Bp of Ox; Glebe, 132 acres; P. C.'s Inc. 220*l* and Ho; Pop. 1393.) Surrogate. [5]

RUSHTON, William, *Brewood, Penkridge, Staffs.*—Trin. Coll. Cam. B.A. 1840, M.A. 1845. 2nd Mast. of Brewood Gr. Sch; Chap. of the Penkridge Union. [6]

RUSSELL, Abraham, *St. Botolph Rectory, 3, George-lane, Eastcheap, London, E.C.*—Dub. A.B. *ad eund.* Cam. 1844; Deac. and Pr. 1845. R. of the united Parishes of St. George's, Botolph-lane and St. Botolph's-by-Billingsgate, Dio. Lon. 1855. (Patrons, Crown and D. and C. of St. Paul's alt; Fire-Act Commutation, 180*l*; R.'s Inc. 360*l* and Ho; Pop. St. George, Botolph-lane, 217, St. Botolph-by-Billingsgate 222.) Formerly C. of St. George and St. Botolph 1851–55. [7]

RUSSELL, Alexander Benn, *Laverton Rectory, Beckington, Bath.*—Emman. Coll. Cam. S.C.L. 1826, B.C.L. 1829; Deac. 1827, Pr. 1828. R. of Laverton, Dio. B. and W. 1858. (Patron, Bp of B. and W; Tithe, 201*l* 15*s*; Glebe, 75 acres; R.'s Inc. 306*l* and Ho; Pop. 164.) Formerly V. of Westbury with Priddy C. Somerset, 1851–58. [8]

RUSSELL, Alfred Oliver, *Leytonstone, Essex, N.E.*—St. John's Coll. Cam. and Theol. Coll. Lichfield; Deac. 1860 by Abp of Cant. Pr. 1861 by Bp of Ely. C. of Leytonstone 1862. Formerly C. of Wombourn, Staffs, 1860–61; Asst. C. of St. John's, Chatham, 1862. Author, *The Perpetual Covenant* (a Sermon at Chatham), 1862, 2*d*; and sundry Parochial Addresses. [9]

RUSSELL, Arthur Tozer, 23, *Upper Parliament-street, Liverpool.*—St. John's Coll. Cam. Hulsean Prizeman 1825, Scho. of St. John's, 1827, B.C.L. 1830; Deac. 1827, Pr. 1830. P. C. of St. Thomas's, Toxteth, Dio. Ches. 1863. (Patron, Right Hon. W. E. Gladstone; Pop. 20,692.) Formerly V. of Caxton, Cambs, 1830, Waddon, Cambs, 1852–63. Author, *The Law a Schoolmaster to lead us to Christ* (Hulsean Prize Essay), 1826; *Sermons on the Festivals and Holy-days*, 1830; *Remarks on Professor Keble's Visitation Sermon*; *Translation of Jewell's Apology, with Notes*, 1834; *Manual of Daily Prayer*, 1842; *Psalm and Hymn Tunes*, 1843; *The Christian Life*, 1837; *Memorials of Dr. Fuller*, 1844; *Psalms and Hymns, partly from the German*, 1851; *Memorials of Bishop Andrewes*, 1860; A New Edition of *Slatter's Old Oxford University and City Guide*; *Letter to Bishop of Oxford upon the Defence of the "Essays and Reviews,"* 1862; *Sermon on the Real Presence*, 1857; *Review of Wordsworth's Hippolytus*; *Advent and other Sermons*, 1855. [10]

RUSSELL, Charles David, *Rossall, Fleetwood.*—St. John's Coll. Cam. 22nd Wrang. B.A. 1865; Deac. 1865 and Pr. 1866 by Bp of Carl. Asst. Mast. at Rossall 1867. Formerly C. of Brathay, Lanc. 1865–66. [11]

RUSSELL, Edward Grant, *Steeple Ashton, Trowbridge, Wilts.*—St. Edm. Hall, Ox. B.A. 1853, M.A. 1861; Deac. 1854 and Pr. 1855 by Bp of Rip. C. of Steeple Ashton 1866. Formerly C. of Calverley, near Leeds, and Tewin, near Hertford, Kyre, Worc. [12]

RUSSELL, Frederick, *Newtown, Southampton.*—Trin. Coll. Cam. B.A. 1848; Deac. 1849, Pr. 1850. P. C. of St. Luke's, Newtown, Dio. Win. 1851. (Patron, Bp of Win; P. C.'s Inc. 300*l*; Pop. 3348.) [13]

RUSSELL, Frederick William, 6, *Victoria-villas, Kentish-town, London, N.W.*—Univ. Coll. Dur. Licen. Theol. and B.A. 1847, M.A. 1850; Deac. 1849 and Pr. 1850 by Bp of Dur. Chap. of Charing Cross Hospital, Lond; Chap. to St. Martin's Workhouse, Wimbledon, 1867. Formerly Fell. of Dur. Univ; C. of St. Botolph's, Aldgate, and Trinity, Kentish-town, Lond. Author, *History of Kett's Rebellion in Norfolk*, 1859, Longmans, 25*s*. [14]

RUSSELL, H. C.—C. of Doncaster, Yorks. [15]

RUSSELL, Harry Vane, *Burneston Vicarage, Bedale, Yorks.*—Univ. Coll. Dur. B.A. 1851, Licen. Theol. 1852, M.A. 1854; Deac. 1854 and Pr. 1855 by Bp of Dur. V. of Burneston, Dio. Rip. 1855. (Patron, Duke of Cleveland; Tithe, Imp. 772*l* 2*s* 8*d*; Glebe, 4 acres; V.'s Inc. 584*l* and Ho; Pop. 774.) Dom. Chap. to the Dowager Duchess of Cleveland. [16]

RUSSELL, Henry, *St. John's College, Cambridge.*—St. John's Coll. Cam. Wrang. and B.A. 1845, M.A. 1848, B.D. 1855. Fell. of St. John's Coll. Cam. [17]

RUSSELL, Henry Lloyd, *St. Andrew's, Deal.*—St. Mary Hall, Ox. Deac. 1864 and Pr. 1865 by Bp of Lich. C. of St. Andrew's, Deal, 1866. Formerly C. of Weston-on-Trent 1864, Rugeley 1864–65, Lichfield 1865–66. [18]

RUSSELL, James, *Wombridge Vicarage, Wellington, Salop.*—St. John's Coll. Cam. B.A. 1852, M.A. 1853; Deac. 1853, Pr. 1854. V. of Wombridge, Dio. Lich. 1857. (Patron, St. J. C. Charlton, Esq; Tithe—Imp. 92*l* 13*s* 6*d*, P. C. 6*s*; Glebe, 10 acres; V.'s Inc. 133*l* and Ho; Pop. 1300.) Formerly C. of St. Stephen's, Wellinghall, Staffs, 1853–54; P. C. of Trinity, Okengate, Salop, 1855–56. Author, *Sermons on Our Lord's Temptations*, 1855, 1*s* 6*d*, Seeleys; *A Suffering Christ*, 1855, 6*d*, Seeleys; *Sound Words for Confirmation; Candidates, A Lecture on the Church Catechism*, 1863, 6*d* and 1*s*; *A Threefold Cord for Colliers*, 2*d* or 4*d*; *Repent To-day*, 1857, 6*d*, Seeleys; Sermons, Tracts, Hymns; etc. [19]

RUSSELL, John, *Holland-Fen Parsonage, Boston, Lincolnshire.*—Jesus Coll. Cam. B.A. 1846, M.A. 1849; Deac. 1846, Pr. 1847. P. C. of Holland-Fen, Dio. Lin. 1848. (Patron, Rev. B. Berridge; Glebe, 33 acres; P. C.'s Inc. 150*l* and Ho.) Formerly P. C. of Chapel Hill, Boston, 1848. [20]

RUSSELL, John Clarke, *Albion-street, Lewes, Sussex.*—St. Peter's Coll. Cam. 3rd Jun. Opt. and B.A. 1826, M.A. 1831; Deac. 1827 and Pr. 1828 by Bp of Salis. R. of St. Thomas-at-Cliffe, Lewes, Dio. Chich. 1841. (Patron, Abp of Cant; Tithe, 140*l* 10*s*; Glebe, 17 acres; R.'s Inc. 190*l*; Pop. 1568.) Formerly C. of Sutton Courtney, Berks, 1827–28, New Romney, Kent, 1828–33; V. of New Romney 1833–38; C. of East Garston, Berks, 1839–41. [21]

RUSSELL, John Fuller, *Cliff House, Greenhithe, Kent.*—St. Peter's Coll. Cam. S.C.L. 1837, B.C.L. 1838; Deac. 1838 and Pr. 1839 by Abp of Cant. R. of Greenhithe, Dio. Roch. 1856. (Patron, Sid. Coll. Cam; Tithe, 155*l*; R.'s Inc. 250*l*; Pop. 1039.) Fell. of the Soc. of Antiquaries. Formerly C. of St. Peter's, Walworth, Lond. 1838–40; P. C. of St. James's, Enfield, 1841–54. Author, *A Letter to the Right Hon. Henry Goulburn, M.P. on the Morals and Religion of the University of Cambridge*, 1833; *The Exclusive Power of an Episcopally-ordained Clergy to administer the Word and Sacraments, and consequently the Divine Authority of Episcopacy, considered*, 1834; *Judgment of the Anglican Church (posterior to the Reformation) on the Sufficiency* *of Holy Scripture, and the Value of Catholic Tradition, with an Introduction, Notes, and Appendix*, 1838; *The Rubric, its Strict Observance recommended*, 1839; *The City of God* (a Sermon), 1840; *Obedience to the Church in Things Ritual* (a Sermon), 1842; *Lays concerning the Early Church*, 1844; *Lives of Alfred the Great, Sir Thomas More, and John Evelyn*, in *Burns's Fireside Library*, 1845; *Anglican Ordinations Valid—A Refutation of certain Statements in the Validity of Anglican Ordinations Examined, by the Very Rev. P. R. Kenrick, V.G.* 1846; *Life of Dr. Samuel Johnson*, 1847; *The Ancient Knight, or Chapters on Chivalry*, 1849; *Sermons for Saints-days*, 1849; *The Church, a House of Prayer for all Nations* (a Sermon), 1855; *The Claims of the Church on the Love and Reverence of Mankind* (a Sermon), 1856, Masters; several Articles in the *Encyclopædia Metropolitana*. Co-Editor with Dr. Hook, of *The Voice of the Church, or Selections from the Writings of the Divines, and other Members of the Church, in all Ages*, 2 vols. 1840; and with Dr. Irons, of *Tracts of the Anglican Fathers*, 1841; Editor of *The Juvenile Englishman's Historical Library*, Masters. [1]

RUSSELL, John Leckey Forbes, *Freiston Vicarage, near Boston, Lincolnshire.*—Dub. *ad eund.* Corpus Coll. Cam. B.A. 1827, M.A. 1832; Deac. 1831 by Bp of Cloyne, Pr. 1832 by Bp of Killaloe. C. of Freiston with Butterwick, Lin. 1867. Dom. Chap. to the Duke of Grafton and to Viscount Keane. Formerly C. of Great and Little Eversden, Cambs, 1842-55, Eriswell, Suffolk, 1863-65. Author, *Parochial Sermons on the leading Doctrines of the Christian Religion*, 1855; *A Collection of Psalms and Hymns for Public Worship*; *A short Dissertation on the Number 7 in Scripture*; Occasional Sermons, Tracts, etc. Editor, *Sacred Musings, or a Collection of Poems on various subjects connected with the Christian's Experience; by the Rev. John Raven, B.A. Rector of Mundford, Norfolk*; *The Catholic Doctrine of a Trinitarian, by the late Rev. William Jones*, 1866, Rivingtons. [2]

RUSSELL, R. — C. of Kibworth-Beauchamp, Leicestershire. [3]

RUSSELL, Richard Norris, *Beachampton Rectory, near Buckingham.*—Caius Coll. Cam. 6th Wrang. and B.A. 1832, M.A. 1835. R. of Beachampton, Dio. Ox. 1835. (Patron, Caius Coll. Cam; Tithe, 354*l*; Glebe, 31 acres; R.'s Inc. 420*l* and Ho; Pop. 272.) Rural Dean of Stony-Stratford. Formerly Fell. of Caius Coll. Cam. [4]

RUSSELL, Robert, *Ilminster, Somerset.*—Oriel Coll. Ox. B.A. 1863; Deac. 1864 by Bp of B. and W. C. of Ilminster 1864. [5]

RUSSELL, Robert Wane, *Ludlow.*—Dub. A.B. 1845, B.C.L. 1849; Deac. 1845, Pr. 1846. Preacher to the Borough of Ludlow. [6]

RUSSELL, Samuel Henry, *Charlbury Vicarage, Enstone, Oxon.*—St. John's Coll. Ox. 4th cl. Lit. Hum. 1st cl. Math. et Phy, and B.A. 1836, M.A. 1840, B.D. 1845. V. of Charlbury with Shorthampton C. and Chadlington C. Dio. Ox. 1858. (Patron, St. John's Coll. Ox; Tithe—Imp. 1022*l* 0*s* 4*d*, V. 681*l* 10*s* 4*d*; Glebe, 400 acres; V.'s Inc. 886*l* and Ho; Pop. 2398.) Formerly 2nd Mast. in Merchant Taylors' Sch. Lond; C. of St. John's, Hoxton, Lond. [7]

RUSSELL, Sydenham Francis, *Willesborough Vicarage, Ashford, Kent.*—St. John's Coll. Cam. B.A. 1849, M.A. 1852; Deac. 1849 and Pr. 1850 by Bp of Ely. V. of Willesborough, Dio. Cant. 1858. (Patrons, D. and C. of Cant; Tithe, 187*l*; Glebe, 2 acres; V.'s Inc. 197*l* and Ho; Pop. 1750.) Formerly C. of Balsham, Cambs, 1849-57. [8]

RUSSELL, Thomas, *Magdalen College School, Brackley, Northants.*—St. John's Coll. Ox. B.A. 1852, M.A. 1854; Deac. 1853 and Pr. 1855 by Bp of Ox. Mast. of the Brackley Gr. Sch. Formerly C. of Shotteswell, Warwickshire, and Drayton, near Banbury; Mast. of Banbury Gr. Sch. [9]

RUSSELL, William, *Aber-Edw, Builth, Brecon.*—New Inn Hall, Ox. B.A. 1840, M.A. 1848. R. of Aber-Edw with Llanvarith R. Dio. St. D. 1846. (Patron, Bp of St. D; Aber-Edw, Tithe, 249*l* 18*s*; Glebe, 1 acre; Llanvarith, Tithe, 145*l*; R.'s Inc. 395*l*; Pop. Aber-Edw 281, Llanvarith 155.) [10]

RUSSELL, William, *Shepperton (Middlesex), near Chertsey, Surrey.*—Clare Coll. Cam. B.A. 1814; Deac. 1814 and Pr. 1815 by Bp of Win. R. of Shepperton, Dio. Lon. 1817. (Patron, Rev. J. C. Govett; Glebe, 11¾ acres; R.'s Inc. 606*l* and Ho; Pop. 849.) Rural Dean of Hampton 1847. [11]

RUSSELL, William Breighton, *Turvey Rectory (Beds), near Newport Pagnel.*—St. Cath. Coll. Cam. Scho. of B.A. 1821, M.A. 1826; Deac. 1821 and Pr. 1822 by Abp of York. R. of Turvey, Dio. Ely, 1856. (Patron, T. C. Higgins, Esq; Tithe—App. 263*l* 14*s*, R. 458*l* 9*s*; R.'s Inc. 458*l* and Ho; Pop. 1093.) Rural Dean. Formerly C. of Saundby, Notts, 1821; P. C. of St. Paul's, Preston, 1827; C. of All Saints', Northampton, 1829, Turvey 1833-56. [12]

RUSSELL, Lord Wriothesley, *The Cloisters, Windsor Castle*, and *Chenies Rectory, Amersham, Bucks.*—Trin. Coll. Cam. M.A. 1829. R. of Chenies, Dio. Ox. 1829. (Patron, Duke of Bedford; Tithe, 421*l* 6*s* 8*d*; Glebe, 22 acres; R.'s Inc. 467*l* and Ho; Pop. 468.) Can. Res. of the Free Chapel of St. George, Windsor, 1840. (Value, 1000*l* and Res.) Hon. Chap. in Ordinary and Deputy-Clerk of the Closet to the Queen, 1850. [13]

RUSSWURM, Alexander, *Portsmouth.*—Head Mast. of the Portsmouth Gr. Sch. [14]

RUST, Cyprian Thomas, 12, *The Crescent, Norwich.*—Queens' Coll. Cam. S.C.L. 1852, LL.B. 1855; Deac. 1852 and Pr. 1853 by Bp of Nor. R. of Heigham, Dio. Nor. 1865. (Patron, Bp of Nor; Tithe, 250*l*; R.'s Inc. 311*l*; Pop. 12,894.) Formerly C. of Rockland St. Mary 1852-53; P. C. of St. Michael's-at-Thorn, Norwich, 1853. Author, *Essays and Reviews*, a Lecture, 6*d*; *Sermons for Sunday at Home*, 2*s*; *The Three Creeds*, 3*d*. [15]

RUST, George, 31, *Bedford-square, London, W.C.*—Pemb. Coll. Ox. 3rd cl. Lit. Hum. and B.A. 1841, M.A. 1844; Deac. 1844 and Pr. 1845 by Bp of Lon. Cl. Mast. in King's Coll. Sch. Lond. 1849. Formerly C. of St. Giles's-in-the-Fields, Lond. 1844. [16]

RUST, John Cyprian, 12, *The Crescent, Norwich.*—Pemb. Coll. Cam. 12th cl. and 14th Jun. Opt. B.A. 1863, Fell. of Coll. 1865, M.A. 1866; Deac. 1864 and Pr. 1865 by Abp of York. C. of Heigham, Norwich, 1866. Formerly C. of St. James's, Doncaster, and Composition Mast. in the Doncaster Gram. Sch. [17]

RUSTON, James, *Hordle Vicarage, Lymington, Hants.*—Jesus Coll. Cam. Coll. Prizeman, English Essayist, 1849, B.A. 1851, M.A. 1854, M.A. Oxon. 1856; Deac. 1851, Pr. 1852. V. of Hordle, Dio. Win. 1861. (Patron, Queen's Coll. Ox; Tithe, 90*l*; Glebe, 32 acres; V.'s Inc. 90*l* and Ho; Pop. 921.) Garrison Chap. at Hurst Castle. Formerly C. of Fritwell, Oxon, and St. Thomas's, Stamford-hill. [18]

RUTHERFORD, Henry Jackson, *Queen Charlton, near Bristol.*—Literate; Deac. 1851, Pr. 1852. P. C. of Queen Charlton, Dio. B. and W. 1862. (Patroness, Mrs. Elliot; P. C.'s Inc. 66*l*; Pop. 141.) Chap. of the Keynsham Union. Formerly C. of Govilon, Mon. 1851-53, North and South Stoke, near Grantham, 1854-56, Glatton with Holme, Hunts, 1856-57, Keynsham, Somerset, 1859. [19]

RUTHERFORD, Robert, *Newlands Parsonage, Keswick.*—St. Aidan's 1857; Deac. 1857 and Pr. 1858 by Bp of Ches. P. C. of Newlands, Dio. Carl. 1867. (Patron, V. of Crosthwaite; P. C.'s Inc. 100*l* and Ho; Pop. 211.) Formerly C. of Holy Trinity, Birkenhead 1857-60, Elland 1860-61, All Saints', Salterhebble, Halifax, 1861-64; P. C. of Grange 1864-67. [20]

RUTHERFORD, W. A.—Chap. of H.M.S. "Barrosa." [21]

RUTLAND, Robert, 4, *Melbury-terrace, Harewood-square, N.W.*—Emman. Coll. Cam. B.A. 1848, M.A. 1850; Deac. 1849 and Pr. 1850 by Bp of Win. C. of St. Mary's, Bryanston-square, Marylebone, Lond. 1855. Formerly C. of Blendworth, Hants, 1849-52, Godalming, Surrey, 1852-55. [22]

RUXTON, Frederick W., *Willington Parsonage, Durham.*—St. Bees 1851; Deac. 1851, Pr. 1852. P. C. of Willington, Dio. Dur. 1860. (Patron, R. of Brancepeth; P. C.'s Inc. 100*l* and Ho; Pop. 3784.) Formerly C. of Brancepeth, near Durham. [1]

RYCROFT, Dyson, 47, *Peel-street, Toxteth-park, Liverpool.*—St. Aidan's 1853; Deac. 1856 and Pr. 1857 by Bp of Ches. Clerical Superintendent of the Liverpool Church of England Scriptural Readers' Soc. Formerly C. of St. Helens, Lancashire, 2 years; Sen. C. of St. Paul's, Prince's-park, Liverpool, 4 years. [2]

RYDE, John Gabriel, *Melrose, Roxburgh, Scotland.*—St. John's Coll. Ox. B.A. 1846, M.A. 1848; Deac. 1847 and Pr. 1848 by Bp of Lon. [3]

RYDER, Henry Dudley, *Lichfield.*—Oriel Coll. Ox. B.A. 1825, M.A. 1828. Can. Res. of Lichfield Cathl. with the Prebendal Stalls of Ryton and Pipe-Minor annexed, 1833. (Value, 690*l* and Res.) [4]

RYDER, James Octavius, *Welwyn, Herts.*—All Souls' Coll. Ox. 1st cl. Lit. Hum. and B.A. 1849, Ellerton Theol. Prize Essay 1850, M.A. 1852; Deac. and Pr. 1851 by Bp of Ox. Fell. of All Souls' Coll. Ox. 1850–52. R. of Welwyn, Dio. Roch. 1866. (Patron, All Souls' Coll. Ox; Tithe, 625*l*; Glebe, 83 acres; R.'s Inc. 740*l*; Pop. 1700.) Formerly C. of Ampfield, Hants, 1851–52; R. of Elmley, Kent, 1852–66. [5]

RYLE, John Charles, *Stradbroke Vicarage, Wickham Market, Suffolk.*—Ch. Ch. Ox. 1st cl. Lit. Hum. Craven Univ. Scho. B.A. 1837; Deac. 1841 and Pr. 1842 by Bp of Win. V. of Stradbroke, Dio. Nor. 1861. (Patron, Bp of Nor; Tithe, comm. 1050*l*; Glebe, 6 acres; V.'s Inc. 1100*l*; Pop. 1537.) Formerly C. of Exbury, Hants, 1841; R. of St. Thomas's, Winchester, 1843; R. of Helmingham, Suffolk, 1844–61. Author, *Expository Thoughts on the Gospels*, 4 vols; and about 60 Tracts at 2*d* each, published between 1845 and 1867, by W. Hunt, London. [6]

RYLEY, Edward, *Sarratt Rectory, Rickmansworth, Herts.*—Trin. Coll. Ox. B.A. 1853, M.A. 1856; Deac. 1853, Pr. 1854 by Abp of Cant. R. of Sarratt, Dio. Roch. 1859. (Patron, S. Ryley, Esq; R.'s Inc. 275*l* and Ho; Pop. 736.) Formerly C. of Plaxtol, Kent, 1853-59. Author, *Sermon, The Duty and Hope of the Christian Minister*, 1859, 1*d*. [7]

RYND, Henry Nassau.—C. of St. Saviour's, Bath. [8]

RYVES, George Thomas, *Nuthall, Nottingham.*—Brasen. Coll. Ox. Hulme Exhib. B.A. 1857, M.A. 1860; Deac. 1859 and Pr. 1860 by Bp of Lich. C. of Nuthall 1865. Formerly C. of Fauls, near Prees, 1859; Hasfield, near Gloucester, 1861. [9]

SABBEN, James, *Walmgate, York.*—Queens' Coll. Cam. B.A. 1838; Deac. 1838 and Pr. 1839 by Abp of York. R. of St. Denis' with St. George's R. York, Dio. York, 1841. (Patron, Ld Chan; R.'s Inc. 150*l*; Pop. St. Denis' 1463, St. George's 2218.) P. C. of Naburn, Dio. York, 1841. (Patron, Rev. W. L. Palmes; Glebe, 35 acres; P. C.'s Inc. 90*l*; Pop. 471.) [10]

SABIN, John Edward, *Dublin.*—Emman. Coll. Cam. B.A. 1854; Deac. 1854 by Bp of Lin. Pr. 1856 by Bp of Ox. Sen. Chap. to the Forces, Dublin. Formerly Chap. to the Forces, Aldershot; Chap. in the Crimean Campaign 1854–56. [11]

SABINE, Thomas, *Tunstall, near Kirby Lonsdale, Westmoreland.*—C. of Tunstall 1854. [12]

SABINE, Williams, *Hotham, Brough, Yorks.*—Jesus Coll. Cam. B.A. 1844; Deac. 1844 and Pr. 1845 by Bp of Ex. R. of Hotham, Dio. York, 1857. (Patron, Ld Chan; R.'s Inc. 345*l*; Pop. 333.) Formerly R. of Thorne-Coffin 1846–53; R. of Brympton, Somerset, 853–57. [13]

SADLER, Michael Ferrebee, *St. Paul's Vicarage, Bedford.*—St. John's Coll. Cam. Univ. Scho. Tyrrwhitt's Heb. Scho. B.A. 1847, M.A. 1849; Deac. 1846 and Pr. 1847 by Bp of Pet. V. of St. Paul's, Bedford, Dio. Ely, 1864. (Patron, Rev. W. G. Fitzgerald; V.'s Inc. 250*l* and Ho; Pop. 4366.) Preb. of Wells 1863. Formerly P. C. of Hanover Chapel, Regent-street, Lond. 1852–57; V. of Bridgwater 1857–64. Author, *Sacrament of Responsibility*, 1851, 6 eds; *The Second Adam and the New Birth*, 1857, 3 eds; *Doctrinal Revision of the Liturgy considered*, 1862; *Parochial Sermons*, First Series, 1861, Second Series, 1862. [14]

SADLER, Ottiwell, *Brancaster Rectory, Lynn Regis, Norfolk.*—Trin. Coll. Cam. B A. 1837, M.A. 1842; Deac. 1840 and Pr. 1841 by Bp of Rip. R. of Brancaster, Dio. Nor. 1844. (Patron, the present R; Tithe, 824*l* 10*s* 4*d*; Glebe, 7 acres; R.'s Inc. 840*l* and Ho; Pop. 1002.) [15]

SADLER, William, *Coleridge Vicarage, Wembworthy, North Devon.*—Queens' Coll. Cam. B.A. 1843; Deac. 1843 and Pr. 1844 by Bp of Ex. V. of Coleridge, Dio. Ex. 1861. (Patron, Bp of Ex; Tithe, 155*l*; Glebe, 17 acres; V.'s Inc. 180*l* and Ho; Pop. 613.) Formerly C. of St. Columb Major 1843–45, Tor Mohun 1845–46, Highweek 1846–61, Nymet Rowland 1862–66. Author, *How are Persons united before the Registrar to be treated by the Church?* 1854; *The Dignity of Wedlock and the Unlawfulness of Divorce*, 1858; *Our True Safeguard*, a Sermon before the 10th Devon Rifle Volunteers, 1860; *God's Claim to our Love*, a Sermon, 1862; etc. [16]

SAFFORD, James Cutting, *Mettingham Castle, Bungay, Suffolk.*—Caius Coll. Cam. B.A. 1822; Deac. 1823 by Bp of Lin. Pr. 1823 by Bp of Nor. V. of Mettingham, Dio. Nor. 1824. (Patron, the present V; Tithe—App. 2*l* 10*s*, Imp. 280*l*, V. 120*l*; Glebe, 48 acres; V.'s Inc. 220*l* and Ho; Pop. 387.) P. C. of Ilketshall St. Lawrence, Suffolk, Dio. Nor. 1840. (Patron, Rev. R. Maclean; Tithe—App. 41*l* 10*s*, Imp. 219*l* 15*s*; P. C.'s Inc. 66*l*; Pop. 202.) [17]

SAFFORD, William Chartres, *Attleborough Rectory, Norfolk.*—Corpus Coll. Cam. B.A. 1852, M.A. 1855; Deac. 1852 and Pr. 1853 by Bp of Ches. R. of Attleborough, Dio. Nor. 1866. (Patron, Sir W. B. Smijth, Bart; Tithe, 1504*l*; Glebe, 17 acres; R.'s Inc. 1570*l* and Ho; Pop. 2221.) Formerly R. of Ch. Ch. with St. Ewens, Bristol, 1855–59; P. C. of Stoven, Suffolk, 1859–66. [18]

SAGAR, Oates, *Bolton, Bradford, Yorks.*—Dub. A.B. 1866; Deac. 1866 by Bp of Rip. C. of Bolton in Calverley 1866. [19]

SAGE, Charles Arthur, *Brackley Vicarage, Northants.*—Trin. Coll. Cam. B.A. 1810; Deac. 1811, Pr. 1817. V. of Brackley St. Peter with St. James C. Dio. Pet. 1825. (Patron, Earl of Ellesmere; St. Peter, Tithe—Imp. 167*l* 10*s*, V. 238*l* 6*s* 10½*d*; Glebe, 51 acres; St. James, Glebe, 26 acres; V.'s Inc. 430*l* and Ho; Pop. St. Peter 1615, St. James 768.) Rural Dean and Surrogate 1826. [20]

SAGE, William Henry, *Two Mile Hill, near Bristol.*—Trin. Coll. Ox. B.A. 1850, M.A. 1853; Deac. 1851, Pr. 1852. P. C. of Two Mile Hill, St. George's, Dio. G. and B. 1860. (Patrons, Crown and Bp of G. and B. alt; P. C.'s Inc. 160*l* and Ho; Pop. 3622.) Formerly Chap. to the Royal Infirmary, Bristol; C. of St. Peter's, Bristol. [21]

SAINSBURY, Charles, *Wootton Courtney, Somerset.*—Trin. Coll. Cam. B.A. 1860, M.A. 1864; Deac. 1861 and Pr. 1862 by Bp of B. and W. C. of Wootton Courtney 1861. [22]

SAINSBURY, Joseph Popham, *Ugborough, Ivybridge, Devon.*—King's Coll. Lond. Theol. Assoc. 1858; Deac. 1858 by Bp of B. and W. Pr. 1859 by Bp of Wor. C. of Ugborough 1866. Formerly C. of Walcot, Bath, 1858, St. Michael's, Coventry, 1859, St. Mark's, St. John's Wood, Lond. 1864. [23]

SAINSBURY, R., *Kidderminster.*—C. of St. Mary's, Kidderminster, 1867. Formerly C. of St. Michael's, Handsworth, Birmingham. [24]

SAINSBURY, Sainsbury Langford, *Beckington Rectory, Frome.*—Trin. Coll. Ox. B.A. 1853, M.A. 1856; Deac. 1855, Pr. 1856. R. of Beckington with Standerwick R. Dio. B. and W. 1857. (Patron, the present R; Tithe, 506*l* 7*s* 1*d*; Glebe, 72½ acres; Standerwick, Tithe, 81*l* 5*s* 10*d*; Glebe, 14 acres; R.'s Inc. 683*l* and Ho; Pop. Beckington 1036, Standerwick 60.) [1]

SAINSBURY, Thomas Ernest Langford, *Beddington Rectory, Croydon.*—Trin. Coll. Ox. B.A. 1856, M.A. 1859; Deac. 1858 and Pr. 1860 by Bp of Salis. C. of Beddington, Surrey, 1865. Formerly C. of Aldbourne, Wilts, 1858–61, Combe Keynes, Dorset, 1861–64. [2]

SAINT, John James, *Speldhurst Rectory, Tunbridge Wells.*—Brasen. Coll. Ox. B.A. 1822, M.A. 1825; Deac. 1823, Pr. 1825. R. of Speldhurst, Dio. Cant. 1831. (Patron, the present R; Tithe, 500*l*; Glebe, 8½ acres with a Ho; R.'s Inc. 540*l* and Ho; Pop. 1898.) Rural Dean; Dom. Chap. to the Earl of Rosslyn. [3]

ST. ASAPH, The Right Rev. Thomas Vowler SHORT, Lord Bishop of St. Asaph, *The Palace, St. Asaph.*—Ch. Ch. Ox. Double 1st cl. 1812, B.A. 1813, M.A. 1815, B.D. 1824, D.D. 1837; Deac. 1813 and Pr. 1814 by Bp of Ox. Consecrated Bp of Sodor and Man 1841; Translated to St. Asaph 1846. (Episcopal Jurisdiction—the Cos. of Denbigh and Flint, with portions of the Cos. of Montgomery, Carnarvon, Merioneth and Salop; Inc. of See, 4200*l*; Pop. 246.337; Acres, 1,067,583; Deaneries, 12; Benefices, 190, and with Glebe Houses, 159; Curates, 57; Church Sittings, 68,044.) His Lordship was formerly Tut. and Censor of Ch. Ch. Ox. 1816–29; P. C. of Cowley, Oxon, 1816 23; Whitehall Preacher 1821; R. of Stockley-Pomeroy, Devon, 1823–26; R. of King's-Worthy, Hants, 1826–34; R. of St. George's, Bloomsbury, Lond. 1834–41; Deputy Clerk of the Closet to the Queen 1837. Author, *Sermons on some of the Fundamental Truths of Christianity*, 1829; *A Letter to the Dean of Christ Church on the State of the Public Examinations in the University of Oxford*, 1829; *Sketch of the History of the Church of England to the Revolution of* 1688 (6 eds.), 1840–55; *Hints on Teaching Vulgar and Decimal Fractions*, S.P.C.K; *Parochialia, Papers printed for the Use of the Parish of St. George, Bloomsbury*, 1834–41; *What is Christianity?* 1843; *Charges delivered to the Convocation held at Bishop's Court, Isle of Man*, 1842, '43, '44, '45; *A Charge at the Primary Visitation at St. Asaph*, 1847; *Catechising* (*an Appendix to the previous Charge*), 1847; *A Charge*, 1850; *ib.* 1853; subsequent Charges. [4]

ST. AUBYN, Hender Molesworth, *Clowance, Camborne, Cornwall.*—Ex. Coll. Ox. B.A. 1820; Deac. 1821 and Pr. 1822 by Bp of Ex. [5]

ST. AUBYN, William John, *Stoke-Damerel Rectory, Devonport.*—Downing Coll. Cam. B.A. 1824, M.A. 1828; Deac. and Pr. 1828. R of Stoke-Damerel, Dio. Ex. 1828. (Patrons, Trustees of the late Sir John St. Aubyn; Tithe, 643*l*; Glebe, 23½ acres; R.'s Inc. 666*l* and Ho; Pop. 25,732.) [6]

ST. DAVID'S, The Right Rev. Connop THIRLWALL, Lord Bishop of St. David's, *Abergwili Palace, Carmarthen.*—Trin. Coll. Cam. Bell's Scho. 1815, Craven Scho. 1815, Sen. Chancellor's Medallist, Sen. Opt. and B.A. 1818, M.A. 1821, B.D. and D.D. per Literas Regias 1840; Deac. 1827 by Bp of Ely, Pr. 1828 by Bp of Bristol, Consecrated Bp of St. David's 1840. (Episcopal Jurisdiction—the Cos. of Pembroke, Cardigan, Brecknock, 46 Parishes in Radnorshire and Carmarthen, and 26 Parishes in Glamorgan; Inc. of See, 4500*l*; Pop. 435,912; Acres, 2,272,790; Deaneries, 18; Benefices, 397, and with Glebe Houses, 173; Curates, 116; Church Sittings, 118,877.) His Lordship is Dean and Treasurer of Christ's Coll. Ch. Brecon, with the Prebendal Stalls of Llangadock, Llanddoyaant and Llangamarch; Visitor of St. David's Coll. Lampeter. His Lordship was formerly Fell. of Trin. Coll. Cam. Author, *Primitiæ, or Essays and Poems on various Subjects, by C. T., Eleven Years of Age—the Preface by his Father, T. Thirlwall*, 1809; *History of Greece* (in Lardner's Cabinet Cyclopædia), 8 vols. 1835–47; new ed. 8 vols. 1845–52; *Geschichte von Griechenland von L. Haymann*, Bd. 1, 2 (no more published), Bonn, 1839–40; Charges, *A Charge delivered to the Clergy of the Diocese of St. David's*, 1842; do. 1845; do. 1848; do. 1851; do. 1854, *with two Appendixes—On the Dogma of the Immaculate Conception*; and *On the History of the Eucharistic Controversy*, 1857; *Charge*, 1860; *Charge*, 1863. Letters, *A Letter to Thomas Turton, D.D. on the Admission of Dissenters to Academical Degrees*, 1834; *A Letter to the Archbishop of Canterbury on the Statements of Sir B. Hall, Bart. M.P. with Regard to the Collegiate Church of Brecon*, 1851; *A second Letter* (on same subject), 1851; *A Letter to J. Bowstead* (commenting on his Letter) *concerning Education in South Wales*, 2nd ed. 1861. Sermons, *A Sermon preached at St. Mary, Haverfordwest*, 1842, *on Behalf of the Society for the Propagation of the Gospel in Foreign Parts*, 1842; *The Centre of Unity*, 1850; *The Excellence of Wisdom, a Sermon on Laying the Foundation Stone of the Welsh Educational Institution* MDCCCXLIX. 1850; *The Apostolical Commission, an Ordination Sermon*, 1853; *English Education for the Middle Classes, a Sermon preached at Hurstpierpoint Church, on the Occasion of the Opening of St. John's School*, 1853; *A Speech in the House of Lords, May 25th, on a Bill for the Relief of Her Majesty's Subjects professing the Jewish Religion* 1848; *Advantages of Literary and Scientific Institutions for all Classes* (a Lecture), 1850; *Inaugural Address delivered to the Members of the Philosophical Institution, Edinburgh*, 1861. Translator of Niebuhr's *History of Rome*, in conjunction with Dr. Julius Hare, 1831, 1847; etc. [7]

ST. GEORGE, Howard, *Billinge Parsonage, Wigan, Lancashire.*—Dub. A.B. 1846, A.M. 1853; Deac. 1846 and Pr. 1848 by Bp. of Ches. P. C. of Billinge, Dio. Ches. 1853. (Patron, R. of Wigan; Tithe—App. 407*l* 0*s* 6*d*; Glebe, 30 acres; P. C.'s Inc. 443*l* and Ho; Pop. 3066.) Surrogate 1850; Dom. Chap. to the Earl of Gosford 1865. Formerly C. of Haigh 1846; Sen. C. of Wigan 1850. [8]

ST. GEORGE, Leonard Henry, *Southsea, Hants.*—Lampeter, B.D. 1854; Deac. 1838 by Bp of St. D. Pr. 1839 by Bp of Salis. for Bp of Lich. Chap. of H.M. Forces 1865. Formerly P. C. of Tong, Salop, 1839–43; C. of Shroton, Dorset, 1843–46, Semley, Wilts, 1848–55; Chap. to H.M. Forces, Parkhurst, Isle of Wight, 1855–56, Newcastle-on-Tyne 1856–57, Mauritius 1857–58, Hong-Kong, Canton, and Shanghai, China, 1858–61, Cork, 1861-65. [9]

ST. HILL, Thomas, *St. Pierre, Calais.*—Deac. 1848, Pr. 1850. Consular Chap. at Calais, and Chap. at St. Pierre. Formerly C. of St. Matthew's, Birmingham, 1856–58. [10]

ST. JOHN, Edward, *Finchamstead Rectory, Wokingham, Berks.*—Downing Coll. Cam. LL.B. 1831; Deac. 1835 by Bp of Wor. Pr. 1836 by Bp of Nor. R. of Finchampstead, Dio. Ox. (Patron, the present R; Tithe, 578*l*; R.'s Inc. 600*l* and Ho; Pop. 637.) Formerly R. of Barkham, near Wokingham. [11]

ST. JOHN, George, 11, *Saville-place, Clifton.*—Wad. Coll. Ox. B.A. 1821, M.A. 1825; Deac. 1822 and Pr. 1823 by Bp of Wor. R. of Warndon, Worcester, Dio. Wor. 1833. (Patron, R. Berkeley, Esq; Tithe, 126*l* 2*s* 6*d*; Glebe, 17 acres; R.'s Inc. 150*l* 2*s* 6*d*; Pop. 164.) [12]

ST. JOHN, George William, *Woodstock Rectory, Oxon.*—Jesus Coll. Cam. M.A. 1817; Deac. 1819, Pr. 1820. R. of Bladen with Woodstock C. Dio. Ox. 1847. (Patron, Duke of Marlborough; Tithe, 237*l*; Glebe, 170 acres; R.'s Inc. 407*l* and Ho; Pop. Bladon 660, Woodstock 1202.) Dom. Chap. to the Marquis of Ailesbury 1821. [13]

ST. JOHN, Henry St. Andrew, *Hilton Vicarage, Blandford.*—Wad. Coll. Ox. B.A. 1816, M.A. 1819; Deac. 1820 by Bp of Wor. Pr. 1821 by Abp of Cant. V. of Hilton, Dio. Salis. 1838. (Patron, Bp of Salis; Tithe—App. 167*l* and 40 acres of Glebe, V. 343*l*; V.'s Inc. 343*l* and Ho; Pop. 833.) Formerly P. C. of Putsey 1821–34; V. of Addingham 1834–38. [14]

ST. JOHN, H. F., *Kempsford, Fairford, Gloucestershire.*—Trin. Coll. Cam. B.A. 1857, M.A. 1861; Deac. 1859 and Pr. 1861 by Bp of G. and B. C. of Kempsford 1859. [1]

ST. JOHN, Maurice William Ferdinand, *Frampton-on-Severn, Stonehouse, Glouc.*—Dur. B.A. 1850; Deac. 1851, Pr. 1852. V. of Frampton-on-Severn, Dio. G. and B. 1853. (Patron, St. W. Silver, Esq; V.'s Inc. 270*l* and Ho; Pop. 983.) [2]

ST. JOHN, Paulet, *Mottisfont Rectory, Romsey, Hants.*—Downing Coll. Cam. B.C.L. 1837; Deac. 1838, Pr. 1839. R. of Mottisfont with Lockerley C. and Dean C. Dio. Win. 1848. (Patron, the present R; Mottisfont, Tithe, 500*l*; Glebe, 24½ acres; Lockerley, Tithe, 500*l*; Glebe, 8¼ acres; Dean, Tithe, 205*l*; Glebe, 4 acres; R.'s Inc. 1230*l* and Ho; Pop. Mottisfont 496, Lockerley 581, Dean 223.) [3]

ST. LEGER, Edward Frederick, *Scotton, Kirton-in-Lindsey.*—Queen's Coll. Ox. B.A. 1855, M.A. 1858; Deac. 1856 and Pr. 1857 by Bp of Herf. R. of Scotton with East Ferry Chapel, Dio. Lin. 1863. (Patron, Sir R. Frederick, Bart; Tithe, 655*l*; Glebe, 70 acres; R.'s Inc. 750*l* and Ho; Pop. Scotton 300, East Ferry 190.) Formerly C. of Kyre Wyaro, Tenbury, 1856–60, Scotton 1860–63. [4]

ST. LEGER, Richard Arthur, *Bishops Wood, Buckland St. Mary, Chard, Somerset.*—Oriel Coll. Ox. B.A. 1813, M.A. 1816. P. C. of Otterford, near Honiton, Somerset, Dio. B. and W. 1858. (Patron, J. Pashley, Esq; Glebe, 32 acres; P. C.'s Inc. 85*l*; Pop. 476.) Formerly R. of Kenn, Devon, 1855–58. [5]

ST. PATTRICK, Beaufoy James, *Weston Begard, near Hereford.*—St. Mary Hall, Ox. B.A. 1847; Deac. 1848 and Pr. 1850 by Bp of Herf. V. of Weston Begard, Dio. Herf. 1863. (Patrons, D. and C. of Herf; Tithe—Imp. 65*l*, V. 130*l*; Glebe, 2½ acres; V.'s Inc. 165*l*; Pop. 372.) [6]

ST. PATTRICK, Reginald.—Queen's Coll. Ox. B.A. 1858; Deac. 1862 by Bp of Man. Pr. 1863 by Bp of Herf. Formerly C. of St. Mary Magdalene's, Bridgnorth, 1862. [7]

ST. QUINTIN, George Darby, *St. Leonards, Sussex.*—Trin. Coll. Cam. B.A. 1826, M.A. 1829; Deac. 1827, Pr. 1828. Dom. Chap. to the Marquis of Salisbury. [8]

ST. QUINTIN, John Whitby, *Hatley Rectory, Caxton, Cambs.*—Emman. Coll. Cam. B.A. 1838, M.A. 1848. R. of Hatley, Dio. Ely, 1850. (Patron, T. St. Quintin, Esq; Tithe, 165*l*; Glebe, 9 acres; R.'s Inc. 177*l* and Ho; Pop. 164.) [9]

SALE, Charles Hanson, *Kirby-on-the-Moor, Boroughbridge, Yorks.*—Brasen. Coll. Ox. B.A. 1840, M.A. 1843; Deac. 1842 and Pr. 1843 by Bp of Wor. V. of Kirby-on-the-Moor, Dio. Rip. 1859. (Patron, Ld Chan; Glebe, 100 acres; V.'s Inc. 400*l* and Ho; Pop. 650.) Formerly C. of Newton Regis, Warwickshire, 1842–59. [10]

SALE, Charles John, *Holt Rectory, Worcester.*—Lin. Coll. Ox. 3rd cl. Lit. Hum. 1840; Deac. 1841 and Pr. 1842 by Bp of Lich. R. of Holt with Little Witley C. Dio. Wor. 1847. (Patron, Earl of Dudley; Tithe, 584*l*; Glebe, 47 acres; R.'s Inc. 622*l* and Ho; Pop. Holt 295, Little Witley 208.) Formerly C. of Eccleshall 1842, Caverswall 1844. [11]

SALE, Edward Townsend, *Rugby.*—Emman. Coll. Cam. 9th Wrang. and B.A. 1850, M.A. 1853, B.D. 1860, Fell. of Emman. Coll. 1852; Deac. 1853 and Pr. 1855 by Bp of Ely. C. of St. Andrew's and Trinity, Rugby, 1860. Formerly C. of Ch. Ch. Doncaster, and Calthorpe, Leic. [12]

SALE, Richard, *St. Lawrence, Ramsgate.*—St. John's Coll. Cam. B.A. 1833, M.A. 1839; Deac. 1834, Pr. 1835. [13]

SALE, Thomas, *The Vicarage, Sheffield.*—Magd. Coll. Ox. 2nd cl. Lit. Hum. and B.A. 1825, M.A. 1827, D.D; Deac. 1827, Pr. 1828. V. of Sheffield, Dio. York, 1851. (Patrons, Mrs. Thornhill and A. S. Lawson, Esq. alt; Tithe, 3*l*; Glebe, 2 acres; V.'s Inc. 504*l* and Ho; Pop. 33,425.) Hon. Can. and Preb. of York 1855; Rural Dean. Formerly Fell. of Magd. Coll. Ox. [14]

SALE, Thomas Townsend, *Norton (Derbyshire), near Sheffield.*—Ch. Coll. Cam. 18th Wrang. and B.A. 1852, M.A. 1855; Deac. 1852 by Bp of Lich. Pr. 1853 by Bp of Man. C. of Norton; Fell. of Ch. Coll. Cam. 1853. [15]

SALE, Thomas Walker, *Attercliffe, Sheffield.*—Wad. Coll. Ox. B.A. 1858; Deac. 1859 and Pr. 1860 by Bp of Lin. P. C. of Attercliffe, Dio. York, 1864. (Patron, V. of Sheffield; Glebe, 5 acres; P. C.'s Inc. 300*l* and Ho; Pop. 3000.) Formerly C. of Boston 1859. [16]

SALISBURY, The Right Rev. Walter Kerr HAMILTON, Lord Bp of Salisbury, *The Palace, Salisbury.*—Ch. Ch. Ox. 1st cl. Lit. Hum. and B.A. 1830, M.A. 1833, D.D. 1854. Consecrated Bp of Salis. 1854. (Episcopal Jurisdiction—some parts of Wilts and the whole of the Co. of Dorset; Inc. of See, 5000*l*; Pop. 377,337; Acres, 1,309,617; Deaneries, 13; Benefices, 472, and with Glebe Houses, 394; Curates, 206; Church Sittings, 155,000.) His Lordship is Provincial Precentor of the Province of Canterbury. His Lordship was formerly Fell. of Mert. Coll. Ox. 1833–37; V. of St. Peter's-in-the-East, Oxford, 1837–43; Exam. Chap. to the late Bp of Salis. 1837–54; Can. Res. and Precentor of Salis. Cathl. 1843–54. Author, *Family Prayers, or Morning and Evening Services for every Day in the Week,* 1842; *Prayers which, in the present Distress, may be used in the Chamber, the Family, or privately in the Church,* 1853; *In the midst of Life we are in Death* (Funeral Sermon for the late Bishop of Salis.), 1854; *Cathedral Reform* (a Letter to the Members of his Diocese, together with a Reprint of his former Letter to the Dean of Salis. in 1853, and the Scheme for the Reform of their own Cathedral suggested by the D. and C. of Salis. to the Cathedral Commission, to which are appended two Letters to the Commissioners by the late Bishop Denison), 1855; *A Charge* (at his Lordship's Primary Visitation), 1855; *A Charge,* 1867. [17]

SALISBURY, Edward, *Leamington.*—Magd. Coll. Cam. Scho. 1849, B.A. 1852, M.A. 1855; Deac. 1856. [18]

SALISBURY, Edward Lister, *Biscovey, Par Station, Cornwall.*—Trin. Hall, Cam. Jun. Opt. Math. Hons. B.A. 1853; Deac. 1857 by Bp of Wor. Pr. 1858 by Bp of Ex. P. C. of Par with Biscovey, Dio. Ex. 1859. (Patrons, the Crown and Bp of Ex. alt; P. C.'s Inc. 150*l*; Pop. 2327.) Formerly C. of St. George's, Truro, 1857–58, Camborne 1858–59. Author, Sermons and Letters to Parishioners on Church-rates and Observance of Good Friday. [19]

SALISBURY, Elijah Edward Baylee, *Thundersley Rectory, Rayleigh, Essex.*—Queens' Coll. Cam. B.D. 1860; Deac. 1851 and Pr. 1852 by Bp of Pet. C. of Thundersley 1854. Formerly C. of Desford 1851, Thaxted 1854. Author, *The Good Churchman,* 1855; 2nd ed. 1857; *Education* (a Sermon), 1858. [20]

SALKELD, Edward, *Aspatria, Carlisle.*—Trin. Coll. Cam. 20th Wrang. and B.A. 1826, M.A. 1831; Deac. 1828 and Pr. 1829 by Bp of Lich. V. of Aspatria, Dio. Carl. 1838. (Patron, Bp of Carl; Tithe—App. 517*l*, V. 52*l* 8*s* 9*d*; Glebe, 192 acres; V.'s Inc. 250*l* and Ho; Pop. 2305.) Surrogate. Formerly C. of Bulkington, Warwickshire, 1828; P. C. of Trinity, Carlisle, and V. of Crosby-on-Eden 1832–38. [21]

SALL, Ernest Augustus, *Panama.*—Dub; Deac. 1843, Pr. 1844. Chap. to the English Residents at Panama. [22]

SALMAN, William Senior, *Brougham Rectory, Penrith.*—St. John's Coll. Cam. B.A. 1836, M.A. 1839; Deac. 1837 by Bp of Dur. Pr. 1838 by Abp of York. R. of Brougham, Dio. Carl. 1864. (Patron, Sir Richard Tufton, Bart; Tithe, 91*l* 5*s*; Glebe, 185 acres; R.'s Inc. 366*l* and Ho; Pop. 227.) Formerly Chap. of Shire Oaks Chapel, Notts, 1837–64; V. of Elmton, Derbyshire, 1843–64. [23]

SALMON, Edwin Arthur, *Martock Vicarage, Somerset.*—Wad. Coll. Ox. B.A. 1853, M.A. 1856; Deac.

1854 by Bp of G. and B. Pr. 1855 by Bp of B. and W. V. of Martock with Long Load C. Dio. B. and W. 1859. (Patron, Treasurer of Wells Cathl; Tithe, 316*l*; Glebe, 81 acres, 141*l*; V.'s Inc. 457*l* and Ho; Pop. 2650.) Surrogate; Rural Dean. Formerly C. of Christian Malford, Wilts, 1854–59. [1]

SALMON, Frederick Thomas, *Maiden Newton, Dorchester.*—C. of Maiden Newton. Formerly C. of Bradford Abbas, Dorset. [2]

SALMON, George, *Shustock Vicarage, Coleshill, Warwickshire.*—Clare Coll. Cam. B.A. 1813, M.A. 1816. V. of Shustock with Bentley C. Dio. Wor. 1831. (Patron, Ld Chan; Shustock, Tithe—Imp. 408*l*, V. 244*l* 10*s*; Glebe, 24 acres; V.'s Inc. 263*l* and Ho; Pop. Shustock 325, Bentley 233.) [3]

SALMON, Gordon, *Nun Monkton, York.*—Dur. Licen. in Theol; Deac. 1856 by Bp of Man. Pr. 1857 by Bp of Dur. V. of Nun Monkton, Dio. Rip. 1865. (Patron, Isaac Crawhall, Esq; V.'s Inc. 100*l* and Ho; Pop. 323.) Formerly C. of Norham 1856, Croft 1859. [4]

SALMON, Henry, *Swarraton Rectory, Alresford, Hants.*—Emman. Coll. Cam. B.A. 1822, M.A. 1825; Deac. 1822 and Pr. 1823 by Bp of Win. R. of Swarraton, 1831, with Northington C. annexed, 1847, Dio. Win. (Patron, Lord Ashburton; Tithe, 112*l*; Glebe, 15 acres; R.'s Inc. 152*l* and Ho; Pop. Swarraton 100, Northington 283.) Formerly V. of Hartley, Wintney, Hants. [5]

SALMON, Henry Thomas, *Milford Parsonage, Godalming.*—Ex. Coll. Ox. B.A. 1848, M.A. 1851; Deac. 1849 and Pr. 1850 by Bp of Nor. P. C. of Milford, Dio. Win. 1865. (Patron, Rev. J. Chandler; Tithe, 97*l* 16*s*; P. C.'s Inc. 97*l* 16*s* and Ho; Pop. 838.) Formerly C. of Barwell, Leic. [6]

SALMON, Henry Wilson, *Oldberrow Rectory, Henley-in-Arden, Worcestershire.*—St. John's Coll. Cam. B.A. 1812, M.A. 1815; Deac. 1813, Pr. 1814. R. of Oldberrow, Dio. Wor. 1859. (Patron, Rev. S. Peshall; Tithe, 208*l*; Glebe, 12 acres; R.'s Inc. 230*l* and Ho; Pop. 52.) Formerly C. of Long Compton, Warwickshire. [7]

SALMON, Robert Ingham.—C. of St. Michael's, Paddington, Lond. [8]

SALT, Francis Gardner, *Bishopswood Parsonage, Penkridge, Staffs.*—St. John's Coll. Cam. B.A. 1852; Deac. 1853, Pr. 1854. P. C. of Bishopswood, Dio. Lich. 1867. (Patron, V. of Brewood; P. C.'s Inc. 80*l* and Ho; Pop. 588.) Formerly C. of Heydon, Norfolk, Southtown, Suffolk, and Harleston, Norfolk. [9]

SALT, George, *Stoke-Gifford, near Bristol.*—Ch. Ch. Ox. B.A. 1821, M.A. 1824; Deac. 1822, Pr. 1823. V. of Stoke-Gifford, Dio. G. and B. 1859. (Patron, Duke of Beaufort; Tithe—Imp. 390*l*, V. 23*l* 6*s*; V.'s Inc. 60*l*; Pop. 445.) Formerly V. of St. George, Glouc. 1842–57. [10]

SALT, George, *St. Bridget's Rectory, Chester.*—Trin. Coll. Cam. B.A. 1850, M.A. 1854; Deac. 1850 and Pr. 1851 by Bp of Ches. R. of St. Bridget's with St. Martin's, City and Dio. Ches. 1855. (Patron, Bp of Ches; Tithe, 39*l*; Glebe, 49 acres; R.'s Inc. 140*l*; Pop. St. Bridget's 1040, St. Martin's 694.) Dioc. Organising Sec. for the National Soc; Surrogate. [11]

SALT, G. C., *Temple, Bristol.*—C. of Temple. [12]

SALT, Samuel, *Dresden, Stoke-on-Trent.*—Literate; Deac. 1863 and Pr. 1864 by Bp of Lich. P. C. of Dresden, Dio Lich. 1867. (Patron, P. C. of Blurton; P. C.'s Inc. 29*l*.) Formerly C. of Blurton, Staffs, 1863–66. [13]

SALT, Thomas Fosbrooke, *Bolton-le-Moors.*—Oriel Coll. Ox. 2nd cl. Lit. Hum. 1864, B.A. 1865; Deac. 1865 by Bp of Ches. for Bp of Lich. Pr. 1866 by Bp of Man. C. of St. Paul's, Bolton, 1866. Formerly C. of Buxton 1865. [14]

SALTER, David Mede, *South Fambridge, Rochford, Essex.*—R. of South Fambridge, Dio. Roch. 1865. (Patron, E. Stephenson, Esq; R.'s Inc. 480*l*; Pop. 104.) [15]

SALTER, Frederick, *Hethe Rectory, Bicester.*—Ex. Coll. Ox. B.A. 1835, M.A. 1866; Deac. 1836, Pr. 1837. R. of Hethe, Dio. Ox. 1854. (Patron, Ld Chan; Glebe, 167 acres; R.'s Inc. 198*l* and Ho; Pop. 442.) Surrogate. [16]

SALTER, John, *Iron Acton, near Bristol.*—Ch. Ch. Ox. B.A. 1814, M.A. 1817; Deac. 1819 and Pr. 1820 by Bp of Ox. R. of Iron Acton. (Patrons, D. and C. of Ch. Ch. Ox; Tithe, 714*l*; Glebe, 60 acres; R.'s Inc. 780*l* and Ho; Pop. 1250.) Hon. Can. of Bristol. [17]

SALTER, William Charles, *St. Alban's Hall, Oxford.*—Ball. Coll. Ox. Fell. of, B.A. 1846, M.A. 1851; Deac. 1849 and Pr. 1860 by Bp of Ox. Prin. of St. Alban's Hall, Ox. 1861; R. of Brattleby, Dio. Lin. 1861. (Patron, Ball. Coll; R.'s Inc. 260*l*; Pop 153.) [18]

SALTHOUSE, Robert, 89, *Roscommon-street, Everton, Liverpool.*—St. Bees; Deac. 1865 and Pr. 1866 by Bp of Ches. C. of All Saints', Liverpool, 1865. [19]

SALTS, Alfred, *Rochdale.*—St. John's Coll. Cam. 2nd cl. Moral Sci. Trip. B.A. 1859, LL.M. 1863; Deac. 1862 and Pr. 1863 by Bp of Rip. C. of Rochdale 1865. Formerly C. of St. Jude's and St. John's, Leeds, 1862–63; Dent (sole charge) 1864. [19]

SALUSBURY, Augustus Pemberton, *Netley, Eling, Southampton.*—Ex. Coll. Ox. B.A. 1849, M.A. 1853; Deac. 1849 and Pr. 1850 by Bp of Lich. P. C. of Netley, Dio. Win. 1854. (Patroness, Miss Sturges Bourne; P. C.'s Inc. 125*l* and Ho; Pop. 1061.) Formerly C. of Trinity, Burton-on-Trent, 1849–52; P. C. of St. Paul's, Halliwell, Lanc. 1852–54. [20]

SALUSBURY, Sir Charles, Bart., *Caerleon, Monmouthshire.*—Deac. 1812, Pr. 1813. R. of Llanwern, Monmouthshire, Dio. Llan. 1816. (Patron, the present R; Tithe, 84*l* 3*s* 9*d*; Glebe, 16½ acres; R.'s Inc. 106*l*; Pop. 15.) [21]

SALUSBURY, C. T., *Chiseldon, Swindon, Wilts.*—C. of Chiseldon. [22]

SALUSBURY, George Augustus, *Westbury Rectory, Shrewsbury.*—Magd. Coll. Cam. LL.B. 1849; Deac. 1849 and Pr. 1850 by Bp of Ches. R. of Westbury-in-Dextra-Parte, Dio. Herf. 1852. (Patron, E. W. S. Owen, Esq; Tithe—Imp. 404*l* 8*s* 6*d*, R. of Sinistra-Parte, 649*l* 10*s* 8*d*, R. of Dextra-Parte, 674*l* 10*s* 8*d*; Glebe, 20 acres; R.'s Inc. 738*l* and Ho; Pop. 1652.) Formerly C. of Westbury-in-Sinistra-Parte. [23]

SALUSBURY, Thelwall, *Offley Vicarage, Hitchin, Herts.*—Trin. Hall, Cam. LL.B. 1791. V. of Offley, Dio. Roch. (Patroness, Lady Salusbury; Tithe, 2*l* 10*s*; V.'s Inc. 300*l* and Ho; Pop. 1215.) [24]

SALVIN, Joseph, *Castlegate Rectory, York.*—Deac. and Pr. 1828 by Abp of York. R. of St. Mary's, Castlegate, York, Dio. York, 1831. (Patron, Ld Chan; R.'s Inc. 120*l* and Ho; Pop. 994.) [25]

SALWEY, Henry, *Church Mission House, London, E.C.*—Ch. Ch. Ox. Stud. of, B.A. 1859, M.A. 1862; Deac. 1860 by Bp of Ox. Pr. 1861 by Bp of Herf. Assoc. Sec. to the Ch. Miss. Soc. Formerly C. of Iron Bridge, Salop, 1860–62, Tidenham, Gloucestershire, 1862–63, St. Saviour's, Upper Chelsea, 1864–66. [26]

SALWEY, John, *The Vicarage, Ewell, Surrey.*—Trin. Coll. Cam. B.A. 1859, M.A. 1863; Deac. 1861 by Bp of Ches. Pr. 1862 by Bp of Herf. C. of Ewell 1866. Formerly C. of Hope-under-Dinmore 1861, St. James's, Bath, 1863. [27]

SALWEY, Richard, *Ash Rectory, Sevenoaks, Kent.*—Ch. Ch. Ox. B.A. 1824; Deac. 1825, Pr. 1826. R. of Fawkham, Kent, Dio. Roch. 1829. (Patrons, Philip Pusey and C. Adams, Esqrs; Tithe, 264*l* 10*s*; Glebe, 1½ acres; R.'s Inc. 266*l* and Ho; Pop. 233.) R. of Ash, Dio. Roch. 1841. (Patron, Malton Lambarde, Esq; R.'s Inc. 650*l* and Ho; Pop. 587.) [28]

SALWEY, Thomas, *Shanklin, Isle of Wight.*—St. John's Coll. Cam. 1810, Sen. Opt. and B.A. 1815, M.A. 1818, B.D. 1827; Deac. 1815, Pr. 1816. V. of Oswestry, Dio. St. A. 1823. (Patron, Earl Powis; Tithe, App. 94*l* 14*s*, Imp. 2058*l* 1*s* 6*d*, V. 327*l* 3*s* 8*d*; Glebe, 50 acres; V.'s Inc. 480*l*; Pop. 4468.) Sinecure R. of St. Florence, Pembrokeshire, Dio. St. D. 1828. (Patron, St John's Coll. Cam; Tithe—V. 80*l* and 10 acres of Glebe; Sinecure R. 160*l*; Glebe, 20 acres; Sinecure R.'s Inc. 198*l*.) Formerly Fell. of St. John's Coll. Cam.

1817–23. Author, *Sermon on the Duties of the Christian Magistrate*, 1825; *Duties and Privileges of Baptism*, 1830, 4*d*; *Gospel Hymns*, 1847, 4*s* 6*d*. [1]

SAMBORNE, Richard Lane Palmer, *Ashreigney Rectory, Chumleigh, Devon.*—Ball. Coll. Ox. B A. 1850, M.A. 1854; Deac. 1851 and Pr. 1852 by Bp of Salis. R. of Ashreigney, Dio. Ex. 1855. (Patron, Rev. J. T. Johnson; Tithe, 460*l*; Glebe, 70 acres; R.'s Inc. 530*l* and Ho; Pop. 842.) [2]

SAMLER, John Harman, *Swallowcliffe Vicarage, Salisbury.*—Pemb. Coll. Ox. B.A. 1833, M.A. 1837; Deac. 1833 by Bp of B. and W. Pr. 1835 by Bp of Bristol. P. C. of Swallowcliffe, Dio. Salis. 1846. (Patron, Bp of Salis; Tithe—App. 301*l*, P. C. 74*l*; Glebe, 2 acres 5 perches; P. C.'s Inc. 80*l* and Ho; Pop. 317.) P. C. of Anstey, Dio. Salis. 1846. (Patron, Lord Arundel; Tithe, 20*l* 16*s*; P. C.'s Inc. 22*l*; Pop. 298.) Formerly C. of Ashmore, Dorset, 1834–39. [3]

SAMMONS, John Coulson, *Kilvington, Elton, Notts.*—St. John's Coll. Cam. B.A. 1848, M.A. 1851; Deac. 1848 and Pr. 1850 by Bp of Nor. R. of Kilvington, Dio. Lin. 1858. (Patron, J. Lambert, Esq; R.'s Inc. 245*l* and Ho; Pop. 45.) P. C. of Cotham, Notts, Dio. Lin. 1865. (Patron, Duke of Portland; P. C.'s Inc. 40*l*; Pop. 100.) [4]

SAMPSON, Daniel Dod, *Kingston, Caxton, Cambs.*—Trin. Hall, Cam. B.A. 1830, M.A. 1834; Deac. 1831, Pr. 1832. R. of Kingston, Dio. Ely, 1837. (Patron, King's Coll. Cam; R.'s Inc. 430*l*; Pop. 313.) [5]

SAMPSON, Henry, *Cudham, Bromley, Kent.*—Trin. Hall, Cam. LL.B. 1814. V. of Cudham, Dio. Cant. 1830. (Patron, Ld Chan: Tithe—Imp. 665*l*, V. 306*l* 8*s* 9*d*; V.'s Inc. 336*l*; Pop. 988.) [6]

SAMPSON, John Edward, *York.*—Literate; Deac. 1852 and Pr. 1853 by Bp of Rip. P. C. of St. Thomas's, City and Dio. York, 1857. (Patron, Abp of York; Endow. 30*l*, Pew-rents, 120*l*; P. C.'s Inc. 150*l*; Pop. 3669.) Author, *Happy Hours with the Church Catechism*, 4*d*; *An Infant's Death*, Macintosh, 1*d*. [7]

SAMPSON, Lewis William, *Prescot, Lancashire.*—King's Coll. Cam. 1826, B.A. 1830, M.A. 1833; Deac. 1831, Pr. 1833. V. of Prescot, Dio. Ches. 1849. (Patron, King's Coll. Cam; Tithe—App 2*l*, V. 13*s*; Glebe, 3 acres; V.'s Inc. 1152*l* and Ho; Pop. 7773.) Surrogate. Formerly Fell. of King's Coll. Cam. 1829. [8]

SAMPSON, Richard King, *Pevensey, Eastbourne, Sussex.*—Jesus Coll. Cam. B.A. 1828; Deac. 1828 and Pr. 1830 by Bp of Chich. Formerly C. of Pevensey. [9]

SAMPSON, Samuel, 44, *Mount-pleasant, Liverpool.*—St. Aidan's; Deac. 1854 and Pr. 1855 by Bp of Ches. P. C. of St. Timothy's, Walton-on-the-Hill, Dio. Ches. 1862. Formerly C. of St. Augustine's, Everton. [10]

SAMS, Barwick John, *Grafton-Regis Rectory, Stony-Stratford.*—Ch. Coll. Cam. B.A. 1824, M.A. 1828; Deac. 1827, Pr. 1828. R. of Alderton with Grafton-Regis, Dio. Pet. 1837. (Patron, Ld Chan; Tithe, 70*l*; Glebe, 120 acres; R.'s Inc. 277*l* and Ho; Pop. Alderton 131, Grafton-Regis 232.) [11]

SAMUEL, John, *Heythrop, Chipping-Norton.*—Jesus Coll. Ox. B.A. 1831; Deac. 1837 by Bp of Salis. Pr. 1839 by Bp of Ox. R. of Heythrop, Dio. Ox. 1845. (Patron, Earl of Shrewsbury; Tithe, 150*l*; R.'s Inc. 160*l*; Pop. 122.) Chap. to Viscount Dillon 1843; Chap. to Chipping-Norton Union. [12]

SANCTUARY, The Ven. Thomas, *Powerstock, Bridport.*—Ex. Coll. Ox. B.A. 1844, M.A. 1846; Deac. 1845 and Pr. 1846 by Bp of Ox. V. of Powerstock with West Milton C. Dio. Salis. 1848. (Patrons, D. and C. of Salis; Tithe—App. 313*l* and 70 acres of Glebe, V. 230*l*; V.'s Inc. 230*l*; Pop. 1025.) R. of North Poorton, Dio. Salis. 1852. (Patroness, Mrs. Jenkyns; Tithe, 79*l*; Glebe, 1 acre; R.'s Inc. 83*l*; Pop. 92.) Archd. of Dorset; Rural Dean 1854. Formerly Archidiaconal Sec. to the S.P.G. [13]

SANDBERG, Paul Lewis, *St. John's Parsonage, Birkenhead.*—Ch. Coll. Cam. Tyrrwhitt Univ. Scho. B.A. 1850, M.A. 1859; Deac. 1842 and Pr. 1843 by Bp of Lon. P. C. of St. John's, Birkenhead, Dio. Ches. 1860. (Patrons, Trustees; P. C.'s Inc. 165*l* and Ho; Pop. 5573.) Formerly P. C. of Kimberworth 1852. Author, *God's Way with Man in the Olden Time, or Gospel Teaching of the Book of Genesis*, Birkenhead, 3*s* 6*d*. [14]

SANDBURN, H. R. P., *Privy Council Office, Downing-street, Westminster, S.W.*—Asst. Inspector of Schs. [15]

SANDERS, Francis G., 2, *Lansdowne-terrace, Brixton, S.*—St. John's Coll. Cam. B.A. 1860, M.A. 1864; Deac. 1861 and Pr. 1862 by Bp of Ches. Sen. C. of St. Matthew's, Brixton, Surrey, 1864. Formerly C. of Ch. Ch. Southport, Lancashire, 1861–64. [16]

SANDERS, Henry, *Sowton Rectory, Exeter.*—Ch. Ch. Ox. Stud. of, 2nd cl. Lit. Hum. and B.A. 1828, M.A. 1830; Deac. 1830 and Pr. 1831 by Bp of Ox. R. of Sowton, Dio. Ex. 1847. (Patron, Bp of Ex; Tithe, 268*l* 10*s*; Glebe, 18 acres; R.'s Inc. 300*l* and Ho; Pop. 362.) Rural Dean of Aylesbeare 1851; Preb. of Ex. 1867. Formerly Head Mast. of Blundell's Sch. Tiverton, 1834–47. [17]

SANDERS, Henry Martyn, *Skidby Parsonage, Beverley, Yorks.*—Emman. Coll. Cam. Sen. Opt. B.A. 1855, M.A. 1858; Deac. 1856 and Pr. 1857 by Abp of Cant. P. C. of Skidby, Dio. York, 1860. (Patron, V. of Cottingham; P. C.'s Inc. 105*l* and Ho; Pop. 364.) Formerly C. of Bexley, Kent, 1856–57. [18]

SANDERS, James, *Ripponden Parsonage, Halifax.*—Queens' Coll. Cam. B.A. 1830, M.A. 1839; Deac. 1830 and Pr. 1831 by Abp of Cant. P. C. of Ripponden, Dio. Rip. 1847. (Patron, V. of Halifax; P. C.'s Inc. 174*l* and Ho.) Surrogate. Author, *The Influence of the Holy Spirit* (a Sermon); *The Errors of Unitarianism* (a Pamphlet); *The Death of Queen Adelaide, of Blessed Memory* (a Sermon), 1849; various other Sermons and Pamphlets. [19]

SANDERS, Lewis, *Wythop, Cockermouth.*—C. of Wythop, Cumberland. [20]

SANDERS, Lloyd, *Whimple Rectory, Exeter.*—Ch. Ch. Ox. B.A. 1837, M.A. 1843; Deac. 1838 by Bp of Salis. Pr. 1839 by Bp of Ex. R. of Whimple, Dio. Ex. 1843. (Patroness, Mrs. Sanders; Tithe, 335*l*; Glebe, 67 acres; R.'s Inc. 440*l*; Pop. 736.) [21]

SANDERS, Robert, *Cropthorne, Pershore, Worcestershire.*—Magd. Hall, Ox. B.A. 1825, M.A. 1826. V. of Cropthorne, Dio. Wor. 1853. (Patrons, D. and C. of Wor; Tithe, App. 136*l* 12*s*, V. 84*l* 8*s* 2*d*; V.'s Inc. 85*l*; Pop. 839.) Min. Can. of Wor. 1825. [22]

SANDERS, Thomas, *Moulton Vicarage, near Northampton.*—Pemb. Coll. Cam. Sen. Opt. B.A. 1827; Deac. 1827, Pr. 1828. V. of Moulton, Dio. Pet. 1838. (Patron, E. S. Burton, Esq; Tithe, 3*l* 18*s* 4*d*; Glebe, 188 acres; V.'s Inc. 420*l* and Ho; Pop. 1840.) [23]

SANDERS, T., *Coventry.*—Chap. of the Gaol, Coventry. [24]

SANDERS, William, *The Grammar School, Woodstock, Oxon.*—Magd. Coll. Ox. B.A. 1856, M.A. 1857, M.A. Ch. Ch. (non-foundation) 1862; Deac. 1857 and Pr. 1858 by Bp of Ox. Mast. of the Gr. Sch. Woodstock; Chap. to the Woodstock Union. Formerly Chorister, etc. of Magd. Coll. Ox. 1846–58; Chap. of Ch. Ch. Oxford, 1857–62; C. of Bletchingdon, Oxon. 1860–67. Author, numerous articles in *Temple Bar*, *Argosy*, *All the Year Round*; etc. [25]

SANDERS, William Frederick, *Newhaven, Sussex.*—St. John's Coll. Cam. Scho. of, Prizeman, Sen. Opt. and B.A. 1833; Deac. 1835 and Pr. 1836 by Bp of Lich. R. of Tarring Neville with South Heighton, Dio. Chich. 1866. (Patroness, Mrs. Fothergill; Glebe, 16 acres; R.'s Inc. 406*l* 10*s* and Ho; Pop. Tarring Neville 84, South Heighton 104.) Formerly V. of Watford, Northants, 1854–66.) [26]

SANDERS, William Skipsey, *Trinity Parsonage, Gosport.*—Ex. Coll. Ox. 2nd cl. Lit. Hum. and B.A. 1846, M.A. 1849; Deac. 1848 and Pr. 1849 by Bp of Ox. P. C. of Trinity, Gosport, Dio. Win. 1859. (Patron, R. of Alverstoke, Hants; P.C.'s Inc. 240*l* and Ho; Pop. 3432.) Formerly C. of Finstock, Oxon. 1848–50, Faringdon, Berks, 1850-52, Adderbury, Oxon. 1852-58, St. Botolph's, Bishopsgate, Lond. 1858-59. [1]

SANDERSON, Alfred Poyntz, *Aspenden Rectory, Buntingford, Herts.*—Jesus Coll. Cam. Coll. Scho. and Prizeman of, B.A. 1847, M.A. 1850; Deac. 1850 and Pr. 1851 by Bp of Ely. R. of Aspenden, Dio. Roch. 1856. (Patroness, Countess of Mexborough; Tithe, comm. 408*l*; Glebe, 22 acres; R.'s Inc. 428*l* and Ho; Pop. 577.) Dioc. Inspector of Schs. Formerly C. of Aspenden. [2]

SANDERSON, Edgar.—Formerly C. of Melcombe Regis, and 2nd Mast. of the Gr. Sch. Weymouth. [3]

SANDERSON, Edward, *Acton, London, W.*—C. of Acton, Middlesex. [4]

SANDERSON, Edward Swinden, *Grammar School, Retford, Notts.*—Corpus Coll. Cam. Sen. Opt. 1st in 2nd cl. Cl. Trip. and B.A. 1854, M.A. 1859; Deac. 1856 by Bp of Man, Pr. 1859 by Bp of Wor. Head Mast. of Retford Gr. Sch. 1866; Chap. to the East Retford Union. Formerly Head Mast. of Atherstone Gr. Sch. 1857-64. [5]

SANDERSON, Lancelot, *Harrow School, Middlesex, N.W.*—Clare Coll. Cam. 2nd in 2nd cl. Cl. B.A. 1861; Deac. 1862 and Pr. 1864 by Bp of Ex. Asst. Cl. Mast. of Harrow Sch. Formerly C. of St. Mary Magdalen's, Torquay, 1862-64. [6]

SANDERSON, Robert Edward, *Lancing College, near New Shoreham, Sussex.*—Lin. Coll. Ox. 2nd cl. Lit. Hum. and B.A. 1850, M.A. 1853; Deac. 1851 and Pr. 1857 by Bp of Ox. Head Mast. of St. Mary and St. Nicolas' Sch. Lancing. Formerly C. of St. Mary's, Oxford, 1851; Head Mast. of St. Andrew's Coll. Bradfield, 1851-59. [7]

SANDERSON, Robert Nicholas, 2, *Arboretum-terrace, Ipswich.*—Magd. Hall, Ox. B.A. 1857, M.A.; Deac. 1857, Pr. 1858. Asst. Mast. of Ipswich Gr. Sch. Formerly C. of St. Mary Elms, Ipswich. [8]

SANDERSON, Thomas, *Wellingborough, Northants.*—Magd. Hall, Ox. B.A. 1825, M.A. 1830, D.D. 1852; Deac. 1825, Pr. 1826. V. of Great Doddington, Dio. Pet. 1851. (Patron, Ld Chan; Glebe, 105 acres; V.'s Inc. 165*l*; Pop. 580.) Formerly Head Mast. of the Wellingborough Gr. Sch. 1825. Author, *A Sermon on Occasion of a General Election,* 1835. [9]

SANDFORD, Charles Waldegrave, *Christ Church, Oxford.*—Ch. Ch. Ox. 1st cl. Lit. Hum. and B.A. 1851, M.A. 1853; Deac. 1855 and Pr. 1856 by Bp of Ox. Chap. to Bp of Lon; Sen. Censor of Ch. Ch. Ox. Whitehall Preacher 1862-64. [10]

SANDFORD, Edward, *Elland Parsonage, Halifax.*—St. Bees; Deac. 1845 and Pr. 1846 by Bp of Lich. P. C. of Elland, Dio. Rip. 1853. (Patron, V. of Halifax; P. C.'s Inc. 310*l* and Ho; Pop. 8000.) Surrogate. Formerly P. C. of Bicton, Shrewsbury, 1851-53. [11]

SANDFORD, E. G., *Alvechurch, Birmingham.*—C. of Alvechurch, Worcestershire. [12]

SANDFORD, George, *Eldon Parsonage, Chantrey-road, Sheffield.*—Magd. Coll. Cam. 1837, Jun. Opt. 2nd cl. Cl. Trip. and B.A. 1840, M.A. 1843; Deac. 1840, Pr. 1841. P. C. of St. Jude's, Eldon, Sheffield, Dio. York, 1846. (Patrons, the Crown and Abp of York alt; P. C.'s Inc. 305*l* and Ho; Pop. 6030.) Chap. to the Sheffield Cemetery 1850. [13]

SANDFORD, Henry Ryder Poole, *Privy Council Office, Downing-street, London, S.W.*—Magd. Hall, Ox. B.A. 1849, M.A. 1852. One of H.M. Inspectors of Schs. [14]

SANDFORD, Holland, *Eaton Vicarage, Church Stretton, Salop.*—St. John's Coll. Cam. B.A. 1847, M.A. 1850; Deac. 1852 and Pr. 1853 by Bp of Lich. V. of Eaton, Dio. Herf. 1860. (Patron, Humphrey Stretton, Esq; Tithe, comm. 192*l*; Glebe, 147 acres with rent of 179*l*; V.'s Inc. 371*l* and Ho; Pop. 580.) Formerly C. of Prees, Salop, 1852-58; 2nd Mast. of the Free Gr. Sch. Whitchurch, 1847-58; C. of Ripponden 1859. [15]

SANDFORD, The Ven. John, *Alvechurch Rectory, Bromsgrove.*—Ball. Coll. Ox. 1st cl. Lit. Hum. and B.A. 1824, M.A. 1838, B.D. 1840; Deac. 1824 by Bp of Lich. Pr. 1826 by Bp of B. and W. Archd. of Coventry 1851. (Value, 200*l*.) Hon. Can. of Wor. 1844; R. of Alvechurch, Dio. Wor. 1854. (Patron, Bp of Wor; Tithe, 1083*l* 11*s*; Glebe, 92 acres; R.'s Inc. 1200*l* and Ho; Pop. 1581.) Exam. Chap. to the Bp of Wor. 1853; Bampton Lect. 1861; Member of Royal Commission on Clerical Subscription 1864. Author, *Remains of Bishop Sandford,* 2 vols. 21*s*; *Parochialia, or Church, School, and Parish,* 16*s*; *Vox Cordis* (a Manual of Devotions), 2*s* 6*d*; *Charges in* 1852, '53, '56, '58, '60, '62, '63, '64, '66, *and* '67; *Bampton Lectures,* 1861; *The Mission and Extension of the Church at Home;* Visitation and other Sermons, Lectures, Speeches. [16]

SANDFORD, William, *The Rectory, Crook, Darlington.*—St. Bees 1831; Deac. 1831, Pr. 1832. R. of Crook, Dio. Dur. 1850. (Patron, R. of Brancepeth; R.'s Inc. 300*l* and Ho; Pop. 10,000.) [17]

SANDFORD, William, *Kingswood Parsonage, Bristol.*—Clare Hall, Cam. B.A. 1844; Deac. 1844, Pr. 1845. P. C. of Kingswood, Dio. G. and B. 1854. (Patron, Bp of G. and B; P. C.'s Inc. 300*l* and Ho; Pop. 4699.) [18]

SANDFORD, William, *Bicton, Shrewsbury.*—St. John's Coll. Cam. B.A. 1851, M.A. 1854; Deac. 1851 and Pr. 1852 by Bp of Lich. P. C. of Bicton, Dio. Lich. 1853. (Patron, V. of St. Chad's; P. C.'s Inc. 140*l*; Pop. 569.) Formerly C. of Colwich 1851-53. [19]

SANDHAM, Henry Mullins, 27, *Hans-place, Sloane-street, London, S.W.*—St. John's Coll. Ox. B.A. 1845, M.A. 1847. P. C. of St. John's Chapel, Marylebone, Dio. Lon. 1855. (Patron, the Crown; P. C.'s Inc. 250*l* and Ho.) [20]

SANDHAM, J. M., *Waltham Parsonage, Petworth, Sussex.*—P. C. of Cold Waltham, Dio. Chich. 1846. (Patron, Bp of Chich; P. C.'s Inc. 56*l* and Ho; Pop. 447.) R. of Hardham, Dio. Chich. 1846. (Patron, Bp of Chich; V.'s Inc. 70*l*; Pop. 87.) [21]

SANDILANDS, Percival Richard Renorden, *Denford Vicarage, Thrapston, Northants.*—Jesus Coll. Cam. B.A. 1848, M.A. 1851; Deac. 1849 by Bp of B. and W. Pr. 1851 by Bp of Ex. V. of Denford with Ringstead V. Dio. Pet. 1863. (Patroness, Miss Leggatt; Tithe, 145*l*; Glebe, 85 acres; V.'s Inc. 230*l* and Ho; Pop. Denford 420, Ringstead 835.) Chap. of Thrapston Union 1866. Formerly 2nd Mast. of Crewkerne Gr. Sch. 1848-50; C. of Chaffcombe, Somerset, 1849-50, Seavington St. Mary, Somerset, 1851-53; Cl. Mast. Cheltenham Coll. 1853-63. [22]

SANDLANDS, John Poole, *Paxton Cottage, Northwood, Hanley, Staffs.*—Theol. Coll. Lichfield; Deac. 1866 and Pr. 1867 by Bp of Lich. C. of Hanley 1867. Formerly C. of Wellington, Staffs, 1866.' [23]

SANDS, Henry Bethune, *Northwood, Rickmansworth.*—Trin. Coll. Cam. B.A. 1845, M.A. 1849; Deac. 1848 by Abp of York, Pr. 1849 by Bp of Ely. P. C. of Northwood, Middlesex, Dio. Lon. 1854. (Patron, Lord Ebury; Glebe, 2¼ acres; P. C.'s Inc. 125*l*; Pop. 451.) Formerly C. of Ingleby, Yorks, 1848-49; Chap. of Trin. Coll. Cam. 1849-52; C. of Kilmington, Devon, 1849-52. [24]

SANDWITH, Henry, *Todwick, near Rotherham.*—St. Cath. Coll. Cam. B.A. 1851; Deac. 1852 by Abp of York, Pr. 1853 by Bp of Ox. R. of Todwick, Dio. York, 1866. (Patroness, Miss Fox; Tithe, 75*l*; Glebe, 68 acres; R.'s Inc. 163*l* and Ho; Pop. 187.) Formerly C. of Adlingfleet 1852, Cholesbury 1853, Harthill 1855; P. C. of Norley 1859; C. of Cawthorne 1862. [25]

SANDYS, John, *Rockland St. Mary Rectory, Norwich.*—Queens' Coll. Cam. 18th Wrang. B.A. 1823, M.A. 1826; Deac. 1823 by Bp of Ely, Pr. 1824 by Bp of Lin. R. of Rockland St. Mary, Dio. Nor. 1865. (Patron, Queens' Coll. Cam; Tithe, 412*l* 1*s*; Glebe, 32 acres; R.'s Inc. 444*l* and Ho; Pop. 480.) Formerly Fell. of Queens' Coll. Cam; P. C. of St. Paul's, Islington, 1828-61; R. of Pakefield, Suffolk, 1861-65. Author, *What is the true Sense of the Baptismal Service?* 2nd ed. 1*s*. [26]

SANDYS, Joseph Samuel, *Tydd St. Giles's, Wisbech.*—Corpus Coll. Cam. Scho. of, B.A. 1859; Deac. 1861 and Pr. 1862 by Bp of Pet. C. of Tydd St. Giles's 1867. Formerly C. of St. Mary's, Peterborough,

1861–63, Horsford and Horsham St. Faith's, Norwich, 1863–67; Asst. Chap. of Peterborough Union and St. Faith's Union. [1]

SANDYS, William Travis, *Burton Coggles Rectory, Colsterworth, Lincolnshire.*—Pemb. Coll. Cam. B.A. 1824, M.A. 1827. R. of Burton Coggles, Dio. Lin. 1856. (Patron, Ld Chan; Tithe, 552*l* 14*s*; Glebe, 104 acres; R.'s Inc. 650*l* and Ho; Pop. 288.) [2]

SANFORD, Edward Ayshford, *Combe Florey Rectory, Taunton.*—Trin. Coll. Cam. B.A. 1842, M.A. 1845. R. of Combe Florey, Dio. B. and W. 1851. (Patron, Ld Chan; Tithe—Imp. 44*l* 1*s* 3*d*, R. 230*l*; Glebe, 70½ acres; R.'s Inc. 370*l* and Ho; Pop. 383.) [3]

SANFORD, George William, *Weddington Rectory, Nuneaton, Warwickshire.*—Trin. Coll. Cam. B.A. 1828, M.A. 1831; Deac. 1829, Pr. 1830. R. of Weddington, Dio. Wor. 1834. (Patron, Rev. B. H. Hall; Tithe, 176*l* 19*s*; Glebe, 45 acres; R.'s Inc. 300*l* and Ho; Pop. 74.) Formerly C. of Caldecote. [4]

SANGAR, Benjamin Cox, *Hythe, Kent.*—Dub. A.B. 1838, A.M. 1841, *ad eund.* Ox. 1842; Deac. 1839, Pr. 1840. P. C. of Hythe, Dio. Cant. 1862. (Patron, R. of Saltwood; P. C.'s Inc. 175*l*; Pop. 2871.) Formerly R. of St. Paul's, Shadwell, Lond. 1846. [5]

SANGAR, James Mortimer, *Swansea.*—C. of Swansea. [6]

SANGER, George, *Carlton-in-Cleveland, Northallerton, Yorks.*—St. Aidan's; Deac. 1862 and Pr. 1863 by Bp of Dur. P. C. of Carlton, Dio. York, 1866. (Patron, J. R. Reeve, Esq; Tithe, 4*l* 16*s*; Glebe, 18 acres; P. C.'s Inc. 82*l* and Ho; Pop. 242.) Formerly C. of Low Town and of Ch. Ch. Tynemouth, and Stokesley, Yorks. [7]

SANGSTER, Charles, *Darton Vicarage, Barnsley.*—St. John's Coll. Cam. Chancellor's English Medallist 1839; Browne's Medallist for Greek and Latin Epigrams 1840, 20th Wrang. 6th in 2nd cl. Cl. Trip and B.A. 1841, M.A. 1845; Deac. 1844 and Pr. 1845 by Bp of Rip. V. of Darton, Dio. Rip. 1855. (Patron, W. B. Beaumont, Esq; Tithe—Imp. 78*l* 1*s* 1*d*, V. 70*l*; Glebe, 80 acres; V.'s Inc. 210*l* and Ho; Pop. 3171.) Rural Dean of Silkstone 1855. Formerly C. of High Hoyland, 1844. Author, *Servants' Claim upon the Christian Master*, 1*s*. [8]

SANKEY, John, *Stony-Stanton Rectory, Hinckley, Leicestershire.*—St. Edm. Hall, Ox. B.A. 1820, M.A. 1823; Deac. 1820 and Pr. 1821 by Bp of Lin. R. of Stony-Stanton, Dio. Pet. 1842. (Patron, T. Frewen, Esq; Glebe, 210 acres; R.'s Inc. 450*l* and Ho; Pop. 703.) Author, single Sermons. [9]

SANKEY, Philip Menzies, *Highclere Rectory, Newbury, Berks.*—Corpus Coll. Ox. B.A. 1852; Deac. 1853, Pr. 1854. R. of Highclere, Dio. Win. 1859. (Patron, Earl of Carnarvon; Tithe, 324*l* 3*s* 6*d*; Glebe, 85 acres; R.'s Inc. 425*l* and Ho; Pop. 446.) Formerly C. of St. Alphege with St. Mary Northgate, Canterbury; 3rd Mast. in the King's Sch. Canterbury. Author, *Catechetical and Devotional Manual*; *Catechism of Old Testament History.* [10]

SANKEY, Richard Boyer, 45, *Steep-hill, near Lincoln.*—Magd. Hall, Ox. Bachelor in Music 1859, B.A. and M.A. 1865; Deac. 1866 and Pr. 1867 by Bp of Lin. C. of Bracebridge 1866. Author, *Responses to the Commandments*, Metzler and Co. [11]

SANKEY, William Thompson, *Stony-Stratford Parsonage, Bucks.*—Ex. Coll. Ox. B.A. 1852, M.A. 1854; Deac. 1853 and Pr. 1855 by Bp of Roch. P. C. of Stony-Stratford, Dio. Ox. 1859. (Patron, Bp of Ox; P. C.'s Inc. 150*l* and Ho; Pop. 2005.) Formerly C. of St. Stephen's, near St. Albans. [12]

SANSOM, John, *Buslingthorpe, Market Rasen.*—Queen's Coll. Ox. B.A. 1836. R. of Buslingthorpe, Dio. Lin. 1855. (Patrons, Governors of the Charterhouse, Lond; Tithe, 235*l*; R.'s Inc. 250*l*; Pop. 55.) [13]

SAPTE, John Henry, *Cranley Rectory, near Guildford.*—Emman. Coll. Cam. B.A. 1845; Deac. 1845, Pr. 1846. R. of Cranley, Dio. Win. 1847. (Patron, the present R; Tithe, 1450*l*; R.'s Inc. 1450*l* and Ho; Pop. 1393.) [14]

SABEL, Henry Rule, *Balcombe Rectory, Cuckfield, Sussex.*—Trin. Coll. Cam. B.A. 1814, M.A. 1817; Deac. 1814, Pr. 1815. R. of Balcombe, Dio. Chich. 1819. (Patron, Rev. G. C. Bethune; Tithe, 450*l*; Glebe, 70 acres; R.'s Inc. 510*l* and Ho; Pop. 851.) Rural Dean. [15]

SARGEANT, William St. George, *Kimberley, Greasley, Nottingham.*—Dur. B.A. 1848. P. C. of Kimberley, Dio. Lin. 1852. (Patron, V. of Greasley; P. C.'s Inc. 70*l*; Pop. 2821.) Dom. Chap. to Lord Elibank. [16]

SARGENT, Henry John, *Bentinck House,* 32, *Belsize-park-road, London, N.W.*—Trin. Coll. Cam. B.A. 1858; Deac. 1858 and Pr. 1859 by Bp of Lon. C. of St. Peter's, Belsize-park, Hampstead, 1861; Aft. Lect. at St. John's, Fitzroy-square, 1865. Formerly C. of St. John's, Hampstead, Middlesex, 1858–61. [17]

SARGENT, John Paine, 7, *Edwards-terrace, Victoria-park, London, N.E.*—Dub. 1st cl. Cl. and A.B. 1825, A.M. 1832; Deac. 1830 by Bp of Down and Connor, Pr. 1831 by Bp of Win. C. and Min. of the Mission Church of St. Bartholomew, Bethnal-green. Author, a Series of Letters on the Study of the Hebrew Language in the *Clerical Journal*; *Dissertation on the Hebrew Words occurring in the New Testament*; several Introductory Works on the Hebrew, Greek, and Latin Languages. [18]

SARJANT, Samuel Crusha, *Holton House, Full-street, Derby.*—Univ. of Glasgow, B.A. 1852; Deac. 1859 and Pr. 1860 by Bp of Nor. Formerly C. of Halesworth with Chediston, Suffolk, 1859–63; St. Michael's and St. Andrew's, Derby, 1863–65. [19]

SATCHELL, William Fletcher, *Merston House School, Seaforth, Liverpool.*—Univ. Coll. Lond. LL.B; Deac. 1857 and Pr. 1858 by Bp of Ches. [20]

SATTERTHWAITE, Charles James, *Disley, Stockport.*—Jesus Coll. Cam. Wrang. B.A. 1857, M.A. 1860; Deac. 1858 and Pr. 1859 by Bp of Ches. P. C. of Disley, Dio. Ches. 1859. (Patron, W. J. Legh, Esq; P. C.'s Inc. 117*l*; Pop. 2265.) [21]

SAUL, Edward William, *Isle Abbotts, Taunton.*—Dub. A.B. 1847. V. of Isle Abbotts, Dio. B. and W. 1858. (Patrons, D. and C. of Bristol; Tithe—App. 210*l*; V.'s Inc. 75*l*; Pop. 397.) Formerly C. of St. Nicholas and St. Leonard's, Bristol. [22]

SAULEZ, Edmund C. P., *Tadley, Basingstoke, Hants.*—C. of Tadley. [23]

SAULEZ, George Alfred Frederick, *Exton Rectory, Bishops Waltham, Hants.*—Magd. Hall, Ox. B.A. 1841, M.A. 1862; Deac. 1840 and Pr. 1841 by Bp of Win. R. of Exton, Dio. Win. 1861. (Patron, Bp of Win; Tithe, 473*l*; Glebe, 9 acres; R.'s Inc. 473*l* and Ho; Pop. 257.) P. C. of Corhampton, Hants, Dio. Win. 1865. (Patron, J. Campbell Wyndham, Esq; Glebe, 70 acres; P. C.'s Inc. 243*l*; Pop. 189.) Formerly C. of St. John's, Newport, Isle of Wight, 1841, Herriard, Hants, 1842; Chap. East India Co. at Allahabad 1843, Nainee Tal 1846, Ghazeepore 1850; C. of Overton, Hants, 1852. Author, *Eight Sermons*, Calcutta, 1847; *Sympathy of Jesus*, Macintosh, 1867, 1*s*. [24]

SAULEZ, Theophilus, 3, *Richmond-villas, Islington, London, N.*—Deac. 1841, Pr. 1842. P. C. of All Saints', Islington, Dio. Lon. 1853. (Patron, P. C. of Trinity, Islington; P. C.'s Inc. 300*l*; Pop. 17,489.) Hon. Chap. to the Great Northern Hospital. [25]

SAULEZ, Vincent, *The Rectory, Canton, Cardiff.*—St. Bees; Deac. 1856 and Pr. 1857 by Bp of Rip. R. of Canton, Dio. Llan. 1863. (Patron, Bp of Llan; Tithe, 140*l*; R.'s Inc. 300*l* and Ho; Pop. 3929.) Formerly C. of Hornby, Yorks. 1856, Odiham, Hants, 1858, St. Paul, near Penzance, 1860, Charles, Plymouth, 1861; Chap. to H.M.S. "Akbar," 1862. Author, *Isabel Gray, the Orphan Missionary*, 1*s*. [26]

SAULL, James Edward, *Mungrisdale, Penrith.*—Deac. 1862 by Bp of Carl. Pr. 1863 by Bp of Dur. P. C. of Mungrisdale, Dio. Carl. 1863. (Patron, R. of Greystock; P. C.'s Inc. 132*l* and Ho; Pop. 302.) Formerly C. of Mungrisdale 1862–63. [27]

SAUMAREZ, Paul, *Great Easton Rectory, Dunmow, Essex.*—Trin. Coll. Ox. B.A. 1819; Deac. 1819 and

Pr. 1820 by Bp of Glouc. R. of Great Easton, Dio. Roch. 1827. (Patron, Viscount Maynard; Tithe, 765*l*; R.'s Inc. 776*l* and Ho; Pop. 891.) [1]

SAUNDERS, Arthur Cardinal, *Magor, Caerleon, Monmouthshire.*—Pemb. Coll. Ox. Scho. of, B.A. 1845, M.A. 1848; Deac. 1847 and Pr. 1848 by Bp of Ox. V. of Magor with Redwick V. Dio. Llan. 1860. (Patron, Duke of Beaufort; Magor, Tithe—Imp. 38*l* 10*s* 6*d*, V. 125*l* 10*s*; Redwick, Tithe—Imp. 14*l* 10*s*, V. 165*l* 2*s* 6*d*; V.'s Inc. 344*l*; Pop. 740.) Formerly C. of Great Barrington, Oxon, and Washingborough. [2]

SAUNDERS, The Very Rev. Augustus Page, *The Deanery, Peterborough.*—Ch. Ch. Ox. Double 1st cl. and B.A. 1824, M.A. 1826, B.D. and D.D. 1842; Deac. and Pr. 1825 by Bp of Ox. Dean of Peterborough 1853. (Value, 1000*l* and Res.) Formerly Head Mast. of the Charterhouse Sch. Lond. Fell. of the Royal Soc. Author, various Tracts and Pamphlets, many of them anonymous, on University Economics and Educational Reform, 1831–32; Newly-adapted Editions of the Series of *Charterhouse Grammars, Selected Authors, &c.* 1832–52; *Cathedral Reforms, specially with a View to Enlargement of their scholastic and other public uses,* 1845–53. [3]

SAUNDERS Cossley Diggle, *Tarrant Hinton Rectory, Blandford.*—Wad. Coll. Ox. B.A. 1838; Deac. 1840 and Pr. 1841 by Bp of B. and W. R. of Tarrant Hinton, Dio. Salis. 1842. (Patron, Pemb. Coll. Cam; Tithe, 335*l*; Glebe, 80 acres; R.'s Inc. 420*l* and Ho; Pop. 258.) [4]

SAUNDERS, David Arthur Fosbroke, *The Green, Frampton, Stonehouse, Gloucestershire.*—King's Coll. Lond. Theol. Assoc. 1867; Deac. 1867 by Bp of G. and B. C. of Saul and Moreton-Valence 1867. [5]

SAUNDERS, George Eveleigh, *Maperton Rectory, Wincanton, Somerset.*—Wad. Coll. Ox. B.A. 1842, M.A. 1847; Deac. 1846 and Pr. 1847 by Bp of Ox. R. of Maperton, Dio. B. and W. 1857. (Patron, Wad. Coll. Ox; R.'s Inc. 450*l* and Ho; Pop. 207.) Formerly Fell. of Wad. Coll. Ox; C. of Much Marcle, Herefordshire. [6]

SAUNDERS, James, *Week St. Mary, Stratton, Cornwall.*—Sid. Coll. Cam. 16th Wrang. and B.A. 1824, M.A. 1828, B.D. 1835; Deac. 1827 by Bp of Nor. Pr. 1830 by Bp of Lin. R. of Week St. Mary, Dio. Ex. 1852. (Patron, Sid. Coll. Cam; Tithe, 450*l*; Glebe, 86 acres; R.'s Inc. 539*l*; Pop. 611.) [7]

SAUNDERS, John, *St. Luke's Rectory, Old-street, London, E.C.*—St. John's Coll. Cam. B.A. 1829, M.A. 1835. R. of St. Luke's, Old-street, Dio. Lon. 1845. (Patrons, D. and C. of St. Paul's; R.'s Inc. 580*l* and Ho; Pop. 25,259.) [8]

SAUNDERS, John Charles Kitching, *Semperingham Vicarage, Folkingham, Lincolnshire.*—St. Edm. Hall, Ox. B.A. 1850, M.A. 1854; Deac. and Pr. 1851 by Abp of York. V. of Semperingham with Pointon, Dio. Lin. 1861. (Patron, Earl Fortescue; Tithe—Imp. 7*l*; V.'s Inc. 131*l*; Pop. Semperingham 122, Pointon 510.) Formerly C. of Withernwick, Hull, 1851–52; C. of South Molton and Chap. of the South Molton Union 1853–61. Author, *A Form of Sound Words; Three Sermons on the Lawfulness and Expediency of a Precomposed Form of Prayer,* 1858, 3*d*. [9]

SAUNDERS, John Goulding, *North Stoke Rectory, Bristol.*—R. of North Stoke, Dio. B. and W. 1862. (Patron, Ld Chan; R.'s Inc. 190*l*; Pop. 160.) Formerly C. of Stowmarket 1859; R. of Stowmarket with Stowupland 1859. [10]

SAUNDERS, Morley Benjamin, *Weston-super-Mare.*—Dub. A.B. 1854, A.M. 1858; Deac. 1855 and Pr. 1857 by Bp of Wor. C. of Ch. Ch. Weston-super-Mare 1866. Formerly C. of St. Matthew's, Rugby, 1855, Bottesford 1859, Broseley 1863, Bushbury 1864. [11]

SAUNDERS, Samuel Walker, *St. Ishmael's Vicarage, Milford Haven.*—Deac. 1828 and Pr. 1829 by Bp of St. D. V. of St. Ishmael's, Dio. St. D. 1832. (Patron, Ld Chan; Tithe—Imp. 170*l* 6*s* 8*d*, V. 90*l*; Glebe, 7 acres; V.'s Inc. 100*l* and Ho; Pop. 1211.) P. C. of Dale, Pembrokeshire, Dio. St. D. 1832. (Patron, J. P. L. A. Philipps, Esq; Tithe, Imp. 8*l* 12*s*; P. C.'s Inc. 58*l*; Pop. 463.) Surrogate 1840. [12]

SAUNDERS, William, *Langar, Nottingham.*—St. Bees; Deac. 1857 and Pr. 1858 by Bp of Carl. C. of Langar. Formerly C. of Maryport 1857, St. Michael's, Stockwell, Surrey, 1862. [13]

SAVAGE, Robert Chapman, *Nuneaton Vicarage, Warwickshire.*—St. John's Coll. Cam. B.A. 1835, M.A. 1839; Deac. 1835 and Pr. 1836 by Bp of Lich. V. of Nuneaton, Dio. Wor. 1845. (Patron, the Crown; Tithe, 400*l*; Glebe, 222 acres; V.'s Inc. 900*l* and Ho; Pop. 4664.) Hon. Can. of Wor. 1849; Surrogate; Rural Dean 1846; Dioc. Inspector of Schs; Dom. Chap. to Viscount Lifford. Formerly V. of Tamworth, Staffs. Author, *An Ordination Sermon* (at Worcester); *A Sermon on the Death of Rev. J. Bickersteth; A Protestant Catechism for Members of the Church of England; A Short Catechism "on Oaths."* [14]

SAVAGE, William, *Tarrant Hinton, Blandford, Dorset.*—Queen's Coll. Ox. B.A. 1842, M.A. 1845; Deac. 1843 and Pr. 1844 by Bp of Ex. C. of Tarrant Hinton 1862. [15]

SAVELL, William James, *Houghton-street, London, W.C.*—St. John's Coll. Cam. B.A. 1858, M.A. 1861; Deac. 1860 by Bp of Lon. Pr. 1861 by Bp of Wor. Head Mast. of St. Clement Danes Gr. Sch. Lond. Formerly Math. Lect. of Wor. Dioc. Training Coll. Saltley. [16]

SAVILE, The Hon. Arthur, *Foulmire Rectory, Royston, Cambs.*—Trin. Coll. Cam. M.A. 1841; Deac. 1843 by Bp of Lon. Pr. 1844 by Bp of Wor. R. of Foulmire, Dio. Ely, 1850. (Patron, Earl of Hardwicke; Tithe, 640*l*; Glebe, 81 acres; R.'s Inc. 668*l* and Ho; Pop. 560.) Rural Dean of Barton 1867. Author, *Six Sermons on the Lord's Prayer.* [17]

SAVILE, Bouchier Wrey, *Dawlish, Devon.*—Emman. Coll. Cam. B.A. 1839, M.A. 1842; Deac. 1840 by Bp of Wor. Pr. 1841 by Bp of Win. C. of Dawlish 1867; Chap. to Earl Fortescue 1844. Formerly C. of Halesowen 1840, Okehampton 1841, Newport 1848, Tawstock 1855, Tattingstone 1860. Author, *Meetness for Heaven,* 1850; *The Apostasy,* 1853; *The First and Second Advent,* 1858; *Introduction of Christianity into Britain,* 1861; *Lyra Sacra,* 1862; *Revelation and Science,* 1862; *Man, or the Old and New Philosophy,* 1863; *Egypt's Testimony to Sacred History,* 1866; etc. [18]

SAVILE, Frederick Alexander, *Ardmore, Torquay.*—Trin. Coll. Cam. B.A. 1843, M.A. 1858; Deac. 1843 by Bp of Win. Pr. 1844 by Bp of Wor. J. P. for Devon 1866. Formerly C. of Holy Rhood, Southampton, 1843–45; R. of King's Nympton 1845–54, North Huish 1854-60; C. of St. Thomas's, Exeter, 1860-66. [19]

SAVILE, The Hon. Philip Yorke, *Methley Rectory, Wakefield.*—Trin. Coll. Cam. M.A. 1834; Deac. and Pr. 1837 by Bp of Lin. R. of Methley, Dio. Rip. 1842. (Patron, Duchy of Lancaster; Glebe, 375 acres; R.'s Inc. 912*l* and Ho; Pop. 2472.) [20]

SAVORY, Edmund, *Binfield Rectory, Bracknell, Berks.*—Oriel Coll. Ox. B.A. 1847, M.A. 1850; Deac. 1851 and Pr. 1853 by Bp of Ox. R. of Binfield, Dio. Ox. 1859. (Patron, Ld Chan; Tithe, 800*l*; Glebe, 20 acres; R.'s Inc. 840*l* and Ho; Pop. 1371.) Formerly C. of Binfield 1853–59. [21]

SAVORY, Henry Stiles, *Cameley, Temple Cloud, Bristol.*—Oriel Coll. Ox. B.A. 1846, M.A. 1850; Deac. 1847, Pr. 1848. R. of Cameley, Dio. B. and W. 1852. (Patron, H. Hippesley, Esq; Tithe, 205*l*; Glebe, 120*l* 10*s*; R.'s Inc. 325*l* 10*s* and Ho; Pop. 526.) Formerly C. of Copgrove, Yorks, 1847–49, High Littleton, Somerset, 1850–52. [22]

SAWBRIDGE, Charles, *Almer, near Blandford,* St. Peter's Coll. Cam. B.A. 1832, M.A. 1839; Deac. 1834, Pr. 1836. R. of Almer, Dio. Salis, 1836. (Patron, T. S. Drax, Esq; Tithe, 275*l*; Glebe, 33 acres; R.'s Inc. 298*l* and Ho; Pop. 155.) R. of Charborough, Dio. Salis. 1836. (Patroness, Mrs. Drax; Tithe, 100*l*; R.'s Inc. 82*l*; Pop. 185.) [23]

SAWBRIDGE, Edward Henry, *Thelnetham Rectory, near Harling, Suffolk.*—Ball. Coll. Ox. 2nd cl. Lit. Hum. and B.A. 1835, M.A. 1838; Deac. 1839, Pr. 1840. R. of Thelnetham, Dio. Ely, 1860. (Patron, the present R; Tithe—App. 37*l* 10*s*, R. 528*l* 2*s* 9*d*; R.'s Inc. 534*l*; Pop. 516). Formerly C. of Thelnetham. [1]

SAWBRIDGE, John Sikes, *St. John's Parsonage, Aylesbury.*—Brasen. Coll. Ox. B.A. 1864; Deac. 1865 and Pr. 1866 by Bp of Ox. C. of Aylesbury 1866. Formerly C. of Brill, Bucks, 1865. [2]

SAWERS, William, *South Perrot, Dorset.*—C. of South Perrot with Mosterton. [3]

SAWYER, Duncombe Herbert, *Hammoon Rectory, Blandford, Dorset.*—Trin. Coll. Cam. 2nd cl. Theol. Trip. B.A. 1859, M.A. 1862; Deac. 1860 and Pr. 1862 by Bp of Ox. C. of Hammoon 1867. Formerly C. of Hambleden, Bucks, West Harnham, Wilts, and Farnham, and Chettle, Dorset. [4]

SAWYER, George Herbert, *Heywood Lodge, Maidenhead.*—Trin. Hall. Cam. LL.B. 1850; Deac. 1849, Pr. 1850. Formerly R. of Sunningwell, Dio. Ox. 1854–66. [5]

SAWYER, J. W., *Shillington, Hitchin.*—C. of Shillington, Beds. [6]

SAWYER, Walter James, *Pencoed, Ross, Herefordshire.*—Queen's Coll. Ox. B.A. 1853; M.A. 1856; Deac. 1854 by Bp of Herf. Pr. 1855 by Bp of Wor. Formerly P. C. of Harewood, Dio. Herf. 1858. [7]

SAWYER, William George, *Little Milton, Tetsworth, Oxon.*—Trin. Hall, Cam. B.A. 1852, M.A. 1855; Deac. 1852 by Bp of Salis. Pr. 1854 by Bp of Ox. P. C. of Little Milton, Dio. Ox. 1860. (Patron, Bp of Ox, P. C.'s Inc. 250*l* and Ho; Pop. 431.) Formerly C. of Wilton 1852, Wantage 1854. [8]

SAWYER, William G., *Dalby-on-the-Wolds, Melton Mowbray.*—Chap. of the Don. of Dalby-on-the-Wolds 1830. (Patron, the present Chap; Chap.'s Inc. 40*l*; Pop. 359.) [9]

SAXBY, Stephen Henry, *East Clevedon, Somerset.*—Caius Coll. Cam. B.A. 1855, M.A. 1859; Deac. 1856 and Pr. 1857 by Bp of Lon. P. C. of East Clevedon, Dio. B. and W. 1860. (Patron, Sir A. H. Elton, Bart; P. C.'s Inc. 120*l* and Ho; Pop. 900.) Chap. to Earl of Carnwath. Author, *Heidelberg Sermons*, 1860, 6*s*; *The English Pew System* (a Prize Essay), Rivingtons, 1866; *The Thankfulness of the Just* (a Sermon), Saunders, Otley, and Co. 1866. [10]

SAXTON, Charles Waring, *Newport, Salop.*—Ch. Ch. Ox. 2nd cl. Cl. 1st cl. Math. et Phy. and B.A. 1827, M.A. 1830, B D. and D.D. 1847; Deac. 1831, Pr. 1832. Head Mast. of the Newport Gr. Sch. 1846. Formerly Exam. under the Board of Control of Candidates for admission to Haileybury Coll. Author, *The Agricola of Tacitus*; *The Catiline War of Sallust, reduced to Latin Exercises, with Preliminary Remarks*; *The Epistles and Gospels of the Year translated into the two Celtic Languages of Great Britain and into the two Breton Languages*, Trübner and Co. [11]

SAY, Francis Henry Stoddart, *Braughing Vicarage, Ware, Herts.*—St. John's Coll. Cam. B.A. 1826, M.A. 1829; Deac. 1827 and Pr. 1828 by Bp of Lon. V. of Braughing, Dio. Roch. 1846. (Patrons, Heirs of the late Rev. W. Tower; Glebe, 200 acres; V.'s Inc. 280*l* and Ho; Pop. 1180) Formerly C. of Braughing 1827–46. [12]

SAYCE, Henry Samuel, *Woolley, Bath.*—Pemb. Coll. Ox. B.A. 1828, M.A. 1832; Deac. 1829, Pr. 1830. C. of Woolley. Formerly P. C. of Shirehampton, near Bristol, 1843–58. [13]

SAYE AND SELE, The Ven. and Right Hon. Lord (TWISLETON - WYKEHAM-FIENNES), 18th Baron, *Hereford.*—New Coll. Ox. B C.L. 1825, D.C.L. 1832; Deac. and Pr. 1823 by Bp of Herf. Preb. of Eigne in Herf. Cathl. 1825. (Value, 25*l*.) Treasurer of Herf. Cathl. 1832; Canon Res. of Herf. Cathl. 1840. (Value, 600*l* and Res.) Mast. of St. Ethelbert's Hospital 1844. (Value, 90*l*.) Archd. of Herf. 1863. (Value, 200*l*.) Formerly R. of Broadwell and Adlestrop, Glouc. 1825–52. Editor of Archbishop Wake's *Church Catechism, with Scripture Proofs*, 1827. [14]

SAYER, Edward Lane, *Weston, Thames Ditton, Surrey.*—St. John's Coll. Cam. B.A. 1829, M.A. 1832; Deac. 1829 and Pr. 1830 by Bp of Lon. Formerly V. of Pulloxhill, Beds, 1844–53. [15]

SAYER, William Carlisle, *Thaxted, Dunmow, Essex.*—Trin. Coll. Cam. B.A. 1860, M.A. 1863; Deac. 1860 and Pr. 1861 by Bp of Roch. C. of Thaxted 1860. [16]

SAYERS, Andrew, *Upleadon Parsonage, Newent, Glouc.*—St. Mary Hall, Ox. B.A. 1831. P. C. of Upleadon, Dio. G. and B. 1834. (Patron, Bp of G. and B; Tithe—App. 364*l* 13*s* 10*d*; P. C.'s Inc. 83*l* and Ho; Pop. 237.) R. of St. Mary-de-Crypt with All Saints and St. Owen (no Church) R.'s Gloucester, Dio. G. and B. 1841. (Patron, Ld Chan; R.'s Inc. 130*l*; Pop. St Mary-de-Crypt 953, All Saints and St. Owen 830.) Chap. to Viscount Avonmore; Surrogate. [17]

SAYERS, Henry, *Gilda-Brook, Eccles, Manchester.*—Dub. A.B. 1851, A.M. 1857, *ad eund.* Ox. 1857; Deac. 1851 and Pr. 1853 by Bp of Man. P. C. of St. James's Hope, Manchester, Dio. Man 1861. (Patrons, Trustees; P. C.'s Inc. 350; Pop. 1000.) Formerly C. of St. John's, Manchester, 1851–57, Eccles 1857–61. [18]

SAYERS, Robert, *Roughton Lodge, Norwich.*—Dub. Hebrew Entrance Prem. 1848, A.B. 1851; Deac. 1852 and Pr. 1853 by Bp of Ches. R. of Roughton, Dio. Nor. 1862. (Patron, Bp of Nor; Tithe, 296*l*; Glebe, 30 acres; R.'s Inc. 341*l*; Pop 420.) Formerly C. of St. Simon's, Liverpool, 1852–53, Tittleshall, Norfolk, 1853–62. [19]

SAYERS, W., *Whitby, Yorks.*—Dub. A.B. 1849. C. of Whitby. [20]

SAYRES, Edward, *Cold Ashton Rectory, Marshfield, near Chippenham.*—Trin. Coll. Cam. B.A. 1844, M.A. 1848; Deac. 1845 and Pr. 1846 by Bp of Nor. R. of Cold Ashton, Dio. G. and B. 1851. (Patron, the present R; Tithe, 470*l*; R.'s Inc. 508*l* and Ho; Pop. 508.) [21]

SCALE, John, *Kintbury, Hungerford.*—St. Aidan's; Deac. 1860 by Bp of Pet. C. of Kintbury. Formerly C. of Woodford-cum-Membris 1860. [22]

SCAMMELL, Francis, *Victoria-terrace, Kendal.*—Corpus Coll. Cam. B.A. 1865; Deac. 1865 and Pr. 1866. C. of Kendal 1865. [23]

SCARD, Thomas, *Durley Lodge, Bishops Waltham, Hants.*—Magd. Hall, Ox. B.A. 1823, M.A. 1829; Deac. 1823 by Bp of Lin. Pr. 1823 by Bp of Win. V. of Durley, Dio. Win. 1855. (Patron, Bp. of Win. Tithe, 410*l*; V.'s Inc. 410*l*; Pop. 411.) Surrogate; Chap. to H.R.H. the Duke of Cambridge. Author, *Sermons for Schools*, 2 vols. 1829. [24]

SCARGILL, John James, *Hyson-green, Nottingham.*—Clare Coll. Cam. B.A. 1855; Deac. 1855 and Pr. 1857 by Bp of Man. C. of Hyson-green 1865. Formerly C. of Heywood, Lancashire, 1855–58, Lever Bridge and Ratcliffe 1858–59, Rugby 1859–60, Kyre, Worcestershire (sole charge), 1861–64. [25]

SCARR, Grover, *Ruskington, Sleaford, Lincolnshire.*—Dur. B.A. 1860; Deac. 1860 and Pr. 1861 by Bp of Lin. V. of 2nd Mediety of Ruskington, Dio. Lin. 1867. (Patron, Ld Chan; Glebe, 64 acres; V.'s Inc. 140*l*; Pop. 1080.) C. of 1st Mediety of Ruskington. Formerly C. of Caistor 1860, Steeple Morden 1862, Ruskington, 1st and 2nd Mediety, 1865. [26]

SCARSBROOK, George, *Woolwich.*—Min. of St. John's, Woolwich. [27]

SCARSDALE, The Right Hon. Alfred Nathaniel Holden Curzon, Baron Scarsdale, *Kedleston Hall, near Derby.*—Mert. Coll. Ox. M.A. 1865, Deac. 1854, and Pr. 1855. R. of Kedleston, Dio. Lich. 1856. (Patron, the present R; R.'s Inc. 150*l*; Pop. 114.) Patron of Mickleover V. and of Quarndon P. C. Derbyshire, and of Worthington P. C. Leicestershire. [28]

SCARTH, Harry Mengden, 15, *Bathwick-hill, Bath.*—Ch. Coll. Cam. B.A. 1837, M.A. 1840; Deac. 1837 and Pr. 1838 by Bp of Lich. R. of Bathwick with Woolley C. Dio. B. and W. 1841. (Patron, Duke of

Cleveland; Bathwick, Tithe, 105*l*; Glebe, 3 acres; Woolley, Tithe, 110*l* 11*s* 6*d*; Glebe, 2 acres; R.'s Inc. 318*l*; Pop. Bathwick 5266, Woolley 71.) Preb. of Combe the 5th in Wells Cathl. 1848. Author, *Aquæ Solis, or Roman Bath*, and sundry papers in *Journal of Archæological Institution*; etc. [1]

SCARTH, John, *Cumberland Villas, Milton-next-Gravesend, Kent.*—King's Coll. Lond. Theol. Assoc; Deac. 1865 and Pr. 1866 by Bp of Roch. C. of Trinity, Milton-next-Gravesend, 1865. Formerly Asst. Chap. to St. Andrew's Waterside Ch. Mission, Gravesend. [2]

SCHNEIDER, Henry, *Carlton Scroop, Grantham.*—St. John's Coll. Cam. B.A. 1822, M.A. 1826; Deac. and Pr. 1824 by Bp of Lin. R. of Carlton Scroop, Dio. Lin. 1830. (Patrons, Earl Brownlow, two turns, and W. Andrews, Esq. one turn; Tithe, 360*l*; Glebe, 38½ acres; R.'s Inc. 450*l* and Ho; Pop. 266.) Rural Dean. [3]

SCHNIBBEN, William Mangles, *Bromfield, Aspatria, Cumberland.*—Literate; Deac. 1847, Pr. 1848. C. of Bromfield 1852. [4]

SCHOFIELD, A., *Sutton, Macclesfield.*—C. of St. George's, Sutton. [5]

SCHOFIELD, James, *Felling, Gateshead.*—St. Bees; Deac. 1853 and Pr. 1854 by Bp of Ches. P. C. of Felling, Dio. Dur. 1866. (Patrons, Five Trustees; P. C.'s Inc. 300*l* and Ho; Pop. 5105.) Formerly C. of St. Paul's, Portwood, Cheshire, 1853–57, St. Matthias', Salford, 1857–58, Felling 1858–66. [6]

SCHOLEFIELD, Arthur Frederick Heber, *Grove House, Highgate, London, N.*—Trin. Coll. Ox. B.A. 1847; Deac. 1848 and Pr. 1849 by Bp of Roch. Chaplain of the Cemetery, Highgate, 1860. Formerly C. of Upminster, Essex, 1851–60. [7]

SCHOLEFIELD, Joshua, *Billesdon Vicarage, near Leicester.*—Corpus Coll. Cam. B.A. 1825; Deac. 1825, Pr. 1826. V. of Billesdon with Goadby and Rolleston Chapelries, Dio. Pet. 1846. (Patron, H. Greene, Esq; Billesdon, Tithe, 2*l*, Goadby, Tithe—Imp. 12*l*, V. 77*l*; Rolleston, Tithe—Imp. 4*l*, V. 45*l*; V.'s Inc. 290*l* and Ho; Pop. Billesdon 909, Goadby 134, Rolleston 42.) Surrogate; Chap. of the Billesdon Union. [8]

SCHOLEFIELD, Richard Brown, *West Newton Rectory, Lynn Regis.*—Trin. Coll. Cam. B.A. 1838, M.A. 1841; Deac. 1840 and Pr. 1841 by Bp of Nor. R. of West Newton, Dio. Nor. 1859. (Patron, Ld Chan; Tithe, 161*l* 6*s*; Glebe, 5¾ acres; R.'s Inc. 200*l* and Ho; Pop. 268.) V. of Appleton, Lynn, Dio. Nor. 1864. (Patron, Edmund Kent, Esq; V.'s Inc. 8*l*.) Formerly C. of Reymerstone and Southborough, Norfolk, 1849–59. [9]

SCHOLFIELD, Charles Richard, *Madehurst Vicarage, Arundel.*—Trin. Coll. Cam. B.A. 1855, M.A. 1858; Deac. 1857, Pr. 1858. V. of Madehurst, Dio. Chich. 1866. (Patron, J. C. Fletcher, Esq; Glebe, 22 acres; V.'s Inc. 100*l* and Ho; Pop. 208.) Formerly C. of Harrowden, Northants, 1857–59; P. C. of Low Dunsforth, Boroughbridge, 1859; C. of Maiden Bradley, Wilts, 1863. [10]

SCHOLFIELD, Philip, *Goulsby, Horncastle, Lincolnshire.*—V. of Goulsby, Dio. Lin. 1853. (Patron, Rev. J. M. Lister; V.'s Inc. 145*l*; Pop. 344.) [11]

SCHON, James F.—Chap. of the Royal Marine Infirmary, Chatham. [12]

SCHREIBER, John Edward Lemuel, *Barham Rectory, Ipswich.*—Ball. Coll. Ox. B.A. 1839, M.A. 1842. R. of Barham, Dio. Nor. 1850. (Patron, F. W. Schreiber, Esq; Tithe, 417*l* 11*s* 1*d*; R.'s Inc. 421*l* and Ho; Pop. 568.) [13]

SCHWABE, William Hermann, *Great Cheverell, Devizes, Wilts.*—Caius Coll. Cam. B.A. 1835. C. of Great Cheverell. Formerly Chap. Bombay Presidency. [14]

SCOBELL, George B., *Madron, Penzance.*—C. of Madron, Cornwall. [15]

SCOBELL, Sanford George, *Burgh-on-Baine Vicarage, Louth, Lincolnshire.*—Oriel Coll. Ox. B.A. 1843; Deac. 1844 by Bp of Lin. Pr. 1845 by Bp of Ox. V. of Burgh-on-Baine, Dio. Lin. 1865. (Patron, J. W. Fox, Esq; V.'s Inc. 190*l* and Ho; Pop. 203.) Surrogate. Formerly V. of Market Rasen, Lincolnshire, 1846–65. [16]

SCOONES, William Dalton, *Langley-Marsh, Colnbrook, Bucks.*—Trin. Coll. Ox. B.A. 1843. P. C. of Langley-Marsh, Dio. Ox. 1856. (Patron, V. of Wraysbury; Tithe—Imp. 730*l* 19*s* 6*d*, App. 275*l* 13*s* 3*d*; P. C.'s Inc. 145*l*; Pop. 1375.) [17]

SCOT, Robert F., *Farnborough Rectory, Hants.*—R. of Farnborough, Dio. Win. 1862. (Patron, Wm. Scot, Esq; Tithe, 152*l*; Glebe, 22 acres; R.'s Inc. 238*l* and Ho; Pop. 5529.) [18]

SCOTT, Charles, *East Molesey Parsonage, Kingston-on-Thames, S.W.*—St. John's Coll. Cam. Coll. Prizeman, Wrang. and B.A. 1847, M.A. 1850. P. C. of St. Paul's, East Molesey, Dio. Win. 1856. (Patron, J. F. Kent, Esq; P. C.'s Inc. 100*l*; Pop. 887.) One of the Masters of Merchant Taylors' Sch. 1856. [19]

SCOTT, Charles Brodrick, 19, *Dean's-yard, Westminster, S.W.*—Trin. Coll. Cam. Pitt Scho. 1847, Sen. Chan.'s Medallist 1848, Wrang. 1st in 1st cl. Cl. Trip. and B.A. 1848, M.A. 1851, B.D. 1861, D.D. 1867; Deac. 1854 by Bp of Ely, Pr. 1855 by Bp of Wor. Head Master of Westminster Sch. Formerly Fell. and Asst. Tut. of Trin. Coll. Cam. [20]

SCOTT, Charles Thomas, *Shadingfield, Wangford, Suffolk.*—Deac. and Pr. 1835. R. of Shadingfield, Dio. Nor. 1839. (Patron, Lord Braybrooke; Tithe—Imp. 6*l* 14*s*, R. 305*l*; Glebe, 7½ acres; R.'s Inc. 309*l* and Ho; Pop. 209.) [21]

SCOTT, Edward, *Douglas, Isle of Man.*—C. of St. Thomas's, Douglas. [22]

SCOTT, Edward Thomas, *Mundsley Rectory, North Walsham, Norfolk.*—Deac. and Pr. 1844 by Bp of Lon. R. of Mundsley, Dio. Nor. 1858. (Patron, Duchy of Lancaster; Tithe, comm. 170*l*; Glebe, 6 acres; R.'s Inc. 185*l*; Pop. 437.) Formerly P. C. of Stoke Ferry, Norfolk, 1856–58. [23]

SCOTT, Francis Caleb, *The Vicarage, Goring St. Mary, Sussex.*—St. John's Coll. Ox. B.A. 1842, M.A. 1856; Deac. 1843, Pr. 1844. V. of Goring St. Mary, Dio. Chich. 1861. (Patron, David Lyon, Esq; Tithe, 164*l* 10*s* 6*d*; Glebe, 7½ acres; V.'s Inc. 179*l* 10*s* 6*d* and Ho; Pop. 533.) Formerly R. of Skinnand, Linc. 1844; Sequestrator of St. Martin's, Chichester, 1855–59. [24]

SCOTT, Francis John, *Tewkesbury.*—Dub. A.B. 1849, A.M. 1852; Deac. 1848 and Pr. 1849 by Bp of G. and B. P.C. of Trinity, Tewkesbury, Dio. G. and B. 1849. (Patrons, Trustees; P. C.'s Inc. 320*l*.) P.C. of Tredington, Dio. G. and B. 1857. (Patron, Bp of G. and B; Tithe—App. 346*l* 10*s*; Glebe, 2 acres; P. C.'s Inc. 60*l* and Ho; Pop. 117.) [25]

SCOTT, Frederick Thomas, *Sibertswold Vicarage, Dover.*—Wor. Coll. Ox. B.A. 1834, M.A. 1837; Deac. 1835, Pr. 1836. V. of Sibertswold with Coldred, Dio. Cant. 1853. (Patron, Abp of Cant; Sibertswold, Tithe—App. 430*l*, V. 135*l* 6*s* 4*d*; Glebe, 6 acres; Coldred, Tithe—App. 242*l* 12*s* 10*d*, Imp. 40*l*. 12*s*, V. 139*l* 8*s* 2*d*; Glebe, 4 acres; V.'s Inc. 306*l* and Ho; Pop. Sibertswold 411, Coldred 134.) [26]

SCOTT, George, *Coxwold, Easingwold, Yorks.*—Trin. Coll. Cam. B.A. 1837, M.A. 1840; Deac. 1837, Pr. 1838. P. C. of Coxwold with Yearsley C. Dio. York, 1843. (Patron, Trin. Coll. Cam; Tithe—App. 64*l* 2*s*, Imp. 1659*l* 8*s*; P. C.'s Inc. 350*l*; Pop. 1165.) P. C. of Husthwaite, Yorks, Dio. York, 1843. (Patron, Trin. Coll. Cam; Tithe—Imp. 467*l* 16*s* 6*d* and 7 acres of Glebe; P. C.'s Inc. 100*l*; Pop. 616.) [27]

SCOTT, George Henry, *Rhôs-Crowther Rectory, near Pembroke.*—Ex. Coll. Ox. 4th cl. Lit. Hum. and B.A. 1831, M.A. 1858; Deac. 1834 and Pr. 1835 by Bp of Chich; R. of Rhôs-Crowther, Dio. St. D. 1850. (Patron, Ld. Chan; Tithe, 280*l*; Glebe, 75 acres; R.'s Inc. 392*l* and Ho; Pop. 202.) Formerly V. of Ifield, near Crawley, Sussex, 1842–50. Author, *Is the Lord with us?* (a Tract), Masters, 1855. [28]

SCOTT, G. Hopton, *Gringley-on-the Hill Vicarage, Bawtry, Yorks.*—Deac. 1858, Pr. 1859. V. of Gringley-on-the-Hill, Dio. Lin. 1861. (Patron, Duke of Rutland; Glebe, 185 acres; V.'s Inc. 300*l* and Ho; Pop. 875.) Chap. to the Earl of Gosford 1865. Formerly C. of Sedgebrooke, Lincolnshire, 1858–61. [29]

SCOTT, George Philip William, *Hilton House, St. Ives, Hunts.*—Brasen. Coll. Ox. B.A. 1857, M.A. 1860; Deac. 1863 and Pr. 1864 by Bp of Ely. C. of King's Ripton and Great Stukeley, Hunts, 1863. [1]

SCOTT, Honeywood D'Obyns Yate, *Tibberton, Newent, Glouc.*—Trin. Coll. Cam. B.A. 1844. R. of Tibberton, Dio. G. and B. 1852. (Patron, H. D. Y. Scott, Esq; Tithe, 328*l* 4*s* 6*d*; Glebe, 5½ acres; R.'s Inc. 353*l*; Pop. 301). Dom. Chap. to the Duke of Richmond. [2]

SCOTT, John, *Hull.*—Trin. Coll. Cam. B.A. 1859, M.A. 1862; Deac. 1860 and Pr. 1861 by Bp of Carl. P. C. of St. Mary's, Hull, Dio. York, 1865. (Patrons, Family of late Rev. John Scott; P. C.'s Inc. 300*l*; Pop. 5210.) Formerly C. of Kendal 1860, Hornsey, Lond. 1862. [3]

SCOTT, John, *Surlingham Vicarage, near Norwich.*—Trin. Coll. Cam. B.A. 1831, M.A. 1834; Deac. 1833 and Pr. 1834 by Bp of Bristol. V. of Surlingham with St. Saviour P. C. Dio. Nor. 1836. (Patron, Bp of Nor; Tithe—Imp. 309*l*, V. 101*l*; Glebe, 3½ acres; V.'s Inc. 132*l* and Ho; Pop. 465.) Author, *Sermon on the Being of a God*, 1850; *Treatise on the Parental and Filial Relations*, 1851, 2*s* 6*d*; *Treatise on the Philosophy of the Two Sacraments*, 1854, 5*s*. [4]

SCOTT, John, *Tydd St. Giles' Rectory, Wisbech.*—Caius Coll. Cam. 36th Wrang. B.A. 1846, M.A. 1849; Deac. 1846 by Bp of Lich. Pr. 1847 by Bp of Ely. R. of Tydd St. Giles', Dio. Ely, 1862. (Patron, Bp of Ely; Tithe, 1050*l*; Glebe, 25*l*; R.'s Inc. 1075*l* and Ho; Pop. 924.) Formerly P. C. of St. Paul's, Cambridge, 1847–62. [5]

SCOTT, John Anker, *Wigton, Cumberland.*—St. Aidan's; Deac. 1862 and Pr. 1863 by Bp of Rip. C. of Wigton 1864. Formerly C. of Longwood 1862. [6]

SCOTT, John Arthur Henry, *Horsham, Sussex.*—Magd. Hall, Ox. B.A. 1858, M.A. 1865; Deac. 1858, Pr. 1860. C. of Horsham 1858. [7]

SCOTT, John Aubrey, *West Tytherley Rectory, Stockbridge, Hants.*—Ball. Coll. Ox. B.A. 1843; Deac. 1845, Pr. 1846. R. of West Tytherley, Dio. Win. 1850. (Patron, C. B. Wall, Esq; Tithe, 309*l*; Glebe, 30 acres; R.'s Inc. 339*l* and Ho; Pop. 469.) [8]

SCOTT, John Haigh, *Frosterley Parsonage, Darlington.*—Wad. Coll. Ox. B.A. 1849, M.A. 1851; Deac. 1850 by Bp of Ches. Pr. 1851 by Bp of Pet. P. C. of Frosterley, Dio. Dur. 1866. (Patron, Bp of Ches; Glebe, 2 acres; P. C.'s Inc. 400*l* and Ho; Pop. 1250.) Formerly Chap. of Liverpool Workhouse 1859–66. Author, *Hymns for the Public Worship of the Church*, 1853, 1*s* 6*d*. [9]

SCOTT, John James, *Bulford, near Salisbury.*—Ex. Coll. Ox. B.A. 1829, M.A. 1831; Deac. 1835 and Pr. 1836 by Bp of Ex. C. in sole charge of Bulford 1863. Author, *Selections from the Old and New Versions of the Psalms*, 1859; *Canticles and Psalters for Chanting in Cathedrals*, 1848. [10]

SCOTT, John Pendred, *Staplegrove Rectory, Taunton.*—Ball. Coll. Ox. B.A. 1837, M.A. 1845; Deac. 1840 and Pr. 1841 by Bp of Ches. R. of Staplegrove, Dio. B. and W. 1846. (Patron, Richard Fort, Esq; Tithe, 205*l*; Land, 10 acres; R.'s Inc. 213*l* and Ho; Pop. 469.) Chap. to the Earl of Meath. [11]

SCOTT, John Richard, *Earsdon, Newcastle-on-Tyne.*—St. Bees; Deac. 1865, Pr. 1867. C. of Earsdon. [12]

SCOTT, Melville Horne, *Ockbrook Vicarage, Derbyshire.*—Caius Coll. Cam. Scho. of, 4th Sen. Opt. and B.A. 1850; Deac. 1850 and Pr. 1851 by Bp of Lich. V. of Ockbrook, Dio. Lich. 1852. (Patron, Thomas Henry Pares, Esq; Glebe, 65 acres; V.'s Inc. 160*l* and Ho; Pop. 1506.) [13]

SCOTT, Richard Folliott, *Arlesey Vicarage, Baldock, Beds.*—Emman. Coll. Cam. B.A. 1858, M.A. 1861; Deac. and Pr. 1859 by Bp of Lich. R. of Astwick with Arlesey V. Dio. Ely, 1860. (Patron, the present V; Glebe, 260 acres; R.'s Inc. 450*l* and Ho; Pop. Astwick 68, Arlesey 1401.) Formerly C. of Fradswell 1859. [14]

SCOTT, Robert, *Balliol College, Oxford.*—Ch. Ch. Ox. Craven Scho. 1830, Ireland Scho. 1833, 1st cl. Lit. Hum. B.A. 1833; Ball. Coll. Ox. M.A. 1836, Denyer Theol. Essay, 1838, B.D. and D.D. 1854; Deac. 1835 and Pr. 1836 by Bp of Ox., Mast. of Ball. Coll. 1854; Member of Hebdomadal Council (under 17 & 18 Vict.) 1854, '57, '63; Delegate of the Press 1855; Prof. of Exegesis of Scripture, Oxford, 1861. Formerly Fell. and Tut. of Ball. Coll. 1835–40; Preb. of Ex. 1845–66; R. of Duloe, Cornwall, 1840–50; R. of South Luffenham, Rutland, 1850–54; Select Preacher 1853. Author (in conjunction with Dr. Liddell), *A Greek-English Lexicon*, 5th ed. 1861, 31*s* 6*d*; *Twelve Sermons*, 1851, 7*s*; *University Sermons*, 1860, 8*s* 6*d*; single Sermons and Tracts. [15]

SCOTT, Robert Allan, *Cranwell Vicarage, Sleaford, Lincolnshire.*—Ball. Coll. Ox. B.A. 1828, M.A. 1831. V. of Cranwell, Dio. Lin. 1846. (Patron, Bp of Lin; Tithe—Imp. 342*l*, V. 170*l*; V.'s Inc. 370*l* and Ho; Pop. 233.) Dom. Chap. to Duke of Montrose. [16]

SCOTT, Robert Hilton, *Wootton Rectory, Isle of Wight.*—Literate; Deac. 1814 and Pr. 1816 by Bp of Dur. R. of Wootton, Dio. Win. 1855. (Patron, F. White Popham, Esq; Tithe, 104*l*; R's Inc. 240*l* and Ho; Pop. 79.) Author, Tracts. [17]

SCOTT, Samuel Cooper, *Wisbech, Cambs.*—Trin. Coll. Cam. B.A. 1866; Deac. 1866 by Bp of Lin. Pr. 1867 by Bp of Ely. C. of St. Peter and St. Paul's, Wisbech, 1866. [18]

SCOTT, Thomas, *London Hospital, E.*—Caius Coll. Cam. Whewell's Moral Philosophy Sen. Prizeman, B.A. 1854, M.A. 1857; Deac. 1854 and Pr. 1855 by Bp of Chich. Chap. of Lond. Hospital 1860. Formerly C. of All Souls', Brighton, 1854–60. [19]

SCOTT, Thomas, *Wappenham Rectory, Towcester.*—Deac. 1830, Pr. 1831. R. of Wappenham, Dio. Pet. 1835. (Patron, Bp of Pet; Glebe, 315 acres; R.'s Inc. 426*l* and Ho; Pop. 650.) Formerly Fell. of Queens' Coll. Cam. [20]

SCOTT, Thomas James, *Malaga.*—Ex. Coll. Ox. B.A. 1851, M.A. 1856; Deac. 1853 and Pr. 1855 by Bp of Salis. Consular Chap. at Malaga 1867. Formerly C. of Scampston and Shapwicke, Dorset, and Devizes, Wilts. [21]

SCOTT, Thomas Scard, *South Penge, Surrey, S.E.*—Wor. Coll. Ox. B.A. 1859; Deac. 1859 and Pr. 1860 by Bp of Win. R. of Skinnand, Dio. Lin. 1862. (Patron, S. Nicholls, Esq; R.'s Inc. 181*l*; Pop. 18; no church.) Min. of Trinity (temporary church), Penge, 1866. Formerly C. of Penge 1859–66. [22]

SCOTT, Walter, *Warton, Lytham, Lancashire.*—C. of Warton and Freckelton. [23]

SCOTT, Walter Henry, *Highworth, Wilts.*—C. of Highworth. [24]

SCOTT, William, *Shapwicke Vicarage, near Blandford.*—St. Peter's Coll. Cam. B.A. 1827, M.A. 1831; Deac. 1827 and Pr. 1828 by Bp of Chich. V. of Shapwicke, Dio. Salis. 1834. (Patron, E. G. Banks, Esq; Tithe—Imp. 491*l* 11*s* 9*d*, V. 425*l*; V.'s Inc. 425*l* and Ho; Pop. 446.) [25]

SCOTT, William, *The Observatory, Sydney, New South Wales.*—Sid. Coll. Cam. B.A. 1848, M.A. 1852; Deac. 1849 and Pr. 1850 by Bp of Ely. Professor of Astronomy in Sydney, New South Wales, 1856. Formerly Fell. and Math. Lect. of Sid. Coll. Cam. Author, *Elementary Treatise on Plane Co-ordinate Geometry, with its Application to Curves of the Second Order*, 5*s* 6*d*. [26]

SCOTT, William, *The Vicarage, New Seaham, Durham.*—Dub. A.B. 1844, A.M. 1856; Deac. 1844 by Bp of Ossory, Pr. 1844 by Bp of Tuam. V. of New Seaham, Dio. Dur. 1857. (Patron, Earl Vane; V.'s Inc. 380*l* and Ho; Pop. 3500.) Formerly Chap. to the Woodstock Union, and C. of Bladon and Woodstock, Oxon. [27]

SCOTT, William, *St. Olave's Rectory, London, E.C.*—Queen's Coll. Ox. 2nd cl. Lit. Hum. and B.A. 1835, M.A. 1839; Deac. 1836 and Pr. 1837 by Bp of Lin. V. of St. Olave's, Jewry, with St. Martin Pomeroy, Dio. Lon. 1860. (Patron, Ld Chan; V.'s Inc. 420*l* and Ho; Pop. St. Olave 143, St. Martin 185.) Formerly P. C. of Ch. Ch. Hoxton, Lond. 1839. Author, *National Neglect in Religion* (a Sermon), 1839; *Vindication of*

Teaching and Services of the Church from Imputation of Romanism (a Sermon), 1841; *Plain Words for Plain People*; *Appeal to Members of the S.P.C.K.* 1844; *Duty of continued Obedience to the Church's Law of Custom* (a Sermon); *A Letter to the Rev. Daniel Wilson, occasioned by his Recent "Appeal," &c.* 4 eds. 1850. Editor of Lawrence's *Lay Baptism Invalid*, 1841; *Archbishop Laud's Works*, in *Library of Anglo-Catholic Theology*; and Editor of the *Christian Remembrancer*. [1]

SCOTT, William, *Exhall Vicarage, Coventry.*—St. Mark's Coll. Chelsea; Deac. 1856 and Pr. 1861 by Bp of Lon. V. of Exhall, Dio. Wor. 1864. (Patrons, Earl and Countess of Aylesford; Tithe, Modus of 21*l*; Glebe, 58 acres; V.'s Inc. 143*l* and Ho; Pop. 964.) Formerly C. of St. Mary's, Westminster, 1856–62, St. James's the Less 1862–63, St. Peter's, Vauxhall, 1863–64. [2]

SCOTT, William, *Forest House, Llandovery, Carmarthenshire.*—Wor. Coll. Ox. B.A. 1855; Deac. 1860 by Bp of St. D. C. of Caledfwlch Chapel, Llandillo, 1860. [3]

SCOTT, The Hon. William Hugh, *Maiden-Newton Rectory, near Dorchester.*—St. John's Coll. Cam. B.A. 1821, M.A. 1822; Deac. 1836, Pr. 1837. R. of Maiden-Newton, Dio. Salis. 1837. (Patron, Earl of Ilchester; Tithe, 496*l*; Glebe, 111 acres; R.'s Inc. 608*l* and Ho; Pop. 844.) Preb. of Salis. 1848; Chap. to the Bp of Salis. [4]

SCOTT, William Langston, *Great Dunmow, Essex.*—Caius Coll. Cam. 30th Wrang. B.A. 1840, M.A. 1845; Deac. 1840 and Pr. 1841 by Bp of Pet. V. of Great Dunmow, Dio. Roch. 1863. (Patron, Bp. of Pet; Tithe, comm. 580*l*; V.'s Inc. 580*l* and Ho; Pop. 2976.) Chap. to Dunmow Union 1864. Formerly C. in sole charge of St. Katharine's, Northampton, 1840; C. of St. Giles's and Chap. to Union, Northampton, 1843; V. of Abthorpe 1854. [5]

SCOTT, William Quested, *Vicarage, Bishop Burton, Beverley, Yorks.*—Queens' Coll. Cam. B.A. 1837; Deac. 1841 by Bp of Ches. Pr. 1849 by Bp of Herf. C. in sole charge of Bishop Burton 1866. Author, *Lectures* in numbers; and a Treatise on the Thirty-nine Articles. [6]

SCOTT, W. B.—Mission C. of St. Mark's, Whitechapel, Lond. [7]

SCOWCROFT, James Hamer, *St. Matthew's Parsonage, Aston, Birmingham.*—Magd. Coll. Cam. S.C.L. 1854, B.A. 1855, M.A. 1860; Deac. 1854 and Pr. 1855 by Bp of Wor. P. C. of St. Matthew's Duddleston-cum-Nechells, Dio. Wor. 1857. (Patrons, Trustees; P. C.'s Inc. 300*l* and Ho; Pop. 18,571.) [8]

SCRAGG, William, *Kirk Ireton, Wirksworth, Derbyshire.*—Literate; Deac. 1857 and Pr. 1858 by Bp of Rip. C. of Kirk Ireton 1860. Formerly C. of Sandal Magna, Yorks, 1857–60. [9]

SCRATCHLEY, Charles James, *Lydiard St. Lawrence, near Taunton.*—Brasen. Coll. Ox. B.A. 1838. C. of Lydiard St. Lawrence. Formerly C. of Hound, near Southampton. [10]

SCRATTON, George, *Stickney, Boston, Lincolnshire.*—St. Bees 1850; Deac. 1851 by Bp of Lich. Pr. 1854 by Abp of Cant. C. of Stickney 1855. Author, *Architectural Economics*, Longmans, 1857; *Manual of Country Building*, Rivingtons, 1867. [11]

SCRATTON, William, *St. Mary's, Platt, Sevenoaks, Kent.*—Ch. Ch. Ox. Stud. of, B.A. 1851, M.A. 1854; Deac. 1853 by Bp of Ox. Pr. 1854 by Abp of Cant. C. of St. Mary's, Platt, 1865. Formerly C. of Tenterden and Smallhythe 1853, Gunthorpe 1859. [12]

SCRIVEN, Charles, *Martinhoe Rectory, Parracombe, Devon.*—Wor. Coll. Ox. 3rd cl. Lit. Hum. and B.A. 1835, M.A. 1838; Deac. 1837 and Pr. 1838 by Bp of Ox. R. of Martinhoe, Dio. Ex. 1857. (Patron, Sir N. W. G. Throckmorton; Tithe, 120*l*; Glebe, 35 acres; R.'s Inc. 150*l* and Ho; Pop. 219.) R. of Trentishoe, Devon, Dio. Ex. 1859. (Patroness, Miss Griffiths; Tithe, 80*l*; Glebe, 42 acres; R.'s Inc. 118*l*; Pop. 123.) Formerly C. of Cogenhoe, Northants; Fell. of Wor. Coll. Ox. [13]

SCRIVEN, Henry Valentine, 1, *Old Town, Stratford-on-Avon.*—Jesus Coll. Cam. B.A. 1853; Deac. 1853, Pr. 1854. P. C. of Preston-on-Stour, Dio. G. and B. 1857. (Patron, James Robert West, Esq; P. C.'s Inc. 55*l*; Pop. 421.) Chap. of Stratford-on-Avon 1856. Formerly C. of Bidford and Salford, Warwickshire, 1853–56. [14]

SCRIVENER, Frederick George, *Arlingham, Stonehouse, Gloucestershire.*—Ex. Coll. Ox. B.A. 1864; Deac. 1866 by Bp of G. and B. C. of Arlingham 1867. [15]

SCRIVENER, Frederick Henry Ambrose, *St. Gerrans Rectory, Grampound, Cornwall.*—Trin. Coll. Cam. Scho. of, 1834, 3rd in 2nd cl. Cl. Trip. B.A. 1835, M.A. 1838; Deac. 1838 and Pr. 1839 by Bp of B. and W. R. of St. Gerrans, Dio. Ex. 1861. (Patron, Bp of Ex; Tithe, 305*l*; Glebe, 2 acres; R.'s Inc. 310*l* and Ho; Pop. 935.) Formerly C. of Sandford Oreas, Somerset, 1838; P. C. of Penwerris, Falmouth, 1846. Author, *Notes on the Authorised Version of the New Testament*, 1845, 10*s* 6*d*; *Collation of Twenty Greek Manuscripts of Holy Gospels*, 1853, 6*s*; *Codex Augiensis and Fifty other Manuscripts*, 1859, 26*s*; *Novum Testamentum Textus Stephanici*, 1860, 3rd ed. 1867, 4*s* 6*d*; *Plain Introduction to the Criticism of the New Testament*, 1861, 15*s*; *Collation of the Codex Sinaiticus*, 1863, 2nd ed. revised, 1867, 5*s*; *Bezæ Codex Cantabrigiensis*, 1864, 26*s*. [16]

SCRIVENOR, Arthur, *Alvingham, Louth, Lincolnshire.*—Wor. Coll. Ox. B.A. 1853, M.A. 1855; Deac. 1854 and Pr. 1855 by Bp of Lin. P. C. of Alvingham with Cockerington St. Mary, Dio. Lin. 1857. (Patron, Bp of Lin; P. C.'s Inc. 300*l* and Ho; Pop. Alvingham 350, Cockerington 265.) Formerly C. of St. John the Baptist's, Nottingham. [17]

SCROGGS, Sydney M., *Bishopsteignton, Teignmouth, Devon.* [18]

SCUDAMORE, Edward Toke, *The Marlons, Elstree, Herts.*—St. Cath. Hall, Cam. B.A. 1852; Deac. 1854 and Pr. 1855 by Bp of G. and B. C. of Elstree 1864. Formerly C. of Broome, Norfolk. [19]

SCUDAMORE, William Edward, *Ditchingham Rectory, near Bungay, Suffolk.*—St. John's Coll. Cam. B.A. 1835, M.A. 1838; Deac. 1838, Pr. 1839. R. of Ditchingham, Dio. Nor. 1839. (Patron, George Shaw, Esq; Tithe, 556*l*; Glebe, 32¾ acres; R.'s Inc. 602*l* and Ho; Pop. 1100.) Warden of the Sisterhood of All Hallows, Ditchingham. Formerly Fell. of St. John's Coll. Cam. Author, *Essay on the Office of the Intellect in Religion*, 1850, 8*s*; *Letters to a Seceder from the Church of England to the Communion of Rome*, 1851, 6*s* 6*d*; *England and Rome, the Principal Doctrines and Passages of History discussed between England and Rome*, 1855, 10*s* 6*d*; *The Communion of the Laity* (an Essay), 1855, 4*s* 6*d*; *Words to take with us, a Manual of Daily and Occasional Prayers*, 1859; *Steps to the Altar, Devotions for the Blessed Eucharist*, 42nd ed. [20]

SCULTHORPE, Clement Fisher, *Beoley Vicarage, Redditch, Worcestershire.*—St. John's Coll. Cam. B.A. 1833, M.A. 1836; Deac. 1837, Pr. 1838. V. of Beoley, Dio. Wor. 1839. (Patron, W. Holmes, Esq; Tithe, 70*l* 16*s* 1½*d*; Glebe, 2 acres; V.'s Inc. 100*l* and Ho; Pop. 682.) [21]

SCULTHORPE, H. Clement, *Beeley Parsonage, Bakewell, Derbyshire.*—P. C. of Beeley, Dio. Lich. (Patron, Duke of Devonshire; P. C.'s Inc. 150*l* and Ho; Pop. 420.) [22]

SCURR, Jonathan, *Ninebanks Parsonage, Haydonbridge, Northumberland.*—St. Bees 1837; Deac. 1838 by Bp of Dur. Pr. 1839 by Bp of Carl. P. C. of Ninebanks, Dio. Dur. 1837. (Patron, P. C. of Allendale; P. C.'s Inc. 134*l* and Ho.) [23]

SEACOMBE, A. H., *Northfield, Birmingham.*—C. of Northfield. [24]

SEAGER, John Osborne, *Stevenage, Herts.*—Trin. Coll. Cam. Sen. Opt. and 2nd cl. Cl. Trip. B.A. 1835, M.A. 1839; Deac. 1835 and Pr. 1836 by Bp of Pet. Formerly C. of Pickworth 1835, Stevenage 1836. [25]

SEAGRAVE, John Young, *Wellfield House, Bedford.*—Ch. Ch. Ox; Deac. 1849, Pr. 1850. Formerly V. of Bramham, Yorks, 1852–62. [26]

SEALE, Edward Taylor, *Morleigh Rectory, Devon.*—Trin. Coll. Cam. B.A. 1839. R. of Morleigh, Dio. Ex. 1841. (Patron, H. M. Stockdale, Esq; Tithe, 150*l*; Glebe, 17 acres; R.'s Inc. 180*l* and Ho; Pop. 122.) Formerly R. of Blackawton, Devon, 1841–61 [1]

SEALE, Frederic S., *Otterington Vicarage, Northallerton, Yorks.*—Trin. Coll. Ox. B.A. 1859; Deac. 1860 and Pr. 1861 by Bp of Ox. V. of North Otterington, Dio. York 1866. (Patron, Ch. Ch. Ox; Glebe, 3 acres; V.'s Inc. 180*l* and Ho; Pop. 650.) Formerly V. of Waterperry, Oxon, 1863–66. [2]

SEALY, E. Mc G., *Worcester.*—C. of St. John's, Bedwardine, Worcester. [3]

SEALY, Sparks Bellett, 19, *Arundel-square, Barnsbury, London, N.*—St. Peter's Coll. Cam. B.A. 1849, M.A. 1852; Deac. 1849 and Pr. 1850 by Bp of Ely. P. C. of St. Michael's, Islington, Dio. Lon. 1866. (Patrons, Trustees; P. C.'s Inc. 200*l* and Pew-rents.) Formerly C. of St. Andrew's-the-Less, Cambridge, 1849–59; V. of West Wratting, Cambs, 1862–66. Author, *Liturgy for Village Sunday Schools*, 1863. [4]

SEALY, William, *Polygon, Southampton.*—St. John's Coll. Ox. M.A.; Deac. 1847 and Pr. 1848 by Bp of Win. P. C. of St. Deunis, Southampton, Dio. Win. 1867. (Patron, Bp of Win; P. C.'s Inc. 150*l*.) Formerly C. of Petersfield, Hants, 1847–57. [5]

SEALY, William Guidott, *West Hill, Winchester.*—St. John's Coll. Cam. B.A. 1823, M.A. 1827; Deac. 1823, Pr. 1824. R. of St. Lawrence's, City and Dio. Win. 1857. (Patron, Ld Chan; R.'s Inc. 60*l*; Pop. 238.) [6]

SEAMAN, J. B., *South Baddesley, Lymington, Hants.*—P. C. of South Baddesley, Dio. Win. 1865. (Patron, P. W. Freeman, Esq; P. C.'s Inc. 100*l*; Pop. 561.) [7]

SEAMAN, Meshach, *Greenstead St. Andrew's Rectory, Colchester.*—Queens' Coll. Cam. 1823, B.D. 1833, D.D. 1839, *ad eund.* Ox. 1844; Deac. 1823 and Pr. 1824 by Bp of Nor. R. of Greenstead, St. Andrew's Dio. Roch. 1849. (Patron, Ld Chan; Tithe, 293*l*; Glebe, 3 acres; R.'s Inc. 308*l* and Ho; Pop. 789.) Chap. to the Colchester Union 1843; Surrogate 1851. Author, *The Scientific Monitor*, 1820, 3*s* 6*d*; *The Christian Preceptor*, 1821, 2*s* 6*d*; *The Bible Advocate*, 1824, 4*s* 6*d*; *The Young Christian Armed against Infidelity*, 1824, 2*s* 6*d*; *The Christian Student's Spelling Assistant*, 1833, 2*s*; *The Churchman's Hymn-book and Popular Psalmody*, 1855, 7*s*; etc. [8]

SEAMAN, Shadrach, *Northwood, Newport, Isle of Wight.*—Queens' Coll. Cam. B.A. 1844, M.A. 1852; Deac. 1844 and Pr. 1845 by Bp of Win. C. of Northwood 1851. [9]

SEARLE, Charles Edward, *Pembroke College, Cambridge.*—Pem. Coll. Cam. 10th Wrang. and B.A. 1851, M.A. 1854. Fell. of Pemb. Coll. Cam. [10]

SEARLE, William George, *Oakington Vicarage, near Cambridge.*—Queens' Coll. Cam. 17th Wrang. and B.A. 1852, M.A. 1855; Deac. 1855 and Pr. 1856 by Bp of Ely. V. of Oakington, Dio. Ely, 1858. (Patron, Queens' Coll. Cam; V.'s Inc. 199*l*; Pop. 592.) Formerly Fellow of Queens' Coll. Cam. [11]

SEATON, Abdiel, *Colton Rectory, near Rugeley, Staffs.*—Queen's Coll. Ox. B.A. 1843; Deac. 1843 by Bp of St. D. Pr. 1844 by Bp of G. and B. R. of Colton, Dio. Lich. 1849. (Patron, Rev. C. W. Landor; Tithe—Imp. 300*l*, R. 423*l*; Glebe, 51 acres; R.'s Inc. 580*l* and Ho; Pop. 629.) [12]

SEATON, Charles Abdiel, *Thame, Oxon.*—King's Coll. Lond. Theol. Assoc. 1862; Deac. 1862 and Pr. 1863 by Bp of Win. C. of Thame 1865. Formerly C. of Trinity, Southampton, 1862–63, St. Paul, Cornwall, 1864, Kingsdown, Bristol, 1864. [13]

SEATON, Douglas, *Bivia House, Goodrich, Ross, Herefordshire.*—Trin. Coll. Cam. B.A. 1862; Deac. 1862 and Pr. 1863 by Bp of Roch. C. of Goodrich 1866. Formerly C. of Bishop's Hatfield, Herts, 1862–64, Chertsey 1864–66; Chap. to Price's Hospital, Hereford, 1866. [14]

SEATON, John, *Cleckheaton, viâ Normanton.*—Deac. 1831 and Pr. 1832 by Abp of York. P. C. of St. John's, Cleckheaton, Dio. Rip. 1832. (Patron, V. of Birstal; Tithe—Imp. 57*l*, App. 57*l*; P. C.'s Inc. 300*l* and Ho; Pop. 5500.) [15]

'**SEATON, John Abdiel,** *Horsforth, Leeds.*—Trin. Coll. Ox. B.A. 1860, M.A. 1863; Deac. 1861 and Pr. 1862 by Bp of Rip. C. of Horsforth 1861. [16]

SEATON, John Montague, *Lichfield.*—Magd. Hall, Ox. B.A. 1858, M.A. 1861; Deac. 1859 and Pr. 1860 by Bp of Lich. Head Mast. of Lich. Gr. Sch. Formerly Asst. Mast. in Repton Gr. Sch; 2nd Mast. in Cheltenham Proprietary Sch. Author, *Twenty-four Chants*, Novello, 1853, 1*s* 6*d*. [17]

SEATON, William, *St. Thomas's Parsonage, Lambeth, Surrey, S.*—Magd. Hall, Ox. B.C.L; Deac. 1836 and Pr. 1837 by Bp of B. and W. P. C. of St. Thomas's, Lambeth, Dio. Win. 1862. (Patrons, Trustees; P. C.'s Inc. 300*l* and Ho; Pop. 9660.) Formerly P. C. of Ch. Ch. Pennington, Lanc. 1854–62. Author, *The Perfection of Christ's Human Nature Vindicated*, 1834, 1*s*; *The Christian Minister's Last Instructions, Warnings, and Encouragements* (a Farewell Sermon), 1847, 1*s*; *Profession without Principle, and Principle with Profession*, 1855, 4*d*; *The Atonement made and the Plague stayed* (a Sermon), 1862, 6*d*; *Ten Invitations to come to Church*, 10th thousand, 1863, 1*d*; *The Doctrine of Baptism of the Church of England Scriptural, and her Catechism, "a Form of Sound Words"* (in Reply to C. H. Spurgeon), 9th ed. 1863, Macintosh, 4*d*. [18]

SEAWELL, Henry Walter, *Little Berkhampstead, Herts.*—Lin. Coll. Ox. B.A. 1828; Deac. 1829, Pr. 1830. R. of Little Berkhampstead, Dio. Roch. 1834. (Patron, Marquis of Salisbury; Tithe, 250*l* 18*s* 4*d*; Glebe, 38½ acres; R.'s Inc. 330*l* and Ho; Pop. 450.) [19]

SECKER, Thomas Jackson, *Hagley-road, Birmingham.*—Ch. Coll. Cam. 1st Sen. Opt. B.A. 1857; M.A. 1860; Deac. 1857 and Pr. 1858 by Bp of Lich. C. of St. Barnabas', Birmingham, 1864. Formerly C. of Kidsgrove, Staffs, 1857, St. Stephen's, Tunbridge, Kent, 1863. [20]

SECKERSON, Edward Barlow, *High Offley Vicarage, Eccleshall, Staffs.*—St. Cath. Coll. Cam. B.A. 1828, M.A. 1831. V. of High Offley, Dio. Lich. (Patron, Bp of Lich; Tithe—App. 300*l*, V. 157*l*; Glebe, 86 acres; V.'s Inc. 315*l* and Ho; Pop. 883.) [21]

SECRETAN, Charles Frederick, *Longdon Vicarage, Tewkesbury.*—Wad. Coll. Ox. Kennicott Heb. Scho. 1843, Pusey and Ellerton Scho. 1844, B.A. 1842, M.A. 1847; Deac. 1844 and Pr. 1845 by Bp of Lon. V. of Longdon with Castle-Morton P. C. Dio. Wor. 1864. (Patrons, D. and C. of Westminster; V.'s Inc. 500*l* and Ho; Pop. 1444.) Formerly P. C. of Trinity, Westminster, 1852–64. Author, *Life and Labours of Robert Nelson*, Murray, 1862; *Sermons preached in Westminster*, Bell, 1861; *Memoirs of Archbishop Leighton*, S. P. C. K. 1865. [22]

SEDDON, Richard, *Pembridge, Leominster.*—C. of Pembridge [23]

SEDDON, William, *Anstey, Thurcaston, Loughborough.*—Emman. Coll. Cam. B.A. 1859; Deac. 1859 and Pr. 1860 by Bp of Lin. P. C. of Anstey, Dio. Pet. 1866. (Patron, R. of Thurcaston; P. C.'s Inc. 150*l*; Pop. 734.) Formerly C. of St. John's, Grantham, and Willingham, Cambridge. [24]

SEDGER, Thomas, *Bracon Ash, near Norwich.*—Queens' Coll. Cam. B.A. 1836, M.A. 1839; Deac. 1837 and Pr. 1838 by Bp of Roch. P. C. of Fundenhall, Dio. Nor. 1862. (Patron, T. Trench Berney, Esq; P. C.'s Inc. 41*l*; Pop. 334.) C. of Bracon Ash 1862. Formerly C. of Cooling, near Gravesend, of Appledore with Ebony, near Tenterden, and of New Buckenham, Norfolk; Chap. of Stafford County Gaol; P. C. of Rusland, near Milnthorpe, Claygate, Surrey, 1852–57. Author, A Literal English Translation, with Grammatical and Exegetical Notes of *De Veritate Religionis Christianæ*, by Grotius, for the Use of Divinity Students, Whittaker, 6*s*; Sermons in the *Pulpit*; etc. [25]

SEDGWICK, Abraham, *Hermon Villa, Freemantle, Southampton.*—St. Bees; Deac. 1848, Pr. 1850. R. of Freemantle, Dio. Win. 1855. (Patron, Bp of Win; Tithe,

50*l*; R.'s Inc. 220*l*; Pop. 3200.) Formerly C. of Stayley 1848, Chorley 1850, St. Thomas's, Preston, 1853–55. [1]

SEDGWICK, Adam, *Trinity College, Cambridge,* and *The Close, Norwich.*—Trin. Coll. Cam. 5th Wrang. B.A. 1808; Deac. 1817 by Bp. of Nor. Pr. 1818 by Bp of Salis. Fell. of Trin. Coll. Cam. 1810; Woodwardian Prof. of Geology 1818; Vice-Mast. of Trin. Coll Cam; Can. of Nor. 1834. Author, *On the Right of Nomination to Professorships* (two Pamphlets), 1823; *Four Letters in Reply to R. M. Beverley, Esq.* 1836; *Discourse on the Studies of the University of Cambridge,* 5th ed. 1850, 12*s*; *Geology of the Lake District,* Kendal, 1853; Preface to Dr Livingstone's *Cambridge Lectures,* 1858. Contributor of various Papers in the *Transactions* of the Cambridge Philosophical Soc; *Transactions* of the Geological Soc. of London; *Proceedings* of the Geological Soc. of London; *Journal* of the Geological Soc. of London; *Annals of Philosophy* and *Philosophical Magazine*; etc. [2]

SEDGWICK, Gordon, 12, *Jesson-street, Coventry.*—Caius Coll. Cam. 6th Sen. Opt. and B.A. 1863, M.A. 1867; Deac. 1866 by Bp of Wor. C. of Trinity, Coventry, 1866. [3]

SEDGWICK, James, *Scalby Vicarage, Scarborough.*—St. John's Coll. Cam. B.A. 1817, M.A. 1823; Deac. 1818 by Bp of Win. Pr. 1818 by Bp of Salis. V. of Scalby with Cloughton, Dio. York, 1840. (Patrons, D. and C. of Nor; Scalby, Tithe, 30*l*; Glebe, 160 acres; Cloughton Glebe, 14 acres; V.'s Inc. 367*l* and Ho; Pop. 1876.) [4]

SEDGWICK, John, *Crook Parsonage, Kendal.*—Deac. 1809 and Pr. 1810 by Bp of Ches. P. C. of Crook, Dio. Carl. 1840. (Patron, V. of Kendal; P. C.'s Inc. 77*l* and Ho; Pop. 258.) [5]

SEDGWICK, John, *Great Houghton Rectory, Northampton.*—Ch. Ch. Ox. 1842, Magd. Coll. 1844, B.A. 1846, M.A. 1848, B D. 1855, D.D. 1859; Deac. 1846 and Pr. 1848 by Bp of Ox. R. of Great Houghton, Dio. Pet. 1862. (Patron, Magd. Coll. Ox; Tithe, 620*l*; Glebe, 40 acres; R.'s Inc. 750*l* and Ho; Pop. 361.) Chap. to Lord Chelmsford 1859, and to Earl of Guilford 1850; Fell. of Magd. Coll. 1855, Bursar of 1859, Vice-Pres. of 1860. Formerly Chap. of High Leigh 1858; C. of Greinton 1864. Author, *History of France,* 1849; *History of Europe,* 1850; *Oremus* (Short Prayers in Verse), 1852; *Hints on the Establishment of Public Industrial Schools,* 1853. [6]

SEDGWICK, John Edmund, *St. Alban's Clergy House, Cheetwood, Manchester.*—Dub. *ad eund.* Ox. B.A. 1852, M.A. 1855; Deac. and Pr. 1853 by Bp of Man. Min. of St. Alban's District, Cheetwood, and Strangeways, Manchester, 1856. Formerly C. of St. Simon's, Salford, 1853. [7]

SEDGWICK, Richard, *Dent (Yorks), Kendal.*—Trin. Coll. Cam. B.A. 1850, M.A. 1853; Deac. 1850 and Pr. 1851 by Bp of Nor. P. C. of Dent, Dio. Rip. 1859. (Patrons, Landowners; P. C.'s Inc. 225*l* and Ho; Pop. 1097.) Formerly P. C. of St. Martin's-at-Oak and St. Giles's, Norwich, 1856. [8]

SELF, William Henry, *St. John's Parsonage, Lytham, Preston.*—St. Bees 1844. P. C. of St. John's, Lytham, Dio. Man. 1848. (Patron, Col. Clifton; P. C.'s Inc. 60*l* and Ho; Pop. 1579.) [9]

SELKIRK, James, *Lister-street, Hull.*—Deac. and Pr. 1825 by Bp of Lon. Chap. of the Borough Gaol and General Cemetery, Hull, 1849. Formerly Miss. of the Ch. Miss. Soc. at Cotta, Ceylon. Author, *Recollections of Ceylon*; *Romanised Singhalese and English Vocabulary,* Cotta Press; small *Treatise on Arithmetic,* and small *Treatise on Geography,* both Singhalese and English, Cotta; one of the Translators of the Scriptures and the Book of Common Prayer into Singhalese. [10]

SELLAR, W. Y.—Fell. of Oriel Coll. Ox. Formerly Tut. in Dur. Univ. [11]

SELLER, Henry Charles, *Trull Parsonage, Taunton.*—St. John's Coll. Cam. B.A. 1840; Deac. 1840, Pr. 1841. P. C. of Trull, Dio. B. and W. 1863. (Patron, F. W. Newton, Esq; P. C.'s Inc. 150*l* and Ho; Pop. 779.) Formerly P. C. of same 1854–58. [12]

SELLON, Edmond, *Caerwood, Tidenham, Chepstow.*—St. Edm. Hall, Ox. M.A.; Deac. 1863 and Pr. 1864 by Bp of G. and B. C. of Tidenham 1866. Formerly C. of St. Paul's, Bedminster, 1863–65. [13]

SELLON, William Edward, *Llangua, Abergavenny.*—Ex. Coll. Ox. 3rd cl. Math. et Phy. and B.A. 1840; Deac. 1841 and Pr. 1842 by Bp of Llan. R. of Llangua, Monmouthshire, Dio. Llan. 1843. (Patron, J. L. Scudamore, Esq; Tithe, 77*l* 8*s*; R.'s Inc. 120*l*; Pop. 114.) R. of Kentchurch, Herefordshire, Dio. Herf. 1858. (Patron, Ld Chan; R.'s Inc. 280*l* and Ho; Pop. 325.) Author, *Essay on Sisterhoods,* Masters, 1*s*. [14]

SELLS, Alfred, *Polygon House, Southampton.*—Clare Hall, Cam. 2nd cl. Cl. Trip. Sen. Opt. B.A. 1844, M.A. 1847; Deac. 1846, Pr. 1847. Formerly one of the Senior Asst. Masts. of Marlborough Coll. Wilts. [15]

SELLWOOD, Charles, *Hope-under-Dinmore, Hereford.*—C. of Hope-under-Dinmore. [16]

SELLWOOD, D., *Northampton.*—C. of All Saints', Northampton. [17]

SELLWOOD, John Binford, *Shute Parsonage, Axminster, Devon.*—St. John's Coll. Ox. 3rd cl. Lit. Hum. and B.A. 1852, M.A. 1853; Deac. 1853 by Bp of Ox. Pr. 1854 by Bp of B. and W. V. of Shute, Dio. Ex. 1860. (Patrons, D. and C. of Ex; Tithe, 180*l*; Glebe, 1½ acres; V.'s Inc. 250*l*; Pop. 610.) Formerly C. of Bicknoller, Somerset, 1853–54. [18]

SELWYN, Congreve, *Hyssington, Bishop's Castle, Montgomeryshire.*—C. of Hyssington and Snead. [19]

SELWYN, Edward John, *The Parsonage, Bickley, Bromley, Kent, S.E.*—Trin. Coll. Cam. Bell's Univ. Scho. B.A. 1846, M.A. 1849; Deac. 1847 and Pr. 1848 by Bp of Lon. P. C. of Bickley, Dio. Cant. 1867. (Patron, George Wythes, Esq; Endow. 50*l*; Pop. 1200.) Formerly Prin. of the Blackheath Proprietary Sch. 1847–64; Asst. C. of St. Margaret's, Lee, Kent, 1859–64; R. of St. Paul's, Wokingham, Berks, 1864–67. Author, *The Love and Pursuit of Heavenly Wisdom* (a Funeral Sermon), 1858; *For God and for England* (a Sermon preached to the 3rd Kent Rifle Volunteers), 1860; "*Remember*" (a Funeral Sermon), 1864. [20]

SELWYN, Sydney George, *Milton Clevedon Vicarage, Evercreech, Bath.*—New Coll. Ox. Fell of, B.A. 1844, M.A. 1846; Deac. 1844 and Pr. 1851 by Bp of Ox. V. of Milton Clevedon, Dio. B. and W. 1853. (Patron, Earl of Ilchester; Tithe, 202*l* 9*s*; Glebe, 62 acres; V.'s Inc. 312*l* 9*s*; Pop. 210.) Preb. of Wells; Rural Dean; District Inspector of Schs. [21]

SELWYN, William, *The College, Ely.*—St. John's Coll. Cam. Chan. Cl. Medal 1828, B.A. 1828, M.A. 1831, B.D. 1849, D.D. 1864; Deac. 1829 by Bp of Ely, Pr. 1831 by Bp of Roch. 6th Can. Res. of Ely Cathl. 1833. (Value, 600*l* and Res.) Lady Margaret's Reader in Theol. Cam. 1855; Chap. in Ordinary to the Queen 1859. Formerly R. of Branstone, Leicestershire, 1831–46; V. of Melbourn, Cambs, 1846–53. Author, *Principles of Cathedral Reform,* Part I. and II. 1840, 5*s*; *Horæ Hebraicæ on Isaiah* ix. 4to, 8*s*; *Two Charts of Prophecy* (in sheets), 2*s* and 1*s*; *Notes on the Revision of the Authorised Version of the Holy Scriptures,* 1856, 1*s*; *Notæ Criticæ in Versionem Septuagintaviralem*—Exodus i.-xxiv. 1856, *Numeri,* 1857, *Deuteronomium,* 1858, *M.P. and Canon Conversations on Ecclesiastical Legislation,* 1858–59; *Reasons for not signing the Oxford Declaration,* 1864; *Winfrid,* 1864, 2*s*; *Waterloo* (with Plans), 2nd ed. 1865, 3*s*; *Errors of Commission,* 1866; all published by Bell and Daldy. [22]

SELWYN, William, *Bromfield Vicarage, Salop.*—St. John's Coll. Cam. B.A. 1862, M.A. 1865; Deac. 1864 and Pr. 1865 by Bp of Wor. V. of Bromfield, Dio. Herf. 1866. (Patron, R. G. W. Clive, Esq; Tithe, 341*l*; Glebe, 8½ acres; V.'s Inc. 375*l* and Ho; Pop. 750. Formerly C. of Chaddesley Corbett, Worcestershire, 1864–66. [23]

SENDALL, E., *Litton Rectory, Wells, Somerset.*—Caius Coll. Cam. M.A. R. of Litton, Dio. B. and W. 1864. (Patron, Bp of B. and W; R.'s Inc. 290*l* and Ho; Pop. 313.) R. of Litton. [24]

SENDALL, Simon, *Scampston, Rillington, New Malton, Yorks.*—Caius Coll. Cam. B.A. 1824, M.A. 1827. P. C. of Scampston, Dio. York, 1865. (Patron, V. of Rillington; P. C.'s Inc. 80*l*; Pop. 248.) Formerly C. of East Acklam, Yorks. [1]

SENIOR, James, *Compton-Pauncefoot Rectory, Castle Carey, Somerset.*—Emman. Coll. Cam. B.A. 1837; Deac. and Pr. 1838 by Bp of B. and W. R. of Blackford, Somerset, Dio. B. and W. 1838. (Patron, B. Husey Hunt, Esq; Tithe, 156*l* 12*s*; Glebe, 24½ acres; R.'s Inc. 191*l* and Ho; Pop. 164.) R. of Compton-Pauncefoot, Dio. B. and W. 1839. (Patron, B. Husey Hunt, Esq; Tithe, 165*l*; Glebe, 34½ acres; R.'s Inc. 220*l* and Ho; Pop. 253.) [2]

SENIOR, Joseph, *St. Mary's Parsonage, Wakefield.*—Glasgow Univ. LL.D. 1835; Deac. 1832 and Pr. 1833 by Abp of York. P. C. of St. Mary's, Wakefield, Dio. Rip. 1851. (Patrons, the Crown and Bp of Rip. alt; P. C.'s Inc. 150*l* and Ho; Pop. 2340.) Campden Lect. of All Saints', Wakefield, 1844. (Patrons, the Mercers' Co. Lond; Value, 100*l*.) Hon. Chap. of the Wakefield Union; Min. of St. Mary's Chantry, on Wakefield-bridge. Formerly Head Mast. of Batley Free Gr. Sch. [3]

SENIOR, Walter, *Sheffield.*—C. of St. Paul's, Sheffield. [4]

SENKLER, Edmund John, *Barmer, Burnham, Westgate, Norfolk.*—Caius Coll. Cam. B.A. 1824, M.A. 1827. P. C. of Barmer (no Ch.) Dio. Nor. 1829. (Patron, T. Kearslake, Esq; Tithe—Imp. 223*l*, P. C. 5*l*; P. C.'s Inc. 5*l*; Pop. 62.) [5]

SEPHTON, John, *Liverpool Institute, Liverpool.*—St. John's Coll. Cam. 5th Wrang. and B.A. 1862, M.A. 1865; Deac. 1863 by Bp of Win. for Bp of Ely, Pr. 1864 by Bp of Ely. Head Mast. of Liverpool Institute and Prin. of Queen's Coll, Liverpool, 1866. Formerly Fell. of St. John's Coll. Cam; Asst Mast. at Highgate Sch. 1862–65; Clerk in Orders St. Anne's, Soho, Westminster, 1865. Author, *Inauguration Address*, Holden, Liverpool, 1867. [6]

SEPPINGS, Dillingham William, *Bramley, Leeds.*—Caius Coll. Cam. Jun. Opt. B.A. 1859, M.A. 1862; Deac. 1859 and Pr. 1860 by Bp of B. and W. C. of Bramley 1866. Formerly C. of Bridgwater 1859–62, Yarmouth 1862–66. [7]

SEPPINGS, George William, *Ashford, Staines, Middlesex.*—Corpus Coll. Cam. B.A. 1855, M.A. 1858; Deac. 1855 and Pr. 1856 by Bp of Win. V. of Ashford, Dio. Lon. 1859. (Patron, Ld Chan; Tithe, 100*l*; Glebe, 26 acres; V.'s Inc. 184*l*; Pop. 784.) Formerly C. of St. Paul's, Winchmore-hill, and St. Peter's, Southwark. [8]

SERGEANT, E. W., *Winchester.*—Ball. Coll. Ox. B.A. 1858, M.A. 1861; Deac. 1859 and Pr. 1860 by Bp of Ox. Asst. Mast. at Win. Coll. Formerly Assist. Mast. at Wellington Coll; Fell. of St. Peter's Coll. Radley. Author, *Sermons*, Macmillans, 1866, 2*s* 6*d*. [9]

SERGEANT, James Saunderson, *Melksham, Wilts.*—C. of Melksham and Seend. [10]

SERGEANT, Oswald Pattisson, *Syresham Rectory, Brackley.*—Trin. Coll. Cam. B.A. 1853, M.A. 1857; Deac. 1853 and Pr. 1854 by Bp of Ox. R. of Syresham, Dio. Pet. 1859. (Patron, C. C. Dormer, Esq; Tithe, 120*l*; Glebe, 25 acres; R.'s Inc. 210*l* and Ho; Pop. 1050.) Formerly C. of Somerton, Oxon, 1854–56, Milton, Berks, 1858. [11]

SERGISON, William, *Slaugham Rectory, Crawley, Sussex.*—Brasen. Coll. Ox. B.A. 1825, M.A. 1827; Deac. 1826 and Pr. 1827 by Bp of Chich. R. of Slaugham, Dio. Chich. 1839. (Patron, Warden Sergison, Esq; Tithe, 464*l* 19*s* 10*d*; Glebe, 20 acres; R.'s Inc. 465*l* and Ho; Pop. 1518.) Dom. Chap. to the Duke of Richmond 1840; Dom. Chap. to the Bp of Chich. 1844; Surrogate. Author, *Pray*; *Confirmation Sermon*. [12]

SERJEANT, H.—Asst. Chap. Scilly Islands. [13]

SERJEANT, James, *North Petherwin (Devon), near Launceston.*—Queens' Coll. Cam. B.A. 1831; Deac. 1831, Pr. 1832. V. of North Petherwin, Dio. Ex. 1853. (Patron, Duke of Bedford; Tithe—Imp. 194*l* 5*s* 2*d*, V. 142*l*; Glebe, 159 acres; V.'s Inc. 187*l* and Ho; Pop. 945.) [14]

SERJEANT, John Flowers, *Sheffield.*—Deac. 1848 and Pr. 1850 by Bp of S. and M. Min. of All Saints', Sheffield, Dio. York, 1867. Formerly C. of St. Mary's, Bryanston-square, Marylebone, Lond; Asst. Chap. at the English Ch. Rue d'Aguesseau, Paris. Author, *My Sunday School Class*, 1846, 2*s*. 6*d*, 2nd ed. 1*s* 4*d*; *Sunday School Teaching, its Object and Method*, 2*s*, 1851, 2nd ed. 1858; etc. [15]

SERJEANTSON, James Jordan, *Stoke-upon-Trent.*—Trin. Coll. Cam. B.A. 1858, M.A. 1860; Deac. 1859, Pr. 1860. C. of Stoke-upon-Trent. [16]

SERJEANTSON, William, *Acton Burnell Rectory, Shrewsbury.*—Ball. Coll. Ox. B.A. 1858, M.A. 1860; Deac. 1859 and Pr. 1860 by Bp of Herf. R. of Acton Burnell, Dio. Lich. 1862. (Patron, Sir C. F. Smythe; Tithe, 390*l*; R.'s Inc. 400*l* and Ho; Pop. 361.) Formerly C. of Staunton-on-Arrow 1859, Titley 1860. [17]

SERJEANTSON, William James, *Thornton Dale, Pickering, Yorks.*—Univ. Coll. Dur. B.A. 1855, M.A. 1857; Deac. 1856 by Bp of Man. Pr. 1857 by Bp of Dur. C. of Thornton Dale. [18]

SERRELL, Henry Digby, *Podymore-Milton, Ilchester, Somerset.*—R. of Podymore-Milton, Dio. B. and W. 1832. (Patrons, Heirs of W. Melliar, Esq; Tithe, 190*l*; Glebe, 22 acres; R.'s Inc. 244*l*; Pop. 131.) [19]

SERRES, Wyndham Scott, *Kingston, Jamaica.*—Queens' Coll. Cam. B.A. 1845; Deac. 1847 and Pr. 1849 by Bp of Chich. Formerly C. of St. Peter's, Bethnal Green, Lond. 1856; R. of Bepton, Sussex, 1849–63. [20]

SERVANTE, William, *Kempley Vicarage, Ledbury.*—Ex. Coll. Ox. B.A. 1816, M.A. 1821. V. of Kempley, Dio. G. and B. 1839. (Patrons, D. and C. of Herf; V.'s Inc. 230*l* and Ho; Pop. 311.) [21]

SETON, H.—C. of St. Thomas's, Portman-square, Lond. [22]

SEVERNE, Arthur, *Thenford, Banbury.*—Trin. Coll. Ox. B.A. 1849, M.A. 1851; Deac. and Pr. 1853 by Bp of Wor. R. of Thenford, Dio. Pet. 1863. (Patron, Ld Chan; R.'s Inc. 120*l* and Ho; Pop. 112.) Formerly R. of Rock, Worc. 1853–63. [23]

SEVERNE, William, *Whitstone Priory, near Shrewsbury.*—Queen's Coll. Ox. B.A. 1823, M.A. 1831. Formerly R. of Rochford, Herefordshire, 1854–57. [24]

SEVIER, James, *Hasfield Rectory, near Gloucester.*—Ch. Coll. Cam. B.A. 1820, M.A. 1823; Deac. 1820 by Bp of Ches. Pr. 1822 by Bp of Chich. R. of Hasfield, Dio. G. and B. 1833. (Patron, the present R; Glebe, 173 acres; R.'s Inc. 365*l* and Ho; Pop. 299.) [25]

SEVIER, William James, *Gayton, Stafford.*—C. of Gayton and Stowe, Staffs. [26]

SEWELL, Capel John, *Privy Council Office, Downing-street, London, S.W.*—Brasen. Coll. Ox. Hulme's Exhib. 1854, 3rd cl. Lit. Hum. 1856, B.A. 1856; Deac. 1858 and Pr. 1859 by Bp of Ches. One of H.M. Inspectors of Schs. Formerly C. of Astbury, Cheshire, and of St. Michael's, Paddington, Lond. [27]

SEWELL, Henry Doyle, *Headcorn Vicarage, Staplehurst, Kent.*—Trin. Coll. Ox. B.A. 1828, M.A. 1831; Deac. 1837, Pr. 1838. V. of Headcorn, Dio. Cant. 1850. (Patron, Abp of Cant; Tithe—Imp. 943*l* 16*s* 7*d*, V. 806*l* 6*s* 8*d*; V.'s Inc. 409*l* and Ho; Pop. 1389.) Formerly Chap. to Bp of Montreal; Chap. to H.M. Embassy, Constantinople, 1848. [28]

SEWELL, James Edwards, *New College, Oxford.*—New Coll. Ox. B.A. 1832, M.A. 1835; Deac. 1834, Pr. 1835. Warden of New Coll. Ox. 1860. [29]

SEWELL, Thomas, *Swindale, Shap, Westmoreland.*—Deac. 1823 and Pr. 1824 by Bp of Ches. P. C. of Swindale, Dio. Carl. 1830. (Patron, V. of Shap; P. C.'s Inc. 64*l*.) [30]

SEWELL, Thomas Wilder, *Carleton Rectory, Newmarket, Cambs.*—Trin. Coll. Cam. B.A. 1856, M.A. 1859; Deac. 1858 and Pr. 1859 by Bp of Ely. R. of Carleton with Willingham C. Dio. Ely, 1864. (Patron, the Rev. J. M. Wilder, B.D; R.'s Inc. 300*l* and Ho; Pop. 402.) Formerly C. of Swineshead, Hunts, and Sternfield, Suffolk. [31]

SEWELL, William, *Troutbeck, Windermere.*—P. C. of Troutbeck, Dio. Carl. 1856. (Patron, R. of Windermere; P. C.'s Inc. 55*l*; Pop. 428.) [1]

SEWELL, William.—Mert. Coll. Ox. 1st cl. Lit. Hum. and B.A. 1827; Fell. of Ex. Coll. Ox. 1827, English and Latin Essay and M.A. 1829, B.D. 1841; Deac. 1831 by Bp of Bristol, Pr. 1832 by Bp of Win. C. of St. Nicholas-in-the-Castle, Newport, Isle of Wight, Dio. Win. 1831. (Patron, the Governor; C.'s Inc. 25*l*; Pop. 265.) Warden of St. Peter's Coll. Radley, 1852; Whitehall Preacher 1850. Formerly Public Examiner in Lit. Hum. Ox. 1832; Prof. of Moral Philosophy 1836–41. Author, *An Address to a Christian Congregation on the Approach of the Cholera Morbus*; *An Essay on the Cultivation of the Intellect by the Study of the Dead Languages*, 1832; *Horæ Philologicæ, or Conjectures on the Structure of the Greek Language*, 1830; *Sermons on the Application of Christianity to the Human Heart*, 1831; *Parochial Sermons on Particular Occasions*, 1832; *Letters to a Dissenter on the Opposition of the University of Oxford to the Charter of the London College*, 1834; *Thoughts on Subscription* (in a Letter to a Member of Convocation), 1834; *Postscript to Thoughts on Subscription*, 1835; *Sacred Thoughts in Verse*, 1835; *Sermons addressed to Young Men*, 1835; *Thoughts on the Admission of Dissenters to the University of Oxford, and on the Establishment of a State Religion* (in a Letter to a Dissenter), 1836; *Christian Morals*, Vol. X. of *The Englishman's Library*, 1840; *An Introduction to the Dialogues of Plato*, 1841; *A Letter to the Rev. E. B. Pusey on the Publication of No. XC. of Tracts for the Times*, 1841; *The Duty of Young Men in Times of Controversy*, 1843; *Popular Evidences of Christianity*, 1843; *Christian Politics*, 1844; *The Plea of Conscience for seceding from the Catholic Church to the Romish Schism in England* (a Sermon, to which is prefixed *An Essay on the Process of Conscience*), 1845; *The New Speaker and Holiday Task Book, selected from Classical Greek, Latin, and English Writers*, 1846; *Journal of a Residence at the College of St. Colomba, in Ireland, with a Preface*, 1847; *Christian Commission* (a Sermon on laying the First Stone of the Almshouse Chapel of St. Mary Magdalene, Chiswick), 1848; *The Danger and Safeguard of the Young in the present State of Controversy* (a Sermon preached before the University of Oxford), 1848; *The Nation, the Church, and the University of Oxford* (two Sermons), 1849; *A Speech delivered at the Meeting of the Friends of National Education at Willis's Rooms*, 1850; *The Position of Christ's Church in England at the Time as a Witness to Divine Truth* (a Sermon, printed in *Sermons preached at St. Barnabas', Pimlico*), 1850; *Suggestions to Minds perplexed by the Gorham Case* (a Sermon), 2 eds. 1850; *Westminster Churches* (a Sermon), 1850; *The Character of Pilate and the Spirit of the Age* (a course of Sermons), 1850; *Oaths to obey Statutes* (a Sermon preached before the University of Oxford), 1852; *The Servant of Christ* (a Sermon preached with reference to the character of the late Duke of Wellington), 3 eds. 1852; *Collegiate Reform* (a Sermon), 1853; *A Year's Sermons to Boys* (preached in the Chapel of St. Peter's Coll. Radley), 1854. Translator of Virgil's *Georgics*, 1850; Æschylus, *The Agamemnon*, 1846; *The Odes and Epodes of Horace*, 1850; *The Georgics of Virgil literally and rhythmically translated*, 1854. [2]

SEWELL, William, *Huntley, Gloucester.*—New Coll. Ox. Fell. of, B.A. 1860, M.A. 1863; Deac. 1861 and Pr. 1862 by Bp of Win. C. of Huntley 1866. Formerly C. of Kingsclere, Hants, 1862–63. [3]

SEWELL, William Henry, *Yaxley Vicarage, Eye, Suffolk.*—Trin. Coll. Cam. B.A. 1858; Deac. 1859 and Pr. 1860 by Bp. of Roch. V. of Yaxley, Dio. Nor. 1861. (Patron, the present V; Tithe, 139*l*; Glebe, 39 acres; V.'s Inc. 200*l*; Pop. 510.) Formerly C. of Holy Trinity, Halstead, 1859–61. [4]

SEYMOUR, Albert Eden, *Comberton-terrace, Kidderminster.*—Univ. Coll. Ox. M.A. 1867; Deac. 1866 by Bp of Wor. C. of St. Mary's, Kidderminster, 1866. [5]

SEYMOUR, Charles Frederic, *Winchfield Rectory, Hants.*—Univ. Coll. Ox. B.A. 1842, M.A. 1849; Deac. 1843, Pr. 1844. R. of Winchfield, Dio. Win. 1849. (Patron, Sir H. St. John Mildmay, Bart; Tithe, 320*l*; R.'s Inc. 380*l* and Ho; Pop. 329.) [6]

SEYMOUR, Edward, *Bratton Clovelly, Oakhampton, Devon.*—Jesus Coll. Cam. B.A. 1847, M.A. 1850; Deac. 1848, Pr. 1849. R. of Bratton Clovelly, Dio. Ex. 1865. (Patron, Bp of Ex; Tithe, 460*l*; Glebe, 140 acres; R.'s Inc. 560*l* and Ho; Pop. 706.) Formerly C. of St. Burian, Cornwall. V. of Manaccan, Cornwall, 1857–65. [7]

SEYMOUR, Francis Payne, *The Rectory, Havant, Hants.*—Ball. Coll. Ox. B.A. 1837, M.A. 1840; Deac. 1839, Pr. 1840. R. of Havant, Dio. Win. 1859. (Patron, Bp of Win; Tithe, 670*l*; Glebe, 10 acres; R.'s Inc. 680*l* and Ho; Pop. 2216.) R. of Hannington, Hants, 1854–59. Author, *Sacrifice, no Part of the Church's Ministry* (a Sermon), 1853. [8]

SEYMOUR, George Augustus, *Trinity Rectory, Winchester.*—Trin. Coll. Cam. Jun. Opt. B.A. 1846, M.A. 1849; Deac. 1846 and Pr. 1849 by Bp of Win. R. of Trinity, Winchester, Dio. Win. 1854. (Patron, the present R; R.'s Inc. 180*l*; Pop. 1872.) Formerly C. of St. Maurice and St. Mary Kalendar, Winchester. Author, *Christ's Exaltation Foreshown* (a Sermon), 1850; *A Help to Persons preparing for Confirmation*, 2nd ed. 1850; *On the Duty of keeping Ourselves from Idols*, 1852; *The Ordinance of Marriage* (a Sermon on the wedding of the Prince of Wales), 1863. [9]

SEYMOUR, George P., *Tynterfield, near Bristol.* [10]

SEYMOUR, Henry, *Holme-Pierrepont Rectory, Nottingham.*—Ball. Coll. Ox. B.A. 1848; Deac. and Pr. 1851 by Bp of Lin. R. of Holme Pierrepont, Dio. Lin. 1864. (Patron, Earl Manvers; Tithe, 748*l* 16*s* 3*d*; Glebe, 32 acres; R.'s Inc. 816*l* and Ho; Pop. 179.) Formerly P. C. of Westcote, Dorking, 1852–64. [11]

SEYMOUR, Henry Fortescue, *Barking Vicarage, Essex.*—Ball. Coll. Ox. 2nd cl. Math. et Phy. and B.A. 1849; All Souls' Coll. M.A. 1852; Deac. 1852 and Pr. 1853 by Bp of Ox. V. of Barking, Dio. Lon. 1854. (Patron, All Souls' Coll. Ox; Tithe—App. 740*l*, Imp. 2209*l* 13*s* 11*d*, V. 820*l*; Glebe, 5 acres; V.'s Inc. 830*l* and Ho; Pop. 5596.) Formerly Fell. of All Souls' Coll. Ox. [12]

SEYMOUR, Sir John Hobart Culme, Bart., *Northchurch Rectory, Great Berkhampstead, Herts.*—Ex. Coll. Ox. B.A. 1821, M.A. 1824; Deac. 1823, Pr. 1824. Chap. in Ordinary to the Queen 1827; Preb. of Lin. 1827. (Value, 72*l*.) Can. Res. of Glouc. 1829. (Value, 750*l* and Res.) R. of Northchurch, or Berkhampstead, St. Mary, Dio. Roch. 1830. (Patron, Prince of Wales; Tithe, 901*l* 5*s*; R.'s Inc. 910*l* and Ho; Pop. 1638.) [13]

SEYMOUR, Michael Hobart, 27, *Marlborough-buildings, Bath.*—Dub. A.B. 1825, A.M. 1827; Deac. 1825, Pr. 1826. Author, *A Pilgrimage to Rome*, Seeleys, 1849; *Mornings among the Jesuits at Rome*, ib. 1850; *Certainty unattainable in the Church of Rome*, ib. 1852; *Evenings with the Romanists*, ib. 1854. [14]

SEYMOUR, Richard, *Kinwarton Rectory, Alcester, Warwickshire.*—Ch. Ch. Ox. B.A. 1828, M.A. 1832; Deac. 1830, Pr. 1831. R. of Kinwarton with Weethley C. and Great Alne C. Dio. Wor. 1834. (Patron, Bp of Wor; Tithe, 402*l*; Glebe, 30 acres; R.'s Inc. 500*l* and Ho; Pop. Kinwarton 64, Weethley 33, Great Alne 347.) Hon. Can. of Wor. 1846; Rural Dean. Author, *Old and New Friendly Societies, a Comparison between them*, 1839; *The Ministerial Office, its Difficulties and Encouragements*, 1847; *Use of the Weekly Offertory*; *The Unity of Churches* (a Sermon preached at the Consecration of the Bp of Moray and Ross), 1851; *The Divine Mode and Measures of Good Works* (a Visitation Sermon), 1854. [15]

SEYMOUR, William, *Landulph Rectory, Saltash, Cornwall.*—Trin. Hall, Cam. LL.D. 1846. R. of Landulph, Dio. Ex. 1847. (Patron, Prince of Wales; Tithe, 336*l*; Glebe, 42½ acres; R.'s Inc. 396*l* and Ho; Pop. 547.) [16]

SEYMOUR, William, *Ridware, Mavesyn, Staffs.*—C. of Ridware. [17]

SEYMOUR, William Scorer, *Chenies, Rickmansworth, Bucks.*—King's Coll. Lond. Theol. Assoc;

Deac. 1860 by Bp of Win. C. of Chenies. Formerly C. of St. Paul's, Southwark, Lond. 1860. [1]

SHABOE, David.—Queens' Coll. Cam. B.A. 1841, M.A. 1844; Deac. 1842 and Pr. 1843 by Bp of Ches. Asst. Chap. of the Tower Hamlets Cemetery, Lond. 1855. [2]

SHACKELL, Henry William.—Pemb. Coll. Cam. 10th Wrang. 2nd cl. Cl. Trip. 1st cl. Theol. Hon. 1857, B.A. 1857; Deac. 1857 by Abp of Cant. Fell. of Pemb. Coll. Cam; Prin. of Ch. Miss. Coll. Agra, N. India. 1858. [3]

SHACKLEFORD, James Shuckburgh, *Lutterworth, Leicestershire.*—Queens' Coll. Cam. B.A. 1830; Deac. 1831, Pr. 1832. [4]

SHACKLETON, Henry John, *Rothley Vicarage, Loughborough.*—Trin. Coll. Cam. B.A. 1827, M.A. 1830. V. of Rothley with Keyham C. Gaddesby C. Wartnaby C. and Caldwell with Wykeham C.'s, Dio. Pet. 1853. (Patrons, Exors. of the late C. C. Macaulay, Esq; V.'s Inc. 550*l* and Ho; Pop. Rothley 939, Keyham 122, Gaddesby 341, Wartnaby 116, Caldwell and Wykeham 139.) [5]

SHACKLETON, Matthew, *Thetford, Norfolk.*—P. C. of Thetford St. Cuthbert, Dio. Nor. 1863. (Patron, J. Shackleton, Esq; P.C.'s Inc. 63*l*; Pop. 1695.) R. of Thetford St. Peter, Dio. Nor. 1863. (Patron W. P. Snell, Esq; R.'s Inc. 122*l*; Pop. 1257.) [6]

SHACKLETON, T., *Lisset, Hull.*—C. of Lisset, Yorks. [7]

SHADFORTH, Thomas, *Hersham, Walton-on-Thames.*—Univ. Coll. Ox. 2nd cl. Lit. Hum. 1st cl. Math. et Phy. and B.A. 1838, M.A. 1841; Deac. 1839, Pr. 1843. P. C. of Hersham, Dio. Win. 1861. (Patron, V. of Walton-on-Thames; P. C.'s Inc. 100*l*; Pop. 1766.) Formerly Fell. of Univ. Coll. Ox. [8]

SHADGETT, Matthew Cordeux, 34, *Canonbury-park, Islington, London, N.*—Trin. Hall, Cam. B.A. 1847; Deac. 1847, Pr. 1848. Chap. of the Workhouse, St. Mary's, Islington, Lond. Formerly C. of Mariners' Ch. Liverpool, 1847, Flempton, Suffolk, 1849, Whepstead, Suffolk, 1852. [9]

SHADRACH, Benjamin, *Llanboidy, St. Clears, Carmarthenshire.*—C. in sole charge of Henllan Amgoed, Carmarthenshire. [10]

SHADWELL, Arthur Thomas Whitmore, *Langton, near Malton, Yorks.*—Ball. Coll. Ox. 2nd cl. Lit. Hum. B.A. 1843, M.A. 1844; Deac. 1844 and Pr. 1845 by Bp of Ches. R. of Langton, Dio. York, 1850. (Patron, Ld Chan; Tithe, 431*l*; Glebe, 88 acres; R.'s Inc. 600*l* and Ho; Pop. 264.) Formerly C. of Frodsham, Cheshire, 1844–45, Iping, Sussex, 1847–49. [11]

SHADWELL, Julius, *The Rectory, Washington, Durham.*—Ball. Coll. Ox. 2nd cl. Lit. Hum. and B.A. 1843; Deac. 1845 and Pr. 1846 by Bp of Ches. R. of Washington, Dio. Dur. 1865. (Patron, Bp of Man; Tithe, 405*l*; Glebe, 240*l*; R.'s Inc. 832*l* and Ho; Pop. 2304.) Formerly C. of Middleton, near Manchester, 1845–50; P. C. of Heywood 1850–65. [12]

SHAFTO, Arthur Duncombe, *Brancepeth Rectory, Durham.*—Univ. Coll. Dur. Licen. Theol. 1841; Deac. 1841, Pr. 1842. R. of Brancepeth, Dio. Dur. 1854. (Patron, R. E. D. Shafto, Esq; Tithe, 917*l* 7*s*; Glebe, 46 acres; R.'s Inc. 977*l* and Ho; Pop. 3325.) Rural Dean. [13]

SHAKESPEAR, Wyndham Arthur, *The Cottage, Peasemore, near Newbury, Berks.*—Ex. Coll. Ox. B.A. 1860, M.A. 1862; Deac. 1861 and Pr. 1862 by Bp of Ox. C. of Peasemore 1862. Formerly C. of Lambourne, near Hungerford, 1861–62. [14]

SHAKSPEARE, Charles.—C. of St. Stephen's, Paddington, Lond. [15]

SHAND, George, *Heydon Rectory, Norwich.*—Queen's Coll. Ox. B.A. 1842, M.A. 1845; Deac. 1842 and Pr. 1843 by Bp of Nor. R. of Heydon with Irmingland R. Dio. Nor. 1861. (Patron, W. E. L. Bulwer, Esq; R.'s Inc. 300*l* and Ho; Pop. 317.) Formerly V. of Guestwick, Norfolk, 1847–61. [16]

SHAND, Thomas Henry Rodie, *Brasenose College, Oxford.*—Brasen. Coll. Ox. 3rd cl. Lit. Hum. 1st cl. Math. 1848, B.A. 1848, Johnson's Math. Scho. 1849, M.A. 1851; Deac. 1853 and Pr. 1856 by Bp of Ox. Vice-Prin. Fell. and Math. Lect. of Brasen. Coll. Ox. [17]

SHANN, Thomas, *Boston Spa, Tadcaster.*—Univ. Coll. Ox. B.A. 1829, M.A. 1832; Deac. 1832 and Pr. 1833 by Abp of York. Formerly V. of Hampsthwaite, Yorks, 1839–55. [18]

SHANNON, Frederick William, *Quarrington Rectory, Sleaford, Lincolnshire.*—R. of Quarrington, Dio. Lin. 1861. (Patron, Marquis of Bristol; R.'s Inc. 300*l* and Ho; Pop. 299.) [19]

SHANNON, George L., *Pembroke College, Oxford.*—Pemb. Coll. Ox. M.A. 1843 [20]

SHAPCOTE, Edward Gifford, *Philippolis, Orange Free State, South Africa.*—Corpus Coll. Cam. B.A. 1852; Deac. 1852 and Pr. 1853 by Bp of Ex. Formerly C. of Odiham, Hants, and West Lavington, Sussex. [21]

SHAPTER, Henry Dwyer, *Dowland, Dolton, Devon*—Wor. Coll. Ox. B.A. 1850, M.A. 1852; Deac. 1850 and Pr. 1851 by Bp of G. and B. P. C. of Dowland, Dio. Ex. 1858. (Patron, Sir S. H. Northcote; Tithe, 121*l*; P. C.'s Inc. 121*l*; Pop. 205.) Formerly C. of Stratfield-Turgis, Hants. [22]

SHARLAND, George Edward, 16, *Woodbine-street, South Shields.*—Dur. Licen. Theol; Deac. 1867 by Bp of Dur. C. of St. Hilda's, South Shields. [23]

SHARLAND, George Thomas, *Spaldwick Vicarage, Kimbolton, Hunts.*—V. of Spaldwick, Dio. Ely, 1865. Patron, Bp of Ely; V.'s Inc. 270*l* and Ho; Pop. 470.) Formerly P. C. of Ide, Devon, 1856–65. [24]

SHARP, Benjamin Oswald, 4, *Verulam-buildings, Gray's Inn, London, W.C.*—King's Coll. Lond. Theol. Assoc; Deac. 1858 and Pr. 1859 by Abp of York. Dioc. Home Miss. Clerkenwell, 1864. Formerly C. of St. James's, Clerkenwell. [25]

SHARP, Henry Isaac, *Swavesey Vicarage, St. Ives, Hunts.*—Jesus Coll. Cam. 20th Wrang. 2nd cl. Theol. Trip. B.A. 1856, M.A. 1857; Deac. 1857 and Pr. 1858 by Bp of Wor. V. of Swavesey, Dio. Ely, 1863. (Patron, Jesus Coll. Cam; V.'s Inc. 425*l* and Ho; Pop. 1371.) Formerly C. of Kidderminster 1857–63. Author, *Harvest Lessons* (a Sermon), 1863. [26]

SHARP, John, *Horbury Parsonage, Wakefield.*—Magd. Coll. Cam. Scho. of, B.A. 1833, M.A. 1836; Deac. 1833, Pr. 1834. P. C. of Horbury, Dio. Rip. 1834. (Patron, V. of Wakefield; P. C.'s Inc. 230*l* and Ho; Pop. 3246.) [27]

SHARP, John Prior, *Edenham, Bourne, Lincolnshire.*—Caius Coll. Cam. B.A. 1857, M.A. 1860; Deac. 1857 and Pr. 1858 by Bp of Lin. P. C. of Edenham, Dio. Lin. 1867. (Patron, Lord Willoughby de Eresby; P. C.'s Inc. 52*l*; Pop. 644.) Formerly C. of St. James's, Nottingham, 1857, Hawton, Notts, 1859, Bourne 1861, Edenham 1865. [28]

SHARP, Theophilus, *Ansley Vicarage, Atherstone, Warwickshire.*—St. Cath. Coll. Cam. B.A. 1847, M.A. 1851; Deac. 1847 by Bp of Ches. Pr. 1848 by Bp of Man. V. of Ansley, Dio. Wor. 1867. (Patron, the present V; Tithe, 102*l*; Glebe, 25 acres; V.'s Inc. 200*l* and Ho; Pop. 685.) Formerly Sen. C. of St. Martin's, Birmingham, and the Abbey, Bath. [29]

SHARP, William, *Mareham-le-Fen Rectory, Boston, Lincolnshire.*—Magd. Coll. Cam. B.A. 1836; Deac. 1836 by Abp of York, Pr. 1837 by Bp of Rip. R. of Mareham-le-Fen, Dio. Lin. 1855. (Patron, Bp. of Carl; Tithe, 10*l* 14*s*; Glebe, 307 acres; R.'s Inc. 430*l* and Ho; Pop. 937.) [30]

SHARP, William, *Altham Vicarage, Accrington, Lancashire.*—St. Bees; Deac. 1846 and Pr. 1847 by Bp of Ches. V. of Altham, Dio. Man. 1848. (Patron, R. T. R. Walton, Esq; Tithe, 2*l* 1*s*; Glebe, 40 acres; V.'s Inc. 180*l* and Ho; Pop. 410.) [31]

SHARPE, Clement Charles, *Ince Parsonage, Chester.*—Ex. Coll. Ox. B.A. 1850, M.A. 1852; Deac. 1850 and Pr. 1851 by Bp of Lon. P. C. of Ince, Dio. Ches. 1852. (Patron, E. W. P. Yates, Esq; P. C.'s Inc. 250*l* and Ho; Pop. 371.) [32]

SHARPE, Francis William, *Tibshelf Vicarage, Alfreton, Derbyshire.*—Emman. Coll. Cam. B.A. 1825; Deac. 1828, Pr. 1829. P. C. of Temple-Normanton, Derbyshire, Dio. Lich. 1842. (Patroness, Miss Lord; P. C.'s Inc. 55*l*; Pop. 136.) V. of Tibshelf, Dio. Lich. 1849. (Patroness, Miss Lord; Tithe—Imp. 123*l* 15*s* 6*d*, V. 185*l* 18*s* 4*d*; Glebe, 42 acres; V.'s Inc. 260*l* and Ho; Pop. 863.) [1]

SHARPE, George Brereton, *Brecon.*—St. John's Coll. Cam. B.A. 1861; Deac. 1862 and Pr. 1863 by Bp of St. D. C. of Brecon 1865. Formerly C. of Laugharne 1862–64, Tenby, 1864. [2]

SHARPE, Henry, *Peterborough.*—C. of St. John Baptist's, Peterborough. [3]

SHARPE, Joseph William, *Broadwell, near Moreton-in-Marsh, Glouc.*—Corpus Coll. Cam. B.A. 1849; Deac. 1849, Pr. 1850. C. of Broadwell. [4]

SHARPE, Lancelot Arthur, *Tackley Rectory, Oxford.*—St. John's Coll. Ox. 2nd cl. Lit. Hum. and B.A. 1828, M.A. 1832, B.D. 1837; Deac. 1829, Pr. 1831. R. of Tackley, Dio. Ox. 1839. (Patron, St. John's Coll. Ox; Tithe, 750*l*; Glebe, 60 acres; R.'s Inc. 830*l* and Ho; Pop. 626.) Surrogate. Formerly Jun. Proctor 1836–37; Select Preacher 1840; Fell. and Tut. of St. John's Coll. Ox. [5]

SHARPE, Robert Napier, *St. Mary's Vicarage, Rochdale.*—Queen's Coll. Ox. B.A. 1847, M.A. 1851; Deac. 1849 and Pr. 1850 by Bp of Ches. V. of St. Mary's, Hundersfield, Rochdale, Dio. Man 1857. (Patron, V. of Rochdale; V.'s Inc. 300*l* and Ho; Pop. 10,610.) Formerly C. of St. Mark's, Dukinfield, Cheshire, 1849–52; Sen. C. of Rochdale 1852–57. [6]

SHARPE, Thomas Henry, *Codicote Vicarage, Welwyn, Herts.*—St. Cath. Coll. Cam. B.A. 1845, M.A. 1848; Deac. 1845 and Pr. 1846 by Abp of York. V. of Codicote, Dio. Roch. 1848. (Patron, Abp of Cant; Tithe, 150*l*; V.'s Inc. 220*l* and Ho; Pop. 1227.) Formerly C. of St. Mary's, Hull, 1845–47, Rauceby, Sleaford, 1847–49. [7]

SHARPE, Thomas Wetherherd, *Beddington, Croydon, S.*—Trin. Coll. Cam. Bell's Univ. Scho. 12th Wrang. 1st cl. Cl. Trip. and B.A. 1852; Deac. 1853 and Pr. 1854 by Bp of Ely. One of H.M.'s Inspectors of Schs. 1859. Formerly Fell. of Ch. Coll. Cam. 1852. [8]

SHARPE, William Leggatt, *St. Paul's Parsonage, Barton, Isle of Wight.*—St. Bees; Deac. 1848 and Pr. 1850 by Bp of Ches. M.A. by Abp of Cant. 1856. P. C. of Barton, Isle of Wight, Dio. Win. 1854. (Patron, R. of Whippingham; P. C.'s Inc. 190*l* and Ho; Pop. 1314.) [9]

SHARPE, William Robert, 19, *Albion-square, Queen's-road, London, N.E.*—St. Cath. Coll. Cam. late Fell. of, 4th Sen. Opt. and B.A. 1839, M.A. 1842; Deac. 1841 by Bp of Ely, Pr. 1842 by Bp of Lin. P. C. of St. Chad's, Haggerston, Dio. Lon. 1863. (Patrons, Trustees; P. C.'s Inc. 300*l*; Pop. 7000.) Formerly C. of Clareborough, Notts, 1842–47, Uppingham, Rutland, 1848–51; P. C. of St. Gregory's, Norwich, 1851–63. [10]

SHARPIN, Frederick Lloyd, *Bombay.*—Ex. Coll. Ox. B.A. 1860; Deac. 1862 and Pr. 1863 by Bp of Ely. Formerly C. of Northill, Biggleswade, 1862. [11]

SHARPLES, Arthur, *Inskip Parsonage, Preston.*—Queens' Coll. Cam. B.A. 1844; Deac. 1844 and Pr. 1845 by Bp of Pet. P. C. of Inskip, Dio. Man. 1849. (Patron, V. of St. Michael's-on-Wyre; P. C.'s Inc. 105*l* and Ho; Pop. 780.) [12]

SHARPLES, James Hool, *Heversham, Milnthorpe, Westmoreland.*—St. John's Coll. Cam. B.A. 1842, M.A. 1845; Deac. 1842, Pr. 1843. Head Mast. of Heversham Gr. Sch. [13]

SHARROCK, James, *Longhorsley, Morpeth.*—St. Bees; Deac. 1857 and Pr 1858 by Bp of Lich. C. of Longhorsley 1861. Formerly C. of Biddulph, Staffs, 1857–61. [14]

SHARWOOD, John Hodges, *Walsall Vicarage, Staffs.*—St. Edm. Hall, Ox. B.A. 1833, M.A. 1838; Deac. 1833, Pr. 1834. V. of Walsall, Dio. Lich. 1845. (Patron, Earl of Bradford; Tithe—Imp. 445*l* 6*s* 4*d*, V. 300*l*: Glebe, 33 acres; V.'s Inc. 500*l* and Ho; Pop. 16,777.) Rural Dean of Walsall 1845. [15]

QQ

SHAW, Charles, *Hilton, Hunts.*—Ch. Coll. Cam. B.A. 1857; Deac. 1858 and Pr. 1859 by Bp of Lin. C. of Hilton 1866. Formerly C. of Ch. Ch. Marylebone, Lond. 1858 60. [16]

SHAW, Charles Henry, 22, *East India-road, Limehouse. E.*—King's Coll. Lond; Deac. 1863 and Pr. 1864 by Bp of Nor. Miss. C. of St. Andrew's, Limehouse, 1866. Formerly C. of St. Michael's, Beccles, Suffolk, 1863–66. [17]

SHAW, Charles James, *Seaborough Rectory (Somerset), near Crewkerne.*—Trin. Coll. Cam. B.A. 1827. M.A. 1832; Deac. 1828 and Pr. 1829 by Bp of Ches. R. of Seaborough, Dio. B. and W. 1837. (Patron, the present R; Tithe, 130*l*; Glebe, 28 acres, 40*l*; R.'s Inc. 170*l* and Ho; Pop. 120.) R. of Cricket St. Thomas, Somerset, Dio. B. and W. 1846. (Patron, Lord Bridport; Tithe, 87*l* 10*s*; Glebe, 30 acres; R.'s Inc. 106*l*; Pop. 76.) [18]

SHAW, Charles J. K., *Brenzett, Romney, Kent.*—V. of Brenzett, Dio. Cant. 1865. (Patron, Rev. W. Brockman; V.'s Inc. 100*l*; Pop. 270.) [19]

SHAW, Daniel, *Wisbech, Cambs.*—C. of St. Peter and St. Paul's, Wisbech. Formerly C. of Grassendale, near Liverpool. [20]

SHAW, Edward Butterworth, *Narborough Rectory, near Leicester.*—Caius Coll. Cam. Sen. Opt. and B.A. 1819, M.A. 1822; Deac. 1820, Pr. 1821. R. of Narborough, Dio. Pet. 1835. (Patron, Thomas Pares, Esq; Tithe, 439*l*; Glebe, 83 acres; R.'s Inc. 609*l* and Ho; Pop. 1156.) Rural Dean. [21]

SHAW, Edwin, *Church Hill, Selby, Yorks.*—St. Bees; Deac. 1866, Pr. 1867. C. of Selby. [22]

SHAW, George, *Bardney, Wragby, Lincolnshire.*—C. of Bardney. [23]

SHAW, G. F. E., *Edgworth Rectory, Cirencester.*—R. of Edgworth, Dio. G. and B. 1864. (Patron, the present R; R.'s Inc. 350*l* and Ho; Pop. 139.) [24]

SHAW, Glencairn Alexander, *Petton, Salisbury.*—St. John's Coll. Ox. B.A. 1863, M.A. 1867; Deac. 1863 and Pr. 1864 by Bp of Ox. R. of Petton, Dio. Lich. 1866. (Patron, Ld Chan; Tithe, 154*l*; R.'s Inc. 154*l*; Pop. 45.) Formerly C. of Chalfont St. Peter [25]

SHAW, John, 9, *Warwick-place, Leeds.*—St. Cath. Coll. Cam. B.A. 1865; Deac. 1866 by Bp of Rip. C. of St. George's, Leeds, 1866. [26]

SHAW, Morton, *Rougham Rectory, Bury St. Edmunds.*—Brasen. Coll. Ox. B.A. 1842, M.A. 1846. R. of Rougham, Dio. Ely, 1854. (Patron, Philip Bennet, Esq; R.'s Inc. 765*l* and Ho; Pop. 988.) [27]

SHAW, Richard D., *Over, Cambs.*—Lin. Coll. Ox. B.A. 1864; Deac. 1865 and Pr. 1866 by Bp of Lich. C. of St. Mary's, Over, 1867. Formerly Asst. C. of St. James's, Longton, Staffs, 1865–67. [28]

SHAW, Robert Henry, *Caius College, Cambridge.*—Caius Coll. Cam. Wrang. and B.A. 1852, M.A. 1855. Fell. of Caius Coll. Cam. [29]

SHAW, Robert John, *Danehill, Uckfield, Sussex.*—P. C. of Danehill, Dio. Chich. 1861. (Patron, Earl of Sheffield; P. C.'s Inc. 90*l*; Pop. 963.) [30]

SHAW, Robert William, *Cuxton Rectory, Rochester.*—Ch. Ch. Ox. B.A. 1826, M.A. 1831. R. of Cuxton, Dio. Roch. 1831. (Patron, Bp of Roch; Tithe—App. 43*l* 5*s*, Imp. 32*l* 1*s* 6*d*, R. 404*l* 10*s*; R.'s Inc. 419*l* and Ho; Pop. 441.) Hon. Can. of Roch. 1851; Chap. to Lord Gardner. [31]

SHAW, William Francis, *Eastry Vicarage, Sandwich, Kent.*—Caius Coll. Cam. B.A. 1862, M.A. 1865; Deac. 1862 and Pr. 1863 by Bp of Ches. V. of Eastry, Dio. Cant. 1867. (Patron, Abp of Cant.; V.'s Inc. 310*l* and Ho; Pop. 1200.) Formerly C. of Acton, Cheshire, 1862, St. John's, Thanet, 1865, Biddenden, 1866. [32]

SHAW, William Maw, *Yealand Parsonage, near Lancaster.*—Sid. Coll. Cam. B.A. 1838, M.A. 1847; Deac. 1841 and Pr 1842 by Bp of Toronto. P.C. of Yealand Conyers, Dio. Man. 1857. (Patrons, Hyndman's Trustees; Tithe, Imp. 300*l*; Glebe, 2 acres; P. C.'s Inc.

255*l* and Ho; Pop. 480.) Formerly Miss. of S.P.G. at Emily, Canada, 1841–45; C. of St. Michael's, Highgate, Lond. 1845–57. Author, *Letter on the Proposed Union between the Wesleyans and the Church*, 1856; *The Gleaning Grapes when the Vintage is done* (14 Sermons preached at Highgate), 1858. [1]

SHAW, W. Stokes, *Lyncombe, Bath.*—C. of Lyncombe, and of St. Mary Magdalen Chapel, Bath. [2]

SHAWCROSS, Richard, *Ellerburne, Pickering, Yorks.*—King's Coll. Lond. Theol. Assoc. 1st cl. 1848; Deac. 1849 and Pr. 1850 by Bp of Wor. V. of Ellerburne with Wilton, C. Dio. York, 1866. (Patron, Abp of York; V.'s Inc. 175*l*; Pop. Ellerburne 467, Wilton 181.) Formerly C. of Settrington 1852–60, Scarborough 1861–62, Everingham 1863. [3]

SHAYLER, Alexander, J., *Bittern, near Southampton.*—St. Alban Hall, Ox. B.A. 1863; Deac. 1864 and Pr. 1865 by Bp of Win. C. of Bittern 1867. Formerly C. of St. Paul's, Westminster-road, Southwark, 1864–67. [4]

SHEA, Robert Francis Jones, *Henbury Parsonage, Macclesfield.*—Dub. A.B. 1839, A.M. 1842; Deac. 1843, Pr. 1844. P. C. of Henbury, Dio. Ches. 1850. (Patron, Bp of Ches; P. C.'s Inc. 152*l* and Ho; Pop. 1015.) [5]

SHEAN, Harry Shum, *East Chiltington, Hurstpierpoint, Sussex.*—Literate; Deac. 1844 and Pr. 1850 by Bp of Chich. C. of East Chiltington 1861. Formerly C. of Westbourne, Sussex, 1844–59, and Bolney, Sussex, 1860. [6]

SHEARD, William D., *Strubby, Alford, Lincolnshire.*—Sid. Coll. Cam. B.A. 1828, M.A. 1831. V. of Strubby, Dio. Lin. 1860. (Patrons, D. and C. of Lin; V.'s Inc. 150*l*; Pop. 295.) Formerly V. of Burton-Dassett, Warw. 1846–60. [7]

SHEARLY, William James, *Burcot House, Wells, Somerset.*—St. Peter's Coll. Cam. B.A. 1840, M.A. 1843; Deac. and Pr. 1841 by Bp of Ches. P. C. of Henton, Somerset, Dio. B. and W. 1847. (Patron, Bp of B. and W; P. C.'s Inc. 100*l*; Pop. 548.) [8]

SHEARM, John, *Toddington, Beds.*—Pemb. Coll. Ox. B.A. 1863, M.A. 1867; Deac. 1866 and Pr. 1867 by Bp of Ely. C. of Toddington 1866. [9]

SHEARS, Augustus, *Moulmein, Burmah.*—M.A; Deac. 1851, Pr. 1852. Miss. of S.P.G. in the East Indies. Formerly C. of Abbotts Langley, Herts. [10]

SHEBBEARE, Charles Hooper, *Wykeham, Yorks.*—Univ. Coll. Ox. 3rd cl. Lit. Hum. and B.A. 1847, M.A. 1850; Deac. 1849 and Pr. 1850 by Bp of Lon. P. C. of Wykeham, Dio. York, 1853. (Patron, Viscount Downe; Tithe—Imp. 398*l* 17*s* 6*d*; P. C.'s Inc. 270*l* and Ho; Pop. 521.) Formerly Asst. C. of St. James's the Great, Bethnal Green, Lond. and Langham and Egleton, Rutland. [11]

SHEDDEN, Edward Cole, *Clapton Rectory, Thrapstone, Northants.*—Univ. Coll. Ox. St. Mary Hall, Ox. B.A. 1837, M.A. 1840; Deac. 1839, Pr. 1840. R. of Clapton, Dio. Pet. 1845. (Patrons, G. and W. G. Shedden, Esqrs; Tithe, 295*l* 16*s*; Glebe, 46 acres; R.'s Inc. 332*l* and Ho; Pop. 153.) [12]

SHEDDEN, Samuel, *Kilton Vicarage, Bridgwater, Somerset.*—Pemb. Coll. Ox. B.A. 1842, M.A. 1844; Deac. 1842 and Pr. 1843 by Bp of Ox. V. of Kilton, Dio. B. and W. 1856. (Patron, Bp of B. and W; Tithe—Imp. 73*l*, V. 172*l* 1*s* 8*d*; Glebe, 50 acres; V.'s Inc. 234*l* and Ho; Pop. 174.) [13]

SHEDDON, T., *Dudley, Worcestershire.*—C. of St. Edmund's, Dudley. [14]

SHEEN, Samuel, *Stanstead Rectory, Sudbury, Suffolk.*—Theol. Assoc. King's Coll. Lond; Ph.D. and M.A. Univ. Jena, Prussia; Deac. 1855 by Abp of Cant. Pr. 1856 by Bp of Herf. R. of Stanstead, Dio. Ely, 1867. (Patron, the present R; Tithe, 277*l*; Glebe, 24 acres; R.'s Inc. 301*l* and Ho; Pop. 382.) Formerly C. of Middle Rasen Drax and Middle Rasen Tupholme, Lincolnshire. [15]

SHEEPSHANKS, Thomas, *Arthington Hall, near Otley, Yorks.*—Trin. Coll. Cam. Scho. of, 2nd cl. Cl. Trip. B.A. 1842, M.A. 1845; Deac. 1842 by Bp of Lon. Pr. 1843 by Abp of Cant. P. C. of Arthington, Dio. Rip. 1864. (Patron, W. Sheepshanks, Esq; P. C.'s Inc. 150*l*; Pop. 344.) Formerly C. of Ide Hill, Kent, 1842–44; P. C. of High Harrogate, Yorks, 1845–57; P. C. of Bilton, Yorks, 1857–64. [16]

SHEEPSHANKS, Thomas, *Coventry.*—Trin. Coll. Cam. B.A. 1820, M.A. 1823; Deac. and Pr. 1825 by Bp of Ex. R. of St. John's, Coventry, Dio. Wor. 1834. (Patrons, Trustees; Tithe, 65*l*; R.'s Inc. 180*l*; Pop. 4800.) Rural Dean. [17]

SHEFFIELD, Charles, *Flixborough Rectory, Brigg, Lincolnshire.*—Ch. Ch. Ox. B.A. 1820, M.A. 1824. R. of Flixborough with Burton-upon-Stather V. Dio. Lin. 1822. (Patron, Sir R. Sheffield, Bart; Tithe, 556*l*; R.'s Inc. 767*l* and Ho; Pop. Flixborough 236, Burton-upon-Stather, 983.) Rural Dean. [18]

SHEFFIELD, Frank, *Normanby-park, Brigg, Lincolnshire.*—Trin. Hall, Cam. B.A. 1860; Deac. 1862 and Pr. 1863 by Bp of Lin. C. of Burton 1862. [19]

SHEFFIELD, John, *Barnton, Northwich, Cheshire.*—Dub. A.B. 1830, A.M. 1834. P. C. of Barnton Dio. Ches. 1864. (Patron, Bp of Ches; P. C.'s Inc. 120*l* and Ho; Pop. 1431.) Surrogate. Formerly Sen. C. of Rochdale and Head Mast. of the Rochdale Gr. Sch; C. of Hartford, Cheshire. [20]

SHELDON, John, *St. James's Parsonage, Handsworth, Birmingham.*—Trin. Coll. Ox. B.A. 1848, M.A. 1851; Deac. 1848 and Pr. 1849 by Bp of Ox. P. C. of St. James's, Handsworth, Dio. Lich. 1856. (Patron, R. of Handsworth; P. C.'s Inc. 200*l*; Pop. 3691.) [21]

SHELDON, Richard Vincent, *Hoylake, Birkenhead.*—Queens' Coll. Cam. B.A. 1852; Deac. 1852, Pr. 1853. P. C. of Hoylake, Dio. Ches. 1858. (Patron, Bp of Ches; Glebe, 1 acre; P. C.'s Inc. 120*l*; Pop. 1017.) Formerly P. C. of St. Matthias', Liverpool, 1853–58. [22]

SHELDON, Robert William, *Fonthill Bishop Rectory, Tisbury, Salisbury.*—Trin. Coll. Cam. B.A. 1842, M.A. 1845; Deac. 1844 and Pr. 1845. R. of Fonthill Bishop, Dio. Salis. 1866. (Patron, Bp. of Win; Tithe, comm. 259*l*; Glebe, 4½ acres; R.'s Inc. 264*l* and Ho; Pop. 187.) Formerly C. of Fawley and of Millbrook, Hants. [23]

SHELFORD, Leonard Edmund, *Upper Clapton, London, N.E.*—King's Coll. Lond. Theol. Assoc. 1860; Deac. 1860 and Pr. 1861 by Bp of Nor. P. C. of St. Matthew's, Upper Clapton, Dio. Lon. 1866. (Patron, Bp of Lon; P. C.'s Inc. 150*l*.) Formerly C. of Aylsham, Norfolk, 1860–62, St. John's, Hackney, Lond. 1862–66. [24]

SHELLEY, Sir Frederick, Bart., *Beer-Ferris Rectory, Tavistock, Devon.*—Deac. 1835, Pr. 1836. R. of Beer-Ferris, Dio. Ex. 1844. (Patron, Earl of Mount Edgcumbe; Tithe, 750*l*; Glebe, 148 acres; R.'s Inc. 750*l* and Ho; Pop. 2847.) [25]

SHELLEY, John, *Bradley, Penkridge, Staffs.*—St. John's Coll. Cam. B.A. 1841, M.A. 1844; Deac. 1842 and Pr. 1843 by Bp of Wor. P. C. of Bradley, Dio. Lich. 1849. (Patron, Duke of Sutherland; Tithe, Imp. 223*l* 3*s* 8*d*; Glebe, 40 acres; P. C.'s Inc. 110*l*; Pop. 597.) [26]

SHELTON, John Wade, *Stourton-Caundle, Blandford, Dorset.*—Pemb. Coll. Ox. B.A. 1849; Deac. 1850 and Pr. 1851 by Bp of Ex. P. C. of Stourton-Caundle, Dio. Salis. 1864. (Patrons, Sir H. A. Hoare, Bart; P. C.'s Inc. 50*l*; Pop. 395.) R. of Chilcombe, Dorset, Dio. Salis. 1866. (Patroness, Dow. Countess Nelson; R.'s Inc. 100*l*; Pop. 26.) Formerly C. of Pilton, Devon, 1850, Tisbury, Wilts, 1857, Westbury, Wilts, 1858, Sturminster Newton, Dorset, 1861, Durweston and Bryanston, Dorset, 1862. [27]

SHEPARD, James William, *Woods Cottage, Turnham-green, W.*—Ball. Coll. Ox. 1st cl. Lit. Hum. B.A. 1856, M.A. 1858; Deac. 1857 and Pr. 1858 by Bp of Lon. C. of Chiswick, Middlesex. [28]

SHEPHARD, H. J., *Stonesby, Melton Mowbray.*—V. of Stonesby, Dio. Pet. 1862. (Patron, T. Holman, Esq; V.'s Inc. 90*l*; Pop. 271.) [29]

SHEPHARD, John, *Eton College, Windsor.*—Ball. Coll. Ox. B.A. 1860, M.A. 1863; Deac. 1862 and Pr. 1863 by Bp of Ox. Conduct of Eton 1863. Formerly C. of Clewer 1862, Staines 1863. [30]

SHEPHEARD, Samuel Marsh, *Calthorpe Vicarage, Ingworth, Norfolk.*—Corpus Coll. Cam. B.A. 1843; Deac. 1845, Pr. 1846. V. of Calthorpe, Dio. Nor. 1848. (Patron, Sir W. Foster, Bart; Tithe—Imp. 201*l* and 34 acres of Glebe, V. 141*l*; Glebe, 28 acres; V.'s Inc. 183*l* and Ho; Pop. 187.) [1]

SHEPHERD, Charles Pitman, 4, *St. James's-terrace, South Lambeth, London, S.*—Magd. Coll. Camb. Capt. of the Poll and B.A. 1846, Hulsean Prizeman 1847, M.A. 1849; Deac. and Pr. 1848 by Bp of Lich. Incumb. of St. Katherine Cree Ch. Lond. Dio. Lon. 1867. (Patron, Magd. Coll. Cam; Incumb.'s Inc. 300*l*; Pop. 1794) Mast. of St. John's Ho. Westminster, 1853. Author, *The Fitness of the Time of Christ's Coming in Relation to the Moral, Social, Intellectual, and Political Condition of the Heathen* (Hulsean Prize, 1847), 3*s*; *Sins of the Tongue* (Sermon), 6*d*; *The Kingdom of Christ, its Progress, and our Relation thereto,* S P.G. 6*d*; *The Argument of St. Paul's Epistle to the Christians in Rome traced and Illustrated,* 2 vols. 1862-64, 15*s*. [2]

SHEPHERD, Edward John, *Trotterscliffe Rectory, Maidstone.*—Trin. Coll. Cam. Scho. of, B.A. 1826, M.A. 1830; Deac. 1827 by Bp of Lin. Pr. 1827 by Bp of Roch. R. of Trotterscliffe, Dio. Cant. 1827. (Patron, Charles William Shepherd, Esq; Tithe, 356*l* 0*s* 9*d*; Glebe, 6 acres; R.'s Inc. 366*l* and Ho; Pop. 284.) Author, *History of the Church of Rome to the End of the Episcopate of Damascus, A.D.* 384, 1851; *Five Letters* (to the Rev. S. R. Maitland, D.D.) *on the Genuineness of the Writings ascribed to Cyprian, Bishop of Carthage,* 1852, '53, '54; *The Parish Church,* 4to, Lumley. Translator of *The Soliloquy of Egbert, Abbot of Schonauge, near Coblentz.* [3]

SHEPHERD, Francis Burton, *Margaret Roding, Dunmow, Essex.*—Oriel Coll. Ox. B.A. 1856, M.A. 1857; Deac. 1857, Pr. 1858. R of Margaret Roding, Dio. Roch. 1861. (Patrons, the present R. and Trustees; Tithe, 223*l*; Glebe, 27 acres; R.'s Inc. 250*l* and Ho; Pop. 236.) Formerly C. of Frindsbury 1857–58, Whitechapel 1859, Aythorpe Roding 1859–61. [4]

SHEPHERD, Henry, *Chaldon Rectory, Redhill, Surrey.*—Magd. Hall, Ox. B.A. 1851, M.A. 1854; Deac. 1853 and Pr. 1854 by Bp of Ox. R. of Chaldon, Dio. Win. 1856. (Patron, the present R; R.'s Inc. 290*l* and Ho; Pop. 169.) Formerly C. of Whittington, Westmoreland. [5]

SHEPHERD, John, *Treneglos Vicarage, Launceston.*—Dub. A.B. 1852, A.M. 1856; Deac. 1856 and Pr. 1857 by Bp of Wor. V. of Treneglos, Dio. Ex. 1866. (Patron, Prince of Wales; Tithe, 226*l* 10*s*; Glebe, 31½ acres; V.'s Inc. 250*l* and Ho; Pop. 571.) Formerly C. of All Saints', Worcester, 1856, St. Clement's, Worcester, 1857; V. of Arenbury, Herefordshire, 1858–66. [6]

SHEPHERD, Joseph Minnikin, *Walton-le-Dale, near Preston.*—Queens' Coll. Ox. B.A. 1864; Deac. 1865 and Pr. 1866 by Bp of Man. C. of Walton-le-Dale 1867. Formerly C. of Deane 1865–67. [7]

SHEPHERD, Richard, *Woburn, Beds.*—St. Mary Hall, Ox. B.A. 1838, M.A. 1840; Deac. 1839 and Pr. 1840 by Bp of Lin. C. of Woburn 1864. Formerly Min. of St. Margaret's, Ware, 1842; C. of St. Michael's, Stockwell, 1856; R. of Stoke next Guildford 1858. Author, *The Church Catechism Explained in 300 Questions and Answers,* 6th ed. 2*d*; *Short Prayers for Every Day in the Week,* 15th ed. 2*d*; *A Call to the House of God,* 4th ed. 1*d*; *The Sabbath a Day of Blessings,* 4th ed. 1*d*; *Friendly Advice on the Lord's Supper, suitable for Confirmation Candidates,* 3rd ed. 1*d*; *A Friendly Word for Mourners,* 2nd ed. 1*d*; Lond. W. Macintosh and Hatchards. [8]

SHEPHERD, Richard, 133, *Brackenbury-street, Moor-park, Preston.*—St. Bees; Deac. 1866 by Bp of Man. C. of St. Thomas's, Preston, 1866. [9]

SHEPHERD, Robert, *St. Paul's Parsonage, High Elswick, Newcastle-on-Tyne.*—M.A. of East Tennessee 1857; Deac. 1826 by Bp of Dur. Pr. 1827 by Abp of York. P. C. of St. Paul's, High Elswick, Dio. Dur. 1849. (Patrons, Trustees; P. C.'s Inc. 300*l* and Ho; Pop. 22,275.) Formerly C. of St. John's-in-the-Vale, Keswick, 1826–28, Houghton-le-Spring, Durham, 1828–47, St. John's, Newcastle-on-Tyne, 1847–49. Author, *Confirmation.* [10]

SHEPHERD, Robert, jun., *Newcastle-upon-Tyne.*—Deac. 1854, Pr. 1855. Chap. of the Newcastle Town and County Gaol and House of Correction. Formerly C. of All Saints', and Chap. of the Union, Newcastle. Author, *The Succession of the Christian Ministry,* 1858; *An Address on Confirmation,* 1859. [11]

SHEPHERD, Samuel, *Boughton, Monchelsea, Maidstone.*—V. of Boughton, Monchelsea, Dio. Cant. 1857. (Patrons, D. and C. of Roch; V.'s Inc. 400*l* and Ho; Pop. 1190.) [12]

SHEPHERD, S. A., *Coleshill, Warwickshire.*—C. of Coleshill. [13]

SHEPHERD, Thomas, *Wellington Vicarage, near Hereford.*—Ch. Ch. Ox. B.A. 1823. V. of Wellington, Dio. Herf. 1838. (Patron, Bp of Wor; Tithe—Eccles. Commis. 274*l* 13*s* 10*d* and 48½ acres of Glebe, App. 1*l* 12*s*, Imp. 152*l* 1*s* 10*d*, V. 266*l* 8*s* 3*d*; Glebe, ½ acre; V.'s Inc. 267*l* and Ho; Pop. 626.) [14]

SHEPHERD, Thomas Dowker, *Staindrop, Darlington.*—Queen's Coll. Ox. B.A. 1858, M.A. 1861; Deac. 1859 and Pr. 1860 by Bp of Man. C. of Staindrop 1864. Formerly C. of St. James's, Heywood, 1859–61, Bury 1861–64. [15]

SHEPHERD, Thomas Henry, *Clayworth, Bawtry, Notts.*—St. John's Coll. Cam. Wrang. and B.A. 1801; Deac. 1801, Pr. 1802. R. of Clayworth, Dio. Lin. 1810. (Patron, Bp of Lin; Tithe, 3*l* 5*s*; R.'s Inc. 550*l* and Ho; Pop. 538.) R. of South Wheatley, Notts, Dio. Lin. (Patron, Chap. of Southwell Coll. Ch; Tithe, 150*l*; Glebe, 7 acres; R.'s Inc. 157*l* and Ho; Pop. 32.) Preb. of Southwell; Rural Dean. Formerly Fell. of Brasen. Coll. Ox. [16]

SHEPHERD, William, *Long Marton, Kirby-Thore, Westmoreland.*—Deac. 1830, Pr. 1831. P. C. of Bolton-in-Morland, Westmoreland, Dio. Carl. 1834. (Patron, V. of Morland; P. C's Inc. 80*l* and Ho; Pop. 390.) [17]

SHEPHERD, William Bradley, *Walton-le-Dale, Preston.*—Queen's Coll. Ox. B.A. 1856, M.A. 1859; Deac. 1857 and Pr. 1858 by Bp of Man. P. C. of Higher Walton, near Preston, Dio. Man. 1864. (Patron, V. of Blackburn; P. C.'s Inc. 120*l*; Pop. 2000.) Formerly C. of St. Leonard's, Walton-le-Dale, 1857–64. [18]

SHEPHERD, William Mutrie, *Newton Arlosh Parsonage, Wigton, Cumberland.*—All Souls' Coll. Ox; Deac. 1861 and Pr. 1862 by Bp of Carl. P. C. of Newton Arlosh, Dio. Carl. 1865. (Patron, V. of Holm Cultram; P. C.'s Inc. 220*l* and Ho; Pop. 526.) Formerly C. of Askham, Westmoreland, 1861–63; C. in sole charge of Newton Arlosh 1864. [19]

SHEPHERD, William Robert, *Lichfield.*—Caius Coll. Cam. and Lichfield Theol. Coll; Deac. 1864 and Pr. 1865 by Bp of Lich. Librarian of Lichfield Theol. Coll; Asst. C. of Ch. Ch. Lichfield; Chap. of St. John's Hospital, Lichfield, 1867. Formerly a Solicitor 1858; C. of Weeford with Hints, Lichfield, 1864-66, Elford, Tamworth, 1867. Author, *Adventures of Mr. Ambiguous Law,* James Blackwood, 1860, 2*s*. [20]

SHEPPARD, Arthur Francis, *Flimby, Maryport, Cumberland.*—Oriel Coll. Ox. B.A. 1835; Deac. 1836 and Pr. 1837 by Bp of Nor. P. C. of Flimby, Dio. Carl. 1855. (Patrons, Landowners; Glebe, 3½ acres; P. C.'s Inc. 82*l*; Pop. 1178.) [21]

SHEPPARD, Francis, *Patrington Rectory, Yorks.*—Clare Coll. Cam. B.A. 1836, M.A. 1839, B.D. 1847. R. of Patrington, Dio. York, 1858. (Patron, Clare Coll. Cam; Tithe, 18*l* 4*s*; Glebe, 400 acres; R.'s Inc. 678*l* and Ho; Pop. 1724.) Surrogate. Formerly Sen. Fell. of Clare Coll. Cam. [22]

SHEPPARD, George Edmund, *Whittington, Oswestry, Salop.*—Wad. Coll. Ox. B.A. 1862, M.A. 1865; Deac. 1864 and Pr. 1865 by Bp of St. A. C. of Whittington 1864. [23]

SHEPPARD, H. A. G., *Holmwood, Dorking, Surrey.*—C. of Holmwood. [24]

SHEPPARD, Henry Fleetwood, *Kilnhurst Parsonage, Rotherham, Yorks.*—Trin. Hall, Cam. Univ.

Travelling Bachelor 1855, B.A. 1855, M.A. 1858; Deac. 1856 and Pr. 1857 by Bp of Ches. P. C. of Kilnhurst, Dio. York, 1860. (Patron, Earl Fitzwilliam; P. C.'s Inc. 155*l* and Ho; Pop. 1247.) Author, various Musical publications, Novello. [1]

SHEPPARD, Henry Winter, *Emsworth Rectory, Hants.*—Trin. Coll. Cam. 2nd cl. Cl. Trip. 13th Wrang. B.A. 1831, M.A. 1834; Deac. 1833 and Pr. 1834 by Bp of Glouc. R. of Emsworth, Dio. Win. 1844. (Patron, R. of Warblington; R.'s Inc. 300*l* and Ho; Pop. 1655.) Formerly Min. of St. Peter's, Emsworth, 1850. [2]

SHEPPARD, John George, *Grammar School, Kidderminster.*—Wad. Coll. Ox. B.A. 1839, M.A. 1841; Deac. 1841 and Pr. 1842 by Bp of Ox. Head Mast. of Gr. Sch. Kidderminster; Fell. of Wad. Coll. Ox; Select Preacher Univ. of Ox. 1856–57. Author, *St. Paul at Athens* (Prize Poem), Oxford; *Christian Citizenship*, Rivingtons; *Theophrasti Characteres*; *Notes on Thucydides*; *Middle-Class Education*; *The Lawfulness of War* (a Sermon). [3]

SHEPPARD, John Lancelot, *Abdon Rectory, Church Stretton, Salop.*—Wad. Coll. Ox. B.A. 1839, M.A. 1842; Deac. 1840 and Pr. 1841 by Bp of Herf. R. of Abdon, Dio. Herf. 1851. (Patron, Earl of Pembroke; Tithe, 128*l*; Glebe, 44 acres; R.'s Inc. 187*l* and Ho; Pop. 170.) [4]

SHEPPARD, Thomas Henry, *Exeter College, Oxford.*—Oriel Coll. Ox. 2nd cl. Lit. Hum. and B.A. 1837, M.A. 1840, B.D. 1851; Deac. 1842 and Pr. 1843, by Bp of Herf. Fell. and Chap. of Ex. Coll. Ox. [5]

SHEPPERD, James Philip, *St. Thomas's Parsonage, Preston.*—Dur. Licen. Theol. and Exhib. 1850; M.A. by Abp of Cant; Deac. 1851 and Pr. 1852 by Bp of Ches. P. C. of St. Thomas's, Preston, Dio. Man. 1864. (Patrons, Hyndman's Trustees; P. C.'s Inc. 300*l* and Ho; Pop. 8053.) Formerly C. of North Shore, Kirkdale, Liverpool, 1851; P. C. of West Smethwick, Staffs, 1858-64. Author, *The Coming Rest*, 1854; *Sermons for the Working Classes*, 1854; *News from the East*, 1855; *Protestant Conversation Cards*, 1*s*. per pack, Wertheim; *Early Closing*, 1857. [6]

SHERARD, Hugh, *Stourbridge, Worcestershire.*—Dub. A.B. 1850, A.M. 1859; Deac. 1856 by Abp of Dub. Pr. 1857 by Bp. of Wor. P. C. of St. Thomas's, Stourbridge, Dio. Wor. 1858. (Patrons, Householders; P. C.'s Inc. 130*l*; Pop. 8783.) Formerly C. of St. Luke's, Dublin. [7]

SHERINGHAM, John William, *Standish Vicarage, Stonehouse, Gloucestershire.*—St. John's Coll. Cam. 2nd cl. Cl. Trip. Jun. Opt. and B.A. 1842, M.A. 1848; Deac. 1843, Pr. 1844. V. of Standish with Hardwick V. Dio. G. and B. 1864. (Patron, Bp of G. and B; Tithe, 406*l*; Glebe, 97 acres; V.'s Inc. 459*l* and Ho; Pop. 1150.) Chap. to Bp of G. and B. Formerly C. of St. Barnabas', Kensington, 1843–48; V. of Strood, Kent, 1848–64. Author, *Parochial Taxation of the Clergy*, 1858, 1*s*. [8]

SHERLOCK, Edgar, *Bentham Rectory, near Lancaster.*—Emman. Coll. Cam. Coll. Exhib. and Div. Prizeman, B.A. 1847, M.A. 1857; Deac. 1847 by Abp of Cant. Pr. 1856 by Bp of Ches. R. of Bentham, Dio. Rip. 1865. (Patron, the present R; Tithe, 689*l*; Glebe, 30 acres; R.'s Inc. 700*l* and Ho; Pop. 2342.) Formerly C. of Ashton-le-Willows, Lancashire, 1847, Peckleton, Leicestershire, 1863. [9]

SHERLOCK, Harold, *Ashton-le-Willows Rectory, Wigan.*—R. of Ashton-le-Willows, Dio. Ches. 1845. (Patron, R. of Winwick; R.'s Inc. 570*l* and Ho.) [10]

SHERLOCK, Henry, *Ashton Rectory, Wigan.*—Dub. A.B. 1863; Deac. 1864, Pr. 1865. C. in sole charge of Ashton-in-Makerfield 1866. Formerly C. of Buglawton, Cheshire. [11]

SHERSON, Robert, *Yaverland, Brading, Isle of Wight.*—St. Mary Hall, Ox. B.A. 1824, M.A. 1827; Deac. 1825, Pr. 1826. R. of Yaverland, Isle of Wight, Dio. Win. 1830. (Patron, Sir Andrew S. Hamond, Bart; Glebe, 13 acres; R.'s Inc. 230*l* and Ho; Pop. 69.) [12]

SHERVINGTON, Joseph, *Campsall, Doncaster.*—St. Bees 1854; Deac. 1856 by Bp of Carl. Pr. 1857 by Abp of York. C. of Campsall, and Skelbrooke, Yorks. [13]

SHERWEN, Samuel, *Dean Rectory, Cockermouth, Cumberland.*—Deac. 1823 and Pr. 1824 by Bp of Ches. P. C. of Mosser, in the Parish of Brigham, Dio. Carl. 1823. (Patron, Earl of Lonsdale; Tithe, Imp. 10*l*; P. C.'s Inc. 44*l*; Pop. 88.) R. of Dean, Dio. Carl. 1826. (Patron, the present R; R.'s Inc. 320*l* and Ho; Pop. 829.) [14]

SHERWEN, William, *Mosser Mains, Cockermouth, Cumberland.*—Queen's Coll. Ox. B.A. 1854, M.A. 1860; Deac. 1860 and Pr. 1861 by Bp of Ox. C. of Dean and Mosser 1866. Formerly C. of Cold Brafield, Bucks, 1860–62, Bishopwearmouth, Durham, 1863–64, Sedgefield, Durham, 1864–66. [15]

SHERWIN, Ambrose, *Chaplain's Residence, Pentonville Prison, London, N.*—Dub. Prizeman in Lit. Hum. Logic and Math. A.B. 1841; Deac. 1842 by Bp of Kildare, Pr. 1843 by Bp of Down and Connor. Chap. of Pentonville Prison 1859. [16]

SHERWOOD, Henry Martyn, *White Ladies Aston, near Worcester.*—Queen's Coll. Ox. B.A. 1834; Deac. 1836 and Pr. 1837 by Bp of Wor. V. of White Ladies Aston, Dio. Wor. 1839. (Patron, R. Berkeley, Esq; Tithe, 250*l*; Glebe, 1 acre; V.'s Inc. 250*l* and Ho; Pop. 353.) R. of Broughton Hackett, Worc. Dio. Wor. 1843. (Patron, Ld Chan; Land in lieu of Tithe, 63 acres; R.'s Inc. 106*l* and Ho; Pop. 164.) Formerly C. of Rushock, near Kidderminster, 1836–40. Author, *Outward Baptism not a Condition of the Christian Covenant*; *Paul altogether Supreme over the Gentile Churches*, 1857, 2*s* 6*d*. [17]

SHEWELL, William Marten, *Horsted Keynes, East Grinstead, Sussex.*—Wor. Coll. Ox. S.C.L. 1851, B.A. 1852, M.A. 1854; Deac. 1851 and Pr. 1852 by Bp of Ex. C. of Horsted Keynes 1863. Formerly C. of Collumpton, Devon, 1851; Chap. of Royal Berks Hospital 1854; C. of Rotherfield Greys, Oxon, 1858, Mapledurham, Oxon, 1860, Amport, Hants, 1862. [18]

SHICKLE, Charles William, 18, *Raby-place, Bath.*—Corpus Coll. Cam. Jun. Opt. B.A. 1864; Deac. 1865 and Pr. 1867 by Bp of B. and W. C. of Twerton, near Bath, 1865. [19]

SHIELD, George Henry, *Exeter.*—Ex. Coll. and Magd. Hall, Ox. B.A. 1839, M.A. 1841; Deac. 1839 by Bp of Ely, Pr. 1840 by Bp of Wor. R. of Holy Trinity, City and Dio. Ex. 1843. (Patrons, D. and C. of Ex; Tithe, 6*l* 7*s* 8*d*; Glebe, 11*l*; R.'s Inc. 160*l*; Pop. 3841.) Formerly Asst. C. of St. Nicholas', Saltash, 1839–42, Silverton 1842–43. Author, *The Sinfulness of not coming to the Holy Communion*, 1847; *Select Portions of the Psalms of David for Congregational and Family Worship*, 1847; *The Sabbath and the Sanctuary*, 1848; *The Bible and the Bible only the Religion of Protestants, being an Answer to a Lecture on the same Subject by the Rev J. M. Neale, M.A.*, Hamilton, Adams, and Co. 1852; *Words in Season, seventeen Sermons*, Clifford, Exeter, 1864, 5*s*; Single Sermons; etc. [20]

SHIELD, William, *Dishforth, Thirsk, Yorks.*—P. C. of Dishforth and Marton-le-Moor, P. C. Dio. York, 1866. (Patron, V. of Topcliffe; P. C.'s Inc. 170*l*; Pop. Dishforth 401, Marton-le-Moor 205.) [21]

SHIELDS, Richard John, *Hornby, Lancaster.*—Univ. Coll. Dur. B.A. 1844, M.A. 1848; Deac. 1845, Pr. 1846. P. C. of Hornby, Dio. Man. 1850. (Patron, John Foster, Esq; Tithe—App. 733*l* 8*s* 8*d*; Glebe, 44 acres; P. C.'s Inc. 116*l*; Pop. 455.) [22]

SHIELDS, William Thomas, *Westburn Cottage, Hexham, Northumberland.*—Dur. Licen. Theol. 1838; Deac. 1839 and Pr. 1840 by Bp of Dur. R. of Thockrington, Dio. Dur. 1864. (Patron, Bp of Dur; Tithe, 116*l*; Glebe, 70*l*; R.'s Inc. 186*l*; Pop. 166.) Formerly C. of St. Margaret's, Durham, 1838, St. Andrew's, Newcastle, 1841, Morpeth 1844, Ovingham 1853, Warden 1855. [23]

SHIFFNER, Sir George Croxton, Bart., *Coombe-place, Lewes, Sussex.*—Ch. Ch. Ox. B.A. 1842, M.A. 1846; Deac. 1844, Pr. 1845. R. of Hamsey, Dio. Chich. 1848. (Patron, the present R; Tithe, 620*l*; Glebe,

26 acres; R.'s Inc. 650*l* and Ho; Pop. 541.) Rural Dean 1867. [1]

SHILLETO, John Hawtrey Richard, *Hollington, Staffs.*—Ch. Coll. Cam. B.A. 1861; Deac. 1864 by Bp of Man. C. of Checkley with Hollington 1867. Formerly C. of St. Stephen's, Salford, 1864. [2]

SHILLETO, Richard, *King's College, Cambridge.*—Trin. Coll. Cam. B.A. 1832, M.A. 1835. Lect. in Cl. and Maths. King's Coll. Cam. [3]

SHILSON, Charles, *Halton, Tring, Bucks.*—R. of Halton, Dio. Ox. 1865. (Patron, Baron Rothschild; R.'s Inc. 380*l*; Pop. 147.) Formerly C. of North Petherton, Somerset. [4]

SHIPLEY, William Samuel, *Plungar Vicarage, Bottesford, near Nottingham.*—St. John's Coll. Cam. S.C.L. 1856, B.A. 1857; Vice-Chan.'s Prizeman, Trin. Coll. Dub. 1851; Deac. 1857, by Bp of B. and W. Pr. 1858 by Bp of Ex. V. of Plungar, Dio. Pet. 1861. (Patron, Duke of Rutland; Glebe, 60 acres; V.'s Inc. 140*l* and Ho; Pop. 251.) Formerly C. of St. Mary's, Devonport, 1857–59, Harston and West Allington 1859–61, Croxton Kerrial, Leic. 1863. [5]

SHIPMAN, Thomas Trafford, *Nether Denton Rectory, Carlisle.*—St. Cath. Coll. Cam. B.A. 1855, M.A. 1859; Deac. 1856 and Pr. 1857 by Bp of Carl. R. of Nether Denton, Dio. Carl. 1866. (Patron, Bp of Carl; Glebe, 691 acres, partly common; R's Inc. 198*l* and Ho; Pop. 302.) Rural Dean; Sec. to the Dioc. Ch. Building Soc. Formerly C. of Barbon, Westmoreland, 1856–58, Ch. Ch. Carlisle, 1858–59, R. of Scaleby, Carlisle, 1859–66. [6]

SHIPMAN, William, *Soham, Cambridge.*—St. Cath. Coll. Cam. B.A. 1850, M.A. 1855; Deac. 1850 and Pr. 1851 by Bp of Man. Sen. C. of Soham 1857. Formerly Sen. C. of St. Michael's, Coventry, 1852–57. [7]

SHIPTON, George, *Barlow Parsonage, Staveley, Chesterfield.*—Holy Spirit Coll. Isle of Cumbrae, N.B; Deac. 1850 and Pr. 1851 by Bp of Argyll and the Isles. P. C. of Barlow, Dio. Lich. 1856. (Patron, R. of Staveley; Glebe, 4 acres; P. C.'s Inc. 132*l* and Ho; Pop. 682.) [8]

SHIPTON, Perceval Maurice, *Halsham Rectory, Patrington, Yorks.*—Magd. Coll. Cam. LL.B. 1851; Deac. 1852 and Pr. 1853 by Bp of Wor. R. of Halsham, Dio. York, 1860. (Patron, Capt. Shipton, R.N; Tithe, 760*l*; Glebe, 25 acres; R.'s Inc. 760*l* and Ho; Pop. 265.) Formerly C. of Dudley 1852–53; R. of Clapton, Somerset, 1855–60. [9]

SHIRLEY, Arthur George Sewallis, *Stinsford Vicarage, Dorchester.*—Ch. Ch. Ox. B.A. 1833, M.A. 1836; Deac. 1836 and Pr. 1837 by Bp of Wor. V. of Stinsford, Dio. Salis. 1837. (Patron, Earl of Ilchester; Tithe—Imp. 240*l*, V. 190*l*; Glebe, 1 acre; V.'s Inc. 190*l* and Ho; Pop. 357.) [10]

SHIRLEY, James, *Frettenham, Norwich.*—Trin. Coll. Ox. B.A. 1824, M.A. 1827; Deac. 1825 by Bp of Chich. Pr. 1826 by Bp of Lin. R. of Frettenham with Staininghall R. Dio. Nor. 1830. (Patron, Lord Suffield; Tithe, 481*l* 10*s*; Glebe, 21 acres; R.'s Inc. 500*l* and Ho; Pop. 221.) [11]

SHIRREFF, Robert St. John, *Woodham Ferrers Rectory, Great Baddow, Essex.*—Wad. Coll. Ox. B.A. 1837, M.A. 1840; Deac. 1839 and Pr. 1840 by Bp of Rip. R. of Woodham Ferrers, Dio. Roch. 1855. (Patron, Sir B. W. Bridges; Tithe, 926*l*; Glebe, 20 acres; R.'s Inc. 950*l*; Pop. 947.) Formerly V. of Thorley, Isle of Wight, 1850–55. [12]

SHITTLER, Robert, *Dorchester.*—Deac. 1816, Pr. 1817. Formerly V. of Alton Pancras, Dorset, 1842–59. Author, *Children Taught the Fear of the Lord*, 1826, 4*d*; *Millennial Address*, 1831, 1*s* 6*d*; *Christ, the Sin Offering*, 1835, 4*s* 6*d*; *National Religion in Church and State*, 5*s* and 10*s* 6*d*; *Methodism Unveiled*, 1835, 1*s*; *Address on Confirmation*, 1837, 6*d*; *Gems of the Church*, 1840, 2*s*; *The Church of England Vindicated, &c.* 1840, 2*s*; *Popular Tracts on Scripture Doctrines*, 1840, 2*s* 6*d*; *Popular Addresses on Puseyite Errors*, 1841, 2*s*; *The Infidel Refuted*, 6*d*; *Grand Pillar of the Christian Faith*, 1841, 6*d*; *Beams from Heaven* 3*d*; *Preparations for the House of Prayer*, 1845, 5*s*; *Sanctification of the People of God*, 1845, 2*s* 6*d*; *The Soldier's Crown*, 1845, 1*s* 6*d*; *Prayers, &c.* 1852, 1*s* 8*d*; *Record of Grace*, 1852, 2*s* 6*d*; *The Domestic Commentary on the Whole Word of God*, 1854, 2*l* 14*s*. [13]

SHOOTER, Richard Walter, *Buckthorpe Vicarage, Pocklington, Yorks.*—St. Cath. Coll. Cam. B.A; Deac. 1857 and Pr. 1859 by Abp of York. V. of Buckthorpe, Dio. York, 1861. (Patron, Abp of York; V.'s Inc. 240*l*; Pop. 245.) Formerly C. of Bishop Wilton 1857, Skipwith 1858–60. [14]

SHORE, T. Teignmouth, *La Belle Sauvage-yard, Ludgate-hill, E.C.*—Dub. Gold Medal for Eng. Composition, Gold Medal for Oratory, Downes' Div. Prize for Reading Liturgy, Div. Prize for Extempore Speaking, A.B. 1861, A.M. 1865; Ox. M.A. 1865; Deac. 1865 and Pr 1866 by Bp of Lon. C. in charge of St. Paul's (iron church), Kensington, 1867. Formerly C. of St. Jude's, Chelsea, 1865. Author, *Lord Macaulay*, an Essay, Dublin. Editor, *The Quiver*, weekly Magazine, and Cassell's *Biographical Dictionary*; *Munchausen*, illustrated by Doré; *Don Quixote*, illustrated by Doré, and Author of *Life of Cervantes* prefixed thereto. Fell. of the Royal Geographical Soc. etc. [15]

SHORLAND, William Henry, *Silton Rectory, Bourton, Bath.*—Wad. Coll. Ox. B.A. 1856, M.A. 1859; Deac. 1857 and Pr. 1858 by Bp of B. and W. R. of Silton, Dio. Salis. 1859. (Patron, Rev. W. J. Percy; Tithe, 380*l* 11*s*; Glebe, 68 acres; R.'s Inc. 464*l* and Ho; Pop. 306.) Formerly Asst. C. of Drayton and Muchelney, Somerset. [16]

SHORROCK, *Hameringham, near Horncastle, Lincolnshire.*—Clare Coll. Cam. B.A. 1859; Deac. and Pr. 1860. R. of Hameringham with Scrayfield, Dio. Lin. 1866. (Patrons, Exors. of the late Sir Thomas Coltman; Glebe, 240 acres; R.'s Inc. 510*l*; Pop. 210.) Formerly C. of Warton, Warwickshire, 1860, Sutton-le-Marsh 1863–64, Flixton, near Manchester, 1865–66. [17]

SHORT, Ambrose, *The School, Oswestry.*—New Coll. Ox. M.A; Deac. 1857 and Pr. 1858 by Bp of Llan. Head Mast. of Gr. Sch. Oswestry. Formerly Fell. of New Coll. Ox. [18]

SHORT, Henry Hassard, *Stockton-on-the-Forest, York.*—P. C. of Stockton-on-the-Forest, Dio. York, 1861. (Patron, Abp of York; P. C.'s Inc. 160*l*; Pop. 450.) Chap. to Lord Denman. [19]

SHORT, Hugh Martin, *Thornthwaite, Keswick.*—Univ. Coll. Dur. B.A. 1842; Deac. 1843 and Pr. 1844. P. C. of Thornthwaite, Dio. Carl. 1857. (Patrons, V. of Crosthwaite and P. C. of St. John's, Keswick; P. C.'s Inc. 140*l* and Ho; Pop. 530.) Formerly P. C. of Kirkstall, near Leeds, 1848–58. [20]

SHORT, John, *St. Cuthbert's Parsonage, Allonby, Maryport, Cumberland.*—Dub. A.B. 1813, A.M. 1819; Deac. 1815 and Pr. 1816 by Bp of Down and Connor. P. C. of St. Cuthbert's, Dio. Carl. 1852. (Patron, P. C. of Holme Cultram; P. C.'s Inc. 100*l* and Ho; Pop. 821.) [21]

SHORT, John Holbeche, *Temple Balsall, Birmingham.*—Mert. Coll. Ox. 3rd cl. Lit. Hum. B.A. 1833, M.A. 1834; Deac. 1838 and Pr. 1839 by Bp of Ches. P. C. of Temple Balsall, Dio. Wor. 1856. (Patrons, Govs. of Balsall Hospital; P. C.'s Inc. 50*l* and Ho; Pop. 1142.) Mast. of Balsall Temple Hospital 1855. (Patrons, Govs. of the Lady Catherine Leveson's Hospital; Value, 200*l*.) Formerly C. of Lytham 1838–40; P. C. of Whittle-le-Woods 1840–43. [22]

SHORT, Thomas, *Trinity College, Oxford.*—Trin. Coll. Ox. B.A. 1812, M.A. 1814, B.D. 1826; Deac. 1814 by Bp of Lich. Pr. 1821 by Bp of Ox. Fell. of Trin. Coll. Ox; Morning Preacher at St. Nicholas', Abingdon, Berks. [23]

SHORT, Walter Francis, *New College, Oxford.*—Sub-Warden, Fell. and Tut. of New Coll. Ox. [24]

SHORT, William, *Llandrinio Rectory (Montgomeryshire), near Oswestry, Salop.*—Ch. Ch. Ox. Double 1st cl. and B.A. 1814, M.A. 1817; Deac. 1816 by Bp of Ox. Pr. 1817 by Bp of Carl. Preb. of Salis. 1834. (Value, 68*l*.) R. of Llandrinio, Dio. St. A. 1858.

(Patron, Bp of St. A; Tithe, App. 556*l* 3*s*; Glebe, 40 acres; R.'s Inc. 650*l* and Ho; Pop. 741.) Formerly R. of St. George the Martyr's, Lond. 1836–58. Author, *Sermons*, 1849. [1]

SHORTER, Joseph, *Tynemouth, North Shields.*—P. C. of Trinity, Tynemouth, Dio. Dur. 1860. (Patron, Duke of Northumberland; P. C.'s Inc. 200*l*. and Ho; Pop. 4000.) [2]

SHORTLAND, Henry Vincent, *Twinstead Rectory (Essex), near Sudbury.*—Lin. Coll. Ox. M.A. 1830; Deac. and Pr. 1830. R. of Twinstead, Dio. Roch, 1838. (Patron, Ld Chan; Tithe, 300*l*; Glebe, 13 acres; R.'s Inc. 300*l* and Ho; Pop. 193.) Formerly C. of Tilehurst, near Reading, 1833–38. [3]

SHORTT, E., *Byker, Newcastle-on-Tyne.*—C. of Byker. [4]

SHORTT, Jonathan, *Hoghton Parsonage, Preston.*—Dub. A.B. 1848; Deac. 1849, Pr. 1850. P. C. of Hoghton, Dio. Man. 1853. (Patron, V. of Leyland; P. C.'s Inc. 150*l* and Ho; Pop. 1100.) [5]

SHOULTS, W. Arderne, 11, *Buckland-street, New North-road, London, N.*—St. John's Coll. Cam. B.A. 1860, M.A. 1863; Deac. 1863 and Pr. 1864 by Bp of Lon. C. of St. Paul's, Bunhill-row, 1866. Formerly C. of St. Peter's. Walworth, 1863. [6]

SHRIMPTON, Henry, 3, *Nelson-terrace, Bedminster, Bristol.*—King's Coll. Lond; Deac. 1864 and Pr. 1865 by Bp of G. and B. C. of St. John's, Bedminster, 1866. Formerly C. of St. Paul's, Bristol, 1864. [7]

SHRUBB, Charles, *Vicar's-hill, Lymington, Hants.*—Ex. Coll. Ox. B.A. 1812, M.A. 1815; Deac. 1813 by Bp of Win. Pr. 1814 by Bp of Salis. V. of Boldre with Lymington C. Dio. Win. 1818. (Patron, the present V; Boldre, Tithe—Imp. 272*l* 4*s* 7*d*, V. 257*l* 13*s* 2*d*; Glebe, 21 acres; Lymington, Tithe—App. 276*l* 14*s* 4*d*, V. 80*l* 7*s* 10*d*; V.'s Inc. 440*l* and Ho; Pop. Boldre 897, Lymington 4098.) [8]

SHRUBB, Henry, *Brabœuf Manor, Guildford.*—Corpus Coll. Ox. B.A. 1814, M.A. 1818, B.D. 1827; Deac. 1818 and Pr. 1819 by Bp of Ox. [9]

SHUCKBURGH, Charles Blencowe, *Bourton Hall, Rugby.*—Wad. and Lin. Colls. Ox. 1st cl. Math. et Phy. and B.A. 1815, M.A. 1818; Deac. 1816 and Pr. 1817 by Bp of Glouc. Formerly C. of Northleach, Glouc. 1816–35; V. of Marston St. Lawrence 1840–50; C. of Bourton-on-Dunsmore 1850–59. [10]

SHUCKBURGH, Charles Verney, *Langford Rectory, Maldon, Essex.*—Trin. Coll. Ox. B.A. 1825, M.A. 1828. R. of Langford, Dio. Roch. 1841. (Patron, Hon. F. Byron; Tithe, 279*l* 10*s*; Glebe, 32 acres; R.'s Inc. 319*l* and Ho; Pop. 279.) [11]

SHUFFLEBOTHAM, Edwin Charles, 20, *Queen's-road, Liverpool.*—St. Mark's Coll. Chelsea; Deac. 1865 and Pr. 1866 by Bp of Ches. C. of Ch. Ch. Liverpool, 1866. Formerly Head Mast. of Tarvin Gr. Sch. 1856–63; 2nd Mast. of Nuneaton Gr. Sch. 1863–65; C. of St. Stephen's, Liverpool, 1865–66. [12]

SHUKER, Henry, *Wichenford Rectory, Worcester.*—St. John's Coll. Cam. B.A. 1843, M.A. 1846; Deac. and Pr. 1844. R. of Wichenford, Dio. Wor. 1847. (Patrons, D. and C. of Wor; Tithe, 422*l*; Glebe, 8 acres; R.'s Inc. 430*l* and Ho; Pop. 366.) [13]

SHULDHAM, John, *Woodnorton Rectory, Thetford, Norfolk.*—Ch. Ch. Ox. 1st cl. Lit. Hum. and B.A. 1817, M.A. 1820; Deac. 1822 and Pr. 1823 by Bp of Ox. R. of the Consolidated R.'s of Woodnorton with Swanton-Novers, Dio. Nor. 1845. (Patron, Ch. Ch. Ox; Woodnorton, Tithe, 430*l*; Glebe, 60 acres; Swanton-Novers, Tithe, 223*l* 10*s*; Glebe, 31½ acres; R.'s Inc. 792*l* and Ho; Pop. Woodnorton 250, Swanton-Novers 315.) Formerly Tut. of Ch. Ch. Ox. [14]

SHULDHAM, Naunton Lemuel, *The Vicarage, Scawby, Brigg.*—Magd. Coll. Ox. Fell. of, B.A. 1854, M.A. 1856; Deac. 1858 and Pr. 1860 by Bp of Ox. V. of Scawby, Dio. Lin. 1867. (Patron, Rev. R. Sutton; V.'s Inc. 370*l* and Ho; Pop. 1570.) Formerly C. of White Waltham and Shottesbrook, Berks, 1858–60, St. Giles's, Oxford, 1860–62; Conduct and Asst. Mast. in Eton Coll. 1862–67; Cl. Tut. to H.R.H. Prince Leopold 1863–66. [15]

SHUM, Frederick, *Staunton Long, near Much Wenlock, Salop.*—C. of Staunton Long. [16]

SHURLOCK, John Russell, *Bassenthwaite, Keswick.*—Queens' Coll. Cam. B.A. 1832, M.A. 1836; Deac. 1834 and Pr. 1835 by Bp of Lon. P. C. of Bassenthwaite, Dio. Carl. 1856. (Patrons, D. and C. of Carl; P. C.'s Inc. 160*l*; Pop. 570.) Formerly P. C. of East Teignmouth, Devon, 1855–56. [17]

SHUTTE, Albert Shadwell, *Mortlake, Surrey, S.W.*—Clare Coll. Cam. Scho. of, B.A. 1859, M.A. 1863; Deac. 1859 and Pr. 1860 by Bp of Man. P. C. of Mortlake with East Sheen, C. Dio. Lon. 1865. (Patrons, D. and C. of Wor; P. C.'s Inc. 200*l* and Ho; Pop. 3778.) Formerly C. of St. Mary's, Rochdale, 1859–62, St. Philip and St. James's, Cheltenham, 1862–64, Mortlake 1864–65. [18]

SHUTTE, Reginald Neale, *Etall, Ford, Northumberland.*—Caius Coll. Cam. B.A. 1852. P. C. of Etall, Dio. Dur. 1866. Formerly R. of St. Mary-Steps, Exeter, 1854–64. [19]

SHUTTLEWORTH, Edward, *Egloshayle Vicarage, Wadebridge, Cornwall.*—St. John's Coll. Cam. B.A. 1829, M.A. 1844; Deac. 1829 and Pr. 1830 by Bp of Ches. V. of Egloshayle, Dio. Ex. 1849. (Patron, Bp of Ex; Tithe, 405*l*; Glebe, 29 acres; V.'s Inc. 465*l* and Ho; Pop. 1479.) Formerly C. of Kenwyn 1833; P. C. of Penzance 1840. Author, *Edification of the Body of Christ in the Unity of Faith and Knowledge* (a Sermon); etc. [20]

SHUTTLEWORTH, William Starkie, *Elm Grove, Salisbury.*—Trin. Coll. Cam. B.A. 1862, M.A. 1865; Deac. 1862 and Pr. 1863 by Bp of Ox. C. of St. Edmund's, Salisbury, 1865. Formerly C. of Caversham, near Reading, 1862–65. [21]

SIBTHORPE, Richard Waldo, *Lincoln.*—Magd. Coll. Ox. B.A. 1813, M.A. 1816, B.D. 1823; Deac. 1815 by Bp of Lin. Pr. 1817 by Bp of Ox. Chap. and Founder of St. Anne's Bedehouses, Lincoln (for 13 aged widows or single women). Formerly C. of St. Mary's, Hull; P. C. of Tattershall, Linc; P. C. of St. James's, Ryde, Isle of Wight; Fell. of Magd. Coll. Ox. Author, *Notes on Book of Jonah*, 1833; *Domestic Liturgy, or Book of Family Devotion*, 1833; *The Book of Genesis, with Explanatory and Practical Observations*, 1835; *Some Answer to the Inquiry, Why are you become a Catholic?* 2 eds. 1842; *A Further Answer to the Inquiry, Why are you become a Catholic? containing a Notice of the Strictures of the Rev. Messrs. Palmer and Dodsworth*, 1842; Two *Sermons* before the Univ. of Ox. preached at Magd. Coll. 1840–41. [22]

SICKLEMORE, George Wilson, *Nether Court, near Ramsgate.*—Trin. Coll. Cam. B.A. 1825, M.A. 1828; Deac. 1826, Pr. 1827. V. of St. Laurence, Thanet, Dio. Cant. 1836. (Patron, Abp of Cant; Tithe, 36*l* 15*s*; Glebe, 3 acres; V.'s Inc. 162*l* and Ho; Pop. 1936.) Formerly C. of St. Mildred and All Saints', of St. Mary Bredman, and St. Andrews, Canterbury, of Minster, Thanet; R. of St. Alphage with St. Mary Northgate, Canterbury. [23]

SIDDALL, Henry, *Orford, near Warrington.*—Clare Coll. Cam. Scho. of, B.A. 1862; Deac. 1863 and Pr. 1864 by Bp of Rip. Chap. of Don. of Orford, Dio. Ches. 1866. (Patron, W. Beamont, Esq; Chap.'s Inc. 100*l*; Pop. 300.) 2nd Mast. in Warrington Gr. Sch. 1866. Formerly C. of Tong, near Leeds, 1863–66. [24]

SIDEBOTHAM, Henry, *Gibraltar.*—Magd. Hall, Ox. B.A. 1861, M.A. 1863; Deac. 1863 by Bp of Roch. Pr. 1864 by Abp of Cant. Asst. Civil Chap. at Gibraltar 1867. Formerly C. of Chipping Barnet, Herts, 1863–64. [25]

SIDEBOTHAM, John Samuel, *Spring-terrace, Abingdon.*—Ox. B.A. Lin. Coll. 1853, M.A. New Coll. 1855, *ad eund.* M.A. Cam. 1856; Deac. 1853 by Bp of Ox. Pr. 1855 by Bp of Pet. Surrogate; one of the four City Lecturers at St. Martin Carfax, Oxford, 1859. (Patrons, Mayor and Corporation of Oxford.) C. of Marcham with Garford, near Abingdon, 1861; Wriggleworth Lect. at St. Helen's, Abingdon, 1864. Formerly Chap. of New Coll. Ox. 1853–66; Incumb. of Canons Ashby, Northants, 1855–56. Author, *A Description of the Paintings in the Debating Room of the Oxford Union Society*, 1859, 1s; *The Legal Exemption of the Clergy from Turnpike Tolls*, 2 eds. 1863, 1s; *Memorials of the King's School, Canterbury*, 1865, 2s 6d; *The Cave of Adullam* (a Sermon preached at Carfax before the Mayor and Corporation of Oxford, published by request), 1866, 1s. [1]

SIDEBOTHAM, Thomas William, *Monken Hadley, Barnet, London, N.*—Magd. Hall, Ox. B.A. 1861, M.A. 1864; Deac. 1861 and Pr. 1862 by Bp of Lon. Formerly C. of Monken Hadley, Middlesex, 1861–64; C. of Therfield, Herts, 1864–66. [2]

SIDEBOTTOM, Frederick Radclyffe, *Yatton-Keynall Rectory, Chippenham.*—Dur. B.A. 1855; Deac. 1856 and Pr. 1858 by Bp of Lich. R. of Yatton-Keynall, Dio. G. and B. 1864. (Patron, Sir J. Neeld, Bart; R.'s Inc. 500*l* and Ho; Pop. 554.) Formerly C. of Chippenham 1859–64. [3]

SIDEBOTTOM, H., *Teston, near Maidstone.*—C. of Teston. [4]

SIDEBOTTOM, Henry Francis, *Sevenoaks Rectory, Kent.*—St. John's Coll. Ox. B.A. 1817, M.A. 1820; Deac. 1817 and Pr. 1818 by Bp of Ox. R. of Sevenoaks, Dio. Cant. 1861. (Patrons, Trustees of Rev. T. Curteis; R.'s Inc. 1261*l* and Ho; Pop. 3171.) Formerly P. C. of Trinity, Ripon, 1850–61. [5]

SIDEBOTTOM, Kingsford B., *Sevenoaks, Kent.*—C. of Sevenoaks. [6]

SIDGWICK, John Benson, *Copley Parsonage, Halifax.*—Trin. Coll. Cam. B.A. 1858, M.A. 1860; Deac. 1859 by Abp of York, Pr. 1860 by Bp of Wor. P. C. of Copley, Dio. Rip. 1865. (Patron, V. of Halifax; Pop. 1610.) Formerly C. of Alvechurch 1859–61, St. Thomas's, Huddersfield, 1861–62. [7]

SIDGWICK, William Carr, *Merton College, Oxford.*—Corpus Coll. Ox. 1st cl. Lit. Hum. B.A. 1856, M.A. 1859; Deac. 1859 and Pr. 1860 by Bp of Ox. Fell and Tut. of Mert. Coll. Ox. [8]

SIDNEY, Charles William Henry Humphrey, *Gooderstone, Stoke-Ferry, Norfolk.*—Sid. Coll. Cam. B.A. 1847; Deac. 1849 and Pr. 1850 by Bp of Nor. V. of Gooderstone, Dio. Nor. 1853. (Patron, H. R. Micklefield, Esq; Tithe—Imp. 250*l*, V. 133*l*; Glebe, 22 acres; V.'s Inc. 170*l*; Pop. 571.) [9]

SIDNEY, Edwin, *Cornard-Parva Rectory, Sudbury, Suffolk.*—St. John's Coll. Cam. B.A. 1820, M.A. 1824; Deac. 1821 and Pr. 1822 by Bp of Nor. R. of Cornard-Parva, Dio. Ely, 1847. (Patron, Bp of Nor; Tithe, 509*l*; Glebe, 32 acres; R.'s Inc. 600*l* and Ho; Pop. 404.) Dom. Chap. to Viscount Hill. Formerly C. of Lopham and Acle, Norfolk, 1821–24; Rural Dean and Surrogate. Author, *Life of the Rev. Rowland Hill*; *Life of the Rev. S. Walker, of Truro*; *Life of Sir Richard Hill, Bart. M.P*; *Life of General Viscount Hill, G.C.B. &c*; *Sermons preached before University of Cambridge*, 2 vols; several occasional Sermons; *Electricity*; *Food and Nutrition*; *Blights of the Wheat*; *The Field and the Fold*; *Teaching the Idiot*; *Conversations on the Bible and Science*, 1867. [10]

SIELY, Thomas Hurford, *Lackford Rectory, Bury St. Edmunds.*—Caius Coll. Cam. B.A. 1806, M.A. 1810. R. of Lackford, Dio. Ely, 1853. (Patron, Sir C. E. Kent, Bart; Tithe—App. 8*l* 14*s* 6*d*, R. 323*l* 6*s*; Glebe, 26½ acres; R.'s Inc. 347*l* and Ho; Pop. 197.) [11]

SIER, Thomas, 1, *Whitehall Gardens, London, S.W.*—Queen's Coll. Ox. B.A. 1846, M.A. 1848, D.C.L. 1853, LL.D. Cam. 1855; Deac. 1849 and Pr. 1850 by Bp of Roch. Called to the Bar, Middle Temple, 1847; C. of Stoke, Kent; V. of Ravensden, Beds, 1851–63; Min. of St. James's Chapel, Piccadilly, 1864. [12]

SIKES, John Churchill, 9, *Lansdowne-terrace, Pembroke-square, Kensington, W.*—Queens' Coll. Cam. B.A. 1868; Deac. 1864 and Pr. 1865 by Bp of Lich. C. of St. Philip's, Earl's-court, Kensington. Formerly C. of St. Michael's and St. Andrew's, Derby, 1865–67, Edgmond, Salop, 1864–65. Author, *A Plea for reading the Bible privately at least once every Year*, Bemrose, Derby; *A Sermon on the Cattle Plague*, ib. 1866. [13]

SIKES, Thomas, *Chevening Rectory, Sevenoaks, Kent.*—Queens' Coll. Cam. B.A. 1827, M.A. 1830; Deac. 1828 and Pr. 1829 by Bp of Lin. R. of Chevening, Dio. Cant. 1854. (Patron, Abp of Cant; Tithe, 766*l*; Glebe, 25 acres; R.'s Inc. 820*l* and Ho; Pop. 883.) Formerly C. and V. of Luton, Beds, 1828–54, and R. of Puttenham, Herts, 1835–48; Rural Dean; Chap. to Luton Union House 1839–42. [14]

SIKES, Thomas Burr, *Halstead Rectory, Sevenoaks, Kent.*—St. John's Coll. Ox. B.A. 1853, M.A. 1855; Deac. 1854 and Pr. 1855 by Abp of Cant. R. of Halstead, Dio. Cant. 1865. (Patron, Abp of Cant; Tithe, 220*l*; Glebe, 6 acres; R.'s Inc. 240*l* and Ho; Pop. 320.) Formerly C. of Halstead, of Chevening, of Keston, of St. Peter's, Maidstone, and of Hunton. Author of Tracts on the Holy Communion and on Public Worship. [15]

SILL, John Parkinson, *Wetheringsett, Stonham, Suffolk.*—Ch. Coll. Cam. B.A. 1826, M.A. 1831; Deac. 1828 and Pr. 1829 by Bp of Herf. R. of Wetheringsett, with Brockford, Dio. Nor. 1858. (Patron, the present R; Tithe, 713*l*; Glebe, 112 acres; R.'s Inc. 804*l* and Ho; Pop. 1030.) Formerly R. of Westhorpe, Suffolk, 1852–58. [16]

SILLIFANT, Charles William, *Wear-Gifford Rectory, Torrington, Devon.*—St. John's Coll. Ox. B.A. 1854, M.A. 1856; Deac. 1855 and Pr. 1856 by Bp of Nor. R. of Wear-Gifford, Dio. Ex. 1857. (Patron, Earl Fortescue; R.'s Inc. 200*l* and Ho; Pop. 494.) Formerly C. of Filby, near Norwich. [17]

SILVER, Edgar, *Medsted Rectory, Alton, Hants.*—Oriel Coll. Ox. M.A. 1854; Deac. 1853 and Pr. 1854 by Bp of Win. R. of Medstead, Hants, Dio. Win. 1867. (Patron, Bp of Win; Tithe, 580*l*; Glebe, 7 acres; R.'s Inc. 600*l* and Ho; Pop. 490.) Formerly C. of Shirley 1853, Bitterne, Hants, 1855; P. C. of Trinity, West Cowes, 1860–67. [18]

SILVER, Frederick, *Norton-in-Hales Rectory, near Market Drayton, Salop.*—Ox. B.A. 1847, M.A. 1850; Deac. 1847, Pr. 1848. R. of Norton-in-Hales, Dio. Lich. 1850. (Patron, S. W. Silver, Esq; Tithe, 305*l*; Glebe, 15 acres; R.'s Inc. 355*l* and Ho; Pop. 309.) [19]

SIM, Henry, 1, *Charlton-terrace, Dover.*—Pemb. Coll. Cam. Jun. Opt. B.A. 1816, M.A. 1820; Deac. 1816, Pr. 1817. Formerly P. C. of Wingham, Kent, 1844–59. [20]

SIMCOE, Henry Addington, *Penhale, near Launceston.*—Wad. Coll. Ox. B.A. 1821, M.A. 1830; Deac. 1826 and Pr. 1828 by Bp of Ex. P. C. of Egloskerry with Tremayne, Cornwall, Dio. Ex. 1846. (Patron, the present P. C; P. C.'s Inc. 111*l*; Pop. Egloskerry 510, Tremayne 109.) Rural Dean. Author, various Publications printed at the Penhale (private) press. [21]

SIMCOX, Thomas Green, *North Harborne Vicarage, Smethwick, Birmingham.*—Wad. Coll. Ox. 2nd cl. Lit. Hum. 1st cl. Math. et Phy. and B.A. 1831, M.A. 1836; Deac. 1833 and Pr. 1834 by Bp of Lich. V. of North Harborne, Dio. Lich. 1838. (Patrons, D. and C. of Lich; Tithe, 133*l*; Glebe, 1½ acres; V.'s Inc. 300*l* and Ho; Pop. 5550.) Formerly C. of Harborne 1833–38. [22]

SIMEY, George, *Ely.*—Dur. B.A. 1851, Licen. in Theol. 1852, M.A. 1862; Deac. and Pr. 1852. Chap. in Ely Cathl. and P. C. of Stuntney, Dio. Ely, 1861. (Patrons, D. and C. of Ely; P. C.'s Inc. 150*l*; Pop. 250.) [23]

SIMMONDS, E. M. De Lasaux, *Chilcomb, Winchester.*—C. of Chilcomb. [24]

SIMMONDS, Joseph De Lasaux, *Chilcomb Rectory, Winchester.*—St. Edm. Hall, Ox. B.A. 1841, M.A. 1844; Deac. 1841 and Pr. 1842 by Bp of G. and B. R. of Chilcomb, Dio. Win. 1849. (Patron, Bp of Win; Tithe, 161*l*; Glebe, 5 acres; R.'s Inc. 161*l* and Ho; Pop. 276.) Surrogate. Formerly C. of St. Paul's, Cheltenham, 1841, St. Luke's, Chelsea, 1843; P. C. of St. Matthew's, Gosport, 1845. [25]

SIMMONS, Joseph Ford, *Southport, Lancashire.*—Lin. Coll. Ox. B.A. 1863, M.A. 1866; Deac. 1864 and

Pr. 1865 by Bp of Ches. C. of Ch. Ch. Southport, 1863. [1]

SIMMONS, Melmoth Arthur Lintorn, *Chew Magna, near Bristol.*—St. Edm. Hall, Ox. B.A. 1859; Deac. 1860 and Pr. 1861 by Bp of Rip. Asst. C. of Chew Magna 1865. Formerly C. of Kildwick, Yorks, 1860–62, Shipham, Bristol (sole charge), 1863–64, Whilton, Lincolnshire (sole charge), 1864–65. [2]

SIMMONS, Thomas Frederick, *Dalton Holme Rectory, Beverley, Yorks.*—Ox. Merton Postmaster, 1832; Wor. Coll. B.A. 1848, M.A. 1859; Deac. 1848 by Bp of Ox. Pr. 1849 by Abp of York. R. of Dalton Holme, Dio. York, 1861. (Patron, Lord Hotham; R.'s Inc. 462*l* and Ho; Pop. 506.) Formerly C. of Beeford 1848–52; V. of Atwick 1852–53; R. of South Dalton 1853–61; P. C. of Holme-on-the-Wolds 1854–61. [3]

SIMONS, Charles Walker, *Halford Rectory, Shipston-on-Stour.*—Queens' Coll. Cam. B.A. 1848, M.A. 1851; Deac. 1848 and Pr. 1849 by Bp of Lich. R. of Halford, Dio. Wor. 1859. (Patron, Bp of Wor; R.'s Inc. 240*l*; Pop. 314.) Formerly P. C. of Cradley, Worc. 1850–56. [4]

SIMONS, Nicholas, *Bramfield Vicarage, Saxmundham, Suffolk.*—Ch. Coll. Cam. B.A. 1834, M.A. 1837; Deac. 1835 and Pr. 1836 by Bp of G. and B. V. of Bramfield, Dio. Nor. 1846. (Patron, Ld Chan; Tithe—Imp. 420*l*, V. 210*l*; Glebe, 4 acres; V.'s Inc. 220*l* and Ho; Pop. 649.) [5]

SIMONS, William Henry, *Hunstanworth, Gateshead.*—V. of Hunstanworth, Dio. Dur. 1862. (Patrons, J. and E. Joicey, Esqs; V.'s Inc. 260*l* and Ho; Pop. 778.) [6]

SIMPKINSON, John Nassau, *Brington, near Northampton.*—Trin. Coll. Cam. 1st cl. Cl. Trip. and B.A. 1839; Deac. 1840, Pr. 1841. R. of Brington, Dio. Pet. 1855. (Patron, Earl Spencer; R.'s Inc. 445*l*; Pop. 806.) Formerly Asst. Mast. in Harrow Sch. [7]

SIMPSON, Alexander George Kennard, *Harpenden, St. Albans.*—Ch. Coll. Cam. 3rd cl. Cl. Trip. B.A. 1862, M.A. 1865; Deac. 1862 and Pr. 1863 by Bp of Roch. C. of Harpenden 1862. [8]

SIMPSON, Arthur Barwick, *Bexhill, Hastings, Sussex.*—Caius Coll. Cam. Sen. Opt. and B.A. 1850, M.A. 1853; Deac. 1851, Pr. 1853. C. of Bexhill 1860. Formerly C. of Lodsworth, Sussex, 1851, Battle, Sussex, 1857. [9]

SIMPSON, Bolton, *Bossall Vicarage, near York.*—Queen's Coll. Ox. B.A. 1828. V. of Bossall with Buttercrambe C. Dio. York, 1854. (Patrons, D. and C. of Dur; Tithe—App. 1389*l* 6*s* 8*d*, Imp. 115*l*, V. 238*l* 18*s* 2*d*; Glebe, 200 acres; V.'s Inc. 530*l* and Ho; Pop. Bossall 187, Buttercrambe 126.) [10]

SIMPSON, Edward Whitmore, *Strensall, York.*—St. Aidan's; Deac. 1866 by Abp of York. C. of Strensall. [11]

SIMPSON, Forster George, *Upper Hardres Rectory, Canterbury.*—St. Edm. Hall, Ox. B.A. 1843; Deac. 1843 and Pr. 1844 by Bp of Win. Formerly C. of St. Mary Chapel, Lambeth, St. Paul's, Islington, and Ickworth with Harringer, Suffolk; R. of Shotley, Suffolk, 1860–66. Author, *God the King of Nations* (two Sermons), 1847, 1*s*; *The Typical Character of the Jewish Tabernacle, Priesthood and Sacrifices* (Lectures), 1852, 6*s*; *The Heavens a Witness for God* (a Sermon), 1856; "*The Snow's Tribute to its Maker*" (a Sermon), 1859; Essays on the Missionary Spirit, Inspiration, and the Baptism of Young Children in *The Church of England Magazine*; various Sermons, Tracts; etc. [12]

SIMPSON, Francis, *Boynton, Bridlington, Yorks.*—Queens' Coll. Cam. B.A. 1838, M.A. 1841; Deac. and Pr. 1840. V. of Boynton with Carnaby V. and Fraisthorpe P. C. Dio. York, 1856. (Patron, Sir G. Strickland, Bart; Boynton, Tithe, 117*l*; Carnaby, Tithe, 40*l*; Fraisthorpe, Tithe—Imp. 369*l*; V.'s Inc. 157*l* and Ho; Pop. Boynton 128, Carnaby 152, Fraisthorpe 101.) [13]

SIMPSON, Francis, jun., *Foston Rectory, York.*—R. of Foston, Dio. York, 1856. (Patron, Ld Chan; Tithe—Imp. 205*l*, R. 90*l*; Glebe, 300 acres; R.'s Inc. 600*l* and Ho; Pop. 355.) [14]

SIMPSON, Frederick Robinson, *North Sunderland, Belford, Northumberland.*—Trin. Coll. Cam. B.A. 1836; Deac. 1836, Pr. 1838. P. C. of North Sunderland, Dio. Dur. 1843. (Patrons, Trustees of Lord Crewe; Tithe—Imp. 229*l* 13*s*, App. 2*l* 10*s*, P. C. 8*s* 6*d*; Glebe, 26 acres; P. C.'s Inc. 300*l* and Ho; Pop. 1178.) Surrogate 1852. [15]

SIMPSON, George, *Loose, Staplehurst, Kent.*—Ch. Coll. Cam. B.A. 1830, M.A. 1833; Deac. 1832 and Pr. 1833 by Abp of Cant. V. of Loose, Dio. Cant. 1866. (Patron, Abp of Cant; Tithe, 524*l*; V.'s Inc. 560*l* and Ho; Pop. 1530.) Formerly C. of Sutton-Valence, Kent; V. of Northbourne, Kent, 1859–66. [16]

SIMPSON, George Stringer, *Rose Hill, Bobbing, Sittingbourne, Kent.*—Trin. Coll. Cam. B.A. 1838, M.A. 1841; Deac. 1838 and Pr. 1839 by Abp of Cant. V. of Bobbing, Dio. Cant. 1840. (Patron, the present V; Tithe—Imp. 194*l* 12*s*, V. 140*l*; Glebe, ¼ acre; V.'s Inc. 145*l*; Pop. 449.) [17]

SIMPSON, Henry Trail, *Adel Rectory, Leeds.*—Trin. Coll. Cam. B.A. 1831, M.A. 1838; Deac. 1832 and Pr. 1833 by Bp of Bristol. R. of Adel, Dio. Rip. 1858. (Patron, John Murray, Esq; Tithe, 597*l*; Glebe, 197*l*; R.'s Inc. 794*l* and Ho; Pop. 1145.) Formerly R. of Marnhull, Dorset. [18]

SIMPSON, Henry Winckworth, *Bexhill Rectory, Battle, Sussex.*—St. John's Coll. Cam; B.A. 1814, M.A. 1818. R. of Bexhill, Dio. Chich. 1840. (Patron, Bp. of Chich; Tithe, 989*l*; R.'s Inc. 1350*l* and Ho; Pop. 1402.) Preb. of Chich. 1841. Author, *Visitation Sermons*, 1842–52. [19]

SIMPSON, James, *Sankey Parsonage, Warrington.*—Deac. 1813, Pr. 1814. P. C. of Great Sankey, Dio. Ches. 1814. (Patron, Lord Lilford; Tithe—App. 140*l*, Imp. 130*l*; Glebe, 36 acres; P. C.'s Inc. 120*l* and Ho; Pop. 563.) [20]

SIMPSON, James, *Kirkby Stephen, Westmoreland.*—Univ. Coll. Dur. Licen. Theol. 1843; Deac. 1843, Pr. 1844. V. of Kirkby Stephen, Dio. Carl. 1863. (Patron, Earl of Lonsdale; V.'s Inc. 360*l* and Ho; Pop. 2846.) Formerly C. of Morland, near Penrith; V. of Shap, Westmoreland, 1857–63. [21]

SIMPSON, James Harvey, *Bexhill, Hastings.*—Trin. Coll. Cam. B.A. 1846, M.A. 1849; Deac. 1848 and Pr. 1849 by Abp of Cant. R. of St. Mark's, Bexhill, Dio. Chich. 1857. (Patron, Bp of Chich; Tithe, 286*l*; R.'s Inc. 290*l*; Pop. 682.) Formerly C. of Kemsing with Seal, 1848–50, Springfield 1850–52, Bexhill 1852–57. Author, *The Canticles noted for Anglican Chants*, Novello, 1857, 6*d*; *First Steps for Choir Boys*, ib. 1866. [22]

SIMPSON, James William Smart, *Lowton, Warrington.*—Dub. A.B. 1847, A.M. 1851; Deac. 1850 and Pr. 1851 by Bp of Ches. P. C. of St. Mary's, Lowton, Dio. Ches. 1860. (Patroness, Miss M. Leigh; P. C.'s Inc. 130*l* and Ho; Pop. 865.) Formerly Asst. C. of Sankey; Head Mast. of Farnworth Gr. Sch. [23]

SIMPSON, John, *Newton-in-Makerfield, Newton-le-Willows, Lancashire.*—Pemb. Coll. Cam. B.A. 1862; Deac. 1864 by Bp of Man. C. of Newton-in-Makerfield. Formerly C. of Ch. Ch. Blackburn, 1864. [24]

SIMPSON, John, *Alstonfield (Staffs), near Ashbourne.*—St. John's Coll. Cam. 1st cl. Coll. Prizeman, 1818 and 1819, 5th Jun. Opt. and B.A. 1821, M.A. 1824, D.D. 1838; Deac. 1821, Pr. 1822. V. of Alstonfield, Dio. Lich. 1822. (Patron, Sir John H. Crewe, Bart; Tithe, 37*l*; Glebe, 290 acres; V.'s Inc. 350*l* and Ho; Pop. 651.) Surrogate 1822; Rural Dean of Alstonfield 1837. Author, *Sermon on the Death of the Rev. John James Deane*, 6*d*, 1822; *The Power and Mercy of Christ Exhibited*, 6*d*, 1827; *Dipping not necessary to Baptism, an Appeal to Lexicographers, Critics, and the Greek Church, &c. respecting the Meaning of "Baptizo,"* 6*d*, 1841; *A Collection of Psalms and Hymns*, 4th ed. 1*s* 6*d*, 1856; *Twenty Plain Expository Lectures upon the History of Elijah the Prophet*, Seeleys, 1866, 5*s*. [25]

SIMPSON, John Foster, *Carlisle.*—Dub. A.B. 1847; Deac. 1848, Pr. 1849. Chap. to the Co. Gaol and Lunatic Asylum, Carlisle, 1855. Formerly Lect. of St. Cuthbert's, Carlisle. [26]

SIMPSON, Joseph, *Tilsworth Vicarage, Leighton Buzzard.*—Queen's Coll. Ox. 2nd cl. Lit. Hum. B.A. 1822, M.A. 1828; Deac. 1826 and Pr. 1827 by Bp of Ches. V. of Tilsworth, Dio. Ely, 1859. (Patron, Sir E. H. P. Turner, Bart; V.'s Inc. 47*l* and Ho; Pop. 348.) [1]

SIMPSON, J. H., *Upton Magna, Shrewsbury.*—C. of Upton Magna. [2]

SIMPSON, Maltyward, *Mickfield Rectory, Stonham, Suffolk.*—Caius Coll. Cam. B.A. 1827. R. of Mickfield, Dio. Nor. 1829. (Patron, the present R; Tithe, 398*l*; Glebe, 26 acres; R.'s Inc. 467*l* and Ho; Pop. 259.) [3]

SIMPSON, Michael Henry, *Ledsham, Milford Junction, Yorks.*—St. Cath. Coll. Cam. B.A. 1843. Mast. of Ledsham Gr. Sch. [4]

SIMPSON, Ralph Hutchinson, *Kirby-Monks Vicarage, Rugby.*—Trin. Coll. Cam. B.A. 1818, M.A. 1824. V. of Kirby-Monks with Withybrook V. and Copston-Magna C. Dio. Wor. 1839. (Patron, Trin. Coll. Cam; Kirby-Monks, Tithe—Imp. 50*l*, V. 9*s*; Withybrook, Tithe—Imp. 713*l* 6*s* 8*d*; Copston-Magna, Tithe—Imp. 391*l* 2*s* 2*d*, V. 1*l* 12*s* 6*d*; V.'s Inc. 170*l* and Ho; Pop. 2268.) [5]

SIMPSON, Robert, *Ryhope, Sunderland.*—St. Bees; Deac. 1859 and Pr. 1860 by Bp of Man. C. of Ryhope 1864. Formerly C. of Emmanuel, Bolton-le-Moors 1859–64. [6]

SIMPSON, Robert James, *The Vicarage, Slough.*—Oriel Coll. Ox. B.A. 1847, M.A. 1851; Deac. 1847, Pr. 1850. V. of Upton with Chalvey and Slough, Dio. Ox. 1867. (Patron, Bp of Ox; Tithe, 50*l*; Glebe, 300*l*; V.'s Inc. 400*l*; Pop. 6000.) Formerly C. of Whetburn and Haughton-le-Skerne, Durham and Windsor and Kensington. [7]

SIMPSON, Robert James, *Tunbridge House (Preparatory) School, Maidstone.*—Dub. A.B. 1854, A.M. 1857; Deac. 1854 and Pr. 1855 by Bp of Ely. Formerly C. of Boxford, Suffolk, 1854–55, Weybread, Suffolk, 1856–58, Rockland, St. Mary, Norfolk, 1860–62, Banham, Norfolk, 1863, St. Peter's, Maidstone, 1864. [8]

SIMPSON, R. W., *Bayville House, Emsworth, Hants.* [9]

SIMPSON, Samuel, *The Greaves, near Lancaster.*—M.A. by Abp of Cant. 1851, Hon. Ox. 1855; Deac. and Pr. 1851. Formerly P. C. of St. Thomas's, Douglas, Isle of Man. 1851–66. Author, *Short Prayers for Morning and Evening of each Day in our Ecclesiastical Year, by a Layman,* Lancaster, 1846; *The Death of the Righteous Considered,* 1857. [10]

SIMPSON, Thomas Burne, *East Teignmouth, Devon.*—Exhib. of Lin. Coll. Ox. B.A. 1849, M.A. 1852; Deac. 1851 and Pr. 1852 by Bp of Lich. P. C. of East Teignmouth, Dio. Ex. 1856. (Patron, V. of Dawlish; P. C.'s Inc. 150*l*; Pop. 2059.) Formerly P. C. of Bassenthwaite, Cumberland, 1855–56; Surrogate for Dio. of Dur. 1852–56, and Exeter 1857. [11]

SIMPSON, Thomas Wood, *Thurnscoe Rectory, near Doncaster.*—Wor. Coll. Ox. B.A. 1806, M.A. 1809; Deac. 1807 and Pr. 1808 by Bp of Ox. R. of Thurnscoe, Dio. York, 1815. (Patron, Earl Fitzwilliam; Tithe, 186*l*; Glebe, 183¼ acres; R.'s Inc. 346*l* and Ho; Pop. 196.) [12]

SIMPSON, William, *Dobcross Parsonage, Rochdale.*—V. of Dobcross, Dio. Man. 1844. (Patron, V. of Rochdale; V.'s Inc. 155*l* and Ho; Pop. 1972.) [13]

SIMPSON, William.—C. of Quiddenham, Norfolk. [14]

SIMPSON, William Bridgeman, *Babworth Rectory, East Retford, Notts.*—Trin. Coll. Cam. B.A. 1838, M.A. 1842. R. of Babworth, Dio. Lin. (Patron, Hon. B. J. Simpson; Tithe, 815*l*; Glebe, 20 acres; R.'s Inc. 855*l* and Ho; Pop. 701.) [15]

SIMPSON, William Hurst, *Stretton, Stamford, Lincolnshire.*—R. of Stretton, Dio. Pet. 1864. (Patron, Lord Aveland; R.'s Inc. 300*l* and Ho; Pop. 189.) [16]

SIMPSON, William Sparrow, *St. Matthew's Rectory, Friday-street, Cheapside, London, E.C.*—Queens' Coll. Cam. Librarian and Scho. of, 1850, B.A. 1851, M.A. 1854, *ad eund.* Ox. 1855; Deac. 1851 and Pr. 1852 by Bp of Win. R. of St. Matthew's, Friday-street, with St. Peter-le-Cheap R. City and Dio. Lon. 1857. (Patrons, Bp of Lon. and Duke of Buccleuch alt; R.'s Inc. 254*l* and Ho; Pop. St. Matthew's, Friday-street, 167, St. Peter-le-Cheap 148.) 9th Min. Can. of St. Paul's 1861. Formerly C. of St. Mark's, Kennington, 1851–56; C. of Great and Little Chesterford 1856–57. Author, *Mormonism, its History, Doctrines, and Practices,* 1853, 1*s*; *Education* (a Sermon), 1858, 1*s*; *Sermons* (preached at St. Matthew's, Friday-street), 1859; Papers in the *Journal of the British Archæological Association*; etc. [17]

SIMS, Frederic, *West Bergholt, Colchester.*—Pemb. Coll. Cam. B.A. 1835; Deac. 1835 by Bp of Lin. Pr. 1836 by Bp of Ely. R. of West Bergholt, Dio. Roch. 1846. (Patron, W. Fisher Hobbs, Esq; Tithe, 600*l*; Glebe, 37 acres; R.'s Inc. 620*l* and Ho; Pop. 906.) [18]

SIMS, H. M., *Hinderwell Rectory, Redcar, Yorks.*—R. of Hinderwell with Roxby C. Dio. York, 1852. (Patron, Robert Barry, Esq; R.'s Inc. 500*l* and Ho; Pop. 2805.) [19]

SIMS, William Francis, *Lee, Blackheath, Kent, S.E.*—Magd. Hall, Ox. B.A. 1839, M.A. 1842; Deac. 1839, Pr. 1840. P. C. of Ch. Ch. Lee, Dio. Lon. 1854. (Patron, R. of Lee; P. C.'s Inc. 300*l* and Ho; Pop. 2333.) Dom. Chap. to Viscount Strangford. Author, *Parochial Sermons,* 1848, 10*s* 6*d*; *Sermons on Justification,* 2nd ed. 1850, 2*s*; *The Christian Sabbath,* 1852, 1*s*; *Almsgiving,* Longmans, 1852, 6*d*; *Anniversary Sermon,* Longmans, 1857, 6*d*. [20]

SINCLAIR, The Ven. John, *The Vicarage, Kensington, London, W.*—Pemb. Coll. Ox. B.A. 1819, M.A. 1822; Deac. 1820 and Pr. 1821 by Bp of Lin. Exam. Chap. to the Bp of Lon. 1839; V. of Kensington, Dio. Lon. 1842. (Patron, Bp of Lon; Tithe, 792*l*; Glebe, 3 acres; Net. Value, 912*l*; Pop. 17,198.) Archd. of Middlesex 1843; Treasurer of the National Soc. Author, *Dissertations vindicating the Church of England,* 1836; *Life and Times of the Right Hon. Sir John Sinclair, Bart.* 2 vols. 1837; *Vindication of the Apostolical Succession*; *Sermon on the Death of the Rev. Archibald Alison*; *Questions illustrating the Catechism of the Church of England*; *Questions on the Orders for Morning and Evening Prayers*; *Essay on Church Patronage*; *Letters and Reports on National Education*; *Remarks on the Discouragements to Religious Teaching in the Report of the Royal Commissioners,* 1861; *Two Letters to the Clergy of the Archdeaconry of Middlesex on the Gorham Case, in Reply to the Bishop of Exeter*; *Essay on Papal Infallibility*; Sermons—*On Divisions in the Church*; *On Hearing God's Word*; and *Brethren Pray for Us* (in St. Paul's Cathedral); *On Religious Ordinances* (in Westminster Abbey); *On the Sublime and Beautiful* and *On Divine Service,* Paris, 1855; *Farewell Sermon,* New York, 1853; *On the General War,* 1854; *The War in* 1855; *Carthaginians and British Mercenaries Compared,* 1857; *Heathen Darkness and Christian Light* (in the Temple, 1864, and published by request of the Benchers); *On the Death of Bishop Blomfield,* 1857; *Charges*—1844, *Duties of Churchwardens*; 1845, *Rubrics and Ruri-Decanal Chapters*; 1849, *National Education and Church Extension*; 1851, *Church Difficulties*; 1852, *Synodal Action Unseasonable and Perilous*; 1853, *Church Questions*; 1855, *Preaching*; 1859, *The Parochial System of England*; 1860, *School-rates in England and America*; 1861, *The Agency of God*; 1863, *How to find out God*; 1865, *The Rights of Bishops, Presbyters and the Laity*; 1866, *On Free Thoughts*; 1867, *On the Morals of the Church of Rome.* [21]

SINCLAIR, William, *Pulborough Rectory, Petworth, Sussex.*—St. Mary Hall, Ox. B.A. 1835, M.A. 1837; Deac. 1835 and Pr. 1836 by Bp of Lich. R. of Pulborough, Dio. Chich. 1857. (Patron, Lord Leconfield; Tithe, 1730*l*; Glebe, 136 acres; R.'s Inc. 1920*l* and Ho; Pop. 1852.) Formerly P. C. of St. George's, Leeds, 1838–57. [22]

SINDEN, Henry.—P. C. of St. Mary's, Johnson-street, St. George's-in-the-East, Dio. Lon. 1864. (Patroness, Dowager Countess of Aberdeen; P. C.'s Inc. 150*l*; Pop. 5515.) [23]

SINDEN, William, *The Parsonage, St. Peter's, Macclesfield.*—St. Aidan's; Deac. 1852 and Pr. 1853 by Bp. of Ches. P. C. of St. Peter's, Macclesfield, Dio. Ches. 1854. (Patrons, the Crown and Bp. of Ches. alt; P. C.'s Inc. 150*l*. and Ho; Pop. 2000.) Formerly C. of St. Paul's, Macclesfield, 1852–53. Author, *The Great Prize Fight*, 1863, 2*d*, Hamilton and Adams. [1]

SINGLETON, John Joseph, *Chesterfield, Derbyshire.*—Pemb. Coll. Cam. Jun. Opt. Deac. 1861, Pr. 1862. Assist. C. of Chesterfield, and C. in sole charge of Calow, Chesterfield, 1861. [2]

SINGLETON, Joseph, *Babraham Vicarage, near Cambridge.*—Queens' Coll. Cam. B.A. 1827, M.A. 1831, Deac. 1827 and Pr. 1828 by Bp of Lin. V. of Babraham, Dio. Ely, 1839. (Patron, Henry John Adeane, Esq; Tithe, 120*l*; Glebe, 3 acres; V.'s Inc. 125*l* and Ho; Pop. 325.) Chap. to the Linton Union. (Salary, 60*l*.) Formerly C. of Trusthorpe, Linc. 1827–39. [3]

SINGLETON, R. C., *York.*—C. of St. Sampson's, York. [4]

SINGLETON, William, *Worlington Rectory (Suffolk), near Soham.*—St. John's Coll. Cam. 17th Wrang. and B.A. 1829, M.A. 1832; Deac. 1830, Pr. 1832. R. of Worlington, Dio. Ely, 1852. (Patrons, Trustees; Glebe, 308 acres; R.'s Inc. 260*l* and Ho; Pop. 349.) Formerly Prin. of Kingston Coll. Hull, 1843–47; P. C. of Trinity, Tunstead, Whalley, 1847–51. [5]

SINKER, Robert, *Trinity College, Cambridge.*—Trin. Coll. Cam. B.A. 1862, M.A. 1865, Wrang. and 2nd cl. Cl. Trip. 1862, 1st cl. Theol. Trip. 1863, Carus Greek Test. Prize 1860–62, Scholefield Prize 1863, Crosse Scho. 1863, Tyrrwhitt Heb. Scho. 1864, Hulsean Prize 1864; Deac. 1863 and Pr. 1864 by Bp of Ely. Chap. of Trin. Coll. 1865. Formerly C. of Coton, Cambs, 1863–66. Author, *The Divine Authority of the New Testament, as shown by a Comparison with preceding Jewish and succeeding Christian Literature* (Hulsean Prize Essay), Cambridge, 1865; *Biblia Sacra Hebraica, sine punctis* (edited jointly with Rev. E. T. Leeke) *Fasciculus* I. 1867, Cambridge. [6]

SINNETT, John, *Bangor Teify Rectory, Newcastle-Emlyn.*—Lampeter, Scho. of, 1853; Deac. 1844 and Pr. 1845 by Bp of St. D. R. of Bangor with Henllan, Dio. St. D. 1850. (Patron, Bp of St. D; Tithe, 113*l* 14*s*; Glebe, 81 acres; R.'s Inc. 200*l* and Ho; Pop. 337.) Formerly C. of Lampeter 1845–50. [7]

SIRR, Joseph D'Arcy, *Winchester.*—Dub. A.B. 1812, A.M. 1823, B.D. 1842, D.D. 1843; Deac. 1818, Pr. 1819. R. of Morestead, Hants, Dio. Win. 1859. (Patron, Bp of Win; R.'s Inc. 180*l* and Ho; Pop. 112.) Asst. Chap. to the Forces, Winchester. Formerly R. of Kilcolman, Ireland, 1823–44; V. of Yoxford, Suffolk, 1844–46; P. C. of St. Mary's, Spital, 1846–50. Author, *Life of Archbishop Usher* (prefixed to *Religion of the Ancient Irish*), 1815; *Funeral Sermon* (Death of George III.); *The Deluge a Type of the Conflagration*, 1832; *The First Resurrection* (Reply to the Rev. H. Gipps), 1833; *Reasons for abiding in the Established Church*, 1836; *A Dissuasive from Separation*, 1836; *Condensed Notes on St. Luke's Gospel*, 1848; *The Law of Sinai and of Zion* (an Act Sermon), 1843; *Memoirs of the last Archbishop of Tuam*, 1843; *Sacrifices Past, Present, and Future*, 1862. [8]

SISSON, John Septimus, *Orton Vicarage (Westmoreland), near Penrith.*—Univ. Coll. Dur. B.A. 1847; Deac. 1847, Pr. 1848. V. of Orton, Dio. Carl. 1850. (Patrons, Landowners; Tithe, 201*l* 8*s* 11*d*; Glebe, 206¼ acres; V.'s Inc. 287*l* and Ho; Pop. 1615.) Surrogate. [9]

SISSON, Joseph Lawson, jun., *Lausanne, Switzerland.*—Jesus Coll. Cam. B.A. 1840. R. of Edingthorpe, North Walsham, Norfolk, Dio. Nor. 1850. (Patron, Duchy of Lancaster; Tithe, 237*l* 7*s*; Glebe, 17½ acres; R.'s Inc. 269*l* and Ho; Pop. 181.) British Chap. at Lausanne. [10]

SISSON, Michael, *Spalding, Lincolnshire.*—St. Bees 1832. P. C. of Moulton Chapel, near Spalding, Dio. Lin. 1838. (Patron, V. of Moulton; P. C.'s Inc. 100*l*.) Head Mast. of Spalding Gr. Sch; Chap. to the Spalding Union. Formerly C. of Weston, Linc. [11]

SISSON, Redman.—St. Bees; Deac. 1854 by Bp of Dur. Pr. 1855 by Bp of Man. C. of Haydon Bridge, near Hexham. Formerly C. of Warden 1855. [12]

SISSON, William, *Slaley, Hexham, Northumberland.*—Univ. Coll. Dur. Licen. Theol. 1840; Deac. 1840 and Pr. 1841 by Bp of Dur. P. C. of Whitley, near Hexham, Dio. Dur. 1841. (Patron, W. B. Beaumont, Esq. M.P; Glebe, 100 acres; P. C.'s Inc. 103*l*; Pop. 907.) P. C. of Slaley, Dio. Dur. 1854. (Patron, W. B. Beaumont, Esq. M.P; Tithe, Imp. 425*l*; Glebe, 53 acres; P. C.'s Inc. 78*l* and Ho; Pop. 561.) Author, *A Farewell Sermon*, 1841. [13]

SITWELL, Albert Hurt, *St. Peter's Parsonage, Stepney, London, E.*—P. C. of St. Peter's, Stepney, Dio. Lon. 1863. (Patron, Bp of Lon; P. C.'s Inc. 350*l* and Ho; Pop. 12,139.) Hon. Chap. to Bp of Lon. [14]

SITWELL, W. D., *Leamington Hastings, Southam, Warwickshire.*—V. of Leamington Hastings, Dio. Wor. 1863. (Patron, A. D. Sitwell, Esq; V.'s Inc. 700*l* and Ho; Pop. 450.) [15]

SKELTON, Robert, *Levisham, Pickering, Yorks.*—Deac. 1814 and Pr. 1815 by Abp of York. R. of Levisham, Dio. York, 1818. (Patron, the present R; R.'s Inc. 125*l*; Pop. 148.) P. C. of Rosedale, near Pickering, Dio. York, 1818. (Patron, the present P. C; Tithe, App. 35*l* 10*s*; P. C.'s Inc. 100*l*; Pop. 446.) [16]

SKENE, William, *Sighill, Dudley Station, Northumberland.*—Univ. Coll. Dur. Heb. Prizeman 1839, B.A. 1843, M.A. 1857, B.D. 1864, D.D. 1866; Deac. 1839 and Pr. 1840 by Bp of Dur. P. C. of Sighill, Dio. Dur. 1855. (Patrons, the Crown and Bp of Dur. alt; P. C.'s Inc. 300*l* and Ho; Pop. 4588.) Formerly C. of Winlaton 1839, Kelloe 1844. Author, *The Consideration of our Latter End* (a Sermon), 1847; *Lectures on the Signs of Thought*, 1848; *Lecture on the Measurement of Time and the Calendar*, 1849; *Consolations in the Early Death of God's Saints* (a Funeral Sermon), 1851; *The Whole Counsel of God* (a Farewell Sermon), 1854; *Our Ignorance of the Future* (a Funeral Sermon), 1856; *The Death of God's Saints precious in his Sight* (a Funeral Sermon), 1866; etc. [17]

SKETCHLEY, Alexander Everingham, *Deptford, Kent, S.E.*—Magd. Hall, Ox. B.A. 1828, M.A. 1831, B.D. and D.D. 1849; Deac. 1828 by Bp of Lon. Pr. 1830 by Bp of Lin. V. of St. Nicholas', Deptford, Dio. Roch. 1836. (Patron, T. T. Drake, Esq; Tithe, App. 519*l*; Glebe, 1 acre; V.'s Inc. 600*l*; Pop. 8139.) Formerly C. of Amersham, Bucks. [18]

SKETCHLEY, Horatio Powis, *Millbrook, Southampton.*—Oriel Coll. Ox. Eveleigh Prize 1863, B.A. 1865; Deac. 1866 by Bp of Win. C. of Millbrook 1866. [19]

SKEY, Frederic Charles, 17, *Pembroke-place, Clifton, Bristol.*—Wor. Coll. Ox. B.A. 1855, M.A. 1857; Deac. 1859 and Pr. 1860 by Bp of Nor. Min. Can. of Bristol Cathl. 1861. (Value, 150*l*.) C. of Ch. Ch. with St. Ewins, Bristol, 1863. Formerly C. of Great Yarmouth 1859–61. Mast. of Bristol Cathl. Gr. Sch. 1861–65. Author, *The Seven Pilgrims, an Allegory.* [20]

SKILTON, William James, *Romford, Essex.*—Corpus Coll. Cam. Scho. of, Sen. Opt. B.A. 1849, M.A. 1852; Deac. 1849 by Bp of Win. Pr. 1850 by Bp of Lich. R. of St. Andrew's, Romford, Dio. Roch. 1862. (Patron, New Coll. Ox; Tithe, 120*l*; R.'s Inc. 300*l*; Pop. 3000.) Formerly C. of Romford 1852–56; P. C. of West Pinchbeck 1856–59; C. of Romford 1859–62. [21]

SKINNER, George, *King's College, Cambridge.*—Jesus Coll. Cam. B.A. 1818, M.A. 1821. Conduct of King's Coll. Cam. Formerly Fell. of Jesus Coll. Cam. [22]

SKINNER, James, *The Warden's Lodge, Newland, Great Malvern.*—Univ. Dur. B.A. 1837, M.A. 1840; Deac. 1841 by Bp of Pet. Pr. 1842 by Bp of Rip. V. of Newland, Dio. Wor. 1861. (Patrons, Trustees of the Beauchamp Charity; V.'s Inc. 60*l*; Pop. 194.) Warden of the Beauchamp Charity. Formerly Fell. of Dur. Univ. 1844–49; Sen. C. of St. Barnabas', Pimlico, Lond. Author, *Warnings and Consolations*, 6*s*; *The Way of the Wilderness by the Red Sea, a Journal in the East*, 10*s* 6*d*; *Perversions to Rome*, 2*s*; *The Revelation of*

Antichrist, 1s 6d; *Guide to Advent*, 2s 6d; *How to keep Lent*, 4s; *Plain Directions for keeping Lent*, 2d; *Why do we prize Externals in the Service of God*, 6d; *The Priest's Call*, 2d; *The Stewards of the Mysteries of God*, 2d; *The Church in the Public School*; *Twenty-one Heads of Christian Duty*, 1s; *The Daily Service Hymnal*, 1s 6d. [1]

SKINNER, Robert, *St. Andrew's, Scotland.*—Bp Hatfield's Hall, Dur. Licen. in Theol; Deac. 1853 and Pr. 1854 by Bp of Dur. Incumb. of St. Andrew's, St. Andrew's. (Inc. 220*l* and Ho.) Formerly C. of Whickham, Durham, 1853–54, St. Andrew's, Aberdeen, 1854–56. [2]

SKINNER, Russell, *Swefling Rectory, Saxmundham, Suffolk.*—Sid. Coll. Cam. Sen. Opt. and B.A. 1825, M.A. 1828; Deac. 1826 and Pr. 1827 by Bp of Lon. R. of Swefling, Dio. Nor. 1835. (Patron, the present R; Tithe, 302*l* 10*s*; Glebe, 10 acres; R.'s Inc. 318*l* and Ho; Pop. 348.) [3]

SKIPPER, John Benson, *Marden Vicarage, Devizes, Wilts.*—Emman. Coll. Cam. B.A. 1829, M.A. 1831; Deac. 1830, Pr. 1831. V. of Marden, Dio. Salis. 1844. (Patrons, D. and C. of Bristol; Tithe—App. 206*l* and 44 acres of Glebe, V. 175*l* 10*s*; Glebe, 1½ acres; V.'s Inc. 170*l* and Ho; Pop 235.) [4]

SKIPSEY, Richard, *St. Thomas's Parsonage, Bishopwearmouth, Sunderland.*—Queen's Coll. Ox. 2nd cl. Math. and B.A. 1828; Deac. 1830 by Bp of Lon. Pr. 1831 by Abp of York. P. C. of St. Thomas's, Bishopwearmouth, Dio. Dur. 1844. (Patron, Bp of Dur; P. C.'s Inc. 300*l* and Ho; Pop. 7413.) Author, *Sermon, after an Explosion at the Iron Works*, Bishopwearmouth, 1846; *Plenary Inspiration of the Bible* (a Sermon), 1852; *The Church founded upon Faith in Jesus Christ*, 1853; *Verification of Holy Scripture*, 1853. [5]

SKIPWITH, Humberston, *Hamstall-Ridware, Rugeley, Staffs.*—Trin. Coll. Cam. S.C.L. 1845; Deac. 1846 and Pr. 1847 by Bp of Wor. R. of Hamstall-Ridware, Dio. Lich. 1866. (Patron, Lord Leigh; R.'s Inc. 300*l*; Pop. 440.) Formerly C. of Marton, Warwick, 1847–49, Bishops Tachbrook 1849–51, Ashow 1851–56; R. of Boothby Graffoe, Lincoln, 1856–63. [6]

SKIPWITH, Randolph, *Whilton Rectory, Daventry, Northants.*—Trin. Coll. Cam. S.C.L. 1843; Deac. 1845 and Pr. 1846 by Bp of Wor. R. of Whilton, Dio. Pet. 1856. (Patron, W. G. Rose, Esq; Glebe, 190 acres; R.'s Inc. 440*l* and Ho; Pop. 350.) Formerly C. of Wolston 1845–56; V. of Marton 1847–56; Surrogate for Dio. Wor. 1848–56. [7]

SKIPWORTH, Arthur Bolland, *Bilsdale Parsonage, Northallerton, Yorks.*—St. Cath. Coll. Cam. Scho. and 1st Prizeman, Math. Hons. and B.A. 1856; Deac. 1857 and Pr. 1858 by Bp of Lin. P. C. of Bilsdale, Dio. York, 1860. (Patron, V. of Helmsley; P. C.'s Inc. 126*l*; Pop. 738.) Formerly C. of Croxby and Beelsby, Lincolnshire. [8]

SKIPWORTH, Grey, *Oakham, Rutland.*—Emman. Coll. Cam. Scho. and Prizeman of, Sen. Opt. 3rd cl. Cl. Trip. B.A. 1858, M.A. 1865; Deac. 1862 and Pr. 1863 by Abp of Armagh. 2nd Mast. and Sub-Warden of Oakham Sch. 1865; Chap. of the County Gaol 1865, and of the Union, Oakham, 1866. Formerly Math. Mast. Lincoln Gr. Sch. 1859–60; Asst. Mast. Royal Sch. Armagh, 1861–65. [9]

SKIRROW, William, *Tolleshunt-Knights, Kelvedon, Essex.*—Univ. Coll. Ox. B.A. 1838, M.A. 1842; R. of Tolleshunt-Knights, Dio. Roch. 1865. (Patron, Ld Chan; R.'s Inc. 488*l* and Ho; Pop. 251.) Formerly V. of Hinckley with Stoke-Golding R. and Dadlington C. Pet. 1849–65. [10]

SKOTTOWE, Charles Mills, *Remenham Rectory, Henley-on-Thames.*—Jesus Coll. Fell. of, Ox. B.A. 1842, M.A. 1845, B.D. 1852; Deac. 1843 and Pr. 1844 by Bp of Ox. R. of Remenham, Dio. Ox. 1866. (Patron, Jesus Coll. Ox; R.'s Inc. 550*l*; Pop. 486.) [11]

SKRIMSHIRE, Arthur James, *Longthorpe, Peterborough.*—St. Bees 1854; Deac. 1856 and Pr. 1857 by Bp of Nor. P. C. of Longthorpe, Dio. Pet. 1860. (Patron, Earl Fitzwilliam; P. C.'s Inc. 80*l*; Pop. 294.) Author, *A Treatise on the Effects of excessive Loss of Blood* (read before the Royal Medical Soc. Edinburgh), 1837; *A Treatise on Chronic Remittent Fever*, 1838; *Original Documents relating to Sudbury* (inserted in the *Proceedings of the West Suffolk Archæological Institute*), 1850. [12]

SKRINE, Clarmont, 20, *Devonshire-terrace, Hyde-park, W.*—King's Coll. Lond. Theol. Assoc. 1855, Ch. Ch. Ox. M.A. by Abp of Cant; Deac. and Pr. 1855 by Abp of Cant. P. C. of St. Peter's Chapel, Charlotte-street, Buckingham-gate, Pimlico. Formerly an Officer in the army; C. of Linton 1855; P. C. of Trent Ch. Enfield, 1856–65. [13]

SKRINE, Harcourt, *Sunbury, Middlesex, S.W.*—Wad. Coll. Ox. B.A. 1840, M.A. 1843; Deac. 1841 and Pr. 1842 by Bp of G. and B. C. of Sunbury 1843. [14]

SKRINE, Wadham Huntley, *Stubbings Parsonage, Maidenhead, Berks.*—Ch. Ch. Ox. B.A. 1841, M.A. 1846; Deac. 1843, Pr. 1844. P. C. of Stubbings, Dio. Ox. 1853. (Patron, Henry Duncan Skrine, Esq; Glebe, 7 acres; P. C.'s Inc. 108*l* and Ho; Pop. 363.) [15]

SLADE, George, *Greenheys, Manchester.*—St. Edm. Hall, Ox. B.A. 1835, M.A. 1838, Dub. LL.D. 1852; Deac. 1835, Pr. 1837 by Abp of Cant. Lect. of St. John's, Manchester, 1865. Formerly C. of Prescot, Lanc. 1835; P. C. of St. Thomas's, Radcliffe, Lanc. 1838; Head Mast. of the Sch. for Eng. Lit. formerly in connection with the Manchester Free Gr. Sch. 1844. [16]

SLADE, George Fitzclarence, *Lewknor Vicarage, Tetsworth, Oxon.*—All Souls' Coll. Ox. 2nd cl. Law and Mod. Hist. B.A. 1854; Deac. 1856 and Pr. 1857 by Bp of Ox. V. of Lewknor, Dio. Ox. 1866. (Patron, All Souls' Coll. Ox; Tithe, 190*l* 10*s*; Glebe, 168*l* 15*s*; V.'s Inc. 280*l* and Ho; Pop. 650.) Formerly Fell. of All Souls' Coll. Ox; C. of St. Nicholas', Great Yarmouth, 1856–58; V. of Alberbury, Herf. 1858–66. [17]

SLADE, Henry Raper, *Wellington, Salop.*—Caius Coll. Cam. LL.B. 1830, Leipsic Univ. D.D. 1843; Deac. 1830 and Pr. 1831 by Bp of B. and W. R. of Kenley, Salop, Dio. Lich. 1841. (Patron, Duke of Cleveland; Tithe, 144*l*; Glebe, 30 acres; R.'s Inc. 169*l*; Pop. 235.) Dom. Chap. to the Earl of Clarendon 1842. Author, *The Necessity of increased Vigilance and Zeal in the Clergy of the Established Church* (a Sermon), 1829; *An Academical Essay on the Doctrine of Types, and its Influence on the Interpretation of the New Testament*, 1830; *An Answer to a Roman Catholic Tract*, entitled *The Surest Way to Salvation*, Wells, 1830; *An Answer to the Protest of William Morshead, a Clergyman, who seceded from the Church of England, calling it Apostate*, Bath, 1833; *Comments upon the Roman Missal and Vesper Office*, 1833; *Four Discourses on the Power of God, the Urgency of Repentance, Spiritual Religion, and the Divinity of Christ*, 1833; *Masonic Didactics*, in a Series of Fifty Moral Essays, and other Literary Papers in the *Freemasons' Quarterly Review*, 1835–47; *The Defence of Socrates, translated from the Original Dialogues of Plato*, 1836; *The Present Times* (a Lent Sermon), 1836; *Pulpit Lectures on the Epistles of the Apostle Paul to Timothy*, 1837; *A Sermon* (in Aid of the Asylum for worthy Aged and Decayed Freemasons), 1839; *Charity, or Brotherly Love* (a Masonic Sermon), 1841; *Dissertatio Academica Inauguralis de Naturâ et Officio Filii Dei inscripta Universitati Pracolyræ*, Leipsic, 1843; *Remarks upon catechising according to the Rubric*, &c. 1844; *Salvation of the Soul the Free Gift of God irrespective of Religious Systems or Modes of Worship* (a Sermon), 1847; etc. [18]

SLADE, James, *Little Lever Parsonage, Bolton-le-Moors.*—St. John's Coll. Cam. B.A. 1842; Deac. 1843 by Bp of Pet. Pr. 1843 by Bp of Ches. P. C. of Little Lever, Dio. Man. 1843. (Patron, V. of Bolton-le-Moors; P. C.'s Inc. 150*l* and Ho; Pop. 3890.) [19]

SLADE, James John, *Netherton, near Dudley.*—St. Edm. Hall, Ox. B.A. 1850, M.A. 1857; Deac. 1850 and Pr. 1851 by Bp of Lich. P. C. of St. Andrew's, Netherton, Dio. Wor. 1857. (Patron, V. of Dudley; P. C.'s Inc. 300*l*; Pop. 10,426.) Formerly C. of St. Mary's, Kingswinford. [20]

SLADEN, Edward, *St. Ives, Hunts.*—Ball. Coll. Ox. 2nd cl. Lit. Hum. 1864; B.A. 1864, M.A. 1866; Deac. 1865 by Bp of Salis. C. of St. Ives 1867. Formerly Asst. C. of St. Neots 1865. [1]

SLADEN, Edward Henry Mainwaring, *Alton-Berners, Marlborough, Wilts.*—Ball. Coll. Ox. B.A. 1837, M.A. 1840; Deac. 1838 and Pr. 1839 by Bp of Chich. C. of Alton-Barnes or Berners 1856. Formerly C. of Ninfield 1838–40 and 1848–53, Bockleton with Leysters 1840–42, Warnford 1843–48, Peterstow 1856, Alton-Priors 1856–62. [2]

SLATER, Edward Bentley, *Pocklington, Yorks.*—St. John's Coll. Cam. 1st cl. Cl. Trip. and B.A. 1843, M.A. 1847; Deac. 1846, Pr. 1847. 2nd Mast. of the Pocklington Gr. Sch. 1849. Formerly Fell. of St. John's Coll. Cam. 1847–49. [3]

SLATER, Francis, *The Grammar School, Sudbury, Suffolk.*—Queens' Coll. Cam. B.A. 1862, M.A. 1866; Deac. 1862 and Pr. 1863 by Bp of Nor. Head Mast. of the Gr. Sch. Sudbury, 1864. Formerly C. of St. Mary-le-Tower, Ipswich, 1862–64. [4]

SLATER, Henry, *Broomhaugh, Riding Mill-on-Tyne.*—Cath. Coll. Cam. B.A. 1847, M.A. 1857, Deac. 1848, Pr. 1849. V. of Bywell St. Andrew, Dio. Dur. 1866. (Patron, W. B. Beaumont, Esq. M.P; Tithe, 100*l*; Glebe, 73*l* 10*s*; V.'s Inc. 174*l* 10*s*; Pop. 509.) Formerly C. of St. Andrew's, Liverpool, 1848–50; Sen. C. of Stanhope and C. of Eastgate, 1850–66. [5]

SLATER, James, *Happisburgh, Norwich.*—Queens' Coll. Cam. B.A. 1847, M.A. 1864, Deac. and Pr. 1847 by Bp of Wor. V. of Happisburgh, Dio. Nor. 1859. (Patron, Bp of Nor; Tithe, App. 226*l* 4*s* 4*d*; V.'s Inc. 300*l* and Ho; Pop. 584.) Formerly C. of St. Peter's, Coventry, 1847; P. C. of Otterford, Somerset, and C. of Ilminster 1848; C. of Acle 1851. [6]

SLATER, Joseph.—C. of St. Lawrence, Southampton. Formerly C. of Trinity, Gosport. [7]

SLATER, Thomas, *Coseley Parsonage, Sedgeley, Staffs.*—Emman. Coll. Cam. B.A. 1857; Deac. 1857 by Bp of Man. P. C. of Coseley, Dio. Lich. 1863. (Patron, Earl of Dudley; P. C.'s Inc. 250*l* and Ho; Pop. 15,796.) [8]

SLATTER, George Maximilian, *Exeter.*—Hertford Coll. Ox. Scho. 1803, *ad eund.* St. Peter's Coll Cam. B.D. 1827, D.D. 1850; Deac. 1816 by Bp. of Glouc. Pr. 1817 by Bp. of Ex. Priest-V. of Ex. Cathl. 1817. (Value, 150*l*.) V. of West Anstey, Devon, Dio. Ex. 1819. (Patrons, D. and C. of Ex; Tithe—App. 78*l*, V. 112*l*; Glebe, 30 acres; V.'s Inc. 167*l* and Ho; Pop. 299.) Dean's V. and Sub-Treasurer of Ex. Cathl. 1830. (Value, 26*l*.) Author, *Brief Sketch of Scripture History*; *Catechetical Instructions on certain Doctrines and Practices of the Church of England*; *Sacred Music*; various Anthems, Services, Psalm Tunes and Chants. [9]

SLATTER, John, *Streatley Vicarage, Reading.*—Lin. Coll. Ox. 3rd cl. Lit. Hum. 1st cl. Math. et Phy. and B.A. 1838, M.A. 1841; Deac. 1840, Pr. 1841. V. of Streatley, Dio. Ox. 1861. (Patron, Bp of Ox; V.'s Inc. 202*l* and Ho; Pop. 552.) [10]

SLATTER, William, *Imber, Heytesbury, Wilts.*—Lin. Coll. Ox. B.A. 1846, M.A. 1849; Deac. 1848 and Pr. 1849 by Bp of Ox. P. C. of Imber, Dio. Salis. 1865. (Patron, Marquis of Bath; P. C.'s Inc. 120*l*; Pop. 382.) Formerly C. of Cowley, Oxon, 1849–50, Warminster, Wilts, 1856–60, Longbridge Deverill with Monkton Deverill, 1860–65. [11]

SLEAP, Edward, *Rossall School, Fleetwood, Lancashire.*—Asst. Mast. in Rossall Sch. [12]

SLEEMAN, Richard, *Whitchurch Vicarage, Tavistock, Devon.*—Ball. Coll. Ox. B.A. 1834; Deac. 1838 and Pr. 1839 by Bp of Ex. V. of Whitchurch, Dio. Ex. 1848. (Patron, the present V; Tithe—Imp. 200*l* 6*s*, V. 192*l* 10*s*; V.'s Inc. 202*l* and Ho; Pop. 1340.) Surrogate 1848. [13]

SLEEMAN, The Ven. Thomas, *Gibraltar,* Deac. 1849 and Pr. 1850 by Bp of Gibraltar. Can. of Gibraltar 1853; British Chap. and Archd. of Gibraltar 1864. Formerly V. of South Tawton, Devon, 1857–60. [14]

SLESSOR, John Henry, *Headbourn-Worthy, Winchester.*—Univ. Coll. Ox. 2nd cl. Lit. Hum. and B.A. 1844, M.A. 1846; Deac. 1850 and Pr. 1851 by Bp of Ox. R. of Headbourn-Worthy, Dio. Win. 1861. (Patron, Univ. Coll. Ox; R.'s Inc. 400*l* and Ho; Pop. 194.) Formerly Asst. C. of Talaton, Devon; Fell. of Univ. Coll. Ox. 1847. [15]

SLIGHT, Alpheus, *Alkmonton, Derby.*—St. John's Coll. Cam. B.A. 1845, M.A. 1848; Deac. 1845 and Pr. 1846 by Bp of Pet. P. C. of Alkmonton, Dio. Lich. 1848. (Patron, Thomas Wm. Evans, Esq. M.P; P. C.'s Inc. 50*l* and Ho; Pop. 175.) C. of Barton Blount, Derbyshire. [16]

SLIGHT, Frederick Goode, *Bury, Lancashire.*—St. John's Coll. Cam. B.A. 1861; Deac. 1863 and Pr. 1865 by Bp of Man. C. of Bury 1865. Formerly C. of St. Michael's, Tonge, 1863–65. [17]

SLIGHT, Henry Spencer, *Ruan Rectory, Grampound, Cornwall.*—Deac. 1837, Pr. 1838. R. of Ruan-Lanihorne, Dio. Ex. 1849. (Patron, Corpus Coll. Ox; Tithe, 420*l*; Glebe, 90 acres; R.'s Inc. 460*l* and Ho; Pop. 325.) Formerly Fell. of Corpus Coll. Ox; Chap. R.N. [18]

SLIGHT, John Bullivant.—St. John's Coll. Cam. Scho. 1857, B.A. 1859; Deac. 1859 and Pr. 1860 by Bp of Chich. Formerly Asst. Mast. of Brighton Coll. [19]

SLIGHT, John Goode, *Taxal Rectory, Stockport, Cheshire.*—St. John's Coll. Cam. B.A. 1839, M.A. 1842; Deac. 1840 and Pr. 1841 by Bp of Pet. R. of Taxal, Dio. Ches. 1844. (Patron, the present R; Tithe, 232*l* 8*s* 10*d*; Glebe, 85 acres; R.'s Inc. 320*l* and Ho; Pop. 1329.) Formerly Fell. of St. John's Coll. Cam; Head Mast. of the Manchester Commercial Schs; C. of Barrow, Leicester. [20]

SLIPPER, Robert Browne, *Coston, Wymondham, Norfolk.*—Caius Coll. Cam. Wrang. and B.A. 1839, M.A. 1842; Deac. 1840, Pr. 1841. R. of Coston, Norfolk, Dio. Nor. 1855. (Patron, Bp of Nor; Tithe, 92*l*; Glebe, 8 acres; Pop. 58.) V. of Runhall, near Wymondham, Dio. Nor. 1859. (Patron, Earl of Kimberley, formerly Lord Wodehouse; V.'s Inc. 60*l*; Pop. 246.) Chap. to the Forehoe Union 1846. Author, *The Country Parish* (a Poem), Parker, 2*s*; *Easter-day* (a Tract). [21]

SLIPPER, William Armine, 1, *Willow-lane, St. Giles', Norwich.*—Emman. Coll. Cam. Math. Exhib. 1843, Scho. 1844, Foundation Scho. 1845, B.A. 1846, M.A. 1849; Deac. 1847 and Pr. 1848 by Bp of Nor. R. of St. Swithin's, Norwich, Dio. Nor. 1865. (Patron, Bp of Nor; R.'s Inc. 105*l*; Pop. 699.) Formerly C. of Catfield 1847, Horsey-next-the-Sea 1851, Ashby with Oby and Thirne 1853, Martham 1858, Ashby with Carlton 1859, St. Michael's with St. Clement's, Nor. 1864. [22]

SLOANE-EVANS, William Sloane, *Kingsbridge, Devon.*—Trin. Coll. Cam. B.A. 1845; Deac. and Pr. 1846. Chap. of the Union and Duncombe Lect. of Kingsbridge 1855; Knight Commander and Chap.-in-Chief of the Order of the Temple 1848; Provincial Grand Chap. of the Freemasons of Devon 1850; Elected Knt.-Commander, Genealogist, 1859, Chap.-General of the Order of St. John of Jerusalem 1865. Formerly P. C. of Trinity, Barnstaple. Author, *Grammar of British Heraldry*; *Original Sacred Music* (Anthems, Services, Chants, Voluntaries, Sanctuses, Kyries and Psalm Tunes), 3 eds; *Outline of Sacred History*; *An Autogenealogiad*, and other small Works. [23]

SLOCOCK, Frederick.—Magd. Hall, Ox. and King's Coll. Lond; Deac. 1851 and Pr. 1852 by Bp of Lon. C. of Warlingham, Surrey. Formerly P. C. of Ruishton, near Taunton, 1852–57. [24]

SLOCOCK, Samuel, *Sulhamstead, Reading.*—Caius Coll. Cam. B.A. 1856, M.A. 1859; Deac. 1856 and Pr. 1857 by Bp of Ox. C. of Sulhamstead, Berks, 1866. Formerly C. of Finchampstead, 1856–60, Silchester 1860–66. [25]

SLOGGETT, Charles, *Stoodleigh, Tiverton.*—Ch. Coll. Cam. B.A. 1846, M.A. 1865; Deac. 1846 and Pr. 1848 by Bp of Ex. C. in sole charge of Stoodleigh 1865. Formerly C. of St. Feock, Cornwall, 1847–48; Chap. H.M. Bengal Service 1848–64. [26]

SLYMAN, Daniel, *Withnell Parsonage, near Chorley, Lancashire.*—Queens' Coll. Cam. B.A. 1837; Deac. 1837 and Pr. 1838 by Bp of Ches. P. C. of St. Paul's, Withnell, Dio. Man. 1854. (Patron, V. of Leyland; Tithe, App. 161*l* 13*s*; P. C.'s Inc. 150*l* and Ho; Pop. 2160.) [1]

SMALL, Harry Alexander, *Clifton Reynes Rectory, Newport-Pagnell, Bucks.*—Downing Coll. Cam. LL.B. 1829; Deac. 1827 by Bp of Lin. Pr. 1828 by Bp of Ely. R. of Clifton Reynes, Dio. Ox. 1832. (Patron, the present R; Tithe, 210*l* 11*s* 8½*d*; Glebe, 107 acres; R.'s Inc. 360*l* and Ho; Pop. 212.) Formerly R. of Haversham, Bucks, 1828–56. [2]

SMALL, Nathaniel Pomfret, *Market Bosworth Rectory, Hinckley, Leicestershire.*—St. Mary Hall, Ox. B.A. 1826, M.A. 1829. R. of Market Bosworth with Barlestone C. Carlton C. Shenton C. and Sutton-Cheney C. Dio. Pet. 1847. (Patron, Sir Alexander Dixie, Bart; Market Bosworth, Tithe, 315*l*; Barlestone, Tithe, 33*l* 4*s* 3*d*; Carlton, Tithe, 75*l*; Shenton, Tithe—App. 114*l* 17*s* 10*d*, R. 220*l*; R.'s Inc. 933*l* and Ho; Pop. Market Bosworth 997, Barlestone 544, Carlton 277, Shenton 206, Sutton-Cheney 352.) Surrogate. [3]

SMALLEY, Cornwall, *Thurrock Parva, Romford, Essex.*—St. John's Coll. Cam. B.A. 1837, M.A. 1840; Deac. 1838, Pr. 1839. R. of Thurrock Parva, Dio. Roch. 1866. (Patron, Rev. H. Prosser; R.'s Inc. 505*l* and Ho; Pop. 294.) Formerly P. C. of St. Matthew's, Bayswater, 1859; Sec. of the Prayer Book and Homily Soc. Editor of *The Whole Book of Common Prayer, with copious Scripture Proofs and References*, Prayer Book and Hom. Soc. [4]

SMALLPIECE, Albert, *Hawley, Farnborough Station, Hants.*—St. John's Coll. Cam. 25th Wrang. 1864; Deac. 1864 and Pr. 1865 by Bp of Win. C. of Hawley 1864. [5]

SMALLPIECE, John, *St. Bees, Whitehaven.*—St. John's Coll. Cam. Sen. Opt. in Math. Trip. 2nd cl. Cl. Trip. B.A. 1853, M.A. 1856; Deac. 1853 and Pr. 1854 by Bp of Chich. Lect. at St. Bees Coll. Formerly Vice-Prin. of Bp Otter's Coll. for Training Schoolmasters, Chichester, 1853–56; Asst. C. of Monk Sherborne, near Basingstoke, 1856 58. [6]

SMALLWOOD, Edward B., *Markfield Grange, Leicester.*—Wor. Coll. Ox. M.A; Deac. 1857 and Pr. 1858 by Bp of Pet. Formerly C. of Kirby Muxloe. [7]

SMALLWOOD, William John, *Naunton-Beauchamp, Pershore.*—R. of Naunton-Beauchamp, Dio. Wor. 1864. (Patron, Ld Chan; R.'s Inc. 96*l* and Ho; Pop. 157.) [8]

SMART, Benjamin, 22, *Widemarsh-street, Hereford.*—Theol. Stud. and Scho. of Queen's Coll. Birmingham; Deac. 1863 by Bp of Lich. Pr. 1864 by Bp of Wor. C. of St. Peter's, Hereford, 1866. Formerly C. of St. Nicholas', Worcester, 1863–66. [9]

SMART, Edward, *Henllan Rectory, Rhyl.*—Jesus Coll. Ox. B.A. 1839, M.A. 1841; Deac. 1839 and Pr. 1840 by Bp of St. A. R. of Henllan, Dio. St. A. 1840. (Patron, Bp of St. A; Tithe, 330*l*; Glebe, 4 acres; V.'s Inc. 350*l* and Ho; Pop. 1048.) [10]

SMART, James, *Meltham, Huddersfield.*—Dub. A.B. 1865; Deac. 1865, Pr. 1866. C. of Meltham. [11]

SMART, John, *Ravenswell, Kingswear, Dartmouth, Devon.*—St. Peter's Coll. Cam. B.A. 1835; Deac. 1835 and Pr. 1836 by Bp of Ex. P. C. of Kingswear, Dio. Ex. 1836. (Patron, V. of Brixham; Tithe—App. 7*l* 15*s*, Imp. 4*l*; P. C.'s Inc. 84*l*; Pop. 274.) [12]

SMART, John Henry, 56, *Lincoln's-inn-fields, London, W.C.*—Trin. Coll. Cam. B.A. 1848, M.A. 1855; Deac. 1850 and Pr. 1851 by Abp of Cant. Assoc. Sec. of the Ch. Miss. Soc. Formerly C. of Holy Trinity, Ely. [13]

SMART, Newton, *Wittersham Rectory, near Staplehurst.*—Univ. Coll. Ox. B.A. 1821, M.A. 1824. R. of Wittersham, Dio. Cant. 1865. (Patron, D. of Cant; Tithe, comm. 732*l*; Pop. 877.) Mast. of Farley Hospital 1836. (Patron, Bp of Salis; Alderbury, Tithe—Imp. 10*s*, V. 80*l*; Pitton and Farley, Tithe—App. 330*l*, V. 103*l*; V.'s Inc. 188*l*; Pop. 1334.) Preb. of Alton Borealis in Salis. Cathl. 1851; a Rural Dean of South Lympne; Chap. to the Abp of Cant. 1836. Formerly V. of Alderbury with Pitton C. and Farley C. Salis. 1843–65. Author, *The Duty of a Christian People under a Divine Visitation*, 1832; *The Duty of a Christian People on the Withdrawal of a Divine Visitation*, 1833; *A Pastoral Address on Confirmation*, 1834, S.P.C.K. 25th ed; *Ecclesiastical Commission considered*, 1839; *A Pastoral Address in Times of grievous Sickness*, 2nd Part, 1849; *A Pastoral Address on the Jubilee of S.P.G. in Foreign Parts*, 1851; *A Pastoral Address on the Indian Mutiny*, 1857; *Prayers for Junior Classes of National Schools*, 1860; *An Address to Soldiers on leaving England for Foreign Service*, 6th ed. 1863; *An Address to Sailors on leaving England for Foreign Service*, 1864; *An Earnest and Affectionate Address to Hospital Patients*, 2nd ed. 1866; *The Cattle Plague a Divine Visitation*, 2nd ed. 1866. [14]

SMART, Thomas Gregory, *Lytham, Preston.*—Trin. Coll. Cam. Scho. of, 1845, B.A. 1849, M.A. 1856; Deac. 1865 and Pr. 1858 by Bp of Lon. C. of St. John's, Lytham. Formerly C. of Banbury 1860, Brill with Boarstall 1861. [15]

SMEATON, James Burn, *Hannington, Highworth, Wilts.*—Queen's Coll. Ox. B.A. 1845; Deac. 1846 and Pr. 1847 by Bp of Ex. V. of Hannington, Dio. G. and B. 1848. (Patrons, Exors. of the late Col. Freke; Tithe, 47*l* 15*s*; Glebe, 60 acres; V.'s Inc. 157*l*; Pop. 378.) [16]

SMEDDLE, John, *Bedlington, Northumberland.*—Univ. Coll. Dur. B.A. and Licen. Theol. 1852, M.A. 1857; Deac. 1852 and Pr. 1853 by Bp of Dur. C. of Bedlington 1865. Formerly C. of Carham, Coldstream, Berwick, and Ch. Ch. Tynemouth. [17]

SMEDLEY, Edward Arthur, *Chesterton, near Cambridge.*—Trin. Coll. Cam. Sen. Opt. and B.A. 1826, M A. 1829; Deac. 1829 by Bp of Ely, Pr. 1830 by Bp of Lin. V. of Chesterton, Dio. Ely, 1836. (Patron, Trin. Coll. Cam; Tithe—Imp. 526*l* and 90 acres of Glebe, V. 198*l*; Glebe, 26 acres; V.'s Inc. 265*l* and Ho; Pop. 2986.) Chap. of Chesterton Union 1841. Formerly Chap. of Trin. Coll. Cam. Author, *A Treatise on Moral Evidence*, 1850, 7*s* 6*d*; *Dramatic Poems on Scriptural Subjects*, 1854, 5*s*. [18]

SMELT, Henry, *Wilcot Vicarage, Marlborough, Wilts.*—Jesus Coll. Cam. B.A. 1849, M.A. 1852; Deac. 1849, Pr. 1850. V. of Wilcot with Oare C. Dio. Salis. 1856. (Patron, Lieut.-Col. Geo. W. Broughton; V.'s Inc. 176*l* and Ho; Pop. 651.) [19]

SMELT, Maurice Allen, *Medstead Rectory, Alton, Hants.*—Caius Coll. Cam. B.A. 1842, M.A. 1846; Deac. 1843 and Pr. 1844 by Bp of Chich. R. of Medstead, Dio. Win. 1863. (Patron, Bp of Win; Tithe, 580*l*; Glebe, 6 acres; R.'s Inc. 586*l* and Ho; Pop. 497.) Formerly C. of Patrixbourne and Bridge, Kent; Sen. C. of Petersfield, Hants; Surrogate. [20]

SMITH, A.—C. of St. Thomas's, Bradley, Woodhouse, Huddersfield. [21]

SMITH, Abraham, *Collegiate House, Huddersfield.*—Queens' Coll. Cam. 4th Sen. Opt. Prizeman, B.A. 1852, M.A. 1857; Deac. 1853 and Pr. 1854 by Bp of Rip. Prin. of the Collegiate Schs. Huddersfield; Min. of Bradley. Formerly C. of Marsden. Author, *Liberation Tactics—The Superstition of the Clergy as narrated by Samuel Morley, Esq. and Rev. J. Thomas*, 6*d*; *The Blasphemy and Superstition of the Clergy as narrated by the same*, 3*d*. [22]

SMITH, Adam Clarke, *St. John's Parsonage, Middlesborough, Yorks.*—Wor. Coll. Ox. 4th cl. Lit. Hum. and B.A. 1850, M.A. 1856; Deac. 1850 and Pr. 1851 by Bp of Ox. P. C. of St. John's, Middlesborough, Dio. York, 1864. (Patron, Abp of York; P. C.'s Inc. 300*l* and Ho; Pop. 23,000.) Formerly C. of Milton Keynes, Bucks, 1850, St. Andrew's, Holborn, Lond. 1853. [23]

SMITH, Albert, *The Waldrons, Croydon.*—Ch. Ch. Coll Ox. B.A. 1862, M.A. 1866; Deac. 1864 and Pr. 1865 by Abp of York. C. of Croydon 1866. Formerly C. of Doncaster 1864–66. [24]

SMITH, Albert, *Sutton Coldfield, Warwickshire.*—Lin. Coll. Ox. B.A. 1856, M.A. 1859; Deac. 1857 and

Pr. 1858 by Bp of Wor. Head Mast. of Sutton Coldfield Gr. Sch. Formerly Asst. Mast. in King Edw. Sch. Birmingham. [1]

SMITH, Alexander, *St. Matthias', Liverpool.*—Dub. A.B. 1850; Deac. 1850 and Pr. 1851 by Bp of Win. P. C. of St. Matthias', Liverpool, Dio. Ches. 1864. (Patron, R. of Liverpool; P. C.'s Inc. 300*l*; Pop. 10,074.) Formerly Min. of St. Andrew's, Jersey. [2]

SMITH, Alfred, *Old Park, near Devizes, Wilts.*—Queen's Coll. Ox. B.A. 1821; Deac. 1823 and Pr. 1824 by Bp of Ox. Formerly P. C. of South Croome, Devizes. [3]

SMITH, Alfred Charles, *Yatesbury Rectory, Calne, Wilts.*—Ch. Ch. Ox. B.A. 1846, M.A. 1848; Deac. 1846 and Pr. 1847 by Bp of B. and W. R. of Yatesbury, Dio. Salis. 1852. (Patron, the present R; Tithe, 510*l*; Glebe, 26 acres; R.'s Inc. 550*l* and Ho; Pop. 230.) Formerly C. of Chewton Mendip, Somerset, 1846–49, Welford, Berks, 1849–50, Milton, Berks, 1851. Author, *Ornithology of Wilts*; *Vestiges of earliest Inhabitants of Wilts*; etc. [4]

SMITH, Alfred Fowler, *Thetford, Norfolk.*—Pemb. Coll. Cam. B.A. 1855, M.A. 1858, *ad eund.* Ox. 1858; Deac. 1856 and Pr. 1857 by Bp of Win. Head Mast. of Thetford Gr. Sch. 1860; Chap. of Thetford Union 1860; R. of St. Mary's, Thetford, Dio. Nor. 1862. (Patrons, Trustees; R.'s Inc. 83*l*; Pop. 1245.) Surrogate; Fell. of Phil. Soc. of Cam. Formerly C. of Twyford, Hants, 1856–60; Asst. Mast. in Ipswich Gr. Sch. 1855–56. [5]

SMITH, Anthony Hart.—C. of Garsdon with Lea, Wilts. [6]

SMITH, Arthur John, *Levens Parsonage, Milnthorpe, Westmoreland.*—Dub. A.B. 1862; Deac. 1863 by Bp of Dur. Pr. 1863 by Bp of Carl. P. C. of Levens, Dio. Carl. 1864. (Patroness, Hon. Mrs. Heward; P. C.'s Inc. 200*l* and Ho; Pop. 804.) Formerly C. of Levens 1863. [7]

SMITH, A. F., *Littlebourne, Sandwich, Kent.*—Pemb. Coll. Cam. 2nd cl. Cl. Trip. B.A. 1854, M.A. 1861; Deac. 1854 and Pr. 1855 by Bp of Lich. C. of Littlebourne 1859. [8]

SMITH, Barnard, *Glaston Rectory, Uppingham,* and *Oriental Club, Hanover-square, London, W.*—Ch. Coll. Cam. 4th Wrang. and B.A. 1839, M.A. 1842; Deac. 1842, Pr. 1843. R. of Glaston, Dio. Pet. 1861. (Patron, St. Peter's Coll. Cam; R.'s Inc. 200*l* and Ho; Pop. 238.) Formerly Fell. Sen. Bursar and Cl. Lect. of St. Peter's Coll. Cam. Author, *Arithmetic and Algebra in their Principles and Application*; *Arithmetic for Schools.* [9]

SMITH, Benjamin Frederick, *Rusthall, Tunbridge Wells.*—Trin. Coll. Cam. Scho. of, 17th Wrang. and B.A. 1842, M.A. 1846; Deac. 1845 by Bp of Win. Pr. 1846 by Bp of Lon. P. C. of Rusthall, Dio. Cant. 1864. (Patron, R. of Speldhurst; P. C.'s Inc. 400*l* from Pew-rents; Pop. 2700.) Dioc. Inspector of Schs. Formerly C. of Trinity, Tunbridge Wells, 1845–50, Rusthall 1850–64. Author, *Reports of Education in the Diocese of Canterbury*, 1853, '55, '56, '59, '61, '62, '63, '64, '65, '66; *Form of Prayer for Opening Schoolrooms*, 1859; *The Schoolmaster Abroad*, 1856; *The Cultivation of the Memory of Children*, 1864; *Sermons—The Great Benefit Society*, 1849; "*Do it with thy Might*," 1862; *John vi. 5*, 1864; *The Old Paths*, 1866; *Prayer and the Cattle Plague*; *Two Sermons*, 1866, 2nd ed. [10]

SMITH, B. J.—C. of Alverstoke, Gosport. Formerly C. of Long Compton. [11]

SMITH, Boteler Chernocke, *Hulcote, Woburn, Beds.*—Trin. Coll. Ox. B.A. 1847; Deac. 1848 and Pr. 1849 by Bp of Ely. R. of Hulcote with Salford V. Dio. Ely, 1865. (Patron, Rev. B. C. Smith; R.'s Inc. 320*l* and Ho; Pop. Hulcote 71, Salford 264.) Formerly C. of Bromham, Beds, 1849–52, Great Bolas, Salop, 1853–55; V. of Biddenham, Beds, 1856–65. [12]

SMITH, Charles, *Bamford Rectory, near Sheffield.*—Ex. Coll. Ox. R. of Bamford, Dio. Lich. 1864. (Patron, W. C. Moore, Esq; Tithe, 35*l*; R.'s Inc. 139*l* and Ho; Pop. 322.) [13]

SMITH, Charles, *Newton, near Sudbury, Suffolk.*—St. Peter's Coll. Cam. B.A. 1819, M.A. 1822, B.D. 1829; Deac. 1821 by Bp of Wor. Pr. 1822 by Bp of Ely. R. of Newton, near Sudbury, Dio. Ely, 1833. (Patron, St. Peter's Coll. Cam; Tithe, 617*l* 10*s*; Glebe, 55 acres; R.'s Inc. 666*l*; Pop. 529.) Formerly Fell. and Tut. of St. Peter's Coll. Cam. Author, *Letters on National Religion to Rev. H. Melvill*, 1832; *The Truths hidden by the False Witness of Convocation* (an Essay), 1834; *An Inquiry into Catholic Truths hidden in the Creed of Rome*, 2 vols; etc. [14]

SMITH, Charles, *Fairfield, Buxton, Derbyshire.*—Trin. Coll. Cam. B.A. 1833, M.A. 1838; Deac. 1833, Pr. 1835. Chap. of D. of Fairfield, Dio. Lich. 1852. (Patrons, Trustees; Tithe—App. 14*l*, Imp. 101*l*; Glebe, 53 acres; Chap.'s Inc. 150*l* and Ho; Pop. 1029.) Formerly C. of Barlow, Derbyshire, 1833, Soham, Cambs, 1838, Horsley, Derbyshire, 1846, Nuthall, Notts, 1849. [15]

SMITH, Charles, *Tarrington Rectory, Ledbury, Herefordshire.*—Magd. Coll. Cam. B.A. 1838, M.A. 1842; Deac. 1843 by Bp of Win. Pr. 1844 by Bp of Lin. R. of Tarrington, Dio. Herf. 1854. (Patroness, Lady Emily Foley; Tithe—App. 20*l*, Imp. 20*l*, R. 440*l*; Glebe, 38½ acres; R.'s Inc. 480*l* and Ho; Pop. 543.) [16]

SMITH, Charles A. J., *Macclesfield.*—P. C. of Macclesfield, Dio. Ches. 1847. (Patrons, Simeon's Trustees; P. C.'s Inc. 225*l* and Ho; Pop. 19,744.) [17]

SMITH, Charles Dunlop, *St. Mary's, Cheltenham.*—Wad. Coll. Ox. B.A. 1866; Deac. 1867 by Bp of G. and B. C. of St. Mary's, Cheltenham. [18]

SMITH, C. E., *Nackington, Canterbury.*—P. C. of Nackington, Dio. Cant. 1865. (Patron, Abp of Cant; P. C.'s Inc. 52*l*; Pop. 165.) [19]

SMITH, Charles Felton, *Crediton Vicarage, Devon.*—Queens' Coll. Cam. B.A. 1839, M.A. 1854; Deac. 1839, Pr. 1841 by Bp of Ches. V. of Crediton, Dio. Ex. 1854. (Patrons, Twelve Govs. of the Church; Tithe, Imp. 1786*l*; Glebe, 1 acre; V.'s Inc. 500*l* and Ho; Pop. 5781.) Dom. Chap. to Viscount Combermere 1840; Preb. of Ex. Cathl. 1856; Rural Dean. Formerly P. C. of St. John's, Rendlesham, 1843. Author, *Holy-week Sermons*, Masters. [20]

SMITH, Charles Francis, *Beeford Rectory, Hull.*—Trin. Coll. Cam. Jun. Opt. and B.A. 1846, M.A. 1855; Deac. 1847 and Pr. 1848 by Bp of Lon. R. of Beeford with Lissett and Dunnington, Dio. York, 1865. (Patron, Abp of York; Tithe, Beeford 91*l*, Dunnington 210*l*; Glebe, Beeford 352 acres, Lissett 135 acres; R.'s Inc. 885*l* and Ho; Pop. Beeford 808, Lissett 111, Dunnington 86.) Formerly C. of St. John's, Westminster, 1847–49, Bishopthorpe 1849–54; V. of Bishopthorpe 1854–65. [21]

SMITH, Charles George, *Carlton-in-Lindrick Rectory, Worksop, Notts.*—St. Bees 1819. R. of Carlton-in-Lindrick, Dio. Lin. 1849. (Patron, Abp of York; R.'s Inc. 587*l* and Ho; Pop. 1085.) Dom. Chap. to Lord Galway. [22]

SMITH, Charles James Eliseo, 15, *Moreton-terrace, Rugby.*—St. John's Coll. Cam. 7th Wrang. B.A. 1860, M.A. 1863; Deac. 1863 and Pr. 1864 by Bp of Ely. Asst. Mast. of Rugby Sch. 1866. Formerly Fell. of St. John's Coll. Cam; Math. Mast. in the King's Sch. Sherborne, 1863. [23]

SMITH, The Ven. Charles John, *Erith, Kent.*—Ch. Ch. Ox. 1838, Bishop Fell's Exhib. 1839, Hon. 4th cl. Lit. Hum. and B.A. 1841, Univ. Theol. Scho. 1843, M.A. 1844; Deac. 1842, Pr. 1843. V. of Erith, Dio. Cant. 1852. (Patron, Lord Wynford; Tithe—Imp. 670*l*, V. 610*l*; Glebe, 9 acres; V.'s Inc. 660*l*; Pop. 3143.) Formerly Archd. and Commissary of Jamaica, and Exam. Chap. to the Bp 1848–52. Author, *An English Grammar for the Use of Schools*; various Sermons. [24]

SMITH, Charles Lesingham, *Little Canfield Rectory, Chelmsford.*—Ch. Coll. Cam. 5th Wrang. and B.A. 1829, M.A. 1832; Deac. 1830, Pr. 1832 by Bp of Lin. R. of Little Canfield, Dio. Roch. 1839. (Patron, Ch. Coll. Cam; Tithe, 410*l*; Glebe, 70 acres; R.'s Inc. 510*l* and Ho; Pop. 315.) Formerly Fell. of Ch. Coll.

1830–35. Author, *Odes and Sonnets*, 1842; *Translation of Tasso's Jerusalem Delivered*, Longmans, 1851. [1]

SMITH, Charles Wyatt, *St. Luke's, Heywood, Manchester.*—Trin. Coll. Ox. B.A. 1864, M.A. 1867; Deac. 1865 and Pr. 1866 by Bp of Man. C. of Conventional District, Gooden, Hopwood, 1866. Formerly C. of St. Luke's, Heywood, 1865. [2]

SMITH, Christopher, *Minto House, Argyll-square, Edinburgh.*—Lond. B.A; Deac. 1859 and Pr. 1860 by Bp of Man. Prin. of the Episcopal Training Coll. Edinburgh, 1862. Formerly 2nd Mast. of the Gr. Sch. Preston. [3]

SMITH, Clement, *Castle Cary, Somerset.*—C. of Castle Cary. [4]

SMITH, Clement Ogle, *Shelfanger Rectory, Diss, Norfolk.*—Corpus Coll. Cam. Scho. of, B.A. 1858, M.A. 1863; Deac. 1858 and Pr. 1860 by Bp of Nor. R. of Shelfanger, Dio. Nor. 1863. (Patron, Albert Smith, Esq; Tithe, 555*l*; Glebe, 90*l*; R.'s Inc. 645*l*; Pop. 370.) Formerly C. of Hingham 1858–61, Lakenham, Norwich, 1861–62. Author, *A Few Plain Words to Labouring Lads*; *Moral Courage*; *Drunkenness*; *Office and Duty of Sponsors*; *Family Prayers.* [5]

SMITH, Ebenezer, *Chapel-le-Dale, Lancaster.*—Magd. Hall, Ox. Exhib. 1852, B.A. 1855; Deac. 1856 by Abp of Cant. Pr. 1857 by Bp of Rip. P. C. of Chapel-le-Dale or Ingleton Fells, Dio. Rip. 1857. (Patron, R. of Bentham; P. C.'s Inc. 122*l* and Ho; Pop. 164.) Formerly C. of Hildenborough 1855. [6]

SMITH, Ebenezer, 144, *Crown-street, Liverpool.*—King's Coll. Lond. Theol. Assoc. 1851; Deac. 1851 and Pr. 1852 by Bp of Lon. Chap. of the Workhouse, Liverpool, 1866. Formerly C. of St. Mary's, Leicester, 1859, Hanley, Staffs, 1856, Ratcliff, Lond. 1854; Miss. C. of St. David's District, Liverpool, 1861. Author, *A Voice from the Tomb of the Duke of Wellington*, 1852; *God is Love* (a Sermon in words of one syllable), 1858. [7]

SMITH, Edgar, *Gorhambury, St. Albans.*—Brasen. Coll. Ox. B.A. 1865; Deac. 1865 by Bp of Roch. C. of St. Michael's, St. Albans, 1865, and Chap. to the Earl of Verulam. [8]

SMITH, Edmund James, *Parson's-lane, Bury, Lancashire.*—Wor. Coll. Ox. B.A. 1847, M.A. 1849; Deac. 1850 and Pr. 1854 by Bp of Ox. P. C. of St. John's, Bury, Dio. Man. 1857. (Patron, R. of Bury; P. C.'s Inc. 180*l*; Pop. 4512.) Formerly C. of Lettcomb-Basset, Berks; previously Fell. of Wor. Coll. Ox. [9]

SMITH, Edward, *Partis College, Bath.*—Wad. Coll. Ox. 2nd cl. Lit. Hum. B.A. 1833, M.A. 1836; Deac. 1837 by Bp of Lin. Pr. 1838 by Bp of Ely. Chap. of Partis Coll. Bath, 1850. Formerly C. of St. Paul's, Bedford, 1837, Bocking, Essex, 1838, Holywell, Northants, 1843; P. C. of Chesterton, Staffs, 1846. Author, *The Church of England before the Reformation*, S.P.C.K. 1840; *An Introduction to the Book of Common Prayer*, ib. 1842. [10]

SMITH, Edward, *Ashley, Newmarket.*—Pemb. Coll. Cam. Sen. Opt. 1825; Deac. 1827, Pr. 1828. R. of Ashley, Dio. Ely, 1835. (Patron, Hon. W. R. J. North; Glebe, 272 acres; R.'s Inc. 400*l* and Ho; Pop. 400.) Formerly C. of Weston, near Chester, and Barkway, Herts. [11]

SMITH, Edward Braithwaite, *Gresford, Denbighshire.*—Brasen. Coll. Ox. B.A. 1851, M.A. 1855, Deac. 1853, Pr. 1854. C. of Gresford 1858. Formerly C. of Huntley, Glouc. 1853–56, Thruxton and Kingston, Herefordshire, 1856–58. [12]

SMITH, E. Digby, *School Lodge, The Close, Norwich.*—Ch. Coll. Cam. Sen. Opt. 1860, B.A. 1860, M.A. 1865; Deac. 1862, Pr. 1865. Math. Mast. of the Norwich Gr. Sch. Formerly C. of St. Michael's at Thorne 1862–64; St. Matthew's, Thorpe Hamlet, 1865–66. [13]

SMITH, Edward Herbert, *Killamarsh, Chesterfield.*—Queens' Coll. Cam. B.A. 1827; Deac. and Pr. 1829 by Bp of Lich. P. C. of Killamarsh, Dio. Lich. 1843. (Patron, the Crown; Tithe, 200*l* 8*s* 7*d*; Glebe, 115 acres; P. C.'s Inc. 400*l* and Ho; Pop. 1053.) Corresponding Member of the Acad. des Sciences de Caen and of the Soc. des Antiquaries de Normandie. Author, *Eloge de Bochart* (inserted in the *Transactions de l'Acad. des Sciences de Caen*), 1833. [14]

SMITH, Edward Langdale, *Chetwode Parsonage, near Buckingham.*—St. John's Coll. Cam. B.A. 1835, M.A. 1838. P. C. of Barton-Hartshorn with Chetwode P. C. Dio. Ox. 1839. (Patron, W. H. Bracebridge, Esq; P. C.'s Inc. 117*l* and Ho; Pop. Barton-Hartshorn 126, Chetwode 177.) [15]

SMITH, Edward Samuel, *Ashcot, Bath.*—St. Aidan's; Deac. 1861 and Pr. 1863 by Bp of Rip. C. of Shapwick with Ashcot 1866. Formerly C. of St. Stephen's, Lindley, Huddersfield, 1861–63; Barrington and Shepton Beauchamp 1863–66. [16]

SMITH, Edwin, *Colchester.*—St. John's Coll. Cam. 3rd Sen. Opt. and B.A. 1838, M.A. 1841; Deac. 1838 and Pr. 1839 by Bp of Ches. Chap. to the Forces, Colchester. Formerly Head Mast. of the Preston Gr. Sch. [17]

SMITH, Edwin Trevelyan, *Cannock Parsonage, Stafford.*—St. John's Coll. Cam. Scho. and Prizeman 1838, B.A. 1839, M.A. 1860; Deac. 1841 and Pr. 1842 by Bp of Win. P. C. of Cannock, Dio. Lich. 1866. (Patrons, D. and C. of Lich; Glebe, 22 acres; P. C.'s Inc. 222*l* and Ho; Pop. 2913.) Surrogate. Formerly C. of St. James's, Bermondsey, 1841; P. C. of St. Paul's, Warwick, 1849–66. [18]

SMITH, Francis, *Moorby Rectory, Boston.*—St. Bees; Deac. 1850 and Pr. 1851 by Bp of Man. R. of Moorby with Wood Enderby P. C. Dio. Lin. 1864. (Patron, Bp of Man; Glebe, 180 acres; R.'s Inc. 229*l* and Ho; Pop. 368.) Formerly C. of St. Paul's, Manchester, 1850–64. Author, *A Proposal for the Extension of the Queen's Park, Manchester*, 1861; *The Advantages of Homœopathy to the Working Classes*, 1859. Editor of *Arminius, a History of the German People and of their Legal and Constitutional Customs from the Days of Julius Cæsar to the Time of Charlemagne*, 1861, 10*s* 6*d*. [19]

SMITH, Francis Alfred, *Rushton Rectory, Blandford, Dorset.*—Corpus Coll. Cam. B.A. 1864; Deac. 1865, Pr. 1866. R. of Tarrant Rushton and Tarrant Rawston, Dio. Salis. 1866. (Patron, Sir William Smith Marriott, Bart; Tithe, 250*l*; Glebe, 70 acres; R.'s Inc. 330*l* and Ho; Pop. 300.) Formerly C. of Lower Mediety, Malpas, Ches. 1865–66. [20]

SMITH, Francis Angel, *The Precincts, Canterbury.*—Queens' Coll. Cam. B.A. 1850, M.A. 1856. R. of St. Peter's with Holy Cross V. Canterbury, Dio. Cant. 1855. (Patrons, Abp and D. and C. of Cant. alt; St. Peter, Tithe, 9*l*; Holy Cross, Tithe, 10*l* 16*s* 4*d*; R.'s Inc. 120*l*; Pop. St. Peter 1188, Holy Cross 1065.) Min. Can. of Cant. Cathl. 1854. (Value, 227*l*.) Surrogate for the Diocese. [21]

SMITH, Francis Edward, *The Rectory, Harlington, Hounslow, Middlesex, W.*—Clare Coll. Cam. 35th Wrang. and B.A. 1852, M.A. 1855; Deac. 1854 and Pr. 1855 by Bp of Ox. C. of Harlington 1863. Formerly Asst. C. of Bracknell, and Chap. to the Easthampstead Union, Berks, 1854–56; C. of Bletchingley, Surrey, 1856–63. [22]

SMITH, Francis Robert, *Radford, Notts.*—C. of Radford. [23]

SMITH, Frederick, *St. Mary's, Aston Brook, Birmingham.*—St. John's Coll. Cam. 13th Sen. Opt. and B.A. 1858, M.A. 1864; Deac. 1858 and Pr. 1859 by Bp of Wor. P. C. of St. Mary's, Aston Brook, Dio. Wor. 1865. (Patrons, Trustees; P. C.'s Inc. 300*l*; Pop. 7000.) Formerly Math. Lect. at the Training Coll. Saltley, 1862. C. of St. Matthew's 1858–61, St. Peter's, Birmingham, 1861–63, Saltley 1863–65. [24]

SMITH, Frederick, *Shelf, Halifax.*—St. John's, Coll. Cam. B.A. 1850, M.A. 1853; Deac. 1850, Pr. 1851. P. C. of Shelf, Dio. Rip. 1857. (Patron, Bp of Rip; P. C.'s Inc. 148*l*; Pop. 3312.) Formerly C. of Huddersfield. [25]

SMITH, Frederick, *Trinity Parsonage, Fareham, Hants.*—St. Cath. Hall, Cam. B.A. 1849; Deac. 1849 and Pr. 1851 by Bp of Win. P. C. of Trinity, Fareham, Dio. Win. 1856. (Patron, Sir H. Thompson; P. C.'s Inc. 100*l*; Pop. 2308.) Formerly C. of Fareham. [26]

SMITH, Frederick George Hume, *Armley, Leeds.*—Trin. Coll. Cam. Sen. Opt. B.A. 1852, M.A. 1855; Deac. 1853 and Pr. 1854 by Bp of Rip. P. C. of Armley, Dio. Rip. 1866. (Patron, V. of Leeds; P. C.'s Inc. 300*l* and Ho; Pop. 6734.) Formerly C. of St. Peter's, Leeds. [1]

SMITH, Frederic Herrmann Bowden, *Fawley, Southampton.*—Trin. Coll. Ox. B.A. 1863, M.A. 1867; Deac. 1864 and Pr. 1866 by Abp of Cant. C. of Fawley 1867. Formerly C. of Marden 1864. [2]

SMITH, Frederick Jeremiah, *Bishop's Hull, Taunton.*—Ball. Coll. Ox. B.A. 1830, M.A. 1836. Preb. of Whitchurch in Wells Cathl. 1848; P. C. of St. John's, Bishop's Hull, Dio. B. and W. 1864. (Patron, the present P. C; Pop. 872.) Surrogate. Formerly P. C. of Trinity, Taunton, and Chap. of the Taunton Union 1842–56. [3]

SMITH, Frederick Webb.—Retired Chaplain R.N. [4]

SMITH, George, 4, *Arundel-street, Panton-square, Haymarket, London, W.*—Min. of St. Peter's, Great Windmill-street, St. James's, Dio. Lon. 1861. (Patron, R. of St. James's, Westminster.) [5]

SMITH, George, *Ottery St. Mary, Devon.*—Ex. Coll. Ox. B.A. 1855, M.A. 1858; Deac. 1857 and Pr. 1859 by Bp of Lich. Chap. of the Coll. Ch. of Ottery St. Mary, Dio. Ex. 1863. (Patrons, Four Govs; Chap.'s Inc. 87*l*; Pop. 3000.) Formerly C. of Weeford, near Lichfield, 1857; Chap. of Canwell, near Tamworth 1861. [6]

SMITH, George Augustus, *Hutton's Ambo, New Malton, Yorks.*—Wad. Coll. Ox. B.A. 1849; Deac. 1850, Pr. 1851 by Abp of York. P. C of Hutton's Ambo, Dio. York, 1861. (Patron, Abp of York; P. C.'s Inc. 250*l* and Ho; Pop. 444.) Formerly C. of Foston, Yorks, 1850–51, Crambe 1851–61. [7]

SMITH, George Crowther, 9, *Grosvenor-park, North Camberwell, S.*—C. of St. Mary's, Newington Butts. Formerly C. of St. Paul's, Chatham, 1865–67. Author, *The Fulness of Jesus,* 1866, Macintosh, 2*s* 6*d*. [8]

SMITH, The Right Rev. George, 3, *Haddo-villas, Blackheath, S.E.*—Magd. Hall, Ox. B.A. 1837, M.A. 1843, D.D. 1849; Deac. 1839 by Bp of Pet. Pr. 1840 by Bp of Rip. C. of Marr, 1839; and Incumb. of Goole, Yorks. 1841. Went to China in 1844 on an Exploratory Mission on behalf of the Ch. Miss. Soc. On his return to England, published in 1847 a *Narrative of an Exploratory Visit to each of the Consular Cities of China and to the Islands of Hong Kong and Chusan in the Years* 1844, 1845, *and* 1846. On May 29, 1849 was consecrated in Cant. Cathl. as first Bp. of Victoria, with jurisdiction over the British colony of Hong Kong, and the Anglican Missionary Clergy and Chaplains in the newly-opened Consular ports on the Chinese coast. Resigned the bishopric in 1865. Author, *The Case of our West-African Cruisers and West-African Settlements fairly considered,* 1848; *Hints for the Times, or the Religions of Sentiment, Form, and Feeling, contrasted with vital Godliness,* 1848; *The Jews at Kaefungfoo* (Introductory Notice), 1851, *Loochoo and the Loochooans* (describing a Visit to that Country), 1852; *The Blood of the Everlasting Covenant* (being an Ordination Sermon preached in St. Paul's Cathedral, Calcutta), 1853; *Journal of a Visit to the Krishnagurh and Tinnevelly Missions* (in Ch. Miss. Soc. *Intelligencer*), 1853; also of a *Visit to Java,* 1855; *Recent Events in China* (the Books of the Taeping Chiefs, in No. XLIII. of the *Calcutta Review*), 1854; *Our National Relations with China* (being Two Speeches on the "Taeping Rebellion," and the "Opium Traffic," in Exeter Hall, London, and in the Free Trade Hall, Manchester), 1857; *The Christian Altar and the Spiritual Sacrifice* (being the Anniversary Sermon of the Colonial and Continental Church Society), 1857; *Ten Weeks in Japan* (being the Narrative of a Visit to that Country), 1861; *Charges* (delivered to the Clergy in China); various Contributions to periodical literature. [9]

SMITH, George Edward, *Owston, near Bawtry.*—St. Cath. Coll. Cam. Scho. of, B.A. 1848, M.A. 1851; Deac. 1848 and Pr. 1849 by Bp of Man. V. of Owston, Dio. Lin. 1863. (Patron, Bp of Ches; Tithe, 30*l*; Glebe, 144*l*; V.'s Inc. 300*l* and Ho; Pop. 1587.) Surrogate. Formerly C. of Standish, Lanc. 1848–50, Owston 1850–62. [10]

SMITH, G. H.—C. of Brewood, Staffs. [11]

SMITH, George Maberly, *Penshurst, Tunbridge, Kent.*—Caius Coll. Cam. 2nd cl. Cl. and Math. Trips. and Sen. Opt. 1854; Deac. 1856 and Pr 1858 by Abp of Cant. Sen. C. of Penshurst 1856. Author, *What shall we Do* (a Sermon to the 23rd Kent Volunteers)? 1863, 1*s*. [12]

SMITH, George Nunn, *Preston, Yeovil*—Sid. Coll. Cam. 11th Wrang. 1831, M.A. 1834; Deac. 1833 by Bp of Ches. Pr. 1834 by Abp of York. C. of Preston and Ashington, near Yeovil. Formerly Head Mast. of Gr. Sch. Preston. [13]

SMITH, Gerard Edwards, *Osmaston, near Ashbourne, Derbyshire.*—St. John's Coll. Ox. B.A. 1828; Deac. 1829 and Pr. 1830 by Abp of Cant. P. C. of Osmaston-next-Ashbourne, Derbyshire, Dio. Lich. 1854. (Patron, Francis Wright, Esq; Pop. 289.) Author, *Phænogamous Plants of South Kent*; etc. [14]

SMITH, Gilbert Edward, *Barton Parsonage, Somerton, Somerset.*—Trin. Coll. Cam. Jun. Opt. B.A. 1853; Deac. 1858, Pr. 1859. P. C. of Barton St. David, Dio. B. and W. 1862. (Patron, Rev. W. Garratt; Tithe, App. 170*l*; Glebe, App. 50 acres; P. C.'s Inc. 61*l* and Ho; Pop. 414.) Formerly C. of Abberley, Worcestershire, 1858–62. [15]

SMITH, Gilbert Nicholas, *Gumfreyston Rectory, Tenby, Pembrokeshire.*—R. of Gumfreyston, Dio. St. D. (Patron, Thomas Meyrick, Esq; Tithe, 160*l*; Glebe, 26 acres; R.'s Inc. 203*l* and Ho; Pop. 118.) C. of Redbarth, Pembrokeshire. [16]

SMITH, Graham, *Scruton, near Bedale, Yorks.*—Clare Coll. Cam. Sen. Scho. of, Sen. Opt. 2nd cl. Cl. Trip. 3rd cl. Theol. Trip. B.A. 1861, M.A. 1864; Deac. 1864 by Bp of Rip. Asst. C. of Kirkby Fleetham 1864. [17]

SMITH, Granville Vincent Vickers, *Melton, near Woodbridge, Suffolk.*—Caius Coll. Cam. Scho. of, 3rd cl. Cl. Trip. B.A. 1861; Deac. 1861 and Pr. 1863 by Bp of Rip. C. of Melton 1865, and Chap. to the Dowager Duchess of St. Albans. Formerly C. of Otley, Yorks, 1861, Welborne, Norfolk, 1863. [18]

SMITH, Harris, *New Shoreham Vicarage, Sussex.*—Oriel Coll. Ox. Scho. 1839, Hertford Scho. 1840, Magd. Coll. Ox. 1841, B.A. 1842, Latin Essay 1844, M.A. 1845, B.D. 1856, D.D. 1857; Deac. 1844 and Pr. 1855 by Bp of Ox. V. of New Shoreham, Dio. Chich. 1856. (Patron, Magd. Coll. Ox; Tithe, 30*l*; V.'s Inc. 500*l* and Ho; Pop. 3351.) Formerly Fell. and Cl. Lect. of Magd. Coll. Ox. [19]

SMITH, Harry, *Crundale Rectory, Canterbury.*—Brasen. Coll. Ox. 2nd cl. Lit. Hum. and B.A. 1812, M.A. 1816; Deac. and Pr. 1817. R. of Crundale, Dio. Cant. 1828. (Patron, Sir E. Filmer, Bart; Tithe—Imp. 23*l* 10*s*, R. 375*l* 7*s* 6*d*; Glebe, 20 acres 2r. 20p; R.'s Inc. 375*l* 7*s* 6*d* and Ho; Pop. 279.) [20]

SMITH, Harry Bennett, *Addington, Croydon, Surrey, S.*—Trin. Coll. Cam. B.A. 1840, M.A. 1845; Deac. 1840 and Pr. 1841 by Bp of Chich. C. of Addington and Shirley. Formerly C. of St. Paul's, Covent-garden, Lond. [21]

SMITH, Henry, *Bankfoot, Bradford, Yorks.*—Queen's Coll. Ox. Bridgman Exhib. 1st cl. Math. and B.A. 1857, M.A. 1861; Deac. 1857 and Pr. 1860 by Bp of Pet. P. C. of Bankfoot, Dio. Rip. 1862. (Patron, J. Hardy, Esq. M.P; P. C.'s Inc. 164*l* and Ho; Pop. 2641.) Formerly C. of Helidon, Northants, 1857–62. [22]

SMITH, Henry, *Firle Vicarage, Lewes.*—Queen's Coll. Ox. B.A. 1839, M.A. 1842; Deac. 1840 and Pr. 1841 by Bp of Chich. V. of Beddingham with West Firle V. Dio. Chich. 1864. (Patrons, Bp and D. and C. of Chich. alt; Beddingham, Tithe—App. 530*l* 17*s* 6*d*, V. 200*l*; West Firle, Tithe—Imp. 434*l* 12*s*, V. 290*l* 8*s*; V.'s Inc. 484*l*; Pop. Beddingham 334, West Firle 631.) Preb. of Mardon in Chich. Cathl. 1863. Formerly P. C.

of Appledram 1842; V. of Chidham 1846; P. C. of Mid Lavant 1857. [1]

SMITH, Henry, *Barnby-in-the-Willows, Newark, Notts.*—Queen's Coll. Ox. B.A. 1828; Deac. 1832 and Pr. 1833 by Abp of York. V. of Barnby-in-the Willows, Notts, Dio. Lin. 1858. (Patron, Southwell Coll. Ch; V.'s Inc. 184*l*; Pop. 302.) Formerly C. of Womersley and Wragby, Yorks. [2]

SMITH, Henry, *Christ Church, St. Albans.*—Sid. Coll. Cam. B.A. 1847, M.A. 1850; Deac. 1847, Pr. 1848. P. C. of Ch. Ch. St. Albans, Dio. Roch. 1859. (Patroness, Mrs. Worley; P. C.'s Inc. 120*l* and Ho; Pop. 670.) Formerly C. of Reigate 1848–49, St. Peter's, Colchester, 1850, Holbrook, Suffolk, 1851–58. Author, *First-Fruits unto the Lord*, 1866, Hunt and Co. 1*s*. [3]

SMITH, Henry, *Easton Maudit, Northampton.*—Ch. Ch. Ox. B.A. 1841, M.A. 1844; Deac. 1842 and Pr. 1843 by Bp of Ox. V. of Easton Maudit, Dio. Pet. 1847. (Patrons, D. and C. of Ch. Ch. Ox; Tithe, 123*l*; Glebe, 28 acres; V.'s Inc. 180*l* and Ho; Pop. 207.) Formerly Stud. of Ch. Ch. Ox. 1837–48; V. of Butlers Marston, Warwickshire, 1844–46. [4]

SMITH, Henry, *Long Stanton, Cambridge.*—Pemb. Coll. Cam. B.A. 1832, M.A. 1835; Deac. 1833, Pr. 1834. V. of Long Stanton, Dio. Ely, 1849. (Patron, Bp of Ely; V.'s Inc. 200*l* and Ho; Pop. 440.) [5]

SMITH, H. B.—C. of Marden, Kent. [6]

SMITH, Henry Fielding, *Lancaster Castle.*—Pemb. Coll. Cam. Exhib. B.A. 1852; Deac. 1853 and Pr. 1854 by Bp of Man. Chap. of Lancaster Castle 1858. Formerly Min. of Dolphinholme 1853–57; Chap. of Lancaster County Asylum 1857–58. [7]

SMITH, Henry John Carter, 21, *Queen's-terrace, Queen's-road, Haverstock-hill, London, N.W.*—Wad. Coll. Ox. B.A. 1836, M.A. 1840. P. C. of St. Andrew's, St. Pancras, Dio. Lon. 1856. (Patron, V. of St. Pancras; P. C.'s Inc. 200*l*.) [8]

SMITH, Henry Percy, *York-town, Farnborough, Surrey.*—Ball. Coll. Ox. 2nd cl. Lit. Hum. B.A. 1848, M.A. 1850; Deac. 1849, Pr. 1850. P. C. of St. Michael's, York-town, Dio. Win. 1851. (Patron, Bp of Win; P. C.'s Inc. 255*l*; Pop. 2200.) [9]

SMITH, Henry Richard Somers, *Little Bentley Rectory, Colchester.*—Trin. Coll. Cam. B.A. 1818; Deac. 1819, Pr. 1820. R. of Little Bentley, Dio. Roch. 1824. (Patron, Emman. Coll. Cam; Tithe, 650*l*; Glebe, 60 acres; R.'s Inc. 750*l* and Ho; Pop. 458.) Rural Dean of Ardleigh 1851. [10]

SMITH, Henry Robert, *Grange Parsonage, Lancashire.*—Brasen. Coll. Ox. B.A. 1844, M.A. 1848; Deac. 1846 and Pr. 1847 by Bp of Ely. P. C. of St. Paul's, Grange, Dio. Carl. 1858. (Patron, Bp of Carl; P. C.'s Inc. 120*l* and Ho.) Rural Dean. Formerly P. C. of St. Mary's, Preston. [11]

SMITH, H. W.—C. of Welton, Lincolnshire. [12]

SMITH, Henry William, *St. White's Villa, Cinderford, Newnham, Glouc.*—St. John's Coll. Cam. 24th Sen. Opt. B.A. 1857, M.A. 1860; Deac. 1862 and Pr. 1864 by Bp of G. and B. C. of St. John's, Forest of Dean, 1862. [13]

SMITH, Herbert, *Norfolk House, Shirley, Southampton.*—Caius Coll. Cam. B.A. 1826; Deac. and Pr. 1828 by Bp of Win. Founder of an Establishment for twenty-four aged persons at Shirley, Southampton. Formerly C. of Stratton 1822–34. Author, *A Sermon and Correspondence*, 1830; *The Lord's Day Record* (a Monthly Periodical), 1836; various Pamphlets on the Poor Laws, 1838 to 1842; *The Advocate for the Restoration of the Order of Deacon*, two numbers, 1847. [14]

SMITH, Herbert Clementi, *Grantham, Lincolnshire.*—St. John's Coll. Cam. 2nd cl. Cl. Trip. Prize Reader, B.A. 1859, M.A. 1862; Deac. 1859 and Pr. 1860 by Bp of Lich. Viscountess Campden's Preacher at Grantham 1867. (Patrons, the Mercers' Company; Stipend 100*l*.) Formerly Asst. Mast. and Chap. to Shrewsbury Sch. 1859–62; C. of Reepham, Norfolk, 1862–64, Battle, Sussex, 1864–67. [15]

SMITH, Hugh William, *Biddlesden, near Brackley, Bucks.*—St. John's Coll. Cam. B.A. 1835, M.A. 1838; Deac. 1838 and Pr. 1839 by Bp of Lin. P. C. of Biddlesden, Dio. Ox. 1851. (Patron, George Morgan, Esq; P. C.'s Inc. 95*l*; Pop. 162.) [16]

SMITH, Isaac, *Crosby Garrett Rectory, Penrith.*—Ch. Miss. Coll. Islington; Deac. 1843 and Pr. 1844 by Bp of Lon. R. of Crosby Garrett, Dio. Carl. 1861. (Patron, William Crawford, Esq; Tithe—Imp. 54*l*, V. 49*l* 14*s* 4*d*; Glebe, 90¾ acres; R.'s Inc. 145*l* and Ho; Pop. 306.) Formerly Miss. of the Ch. Miss. Soc. at Sierra Leone and Abbeokuta 1837–55; C. of Patrixbourne with Bridge, Kent, 1857–61. [17]

SMITH, Isaac Gregory, *Tedstone-de-la-Mere Rectory, Sapey-bridge, Herefordshire.*—Trin. Coll. Ox. B.A. 1849, Brasen. Coll. Ox. M.A. 1854; Deac. 1853 and Pr. 1854 by Bp of Ox. R. of Tedstone-de-la-Mere, Dio. Herf. 1864. (Patron, Brasen. Coll. Ox; Tithe, 246*l* 16*s*; Glebe, 40 acres; R.'s Inc. 300*l* and Ho; Pop. 205.) Formerly Fell. of Brasen. Coll. Ox. Author, *Faith and Philosophy, Essay on some Fallacies of the Day*, 7*s* 6*d*, Longmans; *Epitome of the Life of Our Blessed Saviour*, 2*s*, Rivingtons; *The Conscience Clause, Can it be justified?* 6*d*, Rivingtons. [18]

SMITH, James, *Suffield, Aylsham, Norfolk.*—Queens' Coll. Cam. B.A. 1849; Deac. 1854, Pr. 1855. R. of Suffield, Dio. Nor. 1864. (Patron, Lord Suffield; R.'s Inc. 280*l*; Pop. 212.) Formerly C. of St. Julian's and All Saints', Norwich, and Hethel, Norfolk. [19]

SMITH, James Allan, *Boston, Lincolnshire.*—Wad. Coll. Ox. B.A. 1863, M.A. 1867; Deac. 1864 and Pr. 1865 by Bp of Lon. Lect. of Boston 1866. Formerly C. of Trinity, St. Marylebone, Lond. [20]

SMITH, James Newland, *Maze-hill School, Greenwich-park, Kent, S.E.*—St. John's Coll. Cam. Scho. of, 8th Wrang. and B.A. 1851, M.A. 1854; Deac. 1853 and Pr. 1859 by Bp of Ox. Prin. of Maze-hill Sch. Formerly Asst. C. of the Rural Deanery of Reading, Berks. [21]

SMITH, Jeremiah Finch, *Aldridge Rectory, Walsall, Staffs.*—Brasen. Coll. Ox. Scho. of, and Hulme's Exhib. 3rd cl. Lit. Hum. B.A. 1837, M.A. 1840; Deac. 1839, Pr. 1840. R. of Aldridge, Dio. Lich. 1849. (Patron, St. John's Coll. Cam; Tithe, 500*l*; Glebe, 40 acres; R.'s Inc. 560*l* and Ho; Pop. 1179.) Rural Dean. Formerly C. of St. James's Chapel, Handsworth, 1840–44, Great Wilbraham, Cambs, 1844–45, Ilfracombe and St. Mary Church, Devon, 1845–48. Author, *Plain Statement of the Doctrine of the Church of England on Holy Baptism, with Proofs from Scripture*, Masters, 1850, 6*d*, *Tracts on the Weekly Offertory*; etc. [22]

SMITH, John, *Baldock Rectory, Herts.*—St. John's Coll. Cam. B.A. 1821, M.A. 1836; Deac. 1824 by Bp of Lon. Pr. 1825 by Bp of Nor. R. of Baldock, Dio. Roch. 1832. (Patron, Bp of Roch; Tithe, 63*l*; Glebe, 8 acres; R.'s Inc. 190*l* and Ho; Pop. 1974.) Surrogate. Formerly Dep. Esquire-Bedell to Univ. Cam. 1821–24; C. of St. Clement's, Eastcheap, Lond. 1824, Banham, Norfolk, 1824–32; R. of Pwllcrochan, Pembrokeshire, 1832. Author, *Voyage to Tangier*, 2 vols. 1841, 24*s*; Decipherer of *Pepys' Diary*, 4 vols. 4th ed. 1854, 42*s*. [23]

SMITH, John, *St. John's Parsonage, Chigwell, Essex, N.E.*—St. John's Coll. Cam. B.A. 1829, Heb. Scho. 1831, M.A. 1833; Deac. 1829 and Pr. 1830 by Bp of Lich. P. C. of St. John's, Chigwell, Essex, Dio. Roch. 1848. (Patron, V. of Chigwell; P. C.'s Inc. 75*l* and Ho; Pop. 902.) Chap. to the Earl of Camperdown; Chap. to the Mercers' Company 1840; Head Mast. of the Mercers' Sch. Lond. 1840. Editor of *A Bible giving the various Translations and the Original Passages where they differ from the Authorised Version*. [24]

SMITH, John, *Irchester, Wellingborough, Northants.*—Trin. Coll. Cam. Sen. Opt. B.A. 1830; Deac. 1831 and Pr. 1833 by Bp of Ex. C. of Irchester 1850. Chap. of Wellingborough Union 1851. Formerly C. of Ladock, Talland, and Lanteglos, Cornwall; P. C. of Welcombe, Devon; C. of Holybourne, Hants; Chap. of Alton Union; Surrogate for co. of Southampton. [25]

SMITH, John, *Brisley Rectory, Litcham, Swaffham, Norfolk.*—Ch. Coll. Cam. 14th Wrang. and B.A. 1835, M.A. 1838, B.D. 1846; Deac. and Pr. 1839. R.

of Brisley with Gateley V. Dio. Nor. 1851. (Patron, Ch. Coll. Cam; Brisley, Tithe, 293l 4s; Glebe, 21 acres; Gateley, Tithe—App. 208l 10s 3d, V. 144l 15s 1d; Glebe, 27½ acres; R.'s Inc. 486l and Ho; Pop. Brisley 362, Gateley 134.) Formerly Fell. of Ch. Coll. Cam. [1]

SMITH, John, *Oakworth, near Keighley, Yorks.*—Ch. Coll. Cam. B.A. 1845; Deac. 1845, Pr. 1846. P. C. of Oakworth, Dio. Rip. 1850. (Patrons, the Crown and Bp of Rip. alt; Glebe, 1½ acres; P. C.'s Inc. 150l and Ho; Pop. 1979.) [2]

SMITH, John, *Kington Magna Rectory, Gillingham, Dorset.*—St. Bees; Deac. and Pr. 1852. R. of Kington Magna, Dio. Salis. 1866. (Patron, present R; Tithe, 550l; Glebe, 170 acres; R.'s Inc. 800l and Ho; Pop. 650.) Formerly P. C. of Knutton-heath, Staffs, 1852, Gold-hill, Staffs, 1858–59, Over Tabley, Cheshire, 1859–61, St. John's, Blackburn, 1861–66. [3]

SMITH, John, *Little Hinton Rectory, Shrivenham, Berks.*—Magd. Hall, Ox. 4th cl. Lit. Hum. 4th cl. Math. et Phy. and B.A. 1844, M.A. 1845; Deac. 1842 and Pr. 1843 by Bp of Herf. R. of Little Hinton, Wilts, Dio. G. and B. 1858. (Patron, Bp of Win; Glebe, 2 acres; R.'s Inc. 444l and Ho; Pop. 298.) Formerly C. of Brampton Brian, Shrewsbury, 1842; Chap. to St. John the Baptist's Hospital, Winchester, and Prin. of the Winchester Dioc. Training Sch. 1846–58. [4]

SMITH, John, *Cromwell Rectory, Newark, Notts.*—St. Aidan's; Deac. 1861 and Pr. 1862 by Bp of Ches. C. (sole charge) of Cromwell, 1866. Formerly C. of Middlewich 1861–63; Dodworth (sole charge) 1863–65, Linton (sole charge) 1865–66. [5]

SMITH, J.—C. of St. John's, Bethnal Green, Lond. [6]

SMITH, J.—Asst. Mast. of Harrow Sch. [7]

SMITH, John Bainbridge, *Sotby, Wragby, Lincolnshire.*—St John's Coll. Cam. Sen. Opt. and B.A. 1844, M.A. 1847; Deac. 1845 by Bp of Roch. Pr. 1846 by Bp of Lon. R. of Sotby, Dio. Lin. 1854. (Patron, Ld. Chan; Glebe, 325 acres; R.'s Inc. 290l; Pop. 164.) P. C. of Market Stainton, Dio. Lin. 1868. (Patron, Jonathan Field, Esq; P. C.'s Inc. 82l; Pop. 108.) Formerly Prof. of Math. and Vice-Pres. of King's Coll. Nova Scotia; C. of Randby, Linc. [8]

SMITH, John Boys, *Corsham Vicarage, Wilts.*—Trin. Coll. Cam. Jun. Opt. B.A. 1848, M.A. 1865; Deac. 1848 and Pr. 1849 by Bp of St. D. V. of Corsham, Dio. G. and B. 1866. (Patron, Ld. Methuen; Tithe, comm. 300l, Glebe, 2 acres; V.'s Inc. 330l and Ho; Pop. 3192.) Formerly C. of Tenby 1848–57; Chap. to H.M. Consulate-General, Warsaw, 1857–62; C. of St. Thomas's, Ryde, 1862–63, Corsham, 1863–66. Author, *A Historical Sketch of Tenby.* [9]

SMITH, John Greenwood, *Christ Church Parsonage, Crown Point, Leeds.*—P. C. of Ch. Ch. Meadow Lane, Leeds, Dio. Rip. 1859. (Patron, V. of Leeds; P. C.'s Inc. 260l and Ho; Pop. 7089.) [10]

SMITH, J. F., *Great Baddow, Essex.*—C. of Great Baddow. Formerly C. of Hemel Hempstead. [11]

SMITH, John Henry, *Milverton, Leamington.*—Corpus Coll. Cam. B.A. 1827, M.A. 1831; Deac. 1838 and Pr. 1839 by Bp of Lon. P. C. of Old Milverton with Milverton C. Dio. Wor. 1844. (Patron, Earl of Warwick; P. C.'s Inc. 56l; Pop. 1366.) Author, *Sermons*, 2 vols. [12]

SMITH, John James, *Loddon, Norfolk.*—Caius Coll. Cam. 10th Wrang. and B.A. 1828, M.A. 1831; Deac. 1831, Pr. 1832. V. of Loddon, Dio. Nor. 1849. (Patron, Bp of Nor; Tithe, 300l; V.'s Inc. 315l; Pop. 1165.) Sen. Fell. Proctor, and Tut. of Caius Coll. Cam. Author, Papers in *Transactions* of the Cam. Antiquarian Soc; *Cambridge Portfolio*, 2 vols. 4to, 1840–41; *Catalogue of Coins in Caius College, Cambridge*, 4to, 1840; *Catalogue of MSS. in Caius College, Cambridge*, 1849; *Illustrations of Catalogue of MSS. in Caius College, Cambridge*, 4to, 1853; etc. [13]

SMITH, J. L., *Colchester.*—2nd Mast. of the Gr. Sch. Colchester. Formerly C. of Romford, Essex. [14]

SMITH, John Nathaniel, 7, *St. Margaret's-place, St. Leonard's-on-Sea.*—Pemb. Coll. Ox. B.A. 1863; Deac. 1865, Pr. 1866. C. of St. Leonard's Chapel, 1865. [15]

SMITH, John Tetley, *Repton (Derbyshire), near Burton-on-Trent.*—Queen's Coll. Ox. B.A. 1828; Deac. 1829, Pr. 1830. Chap. of the D. of Bretby in Repton, Dio. Lich. 1832. (Patron, Earl of Chesterfield; Chap.'s Inc. 80l; Pop. 324.) [16]

SMITH, John Thomas Henry, *Manor House, Heyford, near Weedon, Northants.*—Sid. Coll. Cam. B.A. 1832, M.A. 1839; Deac. 1833 and Pr. 1834 by Bp of Pet. Formerly C. of Ashby, St. Leger's, 1833–38, Hardingstone 1838–40, Great Houghton 1840–41, Floore 1841–65. [17]

SMITH, J. Thompson.—Chap. of the Refuge for the Destitute, Dalston, Lond. [18]

SMITH, John William, *Dinsdale Rectory, Darlington.*—Jesus Coll. Cam. B.A. 1834, M.A. 1838; Deac. 1835 and Pr. 1836 by Abp of York. R. of Dinsdale, Dio. Dur. 1859. (Patrons, D. and C. of Dur; Tithe, 194l 10s; Glebe, 70 acres; R.'s Inc. 254l and Ho; Pop. 208.) Formerly C. of Dinsdale. [19]

SMITH, Joseph, *Middlezoy, Bridgwater.*—Dub. A.M. V. of Middlezoy, Dio. B. and W. 1864. (Patron, Bp of Wor; V.'s Inc. 140l; Pop. 658.) [20]

SMITH, Joseph Newton, *Harlow, Essex.*—Trin. Coll. Cam. B.A. 1851, M.A. 1854; Deac. 1851, Pr. 1852. P. C. of St. Mary Magdalen's, Harlow, Dio. Roch. 1863. (Patron, V. of Harlow; Pop. 500.) [21]

SMITH, Kenelm Henry, *Cambridge-road, Ely.*—St. John's Coll. Cam. Scho. of, 1856–58; Deac. 1860 by Bp of B. and W. Pr. 1864 by Bp of Ely. C. of St. Mary's, Ely, 1863, and Asst. Min. of Ely Cathl. 1863. Formerly C. of Colyton and Monkton, Devon, 1860–63. [22]

SMITH, Lister, *St. Peter's, Congleton, Cheshire.*—St. Bees; Deac. 1866 by Bp of Ches. C. of St. Peter's, Congleton, 1866. [23]

SMITH, Merton, *Newport-Pagnell, Bucks.*—Jesus Coll. Cam. Scho. of, Sen. Opt. B.A. 1866; Deac. 1866. C. of Newport Pagnell. [24]

SMITH, Offley, *Leadenham Rectory, Grantham.*—Oriel Coll. Ox. B.A. 1841, M.A. 1846; Deac. 1842, Pr. 1843. R. of Long Leadenham, Dio. Lin. 1843. (Patroness, Mrs. J. Smith; Glebe, 500 acres; R.'s Inc. 750l and Ho; Pop. 686.) [25]

SMITH, O., *Great Gaddesden, Hemel Hempstead, Herts.*—C. of Great Gaddesden. [26]

SMITH, Percy, *Pattiswick, Braintree, Essex.*—Trin. Coll. Cam. B.A. 1827, M.A. 1831; Deac. 1833 and Pr. 1834 by Bp of Chich. P. C. of Pattiswick, Dio. Roch. 1835. (Patron, Bp of Roch; Tithe, 340l; Glebe, 16 acres; P. C.'s Inc. 356l and Ho; Pop. 360.) [27]

SMITH, Percy, *Grinton Vicarage, Richmond, Yorks.*—Univ. Coll. Dur. B.A. 1847, M.A. 1850; Deac. 1847 and Pr. 1848 by Bp of Dur. V. of Grinton, Dio. Rip. 1855. (Patron, Ld Chan; Tithe—Imp. 9l 3s 7d, V. 81l 16s 10d; Glebe, 10 acres; V.'s Inc. 350l and Ho; Pop. 1359.) [28]

SMITH, Peter Parker, *Stanwick St. John, Darlington.*—St. John's Coll. Cam. B.A. 1837; Deac. and Pr. 1838 by Bp of Ex. V. of Stanwick St. John, Dio. Rip. 1866. (Patron, J. Wharton, Esq; V.'s Inc. 61l; Pop. 768.) Formerly Chap. R.N. [29]

SMITH, P. Bowden, *Rugby.*—Univ. Coll. Ox. B.A. 1851, M.A. 1856. Asst. Mast. of Rugby Sch. Formerly Scho. of Univ. Coll. [30]

SMITH, Reginald Southwell, *Stafford Rectory, near Dorchester.*—Ball. Coll. Ox. B.A. 1830, M.A. 1834; Deac. 1834, Pr. 1835. R. of West Stafford, Dio. Salis. 1836. (Patroness, Mrs. E. Floyer; Tithe, 277l; Glebe, 39¼ acres; R.'s Inc. 352l and Ho; Pop. 220.) Author, *Sermons.* [31]

SMITH, Richard, *New Romney, Kent.*—Queens' Coll. Cam. B.D. 1849; Deac. 1831, Pr. 1832. V. of New Romney, Dio. Cant. 1839. (Patron, All Souls Coll. Ox; Tithe—Imp. 45l 7s, V. 87l 18s; Glebe, 27 acres; V.'s Inc. 220l; Pop. 1062.) R. of Hope (no church), Kent, Dio. Cant. 1853. (Patron, Ld Chan; Tithe, 153l; Glebe, 8 acres; R.'s Inc. 166l; Pop. 30.) [32]

SMITH, Richard, 28, *St. James's-street, Brighton.*—Wor. Coll. Ox. B.A. 1855, M.A. 1858; Deac. 1856 by Bp of B. and W. Pr. 1857 by Bp of Chich. C. of St. John's, Brighton, 1864. Formerly C. of East Dean with Friston, Sussex, 1860–61, St. Peter's the Great, Chichester, 1857–59. [1]

SMITH, Richard, *Rushton Parsonage, Leek, Staffs.*—Deac. 1856, Pr. 1858. P. C. of Rushton, Dio. Lich. 1863. (Patron, V. of Leek; P. C.'s Inc. 159*l* and Ho; Pop. 1027.) [2]

SMITH, Richard Chamberlain, *North Tamerton Rectory, Launceston.*—Ex. Coll. Ox. B.A. 1844, M.A. 1847; Deac. 1847 and Pr. 1849 by Bp of Ex. Chap. of D. of North Tamerton, Dio. Ex. 1850. (Patrons, Rev. Roger G. Kingdon and Exors. of Mrs. Smith alt; Tithe—App. 8*l* 15*s* 3*d*, Imp. 25*l* 8*s* 5*d*, R. 284*l*; Glebe, 11 acres; Chap.'s Inc. 300*l* and Ho; Pop. 486.) Formerly C. of St. Ives, 1847–49, North Tamerton, 1849–50. [3]

SMITH, Richard Snowdon, 4, *Atlingworth-street, Brighton.*—Caius Coll. Cam. B.A. 1842, M.A. 1845; Deac. 1841 by Bp of Chich. Pr. 1842 by Bp of Lon. P. C. of All Souls', Brighton, Dio. Chich. 1846. (Patron, V. of Brighton; P. C.'s Inc. 300*l*; Pop. 5000.) Formerly C. of Brighton 1841–46. [4]

SMITH, Robert.—Magd. Hall, Ox. B.A. 1862; Deac. 1863 and Pr. 1864 by Bp of Wor. C. of St. Luke's, Nottingham. Formerly C. of Atherstone 1863. [5]

SMITH, R., *Waterfoot, Bury, Lancashire.*—P. C. of Waterfoot, Dio. Man. 1858. (Patrons, Trustees; P. C.'s Inc. 110*l*.) [6]

SMITH, Robert Crawforth, *Gloucester.*—Pemb. Coll. Ox. B.A. 1820, M.A. 1824; Deac. and Pr. 1821 by Bp of Glouc. V. of St. Catherine's, Gloucester (the Church destroyed at the siege of Gloucester, 1649), Dio. G. and B. 1825. (Patrons, D. and C. of Bristol; Tithe, 10*l*; Glebe, 13 acres; V.'s Inc. 30*l*; Pop. 2084.) R. of Cowley, Cheltenham, Dio. G. and B. 1837. (Patron, Ld Chan; Tithe, 310*l*; Glebe, 70 acres; R.'s Inc. 330*l*; Pop. 311.) Chap. of the Gloucester Union. [7]

SMITH, Robert Frederick, *Vicar's Court, Southwell, Notts.*—Lin. Coll. Ox. 3rd cl. Lit. Hum. B.A. 1855, M.A. 1857; Deac. 1856 and Pr. 1857 by Bp of Lin. P. C. of Halam, Dio. Lin. 1861. (Patrons, Chap. of Southwell Coll. Ch; P. C.'s Inc. 103*l* and Ho; Pop. 382.) Min. Can. of Coll. Ch. of Southwell, Notts, 1863. [8]

SMITH, R. J. French, *Callington, Cornwall.*—C. of Callington. [9]

SMITH, Robert Martin, *Eastham Vicarage, Chester.*—Queens' Coll. Cam. B.A. 1843; Deac. 1843 and Pr. 1844 by Bp of Lon. V. of Eastham, Dio. Ches. 1860. (Patrons, D. and C. of Ches; V.'s Inc. 240*l* and Ho; Pop. 1687.) Formerly C. of Dodleston 1848; Min. Can. of Chester 1853–60. [10]

SMITH, Robert Payne, *Christchurch, Oxford.*—Pemb. and Ch. Ch. Coll. Ox. Boden Sanscrit Scho. 1840, 2nd cl. Lit. Hum. and B.A. 1841, Pusey and Ellerton Heb. Scho. and M.A. 1843; Deac. 1843 by Bp of Ox. Pr. 1844 by Bp of Lin. Canon of Ch. Ch. Ox. and Regius Prof. of Div. 1865; R. of Ewelme, Dio. Ox. 1865. (Attached to Regius Prof. of Div; R.'s Inc. 550*l*; Pop. 684.) Formerly Head Mast. of the Kensington Proprietary Sch. 1853–57; Sub-Librarian of the Bodleian Library, Oxford, 1857–65. Author and Editor, *S. Cyrilli Alex. Commentarii in Lucæ Evangelium quæ supersunt Syriace*, 4to, 1858, 1*l* 2*s*; *St. Cyrill's Commentary on St. Luke's Gospel in English*, 2 vols. 8vo, 1859, 14*s*; *Ecclesiastical History of John, Bishop of Ephesus*, translated into English, 1860, 10*s*; *Catalogus Codicum Syriacorum et Carshunicorum in Bibliotheca Bodleiana*, 4to, 1864, all at the University Press; *The Authenticity and Messianic Interpretation of the Prophecies of Isaiah vindicated*, 10*s* 6*d*. [11]

SMITH, Robert Willan, *Stowmarket, Suffolk.*—Jesus Coll. Ox. Postmaster of Mert. Coll. 1833, Scho. of Jesus Coll. 1834, 3rd cl. Lit. Hum. and B.A. 1835, M.A. 1840; Deac. 1837 and Pr. 1838 by Bp of Ox. Chap. to Viscount Combermere. Formerly P. C. of Stowupland, Suffolk, 1845–62. [12]

SMITH, Roger, 5, *Mulgrave-place, Plymouth.*—Magd. Coll. Cam. M.A. P. C. of Plympton St. Maurice, Dio. Ex. 1866. (Patrons, D. and C. of Windsor; P. C.'s Inc. uncertain; Glebe, 15 acres; Pop. 900.) Formerly R. of Astwick with Arlsey V. 1841–60. [13]

SMITH, Rowland, *Nazing, Waltham Cross, Essex.*—St. John's Coll. Ox. 3rd cl. Lit. Hum. and B.A. 1829; Deac. 1830, Pr. 1831. V. of Nazing, Dio. Roch. 1865. (Patron, Ld Chan; V.'s Inc. 255*l* and Ho; Pop. 763.) Formerly R. of Ilston 1854–65. Author, *Poetical Translation of Ecclesiazusæ of Aristophanes*; *Church Catechism, illustrated by the Book of Common Prayer*, Masters; *Law of the Anglican Church, the Law of the Land*, ib; *Translations of the Greek Romance Writers*, Bohn. [14]

SMITH, Samuel, *Colne-Barrowford, Whalley, Lancashire.*—Magd. Coll. Cam. B.A. 1827, M.A. 1831; Deac. 1829 and Pr. 1830 by Bp of Salis. P. C. of Colne-Barrowford, Dio. Man. 1848. (Patrons, Hulme's Trustees; P. C.'s Inc. 154*l*; Pop. 2796.) [15]

SMITH, Samuel, *Lois-Weedon, Towcester, Northants.*—King's Coll. Cam; Deac. 1819, Pr. 1820. V. of Lois-Weedon, Dio. Pet. 1833. (Patron, King's Coll. Cam; V.'s Inc. 534*l* and Ho; Pop. 555.) Rural Dean. Author, *Hannibal's Passage of the Alps*, 1840; *A Word in Season, or How to grow Wheat with Profit*, 16 eds. 1849–58; *Lois-Weedon Husbandry*, 2 eds. 1856–57; *What I saw in Syria, Palestine and Greece, a Narrative from the Pulpit*, 1864. [16]

SMITH, Samuel, *St. George's Parsonage, Camberwell, London, S.*—Trin. Coll. Cam. B.A. 1827, M.A. 1830; Deac. 1827 and Pr. 1828 by Bp of Lon. P. C. of St. George's, Camberwell, Dio. Win. 1832. (Patron, Sir W. B. Smijth, Bart; P. C.'s Inc. 420*l*; Pop. 20,324.) Friday Even. Lect. at St. Lawrence's, Jewry, Lond. Author, *Eighteen Sermons* (preached as Chap. to the Lord Mayors in the Years 1829, 1830, 1831, 1832, and 1840.) [17]

SMITH, Samuel, *Whitwick Vicarage, near Leicester.*—Dur. Scho. of, 1839, Eng. Essay 1839, Bp Maltby's Math. Prize 1841, Van Mildert Scho. 1843, 1st cl. Math. et Phy. Sci. 2nd cl. Mod. Sci. and Mod. Languages, B.A. 1843, M.A. 1846, B.D. 1858, D.D. 1857; Deac. 1843 and Pr. 1844 by Abp of York. V. of Whitwick, Dio. Pet. 1864. (Patron, Chan. of Duchy of Lanc; Tithe, 175*l*; Glebe, 200 acres; V.'s Inc. 325*l* and Ho; Pop. 3000.) Formerly C. of Whitwick 1846; P. C. of St. George's, Whitwick, 1851. Author, *A Letter to Mr. Kidger in Reply to a Letter from a Roman Catholic Priest*, 1849, Rivingtons, 1*s*; *A Letter to the Inhabitants of Whitwick*, 1842, Rivingtons, 6*d*. [18]

SMITH, Samuel Edward, *Ponder's End, Middlesex, N.*—Wor. Coll. Ox. B.A. 1862; Deac. 1862 by Bp of Rip. Pr. 1863 by Bp of Win. C. of St. James's, Ponder's End, 1867. Formerly C. of Shirley, Southampton, and Pickering, Yorks. [19]

SMITH, Samuel Mountjoy, *Harwell Vicarage, Berks.*—Emman. Coll. Cam. B.A. 1849, M.A. 1852; Deac. 1850, Pr. 1851. V. of Harwell, Dio. Ox. 1856. (Patron, the present V; Tithe, 220*l*; Glebe, 80 acres; V.'s Inc. 375*l* and Ho; Pop. 876.) Formerly C. of Chelwood. [20]

SMITH, Samuel Nicholson, *Davenham, near Northwich, Cheshire.*—Literate; Deac. 1853 by Bp of Rip. Pr. 1854 by Abp of Cant. C. of Davenham 1865. Formerly C. of Penistone 1853, Thurstonland, 1854, Carlton in Lindrick 1857, Darfield 1859, St. Peter's, Oldham-road, Manchester, 1861, Coppenhall, Cheshire, 1864. [21]

SMITH, Sidney Lidderdale, *Brampton-Ash (Northants), near Market Harborough.*—St. John's Coll. Cam. Bell's Univ. Scho. 1837, Sen. Opt. and B.A. 1840, M.A. 1843; Deac. 1843, Pr. 1844. R. of Brampton-Ash, Dio. Pet. 1844. (Patron, Earl Spencer; Tithe, 15*l*; Glebe, 181 acres; R.'s Inc. 400*l* and Ho; Pop. 183.) [22]

SMITH, Solomon, *The College, Ely.*—St. John's Coll. Cam. 23rd Wrang. and B.A. 1829, M.A. 1832; Deac. 1833 by Bp of Lin. Pr. 1833 by Bp of Carl. Min. Can. of Ely Cathl. 1833. (Value, 150*l* and Res.) P. C. of St. Mary's, City and Dio. Ely, 1833. (Patrons, D. and C. of Ely; Tithe, App. 3926*l* 10*s* 3*d*; P. C.'s Inc. 150*l*;

Pop. 2696.) Surrogate. Formerly Fell. of St. John's Coll. Cam. [1]

SMITH, Sydney, *Worth, Sandwich, Kent.*—Trin. Coll. Cam. B.A. 1839, M.A. 1845; Deac. 1839 and Pr. 1840 by Bp of Nor. P. C. of Worth, Dio. Cant. 1854. (Patron, Abp of Cant; Tithe—App. 623*l*, V. 375*l*; Glebe, 52 perches; P. C.'s Inc. 302*l*; Pop. 430.) [2]

SMITH, S. C., *Clapham, Surrey, S.W.*—St. John's Coll. Cam. M.A; Deac. 1852 and Pr. 1854 by Bp of Win. Formerly Chap. in the R.N. [3]

SMITH, Thomas, *Harborne Heath, Birmingham.*—P. C. of St. John's, Harborne Heath, Dio. Lich. 1858. (Patron, the present P. C; P. C.'s Inc. 100*l*; Pop. 2289.) [4]

SMITH, Thomas, 26, *Vincent-square, Westminster, S.W.*—C. of St. Mary's, Tothill Fields, Westminster. [5]

SMITH, Thomas, *Stanton-on-the-Wolds, Notts.*—Deac. 1815 and Pr. 1816 by Abp of York. P. C. of Owthorpe, Notts, Dio. Lin. 1825. (Patron, Sir H. Bromley; P. C.'s Inc. 78*l*; Pop. 112.) R. of Stanton-on-the-Wolds, Dio. Lin. 1848. (Patron, Sir R. Bromley; Glebe, 125 acres; R.'s Inc. 100*l* and Ho; Pop. 158.) [6]

SMITH, Thomas, *Brailes Vicarage (Warwickshire), Shipston-on-Stour, Worcestershire.*—Corpus Coll. Cam. B.A. 1847; Deac. 1848 and Pr. 1849 by Abp of York. V. of Brailes, Dio. Wor. 1856. (Patron, J. Jordan, Esq; Tithe—Imp. 134*l*, V. 62*l*; Glebe, 126 acres; V.'s Inc. 350*l* and Ho; Pop. 1350.) Formerly C. of North Cave, Yorks, 1848–53; P. C. of Ossington, Notts, 1853–56. Author, *Words of Warning to Young Men*, 1864. [7]

SMITH, Thomas, 10, *Wilkinson-street, Sheffield.*—St. Bees; Deac. 1850 and Pr. 1851 by Abp of York. Chap. to the Sheffield General Infirmary 1854; Aft. Lect. at St. Thomas's, Crookes, Sheffield, 1858. [8]

SMITH, Thomas.—Trin. Coll. Cam. B.A. 1855, M.A. 1858; Deac. 1855 and Pr. 1856 by Abp of York. Formerly C. of Balby with Hexthorpe 1855; P. C. of Dunsforth, near Boroughbridge, Yorks, July to Nov. 1864 (resigned through ill-health). [9]

SMITH, Thomas.—Queens' Coll. Cam. Exhib. 15th Jun. Opt. and B.A. 1848, M.A. 1852; Deac. 1849 and Pr. 1850 by Bp of Win. Formerly C. of Chobham, Surrey. [10]

SMITH, Thomas Ayscough, *Tenbury Vicarage, Worcestershire.*—Trin. Coll. Cam. B.A. 1853, M.A. 1856; Deac. and Pr. 1854 by Abp of York. V. of Tenbury, Dio. Wor. 1860. (Patron, the present V; Tithe, 511*l*; V.'s Inc. 744*l* and Ho; Pop. 1581.) Formerly C. of Skipsea, Yorks, 1854–55, Loughborough 1856–60. [11]

SMITH, Thomas Casson, *Nuthall, Nottingham.*—C. of Nuthall. Formerly C. of Ch. Ch. Coseley, Staffs. [12]

SMITH, Thomas Dusautoy Sampson, *Bishopstoke, Southampton.*—St. John's Coll. Cam. B.A. 1845; Deac. 1845 and Pr. 1846 by Bp of Win. C. of Bishopstoke 1849. Formerly C. of Idsworth and Twyford, Dio. Win. Author, *An Enquiry into the Source, Actings and Results of the Divine or Spiritual Life*, Hatchards, 6*s*; *Two Sermons on the Death of Garnier, Dean of Lincoln*, Southampton, 1*s*. [13]

SMITH, Thomas Frederick, *Horsington Rectory, Horncastle, Lincolnshire.*—Queen's Coll. Ox. 4th cl. Lit. Hum. and B.A. 1844, M.A. 1847, B.D. 1854; Deac. 1845, Pr. 1846. R. of Horsington, Dio. Lin. 1856. (Patron, Magd. Coll. Ox; Glebe, 300 acres; R.'s Inc. 350*l* and Ho; Pop. 418.) Formerly Fell. of Magd. Coll. Ox. 1846–56; Pro-proctor of Univ. 1851 and 1854. Author, *Devout Chorister*, Masters, 1848, 3rd ed. 1854; *The Three Nativities* (a Sermon in Magd. Coll. Chapel, partly on the Death of President Routh), 1854. [14]

SMITH, Thomas George, *Winifred House, Sion-hill, Bath.*—Trin. Hall, Cam. Coll. Prize English Essay 1843, Prize Coll. Exam. 1844, B.A. 1846, M.A. 1850; Deac. 1846 and Pr. 1847 by Bp of Roch. Formerly C. of St. Peter's, St. Albans, 1846–48; P. C. of Flax-Bourton, Somerset, 1848–51; Chap. of the Bath Penitentiary and Min. of the Chapel 1851–56. [15]

SMITH, Thomas John, *Sherburn, South Milford, Yorks.*—Lin. Coll. Ox. B.A. 1848; Deac. 1851 by Bp of Win. Pr. 1853 by Bp of Dur. C. of Sherburn and Kirk Fenton. [16]

SMITH, Thomas Sharp, *Mablethorpe, Alford, Lincolnshire.*—C. of Mablethorpe with Stane. [17]

SMITH, Thomas Tunstall, *Wirksworth, Derbyshire.*—St. Peter's Coll. Cam. Sen. Opt. 2nd cl. Cl. Trip. and B.A. 1833, M.A. 1836; Deac. 1834, Pr. 1835. V. of Wirksworth, Dio. Lich. 1851. (Patron, Bp of Lich; Tithe—App. 1095*l* 10*s*, Imp. 6*l*, V. 75*l* 8*s* 2*d*; Glebe, 5 acres; V.'s Inc. 251*l* and Ho; Pop. 5667.) Rural Dean 1851; Surrogate 1851. Formerly V. of Whaplode, Linc. 1842–51. Author, *Sermons*, 2nd ed. 1852, Hatchards, 5*s* 6*d*; *Two Treatises on the Sacraments*, ib. 1845, 3*s*; *Lectures on the Temptation of our Blessed Lord*, 1852, 3*s*. [18]

SMITH, T. W., *Middleton, Manchester.*—C. of Middleton. [19]

SMITH, Urban, *Stony-Middleton, near Sheffield.*—Trin. Coll. Cam. Sen. Opt. and B.A. 1830, M.A. 1833. P. C. of Stony-Middleton, Dio. Lich. 1834. (Patron, V. of Hathersage; Tithe—App. 6*l*, Imp. 30*l*; P. C.'s Inc. 110*l*; Pop. 608.) [20]

SMITH, Villiers Shallet Chernocke, *Husborne-Crawley, Woburn, Beds.*—New Coll. Ox. B.A. 1847, M.A. 1851; Deac. 1847 and Pr. 1848 by Bp of Ox. V. of Husborne Crawley, Dio. Ely. (Patron, Duke of Bedford; V.'s Inc. 50*l* and Ho; Pop. 535.) Formerly Fell. of New Coll. Ox. [21]

SMITH, Vincent, 1, *Stafford-place, S.W.*—King's Coll. Lond. Assoc. 1863; Deac. 1866 and Pr. 1867 by Bp of Lon. Asst. C. of Ch. Ch. Westminster 1866. [22]

SMITH, William, *Fishponds, Bristol.*—Lin. Coll. Ox. 1st cl. Lit. Hum. and B.A. 1843, M.A. 1846; Deac. 1847, Pr. 1848. Prin. of the Stapleton Training Institution for the Dios. of Gloucester, Bristol and Oxford, at Fishponds, 1853. [23]

SMITH, William, *Baydon, Hungerford, Wilts.*—St. John's Coll. Cam. D.D. 1853. P. C. of Baydon, Dio. Salis. 1860. (Patron, Rev. A. Meyrick; P. C.'s Inc. 110*l* and Ho; Pop. 380.) [24]

SMITH, William, *Dry Drayton Rectory, near Cambridge.*—Ch. Ch. Ox. B.A. 1835, M.A. 1839; Deac. 1833 and Pr. 1836 by Bp of Ox. R. of Dry Drayton, Dio. Ely, 1841. (Patron, the present R; Glebe, 340 acres; R.'s Inc. 410*l* and Ho; Pop. 470.) [25]

SMITH, William, *Shadwell Parsonage, near Leeds.*—St. Peter's Coll. Cam. B.A. 1853, M.A. 1856; Deac. 1853 and Pr. 1854 by Bp of Wor. P. C. of Shadwell, Dio. Rip. 1858. (Patron, V. of Thorner, Leeds; P. C.'s Inc. 100*l* and Ho; Pop. 442.) [26]

SMITH, William, *Overbury Vicarage (Worcestershire), near Tewkesbury.*—V. of Overbury with Alston C. Teddington C. and Washbourne C. Dio. Wor. 1839. (Patrons, D. and C. of Wor; V.'s Inc. 425*l* and Ho; Pop. 925.) [27]

SMITH, William, *Cowick Parsonage, Snaith, Selby, Yorks.*—Dub. Heb. Premium 1837, Catechetical Prem. 1839; Deac. 1842, Pr. 1843. P. C. of Cowick Dio. York, 1854. (Patron, Viscount Downe; Glebe, 9 acres; P. C.'s Inc. 193*l* and Ho; Pop. 818.) [28]

SMITH, William, *Bickington, Newton Abbott, Devon.*—Jesus Coll. Cam. Jun. Opt. and B.A. 1855; Deac. 1859 and Pr. 1860 by Bp of Ex. P. C. of Bickington, Dio. Ex. 1864. (Patrons, D. and C. of Ex; P. C.'s Inc. 222*l*; Pop. 294.) Formerly Asst. C. of Heavitree, Devon, 1859; C. of Highampton, N. Devon, 1861; Asst. C. of St. Columb Major, Cornwall, 1863. [29]

SMITH, William, *Biscathorpe Rectory, Louth, Lincolnshire.*—Emman. Coll. Cam. Scho. and Prizeman of, Jun. Opt. B.A. 1859, M.A. 1863; Deac. 1860 and Pr. 1861 by Bp of Lin. C. of Kelstern 1862. Formerly C. of Biscathorpe and Gayton-le-Wold 1860–62. [30]

SMITH, William, *Stewton, Louth, Lincolnshire.*—R. of Stewton, Dio. Lin. 1841. (Patron, the present R; Tithe, 201*l* 19*s*; Glebe, 11 acres; R.'s Inc. 215*l*; Pop. 73.) V. of Keddington, near Louth, Dio. Lin

(Patron, Sir G. E. Welby, Bart; V.'s Inc. 100*l*; Pop. 138.) [1]

SMITH, William Anderton, 6, *Mount Beacon, Lansdown, Bath.*—St. John's Coll. Cam. B.A. 1838, M.A. 1841; Deac. 1839 and Pr. 1840 by Bp of Ely. Chap. to the Bath United Hospital 1855; Chap. to the Bath Mineral Water Hospital 1857. [2]

SMITH, William A., *Swanmore, Ryde, Isle of Wight.*—C. of Swanmore. [3]

SMITH, William Bramwell, *St. John's, Deritend, Aston, Birmingham.*—P. C. of St. John's, Deritend, Dio. Wor. 1842. (Patrons, the Inhabitants; P. C.'s Inc. 200*l*.) [4]

SMITH, William Edmund.—Chap. of H.M.S. "Royal Oak." [5]

SMITH, William George Parks, *Belvedere House, Torquay.*—Trin. Coll. Cam. B.A. 1827, M.A. 1836; Deac. 1837 and Pr. 1838 by Bp of Ex. P. C. of St. John's, Torquay, Dio. Ex. 1839. (Patron, C. Herbert Malloch, Esq; P. C.'s Inc. 205*l*; Pop. 3200.) Formerly Chap. to the Army in the Crimea. [6]

SMITH, William Hart, *St. Minver Vicarage, Wadebridge, Cornwall.*—Brasen. Coll. Ox. B.A. 1848, M.A. 1851; Deac. 1849 and Pr. 1850 by Bp of Ex. V. of St. Minver, Dio. Ex. 1851. (Patroness, Mrs. Stephens; Tithe—Imp. 1000*l* and 21 acres of Glebe, V. 360*l*; Glebe, 45 acres; V.'s Inc. 400*l* and Ho; Pop. 1112.) Rural Dean. Formerly C. of Launceston 1849–51. [7]

SMITH, William Henry, *Dronfield Vicarage, Derby.*—V. of Dronfield, Dio. Lich. 1862. (Patron, Ld Chan; V.'s Inc. 275*l* and Ho; Pop. 4478.) [8]

SMITH, William Joseph, 65, *St. John's Wood-terrace, N.W.*—Queen's Coll. Ox. B.A. 1864; Deac. 1864 and Pr. 1865 by Bp of Lon. C. of St. Stephen's, Avenue-road, Lond. 1866. Formerly C. of St. John's, Charlotte-street, Fitzroy-square, 1864–66. [9]

SMITH, William Lilley, *Dorsington Rectory, Stratford on-Avon.*—Trin. Coll. Cam. Scho. of, B.A. 1849; Deac. 1850 and Pr. 1851 by Bp of Wor. R. of Dorsington, Dio. G. and B. 1866. (Patrons, Trustees; R.'s Inc. 420*l* and Ho; Pop. 115.) Formerly P. C. of Radstone, Northants, 1853–66. [10]

SMITH, William Maxwell, *Tintinhull, Yeovil, Somerset.*—Literate; Deac. 1853 and Pr. 1854 by Bp of S. and M. P. C. of Tintinhull, Dio. B. and W. 1855. (Patron, General Arbuthnot; Tithe—Imp. 396*l* 10*s* and 1 acre of Glebe; P. C.'s Inc. 94*l*; Pop. 437.) R. of Lufton, Dio. B. and W. 1856. (Patron, E. Newman, Esq; Tithe, 110*l*; Glebe, 22½ acres; R.'s Inc. 158*l* and Ho; Pop. 31.) Formerly C. of Kirk Michael, Isle of Man. Author, *Help to District Visitors*, Hatchards, 1858, 3*s* 6*d*; *Home*, Macintosh, 1861, 1*s*. [11]

SMITH, William Ramsden, *Christ Church Parsonage, Bradford, Yorks.*—Queens' Coll. Cam. Scho. of, Cl. and Theol. Prizeman, 24th Sen. Opt. and B.A. 1837, M.A. 1840; Deac. 1837 by Abp of Cant. for Abp of York, Pr. 1838 by Abp of York. P. C. of Ch. Ch. Bradford, Dio. Rip. 1851. (Patron, V. of Bradford; P. C.'s Inc. 275*l* and Ho; Pop. 5626.) Surrogate 1851. Formerly C. of St. George's, Sheffield, 1837–41, Trinity, Holborn, Lond. 1841–42; R. of Hulcott, Bucks, 1842–51. Author, *Baptism for the Dead, an Evidence of the Resurrection*, 1838; *Claims of the S.P.G. upon the English Church* (a Sermon), 1852; *The Motives and Methods of Ministerial Heedfulness* (a Visitation Sermon), 1854. [12]

SMITH, William Robins, *Bath.*—Pemb. Coll. Ox. 1st cl. Lit. Hum. 1854, B.A. 1856, M.A. 1857; Deac. 1858 by Bp of B. and W. Prin. of the Bath Proprietary Coll. [13]

SMITH, William Saumarez, *Trumpington Vicarage, Cambridge.*—Trin. Coll. Cam. 1st cl. Cl. Trip 1858, 1st cl. Theol. Trip. and Scholefield Prize 1859, Carus Greek Testament Prize 1857, Bachelors' Prize 1859, Crosse Theol. Scho. 1859, Tyrrwhitt's Heb. Scho. 1860, Seatonian Prize 1864 and 1866; Deac. 1859 and Pr. 1860 by Bp of Ely. Fell. of Trin. Coll. Cam. 1860; V. of Trumpington, Dio. Ely, 1867. (Patron, Trin. Coll. Cam; V.'s Inc. 250*l* and Ho, Pop. 750.) Formerly C. of St. Paul's, Cambridge, 1859–61; Chap. to Bp of Madras 1861–65; C. of Trinity, Cambridge, 1866. [14]

SMITHARD-HIND, Joseph, *Cramlington, Northumberland.*—Univ. Coll. Dur. Scho. of, B.A. 1849, M.A. 1852, B.C.L. 1866; Deac. 1849 and Pr. 1850 by Bp. of Dur. V. of Cramlington, Dio. Dur. 1860. (Patron, Sir M. W. Ridley, Bart. M.P; Glebe, 40*l*; V.'s Inc. 120*l*. and Ho; Pop. 2430.) Formerly C. of Sunderland; and Chap. R.N. Author, *Sermon on the Visitation of the Cholera at Newcastle*, 1853. [15]

SMITHE, Frederick, *Churchdown Parsonage, near Gloucester.*—St. John's Coll. Cam. M.A. 1857, *ad eund.* Ox; Deac. 1853 and Pr. 1854 by Bp. of G. and B. P. C. of Churchdown, Dio. G. and B. 1856. (Patrons, D. and C. of Bristol; Tithe—App. 1214*l*; Glebe 28 acres; P. C.'s Inc. 100*l* and Ho; Pop. 740.) Fell. of Geol. Soc. Lond. Formerly Fell. of St. Mary's Coll. Windermere, 1853. Author, *The Geology of Churchdown*; *Recent Cephalopoda*; etc. [16]

SMITHE, William Henry, *Sparsholt, Wantage, Berks.*—Corpus Coll. Cam. 2nd cl. Theol. Trip. 1866, B.A. 1865; Deac. 1866 and Pr. 1867 by Bp of Ox. C. of Sparsholt 1866. [17]

SMITHERS, William Henry, 7, *Sussex-terrace, Alpha-road, New Cross, S.E.*—St. John's Coll. Cam. B.A. 1847, M.A. 1859; Deac. 1857 by Bp. of Lin. Pr. 1866 by Bp. of Win. C. of St. Mary Magdalen's, Peckham; Hon. Clerical Sec. to the Church Choral Soc. Formerly Prof. of Mathematics and English Literature at Putney Coll. 1847; Asst. Mast. in City of Lond. School, 1849; Head Mast. of Great Grimsby Gr. Sch. 1850; Prin. of Maze Hill Sch. Greenwich, 1857. [18]

SMITH-MARRIOTT, Hugh Forbes, *Horsmonden Rectory, Staplehurst, Kent.*—Trin. Coll. Cam. B.A. 1863, M.A. 1866; Deac. 1864 and P. R. 1866 by Bp of G. and B. R. of Horsmonden, Dio. Cant. 1866. (Patron, the present R; Pop. 1385.) Formerly C. of Christian Malford, Wilts, 1864. [19]

SMITH-MASTERS, Allan, *Camer, near Gravesend.*—Ex. Coll. Ox. 2nd cl. Lit. Hum. and B.A. 1842, M.A. 1845; Deac. and Pr. 1844. Formerly R. of Humber, Herefordshire, 1844; V. of Tidenham, Gloucestershire, 1855. Mr. Smith-Masters was formerly named Cowburn. [20]

SMITHSON, William, *Sturton Vicarage, East Retford, Notts.*—St. John's Coll. Cam. 20th Sen. Opt. and B.A. 1837, M.A. 1845; Deac. 1837 and Pr. 1838 by Bp of Lin. V. of Sturton, Dio. Lin. 1860. (Patrons, D. and C. of York; Tithe, 40*l*; Glebe, 150 acres; V.'s Inc. 294*l* and Ho; Pop. 583.) P. C. of Littleborough, Dio. Lin. 1854. (Patron, G. S. Foljambe, Esq; Tithe, 3*l* 7*s* 6*d*; Glebe, 50 acres; P. C.'s Inc. 82*l*; Pop. 60.) Formerly C. of Farndon with Balderton, 1837–49, Sturton 1854–60; Math. Mast. and 2nd Cl. Mast. of Newark Gr. Sch. 1837–54. [21]

SMYTH, Charles Bohun, *Alfriston, Lewes, Sussex.*—Wad. Coll. Ox. B.A. 1815; Deac. 1820, Pr. 1821. V. of Alfriston, Dio. Chich. 1832 (Patron, Ld Chan; Tithe—Imp. 452*l* 15*s*. 5*d*, V. 166*l* 16*s*; V.'s Inc. 199*l*; Pop. 522.) Author, *Luther's Councils and Churches* (translated from the German); *Luther's Power of the Keys* (translated from the German); *Voice of the Early Church*, 1850; *Christian Metaphysics*, 1851; *Sicilian Vespers*; *Requiem for the Slain at Alma and Inkermann*, 1855. [22]

SMYTH, Christopher, *Little Houghton, Northampton.*—Trin. Coll. Ox. B.A. 1834; Deac. 1836 and Pr. 1837 by Bp of Lin. V. of Little Houghton with Brayfield-on-the-Green V. Dio. Pet. 1838. (Patron, the present V; V.'s Inc. 386*l* and Ho; Pop. Houghton 578, Brayfield 494.) Formerly C. of Great Linford, near Newport Pagnell 1836–37. [23]

SMYTH, Christopher, *Woodford Rectory, near Thrapstone, Northants.*—Jesus Coll. Cam. B.A. 1850, M.A. 1854; Deac. 1850 and Pr. 1851 by Bp of Nor. R. of Woodford, Dio. Pet. 1857. (Patron, Lord St. John; Glebe, 360 acres; R.'s Inc. 600*l* and Ho; Pop. 912.) Formerly C. of Great Yarmouth. [24]

SMYTH, G. Gordon, *Macclesfield.*—C. of St. Paul's, Macclesfield. [1]

SMYTH, George Watson, *Newick House, Cheltenham.*—Trin. Coll. Cam. B.A. 1834, M.A. 1838; Deac. 1835 and Pr. 1836 by Bp of Win. Cl. Mast. of Cheltenham Coll. Formerly R. of Fyfield, Hants. [2]

SMYTH, Henry Metcalfe, *Whitton, Brigg, Lincolnshire.*—St. Cath. Coll. Cam. Scho. of, B.A. 1855; Deac. 1856 and Pr. 1858 by Bp of Ox. C. of Whitton, Formerly C. of St. Thomas's, Oxford, 1856–58, Baldersby. Thirsk, 1858–60, Thorner 1860–62, Kildwick, Leeds, 1862–64, Halton, Lincolnshire, 1864–66. [3]

SMYTH, Hugh Blagg, *Houghton-Regis Vicarage, Dunstable, Beds.*—Jesus Coll. Cam. B.A. 1845, M.A. 1849; Deac. 1846 by Bp of Dur. Pr. 1847 by Abp of York. V. of Houghton-Regis, Dio. Ely, 1856. (Patron, Duke of Bedford; Tithe—Imp. 63*l* 18*s* 3*d*, V. 8*l* 14*s* 6*d*; Glebe, 205 acres; V.'s Inc. 440*l* and Ho; Pop. 2160.) J. P. for Co. of Bedford. Formerly P. C. of Thornes, Wakefield, 1847–56. Author, *The Present Crisis of the Church*; etc. [4]

SMYTH, Jackson James, 34, *Upper Finchley-road, St. John's-wood, London, N.W.*—Dub. A.B. 1828, A.M. 1831, *ad eund.* Ox. 1831; Deac. 1830 by Bp of Dromore, Pr. 1831 by Bp of Killala and Achonry. [5]

SMYTH, James Grenville, *South Elkington, Louth, Lincolnshire.*—Trin. Coll. Cam. Jun. Opt. and B.A. 1848; Deac. 1848, Pr. 1849. V. of North Elkington with South Elkington V. Dio. Lin. 1854. (Patron, Rev. William Smyth; North Elkington, Tithe—Imp. 159*l* 9*s* 3*d*, V. 99*l* 17*s* 5*d*; Glebe, 6½ acres; South Elkington, Tithe—Imp. 494*l* 17*s* 1*d*, V. 273*l*; Glebe, 10 acres; V.'s Inc. 500*l* and Ho; Pop. North Elkington 108, South Elkington 333.) [6]

SMYTH, J. B.—Chap. of H.M.S. "Brisk." [7]

SMYTH, Joshua, *Keyingham, near Hull.*—Deac. 1818, Pr. 1819. P. C. of Keyingham, Dio. York, 1821. (Patron, Abp of York; Tithe—App. 1000*l* and 450 acres of Glebe; P. C.'s Inc. 300*l* and Ho; Pop. 639.) Formerly V. of Burton Pidsea, Yorks, 1832–63. Author, *A Visitation Sermon*, 6*d*. [8]

SMYTH, Samuel Buxton, *East Hanningfield Rectory, Chelmsford.*—Jesus Coll. Cam. B.A. 1836, M.A. 1839; Deac. 1837 and Pr. 1838 by Bp of Rip. R. of East Hanningfield, Dio. Roch. 1863. (Patron, C. Nottidge, Esq; Tithe, 550*l*; Glebe, 37 acres; R.'s Inc. 550*l* and Ho; Pop. 453.) Formerly C. of Staveley, Yorks, 1837–39, Barling 1839–54; V. of Barling 1854–63; Acting Chap. to Royal Artillery, Shoeburyness, 1855–62. [9]

SMYTH, Stewart, 4, *De Beauvoir-road, London, N.*—Dub. A.B. 1846; Deac. 1847 and Pr. 1848 by Bp of Lich. P. C. of St. Andrew's, Hoxton, Dio. Lon. 1863. (Patrons, Crown and Bp of Lon. alt; P. C.'s Inc. 300*l*; Pop. 3674.) Chap. of the Shoreditch Workhouse. [10]

SMYTH, Thomas, *Hindlip Rectory, Worcester.*—Dub. A.B. 1855; Deac. and Pr. 1856 by Bp of B. and W. R. of Hindlip, Dio. Wor. 1862. (Patron, Viscount Southwell; R.'s Inc. 150*l* and Ho; Pop. 136.) [11]

SMYTH, Thomas Ryle, 16, *Caledonia-place, Clifton.*—Brasen. Coll. Ox. B.A. 1838, M.A. 1842; Deac. 1840 by Bp of Wor. Pr. 1841 by Bp of Chich. Formerly R. of Charlinch, Somerset, 1846–57. [12]

SMYTH, Vere Broughton, *Twickenham, Middlesex, S.W.*—Trin. Coll. Cam. B.A. 1856, M.A. 1859; Deac. 1857 and Pr. 1858 by Bp of Lon. C. of Twickenham. Formerly C. of St. Barnabas', Kensington, 1857. [13]

SMYTH, William, *Elkington, Louth, Lincolnshire.* Brasen. Coll. Ox. M.A. [14]

SMYTHE, Henry Ralph, *Beckbury, Shiffnal, Salop.*—Ch. Ch. Ox. B.A. 1835. R. of Beckbury, Dio. Herf. 1850. (Patron, Ld Chan; Tithe, 333*l*; Glebe, 31 acres; R.'s Inc. 378*l*; Pop. 297.) [15]

SMYTHE, Patrick Murray, *Solihull Rectory, Warwickshire.*—Ch. Ch. Ox. 3rd cl. Lit. Hum. 1826, B.A. 1827, M.A. 1829; Deac. 1828 by Bp of Ox. Pr. 1830 by Bp of Wor. R. of Solihull, Dio. Wor. 1847. (Patron, Rev. Archer Clive; Tithe, 1465*l*; Glebe, 91 acres; R.'s Inc. 1700*l* and Ho; Pop. 1995.) Rural Dean 1848; Hon. Can. of Wor. 1858. Formerly C. of Adderbury, Oxon, 1829, Tanworth, Warwickshire, 1829–47. [16]

SMYTHIES, Edward, *Hathern Rectory, Loughborough.*—Emman. Coll. Cam. Prize Essay 1840, Jun. Opt. and B.A. 1842; Deac. 1843 and Pr. 1844 by Bp of Pet. R. of Hathern, Dio. Pet. 1859. (Patron, the present R; Glebe, 261 acres; R.'s Inc. 550*l* and Ho; Pop. 1112.) Formerly C. of Bitteswell, Leic. 1843–44, Sheepshed 1844–45, Newbold-on-Avon 1845–48, Hathern 1848–59. Author, *Emigration, what to do and where to go* (a Lecture to the Central Farmers' Club), 1867. [17]

SMYTHIES, Henry Raymond, *Bournemouth, Hants.*—Emman. Coll. Cam. B.A. 1837, M.A. 1840; Deac. 1838 and Pr. 1839 by Bp of Ely. Formerly R. of Easthope, Salop, 1858–64. [18]

SMYTHIES, Thomas Gosselin, *Forest of Dean, Newnham, Glouc.*—P. C. of St. John's, Cinderford, Forest of Dean, Dio. G. and B. 1844. (Patron, the Crown; P. C.'s Inc. 150*l*; Pop. 4417.) [19]

SNAPE, Alfred William, *Grove House, Surrey-square, S.*—St. John's Coll. Cam. Prizeman of, B.A. 1848, M.A. 1851; Deac. 1848 and Pr. 1849 by Bp of Ely. P. C. of St. Mary Magdalen's, Southwark, Dio. Win. 1855. (Patron, R. of St. George's, Southwark; P. C.'s Inc. from Pew-rents; Pop. 9283.) Formerly C. of St. John's, Waterloo-road, Lond. Author, *Essential Truths*, 1854, 5*s*; *The Great Adversary*, 1854, 3*s* 6*d*; *The Fountain of Love*, 1855, 3*s* 6*d*; *The Waverer*; *The Procrastinator*; *Lying Abhorred*; *Trouble and its Remedy*; *What Aileth Thee?* (Tracts); *The Broken-hearted*; *Peter Denying, Convicted, Repenting.* [20]

SNAPE, James, *The Grammar School, Newcastle-upon-Tyne.*—Deac. 1852 and Pr. 1853 by Bp of Dur. Head Mast. of the Royal Gr. Sch. Newcastle-upon-Tyne. Author, *English Grammar as a Portion of English Scholastic Education*, 1847; *Mathematics as a Portion of a Liberal Education*, 1847; etc. [21]

SNAPE, Robert William, *Warwick.*—St John's Coll. Cam. Prizeman and Exhib. of, 2nd Jun. Opt. B.A. 1859, M.A. 1862; Deac. 1860 and Pr. 1861 by Bp of Lon. C. of St. Mary's, Warwick. Formerly C. of St. Mary Abbotts, Kensington, 1860–66. [22]

SNEATH, Thomas Aikin, *Bledlow Vicarage, Risborough, Bucks.*—Caius Coll. Cam. 4th Jun. Opt. B.A. 1858, M.A. 1861; Deac. 1858 and Pr. 1859 by Bp of Win. V. of Bledlow with Bledlow Ridge, Dio. Ox. 1867. (Patron, Lord Carington; V.'s Inc. 180*l* and Ho; Pop. 1189.) [23]

SNELL, Alfred, *Feering Vicarage, near Kelvedon, Essex.*—Trin. Coll. Cam. Sen. Opt. B.A. 1857, M.A. 1860; Deac. 1859 and Pr. 1860 by Bp of Lon. V. of Feering, Dio. Roch. 1866. (Patron, Bp of Roch; Tithe, 286*l*; Glebe, 9 acres; V.'s Inc. 350*l* and Ho; Pop. 804.) Formerly C. of Wanstead 1859–65; P. C. of Manningtree 1865–66. [24]

SNELL, Charles, *Oulton, Lowestoft.*—Trin. Coll. Ox. B.A. 1850, M.A. 1852; Deac. 1851 and Pr. 1853 by Bp of G. and B. R. of Oulton, Dio. Nor. 1862. (Patron, Edward Snell, Esq; R.'s Inc. 440*l*; Pop. 747.) Formerly C. of Wheathampstead, Herts. [25]

SNELL, Henry Welsford, *Windermere, Westmoreland.*—Emman. Coll. Cam. Sen. Opt. B.A. 1862, M.A. 1865; Deac. 1863 by Bp of Dur. Pr. 1863 by Bp of Carl. C. of Windermere 1866. [26]

SNELL, William Middleton, *Corpus Christi College, Cambridge.*—Corpus Coll. Cam. Tyrrwhitt Heb. Scho. 11th Wrang. and B.A. 1852, M.A. 1855; Deac. 1854 and Pr. 1856 by Bp of Ely. Fell. of Corpus Coll. Cam. [27]

SNEPP, Charles Busbridge, *Perry Villa, Perry-Barr, Birmingham.*—Caius Coll. Cam. LL.M. 1850; Deac. 1846, Pr. 1847. P. C. of Perry-Barr, Dio. Lich. 1854. (Patron, Lord Calthorpe; P. C.'s Inc. 250*l* and Ho; Pop. 1800.) Author, *Pastoral Addresses* (yearly); *The Healing Balm*; *The Great Physician.* [28]

SNEPP, Edward, *Halifax.*—P. C. of St. Paul's, King's Cross, Halifax, Dio. Rip. 1863. (Patrons, Crown and Bp of Rip. alt; P. C.'s Inc. 180*l* and Ho; Pop. 3782.) [29]

SNEPP, H. S., *Bilston, Wolverhampton.*—V. of St. Mary's, Bilston, Dio. Lich. 1866. (Patron, Bp of Lich; V.'s Inc. 300*l* and Ho; Pop. 9040.) [1]

SNEYD, Henry, *Woodland, Staffs.*—Brasen. Coll. Ox. B.A. 1826; Deac. 1829 and Pr. 1830 by Bp of Lich. P. C. of Wetley Rocks, Dio. Lich. 1834. (Patrons, Children of the late Mrs. Sneyd of Ashcombe; Glebe, 9 acres; P. C.'s Inc. 63*l*; Pop. 950.) [2]

SNEYD, John, *Basford Hall, near Leek, Staffs.*—Brasen. Coll. Ox. B.A. 1820, M.A. 1824; Deac. 1822, Pr. 1823. P. C. of Ipstones, Staffs, Dio. Lich. 1833. (Patrons, Freeholders in Trust; Glebe, 129 acres; P. C.'s Inc. 194*l*; Pop. 1904.) Magistrate for the County of Stafford 1824. [3]

SNEYD, Walter, *Denton House, Wheatley, Oxon.*—Ch. Ch. Ox. B.A. 1831, M.A. 1834; Deac. 1834, Pr. 1835. [4]

SNOOKE, Hargood Bettesworth, *Caen, Normandy.*—Pemb. Coll. Ox. B.A. 1829, M.A. 1832; Deac. 1831 and Pr. 1832 by Bp of Ex. Formerly P. C. of All Saints', Portsea, Hants, 1848–61. [5]

SNOW, Benjamin, *Burton-Pedwardine, Sleaford.*—Trin. Coll. Cam. B.A. 1857, M.A. 1860; Deac. 1857 by Bp of Pet. Pr. 1858 by Bp of Man. V. of Burton-Pedwardine, Dio. Lin. 1859. (Patron, the present V; Tithe, 10*l*; Glebe, 268 acres; V.'s Inc. 308*l* and Ho; Pop. 135.) Dioc. Inspector of Schs. Formerly C. of St. Martin's, Leicester, 1857–59. [6]

SNOW, George D'Oyly.—St. Mary Hall, Ox. B.A. 1840. Formerly C. of Newton-Valence, Hants, and Pimperne, Dorset. Author, *Post Tenebras Lux* (with Prefaces by Rev. F. D. Maurice), Smith, Elder, and Co. 1864, 2*s.* 6*d.* [7]

SNOW, Henry, *Bibury Vicarage, Fairford, Gloucestershire.*—St. John's Coll. Cam. B.A. 1832, M.A. 1836; Deac. 1836 by Abp of Cant. Pr. 1837 by Bp of Lond. V. of Bibury with Winson C. Dio. G. and B. 1843. (Patron, Lord Sherborne; Tithe—Imp. 57*l* 3*s* 2*d*, V. 1015*l* 3*s* 6*d*; V.'s Inc. 1066*l* and Ho; Pop. 1080.) [8]

SNOW, Herbert, *Eton College, Windsor.*—St. John's Coll. Cam. Porson Scho. Browne's Medal, and Camden Medal, B.A. 1857, M.A. 1860; Deac. 1859, Pr. 1860. Asst. Mast. at Eton Coll. [9]

SNOW, James Baynham, *Arreton Vicarage, Newport, Isle of Wight.*—Mert. Coll. Ox. B.A. 1834, M.A. 1841. V. of Arreton, Dio. Win. 1843. (Patron, J. Fleming, Esq; Tithe—App. 39*l*. 5*s*, Imp. 1245*l* 10*s* 4*d*, V. 250*l* 18*s* 1*d*; V.'s Inc. 266*l* and Ho; Pop. 1718.) [10]

SNOW, John Pennell, *Perlethorpe, Ollerton, Notts.*—Trin. Coll. Cam. B.A. 1844, M.A. 1847; Deac. 1852, Pr. 1853. P. C. of Perlethorpe, Dio. Lin. 1862. (Patron, Earl Manvers; P. C.'s Inc. 160*l*; Pop. 98.) Formerly C. of St. Bartholomew's, Sydenham. [11]

SNOW, Thomas, 11, *Rhodes-street, Halifax.*—St. Aidan's; Deac. 1856, Pr. 1857. Chap. of Halifax Union Workhouse and Debtors' Gaol. Formerly C. of Almondbury, Yorks, 1856, Greetland, near Halifax (sole charge), 1857. Author, *Hezekiah breaking in Pieces the Brazen Serpent* (a Sermon), 1859; *Notes on Workhouse Life* in *Leisure Hour.* Editor, *Songs in the Night by the late Grace Dickenson of the Halifax Workhouse,* 1s. [12]

SNOWBALL, Gilbert Francis, *Brook Park, Northop, Flintshire.*—St. John's Coll. Cam. B.A. 1844, M.A. 1847; Deac. 1846, Pr. 1848. [13]

SNOWDEN, Charles Greene, *Milford Vicarage, Morpeth, Northumberland.*—Wor. Coll. Ox. B.A. 1834, M.A. 1838; Deac. 1835 and Pr. 1838 by Bp of Chich. V. of Mitford, Dio. Dur. 1858. (Patron, Bp of Dur; V.'s Inc. 100*l* and Ho; Pop. 646.) Chap. to Northumberland Yeomanry Cavalry. Formerly C. of Hove, Sussex, 1835, Charlton, Dover, 1838, Broadstairs, Kent, 1842, Ramsgate 1844, St. Nicholas', Newcastle-on-Tyne 1849. [14]

SNOWDEN, Edmund, *Huddersfield.*—Univ. Coll. Ox. B.A. 1854. P. C. of St. Thomas's, Huddersfield, Dio. Rip. 1859. (Patroness, Mrs. Starkey; P. C.'s Inc. 170*l*; Pop. 4614.) Formerly C. of St. George's, Hulme, Manchester. [15]

SNOWDEN, John H., 3, *Chester-square, London, S.W.*—Univ. Coll. Ox. B.A. 1851, M.A. 1853; Deac. 1851 and Pr. 1852 by Bp of Lon. P. C. of Trinity, Gough-square, Dio. Lon. 1866. (Patron, Bp of Lon; P. C.'s Inc. 122*l* 5*s* 10*d*; Pop. 3159.) Formerly C. of St. Barnabas', Kensington, 1851–53, Curzon Chapel 1855–56, St. Peter's, Eaton-square, 1856–63. [16]

SNOWDON, James, *Richmond, Yorks.*—St. John's Coll. Cam. 16th Wrang. and 2nd cl. Cl. Trip. Crosse Theol. Scho. 1865, Tyrrwhitt's Heb. Scho. 1866, B.A. 1863, M.A. 1866; Deac. 1866 by Bp of Rip. Fell. of St. John's Coll. Cam. 1866; Asst. Mast. of Richmond Sch. 1866. [17]

SNOWDON, John, *Ilkley Vicarage, near Leeds.*—St. John's Coll. Cam. B.A. 1828, M.A. 1836; Deac. 1829 by Bp of Dur. Pr. 1830 by Bp of Bristol. V. of Ilkley, Dio. Rip. 1842. (Patron, L. L. Hartley, Esq; Tithe, 275*l*; Glebe, ¾ acre; V.'s Inc. 320*l* and Ho; Pop. 1407.) Head Mast. of Ilkley Free Sch. Formerly C. of Sockburn, Durham, 1829–31, Grindon, Durham, 1831–33, Crosby-Garrett 1833–34, Stockton-on-Tees 1834–36, Greatham, Durham, 1836–40, Middleton-Tyas, Yorks, 1840–42. [18]

SNOWDON, Richard Kempley, *Lancing College, Shoreham, Sussex.*—Lin. Coll. Ox. M.A. 1864. Asst. Mast. of St. Mary's and St. Nicolas' Sch. Lancing. [19]

SOAMES, Charles, *Mildenhall, Marlborough, Wilts.*—Caius Coll. Cam. B.A. 1848, M.A. 1851; Deac. 1849 and Pr. 1850 by Bp of Roch. R. of Mildenhall, Dio. Salis. 1861. (Patron, C. Soames, Esq; Tithe, 740*l*; Glebe, 150 acres; R.'s Inc. 900*l* and Ho; Pop. 466.) Formerly C. of Mildenhall. [20]

SOAMES, George Pochin, 39, *Great Titchfield-street, Portland-place, London, W.*—Caius Coll. Cam. B.A. 1861, M.A. 1865; Deac. 1865 and Pr. 1866 by Bp of Lon. C. of All Souls', Langham-place, Marylebone, 1866. Formerly C. of St. Barnabas', Holloway, 1865. [21]

SOCKETT, Francis Parker, *West Bromwich, Staffs.*—Pemb. Coll. Ox. B.A. 1834. P. C. of St. James's, West Bromwich, Dio. Lich. 1844. (Patron, Bp of Lich; P. C.'s Inc. 300*l*; Pop. 8821.) [22]

SOCKETT, Henry, *Sutton Rectory, Petworth, Sussex.*—Ex. Coll. Ox. B.A. 1840. R. of Sutton, Dio. Chich. 1848. (Patron, Lord Leconfield; Tithe, 350*l*; Glebe, 25 acres; R.'s Inc. 399*l* and Ho; Pop. 354.) R. of Bignor, near Petworth, Dio. Chich. 1848. (Patron, Lord Leconfield; Tithe, 201*l*; R.'s Inc. 220*l*; Pop. 167.) [23]

SODEN, Alfred James, *Blockley, near Moreton-in-Marsh, Gloucestershire.*—Deac. 1864 and Pr. 1865 by Bp of Wor. C. of Blockley 1866. Formerly C. of King's Norton, near Birmingham, 1864. [24]

SODEN, Charles William, *Walsgrave Vicarage, Coventry.*—Ch. Coll. Cam. B.A. 1850, M.A. 1854; Deac. 1853 and Pr. 1854 by Bp of Wor. V. of Stoke with Walsgrave V. Dio. Wor. 1866. (Patron, Ld Chan; Tithe, 180*l*; Glebe, 63 acres; V.'s Inc. 400*l* and Ho; Pop. Stoke 1555, Walsgrave 1670.) Formerly C. of Teng; 2nd Mast. of the Gr. Sch. Market Bosworth. [25]

SODEN, George, *Bredon's Norton, Tewkesbury.*—Dub. A.B. 1850; Deac. 1851 by Bp of Man. Pr. 1854 by Bp of Ches. Formerly C. of Bredon's Norton 1863–66. [26]

SODEN, John Jordan, 2, *Barr's Hill-terrace, Coventry.*—Emman. Coll. Cam. Jun. Opt. B.A. 1854, M.A. 1857; Deac. 1855 and Pr. 1856 by Bp of Wor. 2nd Mast. of the Gr. Sch. Coventry. [27]

SODOR AND MAN, The Hon. and Right Rev. Horatio POWYS, Lord Bishop of Sodor and Man, *Bishop's Court, Isle of Man.*—St. John's Coll. Cam. M.A. 1826, D.D. per literas Regias, 1854. Consecrated Bishop of S. and Man. 1854. (Episcopal Jurisdiction—the Isle of Man; Inc. of See, 2000*l*; Pop. 52,469; Acres, 180,000; Benefices, 31; Curates, 14; Church Sittings, 17,210.) His lordship was formerly R. of Warrington, Lancashire, and Rural Dean of Chester 1831–54. [28]

SOLARI, Angelo Antonio Nicolo Francesco, *Ocker Hill, Tipton, Staffs.*—St. John's Coll. Cam. B.A. 1852, M.A. 1855; Deac. 1852 and Pr. 1854 by Bp of Lich. P. C. of Ocker Hill, Dio. Lich. 1854. (Patrons, the Crown and Bp of Lich. alt; P. C.'s Inc. 150*l*; Pop. 3787.) [1]

SOLEY, Thomas Lewis, *Lois-Weedon, Towcester, Northants.*—King's Coll. Cam. Fell of. V. of Lois-Weedon, Dio. Pet. 1866. (Patron, King's Coll. Cam; V.'s Inc. 534*l* and Ho; Pop. 555.) Formerly C. of Prior's Portion, Tiverton. [2]

SOLLIS, William, *Fenton Parsonage, Stoke-upon-Trent.*—Pemb. Coll. Ox. B.A. 1812, M.A. 1814; Deac. 1815 and Pr. 1817 by Bp of Glouc. P. C. of Ch. Ch. Fenton, Dio. Lich. 1839. (Patron, Rev. R. B. Baker; P. C.'s Inc. 300*l* and Ho; Pop. 5348.) Formerly C. of Quinton, Glouc. 1815; R. of West Putford and P. C. of Wolfardisworthy, Devon, 1823. [3]

SOMERSET, Boscawen Thomas George Henry, *Mitchel Troy, Monmouth.*—Oriel Coll. Ox. 3rd cl. Lit. Hum. B.A. 1856, M.A. 1858; Deac. 1858 and Pr. 1859 by Bp of G. and B. R. of Mitchel Troy with Cwmcarvan C. Dio. Llan. 1867. (Patron, Duke of Beaufort; Tithe, 394*l* 13*s* 7*d*; Glebe, 80*l*; R.'s Inc 514*l* 13*s* 7*d* and Ho; Pop. Mitchel Troy 385, Cwmcarvan 382.) Formerly C. of Chipping Campden 1858–63, Trinity, Brompton, Middlesex, 1863–65, Sandhurst, Berks, 1865–66; R. of Widford, Gloucestershire, 1866–67. [4]

SOMERSET, George Henry, *St. Mabyn Rectory, Bodmin, Cornwall.*—St. Mary Hall, Ox. 2nd cl. Lit. Hum. and B.A. 1832, M.A. 1835; Deac. 1833, Pr. 1835. R. of St. Mabyn, Dio. Ex. 1842. (Patron, Viscount Falmouth; Tithe, 780*l*; R.'s Inc. 780*l* and Ho; Pop. 714.) [5]

SOMERSET, Ralph B., *Cambridge.*—Trin. Coll. Cam. Fell. of. Formerly C. of Melbourne, Cambs. [6]

SOMERSET, William, *Wollastone Rectory, Lydney, Glouc.*—Magd. Coll. Cam. S.C.L. 1848, B.C.L. 1851; Deac. 1849 by Bp of Herf. Pr. 1850 by Bp of Llan. R. of Wollastone, Dio. G. and B. 1859. (Patron, Duke of Beaufort; R.'s Inc. 500*l* and Ho; Pop. 1349.) Chap. to the Duke of Beaufort. Formerly P. C. of Rwenny, Glamorganshire, 1855–59. [7]

SOMERVILLE, Dudley, *Southend, Essex.*—Queens' Coll. Cam. Wrang. and B.A. 1844, M.A. 1847; Deac. 1844, Pr. 1845. Chap. to the Forces, Shoeburyness. Formerly Fell. of Queens' Coll. Cam. [8]

SOMERVILLE, Philip, *Milton Parsonage, Lymington, Hants.*—A.B. 1832, A.M. 1835; Deac. and Pr. by Bp of Ex. P. C. of Milton, Dio. Win. 1853. (Patron, V. of Milford; Tithe—Imp. 852*l* 6*s* 4*d*, P. C. 32*l*; Glebe, 5 acres; P. C.'s Inc. 112*l* and Ho; Pop. 1312.) [9]

SOOLE, Seymour Henry, *Christ Church Parsonage, Carlisle.*—St. John's Coll. Cam. B.A. 1865; Deac. 1865 and Pr. 1866 by Bp of Carl. P. C. of Ch. Ch. Carlisle, Dio. Carl. 1867. (Patrons, D. and C. of Carl; P. C.'s Inc. 300*l* and Ho; Pop. 4000.) Formerly C. of Ch. Ch. Carlisle, 1865–67. [10]

SOPER, John, *Crawley Rectory, Sussex.*—Magd. Hall, Ox. 1836, 3rd cl. Lit. Hum. and B.A. 1841; Deac. 1843 and Pr. 1844 by Bp of Lon. R. of Crawley, Dio. Chich. 1856. (Patrons, Heirs of Mrs. Clitherow; R.'s Inc. 116*l* and Ho; Pop. 473.) Formerly Min. of South Lambeth Chapel, Lond. 1852–56. Author, *A Nation's Duty in Time of War* (Fast-day Sermon), 1855. [11]

SORRELL, Joseph, *Pembury Grove, Lower Clapton, N.E.*—King's Coll. Lond. Theol. Assoc. 1863; Deac. 1863 and Pr. 1864 by Bp of Lon. C. of Hackney 1867. Formerly C. of St. John's, Limehouse, 1863–67. [12]

SORSBIE, Robert, *Sutton-Valence, Staplehurst, Kent.*—Univ. Coll. Dur. Licen. Theol. and B.A. 1847, M.A. 1850. Fell. of Univ. Coll. Dur; Min. Can. of Roch. Cathl. 1856. (Value, 150*l* and Res.) V. of Sutton-Valence with East Sutton C. Kent, Dio. Cant. 1866. (Patrons, D. and C. of Roch; V.'s Inc. 350*l* and Ho; Pop. Sutton-Valence 1056, East Sutton 385.) Formerly C. of Oakham, Rutland. [13]

SOTHAM, Francis, *Cove Parsonage, near Farnborough, Hants.*—Magd. Hall, Ox. B.A. 1842, M.A. 1844; Deac. 1843, Pr. 1844. P. C. of Cove, Dio. Win. 1854. (Patron, Bp of Win; P. C.'s Inc. 100*l* and Ho; Pop. 671.) [14]

SOTHEBY, Thomas Hans, *Milverton Vicarage, Wiveliscombe, Somerset.*—V. of Milverton, Dio. B. and W. 1844. (Patron, Archd. of Taunton; Tithe—App. 800*l* 5*s*; V. 425*l* 5*s*; V.'s Inc. 582*l* and Ho; Pop. 1895.) Rural Dean. [15]

SOUTH, Richard M., *East Peckham, Tunbridge, Kent.*—Trin. Coll. Ox. B.A. 1859, M.A. 1862; Deac. 1860 and Pr. 1861 by Abp of York. C. of Mereworth, Kent, 1863. Formerly C. of Rotherham, Yorkshire, 1860–63. [16]

SOUTH, Robert, *Christ's Hospital, London, E.C.*—Pemb. Coll. Cam. Jun. Opt. B.A. 1826, M.A. 1829; Deac. 1827 and Pr. 1828 by Bp of Lon. Lect. of St. Michael Bassishaw, 1854. Formerly C. (1827) and Lect. (1830) of St. Mildred's, Poultry; C. (1838) and Lect. (1838) of St. Bartholomew's Exchange; C. of St. Margaret's, Lothbury, Lond. 1854. [17]

SOUTHBY, Richard William, 4, *Royal Park, Clifton.*—Wad. Coll. Ox. B.A. 1858, M.A. 1861; Deac. 1860 and Pr. 1861 by Bp of Ox. Formerly C. of Colnbrook 1860–62, Kingstone Lisle 1862–64, Sparsholt 1864–65. [18]

SOUTHCOMB, Henry Granger, *Devon-square, Newton Abbot, Devon.*—Pemb. Coll. Ox. B.A. 1860, M.A. 1863; Wells Theol. Coll. 1861; Deac. 1861 and Pr. 1862 by Bp of Ex. Sen. Asst. C. of Wolborough with Newton Abbot, Devon, 1865. Formerly C. of Kilmington, Axminster, 1861–63, Honiton 1863–65. [19]

SOUTHCOMB, John L. H., *Rose-Ash Rectory, South Molton, Devon.*—R. of Rose-Ash, Dio. Ex. 1854. (Patron, Rev. H. G. Southcomb; Tithe, 450*l*; Glebe, 105 acres; R.'s Inc. 600*l* and Ho; Pop. 549.) [20]

SOUTHEY, Charles Cuthbert, *Kingsbury Vicarage, Ilminster, Somerset.*—Queen's Coll. Ox. B.A. 1841, M.A. 1844; Deac. 1842 and Pr. 1843 by Bp of Ches. V. of Kingsbury Episcopi Dio. B. and W. 1855. (Patron, the Chan. of Wells Cathl; Tithe—App. 340*l* and 90 acres of Glebe, V. 360*l*; Glebe, 12 acres; V.'s Inc. 380*l* and Ho; Pop. 1838.) Formerly V. of Ardleigh, Essex, 1851–55. Author, *Life and Correspondence of Robert Southey, LL.D. Poet-Laureate*, 6 vols. Longmans, 1850. [21]

SOUTHEY, Henry Willes, *Lidlington, Beds.*—Caius Coll. Cam. B.A. 1856, M.A. 1859; Deac. 1859 and Pr. 1860 by Bp of Ely. V. of Lidlington, Dio. Ely, 1864. (Patron, Duke of Bedford; V.'s Inc. 174*l* and Ho; Pop. 845.) C. of Woburn 1863. Formerly C. of Thorney Abbey, Cambs. 1859–60, Beddington, Surrey, 1860–63. [22]

SOUTHEY, Thomas Castle, *Queen's College, Oxford.*—Queen's Coll. Ox. 2nd cl. Lit. Hum. and B.A. 1847, M.A. 1850. Fell. of Queen's Coll. Ox. [23]

SOUTHGATE, Frederic, *Northfleet Vicarage, Gravesend, Kent.*—Emman. Coll. Cam. B.A. 1848; Deac. 1849 and Pr. 1850 by Bp of Roch. V. of Northfleet, Kent, Dio. Roch. 1858. (Patron, the Crown; V.'s Inc. 400*l* and Ho; Pop. 4245.) Surrogate. Formerly P. C. of St. Mark's, Rosherville, Kent. [24]

SOUTHOUSE, George Wrenford, *Shanklin Parsonage, Newport, Isle of Wight.*—Oriel Coll. Ox. B.A. 1835, M.A. 1841. P. C. of Shanklin, Dio. Win. 1854. (Patron, F. W. Popham, Esq; Tithe, 47*l* 5*s* 8*d*; Glebe, 53 acres; P. C.'s Inc. 106*l* and Ho; Pop. 479.) Rural Dean. [25]

SOUTHWELL, George, *Yetminster Vicarage, Sherborne, Dorset.*—Trin. Coll. Cam. B.A 1829; Deac. 1837 and Pr. 1838 by Bp of G. and B. V. of Yetminster with Chetnole C. Dio. Salis. 1849. (Patron, Bp of Salis; Tithe, 179*l*; Glebe, 17 acres; V.'s Inc. 206*l* and Ho; Pop. Yetminster 696, Chetnole 269.) Surrogate. [26]

SOUTHWELL, George Bull, *Yetminster, Sherborne, Dorset.*—Trin. Coll. Cam. Cl. Trip. B.A. 1857; Deac. 1857, Pr. 1859. C. of Yetminster 1859, and Stockwood 1860. Formerly C. of Batcombe 1857–59. [27]

SOUTHWELL, H. Glanville.—C. of Croxby and Beelsby, Lincolnshire. [1]

SOUTHWELL, Marcus Richard, *St. Stephen's Vicarage, near St. Albans, Herts.*—Ex. Coll. Ox. B.A. 1826, M.A. 1840; Deac. 1828 by Bp of B. and W. Pr. 1829 by Bp of Ex. V. of St. Stephen's, Dio. Roch. 1830. (Patron, the present V; Tithe—Imp. 1918*l* 17*s*, V. 500*l*; Glebe, 18 acres; V.'s Inc. 535*l* and Ho; Pop. 401.) [2]

SOUTHWOOD, Ebenezer Pleasance, *Newhaven, Lewes, Sussex.*—Trin. Coll. Cam. B.A. 1851, M.A. 1854; Deac. 1851 and Pr. 1852 by Bp of Chich. R. of Newhaven, Dio. Chich. 1856. (Patron, the present R; R.'s Inc. 225*l* and Ho; Pop. 1886.) Formerly C. of Newhaven 1851. [3]

SOUTHWOOD, Thomas Allen, *Cheltenham College.*—Emman. Coll. Cam. B.A. 1843, M.A. 1848. Mast. in Cheltenham Coll. [4]

SOWDEN, George, *Hebden Bridge, Halifax, Yorks.*—Magd. Coll. Cam. B.A. 1845, M.A. 1849; Deac. 1845 by Bp of Pet. Pr. 1846 by Bp of Rip. P. C. of Hebden Bridge, Dio. Rip. 1861. (Patron, V. of Halifax; P. C.'s Inc. 240*l*; Pop. 3385.) Formerly C. of Stainland, Halifax, 1845, Houghton-le-Spring, Durham, 1853. [5]

SOWDON, Frederick, *Oxford and Cambridge University Club, Pall Mall, London, S.W.* and *Dunkerton Rectory, Bath.*—St. Mary Hall, Ox. B.A. 1846, M.A. 1848; Deac. 1847 and Pr. 1848 by Bp of Lich. R. of Dunkerton, Dio. B. and W. 1855. (Patron, the present R; Tithe, 318*l* 16*s* 6*d*; Glebe, 52 acres; R.'s Inc. 410*l* and Ho; Pop. 1060.) [6]

SOWELL, Charles Richard, *St. Feock, Truro.*—Ex. Coll. Ox. B.A. 1852; Deac. 1853 and Pr. 1854 by Bp of Ex. C. of St. Feock. Formerly C. of Paignton, and Marldon, and of Northam, Devon. [7]

SOWERBY, John, *Marlborough, Wilts.*—Trin. Coll. Cam. 1846, 41st Wrang. 6th in 2nd cl. Cl. Trip. and B.A. 1847, M.A. 1850; Deac. 1850 and Pr. 1851 by Bp of Salis. Asst. Mast. in Marlborough Coll. 1849. [8]

SOWERBY, Walter James, *Lewisham, Kent, S.E.*—St. John's Coll. Cam. B.A. 1855. C. of Lewisham. [9]

SOWTER, Joseph, *Warley, Brentwood, Essex.*—King's Coll. Lon. 1st cl. Assoc. 1850; Deac. 1850 by Bp of Win. Pr. 1851 by Bp of Lich. Chap. to the Essex Lunatic Asylum 1853. (Value, 230*l*.) Formerly C. of Findern with Littleover, and Chap. of Derby County Asylum 1850–53. [10]

SPACKMAN, Charles, *Iddesleigh Rectory, Crediton.*—New Inn Hall, Ox. B.A. 1845; Deac. 1847, Pr. 1848. R. of Iddesleigh, Dio. Ex. 1864. (Patron, the present R; Tithe, 332*l* 10*s*; Glebe, 146 acres; R.'s Inc. 486*l* and Ho; Pop. 529.) [11]

SPARKE, Edward Bowyer, *Residentiary Houses, Ely,* and *Feltwell Rectory, Brandon Ferry, Norfolk.*—Pemb. Coll. Cam. B.A. 1826, St. John's Coll. Cam. M.A. 1829. Canon Residentiary of Ely 1829. (Value, 303*l* and Res.) R. of Feltwell, Dio. Nor. 1831. (Patrons, Ld Chan. and Bp of Nor. alt; Tithe, 1296*l*; Glebe, 160 acres; R.'s Inc. 1471*l* and Ho; Pop. 1553.) Registrar of the Dio. of Ely. Formerly Fell. of St. John's Coll. Cam. [12]

SPARKE, Ezekiel, *Tuddenham St. Mary Rectory, Mildenhall, Suffolk.*—Caius Coll. Cam. B.A. 1832, M.A. 1835; Deac. 1835 by Bp of Carl. Pr. 1836 by Bp of Bristol. R. of Tuddenham St. Mary, Dio. Ely, 1852. (Patron, Marquis of Bristol; Tithe, 350*l*; Glebe, 17 acres; R.'s Inc 393*l* and Ho; Pop. 413.) [13]

SPARKE, John Henry, *Gunthorpe, Thetford, Norfolk.*—Pemb. Coll. Cam. 5th Sen. Opt. and B.A. 1815, M.A. 1818; Deac. and Pr. 1818 by Bp of Ely. Can. of Ely 1818. (Value, 307*l* and Res.) R. of Leverington, Cambs, Dio. Ely, 1827. (Patron, Bp of Ely; Tithe, 2100*l*; Glebe, 90 acres; R.'s Inc. 2190*l* and Ho; Pop. 1267.) R. of Gunthorpe with Bale, Norfolk, Dio. Nor. 1831. (Patron, the present R; Gunthorpe, Tithe—App. 2*l* 2*s*, R. 317*l* 18*s*; Glebe, 23 acres; Bale, Tithe, 311*l* 10*s*; Glebe, 20 acres; R.'s Inc. 662*l*; Pop. Gunthorpe 249, Bale 227.) Formerly Fell. of Jesus Coll. Cam. [14]

SPARKS, Richard John, *Alfold Rectory, near Horsham.*—Magd. Hall, Ox; Deac. 1836, Pr. 1837. R. of Alfold, Dio. Win. 1839. (Patron, the present R; Tithe, comm. 360*l*; Glebe, 16 acres; R.'s Inc. 360*l* and Ho; Pop. 535.) [15]

SPARKS, George Davis, *Llangattock, Raglan, Abergavenny.*—Deac. 1837, Pr. 1838. R. of Llansaintfraed, Monmouthshire, Dio. Llan. 1851. (Patroness, Mrs. Jones; Tithe, 49*l*; Glebe, 59 acres; R.'s Inc. 83*l*; Pop. 16.) [16]

SPARLING, John, *Eccleston Rectory, Chorley, Lancashire.*—Oriel Coll. Ox. Hon. 4th cl. Lit. Hum. B.A. 1837, M.A. 1841; Deac. 1838 and Pr. 1840 by Bp of Ches. R. of Eccleston, Dio. Man. 1854. (Patron, Rev. W. Yates; Tithe, 1300*l*; Glebe, 62½ acres; R.'s Inc. 1545*l* and Ho; Pop. 2271.) [17]

SPARROW, John Beridge, *Great Cornard Vicarage, Sudbury, Suffolk.*—Magd. Coll. Cam. B.A. 1851; Deac. 1852 and Pr. 1853 by Bp of Wor. V. of Great Cornard, Dio. Ely, 1858. (Patron, Basil Sparrow, Esq.; Tithe—Imp. 420*l*, V. 167*l*; Glebe, ¾ acre; V.'s Inc. 190*l* and Ho; Pop. 904.) Formerly V. of Offton, with Little Bricett R. Suffolk, 1853–58. [18]

SPARROW, John James Horatio Septimus, *Roll's Court, Whitfield, Dover.*—Clare Coll. Cam. B.A. 1859, M.A. 1864; Deac. by Bp of Win. Pr. by Abp of Cant. V. of West Cliffe, Kent, Dio. Cant. 1866. (Patrons, D. and C. of Cant.; V.'s Inc. 34*l*; Pop. 122.) [19]

SPARROW, Montagu Pennington, *Magdalen Laver Rectory, near Ongar, Essex.*—Clare Coll. Cam. B.A. 1843, M.A. 1848. C. of Magdalen Laver. Formerly Dom. Chap. to the Earl of Mornington. [20]

SPARROW, William Charles, *Grammar School, Ludlow.*—Dub. and Ox. M.A. 1862; Deac. 1856 and Pr. 1858 by Bp of S. and M. Head Mast. of Ludlow Gr. Sch. 1865. Formerly C. of St. Mary's, Castletown; Head Mast. of Ramsey Gr. Sch. Isle of Man, 1858. [21]

SPAWFORTH, J., *Burgh-le-Marsh, Boston.*—C. of Burgh-le-Marsh with Winthorpe, Linc. [22]

SPEARING, Frederic, *Hatcham, Deptford, Kent, S.E.*—King's Coll. Lond. Theol. Assoc; Deac. 1856 and Pr. 1857 by Bp of B. and W. C. of St. James's, Hatcham. Formerly C. of Presteign, Stratton-on-the-Fosse, Somerset. [23]

SPECK, Edward John, *Temple Chambers, London, E.C.*—Sec. to the Ch. Pastoral Aid Soc. Temple-chambers, Fleet-street, Lond. [24]

SPECK, Thomas, *Winston, Darlington.*—St. John's Coll. Cam. Sen. Opt. and B.A. 1833; Deac. and Pr. 1833 by Bp of Chich. R. of Winston, Dio. Dur. 1862. (Patron, Bp of Dur; Tithe, 483*l* 12*s*; Glebe, 88 acres; R.'s Inc. 518*l* and Ho; Pop. 341.) Formerly C. of Gateshead. [25]

SPEDDING, David S., *Hutton Roof Parsonage, Burton, Westmoreland.*—St. Bees; Deac. 1857 and Pr. 1858 by Bp of Ches. P. C. of Hutton Roof, Dio. Carl. 1866. (Patron, V. of Kirkby Lonsdale; Glebe, 50*l*; P. C.'s Inc. 90*l* and Ho; Pop. 284.) Formerly C. of Knutsford, Cheshire, 1857–62, St. Matthew's, Westminster, 1862–66. [26]

SPEDDING, Francis, *Donisthorpe, Ashby-de-la-Zouch.*—Emman. Coll. Cam. B.A. 1843; Deac. 1843, Pr. 1844. P. C. of Donisthorpe, Dio. Lich. 1865. (Patron, Bp of Lich; P. C.'s Inc. 155*l*; Pop. 2132.) Formerly C. of Shiffnal, Salop, for 17 years. [27]

SPEKE, Benjamin, *Dowlish Wake, Ilminster.*—Ch. Ch. Ox. B.A. 1853; Deac. 1853, Pr. 1854. R. of Dowlish Wake with West Dowlish R. Dio. B. and W. 1857. (Patron W. Speke, Esq; Tithe—App. 22*l*, R. 360*l*; Glebe, 34 acres; R.'s Inc. 430*l*; Pop. 371.) Formerly C. of Banbury, 1854–57. [28]

SPEKE, William, *Skenfrith, Monmouthshire.*—Trin. Coll. Ox. B.C.L; Deac. 1846 by Bp of Lich. Pr. 1847 by Bp of Wor. V. of Skenfrith, Dio. Llan. 1855. (Patron, George Speke, Esq; Tithe—App 83*l*, Imp. 85*l* 8*s* 6*d*, V. 166*l*; Glebe, 20 acres; V.'s Inc. 250*l*; Pop. 666.) Chap. to Lord Sandys. [29]

SPENCE, Henry Donald Maurice, *St. David's College, Lampeter, South Wales.*—Corpus Coll.

Cam. 1st cl. Theol. Trip. 1865, B.A. 1864. Carus and Scholefield Univ. Prizeman 1866; Deac. 1865 and Pr. 1866 by Bp of St. D. Prof. of English Literature and Modern Languages, and Hebrew Lecturer at St. David's Coll. Lampeter. [1]

SPENCE, Joseph, *East Keal Rectory, Spilsby.*—Ch. Coll. Cam. B.A. 1840, M.A. 1844. R. of East Keal, Dio. Lin. 1860. (Patron, the present R; R.'s Inc. 495*l* and Ho; Pop. 393.) Formerly C. of Winceby. [2]

SPENCER, Charles, *Great Ellingham, Attleburgh.*—Ch. Coll. Cam. B.A. 1832, M.A. 1839. C. of Great and Little Ellingham. Formerly C. of Cawston. [3]

SPENCER, Charles Christopher, *Benefield Rectory, Oundle, Northants.*—Queen's Coll. Ox. B.A. 1842, M.A. 1846; Deac. 1842 and Pr. 1843 by Bp. of Lon. R. of Benefield, Dio. Pet. 1851. (Patron, J. W. Russell, Esq; Tithe, 18*l* 2*s* 2*d*; Glebe, 490 acres; R.'s Inc. 599*l* and Ho; Pop. 527.) Author, *A Commentary on the Collects; Life and Death, a Series of Meditations.* [4]

SPENCER, The Hon. Charles Frederic Octavius, *Sutton Vicarage, Ely.*—Clare Hall, Cam. Hon. M.A. 1847; Deac. 1848 and Pr. 1849 by Bp of Pet. V. of Sutton, Dio. Ely, 1861. (Patrons, D. and C. of Ely; Tithe, 1175*l*; Glebe, 40 acres; V.'s Inc. 1215*l* and Ho; Pop. 1731.) Formerly C. of Pitsford, Northants, 1848–49; V. of Cumnor, Berks, 1850. [5]

SPENCER, Charles Vere, *Wheatfield Rectory, Tetsworth, Oxon.*—Ch. Ch. Ox. B.A. 1849, M.A. 1852; Deac. 1851 and Pr. 1852 by Bp of Pet. R. of Wheatfield, Dio. Ox. 1852. (Patron, the present R; Tithe, 229*l* 18*s*; Glebe, 30 acres; R.'s Inc. 262*l* and Ho; Pop. 89.) Formerly C. of St. Peter's, Northampton, 1851. [6]

SPENCER, Daniel Hall, *Nuneaton.*—St. John's Coll. Cam. B.A. 1862, M.A. 1865; Deac. 1862 and Pr. 1863 by Bp of Win. C. of Nuneaton 1865. Formerly C. of St. Paul's, Dorking, 1862. [7]

SPENCER, Edward, *Tavistock, Devon.*—Univ. Paris, B.A. 1835; Sid. Coll. Cam. Wrang. and B.A. 1843; Deac. 1846 and Pr. 1847. Chap. to the Earl of Ellesmere 1847; Head Mast. of the Tavistock Gr. Sch. 1854; Lect. of Horrabridge Chapel, Devon. Formerly Lect. of Sid. Coll. Cam. 1843–44; Fell. of same 1844–48. [8]

SPENCER, Henry, *Field Dalling, Holt, Norfolk.*—St. Bees; Deac. 1845 and Pr. 1846 by Bp of Nor. V. of Field Dalling, Dio. Nor. 1859 (Patron, the present V; Tithe, comm. 159*l*; Glebe, 39 acres; V.'s Inc. 217*l* and Ho; Pop. 342.) Formerly C. of Deopham 1845–50, Bagthorpe 1850–57, Ilketshall St. Andrew 1858–59. [9]

SPENCER, Isaac, *Acomb, near York.*—St. Mary Hall, Ox. B.A. 1834, M.A. 1837; Deac. 1834 and Pr. 1835 by Abp of York. V. of Acomb, Dio. York, 1836. (Patron, E. Barlow, Esq; Tithe—App. 135*l*, Imp. 132*l* 3*s* 4*d*; Glebe, 31½ acres; V.'s Inc. 190*l*; Pop. 976.) [10]

SPENCER, James Ogden King, *Turton Parsonage, Bolton-le-Moors.*—St. Bees; Deac. 1853 and Pr. 1855 by Bp of Man. P. C. of Turton, Dio. Man. 1859. (Patron, G. M. Hoare, Esq; P. C.'s Inc. 180*l* and Ho; Pop. 4513.) Formerly C. of St. Anne's, Turton. [11]

SPENCER, John, *Kirby Moorside, Yorks.*—V. of Kirby Moorside with Cocken C. and Gillamoor C. Dio. York 1865. (Patron, Ld Chan; Tithe, 294*l*; Glebe, 105 acres; V.'s Inc. 417*l* and Ho; Pop. 2659.) [12]

SPENCER, John Scott Ellis, *Wilshaw, near Huddersfield.*—Dub. A.B. 1858, A.M. 1863; Deac. 1858, Pr. 1859. P. C. of Wilshaw, Dio. Rip. 1863. (Patron, Joseph Hirst, Esq; P. C.'s Inc. 200*l*; Pop. 500.) Formerly C. of Honley 1858, Meltham, near Huddersfield, 1862. [13]

SPENCER, John Ward, *Wilton Parsonage, Taunton.*—Pemb. Coll. Cam. Sen. Opt. B.A. 1840; Deac. 1841 and Pr. 1842 by Bp of Nor. P. C. of Wilton Dio. B. and W. 1843. (Patron, Hamilton Kinglake, Esq; Tithe—Imp. 225*l* 8*s* and 5¾ acres of Glebe; P. C.'s Inc. 140*l* and Ho; Pop. 909.) Formerly C. of Oxburgh with Foulden, Norfolk, 1841–42, St. Mary Magdalen's, Taunton, 1842–43. [14]

SPENCER, John William, *Dendron, Ulverston.*—St. John's Coll. Cam. B.A. 1859; Deac. 1859 and Pr. 1860 by Bp of Ches. C. in sole charge of Dendron 1866. Formerly C. of Kirkly, Prescot, 1859, Eccleston, 1861. [15]

SPENCER, Josiah, *West Ham, Essex.*—C. of West Ham. [16]

SPENCER, Leigh, *Renhold Vicarage, near Bedford.*—Ch. Coll. Cam. B.A. 1839, M.A. 1845. V. of Renhold, Dio. Ely, 1859. (Patron, F. C. Polhill Turner, Esq; V.'s Inc. 150*l* and Ho; Pop. 513.) Formerly P. C. of Little Linford, near Newport-Pagnell, Bucks, 1852–59. [17]

SPENCER, Matthew Trigg, *Goodnestone Parsonage, Wingham, Kent.*—Caius Coll. Cam. B.A. 1855, M.A. 1859; Deac. 1855 and Pr. 1856 by Abp of Cant. P. C. of Goodnestone-next-Wingham, Dio. Cant. 1865. (Patron, Sir B. W. Bridges; P. C.'s Inc. 240*l* and Ho; Pop. 344.) Formerly C. of Trinity, Margate, 1855–56, St. James's, Croydon, 1856–62, St. Mary's, Brighton, 1863–65. [18]

SPENCER, Robert Franklin, 2, *Devonshire-place, Maida-hill, London, W.*—P. C. of St. Matthew's, Marylebone, Dio. Lon. 1852. (Patrons, Trustees; P. C.'s Inc. 150*l*; Pop. 7972.) [19]

SPENCER, William, *Clare Mount School, Wallasey, near Birkenhead.*—St. John's Coll. Cam. Wrang. B.A. 1840; Deac. 1841 and Pr. 1842, by Bp of Ches. Formerly C. of St. Matthias', Liverpool, 1841–42. [20]

SPENCER, William, *Cheltenham.*—C. of St. James's, Cheltenham. [21]

SPENCER, The Hon. William Henry, *Stoke Clymesland, Callington, Cornwall.*—Ch. Ch. Ox. M.A. 1833; Deac. 1835 and Pr. 1837, by Bp of Salis. R. of Stoke Clymesland, Dio. Ex. 1850. (Patron, Prince of Wales; Tithe, 730*l*; Glebe, 48 acres; R.'s Inc. 790*l* and Ho; Pop. 2554.) Formerly C. of Northleigh 1836; V. of Erehbont 1840. [22]

SPENCER, William Henry, *Daresbury Parsonage, Warrington.*—Ch. Ch. Ox. B.A. 1847; Deac. 1848 and Pr 1849 by Bp of Ox. P. C. of Daresbury, Dio. Ches. 1857. (Patron, G. Greenall, Esq., M.P; P. C.'s Inc. 200*l* and Ho; Pop. 136.) Formerly Chap. of Ch. Ch. 1848–57; C. of South Hinksey, Berks, 1854–57. Author, *Abridgment* of Wall's *History of Infant Baptism.* [23]

SPENCER, William Strutt, *Walpole St. Andrew, Wisbech, Norfolk.*—Queens' Coll. Cam. Sen. Opt. and B.A. 1849; Deac. 1849 and Pr. 1850 by Bp of Nor. C. of Walpole St. Andrew 1863. Formerly C. of Middleton, near Lynn. [24]

SPENCER, Woolley, *Browne's Hospital, Stamford.*—Ch. Coll. Cam. B.A. 1825, M.A. 1828; Deac. 1826 and Pr. 1828 by Bp of Lin. R. of St. Michael's with St. Stephen's and St. Andrew's V. Stamford, Dio. Lin. 1836. (Patron, Marquis of Ex; R. and V.'s Inc. 136*l* and Ho; Pop. 1400.) Confrater of Browne's Hospital, Stamford, 1845. Formerly Sec. and Treas. of S.P.G. 1840; Chap. to High Sheriff of Bucks 1858; Chap. for Marquis of Exeter at Burghley Chapel 1860–64. [25]

SPENCER-STANHOPE, Charles, *Weaverham, Northwick, Cheshire.*—Ch. Ch. Ox. 3rd cl. Lit. Hum. and B.A. 1819; Deac. 1820, Pr. 1821. P. C. of Cawthorne, Yorks, Dio. Rip. 1822. (Patron, J. S. Stanhope, Esq; Tithe—Imp. 44*l* 4*s* 6*d*; Glebe, 10 acres; P. C.'s Inc. 180*l*; Pop. 1283.) V. of Weaverham, Dio. Ches. 1825. (Patron, Bp of Ches; Tithe—App. 469*l* 4*s* 5*d*, Imp. 2*l* 10*s*, V. 329*l* 19*s* 6*d*; Glebe, 30 acres; V.'s Inc. 420*l* and Ho; Pop. 2764.) [26]

SPENS, Andrew Nathaniel Wadham, *Trowbridge, Wilts.*—Bp. Hatfield Hall, Dur. Theol. Schol. 1864, Barry Essay 1866, Licen. in Theol. 1866; Deac. 1867 by Bp of Salis. C. of Trinity, Trowbridge, 1867. [27]

SPERLING, Frederick Hayne, *Papworth St. Agnes, St. Ives, Hunts.*—Trin. Coll. Cam. B.A. 1857; Deac. 1857 by Abp of York, Pr. 1858 by Bp of Ely. R. of Papworth St. Agnes, Cambs, Dio. Ely, 1858. (Patron, Arthur Sperling, Esq; Tithe, 291*l*; Glebe, 79 acres; R's Inc. 411*l* and Ho; Pop. 163.) Formerly C. of Whitby 1857. [28]

SPERLING, John Hanson, *Westbourne Rectory, Emsworth, Sussex.*—Trin. Coll. Cam. B.A. 1848, M.A. 1852, *ad eund.* Ox. 1853; Deac. 1849 and Pr. 1850 by Bp of Lon. R. and V. of Westbourne, Dio. Chich. 1862. (Patron, John Sperling, Esq; R. and V.'s Inc. 450*l* and Ho; Pop. 2165.) Formerly C. of St. Mary Abbotts, Kensington, 1849–56; R. of Wicken Bonant 1856. Author, *Church Walks in Middlesex*, 1st ed. 1849, 2nd ed. 1853, Masters, 3*s* 6*d*; Contributor to the *Ecclesiologist, Churchman's Companion*, and other Periodicals. [1]

SPICER, Newton John, *Byfleet Rectory, Cobham, Surrey.*—Ch. Ch. Ox. B.A. 1844, M.A. 1848; Deac. 1846 and Pr. 1847 by Bp of B. and W. R. of Byfleet, Dio. Win. 1851. (Patron, Ld Chan; Tithe, 295*l*; Glebe, 60 acres; R.'s Inc. 360*l* and Ho; Pop. 770.) Author, *Family Prayers.* [2]

SPICER, William Webb, *Itchen-Abbas, Winchester.*—Ch. Ch. Ox. B.A. 1841, M.A. 1848; Deac. 1845, Pr. 1847. R. of Itchen-Abbas, Dio. Win. 1850. (Patron, J. W. Spicer, Esq; Tithe, 468*l*; Glebe, 48 acres; R.'s Inc. 452*l* and Ho; Pop. 214.) [3]

SPINK, Marshall, *Saltash, Cornwall.*—St. Mary Hall, Ox. B.A. 1849; Deac. 1851 and Pr. 1853 by Bp of Ox. Sub-Chap. of the Chapelry of St. Nicholas, Saltash. Formerly C. of Townednak, Cornwall. [4]

SPITTA, Francis John, 10, *Sutton-place, Hackney, London, N.E.*—St. John's Coll. Cam. 1st cl. and Prizeman, B.A. 1822, M.A. 1828; Deac. 1822 and Pr. 1823 by Bp of Lin. Asst. Min. of Ram's Chapel, Homerton, Middlesex. Formerly C. of Taplow, Bucks, 1822–39. [5]

SPITTAL, John, *St. Andrew's Parsonage, Leicester.*—Trin. Hall, Cam. B.A. 1858, M.A. 1862; Deac. 1859 and Pr. 1860 by Bp of Lon. P. C. of St. Andrew's, Leicester, Dio. Pet. 1861. (Patron, Bp of Pet; P. C.'s Inc. 300*l* and Ho; Pop. 7000.) [6]

SPOONER, Charles.—Magd. Hall, Ox. B.A. 1848, M.A. 1850; Deac. 1845 and Pr. 1846 by Bp of Wor. Reader at Christ Church, Newgate-street, Lond. [7]

SPOONER, Edward, *Heston Vicarage, Hounslow, Middlesex, W.*—Ex. Coll. Ox. B.A. 1843, M.A. 1847; Deac. 1846 and Pr. 1847 by Bp of Lich. V. of Heston, Dio. Lon. 1859. (Patron, Bp of Lon; V.'s Inc. 680*l* and Ho; Pop. 4400.) Formerly P. C. of Holy Trinity, Haverstock Hill, Lond. 1858–59. Author, *Twenty Sermons*, 1860, 2*s* 6*d*; *Parson and People*, 1863, 3*s* 6*d* [8]

SPOONER, George Woodberry, *Inglesham Vicarage, Wilts.*—Magd. Hall, Ox. B.A. 1843; Deac. 1842 and Pr. 1843 by Bp of Wor. V. of Inglesham, Dio. G. and B. 1857. (Patron, Bp of G. and B; V.'s Inc. 300*l*; Pop. 119.) Formerly P. C. of St. Mary's, Dunstall, Staffs, 1853–57. [9]

SPOONER, Isaac, *Edgbaston Vicarage, Birmingham.*—Clare Coll. Cam. B.A. 1831, M.A. 1834; Deac. 1832 by Bp. of Bristol, Pr. 1834 by Bp of B. and W. V. of Edgbaston, Dio. Wor. 1848. (Patron, Lord Calthorpe; Tithe, 307*l*; Glebe, 20 acres; V.'s Inc. 512*l* and Ho; Pop. 2400.) Surrogate 1848; Dom. Chap. to Lord Calthorpe 1851. [10]

SPOONLEY, Richard, *Penley Parsonage, Ellesmere, Salop.*—Jesus Coll. Cam. B.A. 1855, M.A. 1864; Deac. 1855 and Pr. 1856 by Bp of Ches. P. C. of Penley, Dio. Lich. 1865. (Patron, V. of Ellesmere; Tithe, 30*l*; Glebe, 60 acres; P. C.'s Inc. 120*l* and Ho; Pop. 382.) [11]

SPOOR, Robert Boyce, *Ulgham, near Morpeth, Northumberland.*—Deac. 1860 and Pr. 1861 by Bp of Herf. C. of Ulgham. Formerly C. of Chirbury, Salop, 1860–63. [12]

SPOOR, William, *Penshaw Rectory, Fence Houses, Durham.*—Dur; Deac. 1859 and Pr. 1860 by Bp of Dur. C. of Penshaw 1859. [13]

SPRAGUE, W. S., *Much Wenlock, Salop.*—C. of Much Wenlock. [14]

SPRING, Frederick James, *Bombay.*—St. Edm. Hall, Ox. B.A. 1834, M.A. 1838. Chap. on the Bombay Establishment. [15]

SPRINGETT, Robert, *Brafferton Vicarage, Helperby, Yorks.*—King's Coll. Lond. Assoc. 1853; Deac. 1853 and Pr. 1854 by Bp of Win. V. of Brafferton, Dio. York, 1863. (Patron, Ld. Chan., Tithe, 39*l*; Glebe, 118 acres; V.'s Inc. 360*l* and Ho; Pop. 920.) Formerly C. of Horsell, Surrey, 1853, Longstock, Hants, 1855; Asst. C. of Melksham, Wilts, 1861. [16]

SPRINGETT, William John, *Dunkirk Parsonage, Feversham, Kent.*—Wad. Coll. Ox. M.A. 1848; Deac. 1846 and Pr. 1847 by Bp of Ox. P. C. of Dunkirk, Dio. Cant. 1854. (Patron, Abp of Cant; P. C.'s Inc. 123*l* and Ho; Pop. 721.) Formerly C. of Brabourne with Monk's Horton, Kent, 1851–54. [17]

SPROSTON, George, *Trimdon Parsonage, Ferryhill, Durham.*—P. C. of Trimdon, Dio. Dur. 1846. (Patron, Lieut.-Col. Beckwith; Tithe—Imp. 184*l* 17*s* 2*d*; Glebe, 120 acres; P. C.'s Inc. 185*l* and Ho; Pop. 2975.) [18]

SPROSTON, Samuel Thomas, *Wednesfield Heath, Wolverhampton.*—Ch. Coll. Cam. B.D; St. Bees; Deac. 1845, Pr. 1846. P. C. of Wednesfield Heath, Dio. Lich. 1852. (Patron, H. Rogers, Esq; P. C.'s Inc. 160*l*; Pop. 5049.) [19]

SPROULE, George Thomas Patterson, *Messingham Vicarage, Kirton-in-Lindsey.*—Dur. Licen. Theol. 1848. V. of Messingham with Bottesford V. Dio. Lin. 1862. (Patrons, the Bp and D. and C. of Lin. alt; Messingham, Glebe, 295 acres; Bottesford, Tithe—App. 256*l* 10*s*, Imp. 88*l* 17*s* 6*d*, V. 144*l* 9*s* 5*d*; Glebe, 67 acres; V.'s Inc. 650*l* and Ho; Pop. Messingham 1362, Bottesford 1065.) Formerly R. of St. Olave's, Southwark, 1856. [20]

SPROWLE, James William, *Widcombe-crescent, Bath.*—Dub. A.B. 1835, A.M. 1846; Deac. 1838 by Bp of Derry, Pr. 1839 by Bp of Kildare. V. of Lyncombe with St. Mark's C. Bath, Dio. G. and B. 1855. (Patrons, Simeon's Trustees; Tithe, 131*l* 13*s* 2*d*; V.'s Inc. 250*l*.) Min. of St. Mary Magdalene Chapel, Holloway, Bath, 1862. (Patron, Ld Chan.) [21]

SPURGEON, John Norris, *Twyford, near Guist, Norfolk.*—Corpus Coll. Cam. B.A. 1859; Deac. 1859 and Pr. 1860 by Bp of Nor. R. of Twyford and V. of Guist, Dio. Nor. 1861. (Patrons, the present R. and W. Norris, Esq. alt; Rent charge, 332*l*; Glebe, 38 acres; R. and V.'s Inc. 350*l*; Pop. Twyford 60, Guist 361.) [22]

SPURGIN, Arthur Dewing, *Gresham Rectory, Norwich.*—Clare Coll. Cam. Jun. Opt. B.A. 1855; Deac. 1855 and Pr. 1856 by Bp of Roch. R. of Gresham, Dio. Nor. 1857. (Patron, the present R; Tithe, 321*l*; Glebe, 23 acres; R.'s Inc. 356*l* and Ho; Pop. 346.) Chap. to the West Beckham Union House. Formerly C. of Stanstead, Essex. [23]

SPURGIN, John, *Hockham Vicarage, Thetford, Norfolk.*—Corpus Coll. Cam. Prizeman, Wrang. and B A. 1840, M.A. 1843, B.D. 1851; Deac. and Pr. 1842 by Bp of Lich. V. of Great and Little Hockham, Dio. Nor. 1857. (Patron, the present V; Tithe, comm. 275*l*; Glebe, 6 acres; V.'s Inc. 285*l* and Ho; Pop. 629.) Surrogate. Formerly Head Mast. of the Maidstone Gr. Sch. 1844–57; Fell. of Clare Coll. Cam. [24]

SPURLING, John Walter, *Wellington College, Wokingham.*—Trin. Coll. Cam. 1st cl. Cl. Trip; Deac. 1864 and Pr. 1866 by Bp of Ox. Tut. and Asst. Mast. in Wellington Coll. 1863. [25]

SPURRELL, Benjamin, *Drayton-Parslow Rectory, Bletchley, Bucks.*—St. John's Coll. Cam. B.A. 1829, M.A. 1832. R. of Drayton-Parslow, Dio. Ox. 1847. (Patron, the present R; R.'s Inc. 470*l* and Ho; Pop. 468.) [26]

SPURRELL, Frederick, *Faulkbourn Rectory, Witham, Essex.*—Corpus Coll. Cam. B.A. 1847, M.A. 1850; Deac. 1847 and Pr. 1848 by Bp of Chich. R. of Faulkbourn, Dio. Roch. 1854. (Patron, Rev. W. T. Bullock; Tithe, 315*l*; Glebe, 28 acres; R.'s Inc. 355*l* and Ho; Pop. 143.) Formerly C. of Newhaven 1847–48, Barcombe 1850–54; Chap. to the British Residents at Stockholm 1849–50. Author and Editor of *The Architectural History of Fletching Church, Sussex*; *Roman Remains at Newhaven, Sussex*; *Inventory of Household Goods of Cornelius Humphrey of Newhaven* 1697; *Relics of Lewes Priory*; all published in the annual volumes of the Sussex Archæological Society, with drawings by the Author; *On the Seals of the Guilds at Wisby, Sweden,* and other papers in *Archæological Journal.* [1]

SPURRIER, G. H., *Edale Parsonage, Sheffield.*—P. C. of Edale, Derbyshire, Dio. Lich. (Patrons, Trustees; P. C.'s Inc. 130*l* and Ho; Pop. 386.) [2]

SPURRIER, Henry, *Roughton Rectory, Horncastle, Lincolnshire.*—Trin. Coll. Ox. B.A. 1856; Deac. and Pr. by Bp of Lin. R. of Roughton with Haltham, Dio. Lin. 1867. (Patron, the Hon. and Rev. John Dymoke; R.'s Inc. 750*l* and Ho; Pop. Roughton 131, Haltham 215.) Formerly C. in sole charge of Folkingham 1859. [3]

SPURRIER, Horatio, *Shildon, Darlington.*—Oriel Coll. Ox. B.A. 1858, M.A. 1859; Deac. 1858 and Pr. 1859 by Bp of Lin. P. C. of Shildon, Dio. Dur. 1866. (Patron, Bp of Dur; P. C.'s Inc. 300*l* and Ho; Pop. 8000.) Formerly C. of Sleaford 1858–65; Sen. C. of All Souls', Langham-place, Lond. 1865. Author, *Light in Darkness*; and *Our Great Journey.* [4]

SPURWAY, Edward Brian Combe, *Heathfield Rectory, Taunton.*—Trin. Coll. Cam. B.A. 1848, M.A. 1851; Deac. 1849 and Pr. 1850 by Bp of Wor. R. of Heathfield, Dio. B. and W. 1856. (Patron, Rev. T. M. Cornish; Tithe, 200*l*; Glebe, 62 acres; R.'s Inc. 300*l* and Ho; Pop. 124.) [5]

SPURWAY, John, *Pitt's Portion Rectory, Tiverton, Devon.*—Ex. Coll. Ox. B.A. 1813, M.A. 1814; Deac. 1813 by Bp of Ox. Pr. 1815 by Bp of Ex. R. of Pitt's Portion, Tiverton, with Cove C. Dio. Ex. 1821. (Patrons, Earl of Harrowby, Sir W. Carew, Bart. Heirs of Sir R. Vyvyan, and Heirs of the Rev. W. Spurway; Tithe, 850*l*; Glebe, 30 acres; R.'s Inc. 900*l* and Ho.) [6]

SPYERS, Henry Almack, *Vigo House, Weybridge.*—Ball. Coll. Ox. B.A. 1861, M.A. 1864; Deac. 1863, Pr. 1864. C. of Hatchford, Surrey, 1867. Formerly C. of Wisley with Pyrford, 1863–66. [7]

SPYERS, Thomas, *Weybridge.*—St. John's Coll. Cam. B.A. 1827, M.A. 1830, D.D. 1847; Deac. 1833, Pr. 1834. Head Mast. of the Gr. Sch. Weybridge. Author, *A Praxis on the Latin Syntax, a Collection of Sentences from Cicero illustrating each Rule,* 1837; *My Flock, or the Parish Priest's Register,* 1846. [8]

SQUIBB, Arthur.—C. of St. Saviour's, Hoxton, Lond. Formerly C. of Stapleford, Cambs. [9]

SQUIRE, Edward Burnard, *Swansea Vicarage, Swansea.*—St. Bees; Deac. 1841 and Pr. 1842 by Bp of Ches. V. of Swansea, Dio. St. D. 1846. (Patrons, Church Patronage Soc; Tithe, 142*l*; V.'s Inc. 300*l* and Ho; Pop. 28,335.) Rural Dean. Surrogate. Formerly Missionary to China 1836–40; C. of Dolphinholme 1841; C. and Lect. of St. George's, Sheffield, 1842–43; C. in sole charge of Burslem, Staffs. 1844–46. Author, *British Sovereignty in India,* 1846, 1*s*; *Darkness the Characteristic of Papal Rome*; *National Guilt the Cause of National Calamity,* 1*s*; *The Resurrection Hope,* 1*s*; *God's Prolonged Controversy with Britain* (a Sermon on the Indian Mutiny), 1857. [10]

SQUIRE, Graham Harvey, *Sunningwell Rectory, Abingdon.*—Brasen. Coll. Ox. B.A. 1859, M.A. 1862; Deac. 1862 and Pr. 1863 by Bp of Man. R. of Sunningwell, Dio. Ox. 1866. (Patron, Sir George Bowyer, Esq; Tithe, 314*l* 18*s* 5*d*; Glebe, 17 acres; R.'s Inc. 390*l* and Ho; Pop. 290.) Formerly C. of St. James's, Manchester, 1862-63, Sydenham, Kent, 1863-64. [11]

SQUIRE, John.—Chap. of H.M.S. "Bellerophon." [12]

STABLE, B. M., *Shuttington, near Tamworth.*—C. of Shuttington, Warwickshire. [13]

STABLE, George, *Weston, Leamington.*—Dub. A.B. 1833; Deac. 1833, Pr. 1835. V. of Wappenbury, near Leamington, Dio. Wor. 1846. (Patron, Lord Clifford; Tithe—Imp. 3*l* 3*s*; Land purchased, 32 acres; V.'s Inc. 70*l*; Pop. 251.) V. of Weston-under-Wetherley, Warwickshire, Dio. Wor. 1850. (Patron, Lord Clifford; Glebe, 49 acres; V.'s Inc. 95*l*; Pop. 274.) [14]

STACEY, Thomas, *St. John's Vicarage, Cardiff.*—Jesus Coll. Ox. B A. 1820, M.A. 1824; Deac. 1819 by Bp of Ban. Pr. 1820 by Bp of Llan. R. of Coyty with Nolton C. Dio. Llan. 1861. (Patron, Earl of Dunraven; Coyty, Tithe, 550*l*; R.'s Inc. 350*l*; Pop. 2685.) Precentor of Llan. Cathl. 1845; Rural Dean of Cardiff 1835; Surrogate. Formerly C. of St. John the Baptist's, Cardiff; V. of Roath 1823-27; R. of Gelligaer, Glamorgan, 1827; Chap. to the late Earl of Dunraven 1827. [15]

STACKHOUSE, John, *Thwaites Parsonage, Cumberland, near Broughton-in-Furness.*—St. Cath. Coll. Cam. B.A. 1836, M.A. 1839; Deac. 1836 and Pr. 1837 by Bp of Lich. P. C. of Thwaites, Dio. Carl. 1849. (Patrons, the Owners of Five Estates; P. C.'s Inc. 118*l* and Ho; Pop. 350.) Formerly C. of Holmesfield, Derbyshire, 1836, Wormhill 1838, Cottesmore, Rutland, 1841, Uffington, Lincolnshire, 1844. [16]

STACKHOUSE, Jonathan L., *St. Mellion, near Callington, Cornwall.*—C. of St. Mellion. [17]

STACPOOLE, Andrew Douglas, *Writtle Vicarage, Chelmsford.*—New Coll. Ox. B.A. 1829, M.A. 1832. V. of Writtle, Dio. Roch. 1851. (Patron, New Coll. Ox; Tithe—Imp. 2300*l*; V.'s Inc. 620*l* and Ho; Pop. 2374.) Formerly Fell. of New Coll. Ox. [18]

STACYE, John, *Shrewsbury Hospital, Sheffield.*—Ch. Coll. Cam. B.A. 1831, M.A. 1834; Deac. 1833, Pr. 1834. Governor and Chap. of the Hospital of Gilbert, Earl of Shrewsbury, Sheffield, 1850. [19]

STAFFORD, B. H., *Sopley, near Ringwood, Hants.*—C. of Sopley. [20]

STAFFORD, C. E. F., *Dinton, near Salisbury.*—C. of Dinton with Teffont Magna. [21]

STAFFORD, James Charles, *Dinton, near Salisbury.*—Magd. Coll. Ox. B.A. 1816, M.A. 1817, B.D. 1832; Deac. 1817, Pr. 1818. V. of Dinton with Teffont Magna C. Dio. Salis. 1841. (Patron, Magd. Coll. Ox; Tithe—App. 80*l* 10*s* and 2 acres of Glebe, Imp. 390*l*, V. 359*l* 10*s*; Glebe, 49 acres; V.'s Inc. 465*l*; Pop. Dinton 509, Teffont Magna 291.) Formerly Fell. of Magd. Coll. Ox; P. C. of Penkridge, Staffs. Author, *Catechism of the Church*; *Persuasive to Unity*; and other Tracts. [22]

STAFFORD, John Herman, *Liverpool.*—Dub. Univ. Scho. 1824, A B. 1827; Deac. 1828, Pr. 1829. P. C. of St. Paul's, Liverpool, Dio. Ches. 1834. (Patron, G. Ramsden, Esq; P. C.'s Inc. 250*l*; Pop. 7637.) [23]

STAINES, Robert John, *Fort Vancouver, North America.*—Trin. Hall, Cam. B.A. 1845. Chap. to the Hudson's Bay Company; Mast. of Fort Vancouver School. [24]

STAINFORTH, Frederick, *Martley, Worcester.*—Queen's Coll. Cam. B.A. 1857; Deac. 1858 and Pr. 1859 by Bp of Lon. C. of Martley and Chap. of Martley Union. Formerly C. of Spring Grove, Middlesex, 1858–60, St. Barnabas', Holloway, 1860-61, St. Hellier's, Jersey, 1861-63, North Stoke, Bristol, 1863–65, Bures, Suffolk, 1865–66. [25]

STAINFORTH, Richard, *Wheldrake Rectory, York.*—R. of Wheldrake, Dio. York, 1865. (Patron, Abp. of York; Tithe, 178*l*; Glebe, 217 acres; R.'s Inc. 411*l* and Ho; Pop. 678.) [26]

STALLARD, A. G. B., *Pewsey, Wilts.*—C. of Pewsey. [27]

STALLARD, George, *East Grafton, Marlborough, Wilts.*—St. John's Coll. Cam. B.A. 1843, M.A. 1847; Deac. 1843 and Pr. 1844 by Bp of Salis. P. C. of East Grafton, Dio. Salis. 1855. (Patron, V. of Great Bedwyn; P. C.'s Inc. 96*l*; Pop. 1011.) Formerly V. of St. Mary's, Marlborough, 1847; P. C. of Tideford, Cornwall, 1851 [28]

STALLARD, Joseph Orlando, *Heath Vicarage, Leighton Buzzard.*—Lin. Coll. Ox. B.A. 1848, M.A. 1851; Deac. 1850 and Pr. 1851 by Bp of Wor. V. of Heath and Reach, Dio. Ely, 1863. (Patron, V. of Leighton Buzzard; Tithe, 25*l*; Glebe, 1 acre; V.'s Inc. 96*l* and Ho; Pop. 953.) Formerly C. of St. Lawrence's, Evesham, 1850; P. C. of Brockhampton, Herefordshire, 1851. [29]

STALLARD, William Henry, *Bolney Vicarage, Cuckfield, Surrey.*—Dur. B.A. 1853; Deac. 1854, Pr. 1855. V. of Bolney, Dio. Chich. 1860. (Patron, Bp of Chich; Tithe—App. 420*l*, V. 197*l* 3*s* 2*d*; Glebe, 32 acres; V.'s Inc. 300*l* and Ho; Pop. 789.) Formerly C. of Trinity, Leeds. [1]

STAMER, Hugh, *Burnley, Lancashire.*—Dub. A.B. 1839; Deac. 1840 by Bp of Herf. Pr. 1841 by Bp of Rip. P. C. of St. James's, Burnley, Dio. Man. 1844. (Patrons, the Crown and Bp of Man. alt; P. C.'s Inc. 150*l*; Pop. 4420.) Formerly C. of Bradford 1840–42, Elland 1840–43, Chesterfield 1843–44. [2]

STAMER, Sir Lovelace Tomlinson, Bart., *Cliffville, Stoke-upon-Trent.*—Trin. Coll. Cam. 2nd cl. Cl. Trip. B.A. 1853, M.A. 1856; Deac. 1853 by Bp of Lich. Pr. 1855 by Bp of Ely. R. of Stoke-upon-Trent, Dio. Lich. 1858. (Patron, F. W. Tomlinson, Esq; R.'s Inc. 2700*l* and Ho; Pop. 12,337.) Rural Dean. Formerly C. of Clay Cross, Derbyshire, 1853, Turvey, Beds, 1854, Long Melford, Suffolk, 1856. [3]

STAMMERS, Alexander, *Trinity Parsonage, Abergavenny.*—Deac. 1858 and Pr. 1859 by Bp of Llan. P. C. of Trinity, Abergavenny, Dio. Llan. 1866. (Patroness, Miss Rachel Herbert.) Formerly Lect. to the Gelligaer Charity 1858–66. [4]

STAMMERS, Robert, *Quorndon Parsonage, Loughborough.*—St. John's Coll. Cam. Sen. Opt. and B.A. 1827, M.A. 1831; Deac. and Pr. 1828. P. C. of Quorndon, Dio. Pet. 1832. (Patron, V. of Barrow-upon-Soar; P. C.'s Inc. 125*l*; Pop. 1622.) P. C. of Woodhouse, Loughborough, Dio. Pet. 1832. (Patron, V. of Barrow-upon-Soar; P. C.'s Inc. 143*l*; Pop. 1163.) [5]

STAMPER, John G. H., *Burbage, near Buxton, Derbyshire.*—Deac. 1851 and Pr. 1852 by Bp of Ches. P. C. of Burbage, Dio. Lich. 1864. (Patron, Duke of Devonshire; P. C.'s Inc. 120*l* and Ho; Pop. 1200.) Dom. Chap. to the Earl of Courtown. Formerly C. of Portwood, Stockport, 1851, Hurdsfield 1854, Crompton-road, Macclesfield, 1857; P. C. of Salterford 1859. [6]

STANBROUGH, Morris Edgar, *Cleobury North Rectory, Salop.*—Caius Coll. Cam. B.A. 1851, M.A. 1854; Wells Theol. Coll; Deac. 1853, Pr. 1854. R. of Cleobury North, Dio. Herf. 1866. (Patron, Viscount Boyne; Tithe, 138*l* 9*s*; Glebe, 75 acres; R.'s Inc. 238*l* and Ho; Pop. 168.) Formerly C. of North Petherton 1853–54, West Monkton 1854–57, Hanwell 1857–61, Ardingley 1861–62, Redgrave 1862-66. [7]

STANDEN, John Henry, *King's College, London, W.C.*—Trin. Coll. Cam. 9th Sen. Opt. and B.A. 1854, M.A. 1855; Deac. 1853 by Bp of Ox. Pr. 1855 by Bp of B. and W. Asst. Mast. in King's Coll. Sch. Lond. Formerly C. of Runnington, near Wellington. [8]

STANDEN, William, *Binsted, Alton, Hants.*—Emman. Coll. Cam. B.A. 1851, M.A. 1854; Deac. 1852 and Pr. 1853 by Bp of Salis. C. of Binsted. Formerly V. of Tarrant Monkton with Tarrant Launceston, Dorset, 1855–58; C. of East Worldham, and Chap. to the Alton Union, 1859. [9]

STANDIDGE, Arthur, *Sherburn, Milford Junction, Yorks.*—C. of Sherburn. [10]

STANFORD, W. B., *Sherborne, Dorset.*—Asst. Mast. in the King's Sch. Sherborne. [11]

STANHAM, George.—St. John's Coll. Cam. B.A. 1852, M.A. 1855; Deac. 1852 and Pr. 1853 by Bp of Pet. Chap. of the County Lunatic Asylum, Surrey. Formerly C. of Great Snoring 1858. [12]

STANHAM, Louis, 54, *Gibson-square, N.*—St. John's Coll. Cam. Jun. Opt. B.A. 1857, M.A. 1863; Deac. 1857 and Pr. 1858 by Bp of Lon. P.C. of St. Bartholomew's, Islington, Dio. Lon. 1862. (Patrons, Trustees; P. C.'s Inc. 300*l*; Pop. 5200.) Formerly C. of St. Mary's, Islington, 1857–62. [13]

STANHOPE, Berkeley Lionel Scudamore, *Byford Rectory, Hereford.*—All Souls' Coll. Ox. B.A. 1845, M.A. 1851; Deac. 1848 and Pr. 1849 by Bp of Herf. R. of Byford, Dio. Herf. 1866. (Patron, Sir Henry Cotterell, Bart; Tithe, 190*l*; Glebe, 32 acres; R.'s Inc. 200*l* and Ho; Pop. 201.) V. of Mansell Gamage, Dio. Herf. 1866. (Patron, Sir Henry Cotterell, Bart; Tithe, 114*l* 18*s*; Glebe, 1½ acres; V.'s Inc. 115*l*; Pop. 131.) Formerly Fell. of All Souls' Coll. Ox; P. C. of Ballingham 1849–56; V. of Bosbury, Herefordshire, 1856–66. [14]

STANHOPE, The Hon. Henry, *Gawsworth Rectory, Macclesfield.*—R. of Gawsworth, Dio. Ches. 1827. (Patron, Earl of Harrington; Tithe, 700*l*; Glebe, 2 acres; R.'s Inc. 750*l* and Ho; Pop. 713.) [15]

STANHOPE, William Pitt Scudamore, *Holme-Lacy, near Hereford.*—Brasen. Coll. Ox. B.A. 1849, M.A. 1851; Deac. 1850 by Bp of G. and B. Pr. 1851 by Bp of Llan. P. C. of Ballingham, near Hereford, Dio. Herf. 1856. (Patron, Sir E. F. S. Stanhope, Bart; P. C.'s Inc. 200*l*; Pop. 186.) Formerly C. of Stutton, near Ipswich. [16]

STANIFORTH, Thomas, *Storrs Hall, Windermere, Westmoreland.*—Ch. Ch. Ox. B.A. 1830, M.A. 1833; Deac. 1830 and Pr. 1831 by Abp of York. Formerly R. of Bolton-by-Bolland, Yorks, 1831–59. [17]

STANLEY, The Hon. Algernon Charles, *Kidderminster.*—Trin. Coll. Cam. B.A. 1864; Deac. 1866 by Bp of Wor. C. of Kidderminster 1866. [18]

STANLEY, Arthur Penrhyn, *Dean's-yard, Westminster, S.W.*—Ball. Coll. Ox. Ireland Scho. Newdigate Prizeman, 1st cl. Lit. Hum. and B.A. 1837, Latin Essayist 1839, English and Theol. Essayist and M.A. Univ. Coll. 1840; Fell. of Univ. Coll. 1838; Deac. 1839, Pr. 1841. Select Preacher 1845–56. Dean of Westminster 1864. (Value, 2000*l*.) Deputy Clerk of the Closet; Chap. in Ordinary to the Queen; Chap. to the Prince of Wales; and Exam. Chap. to the Bp. of Lon. Formerly Can. of Cant. 1851–58; Regius Prof. of Ecclesiastical History and Can. of Ch. Ch. Ox. 1858–64; Chap. to the late Prince Consort, 1854–62. Author, *Life and Correspondence of Dr. Arnold*, 1844; *Sermons and Essays on the Apostolical Age*, 1846; *Memoir of Bishop Stanley*, 1850; *Lecture on the Study of History*, 1854; *Historical Memorials of Canterbury*, 1854; *Epistles to the Corinthians, with Notes*, 1855; *Sinai and Palestine, in Connection with their History*, 1855; *Three Introductory Lectures on the Study of Ecclesiastical History*, 1857; *Sermons* (preached mostly at Canterbury) *on the Unity of Evangelical and Apostolical Teaching*, 1859; *Follow Paul, Follow Christ* (Sermon preached in St. Paul's), 1859; Sermons—*On Human Corruption*; *Freedom and Labour*; *Great Opportunities*; *A Reasonable, Holy, and Living Sacrifice*, 1858-64; *Lectures on the History of the Eastern Church*, 1860; *Lectures on the History of the Jewish Church*, 2 vols. 1858; *The South-African Controversy in Relation to the Church of England*, Parkers, 1866, 2*s* 6*d*; Articles in *Edinburgh* and *Quarterly Reviews.* [19]

STANLEY, Edward Marmaduke, *Hillmorton, Rugby.*—Wor. Coll. Ox. B.A. 1833, M.A. 1836; Deac. 1833, Pr. 1835. V. of Hillmorton, Dio. Wor. 1864. (Patron, the present V; Tithe—Imp. 10*l* 9*s*, V. 175*l* 9*s* 11*d*; V.'s Inc. 252*l*; Pop. 978.) Surrogate. Formerly C. of Rugby; V. of Middlezoy 1857. [20]

STANLEY, George Sloane, *Branstone Rectory, Grantham.*—Ch. Ch. Ox. B.A. R. of Branstone, Dio. Pet. (Patron, Duke of Rutland; R.'s Inc. 350*l* and Ho; Pop. 297.) [21]

STANLEY, Richard, *Barlings, Lincoln.*—Brasen. Coll. Ox. B.A. 1837, M.A. 1840; Deac. 1839 and Pr. 1840 by Bp of Lin. P. C. of Stainfield, Dio. Lin. 1846. (Patron, T. T. Drake, Esq; Tithe, Imp. 420*l*; P. C.'s Inc. 85*l*; Pop. 164.) P. C. of Apley, Dio. Lin. (no church) 1846. (Patron, T. T. Drake, Esq; Tithe, Imp. 163*l* 18*s* 5*d*; P. C.'s Inc. 26*l*; Pop. 221.) P. C. of Barlings, Dio. Lin. 1851. (Patrons, C. Turnor and T. T. Drake, Esqrs; P. C.'s Inc. 85*l* and Ho; Pop. 475.) Formerly C. of Hackthorn and Cold Hanworth 1839–43, Fiskerton 1843–52. [22]

STANLEY, Robert Rainy Pennington, *Felstead Vicarage, Chelmsford.*—Emman. Coll. Cam. B.A. 1848, M.A. 1851; Deac. 1849 and Pr. 1850 by Bp of Lon. V. of Felstead, Dio. Roch. 1859. (Patrons, Earl Cowley's Trustees; Tithe, 558*l*; Glebe, 55*l*; V.'s Inc. 630*l* and Ho; Pop. 1804.) Formerly C. of Banstead, Surrey. [23]

STANLEY, Thomas Carter, *Plymouth.*—Dub A.B. 1857; Deac. 1857 and Pr. 1858 by Bp of Down and Connor. Chap. to the Forces 1859. Formerly C.

of Holywood, Down, Ireland, 1857-59; Chap. at Aldershot Camp 1859-61, Preston 1861, and Halifax, Nova Scotia, 1862. [1]

STANNING, J. H., *Leigh, Lancashire.*—C. of Leigh. [2]

STANNUS, Beauchamp Walter, *Arrow Rectory, Alcester, Warwickshire.*—Dub. A.B. 1843, A.M. 1849; Deac. 1845 and Pr. 1846 by Bp of Down and Connor. R. of Arrow, Dio. Wor. 1863. (Patron, Marquis of Hertford; Tithe, 693*l* 2*s*; Glebe, 3 acres; R.'s Inc. 700*l* and Ho; Pop. 590.) Formerly C. of Ballinderry, Ireland, 1845-46, Winchester 1846; P. C. of Woodbury-Salterton 1846-63. Author, *The Inquiring Parishioner, or the Plan of Salvation briefly Explained,* 1*d*; *Essay on Preaching*; *Christ is All* (a Visitation Sermon). [3]

STANSBURY, John Adolphus, *Oundle, Northants.*—Lin. Coll. Ox. B.A. 1859, M.A. 1860; Deac. 1860, Pr. 1861. C. of Clapton, Northants, 1860; 3rd Mast. of Oundle Gr. Sch. [4]

STANSBURY, John Fortunatus, *Oundle, Northants.*—Magd. Hall, Ox. B.A. 1830, M.A. 1833, B.D. 1840, D.D. 1844; Deac. 1829 and Pr. 1830 by Bp of Lon. Head Mast. of Oundle Gr. Sch. [5]

STANSFELD, John, *Coniston Cold, Skipton, Yorks.*—St. John's Coll. Cam. Sen. Opt. and B.A. 1842; Deac. 1842, Pr. 1843. P. C. of Coniston Cold, Dio. Rip. 1846. (Patron, Peter Garforth, Esq; P. C.'s Inc. 89*l* and Ho; Pop. 265.) [6]

STANTIAL, Thomas, *College School, Ramsgate.*—Magd. Hall, Ox. M.A. 1856, D.C.L. 1864; Deac. 1852 by Bp of Ex. Pr. 1853 by Bp of Ox. Head Mast. of Coll. Sch. Ramsgate. Formerly Head Mast. of Bridgwater Gr. Sch. 1848-62. Author, *The Test Book for Students,* 1 vol. 7*s* 6*d*, or four parts—*Part I. History and Geography, Part II. Language and Literature, Part III. Mathematics, Part IV. Physics,* 2*s* 6*d* each, London, Bell and Daldy. [7]

STANTON, Arthur Henry, *St. Alban's, Holborn, London, E.C.*—Trin. Coll. Ox. M.A. C. of St. Alban's, Holborn. [8]

STANTON, George Henry.—Magd. Hall, Ox. B.A. 1859, M.A. 1862; Deac. 1858, Pr. 1859. P. C. of Trinity, Lincoln's-inn-fields, Lond. Dio. Lon. 1867. (Patron, R. of St. Giles's.) Formerly C. of Ch. Ch. Rotherhithe, 1858, All Saints', Maidstone, 1862, St. Saviour's, Fitzroy-square, Lond. 1864. [9]

STANTON, Joseph John, *Lovington Parsonage, Castle Cary, Somerset.*—St. John's Coll. Ox. B.A. and M.A. 1858; Deac. 1859 and Pr. 1860 by Bp of B. and W. P. C. of Lovington, Dio. B. and W. 1863. (Patrons, D. and C. of Wells; Glebe, 11 acres; P. C.'s Inc. 74*l* and Ho; Pop. 239.) Formerly C. of Horrington, near Wells. [10]

STANTON, Thomas, *Burbage Vicarage, Marlborough, Wilts.*—Ch. Coll. Cam. Scho. of, Sen. Opt. 3 times Prizeman, B.A. 1831, M.A. 1834; Deac. 1832 by Bp of Lin. Pr. 1834 by Bp of Lon. V. of Burbage, Dio. Salis. 1852. (Patron, Bp of Salis; Tithe—App. 687*l*, V. 863*l*; Glebe, 8 acres; V.'s Inc. 370*l* and Ho; Pop. 1603.) Preb. of Salis; Surrogate; and Rural Dean. Formerly P. C. of St. John's, Buckhurst Hill; R. of Shaftesbury, Dorset. [11]

STANTON, Vincent John, *Halesworth Rectory, Suffolk.*—St. John's Coll. Cam. B.A. 1842, M.A. 1850; Deac. 1842 by Bp of Lon. Pr. 1843 by Bp of Herf. R. of Halesworth with Chediston V. Dio. Nor. 1868. (Patron, Sir T. Fowell Buxton, Bart; Tithe—Halesworth, 393*l*, Chediston, 13*l* 14*s* 6*d*; R.'s Inc. 500*l* and Ho; Pop. 2939.) Formerly C. of St. Peter's, Mile-end, Lond. 1842; Colonial Chap. at Hong Kong 1843-51; P. C. of Southgate, Middlesex, 1851-55. Author, *Jesus First and Last; Mansions in My Father's House,* 1855. [12]

STANTON, William Darke, *Toddington, Winchcombe, Glouc.*—Ex. Coll. Ox. B.A. 1850, M.A. 1853; Deac. 1851 and Pr. 1852 by Bp of Ex. C. of Toddington with Stanley Pontlarge. [13]

STANTON, William Henry, *Haselton Andoversford, near Cheltenham.*—Ex. Coll. Ox. B.A. 1846, M.A. 1848; Deac. 1847 and Pr. 1848 by Bp of G. and B. R. of Haselton with Yanworth, Dio. G. and B. 1860. (Patron, Ld Chan; Yanworth or Yarnworth, Tithe, 256*l*; R.'s Inc. 550*l*; Pop. Haselton 210, Yanworth 123.) Formerly R. of Braceborough 1857. [14]

STANWELL, Charles, *St. John's College, Cambridge.*—St. John's Coll. Cam. Sir W. Browne's Gold Medal for Greek Ode 1856, for Latin Ode 1857, Camden Medal 1857, 14th in 1st cl. Cl. Trip. B.A. 1858, M.A. 1862; Deac. 1862 and Pr. 1863 by Bp of Ox. Fell. of St. John's Coll. Cam. 1862. Formerly Tut. and Asst. Mast. of Wellington Coll. [15]

STAPLETON, Eliot Henry, *Buckhorn Weston Rectory, Wincanton, Dorset.*—Ch. Ch. Ox. B.A. 1859; Deac. 1859 and Pr. 1860 by Abp of Cant. R. of Buckhorn Weston, Dio. Salis. 1861. (Patron, Lady Stapleton; Tithe, 310*l*; Glebe, 63 acres; R.'s Inc. 376*l* and Ho; Pop. 509.) Formerly C. of Mereworth 1859. [16]

STAPLETON, The Hon. Sir Francis Jervis, Bart., *Mereworth Rectory, Maidstone.*—Trin. Coll. Cam. M.A. 1831. R. of Mereworth, Dio. Cant. 1827. (Patroness, Baroness Le de Spencer; Tithe, 932*l*; Glebe, 33½ acres; R.'s Inc. 992*l* and Ho; Pop. 835.) V. of Tudeley with Capel V. Tonbridge, Dio. Cant. 1832. (Patroness, Baroness Le de Spencer; Tudeley, Tithe—Imp. 234*l* 2*s*, V. 225*l* 6*s*; Capel, Tithe—Imp. 229*l* 8*s*, V. 156*l* 8*s*; V's Inc. 365*l* and Ho; Pop. Tudeley 547, Capel 611.) [17]

STAPLETON, Frederick George, *Elvetham, Winchfield, Hants.*—Trin. Hall. Cam. B.A. 1859; Deac. 1860 and Pr. 1861 by Bp of Win. C. of Elvetham. [18]

STAPLETON, John Charles, *Teversall Rectory, Mansfield, Notts.*—Downing Coll. Cam. B.A. 1833, M.A. 1837. R. of Teversall, Dio. Lin. 1837. (Patroness, Dowager Countess of Carnarvon; Tithe, 539*l* 10*s* 7*d*; Glebe, 41¾ acres; R.'s Inc. 589*l* and Ho; Pop. 351.) [19]

STAPLEY, Frederick Anthony.—Wad. Coll. Ox. B.A. 1853; Deac. 1853 and Pr. 1854 by Bp of Ox. C. of St. Andrew's, All Souls', Marylebone, Lond. Formerly Asst. C. of St. John's, Brighton; C. of the Chapelries of Stoke-Mandeville and Buckland, Bucks. [20]

STAPYLTON, Martin, *Barlborough Rectory, Chesterfield.*—Trin. Coll. Cam. B.A. 1822; Deac. 1824 and Pr. 1825 by Abp of York. R. of Barlborough, Dio. Lich. 1827. (Patrons, W. H. De Rodes, Esq; Tithe, 600*l*; Glebe, 73 acres; R.'s Inc. 700*l* and Ho; Pop. 1170.) [21]

STAPYLTON, Martyn, *Hawthorn, Fencehouses, Durham.*—Dur. B.A. 1852, M.A. 1854; Deac. 1853 and Pr. 1854 by Bp of Dur. P. C. of Hawthorn, Dio. Dur. 1864. (Patron, R. L. Pemberton, Esq; Tithe, 27*l*; Glebe, 1 acre; P. C.'s Inc. 150*l* and Ho; Pop. 300.) Pemberton Fell. of Univ. Coll. Dur. Formerly C. of Brancepeth 1853, Bishopton 1856, Eglingham 1858. [22]

STAPYLTON, William Chetwynd, *Malden Vicarage, Kingston, Surrey.*—Mert. Coll. Ox. B.A. 1847; Deac. 1849 and Pr. 1850 by Bp. of Ox. V. of Malden with Chessington, C. Dio. Win. 1850. (Patron, Mert. Coll; Malden, Tithe—Imp. 243*l*, V. 76*l*; Glebe, 15 acres; Chessington, Tithe, 313*l*; Glebe, 20 acres; V.'s Inc. 446*l* and Ho; Pop. Malden 820, Chessington 219.) Formerly Fell. of Mert. Coll. [23]

STAREY, James Richard, *Pennington Parsonage, Manchester.*—St. Bees; Deac. 1846 and Pr. 1847. P. C. of Pennington, Leigh, Dio. Man. 1862. (Patrons, Trustees; P. C.'s Inc. 200*l* and Ho; Pop. 2803.) Formerly P. C. of St Thomas's, Lambeth, 1855. [24]

STARKEY, Alfred, *Oldham.*—St. Bees; Deac. 1855 and Pr. 1856 by Bp of Nor. C. of St. James's, Oldham. Formerly C. of St. Margaret's, King's Lynn, and St. George's, Wolverhampton. [25]

STARKEY, Arthur Brydon Cross, *St. John's College, Oxford.*—St. John's Coll. Ox. B.A. 1839, M.A. 1843, B.D. 1848; Deac. 1840 and Pr. 1841 by Bp of Ox. R. of Bygrave, Herts, Dio. Roch. 1858. (Patron, Marquis of Salisbury; R.'s Inc. 400*l*; Pop. 195.) Formerly P. C. of Northmoor, Oxon, 1855-58; Fell. of St. John's Coll. Ox. [26]

STARKEY, John, *Beverley, Yorks.* [27]

STARKIE, Henry Arthur, *Stainforth, Settle, Yorks.*—Trin. Hall, Cam. B.A. 1860; Deac. 1862 and Pr. 1863 by Bp of Ches. P. C. of Stainforth, Dio. Rip. 1865. (Patrons, Five Trustees; P. C.'s Inc. 100*l* and Ho; Pop. 215.) [1]

STARKY, Andrew Beauchamp, *Rowde Vicarage, Devizes.*—Magd. Coll. Cam. B. A. 1860, M.A. 1864; Deac. 1861, Pr. 1862. V. of Rowde, Dio. Salis, 1864. (Patron, G. Goldney, Esq; Tithe, 320*l*; V.'s Inc. 320*l* and Ho; Pop. 1149.) Formerly Asst. C. of Aylesbury, 1861. [2]

STATHAM, Francis Freeman, *Parsonage, 204, East-street, Walworth, London, S.*—Magd. Coll. Ox. 3rd cl. Math. et Phy. 1842, B.A. 1849; Deac. 1843 and Pr. 1844 by Bp of Win. Chap. of St. Mary's, Newington, 1845; P. C. of St. Peter's, Walworth, Dio. Lon. 1848. (Patron, R. of Newington; P. C.'s Inc. 800*l* and Ho; Pop. 29,000.) Hon. Chap. to the P Division of Police 1848; Fell. of the Geological Soc. Formerly C. of Verulam Episcopal Chapel, Lambeth, 1843–45. Author, *Our Protestant Faith, a Course of Lectures on the Distinctive Errors of Romanism*, 3*s* 6*d*; *The Message of the Spirit* (Sermons on Revelation ii. iii.), 5*s* 6*d*; Editor of *Immortality Unveiled, a Treatise on the Evidences, by the late E. D. Jones, of Walworth, with Biography, Preface and Copious Illustrative Notes*, 4*s* 6*d*; *Loyalty a Christian Duty* (a Sermon on the French Revolution of 1848), 6*d*; *Self-Denial* (a Sermon for Margate Infirmary), 1*s*; *A Sermon on the Death of H.R.H. Prince Albert*, 6*d*; *The Eternity of Things Unseen, a Sermon on the Death of Mrs. Carter, of Walworth.* [3]

STATHAM, F. K.—C. of St. Augustine's, Haggerston, Lond. [4]

STATHAM, George Herbert, *Bury St. Edmunds.*—Ch. Coll. Cam. 2nd cl. Cl. Trip. B.A. 1865; Deac. 1866 and Pr. 1867 by Bp of Ely. C. of St. James's, Bury St. Edmunds, 1866; 2nd Mast. of the Gr. Sch. Bury St. Edmunds, 1865. [5]

STATHAM, John Foster, *Cheetham Hill, Manchester.*—Dub. A.B. 1855, A.M. 1858; Deac. 1855 and Pr. 1857 by Bp of Man. R. of Lower Crumpsall, Dio. Man. 1863. (Patron, Bp of Man; R.'s Inc. 180*l*; Pop. 1400.) Formerly C. of St. Peter's, Manchester. [6]

STATHAM, William, *Ellesmere Port, Chester.*—P. C. of Ellesmere Port, Dio. Ches. 1866. (Patron, Bp of Ches; P. C.'s Inc. 120*l*.) Formerly C. of Swinton, Manchester. [7]

STATTER, James, *Worminghall, Thame, Oxon.*—Dub. A.B. 1830; Deac. 1830 and Pr. 1831 by Bp of Ches. V. of Worminghall, Dio. Ox. 1844. (Patron, Viscount Clifden; V.'s Inc. 124*l* 15*s* 8*d*; Pop. 354.) [8]

STAUNTON, Francis, *Staunton Rectory, Elton, Nottingham.*—St. John's Coll. Cam. B.A. 1862, M.A. 1865; Deac. 1862 and Pr. 1863 by Bp of Ex. R. of Staunton with Flawborough C. Dio. Lin. 1864. (Patron, the present R; R.'s Inc. 134*l* and Ho; Pop. 234.) Formerly C. of St. George, Truro, 1862–64. [9]

STAVELEY, William Brown, *The Rectory, High Halden, Tenterden.*—St. Cath. Coll. Cam. B.A. 1833; Deac. and Pr. 1833 by Bp of Ches. R. of High Halden, Dio. Cant. 1861. (Patron, Abp of Cant; Tithe, 450*l*; Glebe, 2 acres; R.'s Inc. 470*l* and Ho; Pop. 650.) Formerly C. of Ch. Ch. Macclesfield, 1833–34; P. C. of Trinity, Over Darwen, Lanc. 1834–38; C. of Stanmer with Falmer, Sussex, 1838–58; R. of Ruckinge, Kent, 1858–61. Author, *Sermons*, 1840, 10*s* 6*d*. [10]

STAYNER, Thomas Lawrence, *Overbury, Worcestershire.*—Trin. Coll. Cam. B.A. 1859; Deac. 1860 and Pr. 1861 by Bp of Pet. C. of Overbury 1866. Formerly C. of Worthington, Leic. 1860, Hagley, Worc. 1862. [11]

STEAD, Alfred, *Ovingdean Rectory, Brighton.*—Caius Coll. Cam. B.A. 1833, M.A. 1836. R. of Ovingdean, Dio. Chich. 1844. (Patron, the present R; Tithe, 362*l* 5*s*; Glebe, 1½ acres; R.'s Inc. 364*l* and Ho; Pop. 121.) [12]

STEAVENSON, Joseph, *All Saints' Parsonage, Newmarket, Cambs.*—St. John's Coll. Cam. B.A. 1839, M.A. 1842; Deac. 1839 and Pr. 1840 by Bp of Lin. P. C. of All Saints', Newmarket, Dio. Ely, 1853. (Patron, Bp of Nor; P. C.'s Inc. 146*l*; Pop. 1259.) [13]

STEAVENSON, R., *St. Cuthbert's, Stella, Newcastle-on-Tyne.*—C. of St. Cuthbert's, Stella. [14]

STEBBING, Henry, *St. James's Parsonage, Hampstead-road, London, N.W.*—St. John's Coll. Cam. B.A. 1823, M.A. 1827, D.D. 1839. R. of St. Mary Somerset with St. Mary Mounthaw, Dio. Lon. 1857. (Patron, Bp of Lon; R.'s Inc. 350*l*; Pop. St. Mary's Somerset 291, St. Mary's Mounthaw 102.) Chap. to University Coll. Hospital since 1837. Formerly P. C. of St. James's, Hampstead-road, Lond. 1849–57. Author, *The History of the Christian Church, from its Foundation to* A.D. 1492, 2 vols. 1833; *The History of the Reformation*, 2 vols. 1836; *The History of the Church of Christ from* A.D. 1530 *to the Eighteenth Century, in Continuation of Milner's History*, 3 vols. 1839; *Discourse on Death*; *History of Chivalry and the Crusades*, 2 vols; *Jesus, and other Poems*; *Lives of the Italian Poets*, 3 vols; *Sermons.* [15]

STEBBING, Thomas Roscoe Rede, *Tor Crest Hall, Warberry Hill, Torquay.*—King's Coll. Lond. B.A. 1855, Wor. Coll. Ox. B.A. 1857, M.A. 1859; Deac. 1858 and Pr. 1859 by Bp of Ox. Fell. of Wor. Coll. Ox. Formerly Fell. of Radley Coll. Berks; Tut. and Asst. Mast. at Wellington Coll. Berks; Tut. of Wor. Coll. Ox. 1865–67. Author, *Eventide, a Book of Prayer for the Schoolroom*, Bell and Daldy, 1864, 4*d*; *Translation of Longinus on the Sublime*, Shrimptons, Oxford, 1867, 5*s*. [16]

STEDMAN, John, *Colerne, Chippenham, Wilts.*—Pemb. Coll. Ox. B.A. 1851; Deac. 1852 by Bp of Ox. Pr. 1853 by Bp of Ches. C. of Colerne, Wilts. Formerly C. of Scarisbrick, Dolton, and Box. [17]

STEDMAN, Paul, *Thurston Vicarage, Bury St. Edmunds.*—Ch. Coll. Cam. B.A. 1844; Deac. 1844 and Pr. 1846 by Bp of Ely. V. of Thurston, Dio. Ely, 1861. (Patrons, Trustees under the will of the late James Mathew, Esq; Tithe, comm. 217*l*; Glebe, 80 acres; V.'s Inc. 320*l* and Ho; Pop. 750.) Formerly C. of Pulloxhill, Beds, 1844–46, Bromsgrove 1846–48, Stanford-le-Hope 1848–50, Barnham, Suffolk, temporarily in 1850 and again 1852–56. [18]

STEDMAN, W. N., *Hillingdon, Uxbridge.*—C. of Hillingdon, Middlesex. Formerly C. of Hambleden. [19]

STEEDMAN, Samuel Watson, *Fyfield, Andover, Hants.*—Ch. Ch. Ox. B.A. 1842; Deac. 1843, Pr. 1844. R. of Fyfield, Dio. Win. 1854. (Patron, the present R; Tithe, 214*l* 13*s*; Glebe, 34 acres; R.'s Inc. 300*l* and Ho; Pop 222.) [20]

STEEL, Anthony William Wilson, *Scrope-terrace, Cambridge.*—Caius Coll. Cam. 2nd Wrang. and B.A. 1859, M.A. 1862; Deac. 1860 and Pr. 1861 by Bp of Ely. Fell. and Asst. Tut. of Caius Coll. Formerly C. of Whittlesford, Cambs, 1860–62. [21]

STEEL, Francis Chambre, *Llanvetherine Rectory, Abergavenny.*—Jesus Coll. Ox. B.A. 1824, M.A. 1827; Deac. 1825 and Pr. 1826 by Bp of Ox. R. of Llanvetherine, Dio. Llan. 1845. (Patron, Earl of Abergavenny; Tithe, 300*l*; Glebe, 51½ acres; R's. Inc. 365*l* and Ho; Pop. 236.) Rural Dean of Abergavenny 1847. [22]

STEEL, Henry Allen, *Maltby, Rotherham.*—Jesus Coll. Ox. B.A. 1856, M.A. 1858; Deac. 1859 and Pr. 1860 by Bp of Llan. C. of Maltby 1862. Formerly C. of Dingestone and Tregaer 1859–61, Streatley 1861–62. [23]

STEEL, John, *Great Horkesley Rectory, Colchester.*—Ch. Coll. Cam. B.A. 1822; Deac. 1822, Pr. 1824. R. of Great Horkesley, Dio. Roch. 1852. (Patroness, Countess Cowper; Tithe, 1005*l* 17*s* 6*d*; Glebe, 47 acres; R.'s Inc. 1075*l* and Ho; Pop. 769.) Dom. Chap. to Earl Cowper. Formerly P. C. of Cowbit 1827. [24]

STEEL, John, *Great Horkesley, Colchester.*—Ball. Coll. Ox. B.A. 1860, M.A. 1865; Deac. 1860 and Pr. 1861 by Bp of Lin. C. of Great Horkesley 1863. Formerly C. of Welby 1860–63. [25]

STEEL, J., *Hesleden Monk, Castle Eden, Durham.*—C. of Hesleden Monk. [26]

STEEL, Macdonald, *Caerwent Vicarage, Chepstow, Monmouthshire.*—Jesus Coll. Ox. B.A. 1838, M.A.

1844; Deac. 1839, Pr. 1840. V. of Caerwent, Dio. Llan. 1843. (Patrons, D. and C. of Llan; Tithe, 300*l* 18*s*; Glebe, 5 acres; V.'s Inc. 310*l* and Ho; Pop. 445.) P. C. of Llanvair-Discoed, Dio. Llan. 1843. (Patrons, D. and C. of Llan; P. C.'s Inc. 80*l*; Pop. 187.) [1]

STEEL, Thomas Henry, *Harrow-on-the-Hill, Middlesex, N.W.*—Trin. Coll. Cam. Chancellor's Medallist, 20th Wrang. and B.A. 1830, M.A. 1833; Deac. 1831, Pr. 1832. Asst. Cl. Mast. in Harrow Sch. Formerly V. of St. Ippollits with Great Wymondley, Herts, 1837–57. Author, *Sermons at Harrow*, 1842, 4*s* 6*d*; *On the Means of Extending the Utility of Agricultural Societies* (a Letter to Lord Dacre), 1846, 1*s*; *A Plan for the Social Elevation of the Labouring Classes* (a Letter to Lord John Russell), 1848, 6*d*; *Revelations of Astronomy* (a Sermon), 1852, 1*s*; *Sermon for Founders' Day, Harrow*, 1853, 1*s*. [2]

STEELE, Edward, *Great Grimsby, Lincolnshire.*—C. of Great Grimsby. [3]

STEELE, John, *Macclesfield.*—Deac. 1823, Pr. 1824. P. C. of Ch. Ch. Macclesfield, Dio. Ches. 1828. (Patroness, Mrs. Roe; P. C.'s Inc. 320*l*) Author, *Faith, Hope, and Charity* (a Tract for the Times), 1852. [4]

STEELE, Otho William, *Guernsey.*—C. of St. Stephen's, St. Peter Port, Guernsey. [5]

STEELE, Richard Jackson, *East Harlsey, Northallerton, Yorks.*—St. Bees; Deac. and Pr. 1854. P. C. of East Harlsey, Dio. York, 1855. (Patron, J. Beaumont, Esq; Tithe, 16*l*; Glebe, 23 acres; P. C.'s Inc. 74*l* and Ho; Pop. 430.) P. C. of Ingleby-Arncliffe, Yorks, Dio. York. 1855. (Patron, Rev. George Cooper Abbes; Tithe, Imp. 150*l*; Glebe, 25 acres; P. C.'s Inc. 46*l*; Pop. 326.) [6]

STEELE, Thomas, 2, *Bathwick-terrace, Bath.*—Dub. A.B. 1832, LL.D. 1859, Ox. D.C.L. 1860; Deac. 1837 by Bp of Lon. Pr. 1838 by Bp of Australia. Retired Colonial Chap. Formerly Chap. at St. Peter's, Cook's River, near Sydney, 1838–57; Chap. to Governor-General Sir G. Gipps 1837. [7]

STEELE, Thomas James, *Whepstead Rectory, Bury St. Edmunds.*—St. Bees, Librarian; Deac. 1840 by Bp of B. and W. Pr. 1840 by Bp of Dur. R. of Whepstead, Dio. Ely, 1857. (Patron, Adam Rivers Steele, Esq; Tithe, 603*l*; Glebe, 6 acres; R.'s Inc. 640*l* and Ho; Pop. 603.) Dom. Chap. to the Earl of Tankerville 1844. Formerly Sen. C. of Sedgefield, Durham, for ten years. [8]

STEGGALL, Frederick, *Consett, Gateshead.*—Literate; Deac. 1856 and Pr. 1857 by Bp of Carl. P. C. of Consett, Dio. Dur. 1864. (Patrons, Crown and Bp of Dur. alt; P. C.'s Inc. 300*l*; Pop. 5500.) Formerly C. of Trinity, Carlisle; Chap. to the Cumberland Infirmary 1857. [9]

STEGGALL, John, *Great Ashfield, Ixworth, Suffolk.*—P. C. of Great Ashfield, Dio. Ely, 1823. (Patron, Lord Thurlow; P. C.'s Inc. 55*l*; Pop. 408.) Surrogate. [10]

STEGGALL, William, *Hessett, Bury St. Edmunds.*—Jesus Coll. Cam. B.A. 1825, M.A. 1828; Deac. 1826, Pr. 1827. C. of Hessett. [11]

STENNING, George Covey, *Ryde, Isle of Wight.*—Trin. Coll. Cam. B.A. 1862, M.A. 1866; Deac. 1863 and Pr. 1864 by Bp of Win. C. of Trinity, Ryde, 1867. Formerly C. of St. Thomas's, Ryde, 1863–65. [12]

STENT, Henry, *Fairlight, Hastings.*—V. of Fairlight, Dio. Chich. 1857. (Patron, C. Young, Esq; V.'s Inc. 502*l*; Pop. 501.) [13]

STEPHEN, C. J., *Frankby, Cheshire.*—C. of Frankby. [14]

STEPHEN, George Cæsar, *Marown, Isle of Man.*—King William's Coll. Isle of Man, Bp Barrow's Scholarship; Deac. 1840 by Bp of Wor. Pr. 1841 by Bp of St. A. Formerly C. and Chap. of St. James's, Dalby, Dio. S. and M. 1840–56. Author, *The Holiday and Sunday and Prospective Almanac for* 1853,'54,'55,'56 (a Sheet), 8*d*. [15]

STEPHEN, Leslie.—Fell. of Trin. Hall, Cam. [16]

STEPHEN, William Henry George, *St. John's Parsonage, Darlington.*—Univ. Coll. Dur. B.A. 1850. P. C. of St. John's, Darlington, Dio. Dur. 1856. (Patrons, the Crown and Bp of Dur. alt; P. C.'s Inc. 150*l* and Ho; Pop. 3458.) [17]

STEPHENS, Ferdinand Thomas, *St. Mawgan-in-Pydar Rectory, St. Columb, Cornwall.*—Ex. Coll. Ox. B.A. 1838, M.A. 1844. R. of St. Mawgan-in-Pydar, Dio. Ex. 1846. (Patron, H. Willyams, Esq; Tithe, 615*l*; Glebe, 50 acres; R.'s Inc. 665*l* and Ho; Pop. 731.) [18]

STEPHENS, Henry, *Finchley, Middlesex, N.W.*—St. Bees; Deac. 1859 and Pr. 1860 by Bp of Ches. Min. of Ch. Ch. Finchley. Formerly C. of St. Bartholomew's, Liverpool, 1859–61, St. Michael's, Liverpool, 1861, St. Simon Zelotes, Lond. 1862–63. [19]

STEPHENS, J. E., *Wolverhampton.*—C. of St. George's, Wolverhampton. [20]

STEPHENS, John Otter, *Savernake, Marlborough, Wilts.*—Win. Coll. 1842, Hulme Exhib. Brasen. Coll. Ox. 1850, B.A. 1854, M.A. 1857; Deac. 1856 and Pr. 1858 by Bp of Ox. P. C. of Savernake, Dio. Salis. 1861. (Patron, Marquis of Aylesbury; P. C.'s Inc. 150*l*; Pop. 345.) Formerly C. of Belgrave, Leic. and Steeple Aston, Oxon. [21]

STEPHENS, Lawrence Johnstone, *Newbiggin-by-the-Sea, near Morpeth, Northumberland.*—Caius Coll. Cam. B.A. 1851, M.A. 1855; Deac. 1852 and Pr. 1853 by Bp of Wor. Sen. C. of Newbiggin 1867. Formerly C. of All Saints', Worcester, St. Mary's, Glasgow, Alnmouth, Northumberland, and East and West Anstey, Devon, 1865–67. [22]

STEPHENS, Richard, *Belgrave Vicarage, Leicester.*—Brasen. Coll. Ox. 1802, Hulme's Exhib. B.A. 1806, M.A. 1809, B.D. 1816; Deac. 1810 and Pr. 1811 by Bp of Ox. V. of Belgrave with Birstall Chap. Dio. Pet. 1824. (Patron, Bp of Lich; Tithe, Eccles. Commiss. 490*l* 5*s* 3*d*; Glebe, 337 acres; V.'s Inc. 205*l* and Ho; Pop. Belgrave 1510, Birstall 405.) Formerly Fell. and Tut. of Brasen. Coll. Ox. 1810–12; Asst. Mast. of Rugby Sch. 1812–15; Jun. Proctor of the Univ. of Ox. 1815–16. [23]

STEPHENS, Richard, *Frensham, Farnham, Surrey.*—Clare Coll. Cam. B.A. 1831, M.A. 1835. P. C. of Frensham, Dio. Win. 1838. (Patron, Rev. J. Colmer; P. C.'s Inc. 106*l* and Ho; Pop. 1171.) [24]

STEPHENS, Richard Ruding, *Adderbury Vicarage, Banbury.*—New Coll. Ox. B.C.L. 1837, M.A. 1856. V. of Adderbury with Barford C. and Milton C. Dio. Ox. 1858. (Patron, New Coll. Ox; V.'s Inc. 820*l* and Ho; Pop. Adderbury 1251, Barford and Milton 279.) Formerly Fell. and Bursar of New Coll. Ox. [25]

STEPHENS, Thomas Selwood, *St. Erme Rectory, Truro.*—Wor. Coll. Ox. B.A. 1847, M.A. 1850; Deac. 1848 and Pr. 1849 by Bp of Salis. R. of St. Erme, Dio. Ex. 1867. (Patrons, Trustees; Tithe, 514*l*; Glebe, 80 acres; R.'s Inc. 594*l* and Ho; Pop. 554.) Formerly C. of Wanstead, Essex; Downe, Kent, 1850–67. [26]

STEPHENS, William, *Wednesfield, near Wolverhampton.*—V. of Wednesfield, Dio. Lich. 1849. (Patron, Bp of Lich; Tithe—Imp. 1111*l* 16*s* 6*d*; V.'s Inc. 285*l*; Pop. 3504.) [27]

STEPHENS, William Richard Wood, *Earley Court, near Reading.*—Ball. Coll. Ox. 1st cl. Lit. Hum. B.A. 1862, M.A. 1865; Deac. 1864 and Pr. 1865 by Bp of Lon. C. of Purley, near Reading, 1866. Formerly C. of Staines, Middlesex, 1864–66. [28]

STEPHENS, William Robert, *Seaforth, Liverpool.*—Dub. Univ. Scho. 1848, Sen. Mod. and Gold Medallist 1850, Reg. Prof. of Div. Prize 1851; B.A. 1851, M.A. 1862; Deac. 1852 and Pr. 1853 by Bp of Ches. C. of Seaforth 1856. Formerly C. of Ch. Ch. Southport, 1852–54; Lect. at St. Saviour's, Manchester, 1854–56; C. of Rusholme 1855–56. [29]

STEPHENSON, Charles, *Waterden, Fakenham, Norfolk.*—Pemb. Coll. Cam. Jun. Opt. and B.A. 1850, M.A. 1853; Deac. 1851 and Pr. 1852 by Bp of Win. C. of Waterden with Egmore. Formerly C. of Kentish-town Chapel, Lower Craven-place, Lond. 1856. [30]

STEPHENSON, Henry Major, *The College, Liverpool.*—Ch. Coll. Cam. late Fell. of, 9th in 1st cl. Cl.

Trip. B.A. 1861, M.A. 1864; Deac. 1864 by Bp of Ely. Vice-Pres. of Liverpool Coll. [1]

STEPHENSON, John, *St. John's Parsonage, Weymouth.*—Caius Coll. Cam. Scho. of, Sen. Opt. and B.A. 1849, M.A. 1852; Deac. 1849 and Pr. 1850 by Bp of Salis. P. C. of St. John's, Weymouth, Dio. Salis., 1855. (Patron, R. of Melcombe-Regis; P. C.'s Inc. 300*l* and Ho; Pop. 1060.) Formerly C. of Melcombe-Regis 1849-55. [2]

STEPHENSON, John George Rablah, *Cambridge House, Stratford-on-Avon.*—Dub. A.B. 1857, A.M. 1861; Deac. 1857 by Bp of Rip. Pr. 1858 by Bp of Ches. Prin. of the Coll. Sch. Stratford-on-Avon. Formerly C. of Bowes, Yorks, and Tattenhall, Cheshire. [3]

STEPHENSON, Joseph, *Harvington Lodge, near Evesham.*—Dub. A.B. 1864; Deac. 1864 and Pr. 1865 by Bp of Wor. C. of Harvington. Formerly C. of Salford Priors 1864–65, Hanley, Staffs, 1866. [4]

STEPHENSON, Joseph Henry, *Lympsham Rectory, Weston-super-Mare, Somerset.*—Queen's Coll. Ox. B.A. 1841, M.A. 1850; Deac. 1842 and Pr. 1843 by Bp of Ches. R. of Lympsham, Dio. B. and W. 1844. (Patron, the present R; Tithe, 491*l* 15*s*; Glebe, 100 acres; R.'s Inc. 681*l* and Ho; Pop. 496.) District Inspector of Schools for Dio. of B. and W. 1845; Rural Dean of Axbridge 1854; Preb. of Wells 1856. Author, *Brent Knoll* (a Poem), 1837; *Addresses to the Congregation of Lympsham*, 1844 and 1845; *Addresses to Candidates for Confirmation*, 1846; *The Times, their Signals and Obligations*, 1846; *A Collection of Psalms and Hymns*, 1850; *The Fallen Tree*, 1851; *All-Constraining Love*, 1853; *The King and Priest unto God*, 1854; *Jabez, or Pray and Prosper*, 1857; *Poems*, 1864, 2nd ed. 1867; various Pamphlets. [5]

STEPHENSON, Lawrence, *Soulderne Rectory, near Banbury.*—St. John's Coll. Cam. 12th Wrang. and B.A. 1823, M.A. 1826, B.D. 1833. D.D. 1844; Deac. 1826 by Bp of Ely. Pr. 1826 by Bp of Lin. for Bp of Ely. R. of Soulderne, Dio. Ox. 1835. (Patron, St. John's Coll. Cam; Tithe, 428*l* 10*s* 10*d*; Glebe, 125 acres; R.'s Inc. 450*l* and Ho; Pop. 587.) Formerly Fell. of St. John's Coll. and Sadlerian Lect. Cam. 1826-34. [6]

STEPHENSON, Robert, *Ashted, Birmingham.*—St. Bees; M.A. by Abp of Cant. 1863; Deac. 1854 and Pr. 1855 by Abp of York. P. C. of St. James's, Ashted, Dio. Wor. 1859. (Patrons, Trustees; P. C.'s Inc. 160*l*; Pop. 13,392.) Chap. to the Troops, Birmingham. Formerly C. of Trinity, Wicker, Sheffield, and St. George's, Birmingham. [7]

STEPHENSON, T. Nash, *Bromyard, Herefordshire.*—Wor. Coll. Ox. B.A. 1834, M.A. 1837; Deac. 1836 and Pr. 1837 by Bp of Lich. V. of Bromyard, Dio. Herf. 1867. (Patron, Bp of Wor; Tithe, 512*l* 16*s* 6*d*; V.'s Inc. 590*l* and Ho; Pop. 2995.) Formerly C. of Tettenhall 1836, Solihull 1839; P. C. of Shirley, near Birmingham, 1843–67. [8]

STEPHENSON, William, 49, *Prospect-street, Hull.*—Magd. Hall. Ox. B. A. 1854, M.A. 1862; Deac. 1854 by Bp of G. and B. Pr. 1856 by Bp of Lich. C. of Sculcoates, Hull, 1866. Formerly C. of Slymbridge, Glouc. of Longton, Staffs, of Blisworth, Northants, of Eversley, Hants, and Goosnargh, Lancashire. Author, *Twenty-five Village Sermons preached at Eversley*, Simpkin, Marshall, and Co. 1862, 3*s* 6*d*. [9]

STERLAND, Henry Octavius, *St. Edmund's Parsonage, Durham.*—Deac. 1854 by Bp of Lin. P. C. of St. Edmund's, Gateshead, Dio. Dur. 1865. (Patron, Bp of Dur; P. C.'s Inc. 300*l* and Ho; Pop. 3000.) Chap. of King James's Hospital. Formerly C. of St. Mary's, Nottingham, 1854–62, Gateshead 1862–65. Author, *Two Hundred Interesting and Instructive Bible Questions*, 4 series, with Keys, 2*d* each; *A Liturgy for Church of England Sunday Schools*, 25 for 1*s*; *Scripture Lessons* (for Sunday Schs.) [10]

STERRY, Francis.—Ex. Coll. Ox. B.A. 1856, M.A. 1859; Deac. 1858 and Pr. 1859 by Bp of Ox. Formerly C. of Trinity, Windsor, 1858–60; Upminster, Essex, 1860–62; Stockland, Devon (sole charge) 1864–67. [11]

STERT, Arthur Richard, 2, *South-crescent, Walton-on-Naze.*—Ex. Coll. Ox. B.A. 1831, M.A. 1835; Deac. 1832 and Pr. 1834 by Bp of Chich. Formerly C. of Rayleigh, and of Lamarsh, Essex. [12]

STEVENS, Charles Abbot, *Blackheath, Kent, S.E.*—Trin. Coll. Cam. B.A. 1839, M.A. 1842; Deac. 1840 and Pr. 1841 by Bp of Roch. P. C. of All Saints', Blackheath, Dio. Roch. 1864. (Patron, the V. of Lewisham; P. C.'s Inc. 300*l*; Pop. 1827.) Formerly C. of West Farleigh 1840–44, Kensington 1844–51, Oakham 1851–53; Min. of St. Margaret's, Westminster, 1853-55; C. of Oakham 1857–60; V. of Goudhurst 1860–64; Hon. Sec. of United Education Committee (Revised Code) of 1862. Author, *Catalogue of Phænogamous Plants of Great Britain*, 1839; *Practical Remarks on Reformation of Cathedral Music*, 1843; *Rating of Tithe Rent Charge*, 1856; *Conscience Clause Interference*, Rivingtons, 1867. [13]

STEVENS, Enoch, *Brockmoor, Brierley Hill, Staffs.*—St. Bees 1855; Deac. 1856 and Pr. 1857 by Bp of Lich. P. C. of Brockmoor, Dio. Lich. 1862. (Patrons, Crown and Bp of Lich. alt; P. C.'s Inc. 150*l* and Ho; Pop. 3844.) Formerly C. of Brierley Hill 1856–60, St. Edmund's, Dudley, 1861. [14]

STEVENS, George Henry, *St. Alban's, Wood-street, Cheapside, London, E.C.*—Magd. Coll. Cam. B.A. 1840, M.A. 1845. C. of St. Alban's, Wood-street, and St. Olave's, Silver-street, Lond; Asst. Mast. of the Kensington Proprietary Sch. [15]

STEVENS, Henry, *Wateringbury Vicarage, Maidstone.*—Oriel Coll. Ox. B.A. 1830, M.A. 1832; Deac. 1832, Pr. 1833. V. of Wateringbury, Dio. Cant. 1840. (Patrons, D. and C. of Roch; Tithe, comm. 820*l*; Glebe, 5½ acres; V.'s Inc. 850*l* and Ho; Pop. 1370.) [16]

STEVENS, Henry, *Sydenham, Kent, S.E.*—P. C. of Trinity, Sydenham, Dio. Roch. 1866. (Patrons, Trustees.) Sec. to the Lord's Day Observance Soc. [17]

STEVENS, Henry Bingham, *Curridge, Newbury.*—Emman. Coll. Cam. Sen. Opt. B.A. 1857, M.A. 1860; Deac. 1858 and Pr. 1859 by Bp of Ox. C. of Curridge 1861. Formerly C. of Thatcham, Berks, 1858. [18]

STEVENS, John, *Bramley, Basingstoke, Hants.*—Magd. Hall, Ox. B.A. 1835; Deac. 1838 and Pr. 1840 by Bp of Lin. C. of Bramley 1866. [19]

STEVENS, John Robert, *Swadlincote (Derbyshire), near Burton-on-Trent.*—Magd. Hall, Ox. B.A. 1853, M.A. 1865; Deac. and Pr. 1854. P. C. of Swadlincote, Dio. Lich. 1855. (Patron, P. C. of Church-Gresley; P. C.'s Inc. 95*l*; Pop. 1553.) P. C. of Foremark, Dio. Lich. 1855. (Patron, Sir R. Burdett, Bart; P. C.'s Inc. 50*l*; Pop. 238.) [20]

STEVENS, The Very Rev. Robert, *The Vicarage, West Farleigh. Maidstone.*—Trin. Coll. Cam. B.A. 1801, M.A. 1804, B.D. and D.D. 1820; Deac. 1801 by Bp of Nor. Pr. 1802 by Bp of Lon. Preb. of Lin. 1814; Dean of Roch. 1820 (Value, 1966*l* and Ho); V. of West Farleigh, Kent, Dio. Cant. 1820. (Patrons, D. and C. of Roch; Glebe, 14 acres; V.'s Inc. 463*l* and Ho; Pop. 399.) Author, *Sermons on our Duty towards God, our Neighbour and Ourselves*, 1814; *Discourses on the Apostles' Creed*, 1817; *Counsel of God in the Redemption of the World*, 1837. [21]

STEVENS, Robert, 21, *Lion-terrace, Portsea.*—King's Coll. Lond. 1st cl. Assoc; Deac. 1862 and Pr. 1863 by Bp of Win. Even. Lect. of St. Mary's, Portsmouth; Chap. of Portsmouth Union. Formerly C. of St. John's, Portsea. Author, *Hymns of Prayer and Praise selected and arranged to appropriate Tunes*, Macintosh, 1866, 6*d*. [22]

STEVENS, Thomas, *Bradfield, Reading.*—Oriel Coll. Ox. B.A. 1832, M.A. 1835; Deac. 1839 by Bp of Chich. Pr. 1839 by Bp of Win. R. of Bradfield, Dio. Ox. 1843. (Patron, the present R; Tithe, 1147*l* 8*s*; Glebe, 87 acres; R.'s Inc. 1280*l* and Ho; Pop. 1167.) Warden of St. Andrew's Coll. Bradfield; Commissary in England for Bp of Christchurch, New Zealand. Formerly Asst. Poor Law Commr. 1836–39; P. C. of Keele, Staffs, 1839–42. [23]

STEVENS, Thomas, *Woodford, near Thrapstone.*—Magd. Coll. Cam. B.A. 1863, M.A. 1867; Deac. 1865 by Bp of Lon. Pr. 1866 by Bp of Pet. C. of Woodford 1866. Formerly Cl. Mast. at the Charterhouse 1864–66; Asst. C. of St. Mary's, Golden-lane, Lond. [1]

STEVENS, William Everest, *Belgrave-terrace, Durdham Down, Bristol.*—St. John's Coll. Cam. B.A. 1824, M.A. 1827; Deac. and Pr. 1834 by Bp of Ox. R. of Salford and Little Rollright, Dio. Ox. 1836. (Patron, W. N. Skillicorne, Esq; Glebe, 220 acres; R.'s Inc. 350*l* and Ho; Pop. 397.) [2]

STEVENSON, David, *Frostenden, Suffolk.*—Trin. Coll. Cam. B.A. 1849; Deac. 1848, Pr. 1849. C. of Frostenden. Formerly C. of Halesworth, Suffolk. [3]

STEVENSON, George, *Dickleburgh Rectory, Scole, Norfolk.*—Trin. Coll. Cam. 16th Wrang. and B.A. 1816, M.A. 1819; Deac. 1821 by Bp of Ely, Pr. 1823 by Bp. of Lin. R. of Dickleburgh, Dio. Nor. 1838. (Patron, Trin. Coll. Cam; Tithe, 725*l*; Glebe, 109 acres; R.'s Inc. 958*l* and Ho; Pop. 895.) Rural Dean 1841; Hon. Can. of Nor. 1847. Formerly Fell. of Trin. Coll. Cam. Author, *Two Visitation Sermons; A Sermon at the Septennial Meeting of the Diss Provident Society.* [4]

STEVENSON, John, *Patrixbourne Vicarage, near Canterbury.*—V. of Patrixbourne with Bridge Chapelry, Dio. Cant. 1846. (Patron, Marquis of Conyngham; Tithe—Imp. 900*l*, V. 400*l*; V.'s Inc. 442*l* and Ho; Pop. Patrixbourne 228, Bridge 898.) Chap. to the Earl of Kintore. [5]

STEVENSON, John, *Curry Mallet, Somerset.*—C. of Curry Mallet. [6]

STEVENSON, Joseph, *Bath.*—Dur. B.A. 1841, M.A. 1844; Deac. 1841 and Pr. 1842 by Bp of Dur. Formerly V. of Leighton Buzzard 1849; C. of Skegness, Lincolnshire, 1864–66. [7]

STEVENSON, Thomas, 32, *Brompton-crescent, S.W.*—Trin. Coll. Cam. B.A. 1863, M.A. 1867; King's Coll. Lond. B.A. 1853, 1st cl. Theol. Assoc. 1855; Deac. 1856 and Pr. 1857 by Bp of Lon. C. of Park Chapel, Chelsea, 1864. Formerly C. of St. Peter's, Stepney, 1856–60, Meldreth, Cambs, 1861–63, St. Michael's, Chester-square, Lond. 1864. Author, *Pastoral Visitation the Want of the Times*, Rivingtons, 1860, 2nd ed. 1861. [8]

STEVENSON, Thomas Blades, *King Edward's School, Birmingham.*—Ch. Coll. Cam. B.A. 1840, M.A. 1843. Classical Mast. in King Edward's Sch. Birmingham. [9]

STEVENSON, William Allan, *Formby, near Liverpool.*—Queens' Coll. Cam. B A. 1846, M.A. 1849; Deac. and Pr. 1848 by Bp of Ches. P. C. of St. Luke's, Formby, Dio. Ches. 1859. (Patron, R. Formby, Esq. M.D; Glebe, 2 acres; P. C.'s Inc. 32*l* and Ho; Pop. 400.) Formerly C. of Namptwich, Cheshire, 1848–50, Eccleston, Lancashire, 1851–54, Withington 1854–56, Crumpsall (sole charge) 1856–59. Author, "*He is not a Jew who is one outwardly*" (a Sermon), 1863. [10]

STEVENTON, Edwin Horatio, 21, *Eastbourne-terrace, Paddington, London, W.*—Corpus Coll. Cam. 3rd Wrang. and 1st Smith's Prizeman, B.A. 1830, B.D. 1840; Deac. 1834 by Bp of Nor. Pr. 1836 by Bp of Bristol. P. C. of All Saints', Paddington, Dio. Lon. 1847. (Patron, Bp of Lon; P. C.'s Inc. 650*l*; Pop. 6317.) Formerly C. of Paddington 1841–46. [11]

STEWARD, Ambrose Heath, *Godmanchester, Hunts.*—St. John's Coll. Cam. B.A. 1862; Deac. 1863 by Bp of Ely. C. of Godmanchester 1863. [12]

STEWARD, Charles Edward, *Churt, Farnham, Surrey.*—Magd. Coll. Ox. 3rd cl. Lit. Hum. B A. 1861, M.A. 1863; Deac. 1862 and Pr. 1863 by Bp of Win. P. C. of Churt, Dio. Win. 1865. (Patron, Archd. of Surrey; P. C.'s Inc. 150*l*; Pop. 420.) Formerly C. of Farnham 1862–65. [13]

STEWARD, Charles Holden, *Cropthorne, Pershore.*—Oriel Coll. Ox; B.A. 1851, M.A. 1855; Deac. 1851 and Pr. 1852 by Bp of Wor. Formerly C. of Wyre Piddle 1851–52, More 1852–56, Berkswich 1857– [14]

STEWARD, Charles John, *Somerleyton Rectory, Lowestoft.*—Trin. Coll. Cam. B.A. 1861, M.A. 1864; Deac. 1862 and Pr. 1864 by Bp of Nor. R. of Somerleyton, Dio. Nor. 1865. (Patron, C. Lucas, Esq; Tithe, 363*l*; Glebe, 46 acres; R.'s Inc. 400*l* and Ho; Pop. 621.) Formerly C. of Oulton, Suffolk. [15]

STEWARD, Francis, *Barking Rectory, Needham Market, Suffolk.*—Trin. Hall, Cam. B.A. 1829; Deac. 1830 and Pr. 1831 by Bp of Nor. R. of Barking with Darmsden R. Dio. Nor. 1836. (Patron, Earl of Ashburnham; Tithe, 800*l*; Glebe, 4 acres; R.'s Inc. 849*l* and Ho; Pop. Barking 409, Darmsden 64.) [16]

STEWARD, F. Conway, *Salhouse, Norwich.*—C. of Salhouse. Formerly C. of Somerleyton, Suffolk. [17]

STEWARD, George William, *Caister, Yarmouth, Norfolk.*—Corpus Coll. Cam. B.A. 1827, M.A. 1830; Deac. 1828 by Bp of Lich. Pr. 1829 by Bp of Nor. R. of Caister, Dio. Nor. 1829. (Patron, the present R; Tithe, 942*l* 8*s* 11½*d*; Glebe, 5½ acres; R.'s Inc. 977*l* and Ho; Pop. 1203.) Rural Dean; Dioc. Inspector of Schs. [18]

STEWARD, Henry, *Bethel, Wymondham, Norfolk.*—Corpus Coll. Cam. B.A. 1847; Deac. 1847, Pr. 1848. P. C. of Hethel, Dio. Nor. 1863. (Patron, J. Steward, Esq; Tithe, 473*l*; Glebe, 60 acres; P. C.'s Inc. 500*l*; Pop. 196.) Formerly C. of Swardeston 1847. Author, *Pray Read It* (a few Words about Mormonism); *Have You Read It?* (Evidence taken from the Book of Mormon itself, proving it to be the work of an Impostor), 1853. [19]

STEWARD, John, *Edstaston House, near Wem, Salop.*—Wor. Coll. Ox. B.A. 1829; Deac. and Pr. 1832 by Bp of Herf. P. C. of Edstaston, Dio. Lich. 1850. (Patron, R. of Wem; P. C.'s Inc. 150*l*; Pop. 799.) [20]

STEWART, Alexander, *Chilton Cantelos, Ilchester.*—Clare Coll. Cam. B.A. 1848, M.A. 1852; Deac. 1849, Pr. 1850. C. of Chilton Canteloe. Formerly C. of South Cadbury. [21]

STEWART, Charles Desborough, *Southsea, Portsmouth.*—Univ. Coll. Ox. B.A. 1826; Deac. 1827 by Bp. of Lon. Pr. 1828 by Bp of Salis. P. C. of St. Paul's, Southsea, Dio. Win. 1839. (Patron, V. of Portsea; P. C.'s Inc. 150*l*; Pop. 10,674.) Surrogate. [22]

STEWART, Charles Henry, *Royal Arsenal Chapel Parsonage, Plumstead, Kent, S.E.*—Dub. A.B. 1844; Deac. 1844 by Abp of Dub. Pr. 1845 by Bp of Derry. C. of Plumstead, and Royal Arsenal Chap. 1864. [23]

STEWART, Charles James, *New Bury, near Bolton-le-Moors.*—Deac. 1846, Pr. 1848. P. C. of St. James's, New Bury, Dio. Man. 1866. (Patron, Earl of Bradford; P. C.'s Inc. 150*l* and Ho.) Chap. of the Bolton Workhouse 1866. Formerly P. C. of St. John's, Crook-y-Voddy, Isle of Man; C. of Farnworth, Lancashire. [24]

STEWART, David Dale, *The Vicarage, Maidstone.*—Ex. Coll. Ox. B.A. 1840, Ellerton Theol. Essayist 1841, M.A. 1844; Deac. 1841, Pr. 1842. V. of Maidstone, Dio. Cant. 1854. (Patron, Abp of Cant; Tithe—App. 1400*l* 0*s* 4*d*, V. 600*l*; V.'s Inc. 665*l* and Ho; Pop. 3739.) Author, *Memoirs of Rev. James Haldane Stewart; Pastoral Addresses.* [25]

STEWART, David James, *Privy Council Office, Downing-street, London, S.W.*—Trin. Coll. Cam. B.A. 1839, M.A. 1842. One of H.M. Inspectors of Schs. [26]

STEWART, Edward, *Sparsholt, Winchester.*—Oriel Coll. Ox. B.A. 1829, M.A. 1834; Deac. 1841 by Bp of Roch. Pr. 1842 by Bp of Salis. V. of Sparsholt, Dio. Win. 1842. (Patron, Ld Chan; Tithe—Imp. 364*l* 10*s* 5*d*, V. 300*l* 7*s* 8*d*; V.'s Inc. 250*l* and Ho; Pop. 395.) R. of Lainston, Hants, Dio. Win. 1836. (Patron, Sir F. H. Bathurst, Bart; Tithe, 27*l*; Glebe, 23 acres; R.'s Inc. 50*l*; Pop. 33.) [27]

STEWART, James, *Little Stukeley Rectory, Huntingdon.*—Caius Coll. Cam. Hon. M.A. 1842; Deac. 1843 and Pr. 1844 by Bp of Ex. R. of Little Stukeley, Dio. Ely, 1860. (Patron, Duke of Manchester; Glebe, 270 acres; R.'s Inc. 350*l* and Ho; Pop. 385.) Formerly C. of Cury, Cornwall, 1846, [illegible], Suffolk, 1846–60.

Editor, *Sermons by the late Rev. Joseph Parker, M.A. Rector of Wyton*, 6s. [1]

STEWART, James Haldane, *Brightwell Rectory, Wallingford.*—Ex. Coll. Ox. B.A. 1843, M.A. 1846; Deac. 1847 by Bp of Ox. Pr. 1848 by Bp of Win. R. of Brightwell, Berks, Dio. Ox. 1866. (Patron, Bp of Win; Tithe, 747*l*; Glebe, 80 acres; R.'s Inc. 1200*l* and Ho; Pop. 703.) Formerly C. of Limpsfield 1847, Lingfield 1850; P. C. of Crowhurst 1850, all in Surrey; R. of Millbrook, Hants, 1855–66. [2]

STEWART, John, 2, *Claremont Cottage, Upper Grange-road, Bermondsey, S.E.*—Dub. A.B. 1847; Deac. 1848 and Pr. 1849 by Bp of Down and Connor. C. of Bermondsey, Surrey, 1859. [3]

STEWART, John, *The Rectory, West Derby, near Liverpool*—St. John's Coll. Cam. Sen. Opt. and B.A. 1844, M.A. 1847; Deac. 1844 and Pr. 1846 by Bp of Lin. R. of West Derby, Dio. Ches. 1846. (Patron, John Stewart, Esq; Tithe, App. 458*l*; R.'s Inc. 1300*l*; Pop. 31,528.) Rural Dean. Formerly C. of Coddington and Langford, Notts, 1844. [4]

STEWART, John Sinclair, *Stoke-by-Nayland, Colchester.*—Wad. Coll. Ox. B.A. 1858, M.A. 1862; Deac. 1862 and Pr. 1863 by Abp of Cant. C. of Stoke-by-Nayland. Formerly C. of Ashford, Kent, 1862–64. [5]

STEWART, John Vanderstegen, *Portsea Vicarage House, Hants.*—Jesus Coll. Cam. LL.B. 1823; Deac. 1820, Pr. 1821. V. of Portsea, Dio. Win. 1838. (Patron, St. Mary's Coll. Winchester; Tithe—App. 1234*l* 13*s*, V. 272*l* 17*s*; Glebe, 14 acres; V.'s Inc. 656*l* and Ho; Pop. 16,050.) [6]

STEWART, Richard Benson, *Hale, Warrington.*—Caius Coll. Cam 4th Sen. Opt. B.A. 1851, M.A. 1854; Deac. 1852 and Pr. 1853 by Bp of Lin. P. C. of Hale, Dio. Ches. 1857. (Patron, J. Ireland Blackburne, Esq; Tithe, 9*l*; Glebe, 95*l*; P. C.'s Inc. 110*l* and Ho; Pop. 1050.) [7]

STEWART, Thomas Inglis, *Landscove Parsonage, Ashburton, Devon.*—Ex. Coll. Ox. B.A. 1829, M.A. 1832; Deac. 1830, Pr. 1835. P. C. of Landscove, Dio. Ex. 1853. (Patron, V. of Staverton; P. C.'s Inc. 100*l* and Ho; Pop. 399.) [8]

STILES, Robert Canning, *Feltlay Parsonage, Dorking.*—Brasen. Coll. Ox. B.A. 1835, M.A. 1838; Deac. 1857 and Pr. 1858 by Bp of G. and B. C. of Shere, near Guildford, 1864. Formerly C. of Woodchester, near Stroud, 1857, Mere, Wilts, 1859, Wapley with Codrington, Glouc. 1859, Frampton Cotterell 1861. [9]

STILLINGFLEET, Henry James William, *Clehonger, near Hereford.*—Brasen. Coll. Ox. 2nd cl. Lit. Hum. B.A. 1848, M.A. 1850; Deac. 1851, Pr. 1853. C. of Clehonger 1859. Formerly C. of Wantage 1851. [10]

STIMSON, John Henry, *Weedon, Northants.*—Caius Coll. Cam; Deac. 1830 and Pr. 1831 by Bp of Nor. Chap. to the Garrison, and to the District Military Prison, Weedon, 1857. Formerly Chap. of Fort Clarence and Fort Pitt, Chatham, 1847–57. [11]

STIRLING, Charles, *Coombe, Surrey, S.W.*—Ex. Coll. Ox. B.A. 1849; Deac. 1851 and Pr. 1852 by Abp of Cant. P. C. of Ch. Ch. New Malden, Surrey, Dio. Win. 1867. (Patrons, Trustees; P. C.'s Inc. 180*l*; Pop. 1200.) Formerly C. of Hadlow, Kent, 1851–53; St. Mary's Chapel, Reading, 1853–55; nine years (1855–64) Mast. of a Private Sch. Reading, and occasional Preacher in Reading and the neighbourhood. [12]

STIRLING, Waite Hockin, *Keppel Island, West Falklands.*—Ex. Coll. Ox. 4th cl. Lit. Hum. and B.A. 1851; Deac. 1852 and Pr. 1853 by Bp of Lin. Superintendent Miss. at Terra del Fuego of the South American Missionary Soc. Formerly C. of St. Mary's, Nottingham; Sec. of the South-American Missionary Soc. Joint-Author, *The Story of Commander Allen Gardiner, R.N. with Sketches of Missionary Work in South America*, Nisbet, 1867, 2s. [13]

STOBART, Henry, *Warkton Rectory, Kettering.*—Queen's Coll. Ox. B.A. 1847, M.A. 1848; Deac. 1849 and Pr. 1852 by Bp of Ox. R. of Warkton, Dio. Pet. 1866. (Patron, Duke of Buccleuch; Glebe, 248 acres; R.'s Inc. 410*l* and Ho; Pop. 315.) Formerly C. of Burton Agnes, Yorks, 1849–51, St. Mark's, Gloucester, 1858–59, Salehurst, Sussex, 1860–63, Colton 1864. Author, *Daily Services for Christian Households*, 1861, 1*s* 6*d*; republished by S.P.C.K. 1867. [14]

STOBART, William James, *Trinity-square, Southwark, S.*—St. John's Coll. Cam. Sen. Opt. M.A. 1867; Deac. 1865 and Pr. 1866 by Bp of Lon. C. of Trinity, Newington, Surrey, 1865. [15]

STOCK, Edward Peche, *Windermere Rectory, Westmoreland.*—St. John's Coll. Cam. B.A. 1851, M.A. 1854; Deac. 1851 and Pr. 1854 by Bp of Man. R. of Windermere, Dio. Carl. 1857. (Patron, Gen. Le Fleming; Tithe, 87*l*; R.'s Inc. 300*l* and Ho; Pop. 1752.) Surrogate. Formerly C. of Radcliffe, near Manchester, 1854–57. [16]

STOCK, James, *Ventnor-terrace, Lincoln.*—Dub. Hebrew Prizeman, B.A. 1847; Deac. 1847, Pr. 1848. P. C. of Greetwell, City and Dio. Lin. 1860. (Patrons, D. and C. of Lin; P. C.'s Inc. 49*l*; Pop. 60.) Chap. to the Co. Hospital, Lincoln; Chap. to the City Gaol Lincoln. [17]

STOCK, John, 1, *Earl's-terrace, Kensington, London, W.*—St. John's Coll. Cam. B.A. 1815; Deac. and Pr. 1816 by Abp of Cant. Formerly V. of Finchingfield, Essex. Author, *Sermons*, 1841. [18]

STOCK, John, *Chorley, Lancashire.*—Corpus Coll. Cam. B.A. 1846, M.A 1850. P. C. of St. George's, Chorley, Dio. Man. 1850. (Patron, R. of Chorley; P. C.'s Inc. 175*l*; Pop. 9619.) [19]

STOCK, John Russell, 35, *Woburn-place, London, W.C.*—St. John's Coll. Cam. B.A. 1841, M.A. 1844; Deac. 1841 and Pr. 1842 by Bp of Lon. R. of Allhallows the Great with Allhallows the Less, City and Dio. Lon. 1860. (Patron, Abp of Cant; R.'s Inc. 520*l*; Pop. 400.) Sec. to the Clergy Orphan Corporation. Formerly P. C. of St. John's, Finchingfield, 1841–49; P. C. of All Saints', Islington, 1849–53; V. of Finchingfield, Essex, 1853–60. [20]

STOCKDALE, Frederick Septimus, *Havenstreet, near Ryde.*—Emman. Coll. Cam. B.A. 1851; Deac. 1851 and Pr. 1852 by Bp of Wor. P. C. of St. Peter's, Havenstreet, Dio. Win. 1863. (Patron, Rev. F. Kent; P. C.'s Inc. 42*l*; Pop. 394.) Formerly C. of St. John's, Coventry, 1851–53, Alkborough, Lincolnshire, 1853–63. [21]

STOCKDALE, Henry, *Bole, Gainsborough.*—St. Cath. Coll. Cam. B.A. 1841; Deac. 1841 and Pr. 1842 by Bp of Lin. V. of Bole, Dio. Lin. 1858. (Patron, Bp of Lin; Tithe, 125*l*; V.'s Inc. 192*l* 10*s* and Ho; Pop. 230.) Surrogate; Dioc. Inspector of Schs. Formerly P. C. of Misterton, Notts, 1843–58. [22]

STOCKDALE, Jeremiah, *Baslow Parsonage, Bakewell, Derbyshire.*—St. Cath. Hall, Cam. Jun. Opt. and B.A. 1853; Deac. 1853, Pr. 1854. P. C. of Baslow, Dio. Lich. 1859. (Patron, Duke of Devonshire; P. C.'s Inc. 140*l* and Ho; Pop. 2366.) Formerly C. of St. George's, Birmingham, 1853–56; P. C. of St. Matthias', Birmingham, 1856–59. [23]

STOCKDALE, Joseph, *Kingerby Vicarage, Market-Rasen, Lincolnshire.*—Corpus Coll. Cam. B.A. 1807, M.A. 1811; Deac. 1807, Pr. 1808. V. of Kingerby, Dio. Lin. 1811. (Tithe—Imp. 20*l* 14*s* 10*d*, V. 295*l*; Glebe, 10 acres; V.'s Inc. 315*l* and Ho; Pop. 108.) R. of Tetford, Linc. Dio. Lin. 1820. (Patron, Sir M. J. Cholmeley; Land in lieu of Tithe, 309 acres; R.'s Inc. 423*l*; Pop. 793.) Rural Dean of Walscroft 1829, and J. P. [24]

STOCKDALE, Walter, *Morton Vicarage, Bourne, Lincolnshire.*—Trin. Coll. Cam. Jun. Opt. 2nd cl Cl. Trip. and B.A. 1833, M A. 1845; Deac. 1833 and Pr. 1834 by Bp of Lin. V. of Morton with Haceonby, Dio. Lin. 1862. (Patron, Bp of Lin; Land in lieu of Tithe, 209 acres; Glebe, 10 acres; V.'s Inc. 440*l* and Ho; Pop. 1416.) Formerly C. of Linwood, 1835–61; V. of North Willingham 1847–62; Rural Dean 1857–62. [25]

STOCKDALE, William Walter, *Wytchling Rectory, Sittingbourne, Kent.*—Lampeter; Deac. 1846 and

Pr. 1847 by Bp of St. D. R. of Wytchling, Kent, Dio. Cant. 1855. (Patron, H. M. Stockdale, Esq; Tithe, 277*l* 15*s*; Glebe, 27 acres; R.'s Inc. 320*l*; Pop. 147.) [1]

STOCKEN, William Frederick, *Middlesex House of Correction, Cold Bath Fields, W.C.*—Ex. Coll. Ox. B.A. 1856, M.A. 1858; Deac. 1857 and Pr. 1858 by Bp of Lin. Asst. Chap. to Middlesex House of Correction 1866. Formerly C. of Beeston, Notts, 1857, Skirbeck, Lincolnshire, 1860, Kensington 1863. [2]

STOCKER, Charles William, *Draycot Rectory, Cheadle, Staffs.*—St. John's Coll. Ox. 1812, 1st cl. Lit. Hum. 2nd cl. Math. et Phy. and B.A. 1816, M.A. 1820, B.D. and D.D. 1831; Deac. 1816 and Pr. 1817 by Bp of Ox. R. of Draycot-le-Moors, Dio. Lich. 1841. (Patron, Sir E. Vavasour, Bart; Tithe, 423*l* 6*s* 3*d*, Glebe 47 acres; R.'s Inc. 533*l* and Ho; Pop. 451.) Rural Dean of Cheadle 1848; President of the Cheadle Association for Promoting Church Music. Formerly Fell. of St. John's Coll. Ox. 1815; Tut. 1821; Mast. of the Schools 1821; Public Examiner 1823, and again in 1832; Prin. of Elizabeth Coll. Guernsey 1824–29; Vice-Prin. of St. Alban Hall, Ox. 1832–36; Select Preacher 1832; Prof. of Moral Philosophy 1841. Author, *Ode on the Assassination of Right Hon. Spencer Percival*, 1812; *Alma Mater and the Stagyrite*, 1820; *Four Sections*; *Select Passages of Letters and Speeches*, 1832; *Conversations on the Lord's Supper*, 1834, 1*s*; *The Minister of God* (an Assize Sermon), 1836, 1*s* 6*d*. Editor of *Herodotus*; *The Persian Wars*, 2 vols. 1831, 2nd ed. 1843; *Juvenal and Persius*, 1835, '39, '45; *T. Livius* (1st *Decade*), 2 vols. 1846; *T. Livius* (3rd *Decade*), 2 vols. 1838; *Handbook of Twenty-one Tunes for Peculiar Metres, in Four Parts, for the Use of Congregations*, 1856. [3]

STOCKER, Edward Seymour, *Titchwell Rectory, Lynn, Norfolk.*—Dur. B.A. 1850, M.A. 1858; Deac. 1852 and Pr. 1853 by Bp of Ox. R. of Titchwell, Dio. Nor. 1859. (Patron, Eton Coll; Tithe, 413*l*; Glebe, 20 acres; R.'s Inc. 450*l* and Ho; Pop. 146.) Formerly C. of Henley-on-Thames 1852–54; Asst. Chap. to the English Congregation at Rome 1854–59; Fell. of Univ. of Dur. [4]

STOCKER, William Henry Browell, *Horsforth Parsonage, Leeds.*—St. John's Coll. Ox. 2nd cl. Math. and B.A. 1830; Deac. 1833 by Bp of B. and W. Pr. 1834 by Abp of York. P. C. of Horsforth, Dio. Rip. 1837. (Patron, John Spencer Stanhope, Esq; P. C.'s Inc. 155*l* and Ho; Pop. 2671.) [5]

STOCKHAM, John Henry, *Nether Exe, Devon.*—P. C. of Nether Exe, Dio. Ex. 1856. (Patrons, Eight Feoffees; P. C.'s Inc. 68*l*; Pop. 78.) [6]

STOCKS, Samuel Henry, *Shepton Beauchamp, near Ilminster.*—St. Alban Hall, Ox. 4th cl. Lit. Hum. B.A. 1863, M.A. 1867; Deac. 1864 and Pr. 1865 by Bp of Rip. C. of Shepton Beauchamp and Barrington 1866. Formerly C of Penistone, Yorks, 1864–66. [7]

STOCKS, William, *Rishton, Blackburn.*—St. Bees; Deac. 1862 and Pr. 1863 by Bp of Man. C. of Great Harwood 1866. Formerly C. of St. Leonard's, Padiham, 1862–66. Author, *On Amusements, and their Influence upon the People*, 1848, 1*s*. [8]

STOCKWELL, Joseph Samuel, *Wylye Rectory, Heytesbury, Wilts.*—Deac. 1821 and Pr. 1822 by Bp of Salis. R. of Wylye, Dio. Salis. 1840. (Patron, Earl of Pembroke; Glebe, 7 acres; R.'s Inc. 492*l* and Ho; Pop. 489.) [9]

STODDART, Robert Wilson, *Hundon Vicarage, Haverhill, Suffolk.*—Jesus Coll. Cam. Prizeman 1830 and 1831, 4th Sen. Opt. and B.A. 1833, M.A. 1836; Deac. 1833 and Pr. 1834 by Bp of Wor. V. of Hundon, Dio. Ely, 1839. (Patron, Jesus Coll. Cam; Tithe—Imp. 685*l* 5*s* 10*d*, V. 216*l* 13*s* 5*d*; Glebe, 20 acres; V.'s Inc. 236*l* and Ho; Pop. 1132.) Author, *Sermons*. [10]

STODDEN, H. T., *Colnbrook, Bucks.*—C. of Colnbrook. [11]

STOGDON, Abraham Horvill, *Ovington Rectory, Alresford, Hants.*—Trin. Coll. Cam. B.A. 1840, M.A. 1847; Deac. 1839 and Pr. 1840 by Bp of Lich. R. of Ovington, Dio. Win. 1852. (Patron, Bp of Win; Tithe, 7*l* 7*s*; Glebe, 240 acres; R.'s Inc. 207*l* and Ho; Pop. 152.) Surrogate. [12]

STOKER, Henry, *Pittington Vicarage, Durham.*—Univ. Coll. Dur. 3rd cl. Lit. Hum. 4th cl. Math. et Phy. and B.A. 1837, 1st cl. Lit. Hum. and M.A. 1838; Deac. and Pr. 1841 by Bp of Dur. V. of Pittington, Dio. Dur. 1862. (Patrons, D. and C. of Dur; Tithe, 571*l*; Glebe, 52 acres; V.'s Inc. 620*l* and Ho; Pop. 3209.) Formerly C. of Shincliffe, Durham; 2nd Mast. of Dur. Gr. Sch. 1840; Fell. of Univ. Dur. [13]

STOKES, George, *St. Stephen's Rectory, Ipswich.*—Deac. 1848 and Pr. 1849 by Abp of York. R of St. Stephen's, Ipswich, Dio. Nor. 1855. (Patron, Ch. Patronage Soc; Tithe, 1*l* 11*s*; R.'s Inc. 150*l* and Ho; Pop. 679.) [14]

STOKES, George, *Hope, Hanley, Staffs.*—P. C. of Hope, Dio. Lich. 1864. (Patrons, Crown and Bp of Lich. alt; P. C.'s Inc. 200*l*; Pop. 4380.) [15]

STOKES, Henry John, *Grindon Rectory, Leek, Staffs.*—St. John's Coll. Cam. B.A. 1843; Deac. 1844 and Pr. 1845 by Bp of Lich. R. of Grindon, Dio. Lich. 1847. (Patroness, Mrs. Bradshaw; Tithe, 365*l*; Glebe, 22 acres; R.'s Inc. 410*l* and Ho; Pop. 371.) [16]

STOKES, Hudleston, *Bembridge, Ryde, Isle of Wight.*—Caius Coll. Cam. 2nd cl. Cl. Trip. 3rd cl. Math; Deac. 1854 and Pr. 1856 by Bp of Win. C. of Bembridge 1861. [17]

STOKES, Oliver William, 122, *Mount Pleasant, Liverpool.*—Dub. A.B. 1863, A.M. 1867; Deac. 1866 by Bp of Ches. C. of St. Andrew's, Liverpool, 1866. [18]

STOKES, William Haughton, *Denver Rectory, Downham-Market, Norfolk.*—Caius Coll. Cam. B.A. 1828, M.A. 1831. R. of Denver, Dio. Nor. 1852. (Patron, Caius Coll. Cam; Tithe, 862*l* 1*s* 11*d*; Glebe, 92 acres; R.'s Inc. 1002*l* and Ho; Pop. 932.) Formerly Fell. of Caius Coll. Cam. [19]

STOKES, W. H., *Goring Vicarage, Reading.*—V. of Goring, Dio. Ox. 1851. (Patron, S. W. Gardiner, Esq; V.'s Inc. 146*l* and Ho; Pop. 535.) [20]

STOKOE, Thomas Henry, *Richmond, Yorks.*—Lin. Coll. Ox. 1st cl. Lit. Hum. 1855, Denyer Theol. Prize 1859, B.A. 1855, M.A. 1857; Deac. 1857 and Pr. 1858 by Abp of York. Head Mast. of Richmond Gr. Sch. (Salary, 250*l*.) P. C. of Trinity, Richmond, Dio. Rip. 1865. (Patron, L. Cooke, Esq; P. C.'s Inc. 120*l*.) Formerly 2nd Mast. of Clifton Coll. 1862–63. Author, *On the Use and Abuse of the Proverb, "Charity begins at Home"* (Denyer Theol. Essay), 1859. [21]

STOLTERFORTH, C. A.—C. of St. Simon and St. Jude's, Manchester. [22]

STONE, Arthur, *Dum Dum, Calcutta.*—New Inn Hall, Ox. B.A. 1850, M.A. 1853. Chap. at Dum Dum. [23]

STONE, Edward Daniel, *Eton College, Windsor.* King's Coll. Cam. M.A. Asst. Mast. in Eton Coll. [24]

STONE, Henry, *Mount Hawke, Truro.*—P. C. of Mount Hawke, Dio. Ex. 1862. (Patrons, Crown and Bp of Ex. alt; P. C.'s Inc. 130*l*; Pop. 2226.) Formerly P. C. of Cury and Gunwalloe. [25]

STONE, John, *Headcorn, Staplehurst, Kent.*—C. of Headcorn. [26]

STONE, Josiah, *Brierley hill, Staffs.*—Jesus Coll. Cam. Sen. Opt. and B.A. 1851; Deac. 1852 and Pr. 1854 by Bp of Lich. R. of Brierley-hill, Dio. Lich. 1867. (Patron, R. of Kingswinford; Tithe, 150*l*; R.'s Inc. 386*l* and Ho; Pop. 10,700.) Formerly C. of Willington, Derbyshire, 1852–53, Christ Church, Coseley, 1854–60, Coseley 1860–67. [27]

STONE, Meade Nisbett, *Coffinswell Vicarage, Newton Abbott, Devon.*—Dub. A.B. 1833, A.M. 1836; Deac. 1838 by Bp of Down and Connor, Pr. 1839 by Abp of Dub. C. in sole charge of Coffinswell 1867. Formerly C. of Miltown, Dublin, 1838–44; Chap. to the H.E.I.C. on the Madras Establishment 1844–62; C. of Churchdown, Gloucester, 1862–64, Acaster-Malbis, York, 1864–67. [28]

STONE, Samuel John, *Windsor.*—Pemb. Coll. Ox. B.A. 1862; Deac. 1862 and Pr. 1863 by Bp of Ox. C. of Windsor 1862. Author, *Lyra Fidelium, or Twelve*

Hymns on Twelve Articles of the Apostles' Creed, Parkers. 2s 6d; *Sinai* (Prize Poem), Mitchell, 2s; etc. [1]

STONE, William, *Cathedral Precincts, Canterbury.*—Brasen. Coll. Ox. 1st cl. Lit. Hum. and B.A. 1822, M.A. 1825; Deac. and Pr. 1825 by Bp of Ox. Can. Res. of Canterbury Cathl. 1853. (Patron, the Crown; Value, 800*l* and Res.) Formerly Fell. of Brasen. Coll. Ox. 1822–30; R. of Ch. Ch. Spitalfields, 1829–56; one of the Examiners of Candidates for Admission to the E. I. Coll. Haileybury, 1841–56; R. of St. George-the-Martyr's with St. Mary Magdalene's, Canterbury, 1858–66. Author, *The Affectionate Character of the Pastoral Relation* (Visitation Sermon, preached at St. Paul's Cathl. 1838); other Sermons, and occasional Publications. [2]

STONE, William, 17, *Pembury-road, Hackney, London, N.E.*—Wad. Coll. Ox. 2nd cl. Lit. Hum. and 3rd cl. Math. and B.A. 1833, M.A. 1835; Deac. 1834, Pr. 1836. P. C. of St. Paul's, Haggerston, Dio. Lon. 1858. (Patron, Bp of Lon; P. C.'s Inc. 120*l*.) Formerly P. C. of Butterton-in-Trentham, Staffs, 1844–58; Chap. to the Refuge for the Destitute, Dalston, 1852–58. Author, *Exposition of the Church Catechism, Festivals, Feasts, &c.*, 1840; *Address to Sponsors*, 1841; *Course of Truth*, 1842; *A Visitation Sermon*, 1844; *Shadows of the New Creation*, 1849; *Manual of Confirmation*, 1858. [3]

STONEHAM, Thompson, *Ketley Parsonage, Wellington, Salop.*—St. Peter's Coll. Cam. Theol. Prizeman 1833, B.A. 1834, M.A. 1840; Deac. 1835 and Pr. 1836 by Bp of Lich. P. C. of Ketley, Dio. Lich. 1838. (Patron, Duke of Sutherland; Tithe—App. 31*l*, Imp. 92*l*; Glebe, 10½ acres; P. C.'s Inc. 168*l* and Ho; Pop. 2000.) [4]

STONES, Wilson, *Moss-side, Manchester.*—St. Aidan's; Deac. 1862 and Pr. 1863 by Bp of Ches. C. of St. Paul's, Hulme, 1864. Formerly C. of All Saints', Liverpool, 1862–64. [5]

STONEY, Edward Sadleir, *Wrea, Kirkham, Lancashire.*—Dub. A.B. 1854, A.M. 1857; *ad eund.* Ox. M.A. 1859; Deac. 1855 and Pr. 1856 by Bp of Cashel. P. C. of Ribby with Rea P. C. Dio. Man. 1866. (Patron, V. of Kirkham; P. C.'s Inc. 120*l* and Ho; Pop. 918.) [6]

STONEY, Robert Baker, *Loughborough.*—Dub. A.B. 1851, A.M. 1865; Deac. 1851 by Bp of Tuam, Pr. 1852 by Bp of Meath. C. of All Saints', Loughborough, 1863. Formerly C. of Bloxwich, Staffs, 1860, St. Paul's, Wolverhampton. 1861. Author, *Church Music in Tonic Solfa Type*, 1858. [7]

STONHOUSE, Arthur, *The Vicarage, Walford, Ross, Herefordshire.*—Wad. Coll. Ox. B.A. 1832; Deac. 1832 and Pr. 1834 by Bp of Salis. V. of Walford 1842. (Patron, Bp of Wor; V.'s Inc. 242*l* and Ho; Pop. 817.) [8]

STONHOUSE, Charles, *Frimley Rectory, Bagshot, Surrey.*—Dur; Deac. 1851 and Pr. 1852 by Bp of Wor. R. of Frimley, Dio. Win. 1852. (Patron, R. of Ash; Tithe, 225*l*; R.'s Inc. 240*l* and Ho; Pop. 1276.) [9]

STONHOUSE, Frederick, *Kenilworth, Warwickshire.*—Oriel Coll. Ox B.A. 1838; Deac. 1840 and Pr. 1841. R. of Honily, near Kenilworth, Dio. Wor. 1854. (Patroness, Mrs. Willes; Tithe, 167*l*; R.'s Inc. 150*l*; Pop. 63.) [10]

STOOKS, Thomas Fraser, *Highgate, Middlesex, N.*—Trin. Coll. Cam. B.A. 1837, M.A. 1845; Deac. 1841 and Pr. 1842 by Bp of Lon. P. C. of St. Anne's, Brookfield, Highgate-rise, St. Pancras, Dio. Lon. 1853. (Patron, Bp of Lon; P. C.'s Inc. 320*l*; Pop. 491.) Preb. of St. Paul's 1863; Hon. Sec. to the London Diocesan Church Building Soc. 1854. [11]

STOPFORD, Arthur Fanshawe, *Hamerton, Huntingdon.*—Ball. Coll. Ox. B.A. 1844, All Souls' Coll. M.A. 1848; Deac. 1845 and Pr. 1846 by Bp of Ox. R. of Hamerton, Dio. Ely, 1850. (Patron, S. Barry, Esq; Tithe, 435*l*; Glebe, 47 acres; R.'s Inc. 495*l*; Pop. 167.) Formerly Fell. of All Souls' Coll. Ox. Editor of *Sermons to a Country Parish.* [12]

STOPFORD, Frederick Manners, *Tichmarsh Rectory, Thrapstone.*—Ch. Ch. Ox. B.A. 1854; Deac. 1855 and Pr. 1856 by Bp of Pet. Deac. of the Cathl. Ch. Peterborough. (Value, 80*l*.) R. of Tichmarsh, Dio. Pet. 1861. (Patron, Lord Lilford; R.'s Inc. 782*l* and Ho; Pop. 893.) Formerly Chap. to the Peterborough Union. [13]

STOPFORD, George Powys, *Barton-Seagrave, Kettering, Northants.*—Ch. Ch. and All Souls' Coll. Ox. B.A. 1823, M.A. 1825; Deac. 1825 and Pr. 1826 by Bp of Ox. R. of Barton-Seagrave, Dio. Pet. 1864. (Patron, Duke of Buccleugh; Tithe, 492*l*; Glebe, 60 acres; R.'s Inc. 515*l* and Ho; Pop. 199.) [14]

STORER, Thomas, *Northampton.*—St. John's Coll. Cam. B.A. 1829; Deac. 1829, Pr. 1831. P. C. of St. Andrew's, Northampton, Dio. Pet. 1843. (Patrons, Hyndman's Trustees; P. C.'s Inc. 86*l*; Pop. 5681.) [15]

STORK, J. H., *Bigby, Brigg, Lincolnshire.*—C. of Bigby. [16]

STORR, C., *Chilham, Canterbury.*—C. of Chilham. [17]

STORR, Francis, *Brenchley Vicarage, Cranbrook.*—Queen's Coll. Ox. 4th cl. Lit. Hum. M.A. 1834; Deac. and Pr. 1833. V. of Brenchley, Dio. Cant. 1854. (Patron, G. C. Courthorpe, Esq; Tithe—Imp. 732*l* 7*s*, V. 950*l*; Glebe, 6 acres; V.'s Inc. 980*l* and Ho; Pop. 2129.) Formerly R. of Otley, Suffolk, 1836; V. of Acton, Cheshire, 1846. Author, *Scripture Characters*, 3s 6d; *The Christian Farmer*, 1855, 1s; Large Type Tracts for the Parish; Tracts for Confirmation, &c. [18]

STORRS, Henry John, *Pishill Parsonage, Henley-on-Thames.*—St. Cath. Coll. Cam. 18th Sen. Opt. Math. Trip. and B.A. 1862; Deac. 1862 and Pr. 1864 by Bp of Ox. P. C. of Pishill, Dio. Ox. 1866. (Patron, Rev. C. E. R. Keene; P. C.'s Inc. 100*l* and Ho; Pop. 14.) Formerly C. of St. John's, Reading, 1862. [19]

STORY, George Jonathan.—King's Coll. Lond. Theol. Assoc. 1853; Deac. 1853 and Pr. 1856 by Bp of Man. C. of St. Anne's, Soho, Westminster. Formerly C. of St. Mary, Redcliff, Bristol, Farnworth, near Manchester, St. Paul's Mission Coll. Lond. and St. James's, Enfield, Middlesex. [20]

STORY, Philip William, *Fawsley Vicarage, Daventry, Northants.*—Ch. Ch. Ox. B.A. 1840; Deac. 1841 and Pr. 1842 by Bp of Pet. V. of Fawsley, Dio. Pet. 1853. (Patron, Sir C. Knightley, Bart; Tithe, 5*l*; V.'s Inc. 105*l* and Ho; Pop. 64.) Formerly C. of Charlwelton, near Daventry. [21]

STOTHERT, Samuel Kelson.—Wor. Coll. Ox. B.A. 1849, M.A. 1856; Glasgow Univ. LL.D. 1858; Deac. 1851 and Pr. 1852 by Bp of Ox. Chap. of H.M.S. "Victoria." Formerly with Naval Brigade at Sebastopol, and Projector and 1st Min. of St. Andrew's, Constantinople. Author, *Short History of Woodspring Priory*; etc. [22]

STOTHERT, William, *Thorpe Hesley, Rotherham.*—St. John's Coll. Cam. B.A. 1832; Deac. 1835, Pr. 1836. P. C. of Thorpe Hesley, Dio. York, 1865. (Patrons, Trustees; P. C.'s Inc. 200*l* and Ho; Pop. 1966.) Formerly P. C. of Forest Chapel with Wildboarclough, Cheshire, 1855–56; P. C. of Emmanuel, Bolton, 1856–65. Author, *Plain Reasons for adhering to the Church of England, by Philalethes*, 1s. [23]

STOTT, E. Nicholson, *Middleton, Chirbury, Salop.*—P. C. of Middleton, Dio. Herf. 1863. (Patron, V. of Chirbury; P. C.'s Inc. 80*l*; Pop. 740.) [24]

STOTT, George, *Worcester College, Oxford.*—Wor. Coll. Ox. 3rd cl. Lit. Hum. and B.A. 1837, M.A. 1840. Fell. of Wor. Coll. Ox. [25]

STOTT, John, *Rawtenstall, Whalley, Lancashire.*—C. of Rawtenstall. [26]

STOVIN, Charles Frederick, *Cobham, Surrey.* [27]

STOWE, Henry, *West Smethwick Parsonage, Birmingham.*—St. Bees; Deac. 1851 and Pr. 1852 by Bp of Man. P. C. of St. Paul's, West Smethwick, Dio. Lich. 1864. (Patrons, five Trustees; P. C.'s Inc. 140*l* and Ho; Pop. 3200.) Formerly C. of Oswaldtwistle 1851; P. C. of St. Mary's, Mellor, 1852. [28]

STOWELL, Hugh Ashworth, *Breadsall Rectory, Derby.*—Brasen. Coll. Ox. B.A. 1852, M.A. 1855; Deac. 1853 and Pr. 1854 by Abp of Cant. R. of Breadsall, Dio. Lich. 1865. (Patron, Sir John Harpur Crewe, Bart; Glebe, 455 acres; R.'s Inc. 680*l* and Ho; Pop. 591.) Formerly C. of Luddenham, Kent, 1853–57; P. C. of Ch. Ch. Maughold, Isle of Man, 1858–63; P. C. of Warslow and Elkstone, Staffs, 1863–65. Author, various papers on Natural History in the *Zoologist*, *Phytologist*, *Leisure Hour*; etc. [1]

STOWELL, John Gruner, *Clifton-villas, Swinbourne-grove, Withington, Manchester.*—Dub. A.B. 1858; Deac. 1858 and Pr. 1860 by Bp of Man. Chap. to the Chorlton Union Workhouse 1867. Formerly C. of St. Peter's, Oldham-road, Manchester, 1858, and of Farnworth; Min. of the Episcopal Chapel, Stockport Moor. [2]

STOWELL, John La Mothe, *Peel, Isle of Man.*—Queen's Coll. Ox. B.A. 1825; Deac. 1825 by Bp of Ox. Pr. 1825 by Bp of Dur. V. of St. German's, Isle of Man, Dio. S. and M. 1839. (Patron, Bp of S. and M; Tithe, 140*l*; Glebe, 31 acres; V.'s Inc. 200*l* and Ho; Pop. 4772.) [3]

STOWELL, Thomas Alfred, *Adelphi, Salford.*—Queen's Coll. Ox. B.A. 1855, M.A. 1856; Deac. 1857 and Pr. 1858 by Bp of Rip. R. of Ch. Ch Salford, Dio. Man. 1865. (Patrons, Five Trustees; R.'s Inc. 600*l*; Pop. 9414.) Formerly C. of Bolton, Calverley, Yorks, 1858–60; P. C. of St. Stephen's, Bowling, Bradford, 1860–65. Author, *Sermon on the Death of the late Rev. Canon Stowell*, Hatchard, 1865, 6*d*. [4]

STOWERS, Henry Mellish, *Wood Walton, Peterborough.*—St. Edm. Hall, Ox. B.A. 1841, M.A. 1844; Deac. 1843 and Pr. 1844 by Bp of G. and B. R. of Wood Walton, Dio. Ely, 1856. (Patron, R. H. Hussey, Esq; Tithe, 534*l* 8*s*; Glebe, 21 acres; R.'s Inc. 564*l*; Pop. 388.) [5]

STRACEY, William James, *Buxton Vicarage, Norfolk.*—Magd. Coll. Cam. B.A. 1843, M.A. 1846; Deac. 1845, Pr. 1846. R. of Oxnead with Skeyton R. and Buxton V. Dio. Nor. 1855. (Patron, Sir Henry Stracey, Bart; Oxnead, Tithe, 180*l*; Skeyton, Tithe, 343*l*; Buxton, Tithe, 110*l* 16*s* 6*d*; Glebe, 95½ acres; R.'s Inc. 789*l* and Ho; Pop. Oxnead 40, Skeyton 341, Buxton 640.) Formerly Norfolk Fell. of Magd. Coll. Cam. [6]

STRANGE, Cresswell, *Hale, near Farnham, Surrey.*—Pemb. Coll. Ox. B.A. 1866; Deac. 1866 and Pr. 1867 by Bp of Win. C. of Hale 1866. [7]

STRANGE, William Alder, *Abingdon, Berks.*—Pemb. Coll. Ox. B.A. 1833, M.A. 1836, B.D. 1843, D D. 1847. Head Mast. of Abingdon Gr. Sch. [8]

STRANGWAYS, Henry Fox, *Cullumpton, Devon.*—Wad. Coll. Ox. B.A. 1849, M.A. 1852; Deac. 1851 and Pr. 1852 by Bp of Ex. R. of Silverton, Dio. Ex. 1866. (Patrons, Earl of Ilchester, 1 turn in 3; Earl of Egremont's Trustees, 2 turns in 3; Tithe, 950*l*; Glebe, 89¼ acres; R.'s Inc. 1200*l* and Ho; Pop. 1260.) Formerly C. of Kea, Cornwall, 1851–53; R. of Kilmington 1853–66. [9]

STRATON, George William, *Aylestone Rectory, near Leicester.*—Corpus Coll. Cam. B.A. 1829; Deac. 1829 and Pr. 1830 by Bp of Lin. R. of Aylestone, Dio. Pet. 1843. (Patron, Duke of Rutland; Tithe, 190*l*; Glebe, 381 acres; R.'s Inc. 845*l* and Ho; Pop. 575.) Surrogate; Chap. to Viscount Powerscourt. [10]

STRATTEN, John Remington, *St. Paul's Parsonage, Park-square, Leeds.*—King's Coll. Lond. Theol. Assoc; Deac. 1848, Pr. 1849. P. C. of St. Paul's, Leeds, Dio. Rip. 1853. (Patron, V. of Leeds; P. C.'s Inc. 150*l* and Ho.) [11]

STRATTON, Freeman Richard, *Laughton, Hurst Green, Sussex.*—Trin. Coll. Cam. Jun. Opt. B.A. 1851, M.A. 1856; Deac. 1851 and Pr. 1853 by Bp of Win. C. of Laughton 1866. Formerly C. of Romsey 1860, Bishopsteignton. [12]

STRATTON, John Young, *Ditton, Maidstone.*—Magd. Coll. Cam. B.A. 1853; Deac. 1853 and Pr. 1855 by Bp of Man. R. of Ditton, Dio. Cant. 1856. (Patron, Earl of Aylesford; Tithe, 452*l*; R.'s Inc. 456*l*; Pop. 255.) [13]

STRATTON, William, *Gressingham, Wray, Lancaster.*—New Coll. Ox. 2nd cl. Law and Mod. Hist. 3rd cl. Lit. Hum. and B.A. 1856; Deac. and Pr. 1857 by Bp of Man. P. C. of Gressingham, Dio. Man. 1857. (Patron, V. of Lancaster; Tithe—Imp. 108*l*, P. C. 25*l* 9*s*; Glebe, 22 acres; P. C.'s Inc. 100*l* and Ho; Pop. 145.) Formerly C. of Capernwray 1857. [14]

STRAWBRIDGE, A., *Clevedon, Somerset.*—C. of Ch. Ch. Clevedon. [15]

STREATFEILD, William Champion, *Howick Rectory, Bitton, Northumberland.*—Trin. Coll. Cam. B.A. 1860, M.A. 1863; Deac. 1863 and Pr. 1864 by Abp of Cant. R. of Howick, Dio. Dur. 1865. (Patron, Bp of Dur; Tithe, 320*l*; Glebe, 3 acres; R.'s Inc. 320*l* and Ho; Pop. 265.) Formerly C. of St. Andrew's, Croydon, 1863, Plaxtol, Kent, 1864–65. [16]

STREET, Arthur Joseph, *Kempley Vicarage, Ledbury*—Queens' Coll. Cam. Scho. of, B.A. 1847; Deac. 1848 and Pr. 1849 by Bp of G. and B. C. of the Sequestrated V. of Kempley 1851. Formerly C. of St. James's, Bristol. [17]

STREET, Benjamin, *Barnet-by-le-Wold Vicarage, Ulceby, Lincolnshire.*—Dub. A.B. 1838; Deac. 1839 and Pr. 1840 by Bp of Lin. V. of Barnet-by-le-Wold, Dio. Lin. 1857. (Patron, Bp of Lin; V.'s Inc. 307*l* and Ho; Pop. 828.) Formerly C. of Grantham. Author, *The Cholera* (Two Sermons), 1849; *The Jubilee of the S.P.G.* 1851; *The Death of the Duke of Wellington*, 1853; *France allied with England*, 1854; *Proper Attitude of a Christian Nation in Time of War* (Sermons), 1854; *Historical Notes on Grantham*, 1857. [18]

STREET, John Chalice, *St. Andrew's Chapelry, Princess-square, Plymouth*—Queens' Coll. Cam. Jun. Opt. and B.A. 1831, M.A. 1845; Deac. 1831 by Bp of Ches. Pr. 1831 by Bp of Lin. P. C. of St. Andrew's Chapel, Plymouth, Dio. Ex. 1845. (Patron, V. of St. Andrew's; P. C.'s Inc. 114*l* and Ho.) Formerly C. of Rampton 1831; Chap. on the Madras Establishment 1832; Dom. Chap to the Bp of Madras 1839. Author, *The Responsibilities of the Ministerial Office* (a Sermon), Madras, 1837; *The Duty of Obedience to Spiritual Rulers* (a Sermon), 1845; *Five Sermons on Confirmation and the Lord's Supper*, 1856. [19]

STREETEN, E. C., *High Littleton, Somerset.*—V. of High Littleton, Dio. B. and W. 1866. (Patron, Rev. H. H. Mogg; V.'s Inc. 120*l* and Ho; Pop. 860.) [20]

STREETER, Charles, *Washington, Durham.*—Deac. 1863, Pr. 1864. C. of Washington 1866. Formerly C. of Crook, Durham. [21]

STREETER, George Thomas Piper, 19, *Wellington-terrace, Lee-park, Lee, Kent, S.E.*—Clare Coll. Cam. 1st Sen. Opt. Math. Trip. 1856, 1st cl. Moral Sci. 1857. B.A. 1856; Deac. 1857 and Pr. 1858 by Bp of Lon. Asst. C. of Bickley, Kent, 1867. Formerly Asst. Mast. of Blackheath Proprietary School 1856–57; C. of Plumstead 1857–64. Author, *What to Read and How to Read it, a Guide to Candidates for the Civil Service*, 1858, 2*s* 6*d*. [22]

STRETCH, Henry, *Clatworthy, Wiveliscombe, Somerset.*—Magd. Hall, Ox. B.A. 1853; Deac. 1850 and Pr. 1851 by Bp of Ox. C. of Clatworthy 1867. Formerly C. of Chastleton 1850–52; Staple-Fitzpaine 1852–62; Huish Champflower 1862–67. [23]

STRETTELL, Alfred Baker, *Genoa.*—Trin. Coll. Cam. B.A. 1841, M.A. 1844. Consular Chap. at Genoa. [24]

STRETTON, Henry, *Royal Grammar School, St. Albans, Herts.*—Magd. Hall, Ox. B.A. 1843, M.A. 1845; Deac. 1843, Pr. 1844. Head Mast. of St. Albans Gram. Sch. 1866. Formerly Asst. C. of St. John's, Westminster, 1843, St. Paul's, Knightsbridge, 1844; C. of Chidcock, Dorset, 1847; P. C. of Hixon, Staffs, 1848; P. C. of St. Mary's, Chiswick, 1852; Prin. of English and Foreign Coll. Highgate, 1858. Author (joint) of *Visitatio Infirmorum, or Offices for the Clergy, &c.* 3 eds. 1848, 16*s*; *The Acts of St. Mary Magdalene*, 1848, 7*s* 6*d*; *Church Hymns*, 1850, 1*s*; *First Truths*, 2 eds. 1850, 1*d*; *Poor Churchman's Friend*, 1851, 6*d*; *Guide to the Infirm, Sick and Dying Members of the Church of England*, 1852, 5*s* 6*d*; *Child's Catechism*, 1853, 1*d*; *The Church Catechism Explained and Annotated, for Catechising in Churches*, 1*s*; *The Church Catechism Ex-*

plained for the Use of Young Persons, 1855, 2*d*; *A Short Spelling Course*, Nat. Soc. 1½*d*, 1854; *Spelling Exercises*, 6*d*; *Scholar's Manual of Devotions and Sacred Formularies*, 2*d*; *Brief Catechism of Scripture History*, 6*d*; *Collects explained in a Catechetical Form*, Part I. 4*d*, 1858; Part II. 6*d*, 1849; *The Church Catechism Explained, &c.* Part II; *The Creed*, 4*s*. [1]

STRICKLAND, Emmanuel, *Brixton-Deverill Rectory, Warminster, Wilts.*—Queens' Coll. Cam. B.A. 1835, M.A. 1838; Deac. 1836 by Bp. of Ches. Pr. 1836 by Abp of York. R. of Brixton Deverill, Dio. Salis. 1858. (Patron, Bp. of Salis; R.'s Inc. 500*l* and Ho; Pop. 225.) Chap. to Marquis of Bath 1858. Formerly P. C. of Horningsham, Wilts, 1848–58. Author, *Death of the late Mrs. Barnes* (a Funeral Sermon), 1842, 1*s*; *Heresy and Schism, What are they?* 1844, 2*s* 6*d*; *The Effect of Sloth and the Fruit of Diligence* (a Sermon), 1845, 6*d*; Essays in *Church of England Magazine*—*The Providence of God*; *The Character of Moses*; *Definitions of Religious Terms*; *The Authority of a Parochial Minister, and its Extent*; *Examination of the Supper, John xiii*; *Baptism*; *Religious Perfection*; *A Sermon on Confirmation*; *The External and Internal Authority of the Apocrypha*; *A Visitation Sermon on the Blessings of God's Ministry in the Church*; *Explanation of the Phrase "That it might be fulfilled;" The Guide of Controversies*; Sermons and Letters in *Church Magazine*; *Trimming the Lamp*, S.P.C.K. 1861; *The Australian Pastor*, 1862, 1*s* 6*d*. [2]

STRICKLAND, John, *St. Jude's Parsonage, Whitechapel, London, E.*—P. C. of St. Jude's, Dio. Lon. 1864. (Patron, Bp of Lon; P. C.'s Inc. 44*l* and Ho; Pop. 6652.) Formerly of the London Diocesan Home Mission. [3]

STRICKLAND, Nathaniel Constantine, *Reighton Vicarage, Bridlington, Yorks.*—Lin. Coll. Ox B.A. 1829, M.A. 1830. V. of Reighton, Dio. York, 1835. (Patron, Sir G. Strickland, Bart; Tithe—Imp. 14*l*, V. 7*l*; V.'s Inc. 178*l* and Ho; Pop. 251.) P. C of Bessingby, near Bridlington, Dio. York. (Patron, H. Hudson, Esq; P. C.'s Inc. 60*l*; Pop. 70.) [4]

STRICKLAND, William Edmund, 24, *Bank street, Carlisle.*—Dub. A.B. 1866; Deac. 1867. C. of St. Stephen's, Carlisle, 1867. [5]

STRONG, Augustus, *Chippenham, Wilts.*—Ex. Coll. Ox. B.A. 1841, M.A. 1846; Deac. 1846 and Pr. 1847 by Bp of B. and W. R. of St. Paul's, Chippenham, Dio. G. and B. 1855. (Patron, Bp of G. and B; Tithe, 50*l*; R.'s Inc. 200*l*; Pop. 1218.) [6]

STRONG, Clement Dawsonne, 1, *York-buildings, Clifton, Bristol.*—Magd. Hall, Ox. B.A. 1828, M.A. 1831; Deac. 1831, Pr. 1833 by Bp of G. and B. V. of All Saints', Bristol, Dio. G. and B. 1866. (Patrons, D. and C. of Bristol; Glebe, 15 acres; V.'s Inc. 162*l* and Ho; Pop. 60.) Chap. of Missions to Seamen. Formerly C. of St. Michael's, Bristol; Chap. to the Asylum for the Blind. [7]

STRONG, Edmond, *Clyst St. Mary Rectory, near Exeter.*—Ex. Coll. Ox. 2nd cl. Lit. Hum. 1824, B.A. 1825, M.A. 1829; Deac. 1827 by Bp of Roch. Pr. 1828 by Bp of B. and W. R. of Clyst St. Mary, Dio. Ex. 1841. (Patron, the present R; Tithe, 150*l*; Glebe, 26 acres; R.'s Inc. 200*l* and Ho, Pop. 176.) [8]

STRONG, Francis, *Rampton Rectory, Cambridge.*—New Inn Hall, Ox. B.A. 1849; Deac. 1850 and Pr. 1851 by Bp of Ex. R. of Rampton, Dio. Ely, 1860. (Patron, Rev. H. Taylor; Tithe, 300*l*; Glebe, 28 acres; R.'s Inc. 330*l*; Pop. 240.) Formerly C. of West Hatch, near Taunton. [9]

STRONG, P. H. S., *Clehonger, Hereford.*—P. C. of Newton-in-Clodock, Dio. Herf. 1860. (Patron, V. of Clodock; P. C.'s Inc. 80*l*; Pop. 263) [10]

STRONG, Robert.—C. of St. John's, Hoxton, Lond. [11]

STRONG, William Arthur, *Ravensthorpe, Northampton.*—Ch. Ch. Ox. B.A. 1853, M.A. 1855; Deac. 1853 by Bp of Ox. Pr. 1855 by Bp of Lon. Student of Ch. Ch. Ox; V. of Ravensthorpe, Dio. Pet. 1865. (Patron, Ch. Ch. Ox; V.'s Inc. 300*l* and Ho; Pop. 700.) Formerly C. of Trinity, Twickenham, Long Preston, Yorks, and Evesham. [12]

STRONG, William Henry, *Withington, Manchester.*—Dub. A.B. 1837; Deac. 1838, Pr. 1839. R. of Withington, Dio. Man. 1862. (Patrons, Trustees; R.'s Inc. 200*l* and Ho; Pop. 2775.) Formerly R. of Newchurch Kenyon with Bury Lane C. 1855. [13]

STROTHER, James Baxter, *St. Mary Steps, Exeter.*—R. of St. Mary Steps, City and Dio. Ex. 1864. (Patroness, Mrs. Strother; Tithe, 14*l*; R.'s Inc. 179*l*; Pop. 1422.) [14]

STROUD, John, *Grammar School, Tunbridge, Kent.*—Mert. Coll. Ox. 1847, Jackson Scho. 1849, 3rd cl. Lit. Hum. 1st cl. Math. et Phy. and B.A. 1851, M.A. 1854; Deac. 1853 by Bp of Ox. Pr. 1855 by Bp of B. and W. Asst. Mast. of the Gr. Sch. Tunbridge. Formerly C. of Chaffcombe; 2nd Mast. of Crewkerne Gr. Sch. [15]

STROVER, Augustus, *Edwalton, Nottingham.*—Dub. A.B. 1852, A.M. 1857; Deac. 1852 and Pr. 1853 by Bp of Herf. P. C. of Edwalton, Dio. Lin. 1859. (Patron, J. C. Musters, Esq; Tithe, 45*l*; P. C.'s Inc. 110*l*; Pop. 115) Formerly C. of Stanton-on-Arrow 1852, Kington 1853, Trinity, Bath, 1855–58, West Bridgford 1859–62. [16]

STRUGNELL, Alfred, *St. Jude's Parsonage, Bethnal Green, N.E.*—Queens' Coll. Cam. Sen. Opt. and B.A. 1854, M.A. 1864; Deac. 1855 and Pr. 1856 by Bp of Win. C. of St. Jude's, Bethnal Green, 1865. Formerly C. of Mortlake and of Ch. Ch. Bermondsey; Sen. C. of St. Clement Danes, Westminster. [17]

STUART, The Hon. Andrew Godfrey, *Cottesmore Rectory, Oakham, Rutland.*—Dub. A.B. 1835, A.M. 1847; Deac. 1842; Pr. 1843. R. of Cottesmore, Dio. Pet. 1844. (Patron, Earl of Gainsborough; R.'s Inc. 900*l* and Ho: Pop. 627.) Hon. Can. of Pet. Cathl. 1850. [18]

STUART, A. Voules, *Nettleham Parsonage, Lincoln.*—P. C. of Nettleham, Dio. Lin. 1859. (Patron, Bp of Lin; P. C.'s Inc. 350*l*; Pop. 919) [19]

STUART, Charles, 2, *Woodfield-road, Harrow-road, London, W.*—Univ. Lond. Cl. Hon. 1863; Deac. 1843 and Pr. 1846 by Bp of Chich. Chap. to Kensal-green Cemetery, Middlesex, 1857; Chap. of the Paddington Workhouse; Chap. of St. Mary's Hospital, Paddington. Formerly C. of Playden with East Guildford 1843–57; Chap. of Rye Union 1852–57. [20]

STUART, Edward, 4, *Munster-square, Regent's-park, London, N.W.*—New Inn Hall, Ox. B.A. 1842, M.A. 1845. P. C. of St. Mary Magdalen's, St. Pancras, Dio. Lon. 1852. (Patron, the present P. C; P. C's Inc. 220*l*; Pop. 5116.) [21]

STUART, Henry Cumberland, *Wragby Parsonage, Wakefield.*—Ch. Coll. Cam. B.A. 1855, M.A. 1859; Deac. 1856 by Bp of Roch. Pr. 1857 by Bp of Lon. Incumb. of Wragby, Dio. York, 1863. (Patron, Charles Winn, Esq; Inc. 120*l* and Ho; Pop. 1009.) Formerly C. of Stow-on-the-Wold. Author, *The Presence of Christ realised by Love* (a Sermon). [22]

STUART, The Hon. Henry Windsor Villiers, *Napton-on-the-Hill, Rugby.*—Univ. Coll. Dur. 2nd cl. Lit. Hum. B.A. 1849, M.A. 1852; Deac. 1850, Pr. 1851. V. of Napton-on-the-Hill, Dio. Wor. 1855. (Patron, Ld Chan; Glebe, 202 acres; V.'s Inc. 460*l* and Ho; Pop. 975.) Formerly C. of King's Bromley; V. of Bulkington, Warwickshire, 1854–55. [23]

STUART, James Hilman, *Ampton, Bury St. Edmunds.*—Trin. Coll. Ox. B.A. 1830, M.A. 1837; Deac. 1831, Pr. 1832. R. of Ampton, Dio. Ely, 1841. (Patron, H. Rodwell, Esq; Tithe, 125*l*; Glebe, 20 acres; R.'s Inc. 175*l* and Ho; Pop. 131.) [24]

STUART, John Francis, *Kirton-in-Lindsey, Lincolnshire.*—Trin. Coll. Ox. B.A. 1830, M.A. 1834; Deac. 1844 and Pr. 1845 by Bp of Salis. V. of Kirton-in-Lindsey, Dio. Lin. 1858. (Patron Bp of Lin; V.'s Inc. 298*l* and Ho; Pop. 2058.) V. of Northorpe, Dio. Lin. 1860. (Patron, Bp of Lin; V.'s Inc. 100*l*; Pop. 194.) Surrogate. Formerly C. of Hitchin, Herts. [25]

STUART, Theodosius Burnett, *Wookey Vicarage, Wells.*—Queens' Coll. Cam. 13th Wrang. and

B.A. 1827, B.D. 1838; Deac. 1829 Pr. 1831. V. of Wookey, Dio. B. and W. 1849. (Patron, Bp of B. and W; Tithe—App. 220*l* 7*s* 6*d*, V. 299*l* 5*s*; Glebe, 5 acres; V.'s Inc. 342*l* and Ho; Pop. 628.) Preb. of Wells Cathl. 1859. Formerly Fell. of Queens' Coll. Cam. [1]

STUART, William, *Maldon, Essex.*—V. of Mundon; Dio. Roch. 1865. (Patron, Duchy of Lanc; V.'s Inc. 160*l*; Pop. 322.) Mast. of the Maldon Gr. Sch; Chap. of the Maldon Union; Plume Lect. Maldon. Formerly C. of Ch. Ch. West Ham, Surrey, and Stoke-next-Guildford 1858, Maldon, Essex. [2]

STUART-MENTEATH, Francis Hastings, *Thorp-Arch Vicarage near Tadcaster, Yorks.*—Magd. Hall Ox. B.A. 1833; Deac. 1833, Pr. 1834. V. of Thorp-Arch, Dio. York, 1834. (Patron, Rev. C. Wheler; Tithe, 386*l* 9*s* 2*d*; Glebe, 2 acres; V.'s Inc. 400*l*; Pop. 350.) [3]

STUART-MENTEATH, Granville Thorold, *Gwynfe House, Llangadock, Carmarthenshire.*—Univ. Coll. Ox. B.A. 1861; Deac. 1861 and Pr. 1863 by Bp of Roch. Formerly C. of Brent Pelham 1862. [4]

STUBBIN, Newman John, *Somersham Rectory, Ipswich.*—St. John's Coll. Ox. B.A. 1821, M.A. 1825; Deac. 1822 and Pr. 1823 by Bp of Nor. R. of Somersham, Dio. Nor. 1833. (Patron, the present R; Tithe, 270*l*; Glebe, 28 acres; R.'s Inc. 300*l* and Ho; Pop. 306.) [5]

STUBBS, Elias Thackeray, *The Deanery, Raphoe, co. Donegal, Ireland.*—Dub. A.B. 1849, A.M. 1859; Deac. 1850 and Pr. 1851 by Abp of Dub. P. C. of Raphoe, Dio. Raphoe, 1858. (Patron, Dean of Raphoe; P. C.'s Inc. 110*l*; Pop. 681.) Min. Can. of Raphoe Cathl; Dom. Chap. to the Earl of Castle Stuart. Formerly C. of Magore, Derry, 1850. [6]

STUBBS, Edward William, *Beckbury, Salop.*—Ex. Coll. Ox. 2nd cl. Lit. Hum. 1852, B.A. 1854, M.A. 1857; Deac. 1854, Pr. 1855. C. of Beckbury 1861. Formerly C. of Hinton St. George and Dinnington, Somerset, and Eversholt, Beds. [7]

STUBBS, George, *Ebchester Rectory, near Durham.*—Literate; Deac. 1820 by Abp of York, Pr. 1821 by Bp of Ox. R. of Ebchester, Dio. Dur. 1838. (Patron, the Mast. of Sherburn Hospital; Glebe, 100 acres; R.'s Inc. 230*l* and Ho; Pop. 537.) [8]

STUBBS, Henry Cuttill, *Warrington, Lancashire.*—Deac. 1848 and Pr. 1849 by Bp. of Lon. Prin. of the Clergy and Training Schs. Warrington. [9]

STUBBS, Joseph Stubbs, *The Parsonage, Crewkerne.*—St. Cath. Coll. Cam. B.A. 1853, M.A. 1857; Deac. 1854 and Pr. 1855 by Bp. of Lich. P. C. of Crewkerne, Dio. B. and W. 1862. (Patrons D. and C. of Win; Tithe—Imp. 1300*l*; P. C.'s Inc. 180*l* and Ho; Pop. 4705.) R. of Eastham, Dio. B. and W. 1866 (Patron, T. Hoskins, Esq; R.'s Inc. 30*l*.) [10]

STUBBS, Phinehas, *Well Vicarage, Bedale, Yorks.*—Dur. Licen. Theol. 1835 (the first Clergyman ordained from the Univ. of Dur); Deac. and Pr. 1835 by Bp of Ches. V. of Well, Dio. Rip. 1835. (Patron, F. A. Milbanke, Esq; Glebe, 44½ acres; V.'s Inc. 310*l* and Ho; Pop. 950.) The V. of Well commenced, and continues, since 1836, a gratuitous service in the Ancient Chapel of Snape Castle, which was repaired for that purpose by M. Milbanke, Esq. [11]

STUBBS, Stewart Dixon, 15, *Wycombe-terrace, Holloway, London, N.*—Pemb. Coll. Cam. B.A. 1856, M.A. 1859; Deac. 1856 by Bp of Win. Pr. 1857 by Bp of Lon. C. of St. John's, Upper Holloway. Formerly C. of St. Mark's, Tollington-park, Islington. [12]

STUBBS, Warden Flood, *Rocester Parsonage (Staffs), near Ashbourne, Derbyshire.*—Dub. A.B. 1852; Deac. 1853, Pr. 1855. P. C. of Rocester, Dio. Lich. 1857. (Patron, W. H. Bainbridge, Esq; P. C.'s Inc. 160*l* and Ho; Pop. 1028.) Formerly C. of Rossdroit, co. Wexford, Ireland, 1853–55, Ballinasloe, Ireland, 1855–57. [13]

STUBBS, William, *Navestock Vicarage, Romford, Essex, E.*—Ch. Ch. Ox. 1st cl. Lit. Hum. 3rd cl. Math. et Phy. and B.A. 1848, M.A. 1851; Deac. 1848 and Pr. 1850 by Bp of Ox. Regius Prof. of Modern History in the Univ. of Ox. 1866; V. of Navestock, Dio. Roch. 1850. (Patron, Trin. Coll. Ox; Tithe—Imp. 570*l*, V. 574*l*; Glebe, 20 acres; V.'s Inc. 600*l* and Ho; Pop. 928) Formerly Librarian to Abp of Cant. and Keeper of the MSS. at Lambeth. Fell. of Trin. Coll. Ox. Author, *Registrum Sacrum Anglicanum*, Oxford University Press, 1858, 8*s* 6*d*; *Chronicles and Memorials of the Reign of Richard I.* Vol. I. 1864. Editor, *Mosheim's Church History*, 1863, 45*s*. [14]

STUDDERT, George, *Market Overton, Rutland.*—C. of Market Overton. [15]

STUDHOLME, Robert, *Goosnargh Parsonage, Kirkham, Lancashire.*—St. Bees 1817. P. C. of Goosnargh, Dio. Man. 1822. (Patron, Ch. Ch. Ox; Tithe, App. 595*l*; P. C.'s Inc. 150*l* and Ho; Pop. 1171.) Surrogate. [16]

STUDHOLME, T. Matthew, *Goosnargh, Kirkham, Lancashire.*—C. of Goosnargh. Formerly C. of Beer Regis, Dorset. [17]

STUKELEY, J. F., *Ashby-de-la-Zouch.*—C. of Ashby-de-la-Zouch. [18]

STUPART, Gustavus.—Ex. Coll. Ox. B.A. 1837. Fell. of Ex. Coll. Formerly V. of Merton, Oxon, 1840–64. [19]

STURDY, Harry Charles, *St. Stephen's Parsonage, Spitalfields, E.*—King's Coll. Lond. Deac. 1866. C. of St. Stephen's, Spitalfields, 1866. [20]

STURGEON, Thomas, *Burley, Leeds.*—Dub. Cl. and Math. Prizeman 1831, Moderator 1832, A.B. 1833, A.M. 1837; Deac. 1837, and Pr. 1838 by Abp of Dub. P. C. of Burley, Dio. Rip. 1849. (Patrons, Trustees; Tithe, 216*l*; Glebe, 1 acre; P. C.'s Inc. 216*l*; Pop. 3600.) [21]

STURGES, Arthur Smith, *Springlands, Henley-on-Thames.*—Trin. Coll. Cam. B.A. 1862, M.A. 1866; Deac. 1864 and Pr. 1865 by Bp of G. and B. C. of Wargrave, Henley-on-Thames, 1866. Formerly C. of Campden, Gloucestershire, 1864. [22]

STURGES, Edward, *Great Milton, near Tetsworth, Oxon.*—King's Coll. Lond. Theol. Assoc. and Emman. Coll. Cam. B.A. 1855, M.A. 1858; Deac. 1854 and Pr. 1855 by Bp of Ox. V. of Great Milton, Dio. Ox. 1866. (Patron, Bp of Ox; V.'s Inc. 300*l* and Ho; Pop. 807.) Formerly C. of Haseley, Oxon, 1855; R. of Kencott, 1857–66. [23]

STURGES, Simon, *Wargrave Vicarage, near Henley-on-Thames.*—Magd. Hall, Ox. B.A. 1845, M.A. 1848; Deac. 1845 and Pr. 1847 by Bp of Ox. V. of Wargrave, Dio. Ox. 1859. (Patron, Lord Braybrooke; Tithe—Imp. 829*l* 10*s* and 43 acres of Glebe, V. 303*l* 5*s*; V.'s Inc. 346*l* and Ho; Pop. 1531.) Formerly P. C. of Knowl-hill, Berks, 1852–59. [24]

STURGIS, Frederick George, *Easthampstead, Berks.*—Chap. of the Union, and C. of Easthampstead. [25]

STURKEY, John, *St. Asaph, Flintshire.*—Lampeter; Burton Sch. and Prizeman B.D. 1853; Deac. 1845, Pr. 1846 by Bp of St. D. V.-Choral of St. Asaph Cathl. and V. of St. A. Dio. St. A. 1858. (Patron, Bp of St. A; V.'s Inc. 179*l*; Pop. 2600.) Formerly Asst. Tut. of Lampeter; C. of Llandyssil, Montgomeryshire, 1844. [26]

STURMAN, Mark Cephas Tutet.—Univ. and King's Coll. Lond. B.A. 1855, A.K.C. 1857; Deac. 1857 and Pr. 1858 by Bp of Lon. C. of St. George's, Camberwell, 1864. Formerly C. of St. Simon Zelotes, Bethnal Green, and St. James's, Bermondsey. [27]

STURMER, Frederick, *Heapham Rectory, Gainsborough.*—Queen's Coll. Ox. B.A. 1830, M.A. 1832; Deac. 1831 by Bp of B. and W. Pr. 1833 by Bp of Lon. R. of Heapham, Dio. Lin. 1845. (Patron, W. Cracroft Amcotts, Esq; Glebe, 200 acres; R.'s Inc. 246*l*; Pop. 121.) Author, *Socialism* (a Pamphlet), 1840; *Prosperity of a Nation* (a Sermon); *Plain Practical Sermons*, 1 vol. 1854. [28]

STURT, Napier Duncan, *Edmondsham, Cranborne, Dorset.*—Ch. Coll. Cam. B.C.L. 1822; Deac. 1823, Pr. 1854. R. of Edmondsham, Dio. Salis. 1834. (Patrons, Earl of Shaftesbury and Hector Monro, Esq; Tithe, 318*l* 15*s*; Glebe, 4 acres; R.'s Inc. 294*l*; Pop. 279.) [29]

STURTON, Jacob, *Little Bedwyn, Wilts.*—Trin. Coll. Ox. B.A. 1856, M.A. 1857; Deac. 1858 and Pr. 1859 by Bp of Salis. V. of Little Bedwyn, Dio. Salis. 1866. (Patron, the Marquis of Ailesbury; V.'s Inc. 280*l* and Ho; Pop. 496.) Formerly C. of Ramsbury 1858–66. [1]

STYLE, Charles M., *South Warborough, Oxon.*—Fell. of St. John's Coll. Ox. R. of South Warborough, Dio. Ox. (Patron, Ch. Ch. Ox; R.'s Inc. 350*l*; Pop. 764.) Formerly C. of Hardwicke, Oxon. [2]

STYLE, Frederic, *Thames Ditton, Kingston-on-Thames, Surrey, S.W.*—St. John's Coll. Ox. 3rd cl. Lit. Hum. and B.A. 1838, M.A. 1841; Deac. 1839, Pr. 1840. Head Mast. of Sch. at Thames Ditton. [3]

STYLE, G., *Cambridge.*—Fell. of Queens' Coll. and C. of St. Botolph's, Cambridge. [4]

SUCKLING, H., *Hackford, Norfolk.*—C. of Hackford. [5]

SUCKLING, Maurice Shelton, *Shipmeadow, Beccles, Suffolk.*—Trin. Coll. Cam. B.A. 1842, M.A. 1846; Deac. 1842, Pr. 1844. R. of Shipmeadow, Dio. Nor. 1850. (Patron, Rev. R. A. Suckling; Tithe, 220*l*; Glebe, 27½ acres; R.'s Inc. 276*l*; Pop. 334.) [6]

SUCKLING, Robert Alfred John, *Rowde Vicarage, Devizes.*—St. Edm. Hall Ox; Deac. 1865 by Bp of Salis. C. of Rowde. [7]

SUGDEN, The Hon. Arthur, *Newdigate Rectory, Dorking, Surrey.*—Dub. A.B. 1851; Deac. 1851 by Bp of Cork, Pr. 1852 by Bp of Llan. R. of Newdigate, Dio. Win. 1852. (Patron, Ld Chan; Tithe, 580*l* 10*s*; Glebe, 3 acres; R.'s Inc. 580*l* 10*s* and Ho; Pop. 605.) Formerly C. of Castlenock and Clonsilla, Dublin, 1851–52. [8]

SUGDEN, Arthur Maitland, *Mollington Parsonage, Banbury.*—Wad. Coll. Ox. B.A. 1850, M.A. 1857; Deac. 1850 by Bp of B. and W. Pr. 1851 by Bp of Salis. P. C. of Mollington, Dio. Ox. 1863. (Patron, Bp of Ox; P. C.'s Inc. 120*l* and Ho; Pop. 372.) Formerly C. of St. George's, Hanover-square, Lond. [9]

SUGDEN, The Hon. Frank, *Hale Magna Vicarage, Sleaford, Lincolnshire.*—Trin. Coll. Cam. B.A. 1839, M.A. 1842; Deac. 1840 by Bp of G. and B. Pr. 1842 by Bp of Nor. V. of Hale Magna, Dio. Lin. 1858. (Patron, Ld Chan; Tithe, 450*l*; Glebe, 140*l*; V.'s Inc. 590*l* and Ho; Pop. 1100.) Dom. Chap. to Lord St. Leonards. Formerly V. of Adlingfleet and Brignall 1855–58. [10]

SULIVAN, Filmer, *Barnet, Middlesex, N.W.*—P. C. of Ch. Ch. Barnet, 1865. [11]

SULIVAN, Henry William, *Yoxall Rectory, Burton-on-Trent.*—Ball. Coll. Ox. Hon. 4th cl. Lit. Hum. and B.A. 1838, M.A. 1840; Deac. 1841 and Pr. 1842 by Bp of Win. R. of Yoxall, Dio. Lich. 1851. (Patron, Ld Chan; Tithe, 294*l*; Glebe, 192 acres; R.'s Inc. 500*l* and Ho; Pop. 1443.) Author, *Parish Sermons*, 1846, 4*s*; *Sermons* (preached in Yoxall Church); *Three Sermons for the S.P.G.*; miscellaneous Pamphlets. [12]

SULLIVAN, Eugene, *Blagdon, Somerset.*—Dub; Deac. 1866 by Bp of B. and W. C. of Blagdon. [13]

SULLIVAN, Frederick, *Kimpton Vicarage, Welwyn, Herts.*—Brasen. Coll. Ox. 2nd cl. Lit. Hum. and B.A. 1817, All Souls Coll. M.A. 1822; Deac. 1820 by Bp of Ches. Pr. 1821 by Bp of Win. V. of Kimpton, Dio. Roch. 1827. (Patron, Lord Dacre; Tithe—Imp. 683*l* 8*s*, V. 440*l*; Glebe, 22 acres; V.'s Inc. 500*l* and Ho; Pop. 1014.) Formerly Fell. of All Souls Coll. Ox. [14]

SULLIVAN, James, *National Club, 1, Whitehall-gardens, London, S.W.* [15]

SULLIVAN, John, *Over Silton, Yorks.*—C. of Over Silton. [16]

SUMMERHAYES, Julius, *Ealing, Middlesex, W.*—Queens' Coll. Cam. B.A. 1859; Deac. 1859 and Pr. 1860 by Bp of Lon. C. of Ealing 1859. [17]

SUMMERS, Walter, *Crondall, near Farnham, Hants.*—C. of Crondall. [18]

SUMMERS, William, *Cartmel Fell Parsonage, Grange, Lancaster.*—Dub. A.B. 1859; Deac. 1861 and Pr. 1862 by Bp of Carl. P. C. of Cartmel Fell, Dio. Carl. 1867. (Patron Bp of Carl; P. C.'s Inc. 140*l* and Ho; Pop. 350.) Formerly C. of St. George's, Kendal, 1861–67. [19]

SUMMERSFORD, Alfred George, *Great Cressingham, Norfolk.*—Deac. 1853 and Pr. 1854 by Bp of Ex. C. of Great Cressingham. Formerly C. of St. Mary's, Chatham; Asst. C. of Mevagissey, Cornwall. [20]

SUMNER, Charles Vernon Holme, *Ringwould Rectory, Dover.*—Trin. Coll. Cam. B.A. 1823. R. of Ringwould, Dio. Cant. 1853. (Patrons, Executors of the late Rev. L. Monins; Tithe, 505*l*; Glebe, 10 acres; R.'s Inc. 520*l* and Ho; Pop. 338.) Chap. in Ordinary to the Queen 1830. [21]

SUMNER, George Henry, *Old Alresford Rectory, Alresford, Hants.*—Ball. Coll. Ox. B.A. 1845, M.A. 1848; Deac. 1847 by Bp of Ox. Pr. 1848 by Bp of Win. R. of Old Alresford, Dio. Win. 1850. (Patron, Bp of Win; Tithe, 740*l*; Glebe, 24 acres; R.'s Inc. 740*l* and Ho; Pop. 540.) Chap. to Bp of Win; Rural Dean; Proctor in Convocation for the Archd. of Win. Formerly C. of Crawley, Winchester. Author, *Assize Sermon* (preached at Lancaster), 1851, 1*s*; *Book-hawking as conducted in Hampshire*, 2 eds. 4*d*; *Address to Sunday School Teachers*, S.P.C.K. 1856; *A Sermon preached at the Consecration of the Bishop of Rochester*, 1*s*; *The Ecclesiastical Commission*, 3rd ed. 1864, 1*s*. [22]

SUMNER, James, *Pott-Shrigley, Macclesfield.*—Trin. Coll. Cam. B.A. 1823, M.A. 1833; Deac. 1824 and Pr. 1825 by Bp of Ches. P. C. of Pott-Shrigley, Dio. Ches. 1829. (Patroness, Miss Turner; P. C.'s Inc. 104*l* and Ho; Pop. 450.) [23]

SUMNER, John Henry Robertson, *Ellesborough, Rectory, Wendover.*—Dur. B.A. 1843, M.A. 1846; Deac. 1846 by Bp of Dur. Pr. 1847 by Bp of Rip. R. of Ellesborough, Dio. Ox. 1863. (Patron, Sir R. G. Russell; R.'s Inc. 285*l* and Ho; Pop. 724.) Formerly Dom. Chap. to Abp of Cant. 1850; R. of Bishopsbourne 1859. [24]

SUMNER, Joseph, *Kirkthwaite, Sedbergh.*—Dur. Licen. in Theol. 1856; Deac. 1856 by Bp of Man. Pr. 1857 by Bp of Dur. P. C. of Kirkthwaite, Dio. Rip. 1864. (Patron Bp of Rip; Pop. 330.) Formerly C. of Sandal Magna 1862; P. C. of Cargill 1864. [25]

SUMNER, John Maunoir, *Buriton, Petersfield, Hants.*—Ball. Coll. Ox. B.A. 1838, M.A. 1841; Deac. 1839, Pr. 1840. R. of Buriton with Petersfield C. Dio. Win. 1845. (Patron, Bp of Win; Buriton, Tithe, 1084*l* 6*s* 11*d*; Glebe, 61¾ acres; Petersfield and Sheet, Tithe, 386*l* 18*s*; R.'s Inc. 1471*l* 4*s* 11*d* and Ho; Pop. Buriton 1050, Petersfield 1950.) Rural Dean. [26]

SUMNER, N. Halliwell, *Little Holbeck, Yorks.*—C. of Little Holbeck. [27]

SUMNER, P. F., *Brandesburton, Beverley, Yorks.*—C. of Brandesburton. [28]

SURTEES, Henry Radcliffe, *Stockland Vicarage, near Honiton, Devon.*—St. Mary Hall, Ox. B.A. 1837; Deac. 1838 and Pr. 1839 by Bp of Nor. V. of Stockland with Dalwood C. Dio. Ex. 1846. (Patrons, Freeholders and Inhabitants; Tithe—Stockland, Imp. 308*l* 19*s* 11*d*, V. 450*l* 5*s*; Glebe, 1 acre; Tithe—Dalwood, Imp. 229*l* 15*s* 5*d*, V. 140*l*; V.'s Inc. 590*l* and Ho; Pop. 1615.) [29]

SURTEES, Richard, *Holtby Rectory, York.*—Deac. 1842, Pr. 1843. R. of Holtby, Dio. York. (Patron, Lord Feversham; Tithe, 191*l*; Glebe, 52 acres; R.'s Inc. 248*l* and Ho; Pop. 165.) [30]

SURTEES, Scott Frederic, *Sprotborough Rectory, Doncaster.*—Univ. Coll. Ox. B.A. 1836; Deac. 1837 and Pr. 1838 by Bp of Ex. R. of Sprotborough with Cadeby C. Dio. York, 1856. (Patron, Sir J. Copley, Bart; Tithe, 780*l*; Glebe, 40½ acres; R.'s Inc. 840*l* and Ho; Pop. 504.) Formerly V. of Newlyn, Cornwall. Author, *Sermons for the People*; *Education for the People, the Ministry of the Word*, Part I. *The Prophets, not the Priests, the Standing Ministry amongst the Jews*; Part II. *Christ's Ministers Successors of the Prophets, not of the Priests*; *Baptism* (a Sermon by Bp Heber, edited with Notes); *Letters on Emigration*; *Julius Cæsar*; *Waifs and Strays of Northumberland History.* [31]

SUTCLIFFE, Daniel, *St. John's, Holme, Whalley, Lancashire.*—St. Cath. Hall, Cam. B.A. 1844, M.A. 1847; Deac. 1844 and Pr. 1845 by Bp of Ches. P. C. of St. John's, Holme, Dio. Man. 1860. (Patron, T. H. Whitaker, Esq; P. C.'s Inc. 150*l*; Pop. 1770.) Formerly C. of Worsthorne 1844–60. Author, *The Sunday-School Teacher rewarded, or the Memoir of a Sunday Scholar,* 6*d*. [1]

SUTCLIFFE, Henry, *Keele Parsonage, Newcastle-under-Lyne, Staffs.*—Deac. 1834, Pr. 1835. P. C. of Keele, Dio. Lich. 1841. (Patron, R. Sneyd, Esq; Tithe—Imp. 250*l*, P. C. 84*l* 2*s* 6*d*; P. C.'s Inc. 200*l* and Ho; Pop. 560.) [2]

SUTCLIFFE, John, *Leven, near Beverley, Yorks.*—C. of Leven, 1867. Formerly C. of St. Mary's, Sowerby, Halifax. [3]

SUTCLIFFE, Thomas, *Rivington Parsonage, Bolton.*—St. Bees; Deac. 1847 by Bp of Ches. Pr. 1848 by Bp of Man. P. C. of Rivington, Dio. Man. 1856. (Patrons, the Inhabitants; P. C.'s Inc. 100*l* and Ho; Pop. 369.) Formerly C. of St. Peter's, Blackburn, 1849–56. [4]

SUTCLIFFE, William, *Bosley Parsonage, Congleton, Cheshire.*—Dub. A.B. 1830, A.M. 1841; Deac. 1831, Pr. 1832. P. C. of Bosley, Prestbury, Dio. Ches. 1833. (Patron, V. of Prestbury; Tithe—Imp. 282*l*; Glebe, 40 acres; P. C.'s Inc. 108*l*; Pop. 461.) Surrogate 1854. Author, *A Sermon on the Progress of the Cholera* (before the Mayor and Corporation of Congleton), 1832; *Family Prayers, with Addresses,* 3rd ed. 1851, 2*s*; *Two Pastoral Addresses to the Parishioners of Bosley*; *An Address to the Railway Labourers,* 1847. [5]

SUTCLIFFE, William, *Middleton Parsonage, Leeds.*—St. Bees; Deac. 1841 and Pr. 1842 by Bp of Ches. P. C. of Middleton, Dio. Rip. 1865. (Patron, V. of Rothwell; Tithe, 438*l*; P. C.'s Inc. 140*l* and Ho; Pop. 1195.) Formerly C. of Farnworth, Blackburn, and Kirkham; V. of Weeton 1861–65. Author, *Sermons on Church Training, Confirmation, Teetotalism, and Drunkenness.* [6]

SUTHERLAND, Charles, *Grammar School, Stepney, London, E.*—Trin. Coll. Cam. B.A. 1856, M.A. 1859; Deac. 1859 and Pr. 1860 by Bp of Lon. Mast. of the Gr. Sch. Stepney. Formerly C. of St. Philip's, Earl's-court, Kensington, Lond. 1859. [7]

SUTHERLAND James, 34, *Halliford-street, Arlington-square, Islington, London, N.*—Queens' Coll. Cam. B.A. 1843. P. C. of St. Philip's, Islington, Dio. Lon. 1856. (Patrons, Trustees; P. C.'s Inc. 355*l*.) [8]

SUTTABY, William Leonard, *Poslingford Vicarage, Clare, Suffolk.*—St. John's Coll. Cam. Sen. Opt. and B.A. 1826, M.A. 1859; Deac. 1826, Pr. 1827. P. C. of Denston, or Denerdistan, Suffolk, Dio. Ely, 1836. (Tithe, Imp. 14*l* 10*s*; Stipend, 25*l*; Queen Anne's Bounty, 26*l*; P. C.'s Inc. 51*l*; Pop. 277.) V. of Poslingford, Dio. Ely, 1838. (Tithe—Imp. 199*l*, V. 100*l*; Glebe, 6½ acres; V.'s Inc. 114*l* and Ho; Pop. 350.) [9]

SUTTHERY, W., *Clifton Reynes, Olney, Bucks.*—Formerly C. of Newton, Sudbury. [10]

SUTTON, Augustus, *West Tofts Rectory (Norfolk), near Brandon, Suffolk.*—Univ. Coll. Ox. B.A. 1847; Deac. 1848, Pr. 1849. R. of West Tofts, Dio. Nor. 1849. (Patron, Sir Richard Sutton, Bart; Tithe 195*l*; R.'s Inc. 200*l*; Pop. 193.) Preb. in Linc. Cathl. 1862. [11]

SUTTON, Frederick Heathcote, *Theddingworth Vicarage, Rugby.*—Magd. Coll. Ox. V. of Theddingworth, Dio. Pet. 1867. (Patron, J. Cook, Esq; V.'s Inc. 137*l* and Ho; Pop. 281.) Formerly C. of Ketton and Tixover. [12]

SUTTON, Henry, 19, *Shaw-street, Everton, Liverpool.*—Dub. A.B. 1861; Deac. 1858 and Pr. 1861. P. C. of St. Augustine's, Everton, Dio. Ches. 1864. (Patron, John Shaw Lee, Esq; P. C.'s Inc. 320*l*; Pop. 15,000.) Formerly C. of Tealby and Legsby, Linc. 1858–61; Assoc. Sec. Ch. Miss. Soc. [13]

SUTTON, James, *Rosliston, Burton-on-Trent.*—P. C. of Rosliston, Dio. Lich. 1863. (Patron, Rev. J. L. Sutton; P. C.'s Inc. 180*l*; Pop. 382.) [14]

SUTTON, John Lucas, *Weekley Vicarage, Kettering, Northants.*—Ball. Coll. Ox. B.A. 1815, M.A. 1818; Deac. 1816, Pr. 1817. V. of Weekley, Dio. Pet. 1818. (Patron, Duke of Buccleuch; V.'s Inc. 126*l* and Ho; Pop. 268.) R. of Oakley-Parva, Northants, Dio. Pet. 1818. (Patron, Duke of Buccleuch; Tithe, 6*l*; R.'s Inc. 112*l* and Ho; Pop. 127.) [15]

SUTTON, John Lucas, *Allesley, Coventry.*—Wad. Coll. Ox. B.A. 1850, M.A. 1855; Deac. 1850, Pr. 1851. C. of Allesley. Formerly C. of Geddington. [16]

SUTTON, Meyrick John, 4, *Spa terrace, Spa-road, Bermondsey, S.E.*—Corpus Coll. Cam. B.A. 1865; Deac. 1866 by Bp of Win. C. of Ch. Ch. Bermondsey, 1866. [17]

SUTTON, Robert, *Westhampnett Vicarage, Chichester.*—Ex. Coll. Ox. B.A. 1855, M.A. 1858; Deac. 1856 and Pr. 1857 by Bp of Lon. V. of Westhampnett, Dio. Chich. 1861. (Patron, Duke of Richmond; Tithe, Imp. 429*l*; V.'s Inc. 43*l* 18*s* 4*d* and Ho; Pop. 380.) Chap. of the Westhampnett Union and Preb. of Chich. Cathl. Formerly C. of St. Botolph's, Aldgate, Lond. 1856–58, St. Leonard's, Aston Clinton, Oxon, 1858–61. [18]

SUTTON, Robert, *Bilsthorpe Rectory, Ollerton, Notts.*—Trin. Coll. Cam. B.A. 1835, M.A. 1838; Deac. 1837 by Abp of York, Pr. 1838 by Bp of Lin. R. of Bilsthorpe, Dio. Lin. 1859. (Patron, Henry Savile, Esq; Tithe, 372*l*; Glebe, 75 acres; R.'s Inc. 450*l* and Ho; Pop. 220.) Formerly C. of Averham with Kelham, Notts, 1837–44; R. of Averham with Kelham 1844–52. [19]

SUTTON, Robert Shuttleworth, *Rype Rectory, Hurst Green, Sussex.*—Ex. Coll. Ox. B.A. 1843, M.A. 1845; Deac. 1842 and Pr. 1843 by Bp. of Ox. R. of Rype, Dio. Chich. 1853. (Patron, Ex. Coll. Ox; Tithe, 480*l*; Glebe, 33 acres; R.'s Inc. 480*l* and Ho; Pop. 358.) Rural Dean. Formerly Fell. of Ex. Coll. Ox. [20]

SUTTON, Stephen Brain, 41, *Everton-brow, Liverpool.*—Univ. Coll. Lond. B.A. 1846; Deac. 1848 and Pr. 1849 by Bp of Ches. P. C. of St. Peter's, Everton, Dio. Ches. 1850. (Patrons, Trustees; P. C.'s Inc. 430*l*; Pop. 19,000.) Formerly C. of St. Mary's, Kirkdale, 1848–49. [21]

SUTTON, Thomas, *Marton Vicarage, Gainsborough.*—St. Edm. Hall, Ox. B.A. 1828; Deac. 1828, Pr. 1829. V. of Marton, Dio. Lin. 1839. (Patron, Bp of Lin; Glebe, 42 acres; V.'s Inc. 115*l* and Ho; Pop. 487.) Chap. to the Gainsborough Union 1838. [22]

SUTTON, Thomas, *Sunk-Island, near Hull.*—Emman. Coll. Cam. B.A. 1836; Deac. 1836, Pr. 1837. P. C. of Sunk-Island, Dio. York, 1858. (Patron, Ld Chan; P. C.'s Inc. 250*l*; Pop. 376.) Formerly Chap. of York Castle 1844–59. [23]

SUTTON, Thomas Theodore, *Dams' District, Macclesfield.*—C. of the Dams' District. [24]

SUTTON, William, *Rugby, Warwickshire.*—Ball. Coll. Ox. B.A. 1814, M.A. 1817; Deac. 1815, Pr. 1816. [25]

SWABEY, Henry, 67, *Lincoln's-inn-fields, London, W.C.*—Pemb. Coll. Ox. 2nd cl. Math. et Phy. and B.A. 1848, M.A. 1851; Deac. 1849, Pr. 1850. Asst. Sec. of the S.P.C.K. Formerly R. of St. Aldate's, Oxford, 1850–56; C. of St. Martin's-in-the-Fields, Lond. 1858–63. [26]

SWAINE, James, *Whaplode Drove, Lincolnshire.*—Wad. Coll. Ox. B.A. 1836; Deac. 1836 and Pr. 1837 by Bp of Lon. C. of Whaplode Drove. Formerly C. of Stewkley. [27]

SWAINSON, Charles, *Crick, Rugby.*—Ch. Ch. Ox. B.A. 1863; Deac. 1864 by Bp of Salisbury. C. of Crick 1865. Formerly C. of Wilton and Netherhampton 1864. [28]

SWAINSON, Charles Anthony, *Cambridge and Chichester.*—Trin. Coll. Cam. B.A. and 6th Wrang. 1841, Ch. Coll. M.A. 1844, D.D. 1864; Deac. 1843 and Pr. 1844 by Bp of Ely. Can. Res. of Chich. Cathl. 1863. (Inc. 500*l*.) Norrissian Prof. of Div. Cam. 1864 (Inc. 135*l*); Prin. of the Theol. Coll. Chich. 1855. Formerly Fell. and Tut. of Ch. Coll. Cam. 1841–47; Whitehall Preacher 1849–50; Hulsean Lect. 1857–58. Author,

Commonplaces read in Christ's College Chapel, 1848, 3s 6d; *The Creeds of the Church in their Relation to the Word of God and the Conscience of the Christian*, 1858, 9s; *The Authority of the New Testament, the Conviction of Righteousness, and the Ministry of Reconciliation*, 1859, 12s 6d (Hulsean Lectures); and sundry Pamphlets. [1]

SWAINSON, Charles Litchfield, *Crick Rectory (Northants), near Rugby.*—St. John's Coll. Ox. B.A. 1819, B.D. 1830; Deac. 1820, Pr. 1821. R. of Crick, Dio. Pet. 1836. (Patron, St. John's Coll. Ox; Tithe, 560*l*; Glebe, 564 acres; R.'s Inc. 930*l* and Ho; Pop. 999.) Rural Dean. Formerly Fell. of St. John's Coll. 1818; Proctor of the Univ. of Ox. 1829; P. C. of Edge-hill, Liverpool, 1823–34; V. of St. Giles', Oxford, 1834–36. [2]

SWAINSON, Edward Christopher, *Wistanstow Rectory, Shrewsbury.*—Wor. Coll. Ox. B.A. 1832, M.A. 1843; Deac. 1835 and Pr. 1836 by Bp of Lich. R. of Wistanstow with Whittingstow C. Dio. Herf. 1855. (Patron, the present R; Tithe, 950*l*; Glebe, 50 acres; R.'s Inc. 980*l* and Ho; Pop. 1121.) [3]

SWAINSON, James Hopkins, *Alresford Rectory, Colchester.*—Brasen. Coll. Ox. B.A. 1830, M.A. 1833; Deac. 1832 and Pr. 1834 by Bp of Ches. R. of Alresford, Dio. Roch. 1843. (Patrons, Hulme's Trustees; Tithe, 356*l*; Glebe, 30 acres; R.'s Inc. 334*l* and Ho; Pop. 248.) Author, *The Churchman's Book of Family Prayer*, 1848; *Visitation Sermon*, 1862. [4]

SWAINSON, John, *High Kilburn, Oswaldkirk, Yorkshire.*—St. Bees 1824; Deac. 1826 and Pr. 1827 by Abp of York. P. C. of Cold Kirby, Dio. York, 1864. (P. C.'s Inc. 64*l*; Pop. 210.) C. of Scawton 1863. Formerly C. of Helmsley, Kirkdale, Old Byland, Bilsdale, Lastingham, Appleton-le-street and Kilburn, all in Yorks. [5]

SWAINSON, John Graindorge, 54, *Albany-street, London, N.W.*—Ch. Ch. Coll. Ox. B.A. 1866; Deac. 1866. C. of St. Mary's, Munster-square, Lond. [6]

SWALE, Hogarth John, *British Embassy, Rue de Faubourg St. Honoré, Paris.*—Queen's Coll. Ox. B.A. 1832, M.A. 1836; Deac. 1833 and Pr. 1835 by Bp of Ches. Chap. to the British Embassy, Paris. [7]

SWALLOW, Francis Richard, *Blackrod, near Chorley.*—St. Aidan's; Deac. 1856 by Bp of S. and M. Pr. 1858 by Bp of Rip. P. C. of Blackrod, Dio. Man. 1861. (Patron, V. of Bolton; Glebe, 26½ acres; P. C.'s Inc. 350*l* and Ho; Pop. 3214.) [8]

SWALLOW, W. H., *Turvey, near Bedford.*—C. of Turvey. Formerly C. of Brington, Bythorne, and Old Weston. [9]

SWAN, Charles Trollope, *Welton-le-Wold Rectory, Louth, Lincolnshire.*—Ch. Coll. Cam. B.C.L. 1849; Deac. and Pr. 1850 by Bp of Lin. R. of Welton-le-Wold, Dio. Lin. 1859. (Patron, Ld Chan; Tithe, 3*l* 10*s*; Glebe, 473 acres; R.'s Inc. 600*l* and Ho; Pop. 335.) Formerly V. of Dunholme, Linc. 1850–57; R. of Brettenham, Suffolk, 1857–59. [10]

SWAN, Francis, *Bennington Rectory, Boston, Lincolnshire.*—Magd. Coll. Ox. B.A. 1807, M.A. 1810, B.D. 1818; Deac. 1810 by Bp of Dur. Pr. 1811 by Bp of Ox. R. of Sausthorpe, Dio. Lin. 1819. (Patron, the present R; R.'s Inc. 220*l*; Pop. 144.) Preb. of Dunholme in Lin. Cathl. 1825. (Value, 19*l*.) R. of Bennington, near Boston, Dio. Lin. 1833. (Patron, Earl of Ripon; R.'s Inc. 805*l* and Ho; Pop. 588.) [11]

SWAN, Francis H., *Aswardby, Spilsby, Lincolnshire.*—R. of Aswardby, Dio. Lin. 1849. (Patron, Rev. Francis Swan; Tithe, 234*l* 6*s* 1*d*; Glebe, 34 acres; R.'s Inc. 290*l*; Pop. 68.) [12]

SWAN, Richard Charles, *Hothfield, Ashford, Kent.*—St. John's Coll. Cam. B.A. 1840, M.A. 1859; Deac. 1842, Pr. 1844. R. of Hothfield, Dio. Cant. 1849. (Patron, Sir R. Tufton, Bart; Tithe, 380*l*; Glebe, 28 acres; R.'s Inc. 340*l* and Ho; Pop 336.) [13]

SWANN, Edward, *The Vicarage, Elm, Wisbech.*—St. John's Coll. Cam. Wrang. B.A. 1828, M.A. 1831; Deac. 1833 and Pr. 1834 by Bp of Lin. V. of Elm, Dio. Ely, 1863. (Patron, Bp of Ely; Tithe, 495*l*; Glebe, 18 acres; V.'s Inc. 525*l* and Ho; Pop. 860.) Formerly C. of St. Paul's, Bedford, 1833–37, Kempston 1839–41; Chap. of the Infirmary 1841–51, of the Asylum 1849–59; Math. Mast. in the Gr. Sch. Bedford, 1829–63. [14]

SWANN, E. H., *Lindley, Huddersfield.*—C. of Lindley. [15]

SWANN, Johnson Fowell, *Hempstead, Essex.*—Caius Coll. Cam. B A. 1860; Deac. 1861 and Pr. 1862 by Bp of Roch. C. of Hempstead 1863. Formerly C. of East Donyland, Essex, 1861–63. [16]

SWANN, Percival Fiennes, *Brandsby, near York.*—Trin. Coll. Cam. B.A. 1862; Deac. 1863 and Pr. 1864 by Bp of Win. C. of Brandsby 1866. Formerly Asst. C. of Icklesham with Rye Harbour 1864. [17]

SWANN, Robert, *Brandsby Rectory, near York.*—Trin. Coll. Cam. B.A. 1819, M.A. 1822; Deac. 1822, Pr. 1823. R. of Brandsby, Dio. York, 1823. (Patron, F. Cholmeley, Esq; Tithe, 588*l*; Glebe, 68¼ acres; R.'s Inc. 720*l* and Ho; Pop. 284.) R. of Cherry-Burton, Yorks, Dio. York, 1837. (Patron, Rev. H. Ramsden; Tithe, 1050*l*; Glebe, 25¾ acres; R.'s Inc. 1082*l* and Ho; Pop. 502.) [18]

SWANN, Samuel Kirke, *Gedling, near Nottingham.*—Ch. Coll. Cam. B.A. 1842, M.A. 1845; Deac. 1843 and Pr. 1844 by Bp of Pet. C. of Gedling. [19]

SWANN, Thomas William, *Biebie-street, Nottingham.*—Caius Coll. Cam. B.A. 1863; Deac. 1864 by Bp of Lin. C. of New Radford, Nottingham. [20]

SWANTON, Francis, *Barton Stacey Vicarage, Stockbridge, Hants.*—Wad. Coll. Ox. B.C.L. 1817. V. of Barton Stacey, Dio. Win. 1845. (Patrons, D. and C. of Win; Tithe—App. 968*l*, V. 272*l*; Glebe, 53 acres; V.'s Inc. 317*l* and Ho; Pop. 516) P. C. of St. John's, City and Dio. Win. 1827. (Patron, Bp of Win; P. C.'s Inc. 82*l*; Pop. 1160.) [21]

SWANWICK, Philip Slater, *Prestbury, Macclesfield, Cheshire.*—Brasen. Coll. Ox. B.A. 1845, M.A. 1848; Deac. 1846 and Pr. 1847 by Bp of Pet. C. of Alderley, near Congleton, Cheshire. [22]

SWATMAN, Philip, *Guy's Hospital, Southwark, S.E.*—Trin. Coll. Cam. B.A. 1846, M.A. 1850; Deac. 1849 and Pr. 1850 by Bp of Nor. C. of Guy's Hospital, Lond. Formerly C. of Lound, Suffolk. [23]

SWAYNE, Charles Brodrick, *Northampton.*—Dub. A.B. 1845; Deac. 1845 by Bp of Kildare, Pr. 1846 by Bp of Killaloe. Assoc. Sec. of the Church Missionary Society 1858. Formerly C. of Kill, Kildare, 1845, Moneymore, Armagh, 1846; V. of Kilgeffin, Dio. Kilmore, 1849; Sec. in London for Malta Protestant College 1852. [24]

SWAYNE, John, 16, *Great Coram-street, Russell-square, London, W.C.*—Magd. Hall, Ox. B.A. 1843, M.A. 1848. P. C. of Ch. Ch. St. Giles's, Dio. Lon. 1847. (Patron, R. of St. Giles's-in-the-Fields; P. C.'s Inc. 220*l*.) [25]

SWAYNE, Robert George, *St. Edmund's Rectory, Salisbury.*—Wad. Coll. Ox. B.A. 1842, M.A. 1844; Deac. 1844 and Pr. 1845 by Bp of G. and B. R. of St. Edmund's, City and Dio. Salis. 1863. (Patron, Bp of Salis; Endowment, 80*l*; R.'s Inc. 270*l* and Ho; Pop. 4458.) Formerly P. C. of Bussage 1852. [26]

SWAYNE, William John, *Whiteparish, Wilts.*—Ch. Ch. Coll. Ox. 1st cl. Law and Mod. Hist. 2nd cl. Nat. Sci. B.A. 1854, M.A. 1857; Deac. 1858 and Pr. 1859 by Bp of Salis. C. of Whiteparish 1860. Formerly C. of Downton 1858. [27]

SWEATMAN, Arthur, *London, Ontario, Canada.*—Ch. Coll. Cam. B.A. 1859; Deac. 1859 and Pr. 1860 by Bp of Lon. Head Mast. of Collegiate Institute, London, Ontario, Dio. Huron, 1865. Formerly C. of Holy Trinity, Islington, Lond. 1859, St. Stephen's, Islington. Mast of the Special Dept. of the Islington Proprietary Sch. Author, *On Youths' Clubs and Institutes*, Ford, Islington. [28]

SWEET, George, *Sampford Arundel, Wellington, Somerset.*—St. Mary Hall, Ox. B.A. 1838, M.A. 1840. V. of Sampford Arundel, Dio. B. and W. 1862. (Patron, the present V; V.'s Inc. 146*l*; Pop. 425.) Formerly C. of Kentisbury. [29]

SWEET, James Bradby, *Colkirk Rectory, Fakenham, Norfolk.*—Ball. Coll. Ox. B.A. 1839, M.A. 1842; Deac. 1841 and Pr. 1842 by Bp of Ches. R. of Colkirk with Stibbard, Dio. Nor. 1857. (Patron, Henry Hoare, Esq; Glebe, 60 acres; R.'s Inc. 788*l* and Ho; Pop. Colkirk 473, Stibbard 451.) Organising Sec. to the Additional Curates Soc. 1854–57. Formerly C. of Macclesfield 1841–43, Ashby-de-la-Zouch 1843–46; P. C. of Woodville 1846–54. Author, *Religious Liberty and the Church in Chains* (a Pamphlet), 1848, 2*s* 6*d*; *Reasons for Refusing to profane the Order for the Burial of the Dead* (a Pamphlet), 1850, 1*s* 6*d*; *A Statement of the Case in Favour of a Restoration of Corrective Discipline, from the Evidence of Scripture, the Church, and Reason,* Rivingtons, 1863, 1*s* 6*d*; *A Letter on Lay Agency, with Rules for Parochial Associations for spiritual Purposes,* 1864, Rivingtons, 3*d*; *Lay Co-operation, a Funeral Sermon on the Work of the late Henry Hoare, with Preface by the Bishop of London,* Cleaver, 1866, 1*s*; *The Failure of Sunday Schools, its Causes and Remedies,* Cleaver, 1867, 6*d*; *A Catechism on the Church and Church Membership,* Cleaver, 1867, 6*d*; *Speculum Parochiale,* 1859, 4*s*; various Tracts, Reviews, and Articles. [1]

SWEET, William Fort, *West Quantoxhead, Somerset.*—Pemb. Coll. Ox. B.A. 1842; Deac. 1843 by Bp of B. and W. Pr. 1844 by Bp of Ely. C. in sole charge of West Quantoxhead 1866. Formerly R. of Kentisbury 1855, P. C. of Withiel-Florey 1863. [2]

SWEETAPPLE, Thomas, *Babcary Rectory, Somerton, Somerset.*—Deac. 1857 and Pr. 1858 by Bp of Lich. R. of Babcary, Dio. B. and W. 1860. (Patron, Rev. W. H. Twenlow; Tithe—Imp. 8*l* 15*s*, R. 400*l*; Glebe, 38 acres; R.'s Inc. 454*l* and Ho; Pop. 426.) Formerly C. of Box. [3]

SWEETING, Alfred, *Amcotts Rectory, Doncaster.*—Pemb. Coll. Cam. 31st Wrang. B.A. 1854, M.A. 1857; Deac. 1855 by Bp of Ox. Pr. 1857 by Bp of Ely. R. of Amcotts, Dio. Lin. 1861. (Patron, the Crown; Glebe, 122 acres; P. C.'s Inc. 260*l* and Ho; Pop. 374.) Formerly Math. Mast. in Trin. Coll. Glenalmond, Perth, 1854–56; C. of Swynshed, Hunts, 1857–58; Vice-Prin. of Dur. Training Coll. 1859–61. [4]

SWEETING, Robert, *Feliskirk, Thirsk.*—C. of Feliskirk. [5]

SWEETING, Walter Debenham, *Minster Precincts, Peterborough.*—Trin. Coll. Cam. Sen. Opt. and B.A. 1861, M.A. 1864; Deac. 1862 and Pr. 1863 by Bp of Pet. 2nd Mast. of the Cathl. Sch. Peterborough 1861. Author, *Historical and Architectural Notes of the Parish Churches in and around Peterborough* (pub. Monthly, with Photographic Illustrations), 1*s* 6*d*, Hamblin, Peterborough. [6]

SWEETING, William, *Skipton Bridge Parsonage, Thirsk, Yorks.*—Dur. B.A. 1841, M.A. 1844. P. C. of Skipton Bridge, Dio. York, 1842. (Patroness, Miss Elsley; P. C.'s Inc. 50*l* and Ho; Pop. 247.) [7]

SWETE, Henry Barclay, *Caius College, Cambridge.*—Caius Coll. Cam. 1st cl. Cl. Trip. 1858, Carus Greek Test. Prize 1855, Member's Prize 1857, B.A. 1859, M.A. 1862; Fell. of Caius Coll. Cam; Deac. 1858 and Pr. 1859 by Bp of B. and W. C. of All Saints', Cambridge, 1866. Formerly C. of Blagdon 1858. Author, *Nine Questions to the Baptists with an Examination of their Reply,* 1860, 6*d*; *What is the Right Method of conducting the Defence of the Old Testament,* 1863, 4*d*; *The Epistles to the Thessalonians, with an Introduction, Explanatory Notes, &c., for Private and Family Use* (written conjointly with Rev. E. Headland), 1863, 4*s*; *The Epistle to the Galatians, with an Introduction, &c.,* 1866, Hatchard and Co. 3*s* 6*d*. [8]

SWETE, John, *Blagdon Rectory, Bristol.*—Dub. A.B. 1808, A.M. B.D. and D.D. 1823; Deac. 1811 by Bp of Salis. Pr. 1812 by Bp of Glouc. R. of Blagdon, Dio. B. and W. 1850. (Patron, W. Fripp, Esq; Tithe, 512*l*; Glebe, 30 acres; R.'s Inc. 540*l* and Ho; Pop. 1083.) Formerly Chap. of Female Orphan Asylum, and Chap. of H. M. Gaol, Bristol. Author, *Family Prayers,* 12 eds. 3*s* 6*d*; *Explanation of the Church Catechism;* various Tracts and Sermons. [9]

SWETTENHAM, Thomas S. E., *Swettenham Rectory, Congleton, Cheshire.*—R. of Swettenham, Dio. Ches. 1814. (Patron, Rev. R. Blencoe; Tithe, 275*l* 10*s*; R.'s Inc. 300*l* and Ho; Pop. 350.) [10]

SWIFT, Benjamin, *Birkdale Parsonage, Southport, Lancashire.*—Queens' Coll. Cam. B.C.L. 1851; Deac. 1848, Pr. 1849. P. C. of Birkdale, Southport, Dio. Ches. 1857. (Patrons, Trustees; P. C.'s Inc. 350*l* and Ho; Pop. 3000.) Formerly C. of North Meols, Lanc. Author, Various Sermons. [11]

SWIFT, Godwin, *Beverley, Yorks.*—Dub. A.B. 1846, A.M. 1851; Deac. and Pr. 1848 by Bp of Meath. Chap. to the House of Correction for East Riding of York, Beverley, 1859. (Salary, 200*l*.) Formerly C. of St. Thomas's, Scarborough, 1850, Christ Church, Bradford, 1851, St. John's Chapel, Beverley, 1854. Author, *The Saviour's Parting Gift to His People* (a Sermon), 1859. [12]

SWIFT, J. S., *Waltham-on-the-Wolds, Leicestershire.*—C. of Waltham-on-the-Wolds. [13]

SWIFT, Thomas Walthew, *St. Mary's-lane, Walton, near Liverpool.*—Wad. Coll. Ox. B.A. 1862; Deac. 1864, Pr. 1865. C. of Walton-on-the-Hill 1865. Formerly C. of Great Budworth, Cheshire, 1864–65. [14]

SWINBOURN, James, *Trent, Enfield, Middlesex.*—P. C. of Ch. Ch. Trent, Enfield. Formerly P. C. of St. Paul's, Bethnal Green, Lond. 1863. [15]

SWINBURN, Frederick Thomas, *The School House, Hall Green, near Birmingham.*—Dub. A.B. 1856, A.M. 1859; Deac. 1857 and Pr. 1858 by Bp of Wor. C. of Yardley 1857; Head Mast. of the Free Sch. Hall Green, Yardley Author, *A School and What it should be,* 1858. [16]

SWINDEN, George, *Pershore, Worcestershire.*—Brasen. Coll. Ox. B.A. 1861, M.A. 1864; Deac. 1861 and Pr. 1862, by Bp of Wor. V. of Defford with Besford, Dio. Wor. 1865. (Patrons, D. and C. of Westminster. V.'s Inc. 186*l*. and Ho; Pop. 627.) Formerly C. of Pershore. [17]

SWINFORD, Smithett, *Ashton Keynes, Cricklade, Wilts.*—V. of Ashton Keynes, Dio. G. and B. 1866. (Patron, J. Swinford, Esq; V.'s Inc. 325*l* and Ho; Pop. 1382.) [18]

SWIRE, Frederick, *Elston Rectory, Newark, Notts.*—Emman. Coll. Cam. B.A. 1850; Deac. 1851. Pr. 1853 by Bp. of G. and B. R. of Elston, Dio. Lin. 1853. (Patroness, Mrs. F. Darwin; Glebe, 178 acres; R.'s Inc. 400*l* and Ho; Pop. 206.) Formerly C. of Stroud, Glouc. [19]

SYDENHAM, Charles St. Barbe, *Brushford Rectory, Dulverton, Somerset.*—Ex. Coll. Ox. B.A. 1846; Deac. 1847 and Pr. 1848 by Bp of B. and W. R. of Brushford, Dio. B. and W. 1858. (Patron, J. W. Sydenham, Esq; Tithe, 316*l*; Glebe, 120 acres; R.'s Inc. 450*l* and Ho; Pop. 328.) Formerly C. of Brushford. [20]

SYDENHAM, John George, *Shebbear Vicarage, Highampton, N. Devon.*—Ex. Coll. Ox. B.A. and M.A. (the same day) 1860; Deac. 1861 and Pr. 1862 by Bp of B. and W. C. of Shebbear with Sheepwash (sole charge) 1864. Formerly C. of Bridgwater 1861–63. [21]

SYDENHAM, John Philip, *Collumpton, Devon.*—Ex. Coll. Ox. B.A. 1825, M.A. 1829; Deac. 1826 and Pr. 1827 by Bp of Ex. R. of Willand near Collampton, Dio. Ex. 1855. (Patron, Charles James Henry Francis Salters, Esq; Tithe, 103*l* 8*s* 9*d*; Glebe, 1¾ acres; R.'s Inc. 105*l* and Ho; Pop. 382.) [22]

SYER, Barrington Blomfield, *Ashdon, Essex.* C. of Ashdon. [23]

SYER, Isaac, *Murton, Penrith.*—P. C. of Murton, Dio. Carl. 1865. (Patron, Bp of Carl; P. C.'s Inc. 99*l*; Pop. 471.) Formerly C. of Preston Patrick, Cumberland. [24]

SYER, William Henry, *Kedington Rectory, Haverhill, Suffolk.*—Jesus Coll. Cam. B.A. 1829; Deac. 1830 and Pr. 1831 by Bp of Nor. R. of Kedington, Dio. Ely, 1844. (Patron, the present R; Tithe, 701*l* 18*s*; Glebe, 116 acres; R.'s Inc. 780*l* and Ho; Pop. 700.) [25]

SYERS, Henry S., *Summertown, Oxford.*—Brasen. Coll. Ox. 3rd cl. Law and Mod. Hist. and B.A. 1861,

M.A. and B.C.L. 1864; Deac. 1864 and Pr. 1865 by Bp of Ox. C. of Summertown 1865. Formerly C. of St. Mary's, Banbury, 1864. [1]

SYKES, Edward John, *Basildon Vicarage, Reading.*—Wor. Coll. Ox. B.A. 1851, M.A. 1854; Deac. 1852, Pr. 1853. V. of Basildon, Dio. Ox. 1859. (Patrons, Rev. W. Sykes and Simeon's Trustees; V.'s Inc. 220*l* and Ho; Pop. 712.) Formerly C. of Timberscombe, Somerset. [2]

SYKES, Frederick Galland, *Dunsforth Parsonage, Ouseburn, York.*—St. John's Coll. Cam. Scho. of, 24th Wrang. B.A. 1857, M.A. 1860; Deac. 1858 by Bp of Win. Pr. 1859 by Bp of Ox. P. C. of Dunsforth, Dio. Rip. 1865. (Patron, V. of Aldborough; Glebe, 24 acres; P. C.'s Inc. 200*l* and Ho; Pop. 250.) Formerly C. of Colnbrook 1858–60, Slough 1860–64. [3]

SYKES, Godfrey Milnes, *Tadlow Vicarage, near Potton, Beds.*—Downing Coll. Cam. B.A. 1837, M.A. 1840; Deac. 1843 and Pr. 1849 by Bp of Ely. R. of East Hatley, Cambs, Dio. Ely, 1854. (Patron, Downing Coll; Tithe, 210*l*; Glebe, 5 acres; R.'s Inc. 300*l* and Ho; Pop. 139.) V. of Tadlow, Dio. Ely, 1851. (Patron, Downing Coll; Tithe, 127*l*; Glebe, 9 acres; V.'s Inc. 200*l* and Ho; Pop. 214.) [4]

SYKES, John Heath, *Bishopton, Stratford-on-Avon.*—Wor. Coll. Ox. B.A. 1857; Deac. 1857 and Pr. 1858 by Bp of Pet. R. of Billesley, Dio. Wor. 1859. (Patrons, Trustees of late M. Miles, Esq; Tithe, 15*l*; Glebe, 200 acres; R.'s Inc. 312*l* 6*s*; Pop. 35.) V. of Haselor, Dio. Wor. 1867. (Patron, Ld Chan; Tithe, 6*l* 10*s*; Glebe, 8½ acres; V.'s Inc. 63*l*; Pop. 355.) Formerly C. of Chipping Warden, Northants, 1857–59. [5]

SYKES, John Poulett, *Rathmell Parsonage, Settle, Yorks.*—Deac. 1860 and Pr. 1861 by Bp of Man. P. C. of Rathmell, Dio. Rip. 1866. (Patron, Bp of Rip; P. C.'s Inc. 106*l* and Ho; Pop. 305.) Formerly C. of St. James's, Burnley, 1860–62, St. Helens, Lanc. 1862–64, Clapham, Yorks, 1864–66. [6]

SYKES, William, *Chatham.*—Oriel Coll. Ox. M.A; Deac. 1852 and Pr. 1853 by Bp of Nor. Chap. to the Forces, Chatham. Formerly Chap. in Crimea 1855, Cape of Good Hope 1857–60. [7]

SYKES, William, *Dorrington Vicarage, Sleaford, Lincolnshire.*—V. of Dorrington or Dirrington, Dio. Lin. 1862. (Patron, Lord Aveland; Tithe—App. 15*l*, V. 9*l*; Glebe, 115 acres; V.'s Inc. 120*l*; Pop. 467.) [8]

SYLVESTER, C. W., *Devonport.*—C. of St. Stephen's, Devonport. [9]

SYLVESTER, Edward T., *Deene, Wansford, Northants.*—C. of Deene; Dom. Chap. to the Earl of Cardigan. [10]

SYLVESTER, Paul D'Ockham, *West Knighton, Dorchester.*—Ex. Coll. Ox. B.A. 1850, M.A. 1853; Deac. 1851 and Pr. 1852 by Bp of G. and B. C. of West Knighton and Broadmayne, Dorset. [11]

SYLVESTER, William Thomas Mainwaring, *Castleford Rectory, Yorks.*—King's Coll. Lond. Theol. Assoc; Deac. and Pr. 1851. R. of Castleford, Dio. York, 1855. (Patron, Duchy of Lancaster; R.'s Inc. 560*l* and Ho; Pop. 4365.) Formerly Asst. C. of Howden, and Hon. Chap. to the Howden Union, Yorks. [12]

SYMES, Richard, *Cleeve, Bristol.*—Jesus Coll. Cam. B.A. 1824, M.A. 1827; Deac. and Pr. 1825. P. C. of Trinity, Cleeve, Yatton, Dio. B. and W. 1843. (Patron, V. of Yatton; Tithe, 47*l* 17*s* 11*d*; P. C.'s Inc. 78*l*; Pop. 282.) Preb. of Ilton in Wells Cathl. 1853; Asst. Rural Dean of Portishead in the Deanery of Chew. [13]

SYMES, Thomas Legg, *Queen Camel, Somerset.*—Trin. Coll. Cam. B.A. 1853, M.A. 1856; Deac. 1855 and Pr. 1856 by Bp of Ex. C. of Queen Camel 1864. Formerly C. of Redruth, Cornwall, 1855–60, Martock, Somerset, 1860–64. [14]

SYMES, John Edward, *College, Bath.*—St. John's Coll. Cam. Scho. of, 23rd Wrang. B.A. 1858, M.A. Vice-Prin. of the Proprietary Coll. Bath. [15]

SYMONDS, George Edward, *Thaxted Vicarage, Essex.*—Lin. Coll. Ox. B.A. 1842, M.A. 1863; Deac. 1843 and Pr. 1844 by Bp of Salis. V. of Thaxted, Dio. Roch. 1859. (Patron, Viscount Maynard; Tithe, 468*l*; V.'s Inc. 600*l* and Ho; Pop. 2311.) Rural Dean 1863. Formerly P. C. of Tilty, Essex, 1856–59. [16]

SYMONDS, Henry, *The Close, Norwich.*—Magd. Hall, Ox. B.A. 1840, M.A. 1842; Deac. 1843, Pr. 1844. Precentor and Min. Can. of Nor. Cathl. 1844. Formerly C. of St. Mary-in-the-Marsh, Norwich. [17]

SYMONDS, Horatio Giles, *Skegness, Burgh, Lincolnshire.*—Magd. Hall, Ox. M.A. 1855; Deac. 1852 by Bp of Win. Pr. 1854 by Bp of Salis. C. (sole charge) of Skegness 1867. [18]

SYMONDS, John, *Baldhu Parsonage, Truro, Cornwall.*—Clare Coll. Cam. B.A. 1839; Deac. and Pr. 1840. P. C. of Baldhu, Dio. Ex. 1855. (Patron, Viscount Falmouth; P. C.'s Inc. 220*l* and Ho; Pop. 2070.) [19]

SYMONDS, M. F.—C. of St. Mark's, Kennington, Surrey. [20]

SYMONDS, Proger Herbert, *Church Withington Vicarage, near Hereford.*—St. Edm. Hall, Ox. B.A. 1831, M.A. 1833; Deac. 1831 and Pr. 1832 by Bp of Herf. V. of Church Withington, Dio. Herf. 1857. (Patron, Bp of Herf; Tithe, 132*l* 7*s*; Glebe, 16 acres and a farm of 100 acres; V.'s Inc. 417*l* 9*s* 7*d* and Ho; Pop. 788.) Formerly C. of Clehonger, Herefordshire. [21]

SYMONDS, Samuel, *Philleigh Rectory, Grampound, Cornwall.*—Clare Hall, Cam. B.A. 1816, M.A. 1819; Deac. 1815, Pr. 1816. R. of Philleigh, or Fellye, Dio. Ex. 1818. (Patron, Rev. W. Fooks; Tithe, 350*l*; Glebe, 21 acres; R.'s Inc. 380*l* and Ho; Pop. 363.) [22]

SYMONDS, William Samuel, *Pendock Rectory, near Tewkesbury.*—Ch. Coll. Cam. B.A. 1840; Deac. 1841, Pr. 1842. R. of Pendock, Dio. Wor. 1844. (Patron, Rev. W. L. Symonds; Tithe, 320*l*; R.'s Inc. 374*l* and Ho; Pop. 329.) Fell. of the Geol. Soc. Author, *Old Stones*, 1855; *Stones of the Valley*, 1857; *Old Bones*, 1864; Articles in *Edinb. New Phil. Journal*, *Journal of Geol. Soc.* and *Phil. Mag.* [23]

SYMONS, Benjamin Parsons, *Wadham College, Oxford.*—Wad. Coll. Ox. B.A. 1805, M.A. 1810, B.D. 1820, D.D. 1831; Deac. 1809 by Bp of Salis. Pr. 1810 by Bp of Glouc; Fell. and Tut. of Wad. Coll. 1811; Select Preacher of Univ. 1813, 1821, 1831; Public Examiner 1819, 1824; Whitehall Preacher 1823; Vice-Chan. of the Univ. of Oxford 1844–48; Warden of Wad. Coll. Ox. 1831. [24]

SYMONS, Edward, *Ringmer Vicarage, Lewes.*—Wad. Coll. Ox. B.A. 1835; Deac. 1837 by Bp of Lin. Pr. 1838 by Bp of Chich. V. of Ringmer, Dio. Chich. 1863. (Patron, Abp of Cant; Tithe—Imp. 585*l*, V. 400*l* 6*s*; V.'s Inc. 420*l* and Ho; Pop. 1522.) Formerly C. of Ringmer, Sussex, 1841. [25]

SYMONS, John Trehane, *Trevalga Rectory, Boscastle, Cornwall.*—Ex. Coll. Ox. B.A. 1809; Deac. 1809 and Pr. 1810 by Bp of Ex. R. of Trevalga, Dio. Ex. 1832. (Patrons, D. and C. of Ex; Tithe, 140*l*; Glebe, 50 acres; R.'s Inc. 220*l* and Ho; Pop. 140.) [26]

SYMPSON, Charles John, *Kirkby-Misperton Rectory, Pickering, Yorks.*—Trin. Coll. Cam. B.A. 1826, M.A. 1829; Deac. 1827 and Pr. 1828 by Abp of York. R. of Kirkby-Misperton, Dio. York, 1845. (Patron, Lord Feversham; Tithe, 840*l*; Glebe, 120 acres; R.'s Inc. 960*l* and Ho; Pop. 1002.) [27]

SYNGE, Alexander Hamilton, *St. Peter's Parsonage, Ipswich.*—Dub. P. C. of St. Peter's, Ipswich, Dio. Nor. 1857. (Patrons, Simeon's Trustees; P. C.'s Inc. 138*l* and Ho; Pop. 3639.) Formerly C. of Ch. Ch. Clifton, and Trinity, Mile-end, Lond; Min. of the Mariner's Ch. Kingstown. Author, *Law and Grace* (Four Lectures refuting errors of Plymouth Brethren), 9*d*; *The Triumph of Grace*, 2*s*; *The Church Ordinances*, 2*s* 6*d*; *Hymns*, 1*s*; all published by Hunt, Holles-street, Cavendish-square. [28]

SYNGE, Francis, 37, *Oakley-square, Chelsea, S.W.*—Trin. Coll. Cam. 2nd cl. Cl. Trip. B.A. 1859, M.A. 1863; Deac. 1860 and Pr. 1861 by Bp of Ely. C. of St. Luke's, Chelsea, 1862. Formerly C. of All Saints', Huntingdon, 1860–62. [29]

SZYRMA, W. S. L., *St. Ive, Liskeard, Cornwall.*—C. of St. Ive. [30]

TABBERER, G., *Coventry.*—P. C. of St. George's, Coventry, Dio. Wor. 1862. (Patron, V. of Holy Trinity; P. C.'s Inc. 300*l* and Ho; Pop. 3809.) [1]

TABOR, Robert Stammers, *Cheam, Surrey.*—Trin. Coll. Cam. B.A. 1842, M.A. 1845; Deac. 1842, Pr. 1844. Head Mast. of Cheam School. Formerly P. C. of Ch. Ch. Enfield, Middlesex. [2]

TABOR, W. C., *Thornton-le-Moor, Lincolnshire.* C. of Thornton-le-Moor. [3]

TADDY, John, *Caldicot Lodge, Biggleswade, Beds.*—Clare Coll. Cam. B.A. 1835, M.A. 1838; Deac. 1885 and Pr. 1836 by Bp of Lin. V. of Dunton, Dio. Ely, 1852. (Patron, Lord Brownlow; Tithe, 104*l* 15*s*; Glebe, 56 acres; V.'s Inc. 267*l* 10*s*; Pop. 518.) [4]

TAGART, W. B., *Crowfield Parsonage, Needham Market, Suffolk.*—Dub. A.B. 1855; Deac. 1858 and Pr. 1859 by Abp of Dublin. C. of Crowfield 1866. Formerly C. of Scissett, Yorks. [5]

TAGERT, John, *Bideford, Devon.*—Dub. A.B. 1838; Deac. 1849 and Pr. 1850 by Bp of Ox. C. of Bideford; Chap. to the Bideford Union. [6]

TAGERT, Samuel William, *Pyworthy Rectory, Holsworthy, Devon.*—Dub. A.B. 1850; Deac. 1851, Pr. 1852. R. of Pyworthy, Dio. Ex. 1862. (Patron, Rev. Mr. Kingdon; R.'s Inc. 360*l* and Ho; Pop. 567.) Rural Dean. Formerly C. of Trewen, Cornwall. [7]

TAGG, John, *Mellis Rectory, Suffolk.*—Pemb. Coll. Cam. B.A. 1841, M.A. 1844; Deac. 1842, Pr. 1843. R. of Mellis, Dio. Nor. 1867. (Patron, Ld Chan; Tithe, 348*l*; Glebe, 10*l*; R.'s Inc. 358*l* and Ho; Pop. 598.) Formerly P. C. of St. John's, Bethnal Green, Lond. 1845–66. Joint Author with the Rev. J. B. Ansted, of *Sermons on the Apostolic Churches*, 1845, 2*s* 6*d*. [8]

TAIT, Thomas Henry, *Hilperton Rectory, Trowbridge, Wilts.*—Trin. Coll. Cam. B.A. 1847, M.A. 1850. R. of Hilperton with Whaddon, Dio. Salis. 1861. (Patron, W. Long, Esq; R.'s Inc. 418*l* and Ho; Pop. Hilperton 880, Whaddon 40.) Formerly P. C. of Mollington, Oxon, 1851–61. [9]

TAIT, Walter James, *Worcester College, Oxford.*—Fell. and Jun. Tutor of Wor. Coll. [10]

TAIT, William, *Pau.*—Univs. of Edin. and St. Andrew's, M.A. 1841; Deac. 1841 and Pr. 1842 by Bp of S. and M. English Chap. at Pau. Formerly P. C. of Trinity, Wakefield, 1843–53; P. C. of St. Matthew's, Rugby, 1856. Author, *Exposition of the Lord's Prayer*, 1849, 4*s* 6*d*; *The Bible, or Rome? The Jew, the Gentile, and the African*; *The Gospel*; *Confirmation Catechism*; *Christ's Ministry the Model of Ours* (Ordination Sermon), 1850; *Serpent in the Wilderness*, 1851; *Slave Trade overruled for the Salvation of Africa*, 1852, 1*s*; *Sermon on the Death of the Duke of Wellington*, 1852; *Salvation and Obedience* (a Farewell Sermon), 1853; *Exposition of the Epistle to the Hebrews*, 1844, 2nd ed. 1854, 2 vols. 17*s*; *Sermon on the Crimean War*, 1855; *Appeal against the Opium Trade*, 1858, 2nd ed. 1859, 6*d*; etc. [11]

TALBOT, The Hon. Arthur Chetwynd, *Ingestric Rectory, near Stafford.*—Ch. Ch. Ox. B.A. 1826, All Souls' Coll. Ox. M.A. 1829; Deac. 1828 and Pr. 1829 by Bp of Wor. R. of Ingestrie, Dio. Lich. 1829. (Patron, Earl of Shrewsbury; Tithe, 212*l* 13*s* 6*d*; Glebe, 326 acres; R.'s Inc. 575*l* and Ho; Pop. 151.) R. of Church Eaton, near Penkridge, Staffs, Dio. Lich. 1829. (Patron, Earl of Shrewsbury; Tithe, 765*l*; Glebe, 89 acres; R.'s Inc. 925*l* and Ho; Pop. 643.) Rural Dean of Lapley and Triezull. Formerly Fell. of All Souls Coll. Ox. [12]

TALBOT, C. H., *Faversham, Kent.*—C. of Faversham. [13]

TALBOT, The Hon. Edward Plantagenet Airey, *Evercreech Vicarage, Bath.*—Dub. A.B. 1850; Deac. 1850, Pr. 1851. V. of Evercreech with Chesterblade C. Dio. B. and W. 1852. (Patroness, Dowager Lady Talbot de Malahide; Tithe—Imp. 150*l*, V. 250*l*; V.'s Inc. 250*l* and Ho; Pop. 1321.) [14]

TALBOT, Ebenezer Rushton, *Broomhall-park, Sheffield.*—Giessen, M.A. and Ph.D. 1848, D.D. 1861; Deac. 1863 and Pr. 1864 by Abp of York. C. of Sheffield, 1863. Author *Expository Sketches in the Gospel Narratives*, 1855, 1*s* 6*d*; *Experimental Christianity*, 1855, 2*s* 6*d*; *Twenty-five Lectures to Sunday-school Teachers*, 1864, 1*s* 6*d*. [15]

TALBOT, The Hon. George Gustavus Chetwynd, *Withington Rectory, Andoversford, Glouc.*—Ch. Ch. Ox. B A. 1831, M.A. 1833. R. of Withington, Dio. G. and B. 1834. (Patron, Bp of G. and B; Tithe, 295*l* 16*s* 8*d*; Glebe, 1080 acres; R.'s Inc. 650*l* and Ho; Pop. 783.) Formerly C. of Ingestre 1833. [16]

TALBOT, James Hale, *Newton Blossomville, Olney, Bucks.*—Pemb. Coll. Ox. B.A. 1830, M.A. 1834; Deac. 1831 and Pr. 1832 by Bp of Lin. R. of Newton Blossomville, Dio. Ox. 1846. (Patron, W. F. Farren, Esq; Glebe, 156 acres; R.'s Inc. 220*l* and Ho; Pop. 277.) Formerly C. of Hardmead, Bucks. [17]

TALBOT, Thomas, *Chapeltown, Sheffield.*—Deac. 1862 and Pr. 1863 by Bp of Rip. C. of Chapeltown 1864. Formerly C. of Clapham, Lancaster, 1862. [18]

TALBOT, The Hon. William Whitworth Chetwynd, *Bishops Hatfield Rectory, Herts.*—Ch. Ch. Ox. B.A 1834; Deac. 1836 by Bp of Lich. Pr. 1837 by Bp of Wor. R. of Bishops Hatfield with Totteridge C. Dio. Roch. 1855. (Patron, Marquis of Salisbury; Bishops Hatfield, Tithe, 1901*l* 17*s*; Glebe, 107 acres; Totteridge, Tithe, 346*l* 15*s*; R.'s Inc. 2100*l* and Ho; Hatfield 3381, Totteridge 573.) [19]

TALFOURD, William Wordsworth, *Winceby, Horncastle, Lincolnshire.*—New Coll. Ox. B.A. 1854. R. of Winceby, Dio. Lin. 1860. (Patron, Ld Chan; R.'s Inc. 390*l*; Pop. 67.) Formerly C. of St. Mary the Virgin's, Soho, Lond. [20]

TALMAGE, John Mayow, *Fifield, Chipping Norton, Oxon.*—Ch. Ch. Ox. 2nd cl. Lit. Hum. B.A. 1834, M.A. 1837; Deac. 1836 and Pr. 1837 by Bp of Ox. P. C. of Fifield, Dio. Ox. 1843. (Patron, Bp of Ox; Tithe—App. 267*l* 10*s*; Glebe, 37½ acres; P. C.'s Inc. 76*l*; Pop. 234.) P. C. of Idbury, Dio. Ox. 1848. (Patron, Bp of Ox; Glebe, 192 acres; P. C.'s Inc. 32*l*; Pop. 233.) [21]

TALMAN, William, *Haddiscoe Rectory, Beccles, Norfolk.*—King's Coll. Cam. B.A. 1843, M.A. 1846; Deac. 1844 by Bp of Lin. Pr. 1845 by Bp of Salis. R. of Haddiscoe with Monks'-Toft R. Dio. Nor. 1860. (Patron, King's Coll. Cam; R.'s Inc. 500*l* and Ho; Pop. 782.) Formerly Fell. of King's Coll. Cam; P. C. of Waltisham, Suffolk. [22]

TALON, Thomas Knox, 29, *Southampton-street, Strand, London, W.C.*, and 31, *Hungerford-road, Holloway, N.*—Dub. 1843; Deac. 1845 and Pr. 1846 by Abp of Dub. Sec. to the Lond. Hibernian Soc; C. of St. James's, Clerkenwell, 1866. Formerly C. of Thornham and Holme-next-the-Sea, Norfolk, 1847–58; Min. of Belgrave Chapel, 1864–65. Author, *Papists' Conspiracy*, 1848; *The Light of the Knowledge of the Glory of God* (a Sermon), 1849; *Sermons preached in Belgrave Chapel*, 1866, Nisbet and Co., 7*s* 6*d*. [23]

TAMPLIN, George Frederick, *Purleigh Rectory, Maldon, Essex.*—St. John's Coll. Ox. B.A. 1847, M.A. 1849, Deac. 1847 by Bp of Salis. Pr. 1848 by Bp of Roch. C. of Purleigh. [24]

TANCOCK, John Keigwin, *Cheam, Surrey.*—Sid. Coll. Cam. 1st Sen. Opt. B.A. 1863, M.A. 1866; Deac. 1865, Pr. 1866. C. of Ch. Ch. Epsom Common, 1865. [25]

TANCOCK, Osborne John, *The Vicarage, Tavistock, Devon.*—Wad. Coll. Ox. B.A. 1830, M.A. 1840, D.C.L. 1841; Deac. 1830 and Pr. 1831 by Bp of Ex. V. of Tavistock, Dio. Ex. 1857. (Patron, Duke of Bedford; Tithe—Imp. 363*l* 11*s*; V.'s Inc. 300*l* and Ho; Pop. 7642.) Surrogate and Rural Dean. Formerly P. C. of St. John's, Kenwyn, Cornwall, 1839–57. Author, *Sermons on the Death of the Dowager Queen Adelaide, and on Everlasting Punishment and Life Eternal, and two Farewell Sermons on Leaving Truro for Tavistock.* [26]

TANCOCK, Osborne William, *King's School, Sherborne, Dorset.*—Ex. Coll. Ox. 2nd cl. Lit. Hum. B.A.

1862; M.A. 1864; Deac. 1864 and Pr. 1865 by Bp of Salis. Asst. Mast. in the King's Sch. Sherborne. [1]

TANDY, Charles Henry, *The Hermitage, Harrow, Middlesex, N.W.*—Dub. Math. Cl. and Div. Prize M.A; Deac. 1859 and Pr. 1860 by Bp of Lon. C. of Harrow 1862. Formerly C. of Pinner, Middlesex, 1859–61. [2]

TANDY, George Mercer, *Lowswater, Whitehaven, Cumberland.*—St. John's Coll. Cam. 37th Wrang. and B.A. 1842; Deac. 1843 and Pr. 1844 by Bp of Carl. P. C. of Lowswater, Dio. Carl. 1866. (Patron, Earl of Lonsdale; P. C.'s Inc. 49*l* and Ho; Pop. 392.) Formerly P. C. of Newlands, 1861. [3]

TANDY, John Mortimore, *Devizes, Wilts.*—St. Peter's Coll. Cam. B.A. 1849, M.A. 1853. Head Mast. of the Gr. Sch. Devizes. Formerly C. of St. Andrew's, Montpelier, Bristol. [4]

TANNER, James, *Gosport, Hants.*—Queen's Coll. Ox. M.A. P. C. of St. Matthew's, Gosport, Dio. Win. 1849. (Patrons, Bp of Win. and R. of Alverstoke, alt; P. C.'s Inc. 200*l*; Pop. 4836.) [5]

TANNER, James Selwood, *Tenby, South Wales.*—C. of Tenby. [6]

TANNER, John Vowler, *Rockcliffe, Carlisle,*—Caius Coll. Cam. B.A. 1854; Deac. 1867 by Bp of Carl. C. of Rockcliffe 1867. [7]

TANNER, John William Newell, *Antrobus Parsonage, Northwich, Cheshire.*—St. Cath. Coll. Cam. B.A. 1846; Deac. 1846, Pr. 1847. P. C. of Antrobus, Dio. Ches. 1850. (Patron, V. of Great Budworth; P. C.'s Inc. 85*l* and Ho; Pop. 800.) Formerly C. of Newton Moor 1846, Mossley Moss, Congleton 1847-50. [8]

TANNER, Thomas Charles, *Burlescombe, Wellington, Somerset.*—Sid. Coll. Cam. S.C.L. 1849, LL.B. 1852; Deac. 1850 and Pr. 1855 by Bp of B. and W. V. of Burlescombe, Dio. Ex. 1866. (Patron, E. A. Sanford, Esq; Tithe, comm, 330*l*; Glebe, 17 acres; V.'s Inc. 330*l* and Ho; Pop. 856.) Min. of Ayshford Chapel, 1866. Formerly C. of Nynehead, Somerset, 1850–66. [9]

TANNER, Thomas Edward, *Hastings, Sussex.*—Min. of the Fishermen's Chapel, Hastings. [10]

TANNER, William Afric, *Ealing, Middlesex, W.*—King's Coll. Lond. Theol. Assoc. 1858; Deac. 1858 and Pr. 1860 by Bp of Win. C. of Ealing 1867. Formerly C. of Stoke d'Abernon, and Coulsdon, Surrey. [11]

TANQUERAY, Truman, *Tingrith Rectory, Woburn, Beds.*—Pemb. Coll. Cam. B.A. 1843, M.A. 1846; Deac. 1844 by Bp of Ely, Pr. 1846 by Abp of York. R. of Tingrith, Dio. Ely, 1847. (Patronesses, the Misses Trevor; Tithe, 240*l*; Glebe, 5½ acres; R.'s Inc. 250*l* and Ho; Pop. 226.) [12]

TAPSFIELD, Edward, *Cloisters, Windsor Castle.*—Min. Can. of St. George's, Windsor, 1861. [13]

TAPSON, Robert, *Camberwell, Surrey, S.*—C. of Camberwell. [14]

TARBUTT, Arthur Charles, *Streatham, S.*—Wad. Coll. Ox. Fell. of, B.A. 1832, M.A. 1835; Deac. 1833 by Bp of Ox. Pr. 1834 by Bp of Chich. P. C. of St. Peter's, Temporary Ch. Streatham, 1866. Formerly P. C. of Southend, Essex, 1847–50; Incumb. of St. John's, Jedburgh, Scotland, 1850–58; C. of Ascot-under-Wychwood, Oxon, 1858–60, St. Paul's, Wilton-place, Belgravia, 1860–66. Author, *Christian Loyalty* (a Sermon), 6*d*; *Observance of Lent* (a Sermon), 6*d*; *Contend for the Faith* (a Sermon), 6*d*; *What is the Papal Supremacy?* (a Tract), 4*d*; *Blessed art Thou among Women* (a Sermon). [15]

TARLETON, William Haigh, *Shepton-Mallett, Somerset.*—St. John's Coll. Cam. B.A. 1861, M.A. 1865; Deac. 1862, Pr. 1863. Sen. C. of Shepton-Mallett 1863. Formerly C. of Cheddon Fitzpaine, Somerset, 1862–63. [16]

TARLTON, Thomas Henry, *Rectory, Horsleydown, Surrey.*—Caius Coll. Cam; Deac. and Pr. 1858. R. of St. John's, Horsleydown, Dio. Win. 1866. (Patron, Ld Chan; R.'s Inc. 360*l* and Ho; Pop. 7971.) Formerly P. C. of Stroud 1858. Author, *Preface to Lectures on Great Men*, 1855, 5*s*. [17]

TARR, Henry, *Ardwick, Manchester.*—Sid. Coll. Cam. B.A. 1844; Deac. 1844, Pr. 1846. [18]

TARVER, Charles Feral, *St. Peter's Vicarage, Thanet.*—King's Coll. Cam. B.A. 1843, M.A. 1846; Deac. 1846 and Pr. 1849 by Bp of Lin. V. of St. Peter's, Thanet, Dio. Cant. 1863. (Patron, Abp of Cant; Tithe, 545*l*; V.'s Inc. 600*l* and Ho; Pop. 1530.) Chap. in Ordinary to the Queen; Hon. Chap. to the Prince of Wales. Formerly Fell. of King's Coll. Cam; Cl. Tut. to the Prince of Wales; R. of St. John's, Ilketshall, 1855–63. [19]

TARVER, Joseph, *Filgrove Rectory, Newport-Pagnell, Bucks.*—Ex. Coll. Ox. B.A. 1848; Deac. 1849, Pr. 1855. R. of Filgrove with Tyringham, Dio. Ox. 1850. (Patron, William B. Praed, Esq; Tithe, 454*l* 3*s* 6*d*; Glebe, 15 acres; R.'s Inc. 454*l* and Ho; Pop. 226.) [20]

TASKER, Henry, *Soham Vicarage, Cambs.*—Pemb. Coll. Cam. B.A. 1816, M.A. 1819. V. of Soham with Barway C. Dio. Ely, 1832. (Patron, Pemb. Coll. Cam; Tithe—Imp. 700*l*, V. 1654*l* 10*s*; V.'s Inc. 1675*l* and Ho; Pop. 4278.) Hon. Can. of Ely. Formerly Fell. of Pemb. Coll. Cam. [21]

TASKER, James, *Carlisle.*—Lampeter 1841; B.D. 1867; Deac. 1845 and Pr. 1846 by Bp of St. D. P. C. of Trinity, City and Dio. Carl. 1855. (Patrons, D. and C. of Carl; Glebe, 23*l*; P. C.'s Inc. 300*l* and Ho; Pop. 8000.) Formerly C. of Walton East 1845–46, Nolton and Roch 1846–55, both in Pembrokeshire; Asst. Tut. Lampeter 1844-45. [22]

TASKER, John Campbell Wheatley, 1, *Upper Lansdown-villas, Bath.*—Pemb. Coll. Cam. B.A. 1846; Deac. 1847 and Pr. 1849 by Bp of Ely. Chap. of Bath Mineral Water Hospital 1862. Formerly C. of Lawshall, Suffolk, 1847–49, Chapel of Ease, Worthing, 1851–52, Weston, near Bath, 1852–53; Chap. of the Bath United Hospital 1858–62. [23]

TASWELL, George, *Bekesbourne Vicarage, near Canterbury.*—Brasen. Coll. Ox. B.A. 1843, M.A. 1846; Deac. 1845 and Pr. 1846 by Abp of Cant. V. of Bekesbourne, Dio. Cant. 1859. (Patron, Abp of Cant; Tithe—App. 285*l* 3*s*, V. 119*l* 8*s*; V.'s Inc. 215*l* and Ho; Pop. 375.) [24]

TATAM, George, *Charles-street, Hackney-road, E.*—St. Cath. Coll. Cam. B.A. 1843, M.A. 1847; Deac. 1843 and Pr. 1844 by Bp of Ches. C. of St. Thomas's, Bethnal Green, Lond. [25]

TATE, Alexander, *Brompton-Regis Vicarage, Dulverton, Somerset.*—Emman. Coll. Cam. B.A. 1833, M.A. 1836; Deac. 1837 by Bp of Salis; Pr. 1839 by Bp of Roch. V. of Brompton-Regis, Dio. B. and W. 1847. (Patron, Emman. Coll. Cam; Tithe—Imp. 176*l*, V. 425*l*; Glebe, 67 acres; V.'s Inc. 460*l* and Ho; Pop. 929.) [26]

TATE, Charles Richmond, *Send Vicarage, Woking Station, Surrey.*—Corpus Coll. Ox. 2nd cl. Cl. 3rd cl. Math. 1835, B.A. 1835, M.A. 1842, B.D. 1849; Deac. 1838 by Bp of Ox. Pr. 1839 by Bp of Win. V. of Send with Ripley C. Dio. Win. 1852. (Patron, Earl Onslow; Tithe, 397*l*; Glebe, 30 acres; V.'s Inc. 367*l* and Ho; Pop. Send 810, Ripley 933.) Formerly Fell. of Corpus Coll. Ox; C. of Witley, Surrey, 1838, West Clandon 1839–52. [27]

TATE, Francis, *Axminster Vicarage, Devon.*—Ball. Coll. Ox. 1836, Univ. Coll. Ox. 1838, 1st cl. Lit. Hum. and B.A. 1840, M.A 1842; Deac. and Pr. 1844. V. of Axminster with Kilmington C. and Membury C. annexed, Dio. Ex. 1855. (Patron, Dean of Llan; Tithe—App. 1035*l* 6*s*, V. 1184*l*; Glebe, ½ acre; V.'s Inc. 1184*l* and Ho; Pop. Axminster 2707, Kilmington 518, Membury 751.) Surrogate. Formerly R. of Girton, Cambs, 1848–50; Incumb. of Berkeley Chapel, St. George's, Hanover-square, Lond. 1850–55. [28]

TATE, Francis Blackburne, *Quebec, Canada.*—Magd. Coll. Cam. B.A. 1831, M.A. 1834; Deac. and Pr. 1833. Chap. to the Forces, Quebec, 1859; V. of Charing, Kent, Dio. Cant. 1838. (Patrons, D. and C. of St. Paul's Cathl; Tithe, 430*l*; V.'s Inc. 460*l* and Ho; Pop. 1285.) [29]

TATE, George Edward, *Widcombe Lodge, Bath.*—St. John's Coll. Cam. Wrang. B.A. 1841, M.A. 1844;

Deac. 1841 and Pr. 1842 by Bp. of Win. V. of Widcombe, Bath, Dio. B. and W. 1856. (Patrons, Simeon's Trustees; Tithe, 129*l*; V.'s Inc. 350*l*; Pop. 4592.) Chap. to Earl of Kintore; District Dioc. Inspector for Bath; Hon. Sec. Ch. of England Education Soc. Formerly C. of Godstone, Surrey, 1841–45, Great Warley, Essex, 1847–49; P. C. of St. Jude's, Southwark, 1849–56. [1]

TATE, James, *Croxton Rectory, Ulceby, Lincolnshire.*—Corpus Coll. Ox. B.A. 1858, M.A. 1860; Deac. 1859 and Pr. 1860 by Bp of Nor. P. C. of Croxton, Dio. Lin. 1865. (Patron, Ld. Chan; Glebe, 24 acres; R.'s Inc. 420*l* and Ho; Pop. 310.) Formerly V. of Marske, Redcar, Yorks; P. C. of Trinity, Richmond, 1863–65. [2]

TATE, William, *School House, Woodbridge, Suffolk.*—Dub. A.B. 1852, A.M. 1857, *ad eund.* Cam. 1858, D.C.L. 1865. Deac. 1856 by Bp of Carl. Pr. 1857 by Abp of York. Head Mast. of the Seckford Gr. Sch. Woodbridge, 1865. Formerly C. of Ecclesall, Sheffield, and Mast. in the Collegiate Sch. Sheffield, 1856–59; Head Mast. of the Aldeburgh Gr. Sch. Suffolk, 1859–65. [3]

TATHAM, Alfred, *Southwell, Notts.*—St. John's Coll. Cam. B.A. 1837, M.A. 1841; Deac. 1839, Pr. 1840. Min. Can. of Southwell Coll. Ch. 1841. (Value, 150*l*.) Formerly P. C. of Halam, Notts, 1854–61. [4]

TATHAM, Arthur, *Broadoak Rectory, Lostwithiel, Cornwall.*—Magd. Coll. Cam. B.A. 1832, M.A. 1835; Deac. 1832 by Bp of Ely, Pr. 1832 by Bp of Ex. R. of Boconnoc with Broadoak R. Dio. Ex. 1832. (Patron, Hon. G. M. Fortescue; Tithe, 390*l*; Glebe, 82 acres; R.'s Inc. 470*l* and Ho; Pop. Boconnoc 323, Broadoak 274.) Preb. of Exeter 1860. Author, *A Church the House of God and Gate of Heaven* (a Sermon); *Prayers for the Use of Members of the Church of England during her present Troubles* (a Tract), 1851. [5]

TATHAM, George Edmund, *Great Ryburgh Rectory, Fakenham, Norfolk.*—Mert. Coll. Ox. 1849, 3rd cl. Lit. Hum. and B.A. 1852, M.A. 1856; Deac. 1853 and Pr. 1854 by Bp of Lon. R. of Great Ryburgh with Little Ryburgh V. Dio. Nor. 1859. (Patron, Meaburn Tatham, Esq; R. and V.'s Inc. 620*l* and Ho; Pop. Great Ryburgh 556, Little Ryburgh 232.) Formerly Asst. Mast. of Sir Roger Cholmeley's Gr. Sch. Highgate, Lond. 1853–57; R. of Hautbois Magna, Norfolk, 1857–59. [6]

TATHAM, George Turner, *Preston.*—St. John's Coll. Cam. B.A. 1856, M.A. 1859; Deac. 1857 and Pr. 1858 by Bp of Wor. Head Mast. of the Preston Gr. Sch. Formerly Math. Mast. in Bromsgrove Sch; Chap. to the Bromsgrove Union 1858. [7]

TATHAM, John, *Rydal, Ambleside, Westmoreland.*—St. John's Coll. Cam. B.A. 1850. P. C. of Rydal, Dio. Carl. 1857. (Patron, General Le Fleming; P. C.'s Inc. 110*l*; Pop. 414.) Formerly C. of Melling, near Lancaster. [8]

TATHAM, Ralph Raisbech, *Dallington Vicarage, near Hurst Green, Sussex.*—St. John's Coll. Cam. 4th Jun. Opt. and B.A. 1844, M.A. 1847; Deac. 1845, Pr. 1846. V. of Dallington, Dio. Chich. 1848. (Patron, Earl of Ashburnham; Tithe, 295*l*; V.'s Inc. 296*l* and Ho; Pop. 580.) [9]

TATLOCK, William, *Gloucester.*—M.A.; Deac. 1848, Pr. 1849. Assoc. Sec. of the Ch. Pastoral Aid Soc. Author, *The Man of Sorrows*, 1850, 1*s* 6*d*, 2nd ed. 1867; *The Lost One, or the Soul Ruined by Sin*, 1850, 4*d*; *Hymns for Sunday Schools*, 1857, 1*d*. [10]

TATTAM, The Ven. Henry, *Stanford-Rivers Rectory, Romford, Essex.*—Dub. LL.D. Göttingen, D.D. Leyden, Ph. D. R. of Stanford-Rivers, Dio. Roch. 1849. (Patron, Chan. of the Duchy of Lancaster; Tithe, 1020*l*; Glebe, 54 acres; R.'s Inc. 1024*l* and Ho; Pop. 992.) Rural Dean; Chap. in Ordinary to the Queen 1853; Fell. of the Royal Soc. Formerly R. of St. Cuthbert's, Bedford; Archd. of Bedford 1845–66. Author, *Helps to Devotion*; *Egyptian Grammar and Lexicon*; *Twelve Minor Prophets* (in Coptic and Latin); *Defence of the Church of England*; *Apostolical Constitutions* (in Coptic and English); *Book of Job* (in Coptic and English); *The Major Prophets* (in Coptic and Latin); *The New Testament* (in Coptic and Arabic), 2 vols. folio; *The Homilies of Macarius* (in Arabic); *Volume of Prayers*; *Reply to Rev. M. Ritchie on the Wines of Scripture*; *Pamphlet on Confession and Absolution, and on Transubstantiation.* [11]

TATTERSALL, John Creassey, 18, *Westgate-hill, Newcastle-on-Tyne.*—King's Coll. Lond. Theol. Assoc. 1857; Deac. 1857 and Pr. 1858 by Bp of Lon. C. of St. John's, Newcastle, 1863. Formerly C. of St. John's, Bethnal Green, 1857–59; Prin. of Victoria Park Coll. Institute 1858–62; C. of St. Thomas's, Chancery-lane, 1859–61, St. Andrew's, Islington, Lond. 1862. [12]

TATTERSALL, William, *Howe Rectory, Brooke, near Norwich.*—Trin. Coll. Ox. B.A. 1836; Deac. 1839 and Pr. 1840 by Bp of Nor. R. of Howe with West Poringland, Dio. Nor. 1840. (Patron, Rev. C. Wheler; Tithe—App. 42*l*, R. 350*l* 6*s*; Glebe, 55 acres; R.'s Inc. 440*l* and Ho; Pop. Howe 113, West Poringland 46.) [13]

TATTERSALL, William Alfred, *Oxton, Birkenhead.*—Pemb. Coll. Ox. B.A. 1853, M.A. 1855; Deac. 1854 and Pr. 1855 by Bp of Ches. P. C. of Oxton, Dio. Ches. 1859. (Patron, R. of Woodchurch; P. C.'s Inc. 220*l*; Pop. 2945.) Surrogate. Formerly C. of Walton-on-the Hill, near Liverpool. [14]

TATUM, William Wyndham, *St. Martin's Rectory, Salisbury.*—Queen's Coll. Ox. B.A. 1827. R. of St. Martin's, Salisbury, Dio. Salis. 1830. (Patron, J. H. C. Wyndham, Esq; R.'s Inc. 191*l*; Pop. 2997.) [15]

TAUNTON, Charles Edward, *Llan Gasty, near Crickhowell, Brecon.*—C. of Llan Gasty. [16]

TAUNTON, Frederick, *Sydenham, Kent.*—C. of St. Bartholomew's, Sydenham. [17]

TAVERNER, Frederick John, *Skegby, near Mansfield, Notts.*—Oriel Coll. Ox. B.A. 1854; Deac. 1854 and Pr. 1855 by Bp of Lin. P. C. of Skegby, Dio. Lin. 1860. (Patron, Bp of Lin; Tithe, 89*l* 19*s* 9*d*; Glebe, 3½ acres; P. C.'s Inc. 315*l* 19*s* 9*d*; Pop. 850.) Formerly C. of Coddington 1854, Great Grimsby 1858. [18]

TAYLER, Archdale Wilson, 2, *Victoria-road, Headingley, Leeds.*—Dub. A.B. 1864; Deac. 1851 by Bp of G. and B. Pr. 1853 by Bp of Ex. Asst. Mast. of Leeds Gr. Sch. 1856. Formerly C. of Morwenstow, Cornwall, 1851, Bordesley, Birmingham, 1853. [19]

TAYLER, Charles Benjamin, *Otley Rectory, Ipswich.*—Trin. Coll. Cam. B.A. 1819, M.A. 1822; Deac. 1821 by Bp of Bristol, Pr. 1823 by Bp of Lon. R. of Otley, Dio. Nor. 1846. (Patron Earl of Abergavenny; Tithe, 650*l*; Glebe, 70 acres; R.'s Inc. 736*l* and Ho; Pop. 615.) Author, *Facts in a Clergyman's Life*; *Memorials of the English Martyrs*; *The Records of a Good Man's Life*; *Thankfulness*; *Earnestness*; *Truth*; *Social Evils and their Remedy*; *Sermons*; *A Letter to one who cannot read it*; *Mark Wilton, or the Merchant's Clerk, &c*; Tracts—*Edward, or almost an Owenite*; *Jared, or quite an Owenite*; *Pshawland*; *The Blind Man and the Pedlar*; *The Beershop*; *The Fool's Pence*; *The Bar of Iron*; *The Vessel of Gold*; *The Password*; etc. [20]

TAYLER, Charles William, *Marlborough College, Wilts.*—Ch. Ch. Ox. B.A. 1845; Deac. 1845, Pr. 1846. Asst. Mast. in Marlborough Coll. [21]

TAYLER, George Wood Henry, *Grayrigg Parsonage, Kendal.*—Trin. Coll. Cam. B.A. 1855, M.A. 1858; Deac. 1855 and Pr. 1856 by Bp of Nor. P. C. of Grayrigg, Dio. Carl. 1866. (Patron, V. of Kendal; P. C.'s Inc. 155*l* and Ho; Pop. 870.) Formerly C. of Otley, near Ipswich, 1855, St. Mary's, Hull, 1857; P. C. of Helsington, Kendal, 1858; C. of Pontefract 1861; P. C. of St. Mark's, Hull, 1862. [22]

TAYLER, Henry Carr Archdale, *Orwell, Arrington, Cambs.*—Trin. Coll. Cam. Browne's Medallist 1848, 4th in 1st cl. Cl. Trip. 14th Jun. Opt. B.A. 1849; Deac. 1853, Pr. 1854. R. of Orwell, Dio. Ely, 1859. (Patron, Trin. Coll. Cam; R.'s Inc. 340*l* and Ho; Pop. 645.) Formerly Fell. of Trin. Coll. Cam. 1851–54; P. C. of St. Mary's the Great, Cambridge, 1854–59. [23]

TAYLER, I. M., *Quendon Rectory, Bishop Stortford, Herts.*—R. of Quendon, Dio. Roch. 1864. (Patron, Capt. H. Byng, R.N; R.'s Inc. 165*l* and Ho; Pop. 165.) [24]

TAYLOR, Alexander, 3, *Blomfield-terrace, Paddington, London, W.*—Queen's Coll. Ox. 3rd cl. Lit. Hum. 1st cl. Math. et Phy. B.A. 1845, Theol. Prize Essay 1846, M.A. 1848; Deac. 1849, Pr. 1850. Fell. of Queen's Coll. Ox. and Reader of Gray's Inn, Lond.. Formerly C. of Trinity, Paddington, Lond. Editor of *Bishop Jeremy Taylor's "Doctor Dubitantium,"* 2 vols. Longmans, 1851–52; *Bishop Patrick's Works*, 9 vols. Oxford Univ. Press, 1851. [1]

TAYLOR, Alfred Roger, *St. Stephen-in-Bramwell Rectory, St. Austell, Cornwall.*—Trin. Coll. Cam. B.A. 1841; Deac. 1842, Pr. 1843. R. of St. Stephen-in-Bramwell, Dio. Ex. 1852. (Patroness, Baroness Grenville; Tithe, 780*l*; Glebe, 5 acres; R.'s Inc. 790*l* and Ho; Pop. 3045.) Formerly C. of Bodmin. Author, *Funeral Sermon* (on Death of Rev. Jno. Cole Grose), 1851; *Farewell Sermon* (on leaving Bodmin), 1852. [2]

TAYLOR, Barrington, *Ashted, Epsom, Surrey.* —C. of Ashted, and Chap. to the Epsom Union. [3]

TAYLOR, Charles, *Great Cressingham Rectory, Thetford, Norfolk.*—Brasen. Coll. Ox. B.A. 1826, M.A. 1831, B.D. 1840; Deac. 1826, Pr. 1827. R. of Great Cressingham with Bodney R. Dio. Nor. 1859. (Patron, Ld Chan; Tithe—Great Cressingham, 519*l*; Glebe, 52 acres; Bodney, 195*l*; R.'s Inc. 820*l* and Ho; Pop. Great Cressingham 530, Bodney 117.) Preb. of Moreton Magna in Heref. Cathl. 1836. Formerly V. of Lydney, Glouc. 1838–59. [4]

TAYLOR, Charles, *St. John's College, Cambridge.* —Fell. of St. John's Coll. Cam. [5]

TAYLOR, Charles Hellins, *St. Giles on-the-Heath, Launceston.*—Emman. Coll. Cam. B.A. 1858, M.A. 1862; Deac. 1859 and Pr. 1860 by Bp of Man. P. C. of St. Giles-on-the-Heath, Devon, Dio. Ex. 1863. (Patrons, Earl of Mount Edgecombe and Marquis of Lothian; P. C.'s Inc. 100*l*; Pop. 345.) Formerly C. of St. John's, Bury, 1860, St. John's, Plymouth, 1862. [6]

TAYLOR, Charles James Fox, 6, *Barnard's-Inn, Holborn, E.C.*—Dub. A.B. 1844; Deac. 1844, Pr. 1845. Chap. of the City of London Cemetery, Ilford; Early Morning Reader at St. Paul's Cathedral. Formerly C. of St. Sepulchre's, Lond. Author, *Typographical Pronouncing System of Reading*, 6d; *Reading Lessons, adapted to the Pronouncing System*, 2 Parts, 4d. each; *Pronouncing Reading Book*, 3d; *Hard Word Spelling Book*, 1d. [7]

TAYLOR, Christopher Tennant, *Wrawby, Brigg, Lincolnshire.*—St. Mary's Hall, Ox. B.A. 1848, M.A. 1849; Deac. 1848 and Pr. 1849 by Bp of Herf. V. of Elsham, Dio. Lin. 1865. (Patron, T. G. Corbett, Esq; V.'s Inc. 50*l*; Pop. 500.) [8]

TAYLOR, Edward, *Temple Sowerby, Penrith.*—Queen's Coll. Birmingham. P. C. of Temple Sowerby, Dio. Carl. 1863. (Patron, Sir R. Tufton, Bart; P. C.'s Inc. 120*l* and Ho; Pop. 400.) [9]

TAYLOR, Fitzwilliam John, *East Ogwell Rectory, Newton-Abbot, Devon.*—Ch. Ch. Ox. B.A. 1839; Deac. 1841 by Bp of Win; Pr. 1842 by Bp of Ex. R. of the United Rs. of West Ogwell 1844, with East Ogwell 1845, Dio. Ex. (Patron, T. W. Taylor, Esq; West Ogwell, Tithe, 110*l*; East Ogwell, Tithe, 245*l*; R.'s Inc. 430*l* and Ho; Pop. West Ogwell 51, East Ogwell 275.) R. of Haccombe, Devon, Dio. Ex. 1849. (Patron, Sir Walter Palk Carew, Bart; Tithe, 7*l* 2*s* 6*d*; R.'s Inc. 348*l* and Ho; Pop. 42.) Rural Dean of the D. of Ipplepen 1865. [10]

TAYLOR, Francis W., *Plymouth, Devon.*—C. of St. Andrew's, Plymouth. [11]

TAYLOR, Frank, *Kirkandrew's Rectory, Longtown, Cumberland.*—Trin. Coll. Cam. B.A. 1858, M.A. 1864; Deac. 1859 and Pr. 1861 by Bp of Man. R. of Kirkandrew's-on-Esk, Dio. Carl. 1866. (Patron, Sir F. N. Graham; Tithe, 854*l*; R.'s Inc. 854*l*; Pop. 1200.) Formerly C. of Radcliffe, Manchester, 1859–62, Kirkby, Lonsdale, 1862–66. [12]

TAYLOR, George, *Maesteg, Glamorganshire.*—Queen's Coll. Ox. B.A. 1852, M.A. 1856; Deac. 1852 and Pr. 1853 by Bp of Ox. C. of Maesteg 1863. Formerly C. of Checkendon, Oxon. 1852, Great Marlow, Bucks, 1853; Chap. to Strode's Charity, Egham, Surrey, 1859. [13]

TAYLOR, George, *Tatsfield Rectory, Westerham, Surrey.*—R. of Tatsfield, Dio. Win. 1857. (Patron, W. L. Gower, Esq; R.'s Inc. 150*l* and Ho; Pop. 182.) [14]

TAYLOR, George, *Dedham Rectory, Colchester.* —Pemb. Coll. Cam. B.A. 1815, M.A. 1821, *ad eund.* St. John's Coll. Ox. 1826, D.C.L. 1827. R. and Lect. of Dedham, Dio. Roch. (Patrons, Govs. of Dedham Gr. Sch; R. and Lect.'s Inc. 438*l* and Ho; Pop. 1734.) Rural Dean of Dedham. [15]

TAYLOR, G.—C. of St. John's, Clerkenwell; Chap. of the Cemetery, St. Giles-in-the-Fields, Lond. [16]

TAYLOR, George John, *White Colne, Halstead, Essex.*—St. John's Coll. Cam. B.A. 1847, M.A. 1850; Deac. 1848, Pr. 1849. C. of White Colne. [17]

TAYLOR, George Richard, *Oakhill, Shepton-Mallet, Somerset.*—St. John's Coll. Cam. B.A. 1850, M.A. 1853; Deac. 1852 and Pr. 1853 by Bp of Pet. P. C. of All Saints', Oakhill, Dio. B. and W. 1866. (Patron, R. of Shepton-Mallet; P. C.'s Inc. 170*l*; Pop. 450.) Formerly C. of Doulting, Somerset, 1859–63; V. of High Littleton, Somerset, 1863–66. [18]

TAYLOR, Haydon Aldersey, *Portland.*—Asst. Chap. of H.M.'s Convict Establishment, Portland. [19]

TAYLOR, Henry, *Keighley, Yorkshire.*—C. of Keighley. [20]

TAYLOR, Henry, 26, *Derby-street, Cheetham, Manchester.*—Deac. 1850, Pr. 1851. C. of St. Paul's, Manchester, 1864. Formerly C. of Wednesbury 1850, Keighley 1856. [21]

TAYLOR, Henry, *Batcombe, Bruton, Somerset.*—C. of Batcombe with Upton Noble; Chap. to the Earl of Powis. [22]

TAYLOR, H. C., *Dover.*—St. John's Mariners' Ch. Dover. [23]

TAYLOR, Henry John, *Dulverton, Somerset.*—C. of Dulverton. [24]

TAYLOR, Henry Walter, *Overton, Marlborough, Wilts.*—Magd. Hall, Ox. B.A. 1850. C. of Overton with Fyfield. Formerly C. of North Nibley, Glouc. [25]

TAYLOR, Henry Willoughby, *St. George's-terrace, Stonehouse, Devon.*—Dub. A.B. 1842, LL.D. 1863; Deac. 1842 by Bp of Kilmore, Pr. 1843 by Bp of Cork. Chap. to the Royal Marines, Plymouth. (Chap.'s Inc. 383*l* 5*s*.) [26]

TAYLOR, Isaac, 10, *Palestine-place, Bethnal Green, London, N.E.*—Trin. Coll. Cam. Silver Oration Cup, 19th Wrang. B.A. 1853, M.A. 1857; Deac. 1857 and Pr. 1858 by Abp of Cant. P. C. of St. Matthias', Bethnal Green, Dio. Lon. 1865. (Patron, Bp of Lon; P. C.'s Inc. 275*l*; Pop. 6400.) Formerly C. of Trottersclifie, Kent, 1857, Kensington, Lond. 1860, St. Mark's, North Audley-street, Lond. 1862–65. Author, *Becker's Charicles: Illustrations of the Private Life of the Ancient Greeks*, J. W. Parker, 1854, 12*s*; *The Liturgy and the Dissenters*, Hatchard and Co. 3 eds. 1860, 1*s*; *Words and Places, or Etymological Illustrations of History, Ethnology, and Geography*, Macmillan and Co. 2 eds. 1864, 12*s* 6*d*; *The Family Pen: Memorials, Biographical and Literary, of the Taylor Family of Ongar*, 2 vols. 1867, Jackson, Walford, and Hodder; *The Burden of the Poor: a Slight Sketch of a Poor District in the East End of London*, 1867. [27]

TAYLOR, Jackson, *Freystrop, Haverfordwest.*—Oriel Coll. Ox. 3rd cl. Lit. Hum. and B.A. 1855, M.A. 1858; Deac. 1856 and Pr. 1858 by Bp of St. D. R. of Freystrop, Dio. St. D. 1860. (Patron, Ld Chan; Tithe 122*l*; Glebe, 27 acres; R.'s Inc. 200*l*; Pop. 576.) P.C. of Harroldston, St. Issell's, Dio. St. D. 1865. (Patron, James Higgon, Esq; P. C.'s Inc. 56*l*; Pop. 281.) Sec. of the Educational Board for Archdy. of St. David's. Formerly C. of St. Peter's, Carmarthen, 1856–58; Vice-Prin. Training Coll. Carmarthen, 1856–60. [28]

TAYLOR, James, *St. Peter's Parsonage, Blackburn.*—Dur. Licen. in Theol; Deac. 1863 and Pr. 1864 by Bp of Ches. C. of Blackburn 1865. Formerly C. of Ince, Lancashire, 1863–64. [29]

TAYLOR, James, *Brigham, Cockermouth.*—C. of Brigham. [1]

TAYLOR, James, *Wakefield.*—Trin. Coll. Cam. B.A. 1843, M.A. 1846; Deac. 1843, Pr. 1844. Head Mast. of Wakefield Gr. Sch; Even. Lect. of St. Andrew's, Wakefield, 1847. Author, *Appeal to the Archbishop of York on the Heresies of Archdeacon Wilberforce*, 1854; *Remonstrance to the Archbishops and Bishops of the United Church of England and Ireland*, 1855; *True Doctrine of the Holy Eucharist in Reply to Archdeacon Wilberforce, and Romish Views in General*, 1855; *Summary of Evidence on the Existence of a Deity*, 1855. [2]

TAYLOR, James Jeremy, *South Shields.*—Univ. Coll. Dur. B.A. 1852, M.A. 1855; Deac. 1853, Pr. 1855. P. C. of St. Mary's, South Shields, Dio. Dur. 1862. (Patrons, D. and C. of Dur.) Formerly C. of St. George's, Newcastle-under-Lyne, and 2nd Master of the Newcastle-under-Lyne Gr. Sch. 1853; C. of Trinity, Ripon. [3]

TAYLOR, John, *Cambridge House, Tunbridge Wells.*—Pemb. Coll. Ox. 2nd cl. Math. B.A. 1858, M.A. 1861; Deac. 1862 by Bp of Ox. Pr. 1863 by Bp of Tasmania. Formerly Math. Mast. of Bromsgrove Sch. 1859–60; Fell. of Pemb. Coll. Ox; C. of Thruxton-with-Kingston 1862–66. [4]

TAYLOR, John, *The Parsonage, St. John's-in-the-Vale, Keswick.*—Dub. A.B. 1847, A.M. 1851; Deac. 1847 and Pr. 1848 by Bp of Rip. P. C. of St. John's-in-the-Vale, Keswick, Dio. Carl. 1855. (Patrons, the Earl of Lonsdale and Landowners alt; Glebe, 93 acres; P. C.'s Inc. 110*l* and Ho; Pop. 280.) Surrogate. Author, *Services for the Use of Sunday Schools.* [5]

TAYLOR, John Fraser, *St. Aubyn's, Cliftonville, Brighton.*—Wad. Coll. Ox. Double Univ. Hons. B.A. 1850, M.A. 1853; Deac. 1851 and Pr. 1852 by Bp of Nor. P. C. of Trinity, Cliftonville, Hove, near Brighton, Dio. Chich. 1864. (Patron, V. of Preston with Hove; P. C.'s Inc. uncertain, from pews.) Formerly C. of Filby, Norfolk, 1851–53; Sen. C. of Preston with Hove 1853–64. Author, *National Crime and National Punishment* (a Sermon on the Russian War), 1*s*; *The Joyful Sound of the Gospel, a Plea for the Employment of Scripture Readers in Populous Towns* (a Sermon, with Notes, Statistics, &c); *The Lord's Hand upon our Cattle*; etc. [6]

TAYLOR, John Pierrepont, *Townsend House, Leominster.*—Lin. Coll. Ox. B.A. 1831, M.A. 1834; Deac. 1831, Pr. 1832. C. of Eye, near Leominster. [7]

TAYLOR, John Rees, *Eglwys-Cummin, St. Clears, Carmarthenshire.*—Lampeter B.D. 1860; Queens' Coll. Cam; Deac. 1837 and Pr. 1838. R. of Eglwys-Cummin, Dio. St. D. 1846. (Patron, Ld Chan; Tithe, 200*l*; Glebe, 3½ acres; R.'s Inc. 203*l*; Pop. 260.) Author, *Sermon on the Chartist Insurrection at Newport, Monmouthshire*, 1839. [8]

TAYLOR, John William, *St. Peter's College, Cambridge.*—St. Peter's Coll. Cam. Jun. Opt. and 1st cl. Cl. Trip. B.A. 1851, M.A. 1854; Deac. 1852 by Bp of Wor. Fell. and Cl. Lect. of St. Peter's Coll. Cam. 1851, Tut. 1856; R. of Exford, Somerset, Dio. B. and W. 1865. (Patron, St. Peter's Coll. Cam; R.'s Inc. 560*l* and Ho; Pop. 546.) R. of Stathern, Leicestershire, Dio. Pet. 1866. (Patron, St. Peter's Coll. Cam; R.'s Inc. 700*l* and Ho; Pop. 524.) [9]

TAYLOR, John William Augustus, *The Rookery, Headington, near Oxford.*—Trin. Coll. Cam. B.A. 1840, M.A. 1848; Deac. 1845 by Abp of Cant. Pr. 1850 by Bp of G. and B. Formerly Theol. Tut. of Cheltenham Coll. 1848–52; C. of Framfield, Sussex. Translator of *Professor Vinet's Sermons on Solitude*, 1842. [10]

TAYLOR, Joseph, *St. Thomas's, Stockport.*—St. John's Coll. Cam. Sen. Opt. 2nd cl. Cl. Trip. B.A. 1833; Deac. 1833 by Bp of Ely, Pr. 1837 by Bp of Nor. P. C. of St. Thomas's, Stockport, Dio. Ches. 1844. (Patron, R. of St. Mary's, Stockport; P. C.'s Inc. 300*l*; Pop. 12,760.) Author, *A Translation of the First Six Books of Homer's Iliad, with Notes, Critical and Explanatory*; *The Mystery of Godliness*; *Liberty, Fraternity, and Equality*; etc. [11]

TAYLOR, Joseph, *Bird-street, Lichfield.*—Trin. Coll. Cam. B.A. 1829, M.A. 1832; Deac. and Pr. 1829. Pr.-Vicar of Lich. Cathl. 1837 (Value, 100*l*); P. C. of Whittington, Staffs, Dio. Lich. 1852. (Patron, Theophilus John Levett, Esq; Tithe—App. 862*l* 9*s* 2½*d*, P. C. 161*l*; Glebe, 46½ acres; P. C.'s Inc. 350*l*; Pop. 819.) [12]

TAYLOR, Peter, *Hull.*—St. Edm. Hall, Ox. B.A. 1821, M.A. 1825; Deac. 1821 and Pr. 1825 by Bp of Lin. [13]

TAYLOR, Richard, *Arlecdon Parsonage, Whitehaven, Cumberland.*—Deac. 1859 and Pr. 1860 by Bp of Carl. P. C. of Arlecdon, Dio. Carl. 1861. (Patron, Bp of Carl; Glebe, 7 acres; P. C.'s Inc. 107*l* and Ho; Pop. 1560.) Formerly C. of Silloth 1859, Houghton 1860–61. [14]

TAYLOR, Richard, *Kemble, Cirencester.*—V. of Kemble, Wilts, Dio. G. and B. 1861. (Patron, R. Gordon, Esq; V.'s Inc. 250*l*; Pop. 436.) [15]

TAYLOR, Richard Thomas Wilson, *St. Mewan Rectory, St. Austell, Cornwall.*—Wad. Coll. Ox. B.A. 1822. R. of St. Mewan, Dio. Ex. 1843. (Patron, R. Taylor, Esq; Tithe, 314*l*; Glebe, 35 acres; R.'s Inc. 349*l* and Ho; Pop. 1227.) [16]

TAYLOR, Richard Vickerman, *Alford, Lincolnshire.*—King's Coll. Lond. B.A. 1859; Deac. 1863 and Pr. 1864 by Bp of Rip. C. of Alford 1867. Formerly Asst. Mast. in Leeds Gr. Sch; C. of Holbeck, Leeds, 1863–65, Wortley, near Leeds, 1865–67. Author, *Biographia Leodiensis, or Worthies of Leeds*, 1865, 5*s* 6*d*, with *Supplement*, 1867, 1*s* 6*d*; *The Churches of Leeds*, Simpkin, Marshall and Co., 1867, 6*s* 6*d*. [17]

TAYLOR, Robert, *Hartlepool.*—Deac. 1815, Pr. 1816. P. C. of Hartlepool, Dio. Dur. 1834. (Patron, V. of Hart; Tithe, 15*l*; Glebe, 130 acres; P. C.'s Inc. 280*l* and Ho; Pop. 7291.) Author, *Key to the Knowledge of Nature*, 1825, 18*s*; *Natural History of Religion*, 1832, 4*s*; *Pagan and Popish Priestcraft identified and exposed*, 1847, 6*s*; *Thoughts on the Existence and Attributes of the Deity*, in *Church of England Magazine*, 1849–50. [18]

TAYLOR, Robert, *Monk Hesleden, Castle Eden, Durham.*—V. of Monk Hesleden, Dio. Dur. 1859. (Patrons, D. and C. of Dur; V.'s Inc. 350*l* and Ho; Pop. 2077.) [19]

TAYLOR, Robert, *Barmby-Moor Vicarage, York.*—V. of Barmby-Moor, Dio. York, 1840. (Patron, Abp of York; V.'s Inc. 80*l* and Ho; Pop. 537.) V. of Kangfoss, near Pocklington, Yorks, Dio. York, 1840. (Patron, Abp of York; Tithe—App. 21*l* 12*s* 6*d*, Imp. 2*l*, V. 2*l*; V.'s Inc. 46*l*; Pop. 170.) [20]

TAYLOR, Robert, *Hazelbank, Wansfell, York.*—Trin. Hall, Cam. Scho. of, English Prizeman 1846, Latin Prizeman 1847, B.A. 1848, M.A. 1851; Deac. 1848 and Pr. 1849 by Bp of Rip. V. of Wansfell, Dio. York, 1861. (Patron, Abp of York; V.'s Inc. 160*l*; Pop. 217.) Formerly C. of Pontefract, Frmlington, and [illegible]; P. C. of Thurgoland; Asst. Chap. at Madeira. Author, *Instructions on Confirmation*; *A Few Words on Cottage Gardens and Home Comforts*. [21]

TAYLOR, Robert Askwith, *Norton-Malreward, Pensford, Somerset.*—Magd. Hall, Ox. B.A. 1838, M.A. 1840; Deac. 1837, Pr. 1838. R. of Norton Malreward, Dio. B. and W. 1867. (Patron, Rev. W. P. Wait; Tithe, 223*l*; Glebe, 65 acres; R.'s Inc. 305*l* and Ho; Pop. 106.) Formerly C. of St. Werburgh's, Bristol. Author, *Letters on Church Rates*, 1850; *Letters to Priests of the Latin Communion in Bristol and Clifton*, 1850; *Letters to Laymen on Mariolatry and the Canon Law*, 1851–52. [22]

TAYLOR, Robert Fetzer, *Scholes, near Cleckheaton, Leeds.*—Brasen. Coll. Ox. B.A. 1835, M.A. 1837; Deac. 1836 by Abp of York, Pr. 1837 by Bp of Rip. P. C. of Whitechapel, Cleckheaton, Dio. Rip. 1837. (Patron, M. Wilson, Esq; P. C.'s Inc. 220*l*; Pop. 1755.) [23]

TAYLOR, Robert Mitford, *Hunmanby Vicarage, Scarborough.*—Ch. Coll. Cam; Deac. 1833 and Pr. 1834 by Bp of Dur. V. of Hunmanby-with-Fordon C. Dio. York, 1843. (Patron, Admiral Mitford; V.'s

Inc. 958*l* and Ho; Pop. Hunmanby 1387, Fordan 88.) Rural Dean of the East Riding of Yorks. Author, *The Holy Communion*, 1841. [1]

TAYLOR, Samuel Barnard, *Kingswood Parsonage, Epsom, Surrey.*—Trin. Coll. Cam. B.A. 1838, M.A. 1842. P. C. of Kingswood, Dio. Win. 1858. (Patrons, Exors. of late Thomas Alcock, Esq; Tithe—App. 230*l*; Glebe, 31 acres; P. C.'s Inc. 190*l* and Ho; Pop. 838.) Formerly C. of Chertsey, Surrey. [2]

TAYLOR, Samuel Benjamin, *West-street, Wareham, Dorset.*—Ch. Coll. Cam. Jun. Opt. and 2nd cl. Theol. Trip. B.A. 1867; Deac. 1867 by Bp of Salis. C. of Wareham with Arne 1867. [3]

TAYLOR, Sedley, *Trinity College, Cambridge.*—Fell. of Trin. Coll. Cam. [4]

TAYLOR, Thomas, *St. Clement's Hill, Norwich.*—Magd. Hall, Ox. B.A. 1834, M.A. 1838; Deac. 1835 and Pr. 1836 by Bp of Wor. R. of St. Edmund's, Norwich, Dio. Nor. 1864. (Patron, the present R; R.'s Inc. 195*l* and Ho; Pop. 753.) Formerly Head Mast. of the Gr. Sch. Colwall, Herefordshire, 1845–53; P. C. of Little Malvern 1845–62; C. of St. Edmund's, Norwich, 1862–64. [5]

TAYLOR, Thomas, *Boscombe, near Salisbury.*—St. Cath. Hall, Cam. Sen. Opt. and B.A. 1823, M.A. 1827; Deac. 1823, Pr. 1824. R. of Boscombe, Dio. Salis. 1852. (Patron, Bp of Salis; Tithe—Imp. 94*l* 10*s*, R. 240*l*; Glebe, 17 acres; R.'s Inc. 330*l* and Ho; Pop. 143.) [6]

TAYLOR, Thomas Thornely, *Dodworth, Barnsley, Yorks.*—Trin. Coll. Cam. B.A. 1863; Deac. 1864 and Pr. 1865 by Bp of Pet. Formerly C. of Bottesford, Leicestershire, 1864–67. [7]

TAYLOR, Vernon Pearce, *The Parsonage, Pitcombe, Castle Cary, Somerset.*—Ch. Ch. Ox. B.A. 1832, M.A. 1835; Deac. 1833 and Pr. 1834 by Bp of Lin. P. C. of Wyke-Champflower, Dio. B. and W. 1846. (Patron, Sir Henry A. Hoare; P. C.'s Inc. 64*l*; Pop. 99.) P. C. of Pitcombe, Somerset, Dio. B. and W. 1846. (Patron, Sir Henry A. Hoare; P. C.'s Inc. 85*l*; Pop. 443.) Formerly C. of Little Kimble and Little Hampden, Bucks, 1833, Amersham, Bucks, 1836. [8]

TAYLOR, William, *Swynnerton Rectory, Stone, Staffs.*—Univ. Coll. Ox. B.A. 1851; Deac. 1852, Pr. 1853. R. of Swynnerton, Dio. Lich. 1853. (Patron, the present R; Tithe, 1070*l*; Glebe, 70 acres; R.'s Inc. 1170*l* and Ho; Pop. 661.) [9]

TAYLOR, William, *Newton Bromswold Rectory, Higham Ferrers, Northants.*—All Souls Coll. Ox. B.A. 1838, M.A. 1842; Deac. 1838 and Pr. 1840 by Bp of Herf. R. of Newton Bromswold, Dio. Pet. 1848. (Patron, All Souls Coll. Ox; Glebe, 170 acres; R.'s Inc. 225*l* and Ho; Pop. 174.) Formerly C. of Shobdon 1838–45, Titley 1845–49, both in Herefordshire. [10]

TAYLOR, William Addington, *Litchborough Rectory, Weedon, Northants.*—Ex. Coll. Ox. B.A. 1819. R. of Litchborough, Dio. Pet. 1821. (Patron, the present R; Tithe, 570*l* 6*s* 8*d*; Glebe, 21 acres; R.'s Inc. 600*l* and Ho; Pop. 448.) [11]

TAYLOR, William Addington, *Farthinghoe, Brackley, Northants.*—St. Mary Hall, Ox. B.A. 1864; Deac. 1866 by Bp of Pet. C. of Farthinghoe 1866. [12]

TAYLOR, William Francis, *Newbie-terrace, Liverpool.*—Dub. 1st cl. Respondent, Catechetical Prizeman, and Downe's Divinity Prizeman A.B. 1847, A.M. 1850, LL.D. 1855, D.C.L. *ad eund.* Ox. 1856; Deac. and Pr. 1848 by Bp of Ches. P. C. of St. Silas', Liverpool, Dio. Ches. 1861. (Patrons, Trustees; P. C.'s Inc. 500*l*; Pop. 7019.) Formerly C. of Tranmere 1848; Min. of Ch. Ch. Claughton, Birkenhead, 1849–51; P. C. of St. John's, Liverpool, 1851–61. Author, *The Man of Sin*, 1853, 2*s*; *Church and State, an Apology for Christian Legislation*, 1854, 6*d*; *The Prophet's Lamp*, 1860, 1*s*; *The Time is at Hand*, 1862, 1*s*; *The Divine Philosophy of History*, 6*d*; *The Church of the People*, 3*d*; *Lectures on the Seven Churches*, Howell, Liverpool, 1*s*; etc. [13]

TAYLOR, William Henry, *Farnworth Vicarage, Bolton-le-Moors.*—Brasen. Coll. Ox. Scho. of, and Hulmeian Exhib. B.A. 1858, M.A. 1860; Deac. 1860 by Bp of Lon. Pr. 1861 by Bp of Wor. V. of Farnworth with Kearsley, Dio. Man. 1866. (Patrons, Hulme's Trustees; V.'s Inc. 300*l* and Ho; Pop. 9973.) Formerly C. of St. Thomas's, Coventry, 1860–62; Asst. Min. of Sutton Coldfield 1863; Head Mast. of Lower Sch. Rossall, 1864–66. [14]

TAYLOR, William Henry, *Dean Forest, Coleford, Glouc.*—St. John's Coll. Cam. B.A. 1845; Deac. 1845, Pr. 1846. P. C. of Ch. Ch. Dean Forest, Dio. G. and B. 1852. (Patron, the Crown; Glebe, 8 acres; P. C.'s Inc. 167*l* and Ho; Pop. 1777.) [15]

TAYLOR, William Thomas, *Oldbury, near Birmingham.*—St. John's Coll. Cam. 3rd cl. Cl. Trip. B.A. 1858, M.A. 1861; Deac. 1861 and Pr. 1862 by Bp of Wor. C. of Oldbury 1861. [16]

TAYNTON, Francis, *Cowbridge, Glamorganshire.*—Deac. 1822 by Bp of Salis. Pr. 1824 by Bp of G. and B. Formerly P. C. of Ystradowen, Glamorganshire, 1841–66. [17]

TEAGUE, John, *Whitfield Parsonage, Glossop, Derbyshire.*—Emman. Coll. Cam. Scho. and Exhib. of, B.A. 1842; Deac. 1842, Pr. 1843. P. C. of Whitfield, Dio. Lich. 1846. (Patrons, the Crown and Bp of Lich. alt; P. C.'s Inc. 300*l* and Ho; Pop. 13,040.) Surrogate 1846. Formerly C. of Sheffield 1842–46. [18]

TEALE, William, *Clergy House, St. Thomas-the-Martyr, Oxford.*—Ex. Coll. Ox. B.A. 1864, M.A. 1867; Deac. 1866 by Bp of Ox. Asst. C. of St. Thomas-the-Martyr's, Oxford, 1866. [19]

TEALE, William Henry, *Devizes, Wilts.*—St. John's Coll. Cam. B.A. 1834, M.A. 1837; Deac. 1834 and Pr. 1835 by Abp of York. R. of Devizes with St. Mary's C. Dio. Salis. 1861. (Patron, Ld Chan; R.'s Inc. 510*l* and Ho; Pop. Devizes 1906, St. Mary's 2685.) Rural Dean 1865; Surrogate. Formerly V. of Royston Yorks, 1843–61. Author, *Lives of English Laymen*, 1842; *Lives of English Divines*, Masters, 1845; *A Translation of the Confession of Augsburg, with Introduction and Notes*, 1842; *Education in England Historically considered*, 1851; etc. [20]

TEAPE, Douglas William, *Shutford, near Banbury.*—Dub. A.B. 1839; Deac. 1840 by Bp of Killaloe, Pr. 1842 by Bp of Meath. C. of Shutford with Swalcliffe 1861. [21]

TEARLE, Frederick, *Gazeley Vicarage, Newmarket.*—Trin. Hall, Cam. B.A. 1853, M.A. 1856; Deac. 1853 by Bp of Ches. Pr. 1854 by Bp of Ely. V. of Gazeley with Kentford, Dio. Ely, 1866. (Patron, Trin. Hall, Cam; V.'s Inc. 430*l* and Ho; Pop. 280.) Formerly Scho. and Asst. Tut. of Trin. Hall, Cam; Head Mast. of the Gr. Sch. Kettering, 1856; Head Mast. of the Coll. Sch. Leicester. [22]

TEASDALE, Robert Webster, *Thrimby Grange, Penrith.*—Dur; Deac. 1858 and Pr. 1859 by Bp of Dur. P. C. of Thrimby, Dio. Carl. 1863. (Patron, V. of Morland; Glebe, 60 acres; P. C.'s Inc. 85*l*; Pop. 201.) Formerly C. of Barnard Castle 1858–63. [23]

TEBAY, Septimus, *Rivington, Chorley, Lancashire.*—St. John's Coll. Cam. B.A. 1856. Head Mast. of Rivington Gr. Sch. 1857. [24]

TEBBS, William, *Grimsbury, Banbury.*—Queens' Coll. Cam. B.A. 1866; Deac. 1866 by Bp of Ox. C. of South Banbury 1866. [25]

TEBBUTT, Henry Jemson, *Nottingham.*—Trin. Coll. Cam. Sen. Opt. and 3rd cl. Cl. Trip. B.A. 1859, M.A. 1862; Deac. 1860, Pr. 1861. P. C. of St. Anne's, Nottingham, Dio. Lin. 1864. (Patrons, Trustees; P. C.'s Inc. 300*l*; Pop. 10,000.) Formerly C. of St. Mary's, Nottingham, 1860–64. [26]

TEESDALE, Charles Baker, *Lamarsh Rectory, Colchester.*—Ch. Ch. Ox. B.A. 1844, M.A. 1847; Deac. 1845 by Abp of Cant. Pr. 1846 by Bp of Chich. R. of Lamarsh, Dio. Roch. 1850. (Patrons, C. Teesdale and J. H. Spencer, Esqrs; Tithe, 416*l* 10*s*; Glebe, 96 acres; R.'s Inc. 507*l* and Ho; Pop. 329.) [27]

TEESDALE, Francis Barlow, 17, *Gloucester-place, Hyde-park, London, W.*—Ex. Coll. Ox. B.A. 1858, M.A. 1856. Formerly C. of Romsey, Hants. [28]

TEESON, John, 26, *Winchester-street, Pimlico London, S.W.*—Clare Coll. Cam. Wrang. and B.A. 1824, M.A. 1827. Sen. Fell. of Clare Coll. Cam. [1]

TEMPLE, Frederick, *Rugby.*—Ball. Coll. Ox. B.A. 1842, M.A. 1846, D.D. 1858; Deac. 1846, Pr. 1847. Head Mast. of Rugby Sch. 1858; Chap. in Ordinary to the Queen. Author, *Sermons preached in the Chapel of Rugby School in* 1858, '59, *and* '60, Macmillan and Co. 1862, 10*s* 6*d*. [2]

TEMPLE, George William, *Blean, near Canterbury.*—Clare Coll. Cam. Fell. of, Jun. Opt. and 2nd cl. Cl. Trip. B.A. 1849, M.A. 1853; Deac. 1851 and Pr. 1852 by Abp of Cant. V. of Blean, Dio. Cant. 1863. (Patron, Mast. of Eastbridge Hospital, Canterbury; Tithe, 530*l*; Glebe, 3 acres; V.'s Inc. 600*l* and Ho; Pop. 626.) Formerly C. of St. Mary's, Northgate, and St. Alphege's, Canterbury, 1851–55, Herne, near Canterbury, 1855–63. [3]

TEMPLE, Henry, *St. John's Vicarage, Leeds.*—Brasen. Coll. Ox. B.A. 1849, M.A. 1852; Deac. 1850 and Pr. 1851 by Bp of Ox. V. of St. John's, Leeds, Dio. Rip. 1867. (Patrons, Five Trustees; V.'s Inc. 600*l*; Pop. 5198.) Formerly C. of Bucklebury, Berks, 1850; Head Mast. of Worcester Gr. Sch. 1852; Head Mast. of Coventry Gr. Sch. 1857; C. of Stivichall 1866; Even. Lect. at St. Peter's, Coventry, 1866; Dioc. Inspector of Schs. for Coventry Rural Deanery 1866. [4]

TEMPLE, Isaac, *Plemstall, near Chester.*—Queens' Coll. Cam. B.A. 1817, M.A. 1821; Deac. 1816 by Bp of Ches. Pr. 1821 by Bp of Nor. Chap. of the Don. of Plemstall, Dio. Ches. 1832. (Patron, Earl of Bradford; Tithe—Imp. 22*l*, Chap. 360*l*; Glebe, 20 acres; Chap.'s Inc. 420*l*; Pop. 679.) [5]

TEMPLE, John, *Wambrook Rectory, Chard, Dorset.*—Univ. Coll. Dur. B.A. 1852; Deac. 1851 and Pr. 1853 by Bp of Wor. C. of Wambrook 1866. Formerly C. of Welch Bicknor, Herefordshire, 1857–66. [6]

TEMPLE, Joseph Abbott, 3, *Taunton-road-villas, Lee, Kent, S.E.*—King's Coll. Lond. Assoc. of, B.A. 1854, M.A. 1863; Deac. 1852 and Pr. 1853 by Bp of Lon. Formerly C. of St. Bartholomew's, Cripplegate, Lond. 1855, St. Mary's, Devonport, 1856, St. George's-in-the-East, Lond. 1857–58. [7]

TEMPLE, Nicholas John, *Gayton Rectory, Northampton.*—Sid. Coll. Cam. Sen. Opt. and B.A. 1817, M.A. 1820, B.D. 1827, D.D. 1853; Deac. 1819 and Pr. 1820. R. of Gayton, Dio. Pet. 1853. (Patron, Sid. Coll. Cam; Tithe, 532*l* 8*s* 11*d*; Glebe, 92 acres; R.'s Inc. 600*l* and Ho; Pop. 459.) Formerly C. of Lavendon, Bucks, 1819, Condover, Salop, 1823, Chirk, Denbigh, 1825. [8]

TEMPLE, Robert, *Stafford.*—P. C. of St. Mary's, Stafford, Dio. Lich. 1831. (Patron, R. of Stafford; P. C.'s Inc. 170*l*.) [9]

TEMPLE, Robert, *Privy Council Office, Downing-street, London, S.W.*—One of H.M. Inspectors of Schs. [10]

TEMPLE, Robert Charles, *Nantwich, Cheshire.*—Jena, Ph. D. 1860; Deac. 1866 and Pr. 1867 by Bp of Ches. C. of Nantwich 1866. [11]

TEMPLE, Watkin, *Hurstborne Priors, Andover, Hants.*—Deac. 1852 and Pr. 1853. R. of Nymet-Rowland, Dio. Ex. 1853. (Patron, Rev. T. R. Dickinson; Tithe, 75*l* 2*s* 11*d*; R.'s Inc. 168*l*; Pop. 111.) C. of Hurstborne Priors. [12]

TEMPLE, William, *Eastbridge Hospital, Canterbury.*—Corpus Coll. Cam. B.A. 1822; Deac. and Pr. 1823 by Abp of Cant. R. of St. Alphege with St. Mary's, Northgate V. Canterbury, Dio. Cant. 1845. (Patron, Abp of Cant; R. and V.'s Inc. 300*l*; Pop. St. Alphege's 1152, St. Mary's, Northgate, 4865.) Mast. of Eastbridge Hospital, Canterbury, 1850. Formerly C. of Ivychurch 1823, Tenterden 1824, Sandon, Herts, 1831, Whitstable, Kent, 1838, St. Alphege's, Canterbury, 1843. [13]

TEMPLEMAN, Alexander, *Puckington Rectory, Ilminster.*—Queen's Coll. Ox. B.A. 1824, M.A. 1827. R. of Puckington, Dio. B. and W. 1852. (Patron, Lord Portman; Tithe, 110*l*; Glebe, 82½ acres; R.'s Inc. 241*l* and Ho; Pop. 260.) [14]

TEMPLER, Henry Skinner, *Great Coxwel Vicarage, Great Farringdon, Berks.*—New Inn Hall and Ex. Coll. Ox. 1832, 3rd cl. Lit. Hum. 1836, S.C.L. B.A. 1845, M.A. 1847; Deac. 1842 and Pr. 1843 by Bp of Ex. V. of Great Coxwell, Dio. Ox. 1861. (Patron, Bp of Ox; V.'s Inc. 230*l* and Ho; Pop. 371.) Formerly V. of Thornton, Bucks, 1853–61. [15]

TEMPLER, John, *Knowles, Newton Abbot, Devon.*—Ex. Coll. Ox. B.A. 1809, M.A. 1818; Deac. 1811 and Pr. 1812. R. of Teigngrace, Devon, Dio. Ex. 1832. (Patron, Duke of Somerset; Tithe, 160*l*; Glebe, 63 acres; R.'s Inc. 235*l*; Pop. 172.) [16]

TEMPLER, William Christopher, *Burton Bradstock, Bridport, Dorset.*—Trin. Coll. Cam. B.A. 1846, M.A. 1850; Deac. 1846 and Pr. 1847 by Bp of Salis. R. of Burton Bradstock with Shepton George C. Dio. Salis. 1860. (Patron, Lord Rivers; R.'s Inc. 350*l* and Ho; Pop. 1453.) P. C. of Walditch, Bridport, Dio. Salis. 1849. (Patrons, Lord Rolle and J. Bragge, Esq; P. C.'s Inc. 54*l*; Pop. 175.) Formerly C. of Burton Bradstock. Author, *Thy Word is Truth* (Sermon on Papal Aggression), 1852. [17]

TENNANT, William, *St. Stephen's Parsonage, Westminster, S.W.*—Trin. Coll. Cam. B.A. 1834, M.A. 1835; Deac. 1835 by Bp of Lin. Pr. 1836 by Bp of Nor. P. C. of St. Stephen's, Westminster, Dio. Lon. 1847. (Patron, Bp of Lon; P. C.'s Inc. 300*l* and Ho; Pop. 7127.) Author, *No more War* (a Sermon), 1854. [18]

TERROTT, Charles Pratt, *Wispington Vicarage, Horncastle, Lincolnshire.*—Trin. Coll. Cam. B.A. 1826; Deac. 1827, Pr. 1828. V. of Wispington, Dio. Lin. 1838. (Patron, C. Turnor, Esq; Tithe—Imp. 140*l*, V. 70*l*; Glebe, 103 acres; V.'s Inc. 200*l*; Pop. 85.) [19]

TERRY, Charles, *Tostock, Bury St. Edmunds.*—Ex. Coll. Ox. B.A. 1848, M.A. 1850; Deac. 1849, Pr. 1850. R. of Harlestone, Dio. Nor. 1852. (Patron, R. Pettiward, Esq; Tithe, 160*l* 16*s*; R.'s Inc. 175*l*; Pop. 65.) [20]

TERRY, George Thomas, *Full Sutton Rectory, Stamford Bridge, Yorks.*—Dub. A.B. 1833, A.M. and LL.B. 1839, B.D. D.D. and LL.D. 1864; Deac. 1834 and Pr. 1835 by Bp of Ches. R. of Full Sutton, Dio. York, 1845. (Patron, Lord Feversham; Glebe, 114 acres; R.'s Inc. 150*l* and Ho; Pop. 174.) Formerly Head Mast. of the Bedale Gr. Sch. 1834–40; Head Mast. of Lady Lumley's Gr. Sch. and C. of Thornton Dale, near Pickering, 1840–45. [21]

TERRY, Michael, *Awsworth Parsonage, Nottingham.*—P. C. of Awsworth, Dio. Lin. 1866. (Patron, R. of Nuthall; P. C.'s Inc. 110*l*.) Formerly V. of Kelstern, Lincolnshire, 1864–66. [22]

TERRY, Stephen, *Weston Rectory, Odiham, Hants.*—Trin. Coll. Ox. B.A. 1833, M.A. 1842; Deac. 1835 and Pr. 1836 by Bp of Win. R. of Weston Patrick, Dio. Win. 1864. (Patrons, Ecc. Commissioners; Tithe, 175*l*; R.'s Inc. 200*l*; Pop. 210.) Formerly C. of Dummer, Hants. [23]

TERRY, Thomas Hughes, *Pocklington, York.*—St. John's Coll. Cam. B.A. 1830; Deac. 1833 by Bp of Roch. Pr. 1833 by Abp of York. P. C. of Seaton-Ross, Yorks, Dio. York, 1839. (Patron, Lord Herries; Glebe, 43 acres; P. C.'s Inc. 95*l*; Pop. 549.) Formerly C. of North Newbald, Yorks, 1833–39, Everingham 1841–42, Muston 1853–59, Ferrybridge 1859–61, Beeston St. Lawrence with Ashmanhaugh, Norfolk, 1861–62. [24]

TEULON, Josiah Sanders, *Beddington Corner, near Mitcham.*—Lin. Coll. Ox. 3rd cl. Lit. Hum. B.A. 1862, M.A. 1864; Deac. 1865 and Pr. 1867 by Bp of Win. C. of Beddington 1865. [25]

TEUTSCHEL, Anthony Sigismund, *East Hardwick, Pontefract.*—Univ. of Padua, Ph.D. and St. Aidan's; Deac. 1859 and Pr. 1860 by Abp of York. P. C. of East Hardwick, Dio. York, 1865. (Patrons, Trustees; P. C's Inc. 100*l* and Ho; Pop. 213.) C. of Skelbrooke. Formerly C. of Askern, Yorks. [26]

TEW, Edmund, *Patching Rectory, Arundel.*—Magd. Hall, Ox. B.A. 1843. R. of Patching, Dio. Chich. 1848. (Patron, Abp of Cant; Tithe, 218*l*; R.'s Inc. 223*l* and Ho; Pop. 275.) [27]

THACKERAY, Frederick, *Southend, Essex.*—Caius Coll. Cam. B.A. 1840, M.B. 1842, M.A. 1843; Deac. 1844 and Pr. 1845 by Bp of Ches. V. of Shopland, Dio. Roch. 1847. (Patroness, Mrs. Harriett Aiken; V.'s Inc. 106*l*; Pop. 80.) Formerly C. of St. Thomas's, Stockport, 1844–46. [1]

THACKERAY, F. St. John, *Eton, Windsor.*—Mert. Coll. Ox. 1st cl. Lit. Hum. 1856, 2nd cl. Law and Mod. Hist; Fell. of Lin. Coll. 1857; Deac. 1858. Asst. Mast. at Eton Coll. Editor, *Anthologia Latina*, 1865, 6*s* 6*d*; *Anthologia Græca*, Bell and Daldy, 1867, 7*s* 6*d*. [2]

THACKERAY, George, *Hemingby Rectory, Horncastle, Lincolnshire.*—King's Coll. Cam. B.A. 1830, M.A. 1833; Deac. 1831, Pr. 1833. R. of Hemingby, Dio. Lin. 1840. (Patron, King's Coll. Cam; R.'s Inc. 355*l* and Ho; Pop. 473.) Formerly Fell. of King's Coll. Cam. [3]

THACKERAY, Joseph, *Coltishall Rectory, near Norwich.*—King's Coll. Cam. B.A. 1829, M.A. 1832. R. of Coltishall, Dio. Nor. 1846. (Patron, King's Coll. Cam; Tithe, 348*l*; Glebe, 27 acres; R.'s Inc. 388*l* and Ho; Pop. 978.) R. of Horstead, near Coltishall, Dio. Nor. 1856. (Patron, King's Coll. Cam; Tithe, 590*l* 15*s* 4*d*; R.'s Inc. 604*l* and Ho; Pop. 608.) Formerly Fell. of King's Coll. Cam. [4]

THACKERAY, Thompson, *Usworth, near Gateshead-on-Tyne.*—Queens' Coll. Cam. B.A. 1846, M.A. 1849; Deac. and Pr. 1847 by Bp of Dur. R. of Usworth, Dio. Dur. 1853. (Patron, R. of Washington, Tithe, 30*l*; R.'s Inc. 180*l* and Ho; Pop. 3677.) Formerly 2nd Mast. of Richmond Gr. Sch. Yorks, 1846–47; Head Mast. of Gr. Sch. and C. of St. Ann's, Bishop Auckland, Durham, 1847–53. [5]

THACKWELL, Stephen, *Little Birch Rectory, Ross, Herefordshire.*—Pemb. Coll. Ox. B.A. 1831, M.A. 1834; Deac. 1832 and Pr. 1833 by Bp of Wor. R. of Little Birch, Dio. Herf. 1855. (Patron, the present R; Tithe, comm. 160*l*; Glebe, 14 acres; R.'s Inc. 178*l* and Ho; Pop. 336.) P. C. of Aconbury, Herefordshire, Dio. Herf. 1855. (Patron, the present P. C; P. C.'s Inc. 40*l*; Pop. 183.) [6]

THACKWELL, W. H., *Kinwarton, near Alcester, Warwickshire.*—C. of Kinwarton. [7]

THARP, Augustus James, *Snailwell Rectory, Newmarket, Cambs.*—Ch. Coll. Cam. B.A. 1828; Deac. and Pr. 1829 by Bp of Nor. R. of Snailwell, Dio. Ely, 1854. (Patron, J. Tharp, Esq; Tithe, 514*l*; Glebe, 100 acres; R.'s Inc. 639*l* and Ho; Pop. 257.) V. of Chippenham, Cambs, Dio. Ely. (Patron, John Tharp, Esq; V.'s Inc. 240*l* and Ho; Pop. 796.) Chap. to Lord Keane. [8]

THEED, Edward Reed, *Sampford-Courtenay Rectory, Crediton, Devon.*—King's Coll. Cam. B.A. 1835, M.A. 1838. R. of Sampford-Courtenay with Sticklepath C. Dio. Ex. 1859. (Patron, King's Coll. Cam; Tithe, 650*l*; R.'s Inc. 720*l* and Ho; Pop. 991.) Sen. Fell of King's Coll. Cam. [9]

THEED, Joseph Vernon, *Irthlingboro', Higham-Ferrers, Northants.*—St. John's Coll. Cam. B.A. 1852, M.A. 1855; Deac. 1853 and Pr. 1854 by Bp of Pet. R. of Irthlingboro', Dio. Pet. 1865. (Patron, the Hon. G. W. Fitzwilliam; Glebe, 81 acres; R.'s Inc. 275*l*; Pop. 1800.) Formerly V. of Great Gidding, Hunts, 1855–65. [10]

THEED, Thomas Maylin, *Weston Vicarage, Otley, Yorks.*—St. John's Coll. Cam. LL.B. 1852; Deac. 1857, Pr. 1858. V. of Weston, Dio. Rip. 1861. (Patron, Christopher H. Dawson, Esq; V.'s Inc. 120*l* and Ho; Pop. 450.) Formerly C. of Bishop Middleham, Durham, 1859–61. [11]

THEED, William, *Great Orton, Carlisle.*—Clare Coll Cam. B.A. 1843, M.A. 1846; Deac. 1843 and Pr. 1844 by Bp of Lin. R. of Great Orton, Dio. Carl. 1859. (Patron, Sir W. Briscoe; R.'s Inc. 400*l* and Ho; Pop. 463.) [12]

THELWALL, Edward, *Llanbedr Rectory, Ruthin, Denbighshire.*—Jesus Coll. Ox. B.A. 1804, M.A. 1806; Deac. 1804 and Pr. 1805 by Bp of Ban. R. of Llanbedr-Dyffryn-Clwyd, Dio. Ban. 1834. (Patron, Bp of Ban; Tithe, 415*l*; Glebe, 11½ acres; R.'s Inc. 450*l* and Ho; Pop. 431.) Formerly C. of Llangwyfan 1804–19; R. of Efenechtyd 1819–34. [13]

THELWALL, John Hampden, *Oving, Aylesbury, Bucks.*—Trin. Coll. Cam. B.A. 1823, M.A. 1826. R. of Oving, Dio. Ox. 1831. (Patron, Ld Chan; Tithe, 362*l*; R.'s Inc. 366*l*; Pop. 436.) [14]

THELWALL, Sydney, 43, *St. Aubyn-street, Devonport.*—Ch. Coll. Cam. 2nd cl. Cl. Trip. B.A. 1865; Deac. 1865 by Bp of Ex. Pr. 1866 by Bp of Newfoundland for Bp of Ex. Asst. C. of St. Paul's, Devonport, and Cl. Mast. in Plymouth Gr. Sch. 1865. [15]

THEOBALD, Charles, *Chale Rectory, Isle of Wight.*—Trin. Coll. Ox. B.A. 1854, M.A. 1861; Deac. 1854 and Pr. 1855 by Bp of Win. R. of Chale, Dio. Win. 1862. (Patron, James Theobald, Esq; Tithe, 347*l*; Glebe, 39 acres; R.'s Inc. 390*l* and Ho; Pop. 584.) Formerly V. of Grays Thurrock, Essex, 1856–62. [16]

THEOBALD, Frederick, *Drayton, Berks.*—Trin. Coll. Ox. B.A. 1863; Deac. 1864 and Pr. 1865 by Bp of Ox. C. of Drayton 1864. [17]

THEOBALD, Thomas John, *Nunney Rectory, Frome, Somerset.*—Ch. Coll. Cam. B.A. 1829, M.A. 1832; Deac. and Pr. 1830. R. of Nunney, Dio. B. and W. 1830. (Patron, T. Theobald, Esq; Tithe, 374*l* 10*s* 6*d*; Glebe, 58 acres; R.'s Inc. 464*l* and Ho; Pop. 1088.) Formerly Dom. Chap. to Viscount Palmerston. [18]

THEODOSIUS, James Henry, *Stafford.*—Ch. Coll. Cam. B.A. 1847, M.A. 1855; Deac. 1848 by Bp of Nor. Pr. 1849 by Bp of Lich. V. of Ronton, Dio. Lich. 1849. (Patron, Earl of Lichfield; Glebe, 62 acres; V.'s Inc. 100*l*; Pop. 283.) Chap. to the Stafford Union; Chap. to the Coton Hill Institution for the Insane 1858. [19]

THEOPHILUS, Thomas, *Llanelly, Carmarthenshire.*—Lampeter, B.A. 1865; Deac. 1865 and Pr. 1866 by Bp of St. D. C. of St. Paul's, Llanelly, 1865. [20]

THEXTON, Joseph, *Torpenhow, Aspatria, Carlisle.*—Dub. A.B. 1830; Deac. 1831 by Bp of Roch. Pr. 1831 by Bp of Carl. V. of Torpenhow, Dio. Carl. 1854. (Patron, Bp of Carl; Glebe, 10 acres; V.'s Inc. 284*l* and Ho; Pop. 1083.) Formerly C. of Torpenhow 1831–54. [21]

THICKINS, William, *Keresley House, Coventry.*—Trin. Coll. Cam. B.A. 1824, M.A. 1837; Deac. 1826, Pr. 1827. P. C. of Keresley and Coundon, Dio. Wor. 1847. (Patron, Bp of Wor; Glebe, 3 acres; P. C.'s Inc. 140*l*; Pop. 792.) [22]

THICKNESSE, Francis Henry, *Deane Vicarage, Bolton-le-Moors.*—Brasen. Coll. Ox. Lord Mordaunt's Scho. and Hulme's Exhib. B.A. 1851, M.A. 1854; Deac. 1853, Pr. 1854. V. of Deane, Dio. Man. 1855. (Patron, Ld Chan; Tithe—App. 65*l* 17*s* 9*d*, Imp. 219*l* 2*s* 0½*d*; V.'s Inc. 250*l* and Ho; Pop. 4053.) Rural Dean of Bolton-le-Moors 1857; Hon. Can. of Man. 1863. [23]

THIRLWALL, Thomas James, *The Vicarage, Nantmel, Radnorshire.*—Emman. Coll. Cam. B.A. 1850, M.A. 1854; Deac. 1851 by Bp of Wor. Pr. 1852 by Bp of Ex. V. of Nantmel, Dio. St. D. 1858. (Patron, Bp of St. D; Tithe—App. 410*l*, V. 410*l*; V.'s Inc. 410*l* and Ho; Pop. 1453.) Rural Dean. Formerly C. of St. Chad's and St. Mary's, Shrewsbury; P. C. of North Moor-green, Bridgwater. [24]

THOMAS, Abraham, *Beguildy, Knighton, Radnorshire.*—Lampeter; Deac. 1849, Pr. 1850. V. of Beguildy, Dio. St. D. 1852. (Patron, Bp of St. D; Tithe—App. 400*l*, V. 191*l*; V.'s Inc. 195*l* and Ho; Pop. 1203.) [25]

THOMAS, Arthur, *Rottingdean, Brighton.*—Trin. Coll. Cam. B.A. 1839, M.A. 1842; Deac. 1840, Pr. 1841. V. of Rottingdean, Dio. Chich. 1848. (Patron, Earl of Abergavenny; Tithe—Imp. 240*l* 10*s*, V. 400*l*; Glebe, 3 acres; V.'s Inc. 405*l* and Ho; Pop. 1016.) [26]

THOMAS, Arthur Ralph Green, 20, *Camden-square, London, N.W.*—Corpus Coll. Cam. B.A. 1837, M.A. 1849; Deac. 1837 by Bp of Ches. Pr. 1838 by Bp of Chich. P. C. of St. Paul's, Camden-square, Dio. Lon. 1846. (Patrons, D. and C. of St. Paul's; P. C.'s Inc. 350*l*; Pop. 5145.) [27]

THOMAS, Benjamin, *Slebech, Haverfordwest.*—St. Bees; Deac. 1860 and Pr. 1861 by Bp of Lich. C. of Slebech 1861. Formerly C. of Brockmoor, near Dudley, 1860. [1]

THOMAS, C., *Bradford, Yorks.*—C. of Bradford. [2]

THOMAS, Charles Ascanius Neville, *Chudleigh Vicarage, Devon.*—Ex. Coll. Ox. B.A. 1833, M.A. 1843; Deac. 1834 and Pr. 1835 by Bp of Ex. C. of Chudleigh; Surrogate. [3]

THOMAS, Charles Edward, *Warmsworth Rectory, Doncaster.*—Univ. Coll. Dur; Deac. 1846 and Pr. 1847. R. of Warmsworth, Dio. York, 1848. (Patron, W. B. Wrightson, Esq; Tithe—App. 62*l* 2*s*, Imp. 49*l* 16*s* 3*d*, R. 120*l* 12*s* 9*d*; Glebe, 44 acres; R.'s Inc. 175*l* and Ho; Pop. 361.) [4]

THOMAS, David, *Llandawcke Rectory, near Langharne, Carmarthenshire.*—Deac. 1826 and Pr. 1827. R. of Llandawcke with Pendine, Dio. St. D. 1834. (Patron, Col. Powell; Llandawcke, Tithe, 55*l*; Glebe, 2 acres; Pendine, Tithe, 67*l*; R.'s Inc. 120*l*; Pop. Llandawcke 38, Pendine 204.) [5]

THOMAS, David, *Margam, Taibach, South Wales.*—Trin. Coll. Ox. Fell. of, Jun. Math. Scho. 1856, Sen. Math. Scho. and Johnson Math. Scho. 1859, B.A. 1858, M.A. 1861, Scho. of Jesus Coll; Deac. 1861 and Pr. 1862 by Bp of Ox. P. C. of Margam with Taibach C. Dio. Llan. 1864. (Patron, C. R. M. Talbot, Esq. M.P; P. C.'s Inc. 109*l*; Pop. 5528.) [6]

THOMAS, David, *Llanycevn, Narberth, Pembrokeshire.*—C. of Llancevyn and of Mynachlogdu, Pembrokeshire. [7]

THOMAS, David, *St. George Rectory, near Cardiff.*—R. of St. George, Dio. Llan. 1854. (Patroness, Mrs. Traherne; Tithe, 91*l*; R.'s Inc. 125*l* and Ho; Pop. 213.) [8]

THOMAS, David, *Usk, Monmouthshire.*—C. of Usk. [9]

THOMAS, David, *Ystrad Meurig, Cardigan.*—Asst. Mast. of the Gr. Sch. Ystrad Meurig. [10]

THOMAS, D. G., *Heywood, Manchester.*—C. of Heywood. [11]

THOMAS, David Morgan, *Llanelian Rectory, Abergele.*—Jesus Coll. Ox. B.A. 1851, M.A. 1854; Deac. 1853 by Bp of Herf. Pr. 1854 by Bp of St. D. R. of Llanelian, Dio. St. A. 1867. (Patron, Bp of St. A; Tithe, 327*l*; Glebe, 3 acres; R.'s Inc. 330*l* and Ho; Pop. 580.) Formerly C. of Pontyberem 1853–55, Aberystwith 1855, Llanrwst 1856–60; R. of Llanycil with Bala 1860–67. [12]

THOMAS, David Parry, *Llanmaes Rectory, Cowbridge, Glamorganshire.*—Jesus Coll. Ox. B.A. 1839; Deac. 1839, Pr. 1840. R. of Llanmaes, Dio. Llan. 1850. (Patrons, Trustees of the Marquis of Bute; Tithe, 275*l* 6*s*; Glebe, 72½ acres; R.'s Inc. 359*l* and Ho; Pop. 164.) [13]

THOMAS, David Richard, *Cefn Rectory, St. Asaph.*—Jesus Coll. Ox. 3rd cl. Lit. Hum. B.A. 1856, M.A. 1865; Deac. 1857 and Pr. 1858 by Bp of St. A. R. of St. Mary's, Cefn, Dio. St. A. 1864. (Patron, Bp of St. A; Tithe, comm. 292*l*; R.'s Inc. 292*l*; Pop. 613.) Formerly C. of Rhuddlan and St. Asaph 1857–59, Selattyn 1859–64. Author, *A Sermon on the Burial Service*, Oswestry, 1863; *Two Memorial Sermons*, St. Asaph, 1864. [14]

THOMAS, David Thomas, *Trelech Vicarage, Carmarthenshire.*—Deac. 1825, Pr. 1826. V. of Trelechar-Bettws, Dio. St. D. 1828. (Patron, Bp of St. D; Tithe, Imp. 390*l* and 40½ acres of Glebe, V. 95*l*; Glebe, 32 acres; V.'s Inc. 183*l* and Ho; Pop. 1496.) V. of Clydey, Pembrokeshire, Dio. St. D. 1827. (Patron, Bp of St. D; Tithe—App. 250*l*, Imp. 12*l*, V. 125*l*; V.'s Inc. 180*l*; Pop. 1074.) [15]

THOMAS, David Walter, *St. Ann's Parsonage, near Bangor.*—Jesus Coll. Ox. Scho. of, and Powis Scho. 3rd cl. Lit. Hum. B.A. 1851, M.A. 1853; Deac. 1852 by Bp of Ox. Pr. 1853 by Bp of Ban. P. C. of St. Ann's, Llandegai, Dio. Ban. 1859. (Patron, Lord Penrhyn; P. C.'s Inc. 240*l* and Ho; Pop. 1745.) Formerly C. of Pwllheli 1853; Dioc. Inspector of Schs. 1862–64; Chap. of Tremadock 1854–55; R. of Penmachno 1856–59; Organizing Sec. of S.P.G. 1865; Hon. Sec. of Bangor Tract Soc. 1863. [16]

THOMAS, Edmund, *Colwinstone Vicarage, near Cowbridge, Glamorganshire.*—Magd. Hall, Ox. 3rd cl. Math. B.A. 1857, M.A. 1860; Deac. 1858 and Pr. 1859 by Bp of Llan. V. of Colwinstone, Dio. Llan. 1864. (Patron, Hubert De Burgh Thomas, Esq; V.'s Inc. 150*l* and Ho; Pop. 274.) Formerly C. of Aberystwith 1858–59; P. C. of Bonvilstone 1859–64. [17]

THOMAS, Edward, *Neath Abbey, Neath, Glamorganshire.*—Abergavenny Sch; Deac. 1847 and Pr. 1848 by Bp of Llan. P. C. of Skewen, Glamorganshire, Dio. Llan. 1852. (Patrons, the Crown and Bp of Llan. alt; P. C.'s Inc. 170*l*; Pop. 3173.) Formerly C. of Cadoxton-juxta-Neath, 1847–52. [18]

THOMAS, Edward Thomas Watson, *Nailsworth, Gloucestershire.*—Caius Coll. Cam. 6th Sen. Opt. B.A. 1854, M.A. 1861; Deac. 1854 and Pr. 1855 by Bp of Ely. Chap. of St. George's Chapel, Nailsworth, 1864. Formerly C. of St. Mary's, Bury St. Edmunds, 1854–56, Melksham 1857–64. [19]

THOMAS, Evan, *Bradley, Ashbourne, Derbyshire.*—Literate; Deac. 1819 and Pr. 1820 by Bp of St. D. R. of Bradley, Dio. Lich. 1858. (Patron, Bp of Lich; R.'s Inc. 260*l* and Ho; Pop. 253.) Formerly Lect. of Ashbourne 1831–44; C. of Bradley. [20]

THOMAS, Evan Price, *Whitchurch, Cardiff.*—Deac. by Bp of Win. Pr. by Bp of Llan. P. C. of Whitchurch, Dio. Llan. 1845. (Patron, Bp of Llan; Tithe—App. 493*l* and 60 acres of Glebe, V. 133*l*; P. C.'s Inc. 300*l* and Ho; Pop. 2274.) Formerly one of the V.'s of Llandaff Cathl. 1843–57. [21]

THOMAS Francis, *Harroldston West, Haverfordwest, Pembrokeshire.*—Pemb. Coll. Ox. B.A. 1831, M.A. 1834; Deac. 1833, Pr. 1834. P. C. of Harroldston West, Dio. St. D. 1842. (Patron, Pemb. Coll. Ox; Tithe, 121*l* 10*s*; Glebe, 15 acres; P. C.'s Inc. 135*l*; Pop. 149.) P. C. of Lambston, Pembrokeshire, Dio. St. D. 1842. (Patron, Pemb. Coll. Ox; Tithe, 140*l*; Glebe, 13½ acres; P. C.'s Inc. 150*l*; Pop. 216.) [22]

THOMAS, George, *St. Philip's Parsonage, Leeds.*—Trin. Coll. Cam. B.A. 1830; Deac. 1830 and Pr. 1831 by Bp of Ches. P. C. of St. Philip's, Leeds, Dio. Rip. 1851. (Patrons, the Crown and Bp of Rip. alt; P. C.'s Inc. 216*l* and Ho; Pop. 3512.) Formerly C. of Thornton, Bradford, Yorks, 1839.) Author, *National Duties*, 1840, 2*s* 6*d*; *Ministry of the Holy Angels*, 1847, 2*s* 6*d*; *A few Remarks on the Principles of the Established Church as compared with those of Dissent*, 1840; *Thoughts of Peace, or Texts bearing on the Unity and Peace of the Church in Reference to Church Extension*, 1864. [23]

THOMAS, George Fuller, *Butlers-Marston, Kineton, Warwickshire.*—Wor. Coll. Ox. B.A. 1820, M.A. 1824, Deac. 1827 and Pr. 1828 by Bp of Ox. V. of Butlers-Marston, Dio. Wor. 1846. (Patron, Ch. Ch. Ox; Tithe, 2*l* 13*s* 4*d*; Glebe, 60 acres; V.'s Inc. 170*l* and Ho; Pop. 271.) [24]

THOMAS, Griffith, *St. Mary's Vicarage, Cardigan.*—Literate; Deac. 1813 and Pr. 1814 by Bp of St. D. V. of St. Mary's, Cardigan, Dio. St. D. 1824. (Patron, Ld Chan; Tithe—Imp. 300*l*, V. 10*l*; V.'s Inc. 150*l*; Pop. 2706.) Surrogate 1822; Preb. of Llandegley in the Coll. Ch. of Brecon 1832 (Value 12*l*); Chap. of the Cardigan Gaol 1815 (Stipend 40*l*). Formerly Dom. Chap. to H.R.H. the Duke of Clarence (William IV.) 1819. [25]

THOMAS, Henry, *Lower Halstow, Sittingbourne, Kent.*—St. Bees 1848. V. of Lower Halstow, Dio. Cant. 1863. (Patrons, D. and C. of Cant; V.'s Inc. 250*l*; Pop. 399.) Formerly P. C. of Bredhurst, Kent, 1858–68. [26]

THOMAS, Horatio James, *Pentyrch, Cardiff.*—Literate; Deac. 1828 and Pr. 1829 by Bp of Llan. P. C. of Llantwit-Vairdre, Glamorganshire, Dio. Llan. 1829. (Patron, V. of Llantrisant; Tithe—App. 22*l*; P C.'s Inc. 100*l*; Pop. 1233.) V. of Pentyrch, Dio. Llan. 1835. (Patrons, Bp and D. and C. of Llan. alt; Tithe—App. 219*l* 5*s*, V. 182*l* 2*s*; V's Inc. 260*l*; Pop. 2110.) [27]

THOMAS, Hugh, *Old Newton Vicarage, Stowmarket, Suffolk.*—Magd. Coll. Cam. B.A. 1858, M.A.

1861; Deac. and Pr. 1858 by Bp of Chich. V. of Old Newton, Dio. Nor. 1860. (Patron, The Ch. Patronage Trust; Tithe, 166*l* 14*s*; Glebe, 12 acres; V.'s Inc. 260*l* and Ho; Pop. 718.) [1]

THOMAS, Hugh Percy, *Nash Rectory, near Pembroke.*—Lampeter; Deac. 1840 and Pr. 1841 by Bp of Ches. R. of Nash with Upton C. Dio. St. D. 1853. (Patron, Charles Tasker Evans, Esq; Tithe, 80*l*; Glebe, 28½ acres; R.'s Inc. 126*l* and Ho; Pop. Nash 147, Upton 24.) [2]

THOMAS, James, *Lingfield Parsonage, East Grinstead, Surrey.*—P. C. of Lingfield, Dio. Win. 1863. (Patron, Thomas Alcock, Esq; P. C.'s Inc. 150*l* and Ho; Pop. 2202.) [3]

THOMAS, James, *Herbranston Rectory, Milford, Pembrokeshire.*—R. of Herbranston, Dio. St. D. 1865. (Patron, J. D. Brown, Esq; R.'s Inc. 240*l* and Ho; Pop. 257.) [4]

THOMAS, John, *Altcar Parsonage, near Liverpool.*—Deac. 1855 and Pr. 1856 by Bp of Ches. P. C. of Altcar, Dio. Ches. 1862. (Patron, Earl of Sefton; Tithe, 64*l* 8*s* 10*d*; Glebe, 1 acre; P. C.'s Inc. 250*l* and Ho; Pop. 540.) Formerly C. of Congleton 1855–59, Workington 1859–61; P. C. of St. John's, Workington, 1861–62 [5]

THOMAS, John, *Canterbury.*—Trin. Coll. Ox. Wadl. Coll. Exhib. 1828, Craven Scho. 1829, B.A. 1833, B.C.L. 1837, D.C.L. 1846; Deac. and Pr. 1844 by Bp of Ches. V. of Allhallows, Barking, Dio. Lon. 1852. (Patron, Abp of Cant; V.'s Inc. 2000*l*; Pop. 1679.) Can. of Cant. 1862. Formerly Fell. and Tut. of Univ. Coll. Dur. 1836–41; Commissary of part of the Archd. of Richmond 1846–47; Dom. Chap. to Abp of Cant. 1850–62. [6]

THOMAS, John, *Attleborough Parsonage, Nuneaton.*—Trin. Coll. Cam. M.A. P. C. of Attleborough, Dio. Wor. 1864. (Patron, V. of Nuneaton; P. C.'s Inc. 200*l* and Ho; Pop. 1392.) [7]

THOMAS, The Ven. John Harries, *Capetown.*—Trin. Coll. Cam. B.A. 1844, M.A. 1848; Deac. 1844 and Pr. 1845 by Bp of Lon. Pr. in Ordinary to her Majesty 1850 (Value, 58*l*); Archd. of Capetown 1863. Formerly Min. of Abp Tenison's Chapel, St. James's, Lond. 1851–56; R. of Millbrook, Beds, 1856–63. [8]

THOMAS, J. S.—Asst. Mast. in Marlborough Coll. [9]

THOMAS, John William, *Stanstead-Abbotts Vicarage, Ware, Herts.*—Mert. Coll. Ox. B.A. 1860, M.A. 1844. V. of Stanstead-Abbotts, Dio. Roch. 1847. (Patron, W. K. Thomas, Esq; Tithe—Imp. 301*l* 10*s*, V. 92*l*; Glebe, 39½ acres; V.'s Inc. 146*l* and Ho; Pop. 980.) [10]

THOMAS, Lewis, *Trefriw Rectory, Conway, Carnarvonshire.*—Ox; Deac. 1852 and Pr. 1853 by Bp of Llan. R. of Trefriw with Llanrhychwyn C. Dio. Ban. 1863. (Patron, Bp of Llan; Glebe, 1 acre; R.'s Inc. 208*l* and Ho; Pop. 1015.) [11]

THOMAS, Lewis Frederic, *St. James's, Toxteth-park, Liverpool.*—Queens' Coll. Cam. B.A. 1844. P. C. of St. James's, Toxteth-park, Dio. Ches. 1856. (Patron, R. of Walton-on-the-Hill; P. C.'s Inc. 300*l*; Pop. 8845.) [12]

THOMAS, Llewelyn Lloyd, *Newport Rectory, Pembrokeshire.*—Lampeter; Deac. 1822 and Pr. 1823 by Bp of St. D. R. of Newport, Dio. St. D. 1824. (Patron, Thomas Lloyd, Esq; Tithe, 262*l* 17*s* 6*d*; Glebe, 53 acres; R.'s Inc. 310*l* and Ho; Pop. 1575.) R. of Morvil, Pembrokeshire, Dio. St. D. 1844. (Patron, Lord Milford; Tithe, 68*l*; Glebe, 112 acres; R.'s Inc. 120*l*; Pop. 125.) Rural Dean of Upper Kemes 1833. [13]

THOMAS, Morris, *Trinity Clergy House, Great Portland-street, London, W.*—Trin. Coll. Cam. B.A. 1849, M.A. 1854; Deac. 1850 by Bp of Wor. Pr. 1851 by Bp of Chich. C. of Trinity, Marylebone, Lond. Formerly C. of Hartfield. [14]

THOMAS, Owen Davies, *Bettws-Garmon, Carnarvon.*—Lampeter, Scho. of; Deac. 1860. P. C. of Bettws-Garmon, Dio. Ban. 1866. (Patron, Bp of Llan; P. C.'s Inc. 80*l*; Pop. 94.) Formerly C. of Penydarran, Merthyr Tydvil. Author, *Justice to Wales, a University for Wales*, 1863. [15]

THOMAS, Richard James Francis, *Yeovil Vicarage, Somerset.*—Ch. Ch. Ox. 3rd cl. Lit. Hum. and S.C.L. 1834, M.A. 1839; Deac. 1835 and Pr. 1836 by Bp of G. and B. V. of Yeovil with Preston C. Dio. B. and W. 1855. (Patron, G. Harbin, Esq; Yeovil, Tithe—Imp. 506*l*, V. 550*l*; V.'s Inc. 550*l* and Ho; Pop. Yeovil 4489, Preston 363.) Formerly Head Mast. and Chap. of Bancroft's Hospital, Stepney, Middlesex, 1840–55. [16]

THOMAS, Robert, *Llandegvan, Anglesey.*—Queens' Coll. Cam. B.A. 1852; Deac. 1854 and Pr. 1855 by Bp of Ban. C. of Llandegvan, Anglesey; Head Mast.'s Asst. Cl. Mast. and Math. Mast. of the Beaumaris Gr. Sch. [17]

THOMAS, Robert Davies, *Heywood Lodge, Chester.*—St. Cath. Coll. Cam. B.A. 1836; Deac. 1836 and Pr. 1837 by Bp of Ches. P. C. of Ch. Ch. City and Dio. Ches. 1851. (Patron, Bp of Ches; P. C.'s Inc. 300*l*; Pop. 5242.) [18]

THOMAS, R. J. H., *Hodgeston, Pembroke.*—R. of Hodgeston, Dio. St. D. 1858. (Patron, R. E. Arden, Esq; R.'s Inc. 103*l*; Pop. 48.) Surrogate; Chap. to Lord Leigh. [19]

THOMAS, Samuel, *Llandowror Rectory, St. Clears, Carmarthenshire.*—Magd. Hall, Ox. B.A. 1859; Deac. 1860 and Pr. 1861 by Bp of Llan. R. of Llandowror, Dio. St. D. 1867. (Patron, Lord Milford; Tithe, 120*l*; Glebe, 18 acres; R.'s Inc. 160*l* and Ho; Pop. 339.) Formerly C. of Margam 1860, Aberystwith 1863; R. of Llanllawer with Llanychllwydog 1865–67. [20]

THOMAS, Samuel Webb, *Southease Rectory, Lewes.*—Wor. Coll. Ox. B.A. 1854, M.A. 1860; Deac. 1855 and Pr. 1856 by Bp of St. D. R. of Southease, Dio. Chich. 1864. (Patron, the present R; Tithe, 210*l*; Glebe, 12 acres; R.'s Inc. 250*l* and Ho; Pop. 86.) Formerly C. of Southease 1860–64, Glentworth, Lincoln, 1859–60; P. C. of Harroldston St. Issell's, Pembrokeshire, 1856–58; Asst. C. of St. Mary's, Haverfordwest, Pembrokeshire, 1855–56. [21]

THOMAS, Thomas, *Llanrhaiadr Vicarage, Denbigh.*—Jesus Coll. Ox. 1827; Deac. 1828, Pr. 1829. V. of Llanrhaiadr-in-Kinmerch, Dio. St. A. 1862. (Patron, Bp of St. A; Tithe, 650*l*; Glebe, 17 acres; V.'s Inc. 800*l* and Ho; Pop. 1409.) Can. Res. of Ban. Cathl. 1864. (Value, 350*l*.) Formerly C. of Llanfair Caereinion, Montgomeryshire, 1828–31, Ruabon, Denbighshire, 1831–35; V. of Llanbeblig and Carnarvon, 1835–59; V. of Ruabon 1859–62. Author, *A Visitation Sermon in the Cathedral of Bangor*, 1842. [22]

THOMAS, Thomas, *Hundred House, Radnor.*—Lampeter; Deac. 1831 and Pr. 1832 by Bp of St. D. R. of Cregrina with Llanbadarn-y-garreg P. C. Dio. St. D. 1838. (Patron, Bp of St. D; Cregrina, Tithe, 126*l*; Llanbadarn-y-garreg, Tithe, 64*l*; R.'s Inc. 190*l*; Pop. Cregrina 124. Llanbadarn y-garreg 59.) Formerly C. of Nantcwnlle, Cardiganshire, 1831, Llanelwedd with Alltmawr 1833. [23]

THOMAS, Thomas, *Cwmamman Parsonage, Llanelly, Carmarthenshire.*—Lampeter, B.D. 1855; Deac. 1830 and Pr. 1831 by Bp of St. D. P. C. of Christ Church, Cwmamman, Dio. St. D. 1853. (Patron, Bp of St. D; Glebe, ½ acre; P. C.'s Inc. 150*l* and Ho; Pop. 4353.) Formerly C. of Mothvey 1830–51, Llanddausant 1838–49, Dowlais 1852–53. [24]

THOMAS Thomas, *Denbigh.*—Jesus Coll. Ox. 2nd cl. Math. and B.A. 1856, M.A. 1858; Deac. 1857 and Pr. 1858 by Bp of St. D. C. of Denbigh 1861. Formerly Asst. Mast. Gr. Sch. Llandovery, 1856–61. [25]

THOMAS, Thomas, *Knock, Wiston, Pembrokeshire.*—Deac. 1820 and Pr. 1821 by Bp of St. D. R. of New Moat, Dio. St. D. 1839. (Patron, the present R; R.'s Inc. 200*l*; Pop. 311.) R. of Clarbeston, Dio. St. D. 1843. (Patron, the present R; R.'s Inc. 80*l*; Pop. 168.) Formerly C. of Llanycefn 1820, Lysyfran 1821.) [26]

THOMAS, Thomas, *Talley, Llandilo, Carmarthenshire.*—Lampeter 1846–49; Deac. 1849, Pr. 1851. P. C. of Talley, Dio. St. D. 1854. (Patron, Rev. W. T. Nicholls; P. C.'s Inc. 148*l*; Pop. 1022.) Formerly

2nd Mast. of Queen Elizabeth's Gr. Sch. Carmarthen, 1849-54. [1]

THOMAS, Thomas, *Glanhowey, Builth, Brecknockshire.*—Deac. 1822, Pr. 1823. R. of Disserth with Bettws Chapelry, Radnorshire, Dio. St. D. 1832. (Patron, Bp of St. D; Disserth, Tithe, 300*l*; Glebe, ¾ acre; Bettws, Tithe, 74*l*; R.'s Inc. 374*l*; Pop. Disserth 521, Bettws 130.) [2]

THOMAS, Thomas, *Ystalyfera, Swansea.*—Jesus Coll. Ox. B.A. 1861, M.A. 1863; Deac. 1863 and Pr. 1865 by Bp of Ches. C. of Ystalyfera 1866. Formerly C. of Rostherne, Cheshire, 1863-66. [3]

THOMAS, Thomas Kearsey, *Winforton Rectory, near Hereford*—St. John's Coll. Ox. B.A. 1836, M.A. 1837; Deac. 1839 and Pr. 1840 by Bp of Llan. R. of Winforton, Dio. Herf. 1860. (Patron, the Rev. Henry Blisset; Tithe, comm. 260*l*; Glebe, 16 acres; R.'s Inc. 280*l* and Ho; Pop. 162.) Formerly C. of Cusop, Herefordshire. [4]

THOMAS, Thomas Vaughan, *Disserth, Radnorshire.*—Lin. Coll. Ox. B.A. 1861, M.A. 1865; Deac. 1862 and Pr. 1863 by Bp of St. D. Asst. C. of Disserth 1862. [5]

THOMAS, William, *Sithney Vicarage, near Helston, Cornwall.*—Jesus Coll. Cam. B.D. 1829; Deac. 1819, Pr. 1821. V. of Sithney, Dio. Ex. 1839. (Patron, Bp of Ex; Tithe—Imp. 532*l* 1*s* and 104½ acres of Glebe, V. 436*l* 19*s*; Glebe, 14½ acres; V.'s Inc. 460*l* and Ho; Pop. 2047.) Formerly C. of Dartmouth 1819, St. Issey, Cornwall, 1821-31, Stoke Climsland 1831, Altarnon 1831-38; V. of Manaccan 1838. [6]

THOMAS, William, *Alverdiscott, Barnstaple, Devon.*—R. of Alverdiscott or Alscott, Dio. Ex. 1862. (Patron, Rev. W. M. Lee; R.'s Inc. 200*l* and Ho; Pop. 336.) [7]

THOMAS, William, *Llancynfelin, Glandovey, viâ Shrewsbury.*—Lampeter, Sen. Scho. B.D. 1864; Deac. 1852 by Bp of Wor. Pr. 1853 by Bp of St. D. P. C. of Llancynfelin, Dio. St. D. 1865. (Patrons, Sir. A. P. Bruce Chichester, Bart; P. C.'s Inc. 90*l* and Ho; Pop. 967.) Formerly C. in sole charge of Coychurch, Glamorganshire, of Llanwenog, Cardiganshire, and of Llangorse, Breconshire. [8]

THOMAS, William, *Henllan, Rhyl, Denbighshire.*—C. of Henllan. [9]

THOMAS, William Atterbury, *Dolfor, Newtown, Montgomeryshire.*—Lampeter; Burton, Phillips, Salsbury and Sen. Scholarships, and English Reading Prize 1863, B.A. 1865; Deac. 1864 and Pr. 1865 by Bp of St. A. C. of St. Paul's, Dolfor, Kerry. [10]

THOMAS, William Beach, *Steynton Vicarage, near Milford Haven.*—Pemb. Coll. Ox. 1st cl. Lit. Hum. and B.A. 1821, M.A. 1823; Deac. 1823 and Pr. 1824 by Bp of Ox. R. of Johnston with Steynton V. annexed, Dio. St. D. 1846. (Patron, Ld Chan; Steynton, Tithe, 205*l*; Glebe, 10 acres; Johnston, Tithe, 105*l*; Glebe, 25 acres; R. and V.'s Inc. 370*l* and Ho; Pop. Johnston 275, Steynton 3710.) Exam. Chap. to the Bp of St. D. Author, *Sermon at the Primary Visitation of the Bishop of St. David's*, 1842. [11]

THOMAS, William Garnett, *Burtonwood, Warrington.*—Trin. Coll. Cam. B.A. 1822, M.A. 1825; Deac. 1826 and Pr. 1827 by Bp of Ches. P. C. of Burtonwood, Dio. Ches. 1829. (Patron, R. of Warrington; P. C.'s Inc. 104*l*; Pop. 990.) Formerly C. of Astley, near Leigh, 1826. [12]

THOMAS, William Jones, *Llanigan, Hay, Brecknockshire.*—St. Peter's Coll. Cam. B.A. 1835, M.A. 1838; Deac. 1836 and Pr. 1837 by Bp of Ex. V. of Llanigan, Dio. St. D. 1859. (Patron, Ld Chan; Tithe, 237*l* 10*s*; Glebe, 8*l* 10*s*; V.'s Inc. 246*l*; Pop. 484.) Formerly P. C. of Llanelwedd, Radnorshire, 1838-56; R. of Gladestoy, Herefordshire, 1856-59. [13]

THOMAS, William Mathew, *Tanfield, Bedale, Yorks.*—St. John's Coll. Cam. Jun. Opt. B.A. 1858; Deac. 1859 and Pr. 1861 by Bp of G. and B. C. of Tanfield 1863. Formerly C. of Woolastone, Alvington and Lancant, Gloucestershire, 1859. Author, *Lent Lectures and Sermons*, Simpkin, Marshall and Co. Editor, *West Coast of Africa by C. W. Thomas*, Binns and Goodwin. [14]

THOMAS, William Robert, *St. Mary's Parsonage, Peterborough.*—St. Cath. Coll. Cam. B.A. 1849, M.A. 1852; Deac. 1849, Pr. 1850. P. C. of St. Mary's, Peterborough, Dio. Pet. 1856. (Patron, Earl Fitzwilliam; P. C.'s Inc. 150*l*; Pop. 4034.) Surrogate. Formerly first R. of Akarou, Bank's Peninsula, New Zealand; C. of Hemingford Grey, Hunts. [15]

THOMAS, William Samuel, *Thorn St. Margaret, Wellington, Somerset.*—King's Coll. Lond. Theol. Assoc. 1858; Deac. 1858 by Bp of Ex. Pr. 1859 by Bp of B. and W. C. of Thorn St. Margaret. Formerly 2nd Mast. of Aychford's Gr. Sch. Uffculme, 1858; C. of Stamford Arundell, near Wellington, 1859. [16]

THOMASON, William Stephen, *Burgh-le-Marsh, Boston.*—Trin. Coll. Cam. B.A. 1859, M.A. 1862; Deac. 1860 and Pr. 1861 by Bp of Ox. V. of Burgh Marsh with Winthorpe V. Dio. Lin. 1863. (Patron, Bp of Lin; V.'s Inc. 120*l* and Ho; Pop. 1528.) [17]

THOMLINSON, Jeremiah Sharp, *Thorganby, near York.*—Queen's Coll. Ox. Bp. Thomas Exhib. B.A. 1856; Deac. 1860 and Pr. 1861 by Bp of Carl. C. of Thorganby 1864. Formerly C. of St. James's, Whitehaven, 1860-64. [18]

THOMLINSON, Joseph, *Crosby-upon-Eden Vicarage, near Carlisle.*—St. Bees; Deac. 1821 and Pr. 1822 by Bp of Ches. V. of Crosby-upon-Eden, Dio. Carl. 1838. (Patron, Bp of Carl; Tithe, 80*l*; Glebe, 43 acres; V.'s Inc. 140*l* and Ho; Pop. 426.) [19]

THOMPSON, Abraham Kerr, *Bideford, Devon.*—Queen's Coll. Ox. B.A. 1835, M.A. 1842, D.D. 1855; Deac. 1840, Pr. 1841. Head Mast. of Bideford Gr. Sch. 1854; Lect. of Bideford Ch. 1854. Formerly Sen. Asst. Mast. of King Edw. VI.'s Free Gr. Sch. Birmingham; Head Mast. of Dudley Gr. Sch. Author, *The Fasti of Ovid*; *A Parallel, Historical and Genealogical Scale of the several Dynasties of France and England*; *A Map of the Holy Land, containing a complete Harmony of the Gospels, including the Journeys, Miracles and Chief Facts in the History of our Lord* (for the use of King Edw. VI.'s Sch. Birmingham); *A complete Parallel Scale of History from* B.C. 900 *to* A.D. 500; *A comprehensive Series of Rules for the Genders of Latin Nouns, metrically arranged* (for the use of Bideford Gr. Sch.) [20]

THOMPSON, Archer, *Brimpton Rectory, Yeovil, Somerset.*—R. of Brimpton, Dio. B. and W. 1856. (Patroness, Miss Elizabeth Morris; R.'s Inc. 180*l* and Ho; Pop. 135.) [21]

THOMPSON, Archibald Douglas Cavendish, *Wormley Rectory, Hoddesdon, Herts.*—Dur. B.A. 1859, M.A. 1862; Deac. 1859 and Pr. 1860 by Abp of York. R. of Wormley, Dio. Roch. 1865. (Patron, Earl Brownlow; R.'s Inc. 260*l* and Ho; Pop. 572.) Formerly C. of Appleton-le-Street, 1859-61, and Sigglesthorne, Yorks, 1861-65. [22]

THOMPSON, Arthur Steinkopff, *St. Petersburg.*—Wad. Coll. Ox. B.A. 1858; Deac. 1859 and Pr. 1860 by Bp of Lon. Asst. Chap. at St. Petersburg. Formerly C. of St. Mary's, Marylebone, Lond. 1859. [23]

THOMPSON, Barnard Tyrrell, *Hollingwood, Manchester.*—King's Coll. Lond. Assoc. of Gen. Lit. and Sci. 1861, Theol. Assoc. 1864; Deac. 1864 and Pr. 1866 by Bp of Man. C. of Hollingwood 1864. [24]

THOMPSON, Benjamin Peile, *Kemsing, near Sevenoaks, Kent.*—C. of Kemsing. [25]

THOMPSON, Charles, *South Mimms Vicarage, Barnet, Middlesex, N.*—V. of South Mimms, Dio. Lon. 1852. (Patron, W. P. Hammond, Esq; Tithe—Imp. 744*l* 10*s*, V. 295*l* 10*s* 6*d*; V.'s Inc. 310*l* and Ho; Pop. 2279.) [26]

THOMPSON, C.—C. of St. Bartholomew's, Little Moorfields, Lond. [27]

THOMPSON, Charles Edward, *Westbury, near Buckingham.*—Trin. Coll. Ox. Hon. 4th cl. Lit. Hum. Hon. 4th cl. Math. et Phy. and B.A. 1841; Deac. 1841, Pr. 1842. C. of Westbury. [28]

THOMPSON, Charles James, *Magdalen Hall, Oxford.*—King's Coll. Lond. Assoc. 1862; Deac. 1862 and Pr. 1863 by Bp of Win. Formerly C. of Ch. Ch. Rotherhithe, 1862–64, All Saints', Gordon-square, Lond. 1864 65, Ch. Ch. Lee, Kent, 1866–67. [1]

THOMPSON, Christopher, *Walker Parsonage, Newcastle-upon-Tyne.*—St. Bees; Deac. 1842 and Pr. 1843 by Bp of Rip. P. C. of Walker, Dio. Dur. 1846. (Patrons, the Crown and Bp. of Dur. alt; P. C.'s Inc. 300*l* and Ho; Pop. 5843.) Formerly C. of Giggleswick, Yorks, 1842–45. [2]

THOMPSON, Christopher, *Brighton.*—C. of St. Paul's, Brighton. [3]

THOMPSON, Cornelius, *Kirton Rectory, Ollerton, Notts.*—Trin. Coll. Cam. B.A. 1828; Deac. 1828, Pr. 1829. R. of Kirton, Dio. Lin. 1848. (Patron, Duke of Newcastle; Land, in lieu of Tithe, 181 acres; R.'s Inc. 301*l* and Ho; Pop. 170.) Formerly V. of Elkesley, Notts. [4]

THOMPSON, Cyprian, *Fazeley, near Tamworth, Staffs.*—Deac. 1812 and Pr. 1813 by Bp of Carl. P. C. of Fazeley, Dio. Lich. 1818. (Patron, Sir Robert Peel, Bart; Glebe, 6 acres; P. C.'s Inc. 220*l* and Ho; Pop. 1652.) Formerly C. of Sebergham, 1812, Tamworth 1816. [5]

THOMPSON, Edmund, *Clipston Rectory, Northampton.*—Ch. Coll. Cam. B.A. 1840, M.A. 1843; Deac. 1841 and Pr. 1842 by Bp of Ely. R. of Clipston, Dio. Pet. 1867. (Patron, Ch. Coll. Cam; Glebe, 500 acres; R.'s Inc. 400*l* and Ho; Pop. 877.) Fell. of Ch. Coll. Cam. Formerly C. of Islip 1843–49, Pilton, Northants, 1849–52, Faringdon, Berks, 1852–60. [6]

THOMPSON, Edward, *Chaddleworth Vicarage, Wantage, Berks.*—Clare Coll. Cam. B.A. 1832, M.A. 1835, B.D. 1847. V. of Chaddleworth, Dio. Ox. 1851. (Patrons, D. and C. of Westminster; Tithe—App. 553*l* and 3½ acres of Glebe, V. 269*l* 8*s*; Glebe, 19½ acres; V.'s Inc. 294*l* and Ho; Pop. 539.) [7]

THOMPSON, Edwin.—P. C. of St. John's, Battersea, Dio. Win. 1863. (Patron, V. of Battersea; P. C.'s Inc. 300*l*; Pop. 6000.) Formerly Sec. of London Soc. for Promoting Christianity amongst the Jews; R. of Middleton, Salop. [8]

THOMPSON, Francis, *St. Giles's Vicarage, Durham.*—Dur. B.A. 1836, M.A. 1840; Deac. 1838 and Pr. 1839 by Bp of Dur. V. of St. Giles's, Dio. Dur. 1841. (Patron, Earl Vane; Tithe—Imp. 284*l*, V. 42*l*; Glebe, 120 acres; V.'s Inc. 190*l* and Ho; Pop. 2798.) Formerly C. of Warden 1838, Humshaugh 1839, Easington 1840, all in Dio. Dur. [9]

THOMPSON, Francis Edward, *Old Brentford, Middlesex, W.*—Trin. Coll. Cam. B.A. 1826; Deac. 1828, Pr. 1829. P. C. of Old Brentford, Dio. Lon. 1830. (Patron, V. of Ealing; P. C.'s Inc. 300*l*; Pop. 2591.) Author, *Solutions of Bland's Equations*, 1827; *Sermon* (for Church-Building Soc.), 1829; *The Death of George IV.* (a Sermon), 1830; *Literary and Scientific Studies* (a Lecture), 1837; *Lent Lectures*, 1845; *The Papal Aggression* (two Sermons), 1850; etc. [10]

THOMPSON, Frederick Brewster, *Benfieldside Parsonage, Gateshead.*—Univ. Coll. Dur. B.A. 1838; Deac. 1839, Pr. 1841. P. C. of Benfieldside, Dio. Dur. 1848. (Patrons, the Crown and Bp of Dur. alt; P. C.'s Inc. 300*l* and Ho; Pop. 3723.) [11]

THOMPSON, George, 2, *Victoria-crescent, St. Heliers, Jersey.*—Dub. A.B. 1862; Deac. 1863 and Pr. 1865 by Bp of Win. Asst. C. of St. Mark's District Church, Jersey; Math. Mast. in St. James's Coll. Sch. Jersey. Formerly C. of St. Saviour's, Jersey, 1864–66. [12]

THOMPSON, George, *Wisbech.*—Magd. Hall, Ox. Scho. of, B.A. 1829; Deac. 1830 by Bp of B. and W. Pr. 1838 by Bp of Nor. Mast. of Wisbech Gr. Sch. 1831; Chap. to the Wisbech House of Correction 1852. Formerly Mast. of North Walsham Gr. Sch; Mast. of Wells. Coll. Gr. Sch; C. of Elm with Emneth for 15 years. Author, *Young Protestant Champion of the University of Oxford*; *School Prayers.* Editor of, and Author of Papers in, *Wrangler Magazine*; Joint-Editor with Mr. Bissett of *Horace, Virgil, &c*; *Twenty-five Questions on Confirmation*; etc. [13]

THOMPSON, George, *Leigh Vicarage, Sherborne, Dorset.*—Oriel Coll. Ox. B.A. 1850, M.A. 1858; Deac. 1853 by Bp of Ox. Pr. 1854 by Bp of B. and W. V. of Leigh, Dio. Salis. 1854. (Patron, Bp of Salis; Tithe, Imp. 172*l*; V.'s Inc. 250*l* and Ho; Pop. 465.) [14]

THOMPSON, Grammer, *Horsley, near Derby.*—Lin. Coll. Ox. B.A. 1851, M.A. 1854; Deac. 1852 and Pr. 1853 by Bp of Lich. C. of Horsley. [15]

THOMPSON, Sir Henry, Bart., *Frant Rectory, near Tunbridge Wells.*—Oriel Coll. Ox. B.A. 1818, M.A. 1820; Deac. 1819 by Bp of Herf. Pr. 1827 by Bp of B. and W. R. of Frant, Dio. Chich. 1844. (Patron, Earl of Abergavenny; Tithe, 800*l*; Glebe, 75 acres; R.'s Inc. 850*l* and Ho; Pop. 2276.) Preb. of Chich. 1854; Rural Dean; Proctor in Convocation for Archd. of Lewes. Author, *An Assize Sermon* (at Winchester); *An Ordination Sermon* (at Chichester); *A Visitation Sermon* (at Lewes); *Diocesan Inspection* (a Pamphlet); *Sermon* (preached before the Chich. Dioc. Assoc.), 1856. [16]

THOMPSON, Henry, *The Vicarage, Chard, Somerset.*—St. John's Coll. Cam. Scho. of, Browne's Medal for Latin Ode, 1st Members' Prize for Latin Essay, B.A. 1822, M.A. 1825; Deac. 1823 by Bp of Ex. Pr. 1827 by Bp of Win. V. of Chard, Dio. B. and W. 1853. (Patron, Bp of B. and W; Tithe, comm. 520*l*; Glebe, 3 acres; V.'s Inc. 520*l* and Ho; Pop. 4387.) Formerly C. of St. George's, Camberwell, Surrey, 1824, St. Mary's, Salehurst, Sussex, 1827, Wrington, Somerset, 1828-53. Author, *Davidica—Sermons on the Life and Character of David*, 1827; *Pastoralia—a Manual of Helps for the Parochial Clergy*, 1830 and 1832; *The Life of Hannah More, with Notices of her Sisters*, 1837; *The Maid of Orleans, translated from the German of Schiller, with a Critical Preface*, 1845; *German Ballads* (a Contributor to), 1845; *Original Ballads by Living Authors* (Editor of and Contributor to), 1850; Contributor of Articles on *Greek and Latin Literature* to the *Encyclopædia Metropolitana* published in 1824, and improved and issued in separate volumes by R. Griffin and Co. in 1850; *The Lives of Virgil and Horace* adapted from the *Encyclopædia Metropolitana* and prefixed to Griffin's editions of those poets; *Concionalia—Outlines of Sermons for the Christian Year*, Masters, 1853 and 1862; *The Sunday School* (a Lecture), Masters, 1854; Sermons, Tracts, etc. Contributor to *Lyra Sanctorum*, *Lyra Messianica*, *Lyra Eucharistica*, *Lyra Mystica*, and various Collections and Periodicals. [17]

THOMPSON, Henry, *Stockwell, Surrey, S.*—King's Coll. Lond; Deac. 1854 and Pr. 1855 by Bp of Win. P. C. of St. Michael's, Stockwell, Dio. Win. 1859. (Patron, P. C. of St. Mark's, Kennington; P. C.'s Inc. 360*l*; Pop. 3765.) Formerly C. of St. Michael's, Stockwell. [18]

THOMPSON, Henry, *Garsdale Parsonage (Yorks), near Kendal.*—P. C. of Garsdale, Dio. Rip. 1838. (Patron, Ld Chan; P. C.'s Inc. 77*l* and Ho; Pop. 618.) [19]

THOMPSON, Henry, *Cartmel (Lancashire), near Milnthorpe.*—Mast. of Cartmel Gr. Sch. [20]

THOMPSON, Henry.—C. of Ch. Ch. Lee, Kent. [21]

THOMPSON, Henry Bell, *Tatworth, near Chard, Somerset.*—Wor. Coll. Ox. B.A. 1851; Deac. 1851 and Pr. 1852 by Bp of Lon. P. C. of Tatworth, Dio. B. and W. 1836. (Patron, V. of Chard; Glebe, 3½ acres; P. C.'s Inc. 290*l* and Ho; Pop. 925.) Formerly C. of Bromley-by-Bow, Middlesex, 1851–53, Chard, Somerset, 1854-66. [22]

THOMPSON, Henry John, *Dodford Vicarage, Weedon, Northants.*—Queen's Coll. Ox. B.A. 1853, M.A. 1856; Deac. 1854 and Pr. 1856 by Bp of Wor. V. of Dodford, Dio. Pet. 1859. (Patron, Rev. T. C. Thornton; Glebe, 139 acres; V.'s Inc. 260*l* and Ho; Pop. 238.) Formerly C. of St. Mary's, Warwick, 1854–57. Author, *Praise and Thanksgiving* (a Sermon), Church Press Company, 4*d*. [23]

THOMPSON, Henry Thomas, *Bury St. Edmunds.*—St. John's Coll. Cam. B.A. 1817, M.A. 1823; Deac. 1828 and Pr. 1829 by Bp of Nor. C. of Fornham with Westley, Suffolk. [24]

THOMPSON, James, *Bridlington Quay, Yorks.*—Lin. Coll. Ox. B.A. 1839, M.A. 1842; Deac. 1839 and Pr. 1840 by Abp of York. P. C. of Ch. Ch. Bridlington Quay, Dio. York, 1841. (Patron, the P. C. of Bridlington; Glebe, 6½ acres; P. C.'s Inc. 210*l* and Ho; Pop. 2677.) Formerly C. of Bessingby, Yorks. [1]

THOMPSON, John, *Easby Vicarage, Richmond, Yorks.*—Dub. A.B. 1844; Deac. 1845 and Pr. 1846 by Bp of Ches. V. of Easby with Brompton-on-Swale C. Dio. Rip. 1849. (Patron, Leonard Jaques, Esq; Glebe, 47 acres; V.'s Inc. 160*l* and Ho; Pop. 800.) [2]

THOMPSON, John, *Bristol.*—Dub. A.B; C. of Trinity, St. Philip and St. Jacob's, Bristol. [3]

THOMPSON, John, *Trinity Cottage, Ripon.*—St. Aidan's; Deac. 1866 by Bp of Rip. C. of Trinity, Ripon, 1866. [4]

THOMPSON, John, *Patrick Brompton, Bedale, Yorks.*—P. C. of Brompton Patrick with Brompton Hunton P. C. Dio. Rip. 1866. (Patron, Bp of Rip; P. C.'s Inc. 200*l*; Pop. 1129.) Formerly C. of Easby Yorks. [5]

THOMPSON, John Cambage, 1, *Peckitt-street, York.*—Literate; Deac. 1848 and Pr. 1849 by Bp of Rip. Chap. of York Castle. Formerly C. of Easby, Yorks, 1849, Wycliffe 1850, Beverley Minster 1853; Chap. of the East Riding House of Correction, Beverley, 1859; Even. Lect. of St. Margaret's, York, 1859. [6]

THOMPSON, John Elijah, *Offton Vicarage, Needham Market.*—St. John's Coll. Cam. B.A. 1854, M.A. 1857; Deac. 1856 and Pr. 1857 by Bp of Ely. V. of Offton with Little Bricett R. Dio. Nor. 1858. (Patron, J. G. Sparrow, Esq; Tithe—Imp. 218*l*, V. 188*l* 10*s*; Glebe, 27 acres; V.'s Inc. 215*l*; Pop. 394.) Formerly C. of Hitcham, Suffolk. [7]

THOMPSON, John Metcalfe, *York.*—Deac. 1863 and Pr. 1864 by Abp of York. C. of St. Crux, York, and of Heslington, near York, 1863. [8]

THOMPSON, Joseph, *Satley Parsonage, Darlington.*—St. Bees; Deac. 1828, Pr. 1829. P. C. of Satley, Dio. Dur. 1832. (Patron, Bp of Dur; Glebe, 30 acres; P. C.'s Inc. 300*l* and Ho; Pop. 1089.) [9]

THOMPSON, Joseph, *Keston Rectory, Bromley, Kent.*—St. Aidan's; Deac. 1850 and Pr. 1851 by Abp of Cant. R. of Keston, Dio. Cant. 1858. (Patron, Abp of Cant; Tithe, 270*l*; Glebe, 9 acres; R.'s Inc. 320*l* and Ho; Pop. 690.) Formerly C. of Cudham, Kent, 1850–58. [10]

THOMPSON, Joseph Hesselgrave, *Cradley, near Brierley-hill, Worcestershire.*—Magd. Hall, Ox. 4th cl. Lit. Hum. and B.A. 1845; Deac. 1845, Pr. 1846. P. C. of Cradley, Dio. Wor. 1856. (Patron, V. of Hales-Owen; P. C.'s Inc. 390*l*; Pop. 4071.) Formerly C. of Hales-Owen. [11]

THOMPSON, Josiah, *Crowle, Lincolnshire.*—C. of Crowle. [12]

THOMPSON, J. Henry, *Windsor.*—Ch. Coll. Cam. B.A. 1845, M.A. 1848; Deac. 1848 and Pr. 1849, by Bp of Rip. C. of Windsor, Berks, 1866. Formerly P. C. of Middleton, Leeds, 1849; Sen. C. and Even. Lect. of St. Nicholas', Newcastle-on-Tyne, 1853; Prof. of Div. and Heb. Bishop's Coll. Lenoxville, Canada East, 1855; Can. of the Cathl. Montreal and Exam. Chap. to Bp of Montreal, 1861. Author, *The Presence of Christ in Church Synods*, Quebec, 1858; *The Angel of the Church* (Sermon at the Consecration of the Bishop of Quebec), Montreal, 1863; *Revelation and Science* (Commemoration Sermon), Lenoxville, 1864. [13]

THOMPSON, Matthew Carrier, *Alderminster Lodge, Stratford-on-Avon.*—R. of Woodstone, near Peterborough, Dio. Ely, 1829. (Patron, R. J. Thompson, Esq; R.'s Inc. 350*l* and Ho; Pop. 347.) V. of Alderminster, Dio. Wor. 1830. (Patron, Ld. Chan; Tithe—Imp. 188*l* 4*s* 6*d*, V. 160*l* 19*s* 6*d*; Glebe, 28 acres; V.'s Inc. 190*l* and Ho; Pop. 520.) [14]

THOMPSON, Moorhouse, *Lucker Parsonage, Chat-hill, Northumberland.*—Univ. Coll. Dur. 1835, B.A. 1838, M.A. 1839; Deac. 1840, Pr. 1841. P. C. of Lucker, Dio. Dur. 1854. (Patron, Duke of Northumberland; Glebe, 36 acres; P. C.'s Inc. 93*l* and Ho; Pop. 281.) [15]

THOMPSON, Philip, *Droylesden, near Manchester.*—St. Cath. Coll. Cam. B.A. 1843. P. C. of Droylesden, Dio. Man. 1844. (Patrons, the Crown and Bp of Man. alt; P. C.'s Inc. 130*l*; Pop. 8798.) [16]

THOMPSON, Robert, *Musbury, Bury, Lancashire.*—St. Bees; Deac. 1841 and Pr. 1842 by Bp of Ches. P. C. of Musbury, Dio. Man. 1845. (Patrons, the Crown and Bp of Man. alt; P. C.'s Inc. 150*l*; Pop. 2724.) [17]

THOMPSON, Robert, *Shotley Vicarage, Northumberland.*—Dub. A.B. 1832; Deac. 1824 and Pr. 1825 by Bp of Ox. V. of Shotley, Dio. Dur. 1842. (Patrons, Bp Crewe's Trustees; Tithe—Imp. 455*l* 6*s* 6*d*, V. 15*l*; Glebe, 10 acres; V.'s Inc. 300*l* and Ho; Pop 706.) Formerly C. of Stanhope 1824–42. [18]

THOMPSON, Robert, *Skipsea, Hull.*—Pemb. Coll. Cam. B.A. 1856; Deac. 1857 and Pr. 1858 by Bp of Lin. V. of Skipsea, Dio. York, 1864. (Patron, Abp of York; Glebe, 15 acres; V.'s Inc. 300*l* and Ho Pop. 844.) [19]

THOMPSON, Robert Anchor, *St. Mary-the-Virgin Hospital, Newcastle-on-Tyne.*—St. Cath. Coll. Cam. 20th Wrang. and B.A. 1844, M.A. 1850; Deac. 1845 by Bp of Ches. Pr. 1847 by Bp of Dur. Mast. of the Hospital of St. Mary-the-Virgin, Newcastle, an ancient foundation, consisting of a Master and eight Brethren, with a public Chapel. Formerly Astronomical Observer at Durham 1846–49; C. of Louth 1849–53; Binbrook 1854–58. Author, *Sermons*, 1853; *Christian Theism* (Burnett Prize Treatise), 1855, 21*s*, new ed. 1863, 10*s* 6*d*; *Principles of Natural Theology*, 3*s*; *The Oxford Declaration, a Letter to the Oxford Committee*, 1864, 1*s*. [20]

THOMPSON, R. B., *Longwood, Huddersfield.*—C. of St. Mark's, Longwood. [21]

THOMPSON, Robert Oliver, *Bristol.*—Dub. A.B; Deac. 1862 and Pr. 1863 by Bp of G. and B. C. of St. Clement's, Bristol. [22]

THOMPSON, Thomas Bowser Harrison, *Weyhill Rectory, Andover, Hants.*—Queen's Coll. Ox. B.A. 1833, M.A. 1837; Deac. 1834 by Bp of Ox. Pr. 1835 by Bp of Win. R. of Weyhill, Dio. Win. 1854. (Patron, Queen's Coll. Ox; Tithe, 501*l* 18*s*; Glebe, 22½ acres; R.'s Inc. 527*l* and Ho; Pop. 444.) [23]

THOMPSON, Thomas Charles, *Ripley Rectory, Yorks.*—Trin. Coll. Cam. B.A. 1834, M.A. 1837. R. of Ripley, Dio. Rip. 1848. (Patron, Sir W. A. Ingilby, Bart; Tithe, 450*l* 15*s* 9*d*; Glebe, 56½ acres; R.'s Inc. 555*l* and Ho; Pop. 1558.) [24]

THOMPSON, Thomas Henry, *Cassop House, Ferry Hill, Durham.*—Dur. Barrington Scho. Crewe Exhib. 3rd cl. Math. et Phy. B.A. 1851; Licen. in Theol. 1852, M.A. 1854; Deac. 1854 by Bp of Dur. Pr. 1855 by Bp of Man. P. C. of Cassop with Quarrington, Dio. Dur. 1865. (Patrons, Crown and Bp of Dur. alt; P. C.'s Inc. 300*l*; Pop. 2134.) Formerly Sen. C. of Tynemouth 1854–61; C. in sole charge of Alston, Cumberland, 1861–62; C. of St. Paul's District, Darlington 1862–65; Surrogate for Dio. Dur. 1856. [25]

THOMPSON, Thomas William, *Tibenham Vicarage, Long Stratton, Norfolk.*—Pemb. Coll. Cam. B.A. 1844, M.A. 1852; Deac. 1844 by Bp of Lich. Pr. 1845 by Bp of Nor. V. of Tibenham, Dio. Nor. 1863. (Patron, Bp of Nor; Tithe, comm. 325*l*; Glebe, 21 acres; V.'s Inc. 380*l* and Ho; Pop. 729.) Surrogate. Formerly C. of Bobbington, Staffs, 1844; C. 1845 and P. C. 1847 of New Buckenham, Norfolk. [26]

THOMPSON, William, *Addingham Rectory, Yorks.*—Jesus Coll. Cam. B.A. 1838; Deac. 1839 and Pr. 1840 by Bp of Rip. R. of Addingham, Dio. Rip. 1840. (Patron, the present R; Tithe, 220*l*; Glebe, 20 acres; R.'s Inc. 400*l* and Ho; Pop. 1938.) [27]

THOMPSON, William Dent, 24, *East View, Preston.*—Queen's Coll. Birmingham; Deac. 1862 and Pr. 1864 by Bp of Lich. C. of St. Saviour's, Preston, 1864. Formerly C. of Bloxwich, Staffs. [28]

THOMPSON, William Hamilton, *Stoke Dry Rectory, Uppingham, Rutland.*—Dub. A.B. 1835; Deac. 1843 and Pr. 1844 by Bp of Llan. R. of Stoke Dry,

Dio. Pet. 1854. (Patron, Marquis of Exeter; Tithe, 350*l*; Glebe, 33 acres; R.'s Inc. 400*l* and Ho; Pop. 53.) [1]

THOMPSON, William Hepworth, *The Lodge, Trinity College, Cambridge.*—Trin. Coll. Cam B.A. 1832, M.A. 1835, D.D. 1867; Deac. 1837, Pr. 1868. Mast. of Trin. Coll. 1866; Hon. Can. of Ely 1867. Formerly Regius Professor of Greek, Cam. 1853; Fell. and Tut. of Trin. Coll. [2]

THOMPSON, William Joseph, *Royal Naval School, New Cross, Kent, S.E.*—Bp Hatfield's Hall, Dur. Fell. of, 1858, 1st cl. B.A. 1855, M.A. 1858; Deac. 1857 and Pr. 1858 by Abp of York. 2nd Cl. Mast. and Asst. Chap. of the Royal Naval Sch. New Cross, 1861. Formerly 4th Cl. Mast. of St. Peter's Sch. York. [3]

THOMPSON, William Oswell, *Spelsbury, Enstone, Oxon.*—Ex. Coll. Ox. Hon. 4th cl. Nat. Sci. and B.A. 1862, M.A. 1865; Deac. 1863 and Pr. 1864 by Bp of Ox. C. in sole charge of Spelsbury 1866. Formerly C. of Old Windsor, Berks, 1863–66. [4]

THOMSON, Anthony Francis.—British Chap. at Avranches. [5]

THOMSON, Frederick Forsyth, *Woolwich.*—Sid. Coll. Cam. B.A. 1846. Chap. to the Forces. Formerly Chap. to the Dover Gaol. [6]

THOMSON, George, *Chislehurst, Kent, S.E.*—St. Peter's Coll. Cam. B.A. 1838, M.A. 1851; Deac. 1839 and Pr. 1840 by Bp of Ex. [7]

THOMSON, George Selby, *Acklington Parsonage, Northumberland.*—Jesus Coll. Cam. Scho. of, Coll. Prizeman Cl. and Maths. 1828, '29, '30, Sen. Opt. and B.A. 1831, M.A. 1834; Dur. Licen. in Theol; Deac 1835 by Bp of G. and B. Pr. 1837 by Bp of Dur. P. C. of Acklington, Dio. Dur. 1865. (Patron, Duke of Northumberland; P. C.'s Inc. 250*l* and Ho; Pop. 635.) Formerly C. of Rothbury 1836–48; V. of Alnham 1848–65. [8]

THOMSON, James, *Christ's Hospital, Newgate-street, London, E.C.*—St. John's Coll. Cam. Sen. Opt. 2nd cl. Cl. Trip. and B.A. 1840, M.A. 1843; Deac. 1842 and Pr. 1843 by Bp of Lon. 2nd Mast. of the Upper Sch. Christ's Hospital. Formerly C. of St. Mary Aldermary, and St. Thomas's, Lond. 1854–59. [9]

THOMSON, John, *Hemley Rectory, Woodbridge, Suffolk.*—Dur; Deac. 1835 by Bp of Lon. Pr. 1837 by Bp of Madras. R. of Hemley, Dio. Nor. 1867. (Patron, Ld Chan; Tithe, 194*l*; R.'s Inc. 250*l* and Ho; Pop. 75.) Formerly C. of Tincleton and Woodsford, Dorset, 1844–46; C. in sole charge of Broad Hinton, Wilts, 1846–66; Miss. of S.P.G. to South India. Author, *A Translation of the Thirty-nine Articles into the Tamil Language*, Vepery Mission Press of S.P.C.K. 1839; *Summary of Facts on Physical Science, for Native Youth*, in Tamil, 1840; *History of St. Paul*, in Tamil, 1841; *Translation of Marsh on the Collects* into Tamil, ib. 1842; Sermons, in *The Tamil Magazine*; etc. [10]

THOMSON, John, *Barnham Broom, Wymondham, Norfolk.*—Pemb. Coll. Cam. B.A. 1854; Deac. 1856 and Pr. 1858 by Bp of Nor. C. of Barnham Broom. [11]

THOMSON, J. R.—C. of the Octagon Chapel, Bath. [12]

THOMSON, William Stephen, *Horndon-on-the-Hill, Essex.*—Queens' Coll. Cam. B.A. 1839, M.A. 1842. R. of Fobbing, Essex, Dio. Roch. 1850. (Patron, the Crown; Tithe, 753*l* 12*s* 4*d*; R.'s Inc. 760*l* and Ho; Pop. 393.) Formerly British Chap. at Heidelberg. [13]

THOMSON, William Yalden.—Literate; Deac. 1859 and Pr. 1860 by Bp of G. and B. P. C. of St. Matthew's, Newington, Lond. Dio. Lon. 1867. (Patrons, Trustees; P. C.'s Inc. 300*l*.) Formerly P. C. of Percy, North Shields, 1860. [14]

THORESBY, Thomas, *Pen-y-bont, Radnorshire.*—St. John's Coll. Cam. B.A. 1817. P. C. of Llandrindod, near Pen-y-bont, Dio. St. D. 1845. (Patron, the Preb. of Llandrindod in St. D.'s Cathl; Tithe—App. 100*l* and 1½ acres of Glebe; P. C.'s Inc. 48*l*; Pop. 243.) R. of Kevenlleece, near Pen-y-bont, Dio. St. D. 1848. (Patron, Bp of St. D; R.'s Inc. 136*l*; Pop. 395.) [15]

THORN, John Thomas, 5, *Oriel-terrace, Cheltenham.*—Ch. Ch. Ox. Fell. Exhib. B.A. 1854, M.A. 1856; Deac. 1855 and Pr. 1857 by Bp of Herf. 2nd Mast. of Jun. Department, Cheltenham Coll. Formerly C. of Willey and Barrow, Salop, 1855–57; Dom. Chap. to Sir M. R. Shaw-Stewart, Bart. at Ardgowan, Renfrewshire, 1857–66. [16]

THORN, M., *Ashbrittle, Wellington, Somerset.*—C. of Ashbrittle. [17]

THORNE, Joseph, *Bishop-Nympton Vicarage, South Molton, Devon.*—Ex. Coll. Ox. B.A. 1818, M.A. 1859; Deac. and Pr. 1821 by Bp of Ex. V. of Bishop-Nympton, Dio. Ex. 1835. (Patron, Bp of Ex; Tithe—Imp. 421*l*, V. 379*l*; Glebe, 2½ acres; V.'s Inc. 390*l* and Ho; Pop. 1197.) Formerly C. of Michaelstow, Cornwall, 1821, Filleigh, Devon, 1822–23, Rose Ash and Meshaw, 1823–25, Topsham 1825–26, Bishop-Nympton 1826–35. [18]

THORNE, J. P., *Everton, Liverpool.*—C. of Ch. Ch. Everton. [19]

THORNE, Michael, *Tiverton, Devon.*—Lin. Coll. Ox. B.A. 1827; Deac. 1828 and Pr. 1829 by Bp of Ex. Formerly C. of Butterleigh. [20]

THORNEWILL, Charles Francis, 6, *Richmond-street, Leicester.*—Corpus Coll. Ox. 2nd cl. Nat. Sci. and B.A. 1863, M.A. 1866; Deac. 1864 and Pr. 1865 by Bp of Man. C. of St. Mary's, Leicester, 1867. Formerly C. of Trinity, Habergham Eaves, Burnley, 1864. [21]

THORNHILL, H. B., *Eatington, Stratford-on-Avon.*—C. of Eatington 1867. Formerly C. of Huntley, Gloucester. [22]

THORNHILL, John, *Boxworth Rectory, Caxton, Cambs.*—St. John's Coll. Cam. B.A. 1838, M.A. 1841. R. of Boxworth, Dio. Ely. (Patron, G. Thornhill, Esq; Tithe, 490*l*; Glebe, 126 acres; R.'s Inc. 595*l* and Ho; Pop. 347.) [23]

THORNHILL, William, *Offord D'Arcy, Buckden, Hunts.*—St. Cath. Hall, Cam. B.A. 1842, M.A. 1845; Deac. and Pr. 1846 by Abp of Cant. R. of Offord D'Arcy, Dio. Ely 1856. (Patron, G. Thornhill, Esq; Tithe, 42*l*; Glebe, 340 acres; R.'s Inc. 406*l* and Ho; Pop. 437.) [24]

THORNLEY, John James, *Workington, Cumberland.*—St. John's Coll. Cam. B.A. 1866; Deac. 1866 by Bp of Carl. C. of Workington 1866. [25]

THORNTON, Charles, *Bayford, near Hertford.*—Clare Coll. Cam. B.A. 1839, M.A. 1842; Deac. 1839, Pr. 1840. P. C. of Bayford, Dio. Roch. 1867. (Patron, W. R. Baker, Esq; P. C.'s Inc. 150*l* and Ho; Pop. 320.) Formerly C. of Bayford for 28 years. [26]

THORNTON, Francis Vansittart, *South-hill Rectory, Callington, Cornwall.*—Trin. Coll. Cam. B.A. 1838, M.A. 1841. R. of South-hill with Callington R. Dio. Ex. 1864. (Patrons, Trustees of the late Lord Ashburton; Tithe, 750*l*; Glebe, 250 acres; R.'s Inc. 960*l* and Ho; Pop. South-hill 691, Callington 2202.) Formerly R. of Brown Candover, Hants. [27]

THORNTON, George, *Sharnbrook Vicarage, Beds.*—Trin. Coll. Cam. B.A. 1827, M.A. 1830; Deac. 1827, Pr. 1829. V. of Sharnbrook, Dio. Ely, 1844. (Patron, Ld Chan; Glebe, 96 acres; V.'s Inc. 160*l* and Ho; Pop. 867.) [28]

THORNTON, George Wright, *Holsworthy, Devon.*—Dub. 1847; St. Bees 1850–51; Deac. 1851, Pr. 1853. C. and Patron of Holsworthy; Surrogate. Formerly C. of Eccleston, Lancashire. [29]

THORNTON, Henry Woffenden, *Guilden Morden, near Royston, Cambs.*—C. of Guilden Morden. [30]

THORNTON, John, *Aston-Abbotts Vicarage, Aylesbury, Bucks.*—St. Cath. Coll. Cam. Skerne Scho. B.A. 1840, M.A. 1848; Deac. 1840 and Pr. 1841 by Bp of Pet. V. of Aston-Abbotts, Dio. Ox. 1853. (Patron, Lord Overstone; Glebe, 99 acres; V.'s Inc. 150*l* and Ho; Pop. 311.) Formerly Chap. to the General Asylum and Infirmary, Northampton, 1842–47; Head Mast. of the Gr. Sch. Kimbolton, Hunts, 1847–53. [31]

THORNTON, Philip, *Brockhall Rectory, Weedon, Northants.*—Sid. Coll. Cam. B.A. 1804, M.A. 1807; Deac. 1805, Pr. 1806. R. of Brockhall, Dio. Pet. 1806. (Patron, T. R. Thornton, Esq; Tithe, 160*l* 7*s* 6*d*; Glebe,

50 acres; R.'s Inc. 228*l* and Ho; Pop. 54.) Hon. Can. of Pet. 1844. [1]

THORNTON, Robinson, *The College, Epsom, Surrey.*—St. John's Coll. Ox. Jun. Math. Scho. 1845, 1st cl. Lt. Hum. 2nd cl. Math. B.A. 1847, M.A. 1851, B.D. 1856, D.D. 1860; Deac. 1849 and Pr. 1852 by Bp of Ox. Head Mast. and Chap. of Epsom College, 1855. Formerly Asst. C. of St. Thomas's, Oxford, 1849–51; Fell. and Lect. of St. John's Coll. Ox. till 1855. Author, *Comparative Philology with Reference to the Theories of Man's Origin* and *The Logic of Scepticism* (two papers read before the Victoria Institute, and published in the *Transactions* of that Society). Joint-Editor, *Fasciculus* (a collection of Latin verse translations), Parkers, 1866. [2]

THORNTON, Samuel, *St. George's, Birmingham.*—Queen's Coll. Ox. Michel Fell. of, 2nd cl. Lit. Hum. and 2nd cl. Nat. Sci. B.A. 1856, M.A. 1858; Deac. 1858 by Bp of Ox. Pr. 1859 by Bp of Lon. R. of St. George's, Birmingham, Dio. Wor. 1864. (Patrons, Trustees; Tithe, 15*l*; Glebe, 185*l*; R.'s Inc. 620*l*; Pop. 17,138.) Surrogate. Formerly Miss. C. in Bethnal Green 1858; London Dioc. Home Miss. 1858; P. C. of St. Jude's, Whitechapel, 1860. [3]

THORNTON, Thomas, *Bywell St. Peter, Gateshead.*—C. of Bywell St. Peter; Fell. of Dur. Univ. [4]

THORNTON, Thomas Cooke, *Brockhall, Weedon, Northants.*—Clare Coll. Cam. B.A. 1822, M.A. 1825; Deac. 1823, Pr. 1824. [5]

THORNTON, William, *Brockhall, Weedon, Northants.*—Corpus Coll. Cam. B.A. 1828, M.A 1831; Deac. 1830, Pr. 1831. Formerly V. of Dodford, Northants, 1837–59. Author, *Householders' Manual of Family Prayer*, 1853. [6]

THORNTON, William Henry, *North Bovey Rectory, Exeter.*—Trin. Coll. Cam. B.A. 1853, M.A. 1857; Deac. 1853 and Pr. 1855 by Bp of Ex. R. of North Bovey, Dio. Ex. 1867. (Patron, Earl of Devon; Tithe, 325*l*; Glebe, 21 acres; R.'s Inc. 350*l* and Ho; Pop. 520.) Formerly C. of Lynton and Countisbury 1853; P. C. of Exmoor 1856; V. of Dunsford 1861. [7]

THORNTON, William Wheeler, *Godstone, Surrey.*—Trin. Coll. Ox. B.A. 1844, M.A. 1848; Deac. 1847 and Pr. 1848 by Bp of Lin. R. of Horne, Dio. Win. 1867. (Patron, the present R; Tithe—600*l*; R.'s Inc. 600*l*; Pop. 637.) Formerly C. of Benenden, Kent, 1851–58, Worplesdon, Surrey, 1858–67. [8]

THORNYCROFT, John, *Thornycroft Hall, Congleton, Cheshire.*—Brasen. Coll. Ox. B.A. 1831, M.A. 1832; Deac. 1833 and Pr. 1835 by Bp of Ches. Rural Dean of South Macclesfield. [9]

THOROLD, Anthony Wilson, 16, *Portland-place, London, W.*—Queen's Coll. Ox. B.A. 1847, M.A. 1850. R. of St. Giles's-in-the-Fields, Dio. Lon. 1857. (Patron, Ld Chan; R.'s Inc. 663*l*; Pop. 36,684.) Chap. to Abp of York. [10]

THOROLD, Henry Baugh, *Hougham Rectory, Grantham.*—Trin. Coll. Ox. B.A. 1827; Deac. 1828 and Pr. 1829 by Bp of Lin. R. of Hougham with Marston, Dio. Lin. 1836. (Patron, Sir J. C. Thorold, Bart; Tithe, 110*l*; Glebe, 389 acres; R.'s Inc. 730*l* and Ho; Pop. Hougham 349, Marston 403.) [11]

THOROLD, John, *Lincoln.*—Emman. Coll. Cam. Scho. and Exhib. of, B.A. 1840, M.A. 1843; Deac. 1841 and Pr. 1843 by Bp of Lin. R. and V. of St. Mary-le-Wigford, City and Dio. Lin. 1855. (Patron, Bp of Lin; Tithe, 80*l* 10*s*; Glebe, 8 acres; V.'s Inc. 120*l*; Pop. 1746.) Sunday and Wednesday Even. Lect. of same 1852; Surrogate for Lincolnshire and Notts. Formerly Sunday and Wednesday Even. Lect. at St. Peter's-at-Arches, Lincoln, 1851–52. [12]

THOROLD, William, *Weeton Parsonage, Kirkham, Lancashire.*—P. C. of Weeton, Dio. Man. 1865. (Patron, V. of Kirkham; P. C.'s Inc. 110*l* and Ho; Pop. 1017.) [13]

THOROLD, William, *Warkleigh Rectory, South Molton, Devon.*—Wor. Coll. Ox. B.A. 1833, M.A. 1837; Deac. 1837, Pr. 1838. R. of Warkleigh with Satterleigh, Dio. Ex. 1841. (Patron, the present R; Tithe, 300*l*; Glebe, and Augmentation Lands, 100 acres; R.'s Inc. 450*l* and Ho; Pop. Warkleigh 330, Satterleigh 79.) [14]

THOROTON, Charles, *Rauceby Vicarage, Sleaford, Lincolnshire.*—Univ. Coll. Dur. B.A. 1847, M.A. 1850; Deac. 1848 and Pr. 1849 by Bp of Dur. V. of North and South Rauceby, Dio. Lin. 1854. (Patron, Sir J. C. Thorold, Bart; V.'s Inc. 200*l* and Ho; Pop. North Rauceby 279, South Rauceby 474.) [15]

THORP, Charles, *Ellingham Vicarage, Chat Hill, Northumberland.*—Univ. Coll. Ox. B.A. 1850, M.A. 1853; Deac. and Pr. 1850 by Bp of Dur. V. of Ellingham, Dio. Dur. 1855. (Patrons, D. and C. of Dur; Tithe—App. 872*l* 16*s* 1*d*, V. 390*l* 11*s* 10*d*; Glebe, 162 acres; V.'s Inc. 564*l* and Ho; Pop. 660.) Formerly P. C. of Blanchland, Northumberland, 1850–55. [16]

THORP, Edward, *Castle-street, Bridgwater.*—Magd. Hall, Ox. B.A. 1865; Deac. 1865, Pr. 1866. C. of St. Mary's, Bridgwater, 1865. [17]

THORP, Frederic, *Burton Overy, near Leicester.*—Emman. Coll. Cam. B.A. 1850, M.A. 1853; Deac. 1851 and Pr. 1852 by Bp of Lich. R. of Burton Overy, Dio. Pet. 1852. (Patron, Capt. W. Thorpe, R.N; R.'s Inc. 500*l* and Ho; Pop. 465.) [18]

THORP, Gervase, *Danbury, Chelmsford.*—King's Coll. Lond. Theol. Assoc. 1858; Deac. 1858 and Pr. 1859 by Bp of Nor. C. of Danbury 1860. Formerly C. of St. Margaret's, Ipswich, 1858–60. [19]

THORP, John, *Oxford.*—St. Bees; Deac. 1826 and Pr. 1827 by Bp of Jamaica. Chap. of the Oxford City and County Prisons 1853. Formerly Prin. of the Oxford Dioc. Training Sch. 1840–53. [20]

THORP, John, *Darsham Vicarage, Saxmundham.*—Magd. Hall, Ox. B.A. 1859, M.A. 1860; Deac. 1860 and Pr. 1861 by Bp of St. A. V. of Darsham, Dio. Nor. 1866. (Patron, Lord Stradbroke; Tithe, 80*l*; Glebe, 6 acres; V.'s Inc. 101*l* and Ho; Pop. 409.) Formerly C. of Chirk, N. Wales, 1860–64, St. Andrew's, Watford, 1864–65. [21]

THORP, The Ven. Thomas, *Kemerton Rectory, Tewkesbury, Glouc.*—Trin. Coll. Cam. 8th Wrang. Sen. Medallist. B.A. 1819, M.A. 1822, B.D. 1842; Deac. and Pr. 1829. Archd. of Bristol 1836. (Inc. 200*l*.) R. of Kemerton, Dio. G. and B. 1839. (Patron, Bp of G. and B; Glebe, 300 acres; R.'s Inc. 600*l* and Ho; Pop. 559.) Formerly Fell. Tut. and Vice-Master of Trin. Coll. Cam. Twice University Select Preacher. Author, various Sermons and Charges. [22]

THORP, W., *Northampton.*—C. of All Saints', Northampton. [23]

THORP, William Tudor, *Ponteland, Newcastle-on-Tyne.*—Univ. Coll. Ox. B.A. 1862; Deac. 1864 and Pr. 1865 by Bp of Dur. C. of Ponteland 1867. Formerly C. of Cramlington 1864–67. [24]

THORPE, George Villiers, *Thurlby Vicarage, Bourne, Lincolnshire.*—St. John's Coll. Ox. B.A. 1833; Deac. 1838 by Bp of Ely, Pr. 1839 by Bp of Pet. V. of Thurlby, Dio. Lin. 1864. (Patron, Eton Coll; Tithe—Imp. 204*l* 4*s* 10*d*; Glebe, 215 acres; V.'s Inc. 553*l* and Ho; Pop. 833.) Formerly C. of Churchill, Bristol, and Chilton Cantelo, Yeovil. Author, *A Sermon, occasioned by the Death of Lady Pilkington*, Crewe, 1855. [25]

THORPE, Henry, *Aston-le-Walls, Leamington.*—St. John's Coll. Ox. B.A. 1827, M.A. 1830; Deac. 1826, Pr. 1828. R. of Aston-le-Walls, Northants, Dio. Pet. 1831. (Patron, St. John's Coll. Ox; Tithe, 240*l*; Glebe, 142 acres; R.'s Inc. 540*l* and Ho; Pop. 221.) [26]

THORPE, John Frederic, *Hernhill, near Faversham, Kent.*—King's Coll. Lond. Theol. Assoc; Deac. 1852 and Pr. 1853 by Abp of Cant. V. of Hernhill, Dio. Cant. 1866. (Patron, Abp of Cant; Tithe, 350*l*; Glebe, 17 acres; V.'s Inc. 350*l*; Pop. 701.) Formerly C. of Ash-next-Sandwich 1852–64; Chap. to Maidstone Union 1854–60; C. of Graveney with Goodnestone 1860–64, Hollingbourne 1864–66. Author, *Flowers of Friendship* (Original and Selected Poems on Christian Friendship), 4to, 1857, 10*s* 6*d*; *Essay on Young Men's Societies*, Maidstone, 1859; *A Few Thoughts on the Best Means of rendering Ourselves Useful to the Church of Christ*, ib. 1859. [27]

THORPE, Richard Oscar Tugwell, *Park-road, Red-hill, Surrey.*—Ch. Coll. Cam. 9th Wrang. B.A. 1853, M.A. 1856; Deac. 1853 by Bp of Wor. Pr. 1854 by Bp of Ely. C. of St. Matthew's, Red-hill, 1866. Formerly Fell. of Ch. Coll. Cam. 1853-60; V. of St. Clement's, Cambridge, 1855–60; Chap. of Campbell Town and Ross, Tasmania, 1860–62; C. of Trinity, Marylebone, 1864; Ch. Ch. Newgate-street, Lond. 1865. [1]

THORPE, Saint-John Wells, *Manuden Vicarage (Essex), near Bishop Stortford, Herts.*—Queens' Coll. Cam. B.A. 1840; Deac. 1840 and Pr. 1841 by Bp of Ches. V. of Manuden, Dio. Roch. 1850. (Patron, the present V; Tithe, 215*l*; Glebe, 3 acres; V.'s Inc. 225*l* and Ho; Pop. 740.) Surrogate. Author, *Sermons on the Death of a Drunkard*; *The Triumphs of Religion*; *The Game Laws: their Injustice, Tyranny, Oppression, Cruelty, and Selfishness*; etc. [2]

THORPE, William, *Weeley Rectory, Colchester.*—Mert. Coll. Ox. B.A. 1824, M.A. 1828; Deac. 1824 and Pr. 1825 by Bp of Lon. R. of Weeley, Dio. Roch. 1849. (Patron, Brasen. Coll. Ox; Tithe, 580*l*; Glebe, 8 acres; R.'s Inc. 600*l* and Ho; Pop. 630.) Surrogate. Formerly V. of Chattisham, Suffolk, 1830-39; V. of Wookey, Somerset, 1839–49. [3]

THORPE, William Smyth, *Shropham Villa, Larlingford, Norfolk.*—Wad. Coll. Ox. B.A. 1843; Deac. 1844 and Pr. 1845 by Bp of Nor. P. C. of Breckles, Norfolk, Dio. Nor. 1850. (Patron, Sir E. Kerrison, Bart; Tithe—Imp. 239*l* 10*s*; P. C.'s Inc. 46*l*; Pop. 130.) P. C. of Thompson, Norfolk, Dio. Nor. 1860. (Patrons, Hemsworth Trustees; P. C.'s Inc. 49*l*; Pop. 475.) Formerly C. of Thompson 1844–50. [4]

THRESHER, James Henville, *Andover, Hants.*—New Coll. Ox. B.A. 1864; Deac. 1866 and Pr. 1867 by Bp of Win. Asst. C. of Andover 1866. [5]

THRESHER, Philip, *Fareham, Hants.*—Univ. Coll. Ox. B.A. 1824, M.A. 1827; Deac. 1825, Pr. 1826. Formerly Chap. to Fareham Union. [6]

THRING, Edward, 2, *Rock-villas, Rock Ferry, Birkenhead.*—St. Bees; Deac. 1851 and Pr. 1852 by Abp of York. Chap. on the Mersey. [7]

THRING, Edward, *Uppingham, Rutland.*—King's Coll. Cam. Porson Prizeman 1843, B.A. 1844, M.A. 1847; Deac. 1846, Pr. 1847. Head Mast. of Uppingham Gr. Sch. 1853. Author, *Elements of Grammar taught in English*, 2*s*; *Education and School*, 1864, 2nd ed. 1867, 6*s* 6*d*. [8]

THRING, Godfrey, *Hornblotton Rectory, Castle Cary, Somerset.*—Ball. Coll. Ox. B.A. 1845, M.A. 1846; Deac. 1846 and Pr. 1847 by Bp of Win. R. of Alford with Hornblotton, Dio. B. and W. 1858. (Patron, Rev. John Gale Thring; Tithe, Alford, 140*l* and Glebe, 40 acres, Hornblotton, 205*l* and Glebe, 106 acres; R.'s Inc. 535*l* 10*s* and Ho; Pop. Alford 110, Hornblotton 93.) Rural Dean; Hon. Sec. to Mid. Somerset Book Hawking Association. Formerly C. of Stratfield-Turgis 1846, Strathfieldsaye 1850. Author, *Hymns and Verses*, Rivingtons, 1866, 5*s*; *Hymns, Congregational, and others*, ib. 2*s*. [9]

THRING, John Gale Dalton, *Alford House, Castle Cary, Somerset.*—St. John's Coll. Cam. LL.B; Deac. 1807, Pr. 1808. Patron, and formerly R. of Alford with Hornblotton, Somerset, 1808–58. [10]

THRUPP, Edward, *Feltham Vicarage, Hounslow, Middlesex, W.*—Wad. Coll. Ox. B.A. 1830, M.A. 1834; Deac. 1833 and Pr. 1834 by Bp of Wor. V. of Feltham, Dio. Lon. 1848. (Patron, C. E. Jemmett, Esq; Glebe, 129 acres; V.'s Inc. 305*l* and Ho; Pop. 1837.) [11]

THRUPP, Horace William, *Musbury, Axminster, Devon.*—Ex. Coll. Ox. B.A. 1847, M.A. 1850; Deac. 1847, Pr. 1848. R. of Musbury, Dio. Ex. 1863. (Patron, Rev. J. V. Payne; R.'s Inc. 365*l*; Pop. 493.) Formerly C. of Pleasley, Derbyshire. [12]

THURLAND, Francis Edward, *Thurstaston Rectory, Neston, Cheshire.*—New Coll. Ox. 4th cl. Lit. Hum. and B.A. 1841, M.A. 1846; Deac. and Pr. 1843 by Bp of Ox. R. of Thurstaston, Dio. Ches. 1858. (Patrons, D. and C. of Ches; Tithe, 186*l*; Glebe, 32 acres; R.'s Inc. 258*l* and Ho; Pop. 162.) Formerly Min. Can. and Precentor of Ches. Cathl. 1850–58. [13]

THURLOW, Charles Augustus, *Upper Rectory, Malpas, Cheshire.*—Ball. Coll. Ox. B.A. 1824, M.A. 1828; Deac. and Pr. 1827. Chancellor of the Dio. of Ches. 1854; R. of Malpas with Whitewell C. Dio. Ches. 1840. (Patrons, Marquis of Cholmondeley and T. T. Drake, Esq. alt; Tithe, 714*l*; Glebe, 94 acres; R.'s Inc. 1050*l* and Ho; Pop. 3370.) Hon. Can. of Ches. 1844. [14]

THURLOW, Thomas, *Cranley, Godalming, Surrey.*—St. John's Coll. Cam. B.A. 1811, M.A. 1816; Deac. 1813, Pr. 1814. [15]

THURNELL, George, *The Parsonage, Eye, near Peterborough.*—St. John's Coll. Cam. B.A. 1850, M.A. 1857; Deac. 1852 by Bp of Rip. Pr. 1853 by Bp of Dur. P. C. of Eye, Dio. Pet. 1862. (Patron, Bp of Pet; Glebe, 30 acres; P. C.'s Inc. 350*l* and Ho; Pop. 1252.) Formerly V. of Newbottle with Charlton, Northants. [16]

THURSBY, Matthew William Frederic, *Abington Rectory, near Northampton.*—Lin. Coll. Ox. B.A. 1843; Deac. 1846 and Pr. 1847 by Bp of Wor. R. of Abington, Dio. Pet. 1847. (Patron, Lord Overstone; Tithe, 313*l*; Glebe, 47 acres; R.'s Inc. 439*l* and Ho; Pop. 164.) [17]

THURSBY, Walter, *Wolston, Coventry.*—C. of Wolston. [18]

THURSBY, William, *Ormerod House, Burnley, Lancashire.*—Oriel Coll. Ox. B.A. 1818, M.A. 1820; Deac. 1819 and Pr. 1820 by Bp of Pet. P. C. of Worsthorne, Whalley, Dio. Man. 1836. (Patrons, Hulme's Trustees; Tithe—App. 3*l* 10*s*, Imp. 9*l*; P. C.'s Inc. 120*l*; Pop. 1015.) Formerly V. of Hardingstone and All Saints', Northampton, and Dom. Chap. to the Duke of Cambridge. [19]

THURSBY, William Ford, *Burgh Apton, Norwich.*—Emman. Coll. Cam. S.C.L. 1851, B.C.L. 1855; Deac. 1854 and Pr. 1856 by Bp of Man. R. of Burgh Apton with Holverstone R. Dio. Nor. 1864. (Patron, Earl of Abergavenny; R.'s Inc. 600*l* and Ho; Pop. 572.) Formerly C. of Worsthorne, Lancashire. [20]

THURSBY-PELHAM, Augustus, *Cound Rectory, Shrewsbury.*—Univ. Coll. Ox. 3rd cl. Law and History, B.A. 1855, M.A. 1858; Deac. 1857 and Pr. 1858 by Bp of Lich. R. of Cound, Dio. Lich. 1864. (Patron, the Rev. Henry Thursby-Pelham; Tithe, 622*l*; Glebe, 88 acres; R.'s Inc. 748*l* and Ho; Pop. 552.) [21]

THURSBY-PELHAM, Henry, *Cound Hall, Shrewsbury.*—Oriel Coll. Ox. B.A. 1821, M.A. 1824; Deac. 1824 and Pr. 1825 by Bp. of Pet. Formerly C. of Abington, Northants, 1824–25; R. of Isham, Inferior Portion, 1825–39; C. of Penn, Staffs, 1827–36; R. of Cound 1839–64. [22]

THURSFIELD, Richard, *Henley-in-Arden.*—Caius Coll. Cam. B.A. 1854; Deac. 1854 by Bp of Ches. Pr. 1860 by Abp of Cant. V. of Ullenhall, Dio. Wor. 1862. (Patron, T. H. G. Newton, Esq; V.'s Inc. 130*l*; Pop. 470.) Author, *Rest in Jesus*, 2nd ed. 1866, 1½*d*. [23]

THURSFIELD, R. P., *Sidbury Rectory, Bridgnorth, Salop.*—R. of Sidbury, Dio. Herf. 1851. (Patron, Ear of Shrewsbury; R.'s Inc. 250*l* and Ho; Pop. 160.) [24]

THURTELL, Alexander, *Oxburgh, Stoke-Ferry, Norfolk.*—Caius Coll. Cam. 4th Wrang. and B.A. 1829, M.A. 1832; Deac. 1830, Pr. 1837. R. of Oxburgh with Foulden V. Dio. Nor. 1848. (Patron, Caius Coll. Cam; Oxburgh, Tithe—471*l* 12*s* 6*d*; Glebe, 48½ acres; Foulden, Tithe—Imp. 267*l* 16*s* and 3¾ acres of Glebe, V. 178*l* 16*s*; Glebe, 2¾ acres; R.'s Inc. 720*l* and Ho; Pop. Oxburgh 225, Foulden 517.) R. of Caldecot (no church) Norfolk, Dio. Nor. 1851. (Patron, Sir H. R. P. Bedingfield, Bart; Tithe, 6*l* 13*s* 4*d*; Pop. 39.) Rural Dean, Formerly one of H.M. Inspectors of Schs; previously Fell. and Tut. of Caius Coll. Cam. [25]

THWAITES, Edgar Nembhand, *Blaisdon Rectory, Gloucestershire.*—Deac. 1862 by Bp of Carl. Pr. 1865 by Bp. of G. and B. R. of Blaisdon, Dio. G. and B. 1866. (Patron, Henry Crawshay, Esq; Tithe, 199*l* 19*s*;

Glebe, 19 acres; R.'s Inc. 210*l* and Ho; Pop. 270.) Formerly C. of St. John's, Keswick. [1]

THWAITES, Henry Graham, 90, *Park-road, Nechells, Birmingham.*—St. Aidan's; Deac. 1863, Pr. 1864. C. of St. Clements, Nechells, 1863. Author, *Do you ever Pray?* Tract, S.P.C.K. [2]

THWAYTES, James, *Caldbeck Rectory, near Carlisle.*—St. Bees; Deac. 1836 and Pr. 1837 by Bp of Carl. R. of Caldbeck, Dio. Carl. 1855. (Patron, Bp of Carl; Tithe, 348*l*; Glebe, 186½ acres; R.'s Inc. 485*l* and Ho; Pop. 1560.) Surrogate; Lord of the Manor of Kirkland; Proctor in Convocation for the Archd. of Carlisle. Formerly C of Wetheral 1836–38; P. C. of Trinity, Carlisle, 1838–55; Chap. of County Gaol 1840–55, and of County Infirmary 1839–55. Author, *Baptismal Regeneration shown to be the Doctrine of the Catholic and Apostolical Church of England by a Chain of Extracts from her Articles, Homilies, and Liturgy,* Rivingtons, 1st ed. 1840, 2nd ed. 1846, 6*d*. [3]

THWAYTES, Thomas.—Queen's Coll. Ox. B.A. 1863; Deac. 1865 and Pr. 1866 by Bp of Rip. Formerly C. of Kirksall, Yorks, 1865–66. [4]

THYNNE, Arthur B.—C. of Thames Ditton, Surrey. [5]

THYNNE, Arthur Christopher, *Kilkhampton Rectory, Stratton, Cornwall.*—Ball. Coll. Ox. B.A. 1854, M.A. 1850; Deac. 1857 and Pr. 1866 by Bp of Wor. R. of Kilkhampton, Dio. Ex. 1859. (Patron, Rev. Lord John Thynne; Tithe—Imp. 50*l*, R. 612*l*; Glebe, 107 acres; R.'s Inc. 712*l* and Ho; Pop. 1198.) Preb. of Ex. [6]

THYNNE, Lord John, *The Cloisters, Westminster Abbey, S.W.*—St. John's Coll. Cam. M.A. 1819, D.D. 1838; Deac. and Pr. 1822. Can. and Sub-Dean of Westminster 1831; Sinecure R. of Backwell, Somerset, Dio. B. and W. 1823. (Patron, Marquis of Bath; Tithe—Imp. 8*l* 15*s*, Sinecure R. 167*l* 7*s* 1½*d*, V. 167*l* 7*s* 1½*d*; Sinecure R.'s Inc. 166*l*.) Formerly Sub-Dean of Lin. Cathl. 1828–31. [7]

TIARKS, John Gerhard, *Macclesfield.*—St. John's Coll. Cam. B.A. 1853, M.A. 1856; Deac. 1856 and Pr. 1857 by Bp of Ches. 2nd Mast. of Gr. Sch. Macclesfield; Private Chap. at Birtles, Congleton; C. of Alderley, Cheshire. [8]

TIBBITS, Newman.—C. of St. John's, Clifton, Bristol. [9]

TIBBS, Henry Wall, *Bobbington, Bridgnorth.*—Dub. Univ. Scho. 1835, six Honours and Prizes, A.B. 1839, *ad eund.* Univ. Coll. Dur. 1840, Hebrew Prizeman and Licen. Theol. of Univ. Coll. Dur. 1841, Dub. A.M. 1842, *ad eund.* Ox. 1860; Deac. 1841 and Pr. 1842 by Bp of Dur. P. C. of Bobbington, Dio. Herf. 1862. (Patron, T. C. Whitmore, Esq; Tithe—Imp. 460*l*; P. C.'s Inc. 99*l*; Pop. 431.) Mem. Royal Irish Academy; Fell. of Soc. of Antiquarians of Scotland; Member of the Syro-Egyptian Soc. Lond. &c. Formerly C. of Oxton, Notts, 1850–59, Shelford, Notts, 1859–62. Author, *The Bible only* (a Tract); *Uniformity in Matters of Faith* (a Tract), 1854; *Individual and National Sins* (a Sermon), 1855; *Speculation* (a Sermon), 1856; *What the Bible says of Unity and of Dissensions in Religion,* 1857; *Vita della B.V.M. Madre del Nostro Signore Gesù Cristo, estratta dal Nuovo Testamento e raccontata nelle medesime parole della Sacra Scrittura, con una breve Introduzione* (compiled for the Anglo-Continental Assoc.), 1857; the same work in Portuguese, 1859; *Lectures on the Four Ages of Human Life,* 1857; *The Poor exalted in Christ* (a Sermon for Christmas-day), 1858; *The Poor Man's Daily Companion, a Rule of Life, with Short Prayers and other Devotions for Poor Persons,* 1860, 2nd ed. 1869; and numerous Articles and Reviews contributed to Church papers. [10]

TICKELL, Thomas, *Ashton-under-Lyne.*—St. Bees 1849; Deac. 1851 and Pr. 1852 by Abp of York. C. of Ashton-under-Lyne 1865. Formerly C. of St. Sampson's, York, 1851–54, Doncaster 1854–61, Gainsborough, Lincolnshire (sole charge), 1861–64. [11]

TIDCOMBE, George Henry.—C. and Lect. of St. Matthew's, Bethnal Green, Lond. [12]

TIDDEMAN, E. Spencer, *Childerditch Vicarage, Brentwood, Essex.*—V. of Childerditch, Dio. Roch. 1866. (Patron, Lord Petre; V.'s Inc. 180*l* and Ho; Pop. 239.) [13]

TIDDEMAN, Richard Philip Goldesworthy, *Ibstone, Henley-on-Thames.*—Magd. Hall, Ox. B.A. 1824, M.A. 1825. R. of Fingest with Ibstone, Dio. Ox. 1866. (Patrons, Bp. of Ox. and Mert. Coll. Ox. alt; R.'s Inc. 380*l*; Pop. Fingest 33, Ibstone 325.) Surrogate. Formerly P. C. of North Hinksey, Berks, 1841–66. [14]

TIEN, Antonio, *Burnt Ash-lane, Lee, S.E.*—St. Augustine's Coll. Canterbury; Deac. 1860 and Pr. 1862 by Bp of Gibraltar. Min. of St. Peter's, Lee, Dio. Roch. 1867. Formerly Chap. to Bp of Gibraltar; Chap. at Constantinople; C. of All Saints', Dalston, Lond. [15]

TIGHE-GREGORY, A., *Bawdsey Vicarage, Woodbridge, Suffolk.*—Dub. Hons. in Div. LL.B. and M.A; Deac 1843 and Pr. 1844 by Bp of Nor. V. of Bawdsey, Dio. Nor. 1847. (Patron, Ld Chan; Tithe—Imp. 304*l* 16*s* 6*d*, V. 193*l* 0*s* 3*d*; Glebe, 2 acres; V.'s Inc. 248*l* and Ho; Pop. 462.) [16]

TILBURY, Robert, *Totworth, Wotton-under-Edge, Gloucestershire.*—Emman. Coll. Cam. B.A. 1860; Deac. 1860 by Bp of Ox. C. of Totworth and Chap. to Earl of Ducie. Formerly C. of Langford with Little Farringdon, Berks, 1860. [17]

TILEY, C. P., *Bengeo, Hertford.*—C. of Bengeo. [18]

TILL, John, *Gnosall Parsonage, Stafford.*—Queens' Coll. Cam. B.A. 1840, M.A. 1845; Deac. 1840, Pr. 1842. P. C. of Gnosall with Knightley C. Dio. Lich. 1846. (Patron, Bp of Lich; Glebe, 46 acres; P. C.'s Inc. 142*l* and Ho; Pop. 1721.) Formerly C. of Adbaston 1840, Standon 1842 [19]

TILL, Lawrence William, *Chertsey Vicarage, Surrey.*—Pemb. Coll. Ox. B.A. 1852, M.A. 1856; Deac. 1852 and Pr. 1853 by Bp of Lon. V. of Chertsey, Dio. Win. 1857. (Patron, the Haberdashers' Company; Tithe, 108*l*; Glebe, 100*l*; V.'s Inc. 230*l* and Ho; Pop. 3500.) [20]

TILLARD, James Arthur, *Conington, St. Ives, Cambs.*—St. John's Coll. Cam. B.A. 1835, M.A. 1836; Deac. 1836, Pr. 1837. R. of Conington, Dio. Ely, 1841. (Patron, Bp of Ely; Glebe, 270 acres; R.'s Inc. 396*l* and Ho; Pop. 283.) [21]

TILLARD, Richard H., *Blakeney, Thetford, Norfolk.*—R. of Blakeney with Glandford P. C. and Cockthorpe R. Dio. Nor. 1858. (Patron, Lord Calthorpe; R.'s Inc. 550*l* and Ho; Pop. Blakeney 961, Glandford 74, Cockthorpe 42.) [22]

TILLBROOK, William John, *Barrington Hall, Royston, Herts,* and *United University Club, Pall Mall, S.W.*—St. John's Coll. Ox. B.A. 1856, M.A. 1859; Deac. 1860 by Bp of Ox. Pr. 1862 by Bp of Chich. V. of Comberton, Dio. Ely, 1867. (Patron, Jesus Coll. Cam; Tithe, 168*l*; Glebe, 8 acres; V.'s Inc. 183*l* and Ho; Pop. 562.) Formerly C. of Lacey Green, Bucks, 1859; Fell. and Tut. of St. Augustine's Coll. Canterbury, 1861–62; C. of Barlavington, Sussex, 1863. [23]

TILSON, T.—C. of St. Stephen's, South Shields, Durham. [24]

TILSON-MARSH, Sir William Tilson, Bart., *Stretham Manor, Cambs.*—Oriel. Coll. Ox. B.A. 1838, M.A. 1843; Deac. 1839 by Bp of Wor. Pr. 1840 by Bp of Roch. Dom. Chap. to the Marquis of Cholmondeley, and to the Earl of Carnwath. Formerly C. of St. James's, Ryde, Isle of Wight, 1850–57; P. C. of St. Leonard's-on-Sea 1857–64. Author, *Letter to Sir R. Peel on the Church in Ireland,* 1843, 1*s*; *The Church and State of England,* 1849, 7*s*; Tracts, *The Day of Rest*; *Oil in the Lamp at Midnight*; *The Present Crisis*; etc. [25]

TIMINS, John Henry, *West Malling, Kent.*—Trin. Coll. Cam. Sen. Opt. B.A. 1836, M.A. 1839. V. of West Malling, Dio. Cant. (Patron, T. A. Douce, Esq; Tithe—Imp. 150*l*, V. 283*l*; V.'s Inc. 340*l* and Ho; Pop. 2086.) Surrogate. Formerly C. of Grosvenor Chapel, Hanover-square, Lond. [26]

TINDALL, Henry Woods, *Margate.*—Sid. Coll. Cam. 3rd cl. Theol. Trip. B.A. 1856, M.A. 1861; Deac.

1857 and Pr. 1858 by Bp of Lon. Lect. of Trinity, Margate, 1862; Chap. Royal National Hospital, Margate, 1866. Formerly Sen. C. of St. James's, Clerkenwell, Lond. 1857. [1]

TINDALL, Richard Abbey, *St. Stephen's Rectory, Chorlton-on-Medlock, Manchester.*—Bp. Hat. Hall, Dur. Licen. Theol. 1859, B.A. 1860, M.A. 1866; Deac. 1860 and Pr. 1861 by Bp of Dur. R. of St. Stephen's, Chorlton-on-Medlock, Dio. Man. 1865. (Patrons, Trustees; R.'s Inc. 350*l* and Ho; Pop. 6379.) Formerly C. of Brighouse 1860; P. C. of St. Gregory's, Canterbury, 1861–65. Author, *The Jewish Ritual not a Model for Christian Worship* (a Sermon), 1865; *Apostolic Absolution* (a Sermon), 1867. [2]

TINK, Charles Frederick, *Shepton Montague, near Castle Cary, Bath.*—Ex. Coll. Ox. B.A. 1849, M.A. 1856; Deac. 1850 and Pr. 1851 by Bp of Salis. V. of Shepton Montague Dio. B. and W. 1860. (Patron, Earl of Ilchester; V.'s Inc. 62*l* and Ho; Pop. 438.) Formerly P. C. of Berwick Bassett, Wilts, 1850–54; C. of St. Peter Tavy, Devon, 1854–55, Alford, Somerset, 1855–60; P. C. of Lovington, Somerset, 1857–58.) [3]

TINKLER, John, *Landbeach Rectory, near Cambridge.*—Corpus Coll. Cam. 9th Wrang. B.A. 1827, M.A. 1830, B.D. 1837; Deac. 1830 by Bp of Chich. Pr. 1831 by Bp of Roch. R. of Landbeach Dio. Ely, 1843. (Patron, Corpus Coll. Cam; Glebe, 488 acres; R.'s Inc. 800*l* and Ho; Pop. 441.) Formerly C. of Grantchester, 1836–42. Author, *Scripture and Tradition*, 1856. [4]

TINKLER, John, *Whiston, near Prescot, Lancashire.*—St. John's Coll. Cam. 1st cl. and Latin Essay Prizeman, B.A. 1855, M.A. 1860; Deac. 1856 and Pr. 1857 by Bp of Man. C. of Whiston 1862. Formerly C. of Newton Heath, 1856–61, St. John's, Manchester, 1862. Author, *A Carol for Epiphany-Tide set to Music*, Manchester, 1860, 2*s* 6*d*. [5]

TINLING, Edward Douglas, 8, *Cornwall-gardens, Queen's-gate, London, W.*—Ch. Ch. Ox. B.A. 1837, M.A. 1840; Deac. 1838, Pr. 1839. One of H.M.'s Inspectors of Schs. 1847; Preb. of Wells 1863; Can. of Gloucester 1867. Formerly R. of West Worlington, Devon, 1844–47. [6]

TINNISWOOD, William, *Edwinstowe, near Ollerton, Notts.*—Clare Coll. Cam. B.A. 1855; Deac. 1856 and Pr. 1857 by Bp of Lin. C. of Edwinstowe 1860. Formerly C. of Gaistor 1856. [7]

TIPPER, John Gore, *The Parsonage, Horsham St. Faith's, Norwich.*—Emman. Coll. Cam. B.A. 1855, M.A. 1866; Deac. 1855 and Pr. 1856 by Bp of Win. C. in sole charge of Horsham St. Faith's 1867. Formerly C. of Camden Chapel, Camberwell, 1855–57; C. in sole charge of Fobbing, Essex; C. of St. Paul's, Lisson-grove, Marylebone, 1865–67; Prin. of the Operative Jewish Converts' Institution, Bethnal Green, 1861–65. [8]

TIPPET, Edward, *Perran Porth, Truro.*—St. Peter's Coll. Cam. B.A. 1834; Deac. 1835 and Pr. 1836 by Bp of Ex. Chap. of the Union, Truro. Formerly Asst. C. of St. Allen, Truro, 1836–41, Philleigh, Grampound, 1841–51; Chap. of Truro Union 1842–48; Chap. of Royal Cornwall Infirmary 1842–52; C. of Cornworthy, Totnes, 1862–63. [9]

TIPPING, Vernon, *Church-Lawton Rectory, Cheshire.*—Brasen. Coll. Ox. B.A. 1836; Deac. 1837 and Pr. 1838 by Bp of Ches. R. of Church Lawton, Dio. Ches. 1839. (Patron, C. B. Lawton, Esq; Tithe 265*l*; Glebe, 66 acres; R.'s Inc. 366*l* and Ho; Pop. 724.) [10]

TIREMAN, Frederick Stainton, *Wilton Vicarage, Redcar, Yorks.*—Univ. Coll. Ox. B.A. 1851, M.A. 1854; Deac. 1852 and Pr. 1853 by Bp of Rip V. of Wilton, Dio. York, 1861. (Patron, Sir J. H. Lowther, Bart.; Tithe, 10*l* 2*s* 3*d*; Glebe, 128 acres; V.'s Inc. 247*l* and Ho; Pop. 927.) Formerly C. of Kildwick in Craven 1853–54; Min. Can. of Carlisle 1855–61; Precentor of Carlisle Cathl. 1858–61. [11]

TIREMAN, William Walter, *Bowers Gifford Rectory, Rayleigh, Essex.*—Magd. Coll. Ox. Newdigate Prize 1826, B.A 1829, M.A. 1832; Deac. 1834, Pr. 1835. R. of Bowers Gifford, Dio. Roch. 1841. (Patroness, Mrs. Curtis; Tithe, 703*l* 6*s* 9*d*; Glebe, 32 acres; R.'s Inc. 690*l*; Pop. 259.) Rural Dean. Formerly Fell. of Magd. Coll. Ox. [12]

TITCOMB, Jonathan Holt.—St. Peter's Coll. Cam. B.A. 1841, M.A. 1844; Deac. 1842 and Pr. 1843 by Bp of Down and Connor. P. C. of St. Stephen's, South Lambeth, Dio. Win. 1861. (Patron, Rev. C. Kemble; Pop. 3500.) Formerly P. C. of St. Andrew's the-Less, Cambridge. Author, *Heads of Prayer for Daily Private Devotion*; *Parochial Open-Air Preaching*, Seeleys; *Bible Studies*. [13]

TITE, Henry, *Church-street, Luton, Beds.*—King's Coll. Lond. Theol. Assoc; Deac. by Bp of Roch. Pr. by Bp of Herf. C. of Luton 1867. Formerly C. of Chatham, of Upminster, and of Madely, Salop. [14]

TITLEY, Edward, *Peckforton, Tarporley, Cheshire.*—New Inn Hall, Ox. B.A. 1837; Deac. 1838 and Pr. 1839 by Bp of Ches. P. C. of Burwardsley, Bunbury, Cheshire, Dio. Ches. 1849. (Patron, Bp of Ches; Tithe, Imp. 100*l*; P. C.'s Inc. 46*l*; Pop. 560.) C. of Peckforton; Chap. to J. Tollemache, Esq. 1850. [15]

TITLEY, Richard, *Barwell Rectory, Hinckley.*—Trin. Coll. Cam. B.A. 1856, M.A. 1859; Deac. 1856 and Pr. 1857 by Bp of Lich. R. of Barwell with Stapleton and Marston, Dio. Pet. 1865. (Patron, the present R.; Tithe, 750*l*; Glebe, 168 acres; R.'s Inc. 1000*l* and Ho; Pop. 1638.) Formerly C. of Tamworth, Staffs, 1856–59, St. Nicholas', Liverpool, 1859–65. [16]

TITLOW, Samuel, 16, *Crescent, Norwich.*—St. John's Coll. Cam. Scho. of, 7th Wrang. and B.A. 1817, M.A. 1820; Deac. 1817 and Pr. 1818 by Dr. Howley, Bp. of Lon; P. C. of St. John's, Timberhill, Norwich, Dio. Nor. 1831. (Patrons, D. and C. of Nor; P. C.'s Inc. 120*l*; Pop. 1302.) R. of St. Peter's, Hungate, Norwich, Dio. Nor. 1838. (Patron, the Crown; R.'s Inc. 55*l*; Pop. 399.) Formerly C. of Broxbourne, Herts, 1817, St. Clement's, Norwich, 1819, St. Gregory's, Norwich, 1822. Author, *Fractions, with Application to Rules in Arithmetic*, 1844, *Selection of Psalms and Hymns, adapted to the Morning and Evening Prayer of the Church of England*, 5th ed. 1866. [17]

TODD, Edward Hallett, *Aldsworth, Northleach, Gloucestershire.*—Wor. Coll. Ox. B.A. 1859, M.A. 1861; Deac. 1860 and Pr. 1861 by Bp of Lon. P. C. of Aldsworth, Dio. G. and B. 1866. (Patrons, Dean and Chap. of Ch. Ch. Ox; Glebe, 26 acres; P. C.'s Inc. 138*l* and Ho; Pop. 451.) Formerly C. of All Saints', Blackheath, Kent, 1860–63, Sherborne with Windrush 1863–66. [18]

TODD, Edward James, *Sherborne, Burford, Oxon.*—Wor. Coll. Ox. B.A. 1825; Deac. 1825 and Pr. 1826 by Bp of Ex. V. of Sherborne with Windrush, Dio. G. and B. 1843. (Patron, Lord Sherborne; V.'s Inc. 228*l* and Ho; Pop Sherborne 584, Windrush 290.) [19]

TODD, Fortescue, *St. Austell Vicarage, Cornwall.*—Jesus Coll. Cam. LL.B. 1815; Deac. 1816 and Pr. 1817 by Bp of Ex. V. of St. Austell, Dio. Ex. 1838. (Patron, the Crown; Tithe—Imp. 502*l*, V. 587*l* 10*s*; Glebe, 1 acre; V.'s Inc. 540*l* and Ho; Pop. 6417.) [20]

TODD, George Augustus, *Morton Baggott, Bromsgrove, Warwickshire.*—St. Bees; Deac. 1853 and Pr. 1854 by Bp of Ches. R. of Morton-Baggott, Dio. Wor. 1859. (Patron, T. Walker, Esq; R.'s Inc. 160*l*; Pop. 129.) Formerly P. C. of St. Thomas's, Islington, Lond. 1855–59. [21]

TODD, Horatio, *Occold Rectory, Eye, Suffolk.*—Queen's Coll. Ox. B.A. 1825, M.A. 1828; Deac. 1825 and Pr. 1827 by Bp of Ex. R. of Occold, Dio. Nor 1845. (Patron, the present R; Tithe, 495*l*; Glebe, 46 acres; R.'s Inc. 463*l* and Ho; Pop. 570.) Formerly C. of St. Endellion 1826–28, St. Austell 1842–45, both in Cornwall. Author, various Sermons. [22]

TODD, Horatio Lovell, *Aylsham, Norfolk.*—Pemb. Coll. Ox. B.A. 1856, M.A. 1859; Deac. 1857 and Pr. 1858 by Bp of Nor. Asst. C. of Aylsham 1867. Formerly C. of Barsham, Suffolk, and Great Amwell, Herts, 1860–61; Asst. C. of Greenwich 1861–65; C. of Great Yarmouth and Even. Lect. at St. Peter's 1865–67. Author, *The History of our English Bible* (a Lecture). [23]

TODD, Isaac, *Shincliffe Rectory, Durham.*—St. Bees; Deac. 1824 and Pr. 1826 by Bp of Ches. R. of Shincliffe, Dio. Dur. 1826. (Patrons, D. and C. of Dur; Tithe, 277l 15s 7d, V. 4l 9s 7d; Glebe, 3 acres; R.'s Inc. 385l and Ho; Pop. 2000.) [1]

TODD, James, *Ardleigh Vicarage, Colchester.*—V. of Ardleigh, Dio. Roch. 1855. (Patron, Ld Chan; Tithe—App. 1370l 18s 6d, V. 382l 14s 6d; Glebe, 5 acres; V.'s Inc. 385l and Ho; Pop. 1300.) [2]

TODD, John, *North Cowton, Northallerton, Yorks.*—Caius Coll. Cam. Sen. Opt. and B.A. 1828; Deac. 1828 and Pr. 1829 by Bp of Ches. P. C. of South Cowton, Dio. Rip. 1840. (Patron, V. of Gilling; Tithe—Imp. 22l 10s, App. 50l; Glebe, 64 acres; P. C.'s Inc. 52l; Pop. 479.) P. C. of Eryholme, Dio. Rip. 1840. (Patron, V. of Gilling; Tithe—App. 1l 6s 8d, P. C. 14l 7s 9d; Glebe, 28 acres; P. C.'s Inc. 43l and Ho; Pop. 176.) Chap. to Lord Alvanley. [3]

TODD, Richard Utten, *Longbridge Deverill, Warminster.*—Trin. Coll. Cam. B.A. 1860, M.A. 1863; Deac. 1861 and Pr. 1862 by Bp of Ex. C. of Longbridge 1865. Formerly C. of Broad Clyst, Exeter, 1861–65. [4]

TODD, Thomas, *Newton Rectory, Folkingham, Lincolnshire.*—Queen's Coll. Ox. B.A. 1839, M.A. 1853; Deac. 1840 and Pr. 1841 by Bp of Carl. R. of Newton, Dio. Lin. 1858. (Patron, Sir G. E. Welby Gregory, Bart; Glebe, 228 acres; R.'s Inc. 350l and Ho; Pop. 228.) Formerly R. of Trinity, Hulme, Manchester, 1843–58. Author, *Whose is the Bible?* (a Letter to Lord Shaftesbury on the Jubilee of the Bible Soc.) 2nd ed. Masters, 6d; *Creeds, Articles, and Homilies,* a Pamphlet, Masters; *The Offertory* (a Sermon), *The Feast* (a Harvest Home Sermon). [5]

TODD, W., *Bulmer, New Malton, Yorks.*—C. of Bulmer and Whenby. [6]

TOKE, Richard Roundell, *Barnston Rectory, Dunmow, Essex.*—Corpus Coll. Cam. B.A. 1829. R. of Barnston, Dio. Roch. (Patron, the present R; Tithe, 415l; R.'s Inc. 422l and Ho; Pop. 192.) P. C. of Little Dunmow, Essex, Dio. Roch. (Patron, the present P. C; Tithe—Imp. 515l 18s 9d; P. C.'s Inc. 75l; Pop. 379.) [7]

TOLLEMACHE, Augustus Francis, 6, *Goldsmith-square, Stoke Newington, N.*—Ex. Coll. Ox. B.A. 1861; Deac. 1862 and Pr. 1863 by Bp of Rip. C. of St. Matthias', Stoke Newington, 1864. Formerly C. of Penistone, Sheffield, 1862–64. [8]

TOLLEMACHE, The Hon. Hugh Francis, *Harrington Rectory, near Northampton.*—St. Peter's Coll. Cam. B.A. 1831. R. of Harrington, Dio. Pet. 1831. (Patron, John Tollemache, Esq; Tithe, 535l; R.'s Inc. 571l and Ho; Pop. 222.) [9]

TOLLEMACHE, Ralph William Lyonel, *South Witham Rectory, Grantham, Lincolnshire.*—St. Peter's Coll. Cam. B.A. 1849, M.A. 1854, *ad eund.* Ox. 1854; Deac. 1849 by Bp of Man. Pr. 1850 by Bp of Lin. R. of South Witham, Dio. Lin. 1850. (Patron, Earl of Dysart; Glebe, 150 acres; R.'s Inc. 220l and Ho; Pop. 531.) Formerly C. of Admarsh in Bleasdale, Lanc. 1849. [10]

TOLMING, Thomas, *Coniston, Ulverston.*—P. C. of Coniston, Dio. Ches. 1840. (Patron, Rev. A. Peache; Tithe—Imp. 87l 14s 8d; P. C.'s Inc. 108l and Ho; Pop. 1324.) [11]

TOLPUTT, Martin Cramp, *Home Cottage, The Chase, Enfield, Middlesex, N.*—Sid. Coll. Cam. B.A. 1825; Deac. 1825 and Pr. 1826 by Bp of Lon. Formerly C. of Leigh 1825, South Shoebury 1827, Rayleigh and South Fambridge 1830, in Essex. [12]

TOM, Edward Nicolls, *Kingsthorpe, Northampton.*—St. John's Coll. Cam. Exhib. Prizeman and Sen. Opt. B.A. 1858, M.A. 1863; Deac. 1858 and Pr. 1859 by Bp of Nor. C. of Kingsthorpe 1860. Formerly C. of Marham, Norfolk, 1858–60. [13]

TOMBS, Joseph, *Burton Rectory, Haverfordwest, Pembrokeshire.*—Queen's Coll. Ox. B.A. 1845; Deac. 1846 and Pr. 1847 by Bp of Rip. R. of Burton, Dio. St. D. 1858. (Patron, Earl of Cawdor; Glebe, 40 acres; R.'s Inc. 230l and Ho; Pop. 1029.) Formerly Asst. C. of St. Paul's, Huddersfield, 1846–48; C. of St. Thomas's, Haverfordwest, 1848–51; V. of Llanstadwell 1851–58. Author, *Sowing and Reaping* (a Sermon), 1855; *Concerning Pembrokeshire* (a Lecture), 1863. [14]

TOMES, Robert, *Coughton, Alcester, Warwickshire.*—Magd. Hall, Ox. B.A. 1830. V. of Coughton, Dio. Wor. 1831. (Patron, Sir R. Throckmorton, Bart; Tithe—Imp. 245l, V. 45l; Glebe, 1½ acre; V.'s Inc. 163l; Pop. 883.) [15]

TOMKIN, James Wright, *Raydon, near Hadleigh, Suffolk.*—Wad. Coll. Ox. B.A. 1847, M.A. 1849; Deac. 1847 and Pr. 1848 by Abp of Cant. R. of Raydon, Dio. Nor. 1865. (Patron, the present R; Tithe, 500l; Glebe, 50 acres; R.'s Inc. 600l and Ho; Pop. 555.) Formerly C. of Hadleigh, Suffolk, 1847–51; P. C. of Lindsey, Suffolk, 1851–65. [16]

TOMKINS, Gerard William, *Lavendon Rectory, Newport-Pagnell, Bucks.*—Jesus Coll. Cam. B.A. 1864; Deac. 1866 by Bp of Win. Pr. 1867 by Bp of Ox. R. of Lavendon with Brafield, Dio. Ox. 1867. (Patron, present R; R.'s Inc. 284l and Ho; Pop. Lavendon 830, Brafield 99.) Formerly Mast. in Epsom College. [17]

TOMKINS, Henry George, *Exeter.*—Trin. Coll. Cam; Deac. 1857 and Pr. 1858 by Bp of Pet. R. of St. Paul's, Exeter, Dio. Ex. 1866. (Patrons, D. and C. of Ex; R.'s Inc. 115l; Pop. 1308.) Formerly C. of Kegworth 1857, St. Michael's, Derby, 1858, West Coker 1860, St. Mary Church, Devon, 1863; C. in sole charge of Woodbury Salterton, 1864. Author, *Abingdon in 1644* (a Lecture), Abingdon, 1845; *A Remembrance of Drachenfels and other Poems* (with Rev. W. S. Tomkins), Nisbet, 1855; Hymns in *Lyra Anglicana*; Sermons—*God the Ordainer of Human Justice* (on the death of a Police Constable from wounds received in the discharge of his duty), 1862, 3d; *Misericordias Domini* (at the Tercentenary of Abingdon Sch.), 1863, 6d; *The Spirits of the Just*, 1864, 6d, all published by Bell and Daldy; *The Home Soldier* (to Volunteers), 1865, 3d; also *Hymn for Volunteers* (with music of the time of the Armada), Novello, 1865, 3d. [18]

TOMKINS, James P. O., *Foston, Leicestershire.*—St. John's Coll. Cam. Sen. Opt. B.A. 1852; Deac. 1853 and Pr. 1854 by Bp of Ches. C. of Foston 1865. Formerly C. of St. Nicholas', Liverpool, 1853–55, Duffield 1855–58, Lutterworth 1858–63. [19]

TOMKINS, Peter Tivey, 39, *Lancaster-road East, Notting-hill, W.*—St. Aidan's; Deac. 1862 and Pr. 1863 by Bp of Ches. Asst. Chap. Lock Hospital 1865. Formerly C. of St. Andrew's, Liverpool, 1862–65. [20]

TOMKINS, William, *Barford, Warwick.*—St. John's Coll. Cam. B.A. 1863, M.A. 1867; Deac. 1864 and Pr. 1865 by Bp of Win. C. of Barford 1865. Formerly C. of Frensham, Surrey, 1864–65. [21]

TOMKINS, William, *Bath.*—St. Cath. Hall, Cam. B.A. 1830, M.A. 1833; Deac. 1830 and Pr. 1831 by Bp of Lin. R. of St. Saviour's, Bath, 1867. (Patrons, Reps. of Rev. Dr. Stamer; R.'s Inc. 390l; Pop. 4107.) Formerly R. of Lavendon with Cold Brafield, Oxon. 1838. [22]

TOMKINS, William Smith, *West Monkton, Taunton.*—King's Coll. Lond. Theol. Assoc. 1859; Deac. 1859, Pr. 1860. P. C. of Durston, Dio. B. and W. 1862. (Patron, Lord Portman; Tithe, 170l; P. C.'s Inc. 174l; Pop. 223.) Formerly Asst. C. of Crewkerne, Somerset, 1859–61. Author, *The Relation of the Church of England to the Dissenting Communities*, Rivingtons, 6d. [23]

TOMKINSON, Robert, *Kirtlinge Vicarage, near Newmarket, Cambridgeshire.*—St. Bees; Deac. 1852 and Pr. 1853 by Abp of York. V. of Kirtlinge, Dio. Ely, 1864. (Patron, the Hon. W. H. J. North; Glebe, 173 acres; V.'s Inc. 160l and Ho; Pop. 820.) Formerly C. of St. James's, Hull, 1852–58; C. in sole charge of Ashley, near Newmarket, 1858–64; C. of Downham-in-the-Isle 1864. [24]

TOMKYNS, John, *Little Hereford Vicarage (Herefordshire), near Tenbury.*—Queens' Coll. Cam. B.A. 1806, M.A. 1809. R. of Little Hereford with Ashford Carbonell V. Dio. Herf. 1844. (Patron, the Chan. of Herf. Cathl; Little Hereford, Tithe—App. 325l, V. 170l; Ashford Carbonell, Tithe—App. 325l; V.'s Inc. 234l and Ho; Pop. Little Hereford 458, Ashford Carbonell 282.) Formerly Fell. of Queens' Coll. Cam. [1]

TOMLIN, Alfred John, *Wallasey, Cheshire*—Queens' Coll. Cam. B.A. 1844; Deac. 1844 by Abp of York, Pr. 1845 by Bp of Rip. C. of Liverpool 1846; Surrogate; Dioc. Sec. Additional Curates' Society 1851. Formerly C. of Bradford, Yorks, 1844. [2]

TOMLIN, Jacob Haverbrack, *Milnthorpe, Westmoreland.*—St. John's Coll. Cam. B.A. 1818; Deac. 1845 and Pr. 1846 by Bp of Ches. Formerly C. of St. Augustine's, Liverpool, 1845–46; C. in sole charge of Tunstal, near Kirkby Lonsdale, 1847–49, Tankersley 1849–53, Great Coates 1854–56, Brodsworth 1860–61; C. of Cronall 1865–66. Author, *Missionary Journals and Letters during Eleven Years amongst Chinese and Siamese, &c; Shang-te, or proper Rendering of Elohim and Theos into Chinese; Critical Remarks on Medhurst's Translation of the New Testament into Chinese; Comparative Vocabulary in Forty-eight Languages; Proposed Improved Renderings of difficult Passages in the Authorised Translation from the Hebrew and Greek; Critical Remarks on Dr. Tregelles's Greek Text of the Revelation.* [3]

TOMLINS, Richard.—Chap. of the City Gaol, Manchester, 1864. Formerly C. of Penwortham 1840, Uttoxeter 1846. Author, *Poems*, Rivingtons, 1844, 3s; *Sermons for the Church's High Days, &c.* 2nd ed. Masters, 1851, 5s; *Four Advent Sermons*, 1851, 1s 6d; *The Four Night Watches* (2nd Series of Advent Sermons), 1852, 1s 6d, 2nd ed. of both in 1 vol. 1863, 2s 6d; *The Dream that was really Dreamt*, Masters, 1851, 1s 6d; Contributor to the *Churchman's Companion, Lays of the Sanctuary, Lyra Mystica, Hymns*; etc. [4]

TOMLINSON, Charles Henry, *Worcester College, Oxford.*—Wor. Coll. Ox. B.A. 1857, M.A. 1860; Deac. 1859 and Pr. 1860 by Bp of Ox. Tutor and Chap. of Wor. Coll. Ox. [5]

TOMLINSON, Edward, *Hope Parsonage, near Minsterley, Shrewsbury.*—Trin. Coll. Ox. B.A. 1843, M.A. 1847; Deac. 1844, Pr. 1845 by Bp of Ches. R. of Hope, Dio. Herf. 1860. (Patron, New Coll. Ox; Tithe, 235*l*; Glebe, 10 acres; R.'s Inc. 260*l* and Ho; Pop. 1829.) Formerly C. of Worthen and Hope, near Shrewsbury, 1847–60. [6]

TOMLINSON, Edward Murray, *Great Yarmouth.*—Trin. Coll. Cam. B.A. 1864; Deac. 1866, Pr. 1867. Asst. C. of Great Yarmouth 1866. [7]

TOMLINSON, John, *West Felton Rectory, Salop.*—Wad. Coll. Ox. B.A. 1859, M.A. 1861; Deac. 1860, Pr. 1861. C. in sole charge of West Felton. Formerly Chap. to the Bp of Brisbane, Australia. [8]

TOMLINSON, Lewis, *Cameswortk, Bridport.*—Wad. Coll. Ox. B.A. 1829, M.A. 1832; Deac. and Pr. 1830 by Bp of Salis. P. C. of Melplaish, Dio. Salis. 1863. (Patron, Bp. of Salis; P. C.'s Inc. 305*l* and Ho; Pop. 464.) Formerly Chap. to the Salisbury Union 1843. Author, *Recreations in Astronomy*, 4th ed. 1840, 4s. Editor of *Moon's Western Almanac.* [9]

TOMLINSON, Routh, *Lutterworth Rectory, Leicestershire.*—Clare Coll. Cam. Cl. Hons. 1863, B.A. 1863, M.A. 1866; Deac. 1863 and Pr. 1864 by Bp of Pet. C. in sole charge of Lutterworth 1866. Formerly C. of St. Mary's, Peterborough, 1863–66, Wrotham, Kent, 1866. [10]

TOMLINSON, William Bannister, *Horton, Settle, Yorkshire.*—Dub. A.B. 1861; Deac. 1858 and Pr. 1865 by Bp of Rip. Head Mast. of the Gram. Sch. Horton, 1858. (Patrons, the Trustees; Inc. 204*l* and Ho.) Formerly C. of Clapham 1858, Horton 1865. [11]

TOMLINSON, William Robert, *Sherfield English Rectory, Romsey, Hants.*—St. John's Coll. Cam B.A. 1833, M.A. 1836; Deac. 1835 and Pr. 1837 by Bp of Chich. R. of Sherfield English, Dio. Win. 1837 (Patron, R. Bristow, Esq; Tithe, 291*l*; Glebe, 38 acres; R.'s Inc. 321*l* and Ho; Pop. 342.) V. of Whiteparish, Wilts, Dio. Salis. 1837. (Patron, R. Bristow, Esq; Tithe—Imp. 898*l*, V. 200*l*; Glebe, ½ acre; V.'s Inc. 200*l*; Pop. 1225.) [12]

TOMPKINS, P. T.—Asst. Chap. of the Lock Hospital, Paddington. [13]

UU

TOMPKINS, Richard Francis, *Arundel, Sussex.*—St. John's Coll. Cam. B.A. 1844; Deac. 1846 and Pr. 1847 by Bp of Chich. V. of Tortington, Dio. Chich. 1854. (Patron, Duke of Norfolk; Tithe, 175*l*; V.'s Inc. 190*l*; Pop. 112.) [14]

TOMPSON, Edward John, *Denham Parsonage, Bury St. Edmunds.*—Ch. Ch. Ox. Careswell Exhib. B.A. 1851, M.A. 1854; Deac. 1853 and Pr. 1854 by Bp of Lich. P. C. of Denham, Dio. Ely, 1860. (Patron, Captain Farmer; P. C.'s Inc. 100*l*; Pop. 198.) Formerly Divinity Lect. of Ashbourne 1855; P. C. of Brassington 1855. [15]

TOMPSON, Frederic Henry, *Llanllwchaiarn Vicarage, Newtown, Montgomeryshire.*—Queen's Coll. Ox. B.A. 1826, M.A. 1843; Deac. 1827, Pr. 1828. V. of Llanllwchaiarn, Dio. St. A. 1851. (Patron, Bp. of St. A; Tithe—Imp. 220*l*, V. 250*l*; Glebe, 33 acres; V.'s Inc. 360*l* and Ho; Pop. 2394.) Rural Dean. [16]

TOMPSON, John Edward, *Sealand, Hawarden, Flintshire.*—C. of Sealand. Formerly C. of Castle Caereinion, Montgomery. [17]

TOMPSON, Matthew Carrier, *Alderminster Vicarage, Stratford-on-Avon.*—Trin. Coll. Ox. B.A. 1822, M.A. 1830. V. of Alderminster, Dio. Wor. 1830. (Patron, Ld Chan; Tithe—Imp. 188*l* 4s 6d, V. 161*l* 13s 6d; Glebe, 28 acres; V.'s Inc. 191*l* and Ho; Pop. 520.) Rural Dean of Kineton. [18]

TOMS, Humphry William, *Combmartin Rectory, Ilfracombe, Devon.*—Ex. Coll. Ox. B.A. 1841, M.A. 1846; Deac. 1841 and Pr. 1842 by Bp of Ex. R. of Combmartin, Dio. Ex. 1842. (Patron, the present R; Tithe, 400*l*; Glebe, 70 acres; R.'s Inc. 500*l* and Ho; Pop. 1484.) [19]

TONGE, George, 3, *New Inn Hall-street, Oxford.*—Lin. Coll. Ox. 2nd cl. Lit. Hum. and B.A. 1860, M.A. 1863; Deac. 1861 and Pr. 1862 by Bp of Ox. C. of St. Peter-le-Bailey, Oxford, 1864; Jun. Examining Chap. to Bp of Carl. 1866. Formerly C. of Middle Claydon, Bucks, 1861–63. [20]

TONGE, Richard, *The Rectory, Heaton Mersey, Manchester.*—St. John's Coll. Cam. 1st Jun. Opt. B.A. 1854, M.A. 1857; Deac. 1855 and Pr. 1856 by Bp of Man. R. of St. John's, Heaton Mersey, Dio. Man. 1867. (Patron, Bp of Man; R.'s Inc. 220*l*; Pop. 1875.) Formerly C. of St. Luke's, Cheetham Hill, 1855–61; Clerical Sec. of the Manchester Dio. Ch. Build. Soc. 1861–67. [21]

TONKIN, Franklin.—Corpus Coll. Cam. B.A. 1844, M.A. 1862; Deac. 1845, Pr. 1846. C. of St. Matthew's, Spring Gardens, Lond. 1861. Formerly C. of West Lulworth, Dorset, 1845; Miss. Chap. to the Bp of Edinburgh 1847; P. C. of St. Ives, Cornwall, 1855. [22]

TONKIN, Uriah, *Lelant, Hayle, Cornwall.*—Ex. Coll. Ox. B.A. 1811. V. of Lelant with Towednack C. Dio. Ex. 1832. (Patron, Bp of Ex; Lelant, Tithe—Imp. 252*l*, V. 207*l*; Towednack, Tithe—Imp. 118*l*, V. 150*l*; V.'s Inc. 441*l*; Pop. Lelant 2319, Towdenack 1007.) [23]

TOOGOOD, Jonathan James, *Kirkby-Overblow Rectory, Wetherby, Yorks.*—Ball. Coll. Ox. B.A. 1832, M.A. 1834; Deac. 1832 and Pr. 1833 by Bp of B. and W. Preb. of Combe the 10th in Wells Cathl. 1840; R. of Kirkby-Overblow, Dio. Rip. 1858. (Patron, Lord Leconfield; Tithe, 578*l*; Glebe, 71½ acres; R.'s Inc. 964*l* and Ho; Pop. 1326.) Formerly R. of St. Andrew's, Holborn, Lond. 1850–57. [24]

TOOKE, John Hales, *Scawby Vicarage, Brigg, Lincolnshire.*—V. of Scawby, Dio. Lin. 1846. (Patron, Sir J. Nelthorpe, Bart; V.'s Inc. 340*l* and Ho; Pop. 1570.) [25]

TOOKE, Thomas Hammond, *Monkton Farley, Bradford-on-Avon, Wilts.*—Trin. Coll. Cam. B.A. 1848, M.A. 1851; Deac. 1848 and Pr. 1849 by Bp of Ox. R. of Monkton Farley, Dio. Salis. 1865. (Patron, Bp of Salis; R.'s Inc. 196*l* and Ho; Pop. 356.) Formerly C. of Iver 1848, Upton and Chelvey 1850–58; R. of St. Edmund's, Salisbury, 1858–63. [26]

TOOLIS, John Daniel, 6, *Park-terrace, Glastonbury, Somerset.*—St. Aidan's; Deac. 1864 by Abp of York, Pr. 1866 by Bp of B. and W. C. of St. Benedict's, Glastonbury, 1866. Formerly C. of Hull 1864;

C. in sole charge of Cannington, near Bridgwater, 1865. [1]

TOOTH, Arthur, *Mission House, Chiswick, W.*—Trin. Coll. Cam. B.A. 1861, M.A. 1865; Deac. 1863 by Bp of Win. Pr. 1864 by Abp of Cant. Minister of St. Mary's Mission Chapel, Chiswick, 1865. Formerly C. of St. Mary's-the-Less, Lambeth, 1863, St. Mary's, Folkestone, 1864. [2]

TOOTH, Charles, *Falfield, Berkeley, Gloucestershire.*—Downing Coll. Cam. B.A. 1862. Deac. 1863 and Pr. 1864 by Bp of Lon. P. C. of Falfield, Dio. G. and B. 1865. (Patrons, D. and C. of Ch. Ch. Ox; Tithe, 120*l* 5*s* 7*d*; Glebe, 1 acre 3 roods; P. C.'s Inc. 155*l* 6*s* 3*d*; Pop. 700.) [3]

TOOTH, George Chinnery, *Codsall, Wolverhampton.*—Wor. Coll. Ox. B.A. 1843; Deac. 1844, Pr. 1845. P. C. of Codsall, Dio. Lich. 1867. (Patron, Lord Wrottesley; P. C.'s Inc. 150*l*; Pop. 1204.) Formerly P. C. of Longstone, Derbyshire, 1855. [4]

TOOTH, William Augustus, 25, *Crooms-hill, Greenwich.*—Trin. Coll. Cam. B.A. 1860, M.A. 1863; Deac. 1863 and Pr. 1864 by Bp of Wor. C. of St. Alphege with St. Mary's, Greenwich, 1866. Formerly C. of St. Matthew's, Rugby, 1863–65, Sutton-Valence, Staplehurst, Kent, 1865–66. [5]

TOPHAM, Edward Charles, *Ladbroke Rectory, near Southam, Rugby.*—Univ. Coll. Dur. B.A. 1846, M.A. 1850; Deac. 1847 by Bp of Salis; Pr. 1848 by Bp of B. and W. R. of Ladbroke, Dio. Wor. 1858. (Patron, the present R; Tithe, 431*l* 10*s*; Glebe, 40 acres; R.'s Inc. 490*l* and Ho; Pop. 274.) R. of Radbourne, Warw. Dio. Wor. 1863. (Patron, the present R.; Tithe, 40*l*; R.'s Inc. 40*l*; Pop. 32.) Formerly C. of Ticehurst, Sussex, 1851–58. Author, *Philosophy of the Fall*, Bosworth, 1855, 8*s* 6*d*. [6]

TOPHAM, John, *St. Andrew's Rectory, Droitwich, Worcestershire.*—St. John's Coll. Cam. B.A. 1818, M.A. 1822; Deac. 1818, Pr. 1819. R. of the United R.'s of St. Andrew's, St. Mary's Witton and St. Nicholas', Droitwich, Dio. Wor. 1828. (Patron, Ld Chan; St. Andrew's and St. Mary's Witton, Tithe, 208*l*; Glebe, 20 acres; St. Nicholas', Tithe—Imp. 50*l*; R.'s Inc. 330*l*; Pop. St. Andrew's and St. Mary's Witton 1008, St. Nicholas' 707.) Formerly Head Mast. of King Edward VI.'s Gr. Sch. Bromsgrove, Worcestershire. Author, *Evidences of Religion*: Sermons—*On the Use of Music in Devotional Exercises*; *The Holy Communion*; *The Office of the Priesthood*; *The Visitation of the Cholera*; *The Union of Religious and Useful Learning* (to the 18th Worcestershire V. R. C.); *Chemistry Made Easy for Agriculturists.* [7]

TOPHAM, John, *Gosberton, Spalding, Lincolnshire.*—Wor. Coll. Ox. B.A. 1838, M.A. 1841; Deac. 1839, Pr. 1840. V. of Gosberton, Dio. Lin. 1853. (Patrons, D. and C. of Lin; Tithe—Imp. 600*l*; Glebe, 2 acres; V.'s Inc. 150*l* and Ho; Pop. 2107.) Author, *A Farewell Sermon*, 1843; *The Advantages of Knowledge* (a Lecture delivered at the Opening of the Spalding Mechanics' Institute), 1851. [8]

TOPHAM, Robert, *Etruria Parsonage, Stoke-upon-Trent.*—Literate; Deac. 1851, Pr. 1852 by Abp of Cant. P. C. of Etruria, Dio. Lich. 1864. (Patrons, Crown and Bp of Lich. alt; P. C.'s Inc. 150*l* and Ho; Pop. 4000.) Chap. to the North Staff. Infirmary (stipend, 50*l*). Formerly C. of Penistone 1851–57, St. John's, Sheffield, 1858; P. C. of Biggin, Derbyshire, and Chap. to the Duke of Devonshire, 1860–64. [9]

TOPHAM, Samuel, *Tonge, Middleton, Manchester.*—St. Aidan's; Deac. 1864, Pr. 1865. C. of Tonge with Alkrington 1866. Formerly C. of Lastingham, Yorks, 1864–66. [10]

TOPPIN, George Pilgrim, *Cannings Episcopi, Devizes, Wilts.*—Ch. Coll. Cam. B.A. 1858, M.A. 1862; Deac. 1860 and Pr. 1861 by Bp of B. and W. C. of Cannings Episcopi 1864. Formerly C. of Vobster, Somerset, 1860–62, The Lea, Glouc. 1864. [11]

TOPPING, George, *Hayton Parsonage, Carlisle.*—Literate; Deac. 1817, Pr. 1818. P. C. of Hayton with Talkin C. Dio. Carl. 1836. (Patrons, D. and C. of Carl; Tithe, App. 285*l*; P. C.'s Inc. 150*l* and Ho; Pop. 1015.) [12]

TOPPING, George, *Rockcliffe, near Carlisle.*—Deac. and Pr. 1813 by Bp of Carl. P. C. of Rockcliffe, Dio. Carl. 1833. (Patrons, D. and C. of Carl; Tithe—App. 294*l*; Glebe, 2 acres; P. C.'s Inc. 97*l*; Pop. 949.) [13]

TORLESSE, Charles Martin, *Stoke-by-Nayland Vicarage (Suffolk), near Colchester.*—Trin. Coll. Cam. B.A. 1817, M.A. 1821; Deac. 1821 and Pr. 1822 by Bp of Lin. V. of Stoke-by-Nayland, Dio. Ely, 1832. (Patron, Sir C. Rowley; Tithe—Imp. 1254*l* 7*s* 6*d*, V. 355*l*; Glebe, ½ acre; V.'s Inc. 365*l* and Ho; Pop. 755.) [14]

TORR, Thomas Joseph, *Dummer House, Basingstoke, Hants.*—Trin. Coll. Cam. M.A. 1859; Deac. 1857 and Pr. 1859 by Bp of B. and W. C. of Dummer, near Basingstoke, 1866. Formerly C. of Exmoor, Somerset, 1857–59, St. John's, Brighton, 1859–60, South Hanningfield, Chelmsford, 1860–61; R. of Bisley, Bagshot, Surrey, 1861–66. [15]

TORRE, William Fox Whitbread, *The Priory, Leeds.*—St. John's Coll. Cam. Jun. Opt. and B.A. 1851, M.A. 1854; Deac. 1852 and Pr. 1853 by Bp of Wor. Formerly C. of Leeds, P. C. of Headingley, Leeds, 1863. [16]

TORRY, Alfred Freer, *St John's College, Cambridge.*—St. John's Coll. Cam. 4th Wrang. B.A. 1862, M.A. 1865; Deac. 1864 and Pr. 1865 by Bp of Ely. Fell. of St. John's Coll. Cam. [17]

TOTHILL, Charles William Edward, *St Mary's, Tedburn, Exeter.*—King's Coll. Lond. Theol. Assoc. 1856; Deac. 1856 and Pr. 1857 by Bp of B. and W. R. of Tedburn, Dio. Ex. 1865. (Patron, T. C. Tothill, Esq; Tithe, 410*l*; Glebe, 43 acres; R.'s Inc. 450*l* and Ho; Pop. 750.) Formerly C. of Sampford-Brett, Somerset, Filleigh, North Devon, and Tedburn. [18]

TOTTENHAM, R. L., *Florence.*—Chap. to the Bp of Gibraltar. Formerly British Chap. at Turin. [19]

TOTTON, W. A., *Couldson, Croydon, Surrey, S.*—C. of Couldson. [20]

TOUZEL, Helier, *Martyr Worthy Rectory, Winchester.*—Sid. Coll. Cam. B.A. 1831, M.A. 1840; Deac. 1832 and Pr. 1833 by Bp of Win. R. of Martyr Worthy, Dio. Win. 1866. (Patron, Bp of Win; Tithe, 488*l* 15*s* 9*d*; Glebe, 11½ acres; R.'s Inc. 502*l* and Ho; Pop. 259.) Formerly R. of Bram Dean, Hants, 1845–66. [21]

TOVEY, J. D., *Owston, Doncaster.*—C. of Owston. [22]

TOWER, Charles, *Chilmark Rectory, Salisbury.*—St. John's Coll. Cam. B.A. Jun. Opt. 2nd cl. Cl. Trip. 1837, M.A. 1839; Deac. 1838 and Pr. 1839 by Bp of Lon. R. of Chilmark, Dio. Salis. 1843. (Patron, Earl of Pembroke; Tithe, 473*l*; Glebe, 24 acres; R.'s Inc. 509*l* and Ho; Pop. 642.) Rural Dean of Chalke 1863. [23]

TOWER, Ferdinand Ernest, *Earl's Shilton, Hinckley, Leicestershire.*—St. John's Coll. Cam. B.A. 1843, M.A. 1846; Deac. 1844, Pr. 1845. R. of Elmsthorpe with Earl's Shilton P. C. Dio. Pet. 1854. (Patrons, Trustees; Elmsthorpe, Tithe, 56*l*; Earl's Shilton, Tithe, 6*l*; Glebe, 83 acres; R.'s Inc. 240*l*; Pop. Elmsthorpe 45, Earl's Shilton 2176.) [24]

TOWER, Robert Beauchamp, *Moreton Rectory, Chipping-Ongar, Essex.*—Univ. Coll. Dur. 3rd cl. Math. and B.A. 1837, M.A. 1841; Deac. 1839, Pr. 1840. R. of Moreton, Dio. Roch. 1840. (Patron, St. John's Coll. Cam; Tithe, 375*l*; Glebe, 90 acres; R.'s Inc. 475*l* and Ho; Pop. 497.) [25]

TOWERS, Grainger Lawrence, *Tunbridge, Kent.*—St. John's Coll. Cam. B.A. 1847; Deac. 1847 by Bp of Lich. Pr. 1848 by Bp of Chich. Travelling Sec. of S.P.G. 1857. Formerly C. of Burwash, Sussex. [26]

TOWERS, Myles Hodgson, 40, *Byrom-street, Manchester.*—Pemb. Coll. Cam. B.A. 1862; Deac. 1864 and Pr. 1866 by Bp of Man. C. of Stretton, near Warrington, Cheshire. Formerly C. of St. Matthew's, Manchester, 1864. [27]

TOWERS, William Thornton, *Grimoldby, Louth, Lincolnshire.*—St. Bees; Deac. 1860 and Pr. 1861 by Bp of Ches. C. in sole charge of Grimoldby 1862. Formerly C. of Hollinfare, near Warrington, 1860–62. [1]

TOWLE, Charles Seymour, *Lamborne, Berks.*—St. John's Coll. Cam. B.A. 1866; Deac. 1866. C. of Lamborne, 1866. [2]

TOWN, Benjamin, *The Parsonage, Mount Pellon, Halifax, Yorks.*—St. Bees; Deac. 1853 and Pr. 1855 by Bp of Man. P. C. of Mount Pellon, Dio. Rip. 1862. (Patron, V. of Halifax; P. C.'s Inc. 120*l* and Ho; Pop. 2021.) Formerly C. of St. Bartholomew's, Salford, Great Harwood, Lancashire, 1855, Huddersfield 1857, Mount Pellon 1859. [3]

TOWN, Jonathan Ward, *Parsonage, Lindley, Huddersfield*—St. Bees 1848; Deac. 1850 and Pr. 1851 by Bp of Man. P. C. of Lindley with Quarmby, Dio. Rip. 1858. (Patron, V. of Huddersfield; P. C.'s Inc. 180*l* and Ho; Pop. 4259.) Formerly Sen. C. of Huddersfield. [4]

TOWNE, Ernest Josiah, *Ewell, Surrey.*—Trin. Coll. Cam. B.A. 1852; Deac. 1853. Formerly C. of Chester-le-Street, Durham. [5]

TOWNE, Lyndhurst B., *Darlington.*—C. of St. Cuthbert's, Darlington. [6]

TOWNEND, Alfred John, 154, *Chester-road, Hulme, Manchester.*—Trin. Coll. Cam. Jun. Opt. Silver Declamation Cup, B.A. 1861; Deac. 1863 and Pr. 1864 by Bp of Man. C. of St. George's, Hulme, 1863. [7]

TOWNEND, Henry, *Loddiswell Vicarage, Kingsbridge, Devon.*—V. of Loddiswell with Buckland-Tout-Saints, Dio. Ex. 1867. (Patron, the present V; Tithe, 344*l* 5*s* 6*d*; V.'s Inc. 570*l* and Ho; Pop. 950.) [8]

TOWNLEY, Charles, *Hadstock Rectory, Linton, Essex.*—Trin. Coll. Cam. B.A. 1817, M.A. 1820. R. of Hadstock, Dio. Roch. 1838. (Patron, Abp of Cant; R.'s Inc. 270*l* and Ho; Pop. 511.) V. of Little Abington, Dio. Ely, 1859. (Patron, T. Mortlock, Esq; V.'s Inc. 87*l* and Ho; Pop. 316.) Dom. Chap. to the Duke of Leeds. [9]

TOWNLEY, Edmund Townhead, *Newton-in-Cartmel, Lancashire.*—Deac. 1827, Pr. 1828. Formerly P. C. of Staveley-in-Cartmel, Lancashire, 1828–64. [10]

TOWNLEY, William Gale, *Beaupré Hall, Wisbech.*—Trin. Coll. Cam; Deac. 1855 by Bp of Roch. Pr. 1856 by Abp Sumner. R. of Upwell, St. Peter, Dio. Nor. 1862. (Patron, C. W. Townley, Esq; R.'s Inc. 3058*l* and Ho; Pop. 3000.) Formerly C. of Bexley, Maidstone, 1855–62. [11]

TOWNSEND, Aubrey, *Wick St. Lawrence, Weston-super-Mare.*—Dub. A.B. 1836, A.M. 1839, B.D. 1847; Deac. 1837 by Bp of Win. Pr. 1838 by Bp of Lin. C. of Wick St. Lawrence. Formerly C. of St. Michael's, Bath. Editor of *The Writings of the Martyr Bradford*, 2 vols. Cam. Univ. Press, for the Parker Soc. 1848 and 1853. [12]

TOWNSEND, Charles, *Kingston-by-Sea Rectory, New Shoreham, Sussex.*—Emman. Coll. Cam. B.A. 1813, M.A. 1817; Deac. 1813 and Pr. 1814 by Bp of Chich. R. of Kingston-by-Sea, Dio. Chich. 1837. (Patron, Lord Leconfield; Tithe, 248*l* 13*s* 7*d*; Glebe, 22 acres; R.'s Inc. 271*l* and Ho; Pop. 93.) [13]

TOWNSEND, Charles Henry, *Mere Vicarage, Bath.*—Lin. Coll. Ox. B.A. 1850, M.A. 1852; Deac. 1851 and Pr. 1852 by Bp of Salis. V. of Mere, Wilts, Dio. Salis. 1861. (Patron, Bp of Salis; V.'s Inc. 330*l* and Ho; Pop. 2370.) Formerly C. of Laverstock. [14]

TOWNSEND, George Fyler, *St. Michael's Parsonage, Burleigh-street, Covent-garden, London, W.C.*—Trin. Coll. Cam. B.A. 1837, M.A. 1840; Deac. 1837, Pr. 1838. P. C. of St. Michael's, Burleigh-street, Covent-garden, Dio. Lon. 1862. (Patron, V. of St. Martin's-in-the-fields, Westminster; Pop. 3500.) Formerly Chap. to the Duke of Northumberland, and to the Bp of Tasmania; V. of Brantingham, Yorks, 1842–57; V. of Leominster 1857–62. Author, *The Churchman's Year*, 2 vols. Rivingtons, 1842, 18*s*; *The Christian Pilgrimage, from the Cradle to the Grave*, ib. 5*s*; *Warnings from the Past, or Sermons vindicating the Providence of God*, Rivingtons, 5*s*; *History of Town and Borough of Leominster*, Partridge, Leominster, 15*s*; *A new Translation of Three Hundred Æsop's Fables*, Routledge, 5*s*. [15]

TOWNSEND, Henry, *Honington Hall, Shipston-on-Stour, Worcestershire.*—Mert. Coll. Ox. B.A. 1805, M.A. 1808; Deac. 1806, Pr. 1807. [16]

TOWNSEND, John, *Hockley House, Hockley-heath, Warwickshire.*—King's Coll. Lond. Theol. Assoc; Deac. 1854, Pr. 1856. C. of Nuthurst, Hampton-in-Arden, Warwickshire, 1854. [17]

TOWNSEND, Maurice Fitzgerald, *Thornbury Vicarage, Glouc.*—Ch. Ch. Ox. B.A. 1812, M.A. 1815. V. of Thornbury, Dio. G. and B. 1823. (Patron, Ch. Ch. Ox; Tithe—App. 450*l* 10*s* and $1\frac{1}{2}$ acres of Glebe, V. 621*l* 10*s*; Glebe, 3 acres; V.'s Inc. 623*l* and Ho; Pop. 2544.) [18]

TOWNSEND, Samuel Thomas, 5, *Harley-place, Upper Harley-street, London, W.*—Trin. Coll. Cam. B.A. 1824, M.A. 1825; Deac. 1828, Pr. 1829. [19]

TOWNSEND, Thomas, *Aston Blank Vicarage, Northleach, Glouc.*—V. of Aston Blank, Dio. G. and B. 1845. (Patron, Ld. Chan; V.'s Inc. 188*l* and Ho; Pop. 325.) [20]

TOWNSEND, Thomas Jackson Milnes, *Searby Vicarage, near Brigg, Lincolnshire.*—Lin. Coll. Ox. B.A. 1841; Deac. 1842 and Pr. 1843 by Bp of Lin. V. of Searby with Owmby, Dio. Lin. 1845. (Patrons, D. and C. of Lin; Tithe, 96*l*; Glebe, 62 acres; V.'s Inc. 220*l* and Ho; Pop. 263.) Formerly C. of Scarle, Lin. 1842–45. [21]

TOWNSEND, William Lawrence, *Bishops Cleeve, Cheltenham.*—Wor. Coll. Ox; Deac. 1820, Pr. 1821. R. of Bishops Cleeve, Dio. G. and B. 1830. (Patron, the present R; Tithe—Imp. 1322*l* 19*s*, R. 60*l*; Glebe, 508 acres; R.'s Inc. 1600*l* and Ho; Pop. 1970.) [22]

TOWNSEND, William Manifold, *Tavern-street, Stowmarket, Suffolk.*—Queens' Coll. Cam. B.A. 1837, M.A. 1840, Deac. 1838 by Bp of Win; Pr 1840 by Bp of Lich. V. of Finborough-Parva, Dio. Nor. 1858. (Patron, King's Coll. Cam; Tithe, Imp. 96*l*; V.'s Inc. 150*l*; Pop. 62.) Chap. of Stow Union 1858. Formerly C. of Barningham-cum-Coney Weston 1851. [23]

TOWNSHEND, George Henry, *Pleck, Walsall, Staffs.*—King's Coll. Lond. Theol. Assoc; Deac. 1860 by Bp of Wor. P. C. of Pleck with Bescot P. C. Dio. Lich. 1863. (Patron, V. of Walsall; P. C.'s Inc. 120*l* and Ho; Pop. 3220.) Formerly C. of St. Thomas's, Birmingham, 1860–63. [24]

TOWNSON, John, *Strensham Rectory, Tewkesbury.*—Univ. Coll. Dur. B.A. 1845, M.A. 1848; Deac. 1846, Pr. 1847. R. of Strensham, Dio. Wor. 1862. (Patron, J. A. Taylor, Esq; R.'s Inc. 330*l* and Ho; Pop. 270.) Formerly Fell. of Univ. Coll. Dur; C. of All Saints', Dorchester. [25]

TOWNSON, Robert, *Allthwaite, near Ulverston, Lancashire.*—Queen's Coll. Ox. Scho. of, 2nd and 3rd cl. in Hons. B.A. 1854, M.A. 1857; Deac. 1855 by Bp of Pet. Pr. 1858 by Bp of Carl. P. C. of Allthwaite, Dio. Carl. 1866. (Patron, Bp of Ches; P. C.'s Inc. 150*l* and Ho; Pop. 480.) Formerly Asst. Cl. Mast. at Rossall Sch; P. C. of Grayrigg, Kendal, 1860–66. [26]

TOYE, Joseph Theophilus, *Victoria-terrace, Exeter.*—Queen's Coll. Ox. B.A. 1829, M.A. 1845; Deac. 1832 and Pr. 1833 by Bp of Salis. P. C. of St. David's, City and Dio. Ex. 1862. (Patrons, D. and C. of Ex; P. C.'s Inc. 180*l*; Pop. 4486.) Formerly R. of St. Stephen's, Exeter, 1837–62. [27]

TOZER, Henry Fanshawe, *Exeter College, Oxford.*—Ex. Coll. Ox. B.A. 1853; Deac. 1852 and Pr. 1853 by Bp of Ox. Fell. of Ex. Coll. Ox. [28]

TOZER, Samuel Thomas, *St. John's, Tipton, Staffs.*—St. Bees; Deac. 1862, Pr. 1863. P. C. of St. John's, Tipton, Dio. Lich. 1863. (Patron, Bp of Lich; P. C.'s Inc. 40*l*; Pop. 2856.) [29]

TRACEY, John, *Dartmouth Vicarage, Devon.*—Wad. Coll. Ox. B.A. 1834, M.A. 1841; Deac. 1835, Pr. 1836. V. of Townstall with St. Saviour's C. Dio. Ex. 1837. (Patron, Sir H. P. Seale, Bart; Tithe—Imp. 294*l* 17*s* 6*d*,

V. 18*l* 6*s* 8*d*, and Endow. from Queen Anne's Bounty; V.'s Inc. 150*l*; Pop. Townstall 1342, St. Saviour's 2017.) [1]

TRACY, Frederick Francis, *Chichester.*—Ch. Coll. Cam. B.A. 1852, M.A. 1855; Deac. 1853 and Pr. 1857 by Bp of Chich. R. of St. Pancras, Chichester, 1865. (Patrons, Simeon's Trustees; R.'s Inc. 95*l* and Ho; Pop. 1087.) Formerly C. of Shermanbury, Sussex, 1853, Icclesham 1855, All Souls', Brighton, 1857; V. of Worth Maltravers, Dorset, 1857–65. Author, *The Parish Choir and Congregation* (a Sermon), 1864. [2]

TRAFFORD, William, *Uffculme, Devon.*—Ch. Coll. Cam. Sen. Opt. and 2nd cl. Cl. Trip. B.A. 1859; Deac. 1862 and Pr. 1863 by Bp of Dur. Head Mast. of Uffculme Gr. Sch. Formerly 1st Asst. Mast. in Durham Sch. [3]

TRAGETT, Thomas Heathcote, *Awbridge-Danes, Romsey, Hants.*—Corpus Coll. Ox. B.A. 1819, M.A. 1822; Deac. 1823 and Pr. 1824 by Bp of Ox Formerly Fell. of Ch. Ch. Ox. P. C. of Ch. Ch. Coventry, 1832–36; P. C. of Timsbury, Hants, 1843-53. [4]

TRAILL, Francis Robert, *Stanway Vicarage, Winchcomb, Glouc.*—Corpus Coll. Cam. B.A. 1848, M.A. 1851; Deac. 1848, Pr. 1849. V. of Stanway, Dio. G. and B. 1854. (Patron, Earl of Wemyss; Glebe, 159 acres; V.'s Inc. 220*l* and Ho; Pop. 378.) Dom. Chap. to the Earl of Wemyss and March; C. of Cutsdean 1863. [5]

TRANEKER, George Sutton, *Poole, Dorset.*—St. Bees; Deac. 1846 and Pr. 1847 by Bp of Lich. C. of St. James's, Poole. Formerly C. of West Buckland 1862. [6]

TRAPP, Benjamin, *Thurleigh Vicarage, near Bedford.*—Clare Coll. Cam. B.A. 1836, M.A. 1839; Deac. 1836 and Pr. 1837 by Abp of York. V. of Thurleigh, Dio. Ely, 1839. (Patron, S. Crawley, Esq; Land in lieu of Tithe, 236 acres; V.'s Inc. 208*l* and Ho; Pop. 666.) [7]

TRAVERS, Charles Henry, *Stewkley Vicarage, Leighton Buzzard.*—Queen's Coll. Ox. M.A; Deac. 1847 and Pr. 1848 by Bp of Ex. V. of Stewkley, Beds, Dio. Ox. 1859. (Patron, Bp of Ox; V.'s Inc. 320*l* and Ho; Pop. 1453.) Formerly C. of Buckerell and Combeinteignhead, Devon, Maids Morton, Bucks, Old Wolverton, Hungerford, Deddington, and Buckingham. [8]

TRAVERS, John Benward, *Mumby Vicarage, Alford, Lincolnshire.*—Ch. Coll. Cam. Sen. Opt. and B.A. 1833, M.A. 1836; Deac. 1833, Pr. 1834. V. of Mumby, Dio. Lin. 1840. (Patron, Bp of Lin; Tithe, 2*l* 9*s*; Glebe, 84 acres; V.'s Inc. 280*l* and Ho; Pop. Mumby St. Peter's 394, Mumby St. Leonard's 392.) Rural Dean. [9]

TRAVERS, Robert Duncan, *Swanage Rectory, Dorset.*—Caius Coll. Cam. Sen. Opt. and B.A. 1845, M.A. 1848; Deac. 1846 and Pr. 1848 by Bp of Ches. R. of Swanage, Dio. Salis. 1853. (Patron, J. H. Calcraft, Esq; Tithe, 400*l*; Glebe, 19 acres; R.'s Inc. 557*l* and Ho; Pop. 2004.) [10]

TRAVIS, James, *Godmanchester, Hunts.*—Ex Coll. Ox. B.A. 1865; Deac. 1866, Pr. 1867. C. of Godmanchester 1866. [11]

TREACHER, Joseph Skipper, *Merton College, Oxford.*—B.A. 1846, M.A. 1853; Deac. 1847 and Pr. 1848 by Bp. of Ex. Chap. of Merton Coll. Ox. [12]

TREBECK, J. J., *Great Grimsby, Lincolnshire.*—C. of Great Grimsby. Formerly C. of Ch. Ch. St. Pancras, Lond. [13]

TREES, Enoch, *Ossington Parsonage, Newark, Notts.*—Bp Hat. Hall, Dur. Licen. Theol. 1850; Deac. 1850 and Pr. 1851 by Bp of Lich. P. C. of Ossington, Dio. Lin. 1858. (Patron, Right Hon. J. E. Denison; Tithe—Imp. 13*l*; P. C.'s Inc. 105*l* and Ho; Pop. 231.) Formerly C. of North Scarle, Linc. [14]

TREFFRY, Edward John, *Fowey, Cornwall.*—Ex. Coll. Ox. Scho. of, Lin. Coll. 4th cl. Lit. Hum. 1831, B.A. 1832, M.A. 1842, D.C.L. 1864; Deac. 1833 and Pr. 1834. Formerly P. C. of Scilly Islands 1835–41; Head Mast. of the Great Berkhampstead Gr. Sch. 1842–50; V. of Fowey, Cornwall, 1863–67. Author, *Family Prayers*, 1835; Two *Assise Sermons*, 1839. [15]

TREFUSIS, R. E., *Chittlehampton, South Molton, Devon.*—V. of Chittlehampton, Dio. Ex. 1867. (Patrons, Trustees of Lord Rolle; Tithe—Imp. 675*l*, V. 575*l*; Glebe, 41 acres; V.'s Inc. 575*l* and Ho; Pop. 1343.) Formerly C. of Buckingham. [16]

TREGARTHYN, William Francis, *Privy Council Office, Downing-street, London, S.W.*—King's Coll. Lond. 1st cl. and Theol. Assoc. 1855; Deac. 1855 by Bp of B. and W. Pr. 1856 by Bp of G. and B. One of H.M.'s Inspectors of Schs. Formerly C. of Tewkesbury and Walton, Cardiff, and Osmington, Dorset. [17]

TRELAWNY, Charles Trelawny Collins, *Ham, near Plymouth.*—Ball. Coll. Ox. B.A. 1815, M.A. 1821; Deac. 1821 and Pr. 1823 by Bp of Ox. P. C. of North Newton, Somerset, Dio. B. and W. 1828. (Patron, Sir Thomas Dyke Acland, Bart; P. C.'s Inc. 70*l*; Pop. 360.) C. of Penny Cross, Devon. Formerly Fell. of Ball. Coll. Ox. 1820–25; R. of Timsbury 1825–41. Author, *A Visitation Sermon*, 1838; *Summary of Mosheim's "Ecclesiastical History," with Continuation*, 2 vols. 1839; *Peranzabuloe, or the Lost Church Found*, 5th ed; *Appeal to Masters of Families on the Duty of Family Prayer*; etc. [18]

TREMLETT, Francis William, *Belsize-park, Hampstead, London, N.W.*—Mass. United States, M.A. and LL.D. Hon. Ph.D. of Jena; Deac. 1846 and Pr. 1847 by Bp Field. P. C. of St. Peter's, Belsize-park, Hampstead, Dio. Lon. 1859. (Patrons, D. and C. of Westminster; P. C.'s Inc. 1000*l*; Pop. 2000.) Dom. Chap. to Lord Waterpark. Author, *Philosophy of Organic Life*, Berlin, 1859; *Essay on Comets*; and various Sermons and Pamphlets. [19]

TRENCH, Francis, *Islip Rectory, Oxon.*—Oriel Coll. Ox. 2nd cl. Lit. Hum. and B.A. 1828; Deac. 1835 by Bp of Win. Pr. 1836 by Bp of Salis. R. of Islip, Dio. Ox. 1857. (Patrons, D. and C. of Westminster; V.'s Inc. 400*l* and Ho; Pop. 688.) Formerly C. of St. Giles', Reading; P. C. of St. John's, Reading, 1837–57. Author, *Life and Character of St. John the Evangelist*; *Sermons* (preached at Reading); *Portrait of Charity*; *Lectures on Conversation*, and on *Good and Bad Reading*; *Travels in France and Spain*, 1845; *Travels in Scotland*, 1845; *Walk round Mont Blanc*, 1847; *Theological Works*, 3 vols. 1857; *Brief Notes on the Greek of the New Testament, chiefly for English Readers*, 6*s*; *Four Assize Sermons* (preached in York Minster and Leeds Parish Church). 1865; published by Macmillan and Co. [20]

TREND, John Bowden, *St. Augustine's College, Canterbury.*—St. Mary Hall, Ox. Hon. 4th cl. Math. B.A. 1859, M.A. 1863; Deac. 1859 and Pr. 1860 by Bp of Ox. Fell. of St. Augustine's Coll. 1862. Formerly C. of St. Giles', Oxford, 1859–61; Min. of Lundin Links, Fife, Scotland, 1861; C. of Holywell, Oxford, 1861–62. Author, *Hymnal for Use in the Church of England*, Rivingtons. [21]

TRENDELL, William Henry, 114, *Cheshire-view, Pendleton, Manchester.*—St. Aidan's; Deac. and Pr. 1855 by Abp of York. English Lect. at Maentwrog; Dom. Chap. to Mrs. Oakeley, Tan y Bwlch; Travelling Sec. for Curates' Augmentation Fund. Formerly C. of Whitby, Yorks, 1855–57; Asst. Min. Christ's Chapel, Maida-hill, Lond. 1857–58. Author, *Sermons on the Lord's Day.* [22]

TRENOW, Thomas Thompson, *Grafham, Guildford, Surrey.*—King's Coll. Lond. 1st cl. 1853, Theol. Assoc. 1853; Deac. 1853 and Pr. 1854 by Bp of Salis. P. C. of Grafham, Dio. Win. 1863. (Patron, H. Woodyer, Esq; P. C.'s Inc. 50*l*.) Formerly R. of Langton-Herring, Dorset, 1855–58; P. C. of Seavington St. Mary, Somerset, 1858–63. [23]

TRENTHAM, Thomas Braithwaite, *North Petherwin Vicarage, Launceston, Cornwall.*—Emman. Coll. Cam. B.A. 1851; Deac. 1854 and Pr. 1855 by Bp of Ex. V. of North Petherwin, Dio. Ex. 1867. (Patron, Duke of Bedford; Tithe, 145*l*; Glebe, 159 acres; V.'s Inc. 145*l* and Ho, Pop. 900.) Formerly C. of St. Mary Steps, Exeter, and Sithney; C. in sole charge of St. Columb Major, Cornwall. [24]

TREVELYAN, Edward Otto, *Stogumber Vicarage, Taunton.*—Corpus Coll. Ox. 3rd cl. Lit. Hum.

B.A. 1831, M.A. 1840; Deac. and Pr. 1836. C. of Stogumber 1841. [1]

TREVELYAN, George, *Stogumber, Taunton.*—Ball. Coll. Ox. B.A. 1818, M.A. 1820; Deac. and Pr. 1820. V. of Stogumber, Dio. B. and W. 1821. (Patrons, D. and C. of Wells; Tithe—App. 730*l*, V. 325*l*; V.'s Inc. 250*l* and Ho; Pop. 1398.) [2]

TREVELYAN, Walter Henry, *Mawgan Rectory, Helston, Cornwall.*—Ch. Coll. Cam. B.A. 1861; Deac. 1863, Pr. 1864. R. of Mawgan and St. Martin-in-Meneage, Dio. Ex. 1865. (Patron, W. H. Trevelyan; Tithe, 911*l*; Glebe, 23 acres; R.'s Inc. 911*l* and Ho; Pop. 1400.) Formerly C. of East Pennard, Shepton-Mallet, Somerset. [3]

TREVELYAN, William Pitt, *Calverton Rectory, Stony Stratford, Bucks.*—Wor. Coll. Ox; Deac. 1852, Pr. 1853. V. of Wolverton, Dio. Ox. 1856. (Patrons, Trustees of the late Dr. Radcliffe; V.'s Inc. 55*l* and Ho; Pop. 577.) R. of Calverton, Bucks, Dio. Ox. (Patron, Earl of Egmont; R.'s Inc. 360*l* and Ho; Pop. 595.) Formerly P. C. of Broomfield, Somerset, 1853–56. [4]

TREVENEN, Thomas John, *St. Barnabas' College, Pimlico, London, S.W.*—Magd. Hall, Ox. B.A. 1857, M.A. 1860; Deac. 1858 and Pr. 1859 by Bp of Ex. C. of St. Barnabas', Pimlico, 1860. Formerly C. of St. Mary Church, Devon, 1858–60. [5]

TREVITT, James, *The Parsonage, St. Philip's, Bethnal Green, London, E.*—St. Alban Hall, Ox. S.C.L. M.A; Deac. 1843 and Pr. 1844 by Bp of Lon. P. C. of St. Philip's, Bethnal Green, Dio. Lon. 1852. (Patron, Bp of Lon; P. C.'s Inc. 300*l* and Ho; Pop. 13,500.) Formerly C. of Horndon-on-the-Hill, Essex, 1843–51. [6]

TREVOR, George, *All Saints' Rectory, York.*—Magd. Hall, Ox. S.C.L. 1834, Hon. 4th cl. Lit. Hum. 1836, B.A. 1846, M.A. 1847; Deac. 1835 and Pr. 1836 by Bp of Lin. R. of All Saints', Pavement, City and Dio. York, 1847. (Patron, Ld Chan; R.'s Inc. 120*l* and Ho; Pop. 794.) Preb. and Can. of Apesthorpe in York Cathl. 1847 (no Emolument); Proctor for the Chapter in the Convocation of the Province of York 1847, and for the Archd. of York, in the same, 1852; Chap. on Queen Mary's Foundation in the Parish of Sheffield 1850. (Value, 400*l*.) Formerly Chap. to the H.E.I.C. on the Madras Establishment 1836–46; Res. Deputy of the S P.G. in the Province of York 1846–47. Author, *Christ in His Passion* (Daily Lectures on the Principal Events in the Holy-week), 1847, 2*s* 6*d*; *Parochial Missionary Magazine*, 1849–50; *Sermons on Doctrines and Means of Grace*, 1850, 8*s*; *Party Spirit* (a serious Expostulation with the Vicar of Sheffield), 1851; *The Convocations of the Two Provinces* (their Origin, Constitution, and Forms of Proceeding, with a Chapter on their Revival), 1852, 5*s*; *Church Synods, the Institution of Christ* (Sermon in York Minster), 1852; *India, an Historical Sketch*, 1858, *India, its Natives and Missions*, 1859, *Russia, Ancient and Modern*, 1862, and *Ancient Egypt*, 1863, *Egypt from the Conquest of Alexander*, 1865, *Rome from the Fall of the West*, all four published by the R.T.S; *Types and the Antitype* (two courses of Lent Lectures), Mozley, 1864; several single Sermons. [7]

TREW, J., *Cheltenham.*—C. of St. Peter's, Cheltenham. [8]

TREWEEKE, George, *Swithland Rectory, Loughborough.*—R. of Swithland, Dio. Pet. 1858. (Patron, Ld Chan; Tithe, 3*l*; Glebe, 180 acres; R.'s Inc. 320*l* and Ho; Pop. 255.) [9]

TREWMAN, Arthur Henry Peill, *Ilminster Vicarage, Somerset.*—Queens' Coll. Cam. B.A. 1847, M.A. 1851; Deac. 1847 and Pr. 1848 by Bp of B. and W. V. of Ilminster, Dio. B. and W. 1858. (Patroness, Mrs. Scott Gould; V.'s Inc. 550*l* and Ho; Pop. 3241.) Formerly V. of North Petherton, Somerset, 1851–58. [10]

TRIBE, Walter Harry.—Wad. Coll. Ox. B.A. 1854, M.A. 1859; Deac. 1856 and Pr. 1857 by Bp of Win. Formerly C. of Broughton, Hants, 1856–60; R. of Stockbridge 1860–67. [11]

TRIGGE, John Davies, *Brighton.*—C. of Brighton. [12]

TRIGGS, George Charles.—C. of Stockwell Chapel, Kennington, Surrey. [13]

TRIM, William Hewlett, *Sandford-Orcas (Somerset), near Sherborne.*—Wad. Coll. Ox. B.A. 1817, M.A. 1819; Deac. 1820, Pr. 1821. R. of Sandford-Orcas, Dio. B. and W. 1832. (Patroness, Mrs. Cookworthy; Tithe, 260*l*; Glebe, 47 acres; R.'s Inc. 360*l* and Ho; Pop. 318.) [14]

TRIMMER, Barrington J.—Dom. Chap. to the Duke of Sutherland. [15]

TRIMMER, Charles, *Corpus Christi College, Oxford.*—Corpus Coll. Ox. Hon. 4th cl. Lit. Hum. and B.A. 1847, M.A. 1850; Deac. and Pr. 1853 by Bp of Ox. Fell. of Corpus Coll. Ox. Formerly C. of Taverton, Somerset, 1856. [16]

TRIMMER, Henry Syer, *Marston-on-Dove Vicarage (Derbyshire), near Burton-on-Trent.*—Mert. Coll. Ox. B.A. 1828; Deac. 1829 and Pr. 1830 by Bp of Lon. V. of Marston-on-Dove, Dio. Lich. 1840. (Patron, Duke of Devonshire; Tithe—Imp. 4*l* 11*s*, V. 1*l* 10*s* 4*d*; Glebe, 76 acres; V.'s Inc. 230*l* and Ho; Pop. 1211.) Dom. Chap. to Earl Granville. [17]

TRIMMER, Kirby, *St. George's Tombland, Norwich.*—St. Alban Hall, Ox. B.A. 1828. P. C. of St. George's Tombland, City and Dio. Nor. 1842. (Patron, Bp of Nor; P. C.'s Inc. 146*l*; Pop. 687.) [18]

TRIMMER, Robert, *Guildford, Surrey.*—Wad. Coll. Ox. 2nd cl. Lit. Hum. and B.A. 1842, M.A. 1845, Denyer's Theol. Prizeman 1846; Deac. 1844 and Pr. 1845 by Bp of Ox. R. of Trinity with St. Mary's, Guildford, Dio. Win. 1862. (Patron, Ld Chan; Tithe, 136*l*; R.'s Inc. 220*l* and Ho; Pop. Trinity, 1708 St. Mary 1713.) Formerly Fell. and Tut. of Wad. Coll. Ox. 1846–52; R. of Hamstall-Ridware, Lichfield, 1852–58; V. of Stoneleigh, Warw. 1858–62. [19]

TRINDER, Daniel, *Teddington Parsonage, Twickenham, Middlesex, S.W.*—Ex. Coll. Ox. 2nd cl. Lit. Hum. Ellerton Theol. Prize, B.A. and M.A. 1855; Deac. 1852 by Bp of Ex; Pr. 1856, by Bp of Ox. P. C. of Teddington, Dio. Lon. 1857. (Patron, Earl of Bradford; P. C.'s Inc. 65*l* and Ho; Pop. 2500.) Formerly C. of Probus, Cornwall, 1852–54, St. Paul's, Oxford, 1854–57. [20]

TRINGHAM, William, *Busbridge Rectory, Godalming, Surrey.*—St. John's Coll. Ox. M.A. 1857; Deac. 1856 and Pr. 1857 by Bp of Win. R. of Busbridge, Dio. Win. 1865. (Patron, J. C. Ramsden, Esq; Tithe, 300*l*; Glebe, 4½ acres; R.'s Inc. 426*l* and Ho; Pop. 580.) Formerly R. of Wotton Fitzpaine, Dorset, 1858–64. [21]

TRIPP, George, 11, *Taymouth-terrace, Philpot-street, Commercial-road, London, E.*—King's Coll. Lond. Theol. Assoc. 1862; Deac. 1862, Pr. 1863. C. of St. Paul's, Whitechapel, 1862. [22]

TRIPP, Henry, *Winford Rectory, near Bristol.*—Wor. Coll. Ox. 2nd cl. Lit. Hum. and B.A. 1839, M.A. 1841; Deac. 1842, Pr. 1851. R. of Winford, Dio. B. and W. 1858. (Patron, Wor. Coll. Ox; Tithe, 480*l*; Glebe and Ho; Pop. 934.) Formerly Fell of Wor. Coll. Ox. Sub-Warden of St. Columba's Coll. Ireland. Author, *Sermon on the Opening of the Girls' School, Silverton*, 1848; *Selections from Percy's Reliques*, Bell and Daldy, 2*s* 6*d*; *Hymns for Young and Old*, 8*d*; *Scripture Catechism on Religious Error* (Dissent), 1*d*. [23]

TRIPP, James, *Spofforth Rectory, Wetherby, Yorks.*—Ch. Coll. Cam. B.A. 1809; Deac. 1810 and Pr. 1811 by Bp of Win. R. of Spofforth, Dio. Rip. 1847. (Patron, Lord Leconfield; Tithe, 1617*l* 12*s* 8*d*; Glebe, 62 acres; R.'s Inc. 1670*l* and Ho; Pop. 2051.) Rural Dean. [24]

TRIPP, John, *The Rectory, Sampford Brett, Williton, Taunton, Somerset.*—Ox. B.A. 1844, Stud. of Wells Theol. Coll. 1844–45; Deac. 1845 and Pr. 1846 by Bp of B. and W. R. of Sampford Brett, Dio. B. and W. 1865. (Patrons, Trustees of Charles Tripp, D.D. of Silverton, Devon; Tithe, comm. 300*l*; Glebe, 39 acres; R.'s Inc. 400*l* and Ho; Pop. 280.) Chap. of the Williton Union 1848. Formerly C. of Carhampton with Road Huish, Somerset [25]

TRIPP, Robert Henry, *Alternun Vicarage, Launceston.*—Ex. Coll. Ox. 2nd cl. Lit. Hum. and B.A. 1822, M.A. 1826; Deac. 1824 and Pr. 1825 by Bp of Ex. V. of Alternun, Dio. Ex. 1842. (Patrons, D. and C. of Ex; Tithe—App. 264*l*, V. 330*l*; Glebe, 113 acres; V.'s Inc. 400*l* and Ho; Pop. 1206.) Formerly P. C. of St. Sidwell's, Exeter, 1828–42. Author, Single Sermons and Tracts. [1]

TRIPP, Robert Henry, Jun., *Herriard, Hants.*—Magd. Hall. Ox. B.A. 1858; Deac. 1859 and Pr. 1860 by Bp of Win. C. of Herriard 1861. Formerly C. of Old Alresford, and East Worldham, Hants. [2]

TRIST, Jeremiah, 21, *Regent-street, Plymouth.*—Lin. Coll. Ox. B.A. 1853, M.A. 1856; Deac. 1854 and Pr. 1855 by Bp of Ex. Formerly Asst. C. of Sutton-on-Plym, Plymouth, 1863–66. [3]

TRIST, Samuel, Peter John, *Veryan Vicarage, Grampound, Cornwall.*—Oriel Coll. Ox. 2nd cl. Lit. Hum. and B.A. 1812, M.A. 1815; Deac. 1816 and Pr. 1817 by Bp of Ex. V. of Veryan, Dio. Ex. 1829. (Patrons, D. and C. of Ex; Tithe—App. 773*l*, V. 367*l* 11*s* 6*d*; Glebe, 60 acres; V.'s Inc. 450*l* and Ho; Pop. 1399.) Author, A Paper on the Limestone of Veryan, in *Cornwall Geological Transactions*; *A Sermon* (addressed to the Members of the Friendly Soc. Truro). [4]

TRISTRAM, Henry Baker, *Greatham Vicarage, Stockton-on-Tees.*—Lin. Coll. Ox. 2nd cl. Lit. Hum. B.A. 1844, M.A. 1846; Deac. 1845 and Pr. 1846 by Bp of Ex. Mast. of the Hospital of God in Greatham, Dio. Dur. 1860. (Patron, Bp of Dur; Mast.'s Inc. 350*l*.) V. of Greatham, Dio. Dur. 1860. (Patron, Mast. of Greatham Hospital; Tithe—Imp. 289*l*, V. 65*l*; Glebe, 32 acres; V.'s Inc. 190*l* and Ho; Pop. 779.) Surrogate; Chap. to the Earl of Donoughmore; F.L.S. Formerly C. of Morchard Bishop, Devon, 1845–46; Lect. of Pembroke, Bermuda, and acting Naval Chap. Dockyard, Bermuda, 1847–49; R. of Castle Eden, Durham, 1849–60. Author, *The Great Sahara*, Murray, 1860, 15*s*; *The Land of Israel, Journal of Travels with Reference to its Physical History*, S.P.C.K. 1865, 21*s*, 2nd ed. revised, 1866; *Natural History of the Bible*, S.P.C.K. 1867, 7*s* 6*d*; *Ornithology of Palestine*, with coloured plates, Van Voorst, 1866; *Winter Ride in Palestine, Vacation Tourists*, Macmillan, 1864; *The Liberation Society and Church Endowments*, 1862, 6*d*; *Address to Tyneside Naturalists*, Newcastle, 1862, 1*s* 6*d*; Papers in the *Journal* of the Linnean Society, the Zoological Society's *Proceedings, The Ibis, Contemporary Review, Sunday Magazine, Sunday at Home*, and other theological and natural history publications; various Sermons and Lectures; A Contributor to Dr. Smith's *Dictionary of the Bible.* [5]

TRITTON, Robert, *Morden Rectory, Mitcham, Surrey, S.*—St. John's Coll. Cam. B.A. 1817, M.A. 1818; Deac. 1817 by Bp of Ely, Pr. 1818 by Bp of Herf. R. of Morden, Dio. Win. 1835. (Patron, Rev. R. Garth; Tithe, 425*l*; Glebe, 14½ acres; R.'s Inc. 450*l* and Ho; Pop. 654.) Surrogate; Rural Dean 1835. Formerly C. of Titsey and Tattersfield, Surrey, 1817–33. Author, *Reflections on the Office and Duties of the Clergy* (a Visitation Sermon), 1837. [6]

TRITTON, Robert Biscoe, *Otford Parsonage, Sevenoaks, Kent.*—Trin. Coll. Cam. B.A. 1841, M.A. 1844; Deac. 1842 and Pr. 1843 by Bp of Lon. P. C. of Otford, Dio. Cant. 1845. (Patrons, D. and C. of Westminster; Tithe—App. 666*l*; P. C.'s Inc. 174*l* and Ho; Pop. 804.) [7]

TROCKE, Thomas, *Pembroke Lodge, Brighton.*—Pemb. Coll. Cam. B.A. 1823, M.A. 1826; Deac. 1825 and Pr. 1826 by Bp of Lin. Min. of the Chapel Royal, Brighton, Dio. Chich. 1834. (Patron, V. of Brighton; Min.'s Inc. 120*l* from pew rents, 680 sittings let, 122 free.) Surrogate for Archdeaconry of Lewes 1856. Formerly C. of Brighton 1832–34; Chap. to H.M. Troops at Brighton 1836–51. [8]

TROLLOPE, A. B., *Cowlam, Driffield, Yorks.*—R. of Cowlam, Dio. York, 1862. (Patron, Rev. T. F. Foord Bowes; R.'s Inc. 300*l*; Pop. 69.) [9]

TROLLOPE, Charles, *St. Cuthbert's Rectory, Bedford.*—Deac. 1845, Pr. 1846. R. of St. Cuthbert's, Bedford, Dio. Ely, 1852. (Patron, Ld Chan; Glebe, 36 acres; R.'s Inc. 146*l* and Ho; Pop. 787.) [10]

TROLLOPE, The Ven. Edward, *Leasingham Rectory, Sleaford, Lincolnshire.*—Ch. Ch. Ox. B.A. 1839, M.A. 1855; Deac. 1840 and Pr. 1841 by Bp of Lin. R. of Leasingham with Roxholm, Dio. Lin. 1843. (Patron, Sir J. Thorold, Bart; Leasingham, Tithe, 642*l*; Glebe, 40 acres; Roxholm, Tithe, 255*l*; R.'s Inc. 977*l* and Ho; Pop. 473.) Preb. of Lincoln 1861; Archd. of Stow 1867; Dom. Chap. to Earl Somers; Fell. of the Soc. of Antiquaries. Author, *Illustrations of Ancient Art*, 4to, 1854, 25*s*; *Life of Pope Adrian IV.* 4to, 1856; *The Captivity of John, King of France*, 1857; *A Handbook of Lincoln*, 1857; *Temple Bruer and the Templars*, 1857; *The Introduction of Christianity into Lincolnshire*, 1857; *Labyrinths Ancient and Mediæval*, 1858; *Sepulchral Memorials*, sm. 4to, 1858; *Fens and Submarine Forests*, 1859; *The Danes in Lincolnshire*, 1859; *Memorabilia of Grimsby*, 1859; *The Use and Abuse of Red Bricks*, 1859; *The Roman House at Apethorpe*, 1859; *The History of Worksop*, 1860; *Monastic Gatehouses*, 1860; *The Life of the Saxon Hereward*, 1861; *History of Anne Askewe*, 1862; *Battle of Bosworth Field*, 1862; *Shadows of the Past*, 1863; *The Raising of the Royal Standard at Nottingham*, 1864; *Spilsby and other Churches*, 1865; *Gainsborough and other Churches*, 1866; *The Norman Sculptures of Lincoln Cathedral*, 1866. [11]

TROLLOPE, John, *Crowmarsh Rectory (Oxon), near Wallingford, Berks.*—Wad. Coll. Ox. B.A. 1824, M.A. 1826; Deac. 1824 and Pr. 1825 by Bp of Lin. R. of Crowmarsh Gifford, Dio. Ox. 1844. (Patron, Lord Barrington; Tithe, 247*l*; R.'s Inc. 247*l* and Ho; Pop. 342.) [12]

TROLLOPE, John Joseph, *Wigmore, near Leominster.*—Pemb. Coll. Ox. Hon. 4th cl. Lit. Hum. and B.A. 1840; Deac. 1840, Pr. 1841. V. of Wigmore, Dio. Herf. 1842. (Patron, Bp of Herf; Tithe—App. 172*l*, V. 155*l*; Glebe, 1½ acres; V.'s Inc. 200*l*; Pop. 499.) P. C. of Leinthall-Starkes, Herefordshire, Dio. Herf. 1842. (Patron, A. R. B. Knight, Esq; Tithe—App. 140*l* 1*s* 9*d*; P. C.'s Inc. 50*l*; Pop. 144.) [13]

TROTMAN, Edward Fiennes, *South Burcombe Parsonage, near Salisbury.*—New Coll. Ox. B.C.L. 1855. P. C. of South Burcombe, Dio. Salis. 1858. (Patron, Mast. of St. John's Hospital, Wilton; P. C.'s Inc. 60*l* and Ho; Pop. 374.) Fell. of New Coll. Ox. [14]

TROTTER, Charles Dale, *Haverton Hill, Billingham, Durham.*—Dur. B.A. 1853, M.A. 1856; Deac. 1854 by Bp of Dur. Pr. 1856 by Bp of Man. for Bp of Dur. P. C. of Haverton Hill, Dio. Dur. 1862. (Patrons, D. and C. of Dur; P. C.'s Inc. 330*l* and Ho; Pop. 800.) Formerly C. of Brancepeth, Durham, 1854–56, Egglescliffe 1856–63. [15]

TROTTER, Coutts.—Trin. Coll. Cam. 36th Wrang. and 18th Cl. 2nd in 2nd cl. Cl. Trip. 1859, B.A. 1859, M.A. 1862; Deac. 1863 and Pr. 1864 by Bp of Ely. Fell. of Trin. Coll. Cam. 1861. Formerly C. of St. Mary's, Kidderminster, 1863; St. George's, Kidderminster. 1864. [16]

TROTTER, Edward Bush, *Habergham Eaves, Burnley.*—Ch. Coll. Cam. Jun. Opt. 3rd cl. Theol. Trip. and B.A. 1865; Deac. 1866 and Pr. 1867 by Bp of Man. C. of Trinity, Habergham Eaves, 1866. Author, *Cambridge Children's Hymnal*, Macintosh, 1868, 2nd ed. 1867, 2*d*; *Experiences of a Sunday School Teacher*, Ch. of Eng. Sunday School Institute, 1*d*; etc. [17]

TROTTER, Thomas Lewis, *Great Stainton Rectory, Bishopton, Stockton-on-Tees.*—Lin. Coll. Ox. B.A 1832, M.A. 1836; Deac. 1833, Pr. 1834. R. of Great Stainton, Dio. Dur. 1841. (Patron, Ld Chan; Tithe, 270*l*; Glebe, 48 acres; R.'s Inc. 355*l* and Ho; Pop. 140.) [18]

TROUGHTON, George, *Higher Bebington Parsonage, Birkenhead.*—Queens' Coll. Cam. LL.B. 1851; Deac. 1851 and Pr. 1852 by Bp of Man. P. C. of Ch. Ch. Higher Bebington, Dio. Ches. 1859. (Patron, the present P. C.) [19]

TROUGHTON, John Ellis, *Aberhafesp, Newtown, Montgomeryshire.*—Corpus Coll. Cam. B.A. 1835,

M.A. 1840. R. of Aberhafesp, Dio. St. A. 1864. (Patron, Bp of St. A; R.'s Inc. 360*l* and Ho; Pop. 486.) Formerly C. of St. John's, Hawarden, Flints. [1]

TROUSDALE, Robert, *Stretford, near Manchester.*—St. John's Coll. Cam. B.A. 1865; Deac. 1866 by Bp of Man. C. of Stretford 1866. [2]

TROUTBECK, John, *Cathedral, Manchester.*—Univ. Coll. Ox. B.A. 1856, M.A. 1858; Deac. 1855 and Pr. 1857 by Bp of B. and W. Min. Can. and Precentor of Man. Cathl. 1864 (Inc. 250*l*); Surrogate. Formerly C. of St. Cuthbert's, Wells, Somerset, 1855–58; V. of Dacre, Cumberland, 1858–64. [3]

TROW, Isaac William, *Bray, Maidenhead.*—Jesus Coll. Cam. B.A. 1856. C. of Bray 1864. Formerly C. of Wellington, Salop, 1856–59; P. C. of Bishop and C. of St. James's, Stratford-on-Avon 1859–62; C. of Kinwarton 1863–64. [4]

TRUEMAN, Edward, *North Grimston, Malton, Yorks.*—Wor. Coll. Ox. B.A. 1825, M.A. 1826; Deac. 1826, Pr. 1827. V. of North Grimston, Dio. York, 1827. (Patron, Abp of York; Modus, 6*l* 12*s*; Glebe, 156 acres; V.'s Inc. 160*l* and Ho; Pop. 181.) V. of Langtoft with Cotton, P. C. Dio. York, 1827. (Patron, Abp of York; Langtoft with Cotton, Tithe, 149*l*; Glebe, 320 acres; V.'s Inc. 479*l* and Ho; Pop. Langtoft 688, Cotton 95.) [5]

TRUEMAN, Samuel, *Nempnett, near Bristol.*—St. John's Coll. Cam. B.A. 1847, M.A. 1850; Deac. 1849 and Pr. 1852 by Bp of Nor. R. of Nempnett, Dio. B. and W. 1859. (Patron, the present R; Tithe, 265*l*; Glebe, 35*l*; R.'s Inc. 300*l* and Ho; Pop. 259.) Formerly C. of Banningham, Norfolk; Head Mast. of the Free Gr. Sch. Ormskirk, Lancashire; Asst. Mast. of King Edward VI.'s Sch. Bath. [6]

TRUMAN, George William Harrison, *Allonby Parsonage, Maryport, Cumberland.*—Queens' Coll. Cam. B.A. 1860; Deac. 1860 by Bp of Carl. P. C. of Allonby, Dio. Carl. 1863. (Patron, V. of Bromfield; P. C.'s Inc. 94*l* and Ho; Pop. 580.) Formerly C. of Wythop, Cumberland, 1860.) [7]

TRUMAN, John, *Mintern-Magna Rectory, Cerne, Dorset.*—St. Cath. Coll. Cam. 1824, M.A. 1827; Deac. 1823 and Pr. 1824 by Bp of Ex. R. of Mintern-Magna, Dio. Salis. 1835. (Patron, Henry Gerard Sturt, Esq. M.P; Tithe, 130*l*; Glebe, 5 acres; R.'s Inc. 150*l* and Ho; Pop. 330.) C. of Hillfield, Dorset, 1857. Formerly C. of Warbstow and Treneglos 1823, Mary-Tavy 1824, Whimple 1828, More-Critchill 1831. [8]

TRUMAN, John Morley, *Woodlands, near Wimborne, Dorset.*—Caius Coll. Cam. B.A. 1858; Deac. 1858 and Pr. 1859 by Bp of Ches. C. of Horton with Woodlands 1865. Formerly C. of St. Mary's, Bootle, near Liverpool, 1858, Wimberne St. Giles, near Salisbury, 1862. [9]

TRUMPER, William, *Clifford Vicarage, Hay, Herefordshire.*—V. of Clifford, Dio. Herf. 1818. (Patron, the present V; Tithe—App. 503*l* 16*s* 3*d*, Imp. 205*l* 8*s*, V. 337*l* 10*s*; V.'s Inc. 351*l* and Ho; Pop. 895.) [10]

TRUSS, William Nicholas, *Donington, Albrighton, near Wolverhampton.*—Caius Coll. Cam. 2nd cl. Civil Law S.C.L. 1856, Theol. Coll. Wells 1857; Deac. 1857 and Pr. 1858 by Bp of B. and W. C. of Donington 1864. Formerly C. of Paulton, near Bristol, 1858–59, Guilsborough, Northants, 1859–64. Author, *Sermon* (on the death of the Rev. J. D. Watson, thirty years Vicar of Guilsborough). Editor of *Relations of Science* by Rev. J. M. Ashley. [11]

TRYE, Charles Brandon, *Leckhampton Rectory, Cheltenham.*—Brasen. Coll. Ox. B.A. 1828, M.A. 1831; Deac. 1829 and Pr. 1830 by Bp of Glouc. R. of Leckhampton, Dio. G. and B. 1830. (Patron, the present R; Glebe, 170 acres; R.'s Inc. 470*l* and Ho; Pop. 2523.) [12]

TRYE, John Rawlin, *Great Whitcombe Rectory, near Gloucester.*—Jesus Coll. Ox. B.A. 1834, M.A. 1837. R. of Great Whitcombe, Dio. G. and B. 1845. (Patrons, Trustees; Tithe, 132*l* 5*s* 9*d*; Glebe, 1 acre; R.'s Inc. 134*l* and Ho; Pop. 165.) [13]

TRYE, R. E., *Cam, Dursley, Gloucestershire.*—C. of Cam. [14]

TRYER, Henry, *Goodwood, Petworth, Sussex.*—Dom. Chap. to the Duke of Richmond. [15]

TRYON, Charles Alsager, *Alsager, Stoke-on-Trent.*—St. John's Coll. Cam. B.A. 1842; Deac. 1844 and Pr. 1845 by Bp of Lon. P. C. of Alsager, Dio. Ches. 1846. (Patrons, Lords and Ladies of the Manor; Tithe—App. 240*l*; Glebe, 50 acres; P. C.'s Inc. 240*l* and Ho; Pop. 708.) [16]

TUBBS, George Ibberson, *Reading.*—Deac. 1847, Pr. 1848. Min. of St. Mary's, Reading, Dio. Ox. 1852. (Patrons, fifteen Trustees; Min.'s Inc. 580*l*.) [17]

TUCK, George Robert, *Wallington Rectory, Baldock, Herts.*—Emman. Coll. Cam. 9th Wrang. and B.A. 1828, M.A. 1831; Deac. 1831, Pr. 1832. R. of Wallington, Dio. Roch. 1838. (Patron, the Mast. of Emman. Coll. Cam. in trust for the Fellows; Tithe, comm. 430*l* 10*s* 6*d*; Glebe, 20 acres; R.'s Inc. 456*l* 15*s* 6*d* and Ho; Pop. 238.) Formerly Fell. and Tut. of Emman. Coll. Cam. [18]

TUCK, John Johnson, *Little Wymondley, Stevenage, Herts.*—Emman. Coll. Cam. B.A. 1809, M.A. 1814; Deac. 1811, Pr. 1812. [19]

TUCK, Richard Holmes, *Vicarage, Ringwood, Hants.*—King's Coll. Cam. B.A. 1840, M.A. 1843; Deac. 1844 and Pr. 1845 by Bp of Lin. V. of Ringwood with Harbridge C. Dio. Win. 1862. (Patron, King's Coll. Cam; Tithe, 1300*l*; Glebe, 9 acres; V.'s Inc. 1300*l* and Ho; Pop. Ringwood 3750, Harbridge 240.) Rural Dean of Fordingbridge West 1866; Surrogate 1862. Formerly C. of Moulton, Suffolk, 1845–46, S. Mimms, Herts, 1846–47, St. Neots, Hunts, 1847–48, Ewhurst, Sussex, 1848–62. [20]

TUCK, Thomas Ridout, *Epping, Essex.*—Caius Coll. Cam. B.M. 1836; Deac. 1848, Pr. 1849. P. C. of St. John's, Epping, Dio. Roch. 1852. (Patrons, Trustees; P. C.'s Inc. 120*l*; Pop. 2105.) [21]

TUCK, William Gilbert, *Tostock House, Woolpit, Suffolk.*—Jesus Coll. Cam. B.A. 1833, Emman. Coll. Cam. M.A. 1834; Deac. 1834, Pr. 1835. R. of Tostock, Dio. Ely, 1861. (Patron, the present R; R.'s Inc. 240*l* and Ho; Pop. 382.) Formerly C. of Tostock. [22]

TUCKER, Charles, *Charminster, Dorchester.*—Wad. Coll. Ox. 2nd cl. Lit. Hum. and B.A. 1823, M.A. 1827; Deac. 1825, Pr. 1826. P. C. of Charminster with Stratton V. Dio. Salis. 1838. (Patron, Rev. G. Pickard; Tithe—App. 510*l*, Imp. 155*l*, P. C. 12*l*; Stratton, Tithe—Imp. 275*l* 10*s* 7*d*, P. C. 5*l* 12*s*; P. C.'s Inc. 157*l*; Pop. Charminster 1020, Stratton 351.) [23]

TUCKER, Dennis, *Sandon Vicarage, Royston, Herts.*—St. Peter's Coll. Cam. B.A. 1829, M.A. 1835; Deac. 1829, Pr. 1830. V. of Sandon, Dio. Roch. 1841. (Patron, Bp of Roch; Tithe—App. 604*l* 3*s*, V. 249*l* 7*s*; Glebe, 2 acres; V.'s Inc. 280*l* and Ho; Pop, 771.) Author, *Memoir of an only surviving beloved Son.* [24]

TUCKER, Frederick Henry, *Tavistock, Devon.*—St. John's Coll. Cam. M.A; Deac. 1855 by Bp of Llan. Pr. 1856 by Bp of Ex. P. C. of Horrabridge, Dio. Ex. 1867. (Patron, Bp of Ex; Tithe, 40*l*; P. C.'s Inc. 140*l*; Pop. 1500.) Formerly C. of Dawlish, and South Brent, Devon. [25]

TUCKER, George Windsor, *The Parsonage, Forest-row, near East Grinstead, Sussex.*—Trin. Coll. Ox. B.A. 1855; Deac. 1857 and Pr. 1859 by Bp of Ches. C. in sole charge of Forest-row 1864. Formerly C. of Tattenhall 1857, Great Crosby, near Liverpool, 1858, East Grinstead 1862. [26]

TUCKER, Henry Tippetts, *Leigh Court, Angersleigh, Wellington, Somerset.*—St. John's Coll. Ox. B.A. 1820, M.A. 1823. R. of Angersleigh, Dio. B. and W. 1842. (Patron, the present R; Tithe, 103*l*; Glebe, 17 acres; R.'s Inc. 151*l*; Pop. 30.) R. of Clayhidon, Devon, Dio. Ex. 1848. (Patron, G. Burnand, Esq; Tithe, 615*l*; Glebe, 110 acres; R.'s Inc. 715*l* and Ho; Pop. 619.) Rural Dean of Dunkeswell. [27]

TUCKER, Henry William, 5, *Park-place, St. James's-street, S.W.*—Magd. Coll. Ox. B.A. 1854, M.A. 1859; Deac. 1854, Pr. 1855. Asst. Sec. to the S.P.G. 1865. Formerly C. of Chantry, Somerset, 1854–56, West Buckland 1856–60, Devoran, Cornwall, 1860–65. [28]

TUCKER, John, *West Hendred Vicarage, Wantage, Berks.*—Corpus Coll. Ox. B.A. 1813, M.A. 1817, B.D. 1825; Deac. 1818, Pr. 1819. V. of West Hendred, Dio. Ox. 1852. (Patron, Corpus Coll. Ox; Tithe—App. 15s. Imp. 549*l* 1*s* 7*d*, V. 134*l* 8*s* 2*d*; V.'s Inc. 662*l* and Ho; Pop. 351.) Formerly Fell. of Corpus Coll. Ox. [1]

TUCKER, John, *Lannarth Parsonage, Redruth, Cornwall.*—Literate; Deac. and Pr. 1827. P. C. of Lannarth, Dio. Ex. 1845. (Patron, the present P. C; Glebe, ¾ acre; P. C.'s Inc. 208*l* and Ho; Pop. 2615.) Formerly R. of St. Peter's, in British Guiana. Author, *Twenty Sermons on some of the Principal Doctrines and Duties of Christianity*, 1830; *An Answer to a Letter from the Rev. Leonard Strong, late Rector of St. Matthew's, Demerara, on his Secession from the Established Church*, Demerara, 1839; *Spiritual Counsel, or the Christian Pastor's Solemn Address to his Parishioners*; *The Apparition, or the Ghost of Archbishop Cranmer, Deciding the Baptismal and Predestinarian Controversy*, 1851; *Scriptural contrasted with Fanatical Conversion, a Reply to a Letter of the Rev. W. Haslam, addressed to the Ven. the Archdeacon of Cornwall, in which the Ministerial Character of the Clergy of the Church of England is falsely aspersed*, Truro, 1853. [2]

TUCKER, John Kinsman, *Pettaugh Rectory, Stoneham, Suffolk.*—St. Peter's Coll. Cam. B.A. 1840; Deac. 1841, Pr. 1842. R. of Pettaugh, Dio. Nor. 1844. (Tithe, 194*l* 10*s*; Glebe, 18 acres, R.'s Inc. 240*l* and Ho; Pop. 275.) Author, *A Short Catechism on Confirmation*; *Church Catechism explained and illustrated by Anecdotes and Examples* (by a Country Clergyman). [3]

TUCKER, Marwood, *Widworthy Rectory, Honiton, Devon.*—Ball. Coll. Ox. Scho. of, Ex. Coll. Fell. of, B.A. 1825, M.A. 1828; Deac. 1826 and Pr. 1827 by Bp of Ex. R. of Widworthy, Dio. Ex. 1852. (Patron, Sir E. M. Elton, Bart; Tithe, 200*l*; Glebe, 30 acres; R.'s Inc. 240*l* and Ho; Pop. 188.) [4]

TUCKER, Richard Thomas, *Bermuda.*—Queens' Coll. Cam. B.A. 1828; Deac. 1830, Pr. 1831. R. and Rural Dean of St. George's, Bermuda. [5]

TUCKER, Samuel, *Trieste.*—Deac. 1848 by Bp of Pet. Pr. 1856 by Bp of Win. Consular Chap. at Trieste. [6]

TUCKER, William Guise, *Greenwich.*—St. Peter's Coll. Cam. B.A. 1835; Deac. 1835, Pr. 1836. Chap. of Greenwich Hospital. Formerly C. of Charlton Kings 1835–36, Springfield 1836–44; Chap. to H.M.'s Dockyard and Naval Hospital, Malta, 1844–49; Miss. in Canada under the S.P.G. 1850–52. Author, *Argumentative Sermons exhibiting the Truth of Christianity, in a Review of Our Lord's consistent Life and Method of preaching*, Rivingtons, 1844, 3*s* 6*d*. [7]

TUCKER, W. H., *Dunton Waylett Rectory, Brentwood, Essex.*—R. of Dunton Waylett, Dio. Roch. 1845. (Patron, King's Coll. Cam; R.'s Inc. 380*l* and Ho; Pop. 174.) [8]

TUCKWELL, Henry, *Headingley Parsonage, Leeds.*—St. Bees; M.A. by Abp of Cant. 1853; Deac. 1845 and Pr. 1846 by Bp of Newfoundland. P. C. of Headingley, Dio. Rip. 1865. (Patron, V. of Leeds; P. C.'s Inc. 290*l* and Ho; Pop. 1450.) Formerly Head Mast. of the Coll. Sch. and Prin. of the Theol. Coll. St. John's, Newfoundland, 1854–55; C. of Blockley, Worcestershire, 1854–55, and Woodhouse, Leeds, 1855–57; Chap. of the Borough Gaol, Leeds, 1857–64; V. of Little Ouseburn 1864–65. [9]

TUCKWELL, Lewis Stacey, *Magdalen College, Oxford.*—Magd. Coll. Ox. M.A. 1864; Deac. 1864 and Pr. 1866 by Bp of Lin. Chap. of Magd. Coll. and C. of Headington, Oxford. Formerly C. of Frampton, Lincolnshire, 1864–67. [10]

TUCKWELL, William, *The College School, Taunton.*—New Coll. Ox. B.A. 1852, M.A. 1855; Deac. 1854 and Pr. 1858 by Bp of Ox. Head Mast. of the Coll. Sch. Taunton. Formerly Asst. Mast. at St. Columba's Coll. Ireland, 1853; C. of St. Mary Magdalen's, Oxford, 1856; Head Mast. of New Coll. Sch. Oxford, 1857; Chap. and Precentor of New Coll. Ox. 1860. Author, *First Latin Grammar, Part I. Accidence*, Oxford, 1862; *Latin Vocabulary*, 1862; *The Aim of a Liberal Education* (a Sermon in New Coll. Chapel), Parkers, 1864; *Practical Remarks on the teaching of Physical Science in Schools*, Rivingtons, 6*d*. [11]

TUDBALL, Thomas, *Tiverton, Devon.*—Emman. Coll. Cam. B.A. 1841, M.A. 1845; Deac. 1842 by Bp of G. and B. Pr. 1844 by Bp of Salis. Formerly P. C. of St. Peter's, Marland, N. Devon. [12]

TUDOR, C., *Kirkdale, Helmesley, Yorks.*—P. C. of Kirkdale, Dio. York, 1863. (Patron, Univ. of Ox; P. C.'s Inc. 200*l*; Pop. 1043.) [13]

TUDOR, Richard, *Frampton Vicarage, Dorchester.*—Magd. Hall, Ox. B.A. 1851; Deac. 1851 by Bp of Ox. Pr. 1853 by Bp of Salis. V. of Frampton, Dio. Salis. 1866. (Patrons, R. B. Sheridan, Esq. M.P. and Marcia Maria Sheridan; Tithe, 46*l* 13*s* 4*d*; Glebe, 117*l* 17*s*; V.'s Inc. 164*l* 10*s* 4*d* and Ho; Pop. 435.) Formerly C. of Yarnton, Oxon, 1851, Marshwood, Dorset, 1853, Helston, Cornwall, 1857. Author, *The Decalogue viewed as the Christian's Law with special Reference to the Questions and Wants of the Times*, 1860, 10*s* 6*d*; *England's Night Song at Christmas* (a Sermon on the day of the funeral of the Prince Consort); *Almsgiving in Relation to Church Finance considered in two Sermons*, Macmillans, 1864. [14]

TUDOR, Thomas Owen, *Wyesham, near Monmouth.*—Ex. Coll. Ox. B.A. 1848, M.A. 1852; Deac. 1850 and Pr. 1851 by Bp of G. and B. C. of Llantsenor, Monmouth, 1862. Editor, *Thoughts of Comfort for the Sick and Sorrowful* (Poems by E. L.), Monmouth, 1863, 4*d*; Composer of Music to *Hymn for Eventide*, Novello, 1864. [15]

TUDOR, William Henry, *Syderstone Rectory, Fakenham, Norfolk.*—Trin. Coll. Cam. B.A. 1829, M.A. 1833; Deac. 1830, Pr. 1831. R. of Syderstone, Dio. Nor. 1844. (Patron, Marquis of Cholmondeley; Tithe, 562*l*; Glebe, 50 acres; R.'s Inc. 617*l* and Ho; Pop. 528.) Chap. to the Marquis of Cholmondeley. [16]

TUFNELL, Edward, *Easebourne, Midhurst, Sussex.*—Trin. Hall. Cam. B.A. 1855, M.A. 1859; Deac. 1857 by Bp of Pet. Pr. 1858 by Bp of Man. P. C. of Easebourne, Dio. Chich. 1863. (Patron, Earl of Egmont; P. C.'s Inc. 106*l* and Ho; Pop. 859.) Formerly C. of Wootton 1857, Midhurst 1861. [17]

TUFNELL, George, *Thornton-Watlass Rectory, Bedale, Yorks.*—Emman. Coll. Cam. B.A. 1824; Deac. and Pr. 1825. R. of Thornton-Watlass, Dio. Rip. 1852. (Patron, Mark Milbank, Esq; Tithe, 400*l*; Glebe, 45 acres and 3 houses; R.'s Inc. 500*l* and Ho; Pop. 440.) [18]

TUFNELL, George Cressner, *Takeley Vicarage, Essex.*—Wad. Coll. Ox. B.A. 1844, M.A. 1848; Deac. 1849, Pr. 1850. V. of Takeley, Dio. Roch. 1855. (Patron, Bp of Roch; V.'s Inc. 227*l* and Ho; Pop. 1000.) Formerly C. of Denton. [19]

TUFNELL, Thomas Pilkington, *Wormingford Vicarage, Colchester.*—Wad. Coll. Ox. B.A. 1841, M.A. 1846; Deac. 1844, Pr. 1845. V. of Wormingford, Dio. Roch. 1845. (Patron, J. J. Tufnell, Esq; Tithe, Imp. 496*l* 17*s* 6*d*, V. 369*l*; Glebe, 4¾ acres; V.'s Inc. 404*l* and Ho; Pop. 503.) [20]

TUGWELL, Frederick, *St. Andrew's Parsonage, 23, Upper Stamford-street, Blackfriars, S.*—P. C. of St. Andrew's, Lambeth, Dio. Win. 1865. (Patrons, Trustees; P. C.'s Inc. 300*l* and Ho; Pop. 8467.) Surrogate. Formerly C. of Cleator, Cumberland. [21]

TUGWELL, George, *Osborne House, Ilfracombe, Devon.*—Oriel Coll. Ox. B.A. 1852, M.A. 1856; Deac. 1853 and Pr. 1862 by Bp of Ex. Sen. C. of Ilfracombe with sole charge of St. Matthew's, Lee; Sec. to the North Devon Choral-Union 1863. Author, *The Four Seasons of Architecture*, 1853; *Woodleigh, or Life and Death*, 1855; *The Church in the Household* (a Manual of Family Devotion selected from the Book of Common Prayer), 1855; *A Manual of the Sea Anemones commonly found on the English Coast*, J. Van Voorst, 1856, 7*s* 6*d*; *The North Devon Handbook*, 1857, 2nd ed. 1860, 4*s*; *Guide to North Devon*, 1857, 2*s* 6*d*; *The Indian Mutiny of 1857* (a Sermon); *A Book of Verses by a Versemaker*, 1858,

1s 6d; *The Canticles for Morning and Evening Prayer Pointed for Chanting*, Ilfracombe, 1858; *On the Mountain* (North Wales, Notes on its Botany, Geology, Fisheries, &c.), Bentley, 1862, 7s 6d; *The North Devon Scenery Book* (illustrated in chromo-lithography), Simpkin, Marshall and Co. 1863, 10s 6d. [1]

TUGWELL, Lewen, *Bermondsey Rectory, S.E.*—St. Edm. Hall, Ox. B.A. 1850, M.A. 1853; Deac. 1851 and Pr. 1852 by Bp of Nor. R. of Bermondsey, Surrey, Dio. Win. 1865. (Patroness, Mrs. Ram; Tithe, 17l; R.'s Inc. 350l and Ho; Pop. 23,574.) Formerly C. of St. Stephen's, Ipswich, 1851, Christchurch, Dover, 1853; Chap. to the Royal Sea Bathing Infirmary, Margate, and C. of Garlinge, near Margate, 1854–58, P. C. of St. Andrew's, Lambeth, 1858–65. [2]

TUKE, Francis Edward, *Borden Vicarage, Sittingbourne, Kent.*—Brasen. Coll. Ox. B.A. 1846, M.A. 1863; Deac. 1848 and Pr. 1849 by Abp of Cant. C. of Borden 1866. Formerly C. of St. Martin's, Canterbury, 1848–51, Bishopsbourne 1851–52, Upper Deal 1852–53, Willesborough 1854–57; P. C. of Wye 1858–66. [3]

TUNNARD, John, *Frampton House, near Boston.*—Ex. Coll. Ox. B.A. 1837, M.A. 1845; Deac. 1837 and Pr. 1838 by Bp of Pet. V. of Frampton, Dio. Lin. 1840. (Patron, the present V; V.'s Inc. 184l; Pop. 843.) [4]

TUPHOLME, Benjamin Seymour, *Ealing, Middlesex, W.*—Magd. Hall, Ox. Lusby Scho. Double 3rd and B.A. 1859, M.A. 1861; Deac. 1860 and Pr. 1861 by Bp of G. and B. C. of Ch. Ch. Ealing, 1862. Formerly C. of Tortworth, Glouc. 1860–62. [5]

TURING, John Robert, *Trinity College, Cambridge.*—Trin. Coll. Cam. B.A. 1848, M.A. 1851; Deac. 1848 and Pr. 1849 by Bp of Ex. Chap. of Trin. Coll. Cam. 1859; C. of Tydd St. Mary, Lincolnshire. Formerly C. of Axminster, Devon, 1848–51; P. C. of Trinity, Rotherhithe, Lond. 1851–59. [6]

TURLE, William Honey, *The Cloisters, Westminster Abbey, London, S.W.*—New Coll. Ox. 4th cl. Lit. Hum. and B.A. 1851, M.A. 1855; Deac. 1854 and Pr. 1855 by Bp of Lon. P. C. of St. Matthew's, Great Peter-street, Westminster, Dio. Lon. 1866. (Patron, R. of St. John's, Westminster; P. C.'s Inc. 500l; Pop. 7536.) Formerly C. of St. Stephen's, Westminster. [7]

TURNBULL, John, *Gateacre, Liverpool.*—Trin. Coll. Cam. 2nd cl. Cl. Trip. and B.A. 1861; Deac. 1862 and Pr. 1863 by Bp of S. and M. C. of St. Jude's, West Derby, Liverpool. Formerly C. of Malew, Isle of Man, 1862–64; Vice-Prin. of King William's Coll. Isle of Man, 1861–64. [8]

TURNBULL, Joseph Corbett, *The College, Cheltenham.*—Trin. Coll. Cam. 1840, Wrang. and B.A. 1841, M.A. 1844; Deac. 1841 and Pr. 1842 by Bp of G. and B. Sen. Math. Mast. of Cheltenham College 1841. [9]

TURNBULL, Robert, *Wybunbury Vicarage, Nantwich, Cheshire.*—St. John's Coll. Cam. B.A. 1848; Deac. 1848 and Pr. 1849 by Bp of Rip. V. of Wybunbury, Dio. Ches. 1858. (Patron, Bp of Lich; Tithe—App. 1761l, V. 329l 5s 7d; Glebe, 12 acres; V.'s Inc. 430l and Ho; Pop. 3746.) Surrogate. Formerly C. of Whitchurch, Salop. [10]

TURNBULL, Thomas Smith, *Blofield Rectory, Norwich.*—Caius Coll. Cam. Wrang. and B.A. 1816, M.A. 1819; Deac. 1822 by Bp of Nor. Pr. 1822 by Bp of Ely. R. of Blofield, Dio. Nor. 1847. (Patron, Caius Coll. Cam; Tithe—App. 10s, R. 945l; Glebe, 54 acres; R.'s Inc. 1030l and Ho; Pop. 1155.) Fell. of the Royal Soc. [11]

TURNBULL, William Stephenson, *Penistone Vicarage, Sheffield.*—St. Peter's Coll. Cam. B.A. 1850, M.A. 1853; Deac. and Pr. 1852 by Bp of Lin. V. of Penistone, Dio. Rip. 1855. (Patron, G. W. B. Bosville, Esq; V.'s Inc. 155l and Ho; Pop. 4887.) P. C. of Midhope, Dio. York, 1855. (Patron, G. W. B. Bosville, Esq; Tithe—App. 14l 10s, Imp. 11l 10s; P. C.'s Inc. 73l; Pop. 340.) Surrogate for Wills in the province of York, and for Marriages in the Dio. of Rip; Dom. Chap. to the Duke of St. Albans. [12]

TURNER, Alfred, *Whitchurch Vicarage, Aylesbury.*—St. John's Coll. Ox. B.A. 1837, M.A. 1840. V. of Whitchurch, Dio. Ox. 1843. (Patron, Ld Chan; V.'s Inc. 60l and Ho; Pop. 884.) [13]

TURNER, Alfred, *Fitzwilliam-terrace, Huddersfield.*—Ch. Coll. Cam. B.A. 1862, M.A. 1865; Deac. 1863 and Pr. 1865 by Bp of Rip. C. of Trinity, Huddersfield, 1865. Formerly C. of St. John's, Huddersfield, 1863–65. [14]

TURNER, Andrew, *St. Giles's, Norwich.*—Trin. Hall, Cam. 2nd cl. Cl. Trip. B.A. 1852, M.A. 1855; Deac. 1852 and Pr. 1853 by Bp of Chich. Formerly C. of Ch. Ch. Brighton, 1852–55; R. of Burnham Deepdale, Norfolk, 1855–63, Chap. at Pau; C. of St. Margaret's Ipswich, 1865–67. [15]

TURNER, Charles, *Grasby Vicarage, Brigg, Lincolnshire.*—Trin. Coll. Cam. Bell's Scho. 1828, B.A. 1830; Deac. and Pr. 1835 by Bp of Lin. V. of Grasby, Dio. Lin. 1835. (Patron, the present V; Glebe, 154 acres; V.'s Inc. 224l and Ho; Pop. 433.) [16]

TURNER, Charles, 17, *Crescent, Norwich.*—St. John's Coll. Cam. B.A. 1832, M.A. 1835; Deac. 1833, Pr. 1834. P. C. of St. Peter Mancroft, Norwich, Dio. Nor. 1848. (Patrons, Parishioners; P. C.'s Inc. 90l; Pop. 2575.) Formerly P. C. of Cringleford, Norfolk, 1835; P. C. of St. Michael-at-Thorn, Norwich, 1837. [17]

TURNER, Charles, *Chesterton, Kineton, Warwickshire.*—P. C. of Morton Morrell, near Kineton, Dio. Wor. 1856. (Patron, W. Little, Esq; Tithe—Imp. 88l 14s 1d; P. C.'s Inc. 120l; Pop. 266.) C. of Chesterton. [18]

TURNER, Charles Beresford, *Bartley, near Southampton.*—Ball. Coll. Ox. B.A. 1839; Deac. 1843 and Pr. 1844 by Bp of Wor. V. of North Eling, Dio. Win. 1863. (Patrons, Trustees; Tithe, 250l; V.'s Inc. 260l; Pop. 1239.) [19]

TURNER, Charles Charretie, *St. Mary Major Rectory, Exeter.*—Trin. Coll. Cam. B.A. 1850, M.A. 1853; Deac. 1853 and Pr. 1855 by Bp of Ex. R. of St. Mary's Major, Exeter, Dio. Ex. 1856. (Patrons, D. and C. of Ex; R.'s Inc. 203l; Pop. 3409.) Formerly C. of St. Mary Magdalene's, Upton, Torquay. [20]

TURNER, Charles Edgar, *Egg Buckland Vicarage, Plymouth.*—Magd. Coll. Cam. B.A. 1850; Deac. 1850, Pr. 1851. V. of Egg Buckland, Dio. Ex. 1861. (Patron, Ld Chan; V.'s Inc. 500l and Ho; Pop. 1348.) Formerly P. C. of All Saints', Little Bolton, Lancashire, 1854–61. [21]

TURNER, Charles Michael, *Aldford Rectory, Chester.*—Caius Coll. Cam. B.A. 1837; Deac. 1837 by Bp of Salis. Pr. 1838 by Bp of Lin. R. of Aldford, Dio. Ches. 1862. (Patron, Marquis of Westminster; Tithe, 317l 16s; Glebe, 21 acres; R.'s Inc. 385l and Ho; Pop. 731.) Formerly V. of Horndon-on-the-Hill 1843; P. C. of Tong 1856. [22]

TURNER, C. S.—C. of St. James's, Enfield, Middlesex. [23]

TURNER, D. P., *Cambridge.*—C. of St. Andrew's-the-Less, Cambridge. [24]

TURNER, Dawson William, *Royal Institution School, Liverpool.*—Magd. Coll. Ox. 2nd cl. Lit. Hum. Exhib. Scho. and Prizeman, B.A. 1838, M.A. 1840, D.C.L.; Deac. 1840. Head Mast. of the Royal Inst. Sch. Liverpool. Author, *Analyses of English, French, Greek and Roman History*, Longmans; *Notes on Herodotus*; *Translation of Pindar*, Bohn; *Ahn's German Grammar* (new ed.) Trübner; *First Italian Teaching Book*, Rivingtons; *The Knights Acharnians, and Birds of Aristophanes with English Notes*, J. H. and J. Parker; *German Handbook*, Routledge. [25]

TURNER, Edward, *Maresfield Rectory, Uckfield, Sussex.*—Ball. Coll. Ox. B.A. 1815, M.A. 1817; Deac. 1817 and Pr. 1818 by Bp of Chich. R. of Maresfield, Dio. Chich. 1837. (Patron, C. S. Butler, Esq; Tithe, 500l; Glebe, 1½ acres; R.'s Inc. 630l and Ho; Pop. 1180.) Formerly R. of Wiggonholt with Greatham 1834–37. [26]

TURNER, Edward Blomfield, *Offord-Cluny Rectory, near Huntingdon.*—Ch. Coll. Cam. Prizeman,

Sen. Opt. and B.A. 1838; Deac. 1839 and Pr. 1840 by Bp. of Lin. R. of Offord-Cluny, Dio. Ely, 1850. (Patron, Bp of Pet; Glebe, 250 acres; R.'s Inc. 400*l* and Ho; Pop. 326.) Author, *Short Family Prayers for my Parishioners*, 1852. [1]

TURNER, Edward Tindal, *Brasenose College, Oxford.*—Trin. Coll. Ox. Scho. 1840, Brasen. Coll. Ox. B.A. 1844, M.A. 1847; Deac. 1852 and Pr. 1853. Fell. and Tut. of Brasen. Coll. Ox; Sen. Proctor of the Univ. of Ox. 1859; Member of the Hebdomadal Council 1860 and 1866. [2]

TURNER, George Francis, *Rede Rectory, Bury St. Edmunds.*—Trin. Coll. Ox. B.A. 1840, M.A. 1844; Deac. 1841 and Pr. 1842 by Bp of Nor. R. of Rede, Dio. Ely, 1848. (Patron, Ld Chan; Tithe, 293*l*; Glebe, 26 acres; R.'s Inc. 320*l* and Ho; Pop. 245.) Formerly Dom. Chap. to the Duke of Cambridge 1841–46; R. of St. Lawrence's, Exeter, 1846–48. [3]

TURNER, George Richard, *Kelshall Rectory, Royston, Herts.*—Caius Coll. Cam. Sen. Opt. B.A. 1847, M.A. 1850; Deac. 1848 and Pr. 1849, by Bp of Ex. R. of Kelshall, Dio. Roch. 1866. (Patron, Ld Chan; Corn Rent, 368*l*; Glebe, 18 acres; R.'s Inc. 395*l* and Ho; Pop. 318.) Formerly C. of Marlborough, Devon, 1848–52. West Tisted, Hants, 1852–54, R. of New Radnor, S. Wales, 1844–66. [4]

TURNER, George Thomas, *Kettleburgh Rectory, Woodbridge, Suffolk.*—Jesus Coll. Cam. B.A. 1816; Deac. 1817 by Bp of Nor. Pr. 1821 by Bp of Salis. R. of Kettleburgh, Dio. Nor. 1840. (Patron, the present R; Tithe, 405*l*; Glebe, 15 acres; R.'s Inc. 420*l* and Ho; Pop. 359.) [5]

TURNER, Herbert Charles, *Heydon, near Royston, Herts.*—Magd. Coll. Cam. Scho. of, Jun. Opt. B.A. 1865; Deac. 1865 and Pr. 1866 by Bp of Roch. C. of Heydon with Little Chishall 1865. [6]

TURNER, Isaac Biass, *Marsworth Vicarage (Bucks), Tring, Herts.*—Trin. Coll. Cam. 7th Sen. Opt. 1st in 2nd cl. Cl. Trip. and B.A. 1841, M.A. 1845; Deac. 1843, Pr. 1845. V. of Marsworth, Dio. Ox, 1847. (Patrons, Trin. Coll. Cam; Glebe, 79 acres; V.'s Inc. 156*l* and Ho; Pop. 549.) [7]

TURNER, James, *Deddington, Oxon.*—Dub. A.B. 1848; Deac. 1848 and Pr. 1849 by Bp of Dur. V. of Deddington with Clifton C. Dio. Ox. 1864. (Patrons, D. and C. of Windsor; V.'s Inc. 190*l* and Ho; Pop. 2024.) Formerly P. C. of Warmley, Glouc. 1859–60. [8]

TURNER, James, *Hart-road, West Hartlepool.*—Sid. Coll. Cam. 4th Sen. Opt. B.A. 1863; Deac. 1863 and Pr. 1865 by Bp of Dur. Sen. C. of West Hartlepool 1867. Formerly C. of Hartlepool 1863. [9]

TURNER, James Francis, *North Tidworth, Marlborough, Wilts.*—Univ. Coll. Dur. B.A. 1851, M.A. 1854; Deac. 1852 and Pr. 1853 by Bp of Dur. R. of North Tidworth, Dio. Salis. 1858. (Patron, Ld Chan; Tithe, 320*l*; Glebe, 15 acres; R.'s Inc. 331*l* and Ho; Pop. 330.) [10]

TURNER, John, *Glenalmond, Perth.*—Asst. Mast. in Trin. Coll. Glenalmond. [11]

TURNER, John Bowman, *Barford, Wymondham, Norfolk.*—Caius Coll. Cam. B.A. 1842, M.A. 1845. R. of Barford, Dio. Nor. 1859. (Patron, Skinner Turner, Esq; R.'s Inc. 300*l*; Pop. 419.) Formerly C. of Barford. [12]

TURNER, John Fisher, *Winkleigh Vicarage, Crediton, Devon.*—Wor. Coll. Ox. 3rd cl. Lit. Hum. and B.A. 1828, M.A. 1833; Deac. 1828, Pr. 1829. V. of Winkleigh, Dio. Ex. 1856. (Patrons, D. and C. of Ex; Tithe—App. 427*l* 12*s*, V. 312*l*; V.'s Inc. 340*l* and Ho; Pop. 1425.) Formerly R. of St. Mary's Major, Exeter, 1829–56; Bodleian Lect. 1856. [13]

TURNER, John James, *Pentrekeylin, Oswestry.*—St. John's Coll. Cam. B.A. 1853, M.A. 1856; Deac. 1854 and Pr. 1855 by Bp of St. A. Formerly C. of Berriew and Aberhafesp. [14]

TURNER, John Jervis William, *Crowborough, Tunbridge Wells.*—St. Peter's Coll. Cam. B.A. 1822; Deac. 1822 and Pr. 1823 by Bp of Nor. Chap. on Sir Henry Fermor's Foundation at Crowborough 1832. [15]

TURNER, John Leaming, 9, *Napier-terrace, Hackney, London, N.E.*—Formerly Lect. of St. Giles's, Cripplegate. Lond. for 32 years. [16]

TURNER, John Richard, *The Vicarage, Wootton-under-Edge, Glouc.*—St. Peter's Coll. Cam. B.A. 1847, M.A. 1850; Deac. 1848 and Pr. 1849 by Bp of Man. C. of Wootton-under Edge 1863. Formerly C. of St. Andrew's, Ancoats, Manchester, 1848, Foxearth, Essex, 1850, Wheplode Drove, Linc. 1854, Spalding, Linc. 1859. [17]

TURNER, John Wilkinson, *Congleton, Cheshire.*—St. Bees; Deac. 1818, Pr. 1819. Chap. to the Congleton Union 1837. [18]

TURNER, Joseph, *The Vicarage, Lancaster.*—Corpus Coll. Cam. B.A. 1824, M.A. 1828; Deac. 1824, Pr. 1825. V. of St. Mary's with Fulwood C. Lancaster, Dio. Man. 1844. (Patron, George Marton, Esq; Tithe—App. 451*l* 7*s*, Imp. 2493*l* 4*s* 10*d*, V. 311*l* 10*s*; Glebe, 20 acres; V.'s Inc. 1824*l* and Ho; Pop. 10,977.) Hon. Can. of Man. 1853; Rural Dean of Lancaster, Surrogate. Formerly R. of Fen-Ditton, Cambs, 1842–44. [19]

TURNER, Joseph Kirby, *Stalmine, Poulton-le-Fylde, Lancashire.*—Trin. Coll. Cam. B.A. 1857; Deac. 1859 and Pr. 1860 by Bp of Ches. P. C. of Stalmine, Dio. Man. 1864. (Patron, V. of Lancaster; Tithe, 260*l*; Glebe, 69 acres; P. C.'s Inc. 370*l*; Pop. 1280.) Formerly C. of Prestbury, Cheshire, 1859–60, Lawton 1860; Asst. Civil Chap. at Gibraltar 1863. [20]

TURNER, Michael, *Cotton Rectory, Stowmarket, Suffolk.*—Emman. Coll. Cam. B.A. 1840, M.A. 1843; Deac. 1841 and Pr. 1842 by Bp of Nor. R. of Cotton, Dio. Nor. 1847. (Patron, the present R; Tithe, 485*l*; Glebe, 18½ acres; R.'s Inc. 510*l* and Ho; Pop. 542.) [21]

TURNER, Power, *Cherrington Rectory, Warwickshire, near Shipston-on-Stour.*—Pemb. Coll. Ox. B.A. 1828, M.A. 1831; Deac. 1831, Pr. 1832. R. of Cherrington, Dio. Wor. 1841. (Patron, the present R; Tithe, 1*l* 2*s* 6*d*; Glebe, 216 acres; R.'s Inc. 340*l* and Ho; Pop. 311.) [22]

TURNER, Reginald Pyndar, *Churchill Rectory, Kidderminster.*—Ball. Coll. Ox. B.A. 1831, M.A. 1834; Deac. 1833, Pr. 1834. R. of Churchill, Dio. Wor. 1841. (Patron, Lord Lyttelton; Tithe, 180*l*; Glebe, 103 acres; R.'s Inc. 308*l* and Ho; Pop. 181.) Formerly C. of Hagley 1833, Frankley 1838. [23]

TURNER, Robert, *Rawcliffe Parsonage, Howden, Yorks.*—St. Bees; Deac. 1829, Pr. 1830. R. of Rawcliffe, Dio. York, 1860. (Patron, G. J. Yarburgh, Esq; P. C.'s Inc. 120*l* and Ho; Pop. 1630.) [24]

TURNER, Rupert, 3, *St. John's-road, New Town, Deptford, Kent, S.E.*—St. Bees; Deac. 1856 and Pr. 1857 by Abp of York. C. of St. Paul's, Deptford, 1860. Formerly C. of Howden, and Lect. of Barmby-upon-the-Marsh, Yorks, 1856–60. [25]

TURNER, Samuel, *Collingham, Newark, Notts.*—St. Bees; Deac. 1845 and Pr. 1846 by Bp of Lich. V. of North Collingham, Dio. Lin. 1858. (Patrons, D. and C. of Pet; V.'s Inc. 300*l*; Pop. 1010.) Formerly C. of Cromwell, Notts. [26]

TURNER, Samuel, *Nettleton, Caistor, Lincolnshire.*—R. of Nettleton, Dio. Lin. 1823. (Patron, the present R; R.'s Inc. 377*l*; Pop. 536.) V. of Cadney, near Kirton-in-Lindsey, Dio. Lin. 1823. (Patron, Earl of Yarborough; Tithe—Imp. 54*l* 18*s*, V. 357*l* 12*s* 6*d*; V.'s Inc. 362*l*; Pop. 570.) [27]

TURNER, Samuel Blois, *South Elmham, Bungay, Suffolk.*—Pemb. Coll. Cam. B.A. 1828. R. of All Saints' with St. Nicholas R. South Elmham, Dio. Nor. 1861. (Patron, Sir R. Adair, Bart; R.'s Inc. 300*l*; Pop. 380.) Formerly P. C. of Little Linstead 1832-61, and Great Linstead 1838–61. [28]

TURNER, Sydney, 15, *Parliament-street, London, S.W.* and *Reigate, Surrey.*—Trin. Coll. Cam. 18th Wrang. and B.A. 1836; Deac. 1837, Pr. 1838. Inspector of Prisons and Reformatories, and Res. Chap. to the Philanthropic Society for the Reformation of Juvenile Offenders. Author, *Mettray*, 1846; *Reformatory Schools*, 1855. [29]

TURNER, Thomas, *Norton Parsonage, near Gloucester.*—Ex. Coll. Ox. B.A. 1834, M.A. 1836; Deac. 1835 and Pr. 1836 by Bp of Win. P. C. of Norton, Dio. G. and B. 1855. (Patrons, D. and C. of Bristol; Tithe—App. 55*l* and 238½ acres of Land in lieu of Tithe; Glebe, 5 acres; P. C.'s Inc. 51*l*; Pop. 458.) [1]

TURNER, Thomas Day, *Denton, Harleston, Norfolk.*—Caius Coll. Cam. B.A. 1862; Deac. 1862 and Pr. 1863 by Bp of G. and B. C. of Denton 1865. Formerly C. of Bishopsworth, near Bristol, 1862–64. [2]

TURNER, Vaughan Charles, *Powerstock, Bridport, Dorset.*—Stud. at the Salis. Theol. Coll; Deac. 1864 by Bp of Salis. C. of Powerstock with West Milton and North Poorton 1864. [3]

TURNER, Walter N., *Gilling Rectory, near York.*—Dub. A.B. 1852, A.M. 1862; Deac. 1857 and Pr. 1858 by Bp of Rip. C. of Gilling 1866. Formerly C. of Pannal, Yorks, 1857–59, East Ilsley, Berks, 1859–66. [4]

TURNER, William, *Barholme, Stamford, Lincolnshire.*—St. John's Coll. Cam. 18th Wrang. and B.A. 1822, M.A. 1825; Deac. 1822 and Pr. 1823 by Bp of Pet. V. of Barholme with Stowe V. Dio. Lin. 1847. (Patrons, the Govs. of Oakham and Uppingham Schs; Barholme, Tithe—Imp. 45*l*, V. 45*l*; Glebe, 70 acres; V.'s Inc. 175*l*; Pop. Barholme 192, Stowe 11.) Author, occasional Contributions to *The Zoologist.* [5]

TURNER, William Hamilton, *Banwell Vicarage, Weston-super-Mare.*—Pemb. Coll. Cam. B.A. 1824, M.A. 1827; Deac. 1826 and Pr. 1827 by Bp of Nor. V. of Banwell, Dio. B. and W. 1838. (Patrons, D. and C. of Bristol; Tithe—App. 225*l*, V. 702*l*; V.'s Inc. 740*l* and Ho; Pop. 1853.) [6]

TURNER, William Henry, *Trent Rectory, Somerset, near Sherborne.*—Corpus Coll. Ox. B.A. 1806, M.A. 1809, B.D. 1812; Deac. 1808, Pr. 1809. R. of Trent, Dio. B. and W. 1835. (Patron, Corpus Coll. Ox; Tithe, 402*l*; Glebe, 48 acres; R.'s Inc. 480*l* and Ho; Pop. 512.) Preb. of Wells 1813. Formerly Fell. of Corpus Coll. Ox. [7]

TURNER, William Jacob, *Litherland, near Liverpool.*—Dur. B.A. 1860; Deac. 1859, Pr. 1860. P. C. of Litherland, Dio. Ches. 1863. (Patrons, Trustees; P. C.'s Inc. 326*l*; Pop. 1600.) Formerly C. of Bedale and Sefton. Author, *The Gospel suited to Man's Need,* Mozley, 1*s.* [8]

TURNER, William Twiss, *Ore Rectory, Hastings, Sussex.*—Trin. Coll. Cam. Wrang. and B.A. 1836, M.A. 1839; Deac. 1839, Pr. 1840. R. of Ore, Dio. Chich. 1847. (Patrons, Trustees; Tithe, 531*l* 3*s* 2*d*; Glebe, 7½ acres; R.'s Inc. 603*l* and Ho; Pop. 1636.) [9]

TURNER, William Vlako, *Spilsby, Lincolnshire.*—Magd. Coll. Cam. B.A. 1848, M.A. 1856; Deac. 1849 and Pr. 1850 by Abp of Cant. P. C. of Spilsby, Dio. Lin. 1854. (Patron, Lord Willoughby D'Eresby; Tithe, 200*l*; Glebe, 30 acres; P. C.'s Inc. 255*l*; Pop. 1467.) Surrogate; Chap. to the Spilsby Ho. of Correction 1856. Formerly C. of St. James's, Dover. [10]

TURNOCK, James Robert, *St. Mary-le-Tower Parsonage, Ipswich.*—Magd. Hall. Ox. B.A. 1851, M.A. 1853; Deac. 1851 and Pr. 1852 by Bp of Wor. P. C. of St. Mary-le-Tower, Ipswich, Dio. Nor. 1861. (Patron, G. C. E. Bacon, Esq; P. C.'s Inc. 90*l* and Ho; Pop. 960.) Formerly C. of St. Lawrence's, Evesham, St. Mary's, Stafford, and Ch. Ch. St. Pancras, Lond; Incumb. of St. John's, Jedburgh, Scotland. Author, *Sermons addressed to the Congregation of St. Mary-le-Tower, Ipswich,* Parkers, 5*s*; etc. [11]

TURNOUR, Adolphus Augustus, *Ellenhall Parsonage, Eccleshall, Staffs.*—P. C. of Ellenhall, Dio. Lich. 1861. (Patron, Earl of Lichfield; P. C.'s Inc. 91*l* and Ho; Pop. 300.) [12]

TURPIN, Digby, *Brackley, Northants.*—Dub. A.B. 1854; Deac. 1855 and Pr. 1856 by Bp of Rip. C. of Brackley 1865. Formerly C. of St. James's, Taunton, 1857–62, Cheshunt, Herts, 1864. [13]

TURQUAND, Alexander Peter, *Ottery St. Mary, Devon.*—Ex. Coll. Ox. B.A. 1853; Deac. 1853 and Pr. 1854 by Bp of Ex. P. C. of St. Michael's, Ottery St. Mary, Dio. Ex. 1863. (Patron, V. of Ottery; P. C.'s Inc. 80*l*; Pop. 300.) Formerly Sen. C. of Ottery St. Mary. [14]

TURTON, Henry Meysey, 15, *Cornwallis-crescent, Clifton.*—Trin. Coll. Ox. M.A. 1846; Deac. 1848 and Pr. 1849 by Abp of Cant. C. of District of Knowle, Bedminster, Bristol. Formerly V. of Great Milton, Oxon, 1857–59. [15]

TURTON, William Price, *Ravensden Vicarage, near Bedford.*—Wor. Coll. Ox. B.A. 1851; Deac. 1853 and Pr. 1854 by Bp of Wor. V. of Ravensden, Dio. Ely, 1864. (Patron, Rev. Dr. Sier; Glebe, 80 acres; V.'s Inc. 120*l* and Ho; Pop. 470.) Formerly C. of Alfrick and Lulsley 1853–58, Withernwick 1859–64. [16]

TUSON, Frederick Edward, *Oldham Parsonage, Bristol.*—St. John's Coll. Cam. B.A. 1836, M.A. 1839; Deac. 1837 and Pr. 1838 by Bp of B. and W. P. C. of Oldham, Dio. G. and B. 1862. (Patron, V. of Bitton; P. C.'s Inc. 43*l* and Ho; Pop. 1618.) Hon. Can. of Bristol 1852; Dom. Chap. to the Earl of Huntingdon; Dioc. Inspector of Schs. Formerly V. of Minety and Rural Dean of Marlborough, Wilts, 1843–58. Author, *Sermons for Parochial and Family Use,* 1843. [17]

TUSON, George Bailey, *The Grange, Henham, Bristol.*—Trin. Hall, Cam. B.D. 1825. R. of Little Stanmore, Dio. Lon. 1850. (Patroness, Mrs. Dorothy Norman; Tithe—Imp. 36*l* 10*s*, R. 415*l* 5*s* 10*d*; Glebe, 1 acre; R.'s Inc. 416*l* and Ho; Pop. 891.) [18]

TUTE, John Stanley, *Markington, Ripley, Yorks.*—St John's Coll. Cam. B.A. 1846; Deac. 1846 by Bp of Lich. Pr. 1847 by Bp of Rip. P.C. of Markington, Dio. Rip. 1849. (Patron, Bp of Rip; Tithe—App. 44*l*, Imp. 166*l*; Glebe, 1¾ acres; P. C.'s Inc. 73*l*; Pop. 535.) Author, *Holy Times and Scenes,* 1st and 2nd Series, Masters, 3*s.* [19]

TUTHILL, Henry C., *Worcester.*—C. of St. Clement's and Waterman's Ch. Worcester, 1866. Formerly C. of Aldsworth, Gloucestershire. [20]

TUTIN, William, *Morley, Leeds.*—Queen's Coll. Ox. B.A. 1862, M.A. 1866; Deac. 1864 and Pr. 1865 by Bp of Rip. C. of Morley 1866. [21]

TUTTIETT, Laurence, *Lea-Marston Parsonage, Birmingham.*—King's Coll. Lond. Theol. Assoc. 1st cl. 1848; Deac. 1848 and Pr. 1849 by Bp of Lon. P. C. of Lea-Marston, Dio. Wor. 1854. (Patron, C. B. Adderley, Esq. M.P; P. C.'s Inc. 150*l* and Ho; Pop. 261.) Author, *Counsels of a Godfather,* Morgan; *Germs of Thought on the Sunday Services,* ib; *Plain Forms of Household Prayers,* ib; *Household Prayers for Working Men,* ib; *Tracts for the Family,* ib; *Through the Clouds, Thoughts in Plain Verse,* Whittaker; etc. [22]

TWAMLEY, James, *Staincliffe, near Dewsbury.*—Dub. A.B. 1857, A.M. 1862; Deac. 1857 and Pr. 1858 by Bp of Rip. P. C. of Ch. Ch. Staincliffe, Dio. Rip. 1867. (Patron, V. of Batley; Pop. 5500.) Formerly C. of Battershaw 1857–59, Chapelthorpe 1860–61, Brighouse 1862, Teignmouth 1862–67. [23]

TWEDDALE, C., *Evesham.*—C. of Evesham. [24]

TWEDDLE, Christopher, *Chesterton, Peterborough.*—C. of Chesterton with Haddon, Hunts. [25]

TWEDDLE, Thomas, *Fring, King's Lynn, Norfolk.*—St. John's Coll. Cam. B.A. 1854, M.A. 1857; Deac. 1859 and Pr. 1860 by Bp of Ox. P. C. of Fring, Dio. Nor. 1866. (Patrons, D. and C. of Nor; P. C.'s Inc. 100*l* and Ho; Pop. 173.) Formerly C. of East Rudham, Norfolk. [26]

TWEED, Henry Earle, *Coleby, near Lincoln.*—Ox. Trin. and Oriel Colls. 1st cl. Lit. Hum. 1850, Chan.'s Latin Essay, 1851, B.A. 1850, M.A. 1853; Deac. 1855, Pr. 1856. V. of Coleby, Dio. Lin. 1862. (Patron, Oriel Coll. Ox; Tithe, 80*l*; Glebe, 13 acres; V.'s Inc. 155*l* and Ho; Pop. 458.) Formerly Fell. and Tut. of Oriel Coll. Ox. Author, *The Apostles and the Offertory,* 1860, 1*s*; *The Church the Consoler,* 1862, 1*s* (both Sermons). [27]

TWEED, Henry Wilson, *Bridstow Vicarage, Ross, Herefordshire.*—Ex. Coll. Ox. B.A. 1846, M.A. 1848; Deac. 1848 and Pr. 1849 by Bp of Lon. V. of Bridstow, Dio. Herf. 1858. (Patron, Bp of Herf; Tithe-

—App. 355*l*, V. 230*l*; Glebe, 52 acres; V.'s Inc. 335*l* and Ho; Pop. 717.) Formerly C. of Richard's Castle, Herefordshire. [1]

TWEED, James, *Stratton Audley, Bicester, Oxon.*—Corpus Coll. Cam. three Coll. Prizes, Sen. Opt. and B.A. 1815, M.A. 1818; Deac. 1815 and Pr. 1817 by Bp of Lon. Author, *Translation of St. Chrysostom's Homilies on the Pastoral Epistles*, &c. for the Oxford Edition of the Fathers, 1843. [2]

TWEED, James Peers, *Little Waltham Rectory, Chelmsford.*—Pemb. Coll. Ox. 1838, Ireland Scho. 1841, B.A. Exam. and 1st cl. Lit. Hum. 1842, M.A. 1845; Deac. 1843, Pr. 1845. R. of Little Waltham, Dio Roch. 1863 (Patron, Ex. Coll. Ox; R.'s Inc. 650*l* and Ho; Pop. 684) Formerly Fell. and Tut. of Ex. Coll. Ox. [3]

TWEED, John Edward, *Stratton Audley Parsonage, Bicester, Oxon.*—Ch. Ch. Ox. B.A. 1845, M.A. 1847. P. C. of Stratton Audley, Dio. Ox. 1857. (Patron, Ch. Ch. Ox; P. C.'s Inc. 136*l* and Ho; Pop. 424) [4]

TWEED, Joseph Barthorp, *Capel Rectory, Ipswich.*—Corpus Coll. Cam. B.A. 1855; Deac. 1855 and Pr. 1857 by Bp of Nor. R. of Capel St. Mary with Wenham Parva R. Dio. Nor. 1867. (Patron, the present R; Capel St. Mary, Tithe, 525*l*; Glebe, 22 acres; Wenham Parva, Tithe, 260*l*; Glebe, 14 acres; R.'s Inc. 826*l* and Ho; Pop. Capel St. Mary 670, Wenham Parva 45.) Formerly C. of Chartham, Kent, 1861–62, Monk's Eleigh, Suffolk, 1865–66. [5]

TWEED, Robert, *Ascot-under-Wychwood, Enstone, Oxon.*—P. C. of Ascot-under-Wychwood, Dio. Ox. 1860. (Patron, Bp of Ox; P. C.'s Inc. 80*l*; Pop. 458.) [6]

TWELLS, Henry, *Godolphin Grammar School, Hammersmith, Middlesex, W.*—St. Peter's Coll. Cam. B.A. 1848, M.A. 1851, *ad eund.* Ox. 1853; Deac. 1849, Pr. 1850. Head Mast. of the Godolphin Gr. Sch. Hammersmith. (Patrons, Trustees.) Formerly Mast. of St. Andrew's House Sch. Mells, Somerset. [7]

TWELLS, John, *Gamston Rectory, Retford, Notts.*—Trin. Coll. Cam. B.A. 1829, M.A. 1832; Deac. 1829 and Pr. 1830 by Abp of York. V. of Eaton, near Retford, Dio. Lin. 1840. (Patron, Bp of Man; Glebe, 56 acres; V.'s Inc. 78*l*; Pop. 184.) R. of Gamston, Dio. Lin. 1851. (Patron, Ld Chan; Glebe, 289 acres; R.'s Inc. 328*l* and Ho; Pop. 282.) Rural Dean of Retford 1854; Hon. Preb. Sanctæ Crucis of Lin. 1860.) Author, *Visitation Sermon*, 1842; *Gold Standard*, 1848; and various Pamphlets and Speeches on the Currency and the Bank Charter Act. [8]

TWEMLOW, Francis Cradock, *Forton Rectory, Newport, Staffs.*—Oriel Coll. Ox. B.A. 1840, M.A. 1843; Deac. 1841, Pr. 1842. R. of Forton, Dio. Lich. 1853. (Patron, Sir Thomas E. F. Boughey, Bart; Tithe, 458*l*; Glebe, 46 acres; R.'s Inc. 505*l* and Ho; Pop. 729.) [9]

TWENTYMAN, John, *King's College, London, W.C.*—Ch. Coll. Cam. Fell. of, B.A. 1861, M.A. 1864; Deac. 1861 by Bp of Win. Pr. 1862 by Bp of Roch. Vice-Mast. in King's Coll. Sch. Formerly Divinity Lect. Ch. Coll. Cam; Asst. Cl. Mast. in Cheltenham Coll. [10]

TWIGG, Richard, *St. James's Rectory, Wednesbury, Staffs.*—Univ. Coll. Dur. Prizeman and Barry Scho. Licen. in Theol. 1850; Deac. 1850 and Pr. 1851 by Bp of Dur. R. of St. James's, Wednesbury, Dio. Lich. 1856. (Patron, J. N. Bagnall, Esq; Tithe, 100*l*; R.'s Inc. 300*l* and Ho; Pop. 6631.) Formerly C. of Bywell St. Peter's, Northumberland, and St. James's, Wednesbury. [11]

TWIGG, Robert, *Tilmanstone Vicarage, Sandwich, Kent.*—St. Peter's Coll. Cam. B.A. 1826, M.A. 1830. V. of Tilmanstone, Dio. Cant. 1842. (Patron, Abp of Cant; Tithe—App. 160*l* and 27½ acres of Glebe, V. 263*l*; Glebe, ¾ acre; V.'s Inc. 264*l* and Ho; Pop. 405.) [12]

TWINING, George Brewster, *Twickenham, Middlesex, S.W.*—Univ. Coll. Ox. B.A. 1832, M.A. 1835; Deac. 1833, Pr. 1834. Formerly P. C. of Trinity, Tottenham, Middlesex, 1844–61. [13]

TWINING, James, *Little Casterton (Rutland), Stamford.*—Trin. Coll. Cam. 8th Wrang. and B.A. 1843, M.A. 1846; Deac. 1846 and Pr. 1847 by Bp of Win. R. of Little Casterton with Tolethorpe C. Dio. Pet. 1862. (Patron, Lord Chesham; R.'s Inc. 176*l* and Ho; Pop. 118.) Formerly P. C. of Trinity, Twickenham, 1851–62. [14]

TWISADAY, John, *Iford, Lewes, Sussex.*—St. John's Coll. Cam. B.A. 1842, M.A. 1845; Deac. 1842, Pr. 1843. C. of Iford with Kingston. [15]

TWISDEN, John Francis, *Staff College, near Farnborough Station, Hants.*—Prof. of Mathematics on the Staff College. [16]

TWISS, Alexander.—C. of St. Bartholomew's, Bethnal Green, 1867. [17]

TWISS, Christopher Beckett, *St. Ann's, Willenhall, Staffs.*—Univ. of Edinburgh and St. Bees; Deac. 1850 by Abp of York, Pr. 1851 by Bp of Lich. P. C. of St. Ann's, Willenhall, Dio. Lich. 1861. (Patrons, Messrs. Jevons and Mitchell; Pop. 4000.) [18]

TWISS, Martin, *Mawdesley Rectory, Ormskirk, Lancashire.*—Dub. A.B. 1838; Deac 1840 and Pr. 1841 by Bp of Ches. R. of Mawdesley with Bispham, Dio. Man. 1843. (Patron, R. of Croston; R.'s Inc. 170*l* and Ho; Pop. 1189.) Formerly C. of Mawdesley. [19]

TWISS, William Christopher, *Wrestlingworth Rectory, Potton, Beds.*—Caius Coll. Cam. B.A. 1824, M.A. 1828; Deac. 1825 by Bp of Nor. Pr. 1827 by Bp of Lin. R. of Wrestlingworth, Dio. Ely, 1836. (Patron, Ld Chan; R.'s Inc. 150*l* and Ho; Pop. 657.) V. of Eyeworth, Dio. Ely, 1840. (Patron, Lord Ongley; Tithe—Imp. 275*l*, V. 115*l*; V.'s Inc. 116*l*; Pop. 194.) [20]

TWIST, John James, *Birch-in-Rusholme, Manchester.*—Magd. Coll. Cam. 2nd cl. Cl. Trip. M.A; Deac. 1862 and Pr. 1863 by Bp of Man. C. of St. James's, Birch, 1862. [21]

TWOPENY, David, *Stockbury, Sittingbourne, Kent.*—Oriel Coll. Ox. B.A. 1824, M.A. 1827. V. of Stockbury, Dio. Cant. 1831. (Patrons, D. and C. of Roch; Tithe—App. 472*l* 14*s* 3*d*, Imp. 35*l*, V. 275*l* 12*s* 3*d*; V.'s Inc. 300*l*; Pop. 627.) [22]

TWOPENY, Richard, *Ipsden Vicarage, near Wallingford.*—St. John's Coll. Cam. 8th Wrang. and B.A. 1816, M.A. 1819, B.D. 1826; Deac. 1824 by Bp of Ely, Pr. 1824 by Bp. of Lin. V. of North Stoke with Ipsden and Newnham, Dio. Ox. 1829. (Patron, St. John's Coll. Cam; Glebe, 23 acres; V.'s Inc. 800*l* and Ho; Pop. Ipsden 290, North Stoke 140, Newnham 130.) Formerly Fell. of St. John's Coll. Cam. Author, *Infant Baptism and the Mode of Administering it*, 1848, 1*s*; *Lectures for a Village Night-School*, 1863, 1*s*. [23]

TWYCROSS, John, *Charterhouse, London, E.C.*—Dub. and Cam. B.A. Dub. 1818, Cam. M.A. 1827; Deac. and Pr. 1819 by Bp of Ches. Formerly C. of St. Olave's, Southwark, 1819; C. and Lect. of St. Peter-le-Poor, Lond. 1829. Author, articles in *The British Critic*, 1820, and in *Dublin University Magazine*, 1853–56; Editor of *Works of Edmund Burke, with Index*, 12 vols. 1828; *The Penny Sunday Reader*, 8 vols. 1837–38; First, Second, Third, and Fourth *Reports of the Inspectors of Prisons in England for the Home Department*, 1837–40; various Publications edited for the S.P.C.K. among which were *Barrow on the Pope's Supremacy*, *Waterland on the Athanasian Creed*, *Select Sermons of Bishop Beveridge*, and *Jones of Nayland on the Trinity*; *The Bible with Commentary wholly Biblical*, 3 vols. 4to, Bagster, 1856; *Rose's New General Biographical Dictionary*, vols. v.–xii. 1843–47. [24]

TWYNE, William, *Rayleigh Rectory, Essex.*—Magd. Coll. Cam. B.A. 1842, M.A. 1849; Deac. 1842, Pr. 1843. R. of Rayleigh, Dio. Roch. 1843. (Patron, R. Bristow, Esq; Tithe, 940*l*; R.'s Inc. 1000*l* and Ho; Pop. 1433.) [25]

TWYNING, William Henry, *Grosmont Rectory, Hereford.*—Jesus Coll. Ox. B.A. 1833. R. of Grosmont, Dio. Llan. 1855. (Patrons, the present R. and Mrs. Twyning; Tithe—App. 12*l* 10*s*, Imp. 253*l*, R. 201*l* 17*s* 6*d*; R.'s Inc. 211*l* and Ho; Pop. 743.) [26]

TWYSDEN, Thomas, *Charleton Rectory, Kingsbridge, Devon.*—Mert. Coll. Ox. B.A. 1824, M.A. 1826. R. of Charleton, Dio. Ex. 1842. (Patroness, Mrs.

Isabella Twysden; Tithe, 557*l*; Glebe, 30 acres; R.'s Inc. 587*l* and Ho; Pop. 568.) Rural Dean. [1]

TYACKE, Joseph Sidney, *St. Levan, Penzance.*—Ex. Coll. Ox. B.A. 1857, M.A. 1859; Deac. 1858 and Pr. 1859 by Bp of Salis. R. of St. Levan, Cornwall, Dio. Ex. 1864. (Patron, the Prince of Wales; R.'s Inc. 234*l*; Pop. 447.) Formerly Asst. Mast. in Marlborough Coll. 1857–61; Asst. C. of Tor-Mohun, Torquay, 1863–64. [2]

TYACKE, Richard, *Padstow Vicarage, Cornwall.*—St. John's Coll. Cam. B.A. 1827; Deac. 1831 by Bp of Bristol, Pr. 1831 by Bp of Ex. V. of Padstow, Dio. Ex. 1837. (Patron, C. P. Brune, Esq; Tithe—Imp. 440*l*. V. 245*l*; Glebe, 18 acres; V.'s Inc. 260*l* and Ho; Pop 2489.) Surrogate. [3]

TYACKE, Richard Frederick, *St. Ives, Hayle, Cornwall.*—Dub. A.B. 1857, A.M. 1866; Deac. 1857, Pr. 1859. P. C. of St. Ives, Dio. Ex. 1861. (Patron, V. of Lelant; P. C.'s Inc. 300*l* and Ho; Pop. 5087.) Formerly C. of St. Stephen's by Launceston, and St. Mary Magdalen's, Launceston, 1857, Morvah 1858. [4]

TYAS, Robert, *Kingsley Parsonage, Frodsham, Cheshire.*—Queens' Coll. Cam. B A. 1848, M.A. 1856; Deac. 1848 and Pr. 1849 by Bp of Win. P. C. of Kingsley, Dio. Ches. 1851. (Patron, V. of Frodsham; Tithe, App. 331*l*; Glebe, 1¼ acres; P.C.'s Inc. 90*l* and Ho; Pop. 1130.) Author, *Lectures in Holy-week*, 3*s*; *Parochial Sermons*, Bell and Daldy, 7*s* 6*d*; *Favourite Field Flowers*, 2 vols. Houlston and Co. 7*s* 6*d*; *Flowers from the Holy Land*, ib. 7*s* 6*d*. [5]

TYLDEN, William, *Stanford, Hythe, Kent.*—Ball. Coll. Ox. B.A. 1841, M.A. 1844. P. C. of Stanford, Dio. Cant. 1853. (Patron, the present P. C; Tithe, 170*l* 11*s*; Glebe, 9 acres; P. C.'s Inc. 190*l*; Pop. 294.) [6]

TYLECOTE, Thomas, *Marston-Moretaine Rectory, Ampthill, Beds.*—St. John's Coll. Cam. Fell. of 7th Wrang. B.A. 1821, M.A. 1824, B.D. 1830; Deac. 1826 and Pr. 1829 by Bp of Ely. R. of Marston-Moretaine, Dio. Ely, 1837. (Patron, St. John's Coll. Cam; Tithe, 1120*l*; Glebe, 68 acres; R.'s Inc. 1200*l* and Ho; Pop. 1280.) Rural Dean. Author, *True Development of the Binomial Theorem*, 1824. [7]

TYLEE, Mortimer, *Sewerby, Bridlington, Yorks.*—St. Edm. Hall, Ox. B.A. 1841; Deac. 1841 and Pr. 1842 by Bp of Ex. P. C. of Sewerby with Marton and Grindale P. C. Dio. York, 1854. (Patron, Rev. Y. Lloyd; P. C.'s Inc. 210*l* and Ho; Pop. 560.) Formerly C. of Hatherleigh 1841, Lyndhurst 1843, Bridlington 1850. [8]

TYLER, Charles Henry, *Chelwood Rectory, Bristol.*—Trin. Coll. Ox. B.A. 1835, M.A. 1840; Deac. 1835 and Pr. 1836 by Bp of Lin. R. of Chelwood, Dio. B. and W. 1857. (Patron, Bp of B. and W; Tithe, 183*l*; Glebe, 44 acres; R.'s Inc. 233*l* and Ho; Pop. 183.) Formerly C. of Worminghall, Bucks, 1835, Chard, Somerset, 1837–38, Stanton Drew with St. Thomas in Pensford, Somerset, 1838–57. [9]

TYLER, Edward Octavius, *Portbury Vicarage, near Bristol.*—Trin. Coll. Cam. B.A. 1853, M.A. 1857; Deac. 1854 and Pr. 1855 by Bp of Wor. V. of Portbury, Dio. B. and W. 1859. (Patron, Bp of Wor; Tithe—App. 320*l*, V. 279*l*; V.'s Inc. 400*l* and Ho; Pop. 477.) Formerly C. of Blockley, Worcestershire. [10]

TYLER, Owen Blathwayte, *Dinder, Wells.*—Trin. Coll. Ox. Exhib. B.A. 1843, M.A. 1845; Deac. 1844 and Pr. 1845 by Bp of B. and W. P. C. of North Wootton with Worminster C. Somerset, Dio. B. and W. 1845. (Patron, V. of Pilton; Tithe—App. 149*l* 15*s*; P. C. 50*l*; P. C.'s Inc. 305*l*; Pop. 407.) Formerly C. of Paulton, Somerset, 1844. Author, *Sermons*, *Wisdom of this World and Spiritual Wisdom compared*; *The Sin of being Glad at Calamities*, Rivingtons, 1849; *Doctrine and Practice* (volume of Sermons), Rivingtons, 2nd ed. 1865. [11]

TYLER, Robert Trevor, *Llantrithyd Rectory, Cowbridge, Glamorganshire.*—Univ. Coll. Ox. B.A. 1823, M.A. 1827; Deac. 1824 by Bp of Bristol, Pr. 1825 by Bp of Llan. P. C. of Monachlogddû, Pembrokeshire, Dio. St. D. 1836. (Patron, Lord Milford; Tithe, 52*l*; P. C.'s Inc. 221*l*; Pop. 471.) R. of Llantrithyd, Dio. Llan. 1838. (Patron, Sir T. D. Aubrey, Bart; Tithe, 132*l* 17*s* 9*d*; Glebe, 52 acres; R.'s Inc. 240*l* and Ho; Pop. 204.) Rural Dean. Formerly Dom. Chap. to His Majesty King William IV. when Duke of Clarence. [12]

TYNDALE, Henry Annesley, *Holton Rectory, Wheatley, Oxon.*—Wad. Coll. Ox. B.A. 1838, M.A. 1840; Deac. 1839 and Pr. 1840 by Bp of Ox. R. of Holton, Dio. Ox. 1856. (Patron, Rev. F. Biscoe; Tithe, 420*l*; Glebe, 25 acres; R.'s Inc. 450*l* and Ho; Pop. 245.) Formerly R. of Tatsfield, Surrey, 1842-56. [13]

TYRRELL, Francis.—Dom. Chap. to the Earl of Albemarle. [14]

TYRRELL, G. W.—Dom. Chap. to the Marquis of Donegal. [15]

TYRRELL, Walter, 20, *Lancaster-street, Leicester.*—St. Bees; Deac. 1856 and Pr. 1857 by Abp of York. C of Trinity, Leicester, 1866. Formerly C. of St. Matthew's, Sheffield, 1856-58, Maltby and Stainton, Yorks, 1858–61; Chap. to Earl of Scarborough 1858–61; Lect. of Ashby-de-la-Zouch 1861. [16]

TYRWHITT, James Bradshaw, *Wilksby, Horncastle, Lincolnshire.*—Jesus Coll. Cam. B.A. 1828. R. of Wilksby, Dio. Lin. 1833. (Patron, Hon. H. Dymoke; R.'s Inc. 125*l*; Pop. 57.) [17]

TYRWHITT, Richard St. John, 31, *Beaumont-street, Oxford.*—Ch. Ch. Ox. 2nd cl. Lit. Hum. B.A. 1849, M.A. 1852; Deac. 1851, Pr. 1852. V. of St. Mary Magdalen's with St. George-the-Martyr's, V. Oxford, Dio. Ox. 1858. (Patron, Ch. Ch. Ox; V.'s Inc. 170*l*; Pop. 2680.) Formerly Stud. Tut. and Rhetoric Reader Ch. Ch. Ox. Author, *The Schooling of Life*, *Essays*, 1864. [18]

TYSON, John, *Wolstanton Vicarage, Newcastle-under-Lyne.*—Queens' Coll. Cam. B.A. 1834; Deac. 1834, Pr. 1835. V. of Wolstanton, Dio. Lich. 1837. (Patron, R. Sneyd, Esq; Tithe—Imp. 896*l* 3*s*, V. 348*l* 1*s* 6*d*; Glebe, 36½ acres; V.'s Inc. 470*l* and Ho; Pop. 2804.) [19]

TYSON, Joshua, *Distington, Whitehaven, Cumberland*—St. Bees; Deac. 1860 and Pr. 1861 by Bp of Carl. C. of Distington 1860. [20]

TYSSEN, Ridley Daniel, *Hope, near Sheffield.*—Oriel Coll. Ox. B.A. 1863, M.A. 1866; Deac. 1865 and Pr. 1866 by Bp of Lich. C. of Hope 1865. [21]

UGLOW, Theodore Sebastian, *Toretto, Cheltenham.*—Dub. A.B. 1861; Deac. 1864 and Pr. 1865 by Bp of Wor. Formerly C. of St. Andrew's, Droitwich, 1864–67. [22]

UNDERWOOD, Charles Edward, *Crofton Rectory, Bromfield, Salop.*—Ball. Coll. Ox. Greek Exhib. B.A. 1853, M.A. 1856; Deac. 1854 by Bp of Ex. Pr. 1856 by Bp of Ely. V. of Diddlebury, Dio. Herf. 1860. (Patrons, D. and C. of Herf; Tithe, 343*l* 14*s* 2*d*; Glebe, 56 acres; V.'s Inc. 400*l* and Ho; Pop. 800.) Formerly 2nd Mast. of Ilminster Sch. with C. of Knowle St. Giles, 1854–55; C. of Great Saxham, Suffolk, 1855–58, Linton, Heref. 1858–60. [23]

UNDERWOOD, Charles White, *Histon, near Cambridge.*—St. John's Coll. Cam. B.A. 1844, M.A. 1847; Deac. 1844, Pr. 1845. V. of Histon St. Andrew, Dio. Ely 1865. (Patron, Rev. C. W. Underwood; Glebe 218 acres; V.'s Inc. 580*l* and Ho; Pop. 941.) Formerly Vice-Prin. of Liverpool Coll. Institution 1853. [24]

UNDERWOOD, John Grayson, *All Saints' Parsonage, Huntspill, Bridgwater, Somerset.*—St. John's Coll. Cam. B.A. 1842; Deac. 1843, Pr. 1844. P. C. of All Saints', Huntspill, Dio. B. and W. 1846. (Patron, R. of Huntspill; Glebe, 3 acres; P. C.'s Inc. 102*l* and Ho; Pop. 678.) [25]

UNDERWOOD, Richard, *All Saints' Vicarage, Hereford.*—St. John's Coll. Ox. M.A; Deac. 1841 and Pr. 1842 by Bp of G. and B. V. of All Saints', Hereford, Dio. Herf. 1859. (Patrons, D. and C. of Windsor; Tithe, 115*l*; V.'s Inc. 300*l* and Ho; Pop. 4525.) [26]

UNDERWOOD, William D., *West Wittering Vicarage, Chichester.*—St. Bees; Deac. 1853 and Pr. 1854 by Bp of Chich. V. of West Wittering, Dio. Chich. 1867. (Patron, Preb. of Wittering; Tithe, App. 716*l*; V. 172*l* 10*s*; Glebe, 21 acres; V.'s Inc. 180*l* and Ho; Pop. 616.) Formerly C. of Maresfield, Sussex, 1853–58; C. in sole charge of West Wittering 1858–67. [1]

UNDERWOOD, W. J., *Wareham, Dorset.*—C. of Wareham. [2]

UNWIN, John W., *Thorney Abbey, Cambridgeshire.*—C. of Thorney Abbey. [3]

UNWIN, Samuel Hope, *Cheddon-Fitzpaine Rectory, Taunton.*—Wor. Coll. Ox. B.A. 1841, M.A. 1844; Deac. 1842, Pr. 1843 by Bp of Win. R. of Cheddon-Fitzpaine, Dio. B. and W. 1854. (Patron, John Henry Warre, Esq; Tithe, 323*l* 4*s*; Glebe, 79 acres; R.'s Inc. 524*l* and Ho; Pop. 338.) Formerly C. of Richmond, Surrey, 1842–45, Chepstow, Mon. 1845–48; P. C. of Tilstone-Fearnall, Ches. 1848–50; Director of Ch. Miss. Children's Home, Highbury, Lond. 1850–53. [4]

UPCHER, Abbot, *Kirby-Cane Rectory (Norfolk), near Bungay.*—Trin. Coll. Cam. B.A. 1837; Deac. and Pr. 1838. R. of Kirby-Cane, Dio. Nor. 1851. (Patron, Lord Berners; Tithe, 425*l*; Glebe, 40¾ acres; R.'s Inc. 485*l* and Ho; Pop. 448.) Rural Dean of Brooke, East Division; Dom. Chap. to Lord Berners. [5]

UPCHER, Arthur Wilson, *Wreningham, Wymondham, Norfolk.*—Trin. Coll. Cam. Sen. Opt. and B.A. 1837, M.A. 1842; Deac. 1839, Pr. 1840. R. of Ashwelthorpe with Wreningham, Dio. Nor. 1853. (Patron, Lorp Berners; Ashwelthorpe, Tithe, 340*l*; Wreningham, 400*l*; Glebe, 85 acres; R.'s Inc. 782*l* and Ho; Pop. Ashwelthorpe 409, Wreningham 437.) [6]

UPJOHN, Francis, *Gorleston, near Great Yarmouth.*—Queens' Coll. Cam. B.A. 1830, M.A. 1833; Deac. 1830 and Pr. 1831 by Bp of Lin. V. of Gorleston, with Southtown R. and West Town R. Dio. Nor. 1841. (Patrons, Exors. of James Salter, Esq; Gorleston, Tithe—Imp. 243*l* 17*s*, V. 214*l* 15*s* 1*d*; Southtown with West Town, Tithe, 110*l*; from Par. of Runham, 32*l* 4*s* 7*d*; V.'s Inc. 406*l*; Pop. 4472.) [7]

UPTON, Archer, *Coundon Parsonage, Bishops Auckland, Durham.* — Wad. Coll. Ox. B.A. 1853, M.A. 1855; Deac. 1853 and Pr. 1854 by Bp of Dur. P. C. of Coundon, Dio. Dur. 1856. (Patron, Bp of Dur; Glebe, 4 acres; P. C.'s Inc. 330*l* and Ho; Pop. 3095.) Formerly C. of St. Anne's, and St. Andrew's, Auckland. [8]

UPTON, Robert, *Moreton-Say, Market-Drayton, Salop.*—Trin. Coll. Cam. B.A. 1823; Deac. 1824, Pr. 1825. V. of Moreton-Say, Dio. Lich. 1831. (Patron, R. of Hodnet; Tithe—App. 550*l*, P. C. 90*l*; Glebe, 48 acres; V.'s Inc. 195*l*; Pop. 679.) Chap. to the Market-Drayton Union. [9]

UPTON, William Judd, *Fletton Rectory, near Peterborough.*—New Coll. Ox. B.A. 1839, M.A. 1843; Deac. 1841, Pr. 1842. R. of Fletton, Dio. Ely, 1856. (Patron, Earl Fitzwilliam; R.'s Inc. 92*l* and Ho; Pop. 1449.) Formerly P. C. of Greasborough 1850. [10]

UPWOOD, Thomas Thorogood, *Terrington, King's Lynn, Norfolk.*—Clare Hall and Pemb. Coll. Cam. B.A. 1817, Clare Coll. Cam. B.A. 1820; Deac. 1818 and Pr. 1819 by Bp of Nor. V. of St. Clement's-Terrington, Dio. Nor. 1843. (Patron, the Crown; Tithe—Imp. 2402*l* and 6¾ acres of Glebe, V. 661*l*; Glebe, 7½ acres; V.'s Inc. 670*l*; Pop. 2303.) Formerly Fell. of Clare Coll. Cam. [11]

URQUHART, E. W., *Bovey Tracey, Newton Abbott, Devon.*—C. of Bovey Tracey 1867. Formerly C. of St. Philip and St. James's, Oxford. [12]

URQUHART, John, *Chapel-Allerton, Leeds.*—P. C. of Chapel-Allerton, Dio. Rip. 1835. (Patron, V. of Leeds; Tithe—App. 288*l*; P. C.'s Inc. 370*l*; Pop. 3083.) [13]

URQUHART, William, *Broadmayne Rectory, Dorchester.*—Wor. Coll. Ox. B.A. 1852; Deac. 1853 and Pr. 1855 by Bp of Salis. R. of West Knighton with Broadmayne R. Dio. Salis. 1860. (Patron, the present R; West Knighton, Tithe, 142*l* 10*s*; Glebe, 110 acres; Broadmayne, Glebe, 250 acres; R.'s Inc. 580*l* and Ho; Pop. West Knighton 260, Broadmayne, 503.) Formerly C. of West Knighton and Broadmayne. [14]

URWIN, James, *Corsenside Rectory, Hexham.*—Literate; Deac. 1820 by Abp of York, Pr. 1822 by Bp of Ox. R. of Corsenside, Dio. Dur. 1864. (Patron, W. Bewicke, Esq; Tithe, 192*l*; Glebe, 80 acres; R.'s Inc. 300*l* and Ho; Pop. 1000*l*.) Formerly Mast. of the Gr. Sch. Hexham, 1826–61; P. C. of Thockrington with Kirkheaton 1861–64. [15]

USBORNE, Henry, *Bitterne, near Southampton.*—Ball. Coll. Ox. B.A. 1832. P. C. of All Souls, Bitterne, Dio. Win. 1852. (Patron, Bp of Win; P. C.'s Inc. 204*l*.) [16]

USHER, Henry, *St. Clement's Rectory, Saltfleetby, Louth.*—St. Bees; Deac. 1846 and Pr. 1847 by Bp of Wor. R. of St. Clement's, Saltfleetby, Dio. Lin. 1867. (Patron, Hon. C. H. Cust; R.'s Inc. 210*l* and Ho; Pop. 150.) Formerly C. of St. James's, Birmingham, 1846–48, Oddington, Glouc. 1848–56, Broadwell, Glouc. 1856–63, Barrowby, Linc. 1863–67. Author, *The Christian Embassy* (a Pamphlet), 1863, and various Sermons. [17]

USHER, John Harrison, *Bedlington, Northumberland.*—Dur. B.A. 1851, M.A. 1862; Deac. 1852 and Pr. 1853 by Bp of Dur. P. C. of Cambois, Dio. Dur. 1863. (Patrons, D. and C. of Dur; P. C.'s Inc. 300*l*; Pop. 900.) Formerly C. of Monk Hesleton, Durham, 1852–60, Bedlington 1860-63. [18]

USILL, James Harley, *Fulbourn All Saints', near Cambridge.*—Trin. Coll. Cam. Sen. Opt. and B.A. 1852, M.A. 1855; Deac. 1852, Pr. 1853. V. of Fulbourn All Saints', Dio. Ely, 1856. (Patron, Bp. of Pet; V.'s Inc. 275*l*; Pop. 825.) Formerly C. of St. Giles's, Northampton. Author, *Twelve Sermons.* [19]

UTHWATT, Eusebius Andrewes, *Buckingham.*—St. John's Coll. Cam. B.A. 1830; Deac. 1831, Pr. 1832. R. of Foxcote, near Buckingham, Dio. Ox. 1843. (Patron, Lawrence Hall, Esq; Tithe, 172*l*; R.'s Inc. 258*l*; Pop. 90.) [20]

UTHWATT, William, *Maids' Moreton, Buckingham.*—R. of Maids' Morton, Dio. Ox. 1848. (Patron, Rev. J. L. Long; R.'s Inc. 294*l*; Pop. 543.) V. of Stowe, Bucks, Dio. Ox. 1833. (Patron, Duke of Buckingham; V.'s Inc. 95*l*; Pop. 352.) [21]

UTTERSON, Ferris, 36, *Duffield-road, Derby.*—St. John's Coll. Ox. B.A. 1862, M.A. 1865; Deac. 1863 by Bp of Lich. Pr. 1864 by Bp of Pet. C. of St. Alkmund's, Derby, 1863. [22]

UTTERTON, The Ven. John Sutton, *Castle Hill House, Farnham, Surrey,* and *The Close, Winchester.*—Oriel Coll. Ox. Scho. of and 1st cl. Lit. Hum. and B.A. 1836; Deac. 1838, Pr. 1839. Archd. of Surrey 1859 (Value, 130*l*); Can. of Win. 1860 (Value, 60*l*); R. of Farnham, Dio. Win. 1853. (Patron, Bp of Win; Tithe—App. 2331*l* 7*s* 0¾*d*, Imp. 8*s*, V. 300*l* 9*s* 8½*d*; V.'s Inc. 800*l*; Pop. 4693.) Formerly P. C. of Holmwood, Dorking, 1838–51; R. of Calbourne, Isle of Wight, 1851–53. Author, sundry Charges, Sermons (principally on the Ministry); etc. [23]

UWINS, John Geale, *Cainscross Parsonage, near Stroud.*—St. John's Coll. Cam. 24th Wrang. and B.A. 1836, M.A. 1839; Deac. 1836 by Bp of Ches. Pr. 1837 by Bp of Rip. P. C. of Cainscross, Dio. G. and B. 1841. (Patroness, Mrs. Croome; P. C.'s Inc. 130*l* and Ho; Pop. 1916.) Formerly C. of High Harrogate, Yorks, 1836–38, Richmond, Surrey, 1838–41. [24]

VACHELL, Harvey, *Millbrook Rectory, Ampthill, Bedford.*—R. of Millbrook, Dio. Ely, 1866. (Patron, Ld Chan; R.'s Inc. 290*l* and Ho; Pop. 450.) Formerly R. of St. John's, Horselydown, Lond. 1854–66. [25]

VADE, Vicesimus Knox, 4, *Lower Berkeley-street, Portman-square, London, W.*—Trin. Coll. Cam. B.A. 1845, M.A. 1848; Deac. 1845 and Pr. 1847 by Bp of Lon. [26]

VAILE, John, *Coley, near Halifax.*—St. Cath. Coll. Cam. B.A. 1860; Deac. 1864 by Bp of Rip. C. of Coley 1864. [1]

VALE, John Bartholomew, *Crostwight, Smallburgh, Norfolk.*—Emman. Coll. Cam. B.A. 1845, M.A. 1849; Deac. 1846 and Pr. 1847 by Bp of Chich. R. of Crostwight, Dio. Nor. 1855. (Patron, M. Shepheard, Esq; Tithe, 150*l*; Glebe, 13 acres; R.'s Inc. 167*l* 10*s*; Pop. 69.) Chap. of Smallburgh Union 1859. [2]

VALE, William Scarlett, *Mathon, Great Malvern.*—Deac. and Pr. 1840 by Bp of Herf. P. C. of Wisteston, Dio. Herf. 1846. (Patron, the present P. C; P. C.'s Inc. 50*l*.) [3]

VALENTINE, George Thomas, *Nottingham.*—St. John's Coll. Cam. B.A. 1857; Deac. 1857 and Pr. 1859 by Bp of Roch. C. of St. Nicholas', Nottingham, 1867. Formerly C. of Hempstead, Essex, 1857, St. Paul's, High Elswick, Newcastle, 1863, Heighington, Darlington, 1864. [4]

VALENTINE, John Withers, *Odcombe, South Petherton, Somerset.*—Wad. Coll. Ox. Hebrew Exhib. B.A. 1854; Deac. 1854 and Pr. 1855 by Bp of Lich. C. of Odcombe. Formerly British Chap. on the Moselle, Germany; C. of All Saints', Derby. [5]

VALENTINE, William, *St. Thomas's Parsonage, Stepney, London, E.*—Trin. Coll. Cam. B.A. 1815, M.A. 1819; Deac. 1815 by Bp of Ches. Pr. 1816 by Bp of Ex. P. C. of St. Thomas's, Arbour-square, Stepney, Dio. Lon. 1842. (Patron, Bp of Lon; P. C.'s Inc. 300*l* and Ho; Pop. 14,000.) Formerly C. of Culmstock and Walkhampton, Devon, 1815–18; Chap. and House Governor of the London Hospital, 1818–42. Author, *Sermon preached before the University of Cambridge,* 1829, Rivingtons; *Sermon on Death of Duke of Gloucester,* 1834, Hatchards. [6]

VALENTINE, William, *Whixley Vicarage, near York.*—Wor. Coll. Ox. B.A. 1850, M.A. 1857; Deac. 1850 and Pr. 1851 by Bp of Lin. V. of Whixley, Dio. Rip. 1853. (Patrons, Trustees of C. B. Massingberd Mundy, Esq; V.'s Inc. 75*l* and Ho; Pop. 954.) P. C. of Allerton-Mauleverer 1853. (Patron, Lord Stourton; P. C.'s Inc. 61*l*; Pop. 283.) [7]

VALLACK, Benjamin William Salmon, *St. Budeaux Vicarage, Plymouth.*—Ex. Coll. Ox. 1st cl. Math. et Phy. and B.A. 1825; Deac. 1829 by Bp of Nor. Pr. 1830 by Bp of Win. V. of St. Budeaux with Knackersknowle Chapel, Dio. Ex. 1832. (Patron, V. of St. Andrew's, Plymouth; Tithe, 60*l*; Glebe, 3 acres; V.'s Inc. 125*l* and Ho; Pop. 1376.) Formerly C. of Wareham, Dorset, 1829–30, St. Andrew's, Plymouth, 1831–32; Chap. to the High Sheriff of Devon 1853. [8]

VALLANCE, William, *South Church Rectory, Rochford, Essex.*—Univ. Coll. Ox. B.A. 1819, M.A. 1821; Deac. and Pr. 1821 by Abp of Cant. R. of South Church, Dio. Roch. 1854. (Patron, Abp of Cant; Tithe, comm. 830*l*; Glebe, 60 acres; R.'s Inc. 925*l* and Ho; Pop. 494.) Rural Dean. Formerly one of the six Preachers of Cant. Cathl. 1840–66; P. C. of Maidstone 1842–54. [9]

VALLANCY, Henry Edward Francis, *Sutton, St. Helens, Lancashire.*—King's Coll. Cam. B.A. 1831, M.A. 1834; Deac. 1831 by Bp of Lin. Pr. 1835 by Bp of Chich. V. of Sutton, St. Helens, Dio. Ches. 1849. (Patron, King's Coll. Cam; Tithe, 715*l*; Glebe, 1 acre; V.'s Inc. 716*l*; Pop. 4071.) Formerly Fell. of King's Coll. Cam. [10]

VALLINGS, Frederic Ross, *Calcutta.*—Trin. Coll. Cam. 2nd Sen. Opt. and B.A. 1848, M.A. 1851; Deac. 1857 and Pr. 1858 by Bp of Salis. Chap. to the Bp of Calcutta. Formerly C. of Maddington, Wilts. [11]

VALPY, Antony Bird, *Stanford-Dingley Rectory, Reading.*—Ch. Miss. Coll. Islington; Deac. 1855 by Bp of Lich. Pr. 1859 by Bp of Madras. R. of Stanford-Dingley, Dio. Ox. 1864. (Patron, the present R; Tithe, 276*l*; Glebe, 23 acres; R.'s Inc. 316*l* and Ho; Pop. 145.) Formerly Miss. of C.M.S. in Tinnevelly, S. India, 1855–63; C. of St. Andrew's the Less, Cambridge, 1863–64. [12]

VALPY, Francis Edward Jackson, *Garveston Rectory, Attleborough, Norfolk.*—Trin. Coll. Cam. Bell's Univ. Scho. 1816, M.A. 1819; Deac. 1826, Pr. 1827. R. of Garveston, Dio. Nor. 1845. (Patron, the present R; Tithe, 243*l*; Glebe, 16 acres; R.'s Inc. 220*l* and Ho; Pop. 383.) Author, *The Primitives and Leading Words of the Greek Language,* 5*s*; *A Manual of Latin Etymology,* 5*s*; *The Etymology of the Words of the Greek Language,* 5*s*; *The Third Greek Delectus,* 15*s* 6*d*; *The Second Greek Delectus,* 9*s* 6*d*; *Greek Exercises,* 6*s* 6*d*; *A Key,* 3*s*; *Electa ex Ovidio et Tibullo, with English Notes,* 6*s*; *Epitome Sacræ Historiæ, with English Notes,* 2*s*; *The Course of Nature, urged on Principles of Analogy, in Vindication of Scripture,* 5*s*, Longmans. [13]

VALPY, Gabriel, *Bucklebury, Reading.*—Queens' Coll. Cam. B.A. 1812, M.A. 1815; Deac. 1811, Pr. 1814. V. of Bucklebury with Marleston C. Dio. Ox. 1849. (Patron, W. H. H. Hartley, Esq; Bucklebury, Tithe—Imp. 75*l* 10*s*, V. 340*l*; Marleston, Tithe, 226*l* 18*s* 7*d*; V.'s Inc. 566*l* and Ho; Pop. Bucklebury 1178.) Rural Dean; Surrogate. [14]

VALPY, John C. W., *Sneyd, Burslem, Staffordshire.*—C. of Sneyd. [15]

VALPY, John Montagu, *St. John's Parsonage, Nottingham.*—Trin. Coll. Cam. B.A. 1846, M.A. 1850; Deac. 1846, Pr. 1847. P. C. of St. John the Baptist's, Leenside, Nottingham, Dio. Lin. 1853. (Patron, Bp of Lin; P. C.'s Inc. 300*l* and Ho; Pop. 5892.) Surrogate. [16]

VALPY, Julius John Culpeper, *Elsing, East Dereham, Norfolk.*—Clare Coll. Cam. B.A. 1850; Deac. 1851 and Pr. 1852 by Bp of Ely. R. of Elsing, Dio. Nor. 1852. (Patron, R. C. Browne, Esq; Tithe, 336*l*; Glebe, 18 acres; R.'s Inc. 360*l* and Ho; Pop. 392.) [17]

VALPY, Thomas Roworth, *Garveston Rectory, Attleborough, Norfolk.*—St. Bees; Deac. 1854 and Pr. 1855 by Bp of Nor. C. of Garveston 1865. Formerly C. of Sheepshed, Leicester, 1856, West Rudham, Norfolk, 1861, Blickling, Norfolk, 1862, Buxton, Norfolk, 1863. [18]

VANCE, John G., *St. Michael's Rectory, Manchester.*—R. of St. Michael's, City and Dio. Man. 1844. (Patrons, D. and C. of Man; R.'s Inc. 155*l*; Pop. 11,525.) [19]

VANCE, Richard, *Ravenfield, Rotherham.*—Dub; Deac. and Pr. 1832 by Abp of Dub. P. C. of Ravenfield, Dio. York, 1860. (Patron, T. B. Bosville, Esq; P. C.'s Inc. 150*l*; Pop. 183.) Chap. to the Earl of Glengall. Formerly C. in sole charge of Ravenfield. [20]

VANDERMEULEN, Frederick, *Thorley Rectory (Herts), near Bishop Stortford.*—Trin. Coll. Cam. B.A. 1834, M.A. 1837; Deac. 1836 and Pr. 1837 by Bp of Win. R. of Thorley, Dio. Roch. 1853. (Patron, Bp of Roch; Tithe, 535*l*; Glebe, 50 acres; R.'s Inc. 535*l* and Ho; Pop. 388.) [21]

VANE, John, *Wrington Rectory, Somerset.*—Trin. Coll. Cam. B.A. 1814, Magd. Coll. Cam. M.A. 1817. R. of Wrington, Dio. B. and W. 1828. (Patron, Duke of Cleveland; Tithe, 600*l*; Glebe, 54 acres; R.'s Inc. 660*l* and Ho; Pop. 1617.) P. C. of Burrington, Wrington, 1831. (Patrons, the Inhabitants; P. C.'s Inc. 147*l* and Ho; Pop. 477.) Deputy Clerk of the Closet to the Queen. Formerly Fell. of Magd. Coll. Cam. [22]

VAN STRAUBENZEE, A., *Stainton, Yorkshire.*—C. of Stainton. [23]

VARDY, Albert Richard, 37, *Spurstowe-road, Hackney, N.E.*—Trin. Coll. Cam. 1st cl. Cl. Trip. Sen. Opt. Carus Greek Test. 2nd Chancellor's Cl. Medal, B.A. 1864, M.A. 1867; Deac. 1866 by Bp of Ely. Fell. of Trin. Coll. [24]

VASSALL, William, *Hardington-Mandeville Rectory, Yeovil, Somerset.*—St. John's Coll. Cam. B.A. 1846, M.A. 1851; Deac. 1851 and Pr. 1852 by Abp of York. R. of Hardington-Mandeville, Dio. B. and W. 1856. (Patron, Alfred Cox, Esq; Tithe, 359*l* 14*s* 7*d*; Glebe, 108 acres; R.'s Inc. 533*l* and Ho; Pop. 668.) Formerly C. of Church Fenton 1851–54. [25]

VAUDREY, John Howard, *Leek, Staffs.*—St. Aidan's; Deac. 1858 and Pr. 1859 by Bp of Ches. C. of Leek 1864. Formerly C. of Hurdsfield, Macclesfield, 1858–64. [26]

VAUDREY, J. T., *Melcombe Regis, Weymouth.*—C. of St. John's, Melcombe Regis. [1]

VAUGHAN, Arthur O. Chambra, *Greenhead, Haltwhistle, Carlisle.*—Worc. Coll. Ox. M.A. 1860; Deac. 1857 and Pr. 1858 by Bp of Lich. P. C. of Greenhead, Dio. Dur. 1862. (Patron, V. of Haltwhistle; P. C.'s Inc. 50*l* and Ho; Pop. 800.) Chap. of Don. of Lambley, Dio. Dur. 1866. (Patron, J. L. H. Allgood, Esq; Pop. 700.) Formerly C. of Uttoxeter, Staffs, 1857; P. C. of Featherstone Chapel, and C. of Greenhead, Dur. 1861. [2]

VAUGHAN, Charles, *Crickadarn Vicarage, near Brecon.*—Wad. Coll. Ox. B.A. 1831. V. of Crickadarn with Llandevalley V. Dio. St. D. 1842. (Patron, Col. L. V. Watkins; Crickadarn, Tithe, 240*l*; Llandevalley, Tithe, 560*l*; V.'s Inc. 800*l* and Ho; Pop. Crickadarn 448, Llandevalley 687.) [3]

VAUGHAN, Charles, *Barwell, near Hinckley, Leicestershire.*—C. of Barwell. [4]

VAUGHAN, Charles John, *The Vicarage, Doncaster.*—Trin. Coll. Cam. Craven Univ. Scho. Porson Prizeman 1836 and 1837, Browne's Medallist for Greek Ode, Epigrams, and Latin Essay 1837, Chancellor's Medallist and B.A. 1838, Fell. of Trin. Coll. 1839, M.A. 1841, D.D. 1845; Deac and Pr. 1841. Chap. in Ordinary to the Queen 1859. (Stipend, 30*l*.) V. of Doncaster, Dio. York, 1860. (Patron, Abp of York; Tithe, App. 1805*l* 2*s*; V.'s Inc. 460*l* and Ho; Pop. 6419.) Hon. Chan. of York Cathl. 1860; Rural Dean. Formerly V. of St. Martin's, Leicester, 1841–44; Head Mast. of Harrow Sch. 1844–59. Author, *Sermons preached in the Chapel of Harrow School* (First Series), 1847; *Nine Sermons for Advent, Easter, &c.* 1849; *Two Letters on the late Post-office Agitation*, 1849–50; *The Personality of the Tempter, and other Sermons*, 1851; *Sermons preached in the Parish Church of St. Martin's, Leicester*, 1852; *Sermons preached in the Chapel of Harrow School* (Second Series), 1853; *Independence and Submission* (Two Addresses), 1853; *A Few Words on the Crystal Palace Question*, 1853; *A Letter to Lord Palmerston on the Monitorial System of Harrow School*, 1854; *A Discourse on Church Discipline and the Burial Service*, 1854; *Passages from the Life of Cicero* (a Lecture delivered in Exeter Hall), 1854; *Two Sermons on the War*, 1854; *Memorials of Harrow Sundays*, Macmillan, 1859, 10*s* 6*d*; *Revision of the Liturgy*, 4*s* 6*d*; *Notes for Lectures on Confirmation*, 1*s* 6*d*; *Epistle to the Romans, with English Notes*, 7*s* 6*d*; *Epiphany, Lent and Easter: Sermons preached in St. Michael's Church, Chester-square*, 1860, 7*s* 6*d*; *Lectures on the Epistle to the Philippians*, 7*s* 6*d*; *Lectures on the Revelation of St. John*, 2 vols. 15*s*; *The Book and the Life, and other Sermons preached before the University of Cambridge*, 2nd ed. 4*s* 6*d*; *Lessons of Life and Godliness* (Sermons preached at Doncaster), 2nd ed. 4*s* 6*d*; *Words from the Gospels* (a Second Series of Doncaster Sermons), 4*s* 6*d*; etc. [5]

VAUGHAN, Charles Lyndhurst, *St. John's Villa, St. Leonards-on-Sea.*—Oriel Coll. Ox. B.A. 1850, M.A. 1854; Deac. 1851 and Pr. 1852 by Bp of Wor. P.C. of Ch. Ch. with St. John's, St. Leonards-on-Sea, Dio. Chich. 1864. Formerly V. of St. Neots 1854–65; Rural Dean 1860–65. [6]

VAUGHAN, David, *Bryngwyn, Kington, Radnorshire.*—Lampeter; Deac. 1849, Pr. 1851. R. of Bryngwyn, Dio. St. D. 1865. (Patron, Bp of St. D; R.'s Inc. 294*l*; Pop. 334.) Formerly C. of Newchurch and Bryngwyn. [7]

VAUGHAN, David James, *St. Martin's Vicarage, Leicester.*—Trin. Coll. Cam. Bell's Scho. 1845, Browne's Medallist 1847, Members' Prizeman 1847 and 1848, B.A. 1848, M.A. 1851; Deac. 1853 and Pr. 1854 by Bp of Pet. V. of St. Martin's, Leicester, Dio. Pet. 1860. (Patron, Ld Chan; V.'s Inc. 160*l* and Ho; Pop. 2778.) Formerly C. of St. John's, Leicester; P. C. of St. Mark's Whitechapel, Lond. 1856–60; previously Fell. of Trin. Coll. Cam. Author, *The Republic of Plato, translated into English, with an Introduction, Analysis, and Notes*, 1852, 7*s* 6*d*; *A Few Words about Private Tuition, by a Private Tutor*, 1852, 6*d*; *Sermons preached in St. John's Church, Leicester, during the Years* 1855 *and* 1856, 5*s* 6*d*; *Sermons on the Resurrection*, 3*s*; *Three Sermons on the Atonement*, 1*s* 6*d*; *Sermons on Sacrifice and Propitiation*, 2*s* 6*d*, Macmillans; **The Elements of our Christian Faith*, 1*s*; *Christian Evidences and the Bible*, 2nd ed. 5*s* 6*d*, Macmillans. [8]

VAUGHAN, Edward Protheroe, *Wraxall Rectory, near Bristol.*—Ball. Coll. Ox. 1st cl. Math. 2nd cl. Lit. Hum. and B.A. 1832, M.A. 1835; Deac. 1833, Pr. 1834. R. of Wraxall, Dio. B. and W. 1857. (Patron, the present R; Tithe, 520*l*; Glebe, 76 acres; R.'s Inc. 600*l* and Ho; Pop. 912.) Dioc. Inspector of Schools for Dio. of B. and W. Formerly C. of Wraxall 1836–57. Author, Pamphlets on Education. [9]

VAUGHAN, Edward Thomas, *Harpenden Rectory, St. Albans.*—Ch. Coll. Cam. Bell's Univ. Scho. 1831, Members' Prizeman 1833 and 1835, 29th Wrang. 7th in 1st cl. Cl. Trip. and B.A. 1834, M.A. 1837; Deac. 1836 and Pr. 1837 by Bp of Lin. R. of Harpenden, Dio. Roch. 1859. (Patron, Bp of Pet; Tithe, 809*l*; Glebe, 2¼ acres; R.'s Inc. 830*l*; Pop. 2164.) Hon. Can. of Pet. 1846. Formerly Fell. of Ch. Coll. Cam. 1837–39; C. of St. George's, Leicester, 1836, Hathern, Leicestershire, 1838, Hodnet, Salop, 1841; V. of St. Martin's, Leicester, 1845–59. Author, *Sermons, University and Parochial*, 1850, 6*s*, Rivingtons; occasional Sermons. [10]

VAUGHAN, Edward Thomas, *Tring, Herts.*—Pemb. Coll. Ox. 2nd cl. Law and Mod. Hist. B.A. 1853; Deac. 1863 and Pr. 1864 by Bp of Roch. C. of Tring 1867. Formerly C. of Great Berkhampsted 1863–67. [11]

VAUGHAN, Edward William, *Llantwit Vicarage, Cowbridge, Glamorganshire.*—St. John's Coll. Ox. B.A. 1835; Deac. 1835, Pr. 1836 by Bp of Roch. V. of Llantwit-Major with Lisworney R. Dio. Llan. 1845. (Patrons, D. and C. of Glouc; Llantwit-Major—Tithe, App. 481*l* 7*s* 11*d*; Imp. 70*l*, V. 220*l*; Lisworney, Tithe, 190*l* 3*s*; Glebe, 1 acre; V.'s Inc. 416*l* and Ho; Pop. Llantwit-Major 1020, Lisworney 180.) [12]

VAUGHAN, Hugh, *Llansaintfraid-in-Elvel (Radnorshire), near Builth.*—Jesus Coll. Ox. B.A. 1825, M.A. 1828; Deac. 1825, Pr. 1826. V. of Llansaintfraid-in-Elvel, Dio. St. D. 1838. (Patron, Bp of St. D; Tithe, 198*l*; V.'s Inc. 200*l*; Pop. 340.) Rural Dean of North Elvel 1852. [13]

VAUGHAN, James, 73, *Montpelier-road, Brighton.*—Ball. Coll. Ox. 1st cl. Lit. Hum. B.A. 1827, M.A. 1829; Deac. 1830 and Pr. 1831 by Bp of Salis. P. C. of Ch. Ch. Brighton, Dio. Chich. 1838. (Patron, V. of Brighton; P. C.'s Inc. 430*l*.) [14]

VAUGHAN, James Stuart, *Blackawton, Dartmouth.*—Ball. Coll. Ox. B.A. 1848, M.A. 1850; Deac. 1848 and Pr. 1849 by Bp of Wor. C. of Blackawton with Street. Formerly V. of Stockland-Bristol 1851–57. [15]

VAUGHAN, John James, *Gotham Rectory, (Notts), near Kegworth, Leicestershire.*—Mert. Coll. Ox. B.A. 1829, M.A. 1832; Deac. 1832 and Pr. 1833 by Bp of Salis. R. of Gotham, Dio. Lin. 1836. (Patrons, Earl Howe, Lord St. John and G. S. Foljambe, Esq. in rotation; Glebe, 450 acres; R.'s Inc. 680*l* and Ho; Pop. 771.) V. of Ratcliffe-on-Soar, Notts, Dio. Lin. 1836. (Patron, Earl Howe; Tithe—Imp. 200*l*, V. 40*l*; V.'s Inc. 72*l*; Pop. 165.) [16]

VAUGHAN, Joseph Marychurch.—Trin. Hall, Cam. and King's Coll. Lond. Theol. Assoc. 1858; Deac. 1859, Pr. 1860. C. of St. George's-in-the-East, Lond. Formerly C. of Shildon, Durham, 1859–60. [17]

VAUGHAN, Matthew, *Finchingfield Vicarage, Braintree.*—St. Peter's Coll. Cam. 1st cl. Law Trip. B.C.L.; Deac. 1846, Pr. 1847. V. of Finchingfield, Dio. Roch. 1864. (Patron, Rev. J. Stock; Tithe—Imp. 1506*l* 5*s* and 38 acres of Glebe, V. 719*l*; V.'s Inc. 719*l* and Ho; Pop. 1834.) Formerly P. C. of St. John's, Brixton, Lond. 1853. [18]

VAUGHAN, Robert Charles, 3, *Manor-terrace, East-India-road, London, E.*—Caius Coll. Cam. B.A. 1830, M.A. 1833; Deac. 1830, Pr. 1831. C. of All Saints', Poplar, 1833; Chap. to the Poplar Union 1837; Lect. of All Saints', Poplar, 1841. [19]

VAUGHAN, Samuel, *St. Mark's, Dewsbury, Yorkshire.*—M.A. of the Univ. of Rostock, Mecklenburg-Schwerin, Prussia; and Theol. Assoc. of King's Coll. Lond; Deac. 1852 and Pr. 1853 by Bp of Lon. P. C. of St. Mark's, Dewsbury, Dio. Rip. 1865. (Patron, Bp of Rip; Glebe, ½ an acre; Ho; Pop. 4000.) Formerly C. of St. Thomas', Charterhouse, Lond. 1852–54, St. Thomas's, Ardwick and New District of St. Saviour's, Manchester, 1854–58, St. Paul's, Huddersfield, 1863. Author, *An Essay on the Inspiration and Interpretation of Holy Scripture.* [1]

VAUGHAN, Thomas Browne, *Heath, near Chesterfield.*—St. Cath. Coll. Cam. B.A. 1862, M.A. 1865; Deac. 1862 and Pr. 1863 by Bp of Lich. C. of Heath and Hault Hucknall, Derbyshire, 1862. [2]

VAUGHAN, Thomas Charles, *Castle Carrock Rectory, near Carlisle.*—Magd. Hall, Ox. B.A. 1831; Deac. 1833 and Pr. 1834 by Bp of Wor. R. of Castle-Carrock, Dio. Carl. 1834. (Patrons, D. and C. of Carl; Glebe, 280 acres; R.'s Inc. 200*l* and Ho; Pop. 337.) [3]

VAUGHAN, Walter Arnold, *Chart-Sutton Vicarage, Staplehurst, Kent.*—Ch. Ch. Ox. B.A. 1831, M.A. 1835; Deac. 1833 by Bp of Chich. Pr. 1836 by Abp of Cant. V. of Chart Sutton, Dio. Cant. 1836. (Patrons, D. and C. of Roch; Tithe, 250*l*; Glebe, 8 acres; V.'s Inc. 300*l* and Ho; Pop. 700.) Dom. Chap. to Viscount Barrington 1834. Author, *Baptism*, 1860, 1*s*; *Laying on of Hands*, 1863, 1*s*. [4]

VAUGHAN, Walter William, *Llandegley Vicarage, Pen-y-bont, Rhayader, Radnor.*—Lampeter, Scho. 1854; Deac. 1856 and Pr. 1858 by Bp of St. D. V. of Llandeglay, Dio. St. D. 1862. (Patron, Bp of St. D; Tithe, 116*l* 10*s*; Glebe, 25 acres; V.'s Inc. 158*l* and Ho; Pop. 382.) Formerly C. of Steynton, Pembrokeshire, 1856–59, Castle-Caereinion 1860–61. [5]

VAUGHTON, Roger Ryland, *Westborough, Grantham.*—Emman. Coll. Cam. M.A; Deac. 1813 by Bp of Ches. Pr. 1814 by Bp of Lich. R. of Westborough, 1st Med. with Dry Doddington, 2nd Med. Dio. Lin. 1861. (Patrons, Trustees of Rev. Robert Hall; R.'s Inc. 600*l* and Ho; Pop. Westborough 265, Dry Doddington 283.) [6]

VAUTIER, Richard, *Kenwyn Vicarage, Truro.*—St. Peter's Coll. Cam. B.A. 1845, M.A. 1858; Deac. 1845 and Pr. 1846 by Bp of Ex. V. of St. Kenwyn with St. Kea V. Dio. Ex. 1857. (Patron, Bp of Ex; St. Kenwyn, Tithe—App. 9*l* 5*s* 10*d*, Imp. 538*l*, V. 524*l* 11*s* 2*d*; Glebe, 11 acres; St. Kea, Tithe—Imp. 500*l*, V. 242*l* 15*s* 10½*d*; Glebe, 16 acres; V.'s Inc. 790*l* and Ho; Pop. St. Kenwyn 970, St. Kea 856.) Lect. of St. Gluvias, Cornwall, 1857; Surrogate; Chap. to the Bp of Ex. Formerly V. of Yealmpton, Devon, 1856–57. [7]

VAUX, Bowyer, *St. Peter's Parsonage, Great Yarmouth.*—Trin. Coll. Ox. B.A. 1832, M.A. 1836. P. C. of St. Peter's, Great Yarmouth, Dio. Nor. 1846. (Patron, P. C. of Great Yarmouth; P. C.'s Inc. 190*l* and Ho.) Chap. of the Military Asylum, Great Yarmouth. [8]

VAUX, James Edward, *Cavendish Club, Regent-street, London, W.*—Trin. Coll. Cam. B.A. 1851, M.A. 1856; Deac. 1851 and Pr. 1852 by Bp of Wor. C. of St. Philip's, Clerkenwell, 1867. Formerly Assist. C. of Trinity, Westminster, 1855; Chap. to Westminster Hospital, 1856; Asst. C. of St. Mary's, Munster-square, Lond. 1859. Author, *The Presence of the whole Congregation at the Holy Eucharist the Rule of Antiquity and the Intention of the Church of England*, 1861, 1*s*; Article on *Clerical Celibacy* in *The Church and the World*, 1866; *Sermons on the Atonement*, 1867. [9]

VAVASOUR, John Francis Stukeley, *Ashby-de la-Zouch, Leicestershire.*—Brasen. Coll. Ox. Hulmeian Exhib. B.A. 1862, M.A. 1864; Deac. 1863 and Pr. 1864 by Abp of York. C. of Ashby-de-la-Zouch. Formerly C. of Scalby 1863. [10]

VAVASOUR, Marmaduke, *Ashby-de la-Zouch Vicarage, Leicestershire.*—Brasen. Coll. Ox. 2nd cl. Lit. Hum. and B.A. 1820, M.A. 1821; Deac. 1822 and Pr. 1823 by Bp. of Glouc. V. of Ashby-de-la-Zouch, Dio. Pet. 1833. (Patron, Marquis of Hastings; Tithe—Imp. 308*l* 1*s*; Glebe, 185 acres; V.'s Inc. 400*l* and Ho; Pop. 2847.) P. C. of Smisby, Dio. Lich. (Patron, Marquis of Hastings; P. C.'s Inc. 58*l*; Pop. 304.) Surrogate 1834; Rural Dean of Ackley 1847; Hon. Can. of Peterborough 1851. [11]

VAWDREY, Alexander Allen, *St. Agnes Vicarage, Truro, Cornwall.*—St. John's Coll. Cam. Scho. and Exhib. Jun. Opt. 3rd Cl. Trip. and B.A. 1831, M.A. 1834; Deac. 1833 by Bp of Roch. Pr. 1834 by Bp of B. and W. V. of St. Agnes, Dio. Ex. 1845. (Patrons, D. and C. of Ex; Tithe—App. 253*l*; V. 150*l*; V.'s Inc. 400*l* and Ho; Pop. 6539.) Rural Dean. Formerly C. of St. Erth 1833; P. C. of St. Day, Cornwall, 1834. [12]

VAWDREY Daniel, *North Darley Rectory, Matlock, Derbyshire.*—Brasen. Coll. Ox. B.A. 1830, M.A. 1832. R. of North and South Darley, Dio. Lich. 1847. (Patron, Bp of Lich; Tithe, 351*l*; R.'s Inc. 435*l* and Ho; Pop. 1418.) Formerly P. C. of St. Mary's, Cross-green, South Darley. [13]

VAWDREY, William Seaman, *Pannall Vicarage, Wetherby, York.*—V. of Pannall, Dio. Rip. 1862. (Patron, the present V; Tithe, 8*l*; Glebe, 109 acres; V.'s Inc. 318*l* and Ho; Pop. 594.) [14]

VEALE, Henry, *Newcastle-under-Lyne Rectory, Staffs.*—Dur. B.A. 1846; Deac. 1846, Pr. 1847. R. of Newcastle-under-Lyne, Dio. Lich. 1853. (Patrons, Simeon's Trustees; Tithe, 150*l*; Glebe, 8 acres, R.'s Inc. 300*l* and Ho; Pop. 5831.) [15]

VEALE, William, *Gulval, Penzance, Cornwall.*—New. Coll. Ox. B.A. 1806, M.A. 1810; Deac. 1808, Pr. 1809. [16]

VEALE, W. C., *Boxmoor, Herts.*—C. of Boxmoor. [17]

VEASEY, Frederick, *Great Brickhill, Fenny Stratford.*—C. of Great Brickhill. [18]

VEITCH, Andrew, *The Rectory, South Ferriby, Barton-on-Humber.*—R. of South Ferriby, Dio. Lin. 1862. (Patron, Bp of Lin; R.'s Inc. 192*l* and Ho; Pop. 573.) [19]

VEITCH, H. G. F., *Kilmersdon Vicarage, Bath.*—Ball. Coll. Ox. B.A. 1856; Deac. 1857, Pr. 1858. V. of Kilmersdon, Dio. B. and W. 1864. (Patron, Rev. T. R. Joliffe; Tithe, 244*l*; V.'s Inc. 214*l* and Ho; Pop. 807.) [20]

VEITCH, William Douglas, 2, *Warrington-terrace, Maida-hill, London, N.W.*—Ox. B.A. 1823, M.A. 1827; Deac. 1824, Pr. 1826. P. C. of St. Saviour's Paddington, Dio. Lon. 1862. (Patron, Bp of Lon; Pop. 5787.) Chap. to the Bp of Jerusalem. [21]

VENABLES, Edmund, *Precentory, Lincoln.*—Pemb. Coll. Cam. Wrang. 2nd cl. Cl. Trip. and B.A. 1842, M.A. 1845; Deac. 1844 by Bp of Chich. Pr. 1846 by Bp of Nor. Exam. Chap. to Bp of Lin; Canon Res. and Precentor of Lin. 1867. Formerly C. of Herstmonceux, Sussex, 1844–53, Bonchurch, Isle of Wight, 1853–55. Author, *History of Herstmonceux Castle*, 1851; *History of the Church of Great St. Mary, Cambridge*, 1855; *History of the Isle of Wight*, 1860; Translator of Wieseler's *Synopsis Evangelica*, 1864. [22]

VENABLES, George, *Friezland Vicarage, Greenfield, near Manchester.*—St. Edm. Hall, Ox. S.C.L. 1850; Deac. 1850 and Pr. 1852 by Bp of Ox. V. of Friezland, Dio. Man. 1858. (Patron, R. R. Whitehead, Esq; Glebe, ½ an acre; V.'s Inc. 300*l* and Ho; Pop. 2500.) Surrogate. Formerly C. of Nether Worton and Deddington, Oxon, 1850–53, Broadwater, Sussex, with Chap. of Shoreham Union Poorhouse, 1853–54; V. of St. Paul's, Chatham, 1854–58. Author, *Sermons on Romanism* and *Deddington Tracts*, 1851–53; *Church Endowments for New Parishes, How we may at once provide for them*, 1853, 6*d*; *Church Orders*, 1855, 1*s*; *How did they get there? a Tract for* 1862, 2*d*; *Spiritual Destitution*; *Your Child's Baptism*, 6*d*; *Counsels for Communicants*, 1*s*; *Our Church and Our Country*, 6*d* (Mackintosh); *The Good News is true*, 1*s* (Hatchard); *An additional Office for Use in Churches*; Many Sermons in *The Pulpit* and *Penny Pulpit*; etc. [23]

VENABLES, Henry, *Chester.*—Jesus Coll. Cam. B.A. 1846, M.A. 1849; Deac. 1846 and Pr. 1848 by Bp of

Ches. Min. Can. and Precentor of Ches. Cathl. 1857. (Value, 150*l*.) [1]

VENABLES, Richard Lister, *Clyro, Hay, Radnorshire.*—Emman. Coll. Cam. B.A. 1831, M.A. 1835; Deac. 1832, Pr. 1833. V. of Clyro with Bettws Clyro, Dio. St. D. 1847. (Patron, Bp of St. D; Tithe—Eccles. Commis. 676*l*; Glebe, 712 acres; V.'s Inc. 300*l* and Ho; Pop. 888.) [2]

VENESS, Henry Thomas, *Rusholme, Manchester.*—Queens' Coll. Cam. B.A. 1841; Deac. 1842 and Pr. 1843 by Bp of Nor. R. of Rusholme, Dio. Man. 1860. (Patron, C. Worsley, Esq; Pop. 2508.) Formerly Lect. of Trinity, Margate, 1854. [3]

VENN, Henry, *Church Missionary Society, Salisbury-square, Fleet-street, London, E.C.*—Queens' Coll. Cam. B.A. 1818, M.A. 1821, B.D. 1828. Preb. of Caddington Minor in St. Paul's Cathl. 1846. (Value, 2*l*.) Hon. Sec. to the Ch. Miss. Soc. Formerly Fell. of Queen's Coll. Cam. [4]

VENN, Henry Knott, *Combe Rawleigh, Devon.*—St. Peter's Coll. Cam. Jun. Opt. and B.A. 1838; Deac. 1839, Pr. 1840. C. of Coombe Rawleigh and Sheldon; Surrogate. Formerly C. of Monkton; Chap. to the Honiton Union. [5]

VENN, John, *Hereford.*—Queens' Coll. Cam. Bell's Scho. 1824, 12th Wrang. and B.A. 1827; Deac. 1828, Pr. 1829. V. of St. Peter's with St. Owen's R. City and Dio. Herf. 1833. (Patrons, Simeon's Trustees; St. Peter's, Tithe, 4*l* 2*s*; Glebe, 190 acres; St. Owen's, Tithe—App. 15*l* 2*s* 6*d*, R. 75*l*; Glebe, 50 acres; V.'s Inc. 413*l*; Pop. St. Peter's 3053, St. Owen's 2171.) Preb. of Withington Parva in Herf. Cathl. 1843. Formerly Fell. of Queens' Coll. Cam. 1828. [6]

VENN, John.—Caius Coll. Cam. 6th Wrang. B.A. 1857; Deac. 1858 and Pr. 1859 by Bp of Ely. Fell. of Caius Coll. Cam. Formerly C. of Mortlake, and Cheshunt, Herts. [7]

VENN, John Cook, *Buckerell, Devon.*—St. Bees 1844; Deac. 1845, Pr. 1846. C. of Buckerell. Formerly C. of Luppitt, Devon. [8]

VENN, William, *Bishops Waltham, Hants.*—St. Aidan's; Deac. 1864 by Bp of Win. C. of Bishops Waltham, and Head Mast. of the Gr. Sch. Bishops Waltham. [9]

VENTRIS, Edward, 4, *Causeway, Cambridge.*—St. Peter's Coll. Cam. B.A. 1825, M.A. 1828; Deac. 1825 by Bp of Lin. Pr. 1825 by Bp of Ely. P. C. of Stow-cum-Quy, near Cambridge, Dio. Ely, 1825. (Patron, Bp of Ely; Tithe—App. 520*l*; Glebe, 64½ acres; P. C.'s Inc. 52*l*; Pop. 368.) Chap. to Lord St. Leonards; Surrogate; Chap. of the Cambridge County Gaol. Author, *Notes upon Chantries and Free Chapels*, Cam. Antiq. Soc. 1856; Contributor to Vols. 3, 4 and 5 of the Catalogue of the Cam. Univ. Lib. MSS. 1858–59. [10]

VENTRIS, Edward Favell, *Aston Rectory, Newport, Salop.*—Emman. Coll. Cam. B.A. 1847, M.A. 1850; Deac. 1848 by Bp of Lich. Pr. 1850 by Bp of Ches. R. of St. Andrew's, Aston, Dio. Lich. 1863. (Patron, Rev. C. F. C. Pigott; Tithe, 112*l* 17*s* 9*d*; R.'s Inc. 150*l* and Ho; Pop. 1005.) Formerly V. of West Mersea, Essex, and Surrogate for Dio. Roch. 1859–63. Author, *Sermon on the Cattle Plague*, 1866. [11]

VENTRIS, Henry Laurence, *North Whetstone, Finchley, Middlesex, N.*—Queens' Coll. Cam. 7th Sen. Opt. and B.A. 1831; Deac. 1833 and Pr 1834 by Bp of Lon. P. C. of St. John's, Whetstone, Dio. Lon. 1833. (Patron, Bp of Lon; P. C.'s Inc. 170*l*; Pop. 1801.) [12]

VERITY, Edward Arundel, *Habergham, Whalley, Lancashire.*—Lampeter, B.D. 1853; Deac. and Pr. 1845 by Bp of Ches. P.C. of All Saints', Habergham, Dio. Man. 1845. (Patrons, the Crown and Bp of Man. alt; P. C.'s Inc. 220*l*; Pop. 2822.) Formerly Miss. elect and Travelling Sec. S. American Soc. 1845–46; Army Chap. in Crimea 1855–56. Author, *Blessings of a Christian Government and Constitution*, 1846; *The Prayer Book, the Parochial System and the Common People*, 1853; various Tracts, Sermons; etc. [13]

VERNON, Courtenay John, *Grafton Underwood Rectory, Kettering, Northants.*—Trin. Coll. Cam. B.A. 1851. R. of Grafton Underwood, Dio. Pet. 1854. (Patron, Lord Lyveden; R.'s Inc. 260*l* and Ho; Pop. 294.) [14]

VERNON, Evelyn Hardolph Harcourt, *Cotgrave, near Nottingham.*—Univ. Coll. Ox. S.C.L. 1843; Deac. 1845 by Bp of Rip. Pr. 1846 by Bp. of Lin. R. of Cotgrave, Dio. Lin. 1859. (Patron, Earl Manvers; Glebe, 557 acres; R.'s Inc. 628*l* and Ho; Pop. 850.) Preb. of Lin; Rural Dean of Bingham, District No. 3. Formerly R. of Grove, and Sinecure R. and V. of Headon with Upton, Notts, 1846–59. [15]

VERNON, Frederick, *Maulden, near Ampthill, Beds.*—St. John's Coll. Ox. 3rd cl. Cl. B.A. 1860. Deac. 1863 and Pr. 1864 by Bp of Ely. C. of Maulden 1864. Formerly C. of Cranfield, Beds, 1863–64. [16]

VERNON, F. W., *Mucklestone, Market Drayton, Salop.*—C. of Mucklestone. [17]

VERNON, Henry George, *Liverpool.*—St. Aidan's; M.A. 1856; Deac. 1853 and Pr. 1854 by Bp of Ches. Res. Chap. Bursar and Sec. to the Council of St. Aidan's Coll; P. C. of St. Stephen's, Liverpool, Dio. Ches. 1859. (Patron, R. of Liverpool; P. C.'s Inc. 320*l*.) Surrogate. Formerly C. of Trinity, Birkenhead; Pop. 1449.) [18]

VERNON, Henry John, 5, *Park-place, St. James's-street, S.W.*—Magd. Hall, Ox. B.A. 1838. Asst. Sec. to the S.P.G. 79, Pall-mall, Lond. [19]

VERNON, James Edmund, *Middleton Court, Washford, near Taunton, Somerset.*—Wad. Coll. Ox. B.A. 1859, M.A. 1865; Deac. 1863 and Pr. 1864 by Bp of Lon. P. C. of Withiel Florey, Dio. B. and W. 1867. (Patron, Ambrose Lethbridge, Esq; Glebe, 19*l*; Qu. Anne's Bounty, 20*l*; Endow., 20*l*; P. C.'s Inc. 59*l*; Pop. 150.) C. in sole charge of Miss. Ch. Brendon-hill, Somerset, 1867. (Stipend, 100*l*.) Formerly C. of Leyton 1863–67. [20]

VERNON, John, *Eckington, near Pershore, Worcestershire.*—V. of Eckington, Dio. Wor. 1866. (Patrons, D. and C. of Westminster; V.'s Inc. 215*l* and Ho; Pop. 748.) [21]

VERNON, John Richard, *Newington, Hythe, Kent.*—Magd. Hall. Ox. B.A. 1859, M.A. 1863; Deac. 1860 and Pr. 1861 by Abp of Cant. C. of Newington, Hythe, 1867. Formerly C. of Sellinge, and Cheriton 1865. Author, *A Committee on Pews*, Bosworth, Regent-street; Sermon, *The Sorrow not without Hope*, at the Funeral of the Rev. T. C. Maule, Rivingtons. [22]

VERNON, The Hon. John Venables, *Nuthall Rectory, near Nottingham.*—Ch. Ch. Ox. B.A. 1820, M.A. 1823; Deac. 1821 by Abp of York, Pr. 1822 by Bp of Ches. R. of Kirkby-in-Ashfield, Notts, Dio. Lin. 1829. (Patron, Duke of Portland; R.'s Inc. 738*l* and Ho; Pop. 2886.) R. of Nuthall, Dio. Lin. 1837. (Patron, R. Holden, Esq; Tithe, 344*l* 12*s*; Glebe, 52 acres; R.'s Inc. 430*l* and Ho; Pop. 842.) [23]

VERNON, Marcus Henry, *Westfield Vicarage, Battle, Sussex.*—Trin. Coll. Cam. B.A. 1817, M.A. 1822. V. of Westfield, Dio. Chich. 1836. (Patron, Bp of Chich; Tithe—App. 492*l* 8*s* 2*d*, V. 559*l* 1*s* 5*d*; V.'s Inc. [illegible] and Ho; Pop. 883.) [24]

VERNON, W., *Mossley, Ashton-under-Lyne.*—C. of Mossley. [25]

VERNON, William Foley, *Shrawley Rectory, Stourport.*—Emman. Coll. Cam. B.A; Deac. 1851 by Bp of Wor. R. of Shrawley, Dio. Wor. 1863. (Patron, H. F. Vernon, Esq; Tithe, 355*l*; Glebe, 63 acres; R.'s Inc. 350*l* and Ho; Pop. 549.) [26]

VERNON, William George, *Great Barr Parsonage, Birmingham.*—Corpus Coll. Cam. B.A. [illegible]; Deac. 1863 and Pr. 1864 by Bp of St. A. C. in sole charge of Great Barr 1867. Formerly C. of Kerry, Newtown, Montgomeryshire, 1863–66. [27]

VERNON, William Hardy, *Leytonstone Parsonage, Essex, N.E.*—Magd. Hall, Ox. M.A. [illegible]; Deac. and Pr. 1828 by Bp of Lin. P. C. of Leytonstone, Dio. Lon. 1864. (Patron, J. Pardoe, Esq; P. C.'s Inc. [illegible] and Ho; Pop. 2000.) Formerly R. of Carshalton, Surrey, 1835–45; C. of Sutton 1846 and Surrogate. [illegible]

Sermons, 1 vol. 1846; Author, several Occasional Sermons. [1]

VERNON, William Tassie, *Kirk-Ella, near Hull.*—Magd. Hall, Ox. B.A. 1844, M.A. 1864; Deac. 1844 and Pr. 1845 by Bp of Herf. V. of Kirk-Ella, Dio. York, 1858. (Patron, R. Sykes, Esq; Tithe, 14*l* 16*s* 7*d*; Glebe, 133 acres; V.'s Inc. 252*l* and Ho; Pop. 1148.) Formerly C. of Monkland 1844, Ballingham and Bolstone 1847, Pembridge 1849, Madley 1850; P. C. of Hope-under-Dinmore 1852, all in Herefordshire. Author, single Sermons and Pamphlets. [2]

VESEY, Francis Gerald, *Huntingdon.*—Trin. Coll. Cam. B.A. 1855. R. of All Saints' with St. John's V. Huntingdon, Dio. Ely, 1858. (Patron, the present R. and V; R. and V.'s Inc. 250*l*; Pop. All Saints' 430, St. John's 1462.) Rural Dean. Formerly C. of Great St. Mary's, Cambridge. [3]

VEYSIE, Daniel, *Daventry Parsonage, Northants.*—Ch. Ch. Ox. B.A. 1818, M.A. 1821, B.D. 1831; Deac. 1824 and Pr. 1825 by Bp of Ox. P. C. of Daventry, Dio. Pet. 1833. (Patron, Ch. Ch. Ox; Glebe, 14 acres; P. C.'s Inc. 362*l* and Ho; Pop. 4124.) [4]

VIBERT, John Pope, 1, *Alexandra-place, Penzance.*—Magd. Hall, Ox. B.A. 1849; Deac. 1849 and Pr. 1851 by Bp of Ox. P. C. of Newlyn St. Peter, Dio. Ex. 1856. (Patrons, Crown and Bp of Ex. alt; P. C.'s Inc. 150*l*; Pop. 3200.) Formerly C. of Witley, Surrey, 1849, Finstock and Ramsden, Oxon, 1851, Chadlington, Oxon, 1851, Morvah, Cornwall, 1854. [5]

VICARS, John, *Lapford Rectory, Morchard Bishop, Devon.*—Ch. Coll. Cam. B.A. 1854, M.A. 1857; Deac. 1856, Pr. 1858. R. of Lapford, Dio. Ex. 1861. (Patron, Rev. John Vicars; Tithe, 422*l* 16*s* 2*d*; Glebe, 158 acres; R.'s Inc. 600*l* and Ho; Pop. 677.) Formerly C. of St. Mary's Episcopal Chapel, Walcot, Bath, 1860; and Stapleton, Iwerne, Dorset; Head Mast. of the Bath Rectory Middle Sch. [6]

VICARY, J., *Berwick Bassett, Swindon, Wilts.*—P. C. of Berwick Bassett, Dio. Salis. 1861. (Patron, Bp of Salis; P. C.'s Inc. 40*l*; Pop. 171.) [7]

VICKERS, Randall William, *St. John's-park, Ryde, Isle of Wight.*—Ex. Coll. Ox. B.A. 1862, M.A. 1865; Deac. 1863 by Bp of Ox. Pr. 1865 by Bp of Win. C. of Trinity, Ryde, 1865. Formerly C. of St. Philip and James's, Oxford, 1863. [8]

VICKERS, Valentine S., *Eastry, Sandwich, Kent.*—King's Coll. Lond; Deac. 1867 by Abp of Cant. C. of St. Mary's, Eastry, 1867. [9]

VIDAL, Francis, *Beachley, Gloucestershire.*—P. C. of Beachley, Dio. G. and B. 1866. (Patron, V. of Tidenham; P. C.'s Inc. 16*l*; Pop. 188.) [10]

VIDAL, Francis Furse, *Eton College.*—Trin. Hall, Cam. B.A. 1863; Deac. 1864 by Bp of Ox. C. of Clewer, near Windsor, 1864. [11]

VIDAL, James Henry, *Chiddingly Vicarage, Hurst Green, Sussex.*—St. John's Coll. Cam. B.A. 1842, M.A. 1845; Deac. 1842 and Pr. 1843 by Bp of Chich. V. of Chiddingly, Dio. Chich. 1847. (Patrons, the Earl and Countess De la Warr; Tithe—Imp. 555*l* 12*s* and 34 acres of Glebe, V. 256*l* 13*s*; Glebe, 7 acres; V.'s Inc. 263*l* and Ho; Pop. 992.) [12]

VIGERS, Duncan Fermin, *Notgrove Rectory, Northleach, Glouc.*—Trin. Coll. Cam. Sen. Opt. and B.A. 1839, M.A. 1842; Deac. 1841 and Pr. 1842 by Bp of Lon. R. of Notgrove, Dio. G. and B. 1858. (Patron, Ld Chan; Glebe, 309 acres; R.'s Inc. 356*l* and Ho; Pop. 140.) Formerly C. of Kelvedon. [13]

VIGNE, Henry, *Sunbury Vicarage, Middlesex, S.W.*—St. Peter's Coll. Cam. B.A. 1838, M.A. 1847; Deac. 1840, Pr. 1841. V. of Sunbury, Dio. Lon. 1842. (Patrons, D. and C. of St. Paul's; V.'s Inc. 350*l* and Ho; Pop. 2333.) [14]

VIGNOLES, Olinthus John, *Anerley, Norwood, Surrey, S.*—Dub. Regius Prof. of Div. Sen. Prizeman, A.B. 1852, A.M. 1860; Deac. 1853 by Bp of Cork, Pr. 1855 by Bp of Ches. Chap. of the North Surrey Dist. Schs. Anerley, 1857. (Stipend, 250*l*.) Formerly C. of Percy Chapel, Fitzroy-square, Lond. [15]

VIGOR, William Edward, *Botus Fleming Rectory, Saltash, Cornwall.*—Wor. Coll. Ox. B.A. 1842; Deac. 1842 and Pr. 1843 by Bp of Ex. R. of Botus Fleming, Dio. Ex. 1851. (Patron, the present R; Tithe, 228*l*; Glebe, 60 acres; R.'s Inc. 300*l* and Ho; Pop. 237.) Formerly Dioc. Inspector of Schs. 1862–65. [16]

VIGORS, Richard William, *Aust, Bristol.*—C. of Aust and Northwich, Bristol. [17]

VILLAR, John Gaspard, *Hoggeston Rectory, Winslow, Bucks.*—Wor. Coll. Ox. B.A. 1809, M.A. 1812; Deac. 1812 and Pr. 1813 by Bp of Ox. R. of Hoggeston, Dio. Ox. 1840. (Patron, Wor. Coll. Ox; Tithe, 375*l*; Glebe, 80 acres; R.'s Inc. 430*l* and Ho; Pop. 207.) [18]

VILLIERS, H. M., *Adisham Rectory, Wingham, Kent.*—R. of Adisham with Staple P. C. Dio. Cant. 1862. (Patron, Abp of Cant; Adisham, Tithe, 747*l*; Glebe, 18 acres and Ho; Staple, Tithe, 600*l*; R.'s Inc. 1382*l* and Ho; Pop. Adisham 492, Staple 520.) [19]

VILLIERS, William Richard, *Brooksby, Torquay.*—Ch. Coll. Cam. S.C.L. 1852, B.C.L. 1855; Deac. 1852 by Bp of Wor. Pr. 1853 by Bp of Herf. C. of St. John's, Torquay, 1867. Formerly P. C. of Shireshead, Lancashire; Dom. Chap. to Lord De Tabley. [20]

VINALL, Edward, *Tunbridge, Kent.*—St. Cath. Hall, Cam. Schs. and Prizeman, 2nd cl. Cl. and B.A. 1827, M.A. 1831. P. C. of Hildenborough-next-Tunbridge, Dio. Cant. 1844. (Patron, V. of Tunbridge; Glebe, 6 acres; P. C.'s Inc. 120*l* and Ho; Pop. 1049.) Surrogate. [21]

VINCENT, Frederick, *Slinfold Rectory, Horsham, Sussex.*—Brasen. Coll. Ox. 3rd cl. Lit. Hum. B.A. 1819, M.A. 1823. R. of Slinfold, Dio. Chich. 1844. (Patron, Bp of Chich; Tithe—Imp. 10*l* 5*s*, R. 728*l* 9*s* 3*d*; Glebe, 2 acres; R.'s Inc. 730*l* and Ho; Pop. 755.) Preb. of Seaford in Chich. Cathl. 1860; Chap. to the Bp of Chich; Proctor in Convocation for Archd. of Chich. Author, *Letter to the Rev. H. E. Manning (sometime Archdeacon of Chichester) on the Jurisdiction of the Crown in Matters Spiritual*, 1851. [22]

VINCENT, Frederick Augustus, *Ladbroke Rectory, Southam, Warwickshire.*—Dub. A.B. 1842, A.M. 1847, *ad eund.* Ox. 1847, B.D. Dub. and Dur. 1851; Deac. 1842, Pr. 1843 by Bp of Win. R. of Ladbroke, Dio. Wor. 1866. (Patron, present R; Tithe, R. 431*l* 10*s*; Glebe, 40 acres; R.'s Inc. 500*l* and Ho; Pop. 275.) R. of Sinecure R. of Radborne, 1866. (Patron, next turn, Bolton King, Esq; Tithe, 40*l*; no Ch. or Ho; Pop. 23.) Formerly P. C. of St. Matthew's, Jersey, and Vice-Regent of St. Anastasius Gr. Sch. Jersey, 1842–47; Sen. Cl. Mast. Leamington Coll. 1847–51; Mast. of Batley Gr. Sch. 1851–60; V. of St. Chad's, Stafford, 1860–66. [23]

VINCENT, Henry J., *St. Dogmael's (Pembrokeshire), near Cardigan.*—V. of St. Dogmael's with Llantwyd V. and Monington V. Dio. St. D. 1826. (Patron, Ld Chan; St. Dogmael's, Tithe—Imp. 408*l* 11*s*, V. 70*l*; Llantwyd, Tithe—Imp. 125*l*, V. 32*l*; Monington, Tithe—Imp. 45*l*, V. 35*l*; V.'s Inc. 139*l*; Pop. St. Dogmael's 2438, Llantwyd 264, Monington 120.) [24]

VINCENT, James Crawley, *The Vicarage, Carnarvon.*—Jesus Coll. Ox. B.A. 1849, M.A. 1853; Deac. 1852 and Pr. 1853 by Bp of Ban. V. of Llanbeblig with Carnarvon C. and Waenfawr C. Dio. Ban. 1859. (Patron, Bp of Ches; Tithe—App. 486*l* 9*s* 1*d*, Imp. 10*s*, V. 318*l* 9*s*; Glebe, 1 acre; V.'s Inc. 408*l* and Ho; Pop. 10,200.) Rural Dean 1859. Formerly C. of Llantrisaint, Anglesey, 1852–54, Dyserth 1854–56; P. C. of St. Anne's, Llandegan, 1857–59. [25]

VINCENT, The Very Rev. James Vincent, *Bangor.*—Jesus Coll. Ox. B.A. 1815, M.A. 1818; Deac. 1815, Pr. 1816. Dean of Ban. 1862. (Value, 700*l*.) Formerly R. of Llanfair-fechan 1834; Rural Dean 1842; Hon. Can. of Ban. Cathl. 1851; Proctor in Convocation for the Dio. of Ban; Hon. Sec. to the Ban. Diocesan Board of Education; Fell. of Jesus Coll. Ox. Author, *Christian Unity, and the Injurious Effects of Division in preventing the Extension of the Gospel* (a Sermon, in Welsh); occasional Tracts, in Welsh; Addresses to the Church Lay Association, in Welsh. [26]

VINCENT, John, *Jacobstow Rectory, Hatherleigh, Devon.*—Wor. Coll. Ox. B.A. 1832, M.A. 1837; Deac. 1832, Pr. 1837. R. of Jacobstow, Dio. Ex. 1847. (Patron, L. Burton, Esq; Tithe, 160*l*; Glebe, 90 acres; R.'s Inc. 280*l* and Ho; Pop. 232.) [1]

VINCENT, John Charles Frederick, *Longdon Vicarage, Rugeley, Staffs.*—Dub. A.B. 1842, A.M. 1845, LL.D. 1849; Deac. 1842, Pr. 1843. V. of Longdon, Dio. Lich. 1861. (Patron, Bp of Lich; V.'s Inc. 180*l* and Ho; Pop. 900.) Formerly Head Mast. of Henry VII.'s Gr. Sch. of St. Anastasius 1842–44; Prin. of the Coll. at Roseau 1844–45; Min. of St. Aubin's and Lect. of St. Peter's, Jersey, 1845–52; Head Mast. of the Norwich Sch. 1852–59; R. of Morborne 1859. [2]

VINCENT, Osman Parke, 31, *St. Augustine-road, Camden-square, London, N.W.*—Magd. Coll. Cam. B.A. 1839, M.A. 1842. C. in sole charge of St. Paul's, Camden-square, St. Pancras, Lond. Formerly C. of St. Margaret's with St. Nicholas', Lynn Regis. [3]

VINCENT, Thomas, *Wantage, Berks.*—St. John's Coll. Cam. B.A. 1842, M.A. 1845; Deac. 1842 and Pr. 1843 by Bp of Win. Chap. of the St. Mary's Home for Penitents, Wantage, 1850. Author, *Account and Reports of the St. Mary's Home from* 1850. [4]

VINCENT, William, *Chipperfield Parsonage, Rickmansworth, Herts.*—Ch. Ch. Ox. 3rd cl. Lit. Hum. B.A. 1832, M.A. 1850; Deac. 1833 and Pr. 1834 by Bp of Chich. P. C. of Chipperfield, Dio. Roch. 1864. (Patrons, Trustees; P. C.'s Inc. 174*l* and Ho; Pop. 1200.) Formerly C. of Cowfold, Sussex, 1833–38, Bolney 1838–40; V. of Steventon, Berks, 1840–51; P. C. of Trinity, Islington, 1851–64. Author, *Three Sermons on Baptismal and Spiritual Regeneration*, 1846, Wertheim and Mackintosh, 6*d* and 1*s*; and various other Sermons. [5]

VINCENT, William, *Postwick Rectory, Norwich.*—Ch. Ch. Ox. B.A. 1857, M.A. 1858; Deac. 1858 and Pr. 1859 by Bp of Win. R. of Postwick, Dio. Nor. 1864. (Patron, Earl of Rosebery; Tithe, 490*l*; Glebe, 50 acres; R.'s Inc. 550*l* and Ho; Pop. 291.) Formerly C. of Egham 1859–63, Betshanger (sole charge) 1863–64 [6]

VINCENT, William Philip, *Stafford.*—Dub. A.B. 1851, Dur. Licen. Theol. 1852; Deac. 1852 and Pr. 1853 by Bp of Rip. Chap. of the Stafford Co. Gaol 1859 (Stipend, 350*l*); Hon. Sec. to North and South Dist. Prisoners' Aid Soc; Dom. Chap. to Viscount St. Vincent. Formerly C. of Cumberworth, Yorks, 1852–55; P. C. of Thurgoland, Yorks, 1855–58; Asst. Chap. at Stafford Co. Gaol 1858–59. [7]

VINE, Marshall Hall, 59, *Highbury-hill, London, N.*—Univ. Coll. Ox. B.A. 1835, M.A. 1865. R. of St. Mary-le-Bow with St. Pancras, Soper-lane R. and Allhallows, Honey-lane R. City and Dio. Lon. 1851. (Patron, Abp of Cant. 2 turns, and the Grocers' Company 1 turn; Tithe, 333*l* 6*s* 8*d*; Glebe, 350*l*; R.'s Inc. 683*l* 6*s* 8*d*; Pop. St. Mary-le-Bow 317, St. Pancras, Soper-lane, 76, Allhallows, Honey-lane, 65.) [8]

VINE, T., *Patrixbourne, Canterbury.*—C. of Patrixbourne. [9]

VINER, Alfred William Ellis, *Badgeworth Vicarage, Cheltenham.*—Univ. Coll. Ox. B.A. 1845; Deac. 1847 by Bp of Ex. Pr. 1848 by Bp of G. and B. V. of Badgeworth with Great Shurdington C. Dio. G. and B. 1849. (Patron, J. E. Viner, Esq; Tithe—App. 6*l*, Imp. 509*l* 10*s* 9*d*, V. 339*l* 13*s* 7*d*; V.'s Inc. 339*l* 13*s* 7*d* and Ho; Pop. Badgeworth 1048, Great Shurdington 164.) [10]

VINER, George Barber Peregrine, *Enfield, Middlesex, N.*—Trin. Coll. Toronto, Canada West, B.A. 1857; Deac. 1857 and Pr. 1858 by Bp of Toronto. P. C. of St. John's, Enfield, Dio. Lon. 1866. (Patron, V. of Enfield; Glebe, 2 acres; Endowment not completed; Ho; Pop. 600.) Formerly Travelling Miss. in Co. Ontario, C. W. 1857–60; Incumb. of St. George's, Duffin's Creek, with St. Paul's, Whitby, C. W. 1860–62; C. of Christ Church, Marylebone, Lond. 1862–63, St. John's, Enfield, 1863–66. [11]

VINES, Thomas Hotchkin, *Birlingham, Pershore, Worcestershire.*—Corpus Coll. Cam. B.A. 1860; Deac. 1860 and Pr. 1861 by Abp of York. C. of Little Comberton, Pershore, 1864. Formerly C. of Easingwold 1860, and St. Lawrence's, Evesham. [12]

VINTER, Frederick William, *Royal Military College, Sandhurst, Farnborough, Hants.*—St. John's Coll. Cam. 3rd Wrang. and B.A. 1847, M.A. 1850; Deac. 1849 and Pr. 1850 by Bp of Ely. Professor of Mathematics, R.M. Coll. Sandhurst, 1858. Formerly Fell. of St. John's Coll. Cam; Math. Mast. R.M. Academy, Woolwich 1851–58. [13]

VIVIAN, Francis Henry, *Stoughton Vicarage, Emsworth, Sussex.*—Trin. Coll. Cam. M.A. 1854; Deac. 1851, Pr. 1852. V. of Stoughton, Dio. Chich. 1863. (Patron, Bp of Lon; Tithe, 260*l*; V.'s Inc. 260*l*; Pop. 350.) Formerly C. of St. Thomas's, Bethnal Green, 1851–53; P. C. of St. Bartholomew's, Bethnal Green, 1853–61; P. C. of St. Peter's, Stepney, 1861–63. [14]

VIVIAN, James William, 56, *Guildford-street, London, W.C.*—All Souls Coll. Ox. B.A. 1807, M.A. 1810, B.D. and D.D. 1823. Pr. in Ordinary to the Queen 1815 (Value 58*l*); 6th Min. Can. of St. Paul's Cathl. 1816 (Value, 210*l*). R. of St. Peter-le-Poer with St. Benet-Fink P.C. City and Dio. Lon. 1842. (Patrons, D. and C. of St. Paul's; R.'s Inc. 1100*l*; Pop. St. Peter-le-Poer 540, St. Benet-Fink 213.) [15]

VIVIAN, John Vivian, *Cardynham Rectory, Bodmin, Cornwall.*—Trin. Coll. Cam. B.A. 1841, M.A. 1844; Deac. 1842 and Pr. 1843 by Bp of Ex. R. of Cardynham, Dio. Ex. 1845. (Patron, Rev. J. Vivian Vivian; Tithe, 515*l*; Glebe, 216 acres; R.'s Inc. 625*l* and Ho; Pop. 717.) [16]

VIZARD, Henry Brougham, *Spetisbury Rectory, Blandford, Dorset.*—Trin. Coll. Cam. B.A. 1849, M.A. 1859. R. of Spetisbury with Charlton-Marshall C. Dio. Salis. 1855. (Patron, J. S. E. Drax, Esq; Spetisbury, Tithe, 453*l*; Glebe, 51 acres; R.'s Inc. 521*l* and Ho; Pop. Spetisbury 688, Charlton-Marshall 553.) [17]

VIZE, John Edward, *St. Mary's, Hulme, Manchester.*—Dub. A.B. 1858, A.M. 1863; Deac. 1859 by Abp of Dub. Pr. 1860 by Bp of Ches. C. of St. Mary's, Hulme, 1866. Formerly C. of Bray, Wicklow, 1859, Trowbridge, Wilts, 1861, Bath 1864. [18]

VLIELAND, Jerome Nicholas, *Stalisfield Vicarage, Feversham, Kent.*—Theol. Assoc. King's Coll. Lond; Deac. 1848 and Pr. 1849 by Bp of Lon. V. of Stalisfield, Dio. Cant. 1858. (Patron, Abp of Cant; Tithe—App. 362*l* and 134 acres of Glebe, V. 174*l* 13*s*; Glebe, 3 acres; V.'s Inc. 240*l* and Ho; Pop. 332.) Formerly P. C. of Ch. Ch. Chiswick, 1854–58. [19]

VOGAN, Andrew, *East Marden Vicarage, near Petersfield.*—Deac. 1845 and Pr. 1846 by Bp of Chich. R. of North Marden, Dio. Chich. 1858. (Patron, Sir Phipps Hornby; R.'s Inc. 80*l*; Pop. 28.) C. of East Marden. Formerly C. of West Whittering. [20]

VOGAN, Thomas Stuart Lyle, *Walberton Vicarage, Arundel, Sussex.*—St. Edm. Hall, Ox. B.A. 1824, M.A. 1827; Deac. 1825 by Bp of Lich. Pr. 1827 by Bp. of Wor. V. of Walberton with Yapton, Dio. Chich. 1843. (Patron, Bp of Chich; Walberton, Tithe, 368*l* 19*s* 2*d*; Glebe, $26\frac{1}{2}$ acres; Yapton, Tithe, 188*l* 6*s* 9*d*; Glebe, $22\frac{1}{4}$ acres; R.'s Inc. 555*l* 7*s* 11*d* and Ho; Pop. Walberton 588, Yapton, 589.) Can. and Preb. of Wightering in Chich. Cathl. 1842; Rural Dean of Walberton 1852. Formerly Asst. C. of Walsall 1825, St. Clement's, Worcester, 1827, Newport, Monmouthshire, 1828, Worthing, Sussex, 1829, Weston-Longville, Norfolk, 1832, Swaffham 1840; V. of Potter Heigham, Norfolk, 1834. Author, *The Principal Objections against the Doctrine of the Trinity, and a Portion of the Evidence on which that Doctrine is received by the Catholic Church, Reviewed* (Bampton Lectures), 1837, 12*s*; *Sermons*, 1837, 6*s*; *The Doctrine of the Apostolical Succession Developed and Proved* (a Visitation Sermon), 1838, 2*s*; *Lectures on the Holy Sacrament of the Lord's Supper* (Theol. Lectures, Chich. Cathl.), 1849; *Lights on the Altar not in Use in this Church of England by Authority of Parliament, in the 2nd of Edward VI. with Remarks upon Conformity*, 1851, 2*s*; *The Case of Church-rates and the Way to settle it*, 6*d*; *The Use of the Burial Service as required by Law.* [21]

VOIGT, George, *Dulwich College, Surrey, S.*—Clare Coll. Cam. Scho. of, B.A. 1849, M.A. 1855; Deac. 1852 and Pr. 1853 by Bp of Wor. Sen. Asst. Mast. in Upper Sch. of Dulwich Coll. 1861. Formerly Asst. Mast. in Classical Department of King Edward's Sch. Birmingham, 1851. [1]

VON HUBE, Rodolph, *Greasley, Nottingham.*—Continental Universities; Deac. 1857 and Pr. 1860 by Bp of Grahamstown. V. of Greasley, Dio. Lin. 1866. (Patroness, Lady Palmerston; V.'s Inc. 300*l* and Ho; Pop. 2263.) Formerly C. of Eastwood, Derbyshire, 1863–64, Ironville, Codnor-park, 1864. [2]

VORES, Thomas, *Hastings, Sussex.*—Wad. Coll. Ox. 1st cl. Lit. Hum. 2nd cl. Math. et Phy. and B.A. 1825, M.A. 1828; Deac. 1832, Pr. 1833. P. C. of St. Mary's-in-the-Castle, Hastings, Dio. Chich. 1841. (Patron, Earl of Chichester; P. C.'s Inc. 230*l*; Pop. 4809.) [3]

VOSS, William Anthony, *Bowness, Cumberland.*—Deac. 1853 and Pr. 1854 by Bp of Llan. C. of Bowness. Formerly C. of Tintern Parva, Monmouthshire, and Barford St. Martin 1857, Torpenhow, Cumberland. [4]

VOULES, Francis Plimley, *Middle Chinnock Rectory, Ilminster, Somerset.*—Wad. Coll. Ox. B.A. 1837; Deac. 1837 and Pr. 1838 by Bp of Ox. R. of Middle Chinnock, Dio. B. and W. 1841. (Patron, Earl of Ilchester; Tithe, 142*l* 12*s* 7*d*; R.'s Inc. 190*l* and Ho; Pop. 238.) [5]

VOULES, Stirling Cookesley, *Rectory, Bridestowe, Devon.*—Lin. Coll. Ox. B.A. 1866; Deac. 1866 by Bp of Ex. C. of Bridestowe 1867. [6]

VOULES, Tom Arthur, *Ash-hill, Ilminster, Somerset.*—St. Alban Hall, Ox. B.A. 1848, M.A. 1852; Deac. and Pr. 1848. R. of Beer-Crocombe, Dio. B. and W. 1849. (Patron, Earl of Egremont; Tithe, 195*l*; Glebe, 95*l*; R.'s Inc. 260*l*; Pop. 175.) R. of North and South Bradon, Dio. B. and W. 1865. (Patron, Earl of Egremont; Tithe, 120*l*; Glebe, 25*l*; R.'s Inc. 145*l*; Pop. 32.) Surrogate; Dom. Chap. to Viscount Dillon. Formerly Asst. C. of Cheddon-Fitzpaine, near Taunton, 1848. [7]

VOWLER, Samuel Nicholson, *Mancroft, Norwich.*—Trin. Coll. Cam. B.A. 1850; Deac. 1851, Pr. 1852. C. of St. Peter's, Mancroft. Formerly C. of Brent-Eleigh, Suffolk. [8]

VOYSEY, Charles, *Healaugh Parsonage, Tadcaster.*—St. Edm. Hall, Ox. B.A. 1851; Deac. 1852 and Pr. 1853 by Abp of York. P. C. of Healaugh, Dio. York, 1864. (Patron, Rev. Edward Hawke Brooksbank; Glebe, 20 acres; P. C.'s Inc. 100*l* and Ho; Pop. 260.) Formerly C. of Hessle, Yorks, 1852–59; Stip. C. of Craigton, Jamaica, 1859–60; C. of Great Yarmouth 1861, St. Mark's, Whitechapel, 1861–63, St. Mark's, Victoria Docks, 1863, Healaugh 1863. Author, *Sling and Stone*; etc. [9]

VYNER, William Phillips, *Withern, near Alford, Lincolnshire.*—Univ. Coll. Ox. B.A. 1829; Deac. 1829, Pr. 1831. R. of Awthorpe, Linc. Dio. Lin. 1836. (Patron, R. Vyner, Esq; Tithe, 158*l*; Glebe, 28 acres; R.'s Inc. 165*l*; Pop. 134.) R. of Withern, Dio. Lin. 1836. (Patron, R. Vyner, Esq; Tithe, 484*l* 2*s* 1*d*; Glebe, 49 acres; R.'s Inc. 445*l* and Ho; Pop. 528.) Rural Dean. [10]

VYSE, Granville Sykes Howard, *Boughton, near Northampton.*—Ch. Ch. Ox. B.A. 1848, M.A. 1851; Deac. and Pr. 1842 by Bp of Pet. R. of Pitsford, Northants, Dio. Pet. 1842. (Patron, Lieut.-Colonel Howard Vyse; Glebe, 194 acres; R.'s Inc. 349*l*; Pop. 609.) R. of Boughton, Dio. Pet. 1843. (Patron, Lieut.-Col. Howard Vyse; Glebe, 184 acres; R.'s Inc. 336*l*; Pop. 372.) [11]

VYVYAN, Thomas G.—Fell. of Caius Coll. Cam. Math. Mast. of Charterhouse Sch. Lond. Author, *Elementary Analytical Geometry*, 1861. Editor of *Goodwin's Problems and Examples in Mathematics, with Solutions*, Deighton and Bell, Cambridge, 1863. [12]

VYVYAN, Vyell Donnithorne, *The Vicarage, Broad Hinton, Swindon, Wilts.*—St. John's Coll. Cam. and St. Aidan's; Deac. 1854 and Pr. 1855 by Bp of Herf. V. of Broad Hinton, Dio. Salis. 1866. (Patron, The Mast. of St. Nicholas' Hospital, Salis; Tithe, 382*l*; Glebe, 26 acres; V.'s Inc. 413*l* and Ho; Pop. 436.) Formerly C. of Churchstoke, Montgomeryshire; R. of Winterbourne-Monkton, Dorchester, 1856–66. [13]

VYVYAN, Vyell Francis, *Withiel Rectory, Bodmin, Cornwall.*—Trin. Coll. Cam. B.A. 1826, M.A. 1839; Deac. and Pr. 1825. R. of Withiel, Dio. Ex. 1825. (Patron, Sir R. R. Vyvyan, Bart; Tithe, 332*l* 5*s*; Glebe, 60 acres; R.'s Inc. 413*l* and Ho; Pop. 367.) Author, Pastoral Tracts and Sermons; *On the Proposed Bishopric of Cornwall* (a Pamphlet). [14]

WACE, Henry, 1, *Duchess-street, Portland-place, W.*—Brasen. Coll. Ox. 2nd cl. Lit. Hum. 2nd cl. Math. et Phy. B.A. 1860; Deac. 1861, Pr. 1862. C. of St. James's, Piccadilly, Westminster, 1864. Formerly C. of St. Luke's, Berwick-street, Lond. 1861–64. [15]

WACE, Richard Henry, *Hill House, Wadhurst, Hurst Green, Sussex.*—Trin. Coll. Cam. B.A. 1828, M.A. 1832; Deac. 1828 and Pr. 1829 by Abp of York. [16]

WADDELL, William Dudley, *Welford, near Stratford-on-Avon.*—Trin. Coll. Cam. Jun. Opt. B.A. 1860, M.A. 1863, Cuddesdon Theol. Coll; Deac. 1860 and Pr. 1863 by Bp of Ox. C. of Welford and Weston-on-Avon 1866. Formerly C. of East and West Challow, Berks, 1861, Colnbrook 1863, All Saints', Margaret-street, Lond. 1864. [17]

WADDELOW, Samuel Robinson, *Bournemouth, Hants.*—St. Peter's Coll. Cam. M.A. C. of Bournemouth. [18]

WADDINGTON, George.—Emman. Coll. Cam. B.A. 1848; Deac. and Pr. 1851. Formerly Chap. to the Forces in the Crimea; C. of West Tytherley, Hants. [19]

WADDINGTON, The Very Rev. George, *The Deanery, Durham.*—Trin. Coll. Cam. Browne's Medallist 1811, Univ. Scho. and Chan. Medallist for English Verse 1813, B.A. and Sen. Chan. Medallist 1815, Univ. of Dur. D.D. 1840. Dean of Dur. 1840. (Value, 3000*l* and Res.) Formerly Fell. of Trin. Coll. Cam. Author, *A Visit to Ethiopia*, 1822; *A Visit to Greece*, 1825; *A Commemoration Sermon*, 1823; *The Present Condition and Prospects of the Greek or Oriental Church, with some Letters written from the Convent of the Strophades*, 1829; *History of the Church from the Earliest Ages to the Reformation*, 3 vols. 1835, 2 eds; *A History of the Reformation on the Continent*, 3 vols. 1841; *Lectures on National Education*, 1845. [20]

WADDINGTON, Herbert, *The Vicarage, Steventon, Berks.*—Trin. Coll. Cam. B.A. 1851, M.A. 1854; Deac. 1852, Pr. 1853. V. of Steventon, Dio. Ox. 1862. (Patrons, D. and C. of Westminster; V.'s Inc. 160*l* and Ho; Pop. 886.) Formerly C. of Newington-next-Hythe. [21]

WADDINGTON, John Barton, *Clitheroe, Lancashire.*—St. Bees; Deac. 1863 and Pr. 1864 by Bp of Rip. Incumb. of New District of St. Paul's, Low Moor, Clitheroe, 1866. Formerly C. of Slaidburn, Yorks, 1863, Ch. Ch. Burton-on-Trent 1865. [22]

WADE, Albert, *Claughton-villa, Brincliffe Edge, near Sheffield.*—Dur. B.A. 1863, M.A. 1866; Deac. 1864 and Pr. 1865 by Bp of Rip. C. of Eccleshall 1866. Formerly C. of St. James's, Bradford, Yorks, 1864. [23]

WADE, Arthur John, *Ryde, Isle of Wight.*—Dub. A.B. 1834, A.M. 1837; Deac. 1834 by Bp of Down and Connor, Pr. 1836 by Abp of Tuam. P. C. of Trinity, Ryde, Dio. Win. 1846. (Patron, V. of Ryde; P. C.'s Inc. 200*l*; Pop. 3051.) Surrogate. Formerly C. of Lavy, Dio. Kilmore, 1834–35, Clongish, Dio. Ardagh, 1835–40, St. James's, Bristol, 1840–42, St. Paul's, Bunhill-row, Lond. 1842–44, St. Thomas's, Ryde, 1844–46. [24]

WADE, Charles James, *Lower Gravenhurst Rectory, Ampthill, Beds.*—Jesus Coll. Cam. B.A. 1830, M.A. 1838; Deac. 1833, Pr. 1834. P. C. of Upper Gravenhust, Dio. Ely, 1840. (Patrons, the Parishioners; Glebe, 17 acres; P. C.'s Inc. 55*l*; Pop. 337.) R. of

Lower Gravenhurst, Dio. Ely, 1842. (Patron, Ld Chan; Glebe, 58 acres; R.'s Inc. 237*l* and Ho; Pop. 60.) [1]

WADE, Frederick, *Kidsgrove Parsonage, Stoke-upon-Trent, Staffs.*—Dub. Downe's Div. Prizeman, A.M. *ad eund.* Ox; Deac. and Pr. 1835. Preb. of Lich. 1855; P. C. of Kidsgrove, Dio. Lich. 1837. (Patroness, Mrs. Kinnersley; P. C.'s Inc. 208*l* and Ho; Pop. 3700.) Surrogate; Chap. to Earl of Albemarle. [2]

WADE, Garrod, *Coney-Weston Lodge, Ixworth, Suffolk.*—Jesus Coll. Cam. B.A. 1825, M.A. 1828; Deac. 1825, Pr. 1826. [3]

WADE, George Frederick, *Eastoft Parsonage, near Goole, Yorks.*—St. John's Coll. Cam. Jun. Opt. and B.A. 1852, M.A. 1866; Deac. 1852, Pr. 1854. P. C. of Eastoft, Dio. York, 1855. (Patron, H. S. Constable, Esq; P. C.'s Inc. 150*l* and Ho; Pop. 624.) Organising Sec. of S.P.G. in the Archdeaconry of York. Formerly C. of Withernwick, Yorks, 1852–55. [4]

WADE, John, *Haworth Parsonage, Keighley, Yorks.*—P. C. of Haworth, Dio. Rip. 1861. (Patrons, V. of Bradford and Trustees; P. C.'s Inc. 170*l* and Ho; Pop. 3016.) [5]

WADE, Nugent, *Rectory House, 28, Soho-square, London, W.*—Dub. Cl. and Sci. Prem. Scho. Heb. Prem. Cl. Gold Medallist 1828, A.B. 1829, A.M. 1832; Deac. 1832 and Pr. 1833 by Bp of Kilmore. R. of St. Anne's, Soho, Dio. Lon. 1846. (Patron, Bp of Lon; R.'s Inc. 786*l* and Ho; Pop. 11,423.) [6]

WADE, Robert, *West-parade, Norwich.*—Dub. A.B. 1831; Deac. and Pr. 1836. P. C. of Ch. Ch. St. Clement's, Norwich, Dio. Nor. 1852. (Patron, R. of St. Clement's; P. C.'s Inc. 160*l*; Pop. 2991.) Chap. of Norwich Prison. (Salary, 100*l*.) [7]

WADE, Thomas, 8, *Belgrave-terrace, Lee, Kent, S.E.*—Ex. Coll. Ox. 2nd cl. Lit. Hum. 3rd in Math. B.A. 1850, M.A. 1853; Deac. and Pr. 1853 by Bp of Man. Asst. C. of St. Andrew's, Wells-street, Marylebone, 1863; Head Mast. of the Lower Proprietary Sch. Blackheath, 1857. Formerly 2nd Mast. of Wakefield Gr. Sch. Author, *Notes on St. John's Gospel*, Parker, 1857. [8]

WADE, William Serocold, *Redbourn Vicarage, St. Albans.*—St. John's Coll. Ox. B.A. 1824, M.A. 1827. V. of Redbourn, Dio. Roch 1830. (Patron, Earl Verulam; Tithe—Imp. 1053*l* 12*s* 6*d*, V. 315*l*; V.'s Inc. 321*l* and Ho; Pop. 2043.) [9]

WADHAM, John, *The Rectory, Weston-on-Trent, Derby.*—Wad. Coll. Ox. B.A. 1844, M.A. 1850; Deac. 1845 and Pr. 1846 by Bp of Lich. R. of Weston-on-Trent, Dio. Lich. 1863. (Patron, Sir R. Wilmot, Bart; R.'s Inc. 594*l* and Ho; Pop. 321.) Formerly C. of Chew Magna, Somerset. [10]

WADLEY, Thomas Procter, *Bidford, Warwickshire.*—Queens' Coll. Cam. Found. Scho. of, B.A. 1851, M.A. 1857; Deac. 1853 by Bp of Ox. Pr. 1855 by Bp of B. and W. [11]

WADMORE, Henry Robinson.—Pemb. Coll. Ox. 4th cl. Lit. Hum. 1845, and B.A. 1846; Deac. 1847 and Pr. 1849 by Bp of Roch. P. C. of All Souls', Hampstead, Dio. Lon. 1865. (Patron, the present P. C; Pop. 1330.) Formerly C. of St. Barnabas', King's-square, Goswell-road, Lond. Author, *Poems by a Country Curate*, 2*s*. [12]

WADSWORTH, John, *York.*—King's Coll. Lond. Deac. 1800 by Bp. of S. and M. Pr. 1865 by Bp of Llan. Assoc. Sec. to the Colonial and Continental Ch. Soc. 1867. Formerly Head Mast. of the Gr. Sch. Castletown, Isle of Man, and Asst. Govt. Chap. 1860–61; C. of St. Paul's, Newport, Monmouthshire, 1861–67. [13]

WAGNER, Arthur Douglas, *The Vicarage, Brighton.*—Trin. Coll. Cam. B.A. 1846, M.A. 1849; Deac. 1846, Pr. 1849. R. of St. Paul's, and St. Mary Magdalene's, Brighton, Dio. Chich. 1850. (Patron, V. of Brighton; R.'s Inc. 200*l*.) [14]

WAGNER, Henry Michell, *The Vicarage, Brighton.*—King's Coll. Cam; Deac. 1823, Pr. 1824. V. of Brighton with West Blatchington R. Dio. Chich. 1824. (Patron, Bp of Chich; Brighton, Tithe—Imp. 120*l*; V. 186*l*; West Blatchington, Tithe, 200*l*; V.'s Inc. 900*l* and Ho; Pop. 77,752. Treasurer of Chich. Cathl. 1834. (Value, 200*l*.) Surrogate. Formerly Fell. of King's Coll. Cam. [15]

WAGSTAFF, Charles, *Studham, near Dunstable.*—Trin. Coll. Cam. B.A. 1837, M.A. 1840; Deac. 1837 and Pr. 1838 by Bp of Ches. V. of Studham, Dio. Ely, 1850. (Patron, Ld Chan; Tithe, 140*l*; Glebe, 5 acres; V.'s Inc. 188*l*; Pop. 382.) Formerly C. of Preston, Lancashire, 1837–39, Arundel, Sussex, 1839–44; Incumb. of St. Andrew's, Aberdeen, 1844–50. [16]

WAINEWRIGHT, Arnold W., *Iken Rectory, Saxmundham.*—R. of Iken, Dio. Nor. 1863. (Patroness, Mrs. Louisa Wainewright; Tithe, 430*l*; Glebe, 20½ acres; R.'s Inc. 455*l* and Ho; Pop. 336.) [17]

WAINWRIGHT, Charles Henry, *Christ Church Parsonage, Blackpool, Preston.*—Trin. Coll. Cam. B.A. 1855, M.A. 1864; Deac. 1855 by Bp of Lich. Pr. 1856 by Bp of Nor. P. C. of Ch. Ch. Blackpool, Dio. Man. 1861. (Patrons, Trustees; P. C.'s Inc. 160*l* and Ho; Pop. 1500.) Formerly Sen. C. of St. Margaret's, Ipswich, 1855–58, St. James's, Manchester, 1858–60. [18]

WAINWRIGHT, Frederick, *Altrincham, Cheshire.*—Trin. Coll. Cam. Scho. of, B.A. 1860; Deac. 1861 and Pr. 1862 by Bp of Ches. P. C. of St. John's, Altrincham, Dio. Ches. 1866. (Patron, Bp of Ches; Pop. 2800.) Formerly C. of St. Jude's, Liverpool, 1861–63, Ch. Ch. Everton, 1863, Bowdon, Cheshire, 1864–66. [19]

WAINWRIGHT, S., *Trinity Vicarage, York.*—V. of Trinity in Micklegate, York, Dio. York, 1860. (Patron, Ld Chan; V.'s Inc. 90*l* and Ho; Pop. 1652. [20]

WAIT, William Piguenit, *Chewstoke Rectory, Chew Magna, Somerset.*—Deac. and Pr. 1816. R. of Chewstoke, Dio. B. and W. 1819. (Patron, the present R; Tithe—App. 8*l* 8*s*, R. 270*l* 12*s*; Glebe, 14 acres; R.'s Inc. 305*l* and Ho; Pop. 758.) [21]

WAIT, William W., *Sydney Villa, Bath.*—C. of Limpley Stoke, Wilts. [22]

WAITE, John, *Tathwell Vicarage, Louth, Lincolnshire.*—St. John's Coll. Cam. 7th Sen. Opt. and B.A. 1803, M.A. 1806; Deac. 1803 and Pr. 1805 by Bp of Lin. V. of Tathwell, Dio. Lin. 1841. (Patron, Bp of Lin; Tithe—App. 625*l* and 78 acres of Glebe, V. 425*l* 8*s*; Glebe, 9 acres; V.'s Inc. 435*l* and Ho; Pop. 405.) Rural Dean of Louthesko 1829. Formerly R. of Stewton 1818–41; Head Mast. of King Edw. VI.'s Gr. Sch. Louth, 1814–51. [23]

WAITE, John Deane, *Manby Rectory, near Louth, Lincolnshire.*—Clare Hall, Cam. B.A. 1828; Deac. 1828 and Pr. 1829 by Bp of Lin. R. of Manby, Dio. Lin. 1852. (Patron, F. Dickinson Hall, Esq; Glebe, 327 acres; R.'s Inc. 550*l* and Ho; Pop. 210.) [24]

WAITE, Joseph, *Durham.*—Mast. of Univ. Coll. Durham. Formerly Fell. and Tut. of Univ. Coll. Durham. [25]

WAITES, John Bentley, *South Stainley, Ripon.*—P. C. of South Stainley, Dio. Rip. 1841. (Patron, R. Reynard, Esq; P. C.'s Inc. 75*l*; Pop. 259.) [26]

WAKE, Baldwyn Eyre, *Sutton-on-the-Forest, near York.*—Trin. Coll. Ox. B.A. 1862, M.A. 1866; Deac. 1865 and Pr. 1866 by Abp of York. C. of Sutton-on-the-Forest 1865. [27]

WAKE, James Hare, *Sutton-on-the-Forest, near York.*—Queen's Coll. Ox. B.A. 1828; Deac. 1829, Pr. 1830. V. of Sutton-on-the-Forest, Dio. York, 1834. (Patron, Abp of York; Tithe—App. 155*l*, Imp. 33*l* 19*s*, V. 403*l* 6*s* 5½*d*; V.'s Inc. 405*l* and Ho; Pop. 1224.) [28]

WAKEFIELD, Joah Bates, *South Shore, Blackpool, Lancashire.*—Magd. Hall, Ox. and St. Bees 1847; Deac. 1849 and Pr. 1850 by Bp of Man. P. C. of South Shore with Great Marton Moss, Dio. Man. 1853. (Patron, Col. Clifton; Endow. 38*l*; P. C.'s Inc. 120*l* and Ho.) [29]

WAKEFIELD, John, *Hughley Rectory, Much Wenlock, Salop.*—St. Edm. Hall, Ox. B.A. 1824, M.A. 1827; Deac. and Pr. 1824 by Bp of Lich. R. of Hughley, Dio. Herf. 1851. (Patron, Earl of Bradford; Tithe, 73*l* 0*s* 10*d*; Glebe, 88 acres; R.'s Inc. 165*l* and Ho; Pop. 98.) P. C. of Church Preen, Salop, Dio. Herf. 1852. (Patron, Arthur Sparrow, Esq; P. C.'s Inc. 82*l*; Pop. 97.) Author, *The Solitary Christian*, R.T.S. 1853. [30]

WAKEFIELD, William, *Curdworth Vicarage, Birmingham.*—St. John's Coll. Ox. B.A. 1812, M.A. 1815; Deac. 1814, Pr. 1815. V. of Curdworth, Dio. Wor. 1817. (Patrons, B. Noel, Esq. two turns, Right Hon. C. B. Adderley, and the present V. alt; Tithe, 200*l*; V.'s Inc. 300*l* and Ho; Pop. 649.) [1]

WALBRAN, William, *Radcliffe, near Manchester.*—Pemb. Coll. Cam. B.A. 1860; Deac. 1862 and Pr. 1864 by Bp of Man. C. of Radcliffe. [2]

WALCOT, Charles, *Bitterley Court, Ludlow, Salop.*—Trin. Coll. Ox. B.A. 1817, M.A. 1826; Deac. 1819, Pr. 1820. R. of Bitterley, Dio. Herf. (Patron, the present R; Tithe, 740*l*; Glebe, 56 acres; R.'s Inc. 840*l* and Ho; Pop. 704.) [3]

WALCOT, John, *Ribbesford Rectory, Bewdley.*—Lin. Coll. Ox. B.A. 1845; Deac. and Pr. 1845 by Bp of Wor. R. of Ribbesford, Dio. Herf. 1854. (Patron, Rev. E. W. Ingram; Tithe, 310*l* 4*s* 6*d*; Glebe, 60 acres; R.'s Inc. 400*l* and Ho; Pop. 1849.) [4]

WALCOTT, Mackenzie Edward Charles, *Oxford and Cambridge Club, Pall-mall, London, S.W.*—Ex. Coll. Ox. 3rd cl. Lit. Hum. and B.A. 1844, M.A. 1847; Deac. 1844 and Pr. 1845 by Bp of Lon. Precentor and Preb. of Chich. Cathl. 1863; Dom. Chap. to Lord Lyons; Morning Preacher at Berkeley Chapel, May Fair, Lond; F.R.S.L. F.S.A. F.R.S.N.A. &c; and Member of several foreign Learned Societies. Formerly C. of St. Margaret's, Westminster, 1847–50, St. James's, Westminster, 1850–53, Enfield 1845–47. Author, *History of St. Margaret's Church, Westminster*, 1847, 7*s* 6*d*; *Plain Persuasive to the Holy Communion*, 1850, 1*s*; *Memorials of Westminster*, 1850, 14*s*; *The English Ordinal, its History, Validity, and Catholicity*, 1851, 7*s* 6*d*; *William of Wykeham and his Colleges*, 1852, 1*l* 1*s*; *Handbook to St. James's, Westminster*, 1852, 2*s* 6*d*; *Handbook of Winchester Cathedral*, 1854; *The South Coast of England from the North Foreland to the Land's End, with a Glance at the Southern Shore of the Bristol Channel*, 1859, 5*s*; *The Cathedrals of the United Kingdom*, 1860; *The Ministers of the United Kingdom*, 1860. [5]

WALDO, Joseph Peter, 90, *Albert-street, Regent's-park, London, N.W.*—Dub. A.B. 1848; Deac. 1844, Pr. 1840. Min. of Trinity Chapel, Conduit-street. Formerly Min. of St. James's Chapel, Hampstead, Lond. 1858, Woburn Chapel, St. Pancras, Lond. 1855–57; C. of St. John's, Stratford. [6]

WALDRON, Frederick William, *Woolwich Common, Kent, S.E.*—St. John's Coll. Cam. Coll. Prizeman, Sen. Opt. and B.A. 1845; Deac. 1845 and Pr. 1846 by Bp of Lich. Formerly Head Mast. of the Gr. Sch. of Sir John Sedley, Wymondham. [7]

WALDRON, George H., *Salisbury House, Potter's Bar, Middlesex, N.* [8]

WALDY, Charles Richard William, *Gussage All Saints', Salisbury.*—Univ. Coll. Ox. B.A. 1849, M.A. 1854; Deac. 1853 and Pr. 1854 by Bp of Salis. V. of Gussage All Saints', Dio. Salis. 1857. (Patron, Archd. of Dorset; Tithe, 100*l*; Grant from Ecc. Commissioners, 198*l*; Glebe, 10 acres; V.'s Inc. 330*l* and Ho; Pop. 496.) Formerly C. of St. Mary's, Longfleet, Dorset. Author, *Poems*, Mackintosh, 1867. [9]

WALDY, Richard, *Affpuddle, Dorchester.*—Clare Coll. Cam. Scho. of, 1815, B.A. 1818, M.A. 1821; Deac. 1819 by Bp of Herf. Pr. 1819 by Bp of Salis. R. of Turnerspuddle with Affpuddle, Dio. Salis. 1824. (Patron, Henry Frampton, Esq; Glebe, 4 acres; R.'s Inc. 250*l* and Ho; Pop. 597.) Preb. of Salis. 1849. Formerly C. of Christchurch, Hants; Dom. Chap. to Dow. Lady Vernon 1821. [10]

WALE, Alexander Malcolm, *Sunninghill Vicarage (Berks), near Chertsey.*—St. John's Coll. Cam. 2nd Chancellor's Medallist, 16th Wrang. and B.A. 1819, M.A. 1822, B.D. 1829; Deac. 1827 by Bp. of Lin. Pr. 1829 by Bp of Ely. V. of Sunninghill, Dio. Ox. 1830. (Patron, St. John's Coll. Cam; Tithe—Imp. 146*l*, V. 137*l* 10*s* 6*d*; Glebe, 40 acres; V.'s Inc. 360*l* and Ho; Pop. 1435.) Formerly Fell. of St. John's Coll. Cam. 1821. [11]

WALE, Henry John, *The Rectory, Folkesworth, Peterborough.*—Magd. Coll. Cam. Deac. 1861 and Pr. 1862 by Bp of Salis. R. of Folkesworth, Hunts, Dio. Ely, 1865. (Patroness, Mrs. Sarah Freeman; Tithe, 52*l*; Glebe, 111 acres; R.'s Inc. 235*l* and Ho; Pop. 207.) Formerly C. of Ringwood, Hants. [12]

WALES, William, *Uppingham Rectory, Rutland.*—St. Cath. Hall, Cam. B.A. 1827, M.A. 1833; Deac. 1827, Pr. 1828. R. of Uppingham, Dio. Pet. 1859. (Patron, Bp of Pet; Glebe, 266 acres; R.'s Inc. 600*l* and Ho; Pop. 2186.) Hon. Can. of Pet. 1846; Chancellor of the Dio. of Pet. 1850. Formerly V. of All Saints', Northampton, 1832–59. [13]

WALFORD, Edward, 17, *Church-row, Hampstead, London, N.W.*—Ball. Coll. Ox. Scho. 1841, Chan. Prize 1843, B.A. and 3rd cl. Lit. Hum. 1845, Denyer Theol. Prize 1848 and 1849, M.A. 1847; Deac. 1846 and Pr. 1847 by Bp of Ox. Fell. of the Genealogical and Hist. Soc. of Great Britain. Formerly Asst. Mast. of Tunbridge Sch. Author, *Grammar of Latin Poetry*, 1*s*; *Progressive Exercises in Latin Elegiac Verse*, 2 Series, 2*s* 6*d* each; *Hints on Latin Writing*, 2nd ed. 1*s* 6*d*; *Progressive Exercises on Latin Prose Composition*, 2*s* 6*d*; *Shilling Latin Grammar*, 1*s*; *Palaestra Musarum* (a Series of Classical Examination Papers), 7*s* 6*d*; *Handbook of the Greek Grammar*, 6*s*; 11 *Classical Cards*, 1*s* each; *In what sense is it a New Commandment that Christians should love one another?* (Denyer Theol. Prize Essay, 1848), 2*s* 6*d*; *On Original, or Birth Sin* (ib. 1849), 1*s* 6*d*; *A Georgic on Horticulture* (Gold Medal Lat. Hexam. Verse, Charterhouse, 1841), 1*s*; *Venetiæ* (Carmen Latinum, Chan. Prize, 1843; *The Shilling Peerage*, *The Shilling Baronetage*, *The Shilling Knightage*, *The Shilling House of Commons*, Hardwicke (published annually, 1*s* each; *Electoral Representation of the United Kingdom*, 1*s*; *The Annual Biography*, 4*s* 6*d*; *Titles of Courtesy*, 2*s* 6*d*; *County Families*, 4th ed. 1867, 42*s*; *Outlines of Grecian History* and *of Roman History* (Ince's Series), 1*s* each; *Blue Books for the People*, No. 1, *Army Education*, 1857; *Photographic Portraits of Living Characters*, 4to; *Records of the Great and Noble*; *Men of the Time*, 1862; *Life of the Prince Consort*, 1862; Articles in *Dublin Review*; *Tracts for the Christian Seasons*; *Gentleman's Magazine*; Biographies in the *Times*, *Morning Post*, *Illustrated London News*, &c; Editor of *Butler's Analogy and Sermons*, Bohn's Stand. Lib. 3*s* 6*d*; *Mackenzie's Educational Series*, Hardwicke; Translator of *Aristotle's Politics and Economics*, Bohn's Class. Lib; *Socrates' Ecclesiastical History*, Bohn's Eccles. Lib. 5*s*; *Sozomen's Ecclesiastical History*, ib. 5*s*; *Ecclesiastical History of Theodoret and Evagrius*, ib. 5*s*; etc. [14]

WALFORD, Ellis, *Dallinghoe Rectory, Wickham Market.*—Corpus Coll. Cam. B.A. 1825, M.A. 1828; Deac. 1826 and Pr. 1827 by Bp of Nor. R. of Bucklesham, Dio. Nor. 1833. (Patron, the present R; Tithe, 520*l*; Glebe, 50 acres; R.'s Inc. 595*l* and Ho; Pop. 390.) R. of Dallinghoe, Dio. Nor. 1830. (Patron, the present R; Tithe, 410*l*; Glebe, 37 acres; R.'s Inc. 466*l* and Ho; Pop. 385.) Rural Dean of Wilford 1842. [15]

WALFORD, Humphry Thomas, *Sittingbourne Vicarage, Kent.*—St. Cath. Hall, Cam. B.A. 1824, M.A. 1828; Deac. 1824 and Pr. 1825 by Bp of Nor. V. of Sittingbourne, Dio. Cant. 1846. (Patron, Abp of Cant; Tithe—App. 345*l*. and 5½ acres of Glebe, V. 192*l*; Glebe, 2½ acres; V.'s Inc. 305*l* and Ho; Pop. 4301.) P. C. of Iwade, Kent, Dio. Cant. 1846. (Patron, Archd. of Cant; Tithe—App. 533*l* 16*s* 3*d* and 3¾ acres of Glebe; P. C.'s Inc. 85*l*; Pop. 182.) Formerly C. of Horsham 1829–31, East Peckham 1831–46. Author, *Unitarian Controversy* (a Tract); *True Tale of Repentance* (a Tract), S.P.C.K. [16]

WALFORD, William Luke, *Fulham, S.W.*—C. of All Saints', Fulham. [17]

WALKE, Nicholas, *Camborne, Cornwall.*—Wor. Coll. Ox. B.A; Deac. 1863 by Bp of Ex. C. of St. Peter's, Plymouth, 1865. [18]

WALKEM, George, *Abingdon, Berks*—New Inn Hall, Ox. B.A. 1847; Deac. 1848, Pr. 1849. Chap. of the County Gaol and of the Union, Abingdon. Formerly C. of Betley, Staffs. [1]

WALKER, Arthur, *Easton-in-Gordano, Bristol.*—Trin. Coll. Cam. B.A. 1862, M.A. 1866; Deac. 1864 and Pr. 1865 by Bp of Wor. V. of Easton-in-Gordano, Dio. B. and W. 1867. (Patron, Bp of Lon; Tithe, 270*l*; V.'s Inc. 295*l* and Ho; Pop. 526.) Surrogate. Formerly C. of Alvechurch 1864, St. Paul's, Hammersmith, 1866. [2]

WALKER, Charles, *Connaught House, Brighton.*—Trin. Coll. Cam. B.A. 1861, M.A. 1865; Deac. 1863 and Pr. 1864 by Bp of Chich. Asst. C. of St. Michael's, Brighton, 1863. [3]

WALKER, Charles Harry, *St. Gennys Vicarage, Stratton, Cornwall.*—Wor. Coll. Ox. B.A. 1838, M.A. 1841; Deac. 1841 and Pr. 1843 by Bp of Ex. V. of St. Gennys, Cornwall, Dio. Ex. 1862. (Patron, Earl of St. Germans; Tithe, 162*l*; Glebe, 27 acres; V.'s Inc. 185*l* and Ho; Pop. 572.) Formerly C. of Warrington 1841–44, North Taunton 1844–48, West Buckland 1848–52, Chivelstone, Devon, 1852–62. [4]

WALKER, Charles, H., *Walkhampton Vicarage, Horrabridge, Devon.*—V. of Walkhampton, Dio. Ex. 1863. (Patron, Sir M. Lopes, Bart; V.'s Inc. 150*l* and Ho; Pop. 831.) Rural Dean. [5]

WALKER, C. J. S., *Prescot, Lancashire.*—Mast. of the Prescot Gr. Sch. [6]

WALKER, Edward, *The Rectory, Cheltenham.*—Lin. Coll. Ox. B.A. 1846, M.A. 1849, D.C.L. 1865; Deac. 1846 by Bp of Ches. Pr. 1848 by Bp of Man. R. of Cheltenham, Dio. G. and B. 1857. (Patrons, Simeon's Trustees; Tithe, 6*l*; R.'s Inc. 500*l* and Ho; Pop. 39,000.) Surrogate. Formerly C. of St. George's, Manchester, 1846, Silverdale, Lancaster, 1848; P. C. of St. Jude's, Manchester, 1849, St. Matthias', Salford, 1853. Author, various Sermons and Lectures. [7]

WALKER, Edward, 3, *Belvidere-terrace, Brighton.*—Sid. Coll. Cam. B.A. 1861, M.A. 1865; Deac. 1864 and Pr. 1865 by Bp of Chich. C. of Trinity, Cliftonville, Brighton. [8]

WALKER, Edward Martin, 4, *Lambeth-terrace, Lambeth, S.*—Wor. Coll. Ox. B.A. 1852; Deac. 1854, Pr. 1855. C. of St. Clement's Mission District, Lambeth. [9]

WALKER, F. A.—C. of St. Botolph's, Aldgate, Lond. [10]

WALKER, Frederick John, *Drewsteignton, Chagford, Devon.*—Dub. A.B. 1838, A.M. 1841; Deac. 1840 and Pr. 1831 by Bp of Ches. C. of Drewsteignton 1847. Formerly C. of Oswaldtwistle 1840, Eccles 1842, Cheetham Hill, Manchester, 1843, West Teignmouth, Devon, 1846. [11]

WALKER, George, *Belford, Northumberland.*—Aberdeen M.A. Dub. Licen. Theol; Deac. 1842 and Pr. 1843. P. C. of Belford, Dio. Dur. 1843. (Patron, Rev. J. D. Clark; Tithe—Imp. 208*l* 13*s* 4*d*; P. C.'s Inc. 150*l* and Ho; Pop. 1724.) Surrogate. [12]

WALKER, George Alfred, *Chidham Vicarage, Emsworth, Sussex.*—Wad. Coll. Ox. B.A. 1851, M.A. 1854; Deac. 1853 by Bp of Ox. Pr. 1854 by Bp. of Pet. V. of Chidham, Dio. Chich. 1858. (Patron, the present V; V.'s Inc. 200*l* and Ho; Pop. 307.) Formerly C. of Pattishall, 1st Mediety. [13]

WALKER, George Edmund, *Stoulton Parsonage, Worcester.*—St. Edm. Hall, Ox. M.A. 1848; Deac. 1849 and Pr. 1850 by Bp of Wor. P. C. of Stoulton, Dio. Wor. 1860. (Patron, Earl Somers; Tithe, 37*l*; Glebe, 27 acres; P. C.'s Inc. 70*l* and Ho; Pop. 410.) Formerly C. of Bushbury, Staffs, 1851–60. [14]

WALKER, George Edward Cooper, *Farley, Croydon, Surrey, S.*—Mert. Coll. Ox. B.A. 1831. R. of Farley, Dio. Win. 1835. (Patron, Mert. Coll. Ox; Tithe, 182*l* 4*s* 9*d*; Glebe, 28 acres; R.'s Inc. 199*l*; Pop. 105.) R. of Woldingham, Godstone, Surrey, Dio. Win. 1849. (Patron, Captain Howard; Tithe, 120*l*; R.'s Inc. 125*l*; Pop. 67.) [15]

WALKER, Henry, *Ludham, Norwich.*—Sid. Coll. Cam. 35th Wrang. and B.A. 1842, M.A. 1845; Deac. 1844, Pr. 1846. V. of Ludham, Dio. Nor. 1855. (Patron, Bp of Nor; Tithe—App. 640*l*, V. 300*l*; Glebe, 26 acres; V.'s Inc. 360*l* and Ho; Pop. 884.) [16]

WALKER, Henry, *St. Andrew's Parsonage,* 30, *Ashley-place, S.W.*—Ch. Ch. Ox. 3rd cl. Lit. Hum. B.A. 1831, M.A. 1835; Deac. 1833 and Pr. 1834 by Bp of Ox. P. C. of St. Andrew's, Ashley-place, Dio. Lon. 1855. (Patron, R. of St. Margaret's, Westminster; P. C.'s Inc. 500*l* and Ho; Pop. 4029.) [17]

WALKER, Henry Aston, *Brooke-street, Holborn, London, E.C.*—C. of St. Alban's, Holborn, 1864. [18]

WALKER, Henry John, *Burythorpe Rectory, Malton, Yorks.*—St. John's Coll. Cam. B.A. 1853; Deac. 1853 and Pr. 1854 by Abp of York. R. of Burythorpe, Dio. York, 1855. (Patron, Ld Chan; Tithe, 270*l*; Glebe, 25 acres; R.'s Inc. 320*l* and Ho; Pop. 265.) Formerly C. of Slingsby 1853–55. [19]

WALKER, James Harold, *Dilhorne Vicarage, Stone, Staffs.*—V. of Dilhorne, Dio. Lich. 1863. (Patrons, D. and C. of Lich; V.'s Inc. 198*l* and Ho; Pop. 849.) [20]

WALKER, Jeremiah, *Ulpha Parsonage, Ravenglass, Cumberland.*—St. Bees 1817. P. C. of Ulpha, Dio. Carl. 1828. (Patron, V. of Milton; Tithe—Imp. 9*l* 12*s*; P. C.'s Inc. 55*l* and Ho; Pop. 360.) Surrogate. [21]

WALKER, John, *Bradwell Rectory, near Great Yarmouth.*—St. John's Coll. Cam. Scho. B.A. 1844, M.A. 1847; Deac. 1844 and Pr. 1845 by Abp of York. R. of Bradwell, Dio. Nor. 1864. (Patron, J. Walker, Esq; R.'s Inc. 550*l* and Ho; Pop. 387.) Formerly P. C. of Old Malton 1855. [22]

WALKER, John, *Linton, Skipton, Yorks.*—Deac. 1817, Pr. 1818. R. of the 2nd Mediety of Linton, Dio. Rip. 1850. (Patron, the Crown; Tithe—R. of 1st Mediety, 134*l* 10*s*, R. of 2nd Mediety, 134*l* 10*s*; Glebe, 26 acres; R.'s Inc. 230*l* and Ho; Pop. 1911.) [23]

WALKER, John, *The Hill House Grammar School, Enfield, N.*—Oriel Coll. Ox. B.A. 1855, M.A. 1859; Deac. 1856 by Bp of Ox. Pr. 1857 by Bp of G. and B. Head Mast. of the Hill House Gr. Sch. Enfield, 1864. Formerly C. of Hatherop, Fairford, 1856, Hundleby, Spilsby, 1860, Norwell with Carlton, Notts, 1862. [24]

WALKER, John, 57, *St. George's-square, Pimlico, S.W.*—St. John's Coll. Cam. M.A; Deac. 1845 and Pr. 1846 by Bp of Ches. P. C. of St. Saviour's, Pimlico, Dio. Lon. 1864. (Patron, Marquis of Westminster; Pop. 8000.) [25]

WALKER, John Mills, *Trinity Clergy House, Great Portland-street, W.*—St. John's Coll. Cam. B.A. 1866; Deac. 1866 by Bp Anderson for Bp of Lon. C. of Trinity, Marylebone, 1866. [26]

WALKER, John Russell, *Walmersley Parsonage, Bury.*—Univ. Coll. Ox. 2nd cl. Lit. Hum. B.A. 1859, M.A. 1862; Wells Theol. Coll. 1861; Deac. 1862, Pr. 1863. P. C. of Walmersley, Dio. Man. 1865. (Patrons, Five Trustees; Tithe, 25*l*; P. C.'s Inc. 100*l* and Ho; Pop. 3200.) Formerly C. of Middleton 1862–65. [27]

WALKER, John Thomas, *Ashdon Rectory, Linton, Essex.*—Caius Coll. Cam. Wrang. and B.A. 1838, M.A. 1841; Deac. 1846, Pr. 1848. R. of Ashdon, Dio. Roch. 1852. (Patron, Caius Coll. Cam; Tithe, 909*l*; Glebe, 150 acres; R.'s Inc. 1059*l* and Ho; Pop. 1011.) Formerly Fell. of Caius Coll. Cam. [28]

WALKER, John Tyrwhitt, *Coltishall Rectory, Norwich.*—Dub. Lit. Hum. Hons. in Cl. 1834, A.B. 1837, A.M. 1848; Deac. 1850 and Pr. 1851 by Bp of Lin. C. of Coltishall (sole charge) 1852. Formerly C. of Haltham-upon-Bain, Linc. 1850–52. Author, Funeral Sermons, Lectures, Tracts, Music. [29]

WALKER, Joseph, *Averham Rectory, Newark, Notts.*—Brasen. Coll. Ox. B.A. 1850, M.A. 1853; Deac. 1851 and Pr. 1852 by Bp of Ches. R. of Averham with Kelham R. Dio. Lin. 1856. (Patron, J. H. M. Sutton, Esq; Averham, Tithe, 805*l* 15*s* 8*d*; Glebe, 57½ acres; Kelham, Tithe—App. 103*l* 15*s* 6*d*, R. 486*l* 4*s* 6*d*; R.'s Inc. 1475*l* and Ho; Pop. 420.) [30]

WALKER, Joseph, *Great Billing Rectory, Northampton.*—Trin. Coll. Cam. Scho. of, 8th Wrang. and B.A. 1830, M.A. 1832; Deac. 1833 and Pr. 1834 by Bp of Ox. R. of Great Billing, Dio. Pet. 1843. (Patron, Brasen.

Coll. Ox; Glebe, 296 acres; R.'s Inc. 540*l* and Ho; Pop. 425.) Formerly Fell. of Brasen. Coll. Ox. 1832; Whitehall Preacher 1839–40; Tut. Math. Lect. and Vice-Prin. of Brasen. Coll. resigned 1843. [1]

WALKER, Joseph, *Southrop Vicarage, Lechlade, Glouc.*—Wad. Coll. Ox. B.A. 1833, M.A. 1839; Deac. 1839, Pr. 1840. V. of Southrop, Dio. G. and B. 1848. (Patron, Wad. Coll. Ox; Tithe—Imp. 313*l* 17*s* 9*d*, V. 210*l* 2*s*; V.'s Inc. 252*l* and Ho; Pop. 362.) Chap. of Wad. Coll. Ox. [2]

WALKER, Joseph, *Kirk-Whelpington Vicarage (Northumberland), near Newcastle-upon-Tyne.*—V. of Kirk-Whelpington, Dio. Dur. (Patron, Ld Chan; Tithe—Imp. 246*l* 18*s* 8*d*, V. 184*l* 16*s*; V.'s Inc. 290*l* and Ho; Pop. 644.) [3]

WALKER, Josiah, *Wood-Ditton Vicarage, Newmarket, Cambs.*—Trin. Hall, Cam. S.C.L. 1836, 2nd Tyrrwhitt's Heb. Scho. and B.C.L. 1839; Deac. 1836, Pr. 1837. V. of Wood-Ditton, Dio. Nor. 1847. (Patron, Duke of Rutland; Glebe, 175 acres; V.'s Inc. 242*l* and Ho; Pop. 1375.) [4]

WALKER, Paul Marland, *Edensor, Longton, Staffs.*—Dub. A.B. 1844; Deac. 1844 and Pr. 1845 by Bp of Kildare. P. C. of Edensor, Dio. Lich. 1848. (Patrons, the Crown and Bp of Lich. alt; P. C.'s Inc. 300*l* and Ho; Pop. 4943.) Author, *Origin of the Temporal Power of the Pope,* Stafford; *The Lord's Supper, its True Nature, &c.* ib. [5]

WALKER, Richard, *Seathwaite, Broughton-in-Furness, Lancaster.*—New Coll. Ox. B.A. 1830, M.A. 1837; Deac. 1833 and Pr. 1835 by Bp of Ox. P. C. of Seathwaite, Dio. Carl. 1861. (Patron, Major Rawlinson; P. C.'s Inc. 74*l* and Ho; Pop. 172.) [6]

WALKER, Richard Ashwin, *Lower Guyting, Cheltenham.*—V. of Lower Guyting with Farmcote C. Dio. G. and B. 1865. (Patron, J. Walker, Esq; V.'s Inc. 150*l*; Pop. 647.) [7]

WALKER, Richard Zouche, *Boyton Rectory, Heytesbury.*—Magd. Coll. Ox. B.A. 1850, M.A. 1853; Deac. 1852, Pr. 1854. R. of Boyton, Dio. Salis. 1861. (Patron, Magd. Coll. Ox; Tithe, 517*l*; R.'s Inc. 550*l* and Ho; Pop. 410.) Formerly C. of Sparsholt and Kingston-Lisle 1853. [8]

WALKER, Robert, *Wymeswold Vicarage, Loughborough, Leicestershire.*—Trin. Coll. Cam. 2nd Wrang. and B.A. 1847, M.A. 1850; Deac. 1851 by Abp of York, Pr. 1852 by Bp of Ely. V. of Wymeswold, Dio. Pet. 1856. (Patron, Trin. Coll. Cam; Tithe—Imp. 10*s*, V. 15*s* 3*d*; Glebe, 74 acres; V.'s Inc. 170*l* and Ho; Pop. 1209.) Formerly Fell. of Trin. Coll. Cam; C. of Bradfield St. Clare, Suffolk; V. of Helion Bumpsted, Essex, 1854. Author, *Rationalism Unphilosophical and Faith the Gift of God,* Mackintosh, 1863. [9]

WALKER, Robert Graves, *Hindon, Wilts.*—P. C. of Hindon, Dio. Salis. 1855. (Patron, Ld Chan; Tithe, App. 70*l*; P. C.'s Inc. 75*l*; Pop. 604.) [10]

WALKER, Robert Holdsworth.—Math. Mast. at the Royal Military Coll. Farnborough, Hants. [11]

WALKER, Saint George.—Formerly C. of Arthuret, Cumberland. [12]

WALKER, Samuel, *Trafalgar-road, Ipswich.*—Queen's Coll. Birmingham; Deac. 1860 and Pr. 1861 by Bp. of Wor. C. of St. John's Chapel-of-Ease to St. Margaret's, Ipswich, 1864. Formerly C. of St. Matthias', Birmingham, 1860, St. Matthew's, Gosport, 1862. Author, *Gold or Grace, which is best?* 1862. [13]

WALKER, Samuel, *West Bromwich, Staffs.*—C. of St. Peter's, West Bromwich. [14]

WALKER, Samuel Abraham, 23, *Berkeley-square, Bristol.*—Dub. A.B. 1832, A.M. 1833; Deac. 1832 and Pr. 1833 by Bp of Kildare. R. of St. Mary-le-Port, Bristol, Dio. G. and B. 1857. (Patron, Geo. Cooke, Esq. Clifton; R.'s Inc. 300*l*; Pop. 196.) Formerly R. of Gallow, co. Meath, Ireland, 1837–48; C. of St. Mark's, Dublin, 1837–39; Min. of St. Paul's Chapel, Aberdeen, 1848–53. Author, *Missions in Africa,* 12*s*, 1845; *Missions in Sierra Leone,* 12*s*, 1847; *Abraham's Bosom,* 5*s*; *Things New and Old,* 2 vols. 4*s*; *The Papacy, its Author and Aim,* 1*s* 6*d*; *Address to Servants,* 2*d*; *Address to Masters and Mistresses,* 2*d*; *Romanising Tendencies,* 2*d*; *A Few Words of Truth spoken in Love to Religious Liberators and Church Defenders,* 3*d*; *The Christian Soldier Ready,* 3*s* 6*d*; Sermon on *The Marriage of the Princess Royal,* and on *The Marriage of the Prince of Wales*; *How Long will the Laity bear it? a Question for the Sheep against the Shepherds,* 1*s*; Three Series of Annual Lectures to the Working Classes, 1*s* 6*d* each; etc. [15]

WALKER, Samuel Edmund, *St. Columb Major Rectory, Cornwall.*—Trin. Coll. Cam. B.A. 1838, M.A. 1834, B.D. 1841, D.D. 1846. R. of St. Columb Major, Dio. Ex. 1841. (Patron, the present R; Tithe, 1515*l*; Glebe, 30 acres; R.'s Inc. 1545*l* and Ho; Pop. 2879.) Chap. to Viscount Valentia. [16]

WALKER, Samuel Henry, *Harpford, near Ottery St. Mary, Devon.*—Ball. Coll. Ox. Fell. of, 1831–1836, B.A. 1832, M.A. 1835; Deac. 1834 by Bp of Ox. Pr. 1835 by Bp of Ex. P. C. of Newton-Poppleford, Dio. Ex. 1863. (Patron, V. of Aylesbeare; P. C.'s Inc. 28*l*; Pop. 66.) Formerly Asst. C. of Bampton, Devon, 1834–39; Min. of Horrabridge Chapel, Buckland Monachorum, Devon, 1841–55; C. of Newton Poppleford 1855–63. [17]

WALKER, Samuel Masterson, *St. Enoder Rectory, Grampound, Cornwall.*—Caius Coll. Cam. B.A. 1825, M.A. 1843, *ad eund.* Ox. 1851; Deac. 1826, Pr. 1827. R. of St. Enoder, Dio. Ex. 1828. (Patron, Bp of Ex; Tithe—Imp. 463*l*, R. 320*l* 6*s*; Glebe, 38*l*; R.'s Inc. 373*l* and Ho; Pop. 1150.) Surrogate. [18]

‡**WALKER, Sydney Richard Maynard,** *Ross, Herefordshire.*—Ch. Ch. Ox. B.A. 1861; Deac. 1862 by Bp of Ex. Pr. 1864 by Bp of Herf. Asst C. of Ross 1866. [19]

WALKER, Thomas, *Abbotts Moreton, Bromsgrove.*—R. of Abbotts Moreton, Dio. Wor. 1861. (Patron, G. J. A. Walker, Esq; Glebe, 167 acres; R.'s Inc. 159*l*; Pop. 245.) [20]

WALKER, Thomas, *Clipston Rectory (Northants), near Market Harborough.*—Ch. Coll. Cam. B.A. 1831, M.A. 1834. R. of Clipston, Dio. Pet. 1842. (Patron, Ch. Coll. Cam; R.'s Inc. 335*l* and Ho; Pop. 877.) Formerly Fell. of Ch. Coll. Cam. [21]

WALKER, Thomas, *Sleights Parsonage, Whitby, Yorks.*—St. John's Coll. Cam. 1845, 1st cl. and B.A. 1849, M.A. 1852; Deac. 1849, Pr. 1850. P. C. of Eskdaleside with Ugglesbarnby, Dio. York, 1854. (Patron, the present P. C.; Tithe—App. 520*l*; P. C.'s Inc. 320*l* and Ho; Pop. Eskdaleside 417, Ugglebarnby 437.) [22]

WALKER, Thomas Andrew, *Filey, Yorks.*—St. John's Coll. Ox. B.A. 1845, M.A. 1851; Deac. 1846 and Pr. 1847 by Bp of Ox. [23]

WALKER, Walter Nathaniel, 147, *Gower-street, London, W.C.*—Oriel Coll. Ox. B.A. 1853, M.A. 1856; Deac. 1854 and Pr. 1855 by Bp of Ox. C. of All Saints', Gordon-square, 1866. Formerly C. of Chesham, Bucks. [24]

WALKER, William, *Bardney Vicarage, Wragby, Lincolnshire.*—Dub. A.M. 1842, *ad eund.* Cam. 1847; Deac. 1842, Pr. 1843. V. of Bardney, Dio. Lin. 1852. (Patron, Bp of Lin; Tithe—App. 280*l*, Imp. 130*l*, V. 15*l*; Glebe, 1½ acres; V.'s Inc. 140*l* and Ho; Pop. 1425.) Surrogate 1852. [25]

WALKER, William Henry, *Necton Rectory, Thetford.*—St. John's Coll. Cam. B.A. 1854, M.A. 1857, Theol. Assoc. King's Coll. Lond. 1850; Deac. 1854 and Pr. 1855 by Bp of Lin. R. and V. of Necton, Dio. Nor. 1861. (Patron, M. C. Walker, Esq; Tithe, 905*l*; Glebe, 26 acres; R.'s Inc. 645*l* and Ho; Pop. 948.) Formerly C. of South Collingham, and Langford, Notts, and St. Paul's, Herne-hill, Dulwich. Author, *Sermon.* [26]

WALKEY, Charles Collyns, *Lucton, Leominster.*—Ball. Coll. Ox. 1821, Wor. Coll. 1823, 2nd cl. Lit. Hum. and B.A. 1825, M.A. 1827; Deac. 1828, Pr. 1829. P. C. of Lucton, Dio. Herf. 1831. (Patrons, Governors of Lucton School; Tithe—Imp. 135*l*; P. C.'s Inc. 150*l* and Ho; Pop. 174.) Head Mast. of the Lucton Free Gr. Sch. 1831. Formerly Fell. of Wor. Coll. Ox. 1826. [27]

WALKEY, Charles John Elliott, *Llantrisent Vicarage, Llangibby, Newport.*—Lin. Coll. Ox. Huish Scho. B.A. 1857, M.A. 1858; Deac. 1857 and Pr. 1858 by Bp of Herf. V. of Llantrissent with Pertholey V. Dio. Llan. 1861. (Patron, the present V; Tithe, 152*l*; Glebe, 30 acres; V.'s Inc. 180*l* and Ho; Pop. 308.) Formerly C. of Bayton with Mamble 1857, Cusop 1860. [1]

WALL, Charles Joseph, *Sproatley Rectory, Hull.*—St. Peter's Coll. Cam. B.A. 1848, M.A. 1851; Deac. 1849 and Pr. 1850 by Bp of Nor. R. of Sproatley, Dio. York, 1858. (Patron, Sir Clifford Constable, Bart; R.'s Inc. 250*l* and Ho; Pop. 455.) Rural Dean. Formerly C. of Sproatley; Dom. Chap. to Lord Blayney. [2]

WALL, George William, *Burnside, Kendal.*—P. C. of Burnside, Dio. Carl. 1859. (Patrons, Trustees; P. C.'s Inc. 120*l*; Pop. 105.) [3]

WALL, Henry, *Balliol College, Oxford.*—St. Alban Hall, Ox. 1st cl. Lit. Hum. Chan.'s Eng. Essay 1833, B.A. 1833, M.A. 1836; Deac. 1838 and Pr. 1839 by Bp of Ox. Fell. of Ball. Coll; Prof. of Logic; Member of Hebdomadal Council; Vice-Prin. of St. Alban Hall, Ox. 1837–51; Public Examiner 1839 and 1860. [4]

WALL, Richard, *Brewood, Staffs.*—St. John's Coll. Cam. Wrang. and B.A. 1844, M.A. 1848; Deac. 1844, Pr. 1846. Head Mast. of the Gr. Sch. Brewood. Formerly P. C. of St. Anne's, Birkenhead, 1849. [5]

WALL, Thomas, *Edgware Vicarage, Middlesex, N.W.*—Caius Coll. Cam. Wrang. and B.A. 1830, M.A. 1833; Deac. 1835 by Bp of Lin. Pr. 1836 by Bp of Roch. V. of Edgware, Dio. Lon. 1847. (Patrons, Exors. of John Lee, LL.D; Tithe—Imp. 25*l*, V. 450*l*; Glebe, 9 acres; V.'s Inc. 475*l* and Ho; Pop. 705.) [6]

WALL, William, *Belmont Parsonage, Bolton-le-Moors.*—Jesus Coll. Cam. B.A. 1832, M.A. 1836; Deac. and Pr. by Bp of Ex. P. C. of Belmont, Dio. Man. 1860. (Patron, Thomas Wright, Esq; P. C.'s Inc. 120*l* and Ho; Pop. 1033.) Formerly C. of King's Kerswell, Devon; Asst. Min. of Percy Chapel, and Aft. Lect. of St. James's, Pentonville, Lond; Asst. Min. of St. Stephen's, Westbourne-park, Lond. [7]

WALL, William Ellis, *Wheatfields, Powick, Worcester.*—Trin. Coll. Ox. B.A. 1825, M.A. 1830; Deac. 1827, Pr. 1828. [8]

WALLACE, Allen, *Newport, Isle of Wight.*—Pemb. Coll. Cam Jun. Opt. and B.A. 1839, M.A. 1843; Deac. 1841 and Pr. 1842 by Bp of Ches. Head Mast. of the Free Gr. Sch. Newport, 1843; Surrogate. Formerly Garrison Chap. Parkhurst. [9]

WALLACE, Arthur Capel Job, *Monks Eleigh Rectory, Bildestone, Suffolk.*—Corpus Coll. Cam. Jun. Opt. B.A. 1822, M.A. 1825; Deac. 1823 and Pr. 1824 by Bp of Lon. R. of Monks Eleigh, Dio. Ely, 1845. (Patron, Abp of Cant; Tithe, comm. 570*l*; Glebe, 16 acres; R.'s Inc. 590*l* and Ho; Pop. 678.) [10]

WALLACE, Charles Hill, 20, *Sion-hill, Clifton, Bristol.*—Pemb. Coll. Ox. B.A. 1855, M.A. 1858; Deac. 1857 and Pr. 1858 by Bp of G. and B. C. of Trinity, Clifton, 1857. [11]

WALLACE, C. Stebbing, *Monk's Eleigh, Bildestone, Suffolk.*—C. of Monk's Eleigh. [12]

WALLACE, George, *Burghclere Rectory (Hants), near Newbury, Berks.*—Trin. Coll. Cam. B.A. 1831; Deac. 1833, Pr. 1836. R. of Burghclere, with Newtown C. Dio. Win. 1859. (Patron, Earl of Carnarvon; Tithe, Burghclere, 1100*l*; Glebe, 118½ acres; Newtown, Tithe, 100*l* 13*s*; R.'s Inc. 1340*l* and Ho; Pop. Burghclere 819, Newtown 276.) Formerly Head Mast. of the King's Sch. Canterbury, 1833–59. Author, Sermons—*The Glory of God the End of all Education*, 1860; *The Lord the Builder-up of Jerusalem*, 1861; *Eagle Nurture*, 1862; *The Christian Mourner*, 1863; *The Love of God the Source of the Love of Man*, 1865; *Measure the Pattern*; *The Reward of the Meek on Earth and in Heaven*, 1866. [13]

WALLACE, James, *Grammar School, Loughborough.*—Jesus Coll. Cam. Sen. Opt. 2nd cl. Cl. Trip. and B.A. 1851, M.A. 1854; Deac. 1852 and Pr. 1858 by Bp of Roch. Head Mast. of the Gr. Sch. Loughborough. Formerly Head Mast. of the Cathl. Sch. Pet; Chap. in Crimea 1855–56. Author, *Introductory Questions on Scripture History*, 2 eds. [14]

WALLACE, Neason William Adams, *Forest of Dean, Gloucestershire.*—Dub. A.B. 1850; Deac. 1853, Pr. 1854. C. of Ch. Ch. Forest of Dean. Formerly C. of Macclesfield. [15]

WALLACE, Robert James, *Ravenhead, St. Helens, Lancashire.*—Dub. A.M; Deac. and Pr. 1856. C. of Ravenhead, St. Helens. Formerly C. of Kiltnbride 1856–61, St. Paul's, Blackburn, 1861. [16]

WALLACE, William, *St. Helens, Lancashire.*—C. of St. Helens. [17]

WALLACE, William, *Thorpe Abbotts Rectory, Scole, Norfolk.*—Jesus Coll. Cam. B.A. 1832; Deac. 1835, Pr. 1837. R. of Thorpe Abbotts, Dio. Nor. 1838. (Patron, J. Page Reade, Esq; Tithe, 334*l* 4*s*; Glebe, 17 acres; R.'s Inc. 332*l*; Pop. 255) [18]

WALLAS, Gilbert Innes, *Barnstaple Vicarage, Devon.*—Trin. Coll. Cam. B.A. 1844, M.A. 1847; Deac. 1847 and Pr. 1848 by Bp of Dur. V. of Barnstaple, Dio. Ex. 1860. (Patron, Lord Wharncliffe; Tithe, 245*l*; V.'s Inc. 220*l* and Ho; Pop. 3733.) Surrogate. Formerly C. of Bishopwearmouth 1849–58, St. Andrew's, Auckland, 1858–60. [19]

WALLAS, John, *Crosscrake, Milnthorpe, Westmoreland.*—Queen's Coll. Ox. B.A. 1838, M.A. 1844; Deac. 1839 and Pr. 1841 by Bp of Ches. P. C. of Crosscrake, Dio. Carl. 1844. (Patron, V. of Heversham; P. C.'s Inc. 158*l* and Ho; Pop. 350.) [20]

WALLER, Charles Blackmore, *Woodford Bridge, Essex, N.E.*—Wor. Coll. Ox. B.A. 1846, M.A. 1848; Deac. 1846 and Pr. 1847 by Bp of Win. P. C. of St. Paul's, Woodford, Dio. Lon. 1855. (Patron, R. of Woodford; P. C.'s Inc. 130*l*; Pop. 844.) [21]

WALLER, C. E., *Humberstone Vicarage, Leicester.*—V. of Humberstone, Dio. Pet. 1861. (Patron, the present V; V.'s Inc. 200*l* and Ho; Pop. 515.) [22]

WALLER, Charles Henry, *St. John's Hall, Highbury, N.*—Univ. Coll. Ox. Scho. of 2nd cl. Lit. Hum. 3rd cl. Math. 1st Denyer and Johnson's Theol. Scho. 1866; B.A. 1863, M.A. 1867; Deac. 1864 and Pr. 1865 by Bp of Lon. C. of Ch. Ch. Mayfair, 1865; Tut. of the Lond. Coll. of Divinity, St. John's Hall, Highbury, 1865. Formerly C. of St. Jude's, Islington, 1864. Author, *Letter to Everyone who will know his Bible*, Rivingtons, 1864. [23]

WALLER, Daniel, *St. Paul's Parsonage, Dane Bridge, Northwich, Cheshire.*—St. Peter's Coll. Cam. B.A. 1842, M.A. 1846; Deac. 1842 and Pr. 1843 by Bp of Ches. P. C. of Dane Bridge, Dio. Ches. 1846. (Patron, Crown and Bp of Ches. alt; P. C.'s Inc. 150*l* and Ho; Pop. 2315.) Chap. of Northwich Union (Salary, 50*l*.) Formerly C. of Oldham St. Mary 1842–46. [24]

WALLER, Robert, *Bourton-on-the-Water Rectory, Stow-on-the-Wold, Glouc.*—Brasen. Coll. Ox. B.A. 1832, M.A. 1835. R. of Bourton-on-the-Water with Lower-Slaughter C. and Clapton-on-the-Hill C. Dio. G. and B. 1836. (Patron, Wad. Coll. Ox; Bourton-on-the-Water and Clapton-on-the-Hill, Tithe—App. 16*l* 12*s* 10*d*, Imp. 8*l* 19*s* 2½*d*, R. 99*l* 11*s* 4*d*; Glebe, 81½ acres; R.'s Inc. 496*l* and Ho; Pop. Bourton-on-the-Water 1011, Lower-Slaughter 212, Clapton-on-the-Hill 123.) [25]

WALLER, Robert Plume, *Stratton Vicarage, Cornwall.*—Jesus Coll. Cam. B.A. 1839, M.A. 1842; Deac. 1839 by Abp of Cant. Pr 1839 by Abp of York. V. of Stratton, Dio. Ex. 1858. (Patron, Prince of Wales; Glebe, 3 acres; V.'s Inc. 200*l* and Ho; Pop. 989.) [26]

WALLER, Stephen Richard, *Bedford.*—Brasen. Coll. Ox. B.A. 1834, M.A. 1838; Deac. 1836 by Bp of Ban. Pr. 1837 by Bp of Lich. Formerly P. C. of Mitton 1849. [27]

WALLER, Thomas Henry, *Waldringfield Rectory, near Woodbridge.*—Clare Coll. Cam. B.A. 1857; Deac. 1860 and Pr. 1861 by Bp of Nor. R. of Waldringfield, Dio. Nor. 1862. (Patron, the present R; Tithe, comm. 170*l*; Glebe, 38 acres; R.'s Inc. 239*l* and Ho; Pop. 205.) [28]

WALLER, William, *Whittlesey, Cambs.*—St. Cath. Coll. Cam. 1840, M.A. 1845; Deac. 1840, Pr. 1841. V. of Whittlesey St. Mary, Dio. Ely, 1856. (Patron, J. W. Childers, Esq; Tithe—Imp. 3954*l* 6*s* 8½*d*; V.'s Inc. 255*l*; Pop. 5572.) Formerly C. of Soham, near Cambridge; P. C. of St. John's, Dukenfield, Cheshire, 1844–56. [1]

WALLICH, Leonard Calder, *Poringland Rectory, Norwich.*—Trin. Coll. Cam. Jun. Opt. B.A. 1846, M.A. 1849; Deac. 1847 and Pr. 1848 by Bp of Nor. R. of Poringland, Dio. Nor. 1861. (Patron, Henry Birkbeck, Esq; Tithe, 214*l*; Glebe, 18½ acres; R.'s Inc. 254*l* and Ho; Pop. 464.) Formerly C. of Poringland, 1846–61. [2]

WALLINGER, William, *Chichester.*—Univ. Coll. Ox. B.A. 1816, M.A. 1825; Deac. 1820, Pr. 1821. Preb. of Chich. 1847. [3]

WALLIS, G. F. Winstanley, *Watton Vicarage, Thetford, Norfolk.*—V. of Watton, Dio. Nor. 1865. (Patron, Rev. W. H. Hicks; V.'s Inc. 200*l* and Ho; Pop. 1365.) [4]

WALLIS, Joseph, 12, *Lansdowne-circus, Stockwell, S.*—Lond. B.A. 1844; Caius Coll. Cam. Scho. of, B.A. 1850, M.A. 1853; Deac. 1850 and Pr. 1852 by Bp of Ex. Min. of Stockwell Chapel, Dio. Win. 1859. (Patrons, Trustees; Min.'s Inc. 300*l*.) Surrogate; Sec. of Surrey Church Association. Formerly C. of St. Andrew's, Plymouth, 1850–52, Margate 1852–53, St. Clement's, Hastings, 1853–56, Allhallows, Barking, 1856–59. [5]

WALLIS, Robert Ernest, *Coxley Parsonage, near Wells.*—Ph. D. and M.A. of Rostock 1865; Deac. 1849 and Pr. 1851 by Bp of Ex. P. C. of Coxley at Wells, Dio. B. and W. 1863. (Patron, V. of Wells; P.C.'s Inc. 300*l* and Ho; Pop. 425.) Sen. Pr. V. of Wells Cathl. 1858; Surrogate. Formerly C. of St. Mary Magdalen's, Taunton; P. C. of Blackford, Somerset; Sen. C. and Sunday Even. Lect. of St. Cuthbert's, Wells. Author, *The Christian Minister not a Priest, but a Preacher* (a Sermon); *Baptism* (a pamphlet), Rivingtons, 1864; Translation of vol. iv. of Lange's *Life of Christ*, T. and T. Clark, Edinburgh, 1864, and of Delitzsch's *Biblical Psychology*, ib. 1867. [6]

WALLIS, William, *Melford Rectory, near Sudbury, Suffolk.*—Magd. Coll. Cam. Sen. Opt. afterwards Bye-Fellow, B.A. 1811, M.A. 1814; Deac. 1811 by Bp of Ely, Pr. 1812 by Bp of Lon. R. of Long Melford, Dio. Ely, 1861. (Patron, J. C. Cobbold, Esq. M.P; Tithe, and 120 acres of Glebe, 1100*l*; R.'s Inc. 1100*l* and Ho; Pop. 3000.) Formerly C. of Wathington, Lynn Regis, 1839–60. Author, Small Terrestrial Globe on a Novel Principle, with Movable Horizon for Schools, 10*s*, with Explanatory Tract, 6*d*. [7]

WALLS, Richard George, *Great Steeping Vicarage, Spilsby.*—Brasen. Coll. Ox. B.A. 1841, M.A. 1844; Deac. 1842 and Pr. 1843 by Bp of Lin. R. of Firsby with Great Steeping V. Dio. Lin. 1844. (Patron, the present R; Firsby, Tithe—Imp. 19*l* 10*s*, App. 2*l* 18*s* 8*d*, R. 185*l*; Glebe, 11 acres; Great Steeping, Tithe—App. 9*s*, Imp. 160*l*, V. 130*l*; Glebe, 4 acres; R.'s Inc. 342*l* and Ho; Pop. Firsby 237, Great Steeping 334.) [8]

WALMISLEY, Horatio, *Odd Rode Rectory, Lawton, Cheshire.*—Trin. and Sid. Coll. Cam. B.A. 1847, M.A. 1850; Deac. 1848 and Pr. 1849 by Bp of Nor. R. of Odd Rode, Dio. Ches. 1867. (Patron, R. of Astbury, Cheshire; R.'s Inc. 300*l* and Ho; Pop. 2476.) Formerly C. of Clehonger, Herefordshire, and Holme, Wakefield; P. C. of St. Briavels, Gloucestershire, 1859–67. [9]

WALPOLE, Joseph K., *Coaley, Dursley, Glouc.*—V. of Coaley, Dio. G. and B. 1862. (Patron, Ld Chan; V.'s Inc. 156*l* and Ho; Pop. 777.) [10]

WALPOLE, Robert Seymour, *Balderton, near Newark, Notts.*—St. Bees; Deac. 1851 by Bp of Nor. Pr 1852 by Bp of Lin. V. of Balderton, Dio. Lin. 1852. (Patron, Bp of Lin; V.'s Inc. 300*l* and Ho; Pop. 1500.) Formerly C. of Itteringham, Norfolk, 1851. [11]

WALPOLE, Thomas, *Alverstoke Rectory, Gosport, Hants.*—Ball. Coll. Ox. B.A. 1826, M.A. 1829. R. of Alverstoke with Anglesey C. Dio. Win. 1845. (Patron, Bp of Win; Tithe, 1270*l*; Glebe, 45 acres; R.'s Inc. 1345*l* and Ho; Pop. 6450.) Rural Dean. [12]

WALROND, Francis Frederick, *University College, Durham.*—Univ. Coll. Dur. B.A. 1851, Licen. in Theol. 1852, M.A. 1854; Deac. 1853 and Pr. 1854 by Bp of Dur. Registrar of the Univ. 1865; Bursar of Univ. Coll. 1865. Formerly Censor of Bp Hatfield's Hall, Dur. 1852; Vice-Prin. of same 1861. [13]

WALROND, Lloyd Baker, *St. Ann's-street, Salisbury.*—Deac. 1852, Pr. 1853. C. of St. Martin's, Salisbury, 1854. Formerly C. of Gawber, Yorks. 1852–54. [14]

WALROND, M. S. A.—P. C. of St. Mary's, Charterhouse, St. Luke's, Lond. Dio. Lon. 1862. (Patrons, the Crown and Bp of Lon. alt; P. C.'s Inc. 350*l* with 120*l* for curate; Pop. 7000.) [15]

WALROND, Theodore Augustus, 11, *Buckingham-street, Adelphi, London, W.C.*—Sec. of the Soc. for Missions to Seamen, Lond. [16]

WALROND, William Henry, *Ninehead Vicarage, Wellington, Somerset.*—Dub. 1853, Licen. Theol. of Dur. 1853; Deac. 1853, Pr. 1854. V. of Ninehead, Dio. B. and W. 1866. (Patron, G. E. A. Sandford, Esq; Tithe, 185*l*; Glebe, 30*l*; V.'s Inc. 215*l* and Ho; Pop. 321.) Formerly C. of St. John's, Brighton; P. C. of Langford Budville, Somerset, 1863–66. [17]

WALSH, Charles Bingham, *Kingsley, Alton, Hants.*—Dub. A.B. 1841; Deac. and Pr. 1844. V. of Binsted with Kingsley, near Alton, Dio. Win. 1854. (Patrons, D. and C. of Win; Binsted, Tithe—App. 761*l* 2*s* 3*d*, Imp. 136*l* 16*s*, V. 345*l* 11*s* 1*d*; Kingsley, Tithe—App. 282*l* 12*s* 8*d*, V. 114*l* 15*s* 11*d*; V.'s Inc. 480*l* and Ho; Pop. Binsted, 1195, Kingsley, 441.) [18]

WALSH, Digby, *Trinity Parsonage, Trowbridge, Wilts.*—Ball. Coll. Ox. B.A. 1851, M.A. 1856; Deac. 1853 and Pr. 1854 by Bp of Chich. P. C. of Trinity, Trowbridge, Dio. Salis. 1858. (Patron, R. of Trowbridge, P. C.'s Inc. 230*l* and Ho; Pop. 2373.) Surrogate; Dom. Chap. to the Earl of Stamford and Warrington. [19]

WALSH, E. L., *Warley, Essex.*—Chap. to the Forces, 3rd class. Served at Mauritius, at Colchester 3 years, and at Parkhurst 5 years. [20]

WALSH, Francis Clarke, 1, *Waterloo-place, Leamington.*—Univ. Coll. Ox. B.A. 1845, M.A. 1867; Deac. 1845, and Pr. 1846 by Bp of Wor. Mast. of a Preparatory Sch. [21]

WALSH, George Richard Dallas, *Wellesbourne, Warwick.*—Dub. A.B. 1852; Deac. 1852 and Pr. 1853 by Bp of Ches. C. of Wellesbourne; Dom. Chap. to the Dowager Baroness Vivian. Formerly C. of Barthomley, Cheshire, and Ditcheat. [22]

WALSH, Henry George, *St. John's Parsonage, Redland, Bristol.*—Corpus Coll. Cam. 14th Wrang. B.A. 1830, M.A. 1833; Deac. 1831 and Pr. 1832 by Bp of Lin. Min. of St. John's, Clifton, Dio. B. and W. 1841. (Patron, Bp of G. and B; Min.'s Inc. 263*l* and Ho; Pop. 4377.) [23]

WALSH, John Henry Arnold, *Bishopstrow Rectory, near Warminster, Wilts.*—Ball. Coll. Ox. 3rd cl. Lit. Hum. B.A. 1826, M.A. 1829; Deac. 1827 and Pr. 1829 by Bp of Salis. R. of Bishopstrow, Dio. Salis. 1859. (Patron, Sir F. D. Ashley, Bart; Tithe, 241*l*; Glebe, 23*l* 10*s*; R.'s Inc. 270*l* and Ho; Pop. 268.) Formerly C. of Warminster 1827; P. C. of Ch. Ch. Warminster 1831–59. Author, *Practical Commentary on the Four Gospels, in the Form of Lectures, designed to assist Family Devotion* (privately printed in 1846, since sold in aid of the funds of the Ch. Pastoral Aid. Soc.) [24]

WALSH, Joseph Neate, *Kington, Herefordshire.*—St. John's Coll. Ox. 3rd cl. Lit. Hum. 1st cl. Math. et Phy and B.A. 1825, M.A. 1828; Deac. 1828 and Pr. 1829 by Bp of Salis. Head Mast. of Kington Gr. Sch. 1835; Lect. of Kington 1835. [25]

WALSH, Perceval William, *Stanton Harcourt, Witney, Oxon.*—Wor. Coll. Ox. B.A. 1840, M.A. 1844; Deac. 1841 and Pr. 1842. V. of Stanton Harcourt with Chapelry of Southleigh, Dio. Ox. 1845. (Patron,

Bp of Ox;] Tithe, 160*l*; Glebe, 20 acres; V.'s Inc. 140*l*; Pop. Stanton Harcourt 661, Southleigh 319.]

WALSH, Thomas Harris, *Riddings Parsonage, Alfreton, Derbyshire.*—St. Bees; Deac. 1850 and Pr. 1851 by Bp of Rip. P. C. of Riddings with Somercotes C Dio. Lich. 1863. (Patron, V. of Alfreton; P C.'s Inc. 150*l* and Ho; Pop. 4145.) Formerly C. of St. Peter's, Oldham; P. C. of Ashton-Hayes 1857 [2]

WALSH, Walter, *South Ormsby, near Alford, Lincolnshire.*—Emman. Coll. Cam. Scho. of, 36th Wrang. B.A. 1860, M.A. 1863; Deac. 1860 and Pr. 1861 by Bp of Lich. C. of South Ormsby-with-Ketsby 1863. Formerly C. of St. Mary's, Wolverhampton, 1860–63. [3]

WALSH, William, *Great Tey Rectory, Kelvedon, Essex.*—St. John's Coll. Cam. B.A. 1839, M.A. 1842. Sinecure R. and V. of Great Tey, Dio. Roch. 1854. (Patron, the present R; Tithe—Sinecure: 52*l* 4*s* and 7 acres of Glebe, V. 236*l* 11*s* and acres of Glebe; Sinecure R.'s and V.'s Inc. 816*l* and Ho; Pop. 818.) [4]

WALSH, William, *Norton Villa, Wellesley-road, Croydon, S.*—St. Alban Hall, Ox. B.A. 1859, M.A. 1862; Deac. 1860 and Pr. 1861 by Bp of Win. Assoc. Sec. Ch. Miss. Soc. for Kent, Surrey, and Sussex. Formerly C. of Horsell, Surrey, and Upper Chelsea, Lond. [5]

WALSHAM, Charles, *The Vicarage, Sculcoates, Hull.*—Magd. Coll. Cam. Cl. Hons. B.A. 1860, M.A. 1864; Deac. 1861 and Pr. 1862 by Bp of Ely. V. of Sculcoates, Dio. York, 1866. (Patron, Ld Chan; V.'s Inc. 400*l* and Ho; Pop. 17,687.) Chap. to the Mast. of the Rolls; Surrogate. Formerly C. of Trinity, Ely, and Dep. Min. Can. of Ely Cathl; C. of Trinity, Paddington, Lond. 1863–66. Author, *The Christian Rest*; *Treatise on the Catechism*; *Tract on Sunday*; *Confirmation Invitation*; *Confirmation Addresses*, 1864–65; *Sown in Weakness*; *Preparation for the Eucharist*; *The True Light*; *Follow Me*; *I will, Be thou clean*; *We must needs die*; *Sorrowers for Christ*; *Bartimaeus*; *Pilate and his Prisoner*; *Justified by His Grace.* [6]

WALSHAM, Francis, *Nunnington, Oswald, Kirk, Yorks.*—R. of Knill, Herefordshire, Dio. Herf. 1860. (Patron, Sir J. J. Walsham, Bart; R.'s Inc. 90*l*; Pop. 84.) C. of Nunnington; Chap. to the Northumberland Reformatory. [7]

WALSHAW, Joseph Renatus, *Chatham.*—Dub. A.B. 1848, A.M. 1860; Deac. 1848 by Bp of Rip. Pr. 1850 by Bp of Ches. Asst. Chap. of the Convict Prison, Chatham. [8]

WALTER, Arthur, *Gautby Rectory, Horncastle.*—Caius Coll. Cam. B.A. 1853; Deac. 1853 and Pr. 1854 by Bp of Wor. R. of Gautby, Dio. Lin. 1865. (Patron, Ld Chan; Tithe, comm. 90*l*; Glebe, 80 acres; R.'s Inc. 210*l* and Ho; Pop. 113.) Formerly C. of Stourbridge 1853–56, Fenny Compton 1856–65. [9]

WALTER, Edward, *Langton Rectory, Horncastle.*—Ch. Coll. Cam. Sen. Opt. 1824; Deac. 1824, Pr. 1825. R. of Langton with Woodhall V. Dio. Lin. 1828. (Patron, Bp of Lin; Langton, Glebe, 160 acres; R.'s Inc. 168*l* and Ho; Pop. 85; Woodhall, V.'s Inc. 90*l*; Pop. 177.) Author, *A Help to the profitable Reading of the Psalms for Christian People*, 1854, 4*s*; *Old Black Oak* (a Tract), 1854, 2*d*. [10]

WALTER, Frederick Morton, *St. Petrox, Dartmouth, Devon.*—St. John's Coll. Cam. B.D. 1844, *ad eund.* Ox. 1847. P. C. of St. Petrox, Dio. Ex. 1836. (Patron, R. of Stoke Fleming; Glebe, 22 acres; P. C.'s Inc. 120*l*; Pop. 885.) [11]

WALTER, James Conway.—St. Cath. Coll. Cam. B.A. 1853; Deac. 1855 and Pr. 1856 by Bp of Chich. Formerly C. of Patcham, Sussex, 1855–57. Author, *Letters from the Highlands*, 1859, 1*s*; *Forays among Salmon and Deer*, 1861, 5*s*; *The Genuineness of the Book of Daniel asserted on Evidence external and internal*, 1863, 5*s*. [12]

WALTER, William Hampson, *Durham.*—Dur. B.A. 1850, M.A. 1853; Deac. 1852 and Pr. 1853 by Bp of Dur. R. of St. Mary-le-Bow, Durham, Dio. Dur. 1867. (Patron, Archd. of Northumberland; Glebe, 70 acres; R.'s Inc. 310*l*; Pop. 280.) Prin. of Female Training College, Durham. Formerly C. of Sedgefield, and of St. Mary-le-Bow, Durham. [13]

WALTERS, Alfred Vaughan, *Fulflood, Wyke, Winchester*—Magd. Hall, Ox. B.A. 1852; Deac. 1853 and Pr. 1854 by Bp of Salis. C. of Wyke 1861. Formerly C. of Allington and Amesbury, Wilts, 1853–55, Washingborough, Linc. 1855–57, Lea, Linc. 1858–59, Lythe, Yorks, 1860. [14]

WALTERS, Charles, *Farm School, Red-hill, Surrey.*—Primate's Heb. Prizeman 1848, 1st Abp King's Div. Prizeman 1850, 1st Cl. and A.B. 1851, A.M. 1856; Deac. 1852 and Pr. 1853 by Bp of Lich. Res. Chap. to the Philanthropic Society for the Reformation of Juvenile Offenders, Farm School, Red-hill. Formerly C. of St. John's Hanley 1852–56, St. Mark's, Shelton, 1856–57. Author *Reports of Philanthropic Society's Farm School.* [15]

WALTERS, Charles, *Wardington Parsonage, Banbury.*—Mert. Coll. Ox. B.A. 1833, M.A. 1836; Deac. 1834 and Pr. 1835 by Bp of Win. P. C. of Wardington, Dio. Ox. 1851. (Patron, Bp of Ox; Tithe, 13*l* 14*s*, Modus, 59*l* 16*s*; Glebe 24 acres; P. C.'s Inc. 135*l* and Ho; Pop. 732.) [16]

WALTERS, Charles, *Wyke Rectory, near Winchester*—Magd. Hall, Ox. B.A. 1808, M.A. 1812; Deac. and Pr. 1808 by Bp of Win. R. of Wyke, or Weeke, Dio. Win. 1845. (Patron, Bp of Win; Tithe, 265*l*; Glebe, 1 acre; R.'s Inc. 255*l*; Pop. 529.) Chap. of the Wyke Union; Surrogate. Author, *The History of the Town, &c. of Bishops Waltham, Hants*; *A Visitation Sermon*; Pamphlets; etc. [17]

WALTERS, Henry, *Abertylery, Newport, Monmouthshire.*—Lampeter; Deac. 1846 by Bp of St. D. Pr. 1847 by Bp of Llan. C. of St. Michael's, Abertylery, 1862. [18]

WALTERS, Henry Littlejohn Master, *Littlemore, Oxford.*—Ch. Ch. Ox. B.A. 1842, M.A. 1846; Deac. 1843 by Bp of G. and B. Pr. 1844 by Bp of Salis. Chap. of the Littlemore Asylum 1867. Formerly C. of Chilton Cantelo, 1844, in sole charge for 15 years; C. and Lect. of Aust with Northwick, Henbury, 1845; C. of Forton, Hants, 1864. Author, *On the Mischiefs of Lotteries*, 1853; *Footprints by Severn-Side* (a Legendary Ballad), 1858; *Sebastopol and the Harvest* (Thanksgiving-day Sermon); *Arab Life*; *Hints on Confirmation*; various Sermons. [19]

WALTERS, John Thomas, *Ide Vicarage, near Exeter.*—St. John's Coll. Cam. B.A. 1850; Deac. and Pr. 1850. V. of Ide, Dio. Ex. 1865. (Patrons, D. and C. of Ex; V.'s Inc. 200*l* and Ho; Pop. 665.) Formerly R. of Stradishall, Suffolk, 1853–59, Freystrup 1859, V. of Spaldwick, Dio. Ely, 1861–65. [20]

WALTERS, John Vodin.—C. of St. Matthew's, City-road, Lond. [21]

WALTERS, Nicholas, *St. Peter's Rectory, Stamford.*—Trin. Coll. Cam. B.A. 1822, M.A. 1826; Deac. 1824 by Bp of Win. Pr. 1826 by Bp of Lon. R. of All Saints' with St. Peter's, Stamford, Dio. Lin. 1836. (Patrons, Marquis of Exeter 2 turns, and Ld Chan. 1 turn; Tithe—App. 7*l* 1*s*, V. 467*l* 5*s* 7*d*; V.'s Inc. 477*l* and Ho; Pop. 2044.) Rural Dean 1839. Formerly C. of All Saints', Stamford. [22]

WALTERS, Spencer, *St. Peter's Rectory, Stamford.*—St. John's Coll. Cam. B.A. 1854, M.A. 1867. C. in sole charge of All Saints', Stamford, 1867. Formerly C. of Biggleswade 1859–67. [23]

WALTERS, Thomas, *Maenclochog Vicarage, Haverfordwest.*—Lampeter; Deac. 1849 and Pr. 1850 by Bp of St. D. V. of Maenclochog and P. C. of Llangolman and Llandilo, Dio. St. D. 1863. (Patron, George Le Hunte, Esq. Wexford, Ireland; Tithe, 100*l*; Glebe, 62*l* 10*s*; V.'s Inc. 219*l* 16*s* and Ho; Pop. 396.) Formerly C. of Lampeter Velfrey 1852, Talley, Carmarthenshire, 1853–55, Llangan 1855–63. [24]

WALTERS, Thomas, *Ystradgunlais, Swansea.*—Corpus Coll. Cam. B.D. 1863; Deac. 1846 by Bp of St. D. Pr. 1847 by Bp of Llan. R. of Ystradgunlais, Dio. St. D. 1856. (Patron, R. D. Gough, Esq; Tithe, 372*l*; R.'s Inc. 400*l* and Ho; Pop. 4346.) Formerly C. of

Bedwellty, Mon. 1846–48, Ystradgunlais 1848–51, Kilvey, Swansea, 1851–53; Assoc. Sec. for the Ch. Pastoral Aid Soc. for Wales, 1853–55. Author, *A Catechism designed for the Use and Instruction o Candidates for Confirmation* (in English and Welsh); *On Prophetic Scriptures and their Divine Inspiration* (a Sermon preached before the University of Cambridge), 1863; *The Common Lo* :(a Tract), 1864; several Letters on the necessity of appointing Welsh-speaking Chaplains to the Gaols in Glamorganshire, 1859; etc. [1]

WALTERS, William, *Oldham.*—Ch. Ch. Ox. B.A. 1854, M.A. 1857; Deac. 1857 and Pr. 1858 by Bp of Wor. P. C. of Oldham, Dio. Man. 1864. (Patron, R. of Prestwich; P. C.'s Inc. 300*l*; Pop. 16,576.) Formerly C. of Pershore, Worcestershire, 1857–60, Hanley-Castle 1860. [2]

WALTHAM, Joshua, *Broomfleet, Brough, Yorks.*—St. John's Coll. Cam. B.A. 1834; Deac. 1835, Pr. 1836. P. C. of Broomfleet, Dio. York, 1866. (Patroness, Mrs. Barnard; Tithe, 113*l*; P. C.'s Inc. 140*l* and Ho; Pop. 600.) Formerly V. of Skredington, Linc. 1851. Author, *Evangelium Matthæi Syriacum, cum Lexico Syriaco*; etc. [3]

WALTON, C. Bailey, *London-street, Derby.*—Deac. 1864 and Pr. 1865 by Bp of Lich. C. of St. James's the Greater, Derby, 1866. Formerly C. of St. Mary's, Stafford, 1864. [4]

WALTON, Henry Baskerville, *Merton College, Oxford.*—Pemb. Coll. Ox. 1st cl. Cl. and B.A. 1846, M.A. 1849; Deac. 1850, Pr. 1851. P. C. of St. Cross, Oxford, Dio. Ox. 1851. (Patron, Mert. Coll. Ox; P. C.'s Inc. 142*l*; Pop. 943.) Formerly Fell. Sub-Warden and Tut. of Mert. Coll. Ox. [5]

WALTON, James Hatton, *Robert Town, Mill Bridge, Leeds.*—St. Bees; 1st Cl. 1844; Deac. 1845, Pr. 1846. P. C. of Robert Town, Dio. Rip. 1846. (Patron, V. of Birstal; Glebe, 3 roods; P. C.'s Inc. 68*l*; Pop. 2256.) [6]

WALTON, John, *Leigh, Lancashire.*—Marischal Coll. Aberdeen and St. Aidan's; Deac. 1861, Pr. 1862 C. of Leigh 1867. Formerly C. of Codnor 1861, and Mapperley, Derbyshire, 1866. [7]

WALTON, John Leidger, *Silkstone Vicarage, Barnsley, Yorks.*—Trin. Coll. Cam. B.A. 1830, M.A. 1834; Deac. 1830, Pr. 1831. V. of Silkstone, Dio. Rip. 1850. (Patron, Bp of Rip; Tithe—App. 2*l* 14*s*, Imp. 559*l* 18*s*, V. 118*l*; V.'s Inc. 270*l* and Ho; Pop. 1843.) Surrogate; Chap. to Lord Lovat 1839. [8]

WALTON, Joseph, *Alverthorpe, Wakefield.*—Ch. Coll. Cam. B.A. 1844, M.A. 1847; Deac. 1845 and Pr. 1846 by Bp of Rip. P. C. of Alverthorpe, Dio. Rip. 1853. (Patron, V. of Wakefield; P. C.'s Inc. 300*l*; Pop. 4771.) [9]

WALTON, Nicholas, *Adlingfleet Vicarage, Goole, Yorks.*—Literate; Deac. 1836 and Pr. 1837 by Abp of York. C. in sole charge of Adlingfleet 1867. Formerly C. of North Cave, Yorks, 1836; P. C. of Sutton, near Hull, 1339–47; C. in sole charge of Westow ,near Malton, 1848–52; C. of Kirby Moorside 1856. [10]

WALTON, Stanley, *Fenstanton, St. Ives, Hunts.*—Trin. Hall, Cam. Wrang. and B.A. 1850, M.A. 1853; Deac. 1851, Pr. 1852. V. of Fenstanton with Hilton C. Dio. Ely, 1853. (Patron, Trin. Hall, Cam; Fenstanton, Glebe, 90 acres; Hilton, Tithe—Imp. 252*l*, V. 101*l* 1*s*; Glebe, 5¾ acres; V.'s Inc. 340*l*; Pop. Fenstanton 1120, Hilton 387.) Formerly Fell. and Asst. Tut. of Trin. Hall, Cam. [11]

WALTON, S. S., 8, *Reed-street, Hull.*—Fell. of St. John's Coll. Cam. [12]

WALTON, Thomas Isaac, *St. Andrew's, Hillingdon.*—St. John's Coll. Cam. B.A. 1855, M.A. 1858; Deac. 1865 by Bp of Lon. C. of St. Andrew's ,Hillingdon, 1865. [13]

WALTON, T. J.—C. of St. Andrew's, Hillingdon, Middlesex. [14]

WAMBEY, Cornelius Copner, *Croydon Hall, Roadwater, Taunton.*—Magd. Hal Ox. B.A. 1859 :Deac. 1860 and Pr. 1861 by Bp of Ches. P. C. o Leighland, Dio. B. and W. 1864. (Patron, V. o Old Cleeve P. C.'s Inc. 86*l* Pop. 500.) Formerly Professor of Cl. and Div. Lect. at Gothic House Coll. Clapham, 1854–56; C. of Upholland, Wigan, 1860–62, Warburton and Lymm, Cheshire, 1862 .Brompton Ralph, Somerset, 1863–64. Author, *Heaven and other Sermons*, 1865. [15]

WANKLYN, Edward, *The Glen, Bournemouth.*—Queen's Coll. Ox. B.A. 1856; Deac. 1859 and Pr. 1860 by Bp of Man. Formerly C. of Pendleton 1859–61, Oldham 1861. [16]

WANKLYN, Hibbert, *Deopham, Wymondham.*—Dur. Licen. Theol. 1852. V. of Deopham, Dio. Nor. 1861. (Patrons, D. and C. of Cant; V.'s Inc. 240*l*; Pop. 483.) Formerly R. of Fleet-Marston 1855. [17]

WANKLYN, James Hibbert, *Bournemouth, Hants.*—Chap. of the Sanatorium, Bournemouth. [18]

WANNOP, Thomas Nicholas, *The Parsonage, Haddington, Scotland.*—Dur. Licen. Theol. 1849; Deac. 1849 and Pr. 1850 by Bp of Dur. Min. of Episcopal Chapel, Haddington, 1855. Formerly C. of Pittington, Durham, 1849–55. [19]

WANNOP, William, *Burscough Parsonage, Ormskirk, Lancashire.*—Dub. A.B. 1830; Deac. 1833, Pr. 1834. P. C. of Burscough Bridge, Dio. Ches. 1840. (Patron, V. of Ormskirk; Tithe—Imp. 1200*l*; P C.'s Inc. 200*l* and Ho; Pop. 3175.) [20]

WANSTALL, Richard, *Norton Rectory, Stafford.*—St. Edm. Hall, Ox. B.A. 1834; Deac. 1834 and Pr. 1835 by Bp of Lich. R. of Norton-Canes, Staffs. Dio. Lich. 1855. (Patron, Bp of Lich; Glebe, 7 acres; R.'s Inc. 330*l* and Ho; Pop. 845.) Formerly C. of Burton-upon-Trent, of Walton, of Rocester, and of Kingsley, Staffs. [21]

WARBRECK, Edmund, *St. George's-road, Bolton-le-Moors*—Dub. A.B. 1863; Deac. 1863 and Pr. 1864 by Bp of Man. C. of Bolton 1863. [22]

WARBURTON, Henry, *Sible Hedingham Rectory, Halstead, Essex.*—Ex. Coll. Ox. B.A. 1846; Deac. 1847 by Bp of Ches. Pr. 1848 by Bp of Salis. R. of Sible Hedingham, Dio. Roch. 1848. (Patrons, Trustees; Tithe, comm. 1515*l*; Glebe, 72 acres; R.'s Inc. 1600*l* and Ho; Pop. 2123.) Formerly C. of St. John's, Cheltenham, 1847–48. [23]

WARBURTON, John, *South Malling Parsonage, Lewes.*—Ch. Miss. Coll. Islington; Deac. and Pr. 1840 by Bp of Lon. P. C. of South Malling, Dio. Chich. 1851. (Patron, George Campion Courthorpe, Esq; P. C.'s Inc. 150*l* and Ho ;Pop. 718.) Formerly Missionary at Sierra Leone. [24]

WARBURTON, Mark, *Kilmington Rectory, Bath.*—Queen's Coll. Ox. 3rd cl. Lit. Hum. and B.A. 1843, M.A. 1851, B.D. 1858; Deac. 1847 and Pr. 1848 by Bp of Lich. R. of Kilmington, Dio. B. and W. 1866. (Patron, Earl of Ilchester; Tithe, 520*l*; Glebe, 50 acres; R.'s Inc. 625*l* and Ho; Pop. 570.) Dom. Chap. to Earl of Mansfield. Formerly C. of Wirksworth, Derbyshire, 1847; C. in sole charge of Bromley Regis, Staffs, 1848; Chap. to Earl of Ellesmere 1853; P. C. of Revesby, Lincolnshire, 1857–66. [25]

WARBURTON, Peter, *Padiham, near Burnley.*—Brasen. Coll. Ox. B.A. 1860; Deac. 1861 and Pr. 1862 by Bp of Ches. C. of Hapton District of Padiham 1865. Formerly C. of Halewood 1861–62, Leverbridge 1863–64. [26]

WARBURTON, Thomas Acton, *Iffley Rectory, Oxford.*—Dub. D.C.L. *ad eund.* Ox. 1852; Deac. 1851 and Pr. 1852 by Bp of Ox. P. C. of Iffley, Dio. Ox. 1853 (Patron, Archd. of Ox; Glebe, 16 acres; P. C.'s Inc. 315*l* and Ho; Pop. 1001.) [27]

WARBURTON, William, *The Close, Winchester, and Athenæum Club, Pall-Mall, London, S.W.*—Ball. Coll. Ox. 1st cl. Cl. and B.A. 1849, M.A. 1853; Deac. 1851 by Bp of Ox. Pr. 1856 by Abp of Cant. H.M.'s Inspector of Schs. for Berks, Wilts, Hants, and Isle of Wight, 1850. Formerly Fell. of All Souls Coll. Ox. 1849. [28]

WARD, A., *Hollinfare, Warrington.*—C. of Hollinfare. [29]

WARD, Arthur Hawkins, *Bedminster, Somerset.*—Pemb. Coll. Cam. B.A. 1855; Deac. 1856 and Pr.

1857 by Bp of Lin. Chap. of St. Gabriel's Almshouses, Bedminster; Warden of St. Raphael's (Sailors') Coll. Bristol; Dom. Chap. to Earl of Limerick. Formerly C. of Edwinstowe, Notts. [1]

WARD, Arthur Robert, *St. John's College, Cambridge.*—St. John's Coll. Cam. B.A. 1855, M.A. 1858; Deac. and Pr. 1856 by Bp of Ely. V. of St. Clement's, Cambridge, Dio. Ely, 1860. (Patron, Jesus Coll. Cam; V.'s Inc. 56*l*; Pop. 907.) Formerly C. of All Saints', Cambridge. [2]

WARD, Benjamin, *Meesden Rectory, Buntingford, Herts.*—Deac. and Pr. 1817. Hon. Can. of Carl. 1857; R. of Meesden, Herts, Dio. Roch. 1859. (Patron, W. G. Whatman, Esq; R.'s Inc. 250*l* and Ho; Pop. 163.) Formerly Missionary to Ceylon. [3]

WARD, Charles, *Maulden Rectory, Ampthill, Beds.*—Brasen. Coll. Ox. 2nd cl. Math et Phy. and B.A. 1820, M.A. 1822; Deac. 1822 by Bp of Lon. Pr. 1823 by Bp of Ches. R. of Maulden, Dio. Ely, 1825. (Patron, Marquis of Ailesbury; Tithe, 379*l* 10*s* 4*d*; Glebe, 60 acres; R.'s Inc. 470*l* and Ho; Pop. 1563.) Rural Dean of Fleete 1838. [4]

WARD, Charles, *Woodbridge-road, Ipswich.*—Magd. Coll. Cam. B.A. 1839, M.A. 1842; Deac. 1842 and Pr. 1843 by Bp of Ely. P. C. of St. Nicholas', Ipswich, Dio. Nor. 1853. (Patrons, the Parishioners; Glebe, 27 acres; P. C.'s Inc. 150*l*; Pop. 1912.) [5]

WARD, Charles, *The Rectory, Farleigh Hungerford, Bath.*—Ex. Coll. Ox. B.A. 1843, M.A. 1846; Deac. 1844 and Pr. 1845 by Bp of Salis. C. in sole charge of Farleigh Hungerford 1862. Formerly C. of Milton Lilborne, Wilts, 1844–45; V. of Wadworth, Yorks, 1847–61. [6]

WARD, Charles Bruce, *Middleton, Manchester.*—Oriel Coll. Ox. B.A. 1860, M.A. 1863; Deac. 1861 by Bp of Pet. Pr. 1862 by Bp of Lich. C. and Parish Clerk of Middleton 1865. Formerly C. of Uttoxeter 1861–62, Oakamoor, Staffs, 1862–65. [7]

WARD, Charles Cotterill, *Lymm, Warrington.*—Queens' Coll. Cam. B.A. 1854, M.A. 1866; Deac. 1857 and Pr. 1858 by Bp of Win. Head Mast. of Lymm Gr. Sch. 1865. Formerly C. of Niton, Isle of Wight; 2nd Mast. of Sutton Valence Gr. Sch; Sen. Math. Mast. of Royal Naval and Military Academy, Gosport. [8]

WARD, Charles Glegg, *Valley End Parsonage, Bagshot.*—Emman. Coll. Cam. B.A. 1864, M.A. 1867; Deac. 1865 and Pr. 1866 by Abp of Cant. P. C. of St. Saviour's (first Incumb. of), Valley End, Chobham, Dio. Win. 1867. (Patron, Bp of Win; Glebe, 2 acres; P. C.'s Inc. 100*l* and Ho; Pop. 200.) Formerly C. of Brenchley, Kent, 1865–66, Chobham, Surrey, 1867. [9]

WARD, Edward, *Haughley Vicarage, Stowmarket, Suffolk.*—Jesus Coll. Cam. Jun. Opt. and B.A. 1809, M.A. 1812; Deac. 1810 and Pr. 1811 by Bp of Nor. V. of Haughley, Dio. Nor. 1812. (Patrons, Trustees; Tithe—Imp. 463*l* and 33 acres of Glebe, V. 301*l*; V.'s Inc. 310*l* and Ho; Pop 987.) [10]

WARD, Edward, *Blacktoft Parsonage, Howden, Yorks.*—Deac. 1821 and Pr. 1822 by Abp of York. P. C. of Blacktoft, Dio. York, 1838. (Patrons, D. and C. of Dur; Glebe, 28 acres; P. C.'s Inc. 229*l* and Ho; Pop. 534.) [11]

WARD, Edward, *Long Benton, Newcastle-on-Tyne.*—Ch. Coll. Cam. 24th Wrang. B.A. 1856, M.A. 1859; Deac. 1857 by Bp of Rip. Pr. 1858 by Abp of York. C. of Long Benton, Northumberland, 1865. Formerly C. of St. John's, Ousebridge, York, 1857–59, Garforth, Leeds, 1859–65. [12]

WARD, Edward Ditcher, *Acacia-road, St. John's-wood, Regent's-park, N.W.*—St. John's Coll. Cam. 21st Wrang. and B.A. 1847, M.A. 1850; Deac. 1849 and Pr. 1850 by Abp of Cant. Head Mast. of St. John's-wood Proprietary School, Acacia-road. Formerly Prin. of the Coll. Sch. Sheffield, 1856. [13]

WARD, Edward John, *East Clandon Rectory, Guildford.*—Trin. Coll. Ox. B.A. 1826, M.A. 1829; Deac. 1827, Pr. 1828. R. of East Clandon, Dio. Win. 1832. (Patron, Earl of Lovelace; Tithe, 255*l* 4*s* 6*d*; R.'s Inc. 268*l* and Ho; Pop. 283.) [14]

WARD, Edward Langton, *Blendworth Rectory, Horndean, Hants.*—Wad. Coll. Ox. B.A. 1831, M.A. 1834; Deac. and Pr. 1834 by Bp of Lin. R. of Blendworth, Dio. Win. 1834. (Patron, the present R; Tithe—App. 130*l*, R. 244*l* 10*s*; Glebe, 6 acres; R.'s Inc. 251*l* and Ho; Pop. 219.) [15]

WARD, George Andrew, *Christ Church, Oxford.*—Ch. Ch. Ox. B.A. 1840, M.A. 1843. Stud. of Ch. Ch. [16]

WARD, George Sturton, *Magdalen Hall, Oxford.*—Magd. Hall, Ox. 1st cl. Math. et Phy. and B.A. 1850; Deac. 1853 and Pr. 1856 by Bp of Ox. Math. Lect. at Magd. Hall, Ox. Author, *The Propositions of the Fifth Book of Euclid proved Algebraically, with an Introduction, Notes, and Questions,* 1862, 2*s* 6*d*. [17]

WARD, George Thompson, *Stanton St. Bernard Vicarage, Pewsey, Wilts.*—V. of Stanton St. Bernard, Dio. Salis. 1839. (Patron, Earl of Pembroke; Tithe—App. 400*l* V. 170*l*; V.'s Inc. 240*l* and Ho; Pop. 358.) [18]

WARD, Henry, *Aldwinckle, Thrapstone.*—R. of St. Peter's, Aldwinckle, Dio. Pet. 1851. (Patron, Lord Lifford; R.'s Inc. 230*l*; Pop. 222.) [19]

WARD, Henry, *St. Barnabas' Parsonage, King-square, London, E.C.*—Queens' Coll. Cam. B.A. 1836, M.A. 1840; Deac. 1838 and Pr. 1839 by Bp of Salis. P. C. of St. Barnabas', King-square, Dio. Lon. 1852. (Patron, R. of St. Luke's; P. C.'s Inc. 400*l* and Ho; Pop. 9125.) Formerly Preacher at the Magdalen, Lond. [20]

WARD, Horatio James, *Bridgnorth, Salop.*—Emman. Coll. Cam. Sen. Opt. and B.A. 1854, M.A. 1857; Deac. 1856 by Bp of Win. Pr. 1857 by Bp of Lon. Head Mast. of the Gr. Sch. Bridgnorth, 1860. Formerly C. of St. Stephen's, Paddington, 1856–59, and 2nd Mast. of Westbourne College, Bayswater, Lond. 1855–59. [21]

WARD, Horatio Nelson, *Radstock, near Bath.*—Pemb. Coll. Cam. B.A. 1847; Deac. 1848, Pr. 1849. R. of Radstock, Dio. B. and W. 1853. (Patroness, Countess of Waldegrave; Tithe, 260*l*; Glebe, 35½ acres; R.'s Inc. 324*l* and Ho; Pop. 2227.) [22]

WARD, James R., *Basford, Nottingham.*—C. of Basford. [23]

WARD, John, *Scarisbrick, Ormskirk.*—Queens' Coll. Cam. B.A. 1863, M.A. 1866; Deac. 1863 and Pr. 1864 by Bp of Ches. C. of Scarisbrick 1863. [24]

WARD, John, *Colne, St. Ives, Hunts.*—St. Cath. Coll. Cam. B.A. 1851, M.A. 1853; Deac. 1851, Pr. 1852. C. of Colne. [25]

WARD, John, *Nice.*—Asst. Chap. at Nice. [26]

WARD, J. B., *Cheriton, Kent.*—C. of Cheriton and Chap. of the Eltham Union, Kent. [27]

WARD, J. Heald, *Baverstock, Salisbury.*—Trin. Coll. Cam. B A. 1862, M.A. 1866; Deac. and Pr. by Bp of Salis. C. of Baverstock, Wilts, 1866. [28]

WARD, John Henry Kirwan, *Marlborough, Wilts.*—Trin. Coll. Cam. Sen. Opt. and 2nd cl. Cl. Trip. B.A. 1854, M.A. 1857; Deac. 1858 and Pr. 1860 by Bp of Salis. C. of St. Mary's, Marlborough, 1867. Formerly C. of St. Mary's, Marlborough, 1858, Tisbury, Wilts, 1861, Folke, Dorset, 1864, Trinity, Gosport, 1865. [29]

WARD, John Meire, 44, *Canonbury-square, Islington, London, N.*—Dub. A.B. 1840; Deac. 1841, Pr. 1842. P. C. of St. Stephen's, Islington, Dio. Lon. 1862. (Patron, V. of Islington; P. C.'s Inc. 400*l*; Pop. 7321.) Formerly C. of Claypole, near Newark, and Chap. to the Newark Union, Notts; V. of Hampsthwaite 1855. [30]

WARD, John William, *Ruishton, Taunton.*—St. John's Coll. Cam; Deac. 1843 by Bp of Ex. Pr. 1845 by Bp of B. and W. V. of Ruishton, Dio. B. and W. 1856. (Patrons, Trustees; Tithe—Imp. 137*l* 2*s* 6*d*, V. 70*l*; Glebe, 17 acres; V.'s Inc. 105*l*; Pop. 506.) [31]

WARD, Joseph M., *Canterbury.*—C. of St. Mildred's, Canterbury. [32]

WARD, Joseph Preston, *St. John's Vicarage, Little Holbeck, Leeds.*—St. Aidan's; Deac. 1849, Pr. 1850. V. of St. John's, Little Holbeck, Dio. Rip. 1855. (Patrons, J. G. and H. C. Marshall, Esqrs; Glebe, 1 acre; V.'s Inc. 280*l* and Ho; Pop. 2612.) [33]

WARD, Richard, 12, *Eaton-square, Pimlico, S.W.*—Trin. Coll. Cam. Craven Scho. 1806, 2nd Chan. Medallist and B.A. 1808, M.A. 1811; Deac. 1812 and Pr. 1813 by Bp of Bristol. Formerly Fell. of Trin. Coll. Cam. [1]

WARD, Richard Charles, *Gamston, Retford, Notts.*—Emman. Coll. Cam. B.A. 1859; Deac. 1859 and Pr. 1860 by Bp of Lin. C. of Eaton and Gamston 1859. [2]

WARD, Robert Fawssett, *Coningsby, Lincolnshire.*—St. Peter's Coll. Cam. S.C.L. 1856; Deac. 1857 and Pr. 1858 by Bp of Ches. C. of Wilksby. Formerly C. of Mottram, Cheshire. [3]

WARD, Robert John, *Old Basing, Basingstoke, Hants.*—Caius Coll. Cam. B.A. 1837, M.A. 1840; Deac. 1837 and Pr. 1839 by Bp of Lin. Formerly C. of Old Basing and Upper Nately. [4]

WARD, Stephen Haisty, *Shirburn, Tetsworth, Oxon.*—C. of Shirburn. [5]

WARD, Stephen U., *North Gosforth, Newcastle-on-Tyne.*—P. C. of North Gosforth, Dio. Dur. 1865. (Patron, T. E. Smith, Esq; P. C.'s Inc. 150*l*; Pop. 1667.) [6]

WARD, Thomas, *Rowley-Regis, Dudley, Worcestershire.*—Deac. 1851 and Pr. 1852 by Bp of Lich V. of Rowley-Regis, Dio. Wor. 1858. (Patron, Ld Chan; V.'s Inc. 300*l*; Pop. 9436.) Formerly C. of King's Hill, Wednesbury, and West Coseley, Staffs. [7]

WARD, William Craig, *Honingham, Norwich.*—All Souls Coll. Ox. B.A. 1833; Deac. 1842 and Pr. 1843 by Bp of Nor. C. of Honingham and East Tuddenham 1848. Formerly C. of Brome and Oakley, Suffolk, 1842. [8]

WARD, William Harry Perceval, *Compton-Valence, Dorchester.*—Oriel Coll. Ox. B.A. 1834, M.A. 1836; Deac. and Pr. 1836 by Bp of S. and M. R. of Compton-Valence, Dio. Salis. 1838. (Patron, R. Williams, Esq. Bridehead, Dorset; Tithe, 235*l*; Glebe, 107½ acres; R.'s Inc. 335*l* and Ho; Pop. 136.) Author, *Records and Documents of the Isle of Man, and Diocese of Sodor and Man*; *Jesuits of Naples in* 1848 (a Letter); *The Union of the Spiritual and Temporal Authorities in one and the same Ecclesiastical Court* (a Letter); *Book of Domestic Offices and Litanies*; *Divine Service* (a Letter); *Cathedrals* (an Essay). [9]

WARD, W. L.—C. of St. Stephen's, Birmingham. [10]

WARD, William Sparrow, *Iver Parsonage, (Bucks), near Uxbridge.*—Corpus Coll. Cam. Sen. Opt. and B.A. 1833; Deac. and Pr. 1835. P. C. of Iver, Dio. Ox. 1835. (Patron, C. Meeking, Esq; Tithe—Imp. 1149*l* 4*s* 11*d*; P. C.'s Inc. 120*l* and Ho; Pop. 1514.) [11]

WARDALE, Charles Bradford, *Higher Greenham, Crewkerne.*—St. Cath. Coll. Cam. B.A. 1857, M.A. 1861; Deac. 1858 and Pr. 1859 by Bp of Roch. C. of Broadwindsor, Dorset, 1866. Formerly Asst. Mast. of Felstead Gr. Sch. Essex, 1857; Min. of Blackchapel, Essex, 1858, Head Mast. and Chap. of Trowbridge Gr. Sch. 1860–66. [12]

WARDALE, John, *Orcheston St. Mary Rectory, Devizes, Wilts.*—Clare Coll. Cam. 21st Wrang. and B.A. 1846, M.A. 1849; Deac. 1848, Pr. 1852. R. of Orcheston St. Mary, Dio. Salis. 1852. (Patron, Clare Coll. Cam; Tithe, 350*l*; Glebe, 19 acres; R.'s Inc. 380*l* and Ho; Pop. 177.) [13]

WARDALE, Joseph Williams, *Eakring Rectory, near Ollerton, Notts.*—Dur. Licen. Theol. 1855; formerly a solicitor examined and admitted, 1840; Deac. 1856 and Pr. 1858 by Bp of Rip. R. of Eakring, Dio. Lin. 1864. (Patrons, Earl Manvers and Henry Savile, Esq. alt; Tithe, 590*l*; Glebe, 40 acres; R.'s Inc. 660*l* and Ho; Pop. 710.) Formerly P. C. of Gawber, Barnsley, 1856; C. of Allerton, Notts (sole charge), 1858, Eakring 1860. [14]

WARDE, Augustus William, *Little Horsted Rectory, Uckfield, Sussex.*—New Inn Hall, Ox. B.A. 1843, M.A. 1844. R. of Little Horstead, Dio. Chich. 1856. (Patron, F. Barchard, Esq; Tithe, 425*l*; R.'s Inc. 445*l* and Ho; Pop. 296.) [15]

WARDE, William, *Hooton Pagnell Hall, near Doncaster.*—Wor. Coll. Ox. B.A. 1823; Deac. and Pr. 1823 by Abp of York. [16]

WARDELL, Henry, *Winlaton Rectory, Newcastle-on-Tyne.*—Trin. Coll. Cam. B.A. 1823, M.A. 1827; Deac. 1823 and Pr. 1824 by Bp of Dur. R. of Winlaton, Dio. Dur. 1833. (Patron, Bp of Ches; Tithe, 352*l* 6*s* 8*d*; Glebe, 21 acres; R.'s Inc. 385*l* and Ho; Pop. 4163.) [17]

WARDELL, Henry John, *Forest, Walthamstow.*—Emman. Coll. Cam. Scho. of, B.A. 1853, M.A. 1858; Deac. 1853 and Pr. 1854 by Bp of Dur. Resident Mast. in Forest Sch. Walthamstow, Essex. Formerly C. of Winlaton, Durham, 1853–59. Author, *Church Psalm Tunes*, 2*s* 6*d*. [18]

WARDELL, William Henry, *Rochford, Essex.*—Dur. B.A. 1857, M.A. 1862; Deac. 1860 and Pr. 1862 by Bp of Rip. C. of Rochford and South Fambridge 1867. Formerly C. of Bedale, Yorks, 1860–65, Winlaton, Durham, 1865–67. [19]

WARDROPER, Cutfield, *Woodsome Hall, near Huddersfield.*—Trin. Hall, Cam. B.A. 1843, M.A. 1847; Deac. 1843, Pr. 1848. P. C. of Farnley-Tyas, Dio. Rip. 1848. (Patron, Earl of Dartmouth; Tithe—App. 25*l*, Imp. 10¾*d*; P. C.'s Inc. 100*l*; Pop. 702.) Dom. Chap. to the Earl of Dartmouth. [20]

WARE, Charles, *Astwood Vicarage, Newport-Pagnell, Bucks.*—Trin. Coll. Cam. B.A. 1855, M.A. 1858; Deac. and Pr. 1856 by Bp of Ox. V. of Astwood Dio. Ox. 1856. (Patron, Ld Chan; Tithe, 196*l* 15*s* 3*d*; Glebe, 12 acres; V.'s Inc. 221*l* 13*s* 11*d* and Ho; Pop. 246.) [21]

WARE, Frederick Lloyd, *Kilkhampton, Stratton, Cornwall.*—Caius Coll. Cam. 3rd cl. Math. B.A. 1864, M.A. 1867; Deac. 1864 by Bp of Ox. Pr. 1866 by Bp Chapman for Bp of Ex. C. of Kilkhampton 1866. Formerly C. of Chesham, Bucks, 1864. [22]

WARE, George, *Winsham Vicarage, Chard.*—St. Peter's Coll. Cam. B.A. 1823, M.A. 1831; Deac. 1823 by Bp of Ches. Pr. 1823 by Bp of Lich. V. of Winsham, Somerset, Dio. B. and W. 1831. (Patron, Bp of Wor; Tithe—App. 142*l*, V. 340*l*; Glebe, 31 acres; V.'s Inc. 380*l* and Ho; Pop. 1033.) Formerly R. of Ashton, Dio. Ex. 1832. [23]

WARE, Henry, *The Vicarage, Kirkby Lonsdale, Westmoreland.*—Trin. Coll. Cam. Wrang. and 1st cl. Cl. Trip. B.A. 1853, M.A. 1856; Deac. 1860 and Pr. 1862 by Bp of Ely. V. of Kirkby Lonsdale, Dio. Carl. 1862. (Patron, Trin. Coll. Cam; Tithe, 300*l*; Glebe, 259*l*; V.'s Inc. 608*l* and Ho; Pop. 1956.) Rural Dean; Surrogate. Formerly Fell. and Asst. Tut. of Trin. Coll. Cam. [24]

WARE, Henry Ryder, *Olveston, Glouc.*—Corpus Coll. Cam. B.A. 1858; Deac. 1859 and Pr. 1860 by Bp of Ex. C. of Olveston. Formerly C. of Topsham 1859. [25]

WARE, John Middleton, *Ullingswick Rectory, Bromyard, Herefordshire.*—Corpus Coll. Cam. LL.B. 1847; Deac. 1848 and Pr. 1849 by Bp of Wor. R. of Ullingswick with Cowarne Parva C. Dio. Herf. 1854. (Patron, Bp of Wor; Ullingswick, Tithe, 200*l*; Glebe, 25 acres; Cowarne Parva, Tithe, 135*l*; Glebe, 27 acres; R.'s Inc. 385*l* and Ho; Pop. Ullingswick 318, Cowarne Parva 186.) [26]

WARE, Samuel, *Rochdale.*—Deac. 1861 and Pr. 1862 by Bp of Man. Formerly C. of Todmorden 1861–64. [27]

WARE, Wilmot Westmoreland, *Adwick-le-street Rectory, Doncaster.*—Jesus Coll. Cam. B.A. 1855, M.A. 1859; Deac. 1855 and Pr. 1856 by Bp of Lin. R. of Adwick-le-Street, Dio. York, 1859. (Patron, John Fullerton, Esq; Tithe, 442*l*; Glebe, 5 acres; R.'s Inc. 450*l* and Ho; Pop. 440.) Formerly R. of Morborne, Hunts; Chap. to High Sheriff of Yorks 1866. [28]

WARING, The Ven. William, *Hereford.*—Magd. Coll. Cam. Wrang. and B.A. 1823, M.A. 1826. Archd. of Salop 1831. (Value, 200*l*.) Chap. to the Bp of Herf; R. of Burwarton, Salop, Dio. Herf. 1865.

(Patron, Viscount Boyne; R.'s Inc. 150*l* and Ho; Pop. 156.) Formerly Fell. of Magd. Coll. Cam. [1]

WARLEIGH, Henry Smith, *St. Andrew's Rectory, Hertford.*—St. Bees; Deac. 1838 by Bp of Roch. Pr. 1839 by Abp of York. R. of St. Andrew's with St. Mary's R. and St. Nicholas' V. Hertford, Dio. Roch. 1861. (Patron, Duchy of Lanc; Tithe, 300*l*; Glebe, 1½ acres; R.'s Inc. 360*l* and Ho; Pop. 2200.) Formerly Chap. of Parkhurst Prison 1846–62. Author, *The Destitution and Miseries of the Poor disclosed, and their Remedies suggested* (Prize Essay), 3*s* 6*d*; *The Doctrine of Baptismal Regeneration examined by the Bible and Prayer Book*, 2*s* 6*d*; *The Garment of Praise for the Spirit of Heaviness*, 2*s* 6*d*; *The Early British Church*, 1851, 6*d*; *The Principles of Mental and Moral Training*, 5*s*; *Portrait of Antichrist*, 6*d*; *Words of Counsel at Parting*; *Ezekiel's Temple, its Architecture displayed and its Design unfolded*, 1857, 7*s* 6*d*; *The Merchants of Tarshish and Young Lions thereof, are they not England and her Colonies?* 1859, 6*d*; various Papers, Lectures; etc. [2]

WARLOW, George, *Secunderabad, Madras.*—St. John's Coll. Cam. B.A. 1860; Deac. 1860 by Bp of Lon. Chap. at Secunderabad 1863. Formerly C. of Ch. Ch. Lee, Kent, 1860. [3]

WARLOW, William Meyler, *Ashby-de-la-Zouch, Leicestershire.*—Queens' Coll. Cam. 13th Jun. Opt. B.A. 1857; Deac. 1861 and Pr. 1862 by Bp of Pet. C. of Swepston with Snareston 1863. Formerly C. of Donisthorpe. [4]

WARMOLL, Sayer Stone, *Sotterley Rectory, Wangford, Suffolk.*—Queen's Coll. Ox. B.A. 1829; Deac. 1832, Pr. 1833. R. of Sotterley, Dio. Nor. 1849. (Patron, F. Barne, Esq; Tithe, 295*l*; Glebe, 23 acres; R.s Inc. 314*l*; Pop. 231.) Formerly C. of Rushmere, near Lowestoft, 1832, Alphamstone, Essex, 1836, Wormingford 1838, Sotterley 1840. [5]

WARNEFORD, John Henry, *Salterhebble, Halifax.*—Wor. Coll. Ox. Hon. 4th cl. Lit. Hum. and B.A. 1841; Deac. 1843 and Pr. 1844 by Bp of Herf. P. C. of Salterhebble, Dio. Rip. 1846. (Patrons, the Crown and Bp of Rip. alt; P. C.'s Inc. 150*l*; Pop. 4258.) Formerly 2nd Mast. of Lucton Gr. Sch. Author, several Tracts, published by Whitley and Booth, Halifax. [6]

WARNER, A. G.—C. of St. John's, Westminster. [7]

WARNER, Charles, *Henley-on-Thames.*—Wor. Coll. Ox. B.A. 1846, M.A. 1849; Deac. 1846 and Pr. 1847 by Bp of Ox. R. of Henley-on-Thames, Dio. Ox. 1863. (Patron, Bp of Ox; R.'s Inc. 450*l* and Ho; Pop. 3533.) Formerly C. of St. Aldate's, Oxford, 1847–49; C. of Kidderminster and P. C. of Wribbenhall 1849–63. [8]

WARNER, D. F., *Hoo St. Werburgh, Rochester.*—V. of Hoo St. Werburgh, Dio. Roch. 1836. (Patrons, D. and C. of Roch; V.'s Inc. 395*l*; Pop. 1065.) [9]

WARNER, John, *Bradwell-juxta-Mare, Maldon, Essex.*—St. Mary Hall, Ox. B.A. 1849, M.A. 1851; Deac. 1850 and Pr. 1851 by Abp of York. R. of Bradwell-juxta-Mare, Dio. Roch. 1855. (Patron, W. M. Warner, Esq; Tithe, 1373*l*; Glebe, 252 acres; R.'s Inc. 1800*l* and Ho; Pop. 1071.) Rural Dean. Formerly C. of Northallerton, Yorks, Herne Hill, Dulwich, and Wickham Bishops, Essex. [10]

WARNER, Richard Edward, *Snitterby Rectory, Kirton-in-Lindsey.*—Ex. Coll. Ox. Hon. 4th cl. in Law and Mod. Hist. 1858, M.A. 1860; Deac. 1859 by Bp of Man. Pr. 1860 by Bp of Pet. R. of Snitterby, Dio. Lin. 1862. (Patron, the Crown; Glebe, 260 acres allotted in lieu of Tithes; R.'s Inc. 400*l* and Ho; Pop. 286.) Formerly C. of Finedon, Northants, 1859–61. [11]

WARNER, Simon Burney, *Clyst St. Mary Rectory, Exeter.*—New Inn Hall, Ox. B.A. 1845. R. of Clyst St. Mary, Dio. Ex. 1867. (Patron, the present R; Tithe, 150*l*; Glebe, 26 acres; R.'s Inc. 200*l* and Ho; Pop. 176.) Formerly R. of Little Cressingham, Norfolk, 1848 59; C. of Coffinswell, Devon, 1860–67. [12]

WARR, George Winter, *St. Saviour's Parsonage, Liverpool.*—Deac. 1841, Pr. 1842. P. C. of St. Saviour's, Liverpool, Dio. Ches. 1846. (Patrons, Trustees; P. C.'s Inc. 500*l*.) Surrogate. Author, *Canada as it is*; *The Church of England* (a Lecture delivered before the Liverpool Church of England Institute); etc. [13]

WARRE, Francis, *Bere Regis, Blandford, Dorset.*—Ball. Coll. Ox. B.A. 1857, M.A. 1860; Deac. 1858 and Pr. 1859 by Bp of G. and B. V. of Bere Regis with Chapelry of Winterbourne Kingston, Dio. Salis. 1864. (Patron, Ball. Coll. Ox; Tithe, 426*l*; V.'s Inc. 535*l* and Ho; Pop. 2213.) Formerly C. of Olveston, near Bristol, 1859–63. [14]

WARRE, Francis, *Bishops Lydeard Vicarage, Taunton.*—Oriel Coll. Ox. B.A. 1828, M.A. 1831; Deac. 1829, Pr. 1830. V. of Bishops Lydeard, Dio. B. and W. 1836. (Patrons, D. and C. of Wells; Tithe—App. 729*l*; Glebe, 1 acre; V.'s Inc. 206*l* and Ho; Pop. 1459.) P. C. of Cothelstone, Somerset, Dio. B. and W. 1855. (Patron, V. of Kingston; P. C.'s Inc. 58*l*; Pop. 107.) [15]

WARREN, Charles, *Over Vicarage (Cambs), near St. Ives.*—Trin. Coll. Cam. B.A. 1831, M.A. 1834; Deac. 1832 and Pr. 1833 by Bp of Pet. V. of Over, Dio. Ely, 1839. (Patron, Trin. Coll. Cam; Glebe, 5 acres; V.'s Inc. 170*l* and Ho; Pop. 1146.) Author, *The Lord's Table the Christian Altar*; *The Ministry of the Word for Absolution*; five *Sermons* for the Nat. Soc; *The Ely Substitute for Diocesan Synods*, Deighton, Bell and Co. 1866; *The Presbyterate in Synod*, ib. 1866; Editor of *Synodalia*, a Journal of Convocation. [16]

WARREN, Edward Blackburn, *St. Mary's Vicarage, Marlborough, Wilts.*—Queens' Coll. Cam. B.A. 1832, M.A. 1835. V. of St. Mary's, Marlborough, Dio. Salis. 1851. (Patron, Bp of Salis; Tithe, 25*l* 15*s*. V.'s Inc. 100*l* and Ho; Pop. 1903.) [17]

WARREN, Edward Walpole, *The Cottage, Diss, Norfolk.*—Magd. Coll. Cam. Scho. of, B.A. 1861; Deac. 1862 and Pr. 1863 by Bp of B. and W. C. of Diss 1867. Formerly C. of Clandown 1862, C. in sole charge of East and West Cranmore 1864–66. Author, *The Unbidden Guest* (a Sermon), Diss, 2*d*. [18]

WARREN, Frederick Edward, *St. John's College, Oxford.*—St. John's Coll. Ox. 2nd cl. Lit. Hum. B.A. 1865; Deac. 1866 and Pr. 1867 by Bp of Ox. Fell. of St. John's Coll. Ox. [19]

WARREN, Frederick King, *Exton, near Dulverton, Somerset.*—Oriel Coll. Ox. Hon. 4th cl. Math. B.A. 1858, M.A. 1861; Deac. 1859 and Pr. 1860 by Bp of Ex. R. of Exton, Dio. B. and W. 1864. (Patron, Rev. G. B. Warren; Tithe, 325*l*; Glebe, 73 acres; R.'s Inc. 420*l* and Ho; Pop. 410.) Formerly C. of Heavitree, Devon, 1859–64. [20]

WARREN, George Bodley, 7, *Mont-le-grand, Heavitree, Devon.*—Wor. Coll. Ox. B.A. 1827; Deac. 1828, Pr. 1829. Formerly C. of Brushford, Somerset, 1828–34, Dulverton, Somerset, 1834–38. [21]

WARREN, Henry, *Flixton Vicarage, Bungay.*—Jesus Coll. Cam. B.A. 1829, M.A. 1832; Deac. 1831 and Pr. 1835 by Bp of Chich. V. of Flixton, Dio. Nor. 1860. (Patron, Sir R. S. Adair, Bart; Tithe, comm. 144*l*; Glebe, 29 acres; V.'s Inc. 180*l*; Pop. 146.) Formerly C. of Storrington; R. of Sullington, Sussex, 1859. [22]

WARREN, John, *Bawdrip Rectory, Bridgwater, Somerset.*—Ex. Coll. Ox. B.A. 1836; Deac. 1837 and Pr. 1838 by Bp of Ex. R. of Bawdrip, Dio. B. and W. 1855. (Patron, the present R; Tithe, 340*l*; Glebe, 38 acres; R.'s Inc. 400*l* and Ho; Pop. 472.) Rural Dean of Pawlett 1859. [23]

WARREN, John M., *Wellow, Bath.*—Ex. Coll. Ox. M.A; Deac. and Pr. by Bp of B. and W. C. of Wellow 1867. Formerly C. of Vobster, Somerset. [24]

WARREN, John Shrapnel, *Langtoft Vicarage, Market Deeping, Lincolnshire.*—St. Cath. Coll. Cam. B.A 1852, M.A. 1855; Deac. 1853 and Pr. 1854 by Abp of York. V. of Langtoft, Dio. Lin. 1857. (Patron, Lord Aveland; Glebe, 131 acres; V.'s Inc. 300*l* and Ho; Pop. 746.) Formerly C. of North Cave, Yorks, and Folkingham, Lincolnshire. [25]

WARREN, Richard, *Birdbrook, Halstead, Essex.*—C. of Birdbrook. [26]

WARREN, Richard Peter, *Hyde Parsonage, Fordingbridge, Hants.*—Ex. Coll. Ox. Hon. 4th cl. Lit.

Hum. 1831, B.A. 1832, M.A. 1835; Deac. 1833 by Bp of Ex. Pr. 1834 by Bp of B. and W. P. C. of Hyde, Dio. Win. 1855. (Patron, the present P. C; Glebe, 5 acres; P. C.'s Inc. 194*l* 6*s* and Ho; Pop. 837.) Formerly P. C. of Slapton, Devon, 1838–41; R. of Tregony, Cornwall, 1847-51; Asst. C. of Ibsley, Hants, 1852–58. Author, *The Minister of Christ not to seek to please Men, but God* (a Sermon), 1843, 6*d*. [1]

WARREN, Robert Edward, *Mindtown, Bishops Castle, Salop.*—Dub. A.B; Deac. by Bp of Killaloe, Pr. by Abp of Dub. R. of Mindtown, Dio. Herf. 1863. (Patron, Earl of Powis; Tithe, 50*l*; Glebe, 85*l*; R.'s Inc. 135*l* and Ho; Pop. 48.) Formerly P. C. of Middletown, Chirbury, 1849. [2]

WARREN, Samuel, *Neenton Rectory, Bridgnorth, Salop.*—R. of Neenton, Dio. Herf. 1865. (Patroness, Lady Charles Lyster; R.'s Inc. 200*l* and Ho; Pop. 110.) [3]

WARREN, Samuel L., *Kennington, Oxford.*—Wad. Coll. Ox. B.A. 1859, M.A. 1863; Deac. 1859, Pr. 1860. P. C. of Kennington, Berks, Dio. Ox. 1865. (Patron, Bp of Ox; Pop. 138.) Fell. of Wadham Coll. Ox. Formerly C. of Little Torrington, N. Devon, and C. of Broadwinsor with Blackdown, Dorset, 1863–65. [4]

WARREN, W.—Min. of Jews' Episcopal Chapel, Bethnal Green. [5]

WARREN, William, *Wroot Rectory, Bawtry, Lincolnshire.*—Jesus Coll. Cam. B.A. 1826, M.A. 1829; Deac. 1827 and Pr. 1828 by Bp of Ban. R. of Wroot, Dio. Lin. 1832. (Patron, Ld Chan; Tithe, 430*l* 8*s* 6*d*; Glebe, 96 acres; R.'s Inc. 500*l* and Ho; Pop. 392.) Formerly P. C. of Llanfihangel, and Llanfinon, Anglesey, 1828–32. [6]

WARREN, William, *Trowbridge, Wilts.*—C. of Trowbridge. [7]

WARRENER, R., *Snargate, New Romney, Kent.*—R. of Snargate with Snave, Dio. Cant. 1840. (Patron, Abp of Cant; R.'s Inc. 250*l*; Pop. Snargate 71, Snave 97.) [8]

WARRINER, George, *Bloxham Grove, Banbury.*—St. Edm. Hall, Ox. B.A. 1838, M.A. 1841; Deac. 1839, Pr. 1840. [9]

WARTER, Edward, *Hanwood Rectory, Shrewsbury.*—Magd. Coll. Cam. Sen. Opt. 4th in 1st cl. Cl. B A. 1834, M.A. 1837; Deac. 1837, Pr. 1840. R. of Aldrington, Sussex, Dio. Chich. 1852. (Patron, Magd. Coll. Cam; Tithe, 267*l* 7*s* 6*d*; Glebe, 16 acres; R.'s Inc. 290*l*; Pop. 7.) C. of Great Hanwood. Formerly Tut. and President of Magd. Coll. Cam. [10]

WARTER, John Wood, *West Tarring Vicarage, Worthing, Sussex.*—Ch. Ch. Ox. B.A. 1827, M.A. 1834, B.D. 1845; Deac. and Pr. 1830 by Bp of Lon. V. of West Tarring with Heene and Durrington, Dio. Chich. 1834. (Patron, Abp of Cant; Tithe—Eccles. Commis. 699*l* 10*s*, V. 145*l* 18*s* 4*d*; Glebe, 2 acres; V.'s Inc. 525*l* and Ho; Pop. 1100.) Surrogate. Formerly British Chap. to the Embassy at Copenhagen 1829–33. Author, *A Sermon* (preached at the Reopening of Patching Church), 1833; *The Sun shall be turned into Darkness* (a Sermon preached on the occasion of the Eclipse, 1836); *Holy Matrimony*, a Sermon, *with Notes and Appendix*, 1837; *Plain Practical Sermons*, 2 vols. 1844, 23*s*; *The Teaching of the Prayer Book*, 1845, 6*s* 6*d*; *Assize Sermons* (preached at the Lent and Summer Assizes), 1845, 2*s* 6*d*; *No Prophecy of the Scripture is of any Private Interpretation* (a Visitation Sermon), 1849, 1*s* 6*d*; *And the Sea gave up the Dead that were in it* (a Sermon preached at West Tarring), 1850, 2*d*; *Pastoral Letter on the New Roman Catholic Aggression after the Old Fashion*, 2nd ed. 1850, 2*d*; *A Plain Christian's Manual, or Six Sermons on Early Piety, the Sacraments and Man's Latter End*, 2*s*; *A Plain Protestant's Manual, or certain Plain Sermons on the Scriptures, the Church and the Sacraments, &c. in which the Corruptions of the Romish Church are evidently set forth*, 1851, 3*s*; *The Uncontroversial Preaching of the Parochial Clergy enforced from the Beatitudes*, 1*s* 6*d*; *The Last of the Old Squires*, 2nd ed. 3*s* 6*d*; *The Sea Board and the Down*, 2 vols. sm. 4to, *with Illustrations of Tarring Church, St. Thomas à Becket's Palace, Heene and Durrington Chapels*, 28*s*; *Clerical Synods, Convocation, &c.* Editor of *The Doctor, &c.* by Robert Southey, vol. VI. 10*s* 6*d*; vol. VII. 14*s*; in one vol. 20*s*; *Southey's Commonplace-book*, 1st Series, *Choice Passages*, 18*s*; 2nd Series, *Special Collections*, 18*s*; 3rd Series, *Analytical Readings*, 21*s*; 4th Series, *Original Memoranda*, 21*s*; *Southey's Letters*, 2nd Series; *Parochial Fragments, &c. with Lives of Thomas à Becket and John Selden*, 10*s* 6*d*. [11]

WARWICK, John Croft Bridges Warwick, *Northampton.*—Magd. Coll. Cam. B.A. 1859, M.A. 1862; Deac. 1861 and Pr. 1862 by Bp of Pet. Asst. C. of St. Peter's, Northampton with Upton. [12]

WASEY, John Spearman, *Compton-Parva Vicarage, Newbury, Berks.*—Trin. Coll. Ox. B.A. 1844, M.A. 1845; Deac. 1845 by Bp of Lin. Pr. 1846 by Bp of Roch. V. of Compton-Parva, Dio. Ox. 1853. (Patron, J. T. Wasey, Esq; Tithe—Imp. 775*l* 12*s* 6*d*, V. 370*l*; Glebe, 6 acres; V.'s Inc. 370*l* and Ho; Pop. 590.) Dom. Chap. to Viscountess Hood. [13]

WASEY, William George Leigh, *The Knowle Sands, Bridgnorth, Salop.*—Ch. Ch. Ox. B.A. 1833, M.A. 1836; Deac. 1834 and Pr. 1835 by Bp of Ox. P. C. of Quatford, Salop, Dio. Herf. 1840. (Patron, Lord Sudeley; Glebe, 7 acres; P. C.'s Inc. 52*l* and Ho; Pop. 598.) P. C. of Morville with Aston Eyre P. C. Dio. Herf. 1840. (Patron, Lord Sudeley; P. C.'s Inc. 227*l* 10*s* 6*d*; Pop. 505.) Dom. Chap. to Lord Bridport 1835. Formerly C. of Mollington, Oxon, 1834–36, Condover, Salop, 1836–39, Herstmonceux, Sussex, 1839–40. Author, *Our Ancient Parishes*, 1859; *The Spirituality and Reasonableness of Church of England Public Prayers* (a Sermon preached at Cannes, France), 1861. [14]

WASHBOURN, John Addison Russell, *Grammar School, Wakefield.*—Pemb. Coll. Ox. 2nd cl. Lit. Hum. B.A. 1863; Deac. 1864 by Bp of Rip. C. of St. Mary's, Wakefield, 1864; 2nd Mast. of Gr. Sch. Wakefield. [15]

WASHINGTON, Adam, *Kersal, Manchester.*—St. John's Coll. Cam. B.A. 1856, M.A. 1859; Deac. 1857 and Pr. 1858 by Bp of Salis. C. of Kersal 1866. Formerly C. of Melcombe Regis 1857–62, Stradbroke 1862–65. [16]

WASHINGTON, G., *Yalding, Staplehurst, Kent.*—C. of Yalding. Formerly C. of Charlton-by-Dover. [17]

WASHINGTON, Robert, *Stradbroke, Wickham Market.*—Trin. Coll. Cam. B.A. 1864; Deac. 1866 by Bp of Nor. C. of Stradbroke, Suffolk, 1866. [18]

WASON, John, 46, *Montagu-square, London, W.* [19]

WASSE, Gervase, *Worsthorne Parsonage, Burnley.*—St. John's Coll. Cam. B.A. 1855, M.A. 1858; Deac. 1855 and Pr. 1856 by Bp of Lich. C. of Worsthorne 1864. Formerly C. of Melbourne, Derby, 1855–64. [20]

WASSE, Henry Watson, *Prestwold, Loughborough.*—Magd. Coll. Cam. B.A. 1856, M.A. 1859; Deac. 1856 and Pr. 1857 by Bp of Pet. P. C. of Prestwold with Hoton, Dio. Pet. 1861. (Patron, C. W. Packe, Esq; P. C.'s Inc. 18*l*; Pop. 969.) Formerly C. of Hungerton with Twyford and Thorp Satchville, Leic. [21]

WASTELL, Henry, *Newborough, Northumberland.* [22]

WATERFALL, George Howard, *Tollard Royal Rectory, Salisbury.*—Wor. Coll. Ox. B.A. 1854, M.A. 1856; Deac. 1855 and Pr. 1856 by Bp of Herf. R. of Tollard Royal, Dio. Salis. 1865. (Patron, Rev. J. H. Austen; Tithe, 570*l*; Glebe, 80 acres; R.'s Inc. 700*l* and Ho; Pop. 665.) Formerly C. of Leverbridge, near Bolton, Evesbatch, Herefordshire, and Pewsey, Wilts. [23]

WATERHOUSE, Charles James, *Singapore.*—St. John's Coll. Cam. B.A. 1850, M.A. 1854; Deac. 1850 and Pr. 1851 by Bp of Roch. Formerly C. of Egham, Surrey. [24]

WATERS, Edmund Thomas, *Highclere Rectory, Newbury.*—Wor. Coll. Ox. B.A. 1843, M.A. 1846; Deac. 1844, Pr. 1846. R. of Highclere, Hants, Dio. Win. 1867. (Patron, Earl of Carnarvon; Tithe, 324*l*; Glebe,

85 acres; R.'s Inc. 425*l* and Ho; Pop. 446.) Formerly R. of Wivenhoe, Essex, 1846–67. [1]

WATERS, Henry Harcourt, *Redbrook villa, near Monmouth.*—Trin. Coll. Toronto, Found. Scho. and Burnside Scho. of, B.A. 1867; Deac. 1867 by Bp of G. and B. Asst. C. of Newland, Dio. G. and B. 1867. [2]

WATERS, Richard, *Hunslet, Leeds.*—King's Coll. Lond. Assoc. 1859; Deac. 1859 and Pr. 1860 by Bp of Lich. V. of St. Jude's, Hunslet, Dio. Rip. 1867. (Patrons, Crown and Bp of Rip. alt; V.'s Inc. 300*l* and Ho; Pop. 6052,) Formerly C. of St. John's, Burslem, 1859; Sen. C. of St. James's, Bristol, 1861–63; Assoc. Sec. to Ch. Pastoral Aid Soc. 1863–67. [3]

WATERS, Robert, *South Hetton Parsonage, Fence Houses, Durham.*—King's Coll. Lond. Assoc; Deac. 1858 and Pr. 1859 by Bp of G. and B. P. C. of South Hetton, Dio. Dur. 1864. (Patron, Bp of Dur; P. C.'s Inc. 300*l* and Ho; Pop. 2200.) Formerly Chap. of Mariners' Chapel, Gloucester, 1858–63. [4]

WATERS, Thomas, *Maiden Bradley, Bath.*—Ch. Ch. Ox. Stud. of, B.A. 1862, M.A. 1865; Deac. 1863 and Pr. 1864 by Bp of Ox. P. C. of Maiden Bradley, Dio. Salis. 1864. (Patron, Ch. Ch. Ox; Tithe, 80*l*; Glebe, 4 acres; P. C.'s Inc. 155*l* and Ho; Pop. 653.) Formerly C. of Shippon, Abingdon. [5]

WATERS, William Roe, *West Bridgford, Nottingham.*—Corpus Coll. Cam. B.A. 1835; Deac. 1835 and Pr. 1836 by Bp of Lin. R. of West Bridgford, Dio. Lin. 1862. (Patron, J. Chaworth Musters, Esq; R.'s Inc. 640*l*; Pop. 390.) [6]

WATERS, W. T.—Dom. Chap. to the Earl of Saltoun. [7]

WATHEN, John Bateman, *Guarlford Rectory, Great Malvern.*—Queen's Coll. Ox. B.A. 1847, M.A. 1850; Deac. 1847 and Pr. 1849 by Bp of G. and B. R. of Guarlford, Dio. Wor. 1857. (Patron, Earl Beauchamp; Tithe, 307*l*; Glebe, 2 acres; R.'s Inc. 337*l* and Ho; Pop. 628.) Formerly C. of Prestbury, Gloucestershire, 1847–57. [8]

WATHERSTON, John, *Horsington, Wincanton.*—St. Edm. Hall, Ox. B.A. 1863; Deac. 1864, Pr. 1865. C. of Horsington 1867. [9]

WATHERSTON, John Dundas, *The Grammar School, Monmouth.*—St. John's Coll. Cam. B.A. 1843, M.A. 1856. V. of Llanrothal, near Monmouth, Dio. Herf. 1848. (Patron, Joseph Price, Esq; Tithe, 192*l*; Glebe, 12 acres; V.'s Inc. 207*l*; Pop. 107.) Lect. of Monmouth; Surrogate. Formerly Head Mast. of the Monmouth Gr. Sch. [10]

WATKIN, John Woodlands, *Stixwold Vicarage, Horncastle, Lincolnshire.*—St. Edm. Hall, Ox. B.A. 1847, M.A. 1851, D.C.L. 1860; Deac. 1847 and Pr. 1848 by Bp of Dur. V. of Stixwold, Dio. Lin. 1852. (Patron, C. Turnor, Esq; V.'s Inc. 105*l*; Pop. 269.) Author, *National Greatness a Reason for National Thankfulness* (suggested by the Great Exhibition), 1851; *Sermons for Ember-days* in *Church of England Magazine*; *A Brief Reply to Mr. Commissioner Phillips's "Vacation Thoughts on Capital Punishments,"* 1858. [11]

WATKIN, J. W. S., *Shipbourne, Tunbridge, Kent.*—Chap. of the Don. of Shipbourne, Dio. Cant. 1860. (Patron, J. Ridgway, Esq; Pop. 476.) [12]

WATKINS, Bernard Edward, *Treeton Rectory, Rotherham, Yorks.*—Wad. Coll. Ox. B.A. 1844; Deac. 1846 by Bp. of Chich. Pr. 1846 by Bp of Nor. R. of Treeton, Dio. York, 1846. (Patron, the present R; Tithe, 473*l* 16*s*; Glebe, 232*l* 15*s*; R.'s Inc. 715*l* 8*s* and Ho; Pop. 368.) Formerly C. of Udimore, near Rye, Sussex, 1846. [13]

WATKINS, Charles Frederic, *Brixworth Vicarage, near Northampton.*—Deac. and Pr. 1818 by Bp of Salis. V. of Brixworth, Dio. Pet. 1832. (Patron, Bp of Pet; Glebe, 160 acres; V.'s Inc. 400*l* and Ho; Pop. 1253.) Chap. to the Brixworth Union 1849. (Salary, 40*l*.) Formerly C. of Downton, Wilts, 1818–19, Windsor (sole charge) 1820–21, Warden of Farley Hospital and C. of West Grinstead and Plaisford, 1822–32. Author, *Human Hand and other Poems*, 1828, 2nd ed. 1852; *A Treatise on the Origin of Pleasure and Delight in the Human Mind, especially as relating to the Faculty of Taste, and the Sublime and Beautiful*, 1841; *Introduction to Geology*, 1839; *Clerical Subscription, an Appeal to Clergy and Laity*, 1863; Essays on Gravitation, Aerolites, Agriculture, Meteorology; etc. [14]

WATKINS, D., *Thornborough, near Buckingham.*—V. of Thornborough, Dio. Ox. 1834. (Patron, Sir H. Verney, Bart; V.'s Inc. 127*l*; Pop. 694.) Chap. to the Buckingham Union. [15]

WATKINS, Edwin Arthur, *Benhall, Suffolk.*—Deac. 1851 and Pr. 1852 by Bp of Lon. C. of Benhall 1864. Formerly Miss. of Ch. Miss. Soc. in N. W. America. Author, *A Dictionary of the Cree Language*, S.P.C.K. 1865. [16]

WATKINS, Frederick, *Thrybergh, Rotherham.*—Emman. Coll. Cam. Sen. Opt. 2nd cl. Cl. Trip. and B.A. 1830, M.A. 1833, B.D. 1840. One of Her Majesty's Inspectors of Schs. Formerly Fell. of Emman. Coll. Cam. [17]

WATKINS, Frederick Ball, *Woolton, Liverpool.*—St. John's Coll. Cam. 13th Cl. Trip. B.A. 1853, M.A. 1861; Deac. 1855 and Pr. 1856 by Bp. of Llan. C. of St. Peter's, Woolton, 1859. Formerly 2nd Mast. Royal Sch. Armagh, 1853. [18]

WATKINS, G. T. N., *Deptford, Kent, S.E.*—C. of St. Nicholas', Deptford. [19]

WATKINS, Henry George, *St. John's Parsonage, Potter's Bar, Barnet, Middlesex, N.*—Wor. Coll. Ox. B.A. 1831, M.A. 1833, Deac. 1831 and Pr. 1832 by Bp of Lon. P. C. of St. John's, Potter's Bar, Dio. Lon. 1835. (Patron, Bp of Lon; P. C.'s Inc. 174*l* and Ho; Pop. 959.) [20]

WATKINS, Morgan George, *Barnoldby-le-Beck Rectory, Grimsby.*—Ex. Coll. Ox. 2nd cl. Lit. Hum. and B.A. 1856, M.A. 1859; Deac. 1858 and Pr. 1859 by Bp of Wor. R. of Barnoldby-le-Beck, Dio. Lin. 1861. (Patron, Chapter of Southwell Coll. Ch; Glebe, 218 acres; R.'s Inc. 270*l* and Ho; Pop. 242.) Formerly 2nd Mast. of Gr. Sch. and C. of Ottery St. Mary 1858–61. [21]

WATKINS, Robert, *Bartlow Rectory, Linton, Cambs.*—R. of Bartlow, Dio. Ely, 1866. (Patron, the present R; R.'s Inc. 300*l* and Ho; Pop. 120.) [22]

WATKINS, Thomas, *Llanswintfread Rectory, Aberystwith.*—Queens' Coll. Cam. B.A. 1828, M.A. 1831; Deac. 1828 and Pr. 1829 by Bp of Herf. R. of Llanswintfread, Dio. St. D. 1836. (Patron, Thomas Watkins, Esq; Tithe—Imp. 2*l* 5*s*, R. 267*l*; Glebe, 26 acres; R.'s Inc. 295*l* and Ho; Pop. 255.) [23]

WATKINS, Watkin Morgan, *Llanddewi, Llanrwst, N. Wales.*—Lampeter, Philips and Senior Scho; Deac. 1857 by Bp of Ban. Pr. 1858 by Bp of St. A. R. of Llanddewi, Dio. St. A. 1867. (Patron, Bp of St. A.) Formerly C. of Llangerniew 1861. [24]

WATKINS, William, *Welsh Collegiate Institution, Llandovery.*—Caius Coll. Cam. 17th Wrang. B.A. 1860, M.A. 1862; Deac. and Pr. 1861 by Bp of Ox. Warden and Head Mast. of the Welsh Coll. Institution, Llandovery. Formerly Asst. Math. Mast. at Eton. [25]

WATKINSON, Robert, *Earls Colne, Halstead, Essex.*—Emman. Coll. Cam. B.A. 1798, M.A. 1801, B.D. 1808; Deac. 1801 and Pr. 1802 by Bp of Nor. V. of Earls Colne, Dio. Roch. 1829. (Patron, H. H. Carwardine, Esq; Tithe—Imp. 242*l* 14*s* 9*d*, V. 670*l* 15*s*; Glebe, 4½ acres; V.'s Inc. 614*l*; Pop. 1540.) Rural Dean of Colne 1834. Formerly 2nd Mast. of the Charterhouse Sch. Lond; Fell. of Emman. Coll. Cam. [26]

WATLING, Charles Henry, *Tredington Rectory, Shipston-on-Stour, Worcestershire.*—Mert. Coll. Ox. 1813, Jesus Coll. B.A. 1818, M.A. 1820, B.D. [illegible]; Deac. and Pr. 1818. R. of Tredington, Dio. Wor. [illegible] (Patron, Jesus Coll. Ox; Tithe, 622*l*; Glebe, 110 acres; R.'s Inc. 558*l* and Ho; Pop 602.) Formerly Fell. and Tut. of Jesus Coll. Ox. [27]

WATSON, Albert, *Brasenose College, Oxford.*—Wad. Coll. Ox. 1st cl. Lit. Hum. and B.A. 1851, M.A. 1853; Deac. 1853 and Pr. 1856 by Bp of Ox. Fell. of Brasen. Coll. 1852; Tut. 1854. [28]

WATSON, Andrew.—St. Cath. Coll. Cam. B.A. 1829, M.A. 1833. Chap. R.N. 1829. [29]

WATSON, Anthony, *Holy Island Parsonage, (Durham), Berwick-upon-Tweed.*—St. Bees; Deac. 1817 and Pr. 1819 by Bp of Ches. P. C. of Holy Island, Dio. Dur. 1822. (Patrons, D. and C. of Dur; Tithe—Imp. 1038*l* 7*s* 8*d*; Glebe, 6 acres; P. C.'s Inc. 236*l* and Ho; Pop. 935.) [1]

WATSON, B. Lucas, *Dorchester.*—Chap. of the County Prison, Dorchester. [2]

WATSON, Charles, *York.*—Deac. 1836, Pr. 1837. P. C. of Rufforth, near York, Dio. York, 1854. (Patroness, Mrs. Siddall; Tithe—Imp. 5*s* 8*d*; P. C.'s Inc. 110*l*; Pop. 297.) Chap. of the York Co. Hospital. [3]

WATSON, Christopher George, *Melton, Woodbridge, Suffolk.*—Pemb. Coll. Cam. B.A. 1810, M.A. 1814. R. of Melton, Dio. Nor. 1814. (Patrons, D. and C. of Ely; Tithe, 395*l* 3*s* 5*d*; Glebe, 8½ acres; R.'s Inc. 402*l*; Pop. 1084.) Formerly R. of Salcott, near Colchester, 1832–59. [4]

WATSON, C. S., *Sundridge, Sevenoaks, Kent.*—C. of Sundridge. Formerly C. of All Souls, Brighton. [5]

WATSON, C. T., *Broughton, Manchester.*—C. of Broughton. [6]

WATSON, Edward Collis, *Meltham Mills, Huddersfield.*—St. Aidan's; Deac. 1859, Pr. 1860. P. C. of Meltham, Dio. Rip. 1863. (Patron, V. of Almondbury; P. C.'s Inc. 260*l* and Ho; Pop. 3456.) Formerly Asst. C. of Meltham Mills 1859. [7]

WATSON, Fisher, *Hove, Brighton.*—St. John's Coll. Cam. B.A. 1812, M.A. 1815; Deac. 1812, Pr. 1813. Formerly Min. of St. George's Chapel, Great Yarmouth; V. of Lancing 1834–60. [8]

WATSON, Frederick, *Salcott, near Colchester.*—Caius Coll. Cam. B.A. 1856. R. of Salcott, Dio. Roch. 1859. (R.'s Inc. 130*l*; Pop. 188.) Formerly C. of Aslacton, Norfolk. [9]

WATSON, Frederick Fisher, *Lancing Vicarage, Shoreham, Sussex.*—Caius Coll. Cam. Sen. Opt. B.A. 1855, M.A. 1858; Deac. and Pr. 1856 by Bp of Chich. V. of Lancing, Dio. Chich. 1860. (Patron, Bp of Lon; Tithe, 151*l*; Glebe, 4½ acres; V.'s Inc. 151*l* and Ho; Pop. 950.) Formerly C. of Lancing. [10]

WATSON, George, *Sutton Rectory, Rochford, Essex.*—St. John's Coll. Cam. B.A. 1847; Deac. 1847 and Pr. 1848 by Bp of Rip. R. of Sutton, Dio. Roch. 1866. (Patron, the present R; R.'s Inc. 280*l* and Ho; Pop. 148.) Formerly C. of East Tuddenham, Norfolk, and Norton, Northants. [11]

WATSON, George, *Bolton Rectory, Wigton, Cumberland.*—Emman. Coll. Cam. B.A. 1855; Deac. 1856 by Bp of Ex. Pr. 1857 by Bp of B. and W. C. of Bolton 1862. Formerly C. of Stoke Clymsland 1856–58, Acklington-with-Chevington 1859–62. [12]

WATSON, George Augustus Frederick, *Bombay.*—Deac. 1845 and Pr. 1847 by Bp of Bombay. Formerly Head Mast. of the Bombay Education Society's Central School, Bombay, 1845–51; C. of Islip, Northants, 1851–55. Author, *Four Sermons to Soldiers on the Duty of being Religious Men,* Bombay. [13]

WATSON, George Bowes, *The Vicarage, St. Neots, Hunts.*—Trin. Coll. Cam. B.A. 1862, M.A. 1866; Deac. 1863, Pr. 1864. V. of St. Neots, Dio. Ely, 1866. (Patron, G. W. Rowley, Esq; Glebe, 45 acres; V.'s Inc. 216*l* and Ho; Pop. 3321.) Formerly C. of Cuckfield, Sussex, 1863–65. [14]

WATSON, Henry, *Langton Rectory, Spilsby, Lincolnshire.*—Wad. Coll. Ox. B.A. 1843, M.A. 1846; Deac. 1845 and Pr. 1846 by Bp of Salis. R. of Langton, Dio. Lin. 1856. (Patron, B. R. Langton, Esq; Tithe, 340*l*; Glebe, 28 acres; R.'s Inc. 388*l* and Ho; Pop. 190.) [15]

WATSON, Henry Campbell, *Croydon, Surrey, S.*—Corpus Coll. Cam. 3rd cl. Cl. Trip. with Math. Hons. B.A. 1852, M.A. 1855; Deac. 1853 by Bp of Chich. Pr. 1855 by Abp of Cant. P. C. of St. James's, Croydon, Dio. Cant. 1865. (Patron, V. of Croydon; P. C.'s Inc. 430*l*; Pop. 10,600.) Chap. of Whitgift's Hospital, Croydon, 1865. (Patron, Abp of Cant.) Formerly C. of Mayfield, Sussex, 1853; Cl. Mast. of the Ordnance Sch. Carshalton, 1854–56; C. of Croydon 1854–64. [16]

WATSON, Henry George, *Tring, Herts.*—St. John's Coll. Ox. Pusey and Ellerton Heb. Scho. 1859, B.A. 1860, M.A. 1863; Deac. 1861 and Pr. 1862 by Bp of Roch. C. of Tring 1861. [17]

WATSON, Henry Lacon, *Sharnford Rectory, Hinckley, Leicestershire.*—Caius Coll. Cam. 7th Sen. Opt. B.A. 1846, M.A. 1849; Deac. 1846 and Pr. 1847 by Bp of Chich. R. of Sharnford, Dio. Pet. 1850. (Patron, Ld Chan; Tithe, 2*l* 15*s*; Glebe, 228 acres; R.'s Inc. 450*l* and Ho; Pop. 589.) Formerly C. of Tangmere, near Chichester, 1847, Bexhill, near Hastings, 1847–50. [18]

WATSON, H. S., *Rudston, Bridlington, Yorks.*—C. of Rudston 1867. Formerly C. of Trinity, Salford. [19]

WATSON, Henry William, *Berkeswell Rectory, Coventry.*—Trin. Coll. Cam. 2nd Wrang. Prizeman and B.A. 1850, M.A. 1853; Deac. 1856 by Bp of Ely, Pr. 1858 by Bp of Lon. R. of Berkeswell with Barston P. C. Dio. Wor. 1865. (Patronesses, Misses Shirreffs; Berkeswell, Tithe, 798*l* 16*s* 10*d*; Barston, Tithe, 180*l* 5*s*; R.'s Inc. 984*l* and Ho; Pop. Berkeswell 1624, Barston 336.) Formerly Fell. and Asst. Tut. Trin. Coll. Cam; Math. Mast. in Harrow Sch. 1856–65. [20]

WATSON, James, *All Saints' Parsonage, Upper Norwood, Surrey, S.*—Corpus Coll. Cam. 16th Wrang. and B.A. 1848, M.A. 1851; Deac. 1849 and Pr. 1850 by Abp of Cant. P. C. of All Saints', Upper Norwood, Dio. Cant. 1856. (Patron, V. of Croydon; P. C.'s Inc. 350*l* and Ho; Pop. 4060.) Formerly C. of Cheriton with Newington, Kent, 1849, Carshalton 1851; Sen. Math. Mast. in Ordnance Sch. Carshalton, 1851. Author, *Progressive Course of Examples in Arithmetic,* 1853. [21]

WATSON, James, *Marr, Doncaster.*—Caius Coll. Cam. B.A. 1834; Deac. 1837 and Pr. 1838 by Bp of Lin. P. C. of Marr, Dio. York, 1842. (Patrons, Trustees of Peter J. Thellusson, Esq; Tithe, 150*l*; Glebe, 30 acres; P. C.'s Inc. 170*l*; Pop. 222.) [22]

WATSON, James Harrison, *Deaf and Dumb Asylum, Old Kent-road, London, S.*—Pemb. Coll. Cam. B.A. 1851, M.A. 1854, Deac. 1852, Pr. 1853. Prin. of the Deaf and Dumb Asylum. [23]

WATSON, John, 24, *Upper Brook street, Manchester.*—Literate; Deac. 1864 by Bp of Ches. Pr. 1865 by Bp of St. A. C. in sole charge of St. Matthias' Sch. Ch. Saville-street, Chorlton-on-Medlock. Formerly C. of Trinity, St. Helens, 1864, Ch. Ch. Bradford-cum-Beswick, Manchester, 1866. [24]

WATSON, John, *Orton-Longueville Rectory, Peterborough.*—St. John's Coll. Cam. B.A. 1838, M.A. 1841; Deac. 1838, Pr. 1839. R. of Orton-Longueville with Botolph-bridge R. Dio. Ely, 1863. (Patron, Marquis of Huntly; R.'s Inc. 332*l* and Ho; Pop. 311.) [25]

WATSON, John Bodden, *Portishead, Somerset.*—St. Aidan's; Deac. 1856 and Pr. 1857 by Bp of Ches. C. of Portishead 1866. Formerly C. of Bickerton, Chester, 1856, Wendover, Bucks, 1857–61, St. Luke's, Barton Hill, Bristol, 1861–65. [26]

WATSON, John R. B.—C. of St. Philip's, Lambeth. [27]

WATSON, John Selby, *Proprietary Grammar School, Stockwell, Surrey, S.*—Dub. Gold Medal in Classics, A.B. 1838, A.M. 1844, *ad eund.* Ox. 1854; Deac. 1839 and Pr. 1840 by Bp of B. and W. Head Mast. of the Stockwell Proprietary Gr. Sch. 1844. Formerly C. of Langport, Somerset, 1839–41. Author, *Geology, A Poem in Seven Books,* 1844; nine volumes of translations in Bohn's Classical Library, comprising Lucretius, Sallust, Justin, Quintilian, Xenophon, and other authors, 1851–56; *Pope's Homer's Iliad, with Notes and Preface,* Bohn, 1857; *Pope's Homer's Odyssey,* ib. 1858; *Life of George Fox,* 1860; *Sons of Strength, Wisdom, Patience,* 1861; *Story of Sir William Wallace,* 1861; *Life of Richard Porson,* 1861; *Life of Bishop Warburton,* 1863; *Sallust, with English Notes,* Tegg, 1865; *Terence's Andria, with English Notes,* ib. 1866; *Reasoning Power in Animals,* Reeve and Co. 1867. [28]

WATSON, John Sikes, *Canterbury.*—P. C. of St. Gregory's, Canterbury, Dio. Cant. 1860. (Patron, Abp of Cant; Pop. 1426.) Formerly C. of Buckland Newton, Dorset. [29]

WATSON, John William, *Kemberton Rectory, near Shiffnall, Salop.*—Trin. Coll. Cam. B.A. 1835, M.A. 1846; Deac. 1836 by Abp of Cant. Pr. 1837 by Abp of York. R. of Kemberton with Sutton-Maddock V. annexed, Dio. Lich. 1860. (Patrons, Miss Slaney and others; Tithe, 540*l*; Glebe, 60 acres; R.'s Inc. 650*l*, with R. Ho. at Kemberton and V. Ho. at Sutton-Maddock; Pop. 640.) Formerly C. of Scampston, Yorks, 1836; V. of Ellerburne 1837; P. C. of St. Mary's, Preston, 1841; Min. of Beresford Chapel, Walworth, 1843; English Chap. at Thun and at Mannheim 1853; P. C. of St. Paul's, Tiverton, 1854, Trinity, Tulse Hill, Surrey, 1856. Author, *Ministerial First Fruits* (Sermons), 1840, 6*s*; *Lazarus of Bethany*, 1846, 3*s*; *The Catholic Church*, 1856, 6*d*; several single Sermons. [1]

WATSON, Robert Lancaster, *Covington Rectory, Kimbolton, Hunts.*—Ex. Coll. Ox. B.A. 1832. R. of Covington, Dio. Ely, 1865. (Patron, Hon. G. W. Fitzwilliam; R.'s Inc. 270*l* and Ho; Pop. 188.) Formerly Head Mast. of Kimbolton Gr. Sch; C. of Pertenhall, Beds. [2]

WATSON, R. M., 4, *St. Aubyn's-place, Brighton.* [3]

WATSON, Shepley W., *Plumbland, Carlisle.*—C. of Plumbland. [4]

WATSON, Thomas, *East Farleigh Vicarage, Maidstone.*—St. Edm. Hall, Ox. B.A. 1823, M.A. 1839; Deac. and Pr. 1824. V. of East Farleigh, Dio. Cant. 1850. (Patron, Ld Chan; Tithe—Imp. 92*l* 4*s*, V. 928*l* 9*s* 2*d*; Glebe 2 acres; V.'s Inc. 1020*l* and Ho; Pop. 1365.) Author, *Christ, not Anti-Christ, or Papal Heresies*, 3rd ed. 1851; *The Two Cities in the Visions of Ezekiel and St. John Explained and Harmonised*, 1*s*; *The Hill of Zion, or the First and Last Things illustrative of the present Dispensation*, 2nd ed. 3*s* 6*d*; *Shiloh's Sceptre, or the Signs of the Times in Connexion with the Pre-Millennial Advent of Christ*, 2nd ed. 3*s* 6*d*; *Discourses, Practical and Experimental, on the Epistle to the Colossians*, 3rd ed. 10*s* 6*d*; *Spiritual Life Delineated*, 6*s*; *The Baptism of the Spirit*, 3rd ed. 1*s*; *The Axe laid to the Root of the Tree*; *The Flaming Sword*; various other Tracts. [5]

WATSON, Thomas H., *Trinity Parsonage, Tulse-hill, S.*—Dub. A.M. 1858; Deac. 1853, Pr. 1854. P. C. of Trinity, Tulse-hill, Dio. Win. 1865. (Patron, Jonah Cressingham, Esq; P. C.'s Inc. 700*l* and Ho; Pop. 2391.) Formerly C. of St. James's, Croydon Common, and Mitcham, Surrey. [6]

WATSON, William, *Cotterstock Vicarage, Oundle, Northants.*—Corpus Coll. Cam. 22nd Wrang. B.A. 1850, M.A. 1853; Deac. 1851 and Pr. 1852 by Bp of Pet. V. of Cotterstock with Glapthorn, Dio. Pet. 1856 (Patron, Lord Melville; Glebe, 35 acres; V.'s Inc. 105*l* and Ho; Pop. Cotterstock 211, Glapthorn 396.) Formerly 2nd Mast. of Oundle Gr. Sch. 1853–55. [7]

WATSON, William, *Loughton, Essex, N.E.*—St. John's Coll. Cam. B.A. 1832, M.A. 1835; Deac. 1834 and Pr. 1836 by Bp of Ox. Asst. C. of Loughton 1858; Surrogate. Formerly C. of Cottisford, Oxon, 1834–36; P. C. of St. Paul's, High Beech, Essex, 1836–41; P. C. of St. John's, Chigwell, 1846–47. [8]

WATSON, W., *Worplesdon, near Guildford.*—C. of Worplesdon, Surrey. [9]

WATSON, William Frederick Wilcocks, *Ickleford Rectory, Hitchin, Herts.*—Emman. Coll. Cam. 3rd cl. Cl. Trip. 3rd cl. Math. and B.A. 1839, M.A. 1844; Deac. 1841 and Pr. 1843 by Bp of Chich. R. of Ickleford, Dio. Roch. 1855. (Patrons, Reps. of Ralph Lindsay, Esq; R.'s Inc. 300*l* and Ho; Pop. 546.) [10]

WATSON, William Richards, *Saltfleetby-St. Peter's, Louth, Lincolnshire.*—Oriel Coll. Ox. 3rd cl. Lit. Hum. 1850, B.A. 1851, M.A. 1853; Deac. 1851 by Bp of Llan. Pr. 1852 by Bp of Ex. R. of Saltfleetby-St. Peter's, Dio. Lin. 1856. (Patron, Oriel Coll. Ox; R.'s Inc. 249*l*; Pop. 308.) Formerly C. of Kilmington and Axminster. [11]

WATT, John Alexander, *Bath.*—P. C. of St. Luke's, Lyncombe, Bath, Dio. B. and W. 1866. [12]

WATT, Robert, *Cheadle Rectory, Staffs.*—Trin. Coll. Cam. 13th Wrang. and B.A. 1840, M.A. 1843; Deac. 1843 and Pr. 1844 by Bp of Ely. R. of Cheadle, Dio. Lich. 1847. (Patron, Trin. Coll. Cam; Tithe, 400*l*; Glebe, 15 acres; R.'s Inc. 464*l* and Ho; Pop. 4160.) Surrogate. Formerly Fell. of Trin. Coll. Cam. 1842–48; C. of Moulton, Suffolk, 1843–45. [13]

WATTERS, John, 6, *Ainslie's Belvedere, Bath.*—Dub. A.B. 1833, A.M. 1839, LL.D. 1861; Deac. 1833 by Bp of Killaloe, Pr. 1834 by Bp of Limerick. Formerly C. of Kilbeacon 1833–37, Kilkenny 1837–41, Bangor, co. Down, 1842–48, Corn-street Chapel, Bath, 1854; and many temporary charges. [14]

WATTON, Alfred, *Babworth, East Retford, Notts.*—C. of Babworth. [15]

WATTON, Timothy George, *Edgbaston, Birmingham.*—Emman. Coll. Cam. B.A. 1863, M.A. 1867; Deac. 1865 and Pr. 1866 by Bp of Wor. C. of Ch. Ch. Birmingham, 1865. [16]

WATTS, Edmund Thomas, *Dyserth Parsonage, St. Asaph.*—Dub. A.B. 1854, A.M. 1857; Deac. 1855 and Pr. 1856 by Bp of St. A. P. C. of Dyserth, Dio. St. A. 1860. (Patron, Bp of St. A; P. C.'s Inc. 113*l* and Ho; Pop. 1095.) Formerly C. of Llannefydd. [17]

WATTS, George, *Birchanger Rectory, Bishop Stortford.*—Queens' Coll. Cam. B.A. 1831, M.A. 1835; Deac. 1833 and Pr. 1834 by Bp of Chich. R. of Birchanger, Dio. Roch. 1864. (Patron, New Coll. Ox; Tithe, 310*l*; Glebe, 28 acres, 63*l*; R.'s Inc. 373*l* and Ho; Pop. 357.) Formerly C. of Ewhurst, Sussex, 1833–48; V. of Brockworth, Glouc. 1847–64. [18]

WATTS, Henry, *Titchborne, Alresford, Hants.*—C. of Titchborne. [19]

WATTS, James, *Bredhurst Parsonage, Chatham.*—Ch. Coll. Cam. Scho. of, 11th Jun. Opt. B.A. 1856, M.A. 1859; Deac. 1856 and Pr. 1857 by Abp of Cant. C. in sole charge of Bredhurst 1867. Formerly C. of Seal, Kent, 1856–59, Woodchurch, 1860–61, Hollingbourne (sole charge) 1861–64, Rotherfield, Sussex, 1865–66. [20]

WATTS, James George, *Fulletby Rectory, Horncastle.*—Ball. Coll. Ox. B.A. 1841, M.A. 1845; Deac. 1840 and Pr. 1841 by Bp of Herf. R. of Fulletby, Dio. Lin. 1860. (Patron, Rev. John Jackson; Allotment in lieu of Tithes, 290 acres; Glebe, 2 acres; R.'s Inc. 460*l* and Ho; Pop. 303.) Formerly V. of Ledbury 1847–60. [21]

WATTS, John, *Tarrant-Gunville Rectory, Blandford, Dorset.*—Univ. Coll. Ox. 1st cl. Math. et Phy. 2nd cl. Lit. Hum. and B.A. 1816, M.A. 1819; Deac. 1818 and Pr. 1820 by Bp of Ox. R. of Tarrant-Gunville, Dio. Salis. 1828. (Patron, Univ. Coll. Ox; Tithe, 480*l*; Glebe, 50 acres; R.'s Inc. 520*l* and Ho; Pop. 441.) Rural Dean of Pimperne 1835; Surrogate and Official to the Chan. of the Dio. of Salis. 1836; Official to the Archd. of Dorset 1841; Preb. of Salis. 1846. Formerly Fell. of Univ. Coll. Ox. 1817–21; Tutor of Univ. Coll. 1821–27; Chap. to the Earl of Bessborough 1821; Whitehall Preacher 1824; Proctor 1825–28. [22]

WATTS, John William, *The Vicarage, Bicester.*—Magd. Hall Ox. B.A. 1828, M.A. 1838; Deac. 1829 and Pr. 1831 by Bp of B. and W. V. of Bicester, Dio. Ox. 1843. (Patron, Sir E. Page Turner, Bart; Glebe, 126 acres; V.'s Inc. 290*l* and Ho; Pop. 3400.) Surrogate. Chap. to the Bicester Union 1852. Formerly Min. of St. James's, Guernsey, 1834–38; P. C. of Downside, near Bath, 1838–40. Author, *Christ the Consolation of His People*; various single Sermons. [23]

WATTS, Langford Lovell, *The Royd, Stainland, Halifax.*—St. Aidan's; Deac. 1857 and Pr. 1858 by Bp of Rip. P. C. of Stainland, Dio. Rip. 1860. (Patron, V. of Halifax; Glebe, 5½ acres; P. C.'s Inc. 300*l*; Pop. 4660.) Formerly C. of Sowerby Bridge. [24]

WATTS, Percival James, *Nether Witton, Morpeth, Northumberland.*—New Inn Hall, Ox. B.A. 1861; Deac. 1861 and Pr. 1862 by Bp of Pet. P. C. of Nether Witton, Dio. Dur. 1863. (Patron, V. of Hartburn; P. C.'s Inc. 170*l* and Ho; Pop. 450.) Formerly C. of Horton with Piddington, Northants, 1861–63, Morpeth with Ulgham 1863. [25]

WATTS, Peter Robert, *Teffont Magna, Salisbury.*—Ch. Coll. Cam. B.A. 1859; Deac. 1859 and Pr.

1861 by Bp of Man. C. of Dinton with Teffont Magna 1865. Formerly C. of Rushock, Worc. 1859, Pitcombe and Wyke Champflower, Somerset, 1864. [1]

WATTS, Richard, *Nailstone Rectory, Hinckley, Leicestershire.*—Magd. Hall, Ox. B.A. 1842; Deac. 1842 and Pr. 1843 by Bp of Pet. R. of Nailstone with Barton-in-the-Beans, Dio. Pet. 1852. (Patron, the Crown; Tithe, 400*l*; Glebe, 56 acres; R.'s Inc. 500*l* and Ho; Pop. Nailstone 461, Barton-in-the-Beans 157.) Formerly C. of Cossington, Leic. 1842–45, Kimbolton, Hunts, 1845–46, Langford with Little Faringdon, Berks, 1846–50, Nailstone 1850–52. [2]

WATTS, Robert Rowley, *Spetisbury, near Blandford, Dorset.*—Univ. Coll. Ox. 3rd cl. Lit. Hum. 2nd cl. Math. et Phy. and B.A. 1852; Deac. 1854 and Pr. 1855 by Bp of Salis. C. of Spetisbury with Charlton. Formerly C. of Maddington, Wilts; Asst. Mast. in Charterhouse Sch. Lond. 1856. [3]

WATTS, Thomas William.—Caius Coll. Cam. M.A; Deac. 1859 and Pr. 1860 by Bp of Ches. Chap. at Mottram Hall and Addington Hall, Cheshire. Formerly C. of Crewe. [4]

WATTS, William Longmore, *St. Osyth, Colchester.*—Theol. Assoc. King's Coll. Lond; Deac. 1863 and Pr. 1864 by Bp of Roch. Chap. of the Don. of St. Osyth, Dio. Roch. 1864. (Patron, J. R. Kirby, Esq; Chap.'s Inc. 100*l* and Ho; Pop. 1700.) Formerly C. of St. Osyth. [5]

WATTSFORD, Henry James, 27, *Soho-square, London, W.*—Dur. B.A. 1853, M.A. 1856; Deac. 1854 by Bp of Rip. Pr. 1855 by Bp of Man. C. of St. Luke's, Berwick-street, Soho. Formerly C. of South Shields 1855–59. [6]

WAUCHOPE, David, *Church Lawford Rectory, Rugby.*—Wad. Coll. Ox. B.A. 1848, M.A. 1851; Deac. 1849 and Pr. 1850 by Bp of Salis. R. of Church Lawford with King's Newnham V. Dio. Wor. 1863. (Patron, Duke of Buccleuch; Tithe, 167*l* 12*s*; Glebe, 82 acres; R.'s Inc. 310*l* and Ho; Pop. 450.) Formerly C. of Stower-Provost, Dorset, 1849–63; Chap. to 10th, 11th, and 12th Dorset Rifle Volunteers 1860–64. [7]

WAUD, Samuel Wilkes, *Rettendon Rectory, Wickford, Essex.*—Magd. Coll. Cam. 5th Wrang. and B.A. 1825, M.A. 1828; Deac. 1827 and Pr. 1828 by Bp of Ely. R. of Rettendon, Dio. Roch. 1843. (Patron, Ld Chan; Tithe, 854*l*; Glebe, 84 acres; R.'s Inc. 938*l* and Ho; Pop. 785.) Formerly Fell. and Tut. of Magd. Coll. Cam. Author, *Algebraical Geometry*, 1835. [8]

WAUDBY, G.—Chap. Royal Navy. [9]

WAUDBY, William Robert Pallet, *Great Wymondley, Herts.*—Deac. 1844, Pr. 1845. C. of Great Wymondley. Formerly C. of Croston. [10]

WAUGH, Arthur Thornhill, *Elmstead Vicarage, Colchester.*—Jesus Coll. Cam. 28th Wrang. 4th in 3rd cl. Cl. Trip. B.A. 1865; Deac. 1866 by Bp of Man. V. of Elmstead, Dio. Roch. 1867. (Patron, Jesus Coll. Cam; Tithe, 310*l*; Glebe, 6 acres; V.'s Inc. 320*l* and Ho; Pop. 960.) Formerly C. of Thornton and Mast. in Rossall Sch. [11]

WAUGH, James Charles, *Wroughton, near Swindon.*—Trin. Coll. Ox. B.A. 1854; Deac. 1855 by Abp of York. C. of Wroughton. Formerly C. of Beaminster, Dorset. [12]

WAUGH, James Hay, *Corsley Rectory, Warminster, Wilts.*—Magd. Hall, Ox. B.A. 1839, M.A. 1843; Deac. 1840 by Bp of Lin. Pr. 1841 by Bp of Salis. R. of Corsley, Dio. Salis. 1845. (Patron, Marquis of Bath; Tithe—App. 3*l*, R. 2*l*; Glebe, 95 acres; R.'s Inc. 180*l* and Ho; Pop. 1235.) [13]

WAWN, Charles Newby, *North Ferriby, Brough, Yorks.*—St. John's Coll. Cam. B.A. 1840; Deac. 1841 and Pr. 1842 by Abp of York. V. of North Ferriby, Dio. York, 1847. (Patron, W. W. Wilkinson, Esq; Glebe, 1 acre; V.'s Inc. 135*l*; Pop. 948.) [14]

WAWN, John Dale, *Kirkleatham Vicarage, Redcar, Yorks.*—Deac. 1854 and Pr. 1855 by Bp of Rip. V. of Kirkleatham, Dio. York, 1867. (Patron, A. H. Turner Newcomen, Esq; Tithe, Imp. 500*l*; Glebe, 13 acres; V.'s Inc. 96*l* and Ho; Pop. 380.) Formerly C. of Cononley 1854–65; P. C. of Dallowgill 1865–67; Chap. to Turner's Hospital 1867. [15]

WAWN, William Hey, *Coley Parsonage, near Halifax.*—St. John's Coll. Cam. B.A. 1841; Deac. 1842, Pr. 1843. P. C. of Coley, Dio. Rip. 1847. (Patron, V. of Halifax; P. C.'s Inc. 150*l* and Ho.) [16]

WAY, Charles John, *Boreham Vicarage, Chelmsford.*—Trin. Coll. Cam. B.A. 1819, M.A. 1822; Deac. 1819, Pr. 1820. V. of Boreham, Dio. Roch. 1850. (Patron, Bp. of Roch; Tithe—App. 688*l* and 21 acres of Glebe, Imp. 6*l* 3*s* 9*d*, V. 445*l*; Glebe, 18 acres; V.'s Inc. 486*l* and Ho; Pop. 989.) Author, *The Pope Bound by the Threefold Cord of Prophecy* (three Sermons), 1851, 2*s*. [17]

WAY, John Hugh, *Henbury Vicarage, Gloucestershire.*—Oriel Coll. Ox. B.A. 1857; Deac. 1859 and Pr. 1860 by Bp of G. and B. V. of Henbury with Aust, Northwick and Hallen Chapelries, Dio. G. and B. 1860. (Patrons, Sir Greville Smyth and Edward Colston, Esq; Tithe, 800*l*; Glebe, 6 acres; V.'s Inc. 850*l* and Ho; Pop. 2500.) Formerly C. of Hallen in Henbury 1859–60. [18]

WAY, John Hyne, *Bath.*—St. Peter's Coll. Cam. B.A. 1832; Deac. 1838 and Pr. 1839 by Bp of Ex. Min. of Ch. Ch. Walcot, Bath, Dio. B. and W. 1849. (Patron, R. of Walcot; Min.'s Inc. 200*l*.) [19]

WAY, Lewis Albert Martin, *Foxley, near Malmesbury, Wilts.*—Magd. Coll. Cam. B.A. 1849; Deac. 1850, Pr. 1851. R. of Foxley, Dio. G. and B. 1862. (Patroness, Lady Holland; R.'s Inc. 261*l* and Ho; Pop. 65.) Formerly C. of Foxley and Bremilham, Wilts, 1852. [20]

WAY, William, *Chrishall Vicarage, Royston.*—Trin. Coll. Cam. B.A. 1843; Deac. 1844 and Pr. 1845 by Bp of Lon. V. of Chrishall, Dio. Roch. 1865. (Patron, Bp of Roch; V.'s Inc. 290*l* and Ho; Pop. 650.) Formerly C. of Inworth, Essex. [21]

WAYET, Fielde, *Otterton Vicarage, Sidmouth, Devon.*—New Inn Hall, Ox. B.A. 1848, M.A. 1849; Deac. 1848 and Pr. 1849 by Bp of Carl. V. of Otterton, Dio. Ex. 1865. (Patrons, Heirs of Lord Rolle; Tithe, 336*l*; Glebe, 25 acres; V.'s Inc. 366*l* and Ho; Pop. 1140.) Formerly C. of Budleigh Salterton, Devon. [22]

WAYET, West, *Pinchbeck Vicarage, Spalding, Lincolnshire.*—Queen's Coll. Ox. B.A. 1831, M.A. 1834; Deac. 1833 and Pr. 1834 by Bp of Lin. V. of Pinchbeck, Dio. Lin. 1834. (Patron, the present V; V.'s Inc. 700*l* and Ho; Pop. 1518.) Rural Dean. [23]

WAYLAND, Charles, *Holcombe Rectory, Stratton-on-the-Fosse, Bath.*—Wad. Coll. Ox. B.A. 1808, M.A. 1811; Deac. 1810 by Bp of Ban. Pr. 1811 by Abp of York. R. of Holcombe, Dio. B. and W. 1845. (Patron, Rev. T. R. Jolliffe; Tithe—Imp. 2*l*, R. 58*l*; Glebe, 18 acres; R.'s Inc. 99*l* and Ho; Pop. 388.) C. of Babington, Somerset, 1850. Formerly C. of Aymestrey, Herf. 1811, Aberford, Yorks, 1812, Bitton, Glouc. 1813, Litton, Somerset, 1815, Stratton-on-the-Fosse and Holcombe, Somerset, 1825. [24]

WAYMAN, William, *Great Thurlow Vicarage, Newmarket.*—Ex. Coll. Ox. 3rd cl. Lit. Hum. and B.A. 1832, M.A. 1834; Deac. 1832 and Pr. 1833 by Bp of Nor. V. of Great Thurlow, Dio. Ely, 1835. (Patrons, Trustees of Lady Harland; Tithe, 497*l* 10*s*; Glebe, 72 acres; V.'s Inc. 518*l* and Ho; Pop. 423.) [25]

WAYNE, William Henry, *Much-Wenlock, Salop.*—St. Peter's Coll. Cam. Sen. Opt. and B.A. 1825, M.A. 1828; Deac. 1827 and Pr. 1828 by Bp of Lich. V. of Much-Wenlock, Dio. Herf. 1842. (Patron, J. Milnes Gaskell, Esq; Tithe, 343*l* 5*s* 7*d*; V.'s Inc. 400*l*; Pop. 2494.) [26]

WAYNE, William Henry, *Tickwood Hall, Wenlock, Salop.*—Trin. Coll. Cam. B.A. 1856; Deac. 1856, Pr. 1857. P. C. of Benthall, Dio. Herf. 1857. (Patron, V. of Much-Wenlock; P. C.'s Inc. 95*l*; Pop. 199.) Formerly C. of Benthall 1856. [27]

WAYTE, Samuel William, *Trinity College, Oxford.*—Trin. Coll. Ox. Double 1st cl. and B.A. 1842, M.A. 1845, B.D. 1854; Deac. 1847, Pr. 1849. Fell. of Trin. Coll. Ox; one of the Math. Examiners 1850, and

Jun. Bursar; one of the Secs. of the Oxford Univ. Commission. [1]

WAYTE, William, *Eton College, Windsor.*—King's Coll. Cam. Craven Scho. and Browne's Medallist 1850, B.A. 1853, M.A. 1856; Deac. 1853 and Pr. 1854 by Bp of Ox. Asst. Mast. at Eton Coll. 1853. Formerly Fell. of King's Coll. Cam; Select Preacher 1862. Author, *Christian Thoughtfulness in Times of Change* (a Sermon before the University of Cambridge), 1860. Editor of Plato's *Protagoras*. [2]

WEALE, Robert Money, *Chingford, Essex.*—Clare Hall, Cam. 18th Jun. Opt. and B.A. 1849, M.A. 1852; Deac. 1849 and Pr. 1850 by Bp of Roch. R. of Chingford, Dio. Lon. 1865. (Patron, R. B. Heathcote, Esq; R.'s Inc. 538*l* and Ho; Pop. 1174.) Formerly C. of Mansfield-Woodhouse 1851. Author, *The Indian Rebellion* (a Sermon). [3]

WEARE, Thomas William, *Isfield Rectory, Uckfield, Sussex.*—Ch. Ch. Ox. Stud of, B.A. 1836, M.A. 1838; Deac. 1839 and Pr. 1840 by Bp of Ox. R. of Isfield, Dio. Chich. 1867. (Patron, Abp of Cant; R.'s Inc. 340*l* and Ho; Pop. 458.) Formerly Second Mast. of Westminster School 1841–61. Author, *Haseley Church*, 2 eds. Oxford Arch. Soc.'s publications; a Paper in Gilbert Scott's *Gleanings from Westminster Abbey*; *Plauti Trinummus, translated into English Verse*, 1860; *Farewell Sermon to the School, preached in Westminster Abbey*, 1861. [4]

WEARING, Timothy, *Otterburn, Newcastle-on-Tyne.*—St. Bees; Deac. 1858 by Bp of Rip. Pr. 1860 by Bp of Dur. P. C. of Otterburn, Dio. Dur. 1860. (Patron, R. of Elsdon; P. C.'s Inc. 200*l*.) Formerly C. of Rothwell. [5]

WEATHERELL, Robert, *Elton Rectory, Nottingham.*—St. Edm. Hall, Ox. B.A. 1842, M.A. 1845; Deac. 1842 and Pr. 1843 by Bp of Lin. R. of Elton-on-the-Hill, Dio. Lin. 1851. (Patron, Count de Pully; Glebe, 191 acres; R.'s Inc. 263*l* and Ho; Pop. 50.) [6]

WEATHERLEY, Charles Thomas, *North Bradley Vicarage, Trowbridge, Wilts.*—King's Coll. Lond. Assoc; Deac. 1855 and Pr. 1856 by Bp of Lon. C. in sole charge of North Bradley 1866. Formerly C. of Harmondsworth and West Drayton 1855–57; Chap. at Morecroft and Sen. C. of 1858–62; Hillingdon Old St. Pancras, Lond. 1862–66. [7]

WEBB, Albert Brooke, *St. Olave's Priory, near Lowestoft, Suffolk.*—Caius Coll. Cam. B.A. 1862; Deac. 1863 and Pr. 1864 by Bp of St. D. Chap. of Don. of Herringfleet, Dio. Nor. 1866. (Patron, Major H. M. Leathes; Chap.'s Inc. 70*l*; Pop. 200.) Formerly Asst. C. of Henllan, Cardiganshire, 1863–64, Merston, near Chich. (sole charge), 1864. [8]

WEBB, Allan Becher, *University College, Oxford.*—Univ. Coll. Ox. B.A. 1862, M.A. 1864; Deac. 1863 and Pr. 1864 by Bp of Ox. Fell. and Asst. Tut. of Univ. Coll. Formerly C. of St. Peter's, Oxford; Vice Prin. of Cuddesdon Theol. Coll. [9]

WEBB, Anthony Spurr, *Ripley, Surrey.*—St. John's Coll. Cam. B.A. 1860; Deac. 1861 and Pr. 1862 by Bp of Win. C. of Ripley Chapel in the Parish of Send with Ripley 1865. Formerly C. of Milton, Portsea, 1861, Widcombe, Bath, 1863. [10]

WEBB, Arthur H., *Wigan.*—Trin. Coll. Cam. B.A. 1857; Deac. 1857 and Pr. 1858 by Bp of Lich. C. of Wigan 1864. Formerly C. of Sheriff-Hales with Woodcote 1857–64. [11]

WEBB, Benjamin, 2, *Chandos-street, Cavendish-square, London, W.*—Trin. Coll. Cam. B.A. 1842, M.A. 1845. P. C. of St. Andrew's, Wells-street, Marylebone, Dio. Lon. 1862. (Patrons, Crown and Bp alt; P. C.'s Inc. 150*l*; Pop. 5143.) Formerly P. C. of Sheen, Staffs, 1851. [12]

WEBB, Charles, *Blyth Vicarage, Worksop, Notts.*—Dub. A.B. 1854, A.M. 1860; Deac. 1854 by Bp of B. and W. Pr. 1856 by Bp of Lich. C. (sole charge) of Blyth 1866. Formerly C. of East Brent 1854, St. John's, Wolverhampton, 1856; Chap. at Codrington Coll. 1864–66. [13]

WEBB, Charles Henry Cole, *Castle End, Kenilworth.*—Queen's Coll. Ox; Deac. 1866 by Bp of Wor. C. of Kenilworth 1866. [14]

WEBB, George Mower, *The Parsonage, Great Horton, Bradford, Yorks.*—Corpus Coll. Cam. B.A. 1847; Deac. 1847, Pr. 1848. P. C. of Horton, Dio. Rip 1860. (Patron, V. of Bradford; P. C.'s Inc. 300*l* and Ho; Pop. 2000.) Chap. of the Cemetery, Bradford. Formerly V. of Aughton, Selby, 1852–60. Author, *A Wreath for the Tomb, being a Selection of Texts and Verses suitable for Epitaphs*, 1862. [15]

WEBB, James, *Clifton, Brighouse, Yorkshire.*—St. Cath. Hall, Cam. B.A. 1853, M.A. 1856; Deac. 1853 and Pr. 1854 by Bp of Salis. P. C. of Hartshead with Clifton, Dio. Rip. 1866. (P. C.'s Inc. 230*l*; Pop. 2700.) Formerly C. of Horton with Woodlands, Dorset, and Dewsbury. [16]

WEBB, John, *Hardwick Parsonage, Hay, South Wales.*—R. of Tretire with Michaelchurch R. Dio. Herf. 1812. (Patron, the present R; Tithe—App. 7*l* 12*s*, R. 260*l*; R.'s Inc. 270*l* and Ho; Pop. 147.) P. C. of Hardwick, Dio. Herf. 1861. (Patroness, Mrs. Penoyre; P. C.'s Inc. 40*l*.) Formerly V. of St. Mary's, Cardiff, 1821. [17]

WEBB, John Blurton, *Old Cleeve Rectory, Taunton.*—Corpus Coll. Cam. B.A. 1841, M.A. 1845; Deac. 1845 and Pr. 1846 by Bp of Herf. R. of Old Cleeve, Dio. B. and W. 1865. (Patron, the present R; Tithe, 603*l* 15*s*; Glebe, 3 acres; R.'s Inc. 620*l* 5*s* and Ho; Pop. 1200.) Formerly R. of Cleobury North, near Bridgnorth, 1849–59; P. C. of Marchington-Woodlands, Uttoxeter, 1860–65. [18]

WEBB, John Cadman, *Linefield, Blackburn, Lancashire.*—St. Bees; Deac. 1866 by Bp of Man. C. of St. Paul's, Blackburn, 1866. [19]

WEBB, John Marshall, *Great Linford, Newport-Pagnell, Bucks.*—Trin. Coll. Ox. B.A. 1850, M.A. 1853; Deac. 1850 and Pr. 1852 by Bp of Pet. C. of Great Linford. [20]

WEBB, John Moss, *Wold Newton Rectory, Great Grimsby, Lincolnshire.*—Clare Coll. Cam. B.A. 1837, M.A. 1841, M.A. Ox. 1863; Deac. 1838 by Bp of Lich. Pr. 1839 by Bp of Lin. R. of Wold Newton, Dio. Lin. 1866. (Patron, Bp of Lich; Glebe, 10 acres; R.'s Inc. 476*l* and Ho; Pop. 180.) Formerly C. of Swarkeston, near Derby, 1838–66. [21]

WEBB, Joseph, *Ravenstone, near Ashby-de-la-Zouch.*—Wad. Coll. Ox. B.A. 1825; Deac. 1825 and Pr. 1827 by Bp of Lich. Mast. of Ravenstone Hospital 1841. [22]

WEBB, Perceval, *St. Luke's, Heywood, Lancashire.*—All Souls Coll. Ox. B.A. 1854, M.A. 1858; Deac. 1856 by Bp of Ex. Pr. 1857 by Bp of B. and W. C. of St. Luke's, Heywood, 1867. Formerly C. of St. Ewe, Cornwall, 1856, Bodmin 1857, Bishop's Hatfield 1860. [23]

WEBB, Richard James, *Friskney, near Boston, Lincolnshire.*—Lin. Coll. Ox. B.A. 1853; Deac. 1854 by Bp of Down and Connor, Pr. 1855 by Bp of Nor. C. of Friskney. Formerly Asst. C. of South Ormsby. [24]

WEBB, Robert Bennett, *East Challow, Wantage, Berks.*—Pemb. Coll. Ox. Hon. 4th cl. Lit. Hum. Hon. 4th cl. Law and Mod. Hist. 1865; Deac. 1865 and Pr. 1866 by Bp of Ox. C. of E. and W. Challow 1865. [25]

WEBB, Robert Chapman, *Billericay, Essex.*—Emman. Coll. Cam. Jun. Opt. and B.A. 1854, M.A. 1857; Deac. 1854 and Pr. 1855 by Bp of Roch. P. C. of Billericay, Dio. Roch. 1865. (Patron, Bp of Roch; P. C.'s Inc. 220*l*; Pop. 1390.) Chap. to the Billericay Union. (Stipend, 50*l*.) Surrogate. Formerly C. of Braintree 1854, Little Waltham 1857, Great Bardfield 1862. [26]

WEBB, Robert Holden, *Essendon, near Hertford.*—Ch. Coll. Cam. B.A. 1828, M.A. 1831; Deac. 1829, Pr. 1830. R. of Essendon with Bayford C. Dio. Roch. 1843. (Patron, Marquis of Salisbury; Essendon, Tithe, 368*l* 10*s*; Glebe, 45 acres; Bayford, Tithe, 282*l*; R.'s Inc. 650*l* and Ho; Pop. Essendon 672, Bayford 297.) Author, *Flora Hertfordiensis*, 12*s* 6*d*. [27]

WEBB, Samuel George Mower, 36, *Broughton-street, Salford.*—St. Cath. Coll. Cam. B.A. 1866; Deac.

1866 by Bp of Man. C. of St. Stephen's, Salford, 1866. [1]

WEBB, Thomas William, *Hardwick, Hay, South Wales.*—Magd. Hall, Ox. 2nd cl. Math. et Phy. and B.A. 1829, M.A. 1832; Deac. 1830 and Pr. 1831 by Bp of Herf. P. C. of Hardwick, Dio. Herf. 1856. (Patron, Mrs. N. Penoyre; P. C.'s Inc. 150*l*; Pop. 424.) Fell. of the Royal Astronomical Soc. Formerly Precentor of Glouc. Cathl; C. of St. Weonard's, Gangrew; V. of Tretire with Michaelchurch. Author, *Celestial Objects for Common Telescopes*, 1859–67, Longmans, 7*s*. [2]

WEBB, William, *Ryton Rectory, Newcastle-on-Tyne.*—Trin. Coll. Cam. B.A. 1826, M.A. 1829; Deac. 1828 and Pr. 1829 by Bp of Dur. R. of Ryton, Dio. Dur. 1862. (Patron, Bp of Dur; Tithe, 770*l*; Glebe, 163 acres; R.'s Inc. 1030*l* and Ho; Pop. 2510.) Formerly R. of Winston 1848. Author, *Sermon* (on the Death of the Rev. R. Gray, Rector of Sunderland), 1838; *Farewell Sermon* (on Removing from the Rectory of Sunderland), 1848. [3]

WEBB, William, *Tixall Rectory, Stafford.*—Trin. Coll. Cam. B.A. 1828, M.A. 1834; Deac. 1829, Pr. 1830. R. of Tixall, Dio. Lich. 1831. (Patron, Earl of Shrewsbury; Tithe, 190*l*; Glebe, 40 acres; R.'s Inc. 240*l* and Ho; Pop. 289.) [4]

WEBB, William James, *Wigan.*—Trin. Coll. Cam. B.A. 1866; Deac. 1867 by Bp of Ches. C. of Wigan 1867. [5]

WEBBER, Edward Alexander, *Bathealton Rectory, Wellington, Somerset.*—St. John's Coll. Cam. B.A. 1828. R. of Runnington, near Wellington, Dio. B. and W. 1836. (Patron, the present R; Tithe, 89*l*; Glebe, 16 acres; R.'s Inc. 115*l* and Ho; Pop. 100.) R. of Bathealton, Dio. B. and W. 1842. (Patron, the present R; Tithe, 195*l*; Glebe, 46 acres; R.'s Inc. 295*l* and Ho; Pop. 136.) [6]

WEBBER, Frederic, *St. Michael Penkevill, Probus, Cornwall.*—Pemb. Coll. Ox. B.A. 1825, M.A. 1865; Deac. and Pr. 1825 by Bp of Ex. R. of St. Michael Penkevill, Dio. Ex. 1842. (Patron, Viscount Falmouth; Tithe, 125*l*; Glebe, 55*l*; R.'s Inc. 180*l* and Ho; Pop. 190.) Formerly Chap. to H.E.I.C. Bombay, 1827–32; P. C. of Merther, Cornwall, 1834–53; Dom. Chap. to the Earl of Falmouth. [7]

WEBBER, William Charles Fynes, 11, *Charterhouse-square, London, E.C.*—Ch. Ch. Ox. B.A. 1837, M.A. 1839; Deac. 1839 and Pr. 1840 by Bp of Ox. Min. Can. of St. Paul's, 1850. (Value 250*l*.) Succentor and Sub-Dean 1859; R. of St. Botolph's, Aldersgate, Dio. Lon. 1845. (Patrons, D. and C. of Westminster; R.'s Inc. 380*l*; Pop. 6190.) [8]

WEBBER, William Thomas Thornhill, 5, *Red Lion-square, London, W.C.*—Pemb. Coll. Ox. B.A. 1859, M.A. 1862; Deac. 1860 and Pr. 1861 by Bp of Lon. C. in sole charge of the Miss. Dist. of St. John, Holborn, 1865. Formerly C. of Chiswick 1860. [9]

WEBSTER, Alexander Rhind, *Chatham.*—St. Mary Hall, Ox. 2nd cl. Lit. Hum. B.A. 1841, M.A. 1844; Deac. 1841 and Pr. 1843 by Bp of Pet. R. of St. Mary's, Chatham, Dio. Roch. 1865. (Patrons, D. and C. of Roch; Tithe, 290*l*; Glebe, 1½ acres; R.'s Inc. 500*l*; Pop. 7000.) Dioc. Inspector of Schools 1864. Formerly C. of South Luffenham, Rutland, 1841; Chap. to Duke of Newcastle and P. C. of Bothamsall, Notts, 1843; P. C. of Bradninch, Devon, 1846; Rural Dean 1849; C. of Crosthwaite, Cumb. 1855. Author of the following works in Arnold's School Series: *Homer's Iliad*, 3rd ed. 1865, 12*s*; *Homer for Beginners*, 3rd ed. 1864, 3*s* 6*d*; *Euripides—Hippolytus and Medea*, 1853, 3*s*; *Virgil's Æneid*, 1852, 6*s*; *Selections from Cicero's Orations*, Part I. 2nd ed. 4*s*; published by Rivingtons. [10]

WEBSTER, E. M., *Loughton, Essex.*—C. of Loughton. [11]

WEBSTER, George Edis, *Grundisburgh, Woodbridge, Suffolk.*—Trin. Coll. Cam. Wrang. and B.A. 1808; Deac. 1811, Pr. 1812. R. of Grundisburgh, Dio. Nor. 1832. (Patron, Trin. Coll. Cam; Tithe, 527*l* 13*s* 4*d*; Glebe, 47 acres; R.'s Inc. 554*l* and Ho; Pop. 836.) Formerly Fell. of Trin. Coll. Cam. [12]

WEBSTER, John, *King's Heath, near Birmingham.*—Queens' Coll. Cam. B.A. 1850, M.A. 1854; Deac. 1850 and Pr. 1851 by Bp of Ches. V. of King's Heath, Dio. Wor. 1866. (Patron, P. C. of Moseley; Tithe, 6*l*, Glebe, 14 acres; V.'s Inc. 230*l*; Pop. 1500.) Formerly C. of Bruera, near Chester. [13]

WEBSTER, John, 37, *Loraine road, Holloway, London, N.*—Caius Coll. Cam. Lyon Exhib. B.A. 1859, M.A. 1866. P. C. of St. Barnabas', Islington, Dio. Lon. 1863. (P. C.'s Inc. 400*l*; Pop. 9000.) Formerly C. of St. Jude's, Mildmay-park, 1860–61, Chapel of Ease, Islington, 1861–63. [14]

WEBSTER, John, *Charnock-Richard, near Chorley, Lancashire.*—St. John's Coll. Cam. B.A. 1857, M.A. 1860; Deac. 1857 and Pr. 1858 by Bp of Ches. P. C. of Charnock-Richard, Dio. Man. 1860. (Patron, James Darlington, Esq; P. C.'s Inc. 140*l* and Ho; Pop. 1047.) Formerly C. of Alderley Edge 1857–58; P. C. of Widnes Dock 1858–59. [15]

WEBSTER, Montagu, *St. James's Parsonage, Hill, Sutton Coldfield.*—Lin. Coll. Ox. 2nd cl. Lit. Hum. and B.A. 1841, M.A. 1844; Deac. 1844 and Pr. 1846 by Bp of Lich. P. C. of St. James's, Hill, Sutton Coldfield, Dio. Wor. 1860. (Patron, R. of Sutton Coldfield; P. C.'s Inc. 150*l* and Ho; Pop. 1246.) Formerly C. of Seale, Leicestershire. [16]

WEBSTER, Rowland, *Kelloe, Ferry Hill, Durham.*—Lin. Coll. Ox. 1st cl. Math. et Phy. and B.A. 1826, M.A. 1833; Deac. 1828 and Pr. 1829 by Bp of Dur. V. of Kelloe, Dio. Dur. 1851. (Patron, Bp of Dur; Tithe—Imp. 172*l* 16*s* 6*d* and 230 acres of Glebe, V. 11*l*; V.'s Inc. 240*l* and Ho; Pop. 7418.) Hon. Can. of Dur. Cathl. 1851; Surrogate; Rural Dean 1858. [17]

WEBSTER, Samuel King, *Ingham Vicarage, near Lincoln.*—Emman. Coll. Cam. Prizeman, Jun. Opt. and B.A. 1842; Deac. 1842 and Pr. 1843 by Bp of Pet. V. of Ingham, Dio. Lin. 1852. (Patron, Col. Nevile; Glebe, 50 acres; V.'s Inc. 90*l* and Ho; Pop. 646.) Author, various Tracts. [18]

WEBSTER, Thomas Calthorp, *River Cottage, Hornsey, London, N.*—Trin. Coll. Cam. B.A. 1863, M.A. 1867; Deac. 1863 by Bp of Man. and Pr. 1865 by Bp of Ches. C. of Hornsey 1866. Formerly C. of St. Anne's, Lancaster, 1863, St. Michael's, Liverpool, 1864. [19]

WEBSTER, William, *Colne Engaine, Essex.*—Trin. Coll. Cam. Wrang and B.A. 1827, M.A. 1831; Deac. 1829, Pr. 1830. R. of Colne Engaine, Dio. Roch. 1865. (Patron, Christ's Hospital; R.'s Inc. 680*l* and Ho; Pop. 627.) Formerly 2nd Math. Mast. of Christ's Hospital, Lond. 1827–34; Head Math. Mast of Christ's Hospital, 1834; Reader at St. James's, Garlick Hythe; Sunday Even. Lect. of St. Mary-le-Bow, Cheapside, 1847. [20]

WEBSTER, William, 3, *Park-villas West, Richmond, Surrey, S.W.*—Queens' Coll. Cam. B.A. 1834, M.A. 1857; Deac. 1835, Pr. 1836. Min. of Twickenham Episcopal Chapel, Dio. Lon. 1854. (Patron, the present Min.) Formerly Fell. of Queens' Coll. Cam; C. and Lect. of St. Olave's, Jewry, Lond. 1838–50. Author, *An Evangelical Ministry the Strength of the Nation*, Seeleys, 2*s* 6*d*; *The Scriptural Obligation of Life Assurance*, ib. 1*s*; *The Sabbath was made for Man*, Wertheim, 4*d*; *Greek Testament, with Notes*, vol. I. 20*s*; vol. II. 24*s*. Longmans; *The Syntax and Synonyms of the Greek Testament*, 1864. 9*s*, Rivingtons. [21]

WEDDALL, William Charles, 35, *Great Smith-street, Westminster, S.W.*—St. John's Coll. Ox. B.A. 1866; Deac. 1866 by Bp of Lon. C. of St. Matthew's, Westminster. [22]

WEDGE, Charles, *Burrough-green, Newmarket, Cambs.*—Caius Coll. Cam. Sen. Opt. and B.A. 1804, M.A. 1807; Deac. and Pr. 1805. R. of Burrough-green, Dio. Ely, 1805. (Patron, Charles Porcher, Esq; Tithe, 437*l*; Glebe, 73 acres; R.'s Inc. 502*l* and Ho; Pop. 427.) [23]

WEDGWOOD, Robert, *Dumbleton Rectory (Glouc.), near Evesham.*—Trin. Coll. Cam. B.A. 1826, M.A. 1826; Deac. 1828, Pr. 1829. R. of Dumbleton,

Dio. G. and B. 1850. (Patron, E. Holland, Esq; Tithe, 43*l* 16*s*; Glebe, 70 acres; R.'s Inc. 345*l* and Ho; Pop. 465.) [1]

WEEKES, Robert, *Coblentz.*—Deac. 1853 by Bp of Ox. Pr. 1854 by Bp of Win. British Chap. at Coblentz. [2]

WEEKS, Sharp, *Oldham.*—St. Bees, Librarian and 1st cl. Prizeman; Deac. 1852 and Pr. 1853 by Bp of Dur. C. of St. James's, Oldham. [3]

WEGG, Robert, *Dickleburgh, Scole, Norfolk.*—St. John's Coll. Cam. Prizeman, B.A. 1831, M.A. 1836; Deac. 1833, Pr. 1834. R. of Frenze, Norfolk, Dio. Nor. 1840. (Patron, S. Smith, Esq; Tithe, 105*l*; Glebe, 3 acres; R.'s Inc. 116*l*; Pop. 49.) Chap. to the Depwade Union 1836. [4]

WEGG, William, *Lymington, Hants.*—King's Coll. Lond. Theol. Assoc; Deac. 1853 and Pr. 1854 by Bp of Herf. Asst. C. of Lymington 1864. Formerly C. of Mordiford 1853–55, Abergavenny 1855–64. [5]

WEIDEMANN, Charles Frederick Stroehlin, *Hamburg.*—Ch. Ch. Ox. B.A. 1840, M.A. 1845; Deac. 1841, Pr. 1842. Chap. to the British Residents at Hamburg 1852. [6]

WEIGALL, Edward Mitford, *Frodingham Vicarage, Brigg, Lincolnshire.*—Pemb. Coll. Ox. Scho. of, B A. 1856, M.A. 1859; Deac. 1857 by Bp of Ox. Pr. 1858 by Bp of G. and B. V. of Frodingham, Dio. Lin. 1859. (Patron, C. Winn, Esq; Tithe, comm. 100*l*; Glebe, 105 acres; V.'s Inc. 270*l*; Pop. 1200.) Formerly C. of Oddington, Glouc. 1857–59. [7]

WEIGHT, Edward, *Calder Vale, Church Town, Garstang.*—Deac. 1851 and Pr. 1852 by Bp of Rip. P. C. of Calder Vale, Church Town, Dio. Man. 1864. (Patrons, V. of Church Town, and J. W. Garnett, Esq. alt; Glebe, 2 acres; P. C.'s Inc. 108*l*; Pop. 1000.) Formerly C. of Heptonstall 1851–58, Cam 1859–61, Ch. Ch. Leeds, 1862–64. [8]

WEIGHTMAN, Richard Turner, *Arlesey, Beds.*—Lin. Coll. Ox. B.A. 1862; Deac. 1866, Pr. 1867. C. of Arlesey 1866. [9]

WEIR, Archibald, *Forty Hill Parsonage, Enfield, Middlesex, N.*—Trin. Coll. Ox. 1st cl. Law and Mod. Hist. 1857, B.A. 1857, M.A. and B. C. L. 1860, D.C.L. 1864; Deac. 1857 and Pr. 1858 by Bp of Lon. P. C. of Jesus Church, Enfield, Dio. Lon. 1863. (Patron, V. of Enfield; Glebe, 6 acres; P. C.'s Inc. 98*l* and Ho; Pop. 1200.) Formerly C. of St. Andrew's Enfield. Author, *Revivalism* (a Pamphlet), 1860; *Revelation and Belief, a Word of Counsel to the Laity in the present Theological Crisis*, 1861; *Righteousness exalteth a Nation, a Sermon on the Death of the Prince Consort*, 1861; *St. Petersburg and Moscow*, in *Vacation Tourists for* 1861; Various Reviews and Articles. [10]

WEIR, John, *Little Horkesley, Essex.*—P. C. of Little Horkesley, Dio. Roch. 1863. (Patron, Thomas Bourdillon, Esq; P. C.'s Inc. 80*l*; Pop. 250.) Formerly C. of Great Horkesley. [11]

WEIR, John Maxwell, *Pilham Rectory, Gainsborough.*—R. of Pilham, Dio. Lin. 1862. (Patron, Ld Chan; R.'s Inc. 230*l* and Ho; Pop. 59.) [12]

WELBURN, Dale John, *Wing, Leighton Buzzard.*—C. of Wing and of Grove, Bucks. [13]

WELBURN, Frederick William, *Osmington, Weymouth, Dorset.*—Jesus Coll. Cam; Deac. 1867 by Bp of Salis. C. of Osmington. [14]

WELBURN, John Edward Brown, *Farnworth, Bolton-le-Moors.*—Cath. Hall Cam. B.A. 1858; Deac. 1859 and Pr. 1860 by Bp of Ox. C. in sole charge of St. Stephen's District, Kearsley Moor, Farnworth. Formerly C. of Ducklington and Alvescott, Oxon, 1859–61. [15]

WELBY, Abraham Adlard, *Crondall, Farnham.*—Magd. Hall, Ox. B.A. 1861, M.A. 1862; Deac. 1861 and Pr. 1862 by Bp. of Ex. C. of Crondall 1867. Formerly C. of St. Blazey, Cornwall, 1861, St. Paul's, Devonport, 1863, Compton, Plymouth 1865. [16]

WELBY, Arthur Earle, *Trinity, Hulme, Manchester.*—Dur. B.A. 1846; Deac. 1847, Pr. 1848. R. of Trinity, Hulme, Dio. Man. 1858. (Patrons, D. and C. of Man; Glebe, 61 acres; R.'s Inc. 350*l* and Ho; Pop. 5667.) Chap. to the Bp of St. Helena. Formerly R. of Newton, Linc. 1848–58. [17]

WELBY, George Earle, *Barrowby Rectory, Grantham, Lincolnshire.*—Trin. Coll. Cam. B.A. 1842; Deac. 1844 and Pr. 1845 by Bp of Pet. R. of Barrowby, Dio. Lin. 1849. (Patron, Duke of Devonshire; Tithe, 590*l*; Glebe, 420 acres; R.'s Inc. 1256*l* and Ho; Pop. 862.) [18]

WELBY, John Earle, *Magdalen College, Oxford.*—Fell. of Magd. Coll. [19]

WELBY, Montague Earle, *Allington House, Grantham, Lincolnshire.*—Emman. Coll. Cam. B.A. 1801, M.A. 1804; Deac. 1802, Pr. 1803. [20]

WELBY, Montague Earle, *Oystermouth, near Swansea.*—Magd. Coll. Ox. B.A. 1850; Deac. 1851 by Bp of Ox. Pr. 1851 by Bp of St. D. P. C. of Oystermouth, Dio. St. D. 1865. (Patroness, Mrs. Perrott; P. C.'s Inc. 80*l*; Pop. 3000.) Formerly P. C. of St. Paul's, Sketty, 1851–65. [21]

WELBY, Philip James Earle, *Grantham, Lincolnshire.*—C. of Grantham. [22]

WELBY, Walter Hugh Earle, *Harston Rectory, near Grantham.*—Corpus Coll. Ox. B.A. 1855, M.A. 1859; Deac. 1856 and Pr. 1857 by Bp of Lin. R. of Harston, Dio. Pet. 1867. (Patron, Ld Chan; Tithe, 241*l*; Glebe, 43½ acres; R.'s Inc. 302*l* and Ho; Pop. 164.) Formerly C. of Stroxton, Linc. 1856–60; R. of Strensham, Worc. 1860–62; R. of Bearwood, Berks, 1862–67. [23]

WELBY, William Wyan, *Bolton-on-Dearne, Rotherham.*—St. Bees; Deac. 1851 and Pr. 1852 by Bp of Rip. V. of Bolton-on-Dearne, Dio. York, 1860. (Patroness, Mrs Hirst; V.'s Inc. 125*l*; Pop. 479.) Formerly C. of Epwell, Oxon, and Newchurch-in-Pendle. [24]

WELCH, Andrew, *St. Mary Cray, Kent.*—King's Coll. Lond; Deac. 1853 and Pr. 1854 by Abp of Cant. C. of St. Mary Cray 1857. Formerly C. of St. Peter's, Maidstone. [25]

WELCH, Henry Forster, *Clive Parsonage, Shrewsbury.*—St. Bees; Deac. 1853 and Pr. 1854 by Bp of Lich. P. C. of Clive, Dio. Lich. 1863. (Patrons, Trustees; P. C.'s Inc. 111*l* and Ho; Pop. 302.) Formerly C. of Bourton, Salop, and Langley, Essex. [26]

WELCH, Thomas Coleman, *Pattishall, Towcester, Northants.*—Lin. Coll. Ox. B.A. 1819. V. of the 2nd Portion of Pattishall, Dio. Pet. (Patron, the present V; V.'s Inc. 300*l*; Pop. 885.) [27]

WELCH, Timothy, *Rolleston-park, Tutbury, Burton on Trent.*—St. Bees; Deac. 1848 and Pr. 1849 by Bp of Lich. P. C. of Anslow, Dio. Lich. 1860. (Patron, Sir Oswald Mosley, Bart; P. C.'s Inc. 146*l*; Pop. 521.) Formerly C. of Repton, Derbyshire, 1848–57, Eggington 1857, Anslow 1857–60. [28]

WELCH, William Frederick, *Stradsett Vicarage, Downham Market, Norfolk.*—Corpus Coll. Cam. Sen. Opt. and B.A. 1847, M.A. 1851; Deac. 1848 and Pr. 1849 by Bp of Nor. V. of Stradsett, Dio. Nor. 1858. (Patron, Sir W. Bagge, Bart; Tithe, 110*l*; Glebe, 2 acres; V.'s Inc. 116*l* and Ho; Pop. 180.) Formerly C. of Hertingfordbury, Herts, and Downham Market, Norfolk. Author, *Use and Authority of Holy Scripture, a Visitation Sermon*, 1861. [29]

WELCH, William John Joseph, *Stourbridge, Worcestershire.*—St. Cath. Coll. Cam. Scho. Prizeman, Librarian, Sen. Opt. and B.A. 1854, M.A. 1857; Deac. 1854 and Pr. 1855 by Bp of Wor. Head Mast. of King Edward VI.'s Free Gr. Sch. Stourbridge, 1858. Formerly C. of Buckland and Stoke Mandeville 1855. [30]

WELD, Joseph, *Tenterden, Kent.*—St. Edm. Hall, Ox. B.A. 1819, M.A. 1831; Deac. and Pr. 1820. Chap. of the Tenterden Union 1837. Author, *A Sermon on the Opening of the Union House at Tenterden.* [31]

WELDON, George Warburton, *Parsonage of St. Andrew the Less, Cambridge.*—Trin. Coll. Cam. B.A. 1850, M.A. 1864; Deac. 1850, Pr. 1851 by Bp of Tuam. P. C. of St. Andrew's the Less, Cambridge, Dio. Ely, 1862. (Patrons, Trustees; P. C.'s Inc. 300*l* and Ho; Pop. 10,000.) Formerly Chap. to the South-West Protestant

Institute, Brompton; C. of St. Stephen the Martyr's, Portland-town, Lond. Author, *Hasael, or the Treachery of the Human Heart* (Prize Essay), 1850; *Sympathy, or a Plea for Ragged Boys*, 1855; *What is Truth* (a Sermon)? 1856; *Thoughts on our Nationa lPrivileges* (a Sermon), 1858; *Balaam, a Lenten Sermon*, 1863; *The Source of England's Greatness, an Address*, 1864; *Address to the Undergraduates of the University of Cambridge*, 1865; *Weekly Collections, or the Offertory Question fairly discussed*, 1864. [1]

WELLDON, Edward Ind, *Tunbridge, Kent.*—Queens' Coll. Cam. B.A. 1844, M.A. 1847; Deac. 1847 and Pr. 1849 by Abp of Cant. 2nd Mast. of Tunbridge School. [2]

WELLDON, James Ind, *Schoo House, Tunbridge.*—St. John's Coll. Cam. 30th Wrang. 5th in 1st cl. Cl. Trip. and B.A. 1834, M.A. 1837, D.C.L. 1845; Deac. 1836 by Bp of Ely, Pr. 1838 by Bp of Lich. Head Mast. of the Tunbridge Gr. Sch. Formerly Fell. of St. John's Coll. Cam. [3]

WELLESLEY, The Hon. and Very Rev. Gerald Valerian, *The Deanery, Cloisters, Windsor Castle.*—Trin. Coll. Cam. M.A. 1830 :Deac. 1830, Pr. 1831. Dean of Windsor 1854. (Value, 2500*l* and Res.) Registrar of the Most Noble Order of the Garter 1854; Chap. of the Chapel Royal, Hampton Court ;Dom. Chap. to Her Majesty. [4]

WELLINGS, E. P., *Ludlow, Salop.*—Second Mast. of Gr. Sch. Ludlow. [5]

WELLINGTON, William, *Upton-Helions Rectory, Crediton, Devon.*—Pemb. Coll. Ox. B.A. 1828. R. of Upton Helions, Dio. Ex. 1831. (Patron, Rev. Samuel Johnson; Tithe, 170*l*; Glebe, 36 acres; R.'s Inc. 240*l* and Ho; Pop. 111.) [6]

WELLS, E., *March, Cambs.*—C. of March; Surrogate. [7]

WELLS, Edward Cornish, *St. Mary's-square, Bury St. Edmunds.*—St. Edm. Hall, Ox. B.A. 1823, M.A. 1826; Deac. 1823, Pr. 1824. Chap. to the County Gaol, Bury St. Edmunds, 1847; Surrogate. [8]

WELLS, Eudo Gresham, *Marlow, Bucks.*—Merton Coll. Ox. M.A. 1867; Deac. 1866 and Pr. 1867 by Bp of Ox. C. of Marlow 1866. [9]

WELLS, George, *Boxford Rectory, Newbury, Berks.*—Magd. Coll. Ox. B.A. 1825, M.A. 1828; Deac. 1826, Pr. 1827. R. of Boxford, Dio. Ox. 1842. (Patron, the present R; Tithe, 880*l*; Glebe, 10¼ acres; R.'s Inc. 900*l* and Ho; Pop. 636.) [10]

WELLS, George Ashton, *Winchester.*—Trin. Coll. Ox. B.A. 1860, M.A. 1863; Deac. 1861, Pr. 1865. C. of St. Maurice's, Win. 1865. Formerly C. of Alton 1861. [11]

WELLS, George Francis, *Woodchurch, Staplehurst, Kent.*—Ch. Ch. Ox. B.A. 1860; Deac. 1860 and Pr. 1861 by Bp of Salis. C. of Woodchurch 1866. Formerly C. of Chisledon, near Swindon, 1860–64, Welford, near Newbury, 1864–66. [12]

WELLS, Gifford, *Stoke, Guildford.*—Sid. Coll. Cam. 8th Sen. Opt. B.A. 1824, M.A. 1827; Deac. 1825 and Pr. 1827 by Bp of Salis. Formerly Head Mast. of Gr. Sch. and Min. of St. Thomas's, Stourbridge, 1833–58. [13]

WELLS, Harry Morland, *Hatfield, Herts,* and *New University Club.*—Emman. Coll. Cam. B.A. 1862; Deac. 1864 and Pr. 1865 by Bp of B. and W. C. of Hatfield 1867. Formerly C. of Alford and Hornblotton, Somerset, 1864–67. [14]

WELLS, Thomas Bury, *Portlemouth Rectory, Kingsbridge, Devon.*—Trin. Hall, Cam. B.A. 1830, M.A. 1833; Deac. 1833 and Pr. 1834 by Bp of Pet. R. of Portlemouth, Dio. Ex. 1839. (Patrons, Duke of Cleveland and Lord Sandwich, jointly ;Tithe, 347*l* Glebe, 32 acres; R.'s Inc. 392*l* and Ho; Pop. 403.) [15]

WELLS, William, *Carbrooke Vicarage, Watton, Norfolk.*—Corpus Coll. Cam. Wrang. 3rd cl. Cl. Trip. and B.A. 1826, M.A. 1829; Deac. 1830, Pr. 1831. V. of Carbrooke, Dio. Nor. 1845. (Patron, R. Dewing, Esq; Tithe—Imp. 517*l* 4*s*, V. 22*l* 4*s*; V.'s Inc. 190*l* and Ho; Pop. 751.) [16]

WELLSTED, Alfred Oliver, *Parsonage House, Charles-street, Hackney-road, London, N.E.*—Jesus Coll. Ox. St. Cath. Hall, Cam. M.A. 1839; Deac. and Pr. 1840 by Bp of Wor. P. C. of St. Thomas's, Bethnal Green, Dio. Lon. 1864. (Patron, Bp of Lon; P. C.'s Inc. 300*l* and Ho; Pop. 8315.) Formerly P. C. of St. Jude's, Bristol, 1850. Author, Sermons, in *The Pulpit.* [17]

WELSFORD, William Clarke, *Saltford Rectory, Bristol.*—Ex. Coll. Ox. M.A. 1847; Deac. 1846 and Pr. 1847 by Bp of Ex. R. of Saltford, Dio. B. and W. 1854. (Patroness, Mrs. Welsford; Tithe, comm. 194*l*; Glebe, 31*l*; R.'s Inc. 225*l* and Ho; Pop. 373.) [18]

WELSH, John William, *Flora Villa, Walton-on-the-Hill, Liverpool.*—Dub. and St. Aidan's; Deac. 1849 and Pr. 1850 by Bp of Ches. C. of St. Nicholas' and Chap. to the Cemetery, Liverpool, 1863. Formerly S.P.G. Chap. to Emigrants 1849–64. Author, various Papers in S.P.G. Annual Reports and Quarterly Papers 1849–64; Hymns for the use of Emigrants; etc. [19]

WELSH, Thomas C., *Slapton, Towcester, Northants.*—R. of Slapton, Dio. Pet. 1820. (Patron, the present R; R.'s Inc. 312*l*; Pop. 240.) [20]

WENHAM, John, *West Clandon Rectory, Guildford, Surrey.*—M.A. 1835; Deac. and Pr. 1823. R. of West Clandon, Dio. Win. 1852. (Patron, Earl of Onslow; Tithe, 160*l*; Glebe, 24 acres; R.'s Inc. 195*l* and Ho; Pop. 329.) P. C. of St. Martha-on-the-Hill, Chilworth, Dio. Win. 1856. (Patron, Earl Percy; P. C.'s Inc. 25*l*; Pop. 168.) Formerly R. of Brockville, Upper Canada, and Chap. to Bp of Quebec; 2nd Chap. in Ceylon; sometime Asst. Sec. to the S.P.G. Author, *Questions on the Collects; Family Prayers; Tract on Baptism; Prayers for the Army and Navy.* [21]

WENN, James B., *Broome Rectory, Bungay, Norfolk.*—R. of Broome, Dio. Nor. 1867. (Patron, Sir W. F. F. Middleton; R.'s Inc. 300*l* and Ho; Pop. 505.) Dom. Chap. to the Duke of Hamilton and Brandon. [22]

WENSLEY, E. B., *Gravesend.*—Deac. 1864 by Bp of Pet. Pr. 1865 by Bp of Roch. C. of Gravesend 1866. Formerly C. of Hoo-Allhallows, Rochester, 1864–66. [23]

WENT, William Pinder, *Redwick, New Passage, near Bristol.*—Christ's Coll. Cam. LL.B. 1863; Deac. 1864 and Pr. 1865 by Bp of G. and B. C. of Almondsbury 1867. Formerly C. of St. John's, Clifton, Bristol, 1864–66. [24]

WERE, Ellis Bowden, *Stamford-Barron (Northants), near Stamford.*—Queen's Coll. Ox. B.A. 1832, M.A. 1836. V. of Stamford-Barron, Dio. Pet. 1842. (Patron, Marquis of Exeter; V.'s Inc. 218*l*; Pop. 1606.) [25]

WERE, T. W., *Leicester.*—C. of All Saints', Leicester. [26]

WERGE, John Ingall, *Somershall-Herbert, Derbyshire.*—R. of Somershall-Herbert, Dio. Lich. 1864. (Patron, Colonel Fitz-Herbert; R.'s Inc. 250*l* and Ho; Pop. 120.) [27]

WESCOE, Henry, *Blackburn.*—Licen. Theol. Dur; Deac. 1854 and Pr. 1855 by Bp of Ches. P. C. of St. Thomas's, Blackburn. (Patron, V. of Blackburn; P. C.'s Inc. 350*l*; Pop. 7000.) Formerly C. of St. Paul's, Huddersfield, St. Thomas's, Wigan, and Blackburn. [28]

WEST, A. W.—Dom. Chap. to the Duke of Leinster. [29]

WEST, B. H., *Olney, Bucks.*—C. of Olney. [30]

WEST, Charles, *Northampton.*—Chap. of the Borough Gaol and Head Mast. of the Endowed Gr. Sch. Northampton. [31]

WEST, Charles Francis Luttrell, *Shenley Rectory, Stony Stratford, Bucks.*—Emman. Coll. Cam. B.A. 1851, M.A. 1854, Wrang; Deac. 1851 and Pr. 1852 by Bp o fPet. R. of Shenley, Dio. Ox. 1866. (Patron, M. Knapp, Esq ; R.'s Inc. 424*l*; Pop. 492.) Formerly C. of A ll Saints', Northampton, and All Saints', Stamford. [32]

WEST, Charles Frederick Cumber, *Vicarage, Leckford, near Winchester.*—St. John's Coll. Ox. Fell. of, 3rd cl. Lit. Hum. and B.A. 1857, M.A. 1861, B.D. 1866; Deac. 1859 and Pr. 1860 by Bp of Ox. V. of Leckford, Dio. Win. 1862. (Patron, Rev. J. S.

Pinkerton; Tithe, 142*l*; V.'s Inc. 142*l* and Ho; Pop. 279.) Formerly C. of Forest Gate, Essex, 1859-62. [1]

WEST, George, *Rothbury, Northumberland.*—Magd. Hall, Ox. B.A. 1853, M.A. 1855; Deac. 1854 and Pr. 1855 by Bp of Lich. C. of Rothbury 1863; Surrogate 1864. Formerly C. of Thaxted; Sen. C. of Wombourn and Trysull, Staffs, and Ryton, Durham. [2]

WEST, Henry, *North Frodingham, Driffield, Yorks.*—Corpus Coll. Cam. B.A. 1854; Deac. 1854 and Pr. 1855 by Bp of Rip. V. of North Frodingham, Yorks, Dio. York, 1856. (Patron, the present V; Glebe, 128 acres; V.'s Inc. 240*l* and Ho; Pop. 857.) Formerly C. of Trinity, Ripon. [3]

WEST, H., *Wraysbury, Bucks.*—C. of Wraysbury. [4]

WEST, James John, *Winchelsea Rectory, near Rye, Sussex.*—Jesus Coll. Cam. B.A. 1829, M.A. 1832; Deac. 1829, Pr. 1830. R. of Winchelsea, Dio. Chich. 1831. (Patron, Sir A. Ashburnham, Bart; Tithe, 235*l* 9*s* 3*d*; Glebe, 3 acres; R.'s Inc. 324*l* and Ho; Pop. 719.) Author, several Sermons in *The Penny Pulpit.* [5]

WEST, John, *Aisholt Rectory, Bridgwater, Somerset.*—Wor. Coll. Ox. B.A. 1826, M.A. 1829; Deac. 1827 and Pr. 1828 by Bp of Llan. R. of Aisholt or Asholt, Dio. B. and W. 1832. (Patron, the present R; Tithe, 210*l*; Glebe, 59 acres; R.'s Inc. 270*l* and Ho; Pop. 181.) [6]

WEST, John Otho, *Revelstoke Rectory, near Ivybridge, South Devon.*—St. John's Coll. Cam. B.A. 1859, M.A. 1862; Deac. 1859 and Pr. 1800 by Bp of Ex. R. of Revelstoke, Dio. Ex. 1866. (Patron, Bp of Ex; Tithe, comm. 245*l*; Glebe, 9½ acres; R.'s Inc. 245*l* and Ho; Pop. 500.) Formerly C. of St. Austell, Cornwall, and Bridport, Dorset. Author, *A Sermon, The Pleasantness of Christ's Religion,* Hatchard, 6*d.* [7]

WEST, John Rowland, *Wrawby Vicarage, Glandford, Brigg, Lincolnshire.*—Trin. Coll. Cam. Scho. of, B.A. 1832, M.A. 1835, Fell. of Clare Coll; Deac. 1834 and Pr. 1835 by Bp of Ely. V. of Wrawby, Dio. Lin. 1837. (Patron, Clare Coll. Cam; Glebe, 216 acres; V.'s Inc. 230*l* and Ho; Pop. 3000.) Formerly V. of Madingley 1835. Author, *Sermons on Chief Truths,* 6*s*; *Tracts on Church Principles,* 1*s* 6*d*; *Questions for Schools,* 1*d*; *Reasons for being a Churchman,* 4*d*; *Some Account of the Chief Service of the Christian Religion,* 6*d.* Masters; *Wrested Texts,* Parts I. and II. 4*d*; *Catechism on the Church,* 9*d*; *Village Dialogues,* Church Press Co. 1*d.* [8]

WEST, John Thomas Eliot, *Stoak Parsonage, near Chester.*—Ch. Coll. Cam. B.A. 1829. P. C. of Stoak, Dio. Ches. 1833. (Patron, Sir H. E. Bunbury, Bart; P. C.'s Inc. 154*l* and Ho; Pop. 431.) [9]

WEST, Joseph, *Magdalen College, Oxford.*—New Coll. Ox. B.A. 1823, M.A. 1826. Chap. of Magd. Coll. Ox; P. C. of Trinity, St. Ebbe's, City and Dio. Ox. (Patrons, the Crown and Bp of Ox. alt; P. C.'s Inc. 150*l*; Pop. 2609.) [10]

WEST, Joseph Ore Masefield, *Wherwell, Hants.*—Deac. 1855 by Bp of B. and W. Pr. 1858 by Bp of Salis. C. of Wherwell. Formerly C. of St. Paul's, Devonport, and Alderbury with Ditton and Farley. [11]

WEST, J. M., *Peterborough.*—C. of St. Mark's, Peterborough. [12]

WEST, Peter Cornelius, *Tockenham, Wootton Bassett, Wilts.*—Deac. 1852 by Bp of Wor. Pr. 1852 by Bp of Salis. C. of Berwick Bassett, near Swindon, 1866. Formerly Min. among the Moravians; C. of Kington St. Michael, and Tockenham, Wilts. [13]

WEST, Richard Temple, 30, *Delamere-terrace, Paddington, London, W.*—Ch. Ch. Ox. Stud. of, B.A. 1849, M.A. 1852; Deac. 1853 and Pr. 1854 by Bp of Ox. P. C. of St. Mary Magdalen's, Paddington, Dio. Lon. 1865. (Patrons, Trustees; P. C.'s Inc. 153*l*; Pop. 5500.) Formerly P. C. of St. Peter's, Leeds, 1853, St. Mary's House, Hampstead, 1854, All Saints', Boyne Hill, 1858, All Saints', Margaret-street, Lond. 1860. [14]

WEST, Temple Walter, *Tetcott Rectory, Holsworthy, Devon.*—Magd. Hall, Ox. S.C.L. 1837, M.A. 1841; Deac. 1840 and Pr. 1841 by Bp of B. and W. R. of Tetcott, Dio. Ex. 1854. (Patrons, Trustees of Sir W. Molesworth; Tithe, 145*l*; Glebe, 64 acres; R.'s Inc. 195*l* and Ho; Pop. 260.) P. C. of Clawton, Dio. Ex. 1862. (Patron, W. W. Melhuish, Esq; P. C.'s Inc. 76*l*; Pop. 459.) Formerly C. of West Monkton, Somerset, 1840, Orchard Portman 1842, St. Mary Magdalen's, Taunton, 1850; R. of Beaworthy, Devon, 1852. [15]

WEST, Thomas, *Fownhope Vicarage, Hereford.*—St. Edm. Hall, Ox. B.A. 1849. M.A. 1853; Deac. 1849 and Pr. 1850 by Bp of Win. V. of Fownhope with Fawley Chapelry, Dio. Herf. 1865. (Patrons, D. and C. of Herf; Tithe, 347*l*; Glebe, 11 acres; V.'s Inc. 360*l* and Ho; Pop. 1300.) Surrogate. Formerly C. of Whitechurch and Laverstoke, Hants, 1849, Christchurch, Bristol, 1851; Sen. C. of Ross and Chap. to the Ross Union 1854. [16]

WEST, Thomas John, *Lewisham, Kent.*—C. of St. Stephen's, Lewisham. [17]

WEST, Washbourne, *Lincoln College, Oxford.*—Lin. Coll. Ox. 3rd cl. Lit. Hum. and B.A. 1834, M.A. 1838; Deac. and Pr. by Bp of Ox. Fell. and Bursar of Lin. Coll. Formerly P. C. of All Saints', Oxford. [18]

WEST, William, 5, *Watt's-terrace, Chatham, Kent.*—King's Coll. Lond. Theol. Assoc. 1865; Deac. 1865 and Pr. 1866 by Bp of Roch. Formerly Asst. C. of Strood 1865; C. of St. John's, Chatham, 1866. [19]

WEST, William De Lancy, *Brentwood, Essex.*—St. John's Coll. Ox. 1st cl. Math. et Phy. 2nd cl. Lit. Hum. and B.A. 1845, M.A. 1848, B.D. and D.D. 1865; Deac. 1845 and Pr. 1847 by Bp of Herf. Head Mast. of the Brentwood Gr. Sch. 1851. Formerly Head Mast. of Hackney Ch. of England Sch. 1847; Dioc. Sch. Inspector (Rochester), 1861. Author, *Liturgical Services for Schools,* 3rd ed. Rivingtons, 1866, 1*s* 6*d.* [20]

WEST, William Henry.—Wor. Coll. Ox. B.A. 1824. Formerly C. of Westbury, Wilts, and Stogursey, Somerset, 1859; R. of Cheddington, Dorset, 1864–67. [21]

WESTALL, William, *Eltham, Kent.*—Queens' Coll. Cam. B.A. 1847, M A. 1850; Deac. 1848, Pr. 1849. C. of Eltham; Chap. to the Earl of Fife. Formerly C. of St. Paul's, Knightsbridge, and Head Mast. of St. Paul's Gr. Sch. Knightsbridge, 1855–59; C. of St. James the Apostle's, Halstead, 1859. [22]

WESTBROOK, Benjamin.—St. Bees 1854. Min. of St. Mary's, Park-street, Lond. Formerly C. of Sunk Island, near Hull, and Chap. to the Patrington Union, Yorks; P. C. of Skeffling 1853; C. of St. Luke's, Marylebone. [23]

WESTBROOK, Francis S., *Huntingdon.*—Wor. Coll. Ox. B.A. 1859; Deac. 1859 by Abp of Cant. Pr. 1861 by Bp of Dur. C. of All Saints' with St John's, Huntingdon, 1865. Formerly 2nd Mast. of the Gr. Sch. and C. of St. Mary's, Huntingdon; 2nd Mast. of the Gr. Sch. St. Albans; C. of St. Oswald and St. Mary's, Bingfield, Northumberland, and St. Andrew's, Bishop Wearmouth. Sunderland. [24]

WESTBURY, Joseph, *Hartshill Parsonage, Stoke-on-Trent.*—Deac. 1861 and Pr. 1862 by Bp of Lich. P. C. of Hartshill 1866. Formerly C. of Bushbury, Wolverhampton, 1861-65; C. in sole charge of Hartshill 1865–66. [25]

WESTCOTT, Brooke Foss, *Harrow, Middlesex, N.W.*—Trin. Coll. Cam. Battie's Univ. Scho. 1846, Browne's Medallist for Greek Ode 1846 and 1847, Latin Essay 1847 and 1849, 1st cl. Cl. Trip. and B A. 1848, M.A. 1851, B.D. 1864; Deac. and Pr. 1851 by Bp of Man. Asst. Mast. of Harrow Sch. Formerly Fell. of Trin. Coll. Cam. Author, *Elements of Gospel Harmony* (Norrisian Essay), 1851, 6*s* 6*d*; *History of the New Testament Canon,* 1855, 12*s* 6*d*; 2nd ed. 1867, 10*s* 6*d*; *Characteristics of the Gospel Miracles* (Sermons preached before the Univ. of Cam.) 1859, 4*s* 6*d*; *Introduction to the Study of the Gospels,* 1860, 10*s* 6*d*; 3rd ed. 1867; *The Bible in the Church,* 1864, 4*s* 6*d*; 2nd ed. 1866; *The Gospel of the Resurrection,* 1866, 4*s* 6*d*; 2nd ed. 1867. [26]

WESTERMAN, Edward, *Elton Parsonage, Bury, Lancashire.*—Queens' Coll. Cam. 17th Sen. Opt. and B.A. 1855; Deac. 1855 and Pr. 1856 by Bp of Man.

P. C. of Elton, Dio. Man. 1858. (Patron, R. of Bury; P. C.'s Inc. 300*l*; Pop. 7716.) Formerly C. of Bury. [1]

WESTHORP, John White, *Long Melford, Suffolk.*—Clare Hall, Cam. B.A. 1841, M.A. 1844. Formerly R. of Hargrave, Suffolk, 1851–58. [2]

WESTHORP, R. A., *Willingdale Doe, Chipping Ongar, Essex.*—C. of Willingdale Doe and Berners Roding. [3]

WESTHORP, Sterling Moseley, *Sibton Vicarage, Yoxford, Suffolk.*—Caius Coll. Cam. B.A. 1818; Deac. 1818 and Pr. 1819 by Bp of Nor. V. of Sibton with Peasenhall P. C. Dio. Nor. 1821. (Patron, J. W. Brooke, Esq; Sibton, Tithe—Imp. 316*l* 3*s* 7*d*, V. 132*l* 12*s* 6*d*; Glebe, 8¾ acres; Peasenhall, Tithe—Imp. 432*l* 11*s*, V. 129*l* 15*s*; V.'s Inc. 273*l* and Ho; Pop. Sibton 489, Peasenhall 875.) [4]

WESTMORE, Henry Holme, *Cheetham Hill-road, Manchester.*—Queens' Coll. Cam. B.A. 1848, M.A. 1852; Deac. 1848 and Pr. 1849 by Bp of Lon. Min. Can. of Man. Cathl. 1853. (Value, 200*l*.) [5]

WESTMORLAND, Thomas, *Brantingham Vicarage, Brough, Yorks.*—Sid. Coll. Cam. Scho. of, B.A. 1837, M.A. 1840; Deac. 1837, Pr. 1838. V. of Brantingham with Ellerker C. Dio. York, 1857. (Patrons, D. and C. of Dur; V.'s Inc. 300*l* and Ho; Pop. 572.) Formerly C. of Selby, Yorks, 1837–39; Chap. to the High Sheriff of Herefordshire 1854; V. of Leominster 1853–57. [6]

WESTOBY, Amos, *Farthingston, Weedon, Northants.*—St. Edm. Hall, Ox. B.A. 1814, M.A. 1817; Deac. 1813 and Pr. 1814 by Bp of Lin. R. of Farthingston, Dio. Pet. 1843. (Patron, Bp of Pet; Tithe, 14*l*; Glebe, 190 acres; R.'s Inc. 260*l* and Ho; Pop. 316.) Formerly Chap. to Earl of Glasgow. Author, *Daily Helps to Devotion,* 1828, 3*s*; *Helps to Repentance* (Six Lectures for Lent), 1834, 3*s*; *Life of the Rev. Thomas Adam, Rector of Winteringham, Lincolnshire*; *An Exposition of the Four Gospels, by Mr. Adam* (the Notes on St. Mark, Luke and John, not before published), 2 vols. 21*s*. [7]

WESTON, Frederick, *Eaton, Norwich.*—St. John's Coll. Cam. B.A. 1849, M.A. 1854; Deac. 1850 and Pr. 1851 by Bp of Salis. V. of Eaton, Dio. Nor. 1865. (Patrons, D. and C. of Nor; V.'s Inc. 87*l*; Pop. 930.) Formerly C. of Biddulph, Cheshire; P. C. of Charsfield, Suffolk, 1859–65. [8]

WESTON, George Frederick, *Crosby Ravensworth (Westmoreland), near Penrith.*—Ch. Coll. Cam. B.A. 1844, M.A. 1847; Deac. 1847, Pr. 1848. V. of Crosby Ravensworth, Dio. Carl. 1848. (Patroness, The Hon. Mary Greville Howard; Tithe—Imp. 97*l* 2*s* 3½*d*, V. 41*l* 5*s* 3½*d*; Glebe, 117 acres; V.'s Inc. 200*l*; Pop. 927.) [9]

WESTON, George Kirk, *Toller-Fratrum, Dorchester.*—Emman. Coll. Cam. Sen. Opt. and B.A. 1845, M.A. 1852; Deac. 1846, Pr. 1847. V. of Toller-Fratrum with Wynford-Eagle, C. Dio. Salis. 1854. (Patron, G. S. Kirk, Esq. Leamington; Toller-Fratrum, Tithe, 37*l*; Wynford-Eagle, Tithe—Imp. 6*l* 10*s*, V. 150*l*; V.'s Inc. 192*l*; Pop. Toller-Fratrum 45, Wynford-Eagle 187.) [10]

WESTON, R. C., *Bolton-le-Moors, Lancashire.*—P. C. of Emmanuel, Bolton-le-Moors, Dio. Man. 1865. (Patron, V. of Bolton; P. C.'s Inc. 300*l* and Ho; Pop. 9329.) Formerly P. C. of Thorpe Hesley, Rotherham, 1862. [11]

WESTON, Thomas Woods, *St. John's Parsonage, Tunbridge Wells, Kent.*—Deac. 1850, Pr. 1851. P. C. of St. John's, Tunbridge Wells, Dio. Cant. 1858. (Patrons, Trustees; P. C.'s Inc. uncertain and Ho; Pop. 1821.) Formerly P. C. of Preston-upon-Stour, Glouc. 1851–58; C. of St. John's, Tunbridge Wells, 1858. [12]

WESTROPP, Charles John, *Wormbridge, Herefordshire.*—Caius Coll. Cam. B.A. 1844; Deac. and Pr. 1844 by Bp of Wor. P. C. of Kenderchurch, Dio. Herf. 1865. (Patroness, Lady Langdale; P. C.'s Inc. 60*l*; Pop. 100.) Formerly P. C. of Ufton, Worc. [13]

WETHERALL, Augustus W., *Stonegrave Rectory, Oswaldkirk, Yorks.*—R. of Stonegrave, Dio. York, 1855. (Patron, the Crown; R.'s Inc. 530*l* and Ho; Pop. 290.) [14]

WETHERALL, C. A., *Toronto.*—Chap. to the Forces, Toronto. [15]

WETHERALL, John Edward, *Brereton Parsonage, Rugeley, Staffs.*—Lin. Coll. Ox. B.A. 1832, M.A. 1835; Deac. 1835, Pr. 1836. P. C. of Brereton, Dio. Lich. 1840. (Patron, V. of Rugeley; Glebe, 9 acres; P. C.'s Inc. 120*l* and Ho; Pop. 1359.) [16]

WETHERED, Florence James, *Hurley Vicarage, Marlow, Bucks.*—King's Coll. Cam. B.A. 1831, M.A. 1834; Deac. 1831 and Pr. 1832 by Bp of Ely. V. of Hurley, Dio. Ox. 1838. (Patron, the present V; Tithe, comm. 250*l*; Glebe, 1 acre; V.'s Inc. 263*l* and Ho; Pop. 609.) Surrogate. Formerly C. of Ibstone, Oxon, 1831 32, Hurley, Berks, 1832–38. [17]

WETHERED, Florence Thomas, *Hurley, Great Marlow, Bucks.*—Ch. Ch. Ox. B.A. 1861, M.A. 1865; Deac. 1863 and Pr. 1864 by Bp of Salis. C. of Hurley 1865. Formerly C. of Warminster 1863. [18]

WETHERELL, Charles, *Byfield Rectory, Daventry, Northants.*—St. Edm. Hall, Ox. B.A. 1811, M.A. 1814; Deac. 1811 and Pr. 1813 by Bp of Lin. R. of Byfield, Dio. Pet. 1819. (Patron, Corpus Coll. Ox; Glebe, 520 acres; R.'s Inc. 1053*l* and Ho; Pop. 901.) [19]

WETHERELL, F. W.—Chap. to the Earl of Mayo. [20]

WETHERELL, J. Cordeux, 14, *Bowyer-terrace, Clapham, Surrey.*—St. John's Coll. Cam. B.A. 1860, M.A. 1864; Deac. 1861 and Pr. 1862 by Bp of Ches. C. of St. John's, Clapham 1867. Formerly C. of Cheadle, Ches. 1861–62, Lymm, Ches. 1863, Camden Ch. Camberwell, 1863–67. Author, *Regeneration,* 1864, Freeman, 1*d*; *Ritualism,* Moorish, 6*d*. [21]

WETHERELL, Thomas May, *Flaxley, Newnham, Glouc.*—Dub. A.B. 1830, M.A. 1837; Deac. 1832, Pr. 1833. P. C. of Flaxley, Dio. G. and B. 1852. (Patron, Sir T. H. Crawley Boevey, Bart; P. C.'s Inc. 80*l*; Pop. 272.) [22]

WHALE, Thomas William, *The Proprietary College, Bath.*—St. John's Coll. Cam. 1849, 13th Wrang. and B.A. 1849, M.A. 1852; Deac. 1850, Pr. 1851. Prin. of Bath Proprietary Coll; R. of Dolton, Devon, Dio. Ex. 1863. (Patron, the present R; R.'s Inc. 450*l* and Ho; Pop. 938.) [23]

WHALEY, William, *West Witton, Bedale, Yorks.*—Ch. Coll. Cam. B.A. 1848; Deac. 1851 and Pr. 1852 by Bp of Rip. P. C. of West Witton, Dio. Rip. 1866. (Patron, Lord Bolton; Tithe, 15*l*; Glebe, 59 acres; P. C.'s Inc. 114*l*; Pop. 658.) Formerly C. of Bolton with Redmire 1851–55, Askham Bryan 1855–62; V. of Askham Bryan 1862–66. [24]

WHALL, William, *Thurning Rectory, Oundle, Northants.*—Emman. Coll. Cam. Wrang. and B.A. 1830, M.A. 1833; Deac. and Pr. 1833 by Bp of Lin. R. of Thurning, Dio. Ely, 1833. (Patron, Emman. Coll. Cam; Tithe, 180*l*; Glebe, 60½ acres; R.'s Inc. 225*l* and Ho; Pop. 214.) R. of Little Gidding, Hunts, Dio. Ely, 1834. (Patron, Ld Chan; Tithe, 135*l*; R.'s Inc. 140*l*; Pop. 45.) [25]

WHALLEY, Daniel Constable, *Great Wenham (Suffolk), near Colchester.*—Pemb. Coll. Cam. B.A. 1832; Deac. 1832, Pr. 1833. R. of Wenham Magna, *alias* Combusta, Dio. Nor. 1842. (Patron, Bp of Nor; Tithe, 273*l*; Glebe, 16½ acres; R.'s Inc. 250*l* and Ho; Pop. 260.) [26]

WHALLEY, David, *Nottingham.*—R. of St. Peter's, Nottingham, Dio. Lin. 1866. (Patron, Ld Chan; R.'s Inc. 200*l*; Pop. 4986.) Surrogate. Formerly P. C. of St. John's, Carrington, Nottingham, 1849–66. [27]

WHALLEY, James, 3, *Edward-terrace, Queen's-park, Manchester.*—St. Bees; Deac. 1859 and Pr. 1861 by Bp of Rip. C. of the Albert Memorial Church, Manchester, 1866. Formerly C. of St. Stephen's, Lindley, Huddersfield, 1859–61, St. Philip's, Manchester, 1861–64, St. Jude's, Manchester, 1864–66. [28]

WHALLEY, James Park, *Wretham Parsonage, Thetford, Norfolk.*—Univ. Coll. Ox. 4th cl. Lit. Hum.

and B.A. 1839; Deac. 1842, Pr. 1843. R. of East Wretham with West Wretham, Dio. Nor. 1850. (Patron, W. Birch, Esq; Tithe, 536*l*; Glebe, 12 acres and Ho; Pop. East Wretham 257, West Wretham 207.) Dioc. Inspector of Schs. [1]

WHALLEY, Richard Ambrose, *Terrington St. Clement, near King's Lynn.*—Magd. Coll. Cam. Scho. and Prizeman of, Jun. Opt. 1853; Deac. 1853 by Bp of Ely, Pr. 1854 by Bp of Nor. C. of Terrington St. Clement 1855. Formerly 2nd Mast. of King's Lynn Gr. Sch. 1853–55. [2]

WHALLEY, Thomas, *Liverpool.*—Dub. A.B. 1846; Deac. 1846 by Bp of G. and B. Pr. 1848 by Bp of Ches. P. C. of St. John's, Liverpool, Dio. Ches. 1861. (Patrons, Rev. H. M'Neile and others; P. C.'s Inc. 250*l*. Pop. 5561.) Formerly P. C. of Trinity, Guernsey, 1850–61. [3]

WHALLEY, William, 6, *Rivers-street, Bath.*—Ch. Ch. Ox. B.A. 1822, M.A. 1830; Deac. 1823 by Bp of Lon. Pr. 1824 by Bp of Ox. V. of Toddington with Stanley-Pontlarge P. C. Glouc. Dio. G. and B. 1843. (Patron, Lord Sudeley; Toddington, Tithe, 12*l* 13*s* 4*d*; V.'s Inc. 200*l* and Ho; Pop. Toddington 153, Stanley-Pontlarge 57.) V. of Didbrook with Pinnock R. and Hailes C. Glouc. Dio. G. and B. 1843. (Patron, C. H. Tracy, Esq; Didbrook, Tithe—Imp. 65*l*, V. 55*l*; Pinnock, Tithe, 150*l*; V.'s Inc. 270*l*; Pop. Didbrook 221, Pinnock and Hailes 102.) [4]

WHARTON, James Charles, *Gilling Vicarage, Richmond, Yorks.*—Ch. Coll. Cam. B.A. 1839, M.A. 1843. V. of Gilling, Dio. Rip. 1843. (Patron, J. T. Wharton, Esq; Tithe—Imp. 555*l* 5*s*; V.'s Inc. 1025*l* and Ho; Pop. 899.) [5]

WHARTON, John, *Stainmore, Brough, Westmoreland.*—P. C. of Stainmore, Dio. Carl. 1866. (Patron, Sir R. Tufton, Bart; P. C.'s Inc. 119*l*; Pop. 672.) Formerly C. of St. Jude's, Manningham, Bradford, Yorks. [6]

WHARTON, John Warburton, 7, *Johnstone-street, Bath.*—St. John's Coll. Cam. Scho. of, 3rd cl Cl. Hons. B.A. 1862; Deac. 1862 and Pr. 1863 by Bp of B. and W. Assist. Mast. of Sidney Coll. Bath. Formerly Asst. Mast. of Rossall Sch. Lancashire; 3rd Mast. of Bath Proprietary Coll. 1862; C. of Laura Chapel, Bath, 1863. [7]

WHARTON, Joseph Crane, *Willesden Vicarage, Middlesex, N.W.*—Wor. Coll. Ox. 3rd cl. Lit. Hum. and B A. 1848; Deac. 1849, Pr. 1850 by Abp of Cant. V. of Willesden, Dio. Lon. 1864. (Patrons, D. and C. of St. Paul's; V.'s Inc. 320*l* and Ho; Pop. 3204.) Formerly C. of Hadlow, Kent, 1849–51; V. of Waldershare, Kent, 1851–53; V. of Bierton and Quarrendon, Bucks, 1853–64. Author, *Duties and Privileges of Holy Communion*, Bell and Daldy; Sermons; etc. [8]

WHARTON, William Fitzwilliam, *Barningham Rectory (Yorks), Barnard Castle, Darlington.*—Ch. Coll. Cam. B.A. 1832, M.A. 1835. R. of Barningham, Dio. Rip. 1840. (Patron, Ld. Chan; Tithe, 370*l*; Glebe, 101½ acres; R.'s Inc. 556*l* and Ho; Pop. 526.) Dom. Chap. to the Earl of Zetland. [9]

WHATELY, Charles, *Taplow Rectory (Bucks), Maidenhead.*—St. Mary Hall, Ox. B.A. 1837, M.A. 1840. R. of Taplow, Dio. Ox. 1850. (Patron, Ld Chan; R.'s Inc. 464*l* and Ho; Pop. 811.) Rural Dean of Burnham. [10]

WHATELY, Henry Thomas, *Kington, Herefordshire.*—Ch. Ch. Ox. B.A. 1845, M.A. 1847; Deac. 1845 and Pr. 1846 by Bp of Wor. V. of Kington with Huntington R. Dio. Herf. 1860. (Patron, Bp of Wor; V.'s Inc. 560*l* and Ho; Pop. Kington 3076, Huntington 279.) Formerly R. of Rodington 1847–60. [11]

WHATELY, John, *Steep, near Petersfield, Hants.*—Dub. A.B. 1849; Deac. 1851 and Pr. 1852 by Bp of Win. C. of Steep. Formerly C. of Ch. Ch. Brixton, St. Barnabas', South Kennington, Surrey. [12]

WHATELY, William Joseph, *Rise, Hull.*—Ch. Ch. Ox. B.A. 1841, M.A. 1843; Deac. 1842, Pr. 1843. R. of Rise, Dio. York, 1850. (Patron, Ld Chan; Tithe, 537*l* 15*s* 1½*d*; Glebe, 54 acres; R.'s Inc. 580*l* and Ho; Pop. 188.) [13]

WHATLEY, Henry Lawson, *Aston-Ingham (Herefordshire), near Lea.*—Pemb. Coll. Ox. B A. 1823; Deac. 1824, Pr. 1825. R. of Aston-Ingham, Dio. Herf. 1835. (Patron, the present R; Tithe, 350*l*; Glebe, 102 acres; R.'s Inc. 450*l* and Ho; Pop. 568.) [14]

WHATLEY, H. L., jun., *North Piddle, Worcester.*—R. of North Piddle, Dio. Wor. 1864. (Patron, Earl Somers; R.'s Inc. 140*l*; Pop. 131.) [15]

WHEAT, Carlos Cony, *Timberland Vicarage, Sleaford, Lincolnshire.*—St. John's Coll. Cam. B.A. 1824; Deac. 1824, Pr. 1825. V. of Timberland, Dio. Lin. 1841. (Patron, Sir Thomas Whichcote, Bart; Tithe—Imp. 412*l* 5*s* 3*d*, V. 158*l*; V.'s Inc. 450*l* and Ho; Pop. 1618.) [16]

WHEAT, Christopher George, *Powerstock, Bridport.*—St. Mary Hall, Ox. B.A. 1861, M.A. 1865; Deac. 1862 and Pr. 1864 by Bp of Salis. C. of Powerstock 1864. Formerly C. of Gillingham, Dorset, 1862–63. [17]

WHEELER, David, *Pulloxhill Vicarage, Ampthill, Beds.*—St. Edm. Hall, Ox. B.A. 1835; Deac. 1835 by Bp of Lich. Pr. 1836 by Bp of Ban. V. of Pulloxhill, Dio. Ely, 1861. (Patroness, Countess Cowper; Tithe, 133*l*; Glebe, 32 acres; V.'s Inc. 230*l* and Ho; Pop. 715.) Formerly P. C. of St. Paul's, Worcester. [18]

WHEELER, George Domvile, *Wolford Vicarage (Warwickshire), near Shipston-on-Stour.*—Wad. Coll. Ox. B.A. 1836, M.A. 1839; Deac. and Pr. 1839. V. of Wolford with Burmington C. Dio. Wor. 1843. (Patron, Mert. Coll. Ox; Wolford, Tithe—App. 467*l* 12*s* 8*d*, V. 139*l* 10*s* 8*d*; Glebe, 36 acres; Burmington, Tithe, 223*l*; Glebe, 31½ acres; V.'s Inc. 483*l* and Ho; Pop. Wolford 534, Burmington 212.) R. of Barcheston, Warwickshire, Dio. Wor. 1846. (Patron, the present R; Tithe, 224*l* 19*s* 6*d*; Glebe, 8 acres; R.'s Inc. 240*l* and Ho; Pop. 190.) Formerly Fell. of Wad. Coll. Ox. 1841. Author, *A Letter to the Bishop of Worcester, in Reply to the Rev. E. S. Foulke's Three Letters on Marriage with a Deceased Wife's Sister*, 1849, 1*s*; *Some Objections to the Revival of Ecclesiastical Synods answered by a Reference to the Circumstance under which the Apostolic Council at Jerusalem was assembled* (a Sermon preached before the Univ. of Ox.), 1852, 1*s*. [19]

WHEELER, G. V., *Whittington, Chesterfield.*—R. of Whittington, Dio. Lich. (Patron, Bp of Lich; R.'s Inc. 302*l* and Ho; Pop. 2636.) Formerly C. of Whittington. [20]

WHEELER, H. N.—Chap. to the Forces, Aldershot. [21]

WHEELER, John Blucher, *Coppenhall Rectory, Crewe, Cheshire.*—St. Aidan's; Deac. 1850, Pr. 1851. R. of Coppenhall, Dio. Ches. 1854. (Patron, Bp of Lich; Tithe, 275*l* 1*s*; Glebe, 8 acres; R.'s Inc. 262*l* and Ho; Pop. 3020.) [22]

WHEELER, Robert Faulding, *The Parsonage, Whitley, North Shields.*—Ch. Coll. Cam. B.A. 1852, M.A. 1855; Deac. 1852, Pr. 1853. P. C. of Cullercoats, N. Shields, Dio. Dur. 1861. (Patron, Duke of Northumberland; P. C.'s Inc. 200*l* and Ho; Pop. 1867.) Formerly C. of Kirkby Overblow, Yorks, 1852–54, St. Mary's, Chatham (sole charge), 1854–58; Sec. of British and Foreign Bible Society 1858–61. Author, *Pastoral Letters to Inhabitants of Cullercoats*, 1861, '62, '63 and 1864; *On British Fisheries*, and other papers in *Transactions of Tyneside Naturalists' Club*, 1863–67. [23]

WHEELER, Robert Thomas, *Minster Vicarage, Ramsgate, Kent.*—Dub. A.B. 1840, M.A. 1844; Deac. 1840 and Pr. 1841 by Bp of Ches. V. of Minster, Dio. Cant. 1851. (Patron, Abp of Cant; Tithe—App. 1231*l* 10*s* and 113 acres of Glebe, V. 740*l*; Glebe, 28 acres; V.'s Inc. 820*l* and Ho; Pop. 1207.) Formerly C. of St. Anne's, Lancaster; P. C. of St. John's, Blackburn. Author, *Distinctive Truth* (a Sermon); *The Spirit and the Flesh* (a Tract on the Lord's Supper), Macintosh; *Visitation Sermons*; etc. [24]

WHEELER, Thomas Littleton, *Broomwich House, Worcester.*—Wor. Coll. Ox. 1822, 3rd cl. Lit. Hum. and B.A. 1826, M.A. 1830; Deac. 1829 and Pr.

1830 by Bp of Wor. Min. Can. of Wor. Cathl. 1833 (Value, 36l); Precentor 1854 (Value, 50l); R. of St. Martin's, City and Dio. Wor. 1851. (Patrons, D. and C. of Wor; Tithe, comm. 326l 1s; R.'s Inc. 400l; Pop. 5601.) [1]

WHEELER, Thomas Littleton, jun., 4, *Lansdowne-crescent, Worcester*.—Wor. Coll. Ox. 1st cl. Math. B.A. 1856, M.A. 1859; Deac. 1857 and Pr. 1858 by Bp of Herf. P. C. of Trinity, City and Dio. Wor. 1865. (Patron, Bp of Worc; P. C.'s Inc. 130l; Pop. 2300.) Formerly C. of St. Michael's, Tenbury, 1857–60; C. of St. Martin's, Worcester, 1860–65. [2]

WHEELER, T. W., *Toxteth, near Liverpool*.—P. C. of St. Silas', Toxteth, Dio. Ches. 1864. (Patrons, Trustees; Pop. 3500.) [3]

WHEELER, William, *St. Anne's Parsonage, Liverpool*.—P. C. of St. Anne's, Liverpool, Dio. Ches. 1849. (Patron, Rev. T. Stringer; P. C.'s Inc. 150l and Ho; Pop. 10,330.) [4]

WHEELER, William Hancock, *Berrow Vicarage, Bridgwater*.—Wad. Coll. Ox. B.A. 1860; Deac. 1860 by Bp of B. and W. V. of Berrow, Somerset, Dio. B. and W. 1863. (Patron, Archd. of Wells; V.'s Inc. 200l and Ho; Pop. 489.) Formerly C. of Winscombe 1860. [5]

WHEELWRIGHT, George, *Crowhurst, Godstone, Surrey*.—P. C. of Crowhurst, Dio. Win. 1858. (Patron, Earl of Cottenham; P. C.'s Inc. 75l; Pop. 211.) [6]

WHELER, Francis, *Dunchurch Vicarage, Warwickshire*.—V. of Dunchurch, Dio. Wor. 1853. (Patron, Bp of Lich; Tithe, 220l; Glebe, 45 acres; V.'s Inc. 350l and Ho; Pop. 1309.) [7]

WHELPTON, Henry Robert, *Eastbourne, Sussex*.—St. John's Coll. Cam. B.A. 1857, M.A. 1860; Deac. 1857, Pr. 1858. P. C. of St. Saviour's, Eastbourne, Dio. Chich. 1867. (Patron, George Whelpton, Esq; P. C.'s Inc. 200l; Pop. 1000.) Formerly C. of All Saints', Dalston, 1857, Upton with Chalvey, Slough, 1859, St. Edmund's, Salisbury, 1862. [8]

WHICHCOTE, Christopher, *Aswarby Rectory, Folkingham, Lincolnshire*.—St. John's Coll. Cam. 21st Wrang. and B.A. 1828, M.A. 1834; Deac. 1829 and Pr. 1830 by Bp of Lin. R. of Aswarby with Swarby V. Dio. Lin. 1850. (Patron, Sir Thomas Whichcote, Bart; Aswarby, Tithe, 327l 12s; Glebe, 47½ acres; Pop. 128; Swarby, Glebe, 49 acres; Pop. 188; R.'s Inc. 490l and Ho.) Rural Dean. [9]

WHIDBORNE, George Ferris, *Hanley Parsonage, Staffs*.—Queen's Coll. Ox. 1827, B.A. 1832, M.A. 1843; Deac. 1832 by Bp of G. and B. Pr. 1834 by Bp of Ex. P. C. of Hanley, Dio. Lich. 1849. (Patrons, 26 Trustees; P. C.'s Inc. 290l and Ho; Pop. 4000) Surrogate. Formerly C. of Charles, Plymouth, 1832, Combeinteignhead 1834; P. C. of Charles, Plymouth, 1839; P. C. of Ch. Ch. Plymouth, 1846. Author, *What is Infant Baptism? by a Clergyman of the Diocese of Exeter*, Seeleys, 1s; *True Religion always Protestant* (a Visitation Sermon), ib. 6d; *The Grounds, the Nature and the Uses of Confirmation*, 3d; etc. [10]

WHIELDON, Edward, *Hales Hall, Cheadle, Staffs*.—St. John's Coll. Cam. B.A. 1847, M.A. 1850; Deac. 1847 and Pr. 1848 by Bp of Lich. C. of Bradley-in-the-Moors, Dio. Lich. 1859. (Patron, Earl of Shrewsbury; P. C.'s Inc. 60l; Pop. 42.) P. C. of Croxden, Dio. Lich. 1863. (Patron, Earl of Macclesfield; P. C.'s Inc. 102l; Pop. 215.) [11]

WHINFIELD, John, *Orton, Westmoreland*.—Deac. 1802 and Pr. 1803 by Bp of Lon. [12]

WHIPHAM, Arthur, *Gidleigh Park, near Chagford, Devon*.—Trin. Coll. Ox. M.A. 1835; Deac. 1834 by Bp of B. and W. Pr. 1835 by Bp of G. and B. R. of Hittisleigh, Dio. Ex. 1865. (Patron, C. B. Calmady, Esq; Tithe, 85l; Glebe, 40 acres; R.'s Inc. 125l; Pop. 100.) Chap. to Lord Dorchester. Formerly C. of Kingsteignton 1834; R. of Gidleigh 1835. [13]

WHISH, George Thomas, *Charlton, Dover*.—C. of Charlton by Dover 1865. Formerly C. of Monkton, Ramsgate, and Bredhurst, Chatham (sole charge). [14]

WHISH, Henry Fulham, *Birchington, Margate, Kent*.—Corpus Coll. Cam. B.A. 1846, M.A. 1849; Deac. 1847 and Pr. 1848 by Abp of Cant. C. of Monkton with Birchington 1847. [15]

WHISH, John Charles, *East Peckham, Tunbridge, Kent*.—Trin. Coll. Cam. Wrang. and B.A. 1839, M.A. 1843; Deac. 1839, Pr. 1840. V. of Trinity, East Peckham, Dio. Cant. 1843. (Patron, V. of East Peckham; V.'s Inc. 300l and Ho; Pop. 1918.) Author, *The Great Exhibition Prize Essay*, 1851; *Additional Catechism before Confirmation*, 1854, 4d; *The First Cause, a Treatise on the Being and Attributes of God*, Seeleys, 1855, 10s 6d; *Paraphrase of Isaiah*, 1862, ib. 2s 6d; *Paraphrase of Minor Prophets*, 1864, ib. 2s 6d. [16]

WHISH, John Matthew Hale, *Blackford, Wells, Somerset*.—Trin. Coll. Cam. B.A. 1845; Deac. 1846, Pr. 1849. P. C. of Blackford, Wedmore, Dio. B. and W. 1858. (Patron, V. of Wedmore; P. C.'s Inc. 165l and Ho; Pop. 677.) Formerly Asst. C. of Crewkerne. [17]

WHISH, Martin Henry, *Alderley Rectory, Wootton-under-Edge, Glouc*.—Corpus Coll. Cam. B.A. 1838, M.A. 1842; Deac. 1839 and Pr. 1840 by Bp of B. and W. R. of Alderley, Dio. G. and B. 1846. (Patron, R. Blagden Hale, Esq; Tithe, 162l; Glebe, 25 acres; R.'s Inc. 200l and Ho; Pop. 97.) Formerly C. of St. John's, Bedminster, 1839, Abbots Leigh 1840; P. C. of St. Peter's, Bishopsworth, 1844. [18]

WHISH, Richard Peter, *Monkton Vicarage, Ramsgate, Kent*.—Emman. Coll. Cam. 1807, B.A. 1811, M.A. 1814; Deac. 1811 and Pr. 1812 by Bp of Lon. Preb. of Ashill in Wells Cathl. 1819. (Value, 10l.) V. of Monkton with Birchington and Acol, Dio. Cant. 1832. (Patron, Abp of Cant; Monkton, Tithe—App. 725l and 38 acres of Glebe, V. 350l; Birchington, Tithe—App. 682l and 4 acres of Glebe, V. 190l 12s; Acol, Tithe—App. 635l, V. 132l; V.'s Inc. 672l and Ho; Pop. Monkton 375, Birchington 813, Acol 260.) Formerly V. of Broxted, Essex, 1812–32. [19]

WHISHAW, Alexander, *Oakhill Park, Liverpool*.—Trin. Coll. Ox. B.A. 1846, M.A. 1849; Deac. 1848, Pr. 1850. Chap. of St. Mary's Blind Sch. Church, Liverpool, 1867. (Patrons, Trustees.) Min. Can. of Glouc. 1866. Formerly P. C. of Ramsgill, Yorks, 1849; C. of Leighton-Buzzard 1849; V. of Chipping-Norton, Oxon, 1850–66. Author, *Hymnbook for Use of Chipping-Norton*, 1859, 2nd ed. 1864; *Spiritual Worship, a Form of Prayers and Preparation for Holy Communion for the Use of Poor People*, 1858, 2nd ed. 1864. [20]

WHISTLER, Rose Fuller, *St. John's Rectory, Bungay, Suffolk*.—Emman. Coll. Cam. B.A. 1849, M.A. 1854; Deac. 1849 and Pr. 1850 by Bp of Chich. R. of St. John's, Ilketshall, Dio. Nor. 1867. (Patron, Ld Chan; Tithe, 265l 10s; Glebe, 56 acres and Ho.) Formerly C. of Battle, Sussex, 1849–52; V. of Bishop's Norton, Linc. 1852–54; R. of Hollington Sussex, 1854–67. [21]

WHISTON, Robert, *Rochester*.—Trin. Coll. Cam. 5th Sen. Opt. 1st in 2nd cl. Cl. Trip. and B.A. 1831, M.A. 1834; Deac. 1840 by Bp of Ely, Pr. 1841 by Bp of Herf. Head Mast. of the Rochester Cathl. Gr. Sch. 1842. Formerly Sen. Fell. of Trin. Coll. Cam. Author, *Cathedral Trusts, and their Fulfilment*, 5 eds. 3s 6d. Contributor to Smith's *Dictionary of Greek and Roman Antiquities*. Editor of *Demosthenes*, in the *Bibliotheca Classica*, vol. I. 8vo, 16s; vol. II. in the Press, Bell and Daldy. [22]

WHITAKER, Edward Wright, *Stanton-by-Bridge, Derby*.—Ch. Ch. Ox. Student of, B.A. 1863, M.A. 1865; Deac. 1864 and Pr. 1866 by Bp of Ox. C. of Stanton-by-Bridge 1866. Formerly C. of Croft, Yorks, 1865. [23]

WHITAKER, Gascoigne Frederick, *Flordon, St. Mary Stratton, Norfolk*.—Wad. Coll. Ox. B.A. 1848, M.A. 1850. R. of Flordon, Dio. Nor. 1856. (Patron, Sir William Robert Kemp, Bart; Tithe, 291l 2s 4d; R.'s Inc. 320l; Pop. 163.) [24]

WHITAKER, George, *Toronto, Canada West*.—Queens' Coll. Cam. Jun. Opt. and B.A. 1833, M.A.

1836. Provost of Trin. Coll. Toronto. Formerly Fell. of Queens' Coll. Cam. [1]

WHITAKER, George Ayton, *Knoddishall Rectory, Saxmundham, Suffolk.*—Emman. Coll. Cam. B.A. 1830, M.A. 1841; Deac. 1830 and Pr. 1831 by Bp of Nor. R. of Knoddishall with Buxlow C. Dio. Nor. 1835. (Patron, the present R; Tithe, 491*l* 8*s*; Glebe, 17 acres; R.'s Inc. 514*l* and Ho; Pop. 442.) R. of Henstead, Dio. Nor. 1862. (Patron, T. B. Sheriffe, Esq; R.'s Inc. 450*l* and Ho; Pop. 534.) Rural Dean of Dunwich; a Magistrate for the Co. of Suffolk. [2]

WHITAKER, George Henry, *Garforth Rectory, Leeds.*—Magd. Coll. Cam. B.A. 1834, M.A. 1837; Deac. and Pr. 1834. R. of Garforth, Dio. Rip. 1834. (Patron, the present R; Tithe—Imp. 3*l* 13*s*, R. 420*l*; Glebe, 56 acres; R.'s Inc. 504*l* and Ho; Pop. 1504.) [3]

WHITAKER, John, *Helperthorpe, Yorkshire.*—C. of Helperthorpe. [4]

WHITAKER, Robert, *Leconfield Rectory, Beverley, East Yorkshire.*—Trin. Coll. Cam. B.A. 1854, M.A. 1857; Deac. 1854 and Pr. 1855 by Abp of York. R. of Scorborough with Leconfield P. C. Dio. York, 1859. (Patron, Lord Leconfield; Tithe, Scorborough, 306*l* 18*s*; Leconfield, Glebe, 27 acres; R.'s Inc. 380*l* and Ho; Pop. Scorborough 89, Leconfield 348.) Formerly C. of Stokesley, Yorks, 1854–58, Cherry Burton, Yorks, 1858–59. [5]

WHITAKER, Robert Nowell, *Whalley Vicarage, Blackburn.*—St. John's Coll. Cam. B.A. 1825, M.A. 1835; Deac. and Pr. 1827 by Bp of Lon. V. of Whalley, Dio. Man. 1840. (Patron, Abp of Cant; Tithe, 9*l*; Glebe, 10*l*; V.'s Inc. 300*l* and Ho; Pop. 5299.) Surrogate. Formerly C. of St. Mary Woolnoth, Lond; P. C. of Langho, Blackburn, Lancashire. [6]

WHITAKER, Samuel, *Penrhôs Parsonage, near Oswestry.*—St. John's Coll. Cam. Scho. of, B A. 1839, M.A. 1842; Deac. 1839 by Abp of York, Pr. 1840 by Bp of Lich. P. C. of the Consolidated Chap. of Penrhôs, Dio. St. A. 1847. (Patroness, Mrs. Ormsby Gore; Glebe, 6 acres; P. C.'s Inc. 161*l* and Ho; Pop. 976.) Formerly C. of Tipton, near Birmingham, 1839–41, Dunnington, near York, 1842–45, Penrhôs 1845–47. [7]

WHITAKER, Thomas Wright, *Stanton-by-Bridge Rectory, Swarkeston, Derbyshire.*—Emman. Coll. Cam. B.A. 1822, M.A. 1825; Deac. 1822 and Pr. 1823 by Bp of Nor. R. of Stanton-by-Bridge, Dio. Lich. 1830. (Patron, Sir John Harpur Crewe, Bart; Land in lieu of Tithe, 174¾ acres; R.'s Inc. 345*l* and Ho; Pop. 185.) R. of Swarkeston, Dio. Lich. 1830. (Patron, Sir John Harpur Crewe, Bart; Tithe, 11*l* 15*s* 7*d*; R.'s Inc. 185*l*; Pop. 307.) Rural Dean of Stanton-by-Bridge 1844; Preb. of Bobenholl in Lich. Cathl. 1852. [8]

WHITBREAD, Edmund Salter, *Strumpshaw Rectory, Burlingham, Norfolk.*—Trin. Hall, Cam. B.A. 1828, M.A. 1832; Deac. 1829 and Pr. 1831 by Bp of Nor. R. of Strumpshaw with Braydeston R. Dio. Nor. 1833. (Patron, the present R; Strumpshaw, Tithe—App. 16*s*, R. 370*l*; Glebe, 52 acres; Braydeston, Tithe, 150*l*; Glebe, 8 acres; R.'s Inc. 630*l* and Ho; Pop. Strumpshaw 386, Braydeston 133.) J. P. for Norfolk. [9]

WHITBY, Richard Vernon, *Lechlade Vicarage, Glouc.*—Emman. Coll. Cam. B.A. 1839, M.A. 1842, B.D. 1854; Deac. 1844 and Pr. 1845 by Bp of Pet. V. of Lechlade, Dio. G. and B. 1854. (Patron, Emman. Coll. Cam; Tithe, 710*l*; V.'s Inc. 730*l* and Ho; Pop. 1328.) Formerly Fell. of Emmanuel Coll. Cam. [10]

WHITBY, Thomas, 18, *St. John's-terrace, Belle Vue-road, Burnley-road, Leeds.*—St. John's Coll. Cam. B.A. 1859, M.A. 1866; Deac. 1859 and Pr. 1860 by Bp of Ches. P. C. of St. Simon's, Leeds, Dio. Rip. 1865. (Patron, Bp of Rip; P. C.'s Inc. 225*l*.) Formerly C. of St. Paul's, Chester, 1859, St. John's, Fairfield, Liverpool, 1861, St. Andrew's, Leeds, 1864. [11]

WHITCOMBE, Charles, *Sherston Vicarage, Malmesbury, Wilts.*—Oriel Coll. Ox. B.A. 1819, M.A. 1834; Deac. and Pr. 1825 by Bp of Glouc. V. of Sherston with Pinkney R. Dio. G. and B. 1830. (Patrons, D. and C. of Glouc; Sherston, Tithe—App. 250*l* and 288½ acres of Glebe, V. 100*l*; Glebe, 6 acres; Pinkney, Tithe—Imp. 178*l* and 65 acres of Glebe; V.'s Inc. 155*l* and Ho; Pop. Sherston 1503, Pinkney 156.) [12]

WHITCOMBE, Philip, *Abbey Foregate, Shrewsbury.*—Brasen. Coll. Ox. B.A. 1826; Deac. 1829 and Pr. 1830 by Bp of Herf. V. of Holy Cross, or the Abbey Ch. Shrewsbury, Dio. Lich. 1857. (Patron, Lord Berwick; V.'s Inc. 400*l*; Pop. 1659.) [13]

WHITE, Adolphus Leighton, *Mortimer West End, Reading.*—Ball. Coll. Ox. B.A. 1845, M.A. 1848; Deac. 1848 and Pr. 1849 by Bp of Ox. Min. of West End, Stratfield Mortimer, Dio. Ox. 1856. (Patron, R. Benyon, Esq; Min.'s Inc. 150*l* and Ho; Pop. 345.) Formerly C. of Arborfield, Berks, 1848–52; P. C. of Lavesden, Herts, 1853–55. [14]

WHITE, Arthur, *Sapiston, Ixworth, Suffolk.*—Magd. Coll. Cam. B.A. 1852, M.A. 1855. P. C. of Sapiston, Dio. Ely, 1856. (Patron, Duke of Grafton; P. C.'s Inc. 100*l*; Pop. 255.) Fell. of Magd. Coll. Cam. [15]

WHITE, Charles, *Haslington Parsonage, Crewe, Cheshire.*—St. John's Coll. Cam. B.A. 1849; Deac. 1849 and Pr. 1850 by Abp of York. P. C. of Haslington, Barthomley, Dio. Ches. 1857. (Patron, Sir H. D. Broughton; P. C.'s Inc. 150*l* and Ho; Pop. 1600.) Formerly C. of Cottesmore, Rutland. [16]

WHITE, Darius James, *Camborne, Cornwall.*—Queens' Coll. Cam. Scho. of B.A. 1865; Deac. 1866 by Bp of Colombo. Pr. 1867 by Bp of Jamaica. C. of Camborne 1866. [17]

WHITE, Edmund Roger Manwaring, *Mendlesham Vicarage, Stonham, Suffolk.*—Emman. Coll. Cam. B.A. 1851, M.A. 1854; Deac. 1851, Pr. 1853. V. of Mendlesham, Dio. Nor. 1861. (Patron, E. White, Esq; V.'s Inc. 550*l* and Ho; Pop. 1316.) Formerly C. of Debenham, Suffolk. [18]

WHITE, Elisha, *Quernmore Rectory, near Lancaster.*—St. Bees; Deac. 1833 by Bp of Dur. Pr. 1834 by Bp of Carl. P. C. of Quernmore, Dio. Man. 1844. (Patron, V. of Lancaster; P. C.'s Inc. 171*l* and Ho; Pop. 563.) Surrogate 1863. Formerly Mast. of Norton Gr. Sch. Durham, 1832; C. of St. Nicholas', Whitehaven, 1837; P. C. of Wray, near Lancaster, 1841. Author, *A Sermon on the Offertory*, 1864. [19]

WHITE, F. *Wolverhampton.*—C. of St. Luke's, Wolverhampton. [20]

WHITE, Francis Gilbert, *Beeford, near Hull.*—Lin. Coll. Ox. Ld. Crewe's Exhib. 3rd cl. Cl. 1844, B.A. 1845, M.A. 1848; Deac. 1847 and Pr. 1848 by Bp of Ox. C. of Beeford with Lisset 1866. Formerly C. of Launton, near Bicester 1847; Chap. to the Bp of Newfoundland, and Vice-Prin. of the Theol. Coll. at St. John's, Newfoundland; Prin. of the Dioc. Coll. Sch. Cape of Good Hope, 1857–60. Author, *The True Nature of the Church*, Bell and Daldy, 1857. [21]

WHITE, Francis Le Grix, *Croxton Parsonage, Eccleshall, Staffs.*—Wor. Coll. Ox. M.A. 1849, F.G.S; Deac. 1849 and Pr. 1850 by Abp of Cant. P. C. of Croxton, Dio. Lich. 1857. (Patron, Bp of Lich; P. C.'s Inc. 51*l* and Ho; Pop. 1100.) Dom. Chap. to Marquis of Drogheda 1851. Formerly C. of Betshanger and of St. Clement's, Sandwich, 1849; British Chap. at Kissingen 1850–51. [22]

WHITE, Frederick William, *Meare Vicarage, Glastonbury, Somerset.*—Pemb. Coll. Cam. B.A. 1843. V. of Meare, Dio. B. and W. 1851. (Patron, W. T. H. Phelps, Esq; Tithe—Imp. 82*l* 5*s*, V. 92*l* 5*s* 6*d*; V.'s Inc. 331*l* and Ho; Pop. 1593.) [23]

WHITE, George Crosby, *St. Barnabas' Parsonage, Pimlico, London, S.W.*—Trin. Coll. Cam. B.A. 1848, M.A. 1851; Deac. 1848 by Bp of Ox. Pr. 1849 by Bp of Lon. P. C. of St. Barnabas', Pimlico, Dio. Lon. 1846. (Patron, P. C. of St. Paul's, Knightsbridge; P. C.'s Inc. 231*l* 5*s*, and Ho; Pop. 5500.) [24]

WHITE, George William, *Darlaston Rectory, Wednesbury, Staffs.*—St. John's Coll. Cam. B.A. 1823, M.A. 1826; Deac. 1823 by Bp of Ches. Pr. 1824 by Bp of Lich. R. of Darlaston, Dio. Lich. 1843. (Patrons, Simeon's Trustees; Tithe, 250*l*; Glebe, 16 acres; R.'s Inc. 400*l* and Ho; Pop. 6601.) [25]

WHITE, Glyd, *Ewelme (Oxon), near Wallingford, Berks.*—Oriel Coll. Ox. 2nd cl. Lit. Hum. and B.A. 1812, M.A. 1815; Deac. 1812 and Pr. 1813 by Bp of Ox. C. of Mongewell, Oxon. [1]

WHITE, Henry, *Censor's Rooms, King's College, London, W.C.*—Deac. 1857 by Bp of Lich. Pr. 1858 by Abp of Cant. Chap. of Chapel Royal, Savoy, Dio. Lon. 1860. (Patron, The Queen, as Duchess of Lancaster; Chap.'s Inc. 350*l*; Pop. 150.) Censor in King's Coll. 1866. Formerly C. of St. James's, Dover, 1858–59. [2]

WHITE, Henry, *Charnes Hall, Eccleshall, Staffs.*—Downing Coll. Cam; Deac. and Pr. by Bp of Pet. [3]

WHITE, H. A., *Burton-on-Trent.*—Dub. A.B. 1863; Deac. 1864, Pr. 1865. C. of Trinity, Burton-on-Trent. [4]

WHITE, Henry Grattan, *Ballaugh, Isle of Man.*—Dub. A.B. 1842, A.M. 1859; Deac. 1854 and Pr. 1855 by Bp of S. and M. C. of Ballaugh 1858. [5]

WHITE, Henry Joseph, *Hilton, St. Ives, Hunts.* Sid. Coll. Cam. Scho. Exhib. and Prizeman of; Deac. 1863 by Abp of Cant. Pr. 1864 by Bp of Ely. Formerly C. of Hilton 1863–66. [6]

WHITE, Henry Master, *Masbrough Parsonage, Rotherham.*—New Coll. Ox. 1st cl. Lit. Hum. 2nd cl. Maths. 1842, Johnson's Math. Scho. 1843, Pusey and Ellerton Hebrew Scho. 1846, B.A. 1843, M.A. 1846; Deac. 1844 and Pr. 1846 by Bp of Ox. P. C. of Masbrough, Dio. York, 1865. (Patron, Abp of York; P. C.'s Inc. 200*l* and Ho; Pop. 6588.) Formerly Fell. and Tut. of New Coll. Ox; Prin. of Dioc. Coll. Sch. Capetown, 1849–57; C. of Andover, Hants, 1857–61, Masbrough 1861–65. Author, *Ramsden Sermon, 30th May*, 1858; *The Church in the Colonies and the Church at Home*, 1858, 1*s*; *Is the Gospel duly preached to the Poor in England?* (a Sermon before the Univ. of Ox.) 1861, 6*d*; *Church Rates*, 1867, 2*d*; *Principles of Trades Unions*, 1867, 2*d*, Mozley. Editor of *South African Church Magazine*, Capetown, 1853–57. [7]

WHITE, Henry Towry, *Wereham, Stoke-Ferry, Norfolk.*—Dub. A.B. 1847, Theol. Test. 1849; Deac. 1850 and Pr. 1852 by Bp of Ox. P. C. of Wereham with Wretton P. C. Dio. Nor. 1859. (Patron, E. R. Pratt, Esq; P. C.'s Inc. 110*l*; Pop. Wereham 597, Wretton 490.) Formerly C. of Newbury and Chap. to the Newbury Union, Berks, 1850–59. [8]

WHITE, Herbert, *Warborough (Oxon), near Wallingford, Berks.*—Corpus Coll. Ox. B.D. P. C. of Warborough, Dio. Ox. 1837. (Patron, Corpus Coll. Ox; Tithe—Imp. 668*l* 1*s*; Glebe, 18 acres and Ho; Pop. 764.) [9]

WHITE, James, *Sloley, Coltishall, Norfolk.*—R. of Sloley, Dio. Nor. 1852. (Patron, the present R; Tithe, 258*l* 4*s*; Glebe, 24 acres; R.'s Inc. 318*l*; Pop. 258.) [10]

WHITE, James, *Bruton, Somerset.*—P. C. of Bruton, Dio. B. and W. 1841. (Patron, Sir H. H. Hoare, Bart; Tithe—Imp. 125*l* 8*s* 6*d*, P. C. 5*s* 10*d*; P. C.'s Inc. 179*l*; Pop. 2072.) [11]

WHITE, James Baker, *Ely.*—St. John's Coll. Ox. B.A. 1864; Deac. 1866 by Bp of Ely. Assist. C. of Trinity, Ely, 1866. [12]

WHITE, James Henry, *Haxby, near York.*—St. Aidan's; Deac. 1861 and Pr. 1863 by Abp of York. C. of Haxby 1863. C. of St. Paul's, York, 1866. Formerly C. of St. Mary's, Hull, 1862–63, Haxby 1863–65; St. Michael le Belfrey, York, 1865–66. [13]

WHITE, John, *Hackington Vicarage, near Canterbury.*—Queen's Coll. Ox. B.A. 1830, M.A. 1833; Deac. 1830 and Pr. 1831 by Abp. of Cant. V. of Hackington, alias St. Stephen's, Dio. Cant. 1840. (Patron, Archd. of Cant; Tithe, 611*l*; Glebe, ½ acre; V.'s Inc. 618*l* and Ho; Pop. 616.) [14]

WHITE, John, *Chevington, Bury St. Edmunds.*—Caius Coll. Cam. Jun. Opt. 2nd cl. Cl. Trip. and B.A. 1851, M.A. 1854; Deac. 1852, Pr. 1853. R. of Chevington, Dio. Ely, 1853. (Patron, the present R; Tithe, 580*l*; Glebe, 32 acres; R.'s Inc. 630*l* and Ho; Pop. 621.) [15]

WHITE, John, *Grayingham Rectory, Kirton-in-Lindsey, Lincolnshire.*—Lin. Coll. Ox. 4th cl. Lit. Hum. and B.A. 1840, M.A. 1843; Deac. 1841 and Pr. 1842 by Bp of Chich. R. of Grayingham, Dio. Lin. 1851. (Patron, Sir J. C. Thorold, Bart; Tithe, 501*l*; Glebe, 28 acres; R.'s Inc. 520*l* and Ho; Pop. 135.) [16]

WHITE, John, *Croydon, Surrey, S.*—Clare Coll. Cam. B.A. 1848, M.A. 1853; Deac. 1849 and Pr. 1850 by Bp of Lon. P. C. of St. Peter's, Croydon, Dio. Cant. 1857. (Patron, V. of Croydon; P. C.'s Inc. 400*l*; Glebe, 2½ acres; Pop. 2932.) Formerly C. of St. Peter's, Margate. [17]

WHITE, John, *Hilton, St. Ives, Hunts.*—C. of Hilton. [18]

WHITE, J. Baker, *Ely.*—C. of Trinity, Ely. [19]

WHITE, John Calcutta, *Rawreth Rectory, near Wickford, Essex.*—Pemb. Coll. Cam. 7th Wrang. 1813; Deac. 1816, Pr. 1818. R. of Rawreth, Dio. Roch. 1821. (Patron, Pemb. Coll. Cam; Tithe, 694*l*; Glebe, 45 acres; R.'s Inc. 245*l* and Ho; Pop. 386.) [20]

WHITE, John Edward, *Chatham.*—V. of St. Paul's, Chatham, Dio. Roch. 1864. (Patron, Bp of Roch; P. C.'s Inc. 200*l* and Ho; Pop. 6302.) [21]

WHITE, John Eva, *West Ham, Essex.*—C. of St. Mark's, Victoria Docks, West Ham. [22]

WHITE, John Tahourdin, *Christ's Hospital, London, E.C.*—Corpus Coll. Ox. Exhib. B.A. 1834, M.A. 1839; B.D. and D.D. 1866; Deac. 1834 by Bp of Lich. Pr. 1839 by Bp of Lon. C. in sole charge of St. Martin's, Ludgate, City of Lond. 1841; First Mast. of Latin Sch. (late Jun. Upp. Gr. Mast.) Christ's Hospital, Lond. 1836. Formerly C. of Swinnerston, Staffs, 1834; Reader at St. Stephen's, Walbrook, 1836; C. of St. Ann's, Blackfriars, 1837. Author or Editor of the following works published by Longman and Co: *Xenophon's Anabasis*, 7*s* 6*d*; *Cicero's Cato Major and Lælius*, 3*s* 6*d*; *Cornelius Nepos*, 3*s* 6*d*; *Phædrus*, 2*s* 6*d*; *Eutropius*, 2*s* 6*d*; *Selections from Ovid*, 4*s* 6*d*; *Dalzell's Analecta Græca Minora*, 7*s* 6*d*; *Valpy's Latin Delectus*, 2*s* 6*d*; *Valpy's Greek Delectus*, 4*s*; *Eton Latin Grammar* (revised and corrected), *with a Second or Large Grammar for the Higher Classes of Schools*, 2*s* 6*d*; *Latin Suffixes*, 5*s*; *Germany and Agricola of Tacitus*, 4*s* 6*d*; *The First Latin Parsing Book*, 2*s*; *The First Latin Exercise Book*, 2*s* 6*d*; *Progressive Latin Reader*, 3*s* 6*d*; *Latin-English Dictionary* (with Rev. J. E. Riddle), 42*s*; *Abridgment of Latin-English Dictionary*, 8vo, 18*s*; ditto, sq. 12mo, 7*s* 6*d*. [23]

WHITE, Joseph, *St. John's School, Bickenshill, Dymock, Gloucestershire.*—St. Nicolas' Coll. Sussex, Assoc. of, 1860; Deac. 1863 and Pr. 1864 by Bp of Chich. C. of Dymock, and Head Mast. of St. John's Middle Class School, Dymock, 1867. Formerly Asst. Mast. of St. Saviour's Sch. New Shoreham, Sussex. [24]

WHITE, Joseph, *Middleton Rectory, Yoxford, Suffolk.*—Dub. A.B. 1832; Deac. 1833 and Pr. 1835 by Bp of S. and M. R. of Fordley with Middleton R. Dio. Nor. 1862. (Patron, Rev. E. Hollond; Tithe, 161*l* 10*s*; Glebe, 12 acres; R.'s Inc. 180*l* and Ho; Pop. 582.) Formerly C. of St. Barnabas', Douglas, Isle of Man, 1833, Milwich, Staffs, 1836–42, Fordley and Middleton 1842–62. [25]

WHITE, Joseph Neville, *Stalham Vicarage, Norfolk.*—Corpus Coll. Cam. Scho. of, B.A. 1850; Deac. 1850 and Pr. 1851 by Bp of Nor. V. of Stalham, Dio. Nor. 1852. (Patron, Rev. James White; Tithe, 198*l*; Glebe, 24 acres; V.'s Inc. 250*l* and Ho; Pop. 760.) Formerly V. of Rushall 1851–52. [26]

WHITE, Lewis Borrett, *St. Mary's Parsonage, Bow-lane, London, E.C.*—Queen's Coll. Ox. 2nd cl. Lit. Hum. 2nd cl. Math. et Phy. and B.A. 1849, M.A. 1852; Deac. 1850, Pr. 1851. R. of St. Mary's Aldermary with St. Thomas's R. Dio. Lon. 1858. (Patrons, Abp of Cant. and D. and C. of St. Paul's alt; R.'s Inc. 500*l*; Pop. St. Mary's Aldermary 232, St. Thomas's 112.) Sec. of the Colonial and Continental Ch. Soc. Formerly Michell Fell. of Queen's Coll. Ox; C. of Trinity, Maidstone. Author, *Parting Thoughts* (a Sermon), Bromsgrove, 1854. [27]

WHITE, Richard, *Littlington Rectory, Lewes.*—Dur. B.A. 1851; Deac. 1852 and Pr. 1853 by Bp of Ches. R. of Littlington, Dio. Chich. 1862. (Patron, Rev. Thomas Scott; Tithe, 220*l*; Glebe, 3 acres; R.'s Inc. 100*l* and Ho; Pop. 134.) Formerly C. of St. Martin's and St. Bridget's, Chester, 1852–53. [1]

WHITE, Richard H., *Little Bardfield, Braintree, Essex.*—Jesus Coll. Cam. R. of Little Bardfield, Dio. Roch. 1864. (Patron, the present R; Tithe, 480*l*; Glebe, 67 acres; R.'s Inc. 640*l* and Ho; Pop. 429.) Formerly C. of Martham, Norfolk. [2]

WHITE, Richard Marsh, *Fairstead Rectory, Witham, Essex.*—Clare Coll. Cam. B.A. 1822, M.A. 1825; Deac. 1823, Pr. 1825. R. of Fairstead, Dio. Roch. 1863. (Patron, Bp of Roch; R.'s Inc. 450*l* and Ho; Pop. 351.) Formerly V. of Aveley, Essex, 1833–63. [3]

WHITE, Robert, *Little Budworth Parsonage, Tarporley, Cheshire.*—P. C. of Little Budworth, Dio. Ches. 1853. (Patron, Bp of Ches; Tithe, App. 164*l*; P. C.'s Inc. 95*l* and Ho; Pop. 582.) [4]

WHITE, Robert More, *Churchstoke Parsonage, near Shrewsbury.*—St. Peter's Coll. Cam. B.A. 1834, M.A. 1838; Deac. 1836. Pr. 1837. P. C. of Churchstoke, Dio. Herf. 1846. (Patron, Earl of Powis; Tithe, Imp. 866*l*; Glebe, 1 acre; P. C.'s Inc. 235*l* and Ho; Pop. 1323.) [5]

WHITE, Samson Henry, *Maidford, Towcester, Northants.*—Mert. Coll. Ox. B.A. 1823. R. of Maidford, Dio. Pet. 1826. (Patron, W. Grant, Esq; Tithe, 30*l* 16*s* 9*d*; R.'s Inc. 300*l* and Ho; Pop. 344.) [6]

WHITE, Samuel, *Seaham Harbour, Durham.*—Bp Hatfield Hall, Dur; Deac. 1865 and Pr. 1866 by Bp of Dur. C. of St. John's, Seaham Harbour, 1867. Formerly C. of Thornley, Durham, 1865–67. [7]

WHITE, Samuel George Booth, *Boughton-under-Blean Vicarage, Feversham, Kent.*—Caius Coll. Cam. B.A. 1836, M.A. 1839; Deac. 1836 and Pr. 1837 by Bp of Lon. V. of Boughton under-Blean, Dio. Cant. 1854. (Patron, Abp of Cant; Tithe—App. 708*l*, Imp. 60*l*, V. 450*l*; Glebe, 1 acre; V.'s Inc. 450*l* and Ho; Pop. 1624.) Chap. to the Duke of Marlborough. [8]

WHITE, Thomas, *Grammar School, King's Lynn, Norfolk.*—St. John's Coll. Cam. Exhib. Prizeman, 13th Wrang. 3rd cl. Cl. Trip. and B.A. 1852, M.A. 1855; Deac. and Pr. 1853 by Bp of Pet. Head Mast. of King's Lynn Gr. Sch. 1858. Formerly 2nd Mast. of the Loughborough Gr. Sch. Author, *To compare the Doctrines of the Love of God and of our Neighbour, as revealed in Scripture, and as deducible from Natural Reason* (Burney Prize Essay), 1853; *The Beloved Disciple* (a Sermon), 1858. [9]

WHITE, Thomas, *Cowthorpe Rectory, Wetherby, Yorks.*—Queens' Coll. Cam. Scho. of, B.A. 1825; Deac. 1827 by Abp of York, Pr. 1829 by Bp of Lin. R. of Cowthorpe, Dio. York, 1855. (Patron, Andrew Montagu, Esq; Tithe, 77*l*; Glebe, 3 acres; R.'s Inc. 130*l* and Ho; Pop. 141.) Formerly P. C. of Kirk Hamerton, Yorks, 1845–62. [10]

WHITE, Thomas, *Horncastle, Lincolnshire.*—2nd Mast. of the Gr. Sch. Horncastle; P. C. of Scamblesby, Dio. Lin. 1860. (Patron, Bp of Lin; P. C.'s Inc. 300*l*; Pop. 471.) [11]

WHITE, Thomas Pritchard, *Dorrington Parsonage, Shrewsbury.*—Corpus Coll. Cam. B.A. 1846, M.A. 1855; Deac. 1846 and Pr. 1847 by Bp of Herf. P. C. of Dorrington, Dio. Lich. 1861. (Patron, T. H. Hope Edwardes, Esq; P. C.'s Inc. 130*l* and Ho; Pop. 382.) Formerly C. of Astbury, Cheshire. [12]

WHITE, Thomas Reader, *Finchley Rectory, Middlesex, N.*—St. John's Coll. Cam. B.A. 1835, M.A. 1838; Deac. 1837 and Pr. 1838 by Bp of Lon. R. of Finchley, Dio. Lon. 1848. (Patron, Bp of Lon; Tithe, 100*l* 10*s*; Glebe, 153 acres; R.'s Inc. 528*l* and Ho; Pop. 1192.) [13]

WHITE, William Ameers, *Northborough Rectory, Market Deeping, Northants.*—St. John's Coll. Cam. 24th Wrang. and B.A. 1846; Deac. 1848 by Bp of Tasmania, Pr. 1852 by Bp of Pet. R. of Northborough, Dio. Pet. 1856. (Patrons, D. and C. of Pet; R.'s Inc. 345*l* and Ho; Pop. 240.) Head Mast. of Peterborough Cathl. Gr. Sch. 1851. Formerly Sub-Warden of Ch. Coll. Tasmania. [14]

WHITE, W. Farren, *Stonehouse Vicarage, Stroud, Glouc.*—V. of Stonehouse, Dio. G. and B. 1861. (Patron, the Crown; V.'s Inc. 530*l* and Ho; Pop. 1511.) [15]

WHITE, William Henry, *Millbrook, near Staleybridge.*—St. Bees; Deac. 1857 and Pr. 1858 by Bp of Ches. P. C. of St. James's, Millbrook, Dio. Ches. 1863. (Patrons, Trustees; P. C.'s Inc. 100*l* and Ho; Pop. 3000.) Formerly C. of St. John's, Dukinfield, 1857–60, St. Paul's, Staleybridge, 1860–62. [16]

WHITE, William Henry, *Debenham, Suffolk.*—Jesus Coll. Cam. B.A. 1846, M.A. 1851; Deac. 1847, Pr. 1848. V. of Kenton, Debenham, Dio. Nor. 1854. (Patron, Lord Henniker; Tithe—Imp. 154*l*, V. 150*l*; Glebe, 32 acres; V.'s Inc. 190*l* and Ho; Pop. 308.) [17]

WHITE, William Spranger, *Potterhanworth Rectory, near Lincoln.*—Trin. Coll. Cam. B.A. 1832, M.A. 1835; Deac. 1833 and Pr. 1834 by Bp of Lin. R. of Potterhanworth, Dio. Lin. 1859. (Patron, Ld Chan. Tithe, 2*l* 10*s*; Glebe, 698 acres; R.'s Inc. 780*l* and Ho; Pop. 413.) Formerly V. of Chaddesley-Corbett, Worcestershire, 1855–59. [18]

WHITECHURCH, W. F. *Luddenham, Kent.*—C. of Luddenham. Formerly C. of Mistley, Essex. [19]

WHITEFORD, John Lyson, *Maidwell Rectory, Northampton.*—St. Bees, 1st Prizeman and Librarian of; Deac. 1849 and Pr. 1850 by Bp of Man. R. of Maidwell, Dio. Pet. 1866. (Patron, H. H. H. Hungerford, Esq; Modus, 70*l*; Glebe, 100 acres; R.'s Inc. 350*l*; Pop. 290.) Formerly C. of Barnley 1849–51, Long Sutton 1851–53; R. of Tadel 1853–55; C. of Kelvedon Hatch 1855–57; C. in sole charge of Taynton, Lincolnshire, 1857–66. Author, *The English Church always a protesting Church* (Pamphlet); various Sermons. [20]

WHITEHEAD, Alfred, 10, *Chapel-place, Ramsgate.*—Ex. Coll. Ox. M.A. 1856; Deac. 1856, Pr. 1857. Min. of St. Mary's, Chapel of Ease to Parish Church, Ramsgate, 1861. (Patron, V. of Ramsgate.) Formerly C. of St. George's, Ramsgate, 1856–61. [21]

WHITEHEAD, C. H., *Warrington, Lancashire.*—C. of Warrington. Formerly C. of West Pennard, Somerset. [22]

WHITEHEAD, Edward, *Chichester.*—Wad. Coll. Ox. B.A. 1836, M.A. 1838; Deac. 1838, Pr. 1839. P. C. of St. John's, City and Dio. Chich. 1859. (Patrons, Trustees; P. C.'s Inc. 100*l*.) Formerly Dom. Chap. to the Bp of Madras 1839–49; R. of Saltford, Somerset, 1849–53; Min. of Laura Chapel, Bath, 1853–59.) Author, *Sketch of the Church in India*, Rivingtons, 1848; Sermons on Indian Mutiny, Ordination and Visitation; etc. [23]

WHITEHEAD, E., *South Warnborough, Hampshire.*—C. of South Warnborough. [24]

WHITEHEAD, Frederick William, *Caius House, Cambridge.*—Emman. Coll. Cam. B.A. 1850, M.A. 1853; Deac. 1850, Pr. 1851. Chap. to the Spinning House, Cambridge, 1854. Formerly C. of St. Mark's, Birmingham, 1850, Hound, Southampton, 1852, Trinity, Cambridge, 1853. [25]

WHITEHEAD, George, *Birmingham.*—C. of All Saints', Birmingham. [26]

WHITEHEAD, Henry, 315, *Mile-end-road, London, E.*—Lin. Coll. Ox. 2nd cl. Lit. Hum. B.A. 1850, M.A. 1854; Deac. 1851 and Pr. 1852 by Bp of Lon. C. of St. Peter's, Stepney, 1867. Formerly C. of St. Luke's, Soho, 1851, St. Matthew's, Westminster, 1856, Trinity, Clapham, 1857, St. Anne's, Highgate Rise, 1864. Author, *Narrative of the Broad-street Cholera*, Hope, Great Marlborough-street; Sermons and Lectures. [27]

WHITEHEAD, Thomas, *Wimbledon, Surrey, S.W.*—Ex. Coll. Ox. B.A. 1847, M.A. 1850; Deac. 1848 and Pr. 1849 by Bp of Ox. C. of Wimbledon. [28]

WHITEHEAD, Thomas Clarke, *Christ's College, Finchley, London, N.*—Wad. Coll. Ox. Hody Exhib. of, Hon. 4th cl. Lit. Hum. and Math. B.A. 1840, M.A. 1844;

Deac. 1842, Pr. 1844. Sub-Warden of Ch. Coll. Finchley. Formerly P. C. of Trinity, Mount Albion, Ramsgate; P. C. of Gawcott, Bucks. Author, *Village Sketches*, 2s 6d, 2nd ed. 1s, Bosworth and Harrison. [1]

WHITEHEAD, Thomas Henry, *Coxhoe, Durham.*—St. Bees, 1st cl. Prizeman, Rupert's Land Prizeman and Librarian; Deac. 1865 by Bp of Carl. Pr. 1867 by Bp of Dur. C. of Kelloe, Durham, 1865. [2]

WHITEHEAD, William Chantler, *Christ Church, Battye Ford, Mirfield, Yorks.*—St. John's Coll. Cam. B.A. 1862, M.A. 1866; Deac. 1863 and Pr. 1864 by Bp of Rip. C. of Ch. Ch. Battye Ford, Mirfield, 1864. Formerly C. of Brighouse 1863–64; 2nd Mast. of Queen Elizabeth's Gr. Sch. Heath, Halifax, 1862–64. [3]

WHITEHOUSE, Ernest Frederic, *Saltney Parsonage, Chester.*—Dub; Deac. 1848 and Pr. 1849 by Bp of Wor. P. C. of Lache with Saltney, Dio. Ches. 1858. (Patron, Bp of Ches; P. C.'s Inc. 74*l* and Ho; Pop. 3000.) Chap. to the Infirmary, Chester, 1849. (Stipend, 40*l*.) Formerly C. of Netherton, Dudley, 1848–54, Brierley-hill 1854–56, Pensnett, Staffs, 1856–58. Author, *A New System of Shorthand*; *Lectures against Socialism.* [4]

WHITEHOUSE, George Lowe, *Manor House, Tuighton, Chester.*—St. Bees; Deac. 1846 by Bp of Ches. Pr. 1848 by Abp of York. C. of Bruera 1866. Formerly C. of Walmsley, Chester, 1846, Keyingham, Yorks, 1848, Bollington, Chester, 1849, Knaresborough 1856. [5]

WHITEHURST, John, *Gayton Rectory, Northampton.*—St. John's Coll. Cam. B.A. 1860, M.A. 1863; Deac. 1861 and Pr. 1862 by Bp of Pet. C. of Gayton 1861. [6]

WHITEHURST, Thomas Beach, *Leamington.*—St. Peter's Coll. Cam. B.A. 1823, M.A. 1827; Deac. 1824, Pr. 1825. [7]

WHITELAW, G., *Upton-on-Severn, Worcestershire.*—C. of Upton-on-Severn. [8]

WHITELEG, William, *Widnes, Warrington, Lancashire.*—Deac. and Pr. 1830. P. C. of Widnes, Dio. Ches. 1867. (Patron, William Wright, Esq; P. C.'s Inc. 130*l* and Ho; Pop. 10,000.) Formerly P. C. of Tilstock, Salop; Morning Lect. of St. Paul's, Bethnal Green, Lond; P. C. of Threlkeld 1858–66. [9]

WHITELEGGE, William, *Hulme, Manchester.*—Queen's Coll. Ox. B.A. 1837, M.A. 1840; Deac. 1838 and Pr. 1839 by Bp of Ches. R. of St. George's, Hulme, Dio. Man. 1842. (Patrons, D. and C. of Man; R.'s Inc. 400*l*; Pop. 18,349.) Formerly C. of St. George's-in-the Fields, Manchester, 1838, St. Mark's, Cheetham Hill, 1841. Author, several single Sermons. [10]

WHITELEY, Edward, *Oporto.*—Jesus Coll. Cam. B.A. 1821, M.A. 1846. British Chap. at Oporto. [11]

WHITELEY, John Henry, *Pedmore Rectory, Worcestershire.*—Trin. Coll. Cam. B.A. 1851, M.A. 1854; Deac. 1851 and Pr. 1853 by Bp of St. D. R. of Pedmore, Dio. Wor. 1855. (Patron, Lord Foley; Tithe, 320*l*; R.'s Inc. 449*l* and Ho; Pop. 297.) [12]

WHITELEY, William, *Whitegate, Northwich, Cheshire.*—Brasen. Coll. Ox. B.A. 1818. V. of Whitegate, Dio. Ches. 1825. (Patron, Lord Delamere; Tithe—Imp. 150*l*, V. 50*l*; V.'s Inc. 164*l*; Pop. 1535.) [13]

WHITELOCK, Benjamin, *Groombridge, near Tunbridge Wells.*—St. John's Coll. Cam. B.A. 1842, M.A. 1845; Deac. 1842 and Pr. 1843 by Abp of Cant. Min. of Groombridge 1848. Formerly C. of Barnes 1842, Egham, Surrey, 1847. [14]

WHITELOCK, Joseph Hutchinson, *Gilcrux Vicarage, Cockermouth.*—St. Bees; Deac. 1830 and Pr. 1831 by Bp of Carl. V. of Gilcrux, Dio. Carl. 1837. (Patron, Bp of Carl; Tithe—Imp. 22*l* 6*s* 9*d*, V. 10*l* 10*s*; Glebe, 75 acres; V.'s Inc. 121*l* and Ho; Pop. 653.) [15]

WHITELOCK, Richard, *Upper Mill, Saddleworth (Yorks), Rochdale.*—Lin. Coll. Ox. Lord Crewe's Exhib. B.A. 1826, M.A. 1829; Deac. 1826, Pr. 1827 by Bp of Lin. V. of Saddleworth, Dio. Man. 1831. (Patron, V. of Rochdale and then Bp of Roch; Glebe, 32a. 3r. 20p; P. C.'s Inc. 300*l* and Ho; Pop. 2954.) Surrogate. [16]

WHITELOCK, William, *Hutton Rectory, Penrith.*—St. John's Coll. Cam. 4th Sen. Opt. and B.A. 1836; Deac. 1836 and Pr. 1837 by Bp of Carl. R. of Hutton-in-the-Forest, Dio. Carl. 1855. (Patrons, D. and C. of Carl, Tithe, 75*l*; Glebe, 40 acres; R.'s Inc. 142*l* and Ho; Pop. 255.) Formerly C. of Hutton-in-the-Forest, near Penrith, 1836–55; Mast. of Penrith Gr. Sch. 1845–57. [17]

WHITER, Charles Walter, *Clown Rectory, Chesterfield.*—Clare Coll. Cam. B.A. 1824, M.A. 1827; Deac. 1825 and Pr. 1826 by Bp of Nor. R. of Clown, Dio. Lich. 1834. (Patron, Ld Chan; Tithe, 330*l*; Glebe, 67 acres; R.'s Inc. 411*l* and Ho; Pop. 704.) [18]

WHITESIDE, Stephen, *Vicarage, Shap, Westmoreland.*—Queen's Coll. Ox. B.A. 1854, M.A. 1857; Deac. 1856 by Bp. of Rip. Pr. 1858 by Bp of Carl. V. of Shap, Dio. Carl. 1863. (Patron, Earl of Lonsdale; Tithe, 5*l* 11*s*; Glebe, 3 acres; V.'s Inc. 92*l* and Ho; Pop. 930.) Formerly C. of Great Smeaton 1856–57, Lindale-in-Cartmel 1858–59; P. C. of Thrimby 1859–63. [19]

WHITESTONE, Nicholas Grattan, *Forest Side House, near Emsworth, Hants.*—Dub. A.B. 1842; A.M. 1863; Deac. 1843 by Bp of Lin. Pr. 1844 by Bp of Tuam. P. C. of Stansted, Dio. Chich. 1858. (Patroness, Mrs. Dixon; P. C.'s Inc. 213*l* and Ho; Pop. 450.) Formerly C. of Blackley, near Manchester, 1850–56; Assist. Min. of Ch. Ch. Greenheys, Manchester, 1856–58. Author, Protestant Tracts, 1857, Pratt and Son, Manchester. [20]

WHITESTONE, William Arthur, *Micheldever, Hants.*—Dub. A.B. 1856; Deac. 1857 by Bp of G. and B. Pr. 1860 by Bp of Chich. C. of Micheldever, 1866. Formerly C. of Trinity, Forest of Dean, Slindon, near Arundel, 1860. [21]

WHITEWAY, Robert Hayman, *Hill House, Ipswich.*—Wor. Coll. Ox. 4th cl. Lit. Hum. and B.A. 1838, M.A. 1841; Deac. 1839, Pr. 1840. R. of St. Clement's with St. Helen's, Ipswich, 1866. (Patrons, Church Patronage Soc; Tithe, 320*l*; R.'s Inc. 505*l* and Houses.) Formerly P. C. of Trinity, Cheltenham, 1842–46, Coleford, Somerset, 1846–65. [22]

WHITFIELD, Frederick.—Dub. A.B. 1859; Deac. 1859, Pr. 1860. Assoc. Sec. for the Irish Ch. Missions for the East Midland Cos. of England (temporary residence, Bedford). Formerly C. of Otley, Yorks, 1859–61; P. C. of Kirkby Ravensworth 1861–65. Author, *Sacred Poems and Prose*, 1860, 6*d*; *Voices from the Valley*, 1861, 3*s* 6*d*; *Spiritual Unfoldings*, 1862, 3*s* 6*d*; *Gleanings from Scripture*, 1864, 3*s* 6*d*; *Truth in Christ*, 1865, 3*s* 6*d*; *The Christian Casket*, 1864, 6*d*; *The Great Attraction*, 1864, 2*d*; *The Threefold Cord*, 1864, 2nd *Destruction! What is it? Treasure in Earthen Vessels*; *Jesus only*; *The Two Coverings*; *Jesus' Love*; "*Jesus said*;" *Paul and Agrippa, or Words of Warning and Counsel*; all published by S. W. Partridge. [23]

WHITFIELD, George Thomas, *Pudleston Rectory, Leominster, Herefordshire.*—St. John's Coll. Ox. B.A. 1831, M.A. 1835. R. of Pudleston with While R. Dio. Herf. 1840. (Patron, Edwin Chadwick, Esq; Tithe, 221*l* 5*s* 6*d*; R.'s Inc. 280*l* and Ho; Pop. 349.) [24]

WHITING, H. B., *Writhlington Rectory, Bath.*—R. of Writhlington, Somerset, Dio. B. and W. 1848. (Patron, Preb. thereof; R.'s Inc. 166*l* and Ho; Pop. 367.) [25]

WHITING, James, *Royston Vicarage, Herts.*—Queens' Coll. Cam. B.A. 1823, M.A. 1841; Deac. 1824 by Bp of G. and B. Pr. 1824 by Bp. of Nor. V. of Royston, Dio. Roch. 1845. (Patron, Lord Dacre; Glebe, 8 acres; V.'s Inc. 154*l* and Ho; Pop. 1882.) Surrogate. Formerly Chap. to the Hon. E.I.C. on the Bengal Establishment for 17 years. [26]

WHITING, John Bradford, *Broomfield Vicarage, Chelmsford.*—Caius Coll. Cam. Exhib. 5th Sen. Opt. and B.A. 1850; Deac. 1851, Pr. 1852. V. of Broomfield, Dio. Roch. 1861. (Patron, Bp of Roch; V.'s Inc. 250*l* and Ho; Pop. 850.) Formerly C. of Saffron Walden. Author, *Great Importance of the Gift of the Holy Spirit* (a Tract), Macintosh, 1*d*. [27]

WHITING, John Scott, *Storrington, Steyning, Sussex.*—Wor. Coll. Ox. B.A. 1838; Deac. 1842 and Pr.

1843 by Bp of Lin. R. of Storrington, Dio. Chich. 1857. (Patron, Duke of Norfolk; Tithe, 600*l*; Glebe, 25 acres; R.'s Inc. 640*l* and Ho; Pop. 1104.) Formerly C. of Ippolyts with Great Wymondley, Herts. [1]

WHITING, Robert, *Ringsfield Rectory, Beccles, Suffolk.*—St. John's Coll. Cam. B.A. 1829, M.A. 1835. R. of Ringsfield with Little Redisham R. Dio. Nor. 1848. (Patron, E. Staples, Esq; Tithe, 480*l* 2*s* 7*d*; R.'s Inc. 591*l* and Ho; Pop. 324.) [2]

WHITING, R. Chapman, *St. Peter's College, Radley, Berks.*—Fell. of Trin. Coll. Cam; Sub-Warden of St. Peter's Coll. Radley. [3]

WHITLEY, Charles Thomas, *Bedlington Vicarage, Morpeth, Northumberland.*—St. John's Coll. Cam. Sen. Wrang. and B.A. 1830, M.A. 1833; Deac. 1835, Pr. 1836. V. of Bedlington, Dio. Dur. 1854. (Patrons, D. and C. of Dur; Tithe—Eccles. Commis. 827*l* 7*s* 8*d*, V. 227*l* 9*s* 2½*d*; Glebe, 236 acres; V.'s Inc. 560*l* and Ho; Pop. 2328.) Hon. Can. of Dur. Cathl. 1849; Rural Dean. Formerly Fell. of St. John's Coll. Cam. 1831. Translator of *Poinsot on Rotatory Motion*, Cambridge, 1834. [4]

WHITLEY, John, *Newton-in-Makerfield Rectory, near Warrington.*—Queens' Coll. Cam. B.A. 1837, M.A. 1840. R. of Newton-in-Makerfield, Dio. Ches. 1846. (Patron, Earl of Derby; Tithe, 300*l*; R.'s Inc. 321*l* and Ho; Pop. 3787.) Surrogate. [5]

WHITLEY, Thomas, *Newton, Warrington.*—Emman. Coll. Cam. Scho. of, Sen. Opt. B.A. 1855, M.A. 1858; Deac. 1856 and Pr. 1857 by Bp of Ely. P. C. of St. Peter's, Newton-in-Makerfield, Dio. Ches. 1864. (Patron, W. J. Legh, Esq; P. C.'s Inc. 188*l*; Pop. 2122.) Formerly C. of Elton, Hunts, 1856–57, Oundle, Northants, 1857–59, Clun, Salop, 1859–64. [6]

WHITLOCK, George, *Leigh Parsonage, Reigate.*—Deac. 1822 and Pr. 1823 by Bp of Ches. P. C. of Leigh, Dio. Win. 1860. (Patrons, the Dendy family; P. C.'s Inc. 140*l* and Ho; Pop. 506.) [7]

WHITLOCK, George Stewart, *Christ Church, Chelsea, London, S.W.*—Brasen. Coll. Ox. B.A. 1847, M.A. 1850; Deac. 1849 and Pr. 1850 by Bp of Lon. P. C. of Ch. Ch. Chelsea, Dio. Lon. 1865. (Patrons, Hyndman's Trustees; P. C.'s Inc. 300*l*; Pop. 6500.) Formerly C. of St. George's, Bloomsbury, 1849–54; R. of Milton-Bryant, Beds, 1854–65. Author, *The Secret of Apostolical and Ministerial Success* (a Visitation Sermon), J. F. Shaw, 1860, 6*d*. [8]

WHITLOCK, John Aston.—Brasen. Coll. Ox. B. A. 1859; Deac. 1859 and Pr. 1860 by Abp of Cant. Assist. Min. of Portman Chapel, Baker-street, Marylebone, Lond. Formerly C. of Plaxtole, Kent, 1859; St. Giles'-in-the-Fields, Lond. [9]

WHITMARSH, Edgar Dyke, 29, *St. Giles', Oxford.*—St. John's Coll. Ox. M.A. 1865, B.C.L. 1866; Deac. 1865 and Pr. 1866 by Bp of Ox. C. of St. Giles', Oxford, 1865. [10]

WHITMARSH, William, *Greystead, Hexham, Northumberland.*—R. of Greystead, Dio. Dur. 1866. (Patrons, Govs. of Greenwich Hospital; R.'s Inc. 150*l* and Ho; Pop. 290.) Formerly Chap. of H.M.S. "St. Vincent." [11]

WHITMORE, George, *Stockton Rectory, Shiffnal, Salop.*—Ch. Ch. Ox. B.A. 1834, M.A. 1836; Deac. 1836 by Bp of Ban. Pr. 1837 by Bp of Lich. R. of Stockton, Dio. Lich. 1857. (Patron, T. C. Whitmore, Esq; Tithe, 635*l* 15*s*; Glebe, 184 acres; R.'s Inc. 900*l*; Pop. 490.) Formerly R. of Kemberton with Sutton Maddock V. Salop, 1840–56. [12]

WHITMORE, Henry, *Paternoster-row, Carlisle.*—Caius Coll. Cam. B.A. 1859, M.A. 1866; Deac. 1859 and Pr. 1861 by Bp of Carl. Min. Can. and Precentor, Carlisle Cathl. 1863; Sacrist 1864. (Value, Minor Canonry, 150*l*; Precentorship, 25*l*; Sacrist, 1*l*.) Formerly C. of Dalton-in-Furness 1859–63. [13]

WHITNEY, Thomas, *Marsden Parsonage, Huddersfield.*—St. Aidan's; Deac. 1849 and Pr. 1850 by Bp. of Ex. P. C. of Marsden, Dio. Rip. 1856. (Patron, V. of Almondbury; P. C.'s Inc. 165*l* and Ho; Pop. 2690.) Formerly C. of Greetland, Yorks. [14]

WHITTAKER, James, *Bredbury, near Stockport.*—Dub. A.B. 1839; Deac. 1839 and Pr. 1840 by Bp of Ches. P. C. of Bredbury, Dio. Ches. 1846. (Patrons, Crown and Bp of Ches. alt; Glebe, ¼ acre; P. C.'s Inc. 200*l*; Pop. 3408.) Formerly C. of St. Jude's, Manchester. [15]

WHITTAKER, Robert, *Leesfield House, Lees, Manchester.*—St. John's Coll. Cam. 8th Sen. Opt. and B.A. 1844, M.A. 1850; Deac. 1844, Pr. 1845. P. C. of Leesfield, Dio. Man. 1846. (Patrons, the Crown and Bp of Man. alt; P. C.'s Inc. 300*l*; Pop. 5358.) [16]

WHITTARD, Thomas Middlemore, *The College, Cheltenham.*—Trin. Coll. Cam. B.A. 1852, M.A. 1855; Deac. 1852. Head Mast. of the Junior Department, Cheltenham Coll. Formerly Prof. of English Literature at Victoria Coll. Jersey, 1852. [17]

WHITTEMORE, William Meynell, *Angell-park, Brixton, S.*—Queens' Coll. Cam; D.D. 1866; Deac. and Pr. 1845. R. of St. James's within Aldgate, City and Dio. Lon. 1851. (Patron, Corporation of Lond; R.'s Inc. 300*l*.) Author, *The Infant Altar*; *The Seventh Head*; *Daily Devotions for the Young*; *The Larger Church Catechism*; *Short Liturgy*; and various minor Works. Editor of *Golden Hours* and *Sunshine*. [18]

WHITTER, Walrond, *Bridford, Chudleigh, Devon.*—C. of Bridford. [19]

WHITTING, William Henry, *King's College, Cambridge.*—King's Coll. Cam. B.A. 1854; Deac. 1856 by Bp of Lin. Pr. 1858 by Abp of York. Fell. of King's Coll. Cam. and Dean of same 1865; C. of St. Benet's, Cambridge, 1866. Formerly C. of Turvey, Beds, 1856–67, Aberford, Yorks, 1857–65. [20]

WHITTINGHAM, Samuel, *Childrey Rectory, Wantage, Berks.*—Corpus Coll. Ox. B.A. 1803, M.A. 1806, B.D. 1815, D.D. 1833; Deac. 1806 and Pr. 1807 by Bp of Ox. R. of Childrey, Dio. Ox. 1840. (Patron, Corpus Coll. Ox; Glebe, 560 acres; R.'s Inc. 569*l* 2*s* 6*d* and Ho; Pop. 504.) [21]

WHITTINGTON, Henry, *Chilcompton, Bath.*—Pemb. Coll. Cam. B.A. 1831; Deac. 1832 and Pr. 1835 by Bp of Lich. V. of Chilcompton, Dio. B. and W. 1855. (Patron, H. S. W. Tooker, Esq; Tithe—Imp. 120*l*, V. 123*l*; Glebe, 11 acres; V.'s Inc. 150*l*; Pop. 730.) [22]

WHITTINGTON, H. F., *Twyford, Hants.*—C. of Twyford. [23]

WHITTINGTON, Henry Gambler, *King's Bromley, Staffordshire.*—St. Peter's Coll. Cam. B.A. 1860; Deac. 1860 by Bp of Pet. C. of King's Bromley 1865. Formerly C. of Irthlingborough, Northants, 1860, Basford, Notts, 1863. [24]

WHITTINGTON, Richard, 18, *Guildford-street, Russell-square, London, W.C.*—Trin. Coll. Cam. Norrisian Prizeman 1849, B.A. 1847, M.A. 1850; Deac. 1848 and Pr. 1849 by Bp of Lon. Asst. Mast. in Merchant Taylors' Sch. 1853; Sunday Even. Lect. at St. Peter's-upon-Cornhill 1849; Townsend Lect. at St. Magnus', London-bridge, 1862; Morning Reader at St. Mark's, Pentonville, Lond. 1859. Formerly C. of St. Peter's, Saffron-hill, 1848, and St. Matthew's, Friday-street, Lond. 1851. Author, *The Inspiration of the Historical Books of the Old Testament* (Norrisian Essay), Rivingtons, 1849, 4*s* 6*d*; *The Christian Sabbath* (a Sermon), ib. 1849, 6*d*. [25]

WHITTINGTON, R. T., *Bothamsall, Ollerton, Notts.*—C. of Bothamsall. [26]

WHITTLE, Charles, *Nassington, Wansford, Northants.*—Trin. Coll. Ox. S.C.L. 1846; Deac. 1848 and Pr. 1849 by Abp of York. C. of Nassington 1861. Formerly P. C. of Greenham, Berks, 1855–59; C. of Stoke Abbas, Dorset, 1859–61. [27]

WHITWORTH, Richard Hisco, *Blidworth, Mansfield, Notts.*—St. Bees; Deac. 1848 and Pr. 1849 by Abp of York. V. of Blidworth, Dio. Lin. 1865. (Patron, Bp of Man; V.'s Inc. 300*l* and Ho; Pop. 1166.) Formerly 2nd Mast. of the Royal Gr. Sch. Reading; Sen. C. of St. Wilfrid's, Standish, Wigan, 1850. [28]

WHITWORTH, Thomas, *Thorpe St. Peter, Wainfleet, Boston.*—Ch. Coll. Cam. B.A. 1829; Deac.

1829 and Pr. 1830 by Bp of Lin. R. of Addlethorpe, Dio. Lin. 1842. (Patron, Ld Chan; Tithe, 140l 10s; Glebe, 7 acres; R.'s Inc. 154l and Ho; Pop. 302.) V. of Thorpe St. Peter, Dio. Lin. 1843. (Patron, William Hopkinson, Esq; Tithe, 34l; V.'s Inc. 336l; Pop. 593.) [1]

WHITWORTH, William, *Bacup, near Manchester.*—St. John's Coll. Cam. B.A. 1838, M.A. 1842; Deac. and Pr. 1838 by Bp of Ches. P. C. of St. Saviour's, Bacup, 1865. (Patron, J. M. Holt, Esq; Pop. 2350.) Surrogate. Formerly R. of St. Jude's, Manchester. [2]

WHITWORTH, William Allen, 77, *Bedford-street South, Liverpool.*—St. John's Coll. Cam. Scho. of Wrangler, B.A. 1862, M.A. 1865; Deac. 1865 and Pr. 1866, by Bp of Ches. Prof. of Math. in Queen's Coll. Liverpool, 1865; C. of St. Luke's, Liverpool, 1866. Formerly C. of St. Anne's, Birkenhead, 1865. Author, *Trilinear Co-ordinates and other Methods of Modern Analytical Geometry*, 1866, Bell and Daldy, 16s; *Choice and Chance, Two Chapters of Arithmetic*, 1867, Bell and Daldy, 3s 6d. Editor of the *Oxford, Cambridge, and Dublin Messenger of Mathematics*, published every term, Macmillan and Co. [3]

WHITWORTH, William Henry, *Chidcock, Bridport, Dorset.*—Corpus Coll. Ox. 2nd cl. Lit. Hum. and B.A. 1831, M.A. 1835; Deac. 1834 and Pr. 1835 by Bp of Ox. C. of Chidcock; Lect. at Stanton St. Gabriel's. Formerly Fell. and Tut. of Corpus Coll. Ox. [4]

WHORWHOOD, Thomas Henry, *Willoughby, near Rugby.*—Magd. Coll. Ox. B.A. 1833, M.A. 1836, B.D. 1843, D.D. 1847; Deac. 1835 by Bp of Ox. Pr. 1836 by Bp of Wor. V. of Willoughby, Dio. Wor. 1849. (Patron, Magd. Coll. Ox; Glebe, 120 acres; V.'s Inc. 217l; Pop. 372.) Formerly Fell. of Magd. Coll. Ox. [5]

WHYLEY, Edward Bower, *King's School, Peterborough.*—Trin. Coll. Cam. Crosse Univ. Scho. and B.A. 1850, Tyrrwhitt's Heb. Prize, and M.A. 1853; Deac. and Pr. 1851 by Bp of Ely. Head Mast. of the Peterborough Gram. Sch. Formerly C. of Cottenham, Cambs, 1851, Oakington, Cambs (sole charge), 1851–53. [6]

WHYLEY, Francis, 3, *Finsbury-circus, London, E.C.*—C. of St. Andrew's Undershaft, Lond. [7]

WHYLEY, Gregory Edward, *Eaton Bray Vicarage, Dunstable.*—Trin. Coll. Cam. B.A. 1821, M.A. 1824; Deac. 1821 by Abp of Cant. Pr. 1822 by Bp of Lon. V. of Eaton Bray, Dio. Ely, 1825. (Patron, Trin. Coll. Cam; Tithe—Imp. 434l, V. 150l, Glebe, 45 acres; V.'s Inc. 260l and Ho; Pop. 1440.) V. of Stanbridge, Beds, Dio. Ely, 1844. (Patron, V. of Leighton-Buzzard; Tithe—App. 393l 14s 4d, P. C. 16l 15s; Glebe, 19 acres; V.'s Inc. 100l; Pop. 554.) Rural Dean 1839. [8]

WHYTE, Charles Alexander Luscombe, *India.*—Pemb. Coll. Ox. B.A. 1853; Deac. 1855 and Pr. 1856 by Bp of Lin. Formerly C. of Worksop, Notts. [9]

WHYTE, James Richard, *Launcells Vicarage, Stratton, Cornwall.*—Oriel Coll. Ox. B.A. 1832; Deac. 1832 and Pr. 1833 by Bp of Ex. V. of Launcells, Dio. Ex. 1844. (Patron, Sir G. S. Stucley, Bart; Tithe, 220l; Glebe, 9 acres; V.'s Inc. 230l and Ho; Pop. 683.) Formerly C. of Launcells 1832–34, Okehampton, Devon, 1834–40, King's Nympton, Devon, 1840–44. [10]

WHYTE, James Richard, *Winestead Rectory, Hull.*—R. of Winestead, Dio. York, 1852. (Patroness, Mrs. Hildyard; Tithe, 18s; Glebe, 230 acres; R.'s Inc. 352l and Ho; Pop. 173.) [11]

WHYTT, James, *High Wycombe, Bucks.*—St. Edm. Hall, Ox. B.A. 1834, M.A. 1837; Deac. 1834, Pr. 1835. Sen. C. of High Wycombe 1866. Formerly C. of Crewkerne 1859–62, St. Margaret's, Lynn, 1862–66. Author, several Poems. [12]

WICKE, John, *Wootton Bassett, Wilts.*—Ch. Coll. Cam. V. of Wootton Bassett, Dio. Salis. 1865. (Patrons, Trustees of Sir Henry Meux, Bart; Tithe, 495l 12s 4d; Glebe, 92½ acres; V.'s Inc. 630l and Ho; Pop. 2191.) Formerly C. of All Saints', Maidstone, of Trinity, Maidstone, of Trinity, Dover, of West Farleigh, Kent, of Wootton, Isle of Wight, and of St. Peter's, Bristol. [13]

WICKENDEN, J. Frederic, *Stoke Bishop, Bristol.*—Trin. Coll. Cam. B.A. 1852, M.A. 1855; Deac. 1853 by Bp of Man. Pr. 1856 by Bp of Wor. Formerly C. of Pershore 1853–57, Horfield 1857–58. Author, *Seven Days in Attica.* [14]

WICKENS, Henry, *Wyken, Coventry.*—Ex. Coll. Ox. B.A. 1836, M.A. 1844. P. C. of Wyken, Dio. Wor. (Patron, Earl of Craven; P. C.'s Inc. 112l 19s 8d; Pop. 148.) Chap. of the Don. of Binley, near Coventry, Dio. Wor. (Patron, Earl of Craven; Chap.'s Inc. 52l 10s; Pop. 196.) [15]

WICKES, John Beck, *Boughton, Northampton.*—St. John's Coll. Ox. B.A. 1838, M.A. 1841; Deac. 1839, Pr. 1840. Formerly C. of Norton and East Haddon, Northants. [16]

WICKES, William, *Huron College, London, Canada West.*—Trin. Coll. Cam. Scho. Prizeman, 28th Wrang. 1840, M.A. 1843; Deac. 1850 and Pr. 1851 by Bp of Quebec. Prin. of Huron College. Formerly C. at Morebath, Devon. [17]

WICKHAM, Edmund Dawe, *Holmwood, Dorking, Surrey.*—Ball. Coll. Ox. 2nd cl. Lit. Hum. and B.A. 1831, M.A. 1833; Deac. 1833, Pr. 1834. P. C. of Holmwood, Dio. Win. 1851. (Patron, Bp of Win; Glebe, 2 acres; P. C.'s Inc. 120l.; Pop. 1211.) [18]

WICKHAM, Edward Charles, *New College, Oxford.*—New Coll. Ox. Chan. Prize Lat. Verse 1856, M.A. 1858; Deac. 1857, Pr. 1858. Fell. and Tut. of New Coll. Ox. [19]

WICKHAM, Frederick Peers, *New College, Oxford.*—Fell. of New Coll. Ox. [20]

WICKHAM, Hill Dawe, *Horsington Rectory, Wincanton, Somerset.*—Ex. Coll. Ox. B.A. 1828, M.A. 1831; Deac. 1831 and Pr. 1832 by Bp of B. and W. R. of Horsington, Dio. B. and W. 1856. (Patron, the present R; Tithe—App. 1l 4s, R. 874l 8s; Glebe, 75½ acres; R.'s Inc. 974l and Ho; Pop. 869)—the present R. is the seventh of his family in succession since 1686. Formerly P. C. of Ch. Ch. Frome, 1845–56. Author, *Historical Sketch of the Italian Vaudois* (for which the Author received a Gold Medal from Frederick-William IV., King of Prussia), Seeleys, 1847, 5s; *Facts from Frome*, Hatchards, 1853, 1s 6d; *Life and Correspondence of the Rev. Dr Whalley*, Bentley, 2 vols. 1863, 30s. [21]

WICKHAM, The Ven. Robert, *Gresford, Wrexham, Denbighshire.*—Ch. Ch. Ox. 2nd cl. Lit. Hum. 1823, B.A. 1824, M.A. 1827; Deac. 1825, Pr. 1826. Archd. of St. Asaph 1854, with Res. Can. attached. (Value, 300l.) V. of Gresford, Dio. St. A. 1847. (Patron, Bp of St. A; Tithe—App. 1955l 18s 9d and 184½ acres of Glebe, Imp. 110l, V. 587l 9s 9d; Glebe, 47 acres; V.'s Inc. 720l and Ho; Pop. 1690.) Chap. to Bp of St. A. 1847. Author, *Is the Offertory without Communion required by the Church?* 1844; *The Rubrics of the Communion Service examined*, 1845. [22]

WICKHAM, Thomas Vowler, *Rossett Parsonage, Wrexham.*—Ch. Ch. Ox. B.A. 1859, M.A. 1863; Deac. and Pr. 1860 by Bp of St. A. P. C. of Ch. Ch. Rossett, Dio. St. A. 1863. (Patrons, Trustees; Glebe, 4 acres; P. C.'s Inc. 80l and Ho; Pop. 1371.) Formerly C. of Ruabon 1860–63.) [23]

WICKS, Frederick William, *St. Nicholas' Vicarage, Whitehaven.*—St. Bees 1842; Deac. 1843 and Pr. 1844 by Bp of Ches. V. of St. Nicholas', Whitehaven, Dio. Carl. 1849. (Patron, Earl of Lonsdale; P.C.'s Inc. 224l; Pop. 3815.) [24]

WICKSTEAD, John Henry, 22, *Story-street, Hull.*—Wor. Coll. Ox. Hon. 4th cl. Math. B.A. 1861, M.A. 1865; Deac. 1863 and Pr. 1864 by Abp of York. C. of Ch. Ch. Sculcoates, Hull. [25]

WIDDOWSON, Thomas, *Kettering, Northants.*—St. John's Coll. Cam. Scho. and Prizeman of, 25th Wrang. B.A. 1859; Deac. 1860 by Bp of St. A. Pr. 1862 by Bp of Pet. Head Mast. of Kettering Gr. Sch. Formerly C. of Wrexham, Wales, and Houghton-on-the-Hill, Leic. [26]

WIDDRINGTON, Sidney Henry, 2, *Castle-villas, Maida-vale, London, W.*—Magd. Coll. Cam. B.A.

1837, M.A. 1840; Deac. 1835 by Bp of Chich. Pr. by Bp of Ex. P. C. of St. Mark's, Hamilton-terrace, St. John's-wood, Dio. Lon. 1863. (Patron, the Crown; P. C.'s Inc. 600*l*; Pop. 4756.) Formerly P. C. of St. Leonard's, and St. Mary Magdalen's, Sussex, 1838–40; R. of Walcot, Bath, 1840-58; V. of St. Michael's, Coventry, 1858–63. Author, various Sermons and Addresses. [1]

WIGAN, Alfred, *Luddesdown Rectory, Gravesend, Kent.*—Deac. 1842, Pr. 1843. R. of Luddesdown, Dio. Roch. 1856. (Patron, J. A. Wigan, Esq; R.'s Inc. 420*l* and Ho; Pop. 279.) Formerly C. of Trottersclifle, Kent. [2]

WIGAN, Septimus, *Faversham, Kent.*—Trin. Coll. Cam. 3rd Sen. Opt. B.A. 1856, M.A. 1859; Deac. 1856 and Pr. 1858 by Abp of Cant. Chap. of the Almshouses at Faversham. Formerly C. of St. Mary's, Dover, 1856–59, Ticehurst 1859–61; P. C. of Fring, Norfolk, 1861–66. Author, *Election, its Nature and Consequences,* 1860. 3*d.* [3]

WIGAN, William Lewis, *The Vicarage, East Malling, Maidstone.*—Ch. Ch. Ox. B.A. 1840, M.A. 1842; Deac. 1840 and Pr. 1841 by Bp of Roch. V. of East Malling, Dio. Cant. 1847. (Patron, J. A. Wigan, Esq; Tithe, 802*l*; Glebe, 21 acres; V.'s. Inc. 837*l* and Ho; Pop. 1974.) Formerly C. of Trottersclifle, Kent. [4]

WIGGIN, William, *Oddington Rectory, near Chipping-Norton.*—Ex. Coll. Ox. B.A. 1841, M.A. 1847; Deac. 1843, Pr. 1844. R. of Oddington, Dio. G. and B. 1844. (Patron, Bp of G. and B; Tithe, 90*l*; Glebe, 188 acres; R.'s Inc. 361*l* and Ho; Pop. 588.) [5]

WIGHT, William, *Harbury Vicarage, Southam, Warwickshire.*—Corpus Coll. Cam. B.A. 1844, M.A. 1847; Deac. 1845 and Pr. 1846 by Bp of Dur. V. of Harbury, Dio. Wor. 1852. (Patrons, Trustees; Glebe, 190 acres; V.'s Inc. 230*l* and Ho; Pop. 1206.) Author, *The Leprous Soul*; *England's Homes*; *England's Charities, their Mischievous and Deteriorating Influence on the National Character, with Thoughts suggestive of a Remedy*; *England's Gin Palaces*; *Advice to the Working Classes*; *Common Sense*; etc. [6]

WIGHTMAN, Charles Edward Leopold, *St. Alkmond's Vicarage, Shrewsbury.*—Lin. Coll. Ox. B.A. 1838, M.A. 1845; Deac. 1839, Pr. 1840. V. of St. Alkmond's, Shrewsbury, Dio. Lich. 1841. (Patron, Ld. Chan; Tithe—Imp. 1065*l* 4*s* 1*d*, V. 185*l* 4*s*; V.'s Inc. 190*l* and Ho; Pop. 1352.) [7]

WIGHTMAN, William Arnett, *York.*—Caius Coll. Cam. B.A. 1854, M.A. 1857; Deac. 1855 and Pr. 1856 by Abp of York. Min. Can. of York 1858; V. of Trinity in King's Court, York, Dio. York, 1866. (Patron, Mast. of Wells Hospital; V.'s Inc. 75*l*; Pop. 599.) Formerly C. of St. Helen's, York, 1855–63, Trinity, 1863–66. [8]

WIGHTWICK, Henry, *Codford St. Peter Rectory, Heytesbury, Wilts.*—Pemb. Coll. Ox. B.A. 1831, M.A. 1835; Deac. and Pr. 1823 by Bp of Ox. R. of Codford St. Peter, Dio. Salis. 1840. (Patron, Pemb. Coll. Ox; Tithe, 462*l* 2*s*; R.'s Inc. 480*l* and Ho; Pop. 359.) [9]

WIGHTWICK, Humphrey Mercer, 39, *De Beauvoir-road, London, N.*—Deac. 1859 and Pr. 1860 by Bp of Lon. P. C. of St. Anne's, Hoxton, Dio. Lon. 1865. (Patrons, Crown and Bp of Lon. alt; P. C.'s Inc. 200*l*; Pop. 5000.) Chap. of the Refuge, Dalston. Formerly C. of Ch. Ch. Spitalfields 1859–61, Lond; Dioc. Home Miss. 1861–65. [10]

WIGHTWICK, John Briddon, *Newton Parsonage, Penrith.*—Dur. Licen. Theol. 1842; Deac. 1842, Pr. 1843. P. C. of Newton Rigney, Dio. Carl. 1846. (Patron, Bp of Carl; P. C.'s Inc. 90*l* and Ho; Pop. 253.) Chap. to the Penrith Union 1853. [11]

WIGNALL, William, *Bamber Bridge, Preston, Lancashire.*—P. C. of Bamber Bridge, Dio. Man. 1837. (Patron, V. of Blackburn; Glebe, 6¼ acres; P. C.'s Inc. 190*l* and Ho; Pop. 2182.) [12]

WIGRAM, Ernest, *Doncaster.*—C. of Doncaster. [13]

WIGRAM, Frederic Edward, *Highfield, Southampton.*—Trin. Coll. Cam. B.A. 1857, M.A. 1860; Deac. 1858 and Pr. 1859 by Bp of Ely. P. C. of Portswood, South Stoneham, Dio. Win. 1864. (Patron, Bp of Win; Tithe, 212*l* 11*s* 8*d*; Glebe, 1½ acres; P. C.'s Inc. 300*l* and Ho; Pop. 1500.) Formerly C. of St. Paul's, Cambridge, 1858–63, Wanstead, Essex, 1863–64. [14]

WIGRAM, Spencer Robert, *Prittlewell Vicarage, Chelmsford.*—Ball. Coll. Ox. B.A. 1859, M.A. 1861; Deac. 1860 and Pr. 1861 by Bp of Win. V. of Prittlewell, Dio. Roch. 1864. (Patron, Bp of Roch; V.'s Inc. 365*l* and Ho; Pop. 1711.) Formerly C. of Farnham, Surrey, 1860–62, Romford, Essex, 1862–64. [15]

WIGRAM, William Pitt, *Latton Vicarage, Harlow, Essex.*—Trin. Coll. Cam. B.A. 1829, M.A. 1832; Deac. 1831, Pr. 1832. V. of Latton, Dio. Roch. 1867. (Patron, L. Arkwright, Esq; Tithe, 385*l*; Glebe, 113 acres; V.'s Inc. 546*l* and Ho; Pop. 196.) Formerly R. of Wanstead, Essex, 1837–67; Chap. to Bp of Roch. [16]

WIGRAM, Woolmore, *Furneaux Pelham, Ware, Herts.*—Trin. Coll. Cam. B.A. 1854, M.A. 1858; Deac. 1855 by Bp of Colombo, Pr. 1856 by Bp of Lon. V. of Brent Pelham with Furneaux Pelham, Dio. Roch. 1864 (Patron, Treas. of St. Paul's Cathl; V.'s Inc. 360*l* and Ho; Pop. 906.) Formerly C. of Hampstead, Middlesex. [17]

WIGSTON, William, *Rushmere, near Ipswich.*—St. John's Coll. Cam. 12th Jun. Opt. B.A. 1839, M.A. 1842; Deac. 1841 and Pr. 1842 by Bp of Lon. V. of Rushmere St. Andrew, Dio. Nor. 1848. (Patron, Marquis of Bristol; Tithe—Imp. 310*l*. V. 170*l*; Glebe, 35 acres; V.'s Inc. 200*l* and Ho; Pop. 678.) [18]

WILBERFORCE, Ernest Roland, *Middleton Stony, Bicester.*—Ex. Coll. Ox. B.A. 1854, M.A. 1865; Deac. 1864, Pr. 1865. R. of Middleton Stony, Dio. Ox. 1866. (Patron, Bp of Ox; Tithe, 390*l*; Glebe, 100 acres; R.'s Inc. 500*l* and Ho; Pop. 259.) Chap. to Bp of Ox. Formerly C. of Cuddesdon 1864, Lea, Lincolnshire, 1865. [19]

WILBERFORCE, William Francis, *Royston Vicarage, Barnsley, Yorks.*—Univ. Coll. Ox. B.A. 1856, M.A. 1858; Deac. 1857 and Pr. 1859 by Bp of Ox. V. of Royston, Dio. York, 1862. (Patron, Abp of York; V.'s Inc. 300*l* and Ho; Pop. 1240.) Formerly C. of St. Giles's, Reading. [20]

WILBRAHAM, Charles Philip, *Audley Vicarage, Newcastle, Staffs.*—St. Peter's Coll. Cam. B.A. 1844, M.A. 1865; Deac. 1844 by Abp of Cant. Pr. 1844 by Bp of Lich. V. of Audley, Dio. Lich. 1844. (Patron, the present V; Tithe, comm. 430*l*; Glebe, 31 acres; V.'s Inc. 500*l* and Ho; Pop. 2813.) Rural Dean. Author, *Palestine,* 9th ed. S.P.C.K. 6*d*; *Holy Sites in Land of Promise,* ib. 4½*d*; *Scenes beyond the Atlantic,* ib. 4½*d*; *Natives of Africa,* ib. 4½*d*; *Descriptions of Canaan,* Parkers, 1*s*. [21]

WILCOCK, Alfred William, *St. Bartholomew's Hospital, London, E.C.*—Queens' Coll. Cam. B.A. 1847, M.A. 1850; Deac. 1847 and Pr. 1848 by Bp of Ex. Asst. Hospitaller to St. Bartholomew's Hospital 1852; Reader at Ch. Ch. Newgate-street, Lond. [22]

WILCOCKS, Horace Stone, 1, *Clarendon-terrace, North-road, Plymouth.*—St. John's Coll. Cam. B. A. 1859, M.A. 1862; Deac. 1859 by Bp of Man. Pr. 1860 by Bp of Ex. Asst. C. of St. Peter's, Plymouth, 1865. Formerly Asst. C. of St. Luke's, Heywood, Lancashire, 1859–60; C. of St. James's, Davenport, 1860–65. [23]

WILCOX, Arthur Marwood, *Twyford School, near Winchester.*—Emman. Coll. Cam. Scho. of, 10th Sen. Opt. 3rd cl. Cl. Trip. 2nd cl. Theol. Trip. B.A. 1865; Deac. and Pr. 1866 by Bp of Pet. 1st Asst. Mast. of Twyford Sch. Formerly C. of Thorpe Mandeville, Banbury, 1866, Lois Weedon, Towcester, 1866. [24]

WILCOX, John, *Hixon Parsonage, Stafford.*—Queens' Coll. Cam. B.A. 1849, M.A. 1860; Deac. 1849, Pr. 1850. P. C. of Hixon, Dio. Lich. 1858. (Patron, Bp of Lich; P. C.'s Inc. 115*l* and Ho; Pop. 710.) [25]

WILD, George John, *Bisley Rectory, Bagshot, Surrey.*—Emman. Coll. Cam. 1st cl. Law Trip. S.C.L. 1848, LL.B. 1853, LL.D. 1859; Deac. 1850, and Pr. 1852 by Bp. of Lich. R. of Bisley, Dio. Win. 1865. (Patroness, Mrs. Wild; Tithe, 180*l*; Glebe, 30 acres; R.'s Inc. 230*l* and Ho; Pop. 318.) Formerly V. of Dodderhill with Elmbridge for 9½ years. Author, *A Brief Defence of "Essays and Reviews,"* Hardwicke. [1]

WILD, John, *Castle Bytham, Stamford.*—Dub. A.B. 1855; Deac. 1855 and Pr. 1857 by Bp of Lin. C. in sole charge of Castle Bytham 1864. Formerly C. of Old Radford, Notts, 1855–58, Great Grimsby 1858–61, East Drayton 1861–63, Heapham 1862–64. Author, *Remarks on the Clerical Supply and Demand in the Church of England,* Stamford, 6d. [2]

WILD, Marshall, *Poynton, Stockport.*—Queen's Coll. Ox. B.A. 1857, M.A. 1860; Deac. 1858 by Bp of Wor. Pr. 1858 by Bp of Lich. P. C. of Poynton, Dio. Ches. 1864. (Patron, Lord Vernon; P. C.'s Inc. 85*l*; Pop. 1977.) Formerly C. of Newark, Notts, and Alton, Staffs. [3]

WILD, Robert Louis, *Herstmonceux Rectory, Hurst Green, Sussex.*—Oriel Coll. Ox. B.A. 1860, M.A. 1862; Deac. 1860 and Pr. 1861 by Bp of Herf. R. of Herstmonceux, Dio. Chich. 1866. (Patron, the present R; Glebe, 160 acres; R.'s Inc. 920*l* and Ho; Pop. 1287.) Formerly C. of Canon Frome, Herefordshire, 1860–62, Cromhall, Glouc. 1862, Yatesbury, Wilts, 1863, Uffington, Shrewsbury, 1864–66. [4]

WILDBORE, Charles, *Wistow, near Selby, Yorks.* —St. Bees 1857; Deac. 1859 and Pr. 1860 by Bp of Dur. C. in sole charge of Wistow 1865. Formerly C. of Hunstanworth, Durham, 1859, Howden, Yorks, 1861, Selby 1863–65. [5]

WILDBORE, Charles, *Humberstone Vicarage, near Great Grimsby.*—Trin. Coll. Cam; Deac. 1829 by Bp of Nor. Pr. 1830 by Bp of Lin. V. of Humberstone, Dio. Lin. 1849. (Patron, Lord Carrington; V.'s Inc. 100*l*; Pop. 277.) Mast. of Humberstone Gr. Sch. Formerly C. of Waithe 1829, Clee 1831; V. of Clee 1835–49. [6]

WILDE, Albert Sydney, *The Rectory, Louth, Lincolnshire.*—Trin. Coll. Cam. Coll. Prizeman, 2nd Sen. Opt. and B.A. 1849; Deac. 1849, Pr. 1850. R. of Louth, Dio. Lin. 1859. (Patron, Bp of Lin; Tithe, 48*l*; Glebe, 147 acres; R.'s Inc. 500*l* and Ho; Pop. 8167.) Preb. of Lin. 1863; Surrogate; Rural Dean of Louthesk 1865; Chap. to Bp of Lin. 1859. Formerly R. of Greatford with Wilsthorpe, Lincolnshire, 1850–59. [7]

WILDE, John Maxwell, *West Ashby, Horncastle.*—P. C. of West Ashby, Dio. Lin. 1866. (Patron, Bp of Carl; P. C.'s Inc. 54*l*; Pop. 526.) Chap. to Lord Muskerry. [8]

WILDE, Ralph, *Bretherton Rectory, Preston.*—Dub. A.B. 1821; Deac. 1824 by Bp of Nor. Pr. 1825 by Bp of Lin. R. of Bretherton, Dio. Man. 1862. (Patron, R. of Croston; Tithe, 32*l*; Endowment, 114*l*; R.'s Inc. 156*l* and Ho; Pop. 775.) Formerly C. of Pakefield, Suffolk, of Hemingford Abbots, Hunts, of St. Thomas's, Birmingham, and of Tarleton, Lancashire. [9]

WILDE, Richard, *St. Jude's Parsonage, Englefield-green, Staines.*—Clare Coll. Cam. B.A. 1855, M.A. 1858; Deac. 1857 and Pr. 1858 by Bp of Lich. C. of St. Jude's, Englefield-green, Egham. Formerly C. of Little Drayton, Salop, Culford and Uggeshall, Suffolk, and Aylesbury, Bucks. [10]

WILDER, John, *Sulham Rectory, Reading,* and *Eton College, Bucks.*—King's Coll. Cam. Medallist 1823, B.A. 1824, M.A. 1828; Deac. 1824, Pr. 1825. R. of Sulham, Berks, Dio. Ox. 1836. (Patron, F. Wilder, Esq; Tithe, 198*l* 12*s* 9*d*; Glebe, 26 acres; R.'s Inc. 224*l* 12*s* 9*d* and Ho; Pop. 118.) Rural Dean of Bradfield; Fell. of Eton Coll. [11]

WILDER, John M'Mahon, *Brandiston, Alderford, Norwich.*—Emman. Coll. Cam. B.A. 1836, M.A. 1839, B.D. 1851; Deac. 1836, Pr. 1837. R. of Brandiston, Dio. Nor. 1850. (Patron, Magd. Coll. Ox; Tithe, 243*l* 10*s*; Glebe, 9 acres; R's. Inc. 290*l*; Pop. 137.) Formerly R. of Thornham, Kent, 1840–50. [12]

WILDING, Charles James, *Upper Arley, Bewdley, Staffs.*—Trin. Coll. Cam. B.A. 1848, M.A. 1851; Deac. 1848, Pr. 1849. P. C. of Upper Arley, Dio. Lich. 1862. (Patrons, Reps. of Viscount Valentia; P. C.'s Inc. 180*l* and Ho; Pop. 886.) Formerly R. of Mindtown, Salop, 1856–62. [13]

WILDMAN, T.—Dom. Chap. to Earl of Galloway. [14]

WILFORD, Edward Russell, *Upwell Rectory, Wisbech.*—Ch. Coll. Cam. B.A. 1859, M.A. 1862; Deac. 1859 by Bp of Win. Pr. 1860 by Bp of Ely. C. of Upwell St. Peter 1861; Surrogate. Formerly C. of Wisbech St. Peter and St. Paul 1859–61. [15]

WILFORD, Robert Crone, *Southowram, Halifax.*—Dub. A.B. 1865; Deac. 1866 and Pr. 1867 by Bp of Rip. C. of St. Anne's-in-the-Grove, Halifax, 1866. [16]

WILGRESS, George Frederick, *Cuddesdon, Oxon.*—Ex. Coll. Ox. Scho. of, B.A. 1851, M.A. 1853; Deac. 1853 and Pr. 1854 by Bp of Ox. Formerly C. of St. Mary the Virgin's, Oxford; P. C. of Headington Quarry, Oxford. [17]

WILKIE, Christopher Hales, *Cranbrook, Staplehurst, Kent.*—Ex. Coll. Ox. B.A. 1862, M.A. 1866; Wells Theol. Coll; Deac. 1864 and Pr. 1865 by Bp of Nor. C. of Cranbrook 1867. Formerly C. of Great and Little Glemham, Suffolk, 1864–66, St. Margaret-next-Rochester 1866–67. [18]

WILKIE, David, St. John's Coll. Ox. B.A. 1863, M.A. 1866. C. of St. Stephen's, Paddington, Lond. 1866. Formerly C. of Acton, Middlesex. [19]

WILKIN, Arthur, *Bootle Rectory, Ravenglass, Cumberland.*—Ch. Coll. Cam. B.A. 1840, M.A. 1843; Deac. 1840 and Pr. 1841 by Bp of Lin. R. of Bootle, Dio. Carl. 1847. (Patron, Earl of Lonsdale; Tithe, 436*l*; Glebe, 14 acres; R.'s Inc. 466*l* and Ho; Pop. 901.) Chap. to the Earl of Lonsdale 1841. [20]

WILKIN, John, *Stagsden, near Bedford.*—C. of Stagsden. [21]

WILKINS, Arthur Drummond, *The Vicarage, Dewsbury, Yorks.*—New Coll. Ox. B.A. 1853, M.A. 1856; Deac. 1853 by Bp of Roch. Pr. 1854 by Bp of Lin. V. of Dewsbury, Dio. Rip. 1864. (Patron, the Crown; Tithe, 43*l*; Glebe, 51*l*; V.'s Inc. 350*l* and Ho; Pop. 7365.) Rural Dean. Formerly Fell. of New Coll. Ox; C. of Croxby with Beelsby, Linc. 1854–57; V. of Sawbridgeworth, Herts, 1857–64. [22]

WILKINS, Cuthbert Sharp, *Dunham, Newark, Notts.*—C. of Dunham. [23]

WILKINS, Edward, *Hempsted Rectory, Stalham, Norfolk.*—King's Coll. Cam. B.A. 1821; Deac. 1822, Pr. 1823. R. of Hempsted with Lessingham, Dio. Nor. 1832. (Patron, King's Coll. Cam; Hempsted, Tithe, 290*l*; Lessingham, Tithe, 240*l* 5*s*; R.'s Inc. 560*l* and Ho; Pop. Hempsted 178, Lessingham 175.) [24]

WILKINS, George, *Wix Parsonage, Manningtree, Essex.*—Deac. 1818, Pr. 1819. P. C. of Wix, Dio. Roch. 1837. (Patron, the present P. C; Tithe—Imp. 1300*l*; Glebe, 4 acres; P. C.'s Inc. 164*l* and Ho; Pop. 752.) [25]

WILKINS, Henry Musgrave, *Merton College, Oxford.*—Trin. Coll. Ox. 1st cl. Lit. Hum. and B.A. 1845, Mert. Coll. M.A. 1850; Deac. 1850 by Bp of Ox. Fell. of Mert. Coll. Ox. Author, *Notes for Latin Lyrics*; *Greek Delectus*; *A Manual of Latin Prose Composition*; *A Manual of Greek Prose Composition*; *Elementary Greek Exercises*; *A Latin Anthology*; *A Greek Anthology*; *Latin Prose Exercises.* [26]

WILKINS, Henry Robert, *Farnsfield, Southwell, Notts.*—Ch. Coll. Cam. Jun. Opt. and B.A. 1845; Deac. 1845, Pr. 1846. V. of Farnsfield, Dio. Lin. 1849. (Patrons, Chap. of Southwell Coll. Ch; V.'s Inc. 165*l*; Pop. 1071.) [27]

WILKINS, John Murray, *The Rectory, Southwell, Notts.*—Trin. Coll. Cam. B.A. 1838, M.A. 1841; Deac. 1839 by Bp of Roch. Pr. 1840 by Bp of Lin. R. of Southwell, Dio. Lin. 1840. (Patron, Preb. of Normanton in Southwell Coll. Ch; Tithe—App. 564*l* 5*s*, R. 3*s* 6*d*; Glebe, 40 acres; R.'s Inc. 450*l* and Ho; Pop. 2617.) Official to Archd. of Nottingham 1853; Rural Dean 1854; Preb. of Lin. 1859. Formerly C. of St. Mary's, Nottingham, 1834–40. Author, *A Visitation Sermon,* 1843; *A Missionary Sermon,* 1853; *Lectures on Early Church History,* Masters, 1854; *Lectures on Church Music,* ib. 1856; etc. [28]

WILKINS, John Sebastian, *Heywood, Westbury, Wilts.*—Queens' Coll. Cam. Scho. of, Sen. Opt. B.A. 1834; Deac. 1834 by Bp of Ches. Pr. 1835 by Bp of B. and W. P. C. of Heywood, Dio. Salis. 1832. (Patrons, Five Trustees; P. C.'s Inc. 300*l* and Ho; Pop. 516.) [1]

WILKINS, Richard, *Swanmore, Ryde, Isle of Wight.*—Magd. Coll. Cam. B.A. 1854; Deac. 1860 by Bp of Salis. Pr. 1861 by Bp of Ex. C. of Swanmore. Formerly C. of St. James's, Exeter, 1860. [2]

WILKINS, Thomas, *Ecclesfield, Sheffield.*—C. of Ecclesfield; Chap. to the Wortley Union. [3]

WILKINS, Thomas Hodsoll, *Darmstadt.*—Emman. Coll. Cam. B.A. 1846; Deac. 1848 and Pr. 1849 by Bp of Pet. British Chap. at Darmstadt. [4]

WILKINSON, Alfred, *St. James's Parsonage, Poole, Dorset.*—Jesus Coll. Cam. Wrang. and B.A. 1833, M.A. 1836; Deac. 1834 by Bp of B. and W. Pr. 1836 by Bp of Bristol. P. C. of St. James's, Poole, Dio. Salis. 1861. (Patrons, Five Trustees; Tithe, 307*l*; Glebe, 2*l* 2*s*; P. C.'s Inc. 309*l* and Ho; Pop. 6815.) Rural Dean 1862; Chap. to the 4th Dorset Rifles 1862. Formerly C. of Winterbourne Zelstone and Anderstone 1835; P. C. of Downside, Somerset, 1841, Teddington, Middlesex, 1847. [5]

WILKINSON, Charles Alix, *South Willingham, Wragby, Lincolnshire.*—King's Coll. Cam. B.A. 1837, M.A. 1841; Deac. 1841 by Bp of Ely, Pr. 1842 by Bp of Win. R. of South Willingham, Dio. Lin. 1864. (Patron, E. Heneage, Esq; R.'s Inc. 450*l* and Ho; Pop. 340.) Dom. Chap. to H. M. King George of Hanover. Formerly Fell. of King's Coll. Cam. [6]

WILKINSON, Charles Edward, *Castle Park-terrace, Kendal.*—St. John's Coll. Cam. B.A. 1867; Deac. 1867 by Bp of Carl. C. of St. George's, Kendal. [7]

WILKINSON, Charles Thomas, *Edgbaston, Birmingham.*—Dub. A.B. 1846, A.M. 1858; Deac. 1846, Pr. 1847. R. of St. Thomas's, Birmingham, Dio. Wor. 1864. (Patrons, Trustees; R.'s Inc. 550*l*; Pop. 20,000.) Surrogate. Formerly P. C. of Attercliffe, Yorks, 1853–64. [8]

WILKINSON, Clennell, *Frampton Cotterell, near Bristol.*—St. John's Coll. Cam. B.A. 1847, M.A. 1850; Deac. 1849 and Pr. 1850 by Bp of Wor. C. in sole charge of Frampton Cotterell 1863. Formerly C. of St. Thomas's, Coventry, 1849–51, Meole Brace 1851–54, Fulbeck 1855–63. [9]

WILKINSON, Edward, *Stockwell, Surrey, S.*—Univ. of Bonn and Heidelberg M.A. and Ph. D; Deac. 1854 by Bp of Salis. Pr. 1856 by Bp. of Pet. C. of St. Michael's, Stockwell, 1867. Formerly C. of Wivenhoe, Essex, 1861. [10]

WILKINSON, Edward Abercrombie, *Mount Pleasant, Ferry Hill, Durham.*—Trin. Coll. Cam. B.A. 1857, M.A. 1860; Deac. 1859 and Pr. 1860 by Bp of Dur. P. C. of Tudhoe, Dio. Dur. 1866. (Patrons, D. and C. of Dur; Tithe, 50*l*; P. C.'s Inc. 300*l*; Pop. 3500.) Formerly C. of Banborough, Northumberland, 1859–66. [11]

WILKINSON, Edward Gleadow, *Riseholme, Lincoln.*—C. of Riseholme and South Carlton. [12]

WILKINSON, Edward Walker, *Linton, Cambs.*—Ch. Coll. Cam. 12th Wrang. and B.A. 1844, M.A. 1847; Deac. 1849 and Pr. 1850 by Bp of Ely. V. of Linton, Dio. Ely, 1859. (Patron, Bp of Ely; Tithe, comm. 267*l* 11*s* 7*d*; Glebe, 9 acres; V.'s Inc. 305*l*; Pop. 1831.) Rural Dean. Formerly Fell. of Ch. Coll. Cam. 1844–50; Asst. Tut. of same 1849–53. Editor of *Sermons by the late Rev. H. W. Wilkinson*, 1852; *Church Hymnal*, 1860. [13]

WILKINSON, Frederick, *Stour Provost, Gillingham, Bath.*—Corpus Coll. Cam. B.A. 1859, M.A. 1862; Deac. 1859 and Pr. 1860 by Bp of Salis. C. of Stour Provost, Dorset, 1866. Formerly C. of Kington Magna 1859–62, Compton Abbas 1862–66. [14]

WILKINSON, F. Paget, *Ruyton, Shrewsbury.*—V. of Ruyton-in-the-Eleven-Towns, Salop, Dio. Lich. 1859. (Patron, Ld Chan; V.'s Inc. 304*l* and Ho; Pop. 1200.) [15]

WILKINSON, George, *Cherry Burton, near Beverley.*—St. John's Coll. Cam. B.A. 1856; Deac. 1857 and Pr. 1858 by Abp of York. C. of Cherry Burton 1859. Formerly C. of Wold Newton with Butterwick 1857–59. [16]

WILKINSON, G. F., *South Croxton Rectory, Leicester.*—R. of South Croxton, Dio. Pet. 1828. (Patron, Duke of Rutland; R.'s Inc. 150*l* and Ho; Pop. 311.) [17]

WILKINSON, George Howard, *The Parsonage, Bishop Auckland.*—Oriel Coll. Ox. B.A. 1855, M.A. 1859; Deac. 1857 and Pr. 1858 by Bp of Lon. P. C. of St. Andrew with St. Ann Auckland, Dio. Dur. 1863. (Patron, Bp of Dur; P. C.'s Inc. 610*l* and Ho; Pop. 12,234.) Formerly P. C. of Seaham Harbour 1859–63. [18]

WILKINSON, George Pearson, *Harperley-park, Darlington.*—Univ. Coll. Dur. B.A. 1844, M.A. 1845; Deac. 1857 and Pr. 1858 by Bp. of Dur. P. C. of Thornley, Dio. Dur. 1857. (Patron, Bp of Ches; P. C.'s Inc. 100*l*; Pop. 3264.) [19]

WILKINSON, Henry, *Castle Hedingham, Halstead, Essex.*—Trin. Coll. Cam. B.A. 1853, M.A. 1856; Deac. 1854 and Pr. 1855 by Bp of Roch. P. C. of Castle Hedingham, Dio. Roch. 1862. (Patron, A. Majendie, Esq; P. C.'s Inc. 100*l* and Ho; Pop. 1203.) Formerly P. C. of Dilton's Marsh, Wilts, 1857–62. [20]

WILKINSON, H. B.—C. of Tulse-hill, Lambeth, Surrey. [21]

WILKINSON, Henry James, *Hooton-Pagnel Vicarage, Doncaster.*—Deac. 1846 and Pr. 1847 by Bp of Rip. V. of Hooton-Pagnel, Dio. York, 1855. (Patrons, Govs. of Charities at Wakefield; Tithe—App. 5*l* 8*s*, Imp. 160*l* 12*s*, V. 212*l* 10*s*; V.'s Inc. 310*l* and Ho; Pop. 342.) Dom. Chap. to the Earl of Ashburnham. Formerly P. C. of Troutbeck, near Windermere. [22]

WILKINSON, Henry Marlow, *Bisterne Parsonage, Ringwood, Hants.*—Wor. Coll. Ox. B.A. 1852; Deac. 1852 by Bp of Rip. Pr. 1853 by Abp of York. C. of St. Paul's, Bisterne, 1855. Formerly C. of St. Luke's, Leeds, 1852, St. Mary's, Bishophill, York, 1853. [23]

WILKINSON, Henry Thomas, *Weston-Market Rectory, East Harling, Suffolk.*—St. Peter's Coll. Cam. B.A. 1825, M.A. 1828. R. of Weston-Market, Dio. Ely, 1833. (Patron, the present R; Tithe, 330*l* 15*s* 1*d*; Glebe, 16 acres; R.'s Inc. 352*l* and Ho; Pop. 303.) [24]

WILKINSON, Hugh James, 11, *Low Hill, Liverpool.* [25]

WILKINSON, James Butler, *Ditton Priors, Bridgnorth, Salop.*—St. Bees 1854, Lond. Univ. 1858; Deac. 1855 and Pr. 1856 by Bp of St. A. V. of Ditton Priors, Dio. Herf. 1862. (Patron, R. Canning, Esq; V.'s Inc. 330*l* and Ho; Pop. 613.) Formerly C. of Hawarden, Flintshire, 1855–57, St. John's, Manchester, 1857–62. [26]

WILKINSON, John, *Broughton Gifford, Melksham, Wilts.*—Mert. Coll. Ox. B.A. 1838, M.A. 1842; Deac. 1839 and Pr. 1840 by Bp of Ex. R. of Broughton Gifford, Dio. Salis. 1848. (Patron, Ld Chan; Tithe, 400*l*; Glebe, 32 acres; R.'s Inc. 550*l* and Ho; Pop. 621.) Preb. of Salis. 1863. Formerly C. of St. Thomas's, Exeter, and of Exmouth, Devon. Author, *Systematic Analysis of Bishop Butler's Analogy*; *Letter to the Bishop of Salisbury on Popular Education*; Report on *Agriculture in Hampshire* in *Royal Agricultural Society's Journal*; one of the translators of the *Library of the Fathers.* [27]

WILKINSON, John, *Devizes.*—Dub. A.B. 1860; Deac. 1861 and Pr. 1862 by Bp. of Salis. for Bp. of Ex. Sen. C. of Devizes 1867. Formerly C. of St. Ives, Cornwall, 1861, St. Peter's, Plymouth, 1864, Sturminster Newton, Dorset, 1865. [28]

WILKINSON, John, *Goodshaw, Manchester.*—Deac. 1865 and Pr. 1866 by Bp of Man. C. of Goodshaw 1865. [29]

WILKINSON, John Bourdieu, *Wyndham-place, Plymouth.*—St. Peter's Coll. Cam. B.A. 1856; Deac. 1856, Pr. 1857. Sen. Asst. C. of St. Peter's, Plymouth, 1866. Formerly C. of Weston-Market, Suffolk, 1856–57, Ch. Ch. Westminster, 1857–60, Haggerston Mission 1860, Lavington, Sussex, 1861–63, Trinity, Portsea, 1863–66. Author, *Mission Sermons*, 1864, 2nd ed. 1867, 3*s* 6*d*; Sermons—*Tribulation*, 2nd ed. 6*d*;

Sympathy, 6*d*; *Danger of Relapse*, 6*d*; *A Few Loving Christian Words*; *All Availing Prayer* (on death of Dr. Neale); *The Corn of Wheat, or Death in Life, Life in Death*, 1867, 6*d*; *Orationes Sacerdotis*; published by Masters or Parkers. [1]

WILKINSON, John Farrar, *Flamborough, near Bridlington.*—St. John's Coll. Cam. B.A. 1854, M.A. 1857; Deac. 1854 and Pr. 1855 by Abp of York. P. C. of Flamborough, Dio. York, 1867. (Patron, Walter Strickland, Esq; P. C.'s Inc. 130*l* and Ho; Pop. 1287.) Formerly C. of Brandesburton, Yorks, 1854–67. [2]

WILKINSON, John Hessay, *Ludborough Rectory, Louth, Lincolnshire.*—Ch. Miss. Coll. Islington; Deac. 1857 by Bp of Lon. Pr. 1859 by Bp of Madras. C. of Ludborough 1867. Formerly Miss. of Ch. Miss. Soc. 1857–66. [3]

WILKINSON, John James, *Lanteglos Rectory, Camelford, Cornwall.*—Queen's Coll. Ox. B.A. 1842, M.A. 1845; Deac. 1842 and Pr. 1848 by Bp of Lin. R. of Lanteglos with Advent, Dio. Ex. 1852. (Patron, Prince of Wales; Lanteglos, Tithe—App. 2*l* 12*s*, Imp. 5*l* 13*s* 6*d*, R. 353*l*; Glebe, 145 acres; Advent, Tithe, 137*l*; Glebe, 64 acres; R.'s Inc. 710*l* and Ho; Pop. Lanteglos 1620, Advent 206.) [4]

WILKINSON, Jonathan, *St. Omer, France.*—St. John's Coll. Cam. B.A. 1818, M.A. 1821; Deac. 1819 by Bp of Ban. Pr. 1821 by Bp of Win. Min. of the English Episcopal Ch. St. Omer, 1836. Formerly Head Mast. of Aldenham Gr. Sch. Herts. [5]

WILKINSON, Joseph, 15, *Colebrooke-row, Islington, N.*—Caius Coll. Cam. B.A. 1856, M.A. 1860; Deac. 1857 and Pr. 1858 by Abp of Cant. P. C. of St. Silas's, Penton-street, Dio. Lon. 1867. (Patron, Bp of Lon; Pop. 9000.) Formerly C. of Ch. Ch. Dover, 1857–61, East Knoyle, Wilts, 1861–62, Minchinhampton, Glouc. 1862–65; Lond. Dioc. Home Miss. 1865–67. [6]

WILKINSON, Joseph Thornton.—King's Coll. Lond; Deac. 1857 and Pr. 1858 by Bp of Pet. Min. of St. Anne's (temporary church), Bermondsey, 1865. Formerly C. of St. Stephen's, Islington, and of St. James's, Curtain-road, Shoreditch. [7]

WILKINSON, Joshua, *Petham, Canterbury.*—C. of Petham. [8]

WILKINSON, Marlow Watts, *Mansion House, Uley, Glouc.*—Wor. Coll. Ox. B.A. 1810, M.A. 1813, B.D. 1825; Deac. 1810 and Pr. 1812 by Bp of Ox. R. of Uley, Dio. G. and B. 1823. (Patron, Ld Chan; Tithe, 236*l* 17*s* 3*d*; Glebe, 16 acres; R.'s Inc. 280*l*; Pop. 1230.) R. of Harescombe with Pitchcombe R. Glouc. Dio. G. and B. 1825. (Patron, R. J. Purnell, Esq; Harescombe, Tithe—Imp. 23*l*, R. 85*l* 16*s* 1*d*; Glebe, 15¾ acres; Pitchcombe, Tithe—Imp. 5*l* 1*s* 8*d*, R. 47*l* 18*s* 9*d*; Glebe, 8½ acres; R.'s Inc. 170*l*; Pop. Harescombe 138, Pitchcombe 178.) [9]

WILKINSON, Matthew, *West Lavington, Devizes, Wilts.*—Clare Coll. Cam. Fell. and Cl. Lect. of, Jun. Opt. 1st cl. Cl. Trip. and B.A. 1835, M.A. 1839, D.D. 1851; Deac. 1835 and Pr. 1836 by Bp of Ely. V. of Bishop's or West Lavington, Dio. Salis. 1852. (Patron, Bp of Salis; Tithe—App. 1825*l*, V. 360*l*; Glebe, 17 acres; V.'s Inc. 420*l*; Pop. 1589.) Formerly C. of Oakington, Cambs, 1836; Head Mast. of Kensington Sch. 1840; Head Mast. of Marlborough Coll. 1843–52; Rural Dean 1861–66; Select Preacher to the Univ. of Cambridge 1865–66. Author, *On the Expenses of Undergraduates* (a Letter to the Bp of Salis); *Marlborough College Sermons*; *Farewell Sermon* (at Marlborough Coll); etc. [10]

WILKINSON, Michael Joseph, *Wessington Parsonage, Alfreton, Derbyshire.*—Trin. Coll. Cam. B.A. 1846, M.A. 1863; Deac. 1847 by Bp of Lon. Pr. 1848 by Bp of Calcutta. P. C. of Wessington, Dio. Lich. 1861. (Patron, V. of Crich; P. C.'s Inc. 132*l* and Ho; Pop. 519.) Formerly C. at Melchbourne, Beds, 1854–56, Penkridge, Staffs, 1856–60. Author, *Memorials of an Indian Missionary*, Macintosh. [11]

WILKINSON, Michael Marlow Umfreville, *Reepham Rectory, Norwich.*—Trin. Coll. Cam. 5th Wrang. and B.A. 1854, M.A. 1857; Deac. 1857 and Pr. 1858 by Bp of Ely. R. of Reepham with Kerdiston R. Dio. Nor. 1864. (Patron, Trin. Coll. Cam; Tithe, 836*l*; Glebe, 70 acres; R.'s Inc. 900*l* and Ho; Pop. 553.) Formerly Fell. and Asst. Tut. of Trin. Coll. Cam. 1855–65, University Moderator 1864, Exam. for the Math. Trip. 1865. [12]

WILKINSON, Octavius, *Sibton Cottage, Yoxford, Suffolk.*—Emman. Coll. Cam. B.A. 1859, M.A. 1862; Deac. 1860 and Pr. 1862 by Bp of Ely. C. of Sibton with Peasenhall 1864. Formerly C. of Barton Mills, Suffolk, 1860, Great Stukeley with King's Ripton, Hunts, 1861, Little Munden, Herts, 1863. [13]

WILKINSON, Robert, *Killington, Kirkby-Lonsdale, Westmoreland.*—St. Bees; Deac. 1827, Pr. 1828. P. C. of Killington, Dio. Ches. 1834. (Patron, V. of Kirkby-Lonsdale; Tithe—App. 1*l* 2*s*, Imp. 27*l*; Glebe, 57 acres; P. C.'s Inc. 103*l* and Ho; Pop. 273.) [14]

WILKINSON, Robert Parker, *Finchley, N.*—Lin. Coll. Ox. Crewe Exhib. 3rd cl. Lit. Hum. B.A. 1846, M.A. 1849; Deac. 1847 and Pr. 1848 by Bp of Lon. Chap. of the Cemeteries of St. Mary, Islington, and St. Pancras; C. of Trinity, Finchley, 1855. Formerly C. of St. Giles'-in-the-Fields, Lond. 1847–52, St. Pancras 1852–54. [15]

WILKINSON, Thomas, *East Hill, Oxsted, Surrey.*—St. John's Coll. Cam. B.A. 1822; Deac. 1822 and Pr. 1823 by Bp of Ox. [16]

WILKINSON, Thomas, *Trinity College, Cambridge.*—Trin. Coll. Cam. Sen. Opt. 1st cl. Cl. Trip. and B.A. 1830, M.A. 1833; Deac. 1833 by Bp. of Ely, Pr. 1833 by Abp of Cant. Fell. of Trin. Coll. Cam. [17]

WILKINSON, Thomas, *Stanwix Vicarage, Carlisle.*—Queen's Coll. Ox. B.A. 1823, M.A. 1825; Deac. 1822 and Pr. 1823 by Bp of Carl. V. of Stanwix, Dio. Carl. 1840. (Patron, Bp of Carl; Tithe—App. 629*l* 4*s* 8½*d*, Imp. 37*l* 0*s* 6*d*, V. 208*l* 1*s* 3½*d*; Glebe, 3 acres; V.'s Inc. 300*l* and Ho; Pop. 1987.) Surrogate; Inspector of Episcopal Schs. in Scotland. [18]

WILKINSON, Thomas Boston, *East Harling, Thetford, Norfolk.*—Corpus Coll. Cam. B.A. 1820, M.A. 1824; Deac. 1821 and Pr. 1822 by B. of Nor. R. of East Harling, Dio. Nor. 1829. (Patroness, Mrs. Wilkinson; Tithe, comm. 591*l*; Glebe, 68 acres; R.'s Inc. 660*l*; Pop. 1109.) Rural Dean. [19]

WILKINSON, Thomas Edward, *Upper Rickinghall Rectory, Suffolk.*—Jesus Coll. Cam. B.A. 1859, M.A. 1863; Deac. 1861 and Pr. 1862 by Bp of Ely. C. of Rickinghall Superior 1864. Formerly C. of Cavendish 1861 [20]

WILKINSON, Thomas Henry, *Lenaden Parsonage, Ashburton.*—Brasen. Coll. Ox. Hon. 4th cl. in Lit. Hum. and Math. B.A. 1850, M.A. 1853; Deac. 1852 and Pr. 1853 by Bp of Pet. P. C. of Lenaden, Dio. Ex. 1863. (Patroness, Mrs. Larpent; Glebe, 27 acres; P. C.'s Inc. 125*l*; Pop. 430.) Formerly C. of Daventry 1852; P. C. of Grosmont, Yorks, 1853–63. Author, *The Discipline of the Churching Service with Authorities*, Rivingtons, 1867, 6*d*. [21]

WILKINSON, Walter George, *Worcester College, Oxford.*—Lin. Coll. Ox. 1850, Scho. of Wor. Coll. 1851, 3rd cl. Lit. Hum. 1852, B.A. and Fell. of Wor. Coll. Ox. 1853; Deac. 1853, Pr. 1854. Formerly C. of St. Maurice and Trinity, Goodramgate, York; P. C. of Lyford, Berks, 1858–63. [22]

WILKINSON, Watts, *Bisterne Parsonage, Ringwood, Hants.*—Wor. Coll. Ox. B.A. 1818, M.A. 1821; Deac. 1818 and Pr. 1819 by Bp of Nor. Formerly C. of Godshill and St. Lawrence, Isle of Wight, 1825, Harescombe with Pitchcombe, Glouc. 1836, Great Cornard, Suffolk, 1839, St. Gregory's and St. Peter's, Sudbury, 1846; Chap. to the Sudbury Union 1844. [23]

WILKINSON, W., *Sutton St. Michael, Hereford.*—Ch. Coll. Cam. Scho. of, B.A. 1855; Deac. 1855 and Pr. 1856 by Bp of Ches. P. C. of Sutton St. Michael, Hereford, Dio. Herf. 1864. (Patrons, Messrs. Allen and Unett; P. C.'s Inc. 60*l*; Pop. 95.) Formerly C. of St. Chrysostom's, Everton, Liverpool, 1855–57 [24]

WILKINSON, William, *Dunsfold, Godalming, Surrey.*—C. of Dunsfold. [1]

WILKINSON, William, *St. Michael's Rectory, Birmingham.*—Dub. A.B. 1839, A.M. 1854, B.D. and D.D. 1866; Deac. 1840, Pr. 1841. R. of St. Martin's, Birmingham, Dio. Wor. 1866. (Patrons, Trustees; R.'s Inc. 1048*l* and Ho; Pop. 17,000.) Formerly C. of Burbage, Leic. 1840–49; P. C. of Trinity, Sheffield, 1851–53, St. Mary's, Sheffield, 1853–66. [2]

WILKINSON, William Farley, *Keith-road, Shepherd's Bush, London, W.*—Corpus Coll. Cam. B.A. 1819, M.A. 1822, B.D. 1830; Deac. 1819, Pr. 1829. [3]

WILKINSON, William Francis, *St. Werburgh's Vicarage, Derby.*—Queen's Coll. Cam. 6th Sen. Opt. 2nd in 2nd cl. Cl. Trip. and B.A. 1834, M.A. 1837; Deac. 1836 by Bp of Roch. Pr. 1837 by Abp of York. V. of St. Werburgh's, Derby, Dio. Lich. 1848. (Patron, Ld Chan; Tithe, 150*l*; Glebe, 9 acres; V.'s Inc. 434*l* and Ho; Pop. 3000.) Even. Lect of St. Werburgh's, Derby. (Value, 10*l*.) Formerly Select Preacher of Univ. Cam. 1846–48; C. of Sheffield 1836–38, Harrow-on-the-Hill 1838–44; Theol. Tut. of Cheltenham Coll. 1844–47. Author, *Rector in search of a Curate*, 1843; *The Parish rescued*, 1845; *Christ, our Gospel* (four Sermons preached before the Univ. of Cam.) 1846, 2*s* 6*d*; *Catechism of Church History*, 1846, 6*s*; *Articles of the Church of England in English and Latin, with Proofs, &c.*, 1850, 1*s* 6*d*; Editor (with Rev. W. Webster) of *The Greek Testament, with Notes Grammatical and Exegetical*, 1855–61; Pamphlets—*Lecture on the Puritans*, 1848, 1*s*; *Christianity in Christ* (Sermon at the Bishop's Visitation), 1849, 6*d*; *Credibility of the Old Testament*, 1853, 6*d*; *A Plea for National Education, with Religion and without Rates*, 1854, 1*s*; *Education, Elementary, and Liberal*, 1862, 2*s*; *Reasons for Belief in the Truth, Inspiration and Mosaic Authorship of the Pentateuch*, 1863, 4*d*; *Testimony of Scripture and Reason to the Doctrines of the Deity of Christ, the Incarnation, &c.*, S.P.C.K. 1867, 2*d*. [4]

WILKINSON, William G., *Bubwith Vicarage, Selby, Yorks.*—P. C. of Ellerton-Priory, near Brough, Yorks, Dio. York, 1841. (Patron, Rev. J. D. Jefferson; Tithe—Imp. 24*l*; P. C.'s Inc. 84*l*; Pop. 338.) V. of Bubwith, Dio. York, 1847. (Patrons, Ld Chan. and D. and C. of York, alt; Tithe—App. 270*l*, Imp. 287*l* 5*s* 6*d*, V. 54*l*; V.'s Inc. 79*l* and Ho; Pop. 1453.) [5]

WILKINSON, William Henry, *Hensingham Parsonage, Whitehaven.*—St. Bees; Deac. 1862 and Pr. 1863 by Bp of Dur. P. C. of Hensingham, Dio. Carl. 1865. (Patron, Earl of Lonsdale; P. C.'s Inc. 130*l* and Ho; Pop. 1538.) Formerly C. of Escomb, Durham. [6]

WILKS, Samuel Charles, *Nursling Rectory, near Southampton.*—St. Edm. Hall, Ox. B.A. 1814, M.A. 1816. R. of Nursling, Dio. Win. 1847. (Patron, Bp of Win; Tithe, 550*l*; R.'s Inc. 600*l* and Ho; Pop. 715.) [7]

WILKS, Theodore Chambers, *Woking, Surrey.*—Trin. Coll. Cam. B.A. 1851, M.A. 1854; Deac. 1851 and Pr. 1852 by Bp of Win. V. of Woking, Dio. Win. 1866. (Patron, Earl of Onslow; V.'s Inc. 250*l* and Ho; Pop. 3819.) Chap. to Bp of Llan. Formerly C. of Nately Scures, Hants. [8]

WILLAN, Albert, *Meltham Mills, Huddersfield.*—Caius Coll. Cam. B.A. 1864; Deac. 1866 by Bp of Rip. C. of Meltham Mills 1866. [9]

WILLAN, Francis Miles, *Aubourn, near Lincoln.*—Ch. Coll. Cam. B.A. 1828, M.A. 1831; Deac. and Pr. 1830. V. of Aubourn, Dio. Lin. 1834. (Patron, H. Neville, Esq; Tithe—Imp. 241*l* 1*s* 6*d*, V. 209*l* 8*s* 11½*d*; Glebe, 20 acres; V.'s Inc. 250*l*; Pop. 376.) [10]

WILLAN, George Arthur, 12, *Story-street, Hull.*—St. John's Coll. Cam. 3rd cl. Cl. Trip. and B.A. 1863; Deac. 1864 and Pr. 1865 by Abp of York. Sen. C. of St. Mary's, Hull, 1866. Formerly Asst. C. of Royston, Barnsley, Yorks, 1864–66. [11]

WILLES, Edmund Henry Lacon, *Ashby Magna, Lutterworth.*—Queen's Coll, Ox. Fell. of, 2nd cl. Lit. Hum. and B.A. 1853, M.A. 1856; Deac. 1855 and Pr. 1856 by Bp of Ox. V. of Ashby Magna, Dio. Pet. 1866. (Patron, Earl of Aylesford; V.'s Inc. 250*l*; Pop. 330.) Formerly C. of Swinbrook, Oxon, 1856–57, King's Sutton, Banbury, 1857–60, R. of St. Swithin's, Winchester, 1863; V. of Helston, Cornwall, 1865. [12]

WILLESFORD, Francis Thomas Bedford, *Awliscombe Vicarage, Honiton, Devon.*—Ex. Coll. Ox; Deac. 1831, Pr. 1832. V. of Awliscombe, Dio. Ex. 1834. (Patron, Duke of Bedford; Tithe—Imp. 170*l*, V. 220*l*; Glebe, 30 acres; V.'s Inc. 294*l* and Ho; Pop. 579.) [13]

WILLETT, Charles Saltren, *Monkleigh Vicarage, Torrington, Devon.*—Oriel Coll. Ox. B.A. 1847, M.A. 1850; Deac. 1848, Pr. 1850. V. of Monkleigh, Dio. Ex. 1850. (Patron, John Saltren Willett, Esq; Tithe—Imp. 167*l* 10*s* 9*d*, V. 150*l*; Glebe, 58 acres; V.'s Inc. 210*l* and Ho; Pop. 627.) [14]

WILLETT, Edmund Austen, *St. Wilfrid's, Cuckfield, Sussex.*—Trin. Coll. Cam. B.A. 1863, M.A. 1867; Deac. 1866 by Bp of Chich. Asst. C. of St. Wilfrid's, Cuckfield, 1866. [15]

WILLETT, Frederic, *West Bromwich, Staffs.*—Trin. Coll. Cam. B.A. 1860, M.A. 1863; Deac. 1861 by Bp of Roch. Pr. 1862 by Bp of Lich. P. C. of West Bromwich, Dio. Lich. 1865. (Patron, Earl of Dartmouth; P. C.'s Inc. 530*l* and Ho; Pop. 6435.) Formerly Sen. C. of St. Peter's, Wolverhampton, 1861–65. [16]

WILLETT, George Thomas, *Little Leigh, Northwich.*—Dub. A.B. 1849; Deac. 1849 and Pr. 1850 by Bp of Rip. P. C. of Little Leigh, Dio. Ches. 1864. (Patron, V. of Great Budworth; Glebe, 32 acres; P. C.'s Inc. 151*l*; Pop. 830.) Formerly C. of Skipton-in-Craven 1849, Arley, Cheshire, 1852, Scotton, Linc. 1857, Bishop Auckland, Durham, 1860. Author, *Canticles accented for Anglican Chants*, Novello, 2*d*. [17]

WILLETT, Wilmer, *Drybridge House, Hereford.*—Magd. Hall, Ox. B.A. 1836; Deac. 1837 by Bp of Ely, Pr. 1838 by Bp of Nor. [18]

WILLEY, Willoughby, *Arlecdon, near Whitehaven.*—C. of Arlecdon. [19]

WILLIAMS, Alexander, *Up Cerne Rectory, Cerne-Abbas, Dorset.*—Trin. Coll. Cam. B.A. 1833, M.A. 1836; Deac. 1835 by Abp. of York, Pr. 1836 by Bp. of B. and W. R. of Up Cerne, Dio. Salis. 1855. (Patron, J. White, Esq; Tithe, 156*l*; R.'s Inc. 160*l* and Ho; Pop. 75.) [20]

WILLIAMS, Alfred, *Culmington Rectory, Bromfield, Shrewsbury.*—King's Coll. Cam. B.A. 1842, M.A. 1845. R. of Culmington, Dio. Herf. 1856. (Patron, W. J. Clement, Esq; Tithe, 685*l*; R.'s Inc. 702*l* and Ho; Pop. 517.) Formerly Fell. of King's Coll. Cam. [21]

WILLIAMS, Alfred Henry, 49, *Gloucester-street, S.W.*—Clare Coll. Cam. B.A. 1854, M.A. 1858; Deac. 1856 by Bp. of Win. Pr. 1857 by Bp of Lon. Sen. C. of St. Peter's, Pimlico, 1860. [22]

WILLIAMS, Alfred Theodore, *Blyth, Northumberland.*—Chap. of Blyth Chapel, Dio. Dur. 1866. (Patron, Sir M. W. Ridley.) Formerly C. of Horton, Northumberland. [23]

WILLIAMS, Arthur Charles Vaughan, *Alverstoke, Gosport, Hants.*—Ch. Ch. Ox. B.A. 1857, M.A. 1860; Deac. 1860 by Bp of Ox. Stud. of Ch. Ch. Ox; C. of Alverstoke. [24]

WILLIAMS, Arthur James, *Drayton Parsonage, Wallingford.*—Ch. Ch. Ox. B.A. 1855, M.A. 1857; Deac. 1855 by Abp of York, Pr. 1856 by Bp of Ox. P. C. of Drayton, Dio. Ox. 1858. (Patron, Ch. Ch. Ox; P. C.'s Inc. 140*l* and Ho; Pop. 827.) Formerly 2nd Mast. of the Cathl. Sch. Oxford; Chap. of Ch. Ch. and Mert. Coll. Ox. [25]

WILLIAMS, Arthur M., *Kirklinton, near Carlisle.*—C. of Kirklinton. [26]

WILLIAMS, Augustin, *Icomb Rectory, Stow-on-the-Wold, Glouc.*—Lampeter 1850; Deac. 1850 and Pr. 1851 by Bp of Llan. R. of Icomb, Dio. G. and B. 1864. (Patrons, D. and C. of Wor; Pop. 164.) Formerly C. of Dudley 1854, St. Martin's, Worcester, 1858. [27]

WILLIAMS, Bennett, *Bramshall, Uttoxeter, Staffs.*—Queen's Coll. Ox. B.A. 1835; Deac. 1834 and

Pr. 1837 by Bp of Ches. R. of Bramahall, Dio. Lich. 1857. (Patroness, Dowager Lady W. de Broke; Tithe, 148*l*; Glebe, 42¾ acres; R.'s Inc. 200*l* and Ho; Pop. 199.) Formerly C. of North Meols 1836; V. of Bispham, Lancashire, 1837. Author, *Reasons why every Christian should Communicate*, Bemrose, Derby. [1]

WILLIAMS, Bennett Hesketh, *Uppingham.*—Trin. Coll. Ox. B.A. 1861; Deac. 1861 and Pr. 1862 by Bp of Lich. Asst. Mast. in Uppingham Gr. Sch. Formerly C. of Gayton with Stowe, near Stafford, 1861–63. [2]

WILLIAMS, Charles, *Worcester College, Oxford.*—Fell. of Wor. Coll. Ox. [3]

WILLIAMS, Charles, *Llanvigan Rectory, Brecon.*—R. of Llanvigan with Glynn C. Dio. St. D. 1847. (Patrons, Trustees of Rev. C. Clifton; R.'s Inc. 500*l* and Ho; Pop. 674.) [4]

WILLIAMS, Charles, *Jesus College, Oxford.*—Hon. Can. of Bangor, 1857; Prin. of Jesus Coll. Ox. 1857. Formerly P. C. of Holyhead, Anglesey, 1845–57. [5]

WILLIAMS, Charles G. H., *Tipton, Staffs.*—C. of St. Paul's, Tipton. Formerly C. of Trinity, Coventry. [6]

WILLIAMS, C. H. D., *Leeds.*—Dub. A.B. 1862; Deac. 1862 and Pr. 1863 by Bp of Rip. C. of St. James's, Leeds; Head Mast. of Modern Department, Leeds Gr. Sch. Formerly C. of Roundhay. [7]

WILLIAMS, Charles Nathaniel, *Ashchurch, Tewkesbury.*—St. Peter's Coll. Cam. B.A. 1857; Deac. 1857 and Pr. 1858 by Bp of Wor. P. C. of Ashchurch, Dio. G. and B. 1863. (Patron, present P. C; P. C.'s Inc. 285*l*; Pop. 781.) Formerly C. of Bredon's Norton 1857-58, Iver Heath, Bucks, 1859–61, Tortworth, Glouc. 1862. [8]

WILLIAMS, Charles Prytherch Middleton, *Porteynon Rectory, Reynoldstone, Swansea.*—Jesus Coll. Ox. 4th cl. Lit. Hum. Exhib. and twice Theol. Prizeman, B.A. 1846; Deac. 1848 and Pr. 1849 by Bp of St. D. V. of Llanddewi, Dio. St. D. 1853. (Patron, Bp of St. D; Tithe, 42*l* 19*s* 6*d*; Glebe, 43*l* 16*s*; V.'s Inc. 100*l*; Pop. 175.) C. of Porteynon 1862. Formerly C. of Cheriton, Glamorganshire, 1848, Maesteg, Glamorganshire, 1854–62. [9]

WILLIAMS, Daniel, *Baughurst Rectory, Basingstoke, Hants.*—R. of Baughurst, Dio. Win. 1846. (Patron, Bp of Win; Tithe, 340*l*; Glebe, 2 acres; R.'s Inc. 343*l* and Ho; Pop. 563.) [10]

WILLIAMS, Daniel Rowland, *Kingston Lisle, Wantage.*—Corpus Coll. Cam. B.A. 1854, M.A. 1859; Deac. 1855 by Bp of B. and W. Pr. 1857 by Bp of Ex. P. C. of Grinshill, Dio. Lich. 1864. (Patron, Rev. J. R. Wood; Glebe, 40 acres; P. C.'s Inc. 135*l*; Pop. 317.) C. of Kingston Lisle, Berks. Formerly C. of Winforton, Hereford. [11]

WILLIAMS, David, *Dingestow, Monmouth.*—C. of Dingestow with Tregare. [12]

WILLIAMS, David, *Alton-Barnes Rectory, Pewsey, Wilts.*—New Coll. Ox. S.C.L. 1821, B.C.L. 1827; Deac. 1824 and Pr. 1825 by Bp of Herf. R. of Alton-Barnes, Dio. Salis. 1835. (Patron, New Coll. Ox; Tithe, 262*l* 10*s*; Glebe, 49¾ acres; R.'s Inc. 300*l* and Ho; Pop. 177.) Editor of *Home Prayers selected from our Liturgy*, Longmans, 1842. [13]

WILLIAMS, David, *Llanvachreth Rectory, Holyhead, Anglesey.*—Jesus Coll. Ox. B.A. 1824; Deac. 1824 and Pr. 1825 by Bp of Ban. R. of Llanvachreth with Llanengbenedl C. and Llanvigael C. Dio. Ban. 1850. (Patron, Bp of Ban; Llanvachreth, Tithe, 264*l*; Glebe, 10 acres; Llanengbenedl, Tithe, 291*l*; Glebe, 4 acres; Llanvigael, Tithe, 83*l*; R.'s Inc. 638*l* and Ho; Pop. 1180.) Formerly C. of Llanvairvechan 1824, Llanrhyddlad 1828; R. of Trawsvynydd 1837. [14]

WILLIAMS, David, *Nannerch Rectory, Mold, Flintshire*—Jesus Coll. Ox. B.A. 1833, M.A. 1840; Deac. 1835 and Pr. 1836 by Bp of St. A. R. of Nannerch, Dio. St. A. 1845. (Patron, Bp. of St. A; Tithe, 327*l*; Glebe, 7 acres; R.'s Inc. 340*l* and Ho; Pop. 333.) Hon. Can. of St. A. 1858. Author, Translator of several Books of the S.P.C.K. into Welsh, *e.g.*, *Book of Nature*; *Schism*; *Spring Morning*, by the Bp of Oxford; Compiler of *Cennadaeth au Eglwysig*, or Church Missions. [15]

WILLIAMS, D.—C. of Ince in Makerfield, Lancashire. [16]

WILLIAMS, David, *Llanedy Rectory, Llanelly, Carmarthenshire.*—Lampeter, B.D. 1855; Deac. 1848 and Pr. 1849 by Bp of St. D. R. of Llanedy, Carmarthenshire, Dio. St. D. 1854. (Patron, St. David's Coll. Lampeter; Tithe, 308*l*; Glebe, 12 acres; R.'s Inc. 403*l* and Ho; Pop. 1087.) Professor of Welsh at Lampeter 1854. [17]

WILLIAMS, David, *Ysceifiog, Holywell.*—Deac. 1861 and Pr. 1862 by Bp of St. A. C. of Ysceifiog 1863. Formerly C. of Northop 1861–63. [18]

WILLIAMS, David, *Millbrook, Carmarthen.*—Jesus Coll. Ox. 2nd cl. Math. B.A. 1865; Deac. 1866 and Pr. 1867 by Bp of St. D. Asst. C. of Merthyr and of St. David's, Carmarthen, 1866. [19]

WILLIAMS, David, *Gwatchmai, Holyhead.*—St. Bees; Deac. 1863 and Pr. 1864 by Bp of Ban. C. of Gwatchmai 1867. Formerly C. of Dolwyddelan 1863–65, Dwygyfylchi 1865–67. [20]

WILLIAMS, the Ven. David Archard, *St. David's Parsonage, Carmarthen.*—Deac. 1820 and Pr. 1821 by Bp of St. D. P. C. of St. David's, Carmarthen, Dio. St. D. 1842. (Patron, V. of Carmarthen; P. C.'s Inc. 166*l*; Pop. 4332.) R. of Merthyr, Dio. St. D. 1843. (Patron, Prince of Wales; Tithe, 165*l*; R.'s Inc 178*l* and Ho; Pop. 287.) Archd. of Carmarthen 1865; Rural Dean 1828. Formerly Head Mast. of Carmarthen Gr. Sch. 1824–60; Chan. of Dio. of St. D. 1857–65. Author, *A Charge*, 1866-67. [21]

WILLIAMS, David Edwards, *St. Paul's Parsonage, Llanelly, Carmarthenshire.*—Lampeter; Deac. 1845 and Pr. 1846 by Bp of St. D. P. C. of St. Paul's, Llanelly, Dio. St. D. 1847. (Patrons, the Crown and Bp of St. D. alt; P. C.'s Inc. 150*l*; Pop. 5009.) · Author, *Church Principles* (in Welsh), Carmarthen. [22]

WILLIAMS, David Lewis, *Llanwnda, Carnarvon.*—V. of Llanwnda with Llanfaglen, Dio. Ban. 1860. (Patron, Bp of Ban; V.'s Inc. 300*l*; Pop. Llanwnda 1660, Llanfaglen 253.) [23]

WILLIAMS, Ebenezer, *Bryneglwys (Denbighshire), near Corwen.*—Deac. 1814, Pr. 1815. P. C. of Bryneglwys, Dio. St. A. 1831. (Patron, Sir W. W. Wynn; Tithe—Imp. 288*l* 10*s*; Glebe, 21 acres; P. C.'s Inc. 60*l* and Ho; Pop. 444.) R. of Llandegla, Denbighshire, Dio. St. A. 1831. (Patron, Bp of St. A; Tithe, 116*l*; Glebe, 6 acres; R.'s Inc. 122*l*; Pop. 425.) [24]

WILLIAMS, Edleston R., *Smallwood Parsonage, near Lawton, Stoke-on-Trent.*—Magd. Hall, Ox. B. A. 1857; Deac. 1858 and Pr. 1859 by Bp of Lich. P. C. of Smallwood, Dio. Ches. 1862. (Patron, R. of Astbury; P. C.'s Inc. 100*l* and Ho; Pop. 590.) Formerly C. of Uffington and Battlefield 1858–60. [25]

WILLIAMS, Edmund George, *Beaumont Villa, Swansea.*—St. Bees; Deac. 1851 and Pr. 1852 by Bp of Ches. Chap. of the Gaol, Swansea, 1859. (Salary 250*l*.) Formerly C. of St. Peter's, Everton, Liverpool, 1851–53, Swansea, 1853–59. Author, *Sermons on the Sunday and Festival Lessons*, 2 vols. Macintosh, 1865–66, 8*s* 6*d* each. [26]

WILLIAMS, Edmund Turberville, *Caldicot, Chepstow, Monmouthshire.*—Ex. Coll. Ox. B.A. 1837, M.A. 1840; Deac. 1839, Pr. 1848. V. of Caldicot, Dio. Llan. 1841. (Patron, the Rev. M. H. Noel; Tithe—Imp. 271*l* 1*s*, V. 190*l*; Glebe, 39¼ acres; V.'s Inc. 240*l* and Ho; Pop. 579.) Rural Dean. [27]

WILLIAMS, Edward, *Beckingham, near Newark, Notts.*—C. of Beckingham. [28]

WILLIAMS, Edward, 86, *Great Brook street, Birmingham.*—Deac. 1848 and Pr. 1851 by Bp of Newcastle. C. of St. Matthew's, Birmingham, 1865. Formerly Incumb. for 12 years of Tamworth, New South Wales; Miss. C. of Trinity, Shrewsbury, 1862; C. of Shipston-on-Stour 1864. Author, *Dialogue on Schism*, Macintosh, 1865, 2*d*. [29]

WILLIAMS, Edward, *Eardisley, Kington, Herefordshire.*—C. of Eardisley. [1]

WILLIAMS, Edward.—C. of St. Andrew's, Montpelier, Bristol. [2]

WILLIAMS, Edward Addams, *Llangibby Rectory, Newport, Monmouthshire.*—Jesus Coll. Ox. 3rd cl. Lit. Hum. and B.A. 1852, Scho. 1853; Deac. 1853 and Pr. 1854 by Bp of Llan. R. of Llangibby, Dio. Llan. 1862. (Patron, W. Addams Williams, Esq; Tithe, 510*l*; Glebe, 77 acres; R.'s Inc. 607*l* and Ho; Pop. 525.) P. C. of Ch. Ch. Coedypane, Dio. Llan. 1861. (Patron, W. Addams Williams, Esq; P. C.'s Inc. 33*l* 7*s* 6*d*.) Formerly C. of Llangibby 1853-62. [3]

WILLIAMS, E. A.—Chap. of H.M.S. "Cadmus." [4]

WILLIAMS, Edward Fraser Vaughan, *Eagle Farm, Batheaston, Bath.*—Trin. Coll. Cam. B.A. 1856; M.A. 1860; Deac. 1862 by Bp of B. and W. Pr. 1866 by Bp Anderson for Bp of B. and W. C. of Batheaston 1862. [5]

WILLIAMS, Edward P., *Chislehurst, Kent, S.E.*—Ch. Coll. Cam. B.A. 1859. C. of Chislehurst. Formerly C. of Fawley, Hants. [6]

WILLIAMS, Edward Stephen, *East Dean, near Salisbury.*—Jesus Coll. Ox. 4th cl. in Lit. Hum. Goldsmith and Coll. Exhib. B.A. 1852, M.A. 1855; Deac. 1853 and Pr. 1854 by Bp of Lich. C. in sole charge of East Dean 1862. Formerly C. of Sheriff Hales with Woodcote 1853-55; Chap. of St. Thomas's, Ferryside, 1856; Min. of Farnborough, Berks, 1857-58; C. of Fryerning, Essex, 1859-61. [7]

WILLIAMS, E. Valentine, *High-street, Camden-town, London, N.W.*—Vice-Prin. of North Lond. Coll. Sch. Camden-town. [8]

WILLIAMS, Eleazar, *Tydweiliog, Pwllheli.*—Dub. A.B. 1850; Deac. 1850 and Pr. 1851 by Bp of Llan. P. C. of Tydweiliog, Dio. Ban. 1860. (Patron, Rev. G. A. Salusbury; P. C.'s Inc. 170*l*; Pop. 371.) [9]

WILLIAMS, Ellis Osborne, *Llanfachreth Parsonage, Dolgelly, Merionethshire.*—Sid. Coll. Cam. B.A. 1849, M.A. 1853; Deac. 1850, Pr. 1851. P. C. of Llanfachreth, Dio. Ban. 1854. (Patron, Sir R. W. Vaughan; Tithe—Imp. 75*l*; P. C.'s Inc. 100*l* and Ho; Pop. 862.) [10]

WILLIAMS, Sir Erasmus H. G., *St. David's, Haverfordwest.*—R. of Rushall, Dio. Salis. 1829. (Patron, Warden of Mert. Coll. Ox. in trust for Sen. Fell. on Jackson's foundation; R.'s Inc. 400*l* and Ho; Pop. 224.) Chan. of St. D.'s Cathl. 1858. (Value, 350*l*.) [11]

WILLIAMS, Francis, *Adelaide, South Australia.*—Lin. Coll. Ox. B.A. 1854; Deac. 1856 by Bp of Roch. Asst. Mast. of St. Peter's Coll. Sch. Adelaide. Formerly Sen. Asst. Mast. of the Grange Sch. Chigwell, Essex. [12]

WILLIAMS, Frederic, *Saltley Parsonage, near Birmingham.*—Corpus Coll. Cam. B.A. 1840; Deac. 1840 and Pr. 1841 by Bp of Lich. P. C. of Saltley, Dio. Wor. 1852. (Patron, the Rt. Hon. C. B. Adderley, M.P; P. C.'s Inc. 250*l* and Ho; Pop. 2850.) Formerly P. C. of Ettingshall, Stafford, 1841-52. [13]

WILLIAMS, Frederick, *Bettiscombe Rectory, Crewkerne.*—Jesus Coll. Ox. B.A. 1864; Deac. 1865 and Pr. 1866 by Bp of Salis. R. of Bettiscombe, Dio. Salis. 1867. (Patron, R. B. Sheridan, Esq. M.P; Tithe, 128*l*, Glebe, 54 acres; R.'s Inc. 200*l* and Ho; Pop. 76.) C. of Pilsdon 1867. Formerly C. of Bettiscombe 1865-66. [14]

WILLIAMS, Frederick Addams, *Llanllowell, Usk, Monmouthshire.*—R. of Llanllowell, Dio. Llan. 1831. (Patron, the present R; R.'s Inc. 130*l*; Pop. 87.) R. of Llandegveth, Monmouthshire, Dio. Llan. (Patron, W. A. Williams, Esq; R.'s Inc. 164*l*; Pop. 116.) [15]

WILLIAMS, Frederick Mackenzie, *Siefton, Culmington, Bromfield.*—Trin. Coll. Cam. Sen. Opt. and 3rd cl. Cl. Trip. B.A. 1862, M.A. 1866; Deac. 1862 and Pr. 1864 by Bp of Herf. C. of Culmington 1862. [16]

WILLIAMS, Garnon, *Brecon.*—Oriel Coll. Ox. B.A. 1851; Deac. 1852, Pr. 1853. Rural Dean. Formerly V. of Llowes and P. C. of Llanddewi-Fach, Radnorshire, 1853-59. V. of St. John's, Brecon, 1859-64. Author, *The Happy Isles* (Poems), 1858, 5*s*. [17]

WILLIAMS, George, *King's College, Cambridge.*—King's Coll. Cam. B.A. 1837, M.A. 1840, B.D. 1848; Deac. 1837 and Pr. 1838 by Bp of Lin. Sen. Fell. of King's Coll. Cam. 1854. Formerly Warden of St. Columba's Coll. Ireland, 1850. Author, *Historical and Topographical Notices of Jerusalem*, 1st ed. 1 vol. 1845, 2nd ed. 2 vols. 1849; *Sermons* (preached at Jerusalem) 1846; various Articles in Smith's *Dictionary of Classical Geography.* [18]

WILLIAMS, George, *Hauxton, near Cambridge.*—Trin. Coll. Cam. B.A. 1832, M.A. 1835; Deac. 1832, Pr. 1833. V. of Hauxton with Newton, Dio. Ely, 1837. (Patrons, D. and C. of Ely; Newton, Tithe—App. 291*l* 13*s*, Imp. 1*l* 11*s* 6*d*, V. 50*l* 15*s* 6*d*; Glebe, 17 acres; V.'s Inc. 164*l*; Pop. Hauxton 262, Newton 216.) [19]

WILLIAMS, George Campbell, *Barracks, Sheffield.*—Dub. A.B. 1847, A.M. 1851. Chap. to the Forces 1859. [20]

WILLIAMS, George Griffith, *Llanfynydd, near Carmarthen.*—Lampeter; Deac. 1847 and Pr. 1849 by Bp of St. D. V. of Llanfynydd, Dio. St. D. 1852. (Patron, Bp of St. D; Tithe, 121*l*; V.'s Inc. 150*l*; Pop. 1230.) [21]

WILLIAMS, Hamilton John, *Kempston Vicarage, Bedford.*—St. John's Coll. Cam. LL.B. 1829, *ad eund.* Ox. 1862; Deac. and Pr. 1829 by Bp of B. and W. V. of Kempston, Dio. Ely, 1846. (Patron, J. D. Allcroft, Esq; Tithe, 6*l* 6*s*; Glebe, 192 acres; V.'s Inc. 406*l* and Ho; Pop. 2191.) Formerly V. of Buckland Dinham, Somerset, 1829-46. [22]

WILLIAMS, Henry, *Overton, near Marlborough.*—Jesus Coll. Ox. 3rd cl. Lit. Hum. B.A. 1851; Deac. 1852 by Bp of Lich. Pr. 1854 by Bp of Wor. C. of Overton and Fifield 1862. Formerly C. of Blockley, Worc. 1859-61, Bishops Cannings, Wilts, 1861-62 [23]

WILLIAMS, H.—Asst. Mast. of the Gr. Sch. Leeds. [24]

WILLIAMS, Henry, *Croxton Vicarage, Thetford, Norfolk.*—Ch. Coll. Cam. B.A. 1848, M.A. 1852; Deac. 1848, Pr. 1849. V. of Croxton, Dio. Nor. 1852. (Patron, Ch. Coll. Cam; V.'s Inc. 98*l*; Pop. 428.) Chap. to the Thetford Borough Gaol. [25]

WILLIAMS, Henry Bayley, *Llanrug, Carnarvonshire.*—Jesus Coll. Ox. B.A. 1828; Deac. 1828, Pr. 1830. R. of Llanrug, Dio. Ban. 1843. (Patron, Bp of Llan; Tithe, 200*l*; R.'s Inc. 184*l*; Pop. 2139.) Formerly C. of Llanberis 1828; and R. of same 1836. [26]

WILLIAMS, Henry Blackstone, *Bradford-Peverell, Dorchester.*—New Coll. Ox. B.A. 1833, M.A. 1837; Deac. 1836 and Pr. 1837 by Bp. of Ox. R. of Bradford-Peverell, Dio. Salis. 1840. (Patron, Win. Coll; R.'s Inc. 275*l* and Ho; Pop. 361.) Fell. of Win. Coll. 1849; Select Preacher 1847-49; Rural Dean of Dorchester 1859. Author, *Seven Sermons* (preached on several occasions before the Univ. of Ox.), 1849, 6*s*. [27]

WILLIAMS, Henry Griffin, *Preston Rectory, Lavenham, Suffolk.*—Emman. Coll. Cam. 27th Wrang. and B.A. 1839, 1st Tyrrwhitt's Heb. Scho. 1840, M.A. 1842, B.D. 1849; Deac. 1842 and Pr. 1843 by Bp of Ely. R. of Preston, Dio. Ely, 1854. (Patron, Emman. Coll. Cam; Tithe, 514*l* 15*s*; Glebe, 6 acres; R.'s Inc. 522*l* and Ho; Pop. 348.) Prof. of Arabic in the Univ. of Cam. 1854. Formerly Fell. of Emman. Coll. Cam. 1842-54. [28]

WILLIAMS, H. Hughes, *Coxwold, Easingwold, Yorks.*—C. of Coxwold with Yearsley. [29]

WILLIAMS, Henry John, *Barrow, Ulceby, Lincolnshire.*—Deac. 1864 and Pr. 1865 by Bp of Lin. C. of Barrow-on-Humber 1867. Formerly C. of Brocklesby with Kirmington 1864. [30]

WILLIAMS, Henry Lewis, *Whitchurch, Salop.*—Trin. Coll. Cam. B.A. 1864; Deac. 1865 and Pr. 1866 by Bp of Lich. C. of Whitchurch 1865. [31]

WILLIAMS, Herbert, *Penboyr Rectory, Newcastle Emlyn, Carmarthenshire.*—R. of Penboyr with Trinity C. Dio. St. D. 1838. (Patron, Earl of Cawdor; Tithe, 310*l*; Glebe, 162 acres; R.'s Inc. 415*l* and Ho;

Pop. 1146.) P. C. of Llandeveisant, near Llandilovawr, Dio. St. D. (Patron, Earl of Cawdor; P. C.'s Inc. 211*l*; Pop. 258.) P. C. of Llanvihangel-Aberbythic, Carmarthenshire, Dio. St. D. 1838. (Patron, Earl of Cawdor; P. C.'s Inc. 72*l*; Pop. 824.) [1]

WILLIAMS, Herbert, *Brecknock, S. Wales.*—Oriel Coll. Ox. M.A. 1862; Deac. 1865 by Bp of Ox. Pr. 1862 by Bp of St. D. V. of St. John's and St. Mary's, Brecknock, Dio. St. D. 1864. (Patrons, Dean of Llandaff and Mrs. Williams; Tithe, 262*l*; V.'s Inc. 415*l* and Ho; Pop. 4163.) Formerly C. of Steynton, Pembrokeshire, 1860–62. [2]

WILLIAMS, Herbert, 9, *Trinity-square, London, E.C.*—St. John's Coll. Cam. Sen. Opt. and B.A. 1850, M.A. 1853; Deac. 1850 and Pr. 1858 by Bp of Roch. Head Mast. of Tower-hill Gr. Sch; C. of St. Katharine Coleman, Fenchurch-street, Lond. Formerly 2nd Mast. of St. Albans Gr. Sch; Head Mast. of Tunbridge Wells Sch; Chap. of City of Lond. Consumption Hospital. [3]

WILLIAMS, Hugh, *Bassaleg Vicarage, Newport, Monmouthshire.*—Jesus Coll. Ox. 2nd cl. Lit. Hum. and B.A. 1816, M.A. 1819; Deac. 1818, Pr. 1819. Chan. of the Dio. of Llan. and Welsh Examining Chap. to Bp. of Llan. 1845; V. of Radir, Glamorgan, Dio. Llan. 1837. (Patron, Earl of Plymouth; Tithe—Imp. 38*l* 0*s* 9*d*, V. 75*l*; V.'s Inc. 135*l*; Pop. 472.) V. of Bassaleg with Henllys, Dio. Llan. 1838. (Patron, Bp of Llan; Tithe—App. 570*l*, Imp. 60*l* 8*s* 1*d*, V. 392*l* 10*s*; Glebe, 3 acres; V.'s Inc. 433*l* 10*s*; Pop. 2169.) Author, Welsh Translation of *Short Addresses to Children of Sunday Schools, by W. Brooke,* S.P.C.K. 1826; also *A Letter on Infant Baptism, by the late Dean of Llandaff,* ib. 1830; translated into Welsh, for the use of the Welsh Dioceses, the *Prayers, and the Fast and Thanksgiving Services, ordered by the King in Council, for Deliverance from the Cholera in the Years* 1831–33. [4]

WILLIAMS, Isaac, *Colwyn, near Conway, N. Wales.*—Jesus Coll. Ox. B.A. 1822; Deac. 1823, Pr. 1824. Formerly C. of Llandryllo-yn-Rhos, Denbighshire. [5]

WILLIAMS, James, *St Giles's Vicarage, Church-street, Camberwell, London, S.*—V. of Camberwell, Dio. Win. 1846. (Patron, Sir W. Bowyer Smyth, Bart; Tithe—Imp. 83*l*, V. 1100*l*; Glebe, 20 acres; V.'s Inc. 2300*l* and Ho; Pop. 14,161.) [6]

WILLIAMS, James, *Tring Park, Herts.* [7]

WILLIAMS, James, *Llanfairynghornwy Parsonage, Holyhead, Anglesey.*—Jesus Coll. Ox. 2nd cl. Lit. Hum. and B.A. 1810, M.A. 1814; Deac. 1813, Pr. 1814. R. of Llanddeusant with Llanbabo C. and Llanfairynghornwy C. Dio. Ban. 1821. (Patron, Bp of Ban; Llanddeusant, Tithe, 250*l* 2*s*; Glebe, ½ acre; Llanbabo, Tithe, 206*l*; Glebe, 5 acres; Llanfairynghornwy, Tithe, 206*l*; Glebe, 46 acres; R.'s Inc. 700*l* and Ho; Pop. Llanddeusant 565, Llanbabo 188, Llanfairynghornwy 293.) Chan. and Hon. Can. of Ban. 1851; Rural Dean. [8]

WILLIAMS, James, *Goldcliff, Newport, Monmouthshire.*—V. of Goldcliff, Dio. Llan. 1823. (Patron, Eton Coll; Tithe—Imp. 18*l*, V. 17*l* 5*s* 6*d*; V.'s Inc. 70*l*; Pop. 250.) P. C. of Bishton, near Caerleon, Dio. Llan. 1828. (Patron, the Archd. of Llandaff; Tithe—App. 73*l*; P. C.'s Inc. 95*l*; Pop. 188.) [9]

WILLIAMS, James Augustus, *Enham House, near Andover, Hants.*—Clare Hall, Cam. B.A. 1842; Deac. 1842, Pr. 1844. Formerly C. of Wrentham, Suffolk, 1842, Ashelworth, Glouc. 1848–52. [10]

WILLIAMS, James Propert, *Whitchurch Vicarage, near Solva, Haverfordwest, Pembrokeshire.*—Deac. 1827 and Pr. 1828. Min. Can. of St. D.'s 1832, (Value, 122*l*); Sub-Dean of St. D.'s Cathl. 1840. (Patron, the Dean.) V. of Whitchurch, Dio. St. D. 1840. (Patrons, D. and C. of St. D; V.'s Inc. 128*l* and Ho; Pop. 1085.) R. of St. Elvis, Haverfordwest, Dio. St. D. (Patrons, D. and C. of St. D; R.'s Inc. 72*l*; Pop. 33.) [11]

WILLIAMS, James Reynold, *Hedsor Rectory, Beaconsfield, Bucks.*—St. John's Coll. Cam. Jun. Opt. Math. Trip. B.A. 1853; Deac. 1853 and Pr. 1854 by Bp of Ox. R. of Hedsor, Dio. Ox. 1860. (Patrons, Lord Boston two turns, Bp of Ox. 1 turn; Tithe, 84*l* 11*s*; Glebe, 2 acres; R.'s Inc. 96*l*; Pop. 180.) Formerly C. of Langley Marsh, Bucks, 1853–54, Kempston, Beds, 1854–55, Upton with Chalvey, Bucks, 1855–59. [12]

WILLIAMS, Jeremiah, *Hope Vicarage, Mold, Flintshire.*—Queen's Coll Ox. B.A. 1843; Deac. 1844 by Bp of St. A. Pr. 1845 by Bp of Ban. V. of Hope, *alias* Estyn, Dio. St. A. 1859. (Patron, Bp of St. A; V.'s Inc. 270*l* and Ho; Pop. 1986.) Formerly C. of Pontblyddyn, Flintshire. [13]

WILLIAMS, John, *Thornbury Rectory, Bromyard, Herefordshire.*—St. Bees; Deac. and Pr. 1821 by Bp of Ches. R. of Thornbury, Dio. Herf. 1843. (Patron, W. L. Childe, Esq; Tithe, 185*l* 18*s* 2*d*; Glebe, 25 acres; R.'s Inc. 220*l* and Ho; Pop. 224.) [14]

WILLIAMS, John, *Rhoscolyn Rectory, Holyhead, Anglesey.*—Lampeter; Deac. 1829 and Pr. 1830 by Bp of St. D. R. of Rhoscolyn with Llanfairyneubwll C. and Llanfihangel-yn-howyn C. Dio. Ban. 1848. (Patron, Bp of Ban; Rhoscolyn, Tithe, 169*l* 17*s*; Glebe, 9a area; Llanfairyneubwll, Tithe, 137*l* 18*s* 8*d*; Glebe, 2 acres; Llanfihangel-yn-howyn, Tithe, 69*l*; Glebe, 1 acre; R.'s Inc. 396*l* and Ho; Pop. Rhoscolyn 462, Llanfairyneubwll 357, Llanfihangel-yn-howyn 222.) [15]

WILLIAMS, John, *Marcross Rectory, Bridgend, Glamorganshire.*—Jesus Coll. Ox. B.A. 1820, M.A. 1824; Deac. 1820, Pr. 1821. R. of Marcross, Dio. Llan. 1833. (Patrons, D. and C. of Llan; Tithe, 163*l* 7*s*; Glebe, 57 acres; R.'s Inc. 240*l* and Ho; Pop. 91.) V. of St. Donnatt's, Glamorganshire, Dio. Llan. 1843. (Patron, J. W. N. Carne, Esq; Tithe, 87*l* 9*s*; Glebe, 12 acres; V.'s Inc. 170*l*; Pop. 126.) [16]

WILLIAMS, John, *Euxton Glebe, Chorley, Lancashire.*—P. C. of Euxton, Dio. Man. 1837. (Patrons, Executors of J. Armetriding, Esq; P. C.'s Inc. 263*l* and Ho; Pop. 1491.) [17]

WILLIAMS, John, *Wigginton Rectory, Banbury.*—Jesus Coll. Ox. 2nd cl. Lit. Hum. and B.A. 1831, M.A. 1833, B.D. 1841; Deac. 1838, Pr. 1840. R. of Wigginton, Dio. Ox. 1843. (Patron, Jesus Coll. Ox; Glebe, 246 acres; R.'s Inc. 400*l* and Ho; Pop. 338.) Formerly Fell. and Tut. of Jesus Coll. Ox. [18]

WILLIAMS, John, *Glan-Flirnant, Bala, Merionethshire.*—St. Mary Hall, Ox. B.A. 1839; Deac. 1839 and Pr. 1840 by Bp of St. A. P. C. of Trinity, Llanfawr, Dio. St. A. 1838. (Patron, Bp of St. A; Glebe, 1 acre; P. C.'s Inc. 144*l*; Pop. 356.) [19]

WILLIAMS, John, *Crinow, Narberth, Pembrokeshire.*—Lampeter; Deac. 1866 by Bp of St. D. C. of Crinow 1866. [20]

WILLIAMS, John.—C. of St. Mary's, Soho, Westminster. [21]

WILLIAMS, John, *Alne, Yorks.*—St. Bees; Deac. 1864 and Pr. 1865 by Abp of York. C. of Alne 1864. [22]

WILLIAMS, John, 58, *Bow-lane, Preston.*—Dub. A.B. 1863, A.M. 1866; Deac. 1866 by Bp of Man. C. of Ch. Ch. Preston 1866. [23]

WILLIAMS, John, *Taliaris Parsonage, Llandilo-Fawr, Carmarthenshire.*—Deac. 1824, Pr. 1825. P. C. of Taliaris, Dio. St. D. 1842. (Patron, William Peel, Esq; Glebe, 8 acres; P. C.'s Inc. 133*l* and Ho.) [24]

WILLIAMS, John, *Dinas Rectory, Pontypridd, Pembrokeshire.*—R. of Dinas, Dio. St. D. 1858. (Patron, Thomas Lloyd, Esq; R.'s Inc. 150*l* and Ho; Pop. 820.) Rural Dean. [25]

WILLIAMS, John, *Peneraig, near Ross, Herefordshire.* [26]

WILLIAMS, John, *Eglwys-Bach, Denbighshire.*—Deac. 1865 and Pr. 1866 by Bp of St. A. C. of Eglwys Bach 1865. [27]

WILLIAMS, John, *Haldon-terrace, Exeter.*—Trin. Coll. Cam. B.A 1847; Deac. 1847 by Bp of Ex. Asst. C. of St. Mary's Major, Exeter, 1865. Formerly C. of Lydford, Devon, All Saints', Bristol, Ashley, Wilts, and Nash and Llanwerne, Monmouthshire. [28]

WILLIAMS, J., *Mathern, near Chepstow.* [29]

WILLIAMS, John Daniel, *Brecknock, South Wales.*—Trin. Coll. Cam. Bell's Univ. Scho. 1848, Coll. Scho. 1849, Browne's Medallist 1849, Sen. Opt. 1st cl. Cl.

Trip. and B.A. 1851, M.A. 1854; Deac. 1854 and Pr. 1855 by Bp of Salis. Head Mast. of Ch. Coll. Sch. Brecknock, 1855. [1]

WILLIAMS, John David, *Farlow Parsonage, Cleobury Mortimer, Salop.*—Queens' Coll. Cam. B.A. 1841; Deac. 1841 and Pr. 1842 by Bp of Herf. P. C. of Farlow, Dio. Herf. 1856. (Patron, Duke of Cleveland; Tithe—Imp. 100*l*; Glebe, 3½ acres; P. C.'s Inc. 123*l* and Ho; Pop. 593.) Chap. of the Union, Cleobury Mortimer. [2]

WILLIAMS, John Haddelsey, *Eaton Vicarage, Grantham.*—St. Mary Hall, Ox. B.A. 1838, M.A. 1846; Deac. 1839 and Pr. 1840 by Bp of Lin. V. of Eaton, Dio. Pet. 1860. (Patron, Ld Chan; Glebe, 74 acres; V.'s Inc. 123*l* and Ho; Pop. 424.) Formerly C. of Legsby, Linc. 1839, Hamworthy, Dorset, 1843, Langton Matravers 1848, Westborough, Linc. 1860. [3]

WILLIAMS, John Hughes, *Llangadwaladr Rectory, Bethel, Anglesey.*—Jesus Coll. Ox. B.A. 1819; Deac. 1822 and Pr. 1823 by Bp. of Ban. R. of Llangadwaladr with Lanfeirian C. Dio. Ban. 1824. (Patron, Ld Chan; Tithe, 245*l* 10*s*; Glebe, 18 acres; R.'s Inc. 239*l* and Ho; Pop. 526.) P. C. of Talyllyn, Anglesey, Dio. Ban. 1845. (Patron, O. F. Meyrick, Esq; Endow. 8 tenements and 122 acres of land; P. C.'s Inc. 88*l*. [4]

WILLIAMS, John Lewis, *Longfleet, Poole, Dorset.*—P. C. of Longfleet, Dio. Salis. 1861. (Patron, Sir I. B. Guest, Bart; P. C.'s Inc. 160*l*; Pop. 1598.) [5]

WILLIAMS, John M., *Burnby Rectory, near Pocklington, York.*—Dub. 1st cl. Div. M.A. 1849; Deac. and Pr. 1850 by Bp of Ox. R. of Burnby, Dio. York, 1861. (Patron, Lord Londesborough; Tithe, 276*l* 19*s*; Glebe, 48 acres; R.'s Inc. 382*l* 2*s* and Ho; Pop. 131.) Formerly C. of Olney, Bucks, 1850–52, Kirby Wharf, Yorks, 1852–57, West Ham, Lond. 1857–61. [6]

WILLIAMS, John Meredith, *Berriew Vicarage, Welshpool, Montgomeryshire.*—Ch. Coll. Cam. B.A. 1827; Deac. 1831, Pr. 1832. C. of Berriew 1838. [7]

WILLIAMS, J. S., *Leamington Priors, Warwickshire.*—C. of Leamington Priors. [8]

WILLIAMS, Joseph, *Gartheli, Lampeter, Cardiganshire.*—C. of Gartheli. [9]

WILLIAMS, Lewis, *Llanfrothen Rectory, Carnarvon.*—St. Bees; Deac. 1862 and Pr. 1863 by Bp of St. A. R. of Llanfrothen, Dio. Ban. 1866. (Patron, Bp. of Ban; Tithe, comm. 100*l*; Glebe, 7 acres; R.'s Inc. 121*l* 10*s* and Ho; Pop. 681.) Formerly C. of Llangadfan, near Welshpool, 1862; Llanrhaiadr, near Denbigh, 1863. [10]

WILLIAMS, Lewis, *Pontyberem, Llanelly, Carmarthenshire.*—Lampeter 1859–62, Burton Scho. 1859, Phillips' Scho. 1860, Creaton Essay Prize 1860, Science Prize 1861; Deac. 1862 and Pr. 1863 by Bp of St. D. C. of St. John's, near Pontyberem, Llanelly, 1862. (Salary, 80*l*.) [11]

WILLIAMS, Llewellyn.—Magd. Hall, Ox. B.A. 1860; Deac. 1861 and Pr. 1862 by Bp of Salis. Formerly C. of Chittoe, Wilts, 1861–63, Crowcombe, Somerset, 1863–66. [12]

WILLIAMS, Morris, *Henry's Moat, Haverfordwest, Pembrokeshire.*—R. of Henry's Moat, Dio. St. D. 1859. (Patron, W. H. Scourfield, Esq; R.'s Inc. 200*l*; Pop. 287.) [13]

WILLIAMS, Morris, *Llanrhyddlad Rectory, near Holyhead.*—Jesus Coll. Ox. 2nd cl. Lit. Hum. and B.A. 1835, M.A. 1840; Deac. 1836 by Bp of Ches. Pr. 1836 by Bp of St. A. R. of Llanrhyddlad with Llanvlewin C. and Llanrhwydrus C. Dio. Ban. 1858. (Patron, Bp of Ban; R.'s Inc. 590*l* and Ho; Pop. Llanrhyddlad 790, Llanvlewin 128, Llanhrhwydrus 136.) Rural Dean; Surrogate. Formerly P. C. of Amlwch, Anglesey, 1847–58. Author, *Y Flwyddyn Eglwysig*, 1843; *A Welsh Translation of Dr. Sutton's "Disce Vivere,"* 1847; *A New Translation of the "Book of Homilies" into Welsh*, 1847; *A Welsh Translation of Dr. Sutton's "Disce Mori,"* 1848; *A Metrical Version in Welsh of the Psalms*, 2nd ed. 1850; several Sermons. Editor of the amended folio *Welsh Prayer Book*, 1845, and of the revised folio *Welsh Bible*, 1852. [14]

WILLIAMS, Owen Ll., *Bodvaen, Nevin, Carnarvonshire.*—R. of Bodvaen, Dio. Ban. 1862. (Patron, Bp of Ban; R.'s Inc. 200*l*; Pop. 382.) [15]

WILLIAMS, Philip, *Rewe Rectory, Exeter.*—New Coll. Ox. 3rd cl. Lit. Hum. 1848, B.C.L. 1851, M.A. 1859; Deac. 1856 and Pr. 1857 by Bp of Lin. R. of Rewe, Dio. Ex. 1860. (Patrons, Earl of Ilchester and Trustees of Earl of Egremont alt; Tithe, comm. 338*l*; Glebe, 50 acres; R.'s Inc. 400*l* and Ho; Pop. 260.) Formerly Asst. C. of Gedling, Notts, 1856; Min. Can. of Ches. 1859; Fell. of New Coll. Ox. [16]

WILLIAMS, Ralph, 9, *Lorimore-square, Walworth, S.*—King's Coll. Lond. Theol. Assoc. 1st cl.; Deac. 1865 and Pr. 1866 by Bp of Lon. Asst. Miss. of St. Matthew's, Newington Butts, 1867. Formerly C. of St. Mary's, St. George's-in-the-East, Lond. 1865–67. [17]

WILLIAMS, Rees, *Verwig, Cardigan.*—Lampeter; Deac. 1862 and Pr. 1863 by Bp of St. D. V. of Verwig, Dio. St. D. 1864. (Patron, Ld Chan; Tithe, 80*l*; V.'s Inc. 96*l*; Pop. 319.) P. C. of Mount, Cardigan, Dio. St. D. 1864. (Patron, the present P. C.; P. C.'s Inc. 65*l*; Pop. 146.) Formerly C. of Llangoedmore, Cardiganshire, 1862–64, Verwig and Mount 1864. [18]

WILLIAMS, Rees, *Vaynor Rectory (Breconshire), near Merthyr Tydvil.*—Lampeter; Deac. 1833 and Pr. 1834 by Bp of St. D. R. of Vaynor, Dio. St. D. 1839. (Patron, Prince of Wales; Tithe, 263*l* 10*s*; Glebe, 28 acres; R.'s Inc. 270*l* and Ho; Pop. 2984.) [19]

WILLIAMS, Rees, *Hyde, Cheshire.*—C. of St. Thomas's, Hyde. [20]

WILLIAMS, Richard, *Ightfield, near Chepstow.*—Deac. 1816 by Bp of B. and W. Pr. 1817 by Bp of Nor. R. of Rogiett with Ifton R. and Llanvihangel R. Dio. Llan. 1839. (Patron, Lord Tredegar; Tithe, 189*l*; Glebe, 100 acres; R.'s Inc. 390*l*; Pop. 56.) [21]

WILLIAMS, Richard Hayward, *Byford, near Hereford.*—Magd. Coll. Cam. B.A. 1838; Deac. 1838 by Bp of Rip. Pr. 1839 by Bp of St. A. V. of Bridge Sollers, Herefordshire, Dio. Herf. 1866. (Patron, Ld Chan; Tithe, 110*l*; Glebe, 15 acres; V.'s Inc. 140*l*; Pop. 65.) Formerly C. of Byford and Mansell Gamage. [22]

WILLIAMS, Richard Hughes, *Bodlondeb, Llangefni, Anglesey.*—Jesus Coll. Ox. B.A. 1860, M.A. 1862; Deac. 1863 and Pr. 1864 by Abp of York. P. C. of Llandrygarn with Bodrog P. C. Dio. Ban. 1864. (Patron, Jesus Coll. Ox; Glebe, 3½ acres; P. C.'s Inc. 228*l* and Ho; Pop. Llandrygarn 359, Bodwrog 319.) Formerly C. of Cookswold with Yearsley, Yorks, 1863–64. [23]

WILLIAMS, Richard Mainwaring, *Sundridge, Sevenoaks, Kent.*—St. Peter's Coll. Cam. B.A. 1860, M.A. 1866; Deac. 1862 and Pr. 1863 by Bp of St. A C. of Sundridge 1867. Formerly C. of Broningtou, Salop, 1862–64, Eaton Bishop, Hereford, 1864–67. [24]

WILLIAMS, Richard Owen, *Holywell, Flintshire.*—C. of Holywell. [25]

WILLIAMS, Robert, *Rhydycroesau Parsonage, near Oswestry.*—Ch. Ch. Ox. 3rd cl. Lit. Hum. and B.A. 1832, M.A. 1836; Deac. 1833, Pr. 1834. P. C. of Llangadwaladr, Denbighshire, Dio. St. A. 1837. (Patron, Bp of St. A; Tithe—App. 92*l*, Imp. 2*l* 10*s*; P. C.'s Inc. 72*l*; Pop. 223.) P. C. of Rhydycroesau, Dio. St. A 1838. (Patron, Bp of St. A; Glebe, 10 acres; P. C.'s Inc. 55*l* and Ho; Pop. 328.) [26]

WILLIAMS, Robert, *Llanfyllin Rectory, Montgomeryshire, near Oswestry.*—Jesus Coll. Ox. 4th cl. Lit. Hum and B.A. 1839, M.A. 1840; Deac. 1840 and Pr. 1841 by Bp of St. A. R. of Llanfyllin, Dio. St. A. 1850. (Patron, Bp of St. A; Tithe—Imp. 142*l* 10*s*, R. 650*l*; R.'s Inc. 650*l* and Ho; Pop. 1880.) Hon. Can. of St. A. 1858; Surrogate; Rural Dean 1861. Formerly C. of Gwernafield, Mold, 1840. [27]

WILLIAMS, Robert, *Llanfaelog Rectory (Anglesey), Bangor.*—Jesus Coll. Ox. B A. 1835, M.A. 1838; Deac. 1837 and Pr. 1838 by Bp of Ban. R. of Llanbeulan with the Chapelries of Llanfaelog, Llechylched and Ceirchiog, Dio. Ban. 1864. (Patron, Bp of Ban; Tithe, comm. 903*l* 19*s*; Glebe, 30 acres; R.'s Inc. 904*l* and Ho; Pop. Llanbeulan 314, Llanfaelog 755, Lechylched 710, Ceirchiog 64.) Formerly C. of Carnarvon 1837–46; R. of Bottwnog and Mellteyrne 1846–48; V. of Clynnog 1848–64; Surrogate 1855. Author, *Sermon on the Christening of the Prince of Wales*; several Sermons and Pamphlets both in English and Welsh. [1]

WILLIAMS, R., *Bristol.*—R. of St. Stephen's, Bristol, Dio. G. and B. 1858. (Patron, Ld Chan; R.'s Inc. 300*l*; Pop. 2680.) [2]

WILLIAMS, R. E., *Hampton Poyle, Woodstock, Oxon.*—C. of Hampton Poyle. [3]

WILLIAMS, Robert Price, *Scartho Rectory, Great Grimsby, Lincolnshire.*—Jesus Coll. Ox. 4th cl. Lit. Hum. and B.A. 1841, M.A. 1844; Deac. 1842, Pr. 1843. R. of Scartho, Dio. Lin. 1845. (Patron, Jesus Coll. Ox; R.'s Inc. 300*l* and Ho; Pop. 188.) Formerly Fell. of Jesus Coll. Ox. [4]

WILLIAMS, Roger, *Lower Chapel, Brecon.*—Lampeter; Deac. 1855 and Pr. 1856 by Bp of St. D. P. C. of Llanfihangelfechan, Dio. St. D. 1861. (Patron, R. of Llandefaelog-fach; P. C.'s Inc. 225*l*; Pop. 400.) P. C. of Garthbrengy, Brecon, Dio. St. D. 1861. (Patron, Bp of St. D; P. C.'s Inc. 102*l*; Pop. 162.) Formerly C. of Lampeter. Author, *A Welsh Church Hymnal, with a few English Hymns added*, Lampeter. [5]

WILLIAMS, Rowland, *Broad Chalke Vicarage, near Salisbury.*—King's Coll. Cam. Battie's Univ. Scho. 1838, B.A. 1841, M.A. 1844, Muir Prizeman 1849, B.D. 1851, D.D. 1857; Deac. 1842 and Pr. 1843 by Bp of Lin. V. of Broad Chalke with Bower Chalke, Dio. Salis. 1859. (Patron, King's Coll. Cam; Broad Chalke, Tithe, 147*l*; Glebe, 73*l* with Ho; Pop. 796; Bower Chalke, Tithe, 100*l* with Ho; Pop. 496.) Formerly Fell. and Tut. of King's Coll. Cam; Examiner at Eton and Cambridge, and Prof. of Hebrew at Lampeter. Author, *Christianity and Hinduism*; *Rational Godliness*, 1855; *Review of Bishop of Llandaff's Charge*, 1857; *A Letter to the Bishop of St. David's, and a Critical Appendix on his Lordship's Reply*, 1861; *Orestes, an Imitation of a Greek Play*; *An Introduction to Despres's Daniel*, 1865; *A New Version of the Hebrew Prophets*, 1866; *Broad Chalke Sermon-Essays*, 1867; Review of Bunsen in *Essays and Reviews*; Reviews of *Welsh Methodism, Welsh Church, Welsh Bards*, and *Stonehenge* in *Quarterly Review*; etc. [6]

WILLIAMS, St. George Armstrong, *Cefn, Pwllheli, Carnarvonshire.*—Jesus Coll. Ox. B.A. 1827, M.A. 1831; Deac. 1827 and Pr. 1828 by Bp of Ban. R. of Llangybi with Llanarmon, Dio. Ban. 1849. (Patron, Bp of Ban; Llangybi, Tithe, 500*l*; R.'s Inc. 500*l*; Pop. Llangybi 622, Llanarmon 556.) Formerly C. of Llanvair-is-gaer and Chap. of the County Gaol 1827–41; P. C. of Bettws Garmon 1828–41; C. of Llanwrda 1831; V. of Pwllheli 1841–49. Editor of English Works of Rev. Eliezer Williams, M.A. (his father). Author, *A Memoir of the Rev. Eliezer Williams*, 1840, 12*s*; Biographical Sketches, and various letters in the *Haul, North Wales Chronicle, Record*; etc. [7]

WILLIAMS, Samuel, *Hardway, Bruton, Somerset.*—Dub. A.B. 1830; Deac. 1840 and Pr. 1841 by Bp of B. and W. P. C. of Brewham, Dio. B. and W. 1854. (Patron, Sir H. Hoare, Bart; P. C.'s Inc. 104*l*; Pop. 850.) P. C. of Redlynch, Dio. B. and W. 1856. (Patron, Sir H. Hoare, Bart; P. C.'s Inc. 50*l*; Pop. 61.) [8]

WILLIAMS, Stephen, *Lamphey, Pembroke.*—Lampeter; Deac. 1862 and Pr. 1864 by Bp of St. D. V. of Lamphey, Dio. St. D. 1867. (Patron, Bp of St. D; Tithe—App. 60*l*, V. 74*l* 15*s*; Glebe, 24 acres; V.'s Inc. 115*l*; Pop. 395.) Formerly C. of Kenarth, Carmarthenshire, 1863, Lamphey 1864–67. [9]

WILLIAMS, Stephen Frederick, *Liverpool College, Liverpool.*—St. John's Coll. Cam. B.A. 1849, M.A. 1854; Deac. 1854 and Pr. 1855 by Bp of Win. Sen. Math. Mast. of Upper Sch. Liverpool Coll. 1865. Formerly C. of Farnham, Surrey, 1854; Math. Mast. of Charterhouse, Lond. 1862. Author, *Elements of Mechanics*, 1854. [10]

WILLIAMS, Theodore, *Hendon, Middlesex, N.W.*—V. of Hendon, Dio. Lon. 1812. (Patron, Duke of Portland; V.'s Inc. 1300*l* and Ho; Pop. 2450.) [11]

WILLIAMS, Thomas, 87, *High-street, Stourbridge.*—St. Edm. Hall, Ox. B.A. 1850; Deac. 1850 and Pr. 1851 by Bp of Wor. P. C. of St. John's, Stourbridge, Dio. Wor. 1861. (Patron, Earl of Dudley; P. C.'s Inc. 187*l*; Pop. 3377.) Formerly C. of St. Thomas's, Stourbridge, 1852; C. of Sherborne, Dorset, and Chap. to Union 1854; C. of Melksham, Wilts, 1857, Old Swinford 1857-61. [12]

WILLIAMS, Thomas, *St. George Rectory, near St. Asaph.*—Lampeter, B.D. 1854; Deac. 1842, Pr. 1843. R. of St. George or Kegidog, Dio. St. A. 1854. (Patron, Prince of Wales; Tithe—App. 100*l* 15*s* 6*d*, R. 279*l*; R.'s Inc. 295*l* and Ho; Pop. 469.) [13]

WILLIAMS, Thomas, *Grammar School, Cowbridge, Glamorganshire.*—Jesus Coll. Ox. M.A. 1846. Mast. of the Cowbridge Gr. Sch. Formerly Fell. of Jesus Coll. Ox; Vice-Prin. of St. Mark's Training Coll. Chelsea. [14]

WILLIAMS, The Very Rev. Thomas, *Llandaff.*—Oriel Coll. Ox. 1st cl. Lit. Hum. and B.A. 1822, M.A. 1825; Deac. 1827 by Bp of St. D. Pr. 1828 by Bp of Dur. Dean of Llandaff 1857. (Value, 700*l*.) Exam. Chap. to the Bp of Llan. Formerly Archd. of Llan. 1843–59. Author, *Letter to the Bishop of Llandaff on the Condition and Wants of the Diocese*, 1849; *Prophetical Office of Christian Ministers* (a Visitation Sermon), Rivingtons; *Convocation—what is it to be, and what is it to do?* (a Charge), J. W. Parker, 1853; *Education—its Progress and Prospects* (a Charge), 1855; various Charges. [15]

WILLIAMS, Thomas, *Northop, Flintshire.*—Jesus Coll. Ox. B.A. 1842, M.A. 1844; Deac. 1843, Pr. 1844; V. of Northop, Dio. St. A. 1865. (Patron, Bp of St. A; V.'s Inc. 500*l* and Ho; Pop. 2235.) Formerly R. of Flint 1850–65. [16]

WILLIAMS, Thomas, *Llangwm Rectory, Haverfordwest.*—Lampeter; Deac. 1828 and Pr. 1829 by Bp of St. D. R. of Llangwm, Dio. St. D. 1833. (Patrons, Proprietors of the Nash Estate and T. H. Powell, Esq; Tithe, comm. 190*l*; Glebe, 31 acres; R.'s Inc. 230*l* and Ho; Pop. 900.) C. of Martletwy 1863. Formerly C. of Llawrenny 1840–52. [17]

WILLIAMS, Thomas, *Llanddeusant, Holyhead.*—Dur. B.A; Deac. 1850 and Pr. 1851 by Bp of Ban. C. of Llanddeusant, Anglesey, 1856. Formerly C. of Pentraeth 1850–56. [18]

WILLIAMS, Thomas, *Llowes, Radnorshire.*—Oriel Coll. Ox. 2nd cl. Law and Mod. Hist. B.A. 1856, M.A. 1858; Deac. 1857 and Pr. 1858 by Bp of Llan. V. of Llowes with Llanddewy-fach V. Dio. St. D. 1859. (Patron, Archd. of Brecknock; V.'s Inc. 132*l*; Pop. 440.) [19]

WILLIAMS, Thomas, *Elloughton, Brough, Yorks.*—Magd. Hall, Ox. B.A. 1818, M.A. 1825; Deac. 1819, Pr. 1821. V. of Elloughton, Dio. York, 1842. (Patron, Abp of York; Glebe, 40 acres; V.'s Inc. 300*l* and Ho; Pop. 688.) [20]

WILLIAMS, Thomas, *Berse Drelincourt, Wrexham.*—King's Coll. Lond. Theol. Assoc. 1854; Deac. 1854 and Pr. 1855 by Bp of B. and W. P. C. of Berse Drelincourt, Dio. St. A. 1860. (Patron, Bp of St. A; P. C.'s Inc. 87*l* and Ho.) Formerly C. of Wellington, Somerset, 1854, Gaerhill, near Frome, 1858, Kirkham, Lancashire, 1860. [21]

WILLIAMS, Thomas, *Llanrwst, Denbigh.*—C. of Llanrwst. [22]

WILLIAMS, T., *Preston, Lancashire.*—C. of Ch. Ch. Preston. [23]

WILLIAMS, T. C., *Heigham, Norwich.*—St. Aidan's; Deac. 1861, Pr. 1862. C. of Heigham 1866. Formerly C. of St. Luke's 1861–65, and All Saints', Birmingham, 1865–66. [24]

WILLIAMS, Thomas John, *Waddesdon Rectory, Aylesbury.*—Univ. Coll. Ox. M.A. 1857; Deac. 1856 and Pr. 1858 by Bp of Ox. R. of Waddesdon, 3rd portion, Dio. Ox. 1867. (Patron, Duke of Marlborough; R.'s

Inc. 300*l* and Ho; Pop. 1786.) C. in sole charge of Waddesdon, 1st and 2nd portions (C.'s Inc. 100*l*.) C. in sole charge of Upper Winchendon, Bucks, 1867. (C.'s Inc. 80*l*.) Formerly C. of Marcham, Berks, 1856–58; P. C. of Heath, Beds, 1858–63; Chap. of Crediton, Devon, 1863–67. [1]

WILLIAMS, Thomas Jones, *Llanfair-Pwllgwyngyll (Anglesey), near Bangor.*—Jesus Coll. Ox. B.A. 1835, M.A. 1838; Deac. 1837, Pr. 1838. Surrogate. Formerly R. of Llanfair-Pwllgwyngyll with Llandysilio 1850–66. [2]

WILLIAMS, Thomas Lewis, *Matherne, near Chepstow.*—Univ. Coll. Ox. M.A; Deac. by Bp of Llan. Pr. by Bp of Win. V. of Matherne, Dio. Llan. 1845. (Patrons, D. and C. of Llan; V.'s Inc. 300*l* and Ho; Pop. 450.) [3]

WILLIAMS, Thomas Lockyer, *Porthleven, Helstone, Cornwall.*—Trin. Coll. Cam. B.A. 1845; Deac. 1847 and Pr. 1848 by Bp of G. and B. P. C. of Porthleven, Dio. Ex. 1851. (Patron, V. of Sithney; P. C.'s Inc. 152*l* 9*s* 6*d*; Pop. 1256.) Formerly C. of Tetbury 1849–51. Author, *Family Prayers*, 1851. [4]

WILLIAMS, Thomas Norris, *Aber Rectory, Bangor.*—Mert. Coll. Ox. B.A. 1831, M.A. 1836; Deac. 1832, Pr. 1833. R. of Aber, Dio. Ban. 1852. (Patron, Sir Richard B. Williams Bulkeley, Bart. M.P; Tithe, 340*l*; Glebe, 19 acres; R.'s Inc. 400*l* and Ho; Pop. 582.) [5]

WILLIAMS, Thomas Prosser, *Tilney St. Lawrence, Lynn, Norfolk.*—Magd. Coll. Ox. B.A. 1826; Deac. 1827 and Pr. 1828 by Bp of Herf. C. of Tilney St. Lawrence. Formerly C. of Stanton-Long and Clee St. Margaret's, Salop. [6]

WILLIAMS, Wadham Pigott, *Bishops Hull, Taunton.*—Lin. Coll. Ox. B.A. 1845; Deac. 1845 and Pr. 1846 by Bp of B. and W. P. C. of Bishops Hull, Dio. B. and W. 1856. (Patron, the present P. C; Tithe—Imp. 392*l* 19*s* 6*d*; Glebe, 60 acres; P. C.'s Inc. 300*l*; Pop. 845.) [7]

WILLIAMS, Walter A., *Osgathorpe Rectory, Loughborough.*—R. of Osgathorpe, Dio. Pet. 1866. (Patron, Marquis of Hastings; R.'s Inc. 200*l* and Ho; Pop. 351.) [8]

WILLIAMS, Watkin, *Llangar Rectory, Corwen, Merionethshire.*—R. of Llangar, Dio. St. A. 1858. (Patron, Bp of St. A; R.'s Inc. 160*l* and Ho; Pop. 211.) [9]

WILLIAMS, William, *Wall, Lichfield.*—Wor. Coll. Ox. M.A; Deac. 1833 and Pr. 1834 by Bp of Llan. P. C. of Wall, Dio. Lich. 1864. (Patron, P. C. of St. Michael's, Lichfield; P. C.'s Inc. 53*l* and Ho; Pop. 243.) Formerly C. of Lyford, Berks, 1839–64. [10]

WILLIAMS, William, *Llanvihangel-Nantmellan, New Radnor.*—P. C. of Llanvihangel-Nantmellan, Dio. St. D. 1831. (Patron, Ld Chan; P. C.'s Inc. 142*l*; Pop. 348.) [11]

WILLIAMS, William, *Llanddyvnan Pentraeth, Anglesey.*—R. of Llanddyvnan with Llanfair-Mathavarneitháv C. Dio. Ban. 1844. (Patron, Bp of Ban; Llanddyvnan, Tithe—App. 157*l* 18*s*; Llanfair-Mathavarneitháv, Tithe—App. 109*l* 19*s* 7*d*; R.'s Inc. 280*l*; Pop. Llanddyvnan 720, Llanfair-Mathavarneitháv 757.) Surrogate. [12]

WILLIAMS, William, *Llanrhaiadr-yn-Mochnant Vicarage (Denbighshire), near Oswestry.*—Jesus Coll. Ox. B.A. 1829, M.A. 1831; Deac. 1830 and Pr. 1831 by Bp of Ches. V. of Llanrhaiadr-yn-Mochnant, Dio. St. A. 1850. (Patron, Bp of St. A; Tithe—App. 982*l* 16*s* 6*d* and 7 acres of Glebe, Imp. 12*l*, V. 402*l*; Glebe, 7½ acres; V.'s Inc. 580*l* and Ho; Pop. 2611.) [13]

WILLIAMS, William, *Aston Rectory, near Ludlow.*—Jesus Coll. Ox. B.A. 1829; Deac. 1831, Pr. 1832. R. of Aston, Dio. Herf. 1842. (Patron, A. R. B. Knight, Esq; Tithe, 48*l* 17*s*; R.'s Inc. 90*l*; Pop. 84.) Surrogate. [14]

WILLIAMS, William, *Llanychan Rectory, Ruthin, Denbighshire.*—St. John's Coll. Cam. B.A. 1836; Deac. 1836 and Pr. 1837 by Bp of St. A. R. of Llanychan, Dio. Ban. 1844. (Patron, Bp of Ban; Tithe, 196*l* 10*s*; Glebe, 8 acres; R.'s Inc. 211*l* and Ho; Pop. 107.) Chap. to the Denbighshire Co. Prison, Ruthin; Exam. of Howell's Sch. Denbigh, 1865. Formerly C. of Llanchydd 1836–40, Ruthin 1840–44; Sunday Even. Lect. of St. Peter's, Ruthin, 1840–51. [15]

WILLIAMS, William, *Cockermouth.*—Ch. Miss. Coll. Islington; Deac. 1862 and Pr. 1864 by Bp of Carl. P. C. of Ch. Ch. Cockermouth, Dio. Carl. 1865. (Patrons, Trustees; Tithe, 6*l*; P. C.'s Inc. 170*l*; Pop. 3603.) Formerly C. of Eskdale, Cumberland, 1863–65, All Saints', Cockermouth, 1865. [16]

WILLIAMS, William, *Cwmdauddwr, Rhayader, Radnorshire.*—V. of Cwmdauddwr, Dio. St. D. 1863. (Patron, Bp of St. D; Tithe, 124*l* 6*s* 8*d*; V.'s Inc. 174*l* 10*s*; Pop. 798.) Rural Dean. [17]

WILLIAMS, William, *Hyde Vicarage, Winchester.*—Corpus Coll. Cam. 7th Sen. Opt. and B.A. 1829, M.A. 1833; Deac. 1830 and Pr. 1831 by Bp of Win. V. of St. Bartholomew's, Hyde, Dio. Win. 1833. (Patron, Ld Chan; V.'s Inc. 160*l* and Ho; Pop. 953.) Mast. of St. Mary Magdalene's Hospital, Winchester. (Patron, Bp of Win; Mast.'s Inc. 40*l*). Surrogate. Formerly C. of West Tisted, and Bramdean, Hants. [18]

WILLIAMS, William, *Llansaintfraid-Glan-Conway Rectory, Conway, Denbighshire.*—R. of Llansaintfraid-Glán-Conway, Dio. St. A. 1837. (Patron, Bp of St. A; Tithe—App. 444*l* 16*s* 4*d*, Imp. 18*l* 15*s* 6*d*, R. 273*l* 9*s* 6*d*; R.'s Inc. 305*l* and Ho; Pop. 1304.) [19]

WILLIAMS, William, *Reedness Vicarage, Goole, Yorks.*—Deac. 1842 and Pr. 1843 by Bp of Wor. P. C. of Whitgift, Yorks, Dio. York, 1848. (Patron, G. J. Yarburgh, Esq; Tithe—Imp. 1054*l* 16*s* 7*d*; Glebe, 88 acres; P. C.'s Inc. 317*l* and Ho; Pop. 1149.) [20]

WILLIAMS, William, *Llanynis, Builth, Brecknockshire.*—R. of Llanynis, Dio. St. D. 1850. (Patron, the present R; Tithe, 103*l*; Glebe, 3 acres; R.'s Inc. 107*l*; Pop. 152.) R. of Maesmynis, Builth, Brecknockshire, Dio. St. D. 1852. (Patron, Bp of St. D; Tithe, 157*l* 5*s*; R.'s Inc. 165*l*; Pop. 239.) [21]

WILLIAMS, William, *Bedwas Rectory (Monmouthshire), near Caerphilly.*—Deac. 1844, Pr. 1845. R. of Bedwas with Rhuddry, Dio. Llan. 1854. (Patron, Ld Chan; Bedwas, Tithe—App. 188*l* and 104 acres of Glebe; Rhuddry, Tithe—App. 100*l* and 1½ acres of Glebe; R.'s Inc. 388*l* and Ho; Pop. Bedwas 1019, Rhuddry 329.) [22]

WILLIAMS, William, *Llanharry Rectory, Cowbridge, Glamorganshire.*—Lampeter; Deac. 1847, Pr. 1848. R. of Llanharry, Dio. Llan. 1855. (Patroness, Mrs. B. Jenkins; Tithe, 210*l*; Glebe, 17 acres; R.'s Inc. 245*l* and Ho; Pop. 275.) [23]

WILLIAMS, William, *Repton Parsonage (Derbyshire), near Burton-on-Trent.*—Dub. A.B. 1841; Deac. and Pr. by Bp of Lich. P. C. of Repton, Dio. Lich. 1857. (Patron, Sir J. H. Crewe, Bart; Tithe—Imp. 200*l*; Glebe, 65 acres; P. C.'s Inc. 142*l* and Ho; Pop. 1853.) [24]

WILLIAMS, William, 17, *Albert-road, Middlesborough.*—Dub. A.B. 1865; Deac. 1866 by Abp of York. C. of St. Hilda's, Middlesborough, 1866. [25]

WILLIAMS, William.—Lect. of Llanstephan, Carmarthen. [26]

WILLIAMS, William, *Menaifron, near Carnarvon.*—St. John's Coll. Cam. B.A. 1819, M.A. 1826; Deac. 1821, Pr. 1822. R. of Llangeinwen with Llangaffo C. Anglesey, Dio. Ban. 1829. (Patron, the present R; Tithe, 745*l*; R.'s Inc. 745*l*; Pop. Llangeinwen 913, Llangaffo 122.) Dom. Chap. to the Earl of Pembroke and Montgomery; Hon. Can. of Ban. 1851; Rural Dean of Menai 1841. [27]

WILLIAMS, William Bunter, *Settrington, Yorks.*—Dub. A.B. 1860, A.M. 1863; Deac. 1860 and Pr. 1861 by Bp of Ches. C. of Settrington 1865. Formerly C. of Witton, Cheshire, 1860. [28]

WILLIAMS, William Charles, *North London Collegiate School, Camden-town, London, N.W.*—Trin. Coll. Cam. B.A. 1845, M.A. 1853, B.D. 1862; Deac. 1845, Pr. 1846. Prin. of the North London Collegiate Sch. Camden-town; P. C. of Ch. Ch. Brondesbury, Willesden, Dio. Lon. 1866. Author, *An English Grammar*;

A Table of English and French Systems of Weights, Measures; etc. [1]

WILLIAMS, William Henry, *Amersham, Bucks.*—Jesus Coll. Ox. B.A. 1861; Deac. 1861 by Bp of St. A. Pr. 1862 by Bp of Ox. Head Mast. of the Gr. Sch. and C. of Amersham 1864. Formerly C. of Mold 1861–62. [2]

WILLIAMS, William John, *Saxilby Vicarage, Lincoln.*—Brasen. Coll. Ox. Scho. of, and Hulme's Exhib. B.A. 1850, M.A. 1853; Deac. 1854 and Pr. 1855 by Bp of Lin. V. of Saxilby with Ingleby, Dio. Lin. 1867. (Patron, Bp of Lin; Glebe, 137 acres; V.'s Inc. 225*l* and Ho; Pop. 1137.) Formerly C. of Barrowby, near Grantham, 1854–56, St. John's, Stamford, 1856–58; P. C. of Longfleet, near Poole, 1858–61; R. of Saltfleet by St. Clements, Louth, Lincolnshire, 1861–67. [3]

WILLIAMS, William Lloyd, *Llanberis, near Carnarvon.*—Jesus Coll. Ox. B.A. 1831; Deac. 1834 and Pr. 1835 by Bp of Ban. R. of Llanberis, Dio. Ban. 1843. (Patron, Bp of Ban; Tithe, 60*l*; Glebe, 180 acres; R.'s Inc. 192*l*; Pop. 1364.) [4]

WILLIAMS, William Maddock, *Llanfechain Rectory, Oswestry.*—Ball. Coll. Ox. 2nd cl. under line, B.A. 1821, M.A. 1828; Deac. and Pr. 1823. R. of Llanfechain, Dio. St. A. 1851. (Patron, Bp. of Llan; Tithe, 562*l*; Glebe, 32 acres; R.'s Inc. 610*l* and Ho; Pop. 600.) Formerly P. C. of Flint 1825; R. of Halken 1839; Surrogate. [5]

WILLIAMS, William Morris Holt, *Park Hill, Frome.*—Dub. A.B. 1823, A.M. 1826; Deac. 1833 by Bp of Carl. Pr. 1834 by Bp. of B. and W. R. of Orchardleigh, near Frome, Dio. B. and W. 1839. (Patron, the present R; Tithe, 144*l* 4*s* 9*d*; R.'s Inc. 180*l*; Pop. 34.) P. C. of Lullington, Dio. B. and W. 1848. (Patron, R. H. Cox, Esq; Tithe—Imp. 135*l* 1*s*; P. C.'s Inc. 120*l* and Ho; Pop. 137.) Formerly C. of Beckington, Somerset, 1833–40; Mast. of Frome Selwood Gr. Sch. [6]

WILLIAMS, William Prosser, *Grove House, New Radnor.*—Asst. C. of Huntingdon, Herefordshire. Formerly C. of New Radnor, and of Laugharne, Carmarthenshire. [7]

WILLIAMS, William Rees, *Bodelwyddan, St. Asaph.*—Sid. Coll. Cam. 21st Wrang. B.A. 1843, M.A. 1847; Deac. 1845 by Bp of Pet, Pr. 1853 by Bp of Ban. P. C. of Bodelwyddan, Dio. St. A. 1865. (Patron, Sir Hugh Williams, Bart; Glebe, 4 acres; P. C.'s (net) Inc. 400*l* and Ho; Pop. 650.) Formerly Prin. of Training Coll. Carnarvon, 1856–65; Chap. to Dowager Lady Willoughby de Broke 1858–66. [8]

WILLIAMS, William Rice Steuart, *Esher-green, Esher, Surrey.*—Jesus Coll. Ox. B.A. 1844, M.A. 1851, *ad eund.* Cam. 1857; Deac. 1846 by Bp of St. D. Pr. 1847 by Bp of St. A. C. of Esher. Formerly C. of Selattyn, Salop. [9]

WILLIAMS, William Venables, *Plas Uchaf, Llangedwyn, Oswestry.*—Jesus Coll. Ox. B.A. 1852, M.A. 1854; Deac. 1852 by Bp of Ban. Pr. 1853 by Bp of St. A. P. C. of Llangedwyn, Dio. St. A. 1859. (Patron, Sir W. Wm. Wynn, Bart; Tithe, App. 332*l* 2*s*; P. C.'s Inc. 140*l*; Pop. 297.) Formerly C. of Rhuabon, Denbighshire, 1852–59. [10]

WILLIAMS, William Wynn, *Menaifron, near Carnarvon.*—St. John's Coll. Cam. B.A. 1847; Deac. 1850 and Pr. 1851 by Bp of Ban. C. of Llangeinwen and Llangaffo 1855. Formerly C. of same 1850, St. Peter's, Congleton, 1852–53, Maryport, Cumberland, 1853–55. [11]

WILLIAMSON, Arthur, *Weedon, Northants.*—Ch. Coll. Cam. B.A. C. of Weedon. [12]

WILLIAMSON, F., *Salcombe, Kingsbridge, Devon.*—P. C. of Salcombe, Dio. Ex. 1861. (Patron, Earl of Devon; P. C.'s Inc. 200*l*; Pop. 1658.) [13]

WILLIAMSON, George Frederick, *Earl Sterndale, Buxton, Derbyshire.*—Trin. Coll. Cam. B. A. 1842, M.A. 1845; Deac. 1843 and Pr. 1844 by Bp of Nor. P. C. of Earl Sterndale, Dio. Lich. 1864. (Patron, Duke of Devonshire; P. C.'s Inc. 150*l*; Pop. 326.) Formerly V. of Selston, Notts. [14]

WILLIAMSON, John, *Theale Parsonage, Wells.*—St. John's Coll. Cam. B.A. 1837, M.A. 1847; Deac. 1832, Pr. 1833. P. C. of Theale, Dio. B. and W. 1837. (Patron, V. of Wedmore; P. C.'s Inc. 180*l* and Ho; Pop. 743.) Author, *Biographical Memoir of Simeon*, 2*s* 6*d*; various Sermons. [15]

WILLIAMSON, John, *Bilston, Staffs.*—Dub. A.B. 1867; Deac. 1864, Pr. 1865. P. C. of St. Martin's, Bilston, Dio. Lich. 1865. (Patrons, Trustees; P. C.'s Inc. 150*l*; Pop. 4000.) [16]

WILLIAMSON, John, *Birmingham.*—Emman. Coll. Cam. B.A. 1853; Deac. 1854. C. of St. Thomas's, Birmingham. [17]

WILLIAMSON, Joseph, *Sellinge, Hythe, Kent.*—Magd. Hall, Ox. B. A. 1860, M.A. 1862; Deac. 1860 and Pr. 1861 by Bp of Pet. Assist. C. of Sellinge 1864. Formerly Asst. C. of Oundle, Northants, 1860–64. [18]

WILLIAMSON, Robert Hopper, *Hurworth Rectory, Darlington.*—Caius Coll. Cam. B.A. 1835, M.A. 1838; Deac. 1836 and Pr. 1837 by Bp of Dur. R. of Hurworth, Dio. Dur. 1865. (Patron, the present R; R.'s Inc. 574*l* and Ho; Pop. 1525.) Formerly P. C. of Lamesley, Gateshead, 1847–65. [19]

WILLIAMSON, Thomas Pym, *Little Brickhill, Fenny Stratford, Bucks.*—St. Bees; Deac. 1852 and Pr. 1854 by Bp of Ox. V. of Little Brickhill, Dio. Ox. 1860. (Patron, Bp of Ox; V.'s Inc. 150*l*; Pop. 423.) Formerly P. C. of Fenny Stratford. [20]

WILLIAMSON, William, *Datchworth, Stevenage, Herts.*—Clare Hall, Cam. 2nd Wrang. 18th in 2nd cl. Cl. Trip. 2nd Smith's Prizeman and B.A. 1825, M.A. 1828, B.D. 1843; Deac. 1841, Pr. 1842. R. of Datchworth, Dio. Roch. 1849. (Patron, Clare Hall, Cam; Tithe, 475*l*; Glebe, 23¾ acres; R.'s Inc. 525*l* and Ho; Pop. 685.) Formerly Fell. and Tut. of Clare Hall, Cam. [21]

WILLIAMSON, William, *Welton, Lincoln.*—St. John's Coll. Cam. B.A. 1825, M.A. 1831; Deac. and Pr. 1825 by Bp of Lin. V. of Welton, Dio. Lin. 1849. (Patrons, Bp of Lin. and Lessees; Glebe, 266 acres; V.'s Inc. 400*l*; Pop. 692.) Formerly C. of Cold Hanworth 1825–37, Dunholme 1837–43 both in conjunction with Welton. [22]

WILLIMOTT, William, *St. Michael Caerhayes, St. Austell, Cornwall.*—Corpus Coll. Cam. B.A. 1847, M.A. 1850; Deac. 1848 and Pr. 1849 by Bp of Ely. R. of St. Michael Caerhayes, Dio. Ex. 1852. (Patron, Hon. G. M. Fortescue; Tithe, 150*l*; Glebe, 30 acres; R.'s Inc. 180*l* and Ho; Pop. 173.) Formerly C. of Hinxton, Cambs, 1848, Great and Little Chesterford, Essex, 1849. [23]

WILLINGTON, Francis Pye, *Rudham Vicarage, Brandon, Norfolk.*—St. John's Coll. Cam. B.A. 1848, M.A. 1851; Deac. 1849 and Pr. 1850 by Bp of Ely. V. of East and West Rudham, Dio. Nor. 1858. (Patron, Marquis Townshend; V.'s Inc. 560*l*; Pop. East Rudham 956, West Rudham 487.) [24]

WILLINGTON, Henry Edward, *St. Alban's Clergy House, Brooke-street, Holborn, E.C.*—Ex. Coll. Ox. B.A. 1861, M.A. 1864; Deac. 1862 and Pr. 1863 by Bp of Lich. C. of St. Alban's, Holborn, 1866. Formerly C. of Ilam, Staffs. [25]

WILLINGTON, John, *St. Matthew's, Stockport.*—Brasen. Coll. Ox. Scho. of, New Inn Hall, B.A. 1844; Deac. 1846 and Pr. 1847 by Bp of Ches. P. C. of St. Matthew's, Stockport, Dio. Ches. 1851. (Patrons, Crown and Bp of Ches. alt; P. C.'s Inc. 150*l*; Pop. 5550.) Formerly C. of St. Thomas's, Stockport, 1846–51. [26]

WILLINGTON, John Ralph, *Torquay.*—Trin. Coll. Cam. B.A. 1859, M.A. 1863; Deac. 1860 and Pr. 1861 by Bp of Lich. Chap. of St. Raphael's Home, Torquay, 1867. Formerly C. of Ashbourne, Derbyshire 1860–64, Berkswich, near Stafford, and All Saints', Margaret-street, Lond. [27]

WILLIS, Alfred, *St. Mark's House, New Brompton, Chatham.*—St. John's Coll. Ox. B.A. 1859; Deac. 1859 and Pr. 1860 by Bp of Roch. P. C. of St. Mark's, New Brompton, Gillingham, Dio. Roch. 1863. (Patron, Brasen. Coll. Ox; P. C.'s Inc. 160*l*; Pop. 6000.) Formerly C. of Strood, Rochester, 1859–62. [28]

WILLIS, C.—Asst. C. of the Wellclose-square Mission, St. George's-in-the-East, Lond. [1]

WILLIS, Charles Francis, *Letcombe-Bassett, Wantage, Berks.*—Brasen. Coll. Ox. 1844, Scho. of Corpus Coll. Ox. 1845, 2nd cl. Lit. Hum. 1848, B.A. 1849, M.A. 1851; Deac. 1853 and Pr. 1854 by Bp of Ox. R. of Letcombe-Bassett, Dio. Ox. 1857. (Patron, Corpus Coll. Ox; Tithe, 9*l*; Glebe, 304 acres; R.'s Inc. 299*l*; Pop. 283.) Formerly Fell. of Corpus Coll. Ox; C. of Aldbourne, Wilts. [2]

WILLIS, Frederick Augustus, *St. Leonard's-on-Sea, Sussex.*—Dub. *ad eund.* Ox. B.A. 1855, M.A. 1858, LL.D. and D.C.L. Ox; Deac. 1855 and Pr. 1857 by Bp of G. and B. Formerly Head Mast. of Peckham Coll. Sch. Surrey, 1850–55; C. of Highworth, Wilts, 1855–64, St. Leonard's-on-Sea 1864–65. [3]

WILLIS, Henry De Laval, *St. John's Parsonage, Bradford, Yorks.*—Dub. A.B. 1837, D.D. 1855; Deac. 1837 and Pr. 1838 by Bp of Kildare. P. C. of St. John's, Bradford, Dio. Rip. 1850. (Patrons, V. of Bradford, with Messrs. Berthon and Preston; P. C.'s Inc. 300*l* and Ho; Pop. 10,248.) [4]

WILLIS, Henry Marcus, *Trimley St. Mary Rectory, near Ipswich.*—R. of Trimley St. Mary, Dio. Nor. 1857. (Patron, Ld Chan; R.'s Inc. 500*l* and Ho; Pop. 385.) Formerly P. C. of Little Dean, Glouc. 1837–57. [5]

WILLIS, J. F., *Romford, Essex.*—C. of Romford. [6]

WILLIS, John Thomas, *Bepton, Midhurst, Sussex.*—R. of Bepton, Dio. Chich. 1863. (Patron, Earl of Egmont; R.'s Inc. 180*l* and Ho; Pop. 211.) [7]

WILLIS, Robert, 23, *York-terrace, Regent's-park, London, N.W.* and 5, *Park-terrace, Cambridge.*—Caius Coll. Cam. Wrang. and B.A. 1826, M.A. 1829; F.R.S. Corres. Mem. of the Royal Acad. of Sci. Turin; Deac. and Pr. 1829 by Bp of Ely. Jacksonian Prof. of Natural and Experimental Philosophy in the Univ. of Cam. 1837; Lect. on Applied Mechanics at the Government School of Mines, Jermyn-street, Lond. 1853; Sir Robert Rede's Lect. at Cambridge 1861; Pres. of the British Association for the Advancement of Science 1862; Board of Visitors of Royal Observatory, Greenwich, 1866. Formerly Fell. of Caius Coll. Cam. Author, *Essay on the Automaton Chess-player*, 1821; *Essay on the Vowel Sounds* (Cam. Phil. Trans. 1829); *On the Mechanism of the Larynx*, ib; *On the Architecture of the Middle Ages*, Cam. 1835; *On the Teeth of Wheels* (Trans. of Civil Engineers, 1838); *On the Vaults of the Middle Ages* (Trans. of Brit. Architects, 1841); *Principles of Mechanism*, 1841; *Architectural Nomenclature of the Middle Ages* (Cam. Antiquarian Soc. Trans. Vol. I.); *Architectural Histories—Of Canterbury*, 1845; *Winchester Cathedral*, 1846; *York Cathedral*, 1848; *Chichester Cathedral*, 1848; *Of the Holy Sepulchre at Jerusalem*, 1849; *Of Worcester Cathedral*, 1864; *Glastonbury Abbey*, 1866; *Sherborne Minster*, 1866; *System of Apparatus for Mechanical Lectures*, 4to, 1851; *Lecture on Tools* (at Soc. of Arts), 1852; *Sketch-book of Wilars de Honecort*, 1859; etc. [8]

WILLIS, Robert C., *Minster Parsonage, Queensborough, Kent.*—P. C. of Minster, Dio. Cant. 1847. (Patron, James Whitchurch, Esq; P. C.'s Inc. 138*l* and Ho; Pop. 2778.) [9]

WILLIS, Robert Francis, *North-street, Romford, Essex, E.*—Caius Coll. Cam. B.A. 1858, M.A. 1862; Deac. 1860 and Pr. 1861 by Bp of Salis. Sen. C. of Romford 1865. Formerly C. of Bradpole, Dorset, 1860–64, Hornchurch, Essex, 1864–65. [10]

WILLIS, Thomas Frederick, 6, *Alma-terrace, Oxford.*—Ex. Coll. Ox. B.A. 1861; Deac. 1862 by Bp of Nor. Pr. 1867. C. of Cowley, near Oxford, 1867. Formerly Asst. C. of Great Yarmouth, 1862; St. Paul's, Brighton, 1865. [11]

WILLIS, William Downes, *Elsted Rectory (Sussex), near Petersfield, Hants.*—Sid. Coll. Cam. B.A. 1813, M.A. 1819; Deac. 1813 and Pr. 1814 by Abp of York. R. of Elsted with Treyford R. and Didling V. Dio. Chich. 1841. (Patroness, Hon. Mrs. V. Harcourt; Tithe—Elsted, 243*l* 6*s* 6*d*; Treyford, 169*l* 3*s* 3*d*; Didling—App. 94*l*, V. 36*l*; R.'s Inc. 458*l* and Ho; Pop. Elsted 174, Treyford 123, Didling 85.) Preb. of Wenstrow in Wells Cathl. 1840. Formerly V. of Kirkby-in-Cleveland 1817-37; Rural Dean of Bath 1830–40. Author, *Sermons for Servants*, Rivingtons, 1829; *Simony, with Appendix, together with some Account of the Puritan Feoffees*, A.D. 1626, *Simeon Trustees*, A.D. 1836, Rivingtons, 1842; etc. [12]

WILLIS-FLEMING, Arthur.—Dom. Chap. to Lord Heytesbury. [13]

WILLMORE, Benjamin, *Holy Trinity Parsonage, West Bromwich, Staffs.*—St. Bees; Deac. 1847, Pr. 1848. P. C. of Holy Trinity, West Bromwich, Dio. Lich. 1848. (Patrons, Archd. of Stafford and others; P. C.'s Inc. 200*l* and Ho; Pop. 4593.) Chap. to the West Bromwich Union. Author, *Letters on Capital Punishment*, 1*s*; *Lectures on the Evidences of Christianity*, 2*s* 6*d*; *Apostolic Admonitions* (a Visitation Sermon), 1855; *Mormonism unmasked*, 1856. [14]

WILLMOTT, Henry, *Kirkley, Lowestoft, Suffolk.*—Pemb. Coll. Ox. B.A. 1856, M.A. 1859; Deac. 1857 and Pr. 1858 by Bp of Nor. R. of Kirkley, Dio. Nor. 1860. (Patron, the present R; Tithe, 142*l* 10*s*; Glebe, 21 acres; R.'s Inc. 163*l*; Pop. 1129.) Formerly C. of Pakefield, near Lowestoft, 1858–60. [15]

WILLOCK, William W.—Fell. of Magd. Coll. Cam. [16]

WILLOUGHBY, Arthur Henry, 26, *Warwick-square, S.W.*—Wor. Coll. Ox. B.A. 1863, M.A. 1866; Deac. 1864 and Pr. 1865 by Bp of Ox. Formerly C. of Lamborne, Berks, 1864–66; North Kelsey, Lincolnshire, 1866-67. [17]

WILLOUGHBY, The Hon. Charles James, *Wollaton Rectory, Nottingham.*—Trin. Coll. Cam. B.A. 1844, M.A. 1858; Deac. 1845 by Abp of York, Pr. 1846 by Bp of Lin. R. of Wollaton with Cossall, Dio. Lin. 1846. (Patron, Lord Middleton; Tithe, 807*l* 15*s* 6*d*; Glebe, 51½ acres; R.'s Inc. 839*l* and Ho; Pop. Wollaton 555, Cossall 256.) [18]

WILLOUGHBY, John Tyndale, *Leamington, Warwickshire.*—Chap. of the Warneford Hospital, Leamington. [19]

WILLOUGHBY, The Hon. Percival George, *Saundby Rectory, Retford, Notts.*—Trin. Coll. Cam. B.A. 1849; Deac. 1850 and Pr. 1851 by Bp of Lin. R. of Saundby with North Wheatley V. Dio. Lin. 1858. (Patron, Lord Middleton; Tithe, Saundby, 320*l*, North Wheatley, 250*l*; R. and V.'s Inc. 610*l*; Pop. Saundby 86, North Wheatley, 461.) Formerly V. of the united V.s of Carlton-le-Moorland and Stapleford, Lincolnshire, 1852. [20]

WILLS, Charles, *Vicarage, Ventnor, Isle of Wight.*—Lond. Univ. M.A. 1850; Deac. 1861 and Pr. 1862 by Bp of Lon. C. in sole charge of Ventnor 1866. Formerly C. of St. Mary's, Bryanston-square, Lond. 1861, St. Mark's, Kennington, Surrey, 1864. Author, *The Bicentury of the Book of Common Prayer* (a Sermon), 1862; *First Lessons in the Life of our Lord Jesus Christ*, 1863; *Two Letters to Mr. Spurgeon on Baptismal Regeneration*, 1864; *The Nature of the Bible considered in Relation to Modern Scepticism*, 1865; *Plague and Special Prayer* (a Sermon), 1865; etc. [21]

WILLS, George William Burrow, *St. Leonard's Rectory, Exeter.*—Wad. Coll. Ox. B.A. 1837, M.A. 1839; Deac. 1837 and Pr. 1838 by Bp of B. and W. R. of St. Leonard's, City and Dio. Ex. 1840. (Patrons, Trustees; Tithe, 164*l*; Glebe, 2½ acres; R.'s Inc. 300*l* and Ho; Pop. 1700.) [22]

WILLS, John, *South Perrott, Crewkerne, Dorset.*—Wad. Coll. Ox. B.A. 1832; Deac. 1835 and Pr. 1836 by Bp of B. and W. R. of South Perrott with Mosterton C. Dio. Salis. 1848. (Patrons, John and James Trevor Esqs. and John Winter, Esq; Tithe, 395*l*; Glebe, 83 acres; R.'s Inc. 556*l* and Ho; Pop. South Perrott 363 Mosterton 380.) Formerly C. of Bradford Peverell, Dorset. [23]

WILLS, Thomas Alfred, *Beverley House, Wickham, Hants.*—St. John's Coll. Ox. B.A. 1848, M.A. 1851;

Deac. 1849 and Pr. 1850 by Bp of B. and W. Formerly P. C. of Headington Quarry, Oxford. [1]

WILLS, William, *Holcombe-Rogus Vicarage (Devon), near Wellington, Somerset.*—Wad. Coll. Ox. M.A; Deac. 1817, Pr. 1818. V. of Holcombe-Rogus, Dio. Ex. 1824. (Patron, R. Wills, Esq; Tithe—Imp. 320*l*, V. 293*l* 16*s* 3*d*; Glebe, 1½ acres; V.'s Inc. 295*l* and Ho; Pop. 704.) [2]

WILLSON, William Wynne, *St. Mary's, near Godalming, Surrey.*—St. John's Coll. Ox. Fell. of, Pusey and Ellerton Heb. Scho. 1855, Kennicott Scho. 1859, Hon. 4th cl. Lit. Hum. and B.A. 1858, M.A. 1861; Deac. 1859 by Bp of Ox. Pr. 1860 by Bp of Win. C. of St. Mary Shackleford, Surrey, 1865. Formerly C. of Farncombe, Surrey, 1859–63, St. Matthew's, Denmark-hill, Surrey, 1863–65. [3]

WILLY, Parkes, *Pontesbury, Salop.*—St. Bees; Deac. 1852 and Pr. 1853 by Bp of Lich. C. of Pontesbury (1st portion), 1866; Surrogate. Formerly C. of Smethcote 1852–55, Stapleton 1855, Quatt 1855–58, all three in Salop, Sedgeberrow, near Evesham, 1864, Petersham, Surrey, 1864–66. [4]

WILLY, Robert Charles, *Abthorpe Vicarage, Towcester, Northants.*—St. John's Coll. Cam. B.A. 1840; Deac. 1841, Pr. 1842. V. of Abthorpe, Dio. Pet. 1863. (Patrons, Bp of Lich. and Trustees of Leeson's Charity alt; V.'s Inc. 230*l* and Ho; Pop. 541.) Formerly C. of North Wingfield, Derbyshire, 1843–63. [5]

WILMSHURST, A. T., *Woodville, Ashby-de-la-Zouch.*—B.A. 1840, M.A. 1844; Deac. 1843 by Bp of Win. Pr. 1844 by Bp of Wor. P. C. of Woodville, Dio. Pet. 1862. (Patron, Bp of Pet; P. C.'s Inc. 116*l* and Ho; Pop. 1408.) Formerly C. of Bromsgrove, Kirby Muxloe, Braunston, Wordsley, Foleshill; V. of Ratley. Author, *Papal Aggression* (a Sermon), 1850; Volume of *Sermons*, 1852, Masters; *Against marrying a Deceased Wife's Sister* (a Sermon), 1855; *Confirmation* (a Tract), 1861. [6]

WILMOT, E. R. Eardley, 10, *Chandos-street, Cavendish-square, London, W.*—R. of All Souls, Marylebone, Dio. Lon. 1855. (Patron, the Crown; R.'s Inc. 850*l*; Pop. 15,268.) Hon. Can. of Wor. Cathl. 1850. [7]

WILMOT, John James T., *Selkirk.*—St. John's Coll. Cam. M.A; Deac. 1857 and Pr. 1858 by Bp. of Ches. Min. of the Episcopal Chapel, Selkirk. (Patrons, Duke of Buccleuch and others; Min's. Inc. 200*l*.) Formerly C. of St. Mary's, Chester, 1857–58, St. Luke's, Cheltenham, 1861–62. Author, *A Few Words on Education*, 4th ed. Macintosh, 1*s* 6*d*; *The Sabbath Question, a Tract for the Times*, Macintosh, 1866, 3*d*; *A Review of the Report of the Royal Commissioners on the Condition of Public Schools*, 1864, Macintosh. [8]

WILMOT, Robert Deedes, *Kennington Vicarage, Ashford, Kent.*—St. John's Coll. Cam. B.A. 1824, M.A. 1828; Deac. 1824 and Pr. 1825 by Bp. of Chich. V. of Kennington, Dio. Cant. 1833. (Patron, Abp of Cant; Tithe—App. 205*l* and 9 acres of Glebe, V. 198*l* 18*s*; Glebe, 6½ acres; V.'s Inc. 235*l* and Ho; Pop. 567.) R. of Falkenhurst (no church), Kent, Dio. Cant. 1843. (Patron, G. W. P. Carter, Esq; Tithe, 65*l* 13*s* 6*d*; Glebe, 23 acres; R.'s Inc. 100*l*; Pop. 46.) [9]

WILSHERE, Edward Chapman, *Willoughton, Kirton-in-Lindsey, Lincolnshire.*—St. John's Coll. Cam. B.A. 1842, M.A. 1849; Deac. 1843 and Pr. 1844 by Bp. of Ex. C. of Willoughton. Formerly R. of St. Andrew's and St. George's, Scarborough, Tobago, West Indies, 1846–48; British Chap. at Gottenburg, Sweden, 1852–58. [10]

WILSON, Albert Marriott, *Ainstable Vicarage, Penrith.*—Queen's Coll. Ox. B.A. 1848, M.A. 1851; Deac. 1848 and Pr. 1849 by Bp of Rip. V. of Ainstable, Dio. Carl. 1853. (Patron, C. Featherstonhaugh, Esq; Tithe—Imp. 324*l*; Glebe, 465 acres; V.'s Inc. 305*l* and Ho; Pop. 550.) Formerly C. of Heptonstall 1848–50, Sawley and Winksley 1850–53. Author, *Christmas Plea for the Distressed Operatives*, 1863, 1*s*. [11]

WILSON, Alexander, *National Society, Sanctuary, Westminster, S.W.*—M.A. 1849; Deac. 1846 and Pr. 1848 by Bp of Lon. Sec. to the National Society, Westminster. [12]

WILSON, Alfred, *New Brompton, Chatham.*—St. Peter's Coll. Cam. B.A. 1865; Deac. 1866 by Bp of Roch. C. of St. Mark's, New Brompton. [13]

WILSON, Alfred William, *Trinity Vicarage, Coventry.*—Queens' Coll. Cam. B.A. 1846, M.A. 1849. V. of Trinity, Coventry, Dio. Wor. 1864. (Patron, Ld Chan; V.'s Inc. 650*l* and Ho; Pop. 9781.) Surrogate. Formerly R. of Sedgebrook, Lincolnshire, 1851–64. [14]

WILSON, Andrew, *Edge Hill, Liverpool.*—Trin. Coll. Cam. Sen. Opt. 2nd cl. Cl. Trip. 1st cl. and Prize in Moral Sci. Trip. B.A. 1851; Deac. 1856 and Pr. 1857 by Bp of Wor. C. of St. Catherine's, Liverpool, 1862. Formerly Asst. Mast. Leamington Coll. 1856–57. Author, *Sermons*, Rivingtons, 1867. [15]

WILSON, Arthur Charles, *St. Nicolas College, Lancing, Sussex.*—Ch. Ch. Ox. late Stud. of, 3rd cl. Lit. Hum. 4th cl. Math. et Phy. and B.A. 1848, M.A. 1851, B.D. 1866; Deac. 1849, Pr. 1850 by Bp of Ox; Fell. of Lancing Coll. 1850; Second Mast. of Lancing Sch. 1851. Joint-Editor with Rev. W. Stubbs, of the *Hymnale secundum usum Sarum*, Littlemore, 1850, 3*s* 6*d*. Author, *Letter to the Archbishop of Canterbury*; *The Daily Services, how may we not revise them?* J. and H. Parker, 1865, 1*s*. [16]

WILSON, A. Newton, *Lochgilphead, N.B.*—Chap. to the Bp of Argyle and the Isles. [17]

WILSON, Benjamin, *Masham, near Bedale, Yorks.*—Ex. Coll. Ox. B.A. 1866; Deac. 1867 by Bp of Rip. C. of Masham 1867. [18]

WILSON, Beverley S., *Duddo, Berwick-on-Tweed.*—P. C. of Duddo, Dio. Dur. 1866. Formerly P. C. of Etall, Durham, 1861. [19]

WILSON, Charles Henry, *The Rectory, Coberley, Cheltenham.*—Trin. Coll. Cam. B.A. 1840, M.A. 1845; Deac. 1841 and Pr. 1842 by Bp of Ches. R. of Coberley, Dio. G. and B. 1866. (Patron, J. H. Elwes, Esq; Tithe, 470*l*; Glebe, 17 acres; Ho; Pop. 361.) Chap. to the Earl of Stair. Formerly C. of Beetham 1841–43, Heysham, Lancashire, 1843–53, Upton Warren 1855–57, St. James's, Cheltenham, 1857–58, Shurdington, Cheltenham, 1859. [20]

WILSON, Charles Maryon, *White Roding Rectory, Chipping Ongar, Essex.*—R. of White Roding, Dio. Roch. 1855. (Patron, J. M. Wilson, Esq; Tithe, 615*l*; Glebe, 63 acres; R.'s Inc. 615*l* and Ho; Pop. 466.) [21]

WILSON, Cornelius William, *Calbourne Rectory, Newport, Isle of Wight.*—Oriel Coll. Ox. B.A. 1852, M.A. 1855; Deac. 1853 and Pr. 1855 by Bp of Win. R. of Calbourne with Newtown C. Dio. Win. 1863. (Patron, Bp of Win; R.'s Inc. 500*l* and Ho; Pop. 728.) Rural Dean. Formerly P. C. of Northam, Hants, 1858–63. [22]

WILSON, Cyril Fitz Roy, *Stowlangtoft Rectory, Bury St. Edmunds.*—Univ. Coll. Ox. B.A. 1864; Deac. and Pr. 1865 by Bp of Ches. R. of Stowlangtoft, Dio. Ely, 1866. (Patron, Fuller Maitland Wilson, Esq; Tithe, 340*l*; Glebe, 65 acres; R.'s Inc. 420*l* and Ho; Pop. 185.) Formerly C. of the Higher Mediety, Malpas, Cheshire, 1865–67. [23]

WILSON, Daniel, 9, *Barnsbury-park, Islington, London, N.*—Wad. Coll. Ox. B.A. 1827, M.A. 1829; Deac. 1828, Pr. 1829. V. of St. Mary's, Islington, Dio. Lon. 1832. (Patrons, Trustees; V.'s Inc. 1500*l*; Pop. 18,218.) Rural Dean. Formerly R. of Upper Worton, Oxon, 1829–32. Author, *The True Doctrine of the Atonement Asserted and Vindicated*; *A Few Thoughts on Religious Revivals*; *The Duty of the Christian Tradesman towards his Apprentices*; *A Revival of Spiritual Religion the only effectual Remedy for the Dangers which now threaten the Church of England*; *Our Protestant Faith in Danger*; *Practical Duties which result from Communion with a Reformed Church*; *The Christian Character illustrated, a Course of Lectures*; *God's Ways Equal*; *A Pastoral Address to the Young*; etc. [24]

WILSON, Daniel, *Seaton Parsonage, Workington, Cumberland.*—Literate; Deac. 1822 and Pr. 1823 by Bp of Ches. P. C. of Camerton, Cumberland, Dio. Carl. 1852. (Patrons, D. and C. of Carl; Tithe—App. 328*l* 14*s* and 24 acres of Glebe, P. C.'s Inc. 94*l*; Pop. 1326.) Author, *A Work upon the Globes*, Carlisle, 1832, 1*s*; *The Passage through the Red Sea*, Keswick, 1*s*; Pamphlet and Letters upon the Poor Law, 1837; Works in General Literature and Mathematics; *A Tour through the Lakes and Mountains of Cumberland and Westmoreland*; many Articles in *Carlisle Patriot*. [1]

WILSON, Daniel Frederic, *Mitcham Vicarage, Surrey, S.*—Wad. Coll. Ox. B.A. 1852, M.A. 1855; Deac. 1853 by Bp of Calcutta, Pr. 1854 by Bp of Salis. V. of Mitcham, Dio. Win. 1859. (Patron, W. Simpson, Esq; Tithe—Imp. 355*l*, V. 435*l*; V.'s Inc. 460*l* and Ho; Pop. 5078.) Formerly C. of Calne, Wilts, and St. Mary's, Islington, Lond. [2]

WILSON, Edward, *Nocton Vicarage, near Lincoln.*—St. John's Coll. Cam. Bell's Univ. Scho. 1822, Wrang. 1st cl. Cl. Trip. and B.A. 1825, M.A. 1828; Deac. and Pr. 1826. V. of Nocton, Dio. Lin. 1846. (Patron, Ld Chan; Tithe—Imp. 742*l* 12*s* 6*d*; V.'s Inc. 575*l* and Ho; Pop. 537.) Preb. of Lincoln 1867. Formerly Fell. of St. John's Coll. Cam. 1826–36. Author, *Parochial Sermons*, 1833, 10*s* 6*d*; *Memoir of the Rev. J. Hamilton Forsyth, with a Selection of his Sermons*, 1st ed. 1847, 2nd. 1848, 3rd ed. 1850, 10*s* 6*d*; etc. [3]

WILSON, Edward, *St. Mary's Vicarage, Hunslet, Leeds.*—V. of Hunslet, Dio. Rip. 1857. (Patron, Bp of Rip; V.'s Inc. 300*l* and Ho; Pop. 17,368.) Formerly C. of St. Andrew's, Leeds. [4]

WILSON, Edward, *Topcroft Rectory (Norfolk), near Bungay.*—R. of Topcroft, Dio. Nor. 1824. (Patron, Bp of Nor; Tithe, 411*l*; Glebe, 48 acres; R.'s Inc. 471*l* and Ho; Pop. 418.) [5]

WILSON, Edward, *Crosthwaite, Milnthorpe.*—St. Bees; Deac. 1853, Pr. 1855. P. C. of Crosthwaite, Dio. Carl. 1862. (Patron, F. A. Argles, Esq; P. C.'s Inc. 160*l* and Ho; Pop. 780.) Formerly C. of Trinity, Bolton-le-Moors, 1860–62. [6]

WILSON, Francis, *Armitage Rectory, near Rugeley, Staffs.*—Queens' Coll. Cam. B.A. 1837, M.A. 1840; Deac. 1837 by Bp of Ely, Pr. 1838 by Bp of Lich. R. of Armitage, Dio. Lich. 1838. (Patron, Bp of Lich; Tithe, App. 336*l*; Glebe, 1½ acres; R.'s Inc. 350*l*; Pop. 937.) [7]

WILSON, Francis Garratt, *Over-Worton, Steeple-Aston, Oxon.*—Corpus Coll. Cam. B.A. 1848; Deac. 1849 by Bp of Wor. Pr. 1850 by Bp of Ox. P. C. of Nether-Worton, Woodstock, Dio. Ox. 1850. (Patron, Sir J. W. Hayes, Bart; P. C.'s Inc. 50*l*; Pop. 61.) R. of Over-Worton, Dio. Ox. (Patron, Rev. Dr. Wilson; R.'s Inc. 208*l* and Ho; Pop. 82.) Surrogate. [8]

WILSON, Frederick, *Bury, Lancashire.*—P. C. of Trinity, Bury, Dio. Man. 1865. (Patron, R. of Bury.) Formerly C. of Bury. [9]

WILSON, Freeman, *East Horsley, Ripley, Surrey.*—St. Edm. Hall, Ox. B.A. 1849; Deac. 1849 and Pr. 1850 by Bp of Rip. R. of East Horsley, Dio. Win. 1865. (Patron, Abp of Cant; Tithe, comm. 296*l*; Glebe, 9 acres; R.'s Inc. 300*l* and Ho; Pop. 207.) Formerly C. of Lockwood 1849–55, North Cray 1855–56, Farningham 1856–61; R. of All Saints', Chichester, 1861–65. [10]

WILSON, George Edwin, *Linthwaite Parsonage, Huddersfield.*—Dub. A.B. 1860, A.M. 1865. P. C. of Linthwaite, Dio. Rip. 1864. (Patron, V. of Almondbury; P. C.'s Inc. 150*l* and Ho; Pop. 3144.) [11]

WILSON, George Leroux, *West-end Villa, Fisherton, Salisbury.*—Ch. Coll. Cam. B.A. 1840, M.A. 1843; Deac. 1841, Pr. 1842. Chap. of the Fisherton House Asylum 1863. Formerly C. of Danehill, Sussex, 1841–43, New Alresford 1843–46, and Bursledon, Hants, 1846–51, Stourton Caundle, Dorset, 1851–62. [12]

WILSON, G. M., *Horsley, near Nailsworth, Gloucestershire.*—C. of Horsley. [13]

WILSON, Henry Bristow, *Great Staughton Vicarage, St. Neots, Hunts.*—St. John's Coll. Ox. Scho. 1821, 2nd cl. Lit. Hum. and B.A. 1825, M.A. 1828, B.D. 1835; Deac. 1826, Pr. 1827. V. of Great Staughton, Dio. Ely, 1850. (Patron, St. John's Coll. Ox; Glebe, 287 acres; V.'s Inc. 480*l* and Ho; Pop. 1312.) Formerly Fell. of St. John's Coll. Ox. 1821–50; Tut. of St. John's 1833–50; Select Preacher 1835 and 1842; Public Exam. 1836 and 1850; Prof. of Anglo-Saxon 1839; Bampton Lect. 1851. Author, *Letter to Churton*, Oxford; *Independence of Particular Churches* (a Sermon); *Communion of Saints* (Bampton Lecture), 1851; *Letter to Lord Derby on University Reform*, 1854, 1*s*; *Schemes of Christian Comprehension*, in *Oxford Essays*, 1857; *The National Church* in *Essays and Reviews*, 1860; *A Speech before the Judicial Committee of H.M. Privy Council in "Wilson v. Fendall,"* 1863. [14]

WILSON, Henry James, *Buckland Dinham, Frome Selwood, Somerset.*—Corpus Coll. Cam. B.A. 1860; Deac. 1862 and Pr. 1863 by Bp of Chich. C. of Buckland Dinham 1866. Formerly Head Mast. of St. Michael's Middle Sch. Ruthin, North Wales. [15]

WILSON, Henry Johnson, *West Hyde, Rickmansworth, Herts.*—Queen's Coll. Ox. B.A. 1833; Deac. 1835 and Pr. 1836 by Bp of Salis. P. C. of St. Thomas's, West Hyde, Dio. Roch. 1848. (Patron, Bp of Roch; P. C.'s Inc. 160*l*; Pop. 466.) [16]

WILSON, Herbert, *Fritton Rectory, Long Stratton, Norfolk.*—Ex. Coll. Ox. B.A. 1846, M.A. 1849; Deac. 1846 and Pr. 1849 by Bp of Nor. R. of Fritton, Dio. Nor. 1849. (Patron, Edward Howes, Esq; Tithe, 286*l*; Glebe, 16 acres; R.'s Inc. 298*l* and Ho; Pop. 235.) [17]

WILSON, Hugh Owen, *Church Stretton, Salop.*—Wor. Coll. Ox. 1842, B.A. 1844, M.A. 1846; Deac. 1848, Pr. 1849. R. of Church Stretton, Dio. Herf. 1849. (Patron, C. O. Childe Pemberton, Esq; Tithe, 560*l*; Glebe, 68 acres; R.'s Inc. 580*l* and Ho; Pop. 1695.) [18]

WILSON, James, *Trinity Parsonage, Trinity-street, Rotherhithe, London, S.E.*—Emman. Coll. Cam. B.A. 1848, M.A. 1854; Deac. 1849 and Pr. 1851 by Bp of St. D. P. C. of Trinity, Rotherhithe, Dio. Win. 1859. (Patron, R. of Rotherhithe; P. C.'s Inc. 190*l* and Ho; Pop. 3448.) Formerly Sen. C. of St. Mary's, Rotherhithe, 1851–59. [19]

WILSON, James, *Barningham Rectory, Hanworth, Norwich.*—Jesus Coll. Cam. B.A. 1858, M.A. 1861; Deac. 1860 and Pr. 1861 by Bp of Nor. R. of Town Barningham, Dio. Nor. 1866. (Patron, J. T. Mott, Esq; Tithe, 136*l*; Glebe, 40 acres; R.'s Inc. 178*l* 10*s* and Ho; Pop. 108.) P. C. of West Beckham, Dio. Nor. 1866. (Patrons, D. and C. of Nor; P. C.'s Inc. 81*l* 10*s*; Pop. 329.) Formerly C. of Denton, Harleston, Norfolk, 1860–63; Newton-in-the-Isle 1863–66. [20]

WILSON, James Allen, *The Rectory, Bolton-by Bolland, near Clitheroe.*—Trin. Coll. Cam. Scho. of, 1850, 22nd Wrang. and B.A. 1851, M.A. 1854; Deac. 1854 and Pr. 1855 by Bp of Rip. R. of Bolton-by-Bolland, Dio. Rip. 1859. (Patroness, Mrs. H. A. Littledale; Tithe, 335*l* 5*s*; Glebe, 100 acres; R.'s Inc. 430*l* and Ho; Pop. 739.) Formerly C. of Hornby, near Catterick, Yorks, 1854, Stanwix, near Carlisle, 1857. [21]

WILSON, James Gilchrist, *West Heslerton, Yorks.*—C. of West Heslerton. Formerly C. of St. Peter's, Great Windmill-street, St. James's, Westmininster. [22]

WILSON, John, *St. James's Parsonage, Preston.*—Clare Coll. Cam. Sen. Opt. B.A. 1847, M.A 1850; Deac. 1847 by Bp of Ches. Pr. 1848 by Bp of Man. P. C. of St. James's, Preston, Dio. Man. 1854. (Patron, V. of Preston; P. C.'s Inc. 300*l* and Ho; Pop. 8052.) Surrogate. Formerly C. of Preston 1847–50, Docking, Norfolk, 1850–54. [23]

WILSON, John.—St. Bees; Deac. 1859 and Pr. 1860 by Abp of York. Chap. of H.M.S. "Princess Charlotte," 1864. Formerly C. of St. John Baptist's, Frome Selwood, 1863. [24]

WILSON, John, *Woodpery House, near Oxford.*—Trin. Coll. Ox. 1st cl. Lit. Hum. 1809, B.A. 1810, M.A. 1814, B D. 1826, D.D. 1852; Deac. 1817, Pr. 1821. Fell. of the Soc. of Antiquaries, London, and Royal Soc. of Northern Antiquaries, Copenhagen. R. of Garsington, Oxon, Dio. Ox. 1850. (Patron, Trin. Coll. Ox; R.'s Inc. 600*l* and Ho; Pop. 643.) Formerly President of Trin. Coll. Ox. [25]

WILSON, John, *Durham House, Chelsea, London, S.W.*—St. Cath. Hall, Cam. D.D. 1854; Deac. 1841, Pr. 1842. Min. of Trinity Chapel, Knightsbridge, Dio. Lon. 1856. (Patrons, D. and C. of Westminster; Pop. 900.) Head Master of St. Peter's Coll. Sch; Chap. to the Earl of Ripon. Author, '*Assize Sermons*; etc. [1]

WILSON, John, *Grimstone, Loughton, Leicestershire.*—P. C. of Grimstone, Dio. Pet. 1840. (Patron, V. of Rothley; P. C.'s Inc. 43*l*; Pop. 190.) C. of Wartnaby. [2]

WILSON, John, *Wigtoft Vicarage, Spalding, Lincolnshire.*—St. Cath. Coll. Cam. B.A. 1827, M.A. 1830; Deac. 1827 and Pr. 1828 by Bp of Lin. V. of Wigtoft with Quadring V. Dio. Lin. 1840. (Patron, Bp of Lin; Glebe, 220 acres; V.'s Inc. 420*l* and Ho; Pop. Wigtoft 732, Quadring 1001.) Formerly C. of Surfleet 1827, Stickney 1828–32, Folkingham 1832–39; V. of Deeping St. James 1838–40. [3]

WILSON, John, *Sudbury, Suffolk.*—Chap. of the Sudbury Union. [4]

WILSON, John, *Whitton, Brigg, Lincolnshire.*—Deac. 1801, Pr. 1802. V. of Aukborough with Brigg, Dio. Lin. 1818. (Patrons, Bp of Lin. and Rev. C. Constable; Tithe, 12*l*; Glebe, 102 acres; V.'s Inc. 209*l*; Pop. Aukborough 497, Whitton 215.) [5]

WILSON, John, *Hampton Meysey Rectory, (Glouc.), near Cricklade, Wilts.*—Corpus Coll. Ox. 2nd cl. Lit. Hum. and B.A. 1834, M.A. 1837, B.D. 1845; Deac. 1835. Pr. 1836. R. of Hampton Meysey, Dio. G. and B. 1853. (Patron, Corpus Coll. Ox; R.'s Inc. 665*l* and Ho; Pop. 352.) [6]

WILSON, John, 2, *Arnold-terrace, Tower-street, Hackney, N.E.*—Dub. A.B; Deac. and Pr. by Bp of Down and Connor and Dromore. C. of St. Paul's, Haggerston, Lond. 1866. Formerly C. of St. Paul's, Bethnal Green, Lond. and St. Mary's, Preston. [7]

WILSON, John Edward, *St. Peter's College School, Eaton-square, London.*—Sec. Mast. of St. Peter's Coll. Sch. Eaton-square, Lond. Formerly C. of Trinity, Knightsbridge, Lond. [8]

WILSON, John Matthias, *Corpus Christi College, Oxford.*—Corpus Coll. Ox. B.A. 1836, M.A. 1839, B.D. 1847; Deac. 1839, Pr. 1846. Fell. of Corpus Coll. Ox; Professor of Moral Philosophy. Formerly Curator of the Taylor Institute; Vice-Pres. and Tut. of Corpus Coll. Ox. [9]

WILSON, John P., *Moxley Parsonage, Staffs.*—Univ. Coll. Dur. Bp of Durham's Prizeman in Hebrew and Hellenistic Greek, B.A. 1846, M.A. 1849; Deac. 1846 and Pr. 1847 by Bp of B. and W. P. C. of Moxley, Staffs, Dio. Lich. 1847. (Patrons, the Crown and Bp of Lich. alt; P. C.'s Inc. 213*l*; Pop. 3857.) Surrogate. Formerly C. of Cannington, Somerset. [10]

WILSON, John Robert, *The Vicarage, Guilden-Morden, Royston, Cambridgeshire.*—Jesus Coll. Cam. B.A. 1865; Deac. 1866 and Pr. 1867 by Bp of Lon. V. of Guilden-Morden, Dio. Ely, 1867. (Patron, Jesus Coll. Cam; V.'s Inc. 380*l* and Ho; Pop. 900.) Formerly C. of Trinity, Knightsbridge, Lond. [11]

WILSON, John Thomas, *Rose Hill, Pemberton, near Wigan.*—Bp Hatfield's Hall, Dur. B.A. 1861; Deac. 1862 and Pr. 1863 by Bp of Ches. C. of Pemberton 1862. [12]

WILSON, Jonathan, *St. James's Parsonage, Congleton, Cheshire.*—St. Cath. Hall, Cam. Scho. of, B.A. 1845, M.A. 1848; Deac. 1845, Pr. 1846. P. C. of St. James's, Congleton, Dio. Ches. 1846. (Patrons, the Crown and Bp of Ches. alt; P. C.'s Inc. 150*l* and Ho; Pop. 4240.) Formerly C. of Bollington, 1845–46. Author, *What makes Sunday-School Teaching a Failure?* [13]

WILSON, Joseph, *Sutterton, Spalding, Lincolnshire.*—Pemb. Coll. Cam. B.A. 1832; Deac. 1832 and Pr. 1833 by Bp of Lin. C. of Algarkirk-cum-Fosdyke, Lincolnshire, 1842. Formerly C. of Bicker, Lincolnshire, 1832–42. [14]

WILSON, Joseph, *Spring Bank, Pemberton, near Wigan.*—Dub. Catech. Prem. 1845, 1st in 1st cl. Divinity 1846, Heb. Prize 1846–48, B.A. 1848; Deac. 1850 and Pr. 1851 by Bp of Ches. C. of Goose-green, Pemberton, 1855; Chap. of the Wigan Union 1854. [15]

WILSON, Lancelot Ion, *Weston, Crewe, Cheshire.*—Literate; Deac. 1818 and Pr. 1821 by Bp of Ches. P. C. of Weston, Dio. Ches. 1844. (Patron, Sir John Delves Broughton, Bart; Tithe, App. 260*l*; Glebe, 3 acres; P. C.'s Inc. 75*l* and Ho; Pop. 673.) Chap. of the Nantwich Union; Dom. Chap. to the Earl of Dunmore. Formerly C. of Coddington and Acton, and Head Mast. of Acton Gr. Sch. 1829–46. [16]

WILSON, Matthew, *Edenfield Parsonage, Bury, Lancashire.*—St. Bees; Deac. 1839, Pr. 1840. P. C. of Edenfield, Dio. Man. 1842. (Patron, R. of Bury; P. C.'s Inc. 120*l* and Ho; Pop. 3726.) Surrogate. [17]

WILSON, Matthew, *Loddington (Leicestershire), near Uppingham, Rutland.*—St. Cath. Hall, Cam. B.A. 1825; Deac. 1825, Pr. 1826 by Bp of Pelham. V. of Loddington, Dio. Pet. 1843. (Patron, Charles Morris, Esq; Tithe—Imp. 90*l*, V. 175*l*; Glebe, 18 acres; V.'s Inc. 220*l* and Ho; Pop. 142.) [18]

WILSON, Morton Eden, *Kirk-Sandal, Doncaster.*—Deac. 1840 and Pr. 1842 by Abp of York. R. of Kirk-Sandal, Dio. York, 1847. (Patron, Ld Chan; Tithe, 120*l*; Glebe, 214 acres; R.'s Inc. 387*l*; Pop. 233.) Dom. Chap. to the Earl of Auckland. [19]

WILSON, Plumpton, *Knaptoft Rectory, Lutterworth, Leicestershire.*—Trin. Hall, Cam. LL.B. 1821; Deac. 1824 and Pr. 1825 by Bp of Pet. R. of Knaptoft with Shearsley C. and Mowsley C. Dio. Pet. 1852. (Patron, Duke of Rutland; Glebe, 594 acres; R.'s Inc. 664*l* and Ho; Pop. 841.) [20]

WILSON, Plumpton Stravenson, *West Pinchbeck, Spalding, Lincolnshire.*—Ex. Coll. Ox. B.A. 1852, M.A. 1854; Deac. 1854, Pr. 1855. P. C. of West Pinchbeck, Dio. Lin. 1863. (Patron, V. of Pinchbeck; P. C.'s Inc. 150*l* and Ho; Pop. 1415.) Formerly C. of Roydon, Norfolk. [21]

WILSON, Richard, 50, *Oakley-street, Chelsea, London, S.W.*—St. John's Coll. Cam. Scho. and Fell. of, Wrang. and B.A. 1824, M.A. 1827, D.D. 1839; Deac. 1828 and Pr. 1829 by Bp of Ely. Chap. of Chelsea Workhouse 1837. Formerly Even. Lect. of Chelsea 1845; Head Mast. of St. Peter's Coll. Sch. Eaton-square; Dean of Coll. of Preceptors for eleven years. Author, *Questions on the Gospels and Acts, in Connection with the Greek Testament,* 1830; *A Treatise on Plane and Spherical Trigonometry,* 1831; various Sermons and Papers on Classical and Mathematical Subjects. [22]

WILSON, Richard, *Catterick, Yorks.*—Dub. A.B. 1836; Deac. and Pr. 1837 by Bp of Rip. P. C. of Hipswell, near Catterick, Dio. Rip. 1837. (Patron, V. of Catterick; Glebe, 64 acres; P. C.'s Inc. 100*l*.) [23]

WILSON, Richard William, *Richmond, Yorks.*—St. Cath. Coll. Cam. B.A. 1858, Deac. 1859 and Pr. 1860 by Bp of Nor. C. of Richmond 1862. Formerly C. of St. Mary's, Woodbridge, Suffolk, 1859. [24]

WILSON, Robert, *Roecliffe, Boroughbridge, Yorkshire.*—Dub. A.B. 1853, A.M. 1863; Deac. and Pr. 1853. P. C. of Roecliffe, Dio. Rip. 1866. (Patron, A. S. Lawson, Esq; Tithe, 100*l* and Ho; Pop. 230.) Formerly C. of Ch. Ch. Clifton. [25]

WILSON, Robert, 14, *Colet-place, Commercial-road East, London, E.*—Trin. Coll. Cam. B.A. 1856; Deac. 1858, Pr. 1859. Miss. C. of Ch. Ch. Mission, St. George's-in-the-East, Lond. 1864. Formerly C. of Edale, 1858–60, St. John's, Walworth, Lond. 1860–63; Miss. C. of Lock's Fields, Walworth, 1863–64. [26]

WILSON, Robert Francis, *Rownhams, Southampton.*—Oriel Coll. Ox. 1st cl. Lit. Hum. 2nd cl. Math. and B.A. 1831, M.A. 1835; Deac. 1834 by Abp of Cant, Pr. 1835 by Bp of Lon. P. C. of Rownhams, Dio. Win. 1863. (Patroness, Mrs. Colt; P. C.'s Inc. 60*l* and Ho; Pop. 400.) Formerly C. of Bocking, Essex, 1834–35, Hursley, Hants, 1836–41; P. C. of Ampfield, Hants, 1841–53, Baldersby, York, 1858–63. [27]

WILSON, Robert Spedding, *Brasenose College, Oxford.*—Brasen. Coll. Ox. 2nd cl. Lit. Hum. B.A. 1852, M.A. 1855; Deac. 1857 and Pr. 1858 by Bp of Ox. Fell. of St. Peter's Coll. Radley, 1856. Fell. of Brasen.

Coll. Ox. Formerly Fell. of St. Peter's Coll. Radley, 1856–66. [1]

WILSON, Roland, *Sheerness, Kent.*—Emman. Coll. Cam. B.A. 1831; Deac. 1831 and Pr. 1832 by Bp of Nor. Chap. to the Sheerness Dockyard 1852. [2]

WILSON, Samuel, *Pocklington, Yorks.*—Deac. 1833 and Pr. 1834 by Abp of York. V. of Warter, near Pocklington, Dio. York, 1837. (Patron, Lord Muncaster; V.'s Inc. 50*l*; Pop. 539.) Asst. Mast. of the Pocklington Gr. Sch. 1849. [3]

WILSON, Stephen Lea, *Prestbury Vicarage, Macclesfield, Cheshire.*—St. Peter's Coll. Cam. B.A. 1841, M.A. 1849; Deac. 1842, Pr. 1843 by Bp of Lin. V. of Prestbury, Dio. Ches. 1858. (Patron, C. R. B. Legh, Esq; Tithe—App. 104*l*, Imp. 4242*l* 13*s* 9*d*, V. 390*l*; Glebe, 23 acres; V.'s Inc. 500*l* and Ho; Pop. 5128.) Surrogate. Formerly Chap. to the High Sheriff for Sussex 1855–58. [4]

WILSON, Sumner, *Preston Candover, Micheldever, Hants.*—Ch Ch. Ox. B.A. 1853, M.A. 1860; Deac. 1855 and Pr. 1856 by Bp of Win. V. of Preston Candover with Nutley C. Dio. Win. 1862. (Patrons, D. and C. of Win; V.'s Inc. 250*l*; Pop. Preston Candover 476, Nutley 141.) Formerly C. in sole charge of Nately Scures, Hants, Durley, Hants. [5]

WILSON, Theodore Percival, *Smethcote Rectory, Leebotwood, Salop.*—Brasen. Coll. Ox. B.A. 1842, M.A. 1847; Deac. 1845, Pr. 1846. R. of Smethcote, Dio. Lich. 1862. (Patrons, Trustees of Hulme's Charity; R.'s Inc. 280*l* and Ho; Pop. 318.) Formerly P. C. of Trinity, Bardsley, Lancashire, 1854–62. [6]

WILSON, Thomas, *Walton, near Tadcaster, Yorks*—St. Bees; Deac. 1824, Pr. 1827. P. C. of Walton, near Wetherby, Dio. York, 1837. (Patron, G. Lane Fox, Esq; P. C.'s Inc. 105*l*; Pop. 196.) [7]

WILSON, Thomas, *Birkle, Bury, Lancashire.*—P. C. of Birkle, Dio. Man. 1850. (Patron, R. of Middleton; P. C.'s Inc. 180*l*; Pop. 2135.) [8]

WILSON, Thomas, *Armley Grange, near Leeds.*—Trin. Coll. Cam. B.A. 1830, M.A. 1833; Deac. 1833, Pr. 1834. V. of Farnley, near Leeds, Dio. Rip. 1836. (Patron, Bp of Rip; Tithe—Imp. 300*l*, V. 14*l* 14*s*; Glebe, 32 acres; V.'s Inc. 204*l* and Ho; Pop. 3064.) [9]

WILSON, Thomas, *Eccles, near Manchester.*—C. of Eccles. [10]

WILSON, Thomas, *Stirling, N.B.*—Queen's Coll. Ox. Hon. 4th cl. Lit. Hum. B.A. 1855, M.A. 1867; Deac. 1855 and Pr. 1856 by Bp of Carl. Jun. Min. of Episcopal Ch. Stirling, 1865. Formerly C. of Buxton, Derbyshire, 1857–65. [11]

WILSON, Thomas Charles, *Kirkby Fleetham Vicarage, Bedale, Yorks.*—Clare Hall, Cam. 3rd Jun Opt. and B.A. 1835; Deac. 1836, Pr. 1837. V. of Kirkby Fleetham with Fencote C. Dio. Rip. 1859. (Patron, Ld Chan; V.'s Inc. 300*l* and Ho; Pop. 606.) Formerly C. of Kirkby-Malzeard, near Ripon, 1840–59. [12]

WILSON, Thomas Daniel Holt, *Hinderclay Rectory, Bury St. Edmunds.*—Trin. Coll Cam. B.A. 1833, M.A. 1840. R. of Hinderclay, Dio. Ely, 1833. (Patron, G. St. Vincent Wilson, Esq; Tithe, 410*l*; R.'s Inc. 420*l* and Ho; Pop. 388.) R. of Redgrave with Botesdale C. near Diss, Norfolk, Dio. Nor. 1844. (Patron, G. St. Vincent Wilson, Esq; Tithe—App. 10*l* 5*s*, R. 905*l* 8*s* 3*d*; R.'s Inc. 935*l* and Ho; Pop. Redgrave 686, Botesdale 580.) [13]

WILSON, William, *Desborough Vicarage, Kettering, Northants.*—Queen's Coll. Ox. Scho. of, B.A. 1836; Deac. 1837 by Bp of Chich. Pr. 1838 by Bp of Ches. V. of Desborough, Dio. Pet. 1846. (Patron, W. C. Thornhill, Esq; V.'s Inc. 166*l* and Ho; Pop. 1428.) Formerly C. of Methley, and Rochdale. [14]

WILSON, William, *Waterbeach Vicarage, Cambridge.*—St. Cath. Coll. Cam. B.A. 1850, M.A. 1853; Deac. 1851 by Bp of Lin. Pr. 1852 by Bp of Pet. V. of Waterbeach, Dio. Ely, 1867. (Patron, Bp of Ely; V.'s Inc. 692*l* and Ho; Pop. 1435.) Formerly C. of Isham, Northants, 1851–53, West Wratting, Cambs, 1855–59; R. of Teversham 1859–67. [15]

WILSON, William, *The Close, Winchester,* and *New Place House, Southampton.*—Queen's Coll. Ox. B.A. 1804, M.A. 1808, B.D. 1820, D.D. 1824; Deac. 1805, Pr. 1806. V. of Holy Rhood, Southampton, Dio. Win. 1824. (Patron, Queen's Coll. Ox; Glebe, 50 acres; V.'s Inc. 235*l*; Pop. 1571.) Can. of Win. Cathl. 1831; Rural Dean. Formerly Sen. Proctor for the Univ. of Ox. 1819–20. C. of Colne Engaine 1808. Author, *Juvenalis Satyræ expurgatæ*, 1815; *Collectanea Theologica, containing Nowell's Larger Catechism in Latin, &c.* 1816; *Nowell's Smaller Catechism in Latin*, 1817; *Parochial Sermons* (preached at St. Ebbes, Oxford), 1822; *The XXXIX. Articles illustrated by the Liturgy, &c.* 3 eds. 1845; *Bible Student's Guide to the right Understanding of the English Version according to the Hebrew*, 4to, 1850, 42*s*; *Brief Examination of Professor Keble's Sermon on Tradition*, 1837; *Ordination Sermon* (preached at Farnham Castle), 1833; *Sermon* (on a calamitous fire at Southampton). 1837; *English, Hebrew, and Chaldee Lexicon and Concordance for the more correct Understanding of our English Translation of the Old Testament, in Reference to the Original Hebrew*, 2nd ed. Macmillan and Co. 1866, 25*s*; *The Antichrists of the Day*; *Five Advent Sermons*, Paul and Son, Southampton, 4*d*; *Light and Life*; *Loving Correction*; *Christ Suffering and Glorified*; *Church and the World* (single Sermons), 1*d* each. [16]

WILSON, William, *Field-Broughton, Newton-in-Cartmel, Lancashire.*—Deac. 1821, Pr. 1822. P. C. of Field-Broughton, Dio. Carl. 1829. (Patron, Duke of Devonshire; Glebe, 26 acres; P. C.'s Inc. 69*l* and Ho; Pop. 534.) [17]

WILSON, William, *Ryhope Parsonage, Sunderland.*—Univ. Coll. Dur. Heb. Prizeman; Deac. 1836, Pr. 1837. P. C. of Ryhope, Dio. Dur. 1843. (Patron, Bp of Dur; Tithe—App. 210*l* 17*s* 10*d*, Imp. 177*l* 18*s* 6*d*; P. C.'s Inc. 300*l* and Ho; Pop. 4000.) C. of Bishop Wearmouth 1836–43. [18]

WILSON, William Greive, *Forncett St. Peter Rectory, Long-Stratton, Norfolk.*—St. John's Coll. Cam. Bell's Univ. Scho 1839, 16th Wrang. 8th in 1st cl. Cl. Trip. and B.A. 1842, M.A. 1845; Deac. 1845 and Pr. 1846 by Bp of Ely. R. of Forncett St. Peter, Dio. Nor. 1847. (Patron, Earl of Effingham; Tithe, 587*l*; Glebe, 47 acres; R.'s Inc. 620*l* and Ho; Pop. 665.) Formerly Fell. of St. John's Coll. Cam. [19]

WILSON, William Henry, *Frome Selwood, Somerset.*—Queens' Coll. Cam. B.A. 1861, M.A. 1865; Deac. 1861 by Bp of Ely, Pr. 1862 by Bp of Lich. C. of Frome Selwood 1865. Formerly C. of Clifton Campville, Tamworth, 1861. [20]

WILSON, William Heron, *Birtley, Hexham, Northumberland.*—New Inn Hall, Ox. B.A. 1849; Deac. 1851, Pr. 1852. P. C. of Birtley, Dio. Dur. 1853. (Patron, Duke of Northumberland; P. C.'s Inc. 75*l* and Ho; Pop. 404.) Formerly C. of Cornsnside, near Birtley, 1851. [21]

WILSON, W., *Bethnal Green, London, E.*—C. of St. Paul's, Bethnal Green. [22]

WILSON, W. Reginald, *The Parsonage, Bolsterstone, Sheffield.*—Trin. Coll. Cam. B.A. 1861, M.A. 1864; Deac. 1862 and Pr. 1863 by Abp of York. P. C. of Bolsterstone, Dio. York, 1867. (Patrons, J. W. Rimington Wilson, Esq. and others; Glebe, 116 acres; P. C.'s Inc. 170*l* and Ho; Pop. 3000.) Formerly C. of Bolsterstone 1862–66, Knaresborough 1866. [23]

WILSON, W. T. H., *Leeds.*—C. of St. George's, Leeds. [24]

WILTON, Charles Turner, *Foy, Ross.*—Ex. Coll. Ox. B.A. 1855, M.A. 1858; Deac. 1856 and Pr. 1857 by Bp of Win. V. of Foy, Dio. Herf. 1862. (Patrons, Trustees; Tithe, 576*l* 5*s*; Glebe, 52 acres; V.'s Inc. 700*l* and Ho; Pop. 318.) Formerly C. of Hambledon, Hants, 1856–59; P. C. of Pill, Somerset, 1859–62. [25]

WILTON, Edward, *West Lavington, Devizes, Wilts.*—Queens' Coll. Cam. B.A. 1820, M.A. 1823; Deac. 1820 by Bp of Salis. Pr. 1821 by Bp of Bristol. Mast. of the West Lavington Gr. Sch. 1832; Chap. to the Earl of Northesk; Surrogate; Officiating Min. of the Chapelry of Earl Stoke, Wilts. [1]

WILTON, Paul Henzell, *Owthorne Vicarage, Patrington, Yorks.*—Trin. Coll. Cam. B.A. 1816; Deac. 1817 and Pr. 1818 by Bp of Lon. V. of Owthorne, Dio. York, 1845. (Patron, Ld Chan; Tithe—Imp. 203*l* 15*s*, V. 229*l* 15*s* 10*d*; Glebe, 40 acres; V.'s Inc. 290*l* and Ho; Pop. 704.) [2]

WILTON, Richard, *Londesborough Rectory, Market Weighton, Yorks.*—St. Cath. Coll. Cam. B.A. 1851; Deac. 1851 and Pr. 1852 by Bp of Herf. R. of Londesborough, Dio. York, 1866. (Patron, Lord Londesborough; R.'s Inc. 800*l* and Ho; Pop. 306.) Dom. Chap. to Lord Londesborough 1860. Formerly C. of Broseley, Salop, 1851–54; P. C. of St. Thomas's, York, and Chap. to the York Union 1854–57, V. of Kirkby Wharfe, Yorks, 1857–66. [3]

WILTON, R., *Londesborough, Market Weighton, Yorks.*—C. of Londesborough. [4]

WILTSHIRE, Thomas, *St. Nicholas Olave's Rectory, Bread-street-hill, London, E.C.*—Trin. Coll. Cam. Sen. Opt. and B.A. 1850, M.A. 1853, *ad eund.* Ox. 1855; Deac. 1850 by Bp of Roch. Pr. 1853 by Bp of Lon. Sunday Even. Lect. and C. of St. Clement's, Eastcheap, Lond. 1865. [5]

WIMBERLEY, Charles, *Scole, Norfolk.*—Emman. Coll. Cam. 2nd Porson Prizeman, 1st cl. Cl. Trip. and B.A. 1825, M.A. 1827; Deac. 1825 by Bp of Bristol, Pr. 1827 by Bp of Calcutta. R. of Scole, Dio. Nor. 1860. (Patron, Sir E. Kerrison, Bart; R.'s Inc. 280*l* and Ho; Pop. 677.) Formerly Chap. of the Hon. E.I.C. [6]

WIMBERLEY, Charles Irvine, *Hartlip Vicarage, Sittingbourne, Kent.*—Univ. Coll. Ox. B.A. 1854, M.A. 1857; Deac. 1855 and Pr. 1856 by Bp of Pet. V. of Hartlip, Dio. Cant. 1866. (Patrons, D. and C. of Roch; Tithe, 180*l* 4*s* 6*d*; Glebe, 1 acre; V.'s Inc. 258*l* 6*s* 2*d* and Ho; Pop. 340.) Formerly C. of Dodford, Northants, and Charlwood, Surrey. [7]

WIMBERLEY, Conrad M., *Donington-on-Bain Rectory, Lincolnshire.*—St. John's Coll. Cam. B.A. 1833, M.A. 1849; Deac. 1833, Pr. 1834. R. of Donington-on-Bain, Dio. Lin. 1836. (Patron, Lord Monson; Glebe, 213 acres; R.'s Inc. 301*l* and Ho; Pop. 552.) V. of Ranby, Lincolnshire, Dio. Lin. 1866. (Patron, Francis Otter, Esq; Glebe, 37 acres; V.'s Inc. 97*l*; Pop. 117.) [8]

WIMBUSH, Samuel, *Terrington Rectory, York.*—Brasen. Coll. Ox. B.A. 1857, M.A. 1860; Deac. 1857 and Pr. 1858 by Abp of York. R. of Terrington, Dio. York, 1865. (Patron, the present R; Tithe, 110*l* 10*s* 10*d*; R.'s Inc. 571*l* 8*s* 6*d* and Ho; Pop. 833.) Formerly C. of Hackness, near Scarborough, 1857, West Heslerton, York, 1861. [9]

WIMPERIS, John James, *Sunderland Bridge, near Durham.*—King's Coll. Lond. Theol. Assoc. 1863; Deac. 1863 by Bp of Dur. C. of Croxdale, Durham. [10]

WINBOLT, Henry Holt, *Stalbridge, Blandford, Dorset.*—Corpus Coll. Cam. B.A. 1866; Deac. 1866 by Bp of Roch. C. of Stalbridge 1867. Formerly C. of Royston, Herts, 1866. [11]

WINBOLT, Thomas Henry, *Sandridge, St. Albans, Herts.*—Pemb. Coll. Cam. B.A. 1824, M.A. 1827; Deac. 1825, Pr. 1826. C. of Sandridge. [12]

WINCHESTER, The Right Rev. Charles Richard SUMNER, Lord Bishop of Winchester, *Winchester House, St. James's-square, London, S.W.* and *Farnham Castle, Surrey.*—Trin. Coll. Cam. B.A. 1814, M.A. 1817, B.D. and D.D. *per Literas Regias*, 1826. Consecrated Bp of Llan. 1826; Translated to Winchester 1827.) Episcopal Jurisdiction—Co. of Hants and greater part of Surrey, the Islands of Wight, Guernsey, Jersey, Alderney and Sark; Inc. of See, 10,417*l*; Pop. 1,267,794; Acres, 1,598,568; Deaneries, 37; Benefices, 654; Curates, 285; Church-sittings, 301,781.) His Lordship is Provincial Sub-Dean of Cant; Prelate of the most noble Order of the Garter; Visitor of New, Magd. Corpus, Trin. and St. John's Colls. Oxford, and also of the Coll. of St. Mary, Winchester. His Lordship was Founder and first Min. of the English Ch. at Geneva, 1814; Preb. of Wor. 1822; Preb. of Cant. 1825; Preb. and Dean of St. Paul's, Lond. 1826. Author, *Two Sermons*, 1822; *The Ministerial Character of Christ practically considered*, 1824, 2nd ed. 1828; *The Duties of a Maritime Power* (a Sermon), 1824; *J. Miltoni Angli de Doctrinâ Christianâ, &c.* 1827; *A Charge* (to the Clergy of Llan.) 4to, 1827; *A Sermon*, for the S.P.G. (printed in the Society's Report), 1829; *The Distinctive Tokens of Christian Communion*, 1829; *A Charge*, to the Clergy of Win. 1834; *A Charge*, 1841; *The Crucifixion* (a Sermon), in Vol. II. of *Practical Sermons*; *Charges*, 1845, 1850, 1854, 1858 and 1862; *God's Appeal to the Members of His Church* (a Sermon), 1850. [13]

WINCKWORTH, John Broomfield, *Great Bircham Rectory, Lynn, Norfolk.*—St. Edm. Hall, Ox. B.A. 1841; Deac. and Pr. 1841 by Bp of Wor. C. in sole charge of Great Bircham 1853. Formerly C. of Kenilworth 1841–44, Trinity, Coventry, 1844–47, Heacham, Norfolk, 1847–53. [14]

WINDER, John Parry.—Dur. B.A. 1858, M.A. 1861; Deac. 1856 and Pr. 1857 by Bp of Man. Formerly C. of St. Stephen's, Salford, and Stockport; P. C. of Chadkirk, Cheshire, 1862–67. [15]

WINDLE, Henry Edward, *Wall-heath, Dudley.*

WINDLE, John, *Horndon-on-the-Hill, Romford, Essex, E.*—Trin. Coll. Cam. 22nd Wrang. and B.A. 1837, M.A. 1840; Deac. 1849 and Pr. 1850 by Bp of Lon. V. of Horndon-on-the-Hill, Dio. Roch. 1856. (Patrons, D. and C. of St. Paul's; Tithe—App. 391*l* 14*s*, Imp. 248*l*, V. 181*l* 6*s*; Glebe, 7 acres; V.'s Inc. 214*l*; Pop. 522.) [16]

WINDLE, Samuel Allen, *Kingstown, Dublin.*—Deac. 1852 and Pr. 1853 by Bp of Lich. Chap. of Mariners' Ch. Kingstown, 1862. Formerly V. of Mayfield, Staffs, 1854–62. Author, *Words of Comfort for the Afflicted Children of God* (30th Thousand); *Stop! Stop!* (40th Thousand;) *Stone Steps through the Slough of Despond*; etc. [17]

WINDLE, William, 53, *Doughty-street, Mecklenburg-square, London, W.C.*—Magd. Hall, Ox. Hon. 4th cl. Math. et Phy. and B.A. 1848, M.A. 1851; Deac. 1849 and Pr. 1850 by Abp of York. R. of St. Stephen's, Walbrook, with St. Benet's Sherehog R. City and Dio. Lon. 1861. (Patrons, Ld Chan and Grocers' Co. alt; Tithe, comm. 200*l*; R.'s Inc. 465*l*; Pop. St. Stephen's 300, St. Benet's 114.) Formerly V. of Kirtling, Cambs, 1855–61. Author, *Jesus Christ and Him Crucified, the Grand Theme of Ministerial Teaching*, 1851; *A Christmas Address to his Parishioners*, 1858; *The Apostolic Decision, the Apostolic Precedent*, 1859. Editor of *The Church and Home Metrical Psalter and Hymnal*, Routledges, 1863; *The St. Stephen's Penny Hymn Book*, Warne, 1866; *Brief Explanations on the Catechism*, ib; *Brief Explanations on the Collects*, ib. [18]

WINDSOR, Henry, *Kensworth Vicarage, Dunstable.*—St. Cath. Coll. Cam. B.A. 1837, M.A. 1840; Deac. 1837, Pr. 1838. V. of Kensworth, Dio. Roch. 1862. (Patrons, D. and C. of St. Paul's; V.'s Inc. 180*l* and Ho; Pop. 925.) Formerly P. C. of Armitage Bridge, Yorks, 1848–62. [19]

WINDSOR, Samuel Bampfylde, *Kingston, Canada West.*—Ch. Ch. Ox. B.A. 1840, M.A. 1845; Deac. 1845 by Bp of Chich. Pr. 1846 by Bp of Tasmania. Chap. to the Forces. Formerly Chap. to the Army in the East; Chap. to Bp of Tasmania; Warden of Ch. Coll. Tasmania. [20]

WING, Charles, *Crundale, near Canterbury.*—St. John's Coll. Cam. B.A. 1850; Deac. 1851 by Bp of Ely, Pr. 1851 by Bp of Lin. C. of Crundale 1866. Formerly R. of Staunton and Flawboro', Notts, Dio. Lin. 1851–64; R. of Frowlesworth, Leicestershire, 1864–65. [21]

WING, John, *Astley Abbotts, Bridgnorth, Salop.*—Queens' Coll. Cam. B.A. 1843; Deac. 1843 and Pr. 1844 by Bp of Pet. R. of Astley Abbotts, Dio. Herf. 1856. (Patron, W. A. Warwick, Esq; Tithe—Imp. 22*l*, R. 243*l* 6*s*; R.'s Inc. 333*l* and Ho; Pop. 668.) Formerly C. of Piddington, Northants, 1843, Astley Abbotts 1845. [22]

WING, William, *Stibbington Rectory (Hunts), near Wansford.*—Clare Coll. Cam. B.A. 1810, M.A. 1813; Deac. 1811, Pr. 1812. P. C. of Sutton St. Edmund, Lincolnshire, Dio. Lin. 1814. (Patron, V. of Long Sutton; Tithe—App. 386*l*, Imp. 1083*l* 18*s*; P. C.'s Inc. 370*l*; Pop. 730.) R. of Stibbington, Dio. Ely, 1832. (Patron, Duke of Bedford; R.'s Inc. 450*l* and Ho; Pop. 721.) [1]

WINGFIELD, Charles Lee, *All Souls College, Oxford.*—Ex. Coll. Ox. B.A. 1854; All Souls Coll. M.A. 1857; Deac. 1858 and Pr. 1859. Fell. and Chap. of All Souls Coll. Ox. 1855. Formerly Under Master of Westminster Sch. 1856–58. [2]

WINGFIELD, George, *Glatton Rectory, Peterborough.*—Emman. Coll. Cam. B.A. 1831, M.A. 1834. R. of Glatton, Dio. Ely. (Patron, J. M. Wingfield, Esq; R.'s Inc. 566*l* and Ho; Pop. 293.) R. of Tickencote, Rutland, near Stamford, Dio. Pet. (Patron, J. M. Wingfield, Esq; Tithe, 163*l*; R.'s Inc. 172*l*; Pop. 104.) [3]

WINGFIELD, Harry Lancelot, *Market Overton Rectory, Oakham, Rutland.*—New Coll. Ox. B.A. 1849, M.A. 1853; Deac. 1850 by Bp of Ox. Pr. 1851 by Bp of Roch. R. of Market Overton, Dio. Pet. 1857. (Patron, J. M. Wingfield, Esq; R.'s Inc. 522*l* and Ho; Pop. 429.) Formerly C. of Strood, Kent, 1851–55; Min. Can. of Roch. 1855–56. [4]

WINGFIELD, John Digby, *Coleshill, Warwickshire.*—Ex. Coll. Ox. B.A. 1820, M.A. 1822; Deac. 1823 by Bp of Lin. Pr. 1824 by Bp of B. and W. V. of Coleshill, Dio. Wor. 1828. (Patron, G. D. W. Digby, Esq; Glebe, 66 acres; V.'s Inc. 900*l* and Ho; Pop. 2053.) Rural Dean. Formerly R. of Geashill, Kildare, 1824–48. [5]

WINGFIELD, William, *Leighton Vicarage, Ironbridge, Salop.*—V. of Leighton, Dio. Lich. 1863. (Patron, C. Wingfield, Esq; V.'s Inc. 230*l* and Ho; Pop. 340.) [6]

WINGFIELD William Wriothesley, *Gulval Vicarage, Penzance.*—Ch. Ch. Ox; Deac. 1838, Pr. 1839. V. of Gulval, Dio. Ex. 1839. (Patron, Ld Chan; Tithe—Imp. 268*l*, V. 355*l*; Glebe, 20 acres; V.'s Inc. 425*l* and Ho; Pop. 1743.) [7]

WINGFIELD-DIGBY, Richard Henry, *Thornford Rectory, by Sherborne, Dorset.*—Trin. Coll. Cam. B.A. 1861, M.A. 1864; Deac. 1862 and Pr. 1864 by Bp of Man. R. of Thornford, Dio. Salis. 1863. (Patron, G. D. Wingfield-Digby, Esq; R.'s Inc. 300*l* and Ho; Pop. 415.) Formerly C. of Prestwich, Lancashire. [8]

WINHAM, Dan, *The Parsonage, Eridge-green, Tunbridge Wells.*—Ch. Coll. Cam. B.A. 1846, M.A. 1851, *ad eund.* Ox. 1853; Deac. 1846 and Pr. 1847 by Bp of Ely. P. C. of Eridge-green, Sussex, Dio. Chich. 1860. (Patron, Earl of Abergavenny; P. C.'s Inc. 150*l* and Ho; Pop. 575.) Formerly C. of Soham with Barway, Cambs, 1846–47; Sen. C. of Trinity, Tunbridge Wells, 1847–51; C. of Frant, Sussex, 1853–54; Asst. Chap. to the Forces in the East 1854–55. [9]

WINLAW, William, 2, *Stephenson-terrace, Preston.*—Edin. and King's Coll. Lond. Theol. Assoc. 1854; Deac. 1855 and Pr. 1856 by Bp of Man. P. C. of St. Luke's, Preston, Dio. Man. 1859. (Patron, J. Bairstow, Esq; P. C.'s Inc. 200*l*; Pop. 5000.) Formerly C. of St. Peter's, Ashton-under-Lyne, 1855, St. Paul's, Preston, 1857. [10]

WINN, John, *Askrigg, Bedale, Yorks.*—St. John's Coll. Cam. B.A. 1822, M.A. 1825; Deac. 1822 and Pr. 1823 by Bp of Ches. V. of Aysgarth, Yorks, Dio. Rip. 1827. (Patron, Trin. Coll. Cam; Tithe—Imp. 1196*l* 7*s* 6*d*; V.'s Inc. 200*l*; Pop. 1895.) Surrogate. [11]

WINNING, Robert, *Ilminster, Somerset.*—Caius Coll. Cam. B.A. 1867; Deac. 1867 by Bp of Nelson for Bp of B. and W. C. of White Lackington with Seavington St. Mary, Somerset, 1867. [12]

WINPENNY, John, *Yarm, Yorks.*—Deac. 1834, Pr. 1835. R. of Yarm, Dio. York, 1840. (Patron, Abp of York; Tithe—App. 265*l*; Glebe, 2 acres; R.'s Inc. 250*l*; Pop. 1401.) [13]

WINSLOW, A., *Arkendale, near Knaresborough.*—C. of Arkendale, Yorks. [14]

WINSLOW, Charles De Blois, *Church-road, Wavertree, Liverpool.*—Caius Coll. Cam. B.A. 1861, M.A. 1864; Deac. 1861 and Pr. 1863 by Bp of Pet. C. of St. Mary's, Wavertree, 1866. Formerly C. of Tugby, Leicester, 1861–62, Trinity, Leicester, 1862–64, Garforth, Leeds, 1864–66. [15]

WINSLOW, Forbes Edward, *Weir House, Chesham, Bucks.*—Trin. Coll. Ox. B.A. 1865; Deac. 1866 by Bp of Ox. C. of Chesham 1866. Author, *The Subjective and Objective Presence of Christ with His Church* (a Sermon), Bosworth, 1867, 6*d*. [16]

WINSLOW, H. J. S., *St. Petersburg.*—Jun. Chap. at St. Petersburg. Formerly C. of Wandsworth, Surrey. [17]

WINSTON, William, *Llwyncynlefin, Sennybridge, Breconshire.*—Lampeter, Theol. Prizeman; Deac. 1829 and Pr. 1830 by Bp of St. D. P. C. of Llandilo-r'-Van, Breconshire, Dio. St. D. 1850. (Patrons, Co-Heirs of W. Jeffreys, Esq; Tithe—Imp. 173*l*; P. C.'s Inc. 107*l*; Pop. 496.) P. C. of Llanvihangel-Nantbran, Breconshire, Dio. St. D. 1850. (Patrons, Co-Heirs of W. Jeffreys, Esq; Tithe—Imp. 227*l*; P. C.'s Inc. 80*l*; Pop. 453.) [18]

WINSTON, David, *Wainfleet, Boston.*—R. of Wainfleet All Saints', Dio. Lin. 1852. (Patron, Ld Chan; Glebe, 23 acres; R.'s Inc. 380*l*; Pop. 1392.) [19]

WINTER, Alfred Litt, *Oare, Faversham, Kent.*—Univ. Coll. Ox. 3rd cl. Lit. Hum. and B.A. 1835, M.A. 1838; Deac. 1837 and Pr. 1838 by Bp of Lon. P. C. of Oare, Dio. Cant. 1848. (Patron, Abp of Cant; Tithe, App. 220*l*; Glebe, 40 acres; P. C.'s Inc. 110*l* and Ho; Pop. 240.) Formerly C. of Springfield, Essex, 1837–40, Calbourne, Isle of Wight, 1840, St. Clement Danes, Lond. 1841, Cranfield, Beds, 1844, Iver, Bucks, 1845. Author, *A Jubilee Sermon*, for the C.M.S. 1849. [20]

WINTER, George Robert, *East Bradenham Rectory, Shipdham, Norfolk.*—Brasen. Coll. Ox. B.A. 1843, M.A. 1851; Deac. 1849 by Bp of Salis. Pr. 1850 by Bp of Nor. R. of East Bradenham, Dio. Nor. 1851. (Patron, H. S. Adlington, Esq; Tithe, 352*l* 9*s*; Glebe, 3¼ acres; R.'s Inc. 360*l* and Ho; Pop. 399.) [21]

WINTER, George William, *Litcham Rectory, Swaffham, Norfolk.*—Univ. Coll. Ox. B.A. 1845, M.A. 1846, Theol. Coll. Wells; Deac. 1845 and Pr. 1847 by Bp of Ex. R. of Litcham with East Lexham, R. Dio. Nor. 1855. (Patron, the present R; Litcham, Tithe, 441*l*; Glebe, 45 acres; East Lexham, Tithe, 214*l*; R.'s Inc. 735*l* and Ho; Pop. Litcham 903, East Lexham 226.) [22]

WINTER, H. L., *Alnmouth, Northumberland.*—C. of Alnmouth. [23]

WINTER, John, *Wednesbury, Staffs.*—Jesus Coll. Cam. Scho. of, B.A. 1841, M.A. 1844; Deac. 1842 and Pr. 1843 by Bp of Herf. R. of St. John's, Wednesbury, Dio. Lich. 1844. (Patroness, Lady Emily Foley; Tithe, 117*l* 10*s*; R.'s Inc. 300*l*; Pop. 3437.) Formerly Asst. C. of Wednesbury 1842–44. [24]

WINTER, John, *Coxwold, Easingwold, Yorks.*—Deac. 1805 and Pr. 1806 by Abp of York. P. C. of Birdforth, Coxwold, Dio. York, 1818. (Patron, Abp of York; Glebe, 50 acres; P. C.'s Inc. 120*l*; Pop. 40.) C. of Husthwaite, near Easingwold, 1807. [25]

WINTER, John, *Postling Vicarage, Hythe, Kent.*—M.A. by Abp of Cant. 1841; Deac. 1816 and Pr. 1817 by Abp of York. V. of Postling, Dio. Cant. 1851. (Patron, Abp of Cant; Tithe, 289*l*; Glebe, 19 acres; V.'s Inc. 317*l* and Ho; Pop. 139.) Formerly Chap. of the County Prisons, Maidstone, 1821–51. [26]

WINTER, J. B., *Chardstock, Dorset.*—Head Mast. of St. Andrew's Coll. Chardstock. [27]

WINTER, John Saumarez, *Weedon-Beck Vicarage, Weedon, Northants.*—Corpus Coll. Cam. Wrang. B.A. 1831, M.A. 1834; Deac. 1832, Pr. 1833. V. of Weedon-Beck, Dio. Pet. 1863. (Patron, T. R. Thornton, Esq; V.'s Inc. 300*l* and Ho; Pop. 2189.) Formerly C. of Tottenham, Middlesex. [28]

WINTER, Seneca William, 17, *Highfield-road, Edgbaston, Birmingham.*—Emman. Coll. Cam. B.A. 1852; Deac. 1852 and Pr. 1853 by Bp of Wor. P. C. of St. Barnabas', Birmingham, Dio. Wor. 1860. (Patron,

Trustees; P. C.'s Inc. 300*l*; Pop. 6982.) Formerly V. of Queeniborough, Leic. 1857–60. Author, *Popery, its Alliance with Paganism*; *The Household of God*, Macintosh, 1*s*; etc. [1]

WINTER, Thomas, *Daylesford, Chipping Norton, Worcestershire.*—Lin. Coll. Ox. B.A. 1819, M.A. 1821; Deac. 1820 by Bp of B. and W. Pr. 1821 by Bp of Wor. R. of Daylesford, Dio. Wor. 1825. (Patroness, Mrs. Hastings; Tithe, 210*l* 10*s*; R.'s Inc. 208*l*; Pop. 108.) Formerly C. of Condicote, Glouc. [2]

WINTER, Thomas, *Condicote, Stow-on-the-Wold, Glouc.*—C. of Condicote. [3]

WINTERBOTHAM, Rayner, *Braintree, Essex.*—Univ. Coll. Lond. B.A. 1861, B. Sc. 1862, LL.B. 1863; Deac. 1865 and Pr. 1866 by Bp of G. and B. C. of Braintree 1867. Formerly C. of St. Paul's, Cheltenham, 1865–67. [4]

WINTERBOTTOM, Edward, *Allerton Bywater, Castleford, Normanton.*—Ch. Coll. Cam. B.A. 1855; Deac. 1856 and Pr. 1858 by Bp of Rip. P. C. of Allerton Bywater, Dio. Rip. 1866. (Patron, V. of Kippax; P. C.'s Inc. 110*l* and Ho; Pop. 1200.) Formerly C. of Middleton, and of Carrington, near Manchester. [5]

WINTLE, Frederic Thomas William, *Maker Vicarage, Devonport.*—Magd. Coll. Ox. 4th cl. Lit. Hum. B.A. 1853, M.A. 1858; Deac. 1859 and Pr. 1860 by Bp of Roch. V. of Maker, Cornwall, Dio. Ex. 1867. (Patron, the Crown; Tithe, 224*l*; Glebe, 10 acres; V.'s Inc. 250*l* and Ho; Pop. 2986.) Formerly C. of St. Stephen's, St. Albans, Herts, 1859–61, Rayleigh, Essex, 1861–63; 2nd Mast. of Candover Gr. Sch. 1863–64; C. of Southhill and Callington, and Head Mast. of Callington Gr. Sch. 1864–66; R. of Rame, Cornwall, 1866–67. [6]

WINTLE, Ogle Richard, *King James's Grammar School, Bridgwater.*—Lin. Coll. Ox. B.A. 1858, M.A. 1862; Deac. 1859 and Pr. 1860 by Bp of G. and B. Head Mast. of King James's Gr. Sch. and C. of Bridgwater 1864. Formerly Asst. Mast. King Edward VI.'s Sch. Sherborne, Dorset, 1857; C. of Lydiard Tregooze, Wilts, 1859, Rayleigh, Essex, 1860; Fell. of St. Peter's Coll. Radley, 1862; Asst. Mast. Uppingham Gr. Sch. 1862. [7]

WINTLE, Thomas Drayton, *Hawthorn Cottage, Stroud.*—Pemb. Coll. Ox. B.A. 1837, M.A. 1839; Deac. 1838, Pr. 1839. [8]

WINTOUR, Fitzgerald Thomas, *Hawerby Rectory, Louth, Lincolnshire.*—Magd. Coll. Cam. B.A. 1851. R. of Hawerby, Dio. Lin. 1856. (Patron, Chapter of the Coll. Ch. of Southwell; Tithe, 253*l* 5*s*; Glebe, 45 acres; R.'s Inc. 320*l* and Ho; Pop. 91.) [9]

WINTOUR, George, *The Parsonage, Ironbridge, Salop.*—Wor. Coll. Ox. 1841; Deac. 1852 by Bp of Ex. Pr. 1856 by Bp of Lin. P. C. of Ironbridge, Dio. Herf. 1867. (Patron, V. of Madeley, Salop; Tithe, comm. 115*l*; P. C.'s Inc. 237*l* 9*s* and Ho; Pop. 3154.) Formerly C. of Shebbear and Sheepwash, Devon, 1852–54, St. Germoe, Cornwall, 1855; V. of Rampton and Laneham, Notts, 1856–57. [10]

WINWOOD, Henry Hoyle, 4, *Cavendish-crescent, Bath.*—Ex. Coll. Ox. B.A. 1852, M.A. 1855; Deac. 1855 and Pr. 1856 by Bp of Win. Formerly C. of Farlington, Hants, 1855–58. [11]

WIRGMAN, Augustus, *Hartington Vicarage, Ashbourne, Derbyshire.*—St. Peter's Coll. Cam. 1st Math. Prize 1830, Scho. 1831, Jun. Opt. and B.A. 1833, M.A. 1836; Deac. 1834 and Pr. 1835 by Bp of Lich. V. of Hartington, Dio. Lich. 1855. (Patron, Duke of Devonshire; Glebe, 238 acres; V.'s Inc. 270*l* and Ho; Pop. 495.) Surrogate. [12]

WISE, John, *Lillington Vicarage, Leamington.*—Wad. Coll. Ox. B.A. 1831, M.A. 1850; Deac. 1832. Pr. 1833. V. of Lillington, Dio. Wor. 1833. (Patron, H. C. Wise, Esq; Tithe, 173*l*; Glebe 40¾ acres; V.'s Inc. 326*l* and Ho; Pop. 480.) [13]

WISE, The Ven. John, *Stanford, near Brandon, Norfolk.*—Clare Coll. Cam. B.A. 1846. V. of Stanford, Dio Nor. 1866. (Patron, Bp of Nor; Tithe, 95*l*; V.'s Inc. 111*l*; Pop. 200.) Formerly C. of Saffron Walden, Essex, 1846–48; Chap. at Newra Ellia, Ceylon, 1848–52; Chap. of Kandy, Ceylon, 1852–63; Commissary of Dio. of Colombo 1861–63; Archd. of Colombo 1862–64; retired on medical certificate 1864. [14]

WISE, John Henry, *Brendon, Lynmouth, Barnstaple, Devon.*—St. Peter's Coll. Cam. B.A. 1839; Deac. 1842 and Pr. 1843 by Bp of Nor. R. of Brendon, Dio. Ex. 1855. (Patron, Frederick Winn Knight, Esq; Tithe, 167*l*; Glebe, 58 acres; R.'s Inc. 220*l*; Pop. 291.) Rural Dean. [15]

WISE, Richard Farquhar, *Ladock Rectory, Grampound, Cornwall.*—St. John's Coll. Cam. B.A. 1837; Deac. 1838 and Pr. 1839 by Bp of Ex. R. of Ladock, Dio. Ex. 1846. (Patron, Richard Wise, Esq. M.D; Tithe, 720*l*; Glebe, 50 acres; R.'s Inc. 780*l* and Ho; Pop. 742.) Formerly C. of Budock and Aft. Lect. at St. Gluvias', Dio. Ex. 1833–46. Author, *Clerical, Papers by One of our Club*, Parkers; various Sermons. [16]

WISE, William John, *Thanington Parsonage Canterbury.*—St. John's Coll. Ox. Fell. of, B.A. 1839, M.A. 1842; Deac. 1840 and Pr. 1841 by Bp of Ox. P. C. of Thanington, Dio. Cant. 1862. (Patron, Abp of Cant. Glebe, 8 acres; P. C.'s Inc. 134*l* and Ho; Pop. 446.) Chap. to St. John's Hospital, Canterbury, 1864. (Salary, 25*l*.) Formerly C. of Beenham Valence, Berks, 1840–42, Stanton Lacey, Salop, 1842–43; V. of Granborough, Warwickshire, 1843–62. [17]

WISKEN, John, 15, *Free School-lane, Cambridge.*—Caius Coll. Cam. 1845, 8th Wrang. and B.A. 1848, M.A. 1851; Deac. 1849 by Bp of Nor. Pr. 1852 by Bp of Ely. Math. Mast. of the Perse Gr. Sch. 1866. Formerly Fell. of Caius Coll. Cam. 1848–50; Mast. of the Newport Gr. Sch. Essex, 1850. [18]

WITHER, Harris Jervoise Bigg, *Worting Rectory, Basingstoke, Hants.*—Oriel Coll. Ox. B.A. 1829, M.A. 1831; Deac. 1831 and Pr. 1832 by Bp of Win. R. of Worting, Dio. Win. 1832. (Patron, Rev. Lovelace Bigg Wither; Tithe, 280*l* 8*s* 4½*d*; Glebe, 5½ acres; R.'s Inc. 290*l*; Pop. 154.) [19]

WITHER, Lovelace Bigg, *Tangier-park, Basingstoke, Hants.*—Oriel Coll. Ox. 2nd cl. Lit. Hum. and B.A. 1826, M.A. 1829; Deac. 1829 and Pr. 1830 by Bp of Win. [20]

WITHER, Walter Bigg, *Wootton Vicarage, Basingstoke, Hants.*—Deac. 1834 by Bp of Ches. Pr. 1835 by Bp of Lich. V. of Herriard, Hants, Dio. Win. 1835. (Patron, F. J. E. Jervoise, Esq; Tithe—Imp. 288*l* 15*s* and 22½ acres of Glebe, V. 200*l*; V.'s Inc. 190*l*; Pop. 439.) V. of Wootton St. Lawrence, Dio. Win. 1841. (Patrons, D. and C. of Win; Tithe—App. 570*l* 18*s* 6*d*, V. 271*l*; Glebe, 35 acres; V.'s Inc. 348*l* and Ho; Pop. 917.) [21]

WITHER, William Henry Walter Bigg, *Otterbourne, near Winchester.*—New Coll. Ox. B.C.L. 1835, M.A. 1856. C. of Otterbourne; Fell. of New Coll. Ox. [22]

WITHERBY, Cornelius, *Bream Parsonage, Lydney, Glouc.*—Lin. Coll. Ox. B.A. 1855; Deac. 1856 and Pr. 1857 by Bp of Lin. P. C. of Bream, Dio. G. and B. 1858. (Patron, Bp of G. and B; P. C.'s Inc. 200*l* and Ho; Pop. 2750.) Formerly C. of Owmby, Lincolnshire, 1856, St. John Baptist's, Nottingham, 1857. [23]

WITHERBY, Herbert, 1, *Eastgate-street, Winchester.*—Trin. Coll. Cam. B.A. 1865; Deac. 1866 and Pr. 1867 by Bp of Win. C. of Trinity, Winchester, 1866. [24]

WITHERBY, Robert, *North Chapel Rectory, Petworth, Sussex.*—St. John's Coll. Cam. B.A. 1823, M.A. 1827; Deac. 1823 and Pr. 1824 by Bp of Ches. R. of North Chapel, Dio. Chich. 1834. (Patron, Lord Leconfield; Tithe, 401*l*; Glebe, 6 acres; R.'s Inc. 404*l* and Ho; Pop. 785.) [25]

WITHERS, Alexander, *Shipston-on-Stour, Worcestershire.*—Corpus Coll. Cam. B.C.L. 1862; Deac. 1862 by Bp of Lich. Pr. 1863 by Abp of York. C. of Shipston-on-Stour 1867. Formerly C. of Rushall, Staffs, 1862–63, Birkin with Haddlesey 1863–67. [26]

WITHERS, George Undy, *Millbrook, near Southampton.*—Trin. Coll. Cam. B.A. 1829, M.A. 1835, D.D. 1845 by Abp of Cant; Deac. 1830 and Pr. 1831 by Bp of Calcutta. Fell. of St. Augustine's Coll. Canterbury, 1852. Formerly Jun. Prof. of Bishop's Coll. Calcutta, 1829–40; Prin. of Bishop's Coll. 1840–51. [1]

WITHERS, Joseph, *Chedgrave, Loddon, Norfolk.*—Dub. A.B. 1859; Deac. 1859 and Pr. 1860 by Bp of Nor. C. of Chedgrave and Langley 1860. [2]

WITHINGTON, Edward, *Rustington, Littlehampton, Sussex.*—Ch. Ch. Ox. B.A. 1860, M.A. 1863; Deac. 1863 and Pr. 1864 by Bp of Chich. C. of Rustington 1863. [3]

WITTS, Edward Francis, *Upper Slaughter Rectory, Stow-on-the-Wold, Glouc.*—Magd. Hall, Ox. B.A. 1838, M.A. 1842. R. of Upper Slaughter, Dio. G. and B. 1854. (Patron, the present R; R.'s Inc. 138*l* and Ho; Pop. 241.) [4]

WITTS, Francis Edward Broome, *Temple Guiting Parsonage, Winchcomb, Gloucestershire.*—Trin. Coll. Ox. B.A. 1861, M.A. 1865; Deac. 1864 and Pr. 1865 by Bp of G. and B. P. C. of Temple Guiting, Dio. G. and B. 1866. (Patron, Ch. Ch. Ox; P. C.'s Inc. 105*l* and Ho; Pop. 584.) Formerly C. of Dumbleton, Glouc. 1864–66. [5]

WITTS, William Frederick, *Uppingham, Rutlandshire.*—King's Coll. Cam. B.A. 1842, Crosse Theol. Scho. 1842, Tyrrwhitt's Heb. Scho. 1844, M.A. 1845; Deac. 1844, Pr. 1851. Chap. to Uppingham Sch. Formerly Fell. of King's Coll. Cam; C. of St. Giles's, Cambridge, 1844–61. [6]

WITTY, John Francis, *St. Matthew's Parsonage, Sheffield.*—Deac. 1832 and Pr. 1833 by Bp of Salis. P. C. of St. Matthew's, Sheffield, Dio. York, 1851. (Patrons, the Crown and Abp of York alt; P. C.'s Inc. 300*l* and Ho; Pop. 4592.) Author, *What is the Sabbath? What is a Christian, and Where is he to be found? Do Christians believe Christianity?* (Tracts) 3*s* per 100; *The Blood of Christ*; *God's Triumphs and the Devil's Trophies*; *Sermon on the Sheffield Atrocities*; etc. [7]

WIX, Joseph, *Littlebury Vicarage, near Saffron Walden.*—St. Peter's Coll. Cam. B.A. 1833, M.A. 1836; Deac. 1836 and Pr. 1837 by Bp of Lich. V. of Littlebury, Dio. Roch. 1840. (Patron, Bp of Roch; Glebe, 140 acres; V.'s Inc. 206*l* and Ho; Pop. 974.) [8]

WIX, Richard Hooker Edward, *Swanmore, Ryde, Isle of Wight.*—New Inn Hall, Ox. B.A. 1853, M.A. 1856; Deac. 1855 and Pr. 1856 by Bp of Ex. P. C. of St. Michael's, Swanmore, Dio. Win. 1866. (Patron, the present P. C; Pop. 900.) Formerly Asst. C. of St. Olave's, Exeter; P. C. of Aldersholt, Dorset, 1857–66. [9]

WODEHOUSE, Algernon, *Easton Rectory, Hants.*—Trin. Coll. Cam. B.A. 1837, M.A. 1847; Deac. 1837, Pr. 1838. R. of Easton, Hants, 1858. (Patron, Bp of Win; R.'s Inc. 539*l* and Ho; Pop. 455.) Dom. Chap. to Duke of Northumberland. [10]

WODEHOUSE, Campbell, *Alderford Rectory, Norwich.*—Ch. Ch. Ox. B.A. 1847; Deac. 1849, Pr. 1850. R. of Alderford with Attlebridge V. Dio. Nor. 1857. (Patrons, D. and C. of Nor; Tithe, Alderford, 139*l*; Attlebridge—Imp. 165*l*, V. 70*l* 15*s*; Glebe, 7 acres; R.'s Inc. 209*l* and Ho; Pop Alderford 29, Attlebridge 93.) Formerly Asst. Chap. to the Hon. E.I.C. on the Bombay Establishment 1851–55; V. of Bacton, Norfolk, 1855–57. Patron of Great Ryburgh, Norfolk. [11]

WODEHOUSE, Charles Nourse, *King's Lynn, Norfolk.*—Trin. Coll. Cam. B.A. 1813, M.A. 1817; Deac. 1814, Pr. 1815. Formerly Can. of Nor. 1817; P. C. of St. Margaret's, King's Lynn, 1850–60. Author, *Dean Prideaux on Revision of the Liturgy, and Archbishop Tenison on the Commission of* 1689, *reprinted with Preface and Notes*, 1834; *Subscription the Disgrace of the English Church*, Longmans, 1843. [12]

WODEHOUSE, Constantine Griffith, *Larling Rectory, Thetford, Norfolk.*—Ex. Coll. Ox. and Cuddesdon Theol. Coll; Deac. 1861 and Pr. 1862 by Bp of Ox. R. of Larling, Dio. Nor. 1863. (Patroness, Lady Nugent; Tithe, 217*l*; Glebe, 40 acres; R.'s Inc. 250*l* and Ho; Pop. 180.) Formerly C. of Shrivenham, Berks. [13]

WODEHOUSE, Frederick Armine, *All Saints', Nottingham.*—Trin. Coll. Cam. B.A. 1865; Deac. 1865 and Pr. 1866 by Bp of Lin. C. of All Saints', Nottingham, 1865. [14]

WODEHOUSE, Nathaniel, *Worle Vicarage, Axbridge, Somerset.*—Mert. Coll. Ox. B.A. 1826, M.A. 1829. V. of Worle, Dio. B. and W. 1829. (Patron, Ld Chan; Tithe—Imp. 90*l* and ½ acre of Glebe, V. 310*l*; Glebe, 5½ acres; V.'s Inc. 322*l* and Ho; Pop. 980.) V. of Dulverton, Somerset, Dio. B. and W. 1829. (Patrons, D. and C. of Wells; Tithe—App. 300*l* 10*s* and 5 acres of Glebe, V. 421*l*; V.'s Inc. 424*l* and Ho; Pop. 1552.) [15]

WODEHOUSE, Philip Cameron, *Teddington, Middlesex, S.W.*—Cuddesdon, and Ex. Coll. Ox. B.A. 1859, M.A. 1862; Deac. 1860 and Pr. 1861 by Bp of Lon. Asst. C. of Teddington 1860. [16]

WODEHOUSE, Philip John, *King's Lynn, Norfolk.*—Caius Coll. Cam. Fell. of, 8th Wrang. B.A. 1859, M.A. 1862; Deac. 1859 and Pr. 1860 by Bp of Ely. R. of North Lynn and P. C. of St. Margaret with St. Nicholas, King's Lynn, Dio. Nor. 1866. (Patrons, D. and C. of Nor; R.'s Inc. 400*l*; Pop. 7500.) Formerly C. of Hales Owen 1859, St. John's, Ladywood, Birmingham, 1860, St. Mary's, Nottingham, 1865. [17]

WODEHOUSE, Thomas, *East Malling, Maidstone, Kent.*—Ball. Coll. Ox. B.A. 1840. C. of East Malling. [18]

WODEHOUSE, Walker, *Elham Vicarage, near Canterbury.*—Ex. Coll. Ox. B.A. 1843, Mert. Coll. M.A. 1846. V. of Elham, Dio. Cant. 1845. (Patron, Mert. Coll. Ox. on nomination of Abp of Cant; Tithe—Imp. 1393*l* 10*s* 4½*d*; V.'s Inc. 408*l* and Ho; Pop. 1159.) [19]

WODEHOUSE, The Hon. William, *Hingham Rectory, Norfolk.*—All Souls Coll. Ox. B.A. 1804, M.A. 1811; Deac. 1806, Pr. 1807. R. of Hingham, Dio. Nor. 1811. (Patron, Lord Wodehouse; Tithe, 248*l* 16*s* 3*d*; R.'s Inc. 1250*l* and Ho; Pop. 1605.) [20]

WODSWORTH, G., *Warlingham Vicarage, Croydon, Surrey, S.*—V. of Warlingham with Chelsham C. Dio. Win. 1862. (Patron, A. W. Wigzell, Esq; V.'s Inc. 500*l* and Ho; Pop. Warlingham 602, Chelsham 401.) [21]

WOLFE, Arthur, *Fornham All Saints, Bury St. Edmunds.*—St. John's Coll. Cam. B.A. 1842, 16th Sen. Opt. and 5th in 1st cl. Cl. Trip; Deac. 1844 by Bp of Roch. Pr. 1848 by Bp of Ely. Fell. of Clare Coll. 1844; Tut. 1856–63; Sen. Proctor 1855–56; Examiner of Cl. Trip. 1856, '57, '60; Lady Margaret's Preacher 1860; Select Preacher 1863–64. R. of Fornham All Saints with Westley R. Dio. Ely, 1862. (Patron, Clare Coll. Cam; Tithe, 756*l* 4*s* 4*d*; Glebe, 40 acres; R.'s Inc. 860*l* and Ho; Pop. 521.) Author, *The Personality of the Evil Spirit*, 1857; *Reasons for not signing the Oxford Declaration*, 1864; *Family Prayers and Scripture Calendar*, 1865; *Reformation the True Road to Unity, a Plea for the Revision of the Prayer Book, and of the Authorized Version of the Bible*, Bell and Daldy, 1866; *Hymns for Public Worship*, 1860; *Hymns for Private Use*, 1861; *Original Psalm and Hymn Tunes*, Macmillans, 1860; *Nine Sermons on the Lord's Supper, with a special Reference to Present Controversies*, Longmans, 1867. [22]

WOLFE, Richard Robbins, *Furze-park, Torquay, Devon.*—Dub. A.B. 1842, A.M. 1844; Deac. and Pr. 1843 by Bp of Rip. R. of Upton, Torquay, Dio. Ex. 1848. (Patron, Sir L. Palk, Bart; Tithe—Imp. 150*l*; P. C.'s Inc. 300*l*; Pop. 6774.) [23]

WOLFENDEN, Edward, *Alvanley, Frodsham, Cheshire.*—Deac. 1835, Pr. 1837. P. C. of Alvanley, Dio. Ches. 1846. (Patrons, Hon. Miss Arden and others; Tithe, App. 165*l*; P. C.'s Inc. 160*l* and Ho; Pop. 550.) Formerly Chap. R.N. 1842. [24]

WOLLASTON, Charles Buchanan, *Felpham, Bognor, Sussex.*—Ex. Coll. Ox. 4th cl. Math. et Phy. and B.A. 1838, M.A. 1841; Deac. 1842 and Pr. 1843 by Bp of Lon. V. of Felpham, Dio. Chich. 1842. (Patrons, D. and C. of Chich; Tithe—App. 734*l* 4*s* 4*d* and 8½ acres of Glebe, V. 200*l* 12*s*; Glebe, ½ acre; V.'s Inc. 200*l*; Pop. 592.) [25]

WOLLASTON, Henry John, *Withington, near Cheltenham.*—Sid. Coll. Cam. B.A. 1829; Deac. 1829, Pr. 1830. [1]

WOLLASTON, Thelwall, *Molash, Ashford, Kent.*—C. of Molash 1867. Formerly C. of Beddingham with West Firle, Sussex. [2]

WOLLASTON, William Charles, *Westbury-on-Trym, near Bristol.*—Trin. Coll. Cam. 17th Sen. Opt. Bell's Scho. B.A. 1816, M.A. 1830; Deac. 1819 and Pr. 1820 by Abp of York. Sinecure R. of East Dereham, Dio. Nor. 1841. (Patron, the present R; Tithe, 826*l* 14*s* 4*d*; Glebe, 2½ acres; R.'s Inc. 830*l* 2*s* 10*d*.) The R. lapses to the Eccles. Commissioners on the first avoidance.) Formerly Under Mast. of Gr. Sch. and P. C. of St. Mary's, Leeds. [3]

WOLLASTON, William Monro, *Merton Vicarage, Bicester.*—Trin. Coll. Ox. 1st cl. Lit. Hum. B.A. 1855, M.A. 1857, Fell. of Ex. Coll; Deac. 1857, Pr. 1860. V. of Merton, Dio. Ox. 1863. (Patron, Ex. Coll. Ox; Glebe, 39 acres; V.'s Inc. 240*l* and Ho; Pop. 204.) Formerly Tut. of Ex. Coll. Ox. 1857–63; Conduct of Eton Coll. Aug. to Dec. 1863. [4]

WOLLEN, James, *Torquay, Devon.*—St. John's Coll. Cam. B.A. 1822, M.A. 1832; Deac. 1822 by Bp of Ches. Pr. 1823 by Bp of Salis. Formerly C. of Trinity, Bridgwater. [5]

WOLLEY, Charles, *Eton College, Bucks.*—King's Coll. Cam. B.A. 1849, M.A. 1852. Asst. Mast. in Eton Coll; Fell. of King's Coll. Cam. [6]

WOLRYCHE - WHITMORE, Francis Henry, *Dudmaston Hall, Bridgnorth.*—Wad. Coll. Ox. B.A. 1843, M.A. 1845; Deac. 1845 and Pr. 1846 by Bp of Wor. R. of Quatt Malvern, Dio. Lich. 1864. (Patron, the present R; Tithe, 430*l*; R.'s Inc. 430*l* and Ho; Pop. 356.) Formerly C. of Forthampton, Glouc. 1848–56, and P. C. of same 1856–63. [7]

WOLSELEY, Robert Warren.—Dub. A.B. 1846; Deac. 1847 by Bp of Cashel, Pr. 1848 by Bp of Ches. Formerly C. of St. Silas', Liverpool. [8]

WOLSTENCROFT, Thomas, *Syde, Cirencester.*—St. Bees; Deac. 1851, Pr. 1852. R. of Syde, Dio. G. and B. 1866. (Patron, John Hall, Esq; Tithe, comm, 100*l*; Glebe, 32½ acres; R.'s Inc. 140*l* and Ho; Pop. 56.) Formerly C. of St. Bartholomew's, Liverpool, 1851, St. Paul's, Bury, 1852, St. Mary's, Rawtenstall, 1855, St. Michael's, Manchester (sole charge) 1861, Holcombe (sole charge) 1863. [9]

WOLSTENHOLME, Joseph, *Christ's College, Cambridge.*—St. John's Coll. Cam. 3rd Wrang. and B.A. 1850, M.A. 1853; Deac. and Pr. 1854 by Bp of Ely. Fell. of St. John's Coll. Cam. 1852; Fell. of Ch. Coll. Cam. 1853. [10]

WOLSTON, Charles, *Torbryan Rectory, near Newton Abbot, Devon.*—St. John's Coll. Cam. S.C.L. 1854, B.C.L. and M.A. 1856; Deac. 1858 and Pr. 1859 by Bp of Wor. R. of Torbryan, Dio. Ex. 1863. (Patrons, Rev. T. Wolston and others; Glebe, 17 acres; R.'s Inc. 344*l*; Pop. 205.) Formerly C. of Cradley, Worc. 1858, Ashbury, Berks, 1860, Chittoe, Wilts, 1860, Tedburn St. Mary, Devon, 1861, Hatherleigh, Devon, 1862. [11]

WOLSTON, Thomas, 11, *Higher-terrace, St. Leonard's, Exeter.*—Caius Coll. Cam. B.A. 1819; Deac. 1824 and Pr. 1825 by Bp of Ex. Chap. of St. Thomas's Union, Exeter, 1857. (Stipend, 80*l*.) Formerly C. of Withycombe Rawleigh, Devon, 1824–27, Charleton, Devon, 1827–31, Southleigh, near Honiton, 1831–40. [12]

WOOD, Albert, *Castlemorton, Tewkesbury.*—Deac. and Pr. 1855 by Bp of Capetown. C. of Castlemorton, Longdon, Worcestershire, 1864. Formerly Asst. Chap. St. George's Cathl. Capetown, 1855–59; Acting Garrison Chap. and Colonial Chap. St. John's, Wynberg, Cape of Good Hope, 1859–61; C. of St. Mary's, Westminster, 1861–62; St. Paul's, West Leigh, Lancashire, 1862–65. Author, *Prayers for the Young and Unconfirmed*, Capetown, 1*s*; *Lent Sermons*, ib; *Grave Stones, Epitaphs, and Cemeteries with Suggestions for their Improvement*, ib. 1*s*; *The Visitation and Communion of the Sick, with Notes thereon*, 4to, Masters, 1867, 1*s*. [13]

WOOD, Alfred, *Wolverhampton.*—Queen's Theol. Coll. Birmingham, 1857; Deac. 1859 and Pr. 1860 by Bp of Lich. C. of St. George's, Wolverhampton, 1867. Formerly C. of St. Matthew's, Wolverhampton, 1859. [14]

WOOD, Alfred Maitland, *Tarvin, Chester.*—C. of Tarvin. [15]

WOOD, Andrew, *Skillington Vicarage, Grantham.*—Trin. Coll. Cam. B.A. 1855, M.A. 1858; Deac. 1856 and Pr. 1857 by Bp of Win. V. of Skillington, Dio. Lin. 1866. (Patron, Christopher Turner, Esq; Corn Rent 62*l*; Glebe, 26 acres; V.'s Inc. 102*l* and Ho; Pop. 466.) Formerly C. of Ruddington, Notts. Author, *Sermons to Children*, S.P.C.K. 1866. [16]

WOOD, Arthur, *Catterick, Yorks.*—Deac. 1849 and Pr. 1850 by Abp of York. C. of Catterick 1853. Formerly C. of Ingleby, Greenhow, near Stokesley, 1849, Bradfield, near Sheffield, 1851. [17]

WOOD, Arthur T., *Hepworth, Huddersfield.*—P. C. of Hepworth, Dio. Rip. 1863. (Patron, V. of Kirkburton; Pop. 3000.) [18]

WOOD, Benjamin, *Buckland Rectory, near Louth, Lincolnshire.*—R. of Buckland with Farforth R. and Maiden-Well V. Dio. Lin. 1855. (Patron, Earl of Yarborough; R. and V.'s Inc. 400*l* and Ho; Pop. Buckland 46, Farforth and Maiden-Well 103. [19]

WOOD, Charles, *Beaford Rectory, Crediton, Devon.*—Oriel Coll. Ox. B.A. 1821, M.A. 1824. R. of Beaford, Dio. Ex. 1848. (Patron, the present R; Tithe, 250*l*; Glebe, 64 acres; R.'s Inc. 315*l* and Ho; Pop. 639.) [20]

WOOD, Charles Claypon, *Broxholme Rectory, Lincoln.*—Ch. Coll. Cam. B.A. 1859, M.A. 1864; Deac. 1860 by Bp of Dur. Pr. 1862 by Bp of Pet. R. of Broxholme, Dio. Lin. 1865. (Patron, James Robinson, Esq; Glebe, 68 acres; R.'s Inc. 295*l* and Ho; Pop. 113.) Formerly C. of Woodhorn, Northumberland, Hinckley, Leicestershire, and Mansfield Woodhouse, Notts; C. in sole charge of Tredington, Worcestershire. [21]

WOOD, Charles Frederick Bryan, *Penmark Vicarage, Cowbridge, Glamorganshire.*—Pemb. Coll. Ox. 3rd cl. Lit. Hum. and B.A. 1829, M.A. 1834; Deac. 1832, Pr. 1833. V. of Penmark, Dio. Llan. 1844. (Patrons, D. and C. of Glouc; Tithe—App. 347*l* 5*s* and 13 acres of Glebe, V. 210*l* 15*s* 3*d*; Glebe, 116 acres; V.'s Inc. 378*l* and Ho; Pop. 529.) [22]

WOOD, Charles Harrison, *Preston.*—Ch. Coll. Cam. LL.B. 1851. P. C. of St. George's, Preston, Dio. Man. 1862. (Patron, V. of Preston; P. C.'s Inc. 180*l*; Pop. 3337.) Formerly C. of St. George's. [23]

WOOD, Charles Henton, *Thurlaston, Hinckley, Leicestershire.*—C. of Thurlaston. [24]

WOOD, Charles James, *Guernsey.*—Fell. of Brasen. Coll. Ox; Prin. of Elizabeth Coll. Guernsey. [25]

WOOD, Cyril William, *Stogursey, Bridgwater.*—Univ. Coll. Dur. B.A. 1842, M.A. 1845; Deac. 1844 and Pr. 1846 by Bp of Ox. V. of Stogursey, Dio. B. and W. 1867. (Patron, Eton Coll; V.'s Inc. 450*l* and Ho; Pop. 1600.) Formerly C. of Finmere, Oxon, 1851; Warden of St. Thomas's Coll. Colombo, Ceylon, 1854; V. of Atwick, Yorks, 1854–67. [26]

WOOD, Edmund, *Bradfield, Sheffield.*—Magd. Hall, Ox. B.A. 1841, M.A. 1842; Deac. 1842, Pr. 1843. P. C. of Bradfield, Dio. York, 1853. (Patron, V. of Ecclesfield; P. C.'s Inc. 240*l* and Ho.) [27]

WOOD, Edmund Gough De Salis, 3, *Malcolm-street, Cambridge.*—Emman. Coll. Cam. 11th Sen. Opt. B.A. 1864, Hulsean Prizeman 1866, M.A. 1867; Deac. 1865 and Pr. 1866 by Bp of Ely. C. of St. Clement's, Cambridge, 1865. Author, *The Province of Faith*, Rivingtons, 1867. [28]

WOOD, Edward, *Skelton Parsonage, Ripon.*—Trin. Coll. Cam. B.A. 1819; Deac. 1819 and Pr. 1821 by Bp of Ex. P. C. of Skelton, Dio. Rip. 1833. (Patrons, D. and C. of Rip; Glebe, 13 acres; P. C.'s Inc. 90*l* and Ho; Pop. 365.) Formerly C. of St. Agnes with Perransabuloe 1819, St. Austell with St. Blazey 1820, Wheldrake 1827. [29]

WOOD, Frederick, *Newent Vicarage, Gloucestershire.*—Trin. Coll. Cam. B.A. 1854, M.A. 1865; Deac. 1854 by Bp of Dur. Pr. 1855 by Bp of Man. V. of

Newent, Dio. G. and B. 1865. (Patroness, Miss Foley; Tithe, 1542*l*; Glebe, 1 acre; V.'s Inc. 1545*l* and Ho; Pop. 3182.) Formerly C. of Berwick-on-Tweed 1855, Bosbury, Herefordshire, 1856, Hopesay, Salop, 1857–58; R. of Little Marcle, Herefordshire, 1858–65. [1]

WOOD, Frederick John, *Leeds.*—Trin. Coll. Cam. 3rd cl. Cl. Trip. B.A. 1856, M.A. 1859; Deac. 1857 and Pr. 1858 by Bp of Rip. C. of St. Peter's, Leeds, 1857, and Clerk in Orders in same, 1864. Formerly Lect. of St. Peter's, Leeds, 1860–64. [2]

WOOD, George, *Stanningfield, Bury St. Edmunds.*—C. of Stanningfield. Formerly C. of Great Waldingfield, Suffolk. [3]

WOOD, Henry, *Passenham Rectory, Stony Stratford, Northants.*—Assoc. of King's Coll. Lond; Deac. 1859, Pr. 1860. R. of Passenham with Denshanger C. Dio. Pet. 1860. (Patron, Viscount Maynard; Tithe, 315*l*; Glebe, 200 acres; R.'s Inc. 750*l* and Ho; Pop. 1105.) Formerly C. of Passenham 1859–60. [4]

WOOD, Henry, *Biddenham Vicarage, Bedford.*—V. of Biddenham, Dio. Ely, 1865. (Patron, Lord Dynever; V.'s Inc. 100*l* and Ho; Pop. 350.) [5]

WOOD, Henry, *Burrowbridge Parsonage, Bridgwater.*—St. Edm. Hall, Ox. B.A. 1837, M.A. 1838; Deac. and Pr. 1838 by Bp of B. and W. P. C. of Burrowbridge, Dio. B. and W. 1838. (Patron, Bp of B. and W; P. C.'s Inc. 80*l* and Ho; Pop. 692.) V. of Lyng, Somerset, Dio. B. and W. 1852. (Patron, R. M. Meade King, Esq; Tithe—Imp. 45*l*, V. 81*l*; V.'s Inc. 60*l*; Pop. 319.) Author, *Songs in the Night*, Hamilton, Adams and Co. 1857, 2*s* 6*d*; *The Memorable Advent*, Macintosh, 1859, 6*d*. [6]

WOOD, Henry Hayton, *Holwell Rectory, Sherborne, Dorset.*—Queen's Coll. Ox. B.A. 1848, M.A. 1851; Deac. 1849 and Pr. 1853 by Bp of Ox. Fell. of Queen's Coll. 1851, Tut. 1852, Librarian 1853, Dean 1856. R. of Holwell, Dio. Salis. 1857. (Patron, Queen's Coll. Ox; Tithe, 450*l*; Glebe, 47 acres; R.'s Inc. 550*l* and Ho; Pop. 495.) Author, *A Reply to "A Short Review of the Recent Charge of the Lord Bishop of Salisbury by Ecclesiastes,"* Rivingtons, 1865, 6d; *On the Theory of Development and the Antiquity of Man: A Letter to J. Phillips, Esq. F.R.S. Professor of Geology in the University of Oxford*, 1865, 1*s*. [7]

WOOD, Henry William, *Wetton (Staffs), near Ashbourne.*—St. Bees; Deac. 1853 and Pr. 1854 by Bp of Lich. P. C. of Wetton, Dio. Lich. 1855. (Patron, G. F. B. Blackett, Esq; Glebe, 49 acres; P. C.'s Inc. 160*l*; Pop. 452.) [8]

WOOD, Horace Seward, *Great Eccleston Parsonage, Garstang, Lancashire.*—New Coll. Ox. B.A. 1847; Deac. 1850 and Pr. 1851 by Bp of Dur. C. of Great Eccleston 1867. Formerly C. of St. Ann's, Newcastle, 1850–53; V. of Dinnington, Northumberland, 1856–64. [9]

WOOD, Hugh, *Blore Ray Rectory (Staffs), near Ashbourne.*—Trin. Coll. Cam. B.A. 1827; Deac. 1828 and Pr. 1829 by Bp of Lich. R. of Blore Ray, Dio. Lich. 1836. (Patron, O. Shore, Esq; Tithe, 121*l* 10*s*; Glebe, 40 acres; R.'s Inc. 181*l* and Ho; Pop. 320.) [10]

WOOD, Hugh Hathorn, *Pakefield, near Lowestoft, Suffolk.*—Wor. Coll. Ox. B.A. 1859, M.A. 1863; Deac. 1860 and Pr. 1863 by Bp of Ox. R. of Pakefield, Dio. Nor. 1867. (Patron, Ch. Patronage Soc; R.'s Inc. 200*l* and Ho; Pop. 768.) Formerly C. of Middle Claydon 1860, Haslemere 1862, Chesham Bois 1864, all three in Bucks, and Hemingford Abbotts, Hunts, 1865. [11]

WOOD, James, 10, *Burlington-street, Bath.*—Magd. Coll. Cam. B.A. 1836, M.A. 1840; Deac. 1837 and Pr. 1838 by Bp of Rip. Min. of Ch. Ch. Bath, 1842; Asst. Rural Dean. Formerly C. of Walcot, Bath. [12]

WOOD, James, *Warnham Vicarage, Horsham, Sussex.*—Ch. Ch. Ox. B.A. 1828, M.A. 1831; Deac. 1829 and Pr. 1830 by Bp of Lich. V. of Warnham, Dio. Chich. 1839. (Patrons, D. and C. of Cant; Tithe—App. 461*l* 1*s* 3*d*, V. 314*l* 18*s* 5*d*; V.'s Inc. 320*l* and Ho; Pop. 1006.) [13]

WOOD, James, *Theddlethorpe All Saints, Alford, Lincolnshire.*—Deac. 1821 and Pr. 1822 by Abp of York. V. of Theddlethorpe All Saints, Dio. Lin. 1831. (Patrons, Exors. of Thomas Alcock, Esq; Tithe, Imp. 400*l*; Glebe, 59 acres; V.'s Inc. 210*l* and Ho; Pop. 350.) R. of Grimoldby, Lincolnshire, Dio. Lin. 1832. (Patron, the present R; Tithe, 34*l*; Glebe, 151 acres; R.'s Inc. 229*l*; Pop. 321.) [14]

WOOD, James Russell, *Eastbourne, Sussex.*—Head Mast. of Eastbourne Coll. [15]

WOOD, John, *Chillenden, Wingham, Kent*—C. of Chillenden. [16]

WOOD, John, *Ripley, Derby.*—Trin. Coll. Toronto, B.A. 1859, M.A. 1864; Deac. 1861 and Pr. 1862 by Bp of Toronto. C. of Ripley 1865. Formerly First Miss. of Northumberland, Canada West; Min. of Ottawa. [17]

WOOD, John, *Wolverton Vicarage, Stony Stratford, Bucks.*—St. John's Coll. Cam. B.A. 1856; Deac. 1856 and Pr. 1857 by Bp of Ox. C. of Wolverton 1866. Formerly C. of Aylesbury 1856–63, Mapperley 1864–66. [18]

WOOD, John Alexander, *Baldock, Herts.*—C. of Baldock 1867. [19]

WOOD, John Cooper, *St. Kenelm's Rectory, Romsley, Hales Owen, Birmingham.*—St. John's Coll. Cam. Scho. of, B.A. 1860, M.A. 1863; Deac. 1861, Pr. 1862. R. of St. Kenelm's in Romsley, Dio. Wor. 1867. (Patron, R. of Hales Owen; Glebe, 2 acres; R.'s Inc. 145*l* and Ho; Pop. 450.) Formerly 2nd Mast. of Wakefield Gr. Sch. 1860–63; C. of St. John's, Wakefield, 1861–62; Head Mast. of Prescot Gr. Sch. 1863; Head Mast. of Hales Owen Gr. Sch. 1863-66. [20]

WOOD, John George, 9, *Erith-road, Belvidere, Kent, S.E.*—Mert. Coll. Ox. Jackson Scho. 1845, B.A. 1848, M.A. 1851; Deac. 1852, Pr. 1854. Formerly C. of St. Thomas', Oxford, 1852–54; Asst. Hospitaller, St. Bartholomew's Hospital, Lond. 1856–62; Reader at Christchurch, Newgate-street, 1858–63. Author, *Illustrated Natural History*, 3 vols; *Common Objects of the Sea Shore*; *Common Objects of the Country*; *Common Objects of the Microscope*; *Sketches and Anecdotes of Animal Life*, two series; *My Feathered Friends*; *Garden Friends and Foes*; *Natural History of Man*, all published by Routledges; *Glimpses into Petland*, Bell and Daldy; *Homes without Hands*, Longmans; etc. [21]

WOOD, John George, *The Vicarage, Conisborough, Rotherham.*—King's Coll. Lond. Theol. Assoc. 1859; Deac. 1859 and Pr. 1860 by Bp of Ches. V. of Conisborough, Dio. York, 1867. (Patron, Abp of York; Tithe—App. 1*l* 11*s* 6*d*, Imp. 280*l*, V. 89*l*; Glebe, 66½ acres; V.'s Inc. 310*l* and Ho; Pop. 1655.) Formerly C. of St. Cross, Knutsford, 1859–61, Doncaster 1861–67. [22]

WOOD, John Ravenshaw, *Penrith.*—Ch. Ch. Ox. 3rd cl. Lit. Hum. and B.A. 1851, M.A. 1854; Deac. 1852, Pr. 1853. P. C. of Ch. Ch. Penrith, Dio. Carl. 1862. (Patron, Bp of Carl; P. C.'s Inc. 200*l*; Pop. 2500.) Formerly V. of Compton Chamberlayne, Salisbury, 1854–62. [23]

WOOD, John Ryle, *The College, Worcester.*—Ch. Ch. Ox. 2nd cl. Lit. Hum. and B.A. 1827, M.A. 1828; Deac. 1829 by Bp of Ely, Pr. 1830 by Bp of Chich. Can. Res. of Wor. Cathl. 1841. (Value, 700*l* and Res.) V. of St. John's, Bedwardine, City and Dio. Wor. 1841. (Patrons, D. and C. of Wor; V.'s Inc. 706*l*; Pop. 2974.) Chap. in Ordinary to the Queen 1837; Select Preacher to the Univ. of Ox. 1839; Chap. to H.R.H. the Duke of Cambridge. Formerly Dom. Chap. to King William IV. and Queen Adelaide. [24]

WOOD, John Spicer, *St. John's College, Cambridge.*—St. John's Coll. Cam. 22nd Wrang, 4th in Cl. Trip. and B.A. 1846, M.A. 1849, B.D. 1857; Deac. and Pr. 1848. Fell. of St. John's Coll. Cam. 1847; Asst. Tut. 1853; Tut. 1860; Jun. Proctor 1855; One of H. M. Preachers at the Chapel Royal, Whitehall, 1867. [25]

WOOD, Joseph, *Clifton Rectory (Westmoreland), near Penrith.*—Queen's Coll. Ox. B.A. 1836, M.A. 1838. R. of Clifton, Dio. Carl. 1847. (Patron, Bp of Carl; R.'s Inc. 156*l* and Ho; Pop. 342.) [26]

WOOD, Joseph, *Cherington Rectory, Shipston-on-Stour.*—Brasen. Coll. Ox. B.A. 1857, M.A. 1860; Deac. 1858, Pr. 1860. R. of Cherington, Dio. G. and B.

1841. (Patron, Rev. W. George; Glebe, 280 acres; R.'s Inc. 350*l* and Ho; Pop. 311.) Formerly C. of St. Mary's, Warwick, 1858–60. [1]

WOOD, Joseph, *Radley College, Abingdon.*—Fell. of St. John's Coll. Ox; Mast. in Radley Coll. Abingdon. [2]

WOOD, Joshua, *Kirkby Hall, Richmond, Yorks.*—Dub. A.B. 1824, A.M. 1838; Deac. 1828, Pr. 1830. Head Mast. of the Kirkby-Ravensworth Free Gr. Sch. Yorks, 1845. [3]

WOOD, Leonard Charles, *Singleton Lodge, Kirkham, Lancashire.*—Jesus Coll. Ox. Scho. and Exhib. of, 1841, B.A. 1842; Deac. 1842 by Bp of Ox. Pr. 1843 by Bp of Ches. P. C. of Great Singleton, Dio. Man. 1843. (Patron, Thomas Horrocks Miller, Esq; Tithe—App. 396*l* 16*s* 6*d*, Imp. 1*l* 5*s*; Glebe, 80 acres; P. C.'s Inc. 205*l* and Ho; Pop. 338.) [4]

WOOD, Matthew, *Evesham.*—V. of All Saints' with St. Lawrence's P. C. Evesham, Dio. Wor. 1855. (Patron, Ld Chan; V.'s Inc. 250*l* and Ho; Pop. 3421.) [5]

WOOD, Peter Almeric Leheup, *Copford Rectory, Colchester.*—Magd. Coll. Cam. B.A. 1841, M.A. 1845; Deac. 1843, Pr. 1844. R. of Copford, Dio. Roch. 1861. (Patron, Ld Chan; R.'s Inc. 700*l* and Ho; Pop. 775.) Can. of St. George's in the Coll. Ch. of Middleham, Yorks, 1844. Formerly R. of St. John's and St. Mary's, Devizes, 1853–61. [6]

WOOD, Richard, *Woodhall-park, Bedale, Yorks.*—Corpus Coll. Cam. B.A. 1822, M.A. 1825; Deac. 1822 and Pr. 1823 by Bp of Ches. P. C. of Askrigg, Yorks, Dio. Rip. 1823. (Patron, V. of Aysgarth; Tithe—App. 84*l*; Glebe, 80 acres; P. C.'s Inc. 110*l*; Pop. 1168.) V. of Wollaston with Irchester V. Northants, Dio. Pet. 1829. (Patron, the present V; Tithe—Imp. 5*l* 6*s* 8*d*, V. 19*s* 4*d*; Glebe, 220 acres; V.'s Inc. 440*l* and Ho; Pop. Wollaston 1443, Irchester 1168.) [7]

WOOD, Richard, jun., *Woodhall-park, Bedale, Yorks.*—Dur. B.A. 1856, M.A. 1858; Deac. 1857 and Pr. 1858 by Bp of Rip. C. of Askrigg, Yorks. [8]

WOOD, Richard, 31, *Leinster-gardens, Bayswater, London, W.*—St. John's Coll. Ox. B.A. 1832, M.A. 1836, B.D. 1841. P. C. of Ch. Ch. Paddington, Dio. Lon. 1855. (Patron, Bp of Lon; P. C.'s Inc. 730*l* and Ho; Pop. 4019.) Formerly Fell. of St. John's Coll. Ox. [9]

WOOD, Richard Mountford, *Aldbury Rectory, Tring, Herts.*—St. John's Coll. Cam. Sen. Opt. and B.A. 1833, M.A. 1837; Deac. 1834, Pr. 1835. R. of Aldbury, Dio. Roch. 1862. (Patron, Earl Brownlow; R.'s Inc. 500*l* and Ho; Pop. 848.) Formerly C. of Aldbury. [10]

WOOD, Richard Nicholson, *Street, Glastonbury, Somerset.*—Jesus Coll. Cam. B.A. 1841, M.A. 1844; Deac. 1845 and Pr. 1846 by Bp of Salis. C. of Street 1851. Formerly C. of St. Martin's, Salisbury, 1845–48. [11]

WOOD, Robert, *Church-hill, Westward, Wigton, Cumberland.*—St. Bees; Deac. 1820, Pr. 1821. P. C. of Westward, Dio. Carl. 1822. (Patrons, D. and C. of Carl; P. C.'s Inc. 120*l* and Ho; Pop. 1136.) Head Mast. of the Westward Ch. Sch. [12]

WOOD, Robert, *Prior-park, Ashby-de-la-Zouch.*—Queen's Coll. Ox. B.A. 1862, M.A. 1864; Deac. 1864 and Pr. 1865 by Bp of Lich. C. of Smisby, Derbyshire, 1865. Formerly C. of Donisthorpe 1864; Lect. at Ashby-de-la-Zouch. [13]

WOOD, Robert, *Reading.*—C. of Ch. Ch. Reading. [14]

WOOD, Robert Faulkner, *Moreton-Corbett Rectory, near Shrewsbury.*—Brasen. Coll. Ox. B.A. 1844, M.A. 1847; Deac. 1844 and Pr. 1845 by Bp of S. and M. R. of Moreton-Corbett, Dio. Lich. 1849. (Patron, Sir Vincent R. Corbett, Bart; Tithe, 340*l*; Glebe, 39 acres; R.'s Inc. 395*l* and Ho; Pop. 255.) [15]

WOOD, Septimus, *West Keal Rectory, Spilsby, Lincolnshire.*—Clare Coll. Cam. Scho. of, B.A. 1848; Deac. 1850 by Bp of Lon. Pr. 1851 by Bp of Lin. R. of West Keal, Dio. Lin. 1855. (Patron, Colonel Cracroft Amcotts; Glebe, 314 acres; R.'s Inc. 480*l* and Ho; Pop. 511.) Formerly C. of St. Thomas's, Charterhouse, Lond. 1850–51; V. of Kealby, Lincolnshire, 1851–55. [16]

WOOD, Thomas, *St. Ninian's, Sandwich, Kent.*—St. John's Coll. Cam. Jun. Opt. B.A. 1838, M.A. 1841; Deac. 1839 and Pr. 1840 by Bp of G. and B. Officiating Min. at Eythorn, Kent. Formerly C. of Cranbrook, Kent, 1840; Chap. at Dinapore, Bengal, and St. Paul's Cathl. Calcutta. [17]

WOOD, William, *St. Paul's Parsonage, Derby.*—Cam. B.A. 1856, M.A. 1859; Deac. 1856 and Pr. 1857 by Bp of Ches. P. C. of St. Paul's, Derby, Dio. Lich. 1863. (Patrons, Crown and Bp of Lich. alt; P. C.'s Inc. 310*l* and Ho; Pop. 2400.) Formerly P. C. of St. Paul's, Warrington, 1858–63. Author, *Sermons*, Mackie, Warrington. [18]

WOOD, William, *Campbelton, Scotland.* [19]

WOOD, William, *Radley College, Abingdon.*—Trin. Coll. Ox. Scho. of, 1847, Hertford Scho. 1848, 2nd cl. Lit. Hum. and B.A. 1851; Deac. 1852 and Pr. 1853 by Bp of Ox. Sub-Warden of Radley Coll. 1853, Warden, 1866. Formerly Lect. of Trin. Coll. Ox. 1852; P. C. of Prestwood, Bucks, 1864–66. [20]

WOOD, William, *Buckland, Buntingford, Herts.*—C. of Buckland. [21]

WOOD, William Hardy, *St. Luke's, Leeds.*—Univ. Coll. Ox. B.A. 1858, M.A. 1861; Deac. 1859 and Pr. 1860 by Bp of Lich. C. of St. Luke's, Leeds, 1865. Formerly C. of St. Peter's, Wolverhampton; temporary Head Mast. of Gr. Sch. Wolverhampton. [22]

WOOD, William Paul, *Saddington Rectory, Market Harborough, Leicestershire.*—St. John's Coll. Ox. B.A. 1843, M.A. 1846; Deac. 1846 and Pr. 1847 by Bp of Salis. R. of Saddington, Dio. Pet. 1852. (Patron, Ld Chan; Glebe, 230 acres; R.'s Inc. 370*l* and Ho; Pop. 259.) [23]

WOOD, William Spicer, *The Grammar School, Oakham, Rutland.*—St. John's Coll. Cam. Browne's Medallist 1839, Chancellor's Medallist, 7th Wrang. 4th in 1st cl. Cl. Trip. and B.A. 1840, M.A. 1843; Deac. 1844 by Bp of Ely, Pr. 1845 by Bp of Herf. Head Mast. of Oakham Gr. Sch. 1846. Formerly Fell. and Jun. Dean of St. John's Coll. Cam; C. of Brooke, near Oakham, 1853–65. [24]

WOOD, William Watson, *Easton Rectory, Wickham Market, Suffolk.*—Sid. Coll. Cam. B.A. 1853; Deac. 1857, Pr. 1858. R. of Easton, Dio. Nor. 1860. (Patron, Duke of Hamilton; Glebe, 25 acres; R.'s Inc. 355*l* and Ho; Pop. 370.) [25]

WOODARD, Nathaniel, *St. Nicolas' College, Shoreham, Sussex.*—Magd. Hall, Ox. B.A. 1840. Provost of St. Nicolas' Coll. Shoreham. [26]

WOODCOCK, Charles, *Chardstock Vicarage, (Dorset), near Chard, Somerset.*—Ch. Ch. Ox. B.A. 1832, M.A. 1860; Deac. 1832, Pr. 1833. V. of Chardstock, Dio. Salis. 1833. (Patron, Bp of Salis; Tithe—Imp. 490*l* and 65 acres of Glebe, V. 416*l*; Glebe, ½ acre; V.'s Inc. 417*l* and Ho; Pop. 1199.) Formerly C. of Ealing, Middlesex, 1833. [27]

WOODCOCK, Edward Walker, *Beeby Rectory, Leicester.*—King's Coll. Lond. Theol. Assoc. 1855; Deac. 1855, Pr. 1856. R. of Beeby, Dio. Pet. 1865. (Patron, the present R; Tithe, 300*l*; Glebe, 36 acres; R.'s Inc. 370*l* and Ho; Pop. 119.) Dioc. Inspector of Schs. Formerly C. of St. Mark's, Lakenham, Norfolk; V. of Thurmaston, Leicester, 1856–65. [28]

WOODCOCK, Frederic Edward, *Northleigh Rectory, Honiton.*—Deac. 1861 by Abp of Cant. Pr. 1863 by Abp of York. R. of Northleigh, Dio. Ex. 1864. (Patron, the present R; Tithe, 175*l* 10*s*; Glebe, 75 acres; R.'s Inc. 250*l* and Ho; Pop. 290.) Formerly C. of Campsall, Yorks, 1861–63, Ch. Ch. Ashton-under-Lyne, 1863–64. [29]

WOODCOCK, George Henry, *Sixhills Vicarage, Market Rasen, Lincolnshire.*—Emman. Coll. Cam. B.A. 1841, M.A. 1844; Deac. 1841, Pr. 1842. V. of Sixhills, Dio. Lin. 1854. (Patron, E. Heneage, Esq; Tithe—Imp. 300*l*, V. 75*l*; V.'s Inc. 75*l* and Ho; Pop. 164.) C. of Hainton, Lincolnshire; V. of North Willingham, Linc. Dio. Lin. 1863. (Patron, H. R. Boucherett, Esq; V.'s Inc. 70*l*; Pop. 203.) [1]

WOODCOCK, T., *Derby.*—C. of St. Peter's with Normanton, Derby. [2]

WOODD, Alexander, *Stutton, Ipswich.*—C. of Stutton. [3]

WOODD, Basil James, *Hasland, Chesterfield.*—Corpus Coll. Cam. B.A. 1844; Deac. 1848 and Pr. 1849 by Bp of Roch. C. of Hasland 1859. [4]

WOODD, Basil K., *Huntingdon.*—C. of All Saints', Huntingdon. [5]

WOODFORD, Adolphus Frederick Alexander, *Swillington Rectory, near Leeds.*—Univ. Coll. Dur. B.A. and Licen. Theol. 1846; Deac. 1846 and Pr. 1847 by Bp of Dur. R. of Swillington, Dio. Rip. 1847. (Patron, Sir J. H. Lowther, Bart; Tithe, 254*l* 4*s* 8*d*; Glebe, 170 acres; R.'s Inc. 425*l* and Ho; Pop. 662.) [6]

WOODFORD, James Russell, *Kempsford, Fairford, Glouc.*—Pemb. Coll. Cam. Sen. Opt. 2nd cl. Cl. Trip. and B.A. 1842, M.A. 1845; Deac. 1843 by Bp of G. and B. Pr. 1845 by Bp of Ex. V. of Kempsford, Dio. G. and B. 1855. (Patron, Bp of G. and B; Glebe, 597 acres; V.'s Inc. 760*l* and Ho; Pop. 1003.) Hon. Can. of Ch. Ch. Ox. 1867; Exam. Chap. to Bp of Ox. Formerly P. C. of St. Mark's, Easton, Bristol; Select Preacher for Univ. of Cam. 1864. Author, *Sermons*, 3 vols. Masters, 1853; *The Church Past and Present* (four Lectures), ib; *Lectures for Holy Week*, ib; *Hymns for Sundays and Holy-days*, ib; *Lectures on the Creed*, ib; *The Church, Past and Present* (four Lectures), ib; *Sermons preached before the University of Cambridge*, Macmillans, 1864: Editor, *Tracts for Christian Seasons*, 3rd series, Parkers. [7]

WOODFORDE, Alexander John, *Ansford, Castle Cary, Somerset.*—Dur. Licen. in Theol. 1863, B.A. 1866; Deac. 1863 and Pr. 1864 by Bp of G. and B. C. of North and South Barrow, Somerset, 1866. Formerly C. of Dymock, Gloucester, 1865. [8]

WOODGATE, George Stephen, *Pembury, Tunbridge, Kent.*—Univ. Coll. Ox. B.A. 1833. V. of Pembury, with Trinity C. Dio. Cant. 1844. (Patron, the present V; Tithe—Imp. 330*l* 8*s*, V. 262*l*; V.'s Inc. 355*l*; Pop. 1257.) [9]

WOODGATE, Henry Arthur, *Belbroughton Rectory, Stourbridge, Worcestershire,* and *Athenæum Club, London, S.W.*—St. John's Coll. Ox. 1st cl. Lit. Hum. and B.A. 1821, M.A. 1824, B.D. 1830; Deac. 1824, Pr. 1825. R. of Belbroughton with Fairfield C. Dio. Wor. 1837. (Patron, St. John's Coll. Ox; Tithe, 1250*l*; Glebe, 34 acres and Ho; Pop. 1990.) Rural Dean of Kidderminster 1843; Hon. Can. of Wor. Cathl. 1847: Proctor for the Clergy of the Dio. of Wor. in Convocation 1841; Select Preacher 1836–38, and 1865–66. Formerly Fell. and Tut. of St. John's Coll. Ox; Public Examiner 1827–28; Bampton Lecturer 1838. Author, *Letter to Viscount Melbourne, on the Appointment of Dr. Hampden as Regius Professor of Divinity*, 2 eds. 1836; *The Study of Morals Vindicated and Recommended*, 1837; *The Authoritative Teaching of the Church shown to be in Conformity with Scripture, Analogy and the Moral Constitution of Man* (the Bampton Lectures for 1838), 1838; *Analysis of the Tracts on "Reserve in communicating Religious Knowledge*, 1842; *Considerations on the Position and Duty of the University of Oxford*, 1843; *Questions submitted to the Members of Convocation*, 1852; *National Faith considered in Reference to Endowments*, 1854; *Sermons on the Sunday Historical Lessons from the Old Testament, throughout the Year*, 2 vols. 1854–55; *Divine Judgments manifested in the Failure of Human Counsels* (Fast-Day Sermon, 1855), 1855; *The Abnormal Condition of the Church considered with Reference to the Analogy of Scripture and of History*, 1857; *"Essays and Reviews," considered with Reference to the current Principles and Fallacies of the Day, with Strictures on Mill's "Essay on Liberty" and his other Works*, 1861; *The Scribe instructed into the Kingdom of Heaven* (Sermon preached at the Consecration of the Bishop of Rochester, 1867). [10]

WOODGATES, James Richard, *Putley Rectory, Ledbury, Gloucestershire.*—Pemb. Coll. Cam. B.A. 1855, M.A. 1865; Deac. 1858 and Pr. 1859 by Bp of Salis. R. of Putley, Dio. Herf. 1865. (Patrons, D. and C. of Herf; Tithe, 119*l*; Glebe, 25 acres; R.'s Inc. 180*l* and Ho; Pop. 167.) Formerly C. of Wingfield, Wilts, 1858–60; Holme Lacy (sole charge) 1860–66. [11]

WOODHAM, Thomas Fielden, *Farley Rectory, Romsey, Hants.*—Wor. Coll. Ox. B.A. 1826. R. of Farley Chamberlayne, Dio. Win. 1850. (Patron, T. Woodham, Esq; Tithe, 335*l*; Glebe, 60 acres; R.'s Inc. 410*l* and Ho; Pop. 179.) [12]

WOODHOUSE, Alfred Joseph, *Idehill Parsonage, Sevenoaks, Kent.*—Caius Coll. Cam. B.A. and M.A. *ad. eund.* Ox; Deac. 1848 and Pr. 1849 by Abp of Cant. P. C. of Idehill, Dio. Cant. 1863. (Patron, R. of Sundridge; P. C.'s Inc. 150*l* and Ho; Pop. 706.) Formerly C. of Pluckley, Kent; P. C. of Trinity, Dover, 1858–63. [13]

WOODHOUSE, C. C. G., *Upper Gornal, Staffordshire.*—C. of Upper Gornal. [14]

WOODHOUSE, Charles Wright, *St. Peter's Parsonage, Blackburn.*—Caius Coll. Cam. 22nd Wrang. and B.A. 1840, Hulsean Prizeman 1841, M.A. 1843; Deac. 1840 by Bp of Lin. Pr. 1841 by Abp of York. P. C. of St. Peter's, Blackburn, Dio. Man. 1858. (Patron, V. of Blackburn; P. C.'s Inc. 249*l* 9*s* and Ho; Pop. 8244.) Formerly C. of St. James's, Sheffield, 1846; Theol. Lect. in St. Bees Coll. 1846–58. Author, *Use and Value of the Ancient Fathers* (Hulsean Prize Essay), 1841, 3*s* 6*d*; *United Intercessory Prayer, a Sermon on Day of Humiliation, 7th Oct.* 1857; *Notes on the Inspiration of Holy Scripture, for St. Bees College Use*; *Systematic Offerings and Lay Co-operation* (two Sermons), 1864. [15]

WOODHOUSE, E., *Slad Parsonage, Stroud, Gloucestershire.*—P. C. of Slad, Dio. G. and B. 1860. (Patron, V. of Painswick; P. C.'s Inc. 150*l* and Ho; Pop. 874.) [16]

WOODHOUSE, Fletcher, *Roseneath, Whitehaven.*—Queen's Coll. Ox. B.A. 1828, M.A. 1833; Deac. 1830 and Pr. 1831 by Bp of Ches. R. of Moresby, Cumberland, Dio. Carl. 1837. (Patron, Earl of Lonsdale; Tithe, 68*l*; Glebe, 71 acres; R.'s Inc. 129*l*; Pop. 1222.) [17]

WOODHOUSE, Frederick Charles, *St. Mary's Rectory, Hulme, Manchester.*—St. John's Coll. Cam. B.A. 1849, M.A. 1853; Deac. 1849 and Pr. 1851 by Bp of Chich. R. of St. Mary's, Moss Side, Hulme, Dio. Man. 1858. (Patron, Lord Egerton; R.'s Inc. 362*l* and Ho; Pop. 6730.) Formerly C. of Old and New Shoreham, Sussex, 1850–56; Min. of Clayton, near Manchester, 1856–58. [18]

WOODHOUSE, George G., *Budleigh Salterton, Exeter.*—Ch. Ch. Ox. 2nd cl. Lit. Hum. Hon. 4th cl. Law and Mod. Hist. Fell. Exhib. B.A; Deac. 1857 and Pr. 1858. P. C. of Upper Gornal, Dio. Lich. 1861. (Patron, V. of Sedgley; Glebe, 1½ acres; P. C.'s Inc. 200*l* and Ho; Pop. 4044.) Formerly C. of Tong, Salop. [19]

WOODHOUSE, George Windus, *Albrighton Vicarage, Shiffnal, Salop.*—St. Mary Hall, Ox. 2nd cl. Lit. Hum. 1824, B.A. 1825, M.A. 1828; Deac. 1824, Pr. 1825. V. of Albrighton, Dio. Lich. 1836. (Patrons, Haberdashers' Company and Christ's Hospital, Lond. alt; Tithe—Imp. 20*l*, V. 625*l*; V.'s Inc. 651*l* and Ho; Pop. 1156.) Author, *Practical Sermons*, 2 vols. 1839–1846; *The Careless Christian*, 1841; *Parochial Sermons*, 1844. [20]

WOODHOUSE, Gervas Harvey, *Finningley Rectory, Bawtry, Notts.*—St. John's Coll. Cam. B.A. 1824, M.A. 1830; Deac. 1824 and Pr. 1826 by Bp of Lich. R. of Finningley, Dio. Lin. 1836. (Patron, J. Harvey, Esq; Tithe, 44*l* 10*s* 4*d*; Glebe, 703 acres; R.'s Inc. 700*l* and Ho; Pop. 896.) Formerly C. of Boulton and St. Werburgh, Derby; P. C. of Boulton. [21]

WOODHOUSE, Henry David, *Himbleton Vicarage, Droitwich, Worcestershire.*—Ch. Coll. Cam. Scho. of, B.A. 1848, M.A. 1851; Deac. 1848 by Bp of Lich. Pr. 1850 by Bp of Ches. V. of Himbleton, Dio. Wor. 1865. (Patrons, D. and C. of Wor; Tithe, 23*l* 16*s*; Glebe, 115 acres; V.'s Inc. 160*l* and Ho; Pop. 404.) Formerly C. of Ponsonby, Cumberland, 1849–53, King's Bromley, Staffs, 1854–65. [22]

WOODHOUSE, John, *Huish-Champflower Rectory, Wiveliscombe, Somerset.*—Sid. Coll. Cam. Jun. Opt. and B.A. 1827; Deac. 1829 and Pr. 1830 by Bp of B. and W. R. of Huish-Champflower, Dio. B. and W. 1836. (Patron, Sir W. C. Trevelyan, Bart; Tithe, 254*l* 6*s* 9*d*; Glebe, 188 acres; R.'s Inc. 445*l* and Ho; Pop. 444.) [1]

WOODHOUSE, John, *Farnley, Leeds.*—St. Bees; Deac. 1852 and Pr. 1854 by Bp of Ches. Min. of the Iron Church, Farnley. Formerly C. of Goosnargh, Lancashire. [2]

WOODHOUSE, Richard, *Tugford Rectory, Ludlow, Salop.*—Wor. Coll. Ox. B.A. 1853; Deac. 1854, Pr. 1855. R. of Tugford, Dio. Herf. 1862. (Patron, Bp of Herf; Tithe, 182*l* 10*s*; Glebe, 17 acres; R.'s Inc. 220*l* and Ho; Pop. 119.) Formerly C. of Little Hereford 1854, Cradley, Herefordshire, 1856–62. [3]

WOODHOUSE, Thomas, *Hay, near Hereford.*—St. John's Coll. Ox. 2nd cl. Lit. Hum. B.A. 1853, M.A. 1859; Deac. 1854 and Pr. 1855 by Bp of Herf. Private Tut. at Eton 1863; C. of Cusop, Hereford, 1865. Formerly C. of Ross 1854–56, Bishopstone, near Hereford, 1859–62, Millbrook, near Southampton, 1862–63. [4]

WOODHOUSE, Thomas, 6, *Ward-terrace, Hunslet-road, Leeds.*—St. Bees; Deac. 1866 by Bp of Rip. C. of St. Jude's, Hunslet, 1866. [5]

WOODHOUSE, Walter Webb, *St. Clement's Rectory, Ipswich.*—R. of St. Clement's with St. Helen's R. Ipswich, Dio. Nor. 1847. (Patron, Ch. Patronage Soc; St. Clement's, Tithe, 280*l*; St. Helen's, Tithe, 64*l* 18*s* 8*d*; Glebe, 4½ acres; R.'s Inc. 353*l* and Ho; Pop. St. Clement's 4735, St. Helen's 748.) [6]

WOODHOUSE, William, *Wootton St. Lawrence, Basingstoke.*—St. Aidan's; Deac. 1867 by Bp of Win. C. of Wootton St. Lawrence 1867. [7]

WOODLAND, Eldred, *Stone Parsonage, Staffs.*—Magd. Hall, Ox. B.A. 1839; Deac. 1839 by Bp of Ches. Pr. 1840 by Bp of Rip. R. of Stone, Dio. Lich. 1854. (Patron, the Crown; Tithe—Imp. 2114*l* 7*s* 1*d*, P. C. 26*l* 2*s*; Glebe, 20 acres; R.'s Inc. 260*l* and Ho; Pop. 2669.) Author, *Sermon on the Occasion of the French Revolution,* 1848; etc. [8]

WOODMAN, Ebener Flood, *Walton West, Haverfordwest.*—Göttingen Univ. M.A; Deac. 1859 and Pr. 1860 by Bp of St. D. R. of Walton West with Talbenny, Dio. St. D. 1860. (Patron, the present R; Tithe, with Glebe, 354*l*; Pop. Walton 391, Talbenny 204.) Surrogate. Author, *Work or Worship, which? an Argument for the Christian Sabbath*; *The People's Common Prayer Book, with the Daily Services arranged as they are said*; Sermons; etc. [9]

WOODMAN, Frederick Thomas, *Bradwell (Oxon), near Lechlade, Gloucestershire.*—Magd. Hall, Ox. B.A. 1846, M.A. 1848; Deac. 1846 and Pr. 1848 by Bp of Ox. V. of Bradwell with Kelmscott C. Dio. Ox. 1855. (Patron, the present V; Bradwell, Glebe, 140 acres; Kelmscott, Glebe, 79 acres; V.'s Inc. 208*l*; Pop. Bradwell 128, Kelmscott 141.) [10]

WOODMAN, John Sibley, *Glanville-Wootton Rectory, Sherborne, Dorset.*—Wor. Coll. Ox. B.A. 1838; Deac. 1840 and Pr. 1841 by Bp. of G. and B. R. of Glanville-Wootton, Dio. Salis. 1857. (Patron, the present R; Tithe, 315*l*; Glebe, 22 acres; R.'s Inc. 350*l* and Ho; Pop. 300.) Formerly C. of Olverton, Glouc. 1840–49, Bincombe, Salisbury, 1849–51, Selsey, Chichester, 1851–54; P. C. of Mid-Lavant, Sussex, 1854–57. [11]

WOODMAN, Richard, *Romsey, Hants.*—Deac. 1843 and Pr. 1844 by Bp of Barbados. Chap. to the Romsey Union 1848. [12]

WOODMAN, William Henry, *Kidbrooke-park, Blackheath, Kent, S.E.*—Wad. Coll. Ox. Hebrew Exhib. B.A. 1860, M.A. 1864; Deac. 1861 and Pr. 1862 by Bp of Ox. R. of Kidbrooke, Dio. Roch. 1867. (Patron, J. Whitaker, Esq; R.'s Inc. 75*l*; Pop. 1400.) Formerly C. of Woburn, Bucks, and Trinity, Lee, 1863. [13]

WOODMASON, James Mathias, *Buttermere, Cockermouth, Cumberland.*—St. Bees; Deac. 1842 and Pr. 1843 by Bp of Ches. P. C. of Buttermere, Cumberland, Dio. Carl. 1843. (Patron, Earl of Lonsdale; Tithe—Imp. 29*l* 12*s*; P. C.'s Inc. 62*l*; Pop. 88.) P. C. of Wythop, Cumberland, Dio. Carl. 1847. (Patrons, Proprietors; Tithe—Imp. 18*l* 9*s* 5*d*; P. C.'s Inc. 57*l*; Pop. 99.) [14]

WOODROFFE, John N.—British Chap. at Madrid. [15]

WOODROFFE, Thomas Henry.—St. Edm. Hall, Ox. B.A. 1840, M.A. 1845; Deac. 1840 and Pr. 1841 by Bp of Lon. P. C. of St. Augustine's, South Hackney, Lond. 1853. Formerly C. of St. Mary's, Putney, Surrey, 1843–44; C. and Lect. of St. Mary's, Stoke Newington, Middlesex, 1850–53. [16]

WOODROOFFE, Henry, *Ryton, Durham.*—C. of Ryton. [17]

WOODROOFE, Thomas, *Peper-Harrow Rectory, Godalming, Surrey,* and *Residentiary Houses, Winchester.*—St. John's Coll. Ox. B.A. 1810, M.A. 1814. Can. Res. of Win. Cathl. 1845. (Value, 755*l* and Residence.) R. of Peper-Harrow, Dio. Win. 1862. (Patron, Viscount Midleton; R.'s Inc. 200*l* and Ho; Pop. 104.) Formerly V. of Alton, Hants, 1854–62. [18]

WOODRUFF, John, *Upchurch Vicarage, Sittingbourne, Kent.*—Mert. Coll. Ox. B.A. 1827; Deac. 1828 and Pr. 1829 by Bp of Lon. V. of Upchurch, Dio. Cant. 1834. (Patron, All Souls Coll. Ox; Tithe—Imp. 419*l* 12*s* 7*d*, V. 243*l* 16*s*; Glebe, 5 acres; V.'s Inc. 280*l* and Ho; Pop. 468.) [19]

WOODRUFF, Thomas, *Wistow Rectory, near Huntingdon.*—St. John's Coll. Ox. B.A. 1828, M.A. 1829; Deac. 1828 and Pr. 1829 by Bp of Lin. R. of Wistow, Dio. Ely, 1840. (Patron, the present R; Corn Rent, 305*l* 13*s* 5*d*; Glebe, 35 acres; R.'s Inc. 358*l* and Ho; Pop. 532.) Rural Dean. [20]

WOODS, Charles Thomas, *British Columbia.*—Dub. A.B. 1849, A.M. 1855; Deac. 1849 and Pr. 1850 by Bp of Wor. Formerly Min. of Woburn Chapel, Tavistock-square, Lond. 1857–62. [21]

WOODS, Edward S., *Trinity Parsonage, Dover.*—Dub. A.B. 1853, A.M. 1866; Deac. 1854, Pr. 1855. P. C. of Trinity, Dover, Dio. Cant. 1867. (Patron, Abp of Cant; P. C.'s Inc. 240*l* and Ho; Pop. 4492.) Formerly C. of Killesher 1854, Kenilworth 1855; Trinity, Tunbridge Wells, 1858. [22]

WOODS, George, *Sully Rectory, Cardiff.*—Univ. Coll. Ox. B.A. 1833, M.A. 1835. R. of Sully, Dio. Llan. 1848. (Patron, Sir J. Guest, Bart; Tithe, 292*l* 15*s*; R.'s Inc. 306*l* and Ho; Pop. 192.) [23]

WOODS, Henry Horatio, *Tidmarsh Rectory, Reading.*—Emman. Coll. Cam. Scho. of, B.A. 1827, M.A. 1830; Deac. and Pr. 1829 by Bp of Win. R. of Tidmarsh, Dio. Ox. 1855. (Patron, John Hopkins, Esq; Tithe, 228*l*; R.'s Inc. 270*l* and Ho; Pop. 179.) [24]

WOODS, John, 4, *Surrey-square, Old Kent-road, London, S.E.*—St. Aidan's; Deac. 1867 by Bp of Win. C. of St. Mary's, Southwark. [25]

WOODS, Richard, *Walsall, Staffs.*—Assoc. of King's Coll. Lond; Deac. 1863 and Pr. 1864 by Bp of Lich. C. of Bayton and Mamble, Worc. 1866. Formerly C. of St. Peter's, Walsall, 1863. [26]

WOODS, Robert M'Clure, *Pen-y-bryn, Whittington, near Oswestry.*—Dub. A.B. 1843; Deac. 1845 and Pr. 1847 by Bp of Ches. Formerly C. of Farnworth, Lancashire. [27]

WOODWARD, Alexander, *Whitchurch, Salop.*—St. Cath. Coll. Cam. B.A. 1840, M.A. 1843; Deac. 1840 and Pr. 1841 by Bp of Ches. Formerly R. of Hopton-Wafers, Salop, 1854–61. [28]

WOODWARD, Charles, 98, *St. Martin's-lane, London, W.C.*—Queens' Coll. Cam. B.C.L. 1831; Deac. 1830 and Pr. 1831 by Bp of Lin. Chap. of the Freemasons' Sch. for Female Children, Battersea Rise; Royal Masonic Instit. for Boys, Wood Green, Tottenham, 1864; Chap. to the Gen. Lying-in Hospital, York-road. Formerly Colonial Chap. Australia; Head Mast. of the Freemason's Boy's Sch. Tottenham. Author, *Paley's Horæ Paulinæ for Schools,* 1837; *Address on opening Mechanics' Institute, Woolwich, Kent,* 1837. [29]

WOODWARD, Edmund Henry, *The College, Brighton.*—St. John's Coll. Cam. 20th Wrang. and B.A. 1852, M.A. 1855. Fell. of St. John's Coll. Cam. [30]

WOODWARD, Henry, *St. Stephen's Parsonage, Albert-square, Clapham-road, London, S.*—Dub. A.B. 1848; Deac. and Pr. 1848. C. of St. Stephen's, South Lambeth, 1864. Formerly P. C. of Thornton, Bradford, Yorks. 1851–54; Min. of St. James's Chapel, Kennington, Surrey, 1854–63. Author, *Divine Echoes from Fallen Churches*; *Glory in its Fulness*; various Sermons and Pamphlets. [1]

WOODWARD, Henry, *Cleobury-Mortimer, Bewdley, Salop.*—P. C. of St. John's, Cleobury-Mortimer, Dio. Herf. 1854. (Patron, B. Botfield, Esq; P. C.'s Inc. 57*l* and Ho; Pop. 356.) [2]

WOODWARD, Herbert, *Windsor, Liverpool.*—St. Aidan's; Deac. 1853 by Abp of York, Pr. 1854 by Bp of Nor. P. C. of St. Clement's, Toxteth-park, Dio. Ches. 1857. (Patrons, Trustees; P. C.'s Inc. 250*l*; Pop. 7637.) Formerly C. of Sheringham, near Cromer, Norfolk. [3]

WOODWARD, John, *The Parsonage, Montrose, N.B.*—Deac. 1861 and Pr. 1862 by Bp of Chich. Min. of Episcopal Chapel, Montrose, Dio. Brechin, 1866. (Patron, Hercules Scott, Esq; Pop. 420.) Formerly Asst. Mast. in St. John's Coll. Hurstpierpoint, Sussex; Asst. Mast. in St. Saviour's Gr. Sch. New Shoreham, 1866. [4]

WOODWARD, John Peckham Skirrow, *Moulsham, Chelmsford.*—Emman. Coll. Cam. B.A. 1864; Deac. 1864, Pr. 1867. C. of Moulsham. [5]

WOODWARD, Matthew, *Folkestone, Kent.*—St. Aidan's; M.A. by Abp of Cant. 1856; Deac. 1849 and Pr. 1850 by Abp of Cant. V. of Folkestone, Dio. Cant. 1851. (Patron, Abp of Cant; V.'s Inc. 300*l* and Ho; Pop. 6669.) Formerly C. of Hythe 1849–51. [6]

WOODWARD, Richard Francis, *Rossall, Fleetwood.*—Trin. Coll. Cam. Scho. of, 2nd cl. Cl. 2nd cl. Theol. B.A. 1862; Deac. 1864 and Pr. 1865 by Bp of Rip. Asst. Mast. in Rossall Sch. 1867. Formerly C. of Chapelthorpe 1864. [7]

WOODWARD, Robert Boraman, *Great Houghton Hall, near Northampton.*—St. John's Coll. Cam. B.A. 1827, M.A. 1835; Deac. 1827 and Pr. 1828 by Bp of Herf. Co-Brother of St. John's Hospital, Northampton 1843. (Patron, Mast. of St. John's Hospital; Inc. 56*l*.) Formerly C. of Kingsthorpe, Northants, 1828–51. [8]

WOODWARD, Samuel, *Hopton-Wafers, Bewdley, Salop.*—Univ. Coll. Dur. B.A. 1859, M.A. 1862; Theol. Licen. 1860; Deac. 1860 by Bp of Wor. Pr. 1861 by Bp of Lon. R. of Hopton-Wafers, Dio. Herf. 1861. (Patron, T. Woodward, Esq; R.'s Inc. 250*l* and Ho; Pop. 440.) Formerly C. of Hanbury, Worc. [9]

WOODWARD, Thomas, *Thundridge Vicarage, Ware, Herts.*—Dub. A.B. 1832; Deac. 1832 by Bp of Kildare, Pr. 1833 by Bp of Elphin. V. of Thundridge, Dio. Roch. 1855. (Patron, R. Hanbury, Esq; Tithe, 105*l*; V.'s Inc. 128*l*; Pop. 393.) Rural Dean. Formerly C. of St. James's, Bath, 1839–55. [10]

WOODWARD, William, *Bidford Grange, Alcester, Warwickshire.*—St. Cath. Coll. Cam. B.A. 1848; Deac. 1848 and Pr. 1849 by Bp of Ex. [11]

WOODWARD, William, *Plumpton Rectory, Hurstpierpoint, Sussex.*—Trin. Coll. Cam. B.A. 1830; Deac. 1830, Pr. 1831. R. of Plumpton, Dio. Chich. 1850. (Patron, the present R; Tithe, 380*l*; Glebe, 18 acres; R.'s Inc. 395*l* and Ho; Pop. 404.) [12]

WOODWARD, William, *Stafford.*—St. Aidan's. C. of Ch. Ch. Stafford. Formerly C. of Selside, Westmoreland, and Claverley, Salop. [13]

WOODYATT, Edward, *Over, Winsford, Cheshire.*—Ch. Ch. Ox. 4th cl. Jurisp. and Mod. History, B.A. 1854, M.A. 1863; Deac. 1856, Pr. 1858. P. C. of St. John's, Over, Dio. Ches. 1863. (Patron, Lord Delamere; P. C.'s Inc. 150*l* and Ho; Pop. 2000.) [14]

WOODYATT, George, *Radston Parsonage, Brackley, Northants.*—St. Peter's Coll. Cam. B.A. 1851; Deac. 1859 and Pr. 1860 by Bp of Worc. P. C. of Radston, Dio. Pet. 1862. (Patron, Rev. C. W. Holbeck; Glebe, 37 acres; P. C.'s Inc. 118*l* and Ho; Pop. 160.) [15]

WOODYEARE, John Fountain Woodyeare, *Crookhill, Rotherham, Yorks.*—Ch. Coll. Cam. B.A. 1830; Deac. 1832 by Bp of Lin. Pr. 1835 by Abp of York. Dom. Chap. to the Countess-Dowager of Cavan. [16]

WOOLER, William George, *South Bailey, Durham.*—Dur. Licen. in Theol. 1865; Deac. 1866 by Bp of Dur. C. of St. Cuthbert's, Durham, 1866. [17]

WOOLLAM, Henry, *Whitby, Yorks.*—C. of Whitby. [18]

WOOLLAM, John, *Cathedral Close, Hereford.*—St. John's Coll. Ox. B.A. 1850, M.A. 1853; Deac. 1854 and Pr. 1855 by Bp of Herf. Head Mast. of the Cathl. Sch. Hereford, 1858. Formerly C. of Pipe and Lyde, Herefordshire, 1854–58. [19]

WOOLLAM, William, *Vicarage, Buslingthorpe, Leeds.*—St. Aidan's; Deac. 1855 by Bp of Ches. Pr. 1856 by Abp of York. P. C. of Buslingthorpe, Dio. Rip. 1862. (Patrons, Trustees; Tithe, 11*l* 16*s*; Glebe, ½ an acre; P. C.'s Inc. 320*l* and Ho; Pop. 5000.) Formerly C. of St. Barnabas's, Liverpool, 1855–56; P. C. of Thorpe Hesley, York, 1856–62. [20]

WOOLLASTON, Thomas Samuel, *Exford Rectory, Minehead, Somerset.*—St. Peter's Coll. Cam. Browne's Univ. Scho. 1837, 1st Jun. Opt. 1st cl. Cl. Trip. and B.A. 1840, M.A. 1843; Deac. 1842 and Pr. 1845 by Bp of Ely. Foundation Fell. of St. Peter's Coll. Cam. 1840; R. of Exford, Dio. B. and W. 1867. (Patron, St. Peter's Coll; Tithe, 250*l*; Glebe, 240 acres; Ho; Pop. 546.) Formerly C. of East Tuddenham with Honingham, Norfolk, 1843–47, Porlock, Somerset, 1843–47. [21]

WOOLLCOMBE, Edward Cooper, *Balliol College, Oxford.*—Oriel Coll. Ox. 1st cl. Lit. Hum. and B.A. 1837, M.A. 1840; Deac. 1840 and Pr. 1841 by Bp of Ox. Fell. and Tut. of Ball. Coll. Ox. 1838–40; Public Exam. in Lit. Hum. 1843 and 1844; Select Preacher to the Univ. of Ox. 1850; one of the Preachers at the Chapel Royal, Whitehall, 1854. [22]

WOOLLCOMBE, George, *Highampton, Devon.*—Ch. Ch. Ox. 4th cl. Lit. Hum. B.A. 1841, M.A. 1842; Deac. 1842 and Pr. 1843 by Bp of Ex. R. of Highampton, Dio. Ex. 1861. (Patron, Archd. Woollcombe; Tithe, 197*l* 10*s*; Glebe, 149 acres; R.'s Inc. 264*l* and Ho; Pop. 366.) Formerly C. of Dittisham 1842–52, Thorverton 1854–58, Highampton 1858–61. Author, *Prohibitions in Marriage easy to be understood and Scriptural*, 2*d*. [23]

WOOLLCOMBE, George Ley, *Sennen, near Penzance.*—Ball. Coll. Ox. 3rd cl. Math. B.A. 1851, M.A. 1854; Deac. 1853 and Pr. 1854 by Bp of Ex. R. of Sennen, Dio. Ex. 1864. (Patron, H.R.H. The Prince of Wales; Tithe, 230*l*; R.'s Inc. 230*l*; Pop. 647.) Formerly C. of Revelstoke, Devon, 1853–57, Kenwyn 1857–64; C. in sole charge of St. Mary's, Truro, 1864–65. [24]

WOOLLCOMBE, the Ven. Henry, *Heavitree, Exeter.*—Ch. Ch. Ox. 1st cl. Lit. Hum. 2nd cl. Math. et Phy. 1834, Johnson's Theol. Prizeman 1835, B.A. 1834, M.A. 1835; Deac. 1838 and Pr. 1839 by Bp of Ox. V. of Heavitree, Dio. Ex. 1858. (Patrons, D. and C. of Ex; Glebe, 8 acres; V.'s Inc. 650*l* and Ho; Pop. 3200.) Can. Res. of Exeter 1861; Chap. to Bp of Ex. 1843. Formerly C. of Sheepwash and Highampton, Devon, 1838–44; V. of Kingsteignton, Devon, 1844–58; Exam. Chap. to Bp of Ex. 1848–61; Coadjutor to the Ven. Archdeacon of Ex. 1860–62; Archdeacon of Barnstaple 1865. Author, *Forms of Prayer shown to be in Accordance with the Holy Scripture*, Tract No. 561, S.P.C.K; *Summary of the Historical Books of the New Testament*, Nat. Soc. 1854; *Our Lord's Temptation, a Comfort to the Tempted* (a Sermon), 1861; *Charge delivered at the Visitation of the Archdeaconry of Exeter* in 1861, and in 1862, Rivingtons; *Charge delivered at the Visitation of the Archdeaconry of Barnstaple* in 1866, Rivingtons. [25]

WOOLLCOMBE, Louis, *Petrockstowe, North Devon.*—Ex. Coll. Ox. 2nd cl. Lit. Hum. B.A. 1836, M.A. 1839; Deac. 1840 and Pr. 1841 by Bp of Ox. R. of Petrockstowe, Dio. Ex. 1845. (Patron, Lord Clinton; Tithe, 271*l*; Glebe, 49 acres; R.'s Inc. 320*l* and Ho; Pop. 614.) Formerly Fell. of Ex. Coll. Ox. 1837–45. [26]

WOOLLCOMBE, Philip, *Christowe Vicarage, Exeter.*—M.A; Deac. and Pr. 1847 by Bp of Salis. V. of Christowe, Dio. Ex. 1861. (Patron, Viscount Exmouth; V.'s Inc. 160*l* and Ho; Pop. 941.) Rural Dean. Formerly C. of West Stafford, Dorset; C. in sole charge of North Bovey, Devon. [1]

WOOLLCOMBE, William Penrose, *Landwater Parsonage, High Wycombe, Bucks.*—Ch. Ch. Ox. B.A. 1850, M.A. 1859; Deac. 1851 and Pr. 1852 by Bp of Ex. P. C. of Landwater, Dio. Ox. 1865. (Patrons, Trustees; P. C.'s Inc. 152*l* and Ho; Pop. 700.) [2]

WOOLLCOMBE, William Walker, *St. Andrew's Parsonage, 1, Manor-street, Ardwick, Manchester.*—Ex. Coll. Ox. 4th cl. Lit. Hum. 1st cl. Math. et Phy. and B.A. 1842, M.A. 1852; Deac. 1844, Pr. 1845 by Bp of Ex. Sen. C. of St. Andrew's, Manchester. Formerly C. of Clayton, Manchester; Sen. C. of Trinity, Salford. [3]

WOOLLCOMBE, William Wyatt, *Wootton Rectory, Northampton.*—R. of Wootton, Dio. Pet. 1854. (Patron, Ex. Coll. Ox; R.'s Inc. 600*l* and Ho; Pop. 837.) Chap. of Hardingstone Union, Northants, 1854. Formerly Fell. and Sub-Rector of Ex. Coll. Ox; P. C. of Iffley, Oxon. [4]

WOOLLEY, Frederick, *Lewes.*—R. of St. Michael's, Lewes, Dio. Chich. 1863. (Patron, Ld Chan; R.'s Inc. 116*l* and Ho; Pop. 1076.) Head Mast. of Lewes Gr. Sch. [5]

WOOLLEY, Joseph, *Royal School of Naval Architecture, South Kensington, London, S.W.*—St. John's Coll. Cam. 3rd Wrang. and B.A. 1840, M.A. 1843. Formerly Fell. and Lect. on Rhetoric in St. John's Coll. Cam. [6]

WOOLLEY, Joseph, *East Bergholt Rectory, Suffolk.*—Emman. Coll. Cam. Wrang. Norrisian Prize. 1843–44, and B.A. 1838, M.A. 1841, B.D. 1848; Deac. 1841 by Bp of Lich. Pr. 1842 by Bp of Ely. R. of East Bergholt, Suffolk, Dio. Nor. 1855. (Patron, Emman. Coll. Cam; Tithe, 820*l*; Glebe, 20 acres; R.'s Inc. 850*l*; Pop. 1400.) Formerly Fell. and Eccles. Lect. of Emman. Coll. Cam; Select Preacher before Univ. 1853–56; Cambridge Preacher at the Chapel Royal, Whitehall, 1854; C. of Feversham 1842; Warden of and Professor of Moral Philos. in Queen's Coll. Birmingham, 1844. Author, *The Writings of the New Testament contain certain Indications that this Portion of the Sacred Canon was intended to be a Complete Record of Apostolical Doctrine*, 1844; *An Introductory Lecture to a Course on Bishop Butler's Analogy* (delivered to the Students of the Queen's Coll. Birmingham, in 1844), 1844; *By one Offering, Christ has perfected for ever them that are Sanctified* (an Essay), 1845; *The Way of Death mistaken for the Way of Life* (a Sermon preached before the Univ. of Cam.), 1855; *Why do not Working Men get on Better?* (a Sermon); *Earnestness in Religion* (a Sermon); *Absent from the Body and Present with the Lord* (a Sermon); *Christ's Presence the Glory of a Church* (a Sermon preached in 1866 at the opening of Brettenham Church). [7]

WOOLLEY, J., *Newton, near Manchester.*—C. of Newton. [8]

WOOLLNOUGH, J. B. W., *Basingstoke, Hants.*—Wor. Coll. Ox. B.A. 1856, M.A. 1859; Deac. 1856, Pr. 1857 by Bp of Win. C. of Basingstoke 1864. Formerly C. of Hawkley 1856, Ch. Ch. Brighton, 1860, Ramsgate 1862. Author, *Scrambles in Serk*, 1861. [9]

WOOLMER, Charles Edward Shirley, *St. Andrew's Rectory, Deal.*—Ex. Coll. Ox. Stephens', Reynolds' and Aclands' Exhib. 4th cl. Lit. Hum. B.A. 1849, M.A. 1851; Stud. of Wells Theol. Coll. 1849–51; Deac. 1851 and Pr. 1852 by Bp of Man. R. of St. Andrew's, Deal, Dio. Cant. 1866. (Patron, Abp of Cant; R.'s Inc. 150*l* and Ho; Pop. 2900.) Formerly C. of Bolton-le Moors 1851-53, Ashton-le-Willows 1853–55, Ramsgate 1855–62; Sen. Chap. of the Kent County Prison 1862–66. [10]

WOOLOCOMBE, John Bidlake, *Stowford Rectory, Lew Down, Devon.*—Trin. Coll. Ox. B.A. 1846, M.A. 1847; Deac. 1848 and Pr. 1849. R. of Stowford, Dio. Ex. 1866. (Patron, the present R; Tithe, 240*l*; Glebe, 42 acres; R.'s Inc. 350*l* and Ho; Pop. 450.) [11]

WOOLRYCH, Humphry Fitzroy, *Maidstone.*—King's Coll. Lond. Heb. Prizeman of the Univ. of Lond. 1858, B.A. 1843, M.A. 1856; Deac. 1846 by Bp of Rip. Pr. 1847 by Bp of Llan. C. of Hucking, Hollingbourne, Kent, 1867; Chap. of the West Kent and Ophthalmic Hospitals; Dom. Chap. to the Earl of Clarendon. Formerly Asst. Chap. of the Kent County Prison, Maidstone, 1862–66; C. of Sunderland 1846–48, South Hetton 1848–54, Watford 1854, Longbenton 1855–57; Chap. to the Watford Union 1858–62. Author, *Aleph versus Colenso*, Maidstone, 1*s*; various Articles in Religious Periodicals. [12]

WOOLRYCH, William Henry, *Crowle Vicarage, Worcestershire.*—Pemb. Coll. Ox. B.A. 1849; Deac. 1850 and Pr. 1851 by Bp of Man. V. of Crowle, Dio. Wor. 1860. (Patron, the present V; V.'s Inc. 300*l* and Ho; Pop. 576.) Formerly C. of Jesus' Chapel, Enfield, Middlesex. [13]

WOOLWARD, Alfred Gott, *Belton Rectory, Grantham.*—Magd. Coll. Ox. B.A. 1841, M.A. 1846; Deac. 1844, Pr. 1845. Dom. Chap. to Earl Brownlow 1854; R. of Belton, Dio. Lin. 1864. (Patron, Earl Brownlow; R.'s Inc. 450*l* and Ho; Pop. 142. [14]

WORCESTER, The Right Rev. Henry

PHILPOTT, Lord Bishop of Worcester, *Hartlebury Castle, Worcestershire.*—St. Cath. Coll. Cam. Sen. Wrang. Smith's Prizeman, 1st cl. Cl. Trip. and B.A. 1829, M.A. 1832, B.D. 1839, D.D. 1847; Deac. 1831, Pr. 1833. Consecrated Bp of Worcester 1861. (Episcopal Jurisdiction—the Counties of Worcestershire and Warwick, with 1 Par. in Gloucestershire and 3 in Staffordshire; Inc. of See, 5000*l*; Pop. 857,775; Acres, 1,037,451; Deaneries, 13; Benefices, 446; Curates, 199; Church Sittings, 211,021.) His Lordship is Co-Visitor with the Bp of Oxford of Wor. Coll. Ox. His Lordship was formerly Mast. of Cath. Coll. Cam. with a Can. of Norwich annexed, 1845–60; Chap. to H.R.H. Prince Albert 1854–60. [15]

WORDSWORTH, The Ven. Christopher, *The Cloisters, Westminster Abbey, S.W.*—Trin. Coll. Cam. Chan. English Medallist 1827–28, Porson Prizeman 1828, Browne's Medallist 1827–28, Craven Scho. 1829, Sen. Opt. and B.A. 1830, M.A. 1833, B.D. and D.D. *per Literas Regias*, 1839; Deac. 1833 by Bp of Lin. Pr. 1835 by Bp of Carl. Can. Res. 1844 and Archd. of Westminster 1865. (Value, 1100*l* and Res.) V. of Stanford-in-the-Vale with Goosey C. Faringdon, Berks, Dio. Ox. 1850. (Patrons, D. and C. of Westminster; Tithe—App. 750*l*, V. 275*l*; Glebe, 14 acres; V.'s Inc. 420*l* and Ho; Pop. Stanford 1075, Goosey 202.) Rural Dean. Formerly Fell. of Trin. Coll. Cam. 1830–36; Public Orator, Cam. 1836; Head Mast. of Harrow Sch. 1836–44; Hulsean Lect. 1847–48. Author, *The Old Testament in the Author's Second Version, with Notes and Introduction* (the parts published in 1867 reach from *Genesis* to the *Psalms*), Rivingtons; Also, 9th ed. 1867 (Abridgment), 2*s*; *The Holy Year, or Original Hymns for Sundays and Holy Days*, 6*d*; Musical ed. 4*s* 6*d*; *On Union with Rome*, 5th ed. 1*s*; *The Church of Ireland, her History and Claims*, 2nd ed. 1*s*; *The Greek Testament, with Prefaces, Introductions and Notes*, 4th ed; *The Four Gospels*, 21*s*, *Acts of the Apostles*, 10*s* 6*d*. *St. Paul's Epistles*, 31*s* 6*d*, *General Epistles, Revelation, and Indexes*, 21*s*; *The Holy Bible with Introductions and Notes—Genesis and Exodus*, 1865, 21*s*; the rest of the Pentateuch in the press, 1865; *Theophilus Anglicanus, or Instruction concerning the Church and the Anglican Branch of it*, 8 eds. 1857, 5*s*; *Inedited Ancient Writings from the Walls of Pompeii*, 1837, 2*s* 6*d*; *Sermons at Harrow School*, 1841; *Discourses on Public Education*, 1844; *Theocritus, Codicum MSS. ope recensitus et emendatus, cum Indicibus locupletissimis*, 13*s* 6*d*; *Latinæ Grammatica Rudimenta, or King Edward VI.'s Grammar*, 12 eds. 3*s* 6*d*; *Correspondence of Richard Bentley, D.D. Master of Trinity College*, 2 vols. 42*s*; *Diary in France*, 2 eds. 5*s* 6*d*;

Letters to M. Gondon, on the Destructive Character of the Church of Rome, both in Religion and Polity, 3 eds. 7s 6d; *Sequel to the Previous Letters*, 2 eds. 6s 6d; *Scripture Inspiration, or On the Canon of Holy Scripture* (Hulsean Lectures for 1847), 2 eds. ib. 1848, 9s; *On the Apocalypse, or Book of Revelation* (Hulsean Lecture for 1848), 1849, 3 eds. 10s 6d; *Harmony of the Apocalypse*, 4s 6d; *The Apocalypse in Greek, with MSS. Coll. &c.*, 10s 6d; *Manual for Confirmation*, 9d; *Memoirs of William Wordsworth*, 2 vols. 1851, 30s; *Athens and Attica*, 4 eds. with plates, 1854; *Greece, Historical, Pictorial and Descriptive*, 5th ed. 28s; *S. Hippolytus and the Church of Rome in the beginning of the Third Century, from the newly-discovered "Philosophumena,"* 1853, 8s 6d; *Notes at Paris*, 1854, 4s 6d; *Tour in Italy*, 2 vols. 2nd ed; Occasional Sermons, preached in Westminster Abbey, 1850–54—*On Baptism*; *On Calvinism*; *On Secessions to Rome*; *Secular Education*; *Use of Catechisms and Creeds in Education*; *On an Education Rate*: *On the History of the Church of Ireland*; *On National Sins and Judgments*; *On the Religious Census*; *On an Increase in the Episcopate*; *On Tithes*; *On Church Rates*; *On Marriage and Divorce*; *On the New Romish Doctrine of the Immaculate Conception*; *On Marriage with a Deceased Wife's Sister*; *On the Doctrine of the Atonement*, 1s each, etc; *Funeral Sermon on Joshua Watson, Esq. D.C.L.* 6d; and other single Sermons. [1]

WORDSWORTH, Cullen Forth, *Fifield-Bavant, near Salisbury.*—Magd. Hall, Ox. B.A. 1844. P. C. of Ebbesbourne-Wake, near Salisbury, Dio. Salis. 1845. (Patron, the Succentor of Salis. Cathl; Tithe—App. 291*l* and 46 acres of Glebe, Imp. 164*l*; P. C.'s Inc. 132*l*; Pop. 326.) Dom. Chap. to the Marchioness of Bath. Formerly R. of Fifield-Bavant 1844–61. [2]

WORDSWORTH, John, *Plumbland Rectory, Carlisle, Cumberland.*—New Coll. Ox. B.A. 1826, M.A. 1830. V. of Brigham, near Cockermouth, Dio. Carl. 1832. (Patron, Earl of Lonsdale; Tithe—App. 7*l*, Imp. 463*l* 1s 5d; V.'s Inc. 201*l*; Pop. 1768.) R. of Plumbland, Dio. Carl. 1840. (Patron, Henry Curwen, Esq; Tithe—Imp. 105*l* 10s, R. 136*l* 14s 6d; R.'s Inc. 374*l* and Ho; Pop. 726.) [3]

WORDSWORTH, William, *Monk Breton, Royston, Yorks.* [4]

WORKMAN, Albert, *Coventry.*—C. of Trinity, Coventry. [5]

WORKMAN, William Ring, *Basingstoke, Hants.*—Wor. Coll. Ox. B.A. 1847, M.A. 1849; Deac. 1848, Pr. 1849. R. of Eastrop, near Basingstoke, Dio. Win. 1850. (Patron, the present R; Tithe, 85*l*; R.'s Inc. 108*l*; Pop. 130.) [6]

WORLLEDGE, Edmund, 21, *Royal Avenue-terrace, Chelsea, London, S.W.*—Clare Hall, Cam. B.A. 1842, M.A. 1847; Deac. 1842, Pr. 1843. Lect. at the Nat. Soc. Training Institution for Schoolmistresses, Chelsea. Formerly C. of Enfield, Middlesex. [7]

WORSFOLD, John Napper, *Wellington Parsonage, Stoke-upon-Trent.*—St. Bees; Deac. 1853 by Bp of Nor. Pr. 1854 by Bp of Lich. P. C. of Wellington (a Peel parish), Dio. Lich. 1860. (Patrons, Crown and Bp alt; P. C.'s Inc. 300*l* and Ho; Pop. 5555.) Formerly C. of Bramford, Suffolk, 1853, Burslem 1854, St. Clement's, Ipswich, 1855, Wolvey, Warwickshire, 1857; V. of Tickenham 1859. Author, *The Doctrine of the Trinity practically and experimentally considered*; *The Fulness and Freeness of the Gospel*; *Wellington Series of Tracts*; etc. [8]

WORSLEY, Henry, *Norwood Rectory, Southhall, Middlesex, W.*—Ex. Coll. Ox. 1839, Michel Scho. of Queen's Coll. Ox. B.A. 1842, M.A. 1845; Deac. 1844 by Bp of Lin. Pr. 1845 by Bp of Ox. R. of Norwood, Dio. Lon. 1860. (Patron, the present R; Glebe, 80 acres; R.'s Inc. 400*l* and Ho; Pop. 4010.) Formerly R. of Easton, Suffolk, 1847–60. Author, *Prize Essay on Juvenile Depravity*, 1849, 5s; *The Life of Martin Luther*, 2 vols. Bell and Daldy, 1856, 24s. [9]

WORSLEY, John Henry, *Leafield, Witney, Oxon.*—Magd. Coll. Ox. B.A. 1836, M.A. 1838; Deac. 1837 and Pr. 1838 by Bp of Ox. P. C. of Leafield with Wychwood, Dio. Ox. 1857. (Patron, Bp of Ox; Glebe, 58 acres; P. C.'s Inc. 138*l* and Ho; Pop. 974.) Formerly C. of Churchill, Oxon. [10]

WORSLEY, Pennyman Ralph, *Wellingborough, Northants.*—Trin. Coll. Cam. B.A. 1864; Deac. 1866 and Pr. 1867 by Bp of Pet. C. of Finedon, Northants, 1866. [11]

WORSLEY, Pennyman Warton, *Little Ponton, Grantham.*—Deac. 1823, Pr. 1824. Can. Res. of Rip. Cathl. 1827. (Value, 500*l*.) R. of Little Ponton, Dio. Lin. 1829. (Patron, Christopher Turnor, Esq; R.'s Inc. 427*l* and Ho; Pop. 208.) Rural Dean. [12]

WORSLEY, Thomas, *Downing College, Cambridge.*—Trin. Coll. Cam. Scho. 1818, 3rd Sen. Opt. and B.A. 1820, M.A. 1824, D.D. 1858; Deac. 1824 and Pr. 1825 by Bp of Ely. R. of Scawton, near Helmsley, Yorks, Dio. York, 1826. (Patron, Sir William Worsley, Bart; Tithe, 140*l*; Glebe, 32½ acres; R.'s Inc. 170*l*; Pop. 148.) Mast. of Downing Coll. Cam; Christian Advocate in the Univ. of Cam. 1844–50; Select Preacher 1845. Author, *The Province of the Intellect in Religion, deduced from Our Lord's Sermon on the Mount, and considered with Reference to Prevalent Errors*, 3 vols. 1846–50. [13]

WORSLEY, William, *Norbury, Stockport.*—Magd. Hall, Ox. 3rd cl. Lit. Hum. 1829, B.A. 1830; Deac. 1831 and Pr. 1832 by Bp of Ches. P. C. of Norbury, Dio. Ches. 1832. (Patron, William John Legh, Esq; Tithe—App. 126*l*; Glebe, 18 acres; P. C.'s Inc. 140*l*; Pop. 994.) [14]

WORSLEY, William, *Bratoft Rectory, Spilsby, Lincolnshire.*—Ch. Coll. Cam. B.A. 1823; Deac. 1824, Pr. 1825. R. of Bratoft, Dio. Lin. 1842. (Patron, Ld Chan; Tithe—Imp. 18*l* 7s 4d, R. 328*l*; Glebe, 37 acres; R.'s Inc. 368*l* and Ho; Pop. 280.) P. C. of Irby-in-the-Marsh, Dio. Lin. 1856. (Patrons, D. and C. of Lin; P. C.'s Inc. 83*l*; Pop. 169.) Formerly C. of Ganby, near Spilsby. [15]

WORTHAM, Walter, *Shephall Parsonage, Stevenage, Herts.*—Magd. Coll. Cam. B.A. 1824; Deac. 1824, Pr. 1825. R. of Shephall, Dio. Roch. 1837. (Patron, Ld Chan; Tithe, 306*l*; Glebe, 1 acre; R.'s Inc. 309*l* and Ho; Pop. 243.) [16]

WORTHINGTON, J., *Shuckburgh, Southam, Warwickshire.*—P. C. of Shuckburgh, Dio. Wor. 1866. (Patron, Major Shuckburgh.) Formerly V. of Little Bedwyn, Wilts, 1862. [17]

WORTHINGTON, James William, *Trinity Rectory*, 27, *John-street, Bedford-row, London, W.C.*—R. of Trinity, Gray's-inn-road, Dio. Lon. 1838. (Patron, R. of St. Andrew's, Holborn; R.'s Inc. 300*l*; Pop. 13,662.) [18]

WORTHINGTON, Thomas, *Fradswell Rectory, Stone, Staffs.*—St. Bees; Deac. 1854 and Pr. 1855 by Bp of Lich. R. of Fradswell, Dio. Lich. 1857. (Patron, Bp of Lich; R.'s Inc. 138*l* and Ho; Pop. 220.) Formerly C. of Sneyd, Staffs. 1854–57. [19]

WORTHINGTON, William Robert, *York.*—C. of St. Lawrence's, York. [20]

WORTHY, Charles, *Ashburton, Devon.*—Queen's Coll. Ox. B.A. 1831; Deac. 1831 by Bp of Win. Pr. 1832 by Bp of Ex. V. of Ashburton with Buckland-in-the Moor, Dio. Ex. 1861. (Patrons, D. and C. of Ex; Tithe, 415*l*; Glebe, 72 acres; Buckland, Tithe, 110*l*; Pop. 3175.) Formerly R. of Allhallows, Exeter, 1851–61; Chap. of the Exeter City Prison 1840–61; Bodleian Lecturer, 1847; Rural Dean 1852–61. Author, *Reply to an Old Incumbent on the Offertory*, Exeter; *The Sin of Schism* (a Tract); *Election of Bishops*; *The Office of a Rural Dean.* [21]

WORTLEY, John, *Lower Close, Norwich.*—Queens' Coll. Cam. B.D. P.C. of St. Gregory's, City and Dio. Nor. 1864. (Patrons, D. and C. of Nor; P. C.'s Inc. 150*l*; Pop. 934.) [22]

WRANGHAM, Digby Strangeways, *South Cave Vicarage, Brough, Yorks.*—St. John's Coll. Ox. B.A. 1854, M.A. 1859; Deac. 1854 by Bp of G. and B. Pr. 1855 by Bp of B. and W. V. of South Cave, Dio. York, 1859. (Patroness, Mrs. Barnard; Tithe, 145*l*; Glebe, 100*l*; V.'s Inc. 260*l* and Ho; Pop. 896.) Formerly C. of Sobworth, Wilts, and Badminton, Glouc. 1854–59. Author, *The Temple of the Faith* (a Visitation Sermon, 1864), Skeffington, London, 6d; *The Loaves and Fishes*, Hull, 1860, 6d; *The Lord of the Harvest* (a Harvest Home Sermon, 1861), Hull, 6d; *Christ the Prisoner, Christ the Advocate, Christ the Judge* (three Assize Sermons), 1862, 6d each. [1]

WRANGHAM, Richard, *Garton Vicarage, Driffield, Yorks.*—St. Bees; Deac. 1856 by Bp of Carl. Pr. 1857 by Abp of York. V. of Garton-on-the-Wolds, Dio. York, 1862. (Patron, Ld Chan; V.'s Inc. 170*l* and Ho; Pop. 572.) Formerly C. of Skelton, near Redcar, 1856–58, and Middleton-on-the-Wolds, Yorks, 1858–62. [2]

WRATISLAW, Albert Henry, *School Hall, Bury St. Edmunds.*—Ch. Coll. Cam. 25th Sen. Opt. 3rd in 1st cl. Cl. Trip. B.A. 1844, M.A. 1847; Deac. 1845 and Pr. 1846 by Bp of Ely. Head Mast. of Bury St. Edmunds Gr. Sch. Formerly Fell. and Tut. of Ch. Coll. Cam; Head Mast. of Felstead Gr. Sch. Author, *Loci Communes, Common Places* (delivered in the Chapel of Ch. Coll. Cam. jointly with the Rev. C. A. Swainson), 1848, 3s 6d; *Bohemian Poems, Ancient and Modern, translated from the Original Slavonic, with an Introductory Essay*, 1849, 5s; *The Queen's Court Manuscript, with other Ancient Bohemian Poems, translated from the Original Slavonic into English Verse*, 1852, 4s; *Ellisian Greek Exercises*, 1855, 4s; several Pamphlets on University Reform; *Barabbas the Scapegoat*, and other Sermons and Dissertations, 1859; *Notes and Dissertations principally on Difficulties in the Scriptures of the New Covenant*, Bell and Daldy, 1863, 7s 6d; *Baron Wratislaw's Adventures translated out of the original Bohemian*, Bell and Daldy, 1862, 6s 6d; *An Enquiry into the Canonisation of St. John Nepomucen in 1729*, ib. 1866, 6d. [3]

WRAY, Cecil, *St. Martin's-in-the-Fields, Liverpool.*—Brasen. Coll. Ox. B.A. 1826, M.A. 1828; Deac. 1830 and Pr. 1831 by Bp of Ches. P. C. of St. Martin's-in-the-Fields with St. James's-the-Less P. C. Liverpool, Dio. Ches. 1836. (Patrons, Simeon's Trustees; P. C.'s Inc. 300*l*; Pop. 26,961.) Author, *The Suppression of any Portion of the Truth in the Work of Education unjustifiable* (a Sermon), 1843; *Catholic Reasons for rejecting the modern Pretensions and Doctrines of the Church of Rome* (a Tract), Masters, 1846, 14s per 100; *Catholic Tradition, or a Reverence for Antiquity the Leading Principle of the Reformation* (a Sermon), 1850; *Four Years of Pastoral Work* (a Memoir of the Rev. E. J. R. Hughes), 1854, 3s 6d; *The Scandal of permitted Heresy*; *Revelation a Reality*; *Sisterhoods on their Trial, or Protestantism, which? Crime and Cholera in Liverpool*, 1866; *The Religious Principles of Sisterhoods*; *a Sister's Love*; *The Ministry of Christ's Priesthood and Sacrifice*; various other Sermons and Tracts. [4]

WRAY, George, *Leven Rectory, Beverley, Yorks.*—Queen's Coll. Ox. B.A. 1802, M.A. 1803; Deac. 1804, Pr. 1805. Chap. to the Earl of Aberdeen 1811; R. of Leven, Dio. York, 1839. (Patron, J. T. Leather, Esq; Tithe, 732*l*; R.'s Inc. 1220*l* and Ho; Pop. 990.) Rural Dean 1843; Preb. of York 1848. Formerly R. of Crosscombe, Somerset, 1805; Lect. of Leeds 1807–38. Author, *Sermons on the Character, Pretensions and Doctrines of our Blessed Lord*, Longmans, 1838. [5]

WRAY, Henry, *Winchester.*—Trin. Coll. Cam. B.A. 1846, M.A. 1849; Deac. 1846 and Pr. 1847 by Bp of Ches. Precentor of Win. Cathl. 1859. Formerly Min. Can. Sacristan and Precentor of Ely Cathl. [6]

WRAY, William Marcus, *Forton, Gosport.*—St. Cath. Coll. Cam. B.A. 1847, M.A. 1851. Chap. R.N. [7]

WREN, Alfred Theodore, *Tur Langton, Kibworth, Leicestershire.*—St. Peter's Coll. Cam. Scho. of, 11th Sen. Opt. B.A. 1867; Deac. 1867 by Bp of Pet. C. of Church Langton, Tur Langton, and Thorpe Langton. [8]

WREN, Thomas, *Heybridge Vicarage, Maldon, Essex.*—V. of Heybridge, Dio. Roch. 1857. (Patrons, D. and C. of St. Paul's; V.'s Inc. 180*l* and Ho; Pop. 1476.) [9]

WRENCH, Frederick, *Stowting Rectory, Hythe, Kent.*—Trin. Coll. Ox. B.A. 1830, M.A. 1834. R. of Stowting, Dio. Cant. (Patron, the present R; Tithe, 314*l* 19s 6d; R.'s Inc. 318*l* and Ho; Pop. 213.) [10]

WRENCH, Harry Ovenden, *Malta.*—Wor. Coll. Ox. S.C.L. 1833, 4th cl. Lit. Hum. 1835, B.C.L. 1836; Deac. 1835 and Pr. 1836 by Bp of Lon. Chap. to the Forces, Malta; Sinecure R. of Stone-next-Faversham, Kent, Dio. Cant. (R.'s Inc. 220*l*; Pop. 91.) Formerly Sec. and Treasurer of the Maelor District Committee of S.P.C.K. 1840; Chap. to the High Sheriffs of Denbighshire 1842–48; Chap. to the High Sheriff of Montgomeryshire 1855; C. of Overton, Flintshire. [11]

WRENCH, Peter Elwin, *Truro.*—Ch. Coll. Cam. Sen. Opt. and B.A. 1845, M.A. 1849, B.D. 1856; Deac. 1846 and Pr. 1847 by Bp of Ches. P. C. of St. George's, Truro, Dio. Ex. 1852. (Patrons, the Crown and Bp of Ex. alt; P. C.'s Inc. 200*l*; Pop. 2846.) Surrogate; Chap. of the Royal Cornwall Infirmary. [12]

WRENCH, Thomas William, *St. Michael's Rectory, Cornhill, London, E.C.*—Corpus Coll. Cam. B.A. 1828, M.A. 1831; Deac. 1828, Pr. 1830. R. of St. Michael's, City and Dio. Lon. 1836. (Patron, Drapers' Company, Lond; R.'s Inc. 390*l*; Pop. 501.) Author, *A Sermon against Suicide*, 1833. [13]

WRENFORD, John Tinson, *St. Paul's Parsonage, Newport, Monmouthshire.*—Rostock, M.A. and Ph. D. 1866; Deac. 1849, Pr. 1850. P. C. of St. Paul's, Newport, Dio. Llan. 1855. (Patron, Bp. of Llan; P. C.'s Inc. 335*l* and Ho; Pop. 5879.) Formerly C. of St. Mary's, Cardiff, 1849–55, Roath 1850–55. Author, Tracts—*The Penny Bank*, 5s 6d *per* 100; *Kind Words to the Flock, viz., About the Sabbath Day*; *About the Sanctuary*; *About Infant Baptism*; *About Confirmation*, 5s *per* 100; *Romanizing the Church of England* (a Sermon), 4d; *Handbook of Geography of England and Wales*, 6d. [14]

WRENFORD, Thomas Brookes.—St. Bees; Deac. 1854 and Pr. 1855 by Bp of Man. Formerly Min. of the Chapel, Stockport Great Moor, 1835. [15]

WRENFORD, William Henry, *Usk, Monmouthshire.*—Dub. A.B. 1851; Deac. 1851 and Pr. 1852 by Bp of Llan. Mast. of the Gr. Sch. Usk, 1850; Chap. to Roger Edwards's Almshouses, Llangeview; C. in sole charge of Llanllowel, near Usk, 1862. Formerly C. of Bettws Newydd, near Usk. [16]

WREY, Arthur Bourchier, *The Rectory, Ashby Parva, Lutterworth.*—Trin. Coll. Cam. B.A. 1854, M.A. 1857; Deac. 1855 and Pr. 1856 by Bp of Roch. R. of Ashby Parva, Dio. Pet. 1864. (Patron, Ld. Chan; Tithe, 200*l*; Glebe, 30 acres; R.'s Inc. 280*l* and Ho; Pop. 160.) Formerly C. of Great Berkhamsted 1855–58, Buckingham 1859–62; P. C. of Knowl Hill, Berks, 1863–64. [17]

WREY, Bourchier William T., *Combeinteignhead, Teignmouth, Devon.*—Trin. Coll. Cam. S.C.L. 1863; Deac. 1854 and Pr. 1855 by Bp of Lich. R. of Combe-inteignhead, Dio. Ex. 1865. (Patrons, J. W. Harding and W. Long, Esqs; R.'s Inc. 350*l* and Ho; Pop. 417.) [18]

WRIGHT, Adam, *Bolton le-Sands, near Lancaster.*—St. Bees; Deac. 1861 and Pr. 1862 by Bp of Carl. C. of Bolton-le-Sands 1863. Formerly C. of Kirk-linton 1861. [19]

WRIGHT, Arthur, *Welton in-the-Marsh, Spilsby, Lincolnshire.*—St. John's Coll. Cam. Scho. of, 2nd cl. Cl. Trip. and B.A. 1853, M.A. 1856; Deac. 1854 and Pr. 1855 by Bp of Lin. P. C. of Welton-in-the-Marsh, Dio. Lin. 1857. (Patron, Charles L. Massingberd, Esq; Glebe, 100 acres; P. C.'s Inc. 167*l*; Pop. 445.) R. of Gunby, Dio. Lin. 1866. (Patrons, Mrs. Hairby, 2 turns, and then C. L. Massingberd, Esq; Tithe, 145*l* 16s; Glebe, 29 acres; Pop. 82.) Dioc. Inspector of Schs. Formerly C. of Ormsby with Driby, Linc. 1853–57. [20]

WRIGHT, Arthur, 17, *Richmond-crescent, Barnsbury-park, N.*—Queens' Coll. Cam. Scho. of, 1864, Fell. of, 1867, 12th in 1st cl. Cl. Trip; Deac. 1867 by Bp of Ely. C. of Trinity, Islington, 1867. [21]

WRIGHT, Arthur, *St. Mary's, Peterborough.*—Clare Coll. Cam. Sen. Opt. B.A. 1865; Deac. 1865 and Pr. 1866 by Bp of Pet. C. of St. Mary's, Peterborough, 1865. [1]

WRIGHT, Barrington Stafford, *Rye Vicarage, Sussex.*—King's Coll. Lond. Theol. Assoc. 1st cl. 1856, and M.A. by Abp of Cant. 1862; Deac. 1856 and Pr. 1857 by Bp of Lich. V. of Rye, Dio. Chich. 1862. (Patron, Duke of Devonshire; Tithe—App. 315*l*, V. 410*l*; V.'s Inc. 490*l* and Ho; Pop. 4500.) Surrogate. Formerly C. of Baslow, Derbyshire, 1856, Matlock, Bath, 1858; Asst. Chap. Parish Church, Sheffield, 1858; P. C. of Brothertoft 1861. [2]

WRIGHT, Benjamin, *St. Matthew's Vicarage, Wolverhampton.*—St. Bees 1844. V. of St. Matthew's, Wolverhampton, Dio. Lich. 1855. (Patrons, the Crown and Bp of Lich. alt; P. C.'s Inc. 175*l* and Ho; Pop. 6451.) [3]

WRIGHT, Buchan Warren, *Norton-Cuckney Vicarage, Mansfield, Notts.*—Clare Coll. Cam. B.A. 1842, M.A. 1845; Deac. 1842 and Pr. 1843 by Bp of Lin. V. of Norton-Cuckney, Dio. Lin. 1853. (Patron, Earl Manvers; Glebe, 20 acres; V.'s Inc. 250*l* and Ho; Pop. 1454.) Chap. of Holbeck-Woodhouse, near Mansfield, Dio. Lin. 1858. (Patron, Duke of Portland; Chap.'s Inc. 35*l*.) Author, *Modern Irreligion and Infidelity*, 1851; *The Late Revolution in Prussia, in its Relationship to the University and the School*, 1853; *The Beacon of Hope*, 1854; *The Centre of Unity*, 1854; *The Suicide*, 1857; etc. [4]

WRIGHT, Charles Henry Hamilton, *Dresden.*—Dub. A.B. 1857; Deac. 1859 by Bp of Rip. British Chap. at Dresden. Formerly C. of Middleton Tyas, Yorks, 1859. Author, *A Grammar of the Modern Irish Language*, 1855; *The Church, her Dangers and Duties*, 1857; *The Book of Genesis, in Hebrew, with a Critically Revised Text, Various Readings, and Grammatical and Critical Notes*, Williams and Norgate, 1859. [5]

WRIGHT, Charles Howard, 16, *Tavistock-street, Bedford-square, W.C.*—Lin. Coll. Ox. B.A. 1862, M.A. 1865; Deac. 1865 and Pr. 1866 by Bp of Lon. C. of St. Giles's-in-the-Fields, Lond. 1865. [6]

WRIGHT, Charles Sieum, *Broomhall-road, Sheffield.*—Dub. A.B. 1862; Deac. 1863 and Pr. 1864 by Abp of York. P. C. of Gillcar, Dio. York, 1866. (Patrons, The Church Burgesses of Sheffield; P. C.'s Inc. 150*l*; Pop. 11,200.) Formerly C. of St. Philip's, Sheffield, 1863–66. [7]

WRIGHT, David, *Stoke Bishop, near Bristol.*—Magd. Hall, Ox. B.A. 1844, M.A. 1847; Deac. 1844 and Pr. 1846 by Bp of Rip. P. C. of Stoke Bishop, Dio. G. and B. 1860. (Patrons, Trustees; Pop. 700.) Formerly Min. Can. of Bristol. Author, Sermons—*The Syrophœnician Woman, her Faith and Victory*, 1864, 1*s*; *The Word of Christ on Earth, not Peace, but a Sword*, 1867, 1*s*. [8]

WRIGHT, Edward Jones, 8, *Lansdown-place East, Bath.*—King's Coll. Lond. Deac. 1851 and Pr. 1854 by Bp of Ex. Chap. of United Hospital, Bath, 1862. Formerly C. of St. Paul's, Devonport, St. George's, Stonehouse, Wooton, Isle of Wight, and Walcot and St. Stephen's, Bath. [9]

WRIGHT, Francis Hill Arbuthnot, *Perran-Arworthal Vicarage, Penryn, Cornwall.*—Dub. A.B. 1844; Deac. 1846, Pr. 1847. V. of St. Stythians with Perran-Arworthal, Dio. Ex. 1847. (Patron, Earl of Falmouth; St. Stythians, Tithe—Imp. 255*l* 7*s* 6*d*, V. 322*l*; Perran-Arworthal, Tithe—Imp. 150*l* 15*s*, V. 100*l*; V.'s Inc. 450*l* and Ho; Pop. St. Stythians 2358; Perran-Arworthal 1517.) [10]

WRIGHT, Frank Bowcher, *Broughton Rectory, Manchester.*—Queen's Coll. Ox. 3rd cl. Lit. Hum. and B.A. 1832, M.A. 1836; Deac. 1833, Pr. 1834. R. of Broughton, Dio. Man. 1849. (Patrons, Trustees; R.'s Inc., arising from Endow. and Pew-rents, 500*l* and Ho; Pop. 7138.) [11]

WRIGHT, Frank Wynyard, 11, *Edmund-street, Horton, Bradford.*—St. John's Coll. Ox. B.A. 1866; Deac. 1867. C. of All Saints', Horton, 1867. [12]

WRIGHT, George, *Conisborough, Rotherham, Yorks.*—Literate; Deac. and Pr. 1812 by Abp of York. V. of Conisborough, Dio. York, 1844. (Patron, Abp of York; Tithe—App. 1*l* 11*s* 6*d*, Imp. 280*l*, V. 89*l*; Glebe, 66½ acres; V.'s Inc. 310*l* and Ho; Pop. 1655.) Author, *Mischiefs Exposed* (a Pamphlet on Mechanics' Institutes), 1826; *The Uncertainty of the Morrow* (a Sermon), 1826; Translator of *Spanheim's Ecclesiastical Annals, with Chronological Tables and Elements of Chronology and Geography of Palestine*, 1829, 2nd ed. 1840. [13]

WRIGHT, George Farncomb, *Overslade, near Rugby.*—Corpus Coll. Cam. 7th Wrang. and B.A. 1852; Deac. 1854 and Pr. 1856 by Bp of Ely. Formerly Fell. of Corpus Coll. Cam. 1852–55; Math. Mast. of Shrewsbury Sch. 1855–59; Math. Mast. of Wellington Coll. 1859. [14]

WRIGHT, George Newnham.—Brasen. Coll. Ox. B.A. 1835; Deac. and Pr. 1818. Formerly Reader of St. Mary Woolnoth, Lombard-street, Lond. and Mast. of the Gr. Sch. Tewkesbury. Author, *Translation of the Eton Greek Grammar*, 7th ed; *Greek Rudiments*, 16th ed. Whittaker; *Greek Sentences*, ib; *Euclid in General Terms*, ib; *Translation of Homer's Iliad*, 4 vols. ib; *Tours and Guides in the United Kingdom*, 4 vols; *London Encyclopædia*, 22 vols. Tegg; *Gorton and Wright's Topographical Dictionary*, 3 vols. Chapman and Hall; *Wright's Comprehensive Gazetteer of the World*, 5 vols. Kelly; *Illustrations of Scotland and Ireland*, 3 vols; *Mediterranean, Picturesque Survey of*, 2 vols; *China in the Nineteenth Century*, 4 vols; *France under Louis Philippe*, 4 vols; *Scenes in Wales, &c.* 2 vols; *The Rhine, Italy and Greece*, 2 vols; *Belgium Illustrated*; *Life of Louis Philippe of France*; *Life of William IV. of England*, 2 vols; *Life of Wellington*, 4 vols; *Cream of Scientific Knowledge*; *Lancashire in the Nineteenth Century*; *The People's Gallery of Art, &c.* 2 vols; *Bishop Berkeley's Works*, first complete collection, 2 vols. Tegg; *Reid's Metaphysical and Moral Essays*, first complete collection, 2 vols. ib; *Dugald Stewart's Philosophy of the Human Mind*, ib; *Goldsmith's England*, 2 vols; *Goldsmith's School Geography*; *Geography and History, by a Lady*; *Mangnall's Questions*; *Sallust, with English Notes*; *Keith's Astronomy*; *Fisher's Colonial Magazine*, 10 vols; *Tegg's London Magazine*, 12 vols; *Uncle Philip's Conversations on Natural History*; *Parley's Lives of the Apostles*; *Parley's Life and Travels of St. Paul*; *Ellis's Latin Exercises*; *Britannicus' Letters on Turkey and the Turks*, 1855. [15]

WRIGHT, Harry, 44, *Lansdown-crescent, Cheltenham.*—Magd. Hall, Ox. B.A. 1847, M.A. 1849; Deac. 1847 and Pr. 1848 by Bp of G. and B. Formerly C. of St. James's, Gloucester, 1847–48, Great Shurdington, near Cheltenham, 1848–59. [16]

WRIGHT, Henry, *Standard Hill, Nottingham.*—Ball. Coll. Ox. 3rd cl. Lit. Hum. 2nd cl. Sci. Nat. B.A. 1856, M.A. 1858; Deac. 1857 and Pr. 1859 by Bp of Lich. R. of St. Nicholas', Nottingham, Dio. Lin. 1867. (Patrons, Trustees; Glebe, 16 acres; R.'s Inc. 300*l* and Ho; Pop. 5154.) Formerly Chap. to the Butterley Co. 1857; P. C. of Swanwick, Derbyshire, 1862–67. Author, *Secret Prayer a Great Reality*, 1862, 3*d*. [17]

WRIGHT, Henry, *Thuxton Rectory, Attleborough, Norfolk.*—St. Cath. Coll. Cam. Scho. of, B.A. 1839, M.A. 1846; Deac. 1839 and Pr. 1840 by Bp of Lich. R. of Thuxton, Dio. Nor. 1846. (Patron, J. O. Taylor, Esq; Tithe—Imp. 12*l*, R. 260*l*; Glebe, 1½ acres; R.'s Inc. 260*l* and Ho; Pop. 139.) Formerly C. of Walsall, Staffs, 1839–40, Heacham, Norfolk, 1840–46; R. of Coston, Norfolk, 1851–55. Author, *Reply to Essays and Reviews*, 1861, 1*s*; *Is Geology antagonistic to Scripture?* 1863, 2*s* 6*d*, enlarged ed. 1864, 5*s*; *A Lecture on Geology in Connection with Scripture and the Antiquity of the Earth*, 1864, 6*d*; Articles, *Stone, Bronze, Iron, and Iron-Clads* in *Once a Week*, vols. I. and III. [18]

WRIGHT, Henry, *Outwell Rectory (Norfolk), near Wisbech, Cambs.*—Ch. Ch. Ox. 2nd cl. Lit. Hum. B.A. 1843, M.A. 1846. R. of Outwell, Dio. Nor. 1859. (Patron, Bp of Nor; R.'s Inc. 450*l* and Ho; Pop. 1265.) Formerly R. of Hambledon, Surrey, 1854–59. [19]

WRIGHT, Henry Edward, *Vange Rectory, Stanford-le-Hope, Essex.*—R. of Vange, Dio. Roch. 1864. (Patron, Major Spitty; R.'s Inc. 300*l* and Ho; Pop. 160.) Formerly R. of Litton, Somerset, 1836–64. [1]

WRIGHT, Henry Henton, 46, *Gell-street, Sheffield.*—King's Coll. Lond. Theol. Assoc; Deac. 1859 and Pr. 1860 by Abp of York. P. C. of St. James's, Sheffield, Dio. York, 1865. (Patron, V. of Sheffield; Pop. 4659.) Formerly C. of Worksop, Notts, and St. George's, Sheffield. [2]

WRIGHT, The Ven. Henry Press.—St. Peter's Coll. Cam. B.A. 1841; Deac. 1841 by Bp of B. and W. Pr. 1842 by Bp of G. and B. Archd. of British Columbia; Chap. to the Duke of Cambridge; Chap. to the Forces, Portsmouth. Formerly P. C. of St. Mary's, Leeds, 1845–46; Chap. to the Forces, Ionian Islands, 1846–53; Chap. to the Forces, Corfu, and Prin. Chap. to the Army in the East, 1854–56. Author, *Recollections of a Crimean Chaplain* and *Story of Prince Daniel and Montenegro*, 1857; *Letter to General Peel, Secretary of State for War, on Matters affecting the Body, Mind, and Soul of the British Soldier*, 1858; various Sermons. [3]

WRIGHT, Henry Wildey, *St. John's Parsonage, Newcastle-on-Tyne.*—Magd. Hall, Ox. B.A. 1832, M.A. 1836; Deac. 1832 by Bp of Roch. Pr. 1833 by Bp of Carl. P. C. of St. John's, Newcastle-on-Tyne, Dio. Dur. 1835. (Patron, V. of Newcastle-on-Tyne; P. C.'s Inc. 340*l* and Ho; Pop. 19,935.) Hon. Chap. to the Institution for the Deaf and Dumb for the four Northern Counties, Newcastle-on-Tyne; Surrogate. Formerly C. of Bedlington, Northumberland, 1832, Gosforth, 1834. [4]

WRIGHT, James Camper, *Bacton Vicarage, North Walsham, Norfolk.*—King's Coll. Cam. Browne's Medallist 1845–46, Camden Medallist 1846–47, B.A. 1848, M.A. 1852; Deac. 1851 and Pr. 1852 by Bp of Lin. V. of Bacton, Dio. Nor. 1858. (Patron, Lord Kimberley; Tithe, 215*l*; Glebe, 30 acres; V.'s Inc. 281*l* and Ho; Pop. 486.) Formerly Fell. of King's Coll. Cam. 1847–54; C. of Barham, Suffolk, 1854–56, Edingthorpe, Norfolk, 1856–58. [5]

WRIGHT, John, *Honington Vicarage, Shipston-on-Stour.*—Ch. Coll. Cam. B.A. 1837, M.A. 1841; Deac. 1837 and Pr. 1838 by Bp of Wor. V. of Honington, Dio. Wor. 1848. (Patron, Rev. H. Townsend; Tithe—Imp. 2*l* 2*s* 6*d*, V. 47*l* 10*s*; Glebe, 52 acres; V.'s Inc. 125*l* and Ho; Pop. 250.) [6]

WRIGHT, John, *Wem, Salop.*—St. John's Coll. Cam. B.A. 1857, M.A. 1860; Deac. 1858 and Pr. 1859 by Bp of Lin. C. of Wem 1865. Formerly C. of Hucknall Torkard, Notts, 1858, Plumtree, Notts, 1860. [7]

WRIGHT, John Adolphus, *Ickham Rectory, Wingham, Kent.*—Ch. Ch. Ox. B.A. 1822, M.A. 1825; Deac. 1827 by Bp of Dur. Pr. 1828 by Abp of York. R. of Ickham, Dio. Cant. 1839. (Patron, Abp of Cant; Tithe, 1000*l*; Glebe, 17 acres; R.'s Inc. 1080*l*; Pop. 588.) Formerly Chap. to the Abp of Cant. Author, *Sermons on the Sabbath.* [8]

WRIGHT, John George, *Carrington, Nottingham.*—Caius Coll. Cam. 2nd cl. Theol. Trip. B.A. 1857, M.A. 1863; Deac. 1858, Pr. 1859. P. C. of St. John's, Carrington, Dio. Lin. 1866. (Patron, Bp of Lin; P. C.'s Inc. 240*l*; Pop. 2426.) Formerly C. of Trinity, Nottingham, 1858. [9]

WRIGHT, John Howard Cressy, *Wolferlow Vicarage, Tenbury.*—St. John's Coll. Cam. Scho. of, 35th Wrang. and B.A. 1844, M.A. 1848; Deac. 1846 and Pr. 1847 by Bp of Ches. V. of Wolferlow, Dio. Herf. 1854. (Patron, the present V; Tithe, 210*l*; Glebe, 2 acres; V.'s Inc. 210*l* and Ho; Pop. 112.) Formerly C. of Stockport 1847–54. Author, *Sermons to Operatives on Strikes*, Stockport, 1853; *Sermon on the Eastern War*, 1854, 6*d*; and various Papers in Periodicals. [10]

WRIGHT, John Marsden, *Tatham Rectory, Wray, near Lancaster.*—Brasen. Coll. Ox. B.A. 1820, M.A. 1823; Deac. 1822, Pr. 1823. R. of Tatham, Dio. Man. 1823. (Patron, Pudsey Dawson, Esq; Tithe, 306*l*; Glebe, 71 acres; R.'s Inc. 356*l* and Ho; Pop. 588.) [11]

WRIGHT, Joseph, *East Halton Vicarage, Ulceby, Lincolnshire.*—Dub. A.B. 1847; Deac. and Pr. 1848. V. of East Halton, Dio. Lin. 1860. (Patron, Earl of Yarborough; V.'s Inc. 180*l* and Ho; Pop. 727.) Formerly C. of Burgh-on-Bain and Biscathorpe. [12]

WRIGHT, Joseph Farrell, *Bolton-le-Moors.*—St. Bees 1849. Lect. of Bolton-le-Moors. Formerly C. of St. Philip's, Sheffield. [13]

WRIGHT, Josiah, *Barham House, St. Leonard's-on-Sea.*—Trin. Coll. Cam. Sen. Opt. 1st cl. Cl. Trip. M.A. 1849; Deac. 1863 by Bp of Wor. Pr. 1865 by Bp of Chich. Author, *Help to Latin Grammar*, 4*s* 6*d*; *Hellenica*, 3*s* 6*d*; *Seven Kings of Rome*, 3*s*; *David, King of Israel*, 5*s*—all published by Macmillans. Translator, *Plato's Phædrus*, Parker, 4*s*. [14]

WRIGHT, Martin, *Ingleton Vicarage, Darlington.*—Literate; Deac. 1812, Pr. 1814. V. of Ingleton, Dio. Dur. 1845. (Patron, V. of Staindrop; V.'s Inc. 300*l* and Ho; Pop. 667. [15]

WRIGHT, Richard Robert, *Marhamchurch Rectory, Stratton, Cornwall.*—Dub. A.B. 1831, A.M. 1840; Deac. 1833 and Pr. 1834 by Bp of Ex. R. of Marhamchurch, Dio. Ex. 1848. (Patron, Rev. J. Kingdon; Tithe, 390*l*; Glebe, 38 acres; R.'s Inc. 450*l* and Ho; Pop. 581.) [16]

WRIGHT, Richard Franklin, *Wrangle Vicarage, Boston.*—St. John's Coll. Ox. B.A. 1842, M.A. 1853; Deac. 1842 and Pr. 1843 by Abp of York. V. of Wrangle, Dio. Lin. 1858. (Patroness, Mrs. Wright; Glebe, 12 acres; V.'s Inc. 760*l* and Ho; Pop. 1198.) Formerly C. of Wrangle 1848–58. [17]

WRIGHT, Robert Blayney, *Frinstead Rectory, Sittingbourne, Kent.*—Wor. Coll. Ox. 1843, 2nd cl. Lit. Hum. and B.A. 1847, M.A. 1850; Deac. 1849 by Bp of Ox. Pr. 1850 by Abp of Cant. R. of Frinstead, Dio. Cant. 1851. (Patron, Lord Kingsdown; Tithe, 280*l*; Glebe, 6¾ acres; R.'s Inc. 285*l* and Ho; Pop. 219.) Fell. of Wor. Coll. Ox. [18]

WRIGHT, Robert John William, *South Thoresby Rectory, Alford, Lincolnshire.*—Trin. Coll. Ox. B.A. 1826, M.A. 1827; Deac. 1826 and Pr. 1827 by Bp of Win. R. of South Thoresby, Dio. Lin. 1864. (Patron, Duchy of Lancaster; R.'s Inc. 230*l* and Ho; Pop. 162.) Formerly C. of Ovington and Itchin-Abbot, Hants, 1826–36; Chap. to the County Gaol at Winchester and to the County House of Correction, 1836–54; C. of Queenshead, Yorks, 1854–56; V. of Selston, Notts, 1856–64. Author, *Winchester Catechetical Tracts*; *A Prayer* (for the General Humiliation). [19]

WRIGHT, Samuel, *Shirley, Solihull, Warwickshire.*—P. C. of St. James's, Shirley, Dio. Wor. 1867. (Patron, R. of Solihull; P. C.'s Inc. 120*l* and Ho; Pop. 1062.) Formerly C. of Solihull. [20]

WRIGHT, Thomas Booth, *Broughton Rectory, Brigg, Lincolnshire.*—Wad. Coll. Ox. B.A. 1837, M.A. 1841; Deac. 1839 and Pr. 1840 by Abp of York. R. of Broughton, Dio. Lin. 1842. (Patron, the present R; Tithe, 1138*l* 10*s*; R.'s Inc. 1370*l* 10*s* and Ho; Pop. 1280.) [21]

WRIGHT, Thomas Preston, *Wray-park, Reigate.*—St. Cath. Hall, Cam. B.A. 1827, M.A. 1830; Deac. 1828, Pr. 1829. Formerly P. C. of St. Philip's, Dalston, Lond. 1844–60. Author, *Urgent Reasons for reviving the Synodal Functions of the Church*, Rivingtons, 1849; *A Letter to the Rev. Dr. Wordsworth in Reference to his Sermon, "On the Authority and Uses of Church Synods,"* ib. 1851. [22]

WRIGHT, Walter Melvill.—S.C.L. Cam. 1836; Deac. 1836, Pr. 1840. Chap. to the Forces, Limerick. Formerly Chap. to the Garrison, Woolwich, 1850–56. Author, *Service of Heaven*, 1844, 3*s* 6*d*; *Funeral Sermons*; *Sermons to Soldiers*; *God's Word the Soldier's Support*; etc. [23]

WRIGHT, William, *Colchester.*—Trin. Coll. Cam. 25th Wrang. B.A. 1833, M.A. 1842, D.C.L. 1850; Deac. 1833 and Pr. 1834 by Bp of Wor. Head Mast. of the Royal Gr. Sch. and Chap. of the Borough Gaol, Colchester, 1851. Formerly Prin. of Huddersfield Coll. 1837–44; Prin. of Leamington Coll. 1844–51. [24]

WRIGHT, William, *St. Peter's, Worcester.*—V. of St. Peter's with Whittington C. Worcester, Dio. 1852. (Patrons, D. and C. of Wor; V.'s Inc. 240*l* and Ho; Pop. St. Peter's 4749, Whittington 309.) [1]

WRIGHT, William, 13, *Hornton-street, Kensington, London, W.*—St. John's Coll. Ox. Pusey and Ellerton Heb. Scho. 1849, Kennicott Scho. 1851, 4th cl. Lit. Hum. and B.A. 1851, M.A. 1854; Deac. 1852 and Pr. 1853 by Bp of Ox. C. of St. Mary Abbott's, Kensington, 1855. Formerly C. of Hornborough, Oxon, 1852-54, South Warnborough, Hants, 1854. [2]

WRIGHT, William Ball, *Pontefract.*—Dub. Erasmus Smith's Exhib. 1862, A.B. 1865; Deac. 1866 by Abp of York. C. of Pontefract 1866. [3]

WRIGHT, William Bourke, *Wooler, Northumberland.*—Dub. Univ. Scho. 1861; Deac. 1866 and Pr. 1867 by Bp of Dur. C. of Wooler 1866. [4]

WRIGHT, William Henry, *Everton, Liverpool.*—St. Bees; Deac. 1845 by Bp of Ches. Pr. 1846 by Bp of Ox. P. C. of Ch. Ch. Everton, Dio. Ches. 1848. (Patron, T. B. Horsfall, Esq; P. C.'s Inc. 400*l*; Pop. 9334.) [5]

WRIGHT, William Henry, *Hemingborough Vicarage, Howden, Yorks.*—Jesus Coll. Cam. B.A. 1844; Deac. 1845, Pr. 1846. V. of Hemingborough, Dio. York, 1865. (Patron, the Crown; V.'s Inc. 100*l* and Ho; Pop. 1826.) Formerly P. C. of Godolphin, Cornwall, 1855–65. Author, *Masonic Discourses.* [6]

WRIGHTSON, Arthur Bland, *Hemsworth Rectory, Pontefract.*—Trin. Coll. Cam. B.A. 1816, M.A. 1820; Deac. 1816, Pr. 1817. R. of Hemsworth, Dio. York, 1840. (Patron, W. B. Wrightson, Esq; Tithe, 575*l*; Glebe, 199 acres; R.'s Inc. 885*l* and Ho; Pop. 975.) Rural Dean 1841; Preb. of York 1843. [7]

WRIGHTSON, William Garmonsway, 2, *Market-place, Bishops Auckland, Durham.*—Caius Coll. Cam. B.A. 1863; Deac. 1864 by Bp of Dur. C. of St. Andrew's and St Ann's, Bishops Auckland, 1864. [8]

WRIGLEY, Alfred, *The Grammar School, Clapham, Surrey, S.*—Glasgow, and St. John's Coll. Cam. Scho. of, Wrang. B.A. 1841, M.A. 1845, M.D. 1841; Deac. 1844 and Pr. 1845, by Abp of Cant. Head Mast. of the Clapham Gr. Sch. 1862; Fell. of the Royal Astron. Soc. 1841. Author, *Examples in Pure and Mixed Mathematics*, 1844, 8*s* 6*d*; *An Arithmetic*, 1862, 3*s* 6*d*; *A Companion to the Examples*, 1861, 16*s*. [9]

WROTH, Charles C., *Lindridge, Tenbury, Worcestershire.*—C. of Lindridge. [10]

WROTTESLEY, Edward John, *Brewood Vicarage, Stafford.*—Univ. Coll. Ox. 3rd cl. Lit. Hum. 1837, B.A. 1838, M.A. 1855; Deac. 1838, Pr. 1810. V. of Brewood, Dio. Lich. 1863. (Patron, Dean of Lich; V.'s Inc. 600*l* and Ho; Pop. 2045.) Formerly C. of Newton-heath, Manchester, 1838–41; P.C. of Tettenhall, Staffs, 1841–62; C. of Totteridge, Herts, 1862–63. [11]

WULFF, James Gee, *Illogan Rectory, Redruth, Cornwall.*—Dub. A.B. 1819; Deac. 1820, Pr. 1821. R. of Illogan with Trevenson C. and Portreath C. Dio. Ex. 1851. (Patron, J. F. Basset, Esq; Tithe, 670*l*; Glebe, 77 acres; R.'s Inc. 778*l* and Ho; Pop. 8342.) [12]

WYATT, Arthur Harvey, *Barton-under-Needwood, Burton-upon-Trent.*—C. of Barton-under-Needwood. [13]

WYATT, Arthur Montagu, *Raglan Vicarage, Monmouth.*—Deac. 1833 by Bp of St. D. Pr. 1834 by Bp of Lich. V. of Raglan, Dio. Llan. 1866. (Patron, Duke of Beaufort; V.'s Inc. 300*l* and Ho; Pop. 905.) V. of Llandenny, Dio. Llan. 1866. (Patron, Duke of Beaufort; V.'s Inc. 50*l*; Pop. 418.) Rural Dean of Abergavenny 1851. Formerly V. of Penrose, Monmouthshire, 1847–66. [14]

WYATT, Charles Francis, *Broughton Rectory, Banbury.*—Jesus Coll. Cam. B.A. 1818, M.A. 1821; Deac. 1818 and Pr. 1819 by Bp of Ox. R. of Broughton, Dio. Ox. 1819. (Patron, the present R; R.'s Inc. 740*l* and Ho; Pop 641.) J. P. for Oxon. [15]

WYATT, Charles Francis, *Forest Hill Parsonage, Oxford.*—Ch. Ch. Ox. B.A. 1842, M.A. 1845. P. C. of Forest Hill, Dio. Ox. 1848. (Patron, Lin. Coll. Ox; P. C.'s Inc. 85*l* and Ho; Pop. 191.) [16]

WYATT, Henry Herbert, 84, *Montpelier-road, Brighton.*—Queen's Coll. Ox. B.A. 1844, M.A. 1847; Deac. 1845 and Pr. 1846 by Bp of G. and B. Chap. of Chich. Dioc. Training Coll. for Schoolmistresses, Brighton, 1863. Formerly Travelling Sec. of S.P.G. 1852-56; Min. of Trinity Chapel, Brighton, 1856-66. Author, *Psalms and Hymns for Public Worship*, 2 eds. Longmans, 1*s*; various Sermons. [17]

WYATT, John Ingram Penfold, *Hawley Parsonage, Farnborough, Hants.*—Magd. Coll. Cam. and Trin. Hall. Cam. B.A. 1840, M.A. 1844; Deac. 1843 and Pr. 1845 by Bp of Chich. P. C. of Hawley, Dio. Win. 1857. (Patrons, Reps. of Rev. J. Randell; P. C.'s Inc. 100*l* and Ho; Pop. 805.) [18]

WYATT, Robert Edward, *St. Wilfred's, Cuckfield, Sussex.*—Ex. Coll. Ox. B.A. 1852, M.A. 1859; Deac. 1852 and Pr. 1853 by Bp of Lich. P. C. of St. Wilfred's, Dio. Chich. 1866. (Patron, V. of Cuckfield; P. C.'s Inc. 145*l*; Pop. 1200.) Formerly C. of Sheen, Staffs, 1852–56. [19]

WYATT, William Hindes, *Sneinton Parsonage, near Nottingham.*—Pemb. Hall, Cam. Sen. Opt. and B.A. 1819, M.A. 1822; Deac. 1821 by Bp. of Ches. Pr. 1821 by Bp of Nor. P. C. of Snenton, Dio. Lin. 1831. (Patron, Earl Manvers; Glebe, 27 acres; P. C.'s Inc. 200*l* and Ho; Pop. 11048.) Rural Dean; Surrogate. [20]

WYATT, William Robert, *Moreton, Oswestry, Salop.*—Brasen. Coll. Ox. 2nd cl. Lit. Hum. and B.A. 1822, M.A. 1825; Deac. 1824 and Pr. 1826 by Bp of St. A. P. C. of Moreton, Salop, Dio. St. A. 1860. (Patron, Ld Chan; P. C.'s Inc. 680*l*; Pop. 823.) Formerly one of the four Vicars of St. A. Cathl. 1836–60; P. C. of Dyserth, Flintshire, 1836–60. [21]

WYATT-EDGELL, Edgell, 2, *Lansdown-terrace, Ladbroke-square, London, W.*—Oriel Coll. Ox. B.A. 1823; Deac. 1824, Pr. 1825. [22]

WYBERG, Christopher Hilton, *Isell Vicarage, Cockermouth, Cumberland.*—Pemb. Coll. Cam. B.A. 1823, M.A. 1826; Deac. 1823 and Pr. 1825 by Bp of Carl. V. of Isell, Dio. Carl. 1826. (Patron, Sir W. Lawson, Bart; Tithe—Imp. 235*l*, V. 6*l* 16*s*; V.'s Inc. 159*l* and Ho; Pop. 492.) V. of Bromfield, Cumberland, Dio. Carl. 1826. (Patron, Bp of Carl; Tithe—App. 3*l* 3*s*, Imp. 102*l* 18*s* 2*d*, V. 157*l*; V.'s Inc. 275*l* and Ho; Pop. 1267.) [23]

WYBROW, F. T., *Sheepshed, Loughborough.*—C. of Sheepshed. [24]

WYBROW, Henry, *The Vicarage, Stretton-on-Dunsmore, Coventry.*—Wor. Coll. Ox. B.A. 1829; Deac. 1829 by Bp of Glouc. Pr. 1830 by Bp of Herf. V. of Stretton-on-Dunsmore, Dio. Wor. 1855. (Patrons, Simeon's Trustees; Tithe—App. 9*l* 8*s* 3*d*, Imp. 421*l* 14*s* 3*d*, V. 142*l*; Glebe, 165 acres; V.'s Inc. 500*l* and Ho; Pop. 1064.) Formerly C. of Winstone, Glouc. Brinsop, Herefordshire, Buraston and Nash, Salop, St. Columb Major, Cornwall, and Beverstone, Glouc; P. C. of St. Paul's, Newport, Monmouthshire. [25]

WYCHE, Cyrill Herbert Eyre, 18, *York-road, Lambeth, S.*—Trin. Coll. Cam. 2nd cl. Theol. Trip. 1857, B.A. 1856, M.A. 1864; Deac. 1857, Pr. 1859. C. of All Saints', Lambeth, 1865. Formerly C. of St. Mark's, Kennington, Lond. 1858. [26]

WYKEHAM-FIENNES, The Hon. Cecil Brownlow Twisleton, *New College, Oxford.*—New Coll. Ox. M.A. 1859; Deac. 1860 and Pr. 1861 by Bp of Pet. Formerly C. of Charlton with Newbottle, Northants, 1860; R. of Hamstall Ridware, Staffs, 1862–66. [27]

WYLD, Thomas John, *North Wraxhall, Chippenham.*—Ch. Ch. Ox. B.A. 1823, M.A. 1826; Deac. 1823, Pr. 1824. R. of North Wraxhall, Dio. G. and B. 1830. (Patron, the present R; Tithe, 391*l* 8*s*; Glebe, 87 acres; R's Inc. 500*l* and Ho; Pop. 466.) [28]

WYLD, W., *Crumpsall Rectory, Manchester.*—R. of Crumpsall, Dio. Man. 1859. (Patron, Bp of Man; Pop. 3306.) [29]

WYLD, William Thomas, *Woodborough, Pusey, Wilts.*—Ch. Ch. Ox. B.A. 1827, M.A. 1831. R. of

Blunsdon St. Andrew, near Highworth, Wilts, Dio. G. and B. 1834. (Patron, J. J. Calley, Esq; Tithe, 305*l*; R.'s Inc. 310*l*; Pop. 84.) R. of Woodborough, Dio. Salis. 1835. (Patron, G. H. Heneage, Esq; Tithe, 311*l* 10*s*; Glebe, 70½ acres; R.'s Inc. 416*l*; Pop. 406.) Rural Dean. [1]

WYLDE, George A., *Colchester.*—St. John's Coll. Cam. Theol. Assoc. King's Coll. Lond. Chap. to the Forces. [2]

WYLDE, John, *West Bromwich, Staffs.*—Magd. Coll. Ox. 2nd cl. Lit. Hum. and B.A. 1863, M.A. 1865; Deac. 1866 by Bp of Lich. C. of West Bromwich 1866. [3]

WYLDE, Robert, *Northfield, Birmingham.*—C. of Northfield 1867. [4]

WYLDE, Robert Henry, *Southwell, Notts.*—St. John's Coll. Cam. B.A. 1834, M.A. 1837; Deac. 1834, Pr. 1835. [5]

WYLIE, George, *Newnham Rectory, Winchfield, Hants.*—Queen's Coll. Ox. B.A. 1826, M.A. 1829. R. of Newnham with Maplederwell C. Dio. Win. 1844. (Patron, Queen's Coll. Ox; Newnham, Tithe, 310*l*; Maplederwell, Tithe, 223*l*; R.'s Inc. 568*l* and Ho; Pop. Newnham 367, Maplederwell 223.) Formerly Fell. of Queen's Coll. Ox. [6]

WYLIE, William John, *Wootton Vicarage, Ulceby, Lincolnshire.*—Trin. Coll. Cam. M.A. 1856; Deac. 1855 and Pr. 1856 by Bp of Ox. V. of Wootton, Dio. Lin. 1859. (Patroness, Mrs. Giffard; Glebe, 154 acres; V.'s Inc. 330*l* and Ho; Pop. 591.) [7]

WYMER, Edward, *Lowestoft, Suffolk.*—St. John's Coll. Cam. B.A. 1827; Deac. 1827, Pr. 1828. R. of Westwick, Norfolk, Dio. Nor. 1828. (Patron, J. B. Petre, Esq; Tithe, 186*l*; Glebe, 16 acres; R.'s Inc. 208*l*; Pop. 204.) P. C. of Ingham, Norfolk, Dio. Nor. 1832. (Patron, Bp of Nor; P. C.'s Inc. 126*l*; Pop. 480.) [8]

WYNCH, John William, *Madras.*—Sid. Coll. Cam. B.A. 1858, M.A. 1861; Deac. 1858 and Pr. 1859 by Bp of Wor. Asst. Chap. H.M. India Service 1861. Formerly C. of All Saints', Birmingham, 1858. [9]

WYNCOLL, Charles, *Margate.*—Deac. 1865 and Pr. 1866 by Abp of Cant. C. of St. John's, Margate, 1865. [10]

WYNDHAM, E., *Bishops Lydeard, Taunton.*—C. of Bishops Lydeard. [11]

WYNDHAM, Francis M., *Mission House, Well-close-square, E.*—Mert. Coll. Ox. B.A. 1861, M.A. 1864; Deac. 1862 and Pr. 1863 by Bp of Herf. C. of St. Saviour's Mission District, St. George's-in-the East. Formerly C. of Kington, Herefordshire, 1862–66. [12]

WYNDHAM, Hugh Henry Wyndham, *Hungerford, Fordingbridge, Hants.*—King's Coll. Lond. Theol. Assoc. 1866; Deac. 1866 by Bp of Win. C. of Hyde, Fordingbridge, 1866. [13]

WYNDHAM, John, *Sutton Mandeville, near Salisbury.*—Magd. Coll. Ox. B.A. 1834, M.A. 1836; Deac. 1839 and Pr. 1840 by Bp of Salis. R. of Sutton-Mandeville, Dio. Salis. 1840. (Patron, W. Wyndham, Esq; Tithe, 252*l*; Glebe, 40 acres; R.'s Inc. 336*l*; Pop. 289.) [14]

WYNN, James, *St. George's, Sowerby, Normanton.*—St. Bees; Deac. 1860 and Pr. 1861 by Bp of Ches. C. of St. George's, Sowerby, 1866. Formerly C. of All Saints', Liverpool, 1860–61, Burmantofts, Leeds, 1861–65, All Saints', Salterbebble, 1865–66. [15]

WYNNE, Charles James, *Wimbledon, Surrey, S.W.*—Jesus Coll. Ox. B.A. 1851, M.A. 1854; Deac. 1854 by Bp of Salis. Pr. 1855 by Bp of Win. Head Mast. of Wimbledon Sch. 1856. Formerly Sen. Asst. Cl. Mast. in Wimbledon Sch. 1851–54; C. of Bremhill with Highway, Wilts, 1854–55, Knebworth, Herts, 1855–56. [16]

WYNNE, Edward, 77, *New Cross-road, Deptford, S.E.*—Dub. 1st Downes Prizeman, A.B. 1857; Deac. 1857 and Pr. 1858 by Bp of Ches. Lond. Dioc. Home Miss. St. James's, Hatcham, New Cross. Formerly C. of St. Catherine's, Wigan, 1857–59; Sen. C. of Walcot, Bath, 1859–63; Min. of Percy Chapel, Charlotte-street, Fitzroy-square, Lond. 1863–65. [17]

WYNNE, Edward, *Park Gate, Rotherham.*—Ch. Miss. Coll. Islington; LL.D. of St. John's, University, Brooklyn, New York; Deac. 1862 by Bp of Lon. Pr. 1864 by Bp of Wor. Min. of the conventional district of Park Gate 1866. (Patron, Abp of York.) Formerly Miss. of C.M.S. in India 1862–64; C. of St. Clement's and Chap. of the Waterman's Church, Worcester, 1864–65. Author, several sacred songs with music; *Dissertation on Church Music with Original Compositions.* [18]

WYNNE, Edward Bristow Philips, *South Shoebury Rectory, Shoeburyness.*—Magd. Coll. Cam. LL.B. 1851. R. of South Shoebury, Dio. Roch. 1858. (Patron, R. Bristowe, Esq; Tithe, comm. 413*l*; R.'s Inc. 410*l* and Ho; Pop. 1502.) [19]

WYNNE, G. H., *Winterbourne Whitchurch, Blandford, Dorset.*—V. of Winterbourne Whitchurch, Dio. Salis. 1865. (Patron, Bp of Salis; V.'s Inc. 100*l* and Ho; Pop. 554.) Formerly C. of Belchalwell, Dorset. [20]

WYNNE, John, *Warnford Rectory, Southampton.*—Queen's Coll. Ox. B.A. 1817, M.A. 1822; Deac. and Pr. 1818 by Bp of Salis. Formerly R. of Warnford 1853–61. [21]

WYNNE, John, *Warnford Rectory, Southampton.*—St. Mary Hall, Ox. B.A. 1853, M.A. 1854; Deac. 1854 and Pr. 1855 by Bp of Salis. R. of Warnford, Dio. Win. 1861. (Patron, the present R; Tithe, 620*l*; Glebe, 20 acres; R.'s Inc. 640*l* and Ho; Pop. 460.) Formerly C. of Netherbury, and of West Lulworth, Dorset. [22]

WYNNE, John, *Corwen, Merionethshire.*—Jesus Coll. Ox. B.A. 1825, M.A. 1827; Deac. 1825 and Pr. 1826 by Bp of St. A. V. of Llandrillo, Dio. St. A. 1826. (Patron, Bp of St. A; Tithe, 329*l*; Glebe, 9¾ acres; V.'s Inc. 340*l*; Pop. 776.) Formerly C. of Llandrillo, 1825–26. [23]

WYNNE, Robert, *Scalford, Melton Mowbray.*—Wad. Coll. Ox. B.A. 1846, M.A. 1849; Deac. 1847 by Bp of Ox. Pr. 1849 by Bp of Win. V. of Scalford, Dio. Pet. 1865. (Patron, Duke of Rutland; V.'s Inc. 375*l* and Ho; Pop. 535.) Formerly C. of Steeple Barton, Oxford, and Wickham, near Fareham, Hants; P. C. of Corhampton, Hants, 1856–65. [24]

WYNTER, Abraham Farley, *Barnardiston, Haverhill, Suffolk.*—St. John's Coll. Ox. 4th cl. Lit. Hum. and B.A. 1833; Deac. 1836 and Pr. 1837 by Bp. of Lin. R. of Barnardiston, Suffolk, Dio. Ely, 1851. (Patron, the present R; Tithe—Imp. 8*l* 15*s*, R. 245*l*; Glebe, 21 acres; R.'s Inc. 270*l* and Ho; Pop. 280.) [25]

WYNTER, James Cecil, *Gatton Tower, Reigate, Surrey.*—St. John's Coll. Ox. B.A. 1827, M.A. 1830; Deac. and Pr. 1831. R. of Gatton, Dio. Win. 1833. (Patron, Lord Monson; Tithe, 226*l*; Glebe, 11¾ acres; R.'s Inc. 200*l*; Pop. 191.) Rural Dean. Author, *Hints on Church Colonisation*; *Discourses on Education and Colonisation*, 1850; etc. [26]

WYNTER, Philip, *St. John's College, Oxford.*—St. John's Coll. Ox. 2nd cl. Lit. Hum. B.A. 1815, M.A. 1819, B.D. 1824, D.D. 1828; Deac. 1816 by Bp of Ches. Pr. 1817 by Bp of Ox. President of St. John's Coll. Ox. 1828. Formerly Fell. of St. John's Coll. 1814–23; Tut. of St. John's 1823–28; Public Examiner 1825–26; Select Preacher 1830 and 1833. Author, *Two Sermons*, 1846. Editor, *Bishop Hall's Works*, Oxford, 1863. [27]

WYON, W. J., *Bilton, near Rugby.*—C. of Bilton. [28]

WYVILL, Christopher Edward, *Riddlesden, Keighley, Yorks.*—Dur. M.A. 1843; Deac. 1843 and Pr. 1844 by Bp. of Dur. C. of St. Mary's, Riddlesden, 1863. Formerly C. of St. Stephen's, South Shields. [29]

WYVILL, Edward, *Fingall Rectory, Bedale, Yorks.*—Brasen. Coll. Ox. B.A. 1816, M.A. 1819; Deac. 1816 and Pr. 1818 by Bp of Ches. R. of Fingall, Dio. Rip. 1820. (Patron, M. Wyvill, Esq; Tithe, 388*l* 5*s*; Glebe, 84 acres; R.'s Inc. 540*l* and Ho; Pop. 406.) R. of Spennithorne, Yorks, Dio. Rip. 1829. (Patron, M. Wyvill, Esq; R.'s Inc. 400*l*; Pop. 461.) Rural Dean of Fingall 1820. [30]

WYVILL, Edward Christopher, *Bedale, Yorks.*—Jesus Coll. Cam. B.A. 1849, M.A. 1853; Deac. 1849, Pr. 1850. [31]

YALDEN, George, *Twywell Rectory, Thrapstone, Northants.*—Ch. Ch. Ox. B.A. 1843; Deac. 1844 and Pr. 1846 by Bp of Pet. R. of Twywell, Dio. Pet. 1850. (Patron, William Alington, Esq; Glebe, 245 acres; R.'s Inc. 380*l* and Ho; Pop. 336.) [1]

YARD, Thomas, *Ashwell Rectory, Oakham, Rutland.*—Ex. Coll. Ox. B.A. 1832, M.A. 1839; Deac. 1834, Pr. 1835. R. of Ashwell, Dio. Pet. 1850. (Patron, Viscount Downe; Tithe, 412*l*; Glebe, 129½ acres; R.'s Inc. 605*l* and Ho; Pop. 206.) [2]

YARDE, Edward, *Porlock, Minehead, Somerset.*—Ex. Coll. Ox. B.A. 1864, M.A. 1867; Deac. 1865 and Pr. 1866 by Bp of B. and W. C. of Porlock 1867. Formerly C. of Luxborough, Somerset, 1865–67. [3]

YARDLEY, John, *Shrewsbury.*—St. John's Coll. Cam. B.A. 1828, M.A. 1831; Deac. and Pr. 1829 by Bp of Herf. V. of St. Chad's, Shrewsbury, Dio. Lich. 1836. (Patron, Ld Chan; V.'s Inc. 350*l*; Pop. 4760.) [4]

YARKER, John, *Isleworth, Middlesex, W.*—P. C. of St. John's, Isleworth, Dio. Lon. 1856. (Patron, V. of Isleworth; P. C.'s Inc. 150*l*; Pop. 1387.) [5]

YARKER, William, *Ravenstonedale Parsonage, Kirkby-Stephen, Westmoreland.*—Caius Coll. Cam. 1st Sen. Opt. and B.A. 1834; Deac. 1836, Pr. 1837. P. C. of Ravenstonedale, Dio. Carl. 1849. (Patron, Earl of Lonsdale; Glebe, 7 acres; P. C.'s Inc. 120*l* and Ho; Pop. 1264.) [6]

YARRANTON, A. J., *Tingrith, Woburn, Beds.*—C. of Tingrith. [7]

YARRANTON, Thomas Cook, *Wythall, Alvechurch.*—Sid. Coll. Cam. 6th Sen. Opt. Taylor's Exhib. B.A. 1843, M.A. 1847; Deac. 1844 and Pr. 1845 by Bp of Ex. P. C. of Wythall, Dio. Wor. 1859. (Patron, P. C. of King's Norton; Glebe, 35 acres; P. C.'s Inc. 170*l* and Ho; Pop. 1020.) Formerly C. of Beoley, Worcestershire. [8]

YATE, Charles Allix, *Long Buckby Vicarage, Rugby.*—St. John's Coll. Cam. 22nd Wrang. B.A. 1845, M.A. 1848; Deac. 1846 and Pr. 1847 by Bp of Lich. V. of Long Buckby, Dio. Pet. 1856. (Patron, Bp of Pet; Tithe, 90*l* 5*s* 4*d*; Glebe, 36 acres; V.'s Inc. 225*l* and Ho; Pop. 2500.) Formerly C. of Trinity, Burton-on-Trent, 1846–48, St. Lawrence's, Reading, 1848–56. [9]

YATE, George Edward, *Madeley Vicarage, Salop.*—St. John's Coll. Cam. Scho. of, B.A. 1848, M.A. 1851; Deac. 1849 and Pr. 1850 by Bp of Lin. V. of Madeley, Dio. Herf. 1859. (Patron, Rev. J. Bartlett; Tithe—Imp. 115*l* 10*s*, V. 226*l*; V.'s Inc. 300*l* and Ho; Pop. 4715.) Surrogate. Formerly Chap. to Hon. E.I.Co. in Bengal. [10]

YATE, George Lavington, *Wrockwardine Vicarage, Wellington, Salop.*—Queens' Coll. Cam. B.A. 1817, M.A. 1820; Deac. 1818 and Pr. 1819 by Bp of Herf. V. of Wrockwardine, Dio. Lich. 1828. (Patron, Earl of Powis; Tithe, comm. 343*l* 19*s*; V.'s Inc. 365*l* and Ho; Pop. 1048.) Rural Dean 1837; Surrogate 1842. [11]

YATE, William, *Dover.*—Deac. 1825 and Pr. 1826 by Bp of Lon. Author, *History of New Zealand*; *Letters on Confirmation.* [12]

YATES, Edmund Telfer, *Aylsham, Norfolk.*—Oriel Coll. Ox. B.A. 1834, M.A. 1836; Deac. 1835, Pr. 1836. V. of Aylsham, Dio. Nor. 1839. (Patrons, D. and C. of Cant; Tithe—App. 730*l*, V. 679*l*; Glebe, 4 acres; V.'s Inc. 683*l* and Ho; Pop. 2623.) Author, *The Rechabites* (a Sermon); *Questions and Answers on the Liturgy.* [13]

YATES, Henry W., 98, *Lansdowne-place, Brighton.* [14]

YATES, Hugh Seymour, *Henlow Vicarage (Beds), near Baldock, Herts.*—St. John's Coll. Cam. B.A. 1825; Deac. 1826, Pr. 1828. V. of Henlow, Dio. Ely, 1843. (Patron, Ld Chan; Tithe, App. 1*l* 5*s*; V.'s Inc. 290*l* and Ho; Pop. 1011.) [15]

YATES, James, *Swanscombe Rectory, Dartford, Kent.*—Pemb. Coll. Cam. 10th Wrang. and B.A. 1844, M.A. 1847, B.D. 1854; Deac. 1847 and Pr. 1848 by Bp of Ely. Fell. of Sid. Coll. Cam. R. of Swanscombe, Dio. Roch. 1867. (Patron, Sid. Coll. Cam; Tithe, 650*l*; Glebe, 40 acres; R.'s Inc. 695*l* and Ho; Pop. 1473.) Formerly Math. Mast. of King Edward's Sch. Birmingham. [16]

YATES, William, *Cottingham Rectory, Rockingham, Northants.*—R. of Cottingham with Middleton, Dio. Pet. 1866. (Patron, Brasen. Coll. Ox; Tithe, 631*l*; Glebe, 60 acres; R.'s Inc. 709*l* and Ho; Pop. 1139.) Formerly Fell. and Tut. of Brasen. Coll. Ox. [17]

YEARSLEY, Ralph Owen, *St. Michael's Rectory, Sutton Bonnington, Notts.*—Trin. Coll. Cam. B.A. 1862, M.A. 1866; Deac. 1864 and Pr. 1865 by Bp of Lon. R. of Sutton Bonnington, Dio. Lin. 1866. (Patrons, D. and C. of Bristol; Tithe, 6*l* 17*s*; Glebe, 243 acres; R.'s Inc. 661*l* 3*s* 10*d* and Ho; Pop. 638.) Formerly C. of St. John Baptist's, Woodlands, Isleworth, Middlesex, 1864–66. [18]

YEATMAN, Edward Kelson, *New South Wales.*—Wad. Coll. Ox. B.A. 1851, M.A. 1854; Deac. 1852, Pr. 1853. Formerly C. of Potterspury, Northants. [19]

YEATS, George, *New Barnet, N.*—St. John's Coll. Cam. Sen. Opt. B.A. 1855, M.A. 1858; Deac. 1855 and Pr. 1856 by Bp of Lon. P. C. of Trinity, New Barnet, Dio. Lon. 1866. Formerly C. of Plumstead, Kent, 1855–57, All Saints', Hertford, 1857–62, South Ockendon, Essex, 1862–66. [20]

YELD, Charles, *Lincoln.*—C. of St. Peter-at-Arches, Lincoln. [21]

YELLOLY, John, *Barsham Rectory, Beccles, Suffolk.*—Trin. Coll. Cam. B.A. 1831, M.A. 1834; Deac. 1832 and Pr. 1833 by Bp of Nor. R. of Barsham, Dio. Nor. 1856. (Patroness, Mrs. Suckling; Tithe, comm. 463*l*; Glebe, 80 acres; R.'s Inc. 550*l* and Ho; Pop. 238.) Formerly P. C. of Tring with Long Marston, Herts, 1845–56. [22]

YEO, Charles Oldham, *Roxby, near Brigg, Lincolnshire.*—Dub. A.B. 1848, A.M. 1856; Deac. 1851 and Pr. 1853 by Abp of Dub. C. in sole charge of Roxby and Risby 1862. Chap. R. N. 1854, retired on half-pay 1862 with medal for service in Baltic 1854–55. [23]

YEO, James Pearse, 6, *Manchester-row, Bury, Lancashire.*—St. Bees; Deac. 1853 and Pr. 1855 by Bp of Man. C. in sole charge of St. Peter's, Bury, 1862. Formerly C. of Standish, Lanc. 1853–55, St. Mary's, Bury, 1855–62. [24]

YEOMAN, Constantine Bernard, *Manfield Vicarage, Darlington.*—Trin. Coll. Cam. Scho. of, 1844, 27th Wrang. 3rd cl. Cl. Trip. B.A. 1845, M.A. 1848; Deac. and Pr. 1848 by Abp of York. V. of Manfield, Dio. Rip. 1860. (Patron, Ld Chan; Tithe, 293*l* 19*s* 4*d*; Glebe, 105 acres; V.'s Inc. 466*l* and Ho; Pop. 405.) Formerly V. of Yeddingham, 1848–54; R. of Marholm, Northants, 1854–60. [25]

YEOMAN, Henry Everard.—Trin. Hall, Cam. B.A. 1850, M.A. 1854. Chap. R. N. [26]

YEOMAN, Henry Walker, *Moor-Monkton, near York.*—Trin. Coll. Cam. Sen. Opt. 2nd cl. Cl. Trip. M.A. 1839; Deac. and Pr. 1840. R. of Moor-Monkton, Dio. York, 1850. (Patron, Ld Chan; Glebe, 672 acres; R.'s Inc. 891*l* 10*s* 6*d*; Pop. 381.) Rural Dean 1850; Preb. of York 1851. [27]

YERBURGH, Richard, *Sleaford Vicarage, Lincolnshire.*—Ch. Coll. Cam. B.A. 1840; Deac. 1841 and Pr. 1842 by Bp of Ches. V. of New Sleaford, Dio. Lin. 1851. (Patron, the present V; Glebe, 169 acres; V.'s Inc. 180*l* and Ho; Pop. 3467.) Chap. of Sir Robert Carre's Bede Houses, Sleaford, 1851; Surrogate 1851; Chap. to the Sleaford Union 1866. [28]

YEWENS, T. P. Leigh, *Coleford Parsonage, Bath.*—Deac. 1846, Pr. 1847. P. C. of Coleford, Dio. B. and W. 1865. (Patron, V. of Kilmersdon; P. C.'s Inc. 120*l* and Ho; Pop. 1387.) Formerly C. of Stoke-upon-Trent 1846-47, St. George's, Brandon Hill, Bristol, 1850–53, Cheshunt 1854, Bowdon, Cheshire, 1854–57, Camborne, Cornwall, 1857-58, Market Drayton, Salop, 1858-60, Ch. Ch. Cheltenham 1860–61, Stalbridge 1861-65; P. C. of Sneyd, Staffs, 1847–50. [29]

YOLLAND, Bartholomew Stephen, *Great Waltham, Chelmsford.*—Lin. Coll. Ox. 1852, B.A. 1857, M.A. 1859; Deac. 1857 and Pr. 1858 by Bp of Roch. C. of Great Waltham 1865. Formerly C. of Trinity, Halstead, Essex. [1]

YOLLAND, John, *Halstead, Essex.*—Queen's Coll. Ox. M.A. 1852; Deac. 1854 and Pr. 1855 by Bp of Lin. C. of Hadleigh, Essex, 1867. Formerly C. of Trinity, Halstead, 1864. [2]

YONGE, Denys Nelson, *Englefield, Reading.*—Ch. Coll. Cam. B.A. 1858; Deac. 1860 and Pr. 1861 by Bp of Ox. C. of Englefield 1865. Formerly C. of Shottesbrooke with White-Waltham, Berks, 1860–64, Lamorbey, Kent, 1864–65. [3]

YONGE, Duke, *Court House, Newton-Ferrers, Ivybridge, Devon.*—Ex. Coll. Ox. B.A. 1846, M.A. 1849; Deac. 1847 and Pr. 1848 by Bp of Ex. C. of Newton-Ferrers 1849. Formerly C. of Thorverton 1847. [4]

YONGE, John, *Puslinch, Yealmpton, Devon.*—Univ. Coll. Ox. B.A. 1812; Deac. and Pr. 1812 by Bp of Ex. R. of Newton-Ferrers, Devon, Dio. Ex. 1813. (Patron, the present R; Tithe, 444*l*; Glebe, 88¾ acres; R.'s Inc. 590*l*; Pop. 670.) Editor of Sermons by the Rev. James Yonge, 3 vols. Rivingtons, 30*s*; *Parochial Tracts*; etc. [5]

YONGE, John Eyre, *Eton College, Bucks.*—King's Coll. Cam. B.A. 1840, M.A. 1843; Deac. 1843 and Pr. 1844 by Bp of Lin. Asst. Mast. Eton Coll; Chap. to Lord de Lisle. [6]

YONGE, Reginald, *Wrockwardine Wood Rectory, Wellington, Salop.*—St. Cath. Hall, Cam. B.C.L. 1837; Deac. 1837 and Pr. 1838 by Bp of Ches. V. of Wrockwardine Wood, Dio. Lich. 1846, constituted a R. 1853. (Patron, Ld Chan; Tithe, 89*l*; Glebe, 5 acres; R.'s Inc. 220*l* and Ho; Pop. 2587.) [7]

YONGE, Richard, *Weston Parsonage, Crewe.*—St. John's Coll. Cam. B.A. 1834, M.A. 1838; Deac. 1836 by Bp of Ban. Pr. 1837 by Bp of Lich. P. C. of Weston, Dio. Ches. 1867. (Patron, Sir H. D. Broughton, Bart; Glebe, 2 acres; P. C.'s Inc. 70*l* and Ho; Pop. 673.) Formerly C. of Sandiacre, Derbyshire, and Lavenham and Brentely, Suffolk; Chap. to the Wolstanton and Burslem Union. [8]

YONGE, Vernon George, *Broughton, Eccleshall, Staffs.*—St. John's Coll. Cam. Scho. of, B.A. 1845; Deac. 1847 and Pr. 1848 by Bp of Herf. C. of Broughton. Formerly C. of Bolas Magna, Salop, 1855–63; P. C. of Doddington, Cheshire, 1863–66. [9]

YONGE, William Johnson, *Rockburne Parsonage, Fordingbridge, Hants.*—King's Coll. Cam. B.A. 1809, M.A. 1815. Chap. of the D. of Rockburne, Dio. Win. 1824. (Patroness, Lady Coote; Tithe—Imp. 80*l*, Chap. 705*l*; Chap.'s Inc. 710*l* and Ho; Pop. 507.) Rural Dean of Fordingbridge. Formerly Fell. of King's Coll. Cam. [10]

YONGE, William Wellington, *White-Waltham, Maidenhead, Berks.*—Ex. Coll. Ox. B.A. 1851; Deac. 1853 and Pr. 1854 by Bp of Nor. R. of White-Waltham with Shottesbrook, Dio. Ox. 1857. (Patron, C. Vansittart, Esq; Tithe, comm. 300*l*; Glebe, 249 acres; R.'s Inc. 600*l* and Ho; Pop. White-Waltham 148, Shottesbrook 917.) [11]

YORK, The Right Hon. and Most Rev. William THOMSON, Lord Archbishop of York, Primate of England and Metropolitan, *Athenæum Club, London, S.W.* and *Bishopthorpe Palace, York.*—Queen's Coll. Ox. 3rd cl. Lit. Hum. and B.A. 1840, M.A. 1843, B.D. and D.D. 1856; Deac. 1842, Pr. 1843. Consecrated Bp of G. and B. 1861, translated to York 1862. (Episcopal Jurisdiction, Yorkshire, except that portion of it allotted to the See of Rip; Inc. of See, 10,000*l*; Pop. 866,322; Acres, 2,261,493; Deaneries, 10; Benefices, 563; Curates, 205; Church Sittings, 225,614.) His Grace is Visitor of Queen's College, Oxford, and King's College, London; Elector of St. Augustine's College, Canterbury: One of the Lords of Her Majesty's Most Hon. Privy Council. His Grace was formerly Fell. Dean, Bursar and Tut. of Queen's Coll. Ox; Preacher to the Hon. Society of Lincoln's Inn, Lond. 1858–59; R. of All Souls', Marylebone, Lond. 1859–61. Author, *Outline of the Laws of Thought*, 1857, 5*s* 6*d*; *The Atoning Work of Christ*, 1854, 8*s*; *An Open College the best for All*, 1854; several Pamphlets and Sermons. [12]

YORK, Thomas, *Little Eversden Rectory, near Cambridge.*—Queens' Coll. Cam. 14th Wrang. and B.A. 1850, M.A. 1853; Deac. 1850 by Bp of Ely, Pr. 1851 by Bp of Llan. R. of Little Eversden, Dio. Ely, 1854. (Patron, Queens' Coll. Cam; Glebe, 172 acres; R.'s Inc. 224*l* and Ho; Pop. 239.) R. of Great Eversden, Dio. Ely, 1863. (Patron, Ld Chan; R.'s Inc. 59*l*; Pop. 314.) Fell. of Queens' Coll. Cam. [13]

YORKE, The Hon. Grantham Munton, *St. Philip's Rectory, Birmingham.*—R. of St. Philip's, Birmingham, Dio. Wor. 1844. (Patron, Bp of Wor; R.'s Inc. 1000*l* and Ho; Pop. 5019.) Preb. of Lich. 1846; Rural Dean of Birmingham; Dom. Chap. to the Bp of Wor. [14]

YORKE, The Hon. and Ven. Henry Reginald, *Wimpole Rectory, Assington, Cambs.*—St. John's Coll. Cam. B.A. 1826, M.A. 1829; Deac. 1827 and Pr. 1828 by Bp of Lin. Archd. of Huntingdon 1856. (Value, 200*l*.) R. of Wimpole, Dio. Ely, 1832. (Patron, Earl of Hardwicke; Tithe, 567*l* 10*s*; Glebe, 1½ acres; R.'s Inc. 569*l* and Ho; Pop. 406.) Can. of Ely, 1859. [15]

YORKE, James, *Marbury Rectory, Whitchurch, Salop.*—Sid. Coll. Cam. Math. and Div. Prizeman, B.A. 1840, M.A. 1843; Deac. 1840 and Pr. 1842 by Bp of Ches. C. in sole charge of Marbury 1849; Dom. Chap. to Viscount Combermere. [16]

YORKE, Richard, *Clanfield Vicarage, Faringdon, Oxon.*—St. Aidan's; Deac. 1854 and Pr. 1855 by Bp of Ches. V. of Clanfield, Dio. Ox. 1864. (Patron, G. H. Elliott, Esq; V.'s Inc. 120*l* and Ho; Pop. 547.) Formerly C. of Horwich, Lancashire, and Ducklington with Hardwick, Oxon. [17]

YORKE, Samuel, *Manor House, Fritwell, Bicester.*—Ex. Coll. Ox. Scho. of, Brasen. Coll. B.A. 1857, M.A. 1859; Deac. 1858 and Pr. 1859 by Bp of Man. V. of Fritwell, Dio. Ox. 1862. (Patron, William Willes, Esq; Glebe, 85 acres; V.'s Inc. 210*l* and Ho; Pop. 604.) Formerly C. of Preston 1858–61. [18]

YORKE, Thomas Henry, *Bishop Middleham Vicarage, Durham.*—Univ. Coll. Ox. B.A. 1804, M.A. 1810; Deac. and Pr. 1809 by Bp of Ox. V. of Bishop Middleham, Dio. Dur. 1813. (Patron, Ld Chan; Tithe—App. 4*s*, Imp. 384*l* 7*s* 6*d*, V. 151*l* 3*s*; Glebe, 55 acres; V.'s Inc. 191*l* 7*s* and Ho; Pop. 2146.) Formerly R. of St. Cuthbert's, Peasholm Green, 1818–58; Chap. to Countess de Grey 1818. Author, *An Introduction to the Sacrament of the Lord's Supper*, 1821. [19]

YOUNG, Charles John, *Mickleton Vicarage, Chipping Campden, Gloucestershire.*—Chich. Theol. Coll; Deac. 1856 and Pr. 1857 by Bp of Chich. V. of Mickleton, Dio. G. and B. 1865. (Patron, Ld Chan; Tithe, 106*l*; Glebe, 95*l*; V.'s Inc. 205*l* and Ho; Pop. 820.) Author, *Tour on the River Amazon and Rio Negro* in "*Vacation Tourists*," 1861. [20]

YOUNG, Edward, *Clifton Park, Bristol.*—Trin. Coll. Cam. Hulsean Prizeman 1827, B.A. 1828, M.A. 1831; Deac. 1828 and Pr. 1829 by Bp of Win. Author, *Protestantism or Popery*, 2 eds. 1843, 1*s*; *Art, its Constitution and Capacities*, 1854, 1*s* 6*d*; *The House of God and the People's Palace*, 7th thousand, 1854; *Pre-Raffaelitism*, 1856, 7*s*; *A Morning Service in German Score*, 4th ed. 1*s*; *The Harp of God, Twelve Letters on Liturgical Music*, 3*s* 6*d*; and various Sermons and Pamphlets. [21]

YOUNG, Edward Augustus, *Yarmouth, Isle of Wight.*—Dub. A.B; Deac. 1863 and Pr. 1864 by Bp of Win. C. of Yarmouth 1867. Formerly C. of Itchen Stoke, Hants. [22]

YOUNG, Edward Newton, *Quainton, Winslow, Bucks.*—Ch. Ch. Ox. B.A. 1818; Deac. 1819 and Pr. 1820 by Bp of Lon. R. of Quainton, Dio. Ox. 1822.

(Patron, Mr. Chalk; Glebe, 4½ acres; R.'s Inc. 565*l* and Ho; Pop. 929.) [1]

YOUNG, Frederick, *Pett Rectory, Hastings, Sussex.*—Ball. Coll. Ox. B.A. 1852, M.A. 1855; Deac. 1853 and Pr. 1854 by Bp of Lon. R. of Pett, Dio. Chich. 1857. (Patron, H. Young, Esq; Tithe, 508*l*; Glebe, 11 acres; R.'s Inc. 490*l* and Ho; Pop. 320.) Formerly C. of Bromley St. Leonard's, Middlesex. [2]

YOUNG, Frederick, *Walton Parsonage, Aylesbury.*—Queen's Coll. Ox. B.A. 1848; Deac. 1848 and Pr. 1850 by Bp of Ox. P. C. of Walton, near Aylesbury, Dio. Ox. 1859. (Patron, the Church Patronage Society; Endowment, 60*l*; P. C.'s Inc. 110*l* and Ho; Pop. 1100.) Formerly C. of Trinity, Reading, 1848–54, St. Paul's, Ball's-pond, Islington, Lond. 1854–56. [3]

YOUNG, Frederic Clement, *Chetwynd Rectory, Newport, Salop.*—Trin. Coll. Cam. B.A. 1861, M.A. 1865; Deac. 1863 and Pr. 1864 by Bp of Ely. R. of Chetwynd, Dio. Lich. 1866. (Patron, J. C. Burton Borough, Esq; Tithe, 600*l*; Glebe, 27 acres; R.'s Inc. 660*l* and Ho; Pop. 510.) Formerly C. of St. Andrew's-the-Less, Cambridge, 1863–66. [4]

YOUNG, Frederick John, *South Milford, Yorks.*—Ch. Coll. Cam. 1st cl. Nat. Sci. Trip. 1852, Jun. Opt. B.A. 1851, M.A. 1854; Deac. 1852 and Pr. 1853 by Abp of York. P. C. of South Milford, Dio. York, 1859. (Patron, Abp of York; Glebe, 51 acres; P. C.'s Inc. 170*l* and Ho; Pop. 1060.) Formerly C. of Sherburn 1852. [5]

YOUNG, James Gavin, *Hursley Vicarage, Winchester.*—Trin. Coll. Cam. Sen. Opt. B.A. 1841, M.A. 1844; Deac. 1842 and Pr. 1843 by Bp of G. and B. V. of Hursley and Otterbourne, Dio. Win. 1866. (Patron, Sir W. Heathcote, Bart. M.P; Hursley, Tithe—App. 1376*l* 2*s* 6*d* and 161 acres Glebe, V. 265*l* 7*s* 6*d*; Glebe, 1½ acres; Otterbourne, Tithe, 312*l*; Glebe, 8½ acres; R.'s Inc. 573*l* and Ho; Pop. Hursley 1022, Otterbourne 573.) Formerly C. of Boxwell 1842–48, Ilfracombe 1848–49, Brigstock 1849–54; Incumb. of St. Columba's, Kilmartin, Argyllshire, 1854–59; V. of Eatington, Stratford-on-Avon, 1860–66. [6]

YOUNG, James Peter, *Great Grimsby.*—Ex. Coll. Ox. B.A. 1866; Deac. 1867. C. of Great Grimsby 1867. [7]

YOUNG, James Reynolds, *Whitnash Rectory, Leamington.*—Caius Coll. Cam. B.A. 1832, M.A. 1840; Deac. and Pr. 1843 by Bp of Wor. R. of Whitnash, Dio. Wor. 1846. (Patron, Lord Leigh; Tithe, 280*l*; Glebe, 52 acres; R.'s Inc. 360*l* and Ho; Pop. 393.) Rural Dean. Author, *Whitnash Tracts* (printed and published at the Whitnash Press). [8]

YOUNG, J., *Wolverhampton.*—C. of St. Peter's, Wolverhampton. [9]

YOUNG, John Edward Mayne, *St. Saviour's Rectory, York.*—Dub. Catechetical Prize, A.B. 1849, A.M. 1860; Deac. 1852 and Pr. 1853 by Abp of York. R. of St. Saviour's, York, Dio. York, 1866. (Patrons, Trustees of Rev. Josiah Crofts; R.'s Inc. 190*l* and Ho; Pop. 3079.) Chap. of York Union Workhouse 1857. Formerly C. of St. Saviour's, York, 1852. [10]

YOUNG, John Fry, *Kingswood, Wootton-under-Edge, Gloucester.*—R. of Kingswood, Dio. G. and B. 1865. (Patrons, the Inhabitants; R.'s Inc. 99*l* and Ho; Pop. 1061.) Formerly C. of St. Peter's, Hereford. [11]

YOUNG, John William, *Great Malvern.*—St. John's Coll. Cam. B.A. 1847, M.A. 1851; Deac. 1853, Pr. 1855. C. of Great Malvern. Formerly C. of Ch. Ch. Lee, Kent. [12]

YOUNG, Julian Charles, *Ilmington Rectory, Shipston-on-Stour.*—Wor. Coll. Ox. B.A. 1829, M.A. 1830; Deac. 1830 by Bp of Bristol, Pr. 1830 by Bp of Chich. R. of Ilmington, Dio. Wor. 1858. (Patron, the present R; Glebe, 390 acres; R.'s Inc. 679*l* 15*s* and Ho; Pop. 920.) Formerly C. of Fairlight, Sussex; R. of Southwick, Sussex, 1844–58. [13]

YOUNG, Newton Barton, *Tilbrook Rectory, Kimbolton, Beds.*—R. of Tilbrook, Dio. Ely, 1865. (Patron, Lord St. John; R.'s Inc. 450*l* and Ho; Pop. 329.) [14]

YOUNG, Peter, *North Witham Rectory, Colsterworth, Lincolnshire.*—R. of North Witham, Dio. Lin. 1861. (Patron, Viscount Downe; R.'s Inc. 550*l* and Ho; Pop. 278.) [15]

YOUNG, Richard, *Riseley Vicarage (Beds), near Higham-Ferrers, Northants.*—New Coll. Ox. B.A. 1822, M.A. 1826; Deac. 1822 and Pr. 1823 by Bp of Herf. V. of Riseley, Dio. Ely, 1832. (Patron, Lord St. John; Tithe—Imp. 44*l*; Glebe, 26 acres; V.'s Inc. 200*l* and Ho; Pop. 1026.) Formerly V. of Melchbourne, Beds, 1841–64. [16]

YOUNG, Robert Goodwin, *Shrewsbury.*—Dub. A.B. 1852; Deac. 1848 and Pr. 1849 by Abp of York. Min. of St. Michael's, Shrewsbury. [17]

YOUNG, Thomas Drake, *St. Matthew's Parsonage, Sutton Bridge, Long Sutton, Lincolnshire.*—Queens' Coll. Cam. B.A. 1833, M.A. 1840; Deac. 1833 by Bp of Nor. Pr. 1836 by Bp of Roch. for Bp of Nor. P. C. of Sutton St. Matthew's, Dio. Lin. 1844. (Patron, Bp of Lin; Tithe, comm. 115*l*; Glebe, 2 acres; P. C.'s Inc. 270*l* and Ho; Pop. 1614.) Formerly C. of Wiggenhall St. Mary, Norfolk, 1833–34, Hickling, Norfolk, 1835–36, Fleet, Lincolnshire, 1837–39, School Room, Sutton Bridge, 1840–44. [18]

YOUNG, Walter, *King's College, Cambridge.*—King's Coll. Cam. B.A. 1840, M.A. 1843; Deac. 1841, Pr. 1842. Sen. Fell. of King's Coll. Cam. [19]

YOUNG, William, *Croxton, Caxton, Cambs.*—Oriel Coll. Ox. B.A. 1828, M.A. 1831, D.C.L. 1836. R. of Croxton, Dio. Ely, 1850. (Patron, G. O. Newton, Esq; R.'s Inc. 203*l* and Ho; Pop. 267.) V. of Eltisley, Cambs, Dio. Ely, 1850. (Patron, G. O. Newton, Esq; Tithe, Imp. 216*l* 9*s* 6*d*; V.'s Inc. 51*l*; Pop. 478.) [20]

YOUNG, William Boyter, *Russell-street, Reading.*—St. John's Coll. Ox. B.A. 1816, M.A. 1819; Deac. 1817, Pr. 1818. Surrogate for the Dios. of Ox. and Salis. [21]

YOUNG, William Edward Allen, 17, *Cannon-place, Brighton.*—Wor. Coll. Ox. B.A. 1856, M.A. 1859; Deac. 1859 and Pr. 1860 by Bp of Chich. C. of Kingston-by-Sea, Sussex, 1863. Formerly C. of Patcham and Asst. Chap. to the Troops at Brighton 1859–63. [22]

YOUNG, William Henry, *Oving Rectory, Aylesbury.*—Pemb. Coll. Ox. B.A. 1853, M.A. 1857; Deac. 1858 and Pr. 1860 by Bp of Ox. C. in sole charge of Oving, Bucks, 1866. Formerly C. of Little Milton 1858, Great Milton 1860, Benson 1860, Sunningwell 1863. [23]

YOUNGE, John Parkinson Bayly, *Wilsford, Grantham.*—Ch. Coll. Cam. B.A. 1842; Deac. 1843 and Pr. 1845 by Bp of Lin. R. of Wilsford, Dio. Lin. 1852. (Patron, the present R; R.'s Inc. 510*l*; Pop. 641.) [24]

YOUNGER, Thomas, *Castle-Sowerby Vicarage, Penrith.*—St. Bees; Deac. 1848 and Pr. 1849 by Bp of Man. V. of Castle-Sowerby, Dio. Carl. 1851. (Patrons, D. and C. of Carl; Tithe, Imp. 8*l*; Glebe, 300 acres; V.'s Inc. 100*l* and Ho; Pop. 906.) Formerly C. of St. Peter's, Preston, 1848–49, St. Mary's, Maryport, 1850–51. [25]

YOUNGHUSBAND, Edward, *Shrewsbury.*—St. Bees; Deac. 1824 by Bp of Ches. Pr. 1825 by Abp of York. Formerly V. of Egmanton, Notts, 1841–58. [26]

YULE, John Carslake Duncan, *Bradford Rectory, Hatherleigh, Devon.*—Jesus Coll. Cam. Foundation Scho. B.A. 1827, M.A. 1842; Deac. 1827 and Pr. 1828 by Bp of Ex. R. of Bradford, Dio. Ex. 1842. (Patrons, the R.s of East Down, Bratton-Fleming, and Goodleigh, as Trustees of Bampfield's Charity; Tithe, 305*l*; Glebe, 70 acres; R.'s Inc. 365*l* and Ho; Pop. 444.) R. of Hollacombe, Devon, Dio. Ex. 1843. (Patron, Ld Chan; Tithe, 70*l* 8*s*; Glebe, 32 acres; R.'s Inc. 94*l*; Pop. 87.) Rural Dean of Holdsworth; Surrogate. Formerly C. of Seaton with Beer, 1827–28, Zeal Monachorum 1828–32, Clannaborough and Down St. Mary, 1832–38; V. of Coleridge 1838–42; P. C. of Brushford 1838–42, all in Devon. Author, *Letter to Bishop of Exeter, proposing a Scheme for Settlement of Church Rate Question,* Exeter, 1861. [27]

WILLWOOD, John Old, *Compton Rectory, near Winchester.*—Wad. Coll. Ox. 2nd cl. Lit. Hum. 1811, B.A. 1813, M.A. 1816; Deac. and Pr. 1812. R. of Compton, Dio. Win. 1831. (Patron, Bp of Win; Tithe, 394*l*; Glebe, 2 acres; R.'s Inc. 400*l* and Ho; Pop. 279.) Author, *The Book of Psalms in the Authorised Verson arranged in Parallelisms, and distinguished as to the respective Speakers according to Bishop Horsley,* 1855. [1]

ZINCKE, Foster Barham, *Wherstead Vicarage, near Ipswich.*—Wad. Coll. Ox. 2nd cl. Lit. Hum. B.A. 1839; Deac. 1840 and Pr. 1841 by Bp of Win. V. of Wherstead, Dio. Nor. 1847. (Patron, the Crown; Tithe, 158*l*; Glebe, 17 acres; V.'s Inc. 180*l* and Ho; Pop. 245.) Chap. in Ordinary to the Queen 1858. Formerly C. of Andover 1840, Wherstead 1841. Author, *The School of the Future,* 1852, 7*s* 6*d*; *The Duty and Discipline of Extemporary Preaching,* Rivingtons, 1867, 5*s*, 2nd ed. enlarged, New York, 1867. [2]

Additions and Corrections.

ACWORTH, Carr Glyn, *St. Paul's, Preston.*—Ch. Ch. Ox. Jun. Stud. of, 2nd cl. Lit. Hum. B.A. 1867; Deac. 1867 by Bp of Man. C. of St. Paul's District, Preston, 1867. [3]

ADAMSON, James Bardell, *Taunton.*—Emman. Coll. Cam. 3rd Sen. Opt. and 2nd cl. Theol. Trip. B.A. 1866; Deac. 1867 by Bp Hobhouse for Bp of B. and W. C. of St. James's, Taunton, 1867. [4]

AITKENS, Charles Haughton, *Aylsham, near Norwich.*—Trin. Coll. and New Inn Hall, Ox. B.A. 1839, M.A. 1842; Deac. and Pr. 1840 by Bp of Wor. V. of Aylsham, Dio. Nor. 1867. (Patrons, D. and C. of Cant; Tithe, 684*l*; Glebe, 4 acres; V.'s Inc. 720*l* and Ho; Pop. 2623.) Formerly P. C. of Castle Church, Stafford, 1846; R. of Mavesyn Ridware, Staffs, 1852. [5]

ALLEN, Peregrine S., *Mainstone, Bishop's Castle, Salop.*—New Inn Hall, Ox. B.A. 1834; Deac. 1836 and Pr. 1837 by Bp of Ches. R. of Mainstone, Dio. Herf. 1867. (Patron, Ld Chan; Tithe, 343*l*; Glebe, 5 acres; R.'s Inc. 343*l*; Pop. 507.) Formerly C. of Ratby-cum-Grooby, Leicestershire. [6]

ALLEN, William Henry, *Quorndon, near Loughborough.*—St. Bees; Deac. 1867 by Bp of Pet. C. of Quorndon 1867. [7]

ALSOP, James Richard, *The Vicarage, Bednall, Stafford.*—Brasen. Coll. Ox. Hon. 4th cl. Lit. Hum. B.A. 1839; Deac. 1840 and Pr. 1841 by Bp of Ches. V. of Acton Trussell with Bednall, Dio. Lich. 1867. (Patrons, Hulme's Trustees; Tithe, comm. 218*l*; V.'s Inc. 270*l* and Ho; Pop. 617.) Formerly P. C. of West Houghton, Lancashire, 1842–67. Author, *Faith and Practice,* 1858, 10*s* 6*d*; and various Tracts and Sermons. [8]

AMORY, Thomas, *St. Teath, by Camelford, Cornwall.*—Wad. Coll. Ox. B.A. 1815; Deac. 1815 and Pr. 1816 by Bp of B. and W. V. of St. Teath, Dio. Ex. 1838. (Patron, Bp of Ex; Tithe, 242*l* 12*s*; Glebe, 30 acres; V.'s Inc. 275*l* and Ho; Pop. 1980.) Formerly C. of Lanteglos and Advent. [9]

ANDREWS, Christopher Robert, *Hough-on-the-Hill, Grantham.*—Emman. Coll. Cam. B.A. 1844; Deac. 1844 and Pr. 1845 by Bp of Lin. V. of Hough-on-the-Hill with Brandon C. Dio. Lin. 1855. (Patron, Earl Brownlow; V.'s Inc. 250*l* and Ho; Pop. 655.) Formerly C. of Manea 1845–55. [10]

ARMES, George Benjamin, *Tebay, Cumberland.*—St. John's Hall, Lond. Coll. of Divinity; Deac. 1867 by Bp of Carl. C. of Orton, Penrith, 1867. [11]

ARMITAGE, Joseph Akroyd, *Whitwood, near Normanton.*—Dub. A.B. 1852, A.M. 1859; Deac. 1852 and Pr. 1853 by Bp of Rip. R. of Whitwood, Dio. York, 1862. (Patron, Abp of York; Tithe, 120*l*; Glebe, 1 acre; R.'s Inc. 200*l*; Pop. 930.) Formerly C. of Farnley, Leeds, 1852–57, Thornley and Tow Law, Durham, 1857–61. [12]

ARUNDELL, Thomas, *Hayton Vicarage, York.*—St. John's Coll. Cam. 1851; Deac. 1852 and Pr. 1853 by Bp of Win. V. of Hayton with Bealby, Dio. York, 1860. (Patron, Abp of York; V.'s Inc. 388*l* and Ho; Pop. Hayton 210, Bealby 268.) Fell. of Geol. Soc; Sec. for the North of England of the Church Education Soc. for Ireland; Local Sec. of S.P.G. for the District of West Harthill. Formerly C. of Ch. Ch. Blackfriars, Lond. 1853–54, All Saints', Gordon-square, and Reader of Ch. Ch. Newgate-street, Lond. 1854–56; P. C. of St. Peter's, Hammersmith, 1856–60. Author, *Address to Parishioners of Hammersmith,* 1860; various Sermons. [13]

ATLAY, Brownlow Thomas.—St. John's Coll. Cam. B.A. 1854, M.A. 1857; Deac. 1856 and Pr. 1857 by Bp of Ely. Chap. on the Bengal Establishment. Formerly C. of Barrow 1856–60, Great Casterton 1860. [14]

AVERY, John Symons, *Budehaven, Cornwall.*—Magd. Hall, Ox. B.A. 1827; Deac. 1829 and Pr. 1830 by Bp of Ex. P. C. of St. Michael's, Budehaven, Dio. Ex. 1842. (Patron, Sir Thomas Dyke Acland, Bart; P. C.'s Inc. 130*l* and Ho; Pop. 766.) Formerly C. of Helland 1829–31, Golant 1831–42; Head Mast. of Lostwithiel Gr. Sch. 1831–42; all in Cornwall. [15]

BADNALL, James, *Endon, Stoke-on-Trent, Staffs.*—Bp Cosin's Hall, Dur. B.A. 1860; Deac. 1862 and Pr. 1863 by Bp of Lich. P. C. of Endon, Dio. Lich. 1864. (Patron, Earl of Macclesfield; P. C.'s Inc. 160*l*; Pop. 1241.) Formerly C. of Ash, Whitchurch, Salop, 1862. Author, *The Raising of Jairus's Daughter, or the Tears of Christian Mourners wiped away* (a Sermon), Leek. [16]

BAGSHAW, Henry Salmon, *Nassington Vicarage, Wansford, Northants.*—C. of Nassington 1867. Formerly C. of Enderby, Leicester. [17]

BAGSHAWE, Alfred Drake, *Shirland Rectory, near Alfreton, Derbyshire.*—Emman. Coll. Cam. B.A. 1858, M.A. 1861; Deac. 1860 and Pr. 1861 by Bp of Lich. C. of Shirland 1864. Formerly C. of Norbury with Snelston 1860, Norton 1863, Beauchieff Abbey 1863. [18]

BARKER, Edward Smack, *Wiesbaden.*—Magd. Hall, Ox. M.A; Deac. 1864 and Pr. 1865 by Bp of Lon. English Chap. at Wiesbaden. Formerly C. of Heston, Middlesex, 1864–67. [19]

BARNETT, Thomas Henry, *Cotham Brow, Bristol.*—Countess of Huntingdon's Coll. Cheshunt, and King's Coll. Lond; Deac. 1867 by Bp of G. and B. C. of St. Philip and St. Jacob's, Bristol, 1867. [20]

BAXTER, Henry Fleming, *Bushbury, Wolverhampton.*—Brasen. Coll. Ox. M.A. 1864; Deac. 1861 and Pr. 1862 by Abp of York. V. of Bushbury, Dio. Lich. 1867. (Patrons, Trustees; Tithe, 60*l*; Glebe, 60*l*; V.'s Inc. 170*l* and Ho; Pop. 2051.) Formerly C. of St. Thomas's, Scarborough, 1861–63, St. Philip's, Kensington,

1863–65, Bromfield, Salop, 1865–66, St. George's, Shrewsbury, 1866, Bushbury 1866–67. [1]

BEATY-POWNALL, Charles Colyear, *Milton Ernest Vicarage, near Bedford.*—Clare Hall, Cam. Sen. Opt. and B.A. 1829, M.A. 1832; Deac. 1831 and Pr. 1832 by Bp of Lin. V. of Milton Ernest, Dio. Ely, 1835. (Patron, Christopher Turner, Esq; Glebe, 246 acres; V.'s Inc. 267*l* and Ho; Pop. 485.) Chap. to the Earl of Portmore 1831; Rural Dean of Clapham 1840; Hon. Sec. to the Bedfordshire Board of Education 1844. Formerly C. of St. Paul's and South Carlton, Lincoln, 1831. [2]

BEAZOR, John Augustine, *Minster Lovell Vicarage, Witney.*—Deac. 1863 and Pr. 1865 by Bp of Ox. C. of Minster Lovell 1867. Formerly C. of Alderbury, Oxon, 1864–65, Witney 1865–67. [3]

BEEDHAM, Maurice John, *Claverley, Bridgnorth, Salop.*—Caius Coll. Cam. B.A. 1857; Deac. 1858 and Pr. 1859 by Bp of Herf. V. of Claverley, Dio. Herf. 1867. (Patron, John Beedham, Esq; Tithe, 12*l*; Glebe, 6½ acres; V.'s Inc. 300*l* and Ho; Pop. 1667.) Formerly C. of Claverley 1858–62, Kirby Moorside 1862–64, Westbury 1864. [4]

BEERS, John Banks, 49, *Chiswick street, Carlisle.*—Dub. A.B. 1865; Deac. 1866, Pr. 1867. C. of St. Mary's, Carlisle, 1866. [5]

BELL, James, *Clun, Salop.*—St. Cath. Coll. Cam. B.A. 1844, M.A. 1848; Deac. 1844 and Pr. 1845 by Abp of York. Warden of Trinity Hospital 1863. (Patron, Earl of Powis.) C. of Chapel Lawn 1863. Formerly C. of Sneaton 1844, Tickhill, 1846, Doncaster 1848; V. of Meole-Brace, Salop, 1854–58; Sen. C. of St. Botolph's, Bishopsgate, Lond. 1859–63. [6]

BENWELL, Henry, *Wimbledon, S.W.*—Ex. Coll. Ox. 3rd cl. Lit. Hum. and B.A. 1858, M.A. 1865; Deac. 1862 and Pr. 1863 by Bp of St. D. C. of Merton, Surrey, 1866. Formerly C. of St. Michael's, Aberystwith, 1862. [7]

BENNETT, John, *The Mount, Wordsley.*—Trin. Coll. Cam. B.A. 1866; Deac. 1866 by Bp of Lich. C. of Kingswinford 1866. [8]

BERESFORD, William, 36, *Duffield-road, Derby.*—Theol. Coll. Lichfield; Deac. 1867 by Bp of Lich. C. of St. Alkmund's, Derby, 1867. [9]

BERRIMAN, Richard, *Llanelly, Abergavenny.*—Lampeter, B.A. 1866; Deac. 1866 by Bp of St. D. C. of Llanelly 1866. [10]

BINGHAM, Samuel Henry, 16, *Belgrave-street, Euston-road N.W.*—C. of St. Jude's, Gray's-inn-road, Lond. 1867. Formerly C. of Sutton-le-Marsh, Lincolnshire, 1865–67. [11]

BIRD, John Joseph Strutt, *Beccles.*—Jesus Coll. Ox. B.A. 1866; Deac. 1867 by Bp of Nor. C. of Beccles 1867. [12]

BISHOP, Francis, *Walkern, Buntingford, Herts.*—Ch. Coll. Cam. B.A. 1861, M.A. 1865; Deac. 1865 and Pr. 1866 by Bp of Salis. C. of Walkern 1867. Formerly C. of Sturminster Marshall, Dorset. [13]

BLACKETT, Henry Ralph.—St. John's Coll. Cam. B.A. 1846, M.A. 1849; Deac. 1846 by Bp of Win. Pr. 1847 by Bp of Ox. P. C. of Ch. Ch. Woburn-square, Dio. Lon. 1867. (Patron, R. of Bloomsbury; P. C.'s Inc. 500*l* from pew-rents.) Formerly C. of Camden Church, Camberwell, 1846, St. George's, Hanover-square, 1848, Kettering 1851; Chap. of St. George's Workhouse, Hanover-square, 1857. [14]

BLAGDEN, Richard Thomas, *The Priory, Slapton, Dartmouth.*—St. John's Coll. Cam. B.A. 1848, M.A. 1852; Deac. 1848 and Pr. 1849 by Bp of Win. C. in sole charge of Street, near Dartmouth, 1867. Formerly P. C. of Claydon, Oxon, 1861–63, King Sterndale, Derbyshire, 1863–67. [15]

BLAIR, Robert Hugh, *The Commandery, Worcester.*—Dub. A.B. 1861, A.M. 1864; Deac. 1862 and Pr. 1863 by Bp of Wor. R. of St. Michael's, Bedwardine, Worcester, Dio. Wor. 1866. (Patrons, D. and C. of Wor; Glebe, 32 acres; R.'s Inc. 90*l*; Pop. 570.) Prin. of Coll. for Blind of the Higher Classes. [16]

BLISS, John Worthington, *Betteshanger Rectory, Sandwich.*—Trin. Coll. Cam. B.A. 1855; Deac. 1857 and Pr. 1858 by Abp of Cant. R. of Betteshanger, Dio. Cant. 1866. (Patron, Sir Walter C. James, Bart; Tithe, 166*l*; R.'s Inc. 166*l* and Ho; Pop. 210.) Formerly C. of Ide Hill, Sevenoaks, 1857–58, Speldhurst, Tunbridge Wells, 1858–63, Betteshanger 1865–66. [17]

BODINGTON, Charles, *St. Ann's, Willenhall, Staffs.*—King's Coll. Lond. Theol. Assoc. 1863; Deac. 1863 and Pr. 1864 by Abp of York. P. C. of St. Ann's, Willenhall, Dio. Lich. 1867. (Patrons, Henry Jevons, Esq. and John Mitchell, Esq; P. C.'s Inc. 140*l*; Pop. 4198.) Formerly C. of St. John's, Middlesborough, 1863–65, St. James's, Wednesbury, 1865–67. [18]

BOUGHEY, Robert, *Stoke-upon-Trent.*—Ch. Ch. Ox. B.A. 1865; Deac. 1866 by Bp of Lich. C. of Stoke-upon-Trent. [19]

BOULBY, Adam, *Aislaby, near Whitby.*—Queens' Coll. Cam. Scho. of, Sen. Opt. B.A. 1860; Deac. 1862 by Bp of Chich. Pr. 1864 by Abp of York. C. in sole charge of Aislaby 1866. Formerly Asst. Mast. in St. John's Coll. Hurstpierpoint 1861–63; C. of Hotham, Yorks, 1864–65. [20]

BOULTBEE, James, *Montpellier-terrace, Wrangthorn, Leeds.*—King's Coll. Lond. Theol. Assoc; Deac. 1852 and Pr. 1853 by Bp of Lin. P. C. of Wrangthorn, Dio. Rip. 1866. (Patrons, Crown and Bp of Rip. alt; P. C.'s Inc. 150*l*; Pop. 2000.) Formerly C. of Trinity, Nottingham, 1852, East Leake, Notts, 1854; Sen. C. of Kingswinford 1859. [21]

BOURKE, Thomas, *Gee Cross, near Manchester.*—Dub. A.B. 1854; Deac. 1858 and Pr. 1859 by Bp of Ex. C. of Gee Cross 1860. Formerly C. of Sampford Courtenay, Devon, 1858-60. [22]

BOURNE, George Hugh, *St. Andrew's College, Chardstock, Chard.*—Corpus Coll. Ox. B.A. 1863, B.C.L. 1866; Deac. 1863 and Pr. 1864 by Bp of Ox. Head Mast. of St. Andrew's Coll. Chardstock, 1867. Formerly C. of Sandford-on-Thames 1863–66. [23]

BOYD, The Very Rev. Archibald Boyd, *Deanery, Exeter.*—Trin. Coll. Cam. B.A. 1823, M.A. 1834. Dean of Exeter 1867. (Inc. 1100*l* and Res.) Formerly P. C. of Ch. Ch. Cheltenham, 1842–59; Hon. Can. of Glouc. 1857; P. C. of Paddington, Lond. 1859–67. [24]

BRAMAH, Joseph West, *Davington Priory, Faversham, Kent.*—Mert. Coll. Ox. Jackson's Scho. of, B.A. 1844, M.A. 1850, *ad eund.* Cam. 1852; Deac. 1845 and Pr. 1846 by Bp of Pet. Chap. of Don. of Davington, Kent, Dio. Cant. 1862. (Patron, Thomas Willement, Esq; Chap.'s Inc. 100*l*; Pop. 149.) Chap. of the Faversham Union (Stipend, 50*l*). Formerly C. of Kibworth Beauchamp, Leic. 1845–46; Usher in Berkhampstead Gr. Sch. Herts, 1846–47; C. of Worth, Sussex, 1847–50, Merton, Surrey, 1850–54; Tut. to the Earl of Strafford 1857–62. Author, Sermons—*The Sin and Danger of Hypocrisy*, 1850, and *The Responsibility of our Present Existence*, 1857. [25]

BRISTOW, Richard Rhodes, *St. Stephen's, Lewisham, S.E.*—St. Mary Hall, Ox. B.A. 1866; Deac. 1866 by Bp of Lon. Asst. C. of St. Stephen's, Lewisham, and Organising Sec. of the English Church Union 1867. Formerly Asst. C. of St. Philip's, Clerkenwell, 1866–67. [26]

BRITTON, James Pownall, *Heywood, near Westbury, Wilts.*—King's Coll. Lond. Assoc. 1864; Deac. 1864 and Pr. 1865 by Bp of Roch. C. of Heywood 1867. Formerly C. of Brightlingsea, Essex, 1864–67. [27]

BROMFIELD, George Henry Worth, 159, *Upper Kennington-lane, S.*—Univ. Coll. Ox. B.A. 1867; Deac. 1867 by Bp of Win. C. of St. Mary's-the-Less, Lambeth, 1867. [28]

BRYANS, Francis Richard, *Elworth Parsonage, Sandbach, Cheshire.*—Brasen. Coll. Ox. B.A. 1858; Deac. 1859 and Pr. 1860 by Bp of Ches. P. C. of St. Peter's, Elworth, Dio. Ches. 1867. (Patron, V. of Sandbach; Tithe, 40*l*; Glebe, 2¼ acres; P. C.'s Inc. 125*l* and Ho; Pop. 1051.) Formerly C. of Rode, Cheshire. [29]

BULSTRODE, George, *Ely.*—Emman. Coll. Cam. B.A. 1855; Deac. 1855 and Pr. 1856 by Bp of

Wor. C. of Trinity, Ely, 1861. Formerly C. of Redditch 1855-57, Gatcombe, Isle of Wight, 1857-61. Author, *Fifteen Sermons preached at Evening Service in Ely Cathedral*, Bell and Daldy, 1866. [1]

BULKELEY, Alexander Charles, *Berkeley Hall, Cheltenham.*—Caius Coll. Cam. B.A. 1863; Deac. 1867 by Bp of G. and B. C. of St. John's, Cheltenham, 1867. [2]

BULL, Charles, *The Parsonage, Stanley, Falklands, South America.*—M.A. by Abp of Cant. 1859; Deac. 1851 by Bp of Capetown, Pr. 1856 by Bp of Win. for Bp of Lon. Chap. of the Falkland Islands 1859. (Chap.'s Inc. 440*l* and Ho; Pop. 520.) Formerly C. of St. Anne's, Soho, of St. Michael's, Burleigh-street, Strand, and Ch. Ch. Endell-street, St. Giles's, Lond; Miss. of the S.P.G. at Plettenbergh Bay and Schoonberg, South Africa. [3]

BULLEN, John Allan, *St. James the Great, Devonport.*—St. Edm. Hall, Ox. B.A. 1861, M.A. 1864; Deac. 1862, Pr. 1863. P. C. of St. James the Great, Devonport, Dio. Ex. 1867. (Patron, the Crown; P. C.'s Inc. 300*l* and Ho; Pop. 7000.) Dioc. Inspector of Schs. Formerly C. in sole charge of Coffinswell, Devon, 1865. [4]

BULLOCK, John Frederic Watkinson, *Radwinter Rectory, Braintree, Essex.*—St. Peter's Coll. Cam. B.A. 1863; Deac. 1863, Pr. 1864. R. of Radwinter, Dio. Roch. 1864. (Patrons, Lord Maynard and Rev. W. T. Bullock; Tithe, 700*l*; Glebe, 62 acres; R.'s Inc. 760*l* and Ho; Pop. 946.) Formerly C. of Swaffham, Norfolk, 1863-64. [5]

BURDER, Frederick Gouldsmith, *Child's Ercall, Market Drayton, Salop.*—St. John's Coll. Cam. B.A. 1859; Deac. and Pr. 1861 by Bp of Lich. C. of Child's Ercall 1862. Formerly C. of Trinity, Shrewsbury, 1861. [6]

BURTON, Charles Henry, *Aigburth Lodge, near Liverpool.*—Corpus Coll. Cam. B.A. 1839, M.A. 1842; Deac. 1840 and Pr. 1841 by Bp of Ches. P. C. of St. Philip's, Liverpool, Dio. Ches. 1846. (Patroness, Miss Tobin; P. C.'s Inc. 500*l*.) Surrogate. Formerly C. of Staleybridge 1840-41, Bradford 1841-43, Leeds 1843-46. Author, Sermons—*Ye see the Distress that we are in* (during the financial panic in Liverpool), 1847; *Concurrent Festivals*, 1848; *The Royal Supremacy*, 1850; *War* (during the Russian war), 1854; *Jephtha's Vow* (to Lancashire Volunteers), 1862; etc. [7]

BURROUGHES, Robert, *Beighton Rectory, Acle, Norfolk.*—Oriel Coll. Ox. B.A. 1859, M.A. 1861; Deac. 1859 and Pr. 1860 by Bp of Pet. R. of Beighton, Dio. Nor. 1867. (Patron, Robert Fellowes, Esq; Tithe, 420*l*; Glebe, 8½ acres; R.'s Inc. 450*l* and Ho; Pop. 365.) Formerly C. of Kelton, Rutland, 1859-61, Pencombe, Herefordshire, 1861-64, Badsworth, Yorks, 1864-67. [8]

BYNG, The Hon. Francis E. C., 20, *Onslow-gardens, South Kensington, S.W.*—Ch. Ch. Ox. 3rd cl. Law and Modern History, B.A. 1857, M.A. 1858; Deac. 1858 and Pr. 1859 by Bp of Man. P. C. of St. Peter's, South Kensington, Dio. Lon. 1867. Formerly P. C. of Trinity, Twickenham, 1862-67. Author, *Sermons for Households*, 1867. [9]

CALTHROP, Francis James, *Wellingborough.*—Bp Hatfield's Hall, Dur. Theol. Scho. 1862, Barry Scho. 1864, Theol. Prizeman 1864, B.A. 1865; Deac. 1865 and Pr. 1866 by Bp of Pet. C. of Wellingborough 1865. [10]

CAMPBELL, David, 17, *Chapter-road, Lorrimore-square, S.*—St. Andrew's, Scotland, B.A. 1849, M.A. 1850; Deac. 1855 and Pr. 1856 by Bp. of Guiana. C. of St. Mary's, Newington, Surrey, 1866; Reader and Lect. at St. Paul's, Herne Hill, 1866. Formerly various appointments in Guiana 1855-65. [11]

CAMPBELL, Sholto Douglas, *Denmark-street, Gateshead.*—Trin. Coll. Cam. B.A. 1863; Deac. 1865 and Pr. 1866 by Bp of Wor. C. of Gateshead. Formerly C. of Nuneaton 1865. [12]

CARGILL, Eben, *Leeds.*—St. John's Coll. Cam. B.A. 1866; Deac. 1867 by Bp of Rip. C. of Leeds 1867. [13]

CARTER, William Adolphus, *Hitcham Rectory, Maidenhead.*—King's Coll. Cam. B.A. 1838, M.A. 1841; Deac. 1843 and Pr. 1844 by Bp of Lin. R. of Hitcham, Dio. Ox. 1866. (Patron, Eton Coll; Glebe, 80 acres; R.'s Inc. 495*l* and Ho; Pop. 210.) Fell. of King's Coll. Cam. Formerly 2nd Mast. of Eton Coll. [14]

CARTWRIGHT, Anson William Henry, 11, *Alderney-road, Mile End, N.E.*—Queens' Coll. Cam. B.A. 1856, M.A. 1864; Deac. 1859 by Bp of Wor. Pr. 1860 by Bp of Salis. C. of St. Augustine's, Stepney, 1867. Formerly C. of St. Michael's, Teignmouth, 1859, St. John's, Hammersmith, 1860, St. Paul's, Bow Common, 1863, St. Peter's, Stepney, 1867. Author, *Sermons on Subjects*, Bosworth, 1867, 2*s* 6*d*. [15]

CHAVASSE, Ludovick Thomas, 12, *Angell Park Villas, Wiltshire-road, Brixton, S.*—St. Peter's Coll. Cam. B.A. 1851, M.A. 1854; Deac. 1852 by Bp of Man. Pr. 1853 by Bp of Wor. P. C. of St. Saviour's, Herne Hill-road, Camberwell, 1867. Formerly V. of Rushall, Staffs, 1842-67. [16]

CHESSHIRE, John Stanley, *Kidderminster.*—Oriel Coll. Ox. B.A. 1864, M.A. 1867; Deac. 1866 by Bp of Wor. C. of Kidderminster 1866. [17]

CHICHESTER, John Chichester Burnard, *Morpeth, Northumberland.*—Trin. Coll. Cam. LL.B; Deac. 1866 by Bp of Dur. C. of Bothal, Morpeth. [18]

CHILD, John, *Jarrow-on-Tyne.*—Dur. Licen. in Theol. 1866; Deac. 1866 by Bp of Dur. C. of Jarrow 1866. [19]

CHILMAN, William Gwillim, *Wetwang, Driffield.*—St. Bees; Deac. 1866 and Pr. 1867 by Abp of York. C. of Wetwang with Fimber 1866. [20]

CHURTON, Matthew, *Newcastle-on-Tyne.*—King's Coll Lond. Theol. Assoc. 1857; Deac. 1857 and Pr. 1858 by Bp of Win. C. of St. John's, Newcastle, 1867. Formerly C. of St. Mary's, Southwark; Incumb. of Ch. Ch. Edinburgh, 1860-67. [21]

CHUTE, John, 11, *Edmund-street, Bradford, Yorks.*—Dub. A.B. 1864, A.M. 1867; Deac. 1866 and Pr. 1867 by Bp of Rip. C. of St. John's, Bradford, 1866. [22]

CLARK, James, *Alpine House, St. Helens, Lancashire.*—Universities of Göttingen and Lond. 1855-59, M.A. and Ph. D; Deac. and Pr. by Bp of Rip. C. of Rainford; Fell. of the Philol. Soc. Lond; F.R.A.S. Formerly Res. Tut. in Huddersfield Coll; C. of St. Stephen's, Lindley, Huddersfield; C. in sole charge of Trinity, South Shields; Sen. C. of Rotherham. Author, *The Spurious Ethics of Sceptical Philosophy*, 1860; *The Church as established in its Relations with Dissent*, Rivingtons, 1866, 5*s*; Sermons—*My Times are in Thy Hand*; *Behold now is the Accepted Time*; and *Take Heed how ye Hear*; *The Epochs of Language in General and of the English Tongue especially*; etc. [23]

CLARKE, Charles, *Esher, Surrey.*—Trin. Coll. Ox. Hon. 4th cl. Lit. Hum. B.A. 1837; Deac. 1840 and Pr. 1841 by Bp of Pet. Chap. to the Earl of Stamford and Warrington 1864. Formerly C. of Hinckley, Leic. 1841, Daventry, Northants, 1842, Norton, by Daventry, 1844-54. Author, *Sermons preached before the Judges at Northampton*; *Letters to an Undergraduate*; Novels—*Charlie Thornhill*; *Which is the Winner? The Beauclercs*; etc. [24]

CLARKE, Thomas, 2, *North-terrace, Wandsworth, S.W.*—Pemb. Coll. Cam. B.A. 1863; Deac. 1863 and Pr. 1864 by Bp of Man. C. of St. Anne's, Wandsworth, 1866. Formerly C. of St. Andrew's, Manchester, 1863. [25]

COATES, Arthur, *Pemberton, Wigan.*—Dub. A.B. 1846, A.M. 1859; Deac. 1846, Pr. 1848. P. C. of Pemberton, Dio. Ches. 1849. (Patron, R. of Wigan; P. C.'s Inc. 330*l*; Pop. 8358.) [26]

COCHRANE, Thomas, *The Rectory, Stapleford Abbotts, near Romford.*—Oriel Coll. Ox. B.A. 1858, M.A. 1860; Wells Theol. Coll. 1858-59; Deac. 1859 and Pr. 1860 by Bp of Lich. R. of Stapleford Abbotts, Essex, Dio. Roch. 1867. (Patron, Ld Chan; Tithe, 520*l*; Glebe, 20 acres; R.'s Inc. 560*l* and Ho; Pop. 502.) Formerly C. of Handsworth, near Birmingham, 1859-61, Acton, Middlesex, 1862; Mast. of Lord Leycester's Hospital, Warwick, 1863-67. [27

COCKERELL, Louis Arthur, *Boughton Aluph, Ashford, Kent.*—Ball. Coll. Ox. B.A. 1860; Deac. 1863 and Pr. 1864 by Bp of Roch. C. of Boughton Aluph 1865. Formerly C. of North Weald, Essex, 1863. [1]

COLBY, Edmund Reynolds, 3, *Wilton-place, Exeter.*—Emman. Coll. Cam. 1854, Ex. Coll. Ox. 2nd cl. Math. and B.A. 1856, M.A; Deac. 1857 by Bp of Ex. Pr. 1857 by Bp of B. and W. Formerly Chap. of H.M.S. "Madagascar," 1858; C. of St. Mary and St. Martin's, Scilly Isles; Chap. of H.M.SS. "Impérieuse" (China Medal), "Cossack," etc; Bodleian Lect. Exeter, 1864–66; Math. Mast. in Exeter Gr. Sch. 1865–66. [2]

COULTON, Richard, *Syerston, Newark, Notts.*—St. Bees; Deac. 1865 and Pr. 1866 by Bp of Lich. C. in sole charge of Syerston and Elston 1867. Formerly C. of Ch. Ch. West Bromwich, 1865–67. [3]

CORFE, Charles John, *St. Michael's College, Tenbury, Worcestershire.*—All Souls Coll. Ox. B.A. 1865; Deac. 1866 and Pr. 1867 by Bp of Herf. Asst. Mast. in St. Michael's Coll. 1865. [4]

CROOK, James Sutcliffe, *Wolverley Vicarage, Kidderminster.*—Dur. B.A; Deac. 1855 and Pr. 1856 by Bp of Wor. C. in sole charge of Wolverley 1867. Formerly C. of St. Matthew's, Smethwick, of Rowley Regis, Staffs, and of Lower Mitton, Worc. 1862–67. [5]

DAIMPRE, Isidore, *St. Ives, Cornwall.*—Dub. A.B. 1866; Deac. 1867 by Bp Chapman for Bp of Ex. C. of St. Ives 1867. [6]

DANIEL, Alfred Edwin, *Stanhope, near Darlington.*—Corpus Coll. Cam. B.A. 1859; Deac. 1866 by Bp of Carl. C. in sole charge of Eastgate, near Stanhope, Durham, 1867. Formerly C. of Ulverston 1867. [7]

DAVIES, John Lewis, *Llangynog Rectory, Oswestry.*—Literate; Deac. 1862 and Pr. 1866 by Bp of St. A. R. of Llangynog, Dio. St. A. 1867. (Patron, Bp of St. A; Tithe, comm. 180*l*; Glebe, 4½ acres; R.'s Inc. 200*l* and Ho; Pop. 721.) Formerly C. of Pennant, Oswestry, 1862–67. [8]

DAVIS, Daniel George, *St. James's-street, Monmouth.*—Jesus Coll. Ox. B.A. 1863; Deac. 1865 and Pr. 1866 by Bp of Herf. C. of Dixton, near Monmouth, 1867. Formerly C. of Kinnersley, Hereford, 1865. [9]

DOWLING, Barre B., *Chilton Rectory, Micheldever.*—Dub. and Magd. Hall, Ox. Heb. Prizeman, 2nd cl. Lit. Hum. B.A. 1849, M.A. 1860; Deac. 1852 and Pr. 1853 by Bp of Lich. R. of Brown Candover with Chilton Candover R. Dio. Win. 1864. (Patron, Lord Ashburton; Tithe, 600*l*; Glebe, 70 acres; R.'s Inc. 690*l* and Ho; Pop. 464.) Formerly C. of Trinity, Burton-on-Trent, 1852–55, St. Thomas's, Winchester, 1855–64. [10]

DRAKE, William, *Sedgebrook Rectory, Grantham.*—St. John's Coll. Cam. Fell. of, Crosse Univ. Scho. 15th Sen. Opt. 4th in 2nd cl. Cl. Trip. and B.A. 1835, M.A. 1838; Deac. 1837 by Bp of Lin. Pr. 1838 by Bp of Nor. R. of Sedgebrook with East Allington, Dio. Lin. 1864. (Patron, Ld. Chan; Tithe, 456*l*; Glebe, 220 acres; R.'s Inc. 850*l* and Ho; Pop. 520.) Hon. Can. of Wor. 1860; Chap. in Ordinary to the Queen 1861; Dioc. Inspector of Schs. for Deanery of North Grantham. Formerly Head Mast. of Collegiate Sch. Leicester, 1838–41; 2nd Mast. of Gr. Sch. and Lect. of St. John's, Coventry, 1841–57; V. of Trinity, Coventry, 1857–64; Rural Dean of Coventry 1859–64; Exam. in Hebrew in the Univ. of Lond. 1840–60; Select Preacher in the Univ. of Camb. 1862. Author, *Notes Critical and Explanatory on Jonah and Hosea*, Macmillans, 1853, 9*s*; *Sermons on Jonah, Amos and Hosea*, Hope and Co., 1853, 7*s* 6*d*; Various Sermons, Pamphlets, etc; contributions to Vol. I. of Smith's *Dictionary of the Bible.* [11]

DRING, Henry, *Streatham Common, S.*—King's Coll. Lond; Deac. 1867 by Bp of Win. C. of Immanuel's, Streatham Common, 1867. [12]

DUNCAN, William Robert, 161, *Islington, Liverpool.*—Sen. C. of St. Peter's, Liverpool, and Surrogate, 1854. [13]

DURNFORD, Henry Fermoy, *Victoria-villas, St. Ann's-road, New Wandsworth, S.W.*—Pemb. Coll. Ox. B.A. and S.C.L. 1866; Deac. 1867 by Bp of Win. C. of St. Mary's, Battersea, 1867. [14]

EARNSHAW, John, *Rock Ferry, Cheshire.*—King's Coll. Lond. Worsley Scho. Theol. Assoc. M.A. by Abp of Cant. 1860; Deac. 1857 and Pr. 1858 by Bp of Rip. Organising Sec. of S.P.G. for the Dio. of Man. and Archdeaconry of Liverpool. Formerly C. of St. John's, Bowling, Yorks; Prin. of the Sawyerpooram College, Madras. [15]

ECKERSLEY, James, *Preston.*—St. Mary Hall, Ox. B.A. 1866; Deac. 1867 by Bp of Man. C. of Preston 1867. [16]

EDWARDS, Edward, *Eglwys Fach, Glandovey, Shrewsbury.*—New Inn Hall, Ox. B.A. 1849; Deac. 1850 and Pr. 1851 by Bp of Wor. P. C. of Eglwys Fach, Dio. St. D. 1865. (Patron, Rev. L. C. Davies; P. C.'s Inc. 86*l*; Pop. 680.) Formerly C. of Bredon 1850, Pembroke 1858, Brecon 1860. [17]

EDWARDS, Edward, *Llangunnog, St. Clears, Carmarthen.*—Lampeter; Deac. 1864, Pr. 1865. C. of Llanstephan with Llangunnog 1864. [18]

EDWARDS, William Owen, *Aberayon Parsonage, Aberystwith.*—Lampeter, Scho. and Prizeman, B.D. 1867; Deac. 1860 and Pr. 1861 by Bp of Llan. P. C. of Aberayon, Dio. St. D. 1867. (Patrons, Inhabitants; P. C.'s Inc. 50*l* and Ho.) [19]

EMERY, The Ven. William, *Maryland Point, Stratford, E.*—Corpus Coll. Cam. B.A. 1847, M.A. 1850; Deac. 1849, Pr. 1850. Archd. of Ely 1864. Formerly Sen. Fell. Bursar and Tut. of Corpus Coll. Cam. Author, *Church Organization and Efficient Ministry* (Primary Charge), Deighton, Bell and Co. Cambridge, 1866. [20]

EVANS, David, *Llansantffraid Rectory, Corwen.*—St. Bees; Deac. 1851 by Bp of Ches. for Bp of St. A. Pr. 1852 by Bp of St. A. R. of Llansantffraid Glyn Dyfrdwy, Dio. St. A. 1862. (Patron, Bp of St. A; Tithe, 191*l*; Glebe, 60 acres; R.'s Inc. 260*l* and Ho; Pop. 400.) Formerly C. of Meifod, Montgomeryshire. [21]

EVANS, John Bagnall, *Union-street, Carmarthen.*—Jesus Coll. Ox. B.A. 1863, M.A. 1864; Deac. 1864 and Pr. 1865 by Bp of St. D. V. of Roch or Rupa, Dio. St. D. 1865. (Patron, Ld Chan; Tithe, 100*l*; V.'s Inc. 140*l*; Pop. 679.) Formerly C. of Llanboidy 1864–65. [22]

FENTON, George Livingstone, *Lucerne, Switzerland.*—Dub. Cl. Hons. and Latin Prize Poem, A.B. 1836; Deac. 1837 by Bp of Limerick, Pr. 1837 by Bp of Lich. English Chap. at Lucerne 1867. Formerly V. of Lilleshall, Salop; Sen. Chap. of Poona, India. [23]

FINDLEY, William, *Willington, near Burton-on-Trent.*—Deac. 1847 and Pr. 1848 by Bp of Ches. V. of Willington, Dio. Lich. 1855. (Patrons, Corporation of Etwall and Repton Gr. Sch; V.'s Inc. 155*l* and Ho; Pop. 477.) Chap. to Derbyshire County Lunatic Asylum. Formerly C. of St. John's, Beckermont, 1847, St. George's, Macclesfield, 1849, Dronfield 1851, Sutton-on-the-Hill 1853. [24]

FLETCHER, Isaac, *Guisborough, Yorks.*—Queen's Coll. Ox. M.A. 1864; Deac. 1865 and Pr. 1866 by Bp of Ely. C. of Guisborough 1867. Formerly C. of Burwell, Cambs, 1865–66. [25]

FOULKES, Francis, *Bawtry, Yorks.*—St. Bees; Deac. 1857 and Pr. 1858 by Abp of York. Chap. of St. Mary Magdalen's Hospital, Harworth, Notts, Dio. Lin. 1859. (Chap.'s Inc. 120*l*.) Formerly C. of Wombwell, Yorks, 1857. [26]

FOWERAKER, Edmund Thomas, *Cathedral School, Exeter.*—Deac. 1864 and Pr. 1867 by Bp of Jamaica for Bp of Ex. C. of St. Mary Major, Exeter, 1864. [27]

FRIPP, Charles Spencer, *St. Paul's Parsonage, Portland-square, Bristol.*—King's Coll. Lond. Theol. Assoc. 1849, Magd. Hall, Ox. B.A. and M.A. 1861; Deac. 1849 and Pr. 1850 by Bp of B. and W. P. C. of St. Paul's, Bristol, Dio. G. and B. 1867. (Patrons, Trustees; P. C.'s Inc. 380*l* and Ho; Pop. 2951.) Formerly C. of Churchill 1849–52, Kingston-Deverill 1853–55; P. C. of Ch. Ch. Nailsea, 1855–60; C. of Portishead 1862–67. [28]

FURMSTON, Edward, *Cockshutt, Shrewsbury.*—Dur. M.A. 1864; Deac. 1862, Pr. 1863. P. C. of Cockshutt, Dio. Lich. 1864. (Patron, V. of Ellesmere; P. C.'s Inc. 86*l*; Pop. 770.) Formerly C. of Denstone, Staffs. [29]

GARRATT, W. F. H., *Lymington, Hants.*—Trin. Coll. Cam. B.A. 1864; Deac. 1867 by Bp of Win. C. of Pennington, near Lymington, 1867. [1]

GEM, Samuel Harvey, *Malvern Wells.*—Univ. Coll. Ox. Hon. 4th cl. Lit. Hum. 1859, 2nd cl. Law and History, Ellerton Theol. Prize Essay 1861, B.A. 1861, M.A. 1864; Deac. 1865 and Pr. 1867 by Bp of Wor. C of St. Peter's, Malvern Wells, 1865. [2]

GOUGH, Frederick, *Cleeve Priors, Evesham.*—St. Aidan's; Deac. 1864 and Pr. 1865 by Bp of Wor. C. in sole charge of Cleeve Priors 1866. Formerly C. of St. Thomas's, Coventry, 1864. [3]

GRAHAM, George, 34, *Claremont-square, Islington, N.*—Corpus Coll. Cam. Scho. of, 1864, 1st cl. Theol. Trip. B.A. 1866; Deac. 1867 by Bp of Lon. C. of St. Michael's, Islington, 1867. [4]

HAIRBY, John, *Lastingham, Pickering, Yorks.*—St. Bees; Deac. 1855 and Pr. 1856 by Bp of Carl. C. of Lastingham 1867. Formerly C. of Bowness, Cumberland. [5]

HANHAM, Abdiel, *Sittingbourne, Kent.*—King's Coll. Lond. Assoc; Deac. 1858 and Pr. 1859 by Bp of Lon. P. C. of Trinity, Sittingbourne, Dio. Cant. 1867; Chap. to the Milton Union. Formerly C. of Ch. Ch. Poplar, Lond. 1858–60, Wareham, Dorset, 1860–63, Lowestoft, Suffolk, 1864–67. [6]

HAVERFIELD, William Robert, 4, *Dunsford-place, Bath.*—Corpus Coll. Ox. B.A. 1849, M.A. 1852; Deac. 1850, Pr. 1852. C. of St. John Baptist's, Bathwick. Formerly C. of Shipston-on-Stour; P. C. of Headington Quarry, Oxon. [7]

HAYNE, Leighton George, *The Vicarage, Helston, Cornwall.*—Queen's Coll. Ox. M.B. 1856, M.D. 1860; Deac. 1861 and Pr. 1862 by Bp of Ox. V. of Helston, Dio. Ex. 1866. (Patron, Queen's Coll. Ox; Tithe, 440*l*; V.'s Inc. 470*l* and Ho; Pop. 3841.) Coryphœus of the Univ. of Ox. 1863. Formerly Precentor of Queen's Coll. Ox; C. of St. John Baptist's, Ox. [8]

HICKMAN, William, *Christ Church Parsonage, Warminster, Wilts.*—Wad. Coll. Ox. 3rd cl. Law and History, B.A. 1857; Deac. 1865, Pr. 1866. P. C. of Ch. Ch. Warminster, Dio. Salis. 1867. (Patron, V. of Warminster; Glebe, 2 acres; P. C.'s Inc. 300*l* and Ho; Pop. 2166.) Formerly C. of Warminster 1865–67. [9]

HILL, William James, *Preston, Bedale, Yorks.*—Queen's Univ. Dub. A.B. 1865, A.M. 1866; Deac. 1867 by Bp of Rip. C. of Wensley, Yorks, 1867. [10]

HOARE, Henry Rosehurst, *Tunbridge Wells.*—Trin. Coll. Cam. B.A. 1848, M.A. 1851; Deac. 1850 and Pr. 1851 by Bp of Wor. Formerly C. of St. Matthew's, Rugby, 1850–53. [11]

HODGSON, John, *Kinver, Stourbridge, Staffs.*—Wad. Coll. Ox. B.A. 1851, M.A. 1856; Deac. 1851 and Pr. 1852 by Bp of Ex. V. of Kinver, Dio. Lich. 1867. (Patrons, Trustees; V.'s Inc. 200*l*; Pop. 3551.) Preacher of Kinver 1867. Formerly C. of Kinver 1854–58, Calstock 1858–61, Bedworth 1861–64, Wolverley 1864–67. [12]

HORTON, Harry Howells, *Handsworth, Birmingham.*—Rostock, Ph. D. and M.A. 1865; Queen's Coll. Birmingham; Deac. 1858, Pr. 1860. C. of Bishop Ryder's Church, Birmingham, 1860. Formerly Asst. Min. of St. Michael's, Birmingham, 1858. [13]

HOUGHTON, William, *Manaccan, near Helston, Cornwall.*—V. of Manaccan, Dio. Ex. 1865. (Patron, Bp of Ex; Tithe, 182*l*; Glebe, 60*l*; V.'s Inc. 255*l* and Ho; Pop. 505.) Author, *An Examination of Calvinism and especially of its Present Modified Forms,* Cleaver, 1836, 2nd ed. 1849; *An Enquiry into the Theology of the Anglican Reformers,* Hope and Co., 1852; *Rationalism in the Church of England,* Masters, 1863, 1*s* 6*d*; *Doctrine of the Church on the Divinity of our Lord,* ib. 1865, 1*s*; *Pauline Theology,* ib. 1866, 1*s* 6*d*. [14]

HUNTER, the Ven. James, 38, *St. Petersburg-place, Bayswater, W.*—Ch. Miss. Coll. M.A. by Abp of Cant. 1855; Deac. 1843 and Pr. 1844 by Bp of Lon. P. C. of St. Matthew's, Bayswater, Dio. Lon. 1867. (Patron, J. D. Allcroft, Esq; Pop. 5513.) Formerly Archd. of Cumberland, Rupert's Land. Author, *The Book of Common Prayer in Cree; The Gospels of St. Matthew, St. Mark and St. John in Cree; The Faith and Duty of a Christian in Cree; God's Charge to Zion's Watchmen* (an Ordination Sermon). [15]

HYSON, John Bezaleel, *Charminster, Dorchester.*—Ch. Miss. Coll; Deac. 1860 and Pr. 1861 by Bp of Lich. Chap. to the Dorset County Asylums 1866. Formerly C. of St. Mark's, Wolverhampton, and Crewkerne, Somerset. [16]

IAGOE, Joshua R., *Meltham Mills, Huddersfield.*—King's Coll. Lond; Deac. 1857 and Pr. 1858 by Bp of Man. P. C. of Meltham Mills, Dio. Rip. 1867. (Patron, Charles Brook, Esq; P. C.'s Inc. 300*l* and Ho; Pop. 1196.) [17]

IRELAND, William Stanley de Courcy, *Chalford Parsonage, Stroud, Gloucestershire.*—Dub. and Ox. B.A. 1852, M.A. 1858; Deac. 1853 and Pr. 1854 by Bp of Ches. P. C. of Chalford, Dio. G. and B. 1864. (Patron, Archd. of Gloucester; Glebe, 1 acre; P. C.'s Inc. 150*l* and Ho; Pop. 2018.) Formerly C. of Crewe Green, and Chap. at Crewe Hall, 1853; C. of Lever Bridge, Lancashire, 1855; Incumb. of St. Mary's, Montrose, Dio. Brechin, 1857; C. in sole charge of Dursley, Glouc. and Chap. of the Dursley Union 1860. Author, *Sermon on Education,* 1857; Contributor to Astronomical Transactions; etc. [18]

IRESON, Samuel Henry, 35, *Kenyon-terrace, Birkenhead.*—Didsbury and St. Aidan's; Jun. Soph. of Trin. Coll. Dub; Deac. 1866 and Pr. 1867 by Bp of Ches. Chap. of St. Aidan's Coll. Birkenhead, 1866. (Chap.'s Inc. 75*l*.) C. of St. George's, Liverpool, 1867. Formerly Chap. to Mariner's Church, Birkenhead, 1866–67. [19]

JANE, John, *St. Austell, Cornwall.*—St. Aidan's; Deac. 1864 and Pr. 1865 by Bp of Win. C. of St. Austell 1866. Formerly C. of St. John's, Richmond, Surrey, 1864–66. [20]

JENKINS, Edward, 1, *Railway-terrace, North Shields.*—Jesus Coll. Ox. B.A. 1867; Deac. 1867 by Bp of Dur. C. of St. Peter's, Tynemouth, 1867. [21]

KEDDLE, Samuel Shering, *Stoke St. Gregory, Somerset.*—Corpus Coll. Ox. B.A. 1859, M.A. 1862; Deac. 1861 and Pr. 1862 by Bp of Wor. C. of Stoke St. Gregory 1864. Formerly Math. Mast. at Bromsgrove Gr. Sch. 1860–64. [22]

KEMPSON, Howard, *Cookley Parsonage, Kidderminster.*—St. John's Coll. Cam. B.A. 1848; Deac. 1848 and Pr. 1849 by Bp of Lich. P. C. of Cookley, Dio. Wor. 1866. (Patron, William Hancocks, Esq; P. C.'s Inc. 206*l* and Ho; Pop. 1454.) Formerly C. of Yoxall 1848, and Great Haywood, Staffs, 1850; R. of St. Kenelm's, Romsley, 1851–66. [23]

LICHFIELD, The Right Rev. George Augustus Selwyn, *Eccleshall Castle, Staffs.*—Born at Hampstead, Middlesex, 1809; Eton, and St. John's Coll. Cam. Jun. Opt. and 1st cl. Cl. Trip. B.A. 1831, M.A. 1834; B.D. and D.D. 1841. Consecrated Bp of New Zealand 1841, translated to Lichfield 1867. (Episcopal Jurisdiction—the Cos. of Derby and Stafford, and a portion of the Co. of Salop; Inc. of See, 4500*l*; Pop. 1,121,404; Acres, 1,740,607; Deaneries, 49; Benefices, 625; Curates, 254; Church sittings, 305,933.) His Lordship was formerly Tut. at Eton and C. of Windsor. [24]

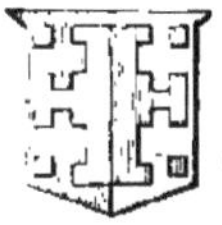

LLOYD, Felix Fitzroy Kelly, *Carlton-in-Lindrick, Worksop, Notts.*—Clare Coll. Cam. B.A. 1866; Deac. 1867 by Bp of Lin. C. of Carlton-in-Lindrick 1867. [25]

LLOYD, Jacob, *Crosswood, Aberystwith.*—Lampeter; Deac. 1856 and Pr. 1857 by Bp of Llan. P. C. of Llanwnws and Llanavan y Trawsgoed P. C. Dio. St. D. 1867. (Patron, Sir A. B. P. Chichester; P. C.'s Inc. 208*l*; Pop. Llanwnws 1295, Llanavan y Trawsgoed 567.) Formerly C. of Gellygaer Charity 1856, Narberth 1858. [26]

LOCK, Campbell, *Clergy Club, St. James's, S.W.*—Trin. Coll. Cam. B.A. 1861, M.A. 1864, M.A. Ox. (*causâ comitatis*) 1866; Deac. 1862 and Pr. 1863 by Bp of Pet. Formerly C. of Barwell, Leic. 1862–63; Sen. C. of Puddletown, Dorset, 1863–65; C. of St. Philip's, Clerkenwell, and St. Mary's, Kilburn, Lond. 1865–67. [1]

LUXMOORE, Charles Coryndon, *Fawley Vicarage, Wantage, Berks.*—Pemb. Coll. Ox. B.A. 1861, M.A. 1864; Deac. 1863, Pr. 1864. V. of Fawley, Dio. Ox. 1866. (Patron, Philip Wroughton, Esq; V.'s Inc. 100*l* and Ho; Pop. 243.) Formerly C. of Lamborne, Berks, 1864–65. [2]

MACDONALD, James Leonard, 18, *Albion-street, Hyde Park, W.*—Dub. A.B. 1860, A.M. 1866; Deac. 1861 and Pr. 1862 by Bp of Ches. C. of All Saints', Hyde Park, 1866. Formerly C. of St. Bride's, Liverpool. [3]

M'KENZIE, Douglas, *Raunds, Thrapstone, Northants.*—St. Peter's Coll. Cam. 33rd Wrang. B.A. 1864, M.A. 1867; Deac. 1864 and Pr. 1865 by Bp of B. and W. C. of Raunds 1866. Formerly 2nd Mast. of Crewkerne Gr. Sch. 1864; C. of Chaffcombe, Somerset, 1864. [4]

MARSTON, William, *Woodfield House, Llangarren, near Ross, Hereford.*—Deac. 1836 by Bp of Lin. Pr. 1836 by Abp of York. [5]

MAUGHAM, Henry Macdonald, *King-street, Sandwich.*—King's Coll. Lond. 1848; Oriel Coll. Ox. 3rd cl. Math. et Phy. and B.A. 1852, M.A. 1855; Deac. 1853 by Bp of Ox. Pr. 1855 by Bp of Win. C. in sole charge of St. Peter's, Sandwich, 1867. Formerly C. of Hazlemere with Tyler's Green, Bucks, 1852, St. Thomas's, Ryde, 1854, Reigate 1855, Chertsey 1858, Kirton, by Boston (sole charge), 1860, Sturry 1867. [6]

MEABY, George Kenneth, 11, *Mount-street, Pendleton, Manchester.*—Queens' Coll. Cam. Scho. of, B.A. 1865; Deac. 1865 and Pr. 1866 by Bp of Rip. C. of St. Thomas's, Pendleton, 1867. Formerly C. of St. Luke's, Bradford, Yorks, 1865. [7]

MIDDLETON, John Douglas, *West Cowes, Isle of Wight.*—Corpus Coll. Ox. 2nd cl. Lit. Hum. B.A. 1855, M.A. 1858; Deac. 1858 and Pr. 1859 by Bp of Win. P. C. of Trinity, West Cowes, with Gurnard C. Dio. Win. 1867. (Patron, Lieut.-Col. Edward Loyd; P. C.'s Inc. 370*l*; Pop. 2500.) Formerly C. of Carisbrook 1858, St. James's, Paddington, Lond. 1860; P. C. of Selsley, Glouc. 1862. [8]

NICOLL, Charles Alfred Samuel, *West Tytherley, Stockbridge, Hants.*—Brasen. Coll. Ox. B.A. 1863, M.A. 1867; Deac. 1865 and Pr. 1867 by Bp of Salis. C. of West Tytherley 1867. Formerly C. of Sherborne, Dorset, 1865. [9]

ORMSBY, G. Albert.—Pr. 1867 by Bp of Dur. Dom. Chap. to the Duke of Manchester 1867. [10]

O'SULLIVAN, Eugene, *Blagdon, Bristol.*—Dub. A.B. 1866; Deac. 1866 by Bp of B. and W. C. of Blagdon 1866 [11]

PALMER, Francis, 21, *Savile-row, Regent-street, W.*—Mert. Coll. Ox. B.A. 1850; Deac. 1855 and Pr. 1856 by Bp of Wor. Min. of St. George's Chapel, Albemarle-street, 1866. Formerly C. of Kidderminster 1855–57, St. Mary's, Dover, 1859–61, St. John's, Paddington, Lond. 1861–64. [12]

PEPLOE, Hanmer William Webb, *Weobley, Herefordshire.*—Pemb. Coll. Cam. B.A. 1859; Deac. and Pr. 1863 by Bp of Herf. V. of King's Pyon with Birley, Dio. Herf. 1866. (Patron, the Rev. John Birch Peploe; Tithe, Pyon, comm. 250*l*, Birley, comm. 125*l*; Glebe, 20*l*; V.'s Inc. 400*l*; Pop. King's Pyon 489, Birley 190.) [13]

PEPLOE, John Birch, *King's Pyon House, Weobley, near Hereford.*—Brasen. Coll. Ox. B.A. 1822, M.A. 1825; Deac. 1824 and Pr. 1825 by Bp of Herf. V. of Weobley, Dio. Herf. 1826. (Patron, Bp of Wor; Tithe—App. 358*l*, V. 250*l*; Glebe, 11 acres; V.'s Inc. 290*l* and Ho; Pop. 849.) Rural Dean. Formerly Preb. of Herf. 1844; V. of King's Pyon with Birley 1825–66. [14]

POPE, W. J., *Langar, Nottingham.*—Deac. 1863 and Pr. 1864 by Bp of Salis. C. of Langar with Barnston 1867. Formerly C. of Osmington, Dorset, 1863–67. [15]

POWER, John Peckleton, *Acton Beauchamp Rectory, Bromyard.*—Queens' Coll. Cam. B.A. 1842, M.A. 1846, *ad eund.* Ox; Deac. 1842 and Pr. 1844 by Bp of Ches. R. of Acton Beauchamp, Dio. Wor. 1867. (Patron, Rev. R. Cowpland; Tithe, 270*l*; Glebe, 36 acres; R.'s Inc. 310*l* and Ho; Pop. 205.) Formerly C. of West Cowes, Isle of Wight; P. C. of Nutley, Sussex. [16]

RANDOLPH, Herbert, *Marcham Vicarage, Abingdon, Berks.*—Ch. Ch. Ox. B.A. 1810, M.A. 1813; Deac. 1813 and Pr. 1814 by Bp of Ox. V. of Marcham with Garford C. Dio. Ox. 1819. (Patron, Ch. Ch. Ox; V.'s Inc. 455*l* and Ho; Pop. 1111.) Formerly P. C. of Hawkhurst, near Staplehurst, Kent, 1815–19. [17]

SEYMOUR, Richard Coxe, *Hurworth-on-Tees, Darlington.*—Brasen. Coll. Ox. Hulmeian Exhib. B.A. 1864, M.A. 1867; Deac. 1866 by Bp of Carl. Pr. 1867 by Bp of Dur. C. of Hurworth. Formerly C. of Woodhorn with Newbiggin, Northumberland. [18]

SLODDEN, Henry Thomas, *Witney.*—Ex. Coll. Ox. B.A. 1866; Deac. 1866 by Bp of Ox. C. of Witney 1867. Formerly C. of Colnbrook, Bucks, 1866–67. [19]

SMITH, Richard, *Winwick, Warrington.*—St. Bees 1857–58; Deac. 1859 and Pr. 1860 by Bp of Ches. C. of Winwick. Formerly C. of St. Thomas's, Norbury, Cheshire. [20]

THOMAS, Lewis Frederick, *Freemantle, Southampton.*—Queens' Coll. Cam. B.A. 1844; Deac. 1844 and Pr. 1845 by Bp of Salis. C. of Ch. Ch. Freemantle. Formerly P. C. of St. James's, Toxteth-park, Liverpool, 1856–66. [21]

WARD, Alfred, *Shutford, near Banbury.*—St. Cath. Coll. Cam. B.A. 1862, M.A. 1867; Deac. 1867 by Bp of Ox. C. of Swalcliffe, Oxon. [22]

WHITEHEAD, Thomas Henry, *Berwick-upon-Tweed.*—St. Bees; Rupert's Land Prizeman, 1st cl. Prizeman, and Librarian; Deac. 1865 by Bp of Carl. for Bp of Dur. Pr. 1867 by Bp of Dur. C. of Berwick-upon-Tweed 1867. Formerly C. of Kelloe, Durham, 1865–67. [23]

WILSON, Beverley S., *Duddo, Norham, Berwick-upon-Tweed.*—Trin. Hall, Cam. B.A. 1858; Deac. 1858, Pr. 1859. V. of Duddo, Dio. Dur. 1866. (Patrons, D. and C. of Dur; Tithe, 398*l*; V.'s Inc. 398*l* and Ho; Pop. 1000.) Formerly C. of Glen Magna, Leicester, 1858–60, Bothal, Northumberland, 1861; P. C. of Etall, Coldstream, 1865; V. of Alnham, Northumberland, 1866. [24]

Established Church of Ireland.

PROVINCE OF ARMAGH.

Comprising the Dioceses of Armagh and Clogher; Meath; Derry and Raphoe; Down, Connor, and Dromore; Kilmore, Elphin, and Ardagh; Tuam, Killala, and Achonry.

United Dioceses of Armagh and Clogher.

Armagh—Four Parishes in Derry, one-third of Tyrone, and nearly all Armagh and Louth;
Clogher—Counties of Monaghan, Fermanagh, and small part of Tyrone, Donegal and Louth.

ARCHBISHOP—The Right Hon. and Most Rev. MARCUS GERVAIS BERESFORD, Primate and Metropolitan of all Ireland, *Armagh Palace*, and 42, *Prince's Gardens, London, W.*
Born, 1801; Trin. Coll. Cam. B.A. 1823; M.A. 1828; D.D. 1840.
Consecrated Bp of Kilmore, 1854; translated to Armagh and Clogher, 1862.
(Armagh—Area, 869,770 acres; Pop. 386,260; Benefices, 71; Perpetual Cures, 37: Total, 108. Clogher—Area, 889,082 acres; Pop. 262,572; Benefices, 44; Perpetual Cures, 33; Total, 77; Inc. of See, 8328*l.*)
His Grace is Prelate of the Order of St. Patrick, Lord Almoner to the Queen, and a Privy Councillor in Ireland.

Diocese of Meath.

Counties of Meath, and West Meath, and part of King's County, and small part of Longford and Cavan.

BISHOP—The Right Hon. and Most Rev. SAMUEL BUTCHER, Premier Bishop of Ireland, *Ardbraccan House, Navan.*
Born, 1811; Dub. A.B. 1834; A.M. 1838; B.D. 1844; D.D. 1849. Consecrated Bp of Meath, 1866.
(Area, 1,264,995 acres; Pop. 253,354; Benefices, 102; Perpetual Cures, 10: Total, 112; Inc. of See, 4308*l.*)
His Lordship was formerly Fell., Prof. of Ecclesiastical History, and Regius Prof. of Divinity in Trin. Coll. Dublin.

United Dioceses of Derry and Raphoe.

Parts of Londonderry, Donegal, and Tyrone, and small part of Antrim.

BISHOP—The Right. Rev. WILLIAM ALEXANDER, *The Palace, Derry.*
Born, 1824; Brasen. Coll. Ox. B.A. 1847; M.A. 1853; D.D. 1867. Consecrated Bp of Derry and Raphoe, 1867.
(Derry—Area, 1,060,466 acres; Pop. 293,251; Benefices, 57; Perpetual Cures, 20: Total, 77.
Raphoe—Area, 885,430 acres; Pop. 169,204; Benefices, 32; Perpetual Cures, 9: Total, 41; Inc. of See, 5500*l.*)
His Lordship was formerly Dean of Emly.

United Dioceses of Down, Connor, and Dromore.

Counties of Down and Antrim, and small part of Armagh and Londonderry.

BISHOP—The Right Rev. ROBERT KNOX, *The Palace, Holywood, and Athenæum Club, London, S.W.*
Born, 1808; Dub. A.B. 1829; A.M. 1834; D.D. 1849. Consecrated Bp of Down, Connor, and Dromore, 1849.
(Down—Area, 356,188 acres; Pop. 163,943; Benefices, 38; Perpetual Cures, 10: Total, 48.
Connor—Area, 785,274 acres; Pop. 386,027; Benefices, 53; Perpetual Cures, 23: Total, 76.
Dromore—Area, 288,512 acres; Pop. 172,215; Benefices, 24; Perpetual Cures, 4: Total, 28; Inc. of See, 4000*l.*)

United Dioceses of Kilmore, Elphin, and Ardagh.

Roscommon, parts of Sligo, Galway, and Mayo, most part of Cavan, Leitrim, part of Fermanagh, all Longford, and part of West Meath.

BISHOP—The Right Rev. HAMILTON VERSCHOYLE, *Kilmore House, Cavan.*
Born, 1803; Dub. A.B. 1826; A.M. 1829; D.D. 1862. Consecrated Bp of Kilmore, Elphin, and Ardagh, 1862.
(Kilmore—Area, 738,503 acres; Pop. 209,714; Benefices, 36; Perpetual Cures, 19: Total, 55.
Elphin—Area, 730,885 acres; Pop. 201,879; Benefices, 36; Perpetual Cures, 5: Total, 41.
Ardagh—Area, 490,232 acres; Pop. 136,298; Benefices, 30; Perpetual Cures, 1: Total, 31; Inc. of See, 5248*l.*)

United Dioceses of Tuam, Killala, and Achonry.

Counties of Galway, Mayo, and small part of Roscommon and Sligo.
BISHOP—The Hon. and Right Rev. CHARLES BRODRICK BERNARD, *Tuam Palace, Galway*.
Born, 1811; Ball. Coll. Ox. B.A. 1832; D.D. 1866.
Consecrated Bp of Tuam, Killala, and Achonry, 1867.
(Tuam—Area, 1,686,986 acres; Pop. 312,961; Benefices, 37; Perpetual Cures, 12: Total, 49.
Killala—Area, 631,361 acres; Pop. 87,075; Benefices, 13; Perpetual Cures, 2: Total, 15.
Achonry—Area, 368,358 acres; Pop. 108,870; Benefices, 10; Perpetual Cures, 2: Total, 12; Inc. of See, 4038*l.*)

PROVINCE OF DUBLIN.

Comprising the Dioceses of Dublin, Glandelagh, and Kildare; Ossory, Ferns, and Leighlin; Cashel, Emly, Waterford, and Lismore; Cork, Cloyne, and Ross; Killaloe, Kilfenora, Clonfert, and Kilmacduagh; Limerick, Ardfert, and Aghadoe.

United Dioceses of Dublin, Glandelagh, and Kildare.

Counties of Dublin, Kildare, Wicklow, small part of Wexford, and part of Queen's and King's Counties.
ARCHBISHOP—The Right Hon. and Most Rev. RICHARD CHENEVIX TRENCH, Primate of Ireland, *The Palace, Stephen's Green, Dublin.*
Born, 1807; Trin. Coll. Cam. B.A. 1829; M.A. 1833; D.D. 1856.
Consecrated Abp. of Dublin and Bp of Glandelagh and Kildare, 1864.
(Dublin and Glandelagh—Area, 777,043 acres; Pop. 513,329; Benefices, 98; Perpetual Cures, 37: Total, 135.
Kildare—Area, 505,117 acres; Benefices, 43; Perpetual Cures, 3: Total, 46; Inc. of See, 7786*l.*)
His Grace is Chan. of the Order of St. Patrick and Visitor of Trin. Coll. Dub.; formerly Hulsean Lect. at Cambridge, 1845-46; Theol. Prof. and Examiner at King's Coll. Lond; Dean of Westminster, 1856-64.

United Dioceses of Ossory, Ferns, and Leighlin.

Counties of Carlow, Kilkenny, Wexford, and part of the Counties of Wicklow, Queen's County, and King's County.
BISHOP—The Right Rev. JAMES THOMAS O'BRIEN, *The Palace, Kilkenny.*
Born, 1792; Trin. Coll. Dub. Consecrated Bp of Ossory, Ferns, and Leighlin, 1842.
(Ossory—Area, 604,281 acres; Pop. 140,086; Benefices, 61; Perpetual Cures, 4: Total, 65.
Ferns—Area, 616,200 acres; Pop. 151,368; Benefices, 53; Perpetual Cures, 10: Total, 63.
Leighlin—Area, 524,766 acres; Pop. 124,889; Benefices, 55; Perpetual Cures, 4: Total, 59; Inc. of See, 3867*l.*)
His Lordship was formerly Fell. of Trin. Coll. Dublin.

United Dioceses of Cashel, Emly, Waterford, and Lismore.

Counties of Tipperary and Waterford, and part of Limerick.
BISHOP—The Right Rev. ROBERT DALY, *See House, Waterford.*
Born, 1783; Dub. A.B. 1803; A.M. 1833; D.D. 1843.
Consecrated Bp. of Cashel, Emly, Waterford, and Lismore, 1843.
(Cashel—Area, 507,323 acres; Pop. 117,855; Benefices, 42.
Emly—Area, 257,786 acres; Pop. 64,352; Benefices, 28; Perpetual Cure, 1: Total, 29.
Waterford—Area, 66,857 acres; Pop. 43,506; Benefices, 12.
Lismore—Area, 573,803 acres; Pop. 145,265; Benefices, 49; Perpetual Cures, 3: Total, 52; Inc. of See, 4402*l.*)

United Dioceses of Cork, Cloyne, and Ross.

County of Cork.
BISHOP—The Right Rev. JOHN GREGG, *The Palace, Cork.*
Born, 1798; Dub. A.B. 1825; A.M. and D.D. 1860. Consecrated Bp of Cork, Cloyne, and Ross, 1862.
(Cork—Area, 659,097 acres; Pop. 239,213; Benefices, 63; Perpetual Cures, 13: Total, 76;
Cloyne—Area, 830,966 acres; Pop. 215,166; Benefices, 89; Perpetual Cures, 2: Total, 91;
Ross—Area, 254,197 acres; Pop. 69,903; Benefices, 28; Perpetual Cure, 1: Total, 29; Inc. of See, 2304*l.*)

United Dioceses of Killaloe, Kilfenora, Clonfert, and Kilmacduagh.

County of Clare, part of Tipperary, King's County, and Limerick, and part of County of Galway.
BISHOP—The Right Rev. WILLIAM FITZGERALD, *Clarisford House, Killaloe.*
Born, 1814; Trin. Coll. Dub. Consecrated Bp of Cork, Cloyne, and Ross, 1857; translated to Killaloe, 1862.
(Killaloe—Area, 1,038,125 acres; Pop. 225,096; Benefices, 65; Perpetual Cures, 2: Total, 67;
Kilfenora—Area, 135,746 acres; Pop. 23,042; Benefices, 7; Perpetual Cures, 1: Total, 8;
Clonfert—Area, 394,320 acres; Pop. 64,143; Benefices, 13;
Kilmacduagh—Area, 139,660 acres; Pop. 42,798; Benefices, 4; Inc. of See, 4041*l.*)
His Lordship was formerly Prof. of Moral Philosophy and Ecclesiastical History in Trin. Coll. Dublin.

United Dioceses of Limerick, Ardfert, and Aghadoe.

Counties of Limerick and Kerry and small part of Clare and Cork.
BISHOP—The Right Rev. CHARLES GRAVES, *The Palace, Limerick.*
Born, 1812; Dub. A.B. 1835; A.M. 1838; D.D. 1857. Consecrated Bp of Limerick, Ardfert, and Aghadoe, 1866.
(Limerick—Area, .06,222 acres; Pop. 172,622; Benefices, 56; Perpetual Cures, 5: Total, 61.
Ardfert and Aghadoe—Area, 1,263,795 acres; Pop. 221,939; Benefices, 48; Perpetual Cures, 1: Total, 49.
Inc. of See, 4377*l.*)
His Lordship was formerly Fell. of Trin. Coll. Dublin, and Dean of Clonfert.

ALPHABETICAL LIST OF THE CLERGY IN IRELAND,

WITH NAME, BENEFICE, DIOCESE, AND POST TOWN.

(Reprinted, by permission, from *Thom's Irish Almanac and Official Directory.*)

The Name of the Diocese is printed in *Italics*.

Abbott, Charles, A.B., Rural Dean, Vicar of Newcastle (*Dublin*), Newtownmountkennedy.
Abbott, Thomas Kingsmill, A.M., Fellow of Trinity College, Dublin.
Acheson, John, A.B., Prebendary and Curate of Elphin (*Elphin*).
Adair, Thomas Benjamin, A.M., Vicar of Templepatrick (*Connor*), Belfast.
Adams, Anthony, A.M., Rural Dean, Rector of Collon (*Armagh*), Collon.
Adams, Benjamin William, D.D., Rector of Cloghran (*Dublin*), Drumcondra.
Adams, James, A.B., Rector of Kilbride (*Meath*), Oldcastle.
Agar, William, Incumbent of Kilcredan (*Cloyne*), Castlemartyr.
Agar, William, jun., A.B., Vicar of Ballynoe (*Cloyne*), Conna.
Alcock, Alexander, A.M., Incumbent of Maculee (*Ossory*), Waterford.
Alcock, Alured H., A.M., Curate of Booterstown (*Dublin*), Blackrock.
Alcock, George A., Curate of Killermogh (*Ossory*), Ballacolla.
Alcock, James, A.M., Vicar of Ringgona (*Lismore*), Dungarvan.
Alcock, Ven. John, A.M., Archdeacon of Waterford, Incumbent of St. Patrick's (*Waterford*), Waterford.
Alcorn, John, D.D., Prebendary of Cashel, Rector of Killardry (*Cashel*), Clonmel.
Aldworth, John, A.B., Prebendary of Cloyne, Rural Dean, and Incumbent of Glanworth (*Cloyne*), Glanworth.
Aldworth, R., A.M., Curate of Carrigrohane (*Cork*), Ballincollig.
Alexander, Charles, A.M., Rural Dean, Rector of Drumcree (*Armagh*), Portadown.
Alexander, John, LL.D., Rector of Carne (*Ferns*), Churchtown, Wexford.
Alexander, John, jun., A.B., Curate of Callan (*Ossory*), Callan.
Alexander, Robert, A.M., Prebendary of Derry, Rector of Aghadoe (*Derry*), Blackhill, Coleraine.
Alexander, Samuel, A.M., Rector of Termonmaguirk (*Armagh*), Omagh.
Allen, Charles, A.B., Perpetual Curate of St. Paul's (*Connor*), Belfast.
Allen, Charles, Curate of Dunany (*Armagh*), Dunleer.
Allen, James, A.B., Incumbent of Creagh (*Ross*), Skibbereen.
Allen, James, A.B., Perpetual Curate of Milford (*Raphoe*), Milford.
Allen, James Hastings, A.M., Registrar of the Dioceses of Killaloe and Kilfenora, Rector of Kiltinanlea (*Killaloe*), Clonlara.
Allen, Robert D., A.B., Perpetual Curate of Ballyscullion (*Connor*), Toome Bridge.
Allen, T., Curate of Fenagh (*Leighlin*), Carlow.
Allison, J. W., A.B., Curate of Aghaderg (*Dromore*), Loughbrickland.
Allman, William, A.B., M.D., Rector of Mevagh (*Raphoe*), Carrigart.
Anderson, Samuel, A.B., Perpetual Curate of Upper Falls, Belfast (*Connor*).

Anderson, Thomas T., Curate of Drumcondra (*Dublin*).
Anderson, William, A.M., Rector of Raymunterdoney (*Raphoe*), Falcarragh.
Andrews, William, A.B., Vicar Choral of St. Canice Cathedral, Kilkenny (*Ossory*).
Anketell, Thomas, A.B., Perpetual Curate of Shanko (*Clogher*), Emyvale.
Annesley, James B., A.B., Curate of Drumkeeran, and Minister of Vaughan School (*Clogher*), Kesh.
Apjohn, Michael Lloyd, A.M., Precentor of Emly, Rector of Ballybrood, Curate of Liscormuck (*Emly*), Caherconlish.
Archbold, Charles, A.M., Vicar of Rathmullan (*Down*), Downpatrick.
Archdall, Charles, A.B., Rector of Clonbeg (*Emly*), Tipperary.
Archdall, H. M., A.M., Perpetual Curate of St. Michael's, Trory (*Clogher*), Enniskillen.
Archdall, John Charles, A.M., Rural Dean, Rector of St Mary's (*Ferns*), Newtownbarry.
Archdall, J., Curate of Templemore (*Cashel*), Templemore.
Archdall, W., Curate of Lislee (*Ross*), Bandon.
Archdall, Mervyn, A.B., Perpetual Curate of Templebredy (*Cork*), Crosshaven.
Archer, Arthur E., Incumbent of Donard (*Dublin*).
Archer, John, A.B., Curate of Clongish (*Ardagh*), Newtownforbes.
Archer, William, A.M., Prebendary of Limerick, Rural Dean, Vicar of Croagh (*Limerick*), Rathkeale.
Ard, A. J., A.B., Perpetual Curate of Magdalen Asylum Belfast (*Connor*), Belfast.
Ardagh, William Johnson, A.B., Incumbent of Rossmire (*Lismore*), Kilmacthomas.
Armstrong, Anthony, A.B., Rector of Killoscully (*Cashel*), Newport-Tipperary.
Armstrong, Sir Edmund F., Bart., Vicar of Skeirke (*Ossory*), Erroll.
Armstrong, George F. A., A.B., Incumbent of Lorum (*Leighlin*), Bagnalstown.
Armstrong, James, A.M., Rector of Fethard (*Ferns*), Fethard.
Armstrong, James, Curate of Tynan (*Armagh*), Tynan.
Armstrong, Thomas Bagot, A.M., Vicar of Ballyvaldon (*Ferns*), Kilmuckridge, Gorey.
Armstrong, William, A.B., Perpetual Curate of Scarvagh (*Dromore*), Scarvagh.
Armstrong, William, A.B., Incumbent of Moydow (*Ardagh*), Longford.
Armstrong, William Bettesworth, Perpetual Curate of Caledon (*Armagh*).
Arthur, Henry, A.M., Rector of Kiltennell (*Ferns*), Gorey.
Ashe, Henry, A.B., Curate of St. John's (*Kilmore*) Belturbet.
Ashe, Henry, Curate of Crossboyne (*Tuam*), Claremorris.
Ashe, Isaac, A.B., Rector of Barronstown (*Armagh*) Dundalk.
Ashe, James, Incumbent of Moore and Drum (*Tuam*), Ballinasloe.
Ashe, Weldon, A.M., Prebendary of Killala, Incumbent of Kilmoremoy (*Killala*), Ballina.
Ashe, William, A.B., Rector of Rossinver (*Kilmore*), Bunderan.

Ashe, William B., A.M., Vicar of Donagh (*Clogher*), Glasslough.

Askin, William Booker, A.M., Incumbent of Harold's Cross (*Dublin*)—residence, 74, Leinster-road, Rathmines.

Askins, W. J., A.B., Curate of Donaghmore (*Dromore*), Loughbrickland.

Atkins, Stephen Hastings, A.M., Rector of Tullylish (*Dromore*), Gilford.

Atkins, William, D.D., Dean of Ferns and Rector of Gorey (*Ferns*).

Atkinson, Hans, A.M., Rector of Fenagh (*Leighlin*), Carlow.

Attwell, William Erskine, D.D., Rector of Clonoe (*Armagh*), Stewartstown.

Auchinleck, John, A.M., Vicar of Dunboyne (*Meath*), Dunboyne.

Ayres, George, A.M., Incumbent of Kilbride (*Dublin*), Brittas.

Babington, David, A.B., Rural Dean, Rector of Glendermot (*Derry*), Derry.

Babington, Hume, A.M., Rural Dean, Rector of Moviddy (*Cork*), Crookstown.

Babington, Richard, A.B., Curate of Glendermot (*Derry*), Derry.

Badham, Henry, Curate of Seagoe (*Dromore*), Portadown.

Badham, Leslie, A.M., Curate of Offerlane (*Ossory*), Mountrath.

Bagge, James, A.B., Incumbent of Templemichael (*Lismore*), Youghal.

Bagot, Daniel, D.D., Dean of Dromore, Official Principal and Vicar General of the Exempt Jurisdiction of Newry and Mourne, and Vicar of Newry (*Dromore*).

Bagot, Richard W., A.B., Rector of Fontstown (*Dublin*), Kildare.

Bailey, William Richey, D.D., Rector of Monaghan (*Clogher*), Monaghan.

Bailie, John, A.M., Rector of Foghart (*Armagh*), Dundalk.

Baillie, Richard E., A.B., Perpetual Curate of Muff (*Derry*).

Bain, John, Curate of Dungarvan and Kilrush (*Lismore*).

Baker, Colpoys Cole, A.M., Perpetual Curate of Portmarnock (*Dublin*), Cloghran.

Baker, Hugh Lefroy, A.M., Rector of Derver (*Armagh*), Dundalk.

Baker, William, A.M., Rector of Shronell and Curate of Kilshane, &c. (*Emly*), Tipperary.

Baldwin, A. B., A.B., Vicar of Rahan (*Cloyne*), Mallow.

Baldwin, W., A.B., Vicar of Kilfaughnabeg (*Ross*), Glandore, Rosscarberry.

Ball, John Gage, A.M., Rector of Killybegs (*Raphoe*).

Banner, Benjamin H., A.M., Precentor of Cashel, Chancellor of Emly, Incumbent of Templeneiry Union (*Cashel*), Bansha, Tipperary.

Barber, Frederick, A.B., Curate of Kilclief (*Down*), Strangford.

Barker, Joseph, A.B., Prebendary of Tuam, Rector of Achill (*Tuam*), Dogort, Achill.

Barklie, John Knox, A.B., Rector of Outragh (*Kilmore*), Ballinamore.

Barlow, James William, A.M., Fellow of Trinity College, Dublin.

Barlow, William, A.M., Treasurer of Armagh, Rector of Creggan (*Armagh*), Crossmaglen.

Barnier, James, LL.D., Vicar of Dungarvan (*Ossory*), Thomastown.

Barton, George T. H., Curate of Monasteroris (*Kildare*), Edenderry.

Barton, George T. U., Curate of Kenure (*Dublin*), Skerries.

Barton, Richard, A.M., Precentor of Christ Church, and Rector of St. George's (*Dublin*)—residence, 17, Temple-street, upper.

Bastable, Robert, A.B., Incumbent of Knocktemple (*Cloyne*), Charleville.

Battersby, John F., Rector of Castletownkindalen (*Meath*), Mullingar.

Battersby, Robert, A.M., Rector of Killeagh (*Meath*), Oldcastle.

Battersby, William Alexander, A.B., Incumbent of Derry (*Derry*).

Batty, Edward, Incumbent of Delvin (*Meath*), Delvin.

Bayley, Charles James, A.B., Rector of Trim (*Meath*), Trim.

Bayly, Edward, A.B., Incumbent of Killegney (*Ferns*), Enniscorthy.

Bayly, Henry Roe, A.M., Rural Dean, Vicar of Ballingarry (*Limerick*).

Beamish, Adam Newman, A.B., Treasurer of Cloyne, Rector of Templenacarriga (*Cloyne*), Midleton.

Beamish, George, Curate of St. Nicholas (*Cork*).

Beatty, John, A.M., Rural Dean, Rector of Killaghtee (*Raphoe*), Dunkineely.

Beatty, Robert, A.B., Curate of Ballymachugh (*Ardagh*), Ballyheelan.

Beauclerk, Charles, A.B., Perpetual Curate of St. Mary's, Belfast (*Connor*), Belfast.

Beaufort, William Augustus, A.M., Rector of Kilrean (*Cork*), Glanmire.

Beere, Francis I., A.B., Vicar of Toomna (*Elphin*), Leitrim.

Beere, Gerald, A.B., Prebendary of Limerick, Rector of Ballycahane (*Limerick*), Limerick.

Beers, James Annesley, A.M., Rector of Drumballyroney (*Dromore*), Rathfriland.

Belcher, Andrew, A.M., Prebendary of Killaloe, Rector of Tomgraney (*Killaloe*), Tomgraney.

Bell, Charles Lucas, A.B., Chaplain R.N., Enniskillen.

Bell, Daniel, A.M., Prebendary of Down, and Rector of Inch (*Down*), Downpatrick.

Bell, Edward, District Curate of Cooley (*Armagh*), Six-mile-Cross.

Bell, James A., A.M., Rector of Ballymore (*Meath*).

Bell, Joseph Samuel, LL.D., Vicar of Beynagh (*Meath*), Banagher.

Bell, Robert, D.D., Incumbent of Tipperary, Treasurer of Waterford, Precentor of Lismore, Bishop's Chaplain (*Cashel*), Tipperary.

Benn, John W., A.B., Rector of Carrigaline (*Cork*), Carrigaline.

Bennett, James, A.M., Rural Dean, Incumbent of Kilmurry (*Killaloe*), Knock.

Bennett, James, A.M., Incumbent of Fedamore (*Limerick*), Bruff.

Bennett, Richard, A.B., Curate of Urney (*Derry*), Strabane.

Bennett, Thomas Glasson, A.B., Rural Dean, Vicar of Kilmacabea (*Ross*), Union-Hall.

Beresford, G. De La Poer, A.B., Rural Dean, Rector of Feenagh (*Ardagh*), Carrick-on-Shannon.

Beresford, William Montgomery, A.M., Rector of Lower Badoney (*Derry*), Gortin.

Bermingham, Joseph Aldrich, A.M., Dean and Incumbent of Kilmacduagh (*Kilmacduagh*), Gort.

Berry, Edward F., Rector of Athlone (*Meath*).

Berry, William Winslow, A.M., Curate of St. Paul's (*Kildare*), Portarlington.

Bevan, Robert Thomas, A.M., Vicar of Street (*Ardagh*), Edgeworthstown.

Bewley, Benjamin Franklin, A.B., Rector of Rathlin (*Connor*), Ballycastle.

Bickerstaffe, Marcus J., A.B., Curate of St. Michan's (*Dublin*).

Bickerstaffe, Roger, A.M., Incumbent of Killead (*Connor*), Crumblin.

Biedermann, W. H., A.M., Chancellor of Connor, Rural Dean, Rector of Ramoan (*Connor*), Ballycastle.

Bindon, William F., A.M., Rural Dean, Rector of Mothel (*Ossory*), Leighlinbridge.

Binney, Richard, D.C.L., Rural Dean, Incumbent of Bangor (*Down*).

Black, Gibson, Incumbent of Inch (*Dublin*), Arklow.

Black, John, A.B., Curate of St. Mary's (*Dublin*), 46, Mountjoy-street.

Black, Samuel, A.B., Curate of Ballyeaston (*Connor*), Ballyclare.

Black, Thomas Ferguson, A.M., Rector of Ballyeaston (*Connor*), Ballyclare.

Blackburne, Anthony, A.B., Rector of Killallon (*Meath*), Clonmellon.

Blacker, Beaver Henry, A.M., Rural Dean, Incumbent of Booterstown (*Dublin*), Rokeby, Southhill-avenue, Blackrock.
Blacker, George, A.M., Prebendary of St. Patrick's, Rector of Maynooth and Taghadoe (*Dublin*), Maynooth.
Blair, Alexander, A.B., Curate of Litter (*Cloyne*), Fermoy.
Bland, Nathaniel, Archdeacon and Rector of Aghadoe, and Rector of Knockane (*Ardfert and Aghadoe*), Killarney.
Bleakley, David Robert, A.M., Perpetual Curate of Benowen (*Meath*), Glasson, Ballymahon.
Bleakley, John, A.M., Vicar of Ballymodan (*Cork*), Bandon.
Blnett, Augustus F. G., A.B., Perpetual Curate of Ballinaclash (*Dublin*), Rathdrum.
Bluett, William Rowley, A.B., Vicar of Clonlea (*Killaloe*), Six-mile-bridge.
Blundell, Robert, A.M., Incumbent of Headford (*Tuam*), Headford.
Bolster, John Abraham, A.M., Prebendary of Cork, Incumbent of Killaspugmullane (*Cork*), Glanmire.
Bolton, Lyndon H., Rector of Drumconrath (*Meath*), Ardee.
Bolton, William, A.B, Curate of Kilfiera (*Killaloe*), Kilkee.
Booker, John, A.M., Rural Dean, Precentor of Ferns, Rector of Templeshambo (*Ferns*), Templeshambo.
Boomer, C. C., A.B., Curate of Killinchy (*Down*).
Booth, Richard, Curate of Navan (*Meath*), Navan.
Bor. James Henry, A.M., Perpetual Curate of Dunlewy (*Raphoe*), Strabane.
Bourchier, J. G., Chaplain, Spike and Haulbowline Islands (*Cloyne*), Queenstown, Cork.
Bourke, John, A.M., Vicar, Kilmeaden (*Waterford*), Portlaw.
Bourke, John, A.M., Curate of Reisk (*Waterford*), Clonmel.
Bourke, John William, A.M., Vicar, Offerlane (*Ossory*), Mountrath.
Bourke, William, Curate of Lackan (*Killala*), Rathlackan.
Bowen, Edward, A.M., Rector of Taughboyne (*Raphoe*), Derry.
Bowens, Thomas S., A.B., Curate of Upper Cumber (*Derry*), Killaloe.
Bowles, John Wright, A.M., Rector of Shinrone (*Killaloe*).
Boyce, James, A.B., Curate of Antrim (*Connor*), Antrim.
Boyce, William George, A.B., Curate of Castlemacadam (*Dublin*), Ovoca.
Boyd, Adam, A.B., Rural Dean, Vicar of Ogonnilloe (*Killaloe*).
Boyd, Charles, A.M., Vicar of Magheradroll (*Dromore*), Ballanahinch, county Down.
Boyton, Charles, A.B., Curate of Tullyagnish (*Raphoe*), Letterkenny.
Brabazon, James, A.M., Rural Dean, Incumbent of Almoritia (*Meath*), Moyvore.
Brabazon, John V., A.B., Perpetual Curate of Rahan (*Meath*), Ballycumber.
Brabazon, William, A.B., Incumbent of Syddan (*Meath*), Ardee.
Braddell, A., A.B., Perpetual Curate of Leny (*Meath*), Balnalack.
Bradley, George, A B., Incumbent of Clanabogan (*Derry*), Omagh.
Bradshaw, Macniven, A.M., Incumbent of Ardamine (*Ferns*), Courtown, Gorey.
Bradshaw, William Hanna, A.M., Curate of Enniskillen (*Clogher*).
Brady, Francis T., A.M., Chancellor of Lismore, Incumbent of St. Mary's, Clonmel (*Lismore*), Clonmel.
Brady, John Westropp, A.B., Rural Dean, Rector of Slane (*Meath*).
Brady, William Maziere, D.D., Rector of Donaghpatrick (*Meath*), Navan.
Brandon, John, Rector of Castlerickard (*Meath*).
Brandon, William, A.B., Treasurer of Ferns, Rector of Leskinfere (*Ferns*), Gorey.
Breakey, Samuel Leslie, A.M., Vicar of Kilmaley (*Killaloe*), Ennis.
Bredin, E., A.B., Curate of Rathdowney (*Ossory*), Rathdowney.

Bredin, James, A.M., Incumbent of Myshall (*Leighlin*), Myshall.
Bree, Martin Stapylton, Incumbent of Kilflyn, &c. (*Ardfert and Aghadoe*), Tralee.
Brenan, Samuel A., A.B., Incumbent of Cushendun (*Connor*), Cushendall.
Brent, J. N., A.B., Perpetual Curate of Penvyle (*Tuam*), Lettertrack.
Brett, Edward E., A.M., Rector of Rathmacknee (*Ferns*), Wexford.
Bridge, John, A.M., Rector of Ballycommon (*Kildare*) Tullamore.
Brien, Ven. Edward H., A.M., Archdeacon of Emly, Rector of Dromkeen and Kilcornan (*Emly*), Cahir.
Brighton, J. G., M.D., Incumbent of Kentstown (*Meath*), Navan.
Brighton, Oliver, Curate of Skyrne (*Meath*), Tara, Navan.
Briscoe, Edward, A.B., Curate of Drumcliff (*Elphin*), Sligo.
Briscoe, Francis, A.M., Incumbent of Kilmessan (*Meath*), Navan.
Briscoe, James R., Vicar of St. Mary's, Drogheda (*Meath*).
Bristow, John, A.B., Rectory of Knockbreda (*Down*), Belfast.
Brooke, Edward Perry, A.M., Precentor of Dromore, Rural Dean, Rector of Magheralin (*Dromore*).
Brougham, Henry, A.B., Rector of Eirke (*Ossory*), Maryborough.
Brougham, John, A.M., Vicar of Timolin (*Dublin*), Ballytore.
Brown, John, A.M., Treasurer of Kildare, Incumbent of Great Connell (*Kildare*).
Browne, A. M. F., Incumbent of Affane (*Lismore*), Cappoquin.
Browne, Dominick Augustus, A.M., Curate of St. George's Chapel, Temple-street (*Dublin*).
Browne, Henry G. C., A.B., Vicar Choral of Lismore, Vicar of Dungarvan (*Lismore*), Dungarvan.
Browne, Hon. and Very Rev. Henry M., A.M., Dean of Lismore, Incumbent of Burnchurch (*Ossory*), Bennetsbridge.
Browne, I. J., Curate of Carlow, Leighlin.
Browne, John, LL.D., Incumbent of Carrick (*Lismore*), Carrick-on-Suir.
Browne, Peter, A.M., Rector of Ahascragh (*Elphin*).
Browne, Robert Wilson, A.B., Perpetual Curate of Derrygortrevy (*Armagh*), Dungannon.
Brownlow, John, A.M., Dean of Clonmacnois, Incumbent of Ardbraccan (*Meath*), Navan.
Brownrigg, David, A.B., Prebendary of Ferns and Incumbent of Kilcommon (*Ferns*), Tinahely.
Brownrigg, George O., Rural Dean, Rector of Ballinrobe (*Tuam*).
Brownrigg, Henry, A.M., Prebendary of St. Patrick's, Rural Dean, Incumbent of Wicklow (*Dublin*).
Brownrigg, Robert Graham, Vicar of Barragh (*Leighlin*), Newtownbarry.
Bruce, C. S., A.B., Curate of Athnowen (*Cork*), Ovens.
Brunker, Brabazon William, A.M., Rural Dean, Rector of Ballymaglassan (*Meath*), Batterstown.
Bruckill, N. R., A.M., Curate of Burnchurch (*Ossory*), Danesfort.
Bruebe, W. H., A.B., Perpetual Curate of Moygounagh (*Killala*), Crossmolina.
Bryan, William Butler, A.M., Incumbent of Castlemacadam, &c. (*Dublin*), Wooden Bridge, Avoca.
Bull, George, A.M., Dean of Connor, Incumbent of Carrickfergus (*Connor*).
Bullen, William Crofts, Vicar of Kilsallaghan (*Dublin*).
Bullick, Alexander, A.M., Rector of Ardkeen (*Down*), Newtownards.
Bunbury, Thomas, A.M., Rural Dean, Rector of Croom (*Limerick*).
Bunbury, William Isaac, A.M., Rector of Shandrum (*Cloyne*), Charleville.
Burdett, Henry, A.B., Perpetual Curate of Newbliss (*Clogher*).
Burke, Francis, Curate of Killaraght (*Achonry*), Boyle.

Burke, H. Anthony, A.M., Rector of Tydavnet (*Clogher*), Monaghan.

Burke, William J., Perpetual Curate of Castlejordan (*Meath*), Edenderry.

Burkett, Francis Hassard, Rural Dean, Incumbent of Killinane (*Clonfert* and *Kilmacduagh*), Loughrea.

Burkett, George, A.B., Incumbent of Kilfiera (*Killaloe*), Kilkee.

Burkitt, James, A.M., Curate of Stillorgan (*Dublin*), Blackrock.

Burnett, James, Vicar of Garristown, and Curate of Clonmethan (*Dublin*), Oldtown, county Dublin.

Burnett, Robert, A.B., Curate of Ballyvalden (*Ossory*), Kilmuckridge.

Burnside, William S., B.D., Rector of Magheracross (*Clogher*), Ballinamallard.

Burroughs, Henry Colclough, A.M., Curate of Quin (*Killaloe*), Quin.

Burroughs, Wolfenden Kenny, A.M., Rector of Grangesylvæ (*Leighlin*), Goresbridge.

Burroughs, W. G., A.B., Incumbent of Kilbeacon (*Ossory*), Mullinavat.

Burrowes, Robert, A.B., Curate of Camus-juxta-Mourne (*Derry*), Strabane.

Burtchael, Somerset B., A.B., Curate of St. Patrick's, Wexford (*Ferns*), and Rector of Killenny (*Leighlin*), Stradbally.

Burton, Charles, Perpetual Curate of Bective (*Meath*), Navan.

Burton, Edward William, A.B., Curate of Bray and Rathmichael (*Dublin*), Bray.

Burton, Robert William, A.M., Rector of Raheny (*Dublin*).

Bury, E. J., A.B., Curate of Monaghan (*Clogher*).

Busby, Samuel E., Curate of Dalkey (*Dublin*).

Bushe, Charles Kendal, A.B., Rural Dean, Incumbent of St. Mary's, New Ross (*Ferns*).

Bushe, John Phillips, Curate of Ballymore (*Armagh*), Tanderagee.

Butler, Edward W., A.B., Vicar of Kiltennell (*Leighlin*), Killedmond.

Butler, Hans, A.B., Vicar Choral, Perpetual Curate of Villierstown (*Lismore*), Cappoquin.

Butler, Theobald, Curate of St. Thomas's (*Dublin*)—residence, 29, Abbey-street, lower.

Butler, T., District Curate of Gweedore (*Raphoe*), Letterkenny.

Butson, Christopher H. Goold, A.M., Archdeacon, and Incumbent of Clonfert (*Clonfert*), Eyrecourt.

Butter, Henry W., A.B., Curate of Lynally (*Meath*), Tullamore.

Byrn, Richard Archibald, A.M., Perpetual Curate of Broomfield (*Clogher*), Castleblayney.

Byrne, James, A.M., Dean of Clonfert, Rector of Cappagh (*Derry*), Omagh.

Callwell, Joseph, A.M., Rector of Aghavea and Curate of Tattykeeran (*Clogher*), Brookborough.

Campbell, Adderley W., A.M., Prebendary of Clogher, Rector of Tullycorbet (*Clogher*), Ballybay.

Campbell, Andrew, A.M., Mariners' Church (*Dublin*).

Campbell, C. D., A.B., Curate of Ballyjamesduff (*Kilmore*), Drumkeeran.

Campbell, Charles, A.B., Rector of Ardglass (*Down*).

Campbell, Charles B., Curate of Ennislannon (*Tuam*), Clifden.

Campbell, Edward George, A.M., Chaplain, Marine School (*Dublin*)—residence, 37, Longwood-avenue.

Campbell, Edward G., A.M., Rector of Kilderry (*Ossory*), and Perpetual Curate of Old Leighlin (*Leighlin*), Kilkenny.

Campbell, Theophilus, A.M., Rural Dean, Rector of Finvoy (*Connor*), Ballymoney (*Connor*), Belfast.

Campion, M., Curate of Liscleary (*Cork*), Douglas.

Campion, M. S., Prebendary of Cork and Rector of Killanully (*Cork*), Monkstown, county Cork.

Campion, Robert D., A.B., Vicar of Knockmourne (*Cloyne*), Tallow.

Card, Robert James, A.M., Rector of Kilcommick (*Ardagh*), Kenagh.

Carey, William, Curate of Glengarriffe (*Cork*), Bantry.

Carleton, Henry, A.M., Vicar of Kilberry (*Dublin*), Athy.

Carleton, James, A.B., Rector of Kildellig (*Ossory*), Leighlinbridge.

Carleton, William, Curate of Fiddown (*Ossory*), Piltown.

Carmichael, Frederick F., A.B., Chaplain, Magdalen Asylum, Leeson-street, Dublin (*Dublin*)—residence, 3, Cullenswood-avenue.

Carpenter, Henry James, Curate of Derryvollan (*Clogher*), Ballinamallard.

Carr, Elliott Elmes, A.B., Rector of Rathsaran (*Ossory*), Rathdowney.

Carr, Francis, Curate of Ballymacward (*Clonfert*), Portumna.

Carr, James W., Curate of Tullamelan (*Lismore*), Clonmel.

Carre, Frederick, A.B., Curate of Inver (*Raphoe*), Donegal.

Carre, Henry, A.M., Prebendary of Raphoe, Rector of Inver (*Raphoe*), Donegal.

Carroll, Charles, A.B., Curate of Ulloe, &c. (*Emly*), Tipperary.

Carroll, Edward A., Rector of Dunmurghill (*Kildare*), Kilcock.

Carroll, Edward A., Curate of Donadea (*Kildare*), Kilcock.

Carroll, Edward C., A.M., Perpetual Curate of Templemartin (*Cork*), Bandon.

Carroll, Henry George, A.M., Perpetual Curate of Glasnevin (*Dublin*).

Carroll, William, Perpetual Curate of Ballycarney (*Ferns*), Ferns.

Carroll, William George, A.M., Perpetual Curate of St. Bride's (*Dublin*),—residence, 27, Wellington-road.

Carson, James, A.M., Incumbent of Caherconlish (*Emly*), Caherconlish.

Carson, James, Rector of Cloghane (*Ardfert and Agadoe*), Dingle.

Carson, Joseph, D.D., Fellow of Trinity College, Dublin.

Carson, Thomas, LL.D., Dean and Vicar-General, Surrogate, Rector of Kilmore (*Kilmore*), Cavan.

Carson, Thomas William, A.M., Curate of Kilmore (*Kilmore*), Cavan.

Carson, William, A.B., Pepetual Curate of Ardmayle (*Cashel*), Cashel.

Carter, Henry, D.D., Rector of Ballintoy (*Connor*), Ballycastle.

Carter, Henry Bryan, Pepetual Curate of Moy (*Armagh*), Moy.

Carter, Leslie, M., Perpetual Curate of Milltown (*Armagh*), Maghera Moy.

Carter, Richard, Rural Dean, Incumbent of Balrathboyne (*Meath*), Kells.

Cather, John, A.M., Archdeacon of Tuam, Rural Dean, Examining Chaplain, Incumbent of Westport (*Tuam*), Westport.

Caulfeild, Thomas Gordon, A.M., Rural Dean, Incumbent of Ballyloughloe (*Meath*), Moate.

Caulfield, Wilberforce, A.M., Incumbent of Odogh (*Ossory*), Kilkenny.

Chadwick, George Alexander, A.B., Assistant Chaplain, Episcopal Chapel, Upper Baggot-street, 31, Leesonpark-avenue.

Chamney, Joseph, A.B., Rector of Dromiskin (*Armagh*), Dromiskin.

Chapman, Joseph, Rector of Kilclonfert (*Kildare*), and St. Kill (*Leighlin*), Bagnalstown.

Chapman, Joseph, Perpetual Curate of Durrow (*Meath*), Tullamore.

Chartres, William, A.B., Curate of Drumragh (*Derry*), Omagh.

Cheevers, Conolly, A.M., Perpetual Curate of Burt (*Derry*), Derry.

Chester, Richard, A.B., Prebendary, Vicar of Ballyclogh, and Curate of Kilmaclenine (*Cloyne*), Mallow.

Chester, William Bennett, A.M., Incumbent of Nenagh (*Killaloe*), Nenagh.

Chichester, G. V., A.M., Vicar of Drummaul (*Connor*), Randalstown.

Chichester, Lord Edward, D.D., Dean of Raphoe, Rector of Raphoe (*Raphoe*).

Chichester, Robert, A.M., Rector of Balteagh (*Derry*), Newtownlimavady.

Childs, Edmond, A.M., Incumbent of Swift's Alley (*Dublin*), residence, 31, Arran-quay.
Chomley, Jonathan, R., A.M., Prebendary of Armagh, Rector of Loughgall (*Armagh*), Loughgall.
Christian, Valentine Duke, A.M., Rector of Drummully (*Clogher*).
Chute, John L., Vicar of Marhin, Perpetual Curate of Dingle (*Ardfert*), Dingle.
Clare, Mervyn Archdall, Curate of Mariners' Church, Kingstown (*Dublin*).
Clark, Frederick J., A.M., Perpetual Curate of Dunnalong (*Derry*), Strabane.
Clarke, Andrew Staples, A.M., Curate of Mullaghadun (*Clogher*), Enniskillen.
Clarke, Benjamin J., A.M., Incumbent of Killererin (*Tuam*), Barnaderg.
Clarke, G. S., Curate of Magheracloonеy (*Clogher*), Kingscourt.
Clarke, James, A.M., Curate of Kildrumferton (*Kilmore*), Kilnaleck.
Clarke, Marshal R., Perpetual Curate of Ardara (*Raphoe*), Ardara.
Clarke, Richard, A.B., Perpetual Curate of Dunseverick (*Connor*), Bushmills.
Clarke, Samuel, A.B., Curate of Glanely (*Dublin*) Ashford, county Wicklow.
Cleland, Andrew, A.B., Rector of Dundonald (*Down*), Belfast.
Clemenger, William Parsons, A.B., Incumbent of Killaloan (*Lismore*), Clonmel.
Cliffe, Allen R., A.M., Rector of Mallow (*Cloyne*).
Clifford, Caleb C., A.B., Rector of Kilnamartery (*Cloyne*), Cloyne.
Close, John Forbes, A.M., Rector of Kilkeel (*Ex. Jur. of Newry and Mourne*), Kilkeel.
Cluff, S. O'Mally, Rector of Timogue (*Leighlin*), Stradbally.
Cobbe, William Power, A.M., Incumbent of Clonegam (*Lismore*), Portlaw.
Cochrane, Henry Stewart, A.B., Rector of Killygarvin (*Raphoe*), Rathmullan, Strabane.
Cochrane, S. J., A.B., Perpetual Curate of Mountcharles (*Raphoe*), Mountcharles.
Coddington, William, A.M., Curate of Lusk (*Dublin*).
Coffey, John T., A.B. Rector of Mogorban (*Cashel*), Fethard, Tipperary.
Coffey, Richard, A.B., Curate of Westport (*Tuam*), Westport.
Coghlan, Augustus C. L., A.M., Perpetual Curate of Nantenan, and Curate of Cappagh (*Limerick*), Limerick.
Coghlan, John Cole, LL.D., Rector of Mourne Abbey (*Cloyne*), Mallow, and Chaplain Lord Lieutenant's Household.
Colburne, William, A.M., Vicar of Aglish (*Cork*), Coachford.
Cole, John H., A.B., Rector of Mogeesha (*Cloyne*), Midleton.
Cole, S., A.B., Curate of Ballyfeard (*Cork*), Kinsale.
Collins, James, D.D., Dean and Rector of Killala (*Killala*).
Collins, John Hurly, A.B., Rector of Ballyheige (*Ardfert and Aghadoe*).
Collins, Thomas R. S., A.M., Curate of St. Mary (*Dublin*), 66, Mountjoy-street, Dublin.
Collis, Maurice Atkin Cooke, D.D., Rector of Clonmel (*Cloyne*), Queenstown.
Colthurst, Henry, A.B., Rector of Termoneeny (*Derry*), Castledawson.
Colthurst, John, Rector of Bovevagh (*Derry*), Dungiven.
Concannon, George B., Incumbent of Dromod (*Ardfert and Aghadoe*), Cahirciveen.
Coneray, John, Perpetual Curate of Moyrus-Beauchamp (*Tuam*), Galway.
Connelly, Richard, A.B., Curate of Clongish (*Ardagh*), Drumlish.
Conner, Richard Mountifort, A.M., Fellow of Trinity College, Dublin.
Connor, Francis, Prebendary of Cloyne, Incumbent of Ballybooly (*Cloyne*), Mallow.
Connor, John, A.B., Curate of Feakle (*Killaloe*), Feakle.
Connor, John, Curate of Lickmolassy (*Clonfert*), Portumna.
Connor, M. L., A.B., Prebendary of Cork, Rector of Dromdaleague (*Cork*), Dunmanway.
Conolly, John, A.M., Prebendary of Cork, Rural Dean, Vicar of Holy Trinity (*Cork*), Cork.
Conroy, John, A.B., Rector, Faughanvale (*Derry*), Eglinton.
Conry, Charles, Chancellor of Ardfert and Aghadoe, Rural Dean, Incumbent of Kilmalkedar (*Ardfert and Aghadoe*), Dingle.
Constable, Henry, A.M., Prebendary of Cork, Rector of Desertmore (*Cork*), Ballincollig.
Constable, John, Curate of Kilcommon (*Killala*), Belmullet.
Cooke, Ambrose, A.B., Curate of Thomastown (*Ossory*).
Cooke, Digby S., A.B., Curate of Bailieborough (*Kilmore*).
Cooke, John, Curate of Holycross (*Cashel*), Holycross.
Cooke, John Digby, A.M., Chaplain Female Orphan House (*Dublin*)—residence, 74, Bushfield-avenue, Donnybrook.
Cooke, John, A.M., Incumbent of Ardfinan (*Lismore*).
Cooke, William, A.B. Rector of Kilnemanagh (*Ferns*), Oulart.
Cooper, Ambrose, A.M., Incumbent of Clane (*Kildare*), Clane.
Cooper, Joseph, A.B., Diocesan Schoolmaster for Down and Dromore (*Down*), Downpatrick.
Cooper, Jonathan S., A.B., Rector of Killann (*Ferns*), Enniscorthy.
Cooper, Robert, A.M., Incumbent of Aghade (*Leighlin*), Tullow.
Cooper, Thomas, A.B., Curate of Agherton (*Connor*), Coleraine.
Coote, Maxwell H. Rural Dean, Perpetual Curate of Clonaslee (*Kildare*).
Coote, Ralph, Incumbent of Fercall (*Meath*), Tullamore.
Corbett, J. E., A.B., Curate of Derrynoose (*Armagh*), Keady.
Corvan, John, D.D., Incumbent of St. Mary's (*Ferns*), Enniscorthy.
Corvan, John, D.D., Curate of Portadown (*Armagh*).
Corvan, William W., A.B., Perpetual Curate of Templeudigan (*Ferns*).
Cory, Henry C., A.M., Missionary Secretary Irish Church Missions, 12, D'Olier-street, Dublin.
Cosby, William, A.M., Rector of Killermogh (*Ossory*), Ballacolla.
Cosgrave, Thomas, A.B., Perpetual Curate of Lambeg (*Connor*), Lisburn.
Costelloe, John Edmund, A.M., Perpetual Curate of Whitehouse (*Connor*), Belfast.
Cotter, Edward, A.B., Curate of Ballycastle (*Antrim*), Ballycastle.
Cotter, George Edmund, A.M., Rector of Monanimy (*Cloyne*), Mallow.
Cotter, Joseph R., A.M., Prebendary of Cloyne, Rector of Donoughmore (*Cloyne*), Coachford.
Cotter, Thomas C., Curate of Athenry (*Tuam*).
Cotter, William, A.M., Perpetual Curate of Lower Falls, Belfast (*Connor*).
Cottingham, Henry, A.M., Vicar of Ballymachugh (*Ardagh*), Mount Nugent.
Cotton, Henry, LL.D., Archdeacon of Cashel, Treasurer of Christ Church, Dublin, Incumbent of Lismalin and Thurles (*Cashel*).
Cotton, Samuel G., A.B., Rector of Carogh (*Kildare*), Naas.
Courtenay, D. Carlisle, A.M., Incumbent of Teckmacrevan (*Connor*), Glenarm.
Courtenay, George F., A.B., Perpetual Curate of Cloughjordan (*Killaloe*), Cloughjordan.
Cousins, J. F., A.B., Curate of Down (*Down*), Downpatrick.
Cowell, George Y., A.B., Curate of Clonmore (*Leighlin*), Hacketstown.
Cowen, Richard, A.B., Incumbent of Ardclare (*Elphin*), Strokestown.
Cox, Michael Bell, A.B., Rural Dean, Perpetual Curate, Glenties (*Raphoe*).
Cox, Samuel O'Neill, A.B., Rector of Glencolumbkille (*Raphoe*), Killybegs.

Craddock, Francis, A.M., Vicar of Whitechurch (*Lismore*), Dungarvan.

Cradock, Thomas, A.M., Marsh's Library (*Dublin*), Upper Kevin-street.

Craig, George, A.M., Rector of Aghanloo (*Derry*), Magilligan, Derry.

Craig, Graham, A.M., Perpetual Curate of Kildalkey (*Meath*), Athboy.

Craig, John Duncan, A.M., Vicar of Kinsale (*Cork*), Kinsale.

Craig, William, A.M., Incumbent of the Free Church (*Derry*), Derry.

Crampton, John F. T., A.B., Prebendary. Rural Dean, Registrar and Surrogate of Clonfert, Rector of Aughrim (*Clonfert*).

Crampton, Josiah, A.M., Rector of Killesher (*Kilmore*), Florence Court.

Crawford, Francis, A.B., Incumbent of Derryloran (*Armagh*), Cookstown.

Crawford, Hugh, A.M., Rural Dean, Incumbent of Killashee (*Ardagh*), Longford.

Crawford, John, A.B., Curate of Clontarf (*Dublin*).

Crawford, Thomas, A.M., Vicar of Drumcliff (*Elphin*), Carney, Sligo.

Crawford, William, A.M., Incumbent of Skerry (*Connor*), Broughshane.

Creek, William, A.M., Curate of Kildallon (*Kilmore*), Ardlogher.

Creeny, H. N., A.M., Curate of Holywood (*Down*), Belfast.

Creery, Audrew, A.B., Prebendary of Connor, Incumbent of Rasharkin (*Connor*), Kilrea.

Cregan, Claud, A.B., Curate of Drumlane (*Kilmore*), Belturbet.

Crofton, James, A.M., Incumbent of Dunleer (*Armagh*).

Crofton, John, A.B., Incumbent of Portloman (*Meath*), Mullingar.

Croghan, Davis George, A.B., Curate of Grangegorman (*Dublin*), 11, Cabra-road.

Croker, Thomas, Vicar of Adare (*Limerick*).

Crookshank, James L., A.B., Perpetual Curate of Rossnowlagh (*Raphoe*), Ballyshannon.

Crommelin, William, Thomas De La Cherois, A.B., Incumbent of Comber (*Down*).

Cross, John A., A.B., Curate of Kells (*Meath*).

Cross, Thomas Henry, A.B., Prebendary of Clonfert, Incumbent of Donanaghta (*Clonfert*), Eyrecourt.

Crossle, Charles, A.M., Rector of Kilclooney (*Armagh*), Markethill.

Crossle, Charles, jun., A.B., Perpetual Curate of Ballymoyer (*Armagh*), Newtownhamilton.

Crossley, John, Perpetual Curate of St. Matthew's, Shankhill, Belfast (*Connor*), Belfast.

Crosthwaite, Charles, A.M., Rural Dean, 3rd Canon and Vicar-General of Kildare, Rector of Rathangan (*Kildare*).

Crowe, Charles, Curate of Drumsnat (*Clogher*), Monaghan.

Crozier, Graham, A.M., Prebendary of Elphin, Incumbent of Taunagh (*Elphin*), Riverstown.

Cumine, James, A.B., Rector of Preban (*Ferns*), Rathdrum.

Cumming, Gordon, A.B., Curate of Boyle (*Elphin*), Boyle.

Cuppage, Adam, Curate of Kilmegan (*Down*), Clough.

Curry, John, A.B., Rector of Desertegny (*Derry*), Buncrana.

Curry, John, Curate of Knappa (*Tuam*), Westport.

Curry, N. B., A.B., Rector of Kilcoleman (*Killaloe*), Parsonstown.

Dalton, Edward, Rector of Drumcannon (*Waterford*), Tramore.

Dalton, G. W., A.M., Perpetual Curate of St. Paul, Glenagcarry (*Dublin*), Kingstown.

Daly, Henry V., A.B. Curate of Creagh (*Clonfert*), Ballinasloe.

Daly, Joseph Morgan, A.M., Rector of Churchtown (*Meath*), Mullingar.

Daly, William, A.M., Incumbent of Kilbride (*Dublin*), Arklow.

Dancer, Hugh W., A.B., Rector of Aghancon (*Killaloe*), Roscrea.

Danford, Henry, A.B., Curate of Conwall (*Raphoe*), Letterkenny.

Darby, Christopher, A.M., Incumbent of Killenaule (*Cashel*), Knocktopher.

Darby, Christopher, A.M., Incumbent of Kells (*Ossory*), Thomastown.

Darby, Christopher L., A.B., Rector of Gowran (*Ossory*).

D'Arcy, Hyacinth, Incumbent of Omey (*Tuam*), Clifden.

D'Arcy, John, A.M., Rector of St. Nicholas (*Tuam*), Galway.

Darley, Ven. John R., A.M., LL.D., Archdeacon of Ardagh, Incumbent of Templemichael (*Ardagh*), Longford.

Darley, William Shaw, A.B., Perpetual Curate of Straffan (*Dublin*).

Daunt, Achilles, M.A., Rector of Stackallan (*Meath*), and Chaplain of St. Matthias (*Dublin*), 21, Leeson park, Dublin.

Davidson, Bennett Clear, A.M., Incumbent of St. John's, Sandymount (*Dublin*).

Davidson, J. H., A.B., Incumbent of Grey Abbey (*Down*).

Davis, John, A.B., Vicar of Kilbrine (*Elphin*), Boyle.

Davy, Humphry, A.B., Perpetual Curate of Crumlin (*Dublin*), Roundtown.

Dawson, A., Perpetual Curate of St. Bartholomew (*Dublin*), Dublin.

Dawson, Abraham, A.M., Perpetual Curate of Knocknamuckly (*Dromore*), Stramore, Gilford.

Dawson, Arthur, A.B., Incumbent of St. Bartholomew's District Church (*Dublin*), and Secretary to the Society for the Propagation of the Gospel, 22, Dawson-street.

Dawson, Thomas, A.M., Vicar of Kilmocar (*Ossory*), Kilkenny.

Day, Edward, A.B., Rural Dean, Incumbent of St. John's (*Elphin*), Sligo.

Day, John Godfrey, A.B., Dean of Ardfert and Aghadoe, Rector of Ratass (*Ardfert and Aghadoe*), Tralee.

Day, John Robert Fitzgerald, Rural Dean, Incumbent of Molahiffe (*Ardfert and Aghadoe*), Killarney.

Day, Maurice Fitzgerald, A.M., Rector of Aughalurcher (*Clogher*), Brookborough.

Day, Maurice, A.B., Curate of Ballymoney (*Cork*), Ballineen.

Day, William, Perpetual Curate of Knocknarea (*Elphin*), Sligo.

Day, William T., A.M., Rector of Rathclarin (*Cork*), Bandon.

Deacon, George, A.B., Perpetual Curate of Cullen (*Cork*), Cork.

Deacon, Isaac Henry, A.B., Perpetual Curate of Trinity Church, Belfast (*Connor*), Belfast.

Deacon, Samuel, A.B., Curate of Templepatrick (*Connor*), Belfast.

De Burgh, Maurice T., A.M., Rural Dean, Vicar of Naas (*Kildare*), Naas.

De Butts, George, A.M., Vicar Choral and Curate of Christ Church, and Minor Canon, St. Patrick's (*Dublin*), 35, Leeson-park.

Deering, William Watkins, A.M., Incumbent of Maguiresbridge (*Clogher*).

Delacour, Robert W., Rector of Killowen (*Cork*), Bandon.

Delap, Alexander, A.B., Rector of Templecrone (*Raphoe*), Dungloe.

Delap, Robert, A.B., Curate of Donaghmore (*Derry*) Strabane.

Delmege, John, A.M., Prebendary of Kilmacduagh and Clonfert, Rector of Youghalarra (*Killaloe*), Nenagh.

De Montmorency, Walter, Dean's Vicar Choral, St. Canice (*Ossory*), Kilkenny.

Deniston, Robert J., A.B., Curate of Raphoe (*Raphoe*).

Dennis, George Morley, A.M., Rural Dean, Incumbent of Enniscoffey (*Meath*), Miltown Pass, Killucan.

Denny, Anthony, Archdeacon of Ardfert, Rector of Kilgobbin (*Ardfert and Aghadoe*).

Denny, Edward, Curate of Blennerville (*Ardfert*), Tralee.

Denny, Henry, Incumbent of Ballynahaglish and St. Anna (*Ardfert and Aghadoe*), Tralee.
De Renzy, John, A.B., Incumbent of Ballynakill (*Waterford*), Waterford.
D'Evelyn, J W., A.M., Rector of Armoy (*Connor*), Ballymoney.
Deverell, Richard, A.B., Rural Dean, Prebendary of Tascoffin, &c. (*Ossory*), Kilkenny.
Devenish, William, Curate of Kilskeery (*Clogher*), Kilskeery.
Dickinson, Daniel, A.M., Rector of Seapatrick (*Dromore*), Banbridge.
Dickinson, Hercules Henry, D.D., Vicar of St. Anne's (*Dublin*)—residence, 58, Pembroke-road.
Dickinson, John A., A.B., Perpetual Curate of Redcross (*Dublin*), Rathdrum.
Dickson, Benjamin, D.D., Fellow of Trinity College, Dublin.
Dickson, Daniel, Curate of Barragh (*Leighlin*), Newtownbarry.
Dickson, Joseph William, A.B., Perpetual Curate of Shillelagh (*Ferns*).
Dickson, William, Curate of St. James (*Dublin*), Conyngham-road.
Dillon, John Jefcott, B.A., Curate of St. Mary, Donnybrook (*Dublin*), Sandymount.
Disney, Brabazon William, B.D., Dean of Armagh (*Armagh*).
Disney, Edward Ogle, A.M., Rector of Killeshil (*Armagh*), Aughnacloy.
Disney, Brabazon Thomas, A.B., Rector of Farrihy (*Cloyne*), Kildorrery.
Disney, James, A.M., Rector of Killyman (*Armagh*), Moy.
Disney, William H., A.B., Incumbent of Ballymacelligott (*Ardfert and Aghadoe*), Tralee.
Dixon, Rob. Vickers, D.D., Rector of Clogherney (*Armagh*), Omagh.
Dobbin, Alexander John, A.M., Curate of St. Mary's, Donnybrook (*Dublin*), Sandymount.
Dobbin, F., A.B., Rector of Castlehaven (*Ross*), Skibbereen.
Dobbin, Orlando Thomas, LL.D., Perpetual Curate of Killochonnigan (*Meath*), Balliver.
Dobbs, Francis, A.M., Rector of Loughguile (*Connor*), Ballymoney.
Dobbyn, William A., A.B., Rural Dean, Incumbent of Cloumore (*Ossory*), Piltown.
Dobbyn, William Peter Hume, A M., Chaplain Steevens' Hospital (*Dublin*).
Dockeray, John W., Curate of Clones (*Clogher*), Clones.
Doherty, A. P., A.B., Perpetual Curate of Newtown Crommelin (*Connor*), Ballymena.
Donnelly, John, A.B., Perpetual Curate of Mountfield (*Derry*), Omagh.
Donovan, Charles, A.B., Prebendary of Ballyhay (*Cloyne*), Charleville.
Donovan, Solomon, A.M., Incumbent of Horetown (*Ferns*), Taghmon.
Dopping, Francis H., Curate of Columbkille (*Ardagh*), Edgeworthstown.
Dorman, Thomas, A.M., Rector of St. Michael (*Cork*), Midleton.
Dougherty, Edward G., A.M., Curate of Lower Fahan (*Derry*), Buncrana.
Dowdall, Launcelot, A.M., Rector of Rathfarnham (*Dublin*), Fortfield-terrace, Templeogue.
Dowling, Frederick, A.M., Incumbent of Bethesda (*Dublin*), Dublin.
Dowse, John Robert, A.B., Rector of Carnew (*Ferns*), Carnew.
Dowse, Richard, A.B., Rector of Clonfadforan (*Meath*), Tyrrells-pass.
Drapes, John L., A.M., Rural Dean, Rector of Tullow (*Leighlin*), Tullow.
Drapes, Vernon R., A.M., Prebendary, Rural Dean, Vicar of Darrow, Rector of Mayne (*Ossory*), Darrow.
Drew, Browning, Incumbent of Kiltallagh (*Ardfert and Aghadoe*), Milltown, Kerry.
Drew, Pierce William, A.B., Rector of Youghal (*Cloyne*).
Drew, Thomas, D.D., Precentor of Down, Rural Dean, Rector of Loughinisland (*Down*), Clough.
Driscoll, Charles, Rector of Ballymacwilliam (*Kildare*), Edenderry.
Drought, Adolphus, A.M., Prebendary, Rector of Clontuskart (*Clonfert*), Ballinasloe.
Drought, Thomas Acton, A.M., Incumbent of Dysart, &c. (*Lismore*), Kilsheelan.
Drought, William, Vicar of Gallen (*Meath*), Cloghan.
Druitt, Joseph, A.B., Vicar of Colpe (*Meath*), Drogheda.
Dubourdieu, Armand, A.M., Curate of Ballyboy (*Meath*), Frankford.
Dudgeon, Alexander, A.M., Curate of Annalong (*Examining Juror of Newry and Mourne*), Kilkeel.
Dudgeon, Walter V. G., A.M., Curate of Skerry and Racavan (*Connor*), Broughshane.
Duffin, William, A.B., Rector of Maghera (*Down*), Clough.
Duke, William C., District Curate of Bilbo (*Leighlin*), Carlow.
Dudley, S. F., A.B., Curate of Seapatrick (*Dromore*), Lurgan.
Dunbar, John, A.B., Rector of Ballybay (*Clogher*).
Dundas, William J., D.D., Rector of Moynalty (*Meath*).
Dunne, Robert Hedges, A.M., Rector of Kilnegarenagh (*Meath*), Ballycumber.
Dunscombe, Nicholas C., A.B., Rector of Macroom (*Cloyne*), Macroom.
Dunseath, James, A.B., Rector of Layde (*Connor*) Cushendall.
Durdin, T. G., Rector of Oldcastle (*Meath*).
Dwyer, Phillip, A.B., Rural Dean, Incumbent of Drumcliffe, &c. (*Killaloe*), Ennis.
Dysart, William, Rector of Tamlaghtard (*Derry*), Magilligan, Newtownlimavady.

Eagar, Edward Charles, A.B., Vicar of Kilronan (*Ardagh*), Keadue.
Eagar, Joseph S., A.B., Rector of Drumgooland (*Dromore*), Ballyward.
Eagar, Robert, Rural Dean (*Ardfert and Aghadoe*), Rector of Brosna, and Curate of Abbeyfeale (*Limerick*), Abbeyfeale.
Eames, Benjamin W., A.M., Rural Dean, Incumbent of Kilconduff (*Achonry*), Swineford.
Eames, William, A.B., Incumbent of Rathgraffe (*Meath*), Castlepollard, 11, Upper Fitzwilliam-street, Dublin.
Eaton, Matthew L., Curate of Ballymureen (*Cashel*), Littleton.
Eaton, Richard E., A.B., Incumbent of Lackagh (*Kildare*), Kildare.
Ebbs, John, A.B., Perpetual Curate of Ballycanew (*Ferns*).
Eccles, John G., Incumbent of St. Peter's (*Armagh*), Drogheda.
Eccles, Robert Gilbert, A.M., Rector of Kilbrogan (*Cork*), Bandon.
Eccles, Samuel, D.D., Chaplain of St. George's, (*Dublin*), Eccles Hall, Delgany.
Edge, John, A.B., Perpetual Curate of Calary (*Dublin*), Enniskerry.
Edmundson, George, A.B., Vicar of Saintfield (*Down*).
Edwards, Arthur William, A.M., Rector of Tamlaght Finlagan (*Derry*), Ballykelly, Derry.
Edwards, Edward, A.B., Perpetual Curate of Derg (*Derry*), Castlederg.
Edwards, William Macklin, A.M., Domestic Chaplain and Secretary to the Lord Bishop of Derry, Rector of Clonleigh (*Derry*), Lifford, Strabane.
Egan, John J., A.B., Vicar, Killinagh (*Kilmore*), Blacklion.
Elliott, Alfred, A.M., Curate of Lurgan (*Kilmore*), Virginia.
Elliott, Charles, A.M., Incumbent of Ballyadams (*Leighlin*), Athy.
Elliott, James, A.B., Rural Dean, Vicar of Clonduff (*Dromore*), Hilltown.
Ellis, Thomas, A.B., Perpetual Curate of Killylea (*Armagh*).
Ellison, Humphrey, A.B., District Curate of Ardoyne (*Leighlin*), Tullow.

Elmes, John, Vicar of St. John's (*Limerick*), Limerick.

Elmes, Thomas, A.B., Rector of Killeely (*Limerick*), Limerick.

Elwood, Harloe, A.B., Curate of Kinawley (*Kilmore*), Ballyconnell.

Emerson, Edward R., A.B., District Curate of St. Edmund's (*Cork*), Cork.

Emerson, J. M., A.B., Vicar of Grangemonk, Curate of Killeban (*Leighlin*), Carlow.

Ensell, Charles H., Perpetual Curate of Lucan (*Dublin*).

Erskine, Henry, A.M., Vicar of Kildumferton (*Kilmore*), Kilnaleck.

Eustace, W. G., A.B., Incumbent of Stradbally (*Leighlin*).

Evans, Edward John, A.M. (*Dromore*), Rostrevor.

Evans, Robert Maunsell, M.A., Archdeacon of Cloyne, and Rector of Gortroe and Dysart (*Cloyne*), Rathcormack.

Evans, Thomas E., A.B., Prebendary of Cork, Rural Dean, Rector of Inniskenny (*Cork*), Cork.

Evans, Tyrrell G., Vicar of Corcomohide (*Limerick*), Newcastle, county Limerick.

Eves, Edmund L., A.B., Curate of Aghold (*Leighlin*), Tullow.

Exshaw, John, A.M., Incumbent of Kinnitty (*Killaloe*).

Eyre, Giles, A.B., Rector of Kilmina (*Tuam*), Westport.

Eyre, Richard Booth, Prebendary, Incumbent of Lickmolassy (*Clonfert*), Portumna.

Eyre, Robt. Hedges Maunsell, Rector of Innishannon (*Cork*).

FAIRTLOUGH, Edward, A.M., Perpetual Curate of Ardagh (*Meath*), Coolderry, Carrickmacross.

Falkiner, Richard, A.B., Vicar of Kilmocomoge (*Cork*), Bantry.

Falkiner, Richard D., A.B., Vicar, Ardcrony (*Killaloe*), Borrisokane.

Falkiner, R. D., A.B., Incumbent of Hollymount (*Tuam*), Hollymount.

Falkner, Robert H., A.M., Prebendary of Cashel, Rector of Newchapel (*Cashel*), Clonmel.

Fallon, John M'Cleland, A.M., Rector of Ballee (*Down*).

Falloon, Charles, A.M., Prebendary of Connor, Rector of Ballynure (*Connor*).

Falloon, John, Perpetual Curate of Ballymore (*Meath*), Moate.

Farmer, Henry Birch, A.M., Rural Dean, Rector of Donaghmore (*Ossory*), Borris-in-Ossory.

Farquhar, Adam, Curate of Crossmolina (*Killala*), Crossmolina.

Farrell, A. T., A.B., Vicar of Tullynakill (*Down*), Killinchy.

Faussett, Henry, A.B., Curate of Donaghmore (*Derry*), Castlefin.

Fawcett, B. C., A.B., Curate of Ballymodan (*Cork*), Bandon.

Fawcett, John, A.M., Curate of Ballymoney (*Connor*), Ballymoney.

Fawcett, Simon, A.B., Curate of Carnmoney (*Connor*), Carnmoney.

Ferguson, Henry, A.B., Curate of Killygarvan (*Raphoe*), Rathmullen, Strabane.

Ferguson, Samuel, A.M., Incumbent of Moyne (*Cashel*), Thurles.

Ferrar, Edward, A.B., Rector of Templescobin (*Ferns*), Enniscorthy.

Ferrar, William Hugh, A.M., Fellow of Trinity College, Dublin.

Fetherstonhaugh, Thomas Orme, A.B., Perpetual Curate of Moyne (*Leighlin*), Rathdrum.

Ffennell, Robert, A.B., Curate of Ballybay (*Clogher*), Ballybay.

Ffolliott, Henry, A.M., Rector of Ballywillan (*Connor*), Portrush.

Ffolliot, James, A.B., Perpetual Curate of Warrenpoint (*Dromore*), Warrenpoint.

Field, James, A.B., Curate of Rathgraffe (*Meath*), Castlepollard.

Finlay, George, A.M., Vicar of Drumcar (*Armagh*), Dunleer.

Finlay, John, A.B., Curate of Clonenagh (*Leighlin*), Mountrath.

Finlayson, Henry, A.B., Minor Canon and Vicar Choral, St. Patrick's (*Dublin*), 22, Pembroke-road.

Finlayson, John, A.M., Vicar Choral and Curate of Christ Church, &c. (*Dublin*), 60, Lower Baggot-street.

Finney, Thomas Henry Cotter, A.B., Vicar of Clondulane (*Cloyne*), Fermoy.

Fishbourne, Edward E., A.B., Curate of St. John Baptist, Cashel (*Cashel*).

Fishbourne, Robert, A.M., Prebendary of Kilrane, Rural Dean, Rector of Kilbride (*Ferns*), Ferns.

Fisher, J. W., A.B., Curate of Abbeyleix (*Leighlin*), Abbeyleix.

Fisher, W. A., A.B., Rector of Kilmoe (*Cork*), Skibbereen.

Fitzgerald, Augustin, A.M., Perpetual Curate of Portadown (*Armagh*), Portadown.

Fitzgerald, Edward Loftus, A.M., Rector of Ardagh (*Cloyne*), Youghal.

Fitzgerald, Frederick, M.A., Rector of Narraghmore (*Dublin*), Ballytore, county Kildare.

Fitzgerald, Gerald, A.B., Incumbent of St. Iberius, Vicar of St. Mullins (*Ferns and Leighlin*), Wexford.

Fitzgerald, James, A.B., Incumbent of Kiltoom (*Elphin*), Athlone.

Fitzgerald, Michael, Incumbent of Kildysart (*Killaloe*).

Fitzgerald, William, A.B., Curate of Kilwatermoy (*Lismore*), Tallow.

Fitzpatrick, Frederick, senior, A.M., Rural Dean, Rector of Lurgan (*Kilmore*), Virginia.

Fitzpatrick, Frederick, junior, A.M., Rector of Cloon, (*Ardagh*).

Fitzpatrick, William, A.B., Vicar of Templemichael, &c. (*Lismore*), Kilsheelan.

Flanagan, John, A.M., Rector of Killeevan (*Clogher*), Clones.

Flavell, J. F., A.M., Prebendary of Armagh, Rural Dean, Rector of Mullabrack (*Armagh*), Markethill.

Fleming, H., A.B., Vicar of Kilcorkey, and Perpetual Curate of Loughglinn (*Elphin*), Frenchpark.

Fleming, Horace T., A.B., Rector of Kilnagross (*Ross*), Clonakilty.

Fleming, John, Curate of Clogh (*Clogher*), Roslea.

Fleming, Harloe Robert, Rector of Ballymacward (*Clonfert*), Aughrim.

Fleming, Thomas H., A.B., Perpetual Curate of Roundstone (*Tuam*).

Flemyng, Robert, A.M., Curate of St. Michael's (*Dublin*), —residence, 18, Fitzwilliam-street, upper.

Flemyng, William Henry, A.M., Rural Dean, Perpetual Curate of St. Philip's, Milltown (*Dublin*), Nullamore, Clonskeagh.

Fletcher, James Samuel, Rector of Innislounagh (*Lismore*), Clonmel.

Fletcher, John Joseph Knox, A.M., Prebendary and Rector of Harristown (*Kildare*), Monasterevan.

Fletcher, R. E., A.B., Perpetual Curate of Cappoquin (*Lismore*), Cappoquin.

Fleury, Charles W., A.B, Curate of St. Nicholas, Galway (*Tuam*).

Fleury, John D., A.B., Perpetual Curate of Garrison (*Clogher*), Ballyshannon.

Flood, Frederick, A.B, Vicar of Kilmood (*Down*), Killinchy.

Floyd, James, A.B., Curate of Leixlip (*Dublin*), Lucan.

Flynn, Hugh John, A.M., Vicar of the Union of Clara (*Meath*).

Foley, Daniel, D.D., Prebendary of Cashel, Incumbent of Templetouhy (*Cashel*), Templemore.

Foley, Patrick, Perpetual Curate of Louisburgh (*Tuam*), Westport.

Foley, Robert P., A.B., Perpetual Curate of Tracton (*Cork*), Cork.

Foot, Frederick, A.M., Rural Dean, Incumbent of Fethard (*Cashel*).

Foot, Simon C., A.M., Incumbent of Knocktopher (*Ossory*).

Forde, Robert, A.M., Rector of Annaclean (*Dromore*), Rathfriland.

Forrest, Thomas, A.B., Rector of Rostellan and Kilteskin (*Cloyne*), Cloyne.

Forster, Thomas, Curate of Rathmolyon (*Meath*), Rathmolyon.

Forster, William Henry, A.B., Curate of Taughboyne (*Raphoe*), St. Johnstown.
Forsythe, James, Perpetual Curate of Ferbane (*Meath*).
Foster, Charles W., A.B., Curate of Templemichael (*Ardagh*), Longford.
Foster, Mark Anthony, A.M., Incumbent of Killedi (*Achonry*). Swineford.
Foster, Nicholas, A.B., Rural Dean, Rector of Ventry (*Ardfert and Aghadoe*), Dingle.
Fowler, James Thomas, A.B., Incumbent of Ballysakeery (*Killala*).
Fowler, Luke, A.M., Prebendary of Ossory, Incumbent of Aghour and Rathcoole (*Ossory*), Freshford.
Fox, John James, A.M., Rural Dean, Rector of Kinawley (*Kilmore*), Ballyconnell.
Frackleton, Samuel Scott, A.M., Perpetual Curate of Magherahamlet (*Dromore*), Ballynahinch.
Franklin, Joseph Uriel, A.B., Prebendary of Leighlin and Rector of Ullard (*Leighlin*), Borris, Kilkenny.
Franks, James S., Curate of Donacavey (*Clogher*), Fintona.
Freeman, Francis E., A.B., District Curate of Bantry (*Armagh*), Dungannon.
Freeman, Robert M. P., Curate of Collon (*Armagh*), Collon.
Freke, James, A.B., Prebendary, Rural Dean, Rector of Murragh (*Cork*), Bandon.
Freke, John Henry, A.M., Treasurer of Down, Rector of Saul (*Down*), Downpatrick.
French, George, Curate of Clontuskart (*Clonfert*), Ballinasloe.
French, St. George, A.M., Curate of Delgany (*Dublin*).
French, Thomas Fitzgerald, A.M., Incumbent of Stradbally (*Killaloe*), Castleconnell.
Frew, John James, A.M., 4th Canon of Kildare (*Kildare*).
Frith, J. B., A.B., Perpetual Curate of Camlough (*Armagh*), Newry.
Frizelle, Richard, A.M., Perpetual Curate of Derralossory (*Dublin*)—residence, 3, Great Charles-street.
Fry, Charles, A.B., Rector of Moyaliffe (*Cashel*), Thurles.
Fry, Henry, A.B., Incumbent of Kilkeedy (*Killaloe*), Gort.
Fry, Henry, Curate of Lismore (*Lismore*).
Fry, William Baker, A.M., Rector of Kilruane (*Killaloe*), Nenagh.
Fuller, Abraham Stritch, A.M., Curate of St. Mark's (*Dublin*)—residence, 7, Fitzwilliam-place, south.
Fullerton, Thomas, A.B., Rector of Stranorlar (*Raphoe*).

Gabbett, Edward, A.M., Perpetual Curate of The Diamond (*Armagh*), Portadown.
Gabbett, Joseph, Curate of Manisternenagh (*Limerick*), Youghal.
Gabbett, Joseph, A.M., Prebendary of Limerick, Rector of Effin (*Limerick*), Kilmallock.
Gabbett, Joseph, Vicar of Bruff (*Limerick*), Bruff.
Gabbett, Joseph, jun., Curate of Kilmallock (*Limerick*).
Gabbett, Robert John, A.M., Rural Dean, Vicar of Shanagolden (*Limerick*).
Gabbett, William, A.M., Prebendary of Cloyne, Incumbent of Inniscarra (*Cloyne*).
Gage, Robert, A.B., Rector of Desertoghill (*Derry*), Garvagh.
Galbraith, George, A.B., Rector of Lower Cumber (*Derry*), Killaloe.
Galbraith, George, A.M., Curate of Kilcommock (*Ardagh*), Kenagh.
Galbraith, Henry, A.M., Rector of Rathdrum (*Dublin*).
Galbraith, John, A.B., Perpetual Curate of Kanturk (*Cloyne*).
Galbraith, Joseph Allen, A.M., F.T.C.D., Dublin.
Galbraith, Richard, A.M., Curate of Drumachose (*Derry*), Stranorlar.
Galway, Charles, A.B., Archdeacon of Derry, Rector of Dunboe (*Derry*), Articlave, Derry.
Galwey, James, A.M., Curate of Callan (*Ossory*).
Garde, Thomas W., A.B., Prebendary of Cloyne, Rector of Coole, Curate of Bohilane (*Cloyne*), Cloyne.
Gardner, Robert, Rector of Ballynure (*Connor*), Ballynure.
Garnet, Charles L., Curate of Carnteel (*Armagh*), Aughnacloy.
Garrett, George, A.B., Prebendary and Incumbent of Lachan (*Killala*).
Garrett, James P., A.B., Rector of Kellistown (*Leighlin*), Carlow.
Garstin, Anthony, A.M., Rector of Mansfieldstown (*Armagh*), Castlebellingham.
Gault, Archibald, A.B., Curate of Christ Church, Belfast (*Connor*), Belfast.
Gaussen, Edmond James, A.B., Curate of Drumglass (*Armagh*), Dungannon.
Gelston, Hugh, A.B., Rural Dean, Rector of Enniskeen (*Meath*), Kingscourt.
Geraghty, James, A.M., Rector of Donaghenry (*Armagh*), Stewartstown.
Gibbings, Richard, A.B., Curate of Shandrum (*Cloyne*), Charleville.
Gibbings, Richard, D.D., Incumbent of Kilcock (*Kildare*), Kilcock.
Gibbs, John, A.M., Rector of Shankill (*Dromore*), Lurgan.
Gibson, Benjamin, A.M., Chaplain, Lying-in Hospital (*Dublin*)—residence, 17, Berkeley-street.
Gilchrist, James, A.M., Curate of Innishargy (*Down*).
Gildea, George Robert, A.M., Prebendary of Tuam, Rural Dean, Incumbent of Kilmaine (*Tuam*), Hollymount.
Gillington, George, A.B., Curate of Ramoan (*Connor*), Ballycastle.
Gillmor, Andrew Todd, LL.D., Incumbent of Killenvoy (*Elphin*), Athlone.
Gilmore, Andrew George, A.M., Perpetual Curate of Carrowdore (*Down*), Donaghadee.
Gilmore, John S., A.M., Prebendary of St. Patrick's, Incumbent of Rathmore and Tipper (*Dublin*), Naas.
Gimlette, Thomas, B.D., Rector of Templeree (*Cashel*), Templemore.
Glenny, Robert Edmund, A.B.
Gloster, Thomas, A.B., Curate of Carrigaline (*Cork*)
Gloster, Thomas, A.M., District Curate, Quivy (*Kilmore*), Belturbet.
Godfrey, Johnston B., A.M., Incumbent of Duneane (*Connor*), Toome Bridge.
Godley, James, A.M., Curate of Carrigallen (*Kilmore*), Carrigallen.
Going, James, Incumbent of Kilgarvan (*Ardfert and Aghadoe*), Kenmare.
Going, Robert James, A.M., Chancellor of Killaloe, Rural Dean, Rector of Ballymackey (*Killaloe*), Ballymackey.
Gollock, James, A.M., Rural Dean, Vicar of Desertserges (*Cork*), Bandon.
Gollock, Thomas H., Curate of Rahan (*Cloyne*), Mallow.
Goodisson, Richard, Rector of Shrule (*Tuam*), Galway.
Goodman, J., Curate of Berehaven (*Ross*), C. T. Berehaven.
Goodman, James, A.B., Vicar of Abbeystrewry (*Ross*), Skibbereen.
Goodman, John, Curate of Ballinacourty (*Ardfert and Aghadoe*), Dingle.
Goodwin, William, Incumbent of Timahoe (*Kildare*), Donadea.
Goodwin, William, A.M., Incumbent of Tullowmoy (*Leighlin*), Abbeyleix.
Goold, Frederick, A.M., Archdeacon of Raphoe, Rector of Raymochy (*Raphoe*), Newtowncunningham.
Goold, Richard, A.B., Vicar of Killard, &c. (*Killaloe*), Kilkee.
Gordon, John Bagwell, A.M., Prebendary and Rector of Doon (*Emly*), Pallasgreen.
Gordon, John Frederick, A.M., Rector of Annahilt (*Dromore*), Lisburn.
Gore, John Ribton, A.M., Rector of Dromard (*Killala*), Collooney.
Gorman, William C., A.B., Vicar Choral, St. Canice Cathedral, Curate of Mayne (*Ossory*), Incumbent of Kilsheelan (*Lismore*), Kilkenny.
Gough, Benjamin B., A.M., Rector of Maghera (*Derry*), Maghera.
Grahame, John, Vicar of Stabannon (*Armagh*), Castlebellingham.
Grant, G. B., A.B., Curate of St. Mary's Shandon (*Cork*).

Grant, James, A.B., Rector of Templemichael de Duagh (*Cork*).
Grant, Jasper A., A.B., Rector of Litter (*Cloyne*), Fermoy.
Grant, J. Brabazon, B.D., Rector of Rathconrath (*Meath*), Ballynacargy.
Graves, James, A.B., Treasurer of Ossory, Rector of Ennisnag (*Ossory*), Stoneyford.
Graves, James William, Incumbent of Castlerobert, and Vicar of Manisternenagh (*Limerick*), Youghal.
Graves, James W., Vicar of Ightermurragh (*Cloyne*), Castlemartyr.
Graves, Richard Hastings, D.D., Prebendary of Cloyne, Rector of Brigown (*Cloyne*), Mitchelstown.
Gray, Thomas Sill, B.D., Incumbent of Stillorgan (*Dublin*), Blackrock.
Gray, Thomas Thompson, A.M., Fellow of Trinity College, Dublin.
Green, John, Perpetual Curate of Monivea (*Tuam*), Athenry.
Green, Thomas W., A.M., Rural Dean, Vicar of Granard (*Ardagh*).
Greene, Godfrey S., A.B., Curate of Tamlaght O'Crilly (*Derry*), Tamlaght, Portglenone.
Greene, Henry, Rector of Ballyclogg (*Armagh*), Stewartstown.
Greene, J. E., A.B., Vicar of Ahamplish (*Elphin*), Churchfield, Grange.
Greene, R. Berkly, A.B., Rector of Killodiernan (*Killaloe*), Nenagh.
Greene, William, A.M., Vicar of Antrim (*Connor*).
Greene, William Conyngham, A.M., Rural Dean, Prebendary of Christchurch Cathedral, Incumbent of St. John's (*Dublin*), 49, Stephen's-green East.
Greer, George Samuel, A.B., Rector of Killencoole (*Armagh*), Castlebellingham.
Greer, John Robert, A.M., Perpetual Curate of Kildarton (*Armagh*), Armagh.
Greer, Samuel, A.B., Precentor of Clogher, Rector of Enniskillen (*Clogher*), Enniskillen.
Greer, William, Curate of Headford (*Tuam*), Headford.
Gregg, James Fitzgerald, A.M., Incumbent of Trinity Church and Rector of St. Lawrence (*Limerick*).
Gregg, John William, LL.B., Curate of Greystones (*Dublin*).
Gregg, Robert Samuel, M A., Precentor of Cork, Incumbent of Carrigrohane (*Cork*), and Domestic Chaplain to the Bishop of Cork, Cork.
Gregg, Tresham Dames, D.D., Chaplain of St. Nicholas Within (*Dublin*), Sandymount.
Gregory, W., Rectory of Killarvey (*Meath*), Ardee.
Gregory, William, A.M., Incumbent of Fiddown (*Ossory*), Pilltown.
Gresson, William R., Incumbent of Bourney (*Killaloe*), Roscrea.
Greyburne, William, Curate of Fenagh (*Leighlin*), Carlow.
Griffin, John Nash, A.M., Incumbent of Trinity Church (*Dublin*)—residence, 16, Kenilworth-square North.
Griffith, George, A.M., Incumbent of Kilkeevin (*Elphin*), Castlerea.
Griffith, James, A.M., Rector and Prebendary of Dysart (*Limerick*)—residence, 50, Rathgar-road, Dublin.
Griffith, Julius H., A.B., Curate of Lurganboy (*Kilmore*), Manorhamilton.
Griffith, Valentine Pole, A.B., Rector of Tullaghobegly (*Raphoe*), Dunfanaghy.
Griffith, William D., Perpetual Curate of Balla (*Tuam*), Ballyglass.
Grogan, Charles James, A.M., Rural Dean, Incumbent of Dunleckny, Bagnalstown (*Leighlin*).
Grogan, John, A.M., Rural Dean, Vicar of Balrothery (*Dublin*), Balbriggan.
Groome, Edward, A.M., Rector of Beaulieu (*Armagh*), Drogheda.
Groome, Thomas M., Prebendary, Incumbent of Kiltormer (*Clonfert*).
Groves, Henry Charles, A.M., Perpetual Curate of Mullavilly (*Armagh*), Tanderagee.
Gubbins, George G., A.B., Incumbent of Kilpeacon (*Limerick*), Limerick.
Gubbins, Henry, A.B., Curate of Kilcrohane (*Ardfert and Aghadoe*), Kenmare.
Gully, James, A.M., Perpetual Curate of St. Peter's, Athlone (*Elphin*).
Gumley, John Stewart, A.B., Prebendary and Rector of Tarmonbarry (*Elphin*), Rusky.
Gumley, Robert, A.B., Perpetual Curate of Corawallen (*Kilmore*), Carigallen.
Gwynn, John, B.D., Rector of Tullyaghnish (*Raphoe*), Letterkenny.
Gwynn, Stephen, A.M., Treasurer of Connor, Rector of Agherton (*Connor*), Coleraine.
Gwynne, George John, A.B, Precentor of Cloyne, Incumbent of Lisgoold (*Cloyne*), Midleton.

Hackett, Cuthbert T., A.M., Rector of Killaney (*Clogher*), Carrickmacross.
Hackett, John Wentrop, A.M. (*Dublin*), St. James's Parsonage, Bray, and 73, Harcourt-street.
Haddock, Edward J., B.A., Curate of Athlone (*Meath*), Athlone.
Haines, John, A.B., Curate of Kinneigh (*Cork*), Bandon.
Halahan, Christopher, A.B., Curate of Carnew (*Ferns*).
Halahan, Hickman Rose, A.M., Perpetual Curate of St. Luke's and St. Nicholas Without (*Dublin*), 29, Harcourt-street.
Halahan, J., A.B., Rector of Berehaven (*Ross*), Castletown, Berehaven.
Halburd, Robert, A.M., Prebendary of Cork, Rector of Kilbrittain (*Cork*), Bandon.
Hall, Alexander Lindsay, A.M., Incumbent of Armaghbreague (*Armagh*), Keady.
Hall, Francis Henry, A.M., Perpetual Curate of Hollymount (*Down*), Clough.
Hallam, Edward, A.M., Prebendary and Incumbent of Toombe (*Ferns*), Camolin.
Hallaran, William, A.M., Prebendary of Cloyne, Incumbent of Castlemartyr (*Cloyne*).
Halloran, Thomas T., Incumbent of Cahir, Rector of Glanbeagh (*Ardfert and Aghadoe*), Cahirciveen.
Hallowell, Alexander B., A.M., Prebendary of Ross, Incumbent of Kilgariffe (*Ross*), Clonakilty.
Hallowell, John, Curate of Rahoon (*Tuam*), Letterfrack.
Hamerton, William, A.M., Rural Dean, Incumbent of Tryvet (*Meath*), Ashbourne.
Hamilton, Alfred, A.B., Rector of Taney (*Dublin and Glendelagh*), Dundrum.
Hamilton, Charles, Curate, Ardstraw (*Derry*), Newtownstewart.
Hamilton, Edward James, A.M., Rector of Kilcronaghan (*Derry*), Tubbermore.
Hamilton, Fitzjohn Stannus, A.M., Incumbent of Ross (*Ross*).
Hamilton, Frederick, A.M., Precentor of Elphin, Incumbent of Creeve (*Elphin*), Boyle.
Hamilton, Frederick C., A.M., Prebendary and Vicar Choral of Limerick, Incumbent of Clonelty (*Limerick*), Newcastle.
Hamilton, Hugh, A.B., Vicar of Balscaddan (*Dublin*).
Hamilton, Hugh, A.M., Rector of Inniamacsaint (*Clogher*), Church-hill.
Hamilton, James Alexander, A.M., Incumbent of Loughcrew (*Meath*), Oldcastle.
Hamilton, John, A.B., Rector of Kilcommon (*Killala*), Belmullet.
Hamilton, John, A.M., Rural Dean, Incumbent of Cloonclare, &c. (*Kilmore*), Manorhamilton.
Hamilton, Joseph R., Rector of Tara (*Meath*), Dunshaughlin.
Hamilton, Richard M., Rector of Killelagh (*Derry*), Maghera.
Hamilton, Robert, Vicar of Moyglare (*Meath*), Maynooth.
Hamilton, Robert, Incumbent of Dundalk (*Armagh*), Dundalk.
Hamilton, Robert P. D., A.M., Rector of Rathkenny, and Vicar of Athlumney (*Meath*), Navan.
Hamilton, Timothy, A.B., Rector of Killorglin (*Ardfert and Aghadoe*.)
Hanan, Denis, Curate of Thurles (*Cashel*), Thurles.
Hand, Thomas, A.M., Rector of Clones (*Clogher*.)
Handcock, E., Curate of Killenny (*Leiglin*), Inistioge.

Handcock, Elias, A.B., Vicar of Dysartenos (*Leighlin*), Stradbally.

Handcock, George Richard, A.M., Perpetual Curate of Corbally (*Killaloe*), Roscrea.

Handcock, Ormsby, A.B., Curate of Bray (*Dublin*), Bray.

Hankin, Frederick Trulock, A.B., Incumbent of Clare (*Armagh*), Tanderagee.

Hanlon, Alexander Patrick, LL.D., Incumbent of Inniscaltra (*Killaloe*), Mountshannon Vicarage, Scariff.

Hanlon, Francis, A.B., Curate of Moira (*Dromore*), Moira.

Hannan, Francis, Perpetual Curate of Tullyallen (*Armagh*), Drogheda.

Hannay, Robert, A.B., Perpetual Curate of Christ Church (*Connor*), Belfast.

Harden, Ralph W., A.B., Curate of St. Iberius (*Ferns*), Wexford.

Harding, Jonathan, A.B., Curate of Tullylish (*Dromore*), Laurencetown.

Hardman, J. W., Curate of Ballycastle (*Connor*).

Hardy, James, A.B., Incumbent of Moylary (*Armagh*), Dunleer.

Hare, Charles, A.M., Prebendary, Incumbent of St. Munchin's.

Hare, George, A.B., Curate of Drumcree (*Meath*), Drumcree.

Hare, George, Chaplain, Royal Hospital, Kilmainham, (*Dublin*.)

Hare, Henry, Curate of Castlecarberry (*Kildare*).

Hare, John, A.M., Minister, Free Church, Great Charles-street (*Dublin*), 8, Mountjoy-place.

Hare, Thomas, Rector of Carnalway (*Kildare*), Kilcullen.

Harley. C., Curate of Fethard (*Cashel*).

Harley, John B., A.B., Incumbent of Ballynakill (*Waterford*), Waterford.

Harman, Samuel T., A.B., Curate of Fermoy (*Cloyne*), Fermoy.

Harman, Thomas, A.B., Rector of The Rower (*Ossory*), New Ross.

Harpur, T. B., Curate of Kildare (*Kildare*).

Harris, John, A.M., Rector of Shercock (*Kilmore*).

Harris, Robert, A.B., Rural Dean, Perpetual Curate of Clareabbey (*Killaloe*), Clarecastle.

Harriron, James, Vicar of Ballykean (*Kildare*), Portarlington.

Hurtley, Percival, Rector of Clonpriest (*Cloyne*), Killeagh.

Hartrick, Edward J., A.M., Perpetual Curate of Magdalene Asylum, Belfast (*Connor*).

Harvey, Alfred, Curate of Trim (*Meath*), Trim.

Harvey, Robert, A.B., Rector of Leck (*Raphoe*), Letterkenny.

Hassard, Edward, D.D., Chancellor of Limerick, Incumbent of Kilscannel and Rathkeale (*Limerick*).

Hastings, Patrick, Curate of St. Patrick's (*Clogher*), Carrickmacross.

Hatchell, Thomas H., A.B., Curate of Clonegall (*Ferns*).

Hatton H., A.B., Curate of Rossdroit (*Ferns*), Enniscorthy.

Haughton, Samuel, A.M., Professor of Geology, and Fellow of Trinity College, Dublin.

Hayes, Francis Carlisle, A.M., Curate of St. Andrew (*Dublin*), 26, Leeson-park, Dublin.

Hayes, Richard, A.B., Incumbent of Nathlash, and Curate of Carrigdowname (*Cloyne*), Kildorrery.

Hayman, Samuel, A.M., Incumbent of Doneraile (*Cloyne*), Doneraile.

Haslewood, G., A.M., Vicar of Monkstown (*Cork*), Cork.

Head, John, D.D., Dean of Killaloe, Incumbent of Ballynaclogh (*Killaloe*), Nenagh.

Head, Jonathan C., A.B., Rector of Terryglass (*Killaloe*), Carrigahorig.

Healy, Robert, A.B., Vicar of Kilcleagh (*Meath*), Moate.

Hearn, Lewis R., A.B., Curate of Pomeroy (*Armagh*), Dungannon.

Hearne, Frederick John, A.M., Curate of Clonca (*Derry*), Malin.

Hearne, St. Julius, A.B, Curate of Cloonclare (*Kilmore*), Manorhamilton.

Heather, George, A.M., Perpetual Curate of Achill Dogort (*Tuam*), Achill-Dogort.

Heatley, Robert Y, Curate of Blackrath (*Ossory*), Kilkenny.

Helps, D., Curate of Kilcolgan (*Kilmacduagh*), Kilcolgan.

Helsham, Henry, A.M., Incumbent of Rosbercon (*Ossory*), New Ross.

Hemphill, John, A.M., Curate of Lismalin (*Cashel*), Killenaule.

Hemphill, Richard, A.M., Minister, North Strand Church, (*Dublin*)—residence, 23, Eglinton-terrace, Seville-place.

Henry, Robert. A.B., Rector of Jonesborough (*Armagh*), Flurrybridge.

Herbert, Edward, Incumbent of Killarney (*Ardfert and Aghadoe*).

Herbert, Henry, A.B., Rural Dean, Incumbent of Rathdowney (*Ossory*).

Herbert, Nicholas, A.M., Prebendary of Lismore, Rector of Dysart (Lismore), and Incumbent of Knockgraffon (*Cashel*).

Herbert, Thomas, Incumbent of Killentierna (*Ardfert and Aghadoe*), Castleisland.

Hewetson, James, A.M., Rector of Haynestown (*Armagh*), Dundalk.

Hewitt, Hon. J. P., Rector of Desertlyn (*Armagh*), Moneymore.

Hewitt, James, A.M, Incumbent of Zion Church, Rathgar (*Dublin*)—residence, 1, Highfield-terrace, Rathgar.

Hewson, Francis, A.M., Second Canon of Kildare, Incumbent of Castlecarberry, &c. (*Kildare*), Carberry.

Hickey, Ambrose, A.B., Incumbent, Ballinaboy (*Cork*), Ballinhassig.

Hickey, John S., Rector of Clonmulsk (*Leighlin*), Carlow.

Hickey, Noah S., Incumbent of Taghmon (*Meath*), Mullingar.

Hickey, William, A.M., Rural Dean, Incumbent of Mulrankin (*Ferns*), Bridgetown.

Hickson, George, A.M., Vicar of Magheracloney (*Clogher*), Kingscourt.

Hickson, James, Curate of Tallow (*Lismore*), Tallow.

Hickson, Robert, Incumbent of Duagh (*Ardfert and Aghadoe*), Listowel.

Hiffernan, George, A.B.. Curate of St. John's, Newport, (*Cashel*), Newport, Tipperary.

Hiffernan, John Michael, A.M., Incumbent of Newport (*Cashel*), Newport, Tipperary.

Hill, Arundel, A.M., Perpetual Curate of Fermoy (*Cloyne*).

Hill, Hugh R., A.B., Rector of Ballybrennan, Incumbent of Ishartmon, and Perpetual Curate of Churchtown (*Ferns*), Wexford.

Hill, John, A.M., Rector of Donaghadee (*Down*).

Hill, Robert, A.M., Incumbent of Magheramesk (*Connor*), and Aghalee (*Dromore*), Lurgan.

Hincks, Thomas, D.D., Archdeacon of Connor and Rector of Billy (*Connor*), Bushmills.

Hinson, Ephraim, A.M., Incumbent of Kilbeevin (*Ferns*), Bannow, New Ross.

Hoare, E. N., A.B., Curate of St. Anne's, Belfast (*Connor*), Belfast.

Hoare, Edward Newenham, A.M., Dean of Waterford, Incumbent of Trinity and St. Olave's (*Waterford*), Waterford.

Hoare, John Newenham, A.M., Rector of Killoskey (*Dublin*), Ashford.

Hobart, William K., A.B., Curate of Templeshambo (*Ferns*), Templeshambo.

Hobson, John Meade, A.M., Incumbent of Maryborough (*Leighlin*).

Hodges, John, A.B., Curate of Ballycotton (*Cloyne*), Cloyne.

Hodson, Hartley, A.M., Prebendary of Connor, Rector of Derrykeighan (*Connor*), Dervock.

Hogan, Henry, Curate of Grangegorman (*Dublin*)—residence, 18, Phibsborough-road.

Hogan, James, A.M., Rector of Magherafelt (*Armagh*).

Hogg, Andrew, LL.D., Rural Dean, Rector of Castleraghan, (*Kilmore*), Ballyjamesduff.

Hogg, John, Vicar of Bruree (Limerick), Bruree.

Holden, G., Perpetual Curate of Ballycroy (*Killala*).

Homan, Knox, A.B., Rector of Termonamongan (*Derry*), Castlederg.

Homan, Richard, A.M., Rector of Cloncha (*Derry*), Culdaff, Derry.

Homan, W. T., A.B., Rector of Modreeny (*Killaloe*), Cloughjordan.

Hoops, Samuel E., A.B., Vicar of Cashel (*Ardagh*), Lanesboro'.

Hope, Ralph James, A.B., Curate of Drung (*Kilmore*).

Hopkins, John Wright, A.B., Rector of Bridgetown (*Cloyne*), Castletownroche.

Hopley, E. H., A.B., Curate of Teampul-na-Inboit (*Cork*), Skibbereen.

Horneck, G. L., A.B., Vicar of Abbeylara (*Ardagh*), Granard.

Horneck, Thomas Little, A.B., Curate of Macollop (*Lismore*), Ballyduff.

Horsford, James Payne, Prebendary of Killaloe, and Rector of Rath (*Killaloe*), Bittern, near Southampton.

Horsford, Thomas Fahie, Rector of Kilrush (*Killaloe*).

Howie, James, A.M., Dean of Cloyne, Rector of Killeagh and Curate of Dingindonovan (*Cloyne*), Cork.

Hoyte, William, A.M., Incumbent of Duleek (*Meath*).

Hudson, John, A.B., Rector of Galloon (*Clogher*), Clones.

Hudson, John, A.M., Rector of Killasnett (*Kilmore*), Sligo.

Hudson, John C., A.B., Chancellor of Clogher, Rector of Galloon, (*Clogher*), Newton-Butler.

Hudson, Thomas, Vicar of Aglish (*Ardfert*), Killarney.

Hughes, Edward, A.M., Rector of Castlane (*Ossory*), Callan.

Hughes, William, A.B., Prebendary of Raphoe, Rural Dean, Rector of Killymard (*Raphoe*), Donegal.

Hume, Quintin Dick, A.B., Incumbent of Rathvilly (*Leighlin*), Baltinglass.

Humphrey, A. S., Curate of Donaghmore (*Derry*), Killygordon.

Humphreys, Robert, A.B., Prebendary of Killaloe, Vicar of Tulloh (*Killaloe*), Tulla.

Hunt, Fitzmaurice, A.M., Vicar-General, Rural Dean, and Incumbent of Athleague (*Elphin*).

Hunt, George, Curate of Drumcree (*Armagh*), Portadown.

Hunt, James, A.B., Prebendary of Elphin, Incumbent of Oran (*Elphin*), Ballymoe.

Hunt, Phineas, A.B., Vicar of Shanrahan (*Lismore*), Clogheen.

Hunter, James S., A.B., Rector of Learmount (*Derry*), Park, Derry.

Hunter, Nathaniel Henry, A.B., Curate of Ballynascreen (*Derry*), Draperstown.

Hurst, F. J., Curate of Tydavnet (*Clogher*), Monaghan.

Hurst, Francis, A.M., Rural Dean, Rector of Currin (*Clogher*), Clones.

Huston, A. Knox, A.B., Rector of Kilmacteige (*Achonry*), Swineford.

Hutchinson, Henry Knox, A.B., Vicar of Rathconnell (*Meath*), Killucan.

Hutchinson, J. Abraham, A.B., Curate of Maryborough and Kilclonbrook (*Leighlin*), Maryborough.

Hutchinson, William Henry, A.B., Curate of Urney and Annagelliff (*Kilmore*), Cavan.

Hyde, Arthur, A.M.. Precentor of Ross (*Ross*).

Hyde, Arthur, jun., A.B., Rector of Tibohine (*Elphin*), Frenchpark.

IRELAND, T. W., A.B., Curate of Drumlummon (*Ardagh*), Scrabby.

Irvine, Aiken, A.B., Curate of Kilbride, Bray (*Dublin*).

Irvine, A. B., A.B., Curate of Coleraine (*Connor*).

Irvine, Christopher, A.M., Incumbent of Trinity Church, Lislemnaghan (*Derry*), Strabane.

Irvine, Gorges, A.B., Rector of Muckno (*Clogher*), Castleblayney.

Irvine, H. C., A.B., Incumbent of Aghavilly (*Armagh*), Armagh.

Irvine, Richard, A.B., Curate of Christchurch (*Connor*), Belfast.

Irvine, William John, A.M., Incumbent of Kilmoon (*Meath*), Ashbourne.

Irving, John, A.M., Rector of Donaghmore (*Derry*), Castlefin.

Irwin, Alexander, A.M., Precentor, Rector of Killevy (*Armagh*).

Irwin, Benjamin, Perpetual Curate of Killukin (*Elphin*), Killukin.

Irwin, Charles King, A.M., Rural Dean, Rector of Loughgilly (*Armagh*), Markethill.

Irwin, Charles King, jun., A.M., Curate of Kilmore (*Armagh*), Armagh.

Irwin, Francis, Incumbent of Donamon (*Elphin*), Athleague.

Irwin, Francis, A.M., Prebendary of Elphin, Rector of Tarmonbarry (*Elphin*), Ruskey.

Irwin, Henry, B.D., Archdeacon of Elphin, Vicar of Aughrim, Rector of Killukin (*Elphin*), Carrick-on-Shannon.

Irwin, Henry, A.B., Perpetual Curate of Newtownmountkennedy (*Dublin*).

Irwin, J. G, A.B., Curate of Clongill (*Meath*), Navan

Irwin, James William, A.M., Curate of Raymochy (*Raphoe*), Manorcunningham.

Irwin, John L., A.M., Vicar Choral, St. Patrick's (*Dublin*), Rector of Thomastown (*Ossory*).

Irwin, Robert, A.B., Vicar of Rathcore (*Meath*), Enfield.

Isaac, Abraham, A.B., Rural Dean, Rector of Killiny (*Ardfert and Aghadoe*), Castlegregory.

JACKSON, James, Perpetual Curate of Tobbercurry (*Achonry*).

Jackson, J. C. M., Curate of Belturbet (*Kilmore*).

Jackson, John, Curate of Syddan (*Meath*), Ardee.

Jackson, John, Incumbent of Tallow and Vicar of Kilwatermoy (*Lismore*), Tallow.

Jackson, John, A.B., Prebendary of Kinvara (*Kilmacduagh*), Curate of New Quay (*Kilfenora*), Burren.

Jackson, John J., A.M., Rector of Ballinderry (*Armagh*), Moneymore.

Jackson, Thomas, A.B., Rural Dean, Rector of Bailieborough (*Kilmore*).

Jackson, William Oliver, A.M., Incumbent of Straid (*Achonry*), Foxford.

Jackson, Ven. William, A.M., Archdeacon of Killala, Rural Dean, Incumbent of Castleconnor (*Killala*), Ballina.

Jacob, Benjamin, A.M., Rural Dean, Rector of St. Patrick's (*Limerick*), and Treasurer of the Diocese, Limerick.

Jacob, John, G., A.B., Curate of Taghmon (*Ferns*).

Jagoe, Abraham, A.B., District Curate of Castlekirke (*Tuam*), Bunakyle, Galway.

James, Albert B., M.A., Perpetual Curate of Clabby (*Clogher*), Fivemiletown.

Jameson, James, A.M., Rector of Killeshin (*Leighlin*), Carlow.

Jameson, Paul, A.M., Curate of Clonfeacle (*Armagh*), Moy.

Jameson, Thomas, A.B., Rural Dean, Vicar of Finglas (*Dublin*), Finglas.

Jameson, William, A.M., Chaplain Female Penitentiary (*Dublin*), Drumcondra.

Jamison, Campbell, A.B., Curate of Killesher (*Kilmore*), Florence-court.

Jamison, Thomas, A.B., Curate of Ballysodare (*Achonry*).

Jebb, Thomas, A.M., Vicar of Larah (*Kilmore*), Stradone.

Jebb, Thomas William, A.B., Incumbent of Lettermacaward (*Raphoe*), Dungloe.

Jeffares, Danby, A.B., Incumbent of Holywood (*Dublin*), Balbriggan.

Jeffares, Richard, A.B., Curate of Connor and Killagan (*Connor*), Ballymena.

Jeffares, Samuel, A.M., Rector of Listerlin (*Ossory*), New Ross.

Jellett, Henry, A.M., Rector of Ahinagh (*Cloyne*), Killanardish.

Jellett, John Hewitt, B.D., Professor of Natural Philosophy and Fellow of Trinity College—residence, 18, Heytesbury-terrace, Dublin.

Jellett, Morgan Woodward, A.M., Curate of St. Peter's (*Dublin*)—residence, 80, Renelagh-road.

Jervois, Robert D., A.B., Incumbent of Kilnaboy (*Killaloe*), Newmarket-on-Fergus, and Kiltoraght (*Kilfenora*), Corofin.

John, William Thomas, A.B., Curate of Free Church, Derry (*Derry*).
Johnson, Benjamin Henry, A.M., Perpetual Curate of Drumcondra (*Dublin*)—residence, 12, Montpelier-hill.
Johnson, Charles, Vicar of Clonagoose (*Leighlin*), Borris.
Johnson, Henry, A.B., Curate of Monkstown (*Dublin*).
Johnson, John, A.B., Perpetual Curate of Old Ross (*Ferns*), New Ross.
Johnson, John Allen, A.B., Curate of Ballinderry (*Connor*).
Johnson, John Evans, D.D., Archdeacon of Ferns, Incumbent of Adamstown (*Ferns*), Enniscorthy, and 70, Harcourt-street, Dublin.
Johnson, William, A.M., Chancellor of Cloyne and Ross, Incumbent of Clenore (*Cloyne*).
Johnston, Henikar, A.M., Rector of Holywood (*Dublin*), Blessington.
Johnston, Henry, A.M., Rector of Ratoath (*Meath*).
Johnston, Richard, A.B., Perpetual Curate of O'Meatle (*Armagh*).
Johnston, Robert, A.M., Rector of Rossorry (*Clogher*), Enniskillen.
Johnston, Walter, A.B., Prebendary and Incumbent of Connor (*Connor*), Ballymena.
Johnston, W. D., A.B., Curate of Ballyscullion (*Derry*).
Johnstone, Henry, A.M., Incumbent of Boyle (*Elphin*), Boyle.
Johnstone, Robert, A.B., Curate of St. George (*Dublin*) - residence, 23, Nelson-street.
Joly, John S., A.M., Rector of Tullamore (*Meath*), Kilbride, Tullamore.
Jones, Andrew A., A.B., Bishop's Chaplain, Rural Dean, Incumbent of Kilmore (*Killaloe*), Silvermines.
Jones, Charles, A.B., Perpetual Curate of Kilteevock (*Raphoe*), Stranorlar.
Jones, E. G., A.M., Incumbent of Kilmurry (*Cork*), Crookstown.
Jones, George, A.B., Prebendary, Incumbent of Whitechurch (*Ferns*), New Ross.
Jones, James, A.M., Chancellor of Armagh, Rector of Kilmore (*Armagh*), Armagh.
Jones, James, junior, A.M., Perpetual Curate of Richhill (*Armagh*).
Jones, Jonas, Curate of Tullagh (*Ross*), Skibbereen.
Jones, Joshua F., A.B., Curate of Clonegam (*Lismore*), Portlaw.
Jones, R., Curate of Youghal (*Cloyne*).
Jones, Richard Bathoe, A.B., Incumbent of Templeharry (*Killaloe*), Cloughjordan.
Jones, Thomas Josiah, A.M., Curate of Ardtrea (*Armagh*), Stewartstown.
Jones, Thomas S., Perpetual Curate of Calry (*Elphin*), Sligo.
Jones, William, A.M., Incumbent of Donabate (*Dublin*), Donabate.
Jordan, Benjamin, A.B., Vicar of Cahercorney (*Emly*), Bruff.
Jordan, Charles, A.B., Curate of Kilcommon (*Killala*), Belmullet.
Jordan, Thomas, B.D., Rector of Arboe (*Armagh*), Stewartstown.
Jordan, William T., A.B., Rector of Templederry (*Killaloe*), Templederry.

Kane, Francis, A.B., Vicar of Shrule (*Ardagh*), Ballymahon.
Kane, John Blackburne, A.B., Perpetual Curate of Annaghmore (*Armagh*), Loughgall.
Kane, Thomas M., Curate of Garvaghy (*Dromore*), Dromore.
Keane, Thomas, A.B., Curate of Trinity and St. Olave (*Waterford*), Waterford.
Kearney, Alexander M., A.B., Curate of Mohill (*Ardagh*).
Kearney, Thomas F., Rector of Kilbeheny (*Emly*), Mitchelstown.
Kearney, Thomas N., LL.D., Rector of Carrigrohanebeg (*Cork*), Ballincollig.
Keatinge, Joseph, A.M., Prebendary of Leighlin, a Vicar Choral, Incumbent of Tecolm (*Leighlin*), Athy.
Keatinge, Michael J., A.M., Dean of Kilfenora, Rector of Kilfenora (*Kilfenora*).
Keene, Martin A., A.B., Curate of Harold's-cross (*Dublin*), —residence, 6, Home-ville, Rathmines.
Kellett, Orange S., A.M., Rural Dean, Rector of Tomregan (*Kilmore*), Ballyconnell.
Kemmis, George, Incumbent of Oregan (*Kildare*), Mountmellick.
Kempston, William A., A.M., Rector of Kilmore (*Meath*), Kilcock.
Kennedy, Henry, A.B., Rector of Upper Langfield (*Derry*), Omagh.
Kennedy, J., Curate of St. Michael's, Trory (*Clogher*), Enniskillen.
Kennedy, L. S., A.M., Incumbent of Holywood (*Down*), Holywood.
Kennedy, Rickard, A.M., Rural Dean, Rector of Kilmacow (*Ossory*), Waterford.
Kennedy, Thomas Le Ban, A.B., Rector of Kilmore (*Clogher*), Monaghan.
Kennedy, William Studdert, A.M., Perpetual Curate, St. Doulagh's (*Dublin*).
Kerin, John, Perpetual Curate of Ardfert and O'Brennan (*Ardfert and Aghadoe*), Ardfert.
Kerr, John Alexander, A.B., Rector of Donegore (*Connor*), Doagh.
Kerr, William Pattison, A.M., Perpetual Curate of Crossduff (*Clogher*), Shantonagh.
Keyburne, George, Curate of Mallow (*Cloyne*).
Kilbride, Henry N., A.B., Curate of Colliery (*Ossory*), Castlecomer.
Kilbride, William, Incumbent of Arran (*Tuam*), Galway.
Kinahan, W. R. L., A.B., Curate of Kiltubbrid (*Ardagh*), Carrick-on-Shannon.
Kincaid, John, A.M., Prebendary of Raphoe, Vicar of Drumholm (*Raphoe*), Ballintra.
King, A. Smyth, A.B., Curate of Dundonald (*Down*), Belfast.
King, Edward, A.B., Curate of Ahoghill, (*Connor*), Ballymena.
King, Francis, Curate of St. Patrick's Chapel of Ease (*Ex. jur. of Newry and Mourne*), Newry.
King, John, A.M., Rural Dean, Rector of Upper Fahan (*Derry*), Fahan.
King, John H., A.M., Rector of Drumglass (*Armagh*), Dungannon.
King, Joseph, A.B., Curate of Drung (*Kilmore*), Drung, Cavan.
King, Richard, Incumbent of Killurin (*Ferns*), Wexford.
King, Robert, A.M., Rector of Kilmore (*Elphin*), Drumsna.
King, Robert W., A.M., Perpetual Curate of Portglenone (*Connor*), Portglenone.
King, William Smyth, A.M., Rural Dean, Incumbent of Clonenagh (*Leighlin*), Mountrath.
Kingsley, Charles, A.B., Curate of Kilmoe (*Cork*), Skibbereen.
Kingsmill, Henry, D.D., Rector of Conwall (*Raphoe*), Letterkenny.
Kingsmore, Robert, A.B., Rector of Tullyniskin (*Armagh*), Dungannon.
Kirby, James, A.B., Incumbent of Kiltegan (*Leighlin*), Baltinglass.
Kirchoffer, Richard B., A.M., Incumbent of Ballyvourney (*Cloyne*), Macroom.
Kirkpatrick, Alexander T., A.B., Curate of Craigs (*Connor*), Cullybackey, Belfast.
Kirkpatrick, George, A.B., Rector of Craigs (*Connor*), Cullybackey, Belfast.
Kirkpatrick, George, A.B., Perpetual Curate of Mayne (*Meath*), Coole, Rathowen.
Kirwan, Anthony Latouch, D.D., Dean of Limerick, Rector of Derrygalvin, and Incumbent of St. Mary's (*Limerick*).
Knott, Thomas, A.B., Incumbent of Ballysumaghan (*Elphin*), Collooney.
Knox, Arthur, A.M., Rector of Castleterra (*Kilmore*) Ballyhaise.
Knox, Charles Beresford, A.B., Treasurer and Rector of Dromore (*Dromore*).

Knox, Denis, A.M., Rector of Muntereonnaught (*Kilmore*), Virginia.

Knox, Denis, A.M., Chaplain of Loughan (*Meath*), Virginia.

Knox, E. D. H., A.B., Rector of Kilflyn (*Limerick*), Kilmallock.

Knox, Edmond, A.B., Archdeacon of Killaloe, Rector of Dorrha and Lorrha (*Killaloe*), Borrisokane.

Knox, George, A.B., Rector of Castleblakeney (*Elphin*), Athleague.

Knox, Thomas, A.M., Vicar-General of Dromore, Precentor of Connor, Rector of Ballymoney (*Connor*), Ballymoney.

Kyle, John Torrens, B.D., Prebendary of Cloyne, Rector of Clondrohid (*Cloyne*), Macroom.

Kyle, Samuel Moore, LL.D., Archdeacon of Cork, Vicar-General and Chancellor of Cork and Cloyne, and Incumbent of St. Peter's (*Cork*), Cork.

Labarte, Richard Burgess, A.B., Curate of Tullylish (*Dromore*) Laurencetown.

Labarte, R., A.B., Curate of Holywood (*Down*).

Labatt, Edward, A.M., Rector of Kilcar (*Raphoe*), Killybegs.

Lamb, Vincent, A.B., Curate of Kilmahon (*Cloyne*), Cloyne.

Lamb, Walter, A.M., Curate of Desertserges (*Cork*), Bandon.

Lambart, Charles J., A.B., Rector of Navan (*Meath*) Balrath, Drogheda.

Lambert, William, Rural Dean, Rector of Killemlagh (*Ardfert and Aghadoe*), Cahirciveen.

Lancaster, James, A.M., Registrar of the Diocese of Tuam, Prebendary of Ossory, Rural Dean, and Incumbent of Inistiogue (*Ossory*), Inistiogue.

Lane, Jeremiah, Rector of Killishee (*Kildare*), Naas.

Lane, Richard C., A.B., Rector of Lisronagh (*Lismore*), Clonmel.

Langley, Charles Seymour, B.D., Incumbent of Kilworth (*Cloyne*).

Latouche, John W., LL.D., Prebendary of St. Patrick's, Rector of Clonmethan (*Dublin*), Oldtown.

Latouche, Peter Digges, Rector of Painstown (*Meath*), Beauparc, Slane.

Lauder, Matthew Nesbitt, A.B., Incumbent of Swanlinbar (*Kilmore*).

Lauder, Robert, LL.D., Incumbent of Agher (*Meath*), Agher.

Lauder, Very Rev. William Bernard, LL.D., Dean of Leighlin and Incumbent of Wells (*Leighlin*), Leighlinbridge.

Law, Robert Samuel, A.B., District Curate of Drumbanagher and Curate of Killeavey (*Armagh*), Newry.

Lawler, Edward F., A.B., Perpetual Curate of Monamolin (*Ferns*).

Lawrence, R. F., A.M., Treasurer of Cashel, Incumbent of Borrisleagh (*Cashel*), Littleton, Thurles.

Lawrenson, William R., A.M., Prebendary of St. Patrick's, Incumbent of Howth (*Dublin*), Sutton House, Howth.

Lawson, Ambrose, A.B., Curate of St. Mary's, Clonmel (*Lismore*).

Lawson, James, A.M., A M., Incumbent of St. Nicholas, Kill (*Waterford*), Passage East.

Leahy, Daniel, Vicar of Kilmactranny (*Elphin*), Ballyfarnon.

Leathley, Joseph Forde, A.M , Incumbent of Termonfeckin (*Armagh*), Drogheda.

Ledger, William C , A.B., Curate of Shinrone (*Killaloe*).

Lee, Alfred T., A.M., Rural Dean, Rector of Ahoghill (*Connor*), Ballymena.

Lee, John, A.M., Rector of Leighmoney (*Cork*), Kinsale.

Lee, Ven. William, D.D., F.T.C.D., Archdeacon of Dublin, Incumbent of St. Peter's (*Dublin*), 24, Merrion-square, south, and Trinity College, Dublin.

Lee, William, A.M.

Leech, Arthur Henry, A.B., Rural Dean, Vicar of Emly and Curate of Ballyscadden (*Emly*).

Leech, John, A.M., Chaplain, Kingston College (*Cloyne*), Mitchelstown.

Leeper, Alexander, B.D., Prebendary of St. Patrickes, Rural Dean, Incumbent of St. Audoen's (*Dublin*), 10, Kildare-street.

Lees, John, A.M., Incumbent of Annaghdown (*Tuam*), Drumgriffin.

Leet, Ambrose W., A.M., Curate of Sandford (*Dublin*), residence, 25, Leeson-park.

Leet, Edward S., Chaplain of Dalkey (*Dublin*), 6, Sandycove-terrace, Kingstown.

Le Fanu, William Joseph Henry, A.M., Rector of St. Paul's (*Dublin*), 5, Blackhall-street.

Lefroy, Henry, A.M., Vicar of Santry (*Dublin*).

Lefroy, Jeffry, A.M., Rural Dean, Rector of Aghaderg (*Dromore*), Loughbrickland.

Le Hunte, Francis, A.M., Chaplain of Dublin Female Penitentiary (*Dublin*), 2, Hardwick-street.

Leonard, Samuel B., A.M., Incumbent of Dromtariff (*Ardfert and Aghadoe*), Banteer.

Le Pan, Louis Augustus, LL.D., Chaplain, King's Hospital (*Dublin*).

Leslie, Charles, A.M., Vicar-General of Ardagh, Incumbent of Drung (*Kilmore*), Cavan.

Leslie, Henry, A.M., Rector of Kilclief (*Down*), Strangford.

Leslie, John, A.M., Fellow of Trinity College, Dublin.

Leslie, R. J. U., A.M., Perpetual Curate of Frankfield (*Cork*), Cork.

L'Estrange, Guy James Carleton, A.M., Rural Dean, Perpetual Vicar of Kilbroney (*Dromore*), Rostrevor.

Lett, Charles, A.M., Rural Dean, Rector of Dunaghby (*Connor*), Ballymena.

Lett, Henry W., A.B., Perpetual Curate of Meigh (*Armagh*), Newry.

Lett, Stephen, A.B., Curate of Kilcommon (*Ferns*), Tinahely.

Lewis, Edmund Jones, A.M., Vicar of Knockmark (*Meath*), Dunshaughlin.

Lewis, John Evans, A.M., Rector of Moyntaghs (*Dromore*), Derrymacash, Lurgan.

Lewis, Samuel Henry, A.B., Vicar of Columbkille (*Ardagh*), Edgeworthstown, and Curate of Shercock (*Kilmore*), Shercock.

Lindsay, Robert, A.B., Curate of Lisburn (*Connor*), Lisburn.

Little, James, Incumbent of Castlemore (*Achonry*), Ballaghadereen.

Lloyd, Edward, A.B., Curate of Bourney (*Killaloe*), Roscrea.

Lloyd, Humphrey, D.D., Vice-Provost and Senior Fellow of Trinity College, Dublin.

Lloyd, Thomas, A.M., Rural Dean, Vicar of Kilglass (*Elphin*), Ruskey.

Lodge, William H., A.B., Curate of Askeaton (*Limerick*), Askeaton.

Logan, Thomas Dawson, A.M., Incumbent of Charlestown (*Armagh*), Ardee.

Lombard, Edmond, A.M., Prebendary of Cork, Rector of Athnowen (*Cork*), Ovens, Cork.

Lombard, John, A.M., Curate of Clonmel (*Cloyne*), Queenstown.

Long, John A., A.B., Rector of Ballysheehan (*Cashel*), Cashel.

Long, Richard Henry, A.B., Incumbent of Rathdrumin (*Armagh*), Dunleer.

Long, Thomas, A.M., Curate of St. John's (*Dublin*), 9, Morehampton-terrace, Donnybrook.

Longfield, George, D.D., Fellow of Trinity College, Dublin.

Longfield, Richard, A.B., Incumbent of Mogeely (*Cloyne*), Tallow.

Longfield, Thomas Hugo, A.M., Rector of St. Paul's (*Cork*), Cork.

Low, John, Curate of Killoughey (*Meath*), Clonaslee.

Lowe, Edward, Incumbent of Kilmacshalgan (*Killala*), Easkey.

Lowe, William, Perpetual Curate of Formoyle (*Derry*), Coleraine.

Luby, Thomas, D.D., Senior Fellow of Trinity College, Dublin.

Lucas, Edward, A.B., Vicar of Killenumery (*Ardagh*), Dromahaire.
Lucas, Frederick John, A.B., Curate of Milltown (*Dublin*), Milltown.
Luther, John F., A.B., Curate of Kilflyn (*Limerick*), Kilmallock.
Lyle, Edward A., A.B., Rural Dean, Perpetual Curate of Kirkcubbin (*Down*), Kirkcubbin.
Lyle, John, A.B., Rector of Kildollagh (*Connor*), Coleraine.
Lymberry, John, A.B., Vicar of Hook (*Ferns*), Fethard.
Lynar, William K., A.M., Rector of Islandmagee (*Connor*), Larne.
Lynch, Brownlow, A.B., Incumbent of Burriscarra (*Tuam*), Ballinrobe.
Lynch, John, A.M., Incumbent of St. John, Monkstown (*Dublin*).
Lynn, John, Curate of St. Patrick's, Wexford (*Ferns*), Wexford.
Lyon, Thomas, A.B., Rural Dean, Vicar of Kilbarron (*Killaloe*), Coulbawn, Roscrea.
Lyons, James, A.B., Curate of Leckpatrick (*Derry*), Strabane.
Lyons, Thomas A., A.M., Rector of Dunmore (*Tuam*).
Lyster, John, Curate of Denn (*Kilmore*), Cavan.
Lyster, William, A.M., Rector of Killucan (*Meath*).

M'Adam, W. H., A.B., Curate of Drummaul (*Connor*), Randalstown.
M'Carthy, Charles Fennell, A.M., Curate of St. Thomas's (*Dublin*), residence, 8, Durham-place, Corrig-road, Kingstown.
M'Carthy, J., A.B., Curate of St. Luke's, (*Cork*), Cork.
M'Causland, A. H., A.B. Incumbent of Groomsport (*Down*), Bangor.
M'Causland, John, Perpetual Curate of Nobber (*Meath*).
M'Causland, John, Conyngham, A.M., Incumbent of Cloonmore (*Armagh*), Dunleer.
M'Causland, Mar., A.M., Rector of Birr (*Killaloe*), Parsonstown.
M'Causland, William C., A.B., Incumbent of Kiltullagh (*Tuam*), Castlerea.
M'Cheane, James Charles, A.M., District Curate of St. Lappens (*Cork*), Glanmire.
M'Cheane, Jeremiah, A.B., Rector of Kilmoganny (*Ossory*), Callan.
M'Cheane, Joseph B., A.B., Curate of Aghour and Ballylarkin (*Ossory*), Freshford.
M'Clellan, Thomas, A.M., Rural Dean, Rector of Camus juxta Bann (*Derry*), Macosquin, Coleraine.
M'Clelland, George, A.B., Rector of Mayo (*Tuam*), Ballyglass.
M'Clelland, William, A.M., Incumbent of Tessaragh (*Elphin*), Mount Talbot.
M'Clintock, H. F., A.M., Rector of Kilmichael (*Cork*), Macroom.
M'Clintock, John S., A.M., Curate of Clonleigh (*Derry*), Lifford.
M'Clintock, Lowry, A.B., Rural Dean, Incumbent of Kilmolara (*Tuam*), Ballinrobe.
M'Clintock, Robert Le P, A.M., Incumbent of Kilsaran (*Armagh*), Castlebellingham.
M'Clure, E., A.M., Curate of St. George (*Connor*), Belfast.
M'Cord, G. M., Curate of Christchurch (*Cork*), Cork.
M'Cormick, James Francis, A.M., Prebendary and Rector of Geashill (*Kildare*), Tullamore.
M'Cormick, Joseph, A.M., Rural Dean, Vicar of Ballinderry (*Connor*).
M'Cready, Christopher, A.M., Curate of St. Audoen's (*Dublin*)—residence 29, Molesworth-street.
M'Creery, Thomas B., A.B., Reader, Cloyne Cathedral (*Cloyne*), Cloyne.
M'Creight, Andrew, A.M., Rural Dean, Bishop's Chaplain, Rector of Belturbet (*Kilmore*).
Macdona, John C., A.M., Rector of Kilbride-Veston (*Meath*), Mullingar.
Macdonald, Henry Francis, Incumbent of Athy (*Dublin*).
Macdonnell, Charles, LL.D., Vicar of Kinneagh (*Dublin*), Castledermot.
Macdonnell, George, A.M., Vicar of Kilgeffin (*Elphin*), Kilrooskey, Longford.
Macdonnell, John Cotter, D.D., Dean of Cashel and Incumbent of St. John the Baptist (*Cashel*), Cashel.
Macdonnell, Ronald, D.D., Rural Dean, Rector of Monkstown (*Dublin*).
M'Donnell, Luke Gardiner, A.M., Rector of Glankeen (*Cashel*), Borrisoleigh.
M'Donogh, A. J., LL.D., Curate of Chapelizod (*Dublin*).
Macdonogh, James D., Curate of Upper Badoney (*Derry*), Plumbridge, Newtownstewart.
M'Donagh, Telford, A.M., Rector of Ettagh (*Killaloe*), Roscrea.
M'Donough, Charles, Rector of Powerscourt (*Dublin*), Enniskerry.
M'Ewen, James, A.B., Rural Dean, Rector of Aghavallin (*Ardfert and Aghadoe*), Listowel.
M'Groarty, John, A.B.
M'Ilwaine, William, A.M., Perpetual Curate of St. George's (*Connor*), Belfast.
M'Kaige, John, Curate of Killegney (*Ferns*), Enniscorthy.
M'Kay, Charles Elrington, A.M., Vicar of Laracor (*Meath*), Kells.
M'Kay, Maurice, LL.D., Rector of Ballyrashane (*Connor*), Coleraine.
M'Kay, Maurice Knox, A.M., Incumbent of St. Matthew's (*Connor*), Lisburn.
M'Kee, Robert, A.B., Precentor of Leighlin, Rector of Nurney, and Curate of Templepeter (*Leighlin*), Bagnalstown.
Macivor, James, D.D., Rector of Ardstraw (*Derry*), Newtownstewart.
Mackesy, William, A.M., Prebendary of Lismore, Rector of Drakestown (*Meath*), Navan.
Mackesy, William P., A.M., Incumbent of Dunkitt (*Ossory*), Waterford.
Maclaughlin, Alexander, A.M., Incumbent of Abington, &c. (*Emly*), Murroe, Limerick.
M'Laurin, John, A.B., Curate of Kiltermon (*Clogher*), Fivemiletown.
Maclean, Henry, Rector of Kilcolman (*Tuam*), Claremorris.
M'Mahon, James Fitzgibbon, A.M., Vicar of Aney (*Emly*), Hospital.
M'Mahon, John Henry, A.M., Curate of St. Werburg's (*Dublin*)—residence, 72, Eccles-street.
M'Nally, Thomas, A.B., Curate of St. Nicholas Without (*Dublin*), 4, Wesley-place.
Macnamara, A. D., A.B., Curate of Free Church, Cork (*Cork*).
Macnamara, Frederick A., A.B.
M'Neece, James, A.M., Curate of Donaghmore (*Armagh*), Dungannon.
M'Neill, George, A.M., Vicar of St. Mark's (*Dublin*)—residence, 4, Corrig-avenue, Kingstown.
M'Neill, Hugh, Curate of Derrykeighan (*Connor*), Ballymoney.
MacNeill, John Gordon Swift, A.M., Curate of St. Catherine's (*Dublin*)—residence, 14, Blackhall-street.
Maconchy, William, A.M., Vicar of Coolock (*Dublin*).
MacSorley, John James, A.M., Curate of St. Kevin's (*Dublin*), 94, Ranelagh-road.
Madden, Hugh Hamilton, A.M., Chancellor of Cashel, Rector of Templemore, Rural Dean (*Cashel*), Templemore.
Madden, Samuel, A.M., Prebendary and Rector of Kilmanagh (*Ossory*), Callan.
Madden, Samuel Owen, A.M., Curate of St. Finbar's, Cork (*Cork*).
Madras, John, Prebendary of Ross, Perpetual Curate of Abbeymahon, Vicar of Donaghmore, and Curate of Templequinlan (*Ross*), Timoleague.
Magee, Samuel, A.M., Vicar of Rathmolyon (*Meath*), Summerhill.
Magee, William Connor, D.D., Dean of Cork, and Dean of the Chapel Royal, Dublin Castle, Dunganstown, Wicklow.
Maginn, Charles Arthur, A.M., Rural Dean, Rector of Castletown (*Cloyne*), Castletownroche.
Maginnis, Charles, A.M., Incumbent of Newtown Saville, (*Clogher*), Omagh.

Magrath, Folliott, A.M., Rector of Corclone (*Leighlin*), Stradbally.
Magrath, W. C., Rector of Baldungen (*Dublin*).
Maguire, Edward, A.M., Rural Dean, Rector of Dunluce (*Connor*), Bushmills.
Maguire, John M., A.M., Rector of Kilkeedy (*Limerick*), Clarina.
Mahaffy, John P., M.A., Fellow Trinity College, Dublin.
Major, William Miller, A.M., Prebendary and Incumbent of Moville, Upper (*Derry*), Moville.
Malet, John Adam, D.D., Fellow of Trinity College, Dublin.
Malone, Savile L'Estrarge, Vicar Choral (*Armagh*), Armagh.
Mangan, James, LL.D., Vicar of Crecora (*Limerick*), Limerick.
Mangan, William Reazon, A.M., Curate of St. Anne, Shandon (*Cork*), Cork
Mansfield, G., A.M., Rector of Kiltubbrid (*Ardagh*), Cashcarrigan.
Mant, Walter Bishop, A.M., Archdeacon of Down, Rector of Hillsborough (*Down*).
Marks, Edward, D.D., Dean's Vicar, Resident Preacher, and Minor Canon of St. Patrick's (*Dublin*), 11, Heytesbury-street.
Marmion, Richard Walton, A.M., Treasurer of Ross, Rector of Kilmeen (*Ross*), Clonakilty.
Marrable, William, A.M., Prebendary and Rector of St. Michan's (*Dublin*), 49, Waterloo-road.
Marsh, Francis, A.B., Perpetual Curate of Multifarnham (*Meath*).
Marshall, James, A.M., Perpetual Curate of St. Mark's, Ballysillan (*Connor*), Belfast.
Marshall, John William M., A.M., Incumbent of Painestown (*Leighlin*), Carlow.
Marshall, Thomas, A.M., Incumbent of Dunshaughlin (*Meath*).
Martin, George Henry, A.B., Incumbent of Killigar (*Kilmore*), Carrigallen.
Martin, Henry, A.M., Incumbent of Kilmacrenan (*Raphoe*), Letterkenny.
Martin, James, A.B., Rector of Finnoe (*Killaloe*), Borrisokane.
Martin, Ven. John Charles, D.D., Archdeacon of Kilmore, Rural Dean, Rector of Killeshandra (*Kilmore*), Killeshandra.
Martin, John C., junior, A.B., Curate of Killeshandra (*Kilmore*).
Martin, John Welply, A.M., Prebendary of Ross, Vicar of Timoleague.
Martin, Nicholas C., A.B., Rector of Donagh (*Derry*), Carndonagh.
Martin, Robert Agnew, A.M., Rector of Moyliskar (*Meath*) Mullingar.
Martin, Samuel, A.B., Perpetual Curate of Convoy (*Raphoe*), Convoy.
Martin, Thomas Fielding, A.M., Incumbent of Tyrella (*Down*), Clough.
Mason, Thomas, Curate of Eglish (*Meath*), Five-alley.
Massey, William E., A.B., Rural Dean, Rector of Rathronan and Curate of Grange (*Limerick*), Newcastle.
Massy, A. H. T., A.B., Curate of Kells (*Ossory*), Thomastown.
Massy, Dawson, A.M., Incumbent of Hacketstown (*Leighlin*), Hacketstown.
Massy, Henry, A.M., Perpetual Curate of Aglishcloghane (*Killaloe*), Borrisokane.
Massy, John M., A.M., Perpetual Curate of Killoughter (*Kilmore*), Redhills.
Masters, Alfred, Incumbent of Killesk (*Ferns*), Arthurstown.
Mathews, John, A.M., Curate of Youghalarra (*Killaloe*), Nenagh.
Maturin, Edward, Curate of Cleenish (*Clogher*), Enniskillen.
Maturin, Henry, A.M., Rector of Gartan (*Raphoe*), Letterkenny.
Maturin, William, A.M., Perpetual Curate of Grangegorman (*Dublin*), Phibsborough, Dublin.

Maunsell, Francis R., Rector of Castleisland (*Ardfert and Aghadoe*).
Maunsell, Horatio, A.M., Rector of Drumbo (*Down*), Lisburn.
Maunsell, Louis Montagu, A.M., Rural Dean, Rector of Kilskeer (*Meath*), Crossakeel.
Maunsell, Robert Augustus, A.M., Rector of Coolbanagher (*Kildare*), Emo.
Maunsell, Warren Cecil, A.M., Incumbent of Thomastown (*Kildare*), Kildare.
Maunsell, William F., A.B., Rural Dean, Perpetual Curate of Kildimo (*Limerick*), Clarina.
Maxwell, Charlton, A.M., Rural Dean, Rector of Leckpatrick (*Derry*), Strabane.
Maxwell, George, Rural Dean, Incumbent of Askeaton (*Limerick*).
Maxwell, Robert W., Prebendary and Incumbent of Balla (*Tuam*), Ballyglass.
Mayers, W. M., A.M., Prebendary of St. Patrick's (*Dublin*).
Mayne, Charles, A.M., Incumbent of Kilmastulla (*Emly*), Killaloe.
Meade, Richard C., A.M., Perpetual Curate of Marmullane (*Cork*), Passage West.
Meade, Robert Henry, A.M., Rector of Rincurran (*Cork*), Kinsale.
Meade, R. T., Rector of Templetrine (*Cork*), Bandon.
Meade, William Edward, A.M., Rector of Ardtrea (*Armagh*), Stewardstown.
Meade, William R., A.B., Incumbent of Inchinabackey (*Cloyne*), Midleton.
Mecredy, James, A.M., Rector of Kilkerrin (*Tuam*), Moylough.
Meighan, James, A.B., Curate of Carrickfergus (*Connor*).
Meredith, Ralph R. A., A.M., Curate of Bray (*Dublin*), Bray.
Meredyth, Francis, M.A. (Oxon), Curate of St. Mary's (*Limerick*).
Meredyth, R. F., A.M., Rector of Ballycualane (*Limerick*), Castleisland.
Meredyth, Richard Graves, A.M., Rector of Knockavilly (*Cork*), Bandon.
Mervyn, W. H., A.B., Curate of Kildallock (*Connor*), Coleraine.
Meyrick, Samuel H., A.M., Prebendary of St. Patrick's, Incumbent of Blessington (*Dublin*), and Vicar Choral of Lismore (*Lismore*).
Miles, Thomas, A.M., Prebendary of Cashel, Rector of Fennor (*Cashel*), Urlingford.
Millar, A. R., Curate of Haggardstown (*Armagh*), Dundalk.
Miller, Alexander Bowley, A.M., Rector of Lissan (*Armagh*), Moneymore.
Miller, Charles, A.M., Rector of Newtownhamilton (*Armagh*), Manorhamilton.
Miller, Thomas Fitzwilliam, D.D., Vicar of Belfast (*Connor*).
Millington, James, Vicar of Kilronan (*Lismore*), Clonmel.
Mills, Charles Edward, A.B., Treasurer of Kilmacduagh, Incumbent of Kilconickny (*Clonfert*), Craughwell.
Mills, Thomas, A.M., Perpetual Curate of St. Jude's (*Dublin*), Inchicore.
Minchin, Augustus H., A.M., Perpetual Curate of Lower Fahan (*Kerry*), Buncrana.
Mitchell, Richard, A.B., Curate of Coolbanagher (*Kildare*), Mountmellick.
Mitchell, Richard H., A.B., Curate of Oregan, (*Kildare*), Mountmellick.
Mitchell, St. John F., A.B., Curate of St. John's, Sandymount (*Dublin*), Sandymount.
Mockler, Edward, A.B., Rector of Maghergal (*Connor*), Lisburn.
Moeran, Edward B., D.D., Rector of Killyleagh (*Down*), Killyleagh.
Moffat, George B., A.M., Rector of Drumlane (*Kilmore*), Belturbet.
Moffat, James, A.B., District Curate of Derryheen (*Kilmore*), Cavan.
Moffett, Robert John, A.M., Incumbent of Kilternan (*Dublin*), Goldenball.
Moinah, Patrick, A.B., Curate of Kilflynn, &c. (*Ardfert and Aghadoe*), Kilflynn, Tralee.

Mollan, Robert, Vicar of Ballinakil (*Tuam*), Clifden.

Molony, Arthur, A.M., Prebendary and Rector of Ballymore (*Armagh*), Tanderagee.

Monahan, James Hunter, B.D., Rector of St. Mary's (*Dublin*), Hilton House, Rathmines.

Monsarratt, J. H., A.M. Incumbent of St. Mark's (*Armagh*), Drogheda.

Montague, Edward, A.B., Curate of Inniscaltra (*Killaloe*), Scariff.

Montgomery, Samuel, A.B., Rural Dean, Rector of Ballynascreen (*Derry*), Tobermore.

Moneypenny, Arthur, A.B., Vicar of Lavey (*Kilmore*), Stradone (*Elphin*), Collooney.

Mooney, Daniel, A.M., Rector of Clondevaddock (*Raphoe*), Ramelton.

Mooney, Peter, Curate of Geashill (*Kildare*), Geashill.

Moore, Arthur, A.M., Incumbent of Emlaghfad (*Achonry*), Ballymote.

Moore, Courtney, A.B., Curate of Brigown (*Cloyne*), Mitchelstown.

Moore, Edward, A.B., Perpetual Curate of Drumnakelly (*Armagh*), Omagh.

Moore, Edwin Lorenzo, A.M., Rector of Cong (*Tuam*).

Moore, E. M., A.B., Curate of Killeshandra (*Kilmore*).

Moore, Henry, A.M., Vicar of Julianstown (*Meath*), Drogheda.

Moore, John L., D.D., Senior Fellow of Trinity College, Dublin.

Moore, Joseph Carson, A.B., Curate of Urney (*Kilmore*), Cavan.

Moore, Ogle William, A.M., Dean and Rector of Clogher (*Clogher*).

Moore, Samuel Matthew, A.M., Curate of St Andrew's (*Dublin*)—residence, 26, Bloomfield-avenue.

Moore, Theodore, Octavius, A.M., Rural Dean, Rector of Annaduff (*Ardagh*), Edgeworthstown.

Moore, Thomas, A.M., Rector of Drumgoon (*Kilmore*), Cootehill.

Moore, Thomas, A.M., Incumbent of Garrane (*Cloyne*), Midleton.

Moore, William, A.B., Vicar of Killerry (*Ardagh*), Ballintogher.

Moran, James Fleming, Provost of Kilmacduagh, Incumbent of Kilcollan (*Kilmacduagh*).

Morewood, Roland S., A.B., Curate of Lis·an (*Armagh*), Moneymore.

Morgan, John, A.M., Rural Dean, Vicar of Cahir (*Lismore*), Cahir.

Morgan, John, A.M., Curate of Killardry (*Cashel*), Clonmel.

Morgan, Thomas P., Rector of Inver (*Connor*), Larne.

Moriarty, Denis, Rural Dean, Rector of Dunurlin (*Ardfert and Aghadoe*), Dingle.

Moriarty, Matthew T., Incumbent of St. Anne's (*Derry*), Draperstown, Tobermore.

Moriarty, Thomas, A.B., Rural Dean, Rector of Tralee (*Ardfert and Aghadoe*), Tralee.

Morphy, Richard, Vicar of Ulloe (*Emly*), Tipperary.

Morse, Edward, Curate of Castledermot (*Dublin*).

Mortimer, William, A.B., Vicar of Garvaghy (*Dromore*), Dromore.

Morton, John F., Curate of Rathronan (*Lismore*), Clonmel.

Morton, Joseph, A.M., Rural Dean, Incumbent of Bumlin (*Elphin*), Strokestown.

Mountmorres, Viscount, LL.D., Dean of Achonry (*Achonry*), Ballymote.

Moutray, John James, Rector of Errigal, Keerogue (*Armagh*), Ballygawley.

Moutray, John Maxwell, A.B., Perpetual Curate of Ballygawley (*Armagh*), Ballygawley.

Moutray, William, A.M., Curate of Portclare (*Clogher*), Aughnacloy.

Mulgan, Mason, LL.D., Perpetual Curate of Lisnadill (*Armagh*), Armagh.

Mulgan, William Edward, A.B., Vicar of Templecorran (*Connor*), Carrickfergus.

Mulholland, Alexander, A.M., Curate of Rathcormack (*Cloyne*), Rathcormack.

Mulloy, Coote, Curate of Finea (*Meath*), Granard.

DDD

Mulloy, William James, A.M., Rural Dean, Rector of Ballysonnon (*Kildare*), Kildare.

Murdock, James C., A.B., Perpetual Curate of Donamore (*Ferns*), Gorey.

Muriel, Hugh E., Rector of Kilconnell (*Clonfert*).

Murphy, Henry C., LL.B., Diocesan Schoolmaster (*Tuam*).

Murphy, Henry, A.M., Incumbent of Traddery (*Killaloe*).

Murphy, Henry, A.M., Rural Dean, Rector of Dromara (*Dromore*), Dromara.

Murphy, John, A.M., Rector of Mogeesha (*Cloyne*), Midleton.

Murphy, John, A.B., Curate of Aghadoe (*Ardfert and Aghadoe*), Killarney.

Murphy, John, A.B., Curate of Kilcoe (*Ross*), Skibbereen.

Murphy, William, A.B, Incumbent of Castleventry (*Ross*), Clonakilty.

Murphy, William Graham, A.B., Curate of Armagh (*Armagh*).

Murray, John E., Vicar of Monasteroris, &c. (*Kildare*), Edenderry.

Murray, John Walton, LL.D., Incumbent of Ballymena (*Connor*).

Mussen, Roberts, A.B., Perpetual Curate of Drumclamph (*Derry*), Castlederg.

Myles, James P., A.B., Vicar of Fanlobbus (*Cork*), Dunmanway.

NANGLE, Edward, A.B., Rural Dean, Rector of Skreen (*Killala*), Dromore, West.

Narton, John G., A.B., Curate of Mullaghbrack (*Armagh*), Markethill.

Nash, Andrew, A.B., Curate of Rathkeale (*Limerick*).

Nash, G. C., A.B., Curate of Dromdaleague (*Cork*), Dunmanway.

Nash, Lewellin C., A.B., Curate of Ringrone (*Cork*), Kinsale.

Nason, William Henry, A.M., Rector of Rathcormack (*Cloyne*).

Neligen, Maurice, A.M., Chaplain, Molyneux Asylum (*Dublin*)—residence, 2, Elgin-road.

Neligan, William Chadwick, LL.D., Incumbent of St. Mary's Shandon (*Cork*), Cork.

Nesbitt, Allan James, Curate of Castlebar (*Tuam*).

Neville, Richard B., A.B., Incumbent of Stradbally (*Lismore*), Piltown.

Neville, William, A., A.M., Chaplain, Royal Hibernian School, Phœnix-park (*Dublin*).

Newbold, James John, A.B., Vicar of Clonbreney (*Ardagh*), Edgeworthstown.

Newenham, Edward H., A.M., Coolmore, Carrigaline.

Newland, Edward, A.B., Perpetual Curate of Collinstown (*Meath*), Ballycomber.

Newman, William, A.M., Rector of Ringrone (*Cork*), Kinsale.

Nichols, Alexander, A.B., Curate of Cloon (*Ardagh*), Mohill.

Nicholson, Alexander J., Curate of Holy Trinity (*Cork*), Cork.

Nickson, Abraham A., A.B., Rector of Clonkeen (*Armagh*), Ardee.

Nisbett, Robert William, A.M., Incumbent of Kilnasoolagh (*Killaloe*), Newmarket-on-Fergus.

Nixon, Arthur N., A.B., Curate of Shankill (*Dromore*) Lurgan.

Nixon, Eckersall, A.B., Incumbent of Aghamart, Curate of Bordwell (*Ossory*), Rathdowney.

Noble, John James, A.M., Youghal.

Noble, Robert, A.M., Rural Dean, Incumbent of Athboy (*Meath*).

Noble, Robert, A.B., Perpetual Curate of Ballydehob, and Curate of Skull (*Cork*), Skull.

Noble, William, A.B., Rural Dean, Incumbent of Tashinny (*Ardagh*), Tashinny.

Noblett, William, A.B., Curate of Skreen (*Killala*), Dromore, West.

Norcott, Robert, A.B., Curate of St. Peter's, Cork (*Cork*).

Norman, Edward, A.M., Rural Dean, Incumbent of Drishane (*Ardfert and Aghadoe*), Millstreet.

Norman, Hugh, A.M., Rector of Aghannushin (*Raphoe*), Letterkenny.

Northmore, Thomas W., Curate of Donaghmore, Derry, Stranorlar.

Norton, Reuben, A.B., Rector of Ballynure (*Leighlin*), The Grange, Athy.

Norton, William, A.M., Rector of Baltinglass (*Leighlin*), Stratford.

Nugent, Edmund, Incumbent of Aharney (*Ossory*), Dublin.

Nugent, Garrett, A.B., Rector of Ardnurcher (*Meath*), Moate.

Nugent, William, Chancellor of Kilmacduagh, Rector of Ardrahan (*Kilmacduagh*), Ardrahan.

Nunn, Loftus, A.B., Prebendary of Ferns, Rector of Clone (*Ferns*), Enniscorthy (*Ferns*), Ferns.

O'Brien, Hon. Henry, A.M., Rural Dean, Vicar of Killersherdiney (*Kilmore*), Cootehill.

O'Brien, Henry J. LL.D., Rector of Kilcully (*Cork*), Cork.

O'Callaghan, John, Incumbent of Ross (*Tuam*), Clonbur, Cong.

O'Callaghan, Robert, D.D., Rector of Castlecomer and Curate of Kilmocar (*Ossory*), Castlecomer.

O'Callaghan, Robert, Curate of Aasleagh (*Tuam*), Westport.

O'Connor, John H., A.B., Perpetual Curate of Cappamore (*Emly*), Cappamore.

O'Connor, William Ised, A.B., Rector of Newton Fertullа (*Meath*), Tyrellspass.

Ogle, Charles D., A.B., Perpetual Curate of Clonmore (*Ferns*), Enniscorthy.

O'Grady, C., Incumbent of Dromin (*Limerick*), Bruff.

O'Grady, Edward G., Vicar of Mungret (*Limerick*).

O'Grady, Thomas, A.B., Rector of Magourney (*Cloyne*), Coachford.

O'Halloran, Stephen, A.B., Rector of Clonmult (*Cloyne*), Midleton.

O'Hara, James Dunn, A.M., Rector of Coleraine (*Connor*).

Olden, Thomas, A.B., Vicar of Tullylease (*Cloyne*), Charleville.

O'Leary, David, A.M., Vicar of Kilshane (*Emly*), Tipperary.

Olphert, Thomas, A.M., Rural Dean, Rector of Lower Moville (*Derry*), Moville.

O'Mahony, Thaddeus, A.M., Professor of Irish in Trinity College, Dublin, and Rector of Feighcullen (*Kildare*), 29, Trinity College.

O'Meara, A.M., Curate of Kilnaughtin (*Ardfert*), Tarbert.

O'Meara, Charles Peter, Curate of Arklow (*Dublin*), Arklow.

O'Meara, Eugene, A.M., Rector of Newcastle-Lyons (*Dublin*), Hazlehatch.

O'Neill, Henry Hugh, A.M., Rural Dean, Rector of Knockbride (*Kilmore*), Bailieborough

O'Regan, John, A.B., Prebendary of St. Patrick's, Dublin, Archdeacon of Kildare, and Incumbent of Dunlavin (*Dublin*).

Orme, Alexander, Curate of Moydow (*Ardagh*), Kenagh.

Ormsby, Edwin, A.B., Vicar of Loughmoe (*Cashel*), Templemore.

Ormsby, H. N., Vicar of Carrigamleary (*Cloyne*), Mallow.

Ormsby, William Gilbert, A.B., Rector of Arklow (*Dublin*).

O'Rorke, John, A.M., Vicar of Killascobe (*Tuam*), Moylough.

O'Rorke, P., A.B., Curate of Berehaven (*Ross*), C. T. Berehaven.

Orpen, Raymond, A.B., Curate of Adare (*Limerick*), Adare.

Orr, Robert Holmes, A.M., Curate of Ahascragh (*Elphin*).

O'Sullivan, Denis, A.B., Vicar of Aghadown (*Ross*), Skibbereen.

Oswald, William H., A.B., Curate of Derrygrath (*Lismore*), Clonmel.

Otway, Cooke, A.M., Rector of Monsea (*Killaloe*).

Oulton, Richard A.M., Rector of Keady (*Armagh*), Keady.

Oulton, Richard C., A.B., Curate of Clogher (*Clogher*).

Owens, James, A.B., Rural Dean, Rector of Inniskeel (*Raphoe*), Ardara.

Owen, Frank, A.B., Incumbent of Killea (*Waterford*), Dunmore, East.

Owen, Frederick, A.M., Prebendary, Rector of Aghold (*Leighlin*), Tullow.

Pack, Richard, A.B., Chancellor of Ossory, Incumbent of Inchyolaghan (*Ossory*), Kilkenny.

Pakenham, Robert, A.M., Rector of Kildrought (*Dublin*), Celbridge.

Palliser, M. W., M.A., Perpetual Curate of Kilnahue (*Ferns*), Gorey.

Palmer, A. S., Curate of Powerscourt (*Dublin*), Enniskerry.

Palmer, Ab. H., Curate of Rathdrum (*Dublin*), Rathdrum.

Palmer, Henry, A M., Rural Dean, Incumbent of Tubrid (*Lismore*), Cahir.

Parker, George, Rector of Templebodan (*Cloyne*), Cork.

Parker, John Frederick, A.B., Prebendary of Kilrossanty, Incumbent of Newtownlenan (*Lismore*), Portlaw.

Paton, James, A.M., Curate of Kilmore (*Armagh*), Armagh.

Patton, G. A. F., A.M., Curate of St. Peter's (*Dublin*), 5, Stamer-street.

Payne, George Thomas, A.M., Rector of Drumbeg (*Down*), Downpatrick.

Payne, Somers H., A.M., Bishop's Chaplain, Vicar-General of Killaloe, Incumbent of Dunkerrin (*Killaloe*), Roscrea.

Peacock, Henry, A.B., Perpetual Curate of St. Michael's (*Limerick*), Limerick.

Peacock, Pryce, A.M., Archdeacon of Limerick, Incumbent of St. Michael's (*Limerick*), Limerick.

Peacock, Ralph, A.B., Prebendary of Down, Rector of Dunsford (*Down*), Ardglass.

Peacocke, George, A.M., Incumbent of Holycross, &c. (*Cashel*).

Peacocke, Joseph F., A.M., Curate of Monkstown (*Dublin*).

Pearson, James M., A.M., Incumbent of Dunmore (*Ossory*), Kilkenny.

Peed, James, A.B., Rural Dean, Incumbent of Wexford (*Ferns*).

Pelly, C. H., A.B., Curate of Omey (*Tuam*), Clifden.

Pennefather, Thomas, A.B., Perpetual Curate of Monart (*Ferns*), Enniscorthy.

Pennefather, William, A.M., Precentor of Cathedral of St. Canice, Rural Dean, Rector of Callan (*Ossory*), Callan.

Penrose, Samuel, A.M., Curate of Rincurran (*Cork*), Kinsale.

Pentland, Thomas, A.B., Rector of Drumreilly (*Kilmore*), Ballinamore.

Pepper, Charles C., A.M., Prebendary of Ossory, Rector of Killamery (*Ossory*), Callan.

Pepper, Edward, A.M., Prebendary of St. Patrick's, Incumbent of Castledermot (*Dublin*).

Percival, Henry, A.B., Rural Dean, Bishop's Chaplain, Rector of Drumlease (*Kilmore*), Drumahair.

Percy, E. J. A., Curate of Mucknoe (*Clogher*), Castleblaney.

Percy, Gilbert, LL.D., Rector of Ballymacormick (*Ardagh*), Longford.

Percy, W. A., A.M., Rector of Kiltoghert (*Ardagh*), Carrick-on-Shannon.

Perrin, Louis, A.M., Incumbent of Garrycloyne (*Cloyne*), Cork.

Perrin, Mark, A.M., Prebendary of Tuam, Rural Dean, Rector of Athenry (*Tuam*).

Perry, Adam Bettesworth, A.M., Surrogate, Rector of Carlow (*Leighlin*), Carlow.

Perry, Henry P., A.M., Treasurer of Lismore, Rector of Tullamelan, and Vicar of Reisk (*Lismore and Waterford*), Clonmel.

Peyton, Walter C., A.B, Incumbent of Billis (*Kilmore*), Virginia.

Phair, George, Curate of Castleconnor (*Killala*), Enniscrone.

Phair, John P., A.B., Incumbent of Buttevant (*Cloyne*).

Phenix, R. A., Curate of Slavin (*Clogher*), Ballyshannon.

Phillips, Thomas George Johnston, A.M., Curate of Mohill (*Ardagh*).

Phillott, James R., A.M., Precentor of Connor (*Connor*).
Phipps, John Hare, A B., Vicar of Drehidtarsna (*Limerick*), Adare.
Phipps, Owen H., A.M., Curate of Shankill (*Dromore*), Lurgan.
Phipps, William, A.M., Assistant Chaplain, Free Church, Great Charles-street (*Dublin*), 30, Upper Gloucester-street.
Pilcher, William Henry, A.M., Rector of Ardclinis (*Connor*), Glenarm.
Pim, John, A.B., Prebendary of Kildare, Incumbent of Nurney (*Kildare*), Kildare.
Pittar, Charles Arthur, A.M., Rector of Newcastle (*Dublin*), Rathcoole.
Plummer, Richard, Rector of Killury (*Ardfert and Aghadoe*), Causeway.
Plummer, Thomas F. G., Rector of Mahoonagh (*Limerick*), Newcastle, Limerick.
Plunket, Hon. and Rev. William Conyngham, A.M., Treasurer of St. Patrick's Cathedral (*Dublin*).
Poole, Hewitt R., A.M., Fellow of Trinity College, Dublin.
Poole, Jonas M., A.M., Incumbent of Athassil, &c. (*Cashel and Emly*), Golden, Cashel.
Pooler, James Galbraith, A.M., Incumbent of New-townards (*Down*).
Porter, John Grey, LL.B., Rural Dean, Rector of Kilskeery (*Clogher*), Kilskeery.
Porter, Thomas Hamblin, D.D., Rector of Desertcreat (*Armagh*), Tullyhogue.
Potter, Samuel G., A.B., Rector of Duncormick (*Ferns*), Wexford.
Potterton, Edward, A.B., Rector of Kilmore, Erris (*Killala*), Belmullet.
Pounden, William Dawson, A.B., Incumbent of Christ-church, Lisburn (*Connor*).
Powell, Dacre H., A.B., Curate of Carrigaline (*Cork*), Carrigaline.
Powell, Edward, A.M., Prebendary of Achrony, Incumbent of Killaraght (*Achonry*), Boyle.
Powell, John Hugh Johnston, A.M., Rural Dean, Incumbent of Clongish (*Ardagh*), Newtownforbes.
Powell, John, A.M., Vicar of Lea (*Kildare*), Ballybrittas.
Powell, W., A.B., Curate of Ballymodan (*Cork*), Bandon.
Power, Ambrose, A.M., Archdeacon and Vicar Choral of Lismore, Rural Dean, Rector of Kilrush (*Lismore*), Lismore.
Power, Thomas, A.B., Rural Dean, Vicar of Clashmore (*Lismore*).
Pratt, Edward O'B., A.B., Curate of Kilkeel (*Ex. Jur. Newry and Mourne*), Kilkeel.
Pratt, James, A.M., Rector of Clontarf (*Dublin*), 4, Walpole-terrace, Clontarf.
Pratt, John, A.B., Rural Dean, Rector of Durrus (*Cork*), Bantry.
Preston, Arthur John, A.M., First Canon and Prebendary of Kildare, Incumbent of Kilmeage (*Kildare*).
Preston, Decimus W., A.B., Vicar of Killinkere (*Kilmore*), Virginia.
Price, T. Blackwood, A.M., Rural Dean, Rector of Bright (*Down*), Downpatrick.
Prior, George, A.B., Curate of Mevagh (*Raphoe*), Carrigart.
Proctor, George A., A.M., Perpetual Curate of Clomantagh (*Ossory*), Urlingford.
Purdon, William John, A.M., Incumbent of Kilmallog (*Ferns*), Castle Ellis.
Puxley, John L., Curate of Kilcoran (*Limerick*), Pallaskenry.
Pyne, John P. L., A.B., Prebendary of Cloyne, Rural Dean, Rector of Inch (*Cloyne*), Whitegate.

Quarry, John, A.M., Prebendary of Cloyne, Rural Dean, Rector of Midleton (*Cloyne*), Midleton.
Quin, Richard, A.M., Rural Dean, Rector of Forkhill (*Armagh*), Forkhill.
Quinn, John Campbell, A.M., Vicar of Donaghmore (*Dromore*), Loughbrickland.

Quintin, James, Curate of St. Catherine's, and Chaplain to Mount Jerome Cemetery (*Dublin*), 2, Parnell-place, Upper.
Quintin, Samuel, Curate of Rathvilly (*Leighlin*), Baltinglass.

Radcliff, John, A M., Incumbent of Innismagrath (*Kilmore*), Drumkeeran.
Radcliff, Richard, A.B., Rector of Skryne (*Meath*), Tara, Navan.
Radcliff, William R., A.M., Prebendary of St. Patrick's, Rector of Donaghmore (*Dublin*), Donard.
Radcliffe, John B., A.M., Curate of Killiney (*Dublin*), Dalkey.
Radcliffe, Stephen, A.B., District Curate of Dowra (*Kilmore*), Carrick-on-Shannon.
Radcliffe, William, A.M., Perpetual Curate of Ballyhuskard (*Ferns*), Enniscorthy.
Rainsford, Joseph Godman, A.B., Curate of Dundalk (*Armagh*), Dundalk.
Rainsford, William G., Curate of Ferns and Kilbride (*Ferns*), Ferns.
Rambaut, Edward F., A.B., Incumbent of Kilfithmore (*Cashel*), Borrisoleigh.
Rankin, J. S., Curate of Kilrush (*Ferns*), Ferns.
Rawlins, Joseph, A.B., Curate of Donagheady (*Derry*), Strabane.
Raymond, William, A.B., Rural Dean, Vicar of Ballyseedy (*Ardfert and Aghadoe*), Tralee.
Reade, David John, A.M., Rural Dean, Prebendary of St. Patrick's, Incumbent of Clondalkin (*Dublin*), Tallaght.
Reade, George Fortescue, A.M., Rector of Magherally (*Dromore*), Banbridge.
Reade, George H., A M., Rural Dean, Rector of Inishkeen (*Clogher*), Dundalk.
Reade, Loftus G., A.M., Prebendary of Clogher, Rector of Devenish (*Clogher*), Enniskillen.
Reddy, Thomas, A.B., Rector of Upper Badoney (*Derry*), Gortin.
Reeves, Boles, A.B., Curate of Rossbarcon (*Ossory*), New Ross.
Reeves Isaac Morgan, A.M., Rector of Myross (*Ross*), Rosscarberry.
Reeves, James Somerville, A.M., Rector of Caheragh (*Cork*), Drimoleague.
Reeves, William, D.D., Rural Dean, Rector of Tynan, Librarian Armagh Library (*Armagh*).
Reichardt, Louis C., Curate of St. Paul's (*Dublin*)—residence, 29, Manor-street.
Reichel, Charles P., D.D., Vicar of Mullingar (*Meath*).
Reid, Samuel, A.B., Vicar of Donegal (*Raphoe*), Donegal.
Revington, John H., A.B., Perpetual Curate of O'Briensbridge (*Killaloe*).
Reynell, William Alexander, A.M., Curate of Leckpatrick (*Derry*), Strabane.
Rhynd, James W., Rector of Galbally (*Emly*), Galbally.
Richards, Edward, A M., Chancellor of Dromore, Rural Dean, Rector of Clonallan (*Dromore*), Warrenpoint.
Richards, George, A.M., Prebendary of Ferns, Rector of Coolstuff, and Curate of Taghmon (*Ferns*), Taghmon.
Richards, James, A.B., Treasurer of Leighlin, Incumbent of Cloydagh (*Leighlin*), Carlow.
Richards, Lewis, A.M., Perpetual Curate of Ashfield (*Kilmore*), Cootehill.
Richardson, Clement, A.M., Curate of Kilscannell (*Limerick*), Rathkeale.
Richey, John, Curate of Tullyniskin (*Armagh*), Coalisland.
Richey, Richard, Curate of Ardmore (*Lismore*), Ardmore.
Richey, Richard John Cockburn, A.M., Vicar of Kilcash, (*Lismore*), Waterford.
Riddall, Walter, A B., Perpetual Curate of Glencraig (*Down*), Glencraig.
Ridgway, Edward, A.M., Incumbent of Mothell (*Lismore*), Carrick-on-Suir.
Ringwood, John Thomas, A.B., Incumbent of Trinity Church (*Kilmore*), Newtonbutler.
Ringwood, William C., A.M., Curate of Ardbraccan (*Meath*), Navan.
Roberts, Samuel, A.B., Vicar of Denn (*Kilmore*), Cavan.

Roberts, William, A.M., Fellow of Trinity College, Dublin.
Robbins, Joseph F., A.M., Incumbent of Castletown-arra (*Killaloe*), Killaloe.
Robinson, Andrew, A.B., Prebendary of Elphin, Rural Dean, Rector of Ardcarn (*Elphin*), Boyle.
Robinson, Charles, A.M., Rural Dean, Incumbent of Kilglass (*Ardagh*), Lenamore.
Robinson, Charles J., A.M., Prebendary, Incumbent of Tynagh (*Clonfert*).
Robinson, George, A.B., Rector of Tartaraghan (*Armagh*), Loughgall.
Robinson, Thomas, LL.D., Vicar of Kilmainhamwood (*Meath*), Kingscourt.
Robinson, Thomas Romney, D.D., Vicar of Carrickmacross (*Clogher*), Armagh.
Robinson, William, A.M., Vicar of Tallaght (*Dublin*).
Robotham, Robert, A.B., Perpetual Curate of Currin (*Clogher*), Clones.
Roe, Edward P., A.B., Incumbent of Gartree (*Connor*). Crumlin.
Roe, Thomas W., A.B., Perpetual Curate of Ballymacarrett (*Down*), Belfast.
Roe, William, A.M., Archdeacon of Kilmacduagh, Vicar-General of Clonfort, Incumbent of Roscrea (*Clonfert, Killaloe, and Kilmacduagh*).
Roe, William Disney, Rural Dean, Incumbent of Burrishoole (*Tuam*), Newport.
Rogers, J. Cecil, A.B., Perpetual Curate of Nohoval (*Cork*), Kinsale.
Rogers, Robert H., A.M., Vicar of St. John's, Kilkenny (*Ossory*), Kilkenny.
Rogers, William, A.M., Prebendary and Registrar of Cloyne, Surrogate, Rector of Kilmahon (*Cloyne*), Cloyne.
Rooke, George W., A.M., Curate of Gorey (*Ferns*), Gorey.
Rooke, Henry, A.M., Curate of Wicklow (*Dublin*).
Ross, Alexander H., Curate of Aghabog (*Clogher*), Newbliss.
Ross, George, A.B., Incumbent of Killinick (*Ferns*), Wexford.
Ross, James, A.B., Perpetual Curate of Castle Archdall, (*Clogher*), Lisnarrick.
Ross, William, A.B., Rural Dean, Vicar of Dungiven (*Derry*).
Royse, Thomas H., Curate of Ballybrood (*Emly*), Caherconlish.
Ruby, James Smith, A.B., Curate of Ightermuragh (*Cloyne*), Castlemartyr.
Rudd, Richard, Vicar of Killannin (*Tuam*), Spiddal.
Rudd, Thomas.
Rush, Edward, A.B., Precentor of Kilmacduagh, Incumbent of Loughrea (*Clonfert*), Loughrea.
Russell, Cecil, A.M., Vicar of Drumcree (*Meath*), Drumcree.
Russell, Charles, A.M., Curate of St. Anne's (*Dublin*)—residence, 2, Hume-street.
Russell, George, A.B., Vicar of Ballingarry (*Cashel*), Callan.
Russell, J. Digby, A.B., Curate of Roscrea (*Killaloe*), Roscrea.
Russell, John, A.B., Perpetual Curate of Clooney (*Derry*), Clooney.
Russell, John, A.B., Perpetual Curate of All Saints (*Raphoe*), Newtowncunningham.
Russell, William G., A.B., Rector of Ematris (*Clogher*), Ballybay.
Rutledge, John Young, D.D., Incumbent of Armagh (*Armagh*).
Ryall, Edward, A.B., Incumbent of Ballingarry (*Killaloe*), Borrisokane.
Ryder, Arthur Gore, D.D., Rector of St. Mary's, Donnybrook (*Dublin*), Donnybrook.
Ryder, Roderick, Curate of Errismore (*Tuam*), Clifden.
Ryland, John Frederick, A.B., Precentor of Lismore (*Lismore*).

Sadleir, Franc, A.M., Curate of Castleknock and Assistant Dean's Vicar of St. Patrick's Cathedral (*Dublin*), Castleknock.
Sadleir, Francis Ralph, D.D., Rector of Raddanstown (*Meath*), Maynooth.
Sadleir, Henry A., A.M., Incumbent of Tessauran (*Meath*), Ferbane.
Sadleir, Ralph, D.D., Prebendary of St. Patrick's, Rural Dean, Vicar of Castleknock (*Dublin*), Mount Hyble, Castleknock.
St. George, Francis de Montmorenci, A.B., Rector of St. Anne, Shandon (*Cork*), Cork.
St. George, Henry L., A.M., Rector of Dromore (*Clogher*), Omagh.
St. George, Howard B. A.B., Incumbent of St. John's (*Down*), Hillsborough.
St. George, Richard, A.M., Prebendary of Killala, Incumbent of Crossmolina (*Killala*).
St. George, William, Curate of Kilcoo and Kilmegan (*Down*), Clough.
Salmon, George, D.D., Fellow of Trinity College, Dublin.
Samuels, A., Curate of Derryaghy (*Connor*), Lisburn.
Sandeforde, E., Rector of Valentia (*Ardfert and Aghadoe*).
Sanders, Francis A., A.B., Rural Dean, Rector of Templeport (*Kilmore*), Bawnboy.
Sandes, Robert, Curate of Aghavallin (*Ardfert and Aghadoe*), Listowel.
Sandes, Samuel Dickson, A.M., Rector of Whitechurch (*Cloyne*), Cork.
Sandford, William, A.M., Rural Dean, Rector of Kilvemnon (*Cashel*), Mullinahone.
Sandiforde, Samuel, A.B, Rector of Ardnageehy (*Cork*), Fermoy.
Sandys, William Robert, A.M., Incumbent of Ballintemple (*Cashel*), Dundrum, Cashel.
Sargent, J. J., A.B., Curate of Monkstown (*Cork*), Monkstown, Cork.
Saunders, William H., A.B., Vicar of Carrigtohill (*Cloyne*), Cork.
Saunderson, Francis, A.M., Rector of Kildallon (*Kilmore*), Ardlober.
Saurin, James, A.M., Archdeacon of Dromore, Rector of Seagoe (*Dromore*), Portadown.
Sayers, George Brydges, A.B., Curate of Ballywillan (*Connor*), Portrush.
Schoales, John W., A.B., District Curate of Derrylane (*Kilmore*), Killeshandra.
Schoales, Peter Henry, A.M., Perpetual Curate of Arvagh (*Kilmore*).
Scott, Edward B., A.B., Curate of Aglishmartin and Polroane (*Ossory*), Waterford.
Scott, Francis M., A.B., Curate of Ardquin (*Down*), Portaferry.
Scott, George, A.M., Incumbent of Banagher (*Derry*), Feeny, Derry.
Scott, Henry, Perpetual Curate of Inch (*Derry*), Derry.
Scott, Henry, A.M., Prebendary of Leighlin, Incumbent of Staplestown (*Leighlin*), Carlow.
Scott, James Bedell, Curate of Banagher (*Derry*), Feeny.
Scott, James George, A.M., Prebendary of Rathmichael, Rector of Bray (*Dublin*), Bray.
Scott, James Leslie Montgomery, A.M., Chancellor of Down, Rector of Ballyphilip (*Down*), Portaferry.
Scott, James Rowland, A.M., Curate of Cappagh (*Derry*), Omagh.
Scott, J. R., A.B., Curate of Dunleckney (*Leighlin*), Bagnalstown.
Scott, John Handcock, A.M., Vicar of Seirkieran (*Ossory*), Parsonstown.
Scott, Richard L, A.B, Vicar of Killaney (*Down*), Lisburn.
Scott, Thomas L., A.M., Curate of Derry (*Derry*).
Scott, William, Incumbent of Kiltyclogher (*Kilmore*), Manorhamilton.
Scott, William, A.M., Rector of Grean, and Curate of Templebreden (*Emly*), Pallasgreen.
Seddall, Henry, Incumbent of Dunany (*Armagh*), Dunleer.
Semple, Edward, A.M., Rector of Drumkeeran (*Clogher*), Kesh.
Seymour, B. Donelan, Perpetual Curate of Drumrasey (*Meath*), Ballymore, Moate.

Seymour, Charles, B.D., Rural Dean, Rector of Urney (*Derry*), Strabane.
Seymour, Charles H., A.M., Dean of Tuam, Rural Dean, Incumbent of Tuam (*Tuam*).
Seymour, Edward, A.M., Prebendary of St. Michael's (*Dublin*)—residence, 4, Kildare-street.
Seymour, John Hobart, A.M., Curate of Trinity Church, Belfast (*Connor*), Belfast.
Seymour, William F., Perpetual Curate of Cahernarry, &c. (*Limerick*), Limerick.
Shaw, Robert J., Curate of Armagh (*Armagh*).
Shaw, William E., A.B., Incumbent of Kinsalebeg (*Lismore*), Youghal.
Shea, E. L., A.B., Curate of Killannin (*Tuam*), Spiddal.
Shea, George, Curate of Sellerna (*Tuam*), Cleggan, Galway.
Shea, John, A.M., Vicar of Abbeylara (*Ardagh*), 6, Webster-place, Dublin.
Shelton, Grantley W., Vicar of Killaliathan (*Limerick*), Drumcolloher.
Sherlock, William, A.M., Curate of Bray (*Dublin*), Bray.
Sherrard, William, A.M., Prebendary of Cork, Rural Dean, Vicar of Castlelyons (*Cloyne*), (*Cork*), Cork.
Sherrard, William Nassau, A.M., Rural Dean, Incumbent of Kilcullen (*Dublin*).
Shire, Loftus Theophilus, A.M., Chaplain of Trinity Church, Rathmines (*Dublin*), 6, Charleston-terrace.
Shone, Samuel, A.M., Rector of Urney and Annagelliff (*Kilmore*), Cavan.
Shortt, Francis, A.M., Rector of Corkbeg (*Cloyne*), Midleton.
Silcock, James, A.B., Perpetual Curate of Ballymakenny (*Armagh*), Drogheda.
Silleto, William Wharton, A.B., Rector of Killowen (*Derry*), Coleraine.
Simpson, J. E. H., A.B., Vicar of Drumsnat (*Clogher*), Monaghan.
Simpson, Samuel, A.M., Rector of Derrynoose (*Armagh*), Keady.
Simpson, Samuel H., Curate of Dromore (*Clogher*), Omagh.
Singer, Paulus Æmilius, A.M., Rector of Ballymoney (*Cork*), Ballineen.
Skipton, William, A.B., Incumbent of Dunfeeney (*Killala*), Killala.
Slacke, William James, A.M., Curate of Newtowngore (*Kilmore*).
Slacke, William R., A.B., Rural Dean, Incumbent of Newcastle (*Down*), Castlewellan.
Sleator, Charles, A.M., Perpetual Curate of Killiney (*Dublin*), Templeville, Ballybrack, Dalkey.
Smith, Francis, A.M., Curate of Derry Cathedral (*Derry*).
Smith, G. K., Curate of St. Michael, Cork (*Cork*).
Smith, George Sidney, D.D., Rector of Drumragh (*Derry*), Omagh.
Smith, George, A.B., Rural Dean, Incumbent of Kilrea (*Derry*), Kilrea.
Smith, George, A.B., Curate of Bangor (*Down*).
Smith, George Sidney, jun.
Smith, Godfrey C. W., A.M., Rural Dean, Rector of Aghabulloge (*Cloyne*), Coachford.
Smith, Horatio Bolton, A.M., Incumbent of Newcastle (*Limerick*).
Smith, James, A.M., Prebendary of Derry, Rector of Upper Cumber (*Derry*), Clady, Derry.
Smith, John B., A.B., Rector of Tullagh (*Ross*), Skibbereen.
Smith, Richard Travers, A.M., Curate of St. Stephen's (*Dublin*), 77, Haddington-road.
Smith, Richard, A.B., Rector of Killea (*Raphoe*), Carrigans.
Smith, Thomas St. Lawrence, A.M., Curate of Carrickmacross (*Clogher*), Carrickmacross.
Smith, W., A.B., Vicar of Marshalstown, Curate of Derryvillane (*Cloyne*), Mitchelstown.
Smullen, Alexander, A.B., District Curate of Ballymeehan (*Kilmore*), Manorhamilton.
Smyly, Andrew Ferguson, A.M., Perpetual Curate of Culmore (*Derry*), Culmore.
Smyly, Cecil, A.B., Perpetual Curate of Grange (*Armagh*), Armagh.
Smyth, Edward Johnson, A.M., Incumbent of Glenavy (*Connor*), Lisburn.
Smyth, Edward, A.M., Rector of Drumgath (*Dromore*), Rathfriland.
Smyth, Henry, A.B., Rural Dean, Incumbent of Cullen (*Emly*), Ulloe.
Smyth, Mitchell, Rector of Errigal (*Derry*), Garvagh.
Smyth, William S. J., A.B., Curate of Glenavy (*Connor*), Lisburn.
Smythe, George Chichester, A.M., Rural Dean, Incumbent of Carnmoney (*Connor*).
Smythe, John Henry, A.M., Rector of Ballyclug (*Connor*).
Sparrow, William, Curate of Desertlyn (*Armagh*), Moneymore.
Spedding, William, A.M., Vicar of Ballyhalbert (*Down*), Kircubbin.
Spring, Edward, A.M., Vicar of Inchigeelah (*Cork*), Macroom.
Sproule, William, A.B., Perpetual Curate of Glenely (*Derry*), Derry.
Stack, Charles M., A.M., Perpetual Curate of Lack (*Clogher*), Kesh.
Stack, Edward William, A.M., Rural Dean, Rector of Graigue (*Leighlin*).
Stack, Thomas, A.M., Fellow of Trinity College, Dublin.
Stack, Thomas Lindsay, A.M. Rector of Lower Langfield (*Derry*), Drumquin, Newtownstewart.
Stamer John, Incumbent of Kilconly, and Curate of Lisselton (*Ardfert and Aghadoe*), Ballybunion.
Standish, Richard Nash, A.B., Curate of Drumlease (*Kilmore*), Dromohair.
Stanford, Bedell, A.B., Curate of Castleraghan (*Kilmore*), Ballyjamesduff.
Stanford, Charles Stuart, D.D., Rector of St. Thomas's (*Dublin*), Park House, Booterstown-avenue.
Stanley, Abraham, LL.D., Curate of Killeban (*Leigh lin*), Carlow.
Stanley, Robert Henry, A.M., Prebendary of Ferns, Incumbent of Edermine (*Ferns*), Taghmon.
Stannus, James, A.M., Dean of Ross, Rector of Lisburn (*Ross and Connor*).
Stanton, James, A.M., Curate of Raddinstown (*Meath*), Kilcock.
Staveley, Robert, B.D., Incumbent of Trinity Church, Killiney (*Dublin and Glendelagh*), Killiney.
Stawell, John Leslie, A.B., Rector of Aghnameadle (*Killaloe*), Toomavara.
Stenson, John O., A.B., Curate of Athea (*Limerick*), Glin.
Stephens, Nathaniel, A.B., Curate of Lower Badoney (*Derry*), Gortin, Omagh.
Stevenson, Henry F., A.B., Rector of Ballyscullion (*Derry*), Bellaghy.
Stevenson, James, A.M., Rector of Brinny (*Cork*), Innishannon.
Stevenson, Joshua, A.B., Rector of Clonfeacle (*Armagh*), Moy.
Stewart, Charles Frederick, A.B., Prebendary of Raphoe, Rector of Clondehorky (*Raphoe*), Dunfanaghy.
Stewart, Henry, A.M., Rural Dean, Incumbent of Leixlip (*Dublin*), Lucan.
Stewart, Henry, A.M., Chancellor of Ferns, Incumbent of Tacumshane (*Ferns*), Tagoat.
Stewart, Henry, A.M., Vicar of Rathbarry (*Ross*), Castlefreke, Clonakilty.
Stewart, Henry, A.M., Vicar of Kilmore (*Down*), Crossgar.
Stewart, Henry, A.M., Rector of Knockbreda (*Down*), Belfast.
Stewart, Henry William, A.B., Incumbent of Russagh (*Ardagh*), Rathowen.
Stewart, John, A.B., Curate of Maghera (*Derry*).
Stewart, Joseph A., A.M., Curate of Derryaghy (*Connor*), Lisburn.
Stewart, Richard, Rector of Killdress (*Armagh*), Cookstown.
Stewart, William, A.B., Curate of Kilbrin (*Cloyne*), Mallow.
Stokes, George Thomas, A.B., Curate of St. Patrick's C. E., Newry (*Ex. Jur. of Newry and Mourne*), Newry.
Stokes, Henry G., A.M., Incumbent of Ardcolm (*Ferns*), Wexford.

Stokes, John Whitley, A.M., Archdeacon of Armagh, Incumbent of Carnteel (*Armagh*), Aughnacloy.

Stokes, Thomas Gabriel, Curate of Carnteel (*Armagh*), Aughnacloy.

Stone, George, A.M., Incumbent of Ballinlanders (*Emly*), Galbally.

Stone, Robert, Curate of Balinlondry (*Emly*), Ballylanders.

Stone, William Henry, A.M., Curate of Kilmore (*Killaloe*), Silvermines.

Stoney, George F., A.B., Curate of Berehaven (*Ross*), C. T. Berehaven.

Stoney, George R., A.B., Prebendary of Killaloe, Vicar of Clondegad (*Killaloe*), Ennis.

Stoney, Robert Baker, A.B., Curate of Taney (*Dublin*), Dundrum.

Stoney, William, A.M., Perpetual Curate of Turlough (*Tuam*), Castlebar.

Stoney, William B., A.M., Rural Dean, Incumbent of Castlebar (*Tuam*).

Stopford, Edward A., A.B., Archdeacon of Meath, Chaplain to the Bishop, Rector of Kells (*Meath*).

Stopford, Hon. Henry Scott, A.M., Archdeacon of Leighlin, Rector of Clonmore and Killeban (*Leighlin*), Hacketstown.

Stopford, Thomas Adderley, Registrar of the Diocese, Incumbent of Clonghill (*Meath*), Navan.

Story, William, A.M., Rural Dean, Rector of Aghabog (*Clogher*), Newbliss.

Stoyte, John, A.B., Rural Dean, Rector of Ballymartle (*Cork*), Kinsale.

Strangways, James Michael Henry, A.M., Vicar Choral (*Armagh*), Armagh.

Streane, Lewis Henry, A.M., Rural Dean, Incumbent of Delgany (*Dublin*), Delgany.

Strong, C. K., A.B., Curate of Kilkeevin (*Elphin*) Castlerea.

Stuart, Alexander, A.M., Archdeacon of Ross, Rector of Kinneigh (*Cork*), Bandon.

Stuart, Alexander George, A.B., Curate of Clondehorky (*Raphoe*), Dunfanaghy.

Stuart, David, A.B., Curate of St. George's (*Dublin*), 35, Nelson-street.

Stuart, George William, A.M., Rural Dean, Rector of Drumachose (*Derry*), Newtownlimavady.

Stubbs, E. Thackeray, A.M., Curate of Raphoe Cathedral (*Raphoe*), Raphoe.

Stubbs, John William, A.M., Fellow of Trinity College, Dublin.

Studdert, Francis P., A.M., Rector of Borrisokane (*Killaloe*).

Studdert, Francis, A.M., Rector of Killeilagh (*Kilfenora*), Borrisokane.

Studdert, George, A.M. Incumbent of Ardee (*Armagh*), Ardee.

Studdert, George, Vicar of Abbeyfeale (*Limerick*).

Studdert, Richard, A.B., Incumbent of Quin (*Killaloe*).

Sullivan, James, A.M., Incumbent of Ballymore Eustace (*Dublin*), Balbriggan.

Swanzy, Henry, A.M., Rector of Kilshannick (*Cloyne*), Mallow.

Swanzy, Henry, jun., A.B., Curate of Kilshannick (*Cloyne*), Mallow.

Swanzy, T. B., A.M., Curate of Newry (*Ex. Jur. of Newry and Mourne*), Newry.

Swene, Eugene, A.B., Curate of Inniskeel (*Raphoe*), Ardara.

Swift, Francis, A.B., Incumbent of Kilbixy (*Meath*), Ballynacarrigy.

Swift, R. M., A.B., Curate of Mountfield (*Derry*), Omagh.

Switzer, Nathaniel, Curate of Kilmanagh (*Ossory*), Callan.

Symmons, Henry Thomas, A.B., Curate of Drumgoon (*Kilmore*), Cootehill.

Symmons, W., A.B., Curate of Dernaclish (*Kilmore*), Cootehill.

Synge, Edward, A.M., Vicar of Lockeene (*Killaloe*), Parsonstown.

Synge, Francis, Incumbent of O'Mallad (*Killaloe*), Carrigahoorig.

TAGERT, Ralph, Vicar of Templetenny (*Lismore*), Clogheen.

Tait, Andrew, LL.B., Rector of Ballyovie (*Tuam*), Hollymount.

Tardy, Elias, A.B., Rector of Aughnamullen (*Clogher*), Ballybay.

Tarleton, John R., A.M., Prebendary of Tyholland, Vicar Choral, St. Patrick's Dublin, Rector of Tyholland (*Clogher*), Monaghan.

Tarleton, J. T., A.B., Perpetual Curate of Rockcorry (*Clogher*), Rockcorry.

Tate, Richard, Curate of Fenagh (*Ardagh*), Carrick-on-Shannon.

Tatton, Arthur, A.B., Archdeacon of Kilfenora, Incumbent of Kilmanaheen (*Kilfenora*), Ennistimon.

Taylor, E. M., A.M., Rural Dean, Vicar of Inishargy (*Down*).

Taylor, Henry, Curate of Faughanvale (*Derry*), Eglinton, Derry.

Taylor, Henry R., A.B., Curate of Mullaghbrack (*Armagh*), Markethill.

Taylor, N. S., A.B., Perpetual Curate of Mullagh (*Kilmore*), Virginia.

Taylor, Thomas, A.B., Curate of Aghadrumsee (*Clogher*), Clones.

Teape, William D., Vicar of Aghavoe (*Ossory*), Ballacolla.

Thacker, Ven. Joseph, A.M., Archdeacon of Ossory, Rural Dean, Rector of Kilfane (*Ossory*), Thomastown.

Thisselton, Alfred C., Incumbent of Episcopal Chapel, Upper Baggot-street (*Dublin*).

Thomas, Edwin, A.B., Vicar of Carlingford (*Armagh*), Carlingford.

Thomas, Francis Heaton, A.M., Incumbent of Carysfort, (*Dublin*), Prince Edward-terrace, Blackrock.

Thomas, George, Curate of Glankeen (*Cashel*), Borrisoleigh.

Thomas, George John, A.B., Rector of Donaghedy (*Derry*), Dunamanagh.

Thompson, Frederick, A.M., Vicar of Kilpatrick (*Ferns*), Kyle, Enniscorthy.

Thompson, George, A.B., Rector of Kilcooly (*Cashel*), Urlingford.

Thompson, John N., A.B., Incumbent of Kilronan (*Elphin*), Ballygar.

Thompson, Matthew N., A.B., Incumbent of Roscommon (*Elphin*).

Thompson, Mungo N., Rector of Clonmany (*Derry*), Clonmany, Derry.

Thornhill, Jonathan, A.M., Perpetual Curate of Bar (*Clogher*), Fintona.

Thornhill, William J., A.M., Prebendary of St. Patrick's, Incumbent of Rathcoole (*Dublin*).

Thorpe, Richard, Curate of Monkstown (*Dublin*).

Tibbs, Philip Grayden, A.M., Curate of Birr (*Killaloe*), Parsonstown.

Tibeando, Oliver, A.B., Curate of Arklow (*Dublin*).

Tickell, Edward A., A.M., Rector of Clonegall (*Ferns*).

Tierney, Matthew, A.B., Rector of Churchtown (*Cloyne*). Buttevant.

Tighe, Hugh Usher, A.M., Dean of Derry, Prebendary of St. Patrick's (*Derry and Dublin*), Derry.

Tighe, William, A.B., Perpetual Curate of Holmpatrick (*Dublin*), Skerries.

Tisdall, Charles Edward, D.D., Chancellor of Christ Church, Incumbent of St. Doulough's (*Dublin*), 63, Upper Gardiner-street.

Todd, Andrew, A.B., Incumbent of Clonmeen, and Curate of Kilcorney (*Cloyne*), Mallow.

Todd, James Henthorn, D.D., Regius Professor of Hebrew and S.F.T.C.D., Precentor of St. Patrick's (*Dublin*), 35, College.

Tombe, Henry Joy, A.M., Incumbent of Glanely (*Dublin*), Ashford, county Wicklow.

Tomes, Charles F., A.B., Perpetual Curate of Finner (*Clogher*), Bundoran.

Tomlinson, Sterling, Curate of St. Mark's (*Dublin*)—residence, 21, Summer-hill.
Tomlinson, Thomas, A.B., Vicar of St. James's (*Dublin*), 21, Summer-hill.
Topham, James, Curate of Drumshambo (*Ardagh*).
Toppin, Richard, A.B., Perpetual Curate of Toem, &c. (*Cashel*), Cappawhite.
Torpy, L., A.M., Vicar of Galtrim (*Meath*), Kilcock.
Torrance, George W., A.M., Curate of St. Anne (*Dublin*).
Torrens, Joseph, Curate of Sallaghy, (*Clogher*), Lisnaskea.
Tottenham, George, A.M., Rector of Inismacsaint (*Clogher*), Church-hill.
Tottenham, Henry, A.M., Prebendary of Clogher, Rector of Donacavey (*Clogher*), Fintona.
Tottenham, Robin L., A.M., Vicar of Donaghmoine (*Clogher*), Carrickmacross.
Townsend, Hamilton, A.B., Rural Dean, Archdeacon of Achonry and Rector of Killoran (*Achonry*), Collooney.
Townsend, Horace T., A.B., Incumbent of Kilcoe (*Ross*), Skibbereen.
Townsend, Richard, A.M., Fellow of Trinity College, Dublin.
Townsend, Somerset Lowry Corry, D.D., Rector of Louth (*Armagh*), Dundalk.
Townsend, Thomas H., A.B., Rector of Aghada (*Cloyne*), Cloyne.
Townsend, Thomas Uniacke, A.M., Incumbent of Fertagh (*Ossory*), Johnstown.
Townsend, William Chambers, A.B., Prebendary of Achonry, Vicar of Ballysodare (*Achonry*).
Treanor, John A.M., Rector of Rabeen (*Tuam*), Galway.
Treanor, Stanley, A.B., Curate of Tuam (*Tuam*).
Tredennick, Nisbett G., A.M., Vicar of Kilbarron (*Raphoe*), Ballyshannon.
Trench, Frederick Fitzwilliam, A.M., Incumbent of Newtown (*Meath*), Kells.
Trench, William Le Poer, D.D., Prebendary of Tuam, Rural Dean, Incumbent of Moylough (*Tuam*).
Trew, R., D.D., Incumbent of Lislee (*Ross*), Bandon.
Triphook, J., A.B., Rector of Skull (*Cork*), Skibbereen.
Triphook, Joseph B., A.B., Precentor of Killaloe, Rector of Lateragh and Curate of Nenagh (*Killaloe*), Nenagh.
Tuckey, Broderick, A.B., Vicar of Kilbonane (*Cork*), Cork.
Tuckey, J. H., A.M., Vicar of Ardfield (*Ross*), Clonakilty.
Turpin, William P., A.M., Vicar of Clara (*Meath*).
Tuthill, James B., A.B., Rector of Belleek (*Clogher*).
Twibill, William, A.B., Curate of Donaghmoine (*Clogher*), Carrickmacross.
Twigg, Samuel, A.M., Rector of Tamlaght (*Armagh*), Moneymore.
Twigg, Thomas, A.M., Rector of Pomeroy (*Armagh*), Dungannon.
Twigg, Thomas, junior, A.M., Rural Dean, Vicar of Swords (*Dublin*), Swords.
Tymons, Frederick, A.B., Curate of St. Bartholomew (*Dublin*), Dublin.
Tyner, Charles, A.B., Curate of Easkey (*Killala*), Easkey.
Tyner, Richard Legg, A.B., Rector of Crossboyne (*Tuam*), Claremorris.
Tyrrell, Gerald Wensley, A.M., Prebendary of Limerick, Rector of Tullabracky (*Limerick*), Bruff.
Tyrrell, William, A.M., Rector of Culdaff (*Derry*), Culdaff.

Vance, Robert, A.M., Rector of St. Catherine's (*Dublin*)—residence, 24, Blackhall-street.
Vandeleur, Gerald O., Curate of Coolbanaghert (*Kildare*), Emo.
Vereker, Henry, Rural Dean, Perpetual Curate of Kilcummin (*Tuam*), Oughterard.
Vereker, Thomas, A.B., Perpetual Curate of Killaloe (*Killaloe*), Killaloe.
Vernon, George, A.M., Prebendary of Elphin (*Elphin*).
Verschoyle, Richard, A.M., Rural Dean and Rector of Derryvollan (*Clogher*), Enniskillen.
Vesey, William, 93, Lower Dorset-street, Assistant Secretary of the Ladies' Irish Association, 17, Upper Sackville-street.

Vignoles, Charles Alexander, A.M., Vicar of Clonmacnois (*Meath*), Athlone.
Vignoles, Charles, D.D., Dean of Ossory, Rector of Urlingford, and St. Patrick's (*Ossory*), Kilkenny.
Vowell, William R., D.D., Vicar of Clonoulty (*Cashel*).

Waddy, Richard, A.B., Rector of Finvoy (*Connor*), Kilrea.
Wade, Benjamin. A.M., Rural Dean, Rector of Donaghmore (*Armagh*), Dungannon.
Wade, Edward John, A.M., Rural Dean, Incumbent of Kenmare (*Ardfert and Aghadoe*), Kenmare.
Wade, George, A.B., Curate of Drumgooland (*Dromore*), Dromore.
Wade, William D., Perpetual Curate of Kilcolman, and Curate of Killarney (*Ardfert and Aghadoe*), Killarney.
Wadsworth, R. P., Curate of Trinity Church (*Dublin*), 3, Gloucester-street, lower.
Wakeham, Henry, A.B., Vicar of Monsea (*Killaloe*), Nenagh.
Wakeham, Thomas, A.B., Curate of Kilbrogan (*Cork*), Bandon.
Walker, Frederick G., A.M., Rector of Kilmaloda (*Ross*), Bandon.
Walker, John Cotton, A.M., Prebendary Incumbent of Creagh (*Clonfert*), Ballinasloe.
Walker, Thomas, A.M., Rector of Tamlaght O'Crilly Upper (*Derry*), Kilrea.
Walker, Thomas, A.M., a Vicar Choral (*Limerick*), Bruff.
Walker, William Clarke, A.M., Treasurer of Cork, Incumbent of Ballinadee (*Cork*), Innishannon.
Wall, Richard Henry, D.D., Chaplain of the Royal Chapel of St. Matthew, Ringsend (*Dublin*), Irishtown.
Wallace, John Bourke, A.B., Incumbent of Ardmore (*Lismore*).
Wallace, Thomas, A.M., Curate of Kill (*Dublin*), Donnybrook.
Waller, Benjamin, A.B., Rector of Rossdroit (*Ferns*), Enniscorthy.
Waller, John Thomas, A.M., Rector of Kilcornan (*Limerick*), Pallaskenry.
Walsh, James, A.M., Rector of Chapel Russell, Bishop's Domestic Chaplain (*Limerick*), Limerick.
Walsh, Robert, A.M, Curate of St. Mary (*Dublin*)—residence, 64, Blessington-street.
Walsh, Robert S, A.B., Incumbent of Kilpipe (*Ferns*), Inch.
Walsh, Spencer William, D.D., Vicar of Clonard (*Meath*), Hill of Down.
Walsh, William Pakenham, A.M., Chaplain of Sandford, and Secretary to the Missionary Society (*Dublin*)—residence, 17, Upper Sackville-street.
Warburton, John, LL.D., Precentor of Limerick, Rector of Dromcliff (*Killaloe*), Kill.
Warburton, John, Incumbent of Kill (*Kildare*), Naas.
Warburton, William, D.D., Dean and Incumbent of Elphin (*Elphin*).
Ward, Charles, A.B., Rector of Kilmurry (*Limerick*).
Ward, Charles, A.M., Rural Dean, Rector of Kilwaughter (*Connor*), Larne.
Ward, Charles, A.M., Rector of Kilwaughter (*Connor*), Larne.
Ward, Hon. Henry, A.M., Rector of Killinchy (*Down*).
Waring, J. Alexander, A.B., Curate of St. Paul's, Cork (*Cork*).
Waring, Arthur Power, Curate of Desertmartin (*Derry*).
Waring, Charles, A M., Perpetual Curate of Eglish (*Armagh*), Moy.
Waring, J. D., A.B., Rector of Lower Tamlaght O'Crilly (*Derry*), Portglenone.
Warner, Gustavus, A.M., Rector of Castlelost (*Meath*), Killucan.
Warren, John Thomas, Perpetual Curate of Ballymascanlan (*Armagh*), Dundalk.
Warren, Latham Coddington, A.M., Incumbent of Bethel Free Church, Kingstown (*Dublin*), Kingstown.
Warren, Robert, A.B., Rector of Cannaway (*Cork*), Crookstown.

Warren, Samuel Percival, A.M., Curate of Balbriggan (*Dublin*).

Warren, Thomas B., Curate of St. Peter (*Cork*), Cork.

Waterson, Francis W., A.M., Vicar of Glynn (*Connor*), Larne.

Watson, Arthur V., Incumbent of Kilcrohane (*Ardfert and Aghadoe*), Kenmare.

Watson, Francis Metcalf, A.M., Prebendary of Kildare, Incumbent of Donadea (*Kildare*), Kilcock.

Watson, George T., A.B., Incumbent of Mullinacuff (*Keighlin*), Tinahely.

Watson, Mahoney V., Curate of Odogh (*Ossory*), Kilkenny.

Weatherhead, Robert, Curate of Dunleckny (*Leighlin*), Bagnalstown.

Webb, Francis, A.M., Vicar of Castlemagner (*Cloyne*), Mallow.

Webb, Matthew, A.B., Incumbent of Drumlummon (*Ardagh*), Granard.

Webb, Richard Francis, A.M., Rector of Dunderrow (*Cork*), Kinsale.

Webb, Ambrose C, A.M., Rector of Dysertgallen (*Leighlin*), Ballinakill.

Webster, George, A.M., Bishop's Chaplain (*Killaloe*), Chancellor of Cork and Rector of St. Nicholas (*Cork*), Cork.

Weir, William, R., A.B., Rector of Edenderry (*Derry*), Omagh.

Weldon, Lewen Burton, A.B., Curate of St. Stephen's (*Dublin*), 77, Haddington-road.

Weldon, Percival Banks, A.M., Rector of Kilcormuck (*Ferns*), Clendaw.

Weldon, Robert Smythe, A.M., Incumbent of Owenduff (*Ferns*), Fethard.

Weldon, Thomas Pyne, Vicar of Kilfergus (*Limerick*), Glin.

Welland, Thomas James, A.M., Assistant Chaplain, Molyneux Asylum (*Dublin*)—residence, 70, Leeson-street, upper.

Wells, J., A.M., Curate of Kilglass (*Ardagh*), Lenamore.

Welsh, Ralph Dawson, A.B., Perpetual Curate of Altedesert (*Armagh*), Pomeroy.

West, Augustus William, A.M., Dean of Ardagh, Chancellor of Kildare, Minor Canon of St. Patrick's, Dublin, Rector of Ardagh, Domestic Chaplain to the Duke of Leinster (*Ardagh and Kildare*), Edgeworthstown.

West, John, D.D., V.G., Dean and Ordinary of Christchurch and St. Patrick's (*Dublin*), 6, Wilton-place.

West, Samuel Maxwell, A.M., Rector of Killough (*Down*).

Westby, Henry H. Jones, A.M., Prebendary of St. Patrick's Cathedral (*Dublin*), 21, Trafalgar-terrace, Monkstown, county Dublin.

Westropp, Thomas, A.M., Prebendary of Limerick, Rector of Ardcanny (*Limerick*), Pallaskenry.

Wetherell, Thomas, A.B., Perpetual Curate of Kinnegad (*Meath*).

Wharton, Joseph James, A.M., Rural Dean, Incumbent of Primult, &c. (*Kildare*), Enfield.

Whately, Edward William, A.M., Chancellor of St. Patrick's, Dublin, and Rector of St. Werburgh's (*Dublin*), 5, Elgin-road.

Wheeler, George Bomford, A.M., Rector of Ballysax (*Kildare*), Curragh Camp.

Wheeler, Trevor W., A.M., Deputation Secretary, Irish Society, 17, Upper Sackville-street, Dublin.

Whelan, Robert W., A.M., Perpetual Curate of Malahide (*Dublin*).

Whitaker, Thomas, A.B., Curate of Stratford-on-Slaney (*Leighlin*), Stratford.

White, Benjamin N., A.M., Chaplain of Ballyfin, and Curate of Clonenagh (*Leighlin*), Mountrath.

White, George P., A.B., Curate of Athassell (*Cashel*), Golden.

White, Henry Grattan, A.M., Prebendary of Clonfert, Rector of Kilmalinoge (*Clonfert*), Ballycrissane.

White, James, Curate of Albert Chapel, Dublin (*Dublin*), —residence, Warwick-terrace.

White, James, Curate of St. Lawrence and Blind Asylum (*Limerick*), Limerick.

White, Newport B., Rector of Kilkenny West (*Meath*), Glasson, Athlone.

White, Richard A., A.B., Curate of St. Peter's, Athlone (*Elphin*).

White, Thomas, A.M., Rector of Powerstown (*Leighlin*), Goresbridge.

White, Thomas Jervis, A.M., Perpetual Curate of Middleton (*Armagh*), Tynan.

Whiteside, James, A.B., Incumbent of Muckamore (*Connor*), Antrim.

Whitfield, Francis, Incumbent of Dunhill (*Lismore*), Curate of Kilbride (*Waterford*), Tramore.

Whitfield, Thomas H., A.B., Vicar of Kilmacahill (*Leighlin*), Gowran.

Whiting, J. F., A.B., Rector of Templeomalus (*Ross*), Clonakilty.

Whitley, John B., A.M., Prebendary of Ross Cathedral, Vicar of Templebryan (*Ross*), Rosscarberry.

Whittaker J., A.B., Curate of Tempo (*Clogher*), Enniskillen.

Whittaker, Mark, A.M., Rector of Bohoe (*Clogher*) Enniskillen.

Whitty, David L., A.B., Curate of Kilfenora (*Kilfenora*).

Whitty, William J. H., Curate of Adamstown (*Ferns*), Enniscorthy.

Wilcocks, J., Curate of St. Lawrence (*Limerick*), Limerick.

Wilkins, William M., A.M., Rural Dean, Rector of Killargue (*Kilmore*), Carrick-on-Shannon.

Wilkinson, Nicholas, A.M., Rural Dean, Vicar of Kilrossanty (*Lismore*), Kilmactoomas.

Wilcocks, James C., A.B., Curate of Ballintemple (*Kilmore*), Ballinagh.

Willcocks, Wm., A.M., Incumbent of Chapelizod (*Dublin*).

Williams, James, A.M., Rector of Templepeter (*Leighlin*), Leighlinbridge.

Williams, John A.B., Rector of Donagheloney (*Dromore*), Waringstown.

Williams, John St. George, A.M., Rector of Clonballoge (*Kildare*), Rathangan.

Williamson, Andrew, A.B., Rector of Magheraculmoney (*Clogher*), Kesh.

Willis, Newcombe, A.B., Treasurer of Kilfenora, Incumbent of Rathdowney (*Kilfenora*), Ballyvaughan.

Willis, Thomas, A.M., Prebendary of Limerick, Rural Dean, Rector of Killeedy (*Limerick*), Ashford, Charleville.

Willock, William Alexander, D.D., Rector of Cleenish (*Clogher*), Enniskillen.

Wills, Freeman C., Curate of Killarney (*Ardfert and Aghadoe*), Killarney.

Wills, James, D.D., Rural Dean, Rector of Attanagh (*Ossory*), Durrow.

Wills, Robert C., A.B., Vicar of Kilfintinan (*Limerick*), Kilrush.

Wills, Samuel Richard, A.M., Incumbent of Kilfinaghty, (*Killaloe*), Bunratty.

Wills, Thomas Burke.

Wilmot, Henry T., A.B., Vicar of Clonfert (*Cloyne*), Kanturk.

Wilson, Alexander B., A.B., Curate of St. Finbar (*Cork*), Cork.

Wilson, Edward, Perpetual Curate of Kilbeggan (*Meath*).

Wilson, Hill, A.B., Rector of Forgney (*Meath*), Ballymahon.

Wilson, Hugh, LL.B., Vicar of Ballywalter (*Down*).

Wilson, John, A.M., Rector of Derrybrusk (*Clogher*), Enniskillen.

Wilson, John, A.B., Rector of Ballyculter (*Down*), Strangford.

Wilson, Mervyn, A.B., Rector of Camus-juxta-Mourne (Derry), Strabane.

Wilson, Richard, A.M., Incumbent of Kilseily (*Killaloe*), Broadford.

Wilson, T. F. M., A.B., Vicar of Rathcline (*Ardagh*), Lanesborough.

Wilson, William, A.M., Rector of Dungourney (*Cloyne*), Midleton.

Wilson, William, A.B., Perpetual Curate of Laghey (*Raphoe*), Laghey.

Windle S. Allan, Incumbent of Mariner's Church, King's-town (*Dublin*), Kingstown.

Wingfield, Hon. William, A.M., Rural Dean, Vicar of Abbeyleix (*Leighlin*).

Wolfe, John Charles, A.B., Archdeacon of Clogher and Rector of Clontibret (*Clogher*), Monaghan.

Wolfenden, Henry, A.B., Rector of Kilfarboy (*Killaloe*), Miltown Malby.

Wolseley, Cadwallader, A.M., Archdeacon of Glandelagh, and Rector of St. Andrew's (*Dublin*), 23, Upper Leeson-street.

Wolseley, Capel, A.B., Incumbent of Lissadill (*Elphin*), Sligo.

Wolseley, John, A.M., Dean of Kildare, Chaplain of St. Michael's (*Kildare*), Portarlington.

Wolseley, William H., A.B., Rector of Kilrush, and Prebendary of Inniscaltra (*Killaloe*), Kilrush.

Wood, Edward B., A.B., Rural Dean, Incumbent of Easkey (*Killala*).

Woodroffe, Henry J., A.M., Rural Deau, Incumbent of Ahern (*Cloyne*), Conna.

Woodroffe, John N., A.B., Curate of St. Finbar (*Cork*), Cork.

Woodroffe, John N., A.M., Prebendary of Cork, Rector of Rathcooney (*Cork*), Glanmire.

Woods, Richard, A.B., Incumbent of Lisgenane (*Lismore*), Youghal.

Woods, William, Chaplain, Magdalen Asylum (*Dublin*)—residence, 113, Gardiner-street, Lower.

Woods, William, A.B., Curate of Geashill (*Kildare*), Geashill.

Woodward, Thomas, A.M., Dean of Down, Rector of Down (*Down*), Downpatrick.

Woodwright, William Henry Edward, A.M., Perpetual Curate of Mullagfad (*Clogher*), Scotstown.

Woolsey, William Myers, Rector of Drinagh (*Cork*), Dunmanway.

Wren, George, A.M., Incumbent of Kilfinane (*Limerick*), Kilmallock.

Wright, Charles E., Perpetual Curate of Muckross (*Ardfert and Aghadoe*), Killarney.

Wright, Robert, A.M., Rural Dean, Rector of Urglin (*Leighlin*), Carlow.

Wright, Richard H., A.B., Rural Dean, Vicar of Kilcaskan (*Ross*), Castletown, Berehaven.

Wrightson, Richard, A.B., Vicar of Lusk (*Dublin*), Lusk.

Wrightson, Thomas Richard, A.B., Rector of Culfeightrin (*Connor*), Ballycastle.

Wrixon, Arthur N., A.B., Senior Curate of Shankill (*Dromore*), Lurgan.

Wrixon, John, A.M., Perpetual Curate of St. John's, Malone (*Connor*), Belfast.

Wrixon, Nicholas, A.M., Prebendary of Cloyne, Rector of Subulter and Union of Kilbrin (*Cloyne*), Mallow.

Wynne, Frederick R., A.M., Prebendary of Ossory and Perpetual Curate of St. Mary's, Kilkenny (*Ossory*), Kilkenny.

Wynne, George Robert, A.B., Perpetual Curate of Whitechurch (*Dublin*), Rathfarnham.

Wynne, Thomas Edward, A.M., Vicar of Killaderry (*Kildare*), Philipstown.

Wynne, William Henry, A.M., Rector of Moira (*Dromore*).

Young, Arthur, Curate of Clogherney (*Armagh*), Omagh.

Young, Francis Charles, A.M., Rector of Kilbride (*Connor*), Kilbride.

Young, Gardiner R., A.M., Vicar of Errigal Trough (*Clogher*), Aughnacloy.

Young, Henry Wray, A.M., Curate of Killeavy (*Armagh*), Newry.

Young, Matthew, A.M., Rector of Ballyroan (*Leighlin*).

Young, Richard P., A.B., Incumbent of Castlewellan (*Down*).

Young, Samuel B., A.M., Rector of Wallstown (*Cloyne*), Doneraile.

Young, Walter, Rector of Templecarn (*Clogher*), Pettigo.

Young, Walter, A.B.

Young, William James M., A.B., Perpetual Curate of Brackaville (*Armagh*), Coal Island.

Young, William F., A.B., Curate of Kilmastulla (*Emly*), Killaloe.

The Episcopal Church in Scotland.

I. United Diocese of Moray, Ross and Caithness.

BISHOP—The Right Rev. ROBERT EDEN, *Hedgefield House, Inverness.*

Ch. Ch. Ox. D.D; Deac. and Pr. 1828 by Bp of G. and B. Consecrated Bp of Moray, Ross and Caithness, 1851; Elected Primus of the Scottish Episcopal Church 1862.

II. Diocese of Edinburgh.

BISHOP—The Right Rev. CHARLES HUGHES TERROT, *Edinburgh.*

Cam. D.D; Deac. 1814. Consecrated Bp of Edinburgh 1841.

CO-ADJUTOR BISHOP—The Right Rev. THOMAS BAKER MORRELL, *Greenhill House, Edinburgh.*

Ball. Coll. Ox. B.A. 1836, M.A. 1839, D.D. 1864; Deac. 1839 and Pr. 1840 by Bp of Ches. Consecrated Co-adjutor Bp of Edinburgh 1863. Formerly R. of Henley-on-Thames 1852–63.

III. United Diocese of Argyll and the Isles.

BISHOP—The Right Rev. ALEXANDER EWING, *Bishopston, Lochgilphead.*

D.D. of Connecticut, LL.D. of Glasgow, D.C.L. of Oxford; Deac. 1838 by Bp of Moray, Pr. 1840 by Bp of Aberdeen. Consecrated Bp of Argyll and the Isles 1847; Incumb. of Ch. Ch. Lochgilphead, 1851.

IV. Diocese of Brechin.

BISHOP—The Right Rev. ALEXANDER PENROSE FORBES, *Dundee.*

Brasen. Coll. Ox. B.A. 1844, D.C.L; Deac. 1844. Consecrated Bp of Brechin 1847; Incumb. of St. Paul's, Dundee. Formerly V. of St. Saviour's, Leeds.

V. United Diocese of St. Andrew's, Dunkeld and Dunblane.

BISHOP—The Right Rev. CHARLES WORDSWORTH, *The Fen House, Perth.*

Ch. Ch. Ox. D.C.L; Deac. 1834 by Bp of Ox. Pr. 1840 by Bp of Win. Consecrated Bp of St. Andrew's, Dunkeld and Dunblane, 1853. Formerly Warden of Trin. Coll. Glenalmond.

VI. United Diocese of Aberdeen and Orkney.

BISHOP—The Right Rev. THOMAS GEORGE SUTHER, *Bon Accord-square, Aberdeen.*

King's Coll. Windsor, Nova Scotia, D.C.L; Deac. 1837. Consecrated Bp of Aberdeen and Orkney 1857; Incumb. of St. Andrew's, Aberdeen.

VII. United Diocese of Glasgow and Galloway.

BISHOP—The Right Rev. WILLIAM SCOT WILSON, *Ayr.*

King's Coll. Aberdeen, M.A. 1827, Dub. LL.D. and D.D. Hobart Coll. U.S.A; Deac. 1827 and Pr. 1829 by Bp of Ross and Argyll. Consecrated Bp of Glasgow and Galloway 1859; Incumb. of Trinity, Ayr, 1832. Formerly Dean of Glasgow and Galloway 1845–59.

ALPHABETICAL LIST OF THE CLERGY IN SCOTLAND.

ADAM, George Robert, *The College, Isle of Cumbrae, Greenock.*—St. Edm. Hall Ox. B.A. 1860, M.A. 1863; Deac. 1861 and Pr. 1862 by Bp of Wor. Formerly C. of Newland 1861, Dorking 1866.

Alexander, John, 7, *Rosebery-crescent, Edinburgh.*—Hobart Coll. New York, D.D; Deac. and Pr. 1842 by Bp of Edinburgh. Incumb. of St. Columbas, Edinburgh, 1846.

Aspinall, George, *Rothesay.*—Heidelberg, Ph.D. and M.A; Deac. 1847 by Bp of Ches. Pr. by Bp. of Man. C. of St. Paul's, Rothesay, 1866.

BADSLY, John Joseph, *Auchindoir.*—Corpus Coll. Cam. B.A. 1856; Deac. 1857 and Pr. 1858 by Bp of B. and W. Incumb. of St. Mary's, Auchindoir.

Ball, Thomas Isaac, *The Cove, by Aberdeen.*—Deac. 1865 and Pr. 1866 by Bp of Brechin. Formerly C. of St. Salvador's, Dundee.

Beckett, Henry Frederick.—St. Cath. Coll. Cam. B.A. 1840, M.A. 1844; Deac. 1840, Pr. 1841. Can. of the Coll. Ch. Isle of Cumbrae, 1852; Orange Free State Mission 1866.

Bell, Walter, *Lochgilphead.*—St. Bees; Deac. 1847 and Pr. 1848 by Bp of Rip. C. of Ch. Ch. Lochgilphead 1867.

Binney, John Erskine, *Drumlanrig Castle, Thornhill.*—Brasen Coll. Ox. B.A. 1858, M.A. 1861; Deac. 1859 and Pr. 1860 by Abp of Cant. Dom. Chap. to Duke of Buccleuch.

Blatch, William, *St. John's Villa, Perth.*—Edinburgh Pantonian Stud. of Divinity; Deac. 1849 and Pr. 1850 by Bp of Edinburgh. Incumb. of St. John's, Perth, 1855; Synod Clerk of the United Diocese of St. Andrew's, Dunkeld and Dunblane.

Bolton, William Henry, *Trinity College, Glenalmond.*—Trin. Coll. Cam. B.A. 1863; Deac. 1864. Asst. Mast. at Trin. Coll. Glenalmond.

Boyce, John Cox, *Chalmers-street, Dunfermline.*—Magd. Hall, Ox. B.A. 1854, M.A. 1859; Deac. 1853 by Bp of Lon. Pr. 1855 by Bp of Wor. Incumb. of Trinity, Dunfermline, 1866.

Boycott, William, *Banchory-Ternan.*—St. John's Coll. Cam. B.A. 1864; Deac. 1866 and Pr. 1867 by Bp of Aberdeen. C. of Banchory-Ternan 1866.

Boyle, John Thomas, *St. Saviour's Parsonage, Bridge of Allan.*—Trin. Coll. Glenalmond; Deac. 1851 by Bp of Edinburgh, Pr. 1853 by Bp of Glasgow. Incumb. of St. Saviour's, Bridge of Allan, 1855.

Bradshaw, John Mills, *Trinity College, Glenalmond.*—Lin. Coll. Ox. B.A. 1858, M.A. 1860; Deac. 1859 and Pr. 1861 by Bp of Llan. Asst. Mast. at Trin. Coll. Glenalmond.

Brigstocke, Decimus, 1, *St. Colme-street, Edinburgh*—Jesus Coll. Ox. B.A. 1862, M.A. 1865; Deac. 1862 and Pr. 1863 by Bp of G. and B. C. of St. Paul's, York-place, Edinburgh, 1866.

Brownjohn, Simeon Dowell, *Bracton College, Inverkip, Greenock.*—Clare Coll. Cam; Deac. 1864 and Pr. 1865 by Bp of Ely. Dom. Chap. to Sir M.R. Shaw Stewart, Ardgowan.

Bruce, Alexander, *Aberdeen.*—Deac. 1810 and Pr. 1812 by Bp of Aberdeen. Formerly Incumb. of St. Andrew's, Banff.

Burton, John, *Meigle House, Meigle.*—Dur. Licen. in Theol. 1847; Deac. 1847 and Pr. 1848 by Bp. of Dur. Incumb. of Alyth and Meigle 1855.

Busfield, Harcourt, *Lonmay Parsonage, by Brucklaw.*—Wor. Coll. Ox.; Deac. 1835 by Bp of Lich. Pr. 1836 by Bp. of Ban. Incumb. of St. Columba's, Lonmay, 1855.

Busbby, William B., *St. Mary's Parsonage, Dalkeith.*—Deac. 1835. Incumb. of St. Mary's, Dalkeith.

Bussell, William John, *Dingwall.*—Pemb. Coll. Ox. B.A. 1826, M.A. 1830; Deac. 1827 and Pr. 1828 by Bp of Ex. Incumb. of St. James's, Dingwall, 1859.

CAVE-BROWN, William Henry, *The Parsonage, Dunmore, Stirlingshire.*—Ch. Ch. Ox. B.A. 1850, M.A. 1853; Deac. 1850 by Bp of Salis. Pr. 1851 by Bp of Roch. Incumb. of St. Andrew's, Dunmore.

Cazenove, John Gibson, *The College, Isle of Cumbrae, Greenock.*—Brasen. Coll. Ox. 2nd cl. Lit. Hum. and 2nd cl. Math. et Phy. B.A. 1843, M.A. 1846; Deac. 1846 and Pr. 1848 by Bp of Rip. Vice-Provost of the Coll. Isle of Cumbrae, 1854-67, Provost 1867; Incumb. of the Collegiate Ch. Isle of Cumbrae.

Chapman, E. W., *Dundee.*—C. of St. Paul's, Dundee.

Cheyne, Patrick, *Aberdeen.*—Formerly Incumb. of St. John's, Aberdeen.

Childs, Henry Horatio, *Aberdeen.*—C. of St. John's, Aberdeen.

Christie, James, *Turriff.*—Marischal College, Aberdeen, M.A; Deac. 1836 and Pr. 1837 by Bp of Aberdeen. Incumb. of Turriff.

Christie, The Very Rev. William, *Fochabers.*—University and King's College, Aberdeen, M.A; Deac. 1839 and Pr. 1840 by Bp of Aberdeen. Incumb. of Fochabers 1855; Dean of the United Diocese of Moray, Ross, and Caithness.

Clarke, Henry James, 6, *Balgillo-terrace, Broughty-Ferry, Dundee.*—Assoc. of King's Coll. Lond; Deac. 1848 and Pr. 1849 by Bp of Lon. Incumb. of St. Mary's, Broughty-Ferry, 1864.

Cole, Charles, *Ardgowan-square, Greenock.*—Clare Hall, Cam. B.A. 1817, B.D.; Deac. and Pr. 1819 by Bp of Lon. Incumb. of St. John's, Greenock.

Cole, Robert, *Greenlaw, Milton Bridge, Edinburgh.*—Queen's Coll. Ox. M.A; Deac. 1840 and Pr. 1841 by Bp of Lon. Chap. to the Military Prison, Greenlaw; Min. at Roslyn Chapel.

Comper, John, 44, *Bon Accord-street, Aberdeen.*—Deac. 1850 and Pr. 1851 by Bp of Brechin. Incumb. of St. John's, Aberdeen.

Crabb, James, *The Parsonage, Church-street, Brechin.*—St. Andrew's, M.A. and Trin. Coll. Glenalmond; Deac. 1853 and Pr. 1854 by Bp of Glasgow and Galloway. Incumb. of St. Andrew's, Brechin, 1866.

Creighton, Alexander Glegg, *The Parsonage, Kilmarnock.*—King's Coll. Aberdeen, and Trin. Coll. Glenalmond; Deac. 1860 by Bp of Glasgow and Galloway. Incumb. of Trinity, Kilmarnock, 1865.

Crowder, Augustus Edward, *The Parsonage, Dunse.*—Dur. Licen. Theol; Deac. 1850 and Pr. 1851 by Bp of Dur. Incumb. of Ch. Ch. Dunse 1852.

Cushnie, Patrick, *Montrose.*—Aberdeen, M.A; Deac. 1800 by Bp of Edinburgh, Pr. 1800 by Bp of Dunkeld. Formerly Incumb. of St. Mary's, Montrose, 1800–45.

DAKERS, John Rose, *The Parsonage, Hawick.*—Glenalmond; Deac. 1852 by Bp of Brechin, Pr. 1854 by Bp of Edinburgh. Incumb of St. Cuthbert's, Hawick, 1854.

Davidson, James, *St. Andrew's Parsonage, Banff.*—Aberdeen, M.A. and Glenalmond; Deac. 1854 by Bp of Glasgow. Incumb. of St. Andrew's, Banff, 1862.

Davies, Alfred Eyles, *Wick.*—St. Mary Hall, Ox. B.A; Deac. 1825 by Bp of Salis. Pr. 1826 by Bp of Ox. C. at Wick.

Douglas, James John, *The Parsonage, Kirriemuir.*—Lampeter, B.D; Deac. 1844 and Pr. 1845 by Abp of York. Incumb. of St. Mary's, Kirriemuir, 1851; Chap. to the Earl of Airlie.

Durno, George, *Port Glasgow.*—Aberdeen, M.A. and Glenalmond; Deac. 1860 and Pr. 1861 by Bp of Glasgow. C. of St. Mary's, Port Glasgow.

ESCHELBACH, Albert, *Dollar*.—Göttingen, M.A; Deac. 1865 by Bp of Dur. Pr. 1866 by Bp Coadjutor of Edinburgh. C. of St. John's, Alloa, and in charge of the Mission at Dollar.

FAITHFULL, Valentine Grantham, 23, *Royal Circus, Edinburgh*.—Corpus Coll. Cam. B.A. 1842, M.A. 1845; Deac. 1845 by Bp of Lin. Pr. 1847 by Bp of Roch. Incumb. of Trinity, Dean Bridge, Edinburgh, 1851.

Ferguson, John, *The Parsonage, Elgin*.—Aberdeen, M.A. and Glenalmond; Deac. 1850 by Bp of Aberdeen, Pr 1853 by Bp of Moray. Chap. to Earl of Fife; Incumb. of Trinity, Elgin, 1853.

Field, Edward Burch, 43, *Moray-place, Edinburgh*.—Sid. Coll. Cam. B.C.L; Deac. 1841 by Bp of Pet. Dom. Chap. to Earl of Rosebery.

Flemyng, Francis Patrick, *Glenfeulan, Helensburgh*.—Magd. Coll. Cam. B.A. 1847, M.A. 1852, LL.D. 1867; Deac. 1847 by Bp of Ches. Pr. 1847 by Bp of Pet. Finance and Corresponding Secretary to the Scottish Episcopal Church Society—Office, 14, Young-street, Edinburgh.

Forbes, George Hay, *Burntisland, Fifeshire*.—Deac. 1848 and Pr. 1849 by Bp of St. Andrew's. Incumb. of Burntisland 1849.

Fortescue, The Very Rev. Edward Bowles Knottesford, *Perth*.—Wad. Coll. Ox. M.A; Deac. 1839 and Pr. 1840 by Bp of Wor. Provost of the Cathedral Church of St. Ninian, Perth, 1850.

Foxton, George, F. H., *Fasque Parsonage, Laurencekirk*.—St. John's Coll. Cam. M.A; Deac. 1848 by Bp of Wor. Incumb. of St. Andrew's, Fasque, 1858.

GAMMACK, James, *The Parsonage, Drumlithie, Fordoun*.—Aberdeen M.A. and Glenalmond; Deac. 1859 and Pr. 1861 by Bp of Aberdeen. Incumb. of St. John's, Drumlithie, 1866.

Gibson, Robert, *Ayr*.—Deac. 1857 and Pr. 1858 by Bp of Glasgow. C. of Trinity, Ayr.

Goalen, Walter Mitchell, *Trinity, near Edinburgh*.—Washington Coll. Mass. U.S.A. M.A; Deac. 1832 and Pr. 1833 by Bp of Moray. Incumb. of Ch. Ch. Trinity, Edinburgh, 1854.

Gordon, James Frederick Skinner, 247, *Bath-street, Glasgow*.—Hobart Episcopal Coll. D.D; Deac. 1843 by Bp of Moray, Pr. 1844 by Bp of Glasgow. Incumb. of St. Andrew's, Glasgow, 1844.

Gordon, Thomas Wilkie, *Aberdeen*.—St. John's Coll. Cam. LL.B; Deac. 1866 by Bp of Aberdeen. Dioc. Chap. to Bp of Aberdeen 1866.

Grant, Alexander Thomson, 1, *Windsor-street, Edinburgh*.—Aberdeen and Glenalmond; Deac. 1864 and Pr. 1866 by Bp Coadjutor of Edinburgh. Dioc. Chap. and Chap to the House of Mercy, Edinburgh, 1867.

Graham, Herbert, *Aberdeen*.—C. of St. Andrew's, Aberdeen.

Green, Samuel Dutton, *Strichen, Aberdeenshire*.—St. Aidan's; Deac. 1854 by Bp of Nova Scotia. Incumb. of Episcopal Church, Stritchen. Formerly Incumb. of Penwortham and Clare, South Australia.

HALLEN, Arthur Washington, *The Parsonage, Alloa*.—St. John's Coll. Cam. B.A. 1858, M.A; Deac. 1858 and Pr. 1859 by Bp of Wor. Incumb. of St. John's, Alloa, 1862.

Harper, Alexander, *Inverurie, by Keith-Hall*.—Aberdeen M.A; Deac. 1841 and Pr. 1842 by Bp of Moray. Incumb. of St. Mary's, Inverurie, 1843.

Hatt, William, *Muchalls, by Stonehaven*.—Aberdeen and Glenalmond; Deac. 1865 by Bp of Brechin, Pr. 1865. by Bp of Aberdeen. Incumb. of St. Ternan's, Muchalls, 1865.

Hay, William, *The Parsonage, Baillieston, Glasgow*.—Aberdeen D.D. and Glenalmond; Deac. 1855 by Bp of Glasgow. Incumb. of St. John's, Baillieston, 1856.

Henderson, The Very Rev. Alexander, *St. Mary's Parsonage, Hamilton*.—Aberdeen, M.A; Deac. 1838 by Bp of Moray, Pr. 1842 by Bp of Glasgow. Incumb. of St. Mary's, Hamilton; Dean of the United Dioc e of Glasgow and Galloway.

Henderson, Robert, *Stirling*.—St. John's Coll. Cam. M.A; Deac. 1822 by Abp of Cant. Incumb. of Trinity, Stirling. 1840.

Henderson, William, *Arbroath*.—Deac. 1827. Incumb. of St. Mary's, Arbroath.

Hill, Thomas Farquhar, *Cally, Gatehouse, Kirkcudbrightshire*.—Deac. 1859; Chap. to H. G. Murray Stewart, Esq. of Cally.

Hood, The Very Rev. Samuel, *Battery-place, Rothesay*.—Deac. 1826 by Bp of Brechin. Incumb. of St. Paul's, Rothesay; Dean of the United Diocese of Argyll and the Isles; Can. of the Coll. Church, I-le of Cumbrae, 1853.

Horwood, Robert, *Birnam, Dunkeld*.—Deac. 1854 by Bp of W. New York. Supernumerary Clergyman for the Dio. of St. Andrew's.

Howard, Henry St. John, *Pitlochrie, Perth*.—Downing Coll. Cam. B.C.L. 1849; Deac. 1849 and Pr. 1850 by Bp of Wor. Incumb. of Trinity, Pitlochrie, 1866.

Humble, Henry, *Perth*.—Dur. B.A. 1837, M.A. 1842; Deac. 1843 and Pr. 1844 by Bp of Dur. Can. and Precentor of the Cathedral of St. Ninian, Perth, 1853; Chap. to Lord Forbes 1844.

Humphrey, William, *Dundee*.—Deac. 1864 and Pr. 1865 by Bp of Brechin. Incumb. of St. Mary Magdalen's, Dundee, 1867.

Hunter, Joseph William, *Laurencekirk*.—Deac. and Pr. 1860 by Bp. of Ox. Incumb. of St. Laurence's, Laurencekirk.

Hutchison, H. Haly, *Stornoway*.—Deac. 1829. Officiating Min. at the Episcopal Church, Stornoway.

Hutton, Robert, *Annan*.—Dur. Licen. in Theol.; Deac. 1856. Incumb. of St. John's, Annan.

INNES, John Brodie, *Milton Brodie, Forres*.—Trin. Coll. Ox. B.A. 1839, M.A. 1842; Deac. 1839 and Pr. 1840 by Bp of Pet. V. of Downe, Kent; licensed clergyman in Diocese of Moray, Ross, and Caithness.

JACKSON, Gildart, *The Parsonage, Leith*.—St. John's Coll. Cam. 16th Sen. Opt. and B.A. 1860, M.A. 1863; Deac. 1861 and Pr. 1862 by Bp of Dur. Chap. to the Forces at Leith Fort and Piershill Barracks; Incumb. of St. James's, Leith, 1865.

Jenkins, Alfred Augustus, *The Parsonage, Galashiels*.—King's Coll. Lond. Theol. Assoc; Deac. 1857 and Pr. 1858 by Bp of Pet. Incumb. of St. Peter's, Galashiels, 1866.

Jenkins, John Gower, *Portobello, near Edinburgh*.—Dur. Licen. in Theol. 1853; Deac. 1853 and Pr. 1854 by Bp of Dur. Incumb. of St. Mark's, Portobello, 1860.

Johnston, Norman, *The Parsonage, Kirkcaldy*.—Dub. A.B. 1832; Deac. 1833 and Pr. 1834 by Bp of Dromore. Incumb. of St. Peter's, Kirkcaldy, 1840; Dom. Chap. to the Countess of Rothes 1859.

Jonas, Edward James, *St. John's Parsonage, Coatbridge*.—Deac. 1850 and Pr. 1851 by Bp of Argyll. Incumb. of St. John's, Coatbridge, 1861.

KEIGWIN, James Philip, *The College, Isle of Cumbrae, Greenock*.—Wad. Coll. Ox. B.A. 1832, M.A. 1838; Deac. 1835 and Pr. 1836 by Bp of Ex. Canon of the Collegiate Church 1854 and Vice Provost 1867; Incumb. of St. Andrew's, Isle of Cumbrae, 1859.

Keith, Charles M'Ghee, *Dalmahoy, Ratho*.—Cumbrae Coll; Deac. 1852 by Bp of Brechin, Pr. 1854 by Bp of Moray. Incumb. of St. Mary's, Dalmahoy, 1862.

Kennedy, William, *Edinburgh*.—Deac. 1850 by Bp of Tuam. Incumb. of St. Paul's, Carruber's Close, Edinburgh, 1865.

LESLIE, Alexander, *The Parsonage, Meiklefolla, Rothie*.—Aberdeen M.A. and Glenalmond; Deac. 1847 and Pr. 1851 by Bp of Aberdeen. Incumb. of St. George's, Meiklefolla, 1852.

Leyland, Leigh, *Lanark.*—Deac. 1848. Incumb. of Episcopal Church, Lanark.

Lingard, R. R., *Dundee.*—Deac. 1852. C. of St. Paul's, Dundee.

Livingston, Ewen Dhu, *Highfield, Beauly.*—Glenalmond; Deac. 1864 by Bp of Moray. Incumb. of Episcopal Church, Highfield.

Low, Alexander, *Longside, Mintlaw.*—Aberdeen, M.A; Deac. 1841 and Pr. 1842 by Bp of Aberdeen. Incumb. of St. John's, Longside, 1842.

Low, William Leslie, *Kincardine O'Neil, Aberdeenshire.*—Aberdeen, A.M. and Glenalmond; Deac. 1863 by Bp of Moray, Pr. 1864 by Bp of Aberdeen. Incumb. of Ch. Ch. Kincardine O'Neil 1865.

MacColl, Hugh, *Kinloch-Moidart, Strontian.*—Glasgow and Glenalmond; Deac. 1864 by Bp of Lon. Pr. 1865 by Bp of Argyll. Missionary Incumb. of Kinloch-Moidart, Strontian, and Mull, 1864.

MacColl, Malcolm, *Glasgow.*—Glasgow and Glenalmond; Deac. 1866 by Bp of Glasgow. C. of Ch. Ch. Glasgow 1866.

Macdonald, J. Ferguson, *Huntly.*—Edinburgh, B.A; Deac. 1846, Pr. 1847. Incumb. of Ch. Ch. Huntly. Synod Clerk of the United Diocese of Moray, Ross, and Caithness.

M'Ewen, Archibald, *The Parsonage, Dumfries.*—Magd. Coll. Cam. B.A. 1840, M.A. 1843; Deac. 1840 and Pr. 1841 by Bp of Salis. Incumb. of St. Mary's, Dumfries, 1846.

M'Gillivray, Archibald, *Strathnairn, Inverness.*—Aberdeen, M.A; Deac. 1858 by Bp of Moray. Incumb. of St. Paul's, Strathnairn.

Mackenzie, Donald, *The Parsonage, Ballachulish, Glencoe.*—Glenalmond; Deac. 1853 and Pr. 1855 by Bp of Glasgow. Incumb. of St. John's, Ballachulish, 1861.

Mackenzie, Duncan, 40, *Dumbarton-road, Glasgow.*—St. Andrew's, M.A; Deac. 1839 and Pr. 1841 by Bp of Moray; Dioc. Chap. of Glasgow and Galloway.

Mackenzie, George William, *The Parsonage, Cupar-Fife.*—Dur. Licen. in Theol; Deac. 1854 by Bp of Dur. Pr. 1855 by Bp of Man. Incumb. of St. James's, Cupar-Fife, 1863.

M'Leod, Nicholas Kenneth, *The Parsonage, Ellon, Aberdeen.*—Aberdeen, M.A; Dur. Licen. in Theol; Deac. 1859 and Pr. 1860 by Bp of Roch. Incumb. of Ellon, 1862.

Macgeorge, Robert Jackson, *Columba-terrace, Oban.*—Deac. 1839 and Pr. 1840 by Bp of Glasgow. Incumb. of St. John's, Oban; Synod Clerk of the United Diocese of Argyll and the Isles.

Macmillan, John, *Birnam, Dunkeld.*—Aberdeen, M.A; Deac. 1826 by Bp of Moray. Incumb. of St. Mary's, Dunkeld, 1845.

Macnamara, Henry, *Dundee.*—Lin. Coll. Ox. M.A; Deac. 1852 by Bp of Lon. C. of St. Paul's, Dundee.

Malcolm, Henry, *The Parsonage, Dunblane.*—St. John's Coll. Cam. B.A; Deac. 1837 by Bp of Dur. Pr. 1840 by Bp of Lich. Incumb. of St. Mary's, Dunblane, 1844.

Mapleton, Reginald John, *Duntroon Castle, Lochgilphead.*—St. John's Coll. Ox. B.A. 1840, M.A. 1857; Deac. 1842 and Pr. 1843 by Bp of Rip. Incumb. of St. Columba's, Kilmartin, 1859.

Martindale, Robert, *St. John's Parsonage, Portsoy.*—St. Bee's; Deac. 1836 and Pr. 1837 by Bp of Ches. Incumb. of St. John's, Portsoy, 1864.

Moffat, Hugh B., *Keith, Banffshire.*—Edin. and Dub. M.A; Deac. 1846 and Pr. 1847 by Bp of Moray. Incumb. of Trinity, Keith, 1850.

Montgomery, James Francis, 7, *Walker-street, Edinburgh.*—Dur. M.A.; Deac. 1856 by Bp of Salis. Incumb. of St. Paul's, Edinburgh, 1864; Synod Clerk of the Dio. of Edinburgh.

Monypenny, Phillips Howard, *The Priory, Pittenweem, Fifeshire.*—Dub. A.B; Deac. 1861 by Bp of Ches. Incumb. of St. John's, Pittenweem, 1866.

Moir, John, *Jedburgh.*—Aberdeen, M.A; Deac. 1836 by Bp of Edinburgh, Pr. 1837 by Bp of Aberdeen. Incumb. of St. John's, Jedburgh, 1861.

Moir, William Young, *Old Meldrum.*—St. Andrew's and Glenalmond; Deac. 1853 by Bp of Brechin, Pr. 1854 by Bp of Glasgow. Incumb. of St. Matthew's, Old Meldrum, 1862.

Morris, Albert A. T., *Muthill, Perthshire.*—Queen's Coll. Ox. B.A. 1854; Deac. 1854 and Pr. 1855 by Bp of Ox. Incumb. of St. James's, Muthill, 1858.

Murdoch, Alexander D., 9, *Viewforth-place, Edinburgh.*—Deac. 1863 and Pr. 1864 by Bp of Ox. C. in charge of St. John's Mission Chapel, Edinburgh, 1863.

Newsam, James, *Mintlaw.*—Deac. 1816. Officiating Clergyman at Pitfour.

Nicolson, James, *Castle Hill, Dundee.*—Aberdeen, M.A. and Glenalmond; Deac. 1856 and Pr. 1857 by Bp. of Brechin. Incumb. of St. Salvador's, Dundee, 1857; Dom. Chap. to Bp of Brechin; Synod Clerk of the Dio. of Brechin.

Oldham, Richard Samuel, 194, *Renfrew-street, Glasgow.*—Wad. Coll. Ox. B.A. 1846, M.A. 1849; Deac. 1846 and Pr. 1847 by Bp of Lon. Incumb. of St. Mary's, Glasgow, 1851.

Orton, Owen, *Trinity College, Glenalmond.*—Corpus Coll. Ox. B.A. 1862, M.A. 1864; Deac. 1862 and Pr. 1864 by Bp of G. and B. Theol. Tut. at Trin. Coll. Glenalmond 1865; Bell Lecturer.

Owen, Edward Henry, *Forres.*—Jesus Coll. Cam. B.A. 1854; Deac. 1855 and Pr. 1856 by Bp of Man. Incumb. of St. John's, Forres, 1859.

Palmer, Henry James, *Stoneyton House, Aberdeen.*—Magd. Hall, Ox. B.A. 1860, M.A. 1867; Deac. 1863 and Pr. 1864 by Bp of Ches. Incumb. of St. Mary's, Aberdeen, 1866.

Penney, John William Watkin, *Stewartville House, Partick, Glasgow.*—Dur. B.A. 1859, M.A. 1862, D.C.L. 1866; Deac. 1860 and Pr. 1861 by Bp of Carl. Incumb. of St. John's, Glasgow, 1865.

Pirie, Henry George, *Dunoon.*—Aberdeen and Edinburgh, M.A; Deac. 1846 and Pr. 1847 by Bp of Glasgow. Incumb. of Trinity, Dunoon, 1848.

Pratt, John Burnett, *Cruden, Ellon.*—Aberdeen, LL.D; Deac. 1821 by Bp of Aberdeen. Incumb. of St. James's, Cruden.

Pressley, Charles, *Fraserburgh.*—Aberdeen, M.A; Deac. 1819 and Pr. 1822 by Bp of Moray. Incumb. of St. Peter's, Fraserburgh, 1838.

Prosser, William, *Leven, Fifeshire.*—Magd. Hall, Ox. M.A; Deac. 1855 and Pr. 1856 by Abp of York. C. in charge at Leven 1863.

Ramsay, The Very Rev. Edward Bannerman, 23, *Ainslie-place, Edinburgh.*—St. John's Coll. Cam. B.A. 1815, M.A. 1831; Deac. 1816 and Pr. 1818 by Bp of B. and W. Incumb. of St. John's, Edinburgh, 1830; Dean of Edinburgh 1841.

Randall, Edward, *Randalstown, Castle Douglas.*—Oriel Coll. Ox. B.A. 1853, M.A. 1858; Deac. 1855 and Pr. 1856 by Bp of Roch. Incumb. of St. Ninian's, Castle Douglas.

Ranken, Arthur, *The Parsonage, Deer, by Brucklaw.*—Aberdeen, M.A. 1826; Deac. 1828 and Pr. 1829 by Bp of Aberdeen. Incumb. of St. Drostane's, Deer; Synod Clerk of the United Diocese of Aberdeen and Orkney.

Ranken, William Arthur, *The Parsonage, Cuminestown, Turriff.*—Glenalmond; Deac. 1864. Incumb. of St. Luke's, Cuminestown.

Rankin, Donald, *Duror Parsonage, Appin.*—Cumbrae; Deac. 1861 and Pr. 1862 by Bp of Argyll. Incumb. of Duror and Portnacroish 1863.

Reid, James Watson, 6, *Abbotsford-place, Glasgow.*—Deac. 1849 and Pr. 1858 by Bp of Glasgow. Incumb. of Ch. Ch. Glasgow, 1857; Chap. to the Forces, Glasgow.

Richardson, Herbert Henley, *Isle of Cumbrae, Greenock.*—St. Mary Hall, Ox. B.A. 1858, M.A. 1861; Deac. 1859 and Pr. 1860 by Abp of Cant. Dom. Chap. to the Countess Dowager of Glasgow 1859; Chap. and Jun. Tut. at Cumbrae College 1863.

Richardson, Walter Hinde, *The Parsonage, Blairgowrie.*—Glenalmond and Cumbrae; Deac. 1863 and Pr. 1864 by Bp of Glasgow. Incumb. of St. Catherine's, Blairgowrie, 1866.

Robertson, Charles, *Tummil Bridge, Pitlochrie.*—Aberdeen, M.A. and Glenalmond; Deac. 1859 and Pr. 1860 by Bp of St. Andrew's. Incumb. of Tummill Bridge, and All Saints, Rannoch, 1859.

Robertson, J. S. S., *Duncrub park, N.B.*—Deac. 1840. Dom. Chap. to Lord Rollo.

Rorison, Gilbert, *Peterhead.*—Glasgow, LL.D; Deac. 1843 and Pr. 1845 by Bp of Glasgow. Incumb. of St. Peter's, Peterhead, 1845.

Roughead, William, *Aberdeen.*—Trin. Coll. Cam. B.A. 1856, M.A. 1859; Theol. Coll. Wells 1858; Deac. 1859 by Bp of B. and W. Pr. 1860 by Bp of Lon. Incumb. of St. John's, Aberdeen, 1867.

Rowbottom, Frederick, 10, *Broughton-place, Edinburgh.*—M.A. by Abp of Cant; Deac. 1858 and Pr. 1860 by Bp of Carl. Incumb. of St. James's, Edinburgh.

Ryde, John Gabriel, *Melrose.*—St. John's Coll. Ox. B.A. 1845, M.A. 1848; Deac. 1847 and Pr. 1848 by Bp of Lon. Incumb. of Trinity, Melrose, 1855; Synod Clerk of the United Dio. of Glasgow and Galloway.

Sandford, Daniel Fox, 14, *Rutland-street, Edinburgh.*—Glenalmond; Deac. 1853 by Bp of Argyll, Pr. 1855 by Bp of Edinburgh. Chap. to the Coadjutor Bp of Edinburgh 1863; Evening Lect. at St. James's, Leith, 1865; C. of St. John's, Edinburgh, 1855.

Scott, Joseph Hill, *Kelso.*—St. Bees; Deac. 1860 by Bp of Ches. Incumb. of St. Andrew's, Kelso, 1862.

Sellar, James Annand, 10, *Salisbury-place, Newington, Edinburgh.*—Aberdeen, M.A. and Glenalmond; Deac. 1851 by Bp of Aberdeen, Pr. 1852 by Bp of Brechin. Incumb. of St. Peter's, Newington, Edinburgh, 1866.

Shaw, William George, *Forfar.*—Glenalmond; Deac. 1853 by Bp of Edinburgh, Pr. 1854 by Bp of St. Andrew's. Incumb. of St. John's, Forfar, 1854.

Simcockes, George Staunton, *Inverness.*—Trin. Coll. Cam. B.A. 1844, M.A. 1850; Deac. 1849, Pr. 1850. Chap. to Bp of Moray 1867.

Simpson, Alexander, *Lochlee, by Brechin.*—Aberdeen, M.A. 1835; Deac. 1838 and Pr. 1840 by Bp of Brechin. Incumb. of Lochlee 1838.

Simpson, William, *Rosse Parsonage, Fortwilliam.*—Queens' Coll. Cam. M.A.; Deac. 1861 and Pr. 1862 by Bp of Argyll. Incumb. of Rosse Church, Fortwilliam, 1862; Registrar of Dio. of Argyll and Isles.

Skinner, Robert, *St. Andrew's.*—Dur. Licen. in Theol; Deac. 1853 and Pr. 1854 by Bp of Dur. Incumb. of St. Andrew's, St. Andrews, 1856.

Smith, Christopher, *Musselburgh.*—Lond. B.A; Deac. 1859 and Pr. 1860 by Bp of Man. Prin. of the Training Coll. Edinburgh, 1862; Incumb. of St. Peter's, Musselburgh, 1866.

Smith, Farquhar, *The Parsonage, Arpafeelie, Inverness.*—Deac. 1862 by Bp of Edinburgh, Pr. 1864 by Bp of Moray. Incumb. of St. John's, Arpafeelie.

Smith, James, *Loches, by Dundee.*—Aberdeen, M.A; Deac. 1838 by Bp of St. Andrew's, Pr. 1840 by Bp of Aberdeen. C. in charge of St. Margaret's, Lochee, 1866.

Stephen, William, *The Parsonage, Dumbarton.*—Lond. and Aberdeen, and Glenalmond; Deac. 1856 and Pr. 1857 by Bp of Glasgow. Incumb. of St. Luke's, Dumbarton, 1859.

Stevenson, James, *Caterline, Stonehaven.*—St. Andrew's, M.A; Deac. and Pr. 1841 by Bp of Moray. Incumb. of St. Philip's, Caterline, 1842.

Stewart, James, *Gallowhill, Paisley.*—Deac. 1842 and Pr. 1843 by Bp of Toronto. Incumb. of Trinity, Paisley, 1851.

Sutcliffe, James C., *Falkirk.*—Dur. Licen. in Theol; Deac. 1859 and Pr. 1860 by Bp of G. and B. Incumb. of Ch. Ch. Falkirk, 1864.

Sutherland, George, *Tillymorgan, by Rothie, Aberdeen.*—Aberdeen, M.A. and Glenalmond; Deac. 1856 and Pr. 1857 by Bp of Aberdeen. Incumb. of St. Thomas's, Tillymorgan, 1865.

Syme, John Stuart, *Helensburgh.*—Glenalmond; Deac. 1857 by Bp of Edinburgh, Pr. 1858 by Bp of Glasgow. Incumb. of St. Michael's, Helensburgh, 1862.

Teape, Charles Richard, 15, *Findhorn-place, Grange, Edinburgh.*—Glenalmond; Deac. 1853 and Pr. 1854 by Bp of Edinburgh. Incumb. of St. Andrew's, Edinburgh, 1856.

Teape, Hudson, *Armadale, Bathgate.*—Dub. A.B; Deac. 1844 and Pr. 1845 by Bp of Down and Connor. Incumb. of St. Paul's, Armadale, 1864.

Temple, Alexander, *Strathtay.*—Aberdeen, M.A. and Glenalmond; Deac. 1853 by Bp of Aberdeen, Pr. 1854 by Bp of St. Andrews. Incumb. of Strathtay 1854.

Temple, William, *Forgue, Huntly.*—Aberdeen, M.A. and Glenalmond; Deac. 1850 by Bp of Aberdeen. Incumb. of Forgue; C. in charge at Aberchirder 1866.

Thom, The Very Rev. Robert Kilgour, *Stonehaven.*—Deac. 1841 and Pr. 1842 by Bp of Brechin. Dean of Brechin; Incumb. of St. James's, Stonehaven, 1865.

Thompson, Henry Morton, 1, *Albany-street, Leith.*—Aberdeen, M.A. and Glenalmond; Deac. 1866 by Bp Coadjutor of Edinburgh. C. of St. James's, Leith.

Torry, The Very Rev. John, *Cupar-Angus.*—Aberdeen, M.A; Deac. 1821 by Bp of Moray, Pr. 1822 by Bp of Dunkeld. Dean of St. Andrews; Incumb. of St. Anne's, Cupar-Angus, 1824.

Troup, Alexander, *Buckie.*—Aberdeen, M.A. and Glenalmond; Deac. 1851 by Bp of Aberdeen, Pr. 1856 by Bp. of Brechin. Incumb. of Arradoul and Buckie 1855.

Turner, John, *Trinity College, Glenalmond, Perthshire.*—King's Coll. Lond. Theol. Assoc. 1856; Deac. 1856 and Pr. 1857 by Bp of Win. Asst. Mast. at Trinity College, Glenalmond, 1859. Formerly C. of St. Mary's-the-Less, Lambeth.

Urquhart, Alexander Jolly, *Largs, Greenock.*—Deac. 1856 by Bp. of Capetown, Pr. 1857 by Bp of Grahamstown. Incumb. of St. Columba's, Largs, 1866.

Walker, Robert, *Lerwick.*—Deac. 1849 by Bp of Brechin, Pr. 1851 by Bp. of Aberdeen. Incumb. of St. Magnus', Lerwick, 1864.

Walker, Thomas, 5, *Rubislaw-place, Aberdeen.*—Aberdeen, M.A; Deac. 1836 by Bp of Aberdeen, Pr. 1838 by Bp of Dunkeld. Licensed Clergyman in Diocese of Aberdeen and Orkney.

Walker, William, *Monymusk, Aberdeen.*—Aberdeen, M.A; Deac. and Pr. 1842 by Bp of Aberdeen. Incumb. of Monymusk 1844.

Walker, William, 101, *St. George's-road, Glasgow.*—St. Andrew's, B.A. and Glenalmond; Deac. 1865 and Pr. 1866 by Bp of Glasgow. C. of St. Mary's, Glasgow, 1865.

Walpole, Thomas Beaumont, *Port-Glasgow.*—St. Bees; Deac. 1851 by Abp of York. Incumb. of St. Mary-the-Virgin's, Port-Glasgow, 1854.

Wannop, Thomas Nicholson, *Haddington.*—Dur. Licen. in Theol. 1849; Deac. 1849 and Pr. 1850 by Bp of Dur. Incumb. of Trinity, Haddington, 1855.

Watson, Alexander E., *Raeburn Cottage, Raeburn-place, Edinburgh.*—Queens' Coll. Cam. M.A; Deac. 1855 by Bp. of Ches. Incumb. of St. George's, Edinburgh, 1855.

Webster, William, *New Pitsligo, Aberdeen.*—Aberdeen, M.A.; Deac. 1834 and Pr. 1835 by Bp of Edinburgh. Incumb. of St. John's, New Pitsligo, 1841.

Weldon, Robert Gascoigne, *Girvan.*—Glasgow, M.A. and Glenalmond; Deac. 1853 and Pr. 1854 by Bp of Glasgow. Incumb. of Girvan and Maybole, 1858.

West, William, *Nairn.*—Dub. A.B. 1856; Deac. 1856 and Pr. 1857 by Bp of Salis. Incumb. of St. Columba's, Nairn, 1864.

Weston, Henry Austen, 95, *Crown-street, Aberdeen.*—Pemb. Coll. Ox.; Deac. 1866 by Bp of Aberdeen.

Head Master of St. Nicholas' Sch. Aberdeen; C. of St. John's, Aberdeen, 1866.

Wildman, Thomas, *Galloway House, Wigtonshire.*—Dub. A.M; Deac. and Pr. 1845 by Bp of St. Andrew's. Dom. Chap. to Earl of Galloway.

Wilson, The Very Rev. David, *Woodhead, Fyvie.*—Aberdeen, M.A.; Deac. 1826 and Pr. 1828. Dean of Aberdeen and Orkney; Incumb. of All Saints', Woodhead, 1828.

Wilson, Thomas, *Stirling.*—Queen's Coll. Ox. B.A; Deac. and Pr. 1855 by Bp of Car. C. of Trinity, Stirling.

Witherby, Robert Hale, *Glenalmond, Perthshire.*—Ex. Coll. Ox. B.A. 1847, M.A. 1852; Deac. 1849 and Pr. 1853 by Bp of Chich. Sub-Warden of Trin. Coll. Glenalmond.

Wood, William, *Campbelton.*—Ox. M.A; Deac. 1834 by Bp of B. and W. Incumb. of St. Kiaran's, Campbelton, 1858.

Woodward, John, *Montrose.*—St. Nicolas Coll. Lancing; Deac. 1861 and Pr. 1862 by Bp of Chich. Incumb. of St. Mary's, Montrose.

Wyer, Thomas Rowland, *Summerfield, Peebles.*—St. John's Coll. Cam. B.A. 1842, M.A. 1846; Deac. 1847 and Pr. 1848 by Bp of Win. Incumb. of St. Peter's, Peebles.

TRINITY COLLEGE, GLENALMOND,

PERTHSHIRE.

WARDEN.

Rev. J. Hannah, D.C.L., late Fell. of Linc. Coll. Ox; Pantonian Professor of Theology.

SUB-WARDEN.

Rev. R. H. Witherby, M.A. Exeter Coll. Ox.

TUTOR IN THEOLOGY.

Rev. O. Orton, M.A., late Scho. of Corpus Coll. Ox; Bell Lecturer.

ASSISTANT MASTERS.

Rev. W. H. Bolton, B.A., late Scho. of Trin. Coll. Cam.

M. T. Park, B.A., late Scho. of Lin. Coll. Ox.

Rev. J. Turner, King's Coll. Lond.

T. Knowles, B.A., St. John's Coll. Cam.

P. Hangen, Ph. D. and M.A., Univ. of Giessen.

COLLEGIATE CHURCH AND COLLEGE,

ISLE OF CUMBRAE.

VISITOR.—The Right Rev. the Bp of Argyll and the Isles 1858

PROVOST.—The Rev. J. G. Cazenove, M.A. ... 1867

CANONS.

The Very Rev. S. Hood, M.A. 1854

Rev. H. F. Beckett, M.A. 1859

Rev. J. P. Kelgwin, M.A., Vice-Provost 1854

The Ven. P. Freeman, M.A. 1854

Rev. J. A. Ewing, M.A. 1854

HONORARY CANONS.

Rev. G. C. White, M.A. 1858

Rev. J. C. Wynter, M.A. 1862

Rev. G. Williams, B.D. 1862

Hon. and Rev. H. Douglas, M.A. 1865

Rev. W. Bright, M.A. 1865

CHAPLAIN.

Rev. H. H. Richardson, M.A. 1863

The Colonial Episcopal Church.

TABLE OF COLONIAL BISHOPS,

SINCE THE ERECTION OF THE FIRST COLONIAL SEE IN 1787.

1. *Nova Scotia.*
Dr. Charles Inglis... 1787
Dr. Robert Stanser 1816
Dr. John Inglis 1825
Dr. H. Binney 1851

2. *Newfoundland.*
Dr. A. G. Spencer 1839
Dr. E. Feild... 1844
Dr. J. B. Kelly (*Coadjutor*)... 1867

3. *Fredericton.*
Dr. J. Medley 1845

4. *Quebec.*
Dr. J. Mountain 1793
Dr. C. J. Stewart... 1825
Dr. J. Mountain 1836
Dr. J. W. Williams 1863

5. *Montreal.*
Dr. F. Fulford 1850

6. *Toronto.*
Dr. J. Strachan 1839

(*Niagara.*)
Dr. A. N. Bethune (*Coadjutor*) 1867

7. *Ontario.*
Dr. J. T. Lewis 1862

8. *Rupert's Land.*
Dr. D. Anderson 1849
Dr. R. Machray 1865

9. *Huron.*
Dr. B. Cronyn 1857

10. *Columbia.*
Dr. G. Hills... 1859

11. *Jamaica.*
Dr. C. Lipscomb 1824
Dr. A. G. Spencer... 1843

(*Kingston.*)
Dr. R. Courtenay (*Coadjutor*) 1856

12. *Barbados.*
Dr. W. H. Coleridge 1824
Dr. Thomas Parry 1842

13. *Antigua.*
Dr. Dan. G. Davis... 1842
Dr. S. J. Rigaud 1858
Dr. W. W. Jackson 1860

14. *Guiana.*
Dr. W. P. Austin... 1842

15. *Nassau.*
Dr. C. Caulfeild 1861
Dr. A. R. P. Venables.... ... 1863

16. *Calcutta.*
Dr. T. F. Middleton 1814
Dr. Reg. Heber 1822
Dr. J. T. James 1827
Dr. J. M. Turner 1829
Dr. Daniel Wilson... 1832
Dr. G. E. L. Cotton 1858
Dr. R. Milman 1867

17. *Bombay.*
Dr. Thomas Carr 1836
Dr. J. Harding 1851

18. *Madras.*
Dr. Daniel Corrie... 1835
Dr. G. T. Spencer... 1837
Dr. Thomas Dealtry 1849
Dr. Fred. Gell 1861

19. *Colombo.*
Dr. James Chapman 1845
Dr. P. C. Claughton 1862

20. *Sydney.*
Dr. W. Broughton... 1836
Dr. F. Barker 1854

21. *Newcastle.*
Dr. W. Tyrrell 1847

22. *Melbourne.*
Dr. Charles Perry... 1847

23. *Adelaide.*
Dr. Augustus Short 1847

24. *Tasmania.*
Dr. F. R. Nixon 1842
Dr. C. H. Bromby... 1864

25. *Perth.*
Dr. M. B. Hale 1857

26. *Brisbane.*
Dr. E. W. Tufnell... 1859

27. *Goulburn.*
Dr. M. Thomas 1863

28. *Grafton and Armidale.*
Dr. W. C. Sawyer... 1867

29. *New Zealand.*
Dr. G. A. Selwyn... 1841

30. *Christ Church.*
Dr. H. J. C. Harper 1856

31. *Nelson.*
Dr. E. Hobhouse 1858
Dr. A. B. Suter 1866

32. *Wellington.*
Dr. C. J. Abraham 1858

33. *Waiapu.*
Dr. W. Williams 1859

34. *Dunedin.*
Dr. H. L. Jenner 1866

35. *Cape Town.*
Dr. Robert Gray 1847

36. *Natal.*
Dr. J. W. Colenso 1853

37. *Graham's Town.*
Dr. J. Armstrong... 1853
Dr. H. Cotterill 1856

38. *Sierra Leone.*
Dr. Owen E. Vidal 1852
Dr. J. W. Weeks 1855
Dr. John Bowen 1857
Dr. E. H. Beckles... 1860

39. *Mauritius.*
Dr. V. William Ryan 1855

40. *St. Helena.*
Dr. P. C. Claughton 1859
Dr. T. E. Welby 1862

41. *Gibraltar.*
Dr. G. Tomlinson... 1842
Dr. W. J. Trower... 1863

42. *Victoria.*
Dr. George Smith... 1849
Dr. C. R. Alford 1867

43. *Labuan and Sarawak.*
Dr. F. T. M'Dougall 1855

MISSIONARY BISHOPS.

Melanesia.
Dr. J. C. Patteson 1861

Africa.
Dr. W. G. Tozer 1862

Honolulu.
Dr. T. N. Staley 1861

Orange River States.
Dr. E. Twells 1863

Africa, Niger Territory.
Dr. S. E. Crowther 1864

EAST INDIES, CHINA, AND THE CAPE OF GOOD HOPE.

Diocese of Calcutta.

CALCUTTA, The Right Rev. Robert MILMAN, Lord Bishop of Calcutta and Metropolitan in India and Ceylon, *Bishop's Palace, Calcutta.*—Ex. Coll. Ox. B.A. 1838, D.D. 1867; Deac. 1839 and Pr. 1840 by Bp of Pet. Consecrated Bp of Calcutta 1867. (Episcopal Jurisdiction, the presidency of Bengal including the N.W. Provinces, Oude, the Punjâb, Assam, Arracan, Tenasserim, Pegu, and the Straits Settlements; Area, 306,012 miles; Pop. 100,000,000; Clergy, 180; Inc. of See, Government allowance, 4600*l.*) His Lordship was formerly V. of Lamborne, Berks, 1851–62, and V. of Great Marlow, Bucks, 1862–67. Author, *Life of Tasso*, 2 vols. 1848; *The Way through the Desert*, 1850; *Meditations of Confirmation* (a Tract), Masters, 3 eds; *Love of the Atonement*, ib. 2 eds.

Abbott, William Henry, Esq., Registrar of the Archdeaconry, and Secretary to the Bishop 1862.

Burge, M. R., M.A., Officiating Domestic Chaplain to the Bishop 1867.

Pratt, The Ven. John Henry, M.A., Archdeacon of Calcutta and Commissary 1849.

Chaplains.

Atlay, Brownlow Thomas, M.A., officiating at Garrison of Fort William and Military Hospital 1867.
Ayerst, William, M.A., Fyzabad 1861.
Baldwin, John Richard, Allahabad 1857.
Baly, Joseph, M.A., Simla 1860.
Beamish, Samuel Henry, B.A., Jullundur 1855.
Behr, Bernhard Martin, B.A. 1867.
Bell, William Charles, Ferozepore 1862.
Blyth, Edward Hamilton, M.A., Europe (on sick leave) 1864.
Blyth, George Francis Popham, M.A., Officiating St. Paul's Cathedral, Calcutta, and Presidency General Hospital 1866.
Bromehead, William Crawford, M.A., St. John's, Calcutta 1859.
Browne, John Cave, M.A., Kidderpore 1851.
Burge, Milward Rodon, M.A., Garrison of Fort William and Military Hospital, Officiating Domestic Chaplain to the Bishop 1852.
Cahusac, Charles William, M.A., Jubbulpore 1845.
Carruthers, George Thomas, Dinapore 1866.
Clough, John, M.A., Tonghoo 1863.
Corbyn, Henry Fisher, M.A., attached to Abyssinian Field Force 1859.
Cowley, William David, M.A., Europe (on sick leave) 1859.
Crofton, Henry Woodward, M.A., Rangoon 1854.
D'Aguilar, John Burton, B.A., Sealkote 1846.
Drawbridge, William Barker, M.A., Darjeeling 1860.
Ellis, Fitz Henry William, M.A., Lucknow 1845.
Fagan, Feltrim Christopher, M.A. 1867.
Firminger, Thomas Augustus Charles, M.A., Gowhatty 1846.
Fynes-Clinton, Dormer, Mussoorie 1860.
Gale, William Henry, B.A. 1867.
Garbett, Charles, M.A., Barrackpore 1839.
Garstin, Anthony, Thyet Myo 1841.
Gavin, Jeremiah Fitz-Austin, B.A., Roorkee 1855.
Godfrey, Edward, M.A., Saugor 1848.
Hamilton, Charles Dillon, M.A., Mhow 1846.
Hardy, Arthur Octavius, M.A., Head Master of the Mussoorie School (Lent to Diocesan Board of Education for three years) 1865.
Hinde, Francis, B.A., Sylhet, Cdachar, and Cherrapoonjee, 1844.
Hocking, John Hocking, M.A., Dhurmsalla and Kangra 1862.
Homer, Frederic William, Delhi 1866.
Horsburgh, Andrew, M.A., Dera Ismael Khan 1859.
Hubbard, Edward James, M.A., Agra 1859.
Irwin, Arthur William, M.A., Rawul Pindee 1860.
James, Henry Daniel, M.A., Mooltan 1856.
Jarbo, Peter John, Ph. D., Calcutta, St. James's 1860.
Kemble, Edward, B.A., Cuttack 1866.
Laing, Malcolm Strickland 1857.
Lovely, George, Calcutta, Old or Mission Church 1855.
Mackay, James, B.D., Penang 1857.
Matthew, Henry James, M.A., Allahabad 1866.
Mazuchelli, Francis Mary Felix Fortunate, D.D., Dacca 1857.
Michell, Francis Rodon, Nowgong and Nagode 1867.
Mills, Michael Edward, Cawnpore 1867.
Mitchell, Andrew Lumsden, Howrah 1866.
Moore, Thomas, B.A., Jhansie 1857.
Moule, Horatio, M.A., Hazareebaugh 1841.
Murray, Henry, M.A., Lucknow Cantonments 1855.
Nicholas, Percy, M.A., Benares 1866.
Nicholls, William Ward, Kussowlie 1862.
Orton, Frederick, B.A. 1867.
Parish, Charles Samuel Pollock, B.A., Moulmein 1852.
Phelps, William Whitmarsh, M.A., Meean Meer 1854.
Pratt, John Henry, M.A., Archdeacon and Commissary 1838.
Richards, Joseph, M.A., Bareilly 1855.
Robberds, Frederick Walter, B.A., Dugshaie 1862.
Robinson, Alexander, M.A., Gwalior 1860.
Rotton, John Edward Wharton, M.A., Umballa 1850.
Sharkey, John, B.A., Europe (on sick leave) 1852.
Sharp, Benjamin, B.A., Subathoo 1861.
Sharpe, James Falconer, B.A., Chunar 1842.
Simpson, William, M.A., Europe (on furlough) 1858.
Spear, Joseph, B.A., Meerut 1865.
Spencer, William, B.A., St. Paul's, Cathedral, Calcutta, and Great Jail 1859.
Spry, Arthur Browne, B.A., Calcutta, St. John's, 1838.
Stamper, John Alexander, B.A., Landour 1860.
Stephenson, John, M.A., Calcutta, St. John's 1866.
Stone, Arthur, M.A., Dum Dum 1860.
Stuart, James Kilbee, M.A., Anarkullee, Lahore 1856.
Symonds, George Davey, B.A., Europe (on sick leave) 1858.
Tandy, Edward Joseph, M.A., Europe (on sick leave) 1859.
Templeman, Edward, B.A., Europe (on furlough) 1858.
Toussaint, Charles Thomas, Muttra 1865.
Tribe, Walter Harry, M.A., Roy Bareilly 1867.
Viret, Francis Charles, M.A., Seetapore 1848.
Wallis, Arthur Wellington, B.A., Berhampore 1846.
Walters, Melmoth Dick Campbell, M.A., Calcutta, Old or Mission Church 1856.
Ward, James Rimington, M.A. 1867.
Warneford, Thomas Lewis John, Port Blair 1866.
Waterhouse, Charles James, M.A., Singapore 1857.
West, William, officiating at Dinapore 1867.
Whyte, Charles Alexander Lascombe, M.A., Shahjehanpore 1858.
Williams, David Payne, M.A., Peshawur 1859.
Willis, Finch D'Anyers 1867.
Wilson, Alexander Newton, officiating at Nowshera 1867.
Young, John William, M.A., Agra Cantonments 1857.

One Vacancy.

Skelton, T., M.A., Principal
Banerjea, K. M., Professor . } Bishop's College, Calcutta.
Coe, J. W. (*pro tem.*) . .

Missionaries of the Society for the Propagation of the Gospel in Foreign Parts.

Bonnaud, R. L. . . .	Hindustani Mission.
Brinckman, Arthur . .	Honorary, Cashmere.
Burrell, S. B.	Cawnpore.
Chand, Tárá	Delhi.

Choudhury, B. C.	Howrah.
Coe, J. W.	Barripore.
Drew, W.	Barripore.
Driberg, C. E.	Tallygunge.
Endle, S.	Tezpore.
Evans, R. W.	Moulmein.
Harrison, H. J.	Barripore.
Hesselmeyer, C. H.	Tezpore.
Hickey, R. W.	Roorkee.
Hill, J. R.	Cawnpore.
Lethbridge, W. M.	Patna.
Lockington, Cornelius	Cawnpore.
Marks, John E.	Rangoon.
Mitter, G. C.	Howrah.
Moor, R.	Patna.
Pall, B. N.	Meerpore.
Sandel, H. H.	Calcutta (Cath. Endt. Fund).
Sells, H.	Roorkee.
Smith, W. O'Brien	Hindustani Mission, Calcutta.
Smithwhite, John	Delhi.
Thomas, P. W.	Tallygunge.
Vallings, F. R.	Secretary to S.P.G. Calcutta.
Varnier, M. J. J.	Patna.
Wheeler, C. E.	Cawnpore.
Whitley, J. C.	Delhi.
Winter, R. R.	Delhi.

Missionaries of the Church Missionary Society.

Abel, F.*	Bareilly.
Ball, William J. B.A.	Europe.
Barton, John, M.A.	Principal of C. M. Coll. Calcutta.
Blumhardt, C. H.	Kishnagur.
Bomwetsch, C.	Calcutta.
Brodie, H.	Peshawur.
Brown, J. M. B.A.	Europe.
Bruce, R. B.A.	Derajat.
Carter, S.	Gorruckpore.
Champion, E.	Jubbulpur.
Clark, Robert, M.A.	Umritsir.
Cooper, J.	Europe.
Davis, B.	Allahabad.
Dœuble, C. G.	Agra.
Drœse, E.	Bhagulpore.
Dyson, Samuel	Calcutta.
Erhardt, James	Lucknow.
Fuchs, J.	Benares.
Geidt, B.	Europe.
Greaves, P., M.A.	Europe.
Handcock, W.	Europe.
Hooper, W., M.A.	Benares.
Hörnle, T.	Meerut.
Hörnle, R. A. F.	Meerut.
Hubbard, H. D. B.A.	Benares.
Hughes, T. P.	Peshawur.
Joseph, Jacob*	Agra.
Kadshu, James*	Kangra.
Keene, W., B.A.	Europe.
Leupolt, C. B.	Benares.
Lincke, J. G.	Bollobpur.
Lockwood, A.	Azimgurh.
Long, James	Calcutta.
M'Carthy, John A.	Europe.
Mallett, W. G.	Umritsir.
Menge, J. P.	Lucknow.
Merk, J. N.	Kangra.
Mohun, D.*	Allahabad.
Neele, A. Peter	Burdwan.
Patterson, H. S.	Europe.
Paul, Tulsi*	Dehra Doon.
Puxley, E. L. M.A.	Europe.
Rebsch, W.	Kotgurh.
Reuther, C.	Fyzabad.
Ridley, W.	Peshawur.
Rozario, De, F. J.	Agurpara, Calcutta.
Sandys, T.	Agurpara, Calcutta.
Sandys, W. Swaytoo*	Kotgurh.
Seal, Modhu S.*	Ruttunpore.
Schneider, F. E.	Agra.
Schurr, F.	Kapasdanga.
Shackell, Henry W. M.A.	Agra.
Smith, W.	Benares.
Solomon, D.*	Benares.
Stern, Henry	Corruckpur.
Stern, Julius, A. L. A.	Burdwan.
Storrs, C. E.	Santhal District.
Storrs, W. T.	Santhal District.
Storrs, Townsend	Umritsur.
Stuart, E. C. B.A.	Secretary, C. M. S. Calcutta.
Stuart, J.	Jubbulpore.
Vaughan, James	Calcutta.
Vines, C. E. M.A.	Principal St. John's College, A.
Wade, T. R.	Peshawur.
Welland, Joseph, B.A.	Calcutta.
Yeates, George, B.A.	Mooltan.

Calcutta Diocesan Additional Clergy Society.

Archer, J. B.	Purreah.
Cardew, F. C.	Mynpoorie.
George, D.	Hissar.
Girling, G.	Europe.
Greenfield, John	Mozufferpore.
Humfrey, Cave	Chittagong.
Ince, J. C.	Raneegunge.
Keene, T. P. LL.B.	Midnapore.
Love, J. C.	Monghyr and Jamalpore.
Mills, M. E.	Bhagulpore.
Norrish, A. A.	Akyab.
Thompson, J. C.	Arrah.
Walshe, A. C.	Midnapore.

Other Clergy in the Diocese.

Acocks, —	Chaplain to Seamen.
Cole, W.	Prin. Laurence Asy., Sanawur.
Lewin, J. R.	Dalhousie.
	Principal, Mussoorie School.
Nesfield, J. C.	Head Mast. of St. Paul's Sch. [Darjeeling.
Slater, S.	Hd. Mst. of the Bp.'s Sch. Simla.
Wood, Henry	Missionary Pastor, Calcutta.

Diocese of Madras.

MADRAS, The Right Reverend Frederick GELL, Lord Bishop of Madras, *Madras.*—Trin. Coll. Cam. Bell's Univ. Scho. 1840, B.A. 1843, M.A. 1846, B.D. 1854, D.D. 1861; Deac. 1843 and Pr. 1844 by Bp of Ely. Consecrated Bp of Madras 1861. (Episcopal Jurisdiction, the Presidency of Madras; Area, 141,923 square miles; Pop. 18,000,000; Clergy, 122; Inc. of See, Government allowance, 2500*l*.) His Lordship was formerly Fell. of Ch. Coll. Cam. 1843–61.

Dealtry, The Ven. Thomas, M.A., Archdeacon of Madras and Commissary, 1861.

Goodhart, Rev. Edward Skelton, B.A., Dom. Chaplain to the Lord Bishop, attached to Abyssinian Field Force, 1866.

Murphy, Rev. Robert, D.C.L., Registrar, 1860.

Chaplains.

Babbington, William Marshall Sargeant, B.A., Vizagapatam 1866.

Bartlett, Arthur Toms, Kurnool 1865.

Clarke, David George, B.A., Poonamallee 1865.

Cooper, William Wright Gilbert, M.A., Bangalore, St. John's 1855.

Dealtry, Thomas, M.A., Archdeacon, St. George's Cathedral 1851.

Deane, Barry O'Meara, B.A., Mercara 1856.

Deane, Charles Henry, M.A., Cannanore 1863.

Dene, Octavius, B.A., Trichinopoly 1861.

Drury, Charles Rous, M.A., St. Thomas's Mount, with charge of Pallaveram, 1856.

English, George, Mysore 1861.

Firth, Richard, M.A., Aurungabad 1850.

Foulkes, Thomas, Vepery 1861.

Gibson, Charles Dockley, M.A., Calicut 1849.

Goodhart, Edward Skelton, B.A., Domestic Chaplain to the Bishop, attached to Abyssinian Field Force, 1865.
Gorton, John, M.A., Fort St. George. Garrison 1846.
Griffiths, John, M.A., St. George's Cathedral 1844.
James, Henry Pigot, B.A., Berar 1855.
Kidd, John Tyrwhit Davy, B.A., Wellington 1854.
Leeming, William, M.A., 1862.
Little, Robert Parker, B.A., Europe (on sick leave) 1856.
Lys, Francis George, M.A., North Black Town, Madras 1864.
McKee, James, B.A., Coonoor 1856.
Murphy, John, LL.D., Rajahmundry 1861.
Murphy, Robert, LL.D., Bangalore, Trinity Church 1854.
Ostrehan, Joseph Duncan, B.A., Vizagapatam 1855.
Ottley, Warner Beckingham, M.A., Berhampore, and Chitterpore 1847.
Pearson, Alleyne Ward, M.A., Europe (on sick leave) 1858.
Pettigrew, Samuel Thomas, M.A., Ootacamund 1855.
Pope, Henry, Vepery 1866.
Powell, William Bassett, Bolarum and Chudderghaut 1866.
Pratt, Thomas Arthur Cooper, M.A., Seetabuldee 1856.
Raban, Richard Charles William, M.A., Secunderabad, St. John's, 1866.
Rhenius, Charles, Bangalore, St. Mark's 1854.
Sayers, James Johnston Brydges, LL D., Vellore and Arcot 1856.
Tanner, James, M.A., Bellary 1866.
Taunton, Charles William Sackville, B.A., Europe (on sick leave), 1865.
Taylor, Alexander, M.A., Kamptee 1861.
Trotman, William Samuel, Trevandrum 1863.
Warlow, George, B A., Trimulgherry 1863.
Wynch, John William, M.A., South Black Town, Madras 1860.

Missionaries of the Church Missionary Society, Madras.

Abraham, J.*	Paneivilei.
Alexander, F. W. N. B.A.	Ellore.
Arden, A. H. M.A. . .	Masulipatam.
Arumanayagam, P.* . .	Asirvadhapuram.
Baker, Henry, jun. . .	Mundakayam.
Bilderbeck, John . . .	Europe—on leave.
Bishop, J. H. B.A. . .	Cottayam.
Bower, F.	Travancore.
Bushanam, Ainala* . .	Masulipatam.
Chandy, Jacob* . . .	Thallawaddi.
Clark, William . . .	On leave.
Collins, R. M.A. . . .	On leave.
Cornelius, Joseph* . .	Sivagasi.
Curean, George* . . .	Cochin.
Darling, Thomas Y. . .	Bezwara.
Devanayagam, V.* . .	Sivagasi.
Devaprasatham, M.* .	Dohnavur.
Devappirasadham, D.* .	Sivagasi.
Dibb, Ashton	Dohnavur.
Dixon, Harding. . . .	Palamcottah.
Eapen, Ittiyerah* . .	Cottayam.
Ellington, William . .	Bezwara.
Fenn, David, M.A. . .	Madras.
Gnanamuttoo, Devasagayam*	Nallur
Gnanamuttoo, S.* . .	Mengnanapuram.
Gordon, G. M. M.A. . .	Madras.
Gray, W. M.A. . . .	On leave.
Harcourt, V.	
Harley, Henry. . . .	Tanjore (on leave).
Harrison, J.	Masulipatam.
Honiss, Nigell	Surandei.
Hope, W.	Pallam.
Jako, Kollata* . . .	Pallam, Travancore.
James, A.*	Surandei.
John, Jesudasau* . . .	Kadachapuram.
Johnson, W.	Travancore.
Johnson, A.	Alleppie.
Joseph, Justus . . .	Mavelicara.
Koshi, Koshi*	Trichur.
Kuruwella, Kuruwella* .	Kodawalania.
Lash, A. H.	Palamcottah.
Macdonald, R. C. B.A. .	Madras.
Maddox, R. H.	Travancore, Mavelicara.
Mamen, O.*	Mallapalli.
Matthan, George* . .	Tiruwella.
Meadows, Robert Rust, M.A.	Sivagasi.
Nallathambi, J.* . . .	Pannikulam.
Perianayagam, M.* . .	Alvarnéri.
Royston, P. S. A.M. . .	Madras (C. M. S. Sec.).
Ratnam, Manchala* . .	Masulipatam.
Samuel, Abraham* . .	Nallur.
Sandosham, Vedamánicum*	Madras.
Sargent, Edward . . .	Palamcottah.
Satthianadhan, Wm. T.*	Madras.
Savarirayan, M.* . . .	Suviseshapuram.
Schaffter, W. P. . . .	Suviseshapuram.
Sell, E.	Madras.
Sharp, John, M.A. . . .	Masulipatam.
Simeon, V.*	Mannaikadu.
Simmons, J. D. . . .	Paneivilei.
Speechly, J. M., M.A. .	Cottayam.
Spratt, T.	Palamcottah.
Tanner, Charles . . .	On leave.
Therien, Jacob* . . .	Kannit.
Thomas, John. . . .	Mengnanapuram.
Thomas J. Davies . .	Mengnanapuram.
Vera Swami, Th.* . .	Madras
Viravagu, D.*. . . .	Satthankulam.
Whitchurch, John . .	Pannikulam.
Wilson, J.	On leave.

Missionaries of the Society for the Propagation of the Gospel in Foreign Parts in Southern India.

Adeikalam, D.* . . .	Aneicadoo.
Adolphus, T. P. . . .	Trichinopoly.
Bower, H.	Madras.
Brotherton, T. M.A. . .	Nazareth.
Caldwell, R. LL.D. . .	Edeyengoody, Tinnevelly.
Clay, J.	Mutialpaud.
Coyle, S. G.	Paumben.
Daniel, Samuel* . . .	Rhadapuram.
David, B.*	St. Thomé.
Devaprasadam, D.* . .	Puthiamputhur.
Devasagayum, S.* . .	Edeyengoody.
Eleazar, John* . . .	Bangalore.
Gnanapragasan, S.* . .	Sawyerpuram.
Guest, J.	Tanjore.
Heyne, G. Y.	Negapatam.
Higgins, J.	On leave.
Hubbard, C.	Canandagudy.
Ignatius, J.*	Combaconum.
Innasi, C.*	Maitooputty, Erungalore.
Job, A.*	Christianagram.
Kearns, J. F.	Puthiamputhur.
Kohlhoff, C. S. . . .	Erungalore.
Leeper, F. J.	Tranquebar.
Martyn, J. D.* . . .	Cuddalore.
Masillamany, A. P.* .	Nangoor.
Naller, A. R. C. . . .	Vediarpuram.
Savarimuttoo, D.* . .	Vepery.
Sebastian, A.* . . .	Ossoor.
Seller, J.	On leave.
Sinnappen, J.* . . .	Alumbaukum.
Solomon, T.*	Madras.
Spencer, J. F. . . .	Kulsapaud.
Strachan, J. M. . . .	On leave.
Symonds, A. R. M.A. .	Prin. of the Missionary Institution and Secretary of Gospel Society.
Taylor, A.	Secunderabad.
Vadakan, A.*	Moodaloor, Palamcottah.
Vedanayagam, K.* . .	Tanjore Fort.
Vethamuttoo, D. . .	Sawyerpuram.
Wyatt, J. L.	Edeyengoody, Palamcottah.

Yesudian, S. G.* . . . . Vypar.
Yesudian, M.*. . . . . Nazareth, Palamacottah.
Kennet, C. E.. . . . . Sec. to the S. P. C. K. Madras.

Clergy of the Colonial and Continental Church Society, Madras.

Shutie, C. C. . . . . . Pulicat.
Webber, P . . . . . . Bangalore.
Welsh, W. . . . . . . Madras (Sec. of C. & C. C. S. Soc.
Wilkinson, J. S. . . . . Nellore.

Clergy not connected with a Society.

Percival, P. . . . . . Madras.
Coultrup, S. W. . . . Madras.
Pope, G. U. D.D. . . . Ootacamund.
Taylor, William. . . . Vallaveram.
Whitehouse, T., B.A. . Ootacamund.
Bamforth J. . . . . . Bishop Cotton's School, Bangalore.
Bliss, T. . . . . . . Bp. Corrie's Gr. School, Bangalore.
Cæmmerer, A. F. . . . Bangalore.
Fennell, J. . . . . . . Mercara.
Godfrey, S. A. . . . . Railway Chaplain.
Stone, A. W. . . . . . Mil. Fem. Asylum, Madras.
Hickey, W. . . . . . Madura.
Franklin, C. . . . . . Bangalore.

Diocese of Bombay.

BOMBAY.—The Right Reverend John HARDING, Lord Bishop of Bombay, *Bombay.*—Wor. Coll. Ox. 3rd cl. Lit. Hum. and B.A. 1826, M.A. 1829, B.D. and D.D. 1851; Deac. 1827 and Pr. 1829 by Bp of Ely. Consecrated Bp of Bombay 1851. (Episcopal Jurisdiction, the Presidency of Bombay; Area, 150,000 square miles; Pop. 18,000,000; Clergy, 53; Inc. of See, Government allowance, 2,500*l.*) His Lordship was formerly R. of St. Andrew's-by-the-Wardrobe with St. Anne's Blackfriars, Lond. 1836–51; and for some years Sec. to the Church Pastoral Aid Society.
Bickersteth, J. P., Esq., Registrar, 1859.
Lye, the Ven. Charles Henry Leigh, M.A., Archdeacon and Commissary, 1865.

Chaplains.

Allen, George Lascomb, Belgaum, visiting Kulludghee and Kolapoor, 1845.
Bagnell, Henry William, B.A., Europe (on sick leave), 1859.
Blunt, James Henry Tomlinson, M.A., Hydrabad and Kotree 1864.
Churchill, John, M.A., Mahableshwur, visiting Sattara, 1843.
Cummins, Henry William, B.A., Aden 1854.
Dickenson, Edw. Newton Dickenson, Rajcote and Bhooj (officiating at Ahmedabad), 1850.
Eames, William Leslie, B.A., Poona, St. Mary's, 1858.
Easum, Robert, B.A., Kirkee 1856.
Ffennell, William Joshua, B.A., Attached to Abyssinian Field Force 1867.
Horsfall, Thomas, 1863.
Hughes, James Henry, M.A., Surat (to visit Baroda, Broach, Bulsar, and Tutbul), 1835.
Jones, William, Upper Scinde 1865.
Laing, Charles, M.A., Malligaum, visiting Dhoolia, Kunhur, and Asseerghur, 1842.
Lye, Charles Henry Leigh, M.A., Poona, Archdeacon and Commissary 1857.
Maule, Ward, S.C.L., Colaba 1859.
Miller, Alexander, B.A., Deesa and Mount Aboo.
Onslow, Alexander Lee, B A., 1863.
Pace, Henry Horatio, 1867.
Polehampton, Arthur, Poona 1864.
Reynell, George Carew, M.A., Byculla and Tanna 1863.
Sharpin, Frederick Lloyd, Nusseerabad, visiting Neemuch 1865.
Spring, Frederick James, M.A., Presidency and Garrison Chaplain 1838.
Stead, Samuel, M.A., Kurrachee 1863.
Streeten, George Bradley 1867.
Walford, Charles, M.A., Rhutnagherry 1863.
Watson, Thomas, B.A., Belgaum 1847.
Watson, George Augustus, Frederick, M.A., Ahmednuggur and Seroor 1855.
Wilson, Charles Thomas, M.A. (Acting at Garrison, Presidency), Ahmedabad and Kaira 1855.
One Vacancy.

Church Missionary Society.

Bappaji, A.* . . . . . Bombay.
Bardsley, Joseph W., B.A. Kurrachee.
Burn, Andrew, B.A. . . On leave.
Cooke, C. . . . . . . Malligaum.
Foote, H. . . . . . . Nassick.
Frost, A. H., M.A. . . . Nassick.
Isenberg, C. . . . . . Hydrabad.
Mengé, Charles C. . . . Malligaum.
Price, William S. . . . Sharanpoor.
Sampson, C. . . . . . Bombay.
Sheldon, James. . . . . Kurrachee.
Schwarz, C. F. . . . . Tooneer.
Shirt, G. . . . . . . Hydrabad.
Weatherhead, T. K., B.A. Bombay.
Wilson, J. . . . . . . Aurungabad.
Deimlar, J. G. . . . . Bombay.
Carss, T. . . . . . . Bombay.

Society for the Propagation of the Gospel in Foreign Parts.

Dingo, J. S. . . . . . Bombay.
Gilder, Charles. . . . . Bombay.
Kirk, C., M.A. . . . . Bombay.
Ledgard, G. . . . . . Bombay.
Taylor, H. . . . . . . Bombay.

Additional Clergy.

Du Bois, W. . . . . . Bombay.
Farnham, J. J. . . . . On leave.
Keer, W. B. . . . . . Bombay Harbour.

Diocese of Colombo.

ISLAND OF CEYLON.

COLOMBO.—The Right Rev. Piers Calveley CLAUGHTON, Lord Bishop of Colombo, *St. Thomas's College, Colombo, Ceylon.*—Brasen Col. Ox., 1st in 1st cl. Lit. Hum. and B.A. 1835, M.A. 1837, Chan.'s Prize for English Essay 1837; Deac. 1837, Pr. 1838. Consecrated first Bp of St. Helena 1859, translated to Colombo 1862. (Episcopal Jurisdiction, the Island of Ceylon; Area 24,448 square miles; Pop. 1,642,062; Clergy, 47; Inc. of See, 2000*l.* from Colonial Funds.) His Lordship was formerly Fell. Tut. and Dean. of Univ. Col. Ox. 1836–42, Public Examiner 1842–43, Select Preacher 1844–45; R. of Elton, Hunts, 1845–59. Author, *Brief Comparison of the XXXIX. Articles with Holy Scriptures* (Printed at the Clarendon Press), 1844; *Letter to the Earl of Derby on the Revival of Convocation*, 1852; various Sermons.

Archdeacon.—The Ven. Edward Mooyaart, M A.

Bishop's Chaplains.

J. B. H. Bailey. J. De Silva (Singhalese).

Arndt, J. C. . . . . . On Pension.
Bacon, J. C. Colombo. Sub-Warden of St. Thomas's Col.
Bailey, J. B. H. Hon. Can. Colombo, Col. Chaplain.
Boake, B., B.A. . . . . Colombo, Prin. of Queen's Col.
Champion, G.* . C.M.S. Nellore.

Christian, T.* . S.P.G. Kurun.
Crampton, E. . S.P.G. Negombo.
David, Christian.* S.P.G. Cotan-china, Colombo.
De Hoedt. . . S.P.G. Badulla
De Mel, F.* . S.P.G. Pantura.
De Levera, J. A.* C.M.S. Cotta.
De Silva, J.* . S.P.G. Mutwal.
Dewasagayam, C.* S.P.G. Kayman's Gate.
Dias, A.* . . . S.P.G. Matura.
Dias, S. W.* Hon. Can. . Colombo, Singh. Col. Chaplain.
Dowbiggen. . C.M.S. Baddagama.
Dunbar, C. . . . . Colombo.
Edrasinghe, P.* . . . Galle.
Edwards, R. . . . . Manaar.
Ellis, W. . . . . . . Komegalle, Diocesan Chaplain.
Glenie, S.O., M.A. . . Trincomalie, Col. Chaplain.
Gomes, C. H.* . S.P.G. Kandy.
Griffiths. . . C.M.S. Kandy, Cooly Mission.
Gunasekara, H.* C.M.S. Baddagama.
Hardy, T. P.* . C.M.S. Nellore.
Hensman, J.* . C.M.S. Copay.
Herat, W.* . . . . . . Kaigalle.
Higgens, E. T. . C.M.S. Baddagama.
Hoole, Elijah.* . C.M.S. Chundicully.
Jayasinhe, C.* . C.M.S. Kandy.
Jones, J. J., B.A. C.M.S. Kornegalle.
Kelly, W. F. . . . . Nuwara Eliya, Chaplain.
Labrooy, E. C. . . Jaffna, Col. Chaplain.
Lovekin, A. P. . . Galle, Col. Chaplain.
Mackenzie, D. C. . . Puselwa, Chaplain.
Maclean, J. . . . . . Colombo.
Mendis, A.* . . . . . Morottoo, Col. Chaplain.
Mooyaart, E. M.A. Hon. Canon . . . . . } Kandy, Col. Chap. & Archd.
Mortimer, T.* . . . . Sutlam.
Nicholas, S.* . . . . . St. Paul's, Colombo, Chaplain.
Oakley, W. . . C.M.S. Kandy.
Ondaatje, S. D. J.* . . Colombo, Tamil Col. Chaplain.
Pickford, John, C.M.S. Kandy, Cooly Mission.
Rowlands, W. E. C.M.S. Colombo.
Sapion, A.* . . . . . Calpentyn.
Schrader, George J. LL.D. Col. Chaplain, Colombo, and Act. Chap. Galle. (On leave.)
Senanayeke, C.* . . . . Galkisse, Col. Chaplain.
Somanader, D.*. S.P.G. Batticaloa.
Taylor, S. T. . . . . . Matelle, Chaplain.
Vethican, A.* . . S.P.G. Chilaw.
Wickremanayake, J.* . Milagryia.

Diocese of Mauritius.

MAURITIUS, The Right Rev. Vincent William RYAN, Lord Bishop of Mauritius, *Mauritius.*—Magd. Hall, Ox. 2nd cl. Lit. Hum. and B.A. 1840, M.A. 1848, B.D. and D.D. 1854. Consecrated Bp of Mauritius 1854. (Episcopal Jurisdiction, the Island of Mauritius and its dependencies; Area, 1400 square miles; Pop. 310,000; Clergy, 13; Inc. of See, an allowance of 750*l* as Sen. Chaplain from Colonial Funds, and interest of 6150*l*, granted by the Colonial Bishoprics' Fund and invested in the Colony.) His Lordship was formerly Principal of the Highbury Ch. Miss. Coll. Islington, Lon; and Head Mast. of the Liverpool Training Institution. Author, *The Influence given to the Christian Ministry* (a Visitation Sermon), 1843; *Lectures on the Book of Amos*, 1850; *The Mercies of God* (a Sermon), 1853; *On the Supplemental Character of the Instruction given in the Bible* (a Lecture to the Ch. of Eng. Sch. Instn.) 1853; *The Liturgy as a Class-book for Teachers*, 1853; *Colonization viewed Historically and Scripturally*, 1854; *The Christian Ministry Entrusted with the Gospel* (a Sermon); *The Communion of Saints, and other Sermons*, 1855.

Ansorgé, P. G. C.M.S. . { Orphan Asylum, Powder Mills, and Incumbent, St. Paul's, Port Louis.
Banks, W. T. B.A. . . . Civil Chaplain, Mahébourg.
Busnell, W. . . . . . St. Thomas', Plaines Wilhems.
Cachemaille, — B.A. . . . St. Barnabas, Pamplemousses.
Bichard, J. G. C.C.C. & S.S. Seamen's Chaplain, Port Louis.
Boyce, R.W. . . . . . Port Louis.
De Joux, J.G. . . . . { Bishop's Commissary and Civil Chaplain, Vacoas.
Fallet, Dr. A. . . . . Civil Chaplain, Port Louis.
Huxtable, Henry, Constantine . . S.P.G. } Secretary to S.P.G.
J. Baptist, (Deac.) S.P.G. Mis. to Tamul-speaking Indns.
Kushalee, Charles.* C.M.S. Mis. to Bengali-speaking Indns.
Mason, Wm. Lewis, M.A. Civil Chaplain, Port Louis.
Mathews, A.D. B.A. . St. John's Church, Moka.
Vandin, A. . . S.P.G. { Missionary and Acting Civil Chaplain, Seychelles.

Diocese of Victoria.

HONG KONG, CHINA.

VICTORIA, The Right Rev. Charles Richard ALFORD, Lord Bishop of Victoria, *Victoria, Hong-Kong.*—Trin. Coll. Cam. B.A. 1839, M.A. 1842, D.D. 1867; Deac. 1839 and Pr. 1840 by Bp of Lin. Consecrated Bp of Victoria 1867. (Episcopal Jurisdiction, the Island of Hong Kong, and the Congregations of the Church of England in China; Clergy, 17; Inc. of See, 1000*l* from Colonial Bishoprics' Fund. His Lordship was formerly C. of Finningley 1839-41; P. C. of St. Matthew's, Rugby, 1841-46; P. C. of Ch. Ch. Doncaster, 1846-54; Prin. of the Metropolitan Training Institution 1854-64; P.C. of Trinity, Islington, 1865-66. Author *The First Principles of the Oracles of God; Private Prayers*; Various Sermons and Pamphlets.

Hong Kong.

Irwin, John James, D.D. Colonial Chaplain. (On leave.) Chaplain to the Forces.
Wilson, John . . . . . Nav. Chap. and Act. Col. Chap.
Warren, C. F. . C.M.S. Missionary.
Piper, John . C.M.S. Missionary.
Lo-Săm-yuen*. C.M.S. Missionary.

Canton.

Gray, John Henry, M.A. . Consular Chaplain.

Amoy.

Consular Chaplain.

Foochow.

Hamilton,— . . . . . Consular Chaplain.
Wolfe, John Richd. C.M.S. Missionary.
Cribbe, A. . . C.M.S. Missionary.

Ningpo.

Bates, James . C.M.S. Missionary.
Russell, W. A. M.A. C.M.S. Missionary. (On leave.)
Gough, Fk. F. M.A. C.M.S. Missionary. (On leave.)
Gretton, Henry C.M.S. Missionary.
Moule, G. E. M.A. C.M.S. Missionary.
Moule, Arthur E. C.M.S. Missionary.
Valentine, J. D. C.M.S. Missionary.

Shanghae.

Butcher, C. H. M.A. . Consular Chaplain.
Kaufmann, Morits . . Chaplain to Seamen.
Dzaw, Tsang Lae* C.M.S. Missionary.

Hankow.

McClatchie, T. M.A. . Consular Chaplain.

Kewkeang.

Pirkis, Daniel . . . Consular Chaplain.

Peking.

Atkinson, C. . C.M.S. Missionary.
Burdon, J. S. . C.M.S. Missionary.
Collins, W. H. . C.M.S. Missionary.

Diocese of Labuan and Sarawak.

BORNEO.

LABUAN, The Right Rev. Francis Thomas MACDOUGALL, Lord Bishop of Labuan, *Labuan, Borneo.*—King's Coll. Lon. Gold Medallist for General Medical Proficiency 1837; Magd. Hall, Ox. D.D. 1855. Consecrated first Bp of Labuan 1853. (Episcopal Jurisdiction, Labuan and its dependencies; Area, 260,000 square miles; Pop. 6,000,000; Clergy, 4; Inc. of See, 360*l* from Colonial Bishoprics' Fund, and 300*l* from the S.P.G. His Lordship was formerly Fell. of the Royal Coll. of Surgeons and Demonstrator of Anatomy in King's Coll. Lond; Missionary to Borneo.

Commissary and Examining Chaplain—W. Chambers.

Colonial Chaplain—J. Moreton.

Walter Chambers, Banting.	J. L. Zehnder, Sarawak.
Julian Moreton, Labuan.	John Richardson, Sadumac.
William H. Gomes, Lundu.	C. W. Hawkins, Mardang.
F. W. Abé, Quop.	Foo Ngien Khoon, Chinese Mission, Sarawak.
W. Crossland, Unclop.	J. Perham, Rejong.
W. R. Mesney, Banting.	

Diocese of Capetown.

Cape of Good Hope.

Capetown, The Right Rev. Robert Gray, Lord Bishop of Capetown and Metropolitan, *Capetown, Cape of Good Hope.*—Univ. Coll. Ox. 4th cl. Lit. Hum. and B.A. 1831, M.A. 1834, B.D. and D.D. 1847; Deac. 1833, Pr. 1834. Consecrated Bp of Capetown 1847. (Episcopal Jurisdiction, Cape Colony; Area, 130,046 square miles; Pop. 225,000; Clergy, 44; Inc. of See, 438*l* from Colonial Bishoprics' Fund, and interest of 8211*l* invested in the Colony.) His Lordship was formerly P.C. of Whitworth, Durham, 1835-45; V. of Stockton-on-Tees, Durham, 1845-47; Hon. Can. of Dur. Cathl, 1846.

Dean—Very Rev. H. A. Douglas, M.A.

Archdeacon of Capetown.—Ven. J. Harries Thomas, M.A.

Archdeacon of George—Ven. H. Badnall, D.D.

Canons.

Archdeacon Badnall, D.D. Archdeacon Merriman, M.A.
G. Ogilvie. E. Judge, M.A. Archdeacon Thomas, M.A.

Rural Deanery of Capetown.

Bebb, W.	St. John's, Capetown.
Belson, W. E. B.A.	Malmesbury.
Browning, T.	Clanwilliam.
Childe, G. F.	S. A. College, Capetown.
Curlewis, J. F.	Lower Paarl.
Curtis, F.	Mast. Gram. School, Capetown.
Douglas, H. A. MA.. (Dean)	St. George's Church, Capetown.
Fisk, G. H. R.	Chaplain to Convicts.
Gething, Guy	Greenpoint.
Gibbs, E.	Petersburg.
Godfrey, J. R.	Curate, Somerset, West.
Glover, E. M.A.	Warden of Kafir Sch. Zonnebloem.
Hancock, J. S.	Curate, Papendorp, Capetown.
Inglis, J.	Paarl.
Jeffrey, A.	Ceres.
Judge, E. M.A.	St. Frances, Simon's Town.
Lamb, R. G. A.B.	Trinity Church, Capetown.
Laurence, G.	D'Urban.
Lightfoot, T. F.	Capetown.
Long, W.	Mowbray.
Maynard, J.	Worcester.
Moore	Curate, Constantia.
Morris, W. J. R.	Namaqua land.
Nichol, R. G.	Curate, St. Hel. Bay Malmsbury.
Ogilvie, G.	Prin. Dioc. Coll. Sch. Woodlands.
Parminter, F.	Precentor, St. George, Capetown, and Mast. of Gr. Sch.
Peters, T. H.	Stellenbosch.
Phillipson, W. W. B. M.A.	St. John's, Wynberg.
Philpott	Dio. College, Woodlands.
Prince, E. B. B.A.	Curate of St. Paul's Rondebosch.
Quinn, J.	Ass. Chaplain to the Forces, Capetown.
Rattle, H.	Vice Principal Dio. Coll.
Thomas, J. H. M.A.	Archdeacon, Rondebosch.
Wilshere, A. R. M.	Claremont.
Wilshere, H. M.	Caledon.

Archdeaconry of George.

Archdeacon—Ven. H. Badnall, D.D.

Badnall, Archd. H. D.D.	St. Mark's, George Town.
Baker, J.	Swellendam.
Bramley, W.	Beaufort.
Brien, R.	Curate, St. John's, Schoonberg.
Eedes, J.	Knysna.
Gibbs, J.	Curate, Plattenberge Bay, Knysna.
Morris, A.	Oudtshoorn.
Mortimer, B. C.	Riversdale.
Samuels, J. C.	Curate, Willowmoor.
Sheard, T.	Mossel Bay.
Taylor, W. F.	Curate, George, and Master of Grammar School.
Walters, T. R.	Victoria West.
Widdicombe, J.	Curate, George.

Diocese of St. Helena.

St. Helena, The Right Rev. Thomas Earle Welby, Lord Bishop of St. Helena, *Jamestown, Island of St. Helena.*—Ch. Coll. Cam. M.A. 1838; Deac. and Pr. 1840 by Bp of Toronto. Consecrated Bp of St. Helena 1862. (Episcopal Jurisdiction, Islands of St. Helena, Ascension, Tristan D'Acunha, Falkland Isles, and English Congregations on the Atlantic Shore of South America; Inc. of See, 800*l*—500*l* from Colonial Funds and interest on 5000*l* collected by the Bp. of Capetown.) His Lordship was formerly R. of Sandwick, Canada West, 1842; in 1845 was presented by his father, Sir William Earle Welby, Bart. of Denton Hale, Lincolnshire, to the Rectory of Newton, Lincolnshire; resigned in 1849 and was collated by the Bp of Capetown to the Rectory of Georgetown, Cape Colony; Can. of St George's Cathl. Capetown and Archd. of George 1856-62.

Canons of the Cathedral—Revs. George Bennett, M.A. and Robert Gray, M.A.

Bishop's Chaplains—Rev. W. H. Earle Welby, M.A.; Rev. Arthur Earle Welby, B.A.

Bennett, George, M.A.	Rector of Jamestown.
Bodily, Henry Jas.	Rector of Longwood.
Bull, Charles,	Falkland Islands.*
Frey, L.	Curate, St. Paul's.
Gray, Robert, M.A.	Head Mast. of the High School, Jamestown, &c.
Pennell, Geo. Barrow, M.A.	Vicar of St. Paul's.
Robinson, James, A.B.	Ascension Island.
Whitehead, Henry	Curate of St. John's, and acting Military Chaplain.

* The Falkland Islands, although subject to Visitation by the Bishop of St. Helena, under authority from the Bishop of London, are not in the Diocese of St. Helena, but still in the Diocese of London.

Diocese of Sierra Leone.

Sierra Leone, The Right Rev. Edward Hyndman Beckles, Lord Bishop of Sierra Leone, *The Christian Institution, Fourah Bay, near Free Town, Sierra Leone.*—Codrington College, Barbados; Deac. 1844 and Pr. 1844 by Bp. of Barbados. Consecrated Bp of Sierra Leone 1860. (Episcopal Jurisdiction, the West Coast of Africa between 20 degrees North and 20 degrees South Latitude, and more especially the Colonies of Sierra Leone, the Gambia, the Gold Coast, and their dependencies; Pop. 45,000; Clergy, 45; Inc. of See, 902*l*—500*l* from Colonial Government, and 402*l* from Colonial Bishoprics' Fund.) His Lordship was formerly R. of St. Peter's, St. Christopher's, West Indies, 1856-59.

Alcock, H. J.	Prin. of the Christian Institution, Fourah Bay.
Allen, William* . . .	Igbein.
Beale, James	Sherbro.
Blake, J.	Colonial Chaplain, Cape Coast Castle. (On leave.)
Brierley, C. H. . . .	Charlotte.
Boston, Henry* . . .	Bullom Mission.
Caiger, G. R.	Freetown.
Campbell, J.* . . .	Chaplain to Colonial Hospital.
Cole, Jacob*	Kissey.
Davis, C.*	Kent.
Davis, J. H.*	Bathurst.
Duport, J. H. A.* . .	Fallangia.
Faulkner, V.	Abbeokuto.
Gollmer, C. A. . . .	On leave.
Hamilton, James . . .	Freetown.
Hartshorn, R. W. M.A. .	Colonial and Garrison Chaplain.
Hinderer, D.	Ibadan.
Johnson, Henry* . .	On leave.
Johnson, James* . . .	Freetown.
Knödler, Charles . . .	Superintendent Quiah Mission.
Lamb, J. A.	Lagos.
Macaulay, George* . .	Wellington.
Macaulay, T. B.* . .	Lagos.
Mann, Adolphus . . .	Lago.
Maser, J. A.	Abbeokuta.
Maurice, J. A.* . . .	
Maxwell, T.*	Wilberforce.
Menzies, A.	Mendi Mission.
Moore, W.*	Oshielle.
Morgan, W.*	Lagos.
Mousa, Samuel* . . .	Bananas.
Nicholson, L.	Lagos.
Nicol, Geo.*	Regent.
Nylander, T. C.* . . .	Gloucester.
Pearce, Moses* . . .	Sherbro.
Oldham, Thomas . . .	Freetown.
Quaker, Jas.*	Mast. of Gram. Sch. Freetown.
Quaker, W.*	York.
Reichardt, Charles . .	Cline Town.
Robbin, J.*	Act. Chaplain at the Gambia.
Smith, Joseph . . .	On leave.
Taylor, M.*	Waterloo.
Thomas, J. J.* . . .	Freetown.
Townsend, H.	Abbeokuta.
Williams, D. G.* . .	Tutor, Fourah Bay Institution.
Wilson, Joseph* . . .	Hastings.
Wood, J. B.	Abbeokuta.

Niger Territory.

Bishop—Right Rev. SAMUEL ADJAI CROWTHER, D.D. 1864.*

Coomber, A. G.* . . .	Idda.
John, Z. C.*	Lokojo.
Taylor, J. C.* . . .	Onitsha.
White, James* . . .	Otta.

Diocese of Natal.

NATAL, The Right Rev. John William COLENSO, Lord Bishop of Natal, *Pieter Maritzburg, Natal.*—St. John's Coll. Cam. 2nd Wrang. Smith's Prizeman and B.A. 1836, M.A. 1839, B.D. and D.D. 1853. Consecrated Bp of Natal 1853. (Episcopal Jurisdiction, the Colony of Natal; Area, 18,000 square miles; Pop. 50,000; Clergy, 14; Inc. of See, 662*l* from Colonial Bishoprics' Fund, and interest of 1100*l* invested in the Colony.) His Lordship was formerly Fell. and Tut. of St. John's Coll. Cam. 1837–46; Math. Mast. of Harrow Sch. 1838–42; R. of Forncett St. Mary, Norfolk, 1846–54. Author, *Miscellaneous Examples in Algebra*, 1848; *The Elements of Algebra adapted for Teachers and Students in the Univ.* 1849; *Elements of Algebra*, 1849, 6 eds; *A Key to Algebra*, 2 parts, 1849, 1850; *Plane Trigonometry*, 1851; *Solutions of Examples in Plane Trigonometry*, 1851; *The Elements of Algebra, for the use of National, Adult, and Commercial Schools*, 1852; *Solutions to the Examples, with answers to the more difficult Questions* (of the preceding work), 1853; *A Text-book of Elementary Arithmetic, designed for National, Adult and Commercial Schools*, 1858; *Progressive Examples in Arithmetic, designed for National, Adult, and Commercial Schools*, 1853; *A Letter to the Archbishop of Canterbury in Reply to a Review of "Village Sermons,"* 1853, 2 eds; *The Good Tidings of Great Joy which shall be to all People* (an Ordination Sermon); *Ten weeks in Natal, a Journal of a First Tour of Visitation among the Colonists and Zulu Kaffirs*, Cam 1855; *The Communion Service, with Selected Readings from the Writings of the Rev. F. D. Maurice*, 1855; *The Pentateuch and Book of Joshua Critically Examined*—Part I. *the Pentateuch examined as an Historical Narrative*, 6*s*, Part II. *the Age and Authorship of the Pentateuch Considered*, 7*s* 6*d*, Part III. *the Book of Deuteronomy*, 8*s*, Part IV. *the First* 11 *Chapters of Genesis examined and separated, with Remarks on the Creation, the Fall, and the Deluge*, 10*s* 6*d*; People's ed. of same in 5 parts, 1*s* each, 1865; a Translation from the Dutch of Professor A. Kuenen's, of Leyden, *The Pentateuch and Book of Joshua critically examined, with Notes by the Translator*, Longmans, 1865, 8*s* 6*d*. Editor of *The Monthly Record of Church Missions*, in connection with the S.P.G. 1852.

Dean of Maritzburg—Very Rev. J. Green, M.A.

Archdeacon of Maritzburg—Vacant.

Archdeacon of Durban—Ven. T. G. Fearne, M.A.

Canons of the Cathedral, Maritzburg—H. Callaway, M.D.; Archdn. Fearne, M.A.

Barker, J.	Umzinto.
Baugh, W.	Umlazi.
Boyd, J. M.A. . . .	Verulam and Mount Moreland.
Callaway, H. M.D. . .	Upper Umkomazi.
De la Mare, F. T. . .	Bluff.
Fearne, T. G. M.A. . .	Byrne.
Gray, R. B.D. . . .	St. Peter's, Maritzburg.
Green, J. M.A. . . .	St. Peter's, Maritzburg.
Jacob, E. H.	Howick and Karkloof.
Lloyd, W. H. C. M.A. .	Durban.
Mason, G. H. M.A. . .	Umhlali.
Newnham, W. O. M.A.	Springvale.
Nisbett, W.	Military Chaplain, Maritzburg.
Robertson, R.	Kwamagwaza, Zululand.
Robinson, E.	Addington and Berea.
Robinson, F. S. M.A. .	St. Andrew's, Maritzburg.
Rolfe, J.	Coedmore.
Samuelson, S. . . .	Zululand.
Taylor, T.	Greytown.
Tönnesen, A.	Umgababa.
Tozer, S. H.	Richmond.
Walton, J.	Pinetown.

Diocese of Grahamstown.

GRAHAMSTOWN, The Right Rev. Henry COTTERILL, Lord Bishop of Grahamstown, *St. Andrew's College, Grahamstown, Cape of Good Hope.*—St. John's Coll. Cam. 1st Smith's Prizeman, Sen. Wrang. 1st cl. Cl. Trip. and B.A. 1835, M.A. by Royal Mandate 1836, D.D. 1850; Deac. 1835 by Bp of Pet. Pr. 1836 by Bp of Bristol. Consecrated Bp of Grahamstown 1856. (Episcopal Jurisdiction, Eastern Province of Cape Colony and British Kaffraria; Area, 45,000 square miles; Pop. 340,000; Clergy, 85; Inc. of See, 604*l* from Colonial Bishoprics' Fund, and interest of 2629*l* invested in the Colony.) His Lordship was formerly Fell. of St. John's Coll. Cam. 1835; Chap. in H.E.I.C.'s service 1836–50; Prin. of Brighton Coll. 1851–56. Author, *Seven Ages of the Church*, 1849. Editor of *The South India Christian Repository*, Madras, 1838–48.

Dean—Very Rev. F. H. Williams, D.D.

Archdeacon of Grahamstown—Ven. N. J. Merriman, M.A.

Archdeacon of British Kaffraria—Ven. Henry Kitton.

Canons of the Cathedral—Ven. N. J. Merryman, M.A.; Ven. Henry Kitton; Rev. W. A. Steabler; Rev. F. Y. St. Leger, B.A.; Rev. T. Henchman; Rev. H. T. Walters.

Chancellor of the Diocese—Vacant.

Aldred, John	Ch. Ch. Adelaide.
Barker, E. W.	Somerset.
Bell, A. B.A.	Military Chap. King William's Town.
Boon, John	Stockenstrom.
Brook, S.	St. Paul's, Port Elizabeth.
Browne, L. S. B.	St. Andrew's Gram. Sch. Grahamstown.
Copeman, P. W. M.A.	Alexandria.
Cotterill, J. M.	St. Andrew's, Grahamstown.
De Kock, S. N.	Colesberg.
Dodd, W.	Mission Station, Tsitsa River.
Every, M. R.	Christ Church, Burghersdorp.
Gordon, John	All Saints, Bashee Mission.
Greenstock, W.	St. Matthew's, Keiskamma Hoek.
Henchman, T.	St. John's, Fort Beaufort.
Johnson, H. I. M.A.	Principal of the Grey Institute and Trinity Church, Port Elizabeth.
Key, B. L.	Mission Station, Tsitsa River.
Kitton, Archdn.	King William's Town.
Lange, C. R.	Port Alfred, Convict Chaplain.
Llewellyn, W. B.A.	Uitenhage.
McCormick, Chas.	Curate of Queenstown.
Maggs, Albert	St. John's Mission, Kabusie, and Komgha.
Meaden, W.	Winterberg.
Merriman, Ven. N. J. M.A.	St. Bartholomew's, Grahamstown.
Mullins, R. J.	Grahamstown Kafir Institution.
Norton, Matthew	Cradock.
Newton, A. J.	St. Peter's Mission, Gwytyn.
Overton, C. F. B.A.	Acting at St. Andrew's, Grahamstown.
Patten, C. F.	St. John Baptist Mission, Bolotwa.
Pickering, E. M.A.	St. Mary's, Port Elizabeth.
Rossiter, W.	St. Paul's, Aliwal North.
Rowe, J. J. M.A.	Keiskamma Hoek, Military Chaplain.
Steabler, W. A.	St. James', Graaff Reinet.
St. Leger, F. Y. B.A.	St. Michael's, Queenstown.
Taberer, C.	Trinity Mission, Fort Beaufort.
Thompson, G. B.A.	Rural District, Grahamstown.
Turpin, W. H.	Grahamstown Kafir Mission.
Wallis, W. C.	East London.
Waters, H. T.	St. Mark's Mission, Kreli's Country.
Williams, F. H. D.D. (Dean)	St. George's, Grahamstown.
Wilson, J. R.	Alice.
Woodrooffe, H. R. B.A.	
Wyld, Samuel	St. Luke's Mission, Newlands.

Orange Free State.

Bishop—Right Rev. Edward Twells, D.D. Bloemfontein, South Africa.

Archdeacon—Ven. N. J. Merriman., M.A. Grahamstown.

First Canon of the Cathedral Church—Rev. Henry Beckett, M.A., Bloemfontein.

Priest Vicar of the Cathedral and Chaplain—Rev. Davis G. Croghan, B.A., Bloemfontein.

Bishop's Commissary in England—Rev. J. G. Cowan, Hammersmith, London.

Beckett, H. M.A.	Bloemfontein.
Clulee, C.	Fauresmith.
Croghan, D. G. B.A.	Bloemfontein.
Mitchell, George	Bloemfontein and Thaba' Nchu.
Richardson, William	Potchefstroom, Trans Vaal.
Wills, J. H.	Travelling Deacon.

BRITISH AMERICA AND THE WEST INDIES.

Diocese of Montreal.

Canada East.

Montreal, The Right Rev. Francis Fulford, Lord Bishop of Montreal, and Metropolitan of Canada, *Montreal.*—Ex. Coll. Ox. 2nd cl. Lit. Hum. and B.A. 1824, M.A. 1838, B.D. and D.D. 1850; Deac. 1825 and Pr. 1826 by Bp of Ox. Consecrated Bp of Montreal 1850; Metropolitan 1860. (Episcopal Jurisdiction, Montreal; Area, 56,258 square miles; Pop. 472,405; Clergy, 66; Inc. of See, 1000*l*, the interest of investments in Canada.) His Lordship was formerly Fell. of Ex. Coll. Ox. 1825–32; R. of Trowbridge, Wilts, 1832–42; R. of Croydon, Cambs, 1842–45; Incumb. of Curzon Chapel, Lond. 1845–50. Author, *A Course of Plain Sermons on the Ministry, Doctrine and Services of the Church of England, with a Preface and Occasional Notes*, 1st vol. 1837, 2nd vol. 1840; *The Interpretation of Law and the Rule of Faith* (an Assize Sermon preached in Win. Cathl.) 1838; *The Progress of the Reformation in England* (to which are added two Sermons by Bp Sanderson), *Of Conformity and Nonconformity*, and *Teaching for Doctrines the Commandments of Men*, 1841; *The Cross and the Glory of the Sons of God*, 1st Series of Sermons *for Sundays, Festivals and Fasts*, 1845; *The Labourers in the Vineyard, Practical Sermons*, Vol. I. 1845; *A Pastoral Letter to the Clergy of his Diocese*, 1851; *An Address delivered in the Chapel of the General Theological Seminary of the Protestant Episcopal Church in the United States*, New York, 1852.

Dean—Very Rev. John Bethune, D.D., LL.D.

Archdeacon—Ven. W. T. Leach, D.C.L.

Senior Canon—Rev. P. W. Loosemore, M.A.

Second Canon—Rev. Lewis P. W. Balch, D.D.

Hon. Canons—Revs. M. Townsend, M.A.; C. Bancroft, D.D.; W. Anderson; W. B. Bond, M.A.

Bishop's Chaplains.

The Ven. the Archdeacon, D.C.L., LL.D.; Rev. Canon Loosemore, M.A.; Rev. Canon Balch, D.D.

Bishop's Examining Chaplain and Secretary—Rev. Canon Loosemore, M.A.

Abbott, C. P.	South Stukeley.
Allan, J.	St. Vincent de Paul.
Anderson, William	Rector of Sorel, Hon. Canon.
Baldwin, M. S. M.A.	St. Luke's, Montreal.
Bancroft, Charles, D.D.	Trinity Church, Montreal, and Honorary Canon.
Bartlett, T. H. M. M.A.	Chaplain to the Forces, Montreal.
Bond, Will. Bennett, M.A.	Rural Dean, Minister of St. George's Church, Montreal, and Hon. Canon.
Borthwick, J. D.	St. Mary's, Hochelaga.
Braithwaite, F. G. C. M.A.	Onslow.

Braithwaite, J. M.A. (Ret.)	Chambly.
Brethour, William, M.A.	Durham, Ormstown.
Brown, W. R.	Aylwin.
Codd, F.	Aylmer.
Constantine, Isaac, M.A.	Stanbridge, East.
Curran, W B. B.A.	St. Stephen's, Montreal.
Daniel, C. A.	Assist. Min. St. John Evangelist, Montreal.
Darnell, Henry F. M.A.	Rector of St. John's.
Dart, W. J.	Lapraire.
Davidson, J. B. B.A.	Rector of Frelighsburg.
Davidson, J. C.	Cowansville.
Dodwell, G. B. M.A.	Rector of Chambly.
Dumoulin, J. P.	Assist. Min. Trinity, Montreal.
Duvernet, E. M.A.	Hemmingford, Rural Dean.
Early, W. T.	Huntingdon.
Ellegood, Jacob, M.A.	Minister of St. James' Church, Montreal.
Evans, H. J. B.A.	Christieville.
Fessenden, E. J.	Assist. Min. Potton.
Fortin, A.	Ely.
Fortin, Octave, B.A.	Assist. Min. Sorel.
Fulton, James, M.A.	Russeltown.
Fyles, T. W.	West Brome.
Godden, J.	Rector of Dunham.
Godden, T. B.A.	Mascouche.
Gribble, J.	Portage du Fort.
Heaton, G. M.A.	Montreal.
Jenkyns, E. S.	Assist. Min. Durham.
Johnson, T. (Ret.)	Abbotsford.
Johnston, John	Hull.
Jones, James (Ret.)	Granby.
Jones, William	Granby.
Kaapcke, Carl J.	Bowman.
Lancaster, C. H.	Assist. Min. Clarenceville.
Leach, Ven. Archd. D.C.L.	Lachine.
Lewis, B.P. B.A.	Sabrevois.
Lindsay, David, M.A.	Waterloo.
Lindsay, Robert, M.A.	Brome.
Lockhart, A.D.	Lacolle.
Lonsdell, Richard, M.A.	Rec. of St. Andrew's, Rural Dean.
McLeod, J. A. M.A.	Montreal.
M'Masters, J.	(Retired.)
Merrick, Joseph	Morin.
Merrick, W. C. M.A.	Berthier.
Montgomery, H.	Rector of Phillipsburgh.
Mussen, T. W. B.A.	West Farnham.
Neve, Frederick Smith	Grenville.
Pyke, James	Pointe à Cavagnol.
Robinson, Frederick, M.A.	Abbotsford.
Robinson, George	Clarendon.
Rollit, John	Clarendon.
Seaborn, W. M.	Rawdon.
Seaman, John	North Wakefield.
Shand, A. LL.B.	New Glasgow.
Slack, George, M.A.	Rural Dean, Bedford.
Smith, J.	Sutton.
Smith, P. W.	Eardley.
Strong, S. S.	Buckingham.
Sutton, Edward George	Edwardstown.
Sullivan, E. B.A.	Assist St. George's, Montreal.
Taylor, A. O.	Gore of Chatham.
Thorndike, C. F.	Chambly.
Townsend, Micajah, M.A.	Rector of Clarenceville, and Hon. Canon.
Whitten, Andrew T.	West Shefford.
Wood, E. M.A.	St. John's the Evangelist, Montrl.
Wright, W. M.D.	Assist. St. James', Montreal.
Wurtele, L. C. B.A.	Upton.
Young, T. Ainslie, M.A.	Côteau du Lac.

Diocese of Quebec.

CANADA EAST.

QUEBEC, The Right Rev. James William WILLIAMS, Lord Bishop of Quebec, *Quebec*.—Consecrated Bp of Quebec 1863. (Episcopal Jurisdiction, Districts of Quebec, Three Rivers, St. Francis, and Gaspé; Area, 153,432 square miles; Pop. 417,856; Clergy, 41; Inc. of See, 1000*l* from Imperial Parliamentary Vote.) Co-Visitor with Bp of Montreal of Bishop's Coll. Lennoxville.

Allen, A. A. B.A.	Stanstead.
Allnatt, F. J. B.	Drummondville.
Ball, T. L. B.A.	North Inverness.
Boydell, James, B.A.	Hatley.
Burrage, Henry G. M.A.	Hatley.
Chapman, Thos. S. M.A.	Dudswell.
Dalziel, John	Port Neuf.
Fortin, O. B.A.	St. Francis.
Foster, John, B.A.	Coaticook.
Fothergill, M. M.	St. Peter's, Quebec.
Hamilton, Chas. M.A.	Quebec, Bishop's Chap. and Sec.
Housman, G. V. M.A.	Rector of Quebec.
Innes, G. M.	Cathedral, Quebec.
Jackson, C.	Hatley (retired).
Jenkins, J. H. B.A.	Frampton.
Kemp, John, B.D.	Compton.
Ker, Matthew	Sandy Beach.
King William	St. Sylvester.
Lyster, W. G. B.A.	Cape Cove.
Merrick, William C. M.A.	Rivière du Loup-en-haut.
Milne, George, M.A.	New Carlisle, Bay of Chaleurs, and Rural Dean.
Mitchell, R.	Stoneham, Lake Beaufort.
Moulpied, J. de	Malbaie, Gaspé.
Mountain, Armine Wale, M.A.	St. Michael's, Quebec; Rur. Dn.
Nicholls, Jasper Hume, D.D.	Principal of Bishop's College, and Chaplain to the Lord Bishop; Rural Dean.
Parker, G. H.	Kingsey.
Parkin, Edward C.	Eaton.
Petry, H. J. B.A.	Danville with Tingwick.
Phillips, S.	Trinity, Quebec.
Plees, Robert George	St. Paul's, Quebec.
Reid, Charles Peter, M.A.	Sherbrooke.
Richardson, T.	Bury.
Richmond, J. P.	Leeds.
Richmond, W. M.A.	Bishop's Coll. Lennoxville.
Robertson, D. M.A.	Lennoxville.
Roe, Henry, B.A.	Incumbent of St. Matthew's, Quebec, and Examining Chap. to the Lord Bishop.
Ross, E. G. W.	Rivière du Loup-en-bas.
Scarth, A. C.	Lennoxville.
Sewell, Edm. Willoughby, M.A.	Minister of Trinity Chapel, Quebec.
Short, Robert	Gaspé Basin.
Smith, Fred. Augustus	Gaspé Basin.
Sykes, J. S.	Chaplain of the Marine Hospital and Harbour of Quebec.
Tambs, R. C. B.A.	Bourg Louis.
Thorneloe, J.	Georgeville.
Tocque, P. M.A.	Hopetown.
Torrance, J.	Three Rivers.
Vial, W. S.	Quebec.
Von Iffland, A.	Val Cartier.
Wainwright, R.	Labrador.
Walker, R. H., M.A.	Rector of Gram. School, Bishop's College, Lennoxville.
Walters, J.	Magdalene Islands.
Ward, R. G.	Lower Ireland.
Wood, Sam. Simpson, M.A.	Upp. Durham & Three Rivers.
Woolryche, A. J.	Ponte Levi.
Wurtele, L. C., B.A.	Acton.

Diocese of Toronto.

CANADA WEST.

TORONTO, The Right Rev. A. N. BETHUNE, Lord Bishop of Toronto, *Toronto*. — Consecrated Coadjutor Bp of Toronto, 1866, and Bp 1867. (Episcopal Jurisdiction, Toronto; Area, 26,000 square miles: Pop. 400,000; Clergy, 102; Inc. of See, 125*l* from Clergy Reverves in Canada West.)

Bishop's Chaplains.

H. Scadding, D.D. | H. J. Grasett, B.D. | S. Givins.

Alexander, J. Lyne	Stoney Creek.
Allen, T. W. M.A.	Cavan, Milbrooke.
Ambrey, J. M.A.	Trinity College, Toronto.
Ardagh, S. Brown, M.A.	Rector of Barrie.
Arnold, R. B.A.	Brampton.
Badgeley, C. H. M.A.	Trinity Coll. School, Weston.
Baldwin, Ed. M.A.	Assist. at St. James', Toronto.
Ballard, J. B.A.	Assistant, Ancaster.
Beaven, James, D.D.	Prof. in the Univ. of Toronto.
Beck, J. W. M.A.	Peterboro'.
Belt, William, M.A.	Scarborough.
Bethune, C. J. S. M.A.	Assist. Cobourg.
Boddy, S. J. A.M.	C. of St. James' Ch., Toronto.
Boyer, R. C.	Brighton.
Brent, Henry	Rector of Newcastle
Briggs, S. M.A.	Walpole.
Broughall, A. J. M.A.	St. Stephen's, Toronto.
Bull, G. Armstrong, B.A.	Barton.
Burnham, Mark, B.A.	Peterborough.
Burt, F.	Minden.
Cary, John, B.D.	Holland Landing.
Cartwright, C. M.A.	Woodbridge.
Cayley, J. M.A.	Whitby.
Chance, James	Indian Mission, Garden River.
Checkley, W. M. M.A.	Grammar School, Barrie.
Cleary, R. B.A.	Mono.
Clementi, V. B.A.	Lakefield.
Cooper, H. Chowell, B.A.	Rector of Etobicoke.
Cooper, H. D. B.A.	Missionary, Beverley.
Cooper, W. E. M.A.	Port Colborne.
Creighton, J.	Welland.
Darling, William Stewart	Asst. Min. Holy Trin., Toronto.
Davidson, J. M.A.	Tecumseth.
Davies, E. R.	Perrytown.
Disbrow, N.	Omemee.
Dixon, Alexander, B.A.	Port Dalhousie.
Drinkwater, C. H. B.A.	R. of St. Thomas, Hamilton.
Farrar, M.	Norwood.
Fidler, A. J. B.A.	Cookstown.
Fletcher, John, B.A.	Oakville.
Flood, John	Dunnville.
Forneri, R. B.A.	Uxbridge.
Fuller, T. B. D.D. D.C.L.	Ru. Dean, St. George's, Toronto.
Geddes, J. Gamble, M.A.	R. of Christ Church, Hamilton.
Gibson, J. D.	Brock.
Givins, Saltern	Incumb. of St. Paul's, Yorkville, Rural Dean.
Grant, W.	Tullamore.
Grassett, Henry Jas. B.D.	Rector of St. James', Toronto.
Greene, Thos. LL.D.	Rector of Wellington Square.
Greenham, H.	Rector, Fort Erie.
Groves, F. J. S.	Seymour.
Hallen, G. B.A.	Penetanguishene.
Harris, R. H. B.A.	Craighurst.
Hebden, John, M.A.	Rect. of the Church of the Ascension, Hamilton.
Henderson, Alex. B.A.	Orangeville.
Hill, Bold Cudmore, M.A.	York.
Hill, G. S. J. M.A.	Markham.
Hilton, John, M.A.	Brockton, Toronto.
Hodge, T. P.	Springfield Credit.
Holland, H. M.A.	St. Catherine's.
Houston, S. B.A.	Mountforest.
Ingles, C. Leycester, B.A.	Drummondville.
Johnson, W. A.	Weston.
Jones, W. M.A.	Trinity College, Toronto.
Langtry, John, M.A.	Assist. St. Paul's, Toronto.
Leeming, Ralph	Dundas (retired).
Lett, Stephen, LL.D.	Collingwood.
Logan, William, B.A.	Cartwright.
Lundy, Francis J. D.C.L.	Rector of Grimsby.
M'Caul, John, LL.D.	President of Toronto University.
McCollum, J. H. M.A.	Aurora.
MacKenzie, J. G. D. M.A.	Inc. of St. John's, Hamilton.
MacLeod, D. J. F. M.A.	Chippewa.
MacMurray, W. D.D. D.C.L.	Rector of Niagara.
Mac Nab, Alex. D.D.	Rector of Bowmanville.
McLeary, J.	Mulmur.
Middleton, J.	Streetsville.
Mitchell, Rd. LL.D.	Rector of York Mills.
Morgan, Edward, M.A.	Assistant Minister, Barrie.
Murphy, E. W.	Innisfil.
Nesbitt, G.	Huston.
O'Meara, Fred. Aug. LL.D.	Georgetown.
Osler, Featherstone Lake, M.A.	Rector of Dundas and Rural Dean.
Osler, Henry Bath	Lloydtown.
Palmer, Arthur, M.A.	Rec. of Guelph, and Rural Dean.
Pentland, John, A.B.	(retired) Whitby.
Phillipps, H. N.	Niagara.
Ramsey, Septimus F. M.A.	Newmarket.
Read, Thos. Bolton, D.D.	Weston.
Ritchie, William, M.A.	Georgina.
Roberts, T. T. M.A.	Rector of Thorold.
Ross, W. M. M.A.	Greenwood.
Ruttan, Charles	Bradford.
Sanson, Alexander	Trinity Church, Toronto.
Scadding, Henry, D.D.	Church of Holy Trinity, Toronto, Bishop's Chap.
Shanklin, Robert	Thornhill.
Sims, J.	Manitowaning.
Smithhurst, J. M.A.	Minto.
Stennett, Walter, M.A.	Keswick.
Stewart, A. M. M.A.	Orillia.
Stimson, E. R.	Jordan.
Strong, S. S. D.D. D.C.L.	(retired) Ottawa.
Thomson, C. E. M.A.	Elora.
Tremayne, Francis, jun.	Milton.
Van Linge, J. B.D.	Grantham.
Vicars, John, B.A.	Lindsay.
Vicars, J.	Guelph.
Warren, P. S. B.A.	Duoro.
Westney, W.	Saltfleet.
Whitaker, George, M.A.	Provost of Trin. Coll. Toronto.
Williams, A. B.A.	Assistant, Yorkville.
Williams, Geo. C. M.A.	Chap. to the Forces, Toronto.
Wilson, John, B.A.	Grafton.
Worrall, J. B.	Oshawa.
Wray, W.	Muskoka.

Diocese of Ontario.

ONTARIO, The Right Rev. John Travers LEWIS, Lord Bishop of Ontario.—Consecrated Bp of Ontario 1862. (Episcopal Jurisdiction, Ontario; Pop. 390,000; Clergy, 56; Inc. of See, interest of 10,000*l.*)

Dean—Very Rev. James Lyster, LL.D.

Archdeacon—Ven. H. Patton, D.C.L. Cornwall.

Examining Chaplains—The Archdeacon; Rev. William Bleasdell, M.A; and Rev. E. J. Boswell, D.C.L.

Anderson, G. A. M.A.	Tyendinaga.
Armstrong, J. G. M.A.	Hawkesbury.
Auston, H. B.A.	Curate, Cornwall.
Baker, E. H. M.	Hillier.
Beaven, E. W. M.A.	Iroquois.
Bell, Chris. Roles, M.B.	Douglas and Eganville.
Bleasdell, W. M.A.	Trenton.
Bogert, J. J. M.A.	Rector of Napanee.
Bogert, D. F. B.A.	Kitley.
Bond, W. B.A.	Roslin.
Boswell, E. J. D.C.L.	Prescott.
Bousfield, T.	In charge of Depository.
Bower, E. C.	Barriefield.
Brown, C.	Ashton.
Burke, J. W. B.A.	Almonte.
Carroll, J.	Gananoque.
Cooke, A. W.	North Augusta.
Denroche, C. T.	Delta.
Dobbs, F. W.	Portsmouth.
Emery, C. P.	Packenham.
Fisher, A.	Finch.
Fleming, W. M.A.	Osgoode.
Forest, C. M.A.	Merrickville.
Fox, C. M. B.A.	Curate, St. Thomas, Belleville.
Garrett, R.	Osnabruck.

Godfrey, J. B.A. . . . Huntley.
Gribble, J. . . . . . Horton.
Grier, J. M.A . . . . Rector, Belleville.
Grout, G. W. G. B.A. . Stirling.
Harding, R. . . . . Rector, Adolphustown.
Harper, W. F. S. . . Rector, Bath.
Harris, J. . . . . . (On leave.)
Henderson, W. M.A. . . Pembroke.
Higginson, G. N. M.A. . New Edinburgh.
Jones, Kearney, B.A. . Madoc.
Jones, S. B.A. . . . Christ Church, West Belleville.
Jones, T. B. LL.D. . . St. Alban's, Ottawa.
Kirkpatrick, F. W. M.A. Wolfe Island.
Lauder, J. S. M.A. . . Ottawa City.
Lewin, William, B.A. . Shannonville.
Lewis, R. M.A. . . . Rector, Maitland.
Loucks, E. . . . . . Rector, Morrisburg.
Lyster, Very Rev. Jas. LL.D. Kingston.
Macaulay, W. . . . . Rector, Picton.
McMorine, J. M.A. . . Lanark.
May, J. M.A. . . . . March.
Merritt, D. P. B.A. . . North Gower.
Morris, E. . . . . . (retired) Carleton Place.
Morris, J. A. . . . . Nepean.
Mulkins, H. . . . . Chap. to the Provincial Penitentiary, Kingston.
Mulock, J. A. . . . . St. Paul's, Kingston.
Nesbitt, W. . . . . Franktown.
O'Loughlin, A. J. . . Sydenham.
Parnell, T. A. . . . Secretary of Synod, Kingston.
Patton, Ven. Arch. D.C.L. Cornwall.
Pettit, C. B. M.A. . . Rector, Richmond.
Philipps, T. D. M.A. . . Ottawa.
Plees, H. E. B.A. . . Carrying Place.
Preston, J. A. M.A. . . Carleton Place.
Rawson, W. B.A. . . Curate, Picton.
Rogers, R. V. M.A. . . St. James's, Kingston.
Rolph, R. . . . . . (retired) Drummondville.
Short, W. . . . . . Amherst Island.
Simpson, J. H. . . . Sebastopol.
Smythe, W. H. . . . Tamworth.
Spencer, A. . . . . Newboro'.
Stannage, John . . . Rector, Kemptville.
Stanton, T. B.A. . . Camden East.
Stephenson, R. L. M.A. . Rector, Perth.
Stephenson, F. L. B.A. . Cumberland.
Street, F. M.A. . . . Curate, Christ Church, Ottawa.
Tane, Frank R. . . . Brockville.
Taylor, Thomas, M.A. . (retired) Richmond.
White, G. W. M.A. . . Smith's Falls.
Wilson, Henry, B.A. . . Kingston.
Williams, S. . . . . Milford.
Windsor, S. B. M.A. . . Chap. to the Forces, Kingston.

Diocese of Huron.

CANADA WEST.

HURON, The Right Rev. Benjamin CRONYN, Lord Bishop of Huron, *London, Canada West.*—Consecrated Bp of Huron 1857. (Episcopal Jurisdiction, Huron; Area, 12,200 square miles; Pop. 277,505; Clergy, 43; Inc. of See, interest on 10,000*l* granted by the Colonial Bishoprics' Fund and invested in the Colony.)

Dean—Very Rev. I. Hellmuth, D.D., Dean of Huron.

Canons.

Rev. William Bettridge, B.D. | Rev. A. Nelles.
Rev. E. L. Elwood, M.A. | Rev. J. C. Usher.

Archdeacon of Huron—Rev. F. W. Sandys, D.D.

Archdeacon of London—Brough, C. C. M.A.

Chaplains to the Bishop.

Brough, C. Crosbie, M.A. | Elwood, E. L. M.A.
Marsh, J. Walker, M.A. | Boomer, M. LL.D.

Appleby, T. H. M.A. . . Clarksburg.
Armstrong, David . . Moore.
Bartlett, H. . . . . Princeton.
Bayly, Benjamin, B.A. . Curate, London.
Belcher, Rev. S. . . . Thamesford.
Bettridge, William, B.D. R. of Woodstock, Rural Dean.
Boomer, Michael, LL.D. . Galt, Rural Dean.
Brookman, W. . . .
Brough, C. Crosbie, M.A. Rector of St. John's, London Township.
Carmichael, J. . . . Clinton.
Caulfield, H. . . . . Mitchell.
Caulfield, St. George, LL.D. St. Thomas, Rural Dean.
Chase, H. P. . . . . Delaware.
Coltworty, W. . . . Mount Pleasant.
Cooper, P. S. . . . . Paisley.
Curran, J. P. . . . . St. Mary's.
Daunt, W. . . . . Dungannon.
Davis, W. . . . . . Birr.
Deacon, D. . . . . Port Rowan.
Des Barres, T. C. M.A. . Eastwood.
Du Bordieu, S. . . . Bayfield.
Elliott, Adam . . . . Tuscarora.
Elliott, F. Gore . . . Sandwich.
Elwood, E. L. M.A. . . Goderich, Rural Dean.
Evans, W. B. B.A. . . Durham.
Falls, A. B.A. . . . Rector of Adelaide.
Fauquier, F. D. . . . South Zorra.
Gibson, J. C. B.A. . . Rector of Warwick.
Grasett, E. M.A. . . . Rector of Simcoe.
Green, W. . . . . . Sombra.
Gunne, John . . . . Florence.
Halpin, H. M.A. . . . Prof. Classics, Huron College, London.
Harding, F. . . . . Aylmer.
Harris, S. . . . . . Waterford.
Hellmuth, Very Rev. Isaac, D.D. . . . . Rector of St. Paul's Cathedral, London.
Hill, R. B.A. . . . . Cornabus.
Hincks, J. P. . . . . Ingersoll.
Hodgskin, T. J. . . . Kincardine.
Hughes, Thomas . . . Dresden.
Hurst, John . . . . Windsor.
Hutchinson, J. . . . Kirkton.
Jamieson, A. . . . . Walpole Island.
Jessopp, H. B. M.A . . Rector of Port Burwell.
Johnson, C. C. . . . Seaforth.
Jones, W. H. M.A. . . Tilsonburg.
Kennedy, John, M.A. . Tryconnell.
Keys, G. . . . . . Exeter.
Low, G. J. . . . . Curate, London.
Mack, F. . . . . . Rector of Amherstburgh.
Marsh, J. W. M.A. . Chaplain to the Bishop, and Secretary to Church Society, London.
Mellish, H. F. . . . Haysville.
Miller, A. C. . . . Listowell.
Mockridge, James, B.A. . Fingal.
Moffett, W. B. . . . Colchester.
Mulholland, A. H. R. . Owen's Sound, Rural Dean.
Mulholland, J. G. M.A. . Victoria.
Murphy, W. . . . . Wingham.
Newman, E. E. . . . Delaware.
Nelles, Abraham . . . Brantford.
Padfield, James . . . Burford.
Patterson, Ephraim, B.A. Stratford.
Patterson, R. S. . . . Stratterdy.
Peake, E. . . . . . Norwich.
Rally, W. B. M.A. . . New Hamburgh.
Revell, Henry, M.A. . . Woodstock (superannuated).
Roberts, R. J. B.A. . . Newport.
Salter, G. J. R. B.A. . Port Sarnia, Rural Dean.
Sanders, T. E. . . . . Lucan.
Sandys, F. W. D.D. . . Chatham.
Smith, J. W. P. . . . Belmont
Smyth, James, B.A. . . London.
Schulte, J. D.D. . . . Port Burwell.
Softley, E. . . . . Walkerton.
Sweatman, Arthur, M.A. Head Master of the Collegiate Institution, London.
Tibbetts, W. . . . . Port Dover.
Tighe, S. B.A. . . . Clinton.

Townley, Adam, D.D.	Paris.
Usher, J. C.	Brantford.
Watson, Thomas	Meaford.
Wickes, William, M.A.	Prin. of Huron College, London.
Wilson, J. D.D.	Morpeth.
Wood, William	St. Williams.
Wright, J. T.	Wardsville.

Diocese of Nova Scotia.

NOVA SCOTIA, The Right Rev. Hibbert BINNEY, Lord Bishop of Nova Scotia, *Halifax, Nova Scotia.*—King's Coll. Lon. and Scho. of Wor. Coll. Ox. 1st cl. Math. et Phy. 2nd cl. Lit. Hum. and B.A. 1842, M.A. 1844, D.D. 1851; Deac. 1842 and Pr. 1843 by Bp of Ox. Consecrated Bp of Nova Scotia 1851. (Episcopal Jurisdiction, Nova Scotia, Cape Breton, and Prince Edward Island; Area, 22,435 square miles; Pop. 411,365; Clergy, 68; Inc. of See, 700*l* from Trust Funds.) Visitor of King's College, Nova Scotia. His Lordship was formerly Hon. Fell. of King's Coll. Lon; and Fell. of Wor. Coll. Ox. 1846–48.

Dean—Very Rev. W. Bullock, D.D.

Archdeacon of Nova Scotia—Ven. George McCawley, D.D.

Archdeacon of Prince Edward's Island—Ven. J. Herbert Read, D.D.

Canons.

Ven. Archdeacon McCawley, D.D. J. C. Cochran, M.A.
J. M. Hensley, D.D. Edwin Gilpin, D.D.

Minor Canon—J. Abbott.

PROVINCE OF NOVA SCOTIA.

Abbott, John	Halifax, St. Luke's.
Alexander, Joseph	St. Mary's River.
Almon, H. F.	St. George's, Halifax.
Almon, H. P. A.B.	Bridgetown.
Ambrose, John, M.A.	Margaret's Bay.
Ancient W. J.	Turn's Bay.
Ansell, Edward, A.B.	Beaver Harbour.
Armstrong, W.	St. Paul's, Halifax.
Avery, Richard	Aylesford.
Axford, F.	St. Mary's.
Ball, E. H.	Melford.
Blackman, T. D.C.L.	Newport.
Boone, W. T.	Windsor.
Bowman, Charles, M.A.	Rawdon.
Breading, James	Falkland.
Brown, John	New Germany.
Bullock, Wm. (Dean) D.D.	Halifax, St. Luke's.
Bullock, W. H. A.B.	Bridgewater.
Burn, C.	Country Harbour.
Burrows, H.	Pugwash.
Campbell, J. R.	Yarmouth.
Cochran, James, C. M.A.	Halifax.
Croucher, J. B.A.	Granville.
De Blois, Henry D. M.A.	Granville.
Dodwell, G. M.A.	Collegiate School, Windsor.
Edghill, R. C.	Garrison Chaplain.
Elliott, Charles, B.A.	Picton.
Filleul, Philip J. B.A.	Weymouth.
Forsyth, Joseph, B.A.	Truro.
Gelling, W. E.	Guysborough.
Genever, H.	Port Medway.
Gilpin, Edwin, D.D.	Halifax.
Godfrey, Wm. M. M.A.	St. Clements.
Gray, Walter, B.A.	Annapolis.
Grindon, Octavius, B.A.	Porter's Lake.
Haire, Robert	Stewiacke.
Hamilton, H.	Manchester, Rural Dean.
Hensley, J. M. D.D.	Windsor Vicinity.
Hill, George William, M.A.	Halifax, St. Pauls.
Hill, L. W. B.A.	Retired.
Hodgson, G. W. M.A.	Lunenburg.
Jamison, Robert	Ship Harbour, Rural Dean.
Jamison, A.D.	Tangier.
Jordan, Abraham	New Dublin.
Kaulbach, J. A. A.B.	River John, Picton.
King, Wm. B. M.A.	Parrsborough.
Maynard, Thomas, M.A.	Windsor.
M'Cawley, G. D.D. (Archdeacon)	Falmouth, President of King's College, Windsor.
Moody, J. T. T. M.A.	Yarmouth.
Moore, David C.	New Ross.
Morris, G. E. W. M.A.	Retired.
Morris, W. T. B.A.	Antigonishe.
Nichols, E. E. B. M.A.	Liverpool.
Owen, Henry L. B.A.	Lunenburg, Rural Dean.
Payne, Robert, B.A.	Blandford.
Pryor, W. F. B.A.	Dartmouth.
Richardson, B.	Dartmouth.
Richey, J. A.	Maitland.
Ritchie, James J. M.A.	Annapolis.
Robertson, James, LL.D.	Wilmot.
Ruggles, R. O. B.A.	Kentville.
Sargent, J. P. B.A.	Antigonistre.
Shannon, W.	Walton.
Shreve, Chas. Jas. B.A.	Chester.
Smith, John S. B.A.	Sackville.
Snyder, William H. M.A.	Mahone Bay.
Spike, H. M., B.A.	New Dublin.
Stamer, Henry	Hubbard's Cove.
Storrs, John	Cornwallis, Rural Dean.
Townshend, George, M.A.	Amherst.
Uniacke, Jas. B. B.A.	Halifax.
Wainwright, H. B.A.	Shelburne.
White, Thomas H. D.D.	Shelburne, Rural Dean.
Wilkins, L.M. B.A.	Albion Mines.
Williams, Hugh	Truro.
Wood, A. C. B.A.	Picton.
Yewens, H. L.	Digby.

CAPE BRETON.

Brine, R. F.	Arichat.
Browne, Alfred, B.A.	Glace Bay.
Jamison, W. H.	Louisburg.
Meek, William	Sydney Mines.
Uniacke, Richard J. D.D.	Sydney, Rural Dean.

PRINCE EDWARD'S ISLAND.

Cox, J. C.	New London.
Dyer, R. W.	Cascumpeque.
Fitzgerald, David.	R. of St. Paul's, Charlotte Town.
Forsythe, Jos. Wm. M.A.	St. Eleanor's.
Jenkins, Louis C. D.C.L.	Charlotte Town (retired).
Parnther, D. B.	Charlotte Town.
Read, J. H. D.D. (Arhd).	Rector of Milton.
Richey, Theoph.	Georgetown.
Sterns, H. B.A.	Crapaud.
Stewart, W. B.A.	Cherry Valley.
Swabey, H. B. B.A.	Port Hill, &c.

Diocese of Fredericton.

FREDERICTON, The Right Rev. John MEDLEY, Lord Bp of Fredericton, *Fredericton, New Brunswick.*—Wad. Coll. Ox. 2nd cl. Lit. Hum. and B.A. 1826, M.A. 1830, D.D. 1845. Consecrated Bp of Fredericton 1845. (Episcopal Jurisdiction, the Province of New Brunswick; Area, 26,000 square miles; Pop. 200,000; Clergy, 55; Inc. of See 1000*l* from Colonial Bishoprics' Fund.) His Lordship was formerly P. C. of St. John's, Truro, 1831–38; V. of St. Thomas's, Exeter, 1838–45; Preb. of Ex. Cathl. 1842–45. Author, *Advice to Teachers in Sunday Schools*, 1833; *The Episcopal Form of Church Government*, 1835; *How are the Mighty Fallen'* (a Sermon), Exeter, 1840; *Elementary Remarks on Church Architecture*, 1841; *The Harvest Field of the World* (a Sermon), 1843; *Sermons* (published by request of many of his late parishioners), 2 eds. 1845; *The Reformation, its Nature, its Necessity, and its Benefits* (a Sermon), 1847; *A Statement respecting the Condition and Wants of his Diocese*, 1848; *A Charge* (at his Primary Visitation), 1848; *A Charge, with a Sermon Preached at the Consecration of the Bishops of South and North Carolina*, 1854. Translator, with the Rev. H. J. Cornish, of *The Homilies of St. John Chrysostom on*

Corinthians, Vol. IV. of *Library of the Fathers*, Oxford, 1838.

PROVINCE OF NEW BRUNSWICK.

Armstrong, George M.	Rector of St. Mark's, St. John.
Armstrong, Wm.	Rector of St. James's, St. John.
Bacon, Samuel	R. of Chatham, and Rural Dean.
Black, John.	R. of King's Clear.
Bliss, Donald M.	Westmoreland.
Boyer, W. N.	Rector of Monkton.
Carey, George T.	R. of Grand Manan.
Coster, Chas. G.	Ast. Min. at Fredericton Cath.
Coster, N. Allen	Rector of Richibucto.
Covert, W. S.	Lancaster.
Cruden, W.	Rector of Blackville, &c.
De Veber, W. H.	Rector of St. Paul's, Portland.
Disbrow, James W.	St. John.
Dinzey, J.	Curate of Woodstock.
Dowling, T.	Rector of Douglas.
Gray, J. W. D. D.D.	R. of Trinity, St. John, Hon. Canon.
Hanford, S. J.	Missionary at Upham.
Hannington, A. W.	Missionary at Prince William and Dumfries.
Harrison, W.	R. of St. Luke's, Portland, Hon. Canon.
Hartin, Thomas	Missionary at Canterbury.
Hill, James	Curate of Trinity, St. John.
Hudson, James	Travelling Missionary.
Jaffrey, W. N.	Rector of St. Mary's.
Jarvis, G. S. D.D.	R. of Shediac.
Ketchum, W. Q.	Rector of St. Andrew's.
Lee, Charles	Rector of Fredericton.
Matthew, C. R.	Curate at St. Mark's, St. John.
Medley, C. S.	R. of Sussex.
M'Kiel, W. Le B.	Missionary at Bathurst.
Milner, Christopher	Retired Missionary, Westfield.
Neales, James	R. of Gagetown.
Neales, William	Curate at Chatham.
Pearson, J.	Sub-Dean of the Cathedral and Missionary at New Maryland.
Pickett, D. W.	Missionary, at Greenwich and Wickham.
Pollard, H.	R. of Maguerville and Burton.
Roberts, G. G.	R. of Sackville and Dorchester.
Rogers, G.	Missionary at Springfield.
Schofield, G.	Rector of Simonds.
Scovil, W.	St. John.
Scovil, W. E.	R. of Kingston.
Shaw, B.	Missionary at Grand Lake.
Sheraton, J. P.	Missionary at Shediac.
Simonds, R.	Missionary at Sussex.
Smith, R. E.	St. Andrew's and Chamcook, Master of Grammar School.
Street, S. D. L.	R. of Woodstock.
Street, W. H.	Missionary at Tobique and Grand Falls.
Swabey, M.	Rector of St. Jude's, Victoria.
Thompson, J. S.	R. of St. David's.
Tilley, Harrison	Curate at Portland, St. John.
Tippett, Henry W.	R. of Queensbury.
Walker, W. W.	R. of Hampton.
Walker, G.	Curate of Hampton.
Walker, W.	Rector of Carleton.
Warneford, E. A.	R. of Norton.
Weeks, A. H.	C. of Cocaigne.
Wetmore, D. J.	Kingston.
Williams, J. S.	Missionary of Campobello.
Wood, Abraham	Retired Missionary.
Woodman, E. S.	Rector of Westfield.

Diocese of Newfoundland.

NEWFOUNDLAND, The Right Rev. E. FEILD, Lord Bishop of Newfoundland and Bermuda.—Queen's Coll. Ox. 1st cl. Math. et Phy. and B.A. 1824, M.A. 1826, D.D. 1844. Consecrated Bp of Newfoundland 1844. (Episcopal Jurisdiction, the Colony of Newfoundland, and the Colony of Bermuda; Newfoundland, Area, 36,022 square miles; Pop. 124,256; Clergy, 40; Bermuda, Area, 22 square miles; Pop. 11,346; Clergy, 8; Inc. of See, 500*l* Imperial Parliamentary Vote, 200*l* from Colonial Funds, and 500*l* from S.P.G; Total, 1200*l*.) His Lordship was formerly Michel Fell. of Queen's Coll. Ox. 1827–33; R. of English and Welsh Bicknor, Glouc. and Heref. 1833–44. Author, *Journal of a Visitation Voyage on the Coast of Labrador and Round the whole Island of Newfoundland*, in *The Church in the Colonies*, 1849.

Coadjutor Bishop—The Right Rev. James B. Kelly, D.D. 1867.

Archdeacon and Commissary—

NEWFOUNDLAND.

Deanery of Avalon.

Caswell, R. C. M.A.	Incumbent of the Cathedral.
Johnson, G. M.	Cathedral, St. John's.
Johnson, R. M.	St. John's Outharbours.
Botwood, E.	St. Mary's (St. John's).
Skinner, H. M.	Ferryland.
Phelps, J. F.	Head Master of the Church of England School, St. John's.
Wood, T. M. (Rural Dean)	St. Thomas' (St. John's).

Deanery of Conception Bay.

Fleet, B.	South Shore.
Harvey, J. C.	Port de Grave.
Hoyles, W. J.	Carbonear.
Jones, B.	Harbor Grace.
Noel, J. M.	Island Cove.
Rouse, O.	Bay de Verd.
Shears, W. C.	Bay Roberts.
Taylor, R. N.	Brigus.

Deanery of Trinity Bay.

Gardner, G.	Heart's Content.
Netten W.	Catalina.
Petley, H. M.A.	New Harbour.
Smith, Benj. (Rural Dean)	Trinity.

Deanery of Bonavista.

Bayly, E. A. C. (Rural Dean)	Bonavista.
Cragg, J. G.	Pinchard's Island.
Kirby, W.	King's Cove.
Milner, W.	Greenspond.
West, C. R.	Salvage.

Deanery of Notre Dame Bay.

Boone, T. (Rural Dean)	Twillingate.
Darrell, J.	Herring Neck.
Hooper, G. H.	Moreton's Harbour.
Oakley, A.	Fogo.
Temple, R.	White Bay.

Deanery of Placentia Bay.

Gabriel, A. E.	Lamaline.
Kingwell, J.	Harbour Buffet.
Rozier, W.	Burin.

Deanery of Fortune Bay.

Chamberlain, G. S.	La Poele.
Colley, E.	Hermitage Cove.
Cunningham, J.	The Burgeos.
Le Gallais, W. W.	Channel.
Lind, H.	St. George's Bay.
Marshall, J.	Belloram.
Bule, U. Z.	Bay of Islands.
White, William K. (Rural Dean)	Harbour Briton.

THE LABRADOR.

Dobie, R. T.	Forteau.
Wilson, M. E.	Battle Harbour.

THE BERMUDAS.

Coombe, C. P. K.	Sandys and Port Royal.
Jenkins, C. B.A	
Lightbourn, J. F., B.A.	Pembroke and Devon.
Lough, J. B. L.	Pagets and Warwick.
Tucker, G. B.A.	Hamilton.
Tucker, R. T. D.D.	St. George's.

Diocese of Rupert's Land.

RUPERT'S LAND, The Right Rev. Robert MACHRAY, Lord Bishop of Rupert's Land.—Sid. Coll. Cam. B.A. 1855, M.A. 1858, D.D. 1865; Deac. 1855 and Pr. 1856 by Bp of Ely. Consecrated Bp of Rupert's Land, 1865. (Episcopal Jurisdiction, the territory of the Hudson's Bay Company; Area, 370,000 square miles; Pop. 200,000; Clergy, 22; Inc. of See, 688*l*, being 300*l*. from Hudson's Bay Company and 388*l* from Leith Bequest.) His Lordship was formerly Fell. of Sid. Coll. Cam. and V. of Madingley, Cambs, 1862–65.

Archdeacon of Assiniboia—Ven. J. McLean, M.A. 1866.

Archdeacon of Cumberland—Ven. Abraham Cowley, 1867.

Commissary in England—Rev. T. T. Perowne, B.D., Rector of Stalbridge, Dorset.

Chaplains to the Bishop.

Ven. Archdeacon McLean, M.A. Exam. Chaplain. Rev. W. H. Taylor.

Native Chaplain—Rev. H. Cochrane.

Registrar—Rev. S. Pritchard.

The Bishop, St. Paul's, Red River.
Bompas, W. C., Ch.M.S., Mackenzie River District.
Budd, Henry, Ch.M.S., Pastor at Devon.
Carrie, J., Col. and Cont. Ch. Soc, Incumbent of Holy Trinity, Headingley, Assiniboine River.
(Vacant), Col. and Cont. Ch. Soc., Incumbent of St. Anne's and St. Margaret's, La Prairie, Assiniboine River.
Cochrane, Henry, Ch.M.S., Pastor of Indian Settlement.
Cook, Thomas, S.P.G., Fort Ellice.
Cowley, Ven. Abraham, Ch.M.S., Incumbent of St. Peter's Church, Red River, and of Mapleton.
Gardiner, Jos. Phelps, Ch.M.S., Incumbent of St. Andrew's Church, Red River (Surrogate).
George, Henry, Ch.M.S, Inc. of St. Mary, La Prairie, Assiniboine River (Surrogate).
Hale, Rev. D. B., Ch.M.S., Fairford.
Horden, John, Ch.M.S., Moose Fort (Surrogate).
Kirkby, W. West, Ch.M.S., Fort Simpson, Mackenzie River.
Macdonald, Robert, Ch.M.S., Fort Youcon.
Mackay, John A., Ch.M.S., Stanley, English River.
McLean, Ven. J. M.A., Warden of St. John's College, Professor of Divinity, and Rector of the Cathedral, Red River.
Mason, William, Ch.M.S., York Fort (Surrogate).
Phair, Robert, Ch.M.S., Lansdowne.
Pritchard, S., Master in the Collegiate School, St. John's College.
Settee, James, Ch.M.S., Swan River District.
Smith, Thomas T., Ch.M.S. (At home.)
(Vacant), S.P.G., Incumbent of St. James's Church, Assiniboine.
Vincent, Thomas, Ch.M.S., Albany, James' Bay.

Diocese of Jamaica.

JAMAICA, The Right Rev. Aubrey George SPENCER, Lord Bishop of Jamaica, *Torquay, Devon.*—Magd. Hall, Ox. D.D. 1839. Consecrated Bp of Newfoundland, 1839, translated to Jamaica, 1843. (Episcopal Jurisdiction, Jamaica, British Honduras, and the Bay Islands; Area, 74,734 square miles; Pop. 418,847; Clergy, 116; Inc. of See, 3000*l*, from the Consolidated Fund.) Author, *Sermons on Various Subjects*, 1827; *The Mourner Comforted* (*Practical Sermons*, Vol. III.), 1845.

KINGSTON, The Right Rev. Reginald COURTENEY, Lord Bishop of Kingston, Co-adjutor of the Bp of Jamaica. —Magd. Hall, Ox. B.A. 1835, M.A. 1838, D.D. 1856. Consecrated Bp of Kingston 1856. (Inc. of See, 1600*l* from the Bp of Jamaica.) Archd. of Middlesex, Jamaica. (Inc. 400*l*.)

Archdeacon and Commissary for Cornwall—The Ven. William Rowe, M.A.

Archdeacon and Commissary for Surrey—The Ven. Thomas Stewart, D.D.

Acting Archdeacon and Commissary for Middlesex—The Rev. J. Williams.

Assistant Commissary for Jamaica and Examining Chaplain of the Bishop—The Rev. Duncan Houston Campbell, M.A.

Commissary for British Honduras—The Ven. William Rowe, M.A.

Bishop's Chaplains.

Ven. Thomas Stewart, D.D.	Rev. D. H. Campbell, M.A.
Ven. William Rowe, M.A.	Rev. F. S. Bradshaw, LL.D.

Domestic Chaplain and Secretary of the Bishop of Kingston—Rev. G. B. Brooks, M.A.

Bishop's Registrar—John James Vidal, Esq.

MIDDLESEX.

St. Catherine.

Webbe, H. Rees, B.C.L., Stipendiary Curate, 300*l*
Williams, J., Rector, 500*l*.
Scotland, H., Island Curate, 340*l*.
Wood, W. J., Curate, 200*l*.
(Vacant), Island Curate, 340*l*.
Cooke, S. H., Island Curate, 340*l*

St. Thomas in the Vale.

Campbell, John, B.A., Rector, 400*l*.
Richards, John G., Island Curate, 340*l*.
Thomson, J. A., Island Curate, 340*l*.

Clarendon.

Downer, G. W., Island Curate, 340*l*.
Hall, Charles Hen., Rector, 400*l*.
MacDermot, H. C. P., Island Curate, 340*l*.

Vere.

Garrett, Thomas, M.A., Rector, 400*l*.
Gray, C. F., Island Curate, 340*l*.
Macdermot, H.M.F., Stipendiary Curate, 300*l*.

Manchester.

Angell, C., Stipendiary Curate, 300*l*.
Forbes, W., Rector, 400*l*.
Key, Edward Bassett, Stipendiary Curate, 300*l*.
Hildebrand, J. S., B.A., Island Curate, 340*l*.
Seymour, A. H., Stipendiary Curate, 300*l*.
Wood, J. S., Island Curate, 340*l*.

St. Mary.

Constantine, M. G., Island Curate, 340*l*.
Sharpe, F. H., Island Curate, 340*l*.
Moore, John H., LL.D., Rector, 400*l*.

St. Ann.

Chandler, Cornelius R., Island Curate, 340*l*.
Hall, G., Island Curate, 340*l*.
Mais, J. L., B.A., Stipendiary Curate, and Master o Walton School, 100*l*.
Melville, H. P. C., Island Curate, 340*l*.
Cheyne, G., Rector, 400*l*.

SURREY.

Kingston.

Campbell, D. H, M.A., Rector, 600*l*.
Nuttall, E., Island Curate, 340*l*.
Serres, W. S., B.A., Chap. to General Penitentiary, 400*l*.
Street, C. P., Island Curate, 340*l*.
Gayleard, J., Stipendiary Curate, 200*l*.

Port Royal.

Fyfe, Charles, Island Curate, 340*l*.
M'Claverty, Colin, M.A., Island Curate, 340.
Bradshaw, F.S., LL.D., Rector, 400*l*.

St. Andrew.

Braine, Geo. Taylor, B.A., Island Curate, 340*l*.
Brooks, G. B., M.A., Stipendiary Curate, 300*l*.
Finlay, A., Island Curate, 340*l*.
Isaacs, H., M.A., Island Curate, 340*l*.
Mayhew, W., M.A., Rector, 450*l*.
Musson, S. C., B.A., Curate,
Stewart, Ven. Archd., D.D., Island Curate, 340*l*.

St. Thomas in the East.

Farquharson, J. S., Rector, 400*l.*
Magnan, C. M., Island Curate, 340*l.*
Sloan, J. W., LL.B., Island Curate, 340*l.*
Douët, C. F., B.A., Island Curate, 340*l.*
King, F. L., Curate.
Harty, T., Curate.
Jackson, Samuel, Island Curate, 340*l.*

Portland.

Orgill, Thomas, T. T., B.A., Island Curate, 340*l.*
Smith, William, Rector, 400*l.*
Foote, A., Island Curate, 340*l.*
Panton, D. B., M.A., Island Curate, 340*l.*

Metcalf.

Browne, H., Rector, 400*l.*

CORNWALL.

St. Elizabeth.

Lynch, R. B., Island Curate, 340*l.*
Ramson, J. L., Island Curate, 340*l.*
Smith, M. H., Island Curate, 340*l.*
Stone, John Campbell, M.A., Rector, 400*l.*
Rowe, D., Stipendiary Curate, 300*l.*
Rowe, Ven. W., M.A., Island Curate, 340*l.*

Westmoreland.

Clarke, Henry, Island Curate, 340*l.*
Cork, J., Rector, 400*l.*
Dunbar, R. K., Island Curate, 340*l.*
Ingle, W. H., B.A., Stipendiary Curate, 300*l.*
Miller, J. E., Stipendiary Curate, 300*l.*
Pierce, W. E., B.A., Island Curate, 340*l.*

Hanover.

Davidson, A. J., Rector, 400*l.*
Lawson, Henry G., Island Curate, 340*l.*

St. James.

Burrell, W. R., B.A., Island Curate, 340*l.*
Garcia del Rio, J. A., Island Curate, 340*l.*
Hepburn, J. K., Island Curate, 340*l.*
Morris, D. R., Rector, 500*l.*

Trelawney.

Hime, M. W., B.A. (Acting), Island Curate, 340*l.*
Littlejohn, David R., Rector, 500*l.*
(Vacant), Island Curate, 340*l.*
Stewart, Ernest A., Island Curate, 340*l.*

Each Rector in the island has either a glebe provided by the parish, independently of his salary from the public treasury, or receives 50*l.* in lieu of a glebe.

The appointments to Rectories and Curacies rest alternately with the Governor and the Bishop.

The undermentioned clergymen have been permitted to retire from the service of the Church in this Diocese, with pensions, on account of their long services and impaired health:—

Rev. W. Hylton, 200*l.*
Rev. E. Jones, 150*l.*
Rev. W. Stearn, 150*l.*
Rev. B. Kingdon, 150*l.*
Rev. T. B. Cahusac, 125*l.*
Rev. J. Stainsby, M.A.

Diocese of Nassau.

NASSAU, The Right Rev. Addington Robert Peel VENABLES, Lord Bishop of Nassau.—Ex. Coll. Ox. B.A. 1848, M.A. 1851, D.D. 1863; Deac. 1849, Pr. 1850. Consecrated Bp of Nassau 1863. (Episcopal Jurisdiction, the Bahamas, Turk's and Caicos Islands; Area, 120,000 square miles; Pop. 36,000; Clergy, 14; Inc. of See, 1125*l.*) His Lordship was formerly C. of St. Paul's, Oxford.

Bishop's Chaplain—C. C. Wakefield, B.A.

BAHAMAS.

New Providence.

Crowther, J., Curate of St. Matthew and Master of the Middle School.
Duncombe, W., Rector of St. Matthew.
Fisher, J. H., Incumbent of St. Agnes'.
Hutcheson, Thomas, St. Matthew's, Western Mission.
Saunders, R., Rector of St. Ann's.
Swann, R., Rector of Christ Church.
Todd, H., M.A., Incumbent of St. Mary's, and Head Master of the Grammar School.

Harbour Island.

Stoombom, W., Rector of St. John's.

Inagua.

Lightbourn, J. F., Incumbent of St. Philip's.

St. Salvador.

Sullivan, A., Incumbent of St. Salvador.

Crooked Island, Long Cay, and Acklin's Island.

Duncombe, W., jun., Incumbent of St. David's.

Abaco, &c.

Weatherstone, T., St. Peter and St. Stephen's.

Long Island and Exuma.

Minns, Sam., Incumbent of St. Andrew and St. Paul, Exuma.

Eleuthera.

Higgs, T. S. T., Incumbent of St. Patrick.

TURK'S ISLANDS.

Grand Cay.

Dillon, M., Rector of St. Thomas.

Salt Cay.

Astwood, Jos., Incumbent of St. John's.

Caicos Islands.

Glanville, W., Incumbent of St. George's.

Diocese of Barbados.

EXPLANATION OF LETTERS AFFIXED.

R. Rectors. C. Curates. M. Ministers. A.C. Assistant Curates. S.C.C. Students at Codrington College who obtained their "testamur." Ch. Bishop's Chaplains.

BARBADOS, The Right Rev. Thomas PARRY, Lord Bishop of Barbados, *Bishop's Court, Barbados.*—Ball. Coll. Ox. 1st cl. Math. et Phy. 2nd cl. Lit. Hum. and B.A. 1816, M.A. 1819, B.D. and D.D. 1842; Deac. 1819 and Pr. 1820 by Bp of Ox. Consecrated Bp of Barbados 1842. (Episcopal Jurisdiction, Barbados, St. Vincent, St. Lucia, Trinidad, Grenada, and Tobago; Area, 3170 square miles; Pop. 308,189; Clergy, 79; Inc. of See, 2500*l.* from Consolidated Fund.) Visitor of Codrington Coll. Barbados. Formerly Fell. of Ball. Coll. Ox. 1819; Archd. of Antigua. Author, *Parochial Sermons*, Oxford, 1828; *Exposition of the Epistle to the Romans*, 1832; *Exposition of the Hebrews*, 1834; *Exposition of Philemon*, 1834; *Christ and His Adversaries, Sermons for Sundays, Festivals, and Fasts*, vol. 1, 1845; *The Christian Stewardship*, vol. 2, 1845; *Ordination Vows practically considered* (a Series of Sermons), 1846; *Episcopal Charges in* 1843, 1845, and 1846; various Sermons.

Archdeacon of Barbados—Ven. H. H. Parry, M.A., 1861.
Archdeacon of Trinidad—Ven. G. Cummins, M.A., 1842.

Allder, W. A., S.C.C., Barbados. St. Stephen's. C.
Anton, J. A., S.C.C., Grenada, St. George. R.
Arrindell, W. M. D, S.C.C., Trinidad, Trin. Par. A.C.
Austin, P. B., B.C.L., Barbados, St. James. R.
Barnett, Edward, Barbados, St. Mark. C.
Beckles, J. A., Tobago, St. Paul and St. Mary. R.
Berkeley, R. F., S.C.C., Grenada, St. John and St. Mark. R. (Rural Dean.)
Bishop, A. H., S.C.C., Barbados, St. John. R.
Bovell, W. H. B., B.A., Barbados, St. Thomas. R.
Bowen, G. T., Barbados, St. Ambrose. C.
Bowen, W. T., S.C.C., Barbados.
Bradshaw, John, M.A. & B.M., Barbados, St. Joseph's. R.
Branch, S. F., S.C.C., St. Patrick and St. David, St. Vincent. R.
Branch, G. W., S.C.C., Granada, St. Paul and St. Clement's. C.
Burgess, W. S., S.C.C., St. Vincent, Charlotte Parish. C.
Carter, Charles, Barbados, Trinity Chapel, C.

Chester, G. J., M.A., Barbados, St. Luke's. A.C.
Clarke, Charles, M.A., Codrington College School.
Clarke, Thomas, M.A., Barbados, St. Michael. R. Ch.
Clinckett, G. M., S.C.C., Barbados, St. Matthew. C.
Collymore, Henry, S.C.C., Barbados, St. Martin. C.
Connell, John, S.S.C., Bequia. R.
Crichlow, Ralph, Trinidad, St. Andrew. R.
Crosby, S. O., S.C.C., Tobago, St. David and St. Patrick. R.
Cummins, C. C., Barbados, St. George. R.
Cummins, Geo., M.A., Trinidad (Archd.) and St. John's. C.
Drayton, J., S.C.C., Barbados, St. Ann's. C.
Dunn, G. G., S.C.C., Cariacou, Christ Church. R.
Eckel, A. E., C.M.S., Trinidad, St. Michael. C.
Eckel, Theodore, Barbados, St. Margaret's. C.
Eversley, Wm., S.C.C., Barbados, St. Barth. C.
Fitzpatrick, F., S.C.C., Grenada, St. Patrick. R.
Frederick, G. M. D., S.C.C., St. Vincent, Charlotte Par. R.
Gillett, C. J., St. A.C., Trinidad, St. Stephen. R.
Gittens, G. Duncan, S.C.C., Barbados, St. Lucy. R.
Graham, T., Trinidad, St. Thomas. C.
Grant, F. B., S.C.C. and M.A., Barbados, St. Mary. C.
Greaves, J. L., S.C.C., Barbados, Middle School. A.C.
Greenidge, N. H., S.C.C., Barbados, Boscobel Chapel. C.
Greenidge, T., S.C.C., Barbados.
Hawkins, E. J., C.M.S., Barbados, St. Patrick. C.
Huggins, H. N., S.C.C., Trinidad, St. Paul's. R.
Hunte, N., S.C.C., Grenada, St. George's. C.
Hutson, Eyre, S.C.C., Barbados, Holy Innocents. C.
Hutson, Henry, S.C.C., Barbados, St. Simons. C.
King, R. F., Barbados, St. Philip. R. (Rural Dean.)
Knight, E. S., St. Vincent, St. David's. C.
Knight, J. G., S.C.C., Trinidad, St. Matthew's. C.
Laborde, H. W., B.A., St. Vincent, St. George, and St. Andrew. R. and Ch. and Rural Dean.
Laurie, G. F., S.C.C., Barbados, Central School Master.
Laurie, W. B., S.C.C., Tobago, St. Andrew and St. George. R. and Rural Dean.
Le Maistre, P., M.A., Trinidad, St. Luke. R.
Matthews, J. W., Trinidad, Christ Church.
Mayers, J. S., B.D., Barbados, St. Mathias. C.
Moe, J. B., King's Coll. and S.C.C., Barbados, Assistant Curate at Cathedral.
Moore, H. W., S.C.C., Barbados, St. Andrew. R.
Norville, B. C., Barbados, St. Augustine's. C.
Parry, H. H., M.A., Barbados (Archdeacon).
Parry, J., M.A., Barbados, Society's Chaplain, and Tutor of Codrington College.
Payne, W. M., Barbados, St. Peter. R.
Petersen, C. L., St. Lucia, Trinity Church. M.
Piggott, Jos. T., Barbados, St. Jude. C.
Pitcher, J. H., A.K.C., Barbados, St. Patrick. A.C.
Redwar, H. R., S.C.C., Barbados, St. Paul. C.
Reece, A., S.C.C., Barbados, Christ Ch. R.
Richards, S. L. B., S.C.C., Trinidad, Holy Trinity, R. (R.D.)
Richards, Henry., S.C.C., Trinidad, St. Mary. R. and Ch.
Roach, E. R., Barbados, St. Saviour's. C.
Rock, Richard J., S.C.C., Grenada, St. David. C.
Rowe, Thomas, Barbados, Chaplain to Prisons.
Sealy, H., S.C.C., Barbados. A.C.
Semper, J., St. Lucia Rivière Dorée. M.
Sinckler, E.G., S.C.C., Barbados, St. Leonard. C.
Sisnett, G. W., Grenada, St. Andrew's and St. David. R.
Skeete, H.B., S.C.C., Barbados, St. Clem. & St. Swithin. C.
Smith, E. L., S.C.C., St. Vincent, St. Paul. M.
Smith, E.P., M.A., Barbados. Formerly Tutor of Codrington College.
Speed, T. L., S.C.C., Trinidad, St. Clement's. C.
Taitt, L. A., S.C.C., St. Vincent, A. C. Mast. of Gr. Sch.
Thomas, E. N., S.C.C. Barbados, St. Silas and St. Alban.
Thorne, E. S., S.C.C. & K.C.A., Barbados, St. Barnabas and St. Giles.
Wall, H. G., S.C.C., Trinidad, All Saints. C.
Watson, J. W. H., S.C.C., Barbados, All Saints. C.
Watson, W. C., S.C.C., Barbados, St. George's. A.C.
Webb, W. T., S.C.C., Barbados, Princ. of Codrington Coll.

Diocese of Antigua.

ANTIGUA, The Right Rev. William Walrond JACKSON, Lord Bishop of Antigua.—Consecrated Bp of Antigua 1860. (Episcopal Jurisdiction, Antigua, Nevis, St. Christopher, Montserrat, Virgin Islands, and Dominica; Area, 751 square miles; Pop. 106,372; Clergy, 35; Inc. of See, 2000*l.* from Consolidated Fund.) His Lordship was formerly Stud. of Codrington Coll. Barbados.

Archdeacons.

Antigua—Ven. George Clarke, M.A. 1849.
St. Christopher's—Ven. George Meade Gibbs, M.A. 1862.

Bishop's Chaplains.

Rev. W. J. Read, M.A. | Rev. E. O. Roach.

Abbott, R. R., R. of St. Peter's, Antigua.
Ambrister, T. A. C., Rector of St. Thomas, Middle Island, St. Kitts.
Barrow, R. H., R. of Holy Trinity, St. Christopher's.
Bindon, R. H., Rector of St. Paul's, Antigua.
Chaplyn, G. R., M.A., Min. of St. George's, Tortola.
Childe, J., Curate of St. Luke's, Antigua.
Collins, J. M., Rector of St. Philip's, Nevis.
Connell, T. G., Rector of St. Paul's, Antigua.
Cowley, William, Minister of Barbuda.
Culpeper, C. C., R. of St. Peter's, St. Christopher's.
Culpeper, A. H., Curate of St. Stephen's, Antigua.
Drinkwater, M. J., Curate of St. Mary's, Antigua.
Elliot, Eb., B.A., R. of Christ Church and St. Mary's, St. Christopher's.
Elliott, Edwin, R. of St. John's, Antigua.
Gibbs, Ven. G. M., M.A., R. of St. George, Basseterre.
Gittens, J. A., R. of St. Ann's, St. Christopher's.
Greenidge, J. W., Curate of St. James', Antigua.
Jemmett, George, B.A., R. of St. George's, Antigua.
Owen, Thomas, Asst. Cur. of St. John's, Antigua.
Paige, W. E., B.A., Curate of All Saints', Antigua, and Master of Grammar School.
Pemberton, J. H., B.A., R. of St. George's and St John's, Nevis.
Pemberton, W., R. of St. John's and St. Paul's, St. Kitt's.
Read, W. J., M.A., R. of St. Mary's, Antigua.
Roper, W. T., R. of St. George's, Dominica.
Sanders, W. A., R. of St. James's, and Minister of St. Thomas', Nevis.
Shervington, J., R. of St. Peter's, Montserrat.
Todd, G. H., R. of St. Anthony's and St. Patrick's, Montserrat.
Warneford, H., Minister of Anguilla.
Yeo, G. E., Curate of the Virgin Islands.

CLERGY OF THE ENGLISH CONGREGATIONS IN DANISH ISLANDS.

Branch, C. J., Rector of St. John's, St. Croix.
Dubois, J. A., Rector of St. Paul's, St. Croix.
Roach, E. O., British Chaplain at St. Thomas'.

Diocese of Guiana.

GUIANA, The Right Rev. William Piercy AUSTIN, Lord Bishop of Guiana, *Kingstown House, Georgetown, Demerara.*—Ex. Coll. Ox. B.A. 1829, M.A. 1835, B.D. and D.D. 1842. Consecrated Bp of Guiana 1842. (Episcopal Jurisdiction, Demerara, Essequibo, and Berbice; Area, 134,000 square miles; Pop. 121,678; Clergy, 33; Inc. of See, 2000*l.* from Consolidated Fund.) His Lordship was formerly Archd. of British Guiana.

Archdeacon of Demerara—Ven. H. Hyndman Jones, M.A.
Archdeacon of Berbice—Vacant.

Allison, J. J., M.A., Rector of St. Swithin's, Demerara.
Austin, William, Rector of St. John's, Essequebo, and Rur. Dean.
Austin, F. W., B.A., Rector of St. Michael's, Berbice.
Austin, W. G. G., M.A., Garrison Chaplain, Bishop's Chaplain, and Inspector of Schools.

Bhose, E. B., Missionary to East Indian Immigrants.
Brett, W. H., Rector of Holy Trinity Parish, and Superintendent of Pomeroon and Moruca Indian Missions.
Butt, G. H., B.A., Curate, Blankenburg, Demerara.
Campbell, W. H., Assistant Curate of St. Philip's, Georgetown.
Dance, C., Missionary, Berbice River.
Donnelly, G. W., Curate of Demerara River.
Drew, W. E., Assistant Curate of St. Mary's, Corentyne.
Drummond, W. R., Assistant Curate of All Saints', New Amsterdam.
Farrar, T., Chaplain H.M. Penal Settlement, and Curate of St. John's, Bartika.
Fox, George, M.A., Principal of Queen's College, and Bishop's Chaplain.
Fox, William, M.A., Incumbent of Christ Church, Georgetown.
Freeman, J., Curate of St. Alban's and St. Jude's, Berbice.
Harris, J. C., Curate of St. Joseph's, Port Mourant, Berbice.
Hillis, Thomas, Curate of St. Paul's and Christ Church, Wakenaam.
Jones, Archdeacon, M.A., Rector of St. George's Cathedral Church.
Large, J. J., Assistant Curate of All Saints' and All Souls', Berbice.
Lathbury, C. E., Curate of St. John's, New Forest, Parish of St. Patrick.
Manning, Samuel, Curate of St. Saviour's, Essequibo.
May, Henry John, Rector of St. Peter's, Essequibo.
Milner, T. R., Curate of St. Mary's, Beterverwagting, Parish of St. Paul.
Morgan, Charles, Curate of St. Bartholomew's, Queenstown, Essequibo.
Payne, J., Assistant Curate of St. Paul's Parish Church, Demerara.
Pieritz, J. A., Rector of St. Patrick's, Berbice.
Smith, David, M.A., Rector of St. Matthew's, Demerara.
Tanner, A. S., Curate of St. Philip's, Georgetown, Demerara.
Veness, W. T., Curate of St. Mary's and St. Margaret's, Berbice.
Walton, R., Assistant Curate of St. Philip's, Georgetown.
Webber, R. L., M.A., Incumbent of St. Philip's, Charles Town, Warden of Bishop's Coll., and Bishop's Chaplain.
Webber, W. J. B., Rector of St. Paul's, Demerara.
Wickham, H. E., Curate of St. Augustine's, Parish of St. Paul.
Wyatt, F. J., Rector of All Saints', Berbice, Rural Dean, and Bishop's Commissary.

Diocese of British Columbia.

COLUMBIA, The Right Rev. George HILLS, Lord Bishop of British Columbia, *Victoria, Vancouver's Island.*—Univ. Coll. Dur; Deac. 1827, Pr. 1829. Consecrated first Bishop of British Columbia 1859. (Episcopal Jurisdiction, British Columbia and Vancouver's Island; Area, 218,000 square miles; Pop. 100,000; Clergy, 15; Inc. of See, 600*l* from Colonial Bishoprics' Fund.) His Lordship was formerly P. C. of St. Nicholas, Great Yarmouth, 1848–59; Hon. Can. of Norwich Cathl. 1830–59. Author, *Christians called to be Saints* (Sermon), 1845; *A Letter of Counsel to the Parishioners of St. Leonard's, Leeds,* 1851.

Dean—The Very Rev. E. Cridge, B.A.
Archdeacon of Columbia—Vacant.
Archdeacon of Vancouver—The Ven. S. Gilson, M.A., Victoria.

Cave, J. B., Nanaimo.
Cridge, Very Rev. Edward, B.A., Rector of Christ Church, Cathedral, Victoria, Vancouver.
Doolan, R. A., B.A., Metlacatla.
Garrett, Alexander Charles, B.A., Principal of Indian Missions, Victoria.
Gilson, Ven. Samuel, M.A., Rector of St. John's, Victoria.
Good, John B., B.A., Yale.
Gribbell, F. B., Metlacatla.
Hayman, W. E., Sapperton.
Jenns, Percival, Nanaimo.
Reece, W. S., Cowichan.
Reynard, J.
Sheepshanks, John, M.A., Rector of Trinity Church, New Westminster, B.C.
Tomlinson, R., B.A.
Woods, T. C., M.A., Principal of Collegiate School, Victoria.

AUSTRALIA AND NEW ZEALAND.

Diocese of Sydney.

NEW SOUTH WALES.

SYDNEY, The Right Rev. Frederic BARKER, Lord Bishop of Sydney, and Metropolitan of Australia, *Sydney, New South Wales.*—Jesus Coll. Cam. B.A. 1829, M.A. 1835, B.D. and D.D. 1854. Consecrated Bp of Sydney 1854. (Episcopal Jurisdiction, the central portion of New South Wales; Area, 50,000 square miles; Pop. 209,144; Clergy, 74; Inc. of See, 2000*l* from Public Worship Fund of the Colony.) His Lordship was formerly P. C. of Upton, Cheshire, 1830–35; P. C. of St. Mary's, Edgehill, Liverpool, 1835–54; P. C. of Baslow, Derbyshire, 1854.

Dean and Archdeacon of Sydney—Very Rev. William Macquarie Cowper, M.A.
Canons—Rev. Robert Allwood, B.A.; Rev. William Horatio Walsh, M.A.
Chaplains—Rev. E. Synge, M.A.; Rev. R. L. King, B.A.

Allworth, William, St. Bartholomew's, Pyrmont.
Allwood, Robert, B.A., Incumbent of St. James's, Sydney.
Bailey, P. R. S., Curate of Mulsoe.
Barlow, W., M.A., Curate of All Saints', Paramatta.
Barnier, Joseph, Forbes.
Barry, Z., Randwick.
Burke, J. A., B.A., St. John's, Carcoar.
Byrnes, W., Paddington.
Carter, J., Picton and the Oaks.
Clarke, W. Brainwhite, M.A., Incumbent of St. Thomas's, Willoughby; with Lane Cove District, near Sydney.

Coombes, W., Dubbo.
Corlette, J. C., M.A., Jamberoo.
Creeny, W. F., B.A., Curate of St. Leonard's.
Cowper, W. M., M.A., Incumbent of St. Philip's, Sydney, Dean and Archdeacon of Sydney.
Donkin, Thomas, B.D., Incumbent of Pennant Hills.
Elder, John, Incumbent of St. Peter's, Richmond, with Kurrajong District.
Ewing, Thomas Campbell, Incumbent of St. Michael's, Wollongong.
Fletcher, J., B.D.
Garnsey, C. F., Windsor.
Gore, William Francis, B.A., Incumbent of All Saints', Parramatta.
Günther, James, Incumbent of St. John Baptist's, Mudgee.
Gurney, G., B.A., Manly.
Hassall, James Samuel, Incumbent of Trinity Ch., Berrima.
Hassall, Thomas, M.A., Colon. Ch., Inc. of St. Paul's, Cobbity, with Narellan.
Hayden, Thomas, M.A., Incumbent of St. John's, Darlinghurst.
Hodgson, William, M.A., Prin. of Moore Theological College, Liverpool, and Incumbent of Holdsworthy.
Horton, Thomas, Sutton Forest and Bong Bong.
Innes, G. A. C., B.A., Orange.
Jagg, F. C., Somerset.
Kemp, Charles Campbell, Incumbent of St. Stephen's, Camperdown, and Chap. to the Ch. of England Cemetery Company, near Sydney.
Kemmis, T., Incumbent of St. Mark's.

King, George, M.A., St. Peter's, Cook's River.
King, Hulton, B.A., Incumbent of St. Michael's, Surrey Hills.
King, R. Lethbridge, B.A., Incumbent of St. John's, Parramatta.
Langley, Henry, Curate of Bathurst.
Lisle, William, Incumbent of Holy Trinity Church, Kelso.
Lumsdaine, W., Ashfield and Burwood.
M'Arthur, George Fairfowl, Macquarie Fields, Liverpool.
Mayne, R. H., B.A., Hartley.
Mitchell, S., Waverley, Randwick, and Coogee.
Moreton, George, Curate of St. James's, Sydney.
Ord, C. R., Bishopthorpe.
O'Reilly, Thomas, St. Andrew's.
Palmer, H. A., Pitt Town and Wilberforce.
Pendrill, J., B.A., Glebe Point.
Priddle, C. F. Durham, Incumbent of St. Luke's, Liverpool.
Rich, C. H., Chaplain to the Jail.
Rogers, Edward, Holy Trinity, Sydney.
Ross, James, B.A., Rylstone.
Salinière, E. M., Waterloo.
Savigny, H., M.A., Bathurst.
Schleicher, J. T., Hunter's Hill, and Lane Cove.
Sharpe, Thomas, M.A., Incumb. of All Saints', Bathurst.
Scott, William, M.A., St. Paul's College.
Simpson, William West, M.A., Inc. of St. Luke's, Dapto.
Smith, Edward, B.A., Campbeltown.
Smith, Elijah, Officiating Min., Penrith and South Creek.
Smith, Percy G., Incumbent of St. Paul's, Canterbury.
Smith, T., St. Barnabas', South Sydney.
Stack, William, B.A., Balmain.
Stephen, Alfred Hewlett, B.A., St. Paul's, Sydney.
Stiles, Henry Tarleton, M.A., Incumb. of St. Matthew's, Windsor, with St. Philip's, Clydesdale.
Stiles, George, B.A., Sofala.
Stone, William, B.A.
Taylor, R., Castle Hill, Dooral and Pennant Hills.
Tingcombe, H., St. John's, Camden.
Tucker, J. K., D.D., Agent for B. and F. B. Society.
Turner, George Edward, S.C.L., St. Anne's, Ryde.
Unwin, T. W., Castlereagh, Emu, and Agnes Bank.
Uzzell, W. F. B., Curate of Dapto.
Vaughan, John, O'Connell Plain, Bathurst.
Vidal, George, B.A., Incumb. of St. Thomas, Mulgoa, with St. Thomas Greendale.
Walsh, Wm. Horatio, M.A., Incumbent of Christ Church, Sydney.
Wilkinson, Thomas Hattam, Appin.
Wilson, Thomas, B.A., Kiama.
Woodd, G. Napoleon, B.A., Denham Court.
Wood, William, Pennant Hills.
Young, R. W., Shoal Haven.

Diocese of Newcastle.

New South Wales.

Newcastle, The Right Reverend William Tyrrell, Lord Bishop of Newcastle, *Newcastle, New South Wales.*—St. John's Coll. Cam. 4th Sen. Opt. and B.A. 1831, M.A. 1834, B.D. and D.D. 1847; Deac. 1832, Pr. 1833. Consecrated Bp of Newcastle 1847. (Episcopal Jurisdiction, the northern part of New South Wales; Area, 500,000 square miles; Pop. 40,000; Clergy, 29; Inc. of See, 500*l* from Colonial Treasury, and interest of 6000*l* invested in the Colony.)

Canons—Rev. J. A. Greaves, M.A; Rev. Coles Child, B.A., Scone.

Commissaries—Rev. R. G. Boodle, M.A., Mells, near Frome; Rev. G. Currey, D.D., Charterhouse, London.

Addams, F. W. . . .	Paterson.
Blackwood, J. B.A. . .	Singleton.
Bode, G. Charles . .	St. John's, Newcastle.
Bode, F. D.	William's River.
Chapman, Robert . .	St. Mary's, West Maitland.
Child, Coles, B.A. . .	Scone.
Colyer, W. K. . . .	Mast. of Gr. Sch. West Maitland.
Curry, C. R.	Namoi River.
Glennie, A.	Lochinvar.
Greaves, J. A. M.A. .	(Absent on leave).
Greenway, C. C. . .	Bundarrah.
Hawkins, W. C. . .	Manning River.
Hungerford, S. . . .	Armidale.
Johnson, J. H. B.A. .	Glen Innes.
Kemp, F. R. . . .	Port Macquarie.
Millard, H. S. M.A. . .	Mast. of Gr. Sch. Newcastle.
Nash, J. J. M.A. . .	Murrurundi.
Norton, J	Lower Hawkesbury.
Selwyn, A. E. . . .	Christ Church, Newcastle.
Shaw, A.	Stroud.
Shaw, Bowyer E. B.A. .	Wollombi.
Shaw, John, B.A. . .	Brisbane Water.
Shaw, T. H.	Richmond River.
Simm, S.	Raymond Terrace.
Thackeray, J. R. . .	St. Paul's, West Maitland.
Tyrrell, L. B.A. . . .	E. Maitland.
Walsh, C.	Morpeth.
Whinfield, J. F. R. . .	Tamworth.
White, W. E. B.A. . .	Muswellbrook.
Wilson, W. S. B.A. . .	Cassilis.
Wood, J. S. . . .	

Diocese of Grafton and Armidale.

Grafton and Armidale, The Right Rev. William Collinson Sawyer, Lord Bishop of Grafton and Armidale.—Oriel Coll. Ox. B.A. 1854, M.A. 1858, D.D. 1867. Consecrated Bp of Grafton and Armidale 1867. (Episcopal Jurisdiction, between 29 and 32 degs. of S. Lat; Area, 140,000 square miles; Pop. 50,000; Inc. of See, interest of 10,000*l*.)

Archdeacon of Grafton—The Ven. W. J. Dampier, M.A.

Chaplain—Rayner Winterbotham, LL.B.

Winterbotham, Rayner, LL.B. Grafton.

Diocese of Goulburn.

New South Wales.

Goulburn, The Right Rev. Mesac Thomas, Lord Bishop of Goulburn.—Trin. Coll. Cam. B.A. 1840, M.A. 1843, D.D. 1813; Deac. 1840 and Pr. 1841 by Bp of Wor. Consecrated Bp of Goulburn 1863. (Episcopal Jurisdiction, part of New South Wales; Area, 50,000 square miles; Pop. 70,000; Clergy, 29; Inc. of See, interest of 14,000*l*. invested in the colony.) His Lordship was formerly P. C. of Attleborough, Warwickshire; V. of Taddenham St. Martin, Suffolk; Sec. to the Colonial Ch. and Sch. Soc.

Chaplain—F. A. C. Lillingston, B.A.

Allan, James, Braidwood.
Byng, C. J., Tumut.
Druitt, Thomas, Cooma.
Earl, R. T., Hay.
Faunce, A.D., Araluen.
Goodwin, T. H., Wentworth and Euston.
Harpur, S. S., B.A., Wagga Wagga.
Hulbert, D. P. M., M.A., Pejar.
Knight, J. L., M.A., Bega, Panbula, Eden.
Jones, D. E., Albury.
Laigh, R., Goulburn, &c.
Lillingston, F. A. C., B.A., Yass.
L'Oste, C. F., Balranald, &c.
Percival, Sam., M.A., Bombala.
Pownall, W. H., Young, &c.
Proctor, E. W., Bungonia.
Puddicombe, A. T., Moruya.
Ross, Henry, Gunning.
Seaborn, F. R., Binda, Bolong, &c.
Seaborn, H. S., Gundagai.
Smith, Pierce Galliard, M.A., Canberra.
Soares, Alberto Dias, Queanbeyan.
Sowerby, William, Goulburn.
Ware, John Maitland, Corowa.

Diocese of Melbourne.

VICTORIA.

MELBOURNE, The Right Rev. Charles PERRY, Lord Bishop of Melbourne, *Melbourne, Victoria*.—Trin. Coll. Cam. Sen. Wrang. 1st cl. Cl. Trip. Sen. Smith's Prizeman and B.A. 1828, M.A. 1831, B.D. and D.D. 1847. Consecrated Bp of Melbourne 1847. (Episcopal Jurisdiction, the Province of Victoria; Area, 80,000 square miles; Pop. 540,322; Clergy, 105; Inc. of See, 1333*l* 6*s* 8*d*—1000*l* allowance from Colonial Treasury, and 333*l* 6*s* 8*d* from Colonial Bishoprics' Fund.) His Lordship was formerly Fell. of Trin. Coll. Cam. Author, *Clerical Education considered with an essential reference to the Universities* (a Letter to the Bp of Lich.) 1841; *The Christian's Light shining to God's Glory* (a Sermon), 1847; *A Charge*, with two Sermons, *On the Church* and *Divisions in the Church*, Lond. 1852; *Five Sermons* (preached before the Univ. of Cam. 1855), 1856, 3*s*.

Dean and Archdeacon of Melbourne—The Very Rev. Hussey Burgh Macartney, D.D.

Archdeacon of Geelong—The Ven. Theodore Carlos Benoni Stretch, M.A.

Archdeacon of Portland—

Archdeacon of Castlemaine—The Ven. A. Crawford, M.A.

Chaplains—The Rev. Septimus Lloyd Chase, M.A; The Rev. George Goodman, M.A.

Adeney, Henry William Howells, Minister of St. Peter's, Ballarat.
Allanby, Christopher Gibson, Minister of Little Bendigo, Brown Hill, and the Forest.
Allnutt, John Charles Parrot, Minister of Carisbrook.
Ashe, Matthew Henry, Curate of Blackwood.
Baker, Louis Alexander, Minister of Tower Hill, &c.
Bardin, Charles Peter Macan, B.A., Incumbent of Brunswick, &c.
Barker, Ralph, Minister of Talbot.
Barlow, John, B.A., Incumbent of St. John's, Melbourne.
Barlow, Robert Borrowes, B.A., Incumbent of St. Mark's, Melbourne.
Beamish, Peter Teulon, LL.D., Incumbent of Warrnambool.
Bean, Willoughby, Chaplain of Lunatic Asylum, Melbourne.
Becher, Michael Henry, B.A., Vicar of St. James', Melbourne.
Booth, Caleb, Minister of Wangaratta.
Beazler, Amos, Minister of Bairnsdale.
Brennan, James Deane, Minister of Maryborough.
Bromby, John Edward, D.D., Principal of Melbourne Grammar School.
Browne, Edwin, Minister of Mansfield.
Carlisle, Joseph, Curate of St. John's, Melbourne.
Carter, William, B.A., Minister of Pentridge.
Chalmers, William, Minister of Inglewood, Newbridge, and Tarnagulla.
Chase, Septimus Lloyd, M.A., Incumbent of St. Paul's, Melbourne.
Cole, Thomas Cornelius, M.A., Minister of Malvern and Oakleigh.
Collins, Robert Reeves, B.A., Minister of Harrow.
Cooper, Astley, Incumbent of St. Paul's, Geelong.
Cooper, William Henry, Itinerating Minister in Interior of Colony.
Crawford, Archibald, M.A., Incumbent of Christchurch, Castlemaine.
Cresswell, Arthur William, M.A., Minister of Woodend and Newham.
Croxton, William Richard, Incumbent of All Saints', Sandhurst.
Cummins, Robert Turner, A.K.C., Incumbent of St. Paul's, Ballarat.
Despard, George Pakenham, B.A., Minister of Dunolly.
Dickinson, Rivers Beachcroft, Incumbent of St. Luke's, Emerald Hill.
Donaldson, Joseph Macafee, Minister of Mortlake, Caramut, and Hexham.

FFF 2

Edwards, Henry John, Minister of Barrabool and Highton.
Fellows, Walter, B.A., Incumbent of St. John's, Toorak.
Firth, John, Minister of Kensington, Point Henry, &c.
Floyd, William, Curate of Christchurch, Ballarat.
Freeman, John, Minister of Benalla.
Fulford, John, Incumbent of St. John's, Belfast.
Garlick, Thomas Boothroyd, Minister of St. Paul's, Gisborne.
Gilbertson, James, Minister of Tallarook, &c.
Glover, James, Minister of Snapper Point and District.
Goodman, George, M.A., Incumbent of Christchurch, Geelong.
Goodwin, Thomas Hill, Missionary to Aborigines.
Gregory, John Herbert, Incumbent of All Saints', St. Kilda.
Guinness, William Newton, M.A., Incumbent of Christchurch, South Yarra.
Hall, John Kay, Minister of Farraville, &c.
Hall, William, Minister of Northcote and Preston.
Handfield, Henry Hewitt Paulet, Incumbent of St. Peter's, Melbourne.
Hayward, Rowland, Minister of Kew.
Heron, Thomas, Incumbent, Parish of Hamilton.
Hollis, Josiah, Minister of Eltham.
Holt, Samuel Bealey, Minister of Fayerstown, &c.
Homan, Philip, B.A., Minister of Ararat.
Hopkins, Francis, B.A., Incumbent of All Saints', Geelong.
Howard William London Corbett, Incumbent of Beechworth.
L'Oste, John William Henry, Minister of Heathcote.
Love, James Graham, Minister of Rutherglen.
Low, John Stanley, Minister of Caulfield.
Lynar, James, B.A., Incumbent of St. John's, Heidelberg.
Macartney, George David, LL.B., Minister of Rosedale, &c.
Macartney, Hussey Burgh, D.D., Dean and Archdeacon of Melbourne.
Macartney, jun., Hussey Burgh, Chaplain of Industrial Schools, &c.
MacCullagh, John Christian, Minister of Lancefield.
McCausland, Anderson John, Minister of Echuca.
Mahalm, Robert, Minister of Woodspoint, &c.
Martin, Matthew Henry, Minister of Camberwell.
May, John Henry, Minister of Yackandandah.
Morris, Henry Charles Edward, Minister of Whittlesea, &c.
Perks, Charles Thomas, Incumbent of St. Stephen's, Richmond.
Perry, Charles Stuart, Curate of St. John's, Melbourne.
Philipps, Thomas M. B., B.A., Minister of Clunes.
Platts, Frederick Charles, Incumbent of Trinity, Sandridge.
Pollard, George, Minister of Daylesford.
Potter, John, B.A., Incumbent of Christ Church, Ballarat.
Potter, Robert, Incumbent of St. Mary's, Melbourne.
Poynder, Robert, Minister of Broadmeadows, &c.
Pryce, Edward Gifford, Minister of White Hills.
Puckle, Edward, Minister of Essendon.
Pyne, Alexander, M.A., Minister of Camperdown.
Radcliffe, E. S., B.A., Minister of Learmouth, &c.
Rupp, Charles Ludwig Herman, Min. of Cranbourne, &c
Russell, Francis Thomas Cusack, D.C.L., Minister of the Wannon River District.
Russell, Garrett John, B.A., Incumbent of Buninyong.
Sabine, J. Coulthard, Minister of Bacchus' Marsh.
Sabine, Thomas, Minister of Birregurra, &c.
Seddon, David, M.A., Incumbent of Christchurch, St. Kilda.
Serjeant, Thomas Woolweck, M.A., Minister of Sale.
Sheldon, John, Minister of Winchelsea.
Singleton, William, M.A., Curate of St. Andrew's, Brighton.
Smith, Frederick, Minister of Station Peak, &c.
Spencer, George, Curate of Buninyong.
Stair, John Bettridge, Minister of St. Arnaud.
Stephens, Richard, Curate of Christchurch, Castlemaine.
Stone, James, Minister of Pleasant Creek and Navarre
Stretch, Theodore Carlos Benoni, M.A., Archdeacon of Geelong.
Stretch, John Cliffe Theodore, B.A., Incumbent of Maldon.
Studdert, George, B.A., Chaplain of Gaols, Melbourne.
Taylor, Samuel, B.A., Incumbent of St. Andrew's, Brighton

Thomson, James, Chaplain to Hospitals and Benevolent Asylum, Melbourne.
Vance, George Oakley, M.A., Incumbent of St. Paul's, Kyneton.
Walker, Barnabas Shaw, Incumbent of St. Philip's, Melbourne.
Walker, Samuel, Minister of Smythesdale and Scarsdale.
*Ware, John Maitland, Minister of Wahgunyah.
Watson, George Wade, Minister of Eagle Hawk.
Watson, Henry Crocker, Minister of Taradale and Malmsbury.
Watson, John, Minister of Prahran.
Watson, James Henry, B.A., Minister of Kilmore, &c.
Wilkinson, George, B.A., Incumbent of Trinity, Williamstown.
Wilkinson, Henry John, Minister of Queenscliff.
Wilson, James Yelverton, Incumbent of St. Stephen's, Portland.
Wollaston, Henry Newton, Incumbent of Trinity, Melbourne.
Wood, William, B.A., Incumb. of Christchurch, Hawthorne.
Yeatman, Edward Kelson, Minister of Avoca, &c.

* This Clergyman is resident in the Diocese of Goulburn, and officiates in the diocese of Melbourne under special arrangements.

Diocese of Adelaide.

SOUTH AUSTRALIA.

ADELAIDE, The Right Rev. Augustus SHORT, Lord Bishop of Adelaide, *Adelaide, South Australia.*—Westminster Sch; Ch. Ch. Ox; 1st cl. Lit. Hum. and B.A. 1824, M.A. 1826, B.D. and D.D. 1847; Deac. 1826, Pr. 1827. Consecrated Bp of Adelaide 1847. (Episcopal Jurisdiction, South Australia; Clergy, 32; Inc. of See, 240*l* from Colonial Bishoprics' Fund, and interest of 13,240*l* invested in the Colony.) His Lordship was formerly V. of Ravensthorpe, Northants, 1835-47; a Rural Dean 1844; Bampton Lecturer 1846. Author, *Sermons principally to Illustrate the Remedial Character of the Christian Scheme*, Oxford, 1838.

Dean—Very Rev. James Farrell, M.A.

Archdeacon of Adelaide—Ven. W. J. Woodcock.

Archdeacon of Flinders—Ven. T. N. Twopeny, M.A.

Honorary Canons.
W. H. Coombs, Rural Dean.
G. H. Farr, Head Master of St. Peter's College School.
C. Marryat, Examining Chaplain.
A. R. Russell, Rural Dean.

Andrews, W.B., Mitcham.
Boake, J. A., B.A., Clare and Penwortham.
Clayfield, W. A., Assistant Minister, Mount Torrens.
Coombs, W. H., Gawler.
Craig, Basil Tudor, M.A., Chaplain to the Bishop.
Dove, G. H., M A., St. Andrew's, Walkerville.
Ewbank, W. W., M.A., Blakiston and Balhannah.
Farrell, Very Rev. J., M.A., Trinity Church, South Adelaide.
Farr, G. H., M.A., Head Master of St. Peter's College School.
Field, T., M.A., Glenelg.
Garratt, F., M.A., All Saints', Hindmarsh.
Green, S., Ginchen Bay.
Hammond, O., Poonindee and St. Thomas's, Port Lincoln.
Howell, E. T., M.A., St. Jude's, Port Elliott.
Howitt, H., Strathalbyn.
Ibbetson, J. D. H., St. John's cum St. Bartholomew's.
Jenkins, E., St. Matthew's, Kensington.
L'Estrange, Savile, Melrose.
Marryat, C., M.A., St. Paul's, Port Adelaide.
Miller, E. K., Willunga and Noalunga.
Mudie, W. H., Glen Osmond.
Needham, R., Mount Gambier.
Neville, T. R., Magill and Campbelton.
Pollit, H. M., Woodville.
Pollitt, James, St. Luke's, South Adelaide.
Reid, R., Assistant Minister, Trinity, South Adelaide.
Russell, A., St. Paul's, South Adelaide.
Simmons, P. K., St. John's, Salisbury.
Smyth, Jasper, Assistant Minister, Mount Gambier.
Stanton, Lionel, M.A., Kooringa.
Titherington, J. B., Riverton and Auburn.
Twopeny, Ven. T. N., M.A., Melrose Mission.
Williams, F., M.A., St. Peter's College School.
Wilson, G. Maryon, M.A., Assistant Minister of Christ Church, Adelaide.

Diocese of Perth.

WESTERN AUSTRALIA.

PERTH, The Right Rev. Matthew Blagden HALE, Lord Bishop of Perth, *Perth, Western Australia.*—Trin. Coll. Cam. B.A. 1835, M.A. 1838, D.D. 1857; Deac. 1836, Pr. 1837. Consecrated Bp of Perth 1857. (Episcopal Jurisdiction, Western Australia; Inc. of See, interest of 4000*l* granted by the Colonial Bishoprics' Fund, and invested in the Colony.) His Lordship was formerly Archd. of Adelaide, South Australia.

Archdeacon of Perth—Ven. James Brown, M.A.

Commissary in England for the Bishop—The Rev. R. N. Russell, M.A., Rector of Beachampton, Bucks.

Alderson, R., M.A., Convict Establishment, Fremantle.
Bostock, G. J., B.A., St. John's Church, Fremantle.
Brown, H. W., B.A., Vasse.
Brown, Ven. James, M.A., Cath. Church of St. George's, Perth.
Clay, Charles, Northam.
Grimaldi, H. B., Guildford.
Harper, C., Toodyay.
Lynch, Frederick, B.A., Beverley District.
Macsorley, A. K., Albany, King George's Sound.
Millett, Edward, B.A., York.
Mitchell, W., Chaplain to the Convicts in Perth.
Price, J. S., B.A., Pinjarrah.
Sadler, George, B.A., Gingin.
Sweeting, G. H., M.A., Upper and Middle Swan.
Tayler, F. T., Head Master of the Perth Collegiate School.
Withers, Joseph, Banbury.

Diocese of Tasmania.

TASMANIA, The Right Rev. Charles Henry BROMBY, Lord Bishop of Tasmania, *Hobart Town, Tasmania.*—St. John's Coll. Cam. B.A. 1837, M.A. 1840, D.D. 1864; Deac. 1838, Pr. 1839. Consecrated Bp of Tasmania 1864. (Episcopal Jurisdiction, Tasmania and Norfolk Island; Area, 24,002 square miles; Pop. 89,977; Clergy, 46; Inc. of See, 1100*l* from the Colonial Treasury, and interest of 5000*l* granted by the Colonial Bishoprics' Fund and invested in the Colony.) His Lordship was formerly P. C. of St. Paul's, Cheltenham, 1843-64; Prin. of Normal Coll. Cheltenham, 1847-64. Author, *The Pupil-Teacher's History and Grammar of the English Language*, 16th edit. 2*s* 6*d*; *The Pupil-Teacher's History, &c. Abridged*, 8*d*; *Papers for the Schoolmaster*, 7 vols. 2*s* 6*d* and 3*s* each; *The Sorrows of Bethany* (Sermons), 1*s* 6*d*; *National Education*, 1837, 2*d*; *The Church, Privy Council, and the Working Classes*, 1*s*; Tracts, *A Sketch of the Book of Common Prayer*, 2nd edit. 4½*d*; *The Rule of Faith*, 3*d*; *Early Church History to the Martyrdom of St. Paul*, 3*d*; *The Antiquity and Original Independence of the British Church*, 3*d*; *Early Church History to the Sixth Century*, 3*d*; *Liturgy and Church History*, 2nd edit. 1*s* 9*d*.

Dean—Very Rev. F. H. Cox, B.A.

Archdeacon of Hobart Town—Ven. Rowland Robert Davies, B.A.

Archdeacon of Launceston—Ven. Thomas Reibey, M.A.

Chaplain to the Bishop—H. B. Bromby, B.A.

Chancellor of the Diocese—Sir Valentine Fleming, Knt., Chief Justice.

Registrar of the Diocese—John Harrison, Esq.

Adams, E. P., Deloraine.
Adams, H. W., Jericho and Coalbrooke Dale.
Arthur, C. R., B.A., Evandale.
Ball, Benjamin, B.A., Broadmarsh.
Barkway, Augustus, St. Paul's, Launceston.
Brammall, C. J., St. John's, Hobart Town.
Bromby, H. B., B.A., Cathedral, Hobart Town.
Browne, W. H., LL.D., St. John's, Launceston.
Brownrigg, Francis, B.A., Paterson's Plains.
Brownrigg, Ross.
Buckland, J. R., B.A., Head Master of Hutchins' School, Hobart Town.
Burrowes, John, M.A., Pontville.
Chambers, John, Fingal.
Cox, Fred. H., B A., St. David's Cathedral, Hobart Town.
Davenport, Arthur, B.A., Trinity, Hobart Town, Secretary to the Synod.
Davies, Arch. R. R., B.A., Without Cure.
Dixon, John, Windermere.
Dobson, Charles, Prosser's Plains.
Drew, H. E., Stanley, Circular Head.
Eastman, George, Port Arthur.
Fereday, John, M.A., Georgetown.
Ffookes, S. B., M.A., Perth.
Freeman, Edward, M.A., Brown's River.
Galer, David, Richmond.
Garrard, Thomas, B.D., Macquarie Plains.
Gellibrand, J. T., M.A., St. John's, Hobart Town.
Hales, Francis, B.A., Trinity, Launceston.
Harris, R. D., M.A., Head Master of the High School, Hobart Town.
Hesketh, W.M., M.A., Bothwell.
Hudspeth, Francis, M.A., St. John the Evangelist, New Town.
Irwin, H. O., M.A., Hagley.
Kane, Henry Plough, M.A., Rostella School.
Martin, C. J., Torquay.
Mason, A. N., Carrick and Hadspen.
Mayson, Joseph, B.A., Swansea.
Mitchell, H., Illawarra.
Murray, W. W. F., M.A., New Norfolk.
Nobbs, G. H., Norfolk Island.
Norman, James, Without Cure.
Norman, J. Marsh, Lake River and Cressey.
Parsons, S., D.D., All Saints, Hobart Town.
Poole, H. J., M.A., Sorell.
Quilter, F. W., M.A., New Town.
Reibey, Archdeacon Thomas, M.A., Carrick.
Richardson, William, B.A., Avoca.
Smales, J. H., Hospitals and Pauper Asylum, Hobart Town.
Smith, George Banks, St. George's, Hobart Town.
Stackhouse, Alfred, M.A., Longford.
Stansfield, T., Franklin.
Symonds, E., D'Entrecasteaux Channel and Bruni Island.
Wayne, A., Greenponds.
Williams, Montague, Westbury.
Wilson, Robert, Clarence Plains and Kangaroo Point.
Wilson, G. M., B.A., Campbell Town.
Wright, George, Hamilton.

Diocese of Brisbane.

QUEENSLAND.

BRISBANE, The Right Rev. Edward Wyndham TUFNELL, Lord Bishop of Brisbane, *Moreton Bay, New South Wales*.—Wad. Coll. Ox. 3rd cl. Lit. Hum. and B.A. 1837, M.A. 1840; Deac. 1837 by Bp of Ox. Pr. 1839 by Bp of Salis. Consecrated first Bp of Brisbane 1859. (Episcopal Jurisdiction, the Province of Queensland; Inc. of See, Interest of 5000*l* from Colonial Bishoprics' Fund.) His Lordship was formerly C. of Broadtown, near Marlborough, 1840–46; R. of Beachingstoke, Wilts, 1846–57; R. of St. Peter's and St. Paul's, Marlborough, 1857–59.

Chancellor—J. Bramston, Esq. D.C.L.

Archdeacon and Examining Chaplain—Ven. Benjamin Glennie, B.A.

Commissary in England.
Rev. Brymer Belcher, St. Gabriel's, Pimlico, London.

Black, James K.	(Licensed without Cure of Souls).
Bliss, John, M.A.	North Brisbane.
Botting, W. J.	
Clayton, Chas. Jas. M.A.	Drayton.
Claughton, H. C. B.A.	Maryborough.
Creyke, Robert, B.A.	Unattached.
Danvers, George Gibberne	Warwick.
Dunning, William Henry	Gayndah.
Glennie, B. B.A. (Archd.)	Warwick.
Harte, William Thomas	
Hoare, John Wm. Deane	South Brisbane.
Jones, Joshua	
Jones, Thomas	North Brisbane.
Matthews, James	Fortitude Valley
Moberley, Edmund G.	Dalby.
Moffatt, Jas. Robt. B.A.	Kangaroo Point.
Moseley, John	Ipswich.
Neville, E. B.	
Searle, C.	Rockhampton.
Tanner, W.	Port Mackay.
Thackeray, Richard, B.A.	Darling Downs.

Diocese of New Zealand,

Bishop and Metropolitan—

Archdeacons—Ven. T. F. Lloyd, Waitemata; Ven. H. Govett, Taranaki.

Examining Chaplain—Ven. Archd. Lloyd.

Ashwell, Benjamin Y.	North Shore.
Baker, C.	Unattached.
Blackburn, Samuel, M.A.	Principal of St. John's College, Auckland.
Bree, E. N.	All Saints', Auckland.
Brown, H. H.	Taranaki.
Burrows, Robert	Unattached.
Chapman, Rev. T.	St. Barnabas', Auckland.
Clarke, E.	Wainate.
Dudley, B. T.	Holy Sepulchre, Auckland.
Duffus, J.	Mango ui.
Dunn, C. B.	Oruru.
Gould, F.	Otahuhu.
Govett, Henry (Archd.)	Taranaki.
Grace, T. S.	Taupo.
Hall, F. H.	Howick.
Heywood, E. H.	Remuera.
Hutton, Thomas B.	(Invalided.)
Jones, D.	St. Matthew's, Auckland.
Kinder, J.	Grammar School, Auckland.
Lloyd, J. F. (Archd.)	St. Paul's, Auckland.
Lush, Vicesimus	District Visitor, Lower Waikato.
Matthews, Joseph	Kaitaia.
Maunsell, Robert, D.D.	St. Mary's, Auckland.
Patiki, P.*	Hokianga.
Pritt, Lonsdale	District Visitor, Upper Waikato.
Purchas, A. G.	Unattached.
Tangata, Leonard*	Mangonui.
Tarawhiti, S.*	Taupiri.
Taupaki, M.*	Bay of Islands.
Te Moanaroa, J.*	Kohanga.

Diocese of Waiapu.

WAIAPU, The Right Rev. William WILLIAMS, Lord Bishop of Waiapu, *Tauranga, New Zealand*.—Magd. Hall, Ox. B.A. 1825, D.C.L. 1851. Consecrated first Bp of Waiapu 1859. (Episcopal Jurisdiction, so much of the Northern Island as lies east of 176° E. long. and north of 39° S. lat; Native Pop. about 16,000; Clergy, 10; Inc.

of See, 450*l* from the Ch. Miss. Soc.) His Lordship was formerly Archd. of Waiapu, and Chap. to the Bp of New Zealand 1844-59.

Archdeacon of Tauranga—Ven. A. N. Brown.

Archdeacon of Waiapu—Ven. W. L. Williams, B.A.

Brown, A. N. (Archd.)	Tauranga.
Huata, T.*	Wairoa.
Kawhia, D.*	Whareponga.
Pahewa, Matiaha*	Tokomaru.
Spencer, S. M.	Tarawera.
Tawhaa, Hare*	Turanga.
Te Ahu, I.*	Maketu.
Te Rangamaro, Rihara*	Tauranga.
Turei, Mohi*	Waiapu.

Diocese of Wellington.

WELLINGTON, The Right Rev. Charles James ABRAHAM, Lord Bp of Wellington, *The College, Wellington, New Zealand.*—Queens' Coll. Cam. B.A. 1837, M.A. 1840, D.D. 1850; Deac. 1838, Pr. 1839. Consecrated first Bp of Wellington 1858. (Episcopal Jurisdiction so much of the Northern Island as lies south of 39° S. latitude; European Pop. about 15,000; Clergy, 10; Inc. of See from a general Church Fund in the Colony.) His Lordship was formerly Fell. of King's Coll. Cam; Archd. of Waitemata, and Chap. to the Bp of New Zealand.

Archdeacon of Kapiti—Ven. O. Hadfield.

Abraham, Thomas	Trentham.
Andrew, J. C.	Unattached.
Desbois, D.	Otaki.
Fancourt, Thomas	Porirua and Karori.
Hadfield, O. (Archd.)	Kapiti.
Herring, John	Inc. of St. James', Lower Hutt, with Christ Church, Taita.
Knell, A.	Wairarapa.
Maxwell, P. Hay, M.A.	St. Paul's, Wellington.
Nicholls, C. H. S.	Whanganui.
Ronaldson, W.	Wairarapa.
St. Hill, H. W.	Kaiwarawara School.
Stock, Arthur, B.A.	St. Peter's, Wellington.
Taylor, B. K. M.A.	Whanganui.
Taylor, Richard, M.A.	Whanganui.
Townsend, John	Ahuriri.
Williams, S.	Ahuriri.

Diocese of Nelson.

NELSON, The Right Rev. Andrew Burn SUTER, Lord Bp of Nelson, *Bishopsdale, Nelson, New Zealand.*—Trin. Coll. Cam. B.A. 1853, M.A. 1856, D.D. 1866. Consecrated Bp of Nelson 1866. (Episcopal Jurisdiction, Middle Island of New Zealand from Cook's Strait to 43° S. lat.; Area, 15,000,000 acres; Pop. 50,000 Colonists and 1000 Natives; Clergy, 12; Inc. of See, 500*l* from a General Church Fund in the Colony.) His Lordship was formerly C. of St. Dunstan's-in-the-West, Fleet-street, Lond. 1856-59; P. C. of All Saints', Spicer-street, Spitalfields, 1859-66.

Chaplain—W. H. Ewald, M.A.

Commissaries in England—Revs. E. Auriol, M.A; M. Gibbs, M.A; and John Patteson, M.A.

Butt, H. F.	Wairau.
Ewald, W. H. M.A.	
Halcombe, C. H. J. B.A.	Golden Bay.
Harvey, B. W. M.A.	
Johnstone, George Henry, B.A. (Commissary)	Nelson.
Lewis, W. D. B.	Waimea, East.
Mackean, C. L.	Second Master, Nelson College.
Muller, C. O. M.A.	
Poole, S. M.A.	Moutucka.
Thorpe, R. J. M.A.	
Twogood, A. B.A.	Waimea, Mid.
Tripp, Francis, B.A.	Waimea, South.
Tudor, T. L.	Picton.

Diocese of Christchurch.

CHRISTCHURCH, The Right Rev. Henry John Chitty HARPER, Lord Bishop of Christchurch, *Christchurch, New Zealand.*—Queen's Coll. Ox. B.A. 1826; M.A. 1840, D.D. 1856; Deac. 1831 by Bp of Roch. Pr. 1832 by Bp of Lin. Consecrated first Bp of Christchurch 1856. (Episcopal Jurisdiction, Middle Island of New Zealand, from 43° S. lat. to its southern extremity, Stewart's Island, the Auckland and all adjacent Islands; Pop 28,000; Clergy, 16; Inc. of See, 600*l* from lands set apart by the Canterbury Association, and interest of 1100*l* invested in the Colony.) His Lordship was formerly Conduct of Eton Coll. 1832-40; V. of Stratfield-Mortimer, near Reading, Berks, 1840-56.

Dean—Very Rev. Henry Jacobs, M.A., Incumbent of St. Michael's and All Angels, Christchurch.

Canons:
- Ven. H. W. Harper, M.A., Archdeacon.
- Rev. B. W. Dudley, Incumbent of Rangiora, Rural Dean.
- Rev. G. Cotterill, B.A., Diocesan Secretary.
- Rev. J. Wilson, M.A., Diocesan Treasurer.

Commissary in England—Rev. T. Stevens, M.A. Bradfield Rectory, Reading.

Aylmer, W. M.A.	Akaroa.
Bagshaw, J. C. M.A.	Avonside.
Bluett, W. J. G. M.A.	Leeston.
Bowen, C.	Riccarton with Halswell.
Brown, L. L. B.A.	Geraldine.
Carpenter, G. M.A.	Assistant Curate of Riccarton with Halswell.
Cholmondeley, G. J.	Heathcote.
Fendall, H. B.A.	Assistant Curate of Ashley.
Foster, G.	Timaru.
Harris, W. C. M.A.	Head Master, Christ's College, Grammar School.
Hoare, J. O'B. M.A.	St. John the Baptist, Christchurch.
Hutchinson, J. B.A.	Ashburton.
Hutchinson, W. B.A.	Not yet settled.
Jackson, R. S.	Prebbleton with Templeton.
Knowles, F.	Lyttelton.
Lingard, E. A.	St. Luke's, Christchurch.
Moore, L. M.A.	Papanui.
O'Callaghan, A. P. M.A.	Oxford with Cust and Eyreton.
Stack, J. W.	Maori Mission.
Torlesse, H.	Governor's Bay.
Turrell, C. M.A.	Leithfield with Ashley.
Willock, W. W. M.A.	Kaiapoi.
Bradley, R. R. B.A.	Unattached.

Diocese of Dunedin.

DUNEDIN, The Right Rev. Henry Lascelles JENNER, Lord Bishop of Dunedin.—Trin. Hall, Cam. LL.B. 1841, D.D. 1867; Deac. 1843 by Abp of Cant. Pr. 1844 by Bp of Ely. Consecrated Bp of Dunedin 1866. (Episcopal Jurisdiction, the Provinces of Otago and Southland in the Middle Island of New Zealand, and the adjacent Islands; Clergy, 8.) His Lordship was formerly C. of Chevening, Kent, 1843-46, St. Columb Major, Cornwall, 1846-49, Antony, Cornwall, 1849-51, Brasted, Kent, 1852; V. of Preston-next-Wingham, Kent, 1854-66.

Dasent, A.	Waikonaiti.
Edwards, E. G. B.A.	St. Paul's, Dunedin; Rural Dean of Otago and Southland.
Gifford, A.	Oamaru.
Granger, E. H. B.A.	All Saints', Dunedin.
Oldham, W. T.	Riverton.
Simmons, W. F. C. M.A.	High School, Dunedin.
Stanford, E. B.A.	Tokomairiro.
Tanner, W. P. M.A.	Invercargill.

Melanesian, or South Pacific Isles.

Missionary Bishop—The Right Rev. J. C. PATTESON, D.D. 1861.

Codrington, R. H. M.A. | Palmer, J. S.
Pritt, Lonsdale, M.A.

Diocese of Honolulu.

Bishop—The Right Rev. Thomas Nettleship STALEY, D.D. 1861.

Archdeacon—Ven. G. Mason, M.A.

Elkington, J. J; Hoapili, W. (Kanai, Hawaii); Turner, C. B; Warren, G; Whipple, G. B. (Wailuku); Williamson, C. G.

THE MEDITERRANEAN.

Diocese of Gibraltar.

GIBRALTAR, The Right Rev. and Hon. Charles Amyand HARRIS, Lord Bishop of Gibraltar.—Oriel Coll. Ox. B.A. 1835, All Souls', M.A. 1837; Deac. 1836 by Bp of Ox. Pr. 1837 by Bp of Lon. Bp Elect of Gibraltar 1868. (Episcopal jurisdiction, Gibraltar, Malta, and the Islands and Countries of the Mediterranean; Clergy, 35; Inc. of See, 1200*l* from Colonial Bishoprics' Fund.) His Lordship was formerly Fell. of All Souls', Ox; P. C. of Rownhams, Southampton, 1855–63; V. of Bremhill, Wilts, 1863–68; Archd. of Wilts 1863–68.

Archdeacon of Gibraltar—(Vacant.)

Archdeacon of Malta—Ven. J. Cleugh, D.D.

Canons of Gibraltar.

T. Sleeman, 1853. | M. Powley, M.A. 1866.
R. Alder, D.D. 1855. | C. Childers, M.A.

Chaplains to the Lord Bishop—Dr. Burbidge, and R. L. Tottenham.

Chaplains at Gibraltar.

Matthew Powley, M.A.	Civil Chaplain.
R. Alder, D.D.	Chap. to the Convict Estab.
Sydney Clarke, M.A.	Chaplain to the Forces.
R. G. Codrington, B.A.	Chap. to the Forces.
H. Sidebotham, M.A.	Asst. Civil Chaplain.
A. Vallespinosa	Spanish Chaplain.

MALTA.

Ven. Archdeacon J. Cleugh, M.A.

John Cleugh, M.A.	Chap. to the Government.
Dr. Burbidge	Holy Trinity.
A. Moodie, M.A.	Chaplain to the Forces.
H. O. Wrench, M.A.	Chaplain to the Forces.
E. Hillman, M.A.	Chaplain to the Forces.
T. W. Burridge, D.C.L.	Chaplain to the Forces.
G. E. Carwithers, M.A.	Naval Chaplain.

FOREIGN JURISDICTION.

SPAIN.

T. W. Scott, M.A.	Malaga.
(Vacant)	Barcelona.
L. S. Tugwell	Seville.
(Vacant)	Puerto Sta. Maria.

FRANCE.

J. B. Hawkins, M.A.	Marseilles.
S. Henning, B.A.	Lyons.
E. F. Neville-Rolfe	Cannes.
J. D. Isaac	Cannes.
W. Barber	Mentone, West Bay.
D. F. Morgan	Mentone, East Bay.
Wm. Brookes	Hyères.
C. Childers, M.A.	Nice.
F. Brodie	Nice.
C. W. Cleeve	Nice.

ITALY.

G. F. Whidborne, M.A.	Bordighera.
Ernest Cowan, M.A.	San Reno.
A. B. Strettell, M.A.	Genoa.
C. Leslie Alexander.	Genoa.
F. H. Snow Pendleton	Florence.
R. L. Tottenham	Chapel of Ease and Spezzia.
W. C. Langdon	Amer. Church.
H. Greene, M.A.	Pisa and Baths of Luca.
B. Sher. Kennedy, M.A.	Pisa.
H. J. Huntington, B.A.	Leghorn.
P. T. Maitland	Naples.
Samuel Tucker	Trieste.
J. D. Mereweather	Venice.
C. B. Brigstocke, M.A.	Turin.
H. J. Garrod, M.A.	Milan.

SICILY.

I. G. Clay, B.A.	Messina.
Charles Wright, M.A.	Palermo.

GREECE.

John Henry Hill, D.D.	Athens.
F. A. Hilner	Syra.
J. Page Sutton	Corfu.
J. O. Bagdon	Zante.

TURKEY.

Constantinople.

C. B. Gribble, B.A.	Chaplain to the Embassy.
Chas. George Curtis, M.A.	Chaplain, S.P.G.
(Vacant)	Missionary, S.P.G.
Dr. Koelle	Missionary, C.M.S.
(Vacant)	Missionary, C.M.S.
R. H. Weakley	Missionary, C.M.S.
S. C. Newman	Missionary to Jews.
C. C. Hanson, B.A.	Missionary to Seamen, C.C.S.

Smyrna.

W. B. Lewis	Chaplain.
J. T. Wolters	Missionary.
T. F. Wolters	Missionary.

AFRICA.

W. Fenner	Missionary, Tunis.
J. Ginsburg	Missionary, Algiers.

Jerusalem.

JERUSALEM, The Right Rev. Samuel GOBAT, Lord Bishop of Jerusalem, *Mission House, Jerusalem.*—Consecrated Bp of Jerusalem 1846. (Inc. of See, 1200*l*, provided, one half by the King of Prussia, and the other half by the Jerusalem Bishopric Fund.) Author, *Journal of a Three Years' Residence in Abyssinia*, Lond. 1847.

Bishop's Chaplains—The Rev. W. Douglas Veitch, M.A. Oxon; T. Smith, M.A. Camb.

Augustus Klein	Jerusalem.
J. Barclay, Hon. Chap. to the Bishop	Jerusalem.
William Bailey	Jerusalem.
E. J. Davies	Alexandria.
John Zeller	Nazareth.
Stephen Carabet	Diarbekir.
Buchanan Chaleel	Nablous.
Elias Benjamin Frankel	Jerusalem.
John Gruhler	Jaffa.
James Samuel Müller	Bethlehem.
Chas. Fred. Hausmann	Cairo.
John Christian Blessing	Khartoom in Nubia.

United States of America.

BISHOPS OF THE PROTESTANT EPISCOPAL CHURCH,

WITH THE DATE OF THEIR CONSECRATION.

Alabama.
Richard H. Wilmer, D.D. ... 1862

Arkansas.
Henry C. Lay, D.D. 1859

California.
Wm. Ingr. Kip, D.D. 1853

Carolina—North.
Thomas Atkinson, D.D.... ... 1853

Carolina—South.
Thomas F. Davis, D.D. 1853

China.
C. M. Williams, D.D, Missionary 1866

Connecticut.
John Williams, D.D. 1851

Colorado.
G. M. Randall, D.D., Missionary 1865

Delaware.
Alfred Lee, D.D. 1841

Florida.
J. F. Young, D.D.... 1867

Georgia.
J. W. Beckwith, D.D. 1867

Illinois.
H. J. Whitehouse, D.D.... ... 1851

Indiana.
George Upfold, D.D., LL.D. ... 1849
J. C. Talbot, D.D., Assist. ... 1865

Iowa.
Henry W. Lee, D.D. 1854

Kansas.
T. H. Vail, D.D. 1865

Kentucky.
Benjamin B. Smith, D.D. ... 1832
G. D. Cummins, D.D., Assist... 1866

Louisiana.
J. P. B. Wilmer, D.D. 1866

Maine.
H. A. Neely, D.D.... 1867

Maryland.
Wm. R. Whittingham, D.D., LL.D.... 1840

Massachusetts.
Manton Eastburn, D.D.... ... 1842

Michigan.
S. A. McCoskry, D.D., D.C.L. Oxford 1836

Minnesota.
Henry Benjamin Whipple, D.D. 1859

Mississippi.
William M. Green, D.D. ... 1850

Missouri.
Cicero Stephens Hawks, D.D. 1844
Horatio Southgate, D.D., Missionary 1844

Montana.
D. S. Tuttle, D.D. 1867

Nebraska.
R. H. Clarkson, D.D., Missionary 1865

New Hampshire.
Carlton Chase, D.D. 1844

New Jersey.
Wm. H. Odenheimer, D.D. ... 1859

New York.
Horatio Potter, D.D., LL.D., D.C.L. 1854

New York—Western.
A. Cleveland Coxe, D D. ... 1864

Ohio.
C. P. McIlvaine, D.D., D.C.L., Oxford 1832
Gregory Thurston Bedell, Assist. 1859

Oregon.
(Vacant).

Pennsylvania.
W. B. Stevens, D.D. 1862

Pittsburgh (Pennsylvania).
J. B. Kerfoot, D.D. 1866

Rhode Island.
Thomas M. Clark, D.D.... ... 1854

Tennessee.
C. T. Quintard, D.D. 1865

Texas.
Alexander Gregg, D.D. 1859

Vermont.
John Henry Hopkins, D.D., LL.D.... 1832

Virginia.
John Jones, D.D. 1842

Western Africa.
John Payne, D.D., Missionary... 1851

Wisconsin.
Jackson Kemper, D.D., LL.D. 1836
W. E. Armitage, D.D., Assist. 1865

Commutation of Tithes.

TITHE COMMISSION.—*Office,* 3, *St. James's-square, S.W.*

Worth of £100 *of Rent Charge for each year since the passing of the Tithe Commutation Act (from* Mr. *Willich's Tables), viz:*

Year	£	s.	d.	Year	£	s.	d.
1837	98	13	9¾	1854	90	19	5
1838	97	7	11	1855	89	15	6¼
1839	95	7	9	1856	93	18	1¼
1840	98	15	9¼	1857	99	13	7¼
1841	102	12	5¼	1858	105	16	3¼
1842	105	8	2¾	1859	108	19	6¼
1843	105	12	2¼	1860	110	17	8¼
1844	104	3	5¼	1861	112	3	4¾
1845	103	17	11¼	1862	109	13	6
1846	102	17	8¾	1863	107	5	2
1847	99	18	10¼	1864	103	3	10¾
1848	102	1	0	1865	98	13	10¼
1849	100	3	7¾	1866	97	7	9¾
1850	98	16	10	1867	98	13	3
1851	96	11	4¾				
1852	93	16	11¼	Total	£3125	2	7¼
1853	91	13	5¾				

General Average for 31 years, £100 16s 2½d.

Appendix.

ADAMS, H. C., *Sandford, Abingdon.*—P. C. of Sandford, Dio. Ox. 1867. (Patron, Bp of Ox; P. C.'s Inc. 150*l* and Ho; Pop. 113.) [1]

ALSTON, Herbert, *Little Bradley, Newmarket.*—R. of Little Bradley, Dio. Ely, 1867. (Patrons, Messrs. E. B. and C. F. Foster; R.'s Inc. 280*l*; Pop. 28.) [2]

ANDREWS, J. N., *Pickworth, Folkingham.*—R. of Pickworth, Dio. Lin. 1867. (Patron, the present R; R.'s Inc. 480*l* and Ho; Pop. 253.) [3]

ARNOTT, Samuel, *Hollington, Hastings.*—R. of Hollington, Dio. Chich. 1867. (Patrons, Exors. of J. Eversfield, Esq; R.'s Inc. 250*l*; Pop. 531.) [4]

ATTHILL, R., *Clenchwharton Rectory, King's Lynn.*—R. of Clenchwharton, Dio. Nor. 1867. (Patron, Sir E. Grogan, Bart; R.'s Inc. 500*l* and Ho; Pop. 599.) [5]

BAIRD, William, *Dymock Vicarage, Gloucester.*—Lin. Coll. Ox. Scho. 1856, B.A. 1859; Deac. 1859 and Pr. 1860 by Bp of Lon. V. of Dymock, Dio. G. and B. 1867. (Patron, Earl Beauchamp; V.'s Inc. 120*l* and Ho; Pop. 1870.) Chap. to Earl Beauchamp. Formerly C. of St. Bartholomew's, Moor-lane, Lond. [6]

BAKER, Arthur, *Addington, Winslow, Bucks.*—Wad. Coll. Ox. B.A. 1840, M.A. 1850, Tunbridge Exhib. of 100*l* per ann; Deac. 1841 and Pr. 1842 by Bp of Lon. R. of Addington, Dio. Ox. 1867. (Patron, J. G. Hubbard, Esq. M.P; R.'s Inc. 250*l* and Ho; Pop. 111.) [7]

BANCKS, Gerard, *Cobham Vicarage, Surrey.*—St. Peter's Coll. Cam. B.A. 1854; Deac. 1855 and Pr. 1856 by Bp of Ches. V. of Cobham, Dio. Win. 1867. (Patron, Charles Coombe, Esq; V.'s Inc. 187*l* and Ho; Pop. 1998.) [8]

BARDSLEY, Samuel, *Christ Church Rectory, Spitalfields, London, E.*—R. of Ch. Ch. Spitalfields, Dio. Lon. 1867. (Patron, T. F. Buxton, Esq; R.'s Inc. 400*l* and Ho; Pop. 15,503.) [9]

BASKERVILLE, C. G., *Lozells, near Birmingham.*—P. C. of St. Silas', Lozells, Dio. Wor. 1867. (Patrons, Trustees; P. C.'s Inc. 31*l*; Pop. 8063.) [10]

BAYLEY, Emilius.—P. C. of St. John's, Paddington, Dio. Lon. 1867. (Patron, P. C. of Paddington; P. C.'s Inc. 1000*l*; Pop. 6123.) [11]

BEARCROFT, Thomas, *Fitz Rectory, Shrewsbury.*—Queen's Coll. Ox. B.A. 1842, M.A. 1846; Deac. 1844 and Pr. 1845 by Bp of Wor. R. of Fitz, Dio. Lich. 1867. (Patron, Ld Chan; R.'s Inc. 300*l* and Ho; Pop. 309.) Formerly C. of Cruckton District in the second portion of Pontesbury Parish, Minsterley, Shropshire. [12]

BECK, Edward Josselyn, *Rotherhithe Rectory, Southwark, S.E.*—R. of Rotherhithe with St. Paul's (Globe-street), C. Dio. Win. 1867. (Patron, Clare Coll. Cam; Tithe, 186*l* 15*s*; R.'s Inc. 775*l* and Ho; Pop. 10,226.) [13]

BEWSHER, William, *Radwell Rectory, Baldock, Herts.*—R. of Radwell, Dio. Roch. 1867. (Patron, F. Pym, Esq; Tithe, 203*l* 6*s*; Glebe 9¼ acres; R.'s Inc. 220*l* and Ho; Pop. 102.) [14]

BLYTHE, Alfred T., *Langwith Rectory, Mansfield.*—R. of Langwith, Dio. Lich. 1867. (Patron, Duke of Devonshire; R.'s Inc. 235*l* and Ho; Pop. 183.) V. of Scarcliff, Dio. Lich. 1867. (Patron, Earl Bathurst; V.'s Inc. 70*l*; Pop. 548.) [15]

BROOKE, Richard England, *Hull.*—Caius Coll. Cam. 3rd Sen. Opt. B.A. 1844, M.A. 1847; Deac. 1844 and Pr. 1845 by Bp of Rip. V. of Hull, Dio. York, 1867. (Patrons, Trustees; V.'s Inc. 700*l* and Ho; Pop. 38,100.) Hon. Can. of Man. 1862 and Exam. Chap. to Bp of Man. 1861. Formerly C. of Kirklinton 1844–46, Great Coates 1846–49; P. C. of Sowerby, Halifax, 1849–52; R of St. Luke's, Cheetham Hill, 1852–63; Rural Dean of Manchester 1860–63; P. C. of St. Mary's, Spring Grove, Middlesex, 1863–67. [16]

BUDD, Joseph, *West Somerton, Norfolk.*—P. C. of West Somerton, Dio. Nor. 1867. (Patron, Thomas Grove, Esq; P. C.'s Inc. 100*l*; Pop. 244.) [17]

BULLEN, John Allan, *Morice Town, Devonport.*—P. C. of St. James's, Morice Town, Dio. Ex. 1867. (Patrons, Crown and Bp of Ex. alt; P. C.'s Inc. 300*l*; Pop. 5997.) [18]

BURGES, Richard Bennett, *St. Paul's Parsonage, Birmingham.*—Dub. A.B. 1851; Deac. 1851 and Pr. 1852. P. C. of St. Paul's, Birmingham, Dio. Wor. 1867. (Patrons, Trustees; P. C.'s Inc. 300*l* and Ho; Pop. 16,817.) Formerly C. of Norton Durham, and Steeple Claydon, Bucks; R. of Waddesdon, Bucks, 1860–67. [19]

BURNABY, Sherrard Beaumont, *Wapping Rectory, London, E.*—Ch. Coll. Cam. Sen. Opt. B.A. 1854, M.A. 1857; Deac. 1857 by Bp of Lon. R. of Wapping, Dio. Lon. 1867. (Patron, Bp of Lon; R.'s Inc. 280*l* and Ho; Pop. 4038.) [20]

CARSON, David, *Soulbury Parsonage, Leighton Buzzard.*—P. C. of Soulbury, Dio. Ox. 1867. (Patroness, Miss Lovett; P.C.'s Inc. 107*l* and Ho; Pop. 589.) [21]

COCKING, R. D.—P. C. of St. John's, Kilburn, Middlesex, Dio. Lon. 1867. (Patrons, Trustees.) [22]

COLING, J., *Chillenden Rectory, Wingham, Kent.*—R. of Chillenden, Dio. Cant. 1867. (Patron, Ld Chan; R.'s Inc. 150*l* and Ho; Pop. 127.) [23]

COLLINGS, P. B., *Sturry Vicarage, Canterbury.*—V. of Sturry, Dio. Cant. 1867. (Patron, Abp of Cant; Tithe, 255*l*; Glebe, 4 acres; V.'s Inc. 267*l* and Ho; Pop. 1044.) [24]

COLLINS, Thomas Farmer, 22, *Lawford-road, Rugby.*—Brasen. Coll. Ox. Hulme Exhib. B.A. 1859, M.A. 1862; Deac. 1861 and Pr. 1862 by Bp of Pet. P. C. of New Bilton, Dio. Wor. 1868. (Patron, R. of Bilton; Tithe, 80*l*; Glebe, 10 acres; P. C.'s Inc. 170*l* and Ho; Pop. 600.) Chap. to the Rugby Union. Formerly C. of Geddington, Northants, 1861, Tring 1862, Bilton 1863. [25]

COLLIS, John Day, *Stratford-on-Avon.*—V. of Stratford-on-Avon, Dio. Wor. 1867. (Patroness, Countess Delawarr; Glebe 12 acres; V.'s Inc. 240*l* and Ho; Pop. 6798.) [26]

COOKES, Thomas Horace, *Tadmarton Rectory, Banbury.*—R. of Tadmarton, Dio. Ox. 1867. (Patron, Wor. Coll. Ox; R.'s Inc. 320*l* and Ho; Pop. 411.) [27]

COOPER, John, *Beaumont Rectory, Colchester.*—Wad. Coll. Ox. B.A. 1837, M.A. 1842; Deac. 1843 R. of Beaumont with Moze R. Dio. Roch. 1867. (Patron

Wad. Coll. Ox; Tithe, 775*l*; Glebe, 46 acres; R.'s Inc. 868*l* and Ho; Pop. 490.) Formerly Fell. and Sub-Warden of Wad. Coll. Ox. [1]

COULSON, A. B., *Carham Vicarage, Coldstream.*—V. of Carham, Dio. Dur. 1867. (Patrons, Heirs of A. Compton, Esq; V.'s Inc. 250*l* and Ho; Pop. 1274.) Formerly C. of Bothal and Hebburn, Northumberland. [2]

COWARD, Ralph John, *Worcester.*—Brasen. Coll. Ox. B.A. 1849, M.A. 1853; Deac. 1853 by Bp of Man. Pr. 1854 by Bp of Chich. P. C. of St. Paul's, Worcester, Dio. Wor. 1867. (Patron, Bp of Wor; P. C.'s Inc. 150*l*; Pop. 2668.) Formerly C. of Lower Beeding, Sussex; Chap. to the Midhurst Union; V. of Mevagissey, Cornwall, 1862–67. [3]

COWIE, William Garden, *The Rectory, Stafford.*—R. of Stafford, Dio. Lich. 1867. (Patron, Ld Chan; R.'s Inc. 375*l* and Ho; Pop. 6448.) Surrogate. [4]

COXHEAD, John James.—P. C. of St. John's, Charlotte-street, Fitzroy-square, London, Dio. Lon. 1867. (Patron, Bp of Lon; P. C.'s Inc. 350*l*; Pop. 12,779.) [5]

CUTTING, William Aubrey, *Gayton, Lynn Regis, Norfolk.*—Corpus Coll. Cam. Jun. Opt. 3rd cl. Cl. Trip. and B.A. 1856, M.A. 1859; Deac. 1857 and Pr. 1858 by Bp of Nor. V. of Gayton, Dio. Nor. 1867. (Patron, Bp of Nor; V.'s Inc. 300*l*; Pop. 920.) Formerly C. of St. Martin's, Norwich, 1857, Lower Sheringham-with-Weyburne 1858–61; R. of Trimingham, Norfolk, 1861–67. [6]

DAVIES, J. H., *Cilian-Aêron, Lampeter.*—R. of Cilian-Aêron, Dio. St. D. 1867. (Patron, Bp of St. D; R.'s Inc. 100*l*; Pop. 301.) [7]

DAVIS, Henry, *Tarrant Monkton, Blandford, Dorset.*—V. of Tarrant Monkton with Tarrant Launceston C. Dio. Salis. 1867. (Patron, J. J. Farquharson, Esq; V.'s Inc. 136*l*; Pop. Tarrant Monkton 243, Tarrant Launceston 107.) [8]

DESBOROUGH, Henry John, *Christchurch Rectory, Southwark, S.*—R. of Ch. Ch. Southwark, Dio. Win. 1867. (Patrons, Marshall's Trustees; R.'s Inc. 600*l* and Ho; Pop. 17,069.) [9]

DICKINSON, C. J., *Bodmin Vicarage, Cornwall.*—V. of Bodmin, Dio. Ex. 1867. (Patron, J. F. Basset, Esq; V.'s Inc. 400*l* and Ho; Pop. 4809.) [10]

DODD, Henry Russell, *Kirk Braddan, Douglas, Isle of Man.*—P. C. of St. Thomas's, Kirk Braddan, Dio. S. and M. 1867. (Patron, Bp of S. and M.; P. C.'s Inc. 200*l*.) [11]

DRAKE, Charles Mackworth, *Seaton Vicarage, Axminster.*—Ex. Coll. Ox. Scho. of, B.A. 1859, M.A. 1862; Deac. 1861 and Pr. 1862 by Bp of Ox. V. of Seaton and Beer, Dio. Ex. 1867. (Patron, Hon. Mark G. K. Rolle; Tithe, 260*l*; Glebe, 14 acres; V.'s Inc. 265*l* and Ho; Pop. 1966.) Formerly C. of Lamborne 1861–62, Great Marlow 1862–63. [12]

DRUITT, William, *Stockbridge, Hants.*—R. of Stockbridge, Dio. Win. 1867. (Patroness, Lady Barker Mill; Tithe, 180*l*; R.'s Inc. 207*l*; Pop. 935.) [13]

EARLE, R. H., *Kencott Rectory, Lechlade, Oxon.*—R. of Kencott, Dio. Ox. 1867. (Patrons, the Hammersley family; R.'s Inc. 260*l* and Ho; Pop. 214.) [14]

EDWARDS, C., *Enderby, Leicester.*—V. of Enderby, Dio. Pet. 1867. (Patron, C. Brook, jun. Esq; V.'s Inc. 200*l*; Pop. 1833.) [15]

ELTON, H. G., *West Hatch, near Taunton.*—V. of West Hatch, Dio. B. and W. 1867. (Patrons, D. and C. of Wells; V.'s Inc. 65*l* and Ho; Pop. 432.) [16]

ERRINGTON, John Launcelot, *Midgham Parsonage, Newbury, Berks.*—P. C. of Midgham, Dio. Ox. 1867. (P. C.'s Inc. 116*l* and Ho; Pop. 233.) [17]

ESPIN, Thomas E., *Wallasey Rectory, Birkenhead.*—R. of Wallasey, Dio. Ches. 1867. (Patron, Bp of Ches; Tithe, 230*l*; Glebe, 30 acres; R.'s Inc. 540*l* and Ho; Pop. 1415.) [18]

EVERETT, E. Hawley, *Whittering Rectory, Stamford.*—R. of Whittering, Dio. Pet. 1867. (Patron, Marquis of Exeter; R.'s Inc. 120*l* and Ho; Pop. 235.) [19]

FAITHFULL, C. H., *Preston Deanery, Northampton.*—V. of Preston Deanery, Dio. Pet. 1867. (Patron, Langham Christie, Esq; V.'s Inc. 200*l*; Pop. 80.) [20]

FARLEY, Henry, *Billbrook, Old Cleeve, Taunton.*—Ex. Coll. Ox. B.A. 1866; Deac. 1867 by Bp Hobhouse for Bp of B. and W. C. of Old Cleeve 1867. [21]

FAUGHT, George Steers, *Bradfield St. Clare, Bury St. Edmunds.*—R. of Bradfield St. Clare, Dio. Ely, 1867. (Patrons, Messrs. W. R. and G. J. Bevan; R.'s Inc. 300*l*; Pop. 233.) [22]

FELLOWES, Thomas Lyon, *Tuddenham Vicarage, Norwich.*—Ch. Ch. Ox. B.A. 1840; Deac. 1841 and Pr. 1842 by Bp of Nor. V. of Honingham with East Tuddenham V. Dio. Nor. 1867. (Patrons, Reps. of Lord Bayning; Honingham—Tithe, 210*l*; Glebe, 1 acre; East Tuddenham—Tithe, 445*l*; Glebe, 102 acres; V.'s Inc. 758*l* and Ho; Pop. Honingham 328, East Tuddenham 512.) Formerly R. of Beighton, Norfolk, 1844–67. Author, *A New Analysis of Aristotle's Rhetoric.* [23]

FIELD, James William, *Braybrook Rectory, Market Harborough.*—R. of Braybrook, Dio. Pet. 1867. (Patron, the present R; Tithe, 33*l* 9*s*; Glebe, 313 acres; R.'s Inc. 600*l* and Ho; Pop. 458.) [24]

FOSTER, Francis Drake, *Dodington Rectory, Chipping Sodbury, Glouc.*—Ball. Coll. Ox. 2nd cl. Lit. Hum. and B.A. 1814, M.A. 1817; Deac. 1817 and Pr. 1818 by Bp of G. and B. R. of Dodington, Dio. G. and B. 1827. (Patron, Sir C. B. Codrington, Bart; Tithe, 245*l*; Glebe, 24 acres; R.'s Inc. 280*l* and Ho; Pop. 126.) [25]

FRANCES, Sandys, *Huddington, Droitwich.*—P.C. of Huddington, Dio. Wor. 1867. (Patron, Earl of Shrewsbury; P.C.'s Inc. 56*l*; Pop. 37.) [26]

FREEMAN, Frederick John, *Manton, Oakham, Rutland.*—V. of Manton, Dio. Pet. 1867. (Patron, E. W. Smyth, Esq; V.'s Inc. 73*l*; Pop. 274.) [27]

FRITH, William Armetriding, *Welby Rectory, Grantham, Lincolnshire.*—Wor. Coll. Ox. B.A. 1849, M.A. 1852; Deac. 1850, Pr. 1851. R. of Welby, Dio. Lin. 1867. (Patron, Bp of Lin; R.'s Inc. 350*l* and Ho; Pop. 499.) Formerly P. C. of Trinity, Gainsborough, 1854–67. [28]

FULLER, Morris J., *Lydford Rectory, Bridestowe, Devon.*—R. of Lydford, Dio. Ex. 1867. (Patron, Prince of Wales; R.'s Inc. 187*l* and Ho; Pop. 2815. [29]

GRASETT, James Elliot, *Allensmore, near Hereford.*—Dur; Deac. 1857 and Pr. 1858 by Bp of Herf. V. of Allensmore, Dio. Herf. 1867. (Patron, Bp of Herf; Tithe, 175*l*; Glebe, 3 acres; V.'s Inc. 190*l* and Ho; Pop. 612.) Formerly C. of Lindridge; P. C. of Kington-on-Teme. [30]

GREEN, Edward Dyer, *Bromborough Rectory, Chester.*—M.A. 1855; Deac. 1844 and Pr. 1845 by Bp of Salis. R. of Bromborough, Dio. Ches. 1860. (Patrons, D. and C. of Ches; Tithe—Imp. 199*l* 19*s*; R. 50*l* 1*s*; Glebe, 6 acres; R.'s Inc. 225*l* and Ho; Pop. 1066.) Surrogate 1863; Hon. Sec. and Treas. of the Bishop Pearson Memorial. Formerly Head Mast. of Langport Gr. Sch; C. of St. Oswald's Cathl. Chester. Author, Poems, Reviews, &c., in various periodicals. [31]

GRIX, William Bevern, *Grammar School, Congleton, Cheshire.*—Queens' Coll. Cam. B.A. 1852, M.A. 1856; Deac. 1855 and Pr. 1856 by Bp of Ches. Head Mast. of the Congleton Gr. Sch. 1856; Chap. of Don. of Somerford, Dio. Ches. 1864. (Patron, Sir C. W. Shakerley, Bart; Chap.'s Inc. 40*l*.) [32]

HANNAH, John Julius, *Grove House, Brill, near Thame.*—Cuddesdon; Ball. Coll. Ox. B.A. 1866; Deac. 1867 by Bp of Ox. C. of Brill with Boarstall. [33]

HADOW, William Elliot, *St. Barnabas' Parsonage, Bristol.*—Ch. Coll. Cam. Found. Scho. and Porteus Gold Medallist, Jun. Opt. and B.A. 1849, M.A. 1852; Deac. 1851 and Pr. 1852 by Bp of Ex. P. C. of St. Barnabas', Bristol, Dio. G. and B. 1867. (Patron, Bp of G. and B; P. C.'s Inc. 150*l* and Ho; Pop. 3735.) Formerly Asst. C. of Tavistock and Brent Tor, Devon, 1851–57; Even. Lect. of Tavistock 1855 57; C. of St. Mary Tavy, Devon, 1857–58, Ebrington, Glouc. 1858–65; V. of Ebrington 1865–67. [34]

HARDWICH, T. F., *Shotton Parsonage, Ferryhill, Durham.*—P. C. of Shotton with Haswell C. Dio. Dur. 1867. (Patron, Bp of Dur; P. C.'s Inc. 300*l* and

Ho; Pop. 3600.) Formerly C. of Shildon and Easington, Durham. [1]

HATCH, Henry John, *Little Stambridge Rectory, Rochford, Essex.*—R. of Little Stambridge, Dio. Roch. 1867. (Patron, Ld Chan; R.'s Inc. 190*l* and Ho; Pop. 125.) [2]

HAYS, John, *Navenby Rectory, Grantham.*—R. of Navenby, Dio. Lin. 1867. (Patron, Ch. Coll. Cam; R.'s Inc. 600*l* and Ho; Pop. 1170.) [3]

HERBERT, Henry, *Hemingford Abbots, St. Ives, Hunts.*—R. of Hemingford Abbots, Dio. Ely, 1867. (Patron, A. Herbert, Esq; Glebe, 510 acres; R.'s Inc. 512*l* and Ho; Pop. 518.) [4]

HEYCOCK, Thomas, *Seaton Rectory, Uppingham.*—R. of Seaton, Dio. Pet. 1867. (Patron, Earl of Harborough; Tithe, 600*l*; R.'s Inc. 650*l* and Ho; Pop. 422.) [5]

HILLS, Thomas Charles, *Bolsover Vicarage, Chesterfield.*—St. Bees; Deac. 1862 and Pr. 1863 by Bp of Lich. V. of Bolsover, Dio. Lich. 1867. (Patron, Duke of Portland; V.'s Inc. 120*l* and Ho; Pop. 1629.) Sec. for North of England and Scotland to the Patagonian or South American Missionary Society. Formerly C. of St. Werburgh's, Derby, 1862–64. [6]

HOARE, Francis, *Derby.*—Deac. 1857, Pr. 1858. P. C. of Trinity, Derby, Dio. Lich. 1867. (Patron, B. West, Esq; Pop. 6989.) Formerly C. of Wigton 1857, Hanley 1859, Shelton 1861, Newcastle 1864–67. [7]

HOLMES, W. R., *Birkby Rectory, North Allerton, Yorks.*—R. of Birkby, Dio. York, 1867. (Patron, the present R; R.'s Inc. 250*l* and Ho; Pop. 169.) [8]

HUNNYBUN, William Martin, *Bicknoller Vicarage, Taunton.*—Caius Coll. Cam. B.A. 1860, M.A. 1864, Deac. 1862 and Pr. 1863 by Bp of St. D. V. of Bicknoller, Dio. B. and W. 1867. (Patron, V. of Stogumber; V.'s Inc. 150*l* and Ho; Pop. 345.) Formerly C. of Steynton, Pembrokeshire; P. C. of Withiell-Florey, Somerset, 1866–67. [9]

JENKINS, J., *Ashby St. Leger's, Rugby.*—V. of Ashby St. Leger's, Dio. Pet. 1867. (Patrons, Messrs. J. A. and W. Senhouse; V.'s Inc. 150*l* and Ho; Pop. 300.) [10]

JOHNSON, Pitt, *Liverpool.*—Min. of District Church of St. Mark, Liverpool, Dio. Ches. 1867. (Patron, P. C. of St. Mark's; Min's. Inc. 120*l*.) [11]

JONES, B. Wilkes, *Nether Whitacre, Coleshill, Warwickshire.*—R. of Nether Whitacre, Dio. Wor. 1867. (Patron, Earl Howe; R.'s Inc. 350*l* and Ho; Pop. 479.) [12]

JONES, Joshua, *Kirk Malew, Douglas, Isle of Man.*—P. C. of St. Thomas's, Kirk Malew, Dio. S. and M. 1866. [13]

JONES, Richard, *Hirnant Rectory, Llanfyllyn, Montgomery.*—R. of Hirnant, Dio. St. A. 1867. (Patron, Bp of St. A; R.'s Inc. 144*l* and Ho; Pop. 293.) [14]

JOPLIN, F., *Debach Rectory, Woodbridge, Suffolk.* R. of Boulge with Debach, Dio. Nor. 1867. (Patron, the present R; Tithe, 264*l*; Glebe, 13 acres; R.'s Inc. 310*l* and Ho; Pop. Boulge 39, Debach 144.) [15]

KEBLE, Thomas, *Bishopworth, Bristol.*—Magd. Coll. Ox. B.A. 1846, M.A. 1849; Deac. 1849 and Pr. 1850 by Bp of Ex. P. C. of St. Peter's, Bishopworth, Dio. G. and B. 1867. (Patron, Bp of G. and B; P. C.'s Inc. 140*l* and Ho; Pop. 1606.) Formerly C. of Bussage, and of Flaxley, Glouc. [16]

KENNEDY, Michael Valentine, *Renwick, Penrith.*—P. C. of Renwick, Dio. Carl. 1867. (Patron, J. Nicholson, Esq; P. C.'s Inc. 96*l*; Pop. 266.) [17]

KENNION, A.—P. C. of St. Mary's, Kilburn, Hampstead, Dio. Lon. 1867. (Patron, Hon. A. Upton; Pop. 2600.) [18]

KIDD, R. Hayward, *Norwich.*—R. of St. Michael Coslany, Norwich, Dio. Nor. 1867. (Patron, Bp of Nor; R.'s Inc. 120*l* and Ho; Pop. 1365.) [19]

KNOLLYS, Erskine William.—P. C. of Trinity, Twickenham, Middlesex, Dio. Lon. 1867. (Patron, Bp of Lon; P. C.'s Inc. 130*l*; Pop. 3285.) [20]

LAMB, James, *Cumrew Parsonage, Carlisle.*—P. C. of Cumrew, Dio. Carl. 1867. (Patrons, D. and C. of Carl; P. C.'s Inc. 81*l* and Ho; Pop. 136.) [21]

LAMBERT, J. J., *Leebotwood, Shrewsbury.*—P. C. of Leebotwood with Longnor P.C. Dio. Lich. 1867. (Patron, P. Corbett, Esq; P.C.'s Inc. 140*l*; Pop. Leebotwood 210, Longnor 244.) [22]

LAMPET, W. E. L., *Great Bardfield Vicarage, Braintree, Essex.*—V. of Great Bardfield, Dio. Roch. 1867. (Patrons, Reps. of Rev. B. E. Lampet; Tithe, 262*l*; V.'s Inc. 270*l* and Ho; Pop. 1065.) Formerly C. of East Pennard, Somerset. [23]

LEE, M. H., *Hanmer Vicarage, Whitchurch, Salop.*—V. of Hanmer, Flints, Dio. St. A. 1867. (Patron, Sir J. Hanmer, Bart; Tithe, 300*l* 16*s*; Glebe, 74 acres; V.'s Inc. 400*l* and Ho; Pop. 1844.) [24]

LEGGE, The Hon. Augustus.—P. C. of St. Bartholomew's, Sydenham, Kent, Dio. Roch. 1867. (Patron, Earl of Dartmouth; P. C.'s Inc. 300*l* and Ho; Pop. 4355.) [25]

LITTLE, R. P., *Chalfield Magna, Melksham.*—R. of Chalfield Magna, Dio. Salis. 1867. (Patroness, Dowager Lady Burrard; R.'s Inc. 180*l*; Pop. 55.) [26]

LLOYD, Charles, *Inglishcombe Vicarage, Bath.*—V. of Inglishcombe, Dio. B. and W. 1867. (Patron, J. W. Gibbs, Esq; Tithe, 170*l*; Glebe 15 acres; V.'s Inc. 190*l* and Ho; Pop. 559.) [27]

LOVETT, R., *Ilsington Vicarage, Chudleigh, Devon.*—V. of Ilsington, Dio. Ex. 1867. (Patrons, D. and C. of Windsor; Tithe, 302*l*; Glebe, 80 acres; V.'s Inc. 372*l* and Ho; Pop. 1209.) [28]

LUKIN, W. Hugo, *Wickford Rectory, Chelmsford.*—R. of Wickford, Dio. Roch. 1867. (Patron, R. B. Berens, Esq; Tithe, 476*l*; Glebe, 47 acres; R.'s Inc. 536*l* and Ho; Pop. 462.) [29]

MACDONOGH, Terence Michael, *Dengie Rectory, Maldon, Essex.*—Deac. and Pr. 1827 by Bp of Llan. R. of Dengie, Dio. Roch. 1867. (Patrons, Trustees; Tithe, 737*l*; Glebe, 15 acres; R.'s Inc. 761*l* and Ho; Pop. 298.) Formerly P. C. of Bransgore, Hants, 1841–67. [30]

M'GILL, George Henry, *Bangor-Monachorum, Wrexham.*—Brasen. Coll. Ox. B.A. 1841, M.A. 1844; Deac. 1841 and Pr. 1842 by Bp of Ches. R. of Bangor-Monachorum with Overton C. Flintshire, Dio. St. A. 1867. (Patron, Marquis of Westminster; Bangor, Tithe, 701*l* 13*s*; Glebe, $\frac{3}{4}$ acre; Overton, Tithe, 551*l* 8*s* 2*d*; R.'s Inc. 1253*l* and Ho; Pop. Bangor 1240, Overton 1897.) Formerly P. C. of Ch. Ch. St. George's-in-the-East, Lond. 1854–67. [31]

MACNAMARA, Richard Yeoville, *Mountnessing, Brentwood, Essex.*—V. of Mountnessing, Dio. Roch. 1867. (Patron, Lord Petre; V.'s Inc. 120*l*; Pop. 844.) [32]

MANDUELL, Matthewman, *Ashby Puerorum, Spilsby, Lincolnshire.*—Queen's Coll. Ox. B.A. 1830; Deac. 1831 and Pr. 1832 by Bp of Lin. V. of Ashby Puerorum, Dio. Lin. 1867. (Patrons, D. and C. of Lin; V.'s Inc. 130*l*; Pop. 149.) Formerly C. of Tetford. [33]

MAY, E., *Parwich, Ashborne, Derbyshire.*—V. of Parwich, Dio. Lich. 1867. (Patron, W. Evans, Esq; V.'s Inc. 129*l*; Pop. 521.) P. C. of Alsop-le-Dale, Dio. Lich. 1867. (Patrons, Freeholders; P. C.'s Inc. 50*l*; Pop. 76). [34]

MAYNE, F. O., *Strood Vicarage, Rochester.*—V. of Strood, Dio. Roch. 1867. (Patrons, D. and C. of Roch; Tithe, 306*l*; Glebe, $1\frac{3}{4}$ acres; V.'s Inc. 400*l* and Ho; Pop. 4057.) [35]

MYRES, William M., *St. Paul's Parsonage, Preston.*—P. C. of St. Paul's, Preston, Dio. Man. 1867. (Patron, V. of Preston; P. C.'s Inc. 300*l* and Ho; Pop. 10,443.) [36]

NORTON, Hector, *Great Bentley Vicarage, Colchester.*—Magd. Coll. Cam. B.A. 1850; Deac. 1850, Pr. 1851. V. of Great Bentley, Dio. Roch. 1867. (Patron, Bp of Roch; V.'s Inc. 360*l* and Ho; Pop. 1033.) Formerly C. of Ecclesfield, near Sheffield, and St. Mary's, Southampton; R. of Longfield, Kent, 1864–67. [37]

OAKLEY, John.—P. C. of St. Saviour's, Hoxton, Lond. Dio. Lon. 1867. (Patrons, Crown and Bp of Lon. alt; P. C.'s Inc. 450*l*; Pop. 5675.) [38]

PAUL, Dolben, *Bearwood Rectory, Wokingham.*—Ch. Ch. Ox. B.A. 1854; Deac. 1856 and Pr. 1857 by Bp of Lin. R. of Bearwood, Dio. Ox. 1867. (Patron, J. Walter, Esq; Glebe, 5 acres; R.'s Inc. 100*l* and Ho; Pop. 814.) Formerly C. of Stevenage, Herts. [1]

POLWHELE, Robert, *Avenbury Vicarage, Bromyard, Herefordshire.*—V. of Avenbury, Dio. Herf. 1867. (Patron, John Freeman, Esq; V.'s Inc. 120*l* and Ho; Pop. 871.) [2]

PROCTER, Charles T., *Richmond, Surrey, S.W.*—V. of Richmond with St. Matthias' C. Dio. Win. 1867. (Patron, King's Coll. Cam; V.'s Inc. 600*l* and Ho; Pop. 6205.) [3]

PYPER, Thomas, *New Radford, Nottingham.*—P. C. of New Radford, Dio. Lin. 1867. (Patrons, Crown and Bp of Lin; P. C.'s Inc. 300*l*; Pop. 5145.) [4]

ROBSON, Thomas, *Marsk, near Redcar, Yorks.*—V. of Marsk, Dio. York. 1867. (Patron, Earl of Zetland; V.'s Inc. 220*l* and Ho; Pop. 1470.) [5]

ROGERS, Robert, *Fordham, Downham Market, Norfolk.*—P. C. of Fordham, Dio. Nor. 1867. (Patron, E. R. Pratt, Esq; P. C.'s Inc. 50*l*; Pop. 211.) C. of West Dereham, Norfolk. [6]

ROUSE, William Archibald, *Darfield Vicarage, York.*—Trin. Coll. Cam. late Scho. of, 24th Wrang. B.A. 1861, M.A. 1864; Deac. and Pr. by Bp of Wor. V. of 2nd Mediety of Darfield, Dio. York, 1866. (Patron, Trin. Coll. Cam; V.'s Inc. 200*l* and Ho.) Formerly Math. Mast. in Leamington Coll; C. of Wath-upon-Dearne. [7]

ST. AUBYN, A. H. Molesworth, *Collingham Vicarage, Wetherby, Yorks.*—V. of Collingham, Dio. Rip. 1867. (Patron, Rev. C. Wheler; V.'s Inc. 445*l* and Ho; Pop. 309.) [8]

SALE, Edward Townsend, *Bodington Rectory, Leamington.*—Emman. Coll. Cam. 9th Wrang. and B.A. 1850, M.A. 1853, B.D. 1860, Fell. of Emman. Coll. 1852; Deac. 1853 and Pr. 1855 by Bp of Ely. R. of Bodington, Northants, Dio. Pet. 1867. (Patron, Emman. Coll. Cam; Tithe, 11*s* 4*d*; Glebe, 468 acres; R.'s Inc. 850*l* and Ho; Pop. 724.) Formerly C. of Ch. Ch. Doncaster, and Calthorpe, Leic; C. of Trinity and St. Andrew's, Rugby, 1860–67. [9]

SALUSBURY, C. T., *Tredunnock Rectory, Llangibby, Monmouthshire.*—R. of Tredunnock, Dio. Llan. 1867. (Patron, C. H. Leigh, Esq; R.'s Inc. 244*l* 10*s* and Ho; Pop. 164.) [10]

SHAW, Charles J. Kenward, *Newington, Hythe, Kent.*—V. of Newington, Dio. Cant. 1867. (Patron, Rev. T. Brockman; Tithe, 235*l*; Glebe, 14 acres; V.'s Inc. 250*l*; Pop. 523.) [11]

SHAW, J. A., *Dallaghgill Parsonage, Ripon.*—P. C. of Dallaghgill, Dio. Rip. 1867. (Patron, V. of Masham; P. C.'s Inc. 150*l* and Ho; Pop. 320.) [12]

SHEWELL, Frank, *Waterperry Vicarage, Wheatley, Oxon.*—V. of Waterperry, Dio. Ox. 1867. (Patron, Right Hon. J. W. Henley; V.'s Inc. 75*l* and Ho; Pop. 230.) [13]

SMITH, Hely Hutchinson A., *Tansley Rectory, Matlock.*—R. of Tansley, Dio. Lich. 1867. (Patron, V. of Crich; R.'s Inc. 200*l* and Ho; Pop. 622.) [14]

SMITH, Oswald, *Crudwell Rectory, Malmesbury.*—R. of Crudwell, Dio. G. and B. 1867. (Patrons, Reps. of Rev. W. Maskelyne; Tithe, 570*l*; Glebe, 68 acres; R.'s Inc. 710*l* and Ho; Pop. 799.) [15]

STRAFFEN, Robert, *Lewes, Sussex.*—R. of All Saints', Lewes, Dio. Chich. 1867. (Patron, C. Goring, Esq; Glebe, 9 acres; R.'s Inc. 200*l*; Pop. 2092.) [16]

TAPP, W. E., *Aldersholt Parsonage, Cranborne, Dorset.*—P. C. of Aldersholt, Dio. Salis. 1867. (Patron, V. of Cranborne; P. C.'s Inc. 120*l* and Ho; Pop. 708.) [17]

TEUTSCHEL, Anthony Sigismund.—V. of Skelbrooke, Dio. York, 1867. (Patron, G. Neville, Esq; V.'s Inc. 80*l*; Pop. 87.) [18]

THEOBALD, Frederick, *Drayton, Abingdon, Berks.*—Trin. Coll. Ox. B.A. 1863; Deac. 1864 and Pr. 1865 by Bp of Ox. P. C. of Drayton, Dio. Ox. 1867. (Patron, Bp of Ox; P. C.'s Inc. 265*l*; Pop. 605.) Formerly C. of Drayton. [19]

THURSBY, Walter, *Handsworth, near Birmingham.*—P. C. of St. Michael's, Handsworth, Dio. Lich. 1867. (Patron, R. of Handsworth; P. C.'s Inc. 320*l*; Pop. 3183.) [20]

TOPHAM, Edward Charles, *Hawkswell Rectory, Bedale, Yorks.*—R. of Hawkswell, Dio. Rip. 1866. (Patroness, Mrs. M. Gale; R.'s Inc. 300*l* and Ho; Pop. 273.) [21]

TOWERS, R.—Min. of St. Paul's Chapel, Kilburn, Middlesex, Dio. Lon. 1867. (Patron, Rev. J. Heming.) [22]

TURNER, Sydney, *Hempstead, near Gloucester.*—R. of Hempstead, Dio. G. and B. 1867. (Patron, J. Higford, Esq; Tithe, 286*l*; Glebe, 5 acres; R.'s Inc. 508*l* and Ho; Pop. 424.) [23]

WATTS, Robert Edward Reginald, *Freefolk, Micheldever Station, Hants.*—Chap. of Don. of Freefolk, Dio. Win. 1867. (Patron, St. Cross Hospital, Winchester; Chap.'s Inc. 60*l*; , Pop. 66.) C. of Laverstoke, Hants. [24]

WATTS, Robert Rowley, *Stourpaine, near Blandford.*—Univ. Coll. Ox. 3rd cl. Lit. Hum. 2nd cl. Math. et Phy. and B.A. 1852; Deac. 1854 and Pr. 1855 by Bp of Salis. V. of Stourpaine, Dio. Salis. 1867. (Patrons, D. and C. of Salis; Tithe, 143*l*; Glebe, 9 acres; V.'s Inc. 154*l* and Ho; Pop. 658.) Formerly C. of Spetisbury with Charlton. [25]

WEBB, Allan Becher, *University College, Oxford.*—Univ. Coll. Ox. B.A. 1862, M.A. 1864; Deac. 1863 and Pr. 1864 by Bp of Ox. Fell. and Asst. Tut. of Univ. Coll. R. of Avon Dasset, near Leamington, Dio. Wor. 1867. (Patron, Rev. R. G. Jeston; Glebe, 270 acres; R.'s Inc. 455*l* and Ho; Pop. 280.) Formerly C. of St. Peter's, Oxford; Vice-Prin. of Cuddesdon Theol. Coll. [26]

WHATELY, J., *Elsenham Vicarage, Stansted Mountfitch, Essex.*—V. of Elsenham, Dio. Roch. 1867. (Patrons, Trustees; V.'s Inc. 92*l* and Ho; Pop. 480.) [27]

WILLIAMS, Alfred, *Kingston-upon-Thames.*—King's Coll. Cam. B.A. 1842, M.A. 1845. V. of Kingston-upon-Thames, Dio. Win. 1867. (Patron, King's Coll. Cam; Tithe, 279*l*; V.'s Inc. 530*l* and Ho; Pop. 6155.) Formerly Fell. of King's Coll. Cam. [28]

WILLIAMS, E., *Edern Rectory, Pwllheli, Carnarvonshire.*—R. of Edern with Carngiwch C. and Pistill C. Dio. Ban. 1865. (Patron, Bp of Ban; R.'s Inc. 400*l* and Ho; Pop. Edern, 613, Carngiwch 130, Pistill 495.) [29]

WILLIAMS, James, *Llandegvan Rectory, Beaumaris.*—R. of Llandegvan with Beaumaris C. Dio. Ban. 1867. (Patron, Sir R. B. W. Bulkeley, Bart; Llandegvan, Tithe, 306*l*; Glebe, 3 acres; Beaumaris, Tithe, 60*l*, Glebe, 2 acres; R.'s Inc. 400*l* and Ho; Pop. Llandegvan 900, Beaumaris 2210.) [30]

WILLIAMS, L. P., *Dodington Rectory, Bridgwater.*—R. of Dodington, Dio. B. and W. 1867. (Patron, Duke of Buckingham; R.'s Inc. 146*l* and Ho; Pop. 98.) [31]

WILLIAMS, T. J., *Llanvaethlu Rectory, Holyhead.*—R. of Llanvaethlu with Llanvwrog C. Dio. Ban. 1866. (Patron, Bp of Ban; Lanvaethlu, Tithe, 359*l* 17*s* 6*d*; Glebe, 27½ acres; Llanvwrog, Tithe, 275*l* 3*s* 1*d*; R.'s Inc. 700*l* and Ho; Pop. Llanvaethlu 445, Llanvwrog 246.) [32]

WOOD, William, *Radley College, Abingdon.*—Chap. of Don. of Radley, Dio. Ox. 1868. (Patron, Sir G. Bowyer, Bart; Pop. 484.) [33]

WOOLLCOMBE, Philip, *Creed Rectory Grampound, Cornwall.*—R. of Creed, Dio. Ex. 1867. (Patron, C. H. T. Hawkins, Esq; Tithe, 450*l*; Glebe, 24 acres; R.'s Inc. 500*l* and Ho; Pop. 743.) [34]

WRIGHT, Adam, *Gilsland, Carlisle.*—St. Bees; Deac. 1861 and Pr. 1862 by Bp of Carl. P. C. of Gilsland with Upper Denton P. C. Dio. Carl. 1867. (Patron, G. G. Mounsey, Esq; P. C.'s Inc. 130*l*; Pop. Gilsland 224, Upper Denton 100.) [35]

INDEX

TO

Benefices in England and Wales.

This Index contains a full list of the Benefices in England and Wales, with references to the PAGE *and* PARAGRAPH *where full particulars are given.*

[NOTE.—Names of places which commence with Great and Little, East and West, North and South, Upper and Lower, &c., are given with the proper name first; *e.g.*, Great Addington *as* Addington, Great; East Allington *as* Allington, East; Little Barford *as* Barford, Little, &c.]

Bettws-Garmon, Ban. P.C 647 15
Bettws-Gwerfi-Goch. St. A. ...R 343 24
Bettws-Leiki, St. D. ... P.C 215 7
Bettws-Newydd, Llan. P.C 536 17
Bettws-Penpont, St. D. P.C 470 7
Bettws-y-Coed, Ban. ... P.C 276 22
Bettws-yn-Rhôs, St. A. ...V 308 6
Bevercotes, Lin. ... ...V 552 18
Beverley, St. John's Chap. P.C 61 12
Beverley-Minster, York P.C 159 15
St. John and St. Martin P.C 61 12
St. Mary's ... ...V 82 8
St. Nicholas ... ...R 82 8
Beverstone, G. and B. ...R 151 23
Bevington, Ches. ... P.C 532 3
Bewcastle, Carl. ... ...R 448 6
Bewdley, Herf. ... ... P.C 235 25
Bexhill, Chich. ... ...R 600 19
St. Mark's ... ... P.C 600 22
Bexley, Cant. ... ...V 291 3
Bexley Heath, Cant. ... P.C 522 19
Bexwell, Nor. ... ...R 340 3
Beyton, Ely ... ...R 308 5
Bibury, G. and B. ... ...V 615 8
Bicester, Ox. ... ...V 692 23
Bickenhall, B. and W. ...R 529 17
Bickenhill, Wor. ... ...V 113 12
Bicker, Lin. ... ...V 232 7
Bickerstaffe, Ches. ... P.C 514 5
Bickerton, Ches. ... P.C 505 19
Bickington, Ex. ... ... P.C 612 29
Bickington, High, Ex. ...R 501 21
Bickleigh, Ex. ... ...R 114 8
V 151 3
Bickley, Cant. ... ... P.C 589 20
Bicknoller, B. and W. ...V 811 9
Bicknor, Cant. ... ...R 68 22
Bicton, Ex. ... ...R 383 1
Bicton, Lich. ... ... P.C 581 19
Bidborough, Cant. ... ...R 58 5
Biddenden, Cant. ... ...R 79 13
Biddenham, Ely ... ...V 730 5
Biddesham, B. and W. ...R 228 22
Biddestone, G. & B. R & V 212 10
Biddlesden, Ox. ... P.C 609 16
Biddulph, Lich. ... ...V 330 24
Biddulph Moor, Lich. P.C 264 16
Bideford, Ex. ... ...R 43 6
Bidford, Wor. ... ...V 74 16
Bidstone, Ches. ... ... P.C 267 9
Bierley, Rip. ... ...V 31 12
Bierton, Ox. ... ...V 16 3
Bigbury, Ex. ... ...R 222 26
Bigby, Lin. ... ...R 34 5
Biggin, Lich. ... ... P.C 477 16
Biggleswade, Ely ... ...V 191 14
Bighton, Win. ... ...R 180 2
Bignor, Chich. ... ...R 615 23
Bilborough, Lin. ... ...R 847 23
Bilbrough, York ... ...R 455 15
Bildeston, Ely ... ...R 250 3
Billericay, Roch. ... P.C 694 26
Billesdon, Pet. ... ...V 585 8
Billesley, Wor. ... ...R 637 5
Billing, Great, Pet. ... ...R 681 1
Billing, Little, Pet. ... ...R 250 15
Billingborough, Lin. ... ...V 393 26
Billinge, Ches. ... ... P.C 577 8
Billingford (Scole), Nor. ...R 148 10
Billingford (Thetford), Nor. R 169 18
Billingham, Dur. ... ...V 573 3
Billinghay, Lin. ... ...V 362 17
Billinghurst, Chich. ... ...V 98 20
Billingsley, Herf. ... ...R 377 19
Billington, Ely ... ...R 80 16
Billockby, Nor. ... ...R 423 1
Bilney, East, Nor. ... ...R 148 24
Bilney, West, Nor. ... P.C 461 24
Bilsby, Lin. ... ...V 444 23

Bilsdale, York ... ... P.C 603 8
Bilsington, Cant. ... P.C 110 26
Bilsthorpe, Lin. .. ..R 634 19
Bilston, Lich. ... ... P.C 232 8
St. Luke's ... ...V 306 10
St. Martin's ... ... P.C 719 16
St. Mary's ... ...V 615 1
Bilton, Rip. ... ... P.C 306 25
Bilton, Wor. ... ...R 18 24
Bilton, York ... ...V 482 16
Binbrooke, St. Gabriel, Lin. V 347 13
St. Mary ... ...R 347 13
Bincombe-with-Broadway, Salis. ... ...R 306 8
Binegar, B. and W. ... ...R 451 18
Binfield, Ox. ... ...R 583 21
Bingham, Lin. ... ...R 457 26
Bingley, Rip. ... ...V 354 17
Binham, Nor. ... ...V 121 7
Binley, Wor. ... ... Chap 707 15
Binsey, Ox. ... ... P.C 589 4
Binstead, Win. ... ...R 314 2
V 683 18
Binsted, Chich ... ...R 71 14
Binton, Wor. ... ...R 198 13
Bintree, Nor. ... ...R 331 4
Birbury, Wor. ... ...R 57 13
Birch, Man. ... ... P.C 383 23
Birch, Roch. ... ...R 297 7
Birch, Little, Herf. ... ...R 645 6
Bircham, Great, Nor. ...R 533 28
Bircham Newton with Bircham Tofts, Nor. ...R 54 8
Birchanger, Roch. ... ...R 692 18
Birchfield, Lich. ... P.C 442 9
Birchington, Cant. ... ...V 701 19
Birch-in-Rusholme, Man. R 14 2
Bircholt, Cant. ... ...R 286 9
Birdbrook, Roch. ... ...R 532 8
Birdforth, York ... P.C 726 25
Birdham, Chich. ... ...R 458 17
Birdsall, York ... ... P.C 210 1
Birkby, York ... ...R 811 8
Birkdale, Ches. ... P.C 636 11
Birkenhead, Ches. ... P.C 393 16
St. Anne's ... ... P.C 36 21
St. James's ... ... P.C 473 2
St. John's ... ... P.C 580 14
St. Paul's ... ... P.C 413 15
Trinity ... ... P.C 42 8
Birkenshaw, Rip. ... P.C 201 7
Birkin, York ... ...R 272 3
Birkle, Man. ... ... P.C 724 8
Birley, Herf. ... ...V 750 13
Birling, Cant. ... .V 66 8
Birlingham, Wor. ... ...R 396 12
Birmingham, All Saints, Wor. R 245 2
Bishop Ryder's Ch. P.C 101 18
Ch. Ch. ... ... P.C 442 27
Immanuel Ch. ... P.C 141 3
St. Barnabas' ... P.C 727 1
St. Bartholomew's P.C 200 13
St. Clement's, Nechells P.C 460 25
St. George's ... ...R 652 3
St. Jude's ... ... P.C 516 25
St. Luke's ... ... P.C 166 13
St. Mark's ... ... P.C 403 28
St. Martin's ... ...R 712 2
St. Mary's ... ... P.C 36 4
St. Mathias' ... ... P.C 83 3
St. Matthew's, Duddlestone-cum-Nechells ... P.C 587 8
St. Michael's ... P.C 553 8
St. Paul's ... ... P.C 809 19
St. Peter's ... ... P.C 440 16
St. Philip's ... ...R 743 14
St. Stephen's ... P.C 552 21
St. Thomas's ... ...R 710 8

Birstal, Rip. ... ...V 306 11
Birstall, Pet. ... ... Chap 624 23
Birstwith, Rip. ... ... P.C 283 8
Birtley, Dur. ... ... P.C 724 21
St. John's ... ... P.C 55 21
Birts-Morton, Wor. ... ...R 522 13
Bisbrooke, Pet. ... ...V 67 19
Biscathorpe, Lin. ... ...R 490 23
Biscovey, Ex. ... ... P.C 578 19
Bisham, Ox. ... ...V 531 22
Bishampton, Wor. ... ...V 485 27
Bishop Burton, York ...V 562 18
Bishop Knoyle, Salis. ...R 458 1
Bishop Middleham, Dur. ...V 743 19
Bishop Monkton, Rip. ...V 527 13
Bishops, or West Lavington, Salis. ... ...V 711 10
Bishopsbourne, Cant. ...R 550 2
Bishops Cannings, Salis. ...V 219 1
Bishops Castle, Herf. ...V 571 8
Bishops Caundle, Salis. ...R 268 3
Bishops Cleeve, G. and B. R 659 22
Bishops Frome, Herf. ...V 334 5
Bishops Hatfield, Roch. ...R 638 19
St. Mary's ... ... P.C 175 3
Bishops Hull, B. and W. P.C 718 7
St. John's (Taunton) P.C 608 3
Bishops Itchington, Wor. ...V 436 13
Bishops Lydeard, B. and W. V 688 15
Bishops Norton, Lin. ...V 73 2
Bishops Nympton, Ex. ...V 651 18
Bishops Stortford, Roch. ...V 552 26
Holy Trinity, Newton P.C 427 8
Bishops Sutton, Win. ...V 433 6
Bishop's Tachbrooke, Wor. V 138 22
Bishop's Tawton, Ex. ...V 156 4
Bishops Teignton, Ex. ...V 491 9
Bishopstoke, Win. ... ...R 247 29
Bishopston, G. and B. ...V 396 9
Bishopston, G. and B. P.C 49 15
Bishopston, St. D. ... ...R 370 14
Bishopstone, Chich. ... ...V 296 11
Bishopstone, Herf. ... ...R 562 13
Bishopstone, Salis. R. and V 403 6
Bishopstrow, Salis. ... ...R 683 25
Bishop's Waltham, Win. ...R 87 11
Bishop's Wood, Lich. P.C 579 9
Bishopswood, Herf. ... P.C 206 12
Bishop Thornton, Rip. P.C 199 6
Bishopthorpe, York ... ...V 378 1
Bishopton, Dur. ... ...V 234 13
Bishopton, Wor. ... P.C 218 7
Bishop Wilton, York ...V 207 14
Bishopwearmouth, Dur. ...R 138 15
St. Thomas's ... ... P.C 603 5
Bishopworth, St. Peter's, G. and B. ... ... P C 811 16
Bishton, Llan. ... ... P.C 715 9
Bisley, G. and B. ... ...V 381 2
Bisley, Win. ... ...R 709 1
Bispham, Man. ... ...V 407 15
R 468 16
Bistre, St. A. ... ... P.C 371 5
Bitchfield, Lin. ... ...V 234 6
Bittadon, Ex. ... ...R 476 11
Bittering, Little, Nor. ...R 572 22
Bitterley, Herf. ... .R 679 3
Bitterne, All Souls, Win. P C 670 16
Bitteswell, Pet. ... ...V 464 6
Bitton, G. and B. ... ...V 207 27
Bix, Ox. ... ...R 511 24
Bixley, Nor. ... ...R 83 15
Bixton, Nor. ... ...R 280 18
Blaby, Pet. ... ...R 336 19
Blackawton, Ex. ... ...V 125 24
Blackborough, Ex. ... ...R 183 2
Blackbourton, Ox. ... ...V 424 19
Blackburn, Man. ... ...V 574 4
Ch. Ch. ... ... P.C 474 14

Blackburn, Man.—*contd.*
St. John's ... ... P.C 27 24
St. Michael's, ... P.C 513 7
St. Paul's ... ... P.C 444 13
St. Peter's ... ... P.C 732 15
St. Thomas's ... P.C 697 28
Trinity ... ... P.C 563 1
Blackford, B. and W. ...R 590 2
P.C 701 17
Blackheath, All Saints', Roch.
P.C 625 13
Morden Coll. ... Chap 290 12
Park Chapel ... ... Min 226 9
Blackheath, St. John's, Lon.
P.C 410 31
Blackland, Salis. ... ...R 428 19
Blackley, Man.... ... ...R 381 13
St. Andrew's ... ...R 502 24
Blackmanstone, Cant. ...R 137 9
Blackmore, Roch. ... P.C 109 26
Black Notley, Roch. .. ...R 496 6
Blackpool, Ch. Ch. Man. P.C 364 14
Blackrod, Man.... ... P.C 635 8
Blacktoft, York ... P.C 686 11
Blackwell, Lich. ... ...V 164 18
Bladen, Ox. ... ...R 577 13
Bladington, G. and B. ...V 318 23
Blaenavon, Llan. ... P.C 373 10
Blaengwrach, Llan. ... P.C 277 8
Blaenpenal, St. D. ... P.C 372 15
Blaen-Porth, St. D. ... P.C 311 19
Blagdon, B. and W. ... ...R 636 9
Blaisdon, G. and B. ... ...R 654 1
Blakemore, Herf. ... ...V 339 16
Blakeney, G. and B.... P.C 89 17
Blakeney, Nor.... ... ...R 654 22
Blakenham, Great, Nor. ...R 17 30
Blakenham, Little, Nor. ...R 336 11
Blakesley, Pet. ... ...V 363 1
Blanchland, Dur. ... P.C 252 14
Blandford Forum, Salis. R & V 544 11
Blandford St. Mary, Salis. R 438 8
Blankney, Lin. ... ...R 85 5
Blaston, St. Giles, Pet. ...R 226 30
Blatchington, East, Chich. R 183 1
Blatchington, West, Chich. R 678 15
Blatherwycke, Pet. ... ...R 23 20
Blawith, Carl. ... ... P.C 507 5
Blaxhall, Nor. ... ...R 40 4
Bleadon, B. and W. ... ...R 400 19
Blean, Cant. ... ...V 644 3
Bleasby, Lin. ... ...V 441 7
Blesdale, Man. ... P.C 81 19
Blechingdon, Ox. ... ...R 167 27
Blechingley, Win. ... ...R 126 4
Bledlow, Ox. ... ...V 614 23
Blendworth, Win. ... ...R 686 15
Bletchley, Ox. ... ...R 51 13
Blethvaugh or Bleddfa, St.D.R 535 23
Bletsoe, Ely ... ...R 179 1
Blewbury, Ox. ... ...V 428 14
Blickling, Nor. ... ...R 165 21
Blidworth, Lin.... ... ...V 706 28
Blindley Heath, Win. P.C 60 9
Blisland, Ex. ... ...R 543 3
Blisworth, Pet.... ... ...R 37 5
Blithfield, Lich. ... ...R 25 5
Blockley, Wor. ... ...V 88 10
Blofield, Nor. ... ...R 665 11
Blo-Norton, Nor. ... ...R 416 24
Bloomsbury, Lon. ... ...R 163 24
Bedford Chapel ... Min 49 1
Ch. Ch., Woburn-sq. P.C 746 14
French Episcopal Ch. Min 476 6
St. George-the-Martyr ...R 23 17
Blore Ray, Lich. ... ...R 730 10
Bloxham, Ox. ... ...V 324 20
Bloxholm, Lin. ... ...R 431 8
Bloxwich, Lich... ... P.C 36 16

Bloxworth, Salis. ... ...R 110 20
Blundeston, Nor. ... ...R 152 17
Blunham, Ely ... ...R 475 12
Blunsdon St. Andrew, G.
& B. ... ...R 741 1
Bluntisham, Ely ... ...R 573 20
Blurton, Lich. ... ... P.C 349 21
Blyborough, Lin. ... ...R 267 22
Blyford, Nor. ... ...R 486 21
Blymhill, Lich.... ... ...R 136 5
Blyth, Dur. ... ... Chap 712 23
Blyth, Lin. ... ...V 545 9
Blyton, Lin. ... ...V 561 14
Boarstall, Ox.... ... P.C 209 24
Bobbing, Cant.... ... ...V 600 17
Bobbington, Herf. ... P.C 654 10
Bocking, Roch.... ...D & R 116 17
Bockleton, Herf. ... P.C 453 13
Boconnoc, Ex. ... ...R 640 5
Bodelwyddan, St. A... ...R 719 8
Bodedeyrn, Ban. ... P.C 342 9
Bodenham, Herf. ... ...V 15 13
Bodewryd, Ban... ... P.C 416 2
Bodham, Nor. ... ...R 57 15
Bodiam, Chich.... ... ...V 502 27
Bodicote, Ox. ... ... P.C 266 13
Bodington, Pet. ... ...R 812 9
Bodle-street Green, Chich. R 180 18
Bodmin, Ex. ... ...V 810 10
Bodney, Nor. ... ...R 641 4
Bodwean, Ban. ... ...R 716 15
Bodvari, St. A.... ... ...R 94 7
Bodwrog, Ban. ... ... P.C 716 23
Bognor, Chich. ... ... P.C 458 10
Bolam, Dur. ... ...V 452 21
Bolas, Great, Lich. ... ...R 318 18
Boldmere, St. Michael's, Wor.
P.C 391 8
Boldon, Dur. ... ...R 271 2
Boldre, Win. ... ...V 598 8
Boldre, East, Win. ... P.C 280 12
Bole, Lin.... ... ...V 627 22
Bolingbroke, Lin. ... ...R 73 13
Bolingbroke, New, Lin. P.C 307 14
Bollington, Ches. ... P.C 555 2
Bolney, Chich.... ... ...V 621 1
Bolnhurst, Ely ... ...R 251 13
Bolsover, Lich. ... ...V 811 6
Bolsterstone, York ... P.C 724 23
Bolton, Carl. ... ...R 422 11
Bolton, Rip. ... ... P.C 508 11
Bolton Abbey, Rip. ... Min. 563 25
Bolton-by-Bolland, Rip. ...R 722 21
Bolton-le-Morland, Carl.
P.C 595 17
Bolton-le-Moors, Man. ...V 531 5
All Saints' ... ... P.C 421 16
Ch. Ch.... ... ... P.C 54 4
Emmanuel Ch. ... P.C 699 11
St. George's ... ... P.C 375 17
St. John's ... ... P.C 122 20
St. Mark's ... ... P.C 189 25
St. Paul's ... ... P.C 320 20
Trinity ... ... P.C 421 10
Bolton-le-Sands, Man. ...V 252 24
Bolton-on-Dearne, York ...V 696 24
Bolton-on-Swale, Rip. P.C 163 3
Bolton Percy, York ... ...R 159 11
Bonby, Lin. ... ...V 390 25
Bonchurch, Win. ... ...R 274 8
Boningale, Lich. ... P.C 354 18
Bonnington, Cant. ... ...R 110 26
Bonsall, Lich. ... ...R 56 7
Bonvilstone, Llan. ... P.C 410 13
Bookham, Great, Win. ...V 308 20
Bookham, Little, Win. ...R 284 5
Boothby Graffoe, Lin. ...R 244 4
Boothby Pagnel, Lin. ...R 482 12
Bootle, Carl. ... ...R 709 20

Bootle, Ch. Ch., Ches. P.C 446 16
St. John's ... ... P.C 31 24
St. Mary's ... ... P.C 162 16
Booton, Nor. ... ...R 211 20
Borden, Cant. ... ...V 289 24
Bordesley, St. Andrew's
Wor.... ... ... P.C 319 21
Trinity ... ... P.C 492 2
Boreham, Roch... ... ...V 693 17
Borley, Roch. ... ...R 98 12
Boroughbridge, Rip.... P.C 497 23
Borrowdale, Carl. ... P.C 482 6
Bosbury, Herf.... ... ...V 126 15
Boscombe, Salis. ... ...R 643 6
Bosham, Chich... ... ...V 461 13
Bosley, Ches. ... ... P.C 634 5
Bossall, York ... ...V 600 10
Bossington, Win. ... ...R 404 27
Boston, Lin. ... ...V 66 1
Chapel of Ease ... P.C 507 18
Boston-Spa, York ... ...V 337 14
Bothal, Dur. ... ...R 210 8
Bothamsall, Lin. ... P.C 135 24
Bothenhampton, Salis. P.C 49 28
Botley, Win. ... ...R 404 14
Botleys, Win. ... ... P.C 565 18
Botolph, Chich.... ... ...V 553 9
Botolphbridge, Ely ... ...R 691 25
Bottesford, Lin. ... ...V 619 20
Bottesford, Pet. ... ...R 487 6
Bottisham, Ely... ... ...V 428 3
Bottisham Lode, Ely P.C 247 3
Botus Fleming, Ex. ... ...R 675 16
Boughrood, St. D. ... ...R 185 3
Boughton, Lin.... ... P.C 385 20
Boughton, Nor.... ... ...R 129 26
Boughton, Pet. ... ...R 677 11
Boughton-Aluph, Cant. ...V 58 14
Boughton-Malherbe, Cant. R 466 11
Boughton Monchelsea, Cant.
V 595 12
Boughton-under-Blean, Cant.
V 704 8
Boulge, Nor. ... ...R 811 15
Boultham, Lin.... ... ...R 483 17
Boulton, Lich. ... ...V 527 11
Bourn, Ely ... ...V 557 18
Bourne, Lin. ... ...V 189 12
Bournemouth, Win. ... P.C 50 2
Bourton, Salis. ... ... P.C 481 23
Bourton-on-Dunsmore, Wor. R 384 9
Bourton-on-the-Hill, G. and B.
R 360 23
Bourton-on-the-Water, G. and
B. ... ...R 682 25
Bovey, North, Ex. ... ...R 652 7
Bovey-Tracey, Ex. ... ...V 154 10
Bovingdon, Roch. ... P.C 89 8
Bovinger, Roch.... ... ...R 492 18
Bow, Ex. ... ...R 265 21
Bow, Lon. ... ...R 194 9
St. Stephen's, Old Ford P.C 505 1
Bow-Brickhill, Ox. ... ...R 356 22
Bow Common, St. Paul's, Lon.
P.C 153 18
Bowden, Great, Pet.... P.C 275 19
Bowden, Little, Pet.... ...R 33 25
Bowden Hill, G. and B. P.C 501 11
Bowdon, Ches. ... ...V 526 21
Bower Chalke, Salis. ...V 717 6
Bowers-Gifford, Roch. ...R 655 12
Bowes, Rip. ... ... P.C 503 13
Bowling, St. John's, Rip. P.C 243 2
St. Stephen's... ... P.C 440 17
Bowness, Carl. ... ...R 563 27
Bowthorpe, Nor. ... ...V 508 24
Box, G. and B.... ... ...V 384 18
Boxford, Ely ... ...R 106 20
Boxford, Ox. ... ...R 697 10

D.

Dringhouses, York ... P.C 221 9
Drinkstone, Ely ... ...R 335 3
Droitwich, St. Andrew's, St. Mary's Witton, and St. Nicholas', Wor.... ...R 658 7
St. Peter's ... ...V 402 14
Dronfield, Lich. ... ...V 613 8
Dropmore, Cant. ... P.C 528 23
Droxford, Win.... ... ...R 144 7
Droylesden, Man. ... P.C 650 16
Dry Doddington, 2nd mediety, Lin. ... ...R 673 6
Dry Drayton, Ely ... ...R 612 25
Drypool, York ... ... P.C 208 2
Ducklington, Ox. ... ...R 222 5
Duckmanton, Lich. ... ...V 345 13
Dudleston, Lich. ... P.C 60 20
Duddleston-cum-Nechells, Wor.... ... ... P.C 587 8
Duddington, Pet. ... P.C 270 22
Duddo, Dur. ... ... P.C 750 24
Dudley, Wor. ... ...V 93 6
St. Edmund's ... P.C 173 14
St. James's ... ... P.C 93 16
St. John's ... ... P.C 486 20
Duffield, Lich. ... ...V 466 17
Dufton, Carl. ... ...R 310 11
Dukinfield, Ches. ... P.C 48 4
St. Mark's ... ... P.C 309 5
Dulas, Herf. ... ... P.C 536 19
Dullingham, Ely ... ...V 30 20
Duloe, Ex. ... ...R 105 24
Dulverton, B. and W. ...V 728 15
Dulwich, East, St. John's, Win.... ... ... P.C 209 9
Dumbleton, G. and B. ...R 696 1
Dummer, Win.... ... ...R 4 3
Dunchideock, Ex. ... ...R 500 20
Dunchurch, Wor. ... ...V 701 7
Duncton, Chich. ... ...R 481 22
Dundry, B. and W.... P.C 75 18
Dunham, Great, Nor. ...R 865 16
Dunham, Little, Nor. ...R 291 22
Dunham Massey, Ches. P.C 389 7
Dunham-on-Trent, Lin. ...V 379 20
Dunholme, Lin. ... ...V 36 3
Dunkerton, B. and W. ...R 617 6
Dunkeswell, Ex. ... P.C 160 21
Dunkeswell Abbey, Ex. P.C 160 21
Dunkirk, Cant. ... P.C 619 17
Dunmow, Great, Roch. ...V 587 5
Dunmow, Little, Roch. P.C 656 7
Dunnington, York ... ...R 546 17
Dunningworth, Nor. ...R 305 20
Dunsby, Lin. ... ...R 381 19
Dunsfold, Win. ... ...R 327 23
Dunsford, Ex.... ... ...V 15 6
Dunsforth, Rip. ... P.C 637 3
Dunstable, Ely ... ...R 335 31
Dunstall, Lich. ... P.C 80 5
Dunster, B. and W.... P.C 425 16
Duns Tew, Ox. ... ...V 435 1
Dunston, Lich.... ... P.C 535 12
Dunston, Lin. ... ...V 160 16
Duuston, Nor. ... ... P.C 418 20
Dunterton, Ex. ... ...R 502 9
Dunton, Ely ... ...V 638 4
Dunton, Nor. ... ...V 191 25
Dunton, Ox. ... ...R 17 24
Dunton Bassett, Pet. ...V 419 8
Dunton Waylett, Roch. ...R 664 8
Duntsbourne Abbots, G. and B. ... ...R 304 19
Duntsbourne Rouse, G. & B. R 260 28
Dunwich, Nor. ... ... P.C 486 21
Durham, St. Cuthbert's P.C 557 7
St. Giles's ... ...V 649 9
P.C 244 20
St. Margaret's ... P.C 163 14

Durham—*contd.*
St. Mary-le-Bow ... ...R 684 13
St. Mary's the Less ...R 273 14
St. Nicholas' ... P.C 238 11
St. Oswald's... ... ...V 199 25
Durleigh, B. and W. Chap 329 24
Durley, Win. ... ...V 584 24
Durlton, Lin. ... ...V 379 20
Durnford, Salis. ... ...V 321 14
Durrington, Chich. ... ...V 689 11
Durrington, Salis. ... P.C 573 6
Dursley, G. and B. ... ...R 432 17
Durston, B. and W.... P.C 656 23
Durweston, Salis. ... ...R 495 4
Duston, Pet. ... ...V 31 9
Duxford, St. John's, Ely ...V 117 5
St. Peter's ... ...R 403 22
Dwygyvylchi, Ban. ... ...V 172 11
Dylife, St. A. ... ... P.C 171 20
Dymchurch, Cant. ... ...R 137 9
Dymock, G. and B. ... ...V 809 6
Dynton, G. and B. ... ...R 136 28
Dyrham, G. and B. ... ...R 564 25
Dyserth, St. A.... ... P.C 692 17

E.

Eagle, Lin. ... ...V 133 4
Eaglescliffe, Dur. ... ...R 344 19
Eakring, Lin. ... ...R 687 14
Ealing, Lon. ... ...V 551 21
Ch. Ch.... ... ... P.C 319 24
St. Paul's ... ... P.C 192 27
Eardisland, Herf. ... ...V 32 21
Eardisley, Herf. ... ...V 500 26
Earlham St. Mary, Nor. ...V 508 24
Earls Barton, Pet. ... ...V 392 1
Earls Colne, Roch. ... ...V 62 9
Earls Croome, Wor. ... ...R 519 22
Earls Heaton, Rip. ... P.C 569 1
Earl Soham, Nor. ... ...R 278 17
Earl Sterndale, Lich.... P.C 719 14
Early, Ox.... ... ... P.C 335 4
Earnley, Chich.... ... ...R 151 27
Earsdon, Dur. ... ...V 445 13
Earsham, Nor. ... ...R 265 2
Eartham, Chich. ... ...V 259 14
Easby, Rip. ... ...V 650 2
Easebourne, Chich. ... P.C 664 17
Easington, Dur. ... ...R 436 23
Easington, Ox. ... ...R 227 31
Easington, York ... ...R 468 12
P.C 434 4
Easingwold, York ... ...V 5 18
Eastbourne, Chich. ... ...V 523 16
Ch. Ch.... ... ... P.C 417 5
St. Saviour's ... ... P.C 701 8
Trinity ... ... P.C 520 27
Eastbridge, Cant. ... ...R 61 8
Eastbury, Ox. ... ... P.C 411 19
Eastchurch, Cant. ... ...R 186 1
Eastdown, Ex. ... ...R 17 11
Easter, High and Good, Roch. V 251 6
Eastergate, Chich. ... ...R 561 7
Eastham, B. and W.... ...R 632 10
Eastham, Ches. ... ...V 611 10
Eastham, Herf.... ... ...R 93 3
Easthampstead, Ox. ... ...R 264 21
Easthope, Herf. ... ...R 543 9
Eastington, G. and B. ...R 316 18
Eastleach Martin, G. & B. R 149 8
Eastleach Turnville, G. and B. P.C 149 8
Eastling, Cant.... ... ...R 562 9
Eastnor, Herf. ... ...R 540 27
Eastoft, York ... ... P C 678 4
Easton, B. and W. ... P.C 451 9

Easton, Ely ... ...V 66 10
Easton, Lower, G. and B. P.C 315 13
Easton, Nor. ... ...R 731 25
V 446 14
Easton, Pet. ... ...R 125 12
Easton, Great, Pet. ... ...V 113 6
Easton, Great, Roch. ...R 583 1
Easton, Little, Roch. ...R 128 1
Easton, Win. ... ...R 728 10
Easton Bavents, Nor. ...R 261 8
Easton Grey, G. and B. ...R 60 2
Easton-in-Gordano, B. & W. V 680 2
Easton Maudit, Pet.... ...V 609 4
Easton Neston, Pet.... ...V 143 10
Easton Royal, Salis.... Chap 415 14
Eastover, B. and W. P.C 143 3
Eastrington, York ... ...V 287 2
Eastrop, Win. ... ...R 736 6
Eastry, Cant. ... ...V 593 32
Eastville, Lin. ... ... P.C 327 20
Eastwell, Cant. ... ...R 498 9
Eastwell, Pet. ... ...R 98 23
Eastwood, Lin.... ... ...R 525 7
Eastwood, Rip.... ... P.C 568 15
Eastwood, Roch. ... ...V 59 16
Eatington, Wor. ... ...V 57 26
Eaton, Ch. Ch., Ches. P.C 229 12
Eaton, Herf. ... ...V 581 15
Eaton, Lin. ... ...V 668 8
Eaton, Little, Lich. ... P.C 398 25
Eaton, Long, Lich. ... P.C 19 25
Eaton, Nor. ... ...V 699 8
Eaton, Pet. ... ...V 716 3
Eaton Bishop, Herf. ...R 156 13
Eaton Bray, Ely ... ...V 707 8
Eaton Constantine, Lich. ...R 45 30
Eaton Hastings, Ox. ...R 353 10
Eaton Socon, Ely ... ...V 334 16
Ebberston, York ... ...V 209 20
Ebbesbourne Wake, Salis. P.C 114 23
Ebchester, Dur. ... P.C 632 8
Ebrington, G. and B. ...V 282 11
Ecchinswell, Win. ... ...V 573 14
Eccles, Man. ... ...V 523 10
Eccles, Nor. ... ...R 422 25
Eccles-next-the-Sea, Nor. ...R 495 1
Ecclesall, York... ... P.C 483 1
Ecclesfield, York ... ...V 249 13
Eccleshall, Lich. ... ...V 261 10
Eccleshill, Rip.... ... P.C 453 20
Eccleston, Ches. ... ...R 419 17
Ch. Ch. ... ... P.C 160 1
St. Thomas's ... P.C 462 12
Eccleston, Man. ... ...R 617 17
Eccleston, Great, Man. P.C 191 23
Eckington, Lich. ... ...R 213 14
Eckington, Wor. ... ...V 674 21
Ecton, Pet. ... ...R 171 12
Edale, Lich. ... ... P.C 620 2
Edburton, Chich. ... ...R 444 3
Eddlesborough, Ox. ... ...V 59 3
Edenbridge, Cant. ... ...V 265 3
Edenfield, Man. ... P.C 723 17
Edengale, Lich. ... P.C 216 3
Edenhall, Carl. ... ...V 529 15
Edenham, Lin. ... P.C 592 [illegible]
Edensor, Lich. ... Chap 265 16
P.C 681 5
Edern, Ban. ... ...R 812 29
Edgbaston, Wor. ... ...V 879 20
St. George's... ... P.C 402 11
St. James's ... ... P.C 93 19
Edgcott, Ox. ... ...R 442 20
Edgcott, Pet. ... ...R 42 11
Edgefield, Nor.... ... ...R 438 15
Edge-hill, St. Catherine's Ches. ... ... P.C 343 7
St. Mary's ... ... P.C 292 12
St. Stephen's ... P.C [illegible] 5

F.

G.

HHH

H.

I.

J.

Jackfield, Herf.... ... ...R 404 10
Jacobstow (Cornwall), Ex. R 39 18
Jacobstow (Devon), Ex. ...R 676 1
Jarrow, Dur. ... ...R 519 18
Jeffreyston, St. D. ... ...V 502 1
Jersey, All Saints, Win. P.C 306 13
Gorea ... ... P.C 56 2
Grouville ... ...R 408 24
Rozel Manor Chapel Min 406 6
St. Aubin's Chapel Chap 407 19
St. Brelade's... ... ...R 221 12
St. Clement's ... ...R 438 22
St. James's Chapel Min 49 7
St. John's ... ...R 408 6
St. Lawrence's ... ...R 493 18
St. Luke's ... ... P.C 279 17
St. Martin's ... ...R 279 19
St. Mary's ... ...R 29 23
St. Matthew's ... P.C 526 2
St. Ouen ... ...R 134 18
St. Paul's ... ... Min 134 13
St. Peter's ... ...R 406 26
St. Saviour's... ... ...R 403 19
Trinity ... ...R 196 14
Jevington, Chich. ... ...R 267 3
Johnston, St. D. ... ...R 648 11
Jordanstone, St. D. ... ...R 480 1

K.

Keal, East, Lin. ... ...R 618 2
Keal, West, Lin. ... ...R 731 16
Kearsley, Man.'... ... ...V 643 14
Keddington, Lin. ... ...V 612 1
Kedington, Ely... ... ...R 636 25
Kedleston, Lich. ... ...R 584 28
Kealby, Lin. ... ...V 330 21
Keele, Lich. ... ... P.C 634 2
Keevil, Salis. ... ...V 527 6
Kegworth, Pet.... ... ...R 130 29
Keighley, Rip. ... ...R 105 19
Keinton Mandeville, B. & W. R 415 7
Kelbrook, Rip. ... ... P.C 497 17
Kelham, Lin. ... ...R 680 30
Kellaways, G. and B. ...R 132 29
Kellet Over, Man. ... ...V 544 10
Kelling, Nor. ... ...R 256 17
Kellington, York ... ...V 437 10
Kelloe, Dur. ... ...V 695 17
Kelly, Ex.... ... ...R 473 8
Kelmarsh, Pet. ... ...R 167 10
Kelsale, Nor. ... ...R 91 11
Kelsall, Ches. ... ... P.C 167 5
Kelsey, North, Lin. ... ...V 123 8
Kelsey, South, Lin. ... ...R 84 9
Kelshall, Roch.... ... ...R 666 4
Kelstern, Lin. ... ...V 221 11
Kelston, B. and W. ... ...R 533 5
Kelvedon, Roch. ... ...V 50 14
Kelvedon Hatch, Roch. ...R 30 11
Kemberton, Lich. ... ...R 692 1
Kemble, G. and B. ... ...V 642 15
Kemerton, G. and B. ...R 652 22
Kemeys Inferior, Llan. ...R 408 10
Kempley, G. and B. ... ...V 590 21
Kempsey, Wor.... ... ...V 239 2
Kempsford, G. and B. ...V 732 7
Kempston, Ely ... ...V 714 22
Kempston, Nor. ... ...V 398 9
Kemsing-with-Seal, Cant. V 62 10
Kenardington, Cant.... ...R 58 14
Kenarth, St. D. ... ...V 172 33
Kenchester, Herf. ... ...R 215 35
Kencott, Ox. ... ...R 810 14
Kendal, Carl. ... ...V 148 24
St. George's ... ... P.C 245 1
Kendal, Carl—*contd.*
St. Thomas's... ... P.C 464 12
Kenderchurch, Herf.... P.C 699 13
Kenilworth, Wor. ... ...V 57 6
St. John's ... ... P.C 318 9
Kenley, Lich. ... ...R 603 18
Kenn, B. and W. ... P.C 2 17
Kenn, Ex.... ... ...R 529 11
Kennerleigh, Ex. ... ...R 212 8
Kennett, Ely ... ...R 261 3
Kennett, East, Salis.... P.C 24 16
Kenninghall, Nor. ... ...V 538 12
Kenningham, Nor. ... ...R 423 5
Kennington, Cant. ... ...V 721 9
Kennington, Ox. ... P.C 689 4
Kennington, St. Barnabas', Win.... ... ... P.C 194 3
St. James's Chapel P.C 384 4
St. Mark's ... ... P.C 416 10
Kensal Green, St. John's, Lon. P.C 512 25
Kensington, Lon. ... ...V 601 21
All Saints (Notting-hill) P.C 412 1
St. Andrew's... ... P.C 562 15
St. Barnabas' ... P.C 313 15
St. James's (Notting-hill) P.C 326 24
St. John's (Notting-hill) P.C 250 18
St. Mark's (Notting-hill) P.C 383 14
St. Philip's ... ... P.C 133 18
Kensington, South, St. Peter's, Lon. ... ... P.C 747 9
St. Stephen's... ... P.C 19 7
Kensworth, Roch. ... ...V 725 19
Kentchurch, Herf. ... ...R 589 14
Kentford, Ely ... ...R 643 22
Kentisbere, Ex.... ... ...R 10 1
Kentisbury, Ex. ... ...R 493 15
Kentish-town, Lon. (*see* St. Pancras).
Kentmere, Ches. ... P.C 305 18
Kenton, Ex. ... ...V 167 22
Kenton, Nor. ... ...V 704 17
Kenvig, Llan. ... ...V 214 10
Kenwyn, Ex. (*see* Truro).
Kerdiston, Nor.... ... ...R 711 12
Keresley, Wor. ... ... P.C 645 22
Kerry, St. A. ... ...V 470 20
Kersall, Man. ... ...R 443 1
Kersey, Ely ... ... P.C 345 15
Kesgrave, Nor. ... ... P.C 142 9
Kessingland, Nor. ... ...R 161 11
Keston, Cant. ... ...R 650 10
Keswick, St. John's, Carl. P.C 41 7
St. John's-in-the-Vale P.C 642 5
Keswick, Nor. ... ...R 187 6
Ketley, Lich. ... ... P.C 629 4
Ketsby, Lin. ... ...R 445 24
Kettering, Pet.... ... ...R 413 1
Ketteringham, Nor. ... ...V 12 29
Kettlebaston, Ely ... ...R 230 24
Kettleburgh, Nor. ... ...R 666 5
Kettleshulme, Ches. ... P.C 108 6
Kettlestone, Nor. ... ...R 464 16
Kettlethorpe, Lin. ... ...R 19 28
Kettlewell, Rip.... ... ...V 299 24
Ketton, Pet. ... ...V 489 3
Kevenlleece, St. D. ... ...R 651 15
Kew, Win. ... ...V 488 24
Kewstoke, B. and W. ...V 301 7
Kexby, York ... ... P.C 434 3
Keyingham, York ... P.C 614 8
Keynsham, B. and W. ...V 563 10
Keysoe, Ely ... ...V 5 24
Keystone, Ely ... ...R 263 9
Keyworth, Lin. ... ...R 530 5
Kibworth Beauchamp, Pet. R 494 21
Kidbrooke, Roch. ... ...R 733 13
Kidderminster, Wor. ...V 79 7
St. George's ... ... P.C 474 25
St. John's ... ... P.C 386 9
Kiddington, Ox. ... ...R 93 15
Kidlington, Ox. ... ...V 412 5
Kidmore End, Ox. ... P.C 137 12
Kidsgrove, Lich. ... P.C 678 2
Kidwelly, St. D. ... ...V 277 23
Kiffig, St. D. ... ... P.C 469 19
Kilburn, Trinity, Lon. P.C 184 4
St. John's ... ... P.C 809 22
St. Mary's ... ... P.C 811 18
St. Paul's Chap. ... Min 812 22
Kilburn, York ... ... P.C 32 26
Kilby, Pet. ... ... P.C 284 3
Kildale, York ... ...V 120 21
Kildwick-in-Craven, Rip. V 224 4
Kilgerran, St. D. ... ...R 214 14
Kilham, York ... ...V 225 26
Kilken, St. A. ... ...V 286 18
Kilkennin, St. D. ... ...V 359 6
Kilkhampton, Ex. ... ...R 654 6
Killamarsh, Lich. ... P.C 607 14
Killingholme, Lin. ... ...V 108 26
Killington, Ches. ... P.C 711 14
Killingworth, Dur. ... P.C 63 17
Killymaenllwyd, St. D. ...R 375 32
Kilmersdon, B. and W. ...V 673 20
Kilmington, B. and W. ...R 685 25
Kilndown, Cant. ... P.C 296 1
Kilnhurst, York ... P.C 596 1
Kilnsea, York ... ...V 434 4
Kilnwick Percy, York ...V 401 20
Kilrhedyn, St. D. ... ...R 312 2
Kilsby, Pet. ... ...V 143 16
Kilton, B. and W. ... ...V 594 13
Kilve, B. and W. ... ...R 275 2
Kilverstone, Nor. ... ...R 467 5
Kilvington, Lin. ... ...R 580 4
Kilvington, South, York ...R 389 8
Kilworth, North, Pet. ...R 47 7
Kilworth, South, Pet. ...R 532 17
Kilwrwg, Llan.... ... P.C 535 22
Kilycwm, St. D. ... ...V 446 24
Kimberley, Lin. ... P.C 582 16
Kimberley, Nor. ... ...V 280 18
Kimberworth, York ... P.C 287 7
Kimble, Great, Ox. ... ...V 494 9
Kimble, Little, Ox. ... ...R 162 21
Kimblesworth, Dur. ... ...R 116 3
Kimbolton, Ely ... ...V 5 15
Kimbolton, Herf. ... P.C 349 14
Kimcote, Pet. ... ...R 156 7
Kimmeridge, Salis. ... Chap 104 18
Kimpton, Roch. ... ...V 633 14
Kimpton, Win. ... ...R 546 14
Kineton, Wor. ... ...V 458 12
Kingerby, Lin. ... ...V 627 24
Kingham, Ox. ... ...R 417 19
Kingsbridge, Ex. ... ...V 321 9
King's Bromley, Lich. P.C 320 19
Kingsbury, Lon. ... ...V 19 11
Kingsbury, Wor. ... ...V 119 7
Kingsbury Episcopi, B. and W. V 616 21
Kingsclere, Win. ... ...V 35 5
King's Cliffe, Pet. ... ...R 198 9
Kingsdon, B. and W. ...R 290 3
Kingsdown, Cant. ... ...R 334 9
P.C 24 14
Kingsdown, Roch. ... ...R 184 26
Kingsey, Ox. ... ...V 357 19
King's Heath, Wor. ... ...V 695 13
King's Kerswell, Ex. P.C 472 2
Kingsland, Herf. ... ...R 216 22
King's Langley, Roch. ...V 324 18
Kingsley, Ches. ... P.C 669 5
Kingsley, Lich. ... ...R 259 18

Llanbadarnfawr (Cardigan), St. D. ... ...V 540 6
Llanbadarnfawr (Radnor), St. D. .. ..R. 375 7
Llanbadarn Treveglwys, St. D. V 350 6
Llanbadarn Vynydd, St. D. P.C 409 25
Llanbadarn-y-garreg, St. D. P.C 647 23
Llanbadrig, Ban. ... ...V 368 5
Llanbeblig, Ban. ... ...V 675 25
Llanbeder, St. D. ... ...R 376 16
Llanbedr, Ban. ... ...R 91 5
Llanbedr-Dyffryn-Clwyd, Ban. R 645 13
Llanbedrog, Ban. ... ...R 497 24
Llanbedr-y-Cenin, Ban. ...R 342 10
Llanberis, Ban.... ... .. R 719 4
Llanbeulan, Ban. ... ...R 717 1
Llanbister, St. D. ... ...V 554 11
Llanblethian, Llan. ... ...V 203 20
Llanboidy, St. D. ... ...V 551 9
Llanbrynmair, Ban. ... ...R 390 3
Llancarvon, Llan. ... ...V 468 18
Llancillo, Herf.... ... P.C 384 6
Llancynfelin, St. D. ... P.C 648 8
Llandanwg, Ban. ... ...R 91 5
Llandarog, St. D. ... P.C 471 25
Llandawcke, St. D. ... ...R 646 5
Llanddeiniol, St. D. ... P.C 215 23
Llanddeiniolen, Ban.... ...R 341 25
Llandderfel, St. A. ... ...R 373 11
Llanddeusant, Ban. ... ...R 715 8
Llanddewi, St. A. ... ...R 690 24
Llanddewi, St. D. ... ...V 713 9
Llanddewi Aberarth, St. D. P.C 343 23
St. Alban's ... .. P.C 371 15
Llanddewi Brevi, St. D. P.C 214 21
Llanddewi-'r-Cwm, St. D. P.C 296 22
Llanddewy Fach, St. D. ...V 717 19
Llanddoget, St. A. ... ...R 175 6
Llanddulas, St. A. ... ...R 173 16
Llanddyvnan, Ban. ... ...R 718 12
Llandebie, St. D. ... ...V 216 2
Llandecwyn, Ban. ... P.C 375 30
Llandefeilog, St. D.... ...V 13 4
Llandegai, Ban. ... P.C 470 18
St. Ann's ... ... P.C 646 16
Llandegla, St. A. ... ...R 713 24
Llandeglay, St. D. ... ...V 673 5
Llandegvan, Ban. ... ...R 812 30
Llandegveth, Llan. ... ...R 714 15
Llandeloy, St. D. ... ...V 176 12
Llandenny, Llan. ... ...V 740 14
Llandevailog Vach, St. D....R 336 8
Llandevalley, St. D. ... ...V 672 3
Llandevand, Llan. ... P.C 408 10
Llandeveisant, St. D.... P.C 715 1
Llandewi Rytherch ... P.C 492 22
Llandewi Velfrey, St. D. ...V 370 16
Llandewi-Ystrad-Ennau, St. D. ... ... P.C 527 10
Llandilo, St. D. ... P.C 684 24
Llandilo Abercowin, St. D. P.C 377 6
Llandilo Graban, St. D. P.C 416 14
Llandilo-'r-Van, St. D. P.C 726 18
Llandilo-tal-y-bont, St. D. V 132 25
Llandilo Vawr, St. D. ...V 277 20
Llandinabo, Herf. ... ...R 45 10
Llandinam, Ban. ... ...V 370 21
Llandingat, St. D. ... ...V 343 2
Llandinorwig, St. D.... P.C 205 4
Llandissilio, St. D. ... ...V 293 17
Llandogo, Llan. ... P.C 227 3
Llandonna, Ban. ... P.C 411 8
Llandough (Cardiff) Llan. R 556 8
Llandough, with St. Mary's Cb. (Cowbridge), Llan. ...R 573 21

Llandow, Llan.... ... ...R 206 20
Llandowror, St. D. ... ...R 647 20
Llandrillo, St. A. ... ...V 741 23
Llandrillo-yn-Rhôs, St. A. V 343 15
Llandrindod, St. D. ... P.C 651 15
Llandrinio, St. A. ... ...R 598 1
Llandrygarn, Ban. ... P.C 716 23
Llandudno, Ban. ... ...R 469 18
Llandugwydd, St. D. P.C 409 24
Llandwrog, Ban. ... ...R 377 14
St. Thomas's ... P.C 539 16
Llandyfodwg, Llan. ... ...V 536 24
Llandyfrydog, Ban. ... ...R 311 20
Llandygwydd, St. D. P.C 204 21
Llandyrnog, St. A. ... ...R 560 5
Llandysilio, Ban. ... ...R 172 5
Llandysilio, St. A. ... ...R 84 11
Llandysilio Gogo, St. D. ...V 373 9
Llandyssil, St. A. ... ...R 227 27
Llandyssil, St. D. ... ...V 468 27
Llandyvriog, St. D. ... ...V 215 15
Llanedarn, Llan. ... ...V 216 13
Llanederne... ... ...V 362 18
Llanedy, St. D. ... ...R 713 17
Llanefydd, St. A. ... ...V 371 4
Llanegryn, Ban. ... P.C 372 1
Llanegwad, St. D. ... ...V 215 3
Llaneilian, Ban. ... ...R 497 4
Llanelian, St. A. ... ...R 646 12
Llanelidan, St. A. ... ...R 560 8
Llanelieu, St. D. ... ...R 373 18
Llanellen, Llan. ... ...V 377 10
Llanellian, St. A. ... ...R 357 1
Llanelltyd, Ban. ... P.C 416 20
Llanelly, St. D. ... ...V 471 25
P.C 277 7
St. Paul's ... ... P.C 713 22
Llanelwedd, St. D. ... P.C 178 1
Llanenddwyn, Ban. ... ...R 377 16
Llanengan, Ban. ... ...R 376 19
Llanerchymedd, Ban. P.C 496 24
Llanervul, St. A. ... ...R 430 11
Llaneugrad, Ban. ... ...R 472 10
Llanfabon, Llan. ... ...V 486 16
Llanfaebreth, Ban. ... P.C 714 10
Llanfaelrhys, Ban. ... P.C 560 24
Llanfaes, Ban. ... ... P.C 374 28
Llanfaglen, Ban. ... ...V 713 23
Llanfaino, Herf. ... P.C 176 3
Llanfair, Ban. ... ...R 445 14
Llanfair Caereinion, St. A. V 539 23
Llanfairfechan, Ban.... ...R 209 30
Llanfairisgaer, Ban. ... P.C 276 24
Llanfair Nant-y-Gof, St. D. R 479 13
Llanfair Orllwyn, St. D. ...R 416 27
Llanfairpwllgwyngyll, Ban. R 172 6
Llanfair Talhaiarn, St. A. R 409 30
Llanfawr, St. A. ... P.C 715 19
Llanfechain, St. A. ... ...R 719 5
Llanfechell, Ban. ... ...R 206 7
Llanfihangel Crucorney, Llan. V 565 21
Llanfihangelfechan, St. D. P.C 717 5
Llanfihangel Lledrod, St. D. P.C 225 15
Llanfihangel Penbedw, St. D. R 567 10
Llanfihangel-Tal-y-Llyn, St. D. R 69 29
Llanfihangel-y-Pennant, Ban. P.C 537 9
Llanfihangel-yng-Nghwnfa, St. A. ... ...R 214 25
Llanfinnan, Ban. ... P.C 376 1
Llanfoist, Llan.... ... ...R 540 2
Llanfor, St. A. ... ...R 470 16
Llanfrothen, Ban. ... ...R 716 10
Llanfrynach, Llan. ... ...V 415 16
Llanfrynach, St. D. ... ...R 535 17

Llanfwrog, St. A. ... ...R 372 23
Llanfyllin, St. A. ... ...R 716 27
Llanfyndd, St. D. ... ...V 714 21
Llanfynydd, St. A. ... P.C 416 30
Llanfyrnach, St. D. ... ...R 339 11
Llangadfan, St. A. ... ...R 205 1
Llangadock Vawr, St. D. ...V 469 30
Llangadwaladr, Ban. ...R 716 4
Llangadwaladr, St. A. P.C 716 26
Llangain, St. D. ... P.C 362 16
Llangammarch, St. D. ...V 363 18
Llangan, Llan.... ... ...R 217 3
Llangan, St. D. ... ...V 215 34
Llangar, St. A.... ... ...R 718 9
Llangarrin, Herf. ... ...V 530 14
Llangasty Tallylln, St. D. R 174 20
Llangathen, St. D. ... ...V 214 20
Llangattock, Llan. ... ...R 151 1
V 205 6
Llangattock, St. D. ... ...R 339 7
Llangattock Llingoed, Llan. V 565 21
Llangattock-Vivon-Avel, Llan. V 515 20
Llangedwyn, St. A. ... P.C 719 10
Llangefni, Ban.... ... ...R 496 22
Llangeinor, Llan. ... P.C 415 16
Llangeinwen, Ban. ... ...R 718 27
Llangeitho, St. D. ... ...R 215 7
Llangeler, St. D. ... ...R 409 9
V 277 15
Llangelynin (Conway), Ban. R 535 8
Llangelynin (Dolgelly), Ban. R 173 28
Llangendeirn, St. D.... P.C 175 22
Llangennech, St. D. ... P.C 470 13
Llangennith, St. D. ... ...V 423 4
Llangenny, St. D. ... ...R 339 7
Llangerniew, St. A. ... ...V 371 11
Llangeview, Llan. ... P.C 68 2
Llangibby, Llan. ... ...R 714 3
Llanginning, St. D. ... P.C 363 12
Llangoed, Ban.... ... P.C 172 32
Llangoedmore, St. D. ...R 488 5
Llangollen, St. A. ... ...V 206 15
Llangolman, St. D. ... P.C 684 24
Llangorse, St. D. ... ...V 469 14
Llangoven, Llan. ... P.C 331 3
Llangower, St. A. ... ...R 215 24
Llangristiolus, Ban. ... ...R 374 8
Llangriville, Lin. ... P.C 385 13
Llangua, Llan. ... ...R 589 14
Llanguick, St. D. ... P.C 370 20
Llangullo, St. D. ... ...R 175 13
Llangunider, St. D. ... ...R 294 12
Llangunllo, St. D. ... ...V 171 25
Llangurig, Ban. ... ...V 216 2
Llangwyllog, Ban. ... P.C 209 11
Llangwm, Llan. ... ...V 536 16
Llangwm, St. A. ... ...V 373 15
Llangwm, St. D. ... ...R 717 17
Llangwstenyn, St. A. P.C 560 12
Llangwyryvon, St. D. P.C 216 19
Llangwyvan, St. A. ... ...R 374 24
Llangybi, Ban.... ... ...R 717 7
Llangyfelach, St. D.... ...V 214 19
Llangynhafal, St. A. ...R 561 18
Llangyniew, St. A. ... ...R 362 20
Llangynog, St. A. ... ...R 748 8
Llangynnog, St. D. ... P.C 214 4
Llangynwyd, Llan. ... ...V 415 18
Llanhamlêch, St. D. ...R 470 7
Llanharry, Llan. ... ...R 718 23
Llanhenog, Llan. ... P.C 531 25
Llanhilleth, Llan. ... ...R 342 8
Llanhowell, St. D. ... ...V 176 12
Llanidan, Ban.... ... ...V 372 20
Llanidloes, Ban. ... ...V 376 9
Llaniestyn, Ban. ... ...R 497 3
Llanigan, St. D. ... ...V 648 13

Llanilar, St. D. ... ...V 410 9
Llanilid, Llan. ... ...R 175 16
Llaniltid, or St. Illtyd, St. D. P.C 469 24
Llanina, St. D.... ... ...V 370 30
Llanishen (Cardiff), Llan. P.C 551 6
Llanishen (Chepstow), Llan. P.C 490 4
Llanllawddog, St. D. P.C 531 7
Llanllechid, Ban. ... ...R 216 7
Llanlleonvel, St. D. ... P.C 566 27
Llanllibio, Ban. ... ...R 540 9
Llanllowell, Llan. ... ...R 714 15
Llanllugan ... ... P.C 358 2
Llanllwch, St. D. ... P.C 362 16
Llanllwchaiarn, St. A. ...V 657 16
Llanllwchaiarn, St. D. ...R 214 15
Llanllwni, St. D. ... ...V 76 1
Llanllynvi, Ban. ... ...R 344 1
Llanmadock, St. D. ... ...R 173 27
Llanmaes, Lan. ... ...R 646 13
Llanmarewig, St. A.... ...R 416 15
Llanmartin, Llan. ... ...R 277 10
Llanmihangel, Llan.... ...R 214 24
Llannon, St. D. ... P.C 471 25
Llanover, Llan.... ... ...V 216 16
Llanpympsaint, St. D. P.C 531 7
Llanreithan, St. D. ... P.C 342 5
Llanrhaiadr - in - Kinmerch, St. A. ... ...V 647 22
St. James's ... ... P.C 343 9
Llanrhaiadr - yn - Mochnant, St. A. ... ...V 718 13
Llanrhidian, St. D. ... ...V 550 29
Llanrhyd, St. A. ... ...R 369 20
Llanrhyddlad, Ban. ... ...R 716 14
Llanrhystid, St. D. ... ...V 217 10
Llanrian, St. D. ... ...V 342 5
Llanrothal, Herf. ... ...V 690 10
Llanrug, Ban. ... ...R 714 26
Llanrwst, St. A. ... ...R 174 12
Llansadurnen, St. D. ...R 296 8
Llansadwrn, Ban. ... ...R 560 29
Llansadwrn, St. D. ... ...V 373 13
Llansaintfraed, Llan. ...R 617 16
Llansaintfraid-in-Elvel, St. D. V 672 13
Llansaintfread, St. D. ...R 690 23
Llansamlet, St. D. ... ...V 470 5
Llansannan, St. A. ... ...V 540 4
Llansannor, Llan. ... ...R 192 13
Llansantffraid-Glân-Conway, St. A. ... ...R 171 27
Llansantffraid-Glyn-Ceiriog, St. A. ... ... P.C 343 6
Llansantffraid-Glyn-Dyfrdwy, St. A. ... ...R 748 21
Llansantffraid-yn-Mechan, St. A. ... ...V 343 11
Llansantffread, St. D. ...V 312 7
Llansawel, St. D. ... ...V 176 9
Llansilin, St. A. ... ...V 377 8
Llansoy, Llan.... ... ...R 217 29
Llanspythid, St. D.... ...V 469 24
Llanstadwell, St. D.... ...V 271 5
Llanstephan (Carmarthenshire), St. D. ... P.C 214 4
Llanstephan (Radnorshire), St. D. ... ... P.C 416 14
Llanstinan, St. D. ... ...R 76 19
Llantewnlle, St. D. ... ...V 215 8
Llanthew, St. D. ... P.C 174 3
Llanthewy Skirrid, Llan. R 222 16
Llanthewy Vach, Llan. P.C 374 13
Llanthony Abbey, Llan. P.C 410 19
Llanthoysaint, St. D. ...V 469 30
Llantillio Crossenny, Llan. V 171 17
Llantillio Pertholey, Llan. P.C 470 15
Llantvisant, Ban. ... ...R 540 9
Llantrisant, Llan. ... ...V 374 22
Llantrissent (Newport), Llan. V 682 1
Llantrithyd, Llan. ... ...R 669 12
Llantwit, Llan.... ... ...R 276 20
Llantwit Major, Llan. ...V 672 12
Llantwit Vairdre, Llan. P.C 646 27
Llantwyd, St. D. ... ...V 675 24
Llantysilio, St. A. ... P.C 370 23
Llanuwchllyn, St. A. P.C 374 27
Llanvaches, Llan. ... ...R 413 4
Llanvachreth, Ban. ... ...R 713 14
Llanvaethlu, Ban. ... ...R 812 32
Llanvair-ar-y-bryn, St. D. V 343 2
Llanvair Discoed, Llan. P.C 624 1
Llanvair-Dyfryn-Clwyd, Ban. V 496 18
Llanvair Kilgidin, Llan. ...R 410 2
Llanvair Nantgwynn, St. D. P.C 217 8
Llanvair Trelygen, St. D ...R 215 15
Llanvair Waterdine, Herf. P.C 387 5
Llanvalteg, St. D. ... ...R 217 6
Llanvanair, Llan. ... P.C 515 20
Llanvapley, Llan. ... ...R 416 16
Llanvarith, St. D. ... ...R 575 10
Llanverres, St. A. ... ...R 497 1
Llanvetherine, Llan.... ...R 623 22
Llanvigan, St. D. ... ...R 713 4
Llanvihangel, Llan. ... ...R 716 21
Llanvihangel Aberbythic, St. D. ... ... P.C 715 1
Llanvihangel-ar-arth, St. D. V 371 14
Llanvihangel Cwmdu, St. D. R 342 17
Llanvihangel-Genen-r-Glyn, St. D. ... ...V 373 16
Llanvihangel-Glyn-Myvyr, St. A. ... ...R 560 13
Llanvihangel Gobion, Llan. R 247 9
Llanvihangel Helygen, St. D. P.C 215 27
Llanvihangel Llantarnam, Llan. ... ... P.C 171 26
Llanvihangel Nantbran, St. D. ... ... P.C 726 18
Llanvihangel Nantmellan, St. D. ... ... P.C 718 11
Llanvihangel - Ponty - Moile, Llan. ... ... P.C 146 5
Llanvihangel-rhyd-Ithan, St. D. ... ... P.C 527 10
Llanvihangel-Tor-y-Mynydd, Llan. ... ...R 535 22
Llanvihangel-vac - Cilvargen, St. D. ... ...R 485 9
Llanvihangel-y-Croyddin, St. D. ... ...V 374 10
Llanvihangel-y-Pennant, Ban. R 505 27
Llanvihangel Yaceiviog, Ban. R 376 1
Llanvihangel-ystern-Llewern, Llan. ... ...R 244 22
Llanvihangel Ystrad, St. D. V 469 1
Llanvihangel-y-Traethan, Ban. P.C 375 30
Llanvillo, St. D. ... ...R 374 1
Llanvrechva, Llan. ... P.C 531 25
Llanwarne, Herf. ... ...R 478 19
Llanwddyn, St. A. ... P.C 342 27
Llanwenarth, Llan. ... ...R 220 25
Llanwenllwyfo, Ban. P.C 560 4
Llanwenog, St. D. ... ...V 225 14
Llanwern, Llan. ... ...R 579 21
Llanwinio, St. D. ... P.C 277 22
Llanwnda, Ban. ... ...V 713 23
Llanwnda, St. D. ... ...V 554 29
Llanwnen, St. D. ... ...V 217 20
Llanwnog, Ban. ... ...V 561 12
Llanwonno, Llan. ... P.C 175 20
Llanwnws, St. D. ... P.C 749 26
Llanwrda, St. D. ... ...V 373 13
Llanwrin, Ban. ... ...R 175 5
Llanwrthwl, St. D. ... ...V 550 25
Llanwyddelan, St. A. ...R 206 11
Llanyblodwell, St. A. ...V 237 1
Llanybri, St. D. ... P.C 377 6
Llanybyther, St. D.... ...V 225 14
Llanychaer, St. D. ... ...R 175 21
Llanychaëron, St. D. P.C 175 7
Llanychaiarn, St. D. P.C 173 13
Llanychan, Ban. ... ...R 718 15
Llanycil, St. A. ... ...R 214 17
Llanymawddwy, Ban. ...R 214 12
Llanymynech, St. A. ...R 425 19
Llanynis, St. D. ... ...R 718 21
Llanynys, Ban.... ... ...V 276 17
Llanyre, St. D.... ... P.C 215 27
Llanystyndwy, Ban.... ...R 553 25
Llan-y-Kevan, St. D. P.C 174 7
Llawhaden, St. D. ... ...V 370 5
Llawr-y-Bettws, St. A. P.C 174 19
Llechgynfarny, Ban. ... ...R 540 9
Llechryd, St. D. ... P.C 496 29
Llowes, St. D. ... ...V 717 19
Llwydiarth, St. A. ... P.C 496 19
Llysfaen, St. A. ... ...R 491 19
Llyswen, St. D.... ... ...R 377 9
Llywell, St. D. ... ...V 536 1
Lockinge, B. and W.... ...V 400 2
Lockinge, East, Ox. ... ...R 407 14
Lockington, Pet. ... ...V 80 18
Lockington, York ... ...R 188 6
Lockwood, Rip.... ... P.C 52 9
Loddington, Pet. ... ...R 257 6
V 723 18
Loddiswell, Ex. ... ...V 659 8
Loddon, Nor. ... ...V 610 13
Loders, Salis. ... ...V. & R 164 4
Lodsworth, Chich. ... P.C 131 23
Lofthouse, Rip.... ... P.C 121 26
Loftus, York ... ...R 317 2
Lois Weedon, Pet. ... ...V 616 2
Lolworth, Ely ... ...R 32 1
Londesborough, York ...R 725 3
London (City of)—
Allhallows, Barking ...V 647 6
Allhallows (Bread-street) R 187 1
Allhallows (Lombard-st.) R 430 17
Allhallows (London-wall) R 394 7
Allhallows the Great ...R 627 20
Allhallows the Less ...R 627 20
Allhallows (Honey-lane) R 676 8
All Saints (Bishopsgate-st.) P.C 344 8
Christ Church (Newgate) V 252 4
St. Alban's (Gray's-inn-lane) P.C 431 13
St. Alban's (Wood-street) R 163 11
St. Alphage's ... ...R 382 14
St. Andrew's (Holborn)...R 68 20
St. Andrew Hubbard ...R 161 24
St. Andrew Undershaft (Leadenhall-street) ...R 67 10
St. Andrew-by-the-Wardrobe ... ... R 125 17
St. Anne's (Blackfriars) R 125 17
St. Anne's and St. Agnes' R 530 22
St. Antholin's ... ...R 459 10
St. Augustine's ... ...R 460 3
St. Bartholomew's (Cripplegate)... ... ... P.C 183 20
St. Bartholomew's (Exchange) ... ...R 572 4

Lutterworth, Pet. ... ...R 367 24
Lutton, Pet. ... ...R 251 18
Luxulyan, Ex. ... ...V 336 7
Lydbrook, G. and B. ... P.C 326 6
Lydbury, North, Herf. ...V 567 20
Lydd, Cant. ... ...V 105 4
Lydden, Cant. ... ...V 398 26
Lyde, Herf. ... ...V 301 14
Lydeard St. Lawrence, B. & W.
R 161 13
Lydford, East, B. and W. R 474 13
Lydford, West, B. and W. R 241 3
Lydford, Ex. ... ...R 810 29
Lydgate, Ely ... ...R 120 26
Lydgate, Man.... ... ...V 155 7
Lydham, Herf. ... ...R 490 3
Lydiard Millicent, G. & B. R 305 22
Lydiate, Ches. ... ... P.C 158 11
Lydlinch, Salis.... ... ...R 311 3
Lydney, G. and B. ... ...V 519 19
Lye, Ch. Ch. Wor. ... P.C 561 29
Lyford, Ox. ... ... P.C 111 6
Lyme Regis, Salis. ... ...V 323 23
Lyminge, Cant. ... R & V 363 14
Lyminster, Chich. ... ...V 212 18
Lymm, Ches. 1st mediety R 82 15
2nd mediety R 44 25
Lympne, Cant.... ... ...V 61 8
Lympsham, B. and W. ...R 625 5
Lympstone, Ex. ... ...R 165 6
Lynby, Lin. ... ...R 537 17
Lynch, Chich. ... ...R 98 15
Linchmere, Chich. ... P.C 506 6
Lyncombe, B. and W. P.C 692 12
Lyncombe, G. and B. ...V 619 21
Lyndhurst, Win. ... ...R 145 1
Lyndon, Pet. ... ...R 494 3
Lyneham, Salis. ... P.C 348 8
Lynesach, Dur. ... P.C 474 6
Lyng, B. and W. ... ...V 730 6
Lyng, Nor. ... ...R 365 14
Lynn, North, Nor. ... ...R 728 17
St. John's ... ... P.C 227 6
Lynn, West, Nor. ... ...R 355 26
Lynn Regis, Nor. ... ...V 405 15
Lynsted, Cant.... ... ...V 287 18
Lynton, Ex. ... ... P.C 401 18
Lyonshall, Herf. ... ...V 270 16
Lyss, Win. ... ... P.C 241 17
Lytchett Matravers, Salis. R 307 15
Lytchett Minster, Salis. ...V 68 19
Lytham, Man.... ... P.C 564 11
St. John's ... ... P.C 589 9
Lythe-cum-Ugthorpe, York V 510 25

M.

Mabe, Ex. ... ...V 322 25
Mablethorpe, Lin. ... ...R 149 13
Mablethorpe St. Peter, Lin. R 384 7
Macclesfield, Ches. ... P.C 606 17
Ch. Ch. ... ... P.C 624 3
St. Paul's ... ... P.C 84 12
St. Peter's ... ... P.C 602 1
Macclesfield Forest, Ches. P.C 241 4
Machen, Llan. ... ...R 468 14
Machynlleth, Ban. ... ...R 276 11
Mackworth, Lich. ... ...V 254 7
Maddington, Salis. ... P.C 50 9
Madehurst, Chich. ... ...V 585 10
Madeley, Herf. ... ...V 742 10
Madeley, Lich. ... ...V 167 17
Madingley, Ely... ... ...V 209 23
Madley, Herf. ... ...V 217 25
Madresfield, Wor. ... ...R 476 28
Madron, Ex. ... ...V 516 17
Maenclochog, St. D.... ...V 684 24
Maentwrog, Ban. ... ...R 204 18
Maesmynis, St. D. ... ...R 718 21
Maghull, Ches.... ... P.C 426 11
Magor, Llan. ... ...V 583 2
Maiden Bradley, Salis. P.C 690 5
Maidenhead, Ox. ... ...V 327 15
St. Mary's ... ... P.C 413 10
Maiden Newton, Salis. ...R 587 4
Maiden Well, Lin. ... ...V 729 19
Maidford, Pet. ... ...R 704 6
Maidstone, Cant. ... ...V 626 25
St. John's ... ... P.C 41 27
St. Paul's ... ... P.C 180 17
St. Peter's ... ... P.C 319 20
St. Philip's ... ... P.C 143 19
Trinity ... ... P.C 299 21
Maidwell, Pet. ... ...R 704 20
Maindee, Llan.... ... P.C 483 8
Mainstone, Herf. ... ...R 745 6
Maisemore, G. and B. P.C 292 23
Maker, Ex. ... ...V 727 5
Malden, Win. .. ..V 622 23
Malden, New, Win. ... P.C 627 12
Maldon, Roch. ... ...V 335 28
St. Mary's ... ...R 84 25
Malin's Lee, Lich. ... P.C 293 18
Mallerstang, Carl. ... P.C 564 14
Malling, East, Cant. ...V 708 4
Malling, West, Cant. ...V 654 24
Malling, South, Chich. P.C 685 26
Mallwyd, Ban. ... ...R 204 19
Malmesbury, G. and B. ...V 523 19
Malpas, Ches. High mediety
R 653 14
Low mediety R 155 13
St. Chad's ... ... P.C 430 21
Maltby, York ... ...V 567 24
Maltby-le-Marsh, Lin. ...R 10 14
Malton, Great, Wor.... ...V 230 23
Malton, New, St. Leonard's,
York... ... ... P.C 208 17
St. Michael's... ... P.C 229 15
Malton, Old, York ... P.C 274 17
Malvern Link, Wor.... P.C 172 10
Malvern, Little, Wor. P.C 386 8
Malvern Wells, St. Peter's,
Wor. ... ... P.C 333 27
Malvern West, St. James's,
Wor.... ... ... P.C 240 25
Mamble, Herf. ... ...V 171 18
Mamhead, Ex. ... ...R 154 11
Mambilad, Llan. ... P.C 146 5
Man, Isle of, Kirk Andreas,
S. and M. ... ...R 467 10
St. Jude's... ... P.C 131 18
Kirk Arbory... ... ...V 543 19
Kirk Ballaugh ... ...R 338 15
Kirk Braddan ... ...V 195 7
St. Barnabas' ... P.C 269 13
St. George's ... P.C 303 22
St. Matthew's ... P.C 112 28
St. Thomas's ... P.C 810 11
Kirk Bride ... ...R 480 17
Jurby ... ...V 291 18
Kirk Christ Lezayre ...V 310 1
Kirk St. Ann ... ...V 298 24
Kirk Christ Rushen ...V 254 17
Kirk German ... ...V 630 3
Cronk-y-Voddee P.C 203 22
St. John's... ... P.C 151 6
Kirk Lonan ... ...V 109 14
Laxey ... ... P.C 48 19
Kirk Malew ... ...V 255 3
St. Mark's ... P.C 5 20
St. Mary's ... P.C 227 9
St. Thomas's ... P.C 611 13
Kirk Marown ... ...V 6 3
Kirk Maughold (Ramsey) V 295 12
St. Paul's... ... P.C 385 9
Kirk Michael ... ...V 352 30
Man, Isle of, S. and M.—*contd.*
Kirk Onchan ... ...V 338 12
Kirk Patrick ... ...V 246 16
St. James's (Dalby) P.C 317 15
Foxdale ... ... P.C 466 18
Manaccan, Ex.... ... ...V 337 18
Manafon, St. A. ... ...R 410 32
Manaton, Ex. ... ...R 362 23
Manby, Lin. ... ...R 678 24
Mancetter, Wor. ... ...V 555 27
Manchester, Albert Memorial
Church, Man. ... ...R 210 15
All Souls, Ancoats ...R 326 19
St. Andrew's Ancoats ...R 556 6
St. Ann's ... ...R 31 22
St. Barnabas' ... P.C 295 2
St. Catherine's ... ...R 303 23
St. Clement's ... P.C 564 21
St. George's ... ... P.C 457 11
St. James's ... ...R 228 20
St. James's Hope... P.C 584 18
St. John's ... ...R 347 11
St. Jude's ... ...R 254 20
St. Luke's (Cheetham)...R 128 14
St. Mark's (Cheetham-hill)
R 213 20
St. Mary's ... ...R 397 4
St. Matthew's ... ...R 52 20
St. Michael's... ... ...R 671 19
St. Paul's ... ...R 395 1
St. Peter's ... ...R 251 9
St. Peter's (Oldham-road)
R 176 8
St. Philip's ... ...R 350 15
St. Simon with St. Jude's
R 490 24
Manerdivy, St. D. ... ...R 417 3
Maner Owen, St. D. ... P.C 554 28
Manfield, Rip. ... ...V 742 25
Mangotsfield, G. and B. P.C 509 9
Manningford Abbotts, Salis. R 218 14
Manningford Bruce, Salis. R 267 29
Manningham, Rip. ... P.C 462 6
Mannington, Nor. ... ...R 211 19
Manningtree, Roch. ... P.C 2 6
Manorbier, St. D. ... ...V 394 29
Mansel Gamage, Herf. ...V 621 14
Mansell Lacy, Herf. ... ...V 319 11
Mansergh, Carl. ... P.C 241 13
Mansfield, Lin. ... ...V 164 18
St. John's ... ... P.C 81 15
Mansfield Woodhouse, Lin. P.C 88 13
Manston, Rip. ... ... P.C 287 14
Manston, Salis.... ... ...R 452 3
Manthorpe, Lin. ... P.C 248 26
Manton, Lin. ... ...R 166 20
Manton, Pet. ... ...V 810 27
Manuden, Roch. ... ...V 653 2
Maperton, B. and W. ...R 583 6
Maple Durham, Ox.... ...V 141 10
Maplestead, Great, Roch ...V 152 8
Maplestead, Little, Roch. P.C 299 8
Mapleton, Lich. ... ...R 212 25
Mapleton, York, ... P.C 234 28
Mapperley, Lich. ... ...V 482 13
Mapperton, Salis. ... ...R 145 3
Mappowder, Salis. ... ...R 9 8
Marbury, Lich.... ... ...R 207 7
Marcham, Ox. ... ...V 750 17
Marchington Woodlands, Lich.
P.C 132 4
Marchwiel, St. A. ... ...R 73 17
Marchwood, Win. ... P.C 196 19
Marcle, Little, Herf.... ...R 535 7
Marcross, Llan.... ... ...R 715 16
Mardale, Carl. ... ... P.C 329 10
Marden, Cant. ... ...V 181 12
Marden, East, Chich. ...V 426 8
Marden, North, Chich. ...R 676 20

Mickleham, Win. ... ...R 102 15
Mickleover, Lich. ... ...V 165 12
Mickleton, G. & B. ... ...V 743 20
Mickley, Dur. ... ... P.C 448 7
Mickley, Rip. ... ... P.C 296 28
Middle, Lich. ... ...R 207 4
Middle Chinnock, B & W. R 677 5
Middleham, Rip. ... ...R 72 21
Middle Littleton, Wor. P.C 223 25
Middlethorpe, York ... ...V 378 1
Middlesborough, St. Hilda's, York ... ... P.C 43 23
St. John's ... ... P.C 605 23
Middlesmoor, Rip. ... P.C 119 19
Middleton, Carl. ... P.C 1 14
Middleton, Chich. ... ...R 145 8
Middleton, Herf. ... P.C 629 24
Middleton, Man. ... ...R 198 28
P.C 40 5
Middleton (Norfolk), Nor. V 385 27
Middleton (Suffolk), Nor....R 703 25
Middleton, Pet. ... ...R 742 17
Middleton, Rip. ... P.C 634 6
Middleton, Roch. ... ...R 549 9
Middleton, Wor. ... P.C 323 17
Middleton, York ... ...V 431 3
P.C 33 24
Middleton - by - Wirksworth, Lich.... ... ... P.C 487 5
Middleton Cheney, Pet. ...R 97 8
Middleton-in-Teasdale, Dur. R 91 2
Middleton-on-the-Hill, Herf. P.C 349 14
Middleton - on - the - Wolds, York... ... ...R 64 15
Middleton Raisen, Lin. ...V 65 4
Middleton St. George, Dur. R 273 19
Middleton Stoney, Ox. ...R 708 19
Middleton Tyas, Rip. ...V 63 11
Middlewich, Ches. ... ...V 264 2
Middlezoy, B. and W. ...V 610 20
Midgham, Ox. ... ... P.C 810 17
Midhope, York ... ... P.C 665 12
Midhurst, Chich. ... P.C 304 12
Midsomer Norton, B. & W. V 472 25
Midville, Lin. ... ... P.C 327 20
Milborne St. Andrew, Salis. V 63 19
Milburne, Carl.... ... P.C 265 15
Milcombe, Ox..... ... P.C 63 14
Milden, Ely ... ...R 286 22
Mildenhall, Ely ... ...V 518 27
Mildenhall, Salis. ... ...R 615 20
Mileham, Nor. ... ...R 35 20
Miles Platting, Man. ...R 555 21
Milford, Lich. ... ... P.C 161 18
Milford, Win. ... ...V 108 23
P.C 579 6
Milford, South, York P.C 744 5
Milford Haven, St. D. P.C 86 1
Milland, Chich. ... P.C 134 4
Millbrook, Ches. ... P.C 704 16
Millbrook, Ely ... ...R 670 25
Millbrook, Ex. ... ... P.C 37 22
Millbrook, Win.... ... ...R 68 17
Mill, New, Rip.... ... P.C 330 5
Mill Hill, Lon. ... ... P C 485 18
Millington, York ... ...V 208 6
Millom Carl. ... ...V 354 11
Mills, New, Lich. ... P.C 558 13
Milnrow, Man.... ... ...V 545 11
Milnsbridge, Rip. ... P.C 416 21
Milnthorpe, Carl. ... P.C 545 6
Milstead, Cant.... ... ...R 320 12
Milston, Salis. ... ...R 544 22
Milton, Cant. ... ...R 55 20
Milton (Sittingbourne), Cant. V 212 15
Milton, Ely ... ...R 124 9
Milton, Ox. ... ...R 135 7
Milton, Great, Ox. ... ...V 632 23
Milton, Little, Ox. ... P.C 584 8
Milton, Pet. ... ...R 385 26
Milton, Roch. ... ... P.C 441 2
Milton (Lymington), Win. P.C 616 9
Milton (Portsea), Win. P.C 42 21
Milton Abbas, Salis.... ...V 561 16
Milton Abbott, Ex. ... ...V 288 5
Milton Bryant, Ely ... ...R 137 17
Milton Clevedon, B. and W. V 589 21
Milton Damerell, Ex. ...R 12 14
Milton Ernest, Ely ... ...V 746 2
Milton Keynes, Ox. ... ...R 167 8
Milton Lilbourne, Salis. ...V 245 16
Milton-next-Gravesend, Roch. R 368 24
Trinity ... ... P.C 562 20
Milverton, B. and W. ...V 616 15
Milverton, Old, Wor. P.C 610 12
Milwich, Lich. ... ...V 402 1
Mimms, North, Roch. ...V 699 9
Mimms, South, Lon.... ...V 648 26
Minchinhampton, G. and B. R 491 20
Mindtown, Herf. ... ...R 689 2
Minehead, B. and W. ...V 425 15
Minera, St. A.... ... P.C 377 3
Minestead, Win. ... ...R 145 1
Minety, G. and B. ... ...V 205 10
Miningsby, Lin. ... ...R 481 20
Minshull Vernon, Ches. ...V 551 20
Minster, Cant.... ... ...V 700 24
P.C 720 9
Minster, Ex. ... ...R 390 6
Minster Lovell, Ox. ... ...V 201 1
Minsterworth, G. and B. ...V 481 5
Mintern Magna, Salis. ...R 663 8
Minting, Lin. ... ...R. & V 39 5
Mirfield, Rip. ... ...V 448 2
Miserden, G. and B.... ...R 459 30
Missenden, Great, Ox. ...V 270 9
Missenden, Little, Ox. ...V 289 22
Misson, Lin. ... ...V 529 23
Misterton, B. and W. ...V 156 2
Misterton, Lin.... ... P.C 466 25
Misterton, Pet.... ... ...R 240 5
Mistley, Roch. ... ...R 305 4
Mitcham, Win.... ... ...V 722 2
Mitchell Troy, Llan.... ...R 616 4
Mitcheldersh, Win.... ...R 449 2
Mitford, Dur. ... ...V 615 14
Mithian, Ex. ... ... P.C 419 23
Mitton, Rip. ... ...V 206 5
Mitton, Lower, Wor.... P.C 251 23
Mixbury, Ox. ... ...R 501 5
Moat, New, St. D. ... ...R 647 26
Moberley, Ches. ... ...R 435 20
Mocças, Herf. ... ...R 152 2
Modbury, Ex. ... ...V 271 1
Moggerhanger, Ely ... P.C 395 5
Molash, Cant. ... ... P.C 545 25
Mold, St. A. ... ...V 173 10
Molesey, East, Win.... P.C 96 24
St. Paul's ... ... P.C 585 19
Molesey, West, Win. ... P.C 484 12
Molesworth, Ely ... ...R 133 13
Molland, Ex. ... ...V 447 14
Mollington, Ox. ... P.C 683 9
Molton, North, Ex. ... ...V 101 11
Molton, South, Ex. ... P.C 434 7
Monachlogddu, St. D. P.C 669 12
Monewden, Nor. ... ...R 419 4
Mongeham, Great, Cant. ...R 513 24
Mongeham, Little, Cant. ...R 299 5
Mongewell, Ox.... ... ...R 198 22
Monington, St. D. ... ...V 675 24
Monk Bretton, York... P.C 395 7
Monken Hadley, Lon. ...R 119 18
Monk Frystone, York P.C 356 8
Monk Hesleden, Dur. ...V 442 19
Monk Hopton, Herf.... P.C 179 12
Monkland, Herf. ... ...V 27 21
Monkleigh, Ex. ... ...V 713 14
Monknash, Llan. ... P.C 206 20
Monk Okehampton, Ex. ...R 466 7
Monk's Eleigh, Ely ... ...R 682 10
Monk's Horton, Cant. ...R 69 22
Monksilver, B. and W. ...R 156 11
Monk Soham, Nor. ... ...R 278 18
Monk's Risborough, Ox. ...R 218 24
Monk's Sherborne, Win. ...V 48 22
Monk's Toft, Nor. ... ...R 686 22
Monkswood, Llan. ... P.C 28 13
Monkton, B. and W.... ...R 368 25
Monkton, Cant. ... ...V 701 19
Monkton, Ex. ... ... P.C 430 14
Monkton Combe, B. & W. P.C 525 18
Monkton Farley, Salis. ...R 657 26
Monkwearmouth, All Saints', Dur. ... ... P.C 364 11
St. Peter's ... ... P.C 457 19
Monkton Wyld, Salis. P.C 408 20
Monmouth, Llan. ... ...V 16 11
St. Thomas's ... P.C 46 3
Monnington-on-Wye, Herf. R 319 1
Montacute, B. and W. ...V 261 24
Montford, Lich.... ... ...V 136 4
Montgomery, Herf. ... ...R 416 19
Monxton, Win. ... ...R 198 26
Monyash, Lich.... ... P.C 284 24
Moor, Low, Rip. ... P.C 419 21
Moor Allerton, Rip. ... P.C 178 2
Moorby, Lin. ... ...R 607 19
Moor Critchill, Salis. ...R 530 1
Moorhouse, Lin. ... ...V 443 12
Moorlinch, B. and W. ...V 425 3
Moor Monkton, York ...R 742 27
Morborne, Ely ... ...R 14 4
Morchard Bishop, Ex. ...R 570 23
Morcott, Pet. ... ...R 348 14
Morden, Salis. ... ...V 569 21
Morden, Win. ... ...R 662 6
Mordiford, Herf. ... ...R 247 21
More, Herf. ... ...R 435 5
Morebath, Ex. ... ...V 53 10
Moresby, Carl. ... ...R 738 17
Morestead, Win. ... ...R 602 18
Moreton, Ches.... ... ...R 224 21
Moreton, Lich.... ... P.C 103 5
Moreton, North, Ox.... ...V 31 26
Moreton, South, Ox.... ...R 456 11
Moreton, Roch.... ... ...R 458 25
Moreton, St. A. ... P.C 748 21
Moreton, Salis.... ... ...R 289 10
Morton Corbet, Lich. ...R 731 15
Moreton Hampstead, Ex....R 180 7
Moreton-in-the-Marsh, G. & B. R 360 23
Moreton Maids, Ox.... ...R 670 21
Moreton-on-Lugg, Herf. ...R 109 2
Morton Say, Lich. ... P.C 670 9
Moreton Valence, G. & B. P.C 274 16
Morland, Carl. ... ...V 439 8
Morleigh, Ex. ... ...R 568 1
Morley, Lich. ... ...R 238 19
Morley, Rip. ... ... P.C 604 10
Morley St. Botolph, Nor. ...R 148 11
Morningthorpe, Nor.... ...R 667 21
Morpeth, Dur. ... ...R 275 8
Morston All Saints, Nor. ...R [illegible]
Mortehoe, Ex. ... ...V 481 2
Mortlake, Lon.... ... P.C 596 18
Morton, Lich. ... ...R 486 1
Morton (Bourne), Lin. ...V 387 25
Morton (Sleasby), Lin. P.C 441 7
Morton (Gainsbro'), Lin. P.C 97 23
Morton, Rip. ... ... P.C 224 7
Morton Baggott, Wor. ...R 455 21

Morton Jeffries, Herf. P.C 60 18
Morton Merrell, Wor.... P.C 665 18
Morton-on-the-Hill, Nor....R 437 4
Morton Pinckney, G. and B.
P.C 371 20
Morvah, Ex. ... ...V 516 17
Morval, Ex. ... ...V 391 2
Morvil, St. D. ... ...V 647 13
Morville, Herf. ... ... P.C 689 14
Morwenstow, Ex. ... ...V 302 7
Moseley, Wor. ... ... P.C 176 28
Mossley, Ches. ... ... P.C 85 16
Mossley, Man. ... ... P.C 371 27
Mosser, Carl. ... ... P.C 596 14
Moss Side, Man. ... ...R 248 14
Moston, Man. ... ...R 441 16
Mostyn, St. A.... ... P.C 560 7
Mothvey, St. D. ... ...V 370 33
Mottisfont, Win. ... ...R 578 3
Mottistone, Win. ... ...R 552 4
Mottram-in-Longdendale, Ches.
V 378 4
Moughtrey, or Mochtre, St. A.
P.C 503 6
Moulsford, Ox.... ... P.C 471 12
Moulsham, Roch. ... P.C 444 22
Moulsoe, Ox. ... ...R 193 13
Moulton, Ely ...R.& V 473 16
Moulton, Lin. ... ...V 356 18
P.C 602 11
Moulton, Nor. ... ...V 49 9
Moulton, Great, Nor.... ...R 476 14
Moulton, Pet. ... ...V 580 24
Mount, St. D. ... ... P.C 716 18
Mount Bures, Roch.... ...R 84 1
Mountfield, Chich. ... ...V 438 23
Mount Hawke, Ex. ... P.C 628 25
Mountnessing, Roch.... ...V 811 32
Mount Pellon, Rip. ... P.C 659 3
Mount Serrel, Pet. ... P.C 198 11
Ch. Ch. ... ... P.C 255 23
Mountain Ash, Llan.... P.C 370 22
Mountfield, Chich. ... ...V 438 23
Mounton, St. D. ... P.C 409 29
Mowcop, Lich. ... ... P.C 564 5
Moxley, Lich. ... ... P.C 728 10
Moylgrove, St. D. ... P.C 468 23
Much Birch, Herf. ... P.C 45 10
Much Cowarne, Herf. ...V 267 12
Much Dewchurch, Herf. ...V 506 15
Muchelney, B. and W. P.C 8 2
Much Hadham, Roch. ...R 546 24
Much Marcle, Herf. ... ...V 125 25
Much Wenlock, Herf. ...V 693 26
Mucking, Roch. ... ...V 178 10
Mucklestone, Lich. ... ...R 320 16
Mudford, B. and W.... ..V 397 16
Muggleswick, Dur. ... P.C 163 13
Muker, Rip. ... ... P.C 203 14
Mulbarton, Nor. ... ...R 423 5
Mumby, Lin. ... ...V 660 9
St. Leonard's ... P.C 95 16
Muncaster, Carl. ... P.C 504 16
Munden, Great, Roch. ...R 447 27
Munden, Little, Roch. ...R 236 9
Mundon, Roch.... ... ...V 632 2
Mundford, Nor.... ... ...R 547 25
Mundham, Nor. ... P.C 104 29
Mundham, North, Chich....V 327 21
Mundsley, Nor.... ... ...R 585 23
Mungrisdale, Carl. ... P.C 582 27
Munsley, Herf.... ... ...R 334 3
Stip.C 11 7
Munslow, Herf.... ... ...R 531 21
Mursley, Ox. ... ...R 161 8
Murston, Cant.... ... ...R 322 14
Murton, Carl. ... ... P.C 636 24
Musbury, Ex. ... ...R 653 12
Musbury, Man.... ... P.C 650 17

Musgrave, Great, Carl. ...R 123 23
Muskham, North, Lin. ...V 344 21
Muskham, South, Lin. ...V 295 18
Muston, Pet. ... ...R 264 17
Muston, York ... ... P.C 272 7
Muswell-hill, Lon. ... P.C 90 3
Mutford, Nor. ... ...V 196 21
Mydrim, St. D.... ... ...V 363 12
Myland, Roch. ... ...R 284 13
Mylor, Ex. ... ...V 322 25
Mynwere, St. D. ... P.C 896 10
Mynyddyslwyn, Llan. P.C 277 18
Mytholmroyd, Rip. ... P.C 29 9
Myton-on-Swale, York... V 491 26

N.

Naeton, Nor. ... ...R 203 4
Nackington, Cant. ... P.C 606 19
Nafferton, York... ... ...V 170 25
Nailsea, B. and W. ... ...R 90 15
Ch. Ch.... ... ... P.C 42 17
Nailstone, Pet. ... ...R 693 2
Nailsworth, Inchbrook Chap.
G and B.... ... Min 169 4
Nannerch, St. A. ... ...R 713 15
Nantddû, St. D. ... P.C 535 20
Nantglyn, St. A. ... ...V 371 8
Nantmel, St. D. ... ...V 645 24
Nantwich, Ches. ... ...R 125 23
Nantyglo, Llan. ... P.C 469 22
Napton-on-the-Hill, Wor....V 631 23
Narberth, St. D. ... ...R 128 20
Narborough, Pet. ... ...R 598 21
Narburgh, Nor. ... ...R 10 5
Narford, Nor. ... ...V 10 5
Naseby, Pet. ... ...V 178 22
Nash, St. D. ... ...R 647 2
Nash, Llan. ... ...V 528 11
Nassington, Pet. ... ...V 413 18
Nately Scures, Win.... ...R 114 29
Nately, Upper, Win. .. ...V 313 17
Natland, Carl. ... P.C 31 3
Naughton, Ely ... ...R 202 21
Naunton, G. and B.... ...R 414 20
Naunton Beauchamp, Wor. R 605 8
Navenby, Lin. ... ...R 811 3
Navestock, Roch. ... ...V 632 14
Nazing, Roch. ... ...V 611 14
Nayland, Ely ... ... P.C 346 7
Neath, Llan. ... ...R 276 20
Neatished, Nor. ... ...V 92 27
Necton, Nor. ... ...R. & V 681 26
Nedging, Ely ... ...R 202 21
Needham, Nor. ... ... P.C 391 25
Needham Market, Nor. P.C 506 25
Needingworth, Ely ... ...R 429 8
Needwood, Lich. ... P.C 226 27
Neen Savage, Herf. ... ...V 138 17
Neen Sollars, Herf. ... ..R 27 29
Neenton, Herf.... ... ...R 689 3
Nefyn, Ban. ... ... P.C 55 15
Nempnett, B. and W. ...R 663 6
Nenthead, Dur. ... P.C 563 17
Nerquis, St. A.... ... P.C 371 3
Ness, Great, Lich. ... ...V 385 2
Neston, Ches. ... ...V 257 22
Netheravon, Salis. ... ...V 65 8
Netherbury, Salis. ... ..V 558 4
Netherfield, Chich. ... P.C 196 19
Netherhampton, Salis. P.C 492 20
Netherthong, Rip. ... P.C 860 1
Netherton, Wor. ... P.C 603 20
Netherwent, Llan. ... ...R 365 8
Netley, Win. ... ... P.C 579 20
Netteswell, Roch. ... ...R 367 22
Nettlebed, Ox. ... Chap 66 9
Nettlecombe, B. and W. ...R 365 2

Nettleden, Ox. ... ... P.C 120 22
Nettleham, Lin.... ... P.C 631 19
Nettlestead, Cant. ... ...R 137 16
Nettlestead, Nor. ... ...R 356 11
Nettleton, G. and B.... ...R 190 4
Newendon, Roch. ... ...R 385 15
Nevern, St. D.... ... ...V 373 14
Newark-upon-Trent, Lin....V 106 12
Ch. Ch.... ... ... P.C 537 8
Newbald, York. ... ...V 298 26
Newbiggin, Carl. ... ...R 563 29
Newbold, Lich.... ... P.C 70 14
Newbold-de-Verdun, Pet....R 273 10
Newbold-on-Avon, Wor. ...V 74 11
Newbold-on-Stour, Wor. ...R 536 25
Newbold Pacey, Wor. ...V 252 20
Newborough, Ban. ... ...R 454 6
Newborough, Lich. ... P.C 333 8
Newborough, Pet. ... P.C 191 3
Newbottle, Dur. ... P.C 68 12
Newbottle, Pet. ... ...V 47 28
Newbourne, Nor. ... ...R 542 7
Newburgh, Ches. ... P.C 168 29
Newburn, Dur.... ... ...V 550 23
Newbury, Ox. ... ...R 546 10
St. John's ... ... P.C 340 19
Newcastle, Herf. ... P.C 159 4
Newcastle, Little, St. D. P.C 554 28
Newcastle, Llan. ... ...V 67 2
Newcastle Emlyn, St. D. P.C 374 23
Newcastle-under-Lyme, Lich.
R 673 15
St. George's... ... P.C 86 25
Newcastle-upon-Tyne, All
Saints, Dur. ... P.C 354 8
Ch. Ch. ... ... P.C 380 18
Jesmond ... ... P.C 4 15
St. Andrew's ... P.C 201 12
St. Ann's ... ... P.C 312 10
St. James's (Benwell) P.C 448 11
St. John's ... ... P.C 789 4
St. Nicholas... ... ...V 465 7
St. Paul's (Elswick) P.C 595 10
St. Peter's ... ... P.C 545 10
St. Thomas's Chapel Min 108 11
Trinity Chapel ... Chap 272 1
Newchapel, Lich. ... P.C 235 8
Newchurch, Cant. ...R. & V 296 27
Newchurch, Ches. ... ...R 62 8
Newchurch, Llan. ... ...V 588 22
Newchurch, St. D ... ...R 108 14
P.C 559 19
Newchurch-in-Pendle, Man.
P.C 251 11
Newchurch-in-Rossendale,
Man.... ... ...R 518 30
Newdigate, Win. ... ...R 683 8
Newenden, Cant. ... ...R 540 11
Newent, G. and B. ... ...V 730 1
Newhall, Lich.... ... P.C 161 15
Newhaven, Chich. ... ...R 617 3
Newick, Chich.... ... ...R 581 20
Newington (Sittingbourne),
Cant... ... ...V 220 7
Newington (Hythe), Cant. V 812 11
Newington, St. Mary's, Lon. R 493 9
St. Matthew's ... P.C. 651 14
Newington, Ox... ... ...R 153 6
Newington, South, Ox. ...V 112 18
Newington Bagpath, G. & B.
R 151 23
Newland, Ches. ... P.C 588 8
Newland, G. and B.... ...V 557 16
Newland, Roch.... ... ...R 119 1
Newland, Wor. ... ...V 603 1
Newland, York... ... P.C 21 2
Newlands, Carl. ... P.C 575 20
Newlyn, Ex. ... ...V 56 24
St. Peter ... ... P.C 675 5

Newmarket, All Saints, Ely P.C 623 13
St. Mary's ... ...R 354 24
Newmarket, St. A. ... P.C 172 20
Newnham, Cant. ... ...V 77 3
Newnham, G. and B. P.C 84 14
Newnham, Ox. ... ...V 668 23
Newnham, Pet. ... ...V 271 28
Newnham, Roch. ... ...V 260 16
Newnham, Win. ... ...R 741 6
Newnton, Long, G. and B. R 213 15
Newnton, North, G. and B. V 544 21
Newnton Longville, Ox. ...R 342 11
Newport, Ex. ... ... P.C 253 11
Newport, Lich. ... ...R 475 14
Newport, Roch.... ... ...V 124 10
Newport, St. D. ... ...R 647 13
Newport, St. Wooloa, Llan. V 302 15
St. Paul's ... ... P.C 737 14
Newport, Win. ... ... P.C 145 19
St. John's ... ... Min 328 12
Newport Pagnell, Ox. ...V 309 6
Newtimber, Chich. ... ...R 264 11
Newton, North, B. & W. P.C 660 18
Newton, West, Carl.... P.C 71 12
Newton, Long, Dur. ... ...R 420 7
Newton (Sudbury), Ely ...R 606 14
Newton (Wisbech), Ely ...R 152 9
V 714 20
Newton, Lin. ... ...R 656 5
Newton, Old, Nor. ... ...V 647 1
Newton, West, Nor. ... ...R 585 9
Newton, Pet. ... ... Chap 152 4
Newton, South, Salis. ...V 514 10
Newton, St. D.... ... P.C 396 10
Newton Arlosh, Carl. P.C 595 19
Newton Blossomville, Ox. R 638 17
Newton Bromswold, Pet. ...R 643 10
Newton-by-Castle-Acre, Nor. V 67 17.
Newton Ferrers, Ex.... ...R 743 5
Newton Flotman, Nor. ...R 418 20
Newton Heath, Man. ...R 349 18
Newton-in-Cleveland, York P.C 351 14
Newton-in-Clodock, Herf. P.C 631 10
Newton-in-Makerfield, Ches. R 706 5
St. Peter's ... ... P.C 706 6
Newton-in-the-Thistles, Wor. R 242 24
Newton Kyme, York ...R 122 13
Newton Moor, Ches.... P.C 76 27
Newton Nottage, Llan. ...R 392 5
Newton Poppleford, Ex. P.C 681 17
Newton Purcell, Ox.... ...R 451 13
Newton Rigney, Carl. P.C 708 11
Newton St. Cyres, Ex. ...V 544 5
Newton St. Loe, B. and W. R 265 9
Newton St. Petrock, Ex. ...R 408 5
Newton Solney, Lich. Chap 257 4
Newton-by-Toft, Lin. ...R 93 4
Newton Tony, Salis. ...R 512 20
Newton Tracey, Ex.... ...R 182 14
Newton-upon-Ouse, York P.C 273 2
Newton-upon-Rawcliffe, York P.C 138 6
Newton-upon-Trent, Lin....V 360 9
Newton Valence, Win. ...V 431 10
Newtown, Rip. ... ... P.C 311 14
Newtown, St. A. ... ...R 205 11
Newtown, Win.... ... P.C 9 23
St. Luke's ... ... P.C 574 13
Newtown Lindford, Pet. Min 443 18
Nibley, North, G. and B. P.C 204 17
Nichol Forest, Carl.... P.C 379 11
Nidd, Rip. ... ...V 436 5
Ninebanks, Dur. ... P.C 587 23
Ninehead, B. and W. ...V 683 17
Ninfield, Chich. ... ...V 545 18
Niton, Win. ... ...R 305 17
Nocton, Lin. ... ...V 722 8
Noke, Ox. ... ...R 246 10
Nolton, St. D. ... ...R 53 23
Nonington, Cant. ... P.C 149 21
Norbiton, Win.... ... P.C 326 8
Norbury, Ches. ... ... P.C 736 14
Norbury, Herf.... ... ...V 567 20
Norbury (Derby), Lich. ...R 89 24
Norbury (Staffs), Lich. ...R 97 20
Norden, Man. ... ... P.C 298 15
Norham, Dur. ... ...V 388 13
Norley, Ches. ... ... P.C 405 20
Normacot, Lich. ... P.C 330 27
Normanby, Lin. ... ...V 39 11
Normanby, York ... ...R 318 14
Normanby-on-the-Wolds, Lin. R 20 15
Normanton, South, Lich....R 191 17
Normanton, Lin. ... ...R 124 15
Normanton, Pet. ... ...R 91 28
Normanton, York ... ...V 396 28
Normanton - le - Heath, Pet. P.C 271 15
Normanton-on-Soar, Lin....R 581 11
Normanton-on-Trent, Lin. V 246 7
Northallerton, York ...V 453 21
Northam, Ex. ... ...V 266 2
Northam, Win.... ... P.C 36 14
Northampton, All Saints', Pet. V 250 4
St. Andrew's... ... P.C 629 15
St. Edmund's ... P.C 93 8
St. Giles' ... ...V 565 6
St. Katharine's ... P.C 388 5
St. Peter's ... ...R 183 32
St. Sepulchre's ... ...V 107 19
Northaw, Roch. ... P.C 410 3
Northborough, Pet. ... ...R 704 14
Northbourne, Cant. ... ...V 51 9
Northchurch, or Berkhamstead, Roch. ... ...R 591 13
Northenden, Ches. ... ...R 366 21
Northfield, Wor. ... ...R 132 3
Northfleet, Roch. ... ...V 616 24
Northiam, Chich. ... ...R 420 1
Northill, Ely ... ...R 530 4
Northleach, G. and B. ...V 335 18
Northleigh, Ex.... ... ...R 731 29
Northmoor, Ox. ... P.C 184 19
Northmoor Green, B. and W. P.C 346 13
Northolt, Lon. ... ...V 288 4
Northop, St. A. ... ...V 717 16
Northorpe, Lin.... ... ...V 631 25
Northover, B. and W. ...V 201 13
Northwich, Ches. ... P.C 415 6
Northwold, Nor. ... ...R 487 4
Northwood, Lich. ... P.C 355 17
Northwood, Lon. ... P.C 581 24
Norton, B. and W. ... ...R 314 5
Norton, Cant. ... ...R 303 21
Norton, Dur. ... ...V 134 21
Norton, Ely ... ...R 185 5
Norton, G. and B. ... ...V 356 17
P.C 667 1
Norton, Herf. ... ...V 317 14
Norton, Lich. ... ...V 510 24
Norton, Roch. ... ...V 521 1
Norton, Wor. ... ...V 41 4
Norton, York ... ... P.C 178 11
Norton Bavant, Salis. ...V 207 22
Norton-by-Daventry, Pet....V 152 12
Norton Canes, Lich.... ...R 685 21
Norton Canon, Herf.... ...V 562 22
Norton Cuckney, Lin. ...V 738 4
Norton Disney, Lin.... ...V 560 17
Norton-in-Hales, Lich. ...R 599 19
Norton-juxta-Kempsey, Wor. P.C 362 10
Norton-juxta-Twycross, Pet. R 388 14
Norton Malreward, B. & W. R 642 22
Norton Mandeville, Roch. P.C 221 18
Norton-on-the-Moors, Lich. R 12 2
Norton St. Philip, B. & W. V 103 23
Norton Subcourse, Nor. ...V 558 23
Norton-under-Hambdon, B. and W.... ... ...R 67 12
Norwell, Lin. ... ...V 449 7
Norwich, All Saints ... ...R 495 22
Ch. Ch. ... ... P.C 678 7
St. Andrew's... ... P.C 150 4
St. Augustine's ... ...R 544 18
St. Benedict's ... P.C 190 3
St. Clement's ... ...R 558 14
St. Edmund's ... ...R 643 5
St. Ethelred's ... P.C 61 26
St. George Colegate P.C 198 18
St. George Tombland P.C 661 18
St. Giles' ... ... P.C 558 28
St. Gregory's ... P.C 736 22
St. Helen's ... ... P.C 507 25
St. James's ... ... P.C 537 11
St. John's (Maddermarket) R 535 14
St. John de Sepulchre P.C 467 23
St. John's (Timberhill) P.C 655 17
St. Julian's ... ...R 493 22
St. Lawrence's ... ...R 320 5
St. Margaret's ... ...R 137 11
St. Martin's-at-Oak P.C 109 23
St. Mary Coslany... P.C 473 4
St. Mary-in-the-Marsh P.C 446 14
St. Michael's-at-Plea ...R 473 4
St. Michael-at-Thorn P.C 171 7
St. Michael Coslany ...R 811 19
St. Paul's ... ...R 146 3
St. Peter Mancroft P.C 665 17
St. Peter's (Hungate) ...R 655 17
St. Peter's (Mountergate) P.C 199 4
St. Peter's (Southgate) R 61 24
St. Saviour's ... ... P.C 147 5
St. Stephen's ... ...V 29 4
St. Swithin's ... ...R 604 22
Norwood, Lon. ... ...R 736 9
Norwood, St. Luke's, Win. P.C 406 19
Norwood, South, St. Mark's, Cant. ... ... P.C 16 14
Norwood, Upper, All Saints, Cant. ... ... P.C 691 21
Nossley ... ... Chap 170 13
Notgrove, G. and B.... ...R 675 13
Nottingham, All Saints', Lin. P.C 281 22
St. Anne's ... ... P.C 643 26
St. James's ... ... P.C 47 19
St. John-the-Baptist's P.C 671 16
St. Luke's ... ... P.C 565 17
St. Mark's ... ... P.C 149 25
St. Mary's ... ...V 473 5
St. Matthew's P.C 197 10
St. Nicholas'... ... ...R 738 17
St. Paul's ... ... P.C 15 24
St. Peter's ... ...R 699 27
St. Saviour's ... ... P.C 210 18
Trinity ... ... P.C 428 15
Notting-hill (*see* Kensington).
Nowton, Ely ... ...R 490 5
Nuffield, Ox. ... ...R 333 26
Nunburnholme, York ...R 472 1
Nuneaton, Wor. ... ...V 583 14
Nuneham Courtenay, Ox. ...R 146 22
Nunkeeling, York ... P.C [illegible] [illegible]
Nun Monkton, Rip. ... ...V 579 4
Nunney, B. and W. ... ...R 645 15

Nunnington, York ... ...R 148 18
Nun Ormsby, Lin. ... ...V 418 1
Nunthorpe-in-Cleveland, York P.C 351 14
Nunton, Salis. ... ...V 508 27
Nursling, Win.... ... ...R 712 7
Nurstead, Roch. ... ...R 203 16
Nutfield, Win. ... ...R 86 10
Nuthall, Lin. ... ...R 674 23
Nuthurst, Chich. ... ...R 427 17
Nutley Lane, Win. ... P.C 449 3
Nymet Rowland, Ex. ...R 644 12
Nympsfield, G. and B. ...R 407 6
Nympton St. George, Ex....R 128 8

O.

Oadby, Pet. ... ...V 274 9
Oakamoor, Lich. ... P.C 386 21
Oake, B. and W. ... ...R 61 23
Oakengates, Lich. ... P.C 23 2
Oakford, Ex. ... ...R 504 6
Oakham, Pet. ... ...V 475 1
Oakhill, B. and W. ... P.C 641 18
Oakington, Ely... ... ...V 588 11
Oakley, Ely ... ...V 141 8
Oakley, Nor. ... ...R 507 11
Oakley, Ox. ... ...V 79 12
Oakley, Roch. ... ...V 101 8
Oakley, Great, Pet. ... Chap 98 17
Oakley, Parva, Pet. ... ...R 634 15
Oakley, Great, Roch.... ...R 440 18
Oakley, Little, Roch.... ...R 102 16
Oakridge, G. and B.... P.C 315 14
Oaksey, G. and B. ... ...R 487 23
Oakwood, Win.... ... P.C 224 18
Oakworth, Rip.... ... P.C 610 2
Oare, B. and W. ... ...R 11 17
Oare, Cant. ... ... P.C 726 20
Oborne, Salis. ... ...V 426 15
Oby, Nor.... ... ...R 70 11
Occold, Nor. ... ...R 655 22
Ockbrook, Lich. ... ...V 586 13
Ockendon, North, Roch. ...R 228 14
Ockendon, South, Roch. ...R 217 31
Ocker Hill, Lich. ... P.C 616 1
Ockham, Win. ... ...R 161 16
Ockley, Win. ... ...R 199 7
Ocle Pitchard, Herf.... ...V 318 10
Odcombe, B. and W. ...R 29 11
Oddingley, Wor. ... ...R 529 6
Oddington, G. and B. ...R 708 5
Oddington, Ox.... ... ...R 516 11
Odd Rode, Ches. ... P.C 683 9
Odell, Ely... ... ...R 346 23
Odiham, Win. ... ...R 133 1
Odstock, Salis.... ... ...R 278 22
Offchurch, Wor. ... ...V 360 25
Offenham, Wor. ... P.C 86 17
Offham, Cant. ... ...R 463 21
Offley, Roch. ... ...V 579 24
Offley, High, Lich. ... ...V 588 21
Offord Cluny, Ely ... ...R 666 1
Offord D'Arcy, Ely ... ...R 651 24
Offton, Nor. ... ...V 650 7
Offwell, Ex. ... ...R 150 6
Ogborne St. Andrew, Salis. V 332 5
Ogborne St. George, Salis. V 528 7
Ogley Hay, Lich. ... P.C 357 8
Ogwell, East, Ex. ... ...R 641 10
Ogwell, West, Ex. ... ...R 641 10
Okeford Fitzpaine, Salis. ...R 347 3
Okehampton, Ex. ... ...V 192 7
Okenbury, Ex. ... ... Chap 321 8
Oldberrow, Wor. ... ...R 579 7
Oldbury, Herf ... ...R 541 17
Oldbury, Wor. ... ... P.C 77 13

Oldbury-on-Severn, G. & B. R 228 8
Oldbury-on-the-Hill, G.&B. R 218 3
Oldcastle, Llan. ... ...R 470 12
Old Cleeve, B. and W. ...R 694 18
Oldham, G. and B. ... P.C 667 17
Oldham, Man. ... ... P.C 685 2
St. James's ... ... P.C 261 19
St. Peter's ... ... P.C 496 15
Oldridge, Ex. ... ... P.C 338 22
Old Weston, Ely ... ...R 47 25
Olney, Ox. ... ...V 397 28
Olveston, G. and B.... ...V 474 7
Ombersley, Wor. ... ...V 20 25
Onecote, Lich. ... ... P.C 485 6
Onehouse, Nor.... ... ...R 543 8
Ongar, High, Roch. ... ...R 200 25
Onibury, Herf. ... ...R 323 27
Openshaw, Man. ... ...R 504 18
Orby, Lin.... ... ...V 367 17
Orchard, East, Salis. ...V 124 20
Orchardleigh, B. and W. ...R 719 6
Orchard Portman, B. and W. R 529 17
Orcheston St. George, Salis. R 422 10
Orcheston St. Mary ...R 687 13
Orcop, Herf. ... ... Chap 268 22
Ordsall, Lin. .. ..R 388 9
Ore, Chich. ... ...R 667 9
Orford, Ches. ... ... Chap 598 24
Orgarswick, Cant. ... ...R 569 5
Orlestone, Cant. ... ...R 567 19
Orleton, Herf. ... ...V 206 17
Orlingbury, Pet. ... ...R 320 13
Ormesby St. Margaret with St. Michael, Nor. ...V 66 23
Ormsby, South, Lin.... ...R 445 25
Ormsby, York ... ...V 354 3
Ormside, Carl. ... ...R 132 28
Ormskirk, Ches. ... ...V 105 23
Orpington, Cant. ... ...V 247 15
Orsett, Roch. ... . R 67 14
Orston, Lin. ... ...V 453 3
Orton, Carl. ... ...V 602 9
Orton, Great, Carl. ... ...R 645 12
Orton, Pet. ... ...V 474 2
Orton Longueville, Ely ...R 691 25
Orton-on-the-Hill, Pet. ...V 149 4
Orton Waterville, Ely ...R 459 18
Orwell, Ely ... ...R 640 23
Osbaldwick, York ... ...V 168 12
Osbournby, Lin. ... ...V 357 9
Osgathorpe, Pet. ... ...R 718 8
Osmaston-next-Ashbourne, Lich.... ... ... P.C 608 14
Osmington, Salis. ... ...V 517 26
Osmotherley, York ... ...V 372 7
Ospringe, Cant. ... ...V 275 20
Ossett, South, Rip. ... P.C 480 10
Ossett-cum-Gawthorpe, Rip. P.C 404 28
Ossington, Lin.... ... P.C 660 14
Oswaldkirk, York ... ...R 144 20
Oswaldtwisle, Man. ... P.C 299 22
Oswestry, St. A. ... ...V 580 1
Trinity ... ... P.C 119 14
Otford, Cant. ... ... P.C 662 7
Otham, Cant. ... ...R 87 16
Othery, B. and W. ... ...V 560 19
Otley, Nor. ... ...R 640 20
Otley, Rip. ... ...V 12 10
Otterbourne, Win. ... ...V 744 6
Otterburn, Dur. ... P.C 694 5
Otterden, Cant. ... ...R 508 18
Otterford, B. and W. P.C 578 5
Otterham, Ex.... ... ...R 177 4
Otterhampton, B. and W. R 218 6
Otterington, North, York V 588 2
Otterington, South, York...R 169 10
Ottershaw, Win. ... P.C 491 24
Otterton, Ex. ... ...V 693 22

Ottery, Upper, Ex. ... ...V 421 5
Ottery St. Mary, Ex. ...V 151 20
Coll. Ch. ... ... Chap 608 6
St. Michael's ... P.C 667 14
Otton Belchamp, Roch. ...R 177 20
Ottringham, York ... P.C 431 2
Oughtibridge, York ... P.C 392 21
Oulton, Nor. ... ...R 614 25
V 346 12
Oulton, Rip. ... ... P.C 287 22
Ousby, Carl. ... ...R 105 21
Oundle, Pet. ... ...V 489 18
Ouse, Little, Ely ... P.C 294 1
Ouseburn, Great, Rip. ...V 20 20
Ouseburn, Little, Rip. ...V 185 22
Out Rawcliffe, Man.... P.C 330 28
Outwell, Nor. ... ...R 738 19
Outwood, Rip. ... ... P.C 246 6
Over, Ches. ... ...V 356 26
St. John's ... ... P.C 734 14
Over, Ely... ... ...V 688 16
Overbury, Wor. ... ...V 612 27
Over Peover, Ches. ... P.C 243 16
Oversilton, York ... P.C 498 12
Overstone, Pet.... ... ...R 59 14
Over Stowey, B. and W. ...V 99 4
Overstrand, Nor. ... ...R 367 20
Over Tabley, Ches. ... P.C 179 19
Overton, Man. ... ... P.C 436 8
Overton, Salis.... ... ...V 13 20
Overton, Win. ... ...R 233 1
Overton, York ... ...V 520 10
Over Wallop, Win. ... . .R 225 27
Oving, Chich. ... ...V 61 10
Oving, Ox. ... ...R 645 14
Ovingdean, Chich. ... ...R 623 12
Ovingham, Dur. ... P.C 57 22
Ovington, Nor.... ... ...R 214 7
Ovington, Roch. ... ...R 229 25
Ovington, Win.... ... ...R 628 12
Owersby, Lin. ... ...V 292 3
Owlpen, G. and B. ... ...R 151 23
Owmby, Lin. ... ...R 271 18
V 659 21
Owsden, Ely ... ...R 428 24
Owslebury, Win. ... P.C 457 25
Owston, Lin. ... ...V 606 10
Owston, Pet. ... ... P.C 114 11
Owston, York ... ...V 146 19
Owthorne, York ... ...V 725 2
Owthorpe, Lin.... ... P.C 612 6
Oxburgh, Nor. ... ...R 653 25
Oxcombe, Lin. ... ...R 122 12
Oxendon Magna, Pet. ...R 503 2
Oxenhall, G. and B.... P.C 414 8
Oxenhope, Rip.... ... P.C 268 7
Oxenton, G. and B.... P.C 154 21
Oxford, All Saints' ... P.C 454 23
Ch. Ch. ... ... Chap 2 15
St. Aldate's ... ...R 129 12
St. Clement's ... ...R 168 30
St. Cross ... ... P.C 685 5
St. Ebbe's ... ...R 289 1
St. George's-the-Martyr V 669 18
St. Giles' ... ...V 532 21
St. Martin's Carfax ...R 345 1
St. Mary Magdalen's ...V 669 18
St. Mary the Virgin ...V 102 7
St. Michael's... ... P.C 455 9
St. Paul's ... ... P.C 281 24
St. Peter's-in-the-East V 387 24
St. Peter-le-Bailey ...R 413 16
St. Philip and St. James's P.C 269 10
St. Thomas's ... ...V 122 18
Trinity ... ... P.C 698 10
Oxhey, Roch. ... ... Chap 359 21
Oxhill, Wor. ... ...R 432 16
Oxnead, Nor. ... ...R 630 6

Oxon, Lich. ... ... P.C 149 3
Oxted, Win. ... ...R 543 14
Oxton, Ches. ... ... P.C 640 14
Oxton, Lin. ... ...V 227 28
Oxwick, Nor. ... ...R 63 20
Oystermouth, St. D.... P.C 696 21
Ozendyke, York ... ...R 140 26
Ozleworth, G. and B. ...R 136 18

P.

Packington, Pet. ... ...V 533 12
Packwood, Wor. ... P.C 367 25
Padbury, Ox. ... ...V 220 10
Paddington, Lon. ... P.C 467 24
All Saints ... ... P.C 626 11
Ch. Ch. ... ... P.C 731 9
St. John's ... ... P.C 809 11
St. Mary's ... ... P.C 97 6
St. Mary Magdalen's P.C 698 14
St. Matthew's ... P.C 749 15
St. Michael's and All Angels ... ... P.C 534 5
St. Peter's ... ... P.C 559 14
St. Saviour's ... ... P.C 673 21
St. Stephen's... ... P.C 89 12
Trinity ... ... P.C 466 9
Paddington, Man. ... P.C 298 1
Paddlesworth, Cant. ... Chap 363 14
Paddock, Rip. ... ... P.C 429 17
Paddock Wood ... ... P.C 528 8
Padgate, Ches. ... ... P.C 85 12
Padiham, Man. ... ... P.C 238 15
Padstow, Ex. ... ...V 669 3
Padworth, Ox. ... ...R 140 22
Pagham, Chich. ... ...V 32 24
Paglesham, Roch. ... ...R 294 18
Paignton, Ex. ... ...V 526 3
Pain's-lane, Lich. ... P.C 9 22
Painswick, G. and B. ...V 57 12
Pakefield, Nor. ... ...R 730 11
Pakenham, Ely... ... ...V 370 2
Palgrave, Nor. ... ...R 111 20
Palgrave, Great and Little, Nor. ... ...R 876 18
Palling, Nor. ... ...V 550 5
Pamber, Win. ... ... P.C 48 22
Pampisford, Ely ... ...V 228 11
Pancras, St. (*see* St. Pancras).
Pancras Wyke, Ex. ... ...V 136 28
Panfield, Roch.... ... ...R 318 1
Pangbourne, Ox. ... ...R 228 25
Pannall, Rip. ... ...V 673 14
Panton, Lin. ... ...R 442 19
Pant-teg, Llan.... ... ...R 358 13
Panxworth, Nor. ... ...R 198 5
Papplewick, Lin. ... P.C 537 17
Papworth Everard, Ely ...R 122 7
Papworth St. Agnes, Ely ...R 618 28
Par, Ex. ... ... P.C 578 19
Parham, Chich.... ... ...R 45 20
Parham, Nor. ... ...V 152 6
Parkstone, Salis. ... P.C 505 5
Parley, West, Salis. 99 1
Parndon, Great, Roch. ...R 3 16
Parndon, Little, Roch. ...R 810 1
Parr, Ches. ... ... P.C 489 5
Parracombe, Ex. ... ...R 543 7
Parson Drove, Ely ... P.C 355 25
Partney, Lin. ... ...R 254 13
Parwich, Lich.... ... ...V 811 34
Passenham, Pet. ... ...R 730 4
Paston, Pet. ... ...R 533 20
Patcham, Chich. ... ...V 9 4
Patching, Chich. ... ...R 644 27
Pateley Bridge, Rip. ... P.C 269 16
Patney, Salis. ... ...R 432 8
Patrington York ... ...R 595 22
Patrixbourne, Cant. ... ...V 626 5
Patshull, Lich. ... ... P.C 273 8
Patterdale, Carl. ... ...R 568 8
Pattesley, Nor. ... ...R 198 8
Pattingham, Lich. ... ...V 273 8
Pattishall (Holy Cross), Pet. V 515 17
2nd portion V 696 27
Pattiswick, Roch. ... P.C 610 27
Paulerspury, Pet. ... ...R 482 3
Paull, York ... ...V 150 21
Paul's Cray, Cant. ... ...R 397 15
Paulton, B. and W. ... P.C 460 24
Pauntley, G. and B. ... P.C 414 8
Pavenham, Ely... ... P.C 545 20
Pawlet, B. and W. ... ...V 161 14
Paxton, Great, Ely ... ...V 484 27
Payhembury, Ex. ... ...V 455 5
Peak Forest, Lich. ... P.C 228 1
Peakirk, Pet. ... ...R 358 17
Peasemore, Ox.... ... ...R 337 5
Peasenhall, Nor. ... P.C 699 4
Peasmarsh, Chich. ... ...V 351 17
Peatling Magna, Pet. ...R 68 10
Peatling Parva, Pet.... ...R 54 9
Pebmarsh, Roch. ... ...R 278 2
Pebworth, G. and B.... ...V 237 9
Peckham, East, Cant. ...V 493 11
Trinity ... ... P.C 701 16
Peckham, West, Cant. ...V 371 6
Peckham, St. Andrew's, Win. P.C 305 26
St. Mary's ... ... P.C 57 28
Peckleton, Pet.... ... ...R 125 22
Pedmore, Wor. ... ...R 705 12
Peel, Man.... ... ... P.C 5 16
Peldon, Roch. ... ...R 295 13
Pelham Brent, Roch.... ...V 708 17
Pelham Furneux, Roch. ...V 708 17
Pelsall, Lich. ... ...V 293 10
Pelton, Dur. ... ... P.C 36 1
Pelynt, Ex. ... ...V 140 11
Pemberton, Ches. ... P.C 747 26
Pembridge, Herf. ... ...R 161 26
Pembroke, St. D. ... ...V 191 1
Pembroke, St. Mary, St. Michael, and St. Nicholas, St. D. V 168 13
Pembroke Dock, St. D. P.C 381 26
Pembury, Cant. ... ...V 732 9
Penally, St. D.... ... ...V 342 15
Penalt, Llan. ... ...V 393 24
Penarth, Llan. ... ...R 506 9
Penboyr, St. D.... ... ...R 715 1
Penbryn, St. D. ... ...V 342 19
Pencarreg, St. D. ... ...V 376 15
Pencombe, Herf. ... ...R 15 12
Pencoyd, Herf. ... ... P.C 139 14
Pendeen, Ex. ... ... P.C 6 21
Penderyn, St. D. .. ...R 449 23
Pendine, St. D.... ... ...R 646 5
Pendlebury, Ch. Ch., Man. P.C 184 27
St. John's ... ... P.C 564 27
Pendleton, Man. ... P.C 396 14
Pendock, Wor. ... ...R 637 23
Pendomer, B. and W. ...R 309 18
Pendoylan, Llan. ... ...V 377 1
Penegoes, St. A. ... ...R 204 23
Penge, Win. ... ... P.C 427 6
St. Paul's ... ... P.C 267 21
Penhow, Llan. ... ...R 433 9
Penhurst, Cant. ... ...R 272 10
Penhurst, Chich. ... ...R 476 30
Penistone, Rip.... ... ...V 665 12
Penkhull, Lich. ... P.C 371 12
Penkridge, Lich. ... P.C 225 19
Penley, Lich. ... ... P.C 619 11
Penmachno, Ban. ... ...R 539 11
Penmaen, Llan. ... P.C 375 25
Penmaen, St. D. ... ...R 358 19
Penmark, Llan. ... ...V 729 22
Penmon, Ban. ... ... P.C 374 28
Penmorva, Ban. ... ...R 518 21
Penmynydd, Ban. ... P.C 372 14
Penn, Lich. ... ...V 500 13
St. Philip's ... ... P.C 167 14
Penn, Ox. ... ...V 267 25
Pennal, Ban. ... ... P.C 171 19
Pennant, St. A. ... ...R 571 7
Pennard, St. D. ... ...V 370 14
Pennard, East, B. and W. V 260 24
Pennard, West, B. and W. P.C 489 11
Pennington, Carl. ... ...V 473 15
Pennington, Man. ... P.C 622 24
Pennington, Win. ... P.C 395 19
Penn Street, Ox. ... P.C 42 16
Penponds, Ex. ... ... P.C 107 21
Penrhos, Ban. ... ... Chap 539 21
Penrhôs, Llan.... ... ...V 225 3
Penrhôs, St. A. ... P.C 702 7
Penrhyn Deudraeth, Ban. P.C 554 28
Penrieth, St. D. ... ...R 339 11
Penrith, Carl. ... ...V 107 10
Ch. Ch. ... ... P.C 730 23
Pensax, Herf. ... ... P.C 121 11
Pen Selwood, B. and W. ...R 408 13
Penshurst, Cant. ... ...R 272 10
Pensnett, Lich.... ... P.C 19 16
Pensthorpe, Nor. ... ...R 196 13
Penstrowed, Ban. ... ...R 312 4
Pentlow, Roch.... ... ...R 98 6
Pentney, Nor.... ... P.C 461 28
Penton Mewsey, Win. ...R 189 8
Pentraeth, Ban... ... P.C 343 4
Pentrevoelas, St. A.... P.C 375 19
Pentrich, Lich. ... ...V 525 21
Pentridge, Salis. ... ...R 111 17
Pentyrch, Llan. ... ...V 646 27
Penwerris, Ex. ... ... P.C 202 18
Penwortham, Man. ... P.C 549 2
Pen-y-Clawdd, Llan. P.C 331 3
Penzance, Ex.... ... P.C 308 27
St. Paul's ... ... P.C 572 28
Peopleton, Wor. ... ...R 146 9
Peover, Lower, Ches. P.C 329 6
Peper Harrow, Win. ... ...R 733 18
Percy, Dur. ... ... P.C 137 2
Perivale, Lon. ... ...R 341 21
Perlethorpe, Lin. ... P.C 615 11
Perran Arworthal, Ex. ...V 738 10
Perran Uthnoe, Ex. ... ...R 19 4
Perranzabuloe, Ex. ... ...V 516 3
Perrott, North, B. and W. ...R 336 15
Perrott, South, Salis. ...R 720 23
Perry Barr, Lich. ... P.C 614 26
Pershore, Wor. ... ...V 33 1
Pertenhall, Ely... ... ...R 476 5
Pertholey, Llan. ... ...V 682 1
Pertwood, Salis. ... ...R 550 19
Peterborough, Pet. ... ...V 319 19
St. Mark's... ... P.C 484 22
St. Mary's ... ... P.C 648 15
Peterchurch, Herf. ... ...V 15 20
Peter's Marland, Ex.... P.C 531 9
Peterstone-super-Ely, Llan. R 410 22
Peterstow, Herf. ... ...R 361 7
Petham, Cant. ... ...V 266 9
Petherick, Little, Ex. ...R 437 18
Petherton, North, B. & W. V 564 7
Petherton, South, B. & W. V 71 3
Petherwin, North, Ex. ...V 660 24
Petherwin, South, Ex. ...V 449 15
Petrockstowe, Ex. ... ...R 739 1
Pett, Chich. ... ...R 744 2
Pettaugh, Nor. ... ...R [illegible] 3
Pettistree, Nor.... ... ...V 196 20
Petton, Lich. ... ...R [illegible] 25
Petworth, Chich. ... ...R 327 19
Pevensey, Chich. ... ...V 96 1

Pevington, Cant. ... ...R 498 7
Pewsey, Salis. ... ...R 548 5
Phillack, Ex. ... ...R 323 12
Philleigh, or Fellye, Ex. ...R 637 22
Piccadilly, Lon. (see Westminster).
Pickenham, North, Nor. ...R 219 10
Pickenham, South, Nor. ...R 111 26
Pickering, York ... ...V 138 6
Pickhill, Rip. ... ...V 445 1
Pickwell, Pet. ... ...R 420 25
Pickworth, Lin... ... ...R 809 3
Pickworth, Pet. ... ...R 524 7
Piddinghoe, Chich. ... ...V 348 20
Piddington, Pet. ... P.C 348 18
Piddle, North, Wor. ... ...R 700 15
Piddle Trenthide, Salis. ...V 316 3
Pightlesthorne, Ox. ... P.C 349 2
Pilgwenlly, Llan. ... P.C 238 20
Pilham, Lin. ... ...R 696 12
Pill, B. and W. ... P.C 394 4
Pillaton, Ex. ... ...R 226 24
Pillerton Hersey, with Pillerton Priors, Wor. ...V 240 23
Pilleth, St. D. ... ...V 171 25
Pilling, Man. ... ... P.C 30 10
Pilsdon, Salis. .. ..R 238 12
Pilton, B. and W. ... ...V 269 9
Pilton, Ex. ... ... P.C 286 1
Pilton (Northants), Pet. ...R 325 6
Pilton (Rutland), Pet. ...R 91 28
Pimlico, Belgrave Chapel, Lon. Min 545 14
St. Andrew's ... P.C 680 17
St. Barnabas' ... P.C 702 24
St. Gabriel's ... P.C 46 35
St. Michael's ... P.C 287 20
St. Peter's ... ... P.C 244 1
St. Peter's Chap. (Charlotte-street) ... P.C 603 13
St. Saviour's ... P.C 680 25
Pimperne, Salis. ... ...R 105 18
Pinchbeck, Lin. ... .. V 693 23
Pinchbeck, West, Lin. P.C 728 21
Pinhoe, Ex. ... ...V 549 25
Pinkney, G. and B. ... ...R 702 12
Pinner, Lon. ... ... P.C 320 28
Pinnock, G. and B. ... ...R 700 4
Pinxton, Lich. ... ...R 496 7
Pipe, Herf. ... ...V 301 14
Pipe Ridware, Lich. P.C 523 13
Pirbright, Win.... ... P.C 498 5
Pirton, Ox. ... ...V 441 22
Pirton, Roch. ... ...V 420 12
Pirton, Wor. ... ...R 354 22
Pishill, Ox. ... ... P.C 629 19
Pitchcombe, G. and B. ...R 452 27
Pitchcott, Ox. ... ...R 486 12
Pitchford, Lich. ... ...R 516 15
Pitcombe, B. and W. P.C 643 8
Pitminster, B. and W. ...V 401 11
Pitney, B. and W. ... ...R 196 6
Pitney Yeovil, B. and W. R 18 26
Pitsea, Roch. ... ...R 360 10
Pitsford, Pet. ... ...R 677 11
Pitsmoor, York... ... P.C 33 18
Pittingdon, Dur. ... ...V 628 13
Pixley, Herf. ... ...R 540 27
Plaistow, Cant.... ... P.C 267 19
Plaistow, Lon. ... ... P.C 441 9
St. Mark's ... ... P.C 78 29
Plaistow, Roch. ... P.C 456 8
Plaitford, Salis.... ... ...R 38 16
Plaxtole, Cant. ... ...R 368 12
Playden, Chich. ... ...R 546 5
Playford, Nor. ... ... P.C 324 13
Pleasley, Lich. ... ...R 268 12
Pleck, Lich. ... ... P.C 659 24
Plemstall, Ches. ... Chap 644 5
Pleshey, Roch. ... ... P.C 190 10

Pluckley, Cant. ... ...R 498 7
Plumbland, Carl. ... ...R 736 3
Plumpton, Carl. ... P.C 296 15
Plumpton, Chich. ... ...R 734 12
Plumpton, Pet.... ... ...R 308 3
Plumstead, Kent, Lon. ...V 427 4
St. Nicholas'... ... P.C 427 5
Plumstead, Nor. ... ...R 398 3
Plumstead, Great, Nor. P.C 140 7
Plumstead, Little, Nor. ...R 514 6
Plumtree, Lin. ... ...R 104 2
Plungar, Pet. ... ...V 597 5
Plymouth, Charles, Ex. ...V 270 6
Charles Chapel ... P.C 154 15
Ch. Ch.... ... ... P.C 51 2
St. Andrew's... ... ...V 300 21
P.C 559 3
St. James's ... ... P.C 66 13
St. Peter's ... ... P.C 539 14
Trinity ... ... P.C 34 20
Plympton St. Mary, Ex. P.C 346 10
Plympton St. Maurice, Ex. P.C 611 13
Plymstock, Ex.... ... P.C 154 4
Plymtree, Ex. ... ...R 190 17
Pocklington, York ... ...V 209 19
Pockthorpe, Nor. ... P.C 537 11
Podington, Ely... ... ...V 250 12
Podymore Milton, B. & W. R 590 19
Pointon, Lin. ... ...V 583 9
Pokesdown, Win. ... P.C 41 8
Polebrook, Pet.... ... ...R 333 13
Polesworth, Wor. ... ...V 432 19
Poling, Chich. ... ...V 405 24
Pollington-cum-Balne P.C 2 12
Polstead, Ely ... ...R 153 20
Poltimore, Ex. ... ...R 235 24
Pond's Bridge, Ely ... P.C 375 33
Ponsonby, Carl. ... P.C 420 8
Pontblyddyn, St. A.... P.C 217 2
Pont Dolanog, St. A. P.C 411 7
Pontefract, York ... ...V 62 3
All Saints' ... ... P.C 67 6
Ponteland, Dur. ... ...V 534 2
Pontesbright, Roch. ... P.C 266 21
Pontesbury, Herf. 1st portion R 297 6
2nd portion 194 28
3rd portion 150 15
Pontnewynydd, Llan.... P.C 469 23
Ponton, Great, Lin. ... ...R 89 14
Ponton, Little, Lin. ... ...R 736 12
Pont Robert, St. A.... ...V 356 15
Pontvaen, St. D. ... P.C 176 18
Pont-y-Rhun, or Pentrebach, Llan.... ... ... P.C 272 5
Pool, South, Ex. ... ...R 7 24
Poole, Rip. ... ... P.C 557 21
Poole, St. James's, Salis. P.C 710 5
St. Paul's ... ... P.C 469 4
Poole Keynes, G. and B. ...R 435 12
Pool Quay, St. A. ... P.C 228 2
Poorton, North, Salis. ...R 580 13
Popham, Win. ... ... P.C 438 9
Poplar, Lon. ... ...R 488 30
Ch. Ch.... ... ... P.C 113 4
St. Matthias'... ... P.C 391 6
Poppleton, Nether with Upper, York... ... ... P.C 273 1
Porchester, Win. ... ...V 106 25
Poringland, Nor. ... ...R 683 2
Poringland, West, Nor. ...R 640 13
Porlock, B. and W. ... ...R 91 21
Portbury, B. and W. ...V 669 10
Port Eynon, St. D. ... ...R 409 28
Porthkerry, Llan. ... ...R 8 20
Porthleven, Ex. ... P.C 718 4
Portisham, Salis. ... ...V 265 22
Portishead, B. and W. ...R 487 3
Portland, Salis.... ... ...R 325 23
St. John's ... ... P.C 364 15

Portlemouth, Ex. ... ...R 697 15
Portsea, Win. ... ...V 627 6
All Saints' ... ... P.C 129 25
St. Bartholomew's P.C 260 1
St. George's ... ... P.C 543 21
St. John's ... ... P.C 391 15
Trinity ... ... P.C 524 16
Portskewett, Llan. ... ...R 409 29
Portslade, Chich. ... ...V 326 9
Portsmouth, Win. ... ...V 429 10
St. Mary's ... ... Min 392 19
Portswood, Win. ... P.C 708 14
Portwood, Ches. ... P.C 148 1
Poslingford, Ely ... ...V 634 9
Postbury, Ex. ... ... P.C 158 26
Postling, Cant.... ... ...V 726 26
Postwick, Nor. ... ...R 676 6
Potterhanworth, Lin. ...R 704 18
Potterne, Salis. ... ...V 452 11
Potter's Bar, Lon. ... P.C 690 20
Potterspury, Pet. ... ...V 158 9
Pottery Field, Rip ... ...V 183 12
Pottesgrove, Ely ... ...R 141 13
Potton, Ely ... ...V 57 18
Pott Shrigley, Ches. ... P.C 633 23
Poughill (Cornwall), Ex. V 115 14
Poughill (Devon), Ex. ...R 452 26
Poulshot, Salis. ... ...R 280 19
Poulton, G. and B. ... P.C 573 15
Poulton-le-Fylde, Man. ...V 131 6
Poulton-le Sands, Man. ...R 436 7
Poundstock, Ex. ... ...V 179 9
Powderham, Ex. ... ...R 479 5
Powerstock, Salis. ... ...V 580 13
Powick, Wor. ... ...V 23 18
Poxwell, Salis.... ... ...R 110 19
Poynings, Chich. ... ...R 328 4
Poyntington, B. and W. ...R 306 15
Poynton, Ches.... ... P.C 709 3
Prees, Lich. ... ...V 9 3
Prendergast, St. D. ... ...R 236 8
Prescot, Ches. ... . V 580 8
Preshute, Salis.... ... ...V 65 23
Prestatyn, St. A. ... P.C 358 21
Prestbury, Ches. ... ...V 724 4
Prestbury, G. and B. ...V 205 12
Presteign, Herf. ... ...R 494 6
Prestolee, Man.... ... P.C 14 23
Preston, Chich. ... ...V 382 4
Preston, East, Chich. ...V 187 9
Preston, Ely ... ...R 714 28
Preston, G. and B. ... ...V 446 2
Preston, Man. ... ...V 505 6
All Saints' ... ... P.C 44 12
Ch. Ch. ... ... P.C 229 16
St. George's ... ... P.C 729 28
St. James's ... ... P.C 722 23
St. Luke's ... ... P.C 726 10
St. Mark's ... ... P.C 368 2
St. Mary's ... ... P.C 8 9
St. Paul's ... ... P.C 811 36
St. Peter's ... .. P.C 124 4
St. Thomas's... ... P.C 596 6
Trinity... ... ... P.C 90 27
Preston, Pet. ... ...R 47 8
Preston, Long, Rip. ... ...V 154 1
Preston, Salis.... ... ...V 28 14
Preston Bagot, Wor.... ...R 118 16
Preston Bissett, Ox.... ...R 70 1
Preston-by-Feversham, Cant. V 516 23
Preston Candover, Win. ...V 724 5
Preston Capes, Pet. ... ...R 392 26
Preston Deanery, Pet. ...V 810 20
Preston Gubbalds, Lich. P.C 101 6
Preston-in-Holderness, York R 26 5
Preston-on-Stour, G. and B. P.C 587 14
Preston-on-Wyre, Herf. ...V 339 16

Benefice			
Rennington, Dur.	P.C	147	19
Renwick, Carl.	P.C	811	17
Repps, Nor.	P.C	318	6
Repps, North, Nor.	R	400	9
Repps, South, Nor.	R	281	17
Repton, Lich.	P.C	718	24
Resolven, Llan.	V	277	8
Reston, North, Lin.	V	356	2
Reston, South, Lin.	R	356	2
Retford, East, Lin.	V	268	23
Retford, West, Lin.	R	331	5
Rettendon, Roch.	R	693	8
Revelstoke, Ex.	R	698	7
Revesby, Lin.	P.C	33	1
Rewe, Ex.	R	716	16
Reydon, Nor.	R	162	6
Reymerston, Nor.	R	280	19
Reynoldston, St. D.	R	173	12
	P.C	502	1
Rhayader, St. D.	P.C	536	30
St. Harmon	V	216	14
Rhes-y-Cae, St. A.	P.C	362	15
Rhiw, Ban.	R	560	18
Rhodes, Man.	P.C	150	18
Rhoscolyn, Ban.	R	715	15
Rhôs Crowther, St. D.	R	585	28
Rhosllanerchrugog, St. A.	P.C	373	27
Rhosmarket, St. D.	V	85	29
Rhossili, St. D.	R	423	4
Rhôstie, St. D.	R	203	25
Rhosymedre, St. A.	P.C	205	14
Rhuddlan, St. A.	V	206	14
Rhuddry, Llan.	R	718	22
Rhydybriew, St. D.	P.C	312	7
Rhydycroesau, St. A.	P.C	716	26
Rhydymwyn, St. A.	P.C	372	22
Rhyl, St. A.	P.C	469	12
Rhymney, Llan.	P.C	217	18
Ribbesford, Herf.	R	679	4
Ribby, Man.	P.C	629	6
Ribchester, Man.	V	299	23
Riby, Lin.	V	180	7
Riccall, York.	V	223	5
Richard's Castle, Herf.	R	396	7
Richmond, Rip.	R	561	13
Trinity	P.C	628	21
Richmond, Win.	V	812	3
St. John's	P.C	283	9
Rickinghall Inferior, Nor.	R	448	13
Rickinghall Superior, Nor.	R	448	13
Rickling, Roch.	V	142	14
Rickmansworth, Roch.	V	32	6
Riddings, Lich.	P.C	684	2
Riddlesworth, Nor.	R	169	2
Ridge, Roch.	V	34	7
Ridgeway, Lich.	P.C	88	7
Ridgewell, Roch.	V	347	20
Ridgmont, Ely	V	26	11
Ridley, Roch.	R	517	20
Ridlington, Nor.	R	231	19
Ridlington, Pet.	R	304	6
Rillington, York	V	428	28
Rimpton, B. and W.	R	304	4
Ringland, Nor.	V	84	17
Ringley, Man.	P.C	426	10
Ringmer, Chich.	V	637	25
Ringmore, Ex.	R	321	8
Ringsfield, Nor.	R	706	2
Ringshall, Nor.	R	502	29
	P.C	183	8
Ringstead, Pet.	V	581	22
Ringstead, Great, Nor.	R	348	11
Ringway, Ches.	P.C	316	23
Ringwood, Win.	V	663	20
Ringwould, Cant.	R	52	2
Ripley, Lich.	P.C	386	1
Ripley, Rip.	R	650	24
Ripon, Rip.	P.C	411	4
Rippingale, Lin.	R	149	16
Ripple, Cant.	R	436	12
Ripple, Wor.	R	135	19
Ripponden, Rip.	P.C	580	19
Risby, Ely	R	2	5
Risby, Lin.	V	34	5
Risca, Llan.	P.C	171	26
Rise, York	R	700	13
Riseholme, Lin.	R	380	20
Riseley, Ely	V	744	16
Rishangels, Nor.	R	102	19
Risington, Great, G. and B.	R	553	7
Risington, Little, G. and B.	R	407	25
Risley, Lich.	P.C	285	1
Riston, Long, York	R	501	25
Rivenhall, Roch.	R	302	11
River, Cant.	V	470	26
Riverhead, Cant.	P.C	102	21
Rivington, Man.	P.C	634	4
Road, B. and W.	R	258	8
Roade, Pet.	V	15	15
Road Hill, Salis.	P.C	509	10
Roath, Llan.	V	470	23
Robert Town, Rip.	P.C	685	6
Robeston, West, St. D.	R	316	16
Robin Hood Gate, Win.	P.C	138	8
Roborough, Ex.	R	281	2
Roby, Ches.	P.C	31	1
Rocester, Lich	P.C	632	13
Roch, St. D.	V	748	22
Rochburne, Win.	Chap	743	10
Rochdale, Man.	V	462	23
St. Alban's	V	503	17
St. Clement's	V	463	3
St. James's	P.C	570	14
Roche, Ex.	R	247	1
Rochester, St. Clement's, Roch.	V	192	29
St. Margaret's	V	192	29
St. Nicholas'	V	73	12
St. Peter's	P.C	518	26
Rochford, Herf.	R	76	3
Rochford, Roch.	R	153	19
Rock, Herf.	R	358	10
Rock, Dur.	P.C	147	19
Rockbeare, Ex.	V	525	24
Rockcliffe, Carl.	P.C	658	18
Rockfield, Llan.	V	218	19
Rockhampton, G. and B.	R	137	7
Rockingham, Pet.	R	57	23
Rockland, All Saints', Nor.	R	310	4
St. Andrew's	R	310	4
St. Mary's	R	581	26
St. Peter's	R	60	13
Rodborne Cheney, G. & B.	V	282	23
Rodborough, G. and B.	R	257	16
Rodden, B. and W.	P.C	203	2
Rode, North, Ches.	P.C	511	16
Roding, High, Roch.	R	449	9
Roding, White, Roch.	R	721	21
Roding Abbess, Roch.	R	163	24
Roding Aythorpe, Roch.	R	423	18
Rodington, Lich.	R	95	24
Rodmarton, G. and B.	R	426	20
Rodmell, Chich.	R	183	25
Rodmersham, Cant.	V	193	21
Roecliffe, Rip.	P.C	723	25
Roehampton, Lon.	P.C	56	3
Rogate, Chich.	V	36	17
Rogiett, Llan.	R	716	21
Rokeby, Rip.	R	76	6
Rollesby, Nor.	R	239	24
Rolleston, Lich.	R	474	10
Rolleston, Pet.	Chap	585	8
Rollestone, Lin.	V	194	24
Rollright, Great, Ox.	R	551	29
Rollright, Little, Ox.	R	626	2
Rollstone, Salis.	R	556	17
Rolvenden, Cant.	V	573	23
Romaldkirk, Rip.	R	135	8
Romansleigh, Ex.	R	450	19
Romford, Roch.	V	238	7
St. Andrew's	P.C	602	21
Romney, New, Cant.	V	610	32
Romney, Old, Cant.	R	234	19
Romsey, Win.	V	54	13
Ronton, Lich.	V	645	19
Rookhope, Dur.	P.C	171	6
Roos, York	R	430	4
Roosdown, Ex.	R	38	5
Ropley, Win.	Chap	433	6
Ropsley, Lin.	R	139	13
Rose Ash, Ex.	R	616	20
Rosedale, York	P.C	465	15
Rosherville, Roch.	P.C	255	19
Rosliston, Lich.	P.C	634	14
Ross, Herf.	R. & V	491	4
Rossett, St. A.	P.C	707	23
Rossington, York	R	76	26
Rostherne, Ches.	V	195	22
Rothbury, Dur.	R	290	14
Rotherfield, Chich.	R	127	19
Rotherfield Greys, Ox.	R	522	23
Trinity	P.C	522	17
Rotherfield Peppard, Ox.	R	552	16
Rotherham, York	V	474	11
Rotherhithe, Win.	R	809	13
All Saints'	P.C	376	4
Ch. Ch.	P.C	461	28
Trinity	P.C	722	19
Rothersthorpe, Pet.	V	114	19
Rotherwick, Win.	R	570	2
Rothley, Pet.	V	592	5
Rothwell, Lin.	R	496	1
Rothwell, Pet.	V	474	2
Rothwell, Rip.	V	47	23
Rottingdean, Chich.	V	645	26
Roudham, Nor.	V	164	15
Rougham, Ely	R	593	27
Rougham, Nor.	V	496	3
Roughton, Lin.	R	620	3
Roughton, Nor.	R	584	19
Roulston, Lin.	V	411	12
Roundhay, Rip.	P.C	176	21
Rounton, East, York	P.C	33	24
Rounton, West, York	R	228	7
Rousham, Ox.	R	512	7
Rouslench, Wor.	R	525	17
Routh, York	R	511	21
Rowberrow, B. and W.	R	313	12
Rowde, Salis.	V	623	2
Rowington, Wor.	V	87	21
Rowley, York	R	317	1
Rowley Regis, Wor.	V	687	7
Rowlstone, Herf.	P.C	384	6
Rowner, Win.	R	117	15
Rownhams, Win.	P.C	723	27
Rowsley, Lich.	P.C	374	2
Rowston, Lin.	V	411	12
Rowton, Lich.	P.C	559	16
Roxby, Lin.	V	34	5
Roxby, Rip.	V	445	1
Roxeth, Lon.	P.C	335	5
Roxham, Nor.	P.C	471	8
Roxholm, Lin.	R	662	11
Roxton, Ely	V	555	18
Roxwell, Roch.	V	307	4
Roydon (Castle Rising), Nor.	R	25	2
Roydon (Diss), Nor.	R	210	27
Roydon, Roch.	V	543	10
Royston, Roch.	V	705	26
Royston, York	V	708	20
Royton, Man.	P.C	319	8
Ruabon, St. A.	V	204	20
Ruan, Major, Ex.	R	564	10
Ruan, Minor, Ex.	R	355	28
Ruan Laniborne, Ex.	R	604	18
Ruardean, G. and B.	V	513	4

S.

Sodbury, Old, G. and B. ...V 479 28
Softley, Dur. ... ... P.C 474 6
Soham, Ely ... ...V 639 21
Solihull, Wor. ... ...R 614 16
Sollers, Hope, Herf. ... ...R 27 27
Somerby, Lin. ... ...R 89 7
Somerby (Brigg), Lin. ...R 374 17
Somerby, Pet. ... ...V 102 22
Somercotes, North, Lin. ...V 94 15
Somercotes, South, Lin. ...R 500 27
Somerford Keynes, G. & B. V 223 28
Somerford Parva, G. and B. R 214 2
Somerleyton, Nor. ... ...R 626 15
Somersby, Lin.... ... ...R 105 9
Somershall Herbert, Lich...R 697 27
Somersham, Ely ... ...R 365 1
Somersham, Nor. ... ...R 632 5
Somerton, B. and W. ...V 278 13
Somerton, Ely ... ...R 234 17
Somerton, East, Nor. ...R 272 11
Somerton, West, Nor. P.C 809 17
Somerton, Ox. ... ...R 536 20
Sompting, Chich. ... ...V 331 10
Sonning, Ox. ... ...V 511 1
Sopley, Win. ... ...V 423 7
Sopworth, G. and B.... ...R 97 7
Sotby, Lin. ... ...R 610 8
Sotherton, Nor.... ... ...R 208 7
Sotterley, Nor.... ... ...R 688 5
Soulbury, Ox. .... P.C 809 21
Soulby, Carl. ... ... P C 349 12
Soulderne, Ox.... ... ...R 625 6
Souldrop, Ely ... ...R 482 2
Sourton, Ex. ... .R 181 25
Southacre, Nor... ... ...R 237 7
Southall Green, Lon. P.C 397 1
Southam, Wor.... ... ...R 320 6
Southampton, All Saints, Win. R 79 31
Holy Rhood ... ...V 724 16
Holy Trinity... ... P.C 105 2
St. Dennis .... P.C 588 5
St. James's ... ... P.C 538 6
St. James's (West-end) P.C 301 5
St. John's ....R 423 2
St. Julian's ... ... Min 198 6
St. Lawrence's ... ...R 423 2
St. Mary's ... ...R 149 2
St. Mary's Extra ... P.C 175 15
St. Matthew's ... P.C 98 24
St. Michael's ... ...V 353 9
St. Paul's .... P.C 119 9
St. Peter's .... P.C 397 26
Southborough, Cant.... P.C 398 7
St. Thomas's... .... P.C 58 6
Southchurch, Roch. ... ...R 671 9
Southease, Chich. ... ...R 647 21
Southend, Lon.... ... Min 473 17
Southend, Roch. .... P.C 312 6
Southery, Nor. ... ...R 380 2
Southfleet, Roch. ....R 259 17
Southgate, Lon. .... P.C 27 3
South-hill, Ex.... ... ...R 651 27
Southleigh, Ex.... ... ...R 359 23
Southleigh, Ox... ... Chap 684 1
Southmere, Nor. ... ...R 41 10
Southminster, Roch.... ...V 53 7
Southoe, Ely ... ...R 467 26
Southport, Ch. Ch., Ches. P.C 131 19
St. Paul's ... . P.C 133 2
Trinity ... . P.C 356 20
Southrop, G. and B.... ...V 681 2
Southsea, St. Jude's, Win. P.C 94 25
St. Luke's ... ... P.C 7 12
St. Paul's ... ... P.C 626 22
St. Simon's ... ... Min 28 23
Southtown, Nor. ... ...R 670 7
St. Mary's Chapel... Min 359 13
Southwark, Ch. Ch., Win. R 610 9

Southwark, Win.—*contd.*
St. George-the-Martyr...R 8 29
St. Jude's ... ... P.C 452 15
St. Mark's (Horsleydown) P.C 245 11
St. Mary Magdalen's P.C 614 20
St. Olave's ... ...R 78 11
St. Peter's ... ... P.C 476 27
St. Saviour's ... Chap 52 6
St. Stephen's ... P.C 11 10
St. Thomas's ... P.C 181 16
Trinity ... ... P.C 475 6
Southwater, Chich. ... P.C 39 2
Southwell, Lin.... ... ...R 709 28
Trinity ... ... P.C 145 14
Southwick, Chich. ... ...R 503 26
Southwick, Dur. ... ...R 142 17
Southwick, Pet. ... ...V 92 6
Southwick, Win. ... Min 420 4
Southwold, Nor. ... P.C 570 6
Southwood, Nor. ... ...R 403 10
Southworth, Ches. ... ...R 390 5
Sowerby, Rip. ... ... P.C 44 4
St. George's ... ... P.C 523 23
St. Mary's .... P.C 557 14
Sowerby, York ... ... P.C 279 15
Sowerby Bridge, Rip... P.C 210 13
Sowton, Ex. ... ...R 580 17
Spalding, Lin. ... ... P.C 466 14
Moulton Chapel ... P.C 602 11
Spaldwick, Ely... ... ...V 592 24
Spanby, Lin. ... .R 391 13
Sparham, Nor. ... ...R 486 25
Sparkford, B. and W. ...R 50 17
Sparsholt, Ox. ... ...V 188 22
Sparsholt, Win. ... ...V 626 27
Spaxton, B. and W. ... ...R 245 29
Speen, Ox. ... ...V 484 9
Speenhamland, Ox. ... P.C 451 22
Speeton, York ... ... P.C 130 21
Speldhurst, Cant. ... ...R 577 3
Spelsbury, Ox. ... ...V 33 2
Spennithorne, Rip. ....R 741 30
Spernall, Wor. ... ...R 189 18
Spetchley, Wor. ....R 207 12
Spetisbury, Salis. ... ...R 676 17
Spexhall, Nor. ... ...R 157 22
Spilsby, Lin. .... P.C 667 10
Spitalfields, All Saints, Lon. P.C 361 1
Ch. Ch. ....R 369 9
St. Mary's (Spital-sq.) P.C 187 15
St. Stephen's... ... P.C 552 20
Spittal, St. D.... .... P.C 363 15
Spixworth, Nor. ... ...R 339 20
Spofforth, Rip. ... ...R 661 24
Spondon, Lich.... ...V 388 19
Sporle, Nor. ....V 376 18
Spratton, Pet. ... ...V 561 4
Spreyton, Ex.... ... ...V 327 8
Spridlington, Lin. ... ...R 350 8
Springfield, Roch. ... ...R 510 10
Spring Grove, Lon..... P.C 88 22
Springthorpe, Lin. ... ...R 56 2
Sproatley, York ....R 682 2
Sprotborough, York... ...R 633 31
Sproughton, Nor. ....R 390 11
Sprowston, Nor. ..... P.C 30 3
Sproxton, Pet.... ... ...V 368 12
Stackpole Bosher, St. D. ...R 9 21
Stackpool Elidur, St. D. ...R 402 15
Stadhampton, Ox. ... P.C 516 8
Stafford, Ch. Ch. Lich. P.C 296 24
St. Chad's .... P.C 132 1
St. Mary's. ... ...R 310 4
P.C 644 9
Stafford, West, Salis... ...R 610 31
Stagsden, Ely ... ...V 87 25
Stainborough ... . Chap 210 26

Stainburn, Rip.... ... P.C 523 3
Stainby, Lin. ... ...R 494 28
Staincliffe, Rip.... ... P.C 667 23
Staindrop, Dur. ... ...V 413 26
Staines, Lon. ... ...V 244 15
Stainfield, Lin.... ... P.C 621 22
Stainforth, Rip. ... P.C 623 1
Staininghall, Nor. ... ...R 597 11
Stainland, Rip.... ... P.C 692 24
Stainley, North, Rip. P.C 361 13
Stainley, South, Rip. P.C 678 26
Stainmore, Carl. ... P.C 700 6
Stainton, Great, Dur. ...R 662 18
Stainton (Rotherham), York V 567 24
Stainton (Stockton-on-Tees), York ... ...V 261 8
Stainton-by-Langworth, Lin. V 567 25
Stainton-le-Vale, Lin. .. R 180 1
Stalbridge, Salis. ... ...R 515 11
Staley, Ches. ... ... P.C 322 18
Staleybridge, New St. George's, Man ... ... P.C 405 21
Old St. George's ... P.C 405 22
Stalham, Nor. ... ...V 703 26
Stalisfield, Cant. ... ...V 676 19
Stallingborough, Lin. ...V 158 21
Stalling Busk, Rip. ... P.C 28 22
Stalmine, Man. ... P.C 666 20
Stambourne, Roch. ... ...R 235 16
Stambridge, Great, Roch....R 513 23
Stambridge, Little, Roch....R 811 2
Stamford, All Saints, Lin....R 684 22
St. Andrew's ... ...V 543 18
St. Clement's and St. John's ... ...R 371 2
St. George with St. Paul's R 94 17
St. Mary's ... ...R 506 7
St. Michael's... ... ...R 491 17
St. Peter's ... ...R 684 22
St. Stephen's ... ...R 543 18
Stamford Barron, Pet. ...V 697 25
Stamfordham, Dur. ... ...V 57 24
Stamford Hill, Lon. ... P.C 369 1
Stanbridge, Ely ... ...V 707 8
Stand, Man. ... ...R 152 12
St. John's ... ... P.C 117 25
Standerwick, B. and W. ...R 377 1
Standish, G. and B.... ...V 596 8
Standish, Man.... ... ...R 82 12
Standlake, Ox.... ... ...R 57 13
Standon, Lich. ... ...R 432 20
Standon, Roch. ... ...V 540 18
Stane, Lin. ... ...R 149 13
Stanfield, Nor. ... ...R 172 21
Stanford, Cant. ... P.C 669 6
Stanford, Nor. ... ...V 727 14
Stanford Bishop, Herf. P.C 72 13
Stanford Dingley, Ox. ...R 671 12
Stanford-in-the-Vale, Ox. V 736 1
Stanford-le-Hope, Roch. ...R 393 6
Stanford-on-Avon, Pet. ...V 413 2
Stanford-on-Soar, Lin. ...R 169 20
Stanford-on-Teme, Herf. ...R 352 25
Stanford Rivers, Roch. ...R 640 11
Stangate, Roch. ... ...V 129 2
Stanground, Ely ... ...V 152 16
Stanhoe, Nor. ... ...R 486 15
Stanhope, Dur.... ... ...R 424 1
Stanley, *alias* Staveley, Rip. R 296 9
Stanley, Ches.... ... P.C 247 10
Stanley, Lich. ... ... P.C 423 6
Stanley, Rip. ... ... P.C 304 6
Stanley Pontlarge, G. & B. P.C 380 4
Stanley St. Leonards, G. and B. ... ... P.C 390 12
Stanmer, Chich. ... ...R 33 14
Stanmore, Great, Lon. ...R 58 19
Stanmore, Little, Lon. ...R 263 16

T.

Toddington, G. and B. ...V 700 4
Todenham, G. and B. ...R 19 6
Todmorden, Man. ... ...V 524 21
Todwick, York ... ...R 581 25
Toft, Ches. ... ... P.C 3 2
Toft, Ely ... ...R 530 26
Toft-next-Newton, Lin. ...R 93 4
Tofts, West, Nor. ... ...R 634 11
Toft Trees, Nor. ... ...V 33 26
Tolland, B. and W. ... ...R 161 13
Tollard Royal, Salis. ...R 689 23
Toller, Great, Salis. .. ...V 360 17
Toller Fratrum, Salis. ...V 699 10
Tollesbury, Roch. ... ...V 41 6
Tolleshunt d'Arcy, Roch. V 194 10
Tolleshunt Knights, Roch. R 603 10
Tolleshunt Major, Roch. ...V 118 29
Tolpuddle, Salis. ... ...V 479 18
Tonbridge (see Tunbridge).
Tong, Lich. ... ... P.C 291 2
Tong, Rip. ... ...V 223 2
Tonge, Cant ... ...V 29 3
Tonge (Bolton-le-Moors), Man.... ... ... P.C 529 10
Tonge (Middleton), Man. P.C 176 26
Tongham, Win. ... P.C 255 25
Tong Street, Rip. ... P.C 236 4
Tooting, Win. ... ...R 270 11
Tooting, Upper, Win. P.C 158 13
Topcliffe, York ... ...V 303 3
Topcroft, Nor. ... ...R 722 5
Toppesfield, Roch. ... ...R 261 2
Topsham, Ex. ... ... P.C 403 4
Torbryan, Ex. ... ...R 729 11
Tormarton, G. and B. ...R 12 1
Tor Mohun, Ex. ... P.C 294 24
Torpenhow, Carl. ... ...V 645 21
Torpoint, Ex. ... ... P.C 193 3
Torquay, St. John's, Ex. P.C 613 6
St. Luke's Chapel... Min 249 6
Trinity Chapel ... Min 224 16
Torrington, Black, Ex. ...R 513 9
Torrington, Great, Ex. ...V 96 20
Torrington, Little, Ex. ...R 279 18
Torrington, East, Lin. ...R 474 17
Torrington, West, Lin. ...V 474 17
Tortington, Chich. ... ...V 657 14
Tortworth, G. and B. ...R 274 25
Torver, Carl. ... ... P.C 210 21
Torwood, Ex. ... ... P.C 826 3
Tosside, Rip. ... ... P.C 400 19
Tostock, Ely ... ...R 663 22
Totham, Great, Roch. ...V 182 27
Totham, Little, Roch. ...R 407 2
Tothill, Lin. ... ...R 275 14
Totnes, Ex. ... ...V 104 9
Tottenham, Lon. ... ...V 283 2
St. Anne's ... ... P.C 409 1
St. Paul's ... ... P.C 432 13
Trinity... ... ... P.C 339 15
Tottenhill, Nor. ... P.C 351 11
Totternhoe, Ely ... ...V 84 28
Tottington, Man. ... P.C 516 5
Tottington, Nor. ... ...V 332 10
Tovil, Cant. ... ... P.C 184 11
Towcester, Pet. ... ...V 412 8
Towersey, Ox. ... ...V 35 16
Towyn, Ban. ... ...V 375 20
Toxteth-park (see Liverpool).
Toynton, All Saints', Lin. P.C 177 27
St. Peter's ... ...R 177 27
Toynton, High, Lin.... P.C 343 20
Toynton, Low, Lin. ... ...V 124 5
Trafford, Old, Man. ... ...R 192 24
Trallong, St. D. ... P.C 293 16
Tranmere, St. Catherine's, Ches. P.C 209 8
St. Paul's ... ... P.C 179 22
Trawden, Man.... ... P.C 345 23

Trawsfynydd, Ban. ... ...R 370 8
Trealee, Man. ... ... P.C 324 6
Treborough, B. and W. ...R 245 13
Tredegar, Llan. ... P.C 407 4
Tredington, G. and B. P.C 585 25
Tredington, Wor. ... ...R 690 27
Treduznock, Llan. ... ...R 812 10
Treeton, York ... ...R 690 13
Trefdraeth, Ban. ... ...R 496 26
Trefelan, St. D. ... ...R 531 27
Trefgarn, Great, St. D. ...R 863 15
Trefriw, Ban. ... ...R 647 11
Trefnant, St. A. ... ...R 409 20
Trefonen, St. A. ... P.C 416 3
Tregaron, St. D. ... ...V 342 14
Tregony, Ex. ... ...V 73 10
Tregynnon, St. A. ... P.C 362 9
Trelech ar Bettws, St. D. ...V 646 15
Treleigh, Ex. ... ... P.C 437 7
Trellech, Llan. ... ...V 893 24
Trelleck Grange, Llan. P.C 490 4
Trelystan, Herf. ... P.C 379 22
Tremain, St. D. ... P.C 311 19
Tremayne, Ex.... ... P.C 599 21
Tremeirchion, St. A.... ...V 498 2
Trenddyn, St. A. ... P.C 173 18
Treneglos, Ex. ... ...V 595 6
Trent, B. and W. ... ...R 667 7
Trent (Enfield), Ch. Ch., Lon. P.C 636 15
Trentham, Lich. ... P.C 204 25
Trentishoe, Ex. ... ...R 587 13
Trent Vale, Lich. ... P.C 91 8
Treslothan, Ex. ... P.C 98 8
Tresmere, Ex. ... ... P.C 470 22
Treswell, Lin. ... ...R 168 9
Tretire, Herf. ... ...R 694 17
Tretower, St. D. ... P.C 535 13
Trevalga, Ex. ... ...R 637 25
Treveglwys, Ban. ... ...V 375 31
Treverbyn, Ex.... ... P.C 51 11
Trevethin, Llan. ... ...V 415 12
Trevor Traian, St. A. P.C 496 28
Treyford, Chich. ... ...R 720 12
Triby, Lin. ... ...R 445 24
Trimdon, Dur. ... ... P.C 619 18
Trimingham, Nor. ... ...R 165 27
Trimley St. Martin, Nor....R 501 22
Trimley St. Mary, Nor. ...R 720 5
Trimpley, Wor. ... P.C 513 11
Tring, Roch. ... ... P.C 298 25
Troedyraur, St. D. ... ...R 416 22
Troston, Ely ... ...R 99 2
Trottersciiffe, Cant. ... ...R 595 3
Trotton, Chich. ... ...R 39 16
Troutbeck, Carl. ... P.C 591 1
Trowbridge, Salis. ... ...R 300 14
Trinity ... ... P.C 683 19
Trowell, Lin. ... ...R 341 2
Trowse, Nor. ... ...V 532 16
Trull, B. and W. ... P.C 589 12
Trumpington, Ely ... ...V 613 14
Trunch, Nor. ... ...R 360 24
Truro, St. Clement's, Ex. V 252 10
St. George's ... ... P.C 737 12
St. John's ... ... P.C 477 14
St. Kea ... ...V 673 7
St. Kenwyn ... ...V 673 7
St. Mary's ... ...R 99 26
St. Paul's ... ... P.C 423 8
Trusham, Ex. ... ...R 278 27
Trusthorpe, Lin. ... ...R 496 21
Trysull, Lich. ... ...V 306 16
Tubney, Ox. ... ...R 107 16
Tucking Mill, Ex. ... P.C 364 4
Tuddenham, Nor. ... ...V 507 16
Tuddenham, North, Nor. ...R 37 4
Tuddenham St. Mary, Ely R 617 13
Tudeley, Cant. ... ...V 622 17

Tudhoe, Dur. ... ... P.C 710 11
Tufton, Win. ... ... P.C 353 20
Tugby, Pet. ... ...V 487 21
Tugford, Herf. ... ...R 733 8
Tulse-hill, Win. ... P.C 692 6
Tunbridge, Cant. ... ...V 437 2
St. Stephen's ... P.C 10 10
Tunbridge Wells, Ch. Ch., Cant. ... ... P.C 557 3
Chapel of Ease ... Min 528 15
St. James's ... ... P.C 510 14
St. John's ... ... P.C 699 12
Trinity ... ... P.C 322 5
Tunstall, Cant.... ... .. R 466 20
Tunstall, Lich. ... ... P.C 302 2
Tunstall, Nor. ... ...R 305 20
P.C 282 4
Tunstall, York ... ...R 1 9
Tunstead, Man. ... P.C 393 26
Tunstead, Nor.... ... ...V 294 7
Tunworth, Win. ... ...R 340 23
Tupsley, Herf. ... ... P.C 112 29
Turkdean, G. and B. ...V 61 14
Turnastone, Herf. ... ...R 531 19
Turnditch, Lich. ... P.C 509 7
Turners Puddle, Salis. ...R 679 10
Turnworth, Salis. ... ...R 414 15
Turton, Man. ... ... P.C 618 11
Turvey, Ely ... ...R 575 12
Turville, Ox. ... ...V 180 8
Turweston, Ox. ... ...R 392 19
Tutbury, Lich. ... ...V 509 8
Tuttington, Nor. ... ...V 823 1
Tuxford, Lin. ... ...V 441 4
Tweedmouth, Dur. ... ...V 538 13
Twerton, B. and W.... ...V 96 23
Twickenham, Lon. ... ...V 258 9
Episcopal Chapel ... Min 695 21
Trinity ... ... P.C 811 20
Twineham, Chich. ... ...R 463 16
Twinstead, Roch. ... ...R 893 3
Twitchen, Ex. ... ... P.C 101 11
Two-Mile-Hill, G. and B. P.C 576 21
Twycross, Pet. ... ... P.C 68 3
Twyford, Nor. ... ...R 619 22
Twyford, Pet. ... ...V 392 6
Twyford, Win. ... ...V 106 15
Twyning, G. and B.... ...V 264 1
Twywell, Pet. ... ...R 742 1
Tydd St. Giles', Ely... ...R 586 5
Tydd St. Mary, Lin.... ...R 420 33
Tydweiliog, Ban. ... P.C 714 9
Tyldesley, Man. ... P.C 553 24
Tyler's Green, Ox. ... P.C 582 6
Tyneham, Salis. ... ...R 71 7
Tynemouth, Dur. ... ...V 550 20
Holy Saviour's ... P.C 225 1
St. Peter's ... ... P.C 316 2
Trinity ... ... P.C 598 2
Tyringham, Ox. ... ...R 839 20
Tysoe, Wor. ... ...V 238 17
Tythby, Lin. ... ... P.C 88 20
Tytherington, G. and B. ...V 559 17
Tytherington, Salis.... P.C 392 14
Tytherley, East, Win. Chap 445 10
Tytherley, West, Win. ...R 536 8
Tytherton, G. and B. ...R 553 15
Tywardreath, Ex. ... ...V 569 12

U.

Ubbeston, Nor.... ... ...V 359 22
Ubley, B. and W. ... ...R 348 15
Uckfield, Chich. ... ...R 113 17
Udimore, Chich. ... ...V 87 14
Uffculme, Ex.... ... ...V 439 6
Uffington, Lich. ... P.C 521 13
Uffington, Lin.... ... ...R 845 26

Y.

Z.

PRINTED BY HORACE COX, WELLINGTON-STREET, STRAND, W.C.

IRISH SOCIETY,

FOR PROMOTING

The Scriptural Education and Religious Instruction of Irish Roman Catholics, chiefly through the medium of their own Language.

ESTABLISHED 1818.

THE attention of the Protestants of England is earnestly called to the following facts in connection with the working of this Society, inasmuch as they are thought to bear largely upon its otherwise obvious claims upon their sympathy and support:—

I. WORK TO BE DONE.

It may be thought that the necessity for such an organisation as the Society purports to employ can be, at the present day at least, but slight; as considering the efforts which have been, and are being put forth to root out the knowledge of the Irish Language, the number of those who speak or understand it must be infinitesimally small. But that this is not the case can be conclusively shewn from the census returns of the years 1851 and 1861. In the year 1861 the following figures represented the Irish-speaking element in the several counties in which the Irish Society's work was being carried on:—

	Speaking Irish only	Speaking English & Irish		Speaking Irish only	Speaking English & Irish
Co. Waterford	10,467	50,642	Co. Donegal	22,156	49.170
,, Clare	7.126	72,074	,, Mayo	32,228	124,148
,, Cork	16.704	185,455	,, Galway	41,512	122,892
,, Kerry	24,971	90,130			

	Speaking Irish only	Speaking English and Irish
Total	155,164	694,511
,, Irish-speaking population		849,675

From the census from which the above numbers are taken it was seen that, during the ten years intervening between 1851 and 1861, this Irish element in the population decreased 4·2 per cent., the percentages being

In 1851	23·3
In 1861	19·1

Supposing, therefore, the rate of decrease for the past six years to have been the same as that of the previous ten years, we would have a further decrease of 2·5 per cent. to record, leaving 16 6 per cent. of the whole population Irish speakers. Supposing, further, this rate of decrease to have spread itself equably over the Irish-speaking districts, and remembering that in the year 1861, according to the above returns, there were 849,675 persons, or 14·6 per cent. of the total population returned as forming an Irish-speaking element in those counties in which the elementary work of the Society was chiefly carried on, we would still have 12·1 per cent., or 701,675 persons to represent the Irish element therein, and this, be it remembered, only in the counties above mentioned, which do not at all exhaust the Irish-speaking element in Ireland.

II. CHARACTER OF THE WORK.

There may be political or there may be social disadvantages connected with this acquaintance, on the part of so many of the people of Ireland, with their native language; but for these (should they exist, which is doubtful) the y is not responsible; it has not been their cause, neither can it be (as it sometimes has been most unjustly) arged with their perpetuation. On the contrary, the blessing of God resting upon the endeavour, it has, through means of this language, effected changes not alone religious or spiritual, but also social and political; for the many who have been brought, through its instrumentality, to know and obey the King of kings and Lord of lords, have at the same time learned to "Honour all men, to love the brotherhood, to honour the king." The test applied to the work by the disturbances of late years places this fact beyond contradiction, so that whatever may have been the disadvantages, whatever the disabilities engendered by the perpetuation of the Irish as a language, it is with confidence that the Protestants of England are bid to see *in its existence, a power* that has been, and can still be, wielded for the temporal as well as the eternal good of their fellow-subjects in Ireland.

III. THE WORK DONE.

It is unnecessary to revert to the past. It can speak for itself, as the results vouchsafed to the working of the Society have been neither few nor insignificant. The present is what has to be thought of, and the following statistics, shewing the number of Roman Catholics reached by the agents of the Society during the year 1866-7, are confidently relied on as exhibiting such an amount of work done as could hardly be expected considering the many and determined efforts from time to time put forth against it, by those whose interest it is to crush, to "stamp" it out:—

New Teachers	11
Total Number of Teachers	261
Relative increase of Pupils about	200
Accession of New Pupils about	3,000
Number of Pupils under instruction about	12,000
" " passed to satisfaction of inspector or re-inspector ...	4,200
" " who have ceased learning	2,800

From these statistics it will be seen that while the relative increase of pupils during the past year amounts to about 200—which is a satisfactory circumstance—the actual accession of new pupils *to supply the places of the* 2,800 who have, through a variety of causes, passed from under instruction, has been about 3,000, which is far more satisfactory still. In estimating, therefore, the actual amount of work done, this constant going out of old and coming in of new pupils, should be taken into account. Doing so for the past and previous years, it is at once seen that there has been an annual average of about 12,000, with an annual incoming of from 2,000 to 3,000 new pupils, which latter fact it is thought opens up to view an extension of the work but seldom, if ever, thought of or accounted for; and which, bearing in mind that the Bible is the only book of instruction in use in the Society's schools, is, in the strongest possible terms, impressed upon all who, valuing the privilege of hearing the message of love from their covenant God in a language they can understand, and therefore that can reach the conscience, are anxious to show their appreciation of this privilege, by endeavouring, while they have time and the opportunity still exists, to extend it to those who as yet enjoy it not. In addition to this agency, which is peculiarly its own, the Society employs—

Ten Missionary Clergymen.
One Re-Inspecting Agent.
24 Inspectors of Irish Schools.
42 Scripture-Readers.
7 Schoolmasters,
3 Schoolmistresses, } in charge of Mission Schools, in which upwards of 420 Children are under instruction.

AND AUXILIARY TO ITS MISSIONARY WORK SUPPORTS—

Four Bedell Irish Scholarships, and a Premium, in the University, for the encouragement of the study of the Irish Language.

IV. INCOME.

For the carrying on of this great work there was received during the past year a sum of about £8,500, of which about £3,700 came from England. It is not supposed that this latter sum, in the collection of which a considerable outlay had to be incurred, represents the value set upon this work by the Protestants of England, it being the rather thought that its claims—the amount of work done, and the real tendency of that work—are still in a measure unknown to them, otherwise the results would be different. It is therefore earnestly hoped that those who may happen on this statement of facts shall not lightly cast it aside, but that, calling to mind their own privileges (not to speak of duties) as Protestants, they shall come forward and, so far as possible, emulate the zeal of their martyred forefathers in giving the Bible to those who have it not; in proclaiming God's truth to those who know it not; in spreading a knowledge of His covenant mercy in, and through Jesus, the Saviour of sinners, amongst those who, by their misguided teachers, are led to trust the keeping of their immortal souls to any other, than to Him who alone "is able to save them to the *uttermost* that come to God by Him."

ANNUAL SUBSCRIPTIONS AND DONATIONS

ARE EARNESTLY SOLICITED, AND WILL BE RECEIVED—

IN ENGLAND—by the National Provincial Bank of England, at their Offices, 112, Bishopsgate-street within, E.C., and 14, Waterloo-place, S.W., London; by the Rev. H. Honywood Dombrain, M.A., Incumbent of St. George's Church, Deal, Ke.. Rev. R. Hayward Kidd, M.A., Rector of St. Michael Coslany, Norwich; or by the Rev. S. Bache Harris, M.A., 32, Sackville-street, London, W.

IN IRELAND (Dublin)—by the Treasurers, Messrs. David La Touche and Co., Castle-street; or by the Secretaries, at the Office of the Society, 17, Upper Sackville-street.

Post-office Orders should be made payable to Mr. Robert Wyon, Accountant of the Society, 17, Upper Sackville-street, Dublin.

Milton Keynes UK
Ingram Content Group UK Ltd.
UKHW021307010823
426148UK00015B/376

9 781015 978126